2017-2018
Thirteenth Edition

Profiles
of
New York State

FOR REFERENCE

A UNIVERSAL REFERENCE BOOK

PUBLISHER: Leslie Mackenzie
EDITORIAL DIRECTOR: Laura Mars
EDITOR: David Garoogian
MARKETING DIRECTOR: Jessica Moody

Grey House Publishing, Inc.
4919 Route 22
Amenia, NY 12501
518.789.8700
FAX 845.373.6390
www.greyhouse.com
e-mail: books @greyhouse.com

Profiles of New York State
2 Volume Set (*New York State Directory* and *Profiles of New York State*)

ISBN: 978-1-68217-364-0
ISBN: 978-1-68217-363-3

Profiles
of
New York State

Table of Contents

Introduction

This is the thirteenth edition of *Profiles of New York State—Facts, Figures & Statistics for 2,570 Populated Places in New York*. As with the other titles in our *State Profiles* series, it was built with content from Grey House Publishing's award-winning *Profiles of America*—a 4-volume compilation of data on more than 43,000 places in the United States. We have included the New York chapter from *Profiles of America*, and added several new chapters of demographic information and ranking sections, so that *Profiles of New York State* is the most comprehensive portrait of the state of New York ever published.

Profiles of New York State provides data on all populated communities and counties in the state of New York for which the US Census provides individual statistics. This edition also includes profiles of 444 unincorporated places and neighborhoods (i.e. Flushing, Queens) based on US Census data by zip code.

This premier reference work includes five major sections that cover everything from **Education** to **Ethnic Backgrounds** to **Climate**. All sections include **Comparative Statistics** or **Rankings**. A section called **About New York** at the front of the book includes detailed narrative and colorful photos and maps. Here is an overview of each section:

1. About New York
This 4-color section gives the researcher a real sense of the state and its history. It includes a Photo Gallery, and comprehensive sections on New York's Government, Timeline of New York History, Land and Natural Resources, New York State Energy Profile and Demographic Maps. These 41 pages, with the help of photos, maps and charts, anchor the researcher to the state, both physically and politically.

2. Profiles
This section, organized by county, gives detailed profiles of 2,570 places plus 62 counties, based on Census 2010 and data from the 2011-2015 American Community Survey. In addition, we have added current government statistics and original research, so that these profiles pull together statistical and descriptive information on every Census-recognized place in the state. Major fields of information include:

Geography	*Housing*	*Education*	*Religion*
Ancestry	*Transportation*	*Population*	*Climate*
Economy	*Industry*	*Health*	

In addition to place and county profiles, this section includes a **Place Name Index**.

3. Comparative Statistics
This section includes tables that compare New York's 100 largest communities by dozens of data points.

4. Community Rankings
This section includes tables that rank the top 150 and bottom 150 incorporated communities with population over 2,500, in dozens of categories.

5. Education
This section begins with an **Educational State Profile,** summarizing number of schools, students, diplomas granted and educational dollars spent. Following the state profile are **School District Rankings** on 16 topics ranging from *Teacher/Student Ratios* to *High School Drop-Out Rates*. Following these rankings are statewide *National Assessment of Educational Progress (NAEP)* results and data from the *New York State Report Card*—an overview of student performance by subject, including easy-to-read charts and graphs.

6. Ancestry and Ethnicity
This section provides a detailed look at the ancestral, Hispanic and racial makeup of New York's 200+ ethnic categories. Data is ranked three ways: 1) by number, based on all places regardless of population; 2) by percent, based on all places regardless of population; 3) by percent, based on places with populations of 50,000 or more. You will discover, for example, that Rochester has the greatest number of *Laotians* in the state (668), and that 13.5% of the population of Harbor Hills are of *Armenian* ancestry.

7. Climate
This section includes a State Summary, colorful maps, and profiles of both National and Cooperative
Weather Stations. In addition, you'll find Weather Station Rankings with hundreds of interesting details,
such as Boonville 2 SSW reporting the highest annual snowfall with 197.5 inches.

This section also includes Significant Storm Event data from January 2000 through December 2009. Here
you will learn that a flash flood caused $250 million in property damage in Delaware County in June 2006
and that excessive heat was responsible for 42 deaths in Southeast New York state in August 2006.

Note: The extensive **User Guide** that follows **About New York** is segmented into four sections and
examines, in some detail, each data field in the individual profiles and comparative sections for all chapters.
It provides sources for all data points and statistical definitions as necessary.

User Guide

Profile Section

Places Covered

All 62 counties.

607 incorporated municipalities. Comprised of 62 cities and 545 villages.

941 Minor Civil Divisions (MCD). Comprise of 924 towns, 5 boroughs, and 12 reservations. These communities are included for states where the Census Bureau has determined that they serve as general-purpose governments. Those states are Connecticut, Maine, Massachusetts, Michigan, Minnesota, New Hampshire, New Jersey, New York, Pennsylvania, Rhode Island, Vermont, and Wisconsin. In some states incorporated municipalities are part of minor civil divisions and in some states they are independent of them.

573 Census Designated Places (CDP). The U.S. Bureau of the Census defines a CDP as "a statistical entity, defined for each decennial census according to Census Bureau guidelines, comprising a densely settled concentration of population that is not within an incorporated place, but is locally identified by a name. CDPs are delineated cooperatively by state and local officials and the Census Bureau, following Census Bureau guidelines.

444 unincorporated communities. The communities included have statistics for their ZIP Code Tabulation Area (ZCTA) available from the Census Bureau. They are referred to as "postal areas." "Postal areas" can span multiple ZCTAs. A ZCTA is a statistical entity developed by the Census Bureau to approximate the delivery area for a US Postal Service 5-digit or 3-digit ZIP Code in the US and Puerto Rico. A ZCTA is an aggregation of census blocks that have the same predominant ZIP Code associated with the mailing addresses in the Census Bureau's Master Address File. Thus, the Postal Service's delivery areas have been adjusted to encompass whole census blocks so that the Census Bureau can tabulate census data for the ZCTAs. ZCTAs do not include all ZIP Codes used for mail delivery and therefore do not precisely depict the area within which mail deliveries associated with that ZIP Code occur. Additionally, some areas that are known by a unique name, although they are part of a larger incorporated place, are also included as "postal areas."

Five communities have a mixed designation of town/village.

For a more in-depth discussion of geographic areas, please refer to the Census Bureau's Geographic Areas Reference Manual at http://www.census.gov/geo/www/garm.html.

IMPORTANT NOTES

- Since the last decennial census, the U.S. Census replaced the long-form sample with the American Community Survey (ACS), which uses a series of monthly samples to produce annually updated estimates for the same areas. ACS estimates are based on data from a sample of housing units and people in the population, not the full population. ACS sampling error (uncertainty of data) is greater for those areas with smaller populations.

- *Profiles of New York State* uses the term "community" to refer to all places except counties. The term "county" is used to refer to counties and county-equivalents. All places are defined as of the 2010 Census.

- If a community spans multiple counties, the community will be shown in the county that contains its largest population.

- Several states, including New York, have incorporated municipalities and minor civil divisions in the same county with the same name. Those communities are given separate entries (e.g. Adams, New York, in Jefferson County will be listed under both the village and town of Adams).

- The city of New York (composed of five coextensive counties/boroughs) has a unique format. Statistical information for the individual counties/boroughs can be found within the New York City entry. The five counties/boroughs are: Bronx County and Borough, Kings County and Brooklyn Borough, New York County and Manhattan Borough, Queens County and Borough, and Richmond County and Staten Island Borough.

- When a county and city are coextensive (occupying the same geographic area and sharing the same government), they are given a single entry.

- In each community profile, only school districts that have schools that are physically located within the community are shown. In addition, statistics for each school district cover the entire district, regardless of the physical location of the schools within the district.

- Special care should be taken when interpreting certain statistics for communities containing large colleges or universities. College students were counted as residents of the area in which they were living while attending college (as they have been since the 1950 census). One effect this may have is skewing the figures for population, income, housing, and educational attainment.

- Some information (e.g. income) is available for both counties and individual communities. Other information is available for just counties (e.g. election results), or just individual communities (e.g. local newspapers). Refer to the "Data Explanation and Sources" section for a complete listing.

- Some statistical information is available only for larger communities. In addition, the larger places are more apt to have services such as newspapers, airports, school districts, etc.

- For the most complete information on any community, users should also check the entry for the county in which the community is located. In addition, more information and services will be listed under the larger places in the county.

Data Explanation and Sources—County Profiles

PHYSICAL AND GEOGRAPHICAL CHARACTERISTICS

Physical Location: Describes the physical location of the county. *Source: Columbia University Press, The Columbia Gazetteer of North America and original research.*

Land and Water Area: Land and water area in square miles. *Source: U.S. Census Bureau, Census 2010*

Latitude and Longitude: Latitude and longitude in degrees. *Source: U.S. Census Bureau, Census 2010*

Time Zone: Lists the time zone. *Source: Original research*

Year Organized: Year the county government was organized. *Source: National Association of Counties*

County Seat: Lists the county seat. If a county has more than one seat, then both are listed. *Source: National Association of Counties*

Metropolitan Area: Indicates the metropolitan area the county is located in. Also lists all the component counties of that metropolitan area. The Office of Management and Budget (OMB) defines metropolitan and micropolitan statistical areas. The most current definitions are as of February 2013. *Source: U.S. Census Bureau*

Climate: Includes all weather stations located within the county. Indicates the station name and elevation as well as the monthly average high and low temperatures, average precipitation, and average snowfall. The period of record is generally 1980-2009, however, certain weather stations contain averages going back as far as 1900. *Source: Grey House Publishing, Weather America: A Thirty-Year Summary of Statistical Weather Data and Rankings, 2010*

POPULATION

Population: Current population. *Source: U.S. Census Bureau, American Community Survey, 2011-2015 Five-Year Estimates*

Population Growth: The increase or decrease in population since 2000. *Source: U.S. Census Bureau, Census 2000; U.S. Census Bureau, American Community Survey, 2011-2015 Five-Year Estimates*

Population Density: Total current population divided by the land area in square miles. *Source: U.S. Census Bureau, Census 2010; U.S. Census Bureau, American Community Survey, 2011-2015 Five-Year Estimates*

Race/Hispanic Origin: Figures include the U.S. Census Bureau categories of White alone; Black/African American alone; Asian alone; American Indian/Alaska Native alone; Native Hawaiian/Other Pacific Islander alone; two or more races; and Hispanic of any race. Alone refers to the fact that these figures are not in combination with any other race. *Source: U.S. Census Bureau, American Community Survey, 2011-2015 Five-Year Estimates*

The concept of race, as used by the Census Bureau, reflects self-identification by people according to the race or races with which they most closely identify. These categories are socio-political constructs and should not be interpreted as being scientific or anthropological in nature. Furthermore, the race categories include both racial and national-origin groups.

- **White.** A person having origins in any of the original peoples of Europe, the Middle East, or North Africa. It includes people who indicated their race(s) as "White" or reported entries such as Irish, German, Italian, Lebanese, Arab, Moroccan, or Caucasian.

- **Black/African American.** A person having origins in any of the Black racial groups of Africa. It includes people who indicated their race(s) as "Black, African Am., or Negro" or reported entries such as African American, Kenyan, Nigerian, or Haitian.

- **Asian.** A person having origins in any of the original peoples of the Far East, Southeast Asia, or the Indian subcontinent, including, for example, Cambodia, China, India, Japan, Korea, Malaysia, Pakistan, the Philippine Islands, Thailand, and Vietnam. It includes people who indicated their race(s) as "Asian" or reported entries such as "Asian Indian," "Chinese," "Filipino," "Korean," "Japanese," "Vietnamese," and "Other Asian" or provided other detailed Asian responses.

- **American Indian/Alaska Native.** A person having origins in any of the original peoples of North and South America (including Central America) and who maintains tribal affiliation or community attachment. This category includes people who indicated their race(s) as "American Indian or Alaska Native" or

reported their enrolled or principal tribe, such as Navajo, Blackfeet, Inupiat, Yup'ik, or Central American Indian groups or South American Indian groups.

- **Native Hawaiian/Other Pacific Islander.** A person having origins in any of the original peoples of Hawaii, Guam, Samoa, or other Pacific Islands. It includes people who indicated their race(s) as "Pacific Islander" or reported entries such as "Native Hawaiian," "Guamanian or Chamorro," "Samoan," and "Other Pacific Islander" or provided other detailed Pacific Islander responses..

- **Two or More Races.** People may choose to provide two or more races either by checking two or more race response check boxes, by providing multiple responses, or by some combination of check boxes and other responses. The race response categories shown on the questionnaire are collapsed into the five minimum race groups identified by OMB, and the Census Bureau's "Some Other Race" category.

- **Hispanic.** The data on the Hispanic or Latino population were derived from answers to a question that was asked of all people. The terms "Spanish," "Hispanic origin," and "Latino" are used interchangeably. Some respondents identify with all three terms while others may identify with only one of these three specific terms. Hispanics or Latinos who identify with the terms "Spanish," "Hispanic," or "Latino" are those who classify themselves in one of the specific Spanish, Hispanic, or Latino categories listed on the questionnaire ("Mexican," "Puerto Rican," or "Cuban") as well as those who indicate that they are "other Spanish/Hispanic/Latino." People who do not identify with one of the specific origins listed on the questionnaire but indicate that they are "other Spanish/Hispanic/Latino" are those whose origins are from Spain, the Spanish-speaking countries of Central or South America, the Dominican Republic, or people identifying themselves generally as Spanish, Spanish-American, Hispanic, Hispano, Latino, and so on. All write-in responses to the "other Spanish/Hispanic/Latino" category were coded. Origin can be viewed as the heritage, nationality group, lineage, or country of birth of the person or the person's parents or ancestors before their arrival in the United States. People who identify their origin as Spanish, Hispanic, or Latino may be of any race.

Average Household Size: Number of persons in the average household. *Source: U.S. Census Bureau, American Community Survey, 2011-2015 Five-Year Estimates*

Median Age: Median age of the population. *Source: U.S. Census Bureau, American Community Survey, 2011-2015 Five-Year Estimates*

Age Under 18: Percent of the total population under 18 years old. *Source: U.S. Census Bureau, American Community Survey, 2011-2015 Five-Year Estimates*

Age 65 and Over: Percent of the total population age 65 and over. *Source: U.S. Census Bureau, American Community Survey, 2011-2015 Five-Year Estimates*

Males per 100 Females: Number of males per 100 females. *Source: U.S. Census Bureau, American Community Survey, 2011-2015 Five-Year Estimates*

Marital Status: Percentage of population never married, now married, separated, widowed, or divorced. *Source: U.S. Census Bureau, American Community Survey, 2011-2015 Five-Year Estimates*

The marital status classification refers to the status at the time of enumeration. Data on marital status are tabulated only for the population 15 years old and over. Each person was asked whether they were "Now married," "Widowed," "Separated," "Divorced," or "Never married." Couples who live together (for example, people in common-law marriages) were able to report the marital status they considered to be the most appropriate.

- **Never married.** Never married includes all people who have never been married, including people whose only marriage(s) was annulled.
- **Now married.** All people whose current marriage has not ended by widowhood or divorce. This category includes people defined as "separated."
- **Separated.** Includes people legally separated or otherwise absent from their spouse because of marital discord. Those without a final divorce decree are classified as "separated." This category also includes people who have been deserted or who have parted because they no longer want to live together, but who have not obtained a divorce.
- **Widowed**. This category includes widows and widowers who have not remarried.
- **Divorced.** This category includes people who are legally divorced and who have not remarried.

Foreign Born: Percentage of population who were not U.S. citizens at birth. Foreign-born people are those who indicated they were either a U.S. citizen by naturalization or they were not a citizen of the United States. *Source: U.S. Census Bureau, American Community Survey, 2011-2015 Five-Year Estimates*

Speak English Only: Percent of population that reported speaking only English at home. *Source: U.S. Census Bureau, American Community Survey, 2011-2015 Five-Year Estimates*

With Disability: Percent of the civilian noninstitutionalized population that reported having a disability. Disability status is determined from from six types of difficulty: vision, hearing, cognitive, ambulatory, self-care, and independent living. For children under 5 years old, hearing and vision difficulty are used to determine disability status. For children between the ages of 5 and 14, disability status is determined from hearing, vision, cognitive, ambulatory, and self-care difficulties. For people aged 15 years and older, they are considered to have a disability if they have difficulty with any one of the six difficulty types. *Source: U.S. Census Bureau, American Community Survey, 2011-2015 Five-Year Estimates*

Veterans: Percent of the civilian population 18 years and over who have served (even for a short time), but are not currently serving, on active duty in the U.S. Army, Navy, Air Force, Marine Corps, or the Coast Guard, or who served in the U.S. Merchant Marine during World War II. People who served in the National Guard or Reserves are classified as veterans only if they were ever called or ordered to active duty, not counting the 4-6 months for initial training or yearly summer camps. All other civilians are classified as nonveterans. Note: While it is possible for 17 year olds to be veterans of the Armed Forces, ACS data products are restricted to the population 18 years and older. *Source: U.S. Census Bureau, American Community Survey, 2011-2015 Five-Year Estimates*

Ancestry: Largest ancestry groups reported (up to five). The data includes persons who report multiple ancestries. For example, if a person reported being Irish and Italian, they would be included in both categories. Thus, the sum of the percentages may be greater than 100%. *Source: U.S. Census Bureau, American Community Survey, 2011-2015 Five-Year Estimates*

The data represent self-classification by people according to the ancestry group or groups with which they most closely identify. Ancestry refers to a person's ethnic origin or descent, "roots," heritage, or the place of birth of the person, the person's parents, or their ancestors before their arrival in the United States. Some ethnic identities, such as Egyptian or Polish, can be traced to geographic areas outside the United States, while other ethnicities such as Pennsylvania German or Cajun evolved in the United States.

The ancestry question was intended to provide data for groups that were not included in the Hispanic origin and race questions. Therefore, although data on all groups are collected, the ancestry data shown in these tabulations are for non-Hispanic and non-race groups. *See* Race/Hispanic Origin for information on Hispanic and race groups.

RELIGION

Religion: Lists the largest religious groups (up to six) based on the number of adherents divided by the population of the county. Adherents are defined as "all members, including full members, their children and the estimated number of other regular participants who are not considered as communicant, confirmed or full members." *Source: American Religious Bodies, 2010 U.S. Religion Census: Religious Congregations & Membership Study*

ECONOMY

Unemployment Rate: Unemployment rate as of October 2016. Includes all civilians age 16 or over who were unemployed and looking for work. *Source: U.S. Department of Labor, Bureau of Labor Statistics, Local Area Unemployment Statistics*

Leading Industries: Lists the three leading industries (excluding government) based on the number of establishments. *Source: U.S. Census Bureau, County Business Patterns 2014*

Farms: The total number of farms and the total acreage they occupy. *Source: U.S. Department of Agriculture, National Agricultural Statistics Service, 2012 Census of Agriculture*

Company Size: The numbers of companies at various employee headcounts. Includes private employers only. *Source: U.S. Census Bureau, County Business Patterns 2014*

- **Employ 1,000 or more persons.** The numbers of companies that employ 1,000 or more persons.
- **Employ 500-999 persons.** The numbers of companies that employ 500 to 999 persons.

- **Employ 100-499 persons.** The numbers of companies that employ 100 to 499 persons.
- **Employ 1-99 persons.** The numbers of companies that employ 1 to 99 persons.

Business Ownership: Number of businesses that are majority-owned by women or various minority groups. *Source: U.S. Census Bureau, 2012 Economic Census, Survey of Business Owners*

- **Women-Owned.** Number of businesses that are majority-owned by a woman. Majority ownership is defined as having 51 percent or more of the stock or equity in the business.
- **Black-Owned.** Number of businesses that are majority-owned by a Black or African American person(s). Majority ownership is defined as having 51 percent or more of the stock or equity in the business. Black or African American is defined as a person having origins in any of the black racial groups of Africa, including those who consider themselves to be "Haitian."
- **Asian-Owned.** Number of businesses that are majority-owned by an Asian person(s). Majority ownership is defined as having 51 percent or more of the stock or equity in the business.
- **American Indian/Alaska Native-Owned.** Number of businesses that are majority-owned by an American Indian or Alaska Native person(s). Majority ownership is defined as having 51 percent or more of the stock or equity in the business.
- **Hispanic-Owned.** Number of businesses that are majority-owned by a person(s) of Hispanic or Latino origin. Majority ownership is defined as having 51 percent or more of the stock or equity in the business. Hispanic or Latino origin is defined as a person of Cuban, Mexican, Puerto Rican, South or Central American, or other Spanish culture or origin, regardless of race.

EMPLOYMENT

Employment by Occupation: Percentage of the employed civilian population 16 years and over in management, professional, service, sales, farming, construction, and production occupations. *Source: U.S. Census Bureau, American Community Survey, 2011-2015 Five-Year Estimates*

- Management, business, and financial occupations include:
  Management occupations
  Business and financial operations occupations

- Computer, engineering, and science occupations include:
  Computer and mathematical occupations
  Architecture and engineering occupations
  Life, physical, and social science occupations

- Education, legal, community service, arts, and media occupations include:
  Community and social service occupations
  Legal occupations
  Education, training, and library occupations
  Arts, design, entertainment, sports, and media occupations

- Healthcare practitioners and technical occupations include:
  Health diagnosing and treating practitioners and other technical occupations
  Health technologists and technicians

- Service occupations include:
  Healthcare support occupations
  Protective service occupations:
      Fire fighting and prevention, and other protective service workers including supervisors
      Law enforcement workers including supervisors
  Food preparation and serving related occupations
  Building and grounds cleaning and maintenance occupations
  Personal care and service occupations

- Sales and office occupations include:
  Sales and related occupations
  Office and administrative support occupations

- Natural resources, construction, and maintenance occupations include:
  Farming, fishing, and forestry occupations
  Construction and extraction occupations
  Installation, maintenance, and repair occupations

- Production, transportation, and material moving occupations include:
  Production occupations
  Transportation occupations
  Material moving occupations

INCOME

Per Capita Income: Per capita income is the mean income computed for every man, woman, and child in a particular group. It is derived by dividing the total income of a particular group by the total population in that group. Per capita income is rounded to the nearest whole dollar. *Source: U.S. Census Bureau, American Community Survey, 2011-2015 Five-Year Estimates*

Median Household Income: Includes the income of the householder and all other individuals 15 years old and over in the household, whether they are related to the householder or not. The median divides the income distribution into two equal parts: one-half of the cases falling below the median income and one-half above the median. For households, the median income is based on the distribution of the total number of households including those with no income. Median income for households is computed on the basis of a standard distribution and is rounded to the nearest whole dollar. *Source: U.S. Census Bureau, American Community Survey, 2011-2015 Five-Year Estimates*

Average Household Income: Average household income is obtained by dividing total household income by the total number of households. *Source: U.S. Census Bureau, American Community Survey, 2011-2015 Five-Year Estimates*

Percent of Households with Income of $100,000 or more: Percent of households with income of $100,000 or more. *Source: U.S. Census Bureau, American Community Survey, 2011-2015 Five-Year Estimates*

Poverty Rate: Percentage of population with income below the poverty level. Based on individuals for whom poverty status is determined. Poverty status was determined for all people except institutionalized people, people in military group quarters, people in college dormitories, and unrelated individuals under 15 years old. *Source: U.S. Census Bureau, American Community Survey, 2011-2015 Five-Year Estimates*

EDUCATIONAL ATTAINMENT

Figures show the percent of population age 25 and over with the following levels of educational attainment. *Source: U.S. Census Bureau, American Community Survey, 2011-2015 Five-Year Estimates*

- **High school diploma or higher.** Includes people whose highest degree is a high school diploma or its equivalent (GED), people who attended college but did not receive a degree, and people who received a college, university, or professional degree.
- **Bachelor's degree or higher.** Includes people who received a bachelor's, master's, doctorate, or professional degree.
- **Graduate/professional degree or higher.** Includes people who received a master's, doctorate, or professional degree.

HOUSING

Homeownership Rate: Percentage of housing units that are owner-occupied. *Source: U.S. Census Bureau, American Community Survey, 2011-2015 Five-Year Estimates*

Median Home Value: Median value in dollars of all owner-occupied housing units as reported by the owner. *Source: U.S. Census Bureau, American Community Survey, 2011-2015 Five-Year Estimates*

Median Year Structure Built: Year structure built refers to when the building was first constructed, not when it was remodeled, added to, or converted. For mobile homes, houseboats, RVs, etc, the manufacturer's model year was assumed to be the year built. The data relate to the number of units built during the specified periods that were still in existence at the time of enumeration. *Source: U.S. Census Bureau, American Community Survey, 2011-2015 Five-Year Estimates*

Homeowner Vacancy Rate: Proportion of the homeowner inventory that is vacant "for sale." It is computed by dividing the number of vacant units "for sale only" by the sum of the owner-occupied units, vacant units that are "for sale only," and vacant units that have been sold but not yet occupied, and then multiplying by 100. This measure is rounded to the nearest tenth. *Source: U.S. Census Bureau, American Community Survey, 2011-2015 Five-Year Estimates*

Median Selected Monthly Owner Costs: Selected monthly owner costs are the sum of payments for mortgages, deeds of trust, contracts to purchase, or similar debts on the property (including payments for the first mortgage, second mortgages, home equity loans, and other junior mortgages); real estate taxes; fire, hazard, and flood insurance on the property; utilities (electricity, gas, and water and sewer); and fuels (oil, coal, kerosene, wood, etc.). It also includes, where appropriate, the monthly condominium fee for condominiums and mobile home costs (personal property taxes, site rent, registration fees, and license fees). Selected monthly owner costs were tabulated for all owner-occupied units, and are shown separately for units "with a mortgage" and for units "not mortgaged." *Source: U.S. Census Bureau, American Community Survey, 2011-2015 Five-Year Estimates*

Median Gross Rent: Median monthly gross rent in dollars on specified renter-occupied and specified vacant-for-rent units. Specified renter-occupied and specified vacant-for-rent units exclude 1-family houses on 10 acres or more. Gross rent is the contract rent plus the estimated average monthly cost of utilities (electricity, gas, and water and sewer) and fuels (oil, coal, kerosene, wood, etc.) if these are paid by the renter (or paid for the renter by someone else). Gross rent is intended to eliminate differentials that result from varying practices with respect to the inclusion of utilities and fuels as part of the rental payment. Contract rent is the monthly rent agreed to or contracted for, regardless of any furnishings, utilities, fees, meals, or services that may be included. For vacant units, it is the monthly rent asked for the rental unit at the time of enumeration. *Source: U.S. Census Bureau, American Community Survey, 2011-2015 Five-Year Estimates*

Rental Vacancy Rate: Proportion of the rental inventory that is vacant "for rent." It is computed by dividing the number of vacant units "for rent" by the sum of the renter-occupied units, vacant units that are "for rent," and vacant units that have been rented but not yet occupied, and then multiplying by 100. This measure is rounded to the nearest tenth. *Source: U.S. Census Bureau, American Community Survey, 2011-2015 Five-Year Estimates*

VITAL STATISTICS

Birth Rate: Estimated number of births per 10,000 population in 2015. *Source: U.S. Census Bureau, Annual Components of Population Change, July 1, 2010 - July 1, 2015*

Death Rate: Estimated number of deaths per 10,000 population in 2015. *Source: U.S. Census Bureau, Annual Components of Population Change, July 1, 2010 - July 1, 2015*

Age-adjusted Cancer Mortality Rate: Number of age-adjusted deaths from cancer per 100,000 population in 2015. Cancer is defined as International Classification of Disease (ICD) codes C00–D48.9 Neoplasms. *Source: Centers for Disease Control, CDC Wonder, 2015*

Age-adjusted death rates are weighted averages of the age-specific death rates, where the weights represent a fixed population by age. They are used because the rates of almost all causes of death vary by age. Age adjustment is a technique for "removing" the effects of age from crude rates, so as to allow meaningful comparisons across populations with different underlying age structures. For example, comparing the crude rate of heart disease in Virginia to that of California is misleading, because the relatively older population in Virginia will lead to a higher crude death rate, even if the age-specific rates of heart disease in Virginia and California are the same. For such a comparison, age-adjusted rates would be preferable. Age-adjusted rates should be viewed as relative indexes rather than as direct or actual measures of mortality risk.

Death rates based on counts of twenty or less (≤ 20) are flagged as "Unreliable". Death rates based on fewer than three years of data for counties with populations of less than 100,000 in the 2000 Census counts, are also flagged as "Unreliable" if the number of deaths is five or less (≤ 5).

HEALTH INSURANCE

Health insurance coverage in the ACS and other Census Bureau surveys define coverage to include plans and programs that provide comprehensive health coverage. Plans that provide insurance for specific conditions or situations such as cancer and long-term care policies are not considered coverage. Likewise, other types of insurance like dental, vision, life, and disability insurance are not considered health insurance coverage.

For reporting purposes, the Census Bureau broadly classifies health insurance coverage as private health insurance or public coverage. Private health insurance is a plan provided through an employer or union, a plan purchased by an individual from a private company, or TRICARE or other military health care. Public health coverage includes the federal programs Medicare, Medicaid, and VA Health Care (provided through the Department of Veterans Affairs); the Children's Health Insurance Program (CHIP); and individual state health plans. The types of health insurance are not mutually exclusive; people may be covered by more than one at the same time. People who had no reported health coverage, or those whose only health coverage was Indian Health Service, were considered uninsured. *Source: U.S. Census Bureau, American Community Survey, 2011-2015 Five-Year Estimates*

- **Have Insurance:** Percent of the civilian noninstitutionalized population with any type of comprehensive health insurance.

- **Have Private Insurance.** Percent of the civilian noninstitutionalized population with private health insurance. A person may report that they have both public and private health insurance, thus, the sum of the percentages may be greater than 100%.

- **Have Public Insurance.** Percent of the civilian noninstitutionalized population with public health insurance. A person may report that they have both public and private health insurance, thus, the sum of the percentages may be greater than 100%.

- **Do Not Have Insurance.** Percent of the civilian noninstitutionalized population with no health insurance.

- **Children Under 18 With No Insurance.** Percent of the civilian noninstitutionalized population under age 18 with no health insurance.

HEALTH CARE

Number of physicians, hospital beds and hospital admission per 10,000 population. *Source: Area Resource File (ARF) 2015-2016. U.S. Department of Health and Human Services, Health Resources and Services Administration, Bureau of Health Professions, Rockville, MD.*

- **Number of Physicians.** The number of active, non-federal physicians (MDs and DOs) per 10,000 population in 2014.

- **Number of Dentists.** The number of dentists per 10,000 population in 2015.

- **Number of Hospital Beds.** The number of hospital beds per 10,000 population in 2013.

- **Number of Hospital Admissions.** The number of hospital admissions per 10,000 population in 2013.

AIR QUALITY INDEX

The percentage of days in 2015 the AQI fell into the Good (0-50), Moderate (51-100), Unhealthy for Sensitive Groups (101-150), Unhealthy (151-200), Very Unhealthy (201-300), and Hazardous (300+) ranges. If a range does not appear, its value is zero. Data is preliminary and covers January 2015 through December 2015. *Source: AirData: Access to Air Pollution Data, U.S. Environmental Protection Agency, Office of Air and Radiation*

The AQI is an index for reporting daily air quality. It tells you how clean or polluted your air is, and what associated health concerns you should be aware of. The AQI focuses on health effects that can happen within a few hours or days after breathing polluted air. EPA uses the AQI for five major air pollutants regulated by the Clean Air Act: ground-level ozone, particulate matter, carbon monoxide, sulfur dioxide, and nitrogen dioxide. For each of these pollutants, EPA has established national air quality standards to protect against harmful health effects.

The AQI runs from 0 to 500. The higher the AQI value, the greater the level of air pollution and the greater the health danger. For example, an AQI value of 50 represents good air quality and little potential to affect public health, while an AQI value over 300 represents hazardous air quality. An AQI value of 100 generally corresponds to the national air quality standard for the pollutant, which is the level EPA has set to protect public health. So, AQI values below 100 are generally thought of as satisfactory. When AQI values are above 100, air quality is considered to be unhealthy—at first for certain sensitive groups of people, then for everyone as AQI values get higher. Each category corresponds to a different level of health concern. For example, when the AQI for a pollutant is between 51 and 100, the health concern is "Moderate." Here are the six levels of health concern and what they mean:

- "Good" The AQI value for your community is between 0 and 50. Air quality is considered satisfactory and air pollution poses little or no risk.

- "Moderate" The AQI for your community is between 51 and 100. Air quality is acceptable; however, for some pollutants there may be a moderate health concern for a very small number of individuals. For example, people who are unusually sensitive to ozone may experience respiratory symptoms.

- "Unhealthy for Sensitive Groups" Certain groups of people are particularly sensitive to the harmful effects of certain air pollutants. This means they are likely to be affected at lower levels than the general public. For example, children and adults who are active outdoors and people with respiratory disease are at greater risk from exposure to ozone, while people with heart disease are at greater risk from carbon monoxide. Some people may be sensitive to more than one pollutant. When AQI values are between 101 and 150, members of sensitive groups may experience health effects. The general public is not likely to be affected when the AQI is in this range.
- "Unhealthy" AQI values are between 151 and 200. Everyone may begin to experience health effects. Members of sensitive groups may experience more serious health effects.
- "Very Unhealthy" AQI values between 201 and 300 trigger a health alert, meaning everyone may experience more serious health effects.
- "Hazardous" AQI values over 300 trigger health warnings of emergency conditions. The entire population is more likely to be affected.

TRANSPORTATION

Commute to Work: Percentage of workers 16 years old and over that use the following means of transportation to commute to work: car; public transportation; walk; work from home. The means of transportation data for some areas may show workers using modes of public transportation that are not available in those areas (e.g. subway or elevated riders in a metropolitan area where there actually is no subway or elevated service). This result is largely due to people who worked during the reference week at a location that was different from their usual place of work (such as people away from home on business in an area where subway service was available) and people who used more than one means of transportation each day but whose principal means was unavailable where they lived (e.g. residents of non-metropolitan areas who drove to the fringe of a metropolitan area and took the commuter railroad most of the distance to work). *Source: U.S. Census Bureau, American Community Survey, 2011-2015 Five-Year Estimates*

Mean Travel Time to Work: Mean travel time to work for workers 16 years old and over. Travel time to work refers to the total number of minutes that it usually took the person to get from home to work each day during the reference week. The elapsed time includes time spent waiting for public transportation, picking up passengers in carpools, and time spent in other activities related to getting to work. *Source: U.S. Census Bureau, American Community Survey, 2011-2015 Five-Year Estimates*

PRESIDENTIAL ELECTION

2016 Presidential election results. *Source: Dave Leip's Atlas of U.S. Presidential Elections*

NATIONAL AND STATE PARKS

Lists National/State parks located in the area. *Source: U.S. Geological Survey, Geographic Names Information System*

ADDITIONAL INFORMATION CONTACTS

General telephone number and website address (if available) of local government.

Data Explanation and Sources—Community Profiles

PHYSICAL AND GEOGRAPHICAL CHARACTERISTICS

Place Type: Lists the type of place (city, town, village, borough, Census-Designated Place (CDP), township, charter township, plantation, gore, district, grant, location, purchase, municipality, reservation, unorganized territory, or unincorporated postal area). *Source: U.S. Census Bureau, American Community Survey, 2011-2015 Five-Year Estimates and U.S. Postal Service, City State File*

ZCTA: *This only appears within unincorporated postal areas.* The statistics that follow cover the corresponding ZIP Code Tabulation Area (ZCTA). A ZCTA is a statistical entity developed by the Census Bureau to approximate the delivery area for a US Postal Service 5-digit or 3-digit ZIP Code in the US and Puerto Rico. A ZCTA is an aggregation of census blocks that have the same predominant ZIP Code associated with the mailing addresses in the Census Bureau's Master Address File. Thus, the Postal Service's delivery areas have been adjusted to encompass whole census blocks so that the Census Bureau can tabulate census data for the ZCTAs. ZCTAs do not include all ZIP Codes used for mail delivery and therefore do not precisely depict the area within which mail deliveries associated with that ZIP Code occur. Additionally, some areas that are known by a unique name, although they are part of a larger incorporated place, are also included as "postal areas."

Land and Water Area: Land and water area in square miles. *Source: U.S. Census Bureau, Census 2010*

Latitude and Longitude: Latitude and longitude in degrees. *Source: U.S. Census Bureau, Census 2010*

Elevation: Elevation in feet. *Source: U.S. Geological Survey, Geographic Names Information System (GNIS)*

HISTORY

Historical information. *Source: Columbia University Press, The Columbia Gazetteer of North America; Original research*

POPULATION

Population: Current population. *Source: U.S. Census Bureau, American Community Survey, 2011-2015 Five-Year Estimates*

Population Growth: The increase or decrease in population since 2000. *Source: U.S. Census Bureau, Census 2000; U.S. Census Bureau, American Community Survey, 2011-2015 Five-Year Estimates*

Population Density: Total current population divided by the land area in square miles. *Source: U.S. Census Bureau, Census 2010; U.S. Census Bureau, American Community Survey, 2011-2015 Five-Year Estimates*

Race/Hispanic Origin: Figures include the U.S. Census Bureau categories of White alone; Black/African American alone; Asian alone; American Indian/Alaska Native alone; Native Hawaiian/Other Pacific Islander alone; two or more races; and Hispanic of any race. Alone refers to the fact that these figures are not in combination with any other race. *Source: U.S. Census Bureau, American Community Survey, 2011-2015 Five-Year Estimates*

The concept of race, as used by the Census Bureau, reflects self-identification by people according to the race or races with which they most closely identify. These categories are socio-political constructs and should not be interpreted as being scientific or anthropological in nature. Furthermore, the race categories include both racial and national-origin groups.

- **White.** A person having origins in any of the original peoples of Europe, the Middle East, or North Africa. It includes people who indicated their race(s) as "White" or reported entries such as Irish, German, Italian, Lebanese, Arab, Moroccan, or Caucasian.
- **Black/African American.** A person having origins in any of the Black racial groups of Africa. It includes people who indicated their race(s) as "Black, African Am., or Negro" or reported entries such as African American, Kenyan, Nigerian, or Haitian.
- **Asian.** A person having origins in any of the original peoples of the Far East, Southeast Asia, or the Indian subcontinent, including, for example, Cambodia, China, India, Japan, Korea, Malaysia, Pakistan, the Philippine Islands, Thailand, and Vietnam. It includes people who indicated their race(s) as "Asian" or reported entries such as "Asian Indian," "Chinese," "Filipino," "Korean," "Japanese," "Vietnamese," and "Other Asian" or provided other detailed Asian responses.

- **American Indian/Alaska Native.** A person having origins in any of the original peoples of North and South America (including Central America) and who maintains tribal affiliation or community attachment. This category includes people who indicated their race(s) as "American Indian or Alaska Native" or reported their enrolled or principal tribe, such as Navajo, Blackfeet, Inupiat, Yup'ik, or Central American Indian groups or South American Indian groups.

- **Native Hawaiian/Other Pacific Islander.** A person having origins in any of the original peoples of Hawaii, Guam, Samoa, or other Pacific Islands. It includes people who indicated their race(s) as "Pacific Islander" or reported entries such as "Native Hawaiian," "Guamanian or Chamorro," "Samoan," and "Other Pacific Islander" or provided other detailed Pacific Islander responses..

- **Two or More Races.** People may choose to provide two or more races either by checking two or more race response check boxes, by providing multiple responses, or by some combination of check boxes and other responses. The race response categories shown on the questionnaire are collapsed into the five minimum race groups identified by OMB, and the Census Bureau's "Some Other Race" category.

- **Hispanic.** The data on the Hispanic or Latino population were derived from answers to a question that was asked of all people. The terms "Spanish," "Hispanic origin," and "Latino" are used interchangeably. Some respondents identify with all three terms while others may identify with only one of these three specific terms. Hispanics or Latinos who identify with the terms "Spanish," "Hispanic," or "Latino" are those who classify themselves in one of the specific Spanish, Hispanic, or Latino categories listed on the questionnaire ("Mexican," "Puerto Rican," or "Cuban") as well as those who indicate that they are "other Spanish/Hispanic/Latino." People who do not identify with one of the specific origins listed on the questionnaire but indicate that they are "other Spanish/Hispanic/Latino" are those whose origins are from Spain, the Spanish-speaking countries of Central or South America, the Dominican Republic, or people identifying themselves generally as Spanish, Spanish-American, Hispanic, Hispano, Latino, and so on. All write-in responses to the "other Spanish/Hispanic/Latino" category were coded. Origin can be viewed as the heritage, nationality group, lineage, or country of birth of the person or the person's parents or ancestors before their arrival in the United States. People who identify their origin as Spanish, Hispanic, or Latino may be of any race.

Average Household Size: Number of persons in the average household. *Source: U.S. Census Bureau, American Community Survey, 2011-2015 Five-Year Estimates*

Median Age: Median age of the population. *Source: U.S. Census Bureau, American Community Survey, 2011-2015 Five-Year Estimates*

Age Under 18: Percent of the total population under 18 years old. *Source: U.S. Census Bureau, American Community Survey, 2011-2015 Five-Year Estimates*

Age 65 and Over: Percent of the total population age 65 and over. *Source: U.S. Census Bureau, American Community Survey, 2011-2015 Five-Year Estimates*

Males per 100 Females: Number of males per 100 females. *Source: U.S. Census Bureau, American Community Survey, 2011-2015 Five-Year Estimates*

Marital Status: Percentage of population never married, now married, separated, widowed, or divorced. *Source: U.S. Census Bureau, American Community Survey, 2011-2015 Five-Year Estimates*

The marital status classification refers to the status at the time of enumeration. Data on marital status are tabulated only for the population 15 years old and over. Each person was asked whether they were "Now married," "Widowed," "Separated," "Divorced," or "Never married." Couples who live together (for example, people in common-law marriages) were able to report the marital status they considered to be the most appropriate.

- **Never married.** Never married includes all people who have never been married, including people whose only marriage(s) was annulled.

- **Now married.** All people whose current marriage has not ended by widowhood or divorce. This category includes people defined as "separated."

- **Separated.** Includes people legally separated or otherwise absent from their spouse because of marital discord. Those without a final divorce decree are classified as "separated." This category also includes people who have been deserted or who have parted because they no longer want to live together, but who have not obtained a divorce.

- **Widowed**. This category includes widows and widowers who have not remarried.

- **Divorced.** This category includes people who are legally divorced and who have not remarried.

Foreign Born: Percentage of population who were not U.S. citizens at birth. Foreign-born people are those who indicated they were either a U.S. citizen by naturalization or they were not a citizen of the United States. *Source: U.S. Census Bureau, American Community Survey, 2011-2015 Five-Year Estimates*

Speak English Only: Percent of population that reported speaking only English at home. *Source: U.S. Census Bureau, American Community Survey, 2011-2015 Five-Year Estimates*

With Disability: Percent of the civilian noninstitutionalized population that reported having a disability. Disability status is determined from from six types of difficulty: vision, hearing, cognitive, ambulatory, self-care, and independent living. For children under 5 years old, hearing and vision difficulty are used to determine disability status. For children between the ages of 5 and 14, disability status is determined from hearing, vision, cognitive, ambulatory, and self-care difficulties. For people aged 15 years and older, they are considered to have a disability if they have difficulty with any one of the six difficulty types. *Source: U.S. Census Bureau, American Community Survey, 2011-2015 Five-Year Estimates*

Veterans: Percent of the civilian population 18 years and over who have served (even for a short time), but are not currently serving, on active duty in the U.S. Army, Navy, Air Force, Marine Corps, or the Coast Guard, or who served in the U.S. Merchant Marine during World War II. People who served in the National Guard or Reserves are classified as veterans only if they were ever called or ordered to active duty, not counting the 4-6 months for initial training or yearly summer camps. All other civilians are classified as nonveterans. Note: While it is possible for 17 year olds to be veterans of the Armed Forces, ACS data products are restricted to the population 18 years and older. *Source: U.S. Census Bureau, American Community Survey, 2011-2015 Five-Year Estimates*

Ancestry: Largest ancestry groups reported (up to five). The data includes persons who report multiple ancestries. For example, if a person reported being Irish and Italian, they would be included in both categories. Thus, the sum of the percentages may be greater than 100%. *Source: U.S. Census Bureau, American Community Survey, 2011-2015 Five-Year Estimates*

The data represent self-classification by people according to the ancestry group or groups with which they most closely identify. Ancestry refers to a person's ethnic origin or descent, "roots," heritage, or the place of birth of the person, the person's parents, or their ancestors before their arrival in the United States. Some ethnic identities, such as Egyptian or Polish, can be traced to geographic areas outside the United States, while other ethnicities such as Pennsylvania German or Cajun evolved in the United States.

The ancestry question was intended to provide data for groups that were not included in the Hispanic origin and race questions. Therefore, although data on all groups are collected, the ancestry data shown in these tabulations are for non-Hispanic and non-race groups. *See* Race/Hispanic Origin for information on Hispanic and race groups.

EMPLOYMENT

Employment by Occupation: Percentage of the employed civilian population 16 years and over in management, professional, service, sales, farming, construction, and production occupations. *Source: U.S. Census Bureau, American Community Survey, 2011-2015 Five-Year Estimates*

- Management, business, and financial occupations include:
    - Management occupations
    - Business and financial operations occupations

- Computer, engineering, and science occupations include:
    - Computer and mathematical occupations
    - Architecture and engineering occupations
    - Life, physical, and social science occupations

- Education, legal, community service, arts, and media occupations include:
    - Community and social service occupations
    - Legal occupations
    - Education, training, and library occupations
    - Arts, design, entertainment, sports, and media occupations

- Healthcare practitioners and technical occupations include:
    - Health diagnosing and treating practitioners and other technical occupations
    - Health technologists and technicians

- Service occupations include:
    Healthcare support occupations
    Protective service occupations:
        Fire fighting and prevention, and other protective service workers including supervisors
        Law enforcement workers including supervisors
    Food preparation and serving related occupations
    Building and grounds cleaning and maintenance occupations
    Personal care and service occupations

- Sales and office occupations include:
    Sales and related occupations
    Office and administrative support occupations

- Natural resources, construction, and maintenance occupations include:
    Farming, fishing, and forestry occupations
    Construction and extraction occupations
    Installation, maintenance, and repair occupations

- Production, transportation, and material moving occupations include:
    Production occupations
    Transportation occupations
    Material moving occupations

INCOME

Per Capita Income: Per capita income is the mean income computed for every man, woman, and child in a particular group. It is derived by dividing the total income of a particular group by the total population in that group. Per capita income is rounded to the nearest whole dollar. *Source: U.S. Census Bureau, American Community Survey, 2011-2015 Five-Year Estimates*

Median Household Income: Includes the income of the householder and all other individuals 15 years old and over in the household, whether they are related to the householder or not. The median divides the income distribution into two equal parts: one-half of the cases falling below the median income and one-half above the median. For households, the median income is based on the distribution of the total number of households including those with no income. Median income for households is computed on the basis of a standard distribution and is rounded to the nearest whole dollar. *Source: U.S. Census Bureau, American Community Survey, 2011-2015 Five-Year Estimates*

Average Household Income: Average household income is obtained by dividing total household income by the total number of households. *Source: U.S. Census Bureau, American Community Survey, 2011-2015 Five-Year Estimates*

Percent of Households with Income of $100,000 or more: Percent of households with income of $100,000 or more. *Source: U.S. Census Bureau, American Community Survey, 2011-2015 Five-Year Estimates*

Poverty Rate: Percentage of population with income below the poverty level. Based on individuals for whom poverty status is determined. Poverty status was determined for all people except institutionalized people, people in military group quarters, people in college dormitories, and unrelated individuals under 15 years old. *Source: U.S. Census Bureau, American Community Survey, 2011-2015 Five-Year Estimates*

EDUCATIONAL ATTAINMENT

Figures show the percent of population age 25 and over with the following levels of educational attainment. *Source: U.S. Census Bureau, American Community Survey, 2011-2015 Five-Year Estimates*

- **High school diploma or higher.** Includes people whose highest degree is a high school diploma or its equivalent (GED), people who attended college but did not receive a degree, and people who received a college, university, or professional degree.
- **Bachelor's degree or higher.** Includes people who received a bachelor's, master's, doctorate, or professional degree.
- **Graduate/professional degree or higher.** Includes people who received a master's, doctorate, or professional degree.

SCHOOL DISTRICTS

Lists the name of each school district, the grade range (PK=pre-kindergarten; KG=kindergarten), the student enrollment, and the district headquarters' phone number. In each community profile, only school districts that have schools that are physically located within the community are shown. In addition, statistics for each school district cover the entire district, regardless of the physical location of the schools within the district. *Source: U.S. Department of Education, National Center for Educational Statistics, Directory of Public Elementary and Secondary Education Agencies, 2014-15*

COLLEGES

Four-year Colleges: Lists the name of each four-year college, the type of institution (private or public; for-profit or non-profit; religious affiliation; historically black), the total estimated student enrollment in 2014, the general telephone number, and the annual tuition and fees for full-time, first-time undergraduate students (in-state and out-of-state). *Source: U.S. Department of Education, National Center for Educational Statistics, IPEDS College Data, 2015-16*

Two-year Colleges: Lists the name of each two-year college, the type of institution (private or public; for-profit or non-profit; religious affiliation; historically black), the total estimated student enrollment in 2014, the general telephone number, and the annual tuition and fees for full-time, first-time undergraduate students (in-state and out-of-state). *Source: U.S. Department of Education, National Center for Educational Statistics, IPEDS College Data, 2015-16*

Vocational/Technical Schools: Lists the name of each vocational/technical school, the type of institution (private or public; for-profit or non-profit; religious affiliation; historically black), the total estimated student enrollment in 2014, the general telephone number, and the annual tuition and fees for full-time students. *Source: U.S. Department of Education, National Center for Educational Statistics, IPEDS College Data, 2015-16*

HOUSING

Homeownership Rate: Percentage of housing units that are owner-occupied. *Source: U.S. Census Bureau, American Community Survey, 2011-2015 Five-Year Estimates*

Median Home Value: Median value in dollars of all owner-occupied housing units as reported by the owner. *Source: U.S. Census Bureau, American Community Survey, 2011-2015 Five-Year Estimates*

Median Year Structure Built: Year structure built refers to when the building was first constructed, not when it was remodeled, added to, or converted. For mobile homes, houseboats, RVs, etc, the manufacturer's model year was assumed to be the year built. The data relate to the number of units built during the specified periods that were still in existence at the time of enumeration. *Source: U.S. Census Bureau, American Community Survey, 2011-2015 Five-Year Estimates*

Homeowner Vacancy Rate: Proportion of the homeowner inventory that is vacant "for sale." It is computed by dividing the number of vacant units "for sale only" by the sum of the owner-occupied units, vacant units that are "for sale only," and vacant units that have been sold but not yet occupied, and then multiplying by 100. This measure is rounded to the nearest tenth. *Source: U.S. Census Bureau, American Community Survey, 2011-2015 Five-Year Estimates*

Median Selected Monthly Owner Costs: Selected monthly owner costs are the sum of payments for mortgages, deeds of trust, contracts to purchase, or similar debts on the property (including payments for the first mortgage, second mortgages, home equity loans, and other junior mortgages); real estate taxes; fire, hazard, and flood insurance on the property; utilities (electricity, gas, and water and sewer); and fuels (oil, coal, kerosene, wood, etc.). It also includes, where appropriate, the monthly condominium fee for condominiums and mobile home costs (personal property taxes, site rent, registration fees, and license fees). Selected monthly owner costs were tabulated for all owner-occupied units, and are shown separately for units "with a mortgage" and for units "not mortgaged." *Source: U.S. Census Bureau, American Community Survey, 2011-2015 Five-Year Estimates*

Median Gross Rent: Median monthly gross rent in dollars on specified renter-occupied and specified vacant-for-rent units. Specified renter-occupied and specified vacant-for-rent units exclude 1-family houses on 10 acres or more. Gross rent is the contract rent plus the estimated average monthly cost of utilities (electricity, gas, and water and sewer) and fuels (oil, coal, kerosene, wood, etc.) if these are paid by the renter (or paid for the renter by someone else). Gross rent is intended to eliminate differentials that result from varying practices with respect to the inclusion of utilities and fuels as part of the rental payment. Contract rent is the monthly rent agreed to or contracted for, regardless of any furnishings, utilities, fees, meals, or services that may be included. For vacant units, it is the

monthly rent asked for the rental unit at the time of enumeration. *Source: U.S. Census Bureau, American Community Survey, 2011-2015 Five-Year Estimates*

Rental Vacancy Rate: Proportion of the rental inventory that is vacant "for rent." It is computed by dividing the number of vacant units "for rent" by the sum of the renter-occupied units, vacant units that are "for rent," and vacant units that have been rented but not yet occupied, and then multiplying by 100. This measure is rounded to the nearest tenth. *Source: U.S. Census Bureau, American Community Survey, 2011-2015 Five-Year Estimates*

HEALTH INSURANCE

Health insurance coverage in the ACS and other Census Bureau surveys define coverage to include plans and programs that provide comprehensive health coverage. Plans that provide insurance for specific conditions or situations such as cancer and long-term care policies are not considered coverage. Likewise, other types of insurance like dental, vision, life, and disability insurance are not considered health insurance coverage.

For reporting purposes, the Census Bureau broadly classifies health insurance coverage as private health insurance or public coverage. Private health insurance is a plan provided through an employer or union, a plan purchased by an individual from a private company, or TRICARE or other military health care. Public health coverage includes the federal programs Medicare, Medicaid, and VA Health Care (provided through the Department of Veterans Affairs); the Children's Health Insurance Program (CHIP); and individual state health plans. The types of health insurance are not mutually exclusive; people may be covered by more than one at the same time. People who had no reported health coverage, or those whose only health coverage was Indian Health Service, were considered uninsured. *Source: U.S. Census Bureau, American Community Survey, 2011-2015 Five-Year Estimates*

- **Have Insurance:** Percent of the civilian noninstitutionalized population with any type of comprehensive health insurance.
- **Have Private Insurance.** Percent of the civilian noninstitutionalized population with private health insurance. A person may report that they have both public and private health insurance, thus, the sum of the percentages may be greater than 100%.
- **Have Public Insurance.** Percent of the civilian noninstitutionalized population with public health insurance. A person may report that they have both public and private health insurance, thus, the sum of the percentages may be greater than 100%.
- **Do Not Have Insurance.** Percent of the civilian noninstitutionalized population with no health insurance.
- **Children Under 18 With No Insurance.** Percent of the civilian noninstitutionalized population under age 18 with no health insurance.

HOSPITALS

Lists the hospital name and the number of licensed beds. *Source: Grey House Publishing, The Comparative Guide to American Hospitals, 2014*; Original research

NEWSPAPERS

List of daily and weekly newspapers with circulation figures. *Source: Gebbie Press, 2015 All-In-One Media Directory*

SAFETY

Violent Crime Rate: Number of violent crimes reported per 10,000 population. Violent crimes include murder, forcible rape, robbery, and aggravated assault. Statistics include the revised definition of forcible rate if available. Otherwise statistics using the legacy definition are used. *Source: Federal Bureau of Investigation, Uniform Crime Reports 2015*

Property Crime Rate: Number of property crimes reported per 10,000 population. Property crimes include burglary, larceny-theft, and motor vehicle theft. *Source: Federal Bureau of Investigation, Uniform Crime Reports 2015*

TRANSPORTATION

Commute to Work: Percentage of workers 16 years old and over that use the following means of transportation to commute to work: car; public transportation; walk; work from home. The means of transportation data for some areas may show workers using modes of public transportation that are not available in those areas (e.g. subway or elevated riders in a metropolitan area where there actually is no subway or elevated service). This result is largely due to people who worked during the reference week at a location that was different from their usual place of work (such as people away from home on business in an area where subway service was available) and people who used more than one

means of transportation each day but whose principal means was unavailable where they lived (e.g. residents of non-metropolitan areas who drove to the fringe of a metropolitan area and took the commuter railroad most of the distance to work). *Source: U.S. Census Bureau, American Community Survey, 2011-2015 Five-Year Estimates*

Mean Travel Time to Work: Mean travel time to work for workers 16 years old and over. Travel time to work refers to the total number of minutes that it usually took the person to get from home to work each day during the reference week. The elapsed time includes time spent waiting for public transportation, picking up passengers in carpools, and time spent in other activities related to getting to work. *Source: U.S. Census Bureau, American Community Survey, 2011-2015 Five-Year Estimates*

Amtrak: Indicates if Amtrak rail or bus service is available. Please note that the cities being served continually change. *Source: National Railroad Passenger Corporation, Amtrak National Timetable, 2017*

AIRPORTS

Lists the local airport(s) along with type of service and hub size. *Source: U.S. Department of Transportation, Bureau of Transportation Statistics*

ADDITIONAL INFORMATION CONTACTS

General telephone number and website address (if available) of local government.

Education Section

State Public School Educational Profile

Schools: Total number of schools in the district. Figures exclude schools with the following status codes: 2 (school has closed since the time of the last report) and 6 (school is temporarily closed and may reopen within three years). *Source: U.S. Department of Education, National Center for Education Statistics, Common Core of Data, Public Elementary/Secondary School Universe Survey: School Year 2013-2014.*

Instructional Level

Primary: Low grade—prekindergarten through 3; high grade—prekindergarten through 8
Middle: Low grade—4 through 7; high grade—4 through 9
High: Low grade—7 through 12; high grade—12 only
Other/Not Reported: Any configuration not falling within the previous three, including ungraded schools

Curriculum

Regular: A regular school is defined as a public elementary/secondary school that does not focus primarily on vocational, special, or alternative education.

Special Education: A special education school is defined as a public elementary/secondary school that focuses primarily on special education, including instruction for any of the following: autism, deaf-blindness, developmental delay, hearing impairment, mental retardation, multiple disabilities, orthopedic impairment, serious emotional disturbance, specific learning disability, speech or language impairment, traumatic brain injury, visual impairment, and other health impairments. These schools adapt curriculum, materials or instruction for students served.

Vocational: A vocational educational school is defined as a public elementary/secondary school that focuses primarily on providing formal preparation for semi-skilled, skilled, technical, or professional occupations for high school-aged students who have opted to develop or expand their employment opportunities, often in lieu of preparing for college entry.

Alternative: A public elementary/secondary school that addresses needs of students which typically cannot be met in a regular school; provides nontraditional education; serves as an adjunct to a regular school; and falls outside of the categories of regular, special education, or vocational education.

Type

Magnet: A special school or program designed to attract students of different racial/ethnic backgrounds for the purpose of reducing, preventing or eliminating racial isolation (50 percent or more minority enrollment); and/or to provide an academic or social focus on a particular theme (e.g., science/math, performing arts, gifted/talented, or foreign language).

Charter: A school providing free public elementary and/or secondary education to eligible students under a specific charter granted by the state legislature or other appropriate authority, and designated by such authority to be a charter school.

Title I Eligible: A school designated under appropriate state and federal regulations as being eligible for participation in programs authorized by Title I of Public Law 103-382.

School-wide Title I: A school in which all the pupils in a school are designated under appropriate state and federal regulations as being eligible for participation in programs authorized by Title I of Public Law 103-382.

Students: A student is an individual for whom instruction is provided in an elementary or secondary education program that is not an adult education program and is under the jurisdiction of a school, school system, or other education institution. *Sources: U.S. Department of Education, National Center for Education Statistics, Common Core of Data, Local Education Agency (School District) Universe Survey: School Year 2013-2014; U.S. Department of Education, National Center for Education Statistics, Common Core of Data, Public Elementary/Secondary School Universe Survey: School Year 2013-2014*

Gender: Percentage of male and female students.

Race/Ethnicity

White: A person having origins in any of the original peoples of Europe, North Africa, or the Middle East. Figures include non-Hispanic whites only.

Black: A person having origins in any of the black racial groups of Africa. Figures include non-Hispanic blacks only.

Asian: A person having origins in any of the original peoples of the Far east, Southeast Asia, and the Indian subcontinent. This includes, for example, China, India, Japan, Korea, and the Philippines. Figures include non-Hispanic Asians only.

American Indian/Alaska Native: A person having origins in any of the original peoples of North America, and who maintains cultural identification through tribal affiliation or community recognition. Figures include non-Hispanic American Indian/Alaska Natives only.

Hawaiian Native/Pacific Islander: A person having origins in any of the original peoples of Hawaii, Guam, Samoa, or other Pacific Islands. Figures include non-Hispanic Hawaiian Native/Pacific Islanders only.

Two or More Races: A person identifying himself or herself as of two or more of the following race groups: White, Black, Asian, Native Hawaiian/Pacific Islander, or American Indian/Alaska Native. Some, but not all, reporting districts use this category. Figures include non-Hispanics, multiple-race students only.

Hispanic: A person of Mexican, Puerto Rican, Cuban, Central or South American, or other Spanish culture or origin, regardless of race.

Special Programs

Individual Education Program (IEP): A written instructional plan for students with disabilities designated as special education students under IDEA-Part B. The written instructional plan includes a statement of present levels of educational performance of a child; statement of annual goals, including short-term instructional objectives; statement of specific educational services to be provided and the extent to which the child will be able to participate in regular educational programs; the projected date for initiation and anticipated duration of services; the appropriate objectives, criteria and evaluation procedures; and the schedules for determining, on at least an annual basis, whether instructional objectives are being achieved. *Source: U.S. Department of Education, National Center for Education Statistics, Common Core of Data, Local Education Agency (School District) Universe Survey: School Year 2013-2014*

English Language Learner (ELL): Formerly referred to as Limited English Proficient (LEP). Students being served in appropriate programs of language assistance (e.g., English as a Second Language, High Intensity Language Training, bilingual education). Does not include pupils enrolled in a class to learn a language other than English. Also Limited-English-Proficient students are individuals who were not born in the United States or whose native language is a language other than English; or individuals who come from environments where a language other than English is dominant; or individuals who are American Indians and Alaskan Natives and who come from environments where a language other than English has had a significant impact on their level of English language proficiency; and who, by reason thereof, have sufficient difficulty speaking, reading, writing, or understanding the English language, to deny such individuals the opportunity to learn successfully in classrooms where the language of instruction is English or to participate fully in our society. *Source: U.S. Department of Education, National Center for Education Statistics, Common Core of Data, Local Education Agency (School District) Universe Survey: School Year 2013-2014*

Eligible for Free Lunch Program: The free lunch program is defined as a program under the National School Lunch Act that provides cash subsidies for free lunches to students based on family size and income criteria. *Source: U.S. Department of Education, National Center for Education Statistics, Common Core of Data, Public Elementary/Secondary School Universe Survey: School Year 2013-2014*

Eligible for Reduced-Price Lunch Program: A student who is eligible to participate in the Reduced-Price Lunch Program under the National School Lunch Act. *Source: U.S. Department of Education, National Center for Education Statistics, Common Core of Data, Public Elementary/Secondary School Universe Survey: School Year 2013-2014*

Adjusted Cohort Graduation Rate (ACGR): The adjusted cohort graduation rate (ACGR) is the percentage of public high school freshmen who graduate with a regular diploma within 4 years of starting 9th grade. Students who are entering 9th grade for the first time form a cohort for the graduating class. This cohort is "adjusted" by adding any

students who subsequently transfer into the cohort and subtracting any students who subsequently transfer out, emigrate to another country, or die. Race categories exclude persons of Hispanic ethnicity. *Source: U.S. Department of Education, Office of Elementary and Secondary Education, Consolidated State Performance Report, 2010-11 through 2013-14.*

Averaged Freshman Graduation Rate (AFGR): Public high school averaged freshman graduation rate (AFGR). The AFGR provides an estimate of the percentage of high school students who graduate within 4 years of first starting 9th grade. The rate uses aggregate student enrollment data to estimate the size of an incoming freshman class and aggregate counts of diplomas awarded 4 years later. *Source: U.S. Department of Education, National Center for Education Statistics, Common Core of Data (CCD), "NCES Common Core of Data State Dropout and Graduation Rate Data file," School Year 2011–12, Preliminary Version 1a.*

Caution in interpreting the AFGR. Although the AFGR was selected as the best of the available alternatives, several factors make it fall short of a true on-time graduation rate. First, the AFGR does not take into account any imbalances in the number of students moving in and out of the nation or individual states over the high school years. As a result, the averaged freshman class is at best an approximation of the actual number of freshmen, where differences in the rates of transfers, retention, and dropping out in the three grades affect the average. Second, by including all graduates in a specific year, the graduates may include students who repeated a grade in high school or completed high school early and thus are not on-time graduates in that year.

Difference between ACGR and AFGR. Both rates measure the percentage of public school students who attain a regular high school diploma within 4 years of starting 9th grade for the first time. However, they differ in important ways. The AFGR is an estimate of the on-time 4-year graduation rate derived from aggregate student enrollment data and graduate counts. The ACGR, on the other hand, uses detailed student-level data to determine the percentage of students who graduate within 4 years of starting 9th grade for the first time. In many states, the data required to produce the ACGR have become available only in recent years. The AFGR estimate is less precise than the ACGR, but it can be estimated as far back as the 1960s.

Event Dropout Rate: The public high school event dropout rate indicates the proportion of students who were enrolled at some time during the school year and were expected to be enrolled in grades 9–12 in the following school year but were not enrolled by October 1 of the following school year. Students who have graduated, transferred to another school, died, moved to another country, or who are out of school due to illness are not considered dropouts. The event dropout rate is not comparable to other dropout rates released by the Department or elsewhere. Status dropout rates, for example, measure the percentage of a population that did not complete high school (e.g., some percentage of young adults aged 18–24 dropped out of high school). *Source: U.S. Department of Education, National Center for Education Statistics, Common Core of Data (CCD), "NCES Common Core of Data State Dropout and Graduation Rate Data file," School Year 2011–12, Preliminary Version 1a.*

Staff

Teachers: Teachers are defined as individuals who provide instruction to pre-kindergarten, kindergarten, grades 1 through 12, or ungraded classes, or individuals who teach in an environment other than a classroom setting, and who maintain daily student attendance records. Numbers reported are full-time equivalents (FTE). The students per teacher ratio is shown in parentheses. *Source: U.S. Department of Education, National Center for Education Statistics, Common Core of Data, Local Education Agency (School District) Universe Survey: School Year 2013-2014.*

Teacher Salary: The average classroom teacher salary in 2015-2016. *Source: National Education Association, Rankings & Estimates: Rankings of the States 2015 and Estimates of School Statistics 2016*

Librarians/Media Specialists: Library and media support staff are defined as staff members who render other professional library and media services; also includes library aides and those involved in library/media support. Their duties include selecting, preparing, caring for, and making available to instructional staff, equipment, films, filmstrips, transparencies, tapes, TV programs, and similar materials maintained separately or as part of an instructional materials center. Also included are activities in the audio-visual center, TV studio, related-work-study areas, and services provided by audio-visual personnel. Numbers reported are full-time equivalents (FTE). The students per librarian/media specialist ratio is shown in parentheses. *Source: U.S. Department of Education, National Center for Education Statistics, Common Core of Data, Local Education Agency (School District) Universe Survey: School Year 2013-2014.*

Guidance Counselors: Professional staff assigned specific duties and school time for any of the following activities in an elementary or secondary setting: counseling with students and parents; consulting with other staff members on learning problems; evaluating student abilities; assisting students in making educational and career choices; assisting students in personal and social development; providing referral assistance; and/or working with

other staff members in planning and conducting guidance programs for students. The state applies its own standards in apportioning the aggregate of guidance counselors/directors into the elementary and secondary level components. Numbers reported are full-time equivalents (FTE). The students per guidance counselor ratio is shown in parentheses. *Source: U.S. Department of Education, National Center for Education Statistics, Common Core of Data, Local Education Agency (School District) Universe Survey: School Year 2013-2014.*

Ratios

Number of Students per Teacher: The number of students divided by the number of teachers (FTE). See Number of Students and Number of Teachers above for more information. *Source: U.S. Department of Education, National Center for Education Statistics, Common Core of Data, Local Education Agency (School District) Universe Survey: School Year 2013-2014.*

Number of Students per Librarian: The number of students divided by the number of library and media support staff. Library and media support staff are defined as staff members who render other professional library and media services; also includes library aides and those involved in library/media support. Their duties include selecting, preparing, caring for, and making available to instructional staff, equipment, films, filmstrips, transparencies, tapes, TV programs, and similar materials maintained separately or as part of an instructional materials center. Also included are activities in the audio-visual center, TV studio, related-work-study areas, and services provided by audio-visual personnel. Numbers are based on full-time equivalents. *Source: U.S. Department of Education, National Center for Education Statistics, Common Core of Data, Local Education Agency (School District) Universe Survey: School Year 2013-2014.*

Number of Students per Counselor: The number of students divided by the number of guidance counselors. Guidance counselors are professional staff assigned specific duties and school time for any of the following activities in an elementary or secondary setting: counseling with students and parents; consulting with other staff members on learning problems; evaluating student abilities; assisting students in making educational and career choices; assisting students in personal and social development; providing referral assistance; and/or working with other staff members in planning and conducting guidance programs for students. The state applies its own standards in apportioning the aggregate of guidance counselors/directors into the elementary and secondary level components. Numbers reported are full-time equivalents. *Source: U.S. Department of Education, National Center for Education Statistics, Common Core of Data, Local Education Agency (School District) Universe Survey: School Year 2013-2014.*

Finances

Note: all financial figures are per student and are calculated by dividing the dollar amount by the fall membership.
Source: U.S. Department of Education, National Center for Education Statistics, Common Core of Data (CCD), National Public Education Financial Survey (State Fiscal), 2012-13 (FY 2013) v.1a

Total Expenditures per Pupil: This is the total expenditures divided by the fall membership as reported in the state finance file. The total expenditures is the subtotal of direct state support expenditures for private schools, debt services expenditures—interest and total expenditures for education.

Total Current Expenditures per Pupil: This is the total current expenditures for public elementary and secondary education divided by the fall membership as reported in the state finance file. The expenditures for equipment, non-public education, school construction, debt financing and community services are excluded from this data item.

Instruction Expenditures per Pupil: This is the total of instructional expenditures divided by the fall membership as reported in the state finance file. Instruction expenditures are for services and materials directly related to classroom instruction and the interaction between teachers and students. Teacher salaries and benefits, textbooks, classroom supplies and extra curricular activities are included in Instruction. Expenditures for the library and in-service teacher training are reported as instruction support services. Guidance counselors and nurses are reported under student support services.

Support Services Expenditures per Pupil: This is the total of support services expenditures divided by the fall membership as reported in the state finance file.

Non-Instruction Expenditures per Pupil: This is the total for food services operations expenditures and enterprise operations expenditures divided by the fall membership as reported in the state finance file. This does not include property or community services expenditures.

Net Current Expenditures per Attendance for Title I: Net current expenditures per average daily attendance (ADA) are calculated by NCES. Net current expenditures are calculated by NCES and are equal to current expenditures minus total exclusions. Computation of ADA is defined by state laws or regulations or by NCES. Net current expenditures per ADA (or state per public expenditures—SPPE) are used to calculate allocations for certain federal education programs, including Title I, impact aid, Indian education and individuals with disabilities.

Total Revenues per Pupil: Total revenues per student are the total revenues from all sources divided by the fall membership as reported in the state finance file.

Federal Revenues per Pupil: Federal revenues per student are federal revenues divided by the fall membership as reported in the state finance file.

State Revenues per Pupil: State revenues per student are revenues received by the LEAs from the state, divided by the fall membership as reported in the state finance file.

Local Revenues per Pupil: Local revenues per student are the total of all local revenue categories divided by the fall membership as reported in the state finance file. Local revenues are raised and allocated by local governments.

Intermediate Revenue per Pupil: Intermediate revenue per pupil are intermediate sources of revenue divided by the student membership as reported on the state finance file. Intermediate sources of revenue are from educational agencies that possess independent fund-raising capabilities and that operate between the state and local government levels.

College Entrance Exam Scores

Scholastic Aptitude Test (SAT). Number of test takers and mean scores for 2015. *Source: The College Board, SAT, 2015 College-Bound Seniors, State Profile Reports*

American College Testing Program (ACT). Participation rate and mean scores for 2015. *Source: ACT, Inc., 2015 ACT National and State Scores*

Note: n/a indicates data not available.

School District Rankings

Number of Schools: Total number of schools in the district. *Source: U.S. Department of Education, National Center for Education Statistics, Common Core of Data, Public Elementary/Secondary School Universe Survey: School Year 2013-2014.*

Number of Teachers: Teachers are defined as individuals who provide instruction to pre-kindergarten, kindergarten, grades 1 through 12, or ungraded classes, or individuals who teach in an environment other than a classroom setting, and who maintain daily student attendance records. Numbers reported are full-time equivalents (FTE). *Source: U.S. Department of Education, National Center for Education Statistics, Common Core of Data, Local Education Agency (School District) Universe Survey: School Year 2013-2014.*

Number of Students: A student is an individual for whom instruction is provided in an elementary or secondary education program that is not an adult education program and is under the jurisdiction of a school, school system, or other education institution. *Source: U.S. Department of Education, National Center for Education Statistics, Common Core of Data, Local Education Agency (School District) Universe Survey: School Year 2013-2014*

Male Students: Percentage of students who are male. *Source: U.S. Department of Education, National Center for Education Statistics, Common Core of Data, Local Education Agency (School District) Universe Survey: School Year 2013-2014*

Female Students: Percentage of students who are female. *Source: U.S. Department of Education, National Center for Education Statistics, Common Core of Data, Local Education Agency (School District) Universe Survey: School Year 2013-2014*

White Students: Percentage of students who are white (a person having origins in any of the original peoples of Europe, North Africa, or the Middle East). Figures include non-Hispanic whites only. *Source: U.S. Department of Education, National Center for Education Statistics, Common Core of Data, Local Education Agency (School District) Universe Survey: School Year 2013-2014*

Black Students: Percentage of students who are black (a person having origins in any of the black racial groups of Africa). Figures include non-Hispanic blacks only. *Source: U.S. Department of Education, National Center for Education Statistics, Common Core of Data, Local Education Agency (School District) Universe Survey: School Year 2013-2014*

Asian Students: Percentage of students who are Asian (a person having origins in any of the original peoples of the Far east, Southeast Asia, and the Indian subcontinent. This includes, for example, China, India, Japan, Korea, and the Philippines). Figures include non-Hispanic Asians only. *Source: U.S. Department of Education, National Center for Education Statistics, Common Core of Data, Local Education Agency (School District) Universe Survey: School Year 2013-2014*

American Indian/Alaska Native Students: Percentage of students who are American Indian/Alaska Native Students (a person having origins in any of the original peoples of North America, and who maintains cultural identification through tribal affiliation or community recognition). Figures include non-Hispanic American Indian/Alaska Natives only. *Source: U.S. Department of Education, National Center for Education Statistics, Common Core of Data, Local Education Agency (School District) Universe Survey: School Year 2013-2014*

Hawaiian Native/Pacific Islander Students: Percentage of students who are Hawaiian Native/Pacific Islander (a person having origins in any of the original peoples of Hawaii, Guam, Samoa, or other Pacific Islands). Figures include non-Hispanic Hawaiian Native/Pacific Islanders only. *Source: U.S. Department of Education, National Center for Education Statistics, Common Core of Data, Local Education Agency (School District) Universe Survey: School Year 2013-2014*

Students who are Two or More Races: Percentage of students who are two or more races (a person identifying himself or herself as of two or more of the following race groups: White, Black, Asian, Native Hawaiian/Pacific Islander, or American Indian/Alaska Native). Some, but not all, reporting districts use this category. Figures include non-Hispanic, multiple-race students only. *Source: U.S. Department of Education, National Center for Education Statistics, Common Core of Data, Local Education Agency (School District) Universe Survey: School Year 2013-2014*

Hispanic Students: Percentage of students who are Hispanic (a person of Mexican, Puerto Rican, Cuban, Central or South American, or other Spanish culture or origin, regardless of race). *Source: U.S. Department of Education, National Center for Education Statistics, Common Core of Data, Local Education Agency (School District) Universe Survey: School Year 2013-2014*

Individual Education Program (IEP) Students: Percentage of students who have an Individual Education Program (IEP) which is a written instructional plan for students with disabilities designated as special education students under IDEA-Part B. The written instructional plan includes a statement of present levels of educational performance of a child; statement of annual goals, including short-term instructional objectives; statement of specific educational services to be provided and the extent to which the child will be able to participate in regular educational programs; the projected date for initiation and anticipated duration of services; the appropriate objectives, criteria and evaluation procedures; and the schedules for determining, on at least an annual basis, whether instructional objectives are being achieved. *Source: U.S. Department of Education, National Center for Education Statistics, Common Core of Data, Local Education Agency (School District) Universe Survey: School Year 2013-2014*

English Language Learner (ELL) Students: Percentage of students who are English Language Learners (ELL). Formerly referred to as Limited English Proficient (LEP). Students being served in appropriate programs of language assistance (e.g., English as a Second Language, High Intensity Language Training, bilingual education). Does not include pupils enrolled in a class to learn a language other than English. Also Limited-English-Proficient students are individuals who were not born in the United States or whose native language is a language other than English; or individuals who come from environments where a language other than English is dominant; or individuals who are American Indians and Alaskan Natives and who come from environments where a language other than English has had a significant impact on their level of English language proficiency; and who, by reason thereof, have sufficient difficulty speaking, reading, writing, or understanding the English language, to deny such individuals the opportunity to learn successfully in classrooms where the language of instruction is English or to participate fully in our society. *Source: U.S. Department of Education, National Center for Education Statistics, Common Core of Data, Local Education Agency (School District) Universe Survey: School Year 2013-2014*

Students Eligible for Free Lunch Program: Percentage of students that are eligible for the free lunch program. The free lunch program is defined as a program under the National School Lunch Act that provides cash subsidies for free lunches to students based on family size and income criteria. *Source: U.S. Department of Education, National Center for Education Statistics, Common Core of Data, Public Elementary/Secondary School Universe Survey: School Year 2013-2014*

Students Eligible for Reduced-Price Lunch Program: Percentage of students that are eligible for the reduced-price lunch program. A student who is eligible to participate in the reduced-price lunch program under the National School Lunch Act. *Source: U.S. Department of Education, National Center for Education Statistics, Common Core of Data, Public Elementary/Secondary School Universe Survey: School Year 2013-2014*

Student/Teacher Ratio: The number of students divided by the number of teachers (FTE). See Number of Students and Number of Teachers above for for information. *Source: U.S. Department of Education, National Center for Education Statistics, Common Core of Data, Local Education Agency (School District) Universe Survey: School Year 2013-2014*

Student/Librarian Ratio: The number of students divided by the number of library and media support staff. Library and media support staff are defined as staff members who render other professional library and media services; also includes library aides and those involved in library/media support. Their duties include selecting, preparing, caring for, and making available to instructional staff, equipment, films, filmstrips, transparencies, tapes, TV programs, and similar materials maintained separately or as part of an instructional materials center. Also included are activities in the audio-visual center, TV studio, related-work-study areas, and services provided by audio-visual personnel. Numbers are based on full-time equivalents. *Source: U.S. Department of Education, National Center for Education Statistics, Common Core of Data, Local Education Agency (School District) Universe Survey: School Year 2013-2014.*

Student/Counselor Ratio: The number of students divided by the number of guidance counselors. Guidance counselors are professional staff assigned specific duties and school time for any of the following activities in an elementary or secondary setting: counseling with students and parents; consulting with other staff members on learning problems; evaluating student abilities; assisting students in making educational and career choices; assisting students in personal and social development; providing referral assistance; and/or working with other staff members in planning and conducting guidance programs for students. The state applies its own standards in apportioning the aggregate of guidance counselors/directors into the elementary and secondary level components. Numbers reported are full-time equivalents. *Source: U.S. Department of Education, National Center for Education Statistics, Common Core of Data, Local Education Agency (School District) Universe Survey: School Year 2013-2014.*

Current Spending per Student: Expenditure for Instruction, Support Services, and Other Elementary/Secondary Programs. Includes salaries, employee benefits, purchased services, and supplies, as well as payments made by states on behalf of school districts. Also includes transfers made by school districts into their own retirement system. Excludes expenditure for Non-Elementary/Secondary Programs, debt service, capital outlay, and transfers to other governments or school districts. This item is formally called "Current Expenditures for Public Elementary/Secondary Education."

Values shown are dollars per pupil per year. They were calculated by dividing the total dollar amounts by the fall membership. Fall membership is comprised of the total student enrollment on October 1 (or the closest school day to October 1) for all grade levels (including prekindergarten and kindergarten) and ungraded pupils. Membership includes students both present and absent on the measurement day. *Source: U.S. Department of Education, National Center for Education Statistics, Common Core of Data, School District Finance Survey (F-33), Fiscal Year 2013.*

Total General Revenue per Student: The sum of revenue contributions emerging from local, state, and federal sources as reported in the district finance file.

Values shown are dollars per pupil per year. They were calculated by dividing the total dollar amounts by the fall membership. Fall membership is comprised of the total student enrollment on October 1 (or the closest school day to October 1) for all grade levels (including prekindergarten and kindergarten) and ungraded pupils. Membership includes students both present and absent on the measurement day. *Source: U.S. Department of Education, National Center for Education Statistics, Common Core of Data, School District Finance Survey (F-33), Fiscal Year 2013.*

Long-Term Debt per Student (end of FY): Includes long-term credit obligations of the school system or its parent government and all interest-bearing short-term (repayable within 1 year) credit obligations. Excludes non-interest bearing short-term obligations, interfund obligations, amounts owed in a trust agency capacity, advances and contingent loans from other governments, and rights of individuals to benefits from school system employee retirement funds.

Values shown are dollars per pupil per year. They were calculated by dividing the total dollar amounts at the end of the fiscal year by the fall membership. Fall membership is comprised of the total student enrollment on October 1 (or the closest school day to October 1) for all grade levels (including prekindergarten and kindergarten) and ungraded pupils. Membership includes students both present and absent on the measurement day. *Source: U.S. Department of Education, National Center for Education Statistics, Common Core of Data, School District Finance Survey (F-33), Fiscal Year 2013.*

Note: n/a indicates data not available.

National Assessment of Educational Progress (NAEP)

The National Assessment of Educational Progress (NAEP), also known as "The Nation's Report Card," is the only nationally representative and continuing assessment of what America's students know and can do in various subject areas. As a result of the "No Child Left Behind" legislation, all states are required to participate in NAEP.

For more information, visit the U.S. Department of Education, National Center for Education Statistics at http://nces.ed.gov/nationsreportcard.

Ancestry and Ethnicity Section

Places Covered

The ancestry and ethnicity profile section of this book covers the state and all counties and places with populations of 50,000 or more. Places included fall into one of the following categories:

Incorporated Places. Depending on the state, places are incorporated as either cities, towns, villages, boroughs, municipalities, independent cities, or corporations. A few municipalities have a form of government combined with another entity (e.g. county) and are listed as special cities or consolidated, unified, or metropolitan governments.

Census Designated Places (CDP). The U.S. Census Bureau defines a CDP as "a statistical entity," defined for each decennial census according to Census Bureau guidelines, comprising a densely settled concentration of population that is not within an incorporated place, but is locally identified by a name. CDPs are delineated cooperatively by state and local officials and the Census Bureau, following Census Bureau guidelines.

Minor Civil Divisions (called charter townships, districts, gores, grants, locations, plantations, purchases, reservations, towns, townships, and unorganized territories) for the states where the Census Bureau has determined that they serve as general-purpose governments. Those states are Connecticut, Maine, Massachusetts, Michigan, Minnesota, New Hampshire, New Jersey, New York, Pennsylvania, Rhode Island, Vermont, and Wisconsin. In some states incorporated municipalities are part of minor civil divisions and in some states they are independent of them.

Note: Several states have incorporated municipalities and minor civil divisions in the same county with the same name. Those communities are given separate entries (e.g. Burlington, New Jersey, in Burlington County will be listed under both the city and township of Burlington). A few states have Census Designated Places and minor civil divisions in the same county with the same name. Those communities are given separate entries (e.g. Bridgewater, Massachusetts, in Plymouth County will be listed under both the CDP and town of Bridgewater).

Source of Data

The ethnicities shown in this book were compiled from two different sources. Data for Race and Hispanic Origin was taken from Census 2010 Summary File 1 (SF1) while Ancestry data was taken from the American Community Survey (ACS) 2006-2010 Five-Year Estimate. The distinction is important because SF1 contains 100-percent data, which is the information compiled from the questions asked of all people and about every housing unit. ACS estimates are compiled from a sampling of households. The 2006-2010 Five-Year Estimate is based on data collected from January 1, 2006 to December 31, 2010.

The American Community Survey (ACS) is a relatively new survey conducted by the U.S. Census Bureau. It uses a series of monthly samples to produce annually updated data for the same small areas (census tracts and block groups) formerly surveyed via the decennial census long-form sample. While some version of this survey has been in the field since 1999, it was not fully implemented in terms of coverage until 2006. In 2005 it was expanded to cover all counties in the country and the 1-in-40 households sampling rate was first applied. The full implementation of the (household) sampling strategy for ACS entails having the survey mailed to about 250,000 households nationwide every month of every year and was begun in January 2005. In January 2006 sampling of group quarters was added to complete the sample as planned. In any given year about 2.5% (1 in 40) of U.S. households will receive the survey. Over any 5-year period about 1 in 8 households should receive the survey (as compared to about 1 in 6 that received the census long form in the 2000 census). Since receiving the survey is not the same as responding to it, the Bureau has adopted a strategy of sampling for non-response, resulting in something closer to 1 in 11 households actually participating in the survey over any 5-year period. For more information about the American Community Survey visit http://www.census.gov/acs/www.

Ancestry

Ancestry refers to a person's ethnic origin, heritage, descent, or "roots," which may reflect their place of birth or that of previous generations of their family. Some ethnic identities, such as "Egyptian" or "Polish" can be traced to geographic areas outside the United States, while other ethnicities such as "Pennsylvania German" or "Cajun" evolved in the United States.

The intent of the ancestry question in the ACS was not to measure the degree of attachment the respondent had to a particular ethnicity, but simply to establish that the respondent had a connection to and self-identified with a particular

ethnic group. For example, a response of "Irish" might reflect total involvement in an Irish community or only a memory of ancestors several generations removed from the respondent.

The Census Bureau coded the responses into a numeric representation of over 1,000 categories. Responses initially were processed through an automated coding system; then, those that were not automatically assigned a code were coded by individuals trained in coding ancestry responses. The code list reflects the results of the Census Bureau's own research and consultations with many ethnic experts. Many decisions were made to determine the classification of responses. These decisions affected the grouping of the tabulated data. For example, the "Indonesian" category includes the responses of "Indonesian," "Celebesian," "Moluccan," and a number of other responses.

Ancestries Covered

Afghan	Palestinian	French, ex. Basque	Scottish
African, Sub-Saharan	Syrian	French Canadian	Serbian
African	Other Arab	German	Slavic
Cape Verdean	Armenian	German Russian	Slovak
Ethiopian	Assyrian/Chaldean/Syriac	Greek	Slovene
Ghanaian	Australian	Guyanese	Soviet Union
Kenyan	Austrian	Hungarian	Swedish
Liberian	Basque	Icelander	Swiss
Nigerian	Belgian	Iranian	Turkish
Senegalese	Brazilian	Irish	Ukrainian
Sierra Leonean	British	Israeli	Welsh
Somalian	Bulgarian	Italian	West Indian, ex.
South African	Cajun	Latvian	Hispanic
Sudanese	Canadian	Lithuanian	Bahamian
Ugandan	Carpatho Rusyn	Luxemburger	Barbadian
Zimbabwean	Celtic	Macedonian	Belizean
Other Sub-Saharan African	Croatian	Maltese	Bermudan
Albanian	Cypriot	New Zealander	British West Indian
Alsatian	Czech	Northern European	Dutch West Indian
American	Czechoslovakian	Norwegian	Haitian
Arab	Danish	Pennsylvania German	Jamaican
Arab	Dutch	Polish	Trinidadian/
Egyptian	Eastern European	Portuguese	Tobagonian
Iraqi	English	Romanian	U.S. Virgin Islander
Jordanian	Estonian	Russian	West Indian
Lebanese	European	Scandinavian	Other West Indian
Moroccan	Finnish	Scotch-Irish	Yugoslavian

The ancestry question allowed respondents to report one or more ancestry groups. Generally, only the first two responses reported were coded. If a response was in terms of a dual ancestry, for example, "Irish English," the person was assigned two codes, in this case one for Irish and another for English. However, in certain cases, multiple responses such as "French Canadian," "Scotch-Irish," "Greek Cypriot," and "Black Dutch" were assigned a single code reflecting their status as unique groups. If a person reported one of these unique groups in addition to another group, for example, "Scotch-Irish English," resulting in three terms, that person received one code for the unique group (Scotch-Irish) and another one for the remaining group (English). If a person reported "English Irish French," only English and Irish were coded. If there were more than two ancestries listed and one of the ancestries was a part of another, such as "German Bavarian Hawaiian," the responses were coded using the more detailed groups (Bavarian and Hawaiian).

The Census Bureau accepted "American" as a unique ethnicity if it was given alone or with one other ancestry. There were some groups such as "American Indian," "Mexican American," and "African American" that were coded and identified separately.

The ancestry question is asked for every person in the American Community Survey, regardless of age, place of birth, Hispanic origin, or race.

Although some people consider religious affiliation a component of ethnic identity, the ancestry question was not designed to collect any information concerning religion. Thus, if a religion was given as an answer to the ancestry question, it was listed in the "Other groups" category which is not shown in this book.

Ancestry should not be confused with a person's place of birth, although a person's place of birth and ancestry may be the same.

Hispanic Origin

The data on the Hispanic or Latino population were derived from answers to a Census 2010 question that was asked of all people. The terms "Spanish," "Hispanic origin," and "Latino" are used interchangeably. Some respondents identify with all three terms while others may identify with only one of these three specific terms. Hispanics or Latinos who identify with the terms "Spanish," "Hispanic," or "Latino" are those who classify themselves in one of the specific Spanish, Hispanic, or Latino categories listed on the questionnaire ("Mexican," "Puerto Rican," or "Cuban") as well as those who indicate that they are "other Spanish/Hispanic/Latino." People who do not identify with one of the specific origins listed on the questionnaire but indicate that they are "other Spanish/Hispanic/Latino" are those whose origins are from Spain, the Spanish-speaking countries of Central or South America, the Dominican Republic, or people identifying themselves generally as Spanish, Spanish-American, Hispanic, Hispano, Latino, and so on. All write-in responses to the "other Spanish/Hispanic/Latino" category were coded.

Hispanic Origins Covered

Hispanic or Latino	Salvadoran	Argentinean	Uruguayan
Central American, ex. Mexican	Other Central American	Bolivian	Venezuelan
Costa Rican	Cuban	Chilean	Other South American
Guatemalan	Dominican Republic	Colombian	Other Hispanic or Latino
Honduran	Mexican	Ecuadorian	
Nicaraguan	Puerto Rican	Paraguayan	
Panamanian	South American	Peruvian	

Origin can be viewed as the heritage, nationality group, lineage, or country of birth of the person or the person's parents or ancestors before their arrival in the United States. People who identify their origin as Hispanic, Latino, or Spanish may be of any race.

Ethnicities Based on Race

The data on race were derived from answers to the Census 2010 question on race that was asked of individuals in the United States. The Census Bureau collects racial data in accordance with guidelines provided by the U.S. Office of Management and Budget (OMB), and these data are based on self-identification.

The racial categories included in the census questionnaire generally reflect a social definition of race recognized in this country and not an attempt to define race biologically, anthropologically, or genetically. In addition, it is recognized that the categories of the race item include racial and national origin or sociocultural groups. People may choose to report more than one race to indicate their racial mixture, such as "American Indian" and "White." People who identify their origin as Hispanic, Latino, or Spanish may be of any race.

Racial Groups Covered

African-American/Black	Crow	Spanish American Indian	Korean
Not Hispanic	Delaware	Tlingit-Haida *(Alaska Native)*	Laotian
Hispanic	Hopi	Tohono O'Odham	Malaysian
American Indian/Alaska Native	Houma	Tsimshian *(Alaska Native)*	Nepalese
Not Hispanic	Inupiat *(Alaska Native)*	Ute	Pakistani
Hispanic	Iroquois	Yakama	Sri Lankan
Alaska Athabascan *(Ala. Nat.)*	Kiowa	Yaqui	Taiwanese
Aleut *(Alaska Native)*	Lumbee	Yuman	Thai
Apache	Menominee	Yup'ik *(Alaska Native)*	Vietnamese
Arapaho	Mexican American Indian	**Asian**	**Hawaii Native/Pacific Islander**
Blackfeet	Navajo	*Not Hispanic*	*Not Hispanic*
Canadian/French Am. Indian	Osage	*Hispanic*	*Hispanic*
Central American Indian	Ottawa	Bangladeshi	Fijian
Cherokee	Paiute	Bhutanese	Guamanian/Chamorro
Cheyenne	Pima	Burmese	Marshallese
Chickasaw	Potawatomi	Cambodian	Native Hawaiian
Chippewa	Pueblo	Chinese, ex. Taiwanese	Samoan
Choctaw	Puget Sound Salish	Filipino	Tongan
Colville	Seminole	Hmong	**White**
Comanche	Shoshone	Indian	*Not Hispanic*
Cree	Sioux	Indonesian	*Hispanic*
Creek	South American Indian	Japanese	

African American or Black: A person having origins in any of the Black racial groups of Africa. It includes people who indicated their race(s) as "Black, African Am., or Negro" or reported entries such as African American, Kenyan, Nigerian, or Haitian.

American Indian or Alaska Native: A person having origins in any of the original peoples of North and South America (including Central America) and who maintains tribal affiliation or community attachment. This category includes people who indicated their race(s) as "American Indian or Alaska Native" or reported their enrolled or principal tribe, such as Navajo, Blackfeet, Inupiat, Yup'ik, or Central American Indian groups or South American Indian groups.

Asian: A person having origins in any of the original peoples of the Far East, Southeast Asia, or the Indian subcontinent, including, for example, Cambodia, China, India, Japan, Korea, Malaysia, Pakistan, the Philippine Islands, Thailand, and Vietnam. It includes people who indicated their race(s) as "Asian" or reported entries such as "Asian Indian," "Chinese," "Filipino," "Korean," "Japanese," "Vietnamese," and "Other Asian" or provided other detailed Asian responses.

Native Hawaiian or Other Pacific Islander: A person having origins in any of the original peoples of Hawaii, Guam, Samoa, or other Pacific Islands. It includes people who indicated their race(s) as "Pacific Islander" or reported entries such as "Native Hawaiian," "Guamanian or Chamorro," "Samoan," and "Other Pacific Islander" or provided other detailed Pacific Islander responses.

White: A person having origins in any of the original peoples of Europe, the Middle East, or North Africa. It includes people who indicated their race(s) as "White" or reported entries such as Irish, German, Italian, Lebanese, Arab, Moroccan, or Caucasian.

Profiles

Each profile shows the name of the place, the county (if a place spans more than one county, the county that holds the majority of the population is shown), and the 2010 population (based on 100-percent data from Census 2010 Summary File 1). The rest of each profile is comprised of all 218 ethnicities grouped into three sections: ancestry; Hispanic origin; and race.

Column one displays the ancestry/Hispanic origin/race name, column two displays the number of people reporting each ancestry/Hispanic origin/race, and column three is the percent of the total population reporting each ancestry/Hispanic origin/race. The population figure shown is used to calculate the value in the "%" column for ethnicities based on race and Hispanic origin. The 2006-2010 estimated population figure from the American Community Survey (not shown) is used to calculate the value in the "%" column for all other ancestries.

For ethnicities in the ancestries group, the value in the "Number" column includes multiple ancestries reported. For example, if a person reported a multiple ancestry such as "French Danish," that response was counted twice in the tabulations, once in the French category and again in the Danish category. Thus, the sum of the counts is not the total population but the total of all responses. Numbers in parentheses indicate the number of people reporting a single ancestry. People reporting a single ancestry includes all people who reported only one ethnic group such as "German." Also included in this category are people with only a multiple-term response such as "Scotch-Irish" who are assigned a single code because they represent one distinct group. For example, the count for German would be interpreted as "The number of people who reported that German was their only ancestry."

For ethnicities based on Hispanic origin, the value in the "Number" column represents the number of people who reported being Mexican, Puerto Rican, Cuban or other Spanish/Hispanic/ Latino (all written-in responses were coded). All ethnicities based on Hispanic origin can be of any race.

For ethnicities based on race data the value in the "Number" column represents the total number of people who reported each category alone or in combination with one or more other race categories. This number represents the maximum number of people reporting and therefore the individual race categories may add up to more than the total population because people may be included in more than one category. The figures in parentheses show the number of people that reported that particular ethnicity alone, not in combination with any other race. For example, in Alabama, the entry for Korean shows 8,320 in parentheses and 10,624 in the "Number" column. This means that 8,320 people reported being Korean alone and 10,624 people reported being Korean alone or in combination with one or more other races.

Rankings

In the rankings section, each ethnicity has three tables. The first table shows the top 10 places sorted by ethnic population (based on all places, regardless of total population), the second table shows the top 10 places sorted by percent of the total population (based on all places, regardless of total population), the third table shows the top 10 places sorted by percent of the total population (based on places with total population of 50,000 or more).

Within each table, column one displays the place name, the state, and the county (if a place spans more than one county, the county that holds the majority of the population is shown). Column one in the first table displays the state only. Column two displays the number of people reporting each ancestry (includes people reporting multiple ancestries), Hispanic origin, or race (alone or in combination with any other race). Column three is the percent of the total population reporting each ancestry, Hispanic origin or race. For tables representing ethnicities based on race or Hispanic origin, the 100-percent population figure from SF1 is used to calculate the value in the "%" column. For all other ancestries, the 2006-2010 five-year estimated population figure from the American Community Survey is used to calculate the value in the "%" column.

Alphabetical Ethnicity Cross-Reference Guide

Afghan see Ancestry–Afghan
African see Ancestry–African, Sub-Saharan: African
African-American see Race–African-American/Black
African-American: Hispanic see Race–African-American/Black: Hispanic
African-American: Not Hispanic see Race–African-American/Black: Not Hispanic
Alaska Athabascan see Race–Alaska Native: Alaska Athabascan
Alaska Native see Race–American Indian/Alaska Native
Alaska Native: Hispanic see Race–American Indian/Alaska Native: Hispanic
Alaska Native: Not Hispanic see Race–American Indian/Alaska Native: Not Hispanic
Albanian see Ancestry–Albanian
Aleut see Race–Alaska Native: Aleut
Alsatian see Ancestry–Alsatian
American see Ancestry–American
American Indian see Race–American Indian/Alaska Native
American Indian: Hispanic see Race–American Indian/Alaska Native: Hispanic
American Indian: Not Hispanic see Race–American Indian/Alaska Native: Not Hispanic
Apache see Race–American Indian: Apache
Arab see Ancestry–Arab: Arab
Arab: Other see Ancestry–Arab: Other
Arapaho see Race–American Indian: Arapaho
Argentinean see Hispanic Origin–South American: Argentinean
Armenian see Ancestry–Armenian
Asian see Race–Asian
Asian Indian see Race–Asian: Indian
Asian: Hispanic see Race–Asian: Hispanic
Asian: Not Hispanic see Race–Asian: Not Hispanic
Assyrian see Ancestry–Assyrian/Chaldean/Syriac
Australian see Ancestry–Australian
Austrian see Ancestry–Austrian
Bahamian see Ancestry–West Indian: Bahamian, except Hispanic
Bangladeshi see Race–Asian: Bangladeshi
Barbadian see Ancestry–West Indian: Barbadian, except Hispanic
Basque see Ancestry–Basque
Belgian see Ancestry–Belgian
Belizean see Ancestry–West Indian: Belizean, except Hispanic
Bermudan see Ancestry–West Indian: Bermudan, except Hispanic
Bhutanese see Race–Asian: Bhutanese
Black see Race–African-American/Black
Black: Hispanic see Race–African-American/Black: Hispanic
Black: Not Hispanic see Race–African-American/Black: Not Hispanic
Blackfeet see Race–American Indian: Blackfeet
Bolivian see Hispanic Origin–South American: Bolivian
Brazilian see Ancestry–Brazilian
British see Ancestry–British

British West Indian *see* Ancestry–West Indian: British West Indian, except Hispanic
Bulgarian *see* Ancestry–Bulgarian
Burmese *see* Race–Asian: Burmese
Cajun *see* Ancestry–Cajun
Cambodian *see* Race–Asian: Cambodian
Canadian *see* Ancestry–Canadian
Canadian/French American Indian *see* Race–American Indian: Canadian/French American Indian
Cape Verdean *see* Ancestry–African, Sub-Saharan: Cape Verdean
Carpatho Rusyn *see* Ancestry–Carpatho Rusyn
Celtic *see* Ancestry–Celtic
Central American *see* Hispanic Origin–Central American, except Mexican
Central American Indian *see* Race–American Indian: Central American Indian
Central American: Other *see* Hispanic Origin–Central American: Other Central American
Chaldean *see* Ancestry–Assyrian/Chaldean/Syriac
Chamorro *see* Race–Hawaii Native/Pacific Islander: Guamanian or Chamorro
Cherokee *see* Race–American Indian: Cherokee
Cheyenne *see* Race–American Indian: Cheyenne
Chickasaw *see* Race–American Indian: Chickasaw
Chilean *see* Hispanic Origin–South American: Chilean
Chinese (except Taiwanese) *see* Race–Asian: Chinese, except Taiwanese
Chippewa *see* Race–American Indian: Chippewa
Choctaw *see* Race–American Indian: Choctaw
Colombian *see* Hispanic Origin–South American: Colombian
Colville *see* Race–American Indian: Colville
Comanche *see* Race–American Indian: Comanche
Costa Rican *see* Hispanic Origin–Central American: Costa Rican
Cree *see* Race–American Indian: Cree
Creek *see* Race–American Indian: Creek
Croatian *see* Ancestry–Croatian
Crow *see* Race–American Indian: Crow
Cuban *see* Hispanic Origin–Cuban
Cypriot *see* Ancestry–Cypriot
Czech *see* Ancestry–Czech
Czechoslovakian *see* Ancestry–Czechoslovakian
Danish *see* Ancestry–Danish
Delaware *see* Race–American Indian: Delaware
Dominican Republic *see* Hispanic Origin–Dominican Republic
Dutch *see* Ancestry–Dutch
Dutch West Indian *see* Ancestry–West Indian: Dutch West Indian, except Hispanic
Eastern European *see* Ancestry–Eastern European
Ecuadorian *see* Hispanic Origin–South American: Ecuadorian
Egyptian *see* Ancestry–Arab: Egyptian
English *see* Ancestry–English
Eskimo *see* Race–Alaska Native: Inupiat
Estonian *see* Ancestry–Estonian
Ethiopian *see* Ancestry–African, Sub-Saharan: Ethiopian
European *see* Ancestry–European
Fijian *see* Race–Hawaii Native/Pacific Islander: Fijian
Filipino *see* Race–Asian: Filipino
Finnish *see* Ancestry–Finnish
French (except Basque) *see* Ancestry–French, except Basque
French Canadian *see* Ancestry–French Canadian
German *see* Ancestry–German
German Russian *see* Ancestry–German Russian
Ghanaian *see* Ancestry–African, Sub-Saharan: Ghanaian
Greek *see* Ancestry–Greek
Guamanian *see* Race–Hawaii Native/Pacific Islander: Guamanian or Chamorro
Guatemalan *see* Hispanic Origin–Central American: Guatemalan
Guyanese *see* Ancestry–Guyanese
Haitian *see* Ancestry–West Indian: Haitian, except Hispanic
Hawaii Native *see* Race–Hawaii Native/Pacific Islander
Hawaii Native: Hispanic *see* Race–Hawaii Native/Pacific Islander: Hispanic

Hawaii Native: Not Hispanic *see* Race–Hawaii Native/Pacific Islander: Not Hispanic

Hispanic or Latino: *see* Hispanic Origin–Hispanic or Latino (of any race)

Hispanic or Latino: Other *see* Hispanic Origin–Other Hispanic or Latino

Hmong *see* Race–Asian: Hmong

Honduran *see* Hispanic Origin–Central American: Honduran

Hopi *see* Race–American Indian: Hopi

Houma *see* Race–American Indian: Houma

Hungarian *see* Ancestry–Hungarian

Icelander *see* Ancestry–Icelander

Indonesian *see* Race–Asian: Indonesian

Inupiat *see* Race–Alaska Native: Inupiat

Iranian *see* Ancestry–Iranian

Iraqi *see* Ancestry–Arab: Iraqi

Irish *see* Ancestry–Irish

Iroquois *see* Race–American Indian: Iroquois

Israeli *see* Ancestry–Israeli

Italian *see* Ancestry–Italian

Jamaican *see* Ancestry–West Indian: Jamaican, except Hispanic

Japanese *see* Race–Asian: Japanese

Jordanian *see* Ancestry–Arab: Jordanian

Kenyan *see* Ancestry–African, Sub-Saharan: Kenyan

Kiowa *see* Race–American Indian: Kiowa

Korean *see* Race–Asian: Korean

Laotian *see* Race–Asian: Laotian

Latvian *see* Ancestry–Latvian

Lebanese *see* Ancestry–Arab: Lebanese

Liberian *see* Ancestry–African, Sub-Saharan: Liberian

Lithuanian *see* Ancestry–Lithuanian

Lumbee *see* Race–American Indian: Lumbee

Luxemburger *see* Ancestry–Luxemburger

Macedonian *see* Ancestry–Macedonian

Malaysian *see* Race–Asian: Malaysian

Maltese *see* Ancestry–Maltese

Marshallese *see* Race–Hawaii Native/Pacific Islander: Marshallese

Menominee *see* Race–American Indian: Menominee

Mexican *see* Hispanic Origin–Mexican

Mexican American Indian *see* Race–American Indian: Mexican American Indian

Moroccan *see* Ancestry–Arab: Moroccan

Native Hawaiian *see* Race–Hawaii Native/Pacific Islander: Native Hawaiian

Navajo *see* Race–American Indian: Navajo

Nepalese *see* Race–Asian: Nepalese

New Zealander *see* Ancestry–New Zealander

Nicaraguan *see* Hispanic Origin–Central American: Nicaraguan

Nigerian *see* Ancestry–African, Sub-Saharan: Nigerian

Northern European *see* Ancestry–Northern European

Norwegian *see* Ancestry–Norwegian

Osage *see* Race–American Indian: Osage

Ottawa *see* Race–American Indian: Ottawa

Pacific Islander *see* Race–Hawaii Native/Pacific Islander

Pacific Islander: Hispanic *see* Race–Hawaii Native/Pacific Islander: Hispanic

Pacific Islander: Not Hispanic *see* Race–Hawaii Native/Pacific Islander: Not Hispanic

Paiute *see* Race–American Indian: Paiute

Pakistani *see* Race–Asian: Pakistani

Palestinian *see* Ancestry–Arab: Palestinian

Panamanian *see* Hispanic Origin–Central American: Panamanian

Paraguayan *see* Hispanic Origin–South American: Paraguayan

Pennsylvania German *see* Ancestry–Pennsylvania German

Peruvian *see* Hispanic Origin–South American: Peruvian

Pima *see* Race–American Indian: Pima

Polish *see* Ancestry–Polish

Portuguese *see* Ancestry–Portuguese

Potawatomi *see* Race–American Indian: Potawatomi

Pueblo *see* Race–American Indian: Pueblo
Puerto Rican *see* Hispanic Origin–Puerto Rican
Puget Sound Salish *see* Race–American Indian: Puget Sound Salish
Romanian *see* Ancestry–Romanian
Russian *see* Ancestry–Russian
Salvadoran *see* Hispanic Origin–Central American: Salvadoran
Samoan *see* Race–Hawaii Native/Pacific Islander: Samoan
Scandinavian *see* Ancestry–Scandinavian
Scotch-Irish *see* Ancestry–Scotch-Irish
Scottish *see* Ancestry–Scottish
Seminole *see* Race–American Indian: Seminole
Senegalese *see* Ancestry–African, Sub-Saharan: Senegalese
Serbian *see* Ancestry–Serbian
Shoshone *see* Race–American Indian: Shoshone
Sierra Leonean *see* Ancestry–African, Sub-Saharan: Sierra Leonean
Sioux *see* Race–American Indian: Sioux
Slavic *see* Ancestry–Slavic
Slovak *see* Ancestry–Slovak
Slovene *see* Ancestry–Slovene
Somalian *see* Ancestry–African, Sub-Saharan: Somalian
South African *see* Ancestry–African, Sub-Saharan: South African
South American *see* Hispanic Origin–South American
South American Indian *see* Race–American Indian: South American Indian
South American: Other *see* Hispanic Origin–South American: Other South American
Soviet Union *see* Ancestry–Soviet Union
Spanish American Indian *see* Race–American Indian: Spanish American Indian
Sri Lankan *see* Race–Asian: Sri Lankan
Sub-Saharan African *see* Ancestry–African, Sub-Saharan
Sub-Saharan African: Other *see* Ancestry–African, Sub-Saharan: Other
Sudanese *see* Ancestry–African, Sub-Saharan: Sudanese
Swedish *see* Ancestry–Swedish
Swiss *see* Ancestry–Swiss
Syriac *see* Ancestry–Assyrian/Chaldean/Syriac
Syrian *see* Ancestry–Arab: Syrian
Taiwanese *see* Race–Asian: Taiwanese
Thai *see* Race–Asian: Thai
Tlingit-Haida *see* Race–Alaska Native: Tlingit-Haida
Tohono O'Odham *see* Race–American Indian: Tohono O'Odham
Tongan *see* Race–Hawaii Native/Pacific Islander: Tongan
Trinidadian and Tobagonian *see* Ancestry–West Indian: Trinidadian and Tobagonian, except Hispanic
Tsimshian *see* Race–Alaska Native: Tsimshian
Turkish *see* Ancestry–Turkish
U.S. Virgin Islander *see* Ancestry–West Indian: U.S. Virgin Islander, except Hispanic
Ugandan *see* Ancestry–African, Sub-Saharan: Ugandan
Ukrainian *see* Ancestry–Ukrainian
Uruguayan *see* Hispanic Origin–South American: Uruguayan
Ute *see* Race–American Indian: Ute
Venezuelan *see* Hispanic Origin–South American: Venezuelan
Vietnamese *see* Race–Asian: Vietnamese
Welsh *see* Ancestry–Welsh
West Indian *see* Ancestry–West Indian: West Indian, except Hispanic
West Indian (except Hispanic) *see* Ancestry–West Indian, except Hispanic
West Indian: Other *see* Ancestry–West Indian: Other, except Hispanic
White *see* Race–White
White: Hispanic *see* Race–White: Hispanic
White: Not Hispanic *see* Race–White: Not Hispanic
Yakama *see* Race–American Indian: Yakama
Yaqui *see* Race–American Indian: Yaqui
Yugoslavian *see* Ancestry–Yugoslavian
Yuman *see* Race–American Indian: Yuman
Yup'ik *see* Race–Alaska Native: Yup'ik
Zimbabwean *see* Ancestry–African, Sub-Saharan: Zimbabwean

Climate Section

SOURCES OF THE DATA

The National Climactic Data Center (NCDC) has two main classes or types of weather stations; first-order stations which are staffed by professional meteorologists and cooperative stations which are staffed by volunteers. All National Weather Service (NWS) stations included in this book are first-order stations.

The data in the climate section is compiled from several sources. The majority comes from the original NCDC computer tapes (DSI-3220 Summary of Month Cooperative). This data was used to create the entire table for each cooperative station and part of each National Weather Service station. The remainder of the data for each NWS station comes from the International Station Meteorological Climate Summary, Version 4.0, September 1996, which is also available from the NCDC.

Storm events come from the NCDC Storm Events Database which is accessible over the Internet at https://www.ncdc.noaa.gov/stormevents.

WEATHER STATION TABLES

The weather station tables are grouped by type (National Weather Service and Cooperative) and then arranged alphabetically. The station name is almost always a place name, and is shown here just as it appears in NCDC data. The station name is followed by the county in which the station is located (or by county equivalent name), the elevation of the station (at the time beginning of the thirty year period) and the latitude and longitude.

The National Weather Service Station tables contain 32 data elements which were compiled from two different sources, the International Station Meteorological Climate Summary (ISMCS) and NCDC DSI-3220 data tapes. The following 13 elements are from the ISMCS: maximum precipitation, minimum precipitation, maximum snowfall, maximum 24-hour snowfall, thunderstorm days, foggy days, predominant sky cover, relative humidity (morning and afternoon), dewpoint, wind speed and direction, and maximum wind gust. The remaining 19 elements come from the DSI-3220 data tapes. The period of record (POR) for data from the DSI-3220 data tapes is 1980-2009. The POR for ISMCS data varies from station to station and appears in a note below each station.

The Cooperative Station tables contain 19 data elements which were all compiled from the DSI-3220 data tapes with a POR of 1980-2009.

WEATHER ELEMENTS (NWS AND COOPERATIVE STATIONS)

The following elements were compiled by the editor from the NCDC DSI-3220 data tapes using a period of record of 1980-2009.

The average temperatures (maximum, minimum, and mean) are the average (see Methodology below) of those temperatures for all available values for a given month. For example, for a given station the average maximum temperature for July is the arithmetic average of all available maximum July temperatures for that station. (Maximum means the highest recorded temperature, minimum means the lowest recorded temperature, and mean means an arithmetic average temperature.)

The extreme maximum temperature is the highest temperature recorded in each month over the period 1980-2009. The extreme minimum temperature is the lowest temperature recorded in each month over the same time period. The extreme maximum daily precipitation is the largest amount of precipitation recorded over a 24-hour period in each month from 1980-2009. The maximum snow depth is the maximum snow depth recorded in each month over the period 1980-2009.

The days for maximum temperature and minimum temperature are the average number of days those criteria were met for all available instances. The symbol ≥ means greater than or equal to, the symbol ≤ means less than or equal to. For example, for a given station, the number of days the maximum temperature was greater than or equal to 90°F in July, is just an arithmetic average of the number of days in all the available Julys for that station.

Heating and cooling degree days are based on the median temperature for a given day and its variance from 65°F. For example, for a given station if the day's high temperature was 50°F and the day's low temperature was 30°F, the median (midpoint) temperature was 40°F. 40°F is 25 degrees below 65°F, hence on this day there would be 25 heating degree days. This also applies for cooling degree days. For example, for a given station if the day's high temperature was 80°F and the day's low temperature was 70°F, the median (midpoint) temperature was 75°F. 75°F is 10 degrees above 65°F, hence on this day there would be 10 cooling degree days. All heating and/or cooling degree

days in a month are summed for the month giving respective totals for each element for that month. These sums for a given month for a given station over the past thirty years are again summed and then arithmetically averaged. It should be noted that the heating and cooling degree days do not cancel each other out. It is possible to have both for a given station in the same month.

Precipitation data is computed the same as heating and cooling degree days. Mean precipitation and mean snowfall are arithmetic averages of cumulative totals for the month. All available values for the thirty year period for a given month for a given station are summed and then divided by the number of values. The same is true for days of greater than or equal to 0.1", 0.5",and 1.0" of precipitation, and days of greater than or equal to 1.0" of snow depth on the ground. The word trace appears for precipitation and snowfall amounts that are too small to measure.

Finally, remember that all values presented in the tables and the rankings are averages, maximums, or minimums of available data (see Methodology below) for that specific data element for the last thirty years (1980-2009).

WEATHER ELEMENTS (NWS STATIONS ONLY)

The following elements were taken directly from the International Station Meteorological Climate Summary. The periods of records vary per station and are noted at the bottom of each table.

Maximum precipitation, minimum precipitation, maximum snowfall, maximum snow depth, maximum 24-hour snowfall, thunderstorm days, foggy days, relative humidity (morning and afternoon), dewpoint, prevailing wind speed and direction, and maximum wind gust are all self-explanatory.

The word trace appears for precipitation and snowfall amounts that are too small to measure.

Predominant sky cover contains four possible entries: CLR (clear); SCT (scattered); BRK (broken); and OVR (overcast).

INCLUSION CRITERIA—HOW STATIONS WERE SELECTED

The basic criteria is that a station must have data for temperature, precipitation, heating and cooling degree days of sufficient quantity in order to create a meaningful average. More specifically, the definition of sufficiency here has two parts. First, there must be 22 values for a given data element, and second, ten of the nineteen elements included in the table must pass this sufficiency test. For example, in regard to mean maximum temperature (the first element on every data table), a given station needs to have a value for every month of at least 22 of the last thirty years in order to meet the criteria, and, in addition, every station included must have at least ten of the nineteen elements with at least this minimal level of completeness in order to fulfill the criteria. We then removed stations that were geographically close together, giving preference to stations with better data quality.

METHODOLOGY

The following discussion applies only to data compiled from the NCDC DSI-3220 data tapes and excludes weather elements that are extreme maximums or minimums.

The data is based on an arithmetic average of all available data for a specific data element at a given station. For example, the average maximum daily high temperature during July for any given station was abstracted from NCDC source tapes for the thirty Julys, starting in July, 1980 and ending in July, 2009. These thirty figures were then summed and divided by thirty to produce an arithmetic average. As might be expected, there were not thirty values for every data element on every table. For a variety of reasons, NCDC data is sometimes incomplete. Thus the following standards were established.

For those data elements where there were 26-30 values, the data was taken to be essentially complete and an average was computed. For data elements where there were 22-25 values, the data was taken as being partly complete but still valid enough to use to compute an average. Such averages are shown in **bold italic** type to indicate that there was less than 26 values. For the few data elements where there were not even 22 values, no average was computed and 'na' appears in the space. If any of the twelve months for a given data element reported a value of 'na', no annual average was computed and the annual average was reported as 'na' as well.

Thus the basic computational methodology used is designed to provide an arithmetic average. Because of this, such a pure arithmetic average is somewhat different from the special type of average (called a "normal") which NCDC procedures produces and appears in federal publications.

Perhaps the best outline of the contrasting normalization methodology is found in the following paragraph (which appears as part of an NCDC technical document titled, CLIM81 1961-1990 NORMALS TD-9641 prepared by Lewis France of NCDC in May, 1992):

Normals have been defined as the arithmetic mean of a climatological element computed over a long time period. International agreements eventually led to the decision that the appropriate time period would be three consecutive decades (Guttman, 1989). The data record should be consistent (have no changes in location, instruments, observation practices, etc.; these are identified here as "exposure changes") and have no missing values so a normal will reflect the actual average climatic conditions. If any significant exposure changes have occurred, the data record is said to be "inhomogeneous," and the normal may not reflect a true climatic average. Such data need to be adjusted to remove the nonclimatic inhomogeneities. The resulting (adjusted) record is then said to be "homogeneous." If no exposure changes have occurred at a station, the normal is calculated simply by averaging the appropriate 30 values from the 1961-1990 record.

In the main, there are two "inhomogeneities" that NCDC is correcting for with normalization: adjusting for variances in time of day of observation (at the so-called First Order stations data is based on midnight to midnight observation times and this practice is not necessarily followed at cooperative stations which are staffed by volunteers), and second, estimating data that is either missing or incongruent.

The editors had some concerns regarding the comparative results of the two methodologies. Would our methodology produce strikingly different results than NCDC's? To allay concerns, results of the two processes were compared for the time period normalized results are available (1971-2000). In short, what was found was that the answer to this question is no. Never the less, users should be aware that because of both the time period covered (1980-2009) and the methodology used, data is not compatible with data from other sources.

POTENTIAL CAUTIONS

First, as with any statistical reference work of this type, users need to be aware of the source of the data. The information here comes from NOAA, and it is the most comprehensive and reliable core data available. Although it is the best, it is not perfect. Most weather stations are staffed by volunteers, times of observation sometimes vary, stations occasionally are moved (especially over a thirty year period), equipment is changed or upgraded, and all of these factors affect the uniformity of the data. The editors do not attempt to correct for these factors, and this data is not intended for either climatologists or atmospheric scientists. Users with concerns about data collection and reporting protocols are both referred to NCDC technical documentation.

Second, users need to be aware of the methodology here which is described above. Although this methodology has produced fully satisfactory results, it is not directly compatible with other methodologies, hence variances in the results published here and those which appear in other publications will doubtlessly arise.

Third, is the trap of that informal logical fallacy known as "hasty generalization," and its corollaries. This may involve presuming the future will be like the past (specifically, next year will be an average year), or it may involve misunderstanding the limitations of an arithmetic average, but more interestingly, it may involve those mistakes made most innocently by generalizing informally on too broad a basis. As weather is highly localized, the data should be taken in that context. A weather station collects data about climatic conditions at that spot, and that spot may or may not be an effective paradigm for an entire town or area.

About New York State

Governor	**Andrew M. Cuomo (D)**
Lt Governor	**Kathleen Courtney "Kathy" Hochul (D)**
State Capital	Albany
Date of Statehood	July 26, 1788 (11th state)
State Nickname	The Empire State
Demonym	New Yorker
Largest City	New York
Highest Point	Mount Marcy (5,344 feet)
Lowest Point	Atlantic Ocean (sea level)
Time Zone	Eastern
State Beverage	2% Milk
State Bird	Eastern bluebird *(sialia sialis)*
State Bush	Lilac bush *(syringa vulgaris)*
State Butterfly	Red-spotted purple/White admiral *(limenitis arthemis)*
State Fish, fresh water	Brook trout *(salvelinus fontinalis)*
State Fish, salt water	Striped bass *(morone saxatilis)*
State Flower	Rose
State Fossil	Sea scorpion *(eurypterus remipes)*
State Fruit	Apple
State Gem	Garnet
State Insect	Nine-spotted ladybug *(coccinella novemnotata)*
State Mammal	Beaver *(castor canadensis)*
State Motto	Excelsior *(Ever upward)*
State Muffin	Apple *(genus malus)*
State Reptile	Common snapping turtle *(chelydra serpentina)*
State Shell	Bay scallop *(argopecten irradians)*
State Slogan	I ♥ NY®
State Song	I Love New York (words and music by Steve Karmen)
State Tree	Sugar maple *(acer saccharum)*

0 mi   200   400   600   800   1000

Times Square, pictured above, is a major commercial intersection and neighborhood in Midtown Manhattan, New York City. At the junction of Broadway and Seventh Avenue, it's brightly adorned by billboards and advertisements. As one of the world's most visited tourist attractions, Times Square is passed through by approximately 330,000 people daily, many of them tourists.

Ellis Island is located in the Upper New York Bay, comprising 27.5 acres. Its main building, shown in the top photo, processed over 12 million immigrants from 1892-1954, the nation's busiest immigrant inspection station at the time. Much of the island has been closed to the general public since 1954. In 2013, the island, including the Immigrant Museum, was reopened after major renovations. Liberty Island, shown in the bottom photo overlooking the Manhattan skyline, is also in the Upper New York Bay just south of Ellis Island. Liberty Island comprises 14.7 acres and is best known as the location of the Statue of Liberty. In 1965, both islands became part of the Statue of Liberty National Monument. In 2016, over 4.5 million visited the islands, a record number.

Long Island, New York, is the longest and largest island in the contiguous United States, with over 400 miles of coastline, from the New York Harbor to Montauk Point. The top photo pictures one of its hundreds of beautiful beaches. Long Island is also home to top wine producing vineyards. The bottom photo shows a vineyard along the north shore of Long Island's eastern end.

Syracuse, shown in the top photo, is a city in and the county seat of Onondaga County in upstate New York, and the fifth most populous city in the state. The city of Buffalo is the second most populous city in New York, after New York City. The bottom photo shows Buffalo's downtown and surrounding area; it's located on the eastern shore of Lake Erie, across from Ontario, Canada.

The site of the 9/11 New York City terrorist attack is now nearly completely rebuilt. Pictured above is the view from North Cove Marina on the Hudson River, showing the Freedom Tower, right (One World Trade Center), and other buildings of the World Financial Center complex.

New York has four distinct seasons. This shows the beauty of autumn at Taughannock Falls, in the Finger Lakes region in central New York.

Albany City Hall was designed by Henry Hobson Richardson in his particular Romanesque style. It opened in 1883, and includes a 202-foot clock tower (detail above) with one of the only municipal carillons in the country. The three-and-a-half story building, which houses the office of the mayor, the Common Council chamber, the city and traffic courts, and other city services, was added to the U.S. National Register of Historic Places in 1972.

A Brief History of New York State

New York harbor was visited by Verrazano in 1524, and the Hudson River was first explored by Henry Hudson in 1609. The Dutch settled here permanently in 1624 and for 40 years they ruled over the colony of New Netherland. It was conquered by the English in 1664 and was then named New York in honor of the Duke of York.

Existing as a colony of Great Britain for over a century, New York declared its independence on July 9, 1776, becoming one of the original 13 states of the Federal Union. The next year, on April 20, 1777, New York's first constitution was adopted.

In many ways, New York State was the principal battleground of the Revolutionary War. The Battle of Saratoga was the turning point of the Revolution leading to the French alliance and eventual victory. New York City, long occupied by British troops, was evacuated on November 25, 1783 where, on December 4 at Fraunces Tavern, General George Washington bade farewell to his officers.

During the Revolutionary War, an election for the first governor took place and George Clinton was inaugurated as Governor at Kingston, July 30, 1777. New York City became the first capital of the new nation, where President George Washington was inaugurated on April 30, 1789. Albany became the capital of the State in January 1797.

In following years, New York's economic and industrial growth encouraged the title "The Empire State," an expression possibly originated by George Washington in 1784.

The Erie Canal, completed in 1825, greatly enhanced the importance of the port of New York and caused populous towns and cities to spring up across the state. The Erie Canal was replaced by the Barge Canal in 1918, and the system of waterways was further expanded by the construction of the St. Lawrence Seaway.

Overland transportation grew rapidly from a system of turnpikes established in the early 1880s to the modern day Governor Thomas E. Dewey New York State Thruway. By 1853, railroads crossed the state in systems like the Erie and New York Central.

Located in New York harbor, the Statue of Liberty was formally presented to the U.S. Minister to France, Levi Parsons on July 4, 1884 by Ferdinand Lesseps, representing the Franco-American Union. President Grover Cleveland dedicated the Statue of Liberty on October 28, 1886, when the last rivet was put into place. Its famous inscription, "Give me your tired, your poor, your huddled masses yearning to breathe free," was the first symbol of America's mission.

The international character of New York City, the principal port for overseas commerce, and later for transcontinental and international airways, has been further enhanced by becoming the home of the United Nations, capital of the free world. Here the people of all nations and races come to discuss and try to solve the world's problems in a free and democratic climate.

As one of the wealthiest states, New York made tremendous strides in industry and commerce. The New York Stock Exchange, founded in 1792, has become the center of world finance. New York City also became a leading national center for art, music and literature, as exemplified by the Metropolitan Museum of Art, The Metropolitan Opera Company, and large publishing houses.

Timeline of New York State History

1524

Explorer Giovanni da Verrazzano, commissioned by the King of France, sailed to the New World, and into what is now New York Harbor; probably accompanied by Jacques Cartier.

1609

After sailing to the New World on the Halve Maen, Henry Hudson explored the mighty river that would later be named for him. Samuel de Champlain explored the northeastern region of the area now called New York and discovered his namesake, Lake Champlain.

1624

The first Dutch settlement was established; for 40 years the Dutch ruled over the colony of New Netherland.

1664

The British army conquered the colony of New Netherland, which was then re-named New York, in honor of the Duke of York.

1754-1763

The French and Indian War, a fierce contest to gain control of the New World, changed the course of history. The British and American colonists fought against the French and Canadians, with Native American allies on both sides. By uniting the colonies and building their military strength and confidence, this war set the stage for the American Revolution.

1765

New York City hosted the first Colonial Congress, a conference called to discuss the King of England's Stamp Act.

1775-1783

The Revolutionary War. On May 10, 1775, Ethan Allen, Benedict Arnold and 83 "Green Mountain Boys" surprised the sleeping British garrison at Fort Ticonderoga and took the fort called the Key to a Continent without firing a shot. This was the first American victory of the Revolutionary War.

1776

After serving as a colony of Great Britain for over a century, New York declared its independence on July 9, becoming one of the original 13 states of the Federal Union.

1777

New York's first constitution was adopted on April 20. George Clinton was elected as New York's first Governor in June. On October 17, the Americans defeated the British at the Battle of Saratoga, one of the decisive battles of the world. This victory marked the turning point of the Revolution, leading to the Americans' alliance with the French and eventual victory.

1783

On November 25, the last British troops evacuated New York City, which had been occupied by the British since September 1776. This was the last British military position in the US. After they departed, US General George Washington entered the city in triumph to the cheers of New Yorkers.

1785-1790

New York City became the first capital of the United States. In 1789, it was the site of George Washington's inauguration as the first US President; it remained the nation's capital until 1790.

1792

The New York Stock Exchange was founded in New York City.

1797

In January, Albany became the capital of New York State.

1802

The US Military Academy opened at West Point.

1807

Robert Fulton's North River Steamboat traveled from New York to Albany. This first voyage of significant distance made by a steamboat began a new era in transportation.

1825

The Erie Canal opened in 1825, linking the Hudson River to the Great Lakes and leading to greater development in the western part of the state.

1827

New York outlawed slavery. At the forefront of the Underground Railroad movement, New York had more anti-slavery organizations than any other state and strong abolitionist leaders such as Harriet Tubman, Frederick Douglass and John Brown. From the early 1800s until the end of the Civil War in 1865, thousands of people passed through New York as they traveled to freedom in Canada.

1837

Martin Van Buren, born in Kinderhook, became the eighth President of the US.

1848

Elizabeth Cady Stanton, Lucretia Mott, and more than 300 women and men gathered in Seneca Falls, for the nation's first women's rights convention.

1850

Millard Fillmore, born in Cayuga County, became the 13th President of the US.

1860s

The State of New York supplied almost one-sixth of all Union forces during the Civil War, which began in 1861.

1883

The Brooklyn Bridge, a wonder of design and engineering, opened. P.T. Barnum led a parade of 21 elephants back and forth across the bridge, to demonstrate its sturdiness to skeptics.

1886

The Statue of Liberty, a gift from France to the United States in honor of the Centennial of the American Declaration of Independence, was dedicated on October 28 in New York Harbor.

1890s-1954

Between 1892 and 1954, more than 12 million immigrants passed through Ellis Island, an immigration facility that is now part of the Statue of Liberty National Monument.

1899

The State Capitol at Albany was completed.

1901

When President William McKinley was assassinated in Buffalo, Theodore Roosevelt (born in New York City), was hurriedly sworn in as the 26th president of the US. Not quite 43 years old, TR became the youngest president in the nation's history.

1902

New York City's first skyscraper was built: the 21-story Flatiron building at 23rd Street and Fifth Avenue.

1904

New York City's first subway line, called the IRT, opened.

1920

On August 26, the 19th Amendment to the US Constitution extended the right to vote to women. After a long struggle, women could vote in the fall elections, including the Presidential election.

1932
Lake Placid hosted the Olympic Winter Games. The Whiteface Lake Placid Olympic Center at the site features an Olympic Museum and Sports Complex.

1931
The Empire State Building and the Chrysler Building were completed, and the George Washington Bridge opened, all adding to the New York City's burgeoning skyline.

1933
Franklin D. Roosevelt, born near Hyde Park, became the 32nd President of the US.

1939
The World's Fair opened in New York City, corresponding to the 150th anniversary of George Washington's inauguration as first President of the US. Many countries around the world participated; over 44 million people attended over two seasons.

1941-1945
World War II. Three WWII ships on display at the Buffalo/Erie County Naval and Military Park include the Destroyer USS The Sullivans, named for five brothers who lost their lives on November 13, 1942 following the Naval Battle of Guadalcanal; the guided missile cruiser USS Little Rock; and the submarine USS Croaker.

1952
New York City became the permanent headquarters of the United Nations.

1956
New York City hosted a Subway Series; a Major League baseball championship between the New York Yankees and the Brooklyn Dodgers.

1961-1975
The Vietnam War. The New York State Vietnam Memorial at the Empire State Plaza in Albany commemorates the military service of New York State residents who served their country in Southeast Asia between 1961 and 1975, including more than 4,000 who lost their lives or were declared missing in action.

1964
The World's Fair opened (again) in New York City.

1969
The three-day Woodstock Music & Art Fair was held on a former dairy farm in Bethel. The open-air festival featured icons of rock music and attracted half a million fans. Today the Bethel Woods Center for the Arts features a1960s museum and presents concerts at the site. The New York Mets won the 1969 World Series.

1973
The World Trade Center was completed. Each of the twin towers measured 1,368 feet in height. Lieutenant Governor Malcom Wilson became Governor of NY upon the resignation of Nelson Rockefeller.

1974 and 1978
Hugh Carey was elected Governor of NY.

1977
The I LOVE NEW YORK tourism campaign was created. Amid a nationwide recession, Governor Hugh Carey and the NY Department of Commerce made a strategic decision—to market tourism as a means to improve the state's economy. It started with four little words. I LOVE NEW YORK—slogan, logo and jingle—created an overall theme that was an instant hit. The clear simple message has endured for more than 35 years, reflecting its universal appeal and New York's cultural and natural wonders.

1977 and 1978
The New York Yankees won the World Series.

1980
Lake Placid hosted the Olympic Winter Games for a second time. The Whiteface Lake Placid Olympic Center at the site features an Olympic Museum and Sports Complex.

1982, 1986, and 1990
Mario Cuomo was elected Governor of NY.

1982
The musical Cats opened on Broadway, beginning a run of nearly 20 years. Winner of the 1983 Tony for Best Musical, this show charmed audiences with spectacular choreography and songs by Andrew Lloyd Webber.

1984
The New York State Vietnam Memorial was dedicated at the Empire State Plaza in Albany. Commemorating the military service of New York State residents who served their country in Southeast Asia between 1961 and 1975, including more than 4,000 who lost their lives or were declared missing in action, the memorial was the first such state effort in the nation.

1986
The New York Mets won the World Series.

1988
The musical Phantom of the Opera, now a multi-Tony Award winner and the longest running show on Broadway, opened.

1989
David Dinkins was elected Mayor of New York City. He was the City's first African-American mayor.

1992
On May 17, the New York Stock Exchange Bicentennial celebrated its 200th anniversary as one of the world's most vital and enduring financial institutions.

1993
On February 26, a terrorist attack at the World Trade Center killed six people and injured over 1000. In 1995, militant Sheik Omar Abdel Rahman and nine others were convicted of conspiracy charges, and in 1998, Ramzi Yousef, believed to have been the mastermind, was convicted of the bombing. Al-Qaeda involvement was suspected.

1994
On January 1, Rudolph Giuliani was sworn in as the 107th Mayor of New York City. He was the City's first Republican mayor in two decades. Among other things, he set out to reduce crime and reinvent the Times Square area as a family-friendly tourist destination.

1994, 1998, and 2002
George Pataki was elected Governor of NY.

1996, 1998, 1999 and 2000
The New York Yankees won the World Series.

2000
Former first lady Hillary Clinton was elected to the US Senate. She was the first female senator to represent New York.

2001
On September 11, terrorist attacks destroyed the World Trade Center. Nearly 3,000 people were killed. The NY Stock Exchange closed for four days—its longest closure since 1933. Symbolizing our nation's strength and resilience, it reopened on September 17, setting a record volume of 2.37 billion shares. Today, the National September 11 Memorial & Museum honors the nearly 3,000 people killed in the terror attacks of September 11, 2001 at the World Trade Center site; near Shanksville, Pennsylvania; and at the Pentagon; as well as the six people killed in the World Trade Center bombing in February 1993.

2006
The National Purple Heart Hall of Honor opened in November at the New Windsor Cantonment State Historic Site in the Hudson Valley. The facility commemorates the extraordinary sacrifices of America's servicemen and servicewomen who were killed or wounded in combat, and shares the stories of America's combat wounded

veterans and those who never returned, all recipients of the Purple Heart. The first beam of the new Freedom Tower was placed at the World Trade Center Memorial Site, now the National September 11 Memorial & Museum.

2007
Eliot Spitzer was sworn in as Governor of NY on January 11.

2008
In March, Lieutenant Governor David Paterson became Governor of NY, upon the resignation of Eliot Spitzer. He is New York's first African-American governor and first legally blind governor, as well as the fourth African-American governor in the US. Governor Paterson is nationally recognized as a leading advocate for the visually and physically impaired.

2009
In January, NY Senator Hilary Clinton was sworn in as US Secretary of State. Appointed by President Barack Obama, she is the first former First Lady to serve in a president's cabinet.

In May, Pedestrian Malls were created at Times Square and Herald Square on Broadway. Beginning on May 22, New York City's Broadway was closed to vehicle traffic for five blocks at Times Square, turning part of the "Crossroads of the World" into a pedestrian mall with cafe tables and benches. A second promenade was created at Herald Square where Macy's, the world's largest store, dominates the intersection. The plan is part of an experiment to create open spaces for tourists and make the city even more pedestrian friendly. The first section of the High Line, from Gansevoort Street to West 20th Street, opened June 9. The unique public park, built on an historic freight rail line elevated above the streets on Manhattan's West Side, offers spectacular views.

2010
Andrew Cuomo was elected Governor of New York on November 2. Governor Andrew Cuomo's father, Mario Cuomo, was New York governor from 1983 to 1994.

2011
On June 24, New York became the sixth state in the nation to legalize same-sex marriage. New adventure parks opened at ski mountains across New York, including the Outdoor Adventure Center at Greek Peak, featuring an Alpine Mountain coaster; the Sky High Adventure Park, Aerial Adventure and Mountain Coaster at Holiday Valley; and the New York Zipline at Hunter Mountain, the longest and highest in North America. On September 22, Jane's Carousel was installed in Brooklyn Bridge Park. The first carousel to be listed on the National Register of Historic Places, it was painstakingly restored by Jane Walentas at her studio in Brooklyn's DUMBO neighborhood. Set beside the East River between the Brooklyn and Manhattan bridges, the elegant 1922 carousel has 48 hand-carved horses and 1200 brilliant lights. Housed in a spectacular Pavilion designed by renowned architect Jean Nouvel, it delights local children and visitors from around the world. The Carousel and Pavilion were a gift from the Walentas family to the people of the City of New York.

2012
Destiny USA, one of the nation's largest shopping centers, opened in Syracuse. The 2.4-million-square-foot tourist destination features luxury retailers, premium outlets, diverse restaurants and unique entertainment like an Ice Museum, WonderWorks and Canyon Climb Adventure. Hurricane Sandy hit New York City on October 29. It was the deadliest and most destructive tropical cyclone of the 2012 Atlantic hurricane season, as well as the second-costliest hurricane in US history. New Yorkers and many other volunteers pulled together to help clean up, supply food, and provide overall assistance in the City's recovery. Volun-tourism focused on the areas hardest hit by Hurricane Sandy. Jane's Carousel (*see* 2011) survived Hurricane Sandy.

Raging waters engulfed the carousel, set on a three-foot-high pavilion that usually stands 30 feet from the river. From seven stories above and a block away, neighbors took a photo of the still-lit pavilion—surrounded by surging tides that threatened to wash it away. Amazingly it survived. The photo of the illuminated carousel surrounded by darkness and crashing waves spread across the Internet, as a symbol of New York City's resilience.

2013
Historic Saratoga Race Course celebrates its 150th Anniversary.

2014

IBM says it's teaming up with the New York Genome Center to help fight brain cancer. Its Watson cloud computing system will be used in partnership with the genetic research center to help sequence DNA for the treatment of glioblastoma, the most common type of brain cancer in US adults.

On June 6, Karen DeCrow (b.1937), former head of NOW (1974-1977), the National Organization for Women, died at her home in Jamesville, NY.

A freakish storm swept off the Great Lakes on November 18 and after 3 days deposited 7 feet of snow and more and left at least 12 people dead.

2015

David Letterman retires as the longest-serving talk show host in history, broadcasting from New York City's Ed Sullivan Theater for 33 years.

NYS Assembly Speaker Sheldon Silver is arrested on Federal corruption charges, the 41st elected New York state official to be accused of misdeeds in the past 12 years.

After thirty-seven years, thoroughbred racehorse American Pharoah joined the elite list of Triple Crown winners with a resounding victory in the Belmont in New York. He is the twelfth Triple Crown winner in American racing history.

2016

A massive snowstorm, January 22-23 broke a snowfall record in Central Park with 27.5 inches of snow, the most seen in New York City since recordkeeping began in 1869. More still—34 inches—fell in Jackson Heights, Queens.

Despite losing the New York State primary to Democratic presidential candidate Hillary Clinton, Donald Trump defeated Clinton to win the White House. Throughout the campaign billionaire Trump appealed to white, working-class Americans and others who felt left behind by the economic recovery following the 2008 recession, and he took traditional Democratic stronghold states such as Michigan, Wisconsin and Pennsylvania. Since taking office, the Trump Towers in New York City has been the scene of much Presidential business.

2017

The first phase of a new New York City subway line—the Second Avenue Subway (SAS) opened in January with three new stations under Second Avenue on the East Side of Manhattan. It will serve an estimated 200,000 riders daily. The full Second Avenue Line, is planned in three additional phases, between 125th Street and Hanover Square, for a total of 8.5 miles, 16 stations, a projected daily ridership of 560,000, and a cost of more than $17 billion.

Source: New York Department of Economic Development; Original research.

An Introduction to New York State Government

Organization

New York's state government contains three branches: legislative, judicial and executive.

The Legislative Branch

The legislative branch consists of a bicameral (two chamber) Legislature—a 62 member Senate and 150 member Assembly that, together, represent the 18 million citizens of the State. All members are elected for two-year terms.

The Judicial Branch

The judicial branch comprises a range of courts (from trial to appellate) with various jurisdictions (from village and town courts to the State's highest court—the Court of Appeals). The State assumes the cost for all but the town and village courts.

The Judiciary functions under a Unified Court System whose organization, administration and financing are prescribed by the State Constitution and the Unified Court Budget Act. The Unified Court System has responsibility for peacefully and fairly resolving civil claims, family disputes, and criminal accusations, as well as providing legal protection for children, mentally-ill persons and others entitled to special protections.

The Executive Branch

The executive branch of New York State government consists of 20 departments—the maximum number allowed by the State Constitution. This limitation came about as a result of constitutional reforms from the 1920s that were designed to make State government more manageable by eliminating many of the independently elected executive officers and curbing the creation of new departments. The 20 departments are:

- **Agriculture and Markets:** Serves agricultural producers and the consuming public. Promotes agriculture through various industry and export development programs; enforces food safety laws.
- **Audit and Control:** Maintains the State's accounts; pays the State's payrolls and bills; invests State funds; audits State agencies and local governments; and administers the State employee retirement system.
- **Banking:** Primary regulator for State-licensed and State-chartered financial entities operating in New York, including: domestic banks, foreign agencies, branch and representative offices, savings institutions and trust companies, mortgage bankers and brokers, check cashers and money transmitters. Ensures the safe and sound conduct of these businesses, maintains public confidence in the banking system and protects the public interest as well as the interests of depositors, creditors and shareholders.
- **Civil Service:** The central personnel agency for the Executive branch of State government. Provides the State of New York with a trained workforce; administers health, dental and insurance programs covering State employees and retirees as well as some local government employees; and provides technical services to the State's 102 municipal service agencies, covering approximately 392,000 local government employees.
- **Correctional Services:** Operates facilities for the custody and rehabilitation of inmates.
- **Economic Development:** Creates jobs and encourages economic prosperity by providing technical and financial assistance to businesses.
- **Education:** Supervises all educational institutions in the State, operates certain educational and cultural institutions, certifies teachers and certifies/licenses 44 other professions.
- **Environmental Conservation:** Administers programs designed to protect and improve the State's natural resources.
- **Executive:** Since the 1920s constitutional reforms, numerous agencies have been created within the Executive Department to accommodate various governmental functions. These include the Division of Veterans' Affairs (which advises veterans on services, benefits and entitlements, and administers payments of bonuses and annuities to blind veterans) and the Office of General Services (which provides centralized data processing, construction, maintenance and design services as well as printing, transportation and communication systems).

- **Family Assistance:** Promotes greater self-sufficiency by providing support services for needy families and adults that lead to, self-reliance.
- **Health:** Protects and promotes the health of New Yorkers through enforcement of public health and related laws, and assurance of quality health care delivery.
- **Insurance:** Supervises and regulates all insurance business in New York State. Issues licenses to agents, brokers and consultants; conducts examinations of insurers; reviews complaints from policyholders; and approves corporate formations, mergers and consolidations.
- **Labor:** Helps New York work by preparing individuals for jobs; administering unemployment insurance, disability benefits and workers' compensation; and ensuring workplace safety.
- **Law:** Protects the rights of New Yorkers; represents the State in legal matters; and prosecutes violations of State law.
- **Mental Hygiene:** Provides services for individuals suffering from mental illness, developmental disabilities and/or substance abuse.
- **Motor Vehicles:** Registers vehicles, licenses drivers and promotes highway safety.
- **Public Service:** Ensures that all New Yorkers have access to reliable and low-cost utility services by promoting competition and reliability in utility services.
- **State:** Known as the keeper of records, the Department of State issues business licenses, enforces building codes, provides technical assistance to local governments and administers fire prevention and control services.
- **Taxation and Finance:** Collects taxes and administers the State's tax laws.
- **Transportation:** Coordinates and assists in the development and operation of highway, railroad, mass transit, port, waterway and aviation facilities.

Elected Officers and Appointed Officials

Only four statewide government officers are directly elected:

- The Governor, who heads the Executive Department, and Lieutenant Governor (who are elected on a joint ballot).
- The State Comptroller, who heads the Department of Audit and Control.
- The Attorney General, who heads the Department of Law.

With a few exceptions, the Governor appoints the heads of all State departments and agencies of the executive branch. The exceptions include:

- The Commissioner of the State Education Department, who is appointed by and serves at the pleasure of the State Board of Regents.
- The Chancellor of the State University of New York, who is appointed by a Board of Trustees.
- The Chancellor of the City University of New York, who is appointed by a Board of Trustees.

Local Governments

Geographically, New York State is divided into 62 counties (five of which are boroughs of New York City). Within these counties are 62 cities (including New York City), 932 towns, 555 villages and 697 school districts (including New York City). In addition to counties, cities, towns and villages, "special districts" meet local needs for fire and police protection, sewer and water systems or other services.

Local governments are granted the power to adopt local laws that are not inconsistent with the provisions of the State Constitution or other general law. The Legislature, in turn, may not pass any law that affects only one locality unless the governing body of that locality has first approved the bill—referred to as a home rule request—or unless a State interest exists.

Source: New York State Division of the Budget, June 2012

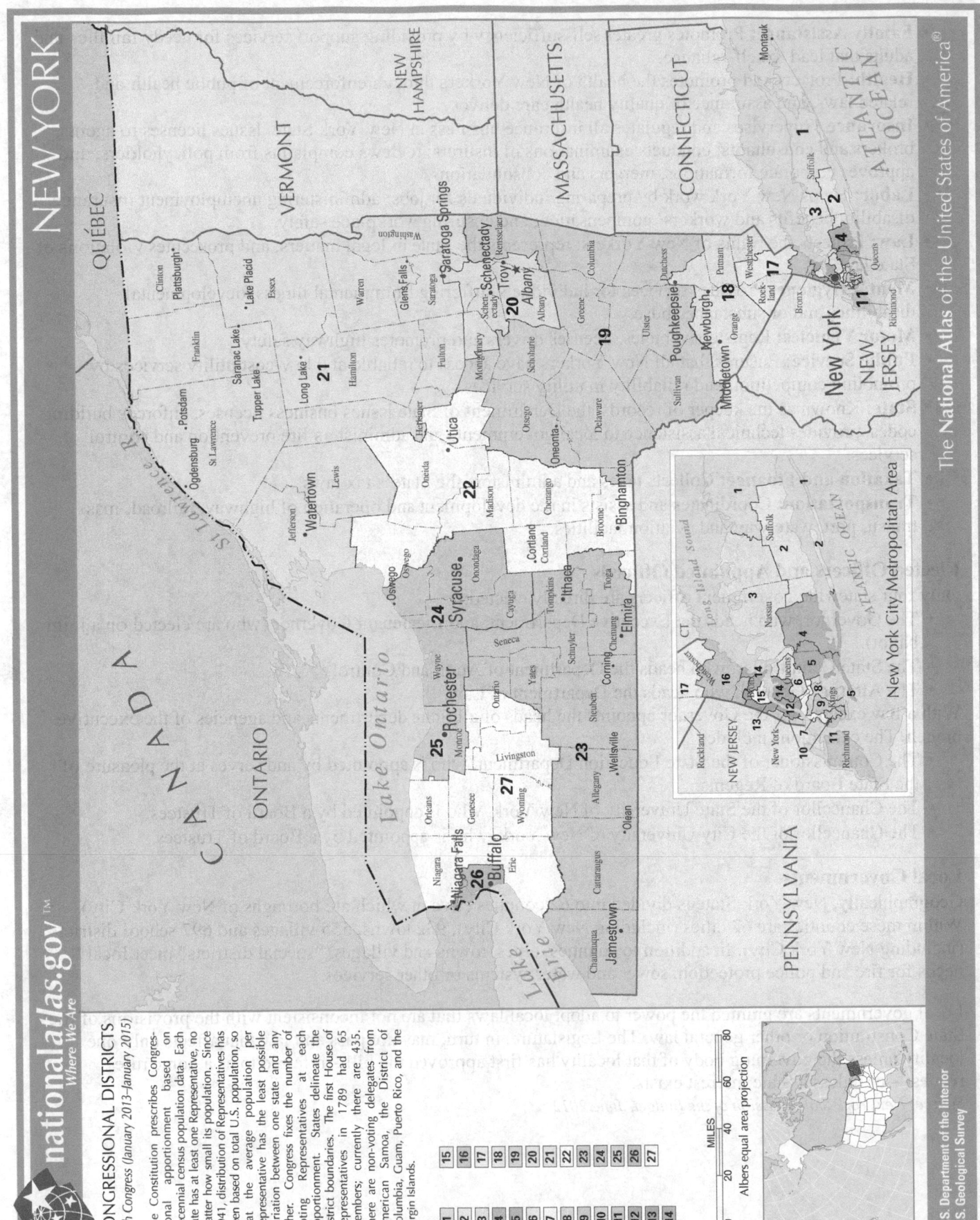

NEW YORK

QUÉBEC

CANADA

NEW HAMPSHIRE

VERMONT

MASSACHUSETTS

CONNECTICUT

NEW JERSEY

PENNSYLVANIA

ATLANTIC OCEAN

Lake Ontario

Lake Erie

St Lawrence River

ONTARIO

New York City Metropolitan Area

Long Island Sound

ATLANTIC OCEAN

nationalatlas.gov™
Where We Are

CONGRESSIONAL DISTRICTS
113th Congress (January 2013–January 2015)

The Constitution prescribes Congressional apportionment based on decennial census population data. Each state has at least one Representative, no matter how small its population. Since 1941, distribution of Representatives has been based on total U.S. population, so that the average population per Representative has the least possible variation between one state and any other. Congress fixes the number of voting Representatives at each apportionment. States delineate the district boundaries. The first House of Representatives in 1789 had 65 members; currently there are 435. There are non-voting delegates from American Samoa, the District of Columbia, Guam, Puerto Rico, and the Virgin Islands.

MILES

0   20   40   60   80

Albers equal area projection

U.S. Department of the Interior
U.S. Geological Survey

The **National Atlas** of the United States of America®

Percent of Population Who Voted for Donald Trump in 2016

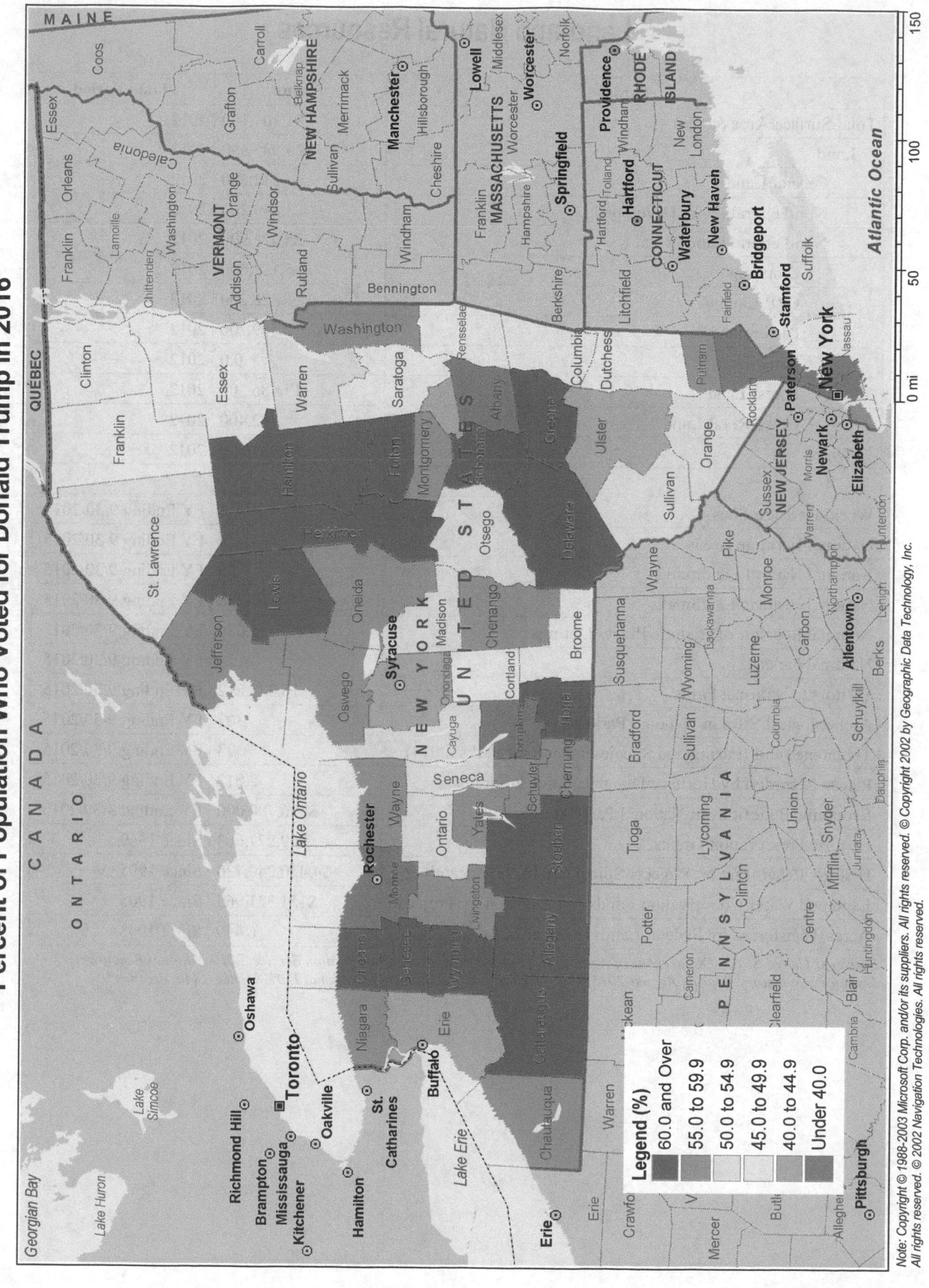

Legend (%)
- 60.0 and Over
- 55.0 to 59.9
- 50.0 to 54.9
- 45.0 to 49.9
- 40.0 to 44.9
- Under 40.0

Land and Natural Resources

Topic	Value	Time Period
Total Surface Area (acres)	31,409,100	2012
Land	29,985,600	2012
Federal Land	212,500	2012
Non-Federal Land, Developed	3,844,200	2012
Non-Federal Land, Rural	25,928,900	2012
Cropland	5,122,600	2012
CRP Land	28,200	2012
Pastureland	2,509,700	2012
Rangeland	0.0	2012
Forest Land	17,486,300	2012
Other Rural Land	782,400	2012
Water	1,423,500	2012
World Heritage Sites	1	FY Ending 9/30/2015
National Heritage Areas	4	FY Ending 9/30/2015
National Natural Landmarks	28	FY Ending 9/30/2015
National Historic Landmarks	268	FY Ending 9/30/2015
National Register of Historic Places Listings	5,630	FY Ending 9/30/2015
National Parks	22	FY Ending 9/30/2015
Visitors to National Parks	16,328,212	FY Ending 9/30/2015
Archeological Sites in National Parks	307	FY Ending 9/30/2015
Threatened and Endangered Species in National Parks (2014)	23	FY Ending 9/30/2015
Places Recorded by Heritage Documentation Programs	2,012	FY Ending 9/30/2015
Economic Benefit from National Park Tourism	$606,700,000	FY Ending 9/30/2015
Historic Preservation Grants	$69,277,663	Since 1969
Historic Rehabilitation Projects Stimulated by Tax Incentives	$4,420,240,720	Since 1995
Land and Water Conservation Funds Appropriated for Projects	$151,321,965	Since 1965
Acres Transferred by Federal Lands to Local Parks	6,449	Since 1948

Sources: *United States Department of Agriculture, Natural Resources Conservation Service, 2012 National Resources Inventory, Summary Report, August 2015; U.S. Department of the Interior, National Park Service, State Profiles*

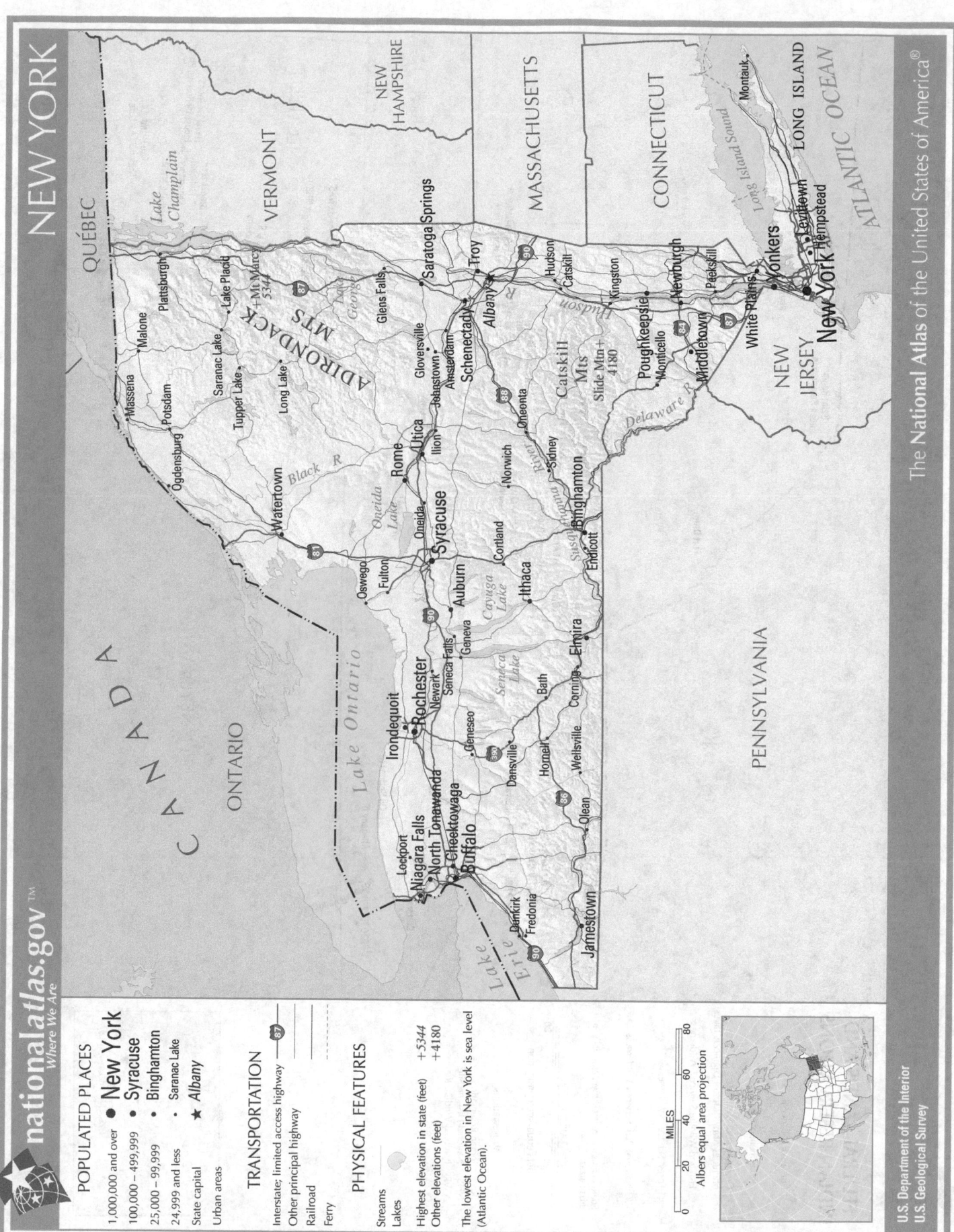

NEW YORK

POPULATED PLACES

1,000,000 and over	● New York
100,000 – 499,999	● Syracuse
25,000 – 99,999	● Binghamton
24,999 and less	• Saranac Lake
State capital	★ Albany
Urban areas	

TRANSPORTATION

Interstate; limited access highway
Other principal highway
Railroad
Ferry

PHYSICAL FEATURES

Streams
Lakes
Highest elevation in state (feet)   +5344
Other elevations (feet)   +4180

The lowest elevation in New York is sea level
(Atlantic Ocean).

MILES
0   20   40   60   80
Albers equal area projection

The National Atlas of the United States of America®

U.S. Department of the Interior
U.S. Geological Survey

QUÉBEC
NEW HAMPSHIRE
VERMONT
MASSACHUSETTS
CONNECTICUT
ATLANTIC OCEAN
LONG ISLAND
NEW JERSEY
PENNSYLVANIA
CANADA
ONTARIO

Lake Champlain
ADIRONDACK MTS
Lake Ontario
Lake Erie
Long Island Sound

Plattsburgh
Massena
Malone
Potsdam
Ogdensburg
Saranac Lake
Lake Placid
+Mt Marcy 5344
Tupper Lake
Long Lake
Watertown
Black R
Oneida Lake
Saratoga Springs
Glens Falls
Troy
Hudson
Catskill
Kingston
Poughkeepsie
Monticello
Newburgh
Peekskill
White Plains
Yonkers
New York
Hempstead
Levittown
Montauk
Gloversville
Johnstown
Amsterdam
Schenectady
Albany
Utica
Rome
Ilion
Oneonta
Sidney
Norwich
Binghamton
Endicott
Catskill Mts
Slide Mtn + 4180
Delaware R
Susquehanna River
Middletown
Syracuse
Oneida
Oswego
Fulton
Auburn
Cortland
Ithaca
Cayuga Lake
Elmira
Corning
Bath
Rochester
Irondequoit
Newark
Seneca Falls
Geneva
Seneca Lake
Geneseo
Dansville
Hornell
Wellsville
Olean
Lockport
Niagara Falls
North Tonawanda
Cheektowaga
Buffalo
Dunkirk
Fredonia
Jamestown

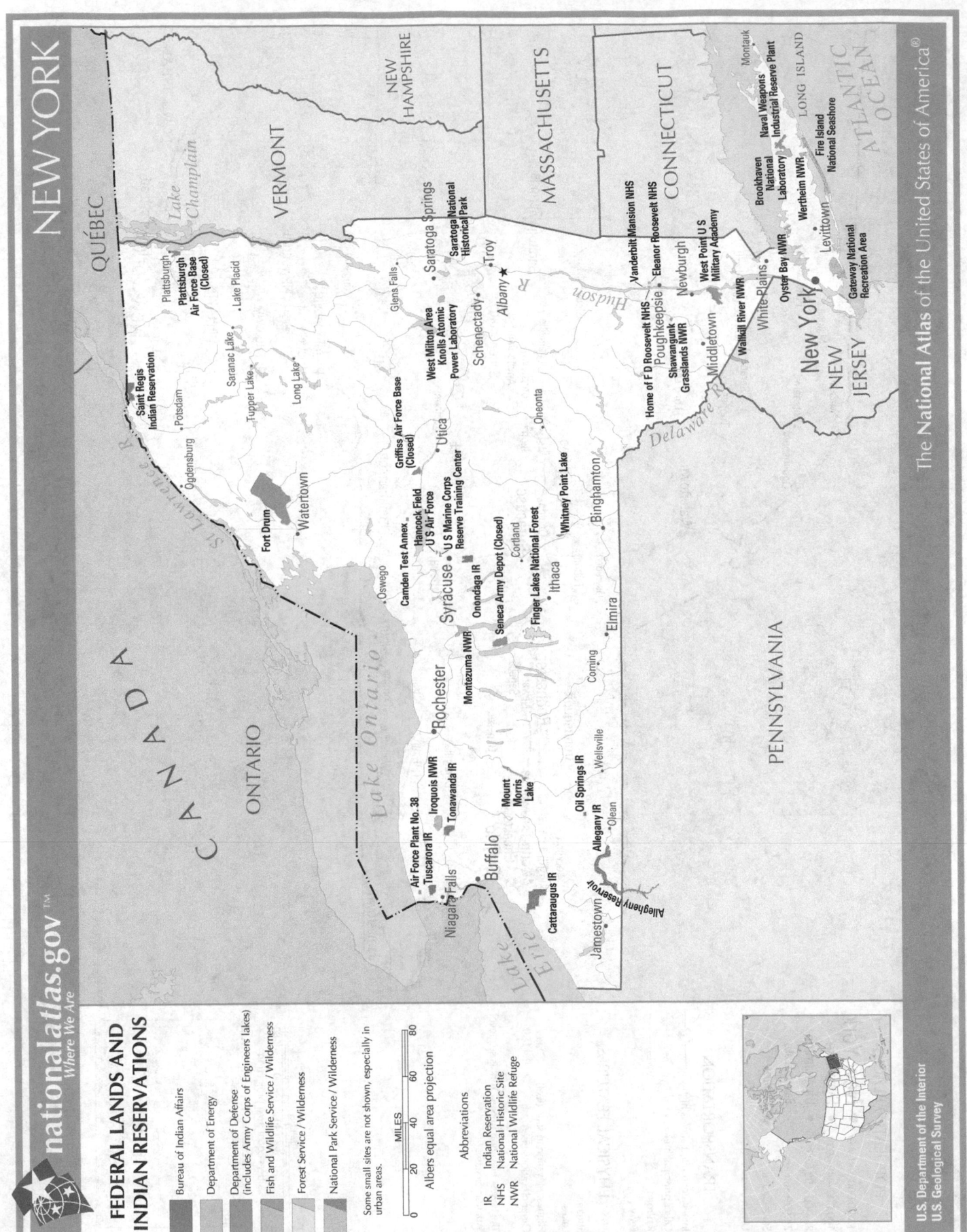

NEW YORK

FEDERAL LANDS AND INDIAN RESERVATIONS

Bureau of Indian Affairs

Department of Energy

Department of Defense
(includes Army Corps of Engineers lakes)

Fish and Wildlife Service / Wilderness

Forest Service / Wilderness

National Park Service / Wilderness

Some small sites are not shown, especially in urban areas.

MILES
0   20   40   60   80

Albers equal area projection

Abbreviations

IR   Indian Reservation
NHS   National Historic Site
NWR   National Wildlife Refuge

nationalatlas.gov ™
Where We Are

The National Atlas of the United States of America®

U.S. Department of the Interior
U.S. Geological Survey

QUÉBEC

VERMONT

NEW HAMPSHIRE

MASSACHUSETTS

CONNECTICUT

CANADA

ONTARIO

PENNSYLVANIA

NEW JERSEY

ATLANTIC OCEAN

LONG ISLAND

Lake Champlain

Lake Ontario

Lake Erie

St. Lawrence River

Plattsburgh
Plattsburgh Air Force Base (Closed)

Lake Placid

Saint Regis Indian Reservation

Potsdam

Ogdensburg

Saranac Lake

Tupper Lake

Long Lake

Watertown

Fort Drum

Oswego

Glens Falls

Saratoga Springs
Saratoga National Historical Park

Troy

West Milton Area
Knolls Atomic Power Laboratory

Schenectady

Albany

Hudson R

Griffiss Air Force Base (Closed)

Utica

Oneonta

Camden Test Annex
Hancock Field
U S Air Force

U S Marine Corps Reserve Training Center

Syracuse

Onondaga IR

Seneca Army Depot (Closed)

Cortland

Finger Lakes National Forest

Ithaca

Whitney Point Lake

Binghamton

Rochester

Montezuma NWR

Elmira

Corning

Delaware R

Vanderbilt Mansion NHS

Eleanor Roosevelt NHS

Home of F D Roosevelt NHS
Poughkeepsie

Shawangunk
Grasslands NWR

Newburgh

West Point U S Military Academy

Middletown

Wallkill River NWR

White Plains

Oyster Bay NWR

New York

Levittown

Montauk

Naval Weapons Industrial Reserve Plant

Brookhaven National Laboratory

Wertheim NWR

Fire Island National Seashore

Gateway National Recreation Area

Air Force Plant No. 38

Tuscarora IR

Iroquois NWR

Tonawanda IR

Mount Morris Lake

Oil Springs IR

Wellsville

Allegany IR

Olean

Cattaraugus IR

Niagara Falls

Buffalo

Jamestown

Allegheny Reservoir

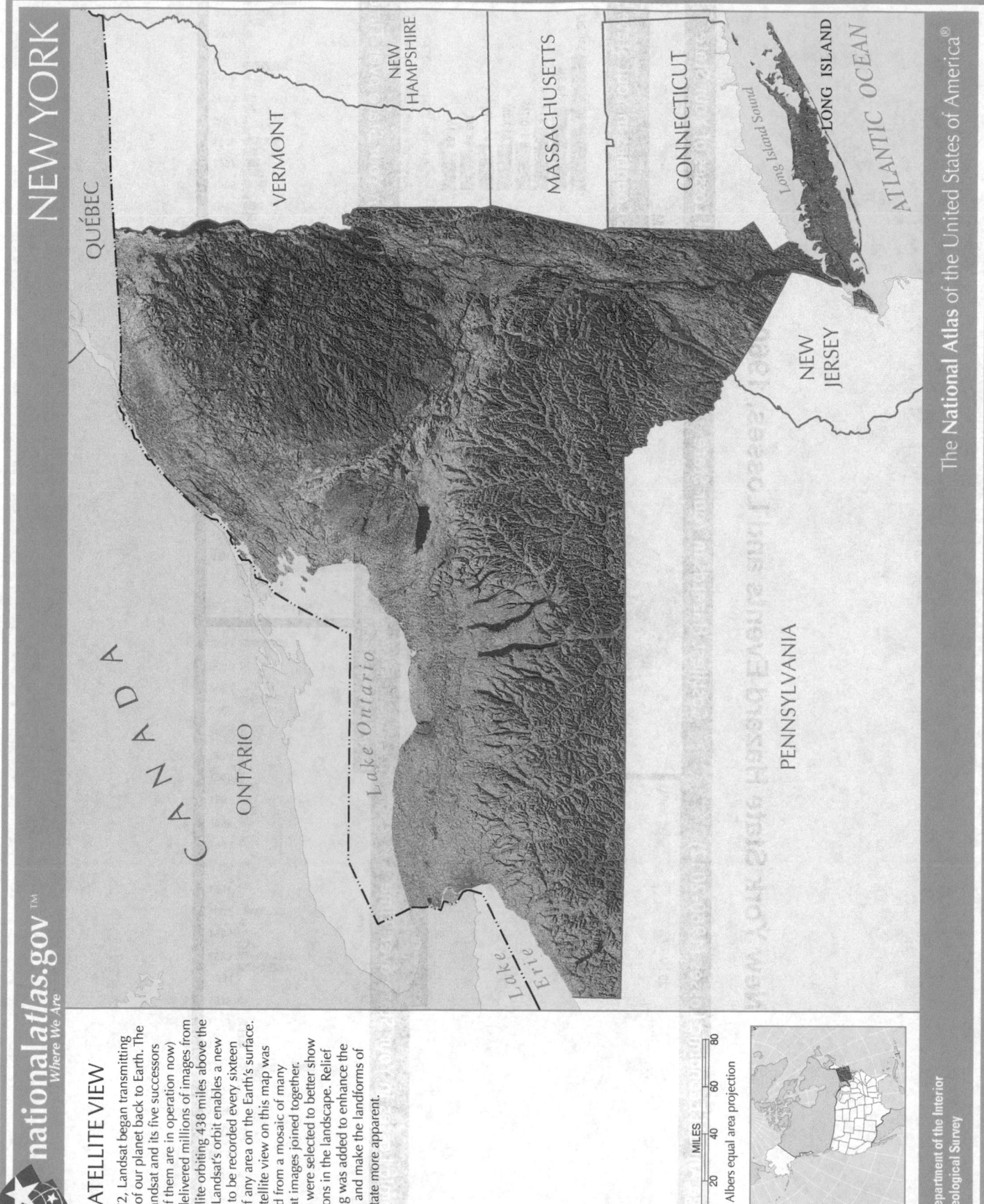

NEW YORK

nationalatlas.gov™
Where We Are

SATELLITE VIEW

In 1972, Landsat began transmitting views of our planet back to Earth. The first Landsat and its five successors (two of them are in operation now) have delivered millions of images from a satellite orbiting 438 miles above the Earth. Landsat's orbit enables a new image to be recorded every sixteen days of any area on the Earth's surface. The satellite view on this map was created from a mosaic of many Landsat images joined together. Colors were selected to better show variations in the landscape. Relief shading was added to enhance the terrain and make the landforms of each state more apparent.

MILES
0   20   40   60   80
Albers equal area projection

U.S. Department of the Interior
U.S. Geological Survey

The **National Atlas** of the United States of America®

QUÉBEC

CANADA

ONTARIO

Lake Ontario

Lake Erie

VERMONT

NEW HAMPSHIRE

MASSACHUSETTS

CONNECTICUT

Long Island Sound

LONG ISLAND

ATLANTIC OCEAN

NEW JERSEY

PENNSYLVANIA

New York State Hazard Events and Losses, 1960-2012

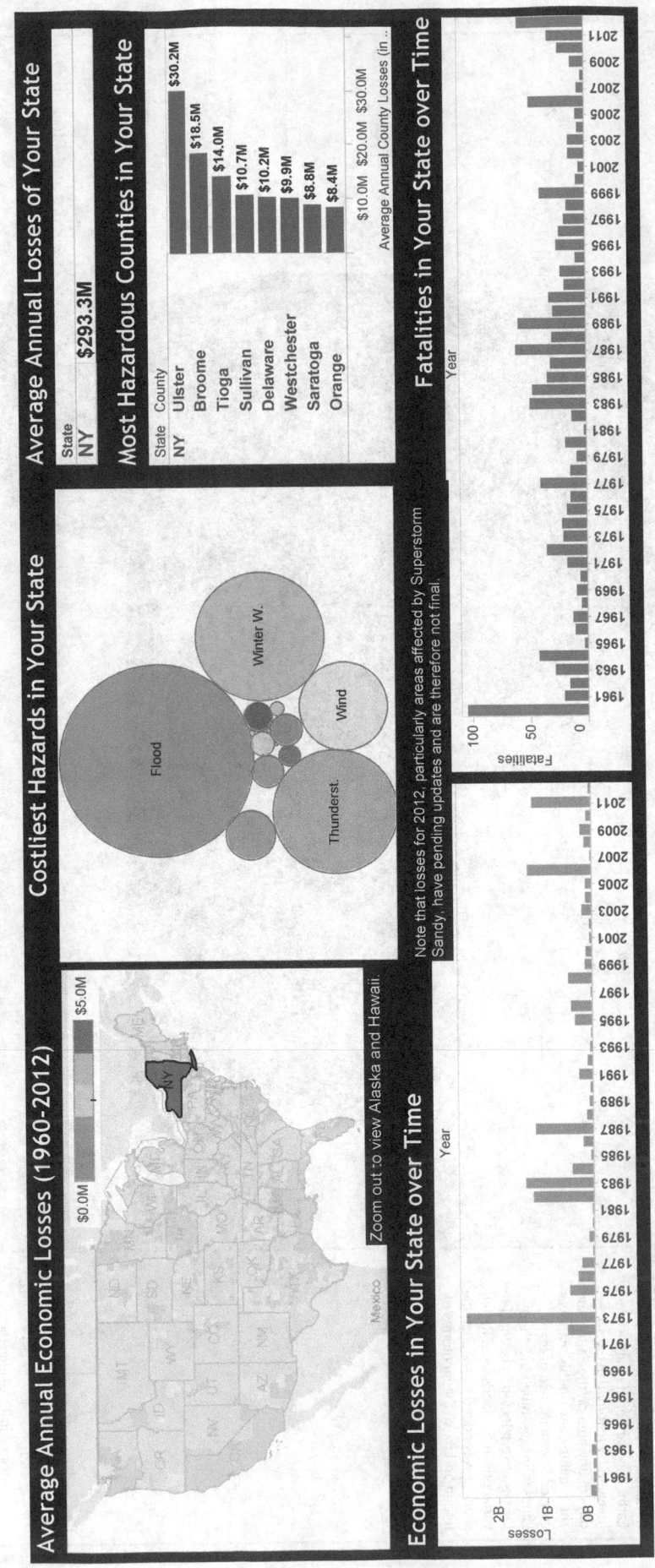

Average Annual Losses of Your State

State	
NY	$293.3M

Most Hazardous Counties in Your State

State	County	
NY	Ulster	$30.2M
	Broome	$18.5M
	Tioga	$14.0M
	Sullivan	$10.7M
	Delaware	$10.2M
	Westchester	$9.9M
	Saratoga	$8.8M
	Orange	$8.4M

$0.0M $10.0M $20.0M $30.0M
Average Annual County Losses (in ..

Costliest Hazards in Your State

Flood · Winter W. · Wind · Thunderst.

Average Annual Economic Losses (1960-2012)

$0.0M $5.0M

Mexico   Zoom out to view Alaska and Hawaii.

Fatalities in Your State over Time

Fatalities · Year

100 · 50 · 0

Note that losses for 2012, particularly areas affected by Superstorm Sandy, have pending updates and are therefore not final.

Economic Losses in Your State over Time

Losses · Year

2B · 1B · 0B

New York State Energy Profile

Quick Facts

- The 2.4-gigawatt Robert Moses Niagara hydroelectric power plant is the fourth-largest hydroelectric power plant in the United States. In 2015, New York produced more hydroelectric power than any other state east of the Rocky Mountains.
- In 2015, New York had the eighth-highest average electricity prices in the United States, down from the fourth-highest price in 2014.
- To curb air pollution, in 2012 New York became the first northeastern state to require that all heating oil be ultra-low sulfur diesel.
- To ensure reliability, New York regulators require electricity-generating units that can burn either fuel oil or natural gas to be ready to switch to fuel oil if natural gas supply is constrained.
- The NY-Sun initiative aims to install 3,000 megawatts of small-scale (less than 200 kilowatts) solar photovoltaic facilities by 2023, and more than 15% of that target was installed by the end of 2015.
- More than half of New York households (53%) use individual window or wall air conditioning units, while only 20% have a central air conditioning system, according to EIA's Residential Energy Consumption Survey. Analysis

Overview

New York state stretches from the Great Lakes to New England and from Canada south to the Atlantic Ocean beaches of Long Island. It includes the densely populated New York City metropolis, rolling agricultural lands, and rugged mountains. The state's climate ranges from the temperate, ocean-moderated southeast to interior plains where Arctic winds sweep in from the Great Lakes and Canada. Because of its large population, New York's total energy consumption ranks among the highest in the nation, but its energy intensity and per capita energy consumption are among the lowest. The state's energy efficiency results in part from the New York City metropolitan region's widely used mass transportation systems. More than half of New York City workers use public transit, and more than one-fourth of state residents do, which is five times the U.S. average.

The commercial sector leads state energy demand, followed by the residential sector and the transportation sector. New York's key businesses—construction, food processing, electronics manufacturing, financial services, professional services, education, and health care—are not among the most energy-intensive industries, and the state's industrial energy consumption is close to the national median.

More than half New York's energy is supplied from other states and Canada. New York has developed a state energy plan to reduce greenhouse gases by 40% from 1990 levels and obtain half of all electricity from renewable sources, both by 2030.9 State emissions from electricity generation have declined since 2000 because of increased natural gas use and because of compliance with the Regional Greenhouse Gas Initiative, a program to reduce power plant emissions in nine northeastern states. In 2013, New York had the lowest carbon dioxide emissions per capita of any state in the nation.

Petroleum

New York is one of the largest consumers of petroleum products, which are used mainly for transportation and home heating. New York was an important center for oil production and refining in the 19th century, supporting the state's industrial regions around New York City and along the Erie Canal from as many as 56 refineries. By the end of the 20th century, all the refineries were closed. The state continues to produce small amounts of crude oil. Petroleum products consumed in New York are supplied by refineries in New Jersey and Pennsylvania, by the Colonial Pipeline system from the Gulf Coast, and by imports, mostly from Canada. New York Harbor, which includes terminals on both the New York and New Jersey shorelines, is the largest petroleum products hub in the Northeast, with bulk storage capacity exceeding 75 million barrels. Petroleum products delivered to the harbor are redistributed by truck or by barge to smaller ports on Long Island and upstate along the Hudson River, and to Connecticut, Rhode Island, and Massachusetts. Western New York receives refined products from Pennsylvania and the Midwest through pipelines and from Canada through the Port of Buffalo.

New York required that ultra-low sulfur diesel replace high-sulfur home heating oil starting in 2012.

More than three-fourths of petroleum products consumed in New York are used in the transportation sector, and much of the rest is used for heating. About one-fourth of New York households are heated with fuel oil. In 2000, after severe winter weather threatened regional shortages of home heating oil in the Northeast, the federal government created the Northeast Home Heating Oil Reserve. In 2011, the government converted the reserve to ultra-low sulfur diesel (ULSD), in part as a result of New York's decision to require consumers heating with petroleum to use ULSD starting in 2012. New York's decision led to a substantial increase in demand for ULSD, and most other northeastern states are phasing in ULSD as well.

To reduce ozone formation, reformulated motor gasoline blended with ethanol is required year-round in New York City and the surrounding metropolitan areas. The rest of the state is required to use a low volatility blend in the summer. New York Harbor is the primary Northeast distribution hub for ethanol supplies. Some ethanol is produced in New York, and Midwest ethanol producers often transport output to New York Harbor and to the Port of Albany by rail. Storage capacity and intermodal shipping capability have been expanded at Albany to distribute ethanol for blending with motor gasoline and also to move crude oil from North Dakota to East Coast refineries.

Natural Gas

The electric power sector, residential sector, and commercial sector consume most of the natural gas used in New York. More than half of New York households heat with natural gas. Western New York has historically produced small amounts of natural gas, but most natural gas consumed in the state is supplied by pipelines from other states and Canada. An increasing share of New York's natural gas comes from Pennsylvania. The Marcellus Shale, a formation extending under parts of New York, Pennsylvania, Ohio, West Virginia, and Maryland, is the largest natural gas field in the United States. There has been no development of natural gas shale resources in New York, and the total amount of retrievable natural gas under the state is unclear. In late 2014, citing health and environmental concerns, the state government banned hydraulic fracturing, a technique used to produce shale gas. New York had maintained a moratorium on the technology since 2008 while state officials explored safety and environmental regulations.

Virtually all major interstate pipelines from the Gulf Coast and Canada reach New York, both to supply in-state customers and to ship supplies onward to Connecticut and Massachusetts. With Pennsylvania natural gas production growing more than seventeen-fold since 2009, pipeline companies are expanding their capabilities to ship Marcellus Shale natural gas to customers in New York and New England. New York has more than two dozen natural gas underground storage facilities, mainly in depleted gas fields. Along with storage in Pennsylvania and West Virginia, those facilities are key to meeting northeastern winter heating demand.

Coal

New York has no coal mining. Coal is transported to New York electricity generating plants by rail, barge, or truck from nearby states, primarily Pennsylvania, and from the Powder River Basin in Wyoming. About 20% of the coal consumed in New York is used by industrial plants. Some steam coal for power generation is imported from Latin America through New York City's port. Coal from eastern U.S. mines is exported to Canada through the Port of Buffalo.

Since 2000, coal has been providing progressively less of New York's net electricity generation because new generating capacity has been mostly natural gas-fired. In recent years, less than 5% of New York's net electricity generation has been fueled by coal. New York has adopted carbon dioxide limits for new generating plants that may constrain future use of coal.

Electricity

New York electricity generators include both regulated electric utilities and independent power producers with diverse energy sources of generation. Natural gas, nuclear power, and hydroelectricity typically provide nine-tenths of net electricity generation, with wind, biomass, coal, and petroleum making up the balance. In 2015, about two-fifths of net electricity generation came from natural gas, one-third from nuclear power, and one-fifth from hydroelectricity.

New York's electricity usually flows east and south because half of the state's power demand is in the New York City region, but only about two-fifths of net electricity generation originates there. New York sometimes imports electricity from neighboring states and Canada, but demand has declined since the 2008 recession. Only about 10% of New York households use electricity for heating, and New Yorkers per capita are among the lowest electricity users in the nation. The New York grid operator says in-state generating resources can meet expected demand, but maintaining capability

to exchange electricity with neighboring grids remains vital to power reliability and system efficiency. More than half of New York's in-state generating capacity can burn either fuel oil or natural gas. To avoid blackouts, New York regulators require units with this dual-fuel capability to be ready to switch to fuel oil in the event of a natural gas supply disruption.

Renewable Energy

About four-fifths of net renewable generation in New York comes from hydroelectricity, with small but growing amounts from wind, biomass, and solar sources. The state is home to the largest hydroelectric power plant in the eastern United States, the 2.4-gigawatt Robert Moses Niagara plant, and produces more hydroelectric power than any other state east of the Rocky Mountains. New York is also among the top states using landfill gas and municipal solid waste to fuel electricity generation.

New York is consolidating its renewable portfolio standard (RPS), energy efficiency portfolio standard (EEPS), and other clean energy mandates under a program called Reforming the Energy Vision (REV). REV is intended to create a flexible utility business model that offers increased incentives for renewable and distributed electricity generation as well as consumer incentives for efficiency and distributed generation. The REV program details were being developed during 2016. The REV sets state goals for 2030 of obtaining half of all electricity sold in the state from renewable sources, reducing energy-related greenhouse gas emissions 40% from 1990 levels, and reducing energy consumption by buildings 23% from 2012 levels. The program sets a further goal of cutting greenhouse gas emissions 80% by 2050. As part of the REV development, a clean energy standard (CES) is replacing the state's expired RPS. The CES may recognize some nuclear power as an eligible clean energy source that reduces greenhouse gas emissions.

Most new renewable electricity has been obtained competitively from utility-scale projects by the New York State Energy Research and Development Authority. Most new power is from wind. The state's first wind farm began operating in 2000. More than two dozen wind farms are operating or are in development around the state. New York has an estimated potential for nearly 140,000 megawatts of onshore wind energy, particularly around Lake Erie and Lake Ontario, on peaks of the Adirondack Mountains and the Catskill Mountains, and along the Long Island shoreline. Some areas off the Long Island coast are also considered suitable for large-scale wind farms. Other new renewable electricity is being obtained from biomass and biogas resources and from hydroelectric facility upgrades. In 2010, New York regulators set a goal of obtaining about 8.5% of new renewable generation from small, customer-sited facilities, such as solar photovoltaic (PV) and solar thermal systems, fuel cells, anaerobic digester systems, and wind installations. Customer systems are generally limited to normal customer load, up to 200 kilowatts of capacity. The state offers consumers incentives for those installations.

In 2014, as part of the state's NY-Sun initiative, New York set a target of installing 3,000 megawatts of solar PV systems by 2023. At the end of 2015, 457 megawatts of solar PV capacity were installed in New York under NY-Sun, and 493 megawatts were in development. New York also encourages customer-sited solar installations, such as rooftop solar, through net metering. With its variety of support programs, the state was fifth in the nation in new solar capacity installed in 2015. Solar PV systems still provided less than 1% of New York's net electricity generation, but solar generation increased by 60% from 2014. The 32-megawatt Long Island Solar Farm is the largest solar PV generator in the eastern United States, but most solar installations in New York are small. Four-fifths of the state's 2015 solar generation came from customer-sited solar panels.

Source: U.S. Energy Information Administration, State Profile and Energy Estimates, July 21, 2016

Household Energy Use in New York

A closer look at residential energy consumption

All data from EIA's 2009 Residential Energy Consumption Survey
www.eia.gov/consumption/residential/

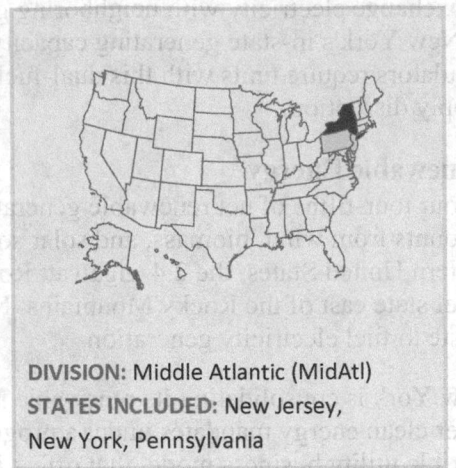

DIVISION: Middle Atlantic (MidAtl)

STATES INCLUDED: New Jersey, New York, Pennsylvania

- New York households consume an average of 103 million Btu per year, 15% more than the U.S. average.
- Electricity consumption in New York homes is much lower than the U.S. average, because many households use other fuels for major energy end uses like space heating, water heating, and cooking. Electricity costs are closer to the national average due to higher than average electricity prices in the state.
- New York homes are typically older and, with a higher percentage of apartments, are smaller on average than homes in other parts of the country.

ALL ENERGY *average per household (excl. transportation)*

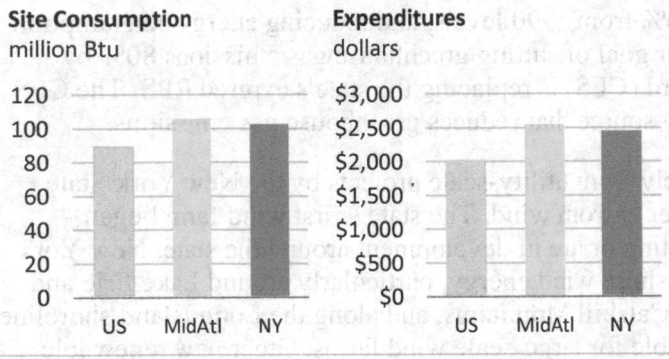

ELECTRICITY ONLY *average per household*

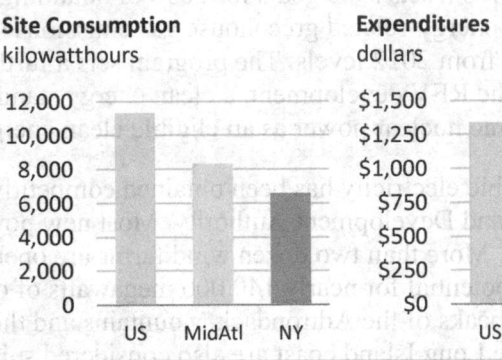

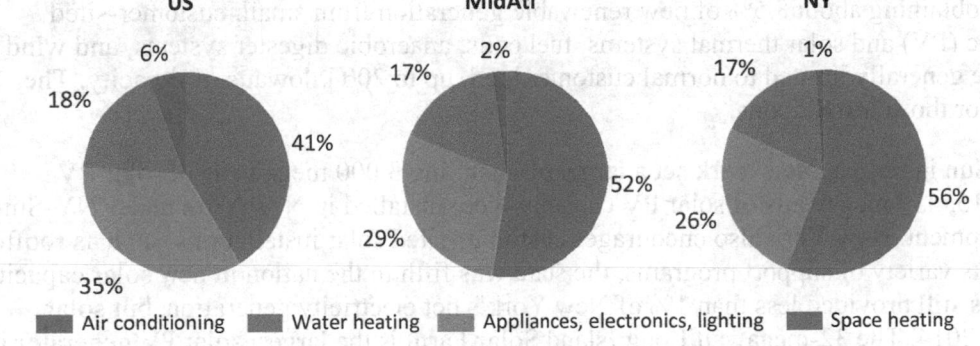

CONSUMPTION BY END USE

Since the weather in New York is cooler than most other areas of the United States, space heating (56%) makes up a greater portion of energy use in homes compared to the U.S. average, and air conditioning makes up only 1% of energy use.

MAIN HEATING FUEL USED

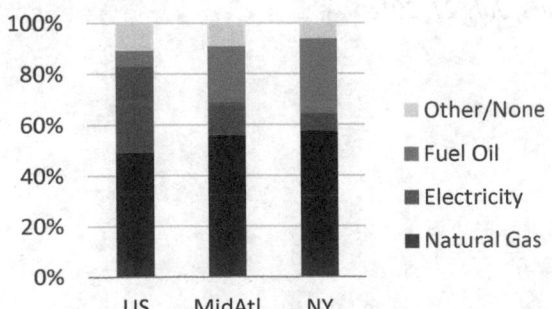

Natural gas provides space heating for 57% of New York households. Fuel oil (29%) is still a popular choice, despite declining usage nationwide.

COOLING EQUIPMENT USED

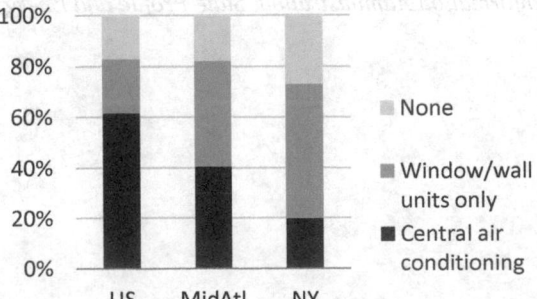

More than half of New York households (53%) use individual window/wall air conditioning units, while only 20% have a central system.

More highlights from RECS on housing characteristics and energy-related features per household...
US = United States | MidAtl = Middle Atlantic | NY = New York

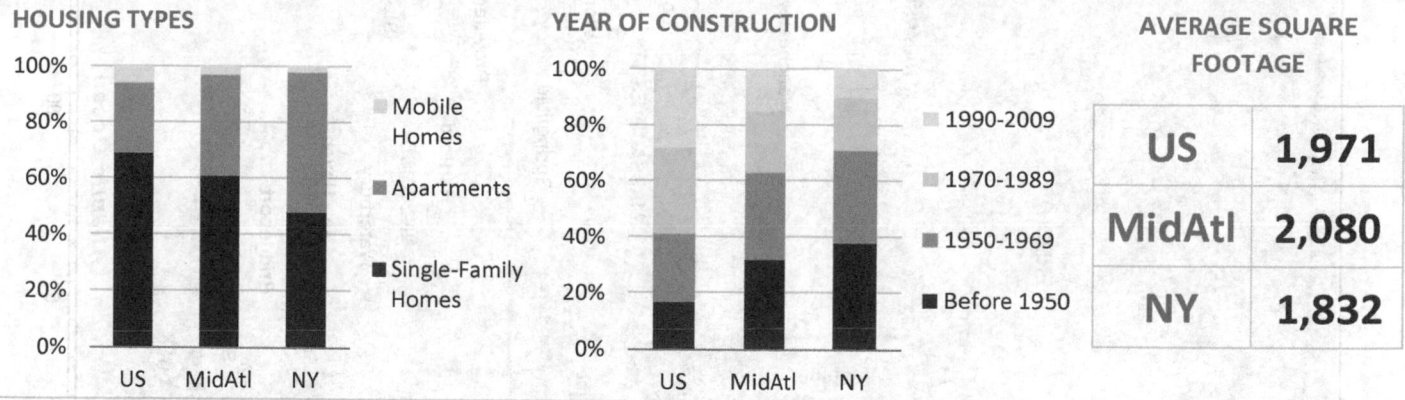

HOUSING TYPES

- Mobile Homes
- Apartments
- Single-Family Homes

YEAR OF CONSTRUCTION

- 1990-2009
- 1970-1989
- 1950-1969
- Before 1950

AVERAGE SQUARE FOOTAGE

US	1,971
MidAtl	2,080
NY	1,832

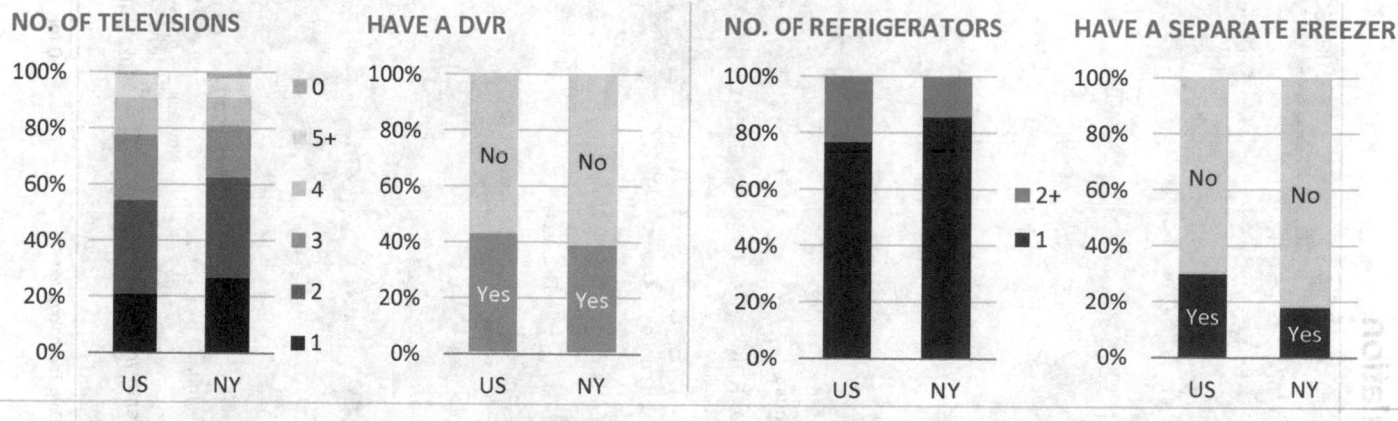

NO. OF TELEVISIONS

- 0
- 5+
- 4
- 3
- 2
- 1

HAVE A DVR

NO. OF REFRIGERATORS

- 2+
- 1

HAVE A SEPARATE FREEZER

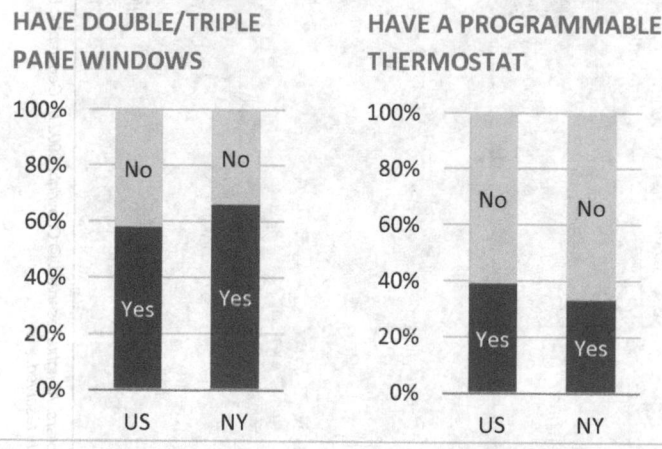

HAVE DOUBLE/TRIPLE PANE WINDOWS

HAVE A PROGRAMMABLE THERMOSTAT

About the Residential Energy Consumption Survey (RECS) Program

The RECS gathers energy characteristics through personal interviews from a nationwide sample of homes, and cost and consumption from energy suppliers.

The 2009 RECS is the thirteenth edition of the survey, which was first conducted in 1978.

Resulting products include:

- Home energy characteristics
- Average consumption & cost
- Detailed energy end-use statistics
- Reports highlighting key findings
- Microdata file for in-depth analysis

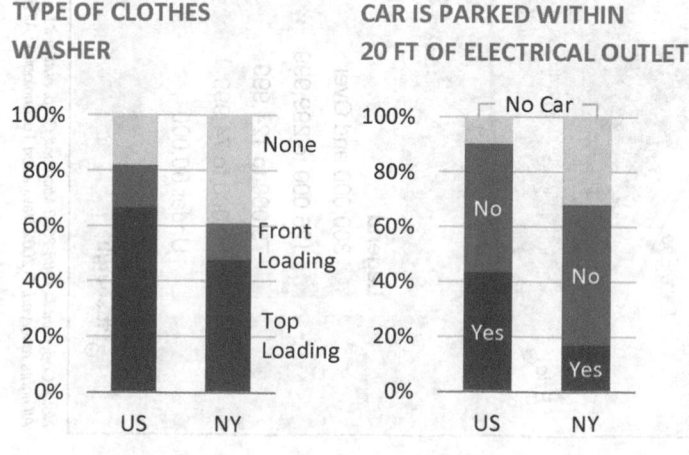

TYPE OF CLOTHES WASHER

- None
- Front Loading
- Top Loading

CAR IS PARKED WITHIN 20 FT OF ELECTRICAL OUTLET

- No Car

www.eia.gov/consumption/residential/

Population

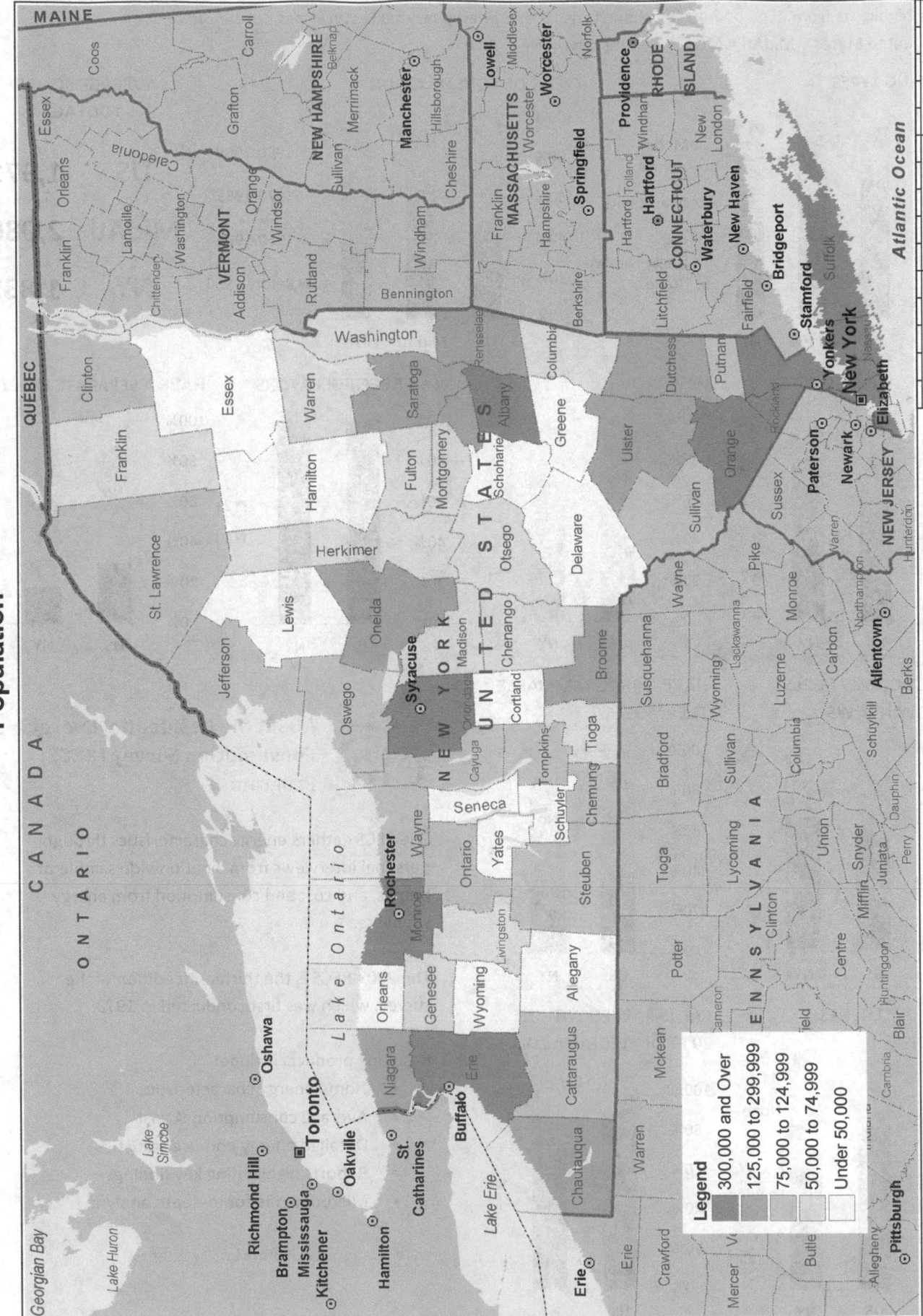

Legend
- 300,000 and Over
- 125,000 to 299,999
- 75,000 to 124,999
- 50,000 to 74,999
- Under 50,000

Percent White

Legend

- 95.0 and Over
- 90.0 to 94.9
- 85.0 to 89.9
- 80.0 to 84.9
- Under 80.0

Percent Black

Legend
- 8.0 and Over
- 6.0 to 7.9
- 4.0 to 5.9
- 2.0 to 3.9
- Under 2.0

Percent Asian

Legend

- 3.0 and Over
- 2.0 to 2.9
- 1.0 to 1.9
- 0.5 to 0.9
- Under 0.5

Percent Hispanic

Legend

■	8.0 and Over
■	6.0 to 7.9
■	4.0 to 5.9
■	2.0 to 3.9
□	Under 2.0

Median Age

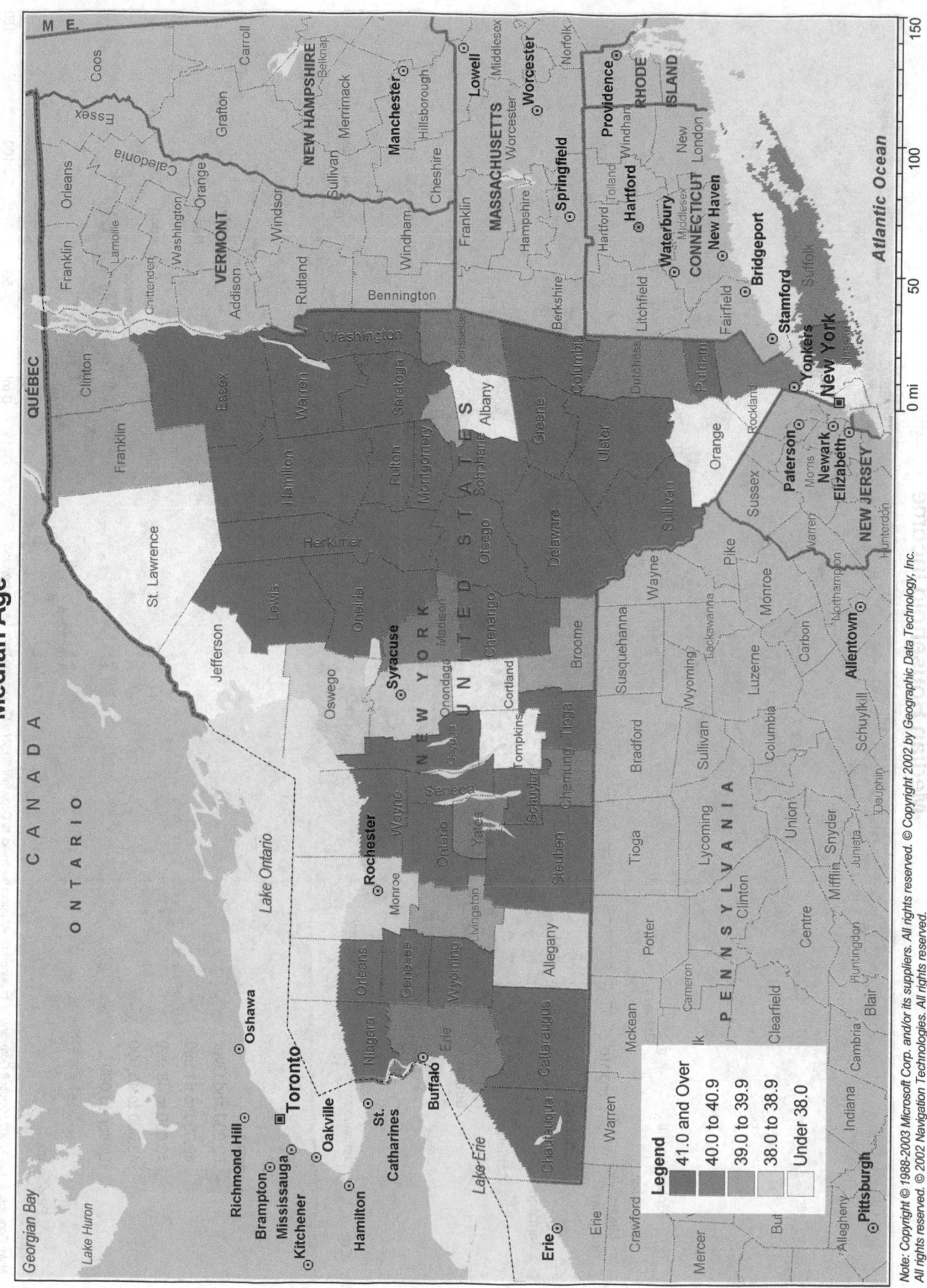

Legend

- 41.0 and Over
- 40.0 to 40.9
- 39.0 to 39.9
- 38.0 to 38.9
- Under 38.0

Median Household Income

Legend

- 52,000 and Over
- 49,000 to 51,999
- 46,000 to 48,999
- 43,000 to 45,999
- Under 43,000

Median Home Value

Legend
- 200,000 and Over
- 175,000 to 199,999
- 150,000 to 174,999
- 125,000 to 149,999
- 100,000 to 124,999
- Under 100,000

High School Graduates*

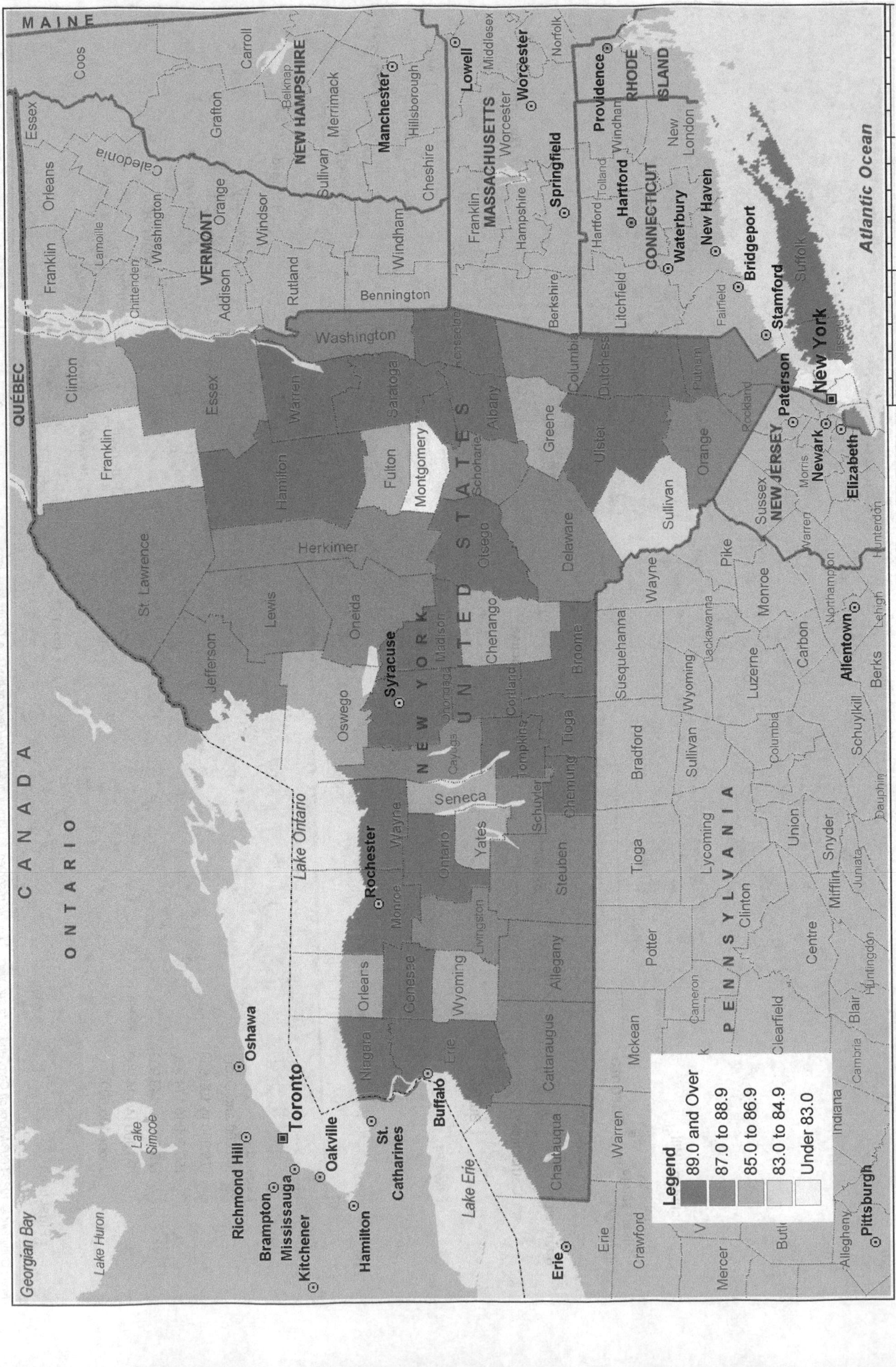

Legend
- 89.0 and Over
- 87.0 to 88.9
- 85.0 to 86.9
- 83.0 to 84.9
- Under 83.0

College Graduates*

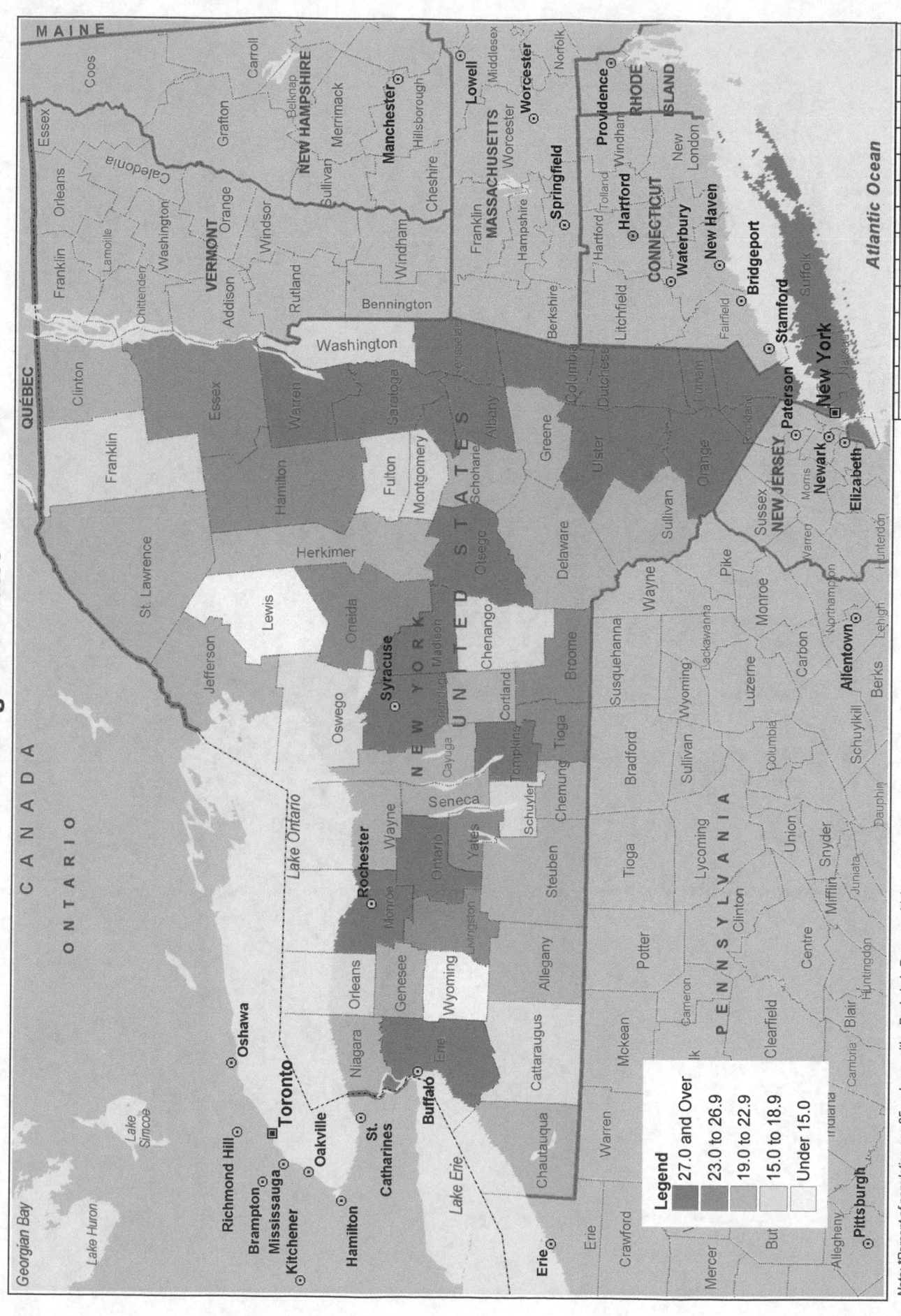

Legend

- 27.0 and Over
- 23.0 to 26.9
- 19.0 to 22.9
- 15.0 to 18.9
- Under 15.0

Profiles

Albany County

Located in eastern New York; bounded on the east by the Hudson River; includes the Helderbergs and part of the Catskills. Covers a land area of 522.804 square miles, a water area of 10.498 square miles, and is located in the Eastern Time Zone at 42.59° N. Lat., 73.97° W. Long. The county was founded in 1683. County seat is Albany.

Albany County is part of the Albany-Schenectady-Troy, NY Metropolitan Statistical Area. The entire metro area includes: Albany County, NY; Rensselaer County, NY; Saratoga County, NY; Schenectady County, NY; Schoharie County, NY

Weather Station: Albany County Arpt   Elevation: 274 feet

	Jan	Feb	Mar	Apr	May	Jun	Jul	Aug	Sep	Oct	Nov	Dec
High	31	35	44	58	70	78	82	81	72	60	48	36
Low	14	17	25	37	47	56	61	60	51	39	31	21
Precip	2.5	2.1	3.3	3.2	3.6	3.8	4.1	3.6	3.3	3.5	3.3	2.9
Snow	17.7	11.5	11.4	2.3	0.1	tr	tr	0.0	tr	0.3	3.2	13.7

High and Low temperatures in degrees Fahrenheit; Precipitation and Snow in inches

Weather Station: Alcove Dam   Elevation: 606 feet

	Jan	Feb	Mar	Apr	May	Jun	Jul	Aug	Sep	Oct	Nov	Dec
High	31	35	42	56	68	76	80	79	71	59	47	36
Low	12	14	22	34	44	53	58	57	49	37	29	19
Precip	2.4	2.1	3.5	3.8	3.5	4.5	3.8	3.5	3.7	3.5	3.5	2.8
Snow	na	na	na	0.4	tr	0.0	0.0	0.0	0.0	0.1	0.4	na

High and Low temperatures in degrees Fahrenheit; Precipitation and Snow in inches

Population: 307,463; Growth (since 2000): 4.4%; Density: 588.1 persons per square mile; Race: 77.0% White, 12.6% Black/African American, 5.7% Asian, 0.1% American Indian/Alaska Native, 0.1% Native Hawaiian/Other Pacific Islander, 3.2% two or more races, 5.5% Hispanic of any race; Average household size: 2.35; Median age: 37.9; Age under 18: 19.2%; Age 65 and over: 14.9%; Males per 100 females: 93.6; Marriage status: 42.4% never married, 42.7% now married, 1.9% separated, 6.0% widowed, 8.9% divorced; Foreign born: 8.8%; Speak English only: 88.2%; With disability: 11.2%; Veterans: 6.7%; Ancestry: 22.4% Irish, 16.5% Italian, 15.0% German, 8.2% English, 5.8% Polish

Religion: Six largest groups: 28.0% Catholicism, 3.1% Non-denominational Protestant, 2.1% Presbyterian-Reformed, 2.0% Methodist/Pietist, 1.7% Judaism, 1.5% Muslim Estimate

Economy: Unemployment rate: 4.0%; Leading industries: 14.1 % retail trade; 12.7 % professional, scientific, and technical services; 11.2 % other services (except public administration); Farms: 494 totaling 63,394 acres; Company size: 10 employ 1,000 or more persons, 19 employ 500 to 999 persons, 259 employ 100 to 499 persons, 9,110 employ less than 100 persons; Business ownership: 7,125 women-owned, 1,179 Black-owned, 821 Hispanic-owned, 1,229 Asian-owned, 75 American Indian/Alaska Native-owned

Employment: 15.5% management, business, and financial, 7.7% computer, engineering, and science, 13.3% education, legal, community service, arts, and media, 6.7% healthcare practitioners, 17.6% service, 26.2% sales and office, 5.6% natural resources, construction, and maintenance, 7.4% production, transportation, and material moving

Income: Per capita: $32,779; Median household: $59,887; Average household: $78,816; Households with income of $100,000 or more: 26.4%; Poverty rate: 13.5%

Educational Attainment: High school diploma or higher: 92.8%; Bachelor's degree or higher: 38.6%; Graduate/professional degree or higher: 18.4%

Housing: Homeownership rate: 58.3%; Median home value: $208,400; Median year structure built: 1958; Homeowner vacancy rate: 1.4%; Median selected monthly owner costs: $1,660 with a mortgage, $608 without a mortgage; Median gross rent: $919 per month; Rental vacancy rate: 6.0%

Vital Statistics: Birth rate: 100.2 per 10,000 population; Death rate: 86.6 per 10,000 population; Age-adjusted cancer mortality rate: 166.3 deaths per 100,000 population

Health Insurance: 94.0% have insurance; 77.7% have private insurance; 30.1% have public insurance; 6.0% do not have insurance; 2.2% of children under 18 do not have insurance

Health Care: Physicians: 59.3 per 10,000 population; Dentists: 8.5 per 10,000 population; Hospital beds: 50.5 per 10,000 population; Hospital admissions: 2,007.0 per 10,000 population

Air Quality Index (AQI): Percent of Days: 84.7% good, 15.1% moderate, 0.3% unhealthy for sensitive individuals, 0.0% unhealthy, 0.0% very unhealthy; Annual median: 35; Annual maximum: 107

Transportation: Commute: 85.3% car, 5.7% public transportation, 4.5% walk, 2.9% work from home; Mean travel time to work: 20.4 minutes

2016 Presidential Election: 34.6% Trump, 60.1% Clinton, 3.5% Johnson, 1.8% Stein

National and State Parks: Thacher State Park

Additional Information Contacts

Albany Government . . . . (518) 447-7300
   http://www.albanycounty.com

Albany County Communities

ALBANY (city). State capital. County seat. Covers a land area of 21.388 square miles and a water area of 0.548 square miles. Located at 42.67° N. Lat; 73.80° W. Long. Elevation is 148 feet.

History: Native American trails running in all directions crossed at the site of Albany. Several ship captains, including Henry Hudson, dropped anchor in the shallows near the present city, and made friends with the inhabitants. The next settlers, who came in 1624, were mostly Walloons from Holland. They built a fort and called it Fort Orange. Dutch, Norwegians, Danes, Germans, and Scots all settled on this land. In 1652, Peter Stuyvesant was sent out by the West India Company to set up a court and he laid out space around Fort Orange for a new village called Beverwyck. In 1685, control was relinquished to the English. The town became a mixture of Dutch and British people and cultures. It was chartered as Albany in 1686. Early fur trade made Albany residents wealthy, but wars plagued the area for almost a century. At the end of the wars, Albany found itself at the crossroad of a developing nation, with travelers coming by land, water, and rail. Lumbering and manufacturing also became important in the 19th century.

Population: 98,468; Growth (since 2000): 2.9%; Density: 4,603.8 persons per square mile; Race: 55.5% White, 29.9% Black/African American, 7.0% Asian, 0.3% American Indian/Alaska Native, 0.1% Native Hawaiian/Other Pacific Islander, 5.0% Two or more races, 9.6% Hispanic of any race; Average household size: 2.19; Median age: 31.2; Age under 18: 17.1%; Age 65 and over: 12.4%; Males per 100 females: 93.6; Marriage status: 60.7% never married, 25.7% now married, 1.8% separated, 5.7% widowed, 7.9% divorced; Foreign born: 11.5%; Speak English only: 84.4%; With disability: 12.1%; Veterans: 4.3%; Ancestry: 15.0% Irish, 13.0% Italian, 9.8% German, 5.2% English, 3.9% Polish

Employment: 12.5% management, business, and financial, 7.1% computer, engineering, and science, 13.9% education, legal, community service, arts, and media, 5.7% healthcare practitioners, 24.2% service, 25.9% sales and office, 4.4% natural resources, construction, and maintenance, 6.3% production, transportation, and material moving

Income: Per capita: $24,912; Median household: $40,949; Average household: $57,274; Households with income of $100,000 or more: 15.2%; Poverty rate: 26.8%

Educational Attainment: High school diploma or higher: 89.6%; Bachelor's degree or higher: 36.4%; Graduate/professional degree or higher: 16.8%

School District(s)

Achievement Academy Charter School (05-08)
   2014-15 Enrollment: n/a . . . . (518) 533-1601
Albany City SD (PK-12)
   2014-15 Enrollment: 8,942 . . . . (518) 475-6010
Albany Community Charter School (KG-05)
   2014-15 Enrollment: 643 . . . . (518) 433-1500
Albany Leadership Charter High School for Girls (09-11)
   2014-15 Enrollment: 369 . . . . (518) 694-5300
Albany Preparatory Charter School (05-08)
   2014-15 Enrollment: n/a . . . . (518) 694-5005
Brighter Choice Charter Middle School for Boys
   2014-15 Enrollment: 213 . . . . (518) 703-6100
Brighter Choice Charter Middle School for Girls
   2014-15 Enrollment: 220 . . . . (518) 694-5550
Brighter Choice Charter School for Boys (KG-04)
   2014-15 Enrollment: 288 . . . . (518) 694-8200
Brighter Choice Charter School for Girls (KG-04)
   2014-15 Enrollment: 277 . . . . (518) 694-4100
Capital Region Boces
   2014-15 Enrollment: n/a . . . . (518) 862-4901

Green Tech High Charter School (09-12)
2014-15 Enrollment: 346 . . . . (518) 694-3400
Guilderland Central SD (KG-12)
2014-15 Enrollment: 4,984 . . . . (518) 456-6200
Henry Johnson Charter School (KG-04)
2014-15 Enrollment: 389 . . . . (518) 432-4300
Kipp Tech Valley Charter School (05-08)
2014-15 Enrollment: 289 . . . . (518) 694-9494
NYS Dept of Corrections
2014-15 Enrollment: 1,363 . . . . (518) 457-8126
New York State Omh
2014-15 Enrollment: 354 . . . . (518) 473-6328
Nys Office for People With Developmental Disabilit
2014-15 Enrollment: n/a . . . . (866) 946-9733
South Colonie Central SD (PK-12)
2014-15 Enrollment: 4,939 . . . . (518) 869-3576

Four-year College(s)
Albany College of Pharmacy and Health Sciences (Private, Not-for-profit)
Fall 2014 Enrollment: 1,563 . . . . (518) 694-7200
2015-16 Tuition: In-state $31,081; Out-of-state $31,081
Albany Law School (Private, Not-for-profit)
Fall 2014 Enrollment: 475 . . . . (518) 445-2311
Albany Medical College (Private, Not-for-profit)
Fall 2014 Enrollment: 823 . . . . (518) 262-3125
Bryant & Stratton College-Albany (Private, For-profit)
Fall 2014 Enrollment: 500 . . . . (518) 437-1802
2015-16 Tuition: In-state $16,042; Out-of-state $16,042
Excelsior College (Private, Not-for-profit)
Fall 2014 Enrollment: 41,527 . . . . (518) 464-8500
Maria College of Albany (Private, Not-for-profit)
Fall 2014 Enrollment: 859 . . . . (518) 438-3111
2015-16 Tuition: In-state $13,340; Out-of-state $13,340
SUNY at Albany (Public)
Fall 2014 Enrollment: 17,273 . . . . (518) 442-3300
2015-16 Tuition: In-state $8,996; Out-of-state $22,116
Siena College (Loudonville) (Private, Not-for-profit, Roman Catholic)
Fall 2014 Enrollment: 3,179 . . . . (518) 783-2300
2015-16 Tuition: In-state $33,415; Out-of-state $33,415
The College of Saint Rose (Private, Not-for-profit)
Fall 2014 Enrollment: 4,499 . . . . (518) 454-5111
2015-16 Tuition: In-state $29,826; Out-of-state $29,826

Two-year College(s)
ITT Technical Institute-Albany (Private, For-profit)
Fall 2014 Enrollment: 232 . . . . (518) 452-9300
2015-16 Tuition: In-state $18,048; Out-of-state $18,048
Memorial College of Nursing (Private, Not-for-profit)
Fall 2014 Enrollment: 131 . . . . (518) 471-3260
2015-16 Tuition: In-state $11,288; Out-of-state $11,288
Mildred Elley School-Albany Campus (Private, For-profit)
Fall 2014 Enrollment: 748 . . . . (518) 786-0855
2015-16 Tuition: In-state $11,205; Out-of-state $11,205

Vocational/Technical School(s)
Albany BOCES-Adult Practical Nursing Program (Public)
Fall 2014 Enrollment: 141 . . . . (518) 862-4800
2015-16 Tuition: $14,105
Austin's School of Spa Technology (Private, For-profit)
Fall 2014 Enrollment: 283 . . . . (518) 438-7879
2015-16 Tuition: $10,375
Branford Hall Career Institute-Albany Campus (Private, For-profit)
Fall 2014 Enrollment: 309 . . . . (518) 456-4464
2015-16 Tuition: $13,140
Center for Natural Wellness School of Massage Therapy (Private, For-profit)
Fall 2014 Enrollment: 45 . . . . (518) 489-4026
2015-16 Tuition: $16,600
New School of Radio and Television (Private, For-profit)
Fall 2014 Enrollment: 65 . . . . (518) 438-7682
2015-16 Tuition: $11,410
Orlo School of Hair Design and Cosmetology (Private, For-profit)
Fall 2014 Enrollment: 66 . . . . (518) 459-7832
2015-16 Tuition: $10,400
Housing: Homeownership rate: 37.5%; Median home value: $171,400; Median year structure built: Before 1940; Homeowner vacancy rate: 2.7%; Median selected monthly owner costs: $1,556 with a mortgage, $599

without a mortgage; Median gross rent: $857 per month; Rental vacancy rate: 6.9%
Health Insurance: 90.8% have insurance; 65.9% have private insurance; 35.9% have public insurance; 9.2% do not have insurance; 2.6% of children under 18 do not have insurance
Hospitals: Albany Medical Center Hospital (651 beds); Albany Memorial Hospital (165 beds); Albany VA Medical Center (156 beds); Saint Peter's Hospital (442 beds)
Safety: Violent crime rate: 80.3 per 10,000 population; Property crime rate: 325.1 per 10,000 population
Newspapers: Metroland (weekly circulation 40,000); Times Union (daily circulation 95,500)
Transportation: Commute: 71.1% car, 14.4% public transportation, 10.3% walk, 2.4% work from home; Mean travel time to work: 19.1 minutes; Amtrak: Train service available.
Airports: Albany International (primary service/small hub)
Additional Information Contacts
City of Albany . . . . (518) 434-5075
http://www.albanyny.org/home.aspx

ALCOVE (unincorporated postal area)
ZCTA: 12007
Covers a land area of 1.213 square miles and a water area of 0.003 square miles. Located at 42.46° N. Lat; 73.93° W. Long. Elevation is 545 feet.
Population: 17; Growth (since 2000): n/a; Density: 14.0 persons per square mile; Race: 100.0% White, 0.0% Black/African American, 0.0% Asian, 0.0% American Indian/Alaska Native, 0.0% Native Hawaiian/Other Pacific Islander, 0.0% Two or more races, 0.0% Hispanic of any race; Average household size: 2.13; Median age: n/a; Age under 18: 0.0%; Age 65 and over: 100.0%; Males per 100 females: 140.0; Marriage status: 0.0% never married, 100.0% now married, 0.0% separated, 0.0% widowed, 0.0% divorced; Foreign born: 0.0%; Speak English only: 100.0%; With disability: 0.0%; Veterans: 0.0%; Ancestry: 100.0% American
Employment: n/a management, business, and financial, n/a computer, engineering, and science, n/a education, legal, community service, arts, and media, n/a healthcare practitioners, n/a service, n/a sales and office, n/a natural resources, construction, and maintenance, n/a production, transportation, and material moving
Income: Per capita: n/a; Median household: n/a; Average household: n/a; Households with income of $100,000 or more: n/a; Poverty rate: n/a
Educational Attainment: High school diploma or higher: 100.0%; Bachelor's degree or higher: n/a; Graduate/professional degree or higher: n/a
Housing: Homeownership rate: 100.0%; Median home value: n/a; Median year structure built: n/a; Homeowner vacancy rate: 75.8%; Median selected monthly owner costs: $0 with a mortgage, $0 without a mortgage; Median gross rent: n/a per month; Rental vacancy rate: 0.0%
Health Insurance: 100.0% have insurance; 100.0% have private insurance; 100.0% have public insurance; 0.0% do not have insurance; 0.0% of children under 18 do not have insurance
Transportation: Commute: n/a car, n/a public transportation, n/a walk, n/a work from home; Mean travel time to work: 0.0 minutes

ALTAMONT (village). Covers a land area of 1.186 square miles and a water area of <.001 square miles. Located at 42.71° N. Lat; 74.03° W. Long. Elevation is 463 feet.
Population: 1,610; Growth (since 2000): -7.3%; Density: 1,357.0 persons per square mile; Race: 97.6% White, 0.7% Black/African American, 0.0% Asian, 0.0% American Indian/Alaska Native, 0.2% Native Hawaiian/Other Pacific Islander, 0.6% Two or more races, 3.3% Hispanic of any race; Average household size: 2.37; Median age: 45.1; Age under 18: 20.4%; Age 65 and over: 15.8%; Males per 100 females: 94.4; Marriage status: 24.4% never married, 58.4% now married, 1.0% separated, 6.6% widowed, 10.7% divorced; Foreign born: 2.8%; Speak English only: 98.4%; With disability: 11.1%; Veterans: 6.5%; Ancestry: 27.3% Irish, 21.6% English, 21.6% German, 16.5% Italian, 7.3% Polish
Employment: 18.6% management, business, and financial, 4.8% computer, engineering, and science, 18.9% education, legal, community service, arts, and media, 7.2% healthcare practitioners, 17.5% service, 23.1% sales and office, 6.0% natural resources, construction, and maintenance, 3.8% production, transportation, and material moving

Income: Per capita: $37,939; Median household: $80,078; Average household: $90,060; Households with income of $100,000 or more: 43.1%; Poverty rate: 6.6%

Educational Attainment: High school diploma or higher: 97.5%; Bachelor's degree or higher: 42.7%; Graduate/professional degree or higher: 24.3%

School District(s)
Guilderland Central SD (KG-12)

   2014-15 Enrollment: 4,984 . . . . (518) 456-6200

Housing: Homeownership rate: 73.3%; Median home value: $250,200; Median year structure built: 1961; Homeowner vacancy rate: 0.0%; Median selected monthly owner costs: $1,977 with a mortgage, $753 without a mortgage; Median gross rent: $927 per month; Rental vacancy rate: 15.4%

Health Insurance: 97.8% have insurance; 85.0% have private insurance; 28.4% have public insurance; 2.2% do not have insurance; 0.0% of children under 18 do not have insurance

Safety: Violent crime rate: 5.8 per 10,000 population; Property crime rate: 63.7 per 10,000 population

Newspapers: Altamont Enterprise (weekly circulation 6,300)

Transportation: Commute: 95.2% car, 0.0% public transportation, 0.5% walk, 2.9% work from home; Mean travel time to work: 28.2 minutes

BERNE (town). Covers a land area of 64.030 square miles and a water area of 0.704 square miles. Located at 42.60° N. Lat; 74.13° W. Long. Elevation is 971 feet.

Population: 2,823; Growth (since 2000): -0.8%; Density: 44.1 persons per square mile; Race: 96.6% White, 0.8% Black/African American, 0.7% Asian, 0.0% American Indian/Alaska Native, 0.6% Native Hawaiian/Other Pacific Islander, 1.0% Two or more races, 0.5% Hispanic of any race; Average household size: 2.39; Median age: 48.0; Age under 18: 18.5%; Age 65 and over: 17.6%; Males per 100 females: 102.3; Marriage status: 24.8% never married, 57.9% now married, 2.7% separated, 6.7% widowed, 10.6% divorced; Foreign born: 3.0%; Speak English only: 96.5%; With disability: 9.5%; Veterans: 8.9%; Ancestry: 26.3% Irish, 24.4% German, 12.9% English, 11.1% Italian, 10.7% Dutch

Employment: 16.5% management, business, and financial, 6.2% computer, engineering, and science, 9.2% education, legal, community service, arts, and media, 6.6% healthcare practitioners, 14.5% service, 21.6% sales and office, 15.6% natural resources, construction, and maintenance, 9.9% production, transportation, and material moving

Income: Per capita: $35,435; Median household: $65,662; Average household: $82,285; Households with income of $100,000 or more: 31.5%; Poverty rate: 9.1%

Educational Attainment: High school diploma or higher: 96.5%; Bachelor's degree or higher: 27.7%; Graduate/professional degree or higher: 10.0%

School District(s)
Berne-Knox-Westerlo Central SD (PK-12)

   2014-15 Enrollment: 844. . . . . (518) 872-1293

Housing: Homeownership rate: 92.5%; Median home value: $187,800; Median year structure built: 1966; Homeowner vacancy rate: 0.0%; Median selected monthly owner costs: $1,510 with a mortgage, $548 without a mortgage; Median gross rent: $745 per month; Rental vacancy rate: 11.1%

Health Insurance: 96.1% have insurance; 82.5% have private insurance; 30.0% have public insurance; 3.9% do not have insurance; 0.8% of children under 18 do not have insurance

Transportation: Commute: 95.8% car, 0.6% public transportation, 1.0% walk, 1.1% work from home; Mean travel time to work: 31.8 minutes

BETHLEHEM (town). Covers a land area of 49.030 square miles and a water area of 0.834 square miles. Located at 42.59° N. Lat; 73.83° W. Long. Elevation is 210 feet.

Population: 34,430; Growth (since 2000): 10.0%; Density: 702.2 persons per square mile; Race: 91.1% White, 2.5% Black/African American, 4.0% Asian, 0.0% American Indian/Alaska Native, 0.0% Native Hawaiian/Other Pacific Islander, 2.0% Two or more races, 1.7% Hispanic of any race; Average household size: 2.55; Median age: 43.3; Age under 18: 23.0%; Age 65 and over: 15.8%; Males per 100 females: 92.2; Marriage status: 27.3% never married, 58.2% now married, 0.9% separated, 6.7% widowed, 7.9% divorced; Foreign born: 6.2%; Speak English only: 92.3%; With disability: 9.9%; Veterans: 7.4%; Ancestry: 28.9% Irish, 19.5% German, 15.6% Italian, 12.9% English, 6.1% American

Employment: 19.4% management, business, and financial, 9.8% computer, engineering, and science, 18.9% education, legal, community service, arts, and media, 8.5% healthcare practitioners, 11.2% service,

22.0% sales and office, 4.8% natural resources, construction, and maintenance, 5.6% production, transportation, and material moving

Income: Per capita: $45,215; Median household: $93,366; Average household: $115,120; Households with income of $100,000 or more: 45.9%; Poverty rate: 4.3%

Educational Attainment: High school diploma or higher: 96.7%; Bachelor's degree or higher: 56.3%; Graduate/professional degree or higher: 32.4%

Housing: Homeownership rate: 78.3%; Median home value: $271,900; Median year structure built: 1974; Homeowner vacancy rate: 1.5%; Median selected monthly owner costs: $2,011 with a mortgage, $777 without a mortgage; Median gross rent: $1,094 per month; Rental vacancy rate: 8.2%

Health Insurance: 97.3% have insurance; 89.5% have private insurance; 22.9% have public insurance; 2.7% do not have insurance; 2.3% of children under 18 do not have insurance

Safety: Violent crime rate: 6.9 per 10,000 population; Property crime rate: 131.6 per 10,000 population

Transportation: Commute: 90.6% car, 1.4% public transportation, 1.1% walk, 5.9% work from home; Mean travel time to work: 20.9 minutes

Additional Information Contacts

Town of Bethlehem . . . . (518) 439-4955
   http://www.townofbethlehem.org

COEYMANS (town). Covers a land area of 50.129 square miles and a water area of 3.038 square miles. Located at 42.49° N. Lat; 73.88° W. Long. Elevation is 59 feet.

History: Coeymans is named after an early settler, who was the patent-holder for the area.

Population: 7,457; Growth (since 2000): -8.5%; Density: 148.8 persons per square mile; Race: 93.9% White, 4.6% Black/African American, 0.5% Asian, 0.1% American Indian/Alaska Native, 0.0% Native Hawaiian/Other Pacific Islander, 0.7% Two or more races, 2.9% Hispanic of any race; Average household size: 2.41; Median age: 43.1; Age under 18: 20.2%; Age 65 and over: 17.0%; Males per 100 females: 99.3; Marriage status: 29.6% never married, 54.2% now married, 1.4% separated, 5.6% widowed, 10.5% divorced; Foreign born: 2.8%; Speak English only: 95.6%; With disability: 11.4%; Veterans: 10.3%; Ancestry: 20.2% German, 18.8% Italian, 17.3% Irish, 17.0% American, 5.7% French

Employment: 14.0% management, business, and financial, 7.3% computer, engineering, and science, 9.8% education, legal, community service, arts, and media, 4.5% healthcare practitioners, 15.3% service, 25.2% sales and office, 9.4% natural resources, construction, and maintenance, 14.5% production, transportation, and material moving

Income: Per capita: $29,024; Median household: $55,429; Average household: $68,309; Households with income of $100,000 or more: 19.1%; Poverty rate: 9.9%

Educational Attainment: High school diploma or higher: 91.3%; Bachelor's degree or higher: 18.4%; Graduate/professional degree or higher: 7.1%

School District(s)
Ravena-Coeymans-Selkirk Central SD (PK-12)

   2014-15 Enrollment: 1,938 . . . . (518) 756-5200

Housing: Homeownership rate: 69.8%; Median home value: $171,000; Median year structure built: 1958; Homeowner vacancy rate: 1.2%; Median selected monthly owner costs: $1,529 with a mortgage, $652 without a mortgage; Median gross rent: $830 per month; Rental vacancy rate: 7.7%

Health Insurance: 92.6% have insurance; 75.6% have private insurance; 32.7% have public insurance; 7.4% do not have insurance; 3.6% of children under 18 do not have insurance

Safety: Violent crime rate: 6.7 per 10,000 population; Property crime rate: 123.5 per 10,000 population

Transportation: Commute: 93.8% car, 1.0% public transportation, 1.1% walk, 1.9% work from home; Mean travel time to work: 25.7 minutes

Additional Information Contacts

Town of Coeymans . . . . (518) 756-6006
   http://www.coeymans.org

COEYMANS HOLLOW (unincorporated postal area)
ZCTA: 12046

   Covers a land area of 15.349 square miles and a water area of 2.081 square miles. Located at 42.51° N. Lat; 73.92° W. Long. Elevation is 413 feet.

Population: 855; Growth (since 2000) -8.5%; Density: 55.7 persons per square mile; Race: 100.0% White, 0.0% Black/African American,

0.0% Asian, 0.0% American Indian/Alaska Native, 0.0% Native Hawaiian/Other Pacific Islander, 0.0% Two or more races, 0.0% Hispanic of any race; Average household size: 2.51; Median age: 40.6; Age under 18: 19.5%; Age 65 and over: 15.7%; Males per 100 females: 97.8; Marriage status: 27.8% never married, 54.2% now married, 0.0% separated, 1.3% widowed, 16.7% divorced; Foreign born: 1.9%; Speak English only: 91.1%; With disability: 9.7%; Veterans: 14.1%; Ancestry: 28.7% German, 15.2% Irish, 11.5% Italian, 9.2% American, 7.4% French
Employment: 18.1% management, business, and financial, 10.7% computer, engineering, and science, 6.1% education, legal, community service, arts, and media, 3.5% healthcare practitioners, 4.6% service, 22.4% sales and office, 7.6% natural resources, construction, and maintenance, 27.0% production, transportation, and material moving
Income: Per capita: $33,872; Median household: $80,129; Average household: $84,054; Households with income of $100,000 or more: 36.3%; Poverty rate: 7.4%
Educational Attainment: High school diploma or higher: 94.0%; Bachelor's degree or higher: 26.7%; Graduate/professional degree or higher: 5.9%
Housing: Homeownership rate: 91.2%; Median home value: $211,700; Median year structure built: 1969; Homeowner vacancy rate: 0.0%; Median selected monthly owner costs: $1,715 with a mortgage, $810 without a mortgage; Median gross rent: n/a per month; Rental vacancy rate: 0.0%
Health Insurance: 95.7% have insurance; 81.6% have private insurance; 23.4% have public insurance; 4.3% do not have insurance; 0.0% of children under 18 do not have insurance
Transportation: Commute: 85.2% car, 2.1% public transportation, 2.1% walk, 7.7% work from home; Mean travel time to work: 26.0 minutes

COHOES (city).
Covers a land area of 3.774 square miles and a water area of 0.463 square miles. Located at 42.77° N. Lat; 73.71° W. Long. Elevation is 98 feet.
History: The world's first power-operated knitting mill was opened here in 1832. Van Schaick Mansion (1735), now a Museum, was used as headquarters by General Horatio Gates during the American Revolution. Settled by Dutch 1665, Incorporated 1869.
Population: 16,281; Growth (since 2000): 4.9%; Density: 4,314.5 persons per square mile; Race: 88.4% White, 3.9% Black/African American, 0.7% Asian, 0.4% American Indian/Alaska Native, 0.0% Native Hawaiian/Other Pacific Islander, 4.9% Two or more races, 5.7% Hispanic of any race; Average household size: 2.22; Median age: 39.7; Age under 18: 18.4%; Age 65 and over: 18.1%; Males per 100 females: 89.7; Marriage status: 38.9% never married, 39.9% now married, 1.8% separated, 8.6% widowed, 12.6% divorced; Foreign born: 4.3%; Speak English only: 94.3%; With disability: 17.4%; Veterans: 8.7%; Ancestry: 22.8% Irish, 16.2% French, 15.8% Italian, 11.7% German, 11.6% Polish
Employment: 12.4% management, business, and financial, 5.3% computer, engineering, and science, 8.3% education, legal, community service, arts, and media, 4.4% healthcare practitioners, 21.9% service, 27.3% sales and office, 8.4% natural resources, construction, and maintenance, 12.1% production, transportation, and material moving
Income: Per capita: $24,976; Median household: $46,226; Average household: $54,322; Households with income of $100,000 or more: 12.1%; Poverty rate: 17.4%
Educational Attainment: High school diploma or higher: 87.3%; Bachelor's degree or higher: 18.5%; Graduate/professional degree or higher: 8.0%
School District(s)
Cohoes City SD (KG-12)
    2014-15 Enrollment: 1,870 . . . . (518) 237-0100
North Colonie CSD
    2014-15 Enrollment: 5,383 . . . . (518) 785-8591
Housing: Homeownership rate: 42.9%; Median home value: $150,000; Median year structure built: 1941; Homeowner vacancy rate: 1.3%; Median selected monthly owner costs: $1,374 with a mortgage, $529 without a mortgage; Median gross rent: $825 per month; Rental vacancy rate: 7.8%
Health Insurance: 91.8% have insurance; 65.3% have private insurance; 40.9% have public insurance; 8.2% do not have insurance; 2.9% of children under 18 do not have insurance
Safety: Violent crime rate: 23.4 per 10,000 population; Property crime rate: 141.8 per 10,000 population
Transportation: Commute: 92.1% car, 2.3% public transportation, 2.4% walk, 1.6% work from home; Mean travel time to work: 20.3 minutes

Additional Information Contacts
City of Cohoes. . . . . (518) 233-2121
  http://www.cohoes.com

COLONIE (town).
Covers a land area of 55.943 square miles and a water area of 1.900 square miles. Located at 42.74° N. Lat; 73.79° W. Long. Elevation is 312 feet.
History: Incorporated 1921.
Population: 82,750; Growth (since 2000): 4.4%; Density: 1,479.2 persons per square mile; Race: 83.1% White, 5.8% Black/African American, 7.2% Asian, 0.0% American Indian/Alaska Native, 0.1% Native Hawaiian/Other Pacific Islander, 2.6% Two or more races, 4.5% Hispanic of any race; Average household size: 2.47; Median age: 41.4; Age under 18: 19.2%; Age 65 and over: 16.4%; Males per 100 females: 92.8; Marriage status: 34.7% never married, 50.0% now married, 2.2% separated, 5.8% widowed, 9.4% divorced; Foreign born: 10.3%; Speak English only: 86.0%; With disability: 11.0%; Veterans: 7.7%; Ancestry: 26.6% Irish, 19.7% Italian, 15.9% German, 8.3% English, 6.7% Polish
Employment: 17.4% management, business, and financial, 7.8% computer, engineering, and science, 10.8% education, legal, community service, arts, and media, 7.4% healthcare practitioners, 15.8% service, 27.9% sales and office, 5.5% natural resources, construction, and maintenance, 7.4% production, transportation, and material moving
Income: Per capita: $35,473; Median household: $71,658; Average household: $88,857; Households with income of $100,000 or more: 32.7%; Poverty rate: 6.9%
Educational Attainment: High school diploma or higher: 93.9%; Bachelor's degree or higher: 39.0%; Graduate/professional degree or higher: 16.8%
Housing: Homeownership rate: 70.8%; Median home value: $219,000; Median year structure built: 1967; Homeowner vacancy rate: 0.6%; Median selected monthly owner costs: $1,637 with a mortgage, $557 without a mortgage; Median gross rent: $1,030 per month; Rental vacancy rate: 2.5%
Health Insurance: 96.2% have insurance; 84.8% have private insurance; 27.1% have public insurance; 3.8% do not have insurance; 2.1% of children under 18 do not have insurance
Safety: Violent crime rate: 9.3 per 10,000 population; Property crime rate: 249.8 per 10,000 population
Transportation: Commute: 91.8% car, 2.3% public transportation, 2.2% walk, 2.4% work from home; Mean travel time to work: 19.4 minutes
Additional Information Contacts
Town of Colonie . . . . (518) 783-2700
  http://www.colonie.org

COLONIE (village).
Covers a land area of 3.242 square miles and a water area of 0.003 square miles. Located at 42.72° N. Lat; 73.83° W. Long. Elevation is 312 feet.
Population: 7,898; Growth (since 2000): -0.2%; Density: 2,436.5 persons per square mile; Race: 86.3% White, 2.2% Black/African American, 6.6% Asian, 0.3% American Indian/Alaska Native, 0.0% Native Hawaiian/Other Pacific Islander, 2.5% Two or more races, 4.2% Hispanic of any race; Average household size: 2.50; Median age: 41.3; Age under 18: 18.8%; Age 65 and over: 18.7%; Males per 100 females: 91.4; Marriage status: 32.0% never married, 47.8% now married, 2.1% separated, 7.3% widowed, 12.9% divorced; Foreign born: 7.3%; Speak English only: 89.7%; With disability: 10.8%; Veterans: 8.7%; Ancestry: 30.3% Irish, 20.7% German, 17.4% Italian, 8.9% English, 8.3% Polish
Employment: 13.2% management, business, and financial, 7.9% computer, engineering, and science, 9.5% education, legal, community service, arts, and media, 5.9% healthcare practitioners, 13.1% service, 35.3% sales and office, 4.6% natural resources, construction, and maintenance, 10.5% production, transportation, and material moving
Income: Per capita: $33,363; Median household: $78,263; Average household: $80,270; Households with income of $100,000 or more: 30.6%; Poverty rate: 4.6%
Educational Attainment: High school diploma or higher: 94.2%; Bachelor's degree or higher: 33.5%; Graduate/professional degree or higher: 13.9%
Housing: Homeownership rate: 77.0%; Median home value: $197,200; Median year structure built: 1962; Homeowner vacancy rate: 0.8%; Median selected monthly owner costs: $1,467 with a mortgage, $526 without a mortgage; Median gross rent: $1,154 per month; Rental vacancy rate: 0.0%

Health Insurance: 95.6% have insurance; 79.8% have private insurance; 33.5% have public insurance; 4.4% do not have insurance; 0.9% of children under 18 do not have insurance
Transportation: Commute: 94.8% car, 0.7% public transportation, 2.4% walk, 1.1% work from home; Mean travel time to work: 15.9 minutes
Additional Information Contacts
Village of Colonie . . . . (518) 869-7562
   http://www.colonievillage.org

DELMAR (unincorporated postal area)
ZCTA: 12054

Covers a land area of 15.447 square miles and a water area of 0.030 square miles. Located at 42.61° N. Lat; 73.86° W. Long. Elevation is 223 feet.
Population: 17,318; Growth (since 2000): 5.5%; Density: 1,121.1 persons per square mile; Race: 91.8% White, 2.5% Black/African American, 2.7% Asian, 0.0% American Indian/Alaska Native, 0.0% Native Hawaiian/Other Pacific Islander, 2.2% Two or more races, 1.7% Hispanic of any race; Average household size: 2.55; Median age: 42.2; Age under 18: 25.1%; Age 65 and over: 14.8%; Males per 100 females: 91.3; Marriage status: 26.7% never married, 58.5% now married, 1.1% separated, 7.3% widowed, 7.6% divorced; Foreign born: 5.1%; Speak English only: 95.3%; With disability: 7.6%; Veterans: 6.1%; Ancestry: 31.9% Irish, 18.7% German, 13.9% English, 13.4% Italian, 7.0% American
Employment: 18.9% management, business, and financial, 10.2% computer, engineering, and science, 22.4% education, legal, community service, arts, and media, 9.6% healthcare practitioners, 9.8% service, 21.4% sales and office, 4.5% natural resources, construction, and maintenance, 3.1% production, transportation, and material moving
Income: Per capita: $46,085; Median household: $96,813; Average household: $117,243; Households with income of $100,000 or more: 48.4%; Poverty rate: 3.7%
Educational Attainment: High school diploma or higher: 97.2%; Bachelor's degree or higher: 64.2%; Graduate/professional degree or higher: 36.3%
School District(s)
Bethlehem Central SD (KG-12)
   2014-15 Enrollment: 4,707 . . . . (518) 439-7098
Housing: Homeownership rate: 76.8%; Median home value: $267,400; Median year structure built: 1962; Homeowner vacancy rate: 1.7%; Median selected monthly owner costs: $2,013 with a mortgage, $767 without a mortgage; Median gross rent: $1,132 per month; Rental vacancy rate: 7.8%
Health Insurance: 98.1% have insurance; 91.2% have private insurance; 20.3% have public insurance; 1.9% do not have insurance; 0.6% of children under 18 do not have insurance
Newspapers: Spotlight LLC (weekly circulation 53,000)
Transportation: Commute: 90.3% car, 1.1% public transportation, 0.8% walk, 6.5% work from home; Mean travel time to work: 19.0 minutes

EAST BERNE (unincorporated postal area)
ZCTA: 12059

Covers a land area of 25.950 square miles and a water area of 0.699 square miles. Located at 42.62° N. Lat; 74.06° W. Long. Elevation is 1,178 feet.
Population: 1,658; Growth (since 2000): -10.0%; Density: 63.9 persons per square mile; Race: 96.4% White, 0.7% Black/African American, 1.3% Asian, 0.0% American Indian/Alaska Native, 0.0% Native Hawaiian/Other Pacific Islander, 1.0% Two or more races, 0.8% Hispanic of any race; Average household size: 2.49; Median age: 48.0; Age under 18: 18.8%; Age 65 and over: 16.5%; Males per 100 females: 105.5; Marriage status: 27.1% never married, 60.4% now married, 2.9% separated, 2.5% widowed, 9.9% divorced; Foreign born: 3.7%; Speak English only: 96.2%; With disability: 9.3%; Veterans: 11.4%; Ancestry: 28.3% Irish, 20.3% German, 16.0% Italian, 13.1% English, 12.2% Dutch
Employment: 25.6% management, business, and financial, 7.4% computer, engineering, and science, 2.4% education, legal, community service, arts, and media, 7.4% healthcare practitioners, 10.1% service, 20.1% sales and office, 17.5% natural resources, construction, and maintenance, 9.4% production, transportation, and material moving
Income: Per capita: $39,932; Median household: $76,250; Average household: $97,467; Households with income of $100,000 or more: 40.2%; Poverty rate: 8.3%

Educational Attainment: High school diploma or higher: 98.2%; Bachelor's degree or higher: 32.8%; Graduate/professional degree or higher: 9.5%
Housing: Homeownership rate: 92.6%; Median home value: $219,800; Median year structure built: 1973; Homeowner vacancy rate: 0.0%; Median selected monthly owner costs: $1,474 with a mortgage, $618 without a mortgage; Median gross rent: $745 per month; Rental vacancy rate: 13.8%
Health Insurance: 95.4% have insurance; 86.6% have private insurance; 25.6% have public insurance; 4.6% do not have insurance; 5.1% of children under 18 do not have insurance
Transportation: Commute: 97.4% car, 0.9% public transportation, 0.6% walk, 0.5% work from home; Mean travel time to work: 33.5 minutes

FEURA BUSH (unincorporated postal area)
ZCTA: 12067

Covers a land area of 21.411 square miles and a water area of 0.197 square miles. Located at 42.56° N. Lat; 73.92° W. Long. Elevation is 266 feet.
Population: 1,594; Growth (since 2000): -14.0%; Density: 74.4 persons per square mile; Race: 100.0% White, 0.0% Black/African American, 0.0% Asian, 0.0% American Indian/Alaska Native, 0.0% Native Hawaiian/Other Pacific Islander, 0.0% Two or more races, 0.6% Hispanic of any race; Average household size: 2.80; Median age: 41.1; Age under 18: 22.1%; Age 65 and over: 18.2%; Males per 100 females: 100.5; Marriage status: 30.2% never married, 60.7% now married, 1.8% separated, 1.7% widowed, 7.4% divorced; Foreign born: 0.0%; Speak English only: 97.7%; With disability: 10.0%; Veterans: 10.4%; Ancestry: 21.8% Irish, 14.9% French, 13.2% American, 11.2% English, 11.2% German
Employment: 12.9% management, business, and financial, 3.9% computer, engineering, and science, 17.0% education, legal, community service, arts, and media, 6.4% healthcare practitioners, 13.3% service, 29.6% sales and office, 9.5% natural resources, construction, and maintenance, 7.4% production, transportation, and material moving
Income: Per capita: $32,512; Median household: $66,875; Average household: $87,422; Households with income of $100,000 or more: 30.5%; Poverty rate: 3.3%
Educational Attainment: High school diploma or higher: 99.0%; Bachelor's degree or higher: 30.1%; Graduate/professional degree or higher: 18.4%
Housing: Homeownership rate: 85.3%; Median home value: $192,300; Median year structure built: 1977; Homeowner vacancy rate: 0.0%; Median selected monthly owner costs: $1,651 with a mortgage, $746 without a mortgage; Median gross rent: $972 per month; Rental vacancy rate: 0.0%
Health Insurance: 100.0% have insurance; 89.4% have private insurance; 33.1% have public insurance; 0.0% do not have insurance; 0.0% of children under 18 do not have insurance
Transportation: Commute: 93.2% car, 0.0% public transportation, 4.0% walk, 1.5% work from home; Mean travel time to work: 23.8 minutes

GLENMONT (unincorporated postal area)
ZCTA: 12077

Covers a land area of 10.086 square miles and a water area of 0.396 square miles. Located at 42.59° N. Lat; 73.78° W. Long. Elevation is 46 feet.
Population: 6,450; Growth (since 2000): 12.8%; Density: 639.5 persons per square mile; Race: 86.2% White, 3.3% Black/African American, 8.3% Asian, 0.0% American Indian/Alaska Native, 0.0% Native Hawaiian/Other Pacific Islander, 2.2% Two or more races, 0.7% Hispanic of any race; Average household size: 2.55; Median age: 45.3; Age under 18: 17.5%; Age 65 and over: 17.9%; Males per 100 females: 95.4; Marriage status: 33.1% never married, 53.6% now married, 0.9% separated, 5.3% widowed, 8.1% divorced; Foreign born: 9.1%; Speak English only: 89.1%; With disability: 11.4%; Veterans: 7.5%; Ancestry: 27.6% Irish, 20.3% German, 13.2% Italian, 10.7% English, 6.3% Polish
Employment: 19.1% management, business, and financial, 14.3% computer, engineering, and science, 13.6% education, legal, community service, arts, and media, 5.6% healthcare practitioners, 14.5% service, 22.6% sales and office, 5.8% natural resources, construction, and maintenance, 4.4% production, transportation, and material moving
Income: Per capita: $42,437; Median household: $95,135; Average household: $109,914; Households with income of $100,000 or more: 44.8%; Poverty rate: 7.7%

Educational Attainment: High school diploma or higher: 97.3%; Bachelor's degree or higher: 51.0%; Graduate/professional degree or higher: 30.3%

School District(s)
Bethlehem Central SD (KG-12)
   2014-15 Enrollment: 4,707 . . . . (518) 439-7098
Housing: Homeownership rate: 77.0%; Median home value: $287,400; Median year structure built: 1988; Homeowner vacancy rate: 3.4%; Median selected monthly owner costs: $2,106 with a mortgage, $864 without a mortgage; Median gross rent: $1,024 per month; Rental vacancy rate: 7.9%
Health Insurance: 94.9% have insurance; 85.2% have private insurance; 28.8% have public insurance; 5.1% do not have insurance; 5.0% of children under 18 do not have insurance
Transportation: Commute: 87.4% car, 2.6% public transportation, 3.3% walk, 6.6% work from home; Mean travel time to work: 21.1 minutes

GREEN ISLAND (town/village).
Covers a land area of 0.747 square miles and a water area of 0.186 square miles. Located at 42.75° N. Lat; 73.69° W. Long. Elevation is 23 feet.
Population: 2,629; Growth (since 2000): 15.4%; Density: 3,518.8 persons per square mile; Race: 91.7% White, 1.0% Black/African American, 3.7% Asian, 0.0% American Indian/Alaska Native, 0.0% Native Hawaiian/Other Pacific Islander, 3.6% Two or more races, 8.6% Hispanic of any race; Average household size: 2.44; Median age: 36.3; Age under 18: 21.5%; Age 65 and over: 13.5%; Males per 100 females: 89.7; Marriage status: 36.4% never married, 47.1% now married, 4.7% separated, 3.1% widowed, 13.5% divorced; Foreign born: 4.6%; Speak English only: 90.3%; With disability: 10.1%; Veterans: 11.1%; Ancestry: 31.8% Irish, 16.7% German, 15.6% Italian, 9.5% French, 9.1% Polish
Employment: 14.6% management, business, and financial, 3.4% computer, engineering, and science, 12.7% education, legal, community service, arts, and media, 8.4% healthcare practitioners, 15.1% service, 31.2% sales and office, 8.4% natural resources, construction, and maintenance, 6.1% production, transportation, and material moving
Income: Per capita: $25,410; Median household: $55,000; Average household: $60,152; Households with income of $100,000 or more: 13.6%; Poverty rate: 10.7%
Educational Attainment: High school diploma or higher: 93.2%; Bachelor's degree or higher: 16.9%; Graduate/professional degree or higher: 5.0%

School District(s)
Green Island Union Free SD (KG-12)
   2014-15 Enrollment: 341. . . . . (518) 273-1422
Housing: Homeownership rate: 33.3%; Median home value: $119,700; Median year structure built: Before 1940; Homeowner vacancy rate: 0.0%; Median selected monthly owner costs: $1,407 with a mortgage, $481 without a mortgage; Median gross rent: $868 per month; Rental vacancy rate: 6.1%
Health Insurance: 91.0% have insurance; 68.3% have private insurance; 37.0% have public insurance; 9.0% do not have insurance; 2.8% of children under 18 do not have insurance
Safety: Violent crime rate: 7.6 per 10,000 population; Property crime rate: 183.3 per 10,000 population
Transportation: Commute: 92.0% car, 0.0% public transportation, 5.8% walk, 2.3% work from home; Mean travel time to work: 17.0 minutes

GUILDERLAND (town).
Covers a land area of 57.902 square miles and a water area of 0.885 square miles. Located at 42.71° N. Lat; 73.96° W. Long. Elevation is 207 feet.
History: Guilderland is a town in Albany County, New York, named for the Gelderland province in the Netherlands.
Population: 35,675; Growth (since 2000): 9.1%; Density: 616.1 persons per square mile; Race: 86.3% White, 4.0% Black/African American, 7.1% Asian, 0.1% American Indian/Alaska Native, 0.1% Native Hawaiian/Other Pacific Islander, 1.4% Two or more races, 2.9% Hispanic of any race; Average household size: 2.36; Median age: 39.8; Age under 18: 19.7%; Age 65 and over: 14.8%; Males per 100 females: 94.0; Marriage status: 34.9% never married, 50.4% now married, 1.6% separated, 5.8% widowed, 8.8% divorced; Foreign born: 8.5%; Speak English only: 90.2%; With disability: 7.8%; Veterans: 6.5%; Ancestry: 23.1% Irish, 19.8% Italian, 18.1% German, 11.9% English, 5.7% Polish
Employment: 16.6% management, business, and financial, 10.3% computer, engineering, and science, 17.3% education, legal, community service, arts, and media, 7.7% healthcare practitioners, 12.7% service,

26.2% sales and office, 4.0% natural resources, construction, and maintenance, 5.3% production, transportation, and material moving
Income: Per capita: $41,460; Median household: $78,131; Average household: $101,141; Households with income of $100,000 or more: 37.4%; Poverty rate: 5.8%
Educational Attainment: High school diploma or higher: 96.8%; Bachelor's degree or higher: 49.1%; Graduate/professional degree or higher: 25.7%

School District(s)
Guilderland Central SD (KG-12)
   2014-15 Enrollment: 4,984 . . . . (518) 456-6200
Housing: Homeownership rate: 68.1%; Median home value: $249,000; Median year structure built: 1975; Homeowner vacancy rate: 1.4%; Median selected monthly owner costs: $1,864 with a mortgage, $662 without a mortgage; Median gross rent: $1,111 per month; Rental vacancy rate: 4.9%
Health Insurance: 96.4% have insurance; 87.6% have private insurance; 22.8% have public insurance; 3.6% do not have insurance; 0.6% of children under 18 do not have insurance
Safety: Violent crime rate: 2.9 per 10,000 population; Property crime rate: 167.7 per 10,000 population
Transportation: Commute: 90.7% car, 1.4% public transportation, 2.6% walk, 3.7% work from home; Mean travel time to work: 21.4 minutes
Additional Information Contacts
Town of Guilderland . . . . (518) 356-1980
   http://www.townofguilderland.org

GUILDERLAND CENTER (unincorporated postal area)
ZCTA: 12085
Covers a land area of 0.176 square miles and a water area of 0 square miles. Located at 42.70° N. Lat; 73.96° W. Long. Elevation is 318 feet.
Population: 601; Growth (since 2000): n/a; Density: 3,423.1 persons per square mile; Race: 86.9% White, 2.5% Black/African American, 0.0% Asian, 0.0% American Indian/Alaska Native, 0.0% Native Hawaiian/Other Pacific Islander, 1.8% Two or more races, 11.3% Hispanic of any race; Average household size: 2.51; Median age: 34.8; Age under 18: 27.3%; Age 65 and over: 16.5%; Males per 100 females: 59.1; Marriage status: 27.7% never married, 41.5% now married, 6.0% separated, 18.7% widowed, 12.0% divorced; Foreign born: 16.1%; Speak English only: 83.0%; With disability: 7.3%; Veterans: 4.8%; Ancestry: 16.1% Italian, 11.5% English, 11.0% German, 6.7% Irish, 5.2% Polish
Employment: 9.7% management, business, and financial, 0.0% computer, engineering, and science, 5.3% education, legal, community service, arts, and media, 4.9% healthcare practitioners, 17.3% service, 54.0% sales and office, 4.4% natural resources, construction, and maintenance, 4.4% production, transportation, and material moving
Income: Per capita: $18,705; Median household: $41,985; Average household: $48,384; Households with income of $100,000 or more: 8.6%; Poverty rate: 7.3%
Educational Attainment: High school diploma or higher: 98.8%; Bachelor's degree or higher: 18.2%; Graduate/professional degree or higher: 5.7%

School District(s)
Guilderland Central SD (KG-12)
   2014-15 Enrollment: 4,984 . . . . (518) 456-6200
Housing: Homeownership rate: 16.8%; Median home value: $210,700; Median year structure built: 1970; Homeowner vacancy rate: 0.0%; Median selected monthly owner costs: $1,635 with a mortgage, $0 without a mortgage; Median gross rent: $974 per month; Rental vacancy rate: 13.2%
Health Insurance: 84.6% have insurance; 70.4% have private insurance; 16.2% have public insurance; 15.4% do not have insurance; 0.0% of children under 18 do not have insurance
Transportation: Commute: 100.0% car, 0.0% public transportation, 0.0% walk, 0.0% work from home; Mean travel time to work: 20.8 minutes

KNOX (town).
Covers a land area of 41.762 square miles and a water area of 0.174 square miles. Located at 42.69° N. Lat; 74.11° W. Long. Elevation is 1,234 feet.
Population: 2,769; Growth (since 2000): 4.6%; Density: 66.3 persons per square mile; Race: 98.2% White, 0.5% Black/African American, 0.1% Asian, 0.0% American Indian/Alaska Native, 0.0% Native Hawaiian/Other Pacific Islander, 0.8% Two or more races, 1.0% Hispanic of any race;

Average household size: 2.84; Median age: 41.9; Age under 18: 23.4%; Age 65 and over: 14.8%; Males per 100 females: 103.2; Marriage status: 28.9% never married, 58.1% now married, 1.0% separated, 3.9% widowed, 9.1% divorced; Foreign born: 2.5%; Speak English only: 95.6%; With disability: 9.8%; Veterans: 10.5%; Ancestry: 28.1% German, 21.6% Irish, 19.6% Italian, 14.2% English, 8.8% Dutch

Employment: 17.1% management, business, and financial, 5.7% computer, engineering, and science, 11.3% education, legal, community service, arts, and media, 5.4% healthcare practitioners, 16.0% service, 21.8% sales and office, 11.8% natural resources, construction, and maintenance, 11.0% production, transportation, and material moving

Income: Per capita: $30,227; Median household: $71,944; Average household: $83,937; Households with income of $100,000 or more: 36.6%; Poverty rate: 6.1%

Educational Attainment: High school diploma or higher: 94.4%; Bachelor's degree or higher: 30.8%; Graduate/professional degree or higher: 11.0%

Housing: Homeownership rate: 86.4%; Median home value: $230,300; Median year structure built: 1972; Homeowner vacancy rate: 2.0%; Median selected monthly owner costs: $1,583 with a mortgage, $650 without a mortgage; Median gross rent: $1,146 per month; Rental vacancy rate: 17.0%

Health Insurance: 93.4% have insurance; 81.2% have private insurance; 27.5% have public insurance; 6.6% do not have insurance; 4.9% of children under 18 do not have insurance

Transportation: Commute: 93.1% car, 0.0% public transportation, 2.4% walk, 3.7% work from home; Mean travel time to work: 30.8 minutes

Additional Information Contacts

Town of Knox . . . . (518) 872-2551
   http://www.knoxny.org

LATHAM (unincorporated postal area)
ZCTA: 12110

Covers a land area of 14.686 square miles and a water area of 0.450 square miles. Located at 42.75° N. Lat; 73.78° W. Long. Elevation is 354 feet.

Population: 22,550; Growth (since 2000): 10.2%; Density: 1,535.5 persons per square mile; Race: 81.4% White, 7.0% Black/African American, 7.5% Asian, 0.0% American Indian/Alaska Native, 0.2% Native Hawaiian/Other Pacific Islander, 2.0% Two or more races, 6.8% Hispanic of any race; Average household size: 2.52; Median age: 40.2; Age under 18: 16.4%; Age 65 and over: 15.3%; Males per 100 females: 94.3; Marriage status: 41.0% never married, 46.0% now married, 3.1% separated, 4.7% widowed, 8.3% divorced; Foreign born: 10.1%; Speak English only: 84.5%; With disability: 11.3%; Veterans: 7.1%; Ancestry: 28.8% Irish, 21.2% Italian, 14.2% German, 7.6% Polish, 7.6% English

Employment: 18.3% management, business, and financial, 7.3% computer, engineering, and science, 12.0% education, legal, community service, arts, and media, 8.3% healthcare practitioners, 14.8% service, 27.4% sales and office, 5.8% natural resources, construction, and maintenance, 6.1% production, transportation, and material moving

Income: Per capita: $32,698; Median household: $73,997; Average household: $91,520; Households with income of $100,000 or more: 33.9%; Poverty rate: 9.2%

Educational Attainment: High school diploma or higher: 95.3%; Bachelor's degree or higher: 43.4%; Graduate/professional degree or higher: 19.2%

School District(s)
North Colonie CSD
   2014-15 Enrollment: 5,383 . . . . (518) 785-8591

Four-year College(s)
Aesthetic Science Institute (Private, For-profit)
   Fall 2014 Enrollment: 66 . . . . (518) 786-0760
John Paolo's Xtreme Beauty Institute-Goldwell Product Artistry (Private, For-profit)
   Fall 2014 Enrollment: 10 . . . . (518) 783-0808

Two-year College(s)
Aesthetic Science Institute (Private, For-profit)
   Fall 2014 Enrollment: 66 . . . . (518) 786-0760
John Paolo's Xtreme Beauty Institute-Goldwell Product Artistry (Private, For-profit)
   Fall 2014 Enrollment: 10 . . . . (518) 783-0808

Vocational/Technical School(s)
Aesthetic Science Institute (Private, For-profit)
   Fall 2014 Enrollment: 66 . . . . (518) 786-0760
   2015-16 Tuition: $7,500
John Paolo's Xtreme Beauty Institute-Goldwell Product Artistry (Private, For-profit)
   Fall 2014 Enrollment: 10 . . . . (518) 783-0808
   2015-16 Tuition: $13,600

Housing: Homeownership rate: 74.2%; Median home value: $232,200; Median year structure built: 1968; Homeowner vacancy rate: 0.6%; Median selected monthly owner costs: $1,661 with a mortgage, $548 without a mortgage; Median gross rent: $1,110 per month; Rental vacancy rate: 1.9%

Health Insurance: 96.7% have insurance; 87.5% have private insurance; 24.4% have public insurance; 3.3% do not have insurance; 2.2% of children under 18 do not have insurance

Transportation: Commute: 89.4% car, 1.3% public transportation, 4.3% walk, 3.0% work from home; Mean travel time to work: 18.3 minutes

MEDUSA (unincorporated postal area)
ZCTA: 12120

Covers a land area of 17.511 square miles and a water area of 0.063 square miles. Located at 42.45° N. Lat; 74.15° W. Long. Elevation is 804 feet.

Population: 614; Growth (since 2000): 13.9%; Density: 35.1 persons per square mile; Race: 97.4% White, 0.8% Black/African American, 0.0% Asian, 0.0% American Indian/Alaska Native, 0.0% Native Hawaiian/Other Pacific Islander, 1.8% Two or more races, 1.8% Hispanic of any race; Average household size: 2.42; Median age: 50.1; Age under 18: 21.2%; Age 65 and over: 24.8%; Males per 100 females: 103.7; Marriage status: 11.7% never married, 72.7% now married, 0.0% separated, 9.2% widowed, 6.4% divorced; Foreign born: 5.4%; Speak English only: 93.1%; With disability: 11.4%; Veterans: 15.3%; Ancestry: 24.4% German, 16.1% Irish, 12.9% Italian, 8.6% American, 8.1% Albanian

Employment: 24.8% management, business, and financial, 8.9% computer, engineering, and science, 7.4% education, legal, community service, arts, and media, 10.7% healthcare practitioners, 17.8% service, 11.5% sales and office, 13.3% natural resources, construction, and maintenance, 5.6% production, transportation, and material moving

Income: Per capita: $31,250; Median household: $56,250; Average household: $77,063; Households with income of $100,000 or more: 28.7%; Poverty rate: 7.3%

Educational Attainment: High school diploma or higher: 90.1%; Bachelor's degree or higher: 21.2%; Graduate/professional degree or higher: 12.8%

Housing: Homeownership rate: 88.2%; Median home value: $201,100; Median year structure built: 1972; Homeowner vacancy rate: 0.0%; Median selected monthly owner costs: $1,771 with a mortgage, $662 without a mortgage; Median gross rent: $1,288 per month; Rental vacancy rate: 0.0%

Health Insurance: 94.1% have insurance; 80.9% have private insurance; 34.0% have public insurance; 5.9% do not have insurance; 0.0% of children under 18 do not have insurance

Transportation: Commute: 81.5% car, 1.2% public transportation, 1.9% walk, 14.2% work from home; Mean travel time to work: 36.2 minutes

MENANDS (village). Covers a land area of 3.058 square miles and a water area of 0.251 square miles. Located at 42.69° N. Lat; 73.73° W. Long. Elevation is 36 feet.

History: Incorporated 1924.

Population: 4,004; Growth (since 2000): 2.4%; Density: 1,309.3 persons per square mile; Race: 68.2% White, 13.0% Black/African American, 11.5% Asian, 0.0% American Indian/Alaska Native, 0.0% Native Hawaiian/Other Pacific Islander, 2.7% Two or more races, 6.3% Hispanic of any race; Average household size: 2.36; Median age: 34.0; Age under 18: 23.3%; Age 65 and over: 10.0%; Males per 100 females: 91.1; Marriage status: 40.8% never married, 48.0% now married, 0.4% separated, 1.7% widowed, 9.5% divorced; Foreign born: 15.1%; Speak English only: 86.0%; With disability: 11.4%; Veterans: 8.9%; Ancestry: 26.2% Irish, 12.8% Italian, 10.0% English, 9.7% German, 5.4% American

Employment: 26.6% management, business, and financial, 12.4% computer, engineering, and science, 11.6% education, legal, community service, arts, and media, 7.0% healthcare practitioners, 7.9% service,

31.1% sales and office, 2.3% natural resources, construction, and maintenance, 1.0% production, transportation, and material moving
Income: Per capita: $35,386; Median household: $62,683; Average household: $81,957; Households with income of $100,000 or more: 26.1%; Poverty rate: 6.4%
Educational Attainment: High school diploma or higher: 95.3%; Bachelor's degree or higher: 53.5%; Graduate/professional degree or higher: 22.8%

School District(s)
Menands Union Free SD (KG-08)
   2014-15 Enrollment: 263 . . . . (518) 465-4561
Housing: Homeownership rate: 36.0%; Median home value: $255,700; Median year structure built: 1965; Homeowner vacancy rate: 0.0%; Median selected monthly owner costs: $1,726 with a mortgage, $683 without a mortgage; Median gross rent: $1,073 per month; Rental vacancy rate: 3.6%
Health Insurance: 97.5% have insurance; 86.7% have private insurance; 21.9% have public insurance; 2.5% do not have insurance; 0.0% of children under 18 do not have insurance
Safety: Violent crime rate: 10.0 per 10,000 population; Property crime rate: 316.9 per 10,000 population
Transportation: Commute: 85.0% car, 7.6% public transportation, 1.3% walk, 5.2% work from home; Mean travel time to work: 16.1 minutes
Additional Information Contacts
Village of Menands . . . . (518) 434-2922
   http://www.villageofmenands.com

NEW SCOTLAND (town).
Covers a land area of 57.499 square miles and a water area of 0.470 square miles. Located at 42.60° N. Lat; 73.94° W. Long. Elevation is 282 feet.
Population: 8,753; Growth (since 2000): 1.5%; Density: 152.2 persons per square mile; Race: 96.3% White, 0.2% Black/African American, 1.3% Asian, 0.2% American Indian/Alaska Native, 0.0% Native Hawaiian/Other Pacific Islander, 1.7% Two or more races, 3.3% Hispanic of any race; Average household size: 2.64; Median age: 43.5; Age under 18: 21.5%; Age 65 and over: 15.0%; Males per 100 females: 98.4; Marriage status: 29.6% never married, 56.4% now married, 1.4% separated, 4.7% widowed, 9.3% divorced; Foreign born: 2.7%; Speak English only: 95.1%; With disability: 7.9%; Veterans: 9.0%; Ancestry: 26.7% Irish, 21.2% German, 16.0% Italian, 10.5% English, 8.5% Polish
Employment: 18.5% management, business, and financial, 6.2% computer, engineering, and science, 15.1% education, legal, community service, arts, and media, 4.4% healthcare practitioners, 13.3% service, 26.8% sales and office, 8.0% natural resources, construction, and maintenance, 7.8% production, transportation, and material moving
Income: Per capita: $37,983; Median household: $80,881; Average household: $98,289; Households with income of $100,000 or more: 35.2%; Poverty rate: 5.9%
Educational Attainment: High school diploma or higher: 95.0%; Bachelor's degree or higher: 43.8%; Graduate/professional degree or higher: 21.9%
Housing: Homeownership rate: 82.2%; Median home value: $238,700; Median year structure built: 1965; Homeowner vacancy rate: 0.8%; Median selected monthly owner costs: $1,801 with a mortgage, $729 without a mortgage; Median gross rent: $951 per month; Rental vacancy rate: 0.0%
Health Insurance: 96.5% have insurance; 86.8% have private insurance; 25.7% have public insurance; 3.5% do not have insurance; 1.2% of children under 18 do not have insurance
Transportation: Commute: 93.2% car, 1.0% public transportation, 1.3% walk, 3.4% work from home; Mean travel time to work: 22.5 minutes
Additional Information Contacts
Town of New Scotland . . . . (518) 439-4865
   http://www.townofnewscotland.com

PRESTON HOLLOW (unincorporated postal area)
ZCTA: 12469
   Covers a land area of 33.905 square miles and a water area of 0.020 square miles. Located at 42.45° N. Lat; 74.24° W. Long. Elevation is 846 feet.
Population: 755; Growth (since 2000): -3.6%; Density: 22.3 persons per square mile; Race: 98.4% White, 0.0% Black/African American, 0.4% Asian, 0.0% American Indian/Alaska Native, 0.0% Native Hawaiian/Other Pacific Islander, 1.1% Two or more races, 0.1% Hispanic of any race; Average household size: 2.23; Median age: 49.7; Age under 18: 13.5%; Age 65 and over: 20.3%; Males per 100 females:

102.7; Marriage status: 26.6% never married, 50.1% now married, 4.5% separated, 8.8% widowed, 14.6% divorced; Foreign born: 10.1%; Speak English only: 90.8%; With disability: 12.2%; Veterans: 14.5%; Ancestry: 19.7% German, 15.6% Irish, 13.1% American, 12.7% Italian, 10.2% English
Employment: 11.2% management, business, and financial, 0.8% computer, engineering, and science, 4.7% education, legal, community service, arts, and media, 6.0% healthcare practitioners, 6.3% service, 26.0% sales and office, 28.5% natural resources, construction, and maintenance, 16.4% production, transportation, and material moving
Income: Per capita: $27,707; Median household: $44,643; Average household: $58,101; Households with income of $100,000 or more: 18.4%; Poverty rate: 13.2%
Educational Attainment: High school diploma or higher: 86.3%; Bachelor's degree or higher: 15.9%; Graduate/professional degree or higher: 6.5%
Housing: Homeownership rate: 93.5%; Median home value: $156,900; Median year structure built: 1958; Homeowner vacancy rate: 12.9%; Median selected monthly owner costs: $1,242 with a mortgage, $523 without a mortgage; Median gross rent: n/a per month; Rental vacancy rate: 0.0%
Health Insurance: 91.0% have insurance; 68.7% have private insurance; 41.3% have public insurance; 9.0% do not have insurance; 0.0% of children under 18 do not have insurance
Transportation: Commute: 89.7% car, 1.9% public transportation, 1.9% walk, 3.1% work from home; Mean travel time to work: 39.4 minutes

---

PRESTON-POTTER HOLLOW (CDP).
Covers a land area of 10.134 square miles and a water area of 0 square miles. Located at 42.43° N. Lat; 74.23° W. Long. Elevation is 860 feet.
Population: 420; Growth (since 2000): 12.3%; Density: 41.4 persons per square mile; Race: 98.1% White, 0.0% Black/African American, 0.7% Asian, 0.0% American Indian/Alaska Native, 0.0% Native Hawaiian/Other Pacific Islander, 1.2% Two or more races, 0.0% Hispanic of any race; Average household size: 2.40; Median age: 47.4; Age under 18: 18.3%; Age 65 and over: 26.0%; Males per 100 females: 95.7; Marriage status: 29.6% never married, 52.1% now married, 0.8% separated, 7.9% widowed, 10.4% divorced; Foreign born: 9.5%; Speak English only: 88.2%; With disability: 11.4%; Veterans: 16.0%; Ancestry: 20.5% American, 16.0% German, 11.9% Irish, 10.5% Italian, 10.0% English
Employment: 14.6% management, business, and financial, 0.0% computer, engineering, and science, 3.8% education, legal, community service, arts, and media, 3.8% healthcare practitioners, 0.0% service, 35.7% sales and office, 32.4% natural resources, construction, and maintenance, 9.7% production, transportation, and material moving
Income: Per capita: $26,780; Median household: $50,875; Average household: $59,159; Households with income of $100,000 or more: 16.6%; Poverty rate: 7.9%
Educational Attainment: High school diploma or higher: 82.5%; Bachelor's degree or higher: 17.8%; Graduate/professional degree or higher: 7.6%
Housing: Homeownership rate: 90.3%; Median home value: $117,600; Median year structure built: 1957; Homeowner vacancy rate: 9.7%; Median selected monthly owner costs: $1,331 with a mortgage, $494 without a mortgage; Median gross rent: n/a per month; Rental vacancy rate: 0.0%
Health Insurance: 91.0% have insurance; 66.4% have private insurance; 45.7% have public insurance; 9.0% do not have insurance; 0.0% of children under 18 do not have insurance
Transportation: Commute: 81.0% car, 3.9% public transportation, 3.9% walk, 4.5% work from home; Mean travel time to work: 39.6 minutes

---

RAVENA (village).
Covers a land area of 1.467 square miles and a water area of 0.005 square miles. Located at 42.48° N. Lat; 73.81° W. Long. Elevation is 230 feet.
History: Incorporated 1914.
Population: 3,289; Growth (since 2000): -2.4%; Density: 2,241.9 persons per square mile; Race: 89.1% White, 8.9% Black/African American, 0.5% Asian, 0.0% American Indian/Alaska Native, 0.0% Native Hawaiian/Other Pacific Islander, 1.5% Two or more races, 4.3% Hispanic of any race; Average household size: 2.33; Median age: 38.0; Age under 18: 22.9%; Age 65 and over: 13.7%; Males per 100 females: 94.2; Marriage status: 34.8% never married, 48.2% now married, 2.5% separated, 4.5% widowed, 12.5% divorced; Foreign born: 4.0%; Speak English only: 96.1%; With disability: 11.9%; Veterans: 8.8%; Ancestry: 20.2% American, 19.7% Irish, 19.5% Italian, 19.0% German, 6.0% Polish

Employment: 14.1% management, business, and financial, 8.2% computer, engineering, and science, 12.0% education, legal, community service, arts, and media, 3.7% healthcare practitioners, 20.5% service, 22.0% sales and office, 5.8% natural resources, construction, and maintenance, 13.8% production, transportation, and material moving
Income: Per capita: $24,694; Median household: $48,895; Average household: $55,473; Households with income of $100,000 or more: 10.8%; Poverty rate: 12.0%
Educational Attainment: High school diploma or higher: 90.8%; Bachelor's degree or higher: 16.0%; Graduate/professional degree or higher: 4.5%
School District(s)
Ravena-Coeymans-Selkirk Central SD (PK-12)
    2014-15 Enrollment: 1,938 . . . . (518) 756-5200
Housing: Homeownership rate: 59.7%; Median home value: $157,300; Median year structure built: 1956; Homeowner vacancy rate: 0.2%; Median selected monthly owner costs: $1,345 with a mortgage, $624 without a mortgage; Median gross rent: $860 per month; Rental vacancy rate: 12.2%
Health Insurance: 87.7% have insurance; 69.1% have private insurance; 33.0% have public insurance; 12.3% do not have insurance; 3.9% of children under 18 do not have insurance
Transportation: Commute: 92.1% car, 0.0% public transportation, 2.0% walk, 1.4% work from home; Mean travel time to work: 24.2 minutes

RENSSELAERVILLE (town). Covers a land area of 61.464 square miles and a water area of 0.420 square miles. Located at 42.48° N. Lat; 74.18° W. Long. Elevation is 1,365 feet.
Population: 1,797; Growth (since 2000): -6.2%; Density: 29.2 persons per square mile; Race: 96.7% White, 0.7% Black/African American, 0.4% Asian, 0.0% American Indian/Alaska Native, 0.0% Native Hawaiian/Other Pacific Islander, 2.2% Two or more races, 0.6% Hispanic of any race; Average household size: 2.44; Median age: 48.7; Age under 18: 20.5%; Age 65 and over: 22.9%; Males per 100 females: 103.6; Marriage status: 22.6% never married, 57.9% now married, 1.9% separated, 9.0% widowed, 10.4% divorced; Foreign born: 5.3%; Speak English only: 94.6%; With disability: 14.5%; Veterans: 12.3%; Ancestry: 22.9% German, 15.0% Irish, 13.8% American, 10.5% Italian, 9.0% English
Employment: 19.9% management, business, and financial, 6.8% computer, engineering, and science, 9.1% education, legal, community service, arts, and media, 4.8% healthcare practitioners, 7.8% service, 21.7% sales and office, 18.9% natural resources, construction, and maintenance, 10.9% production, transportation, and material moving
Income: Per capita: $29,451; Median household: $53,011; Average household: $70,327; Households with income of $100,000 or more: 24.2%; Poverty rate: 15.4%
Educational Attainment: High school diploma or higher: 89.9%; Bachelor's degree or higher: 24.5%; Graduate/professional degree or higher: 14.7%
Housing: Homeownership rate: 90.5%; Median home value: $171,500; Median year structure built: 1964; Homeowner vacancy rate: 6.8%; Median selected monthly owner costs: $1,591 with a mortgage, $586 without a mortgage; Median gross rent: $893 per month; Rental vacancy rate: 0.0%
Health Insurance: 93.5% have insurance; 74.6% have private insurance; 38.9% have public insurance; 6.5% do not have insurance; 2.4% of children under 18 do not have insurance
Transportation: Commute: 87.0% car, 1.3% public transportation, 1.6% walk, 6.9% work from home; Mean travel time to work: 38.0 minutes

SELKIRK (unincorporated postal area)
ZCTA: 12158
    Covers a land area of 30.595 square miles and a water area of 0.943 square miles. Located at 42.54° N. Lat; 73.82° W. Long. Elevation is 161 feet.
Population: 6,915; Growth (since 2000): 19.7%; Density: 226.0 persons per square mile; Race: 95.0% White, 2.5% Black/African American, 0.2% Asian, 0.2% American Indian/Alaska Native, 0.0% Native Hawaiian/Other Pacific Islander, 2.0% Two or more races, 0.9% Hispanic of any race; Average household size: 2.71; Median age: 40.1; Age under 18: 23.7%; Age 65 and over: 11.3%; Males per 100 females: 98.3; Marriage status: 26.8% never married, 59.3% now married, 0.5% separated, 5.7% widowed, 8.2% divorced; Foreign born: 1.9%; Speak English only: 95.0%; With disability: 14.0%; Veterans: 11.2%; Ancestry: 24.9% German, 20.4% Irish, 20.0% Italian, 10.2% English, 8.3% French
Employment: 10.6% management, business, and financial, 6.0% computer, engineering, and science, 13.4% education, legal, community

service, arts, and media, 7.3% healthcare practitioners, 14.2% service, 25.9% sales and office, 9.4% natural resources, construction, and maintenance, 13.1% production, transportation, and material moving
Income: Per capita: $34,113; Median household: $81,006; Average household: $90,419; Households with income of $100,000 or more: 34.5%; Poverty rate: 7.0%
Educational Attainment: High school diploma or higher: 94.4%; Bachelor's degree or higher: 30.2%; Graduate/professional degree or higher: 17.2%
School District(s)
Ravena-Coeymans-Selkirk Central SD (PK-12)
    2014-15 Enrollment: 1,938 . . . . (518) 756-5200
Housing: Homeownership rate: 85.8%; Median home value: $210,200; Median year structure built: 1976; Homeowner vacancy rate: 0.0%; Median selected monthly owner costs: $1,660 with a mortgage, $590 without a mortgage; Median gross rent: $946 per month; Rental vacancy rate: 14.2%
Health Insurance: 96.6% have insurance; 84.3% have private insurance; 24.3% have public insurance; 3.4% do not have insurance; 3.5% of children under 18 do not have insurance
Transportation: Commute: 96.5% car, 0.5% public transportation, 0.0% walk, 2.0% work from home; Mean travel time to work: 28.0 minutes

SLINGERLANDS (unincorporated postal area)
ZCTA: 12159
    Covers a land area of 14.088 square miles and a water area of 0.044 square miles. Located at 42.65° N. Lat; 73.89° W. Long. Elevation is 220 feet.
Population: 8,009; Growth (since 2000): 4.7%; Density: 568.5 persons per square mile; Race: 89.2% White, 2.1% Black/African American, 6.1% Asian, 0.0% American Indian/Alaska Native, 0.0% Native Hawaiian/Other Pacific Islander, 1.9% Two or more races, 2.9% Hispanic of any race; Average household size: 2.41; Median age: 46.3; Age under 18: 23.2%; Age 65 and over: 18.4%; Males per 100 females: 89.1; Marriage status: 28.3% never married, 55.0% now married, 1.9% separated, 7.9% widowed, 8.8% divorced; Foreign born: 8.0%; Speak English only: 89.3%; With disability: 10.1%; Veterans: 5.9%; Ancestry: 29.0% Irish, 17.9% Italian, 15.7% German, 13.1% English, 6.7% American
Employment: 29.6% management, business, and financial, 5.8% computer, engineering, and science, 19.5% education, legal, community service, arts, and media, 8.4% healthcare practitioners, 9.1% service, 21.4% sales and office, 2.4% natural resources, construction, and maintenance, 3.8% production, transportation, and material moving
Income: Per capita: $55,836; Median household: $87,927; Average household: $133,975; Households with income of $100,000 or more: 43.8%; Poverty rate: 3.1%
Educational Attainment: High school diploma or higher: 96.7%; Bachelor's degree or higher: 61.4%; Graduate/professional degree or higher: 35.4%
Housing: Homeownership rate: 74.5%; Median home value: $339,600; Median year structure built: 1986; Homeowner vacancy rate: 0.3%; Median selected monthly owner costs: $2,586 with a mortgage, $1,035 without a mortgage; Median gross rent: $1,004 per month; Rental vacancy rate: 4.2%
Health Insurance: 97.4% have insurance; 90.2% have private insurance; 25.4% have public insurance; 2.6% do not have insurance; 0.6% of children under 18 do not have insurance
Transportation: Commute: 91.8% car, 0.7% public transportation, 2.0% walk, 4.1% work from home; Mean travel time to work: 20.9 minutes

SOUTH BETHLEHEM (unincorporated postal area)
ZCTA: 12161
    Covers a land area of 0.409 square miles and a water area of 0.006 square miles. Located at 42.53° N. Lat; 73.85° W. Long. Elevation is 213 feet.
Population: 91; Growth (since 2000): n/a; Density: 222.4 persons per square mile; Race: 100.0% White, 0.0% Black/African American, 0.0% Asian, 0.0% American Indian/Alaska Native, 0.0% Native Hawaiian/Other Pacific Islander, 0.0% Two or more races, 0.0% Hispanic of any race; Average household size: 2.68; Median age: 41.2; Age under 18: 42.9%; Age 65 and over: 0.0%; Males per 100 females: 102.5; Marriage status: 0.0% never married, 71.2% now married, 0.0% separated, 0.0% widowed, 28.8% divorced; Foreign born: 0.0%; Speak English only: 74.6%; With disability: 0.0%; Veterans: 0.0%; Ancestry:

62.6% Dutch, 62.6% German, 37.4% English, 20.9% French, 16.5% Irish
Employment: 100.0% management, business, and financial, 0.0% computer, engineering, and science, 0.0% education, legal, community service, arts, and media, 0.0% healthcare practitioners, 0.0% service, 0.0% sales and office, 0.0% natural resources, construction, and maintenance, 0.0% production, transportation, and material moving
Income: Per capita: $32,643; Median household: n/a; Average household: n/a; Households with income of $100,000 or more: 55.9%; Poverty rate: n/a
Educational Attainment: High school diploma or higher: 100.0%; Bachelor's degree or higher: 71.2%; Graduate/professional degree or higher: 34.6%
Housing: Homeownership rate: 55.9%; Median home value: n/a; Median year structure built: n/a; Homeowner vacancy rate: 0.0%; Median selected monthly owner costs: $0 with a mortgage, $0 without a mortgage; Median gross rent: n/a per month; Rental vacancy rate: 0.0%
Health Insurance: 83.5% have insurance; 83.5% have private insurance; 0.0% have public insurance; 16.5% do not have insurance; 0.0% of children under 18 do not have insurance
Transportation: Commute: 100.0% car, 0.0% public transportation, 0.0% walk, 0.0% work from home; Mean travel time to work: 0.0 minutes

VOORHEESVILLE (village).
Covers a land area of 2.139 square miles and a water area of 0.005 square miles. Located at 42.65° N. Lat; 73.93° W. Long. Elevation is 338 feet.
Population: 2,820; Growth (since 2000): 4.3%; Density: 1,318.5 persons per square mile; Race: 92.8% White, 0.5% Black/African American, 3.0% Asian, 0.1% American Indian/Alaska Native, 0.0% Native Hawaiian/Other Pacific Islander, 2.5% Two or more races, 6.4% Hispanic of any race; Average household size: 2.62; Median age: 42.0; Age under 18: 23.4%; Age 65 and over: 16.3%; Males per 100 females: 94.8; Marriage status: 25.7% never married, 59.8% now married, 1.4% separated, 5.8% widowed, 8.7% divorced; Foreign born: 4.3%; Speak English only: 92.7%; With disability: 6.8%; Veterans: 9.4%; Ancestry: 27.9% Irish, 22.6% German, 17.8% Italian, 9.8% English, 9.6% Polish
Employment: 18.2% management, business, and financial, 9.3% computer, engineering, and science, 14.4% education, legal, community service, arts, and media, 3.1% healthcare practitioners, 12.5% service, 27.6% sales and office, 6.3% natural resources, construction, and maintenance, 8.6% production, transportation, and material moving
Income: Per capita: $36,327; Median household: $83,500; Average household: $93,167; Households with income of $100,000 or more: 34.5%; Poverty rate: 3.3%
Educational Attainment: High school diploma or higher: 97.9%; Bachelor's degree or higher: 52.6%; Graduate/professional degree or higher: 24.7%

School District(s)
Voorheesville Central SD (KG-12)
   2014-15 Enrollment: 1,182 . . . . (518) 765-3313
Housing: Homeownership rate: 80.0%; Median home value: $231,500; Median year structure built: 1965; Homeowner vacancy rate: 0.0%; Median selected monthly owner costs: $1,741 with a mortgage, $737 without a mortgage; Median gross rent: $948 per month; Rental vacancy rate: 0.0%
Health Insurance: 97.4% have insurance; 87.9% have private insurance; 25.2% have public insurance; 2.6% do not have insurance; 0.0% of children under 18 do not have insurance
Transportation: Commute: 94.1% car, 1.2% public transportation, 0.7% walk, 3.9% work from home; Mean travel time to work: 23.5 minutes

WATERVLIET (city).
Covers a land area of 1.345 square miles and a water area of 0.130 square miles. Located at 42.72° N. Lat; 73.71° W. Long. Elevation is 30 feet.
History: The U.S. Watervliet Arsenal here, which specializes in the production of heavy ordnance, was established 1813. In 1776, Ann Lee founded the first American community of Shakers (United Society of Believers) in Watervliet. Founded by the Dutch 1735, Incorporated as a city 1896.
Population: 10,241; Growth (since 2000): 0.3%; Density: 7,611.3 persons per square mile; Race: 84.2% White, 9.1% Black/African American, 1.9% Asian, 0.0% American Indian/Alaska Native, 0.0% Native Hawaiian/Other Pacific Islander, 4.3% Two or more races, 4.5% Hispanic of any race; Average household size: 2.15; Median age: 36.8; Age under 18: 21.2%; Age 65 and over: 13.3%; Males per 100 females: 92.9; Marriage status: 47.3% never married, 37.6% now married, 5.0% separated, 5.4%

widowed, 9.7% divorced; Foreign born: 4.7%; Speak English only: 93.2%; With disability: 15.7%; Veterans: 9.7%; Ancestry: 33.1% Irish, 18.7% Italian, 14.8% German, 7.5% French, 7.4% English
Employment: 9.8% management, business, and financial, 5.3% computer, engineering, and science, 7.3% education, legal, community service, arts, and media, 6.0% healthcare practitioners, 18.3% service, 31.8% sales and office, 6.8% natural resources, construction, and maintenance, 14.7% production, transportation, and material moving
Income: Per capita: $25,709; Median household: $45,533; Average household: $53,815; Households with income of $100,000 or more: 10.1%; Poverty rate: 14.5%
Educational Attainment: High school diploma or higher: 90.9%; Bachelor's degree or higher: 17.4%; Graduate/professional degree or higher: 5.4%

School District(s)
Watervliet City SD (PK-12)
   2014-15 Enrollment: 1,347 . . . . (518) 629-3201
Housing: Homeownership rate: 40.5%; Median home value: $132,500; Median year structure built: Before 1940; Homeowner vacancy rate: 0.0%; Median selected monthly owner costs: $1,358 with a mortgage, $550 without a mortgage; Median gross rent: $832 per month; Rental vacancy rate: 5.6%
Health Insurance: 89.9% have insurance; 68.5% have private insurance; 34.7% have public insurance; 10.1% do not have insurance; 4.2% of children under 18 do not have insurance
Safety: Violent crime rate: 24.4 per 10,000 population; Property crime rate: 205.3 per 10,000 population
Transportation: Commute: 86.9% car, 7.1% public transportation, 2.6% walk, 2.2% work from home; Mean travel time to work: 18.3 minutes
Additional Information Contacts
City of Watervliet . . . . (518) 270-3800
   http://www.watervliet.com

WESTERLO (town).
Covers a land area of 57.791 square miles and a water area of 0.746 square miles. Located at 42.50° N. Lat; 74.05° W. Long. Elevation is 1,165 feet.
Population: 3,390; Growth (since 2000): -2.2%; Density: 58.7 persons per square mile; Race: 97.6% White, 0.6% Black/African American, 1.8% Asian, 0.0% American Indian/Alaska Native, 0.0% Native Hawaiian/Other Pacific Islander, 0.0% Two or more races, 1.3% Hispanic of any race; Average household size: 2.44; Median age: 47.9; Age under 18: 18.3%; Age 65 and over: 18.7%; Males per 100 females: 102.7; Marriage status: 22.5% never married, 61.0% now married, 0.3% separated, 7.1% widowed, 9.4% divorced; Foreign born: 3.8%; Speak English only: 96.0%; With disability: 9.4%; Veterans: 7.5%; Ancestry: 30.1% German, 21.8% Irish, 17.0% American, 11.4% English, 10.0% Italian
Employment: 21.2% management, business, and financial, 4.8% computer, engineering, and science, 10.3% education, legal, community service, arts, and media, 8.5% healthcare practitioners, 12.3% service, 19.1% sales and office, 11.8% natural resources, construction, and maintenance, 12.0% production, transportation, and material moving
Income: Per capita: $38,851; Median household: $78,375; Average household: $92,312; Households with income of $100,000 or more: 38.1%; Poverty rate: 4.0%
Educational Attainment: High school diploma or higher: 91.5%; Bachelor's degree or higher: 27.6%; Graduate/professional degree or higher: 13.6%
Housing: Homeownership rate: 94.3%; Median home value: $177,900; Median year structure built: 1978; Homeowner vacancy rate: 0.0%; Median selected monthly owner costs: $1,537 with a mortgage, $561 without a mortgage; Median gross rent: n/a per month; Rental vacancy rate: 0.0%
Health Insurance: 98.4% have insurance; 90.2% have private insurance; 24.5% have public insurance; 1.6% do not have insurance; 0.0% of children under 18 do not have insurance
Transportation: Commute: 92.5% car, 0.6% public transportation, 3.5% walk, 2.7% work from home; Mean travel time to work: 32.0 minutes

WESTMERE (CDP).
Covers a land area of 3.171 square miles and a water area of 0.010 square miles. Located at 42.69° N. Lat; 73.87° W. Long. Elevation is 292 feet.
Population: 6,758; Growth (since 2000): -6.0%; Density: 2,131.2 persons per square mile; Race: 80.7% White, 5.4% Black/African American, 11.4% Asian, 0.0% American Indian/Alaska Native, 0.0% Native Hawaiian/Other Pacific Islander, 1.4% Two or more races, 3.3% Hispanic of any race; Average household size: 2.15; Median age: 43.8; Age under 18: 17.8%;

Age 65 and over: 18.0%; Males per 100 females: 94.8; Marriage status: 32.6% never married, 50.6% now married, 2.5% separated, 7.9% widowed, 9.0% divorced; Foreign born: 13.0%; Speak English only: 83.6%; With disability: 8.3%; Veterans: 8.5%; Ancestry: 19.8% Irish, 19.1% Italian, 17.2% German, 12.4% English, 5.7% French

Employment: 18.1% management, business, and financial, 11.0% computer, engineering, and science, 12.4% education, legal, community service, arts, and media, 8.0% healthcare practitioners, 12.8% service, 24.1% sales and office, 4.6% natural resources, construction, and maintenance, 8.9% production, transportation, and material moving

Income: Per capita: $45,036; Median household: $71,949; Average household: $95,590; Households with income of $100,000 or more: 34.7%; Poverty rate: 10.1%

Educational Attainment: High school diploma or higher: 96.0%; Bachelor's degree or higher: 45.1%; Graduate/professional degree or higher: 26.1%

Housing: Homeownership rate: 59.9%; Median home value: $226,100; Median year structure built: 1971; Homeowner vacancy rate: 1.3%; Median selected monthly owner costs: $1,707 with a mortgage, $563 without a mortgage; Median gross rent: $1,147 per month; Rental vacancy rate: 5.9%

Health Insurance: 97.0% have insurance; 89.7% have private insurance; 24.0% have public insurance; 3.0% do not have insurance; 0.0% of children under 18 do not have insurance

Transportation: Commute: 94.1% car, 0.3% public transportation, 0.9% walk, 3.8% work from home; Mean travel time to work: 21.2 minutes

Allegany County

Located in western New York; bounded on the south by Pennsylvania. Covers a land area of 1,029.308 square miles, a water area of 5.079 square miles, and is located in the Eastern Time Zone at 42.25° N. Lat., 78.03° W. Long. The county was founded in 1806. County seat is Belmont.

Weather Station: Alfred   Elevation: 1,770 feet

	Jan	Feb	Mar	Apr	May	Jun	Jul	Aug	Sep	Oct	Nov	Dec
High	31	35	44	57	68	76	80	79	71	59	47	36
Low	13	13	20	31	40	50	54	52	46	35	28	19
Precip	2.2	1.7	2.7	3.0	3.3	4.3	3.9	3.6	3.7	3.3	3.3	2.6
Snow	20.8	16.7	17.1	4.0	0.3	0.0	0.0	0.0	0.0	0.5	8.6	19.6

High and Low temperatures in degrees Fahrenheit; Precipitation and Snow in inches

Weather Station: Angelica   Elevation: 1,444 feet

	Jan	Feb	Mar	Apr	May	Jun	Jul	Aug	Sep	Oct	Nov	Dec
High	32	34	43	56	67	75	79	78	71	59	47	36
Low	13	13	20	31	39	49	53	52	45	35	28	19
Precip	2.2	1.9	2.6	3.1	3.3	4.5	3.9	4.1	3.7	3.3	3.2	2.5
Snow	15.8	11.3	11.8	3.2	0.2	0.0	0.0	0.0	0.0	0.2	7.1	14.1

High and Low temperatures in degrees Fahrenheit; Precipitation and Snow in inches

Population: 48,070; Growth (since 2000): -3.7%; Density: 46.7 persons per square mile; Race: 95.7% White, 1.4% Black/African American, 1.2% Asian, 0.3% American Indian/Alaska Native, 0.0% Native Hawaiian/Other Pacific Islander, 0.9% two or more races, 1.5% Hispanic of any race; Average household size: 2.36; Median age: 38.3; Age under 18: 20.9%; Age 65 and over: 16.4%; Males per 100 females: 101.8; Marriage status: 33.4% never married, 49.8% now married, 2.1% separated, 6.8% widowed, 10.0% divorced; Foreign born: 2.2%; Speak English only: 94.9%; With disability: 15.2%; Veterans: 10.9%; Ancestry: 25.3% German, 17.5% Irish, 15.3% English, 6.9% American, 6.7% Italian

Religion: Six largest groups: 8.8% Catholicism, 6.9% Methodist/Pietist, 3.8% Holiness, 2.8% Non-denominational Protestant, 2.6% Baptist, 1.4% European Free-Church

Economy: Unemployment rate: 4.7%; Leading industries: 17.0 % retail trade; 16.0 % other services (except public administration); 12.2 % health care and social assistance; Farms: 784 totaling 150,383 acres; Company size: 1 employs 1,000 or more persons, 3 employ 500 to 999 persons, 8 employ 100 to 499 persons, 789 employ less than 100 persons; Business ownership: 920 women-owned, n/a Black-owned, 27 Hispanic-owned, 129 Asian-owned, 28 American Indian/Alaska Native-owned

Employment: 9.0% management, business, and financial, 3.0% computer, engineering, and science, 14.6% education, legal, community service, arts, and media, 5.5% healthcare practitioners, 21.0% service, 19.5% sales and office, 11.7% natural resources, construction, and maintenance, 15.8% production, transportation, and material moving

Income: Per capita: $20,940; Median household: $42,776; Average household: $53,610; Households with income of $100,000 or more: 11.3%; Poverty rate: 16.9%

Educational Attainment: High school diploma or higher: 88.6%; Bachelor's degree or higher: 20.0%; Graduate/professional degree or higher: 10.2%

Housing: Homeownership rate: 73.1%; Median home value: $70,300; Median year structure built: 1964; Homeowner vacancy rate: 1.5%; Median selected monthly owner costs: $990 with a mortgage, $442 without a mortgage; Median gross rent: $606 per month; Rental vacancy rate: 4.1%

Vital Statistics: Birth rate: 98.0 per 10,000 population; Death rate: 94.2 per 10,000 population; Age-adjusted cancer mortality rate: 173.6 deaths per 100,000 population

Health Insurance: 90.9% have insurance; 67.8% have private insurance; 38.7% have public insurance; 9.1% do not have insurance; 9.7% of children under 18 do not have insurance

Health Care: Physicians: 8.0 per 10,000 population; Dentists: 2.9 per 10,000 population; Hospital beds: 23.7 per 10,000 population; Hospital admissions: 487.4 per 10,000 population

Transportation: Commute: 83.4% car, 0.6% public transportation, 11.5% walk, 3.0% work from home; Mean travel time to work: 21.4 minutes

2016 Presidential Election: 68.0% Trump, 26.5% Clinton, 4.0% Johnson, 1.5% Stein

Additional Information Contacts

Allegany Government . . . . (585) 268-9222
    http://www.alleganyco.com

Allegany County Communities

ALFRED (town). Covers a land area of 31.476 square miles and a water area of 0.149 square miles. Located at 42.23° N. Lat; 77.80° W. Long. Elevation is 1,765 feet.

History: Alfred is a town in Allegany County, New York, and includes a village of the same name. Alfred University and Alfred State College are located in the Village of Alfred.

Population: 5,119; Growth (since 2000): -0.4%; Density: 162.6 persons per square mile; Race: 83.1% White, 8.2% Black/African American, 5.0% Asian, 0.5% American Indian/Alaska Native, 0.0% Native Hawaiian/Other Pacific Islander, 1.2% Two or more races, 4.6% Hispanic of any race; Average household size: 2.16; Median age: 20.4; Age under 18: 7.8%; Age 65 and over: 4.6%; Males per 100 females: 143.2; Marriage status: 84.3% never married, 12.4% now married, 0.1% separated, 1.2% widowed, 2.1% divorced; Foreign born: 7.9%; Speak English only: 88.5%; With disability: 4.1%; Veterans: 2.1%; Ancestry: 19.7% German, 19.0% Irish, 13.7% Italian, 9.3% English, 5.8% Polish

Employment: 5.6% management, business, and financial, 6.5% computer, engineering, and science, 23.7% education, legal, community service, arts, and media, 1.2% healthcare practitioners, 31.3% service, 21.6% sales and office, 6.0% natural resources, construction, and maintenance, 4.2% production, transportation, and material moving

Income: Per capita: $11,287; Median household: $37,422; Average household: $55,826; Households with income of $100,000 or more: 18.1%; Poverty rate: 27.2%

Educational Attainment: High school diploma or higher: 97.4%; Bachelor's degree or higher: 62.3%; Graduate/professional degree or higher: 40.4%

Four-year College(s)

Alfred University (Private, Not-for-profit)
    Fall 2014 Enrollment: 2,310 . . . . (607) 871-2111
    2015-16 Tuition: In-state $26,261; Out-of-state $26,261
SUNY College of Technology at Alfred (Public)
    Fall 2014 Enrollment: 3,661 . . . . (800) 425-3733
    2015-16 Tuition: In-state $8,057; Out-of-state $14,617

Housing: Homeownership rate: 47.6%; Median home value: $113,200; Median year structure built: 1963; Homeowner vacancy rate: 3.6%; Median selected monthly owner costs: $1,259 with a mortgage, $612 without a mortgage; Median gross rent: $697 per month; Rental vacancy rate: 3.8%

Health Insurance: 95.6% have insurance; 86.5% have private insurance; 15.9% have public insurance; 4.4% do not have insurance; 0.0% of children under 18 do not have insurance

Newspapers: Alfred Sun (weekly circulation 1,000)

Transportation: Commute: 39.1% car, 0.0% public transportation, 57.3% walk, 2.9% work from home; Mean travel time to work: 11.5 minutes

Profiles of New York State

Additional Information Contacts
Town of Alfred . . . . (607) 587-8524
  http://townofalfred.com

ALFRED (village).
Covers a land area of 1.190 square miles and a water area of 0 square miles. Located at 42.25° N. Lat; 77.79° W. Long. Elevation is 1,765 feet.

History: Alfred is a town in Allegany County, New York. The Town of Alfred has a village named Alfred in the center of the town. Alfred University and Alfred State College are located in the Village of Alfred.

Population: 4,314; Growth (since 2000): 9.1%; Density: 3,625.7 persons per square mile; Race: 79.9% White, 9.8% Black/African American, 5.9% Asian, 0.6% American Indian/Alaska Native, 0.0% Native Hawaiian/Other Pacific Islander, 1.4% Two or more races, 5.5% Hispanic of any race; Average household size: 2.19; Median age: 20.2; Age under 18: 5.2%; Age 65 and over: 2.1%; Males per 100 females: 154.7; Marriage status: 93.3% never married, 5.7% now married, 0.0% separated, 0.5% widowed, 0.5% divorced; Foreign born: 9.3%; Speak English only: 86.8%; With disability: 3.8%; Veterans: 0.6%; Ancestry: 19.7% Irish, 18.5% German, 13.0% Italian, 7.8% English, 6.6% Polish

Employment: 3.4% management, business, and financial, 6.5% computer, engineering, and science, 21.5% education, legal, community service, arts, and media, 0.6% healthcare practitioners, 34.2% service, 25.3% sales and office, 6.1% natural resources, construction, and maintenance, 2.4% production, transportation, and material moving

Income: Per capita: $7,780; Median household: $25,469; Average household: $47,223; Households with income of $100,000 or more: 16.6%; Poverty rate: 40.5%

Educational Attainment: High school diploma or higher: 99.4%; Bachelor's degree or higher: 81.4%; Graduate/professional degree or higher: 48.6%

Four-year College(s)
Alfred University (Private, Not-for-profit)
  Fall 2014 Enrollment: 2,310 . . . . (607) 871-2111
  2015-16 Tuition: In-state $26,261; Out-of-state $26,261
SUNY College of Technology at Alfred (Public)
  Fall 2014 Enrollment: 3,661 . . . . (800) 425-3733
  2015-16 Tuition: In-state $8,057; Out-of-state $14,617

Housing: Homeownership rate: 26.9%; Median home value: $115,300; Median year structure built: 1960; Homeowner vacancy rate: 7.4%; Median selected monthly owner costs: $1,292 with a mortgage, $723 without a mortgage; Median gross rent: $766 per month; Rental vacancy rate: 5.0%

Health Insurance: 96.4% have insurance; 89.7% have private insurance; 11.7% have public insurance; 3.6% do not have insurance; 0.0% of children under 18 do not have insurance

Safety: Violent crime rate: 10.0 per 10,000 population; Property crime rate: 80.2 per 10,000 population

Newspapers: Alfred Sun (weekly circulation 1,000)

Transportation: Commute: 28.5% car, 0.0% public transportation, 67.3% walk, 3.4% work from home; Mean travel time to work: 10.7 minutes

Additional Information Contacts
Village of Alfred . . . . (607) 587-9188
  http://www.alfredny.org

ALFRED STATION (unincorporated postal area)
ZCTA: 14803
  Covers a land area of 24.924 square miles and a water area of 0.097 square miles. Located at 42.27° N. Lat; 77.75° W. Long. Elevation is 1,644 feet.

Population: 964; Growth (since 2000): -22.3%; Density: 38.7 persons per square mile; Race: 100.0% White, 0.0% Black/African American, 0.0% Asian, 0.0% American Indian/Alaska Native, 0.0% Native Hawaiian/Other Pacific Islander, 0.0% Two or more races, 0.5% Hispanic of any race; Average household size: 2.13; Median age: 40.5; Age under 18: 22.6%; Age 65 and over: 17.3%; Males per 100 females: 110.0; Marriage status: 26.8% never married, 55.2% now married, 0.4% separated, 5.0% widowed, 13.1% divorced; Foreign born: 1.2%; Speak English only: 97.4%; With disability: 6.1%; Veterans: 8.6%; Ancestry: 27.8% German, 19.8% Irish, 18.5% Italian, 18.0% English, 5.5% American

Employment: 11.8% management, business, and financial, 6.1% computer, engineering, and science, 32.2% education, legal, community service, arts, and media, 3.7% healthcare practitioners, 19.7% service, 7.9% sales and office, 7.2% natural resources, construction, and maintenance, 11.4% production, transportation, and material moving

Income: Per capita: $27,602; Median household: $47,188; Average household: $59,757; Households with income of $100,000 or more: 15.3%; Poverty rate: 14.6%

Educational Attainment: High school diploma or higher: 95.5%; Bachelor's degree or higher: 47.3%; Graduate/professional degree or higher: 29.0%

Housing: Homeownership rate: 65.8%; Median home value: $117,000; Median year structure built: 1973; Homeowner vacancy rate: 1.7%; Median selected monthly owner costs: $1,257 with a mortgage, $571 without a mortgage; Median gross rent: $645 per month; Rental vacancy rate: 0.0%

Health Insurance: 92.0% have insurance; 67.2% have private insurance; 41.7% have public insurance; 8.0% do not have insurance; 2.8% of children under 18 do not have insurance

Transportation: Commute: 86.6% car, 0.0% public transportation, 12.7% walk, 0.7% work from home; Mean travel time to work: 17.6 minutes

ALLEN (town).
Covers a land area of 36.377 square miles and a water area of 0.203 square miles. Located at 42.40° N. Lat; 78.00° W. Long.

Population: 577; Growth (since 2000): 24.9%; Density: 15.9 persons per square mile; Race: 99.7% White, 0.0% Black/African American, 0.0% Asian, 0.0% American Indian/Alaska Native, 0.0% Native Hawaiian/Other Pacific Islander, 0.0% Two or more races, 0.3% Hispanic of any race; Average household size: 3.21; Median age: 29.3; Age under 18: 43.2%; Age 65 and over: 11.6%; Males per 100 females: 111.3; Marriage status: 31.3% never married, 54.4% now married, 1.3% separated, 4.9% widowed, 9.5% divorced; Foreign born: 0.3%; Speak English only: 67.9%; With disability: 8.8%; Veterans: 12.2%; Ancestry: 17.5% German, 14.7% Dutch, 12.8% Pennsylvania German, 8.7% English, 8.0% Swiss

Employment: 7.6% management, business, and financial, 2.5% computer, engineering, and science, 7.6% education, legal, community service, arts, and media, 1.9% healthcare practitioners, 12.7% service, 28.5% sales and office, 15.8% natural resources, construction, and maintenance, 23.4% production, transportation, and material moving

Income: Per capita: $13,240; Median household: $40,972; Average household: $42,629; Households with income of $100,000 or more: 2.8%; Poverty rate: 32.2%

Educational Attainment: High school diploma or higher: 77.1%; Bachelor's degree or higher: 11.1%; Graduate/professional degree or higher: 3.9%

Housing: Homeownership rate: 87.8%; Median home value: $82,200; Median year structure built: 1977; Homeowner vacancy rate: 3.1%; Median selected monthly owner costs: $1,092 with a mortgage, $373 without a mortgage; Median gross rent: $471 per month; Rental vacancy rate: 0.0%

Health Insurance: 50.3% have insurance; 39.5% have private insurance; 21.0% have public insurance; 49.7% do not have insurance; 74.3% of children under 18 do not have insurance

Transportation: Commute: 71.5% car, 0.0% public transportation, 13.9% walk, 9.5% work from home; Mean travel time to work: 33.0 minutes

ALLENTOWN (unincorporated postal area)
ZCTA: 14707
  Covers a land area of 1.987 square miles and a water area of 0 square miles. Located at 42.08° N. Lat; 78.06° W. Long. Elevation is 1,847 feet.

Population: 225; Growth (since 2000): n/a; Density: 113.2 persons per square mile; Race: 100.0% White, 0.0% Black/African American, 0.0% Asian, 0.0% American Indian/Alaska Native, 0.0% Native Hawaiian/Other Pacific Islander, 0.0% Two or more races, 4.9% Hispanic of any race; Average household size: 2.34; Median age: 46.7; Age under 18: 20.4%; Age 65 and over: 26.7%; Males per 100 females: 123.4; Marriage status: 20.9% never married, 63.7% now married, 4.0% separated, 3.0% widowed, 12.4% divorced; Foreign born: 0.9%; Speak English only: 100.0%; With disability: 16.9%; Veterans: 15.6%; Ancestry: 39.6% German, 22.7% Irish, 11.6% American, 10.2% English, 4.9% Italian

Employment: 5.7% management, business, and financial, 0.0% computer, engineering, and science, 8.0% education, legal, community service, arts, and media, 0.0% healthcare practitioners, 42.0% service, 3.4% sales and office, 22.7% natural resources, construction, and maintenance, 18.2% production, transportation, and material moving

Income: Per capita: $24,216; Median household: $57,500; Average household: $61,225; Households with income of $100,000 or more: 13.5%; Poverty rate: 1.3%

Educational Attainment: High school diploma or higher: 92.9%; Bachelor's degree or higher: 5.2%; Graduate/professional degree or higher: n/a

Housing: Homeownership rate: 90.6%; Median home value: $53,400; Median year structure built: Before 1940; Homeowner vacancy rate: 0.0%; Median selected monthly owner costs: $1,141 with a mortgage, $325 without a mortgage; Median gross rent: n/a per month; Rental vacancy rate: 0.0%

Health Insurance: 93.3% have insurance; 70.7% have private insurance; 42.2% have public insurance; 6.7% do not have insurance; 0.0% of children under 18 do not have insurance

Transportation: Commute: 89.4% car, 0.0% public transportation, 4.7% walk, 0.0% work from home; Mean travel time to work: 19.4 minutes

---

ALMA (town). Covers a land area of 36.215 square miles and a water area of 0.301 square miles. Located at 42.05° N. Lat; 78.02° W. Long. Elevation is 1,549 feet.

Population: 797; Growth (since 2000): -5.9%; Density: 22.0 persons per square mile; Race: 99.9% White, 0.0% Black/African American, 0.0% Asian, 0.0% American Indian/Alaska Native, 0.0% Native Hawaiian/Other Pacific Islander, 0.1% Two or more races, 1.6% Hispanic of any race; Average household size: 2.36; Median age: 46.0; Age under 18: 22.5%; Age 65 and over: 15.8%; Males per 100 females: 113.7; Marriage status: 20.3% never married, 59.8% now married, 4.0% separated, 4.7% widowed, 15.1% divorced; Foreign born: 0.9%; Speak English only: 100.0%; With disability: 17.1%; Veterans: 19.1%; Ancestry: 29.9% German, 16.6% Irish, 12.3% English, 11.3% American, 6.5% Polish

Employment: 6.4% management, business, and financial, 2.3% computer, engineering, and science, 8.4% education, legal, community service, arts, and media, 3.9% healthcare practitioners, 18.0% service, 14.1% sales and office, 15.8% natural resources, construction, and maintenance, 31.2% production, transportation, and material moving

Income: Per capita: $22,235; Median household: $46,989; Average household: $53,077; Households with income of $100,000 or more: 10.4%; Poverty rate: 18.0%

Educational Attainment: High school diploma or higher: 89.7%; Bachelor's degree or higher: 7.9%; Graduate/professional degree or higher: 2.0%

Housing: Homeownership rate: 82.2%; Median home value: $53,200; Median year structure built: 1974; Homeowner vacancy rate: 3.4%; Median selected monthly owner costs: $931 with a mortgage, $381 without a mortgage; Median gross rent: $683 per month; Rental vacancy rate: 0.0%

Health Insurance: 95.0% have insurance; 65.9% have private insurance; 47.6% have public insurance; 5.0% do not have insurance; 1.7% of children under 18 do not have insurance

Transportation: Commute: 94.6% car, 0.0% public transportation, 2.7% walk, 1.0% work from home; Mean travel time to work: 30.7 minutes

---

ALMOND (town). Covers a land area of 45.717 square miles and a water area of 0.067 square miles. Located at 42.34° N. Lat; 77.78° W. Long. Elevation is 1,335 feet.

Population: 1,596; Growth (since 2000): -0.5%; Density: 34.9 persons per square mile; Race: 94.8% White, 0.2% Black/African American, 3.3% Asian, 0.0% American Indian/Alaska Native, 0.0% Native Hawaiian/Other Pacific Islander, 1.1% Two or more races, 0.7% Hispanic of any race; Average household size: 2.49; Median age: 40.8; Age under 18: 26.0%; Age 65 and over: 16.2%; Males per 100 females: 99.6; Marriage status: 20.8% never married, 66.2% now married, 1.6% separated, 5.8% widowed, 7.2% divorced; Foreign born: 2.6%; Speak English only: 97.4%; With disability: 13.5%; Veterans: 11.5%; Ancestry: 20.8% German, 16.2% Irish, 13.2% English, 11.8% American, 5.1% Italian

Employment: 10.9% management, business, and financial, 4.6% computer, engineering, and science, 15.9% education, legal, community service, arts, and media, 7.8% healthcare practitioners, 17.4% service, 20.2% sales and office, 12.7% natural resources, construction, and maintenance, 10.4% production, transportation, and material moving

Income: Per capita: $25,512; Median household: $52,401; Average household: $64,988; Households with income of $100,000 or more: 17.9%; Poverty rate: 14.3%

Educational Attainment: High school diploma or higher: 93.9%; Bachelor's degree or higher: 32.4%; Graduate/professional degree or higher: 17.6%

School District(s)

Alfred-Almond Central SD (PK-12)

    2014-15 Enrollment: 666 . . . . (607) 276-6500

Housing: Homeownership rate: 82.4%; Median home value: $81,700; Median year structure built: 1972; Homeowner vacancy rate: 1.7%; Median selected monthly owner costs: $1,107 with a mortgage, $462 without a mortgage; Median gross rent: $665 per month; Rental vacancy rate: 0.0%

Health Insurance: 94.9% have insurance; 74.1% have private insurance; 37.7% have public insurance; 5.1% do not have insurance; 3.9% of children under 18 do not have insurance

Transportation: Commute: 94.3% car, 0.4% public transportation, 2.8% walk, 2.2% work from home; Mean travel time to work: 23.3 minutes

---

ALMOND (village). Covers a land area of 0.564 square miles and a water area of 0 square miles. Located at 42.32° N. Lat; 77.74° W. Long. Elevation is 1,335 feet.

Population: 480; Growth (since 2000): 4.1%; Density: 850.5 persons per square mile; Race: 92.9% White, 0.2% Black/African American, 2.7% Asian, 0.0% American Indian/Alaska Native, 0.0% Native Hawaiian/Other Pacific Islander, 4.2% Two or more races, 1.0% Hispanic of any race; Average household size: 2.61; Median age: 38.0; Age under 18: 29.2%; Age 65 and over: 15.0%; Males per 100 females: 104.4; Marriage status: 20.9% never married, 60.6% now married, 2.7% separated, 8.7% widowed, 9.8% divorced; Foreign born: 1.9%; Speak English only: 95.9%; With disability: 18.1%; Veterans: 15.0%; Ancestry: 19.4% English, 17.9% German, 13.3% Irish, 7.9% Italian, 6.3% American

Employment: 9.6% management, business, and financial, 8.0% computer, engineering, and science, 21.3% education, legal, community service, arts, and media, 4.3% healthcare practitioners, 12.2% service, 23.9% sales and office, 7.4% natural resources, construction, and maintenance, 13.3% production, transportation, and material moving

Income: Per capita: $21,307; Median household: $48,864; Average household: $57,040; Households with income of $100,000 or more: 10.9%; Poverty rate: 20.7%

Educational Attainment: High school diploma or higher: 95.8%; Bachelor's degree or higher: 29.0%; Graduate/professional degree or higher: 16.6%

School District(s)

Alfred-Almond Central SD (PK-12)

    2014-15 Enrollment: 666 . . . . (607) 276-6500

Housing: Homeownership rate: 71.2%; Median home value: $64,300; Median year structure built: Before 1940; Homeowner vacancy rate: 0.0%; Median selected monthly owner costs: $873 with a mortgage, $406 without a mortgage; Median gross rent: $622 per month; Rental vacancy rate: 0.0%

Health Insurance: 93.5% have insurance; 64.6% have private insurance; 42.7% have public insurance; 6.5% do not have insurance; 2.9% of children under 18 do not have insurance

Transportation: Commute: 95.7% car, 1.6% public transportation, 2.1% walk, 0.5% work from home; Mean travel time to work: 22.2 minutes

---

AMITY (town). Covers a land area of 34.442 square miles and a water area of 0.123 square miles. Located at 42.23° N. Lat; 78.00° W. Long. Elevation is 1,391 feet.

Population: 2,253; Growth (since 2000): 0.4%; Density: 65.4 persons per square mile; Race: 95.0% White, 1.8% Black/African American, 0.8% Asian, 0.7% American Indian/Alaska Native, 0.0% Native Hawaiian/Other Pacific Islander, 0.9% Two or more races, 1.3% Hispanic of any race; Average household size: 2.25; Median age: 44.4; Age under 18: 20.4%; Age 65 and over: 17.4%; Males per 100 females: 102.6; Marriage status: 28.9% never married, 53.0% now married, 1.9% separated, 7.5% widowed, 10.6% divorced; Foreign born: 2.0%; Speak English only: 95.3%; With disability: 16.5%; Veterans: 12.8%; Ancestry: 29.4% German, 17.6% Irish, 17.3% English, 8.7% Italian, 6.5% American

Employment: 13.0% management, business, and financial, 1.4% computer, engineering, and science, 12.1% education, legal, community service, arts, and media, 7.2% healthcare practitioners, 19.4% service, 22.5% sales and office, 7.8% natural resources, construction, and maintenance, 16.6% production, transportation, and material moving

Income: Per capita: $21,852; Median household: $42,188; Average household: $51,921; Households with income of $100,000 or more: 10.9%; Poverty rate: 14.3%

Educational Attainment: High school diploma or higher: 89.0%; Bachelor's degree or higher: 14.5%; Graduate/professional degree or higher: 6.2%

Housing: Homeownership rate: 73.3%; Median home value: $65,000; Median year structure built: 1954; Homeowner vacancy rate: 0.0%; Median

selected monthly owner costs: $945 with a mortgage, $445 without a mortgage; Median gross rent: $557 per month; Rental vacancy rate: 0.0%
Health Insurance: 92.0% have insurance; 67.9% have private insurance; 40.3% have public insurance; 8.0% do not have insurance; 5.9% of children under 18 do not have insurance
Transportation: Commute: 94.3% car, 0.7% public transportation, 1.5% walk, 2.8% work from home; Mean travel time to work: 24.7 minutes

ANDOVER (town). Covers a land area of 39.430 square miles and a water area of 0.066 square miles. Located at 42.15° N. Lat; 77.81° W. Long. Elevation is 1,660 feet.

History: Incorporated 1892.
Population: 1,685; Growth (since 2000): -13.4%; Density: 42.7 persons per square mile; Race: 98.2% White, 0.7% Black/African American, 1.1% Asian, 0.0% American Indian/Alaska Native, 0.0% Native Hawaiian/Other Pacific Islander, 0.0% Two or more races, 1.2% Hispanic of any race; Average household size: 2.45; Median age: 42.6; Age under 18: 23.6%; Age 65 and over: 17.9%; Males per 100 females: 96.8; Marriage status: 25.9% never married, 58.6% now married, 2.8% separated, 6.8% widowed, 8.8% divorced; Foreign born: 1.4%; Speak English only: 99.8%; With disability: 15.2%; Veterans: 13.3%; Ancestry: 29.3% German, 19.5% Irish, 17.3% English, 6.8% American, 6.1% Polish
Employment: 6.6% management, business, and financial, 3.4% computer, engineering, and science, 13.3% education, legal, community service, arts, and media, 5.4% healthcare practitioners, 20.5% service, 17.8% sales and office, 15.2% natural resources, construction, and maintenance, 17.9% production, transportation, and material moving
Income: Per capita: $22,394; Median household: $46,838; Average household: $54,682; Households with income of $100,000 or more: 7.7%; Poverty rate: 14.1%
Educational Attainment: High school diploma or higher: 90.8%; Bachelor's degree or higher: 16.5%; Graduate/professional degree or higher: 5.9%

School District(s)
Andover Central SD (PK-12)
    2014-15 Enrollment: 358 . . . . (607) 478-8491
Housing: Homeownership rate: 76.1%; Median home value: $60,800; Median year structure built: 1947; Homeowner vacancy rate: 3.3%; Median selected monthly owner costs: $888 with a mortgage, $408 without a mortgage; Median gross rent: $668 per month; Rental vacancy rate: 3.5%
Health Insurance: 95.8% have insurance; 72.3% have private insurance; 43.9% have public insurance; 4.2% do not have insurance; 1.5% of children under 18 do not have insurance
Transportation: Commute: 91.5% car, 2.2% public transportation, 3.9% walk, 2.4% work from home; Mean travel time to work: 21.7 minutes

ANDOVER (village). Covers a land area of 1.001 square miles and a water area of 0.015 square miles. Located at 42.16° N. Lat; 77.80° W. Long. Elevation is 1,660 feet.

Population: 829; Growth (since 2000): -22.7%; Density: 828.2 persons per square mile; Race: 96.4% White, 1.4% Black/African American, 2.2% Asian, 0.0% American Indian/Alaska Native, 0.0% Native Hawaiian/Other Pacific Islander, 0.0% Two or more races, 0.0% Hispanic of any race; Average household size: 2.36; Median age: 40.5; Age under 18: 22.7%; Age 65 and over: 16.4%; Males per 100 females: 91.2; Marriage status: 23.6% never married, 62.8% now married, 2.7% separated, 6.8% widowed, 6.8% divorced; Foreign born: 2.5%; Speak English only: 100.0%; With disability: 15.3%; Veterans: 12.8%; Ancestry: 35.3% German, 24.1% Irish, 19.5% English, 7.7% American, 5.5% Scottish
Employment: 7.3% management, business, and financial, 3.4% computer, engineering, and science, 14.9% education, legal, community service, arts, and media, 5.0% healthcare practitioners, 20.1% service, 17.5% sales and office, 15.1% natural resources, construction, and maintenance, 16.7% production, transportation, and material moving
Income: Per capita: $22,197; Median household: $48,438; Average household: $52,256; Households with income of $100,000 or more: 6.0%; Poverty rate: 9.5%
Educational Attainment: High school diploma or higher: 94.3%; Bachelor's degree or higher: 19.8%; Graduate/professional degree or higher: 5.7%

School District(s)
Andover Central SD (PK-12)
    2014-15 Enrollment: 358 . . . . (607) 478-8491
Housing: Homeownership rate: 71.5%; Median home value: $57,400; Median year structure built: Before 1940; Homeowner vacancy rate: 0.0%;

Median selected monthly owner costs: $856 with a mortgage, $387 without a mortgage; Median gross rent: $671 per month; Rental vacancy rate: 5.7%
Health Insurance: 97.6% have insurance; 73.7% have private insurance; 44.0% have public insurance; 2.4% do not have insurance; 0.0% of children under 18 do not have insurance
Safety: Violent crime rate: 0.0 per 10,000 population; Property crime rate: 9.9 per 10,000 population
Transportation: Commute: 89.1% car, 3.2% public transportation, 5.3% walk, 2.4% work from home; Mean travel time to work: 21.4 minutes

ANGELICA (town). Covers a land area of 36.394 square miles and a water area of 0.038 square miles. Located at 42.30° N. Lat; 78.02° W. Long. Elevation is 1,434 feet.

History: Oldest village in the county; founded in 1800 by Captain Philip Church, nephew of Alexander Hamilton. Church is buried with his wife at Until the Day Dawns Cemetery. Contingent of French royalists settled here in 1806; one of them became the French ambassador to U.S; another was Victor Marie du Pont de Nemours.
Population: 1,368; Growth (since 2000): -3.0%; Density: 37.6 persons per square mile; Race: 98.3% White, 0.4% Black/African American, 0.8% Asian, 0.0% American Indian/Alaska Native, 0.0% Native Hawaiian/Other Pacific Islander, 0.4% Two or more races, 0.0% Hispanic of any race; Average household size: 2.47; Median age: 42.0; Age under 18: 25.8%; Age 65 and over: 17.9%; Males per 100 females: 111.9; Marriage status: 21.3% never married, 60.1% now married, 2.5% separated, 5.0% widowed, 13.7% divorced; Foreign born: 1.0%; Speak English only: 95.9%; With disability: 15.2%; Veterans: 13.4%; Ancestry: 29.6% German, 20.2% Irish, 14.0% English, 13.8% American, 6.2% Italian
Employment: 14.5% management, business, and financial, 3.8% computer, engineering, and science, 17.2% education, legal, community service, arts, and media, 4.1% healthcare practitioners, 19.6% service, 17.1% sales and office, 10.6% natural resources, construction, and maintenance, 13.1% production, transportation, and material moving
Income: Per capita: $22,176; Median household: $43,125; Average household: $54,453; Households with income of $100,000 or more: 15.4%; Poverty rate: 16.9%
Educational Attainment: High school diploma or higher: 94.2%; Bachelor's degree or higher: 20.1%; Graduate/professional degree or higher: 8.0%
Housing: Homeownership rate: 78.7%; Median home value: $85,500; Median year structure built: 1944; Homeowner vacancy rate: 1.1%; Median selected monthly owner costs: $1,018 with a mortgage, $370 without a mortgage; Median gross rent: $579 per month; Rental vacancy rate: 7.8%
Health Insurance: 92.3% have insurance; 61.8% have private insurance; 43.9% have public insurance; 7.7% do not have insurance; 8.2% of children under 18 do not have insurance
Transportation: Commute: 92.5% car, 1.3% public transportation, 2.4% walk, 2.1% work from home; Mean travel time to work: 23.4 minutes

ANGELICA (village). Covers a land area of 2.152 square miles and a water area of 0 square miles. Located at 42.31° N. Lat; 78.02° W. Long. Elevation is 1,434 feet.

Population: 831; Growth (since 2000): -8.0%; Density: 386.2 persons per square mile; Race: 98.9% White, 0.0% Black/African American, 0.4% Asian, 0.0% American Indian/Alaska Native, 0.0% Native Hawaiian/Other Pacific Islander, 0.7% Two or more races, 0.0% Hispanic of any race; Average household size: 2.42; Median age: 41.4; Age under 18: 23.0%; Age 65 and over: 19.9%; Males per 100 females: 104.5; Marriage status: 18.8% never married, 63.5% now married, 3.5% separated, 6.3% widowed, 11.4% divorced; Foreign born: 0.6%; Speak English only: 99.1%; With disability: 15.0%; Veterans: 12.7%; Ancestry: 31.5% German, 20.5% Irish, 17.1% English, 9.9% Italian, 9.6% American
Employment: 16.3% management, business, and financial, 1.7% computer, engineering, and science, 19.1% education, legal, community service, arts, and media, 4.2% healthcare practitioners, 19.7% service, 15.0% sales and office, 8.6% natural resources, construction, and maintenance, 15.5% production, transportation, and material moving
Income: Per capita: $23,000; Median household: $45,417; Average household: $54,790; Households with income of $100,000 or more: 13.7%; Poverty rate: 12.2%
Educational Attainment: High school diploma or higher: 93.4%; Bachelor's degree or higher: 20.2%; Graduate/professional degree or higher: 8.7%

Housing: Homeownership rate: 75.6%; Median home value: $84,500; Median year structure built: Before 1940; Homeowner vacancy rate: 1.9%; Median selected monthly owner costs: $954 with a mortgage, $394 without a mortgage; Median gross rent: $578 per month; Rental vacancy rate: 0.0%
Health Insurance: 94.2% have insurance; 69.2% have private insurance; 41.0% have public insurance; 5.8% do not have insurance; 2.1% of children under 18 do not have insurance
Safety: Violent crime rate: 0.0 per 10,000 population; Property crime rate: 47.7 per 10,000 population
Transportation: Commute: 90.1% car, 2.0% public transportation, 3.8% walk, 2.3% work from home; Mean travel time to work: 22.8 minutes

BELFAST (CDP). Covers a land area of 1.385 square miles and a water area of 0.027 square miles. Located at 42.34° N. Lat; 78.12° W. Long. Elevation is 1,309 feet.
Population: 907; Growth (since 2000): n/a; Density: 654.9 persons per square mile; Race: 99.4% White, 0.0% Black/African American, 0.0% Asian, 0.0% American Indian/Alaska Native, 0.0% Native Hawaiian/Other Pacific Islander, 0.1% Two or more races, 6.0% Hispanic of any race; Average household size: 2.19; Median age: 33.2; Age under 18: 28.7%; Age 65 and over: 20.1%; Males per 100 females: 87.7; Marriage status: 24.1% never married, 51.0% now married, 1.2% separated, 9.9% widowed, 14.9% divorced; Foreign born: 0.4%; Speak English only: 99.2%; With disability: 15.3%; Veterans: 15.6%; Ancestry: 28.7% Irish, 25.2% German, 12.8% English, 8.2% American, 7.8% Dutch
Employment: 3.4% management, business, and financial, 2.3% computer, engineering, and science, 20.2% education, legal, community service, arts, and media, 3.1% healthcare practitioners, 18.5% service, 22.2% sales and office, 8.3% natural resources, construction, and maintenance, 21.9% production, transportation, and material moving
Income: Per capita: $17,117; Median household: $35,078; Average household: $37,407; Households with income of $100,000 or more: 3.9%; Poverty rate: 14.9%
Educational Attainment: High school diploma or higher: 87.9%; Bachelor's degree or higher: 10.0%; Graduate/professional degree or higher: 4.6%
School District(s)
Belfast Central SD (PK-12)
    2014-15 Enrollment: 373 . . . . (585) 365-9940
Housing: Homeownership rate: 52.5%; Median home value: $56,900; Median year structure built: 1943; Homeowner vacancy rate: 0.0%; Median selected monthly owner costs: $839 with a mortgage, $442 without a mortgage; Median gross rent: $513 per month; Rental vacancy rate: 4.2%
Health Insurance: 90.6% have insurance; 65.4% have private insurance; 42.6% have public insurance; 9.4% do not have insurance; 8.8% of children under 18 do not have insurance
Transportation: Commute: 89.9% car, 0.0% public transportation, 6.3% walk, 3.7% work from home; Mean travel time to work: 23.0 minutes

BELFAST (town). Covers a land area of 36.295 square miles and a water area of 0.249 square miles. Located at 42.30° N. Lat; 78.14° W. Long. Elevation is 1,309 feet.
Population: 1,836; Growth (since 2000): 7.1%; Density: 50.6 persons per square mile; Race: 99.7% White, 0.0% Black/African American, 0.0% Asian, 0.0% American Indian/Alaska Native, 0.0% Native Hawaiian/Other Pacific Islander, 0.1% Two or more races, 2.9% Hispanic of any race; Average household size: 2.44; Median age: 38.8; Age under 18: 27.5%; Age 65 and over: 18.7%; Males per 100 females: 98.0; Marriage status: 20.9% never married, 58.7% now married, 1.9% separated, 6.9% widowed, 13.5% divorced; Foreign born: 1.0%; Speak English only: 88.4%; With disability: 16.1%; Veterans: 13.1%; Ancestry: 33.6% German, 19.6% Irish, 17.9% English, 5.9% American, 5.5% Dutch
Employment: 10.1% management, business, and financial, 2.0% computer, engineering, and science, 16.2% education, legal, community service, arts, and media, 5.2% healthcare practitioners, 15.8% service, 17.0% sales and office, 12.8% natural resources, construction, and maintenance, 20.8% production, transportation, and material moving
Income: Per capita: $18,406; Median household: $42,695; Average household: $45,252; Households with income of $100,000 or more: 5.6%; Poverty rate: 13.9%
Educational Attainment: High school diploma or higher: 81.7%; Bachelor's degree or higher: 12.1%; Graduate/professional degree or higher: 5.6%

School District(s)
Belfast Central SD (PK-12)
    2014-15 Enrollment: 373 . . . . (585) 365-9940
Housing: Homeownership rate: 71.5%; Median home value: $70,300; Median year structure built: 1973; Homeowner vacancy rate: 0.0%; Median selected monthly owner costs: $946 with a mortgage, $448 without a mortgage; Median gross rent: $521 per month; Rental vacancy rate: 3.9%
Health Insurance: 81.2% have insurance; 59.7% have private insurance; 36.8% have public insurance; 18.8% do not have insurance; 29.5% of children under 18 do not have insurance
Transportation: Commute: 85.4% car, 0.0% public transportation, 6.5% walk, 8.1% work from home; Mean travel time to work: 24.9 minutes

BELMONT (village). County seat. Covers a land area of 0.996 square miles and a water area of 0.002 square miles. Located at 42.22° N. Lat; 78.03° W. Long. Elevation is 1,391 feet.
History: Incorporated 1871.
Population: 1,010; Growth (since 2000): 6.1%; Density: 1,014.2 persons per square mile; Race: 98.8% White, 0.3% Black/African American, 0.0% Asian, 0.5% American Indian/Alaska Native, 0.0% Native Hawaiian/Other Pacific Islander, 0.4% Two or more races, 0.5% Hispanic of any race; Average household size: 2.17; Median age: 40.7; Age under 18: 25.6%; Age 65 and over: 17.0%; Males per 100 females: 94.2; Marriage status: 24.8% never married, 52.2% now married, 1.5% separated, 9.5% widowed, 13.5% divorced; Foreign born: 0.4%; Speak English only: 97.4%; With disability: 16.3%; Veterans: 6.1%; Ancestry: 26.2% German, 17.9% Irish, 15.6% Italian, 10.9% English, 4.8% American
Employment: 10.5% management, business, and financial, 0.7% computer, engineering, and science, 16.1% education, legal, community service, arts, and media, 9.3% healthcare practitioners, 24.8% service, 18.0% sales and office, 7.5% natural resources, construction, and maintenance, 13.1% production, transportation, and material moving
Income: Per capita: $20,980; Median household: $40,000; Average household: $46,402; Households with income of $100,000 or more: 11.2%; Poverty rate: 14.4%
Educational Attainment: High school diploma or higher: 93.2%; Bachelor's degree or higher: 21.1%; Graduate/professional degree or higher: 9.3%
School District(s)
Genesee Valley Central SD At Angelica-Belmont (PK-12)
    2014-15 Enrollment: 570 . . . . (585) 268-7900
Housing: Homeownership rate: 65.9%; Median home value: $61,800; Median year structure built: Before 1940; Homeowner vacancy rate: 0.0%; Median selected monthly owner costs: $909 with a mortgage, $461 without a mortgage; Median gross rent: $555 per month; Rental vacancy rate: 0.0%
Health Insurance: 93.2% have insurance; 64.5% have private insurance; 44.5% have public insurance; 6.8% do not have insurance; 6.2% of children under 18 do not have insurance
Transportation: Commute: 93.2% car, 1.0% public transportation, 3.4% walk, 2.4% work from home; Mean travel time to work: 26.5 minutes

BIRDSALL (town). Covers a land area of 35.889 square miles and a water area of 0.171 square miles. Located at 42.40° N. Lat; 77.89° W. Long. Elevation is 1,693 feet.
Population: 163; Growth (since 2000): -39.2%; Density: 4.5 persons per square mile; Race: 100.0% White, 0.0% Black/African American, 0.0% Asian, 0.0% American Indian/Alaska Native, 0.0% Native Hawaiian/Other Pacific Islander, 0.0% Two or more races, 1.2% Hispanic of any race; Average household size: 1.94; Median age: 59.8; Age under 18: 7.4%; Age 65 and over: 35.6%; Males per 100 females: 104.6; Marriage status: 9.3% never married, 63.6% now married, 5.3% separated, 13.9% widowed, 13.2% divorced; Foreign born: 0.0%; Speak English only: 100.0%; With disability: 23.3%; Veterans: 17.9%; Ancestry: 26.4% German, 20.9% Irish, 19.6% English, 8.6% Italian, 4.3% American
Employment: 15.9% management, business, and financial, 8.5% computer, engineering, and science, 3.7% education, legal, community service, arts, and media, 4.9% healthcare practitioners, 13.4% service, 12.2% sales and office, 20.7% natural resources, construction, and maintenance, 20.7% production, transportation, and material moving
Income: Per capita: $25,203; Median household: $45,455; Average household: $48,440; Households with income of $100,000 or more: 7.2%; Poverty rate: 8.6%

Educational Attainment: High school diploma or higher: 84.8%; Bachelor's degree or higher: 11.7%; Graduate/professional degree or higher: 5.5%

Housing: Homeownership rate: 97.6%; Median home value: $63,100; Median year structure built: 1978; Homeowner vacancy rate: 0.0%; Median selected monthly owner costs: $846 with a mortgage, $405 without a mortgage; Median gross rent: n/a per month; Rental vacancy rate: 0.0%

Health Insurance: 93.3% have insurance; 79.1% have private insurance; 57.1% have public insurance; 6.7% do not have insurance; 0.0% of children under 18 do not have insurance

Transportation: Commute: 86.5% car, 0.0% public transportation, 2.7% walk, 5.4% work from home; Mean travel time to work: 55.8 minutes

BLACK CREEK (unincorporated postal area)
ZCTA: 14714

Covers a land area of 18.175 square miles and a water area of 0.081 square miles. Located at 42.30° N. Lat; 78.23° W. Long. Elevation is 1,509 feet.

Population: 500; Growth (since 2000): 44.9%; Density: 27.5 persons per square mile; Race: 96.6% White, 0.0% Black/African American, 0.0% Asian, 2.6% American Indian/Alaska Native, 0.0% Native Hawaiian/Other Pacific Islander, 0.8% Two or more races, 0.0% Hispanic of any race; Average household size: 2.63; Median age: 34.9; Age under 18: 28.2%; Age 65 and over: 15.4%; Males per 100 females: 107.2; Marriage status: 19.0% never married, 62.3% now married, 0.5% separated, 10.2% widowed, 8.6% divorced; Foreign born: 0.4%; Speak English only: 91.5%; With disability: 12.4%; Veterans: 11.4%; Ancestry: 21.2% German, 15.8% Pennsylvania German, 14.2% English, 7.2% Irish, 6.4% American

Employment: 4.0% management, business, and financial, 1.0% computer, engineering, and science, 12.9% education, legal, community service, arts, and media, 8.9% healthcare practitioners, 13.9% service, 11.4% sales and office, 14.4% natural resources, construction, and maintenance, 33.7% production, transportation, and material moving

Income: Per capita: $19,780; Median household: $42,500; Average household: $50,953; Households with income of $100,000 or more: 8.4%; Poverty rate: 6.1%

Educational Attainment: High school diploma or higher: 82.2%; Bachelor's degree or higher: 13.8%; Graduate/professional degree or higher: 5.9%

Housing: Homeownership rate: 84.7%; Median home value: $76,000; Median year structure built: 1973; Homeowner vacancy rate: 1.2%; Median selected monthly owner costs: $1,256 with a mortgage, $495 without a mortgage; Median gross rent: $829 per month; Rental vacancy rate: 0.0%

Health Insurance: 74.0% have insurance; 57.4% have private insurance; 45.8% have public insurance; 26.0% do not have insurance; 43.3% of children under 18 do not have insurance

Transportation: Commute: 82.7% car, 1.5% public transportation, 5.0% walk, 7.4% work from home; Mean travel time to work: 21.8 minutes

BOLIVAR (town). Covers a land area of 35.863 square miles and a water area of 0.010 square miles. Located at 42.03° N. Lat; 78.14° W. Long. Elevation is 1,594 feet.

History: Surrounding region was prominent early petroleum-producing area from late 19th to early 20th century. Incorporated 1882.

Population: 2,239; Growth (since 2000): 0.7%; Density: 62.4 persons per square mile; Race: 97.1% White, 0.5% Black/African American, 0.8% Asian, 0.8% American Indian/Alaska Native, 0.0% Native Hawaiian/Other Pacific Islander, 0.7% Two or more races, 0.1% Hispanic of any race; Average household size: 2.49; Median age: 37.7; Age under 18: 26.9%; Age 65 and over: 13.6%; Males per 100 females: 96.5; Marriage status: 23.4% never married, 59.4% now married, 2.8% separated, 7.8% widowed, 9.4% divorced; Foreign born: 1.9%; Speak English only: 99.6%; With disability: 13.3%; Veterans: 8.7%; Ancestry: 21.1% German, 15.9% Irish, 14.6% English, 8.5% American, 6.0% Italian

Employment: 7.2% management, business, and financial, 1.8% computer, engineering, and science, 17.7% education, legal, community service, arts, and media, 4.1% healthcare practitioners, 15.3% service, 17.2% sales and office, 14.9% natural resources, construction, and maintenance, 21.7% production, transportation, and material moving

Income: Per capita: $21,441; Median household: $41,300; Average household: $52,689; Households with income of $100,000 or more: 9.2%; Poverty rate: 14.6%

Educational Attainment: High school diploma or higher: 87.2%; Bachelor's degree or higher: 14.9%; Graduate/professional degree or higher: 5.7%

School District(s)
Bolivar-Richburg Central SD (PK-12)
   2014-15 Enrollment: 846 . . . . (585) 928-2561

Housing: Homeownership rate: 74.5%; Median home value: $58,900; Median year structure built: 1950; Homeowner vacancy rate: 0.0%; Median selected monthly owner costs: $961 with a mortgage, $493 without a mortgage; Median gross rent: $574 per month; Rental vacancy rate: 14.0%

Health Insurance: 93.7% have insurance; 65.7% have private insurance; 42.2% have public insurance; 6.3% do not have insurance; 4.0% of children under 18 do not have insurance

Transportation: Commute: 91.3% car, 0.2% public transportation, 4.6% walk, 2.1% work from home; Mean travel time to work: 23.8 minutes

BOLIVAR (village). Covers a land area of 0.798 square miles and a water area of 0 square miles. Located at 42.07° N. Lat; 78.17° W. Long. Elevation is 1,594 feet.

Population: 1,123; Growth (since 2000): -4.3%; Density: 1,406.6 persons per square mile; Race: 95.2% White, 0.1% Black/African American, 1.7% Asian, 1.6% American Indian/Alaska Native, 0.0% Native Hawaiian/Other Pacific Islander, 1.4% Two or more races, 0.0% Hispanic of any race; Average household size: 2.33; Median age: 37.9; Age under 18: 23.6%; Age 65 and over: 12.8%; Males per 100 females: 96.8; Marriage status: 28.0% never married, 53.6% now married, 3.8% separated, 7.5% widowed, 10.9% divorced; Foreign born: 2.1%; Speak English only: 99.6%; With disability: 17.3%; Veterans: 10.3%; Ancestry: 23.5% German, 15.9% Irish, 12.7% English, 6.4% American, 4.3% Italian

Employment: 7.1% management, business, and financial, 3.8% computer, engineering, and science, 16.4% education, legal, community service, arts, and media, 7.1% healthcare practitioners, 17.0% service, 10.7% sales and office, 18.7% natural resources, construction, and maintenance, 19.3% production, transportation, and material moving

Income: Per capita: $24,503; Median household: $41,042; Average household: $56,172; Households with income of $100,000 or more: 9.6%; Poverty rate: 13.8%

Educational Attainment: High school diploma or higher: 87.3%; Bachelor's degree or higher: 19.7%; Graduate/professional degree or higher: 7.6%

School District(s)
Bolivar-Richburg Central SD (PK-12)
   2014-15 Enrollment: 846 . . . . (585) 928-2561

Housing: Homeownership rate: 63.8%; Median home value: $60,900; Median year structure built: Before 1940; Homeowner vacancy rate: 0.0%; Median selected monthly owner costs: $948 with a mortgage, $541 without a mortgage; Median gross rent: $547 per month; Rental vacancy rate: 8.9%

Health Insurance: 93.5% have insurance; 65.8% have private insurance; 41.2% have public insurance; 6.5% do not have insurance; 4.2% of children under 18 do not have insurance

Transportation: Commute: 87.4% car, 0.0% public transportation, 8.9% walk, 3.0% work from home; Mean travel time to work: 21.2 minutes

BURNS (town). Covers a land area of 27.220 square miles and a water area of 0.036 square miles. Located at 42.44° N. Lat; 77.78° W. Long. Elevation is 1,197 feet.

Population: 1,436; Growth (since 2000): 15.1%; Density: 52.8 persons per square mile; Race: 96.9% White, 0.0% Black/African American, 0.1% Asian, 0.0% American Indian/Alaska Native, 0.0% Native Hawaiian/Other Pacific Islander, 0.1% Two or more races, 2.7% Hispanic of any race; Average household size: 2.67; Median age: 36.8; Age under 18: 30.2%; Age 65 and over: 11.6%; Males per 100 females: 104.2; Marriage status: 24.7% never married, 59.9% now married, 0.4% separated, 5.2% widowed, 10.2% divorced; Foreign born: 0.7%; Speak English only: 97.9%; With disability: 18.1%; Veterans: 9.5%; Ancestry: 29.7% German, 16.8% Irish, 11.2% English, 7.6% American, 3.5% Italian

Employment: 8.9% management, business, and financial, 2.1% computer, engineering, and science, 3.7% education, legal, community service, arts, and media, 9.9% healthcare practitioners, 19.5% service, 18.6% sales and office, 23.7% natural resources, construction, and maintenance, 13.7% production, transportation, and material moving

Income: Per capita: $18,046; Median household: $40,183; Average household: $47,878; Households with income of $100,000 or more: 6.5%; Poverty rate: 14.8%

Educational Attainment: High school diploma or higher: 90.1%; Bachelor's degree or higher: 10.3%; Graduate/professional degree or higher: 4.9%

Housing: Homeownership rate: 72.9%; Median home value: $76,600; Median year structure built: 1955; Homeowner vacancy rate: 3.7%; Median selected monthly owner costs: $1,095 with a mortgage, $548 without a mortgage; Median gross rent: $758 per month; Rental vacancy rate: 0.0%

Health Insurance: 94.1% have insurance; 72.7% have private insurance; 38.6% have public insurance; 5.9% do not have insurance; 1.4% of children under 18 do not have insurance

Transportation: Commute: 92.6% car, 1.3% public transportation, 3.6% walk, 1.3% work from home; Mean travel time to work: 26.2 minutes

CANASERAGA (village).

Covers a land area of 1.062 square miles and a water area of 0 square miles. Located at 42.46° N. Lat; 77.78° W. Long. Elevation is 1,250 feet.

Population: 600; Growth (since 2000): 1.0%; Density: 564.8 persons per square mile; Race: 97.3% White, 0.0% Black/African American, 0.3% Asian, 0.0% American Indian/Alaska Native, 0.0% Native Hawaiian/Other Pacific Islander, 0.3% Two or more races, 2.8% Hispanic of any race; Average household size: 2.67; Median age: 37.0; Age under 18: 29.0%; Age 65 and over: 12.2%; Males per 100 females: 101.5; Marriage status: 29.8% never married, 48.9% now married, 0.2% separated, 9.3% widowed, 12.0% divorced; Foreign born: 0.3%; Speak English only: 96.6%; With disability: 22.8%; Veterans: 10.1%; Ancestry: 41.2% German, 19.0% Irish, 11.0% American, 11.0% English, 7.2% Scottish

Employment: 11.9% management, business, and financial, 1.4% computer, engineering, and science, 1.9% education, legal, community service, arts, and media, 4.3% healthcare practitioners, 19.0% service, 24.8% sales and office, 19.0% natural resources, construction, and maintenance, 17.6% production, transportation, and material moving

Income: Per capita: $13,886; Median household: $29,875; Average household: $37,002; Households with income of $100,000 or more: 4.9%; Poverty rate: 29.7%

Educational Attainment: High school diploma or higher: 87.3%; Bachelor's degree or higher: 11.4%; Graduate/professional degree or higher: 6.1%

School District(s)
Canaseraga Central SD (PK-12)
   2014-15 Enrollment: 248. . . . . (607) 545-6421

Housing: Homeownership rate: 65.3%; Median home value: $62,200; Median year structure built: Before 1940; Homeowner vacancy rate: 9.3%; Median selected monthly owner costs: $1,072 with a mortgage, $516 without a mortgage; Median gross rent: $708 per month; Rental vacancy rate: 0.0%

Health Insurance: 92.7% have insurance; 55.7% have private insurance; 54.2% have public insurance; 7.3% do not have insurance; 1.1% of children under 18 do not have insurance

Transportation: Commute: 84.4% car, 3.5% public transportation, 7.5% walk, 1.0% work from home; Mean travel time to work: 27.5 minutes

CANEADEA (town).

Covers a land area of 35.649 square miles and a water area of 0.693 square miles. Located at 42.39° N. Lat; 78.13° W. Long. Elevation is 1,253 feet.

Population: 2,573; Growth (since 2000): -4.5%; Density: 72.2 persons per square mile; Race: 91.6% White, 3.3% Black/African American, 2.4% Asian, 0.2% American Indian/Alaska Native, 0.0% Native Hawaiian/Other Pacific Islander, 1.6% Two or more races, 2.4% Hispanic of any race; Average household size: 2.43; Median age: 21.8; Age under 18: 14.0%; Age 65 and over: 16.4%; Males per 100 females: 79.6; Marriage status: 54.9% never married, 36.5% now married, 1.0% separated, 6.2% widowed, 2.4% divorced; Foreign born: 3.3%; Speak English only: 93.5%; With disability: 9.6%; Veterans: 5.3%; Ancestry: 25.6% German, 20.3% English, 17.5% Irish, 6.0% Polish, 5.7% Italian

Employment: 6.5% management, business, and financial, 1.5% computer, engineering, and science, 27.5% education, legal, community service, arts, and media, 3.2% healthcare practitioners, 32.4% service, 16.1% sales and office, 6.5% natural resources, construction, and maintenance, 6.3% production, transportation, and material moving

Income: Per capita: $14,842; Median household: $43,333; Average household: $52,638; Households with income of $100,000 or more: 10.8%; Poverty rate: 12.7%

Educational Attainment: High school diploma or higher: 94.8%; Bachelor's degree or higher: 41.7%; Graduate/professional degree or higher: 24.8%

Housing: Homeownership rate: 70.7%; Median home value: $97,200; Median year structure built: 1964; Homeowner vacancy rate: 0.0%; Median selected monthly owner costs: $1,071 with a mortgage, $506 without a mortgage; Median gross rent: $541 per month; Rental vacancy rate: 0.0%

Health Insurance: 94.7% have insurance; 81.3% have private insurance; 25.6% have public insurance; 5.3% do not have insurance; 2.8% of children under 18 do not have insurance

Transportation: Commute: 55.5% car, 0.4% public transportation, 37.9% walk, 4.6% work from home; Mean travel time to work: 14.4 minutes

CENTERVILLE (town).

Covers a land area of 35.435 square miles and a water area of 0.047 square miles. Located at 42.47° N. Lat; 78.27° W. Long. Elevation is 1,759 feet.

Population: 765; Growth (since 2000): 0.4%; Density: 21.6 persons per square mile; Race: 97.4% White, 0.0% Black/African American, 0.0% Asian, 0.0% American Indian/Alaska Native, 0.0% Native Hawaiian/Other Pacific Islander, 2.6% Two or more races, 0.0% Hispanic of any race; Average household size: 2.65; Median age: 31.5; Age under 18: 28.8%; Age 65 and over: 9.8%; Males per 100 females: 98.1; Marriage status: 30.6% never married, 54.2% now married, 3.7% separated, 4.6% widowed, 10.6% divorced; Foreign born: 1.0%; Speak English only: 76.5%; With disability: 13.6%; Veterans: 7.0%; Ancestry: 41.4% German, 12.2% English, 11.5% Irish, 9.4% Swiss, 8.5% Polish

Employment: 10.7% management, business, and financial, 1.0% computer, engineering, and science, 12.0% education, legal, community service, arts, and media, 3.7% healthcare practitioners, 9.0% service, 11.7% sales and office, 26.3% natural resources, construction, and maintenance, 25.7% production, transportation, and material moving

Income: Per capita: $18,499; Median household: $41,776; Average household: $48,134; Households with income of $100,000 or more: 6.2%; Poverty rate: 19.2%

Educational Attainment: High school diploma or higher: 65.6%; Bachelor's degree or higher: 7.4%; Graduate/professional degree or higher: 4.3%

Housing: Homeownership rate: 82.7%; Median home value: $73,200; Median year structure built: 1979; Homeowner vacancy rate: 0.0%; Median selected monthly owner costs: $933 with a mortgage, $375 without a mortgage; Median gross rent: $688 per month; Rental vacancy rate: 0.0%

Health Insurance: 63.3% have insurance; 42.2% have private insurance; 31.0% have public insurance; 36.7% do not have insurance; 46.8% of children under 18 do not have insurance

Transportation: Commute: 71.6% car, 0.0% public transportation, 6.6% walk, 9.0% work from home; Mean travel time to work: 28.6 minutes

CERES (unincorporated postal area)
ZCTA: 14721

Covers a land area of 3.732 square miles and a water area of 0 square miles. Located at 42.01° N. Lat; 78.27° W. Long. Elevation is 1,453 feet.

Population: 113; Growth (since 2000): 10.8%; Density: 30.3 persons per square mile; Race: 100.0% White, 0.0% Black/African American, 0.0% Asian, 0.0% American Indian/Alaska Native, 0.0% Native Hawaiian/Other Pacific Islander, 0.0% Two or more races, 3.5% Hispanic of any race; Average household size: 1.92; Median age: 27.7; Age under 18: 11.5%; Age 65 and over: 9.7%; Males per 100 females: 98.3; Marriage status: 30.0% never married, 52.0% now married, 0.0% separated, 3.0% widowed, 15.0% divorced; Foreign born: 0.9%; Speak English only: 99.0%; With disability: 17.7%; Veterans: 5.0%; Ancestry: 24.8% Polish, 19.5% German, 13.3% English, 11.5% Ukrainian, 7.1% Welsh

Employment: 6.0% management, business, and financial, 0.0% computer, engineering, and science, 22.4% education, legal, community service, arts, and media, 0.0% healthcare practitioners, 14.9% service, 10.4% sales and office, 9.0% natural resources, construction, and maintenance, 37.3% production, transportation, and material moving

Income: Per capita: $18,479; Median household: n/a; Average household: $35,664; Households with income of $100,000 or more: 5.1%; Poverty rate: 11.5%

Educational Attainment: High school diploma or higher: 100.0%; Bachelor's degree or higher: 5.3%; Graduate/professional degree or higher: n/a

Housing: Homeownership rate: 67.8%; Median home value: $46,200; Median year structure built: 1968; Homeowner vacancy rate: 0.0%; Median selected monthly owner costs: $950 with a mortgage, $317 without a mortgage; Median gross rent: n/a per month; Rental vacancy rate: 0.0%

Health Insurance: 75.2% have insurance; 61.1% have private insurance; 26.5% have public insurance; 24.8% do not have insurance; 0.0% of children under 18 do not have insurance
Transportation: Commute: 89.6% car, 0.0% public transportation, 10.4% walk, 0.0% work from home; Mean travel time to work: 30.1 minutes

CLARKSVILLE (town). Covers a land area of 36.276 square miles and a water area of 0.020 square miles. Located at 42.14° N. Lat; 78.25° W. Long.

Population: 917; Growth (since 2000): -20.0%; Density: 25.3 persons per square mile; Race: 97.5% White, 0.3% Black/African American, 2.2% Asian, 0.0% American Indian/Alaska Native, 0.0% Native Hawaiian/Other Pacific Islander, 0.0% Two or more races, 2.5% Hispanic of any race; Average household size: 2.31; Median age: 47.8; Age under 18: 18.2%; Age 65 and over: 18.4%; Males per 100 females: 101.6; Marriage status: 19.3% never married, 65.8% now married, 2.7% separated, 6.0% widowed, 8.9% divorced; Foreign born: 2.7%; Speak English only: 97.8%; With disability: 19.3%; Veterans: 14.5%; Ancestry: 28.1% German, 22.1% English, 19.2% Irish, 13.0% Polish, 4.8% Dutch
Employment: 5.0% management, business, and financial, 3.7% computer, engineering, and science, 11.9% education, legal, community service, arts, and media, 4.6% healthcare practitioners, 10.6% service, 22.2% sales and office, 10.1% natural resources, construction, and maintenance, 31.9% production, transportation, and material moving
Income: Per capita: $22,345; Median household: $44,659; Average household: $51,064; Households with income of $100,000 or more: 11.5%; Poverty rate: 8.3%
Educational Attainment: High school diploma or higher: 87.8%; Bachelor's degree or higher: 15.2%; Graduate/professional degree or higher: 6.5%
Housing: Homeownership rate: 85.8%; Median home value: $56,900; Median year structure built: 1974; Homeowner vacancy rate: 0.0%; Median selected monthly owner costs: $769 with a mortgage, $387 without a mortgage; Median gross rent: $838 per month; Rental vacancy rate: 0.0%
Health Insurance: 94.0% have insurance; 76.3% have private insurance; 37.5% have public insurance; 6.0% do not have insurance; 0.0% of children under 18 do not have insurance
Transportation: Commute: 94.3% car, 3.3% public transportation, 0.5% walk, 0.9% work from home; Mean travel time to work: 29.2 minutes

CUBA (town). Covers a land area of 35.129 square miles and a water area of 0.763 square miles. Located at 42.21° N. Lat; 78.24° W. Long. Elevation is 1,496 feet.

History: Seneca Oil Spring, where oil was first noted by Jesuit missionaries in early 17th century, is nearby; the spring was the precursor of the "Pennsylvania field," the first oil field in the U.S. Incorporated 1850.
Population: 3,206; Growth (since 2000): -5.5%; Density: 91.3 persons per square mile; Race: 98.0% White, 0.0% Black/African American, 0.4% Asian, 0.0% American Indian/Alaska Native, 0.0% Native Hawaiian/Other Pacific Islander, 1.6% Two or more races, 1.1% Hispanic of any race; Average household size: 2.39; Median age: 44.6; Age under 18: 20.9%; Age 65 and over: 19.8%; Males per 100 females: 91.7; Marriage status: 26.8% never married, 54.7% now married, 2.5% separated, 6.6% widowed, 12.0% divorced; Foreign born: 0.2%; Speak English only: 96.3%; With disability: 16.0%; Veterans: 12.3%; Ancestry: 21.1% German, 18.3% English, 16.3% Irish, 9.3% American, 8.9% Italian
Employment: 9.2% management, business, and financial, 3.3% computer, engineering, and science, 18.7% education, legal, community service, arts, and media, 5.6% healthcare practitioners, 18.3% service, 24.6% sales and office, 8.5% natural resources, construction, and maintenance, 11.7% production, transportation, and material moving
Income: Per capita: $29,215; Median household: $52,026; Average household: $70,528; Households with income of $100,000 or more: 14.9%; Poverty rate: 15.0%
Educational Attainment: High school diploma or higher: 93.6%; Bachelor's degree or higher: 27.0%; Graduate/professional degree or higher: 14.8%
School District(s)
Cuba-Rushford Central SD (PK-12)
  2014-15 Enrollment: 885 . . . . (585) 968-2650
Housing: Homeownership rate: 81.8%; Median home value: $72,000; Median year structure built: 1955; Homeowner vacancy rate: 0.0%; Median selected monthly owner costs: $1,100 with a mortgage, $474 without a mortgage; Median gross rent: $629 per month; Rental vacancy rate: 11.4%

Health Insurance: 89.4% have insurance; 67.8% have private insurance; 36.6% have public insurance; 10.6% do not have insurance; 4.6% of children under 18 do not have insurance
Hospitals: Cuba Memorial Hospital
Safety: Violent crime rate: 9.4 per 10,000 population; Property crime rate: 229.3 per 10,000 population
Newspapers: Patriot & Free Press (weekly circulation 5,000)
Transportation: Commute: 93.2% car, 0.4% public transportation, 3.2% walk, 2.1% work from home; Mean travel time to work: 18.6 minutes

CUBA (village). Covers a land area of 1.216 square miles and a water area of 0 square miles. Located at 42.22° N. Lat; 78.28° W. Long. Elevation is 1,496 feet.

Population: 1,654; Growth (since 2000): 1.3%; Density: 1,359.7 persons per square mile; Race: 96.8% White, 0.1% Black/African American, 0.7% Asian, 0.0% American Indian/Alaska Native, 0.0% Native Hawaiian/Other Pacific Islander, 2.4% Two or more races, 1.4% Hispanic of any race; Average household size: 2.49; Median age: 40.1; Age under 18: 21.7%; Age 65 and over: 18.0%; Males per 100 females: 85.5; Marriage status: 30.3% never married, 48.5% now married, 3.4% separated, 8.3% widowed, 12.9% divorced; Foreign born: 0.4%; Speak English only: 97.9%; With disability: 17.4%; Veterans: 10.6%; Ancestry: 22.9% German, 21.0% Irish, 20.4% English, 8.7% Polish, 8.2% American
Employment: 9.5% management, business, and financial, 4.3% computer, engineering, and science, 18.2% education, legal, community service, arts, and media, 2.8% healthcare practitioners, 25.7% service, 19.4% sales and office, 7.5% natural resources, construction, and maintenance, 12.6% production, transportation, and material moving
Income: Per capita: $22,781; Median household: $46,908; Average household: $57,229; Households with income of $100,000 or more: 14.9%; Poverty rate: 22.3%
Educational Attainment: High school diploma or higher: 95.0%; Bachelor's degree or higher: 25.4%; Graduate/professional degree or higher: 10.6%
School District(s)
Cuba-Rushford Central SD (PK-12)
  2014-15 Enrollment: 885 . . . . (585) 968-2650
Housing: Homeownership rate: 68.2%; Median home value: $67,500; Median year structure built: Before 1940; Homeowner vacancy rate: 0.0%; Median selected monthly owner costs: $1,007 with a mortgage, $470 without a mortgage; Median gross rent: $570 per month; Rental vacancy rate: 13.2%
Health Insurance: 88.9% have insurance; 60.9% have private insurance; 42.1% have public insurance; 11.1% do not have insurance; 4.2% of children under 18 do not have insurance
Hospitals: Cuba Memorial Hospital
Newspapers: Patriot & Free Press (weekly circulation 5,000)
Transportation: Commute: 86.4% car, 0.7% public transportation, 6.5% walk, 4.2% work from home; Mean travel time to work: 18.5 minutes

FARMERSVILLE STATION (unincorporated postal area)
ZCTA: 14060
  Covers a land area of 17.740 square miles and a water area of 0.149 square miles. Located at 42.45° N. Lat; 78.30° W. Long..
Population: 412; Growth (since 2000): -6.6%; Density: 23.2 persons per square mile; Race: 95.1% White, 0.0% Black/African American, 0.0% Asian, 0.0% American Indian/Alaska Native, 0.0% Native Hawaiian/Other Pacific Islander, 4.9% Two or more races, 2.9% Hispanic of any race; Average household size: 2.24; Median age: 49.5; Age under 18: 19.2%; Age 65 and over: 21.1%; Males per 100 females: 113.0; Marriage status: 20.1% never married, 61.6% now married, 4.7% separated, 9.2% widowed, 9.2% divorced; Foreign born: 1.9%; Speak English only: 98.0%; With disability: 22.1%; Veterans: 11.7%; Ancestry: 45.4% German, 35.2% English, 11.7% Irish, 7.3% Polish, 7.0% Italian
Employment: 6.6% management, business, and financial, 0.0% computer, engineering, and science, 9.3% education, legal, community service, arts, and media, 2.6% healthcare practitioners, 27.8% service, 11.3% sales and office, 9.9% natural resources, construction, and maintenance, 32.5% production, transportation, and material moving
Income: Per capita: $20,701; Median household: n/a; Average household: $44,972; Households with income of $100,000 or more: 4.3%; Poverty rate: 8.7%
Educational Attainment: High school diploma or higher: 82.2%; Bachelor's degree or higher: 10.9%; Graduate/professional degree or higher: 7.2%

Housing: Homeownership rate: 95.7%; Median home value: $75,800; Median year structure built: 1957; Homeowner vacancy rate: 0.0%; Median selected monthly owner costs: $1,088 with a mortgage, $527 without a mortgage; Median gross rent: $920 per month; Rental vacancy rate: 0.0%
Health Insurance: 93.9% have insurance; 58.5% have private insurance; 51.7% have public insurance; 6.1% do not have insurance; 0.0% of children under 18 do not have insurance
Transportation: Commute: 98.6% car, 0.0% public transportation, 0.0% walk, 1.4% work from home; Mean travel time to work: 41.9 minutes

FILLMORE (CDP).
Covers a land area of 0.816 square miles and a water area of 0 square miles. Located at 42.47° N. Lat; 78.11° W. Long. Elevation is 1,197 feet.
Population: 596; Growth (since 2000): n/a; Density: 730.6 persons per square mile; Race: 99.7% White, 0.3% Black/African American, 0.0% Asian, 0.0% American Indian/Alaska Native, 0.0% Native Hawaiian/Other Pacific Islander, 0.0% Two or more races, 0.0% Hispanic of any race; Average household size: 2.19; Median age: 41.3; Age under 18: 25.0%; Age 65 and over: 11.6%; Males per 100 females: 91.4; Marriage status: 20.1% never married, 62.7% now married, 8.7% separated, 10.0% widowed, 7.2% divorced; Foreign born: 0.8%; Speak English only: 100.0%; With disability: 14.9%; Veterans: 8.3%; Ancestry: 39.3% German, 16.1% Irish, 11.2% Polish, 10.4% English, 9.6% American
Employment: 6.6% management, business, and financial, 1.2% computer, engineering, and science, 23.4% education, legal, community service, arts, and media, 3.1% healthcare practitioners, 16.0% service, 23.4% sales and office, 14.5% natural resources, construction, and maintenance, 11.7% production, transportation, and material moving
Income: Per capita: $20,077; Median household: $37,500; Average household: $44,759; Households with income of $100,000 or more: 6.3%; Poverty rate: 13.9%
Educational Attainment: High school diploma or higher: 96.9%; Bachelor's degree or higher: 26.1%; Graduate/professional degree or higher: 18.4%

School District(s)
Fillmore Central SD (PK-12)
    2014-15 Enrollment: 683. . . . . (585) 567-2251
Housing: Homeownership rate: 56.3%; Median home value: $74,800; Median year structure built: 1943; Homeowner vacancy rate: 0.0%; Median selected monthly owner costs: $907 with a mortgage, $386 without a mortgage; Median gross rent: $606 per month; Rental vacancy rate: 5.8%
Health Insurance: 91.9% have insurance; 67.6% have private insurance; 36.2% have public insurance; 8.1% do not have insurance; 0.0% of children under 18 do not have insurance
Transportation: Commute: 74.4% car, 0.0% public transportation, 20.3% walk, 4.4% work from home; Mean travel time to work: 22.6 minutes

FRIENDSHIP (CDP).
Covers a land area of 2.889 square miles and a water area of 0 square miles. Located at 42.21° N. Lat; 78.14° W. Long. Elevation is 1,506 feet.
Population: 1,255; Growth (since 2000): 6.7%; Density: 434.5 persons per square mile; Race: 96.8% White, 0.0% Black/African American, 0.0% Asian, 0.0% American Indian/Alaska Native, 0.0% Native Hawaiian/Other Pacific Islander, 3.2% Two or more races, 0.0% Hispanic of any race; Average household size: 2.69; Median age: 30.2; Age under 18: 33.6%; Age 65 and over: 12.0%; Males per 100 females: 93.3; Marriage status: 38.2% never married, 44.4% now married, 7.1% separated, 4.5% widowed, 12.9% divorced; Foreign born: 1.4%; Speak English only: 98.0%; With disability: 20.9%; Veterans: 12.0%; Ancestry: 22.5% Irish, 22.5% German, 15.9% English, 8.8% American, 7.3% Dutch
Employment: 3.0% management, business, and financial, 1.5% computer, engineering, and science, 1.2% education, legal, community service, arts, and media, 3.6% healthcare practitioners, 22.1% service, 45.0% sales and office, 0.0% natural resources, construction, and maintenance, 23.6% production, transportation, and material moving
Income: Per capita: $12,088; Median household: $28,782; Average household: $32,511; Households with income of $100,000 or more: 1.3%; Poverty rate: 36.2%
Educational Attainment: High school diploma or higher: 82.0%; Bachelor's degree or higher: 10.2%; Graduate/professional degree or higher: 4.4%

School District(s)
Friendship Central SD (PK-12)
    2014-15 Enrollment: 392. . . . . (585) 973-3534

Housing: Homeownership rate: 58.7%; Median home value: $40,900; Median year structure built: Before 1940; Homeowner vacancy rate: 0.0%; Median selected monthly owner costs: $836 with a mortgage, $421 without a mortgage; Median gross rent: $705 per month; Rental vacancy rate: 0.0%
Health Insurance: 85.9% have insurance; 38.2% have private insurance; 57.8% have public insurance; 14.1% do not have insurance; 10.0% of children under 18 do not have insurance
Transportation: Commute: 100.0% car, 0.0% public transportation, 0.0% walk, 0.0% work from home; Mean travel time to work: 27.1 minutes

FRIENDSHIP (town).
Covers a land area of 36.215 square miles and a water area of 0.013 square miles. Located at 42.21° N. Lat; 78.13° W. Long. Elevation is 1,506 feet.
History: Incorporated 1898.
Population: 2,029; Growth (since 2000): 5.3%; Density: 56.0 persons per square mile; Race: 98.0% White, 0.0% Black/African American, 0.0% Asian, 0.0% American Indian/Alaska Native, 0.0% Native Hawaiian/Other Pacific Islander, 2.0% Two or more races, 0.0% Hispanic of any race; Average household size: 2.44; Median age: 35.0; Age under 18: 29.6%; Age 65 and over: 16.6%; Males per 100 females: 99.8; Marriage status: 30.9% never married, 47.1% now married, 6.0% separated, 6.4% widowed, 15.6% divorced; Foreign born: 1.6%; Speak English only: 98.5%; With disability: 19.2%; Veterans: 14.0%; Ancestry: 20.7% Irish, 20.6% German, 13.2% English, 8.1% American, 7.7% Italian
Employment: 3.2% management, business, and financial, 1.6% computer, engineering, and science, 2.4% education, legal, community service, arts, and media, 5.5% healthcare practitioners, 27.1% service, 31.5% sales and office, 8.1% natural resources, construction, and maintenance, 20.6% production, transportation, and material moving
Income: Per capita: $15,838; Median household: $29,684; Average household: $39,270; Households with income of $100,000 or more: 3.3%; Poverty rate: 31.2%
Educational Attainment: High school diploma or higher: 86.2%; Bachelor's degree or higher: 10.3%; Graduate/professional degree or higher: 4.7%

School District(s)
Friendship Central SD (PK-12)
    2014-15 Enrollment: 392. . . . . (585) 973-3534
Housing: Homeownership rate: 68.8%; Median home value: $41,300; Median year structure built: 1950; Homeowner vacancy rate: 0.0%; Median selected monthly owner costs: $973 with a mortgage, $386 without a mortgage; Median gross rent: $632 per month; Rental vacancy rate: 0.0%
Health Insurance: 88.1% have insurance; 45.7% have private insurance; 57.2% have public insurance; 11.9% do not have insurance; 11.2% of children under 18 do not have insurance
Transportation: Commute: 100.0% car, 0.0% public transportation, 0.0% walk, 0.0% work from home; Mean travel time to work: 28.3 minutes

GENESEE (town).
Covers a land area of 36.239 square miles and a water area of 0.048 square miles. Located at 42.05° N. Lat; 78.25° W. Long.
Population: 1,403; Growth (since 2000): -22.2%; Density: 38.7 persons per square mile; Race: 97.2% White, 0.0% Black/African American, 1.0% Asian, 0.4% American Indian/Alaska Native, 0.0% Native Hawaiian/Other Pacific Islander, 0.4% Two or more races, 1.6% Hispanic of any race; Average household size: 2.29; Median age: 46.6; Age under 18: 17.0%; Age 65 and over: 20.5%; Males per 100 females: 99.6; Marriage status: 27.9% never married, 57.6% now married, 2.4% separated, 5.6% widowed, 8.9% divorced; Foreign born: 1.7%; Speak English only: 98.4%; With disability: 14.7%; Veterans: 12.5%; Ancestry: 26.9% German, 17.7% Irish, 16.5% English, 10.0% Polish, 5.4% Italian
Employment: 7.2% management, business, and financial, 2.2% computer, engineering, and science, 11.6% education, legal, community service, arts, and media, 4.1% healthcare practitioners, 21.6% service, 20.7% sales and office, 7.7% natural resources, construction, and maintenance, 25.0% production, transportation, and material moving
Income: Per capita: $24,248; Median household: $44,886; Average household: $54,769; Households with income of $100,000 or more: 10.4%; Poverty rate: 13.2%
Educational Attainment: High school diploma or higher: 88.1%; Bachelor's degree or higher: 14.3%; Graduate/professional degree or higher: 5.9%
Housing: Homeownership rate: 84.0%; Median home value: $75,100; Median year structure built: 1974; Homeowner vacancy rate: 0.9%; Median

selected monthly owner costs: $1,097 with a mortgage, $391 without a mortgage; Median gross rent: $571 per month; Rental vacancy rate: 0.0%
Health Insurance: 92.4% have insurance; 72.1% have private insurance; 36.1% have public insurance; 7.6% do not have insurance; 3.3% of children under 18 do not have insurance
Transportation: Commute: 94.0% car, 0.0% public transportation, 1.0% walk, 3.7% work from home; Mean travel time to work: 28.4 minutes

GRANGER (town).
Covers a land area of 31.938 square miles and a water area of 0.100 square miles. Located at 42.48° N. Lat; 78.01° W. Long.
Population: 575; Growth (since 2000): -0.3%; Density: 18.0 persons per square mile; Race: 99.8% White, 0.0% Black/African American, 0.0% Asian, 0.0% American Indian/Alaska Native, 0.0% Native Hawaiian/Other Pacific Islander, 0.0% Two or more races, 0.2% Hispanic of any race; Average household size: 2.64; Median age: 38.7; Age under 18: 24.3%; Age 65 and over: 14.3%; Males per 100 females: 116.1; Marriage status: 18.0% never married, 61.6% now married, 1.3% separated, 6.7% widowed, 13.7% divorced; Foreign born: 1.0%; Speak English only: 96.6%; With disability: 15.7%; Veterans: 13.6%; Ancestry: 25.4% German, 19.7% English, 16.7% Irish, 13.0% French, 10.8% Polish
Employment: 11.7% management, business, and financial, 3.9% computer, engineering, and science, 6.6% education, legal, community service, arts, and media, 8.2% healthcare practitioners, 11.3% service, 14.0% sales and office, 27.2% natural resources, construction, and maintenance, 17.1% production, transportation, and material moving
Income: Per capita: $21,609; Median household: $52,321; Average household: $57,632; Households with income of $100,000 or more: 11.0%; Poverty rate: 8.6%
Educational Attainment: High school diploma or higher: 85.5%; Bachelor's degree or higher: 8.9%; Graduate/professional degree or higher: 4.8%
Housing: Homeownership rate: 88.5%; Median home value: $81,900; Median year structure built: 1977; Homeowner vacancy rate: 6.3%; Median selected monthly owner costs: $1,130 with a mortgage, $388 without a mortgage; Median gross rent: $700 per month; Rental vacancy rate: 0.0%
Health Insurance: 92.0% have insurance; 65.9% have private insurance; 40.5% have public insurance; 8.0% do not have insurance; 0.0% of children under 18 do not have insurance
Transportation: Commute: 94.1% car, 0.0% public transportation, 2.4% walk, 3.5% work from home; Mean travel time to work: 33.3 minutes

GROVE (town).
Covers a land area of 33.366 square miles and a water area of 0.335 square miles. Located at 42.48° N. Lat; 77.89° W. Long. Elevation is 1,627 feet.
Population: 415; Growth (since 2000): -22.1%; Density: 12.4 persons per square mile; Race: 98.1% White, 0.0% Black/African American, 0.0% Asian, 1.0% American Indian/Alaska Native, 0.0% Native Hawaiian/Other Pacific Islander, 1.0% Two or more races, 0.7% Hispanic of any race; Average household size: 2.01; Median age: 53.8; Age under 18: 11.8%; Age 65 and over: 21.0%; Males per 100 females: 113.2; Marriage status: 25.1% never married, 41.9% now married, 1.3% separated, 11.9% widowed, 21.2% divorced; Foreign born: 0.0%; Speak English only: 99.3%; With disability: 17.3%; Veterans: 7.4%; Ancestry: 37.6% German, 28.7% Irish, 23.1% English, 7.7% Italian, 6.5% American
Employment: 16.1% management, business, and financial, 1.8% computer, engineering, and science, 6.9% education, legal, community service, arts, and media, 7.8% healthcare practitioners, 19.8% service, 19.4% sales and office, 8.8% natural resources, construction, and maintenance, 19.4% production, transportation, and material moving
Income: Per capita: $29,001; Median household: $50,833; Average household: $58,345; Households with income of $100,000 or more: 16.6%; Poverty rate: 8.2%
Educational Attainment: High school diploma or higher: 89.1%; Bachelor's degree or higher: 16.0%; Graduate/professional degree or higher: 8.6%
Housing: Homeownership rate: 91.7%; Median home value: $74,200; Median year structure built: 1973; Homeowner vacancy rate: 3.1%; Median selected monthly owner costs: $883 with a mortgage, $470 without a mortgage; Median gross rent: $775 per month; Rental vacancy rate: 29.2%
Health Insurance: 95.2% have insurance; 83.6% have private insurance; 32.5% have public insurance; 4.8% do not have insurance; 0.0% of children under 18 do not have insurance
Transportation: Commute: 92.4% car, 1.4% public transportation, 3.3% walk, 2.8% work from home; Mean travel time to work: 28.9 minutes

HOUGHTON (CDP).
Covers a land area of 2.479 square miles and a water area of 0.010 square miles. Located at 42.43° N. Lat; 78.17° W. Long. Elevation is 1,207 feet.
History: Seat of Houghton College (1923).
Population: 1,747; Growth (since 2000): -0.1%; Density: 704.7 persons per square mile; Race: 89.3% White, 4.8% Black/African American, 3.5% Asian, 0.0% American Indian/Alaska Native, 0.0% Native Hawaiian/Other Pacific Islander, 1.0% Two or more races, 3.2% Hispanic of any race; Average household size: 2.58; Median age: 20.8; Age under 18: 11.6%; Age 65 and over: 12.0%; Males per 100 females: 67.5; Marriage status: 67.6% never married, 25.5% now married, 0.6% separated, 5.9% widowed, 1.1% divorced; Foreign born: 4.5%; Speak English only: 90.6%; With disability: 6.5%; Veterans: 1.6%; Ancestry: 23.2% German, 19.9% English, 17.3% Irish, 5.3% Italian, 4.6% Dutch
Employment: 5.7% management, business, and financial, 1.6% computer, engineering, and science, 33.0% education, legal, community service, arts, and media, 0.9% healthcare practitioners, 33.0% service, 18.5% sales and office, 3.1% natural resources, construction, and maintenance, 4.1% production, transportation, and material moving
Income: Per capita: $12,427; Median household: $51,042; Average household: $60,756; Households with income of $100,000 or more: 17.4%; Poverty rate: 11.9%
Educational Attainment: High school diploma or higher: 97.0%; Bachelor's degree or higher: 67.9%; Graduate/professional degree or higher: 42.7%

Four-year College(s)
Houghton College (Private, Not-for-profit, Wesleyan)
    Fall 2014 Enrollment: 1,073 . . . . (585) 567-9200
    2015-16 Tuition: In-state $29,458; Out-of-state $29,458
Housing: Homeownership rate: 57.3%; Median home value: $119,100; Median year structure built: 1963; Homeowner vacancy rate: 0.0%; Median selected monthly owner costs: $1,177 with a mortgage, $603 without a mortgage; Median gross rent: $526 per month; Rental vacancy rate: 0.0%
Health Insurance: 97.4% have insurance; 92.1% have private insurance; 14.8% have public insurance; 2.6% do not have insurance; 1.5% of children under 18 do not have insurance
Transportation: Commute: 40.5% car, 0.5% public transportation, 51.6% walk, 5.1% work from home; Mean travel time to work: 9.1 minutes

HUME (town).
Covers a land area of 37.890 square miles and a water area of 0.431 square miles. Located at 42.48° N. Lat; 78.12° W. Long. Elevation is 1,273 feet.
Population: 1,973; Growth (since 2000): -0.7%; Density: 52.1 persons per square mile; Race: 98.1% White, 0.7% Black/African American, 0.0% Asian, 0.2% American Indian/Alaska Native, 0.0% Native Hawaiian/Other Pacific Islander, 0.8% Two or more races, 0.4% Hispanic of any race; Average household size: 2.24; Median age: 42.4; Age under 18: 23.1%; Age 65 and over: 14.5%; Males per 100 females: 100.7; Marriage status: 22.9% never married, 59.0% now married, 2.9% separated, 7.5% widowed, 10.6% divorced; Foreign born: 1.1%; Speak English only: 96.8%; With disability: 17.6%; Veterans: 11.5%; Ancestry: 34.5% German, 12.9% Irish, 12.1% English, 9.1% Polish, 9.0% American
Employment: 6.9% management, business, and financial, 0.7% computer, engineering, and science, 13.1% education, legal, community service, arts, and media, 3.8% healthcare practitioners, 19.1% service, 18.4% sales and office, 21.2% natural resources, construction, and maintenance, 16.8% production, transportation, and material moving
Income: Per capita: $20,348; Median household: $37,056; Average household: $45,280; Households with income of $100,000 or more: 4.8%; Poverty rate: 22.9%
Educational Attainment: High school diploma or higher: 84.7%; Bachelor's degree or higher: 19.2%; Graduate/professional degree or higher: 12.4%
Housing: Homeownership rate: 62.8%; Median home value: $76,600; Median year structure built: 1956; Homeowner vacancy rate: 1.6%; Median selected monthly owner costs: $930 with a mortgage, $392 without a mortgage; Median gross rent: $572 per month; Rental vacancy rate: 2.3%
Health Insurance: 91.3% have insurance; 63.5% have private insurance; 40.9% have public insurance; 8.7% do not have insurance; 1.3% of children under 18 do not have insurance
Transportation: Commute: 88.5% car, 0.0% public transportation, 7.0% walk, 2.1% work from home; Mean travel time to work: 24.9 minutes
Additional Information Contacts
Town of Hume . . . . (585) 567-2666
    http://www.humetown.org

INDEPENDENCE (town). Covers a land area of 34.484 square miles and a water area of 0.005 square miles. Located at 42.04° N. Lat; 77.79° W. Long. Elevation is 2,057 feet.

Population: 1,173; Growth (since 2000): 9.2%; Density: 34.0 persons per square mile; Race: 95.9% White, 0.0% Black/African American, 3.8% Asian, 0.0% American Indian/Alaska Native, 0.0% Native Hawaiian/Other Pacific Islander, 0.3% Two or more races, 0.7% Hispanic of any race; Average household size: 2.53; Median age: 40.9; Age under 18: 24.3%; Age 65 and over: 15.6%; Males per 100 females: 105.5; Marriage status: 23.0% never married, 64.9% now married, 2.0% separated, 4.6% widowed, 7.5% divorced; Foreign born: 2.5%; Speak English only: 99.5%; With disability: 13.9%; Veterans: 8.0%; Ancestry: 22.9% Irish, 19.7% German, 13.9% English, 9.1% American, 8.4% Italian
Employment: 13.7% management, business, and financial, 2.1% computer, engineering, and science, 13.6% education, legal, community service, arts, and media, 4.0% healthcare practitioners, 19.0% service, 17.5% sales and office, 14.5% natural resources, construction, and maintenance, 15.6% production, transportation, and material moving
Income: Per capita: $21,480; Median household: $47,143; Average household: $51,666; Households with income of $100,000 or more: 11.7%; Poverty rate: 18.8%
Educational Attainment: High school diploma or higher: 85.6%; Bachelor's degree or higher: 12.1%; Graduate/professional degree or higher: 6.4%
Housing: Homeownership rate: 81.9%; Median home value: $72,100; Median year structure built: 1952; Homeowner vacancy rate: 0.0%; Median selected monthly owner costs: $964 with a mortgage, $426 without a mortgage; Median gross rent: $513 per month; Rental vacancy rate: 4.5%
Health Insurance: 95.4% have insurance; 68.3% have private insurance; 41.3% have public insurance; 4.6% do not have insurance; 0.0% of children under 18 do not have insurance
Safety: Violent crime rate: 0.0 per 10,000 population; Property crime rate: 50.9 per 10,000 population
Transportation: Commute: 81.6% car, 0.6% public transportation, 8.5% walk, 6.6% work from home; Mean travel time to work: 22.0 minutes

LITTLE GENESEE (unincorporated postal area)
ZCTA: 14754

Covers a land area of 16.613 square miles and a water area of 0.014 square miles. Located at 42.02° N. Lat; 78.20° W. Long. Elevation is 1,552 feet.
Population: 569; Growth (since 2000): 4.4%; Density: 34.2 persons per square mile; Race: 100.0% White, 0.0% Black/African American, 0.0% Asian, 0.0% American Indian/Alaska Native, 0.0% Native Hawaiian/Other Pacific Islander, 0.0% Two or more races, 0.7% Hispanic of any race; Average household size: 2.19; Median age: 46.3; Age under 18: 17.2%; Age 65 and over: 20.7%; Males per 100 females: 102.1; Marriage status: 24.9% never married, 60.8% now married, 2.4% separated, 6.8% widowed, 7.4% divorced; Foreign born: 3.7%; Speak English only: 97.3%; With disability: 14.4%; Veterans: 15.5%; Ancestry: 22.1% German, 20.7% Irish, 17.6% English, 10.0% American, 7.6% Polish
Employment: 7.8% management, business, and financial, 3.8% computer, engineering, and science, 6.5% education, legal, community service, arts, and media, 2.4% healthcare practitioners, 16.0% service, 23.5% sales and office, 10.2% natural resources, construction, and maintenance, 29.7% production, transportation, and material moving
Income: Per capita: $21,535; Median household: $43,375; Average household: $46,838; Households with income of $100,000 or more: 7.3%; Poverty rate: 20.9%
Educational Attainment: High school diploma or higher: 83.2%; Bachelor's degree or higher: 6.6%; Graduate/professional degree or higher: 1.0%
Housing: Homeownership rate: 82.7%; Median home value: $57,500; Median year structure built: 1972; Homeowner vacancy rate: 0.0%; Median selected monthly owner costs: $996 with a mortgage, $367 without a mortgage; Median gross rent: $571 per month; Rental vacancy rate: 0.0%
Health Insurance: 86.8% have insurance; 66.4% have private insurance; 39.7% have public insurance; 13.2% do not have insurance; 15.3% of children under 18 do not have insurance
Transportation: Commute: 96.2% car, 0.0% public transportation, 0.0% walk, 3.8% work from home; Mean travel time to work: 28.3 minutes

NEW HUDSON (town). Covers a land area of 36.195 square miles and a water area of 0.124 square miles. Located at 42.29° N. Lat; 78.25° W. Long.

Population: 773; Growth (since 2000): 5.0%; Density: 21.4 persons per square mile; Race: 97.2% White, 0.0% Black/African American, 0.3% Asian, 1.7% American Indian/Alaska Native, 0.0% Native Hawaiian/Other Pacific Islander, 0.9% Two or more races, 0.5% Hispanic of any race; Average household size: 2.61; Median age: 38.3; Age under 18: 28.2%; Age 65 and over: 12.8%; Males per 100 females: 111.1; Marriage status: 17.0% never married, 64.9% now married, 1.0% separated, 7.3% widowed, 10.8% divorced; Foreign born: 1.4%; Speak English only: 93.4%; With disability: 15.0%; Veterans: 15.3%; Ancestry: 24.6% German, 13.1% Irish, 12.0% English, 11.6% Italian, 10.2% Pennsylvania German
Employment: 9.0% management, business, and financial, 2.6% computer, engineering, and science, 10.8% education, legal, community service, arts, and media, 8.7% healthcare practitioners, 15.2% service, 14.6% sales and office, 10.2% natural resources, construction, and maintenance, 28.9% production, transportation, and material moving
Income: Per capita: $21,229; Median household: $42,500; Average household: $54,050; Households with income of $100,000 or more: 13.9%; Poverty rate: 5.1%
Educational Attainment: High school diploma or higher: 85.5%; Bachelor's degree or higher: 15.4%; Graduate/professional degree or higher: 8.9%
Housing: Homeownership rate: 84.8%; Median home value: $77,500; Median year structure built: 1975; Homeowner vacancy rate: 0.8%; Median selected monthly owner costs: $1,229 with a mortgage, $495 without a mortgage; Median gross rent: $921 per month; Rental vacancy rate: 0.0%
Health Insurance: 80.2% have insurance; 59.6% have private insurance; 42.2% have public insurance; 19.8% do not have insurance; 30.3% of children under 18 do not have insurance
Transportation: Commute: 88.0% car, 0.9% public transportation, 2.9% walk, 5.6% work from home; Mean travel time to work: 25.3 minutes

OIL SPRINGS RESERVATION (reservation). Covers a land area of 0.590 square miles and a water area of 0.010 square miles. Located at 42.23° N. Lat; 78.30° W. Long.

Population: 20; Growth (since 2000): n/a; Density: 33.9 persons per square mile; Race: 0.0% White, 0.0% Black/African American, 0.0% Asian, 0.0% American Indian/Alaska Native, 0.0% Native Hawaiian/Other Pacific Islander, 100.0% Two or more races, 0.0% Hispanic of any race; Average household size: 3.33; Median age: n/a; Age under 18: 0.0%; Age 65 and over: 0.0%; Males per 100 females: All males; Marriage status: 70.0% never married, 0.0% now married, 0.0% separated, 30.0% widowed, 0.0% divorced; Foreign born: 100.0%; Speak English only: 0.0%; With disability: 0.0%; Veterans: 0.0%; Ancestry: n/a.
Employment: 0.0% management, business, and financial, 0.0% computer, engineering, and science, 0.0% education, legal, community service, arts, and media, 0.0% healthcare practitioners, 100.0% service, 0.0% sales and office, 0.0% natural resources, construction, and maintenance, 0.0% production, transportation, and material moving
Income: Per capita: n/a; Median household: n/a; Average household: n/a; Households with income of $100,000 or more: n/a; Poverty rate: n/a
Educational Attainment: High school diploma or higher: 100.0%; Bachelor's degree or higher: 100.0%; Graduate/professional degree or higher: n/a
Housing: Homeownership rate: n/a; Median home value: n/a; Median year structure built: 1967; Homeowner vacancy rate: 0.0%; Median selected monthly owner costs: n/a with a mortgage, n/a without a mortgage; Median gross rent: n/a per month; Rental vacancy rate: 0.0%
Health Insurance: 100.0% have insurance; 100.0% have private insurance; 70.0% have public insurance; 0.0% do not have insurance; 0.0% of children under 18 do not have insurance
Transportation: Commute: 100.0% car, 0.0% public transportation, 0.0% walk, 0.0% work from home; Mean travel time to work: 0.0 minutes

RICHBURG (village). Covers a land area of 0.900 square miles and a water area of 0 square miles. Located at 42.09° N. Lat; 78.16° W. Long. Elevation is 1,660 feet.

Population: 615; Growth (since 2000): 37.3%; Density: 683.2 persons per square mile; Race: 100.0% White, 0.0% Black/African American, 0.0% Asian, 0.0% American Indian/Alaska Native, 0.0% Native Hawaiian/Other Pacific Islander, 0.0% Two or more races, 1.3% Hispanic of any race; Average household size: 2.97; Median age: 31.1; Age under 18: 36.3%; Age 65 and over: 7.5%; Males per 100 females: 89.1; Marriage status:

27.2% never married, 53.9% now married, 1.4% separated, 9.0% widowed, 9.9% divorced; Foreign born: 0.0%; Speak English only: 97.5%; With disability: 13.3%; Veterans: 9.7%; Ancestry: 15.9% Irish, 15.6% German, 14.8% English, 7.0% American, 6.2% Italian
Employment: 9.5% management, business, and financial, 3.8% computer, engineering, and science, 13.7% education, legal, community service, arts, and media, 1.4% healthcare practitioners, 17.1% service, 22.7% sales and office, 8.1% natural resources, construction, and maintenance, 23.7% production, transportation, and material moving
Income: Per capita: $15,849; Median household: $38,125; Average household: $48,129; Households with income of $100,000 or more: 10.2%; Poverty rate: 29.3%
Educational Attainment: High school diploma or higher: 87.6%; Bachelor's degree or higher: 9.7%; Graduate/professional degree or higher: 5.8%

School District(s)
Bolivar-Richburg Central SD (PK-12)
    2014-15 Enrollment: 846. . . . . (585) 928-2561
Housing: Homeownership rate: 69.1%; Median home value: $48,000; Median year structure built: 1947; Homeowner vacancy rate: 6.5%; Median selected monthly owner costs: $888 with a mortgage, $506 without a mortgage; Median gross rent: $631 per month; Rental vacancy rate: 7.2%
Health Insurance: 91.9% have insurance; 48.1% have private insurance; 53.3% have public insurance; 8.1% do not have insurance; 6.3% of children under 18 do not have insurance
Transportation: Commute: 94.2% car, 1.0% public transportation, 1.9% walk, 0.0% work from home; Mean travel time to work: 24.9 minutes

RUSHFORD (CDP). Covers a land area of 0.559 square miles and a water area of 0 square miles. Located at 42.39° N. Lat; 78.25° W. Long. Elevation is 1,499 feet.
Population: 327; Growth (since 2000): n/a; Density: 585.4 persons per square mile; Race: 88.1% White, 3.1% Black/African American, 0.0% Asian, 0.0% American Indian/Alaska Native, 0.0% Native Hawaiian/Other Pacific Islander, 8.9% Two or more races, 0.0% Hispanic of any race; Average household size: 2.89; Median age: 34.1; Age under 18: 24.2%; Age 65 and over: 10.7%; Males per 100 females: 81.5; Marriage status: 31.5% never married, 43.5% now married, 0.0% separated, 5.8% widowed, 19.2% divorced; Foreign born: 1.5%; Speak English only: 100.0%; With disability: 16.5%; Veterans: 7.3%; Ancestry: 37.9% German, 18.3% Irish, 9.8% American, 8.3% Polish, 5.2% English
Employment: 2.0% management, business, and financial, 0.0% computer, engineering, and science, 10.1% education, legal, community service, arts, and media, 0.0% healthcare practitioners, 40.9% service, 12.1% sales and office, 14.8% natural resources, construction, and maintenance, 20.1% production, transportation, and material moving
Income: Per capita: $15,003; Median household: $38,563; Average household: $42,958; Households with income of $100,000 or more: 6.2%; Poverty rate: 15.3%
Educational Attainment: High school diploma or higher: 87.1%; Bachelor's degree or higher: 14.9%; Graduate/professional degree or higher: 10.0%

School District(s)
Cuba-Rushford Central SD (PK-12)
    2014-15 Enrollment: 885. . . . . (585) 968-2650
Housing: Homeownership rate: 64.6%; Median home value: $46,500; Median year structure built: Before 1940; Homeowner vacancy rate: 12.0%; Median selected monthly owner costs: $840 with a mortgage, $295 without a mortgage; Median gross rent: $722 per month; Rental vacancy rate: 20.0%
Health Insurance: 89.3% have insurance; 67.6% have private insurance; 40.7% have public insurance; 10.7% do not have insurance; 2.5% of children under 18 do not have insurance
Transportation: Commute: 83.2% car, 6.0% public transportation, 6.7% walk, 4.0% work from home; Mean travel time to work: 22.3 minutes

RUSHFORD (town). Covers a land area of 35.294 square miles and a water area of 0.790 square miles. Located at 42.39° N. Lat; 78.25° W. Long. Elevation is 1,499 feet.
Population: 1,044; Growth (since 2000): -17.1%; Density: 29.6 persons per square mile; Race: 96.3% White, 1.0% Black/African American, 0.0% Asian, 0.0% American Indian/Alaska Native, 0.0% Native Hawaiian/Other Pacific Islander, 2.8% Two or more races, 0.0% Hispanic of any race; Average household size: 2.18; Median age: 49.5; Age under 18: 17.2%; Age 65 and over: 22.2%; Males per 100 females: 104.6; Marriage status:

24.0% never married, 55.7% now married, 1.4% separated, 8.4% widowed, 11.9% divorced; Foreign born: 0.5%; Speak English only: 98.6%; With disability: 16.7%; Veterans: 15.4%; Ancestry: 39.5% German, 21.3% Irish, 19.7% English, 12.5% American, 10.2% Polish
Employment: 14.4% management, business, and financial, 1.2% computer, engineering, and science, 9.5% education, legal, community service, arts, and media, 8.1% healthcare practitioners, 21.7% service, 11.0% sales and office, 12.6% natural resources, construction, and maintenance, 21.5% production, transportation, and material moving
Income: Per capita: $24,116; Median household: $42,891; Average household: $52,912; Households with income of $100,000 or more: 12.8%; Poverty rate: 13.4%
Educational Attainment: High school diploma or higher: 92.0%; Bachelor's degree or higher: 23.2%; Graduate/professional degree or higher: 13.1%

School District(s)
Cuba-Rushford Central SD (PK-12)
    2014-15 Enrollment: 885. . . . . (585) 968-2650
Housing: Homeownership rate: 84.0%; Median home value: $75,700; Median year structure built: 1969; Homeowner vacancy rate: 6.7%; Median selected monthly owner costs: $906 with a mortgage, $475 without a mortgage; Median gross rent: $792 per month; Rental vacancy rate: 11.5%
Health Insurance: 93.6% have insurance; 67.4% have private insurance; 47.9% have public insurance; 6.4% do not have insurance; 1.1% of children under 18 do not have insurance
Transportation: Commute: 85.0% car, 2.7% public transportation, 2.3% walk, 8.7% work from home; Mean travel time to work: 21.5 minutes

SCIO (CDP). Covers a land area of 1.352 square miles and a water area of 0 square miles. Located at 42.17° N. Lat; 77.98° W. Long. Elevation is 1,457 feet.
Population: 508; Growth (since 2000): n/a; Density: 375.7 persons per square mile; Race: 100.0% White, 0.0% Black/African American, 0.0% Asian, 0.0% American Indian/Alaska Native, 0.0% Native Hawaiian/Other Pacific Islander, 0.0% Two or more races, 1.6% Hispanic of any race; Average household size: 2.21; Median age: 49.4; Age under 18: 17.3%; Age 65 and over: 14.4%; Males per 100 females: 102.3; Marriage status: 21.3% never married, 55.5% now married, 1.8% separated, 11.8% widowed, 11.4% divorced; Foreign born: 0.0%; Speak English only: 98.4%; With disability: 18.5%; Veterans: 11.7%; Ancestry: 22.0% English, 20.3% German, 19.1% Irish, 4.3% French, 3.9% Scottish
Employment: 13.8% management, business, and financial, 4.7% computer, engineering, and science, 17.0% education, legal, community service, arts, and media, 6.9% healthcare practitioners, 6.5% service, 23.9% sales and office, 9.4% natural resources, construction, and maintenance, 17.8% production, transportation, and material moving
Income: Per capita: $29,125; Median household: $58,250; Average household: $64,498; Households with income of $100,000 or more: 20.0%; Poverty rate: 14.6%
Educational Attainment: High school diploma or higher: 95.4%; Bachelor's degree or higher: 22.9%; Graduate/professional degree or higher: 13.6%

School District(s)
Scio Central SD (PK-12)
    2014-15 Enrollment: 362. . . . . (585) 593-5076
Housing: Homeownership rate: 82.6%; Median home value: $65,300; Median year structure built: 1955; Homeowner vacancy rate: 0.0%; Median selected monthly owner costs: $882 with a mortgage, $475 without a mortgage; Median gross rent: $688 per month; Rental vacancy rate: 0.0%
Health Insurance: 94.9% have insurance; 75.8% have private insurance; 34.6% have public insurance; 5.1% do not have insurance; 0.0% of children under 18 do not have insurance
Transportation: Commute: 89.1% car, 3.6% public transportation, 5.5% walk, 1.8% work from home; Mean travel time to work: 12.5 minutes

SCIO (town). Covers a land area of 35.295 square miles and a water area of 0.039 square miles. Located at 42.15° N. Lat; 77.99° W. Long. Elevation is 1,457 feet.
Population: 1,594; Growth (since 2000): -16.7%; Density: 45.2 persons per square mile; Race: 99.6% White, 0.4% Black/African American, 0.0% Asian, 0.0% American Indian/Alaska Native, 0.0% Native Hawaiian/Other Pacific Islander, 0.1% Two or more races, 0.5% Hispanic of any race; Average household size: 2.21; Median age: 51.1; Age under 18: 17.1%; Age 65 and over: 21.1%; Males per 100 females: 103.7; Marriage status: 19.2% never married, 57.7% now married, 2.4% separated, 10.3%

widowed, 12.8% divorced; Foreign born: 0.4%; Speak English only: 98.2%; With disability: 18.9%; Veterans: 13.0%; Ancestry: 17.6% Irish, 16.9% English, 16.6% German, 6.9% American, 4.5% Dutch
Employment: 10.0% management, business, and financial, 2.6% computer, engineering, and science, 11.4% education, legal, community service, arts, and media, 4.0% healthcare practitioners, 15.9% service, 22.7% sales and office, 9.6% natural resources, construction, and maintenance, 23.7% production, transportation, and material moving
Income: Per capita: $24,883; Median household: $50,542; Average household: $55,419; Households with income of $100,000 or more: 14.1%; Poverty rate: 12.5%
Educational Attainment: High school diploma or higher: 89.1%; Bachelor's degree or higher: 17.1%; Graduate/professional degree or higher: 9.1%

School District(s)
Scio Central SD (PK-12)
  2014-15 Enrollment: 362 . . . . (585) 593-5076
Housing: Homeownership rate: 79.2%; Median home value: $63,100; Median year structure built: 1968; Homeowner vacancy rate: 0.0%; Median selected monthly owner costs: $883 with a mortgage, $467 without a mortgage; Median gross rent: $652 per month; Rental vacancy rate: 6.9%
Health Insurance: 93.4% have insurance; 72.8% have private insurance; 42.6% have public insurance; 6.6% do not have insurance; 4.4% of children under 18 do not have insurance
Transportation: Commute: 92.7% car, 1.5% public transportation, 2.2% walk, 2.5% work from home; Mean travel time to work: 15.7 minutes

STANNARDS (CDP). Covers a land area of 2.797 square miles and a water area of 0 square miles. Located at 42.07° N. Lat; 77.91° W. Long. Elevation is 1,549 feet.
Population: 841; Growth (since 2000): -3.1%; Density: 300.7 persons per square mile; Race: 100.0% White, 0.0% Black/African American, 0.0% Asian, 0.0% American Indian/Alaska Native, 0.0% Native Hawaiian/Other Pacific Islander, 0.0% Two or more races, 0.6% Hispanic of any race; Average household size: 2.15; Median age: 51.3; Age under 18: 16.9%; Age 65 and over: 22.0%; Males per 100 females: 89.5; Marriage status: 14.3% never married, 53.6% now married, 1.3% separated, 14.5% widowed, 17.6% divorced; Foreign born: 1.4%; Speak English only: 98.7%; With disability: 16.6%; Veterans: 12.0%; Ancestry: 22.1% English, 20.5% German, 17.0% Irish, 8.9% Polish, 6.5% American
Employment: 16.6% management, business, and financial, 1.7% computer, engineering, and science, 19.8% education, legal, community service, arts, and media, 3.4% healthcare practitioners, 24.4% service, 21.2% sales and office, 6.3% natural resources, construction, and maintenance, 6.6% production, transportation, and material moving
Income: Per capita: $27,276; Median household: $36,875; Average household: $58,078; Households with income of $100,000 or more: 23.0%; Poverty rate: 19.7%
Educational Attainment: High school diploma or higher: 85.4%; Bachelor's degree or higher: 25.3%; Graduate/professional degree or higher: 14.1%
Housing: Homeownership rate: 60.2%; Median home value: $76,800; Median year structure built: 1981; Homeowner vacancy rate: 1.3%; Median selected monthly owner costs: $1,010 with a mortgage, $433 without a mortgage; Median gross rent: $611 per month; Rental vacancy rate: 0.0%
Health Insurance: 92.2% have insurance; 69.1% have private insurance; 45.4% have public insurance; 7.8% do not have insurance; 2.8% of children under 18 do not have insurance
Transportation: Commute: 94.8% car, 0.0% public transportation, 4.1% walk, 1.2% work from home; Mean travel time to work: 20.9 minutes

SWAIN (unincorporated postal area)
ZCTA: 14884
  Covers a land area of 19.162 square miles and a water area of 0.324 square miles. Located at 42.48° N. Lat; 77.89° W. Long. Elevation is 1,316 feet.
  Population: 183; Growth (since 2000): -40.8%; Density: 9.6 persons per square mile; Race: 98.4% White, 0.0% Black/African American, 0.0% Asian, 0.0% American Indian/Alaska Native, 0.0% Native Hawaiian/Other Pacific Islander, 1.6% Two or more races, 1.6% Hispanic of any race; Average household size: 1.76; Median age: 54.9; Age under 18: 12.0%; Age 65 and over: 19.7%; Males per 100 females: 108.4; Marriage status: 21.2% never married, 31.8% now married, 2.9% separated, 14.7% widowed, 32.4% divorced; Foreign born: 0.0%; Speak English only: 98.3%; With disability: 16.9%; Veterans: 7.5%; Ancestry:

25.1% English, 24.6% German, 19.1% Irish, 12.6% American, 5.5% Polish
Employment: 8.3% management, business, and financial, 1.9% computer, engineering, and science, 7.4% education, legal, community service, arts, and media, 9.3% healthcare practitioners, 28.7% service, 18.5% sales and office, 10.2% natural resources, construction, and maintenance, 15.7% production, transportation, and material moving
Income: Per capita: $33,220; Median household: $47,500; Average household: $58,506; Households with income of $100,000 or more: 19.2%; Poverty rate: 5.0%
Educational Attainment: High school diploma or higher: 91.0%; Bachelor's degree or higher: 11.0%; Graduate/professional degree or higher: 7.1%
Housing: Homeownership rate: 89.4%; Median home value: $74,800; Median year structure built: 1974; Homeowner vacancy rate: 6.1%; Median selected monthly owner costs: $1,010 with a mortgage, $418 without a mortgage; Median gross rent: n/a per month; Rental vacancy rate: 21.4%
Health Insurance: 94.5% have insurance; 77.6% have private insurance; 35.5% have public insurance; 5.5% do not have insurance; 0.0% of children under 18 do not have insurance
Transportation: Commute: 96.3% car, 0.0% public transportation, 0.0% walk, 3.7% work from home; Mean travel time to work: 32.1 minutes

WARD (town). Covers a land area of 29.175 square miles and a water area of 0.017 square miles. Located at 42.23° N. Lat; 77.90° W. Long.
Population: 378; Growth (since 2000): -3.1%; Density: 13.0 persons per square mile; Race: 97.4% White, 0.5% Black/African American, 0.0% Asian, 0.0% American Indian/Alaska Native, 0.0% Native Hawaiian/Other Pacific Islander, 1.3% Two or more races, 1.3% Hispanic of any race; Average household size: 2.82; Median age: 44.3; Age under 18: 24.3%; Age 65 and over: 15.3%; Males per 100 females: 106.7; Marriage status: 22.1% never married, 52.7% now married, 0.0% separated, 8.7% widowed, 16.4% divorced; Foreign born: 1.6%; Speak English only: 98.9%; With disability: 16.7%; Veterans: 12.6%; Ancestry: 38.4% German, 20.9% Irish, 10.6% English, 5.6% American, 2.9% Scottish
Employment: 11.0% management, business, and financial, 5.5% computer, engineering, and science, 12.9% education, legal, community service, arts, and media, 4.9% healthcare practitioners, 14.1% service, 12.9% sales and office, 16.0% natural resources, construction, and maintenance, 22.7% production, transportation, and material moving
Income: Per capita: $22,830; Median household: $44,167; Average household: $63,531; Households with income of $100,000 or more: 19.4%; Poverty rate: 14.0%
Educational Attainment: High school diploma or higher: 93.0%; Bachelor's degree or higher: 16.6%; Graduate/professional degree or higher: 10.0%
Housing: Homeownership rate: 85.1%; Median home value: $81,000; Median year structure built: 1984; Homeowner vacancy rate: 2.6%; Median selected monthly owner costs: $979 with a mortgage, $463 without a mortgage; Median gross rent: $1,375 per month; Rental vacancy rate: 0.0%
Health Insurance: 92.9% have insurance; 60.8% have private insurance; 50.3% have public insurance; 7.1% do not have insurance; 0.0% of children under 18 do not have insurance
Transportation: Commute: 89.6% car, 2.5% public transportation, 1.2% walk, 2.5% work from home; Mean travel time to work: 24.1 minutes

WELLSVILLE (town). Covers a land area of 36.646 square miles and a water area of 0.037 square miles. Located at 42.12° N. Lat; 77.93° W. Long. Elevation is 1,512 feet.
History: Wellsville was settled in 1795 and named for Gardiner Wells, early settler and chief landowner. Site of David A. Howe Library (1937), with museum and theater. Special museum, Mather Homestead, for visually impaired. Incorporated in 1871.
Population: 7,256; Growth (since 2000): -5.5%; Density: 198.0 persons per square mile; Race: 97.2% White, 0.8% Black/African American, 0.5% Asian, 0.8% American Indian/Alaska Native, 0.0% Native Hawaiian/Other Pacific Islander, 0.6% Two or more races, 1.8% Hispanic of any race; Average household size: 2.16; Median age: 46.7; Age under 18: 18.9%; Age 65 and over: 21.1%; Males per 100 females: 89.8; Marriage status: 26.1% never married, 49.0% now married, 3.4% separated, 11.4% widowed, 13.5% divorced; Foreign born: 2.0%; Speak English only: 95.6%; With disability: 21.4%; Veterans: 14.5%; Ancestry: 23.3% German, 17.6% Irish, 16.1% English, 6.7% American, 6.2% Italian

Employment: 8.7% management, business, and financial, 3.4% computer, engineering, and science, 12.2% education, legal, community service, arts, and media, 8.6% healthcare practitioners, 23.1% service, 18.9% sales and office, 10.4% natural resources, construction, and maintenance, 14.6% production, transportation, and material moving

Income: Per capita: $24,322; Median household: $41,067; Average household: $53,062; Households with income of $100,000 or more: 12.1%; Poverty rate: 17.2%

Educational Attainment: High school diploma or higher: 87.8%; Bachelor's degree or higher: 21.2%; Graduate/professional degree or higher: 9.9%

School District(s)
Wellsville Central SD (PK-12)
    2014-15 Enrollment: 1,303 . . . . (585) 596-2170

Housing: Homeownership rate: 59.2%; Median home value: $69,800; Median year structure built: 1948; Homeowner vacancy rate: 2.0%; Median selected monthly owner costs: $966 with a mortgage, $446 without a mortgage; Median gross rent: $579 per month; Rental vacancy rate: 4.5%

Health Insurance: 91.4% have insurance; 60.3% have private insurance; 48.7% have public insurance; 8.6% do not have insurance; 7.4% of children under 18 do not have insurance

Hospitals: Jones Memorial Hospital (70 beds)

Newspapers: Daily Reporter (daily circulation 4,500)

Transportation: Commute: 91.2% car, 0.8% public transportation, 5.7% walk, 0.6% work from home; Mean travel time to work: 17.7 minutes

Additional Information Contacts
Town of Wellsville . . . . (585) 593-1780
    http://www.townofwellsvilleny.org

WELLSVILLE (village). Covers a land area of 2.424 square miles and a water area of 0 square miles. Located at 42.12° N. Lat; 77.95° W. Long. Elevation is 1,512 feet.

Population: 4,589; Growth (since 2000): -11.3%; Density: 1,893.0 persons per square mile; Race: 97.5% White, 1.2% Black/African American, 0.0% Asian, 0.2% American Indian/Alaska Native, 0.0% Native Hawaiian/Other Pacific Islander, 1.0% Two or more races, 1.9% Hispanic of any race; Average household size: 2.22; Median age: 42.6; Age under 18: 20.3%; Age 65 and over: 18.2%; Males per 100 females: 88.9; Marriage status: 30.8% never married, 45.1% now married, 3.7% separated, 7.6% widowed, 16.5% divorced; Foreign born: 2.0%; Speak English only: 96.7%; With disability: 23.9%; Veterans: 14.7%; Ancestry: 24.4% German, 16.8% English, 16.6% Irish, 7.6% American, 6.7% Italian

Employment: 8.5% management, business, and financial, 2.2% computer, engineering, and science, 12.4% education, legal, community service, arts, and media, 7.7% healthcare practitioners, 25.3% service, 20.0% sales and office, 12.1% natural resources, construction, and maintenance, 11.9% production, transportation, and material moving

Income: Per capita: $22,663; Median household: $39,068; Average household: $50,489; Households with income of $100,000 or more: 11.2%; Poverty rate: 21.1%

Educational Attainment: High school diploma or higher: 89.0%; Bachelor's degree or higher: 22.1%; Graduate/professional degree or higher: 9.9%

School District(s)
Wellsville Central SD (PK-12)
    2014-15 Enrollment: 1,303 . . . . (585) 596-2170

Housing: Homeownership rate: 50.8%; Median home value: $67,900; Median year structure built: Before 1940; Homeowner vacancy rate: 3.6%; Median selected monthly owner costs: $887 with a mortgage, $479 without a mortgage; Median gross rent: $569 per month; Rental vacancy rate: 2.9%

Health Insurance: 89.9% have insurance; 51.2% have private insurance; 54.1% have public insurance; 10.1% do not have insurance; 7.0% of children under 18 do not have insurance

Hospitals: Jones Memorial Hospital (70 beds)

Safety: Violent crime rate: 17.7 per 10,000 population; Property crime rate: 227.5 per 10,000 population

Newspapers: Daily Reporter (daily circulation 4,500)

Transportation: Commute: 88.5% car, 1.1% public transportation, 6.9% walk, 0.7% work from home; Mean travel time to work: 17.8 minutes

Additional Information Contacts
Village of Wellsville . . . . (585) 593-1121
    http://www.wellsvilleny.com

WEST ALMOND (town). Covers a land area of 35.995 square miles and a water area of 0.095 square miles. Located at 42.31° N. Lat; 77.91° W. Long. Elevation is 1,854 feet.

Population: 418; Growth (since 2000): 18.4%; Density: 11.6 persons per square mile; Race: 89.0% White, 0.0% Black/African American, 2.4% Asian, 0.0% American Indian/Alaska Native, 0.0% Native Hawaiian/Other Pacific Islander, 8.4% Two or more races, 1.0% Hispanic of any race; Average household size: 2.90; Median age: 38.8; Age under 18: 30.9%; Age 65 and over: 16.3%; Males per 100 females: 115.5; Marriage status: 22.1% never married, 63.4% now married, 0.3% separated, 7.3% widowed, 7.3% divorced; Foreign born: 3.8%; Speak English only: 84.8%; With disability: 13.6%; Veterans: 14.2%; Ancestry: 25.6% German, 17.9% English, 16.0% Pennsylvania German, 13.4% Irish, 8.6% American

Employment: 26.2% management, business, and financial, 3.0% computer, engineering, and science, 8.5% education, legal, community service, arts, and media, 4.3% healthcare practitioners, 14.6% service, 9.1% sales and office, 20.7% natural resources, construction, and maintenance, 13.4% production, transportation, and material moving

Income: Per capita: $21,500; Median household: $57,500; Average household: $61,260; Households with income of $100,000 or more: 11.8%; Poverty rate: 12.9%

Educational Attainment: High school diploma or higher: 83.8%; Bachelor's degree or higher: 18.1%; Graduate/professional degree or higher: 3.5%

Housing: Homeownership rate: 89.6%; Median home value: $82,600; Median year structure built: 1973; Homeowner vacancy rate: 1.5%; Median selected monthly owner costs: $981 with a mortgage, $463 without a mortgage; Median gross rent: n/a per month; Rental vacancy rate: 0.0%

Health Insurance: 74.9% have insurance; 63.4% have private insurance; 27.8% have public insurance; 25.1% do not have insurance; 34.9% of children under 18 do not have insurance

Transportation: Commute: 81.5% car, 0.0% public transportation, 8.6% walk, 1.2% work from home; Mean travel time to work: 19.8 minutes

WHITESVILLE (unincorporated postal area)
ZCTA: 14897

Covers a land area of 25.532 square miles and a water area of 0.002 square miles. Located at 42.02° N. Lat; 77.79° W. Long. Elevation is 1,716 feet.

Population: 887; Growth (since 2000): -0.3%; Density: 34.7 persons per square mile; Race: 99.5% White, 0.0% Black/African American, 0.0% Asian, 0.0% American Indian/Alaska Native, 0.0% Native Hawaiian/Other Pacific Islander, 0.5% Two or more races, 0.5% Hispanic of any race; Average household size: 2.40; Median age: 44.4; Age under 18: 20.5%; Age 65 and over: 18.6%; Males per 100 females: 103.3; Marriage status: 20.1% never married, 65.8% now married, 0.9% separated, 5.4% widowed, 8.7% divorced; Foreign born: 0.2%; Speak English only: 99.3%; With disability: 17.8%; Veterans: 9.2%; Ancestry: 18.6% Irish, 17.0% German, 14.2% English, 9.7% American, 5.9% Italian

Employment: 11.4% management, business, and financial, 2.7% computer, engineering, and science, 8.6% education, legal, community service, arts, and media, 2.7% healthcare practitioners, 24.0% service, 17.0% sales and office, 16.8% natural resources, construction, and maintenance, 16.8% production, transportation, and material moving

Income: Per capita: $20,976; Median household: $45,789; Average household: $49,306; Households with income of $100,000 or more: 7.6%; Poverty rate: 13.3%

Educational Attainment: High school diploma or higher: 86.2%; Bachelor's degree or higher: 8.9%; Graduate/professional degree or higher: 3.8%

School District(s)
Whitesville Central SD (PK-12)
    2014-15 Enrollment: 256 . . . . (607) 356-3301

Housing: Homeownership rate: 82.2%; Median home value: $67,500; Median year structure built: 1949; Homeowner vacancy rate: 0.0%; Median selected monthly owner costs: $868 with a mortgage, $413 without a mortgage; Median gross rent: $519 per month; Rental vacancy rate: 5.7%

Health Insurance: 92.0% have insurance; 68.9% have private insurance; 41.0% have public insurance; 8.0% do not have insurance; 3.8% of children under 18 do not have insurance

Transportation: Commute: 79.1% car, 0.8% public transportation, 8.8% walk, 7.8% work from home; Mean travel time to work: 21.0 minutes

WILLING (town). Covers a land area of 36.240 square miles and a water area of 0.030 square miles. Located at 42.04° N. Lat; 77.89° W. Long.

Population: 1,490; Growth (since 2000): 8.7%; Density: 41.1 persons per square mile; Race: 99.1% White, 0.3% Black/African American, 0.0% Asian, 0.7% American Indian/Alaska Native, 0.0% Native Hawaiian/Other Pacific Islander, 0.0% Two or more races, 0.3% Hispanic of any race; Average household size: 2.46; Median age: 44.4; Age under 18: 24.0%; Age 65 and over: 19.8%; Males per 100 females: 99.7; Marriage status: 22.5% never married, 61.5% now married, 1.5% separated, 5.0% widowed, 11.0% divorced; Foreign born: 1.0%; Speak English only: 95.5%; With disability: 15.6%; Veterans: 9.5%; Ancestry: 22.8% German, 18.2% English, 14.8% Irish, 8.7% American, 8.3% Pennsylvania German

Employment: 11.4% management, business, and financial, 2.2% computer, engineering, and science, 11.1% education, legal, community service, arts, and media, 8.8% healthcare practitioners, 20.4% service, 21.3% sales and office, 13.7% natural resources, construction, and maintenance, 11.1% production, transportation, and material moving

Income: Per capita: $22,589; Median household: $41,643; Average household: $55,439; Households with income of $100,000 or more: 16.0%; Poverty rate: 22.6%

Educational Attainment: High school diploma or higher: 86.1%; Bachelor's degree or higher: 17.7%; Graduate/professional degree or higher: 7.0%

Housing: Homeownership rate: 76.2%; Median home value: $83,000; Median year structure built: 1967; Homeowner vacancy rate: 1.3%; Median selected monthly owner costs: $976 with a mortgage, $422 without a mortgage; Median gross rent: $605 per month; Rental vacancy rate: 0.0%

Health Insurance: 86.2% have insurance; 65.8% have private insurance; 39.8% have public insurance; 13.8% do not have insurance; 20.4% of children under 18 do not have insurance

Transportation: Commute: 92.4% car, 0.0% public transportation, 2.0% walk, 5.7% work from home; Mean travel time to work: 24.9 minutes

WIRT (town). Covers a land area of 35.938 square miles and a water area of 0.066 square miles. Located at 42.12° N. Lat; 78.13° W. Long. Elevation is 1,877 feet.

Population: 999; Growth (since 2000): -17.8%; Density: 27.8 persons per square mile; Race: 99.9% White, 0.0% Black/African American, 0.0% Asian, 0.1% American Indian/Alaska Native, 0.0% Native Hawaiian/Other Pacific Islander, 0.0% Two or more races, 0.8% Hispanic of any race; Average household size: 2.40; Median age: 46.7; Age under 18: 22.6%; Age 65 and over: 18.6%; Males per 100 females: 94.9; Marriage status: 17.5% never married, 61.3% now married, 0.4% separated, 10.8% widowed, 10.5% divorced; Foreign born: 0.9%; Speak English only: 98.2%; With disability: 19.2%; Veterans: 14.2%; Ancestry: 27.5% German, 16.4% English, 14.2% Irish, 7.9% American, 3.8% Italian

Employment: 13.8% management, business, and financial, 3.8% computer, engineering, and science, 13.5% education, legal, community service, arts, and media, 4.3% healthcare practitioners, 12.5% service, 18.4% sales and office, 12.2% natural resources, construction, and maintenance, 21.4% production, transportation, and material moving

Income: Per capita: $21,911; Median household: $40,909; Average household: $53,265; Households with income of $100,000 or more: 13.7%; Poverty rate: 20.2%

Educational Attainment: High school diploma or higher: 85.9%; Bachelor's degree or higher: 7.8%; Graduate/professional degree or higher: 5.3%

Housing: Homeownership rate: 86.1%; Median home value: $53,800; Median year structure built: 1973; Homeowner vacancy rate: 2.7%; Median selected monthly owner costs: $971 with a mortgage, $449 without a mortgage; Median gross rent: $620 per month; Rental vacancy rate: 0.0%

Health Insurance: 95.5% have insurance; 66.7% have private insurance; 49.4% have public insurance; 4.5% do not have insurance; 3.5% of children under 18 do not have insurance

Transportation: Commute: 91.6% car, 0.0% public transportation, 2.6% walk, 3.4% work from home; Mean travel time to work: 25.2 minutes

Bronx County and Borough

See New York City

Brooklyn Borough

See New York City

Broome County

Located in southern New York; bounded on the south by Pennsylvania. Covers a land area of 705.766 square miles, a water area of 9.749 square miles, and is located in the Eastern Time Zone at 42.16° N. Lat., 75.83° W. Long. The county was founded in 1806. County seat is Binghamton.

Broome County is part of the Binghamton, NY Metropolitan Statistical Area. The entire metro area includes: Broome County, NY; Tioga County, NY

Weather Station: Binghamton Edwin A Link Field								Elevation: 1,600 feet			
	Jan	Feb	Mar	Apr	May	Jun	Jul	Aug	Sep	Oct	Nov	Dec
High	29	33	41	55	66	74	78	77	69	57	45	34
Low	16	17	25	36	46	55	60	58	51	40	31	21
Precip	2.4	2.3	3.1	3.5	3.5	4.3	3.7	3.4	3.6	3.3	3.3	2.8
Snow	21.7	15.9	15.5	4.3	0.1	tr	0.0	tr	tr	1.1	7.0	17.2

High and Low temperatures in degrees Fahrenheit; Precipitation and Snow in inches

Population: 198,093; Growth (since 2000): -1.2%; Density: 280.7 persons per square mile; Race: 86.9% White, 5.4% Black/African American, 4.1% Asian, 0.3% American Indian/Alaska Native, 0.0% Native Hawaiian/Other Pacific Islander, 2.3% two or more races, 3.8% Hispanic of any race; Average household size: 2.37; Median age: 39.9; Age under 18: 19.7%; Age 65 and over: 17.3%; Males per 100 females: 96.2; Marriage status: 36.1% never married, 46.0% now married, 2.2% separated, 6.7% widowed, 11.1% divorced; Foreign born: 6.3%; Speak English only: 90.6%; With disability: 14.4%; Veterans: 8.5%; Ancestry: 19.7% Irish, 16.7% German, 13.2% Italian, 11.9% English, 6.2% Polish

Religion: Six largest groups: 31.0% Catholicism, 7.1% Methodist/Pietist, 3.0% Non-denominational Protestant, 1.9% Holiness, 1.5% Presbyterian-Reformed, 1.4% Lutheran

Economy: Unemployment rate: 5.2%; Leading industries: 17.3 % retail trade; 12.3 % accommodation and food services; 11.9 % other services (except public administration); Farms: 563 totaling 79,676 acres; Company size: 5 employ 1,000 or more persons, 7 employ 500 to 999 persons, 104 employ 100 to 499 persons, 4,145 employ less than 100 persons; Business ownership: 4,461 women-owned, 583 Black-owned, 226 Hispanic-owned, 434 Asian-owned, 98 American Indian/Alaska Native-owned

Employment: 11.0% management, business, and financial, 6.1% computer, engineering, and science, 12.3% education, legal, community service, arts, and media, 6.7% healthcare practitioners, 19.4% service, 24.9% sales and office, 8.3% natural resources, construction, and maintenance, 11.2% production, transportation, and material moving

Income: Per capita: $25,105; Median household: $46,261; Average household: $61,133; Households with income of $100,000 or more: 17.5%; Poverty rate: 17.9%

Educational Attainment: High school diploma or higher: 89.9%; Bachelor's degree or higher: 27.2%; Graduate/professional degree or higher: 12.2%

Housing: Homeownership rate: 65.7%; Median home value: $109,900; Median year structure built: 1956; Homeowner vacancy rate: 2.1%; Median selected monthly owner costs: $1,172 with a mortgage, $484 without a mortgage; Median gross rent: $703 per month; Rental vacancy rate: 6.9%

Vital Statistics: Birth rate: 104.6 per 10,000 population; Death rate: 106.1 per 10,000 population; Age-adjusted cancer mortality rate: 166.6 deaths per 100,000 population

Health Insurance: 93.0% have insurance; 69.2% have private insurance; 38.9% have public insurance; 7.0% do not have insurance; 4.1% of children under 18 do not have insurance

Health Care: Physicians: 30.2 per 10,000 population; Dentists: 6.7 per 10,000 population; Hospital beds: 36.6 per 10,000 population; Hospital admissions: 1,407.2 per 10,000 population

Transportation: Commute: 87.6% car, 3.3% public transportation, 4.5% walk, 3.5% work from home; Mean travel time to work: 19.6 minutes

2016 Presidential Election: 48.2% Trump, 46.2% Clinton, 3.8% Johnson, 1.8% Stein

National and State Parks: Broome State Forest; Chenango Valley State Park; Tracy Creek State Forest

Additional Information Contacts
Broome Government . . . . (607) 778-2109
http://www.gobroomecounty.com/legis

Broome County Communities

BARKER (town). Covers a land area of 41.403 square miles and a water area of 0.376 square miles. Located at 42.27° N. Lat; 75.91° W. Long.
Population: 2,700; Growth (since 2000): -1.4%; Density: 65.2 persons per square mile; Race: 97.9% White, 0.0% Black/African American, 0.1% Asian, 0.0% American Indian/Alaska Native, 0.0% Native Hawaiian/Other Pacific Islander, 0.6% Two or more races, 2.1% Hispanic of any race; Average household size: 2.68; Median age: 43.6; Age under 18: 22.1%; Age 65 and over: 12.6%; Males per 100 females: 104.6; Marriage status: 24.4% never married, 60.8% now married, 3.4% separated, 3.6% widowed, 11.2% divorced; Foreign born: 2.4%; Speak English only: 94.7%; With disability: 16.3%; Veterans: 10.8%; Ancestry: 14.2% American, 14.1% Irish, 13.7% German, 9.4% English, 7.1% Italian
Employment: 11.0% management, business, and financial, 4.9% computer, engineering, and science, 6.8% education, legal, community service, arts, and media, 4.1% healthcare practitioners, 16.3% service, 27.5% sales and office, 10.9% natural resources, construction, and maintenance, 18.5% production, transportation, and material moving
Income: Per capita: $24,684; Median household: $52,868; Average household: $64,538; Households with income of $100,000 or more: 19.0%; Poverty rate: 10.6%
Educational Attainment: High school diploma or higher: 90.6%; Bachelor's degree or higher: 17.7%; Graduate/professional degree or higher: 7.8%
Housing: Homeownership rate: 92.2%; Median home value: $102,000; Median year structure built: 1975; Homeowner vacancy rate: 0.0%; Median selected monthly owner costs: $1,166 with a mortgage, $438 without a mortgage; Median gross rent: $835 per month; Rental vacancy rate: 0.0%
Health Insurance: 93.1% have insurance; 70.5% have private insurance; 35.3% have public insurance; 6.9% do not have insurance; 0.0% of children under 18 do not have insurance
Transportation: Commute: 93.1% car, 0.0% public transportation, 2.0% walk, 4.6% work from home; Mean travel time to work: 26.3 minutes

BINGHAMTON (city). County seat. Covers a land area of 10.489 square miles and a water area of 0.647 square miles. Located at 42.10° N. Lat; 75.91° W. Long. Elevation is 866 feet.
History: Little is known of the Binghamton area before the Revolution. The site was purchased in 1786 by William Bingham, a Philadelphia merchant. Joseph Leonard, first permanent settler, built his log cabin nearby in 1787 and was soon joined by other pioneers, who called the new settlement Chenango. It was later renamed in honor of Bingham, who made liberal donations of land to the settlement. It was incorporated as a village in 1834 and as a city in 1867.
Population: 46,495; Growth (since 2000): -1.9%; Density: 4,432.8 persons per square mile; Race: 75.9% White, 13.9% Black/African American, 4.6% Asian, 0.4% American Indian/Alaska Native, 0.1% Native Hawaiian/Other Pacific Islander, 3.6% Two or more races, 7.0% Hispanic of any race; Average household size: 2.25; Median age: 36.2; Age under 18: 18.6%; Age 65 and over: 16.7%; Males per 100 females: 96.1; Marriage status: 47.6% never married, 31.9% now married, 2.8% separated, 8.0% widowed, 12.5% divorced; Foreign born: 9.1%; Speak English only: 86.3%; With disability: 18.3%; Veterans: 6.9%; Ancestry: 20.3% Irish, 13.6% German, 13.5% Italian, 8.6% English, 4.5% Polish
Employment: 9.2% management, business, and financial, 5.0% computer, engineering, and science, 14.1% education, legal, community service, arts, and media, 5.3% healthcare practitioners, 22.1% service, 27.9% sales and office, 7.2% natural resources, construction, and maintenance, 9.1% production, transportation, and material moving
Income: Per capita: $19,891; Median household: $29,824; Average household: $44,614; Households with income of $100,000 or more: 9.6%; Poverty rate: 33.9%
Educational Attainment: High school diploma or higher: 84.4%; Bachelor's degree or higher: 23.4%; Graduate/professional degree or higher: 10.6%

School District(s)
Binghamton City SD (PK-12)
    2014-15 Enrollment: 5,955 . . . . (607) 762-8100

Broome-Delaware-Tioga Boces
    2014-15 Enrollment: n/a . . . . (607) 766-3802
Chenango Forks Central SD (PK-12)
    2014-15 Enrollment: 1,574 . . . . (607) 648-7543
Chenango Valley Central SD (PK-12)
    2014-15 Enrollment: 1,793 . . . . (607) 762-6801
Susquehanna Valley Central SD (KG-12)
    2014-15 Enrollment: 1,585 . . . . (607) 775-0170
Two-year College(s)
SUNY Broome Community College (Public)
    Fall 2014 Enrollment: 5,944 . . . . (607) 778-5000
    2015-16 Tuition: In-state $4,721; Out-of-state $8,945
Vocational/Technical School(s)
Broome Delaware Tioga BOCES-Practical Nursing Program (Public)
    Fall 2014 Enrollment: 61 . . . . (607) 763-3465
    2015-16 Tuition: $11,900
Ridley-Lowell Business & Technical Institute-Binghamton (Private, For-profit)
    Fall 2014 Enrollment: 146 . . . . (607) 724-2941
    2015-16 Tuition: $13,000
Housing: Homeownership rate: 45.5%; Median home value: $85,300; Median year structure built: 1940; Homeowner vacancy rate: 4.7%; Median selected monthly owner costs: $1,082 with a mortgage, $475 without a mortgage; Median gross rent: $657 per month; Rental vacancy rate: 8.3%
Health Insurance: 91.6% have insurance; 54.4% have private insurance; 49.7% have public insurance; 8.4% do not have insurance; 2.6% of children under 18 do not have insurance
Hospitals: Our Lady of Lourdes Memorial Hospital (161 beds)
Safety: Violent crime rate: 67.3 per 10,000 population; Property crime rate: 454.3 per 10,000 population
Newspapers: Press & Sun-Bulletin (daily circulation 52,000)
Transportation: Commute: 79.1% car, 8.6% public transportation, 7.1% walk, 2.9% work from home; Mean travel time to work: 18.0 minutes
Airports: Greater Binghamton/Edwin A Link Field (primary service/non-hub)
Additional Information Contacts
City of Binghamton . . . . (607) 772-7001
http://www.cityofbinghamton.com

BINGHAMTON (town). Covers a land area of 25.251 square miles and a water area of 0.088 square miles. Located at 42.04° N. Lat; 75.91° W. Long. Elevation is 866 feet.
History: Grew mainly after the Chenango Canal connected it with Utica in 1837. First railroad service began in 1869. State University of N.Y. at Binghamton in the vicinity. Settled 1787, Incorporated as a city 1867.
Population: 4,880; Growth (since 2000): -1.8%; Density: 193.3 persons per square mile; Race: 94.0% White, 1.2% Black/African American, 1.9% Asian, 0.0% American Indian/Alaska Native, 0.0% Native Hawaiian/Other Pacific Islander, 2.9% Two or more races, 1.0% Hispanic of any race; Average household size: 2.57; Median age: 45.2; Age under 18: 19.8%; Age 65 and over: 17.8%; Males per 100 females: 101.6; Marriage status: 26.7% never married, 60.6% now married, 0.6% separated, 4.3% widowed, 8.5% divorced; Foreign born: 4.8%; Speak English only: 94.1%; With disability: 10.6%; Veterans: 7.9%; Ancestry: 25.6% Irish, 17.7% Italian, 16.1% German, 13.5% English, 8.0% Polish
Employment: 14.7% management, business, and financial, 6.3% computer, engineering, and science, 14.3% education, legal, community service, arts, and media, 5.1% healthcare practitioners, 15.5% service, 24.7% sales and office, 9.7% natural resources, construction, and maintenance, 9.6% production, transportation, and material moving
Income: Per capita: $35,752; Median household: $69,100; Average household: $90,855; Households with income of $100,000 or more: 35.0%; Poverty rate: 5.9%
Educational Attainment: High school diploma or higher: 93.8%; Bachelor's degree or higher: 35.1%; Graduate/professional degree or higher: 19.4%
School District(s)
Binghamton City SD (PK-12)
    2014-15 Enrollment: 5,955 . . . . (607) 762-8100
Broome-Delaware-Tioga Boces
    2014-15 Enrollment: n/a . . . . (607) 766-3802
Chenango Forks Central SD (PK-12)
    2014-15 Enrollment: 1,574 . . . . (607) 648-7543
Chenango Valley Central SD (PK-12)
    2014-15 Enrollment: 1,793 . . . . (607) 762-6801

Susquehanna Valley Central SD (KG-12)
  2014-15 Enrollment: 1,585 . . . . (607) 775-0170
                    Two-year College(s)
SUNY Broome Community College (Public)
  Fall 2014 Enrollment: 5,944 . . . . (607) 778-5000
  2015-16 Tuition: In-state $4,721; Out-of-state $8,945
              Vocational/Technical School(s)
Broome Delaware Tioga BOCES-Practical Nursing Program (Public)
  Fall 2014 Enrollment: 61 . . . . (607) 763-3465
  2015-16 Tuition: $11,900
Ridley-Lowell Business & Technical Institute-Binghamton (Private, For-profit)
  Fall 2014 Enrollment: 146 . . . . (607) 724-2941
  2015-16 Tuition: $13,000
Housing: Homeownership rate: 91.2%; Median home value: $139,400; Median year structure built: 1970; Homeowner vacancy rate: 2.1%; Median selected monthly owner costs: $1,423 with a mortgage, $545 without a mortgage; Median gross rent: $802 per month; Rental vacancy rate: 0.0%
Health Insurance: 93.6% have insurance; 77.7% have private insurance; 30.6% have public insurance; 6.4% do not have insurance; 6.3% of children under 18 do not have insurance
Hospitals: Our Lady of Lourdes Memorial Hospital (161 beds)
Newspapers: Press & Sun-Bulletin (daily circulation 52,000)
Transportation: Commute: 95.2% car, 0.8% public transportation, 0.0% walk, 3.6% work from home; Mean travel time to work: 19.3 minutes
Airports: Greater Binghamton/Edwin A Link Field (primary service/non-hub)
Additional Information Contacts
Town of Binghamton . . . . (607) 772-0357
  http://www.townofbinghamton.com

BINGHAMTON UNIVERSITY (CDP). Covers a land area of 0.775 square miles and a water area of 0 square miles. Located at 42.09° N. Lat; 75.97° W. Long.
History: Binghamton is a city in, and the county seat of, Broome County, New York. It is the home of Binghamton University, a state university of New York.
Population: 6,084; Growth (since 2000): n/a; Density: 7,845.4 persons per square mile; Race: 62.4% White, 7.8% Black/African American, 22.9% Asian, 0.1% American Indian/Alaska Native, 0.0% Native Hawaiian/Other Pacific Islander, 3.7% Two or more races, 10.5% Hispanic of any race; Average household size: 0.00; Median age: 19.7; Age under 18: 1.5%; Age 65 and over: 0.0%; Males per 100 females: 109.1; Marriage status: 99.6% never married, 0.4% now married, 0.0% separated, 0.0% widowed, 0.1% divorced; Foreign born: 10.7%; Speak English only: 71.2%; With disability: 4.9%; Veterans: 0.1%; Ancestry: 14.4% Italian, 10.7% Irish, 10.2% German, 4.8% Polish, 3.2% Russian
Employment: 6.1% management, business, and financial, 6.8% computer, engineering, and science, 15.5% education, legal, community service, arts, and media, 0.0% healthcare practitioners, 29.6% service, 35.6% sales and office, 0.0% natural resources, construction, and maintenance, 6.4% production, transportation, and material moving
Income: Per capita: $2,936; Median household: n/a; Average household: n/a; Households with income of $100,000 or more: n/a; Poverty rate: n/a
Educational Attainment: High school diploma or higher: 100.0%; Bachelor's degree or higher: 23.4%; Graduate/professional degree or higher: 23.4%
Housing: Homeownership rate: n/a; Median home value: n/a; Median year structure built: n/a; Homeowner vacancy rate: 0.0%; Median selected monthly owner costs: n/a with a mortgage, n/a without a mortgage; Median gross rent: n/a per month; Rental vacancy rate: 0.0%
Health Insurance: 96.3% have insurance; 86.8% have private insurance; 10.9% have public insurance; 3.7% do not have insurance; 0.0% of children under 18 do not have insurance
Transportation: Commute: 22.9% car, 4.5% public transportation, 58.4% walk, 13.1% work from home; Mean travel time to work: 11.6 minutes

CASTLE CREEK (unincorporated postal area)
ZCTA: 13744
  Covers a land area of 11.587 square miles and a water area of 0.004 square miles. Located at 42.24° N. Lat; 75.91° W. Long. Elevation is 1,050 feet.
  Population: 1,139; Growth (since 2000): -5.2%; Density: 98.3 persons per square mile; Race: 96.3% White, 0.0% Black/African American, 0.0% Asian, 1.8% American Indian/Alaska Native, 0.0% Native

Hawaiian/Other Pacific Islander, 1.8% Two or more races, 2.4% Hispanic of any race; Average household size: 2.22; Median age: 47.6; Age under 18: 17.4%; Age 65 and over: 15.5%; Males per 100 females: 105.2; Marriage status: 21.7% never married, 61.1% now married, 0.4% separated, 7.7% widowed, 9.5% divorced; Foreign born: 4.4%; Speak English only: 98.0%; With disability: 8.1%; Veterans: 7.5%; Ancestry: 16.5% German, 16.2% Irish, 13.0% American, 9.0% Italian, 8.7% Polish
Employment: 12.8% management, business, and financial, 8.7% computer, engineering, and science, 10.1% education, legal, community service, arts, and media, 7.2% healthcare practitioners, 10.1% service, 26.7% sales and office, 8.4% natural resources, construction, and maintenance, 16.0% production, transportation, and material moving
Income: Per capita: $28,472; Median household: $55,395; Average household: $62,937; Households with income of $100,000 or more: 16.9%; Poverty rate: 11.0%
Educational Attainment: High school diploma or higher: 89.0%; Bachelor's degree or higher: 28.3%; Graduate/professional degree or higher: 13.3%
Housing: Homeownership rate: 86.9%; Median home value: $120,600; Median year structure built: 1969; Homeowner vacancy rate: 0.0%; Median selected monthly owner costs: $1,173 with a mortgage, $521 without a mortgage; Median gross rent: $730 per month; Rental vacancy rate: 0.0%
Health Insurance: 92.6% have insurance; 78.4% have private insurance; 29.7% have public insurance; 7.4% do not have insurance; 0.0% of children under 18 do not have insurance
Transportation: Commute: 89.5% car, 0.0% public transportation, 3.9% walk, 6.6% work from home; Mean travel time to work: 22.2 minutes

CHENANGO (town). Covers a land area of 33.834 square miles and a water area of 0.434 square miles. Located at 42.22° N. Lat; 75.90° W. Long.
Population: 11,103; Growth (since 2000): -3.1%; Density: 328.2 persons per square mile; Race: 96.4% White, 1.0% Black/African American, 1.0% Asian, 0.2% American Indian/Alaska Native, 0.0% Native Hawaiian/Other Pacific Islander, 1.3% Two or more races, 1.5% Hispanic of any race; Average household size: 2.51; Median age: 43.8; Age under 18: 20.2%; Age 65 and over: 17.1%; Males per 100 females: 96.5; Marriage status: 27.4% never married, 58.4% now married, 1.8% separated, 5.9% widowed, 8.3% divorced; Foreign born: 3.9%; Speak English only: 93.8%; With disability: 12.1%; Veterans: 8.5%; Ancestry: 24.7% Irish, 20.0% German, 14.0% English, 11.1% Italian, 7.7% Polish
Employment: 15.0% management, business, and financial, 5.1% computer, engineering, and science, 13.2% education, legal, community service, arts, and media, 9.1% healthcare practitioners, 14.1% service, 25.9% sales and office, 7.9% natural resources, construction, and maintenance, 9.6% production, transportation, and material moving
Income: Per capita: $29,854; Median household: $64,678; Average household: $73,740; Households with income of $100,000 or more: 21.5%; Poverty rate: 9.7%
Educational Attainment: High school diploma or higher: 93.5%; Bachelor's degree or higher: 32.3%; Graduate/professional degree or higher: 12.0%
Housing: Homeownership rate: 83.4%; Median home value: $131,100; Median year structure built: 1963; Homeowner vacancy rate: 0.4%; Median selected monthly owner costs: $1,271 with a mortgage, $485 without a mortgage; Median gross rent: $741 per month; Rental vacancy rate: 1.6%
Health Insurance: 95.4% have insurance; 79.6% have private insurance; 31.8% have public insurance; 4.6% do not have insurance; 1.7% of children under 18 do not have insurance
Transportation: Commute: 93.1% car, 0.9% public transportation, 2.4% walk, 3.2% work from home; Mean travel time to work: 20.7 minutes
Additional Information Contacts
Town of Chenango . . . . (607) 648-4809
  http://www.townofchenango.com

CHENANGO BRIDGE (CDP). Covers a land area of 2.448 square miles and a water area of 0.144 square miles. Located at 42.17° N. Lat; 75.86° W. Long. Elevation is 896 feet.
Population: 2,795; Growth (since 2000): n/a; Density: 1,141.6 persons per square mile; Race: 98.6% White, 0.4% Black/African American, 0.7% Asian, 0.0% American Indian/Alaska Native, 0.0% Native Hawaiian/Other Pacific Islander, 0.3% Two or more races, 0.4% Hispanic of any race; Average household size: 2.51; Median age: 45.0; Age under 18: 18.8%; Age 65 and over: 19.3%; Males per 100 females: 96.0; Marriage status:

24.7% never married, 61.2% now married, 0.0% separated, 6.8% widowed, 7.4% divorced; Foreign born: 3.2%; Speak English only: 97.7%; With disability: 12.5%; Veterans: 7.9%; Ancestry: 25.6% Irish, 21.6% German, 16.0% Italian, 13.0% English, 9.2% Polish

Employment: 18.6% management, business, and financial, 5.0% computer, engineering, and science, 15.1% education, legal, community service, arts, and media, 8.9% healthcare practitioners, 13.5% service, 20.2% sales and office, 6.4% natural resources, construction, and maintenance, 12.4% production, transportation, and material moving

Income: Per capita: $32,098; Median household: $71,645; Average household: $80,115; Households with income of $100,000 or more: 22.1%; Poverty rate: 5.8%

Educational Attainment: High school diploma or higher: 94.7%; Bachelor's degree or higher: 37.2%; Graduate/professional degree or higher: 15.0%

Housing: Homeownership rate: 91.4%; Median home value: $131,000; Median year structure built: 1958; Homeowner vacancy rate: 0.0%; Median selected monthly owner costs: $1,247 with a mortgage, $443 without a mortgage; Median gross rent: $644 per month; Rental vacancy rate: 0.0%

Health Insurance: 95.5% have insurance; 87.4% have private insurance; 26.5% have public insurance; 4.5% do not have insurance; 3.0% of children under 18 do not have insurance

Transportation: Commute: 95.3% car, 0.0% public transportation, 2.1% walk, 2.6% work from home; Mean travel time to work: 18.1 minutes

CHENANGO FORKS (unincorporated postal area)

ZCTA: 13746

Covers a land area of 27.735 square miles and a water area of 0.483 square miles. Located at 42.27° N. Lat; 75.88° W. Long. Elevation is 915 feet.

Population: 2,191; Growth (since 2000): -0.5%; Density: 79.0 persons per square mile; Race: 91.1% White, 0.0% Black/African American, 0.8% Asian, 2.3% American Indian/Alaska Native, 0.0% Native Hawaiian/Other Pacific Islander, 4.1% Two or more races, 1.9% Hispanic of any race; Average household size: 2.64; Median age: 43.7; Age under 18: 25.1%; Age 65 and over: 15.9%; Males per 100 females: 104.9; Marriage status: 25.6% never married, 61.5% now married, 1.8% separated, 4.2% widowed, 8.8% divorced; Foreign born: 2.1%; Speak English only: 95.7%; With disability: 13.8%; Veterans: 10.1%; Ancestry: 21.1% Irish, 18.3% English, 13.1% American, 12.5% Italian, 12.3% German

Employment: 11.6% management, business, and financial, 6.5% computer, engineering, and science, 9.7% education, legal, community service, arts, and media, 10.1% healthcare practitioners, 18.1% service, 24.8% sales and office, 7.2% natural resources, construction, and maintenance, 12.1% production, transportation, and material moving

Income: Per capita: $25,408; Median household: $51,793; Average household: $65,672; Households with income of $100,000 or more: 19.6%; Poverty rate: 16.2%

Educational Attainment: High school diploma or higher: 90.9%; Bachelor's degree or higher: 20.9%; Graduate/professional degree or higher: 8.2%

Housing: Homeownership rate: 92.1%; Median home value: $96,300; Median year structure built: 1977; Homeowner vacancy rate: 0.0%; Median selected monthly owner costs: $1,306 with a mortgage, $523 without a mortgage; Median gross rent: $831 per month; Rental vacancy rate: 0.0%

Health Insurance: 97.2% have insurance; 68.4% have private insurance; 40.8% have public insurance; 2.8% do not have insurance; 0.0% of children under 18 do not have insurance

Transportation: Commute: 96.2% car, 1.0% public transportation, 0.0% walk, 2.8% work from home; Mean travel time to work: 26.9 minutes

COLESVILLE (town). Covers a land area of 78.347 square miles and a water area of 0.824 square miles. Located at 42.18° N. Lat; 75.65° W. Long.

Population: 5,168; Growth (since 2000): -5.0%; Density: 66.0 persons per square mile; Race: 98.7% White, 1.2% Black/African American, 0.0% Asian, 0.0% American Indian/Alaska Native, 0.0% Native Hawaiian/Other Pacific Islander, 0.1% Two or more races, 0.3% Hispanic of any race; Average household size: 2.59; Median age: 43.0; Age under 18: 22.6%; Age 65 and over: 16.2%; Males per 100 females: 107.3; Marriage status: 15.7% never married, 59.5% now married, 2.3% separated, 8.9% widowed, 15.9% divorced; Foreign born: 0.4%; Speak English only: 96.7%;

With disability: 18.6%; Veterans: 11.2%; Ancestry: 24.2% Irish, 23.8% German, 13.3% American, 11.3% English, 9.2% Italian

Employment: 7.9% management, business, and financial, 1.3% computer, engineering, and science, 12.3% education, legal, community service, arts, and media, 0.0% healthcare practitioners, 21.2% service, 17.0% sales and office, 14.6% natural resources, construction, and maintenance, 25.7% production, transportation, and material moving

Income: Per capita: $21,850; Median household: $42,958; Average household: $55,934; Households with income of $100,000 or more: 17.6%; Poverty rate: 19.9%

Educational Attainment: High school diploma or higher: 81.6%; Bachelor's degree or higher: 15.0%; Graduate/professional degree or higher: 9.1%

Housing: Homeownership rate: 77.9%; Median home value: $94,300; Median year structure built: 1978; Homeowner vacancy rate: 0.0%; Median selected monthly owner costs: $1,292 with a mortgage, $376 without a mortgage; Median gross rent: $699 per month; Rental vacancy rate: 8.4%

Health Insurance: 86.7% have insurance; 58.5% have private insurance; 42.4% have public insurance; 13.3% do not have insurance; 8.9% of children under 18 do not have insurance

Transportation: Commute: 95.0% car, 0.0% public transportation, 1.5% walk, 3.6% work from home; Mean travel time to work: 24.8 minutes

Additional Information Contacts

Town of Colesville . . . . (607) 693-1174
  http://townofcolesville.org/content

CONKLIN (town). Covers a land area of 24.385 square miles and a water area of 0.504 square miles. Located at 42.04° N. Lat; 75.84° W. Long. Elevation is 869 feet.

Population: 5,340; Growth (since 2000): -10.1%; Density: 219.0 persons per square mile; Race: 98.8% White, 0.8% Black/African American, 0.0% Asian, 0.1% American Indian/Alaska Native, 0.0% Native Hawaiian/Other Pacific Islander, 0.3% Two or more races, 0.7% Hispanic of any race; Average household size: 2.63; Median age: 45.3; Age under 18: 22.7%; Age 65 and over: 16.8%; Males per 100 females: 97.2; Marriage status: 26.7% never married, 53.3% now married, 2.9% separated, 2.2% widowed, 17.8% divorced; Foreign born: 0.7%; Speak English only: 98.6%; With disability: 14.3%; Veterans: 9.5%; Ancestry: 28.5% English, 25.9% Irish, 23.8% German, 10.3% Italian, 6.0% Polish

Employment: 7.5% management, business, and financial, 1.7% computer, engineering, and science, 6.6% education, legal, community service, arts, and media, 6.3% healthcare practitioners, 23.4% service, 25.9% sales and office, 9.3% natural resources, construction, and maintenance, 19.3% production, transportation, and material moving

Income: Per capita: $25,940; Median household: $52,824; Average household: $66,420; Households with income of $100,000 or more: 18.4%; Poverty rate: 12.4%

Educational Attainment: High school diploma or higher: 93.4%; Bachelor's degree or higher: 23.5%; Graduate/professional degree or higher: 8.6%

School District(s)

Susquehanna Valley Central SD (KG-12)
  2014-15 Enrollment: 1,585 . . . . (607) 775-0170

Housing: Homeownership rate: 88.4%; Median home value: $111,500; Median year structure built: 1971; Homeowner vacancy rate: 0.0%; Median selected monthly owner costs: $1,161 with a mortgage, $489 without a mortgage; Median gross rent: $638 per month; Rental vacancy rate: 0.0%

Health Insurance: 88.2% have insurance; 75.4% have private insurance; 26.8% have public insurance; 11.8% do not have insurance; 29.0% of children under 18 do not have insurance

Newspapers: Country Courier (weekly circulation 1,300); Windsor Standard (weekly circulation 1,300)

Transportation: Commute: 96.0% car, 0.0% public transportation, 0.7% walk, 2.7% work from home; Mean travel time to work: 25.9 minutes

Additional Information Contacts

Town of Conklin . . . . (607) 775-3454
  http://www.townofconklin.org

DICKINSON (town). Covers a land area of 4.772 square miles and a water area of 0.105 square miles. Located at 42.13° N. Lat; 75.92° W. Long.

History: Incorporated 1876.

Population: 5,234; Growth (since 2000): -1.9%; Density: 1,096.9 persons per square mile; Race: 92.0% White, 5.2% Black/African American, 0.2% Asian, 0.0% American Indian/Alaska Native, 0.0% Native Hawaiian/Other

Pacific Islander, 2.5% Two or more races, 2.8% Hispanic of any race; Average household size: 2.20; Median age: 43.1; Age under 18: 16.9%; Age 65 and over: 19.9%; Males per 100 females: 103.8; Marriage status: 39.7% never married, 40.2% now married, 3.1% separated, 8.2% widowed, 11.9% divorced; Foreign born: 2.6%; Speak English only: 95.3%; With disability: 19.5%; Veterans: 12.9%; Ancestry: 22.4% Irish, 19.9% German, 12.4% English, 11.6% Italian, 9.3% Polish

Employment: 11.0% management, business, and.financial, 6.0% computer, engineering, and science, 15.4% education, legal, community service, arts, and media, 9.3% healthcare practitioners, 21.0% service, 25.1% sales and office, 5.0% natural resources, construction, and maintenance, 7.2% production, transportation, and material moving

Income: Per capita: $23,933; Median household: $48,105; Average household: $57,983; Households with income of $100,000 or more: 15.7%; Poverty rate: 17.3%

Educational Attainment: High school diploma or higher: 88.8%; Bachelor's degree or higher: 23.1%; Graduate/professional degree or higher: 10.7%

Housing: Homeownership rate: 65.3%; Median home value: $111,100; Median year structure built: 1952; Homeowner vacancy rate: 0.0%; Median selected monthly owner costs: $1,169 with a mortgage, $420 without a mortgage; Median gross rent: $673 per month; Rental vacancy rate: 5.3%

Health Insurance: 96.5% have insurance; 75.4% have private insurance; 39.8% have public insurance; 3.5% do not have insurance; 0.7% of children under 18 do not have insurance

Transportation: Commute: 91.1% car, 2.6% public transportation, 0.9% walk, 3.1% work from home; Mean travel time to work: 15.3 minutes

Additional Information Contacts

Town of Dickinson . . . . (607) 723-9401
　http://www.townofdickinson.com

ENDICOTT (village).
Covers a land area of 3.194 square miles and a water area of 0.004 square miles. Located at 42.10° N. Lat; 76.06° W. Long. Elevation is 840 feet.

History: Settled c.1795; incorporated 1906.

Population: 13,143; Growth (since 2000): 0.8%; Density: 4,115.1 persons per square mile; Race: 86.6% White, 5.6% Black/African American, 2.4% Asian, 0.4% American Indian/Alaska Native, 0.0% Native Hawaiian/Other Pacific Islander, 3.0% Two or more races, 6.0% Hispanic of any race; Average household size: 2.19; Median age: 38.1; Age under 18: 21.3%; Age 65 and over: 16.6%; Males per 100 females: 93.4; Marriage status: 38.0% never married, 40.0% now married, 4.2% separated, 7.1% widowed, 14.9% divorced; Foreign born: 6.2%; Speak English only: 90.9%; With disability: 18.1%; Veterans: 9.1%; Ancestry: 17.8% Italian, 15.7% Irish, 13.7% German, 8.5% English, 7.2% Polish

Employment: 8.5% management, business, and financial, 6.0% computer, engineering, and science, 9.5% education, legal, community service, arts, and media, 4.9% healthcare practitioners, 23.4% service, 25.6% sales and office, 8.2% natural resources, construction, and maintenance, 14.0% production, transportation, and material moving

Income: Per capita: $20,243; Median household: $32,726; Average household: $44,448; Households with income of $100,000 or more: 9.7%; Poverty rate: 23.1%

Educational Attainment: High school diploma or higher: 88.7%; Bachelor's degree or higher: 19.4%; Graduate/professional degree or higher: 7.7%

School District(s)
Union-Endicott Central SD (KG-12)
　2014-15 Enrollment: 3,946 . . . . (607) 757-2103

Housing: Homeownership rate: 42.1%; Median home value: $89,300; Median year structure built: 1941; Homeowner vacancy rate: 3.7%; Median selected monthly owner costs: $1,061 with a mortgage, $451 without a mortgage; Median gross rent: $680 per month; Rental vacancy rate: 8.3%

Health Insurance: 88.8% have insurance; 50.6% have private insurance; 50.5% have public insurance; 11.2% do not have insurance; 1.9% of children under 18 do not have insurance

Safety: Violent crime rate: 51.5 per 10,000 population; Property crime rate: 425.0 per 10,000 population

Transportation: Commute: 81.6% car, 3.2% public transportation, 10.1% walk, 3.3% work from home; Mean travel time to work: 18.0 minutes

Additional Information Contacts

Village of Endicott . . . . (607) 757-5337
　http://www.endicottny.com

ENDWELL (CDP).
Covers a land area of 3.744 square miles and a water area of 0.032 square miles. Located at 42.12° N. Lat; 76.02° W. Long. Elevation is 846 feet.

History: Also called Hooper.

Population: 11,445; Growth (since 2000): -2.2%; Density: 3,057.2 persons per square mile; Race: 92.1% White, 2.3% Black/African American, 2.1% Asian, 0.2% American Indian/Alaska Native, 0.1% Native Hawaiian/Other Pacific Islander, 1.4% Two or more races, 4.4% Hispanic of any race; Average household size: 2.30; Median age: 44.5; Age under 18: 20.9%; Age 65 and over: 18.7%; Males per 100 females: 91.2; Marriage status: 27.1% never married, 54.0% now married, 2.0% separated, 6.8% widowed, 12.1% divorced; Foreign born: 4.6%; Speak English only: 93.7%; With disability: 11.3%; Veterans: 10.9%; Ancestry: 20.5% Italian, 20.5% Irish, 16.9% German, 11.8% English, 8.8% Polish

Employment: 11.4% management, business, and financial, 9.8% computer, engineering, and science, 14.4% education, legal, community service, arts, and media, 5.0% healthcare practitioners, 18.6% service, 26.8% sales and office, 5.3% natural resources, construction, and maintenance, 8.8% production, transportation, and material moving

Income: Per capita: $30,296; Median household: $54,446; Average household: $69,337; Households with income of $100,000 or more: 24.9%; Poverty rate: 8.7%

Educational Attainment: High school diploma or higher: 94.2%; Bachelor's degree or higher: 35.8%; Graduate/professional degree or higher: 14.9%

School District(s)
Maine-Endwell Central SD (PK-12)
　2014-15 Enrollment: 2,474 . . . . (607) 754-1400

Housing: Homeownership rate: 71.2%; Median home value: $128,300; Median year structure built: 1957; Homeowner vacancy rate: 2.2%; Median selected monthly owner costs: $1,236 with a mortgage, $473 without a mortgage; Median gross rent: $699 per month; Rental vacancy rate: 7.1%

Health Insurance: 96.0% have insurance; 78.6% have private insurance; 33.4% have public insurance; 4.0% do not have insurance; 2.0% of children under 18 do not have insurance

Transportation: Commute: 90.1% car, 1.6% public transportation, 1.2% walk, 6.0% work from home; Mean travel time to work: 17.6 minutes

FENTON (town).
Covers a land area of 32.773 square miles and a water area of 0.592 square miles. Located at 42.20° N. Lat; 75.80° W. Long.

Population: 6,554; Growth (since 2000): -5.1%; Density: 200.0 persons per square mile; Race: 95.6% White, 0.3% Black/African American, 0.3% Asian, 1.5% American Indian/Alaska Native, 0.0% Native Hawaiian/Other Pacific Islander, 2.3% Two or more races, 0.0% Hispanic of any race; Average household size: 2.40; Median age: 44.1; Age under 18: 21.7%; Age 65 and over: 16.6%; Males per 100 females: 97.6; Marriage status: 28.9% never married, 51.9% now married, 1.3% separated, 6.7% widowed, 12.4% divorced; Foreign born: 1.6%; Speak English only: 97.9%; With disability: 11.6%; Veterans: 7.9%; Ancestry: 20.1% German, 19.8% English, 19.3% Irish, 11.6% Italian, 9.1% Polish

Employment: 8.4% management, business, and financial, 4.8% computer, engineering, and science, 12.4% education, legal, community service, arts, and media, 5.7% healthcare practitioners, 15.0% service, 24.5% sales and office, 12.5% natural resources, construction, and maintenance, 16.6% production, transportation, and material moving

Income: Per capita: $27,375; Median household: $46,071; Average household: $65,765; Households with income of $100,000 or more: 19.0%; Poverty rate: 15.4%

Educational Attainment: High school diploma or higher: 90.0%; Bachelor's degree or higher: 22.7%; Graduate/professional degree or higher: 8.9%

Housing: Homeownership rate: 85.6%; Median home value: $103,500; Median year structure built: 1962; Homeowner vacancy rate: 2.1%; Median selected monthly owner costs: $1,207 with a mortgage, $437 without a mortgage; Median gross rent: $660 per month; Rental vacancy rate: 0.0%

Health Insurance: 95.9% have insurance; 72.2% have private insurance; 39.6% have public insurance; 4.1% do not have insurance; 0.0% of children under 18 do not have insurance

Transportation: Commute: 97.7% car, 0.0% public transportation, 0.0% walk, 2.3% work from home; Mean travel time to work: 21.0 minutes

Additional Information Contacts

Town of Fenton . . . . (607) 648-4800
　http://www.townoffenton.com

GLEN AUBREY (CDP). Covers a land area of 0.986 square miles and a water area of 0 square miles. Located at 42.26° N. Lat; 76.00° W. Long. Elevation is 991 feet.
Population: 308; Growth (since 2000): n/a; Density: 312.3 persons per square mile; Race: 97.1% White, 1.6% Black/African American, 0.0% Asian, 0.0% American Indian/Alaska Native, 0.0% Native Hawaiian/Other Pacific Islander, 1.3% Two or more races, 0.0% Hispanic of any race; Average household size: 2.32; Median age: 44.5; Age under 18: 17.2%; Age 65 and over: 22.7%; Males per 100 females: 84.4; Marriage status: 33.0% never married, 51.5% now married, 13.3% separated, 4.9% widowed, 10.6% divorced; Foreign born: 0.0%; Speak English only: 100.0%; With disability: 14.0%; Veterans: 20.4%; Ancestry: 12.0% English, 9.1% Dutch, 8.4% American, 7.8% German, 7.5% Irish
Employment: 10.4% management, business, and financial, 1.3% computer, engineering, and science, 2.6% education, legal, community service, arts, and media, 0.0% healthcare practitioners, 26.6% service, 10.4% sales and office, 6.5% natural resources, construction, and maintenance, 42.2% production, transportation, and material moving
Income: Per capita: $26,453; Median household: $58,438; Average household: $58,534; Households with income of $100,000 or more: 6.0%; Poverty rate: 14.3%
Educational Attainment: High school diploma or higher: 87.3%; Bachelor's degree or higher: 10.0%; Graduate/professional degree or higher: n/a
Housing: Homeownership rate: 54.9%; Median home value: $114,800; Median year structure built: 1979; Homeowner vacancy rate: 11.0%; Median selected monthly owner costs: $1,010 with a mortgage, $388 without a mortgage; Median gross rent: $775 per month; Rental vacancy rate: 13.0%
Health Insurance: 94.5% have insurance; 67.2% have private insurance; 46.8% have public insurance; 5.5% do not have insurance; 0.0% of children under 18 do not have insurance
Transportation: Commute: 96.1% car, 3.9% public transportation, 0.0% walk, 0.0% work from home; Mean travel time to work: 28.2 minutes

HARPURSVILLE (unincorporated postal area)
ZCTA: 13787
Covers a land area of 63.639 square miles and a water area of 0.465 square miles. Located at 42.21° N. Lat; 75.67° W. Long. Elevation is 1,024 feet.
Population: 3,903; Growth (since 2000): 7.2%; Density: 61.3 persons per square mile; Race: 98.5% White, 1.1% Black/African American, 0.0% Asian, 0.0% American Indian/Alaska Native, 0.0% Native Hawaiian/Other Pacific Islander, 0.4% Two or more races, 0.5% Hispanic of any race; Average household size: 2.77; Median age: 37.8; Age under 18: 27.3%; Age 65 and over: 11.4%; Males per 100 females: 103.9; Marriage status: 15.8% never married, 61.6% now married, 3.8% separated, 7.1% widowed, 15.5% divorced; Foreign born: 0.1%; Speak English only: 95.8%; With disability: 17.5%; Veterans: 8.5%; Ancestry: 28.4% Irish, 24.6% German, 11.5% Italian, 11.0% English, 9.2% American
Employment: 8.7% management, business, and financial, 1.7% computer, engineering, and science, 12.9% education, legal, community service, arts, and media, 0.0% healthcare practitioners, 18.4% service, 19.4% sales and office, 17.7% natural resources, construction, and maintenance, 21.2% production, transportation, and material moving
Income: Per capita: $19,527; Median household: $39,634; Average household: $53,130; Households with income of $100,000 or more: 15.5%; Poverty rate: 23.9%
Educational Attainment: High school diploma or higher: 80.1%; Bachelor's degree or higher: 13.1%; Graduate/professional degree or higher: 9.6%

School District(s)
Harpursville Central SD (PK-12)
   2014-15 Enrollment: 900 . . . . (607) 693-8101
Housing: Homeownership rate: 72.9%; Median home value: $87,200; Median year structure built: 1981; Homeowner vacancy rate: 0.0%; Median selected monthly owner costs: $1,507 with a mortgage, $345 without a mortgage; Median gross rent: $674 per month; Rental vacancy rate: 9.5%
Health Insurance: 85.1% have insurance; 58.9% have private insurance; 36.6% have public insurance; 14.9% do not have insurance; 9.8% of children under 18 do not have insurance
Transportation: Commute: 92.6% car, 0.0% public transportation, 2.2% walk, 5.2% work from home; Mean travel time to work: 22.3 minutes

JOHNSON CITY (village). Covers a land area of 4.536 square miles and a water area of 0.099 square miles. Located at 42.13° N. Lat; 75.96° W. Long. Elevation is 873 feet.
History: Originally called Lestershire, the area remained rural until a shoe company built a factory here in 1890. The name was changed in 1916. Incorporated 1892.
Population: 14,903; Growth (since 2000): -4.1%; Density: 3,285.2 persons per square mile; Race: 78.6% White, 7.1% Black/African American, 8.6% Asian, 0.0% American Indian/Alaska Native, 0.2% Native Hawaiian/Other Pacific Islander, 3.6% Two or more races, 4.4% Hispanic of any race; Average household size: 2.21; Median age: 36.3; Age under 18: 20.9%; Age 65 and over: 15.9%; Males per 100 females: 92.1; Marriage status: 38.9% never married, 39.8% now married, 2.7% separated, 8.2% widowed, 13.2% divorced; Foreign born: 9.1%; Speak English only: 87.9%; With disability: 14.7%; Veterans: 7.9%; Ancestry: 15.3% Irish, 15.0% German, 11.7% Italian, 8.7% English, 8.5% Polish
Employment: 6.6% management, business, and financial, 5.0% computer, engineering, and science, 13.8% education, legal, community service, arts, and media, 11.6% healthcare practitioners, 22.6% service, 25.2% sales and office, 5.7% natural resources, construction, and maintenance, 9.5% production, transportation, and material moving
Income: Per capita: $23,080; Median household: $38,371; Average household: $51,170; Households with income of $100,000 or more: 11.1%; Poverty rate: 18.8%
Educational Attainment: High school diploma or higher: 89.4%; Bachelor's degree or higher: 24.2%; Graduate/professional degree or higher: 9.9%

School District(s)
Johnson City Central SD (PK-12)
   2014-15 Enrollment: 2,562 . . . . (607) 763-1230
Four-year College(s)
Davis College (Private, Not-for-profit, Undenominational)
   Fall 2014 Enrollment: 396 . . . . (607) 729-1581
   2015-16 Tuition: In-state $13,540; Out-of-state $13,540
Housing: Homeownership rate: 53.1%; Median home value: $84,100; Median year structure built: 1947; Homeowner vacancy rate: 1.7%; Median selected monthly owner costs: $1,022 with a mortgage, $480 without a mortgage; Median gross rent: $730 per month; Rental vacancy rate: 4.3%
Health Insurance: 91.7% have insurance; 65.2% have private insurance; 42.9% have public insurance; 8.3% do not have insurance; 5.2% of children under 18 do not have insurance
Hospitals: United Health Services Hospitals (516 beds)
Safety: Violent crime rate: 48.1 per 10,000 population; Property crime rate: 715.2 per 10,000 population
Transportation: Commute: 82.3% car, 7.3% public transportation, 7.1% walk, 1.7% work from home; Mean travel time to work: 16.2 minutes
Additional Information Contacts
Village of Johnson City . . . . (607) 798-7861
   http://www.villageofjc.com

KILLAWOG (unincorporated postal area)
ZCTA: 13794
Covers a land area of 0.717 square miles and a water area of 0 square miles. Located at 42.39° N. Lat; 76.01° W. Long. Elevation is 1,007 feet.
Population: 25; Growth (since 2000): n/a; Density: 34.8 persons per square mile; Race: 100.0% White, 0.0% Black/African American, 0.0% Asian, 0.0% American Indian/Alaska Native, 0.0% Native Hawaiian/Other Pacific Islander, 0.0% Two or more races, 0.0% Hispanic of any race; Average household size: 2.08; Median age: 55.7; Age under 18: 12.0%; Age 65 and over: 0.0%; Males per 100 females: 114.3; Marriage status: 13.6% never married, 86.4% now married, 0.0% separated, 0.0% widowed, 0.0% divorced; Foreign born: 0.0%; Speak English only: 100.0%; With disability: 0.0%; Veterans: 0.0%; Ancestry: 76.0% German, 24.0% Italian, 12.0% Polish
Employment: 0.0% management, business, and financial, 22.7% computer, engineering, and science, 0.0% education, legal, community service, arts, and media, 0.0% healthcare practitioners, 54.5% service, 0.0% sales and office, 0.0% natural resources, construction, and maintenance, 22.7% production, transportation, and material moving
Income: Per capita: $39,332; Median household: $84,375; Average household: $75,942; Households with income of $100,000 or more: 41.7%; Poverty rate: n/a
Educational Attainment: High school diploma or higher: 100.0%; Bachelor's degree or higher: n/a; Graduate/professional degree or higher: n/a

Housing: Homeownership rate: 100.0%; Median home value: n/a; Median year structure built: 1991; Homeowner vacancy rate: 0.0%; Median selected monthly owner costs: $0 with a mortgage, $0 without a mortgage; Median gross rent: n/a per month; Rental vacancy rate: 0.0%
Health Insurance: 100.0% have insurance; 76.0% have private insurance; 24.0% have public insurance; 0.0% do not have insurance; 0.0% of children under 18 do not have insurance
Transportation: Commute: 59.1% car, 0.0% public transportation, 0.0% walk, 40.9% work from home; Mean travel time to work: 0.0 minutes

KIRKWOOD (town). Covers a land area of 30.795 square miles and a water area of 0.397 square miles. Located at 42.09° N. Lat; 75.80° W. Long. Elevation is 892 feet.
Population: 5,776; Growth (since 2000): 2.2%; Density: 187.6 persons per square mile; Race: 97.1% White, 0.2% Black/African American, 0.5% Asian, 0.3% American Indian/Alaska Native, 0.0% Native Hawaiian/Other Pacific Islander, 1.1% Two or more races, 4.0% Hispanic of any race; Average household size: 2.49; Median age: 45.0; Age under 18: 18.9%; Age 65 and over: 20.1%; Males per 100 females: 97.9; Marriage status: 27.5% never married, 57.7% now married, 3.7% separated, 4.9% widowed, 9.9% divorced; Foreign born: 4.0%; Speak English only: 93.7%; With disability: 20.1%; Veterans: 10.9%; Ancestry: 26.2% Irish, 22.6% German, 17.9% English, 10.8% Italian, 6.6% Polish
Employment: 7.4% management, business, and financial, 4.5% computer, engineering, and science, 7.4% education, legal, community service, arts, and media, 3.5% healthcare practitioners, 22.3% service, 20.8% sales and office, 13.2% natural resources, construction, and maintenance, 21.0% production, transportation, and material moving
Income: Per capita: $29,412; Median household: $51,250; Average household: $71,999; Households with income of $100,000 or more: 20.3%; Poverty rate: 13.0%
Educational Attainment: High school diploma or higher: 83.9%; Bachelor's degree or higher: 16.1%; Graduate/professional degree or higher: 7.1%

School District(s)
Windsor Central SD (PK-12)
  2014-15 Enrollment: 1,769 . . . . (607) 655-8216
Housing: Homeownership rate: 72.2%; Median home value: $99,700; Median year structure built: 1961; Homeowner vacancy rate: 2.4%; Median selected monthly owner costs: $1,045 with a mortgage, $568 without a mortgage; Median gross rent: $665 per month; Rental vacancy rate: 0.0%
Health Insurance: 91.4% have insurance; 72.0% have private insurance; 40.2% have public insurance; 8.6% do not have insurance; 6.8% of children under 18 do not have insurance
Transportation: Commute: 93.6% car, 0.8% public transportation, 0.0% walk, 4.9% work from home; Mean travel time to work: 19.4 minutes
Additional Information Contacts
Town of Kirkwood . . . . (607) 775-1370
  http://www.townofkirkwood.org

LISLE (town). Covers a land area of 46.894 square miles and a water area of 0.090 square miles. Located at 42.38° N. Lat; 76.06° W. Long. Elevation is 974 feet.
Population: 2,709; Growth (since 2000): 0.1%; Density: 57.8 persons per square mile; Race: 97.8% White, 0.0% Black/African American, 0.0% Asian, 0.0% American Indian/Alaska Native, 0.0% Native Hawaiian/Other Pacific Islander, 2.1% Two or more races, 0.8% Hispanic of any race; Average household size: 2.69; Median age: 42.1; Age under 18: 23.9%; Age 65 and over: 14.3%; Males per 100 females: 94.6; Marriage status: 33.2% never married, 50.3% now married, 1.7% separated, 6.4% widowed, 10.0% divorced; Foreign born: 0.2%; Speak English only: 98.3%; With disability: 16.5%; Veterans: 6.7%; Ancestry: 15.8% English, 15.1% Irish, 12.5% American, 12.2% German, 5.8% Italian
Employment: 11.9% management, business, and financial, 3.4% computer, engineering, and science, 10.0% education, legal, community service, arts, and media, 4.2% healthcare practitioners, 19.3% service, 23.0% sales and office, 12.7% natural resources, construction, and maintenance, 15.6% production, transportation, and material moving
Income: Per capita: $23,949; Median household: $50,833; Average household: $63,106; Households with income of $100,000 or more: 16.1%; Poverty rate: 13.0%
Educational Attainment: High school diploma or higher: 89.3%; Bachelor's degree or higher: 14.1%; Graduate/professional degree or higher: 4.9%

Housing: Homeownership rate: 85.4%; Median home value: $89,300; Median year structure built: 1976; Homeowner vacancy rate: 0.0%; Median selected monthly owner costs: $1,137 with a mortgage, $548 without a mortgage; Median gross rent: $755 per month; Rental vacancy rate: 13.6%
Health Insurance: 90.6% have insurance; 65.1% have private insurance; 38.8% have public insurance; 9.4% do not have insurance; 3.2% of children under 18 do not have insurance
Transportation: Commute: 92.2% car, 0.7% public transportation, 1.1% walk, 5.7% work from home; Mean travel time to work: 25.4 minutes

LISLE (village). Covers a land area of 0.936 square miles and a water area of 0 square miles. Located at 42.35° N. Lat; 76.01° W. Long. Elevation is 974 feet.
Population: 257; Growth (since 2000): -14.9%; Density: 274.5 persons per square mile; Race: 99.2% White, 0.0% Black/African American, 0.0% Asian, 0.0% American Indian/Alaska Native, 0.0% Native Hawaiian/Other Pacific Islander, 0.8% Two or more races, 4.3% Hispanic of any race; Average household size: 2.14; Median age: 41.5; Age under 18: 21.4%; Age 65 and over: 19.5%; Males per 100 females: 93.9; Marriage status: 38.5% never married, 39.9% now married, 0.5% separated, 2.9% widowed, 18.8% divorced; Foreign born: 0.0%; Speak English only: 100.0%; With disability: 24.5%; Veterans: 8.9%; Ancestry: 19.1% Irish, 15.6% German, 12.5% English, 8.2% Polish, 7.4% Italian
Employment: 17.0% management, business, and financial, 4.5% computer, engineering, and science, 14.8% education, legal, community service, arts, and media, 3.4% healthcare practitioners, 15.9% service, 18.2% sales and office, 13.6% natural resources, construction, and maintenance, 12.5% production, transportation, and material moving
Income: Per capita: $27,144; Median household: $48,750; Average household: $55,910; Households with income of $100,000 or more: 7.5%; Poverty rate: 21.8%
Educational Attainment: High school diploma or higher: 93.0%; Bachelor's degree or higher: 12.8%; Graduate/professional degree or higher: 5.9%
Housing: Homeownership rate: 62.5%; Median home value: $93,100; Median year structure built: Before 1940; Homeowner vacancy rate: 0.0%; Median selected monthly owner costs: $1,033 with a mortgage, $475 without a mortgage; Median gross rent: $638 per month; Rental vacancy rate: 7.4%
Health Insurance: 85.2% have insurance; 42.0% have private insurance; 59.5% have public insurance; 14.8% do not have insurance; 12.7% of children under 18 do not have insurance
Transportation: Commute: 87.5% car, 4.5% public transportation, 3.4% walk, 4.5% work from home; Mean travel time to work: 26.5 minutes

MAINE (town). Covers a land area of 45.643 square miles and a water area of 0.117 square miles. Located at 42.20° N. Lat; 76.02° W. Long. Elevation is 912 feet.
Population: 5,307; Growth (since 2000): -2.8%; Density: 116.3 persons per square mile; Race: 97.6% White, 0.0% Black/African American, 1.1% Asian, 0.2% American Indian/Alaska Native, 0.0% Native Hawaiian/Other Pacific Islander, 1.1% Two or more races, 0.1% Hispanic of any race; Average household size: 2.96; Median age: 36.8; Age under 18: 24.8%; Age 65 and over: 17.9%; Males per 100 females: 98.0; Marriage status: 32.2% never married, 52.0% now married, 1.9% separated, 6.6% widowed, 9.2% divorced; Foreign born: 2.1%; Speak English only: 95.8%; With disability: 10.9%; Veterans: 8.3%; Ancestry: 22.2% Irish, 17.4% German, 13.0% Italian, 10.8% English, 7.8% Polish
Employment: 10.3% management, business, and financial, 6.0% computer, engineering, and science, 10.4% education, legal, community service, arts, and media, 10.8% healthcare practitioners, 20.1% service, 21.2% sales and office, 11.4% natural resources, construction, and maintenance, 9.8% production, transportation, and material moving
Income: Per capita: $24,651; Median household: $57,430; Average household: $71,907; Households with income of $100,000 or more: 22.2%; Poverty rate: 13.4%
Educational Attainment: High school diploma or higher: 90.0%; Bachelor's degree or higher: 25.8%; Graduate/professional degree or higher: 9.0%

School District(s)
Maine-Endwell Central SD (PK-12)
  2014-15 Enrollment: 2,474 . . . . (607) 754-1400
Housing: Homeownership rate: 84.6%; Median home value: $117,300; Median year structure built: 1962; Homeowner vacancy rate: 1.0%; Median

selected monthly owner costs: $1,264 with a mortgage, $551 without a mortgage; Median gross rent: $809 per month; Rental vacancy rate: 0.0%
Health Insurance: 94.4% have insurance; 72.1% have private insurance; 39.9% have public insurance; 5.6% do not have insurance; 0.0% of children under 18 do not have insurance
Transportation: Commute: 95.4% car, 0.0% public transportation, 1.2% walk, 3.4% work from home; Mean travel time to work: 27.6 minutes
Additional Information Contacts
Town of Maine. . . . . (607) 862-3334
    http://townofmaine.org/content

NANTICOKE (town). Covers a land area of 24.270 square miles and a water area of 0.089 square miles. Located at 42.28° N. Lat; 76.03° W. Long. Elevation is 1,089 feet.

Population: 1,454; Growth (since 2000): -18.8%; Density: 59.9 persons per square mile; Race: 97.5% White, 1.5% Black/African American, 0.0% Asian, 0.3% American Indian/Alaska Native, 0.0% Native Hawaiian/Other Pacific Islander, 0.8% Two or more races, 0.6% Hispanic of any race; Average household size: 2.64; Median age: 45.4; Age under 18: 20.8%; Age 65 and over: 17.5%; Males per 100 females: 102.2; Marriage status: 26.3% never married, 63.3% now married, 3.6% separated, 3.6% widowed, 6.9% divorced; Foreign born: 0.5%; Speak English only: 99.8%; With disability: 15.3%; Veterans: 11.3%; Ancestry: 16.7% German, 12.9% English, 12.6% Irish, 9.2% American, 7.4% Italian
Employment: 8.2% management, business, and financial, 4.5% computer, engineering, and science, 6.2% education, legal, community service, arts, and media, 4.4% healthcare practitioners, 19.3% service, 20.8% sales and office, 13.6% natural resources, construction, and maintenance, 23.0% production, transportation, and material moving
Income: Per capita: $24,349; Median household: $59,063; Average household: $62,091; Households with income of $100,000 or more: 15.0%; Poverty rate: 11.4%
Educational Attainment: High school diploma or higher: 86.9%; Bachelor's degree or higher: 12.7%; Graduate/professional degree or higher: 2.7%
Housing: Homeownership rate: 79.3%; Median home value: $109,600; Median year structure built: 1982; Homeowner vacancy rate: 2.0%; Median selected monthly owner costs: $1,131 with a mortgage, $423 without a mortgage; Median gross rent: $742 per month; Rental vacancy rate: 7.3%
Health Insurance: 95.6% have insurance; 69.5% have private insurance; 44.8% have public insurance; 4.4% do not have insurance; 3.6% of children under 18 do not have insurance
Transportation: Commute: 97.4% car, 0.9% public transportation, 0.6% walk, 1.1% work from home; Mean travel time to work: 27.9 minutes

NINEVEH (unincorporated postal area)
ZCTA: 13813
Covers a land area of 27.856 square miles and a water area of 0.665 square miles. Located at 42.16° N. Lat; 75.55° W. Long. Elevation is 965 feet.
Population: 502; Growth (since 2000): -45.2%; Density: 18.0 persons per square mile; Race: 100.0% White, 0.0% Black/African American, 0.0% Asian, 0.0% American Indian/Alaska Native, 0.0% Native Hawaiian/Other Pacific Islander, 0.0% Two or more races, 0.0% Hispanic of any race; Average household size: 1.76; Median age: 57.8; Age under 18: 6.0%; Age 65 and over: 38.2%; Males per 100 females: 105.3; Marriage status: 11.7% never married, 43.4% now married, 0.0% separated, 10.6% widowed, 34.2% divorced; Foreign born: 2.0%; Speak English only: 93.4%; With disability: 17.7%; Veterans: 20.3%; Ancestry: 30.7% German, 22.1% American, 17.5% Italian, 13.5% Irish, 12.0% English
Employment: 6.4% management, business, and financial, 0.0% computer, engineering, and science, 13.3% education, legal, community service, arts, and media, 3.0% healthcare practitioners, 4.4% service, 10.3% sales and office, 17.2% natural resources, construction, and maintenance, 45.3% production, transportation, and material moving
Income: Per capita: $29,070; Median household: $42,768; Average household: $51,421; Households with income of $100,000 or more: 11.0%; Poverty rate: 20.7%
Educational Attainment: High school diploma or higher: 76.9%; Bachelor's degree or higher: 14.3%; Graduate/professional degree or higher: 8.8%
Housing: Homeownership rate: 75.8%; Median home value: $116,000; Median year structure built: 1983; Homeowner vacancy rate: 16.8%; Median selected monthly owner costs: $1,045 with a mortgage, $457

without a mortgage; Median gross rent: n/a per month; Rental vacancy rate: 0.0%
Health Insurance: 85.3% have insurance; 64.1% have private insurance; 50.8% have public insurance; 14.7% do not have insurance; 0.0% of children under 18 do not have insurance
Transportation: Commute: 100.0% car, 0.0% public transportation, 0.0% walk, 0.0% work from home; Mean travel time to work: 24.3 minutes

PORT CRANE (unincorporated postal area)
ZCTA: 13833
Covers a land area of 35.734 square miles and a water area of 0.150 square miles. Located at 42.20° N. Lat; 75.77° W. Long. Elevation is 889 feet.
Population: 4,345; Growth (since 2000): -2.6%; Density: 121.6 persons per square mile; Race: 97.1% White, 0.0% Black/African American, 0.2% Asian, 2.3% American Indian/Alaska Native, 0.0% Native Hawaiian/Other Pacific Islander, 0.5% Two or more races, 0.0% Hispanic of any race; Average household size: 2.43; Median age: 44.8; Age under 18: 16.6%; Age 65 and over: 16.4%; Males per 100 females: 104.3; Marriage status: 26.5% never married, 55.4% now married, 1.7% separated, 6.4% widowed, 11.8% divorced; Foreign born: 1.0%; Speak English only: 99.3%; With disability: 12.0%; Veterans: 8.1%; Ancestry: 19.4% English, 19.1% German, 13.3% Irish, 8.3% Polish, 7.2% Italian
Employment: 5.5% management, business, and financial, 3.9% computer, engineering, and science, 8.5% education, legal, community service, arts, and media, 3.2% healthcare practitioners, 22.3% service, 20.8% sales and office, 12.5% natural resources, construction, and maintenance, 23.3% production, transportation, and material moving
Income: Per capita: $24,932; Median household: $47,399; Average household: $59,941; Households with income of $100,000 or more: 18.0%; Poverty rate: 16.9%
Educational Attainment: High school diploma or higher: 85.7%; Bachelor's degree or higher: 18.0%; Graduate/professional degree or higher: 5.4%
Housing: Homeownership rate: 86.8%; Median home value: $101,000; Median year structure built: 1974; Homeowner vacancy rate: 1.7%; Median selected monthly owner costs: $1,144 with a mortgage, $424 without a mortgage; Median gross rent: $672 per month; Rental vacancy rate: 0.0%
Health Insurance: 91.7% have insurance; 67.3% have private insurance; 43.1% have public insurance; 8.3% do not have insurance; 0.0% of children under 18 do not have insurance
Transportation: Commute: 97.8% car, 0.0% public transportation, 0.0% walk, 2.2% work from home; Mean travel time to work: 24.3 minutes

PORT DICKINSON (village). Covers a land area of 0.637 square miles and a water area of 0.078 square miles. Located at 42.14° N. Lat; 75.89° W. Long. Elevation is 863 feet.
Population: 1,648; Growth (since 2000): -2.9%; Density: 2,585.2 persons per square mile; Race: 94.5% White, 2.2% Black/African American, 0.4% Asian, 0.0% American Indian/Alaska Native, 0.0% Native Hawaiian/Other Pacific Islander, 2.9% Two or more races, 0.9% Hispanic of any race; Average household size: 2.26; Median age: 38.6; Age under 18: 20.0%; Age 65 and over: 12.5%; Males per 100 females: 83.8; Marriage status: 34.0% never married, 48.6% now married, 4.2% separated, 2.9% widowed, 14.5% divorced; Foreign born: 0.6%; Speak English only: 98.2%; With disability: 11.6%; Veterans: 13.2%; Ancestry: 23.7% German, 19.7% Irish, 15.2% English, 13.3% Italian, 7.1% Polish
Employment: 10.4% management, business, and financial, 6.0% computer, engineering, and science, 14.0% education, legal, community service, arts, and media, 10.2% healthcare practitioners, 18.0% service, 25.9% sales and office, 4.7% natural resources, construction, and maintenance, 10.8% production, transportation, and material moving
Income: Per capita: $26,337; Median household: $49,777; Average household: $58,497; Households with income of $100,000 or more: 14.6%; Poverty rate: 11.0%
Educational Attainment: High school diploma or higher: 96.5%; Bachelor's degree or higher: 28.0%; Graduate/professional degree or higher: 10.6%
Housing: Homeownership rate: 63.4%; Median home value: $105,500; Median year structure built: Before 1940; Homeowner vacancy rate: 0.0%; Median selected monthly owner costs: $1,166 with a mortgage, $482 without a mortgage; Median gross rent: $691 per month; Rental vacancy rate: 0.0%

Health Insurance: 95.3% have insurance; 77.9% have private insurance; 33.0% have public insurance; 4.7% do not have insurance; 1.8% of children under 18 do not have insurance
Safety: Violent crime rate: 6.3 per 10,000 population; Property crime rate: 100.4 per 10,000 population
Transportation: Commute: 92.8% car, 3.6% public transportation, 0.3% walk, 1.7% work from home; Mean travel time to work: 16.8 minutes

SANFORD (town).
Covers a land area of 90.098 square miles and a water area of 0.924 square miles. Located at 42.09° N. Lat; 75.50° W. Long. Elevation is 1,178 feet.
Population: 2,555; Growth (since 2000): 3.1%; Density: 28.4 persons per square mile; Race: 95.9% White, 0.4% Black/African American, 0.7% Asian, 0.0% American Indian/Alaska Native, 0.0% Native Hawaiian/Other Pacific Islander, 2.8% Two or more races, 1.7% Hispanic of any race; Average household size: 2.41; Median age: 46.2; Age under 18: 19.8%; Age 65 and over: 20.5%; Males per 100 females: 101.1; Marriage status: 26.5% never married, 58.3% now married, 1.1% separated, 5.9% widowed, 9.2% divorced; Foreign born: 4.7%; Speak English only: 94.7%; With disability: 17.8%; Veterans: 13.0%; Ancestry: 23.3% Irish, 22.2% German, 13.2% Italian, 12.1% English, 11.5% American
Employment: 6.4% management, business, and financial, 4.8% computer, engineering, and science, 8.6% education, legal, community service, arts, and media, 2.9% healthcare practitioners, 24.4% service, 20.9% sales and office, 16.2% natural resources, construction, and maintenance, 15.8% production, transportation, and material moving
Income: Per capita: $24,446; Median household: $44,516; Average household: $57,881; Households with income of $100,000 or more: 15.9%; Poverty rate: 14.4%
Educational Attainment: High school diploma or higher: 86.4%; Bachelor's degree or higher: 17.4%; Graduate/professional degree or higher: 7.6%
Housing: Homeownership rate: 74.1%; Median home value: $114,500; Median year structure built: 1962; Homeowner vacancy rate: 5.4%; Median selected monthly owner costs: $1,157 with a mortgage, $493 without a mortgage; Median gross rent: $676 per month; Rental vacancy rate: 4.5%
Health Insurance: 87.3% have insurance; 58.1% have private insurance; 44.7% have public insurance; 12.7% do not have insurance; 5.9% of children under 18 do not have insurance
Transportation: Commute: 84.4% car, 1.1% public transportation, 4.7% walk, 7.9% work from home; Mean travel time to work: 26.9 minutes

TRIANGLE (town).
Covers a land area of 37.875 square miles and a water area of 1.907 square miles. Located at 42.36° N. Lat; 75.93° W. Long. Elevation is 1,070 feet.
Population: 2,905; Growth (since 2000): -4.2%; Density: 76.7 persons per square mile; Race: 97.4% White, 0.4% Black/African American, 0.1% Asian, 0.0% American Indian/Alaska Native, 0.2% Native Hawaiian/Other Pacific Islander, 1.4% Two or more races, 2.1% Hispanic of any race; Average household size: 2.64; Median age: 40.7; Age under 18: 24.2%; Age 65 and over: 18.0%; Males per 100 females: 96.4; Marriage status: 23.9% never married, 59.8% now married, 2.5% separated, 5.4% widowed, 11.0% divorced; Foreign born: 1.2%; Speak English only: 96.9%; With disability: 11.9%; Veterans: 11.0%; Ancestry: 17.2% English, 11.8% German, 11.0% Irish, 8.8% American, 3.2% Italian
Employment: 10.4% management, business, and financial, 5.5% computer, engineering, and science, 8.5% education, legal, community service, arts, and media, 4.2% healthcare practitioners, 15.9% service, 28.9% sales and office, 15.2% natural resources, construction, and maintenance, 11.5% production, transportation, and material moving
Income: Per capita: $26,009; Median household: $63,581; Average household: $68,180; Households with income of $100,000 or more: 20.6%; Poverty rate: 11.1%
Educational Attainment: High school diploma or higher: 93.6%; Bachelor's degree or higher: 16.8%; Graduate/professional degree or higher: 7.7%
Housing: Homeownership rate: 81.7%; Median home value: $106,800; Median year structure built: 1974; Homeowner vacancy rate: 0.0%; Median selected monthly owner costs: $1,229 with a mortgage, $537 without a mortgage; Median gross rent: $659 per month; Rental vacancy rate: 6.9%
Health Insurance: 95.8% have insurance; 75.7% have private insurance; 38.0% have public insurance; 4.2% do not have insurance; 0.3% of children under 18 do not have insurance
Transportation: Commute: 92.1% car, 0.0% public transportation, 4.8% walk, 2.8% work from home; Mean travel time to work: 27.8 minutes

UNION (town).
Covers a land area of 35.452 square miles and a water area of 0.538 square miles. Located at 42.13° N. Lat; 76.03° W. Long. Elevation is 846 feet.
Population: 55,474; Growth (since 2000): -1.5%; Density: 1,564.8 persons per square mile; Race: 87.1% White, 4.3% Black/African American, 4.2% Asian, 0.1% American Indian/Alaska Native, 0.1% Native Hawaiian/Other Pacific Islander, 2.8% Two or more races, 3.6% Hispanic of any race; Average household size: 2.26; Median age: 41.1; Age under 18: 20.9%; Age 65 and over: 18.0%; Males per 100 females: 92.3; Marriage status: 32.7% never married, 47.6% now married, 2.5% separated, 7.5% widowed, 12.2% divorced; Foreign born: 6.8%; Speak English only: 91.0%; With disability: 14.0%; Veterans: 9.2%; Ancestry: 17.4% Irish, 16.4% Italian, 15.8% German, 10.6% English, 7.7% Polish
Employment: 10.4% management, business, and financial, 8.0% computer, engineering, and science, 12.3% education, legal, community service, arts, and media, 7.9% healthcare practitioners, 19.5% service, 26.1% sales and office, 5.9% natural resources, construction, and maintenance, 9.9% production, transportation, and material moving
Income: Per capita: $26,540; Median household: $45,958; Average household: $60,123; Households with income of $100,000 or more: 17.7%; Poverty rate: 14.5%
Educational Attainment: High school diploma or higher: 91.9%; Bachelor's degree or higher: 29.6%; Graduate/professional degree or higher: 12.5%
Housing: Homeownership rate: 59.5%; Median home value: $107,800; Median year structure built: 1954; Homeowner vacancy rate: 2.1%; Median selected monthly owner costs: $1,117 with a mortgage, $472 without a mortgage; Median gross rent: $725 per month; Rental vacancy rate: 6.8%
Health Insurance: 92.8% have insurance; 68.1% have private insurance; 40.3% have public insurance; 7.2% do not have insurance; 3.9% of children under 18 do not have insurance
Transportation: Commute: 87.1% car, 3.2% public transportation, 4.9% walk, 3.6% work from home; Mean travel time to work: 17.3 minutes
Additional Information Contacts
Town of Union . . . . (607) 786-2900
   http://www.townofunion.com

VESTAL (town).
Covers a land area of 51.742 square miles and a water area of 0.854 square miles. Located at 42.05° N. Lat; 76.02° W. Long. Elevation is 830 feet.
History: Vestal is home to Binghamton University, which employs more than 3,000 faculty and staff.
Population: 28,243; Growth (since 2000): 6.4%; Density: 545.8 persons per square mile; Race: 81.3% White, 4.3% Black/African American, 11.6% Asian, 0.2% American Indian/Alaska Native, 0.0% Native Hawaiian/Other Pacific Islander, 1.4% Two or more races, 4.7% Hispanic of any race; Average household size: 2.43; Median age: 30.5; Age under 18: 15.8%; Age 65 and over: 16.7%; Males per 100 females: 96.2; Marriage status: 44.8% never married, 43.1% now married, 0.7% separated, 5.4% widowed, 6.7% divorced; Foreign born: 9.9%; Speak English only: 84.5%; With disability: 8.5%; Veterans: 7.0%; Ancestry: 16.7% Irish, 16.3% German, 12.9% Italian, 10.4% English, 5.5% Polish
Employment: 15.9% management, business, and financial, 8.5% computer, engineering, and science, 13.9% education, legal, community service, arts, and media, 8.2% healthcare practitioners, 18.8% service, 22.1% sales and office, 6.8% natural resources, construction, and maintenance, 6.0% production, transportation, and material moving
Income: Per capita: $26,124; Median household: $61,244; Average household: $79,069; Households with income of $100,000 or more: 26.2%; Poverty rate: 10.2%
Educational Attainment: High school diploma or higher: 94.9%; Bachelor's degree or higher: 42.7%; Graduate/professional degree or higher: 22.8%
School District(s)
Vestal Central SD (KG-12)
   2014-15 Enrollment: 3,477 . . . . (607) 757-2241
Four-year College(s)
SUNY at Binghamton (Public)
   Fall 2014 Enrollment: 16,695 . . . . (607) 777-2000
   2015-16 Tuition: In-state $9,053; Out-of-state $22,173
Housing: Homeownership rate: 79.4%; Median home value: $146,900; Median year structure built: 1965; Homeowner vacancy rate: 1.8%; Median selected monthly owner costs: $1,359 with a mortgage, $555 without a mortgage; Median gross rent: $890 per month; Rental vacancy rate: 8.3%

Health Insurance: 96.4% have insurance; 86.2% have private insurance; 25.6% have public insurance; 3.6% do not have insurance; 2.9% of children under 18 do not have insurance
Safety: Violent crime rate: 7.1 per 10,000 population; Property crime rate: 214.2 per 10,000 population
Newspapers: The Reporter (weekly circulation 2,400)
Transportation: Commute: 84.0% car, 2.8% public transportation, 8.2% walk, 4.5% work from home; Mean travel time to work: 19.4 minutes
Additional Information Contacts
Town of Vestal. . . . . (607) 748-1514
   http://www.vestalny.com

WHITNEY POINT (village). Covers a land area of 1.043 square miles and a water area of 0.070 square miles. Located at 42.33° N. Lat; 75.97° W. Long. Elevation is 958 feet.
Population: 1,004; Growth (since 2000): 4.0%; Density: 963.0 persons per square mile; Race: 95.4% White, 1.1% Black/African American, 0.2% Asian, 0.0% American Indian/Alaska Native, 0.0% Native Hawaiian/Other Pacific Islander, 1.7% Two or more races, 4.2% Hispanic of any race; Average household size: 2.55; Median age: 34.8; Age under 18: 26.8%; Age 65 and over: 19.3%; Males per 100 females: 90.9; Marriage status: 28.5% never married, 50.5% now married, 2.5% separated, 7.6% widowed, 13.4% divorced; Foreign born: 0.4%; Speak English only: 94.3%; With disability: 14.0%; Veterans: 8.7%; Ancestry: 20.2% English, 9.6% Irish, 8.6% German, 4.9% American, 2.2% Dutch
Employment: 10.3% management, business, and financial, 6.6% computer, engineering, and science, 9.2% education, legal, community service, arts, and media, 8.1% healthcare practitioners, 18.4% service, 36.4% sales and office, 5.9% natural resources, construction, and maintenance, 5.0% production, transportation, and material moving
Income: Per capita: $22,646; Median household: $44,297; Average household: $57,625; Households with income of $100,000 or more: 21.6%; Poverty rate: 24.9%
Educational Attainment: High school diploma or higher: 94.3%; Bachelor's degree or higher: 20.0%; Graduate/professional degree or higher: 9.2%

School District(s)
Whitney Point Central SD (PK-12)
   2014-15 Enrollment: 1,486 . . . . (607) 692-8202
Housing: Homeownership rate: 63.9%; Median home value: $103,100; Median year structure built: Before 1940; Homeowner vacancy rate: 0.0%; Median selected monthly owner costs: $1,369 with a mortgage, $559 without a mortgage; Median gross rent: $544 per month; Rental vacancy rate: 9.6%
Health Insurance: 97.7% have insurance; 74.8% have private insurance; 41.6% have public insurance; 2.3% do not have insurance; 0.7% of children under 18 do not have insurance
Transportation: Commute: 83.6% car, 0.0% public transportation, 13.2% walk, 3.3% work from home; Mean travel time to work: 24.4 minutes

WINDSOR (town). Covers a land area of 91.743 square miles and a water area of 1.264 square miles. Located at 42.06° N. Lat; 75.67° W. Long. Elevation is 948 feet.
History: Windsor is a town in Broome County, New York. The town is on the south border of the county, east of Binghamton, and includes the village of Windsor, located on the Susquehanna River.
Population: 6,196; Growth (since 2000): -3.5%; Density: 67.5 persons per square mile; Race: 97.5% White, 1.1% Black/African American, 0.4% Asian, 0.3% American Indian/Alaska Native, 0.0% Native Hawaiian/Other Pacific Islander, 0.7% Two or more races, 0.7% Hispanic of any race; Average household size: 2.59; Median age: 44.7; Age under 18: 20.8%; Age 65 and over: 15.0%; Males per 100 females: 102.8; Marriage status: 19.9% never married, 62.2% now married, 2.6% separated, 4.6% widowed, 13.3% divorced; Foreign born: 0.8%; Speak English only: 97.1%; With disability: 14.7%; Veterans: 8.1%; Ancestry: 26.1% Irish, 23.8% German, 20.0% English, 9.2% American, 8.2% Italian
Employment: 11.5% management, business, and financial, 2.8% computer, engineering, and science, 8.1% education, legal, community service, arts, and media, 5.9% healthcare practitioners, 15.0% service, 16.2% sales and office, 16.6% natural resources, construction, and maintenance, 23.9% production, transportation, and material moving
Income: Per capita: $27,498; Median household: $60,181; Average household: $69,618; Households with income of $100,000 or more: 21.4%; Poverty rate: 7.4%

Educational Attainment: High school diploma or higher: 92.5%; Bachelor's degree or higher: 17.4%; Graduate/professional degree or higher: 6.8%

School District(s)
Windsor Central SD (PK-12)
   2014-15 Enrollment: 1,769 . . . . (607) 655-8216
Housing: Homeownership rate: 86.4%; Median home value: $105,800; Median year structure built: 1973; Homeowner vacancy rate: 0.4%; Median selected monthly owner costs: $1,148 with a mortgage, $439 without a mortgage; Median gross rent: $590 per month; Rental vacancy rate: 0.5%
Health Insurance: 91.0% have insurance; 77.7% have private insurance; 29.1% have public insurance; 9.0% do not have insurance; 6.3% of children under 18 do not have insurance
Transportation: Commute: 98.1% car, 0.0% public transportation, 0.8% walk, 1.0% work from home; Mean travel time to work: 22.3 minutes
Additional Information Contacts
Town of Windsor . . . . (607) 655-2023
   http://www.windsorny.org

WINDSOR (village). Covers a land area of 1.095 square miles and a water area of 0.072 square miles. Located at 42.08° N. Lat; 75.64° W. Long. Elevation is 948 feet.
Population: 1,030; Growth (since 2000): 14.3%; Density: 940.7 persons per square mile; Race: 98.3% White, 1.0% Black/African American, 0.2% Asian, 0.0% American Indian/Alaska Native, 0.0% Native Hawaiian/Other Pacific Islander, 0.6% Two or more races, 1.1% Hispanic of any race; Average household size: 2.70; Median age: 39.6; Age under 18: 23.8%; Age 65 and over: 14.2%; Males per 100 females: 92.4; Marriage status: 18.3% never married, 67.1% now married, 2.3% separated, 5.2% widowed, 9.5% divorced; Foreign born: 0.9%; Speak English only: 97.0%; With disability: 10.4%; Veterans: 10.1%; Ancestry: 24.5% German, 23.1% Irish, 22.0% Italian, 15.2% English, 10.6% American
Employment: 9.7% management, business, and financial, 7.4% computer, engineering, and science, 12.8% education, legal, community service, arts, and media, 4.0% healthcare practitioners, 13.7% service, 27.6% sales and office, 9.1% natural resources, construction, and maintenance, 15.8% production, transportation, and material moving
Income: Per capita: $26,354; Median household: $60,536; Average household: $69,512; Households with income of $100,000 or more: 23.3%; Poverty rate: 8.2%
Educational Attainment: High school diploma or higher: 94.6%; Bachelor's degree or higher: 22.6%; Graduate/professional degree or higher: 11.3%

School District(s)
Windsor Central SD (PK-12)
   2014-15 Enrollment: 1,769 . . . . (607) 655-8216
Housing: Homeownership rate: 75.4%; Median home value: $107,500; Median year structure built: 1946; Homeowner vacancy rate: 3.0%; Median selected monthly owner costs: $1,172 with a mortgage, $550 without a mortgage; Median gross rent: $686 per month; Rental vacancy rate: 2.0%
Health Insurance: 88.7% have insurance; 73.5% have private insurance; 28.8% have public insurance; 11.3% do not have insurance; 7.3% of children under 18 do not have insurance
Transportation: Commute: 89.9% car, 0.0% public transportation, 5.8% walk, 3.8% work from home; Mean travel time to work: 21.5 minutes

Cattaraugus County

Located in western New York; bounded on the south by Pennsylvania; crossed by the Allegheny River. Covers a land area of 1,308.350 square miles, a water area of 14.135 square miles, and is located in the Eastern Time Zone at 42.24° N. Lat., 78.68° W. Long. The county was founded in 1808. County seat is Little Valley.

Cattaraugus County is part of the Olean, NY Micropolitan Statistical Area. The entire metro area includes: Cattaraugus County, NY

Weather Station: Allegany State Park   Elevation: 1,500 feet

	Jan	Feb	Mar	Apr	May	Jun	Jul	Aug	Sep	Oct	Nov	Dec
High	30	33	42	55	67	75	78	76	69	57	46	35
Low	13	14	20	32	41	50	54	53	47	36	29	19
Precip	3.0	2.3	3.1	3.5	3.8	4.9	4.6	4.1	4.1	3.8	3.9	3.4
Snow	na	na	10.5	2.1	tr	0.0	0.0	0.0	0.0	0.1	4.3	na

High and Low temperatures in degrees Fahrenheit; Precipitation and Snow in inches

Weather Station: Franklinville										Elevation: 1,549 feet		
	Jan	Feb	Mar	Apr	May	Jun	Jul	Aug	Sep	Oct	Nov	Dec
High	30	32	40	54	66	74	78	77	70	58	46	34
Low	12	12	18	31	39	49	54	53	46	35	28	18
Precip	2.6	2.1	2.9	3.3	3.7	4.4	4.5	4.0	4.4	3.8	3.6	3.1
Snow	27.8	17.7	16.7	4.0	0.2	0.0	0.0	0.0	0.0	0.6	10.2	25.6

High and Low temperatures in degrees Fahrenheit; Precipitation and Snow in inches

Weather Station: Little Valley										Elevation: 1,625 feet		
	Jan	Feb	Mar	Apr	May	Jun	Jul	Aug	Sep	Oct	Nov	Dec
High	30	33	41	54	66	74	78	77	70	58	46	34
Low	13	14	20	32	41	50	55	54	47	37	30	19
Precip	3.2	2.5	3.1	3.6	3.6	4.4	4.5	4.0	4.5	4.3	4.3	3.8
Snow	28.2	19.8	16.7	4.5	0.3	0.0	0.0	0.0	0.0	0.8	12.9	30.3

High and Low temperatures in degrees Fahrenheit; Precipitation and Snow in inches

Population: 78,962; Growth (since 2000): -5.9%; Density: 60.4 persons per square mile; Race: 92.2% White, 1.6% Black/African American, 0.8% Asian, 2.8% American Indian/Alaska Native, 0.0% Native Hawaiian/Other Pacific Islander, 2.1% two or more races, 1.9% Hispanic of any race; Average household size: 2.41; Median age: 41.4; Age under 18: 22.9%; Age 65 and over: 16.6%; Males per 100 females: 97.9; Marriage status: 29.7% never married, 50.7% now married, 2.1% separated, 7.1% widowed, 12.5% divorced; Foreign born: 2.0%; Speak English only: 94.9%; With disability: 15.1%; Veterans: 11.6%; Ancestry: 30.5% German, 18.1% Irish, 12.9% English, 10.8% Polish, 9.0% Italian

Religion: Six largest groups: 15.4% Catholicism, 5.4% Methodist/Pietist, 2.5% Lutheran, 2.2% Holiness, 1.9% Non-denominational Protestant, 1.9% Muslim Estimate

Economy: Unemployment rate: 5.4%; Leading industries: 21.0 % retail trade; 12.9 % accommodation and food services; 12.3 % other services (except public administration); Farms: 1,038 totaling 197,257 acres; Company size: 3 employ 1,000 or more persons, 3 employ 500 to 999 persons, 18 employ 100 to 499 persons, 1,602 employ less than 100 persons; Business ownership: 1,554 women-owned, n/a Black-owned, n/a Hispanic-owned, 161 Asian-owned, 84 American Indian/Alaska Native-owned

Employment: 10.3% management, business, and financial, 2.4% computer, engineering, and science, 9.8% education, legal, community service, arts, and media, 5.1% healthcare practitioners, 20.7% service, 24.6% sales and office, 11.4% natural resources, construction, and maintenance, 15.7% production, transportation, and material moving

Income: Per capita: $22,336; Median household: $42,601; Average household: $54,628; Households with income of $100,000 or more: 12.5%; Poverty rate: 18.3%

Educational Attainment: High school diploma or higher: 87.9%; Bachelor's degree or higher: 17.8%; Graduate/professional degree or higher: 7.5%

Housing: Homeownership rate: 71.3%; Median home value: $84,600; Median year structure built: 1958; Homeowner vacancy rate: 1.9%; Median selected monthly owner costs: $1,056 with a mortgage, $465 without a mortgage; Median gross rent: $617 per month; Rental vacancy rate: 6.2%

Vital Statistics: Birth rate: 115.0 per 10,000 population; Death rate: 104.2 per 10,000 population; Age-adjusted cancer mortality rate: 174.5 deaths per 100,000 population

Health Insurance: 89.8% have insurance; 67.3% have private insurance; 39.8% have public insurance; 10.2% do not have insurance; 9.9% of children under 18 do not have insurance

Health Care: Physicians: 13.2 per 10,000 population; Dentists: 4.1 per 10,000 population; Hospital beds: 23.5 per 10,000 population; Hospital admissions: 756.9 per 10,000 population

Transportation: Commute: 89.3% car, 0.5% public transportation, 5.6% walk, 3.0% work from home; Mean travel time to work: 21.8 minutes

2016 Presidential Election: 63.8% Trump, 30.8% Clinton, 4.0% Johnson, 1.4% Stein

National and State Parks: Allegany State Park; Harry E Dobbins Memorial State Forest

Additional Information Contacts
Cattaraugus Government . . . . (716) 938-9111
   http://www.cattco.org

Cattaraugus County Communities

ALLEGANY (town). Covers a land area of 70.923 square miles and a water area of 0.658 square miles. Located at 42.09° N. Lat; 78.53° W. Long. Elevation is 1,421 feet.

History: Incorporated 1906.

Population: 7,819; Growth (since 2000): -5.0%; Density: 110.2 persons per square mile; Race: 92.1% White, 2.6% Black/African American, 2.3% Asian, 0.3% American Indian/Alaska Native, 0.0% Native Hawaiian/Other Pacific Islander, 0.9% Two or more races, 2.7% Hispanic of any race; Average household size: 2.37; Median age: 35.3; Age under 18: 14.8%; Age 65 and over: 16.6%; Males per 100 females: 90.8; Marriage status: 41.8% never married, 44.4% now married, 0.7% separated, 5.1% widowed, 8.7% divorced; Foreign born: 5.1%; Speak English only: 94.1%; With disability: 11.5%; Veterans: 9.7%; Ancestry: 29.5% German, 21.4% Irish, 15.9% Italian, 11.5% English, 9.2% Polish

Employment: 12.6% management, business, and financial, 4.7% computer, engineering, and science, 11.8% education, legal, community service, arts, and media, 6.6% healthcare practitioners, 15.3% service, 29.8% sales and office, 6.0% natural resources, construction, and maintenance, 13.2% production, transportation, and material moving

Income: Per capita: $21,786; Median household: $48,659; Average household: $61,665; Households with income of $100,000 or more: 17.6%; Poverty rate: 15.2%

Educational Attainment: High school diploma or higher: 94.3%; Bachelor's degree or higher: 27.4%; Graduate/professional degree or higher: 12.7%

School District(s)
Allegany-Limestone Central SD (PK-12)
   2014-15 Enrollment: 1,176 . . . . (716) 375-6600

Housing: Homeownership rate: 75.9%; Median home value: $97,900; Median year structure built: 1966; Homeowner vacancy rate: 2.4%; Median selected monthly owner costs: $1,220 with a mortgage, $515 without a mortgage; Median gross rent: $638 per month; Rental vacancy rate: 1.9%

Health Insurance: 94.3% have insurance; 78.7% have private insurance; 32.2% have public insurance; 5.7% do not have insurance; 0.0% of children under 18 do not have insurance

Transportation: Commute: 85.7% car, 0.6% public transportation, 10.5% walk, 2.3% work from home; Mean travel time to work: 17.0 minutes

Additional Information Contacts
Town of Allegany . . . . (716) 373-0120
   http://www.allegany.org

ALLEGANY (village). Covers a land area of 0.705 square miles and a water area of 0.007 square miles. Located at 42.09° N. Lat; 78.49° W. Long. Elevation is 1,421 feet.

Population: 1,839; Growth (since 2000): -2.3%; Density: 2,606.9 persons per square mile; Race: 93.3% White, 1.8% Black/African American, 1.5% Asian, 0.0% American Indian/Alaska Native, 0.0% Native Hawaiian/Other Pacific Islander, 2.7% Two or more races, 1.0% Hispanic of any race; Average household size: 2.56; Median age: 32.5; Age under 18: 15.9%; Age 65 and over: 13.8%; Males per 100 females: 90.8; Marriage status: 42.7% never married, 45.5% now married, 1.4% separated, 3.9% widowed, 7.9% divorced; Foreign born: 3.2%; Speak English only: 95.2%; With disability: 7.6%; Veterans: 10.2%; Ancestry: 25.2% German, 21.6% Irish, 18.8% Italian, 10.2% Polish, 10.0% English

Employment: 14.0% management, business, and financial, 4.9% computer, engineering, and science, 16.2% education, legal, community service, arts, and media, 7.1% healthcare practitioners, 13.4% service, 30.9% sales and office, 5.4% natural resources, construction, and maintenance, 8.1% production, transportation, and material moving

Income: Per capita: $26,426; Median household: $48,750; Average household: $66,506; Households with income of $100,000 or more: 22.1%; Poverty rate: 26.9%

Educational Attainment: High school diploma or higher: 98.1%; Bachelor's degree or higher: 43.6%; Graduate/professional degree or higher: 22.1%

School District(s)
Allegany-Limestone Central SD (PK-12)
   2014-15 Enrollment: 1,176 . . . . (716) 375-6600

Housing: Homeownership rate: 64.4%; Median home value: $105,200; Median year structure built: 1947; Homeowner vacancy rate: 0.9%; Median selected monthly owner costs: $1,255 with a mortgage, $550 without a mortgage; Median gross rent: $600 per month; Rental vacancy rate: 4.5%

Health Insurance: 92.8% have insurance; 76.7% have private insurance; 29.1% have public insurance; 7.2% do not have insurance; 0.0% of children under 18 do not have insurance
Safety: Violent crime rate: 0.0 per 10,000 population; Property crime rate: 39.9 per 10,000 population
Transportation: Commute: 91.1% car, 1.6% public transportation, 1.1% walk, 4.4% work from home; Mean travel time to work: 16.5 minutes
Additional Information Contacts
Village of Allegany. . . . . (716) 373-1460
http://www.allegany.org

ALLEGANY RESERVATION (reservation). Covers a land area of 36.288 square miles and a water area of 7.380 square miles. Located at 42.12° N. Lat; 78.67° W. Long.
Population: 888; Growth (since 2000): -19.2%; Density: 24.5 persons per square mile; Race: 29.5% White, 0.9% Black/African American, 0.0% Asian, 61.9% American Indian/Alaska Native, 0.0% Native Hawaiian/Other Pacific Islander, 7.7% Two or more races, 0.7% Hispanic of any race; Average household size: 2.42; Median age: 37.0; Age under 18: 27.1%; Age 65 and over: 14.1%; Males per 100 females: 92.8; Marriage status: 35.4% never married, 35.7% now married, 1.0% separated, 8.8% widowed, 20.1% divorced; Foreign born: 0.5%; Speak English only: 81.3%; With disability: 15.8%; Veterans: 8.3%; Ancestry: 14.4% German, 5.5% Irish, 3.6% Italian, 2.5% Dutch, 2.1% English
Employment: 8.0% management, business, and financial, 0.9% computer, engineering, and science, 6.2% education, legal, community service, arts, and media, 1.2% healthcare practitioners, 25.1% service, 34.2% sales and office, 11.2% natural resources, construction, and maintenance, 13.3% production, transportation, and material moving
Income: Per capita: $15,926; Median household: $30,542; Average household: $38,307; Households with income of $100,000 or more: 4.1%; Poverty rate: 27.3%
Educational Attainment: High school diploma or higher: 91.0%; Bachelor's degree or higher: 7.6%; Graduate/professional degree or higher: 3.1%
Housing: Homeownership rate: 71.1%; Median home value: $70,800; Median year structure built: 1973; Homeowner vacancy rate: 0.0%; Median selected monthly owner costs: $686 with a mortgage, $271 without a mortgage; Median gross rent: $511 per month; Rental vacancy rate: 5.0%
Health Insurance: 78.5% have insurance; 43.2% have private insurance; 47.7% have public insurance; 21.5% do not have insurance; 23.7% of children under 18 do not have insurance
Transportation: Commute: 95.8% car, 1.8% public transportation, 2.4% walk, 0.0% work from home; Mean travel time to work: 19.3 minutes

ASHFORD (town). Covers a land area of 51.737 square miles and a water area of 0.164 square miles. Located at 42.44° N. Lat; 78.65° W. Long. Elevation is 1,634 feet.
Population: 2,142; Growth (since 2000): -3.6%; Density: 41.4 persons per square mile; Race: 93.6% White, 0.0% Black/African American, 0.3% Asian, 0.6% American Indian/Alaska Native, 0.0% Native Hawaiian/Other Pacific Islander, 5.6% Two or more races, 1.3% Hispanic of any race; Average household size: 2.39; Median age: 46.2; Age under 18: 21.7%; Age 65 and over: 20.3%; Males per 100 females: 106.4; Marriage status: 27.7% never married, 56.4% now married, 1.5% separated, 3.3% widowed, 12.6% divorced; Foreign born: 3.0%; Speak English only: 99.0%; With disability: 13.2%; Veterans: 12.7%; Ancestry: 48.6% German, 21.0% Irish, 16.6% English, 9.2% Polish, 4.4% Scottish
Employment: 7.0% management, business, and financial, 3.3% computer, engineering, and science, 4.0% education, legal, community service, arts, and media, 5.1% healthcare practitioners, 31.5% service, 24.8% sales and office, 12.6% natural resources, construction, and maintenance, 11.7% production, transportation, and material moving
Income: Per capita: $24,617; Median household: $47,321; Average household: $59,011; Households with income of $100,000 or more: 17.4%; Poverty rate: 11.2%
Educational Attainment: High school diploma or higher: 91.4%; Bachelor's degree or higher: 16.2%; Graduate/professional degree or higher: 5.8%
Housing: Homeownership rate: 81.6%; Median home value: $114,700; Median year structure built: 1974; Homeowner vacancy rate: 1.5%; Median selected monthly owner costs: $1,175 with a mortgage, $646 without a mortgage; Median gross rent: $624 per month; Rental vacancy rate: 2.9%

Health Insurance: 96.4% have insurance; 78.2% have private insurance; 41.0% have public insurance; 3.6% do not have insurance; 0.0% of children under 18 do not have insurance
Transportation: Commute: 93.4% car, 1.2% public transportation, 0.5% walk, 3.6% work from home; Mean travel time to work: 33.7 minutes

CARROLLTON (town). Covers a land area of 42.299 square miles and a water area of 0.041 square miles. Located at 42.06° N. Lat; 78.64° W. Long. Elevation is 1,398 feet.
Population: 1,257; Growth (since 2000): -10.9%; Density: 29.7 persons per square mile; Race: 97.1% White, 0.3% Black/African American, 0.1% Asian, 2.1% American Indian/Alaska Native, 0.0% Native Hawaiian/Other Pacific Islander, 0.5% Two or more races, 1.5% Hispanic of any race; Average household size: 2.30; Median age: 42.6; Age under 18: 23.9%; Age 65 and over: 15.8%; Males per 100 females: 95.3; Marriage status: 22.0% never married, 55.1% now married, 4.1% separated, 10.1% widowed, 12.7% divorced; Foreign born: 1.3%; Speak English only: 98.7%; With disability: 16.1%; Veterans: 15.3%; Ancestry: 31.6% German, 24.5% Irish, 10.6% English, 9.3% Italian, 8.8% Polish
Employment: 7.0% management, business, and financial, 1.0% computer, engineering, and science, 6.9% education, legal, community service, arts, and media, 7.0% healthcare practitioners, 19.6% service, 24.6% sales and office, 15.2% natural resources, construction, and maintenance, 18.6% production, transportation, and material moving
Income: Per capita: $21,310; Median household: $39,063; Average household: $48,490; Households with income of $100,000 or more: 8.6%; Poverty rate: 14.5%
Educational Attainment: High school diploma or higher: 89.2%; Bachelor's degree or higher: 10.6%; Graduate/professional degree or higher: 3.2%
Housing: Homeownership rate: 81.1%; Median home value: $65,800; Median year structure built: 1965; Homeowner vacancy rate: 0.0%; Median selected monthly owner costs: $847 with a mortgage, $338 without a mortgage; Median gross rent: $529 per month; Rental vacancy rate: 0.0%
Health Insurance: 90.5% have insurance; 71.5% have private insurance; 34.6% have public insurance; 9.5% do not have insurance; 9.8% of children under 18 do not have insurance
Transportation: Commute: 92.8% car, 0.0% public transportation, 0.5% walk, 4.1% work from home; Mean travel time to work: 29.5 minutes

CATTARAUGUS (village). Covers a land area of 1.117 square miles and a water area of 0.002 square miles. Located at 42.33° N. Lat; 78.87° W. Long. Elevation is 1,375 feet.
History: Settled 1851 during construction of Erie Railroad; incorporated 1882.
Population: 1,035; Growth (since 2000): -3.7%; Density: 926.2 persons per square mile; Race: 97.6% White, 0.2% Black/African American, 0.0% Asian, 0.4% American Indian/Alaska Native, 0.0% Native Hawaiian/Other Pacific Islander, 1.8% Two or more races, 4.0% Hispanic of any race; Average household size: 2.23; Median age: 43.1; Age under 18: 18.2%; Age 65 and over: 18.6%; Males per 100 females: 94.2; Marriage status: 31.2% never married, 51.1% now married, 2.9% separated, 6.5% widowed, 11.2% divorced; Foreign born: 1.0%; Speak English only: 98.6%; With disability: 17.9%; Veterans: 15.3%; Ancestry: 52.3% German, 16.6% Irish, 10.3% English, 9.9% Polish, 6.6% Italian
Employment: 7.4% management, business, and financial, 0.6% computer, engineering, and science, 7.6% education, legal, community service, arts, and media, 7.0% healthcare practitioners, 31.4% service, 19.3% sales and office, 8.5% natural resources, construction, and maintenance, 18.2% production, transportation, and material moving
Income: Per capita: $22,543; Median household: $41,429; Average household: $49,918; Households with income of $100,000 or more: 10.7%; Poverty rate: 19.2%
Educational Attainment: High school diploma or higher: 90.2%; Bachelor's degree or higher: 16.2%; Graduate/professional degree or higher: 6.0%

School District(s)
Cattaraugus-Little Valley Central SD (PK-12)
    2014-15 Enrollment: 940. . . . . (716) 257-5292
Housing: Homeownership rate: 70.7%; Median home value: $69,500; Median year structure built: Before 1940; Homeowner vacancy rate: 0.0%; Median selected monthly owner costs: $1,009 with a mortgage, $487 without a mortgage; Median gross rent: $465 per month; Rental vacancy rate: 7.5%

Health Insurance: 93.1% have insurance; 67.9% have private insurance; 44.1% have public insurance; 6.9% do not have insurance; 8.0% of children under 18 do not have insurance
Transportation: Commute: 89.0% car, 0.0% public transportation, 8.4% walk, 1.9% work from home; Mean travel time to work: 26.9 minutes

CATTARAUGUS RESERVATION (reservation). Covers a land area of 5.845 square miles and a water area of 0.194 square miles. Located at 42.53° N. Lat; 79.03° W. Long.

Population: 344; Growth (since 2000): n/a; Density: 58.9 persons per square mile; Race: 2.6% White, 0.0% Black/African American, 13.7% Asian, 65.1% American Indian/Alaska Native, 0.0% Native Hawaiian/Other Pacific Islander, 18.6% Two or more races, 0.0% Hispanic of any race; Average household size: 3.66; Median age: 23.6; Age under 18: 43.3%; Age 65 and over: 11.6%; Males per 100 females: 84.7; Marriage status: 53.8% never married, 27.8% now married, 5.6% separated, 13.7% widowed, 4.7% divorced; Foreign born: 7.8%; Speak English only: 62.7%; With disability: 14.8%; Veterans: 4.6%; Ancestry: 14.5% French Canadian, 5.8% Swiss, 2.0% Greek
Employment: 0.0% management, business, and financial, 0.0% computer, engineering, and science, 14.3% education, legal, community service, arts, and media, 0.0% healthcare practitioners, 58.6% service, 12.9% sales and office, 4.3% natural resources, construction, and maintenance, 10.0% production, transportation, and material moving
Income: Per capita: $7,530; Median household: $18,500; Average household: $23,419; Households with income of $100,000 or more: n/a; Poverty rate: 54.7%
Educational Attainment: High school diploma or higher: 77.4%; Bachelor's degree or higher: 6.0%; Graduate/professional degree or higher: 6.0%
Housing: Homeownership rate: 67.0%; Median home value: $34,800; Median year structure built: 1978; Homeowner vacancy rate: 0.0%; Median selected monthly owner costs: $1,261 with a mortgage, $292 without a mortgage; Median gross rent: $963 per month; Rental vacancy rate: 0.0%
Health Insurance: 68.6% have insurance; 54.4% have private insurance; 28.5% have public insurance; 31.4% do not have insurance; 14.8% of children under 18 do not have insurance
Transportation: Commute: 85.7% car, 0.0% public transportation, 0.0% walk, 14.3% work from home; Mean travel time to work: 8.1 minutes

COLDSPRING (town). Covers a land area of 51.464 square miles and a water area of 0.554 square miles. Located at 42.06° N. Lat; 78.84° W. Long. Elevation is 1,407 feet.

Population: 647; Growth (since 2000): -13.8%; Density: 12.6 persons per square mile; Race: 96.6% White, 0.0% Black/African American, 0.0% Asian, 1.4% American Indian/Alaska Native, 0.0% Native Hawaiian/Other Pacific Islander, 2.0% Two or more races, 0.3% Hispanic of any race; Average household size: 2.39; Median age: 47.0; Age under 18: 19.8%; Age 65 and over: 18.2%; Males per 100 females: 108.5; Marriage status: 20.9% never married, 56.5% now married, 1.1% separated, 7.3% widowed, 15.2% divorced; Foreign born: 0.3%; Speak English only: 99.3%; With disability: 18.5%; Veterans: 11.9%; Ancestry: 26.4% German, 20.1% Irish, 18.4% English, 11.9% Swedish, 7.1% American
Employment: 7.3% management, business, and financial, 2.0% computer, engineering, and science, 6.0% education, legal, community service, arts, and media, 7.7% healthcare practitioners, 18.7% service, 10.3% sales and office, 19.3% natural resources, construction, and maintenance, 28.7% production, transportation, and material moving
Income: Per capita: $20,672; Median household: $39,688; Average household: $48,769; Households with income of $100,000 or more: 12.2%; Poverty rate: 16.7%
Educational Attainment: High school diploma or higher: 87.7%; Bachelor's degree or higher: 9.3%; Graduate/professional degree or higher: 4.9%
Housing: Homeownership rate: 84.9%; Median home value: $72,000; Median year structure built: 1954; Homeowner vacancy rate: 0.0%; Median selected monthly owner costs: $1,006 with a mortgage, $415 without a mortgage; Median gross rent: $590 per month; Rental vacancy rate: 0.0%
Health Insurance: 85.2% have insurance; 64.3% have private insurance; 39.3% have public insurance; 14.8% do not have insurance; 18.0% of children under 18 do not have insurance
Transportation: Commute: 90.5% car, 1.8% public transportation, 1.4% walk, 3.9% work from home; Mean travel time to work: 29.0 minutes

CONEWANGO (town). Covers a land area of 36.114 square miles and a water area of 0.022 square miles. Located at 42.23° N. Lat; 79.01° W. Long. Elevation is 1,293 feet.

Population: 1,832; Growth (since 2000): 5.8%; Density: 50.7 persons per square mile; Race: 99.8% White, 0.0% Black/African American, 0.0% Asian, 0.2% American Indian/Alaska Native, 0.0% Native Hawaiian/Other Pacific Islander, 0.0% Two or more races, 0.9% Hispanic of any race; Average household size: 3.20; Median age: 27.9; Age under 18: 37.1%; Age 65 and over: 12.2%; Males per 100 females: 100.8; Marriage status: 22.8% never married, 63.4% now married, 1.5% separated, 4.2% widowed, 9.5% divorced; Foreign born: 0.6%; Speak English only: 63.7%; With disability: 9.7%; Veterans: 5.1%; Ancestry: 22.6% German, 18.4% Pennsylvania German, 11.0% Dutch, 10.3% English, 10.0% Irish
Employment: 18.6% management, business, and financial, 1.6% computer, engineering, and science, 5.8% education, legal, community service, arts, and media, 2.4% healthcare practitioners, 17.9% service, 18.3% sales and office, 15.2% natural resources, construction, and maintenance, 20.2% production, transportation, and material moving
Income: Per capita: $14,169; Median household: $32,500; Average household: $45,006; Households with income of $100,000 or more: 6.6%; Poverty rate: 30.2%
Educational Attainment: High school diploma or higher: 67.4%; Bachelor's degree or higher: 12.0%; Graduate/professional degree or higher: 6.3%
Housing: Homeownership rate: 77.3%; Median home value: $80,900; Median year structure built: 1975; Homeowner vacancy rate: 2.6%; Median selected monthly owner costs: $954 with a mortgage, $294 without a mortgage; Median gross rent: $603 per month; Rental vacancy rate: 10.3%
Health Insurance: 55.0% have insurance; 37.3% have private insurance; 27.5% have public insurance; 45.0% do not have insurance; 61.5% of children under 18 do not have insurance
Transportation: Commute: 79.6% car, 0.0% public transportation, 5.9% walk, 10.7% work from home; Mean travel time to work: 23.5 minutes

CONEWANGO VALLEY (unincorporated postal area)
ZCTA: 14726

Covers a land area of 40.668 square miles and a water area of <.001 square miles. Located at 42.25° N. Lat; 79.02° W. Long..
Population: 2,039; Growth (since 2000): -4.9%; Density: 50.1 persons per square mile; Race: 100.0% White, 0.0% Black/African American, 0.0% Asian, 0.0% American Indian/Alaska Native, 0.0% Native Hawaiian/Other Pacific Islander, 0.0% Two or more races, 1.3% Hispanic of any race; Average household size: 3.46; Median age: 26.0; Age under 18: 38.2%; Age 65 and over: 9.0%; Males per 100 females: 103.0; Marriage status: 26.1% never married, 61.9% now married, 1.9% separated, 4.1% widowed, 8.0% divorced; Foreign born: 0.5%; Speak English only: 64.7%; With disability: 8.5%; Veterans: 3.5%; Ancestry: 24.5% Pennsylvania German, 15.9% German, 9.7% Irish, 9.1% English, 4.8% Italian
Employment: 14.8% management, business, and financial, 1.8% computer, engineering, and science, 6.0% education, legal, community service, arts, and media, 3.9% healthcare practitioners, 15.6% service, 11.4% sales and office, 19.7% natural resources, construction, and maintenance, 26.8% production, transportation, and material moving
Income: Per capita: $12,380; Median household: $34,833; Average household: $42,416; Households with income of $100,000 or more: 5.2%; Poverty rate: 34.1%
Educational Attainment: High school diploma or higher: 62.3%; Bachelor's degree or higher: 8.6%; Graduate/professional degree or higher: 1.3%
Housing: Homeownership rate: 76.4%; Median home value: $67,100; Median year structure built: 1975; Homeowner vacancy rate: 2.0%; Median selected monthly owner costs: $903 with a mortgage, $340 without a mortgage; Median gross rent: $641 per month; Rental vacancy rate: 6.7%
Health Insurance: 50.0% have insurance; 27.1% have private insurance; 27.4% have public insurance; 50.0% do not have insurance; 58.8% of children under 18 do not have insurance
Transportation: Commute: 68.1% car, 0.8% public transportation, 6.6% walk, 13.8% work from home; Mean travel time to work: 28.0 minutes

DAYTON (town). Covers a land area of 35.527 square miles and a water area of 0.618 square miles. Located at 42.38° N. Lat; 79.00° W. Long. Elevation is 1,339 feet.
Population: 2,265; Growth (since 2000): 16.5%; Density: 63.8 persons per square mile; Race: 98.4% White, 0.0% Black/African American, 0.0% Asian, 0.6% American Indian/Alaska Native, 0.0% Native Hawaiian/Other Pacific Islander, 0.6% Two or more races, 2.3% Hispanic of any race; Average household size: 2.70; Median age: 34.4; Age under 18: 26.8%; Age 65 and over: 15.1%; Males per 100 females: 102.6; Marriage status: 33.9% never married, 50.3% now married, 0.8% separated, 6.2% widowed, 9.5% divorced; Foreign born: 0.3%; Speak English only: 94.2%; With disability: 19.0%; Veterans: 9.2%; Ancestry: 32.9% German, 17.8% English, 13.9% Irish, 9.1% Polish, 7.9% Italian
Employment: 6.2% management, business, and financial, 1.2% computer, engineering, and science, 8.7% education, legal, community service, arts, and media, 5.5% healthcare practitioners, 26.9% service, 15.3% sales and office, 20.5% natural resources, construction, and maintenance, 15.8% production, transportation, and material moving
Income: Per capita: $19,592; Median household: $49,954; Average household: $54,071; Households with income of $100,000 or more: 9.3%; Poverty rate: 20.6%
Educational Attainment: High school diploma or higher: 80.6%; Bachelor's degree or higher: 8.4%; Graduate/professional degree or higher: 3.2%
Housing: Homeownership rate: 76.1%; Median home value: $81,300; Median year structure built: Before 1940; Homeowner vacancy rate: 0.5%; Median selected monthly owner costs: $1,069 with a mortgage, $513 without a mortgage; Median gross rent: $641 per month; Rental vacancy rate: 0.0%
Health Insurance: 88.1% have insurance; 65.5% have private insurance; 35.9% have public insurance; 11.9% do not have insurance; 16.9% of children under 18 do not have insurance
Transportation: Commute: 90.7% car, 0.2% public transportation, 2.6% walk, 4.8% work from home; Mean travel time to work: 26.9 minutes

DELEVAN (village). Covers a land area of 0.994 square miles and a water area of 0 square miles. Located at 42.49° N. Lat; 78.48° W. Long. Elevation is 1,424 feet.
Population: 1,076; Growth (since 2000): -1.2%; Density: 1,082.5 persons per square mile; Race: 96.8% White, 0.0% Black/African American, 0.8% Asian, 0.0% American Indian/Alaska Native, 0.0% Native Hawaiian/Other Pacific Islander, 2.3% Two or more races, 0.0% Hispanic of any race; Average household size: 2.45; Median age: 39.4; Age under 18: 24.9%; Age 65 and over: 12.1%; Males per 100 females: 98.7; Marriage status: 34.4% never married, 49.2% now married, 4.6% separated, 7.2% widowed, 9.3% divorced; Foreign born: 0.5%; Speak English only: 98.3%; With disability: 16.1%; Veterans: 8.4%; Ancestry: 38.0% German, 27.9% Irish, 14.8% Polish, 11.4% English, 7.9% Italian
Employment: 5.6% management, business, and financial, 2.0% computer, engineering, and science, 7.4% education, legal, community service, arts, and media, 2.6% healthcare practitioners, 18.3% service, 25.9% sales and office, 14.5% natural resources, construction, and maintenance, 23.7% production, transportation, and material moving
Income: Per capita: $18,133; Median household: $36,172; Average household: $43,683; Households with income of $100,000 or more: 4.8%; Poverty rate: 20.1%
Educational Attainment: High school diploma or higher: 87.9%; Bachelor's degree or higher: 10.3%; Graduate/professional degree or higher: 2.1%

School District(s)
Yorkshire-Pioneer Central SD (PK-12)
   2014-15 Enrollment: 2,585 . . . . (716) 492-9304
Housing: Homeownership rate: 55.4%; Median home value: $87,100; Median year structure built: 1956; Homeowner vacancy rate: 0.0%; Median selected monthly owner costs: $1,102 with a mortgage, $461 without a mortgage; Median gross rent: $485 per month; Rental vacancy rate: 7.6%
Health Insurance: 90.2% have insurance; 65.1% have private insurance; 38.6% have public insurance; 9.8% do not have insurance; 7.1% of children under 18 do not have insurance
Transportation: Commute: 92.0% car, 1.2% public transportation, 5.0% walk, 1.8% work from home; Mean travel time to work: 26.7 minutes

EAST OTTO (town). Covers a land area of 40.070 square miles and a water area of 0.326 square miles. Located at 42.41° N. Lat; 78.74° W. Long. Elevation is 1,427 feet.
Population: 897; Growth (since 2000): -18.8%; Density: 22.4 persons per square mile; Race: 97.9% White, 0.0% Black/African American, 0.4% Asian, 0.4% American Indian/Alaska Native, 0.0% Native Hawaiian/Other Pacific Islander, 1.1% Two or more races, 0.1% Hispanic of any race; Average household size: 2.23; Median age: 49.6; Age under 18: 15.9%; Age 65 and over: 12.2%; Males per 100 females: 113.7; Marriage status: 18.8% never married, 57.7% now married, 1.2% separated, 7.3% widowed, 16.2% divorced; Foreign born: 1.6%; Speak English only: 94.6%; With disability: 13.2%; Veterans: 7.4%; Ancestry: 39.1% German, 12.8% Irish, 9.8% Italian, 8.6% Polish, 8.2% English
Employment: 14.8% management, business, and financial, 1.2% computer, engineering, and science, 6.0% education, legal, community service, arts, and media, 4.3% healthcare practitioners, 23.1% service, 18.3% sales and office, 20.4% natural resources, construction, and maintenance, 12.0% production, transportation, and material moving
Income: Per capita: $30,546; Median household: $58,281; Average household: $68,261; Households with income of $100,000 or more: 13.6%; Poverty rate: 10.9%
Educational Attainment: High school diploma or higher: 91.1%; Bachelor's degree or higher: 14.1%; Graduate/professional degree or higher: 7.3%
Housing: Homeownership rate: 83.7%; Median home value: $94,300; Median year structure built: 1973; Homeowner vacancy rate: 0.0%; Median selected monthly owner costs: $1,170 with a mortgage, $484 without a mortgage; Median gross rent: $606 per month; Rental vacancy rate: 0.0%
Health Insurance: 89.6% have insurance; 72.4% have private insurance; 27.6% have public insurance; 10.4% do not have insurance; 21.4% of children under 18 do not have insurance
Transportation: Commute: 93.0% car, 0.4% public transportation, 1.7% walk, 4.3% work from home; Mean travel time to work: 28.8 minutes

EAST RANDOLPH (CDP). Covers a land area of 1.088 square miles and a water area of <.001 square miles. Located at 42.17° N. Lat; 78.96° W. Long. Elevation is 1,325 feet.
Population: 588; Growth (since 2000): -6.7%; Density: 540.2 persons per square mile; Race: 92.7% White, 1.0% Black/African American, 0.3% Asian, 0.2% American Indian/Alaska Native, 0.0% Native Hawaiian/Other Pacific Islander, 4.9% Two or more races, 3.6% Hispanic of any race; Average household size: 2.53; Median age: 31.7; Age under 18: 31.1%; Age 65 and over: 21.9%; Males per 100 females: 112.3; Marriage status: 30.3% never married, 51.7% now married, 0.2% separated, 5.7% widowed, 12.3% divorced; Foreign born: 0.7%; Speak English only: 97.1%; With disability: 18.5%; Veterans: 10.1%; Ancestry: 27.6% German, 22.1% Irish, 16.2% English, 6.8% Italian, 6.5% Polish
Employment: 9.6% management, business, and financial, 3.4% computer, engineering, and science, 5.8% education, legal, community service, arts, and media, 4.8% healthcare practitioners, 13.9% service, 29.3% sales and office, 13.5% natural resources, construction, and maintenance, 19.7% production, transportation, and material moving
Income: Per capita: $13,777; Median household: $22,708; Average household: $36,284; Households with income of $100,000 or more: 5.6%; Poverty rate: 37.2%
Educational Attainment: High school diploma or higher: 83.5%; Bachelor's degree or higher: 8.3%; Graduate/professional degree or higher: 5.3%
Housing: Homeownership rate: 51.9%; Median home value: $81,700; Median year structure built: 1941; Homeowner vacancy rate: 0.0%; Median selected monthly owner costs: $1,115 with a mortgage, $397 without a mortgage; Median gross rent: $577 per month; Rental vacancy rate: 5.5%
Health Insurance: 91.5% have insurance; 53.5% have private insurance; 64.6% have public insurance; 8.5% do not have insurance; 5.9% of children under 18 do not have insurance
Transportation: Commute: 84.0% car, 1.5% public transportation, 12.1% walk, 2.4% work from home; Mean travel time to work: 19.9 minutes

ELLICOTTVILLE (town). Covers a land area of 45.095 square miles and a water area of 0.093 square miles. Located at 42.31° N. Lat; 78.64° W. Long. Elevation is 1,549 feet.
History: Incorporated 1881.
Population: 1,489; Growth (since 2000): -14.3%; Density: 33.0 persons per square mile; Race: 97.9% White, 0.9% Black/African American, 0.0% Asian, 0.7% American Indian/Alaska Native, 0.0% Native Hawaiian/Other

Pacific Islander, 0.0% Two or more races, 1.5% Hispanic of any race; Average household size: 2.20; Median age: 49.2; Age under 18: 20.0%; Age 65 and over: 24.1%; Males per 100 females: 104.9; Marriage status: 21.2% never married, 63.0% now married, 4.4% separated, 6.7% widowed, 9.0% divorced; Foreign born: 4.2%; Speak English only: 95.3%; With disability: 11.9%; Veterans: 10.7%; Ancestry: 35.7% German, 22.0% Irish, 15.8% English, 14.1% Polish, 6.9% Italian

Employment: 17.7% management, business, and financial, 2.2% computer, engineering, and science, 14.3% education, legal, community service, arts, and media, 2.3% healthcare practitioners, 21.5% service, 20.6% sales and office, 15.0% natural resources, construction, and maintenance, 6.4% production, transportation, and material moving

Income: Per capita: $36,390; Median household: $61,250; Average household: $79,712; Households with income of $100,000 or more: 27.3%; Poverty rate: 6.6%

Educational Attainment: High school diploma or higher: 93.0%; Bachelor's degree or higher: 32.4%; Graduate/professional degree or higher: 13.7%

School District(s)

Ellicottville Central SD (PK-12)

    2014-15 Enrollment: 588 . . . . (716) 699-2368

Housing: Homeownership rate: 79.7%; Median home value: $190,100; Median year structure built: 1984; Homeowner vacancy rate: 6.5%; Median selected monthly owner costs: $1,480 with a mortgage, $555 without a mortgage; Median gross rent: $632 per month; Rental vacancy rate: 7.6%

Health Insurance: 92.6% have insurance; 82.4% have private insurance; 32.8% have public insurance; 7.4% do not have insurance; 0.0% of children under 18 do not have insurance

Safety: Violent crime rate: 0.0 per 10,000 population; Property crime rate: 56.0 per 10,000 population

Transportation: Commute: 90.6% car, 0.0% public transportation, 5.7% walk, 1.9% work from home; Mean travel time to work: 26.9 minutes

ELLICOTTVILLE (village). Covers a land area of 0.820 square miles and a water area of 0.014 square miles. Located at 42.27° N. Lat; 78.67° W. Long. Elevation is 1,549 feet.

Population: 273; Growth (since 2000): -42.2%; Density: 332.7 persons per square mile; Race: 100.0% White, 0.0% Black/African American, 0.0% Asian, 0.0% American Indian/Alaska Native, 0.0% Native Hawaiian/Other Pacific Islander, 0.0% Two or more races, 0.0% Hispanic of any race; Average household size: 1.69; Median age: 59.1; Age under 18: 8.8%; Age 65 and over: 33.7%; Males per 100 females: 106.6; Marriage status: 26.7% never married, 53.7% now married, 0.0% separated, 12.9% widowed, 6.7% divorced; Foreign born: 11.4%; Speak English only: 87.3%; With disability: 18.7%; Veterans: 12.0%; Ancestry: 31.1% German, 22.3% Irish, 17.2% English, 16.1% Polish, 7.3% French

Employment: 28.1% management, business, and financial, 2.7% computer, engineering, and science, 17.8% education, legal, community service, arts, and media, 1.4% healthcare practitioners, 16.4% service, 21.9% sales and office, 7.5% natural resources, construction, and maintenance, 4.1% production, transportation, and material moving

Income: Per capita: $43,873; Median household: $38,125; Average household: $72,616; Households with income of $100,000 or more: 14.2%; Poverty rate: 2.2%

Educational Attainment: High school diploma or higher: 95.9%; Bachelor's degree or higher: 33.1%; Graduate/professional degree or higher: 13.2%

School District(s)

Ellicottville Central SD (PK-12)

    2014-15 Enrollment: 588 . . . . (716) 699-2368

Housing: Homeownership rate: 76.5%; Median home value: $219,000; Median year structure built: Before 1940; Homeowner vacancy rate: 1.6%; Median selected monthly owner costs: $1,554 with a mortgage, $472 without a mortgage; Median gross rent: $703 per month; Rental vacancy rate: 0.0%

Health Insurance: 89.7% have insurance; 78.4% have private insurance; 39.6% have public insurance; 10.3% do not have insurance; 0.0% of children under 18 do not have insurance

Transportation: Commute: 88.9% car, 0.0% public transportation, 8.3% walk, 2.8% work from home; Mean travel time to work: 19.1 minutes

FARMERSVILLE (town). Covers a land area of 47.833 square miles and a water area of 0.138 square miles. Located at 42.38° N. Lat; 78.41° W. Long. Elevation is 1,837 feet.

Population: 1,012; Growth (since 2000): -1.6%; Density: 21.2 persons per square mile; Race: 100.0% White, 0.0% Black/African American, 0.0% Asian, 0.0% American Indian/Alaska Native, 0.0% Native Hawaiian/Other Pacific Islander, 0.0% Two or more races, 2.1% Hispanic of any race; Average household size: 2.24; Median age: 50.3; Age under 18: 18.0%; Age 65 and over: 20.8%; Males per 100 females: 97.5; Marriage status: 18.2% never married, 63.5% now married, 3.0% separated, 7.0% widowed, 11.3% divorced; Foreign born: 0.9%; Speak English only: 95.3%; With disability: 14.6%; Veterans: 10.8%; Ancestry: 32.8% German, 17.1% English, 11.8% Irish, 8.9% Polish, 8.1% Italian

Employment: 11.1% management, business, and financial, 0.9% computer, engineering, and science, 5.9% education, legal, community service, arts, and media, 9.3% healthcare practitioners, 22.9% service, 15.9% sales and office, 13.6% natural resources, construction, and maintenance, 20.4% production, transportation, and material moving

Income: Per capita: $21,815; Median household: $40,125; Average household: $49,518; Households with income of $100,000 or more: 10.7%; Poverty rate: 12.8%

Educational Attainment: High school diploma or higher: 82.9%; Bachelor's degree or higher: 11.7%; Graduate/professional degree or higher: 3.5%

Housing: Homeownership rate: 89.8%; Median home value: $88,100; Median year structure built: 1980; Homeowner vacancy rate: 0.0%; Median selected monthly owner costs: $1,225 with a mortgage, $490 without a mortgage; Median gross rent: $568 per month; Rental vacancy rate: 0.0%

Health Insurance: 84.4% have insurance; 60.9% have private insurance; 42.4% have public insurance; 15.6% do not have insurance; 33.5% of children under 18 do not have insurance

Transportation: Commute: 90.3% car, 0.0% public transportation, 4.1% walk, 3.7% work from home; Mean travel time to work: 35.0 minutes

FRANKLINVILLE (town). Covers a land area of 51.812 square miles and a water area of 0.173 square miles. Located at 42.30° N. Lat; 78.50° W. Long. Elevation is 1,591 feet.

History: Settled 1806, incorporated 1874.

Population: 2,930; Growth (since 2000): -6.3%; Density: 56.6 persons per square mile; Race: 95.6% White, 1.1% Black/African American, 0.9% Asian, 0.4% American Indian/Alaska Native, 0.0% Native Hawaiian/Other Pacific Islander, 1.7% Two or more races, 2.8% Hispanic of any race; Average household size: 2.45; Median age: 38.0; Age under 18: 24.9%; Age 65 and over: 15.3%; Males per 100 females: 98.9; Marriage status: 24.5% never married, 51.0% now married, 1.0% separated, 10.8% widowed, 13.7% divorced; Foreign born: 2.3%; Speak English only: 96.0%; With disability: 16.7%; Veterans: 12.9%; Ancestry: 34.0% German, 16.8% Polish, 14.3% Irish, 13.0% English, 7.4% American

Employment: 10.9% management, business, and financial, 1.7% computer, engineering, and science, 11.8% education, legal, community service, arts, and media, 4.4% healthcare practitioners, 20.0% service, 24.6% sales and office, 12.2% natural resources, construction, and maintenance, 14.4% production, transportation, and material moving

Income: Per capita: $20,827; Median household: $44,412; Average household: $51,119; Households with income of $100,000 or more: 10.6%; Poverty rate: 18.4%

Educational Attainment: High school diploma or higher: 91.2%; Bachelor's degree or higher: 16.9%; Graduate/professional degree or higher: 6.6%

School District(s)

Franklinville Central SD (PK-12)

    2014-15 Enrollment: 736 . . . . (716) 676-8029

Housing: Homeownership rate: 71.4%; Median home value: $70,200; Median year structure built: Before 1940; Homeowner vacancy rate: 3.9%; Median selected monthly owner costs: $961 with a mortgage, $503 without a mortgage; Median gross rent: $665 per month; Rental vacancy rate: 5.6%

Health Insurance: 87.8% have insurance; 60.9% have private insurance; 42.2% have public insurance; 12.2% do not have insurance; 5.5% of children under 18 do not have insurance

Transportation: Commute: 86.4% car, 0.3% public transportation, 9.9% walk, 3.0% work from home; Mean travel time to work: 24.5 minutes

Additional Information Contacts

Town of Franklinville . . . . (716) 676-3077

    http://www.franklinvilleny.org

FRANKLINVILLE (village). Covers a land area of 1.100 square miles and a water area of 0 square miles. Located at 42.33° N. Lat; 78.45° W. Long. Elevation is 1,591 feet.
Population: 1,850; Growth (since 2000): -0.3%; Density: 1,681.8 persons per square mile; Race: 93.0% White, 1.7% Black/African American, 1.4% Asian, 0.6% American Indian/Alaska Native, 0.0% Native Hawaiian/Other Pacific Islander, 2.6% Two or more races, 3.9% Hispanic of any race; Average household size: 2.57; Median age: 33.9; Age under 18: 29.9%; Age 65 and over: 12.6%; Males per 100 females: 95.5; Marriage status: 27.7% never married, 49.5% now married, 1.7% separated, 10.3% widowed, 12.5% divorced; Foreign born: 3.7%; Speak English only: 95.9%; With disability: 15.1%; Veterans: 13.0%; Ancestry: 35.1% German, 16.4% Irish, 15.1% English, 14.9% Polish, 4.8% French
Employment: 8.9% management, business, and financial, 2.9% computer, engineering, and science, 10.1% education, legal, community service, arts, and media, 7.6% healthcare practitioners, 22.7% service, 24.8% sales and office, 10.5% natural resources, construction, and maintenance, 12.4% production, transportation, and material moving
Income: Per capita: $18,661; Median household: $36,726; Average household: $47,842; Households with income of $100,000 or more: 12.7%; Poverty rate: 24.2%
Educational Attainment: High school diploma or higher: 89.7%; Bachelor's degree or higher: 15.8%; Graduate/professional degree or higher: 5.4%
School District(s)
Franklinville Central SD (PK-12)
    2014-15 Enrollment: 736 . . . . (716) 676-8029
Housing: Homeownership rate: 61.1%; Median home value: $64,300; Median year structure built: Before 1940; Homeowner vacancy rate: 7.3%; Median selected monthly owner costs: $888 with a mortgage, $484 without a mortgage; Median gross rent: $619 per month; Rental vacancy rate: 6.8%
Health Insurance: 89.8% have insurance; 59.5% have private insurance; 47.1% have public insurance; 10.2% do not have insurance; 3.6% of children under 18 do not have insurance
Transportation: Commute: 87.0% car, 0.5% public transportation, 6.8% walk, 4.9% work from home; Mean travel time to work: 26.0 minutes
Additional Information Contacts
Village of Franklinville . . . . (716) 676-3010
    http://www.franklinvilleny.org

FREEDOM (town). Covers a land area of 40.987 square miles and a water area of 0.329 square miles. Located at 42.47° N. Lat; 78.38° W. Long. Elevation is 1,801 feet.
Population: 2,251; Growth (since 2000): -9.7%; Density: 54.9 persons per square mile; Race: 98.3% White, 1.6% Black/African American, 0.0% Asian, 0.0% American Indian/Alaska Native, 0.0% Native Hawaiian/Other Pacific Islander, 0.0% Two or more races, 0.1% Hispanic of any race; Average household size: 2.50; Median age: 43.6; Age under 18: 22.3%; Age 65 and over: 16.1%; Males per 100 females: 106.1; Marriage status: 18.6% never married, 64.8% now married, 1.7% separated, 7.8% widowed, 8.8% divorced; Foreign born: 1.7%; Speak English only: 97.6%; With disability: 14.8%; Veterans: 12.9%; Ancestry: 33.9% German, 16.3% Irish, 15.5% English, 14.6% Polish, 6.4% American
Employment: 7.1% management, business, and financial, 1.1% computer, engineering, and science, 5.9% education, legal, community service, arts, and media, 3.0% healthcare practitioners, 19.9% service, 20.0% sales and office, 14.6% natural resources, construction, and maintenance, 28.5% production, transportation, and material moving
Income: Per capita: $21,045; Median household: $43,850; Average household: $52,012; Households with income of $100,000 or more: 14.3%; Poverty rate: 13.1%
Educational Attainment: High school diploma or higher: 83.4%; Bachelor's degree or higher: 9.5%; Graduate/professional degree or higher: 3.0%
Housing: Homeownership rate: 88.2%; Median home value: $111,400; Median year structure built: 1978; Homeowner vacancy rate: 1.8%; Median selected monthly owner costs: $1,123 with a mortgage, $438 without a mortgage; Median gross rent: $578 per month; Rental vacancy rate: 0.0%
Health Insurance: 92.9% have insurance; 67.1% have private insurance; 38.3% have public insurance; 7.1% do not have insurance; 1.6% of children under 18 do not have insurance
Transportation: Commute: 90.3% car, 1.3% public transportation, 4.7% walk, 2.2% work from home; Mean travel time to work: 25.1 minutes

GOWANDA (village). Covers a land area of 1.593 square miles and a water area of 0.016 square miles. Located at 42.46° N. Lat; 78.93° W. Long. Elevation is 761 feet.
Population: 2,656; Growth (since 2000): -6.5%; Density: 1,667.1 persons per square mile; Race: 88.4% White, 0.9% Black/African American, 2.6% Asian, 3.3% American Indian/Alaska Native, 0.0% Native Hawaiian/Other Pacific Islander, 4.8% Two or more races, 0.0% Hispanic of any race; Average household size: 2.20; Median age: 41.3; Age under 18: 22.2%; Age 65 and over: 19.2%; Males per 100 females: 91.7; Marriage status: 36.1% never married, 38.6% now married, 3.8% separated, 8.8% widowed, 16.5% divorced; Foreign born: 2.4%; Speak English only: 95.4%; With disability: 19.0%; Veterans: 7.7%; Ancestry: 40.1% German, 18.9% Irish, 11.9% Polish, 11.0% English, 9.6% Italian
Employment: 11.2% management, business, and financial, 2.5% computer, engineering, and science, 12.8% education, legal, community service, arts, and media, 6.1% healthcare practitioners, 30.3% service, 10.3% sales and office, 9.2% natural resources, construction, and maintenance, 17.7% production, transportation, and material moving
Income: Per capita: $23,873; Median household: $40,386; Average household: $53,594; Households with income of $100,000 or more: 8.9%; Poverty rate: 21.0%
Educational Attainment: High school diploma or higher: 83.2%; Bachelor's degree or higher: 16.3%; Graduate/professional degree or higher: 7.7%
School District(s)
Gowanda Central SD (PK-12)
    2014-15 Enrollment: 1,200 . . . . (716) 532-3325
Housing: Homeownership rate: 58.3%; Median home value: $74,500; Median year structure built: Before 1940; Homeowner vacancy rate: 2.5%; Median selected monthly owner costs: $908 with a mortgage, $398 without a mortgage; Median gross rent: $640 per month; Rental vacancy rate: 5.0%
Health Insurance: 87.5% have insurance; 67.6% have private insurance; 36.3% have public insurance; 12.5% do not have insurance; 7.5% of children under 18 do not have insurance
Hospitals: TLC Health Network (65 beds)
Safety: Violent crime rate: 22.8 per 10,000 population; Property crime rate: 235.4 per 10,000 population
Transportation: Commute: 88.1% car, 1.2% public transportation, 6.8% walk, 2.3% work from home; Mean travel time to work: 27.1 minutes

GREAT VALLEY (town). Covers a land area of 49.635 square miles and a water area of 0.036 square miles. Located at 42.20° N. Lat; 78.64° W. Long. Elevation is 1,460 feet.
Population: 2,262; Growth (since 2000): 5.5%; Density: 45.6 persons per square mile; Race: 98.2% White, 0.4% Black/African American, 0.0% Asian, 1.2% American Indian/Alaska Native, 0.0% Native Hawaiian/Other Pacific Islander, 0.2% Two or more races, 0.4% Hispanic of any race; Average household size: 2.42; Median age: 44.7; Age under 18: 22.5%; Age 65 and over: 19.1%; Males per 100 females: 97.6; Marriage status: 27.2% never married, 54.8% now married, 3.1% separated, 6.3% widowed, 11.7% divorced; Foreign born: 0.8%; Speak English only: 96.7%; With disability: 15.8%; Veterans: 14.9%; Ancestry: 24.5% German, 22.8% Irish, 17.0% Polish, 14.9% English, 7.9% Italian
Employment: 7.7% management, business, and financial, 3.8% computer, engineering, and science, 16.9% education, legal, community service, arts, and media, 2.8% healthcare practitioners, 24.7% service, 21.8% sales and office, 16.9% natural resources, construction, and maintenance, 5.4% production, transportation, and material moving
Income: Per capita: $23,976; Median household: $48,719; Average household: $57,089; Households with income of $100,000 or more: 15.2%; Poverty rate: 15.9%
Educational Attainment: High school diploma or higher: 85.5%; Bachelor's degree or higher: 18.8%; Graduate/professional degree or higher: 7.9%
Housing: Homeownership rate: 81.5%; Median home value: $118,300; Median year structure built: 1980; Homeowner vacancy rate: 1.6%; Median selected monthly owner costs: $1,190 with a mortgage, $512 without a mortgage; Median gross rent: $590 per month; Rental vacancy rate: 13.6%
Health Insurance: 90.2% have insurance; 67.6% have private insurance; 39.6% have public insurance; 9.8% do not have insurance; 0.0% of children under 18 do not have insurance
Transportation: Commute: 91.7% car, 0.0% public transportation, 2.7% walk, 5.1% work from home; Mean travel time to work: 24.1 minutes

HINSDALE (town). Covers a land area of 38.731 square miles and a water area of 0.042 square miles. Located at 42.17° N. Lat; 78.37° W. Long. Elevation is 1,480 feet.

Population: 2,101; Growth (since 2000): -7.4%; Density: 54.2 persons per square mile; Race: 94.8% White, 3.0% Black/African American, 0.0% Asian, 0.0% American Indian/Alaska Native, 0.0% Native Hawaiian/Other Pacific Islander, 1.5% Two or more races, 0.3% Hispanic of any race; Average household size: 2.43; Median age: 41.1; Age under 18: 25.5%; Age 65 and over: 17.8%; Males per 100 females: 98.2; Marriage status: 23.7% never married, 56.8% now married, 2.3% separated, 11.9% widowed, 7.6% divorced; Foreign born: 2.3%; Speak English only: 99.3%; With disability: 19.3%; Veterans: 12.1%; Ancestry: 31.8% German, 15.1% English, 14.9% Irish, 13.9% Italian, 12.8% Polish

Employment: 6.5% management, business, and financial, 1.8% computer, engineering, and science, 12.1% education, legal, community service, arts, and media, 5.0% healthcare practitioners, 17.1% service, 23.1% sales and office, 12.5% natural resources, construction, and maintenance, 22.0% production, transportation, and material moving

Income: Per capita: $19,512; Median household: $40,125; Average household: $47,125; Households with income of $100,000 or more: 6.4%; Poverty rate: 17.4%

Educational Attainment: High school diploma or higher: 85.0%; Bachelor's degree or higher: 14.5%; Graduate/professional degree or higher: 6.5%

School District(s)

Hinsdale Central SD (PK-12)

    2014-15 Enrollment: 466 . . . . (716) 557-2227

Housing: Homeownership rate: 84.5%; Median home value: $73,400; Median year structure built: 1977; Homeowner vacancy rate: 1.7%; Median selected monthly owner costs: $1,088 with a mortgage, $426 without a mortgage; Median gross rent: $720 per month; Rental vacancy rate: 0.0%

Health Insurance: 92.1% have insurance; 66.3% have private insurance; 45.6% have public insurance; 7.9% do not have insurance; 2.4% of children under 18 do not have insurance

Transportation: Commute: 94.3% car, 0.1% public transportation, 1.1% walk, 2.1% work from home; Mean travel time to work: 20.7 minutes

HUMPHREY (town). Covers a land area of 37.136 square miles and a water area of 0.017 square miles. Located at 42.23° N. Lat; 78.50° W. Long. Elevation is 1,617 feet.

Population: 784; Growth (since 2000): 8.7%; Density: 21.1 persons per square mile; Race: 98.0% White, 0.0% Black/African American, 0.0% Asian, 1.5% American Indian/Alaska Native, 0.0% Native Hawaiian/Other Pacific Islander, 0.5% Two or more races, 0.4% Hispanic of any race; Average household size: 2.68; Median age: 38.9; Age under 18: 25.0%; Age 65 and over: 11.5%; Males per 100 females: 113.4; Marriage status: 23.8% never married, 58.9% now married, 2.1% separated, 5.3% widowed, 12.0% divorced; Foreign born: 0.8%; Speak English only: 100.0%; With disability: 14.7%; Veterans: 9.7%; Ancestry: 29.0% Irish, 28.1% German, 8.7% American, 6.9% Polish, 6.3% English

Employment: 20.1% management, business, and financial, 2.8% computer, engineering, and science, 13.8% education, legal, community service, arts, and media, 1.9% healthcare practitioners, 12.4% service, 19.6% sales and office, 13.8% natural resources, construction, and maintenance, 15.7% production, transportation, and material moving

Income: Per capita: $24,569; Median household: $58,750; Average household: $66,572; Households with income of $100,000 or more: 18.5%; Poverty rate: 18.5%

Educational Attainment: High school diploma or higher: 78.1%; Bachelor's degree or higher: 16.4%; Graduate/professional degree or higher: 7.3%

Housing: Homeownership rate: 87.0%; Median home value: $101,700; Median year structure built: 1984; Homeowner vacancy rate: 0.0%; Median selected monthly owner costs: $1,182 with a mortgage, $400 without a mortgage; Median gross rent: $708 per month; Rental vacancy rate: 0.0%

Health Insurance: 90.7% have insurance; 72.6% have private insurance; 34.8% have public insurance; 9.3% do not have insurance; 0.0% of children under 18 do not have insurance

Transportation: Commute: 87.4% car, 0.6% public transportation, 3.4% walk, 8.1% work from home; Mean travel time to work: 29.7 minutes

ISCHUA (town). Covers a land area of 32.377 square miles and a water area of 0.021 square miles. Located at 42.24° N. Lat; 78.38° W. Long. Elevation is 1,542 feet.

Population: 866; Growth (since 2000): -3.2%; Density: 26.7 persons per square mile; Race: 99.3% White, 0.0% Black/African American, 0.0% Asian, 0.0% American Indian/Alaska Native, 0.0% Native Hawaiian/Other Pacific Islander, 0.7% Two or more races, 0.6% Hispanic of any race; Average household size: 2.48; Median age: 46.4; Age under 18: 22.1%; Age 65 and over: 18.2%; Males per 100 females: 116.4; Marriage status: 19.0% never married, 62.2% now married, 2.2% separated, 5.1% widowed, 13.7% divorced; Foreign born: 1.5%; Speak English only: 91.7%; With disability: 14.7%; Veterans: 13.5%; Ancestry: 30.9% German, 15.7% English, 11.8% Irish, 10.0% American, 8.1% Polish

Employment: 11.3% management, business, and financial, 4.8% computer, engineering, and science, 7.4% education, legal, community service, arts, and media, 5.7% healthcare practitioners, 15.0% service, 28.0% sales and office, 9.9% natural resources, construction, and maintenance, 17.8% production, transportation, and material moving

Income: Per capita: $24,000; Median household: $49,659; Average household: $59,313; Households with income of $100,000 or more: 12.6%; Poverty rate: 14.9%

Educational Attainment: High school diploma or higher: 80.7%; Bachelor's degree or higher: 18.7%; Graduate/professional degree or higher: 6.2%

Housing: Homeownership rate: 86.5%; Median home value: $81,200; Median year structure built: 1970; Homeowner vacancy rate: 0.0%; Median selected monthly owner costs: $1,269 with a mortgage, $469 without a mortgage; Median gross rent: $634 per month; Rental vacancy rate: 0.0%

Health Insurance: 90.1% have insurance; 69.2% have private insurance; 34.5% have public insurance; 9.9% do not have insurance; 22.5% of children under 18 do not have insurance

Transportation: Commute: 94.8% car, 0.0% public transportation, 0.0% walk, 5.2% work from home; Mean travel time to work: 26.8 minutes

KILL BUCK (unincorporated postal area)
ZCTA: 14748

Covers a land area of 17.902 square miles and a water area of 0.376 square miles. Located at 42.16° N. Lat; 78.64° W. Long. Elevation is 1,407 feet.

Population: 822; Growth (since 2000): 24.5%; Density: 45.9 persons per square mile; Race: 72.3% White, 0.0% Black/African American, 0.1% Asian, 19.8% American Indian/Alaska Native, 0.0% Native Hawaiian/Other Pacific Islander, 7.8% Two or more races, 0.7% Hispanic of any race; Average household size: 2.54; Median age: 32.6; Age under 18: 27.3%; Age 65 and over: 17.0%; Males per 100 females: 95.8; Marriage status: 34.7% never married, 44.1% now married, 3.2% separated, 5.0% widowed, 16.3% divorced; Foreign born: 0.1%; Speak English only: 94.0%; With disability: 18.2%; Veterans: 15.1%; Ancestry: 31.8% German, 16.2% Irish, 12.9% Polish, 11.7% Italian, 8.6% Greek

Employment: 5.4% management, business, and financial, 0.9% computer, engineering, and science, 4.7% education, legal, community service, arts, and media, 0.0% healthcare practitioners, 25.9% service, 29.0% sales and office, 25.2% natural resources, construction, and maintenance, 8.8% production, transportation, and material moving

Income: Per capita: $18,038; Median household: $35,417; Average household: $45,143; Households with income of $100,000 or more: 8.4%; Poverty rate: 30.3%

Educational Attainment: High school diploma or higher: 79.2%; Bachelor's degree or higher: 9.0%; Graduate/professional degree or higher: 4.6%

Housing: Homeownership rate: 65.1%; Median home value: $81,800; Median year structure built: 1971; Homeowner vacancy rate: 0.0%; Median selected monthly owner costs: $1,039 with a mortgage, $419 without a mortgage; Median gross rent: $535 per month; Rental vacancy rate: 5.0%

Health Insurance: 87.3% have insurance; 55.4% have private insurance; 48.8% have public insurance; 12.7% do not have insurance; 4.5% of children under 18 do not have insurance

Transportation: Commute: 85.9% car, 1.9% public transportation, 5.8% walk, 6.4% work from home; Mean travel time to work: 19.0 minutes

LEON (town). Covers a land area of 36.182 square miles and a water area of 0.027 square miles. Located at 42.30° N. Lat; 79.00° W. Long. Elevation is 1,375 feet.
Population: 1,227; Growth (since 2000): -11.1%; Density: 33.9 persons per square mile; Race: 97.1% White, 0.3% Black/African American, 0.0% Asian, 0.0% American Indian/Alaska Native, 0.0% Native Hawaiian/Other Pacific Islander, 2.6% Two or more races, 0.3% Hispanic of any race; Average household size: 3.31; Median age: 25.8; Age under 18: 37.7%; Age 65 and over: 8.6%; Males per 100 females: 103.1; Marriage status: 26.0% never married, 61.3% now married, 3.6% separated, 3.3% widowed, 9.4% divorced; Foreign born: 0.3%; Speak English only: 76.3%; With disability: 10.5%; Veterans: 5.0%; Ancestry: 21.1% German, 17.2% Pennsylvania German, 13.8% Irish, 11.6% English, 7.5% French
Employment: 9.1% management, business, and financial, 2.6% computer, engineering, and science, 6.0% education, legal, community service, arts, and media, 4.0% healthcare practitioners, 17.7% service, 16.0% sales and office, 28.4% natural resources, construction, and maintenance, 16.3% production, transportation, and material moving
Income: Per capita: $16,720; Median household: $36,058; Average household: $55,415; Households with income of $100,000 or more: 5.6%; Poverty rate: 30.9%
Educational Attainment: High school diploma or higher: 69.5%; Bachelor's degree or higher: 11.0%; Graduate/professional degree or higher: 1.9%
Housing: Homeownership rate: 69.0%; Median home value: $74,100; Median year structure built: 1976; Homeowner vacancy rate: 0.0%; Median selected monthly owner costs: $896 with a mortgage, $517 without a mortgage; Median gross rent: $656 per month; Rental vacancy rate: 11.5%
Health Insurance: 61.7% have insurance; 38.5% have private insurance; 31.4% have public insurance; 38.3% do not have insurance; 42.9% of children under 18 do not have insurance
Transportation: Commute: 68.2% car, 1.2% public transportation, 5.2% walk, 11.9% work from home; Mean travel time to work: 29.4 minutes

LIME LAKE (CDP). Covers a land area of 2.378 square miles and a water area of 0.266 square miles. Located at 42.43° N. Lat; 78.48° W. Long. Elevation is 1,660 feet.
Population: 661; Growth (since 2000): n/a; Density: 278.0 persons per square mile; Race: 98.6% White, 0.8% Black/African American, 0.0% Asian, 0.0% American Indian/Alaska Native, 0.0% Native Hawaiian/Other Pacific Islander, 0.6% Two or more races, 0.0% Hispanic of any race; Average household size: 2.28; Median age: 54.5; Age under 18: 21.2%; Age 65 and over: 34.8%; Males per 100 females: 91.8; Marriage status: 21.2% never married, 46.1% now married, 0.0% separated, 20.6% widowed, 12.1% divorced; Foreign born: 0.0%; Speak English only: 99.4%; With disability: 18.5%; Veterans: 11.3%; Ancestry: 23.9% German, 15.3% Polish, 12.4% English, 9.5% Irish, 6.4% Italian
Employment: 16.3% management, business, and financial, 0.0% computer, engineering, and science, 3.8% education, legal, community service, arts, and media, 20.6% healthcare practitioners, 12.0% service, 20.1% sales and office, 14.4% natural resources, construction, and maintenance, 12.9% production, transportation, and material moving
Income: Per capita: $21,489; Median household: $44,500; Average household: $51,875; Households with income of $100,000 or more: 9.7%; Poverty rate: 16.8%
Educational Attainment: High school diploma or higher: 86.4%; Bachelor's degree or higher: 12.0%; Graduate/professional degree or higher: 4.0%
Housing: Homeownership rate: 74.6%; Median home value: $118,800; Median year structure built: 1960; Homeowner vacancy rate: 0.0%; Median selected monthly owner costs: $1,104 with a mortgage, $393 without a mortgage; Median gross rent: $725 per month; Rental vacancy rate: 18.9%
Health Insurance: 98.3% have insurance; 58.9% have private insurance; 61.8% have public insurance; 1.7% do not have insurance; 0.0% of children under 18 do not have insurance
Transportation: Commute: 87.8% car, 0.0% public transportation, 10.2% walk, 2.0% work from home; Mean travel time to work: 30.8 minutes

LIMESTONE (CDP). Covers a land area of 1.623 square miles and a water area of 0.010 square miles. Located at 42.02° N. Lat; 78.63° W. Long. Elevation is 1,407 feet.
History: The field was the first major oil-producing region in the U.S. When the first well was successfully drilled near Titusville, Pennsylvania, in 1859, Allegany, Cattaraugus, and Chautauqua counties all shared in the prosperity.

Population: 330; Growth (since 2000): -19.7%; Density: 203.3 persons per square mile; Race: 98.8% White, 1.2% Black/African American, 0.0% Asian, 0.0% American Indian/Alaska Native, 0.0% Native Hawaiian/Other Pacific Islander, 0.0% Two or more races, 0.3% Hispanic of any race; Average household size: 2.49; Median age: 35.5; Age under 18: 30.0%; Age 65 and over: 11.8%; Males per 100 females: 87.9; Marriage status: 25.7% never married, 53.4% now married, 1.2% separated, 8.4% widowed, 12.4% divorced; Foreign born: 0.0%; Speak English only: 100.0%; With disability: 14.2%; Veterans: 10.0%; Ancestry: 36.7% German, 19.4% Irish, 13.6% Italian, 10.3% Swedish, 6.4% English
Employment: 4.4% management, business, and financial, 0.0% computer, engineering, and science, 5.1% education, legal, community service, arts, and media, 7.0% healthcare practitioners, 20.9% service, 31.6% sales and office, 15.8% natural resources, construction, and maintenance, 15.2% production, transportation, and material moving
Income: Per capita: $20,352; Median household: $45,227; Average household: $51,965; Households with income of $100,000 or more: 18.4%; Poverty rate: 12.2%
Educational Attainment: High school diploma or higher: 89.8%; Bachelor's degree or higher: 11.2%; Graduate/professional degree or higher: 1.0%
Housing: Homeownership rate: 61.5%; Median home value: $67,100; Median year structure built: 1947; Homeowner vacancy rate: 0.0%; Median selected monthly owner costs: $870 with a mortgage, $342 without a mortgage; Median gross rent: $717 per month; Rental vacancy rate: 0.0%
Health Insurance: 89.2% have insurance; 72.2% have private insurance; 31.8% have public insurance; 10.8% do not have insurance; 6.3% of children under 18 do not have insurance
Transportation: Commute: 94.9% car, 0.0% public transportation, 0.0% walk, 1.3% work from home; Mean travel time to work: 19.4 minutes

LITTLE VALLEY (town). Covers a land area of 29.787 square miles and a water area of 0.006 square miles. Located at 42.22° N. Lat; 78.76° W. Long. Elevation is 1,598 feet.
History: Incorporated 1876.
Population: 1,875; Growth (since 2000): 4.9%; Density: 62.9 persons per square mile; Race: 89.3% White, 3.3% Black/African American, 0.2% Asian, 1.2% American Indian/Alaska Native, 0.0% Native Hawaiian/Other Pacific Islander, 4.3% Two or more races, 5.6% Hispanic of any race; Average household size: 2.57; Median age: 33.2; Age under 18: 28.7%; Age 65 and over: 13.5%; Males per 100 females: 111.7; Marriage status: 32.2% never married, 48.9% now married, 1.4% separated, 8.1% widowed, 10.8% divorced; Foreign born: 1.5%; Speak English only: 96.6%; With disability: 12.3%; Veterans: 10.3%; Ancestry: 31.1% German, 19.0% Irish, 16.3% English, 8.2% Polish, 5.5% American
Employment: 8.9% management, business, and financial, 3.3% computer, engineering, and science, 12.1% education, legal, community service, arts, and media, 3.3% healthcare practitioners, 19.4% service, 23.1% sales and office, 16.4% natural resources, construction, and maintenance, 13.6% production, transportation, and material moving
Income: Per capita: $17,643; Median household: $38,158; Average household: $47,425; Households with income of $100,000 or more: 8.3%; Poverty rate: 20.4%
Educational Attainment: High school diploma or higher: 86.1%; Bachelor's degree or higher: 12.4%; Graduate/professional degree or higher: 3.3%

School District(s)
Cattaraugus-Little Valley Central SD (PK-12)
    2014-15 Enrollment: 940 . . . . (716) 257-5292
Housing: Homeownership rate: 71.9%; Median home value: $85,500; Median year structure built: 1943; Homeowner vacancy rate: 2.0%; Median selected monthly owner costs: $959 with a mortgage, $453 without a mortgage; Median gross rent: $548 per month; Rental vacancy rate: 4.3%
Health Insurance: 89.2% have insurance; 65.8% have private insurance; 39.0% have public insurance; 10.8% do not have insurance; 3.0% of children under 18 do not have insurance
Transportation: Commute: 90.3% car, 0.0% public transportation, 8.9% walk, 0.5% work from home; Mean travel time to work: 23.8 minutes

LITTLE VALLEY (village). County seat. Covers a land area of 1.002 square miles and a water area of 0 square miles. Located at 42.25° N. Lat; 78.80° W. Long. Elevation is 1,598 feet.
Population: 1,276; Growth (since 2000): 12.9%; Density: 1,273.4 persons per square mile; Race: 85.9% White, 4.9% Black/African American, 0.0% Asian, 1.3% American Indian/Alaska Native, 0.0% Native Hawaiian/Other

Pacific Islander, 5.5% Two or more races, 8.2% Hispanic of any race; Average household size: 2.61; Median age: 30.7; Age under 18: 30.4%; Age 65 and over: 12.6%; Males per 100 females: 112.8; Marriage status: 39.9% never married, 40.0% now married, 2.1% separated, 8.4% widowed, 11.6% divorced; Foreign born: 1.6%; Speak English only: 95.0%; With disability: 15.8%; Veterans: 9.7%; Ancestry: 28.5% German, 18.0% Irish, 14.3% English, 6.7% Polish, 6.4% American
Employment: 5.4% management, business, and financial, 2.9% computer, engineering, and science, 11.9% education, legal, community service, arts, and media, 2.7% healthcare practitioners, 24.6% service, 21.9% sales and office, 16.7% natural resources, construction, and maintenance, 13.8% production, transportation, and material moving
Income: Per capita: $15,213; Median household: $31,750; Average household: $42,414; Households with income of $100,000 or more: 7.6%; Poverty rate: 23.1%
Educational Attainment: High school diploma or higher: 81.9%; Bachelor's degree or higher: 8.7%; Graduate/professional degree or higher: 1.0%

School District(s)
Cattaraugus-Little Valley Central SD (PK-12)
   2014-15 Enrollment: 940 . . . . (716) 257-5292
Housing: Homeownership rate: 61.3%; Median home value: $68,800; Median year structure built: Before 1940; Homeowner vacancy rate: 0.0%; Median selected monthly owner costs: $919 with a mortgage, $436 without a mortgage; Median gross rent: $527 per month; Rental vacancy rate: 5.1%
Health Insurance: 87.2% have insurance; 59.7% have private insurance; 43.6% have public insurance; 12.8% do not have insurance; 1.6% of children under 18 do not have insurance
Transportation: Commute: 85.1% car, 0.0% public transportation, 13.7% walk, 0.8% work from home; Mean travel time to work: 22.8 minutes

LYNDON (town). Covers a land area of 33.231 square miles and a water area of 0.036 square miles. Located at 42.31° N. Lat; 78.38° W. Long. Elevation is 2,064 feet.
Population: 793; Growth (since 2000): 20.0%; Density: 23.9 persons per square mile; Race: 97.9% White, 1.0% Black/African American, 0.0% Asian, 0.4% American Indian/Alaska Native, 0.0% Native Hawaiian/Other Pacific Islander, 0.4% Two or more races, 2.6% Hispanic of any race; Average household size: 2.32; Median age: 46.8; Age under 18: 23.8%; Age 65 and over: 18.9%; Males per 100 females: 115.5; Marriage status: 22.1% never married, 62.8% now married, 0.5% separated, 3.6% widowed, 11.6% divorced; Foreign born: 1.8%; Speak English only: 92.2%; With disability: 12.5%; Veterans: 17.1%; Ancestry: 31.1% German, 16.3% Irish, 10.1% Polish, 8.4% English, 6.3% Italian
Employment: 23.1% management, business, and financial, 0.0% computer, engineering, and science, 0.7% education, legal, community service, arts, and media, 6.8% healthcare practitioners, 17.3% service, 15.0% sales and office, 19.0% natural resources, construction, and maintenance, 18.0% production, transportation, and material moving
Income: Per capita: $23,683; Median household: $39,722; Average household: $55,543; Households with income of $100,000 or more: 7.0%; Poverty rate: 16.4%
Educational Attainment: High school diploma or higher: 83.8%; Bachelor's degree or higher: 11.0%; Graduate/professional degree or higher: 4.5%
Housing: Homeownership rate: 84.5%; Median home value: $101,300; Median year structure built: 1983; Homeowner vacancy rate: 2.0%; Median selected monthly owner costs: $1,141 with a mortgage, $548 without a mortgage; Median gross rent: $640 per month; Rental vacancy rate: 0.0%
Health Insurance: 88.0% have insurance; 73.9% have private insurance; 29.8% have public insurance; 12.0% do not have insurance; 15.9% of children under 18 do not have insurance
Transportation: Commute: 96.6% car, 0.0% public transportation, 2.4% walk, 1.0% work from home; Mean travel time to work: 33.6 minutes

MACHIAS (CDP). Covers a land area of 0.865 square miles and a water area of 0.167 square miles. Located at 42.41° N. Lat; 78.49° W. Long. Elevation is 1,680 feet.
Population: 500; Growth (since 2000): n/a; Density: 577.8 persons per square mile; Race: 95.4% White, 0.0% Black/African American, 0.0% Asian, 0.0% American Indian/Alaska Native, 0.0% Native Hawaiian/Other Pacific Islander, 4.6% Two or more races, 0.0% Hispanic of any race; Average household size: 2.69; Median age: 35.7; Age under 18: 23.0%; Age 65 and over: 17.8%; Males per 100 females: 89.9; Marriage status:

34.7% never married, 44.7% now married, 1.8% separated, 5.5% widowed, 15.1% divorced; Foreign born: 0.0%; Speak English only: 100.0%; With disability: 16.8%; Veterans: 8.8%; Ancestry: 50.4% German, 19.8% English, 15.6% Irish, 9.6% American, 6.8% Polish
Employment: 2.0% management, business, and financial, 0.0% computer, engineering, and science, 8.2% education, legal, community service, arts, and media, 9.8% healthcare practitioners, 8.2% service, 38.0% sales and office, 19.6% natural resources, construction, and maintenance, 14.1% production, transportation, and material moving
Income: Per capita: $21,605; Median household: $42,125; Average household: $56,631; Households with income of $100,000 or more: 17.2%; Poverty rate: 11.9%
Educational Attainment: High school diploma or higher: 93.9%; Bachelor's degree or higher: 8.3%; Graduate/professional degree or higher: 8.3%
Housing: Homeownership rate: 75.8%; Median home value: $73,200; Median year structure built: 1963; Homeowner vacancy rate: 0.0%; Median selected monthly owner costs: $961 with a mortgage, $332 without a mortgage; Median gross rent: $757 per month; Rental vacancy rate: 21.7%
Health Insurance: 98.4% have insurance; 76.4% have private insurance; 42.0% have public insurance; 1.6% do not have insurance; 0.0% of children under 18 do not have insurance
Transportation: Commute: 91.8% car, 0.0% public transportation, 8.2% walk, 0.0% work from home; Mean travel time to work: 20.7 minutes

MACHIAS (town). Covers a land area of 40.429 square miles and a water area of 0.649 square miles. Located at 42.40° N. Lat; 78.51° W. Long. Elevation is 1,680 feet.
Population: 2,302; Growth (since 2000): -7.3%; Density: 56.9 persons per square mile; Race: 97.9% White, 0.2% Black/African American, 0.0% Asian, 0.0% American Indian/Alaska Native, 0.0% Native Hawaiian/Other Pacific Islander, 1.9% Two or more races, 0.7% Hispanic of any race; Average household size: 2.70; Median age: 44.2; Age under 18: 23.4%; Age 65 and over: 20.5%; Males per 100 females: 94.4; Marriage status: 31.2% never married, 49.3% now married, 0.7% separated, 8.5% widowed, 11.0% divorced; Foreign born: 1.5%; Speak English only: 97.6%; With disability: 17.2%; Veterans: 11.2%; Ancestry: 35.5% German, 16.4% English, 15.7% Irish, 8.4% Polish, 5.8% American
Employment: 5.2% management, business, and financial, 2.0% computer, engineering, and science, 10.0% education, legal, community service, arts, and media, 8.3% healthcare practitioners, 16.1% service, 22.7% sales and office, 20.1% natural resources, construction, and maintenance, 15.6% production, transportation, and material moving
Income: Per capita: $20,901; Median household: $46,700; Average household: $56,332; Households with income of $100,000 or more: 11.2%; Poverty rate: 11.3%
Educational Attainment: High school diploma or higher: 86.3%; Bachelor's degree or higher: 14.4%; Graduate/professional degree or higher: 6.8%
Housing: Homeownership rate: 84.7%; Median home value: $101,200; Median year structure built: 1969; Homeowner vacancy rate: 0.0%; Median selected monthly owner costs: $1,019 with a mortgage, $551 without a mortgage; Median gross rent: $745 per month; Rental vacancy rate: 18.0%
Health Insurance: 98.2% have insurance; 71.8% have private insurance; 44.7% have public insurance; 1.8% do not have insurance; 0.0% of children under 18 do not have insurance
Transportation: Commute: 92.8% car, 0.5% public transportation, 4.8% walk, 1.9% work from home; Mean travel time to work: 28.5 minutes

MANSFIELD (town). Covers a land area of 40.126 square miles and a water area of 0.031 square miles. Located at 42.30° N. Lat; 78.77° W. Long.
Population: 796; Growth (since 2000): -0.5%; Density: 19.8 persons per square mile; Race: 99.4% White, 0.0% Black/African American, 0.0% Asian, 0.0% American Indian/Alaska Native, 0.0% Native Hawaiian/Other Pacific Islander, 0.6% Two or more races, 0.8% Hispanic of any race; Average household size: 2.38; Median age: 51.3; Age under 18: 18.7%; Age 65 and over: 20.9%; Males per 100 females: 101.5; Marriage status: 18.6% never married, 61.8% now married, 2.8% separated, 9.4% widowed, 10.3% divorced; Foreign born: 4.0%; Speak English only: 92.7%; With disability: 10.7%; Veterans: 10.2%; Ancestry: 37.6% German, 18.1% Irish, 12.9% English, 7.7% Polish, 7.0% Italian
Employment: 16.0% management, business, and financial, 0.8% computer, engineering, and science, 4.9% education, legal, community service, arts, and media, 5.7% healthcare practitioners, 22.2% service,

23.0% sales and office, 15.0% natural resources, construction, and maintenance, 12.4% production, transportation, and material moving
Income: Per capita: $28,080; Median household: $50,735; Average household: $66,034; Households with income of $100,000 or more: 18.9%; Poverty rate: 10.0%
Educational Attainment: High school diploma or higher: 88.3%; Bachelor's degree or higher: 25.6%; Graduate/professional degree or higher: 10.1%
Housing: Homeownership rate: 89.8%; Median home value: $140,600; Median year structure built: 1974; Homeowner vacancy rate: 3.2%; Median selected monthly owner costs: $1,241 with a mortgage, $572 without a mortgage; Median gross rent: $856 per month; Rental vacancy rate: 0.0%
Health Insurance: 82.5% have insurance; 70.1% have private insurance; 32.3% have public insurance; 17.5% do not have insurance; 17.4% of children under 18 do not have insurance
Transportation: Commute: 93.0% car, 0.0% public transportation, 2.9% walk, 3.7% work from home; Mean travel time to work: 23.3 minutes

NAPOLI (town). Covers a land area of 36.375 square miles and a water area of 0.170 square miles. Located at 42.21° N. Lat; 78.88° W. Long. Elevation is 1,732 feet.
Population: 1,190; Growth (since 2000): 2.7%; Density: 32.7 persons per square mile; Race: 98.6% White, 0.0% Black/African American, 0.0% Asian, 0.0% American Indian/Alaska Native, 0.0% Native Hawaiian/Other Pacific Islander, 1.4% Two or more races, 0.0% Hispanic of any race; Average household size: 2.86; Median age: 36.4; Age under 18: 32.7%; Age 65 and over: 12.1%; Males per 100 females: 112.2; Marriage status: 26.2% never married, 57.2% now married, 2.1% separated, 3.5% widowed, 13.0% divorced; Foreign born: 0.0%; Speak English only: 81.6%; With disability: 10.8%; Veterans: 13.6%; Ancestry: 33.9% German, 26.5% English, 12.5% Irish, 8.1% Polish, 5.8% Pennsylvania German
Employment: 8.3% management, business, and financial, 4.0% computer, engineering, and science, 5.9% education, legal, community service, arts, and media, 6.7% healthcare practitioners, 23.8% service, 10.5% sales and office, 25.3% natural resources, construction, and maintenance, 15.4% production, transportation, and material moving
Income: Per capita: $18,097; Median household: $49,946; Average household: $51,815; Households with income of $100,000 or more: 5.9%; Poverty rate: 24.0%
Educational Attainment: High school diploma or higher: 83.8%; Bachelor's degree or higher: 12.7%; Graduate/professional degree or higher: 5.1%
Housing: Homeownership rate: 92.9%; Median home value: $75,000; Median year structure built: 1969; Homeowner vacancy rate: 0.0%; Median selected monthly owner costs: $1,099 with a mortgage, $366 without a mortgage; Median gross rent: $542 per month; Rental vacancy rate: 8.1%
Health Insurance: 77.5% have insurance; 57.8% have private insurance; 32.4% have public insurance; 22.5% do not have insurance; 35.7% of children under 18 do not have insurance
Transportation: Commute: 81.1% car, 1.8% public transportation, 1.2% walk, 11.6% work from home; Mean travel time to work: 26.8 minutes

NEW ALBION (town). Covers a land area of 35.629 square miles and a water area of 0.194 square miles. Located at 42.31° N. Lat; 78.89° W. Long. Elevation is 1,417 feet.
Population: 1,888; Growth (since 2000): -8.7%; Density: 53.0 persons per square mile; Race: 96.3% White, 0.1% Black/African American, 0.0% Asian, 1.0% American Indian/Alaska Native, 0.0% Native Hawaiian/Other Pacific Islander, 2.1% Two or more races, 2.7% Hispanic of any race; Average household size: 2.23; Median age: 47.4; Age under 18: 17.8%; Age 65 and over: 21.2%; Males per 100 females: 98.4; Marriage status: 25.8% never married, 52.9% now married, 3.5% separated, 8.6% widowed, 12.7% divorced; Foreign born: 1.2%; Speak English only: 98.9%; With disability: 19.4%; Veterans: 15.1%; Ancestry: 47.0% German, 14.6% Irish, 13.2% English, 12.3% Polish, 5.9% Italian
Employment: 8.3% management, business, and financial, 1.0% computer, engineering, and science, 7.8% education, legal, community service, arts, and media, 4.4% healthcare practitioners, 27.9% service, 21.2% sales and office, 12.7% natural resources, construction, and maintenance, 16.8% production, transportation, and material moving
Income: Per capita: $22,946; Median household: $41,202; Average household: $50,794; Households with income of $100,000 or more: 9.8%; Poverty rate: 15.5%

Educational Attainment: High school diploma or higher: 86.9%; Bachelor's degree or higher: 12.3%; Graduate/professional degree or higher: 5.6%
Housing: Homeownership rate: 75.4%; Median home value: $73,200; Median year structure built: Before 1940; Homeowner vacancy rate: 0.0%; Median selected monthly owner costs: $987 with a mortgage, $488 without a mortgage; Median gross rent: $496 per month; Rental vacancy rate: 5.1%
Health Insurance: 94.0% have insurance; 70.2% have private insurance; 44.7% have public insurance; 6.0% do not have insurance; 4.5% of children under 18 do not have insurance
Transportation: Commute: 87.1% car, 0.6% public transportation, 6.8% walk, 4.3% work from home; Mean travel time to work: 26.6 minutes

OLEAN (city). Covers a land area of 5.908 square miles and a water area of 0.258 square miles. Located at 42.08° N. Lat; 78.44° W. Long. Elevation is 1,447 feet.
History: Olean came to life as a lumber camp. From their lumber, settlers built rafts to sell to emigrants who gathered to await the spring flood which would float them down the Allegheny and Ohio Rivers to the western frontier.
Population: 14,099; Growth (since 2000): -8.1%; Density: 2,386.6 persons per square mile; Race: 91.6% White, 3.7% Black/African American, 2.0% Asian, 0.8% American Indian/Alaska Native, 0.0% Native Hawaiian/Other Pacific Islander, 1.9% Two or more races, 0.9% Hispanic of any race; Average household size: 2.26; Median age: 40.5; Age under 18: 21.9%; Age 65 and over: 15.2%; Males per 100 females: 92.2; Marriage status: 35.4% never married, 41.9% now married, 2.4% separated, 6.4% widowed, 16.3% divorced; Foreign born: 2.4%; Speak English only: 96.5%; With disability: 16.5%; Veterans: 12.3%; Ancestry: 27.1% German, 20.0% Irish, 14.4% Polish, 13.7% Italian, 11.4% English
Employment: 10.5% management, business, and financial, 2.3% computer, engineering, and science, 12.5% education, legal, community service, arts, and media, 5.4% healthcare practitioners, 19.4% service, 30.7% sales and office, 4.4% natural resources, construction, and maintenance, 14.6% production, transportation, and material moving
Income: Per capita: $24,565; Median household: $38,450; Average household: $55,169; Households with income of $100,000 or more: 12.7%; Poverty rate: 23.7%
Educational Attainment: High school diploma or higher: 91.5%; Bachelor's degree or higher: 25.4%; Graduate/professional degree or higher: 11.0%

School District(s)
Cattaraugus-Allegany-Erie-Wyoming Boces
 2014-15 Enrollment: n/a . . . . (716) 376-8254
Olean City SD (PK-12)
 2014-15 Enrollment: 2,182 . . . . (716) 375-8055
Vocational/Technical School(s)
Cattaraugus Allegany BOCES-Practical Nursing Program (Public)
 Fall 2014 Enrollment: 50 . . . . (716) 376-8268
Continental School of Beauty Culture-Olean (Private, For-profit)
 Fall 2014 Enrollment: 69 . . . . (716) 372-5095
 2015-16 Tuition: $12,440
Housing: Homeownership rate: 52.0%; Median home value: $70,400; Median year structure built: Before 1940; Homeowner vacancy rate: 5.0%; Median selected monthly owner costs: $979 with a mortgage, $482 without a mortgage; Median gross rent: $623 per month; Rental vacancy rate: 8.3%
Health Insurance: 93.7% have insurance; 67.5% have private insurance; 46.8% have public insurance; 6.3% do not have insurance; 2.2% of children under 18 do not have insurance
Hospitals: Olean General Hospital (217 beds)
Safety: Violent crime rate: 18.6 per 10,000 population; Property crime rate: 316.9 per 10,000 population
Newspapers: Times-Herald (daily circulation 14,000)
Transportation: Commute: 85.6% car, 0.4% public transportation, 9.3% walk, 1.9% work from home; Mean travel time to work: 14.8 minutes
Airports: Cattaraugus County-Olean (general aviation)
Additional Information Contacts
City of Olean . . . . (716) 376-5604
 http://www.cityofolean.com

OLEAN (town). Covers a land area of 29.609 square miles and a water area of 0.127 square miles. Located at 42.06° N. Lat; 78.42° W. Long. Elevation is 1,447 feet.

History: Once an oil-based economy emanating from nearby Pennsylvania oil fields. St. Bonaventure University nearby. Major outfitting post for settlers moving west down the Allegheny and Ohio rivers in early 1800s. In 1972 a severe flood associated with Hurricane Agnes flooded large areas and damaged more than 2,900 homes. Settled 1804, Incorporated 1893.

Population: 1,939; Growth (since 2000): -4.4%; Density: 65.5 persons per square mile; Race: 96.1% White, 0.3% Black/African American, 3.2% Asian, 0.0% American Indian/Alaska Native, 0.0% Native Hawaiian/Other Pacific Islander, 0.4% Two or more races, 0.0% Hispanic of any race; Average household size: 2.35; Median age: 50.7; Age under 18: 17.9%; Age 65 and over: 19.1%; Males per 100 females: 103.0; Marriage status: 20.1% never married, 61.6% now married, 0.7% separated, 7.2% widowed, 11.2% divorced; Foreign born: 1.4%; Speak English only: 98.0%; With disability: 11.7%; Veterans: 11.3%; Ancestry: 26.3% German, 17.8% Irish, 14.0% Polish, 12.2% Italian, 8.1% English

Employment: 15.4% management, business, and financial, 3.3% computer, engineering, and science, 11.9% education, legal, community service, arts, and media, 3.6% healthcare practitioners, 14.6% service, 24.1% sales and office, 10.4% natural resources, construction, and maintenance, 16.7% production, transportation, and material moving

Income: Per capita: $27,314; Median household: $51,354; Average household: $63,343; Households with income of $100,000 or more: 17.5%; Poverty rate: 12.2%

Educational Attainment: High school diploma or higher: 89.5%; Bachelor's degree or higher: 21.9%; Graduate/professional degree or higher: 9.5%

School District(s)
Cattaraugus-Allegany-Erie-Wyoming Boces
   2014-15 Enrollment: n/a . . . . (716) 376-8254
Olean City SD (PK-12)
   2014-15 Enrollment: 2,182 . . . . (716) 375-8055

Vocational/Technical School(s)
Cattaraugus Allegany BOCES-Practical Nursing Program (Public)
   Fall 2014 Enrollment: 50 . . . . (716) 376-8268
Continental School of Beauty Culture-Olean (Private, For-profit)
   Fall 2014 Enrollment: 69 . . . . (716) 372-5095
   2015-16 Tuition: $12,440

Housing: Homeownership rate: 82.9%; Median home value: $91,400; Median year structure built: 1958; Homeowner vacancy rate: 0.0%; Median selected monthly owner costs: $1,285 with a mortgage, $507 without a mortgage; Median gross rent: $677 per month; Rental vacancy rate: 0.0%

Health Insurance: 93.9% have insurance; 71.7% have private insurance; 38.2% have public insurance; 6.1% do not have insurance; 3.7% of children under 18 do not have insurance

Hospitals: Olean General Hospital (217 beds)

Newspapers: Times-Herald (daily circulation 14,000)

Transportation: Commute: 94.4% car, 1.4% public transportation, 1.9% walk, 1.2% work from home; Mean travel time to work: 16.3 minutes

Airports: Cattaraugus County-Olean (general aviation)

OTTO (town). Covers a land area of 32.730 square miles and a water area of 0.117 square miles. Located at 42.40° N. Lat; 78.84° W. Long. Elevation is 1,260 feet.

Population: 829; Growth (since 2000): -0.2%; Density: 25.3 persons per square mile; Race: 97.8% White, 1.8% Black/African American, 0.0% Asian, 0.0% American Indian/Alaska Native, 0.0% Native Hawaiian/Other Pacific Islander, 0.4% Two or more races, 1.1% Hispanic of any race; Average household size: 2.49; Median age: 43.8; Age under 18: 20.0%; Age 65 and over: 19.1%; Males per 100 females: 106.1; Marriage status: 24.9% never married, 62.9% now married, 0.9% separated, 3.8% widowed, 8.4% divorced; Foreign born: 1.8%; Speak English only: 93.2%; With disability: 14.2%; Veterans: 12.1%; Ancestry: 46.0% German, 18.7% Irish, 11.8% Polish, 8.6% English, 7.6% Italian

Employment: 10.9% management, business, and financial, 1.0% computer, engineering, and science, 4.1% education, legal, community service, arts, and media, 5.1% healthcare practitioners, 25.4% service, 19.5% sales and office, 21.3% natural resources, construction, and maintenance, 12.7% production, transportation, and material moving

Income: Per capita: $25,296; Median household: $53,667; Average household: $63,525; Households with income of $100,000 or more: 18.4%; Poverty rate: 12.6%

Educational Attainment: High school diploma or higher: 86.2%; Bachelor's degree or higher: 14.3%; Graduate/professional degree or higher: 5.7%

Housing: Homeownership rate: 85.2%; Median home value: $115,400; Median year structure built: 1959; Homeowner vacancy rate: 4.4%; Median selected monthly owner costs: $1,232 with a mortgage, $533 without a mortgage; Median gross rent: $875 per month; Rental vacancy rate: 0.0%

Health Insurance: 90.8% have insurance; 73.6% have private insurance; 34.6% have public insurance; 9.2% do not have insurance; 9.6% of children under 18 do not have insurance

Transportation: Commute: 92.3% car, 0.0% public transportation, 2.3% walk, 5.4% work from home; Mean travel time to work: 31.7 minutes

PERRYSBURG (town). Covers a land area of 28.421 square miles and a water area of 0.126 square miles. Located at 42.48° N. Lat; 79.02° W. Long. Elevation is 1,322 feet.

Population: 1,486; Growth (since 2000): -16.1%; Density: 52.3 persons per square mile; Race: 96.1% White, 0.0% Black/African American, 0.1% Asian, 2.4% American Indian/Alaska Native, 0.0% Native Hawaiian/Other Pacific Islander, 1.4% Two or more races, 4.6% Hispanic of any race; Average household size: 2.35; Median age: 45.6; Age under 18: 20.7%; Age 65 and over: 18.8%; Males per 100 females: 97.3; Marriage status: 22.4% never married, 59.8% now married, 0.7% separated, 5.7% widowed, 12.2% divorced; Foreign born: 2.2%; Speak English only: 97.5%; With disability: 10.1%; Veterans: 10.2%; Ancestry: 32.9% German, 19.8% Irish, 16.3% Polish, 11.7% English, 11.0% Italian

Employment: 13.5% management, business, and financial, 3.1% computer, engineering, and science, 8.4% education, legal, community service, arts, and media, 3.6% healthcare practitioners, 23.8% service, 24.4% sales and office, 10.2% natural resources, construction, and maintenance, 13.0% production, transportation, and material moving

Income: Per capita: $27,904; Median household: $53,750; Average household: $63,651; Households with income of $100,000 or more: 16.8%; Poverty rate: 10.2%

Educational Attainment: High school diploma or higher: 96.5%; Bachelor's degree or higher: 15.8%; Graduate/professional degree or higher: 7.5%

Housing: Homeownership rate: 81.4%; Median home value: $105,900; Median year structure built: 1953; Homeowner vacancy rate: 4.6%; Median selected monthly owner costs: $1,197 with a mortgage, $493 without a mortgage; Median gross rent: $556 per month; Rental vacancy rate: 7.1%

Health Insurance: 93.6% have insurance; 78.7% have private insurance; 34.2% have public insurance; 6.4% do not have insurance; 3.6% of children under 18 do not have insurance

Transportation: Commute: 94.0% car, 0.0% public transportation, 2.4% walk, 3.6% work from home; Mean travel time to work: 26.3 minutes

PERRYSBURG (CDP). Covers a land area of 0.984 square miles and a water area of 0.003 square miles. Located at 42.46° N. Lat; 79.00° W. Long. Elevation is 1,322 feet.

Population: 325; Growth (since 2000): -20.3%; Density: 330.1 persons per square mile; Race: 97.8% White, 0.0% Black/African American, 0.3% Asian, 0.0% American Indian/Alaska Native, 0.0% Native Hawaiian/Other Pacific Islander, 1.8% Two or more races, 2.2% Hispanic of any race; Average household size: 2.29; Median age: 41.1; Age under 18: 21.8%; Age 65 and over: 19.4%; Males per 100 females: 95.6; Marriage status: 24.2% never married, 51.6% now married, 2.7% separated, 8.6% widowed, 15.6% divorced; Foreign born: 4.6%; Speak English only: 97.9%; With disability: 9.2%; Veterans: 4.7%; Ancestry: 39.1% German, 32.9% Irish, 13.8% Italian, 11.7% Polish, 9.8% English

Employment: 8.7% management, business, and financial, 4.3% computer, engineering, and science, 3.6% education, legal, community service, arts, and media, 5.8% healthcare practitioners, 22.5% service, 25.4% sales and office, 10.9% natural resources, construction, and maintenance, 18.8% production, transportation, and material moving

Income: Per capita: $26,726; Median household: $40,714; Average household: $57,330; Households with income of $100,000 or more: 16.9%; Poverty rate: 12.9%

Educational Attainment: High school diploma or higher: 99.0%; Bachelor's degree or higher: 10.6%; Graduate/professional degree or higher: 3.8%

Housing: Homeownership rate: 66.9%; Median home value: $75,000; Median year structure built: Before 1940; Homeowner vacancy rate: 4.0%; Median selected monthly owner costs: $1,188 with a mortgage, $445

without a mortgage; Median gross rent: $517 per month; Rental vacancy rate: 0.0%
Health Insurance: 98.2% have insurance; 82.2% have private insurance; 32.6% have public insurance; 1.8% do not have insurance; 0.0% of children under 18 do not have insurance
Transportation: Commute: 94.2% car, 0.0% public transportation, 2.2% walk, 3.6% work from home; Mean travel time to work: 22.4 minutes

PERSIA (town). Covers a land area of 20.893 square miles and a water area of 0.097 square miles. Located at 42.42° N. Lat; 78.92° W. Long. Elevation is 1,342 feet.
Population: 2,301; Growth (since 2000): -8.4%; Density: 110.1 persons per square mile; Race: 93.0% White, 0.7% Black/African American, 0.7% Asian, 2.8% American Indian/Alaska Native, 0.0% Native Hawaiian/Other Pacific Islander, 2.8% Two or more races, 0.0% Hispanic of any race; Average household size: 2.22; Median age: 43.3; Age under 18: 20.6%; Age 65 and over: 20.4%; Males per 100 females: 96.1; Marriage status: 33.4% never married, 39.8% now married, 3.0% separated, 9.5% widowed, 17.3% divorced; Foreign born: 1.3%; Speak English only: 96.4%; With disability: 15.8%; Veterans: 10.2%; Ancestry: 37.6% German, 21.8% Irish, 15.1% Polish, 14.7% English, 12.1% Italian
Employment: 8.5% management, business, and financial, 2.9% computer, engineering, and science, 10.8% education, legal, community service, arts, and media, 5.9% healthcare practitioners, 30.4% service, 14.5% sales and office, 11.1% natural resources, construction, and maintenance, 15.8% production, transportation, and material moving
Income: Per capita: $22,068; Median household: $40,731; Average household: $50,006; Households with income of $100,000 or more: 9.2%; Poverty rate: 17.9%
Educational Attainment: High school diploma or higher: 89.1%; Bachelor's degree or higher: 13.7%; Graduate/professional degree or higher: 4.6%
Housing: Homeownership rate: 65.8%; Median home value: $75,300; Median year structure built: Before 1940; Homeowner vacancy rate: 2.6%; Median selected monthly owner costs: $883 with a mortgage, $386 without a mortgage; Median gross rent: $669 per month; Rental vacancy rate: 5.2%
Health Insurance: 88.0% have insurance; 70.8% have private insurance; 33.8% have public insurance; 12.0% do not have insurance; 9.3% of children under 18 do not have insurance
Transportation: Commute: 90.8% car, 0.5% public transportation, 5.6% walk, 1.4% work from home; Mean travel time to work: 26.0 minutes

PORTVILLE (town). Covers a land area of 35.580 square miles and a water area of 0.448 square miles. Located at 42.06° N. Lat; 78.35° W. Long. Elevation is 1,430 feet.
History: Incorporated 1895.
Population: 3,662; Growth (since 2000): -7.3%; Density: 102.9 persons per square mile; Race: 98.3% White, 0.2% Black/African American, 0.0% Asian, 0.0% American Indian/Alaska Native, 0.0% Native Hawaiian/Other Pacific Islander, 1.3% Two or more races, 1.8% Hispanic of any race; Average household size: 2.37; Median age: 45.1; Age under 18: 19.1%; Age 65 and over: 22.4%; Males per 100 females: 94.9; Marriage status: 25.7% never married, 53.2% now married, 2.4% separated, 8.6% widowed, 12.4% divorced; Foreign born: 0.8%; Speak English only: 98.0%; With disability: 18.1%; Veterans: 14.4%; Ancestry: 30.4% German, 17.5% English, 16.6% Irish, 6.0% Polish, 5.9% Italian
Employment: 9.7% management, business, and financial, 2.8% computer, engineering, and science, 8.6% education, legal, community service, arts, and media, 6.8% healthcare practitioners, 18.4% service, 26.5% sales and office, 10.7% natural resources, construction, and maintenance, 16.4% production, transportation, and material moving
Income: Per capita: $29,437; Median household: $53,958; Average household: $69,525; Households with income of $100,000 or more: 21.2%; Poverty rate: 9.6%
Educational Attainment: High school diploma or higher: 91.3%; Bachelor's degree or higher: 18.0%; Graduate/professional degree or higher: 9.2%

School District(s)
Portville Central SD (PK-12)
    2014-15 Enrollment: 1,007 . . . . (716) 933-7140
Housing: Homeownership rate: 75.7%; Median home value: $88,500; Median year structure built: 1953; Homeowner vacancy rate: 0.0%; Median selected monthly owner costs: $1,055 with a mortgage, $499 without a mortgage; Median gross rent: $585 per month; Rental vacancy rate: 2.3%

Health Insurance: 92.5% have insurance; 78.3% have private insurance; 39.1% have public insurance; 7.5% do not have insurance; 5.5% of children under 18 do not have insurance
Transportation: Commute: 97.2% car, 0.8% public transportation, 1.1% walk, 0.0% work from home; Mean travel time to work: 20.1 minutes

PORTVILLE (village). Covers a land area of 0.802 square miles and a water area of 0 square miles. Located at 42.04° N. Lat; 78.34° W. Long. Elevation is 1,430 feet.
Population: 1,146; Growth (since 2000): 11.9%; Density: 1,428.8 persons per square mile; Race: 95.6% White, 0.4% Black/African American, 0.0% Asian, 0.0% American Indian/Alaska Native, 0.0% Native Hawaiian/Other Pacific Islander, 3.1% Two or more races, 0.9% Hispanic of any race; Average household size: 2.40; Median age: 39.3; Age under 18: 28.3%; Age 65 and over: 17.4%; Males per 100 females: 86.4; Marriage status: 25.7% never married, 48.7% now married, 1.7% separated, 8.3% widowed, 17.3% divorced; Foreign born: 1.2%; Speak English only: 98.3%; With disability: 13.0%; Veterans: 15.2%; Ancestry: 28.0% German, 22.6% Irish, 12.4% English, 10.0% Italian, 4.9% American
Employment: 11.2% management, business, and financial, 0.0% computer, engineering, and science, 13.7% education, legal, community service, arts, and media, 4.5% healthcare practitioners, 19.2% service, 32.0% sales and office, 7.6% natural resources, construction, and maintenance, 11.8% production, transportation, and material moving
Income: Per capita: $28,428; Median household: $51,010; Average household: $67,563; Households with income of $100,000 or more: 17.2%; Poverty rate: 15.0%
Educational Attainment: High school diploma or higher: 92.0%; Bachelor's degree or higher: 26.4%; Graduate/professional degree or higher: 13.2%

School District(s)
Portville Central SD (PK-12)
    2014-15 Enrollment: 1,007 . . . . (716) 933-7140
Housing: Homeownership rate: 69.2%; Median home value: $84,600; Median year structure built: Before 1940; Homeowner vacancy rate: 0.0%; Median selected monthly owner costs: $1,074 with a mortgage, $438 without a mortgage; Median gross rent: $612 per month; Rental vacancy rate: 5.8%
Health Insurance: 90.1% have insurance; 71.0% have private insurance; 37.3% have public insurance; 9.9% do not have insurance; 9.0% of children under 18 do not have insurance
Transportation: Commute: 95.0% car, 0.0% public transportation, 3.3% walk, 0.0% work from home; Mean travel time to work: 21.6 minutes

RANDOLPH (town). Covers a land area of 36.064 square miles and a water area of 0.223 square miles. Located at 42.13° N. Lat; 79.00° W. Long. Elevation is 1,276 feet.
Population: 2,550; Growth (since 2000): -4.9%; Density: 70.7 persons per square mile; Race: 94.2% White, 0.2% Black/African American, 0.3% Asian, 0.3% American Indian/Alaska Native, 0.0% Native Hawaiian/Other Pacific Islander, 4.8% Two or more races, 3.7% Hispanic of any race; Average household size: 2.55; Median age: 41.6; Age under 18: 29.1%; Age 65 and over: 16.2%; Males per 100 females: 103.6; Marriage status: 26.6% never married, 56.2% now married, 2.5% separated, 6.4% widowed, 10.7% divorced; Foreign born: 1.0%; Speak English only: 97.9%; With disability: 10.2%; Veterans: 11.3%; Ancestry: 26.0% German, 15.9% English, 13.9% Irish, 7.9% Swedish, 7.5% Italian
Employment: 10.5% management, business, and financial, 3.0% computer, engineering, and science, 9.3% education, legal, community service, arts, and media, 5.9% healthcare practitioners, 13.1% service, 29.7% sales and office, 9.3% natural resources, construction, and maintenance, 19.3% production, transportation, and material moving
Income: Per capita: $20,076; Median household: $40,588; Average household: $51,326; Households with income of $100,000 or more: 13.2%; Poverty rate: 16.8%
Educational Attainment: High school diploma or higher: 89.0%; Bachelor's degree or higher: 13.3%; Graduate/professional degree or higher: 5.9%

School District(s)
Randolph Academy Union Free SD (KG-12)
    2014-15 Enrollment: 37 . . . . (716) 358-6866
Randolph Central SD (PK-12)
    2014-15 Enrollment: 946 . . . . (716) 358-7005
Housing: Homeownership rate: 68.9%; Median home value: $78,800; Median year structure built: 1940; Homeowner vacancy rate: 0.0%; Median

selected monthly owner costs: $987 with a mortgage, $427 without a mortgage; Median gross rent: $525 per month; Rental vacancy rate: 4.8%
Health Insurance: 91.9% have insurance; 67.2% have private insurance; 42.9% have public insurance; 8.1% do not have insurance; 6.2% of children under 18 do not have insurance
Transportation: Commute: 90.2% car, 0.3% public transportation, 4.8% walk, 3.7% work from home; Mean travel time to work: 20.4 minutes

RED HOUSE (town).
Covers a land area of 55.668 square miles and a water area of 0.188 square miles. Located at 42.07° N. Lat; 78.74° W. Long. Elevation is 1,339 feet.
Population: 50; Growth (since 2000): 31.6%; Density: 0.9 persons per square mile; Race: 100.0% White, 0.0% Black/African American, 0.0% Asian, 0.0% American Indian/Alaska Native, 0.0% Native Hawaiian/Other Pacific Islander, 0.0% Two or more races, 0.0% Hispanic of any race; Average household size: 3.33; Median age: 32.3; Age under 18: 34.0%; Age 65 and over: 20.0%; Males per 100 females: 123.5; Marriage status: 48.5% never married, 45.5% now married, 3.0% separated, 3.0% widowed, 3.0% divorced; Foreign born: 0.0%; Speak English only: 97.8%; With disability: 2.0%; Veterans: 6.1%; Ancestry: 18.0% Irish, 16.0% German, 10.0% American, 8.0% Italian, 6.0% Polish
Employment: 28.6% management, business, and financial, 0.0% computer, engineering, and science, 7.1% education, legal, community service, arts, and media, 0.0% healthcare practitioners, 7.1% service, 7.1% sales and office, 42.9% natural resources, construction, and maintenance, 7.1% production, transportation, and material moving
Income: Per capita: $19,546; Median household: $48,125; Average household: $57,820; Households with income of $100,000 or more: 13.3%; Poverty rate: 42.0%
Educational Attainment: High school diploma or higher: 68.8%; Bachelor's degree or higher: 18.8%; Graduate/professional degree or higher: 6.3%
Housing: Homeownership rate: 46.7%; Median home value: $77,500; Median year structure built: Before 1940; Homeowner vacancy rate: 0.0%; Median selected monthly owner costs: n/a with a mortgage, $225 without a mortgage; Median gross rent: $588 per month; Rental vacancy rate: 0.0%
Health Insurance: 98.0% have insurance; 80.0% have private insurance; 42.0% have public insurance; 2.0% do not have insurance; 0.0% of children under 18 do not have insurance
Transportation: Commute: 85.7% car, 0.0% public transportation, 14.3% walk, 0.0% work from home; Mean travel time to work: 16.1 minutes

SAINT BONAVENTURE (CDP).
Covers a land area of 1.976 square miles and a water area of 0.152 square miles. Located at 42.08° N. Lat; 78.47° W. Long. Elevation is 1,427 feet.
Population: 2,052; Growth (since 2000): -3.5%; Density: 1,038.4 persons per square mile; Race: 82.1% White, 8.4% Black/African American, 3.0% Asian, 0.0% American Indian/Alaska Native, 0.0% Native Hawaiian/Other Pacific Islander, 0.5% Two or more races, 9.0% Hispanic of any race; Average household size: 1.95; Median age: 20.7; Age under 18: 3.8%; Age 65 and over: 11.7%; Males per 100 females: 85.3; Marriage status: 79.3% never married, 16.0% now married, 0.0% separated, 1.6% widowed, 3.0% divorced; Foreign born: 14.1%; Speak English only: 85.5%; With disability: 7.2%; Veterans: 2.3%; Ancestry: 26.0% Irish, 21.1% German, 18.5% Italian, 7.7% Polish, 7.0% English
Employment: 11.7% management, business, and financial, 0.3% computer, engineering, and science, 21.8% education, legal, community service, arts, and media, 4.9% healthcare practitioners, 28.8% service, 25.9% sales and office, 3.0% natural resources, construction, and maintenance, 3.7% production, transportation, and material moving
Income: Per capita: $9,975; Median household: $34,883; Average household: $53,628; Households with income of $100,000 or more: 13.8%; Poverty rate: 12.3%
Educational Attainment: High school diploma or higher: 89.1%; Bachelor's degree or higher: 37.3%; Graduate/professional degree or higher: 18.3%

Four-year College(s)
St Bonaventure University (Private, Not-for-profit, Roman Catholic)
   Fall 2014 Enrollment: 2,150 . . . . (716) 375-2000
   2015-16 Tuition: In-state $31,389; Out-of-state $31,389
Housing: Homeownership rate: 73.9%; Median home value: $92,700; Median year structure built: 1958; Homeowner vacancy rate: 9.1%; Median selected monthly owner costs: $842 with a mortgage, $459 without a mortgage; Median gross rent: n/a per month; Rental vacancy rate: 0.0%

Health Insurance: 96.9% have insurance; 94.2% have private insurance; 18.7% have public insurance; 3.1% do not have insurance; 0.0% of children under 18 do not have insurance
Transportation: Commute: 54.9% car, 0.7% public transportation, 43.3% walk, 0.9% work from home; Mean travel time to work: 10.1 minutes

SALAMANCA (city).
Covers a land area of 5.994 square miles and a water area of 0.242 square miles. Located at 42.16° N. Lat; 78.74° W. Long. Elevation is 1,381 feet.
Population: 5,686; Growth (since 2000): -6.7%; Density: 948.6 persons per square mile; Race: 69.6% White, 3.7% Black/African American, 0.2% Asian, 17.8% American Indian/Alaska Native, 0.0% Native Hawaiian/Other Pacific Islander, 6.6% Two or more races, 6.9% Hispanic of any race; Average household size: 2.44; Median age: 34.0; Age under 18: 29.5%; Age 65 and over: 14.0%; Males per 100 females: 91.0; Marriage status: 36.5% never married, 39.7% now married, 3.0% separated, 8.6% widowed, 15.3% divorced; Foreign born: 1.7%; Speak English only: 93.9%; With disability: 15.8%; Veterans: 10.4%; Ancestry: 19.4% German, 16.6% Irish, 8.8% Polish, 7.1% English, 6.9% Italian
Employment: 9.4% management, business, and financial, 1.8% computer, engineering, and science, 7.6% education, legal, community service, arts, and media, 3.8% healthcare practitioners, 29.7% service, 25.5% sales and office, 9.2% natural resources, construction, and maintenance, 13.1% production, transportation, and material moving
Income: Per capita: $16,152; Median household: $30,557; Average household: $39,208; Households with income of $100,000 or more: 5.5%; Poverty rate: 28.1%
Educational Attainment: High school diploma or higher: 83.9%; Bachelor's degree or higher: 13.0%; Graduate/professional degree or higher: 3.9%

School District(s)
Salamanca City SD (PK-12)
   2014-15 Enrollment: 1,320 . . . . (716) 945-2400
Housing: Homeownership rate: 51.9%; Median home value: $64,500; Median year structure built: Before 1940; Homeowner vacancy rate: 1.0%; Median selected monthly owner costs: $782 with a mortgage, $353 without a mortgage; Median gross rent: $611 per month; Rental vacancy rate: 8.9%
Health Insurance: 87.5% have insurance; 53.3% have private insurance; 47.3% have public insurance; 12.5% do not have insurance; 9.9% of children under 18 do not have insurance
Safety: Violent crime rate: 39.2 per 10,000 population; Property crime rate: 181.7 per 10,000 population
Newspapers: County Chronicle (weekly circulation 5,000); Salamanca Press (daily circulation 2,000)
Transportation: Commute: 90.8% car, 0.5% public transportation, 5.0% walk, 2.4% work from home; Mean travel time to work: 16.9 minutes
Additional Information Contacts
City of Salamanca . . . . (716) 945-4620
   http://www.salmun.com

SALAMANCA (town).
Covers a land area of 18.391 square miles and a water area of <.001 square miles. Located at 42.17° N. Lat; 78.81° W. Long. Elevation is 1,381 feet.
History: In Allegany Indian Reservation. Allegany State Park is just S. Furniture, plastic and wood prods; printing. Most of the city is built on land that is leased from the Seneca Nation's Allegany Indian Reservation. Settled in 1860s; inc. as city 1913.
Population: 446; Growth (since 2000): -18.0%; Density: 24.3 persons per square mile; Race: 95.5% White, 0.0% Black/African American, 0.0% Asian, 2.0% American Indian/Alaska Native, 0.0% Native Hawaiian/Other Pacific Islander, 2.5% Two or more races, 0.4% Hispanic of any race; Average household size: 2.46; Median age: 53.2; Age under 18: 17.9%; Age 65 and over: 23.1%; Males per 100 females: 114.7; Marriage status: 17.3% never married, 66.4% now married, 2.4% separated, 5.0% widowed, 11.3% divorced; Foreign born: 1.3%; Speak English only: 94.3%; With disability: 17.7%; Veterans: 15.6%; Ancestry: 26.2% German, 22.9% Irish, 16.6% Italian, 16.1% English, 14.6% Polish
Employment: 12.7% management, business, and financial, 3.9% computer, engineering, and science, 14.4% education, legal, community service, arts, and media, 7.2% healthcare practitioners, 20.4% service, 19.9% sales and office, 9.4% natural resources, construction, and maintenance, 12.2% production, transportation, and material moving

Income: Per capita: $25,383; Median household: $47,083; Average household: $60,017; Households with income of $100,000 or more: 18.3%; Poverty rate: 14.1%

Educational Attainment: High school diploma or higher: 88.4%; Bachelor's degree or higher: 15.1%; Graduate/professional degree or higher: 7.8%

School District(s)

Salamanca City SD (PK-12)

    2014-15 Enrollment: 1,320 . . . . (716) 945-2400

Housing: Homeownership rate: 95.6%; Median home value: $89,200; Median year structure built: 1967; Homeowner vacancy rate: 0.0%; Median selected monthly owner costs: $1,102 with a mortgage, $461 without a mortgage; Median gross rent: n/a per month; Rental vacancy rate: 0.0%

Health Insurance: 91.7% have insurance; 71.1% have private insurance; 43.0% have public insurance; 8.3% do not have insurance; 0.0% of children under 18 do not have insurance

Newspapers: County Chronicle (weekly circulation 5,000); Salamanca Press (daily circulation 2,000)

Transportation: Commute: 97.1% car, 0.0% public transportation, 1.1% walk, 1.7% work from home; Mean travel time to work: 19.6 minutes

---

SOUTH DAYTON (village). Covers a land area of 1.006 square miles and a water area of 0 square miles. Located at 42.36° N. Lat; 79.05° W. Long. Elevation is 1,306 feet.

Population: 756; Growth (since 2000): 14.2%; Density: 751.7 persons per square mile; Race: 98.3% White, 0.0% Black/African American, 0.0% Asian, 0.0% American Indian/Alaska Native, 0.0% Native Hawaiian/Other Pacific Islander, 0.7% Two or more races, 3.2% Hispanic of any race; Average household size: 2.60; Median age: 32.0; Age under 18: 32.8%; Age 65 and over: 12.8%; Males per 100 females: 94.4; Marriage status: 31.4% never married, 45.8% now married, 2.0% separated, 9.7% widowed, 13.0% divorced; Foreign born: 0.5%; Speak English only: 97.4%; With disability: 17.2%; Veterans: 9.8%; Ancestry: 42.1% German, 26.5% English, 18.5% Irish, 13.8% Polish, 9.9% Swedish

Employment: 7.7% management, business, and financial, 0.6% computer, engineering, and science, 5.8% education, legal, community service, arts, and media, 8.7% healthcare practitioners, 23.2% service, 20.0% sales and office, 15.2% natural resources, construction, and maintenance, 18.7% production, transportation, and material moving

Income: Per capita: $17,389; Median household: $38,438; Average household: $44,302; Households with income of $100,000 or more: 5.2%; Poverty rate: 14.6%

Educational Attainment: High school diploma or higher: 91.3%; Bachelor's degree or higher: 11.0%; Graduate/professional degree or higher: 4.9%

School District(s)

Pine Valley Central SD (South Dayton) (PK-12)

    2014-15 Enrollment: 644 . . . . (716) 988-3293

Housing: Homeownership rate: 67.7%; Median home value: $64,400; Median year structure built: Before 1940; Homeowner vacancy rate: 1.5%; Median selected monthly owner costs: $1,021 with a mortgage, $545 without a mortgage; Median gross rent: $675 per month; Rental vacancy rate: 0.0%

Health Insurance: 95.2% have insurance; 73.8% have private insurance; 39.7% have public insurance; 4.8% do not have insurance; 0.4% of children under 18 do not have insurance

Transportation: Commute: 92.2% car, 0.0% public transportation, 5.8% walk, 2.0% work from home; Mean travel time to work: 23.7 minutes

---

SOUTH VALLEY (town). Covers a land area of 36.840 square miles and a water area of 0.247 square miles. Located at 42.05° N. Lat; 79.00° W. Long.

Population: 220; Growth (since 2000): -27.2%; Density: 6.0 persons per square mile; Race: 98.6% White, 0.0% Black/African American, 0.0% Asian, 1.4% American Indian/Alaska Native, 0.0% Native Hawaiian/Other Pacific Islander, 0.0% Two or more races, 0.0% Hispanic of any race; Average household size: 1.79; Median age: 59.7; Age under 18: 5.5%; Age 65 and over: 32.7%; Males per 100 females: 123.7; Marriage status: 16.7% never married, 60.3% now married, 1.4% separated, 4.8% widowed, 18.2% divorced; Foreign born: 0.0%; Speak English only: 100.0%; With disability: 25.5%; Veterans: 16.8%; Ancestry: 41.8% German, 18.6% Irish, 10.9% Swedish, 7.7% Polish, 6.8% American

Employment: 15.2% management, business, and financial, 1.1% computer, engineering, and science, 13.0% education, legal, community service, arts, and media, 7.6% healthcare practitioners, 15.2% service,

20.7% sales and office, 7.6% natural resources, construction, and maintenance, 19.6% production, transportation, and material moving

Income: Per capita: $31,955; Median household: $56,250; Average household: $58,099; Households with income of $100,000 or more: 16.3%; Poverty rate: 12.7%

Educational Attainment: High school diploma or higher: 91.9%; Bachelor's degree or higher: 19.7%; Graduate/professional degree or higher: 14.6%

Housing: Homeownership rate: 92.7%; Median home value: $86,400; Median year structure built: 1988; Homeowner vacancy rate: 0.0%; Median selected monthly owner costs: $1,108 with a mortgage, $437 without a mortgage; Median gross rent: $588 per month; Rental vacancy rate: 0.0%

Health Insurance: 95.5% have insurance; 73.2% have private insurance; 49.5% have public insurance; 4.5% do not have insurance; 0.0% of children under 18 do not have insurance

Transportation: Commute: 92.8% car, 0.0% public transportation, 2.4% walk, 1.2% work from home; Mean travel time to work: 44.4 minutes

---

STEAMBURG (unincorporated postal area)

ZCTA: 14783

Covers a land area of 24.917 square miles and a water area of 6.425 square miles. Located at 42.08° N. Lat; 78.89° W. Long. Elevation is 1,407 feet.

Population: 330; Growth (since 2000): -19.9%; Density: 13.2 persons per square mile; Race: 55.5% White, 0.0% Black/African American, 0.0% Asian, 44.5% American Indian/Alaska Native, 0.0% Native Hawaiian/Other Pacific Islander, 0.0% Two or more races, 0.0% Hispanic of any race; Average household size: 2.26; Median age: 44.0; Age under 18: 21.2%; Age 65 and over: 12.1%; Males per 100 females: 113.3; Marriage status: 28.2% never married, 41.4% now married, 0.0% separated, 8.6% widowed, 21.8% divorced; Foreign born: 0.0%; Speak English only: 90.2%; With disability: 12.4%; Veterans: 5.4%; Ancestry: 20.6% German, 16.1% Irish, 12.1% English, 7.0% French, 3.9% American

Employment: 1.7% management, business, and financial, 0.0% computer, engineering, and science, 4.6% education, legal, community service, arts, and media, 2.3% healthcare practitioners, 25.1% service, 21.1% sales and office, 24.6% natural resources, construction, and maintenance, 20.6% production, transportation, and material moving

Income: Per capita: $18,923; Median household: $31,111; Average household: $41,764; Households with income of $100,000 or more: 4.8%; Poverty rate: 27.9%

Educational Attainment: High school diploma or higher: 87.3%; Bachelor's degree or higher: 6.1%; Graduate/professional degree or higher: 4.4%

Housing: Homeownership rate: 85.6%; Median home value: $69,700; Median year structure built: 1968; Homeowner vacancy rate: 0.0%; Median selected monthly owner costs: $910 with a mortgage, $354 without a mortgage; Median gross rent: $429 per month; Rental vacancy rate: 0.0%

Health Insurance: 70.3% have insurance; 47.9% have private insurance; 34.2% have public insurance; 29.7% do not have insurance; 5.7% of children under 18 do not have insurance

Transportation: Commute: 93.5% car, 0.0% public transportation, 2.4% walk, 4.2% work from home; Mean travel time to work: 18.7 minutes

---

VERSAILLES (unincorporated postal area)

ZCTA: 14168

Covers a land area of 0.040 square miles and a water area of 0 square miles. Located at 42.52° N. Lat; 78.99° W. Long. Elevation is 764 feet.

Population: 76; Growth (since 2000): n/a; Density: 1,917.6 persons per square mile; Race: 69.7% White, 0.0% Black/African American, 0.0% Asian, 30.3% American Indian/Alaska Native, 0.0% Native Hawaiian/Other Pacific Islander, 0.0% Two or more races, 51.3% Hispanic of any race; Average household size: 3.30; Median age: 16.9; Age under 18: 51.3%; Age 65 and over: 0.0%; Males per 100 females: 111.8; Marriage status: 22.9% never married, 52.1% now married, 0.0% separated, 0.0% widowed, 25.0% divorced; Foreign born: 0.0%; Speak English only: 100.0%; With disability: 18.4%; Veterans: 0.0%; Ancestry: 28.9% French, 28.9% Swedish, 14.5% Scottish, 3.9% American

Employment: 44.1% management, business, and financial, 0.0% computer, engineering, and science, 0.0% education, legal, community service, arts, and media, 0.0% healthcare practitioners, 23.5% service, 0.0% sales and office, 32.4% natural resources, construction, and maintenance, 0.0% production, transportation, and material moving

Income: Per capita: $17,457; Median household: n/a; Average household: $56,200; Households with income of $100,000 or more: n/a; Poverty rate: 61.8%

Educational Attainment: High school diploma or higher: 100.0%; Bachelor's degree or higher: 21.6%; Graduate/professional degree or higher: n/a

Housing: Homeownership rate: 13.0%; Median home value: n/a; Median year structure built: Before 1940; Homeowner vacancy rate: 0.0%; Median selected monthly owner costs: $0 with a mortgage, $0 without a mortgage; Median gross rent: n/a per month; Rental vacancy rate: 0.0%

Health Insurance: 44.7% have insurance; 7.9% have private insurance; 36.8% have public insurance; 55.3% do not have insurance; 28.2% of children under 18 do not have insurance

Transportation: Commute: 100.0% car, 0.0% public transportation, 0.0% walk, 0.0% work from home; Mean travel time to work: 0.0 minutes

WEST VALLEY (CDP).
Covers a land area of 1.532 square miles and a water area of 0.003 square miles. Located at 42.40° N. Lat; 78.61° W. Long. Elevation is 1,522 feet.

Population: 468; Growth (since 2000): n/a; Density: 305.5 persons per square mile; Race: 92.1% White, 0.0% Black/African American, 0.0% Asian, 0.0% American Indian/Alaska Native, 0.0% Native Hawaiian/Other Pacific Islander, 7.9% Two or more races, 0.0% Hispanic of any race; Average household size: 2.31; Median age: 48.0; Age under 18: 22.4%; Age 65 and over: 24.8%; Males per 100 females: 103.9; Marriage status: 23.7% never married, 58.2% now married, 6.1% separated, 1.3% widowed, 16.8% divorced; Foreign born: 0.0%; Speak English only: 100.0%; With disability: 9.2%; Veterans: 6.1%; Ancestry: 65.8% German, 14.3% Scottish, 12.0% Irish, 9.4% English, 4.3% European

Employment: 3.0% management, business, and financial, 0.0% computer, engineering, and science, 5.6% education, legal, community service, arts, and media, 0.0% healthcare practitioners, 32.1% service, 25.6% sales and office, 11.1% natural resources, construction, and maintenance, 22.6% production, transportation, and material moving

Income: Per capita: $22,452; Median household: $43,024; Average household: $50,698; Households with income of $100,000 or more: 14.8%; Poverty rate: 20.9%

Educational Attainment: High school diploma or higher: 96.6%; Bachelor's degree or higher: 19.9%; Graduate/professional degree or higher: 9.0%

School District(s)
West Valley Central SD (PK-12)
  2014-15 Enrollment: 295 . . . . (716) 942-3293

Housing: Homeownership rate: 70.0%; Median home value: $93,000; Median year structure built: 1954; Homeowner vacancy rate: 0.0%; Median selected monthly owner costs: $1,170 with a mortgage, $620 without a mortgage; Median gross rent: $530 per month; Rental vacancy rate: 0.0%

Health Insurance: 97.9% have insurance; 85.5% have private insurance; 47.0% have public insurance; 2.1% do not have insurance; 0.0% of children under 18 do not have insurance

Transportation: Commute: 85.9% car, 0.0% public transportation, 2.1% walk, 12.0% work from home; Mean travel time to work: 34.5 minutes

WESTON MILLS (CDP).
Covers a land area of 6.669 square miles and a water area of 0.073 square miles. Located at 42.08° N. Lat; 78.37° W. Long. Elevation is 1,463 feet.

Population: 1,527; Growth (since 2000): -5.0%; Density: 229.0 persons per square mile; Race: 97.4% White, 0.1% Black/African American, 1.7% Asian, 0.0% American Indian/Alaska Native, 0.0% Native Hawaiian/Other Pacific Islander, 0.8% Two or more races, 3.7% Hispanic of any race; Average household size: 2.33; Median age: 48.8; Age under 18: 18.3%; Age 65 and over: 24.5%; Males per 100 females: 96.3; Marriage status: 30.2% never married, 49.3% now married, 0.4% separated, 9.9% widowed, 10.6% divorced; Foreign born: 0.3%; Speak English only: 100.0%; With disability: 20.6%; Veterans: 16.1%; Ancestry: 24.1% German, 16.0% Irish, 14.8% English, 7.8% Italian, 6.6% Polish

Employment: 14.0% management, business, and financial, 1.3% computer, engineering, and science, 11.2% education, legal, community service, arts, and media, 9.1% healthcare practitioners, 9.3% service, 25.2% sales and office, 6.8% natural resources, construction, and maintenance, 23.0% production, transportation, and material moving

Income: Per capita: $26,010; Median household: $44,208; Average household: $60,658; Households with income of $100,000 or more: 15.9%; Poverty rate: 8.4%

Educational Attainment: High school diploma or higher: 89.4%; Bachelor's degree or higher: 17.8%; Graduate/professional degree or higher: 10.2%

Housing: Homeownership rate: 71.6%; Median home value: $86,700; Median year structure built: 1958; Homeowner vacancy rate: 0.0%; Median selected monthly owner costs: $1,052 with a mortgage, $515 without a mortgage; Median gross rent: $536 per month; Rental vacancy rate: 0.0%

Health Insurance: 91.6% have insurance; 71.9% have private insurance; 43.8% have public insurance; 8.4% do not have insurance; 3.3% of children under 18 do not have insurance

Transportation: Commute: 96.4% car, 1.5% public transportation, 2.1% walk, 0.0% work from home; Mean travel time to work: 19.2 minutes

WESTONS MILLS (unincorporated postal area)
ZCTA: 14788

Covers a land area of 0.210 square miles and a water area of 0 square miles. Located at 42.06° N. Lat; 78.38° W. Long. Elevation is 1,440 feet.

Population: 222; Growth (since 2000): n/a; Density: 1,055.0 persons per square mile; Race: 99.5% White, 0.5% Black/African American, 0.0% Asian, 0.0% American Indian/Alaska Native, 0.0% Native Hawaiian/Other Pacific Islander, 0.0% Two or more races, 4.5% Hispanic of any race; Average household size: 1.82; Median age: 27.9; Age under 18: 7.2%; Age 65 and over: 39.6%; Males per 100 females: 123.3; Marriage status: 43.9% never married, 36.8% now married, 0.0% separated, 14.6% widowed, 4.7% divorced; Foreign born: 0.0%; Speak English only: 100.0%; With disability: 31.9%; Veterans: 12.1%; Ancestry: 18.0% English, 16.7% German, 13.1% Irish, 13.1% Pennsylvania German, 13.1% Polish

Employment: 0.0% management, business, and financial, 0.0% computer, engineering, and science, 0.0% education, legal, community service, arts, and media, 30.7% healthcare practitioners, 26.1% service, 1.1% sales and office, 11.4% natural resources, construction, and maintenance, 30.7% production, transportation, and material moving

Income: Per capita: $28,335; Median household: $62,188; Average household: $56,123; Households with income of $100,000 or more: n/a; Poverty rate: 15.0%

Educational Attainment: High school diploma or higher: 71.1%; Bachelor's degree or higher: 14.9%; Graduate/professional degree or higher: 14.9%

Housing: Homeownership rate: 25.5%; Median home value: n/a; Median year structure built: 1945; Homeowner vacancy rate: 0.0%; Median selected monthly owner costs: $0 with a mortgage, $0 without a mortgage; Median gross rent: $425 per month; Rental vacancy rate: 0.0%

Health Insurance: 73.2% have insurance; 39.9% have private insurance; 60.6% have public insurance; 26.8% do not have insurance; 100.0% of children under 18 do not have insurance

Transportation: Commute: 100.0% car, 0.0% public transportation, 0.0% walk, 0.0% work from home; Mean travel time to work: 0.0 minutes

YORKSHIRE (CDP).
Covers a land area of 1.845 square miles and a water area of 0.010 square miles. Located at 42.52° N. Lat; 78.48° W. Long. Elevation is 1,434 feet.

Population: 1,093; Growth (since 2000): -22.1%; Density: 592.5 persons per square mile; Race: 96.1% White, 0.0% Black/African American, 0.0% Asian, 0.0% American Indian/Alaska Native, 0.0% Native Hawaiian/Other Pacific Islander, 3.9% Two or more races, 1.0% Hispanic of any race; Average household size: 1.81; Median age: 53.1; Age under 18: 13.3%; Age 65 and over: 19.3%; Males per 100 females: 85.8; Marriage status: 19.4% never married, 49.3% now married, 0.0% separated, 13.2% widowed, 18.1% divorced; Foreign born: 0.0%; Speak English only: 99.0%; With disability: 33.5%; Veterans: 14.3%; Ancestry: 53.1% German, 25.1% English, 23.5% Irish, 10.2% Polish, 7.6% French

Employment: 0.0% management, business, and financial, 0.0% computer, engineering, and science, 1.5% education, legal, community service, arts, and media, 0.0% healthcare practitioners, 12.8% service, 33.3% sales and office, 8.1% natural resources, construction, and maintenance, 44.3% production, transportation, and material moving

Income: Per capita: $19,177; Median household: $22,250; Average household: $34,447; Households with income of $100,000 or more: 1.0%; Poverty rate: 19.2%

Educational Attainment: High school diploma or higher: 74.5%; Bachelor's degree or higher: 9.3%; Graduate/professional degree or higher: 3.7%

Yorkshire-Pioneer Central SD (PK-12)
   2014-15 Enrollment: 2,585 . . . . (716) 492-9304
Housing: Homeownership rate: 73.1%; Median home value: $22,900;
Median year structure built: 1984; Homeowner vacancy rate: 0.0%; Median
selected monthly owner costs: $876 with a mortgage, $288 without a
mortgage; Median gross rent: $646 per month; Rental vacancy rate: 0.0%
Health Insurance: 90.5% have insurance; 56.6% have private insurance;
47.6% have public insurance; 9.5% do not have insurance; 0.0% of
children under 18 do not have insurance
Transportation: Commute: 90.9% car, 0.0% public transportation, 9.1%
walk, 0.0% work from home; Mean travel time to work: 20.1 minutes

YORKSHIRE (town). Covers a land area of 36.249 square miles and a
water area of 0.145 square miles. Located at 42.48° N. Lat; 78.52° W.
Long. Elevation is 1,434 feet.
Population: 3,837; Growth (since 2000): -8.9%; Density: 105.9 persons
per square mile; Race: 98.0% White, 0.0% Black/African American, 0.2%
Asian, 0.0% American Indian/Alaska Native, 0.0% Native Hawaiian/Other
Pacific Islander, 1.8% Two or more races, 1.8% Hispanic of any race;
Average household size: 2.33; Median age: 41.8; Age under 18: 21.9%;
Age 65 and over: 12.6%; Males per 100 females: 99.7; Marriage status:
24.2% never married, 56.1% now married, 2.9% separated, 8.4%
widowed, 11.3% divorced; Foreign born: 0.5%; Speak English only: 98.5%;
With disability: 19.9%; Veterans: 12.3%; Ancestry: 39.9% German, 24.1%
Irish, 14.0% English, 11.6% Polish, 6.1% Italian
Employment: 5.9% management, business, and financial, 0.9% computer,
engineering, and science, 7.2% education, legal, community service, arts,
and media, 4.0% healthcare practitioners, 19.3% service, 23.4% sales and
office, 13.4% natural resources, construction, and maintenance, 25.9%
production, transportation, and material moving
Income: Per capita: $19,723; Median household: $36,369; Average
household: $45,784; Households with income of $100,000 or more: 7.5%;
Poverty rate: 13.2%
Educational Attainment: High school diploma or higher: 82.1%;
Bachelor's degree or higher: 12.9%; Graduate/professional degree or
higher: 4.6%
Yorkshire-Pioneer Central SD (PK-12)
   2014-15 Enrollment: 2,585 . . . . (716) 492-9304
Housing: Homeownership rate: 72.0%; Median home value: $84,900;
Median year structure built: 1978; Homeowner vacancy rate: 0.0%; Median
selected monthly owner costs: $1,085 with a mortgage, $362 without a
mortgage; Median gross rent: $587 per month; Rental vacancy rate: 3.4%
Health Insurance: 87.7% have insurance; 62.9% have private insurance;
40.0% have public insurance; 12.3% do not have insurance; 14.0% of
children under 18 do not have insurance
Transportation: Commute: 90.4% car, 0.4% public transportation, 5.5%
walk, 3.1% work from home; Mean travel time to work: 22.9 minutes

Cayuga County

Located in west central New York; bounded on the north by Lake Ontario;
drained by the Seneca River. Covers a land area of 691.582 square miles,
a water area of 172.089 square miles, and is located in the Eastern Time
Zone at 43.01° N. Lat., 76.57° W. Long. The county was founded in 1799.
County seat is Auburn.

Cayuga County is part of the Auburn, NY Micropolitan Statistical Area. The
entire metro area includes: Cayuga County, NY

Weather Station: Aurora Research Farm   Elevation: 830 feet

	Jan	Feb	Mar	Apr	May	Jun	Jul	Aug	Sep	Oct	Nov	Dec
High	32	34	42	56	68	77	81	80	73	60	48	37
Low	17	18	25	36	46	56	61	59	52	41	33	23
Precip	1.9	1.7	2.6	3.3	3.2	3.8	3.5	3.1	4.1	3.4	3.2	2.3
Snow	14.5	11.8	12.1	4.0	0.2	0.0	0.0	0.0	0.0	0.2	4.9	11.3

High and Low temperatures in degrees Fahrenheit; Precipitation and Snow in inches

Population: 79,173; Growth (since 2000): -3.4%; Density: 114.5 persons
per square mile; Race: 92.3% White, 4.4% Black/African American, 0.4%
Asian, 0.4% American Indian/Alaska Native, 0.0% Native Hawaiian/Other
Pacific Islander, 2.0% two or more races, 2.7% Hispanic of any race;
Average household size: 2.43; Median age: 42.5; Age under 18: 20.7%;
Age 65 and over: 16.5%; Males per 100 females: 104.2; Marriage status:
30.9% never married, 49.8% now married, 3.0% separated, 7.4%

widowed, 11.9% divorced; Foreign born: 2.5%; Speak English only: 94.9%;
With disability: 13.9%; Veterans: 9.9%; Ancestry: 21.4% Irish, 18.2%
German, 16.5% English, 15.3% Italian, 6.3% Polish
Religion: Six largest groups: 29.9% Catholicism, 4.2% Methodist/Pietist,
2.0% Baptist, 1.6% Presbyterian-Reformed, 1.4% Non-denominational
Protestant, 1.0% Holiness
Economy: Unemployment rate: 4.5%; Leading industries: 15.2 % retail
trade; 14.4 % construction; 12.0 % health care and social assistance;
Farms: 891 totaling 238,444 acres; Company size: 0 employ 1,000 or more
persons, 1 employs 500 to 999 persons, 26 employ 100 to 499 persons,
1,626 employ less than 100 persons; Business ownership: 1,511
women-owned, 50 Black-owned, 25 Hispanic-owned, 79 Asian-owned, 38
American Indian/Alaska Native-owned
Employment: 12.6% management, business, and financial, 3.2%
computer, engineering, and science, 11.9% education, legal, community
service, arts, and media, 5.0% healthcare practitioners, 19.9% service,
22.4% sales and office, 10.3% natural resources, construction, and
maintenance, 14.7% production, transportation, and material moving
Income: Per capita: $25,786; Median household: $52,082; Average
household: $63,949; Households with income of $100,000 or more: 18.6%;
Poverty rate: 12.0%
Educational Attainment: High school diploma or higher: 87.7%;
Bachelor's degree or higher: 21.4%; Graduate/professional degree or
higher: 8.8%
Housing: Homeownership rate: 71.1%; Median home value: $113,600;
Median year structure built: 1955; Homeowner vacancy rate: 2.0%; Median
selected monthly owner costs: $1,199 with a mortgage, $509 without a
mortgage; Median gross rent: $673 per month; Rental vacancy rate: 3.9%
Vital Statistics: Birth rate: 94.0 per 10,000 population; Death rate: 88.0
per 10,000 population; Age-adjusted cancer mortality rate: 182.4 deaths
per 100,000 population
Health Insurance: 91.6% have insurance; 71.0% have private insurance;
36.2% have public insurance; 8.4% do not have insurance; 4.8% of
children under 18 do not have insurance
Health Care: Physicians: 8.9 per 10,000 population; Dentists: 4.2 per
10,000 population; Hospital beds: 22.6 per 10,000 population; Hospital
admissions: 579.6 per 10,000 population
Transportation: Commute: 90.1% car, 0.9% public transportation, 3.8%
walk, 4.1% work from home; Mean travel time to work: 22.3 minutes
2016 Presidential Election: 53.1% Trump, 41.3% Clinton, 4.1% Johnson,
1.5% Stein
National and State Parks: Bear Swamp State Forest; Fair Haven Beach
State Park; Fillmore Glen State Park; Howland Island State Wildlife
Management Area; Long Point State Park; Summer Hill State Forest
Additional Information Contacts
Cayuga Government . . . . (315) 253-1211
   http://www.co.cayuga.ny.us

Cayuga County Communities

AUBURN (city). County seat. Covers a land area of 8.336 square miles
and a water area of 0.075 square miles. Located at 42.93° N. Lat; 76.57°
W. Long. Elevation is 686 feet.
History: In 1793, Colonel John Hardenbergh, surveyor and Revolutionary
veteran, built the first cabin on the present site of Auburn and a year later
erected the first gristmill on the Owasco Outlet. At a meeting in 1805 the
present name was taken from Goldsmith's "The Deserted Village."
Transportation facilities and abundant water power attracted industry. A
scythe factory, a carpet factory, and the D. M. Osborne Company, which
was later absorbed by International Harvester, were among its industries.
The Auburn Theological Seminary, chartered by the Presbyterian General
Assembly in 1819, was merged with the Union Theological Seminary in
New York City 120 years later.
Population: 27,264; Growth (since 2000): -4.6%; Density: 3,270.5 persons
per square mile; Race: 85.3% White, 10.0% Black/African American, 0.4%
Asian, 0.6% American Indian/Alaska Native, 0.0% Native Hawaiian/Other
Pacific Islander, 3.3% Two or more races, 3.3% Hispanic of any race;
Average household size: 2.23; Median age: 39.5; Age under 18: 19.4%;
Age 65 and over: 16.3%; Males per 100 females: 102.9; Marriage status:
37.8% never married, 39.4% now married, 4.1% separated, 9.2%
widowed, 13.6% divorced; Foreign born: 3.2%; Speak English only: 91.7%;
With disability: 15.4%; Veterans: 8.6%; Ancestry: 20.9% Irish, 19.9%
Italian, 15.8% German, 13.2% English, 7.2% Polish
Employment: 10.2% management, business, and financial, 2.6%
computer, engineering, and science, 14.4% education, legal, community

service, arts, and media, 4.7% healthcare practitioners, 24.2% service, 23.1% sales and office, 6.9% natural resources, construction, and maintenance, 13.9% production, transportation, and material moving
Income: Per capita: $20,910; Median household: $39,438; Average household: $48,957; Households with income of $100,000 or more: 11.5%; Poverty rate: 17.9%
Educational Attainment: High school diploma or higher: 84.4%; Bachelor's degree or higher: 18.5%; Graduate/professional degree or higher: 7.0%

School District(s)
Auburn City SD (PK-12)
    2014-15 Enrollment: 4,293 . . . . (315) 255-8835
Cayuga-Onondaga Boces
    2014-15 Enrollment: n/a . . . . (315) 253-0361
Two-year College(s)
Cayuga County Community College (Public)
    Fall 2014 Enrollment: 4,290 . . . . (315) 255-1743
    2015-16 Tuition: In-state $4,742; Out-of-state $9,068
Vocational/Technical School(s)
Cayuga Onondaga BOCES-Practical Nursing Program (Public)
    Fall 2014 Enrollment: 34 . . . . (315) 253-0361
    2015-16 Tuition: In-state $9,613; Out-of-state $9,613
Housing: Homeownership rate: 46.6%; Median home value: $96,000; Median year structure built: Before 1940; Homeowner vacancy rate: 2.4%; Median selected monthly owner costs: $1,134 with a mortgage, $491 without a mortgage; Median gross rent: $654 per month; Rental vacancy rate: 4.4%
Health Insurance: 90.0% have insurance; 65.1% have private insurance; 41.0% have public insurance; 10.0% do not have insurance; 4.9% of children under 18 do not have insurance
Hospitals: Auburn Community Hospital (99 beds)
Safety: Violent crime rate: 49.5 per 10,000 population; Property crime rate: 368.1 per 10,000 population
Newspapers: Skaneateles Journal (weekly circulation 5,500); The Citizen (daily circulation 11,600)
Transportation: Commute: 85.1% car, 2.4% public transportation, 6.5% walk, 4.0% work from home; Mean travel time to work: 17.4 minutes
Additional Information Contacts
City of Auburn . . . . (315) 255-4104
    http://www.auburnny.gov

AURELIUS (town). Covers a land area of 30.245 square miles and a water area of 1.749 square miles. Located at 42.93° N. Lat; 76.67° W. Long.
Population: 2,751; Growth (since 2000): -6.3%; Density: 91.0 persons per square mile; Race: 98.9% White, 0.4% Black/African American, 0.0% Asian, 0.1% American Indian/Alaska Native, 0.0% Native Hawaiian/Other Pacific Islander, 0.5% Two or more races, 0.0% Hispanic of any race; Average household size: 2.43; Median age: 47.4; Age under 18: 18.4%; Age 65 and over: 18.9%; Males per 100 females: 100.6; Marriage status: 21.8% never married, 61.8% now married, 2.9% separated, 6.3% widowed, 10.1% divorced; Foreign born: 1.0%; Speak English only: 96.5%; With disability: 14.8%; Veterans: 10.6%; Ancestry: 24.3% English, 23.6% Irish, 19.0% German, 15.4% Italian, 7.8% Polish
Employment: 14.2% management, business, and financial, 1.7% computer, engineering, and science, 11.3% education, legal, community service, arts, and media, 5.1% healthcare practitioners, 18.3% service, 22.9% sales and office, 10.3% natural resources, construction, and maintenance, 16.3% production, transportation, and material moving
Income: Per capita: $28,888; Median household: $55,000; Average household: $69,111; Households with income of $100,000 or more: 23.3%; Poverty rate: 5.1%
Educational Attainment: High school diploma or higher: 89.5%; Bachelor's degree or higher: 20.9%; Graduate/professional degree or higher: 9.5%
Housing: Homeownership rate: 87.9%; Median home value: $125,300; Median year structure built: 1956; Homeowner vacancy rate: 2.3%; Median selected monthly owner costs: $1,194 with a mortgage, $487 without a mortgage; Median gross rent: $611 per month; Rental vacancy rate: 3.5%
Health Insurance: 93.1% have insurance; 76.1% have private insurance; 34.8% have public insurance; 6.9% do not have insurance; 5.5% of children under 18 do not have insurance
Transportation: Commute: 97.6% car, 0.0% public transportation, 1.5% walk, 0.8% work from home; Mean travel time to work: 21.3 minutes

Additional Information Contacts
Town of Aurelius . . . . (315) 255-1894
    http://co.cayuga.ny.us/aurelius/index.html

AURORA (village). Covers a land area of 0.919 square miles and a water area of <.001 square miles. Located at 42.75° N. Lat; 76.70° W. Long. Elevation is 413 feet.
History: Seat of Wells College (1869).
Population: 740; Growth (since 2000): 2.8%; Density: 805.2 persons per square mile; Race: 85.4% White, 8.6% Black/African American, 0.8% Asian, 0.0% American Indian/Alaska Native, 0.0% Native Hawaiian/Other Pacific Islander, 3.5% Two or more races, 8.5% Hispanic of any race; Average household size: 2.11; Median age: 21.8; Age under 18: 5.7%; Age 65 and over: 10.0%; Males per 100 females: 60.5; Marriage status: 68.1% never married, 26.9% now married, 0.6% separated, 1.0% widowed, 4.1% divorced; Foreign born: 9.5%; Speak English only: 85.4%; With disability: 14.5%; Veterans: 2.6%; Ancestry: 23.8% German, 19.6% Irish, 16.6% English, 12.3% Italian, 7.8% Norwegian
Employment: 11.5% management, business, and financial, 5.3% computer, engineering, and science, 26.9% education, legal, community service, arts, and media, 1.4% healthcare practitioners, 26.7% service, 20.5% sales and office, 4.8% natural resources, construction, and maintenance, 3.0% production, transportation, and material moving
Income: Per capita: $22,224; Median household: $70,833; Average household: $75,796; Households with income of $100,000 or more: 28.6%; Poverty rate: 2.9%
Educational Attainment: High school diploma or higher: 92.8%; Bachelor's degree or higher: 48.3%; Graduate/professional degree or higher: 31.5%

School District(s)
Southern Cayuga Central SD (PK-12)
    2014-15 Enrollment: 690 . . . . (315) 364-7211
Four-year College(s)
Wells College (Private, Not-for-profit)
    Fall 2014 Enrollment: 550 . . . . (315) 364-3266
    2015-16 Tuition: In-state $37,500; Out-of-state $37,500
Housing: Homeownership rate: 65.9%; Median home value: $163,000; Median year structure built: Before 1940; Homeowner vacancy rate: 5.3%; Median selected monthly owner costs: $1,281 with a mortgage, $693 without a mortgage; Median gross rent: $758 per month; Rental vacancy rate: 0.0%
Health Insurance: 94.1% have insurance; 79.6% have private insurance; 24.7% have public insurance; 5.9% do not have insurance; 4.8% of children under 18 do not have insurance
Transportation: Commute: 51.3% car, 1.8% public transportation, 37.1% walk, 9.5% work from home; Mean travel time to work: 18.8 minutes

BRUTUS (town). Covers a land area of 22.106 square miles and a water area of 0.394 square miles. Located at 43.05° N. Lat; 76.55° W. Long.
Population: 4,400; Growth (since 2000): -7.9%; Density: 199.0 persons per square mile; Race: 97.8% White, 0.1% Black/African American, 0.9% Asian, 0.1% American Indian/Alaska Native, 0.0% Native Hawaiian/Other Pacific Islander, 1.1% Two or more races, 1.2% Hispanic of any race; Average household size: 2.47; Median age: 42.9; Age under 18: 22.9%; Age 65 and over: 15.4%; Males per 100 females: 94.6; Marriage status: 30.3% never married, 49.8% now married, 3.9% separated, 6.5% widowed, 13.4% divorced; Foreign born: 2.2%; Speak English only: 97.6%; With disability: 16.3%; Veterans: 13.1%; Ancestry: 20.2% English, 20.1% German, 19.7% Irish, 15.2% Italian, 6.5% Polish
Employment: 10.9% management, business, and financial, 3.1% computer, engineering, and science, 8.3% education, legal, community service, arts, and media, 4.8% healthcare practitioners, 19.5% service, 28.8% sales and office, 8.6% natural resources, construction, and maintenance, 16.0% production, transportation, and material moving
Income: Per capita: $25,756; Median household: $54,362; Average household: $62,132; Households with income of $100,000 or more: 19.9%; Poverty rate: 10.8%
Educational Attainment: High school diploma or higher: 89.7%; Bachelor's degree or higher: 21.0%; Graduate/professional degree or higher: 8.9%
Housing: Homeownership rate: 77.9%; Median home value: $107,100; Median year structure built: 1970; Homeowner vacancy rate: 1.6%; Median selected monthly owner costs: $1,260 with a mortgage, $495 without a mortgage; Median gross rent: $708 per month; Rental vacancy rate: 0.0%

Health Insurance: 96.1% have insurance; 78.4% have private insurance; 33.2% have public insurance; 3.9% do not have insurance; 0.0% of children under 18 do not have insurance
Transportation: Commute: 94.9% car, 0.0% public transportation, 1.1% walk, 2.0% work from home; Mean travel time to work: 22.7 minutes
Additional Information Contacts
Town of Brutus . . . . (315) 834-9398
  http://www.townofbrutus.org

CATO (town). Covers a land area of 33.643 square miles and a water area of 2.544 square miles. Located at 43.12° N. Lat; 76.54° W. Long. Elevation is 459 feet.
Population: 2,610; Growth (since 2000): -4.9%; Density: 77.6 persons per square mile; Race: 97.2% White, 1.3% Black/African American, 0.4% Asian, 0.5% American Indian/Alaska Native, 0.0% Native Hawaiian/Other Pacific Islander, 0.6% Two or more races, 0.3% Hispanic of any race; Average household size: 2.62; Median age: 44.1; Age under 18: 20.6%; Age 65 and over: 13.2%; Males per 100 females: 104.3; Marriage status: 26.2% never married, 59.7% now married, 1.3% separated, 5.5% widowed, 8.6% divorced; Foreign born: 2.1%; Speak English only: 94.5%; With disability: 12.8%; Veterans: 9.3%; Ancestry: 28.2% German, 21.0% Irish, 15.5% English, 9.8% Italian, 8.2% French
Employment: 16.1% management, business, and financial, 4.3% computer, engineering, and science, 8.9% education, legal, community service, arts, and media, 7.7% healthcare practitioners, 14.9% service, 20.6% sales and office, 13.1% natural resources, construction, and maintenance, 14.4% production, transportation, and material moving
Income: Per capita: $27,353; Median household: $62,069; Average household: $70,228; Households with income of $100,000 or more: 22.4%; Poverty rate: 6.2%
Educational Attainment: High school diploma or higher: 89.2%; Bachelor's degree or higher: 25.3%; Graduate/professional degree or higher: 7.5%

School District(s)
Cato-Meridian Central SD (PK-12)
  2014-15 Enrollment: 993 . . . . (315) 626-3439
Housing: Homeownership rate: 88.0%; Median home value: $132,000; Median year structure built: 1973; Homeowner vacancy rate: 2.5%; Median selected monthly owner costs: $1,262 with a mortgage, $534 without a mortgage; Median gross rent: $758 per month; Rental vacancy rate: 13.0%
Health Insurance: 91.1% have insurance; 76.3% have private insurance; 26.0% have public insurance; 8.9% do not have insurance; 8.2% of children under 18 do not have insurance
Transportation: Commute: 91.8% car, 0.3% public transportation, 1.4% walk, 5.2% work from home; Mean travel time to work: 26.3 minutes

CATO (village). Covers a land area of 0.989 square miles and a water area of 0.025 square miles. Located at 43.17° N. Lat; 76.57° W. Long. Elevation is 459 feet.
Population: 655; Growth (since 2000): 9.0%; Density: 662.6 persons per square mile; Race: 91.0% White, 0.0% Black/African American, 0.0% Asian, 2.0% American Indian/Alaska Native, 0.0% Native Hawaiian/Other Pacific Islander, 0.0% Two or more races, 0.5% Hispanic of any race; Average household size: 2.86; Median age: 28.7; Age under 18: 31.8%; Age 65 and over: 10.1%; Males per 100 females: 90.0; Marriage status: 34.8% never married, 44.6% now married, 1.2% separated, 6.1% widowed, 14.5% divorced; Foreign born: 0.3%; Speak English only: 98.3%; With disability: 15.0%; Veterans: 11.9%; Ancestry: 18.6% Irish, 13.9% German, 10.2% English, 8.9% Polish, 8.2% French
Employment: 12.7% management, business, and financial, 0.7% computer, engineering, and science, 8.5% education, legal, community service, arts, and media, 8.1% healthcare practitioners, 13.0% service, 30.0% sales and office, 10.7% natural resources, construction, and maintenance, 16.3% production, transportation, and material moving
Income: Per capita: $19,468; Median household: $47,083; Average household: $55,261; Households with income of $100,000 or more: 13.2%; Poverty rate: 10.4%
Educational Attainment: High school diploma or higher: 93.9%; Bachelor's degree or higher: 9.6%; Graduate/professional degree or higher: 6.1%

School District(s)
Cato-Meridian Central SD (PK-12)
  2014-15 Enrollment: 993 . . . . (315) 626-3439
Housing: Homeownership rate: 55.0%; Median home value: $96,900; Median year structure built: Before 1940; Homeowner vacancy rate: 7.6%;

Median selected monthly owner costs: $1,083 with a mortgage, $589 without a mortgage; Median gross rent: $701 per month; Rental vacancy rate: 0.0%
Health Insurance: 90.5% have insurance; 69.2% have private insurance; 30.8% have public insurance; 9.5% do not have insurance; 2.4% of children under 18 do not have insurance
Transportation: Commute: 84.0% car, 0.0% public transportation, 11.4% walk, 4.6% work from home; Mean travel time to work: 25.7 minutes

CAYUGA (village). Covers a land area of 0.904 square miles and a water area of 0.462 square miles. Located at 42.92° N. Lat; 76.73° W. Long. Elevation is 482 feet.
Population: 545; Growth (since 2000): 7.1%; Density: 603.0 persons per square mile; Race: 98.0% White, 1.3% Black/African American, 0.0% Asian, 0.4% American Indian/Alaska Native, 0.0% Native Hawaiian/Other Pacific Islander, 0.4% Two or more races, 0.0% Hispanic of any race; Average household size: 2.33; Median age: 50.9; Age under 18: 18.3%; Age 65 and over: 25.1%; Males per 100 females: 94.7; Marriage status: 22.8% never married, 61.9% now married, 3.1% separated, 5.0% widowed, 10.4% divorced; Foreign born: 0.9%; Speak English only: 99.0%; With disability: 16.3%; Veterans: 11.7%; Ancestry: 34.5% English, 27.3% Irish, 21.8% German, 7.3% Italian, 6.6% French
Employment: 10.4% management, business, and financial, 2.0% computer, engineering, and science, 11.6% education, legal, community service, arts, and media, 6.4% healthcare practitioners, 29.2% service, 18.8% sales and office, 5.2% natural resources, construction, and maintenance, 16.4% production, transportation, and material moving
Income: Per capita: $29,544; Median household: $50,536; Average household: $68,659; Households with income of $100,000 or more: 24.8%; Poverty rate: 2.4%
Educational Attainment: High school diploma or higher: 93.6%; Bachelor's degree or higher: 25.3%; Graduate/professional degree or higher: 5.2%

School District(s)
Union Springs Central SD (KG-12)
  2014-15 Enrollment: 852 . . . . (315) 889-4101
Housing: Homeownership rate: 83.3%; Median home value: $112,900; Median year structure built: 1950; Homeowner vacancy rate: 10.6%; Median selected monthly owner costs: $1,153 with a mortgage, $504 without a mortgage; Median gross rent: $436 per month; Rental vacancy rate: 11.4%
Health Insurance: 98.2% have insurance; 80.0% have private insurance; 42.0% have public insurance; 1.8% do not have insurance; 0.0% of children under 18 do not have insurance
Transportation: Commute: 100.0% car, 0.0% public transportation, 0.0% walk, 0.0% work from home; Mean travel time to work: 25.4 minutes
Additional Information Contacts
Village of Cayuga . . . . (315) 252-1707
  http://co.cayuga.ny.us/cayugavil

CONQUEST (town). Covers a land area of 35.222 square miles and a water area of 1.096 square miles. Located at 43.12° N. Lat; 76.66° W. Long. Elevation is 440 feet.
Population: 1,538; Growth (since 2000): -20.1%; Density: 43.7 persons per square mile; Race: 98.6% White, 0.0% Black/African American, 0.0% Asian, 0.1% American Indian/Alaska Native, 0.0% Native Hawaiian/Other Pacific Islander, 1.1% Two or more races, 1.0% Hispanic of any race; Average household size: 2.49; Median age: 47.6; Age under 18: 21.1%; Age 65 and over: 18.3%; Males per 100 females: 106.7; Marriage status: 17.1% never married, 61.4% now married, 3.6% separated, 5.6% widowed, 15.9% divorced; Foreign born: 0.7%; Speak English only: 99.0%; With disability: 12.4%; Veterans: 7.9%; Ancestry: 23.1% German, 21.1% Irish, 16.0% English, 7.1% American, 7.1% Dutch
Employment: 8.7% management, business, and financial, 3.6% computer, engineering, and science, 3.9% education, legal, community service, arts, and media, 4.1% healthcare practitioners, 17.3% service, 20.5% sales and office, 12.4% natural resources, construction, and maintenance, 29.4% production, transportation, and material moving
Income: Per capita: $23,688; Median household: $49,539; Average household: $57,218; Households with income of $100,000 or more: 11.8%; Poverty rate: 13.0%
Educational Attainment: High school diploma or higher: 83.6%; Bachelor's degree or higher: 12.1%; Graduate/professional degree or higher: 4.9%

Housing: Homeownership rate: 91.1%; Median home value: $86,800; Median year structure built: 1977; Homeowner vacancy rate: 0.0%; Median selected monthly owner costs: $1,054 with a mortgage, $391 without a mortgage; Median gross rent: $817 per month; Rental vacancy rate: 0.0%
Health Insurance: 90.6% have insurance; 68.8% have private insurance; 37.5% have public insurance; 9.4% do not have insurance; 12.7% of children under 18 do not have insurance
Transportation: Commute: 97.6% car, 0.0% public transportation, 0.5% walk, 1.5% work from home; Mean travel time to work: 30.0 minutes
Additional Information Contacts
Town of Conquest . . . . (315) 776-4539
  http://co.cayuga.ny.us/conquest

FAIR HAVEN (village).
Covers a land area of 1.755 square miles and a water area of 1.168 square miles. Located at 43.32° N. Lat; 76.71° W. Long. Elevation is 285 feet.
Population: 700; Growth (since 2000): -20.8%; Density: 398.9 persons per square mile; Race: 95.0% White, 1.3% Black/African American, 0.7% Asian, 0.3% American Indian/Alaska Native, 0.0% Native Hawaiian/Other Pacific Islander, 1.0% Two or more races, 2.1% Hispanic of any race; Average household size: 2.11; Median age: 49.5; Age under 18: 16.0%; Age 65 and over: 24.9%; Males per 100 females: 94.0; Marriage status: 29.2% never married, 48.6% now married, 3.5% separated, 8.1% widowed, 14.0% divorced; Foreign born: 5.7%; Speak English only: 92.9%; With disability: 17.1%; Veterans: 8.5%; Ancestry: 23.3% German, 20.0% Irish, 19.6% English, 10.3% French, 7.7% Dutch
Employment: 11.7% management, business, and financial, 5.0% computer, engineering, and science, 14.7% education, legal, community service, arts, and media, 3.0% healthcare practitioners, 11.7% service, 25.3% sales and office, 5.3% natural resources, construction, and maintenance, 23.3% production, transportation, and material moving
Income: Per capita: $31,057; Median household: $50,208; Average household: $65,786; Households with income of $100,000 or more: 19.5%; Poverty rate: 12.8%
Educational Attainment: High school diploma or higher: 93.7%; Bachelor's degree or higher: 29.0%; Graduate/professional degree or higher: 11.2%
Housing: Homeownership rate: 75.2%; Median home value: $103,600; Median year structure built: 1948; Homeowner vacancy rate: 2.4%; Median selected monthly owner costs: $1,032 with a mortgage, $509 without a mortgage; Median gross rent: $676 per month; Rental vacancy rate: 7.1%
Health Insurance: 90.5% have insurance; 65.6% have private insurance; 44.2% have public insurance; 9.5% do not have insurance; 6.4% of children under 18 do not have insurance
Transportation: Commute: 93.8% car, 0.0% public transportation, 4.9% walk, 1.4% work from home; Mean travel time to work: 30.0 minutes
Additional Information Contacts
Village of Fair Haven . . . . (315) 947-5112
  http://co.cayuga.ny.us/fairhaven

FLEMING (town).
Covers a land area of 21.819 square miles and a water area of 2.480 square miles. Located at 42.87° N. Lat; 76.58° W. Long. Elevation is 902 feet.
Population: 2,617; Growth (since 2000): -1.1%; Density: 119.9 persons per square mile; Race: 96.9% White, 0.2% Black/African American, 0.5% Asian, 0.5% American Indian/Alaska Native, 0.0% Native Hawaiian/Other Pacific Islander, 0.6% Two or more races, 3.2% Hispanic of any race; Average household size: 2.36; Median age: 50.9; Age under 18: 19.0%; Age 65 and over: 21.9%; Males per 100 females: 102.6; Marriage status: 20.8% never married, 65.9% now married, 0.9% separated, 5.3% widowed, 8.0% divorced; Foreign born: 4.4%; Speak English only: 94.3%; With disability: 9.1%; Veterans: 11.6%; Ancestry: 27.2% Irish, 18.0% English, 16.7% Italian, 15.4% German, 12.1% Polish
Employment: 14.1% management, business, and financial, 6.6% computer, engineering, and science, 14.8% education, legal, community service, arts, and media, 6.3% healthcare practitioners, 16.4% service, 19.4% sales and office, 12.6% natural resources, construction, and maintenance, 9.8% production, transportation, and material moving
Income: Per capita: $32,793; Median household: $60,625; Average household: $75,866; Households with income of $100,000 or more: 27.0%; Poverty rate: 2.1%
Educational Attainment: High school diploma or higher: 94.4%; Bachelor's degree or higher: 31.8%; Graduate/professional degree or higher: 16.0%

Housing: Homeownership rate: 85.9%; Median home value: $171,000; Median year structure built: 1967; Homeowner vacancy rate: 1.9%; Median selected monthly owner costs: $1,363 with a mortgage, $604 without a mortgage; Median gross rent: $681 per month; Rental vacancy rate: 0.0%
Health Insurance: 94.6% have insurance; 84.9% have private insurance; 28.9% have public insurance; 5.4% do not have insurance; 4.6% of children under 18 do not have insurance
Transportation: Commute: 92.1% car, 0.3% public transportation, 0.0% walk, 7.1% work from home; Mean travel time to work: 20.5 minutes
Additional Information Contacts
Town of Fleming . . . . (315) 252-8988
  http://co.cayuga.ny.us/fleming

GENOA (town).
Covers a land area of 39.598 square miles and a water area of 3.565 square miles. Located at 42.65° N. Lat; 76.57° W. Long. Elevation is 853 feet.
Population: 1,809; Growth (since 2000): -5.5%; Density: 45.7 persons per square mile; Race: 97.1% White, 0.1% Black/African American, 0.0% Asian, 2.4% American Indian/Alaska Native, 0.0% Native Hawaiian/Other Pacific Islander, 0.4% Two or more races, 8.6% Hispanic of any race; Average household size: 2.64; Median age: 40.4; Age under 18: 25.4%; Age 65 and over: 14.8%; Males per 100 females: 105.6; Marriage status: 26.5% never married, 59.4% now married, 3.4% separated, 4.5% widowed, 9.7% divorced; Foreign born: 1.4%; Speak English only: 93.3%; With disability: 12.5%; Veterans: 7.9%; Ancestry: 21.0% Irish, 20.7% German, 19.8% English, 11.9% Italian, 5.5% Polish
Employment: 16.2% management, business, and financial, 5.2% computer, engineering, and science, 9.7% education, legal, community service, arts, and media, 7.5% healthcare practitioners, 13.4% service, 19.9% sales and office, 12.5% natural resources, construction, and maintenance, 15.6% production, transportation, and material moving
Income: Per capita: $30,330; Median household: $62,500; Average household: $78,561; Households with income of $100,000 or more: 21.2%; Poverty rate: 12.4%
Educational Attainment: High school diploma or higher: 93.5%; Bachelor's degree or higher: 25.2%; Graduate/professional degree or higher: 10.3%
Housing: Homeownership rate: 78.1%; Median home value: $111,300; Median year structure built: 1955; Homeowner vacancy rate: 1.1%; Median selected monthly owner costs: $1,246 with a mortgage, $473 without a mortgage; Median gross rent: $677 per month; Rental vacancy rate: 5.7%
Health Insurance: 94.6% have insurance; 75.0% have private insurance; 31.2% have public insurance; 5.4% do not have insurance; 0.0% of children under 18 do not have insurance
Transportation: Commute: 88.2% car, 0.8% public transportation, 5.5% walk, 4.9% work from home; Mean travel time to work: 23.5 minutes
Additional Information Contacts
Town of Genoa . . . . (315) 364-5505
  http://co.cayuga.ny.us/genoa

IRA (town).
Covers a land area of 34.795 square miles and a water area of 0.103 square miles. Located at 43.21° N. Lat; 76.53° W. Long. Elevation is 489 feet.
Population: 2,266; Growth (since 2000): -6.6%; Density: 65.1 persons per square mile; Race: 95.7% White, 0.8% Black/African American, 0.0% Asian, 0.6% American Indian/Alaska Native, 0.0% Native Hawaiian/Other Pacific Islander, 0.9% Two or more races, 2.2% Hispanic of any race; Average household size: 2.90; Median age: 36.2; Age under 18: 30.0%; Age 65 and over: 12.9%; Males per 100 females: 103.1; Marriage status: 24.3% never married, 61.9% now married, 4.5% separated, 5.0% widowed, 8.8% divorced; Foreign born: 2.2%; Speak English only: 99.0%; With disability: 12.5%; Veterans: 12.9%; Ancestry: 19.5% German, 18.9% Irish, 11.1% French, 10.4% English, 8.5% Italian
Employment: 15.7% management, business, and financial, 5.4% computer, engineering, and science, 9.8% education, legal, community service, arts, and media, 3.3% healthcare practitioners, 10.4% service, 24.4% sales and office, 16.8% natural resources, construction, and maintenance, 14.2% production, transportation, and material moving
Income: Per capita: $25,750; Median household: $60,288; Average household: $73,358; Households with income of $100,000 or more: 22.9%; Poverty rate: 8.6%
Educational Attainment: High school diploma or higher: 90.5%; Bachelor's degree or higher: 25.4%; Graduate/professional degree or higher: 10.4%

Housing: Homeownership rate: 87.2%; Median home value: $113,100; Median year structure built: 1970; Homeowner vacancy rate: 0.7%; Median selected monthly owner costs: $1,100 with a mortgage, $495 without a mortgage; Median gross rent: $704 per month; Rental vacancy rate: 0.0%
Health Insurance: 91.2% have insurance; 71.5% have private insurance; 32.2% have public insurance; 8.8% do not have insurance; 4.9% of children under 18 do not have insurance
Transportation: Commute: 93.2% car, 0.0% public transportation, 2.7% walk, 4.1% work from home; Mean travel time to work: 29.8 minutes
Additional Information Contacts
Town of Ira . . . . (315) 626-6905
  http://co.cayuga.ny.us/ira

KING FERRY (unincorporated postal area)
ZCTA: 13081
Covers a land area of 28.958 square miles and a water area of 0.012 square miles. Located at 42.67° N. Lat; 76.63° W. Long. Elevation is 955 feet.
Population: 1,030; Growth (since 2000): -13.4%; Density: 35.6 persons per square mile; Race: 97.6% White, 0.4% Black/African American, 0.3% Asian, 1.0% American Indian/Alaska Native, 0.0% Native Hawaiian/Other Pacific Islander, 0.8% Two or more races, 1.3% Hispanic of any race; Average household size: 2.35; Median age: 50.4; Age under 18: 16.2%; Age 65 and over: 18.5%; Males per 100 females: 101.6; Marriage status: 23.0% never married, 62.9% now married, 1.7% separated, 4.5% widowed, 9.7% divorced; Foreign born: 2.0%; Speak English only: 97.0%; With disability: 12.9%; Veterans: 8.3%; Ancestry: 23.5% English, 22.2% Irish, 12.0% German, 8.3% Italian, 5.3% Polish
Employment: 15.8% management, business, and financial, 9.2% computer, engineering, and science, 12.1% education, legal, community service, arts, and media, 3.6% healthcare practitioners, 16.8% service, 22.8% sales and office, 10.3% natural resources, construction, and maintenance, 9.2% production, transportation, and material moving
Income: Per capita: $36,924; Median household: $58,173; Average household: $85,633; Households with income of $100,000 or more: 23.5%; Poverty rate: 10.0%
Educational Attainment: High school diploma or higher: 93.1%; Bachelor's degree or higher: 31.0%; Graduate/professional degree or higher: 15.6%
Housing: Homeownership rate: 79.5%; Median home value: $151,700; Median year structure built: 1952; Homeowner vacancy rate: 0.0%; Median selected monthly owner costs: $1,409 with a mortgage, $490 without a mortgage; Median gross rent: $722 per month; Rental vacancy rate: 0.0%
Health Insurance: 94.8% have insurance; 74.1% have private insurance; 37.2% have public insurance; 5.2% do not have insurance; 0.0% of children under 18 do not have insurance
Transportation: Commute: 92.8% car, 0.0% public transportation, 3.9% walk, 2.9% work from home; Mean travel time to work: 28.0 minutes

LEDYARD (town). Covers a land area of 36.112 square miles and a water area of 12.469 square miles. Located at 42.75° N. Lat; 76.67° W. Long. Elevation is 984 feet.
Population: 1,795; Growth (since 2000): -2.0%; Density: 49.7 persons per square mile; Race: 89.2% White, 3.8% Black/African American, 0.8% Asian, 0.0% American Indian/Alaska Native, 0.0% Native Hawaiian/Other Pacific Islander, 1.8% Two or more races, 7.7% Hispanic of any race; Average household size: 2.30; Median age: 36.8; Age under 18: 13.3%; Age 65 and over: 14.5%; Males per 100 females: 84.0; Marriage status: 43.5% never married, 45.3% now married, 1.9% separated, 3.9% widowed, 7.3% divorced; Foreign born: 7.7%; Speak English only: 88.9%; With disability: 14.3%; Veterans: 6.4%; Ancestry: 21.8% Irish, 21.7% German, 18.1% English, 9.9% Italian, 5.8% American
Employment: 15.0% management, business, and financial, 3.8% computer, engineering, and science, 19.2% education, legal, community service, arts, and media, 1.4% healthcare practitioners, 18.7% service, 19.9% sales and office, 12.1% natural resources, construction, and maintenance, 9.9% production, transportation, and material moving
Income: Per capita: $26,395; Median household: $64,219; Average household: $71,711; Households with income of $100,000 or more: 21.5%; Poverty rate: 11.5%
Educational Attainment: High school diploma or higher: 90.9%; Bachelor's degree or higher: 37.6%; Graduate/professional degree or higher: 21.8%

Housing: Homeownership rate: 77.1%; Median home value: $160,300; Median year structure built: 1959; Homeowner vacancy rate: 1.3%; Median selected monthly owner costs: $1,406 with a mortgage, $558 without a mortgage; Median gross rent: $755 per month; Rental vacancy rate: 0.0%
Health Insurance: 90.4% have insurance; 74.1% have private insurance; 31.1% have public insurance; 9.6% do not have insurance; 8.4% of children under 18 do not have insurance
Transportation: Commute: 77.1% car, 0.7% public transportation, 16.3% walk, 5.4% work from home; Mean travel time to work: 25.9 minutes
Additional Information Contacts
Town of Ledyard . . . . (315) 364-5707
  http://co.cayuga.ny.us/ledyard

LOCKE (town). Covers a land area of 24.305 square miles and a water area of 0.105 square miles. Located at 42.65° N. Lat; 76.42° W. Long. Elevation is 791 feet.
History: President Millard Fillmore born here.
Population: 1,802; Growth (since 2000): -5.2%; Density: 74.1 persons per square mile; Race: 99.1% White, 0.8% Black/African American, 0.0% Asian, 0.1% American Indian/Alaska Native, 0.0% Native Hawaiian/Other Pacific Islander, 0.0% Two or more races, 0.3% Hispanic of any race; Average household size: 2.59; Median age: 43.9; Age under 18: 21.9%; Age 65 and over: 18.6%; Males per 100 females: 100.5; Marriage status: 26.6% never married, 49.2% now married, 1.0% separated, 4.6% widowed, 19.6% divorced; Foreign born: 0.5%; Speak English only: 98.3%; With disability: 15.3%; Veterans: 15.6%; Ancestry: 22.1% English, 21.1% German, 18.1% Irish, 12.7% French, 7.5% American
Employment: 11.1% management, business, and financial, 2.8% computer, engineering, and science, 7.6% education, legal, community service, arts, and media, 4.0% healthcare practitioners, 19.3% service, 21.6% sales and office, 7.4% natural resources, construction, and maintenance, 26.2% production, transportation, and material moving
Income: Per capita: $25,679; Median household: $54,922; Average household: $64,035; Households with income of $100,000 or more: 16.6%; Poverty rate: 14.2%
Educational Attainment: High school diploma or higher: 81.9%; Bachelor's degree or higher: 15.6%; Graduate/professional degree or higher: 6.3%
Housing: Homeownership rate: 84.6%; Median home value: $99,300; Median year structure built: 1980; Homeowner vacancy rate: 5.8%; Median selected monthly owner costs: $1,066 with a mortgage, $486 without a mortgage; Median gross rent: $807 per month; Rental vacancy rate: 0.0%
Health Insurance: 91.0% have insurance; 59.6% have private insurance; 45.9% have public insurance; 9.0% do not have insurance; 11.2% of children under 18 do not have insurance
Transportation: Commute: 91.9% car, 0.2% public transportation, 2.7% walk, 4.1% work from home; Mean travel time to work: 25.6 minutes
Additional Information Contacts
Town of Locke . . . . (315) 497-9338
  http://co.cayuga.ny.us/locke

MARTVILLE (unincorporated postal area)
ZCTA: 13111
Covers a land area of 26.607 square miles and a water area of 0.091 square miles. Located at 43.26° N. Lat; 76.61° W. Long. Elevation is 354 feet.
Population: 1,623; Growth (since 2000): -7.2%; Density: 61.0 persons per square mile; Race: 99.0% White, 0.0% Black/African American, 0.0% Asian, 0.0% American Indian/Alaska Native, 0.0% Native Hawaiian/Other Pacific Islander, 1.0% Two or more races, 0.0% Hispanic of any race; Average household size: 2.65; Median age: 43.5; Age under 18: 29.3%; Age 65 and over: 13.7%; Males per 100 females: 109.6; Marriage status: 19.7% never married, 58.4% now married, 0.0% separated, 8.2% widowed, 13.7% divorced; Foreign born: 1.0%; Speak English only: 99.7%; With disability: 11.3%; Veterans: 11.6%; Ancestry: 17.1% German, 13.3% Irish, 10.9% English, 9.8% Italian, 5.2% French
Employment: 20.1% management, business, and financial, 4.3% computer, engineering, and science, 9.1% education, legal, community service, arts, and media, 1.1% healthcare practitioners, 14.3% service, 19.0% sales and office, 18.1% natural resources, construction, and maintenance, 14.0% production, transportation, and material moving
Income: Per capita: $22,369; Median household: $52,019; Average household: $57,992; Households with income of $100,000 or more: 15.2%; Poverty rate: 28.4%

Educational Attainment: High school diploma or higher: 91.2%; Bachelor's degree or higher: 12.0%; Graduate/professional degree or higher: 5.9%

Housing: Homeownership rate: 91.5%; Median home value: $90,000; Median year structure built: 1982; Homeowner vacancy rate: 2.1%; Median selected monthly owner costs: $1,074 with a mortgage, $490 without a mortgage; Median gross rent: $646 per month; Rental vacancy rate: 0.0%

Health Insurance: 88.1% have insurance; 59.8% have private insurance; 45.8% have public insurance; 11.9% do not have insurance; 9.1% of children under 18 do not have insurance

Transportation: Commute: 91.4% car, 0.7% public transportation, 0.0% walk, 8.0% work from home; Mean travel time to work: 31.5 minutes

MELROSE PARK (CDP). Covers a land area of 3.732 square miles and a water area of 0.584 square miles. Located at 42.91° N. Lat; 76.51° W. Long. Elevation is 732 feet.

Population: 2,199; Growth (since 2000): -6.8%; Density: 589.3 persons per square mile; Race: 99.8% White, 0.0% Black/African American, 0.1% Asian, 0.0% American Indian/Alaska Native, 0.0% Native Hawaiian/Other Pacific Islander, 0.0% Two or more races, 0.1% Hispanic of any race; Average household size: 2.47; Median age: 48.8; Age under 18: 18.9%; Age 65 and over: 16.3%; Males per 100 females: 93.8; Marriage status: 22.4% never married, 62.6% now married, 4.1% separated, 7.1% widowed, 8.0% divorced; Foreign born: 1.7%; Speak English only: 99.5%; With disability: 8.9%; Veterans: 10.7%; Ancestry: 38.6% Italian, 24.0% Irish, 17.6% English, 13.3% German, 6.2% Ukrainian

Employment: 16.6% management, business, and financial, 4.9% computer, engineering, and science, 12.9% education, legal, community service, arts, and media, 8.0% healthcare practitioners, 17.2% service, 25.3% sales and office, 8.3% natural resources, construction, and maintenance, 6.8% production, transportation, and material moving

Income: Per capita: $44,659; Median household: $90,078; Average household: $109,562; Households with income of $100,000 or more: 45.5%; Poverty rate: 3.5%

Educational Attainment: High school diploma or higher: 97.3%; Bachelor's degree or higher: 41.2%; Graduate/professional degree or higher: 12.1%

Housing: Homeownership rate: 93.3%; Median home value: $151,500; Median year structure built: 1957; Homeowner vacancy rate: 0.0%; Median selected monthly owner costs: $1,444 with a mortgage, $575 without a mortgage; Median gross rent: $768 per month; Rental vacancy rate: 0.0%

Health Insurance: 97.8% have insurance; 91.3% have private insurance; 22.3% have public insurance; 2.2% do not have insurance; 0.0% of children under 18 do not have insurance

Transportation: Commute: 92.2% car, 0.1% public transportation, 1.5% walk, 4.1% work from home; Mean travel time to work: 24.8 minutes

MENTZ (town). Covers a land area of 16.922 square miles and a water area of 0.260 square miles. Located at 43.04° N. Lat; 76.63° W. Long.

Population: 2,469; Growth (since 2000): 0.9%; Density: 145.9 persons per square mile; Race: 97.9% White, 0.7% Black/African American, 0.0% Asian, 0.0% American Indian/Alaska Native, 0.0% Native Hawaiian/Other Pacific Islander, 1.2% Two or more races, 2.4% Hispanic of any race; Average household size: 2.59; Median age: 38.8; Age under 18: 22.4%; Age 65 and over: 17.5%; Males per 100 females: 95.6; Marriage status: 31.3% never married, 52.3% now married, 1.8% separated, 7.3% widowed, 9.1% divorced; Foreign born: 1.1%; Speak English only: 99.0%; With disability: 14.3%; Veterans: 7.7%; Ancestry: 26.3% Irish, 17.9% German, 16.5% English, 15.7% Italian, 8.5% Polish

Employment: 7.7% management, business, and financial, 0.9% computer, engineering, and science, 7.4% education, legal, community service, arts, and media, 3.6% healthcare practitioners, 22.0% service, 25.1% sales and office, 15.1% natural resources, construction, and maintenance, 18.2% production, transportation, and material moving

Income: Per capita: $21,300; Median household: $49,833; Average household: $54,093; Households with income of $100,000 or more: 12.9%; Poverty rate: 12.1%

Educational Attainment: High school diploma or higher: 88.0%; Bachelor's degree or higher: 12.2%; Graduate/professional degree or higher: 3.9%

Housing: Homeownership rate: 81.5%; Median home value: $79,600; Median year structure built: 1960; Homeowner vacancy rate: 1.4%; Median selected monthly owner costs: $1,117 with a mortgage, $479 without a mortgage; Median gross rent: $694 per month; Rental vacancy rate: 5.2%

Health Insurance: 93.1% have insurance; 69.5% have private insurance; 38.2% have public insurance; 6.9% do not have insurance; 0.5% of children under 18 do not have insurance

Transportation: Commute: 97.6% car, 0.0% public transportation, 1.6% walk, 0.0% work from home; Mean travel time to work: 21.0 minutes

Additional Information Contacts

Town of Mentz . . . . (315) 776-8692
  http://www.townofmentz.com

MERIDIAN (village). Covers a land area of 0.691 square miles and a water area of 0 square miles. Located at 43.16° N. Lat; 76.54° W. Long. Elevation is 453 feet.

Population: 293; Growth (since 2000): -16.3%; Density: 424.2 persons per square mile; Race: 95.6% White, 0.0% Black/African American, 0.0% Asian, 1.4% American Indian/Alaska Native, 0.0% Native Hawaiian/Other Pacific Islander, 3.1% Two or more races, 2.7% Hispanic of any race; Average household size: 2.93; Median age: 37.3; Age under 18: 25.3%; Age 65 and over: 11.3%; Males per 100 females: 103.3; Marriage status: 26.6% never married, 59.5% now married, 0.0% separated, 9.3% widowed, 4.6% divorced; Foreign born: 0.3%; Speak English only: 96.7%; With disability: 10.6%; Veterans: 15.5%; Ancestry: 27.6% Irish, 21.2% Italian, 17.7% English, 17.1% German, 8.5% French

Employment: 20.1% management, business, and financial, 0.0% computer, engineering, and science, 7.6% education, legal, community service, arts, and media, 2.1% healthcare practitioners, 18.8% service, 22.9% sales and office, 11.1% natural resources, construction, and maintenance, 17.4% production, transportation, and material moving

Income: Per capita: $22,326; Median household: $61,042; Average household: $62,807; Households with income of $100,000 or more: 16.0%; Poverty rate: 7.2%

Educational Attainment: High school diploma or higher: 91.1%; Bachelor's degree or higher: 15.8%; Graduate/professional degree or higher: 2.5%

Housing: Homeownership rate: 81.0%; Median home value: $98,500; Median year structure built: Before 1940; Homeowner vacancy rate: 5.8%; Median selected monthly owner costs: $1,202 with a mortgage, $478 without a mortgage; Median gross rent: $817 per month; Rental vacancy rate: 17.4%

Health Insurance: 89.4% have insurance; 76.8% have private insurance; 22.9% have public insurance; 10.6% do not have insurance; 8.1% of children under 18 do not have insurance

Transportation: Commute: 94.8% car, 3.0% public transportation, 0.0% walk, 2.2% work from home; Mean travel time to work: 23.8 minutes

MONTEZUMA (town). Covers a land area of 18.242 square miles and a water area of 0.473 square miles. Located at 43.01° N. Lat; 76.70° W. Long. Elevation is 397 feet.

Population: 1,356; Growth (since 2000): -5.2%; Density: 74.3 persons per square mile; Race: 97.6% White, 0.1% Black/African American, 1.0% Asian, 0.3% American Indian/Alaska Native, 0.0% Native Hawaiian/Other Pacific Islander, 0.1% Two or more races, 3.2% Hispanic of any race; Average household size: 2.73; Median age: 45.3; Age under 18: 18.2%; Age 65 and over: 11.9%; Males per 100 females: 102.7; Marriage status: 28.4% never married, 54.4% now married, 1.0% separated, 5.7% widowed, 11.4% divorced; Foreign born: 2.0%; Speak English only: 99.5%; With disability: 18.1%; Veterans: 11.6%; Ancestry: 27.6% English, 20.4% German, 19.9% Irish, 7.4% Italian, 6.8% French

Employment: 11.5% management, business, and financial, 2.2% computer, engineering, and science, 8.4% education, legal, community service, arts, and media, 3.7% healthcare practitioners, 22.4% service, 17.9% sales and office, 11.1% natural resources, construction, and maintenance, 22.7% production, transportation, and material moving

Income: Per capita: $23,306; Median household: $55,391; Average household: $62,173; Households with income of $100,000 or more: 18.3%; Poverty rate: 13.3%

Educational Attainment: High school diploma or higher: 82.5%; Bachelor's degree or higher: 6.5%; Graduate/professional degree or higher: 3.1%

Housing: Homeownership rate: 83.3%; Median home value: $89,400; Median year structure built: 1981; Homeowner vacancy rate: 0.0%; Median selected monthly owner costs: $1,131 with a mortgage, $397 without a mortgage; Median gross rent: $764 per month; Rental vacancy rate: 0.0%

Health Insurance: 89.9% have insurance; 66.8% have private insurance; 40.7% have public insurance; 10.1% do not have insurance; 2.8% of children under 18 do not have insurance

Transportation: Commute: 96.5% car, 0.0% public transportation, 0.0% walk, 3.5% work from home; Mean travel time to work: 28.9 minutes
Additional Information Contacts
Town of Montezuma . . . . (315) 776-8844
  http://co.cayuga.ny.us/montezuma

MORAVIA (town). Covers a land area of 28.884 square miles and a water area of 0.753 square miles. Located at 42.73° N. Lat; 76.41° W. Long. Elevation is 735 feet.
History: Fillmore Glen State Park and the birthplace of President Millard Fillmore are nearby. Incorporated 1837.
Population: 3,557; Growth (since 2000): -12.0%; Density: 123.1 persons per square mile; Race: 85.3% White, 9.1% Black/African American, 0.5% Asian, 0.3% American Indian/Alaska Native, 0.0% Native Hawaiian/Other Pacific Islander, 3.7% Two or more races, 4.0% Hispanic of any race; Average household size: 2.57; Median age: 40.6; Age under 18: 18.1%; Age 65 and over: 13.2%; Males per 100 females: 173.7; Marriage status: 38.1% never married, 42.3% now married, 3.9% separated, 4.6% widowed, 15.0% divorced; Foreign born: 0.9%; Speak English only: 95.9%; With disability: 13.5%; Veterans: 10.1%; Ancestry: 22.5% Irish, 16.8% German, 13.0% English, 11.0% Italian, 5.3% American
Employment: 11.2% management, business, and financial, 3.1% computer, engineering, and science, 8.7% education, legal, community service, arts, and media, 3.6% healthcare practitioners, 20.3% service, 22.8% sales and office, 10.6% natural resources, construction, and maintenance, 19.8% production, transportation, and material moving
Income: Per capita: $20,610; Median household: $55,625; Average household: $62,138; Households with income of $100,000 or more: 17.4%; Poverty rate: 9.8%
Educational Attainment: High school diploma or higher: 83.7%; Bachelor's degree or higher: 12.6%; Graduate/professional degree or higher: 6.2%

School District(s)
Moravia Central SD (PK-12)
  2014-15 Enrollment: 1,022 . . . . (315) 497-2670
Housing: Homeownership rate: 70.4%; Median home value: $96,700; Median year structure built: 1946; Homeowner vacancy rate: 3.6%; Median selected monthly owner costs: $1,107 with a mortgage, $468 without a mortgage; Median gross rent: $612 per month; Rental vacancy rate: 3.8%
Health Insurance: 94.9% have insurance; 71.0% have private insurance; 37.4% have public insurance; 5.1% do not have insurance; 0.5% of children under 18 do not have insurance
Newspapers: Republican-Register (weekly circulation 1,000)
Transportation: Commute: 95.6% car, 0.1% public transportation, 1.5% walk, 2.7% work from home; Mean travel time to work: 27.0 minutes
Additional Information Contacts
Town of Moravia . . . . (315) 497-1972
  http://co.cayuga.ny.us/townofmoravia

MORAVIA (village). Covers a land area of 1.703 square miles and a water area of 0.021 square miles. Located at 42.71° N. Lat; 76.42° W. Long. Elevation is 735 feet.
Population: 1,521; Growth (since 2000): 11.6%; Density: 893.0 persons per square mile; Race: 95.4% White, 0.0% Black/African American, 1.1% Asian, 0.0% American Indian/Alaska Native, 0.0% Native Hawaiian/Other Pacific Islander, 2.6% Two or more races, 0.9% Hispanic of any race; Average household size: 2.45; Median age: 44.2; Age under 18: 19.9%; Age 65 and over: 19.9%; Males per 100 females: 92.8; Marriage status: 33.4% never married, 42.0% now married, 1.8% separated, 8.8% widowed, 15.8% divorced; Foreign born: 0.9%; Speak English only: 99.5%; With disability: 18.5%; Veterans: 11.2%; Ancestry: 29.5% Irish, 26.0% German, 14.3% English, 13.1% Italian, 6.4% Dutch
Employment: 8.5% management, business, and financial, 4.0% computer, engineering, and science, 10.3% education, legal, community service, arts, and media, 4.2% healthcare practitioners, 23.5% service, 24.9% sales and office, 5.1% natural resources, construction, and maintenance, 19.5% production, transportation, and material moving
Income: Per capita: $24,014; Median household: $51,700; Average household: $56,820; Households with income of $100,000 or more: 13.6%; Poverty rate: 8.9%
Educational Attainment: High school diploma or higher: 85.4%; Bachelor's degree or higher: 18.8%; Graduate/professional degree or higher: 9.3%

School District(s)
Moravia Central SD (PK-12)
  2014-15 Enrollment: 1,022 . . . . (315) 497-2670
Housing: Homeownership rate: 63.0%; Median home value: $95,800; Median year structure built: Before 1940; Homeowner vacancy rate: 0.0%; Median selected monthly owner costs: $1,140 with a mortgage, $430 without a mortgage; Median gross rent: $550 per month; Rental vacancy rate: 0.0%
Health Insurance: 96.1% have insurance; 73.2% have private insurance; 39.1% have public insurance; 3.9% do not have insurance; 0.0% of children under 18 do not have insurance
Safety: Violent crime rate: 0.0 per 10,000 population; Property crime rate: 56.3 per 10,000 population
Newspapers: Republican-Register (weekly circulation 1,000)
Transportation: Commute: 92.9% car, 0.3% public transportation, 3.0% walk, 3.7% work from home; Mean travel time to work: 23.8 minutes
Additional Information Contacts
Village of Moravia . . . . (315) 497-1820
  http://co.cayuga.ny.us/villageofmoravia

NILES (town). Covers a land area of 38.975 square miles and a water area of 4.376 square miles. Located at 42.82° N. Lat; 76.40° W. Long. Elevation is 915 feet.
Population: 1,160; Growth (since 2000): -4.0%; Density: 29.8 persons per square mile; Race: 95.5% White, 1.3% Black/African American, 0.4% Asian, 0.0% American Indian/Alaska Native, 0.0% Native Hawaiian/Other Pacific Islander, 2.0% Two or more races, 1.9% Hispanic of any race; Average household size: 2.56; Median age: 48.2; Age under 18: 19.1%; Age 65 and over: 20.9%; Males per 100 females: 111.7; Marriage status: 21.1% never married, 63.2% now married, 2.3% separated, 6.2% widowed, 9.5% divorced; Foreign born: 1.4%; Speak English only: 97.7%; With disability: 18.7%; Veterans: 11.4%; Ancestry: 22.0% English, 21.4% German, 15.2% Irish, 7.6% Polish, 6.9% Italian
Employment: 15.8% management, business, and financial, 2.5% computer, engineering, and science, 6.4% education, legal, community service, arts, and media, 2.9% healthcare practitioners, 17.9% service, 20.4% sales and office, 15.6% natural resources, construction, and maintenance, 18.5% production, transportation, and material moving
Income: Per capita: $31,899; Median household: $60,926; Average household: $79,723; Households with income of $100,000 or more: 23.2%; Poverty rate: 4.5%
Educational Attainment: High school diploma or higher: 91.3%; Bachelor's degree or higher: 26.1%; Graduate/professional degree or higher: 11.8%
Housing: Homeownership rate: 91.9%; Median home value: $164,800; Median year structure built: 1970; Homeowner vacancy rate: 0.0%; Median selected monthly owner costs: $1,210 with a mortgage, $683 without a mortgage; Median gross rent: $779 per month; Rental vacancy rate: 0.0%
Health Insurance: 89.7% have insurance; 69.1% have private insurance; 41.8% have public insurance; 10.3% do not have insurance; 10.4% of children under 18 do not have insurance
Transportation: Commute: 92.2% car, 0.4% public transportation, 1.2% walk, 5.6% work from home; Mean travel time to work: 26.2 minutes
Additional Information Contacts
Town of Niles. . . . . (315) 497-0066
  http://co.cayuga.ny.us/niles

OWASCO (town). Covers a land area of 20.881 square miles and a water area of 2.594 square miles. Located at 42.89° N. Lat; 76.49° W. Long. Elevation is 892 feet.
Population: 3,761; Growth (since 2000): 0.2%; Density: 180.1 persons per square mile; Race: 99.2% White, 0.0% Black/African American, 0.2% Asian, 0.0% American Indian/Alaska Native, 0.0% Native Hawaiian/Other Pacific Islander, 0.5% Two or more races, 0.3% Hispanic of any race; Average household size: 2.41; Median age: 49.1; Age under 18: 18.3%; Age 65 and over: 19.5%; Males per 100 females: 97.9; Marriage status: 25.8% never married, 59.3% now married, 2.9% separated, 7.6% widowed, 7.3% divorced; Foreign born: 2.2%; Speak English only: 96.5%; With disability: 8.9%; Veterans: 10.4%; Ancestry: 32.4% Italian, 24.7% Irish, 17.9% English, 13.0% German, 5.7% American
Employment: 15.0% management, business, and financial, 5.3% computer, engineering, and science, 15.4% education, legal, community service, arts, and media, 9.8% healthcare practitioners, 18.2% service, 20.6% sales and office, 9.1% natural resources, construction, and maintenance, 6.6% production, transportation, and material moving

Income: Per capita: $44,510; Median household: $83,917; Average household: $106,432; Households with income of $100,000 or more: 41.2%; Poverty rate: 2.6%
Educational Attainment: High school diploma or higher: 93.6%; Bachelor's degree or higher: 43.2%; Graduate/professional degree or higher: 17.4%
Housing: Homeownership rate: 93.8%; Median home value: $191,500; Median year structure built: 1965; Homeowner vacancy rate: 0.0%; Median selected monthly owner costs: $1,525 with a mortgage, $613 without a mortgage; Median gross rent: $773 per month; Rental vacancy rate: 0.0%
Health Insurance: 98.4% have insurance; 89.7% have private insurance; 26.9% have public insurance; 1.6% do not have insurance; 0.0% of children under 18 do not have insurance
Transportation: Commute: 93.1% car, 0.1% public transportation, 1.4% walk, 4.1% work from home; Mean travel time to work: 25.3 minutes
Additional Information Contacts
Town of Owasco . . . . (315) 253-9021
  http://co.cayuga.ny.us/owasco

PORT BYRON (village). Covers a land area of 0.979 square miles and a water area of 0.029 square miles. Located at 43.04° N. Lat; 76.63° W. Long. Elevation is 407 feet.

Population: 1,310; Growth (since 2000): 1.0%; Density: 1,338.4 persons per square mile; Race: 98.3% White, 1.1% Black/African American, 0.1% Asian, 0.0% American Indian/Alaska Native, 0.0% Native Hawaiian/Other Pacific Islander, 0.2% Two or more races, 4.5% Hispanic of any race; Average household size: 2.73; Median age: 35.1; Age under 18: 26.7%; Age 65 and over: 14.8%; Males per 100 females: 90.3; Marriage status: 36.9% never married, 47.9% now married, 1.6% separated, 4.2% widowed, 11.0% divorced; Foreign born: 1.0%; Speak English only: 98.8%; With disability: 13.2%; Veterans: 8.6%; Ancestry: 26.2% Irish, 19.0% English, 14.8% Italian, 14.0% German, 11.1% Polish
Employment: 11.6% management, business, and financial, 1.0% computer, engineering, and science, 8.4% education, legal, community service, arts, and media, 6.1% healthcare practitioners, 23.5% service, 26.1% sales and office, 9.0% natural resources, construction, and maintenance, 14.2% production, transportation, and material moving
Income: Per capita: $21,029; Median household: $48,512; Average household: $55,831; Households with income of $100,000 or more: 17.0%; Poverty rate: 16.3%
Educational Attainment: High school diploma or higher: 89.3%; Bachelor's degree or higher: 12.4%; Graduate/professional degree or higher: 4.9%

School District(s)

Port Byron Central SD (PK-12)
  2014-15 Enrollment: 1,004 . . . . (315) 776-5728
Housing: Homeownership rate: 71.6%; Median home value: $82,300; Median year structure built: Before 1940; Homeowner vacancy rate: 3.1%; Median selected monthly owner costs: $1,209 with a mortgage, $549 without a mortgage; Median gross rent: $691 per month; Rental vacancy rate: 6.5%
Health Insurance: 93.2% have insurance; 69.6% have private insurance; 36.4% have public insurance; 6.8% do not have insurance; 0.9% of children under 18 do not have insurance
Safety: Violent crime rate: 0.0 per 10,000 population; Property crime rate: 24.0 per 10,000 population
Transportation: Commute: 97.3% car, 0.0% public transportation, 2.4% walk, 0.0% work from home; Mean travel time to work: 19.6 minutes
Additional Information Contacts
Village of Port Byron . . . . (315) 776-4321
  http://www.villageofportbyron.com

SCIPIO (town). Covers a land area of 36.558 square miles and a water area of 2.751 square miles. Located at 42.79° N. Lat; 76.57° W. Long.

Population: 1,737; Growth (since 2000): 13.0%; Density: 47.5 persons per square mile; Race: 98.7% White, 0.6% Black/African American, 0.0% Asian, 0.0% American Indian/Alaska Native, 0.0% Native Hawaiian/Other Pacific Islander, 0.7% Two or more races, 1.4% Hispanic of any race; Average household size: 2.76; Median age: 41.3; Age under 18: 23.1%; Age 65 and over: 13.0%; Males per 100 females: 106.4; Marriage status: 25.0% never married, 59.7% now married, 1.4% separated, 5.1% widowed, 10.3% divorced; Foreign born: 0.9%; Speak English only: 98.3%; With disability: 9.2%; Veterans: 10.0%; Ancestry: 25.3% German, 24.4% Irish, 17.3% English, 9.7% Dutch, 6.5% Italian

Employment: 13.2% management, business, and financial, 2.8% computer, engineering, and science, 19.4% education, legal, community service, arts, and media, 5.9% healthcare practitioners, 15.2% service, 20.7% sales and office, 11.9% natural resources, construction, and maintenance, 10.9% production, transportation, and material moving
Income: Per capita: $30,926; Median household: $69,444; Average household: $83,251; Households with income of $100,000 or more: 25.0%; Poverty rate: 8.5%
Educational Attainment: High school diploma or higher: 87.9%; Bachelor's degree or higher: 20.1%; Graduate/professional degree or higher: 8.4%
Housing: Homeownership rate: 82.1%; Median home value: $138,400; Median year structure built: 1972; Homeowner vacancy rate: 3.4%; Median selected monthly owner costs: $1,199 with a mortgage, $517 without a mortgage; Median gross rent: $823 per month; Rental vacancy rate: 0.0%
Health Insurance: 85.9% have insurance; 72.7% have private insurance; 25.8% have public insurance; 14.1% do not have insurance; 21.1% of children under 18 do not have insurance
Transportation: Commute: 80.1% car, 0.0% public transportation, 6.4% walk, 13.5% work from home; Mean travel time to work: 23.0 minutes
Additional Information Contacts
Town of Scipio . . . . (315) 364-5740
  http://co.cayuga.ny.us/scipio

SCIPIO CENTER (unincorporated postal area)
ZCTA: 13147

  Covers a land area of 35.885 square miles and a water area of 0.007 square miles. Located at 42.78° N. Lat; 76.57° W. Long. Elevation is 1,191 feet.
Population: 1,286; Growth (since 2000): 6.8%; Density: 35.8 persons per square mile; Race: 96.9% White, 2.4% Black/African American, 0.0% Asian, 0.0% American Indian/Alaska Native, 0.0% Native Hawaiian/Other Pacific Islander, 0.2% Two or more races, 9.3% Hispanic of any race; Average household size: 2.71; Median age: 41.8; Age under 18: 18.7%; Age 65 and over: 14.5%; Males per 100 females: 113.1; Marriage status: 24.7% never married, 54.9% now married, 2.8% separated, 5.9% widowed, 14.5% divorced; Foreign born: 5.0%; Speak English only: 91.6%; With disability: 12.4%; Veterans: 8.5%; Ancestry: 24.0% Irish, 23.6% German, 20.8% English, 7.9% Dutch, 4.7% American
Employment: 12.2% management, business, and financial, 1.6% computer, engineering, and science, 14.3% education, legal, community service, arts, and media, 3.5% healthcare practitioners, 18.7% service, 18.5% sales and office, 17.0% natural resources, construction, and maintenance, 14.3% production, transportation, and material moving
Income: Per capita: $33,404; Median household: $66,875; Average household: $88,228; Households with income of $100,000 or more: 24.2%; Poverty rate: 6.3%
Educational Attainment: High school diploma or higher: 84.5%; Bachelor's degree or higher: 14.7%; Graduate/professional degree or higher: 5.3%
Housing: Homeownership rate: 80.0%; Median home value: $109,700; Median year structure built: 1946; Homeowner vacancy rate: 2.4%; Median selected monthly owner costs: $970 with a mortgage, $514 without a mortgage; Median gross rent: $766 per month; Rental vacancy rate: 0.0%
Health Insurance: 83.7% have insurance; 66.4% have private insurance; 28.2% have public insurance; 16.3% do not have insurance; 9.5% of children under 18 do not have insurance
Transportation: Commute: 90.7% car, 0.0% public transportation, 1.0% walk, 7.9% work from home; Mean travel time to work: 24.9 minutes

SEMPRONIUS (town). Covers a land area of 29.339 square miles and a water area of 0.379 square miles. Located at 42.74° N. Lat; 76.33° W. Long. Elevation is 1,598 feet.

Population: 935; Growth (since 2000): 4.7%; Density: 31.9 persons per square mile; Race: 98.1% White, 0.0% Black/African American, 0.0% Asian, 1.5% American Indian/Alaska Native, 0.0% Native Hawaiian/Other Pacific Islander, 0.4% Two or more races, 0.3% Hispanic of any race; Average household size: 2.61; Median age: 40.8; Age under 18: 21.5%; Age 65 and over: 12.1%; Males per 100 females: 114.6; Marriage status: 30.5% never married, 53.2% now married, 2.6% separated, 6.3% widowed, 9.9% divorced; Foreign born: 1.3%; Speak English only: 98.3%; With disability: 9.5%; Veterans: 5.6%; Ancestry: 20.2% English, 20.1% German, 13.9% Irish, 12.6% American, 4.5% Polish

Employment: 10.4% management, business, and financial, 1.4% computer, engineering, and science, 5.3% education, legal, community service, arts, and media, 6.5% healthcare practitioners, 15.0% service, 19.1% sales and office, 16.5% natural resources, construction, and maintenance, 25.8% production, transportation, and material moving
Income: Per capita: $23,852; Median household: $55,000; Average household: $61,471; Households with income of $100,000 or more: 17.3%; Poverty rate: 12.7%
Educational Attainment: High school diploma or higher: 86.9%; Bachelor's degree or higher: 12.4%; Graduate/professional degree or higher: 5.6%
Housing: Homeownership rate: 90.5%; Median home value: $95,000; Median year structure built: 1979; Homeowner vacancy rate: 0.0%; Median selected monthly owner costs: $1,028 with a mortgage, $520 without a mortgage; Median gross rent: $715 per month; Rental vacancy rate: 5.6%
Health Insurance: 91.9% have insurance; 66.4% have private insurance; 34.5% have public insurance; 8.1% do not have insurance; 1.0% of children under 18 do not have insurance
Transportation: Commute: 94.5% car, 0.4% public transportation, 2.2% walk, 2.4% work from home; Mean travel time to work: 26.2 minutes
Additional Information Contacts
Town of Sempronius . . . . (315) 496-2376
  http://co.cayuga.ny.us/sempronius

SENNETT (town). Covers a land area of 28.820 square miles and a water area of 0.024 square miles. Located at 42.98° N. Lat; 76.52° W. Long. Elevation is 594 feet.
Population: 3,592; Growth (since 2000): 10.7%; Density: 124.6 persons per square mile; Race: 92.9% White, 3.1% Black/African American, 2.2% Asian, 0.0% American Indian/Alaska Native, 0.0% Native Hawaiian/Other Pacific Islander, 1.8% Two or more races, 1.1% Hispanic of any race; Average household size: 2.51; Median age: 42.9; Age under 18: 23.4%; Age 65 and over: 17.4%; Males per 100 females: 102.8; Marriage status: 28.8% never married, 53.3% now married, 1.0% separated, 10.5% widowed, 7.4% divorced; Foreign born: 3.4%; Speak English only: 97.7%; With disability: 9.5%; Veterans: 8.2%; Ancestry: 22.1% Irish, 19.1% English, 18.6% German, 15.6% Italian, 6.9% Polish
Employment: 26.5% management, business, and financial, 3.8% computer, engineering, and science, 12.9% education, legal, community service, arts, and media, 6.7% healthcare practitioners, 14.7% service, 24.5% sales and office, 4.7% natural resources, construction, and maintenance, 6.2% production, transportation, and material moving
Income: Per capita: $34,635; Median household: $72,409; Average household: $94,158; Households with income of $100,000 or more: 33.9%; Poverty rate: 2.8%
Educational Attainment: High school diploma or higher: 92.3%; Bachelor's degree or higher: 37.1%; Graduate/professional degree or higher: 16.1%
Housing: Homeownership rate: 89.5%; Median home value: $182,800; Median year structure built: 1966; Homeowner vacancy rate: 0.8%; Median selected monthly owner costs: $1,771 with a mortgage, $573 without a mortgage; Median gross rent: $892 per month; Rental vacancy rate: 11.6%
Health Insurance: 95.8% have insurance; 81.9% have private insurance; 29.8% have public insurance; 4.2% do not have insurance; 0.0% of children under 18 do not have insurance
Transportation: Commute: 94.1% car, 0.7% public transportation, 1.5% walk, 2.6% work from home; Mean travel time to work: 22.0 minutes
Additional Information Contacts
Town of Sennett . . . . (315) 253-3712
  http://co.cayuga.ny.us/sennett

SPRINGPORT (town). Covers a land area of 21.399 square miles and a water area of 5.431 square miles. Located at 42.85° N. Lat; 76.67° W. Long.
Population: 2,402; Growth (since 2000): 6.5%; Density: 112.3 persons per square mile; Race: 89.2% White, 1.1% Black/African American, 0.3% Asian, 0.6% American Indian/Alaska Native, 0.0% Native Hawaiian/Other Pacific Islander, 6.2% Two or more races, 6.1% Hispanic of any race; Average household size: 2.43; Median age: 42.9; Age under 18: 19.3%; Age 65 and over: 20.4%; Males per 100 females: 98.9; Marriage status: 28.9% never married, 52.9% now married, 2.3% separated, 8.1% widowed, 10.1% divorced; Foreign born: 3.7%; Speak English only: 96.4%; With disability: 12.7%; Veterans: 10.7%; Ancestry: 25.4% Irish, 20.0% English, 17.0% German, 13.1% Italian, 6.1% Polish

Employment: 13.7% management, business, and financial, 1.9% computer, engineering, and science, 11.3% education, legal, community service, arts, and media, 3.8% healthcare practitioners, 23.6% service, 19.0% sales and office, 11.0% natural resources, construction, and maintenance, 15.8% production, transportation, and material moving
Income: Per capita: $30,155; Median household: $69,688; Average household: $73,934; Households with income of $100,000 or more: 24.3%; Poverty rate: 10.5%
Educational Attainment: High school diploma or higher: 92.5%; Bachelor's degree or higher: 23.4%; Graduate/professional degree or higher: 9.5%
Housing: Homeownership rate: 75.9%; Median home value: $118,900; Median year structure built: 1969; Homeowner vacancy rate: 1.4%; Median selected monthly owner costs: $1,181 with a mortgage, $511 without a mortgage; Median gross rent: $619 per month; Rental vacancy rate: 2.0%
Health Insurance: 89.5% have insurance; 69.7% have private insurance; 37.0% have public insurance; 10.5% do not have insurance; 4.7% of children under 18 do not have insurance
Transportation: Commute: 86.5% car, 0.0% public transportation, 6.4% walk, 6.4% work from home; Mean travel time to work: 22.0 minutes
Additional Information Contacts
Town of Springport . . . . (315) 889-7717
  http://co.cayuga.ny.us/springport

STERLING (town). Covers a land area of 45.454 square miles and a water area of 1.661 square miles. Located at 43.32° N. Lat; 76.66° W. Long. Elevation is 315 feet.
Population: 3,034; Growth (since 2000): -11.6%; Density: 66.7 persons per square mile; Race: 98.6% White, 0.3% Black/African American, 0.2% Asian, 0.1% American Indian/Alaska Native, 0.0% Native Hawaiian/Other Pacific Islander, 0.5% Two or more races, 0.5% Hispanic of any race; Average household size: 2.44; Median age: 45.5; Age under 18: 23.9%; Age 65 and over: 18.6%; Males per 100 females: 102.9; Marriage status: 19.9% never married, 55.8% now married, 1.8% separated, 8.8% widowed, 15.5% divorced; Foreign born: 1.3%; Speak English only: 98.1%; With disability: 14.6%; Veterans: 14.4%; Ancestry: 20.5% German, 18.2% Irish, 14.7% English, 7.5% Italian, 7.0% French
Employment: 14.5% management, business, and financial, 2.6% computer, engineering, and science, 11.4% education, legal, community service, arts, and media, 3.7% healthcare practitioners, 15.6% service, 20.8% sales and office, 16.7% natural resources, construction, and maintenance, 14.7% production, transportation, and material moving
Income: Per capita: $25,841; Median household: $55,182; Average household: $61,651; Households with income of $100,000 or more: 15.3%; Poverty rate: 15.7%
Educational Attainment: High school diploma or higher: 92.2%; Bachelor's degree or higher: 18.8%; Graduate/professional degree or higher: 9.3%
Housing: Homeownership rate: 89.8%; Median home value: $88,800; Median year structure built: 1975; Homeowner vacancy rate: 6.6%; Median selected monthly owner costs: $1,029 with a mortgage, $498 without a mortgage; Median gross rent: $645 per month; Rental vacancy rate: 4.5%
Health Insurance: 89.2% have insurance; 68.3% have private insurance; 38.7% have public insurance; 10.8% do not have insurance; 5.0% of children under 18 do not have insurance
Transportation: Commute: 96.4% car, 0.8% public transportation, 1.2% walk, 1.6% work from home; Mean travel time to work: 29.7 minutes
Additional Information Contacts
Town of Sterling . . . . (315) 947-5666
  http://co.cayuga.ny.us/sterling

SUMMERHILL (town). Covers a land area of 25.861 square miles and a water area of 0.123 square miles. Located at 42.65° N. Lat; 76.32° W. Long.
Population: 1,261; Growth (since 2000): 14.8%; Density: 48.8 persons per square mile; Race: 98.3% White, 0.6% Black/African American, 0.8% Asian, 0.0% American Indian/Alaska Native, 0.0% Native Hawaiian/Other Pacific Islander, 0.3% Two or more races, 1.2% Hispanic of any race; Average household size: 2.91; Median age: 36.6; Age under 18: 26.2%; Age 65 and over: 10.9%; Males per 100 females: 104.2; Marriage status: 32.3% never married, 50.7% now married, 3.5% separated, 6.2% widowed, 10.7% divorced; Foreign born: 0.8%; Speak English only: 96.5%; With disability: 9.0%; Veterans: 12.0%; Ancestry: 13.8% English, 13.6% German, 12.1% Irish, 6.7% Dutch, 6.0% American

Employment: 9.8% management, business, and financial, 6.5% computer, engineering, and science, 5.9% education, legal, community service, arts, and media, 9.5% healthcare practitioners, 16.7% service, 25.5% sales and office, 11.6% natural resources, construction, and maintenance, 14.5% production, transportation, and material moving
Income: Per capita: $25,085; Median household: $57,500; Average household: $69,270; Households with income of $100,000 or more: 18.2%; Poverty rate: 19.8%
Educational Attainment: High school diploma or higher: 90.3%; Bachelor's degree or higher: 18.3%; Graduate/professional degree or higher: 4.8%
Housing: Homeownership rate: 90.6%; Median home value: $113,200; Median year structure built: 1978; Homeowner vacancy rate: 4.6%; Median selected monthly owner costs: $1,305 with a mortgage, $538 without a mortgage; Median gross rent: $692 per month; Rental vacancy rate: 0.0%
Health Insurance: 85.3% have insurance; 56.5% have private insurance; 37.5% have public insurance; 14.7% do not have insurance; 11.8% of children under 18 do not have insurance
Transportation: Commute: 93.8% car, 0.0% public transportation, 3.2% walk, 1.8% work from home; Mean travel time to work: 24.9 minutes
Additional Information Contacts
Town of Summerhill. . . . . (315) 497-3494
   http://co.cayuga.ny.us/summerhill

THROOP (town).
Covers a land area of 18.586 square miles and a water area of 0.111 square miles. Located at 42.98° N. Lat; 76.62° W. Long. Elevation is 548 feet.
Population: 1,988; Growth (since 2000): 9.0%; Density: 107.0 persons per square mile; Race: 96.7% White, 0.9% Black/African American, 0.6% Asian, 0.0% American Indian/Alaska Native, 0.0% Native Hawaiian/Other Pacific Islander, 1.7% Two or more races, 2.7% Hispanic of any race; Average household size: 2.61; Median age: 45.9; Age under 18: 20.6%; Age 65 and over: 19.7%; Males per 100 females: 99.0; Marriage status: 23.9% never married, 57.0% now married, 1.4% separated, 7.6% widowed, 11.6% divorced; Foreign born: 1.2%; Speak English only: 97.0%; With disability: 14.3%; Veterans: 13.4%; Ancestry: 28.8% Irish, 22.8% Italian, 20.1% English, 19.3% German, 10.6% Polish
Employment: 13.0% management, business, and financial, 2.4% computer, engineering, and science, 7.5% education, legal, community service, arts, and media, 4.8% healthcare practitioners, 21.9% service, 25.7% sales and office, 12.7% natural resources, construction, and maintenance, 12.0% production, transportation, and material moving
Income: Per capita: $28,648; Median household: $68,555; Average household: $72,805; Households with income of $100,000 or more: 24.1%; Poverty rate: 6.4%
Educational Attainment: High school diploma or higher: 90.2%; Bachelor's degree or higher: 16.8%; Graduate/professional degree or higher: 5.9%
Housing: Homeownership rate: 94.5%; Median home value: $144,500; Median year structure built: 1962; Homeowner vacancy rate: 1.2%; Median selected monthly owner costs: $1,373 with a mortgage, $591 without a mortgage; Median gross rent: $908 per month; Rental vacancy rate: 0.0%
Health Insurance: 96.1% have insurance; 79.7% have private insurance; 33.5% have public insurance; 3.9% do not have insurance; 1.5% of children under 18 do not have insurance
Transportation: Commute: 91.9% car, 0.0% public transportation, 1.3% walk, 6.5% work from home; Mean travel time to work: 19.0 minutes
Additional Information Contacts
Town of Throop . . . . (315) 252-7373
   http://co.cayuga.ny.us/throop

UNION SPRINGS (village).
Covers a land area of 1.737 square miles and a water area of 0.015 square miles. Located at 42.85° N. Lat; 76.69° W. Long. Elevation is 410 feet.
Population: 1,268; Growth (since 2000): 18.1%; Density: 729.9 persons per square mile; Race: 81.2% White, 2.1% Black/African American, 0.6% Asian, 0.6% American Indian/Alaska Native, 0.0% Native Hawaiian/Other Pacific Islander, 10.6% Two or more races, 11.0% Hispanic of any race; Average household size: 2.41; Median age: 38.8; Age under 18: 21.7%; Age 65 and over: 18.0%; Males per 100 females: 97.5; Marriage status: 32.5% never married, 50.6% now married, 3.6% separated, 8.1% widowed, 8.8% divorced; Foreign born: 6.3%; Speak English only: 93.7%; With disability: 13.9%; Veterans: 12.0%; Ancestry: 23.7% Irish, 17.1% German, 16.2% English, 11.1% Italian, 5.5% French

Employment: 12.0% management, business, and financial, 2.7% computer, engineering, and science, 11.4% education, legal, community service, arts, and media, 2.7% healthcare practitioners, 25.7% service, 18.8% sales and office, 12.8% natural resources, construction, and maintenance, 13.8% production, transportation, and material moving
Income: Per capita: $25,815; Median household: $60,000; Average household: $63,780; Households with income of $100,000 or more: 19.8%; Poverty rate: 15.0%
Educational Attainment: High school diploma or higher: 94.0%; Bachelor's degree or higher: 18.5%; Graduate/professional degree or higher: 6.3%
School District(s)
Union Springs Central SD (KG-12)
   2014-15 Enrollment: 852. . . . . (315) 889-4101
Housing: Homeownership rate: 69.0%; Median home value: $117,000; Median year structure built: 1950; Homeowner vacancy rate: 2.9%; Median selected monthly owner costs: $1,127 with a mortgage, $481 without a mortgage; Median gross rent: $476 per month; Rental vacancy rate: 0.0%
Health Insurance: 87.9% have insurance; 66.3% have private insurance; 35.5% have public insurance; 12.1% do not have insurance; 6.5% of children under 18 do not have insurance
Transportation: Commute: 76.4% car, 0.0% public transportation, 12.3% walk, 10.1% work from home; Mean travel time to work: 20.4 minutes
Additional Information Contacts
Village of Union Springs . . . . (315) 889-7341
   http://unionspringsny.com

VENICE (town).
Covers a land area of 41.088 square miles and a water area of 0.200 square miles. Located at 42.72° N. Lat; 76.54° W. Long.
Population: 1,361; Growth (since 2000): 5.8%; Density: 33.1 persons per square mile; Race: 97.4% White, 2.0% Black/African American, 0.0% Asian, 0.0% American Indian/Alaska Native, 0.0% Native Hawaiian/Other Pacific Islander, 0.1% Two or more races, 11.3% Hispanic of any race; Average household size: 2.61; Median age: 42.1; Age under 18: 21.1%; Age 65 and over: 17.0%; Males per 100 females: 112.8; Marriage status: 28.4% never married, 55.0% now married, 2.1% separated, 4.5% widowed, 12.1% divorced; Foreign born: 6.2%; Speak English only: 90.6%; With disability: 10.7%; Veterans: 8.5%; Ancestry: 22.4% English, 18.1% Irish, 13.8% German, 5.4% Italian, 4.6% Polish
Employment: 11.0% management, business, and financial, 2.5% computer, engineering, and science, 10.7% education, legal, community service, arts, and media, 3.3% healthcare practitioners, 17.4% service, 19.4% sales and office, 22.5% natural resources, construction, and maintenance, 13.2% production, transportation, and material moving
Income: Per capita: $27,850; Median household: $60,395; Average household: $72,072; Households with income of $100,000 or more: 22.5%; Poverty rate: 7.3%
Educational Attainment: High school diploma or higher: 86.2%; Bachelor's degree or higher: 18.8%; Graduate/professional degree or higher: 9.6%
Housing: Homeownership rate: 76.9%; Median home value: $108,700; Median year structure built: Before 1940; Homeowner vacancy rate: 0.0%; Median selected monthly owner costs: $1,113 with a mortgage, $556 without a mortgage; Median gross rent: $700 per month; Rental vacancy rate: 0.0%
Health Insurance: 89.3% have insurance; 69.8% have private insurance; 37.2% have public insurance; 10.7% do not have insurance; 2.8% of children under 18 do not have insurance
Transportation: Commute: 90.4% car, 0.0% public transportation, 0.4% walk, 8.8% work from home; Mean travel time to work: 26.7 minutes
Additional Information Contacts
Town of Venice . . . . (315) 364-9512
   http://co.cayuga.ny.us/venice

VICTORY (town).
Covers a land area of 34.394 square miles and a water area of 0.058 square miles. Located at 43.21° N. Lat; 76.65° W. Long. Elevation is 423 feet.
Population: 1,708; Growth (since 2000): -7.1%; Density: 49.7 persons per square mile; Race: 98.5% White, 0.2% Black/African American, 0.0% Asian, 0.7% American Indian/Alaska Native, 0.0% Native Hawaiian/Other Pacific Islander, 0.6% Two or more races, 0.5% Hispanic of any race; Average household size: 2.64; Median age: 46.1; Age under 18: 24.1%; Age 65 and over: 16.1%; Males per 100 females: 103.7; Marriage status: 22.4% never married, 58.1% now married, 2.8% separated, 6.6% widowed, 12.9% divorced; Foreign born: 1.3%; Speak English only: 98.0%;

With disability: 19.7%; Veterans: 10.3%; Ancestry: 28.6% German, 18.4% English, 18.0% Irish, 7.2% American, 6.5% Italian
Employment: 7.7% management, business, and financial, 4.5% computer, engineering, and science, 8.3% education, legal, community service, arts, and media, 2.8% healthcare practitioners, 20.1% service, 13.1% sales and office, 18.4% natural resources, construction, and maintenance, 25.2% production, transportation, and material moving
Income: Per capita: $22,519; Median household: $50,536; Average household: $57,805; Households with income of $100,000 or more: 11.7%; Poverty rate: 12.4%
Educational Attainment: High school diploma or higher: 85.0%; Bachelor's degree or higher: 11.9%; Graduate/professional degree or higher: 3.6%
Housing: Homeownership rate: 90.9%; Median home value: $98,500; Median year structure built: 1976; Homeowner vacancy rate: 0.0%; Median selected monthly owner costs: $998 with a mortgage, $440 without a mortgage; Median gross rent: $520 per month; Rental vacancy rate: 0.0%
Health Insurance: 84.1% have insurance; 62.3% have private insurance; 36.4% have public insurance; 15.9% do not have insurance; 15.6% of children under 18 do not have insurance
Transportation: Commute: 91.6% car, 0.6% public transportation, 0.6% walk, 6.1% work from home; Mean travel time to work: 30.5 minutes

WEEDSPORT (village).
Covers a land area of 0.976 square miles and a water area of 0 square miles. Located at 43.05° N. Lat; 76.56° W. Long. Elevation is 413 feet.
History: Incorporated 1831.
Population: 1,847; Growth (since 2000): -8.4%; Density: 1,893.1 persons per square mile; Race: 95.9% White, 0.3% Black/African American, 1.5% Asian, 0.2% American Indian/Alaska Native, 0.0% Native Hawaiian/Other Pacific Islander, 2.1% Two or more races, 2.0% Hispanic of any race; Average household size: 2.32; Median age: 45.7; Age under 18: 19.2%; Age 65 and over: 18.2%; Males per 100 females: 89.9; Marriage status: 33.5% never married, 44.1% now married, 4.1% separated, 7.2% widowed, 15.2% divorced; Foreign born: 2.3%; Speak English only: 97.5%; With disability: 18.7%; Veterans: 12.5%; Ancestry: 26.8% English, 24.7% Irish, 23.3% German, 14.9% Italian, 8.1% Polish
Employment: 9.1% management, business, and financial, 3.0% computer, engineering, and science, 12.9% education, legal, community service, arts, and media, 5.6% healthcare practitioners, 15.9% service, 29.1% sales and office, 10.2% natural resources, construction, and maintenance, 14.2% production, transportation, and material moving
Income: Per capita: $27,878; Median household: $53,000; Average household: $62,875; Households with income of $100,000 or more: 21.1%; Poverty rate: 7.9%
Educational Attainment: High school diploma or higher: 90.1%; Bachelor's degree or higher: 24.5%; Graduate/professional degree or higher: 10.8%

School District(s)
Weedsport Central SD (KG-12)
    2014-15 Enrollment: 829 . . . . (315) 834-6637
Housing: Homeownership rate: 63.3%; Median home value: $112,600; Median year structure built: Before 1940; Homeowner vacancy rate: 0.0%; Median selected monthly owner costs: $1,202 with a mortgage, $477 without a mortgage; Median gross rent: $649 per month; Rental vacancy rate: 0.0%
Health Insurance: 96.6% have insurance; 79.4% have private insurance; 34.5% have public insurance; 3.4% do not have insurance; 0.0% of children under 18 do not have insurance
Safety: Violent crime rate: 0.0 per 10,000 population; Property crime rate: 62.0 per 10,000 population
Transportation: Commute: 94.2% car, 0.0% public transportation, 2.7% walk, 2.2% work from home; Mean travel time to work: 20.0 minutes
Additional Information Contacts
Village of Weedsport . . . . (315) 834-6634
    http://villageofweedsport.org

Chautauqua County

Located in western New York; bounded on the northwest by Lake Erie, and on the west and south by Pennsylvania. Covers a land area of 1,060.226 square miles, a water area of 439.957 square miles, and is located in the Eastern Time Zone at 42.30° N. Lat., 79.41° W. Long. The county was founded in 1808. County seat is Mayville.

Chautauqua County is part of the Jamestown-Dunkirk-Fredonia, NY Micropolitan Statistical Area. The entire metro area includes: Chautauqua County, NY

Weather Station: Fredonia   Elevation: 759 feet

	Jan	Feb	Mar	Apr	May	Jun	Jul	Aug	Sep	Oct	Nov	Dec
High	33	36	44	57	68	77	80	79	73	61	50	38
Low	20	20	27	38	48	58	63	62	55	45	36	26
Precip	2.6	2.1	2.7	3.3	3.5	3.7	4.1	3.7	4.6	4.3	4.0	3.4
Snow	25.4	13.3	11.1	2.7	0.3	0.0	0.0	0.0	0.0	0.2	5.9	20.3

High and Low temperatures in degrees Fahrenheit; Precipitation and Snow in inches

Weather Station: Jamestown 4 NE   Elevation: 1,250 feet

	Jan	Feb	Mar	Apr	May	Jun	Jul	Aug	Sep	Oct	Nov	Dec
High	32	35	43	57	67	76	80	79	72	59	48	36
Low	15	15	22	33	42	52	56	55	48	37	31	21
Precip	3.1	2.5	3.0	3.6	3.9	4.8	4.8	4.1	4.4	3.8	4.1	3.5
Snow	24.9	15.6	13.1	2.9	tr	0.0	0.0	0.0	0.0	0.4	8.3	21.4

High and Low temperatures in degrees Fahrenheit; Precipitation and Snow in inches

Weather Station: Westfield 2 SSE   Elevation: 707 feet

	Jan	Feb	Mar	Apr	May	Jun	Jul	Aug	Sep	Oct	Nov	Dec
High	33	35	43	56	67	76	80	78	71	60	48	37
Low	20	21	27	38	49	58	63	62	55	45	35	26
Precip	2.5	2.2	2.9	3.4	3.8	4.1	4.2	4.0	4.9	4.9	4.3	3.4
Snow	21.2	14.0	12.7	2.7	0.4	0.0	0.0	0.0	tr	0.4	8.7	24.4

High and Low temperatures in degrees Fahrenheit; Precipitation and Snow in inches

Population: 132,646; Growth (since 2000): -5.1%; Density: 125.1 persons per square mile; Race: 93.0% White, 2.5% Black/African American, 0.7% Asian, 0.5% American Indian/Alaska Native, 0.1% Native Hawaiian/Other Pacific Islander, 1.7% two or more races, 6.8% Hispanic of any race; Average household size: 2.36; Median age: 41.7; Age under 18: 21.0%; Age 65 and over: 17.6%; Males per 100 females: 97.2; Marriage status: 31.4% never married, 49.7% now married, 2.7% separated, 6.8% widowed, 12.0% divorced; Foreign born: 2.0%; Speak English only: 92.5%; With disability: 15.2%; Veterans: 9.8%; Ancestry: 21.7% German, 15.1% Italian, 14.6% Irish, 13.5% English, 12.1% Swedish
Religion: Six largest groups: 15.5% Catholicism, 8.4% Methodist/Pietist, 3.3% Lutheran, 2.2% Presbyterian-Reformed, 2.1% Holiness, 2.1% Non-denominational Protestant
Economy: Unemployment rate: 5.6%; Leading industries: 17.2 % retail trade; 13.2 % other services (except public administration); 12.1 % accommodation and food services; Farms: 1,515 totaling 236,546 acres; Company size: 3 employ 1,000 or more persons, 3 employ 500 to 999 persons, 57 employ 100 to 499 persons, 2,845 employ less than 100 persons; Business ownership: 2,757 women-owned, 56 Black-owned, 259 Hispanic-owned, 101 Asian-owned, n/a American Indian/Alaska Native-owned
Employment: 10.7% management, business, and financial, 2.5% computer, engineering, and science, 10.5% education, legal, community service, arts, and media, 5.2% healthcare practitioners, 19.9% service, 22.5% sales and office, 9.8% natural resources, construction, and maintenance, 18.9% production, transportation, and material moving
Income: Per capita: $22,903; Median household: $42,993; Average household: $54,880; Households with income of $100,000 or more: 12.3%; Poverty rate: 18.9%
Educational Attainment: High school diploma or higher: 88.2%; Bachelor's degree or higher: 20.9%; Graduate/professional degree or higher: 9.5%
Housing: Homeownership rate: 69.6%; Median home value: $84,500; Median year structure built: 1949; Homeowner vacancy rate: 2.5%; Median selected monthly owner costs: $993 with a mortgage, $445 without a mortgage; Median gross rent: $612 per month; Rental vacancy rate: 7.9%
Vital Statistics: Birth rate: 102.6 per 10,000 population; Death rate: 104.0 per 10,000 population; Age-adjusted cancer mortality rate: 181.7 deaths per 100,000 population
Health Insurance: 92.3% have insurance; 66.5% have private insurance; 41.0% have public insurance; 7.7% do not have insurance; 6.9% of children under 18 do not have insurance
Health Care: Physicians: 12.4 per 10,000 population; Dentists: 5.6 per 10,000 population; Hospital beds: 35.0 per 10,000 population; Hospital admissions: 1,783.4 per 10,000 population
Air Quality Index (AQI): Percent of Days: 89.0% good, 10.7% moderate, 0.3% unhealthy for sensitive individuals, 0.0% unhealthy, 0.0% very unhealthy; Annual median: 35; Annual maximum: 106

Transportation: Commute: 90.5% car, 0.3% public transportation, 4.5% walk, 3.5% work from home; Mean travel time to work: 17.9 minutes
2016 Presidential Election: 58.9% Trump, 35.6% Clinton, 4.1% Johnson, 1.4% Stein
National and State Parks: Lake Erie State Park
Additional Information Contacts
Chautauqua Government . . . . (716) 753-4211
   http://www.co.chautauqua.ny.us

Chautauqua County Communities

ARKWRIGHT (town). Covers a land area of 35.670 square miles and a water area of 0.060 square miles. Located at 42.39° N. Lat; 79.24° W. Long. Elevation is 1,634 feet.
Population: 965; Growth (since 2000): -14.3%; Density: 27.1 persons per square mile; Race: 96.7% White, 0.4% Black/African American, 0.6% Asian, 0.0% American Indian/Alaska Native, 0.0% Native Hawaiian/Other Pacific Islander, 1.9% Two or more races, 0.9% Hispanic of any race; Average household size: 2.38; Median age: 48.5; Age under 18: 16.7%; Age 65 and over: 18.3%; Males per 100 females: 108.4; Marriage status: 29.9% never married, 60.1% now married, 3.6% separated, 4.6% widowed, 5.3% divorced; Foreign born: 0.9%; Speak English only: 98.2%; With disability: 15.6%; Veterans: 10.4%; Ancestry: 23.7% German, 19.5% Polish, 14.5% English, 13.2% Irish, 9.6% Italian
Employment: 12.1% management, business, and financial, 5.2% computer, engineering, and science, 8.4% education, legal, community service, arts, and media, 4.2% healthcare practitioners, 19.6% service, 25.5% sales and office, 12.7% natural resources, construction, and maintenance, 12.3% production, transportation, and material moving
Income: Per capita: $25,380; Median household: $56,563; Average household: $61,130; Households with income of $100,000 or more: 13.9%; Poverty rate: 13.1%
Educational Attainment: High school diploma or higher: 86.2%; Bachelor's degree or higher: 19.9%; Graduate/professional degree or higher: 8.3%
Housing: Homeownership rate: 93.8%; Median home value: $90,000; Median year structure built: 1977; Homeowner vacancy rate: 0.0%; Median selected monthly owner costs: $1,160 with a mortgage, $408 without a mortgage; Median gross rent: n/a per month; Rental vacancy rate: 0.0%
Health Insurance: 94.2% have insurance; 68.7% have private insurance; 41.5% have public insurance; 5.8% do not have insurance; 1.9% of children under 18 do not have insurance
Transportation: Commute: 91.3% car, 0.0% public transportation, 1.3% walk, 4.0% work from home; Mean travel time to work: 21.8 minutes

ASHVILLE (unincorporated postal area)
ZCTA: 14710
   Covers a land area of 48.365 square miles and a water area of 0.057 square miles. Located at 42.09° N. Lat; 79.42° W. Long. Elevation is 1,358 feet.
Population: 3,247; Growth (since 2000): -18.0%; Density: 67.1 persons per square mile; Race: 98.8% White, 0.0% Black/African American, 0.2% Asian, 0.4% American Indian/Alaska Native, 0.0% Native Hawaiian/Other Pacific Islander, 0.3% Two or more races, 1.4% Hispanic of any race; Average household size: 2.45; Median age: 48.3; Age under 18: 19.5%; Age 65 and over: 19.9%; Males per 100 females: 100.0; Marriage status: 21.0% never married, 59.1% now married, 1.2% separated, 5.4% widowed, 14.5% divorced; Foreign born: 1.4%; Speak English only: 97.8%; With disability: 10.7%; Veterans: 8.8%; Ancestry: 20.6% English, 20.3% Swedish, 18.7% German, 18.0% Irish, 8.9% Italian
Employment: 10.8% management, business, and financial, 4.8% computer, engineering, and science, 9.9% education, legal, community service, arts, and media, 7.5% healthcare practitioners, 9.7% service, 23.1% sales and office, 10.7% natural resources, construction, and maintenance, 23.5% production, transportation, and material moving
Income: Per capita: $26,609; Median household: $52,946; Average household: $63,763; Households with income of $100,000 or more: 18.4%; Poverty rate: 11.8%
Educational Attainment: High school diploma or higher: 91.3%; Bachelor's degree or higher: 17.6%; Graduate/professional degree or higher: 9.3%
Housing: Homeownership rate: 89.1%; Median home value: $89,200; Median year structure built: 1956; Homeowner vacancy rate: 4.2%; Median selected monthly owner costs: $1,045 with a mortgage, $441

without a mortgage; Median gross rent: $813 per month; Rental vacancy rate: 0.0%
Health Insurance: 91.3% have insurance; 70.6% have private insurance; 37.7% have public insurance; 8.7% do not have insurance; 1.9% of children under 18 do not have insurance
Transportation: Commute: 91.8% car, 0.3% public transportation, 0.4% walk, 7.4% work from home; Mean travel time to work: 24.8 minutes

BEMUS POINT (village). Covers a land area of 0.436 square miles and a water area of 0 square miles. Located at 42.16° N. Lat; 79.39° W. Long. Elevation is 1,322 feet.
Population: 192; Growth (since 2000): -43.5%; Density: 440.3 persons per square mile; Race: 99.0% White, 1.0% Black/African American, 0.0% Asian, 0.0% American Indian/Alaska Native, 0.0% Native Hawaiian/Other Pacific Islander, 0.0% Two or more races, 0.0% Hispanic of any race; Average household size: 1.94; Median age: 58.4; Age under 18: 17.2%; Age 65 and over: 39.6%; Males per 100 females: 86.7; Marriage status: 21.0% never married, 53.7% now married, 2.5% separated, 14.8% widowed, 10.5% divorced; Foreign born: 1.0%; Speak English only: 98.9%; With disability: 20.8%; Veterans: 11.9%; Ancestry: 25.0% Swedish, 23.4% German, 19.8% Irish, 18.2% English, 15.6% Italian
Employment: 19.4% management, business, and financial, 8.1% computer, engineering, and science, 8.1% education, legal, community service, arts, and media, 22.6% healthcare practitioners, 25.8% service, 6.5% sales and office, 1.6% natural resources, construction, and maintenance, 8.1% production, transportation, and material moving
Income: Per capita: $50,695; Median household: $36,477; Average household: $97,127; Households with income of $100,000 or more: 21.3%; Poverty rate: 18.2%
Educational Attainment: High school diploma or higher: 93.6%; Bachelor's degree or higher: 36.5%; Graduate/professional degree or higher: 17.9%
School District(s)
Bemus Point Central SD (PK-12)
   2014-15 Enrollment: 746 . . . . (716) 386-2375
Housing: Homeownership rate: 55.6%; Median home value: $204,200; Median year structure built: 1965; Homeowner vacancy rate: 41.5%; Median selected monthly owner costs: n/a with a mortgage, n/a without a mortgage; Median gross rent: $396 per month; Rental vacancy rate: 27.9%
Health Insurance: 97.9% have insurance; 73.4% have private insurance; 55.7% have public insurance; 2.1% do not have insurance; 0.0% of children under 18 do not have insurance
Transportation: Commute: 88.7% car, 0.0% public transportation, 6.5% walk, 4.8% work from home; Mean travel time to work: 18.4 minutes

BROCTON (village). Covers a land area of 1.710 square miles and a water area of 0 square miles. Located at 42.39° N. Lat; 79.44° W. Long. Elevation is 735 feet.
History: A short-lived community of the Brotherhood of the New Life was founded here in 1867 by Thomas L. Harris. Incorporated 1894.
Population: 1,518; Growth (since 2000): -1.9%; Density: 887.9 persons per square mile; Race: 96.6% White, 0.9% Black/African American, 0.0% Asian, 0.0% American Indian/Alaska Native, 0.0% Native Hawaiian/Other Pacific Islander, 2.5% Two or more races, 0.4% Hispanic of any race; Average household size: 2.24; Median age: 44.5; Age under 18: 22.1%; Age 65 and over: 18.5%; Males per 100 females: 91.5; Marriage status: 31.0% never married, 40.9% now married, 1.6% separated, 8.5% widowed, 19.6% divorced; Foreign born: 0.0%; Speak English only: 98.7%; With disability: 21.1%; Veterans: 8.0%; Ancestry: 33.9% German, 18.3% Irish, 17.7% Italian, 15.8% Polish, 13.6% English
Employment: 8.0% management, business, and financial, 1.4% computer, engineering, and science, 7.7% education, legal, community service, arts, and media, 2.5% healthcare practitioners, 24.2% service, 18.6% sales and office, 9.1% natural resources, construction, and maintenance, 28.6% production, transportation, and material moving
Income: Per capita: $21,209; Median household: $38,438; Average household: $46,276; Households with income of $100,000 or more: 8.1%; Poverty rate: 18.7%
Educational Attainment: High school diploma or higher: 85.9%; Bachelor's degree or higher: 13.3%; Graduate/professional degree or higher: 6.0%
School District(s)
Brocton Central SD (PK-12)
   2014-15 Enrollment: 601 . . . . (716) 792-2173

Housing: Homeownership rate: 58.8%; Median home value: $70,100; Median year structure built: 1942; Homeowner vacancy rate: 0.7%; Median selected monthly owner costs: $869 with a mortgage, $392 without a mortgage; Median gross rent: $547 per month; Rental vacancy rate: 0.0%
Health Insurance: 94.1% have insurance; 61.3% have private insurance; 44.9% have public insurance; 5.9% do not have insurance; 0.0% of children under 18 do not have insurance
Transportation: Commute: 93.5% car, 0.0% public transportation, 3.8% walk, 2.5% work from home; Mean travel time to work: 17.0 minutes

BUSTI (CDP). Covers a land area of 2.264 square miles and a water area of 0 square miles. Located at 42.04° N. Lat; 79.28° W. Long. Elevation is 1,365 feet.
Population: 477; Growth (since 2000): n/a; Density: 210.7 persons per square mile; Race: 92.0% White, 0.0% Black/African American, 8.0% Asian, 0.0% American Indian/Alaska Native, 0.0% Native Hawaiian/Other Pacific Islander, 0.0% Two or more races, 0.0% Hispanic of any race; Average household size: 3.94; Median age: 25.8; Age under 18: 30.6%; Age 65 and over: 8.0%; Males per 100 females: 100.5; Marriage status: 30.2% never married, 61.8% now married, 0.0% separated, 2.4% widowed, 5.6% divorced; Foreign born: 3.8%; Speak English only: 91.5%; With disability: 15.1%; Veterans: 11.8%; Ancestry: 29.1% English, 15.3% American, 11.5% German, 11.5% Swedish, 9.9% Irish
Employment: 0.0% management, business, and financial, 14.2% computer, engineering, and science, 4.1% education, legal, community service, arts, and media, 0.0% healthcare practitioners, 9.5% service, 22.5% sales and office, 34.3% natural resources, construction, and maintenance, 15.4% production, transportation, and material moving
Income: Per capita: $15,834; Median household: $59,861; Average household: $59,766; Households with income of $100,000 or more: 7.4%; Poverty rate: 8.3%
Educational Attainment: High school diploma or higher: 87.8%; Bachelor's degree or higher: 24.7%; Graduate/professional degree or higher: 2.7%
Housing: Homeownership rate: 91.7%; Median home value: $93,900; Median year structure built: 1953; Homeowner vacancy rate: 0.0%; Median selected monthly owner costs: $906 with a mortgage, $538 without a mortgage; Median gross rent: n/a per month; Rental vacancy rate: 0.0%
Health Insurance: 83.9% have insurance; 47.6% have private insurance; 50.9% have public insurance; 16.1% do not have insurance; 4.8% of children under 18 do not have insurance
Transportation: Commute: 94.3% car, 0.0% public transportation, 0.0% walk, 5.7% work from home; Mean travel time to work: 15.0 minutes

BUSTI (town). Covers a land area of 47.825 square miles and a water area of 0.014 square miles. Located at 42.05° N. Lat; 79.33° W. Long. Elevation is 1,365 feet.
Population: 7,303; Growth (since 2000): -5.9%; Density: 152.7 persons per square mile; Race: 95.6% White, 0.6% Black/African American, 3.0% Asian, 0.0% American Indian/Alaska Native, 0.0% Native Hawaiian/Other Pacific Islander, 0.7% Two or more races, 1.2% Hispanic of any race; Average household size: 2.39; Median age: 46.8; Age under 18: 21.2%; Age 65 and over: 19.9%; Males per 100 females: 98.4; Marriage status: 24.7% never married, 57.6% now married, 2.5% separated, 7.3% widowed, 10.4% divorced; Foreign born: 2.7%; Speak English only: 96.9%; With disability: 13.5%; Veterans: 9.6%; Ancestry: 19.9% German, 19.3% Swedish, 17.3% English, 15.1% Italian, 14.6% Irish
Employment: 15.5% management, business, and financial, 3.6% computer, engineering, and science, 8.6% education, legal, community service, arts, and media, 7.9% healthcare practitioners, 18.1% service, 21.9% sales and office, 10.0% natural resources, construction, and maintenance, 14.4% production, transportation, and material moving
Income: Per capita: $29,018; Median household: $51,632; Average household: $68,407; Households with income of $100,000 or more: 18.2%; Poverty rate: 9.4%
Educational Attainment: High school diploma or higher: 93.0%; Bachelor's degree or higher: 28.6%; Graduate/professional degree or higher: 13.4%
Housing: Homeownership rate: 78.3%; Median home value: $99,500; Median year structure built: 1960; Homeowner vacancy rate: 3.6%; Median selected monthly owner costs: $1,139 with a mortgage, $439 without a mortgage; Median gross rent: $696 per month; Rental vacancy rate: 12.0%
Health Insurance: 93.1% have insurance; 69.0% have private insurance; 40.9% have public insurance; 6.9% do not have insurance; 6.1% of children under 18 do not have insurance

Transportation: Commute: 96.3% car, 0.6% public transportation, 1.2% walk, 2.0% work from home; Mean travel time to work: 18.3 minutes
Additional Information Contacts
Town of Busti. . . . . (716) 763-8561
  http://www.townofbusti.com

CARROLL (town). Covers a land area of 33.320 square miles and a water area of 0.023 square miles. Located at 42.04° N. Lat; 79.10° W. Long.
Population: 3,466; Growth (since 2000): -4.6%; Density: 104.0 persons per square mile; Race: 98.2% White, 0.8% Black/African American, 0.0% Asian, 0.0% American Indian/Alaska Native, 0.0% Native Hawaiian/Other Pacific Islander, 0.7% Two or more races, 0.9% Hispanic of any race; Average household size: 2.33; Median age: 47.9; Age under 18: 16.4%; Age 65 and over: 22.5%; Males per 100 females: 95.5; Marriage status: 25.6% never married, 47.8% now married, 1.7% separated, 8.3% widowed, 18.3% divorced; Foreign born: 2.4%; Speak English only: 99.4%; With disability: 16.1%; Veterans: 9.9%; Ancestry: 33.0% Swedish, 18.1% Irish, 14.0% Italian, 12.3% English, 12.1% German
Employment: 6.9% management, business, and financial, 1.0% computer, engineering, and science, 12.4% education, legal, community service, arts, and media, 5.5% healthcare practitioners, 18.7% service, 26.0% sales and office, 10.0% natural resources, construction, and maintenance, 19.5% production, transportation, and material moving
Income: Per capita: $24,551; Median household: $45,625; Average household: $55,853; Households with income of $100,000 or more: 13.6%; Poverty rate: 9.5%
Educational Attainment: High school diploma or higher: 90.2%; Bachelor's degree or higher: 20.4%; Graduate/professional degree or higher: 10.2%
Housing: Homeownership rate: 80.5%; Median home value: $79,700; Median year structure built: 1962; Homeowner vacancy rate: 4.3%; Median selected monthly owner costs: $1,045 with a mortgage, $538 without a mortgage; Median gross rent: $508 per month; Rental vacancy rate: 0.0%
Health Insurance: 98.0% have insurance; 80.3% have private insurance; 40.4% have public insurance; 2.0% do not have insurance; 0.0% of children under 18 do not have insurance
Safety: Violent crime rate: 0.0 per 10,000 population; Property crime rate: 20.4 per 10,000 population
Transportation: Commute: 99.0% car, 0.0% public transportation, 1.0% walk, 0.0% work from home; Mean travel time to work: 17.5 minutes

CASSADAGA (village). Covers a land area of 0.839 square miles and a water area of 0.217 square miles. Located at 42.34° N. Lat; 79.32° W. Long. Elevation is 1,339 feet.
Population: 709; Growth (since 2000): 4.9%; Density: 845.4 persons per square mile; Race: 98.2% White, 0.0% Black/African American, 1.1% Asian, 0.0% American Indian/Alaska Native, 0.0% Native Hawaiian/Other Pacific Islander, 0.7% Two or more races, 1.3% Hispanic of any race; Average household size: 2.69; Median age: 41.8; Age under 18: 24.3%; Age 65 and over: 21.3%; Males per 100 females: 100.6; Marriage status: 31.5% never married, 51.8% now married, 1.2% separated, 6.4% widowed, 10.3% divorced; Foreign born: 0.7%; Speak English only: 99.0%; With disability: 12.8%; Veterans: 12.3%; Ancestry: 26.7% English, 24.8% German, 11.4% Irish, 8.9% Polish, 7.3% Swedish
Employment: 9.0% management, business, and financial, 0.0% computer, engineering, and science, 9.7% education, legal, community service, arts, and media, 9.0% healthcare practitioners, 19.7% service, 16.1% sales and office, 10.4% natural resources, construction, and maintenance, 26.1% production, transportation, and material moving
Income: Per capita: $22,351; Median household: $52,917; Average household: $56,916; Households with income of $100,000 or more: 10.2%; Poverty rate: 9.3%
Educational Attainment: High school diploma or higher: 91.9%; Bachelor's degree or higher: 19.7%; Graduate/professional degree or higher: 8.5%

School District(s)
Cassadaga Valley Central SD (PK-12)
  2014-15 Enrollment: 971. . . . . (716) 962-5155
Housing: Homeownership rate: 75.8%; Median home value: $108,500; Median year structure built: Before 1940; Homeowner vacancy rate: 0.0%; Median selected monthly owner costs: $1,036 with a mortgage, $405 without a mortgage; Median gross rent: $765 per month; Rental vacancy rate: 0.0%

Health Insurance: 96.6% have insurance; 77.2% have private insurance; 38.2% have public insurance; 3.4% do not have insurance; 1.2% of children under 18 do not have insurance

Transportation: Commute: 91.7% car, 1.0% public transportation, 6.3% walk, 0.3% work from home; Mean travel time to work: 22.5 minutes

CATTARAUGUS RESERVATION (reservation). Covers a land area of 2.446 square miles and a water area of 0.328 square miles. Located at 42.54° N. Lat; 79.09° W. Long.

Population: 78; Growth (since 2000): n/a; Density: 31.9 persons per square mile; Race: 0.0% White, 0.0% Black/African American, 0.0% Asian, 100.0% American Indian/Alaska Native, 0.0% Native Hawaiian/Other Pacific Islander, 0.0% Two or more races, 0.0% Hispanic of any race; Average household size: 3.55; Median age: 11.2; Age under 18: 56.4%; Age 65 and over: 19.2%; Males per 100 females: 123.5; Marriage status: 73.5% never married, 26.5% now married, 0.0% separated, 0.0% widowed, 0.0% divorced; Foreign born: 0.0%; Speak English only: 85.5%; With disability: 7.7%; Veterans: 35.3%; Ancestry: n/a.

Employment: 0.0% management, business, and financial, 0.0% computer, engineering, and science, 76.9% education, legal, community service, arts, and media, 0.0% healthcare practitioners, 23.1% service, 0.0% sales and office, 0.0% natural resources, construction, and maintenance, 0.0% production, transportation, and material moving

Income: Per capita: $5,099; Median household: n/a; Average household: $16,659; Households with income of $100,000 or more: n/a; Poverty rate: 88.5%

Educational Attainment: High school diploma or higher: 55.9%; Bachelor's degree or higher: n/a; Graduate/professional degree or higher: n/a

Housing: Homeownership rate: 40.9%; Median home value: n/a; Median year structure built: 1963; Homeowner vacancy rate: 0.0%; Median selected monthly owner costs: n/a with a mortgage, n/a without a mortgage; Median gross rent: n/a per month; Rental vacancy rate: 0.0%

Health Insurance: 100.0% have insurance; 24.4% have private insurance; 83.3% have public insurance; 0.0% do not have insurance; 0.0% of children under 18 do not have insurance

Transportation: Commute: 100.0% car, 0.0% public transportation, 0.0% walk, 0.0% work from home; Mean travel time to work: 0.0 minutes

CELORON (village). Covers a land area of 0.747 square miles and a water area of <.001 square miles. Located at 42.11° N. Lat; 79.28° W. Long. Elevation is 1,319 feet.

History: Incorporated 1896.

Population: 1,183; Growth (since 2000): -8.6%; Density: 1,582.7 persons per square mile; Race: 97.9% White, 0.0% Black/African American, 1.4% Asian, 0.0% American Indian/Alaska Native, 0.0% Native Hawaiian/Other Pacific Islander, 0.7% Two or more races, 3.9% Hispanic of any race; Average household size: 2.12; Median age: 43.4; Age under 18: 18.7%; Age 65 and over: 18.7%; Males per 100 females: 98.6; Marriage status: 27.7% never married, 46.2% now married, 4.6% separated, 7.9% widowed, 18.3% divorced; Foreign born: 1.0%; Speak English only: 96.7%; With disability: 15.5%; Veterans: 10.6%; Ancestry: 30.1% Swedish, 15.6% German, 11.4% Irish, 10.6% English, 10.1% Italian

Employment: 7.7% management, business, and financial, 0.0% computer, engineering, and science, 3.5% education, legal, community service, arts, and media, 3.7% healthcare practitioners, 28.5% service, 25.7% sales and office, 10.1% natural resources, construction, and maintenance, 20.8% production, transportation, and material moving

Income: Per capita: $23,010; Median household: $42,500; Average household: $47,827; Households with income of $100,000 or more: 8.2%; Poverty rate: 15.1%

Educational Attainment: High school diploma or higher: 81.6%; Bachelor's degree or higher: 12.5%; Graduate/professional degree or higher: 4.8%

Housing: Homeownership rate: 58.2%; Median home value: $61,800; Median year structure built: Before 1940; Homeowner vacancy rate: 3.0%; Median selected monthly owner costs: $876 with a mortgage, $363 without a mortgage; Median gross rent: $669 per month; Rental vacancy rate: 10.9%

Health Insurance: 90.1% have insurance; 58.4% have private insurance; 45.7% have public insurance; 9.9% do not have insurance; 1.8% of children under 18 do not have insurance

Transportation: Commute: 96.6% car, 0.0% public transportation, 2.1% walk, 0.0% work from home; Mean travel time to work: 14.9 minutes

CHARLOTTE (town). Covers a land area of 36.432 square miles and a water area of 0 square miles. Located at 42.30° N. Lat; 79.24° W. Long. Elevation is 1,532 feet.

Population: 1,825; Growth (since 2000): 6.5%; Density: 50.1 persons per square mile; Race: 99.2% White, 0.0% Black/African American, 0.2% Asian, 0.2% American Indian/Alaska Native, 0.0% Native Hawaiian/Other Pacific Islander, 0.2% Two or more races, 1.2% Hispanic of any race; Average household size: 2.66; Median age: 40.6; Age under 18: 25.5%; Age 65 and over: 13.0%; Males per 100 females: 105.3; Marriage status: 25.5% never married, 59.7% now married, 1.2% separated, 6.3% widowed, 8.5% divorced; Foreign born: 0.5%; Speak English only: 96.9%; With disability: 12.3%; Veterans: 9.9%; Ancestry: 23.2% German, 17.4% Irish, 16.9% English, 13.5% Swedish, 12.2% Italian

Employment: 9.8% management, business, and financial, 1.2% computer, engineering, and science, 10.2% education, legal, community service, arts, and media, 4.3% healthcare practitioners, 24.1% service, 15.2% sales and office, 16.8% natural resources, construction, and maintenance, 18.5% production, transportation, and material moving

Income: Per capita: $20,606; Median household: $44,052; Average household: $53,485; Households with income of $100,000 or more: 9.8%; Poverty rate: 20.1%

Educational Attainment: High school diploma or higher: 86.1%; Bachelor's degree or higher: 14.1%; Graduate/professional degree or higher: 5.2%

Housing: Homeownership rate: 83.5%; Median home value: $68,200; Median year structure built: 1972; Homeowner vacancy rate: 1.2%; Median selected monthly owner costs: $1,043 with a mortgage, $518 without a mortgage; Median gross rent: $602 per month; Rental vacancy rate: 0.0%

Health Insurance: 93.0% have insurance; 59.9% have private insurance; 41.3% have public insurance; 7.0% do not have insurance; 0.0% of children under 18 do not have insurance

Transportation: Commute: 89.7% car, 0.5% public transportation, 1.8% walk, 5.6% work from home; Mean travel time to work: 24.3 minutes

CHAUTAUQUA (CDP). Covers a land area of 0.427 square miles and a water area of 0 square miles. Located at 42.21° N. Lat; 79.47° W. Long. Elevation is 1,362 feet.

Population: 594; Growth (since 2000): n/a; Density: 1,391.0 persons per square mile; Race: 90.6% White, 4.0% Black/African American, 3.5% Asian, 0.0% American Indian/Alaska Native, 0.0% Native Hawaiian/Other Pacific Islander, 1.2% Two or more races, 2.4% Hispanic of any race; Average household size: 1.90; Median age: 38.9; Age under 18: 4.7%; Age 65 and over: 39.4%; Males per 100 females: 83.7; Marriage status: 49.1% never married, 45.8% now married, 0.0% separated, 0.0% widowed, 5.1% divorced; Foreign born: 7.4%; Speak English only: 94.6%; With disability: 7.2%; Veterans: 3.2%; Ancestry: 20.4% German, 18.9% Irish, 10.6% Italian, 8.6% Swedish, 7.7% British

Employment: 16.1% management, business, and financial, 4.9% computer, engineering, and science, 9.8% education, legal, community service, arts, and media, 7.0% healthcare practitioners, 39.9% service, 7.0% sales and office, 10.5% natural resources, construction, and maintenance, 4.9% production, transportation, and material moving

Income: Per capita: $58,403; Median household: $95,333; Average household: $194,487; Households with income of $100,000 or more: 42.6%; Poverty rate: 5.3%

Educational Attainment: High school diploma or higher: 96.5%; Bachelor's degree or higher: 85.9%; Graduate/professional degree or higher: 65.0%

Housing: Homeownership rate: 91.4%; Median home value: $579,100; Median year structure built: Before 1940; Homeowner vacancy rate: 0.0%; Median selected monthly owner costs: $1,635 with a mortgage, $1,102 without a mortgage; Median gross rent: n/a per month; Rental vacancy rate: 0.0%

Health Insurance: 91.6% have insurance; 76.8% have private insurance; 44.4% have public insurance; 8.4% do not have insurance; 0.0% of children under 18 do not have insurance

Transportation: Commute: 66.9% car, 2.2% public transportation, 27.9% walk, 2.9% work from home; Mean travel time to work: 10.5 minutes

CHAUTAUQUA (town). Covers a land area of 67.099 square miles and a water area of 0.094 square miles. Located at 42.24° N. Lat; 79.51° W. Long. Elevation is 1,362 feet.

History: Founded as meeting place for Methodist ministers and laity. Chautauqua Institute, founded in 1864, is located here. Famous people connected with the school include U.S. Presidents Garfield, Grant,

McKinley, Harding, and both Roosevelts; explorers Admiral Richard Byrd and Amelia Earhart; inventors Henry Ford and Thomas Edison; Senator Robert Kennedy, William Jennings Bryan, Jane Addams, Ida Tarbell and N.Y. governor Al Smith. Village formerly known as Fair Point.
Population: 4,400; Growth (since 2000): -5.7%; Density: 65.6 persons per square mile; Race: 93.2% White, 3.0% Black/African American, 0.8% Asian, 0.0% American Indian/Alaska Native, 0.2% Native Hawaiian/Other Pacific Islander, 2.3% Two or more races, 1.9% Hispanic of any race; Average household size: 2.25; Median age: 45.3; Age under 18: 12.8%; Age 65 and over: 22.3%; Males per 100 females: 108.3; Marriage status: 29.2% never married, 55.9% now married, 2.8% separated, 4.2% widowed, 10.7% divorced; Foreign born: 3.6%; Speak English only: 89.8%; With disability: 12.1%; Veterans: 10.2%; Ancestry: 23.8% German, 20.9% English, 13.4% Irish, 10.5% Swedish, 8.7% Italian
Employment: 16.3% management, business, and financial, 4.2% computer, engineering, and science, 11.9% education, legal, community service, arts, and media, 4.4% healthcare practitioners, 22.6% service, 14.5% sales and office, 17.9% natural resources, construction, and maintenance, 8.2% production, transportation, and material moving
Income: Per capita: $30,641; Median household: $51,614; Average household: $76,475; Households with income of $100,000 or more: 18.3%; Poverty rate: 13.7%
Educational Attainment: High school diploma or higher: 91.2%; Bachelor's degree or higher: 32.7%; Graduate/professional degree or higher: 15.6%
Housing: Homeownership rate: 80.8%; Median home value: $112,200; Median year structure built: 1954; Homeowner vacancy rate: 4.6%; Median selected monthly owner costs: $953 with a mortgage, $456 without a mortgage; Median gross rent: $657 per month; Rental vacancy rate: 3.0%
Health Insurance: 88.0% have insurance; 70.4% have private insurance; 38.1% have public insurance; 12.0% do not have insurance; 25.5% of children under 18 do not have insurance
Transportation: Commute: 85.4% car, 0.2% public transportation, 4.3% walk, 7.7% work from home; Mean travel time to work: 20.1 minutes
Additional Information Contacts
Town of Chautauqua. . . . . (716) 753-7342
   http://www.townofchautauqua.com

CHERRY CREEK (town). Covers a land area of 36.632 square miles and a water area of 0.013 square miles. Located at 42.30° N. Lat; 79.12° W. Long. Elevation is 1,302 feet.
Population: 957; Growth (since 2000): -16.9%; Density: 26.1 persons per square mile; Race: 98.9% White, 0.2% Black/African American, 0.5% Asian, 0.0% American Indian/Alaska Native, 0.0% Native Hawaiian/Other Pacific Islander, 0.4% Two or more races, 0.1% Hispanic of any race; Average household size: 2.56; Median age: 43.9; Age under 18: 23.9%; Age 65 and over: 17.9%; Males per 100 females: 101.8; Marriage status: 20.4% never married, 63.4% now married, 2.1% separated, 6.1% widowed, 10.1% divorced; Foreign born: 1.1%; Speak English only: 90.6%; With disability: 14.0%; Veterans: 8.9%; Ancestry: 31.9% German, 17.2% Irish, 12.3% Italian, 11.6% English, 10.7% Polish
Employment: 10.3% management, business, and financial, 0.0% computer, engineering, and science, 7.5% education, legal, community service, arts, and media, 7.3% healthcare practitioners, 20.7% service, 20.2% sales and office, 16.4% natural resources, construction, and maintenance, 17.6% production, transportation, and material moving
Income: Per capita: $22,795; Median household: $50,395; Average household: $56,542; Households with income of $100,000 or more: 14.9%; Poverty rate: 10.2%
Educational Attainment: High school diploma or higher: 84.7%; Bachelor's degree or higher: 16.3%; Graduate/professional degree or higher: 7.6%
Housing: Homeownership rate: 81.8%; Median home value: $79,800; Median year structure built: 1951; Homeowner vacancy rate: 0.0%; Median selected monthly owner costs: $1,214 with a mortgage, $477 without a mortgage; Median gross rent: $707 per month; Rental vacancy rate: 0.0%
Health Insurance: 86.9% have insurance; 67.3% have private insurance; 35.3% have public insurance; 13.1% do not have insurance; 20.1% of children under 18 do not have insurance
Transportation: Commute: 90.5% car, 0.0% public transportation, 4.3% walk, 1.9% work from home; Mean travel time to work: 24.6 minutes

CHERRY CREEK (village). Covers a land area of 1.362 square miles and a water area of 0 square miles. Located at 42.30° N. Lat; 79.10° W. Long. Elevation is 1,302 feet.
Population: 447; Growth (since 2000): -18.9%; Density: 328.1 persons per square mile; Race: 99.6% White, 0.0% Black/African American, 0.4% Asian, 0.0% American Indian/Alaska Native, 0.0% Native Hawaiian/Other Pacific Islander, 0.0% Two or more races, 0.2% Hispanic of any race; Average household size: 2.43; Median age: 41.8; Age under 18: 26.6%; Age 65 and over: 15.4%; Males per 100 females: 97.9; Marriage status: 19.7% never married, 63.2% now married, 2.6% separated, 7.1% widowed, 10.0% divorced; Foreign born: 1.1%; Speak English only: 98.4%; With disability: 17.7%; Veterans: 9.5%; Ancestry: 41.8% German, 24.6% Irish, 14.8% Italian, 13.9% English, 13.6% Polish
Employment: 9.1% management, business, and financial, 0.0% computer, engineering, and science, 7.5% education, legal, community service, arts, and media, 15.1% healthcare practitioners, 21.0% service, 15.1% sales and office, 9.7% natural resources, construction, and maintenance, 22.6% production, transportation, and material moving
Income: Per capita: $21,645; Median household: $40,000; Average household: $51,806; Households with income of $100,000 or more: 12.5%; Poverty rate: 17.7%
Educational Attainment: High school diploma or higher: 86.2%; Bachelor's degree or higher: 15.2%; Graduate/professional degree or higher: 5.1%
Housing: Homeownership rate: 68.5%; Median home value: $61,500; Median year structure built: Before 1940; Homeowner vacancy rate: 0.0%; Median selected monthly owner costs: $1,138 with a mortgage, $496 without a mortgage; Median gross rent: $715 per month; Rental vacancy rate: 0.0%
Health Insurance: 92.4% have insurance; 68.9% have private insurance; 41.8% have public insurance; 7.6% do not have insurance; 3.4% of children under 18 do not have insurance
Transportation: Commute: 95.7% car, 0.0% public transportation, 1.1% walk, 1.1% work from home; Mean travel time to work: 26.6 minutes

CLYMER (town). Covers a land area of 36.070 square miles and a water area of 0.093 square miles. Located at 42.05° N. Lat; 79.58° W. Long. Elevation is 1,457 feet.
Population: 1,504; Growth (since 2000): 0.2%; Density: 41.7 persons per square mile; Race: 98.6% White, 0.3% Black/African American, 0.3% Asian, 0.0% American Indian/Alaska Native, 0.0% Native Hawaiian/Other Pacific Islander, 0.8% Two or more races, 0.0% Hispanic of any race; Average household size: 2.76; Median age: 36.0; Age under 18: 31.7%; Age 65 and over: 14.3%; Males per 100 females: 100.0; Marriage status: 26.9% never married, 55.4% now married, 0.9% separated, 8.3% widowed, 9.4% divorced; Foreign born: 0.8%; Speak English only: 67.0%; With disability: 8.9%; Veterans: 5.3%; Ancestry: 23.1% Dutch, 19.2% German, 9.8% English, 9.7% Pennsylvania German, 8.7% Irish
Employment: 18.3% management, business, and financial, 1.4% computer, engineering, and science, 9.7% education, legal, community service, arts, and media, 4.6% healthcare practitioners, 17.5% service, 14.6% sales and office, 15.8% natural resources, construction, and maintenance, 18.1% production, transportation, and material moving
Income: Per capita: $23,511; Median household: $46,027; Average household: $64,139; Households with income of $100,000 or more: 17.4%; Poverty rate: 23.5%
Educational Attainment: High school diploma or higher: 78.1%; Bachelor's degree or higher: 14.1%; Graduate/professional degree or higher: 6.9%

School District(s)
Clymer Central SD (KG-12)
   2014-15 Enrollment: 456. . . . . (716) 355-4444
Housing: Homeownership rate: 84.0%; Median home value: $99,100; Median year structure built: 1959; Homeowner vacancy rate: 0.0%; Median selected monthly owner costs: $973 with a mortgage, $358 without a mortgage; Median gross rent: $765 per month; Rental vacancy rate: 7.4%
Health Insurance: 64.2% have insurance; 50.1% have private insurance; 26.3% have public insurance; 35.8% do not have insurance; 58.5% of children under 18 do not have insurance
Transportation: Commute: 71.5% car, 2.7% public transportation, 11.9% walk, 8.1% work from home; Mean travel time to work: 22.6 minutes

DEWITTVILLE (unincorporated postal area)

ZCTA: 14728

Covers a land area of 26.795 square miles and a water area of 0.047 square miles. Located at 42.26° N. Lat; 79.42° W. Long. Elevation is 1,325 feet.

Population: 758; Growth (since 2000): -29.2%; Density: 28.3 persons per square mile; Race: 99.7% White, 0.0% Black/African American, 0.0% Asian, 0.0% American Indian/Alaska Native, 0.0% Native Hawaiian/Other Pacific Islander, 0.3% Two or more races, 0.0% Hispanic of any race; Average household size: 2.11; Median age: 51.0; Age under 18: 11.7%; Age 65 and over: 28.8%; Males per 100 females: 105.8; Marriage status: 15.5% never married, 66.6% now married, 1.9% separated, 10.2% widowed, 7.7% divorced; Foreign born: 2.8%; Speak English only: 91.8%; With disability: 16.8%; Veterans: 13.5%; Ancestry: 23.1% German, 16.6% English, 12.3% Irish, 11.1% Swedish, 6.2% Polish

Employment: 12.9% management, business, and financial, 2.9% computer, engineering, and science, 16.7% education, legal, community service, arts, and media, 1.8% healthcare practitioners, 17.6% service, 18.2% sales and office, 10.0% natural resources, construction, and maintenance, 19.9% production, transportation, and material moving

Income: Per capita: $33,547; Median household: $47,750; Average household: $67,951; Households with income of $100,000 or more: 25.7%; Poverty rate: 18.5%

Educational Attainment: High school diploma or higher: 81.5%; Bachelor's degree or higher: 29.8%; Graduate/professional degree or higher: 12.6%

Housing: Homeownership rate: 88.0%; Median home value: $97,800; Median year structure built: 1972; Homeowner vacancy rate: 0.0%; Median selected monthly owner costs: $1,035 with a mortgage, $411 without a mortgage; Median gross rent: n/a per month; Rental vacancy rate: 0.0%

Health Insurance: 89.1% have insurance; 73.0% have private insurance; 40.9% have public insurance; 10.9% do not have insurance; 49.4% of children under 18 do not have insurance

Transportation: Commute: 94.5% car, 0.0% public transportation, 2.3% walk, 2.6% work from home; Mean travel time to work: 20.4 minutes

DUNKIRK (city).

Covers a land area of 4.502 square miles and a water area of 0.050 square miles. Located at 42.48° N. Lat; 79.33° W. Long. Elevation is 617 feet.

History: In 1946, it developed a program to help Dunkerque, France (for which it was named), recover from World War II. Other U.S. cities followed, and established a program, called the One World Plan, to aid war-damaged European cities. Founded c.1800, Incorporated as city 1880.

Population: 12,308; Growth (since 2000): -6.3%; Density: 2,734.0 persons per square mile; Race: 87.8% White, 5.3% Black/African American, 0.0% Asian, 0.5% American Indian/Alaska Native, 0.0% Native Hawaiian/Other Pacific Islander, 2.4% Two or more races, 26.6% Hispanic of any race; Average household size: 2.27; Median age: 37.9; Age under 18: 22.1%; Age 65 and over: 14.6%; Males per 100 females: 96.2; Marriage status: 38.5% never married, 42.7% now married, 5.3% separated, 5.3% widowed, 13.5% divorced; Foreign born: 2.3%; Speak English only: 82.1%; With disability: 18.0%; Veterans: 9.3%; Ancestry: 20.8% Polish, 16.8% Italian, 16.5% German, 10.9% Irish, 6.1% English,

Employment: 8.3% management, business, and financial, 1.3% computer, engineering, and science, 9.3% education, legal, community service, arts, and media, 5.6% healthcare practitioners, 19.9% service, 23.3% sales and office, 9.6% natural resources, construction, and maintenance, 22.8% production, transportation, and material moving

Income: Per capita: $20,168; Median household: $38,937; Average household: $45,591; Households with income of $100,000 or more: 8.3%; Poverty rate: 25.0%

Educational Attainment: High school diploma or higher: 85.8%; Bachelor's degree or higher: 15.4%; Graduate/professional degree or higher: 7.9%

School District(s)

Dunkirk City SD (KG-12)
    2014-15 Enrollment: 2,112 . . . . (716) 366-9300

Housing: Homeownership rate: 60.1%; Median home value: $64,700; Median year structure built: Before 1940; Homeowner vacancy rate: 4.8%; Median selected monthly owner costs: $843 with a mortgage, $434 without a mortgage; Median gross rent: $614 per month; Rental vacancy rate: 5.0%

Health Insurance: 94.5% have insurance; 61.1% have private insurance; 47.3% have public insurance; 5.5% do not have insurance; 4.8% of children under 18 do not have insurance

Hospitals: Brooks Memorial Hospital (99 beds)

Safety: Violent crime rate: 31.3 per 10,000 population; Property crime rate: 228.3 per 10,000 population

Newspapers: The Observer (daily circulation 9,100)

Transportation: Commute: 94.0% car, 0.4% public transportation, 3.0% walk, 1.0% work from home; Mean travel time to work: 14.0 minutes; Amtrak: Bus service available.

Additional Information Contacts

City of Dunkirk . . . . (716) 366-3967
    http://www.dunkirkny.org

DUNKIRK (town).

Covers a land area of 6.228 square miles and a water area of 0.054 square miles. Located at 42.47° N. Lat; 79.32° W. Long. Elevation is 617 feet.

Population: 1,305; Growth (since 2000): -5.9%; Density: 209.5 persons per square mile; Race: 93.9% White, 0.6% Black/African American, 1.9% Asian, 0.2% American Indian/Alaska Native, 0.0% Native Hawaiian/Other Pacific Islander, 0.4% Two or more races, 15.7% Hispanic of any race; Average household size: 2.16; Median age: 56.1; Age under 18: 10.9%; Age 65 and over: 32.4%; Males per 100 females: 83.8; Marriage status: 23.4% never married, 47.1% now married, 3.8% separated, 19.1% widowed, 10.5% divorced; Foreign born: 4.0%; Speak English only: 85.0%; With disability: 23.1%; Veterans: 18.4%; Ancestry: 22.0% German, 21.9% Polish, 14.9% Italian, 11.6% English, 10.3% Irish

Employment: 8.4% management, business, and financial, 1.9% computer, engineering, and science, 9.8% education, legal, community service, arts, and media, 10.3% healthcare practitioners, 16.5% service, 24.0% sales and office, 6.0% natural resources, construction, and maintenance, 23.1% production, transportation, and material moving

Income: Per capita: $32,885; Median household: $47,031; Average household: $75,747; Households with income of $100,000 or more: 20.9%; Poverty rate: 10.7%

Educational Attainment: High school diploma or higher: 84.3%; Bachelor's degree or higher: 21.5%; Graduate/professional degree or higher: 8.8%

School District(s)

Dunkirk City SD (KG-12)
    2014-15 Enrollment: 2,112 . . . . (716) 366-9300

Housing: Homeownership rate: 83.5%; Median home value: $89,400; Median year structure built: 1957; Homeowner vacancy rate: 6.3%; Median selected monthly owner costs: $1,192 with a mortgage, $440 without a mortgage; Median gross rent: $647 per month; Rental vacancy rate: 3.5%

Health Insurance: 95.9% have insurance; 72.2% have private insurance; 39.6% have public insurance; 4.1% do not have insurance; 0.0% of children under 18 do not have insurance

Hospitals: Brooks Memorial Hospital (99 beds)

Newspapers: The Observer (daily circulation 9,100)

Transportation: Commute: 95.5% car, 0.0% public transportation, 0.0% walk, 4.5% work from home; Mean travel time to work: 15.7 minutes; Amtrak: Bus service available.

ELLERY (town).

Covers a land area of 47.454 square miles and a water area of 0.117 square miles. Located at 42.19° N. Lat; 79.35° W. Long.

Population: 4,482; Growth (since 2000): -2.1%; Density: 94.4 persons per square mile; Race: 97.6% White, 1.2% Black/African American, 0.0% Asian, 0.2% American Indian/Alaska Native, 0.0% Native Hawaiian/Other Pacific Islander, 1.0% Two or more races, 0.2% Hispanic of any race; Average household size: 2.20; Median age: 49.0; Age under 18: 17.8%; Age 65 and over: 24.0%; Males per 100 females: 95.9; Marriage status: 22.3% never married, 59.4% now married, 2.3% separated, 8.5% widowed, 9.7% divorced; Foreign born: 0.8%; Speak English only: 98.4%; With disability: 11.0%; Veterans: 11.1%; Ancestry: 26.8% German, 25.0% Swedish, 18.9% English, 14.1% Italian, 13.3% Irish

Employment: 14.2% management, business, and financial, 3.0% computer, engineering, and science, 12.4% education, legal, community service, arts, and media, 4.1% healthcare practitioners, 22.0% service, 24.5% sales and office, 7.7% natural resources, construction, and maintenance, 12.0% production, transportation, and material moving

Income: Per capita: $29,799; Median household: $48,027; Average household: $66,587; Households with income of $100,000 or more: 16.8%; Poverty rate: 7.0%

Educational Attainment: High school diploma or higher: 93.0%; Bachelor's degree or higher: 27.2%; Graduate/professional degree or higher: 11.8%

Housing: Homeownership rate: 82.3%; Median home value: $116,800; Median year structure built: 1966; Homeowner vacancy rate: 2.3%; Median selected monthly owner costs: $1,299 with a mortgage, $470 without a mortgage; Median gross rent: $656 per month; Rental vacancy rate: 4.6%

Health Insurance: 92.1% have insurance; 73.0% have private insurance; 36.7% have public insurance; 7.9% do not have insurance; 5.6% of children under 18 do not have insurance

Transportation: Commute: 88.6% car, 0.0% public transportation, 1.5% walk, 9.0% work from home; Mean travel time to work: 20.2 minutes

Additional Information Contacts

Town of Ellery . . . . (716) 386-3465
  http://www.elleryny.org

ELLICOTT (town).
Covers a land area of 30.449 square miles and a water area of 0.024 square miles. Located at 42.13° N. Lat; 79.23° W. Long.

Population: 8,612; Growth (since 2000): -7.2%; Density: 282.8 persons per square mile; Race: 96.7% White, 0.5% Black/African American, 0.8% Asian, 0.3% American Indian/Alaska Native, 0.0% Native Hawaiian/Other Pacific Islander, 1.6% Two or more races, 1.7% Hispanic of any race; Average household size: 2.26; Median age: 46.0; Age under 18: 20.7%; Age 65 and over: 20.0%; Males per 100 females: 94.5; Marriage status: 25.7% never married, 54.9% now married, 2.5% separated, 7.7% widowed, 11.6% divorced; Foreign born: 2.1%; Speak English only: 96.6%; With disability: 15.0%; Veterans: 9.9%; Ancestry: 25.4% Swedish, 20.5% Italian, 18.4% German, 14.5% Irish, 13.2% English

Employment: 10.8% management, business, and financial, 3.1% computer, engineering, and science, 11.6% education, legal, community service, arts, and media, 7.2% healthcare practitioners, 16.9% service, 20.4% sales and office, 7.1% natural resources, construction, and maintenance, 22.9% production, transportation, and material moving

Income: Per capita: $25,490; Median household: $49,286; Average household: $57,322; Households with income of $100,000 or more: 13.8%; Poverty rate: 13.1%

Educational Attainment: High school diploma or higher: 89.7%; Bachelor's degree or higher: 20.2%; Graduate/professional degree or higher: 8.3%

Housing: Homeownership rate: 72.1%; Median home value: $87,400; Median year structure built: 1950; Homeowner vacancy rate: 2.6%; Median selected monthly owner costs: $1,018 with a mortgage, $418 without a mortgage; Median gross rent: $620 per month; Rental vacancy rate: 3.1%

Health Insurance: 95.1% have insurance; 76.5% have private insurance; 35.4% have public insurance; 4.9% do not have insurance; 0.2% of children under 18 do not have insurance

Safety: Violent crime rate: 15.6 per 10,000 population; Property crime rate: 433.2 per 10,000 population

Transportation: Commute: 92.2% car, 0.2% public transportation, 4.4% walk, 2.1% work from home; Mean travel time to work: 14.0 minutes

Additional Information Contacts

Town of Ellicott . . . . (716) 665-5317
  http://www.townofellicott.com

ELLINGTON (town).
Covers a land area of 36.545 square miles and a water area of 0.014 square miles. Located at 42.22° N. Lat; 79.12° W. Long. Elevation is 1,371 feet.

Population: 1,663; Growth (since 2000): 1.5%; Density: 45.5 persons per square mile; Race: 98.0% White, 0.0% Black/African American, 0.0% Asian, 1.4% American Indian/Alaska Native, 0.0% Native Hawaiian/Other Pacific Islander, 0.5% Two or more races, 3.4% Hispanic of any race; Average household size: 2.70; Median age: 40.1; Age under 18: 26.9%; Age 65 and over: 10.8%; Males per 100 females: 105.6; Marriage status: 23.7% never married, 61.2% now married, 0.7% separated, 5.6% widowed, 9.4% divorced; Foreign born: 0.4%; Speak English only: 94.2%; With disability: 10.3%; Veterans: 10.0%; Ancestry: 21.1% German, 16.3% English, 12.6% Swedish, 11.1% Irish, 7.6% Italian

Employment: 12.5% management, business, and financial, 1.2% computer, engineering, and science, 7.6% education, legal, community service, arts, and media, 3.4% healthcare practitioners, 16.4% service, 20.9% sales and office, 9.2% natural resources, construction, and maintenance, 28.9% production, transportation, and material moving

Income: Per capita: $21,806; Median household: $50,667; Average household: $57,413; Households with income of $100,000 or more: 12.7%; Poverty rate: 14.0%

Educational Attainment: High school diploma or higher: 87.7%; Bachelor's degree or higher: 9.5%; Graduate/professional degree or higher: 2.5%

Housing: Homeownership rate: 88.5%; Median home value: $75,400; Median year structure built: 1972; Homeowner vacancy rate: 0.0%; Median selected monthly owner costs: $1,041 with a mortgage, $440 without a mortgage; Median gross rent: $538 per month; Rental vacancy rate: 0.0%

Health Insurance: 88.6% have insurance; 62.4% have private insurance; 37.2% have public insurance; 11.4% do not have insurance; 10.3% of children under 18 do not have insurance

Transportation: Commute: 93.1% car, 1.2% public transportation, 0.4% walk, 5.1% work from home; Mean travel time to work: 24.5 minutes

FALCONER (village).
Covers a land area of 1.093 square miles and a water area of 0 square miles. Located at 42.12° N. Lat; 79.20° W. Long. Elevation is 1,263 feet.

History: Settled 1807, incorporated 1891.

Population: 2,573; Growth (since 2000): 1.3%; Density: 2,354.4 persons per square mile; Race: 96.2% White, 0.0% Black/African American, 1.0% Asian, 0.0% American Indian/Alaska Native, 0.0% Native Hawaiian/Other Pacific Islander, 2.8% Two or more races, 3.1% Hispanic of any race; Average household size: 2.28; Median age: 37.4; Age under 18: 25.1%; Age 65 and over: 17.6%; Males per 100 females: 100.2; Marriage status: 32.4% never married, 46.7% now married, 3.0% separated, 9.1% widowed, 11.8% divorced; Foreign born: 1.7%; Speak English only: 96.8%; With disability: 11.3%; Veterans: 9.7%; Ancestry: 28.2% Swedish, 26.0% Italian, 14.6% German, 13.8% Irish, 11.8% English

Employment: 8.2% management, business, and financial, 1.2% computer, engineering, and science, 12.2% education, legal, community service, arts, and media, 8.3% healthcare practitioners, 11.4% service, 22.5% sales and office, 4.6% natural resources, construction, and maintenance, 31.7% production, transportation, and material moving

Income: Per capita: $19,622; Median household: $37,566; Average household: $43,642; Households with income of $100,000 or more: 7.9%; Poverty rate: 16.5%

Educational Attainment: High school diploma or higher: 92.6%; Bachelor's degree or higher: 16.0%; Graduate/professional degree or higher: 6.6%

School District(s)

Falconer Central SD (PK-12)
  2014-15 Enrollment: 1,229 . . . . (716) 665-6624

Housing: Homeownership rate: 52.4%; Median home value: $66,500; Median year structure built: Before 1940; Homeowner vacancy rate: 2.5%; Median selected monthly owner costs: $909 with a mortgage, $365 without a mortgage; Median gross rent: $554 per month; Rental vacancy rate: 0.9%

Health Insurance: 95.5% have insurance; 73.1% have private insurance; 40.0% have public insurance; 4.5% do not have insurance; 0.0% of children under 18 do not have insurance

Transportation: Commute: 87.9% car, 0.0% public transportation, 9.6% walk, 1.1% work from home; Mean travel time to work: 13.8 minutes

FINDLEY LAKE (unincorporated postal area)
ZCTA: 14736

Covers a land area of 5.226 square miles and a water area of 0 square miles. Located at 42.14° N. Lat; 79.75° W. Long. Elevation is 1,440 feet.

Population: 249; Growth (since 2000): -13.8%; Density: 47.6 persons per square mile; Race: 100.0% White, 0.0% Black/African American, 0.0% Asian, 0.0% American Indian/Alaska Native, 0.0% Native Hawaiian/Other Pacific Islander, 0.0% Two or more races, 0.0% Hispanic of any race; Average household size: 2.17; Median age: 49.1; Age under 18: 20.1%; Age 65 and over: 13.7%; Males per 100 females: 100.0; Marriage status: 17.1% never married, 66.3% now married, 0.0% separated, 5.9% widowed, 10.7% divorced; Foreign born: 0.0%; Speak English only: 100.0%; With disability: 13.7%; Veterans: 11.6%; Ancestry: 29.3% German, 16.5% Irish, 16.1% Italian, 12.9% English, 9.2% American

Employment: 21.3% management, business, and financial, 0.0% computer, engineering, and science, 11.0% education, legal, community service, arts, and media, 0.0% healthcare practitioners, 16.5% service, 31.5% sales and office, 6.3% natural resources, construction, and maintenance, 13.4% production, transportation, and material moving

Income: Per capita: $24,904; Median household: $42,589; Average household: $52,952; Households with income of $100,000 or more: 10.4%; Poverty rate: 11.2%

Educational Attainment: High school diploma or higher: 100.0%; Bachelor's degree or higher: 25.7%; Graduate/professional degree or higher: 13.9%

Housing: Homeownership rate: 67.8%; Median home value: $122,900; Median year structure built: 1977; Homeowner vacancy rate: 0.0%; Median selected monthly owner costs: $1,375 with a mortgage, $464 without a mortgage; Median gross rent: n/a per month; Rental vacancy rate: 0.0%

Health Insurance: 86.7% have insurance; 70.7% have private insurance; 26.5% have public insurance; 13.3% do not have insurance; 0.0% of children under 18 do not have insurance

Transportation: Commute: 80.3% car, 0.0% public transportation, 14.2% walk, 5.5% work from home; Mean travel time to work: 17.4 minutes

FORESTVILLE (village).
Covers a land area of 0.979 square miles and a water area of 0 square miles. Located at 42.47° N. Lat; 79.18° W. Long. Elevation is 932 feet.

Population: 581; Growth (since 2000): -24.5%; Density: 593.2 persons per square mile; Race: 95.0% White, 0.0% Black/African American, 0.5% Asian, 2.4% American Indian/Alaska Native, 0.0% Native Hawaiian/Other Pacific Islander, 2.1% Two or more races, 3.1% Hispanic of any race; Average household size: 2.43; Median age: 38.5; Age under 18: 22.4%; Age 65 and over: 16.9%; Males per 100 females: 112.5; Marriage status: 34.5% never married, 44.1% now married, 2.3% separated, 7.3% widowed, 14.1% divorced; Foreign born: 1.4%; Speak English only: 95.3%; With disability: 20.1%; Veterans: 12.9%; Ancestry: 26.5% German, 20.5% Italian, 19.3% Irish, 11.7% Polish, 10.8% English

Employment: 8.0% management, business, and financial, 0.8% computer, engineering, and science, 11.4% education, legal, community service, arts, and media, 1.5% healthcare practitioners, 20.8% service, 19.3% sales and office, 5.7% natural resources, construction, and maintenance, 32.6% production, transportation, and material moving

Income: Per capita: $21,569; Median household: $45,000; Average household: $52,435; Households with income of $100,000 or more: 5.5%; Poverty rate: 19.7%

Educational Attainment: High school diploma or higher: 90.8%; Bachelor's degree or higher: 17.2%; Graduate/professional degree or higher: 3.8%

School District(s)
Forestville Central SD (PK-12)
    2014-15 Enrollment: 503 . . . . (716) 965-2742

Housing: Homeownership rate: 68.8%; Median home value: $82,800; Median year structure built: Before 1940; Homeowner vacancy rate: 0.0%; Median selected monthly owner costs: $798 with a mortgage, $448 without a mortgage; Median gross rent: $623 per month; Rental vacancy rate: 0.0%

Health Insurance: 93.1% have insurance; 63.3% have private insurance; 46.3% have public insurance; 6.9% do not have insurance; 0.0% of children under 18 do not have insurance

Transportation: Commute: 91.9% car, 0.0% public transportation, 5.2% walk, 2.8% work from home; Mean travel time to work: 18.3 minutes

FREDONIA (village).
Covers a land area of 5.189 square miles and a water area of 0 square miles. Located at 42.44° N. Lat; 79.33° W. Long. Elevation is 722 feet.

History: Incorporated 1829. Was the site of the first gas well in the U.S. The first local unit of the Natioanl Grange (Patrons of Husbandry) Movement was also founded here. State University of N.Y. at Fredonia here.

Population: 10,881; Growth (since 2000): 1.6%; Density: 2,096.9 persons per square mile; Race: 93.5% White, 2.7% Black/African American, 2.1% Asian, 0.0% American Indian/Alaska Native, 0.1% Native Hawaiian/Other Pacific Islander, 0.8% Two or more races, 5.6% Hispanic of any race; Average household size: 2.18; Median age: 25.5; Age under 18: 13.1%; Age 65 and over: 14.9%; Males per 100 females: 88.1; Marriage status: 50.8% never married, 36.9% now married, 1.0% separated, 4.0% widowed, 8.3% divorced; Foreign born: 4.4%; Speak English only: 91.6%; With disability: 9.1%; Veterans: 6.0%; Ancestry: 26.9% Italian, 24.0% German, 18.8% Irish, 15.0% Polish, 13.7% English

Employment: 14.2% management, business, and financial, 3.2% computer, engineering, and science, 18.1% education, legal, community

service, arts, and media, 2.5% healthcare practitioners, 25.4% service, 21.8% sales and office, 4.3% natural resources, construction, and maintenance, 10.5% production, transportation, and material moving

Income: Per capita: $23,962; Median household: $47,910; Average household: $64,981; Households with income of $100,000 or more: 18.3%; Poverty rate: 19.1%

Educational Attainment: High school diploma or higher: 96.2%; Bachelor's degree or higher: 41.4%; Graduate/professional degree or higher: 22.6%

School District(s)
Fredonia Central SD (PK-12)
    2014-15 Enrollment: 1,573 . . . . (716) 679-1581

Four-year College(s)
SUNY at Fredonia (Public)
    Fall 2014 Enrollment: 5,215 . . . . (716) 673-3111
    2015-16 Tuition: In-state $8,074; Out-of-state $17,924

Housing: Homeownership rate: 63.4%; Median home value: $128,300; Median year structure built: 1946; Homeowner vacancy rate: 3.1%; Median selected monthly owner costs: $1,206 with a mortgage, $584 without a mortgage; Median gross rent: $616 per month; Rental vacancy rate: 12.9%

Health Insurance: 95.5% have insurance; 82.5% have private insurance; 26.2% have public insurance; 4.5% do not have insurance; 0.0% of children under 18 do not have insurance

Safety: Violent crime rate: 5.6 per 10,000 population; Property crime rate: 214.3 per 10,000 population

Transportation: Commute: 78.4% car, 0.5% public transportation, 14.2% walk, 5.4% work from home; Mean travel time to work: 13.9 minutes; Amtrak: Train service available.

FRENCH CREEK (town).
Covers a land area of 36.259 square miles and a water area of 0.020 square miles. Located at 42.04° N. Lat; 79.71° W. Long. Elevation is 1,417 feet.

Population: 889; Growth (since 2000): -4.9%; Density: 24.5 persons per square mile; Race: 97.6% White, 0.0% Black/African American, 0.0% Asian, 0.4% American Indian/Alaska Native, 0.0% Native Hawaiian/Other Pacific Islander, 1.9% Two or more races, 0.7% Hispanic of any race; Average household size: 2.71; Median age: 35.4; Age under 18: 24.5%; Age 65 and over: 15.9%; Males per 100 females: 106.4; Marriage status: 27.5% never married, 58.5% now married, 1.7% separated, 4.9% widowed, 9.1% divorced; Foreign born: 0.0%; Speak English only: 97.4%; With disability: 13.8%; Veterans: 10.4%; Ancestry: 31.8% German, 11.4% English, 10.6% Italian, 10.3% Irish, 7.9% Polish

Employment: 9.6% management, business, and financial, 2.6% computer, engineering, and science, 8.6% education, legal, community service, arts, and media, 4.2% healthcare practitioners, 14.3% service, 15.4% sales and office, 18.5% natural resources, construction, and maintenance, 26.8% production, transportation, and material moving

Income: Per capita: $24,562; Median household: $44,318; Average household: $62,760; Households with income of $100,000 or more: 11.6%; Poverty rate: 19.6%

Educational Attainment: High school diploma or higher: 86.0%; Bachelor's degree or higher: 14.9%; Graduate/professional degree or higher: 6.6%

Housing: Homeownership rate: 78.4%; Median home value: $89,600; Median year structure built: 1985; Homeowner vacancy rate: 7.2%; Median selected monthly owner costs: $960 with a mortgage, $424 without a mortgage; Median gross rent: $650 per month; Rental vacancy rate: 22.0%

Health Insurance: 86.3% have insurance; 67.9% have private insurance; 32.4% have public insurance; 13.7% do not have insurance; 28.4% of children under 18 do not have insurance

Transportation: Commute: 93.3% car, 0.0% public transportation, 2.2% walk, 4.6% work from home; Mean travel time to work: 27.0 minutes

FREWSBURG (CDP).
Covers a land area of 3.373 square miles and a water area of 0.015 square miles. Located at 42.06° N. Lat; 79.13° W. Long. Elevation is 1,299 feet.

Population: 2,207; Growth (since 2000): 12.3%; Density: 654.4 persons per square mile; Race: 100.0% White, 0.0% Black/African American, 0.0% Asian, 0.0% American Indian/Alaska Native, 0.0% Native Hawaiian/Other Pacific Islander, 0.0% Two or more races, 0.0% Hispanic of any race; Average household size: 2.33; Median age: 50.7; Age under 18: 12.3%; Age 65 and over: 23.6%; Males per 100 females: 90.0; Marriage status: 24.1% never married, 48.1% now married, 1.6% separated, 8.3% widowed, 19.5% divorced; Foreign born: 2.8%; Speak English only:

100.0%; With disability: 16.0%; Veterans: 7.2%; Ancestry: 35.8% Swedish, 21.9% Irish, 15.6% Italian, 14.9% German, 9.0% Polish
Employment: 5.6% management, business, and financial, 0.0% computer, engineering, and science, 9.6% education, legal, community service, arts, and media, 6.8% healthcare practitioners, 21.4% service, 28.9% sales and office, 7.3% natural resources, construction, and maintenance, 20.5% production, transportation, and material moving
Income: Per capita: $25,317; Median household: $47,773; Average household: $57,471; Households with income of $100,000 or more: 15.9%; Poverty rate: 10.1%
Educational Attainment: High school diploma or higher: 89.1%; Bachelor's degree or higher: 19.3%; Graduate/professional degree or higher: 10.1%

School District(s)
Frewsburg Central SD (PK-12)
    2014-15 Enrollment: 865 . . . . (716) 569-7041
Housing: Homeownership rate: 71.2%; Median home value: $89,400; Median year structure built: 1956; Homeowner vacancy rate: 0.0%; Median selected monthly owner costs: $921 with a mortgage, $701 without a mortgage; Median gross rent: $496 per month; Rental vacancy rate: 0.0%
Health Insurance: 98.6% have insurance; 77.7% have private insurance; 44.0% have public insurance; 1.4% do not have insurance; 0.0% of children under 18 do not have insurance
Transportation: Commute: 100.0% car, 0.0% public transportation, 0.0% walk, 0.0% work from home; Mean travel time to work: 16.4 minutes

GERRY (town). Covers a land area of 36.125 square miles and a water area of 0.018 square miles. Located at 42.22° N. Lat; 79.24° W. Long. Elevation is 1,302 feet.
Population: 2,071; Growth (since 2000): 0.8%; Density: 57.3 persons per square mile; Race: 96.9% White, 0.0% Black/African American, 0.5% Asian, 0.0% American Indian/Alaska Native, 0.0% Native Hawaiian/Other Pacific Islander, 2.4% Two or more races, 0.8% Hispanic of any race; Average household size: 2.61; Median age: 46.8; Age under 18: 19.7%; Age 65 and over: 21.3%; Males per 100 females: 91.8; Marriage status: 25.1% never married, 57.1% now married, 1.2% separated, 9.0% widowed, 8.8% divorced; Foreign born: 1.6%; Speak English only: 98.0%; With disability: 14.4%; Veterans: 14.3%; Ancestry: 23.9% Swedish, 19.1% German, 17.4% Irish, 16.2% English, 7.1% American
Employment: 15.3% management, business, and financial, 3.0% computer, engineering, and science, 5.5% education, legal, community service, arts, and media, 5.3% healthcare practitioners, 17.0% service, 25.2% sales and office, 11.6% natural resources, construction, and maintenance, 17.2% production, transportation, and material moving
Income: Per capita: $25,392; Median household: $51,888; Average household: $65,882; Households with income of $100,000 or more: 18.2%; Poverty rate: 5.7%
Educational Attainment: High school diploma or higher: 89.0%; Bachelor's degree or higher: 16.9%; Graduate/professional degree or higher: 7.1%
Housing: Homeownership rate: 78.6%; Median home value: $83,100; Median year structure built: 1967; Homeowner vacancy rate: 5.5%; Median selected monthly owner costs: $1,056 with a mortgage, $376 without a mortgage; Median gross rent: $618 per month; Rental vacancy rate: 10.6%
Health Insurance: 93.6% have insurance; 73.0% have private insurance; 34.2% have public insurance; 6.4% do not have insurance; 4.9% of children under 18 do not have insurance
Transportation: Commute: 90.8% car, 0.0% public transportation, 2.1% walk, 6.2% work from home; Mean travel time to work: 20.2 minutes

GREENHURST (unincorporated postal area)
ZCTA: 14742
    Covers a land area of 0.225 square miles and a water area of 0 square miles. Located at 42.12° N. Lat; 79.31° W. Long. Elevation is 1,319 feet.
Population: 296; Growth (since 2000): n/a; Density: 1,318.1 persons per square mile; Race: 73.0% White, 8.8% Black/African American, 0.0% Asian, 3.0% American Indian/Alaska Native, 0.0% Native Hawaiian/Other Pacific Islander, 15.2% Two or more races, 0.0% Hispanic of any race; Average household size: 1.98; Median age: 58.9; Age under 18: 0.0%; Age 65 and over: 39.5%; Males per 100 females: 67.9; Marriage status: 22.0% never married, 50.7% now married, 0.0% separated, 15.2% widowed, 12.2% divorced; Foreign born: 3.0%; Speak English only: 96.3%; With disability: 0.0%; Veterans: 22.6%; Ancestry: 41.2% Swedish, 11.8% German, 9.1% English, 7.1% Polish, 5.7% Irish

Employment: 22.2% management, business, and financial, 0.0% computer, engineering, and science, 7.6% education, legal, community service, arts, and media, 0.0% healthcare practitioners, 45.8% service, 6.3% sales and office, 0.0% natural resources, construction, and maintenance, 18.1% production, transportation, and material moving
Income: Per capita: $25,666; Median household: $78,988; Average household: $71,280; Households with income of $100,000 or more: n/a; Poverty rate: n/a
Educational Attainment: High school diploma or higher: 100.0%; Bachelor's degree or higher: 13.9%; Graduate/professional degree or higher: 10.6%
Housing: Homeownership rate: 86.4%; Median home value: $97,100; Median year structure built: 1944; Homeowner vacancy rate: 0.0%; Median selected monthly owner costs: $0 with a mortgage, $0 without a mortgage; Median gross rent: n/a per month; Rental vacancy rate: 0.0%
Health Insurance: 100.0% have insurance; 100.0% have private insurance; 5.0% have public insurance; 0.0% do not have insurance; 0.0% of children under 18 do not have insurance
Transportation: Commute: 100.0% car, 0.0% public transportation, 0.0% walk, 0.0% work from home; Mean travel time to work: 14.4 minutes

HANOVER (town). Covers a land area of 49.178 square miles and a water area of 0.284 square miles. Located at 42.49° N. Lat; 79.12° W. Long.
Population: 6,974; Growth (since 2000): -8.7%; Density: 141.8 persons per square mile; Race: 95.1% White, 0.9% Black/African American, 0.0% Asian, 1.8% American Indian/Alaska Native, 0.0% Native Hawaiian/Other Pacific Islander, 1.3% Two or more races, 3.6% Hispanic of any race; Average household size: 2.41; Median age: 43.7; Age under 18: 21.2%; Age 65 and over: 19.2%; Males per 100 females: 97.3; Marriage status: 29.0% never married, 50.2% now married, 4.0% separated, 7.6% widowed, 13.2% divorced; Foreign born: 1.5%; Speak English only: 97.4%; With disability: 17.4%; Veterans: 10.9%; Ancestry: 35.8% German, 18.7% Irish, 16.6% Italian, 16.4% Polish, 16.3% English
Employment: 9.6% management, business, and financial, 1.3% computer, engineering, and science, 8.2% education, legal, community service, arts, and media, 3.4% healthcare practitioners, 25.9% service, 20.6% sales and office, 12.2% natural resources, construction, and maintenance, 18.8% production, transportation, and material moving
Income: Per capita: $23,742; Median household: $50,890; Average household: $56,551; Households with income of $100,000 or more: 9.9%; Poverty rate: 15.1%
Educational Attainment: High school diploma or higher: 88.8%; Bachelor's degree or higher: 17.9%; Graduate/professional degree or higher: 7.2%
Housing: Homeownership rate: 78.4%; Median home value: $92,100; Median year structure built: 1954; Homeowner vacancy rate: 2.0%; Median selected monthly owner costs: $1,001 with a mortgage, $480 without a mortgage; Median gross rent: $685 per month; Rental vacancy rate: 8.0%
Health Insurance: 92.2% have insurance; 69.1% have private insurance; 41.7% have public insurance; 7.8% do not have insurance; 2.2% of children under 18 do not have insurance
Transportation: Commute: 94.2% car, 0.0% public transportation, 3.1% walk, 2.7% work from home; Mean travel time to work: 22.7 minutes
Additional Information Contacts
Town of Hanover . . . . (716) 934-2273
    http://townofhanover.org/content

HARMONY (town). Covers a land area of 45.400 square miles and a water area of 0.161 square miles. Located at 42.05° N. Lat; 79.46° W. Long.
Population: 2,179; Growth (since 2000): -6.8%; Density: 48.0 persons per square mile; Race: 97.7% White, 0.0% Black/African American, 0.0% Asian, 0.7% American Indian/Alaska Native, 0.0% Native Hawaiian/Other Pacific Islander, 0.6% Two or more races, 1.6% Hispanic of any race; Average household size: 2.53; Median age: 43.8; Age under 18: 23.6%; Age 65 and over: 17.9%; Males per 100 females: 97.3; Marriage status: 22.0% never married, 60.2% now married, 3.8% separated, 4.7% widowed, 13.1% divorced; Foreign born: 0.6%; Speak English only: 96.1%; With disability: 12.3%; Veterans: 8.8%; Ancestry: 22.3% Swedish, 19.8% English, 19.7% German, 12.1% Irish, 8.5% Italian
Employment: 4.8% management, business, and financial, 2.6% computer, engineering, and science, 11.4% education, legal, community service, arts, and media, 7.8% healthcare practitioners, 12.3% service, 24.3% sales and

office, 15.2% natural resources, construction, and maintenance, 21.5% production, transportation, and material moving
Income: Per capita: $22,108; Median household: $47,250; Average household: $54,728; Households with income of $100,000 or more: 12.2%; Poverty rate: 12.4%
Educational Attainment: High school diploma or higher: 89.5%; Bachelor's degree or higher: 16.3%; Graduate/professional degree or higher: 6.9%
Housing: Homeownership rate: 84.2%; Median home value: $79,300; Median year structure built: 1962; Homeowner vacancy rate: 0.0%; Median selected monthly owner costs: $1,001 with a mortgage, $372 without a mortgage; Median gross rent: $638 per month; Rental vacancy rate: 5.6%
Health Insurance: 88.8% have insurance; 66.7% have private insurance; 36.5% have public insurance; 11.2% do not have insurance; 7.6% of children under 18 do not have insurance
Transportation: Commute: 94.1% car, 0.5% public transportation, 0.8% walk, 4.0% work from home; Mean travel time to work: 22.6 minutes

JAMESTOWN (city).
Covers a land area of 8.935 square miles and a water area of 0.128 square miles. Located at 42.10° N. Lat; 79.24° W. Long. Elevation is 1,378 feet.
History: The founder of the Jamestown settlement was James Prendergast, who purchased 1,000 acres of land his brother had earlier bought from the Holland Land Company. Among the early settlers were a number of skilled woodworkers, who began to make furniture to supply the needs of the pioneers of the region. In 1849, some Swedish immigrants appeared. After the close of the Civil War, many others joined them. Most of them were cabinet makers attracted by the furniture factories. In 1888, two years after Jamestown had become officially a city, construction of metal furniture was begun.
Population: 30,546; Growth (since 2000): -3.7%; Density: 3,418.9 persons per square mile; Race: 87.7% White, 4.7% Black/African American, 0.7% Asian, 0.8% American Indian/Alaska Native, 0.1% Native Hawaiian/Other Pacific Islander, 3.1% Two or more races, 9.2% Hispanic of any race; Average household size: 2.30; Median age: 37.3; Age under 18: 24.5%; Age 65 and over: 15.4%; Males per 100 females: 94.6; Marriage status: 34.1% never married, 43.5% now married, 3.3% separated, 7.6% widowed, 14.8% divorced; Foreign born: 1.6%; Speak English only: 91.3%; With disability: 18.6%; Veterans: 9.5%; Ancestry: 16.3% German, 15.6% Swedish, 14.7% Italian, 14.4% Irish, 10.8% English
Employment: 8.8% management, business, and financial, 2.5% computer, engineering, and science, 10.1% education, legal, community service, arts, and media, 4.5% healthcare practitioners, 20.9% service, 25.5% sales and office, 8.4% natural resources, construction, and maintenance, 19.3% production, transportation, and material moving
Income: Per capita: $18,796; Median household: $30,950; Average household: $42,948; Households with income of $100,000 or more: 7.4%; Poverty rate: 29.3%
Educational Attainment: High school diploma or higher: 85.9%; Bachelor's degree or higher: 18.3%; Graduate/professional degree or higher: 7.5%
School District(s)
Jamestown City SD (PK-12)
    2014-15 Enrollment: 5,188 . . . . (716) 483-4420
Southwestern Central SD At Jamestown (PK-12)
    2014-15 Enrollment: 1,438 . . . . (716) 484-1136
Four-year College(s)
Jamestown Business College (Private, For-profit)
    Fall 2014 Enrollment: 318 . . . . (716) 664-5100
    2015-16 Tuition: In-state $12,300; Out-of-state $12,300
Two-year College(s)
Jamestown Community College (Public)
    Fall 2014 Enrollment: 5,065 . . . . (716) 338-1000
    2015-16 Tuition: In-state $5,360; Out-of-state $9,880
Housing: Homeownership rate: 51.1%; Median home value: $63,600; Median year structure built: Before 1940; Homeowner vacancy rate: 1.8%; Median selected monthly owner costs: $876 with a mortgage, $393 without a mortgage; Median gross rent: $587 per month; Rental vacancy rate: 10.5%
Health Insurance: 92.3% have insurance; 54.8% have private insurance; 51.3% have public insurance; 7.7% do not have insurance; 5.7% of children under 18 do not have insurance
Hospitals: Woman's Christian Association (342 beds)
Safety: Violent crime rate: 78.3 per 10,000 population; Property crime rate: 334.4 per 10,000 population

Newspapers: Post-Journal (daily circulation 18,600)
Transportation: Commute: 89.3% car, 0.4% public transportation, 6.0% walk, 2.3% work from home; Mean travel time to work: 14.7 minutes; Amtrak: Bus service available.
Airports: Chautauqua County/Jamestown (commercial service–non-primary)
Additional Information Contacts
City of Jamestown . . . . (716) 483-7612
    http://www.jamestownny.net

JAMESTOWN WEST (CDP).
Covers a land area of 2.517 square miles and a water area of 0 square miles. Located at 42.09° N. Lat; 79.28° W. Long.
Population: 2,267; Growth (since 2000): -10.6%; Density: 900.7 persons per square mile; Race: 95.1% White, 1.4% Black/African American, 0.4% Asian, 0.0% American Indian/Alaska Native, 0.0% Native Hawaiian/Other Pacific Islander, 2.8% Two or more races, 1.1% Hispanic of any race; Average household size: 2.18; Median age: 52.5; Age under 18: 15.2%; Age 65 and over: 27.0%; Males per 100 females: 86.7; Marriage status: 26.5% never married, 55.4% now married, 1.5% separated, 9.5% widowed, 8.7% divorced; Foreign born: 4.4%; Speak English only: 94.8%; With disability: 21.5%; Veterans: 7.3%; Ancestry: 20.4% German, 19.7% Swedish, 19.5% Italian, 17.3% Irish, 16.1% English
Employment: 15.1% management, business, and financial, 5.7% computer, engineering, and science, 14.2% education, legal, community service, arts, and media, 7.2% healthcare practitioners, 11.5% service, 23.8% sales and office, 3.8% natural resources, construction, and maintenance, 18.6% production, transportation, and material moving
Income: Per capita: $30,273; Median household: $64,094; Average household: $67,976; Households with income of $100,000 or more: 19.5%; Poverty rate: 6.4%
Educational Attainment: High school diploma or higher: 85.5%; Bachelor's degree or higher: 29.8%; Graduate/professional degree or higher: 9.2%
Housing: Homeownership rate: 89.7%; Median home value: $100,700; Median year structure built: 1956; Homeowner vacancy rate: 0.0%; Median selected monthly owner costs: $980 with a mortgage, $413 without a mortgage; Median gross rent: $699 per month; Rental vacancy rate: 0.0%
Health Insurance: 98.2% have insurance; 77.9% have private insurance; 39.7% have public insurance; 1.8% do not have insurance; 0.0% of children under 18 do not have insurance
Transportation: Commute: 91.7% car, 0.8% public transportation, 3.2% walk, 3.5% work from home; Mean travel time to work: 14.5 minutes

KENNEDY (CDP).
Covers a land area of 2.035 square miles and a water area of 0 square miles. Located at 42.16° N. Lat; 79.10° W. Long. Elevation is 1,266 feet.
Population: 504; Growth (since 2000): n/a; Density: 247.6 persons per square mile; Race: 96.8% White, 0.0% Black/African American, 0.0% Asian, 0.0% American Indian/Alaska Native, 0.0% Native Hawaiian/Other Pacific Islander, 3.2% Two or more races, 0.0% Hispanic of any race; Average household size: 2.25; Median age: 52.6; Age under 18: 7.3%; Age 65 and over: 28.6%; Males per 100 females: 97.0; Marriage status: 21.2% never married, 56.3% now married, 2.4% separated, 7.1% widowed, 15.4% divorced; Foreign born: 0.0%; Speak English only: 98.0%; With disability: 13.5%; Veterans: 13.3%; Ancestry: 19.4% Swedish, 16.1% German, 13.7% American, 13.3% English, 12.5% Irish
Employment: 6.6% management, business, and financial, 1.9% computer, engineering, and science, 8.5% education, legal, community service, arts, and media, 0.0% healthcare practitioners, 14.7% service, 30.9% sales and office, 5.0% natural resources, construction, and maintenance, 32.4% production, transportation, and material moving
Income: Per capita: $22,961; Median household: $38,500; Average household: $51,196; Households with income of $100,000 or more: 6.7%; Poverty rate: 16.9%
Educational Attainment: High school diploma or higher: 85.5%; Bachelor's degree or higher: 7.0%; Graduate/professional degree or higher: 2.5%
School District(s)
Falconer Central SD (PK-12)
    2014-15 Enrollment: 1,229 . . . . (716) 665-6624
Housing: Homeownership rate: 74.1%; Median home value: $69,000; Median year structure built: Before 1940; Homeowner vacancy rate: 0.0%; Median selected monthly owner costs: $776 with a mortgage, $381 without

a mortgage; Median gross rent: $545 per month; Rental vacancy rate: 0.0%
Health Insurance: 97.2% have insurance; 67.5% have private insurance; 49.4% have public insurance; 2.8% do not have insurance; 0.0% of children under 18 do not have insurance
Transportation: Commute: 98.4% car, 0.0% public transportation, 1.6% walk, 0.0% work from home; Mean travel time to work: 19.3 minutes

KIANTONE (town).
Covers a land area of 18.397 square miles and a water area of 0.140 square miles. Located at 42.03° N. Lat; 79.19° W. Long. Elevation is 1,503 feet.
Population: 1,566; Growth (since 2000): 13.1%; Density: 85.1 persons per square mile; Race: 98.4% White, 1.1% Black/African American, 0.0% Asian, 0.0% American Indian/Alaska Native, 0.0% Native Hawaiian/Other Pacific Islander, 0.5% Two or more races, 1.3% Hispanic of any race; Average household size: 2.65; Median age: 42.7; Age under 18: 28.6%; Age 65 and over: 12.7%; Males per 100 females: 96.8; Marriage status: 19.8% never married, 65.2% now married, 1.6% separated, 6.5% widowed, 8.5% divorced; Foreign born: 1.8%; Speak English only: 98.5%; With disability: 10.0%; Veterans: 9.7%; Ancestry: 24.8% Swedish, 21.5% German, 13.7% Irish, 13.4% Italian, 12.6% English
Employment: 11.4% management, business, and financial, 3.2% computer, engineering, and science, 13.7% education, legal, community service, arts, and media, 8.0% healthcare practitioners, 15.7% service, 21.4% sales and office, 11.4% natural resources, construction, and maintenance, 15.3% production, transportation, and material moving
Income: Per capita: $26,610; Median household: $57,115; Average household: $69,596; Households with income of $100,000 or more: 20.2%; Poverty rate: 8.4%
Educational Attainment: High school diploma or higher: 94.0%; Bachelor's degree or higher: 25.9%; Graduate/professional degree or higher: 13.1%
Housing: Homeownership rate: 89.8%; Median home value: $120,400; Median year structure built: 1962; Homeowner vacancy rate: 0.0%; Median selected monthly owner costs: $1,201 with a mortgage, $446 without a mortgage; Median gross rent: $500 per month; Rental vacancy rate: 0.0%
Health Insurance: 95.7% have insurance; 84.4% have private insurance; 24.5% have public insurance; 4.3% do not have insurance; 2.9% of children under 18 do not have insurance
Transportation: Commute: 92.7% car, 0.0% public transportation, 2.1% walk, 5.2% work from home; Mean travel time to work: 15.5 minutes

LAKEWOOD (village).
Covers a land area of 1.976 square miles and a water area of 0 square miles. Located at 42.10° N. Lat; 79.32° W. Long. Elevation is 1,325 feet.
History: Settled 1809, incorporated 1893.
Population: 2,951; Growth (since 2000): -9.4%; Density: 1,493.3 persons per square mile; Race: 94.3% White, 0.9% Black/African American, 4.5% Asian, 0.0% American Indian/Alaska Native, 0.0% Native Hawaiian/Other Pacific Islander, 0.0% Two or more races, 1.9% Hispanic of any race; Average household size: 2.18; Median age: 47.4; Age under 18: 21.9%; Age 65 and over: 21.7%; Males per 100 females: 92.4; Marriage status: 27.0% never married, 51.4% now married, 3.5% separated, 9.2% widowed, 12.4% divorced; Foreign born: 1.9%; Speak English only: 97.5%; With disability: 14.0%; Veterans: 11.0%; Ancestry: 23.1% German, 20.5% Italian, 17.4% Swedish, 15.9% English, 15.3% Irish
Employment: 22.1% management, business, and financial, 5.8% computer, engineering, and science, 7.8% education, legal, community service, arts, and media, 7.8% healthcare practitioners, 20.7% service, 17.9% sales and office, 7.8% natural resources, construction, and maintenance, 9.9% production, transportation, and material moving
Income: Per capita: $30,675; Median household: $47,143; Average household: $65,698; Households with income of $100,000 or more: 20.8%; Poverty rate: 10.5%
Educational Attainment: High school diploma or higher: 93.9%; Bachelor's degree or higher: 31.9%; Graduate/professional degree or higher: 16.2%
Housing: Homeownership rate: 65.2%; Median home value: $94,000; Median year structure built: 1957; Homeowner vacancy rate: 9.3%; Median selected monthly owner costs: $1,098 with a mortgage, $428 without a mortgage; Median gross rent: $718 per month; Rental vacancy rate: 16.1%
Health Insurance: 91.4% have insurance; 67.7% have private insurance; 40.1% have public insurance; 8.6% do not have insurance; 7.3% of children under 18 do not have insurance

Transportation: Commute: 96.6% car, 0.7% public transportation, 1.5% walk, 1.2% work from home; Mean travel time to work: 15.6 minutes

LILY DALE (unincorporated postal area)
ZCTA: 14752
Covers a land area of 0.251 square miles and a water area of 0 square miles. Located at 42.35° N. Lat; 79.32° W. Long. Elevation is 1,332 feet.
Population: 196; Growth (since 2000): n/a; Density: 781.6 persons per square mile; Race: 100.0% White, 0.0% Black/African American, 0.0% Asian, 0.0% American Indian/Alaska Native, 0.0% Native Hawaiian/Other Pacific Islander, 0.0% Two or more races, 0.0% Hispanic of any race; Average household size: 1.69; Median age: 54.3; Age under 18: 19.9%; Age 65 and over: 31.6%; Males per 100 females: 65.7; Marriage status: 32.6% never married, 30.9% now married, 0.0% separated, 4.5% widowed, 32.0% divorced; Foreign born: 16.3%; Speak English only: 95.4%; With disability: 29.1%; Veterans: 5.7%; Ancestry: 40.8% German, 28.6% Italian, 17.3% Irish, 15.8% English, 12.2% Czech
Employment: 19.6% management, business, and financial, 19.6% computer, engineering, and science, 0.0% education, legal, community service, arts, and media, 0.0% healthcare practitioners, 0.0% service, 60.9% sales and office, 0.0% natural resources, construction, and maintenance, 0.0% production, transportation, and material moving
Income: Per capita: $26,362; Median household: n/a; Average household: $44,236; Households with income of $100,000 or more: 13.0%; Poverty rate: 25.0
Educational Attainment: High school diploma or higher: 93.8%; Bachelor's degree or higher: 35.4%; Graduate/professional degree or higher: 22.2%
Housing: Homeownership rate: 100.0%; Median home value: $79,700; Median year structure built: Before 1940; Homeowner vacancy rate: 0.0%; Median selected monthly owner costs: $0 with a mortgage, $380 without a mortgage; Median gross rent: n/a per month; Rental vacancy rate: 0.0%
Health Insurance: 96.9% have insurance; 80.6% have private insurance; 46.9% have public insurance; 3.1% do not have insurance; 0.0% of children under 18 do not have insurance
Transportation: Commute: 80.4% car, 0.0% public transportation, 0.0% walk, 19.6% work from home; Mean travel time to work: 0.0 minutes

MAPLE SPRINGS (unincorporated postal area)
ZCTA: 14756
Covers a land area of 0.137 square miles and a water area of 0 square miles. Located at 42.20° N. Lat; 79.42° W. Long. Elevation is 1,312 feet.
Population: 184; Growth (since 2000): n/a; Density: 1,341.9 persons per square mile; Race: 100.0% White, 0.0% Black/African American, 0.0% Asian, 0.0% American Indian/Alaska Native, 0.0% Native Hawaiian/Other Pacific Islander, 0.0% Two or more races, 0.0% Hispanic of any race; Average household size: 1.80; Median age: 45.8; Age under 18: 0.0%; Age 65 and over: 10.3%; Males per 100 females: 89.7; Marriage status: 52.7% never married, 47.3% now married, 27.2% separated, 0.0% widowed, 0.0% divorced; Foreign born: 0.0%; Speak English only: 100.0%; With disability: 9.8%; Veterans: 10.3%; Ancestry: 66.8% Swedish, 39.7% German, 37.0% English, 22.8% Italian, 10.3% Irish
Employment: 0.0% management, business, and financial, 0.0% computer, engineering, and science, 70.2% education, legal, community service, arts, and media, 0.0% healthcare practitioners, 29.8% service, 0.0% sales and office, 0.0% natural resources, construction, and maintenance, 0.0% production, transportation, and material moving
Income: Per capita: $21,558; Median household: n/a; Average household: $38,516; Households with income of $100,000 or more: 8.8%; Poverty rate: n/a
Educational Attainment: High school diploma or higher: 100.0%; Bachelor's degree or higher: 82.8%; Graduate/professional degree or higher: n/a
Housing: Homeownership rate: 100.0%; Median home value: $90,300; Median year structure built: 1946; Homeowner vacancy rate: 0.0%; Median selected monthly owner costs: n/a with a mortgage, n/a without a mortgage; Median gross rent: n/a per month; Rental vacancy rate: 0.0%
Health Insurance: 100.0% have insurance; 72.8% have private insurance; 37.5% have public insurance; 0.0% do not have insurance; 0.0% of children under 18 do not have insurance

Transportation: Commute: 100.0% car, 0.0% public transportation, 0.0% walk, 0.0% work from home; Mean travel time to work: 0.0 minutes

MAYVILLE (village). County seat. Covers a land area of 1.991 square miles and a water area of 0.002 square miles. Located at 42.25° N. Lat; 79.50° W. Long. Elevation is 1,453 feet.

History: Incorporated 1830.
Population: 1,413; Growth (since 2000): -19.5%; Density: 709.6 persons per square mile; Race: 87.5% White, 6.4% Black/African American, 0.4% Asian, 0.0% American Indian/Alaska Native, 0.0% Native Hawaiian/Other Pacific Islander, 4.5% Two or more races, 3.6% Hispanic of any race; Average household size: 2.10; Median age: 40.2; Age under 18: 15.3%; Age 65 and over: 16.2%; Males per 100 females: 116.3; Marriage status: 33.3% never married, 47.2% now married, 5.6% separated, 4.8% widowed, 14.6% divorced; Foreign born: 2.2%; Speak English only: 92.8%; With disability: 14.5%; Veterans: 10.4%; Ancestry: 29.8% German, 19.6% English, 15.0% Swedish, 12.0% Irish, 11.4% Italian
Employment: 11.3% management, business, and financial, 3.9% computer, engineering, and science, 10.4% education, legal, community service, arts, and media, 8.4% healthcare practitioners, 23.2% service, 18.1% sales and office, 17.6% natural resources, construction, and maintenance, 7.0% production, transportation, and material moving
Income: Per capita: $21,754; Median household: $48,542; Average household: $53,866; Households with income of $100,000 or more: 10.4%; Poverty rate: 17.2%
Educational Attainment: High school diploma or higher: 87.3%; Bachelor's degree or higher: 19.2%; Graduate/professional degree or higher: 7.6%

School District(s)
Chautauqua Lake Central SD (PK-12)
   2014-15 Enrollment: 925 . . . . (716) 753-5808
Housing: Homeownership rate: 64.7%; Median home value: $101,800; Median year structure built: 1945; Homeowner vacancy rate: 4.4%; Median selected monthly owner costs: $975 with a mortgage, $464 without a mortgage; Median gross rent: $517 per month; Rental vacancy rate: 5.0%
Health Insurance: 95.4% have insurance; 69.3% have private insurance; 43.2% have public insurance; 4.6% do not have insurance; 0.0% of children under 18 do not have insurance
Transportation: Commute: 92.7% car, 0.0% public transportation, 3.2% walk, 3.6% work from home; Mean travel time to work: 21.2 minutes

MINA (town). Covers a land area of 35.817 square miles and a water area of 0.511 square miles. Located at 42.12° N. Lat; 79.70° W. Long. Elevation is 1,594 feet.

Population: 1,063; Growth (since 2000): -9.6%; Density: 29.7 persons per square mile; Race: 100.0% White, 0.0% Black/African American, 0.0% Asian, 0.0% American Indian/Alaska Native, 0.0% Native Hawaiian/Other Pacific Islander, 0.0% Two or more races, 0.0% Hispanic of any race; Average household size: 2.51; Median age: 44.6; Age under 18: 21.4%; Age 65 and over: 10.4%; Males per 100 females: 97.9; Marriage status: 29.4% never married, 53.7% now married, 0.3% separated, 5.2% widowed, 11.7% divorced; Foreign born: 0.3%; Speak English only: 99.7%; With disability: 9.0%; Veterans: 14.1%; Ancestry: 22.6% German, 14.3% English, 9.1% Irish, 9.0% American, 8.9% Polish
Employment: 14.9% management, business, and financial, 2.4% computer, engineering, and science, 7.0% education, legal, community service, arts, and media, 8.8% healthcare practitioners, 18.2% service, 20.8% sales and office, 14.8% natural resources, construction, and maintenance, 13.1% production, transportation, and material moving
Income: Per capita: $24,769; Median household: $50,598; Average household: $62,181; Households with income of $100,000 or more: 16.0%; Poverty rate: 13.5%
Educational Attainment: High school diploma or higher: 93.7%; Bachelor's degree or higher: 19.0%; Graduate/professional degree or higher: 9.2%
Housing: Homeownership rate: 84.6%; Median home value: $125,000; Median year structure built: 1959; Homeowner vacancy rate: 4.5%; Median selected monthly owner costs: $981 with a mortgage, $504 without a mortgage; Median gross rent: $746 per month; Rental vacancy rate: 12.2%
Health Insurance: 83.3% have insurance; 70.5% have private insurance; 22.6% have public insurance; 16.7% do not have insurance; 22.4% of children under 18 do not have insurance
Transportation: Commute: 89.8% car, 0.0% public transportation, 5.9% walk, 3.5% work from home; Mean travel time to work: 22.3 minutes

NORTH HARMONY (town). Covers a land area of 42.133 square miles and a water area of 0.023 square miles. Located at 42.13° N. Lat; 79.46° W. Long.

Population: 2,115; Growth (since 2000): -16.1%; Density: 50.2 persons per square mile; Race: 98.2% White, 0.0% Black/African American, 0.5% Asian, 0.7% American Indian/Alaska Native, 0.0% Native Hawaiian/Other Pacific Islander, 0.2% Two or more races, 3.4% Hispanic of any race; Average household size: 2.41; Median age: 48.1; Age under 18: 19.0%; Age 65 and over: 22.0%; Males per 100 females: 104.1; Marriage status: 23.0% never married, 60.5% now married, 0.9% separated, 5.6% widowed, 10.8% divorced; Foreign born: 3.6%; Speak English only: 95.7%; With disability: 11.7%; Veterans: 8.3%; Ancestry: 22.0% English, 19.9% Irish, 19.8% German, 15.8% Swedish, 7.8% Italian
Employment: 13.9% management, business, and financial, 6.6% computer, engineering, and science, 8.4% education, legal, community service, arts, and media, 6.8% healthcare practitioners, 12.0% service, 21.9% sales and office, 10.9% natural resources, construction, and maintenance, 19.5% production, transportation, and material moving
Income: Per capita: $27,032; Median household: $51,722; Average household: $63,997; Households with income of $100,000 or more: 19.2%; Poverty rate: 13.3%
Educational Attainment: High school diploma or higher: 94.0%; Bachelor's degree or higher: 21.2%; Graduate/professional degree or higher: 12.6%
Housing: Homeownership rate: 85.4%; Median home value: $115,000; Median year structure built: 1957; Homeowner vacancy rate: 6.5%; Median selected monthly owner costs: $1,141 with a mortgage, $491 without a mortgage; Median gross rent: $833 per month; Rental vacancy rate: 10.5%
Health Insurance: 90.3% have insurance; 74.4% have private insurance; 34.6% have public insurance; 9.7% do not have insurance; 9.5% of children under 18 do not have insurance
Transportation: Commute: 88.2% car, 0.0% public transportation, 1.1% walk, 10.7% work from home; Mean travel time to work: 24.3 minutes

PANAMA (village). Covers a land area of 2.200 square miles and a water area of 0.006 square miles. Located at 42.07° N. Lat; 79.49° W. Long. Elevation is 1,552 feet.

History: Panama Rocks, a 25-acre park with a 60-foot high rock outcropping containing abundant early Paleozoic marine fossils, is 1 mile West Southwest.
Population: 503; Growth (since 2000): 2.4%; Density: 228.6 persons per square mile; Race: 99.6% White, 0.0% Black/African American, 0.0% Asian, 0.0% American Indian/Alaska Native, 0.0% Native Hawaiian/Other Pacific Islander, 0.2% Two or more races, 0.8% Hispanic of any race; Average household size: 2.43; Median age: 41.9; Age under 18: 26.8%; Age 65 and over: 21.7%; Males per 100 females: 94.7; Marriage status: 22.6% never married, 60.8% now married, 4.6% separated, 7.2% widowed, 9.5% divorced; Foreign born: 0.6%; Speak English only: 99.0%; With disability: 18.7%; Veterans: 7.9%; Ancestry: 20.1% Irish, 17.3% English, 15.3% German, 10.9% Swedish, 8.5% Dutch
Employment: 15.1% management, business, and financial, 1.6% computer, engineering, and science, 7.6% education, legal, community service, arts, and media, 4.9% healthcare practitioners, 19.5% service, 23.8% sales and office, 8.6% natural resources, construction, and maintenance, 18.9% production, transportation, and material moving
Income: Per capita: $20,233; Median household: $36,691; Average household: $48,426; Households with income of $100,000 or more: 13.1%; Poverty rate: 11.0%
Educational Attainment: High school diploma or higher: 88.7%; Bachelor's degree or higher: 19.3%; Graduate/professional degree or higher: 8.3%

School District(s)
Panama Central SD (PK-12)
   2014-15 Enrollment: 538 . . . . (716) 782-4445
Housing: Homeownership rate: 70.5%; Median home value: $85,200; Median year structure built: 1946; Homeowner vacancy rate: 0.0%; Median selected monthly owner costs: $1,019 with a mortgage, $348 without a mortgage; Median gross rent: $547 per month; Rental vacancy rate: 11.6%
Health Insurance: 88.9% have insurance; 63.8% have private insurance; 44.5% have public insurance; 11.1% do not have insurance; 11.9% of children under 18 do not have insurance
Transportation: Commute: 89.2% car, 0.0% public transportation, 4.3% walk, 5.4% work from home; Mean travel time to work: 25.2 minutes

POLAND (town). Covers a land area of 36.617 square miles and a water area of 0.266 square miles. Located at 42.13° N. Lat; 79.12° W. Long.

Population: 2,110; Growth (since 2000): -14.5%; Density: 57.6 persons per square mile; Race: 97.1% White, 0.2% Black/African American, 0.2% Asian, 0.0% American Indian/Alaska Native, 0.0% Native Hawaiian/Other Pacific Islander, 1.2% Two or more races, 1.6% Hispanic of any race; Average household size: 2.37; Median age: 49.3; Age under 18: 15.3%; Age 65 and over: 21.3%; Males per 100 females: 102.6; Marriage status: 22.5% never married, 60.0% now married, 1.1% separated, 6.9% widowed, 10.7% divorced; Foreign born: 0.6%; Speak English only: 95.7%; With disability: 15.0%; Veterans: 12.4%; Ancestry: 20.9% Swedish, 19.6% German, 17.0% English, 13.1% Italian, 11.0% Irish

Employment: 13.1% management, business, and financial, 2.2% computer, engineering, and science, 10.0% education, legal, community service, arts, and media, 7.9% healthcare practitioners, 14.4% service, 21.1% sales and office, 8.2% natural resources, construction, and maintenance, 23.0% production, transportation, and material moving

Income: Per capita: $24,007; Median household: $41,893; Average household: $55,604; Households with income of $100,000 or more: 14.1%; Poverty rate: 10.6%

Educational Attainment: High school diploma or higher: 85.8%; Bachelor's degree or higher: 12.8%; Graduate/professional degree or higher: 5.3%

Housing: Homeownership rate: 85.8%; Median home value: $77,800; Median year structure built: 1961; Homeowner vacancy rate: 2.2%; Median selected monthly owner costs: $1,059 with a mortgage, $427 without a mortgage; Median gross rent: $491 per month; Rental vacancy rate: 0.0%

Health Insurance: 97.5% have insurance; 73.6% have private insurance; 40.1% have public insurance; 2.5% do not have insurance; 2.5% of children under 18 do not have insurance

Transportation: Commute: 94.5% car, 1.8% public transportation, 2.2% walk, 1.5% work from home; Mean travel time to work: 17.9 minutes

POMFRET (town). Covers a land area of 43.855 square miles and a water area of 0.334 square miles. Located at 42.41° N. Lat; 79.33° W. Long.

Population: 14,579; Growth (since 2000): -0.8%; Density: 332.4 persons per square mile; Race: 92.1% White, 3.1% Black/African American, 1.7% Asian, 0.1% American Indian/Alaska Native, 0.3% Native Hawaiian/Other Pacific Islander, 0.8% Two or more races, 7.2% Hispanic of any race; Average household size: 2.24; Median age: 30.8; Age under 18: 15.1%; Age 65 and over: 15.9%; Males per 100 females: 90.5; Marriage status: 45.4% never married, 41.4% now married, 1.1% separated, 4.3% widowed, 8.9% divorced; Foreign born: 4.0%; Speak English only: 92.0%; With disability: 10.7%; Veterans: 8.0%; Ancestry: 25.4% Italian, 24.0% German, 17.7% Irish, 15.3% Polish, 12.7% English

Employment: 12.1% management, business, and financial, 2.9% computer, engineering, and science, 17.4% education, legal, community service, arts, and media, 4.2% healthcare practitioners, 23.5% service, 22.2% sales and office, 4.9% natural resources, construction, and maintenance, 12.8% production, transportation, and material moving

Income: Per capita: $24,110; Median household: $49,186; Average household: $64,192; Households with income of $100,000 or more: 18.6%; Poverty rate: 18.9%

Educational Attainment: High school diploma or higher: 94.4%; Bachelor's degree or higher: 36.6%; Graduate/professional degree or higher: 19.8%

Housing: Homeownership rate: 69.4%; Median home value: $123,100; Median year structure built: 1949; Homeowner vacancy rate: 2.1%; Median selected monthly owner costs: $1,162 with a mortgage, $555 without a mortgage; Median gross rent: $643 per month; Rental vacancy rate: 11.5%

Health Insurance: 94.5% have insurance; 78.9% have private insurance; 30.5% have public insurance; 5.5% do not have insurance; 1.0% of children under 18 do not have insurance

Transportation: Commute: 82.5% car, 0.4% public transportation, 11.3% walk, 4.5% work from home; Mean travel time to work: 15.4 minutes

Additional Information Contacts

Town of Pomfret . . . . (716) 672-7496
  http://townofpomfretny.org/content

PORTLAND (town). Covers a land area of 34.116 square miles and a water area of 0.064 square miles. Located at 42.37° N. Lat; 79.46° W. Long. Elevation is 761 feet.

Population: 4,862; Growth (since 2000): -11.6%; Density: 142.5 persons per square mile; Race: 87.7% White, 7.2% Black/African American, 0.1% Asian, 0.0% American Indian/Alaska Native, 0.0% Native Hawaiian/Other Pacific Islander, 3.0% Two or more races, 5.3% Hispanic of any race; Average household size: 2.37; Median age: 40.9; Age under 18: 16.4%; Age 65 and over: 17.3%; Males per 100 females: 126.6; Marriage status: 37.2% never married, 40.6% now married, 1.9% separated, 7.0% widowed, 15.1% divorced; Foreign born: 2.8%; Speak English only: 90.5%; With disability: 19.2%; Veterans: 7.6%; Ancestry: 28.7% German, 19.1% Italian, 16.8% Irish, 13.7% English, 8.2% Polish

Employment: 7.7% management, business, and financial, 1.4% computer, engineering, and science, 9.3% education, legal, community service, arts, and media, 2.5% healthcare practitioners, 27.2% service, 22.7% sales and office, 6.0% natural resources, construction, and maintenance, 23.2% production, transportation, and material moving

Income: Per capita: $19,483; Median household: $40,142; Average household: $51,835; Households with income of $100,000 or more: 10.3%; Poverty rate: 18.7%

Educational Attainment: High school diploma or higher: 80.4%; Bachelor's degree or higher: 14.2%; Graduate/professional degree or higher: 7.1%

Housing: Homeownership rate: 73.8%; Median home value: $82,900; Median year structure built: 1958; Homeowner vacancy rate: 2.2%; Median selected monthly owner costs: $1,074 with a mortgage, $429 without a mortgage; Median gross rent: $556 per month; Rental vacancy rate: 0.0%

Health Insurance: 89.5% have insurance; 62.0% have private insurance; 40.8% have public insurance; 10.5% do not have insurance; 9.6% of children under 18 do not have insurance

Transportation: Commute: 92.2% car, 0.1% public transportation, 2.7% walk, 5.0% work from home; Mean travel time to work: 20.2 minutes

Additional Information Contacts

Town of Portland . . . . (716) 792-9614
  http://www.town.portland.ny.us

RIPLEY (CDP). Covers a land area of 1.372 square miles and a water area of 0 square miles. Located at 42.27° N. Lat; 79.71° W. Long. Elevation is 735 feet.

Population: 966; Growth (since 2000): -6.2%; Density: 704.1 persons per square mile; Race: 98.6% White, 0.8% Black/African American, 0.0% Asian, 0.0% American Indian/Alaska Native, 0.0% Native Hawaiian/Other Pacific Islander, 0.6% Two or more races, 0.7% Hispanic of any race; Average household size: 2.32; Median age: 34.3; Age under 18: 23.3%; Age 65 and over: 14.5%; Males per 100 females: 95.1; Marriage status: 26.7% never married, 53.3% now married, 1.6% separated, 9.1% widowed, 10.8% divorced; Foreign born: 0.0%; Speak English only: 99.7%; With disability: 20.9%; Veterans: 16.1%; Ancestry: 28.6% Irish, 25.1% German, 15.3% English, 14.5% Italian, 8.1% Polish

Employment: 5.1% management, business, and financial, 2.0% computer, engineering, and science, 4.7% education, legal, community service, arts, and media, 4.9% healthcare practitioners, 26.3% service, 15.4% sales and office, 15.4% natural resources, construction, and maintenance, 26.1% production, transportation, and material moving

Income: Per capita: $18,329; Median household: $30,152; Average household: $41,425; Households with income of $100,000 or more: 3.6%; Poverty rate: 20.3%

Educational Attainment: High school diploma or higher: 83.7%; Bachelor's degree or higher: 12.5%; Graduate/professional degree or higher: 5.3%

School District(s)

Ripley Central SD (PK-12)
  2014-15 Enrollment: 177 . . . . (716) 736-6201

Housing: Homeownership rate: 71.2%; Median home value: $57,800; Median year structure built: 1953; Homeowner vacancy rate: 9.3%; Median selected monthly owner costs: $950 with a mortgage, $343 without a mortgage; Median gross rent: $573 per month; Rental vacancy rate: 0.0%

Health Insurance: 90.3% have insurance; 54.2% have private insurance; 44.8% have public insurance; 9.7% do not have insurance; 0.0% of children under 18 do not have insurance

Transportation: Commute: 89.3% car, 0.0% public transportation, 8.5% walk, 2.2% work from home; Mean travel time to work: 26.5 minutes

RIPLEY (town). Covers a land area of 48.763 square miles and a water area of 0.104 square miles. Located at 42.23° N. Lat; 79.70° W. Long. Elevation is 735 feet.

Population: 2,245; Growth (since 2000): -14.8%; Density: 46.0 persons per square mile; Race: 98.5% White, 0.6% Black/African American, 0.0% Asian, 0.0% American Indian/Alaska Native, 0.0% Native Hawaiian/Other Pacific Islander, 0.3% Two or more races, 4.2% Hispanic of any race; Average household size: 2.43; Median age: 41.8; Age under 18: 22.2%; Age 65 and over: 15.8%; Males per 100 females: 101.6; Marriage status: 23.2% never married, 62.0% now married, 1.2% separated, 6.5% widowed, 8.2% divorced; Foreign born: 2.2%; Speak English only: 96.3%; With disability: 16.4%; Veterans: 15.3%; Ancestry: 23.8% German, 17.2% Irish, 14.6% English, 8.8% Italian, 8.6% American

Employment: 8.5% management, business, and financial, 2.1% computer, engineering, and science, 5.3% education, legal, community service, arts, and media, 6.0% healthcare practitioners, 19.4% service, 21.6% sales and office, 16.3% natural resources, construction, and maintenance, 20.8% production, transportation, and material moving

Income: Per capita: $22,207; Median household: $41,420; Average household: $53,043; Households with income of $100,000 or more: 9.9%; Poverty rate: 14.1%

Educational Attainment: High school diploma or higher: 84.9%; Bachelor's degree or higher: 10.5%; Graduate/professional degree or higher: 2.8%

School District(s)
Ripley Central SD (PK-12)
    2014-15 Enrollment: 177 . . . . (716) 736-6201

Housing: Homeownership rate: 77.0%; Median home value: $68,400; Median year structure built: 1953; Homeowner vacancy rate: 4.2%; Median selected monthly owner costs: $943 with a mortgage, $403 without a mortgage; Median gross rent: $579 per month; Rental vacancy rate: 0.0%

Health Insurance: 90.1% have insurance; 61.8% have private insurance; 40.0% have public insurance; 9.9% do not have insurance; 3.6% of children under 18 do not have insurance

Transportation: Commute: 91.0% car, 0.0% public transportation, 4.7% walk, 3.8% work from home; Mean travel time to work: 25.8 minutes

SHERIDAN (town). Covers a land area of 37.252 square miles and a water area of 0.051 square miles. Located at 42.49° N. Lat; 79.23° W. Long. Elevation is 748 feet.

Population: 2,622; Growth (since 2000): -7.6%; Density: 70.4 persons per square mile; Race: 95.3% White, 0.7% Black/African American, 1.1% Asian, 0.6% American Indian/Alaska Native, 0.0% Native Hawaiian/Other Pacific Islander, 0.8% Two or more races, 4.8% Hispanic of any race; Average household size: 2.40; Median age: 48.6; Age under 18: 20.3%; Age 65 and over: 17.6%; Males per 100 females: 98.9; Marriage status: 23.6% never married, 51.5% now married, 3.7% separated, 8.3% widowed, 16.6% divorced; Foreign born: 1.8%; Speak English only: 94.0%; With disability: 16.2%; Veterans: 8.8%; Ancestry: 24.8% German, 23.3% Polish, 21.7% English, 12.7% Irish, 9.2% Italian

Employment: 10.4% management, business, and financial, 3.2% computer, engineering, and science, 9.6% education, legal, community service, arts, and media, 5.8% healthcare practitioners, 16.3% service, 20.6% sales and office, 13.1% natural resources, construction, and maintenance, 21.0% production, transportation, and material moving

Income: Per capita: $25,861; Median household: $52,112; Average household: $61,636; Households with income of $100,000 or more: 14.1%; Poverty rate: 12.9%

Educational Attainment: High school diploma or higher: 91.3%; Bachelor's degree or higher: 15.8%; Graduate/professional degree or higher: 6.5%

Housing: Homeownership rate: 86.0%; Median home value: $117,900; Median year structure built: 1960; Homeowner vacancy rate: 0.0%; Median selected monthly owner costs: $1,161 with a mortgage, $519 without a mortgage; Median gross rent: $699 per month; Rental vacancy rate: 0.0%

Health Insurance: 95.7% have insurance; 80.4% have private insurance; 32.9% have public insurance; 4.3% do not have insurance; 0.0% of children under 18 do not have insurance

Transportation: Commute: 94.3% car, 0.3% public transportation, 0.7% walk, 3.1% work from home; Mean travel time to work: 19.0 minutes

SHERMAN (town). Covers a land area of 36.271 square miles and a water area of 0.130 square miles. Located at 42.14° N. Lat; 79.58° W. Long. Elevation is 1,539 feet.

Population: 1,802; Growth (since 2000): 16.0%; Density: 49.7 persons per square mile; Race: 99.6% White, 0.0% Black/African American, 0.0% Asian, 0.0% American Indian/Alaska Native, 0.0% Native Hawaiian/Other Pacific Islander, 0.4% Two or more races, 0.9% Hispanic of any race; Average household size: 3.31; Median age: 28.5; Age under 18: 35.0%; Age 65 and over: 11.0%; Males per 100 females: 100.1; Marriage status: 30.7% never married, 54.5% now married, 1.5% separated, 5.0% widowed, 9.8% divorced; Foreign born: 0.3%; Speak English only: 70.2%; With disability: 11.4%; Veterans: 6.1%; Ancestry: 38.0% German, 10.4% Dutch, 10.2% Swedish, 10.2% English, 8.2% American

Employment: 14.7% management, business, and financial, 0.3% computer, engineering, and science, 4.9% education, legal, community service, arts, and media, 2.3% healthcare practitioners, 17.9% service, 16.6% sales and office, 29.6% natural resources, construction, and maintenance, 13.7% production, transportation, and material moving

Income: Per capita: $16,668; Median household: $39,500; Average household: $52,202; Households with income of $100,000 or more: 13.8%; Poverty rate: 23.5%

Educational Attainment: High school diploma or higher: 72.1%; Bachelor's degree or higher: 14.1%; Graduate/professional degree or higher: 6.3%

School District(s)
Sherman Central SD (PK-12)
    2014-15 Enrollment: 424 . . . . (716) 761-6122

Housing: Homeownership rate: 80.1%; Median home value: $78,800; Median year structure built: Before 1940; Homeowner vacancy rate: 0.0%; Median selected monthly owner costs: $954 with a mortgage, $355 without a mortgage; Median gross rent: $550 per month; Rental vacancy rate: 8.5%

Health Insurance: 65.0% have insurance; 45.4% have private insurance; 28.5% have public insurance; 35.0% do not have insurance; 49.8% of children under 18 do not have insurance

Transportation: Commute: 83.3% car, 0.0% public transportation, 5.3% walk, 8.4% work from home; Mean travel time to work: 23.9 minutes

SHERMAN (village). Covers a land area of 0.854 square miles and a water area of 0 square miles. Located at 42.16° N. Lat; 79.59° W. Long. Elevation is 1,539 feet.

Population: 681; Growth (since 2000): -4.6%; Density: 797.7 persons per square mile; Race: 99.0% White, 0.0% Black/African American, 0.0% Asian, 0.0% American Indian/Alaska Native, 0.0% Native Hawaiian/Other Pacific Islander, 1.0% Two or more races, 2.3% Hispanic of any race; Average household size: 2.38; Median age: 37.6; Age under 18: 24.2%; Age 65 and over: 18.8%; Males per 100 females: 97.3; Marriage status: 22.0% never married, 58.7% now married, 2.4% separated, 9.7% widowed, 9.5% divorced; Foreign born: 0.3%; Speak English only: 97.4%; With disability: 14.0%; Veterans: 11.4%; Ancestry: 35.7% German, 20.0% English, 12.0% Dutch, 9.4% Swedish, 8.8% Irish

Employment: 9.2% management, business, and financial, 0.7% computer, engineering, and science, 7.5% education, legal, community service, arts, and media, 2.4% healthcare practitioners, 25.9% service, 17.3% sales and office, 21.8% natural resources, construction, and maintenance, 15.3% production, transportation, and material moving

Income: Per capita: $19,904; Median household: $35,238; Average household: $44,087; Households with income of $100,000 or more: 7.3%; Poverty rate: 14.0%

Educational Attainment: High school diploma or higher: 85.8%; Bachelor's degree or higher: 20.4%; Graduate/professional degree or higher: 9.2%

School District(s)
Sherman Central SD (PK-12)
    2014-15 Enrollment: 424 . . . . (716) 761-6122

Housing: Homeownership rate: 69.6%; Median home value: $66,700; Median year structure built: Before 1940; Homeowner vacancy rate: 0.0%; Median selected monthly owner costs: $894 with a mortgage, $388 without a mortgage; Median gross rent: $439 per month; Rental vacancy rate: 0.0%

Health Insurance: 90.7% have insurance; 64.0% have private insurance; 43.2% have public insurance; 9.3% do not have insurance; 7.3% of children under 18 do not have insurance

Transportation: Commute: 90.3% car, 0.0% public transportation, 7.4% walk, 2.3% work from home; Mean travel time to work: 20.1 minutes

SILVER CREEK (village). Covers a land area of 1.160 square miles and a water area of 0 square miles. Located at 42.54° N. Lat; 79.17° W. Long. Elevation is 587 feet.

History: Annual grape festival held here in October. Incorporated 1848.
Population: 2,598; Growth (since 2000): -10.3%; Density: 2,239.3 persons per square mile; Race: 97.3% White, 0.4% Black/African American, 0.0% Asian, 0.6% American Indian/Alaska Native, 0.0% Native Hawaiian/Other Pacific Islander, 1.4% Two or more races, 1.9% Hispanic of any race; Average household size: 2.53; Median age: 37.1; Age under 18: 26.9%; Age 65 and over: 13.5%; Males per 100 females: 95.9; Marriage status: 26.4% never married, 54.0% now married, 4.5% separated, 7.6% widowed, 12.1% divorced; Foreign born: 1.9%; Speak English only: 98.3%; With disability: 15.7%; Veterans: 10.7%; Ancestry: 35.6% German, 22.3% Italian, 21.4% Irish, 18.4% Polish, 17.9% English
Employment: 10.2% management, business, and financial, 3.2% computer, engineering, and science, 10.7% education, legal, community service, arts, and media, 4.1% healthcare practitioners, 24.4% service, 19.0% sales and office, 9.5% natural resources, construction, and maintenance, 19.0% production, transportation, and material moving
Income: Per capita: $21,345; Median household: $45,089; Average household: $52,906; Households with income of $100,000 or more: 9.7%; Poverty rate: 20.4%
Educational Attainment: High school diploma or higher: 92.0%; Bachelor's degree or higher: 24.3%; Graduate/professional degree or higher: 9.5%

School District(s)
Silver Creek Central SD (PK-12)
    2014-15 Enrollment: 1,098 . . . . (716) 934-2603
Housing: Homeownership rate: 74.6%; Median home value: $75,300; Median year structure built: Before 1940; Homeowner vacancy rate: 2.6%; Median selected monthly owner costs: $1,060 with a mortgage, $516 without a mortgage; Median gross rent: $700 per month; Rental vacancy rate: 9.6%
Health Insurance: 90.6% have insurance; 66.7% have private insurance; 41.2% have public insurance; 9.4% do not have insurance; 4.6% of children under 18 do not have insurance
Transportation: Commute: 94.0% car, 0.0% public transportation, 4.5% walk, 1.5% work from home; Mean travel time to work: 22.7 minutes

SINCLAIRVILLE (village). Covers a land area of 1.612 square miles and a water area of 0 square miles. Located at 42.27° N. Lat; 79.26° W. Long. Elevation is 1,401 feet.
Population: 644; Growth (since 2000): -3.2%; Density: 399.5 persons per square mile; Race: 99.2% White, 0.0% Black/African American, 0.0% Asian, 0.3% American Indian/Alaska Native, 0.0% Native Hawaiian/Other Pacific Islander, 0.5% Two or more races, 0.8% Hispanic of any race; Average household size: 2.72; Median age: 37.8; Age under 18: 30.9%; Age 65 and over: 13.2%; Males per 100 females: 102.1; Marriage status: 25.5% never married, 59.8% now married, 1.1% separated, 6.3% widowed, 8.4% divorced; Foreign born: 0.9%; Speak English only: 97.9%; With disability: 15.8%; Veterans: 10.1%; Ancestry: 20.3% Swedish, 20.0% German, 15.7% English, 14.3% Irish, 11.3% Italian
Employment: 7.6% management, business, and financial, 2.2% computer, engineering, and science, 5.8% education, legal, community service, arts, and media, 0.0% healthcare practitioners, 29.3% service, 23.6% sales and office, 14.5% natural resources, construction, and maintenance, 17.0% production, transportation, and material moving
Income: Per capita: $17,645; Median household: $42,344; Average household: $47,362; Households with income of $100,000 or more: 5.1%; Poverty rate: 21.1%
Educational Attainment: High school diploma or higher: 89.4%; Bachelor's degree or higher: 9.7%; Graduate/professional degree or higher: 0.5%

School District(s)
Cassadaga Valley Central SD (PK-12)
    2014-15 Enrollment: 971 . . . . (716) 962-5155
Housing: Homeownership rate: 78.9%; Median home value: $65,500; Median year structure built: Before 1940; Homeowner vacancy rate: 0.0%; Median selected monthly owner costs: $1,020 with a mortgage, $419 without a mortgage; Median gross rent: $405 per month; Rental vacancy rate: 0.0%
Health Insurance: 94.4% have insurance; 55.1% have private insurance; 49.2% have public insurance; 5.6% do not have insurance; 0.0% of children under 18 do not have insurance

Transportation: Commute: 91.7% car, 1.4% public transportation, 0.7% walk, 3.6% work from home; Mean travel time to work: 21.9 minutes

STOCKTON (town). Covers a land area of 47.160 square miles and a water area of 0.489 square miles. Located at 42.30° N. Lat; 79.36° W. Long. Elevation is 1,325 feet.
Population: 2,403; Growth (since 2000): 3.1%; Density: 51.0 persons per square mile; Race: 97.8% White, 0.0% Black/African American, 0.3% Asian, 0.0% American Indian/Alaska Native, 0.0% Native Hawaiian/Other Pacific Islander, 1.8% Two or more races, 1.2% Hispanic of any race; Average household size: 2.82; Median age: 34.9; Age under 18: 28.2%; Age 65 and over: 16.5%; Males per 100 females: 98.4; Marriage status: 28.7% never married, 54.9% now married, 1.4% separated, 5.9% widowed, 10.5% divorced; Foreign born: 1.0%; Speak English only: 99.6%; With disability: 18.9%; Veterans: 10.9%; Ancestry: 27.1% German, 21.1% English, 16.5% Irish, 11.8% Polish, 11.7% Italian
Employment: 4.7% management, business, and financial, 4.5% computer, engineering, and science, 10.3% education, legal, community service, arts, and media, 4.2% healthcare practitioners, 18.9% service, 21.7% sales and office, 11.4% natural resources, construction, and maintenance, 24.4% production, transportation, and material moving
Income: Per capita: $19,050; Median household: $48,102; Average household: $51,920; Households with income of $100,000 or more: 9.7%; Poverty rate: 25.9%
Educational Attainment: High school diploma or higher: 83.2%; Bachelor's degree or higher: 18.5%; Graduate/professional degree or higher: 6.0%
Housing: Homeownership rate: 69.6%; Median home value: $93,500; Median year structure built: 1962; Homeowner vacancy rate: 0.0%; Median selected monthly owner costs: $893 with a mortgage, $429 without a mortgage; Median gross rent: $767 per month; Rental vacancy rate: 0.0%
Health Insurance: 97.0% have insurance; 62.1% have private insurance; 47.5% have public insurance; 3.0% do not have insurance; 1.5% of children under 18 do not have insurance
Transportation: Commute: 94.1% car, 0.3% public transportation, 2.4% walk, 2.4% work from home; Mean travel time to work: 24.8 minutes

SUNSET BAY (CDP). Covers a land area of 0.661 square miles and a water area of 0.044 square miles. Located at 42.56° N. Lat; 79.13° W. Long. Elevation is 577 feet.
Population: 781; Growth (since 2000): n/a; Density: 1,182.1 persons per square mile; Race: 85.0% White, 2.7% Black/African American, 0.0% Asian, 7.4% American Indian/Alaska Native, 0.0% Native Hawaiian/Other Pacific Islander, 0.0% Two or more races, 5.2% Hispanic of any race; Average household size: 2.11; Median age: 51.9; Age under 18: 18.4%; Age 65 and over: 25.4%; Males per 100 females: 91.9; Marriage status: 36.3% never married, 43.6% now married, 1.1% separated, 8.3% widowed, 11.8% divorced; Foreign born: 0.0%; Speak English only: 100.0%; With disability: 14.0%; Veterans: 12.2%; Ancestry: 39.6% German, 23.7% Polish, 20.0% Irish, 12.8% English, 9.5% Italian
Employment: 9.6% management, business, and financial, 0.0% computer, engineering, and science, 0.0% education, legal, community service, arts, and media, 0.0% healthcare practitioners, 52.0% service, 22.1% sales and office, 10.3% natural resources, construction, and maintenance, 5.9% production, transportation, and material moving
Income: Per capita: $25,922; Median household: $58,527; Average household: $62,161; Households with income of $100,000 or more: 12.3%; Poverty rate: 5.3%
Educational Attainment: High school diploma or higher: 80.7%; Bachelor's degree or higher: 11.7%; Graduate/professional degree or higher: 2.9%
Housing: Homeownership rate: 64.2%; Median home value: $113,500; Median year structure built: 1961; Homeowner vacancy rate: 0.0%; Median selected monthly owner costs: $1,047 with a mortgage, $563 without a mortgage; Median gross rent: $859 per month; Rental vacancy rate: 0.0%
Health Insurance: 86.9% have insurance; 71.9% have private insurance; 25.6% have public insurance; 13.1% do not have insurance; 0.0% of children under 18 do not have insurance
Transportation: Commute: 96.9% car, 0.0% public transportation, 3.1% walk, 0.0% work from home; Mean travel time to work: 17.5 minutes

VILLENOVA (town). Covers a land area of 36.093 square miles and a water area of 0.111 square miles. Located at 42.39° N. Lat; 79.12° W. Long.

Population: 940; Growth (since 2000): -16.1%; Density: 26.0 persons per square mile; Race: 95.5% White, 0.0% Black/African American, 0.0% Asian, 1.8% American Indian/Alaska Native, 0.0% Native Hawaiian/Other Pacific Islander, 2.0% Two or more races, 0.9% Hispanic of any race; Average household size: 2.49; Median age: 50.9; Age under 18: 19.5%; Age 65 and over: 19.4%; Males per 100 females: 97.5; Marriage status: 21.3% never married, 64.0% now married, 2.8% separated, 3.6% widowed, 11.0% divorced; Foreign born: 0.7%; Speak English only: 99.5%; With disability: 11.2%; Veterans: 12.7%; Ancestry: 38.1% German, 15.3% Irish, 14.4% English, 13.5% Polish, 11.5% Italian

Employment: 5.6% management, business, and financial, 2.6% computer, engineering, and science, 7.7% education, legal, community service, arts, and media, 5.6% healthcare practitioners, 17.5% service, 15.6% sales and office, 25.2% natural resources, construction, and maintenance, 20.3% production, transportation, and material moving

Income: Per capita: $23,802; Median household: $44,191; Average household: $58,263; Households with income of $100,000 or more: 10.6%; Poverty rate: 10.2%

Educational Attainment: High school diploma or higher: 90.1%; Bachelor's degree or higher: 15.2%; Graduate/professional degree or higher: 5.6%

Housing: Homeownership rate: 90.2%; Median home value: $85,100; Median year structure built: 1974; Homeowner vacancy rate: 0.0%; Median selected monthly owner costs: $1,118 with a mortgage, $462 without a mortgage; Median gross rent: $508 per month; Rental vacancy rate: 0.0%

Health Insurance: 94.8% have insurance; 71.7% have private insurance; 41.6% have public insurance; 5.2% do not have insurance; 0.0% of children under 18 do not have insurance

Transportation: Commute: 94.0% car, 0.0% public transportation, 1.4% walk, 4.5% work from home; Mean travel time to work: 27.9 minutes

WESTFIELD (town). Covers a land area of 47.185 square miles and a water area of 0.066 square miles. Located at 42.27° N. Lat; 79.60° W. Long. Elevation is 745 feet.

History: In 1873 Thomas and Charles Bradwell Welch, ardent Prohibitionists, devised method of pressing Concord grapes into unfermented wine. Settled 1800, incorporated 1833.

Population: 4,812; Growth (since 2000): -8.0%; Density: 102.0 persons per square mile; Race: 99.5% White, 0.3% Black/African American, 0.0% Asian, 0.0% American Indian/Alaska Native, 0.0% Native Hawaiian/Other Pacific Islander, 0.0% Two or more races, 5.9% Hispanic of any race; Average household size: 2.34; Median age: 45.9; Age under 18: 19.2%; Age 65 and over: 23.5%; Males per 100 females: 93.8; Marriage status: 26.4% never married, 54.8% now married, 3.6% separated, 10.0% widowed, 8.8% divorced; Foreign born: 0.1%; Speak English only: 96.7%; With disability: 11.6%; Veterans: 11.0%; Ancestry: 29.6% German, 16.0% English, 12.9% Irish, 11.7% Polish, 8.7% Italian

Employment: 13.3% management, business, and financial, 1.4% computer, engineering, and science, 7.6% education, legal, community service, arts, and media, 6.1% healthcare practitioners, 13.3% service, 23.7% sales and office, 6.4% natural resources, construction, and maintenance, 28.2% production, transportation, and material moving

Income: Per capita: $21,978; Median household: $44,882; Average household: $50,804; Households with income of $100,000 or more: 7.2%; Poverty rate: 14.6%

Educational Attainment: High school diploma or higher: 88.7%; Bachelor's degree or higher: 23.0%; Graduate/professional degree or higher: 10.7%

School District(s)

Westfield Central SD (KG-12)
    2014-15 Enrollment: 668 . . . . (716) 326-2151

Housing: Homeownership rate: 73.8%; Median home value: $89,900; Median year structure built: Before 1940; Homeowner vacancy rate: 0.0%; Median selected monthly owner costs: $913 with a mortgage, $445 without a mortgage; Median gross rent: $617 per month; Rental vacancy rate: 6.6%

Health Insurance: 95.3% have insurance; 71.9% have private insurance; 39.0% have public insurance; 4.7% do not have insurance; 1.1% of children under 18 do not have insurance

Hospitals: Westfield Memorial Hospital (32 beds)

Newspapers: Westfield Republican (weekly circulation 1,400)

Transportation: Commute: 89.7% car, 0.0% public transportation, 6.6% walk, 3.7% work from home; Mean travel time to work: 21.7 minutes

Additional Information Contacts

Town of Westfield . . . . (716) 326-3211
    http://www.townofwestfield.org

WESTFIELD (village). Covers a land area of 3.822 square miles and a water area of 0 square miles. Located at 42.32° N. Lat; 79.57° W. Long. Elevation is 745 feet.

Population: 3,466; Growth (since 2000): -0.4%; Density: 906.8 persons per square mile; Race: 99.6% White, 0.4% Black/African American, 0.0% Asian, 0.0% American Indian/Alaska Native, 0.0% Native Hawaiian/Other Pacific Islander, 0.0% Two or more races, 7.3% Hispanic of any race; Average household size: 2.47; Median age: 40.3; Age under 18: 23.1%; Age 65 and over: 21.1%; Males per 100 females: 89.3; Marriage status: 29.4% never married, 49.4% now married, 2.8% separated, 11.0% widowed, 10.2% divorced; Foreign born: 0.2%; Speak English only: 95.8%; With disability: 9.6%; Veterans: 10.9%; Ancestry: 32.3% German, 16.8% English, 11.5% Polish, 10.4% Irish, 8.9% American

Employment: 13.8% management, business, and financial, 1.0% computer, engineering, and science, 7.9% education, legal, community service, arts, and media, 7.7% healthcare practitioners, 14.1% service, 20.4% sales and office, 5.3% natural resources, construction, and maintenance, 29.8% production, transportation, and material moving

Income: Per capita: $21,619; Median household: $46,370; Average household: $53,006; Households with income of $100,000 or more: 8.5%; Poverty rate: 13.5%

Educational Attainment: High school diploma or higher: 88.5%; Bachelor's degree or higher: 27.9%; Graduate/professional degree or higher: 12.8%

School District(s)

Westfield Central SD (KG-12)
    2014-15 Enrollment: 668 . . . . (716) 326-2151

Housing: Homeownership rate: 71.8%; Median home value: $87,200; Median year structure built: Before 1940; Homeowner vacancy rate: 0.0%; Median selected monthly owner costs: $898 with a mortgage, $435 without a mortgage; Median gross rent: $623 per month; Rental vacancy rate: 8.7%

Health Insurance: 95.6% have insurance; 74.4% have private insurance; 34.4% have public insurance; 4.4% do not have insurance; 0.0% of children under 18 do not have insurance

Hospitals: Westfield Memorial Hospital (32 beds)

Safety: Violent crime rate: 6.4 per 10,000 population; Property crime rate: 16.1 per 10,000 population

Newspapers: Westfield Republican (weekly circulation 1,400)

Transportation: Commute: 91.8% car, 0.0% public transportation, 7.2% walk, 1.0% work from home; Mean travel time to work: 22.1 minutes

Chemung County

Located in southern New York; hilly area bounded on the south by Pennsylvania; cut by the Chemung River Valley. Covers a land area of 407.352 square miles, a water area of 3.427 square miles, and is located in the Eastern Time Zone at 42.16° N. Lat., 76.75° W. Long. The county was founded in 1836. County seat is Elmira.

Chemung County is part of the Elmira, NY Metropolitan Statistical Area. The entire metro area includes: Chemung County, NY

Weather Station: Elmira										Elevation: 844 feet	
	Jan	Feb	Mar	Apr	May	Jun	Jul	Aug	Sep	Oct	Nov	Dec
High	33	36	44	58	70	78	82	81	73	61	49	37
Low	16	17	23	34	44	53	58	57	49	38	31	21
Precip	1.9	1.8	2.9	3.2	3.0	4.2	3.7	3.6	3.5	2.8	3.0	2.3
Snow	10.6	8.2	9.4	1.3	0.0	0.0	0.0	0.0	0.0	0.2	2.7	7.8

High and Low temperatures in degrees Fahrenheit; Precipitation and Snow in inches

Population: 88,267; Growth (since 2000): -3.1%; Density: 216.7 persons per square mile; Race: 88.5% White, 5.9% Black/African American, 1.5% Asian, 0.4% American Indian/Alaska Native, 0.0% Native Hawaiian/Other Pacific Islander, 3.4% two or more races, 2.9% Hispanic of any race; Average household size: 2.35; Median age: 40.9; Age under 18: 22.0%; Age 65 and over: 16.3%; Males per 100 females: 98.9; Marriage status: 31.4% never married, 51.0% now married, 2.7% separated, 7.3% widowed, 10.3% divorced; Foreign born: 2.7%; Speak English only: 96.3%;

With disability: 13.5%; Veterans: 9.5%; Ancestry: 18.5% Irish, 18.1% German, 13.4% American, 12.0% Italian, 11.2% English
Religion: Six largest groups: 16.4% Catholicism, 5.3% Methodist/Pietist, 2.4% Non-denominational Protestant, 1.9% Holiness, 1.9% Baptist, 1.9% Muslim Estimate
Economy: Unemployment rate: 5.3%; Leading industries: 19.1 % retail trade; 11.9 % accommodation and food services; 11.5 % health care and social assistance; Farms: 372 totaling 58,114 acres; Company size: 2 employ 1,000 or more persons, 1 employs 500 to 999 persons, 41 employs 100 to 499 persons, 1,766 employ less than 100 persons; Business ownership: 1,877 women-owned, 213 Black-owned, 105 Hispanic-owned, 171 Asian-owned, n/a American Indian/Alaska Native-owned
Employment: 11.5% management, business, and financial, 4.1% computer, engineering, and science, 12.0% education, legal, community service, arts, and media, 6.9% healthcare practitioners, 20.4% service, 23.1% sales and office, 8.2% natural resources, construction, and maintenance, 13.9% production, transportation, and material moving
Income: Per capita: $26,262; Median household: $50,320; Average household: $65,467; Households with income of $100,000 or more: 19.0%; Poverty rate: 15.8%
Educational Attainment: High school diploma or higher: 89.7%; Bachelor's degree or higher: 23.4%; Graduate/professional degree or higher: 10.7%
Housing: Homeownership rate: 69.1%; Median home value: $100,400; Median year structure built: 1953; Homeowner vacancy rate: 1.1%; Median selected monthly owner costs: $1,098 with a mortgage, $437 without a mortgage; Median gross rent: $713 per month; Rental vacancy rate: 4.5%
Vital Statistics: Birth rate: 105.7 per 10,000 population; Death rate: 105.8 per 10,000 population; Age-adjusted cancer mortality rate: 196.8 deaths per 100,000 population
Health Insurance: 93.3% have insurance; 68.8% have private insurance; 39.0% have public insurance; 6.7% do not have insurance; 2.8% of children under 18 do not have insurance
Health Care: Physicians: 24.5 per 10,000 population; Dentists: 5.4 per 10,000 population; Hospital beds: 63.9 per 10,000 population; Hospital admissions: 1,847.5 per 10,000 population
Transportation: Commute: 91.4% car, 2.0% public transportation, 3.3% walk, 2.3% work from home; Mean travel time to work: 19.5 minutes
2016 Presidential Election: 56.2% Trump, 38.5% Clinton, 4.0% Johnson, 1.3% Stein
Additional Information Contacts
Chemung Government . . . . (607) 737-2920
   http://www.chemungcounty.com

Chemung County Communities

ASHLAND (town). Covers a land area of 14.182 square miles and a water area of 0.355 square miles. Located at 42.02° N. Lat; 76.75° W. Long.
Population: 1,533; Growth (since 2000): -21.4%; Density: 108.1 persons per square mile; Race: 97.0% White, 0.4% Black/African American, 0.0% Asian, 0.1% American Indian/Alaska Native, 0.0% Native Hawaiian/Other Pacific Islander, 2.5% Two or more races, 0.6% Hispanic of any race; Average household size: 2.28; Median age: 43.0; Age under 18: 22.3%; Age 65 and over: 18.3%; Males per 100 females: 98.9; Marriage status: 27.4% never married, 55.8% now married, 3.0% separated, 7.7% widowed, 9.1% divorced; Foreign born: 1.9%; Speak English only: 97.3%; With disability: 11.4%; Veterans: 9.7%; Ancestry: 23.4% Irish, 21.3% American, 19.1% German, 10.0% English, 8.0% Italian
Employment: 9.1% management, business, and financial, 1.9% computer, engineering, and science, 6.3% education, legal, community service, arts, and media, 7.1% healthcare practitioners, 25.7% service, 16.0% sales and office, 9.2% natural resources, construction, and maintenance, 24.6% production, transportation, and material moving
Income: Per capita: $21,920; Median household: $38,750; Average household: $49,978; Households with income of $100,000 or more: 9.7%; Poverty rate: 22.3%
Educational Attainment: High school diploma or higher: 87.0%; Bachelor's degree or higher: 12.3%; Graduate/professional degree or higher: 6.4%
Housing: Homeownership rate: 86.0%; Median home value: $69,200; Median year structure built: 1969; Homeowner vacancy rate: 1.0%; Median selected monthly owner costs: $963 with a mortgage, $381 without a mortgage; Median gross rent: $675 per month; Rental vacancy rate: 21.7%

Health Insurance: 93.8% have insurance; 60.8% have private insurance; 53.2% have public insurance; 6.2% do not have insurance; 3.3% of children under 18 do not have insurance
Transportation: Commute: 94.8% car, 0.5% public transportation, 1.3% walk, 1.5% work from home; Mean travel time to work: 24.2 minutes

BALDWIN (town). Covers a land area of 25.716 square miles and a water area of 0.020 square miles. Located at 42.10° N. Lat; 76.66° W. Long.
Population: 799; Growth (since 2000): -6.3%; Density: 31.1 persons per square mile; Race: 98.1% White, 0.0% Black/African American, 0.4% Asian, 0.0% American Indian/Alaska Native, 0.0% Native Hawaiian/Other Pacific Islander, 1.5% Two or more races, 0.0% Hispanic of any race; Average household size: 2.15; Median age: 48.2; Age under 18: 15.3%; Age 65 and over: 19.8%; Males per 100 females: 108.5; Marriage status: 25.1% never married, 52.4% now married, 3.6% separated, 7.8% widowed, 14.7% divorced; Foreign born: 1.5%; Speak English only: 99.1%; With disability: 14.5%; Veterans: 11.7%; Ancestry: 24.9% Irish, 23.9% German, 13.1% American, 11.4% English, 7.5% Italian
Employment: 16.1% management, business, and financial, 2.4% computer, engineering, and science, 9.3% education, legal, community service, arts, and media, 4.6% healthcare practitioners, 18.6% service, 15.2% sales and office, 13.7% natural resources, construction, and maintenance, 20.0% production, transportation, and material moving
Income: Per capita: $29,174; Median household: $54,688; Average household: $63,560; Households with income of $100,000 or more: 15.3%; Poverty rate: 7.8%
Educational Attainment: High school diploma or higher: 90.5%; Bachelor's degree or higher: 9.5%; Graduate/professional degree or higher: 2.8%
Housing: Homeownership rate: 86.5%; Median home value: $88,600; Median year structure built: 1975; Homeowner vacancy rate: 0.0%; Median selected monthly owner costs: $988 with a mortgage, $459 without a mortgage; Median gross rent: $571 per month; Rental vacancy rate: 0.0%
Health Insurance: 94.0% have insurance; 81.2% have private insurance; 31.4% have public insurance; 6.0% do not have insurance; 5.7% of children under 18 do not have insurance
Transportation: Commute: 99.0% car, 0.0% public transportation, 0.0% walk, 1.0% work from home; Mean travel time to work: 22.7 minutes

BIG FLATS (CDP). Covers a land area of 16.300 square miles and a water area of 0.077 square miles. Located at 42.16° N. Lat; 76.91° W. Long. Elevation is 902 feet.
Population: 5,303; Growth (since 2000): 113.7%; Density: 325.3 persons per square mile; Race: 96.5% White, 0.5% Black/African American, 2.9% Asian, 0.0% American Indian/Alaska Native, 0.0% Native Hawaiian/Other Pacific Islander, 0.0% Two or more races, 1.4% Hispanic of any race; Average household size: 2.34; Median age: 44.8; Age under 18: 21.8%; Age 65 and over: 18.5%; Males per 100 females: 97.6; Marriage status: 23.9% never married, 56.8% now married, 1.2% separated, 7.6% widowed, 11.8% divorced; Foreign born: 3.4%; Speak English only: 96.0%; With disability: 9.4%; Veterans: 10.3%; Ancestry: 27.0% German, 23.0% Irish, 16.1% Italian, 15.4% English, 7.5% Polish
Employment: 20.2% management, business, and financial, 5.8% computer, engineering, and science, 14.1% education, legal, community service, arts, and media, 7.2% healthcare practitioners, 13.8% service, 20.9% sales and office, 9.4% natural resources, construction, and maintenance, 8.6% production, transportation, and material moving
Income: Per capita: $34,163; Median household: $65,269; Average household: $80,863; Households with income of $100,000 or more: 33.4%; Poverty rate: 5.5%
Educational Attainment: High school diploma or higher: 96.7%; Bachelor's degree or higher: 39.3%; Graduate/professional degree or higher: 19.2%
School District(s)
Horseheads Central SD (PK-12)
   2014-15 Enrollment: 4,156 . . . . (607) 739-5601
Housing: Homeownership rate: 86.1%; Median home value: $145,200; Median year structure built: 1970; Homeowner vacancy rate: 4.3%; Median selected monthly owner costs: $1,227 with a mortgage, $515 without a mortgage; Median gross rent: $924 per month; Rental vacancy rate: 0.0%
Health Insurance: 94.7% have insurance; 82.3% have private insurance; 27.2% have public insurance; 5.3% do not have insurance; 4.3% of children under 18 do not have insurance

Transportation: Commute: 94.6% car, 0.4% public transportation, 1.6% walk, 3.0% work from home; Mean travel time to work: 16.4 minutes

BIG FLATS (town). Covers a land area of 44.484 square miles and a water area of 0.581 square miles. Located at 42.14° N. Lat; 76.91° W. Long. Elevation is 902 feet.

Population: 7,793; Growth (since 2000): 7.9%; Density: 175.2 persons per square mile; Race: 96.7% White, 1.0% Black/African American, 2.0% Asian, 0.0% American Indian/Alaska Native, 0.0% Native Hawaiian/Other Pacific Islander, 0.2% Two or more races, 0.9% Hispanic of any race; Average household size: 2.32; Median age: 45.4; Age under 18: 21.6%; Age 65 and over: 17.1%; Males per 100 females: 97.9; Marriage status: 25.5% never married, 59.3% now married, 1.8% separated, 6.1% widowed, 9.1% divorced; Foreign born: 3.0%; Speak English only: 96.4%; With disability: 9.4%; Veterans: 10.3%; Ancestry: 23.8% German, 21.8% Irish, 15.3% English, 14.8% Italian, 8.4% American
Employment: 18.5% management, business, and financial, 5.6% computer, engineering, and science, 14.3% education, legal, community service, arts, and media, 6.7% healthcare practitioners, 14.5% service, 20.3% sales and office, 11.0% natural resources, construction, and maintenance, 9.1% production, transportation, and material moving
Income: Per capita: $35,348; Median household: $65,893; Average household: $82,905; Households with income of $100,000 or more: 30.3%; Poverty rate: 6.6%
Educational Attainment: High school diploma or higher: 95.4%; Bachelor's degree or higher: 37.9%; Graduate/professional degree or higher: 19.3%

School District(s)
Horseheads Central SD (PK-12)
    2014-15 Enrollment: 4,156 . . . . (607) 739-5601
Housing: Homeownership rate: 87.9%; Median home value: $145,800; Median year structure built: 1969; Homeowner vacancy rate: 2.9%; Median selected monthly owner costs: $1,300 with a mortgage, $499 without a mortgage; Median gross rent: $929 per month; Rental vacancy rate: 11.0%
Health Insurance: 95.5% have insurance; 83.1% have private insurance; 27.1% have public insurance; 4.5% do not have insurance; 3.0% of children under 18 do not have insurance
Transportation: Commute: 93.5% car, 1.0% public transportation, 1.1% walk, 4.0% work from home; Mean travel time to work: 17.6 minutes
Additional Information Contacts
Town of Big Flats. . . . . (607) 562-8443
    http://www.bigflatsny.gov/pmwiki.php

BREESPORT (CDP). Covers a land area of 1.628 square miles and a water area of 0.012 square miles. Located at 42.18° N. Lat; 76.74° W. Long. Elevation is 1,099 feet.

Population: 738; Growth (since 2000): n/a; Density: 453.2 persons per square mile; Race: 95.7% White, 0.0% Black/African American, 1.9% Asian, 0.0% American Indian/Alaska Native, 0.0% Native Hawaiian/Other Pacific Islander, 2.4% Two or more races, 0.0% Hispanic of any race; Average household size: 2.92; Median age: 34.4; Age under 18: 32.1%; Age 65 and over: 7.5%; Males per 100 females: 108.0; Marriage status: 12.0% never married, 67.6% now married, 3.1% separated, 9.9% widowed, 10.5% divorced; Foreign born: 0.0%; Speak English only: 97.8%; With disability: 8.1%; Veterans: 7.4%; Ancestry: 20.2% Italian, 19.2% English, 18.8% German, 12.6% Irish, 9.2% Polish
Employment: 4.2% management, business, and financial, 0.0% computer, engineering, and science, 19.8% education, legal, community service, arts, and media, 15.9% healthcare practitioners, 13.8% service, 18.0% sales and office, 18.6% natural resources, construction, and maintenance, 9.6% production, transportation, and material moving
Income: Per capita: $22,768; Median household: $57,750; Average household: $65,854; Households with income of $100,000 or more: 29.2%; Poverty rate: 4.3%
Educational Attainment: High school diploma or higher: 96.7%; Bachelor's degree or higher: 29.5%; Graduate/professional degree or higher: 6.8%
Housing: Homeownership rate: 100.0%; Median home value: $138,200; Median year structure built: 1973; Homeowner vacancy rate: 0.0%; Median selected monthly owner costs: $1,265 with a mortgage, $460 without a mortgage; Median gross rent: n/a per month; Rental vacancy rate: 0.0%
Health Insurance: 93.6% have insurance; 87.8% have private insurance; 26.4% have public insurance; 6.4% do not have insurance; 0.0% of children under 18 do not have insurance

Transportation: Commute: 100.0% car, 0.0% public transportation, 0.0% walk, 0.0% work from home; Mean travel time to work: 32.4 minutes

CATLIN (town). Covers a land area of 37.989 square miles and a water area of 0.027 square miles. Located at 42.23° N. Lat; 76.90° W. Long.

Population: 2,620; Growth (since 2000): -1.1%; Density: 69.0 persons per square mile; Race: 96.1% White, 2.0% Black/African American, 0.7% Asian, 0.2% American Indian/Alaska Native, 0.0% Native Hawaiian/Other Pacific Islander, 0.2% Two or more races, 1.6% Hispanic of any race; Average household size: 2.50; Median age: 41.0; Age under 18: 22.7%; Age 65 and over: 11.5%; Males per 100 females: 101.7; Marriage status: 21.7% never married, 65.2% now married, 4.0% separated, 5.2% widowed, 7.8% divorced; Foreign born: 1.6%; Speak English only: 97.7%; With disability: 9.1%; Veterans: 7.8%; Ancestry: 25.0% American, 23.6% German, 15.0% Irish, 12.3% English, 10.4% Italian
Employment: 7.5% management, business, and financial, 7.2% computer, engineering, and science, 8.1% education, legal, community service, arts, and media, 4.8% healthcare practitioners, 17.1% service, 24.1% sales and office, 9.2% natural resources, construction, and maintenance, 22.0% production, transportation, and material moving
Income: Per capita: $29,888; Median household: $59,918; Average household: $74,236; Households with income of $100,000 or more: 26.3%; Poverty rate: 10.6%
Educational Attainment: High school diploma or higher: 90.0%; Bachelor's degree or higher: 21.5%; Graduate/professional degree or higher: 9.1%
Housing: Homeownership rate: 88.8%; Median home value: $103,700; Median year structure built: 1970; Homeowner vacancy rate: 0.0%; Median selected monthly owner costs: $1,136 with a mortgage, $548 without a mortgage; Median gross rent: $631 per month; Rental vacancy rate: 0.0%
Health Insurance: 96.7% have insurance; 80.3% have private insurance; 26.8% have public insurance; 3.3% do not have insurance; 0.0% of children under 18 do not have insurance
Transportation: Commute: 97.0% car, 0.3% public transportation, 0.0% walk, 2.2% work from home; Mean travel time to work: 24.1 minutes

CHEMUNG (town). Covers a land area of 49.479 square miles and a water area of 0.562 square miles. Located at 42.06° N. Lat; 76.61° W. Long. Elevation is 846 feet.

Population: 2,551; Growth (since 2000): -4.3%; Density: 51.6 persons per square mile; Race: 98.3% White, 0.4% Black/African American, 0.3% Asian, 0.0% American Indian/Alaska Native, 0.0% Native Hawaiian/Other Pacific Islander, 1.0% Two or more races, 1.6% Hispanic of any race; Average household size: 2.55; Median age: 45.8; Age under 18: 18.9%; Age 65 and over: 16.3%; Males per 100 females: 98.8; Marriage status: 24.7% never married, 62.9% now married, 1.6% separated, 4.2% widowed, 8.2% divorced; Foreign born: 2.0%; Speak English only: 99.5%; With disability: 17.2%; Veterans: 11.4%; Ancestry: 19.9% German, 17.6% American, 11.4% Irish, 9.6% English, 9.5% Italian
Employment: 8.7% management, business, and financial, 2.2% computer, engineering, and science, 9.2% education, legal, community service, arts, and media, 6.6% healthcare practitioners, 22.2% service, 22.3% sales and office, 16.3% natural resources, construction, and maintenance, 12.3% production, transportation, and material moving
Income: Per capita: $24,587; Median household: $45,288; Average household: $62,672; Households with income of $100,000 or more: 20.5%; Poverty rate: 11.1%
Educational Attainment: High school diploma or higher: 90.9%; Bachelor's degree or higher: 15.3%; Graduate/professional degree or higher: 6.9%

School District(s)
Waverly Central SD (PK-12)
    2014-15 Enrollment: 1,671 . . . . (607) 565-2841
Housing: Homeownership rate: 87.8%; Median home value: $97,600; Median year structure built: 1968; Homeowner vacancy rate: 0.0%; Median selected monthly owner costs: $1,113 with a mortgage, $417 without a mortgage; Median gross rent: $769 per month; Rental vacancy rate: 0.0%
Health Insurance: 93.5% have insurance; 74.6% have private insurance; 34.3% have public insurance; 6.5% do not have insurance; 3.5% of children under 18 do not have insurance
Transportation: Commute: 92.8% car, 1.4% public transportation, 1.2% walk, 4.2% work from home; Mean travel time to work: 18.6 minutes
Additional Information Contacts
Town of Chemung. . . . . (607) 529-3532
    http://townofchemung.com

ELMIRA (city). County seat. Covers a land area of 7.249 square miles and a water area of 0.326 square miles. Located at 42.09° N. Lat; 76.81° W. Long. Elevation is 853 feet.

History: The Sullivan-Clinton Expedition entered the region of Elmira in 1779. Most of the early settlers were emigrants from Wyoming and Wilkes-Barre, Pennsylvania. In 1789 a famine struck the valley as the result of a frost. The only deaths that occurred resulted not from starvation but from overeating when food was finally obtained. The present name was adopted in 1828. According to local tradition, Nathan Teall, an early settler, had a daughter named Elmira, for whom her mother called in a shrill, far-reaching voice. When it was decided to adopt a new name, several people suggested the one they had heard so often when Elmira was a child.

Population: 28,817; Growth (since 2000): -6.9%; Density: 3,975.4 persons per square mile; Race: 77.7% White, 14.5% Black/African American, 0.5% Asian, 0.2% American Indian/Alaska Native, 0.0% Native Hawaiian/Other Pacific Islander, 6.3% Two or more races, 5.4% Hispanic of any race; Average household size: 2.36; Median age: 33.4; Age under 18: 24.0%; Age 65 and over: 11.4%; Males per 100 females: 102.4; Marriage status: 46.2% never married, 35.1% now married, 3.7% separated, 7.1% widowed, 11.7% divorced; Foreign born: 2.3%; Speak English only: 95.8%; With disability: 16.5%; Veterans: 6.8%; Ancestry: 17.2% Irish, 16.0% German, 15.5% American, 11.0% Italian, 7.3% English

Employment: 7.2% management, business, and financial, 3.1% computer, engineering, and science, 10.4% education, legal, community service, arts, and media, 6.2% healthcare practitioners, 27.0% service, 24.5% sales and office, 7.6% natural resources, construction, and maintenance, 14.0% production, transportation, and material moving

Income: Per capita: $16,326; Median household: $29,295; Average household: $43,762; Households with income of $100,000 or more: 7.8%; Poverty rate: 32.1%

Educational Attainment: High school diploma or higher: 82.8%; Bachelor's degree or higher: 14.0%; Graduate/professional degree or higher: 6.0%

School District(s)
Elmira City SD (PK-12)
    2014-15 Enrollment: 6,582 . . . . (607) 735-3010
Four-year College(s)
Elmira College (Private, Not-for-profit)
    Fall 2014 Enrollment: 1,482 . . . . (607) 735-1800
    2015-16 Tuition: In-state $39,950; Out-of-state $39,950
Two-year College(s)
Arnot Ogden Medical Center (Private, Not-for-profit)
    Fall 2014 Enrollment: 70 . . . . (607) 737-4153
Elmira Business Institute (Private, For-profit)
    Fall 2014 Enrollment: 400 . . . . (607) 733-7177
    2015-16 Tuition: In-state $20,780; Out-of-state $20,780
Vocational/Technical School(s)
Schuyler Steuben Chemung Tioga Allegany BOCES (Public)
    Fall 2014 Enrollment: 144 . . . . (607) 739-3581
    2015-16 Tuition: $11,595

Housing: Homeownership rate: 44.2%; Median home value: $68,800; Median year structure built: Before 1940; Homeowner vacancy rate: 1.8%; Median selected monthly owner costs: $926 with a mortgage, $427 without a mortgage; Median gross rent: $670 per month; Rental vacancy rate: 3.0%

Health Insurance: 91.3% have insurance; 47.9% have private insurance; 53.2% have public insurance; 8.7% do not have insurance; 3.9% of children under 18 do not have insurance

Hospitals: Arnot Ogden Medical Center (256 beds); Saint Joseph's Hospital (295 beds)

Safety: Violent crime rate: 29.5 per 10,000 population; Property crime rate: 306.1 per 10,000 population

Newspapers: Star-Gazette (daily circulation 26,300)

Transportation: Commute: 83.8% car, 5.8% public transportation, 7.2% walk, 2.1% work from home; Mean travel time to work: 18.5 minutes

Airports: Elmira/Corning Regional (primary service/non-hub)

Additional Information Contacts
City of Elmira . . . . (607) 737-5672
    http://www.cityofelmira.net

ELMIRA (town). Covers a land area of 22.212 square miles and a water area of 0.329 square miles. Located at 42.09° N. Lat; 76.78° W. Long. Elevation is 853 feet.

History: Formerly Newtown, renamed for Elmira Teall, an innkeeper's daughter. The Treaty of Painted Post, ending warfare between settlers and the Iroquois confederation, was signed here in 1791. Site of a Confederate prison camp in 1864-1865 and 3,000 Confederate prisoners are buried here. The well-known Elmira Correctional Facility (est. 1876) led the way in prison reform. Mark Twain spent many summers in Elmira and is buried here. Settled 1788, Incorporated 1864.

Population: 6,861; Growth (since 2000): -4.7%; Density: 308.9 persons per square mile; Race: 92.6% White, 2.1% Black/African American, 0.9% Asian, 0.3% American Indian/Alaska Native, 0.0% Native Hawaiian/Other Pacific Islander, 4.1% Two or more races, 0.0% Hispanic of any race; Average household size: 2.33; Median age: 46.4; Age under 18: 23.0%; Age 65 and over: 19.8%; Males per 100 females: 90.0; Marriage status: 21.5% never married, 62.6% now married, 1.6% separated, 8.6% widowed, 7.3% divorced; Foreign born: 3.3%; Speak English only: 97.6%; With disability: 9.2%; Veterans: 11.5%; Ancestry: 28.7% Irish, 18.8% Italian, 15.9% German, 11.1% English, 9.6% Polish

Employment: 17.9% management, business, and financial, 2.6% computer, engineering, and science, 18.9% education, legal, community service, arts, and media, 6.2% healthcare practitioners, 7.4% service, 29.8% sales and office, 5.4% natural resources, construction, and maintenance, 11.6% production, transportation, and material moving

Income: Per capita: $47,656; Median household: $76,613; Average household: $114,449; Households with income of $100,000 or more: 34.1%; Poverty rate: 3.4%

Educational Attainment: High school diploma or higher: 97.1%; Bachelor's degree or higher: 44.6%; Graduate/professional degree or higher: 21.4%

School District(s)
Elmira City SD (PK-12)
    2014-15 Enrollment: 6,582 . . . . (607) 735-3010
Four-year College(s)
Elmira College (Private, Not-for-profit)
    Fall 2014 Enrollment: 1,482 . . . . (607) 735-1800
    2015-16 Tuition: In-state $39,950; Out-of-state $39,950
Two-year College(s)
Arnot Ogden Medical Center (Private, Not-for-profit)
    Fall 2014 Enrollment: 70 . . . . (607) 737-4153
Elmira Business Institute (Private, For-profit)
    Fall 2014 Enrollment: 400 . . . . (607) 733-7177
    2015-16 Tuition: In-state $20,780; Out-of-state $20,780
Vocational/Technical School(s)
Schuyler Steuben Chemung Tioga Allegany BOCES (Public)
    Fall 2014 Enrollment: 144 . . . . (607) 739-3581
    2015-16 Tuition: $11,595

Housing: Homeownership rate: 85.1%; Median home value: $123,200; Median year structure built: 1950; Homeowner vacancy rate: 0.0%; Median selected monthly owner costs: $1,216 with a mortgage, $508 without a mortgage; Median gross rent: $975 per month; Rental vacancy rate: 0.0%

Health Insurance: 94.1% have insurance; 83.9% have private insurance; 26.9% have public insurance; 5.9% do not have insurance; 1.1% of children under 18 do not have insurance

Hospitals: Arnot Ogden Medical Center (256 beds); Saint Joseph's Hospital (295 beds)

Safety: Violent crime rate: 0.0 per 10,000 population; Property crime rate: 1.7 per 10,000 population

Newspapers: Star-Gazette (daily circulation 26,300)

Transportation: Commute: 93.3% car, 1.0% public transportation, 3.2% walk, 1.5% work from home; Mean travel time to work: 16.8 minutes

Airports: Elmira/Corning Regional (primary service/non-hub)

Additional Information Contacts
Town of Elmira . . . . (607) 734-2031
    http://www.townofelmira.com

ELMIRA HEIGHTS (village). Covers a land area of 1.146 square miles and a water area of 0 square miles. Located at 42.13° N. Lat; 76.83° W. Long. Elevation is 879 feet.

Population: 3,945; Growth (since 2000): -5.4%; Density: 3,441.1 persons per square mile; Race: 89.7% White, 2.7% Black/African American, 3.4% Asian, 0.6% American Indian/Alaska Native, 0.0% Native Hawaiian/Other Pacific Islander, 3.7% Two or more races, 0.0% Hispanic of any race; Average household size: 2.38; Median age: 33.1; Age under 18: 26.0%;

Age 65 and over: 14.7%; Males per 100 females: 93.3; Marriage status: 34.4% never married, 46.6% now married, 1.2% separated, 9.4% widowed, 9.6% divorced; Foreign born: 1.6%; Speak English only: 96.2%; With disability: 12.9%; Veterans: 12.5%; Ancestry: 20.5% Irish, 15.2% German, 14.3% Italian, 10.7% American, 8.2% English

Employment: 7.1% management, business, and financial, 5.1% computer, engineering, and science, 12.9% education, legal, community service, arts, and media, 3.7% healthcare practitioners, 24.8% service, 24.7% sales and office, 4.3% natural resources, construction, and maintenance, 17.4% production, transportation, and material moving

Income: Per capita: $20,779; Median household: $41,299; Average household: $49,870; Households with income of $100,000 or more: 8.2%; Poverty rate: 12.4%

Educational Attainment: High school diploma or higher: 89.7%; Bachelor's degree or higher: 14.4%; Graduate/professional degree or higher: 5.9%

School District(s)

Elmira Heights Central SD (PK-12)

   2014-15 Enrollment: 1,081 . . . . (607) 734-7114

Housing: Homeownership rate: 53.5%; Median home value: $77,000; Median year structure built: 1943; Homeowner vacancy rate: 0.0%; Median selected monthly owner costs: $956 with a mortgage, $503 without a mortgage; Median gross rent: $630 per month; Rental vacancy rate: 0.0%

Health Insurance: 95.6% have insurance; 68.8% have private insurance; 40.3% have public insurance; 4.4% do not have insurance; 0.0% of children under 18 do not have insurance

Safety: Violent crime rate: 7.5 per 10,000 population; Property crime rate: 150.5 per 10,000 population

Transportation: Commute: 89.1% car, 2.1% public transportation, 4.4% walk, 1.7% work from home; Mean travel time to work: 18.1 minutes

Additional Information Contacts

Village of Elmira Heights . . . . (607) 734-7156

  http://www.elmiraheights.org

ERIN (CDP). Covers a land area of 0.747 square miles and a water area of 0.010 square miles. Located at 42.18° N. Lat; 76.67° W. Long. Elevation is 1,263 feet.

Population: 357; Growth (since 2000): n/a; Density: 477.7 persons per square mile; Race: 96.1% White, 2.0% Black/African American, 0.0% Asian, 0.8% American Indian/Alaska Native, 0.0% Native Hawaiian/Other Pacific Islander, 1.1% Two or more races, 0.0% Hispanic of any race; Average household size: 1.96; Median age: 47.9; Age under 18: 10.9%; Age 65 and over: 12.9%; Males per 100 females: 104.7; Marriage status: 25.5% never married, 52.5% now married, 8.0% separated, 8.0% widowed, 13.9% divorced; Foreign born: 0.0%; Speak English only: 100.0%; With disability: 23.8%; Veterans: 18.9%; Ancestry: 31.1% American, 30.0% German, 20.7% Irish, 15.4% Dutch, 3.9% English

Employment: 5.9% management, business, and financial, 0.0% computer, engineering, and science, 8.9% education, legal, community service, arts, and media, 2.4% healthcare practitioners, 23.1% service, 23.7% sales and office, 17.8% natural resources, construction, and maintenance, 18.3% production, transportation, and material moving

Income: Per capita: $19,684; Median household: $32,292; Average household: $38,527; Households with income of $100,000 or more: 2.2%; Poverty rate: 12.3%

Educational Attainment: High school diploma or higher: 89.7%; Bachelor's degree or higher: 6.6%; Graduate/professional degree or higher: 1.0%

Housing: Homeownership rate: 100.0%; Median home value: $50,000; Median year structure built: 1980; Homeowner vacancy rate: 0.0%; Median selected monthly owner costs: $1,034 with a mortgage, $253 without a mortgage; Median gross rent: n/a per month; Rental vacancy rate: 0.0%

Health Insurance: 83.5% have insurance; 57.4% have private insurance; 42.6% have public insurance; 16.5% do not have insurance; 0.0% of children under 18 do not have insurance

Transportation: Commute: 97.6% car, 0.0% public transportation, 0.0% walk, 0.0% work from home; Mean travel time to work: 25.1 minutes

ERIN (town). Covers a land area of 44.247 square miles and a water area of 0.221 square miles. Located at 42.18° N. Lat; 76.67° W. Long. Elevation is 1,263 feet.

Population: 2,014; Growth (since 2000): -1.9%; Density: 45.5 persons per square mile; Race: 98.4% White, 0.3% Black/African American, 0.0% Asian, 0.5% American Indian/Alaska Native, 0.0% Native Hawaiian/Other Pacific Islander, 0.7% Two or more races, 3.8% Hispanic of any race;

Average household size: 2.46; Median age: 43.2; Age under 18: 21.9%; Age 65 and over: 13.2%; Males per 100 females: 106.5; Marriage status: 23.0% never married, 59.7% now married, 1.8% separated, 4.1% widowed, 13.1% divorced; Foreign born: 1.0%; Speak English only: 98.5%; With disability: 12.2%; Veterans: 12.3%; Ancestry: 22.3% American, 21.7% German, 18.1% Irish, 10.8% English, 7.1% Italian

Employment: 10.8% management, business, and financial, 3.5% computer, engineering, and science, 9.5% education, legal, community service, arts, and media, 5.0% healthcare practitioners, 21.0% service, 20.7% sales and office, 10.3% natural resources, construction, and maintenance, 19.2% production, transportation, and material moving

Income: Per capita: $25,661; Median household: $54,605; Average household: $62,513; Households with income of $100,000 or more: 18.5%; Poverty rate: 9.4%

Educational Attainment: High school diploma or higher: 91.3%; Bachelor's degree or higher: 15.4%; Graduate/professional degree or higher: 6.0%

Housing: Homeownership rate: 93.5%; Median home value: $90,200; Median year structure built: 1978; Homeowner vacancy rate: 2.4%; Median selected monthly owner costs: $1,215 with a mortgage, $352 without a mortgage; Median gross rent: $820 per month; Rental vacancy rate: 0.0%

Health Insurance: 92.7% have insurance; 78.4% have private insurance; 26.9% have public insurance; 7.3% do not have insurance; 1.6% of children under 18 do not have insurance

Transportation: Commute: 96.5% car, 0.0% public transportation, 0.0% walk, 2.4% work from home; Mean travel time to work: 24.6 minutes

HORSEHEADS (town). Covers a land area of 35.606 square miles and a water area of 0.314 square miles. Located at 42.16° N. Lat; 76.78° W. Long. Elevation is 896 feet.

History: Settled 1789, incorporated 1837.

Population: 19,630; Growth (since 2000): 0.4%; Density: 551.3 persons per square mile; Race: 92.2% White, 1.6% Black/African American, 4.3% Asian, 0.1% American Indian/Alaska Native, 0.0% Native Hawaiian/Other Pacific Islander, 1.8% Two or more races, 1.7% Hispanic of any race; Average household size: 2.35; Median age: 43.1; Age under 18: 22.0%; Age 65 and over: 20.6%; Males per 100 females: 90.3; Marriage status: 25.0% never married, 56.1% now married, 2.0% separated, 9.2% widowed, 9.7% divorced; Foreign born: 4.5%; Speak English only: 93.6%; With disability: 12.5%; Veterans: 10.5%; Ancestry: 17.0% German, 16.7% Irish, 13.5% Italian, 12.0% English, 10.6% American

Employment: 13.0% management, business, and financial, 3.9% computer, engineering, and science, 14.0% education, legal, community service, arts, and media, 9.0% healthcare practitioners, 18.5% service, 21.6% sales and office, 8.1% natural resources, construction, and maintenance, 12.0% production, transportation, and material moving

Income: Per capita: $29,439; Median household: $55,885; Average household: $70,265; Households with income of $100,000 or more: 23.3%; Poverty rate: 8.7%

Educational Attainment: High school diploma or higher: 93.6%; Bachelor's degree or higher: 29.2%; Graduate/professional degree or higher: 12.9%

School District(s)

Horseheads Central SD (PK-12)

   2014-15 Enrollment: 4,156 . . . . (607) 739-5601

Housing: Homeownership rate: 69.2%; Median home value: $116,100; Median year structure built: 1960; Homeowner vacancy rate: 1.3%; Median selected monthly owner costs: $1,186 with a mortgage, $427 without a mortgage; Median gross rent: $805 per month; Rental vacancy rate: 5.1%

Health Insurance: 94.9% have insurance; 78.3% have private insurance; 33.8% have public insurance; 5.1% do not have insurance; 1.9% of children under 18 do not have insurance

Transportation: Commute: 93.6% car, 0.7% public transportation, 2.2% walk, 2.5% work from home; Mean travel time to work: 18.6 minutes

Additional Information Contacts

Town of Horseheads . . . . (607) 739-8783

  http://townofhorseheads.org

HORSEHEADS (village). Covers a land area of 3.887 square miles and a water area of 0.015 square miles. Located at 42.17° N. Lat; 76.83° W. Long. Elevation is 896 feet.

Population: 6,594; Growth (since 2000): 2.2%; Density: 1,696.4 persons per square mile; Race: 93.2% White, 1.1% Black/African American, 3.2% Asian, 0.2% American Indian/Alaska Native, 0.0% Native Hawaiian/Other Pacific Islander, 2.3% Two or more races, 2.3% Hispanic of any race;

Average household size: 2.17; Median age: 42.1; Age under 18: 21.6%; Age 65 and over: 24.1%; Males per 100 females: 82.8; Marriage status: 28.5% never married, 50.6% now married, 2.7% separated, 10.8% widowed, 10.1% divorced; Foreign born: 5.1%; Speak English only: 93.8%; With disability: 13.5%; Veterans: 10.6%; Ancestry: 18.5% Irish, 17.8% German, 15.3% English, 13.8% American, 12.1% Italian

Employment: 17.1% management, business, and financial, 4.4% computer, engineering, and science, 15.4% education, legal, community service, arts, and media, 9.7% healthcare practitioners, 17.7% service, 21.5% sales and office, 7.5% natural resources, construction, and maintenance, 6.9% production, transportation, and material moving

Income: Per capita: $28,992; Median household: $53,435; Average household: $63,673; Households with income of $100,000 or more: 18.3%; Poverty rate: 9.6%

Educational Attainment: High school diploma or higher: 93.8%; Bachelor's degree or higher: 28.9%; Graduate/professional degree or higher: 11.7%

School District(s)

Horseheads Central SD (PK-12)

2014-15 Enrollment: 4,156 . . . . (607) 739-5601

Housing: Homeownership rate: 58.7%; Median home value: $102,700; Median year structure built: 1957; Homeowner vacancy rate: 1.0%; Median selected monthly owner costs: $1,007 with a mortgage, $406 without a mortgage; Median gross rent: $839 per month; Rental vacancy rate: 3.5%

Health Insurance: 94.4% have insurance; 75.0% have private insurance; 40.1% have public insurance; 5.6% do not have insurance; 2.9% of children under 18 do not have insurance

Safety: Violent crime rate: 0.0 per 10,000 population; Property crime rate: 132.2 per 10,000 population

Transportation: Commute: 94.2% car, 0.7% public transportation, 3.8% walk, 0.9% work from home; Mean travel time to work: 16.3 minutes

Additional Information Contacts

Village of Horseheads . . . . (607) 739-5691
   http://www.horseheads.org

HORSEHEADS NORTH (CDP). Covers a land area of 2.211 square miles and a water area of 0.029 square miles. Located at 42.20° N. Lat; 76.80° W. Long.

Population: 2,755; Growth (since 2000): -3.4%; Density: 1,245.8 persons per square mile; Race: 97.4% White, 0.5% Black/African American, 2.1% Asian, 0.0% American Indian/Alaska Native, 0.0% Native Hawaiian/Other Pacific Islander, 0.0% Two or more races, 6.0% Hispanic of any race; Average household size: 2.47; Median age: 41.0; Age under 18: 18.1%; Age 65 and over: 15.6%; Males per 100 females: 89.3; Marriage status: 23.7% never married, 67.0% now married, 1.8% separated, 3.3% widowed, 6.0% divorced; Foreign born: 2.9%; Speak English only: 94.8%; With disability: 11.9%; Veterans: 11.1%; Ancestry: 20.4% German, 19.2% Irish, 14.3% Polish, 10.7% Italian, 9.9% American

Employment: 17.9% management, business, and financial, 5.0% computer, engineering, and science, 14.6% education, legal, community service, arts, and media, 4.7% healthcare practitioners, 16.5% service, 17.9% sales and office, 11.8% natural resources, construction, and maintenance, 11.6% production, transportation, and material moving

Income: Per capita: $34,197; Median household: $72,313; Average household: $83,812; Households with income of $100,000 or more: 35.6%; Poverty rate: 5.0%

Educational Attainment: High school diploma or higher: 99.2%; Bachelor's degree or higher: 36.4%; Graduate/professional degree or higher: 13.6%

Housing: Homeownership rate: 82.5%; Median home value: $146,200; Median year structure built: 1967; Homeowner vacancy rate: 3.9%; Median selected monthly owner costs: $1,414 with a mortgage, $456 without a mortgage; Median gross rent: $1,029 per month; Rental vacancy rate: 0.0%

Health Insurance: 97.9% have insurance; 87.5% have private insurance; 27.1% have public insurance; 2.1% do not have insurance; 0.0% of children under 18 do not have insurance

Transportation: Commute: 97.8% car, 0.0% public transportation, 0.0% walk, 2.2% work from home; Mean travel time to work: 18.0 minutes

LOWMAN (unincorporated postal area)
ZCTA: 14861
   Covers a land area of 34.223 square miles and a water area of 0.261 square miles. Located at 42.09° N. Lat; 76.69° W. Long. Elevation is 840 feet.

Population: 1,294; Growth (since 2000): -11.3%; Density: 37.8 persons per square mile; Race: 99.7% White, 0.0% Black/African American, 0.0% Asian, 0.0% American Indian/Alaska Native, 0.0% Native Hawaiian/Other Pacific Islander, 0.3% Two or more races, 0.0% Hispanic of any race; Average household size: 2.20; Median age: 49.2; Age under 18: 15.5%; Age 65 and over: 20.1%; Males per 100 females: 100.6; Marriage status: 23.2% never married, 56.3% now married, 4.3% separated, 7.4% widowed, 13.1% divorced; Foreign born: 1.0%; Speak English only: 99.1%; With disability: 12.7%; Veterans: 13.2%; Ancestry: 22.3% American, 17.5% Irish, 14.6% German, 10.0% English, 6.3% Italian

Employment: 15.6% management, business, and financial, 1.9% computer, engineering, and science, 8.9% education, legal, community service, arts, and media, 5.2% healthcare practitioners, 23.8% service, 15.2% sales and office, 12.0% natural resources, construction, and maintenance, 17.3% production, transportation, and material moving

Income: Per capita: $28,449; Median household: $49,688; Average household: $62,472; Households with income of $100,000 or more: 17.4%; Poverty rate: 12.3%

Educational Attainment: High school diploma or higher: 89.8%; Bachelor's degree or higher: 12.3%; Graduate/professional degree or higher: 7.1%

Housing: Homeownership rate: 87.9%; Median home value: $87,100; Median year structure built: 1974; Homeowner vacancy rate: 1.9%; Median selected monthly owner costs: $1,121 with a mortgage, $388 without a mortgage; Median gross rent: $802 per month; Rental vacancy rate: 0.0%

Health Insurance: 94.9% have insurance; 80.4% have private insurance; 31.1% have public insurance; 5.1% do not have insurance; 2.5% of children under 18 do not have insurance

Transportation: Commute: 94.6% car, 0.0% public transportation, 0.0% walk, 5.4% work from home; Mean travel time to work: 21.3 minutes

MILLPORT (village). Covers a land area of 0.348 square miles and a water area of 0 square miles. Located at 42.27° N. Lat; 76.84° W. Long. Elevation is 718 feet.

Population: 355; Growth (since 2000): 19.5%; Density: 1,020.0 persons per square mile; Race: 94.9% White, 0.0% Black/African American, 0.0% Asian, 0.0% American Indian/Alaska Native, 0.0% Native Hawaiian/Other Pacific Islander, 5.1% Two or more races, 0.6% Hispanic of any race; Average household size: 2.82; Median age: 34.1; Age under 18: 20.0%; Age 65 and over: 10.7%; Males per 100 females: 98.7; Marriage status: 36.8% never married, 41.6% now married, 4.1% separated, 6.2% widowed, 15.5% divorced; Foreign born: 0.8%; Speak English only: 98.5%; With disability: 12.1%; Veterans: 9.9%; Ancestry: 22.0% German, 20.6% Irish, 18.3% English, 17.7% American, 10.4% Italian

Employment: 2.8% management, business, and financial, 4.2% computer, engineering, and science, 14.6% education, legal, community service, arts, and media, 2.1% healthcare practitioners, 31.9% service, 16.7% sales and office, 4.9% natural resources, construction, and maintenance, 22.9% production, transportation, and material moving

Income: Per capita: $17,850; Median household: $45,000; Average household: $51,033; Households with income of $100,000 or more: 7.1%; Poverty rate: 19.0%

Educational Attainment: High school diploma or higher: 84.3%; Bachelor's degree or higher: 6.8%; Graduate/professional degree or higher: 4.7%

Housing: Homeownership rate: 84.1%; Median home value: $66,000; Median year structure built: Before 1940; Homeowner vacancy rate: 4.5%; Median selected monthly owner costs: $1,013 with a mortgage, $350 without a mortgage; Median gross rent: $850 per month; Rental vacancy rate: 0.0%

Health Insurance: 89.0% have insurance; 49.0% have private insurance; 48.7% have public insurance; 11.0% do not have insurance; 5.6% of children under 18 do not have insurance

Transportation: Commute: 93.8% car, 0.0% public transportation, 1.4% walk, 4.2% work from home; Mean travel time to work: 25.5 minutes

PINE CITY (unincorporated postal area)
ZCTA: 14871
   Covers a land area of 57.175 square miles and a water area of 0.499 square miles. Located at 42.04° N. Lat; 76.91° W. Long. Elevation is 1,001 feet.

Population: 5,474; Growth (since 2000): 11.5%; Density: 95.7 persons per square mile; Race: 93.1% White, 6.2% Black/African American,

0.1% Asian, 0.2% American Indian/Alaska Native, 0.0% Native Hawaiian/Other Pacific Islander, 0.2% Two or more races, 2.6% Hispanic of any race; Average household size: 2.32; Median age: 47.9; Age under 18: 17.5%; Age 65 and over: 19.8%; Males per 100 females: 131.8; Marriage status: 24.8% never married, 59.2% now married, 2.5% separated, 7.8% widowed, 8.2% divorced; Foreign born: 1.1%; Speak English only: 98.7%; With disability: 10.5%; Veterans: 10.5%; Ancestry: 16.9% English, 16.8% Irish, 15.0% German, 13.2% American, 9.1% Italian

Employment: 9.4% management, business, and financial, 3.9% computer, engineering, and science, 11.3% education, legal, community service, arts, and media, 6.7% healthcare practitioners, 21.4% service, 22.9% sales and office, 9.9% natural resources, construction, and maintenance, 14.4% production, transportation, and material moving

Income: Per capita: $26,885; Median household: $62,212; Average household: $69,404; Households with income of $100,000 or more: 22.1%; Poverty rate: 4.1%

Educational Attainment: High school diploma or higher: 88.1%; Bachelor's degree or higher: 20.8%; Graduate/professional degree or higher: 11.2%

School District(s)

Elmira City SD (PK-12)

   2014-15 Enrollment: 6,582 . . . . (607) 735-3010

Housing: Homeownership rate: 88.1%; Median home value: $123,600; Median year structure built: 1957; Homeowner vacancy rate: 0.0%; Median selected monthly owner costs: $1,177 with a mortgage, $404 without a mortgage; Median gross rent: $776 per month; Rental vacancy rate: 0.0%

Health Insurance: 98.5% have insurance; 85.9% have private insurance; 32.2% have public insurance; 1.5% do not have insurance; 0.0% of children under 18 do not have insurance

Transportation: Commute: 97.9% car, 0.0% public transportation, 0.0% walk, 1.2% work from home; Mean travel time to work: 23.3 minutes

PINE VALLEY (CDP).

Covers a land area of 1.204 square miles and a water area of 0.014 square miles. Located at 42.23° N. Lat; 76.85° W. Long. Elevation is 932 feet.

Population: 774; Growth (since 2000): n/a; Density: 642.7 persons per square mile; Race: 94.7% White, 5.3% Black/African American, 0.0% Asian, 0.0% American Indian/Alaska Native, 0.0% Native Hawaiian/Other Pacific Islander, 0.0% Two or more races, 0.8% Hispanic of any race; Average household size: 2.06; Median age: 48.1; Age under 18: 10.3%; Age 65 and over: 13.4%; Males per 100 females: 96.9; Marriage status: 21.3% never married, 60.8% now married, 3.7% separated, 3.7% widowed, 14.2% divorced; Foreign born: 7.2%; Speak English only: 100.0%; With disability: 14.0%; Veterans: 9.8%; Ancestry: 26.2% German, 18.5% American, 17.8% Italian, 15.2% English, 11.9% Irish

Employment: 9.9% management, business, and financial, 1.2% computer, engineering, and science, 0.0% education, legal, community service, arts, and media, 8.5% healthcare practitioners, 10.8% service, 19.5% sales and office, 19.8% natural resources, construction, and maintenance, 30.4% production, transportation, and material moving

Income: Per capita: $27,128; Median household: $50,583; Average household: $55,724; Households with income of $100,000 or more: 18.6%; Poverty rate: 25.3%

Educational Attainment: High school diploma or higher: 84.7%; Bachelor's degree or higher: 12.9%; Graduate/professional degree or higher: n/a

Housing: Homeownership rate: 78.7%; Median home value: $108,300; Median year structure built: 1972; Homeowner vacancy rate: 0.0%; Median selected monthly owner costs: $1,114 with a mortgage, $398 without a mortgage; Median gross rent: $636 per month; Rental vacancy rate: 0.0%

Health Insurance: 99.1% have insurance; 83.1% have private insurance; 29.7% have public insurance; 0.9% do not have insurance; 0.0% of children under 18 do not have insurance

Transportation: Commute: 97.1% car, 0.0% public transportation, 0.0% walk, 0.0% work from home; Mean travel time to work: 22.5 minutes

SOUTHPORT (CDP).

Covers a land area of 6.377 square miles and a water area of 0.239 square miles. Located at 42.06° N. Lat; 76.82° W. Long. Elevation is 889 feet.

History: Southport is a town in Chemung County, New York, first settled around 1788. The town of Southport was formed from the town of Elmira in 1822.

Population: 7,001; Growth (since 2000): -5.3%; Density: 1,097.9 persons per square mile; Race: 90.1% White, 0.8% Black/African American, 0.5% Asian, 3.9% American Indian/Alaska Native, 0.0% Native Hawaiian/Other Pacific Islander, 4.6% Two or more races, 3.5% Hispanic of any race; Average household size: 2.10; Median age: 48.3; Age under 18: 18.4%; Age 65 and over: 20.2%; Males per 100 females: 93.4; Marriage status: 26.2% never married, 52.6% now married, 3.3% separated, 7.7% widowed, 13.5% divorced; Foreign born: 0.6%; Speak English only: 98.9%; With disability: 19.0%; Veterans: 13.2%; Ancestry: 22.6% Irish, 15.8% American, 15.1% German, 15.0% English, 10.0% Italian

Employment: 7.6% management, business, and financial, 3.1% computer, engineering, and science, 5.1% education, legal, community service, arts, and media, 6.2% healthcare practitioners, 33.1% service, 24.4% sales and office, 4.7% natural resources, construction, and maintenance, 15.8% production, transportation, and material moving

Income: Per capita: $25,192; Median household: $42,287; Average household: $53,322; Households with income of $100,000 or more: 9.6%; Poverty rate: 16.0%

Educational Attainment: High school diploma or higher: 88.2%; Bachelor's degree or higher: 11.2%; Graduate/professional degree or higher: 3.2%

Housing: Homeownership rate: 70.2%; Median home value: $76,100; Median year structure built: 1949; Homeowner vacancy rate: 0.0%; Median selected monthly owner costs: $868 with a mortgage, $373 without a mortgage; Median gross rent: $725 per month; Rental vacancy rate: 11.0%

Health Insurance: 89.3% have insurance; 63.5% have private insurance; 43.1% have public insurance; 10.7% do not have insurance; 5.2% of children under 18 do not have insurance

Transportation: Commute: 92.3% car, 1.1% public transportation, 4.1% walk, 1.6% work from home; Mean travel time to work: 19.3 minutes

SOUTHPORT (town).

Covers a land area of 46.414 square miles and a water area of 0.426 square miles. Located at 42.05° N. Lat; 76.88° W. Long. Elevation is 889 feet.

Population: 10,726; Growth (since 2000): -4.1%; Density: 231.1 persons per square mile; Race: 90.1% White, 3.7% Black/African American, 0.3% Asian, 2.7% American Indian/Alaska Native, 0.0% Native Hawaiian/Other Pacific Islander, 3.1% Two or more races, 3.6% Hispanic of any race; Average household size: 2.24; Median age: 47.2; Age under 18: 18.1%; Age 65 and over: 19.1%; Males per 100 females: 111.5; Marriage status: 27.0% never married, 54.3% now married, 2.9% separated, 7.1% widowed, 11.6% divorced; Foreign born: 0.9%; Speak English only: 98.7%; With disability: 15.8%; Veterans: 11.7%; Ancestry: 20.1% Irish, 16.6% German, 15.6% English, 14.2% American, 9.4% Italian

Employment: 8.1% management, business, and financial, 3.3% computer, engineering, and science, 7.4% education, legal, community service, arts, and media, 6.3% healthcare practitioners, 29.3% service, 23.9% sales and office, 5.5% natural resources, construction, and maintenance, 16.3% production, transportation, and material moving

Income: Per capita: $25,171; Median household: $50,426; Average household: $59,623; Households with income of $100,000 or more: 15.1%; Poverty rate: 11.5%

Educational Attainment: High school diploma or higher: 88.3%; Bachelor's degree or higher: 16.2%; Graduate/professional degree or higher: 6.9%

Housing: Homeownership rate: 75.9%; Median home value: $87,600; Median year structure built: 1951; Homeowner vacancy rate: 0.0%; Median selected monthly owner costs: $972 with a mortgage, $387 without a mortgage; Median gross rent: $744 per month; Rental vacancy rate: 10.1%

Health Insurance: 92.0% have insurance; 71.9% have private insurance; 38.1% have public insurance; 8.0% do not have insurance; 3.5% of children under 18 do not have insurance

Transportation: Commute: 94.2% car, 0.7% public transportation, 2.8% walk, 1.3% work from home; Mean travel time to work: 19.8 minutes

Additional Information Contacts

Town of Southport . . . . (607) 734-1548
  http://www.townofsouthport.com

VAN ETTEN (town).

Covers a land area of 41.446 square miles and a water area of 0.124 square miles. Located at 42.23° N. Lat; 76.58° W. Long. Elevation is 1,017 feet.

Population: 1,628; Growth (since 2000): 7.2%; Density: 39.3 persons per square mile; Race: 98.3% White, 0.4% Black/African American, 0.0% Asian, 0.0% American Indian/Alaska Native, 0.0% Native Hawaiian/Other Pacific Islander, 1.1% Two or more races, 0.4% Hispanic of any race;

Average household size: 2.51; Median age: 45.4; Age under 18: 21.3%; Age 65 and over: 16.7%; Males per 100 females: 99.4; Marriage status: 24.1% never married, 56.8% now married, 2.2% separated, 7.0% widowed, 12.1% divorced; Foreign born: 1.0%; Speak English only: 97.2%; With disability: 14.1%; Veterans: 11.8%; Ancestry: 22.5% German, 16.5% Irish, 16.2% American, 11.3% English, 8.0% Italian
Employment: 13.4% management, business, and financial, 5.7% computer, engineering, and science, 9.5% education, legal, community service, arts, and media, 1.8% healthcare practitioners, 17.1% service, 19.8% sales and office, 11.7% natural resources, construction, and maintenance, 20.9% production, transportation, and material moving
Income: Per capita: $24,800; Median household: $50,625; Average household: $61,497; Households with income of $100,000 or more: 15.5%; Poverty rate: 13.5%
Educational Attainment: High school diploma or higher: 88.3%; Bachelor's degree or higher: 18.2%; Graduate/professional degree or higher: 5.9%

School District(s)
Spencer-Van Etten Central SD (PK-12)
   2014-15 Enrollment: 924 . . . . (607) 589-7100
Housing: Homeownership rate: 82.7%; Median home value: $98,800; Median year structure built: 1965; Homeowner vacancy rate: 0.6%; Median selected monthly owner costs: $1,179 with a mortgage, $462 without a mortgage; Median gross rent: $744 per month; Rental vacancy rate: 0.0%
Health Insurance: 91.4% have insurance; 63.7% have private insurance; 40.3% have public insurance; 8.6% do not have insurance; 1.7% of children under 18 do not have insurance
Transportation: Commute: 92.3% car, 0.5% public transportation, 3.9% walk, 2.3% work from home; Mean travel time to work: 29.9 minutes

VAN ETTEN (village). Covers a land area of 0.869 square miles and a water area of <.001 square miles. Located at 42.20° N. Lat; 76.55° W. Long. Elevation is 1,017 feet.
Population: 602; Growth (since 2000): 3.6%; Density: 692.5 persons per square mile; Race: 97.5% White, 0.7% Black/African American, 0.0% Asian, 0.0% American Indian/Alaska Native, 0.0% Native Hawaiian/Other Pacific Islander, 1.3% Two or more races, 1.2% Hispanic of any race; Average household size: 2.54; Median age: 37.7; Age under 18: 24.9%; Age 65 and over: 11.3%; Males per 100 females: 96.7; Marriage status: 31.3% never married, 47.8% now married, 2.9% separated, 4.1% widowed, 16.8% divorced; Foreign born: 0.5%; Speak English only: 98.9%; With disability: 16.1%; Veterans: 12.6%; Ancestry: 28.9% German, 21.9% Irish, 14.0% American, 12.3% English, 11.5% Italian
Employment: 16.2% management, business, and financial, 3.6% computer, engineering, and science, 10.8% education, legal, community service, arts, and media, 4.0% healthcare practitioners, 15.5% service, 21.6% sales and office, 14.0% natural resources, construction, and maintenance, 14.4% production, transportation, and material moving
Income: Per capita: $25,100; Median household: $49,875; Average household: $62,895; Households with income of $100,000 or more: 14.7%; Poverty rate: 14.5%
Educational Attainment: High school diploma or higher: 89.0%; Bachelor's degree or higher: 17.8%; Graduate/professional degree or higher: 2.9%

School District(s)
Spencer-Van Etten Central SD (PK-12)
   2014-15 Enrollment: 924 . . . . (607) 589-7100
Housing: Homeownership rate: 73.0%; Median home value: $90,800; Median year structure built: Before 1940; Homeowner vacancy rate: 1.7%; Median selected monthly owner costs: $1,250 with a mortgage, $523 without a mortgage; Median gross rent: $740 per month; Rental vacancy rate: 0.0%
Health Insurance: 92.0% have insurance; 66.9% have private insurance; 38.5% have public insurance; 8.0% do not have insurance; 4.0% of children under 18 do not have insurance
Transportation: Commute: 96.0% car, 0.0% public transportation, 3.3% walk, 0.7% work from home; Mean travel time to work: 26.7 minutes

VETERAN (town). Covers a land area of 38.327 square miles and a water area of 0.143 square miles. Located at 42.25° N. Lat; 76.79° W. Long.
Population: 3,295; Growth (since 2000): 0.7%; Density: 86.0 persons per square mile; Race: 96.2% White, 0.2% Black/African American, 2.3% Asian, 0.0% American Indian/Alaska Native, 0.0% Native Hawaiian/Other Pacific Islander, 1.3% Two or more races, 0.1% Hispanic of any race;

Average household size: 2.48; Median age: 49.8; Age under 18: 19.2%; Age 65 and over: 19.4%; Males per 100 females: 95.5; Marriage status: 19.0% never married, 68.7% now married, 1.6% separated, 4.9% widowed, 7.4% divorced; Foreign born: 4.4%; Speak English only: 98.7%; With disability: 11.1%; Veterans: 9.8%; Ancestry: 26.6% German, 18.8% English, 11.7% Italian, 11.1% Irish, 9.9% American
Employment: 13.3% management, business, and financial, 12.1% computer, engineering, and science, 13.6% education, legal, community service, arts, and media, 8.1% healthcare practitioners, 8.7% service, 21.3% sales and office, 7.4% natural resources, construction, and maintenance, 15.6% production, transportation, and material moving
Income: Per capita: $32,565; Median household: $68,365; Average household: $81,387; Households with income of $100,000 or more: 34.2%; Poverty rate: 8.0%
Educational Attainment: High school diploma or higher: 93.9%; Bachelor's degree or higher: 30.9%; Graduate/professional degree or higher: 16.5%
Housing: Homeownership rate: 91.9%; Median home value: $130,700; Median year structure built: 1972; Homeowner vacancy rate: 0.4%; Median selected monthly owner costs: $1,203 with a mortgage, $525 without a mortgage; Median gross rent: $675 per month; Rental vacancy rate: 0.0%
Health Insurance: 95.1% have insurance; 85.7% have private insurance; 29.9% have public insurance; 4.9% do not have insurance; 3.2% of children under 18 do not have insurance
Transportation: Commute: 96.1% car, 0.7% public transportation, 0.7% walk, 1.8% work from home; Mean travel time to work: 25.0 minutes

WELLSBURG (village). Covers a land area of 0.568 square miles and a water area of 0.009 square miles. Located at 42.01° N. Lat; 76.73° W. Long. Elevation is 827 feet.
Population: 573; Growth (since 2000): -9.2%; Density: 1,008.6 persons per square mile; Race: 96.3% White, 0.2% Black/African American, 0.0% Asian, 0.0% American Indian/Alaska Native, 0.0% Native Hawaiian/Other Pacific Islander, 3.5% Two or more races, 0.0% Hispanic of any race; Average household size: 2.48; Median age: 37.9; Age under 18: 23.2%; Age 65 and over: 15.5%; Males per 100 females: 106.4; Marriage status: 33.2% never married, 51.5% now married, 1.5% separated, 3.1% widowed, 12.2% divorced; Foreign born: 3.8%; Speak English only: 95.5%; With disability: 16.8%; Veterans: 10.0%; Ancestry: 20.9% German, 18.7% Irish, 14.8% American, 9.2% Italian, 7.7% English
Employment: 9.3% management, business, and financial, 0.0% computer, engineering, and science, 2.2% education, legal, community service, arts, and media, 15.0% healthcare practitioners, 33.6% service, 16.4% sales and office, 6.2% natural resources, construction, and maintenance, 17.3% production, transportation, and material moving
Income: Per capita: $20,629; Median household: $40,521; Average household: $50,807; Households with income of $100,000 or more: 10.6%; Poverty rate: 26.9%
Educational Attainment: High school diploma or higher: 91.8%; Bachelor's degree or higher: 16.5%; Graduate/professional degree or higher: 5.1%
Housing: Homeownership rate: 82.4%; Median home value: $81,000; Median year structure built: 1951; Homeowner vacancy rate: 3.1%; Median selected monthly owner costs: $928 with a mortgage, $407 without a mortgage; Median gross rent: $615 per month; Rental vacancy rate: 18.6%
Health Insurance: 94.8% have insurance; 66.8% have private insurance; 51.1% have public insurance; 5.2% do not have insurance; 3.8% of children under 18 do not have insurance
Transportation: Commute: 96.3% car, 1.4% public transportation, 0.0% walk, 1.4% work from home; Mean travel time to work: 25.6 minutes

WEST ELMIRA (CDP). Covers a land area of 3.038 square miles and a water area of 0.116 square miles. Located at 42.09° N. Lat; 76.84° W. Long. Elevation is 886 feet.
Population: 5,160; Growth (since 2000): 0.5%; Density: 1,698.3 persons per square mile; Race: 92.0% White, 2.8% Black/African American, 1.0% Asian, 0.0% American Indian/Alaska Native, 0.0% Native Hawaiian/Other Pacific Islander, 4.2% Two or more races, 0.0% Hispanic of any race; Average household size: 2.36; Median age: 47.1; Age under 18: 23.3%; Age 65 and over: 21.9%; Males per 100 females: 89.4; Marriage status: 18.9% never married, 66.3% now married, 0.9% separated, 7.7% widowed, 7.2% divorced; Foreign born: 3.4%; Speak English only: 97.8%; With disability: 8.7%; Veterans: 10.5%; Ancestry: 29.4% Irish, 20.4% Italian, 14.1% German, 10.7% English, 10.0% Polish

Employment: 18.7% management, business, and financial, 2.1% computer, engineering, and science, 20.7% education, legal, community service, arts, and media, 6.0% healthcare practitioners, 5.7% service, 32.7% sales and office, 3.8% natural resources, construction, and maintenance, 10.3% production, transportation, and material moving
Income: Per capita: $51,318; Median household: $81,475; Average household: $125,229; Households with income of $100,000 or more: 39.2%; Poverty rate: 2.2%
Educational Attainment: High school diploma or higher: 99.1%; Bachelor's degree or higher: 51.9%; Graduate/professional degree or higher: 25.3%
Housing: Homeownership rate: 86.6%; Median home value: $132,300; Median year structure built: 1951; Homeowner vacancy rate: 0.0%; Median selected monthly owner costs: $1,246 with a mortgage, $508 without a mortgage; Median gross rent: $1,383 per month; Rental vacancy rate: 0.0%
Health Insurance: 94.4% have insurance; 87.1% have private insurance; 24.6% have public insurance; 5.6% do not have insurance; 1.4% of children under 18 do not have insurance
Transportation: Commute: 96.1% car, 0.6% public transportation, 1.6% walk, 0.9% work from home; Mean travel time to work: 16.8 minutes

Chenango County

Located in central New York; bounded on the east by the Unadilla River; drained by the Susquehanna, Otselic, and Chenango Rivers. Covers a land area of 893.548 square miles, a water area of 5.082 square miles, and is located in the Eastern Time Zone at 42.49° N. Lat., 75.60° W. Long. The county was founded in 1798. County seat is Norwich.

Weather Station: Norwich											Elevation: 1,020 feet	
	Jan	Feb	Mar	Apr	May	Jun	Jul	Aug	Sep	Oct	Nov	Dec
High	32	35	44	57	69	77	81	79	72	60	48	36
Low	13	14	22	33	43	52	57	56	48	37	29	19
Precip	2.9	2.6	3.3	3.6	3.7	4.3	3.8	3.8	4.0	3.6	3.6	3.3
Snow	17.9	14.1	11.5	2.7	tr	0.0	0.0	0.0	0.0	0.5	5.6	15.4

High and Low temperatures in degrees Fahrenheit; Precipitation and Snow in inches

Weather Station: Sherburne 2 S											Elevation: 1,080 feet	
	Jan	Feb	Mar	Apr	May	Jun	Jul	Aug	Sep	Oct	Nov	Dec
High	32	34	42	56	68	77	81	80	72	60	48	36
Low	13	12	20	32	42	53	56	55	47	37	29	19
Precip	2.2	2.0	2.9	3.3	3.5	4.5	3.8	3.4	3.8	3.5	3.3	2.6
Snow	16.9	14.1	13.1	2.9	tr	0.0	0.0	0.0	tr	0.5	6.0	14.5

High and Low temperatures in degrees Fahrenheit; Precipitation and Snow in inches

Population: 49,549; Growth (since 2000): -3.6%; Density: 55.5 persons per square mile; Race: 96.2% White, 0.8% Black/African American, 0.5% Asian, 0.3% American Indian/Alaska Native, 0.0% Native Hawaiian/Other Pacific Islander, 1.6% two or more races, 2.1% Hispanic of any race; Average household size: 2.49; Median age: 43.8; Age under 18: 21.4%; Age 65 and over: 18.3%; Males per 100 females: 99.2; Marriage status: 27.4% never married, 53.1% now married, 2.9% separated, 7.1% widowed, 12.5% divorced; Foreign born: 1.8%; Speak English only: 96.8%; With disability: 17.7%; Veterans: 9.5%; Ancestry: 18.7% German, 18.5% Irish, 17.4% English, 10.4% Italian, 9.5% American
Religion: Six largest groups: 11.0% Catholicism, 5.7% Methodist/Pietist, 2.9% Episcopalianism/Anglicanism, 2.1% Baptist, 2.1% Presbyterian-Reformed, 2.0% Non-denominational Protestant
Economy: Unemployment rate: 4.7%; Leading industries: 17.5 % retail trade; 12.2 % other services (except public administration); 11.6 % health care and social assistance; Farms: 828 totaling 167,226 acres; Company size: 1 employs 1,000 or more persons, 2 employ 500 to 999 persons, 19 employ 100 to 499 persons, 911 employs less than 100 persons; Business ownership: 1,075 women-owned, n/a Black-owned, 57 Hispanic-owned, n/a Asian-owned, n/a American Indian/Alaska Native-owned
Employment: 12.3% management, business, and financial, 2.9% computer, engineering, and science, 11.2% education, legal, community service, arts, and media, 4.9% healthcare practitioners, 18.6% service, 22.0% sales and office, 10.0% natural resources, construction, and maintenance, 18.1% production, transportation, and material moving
Income: Per capita: $23,036; Median household: $45,668; Average household: $56,345; Households with income of $100,000 or more: 13.8%; Poverty rate: 15.9%

Educational Attainment: High school diploma or higher: 87.2%; Bachelor's degree or higher: 17.4%; Graduate/professional degree or higher: 7.9%
Housing: Homeownership rate: 75.3%; Median home value: $91,700; Median year structure built: 1963; Homeowner vacancy rate: 2.8%; Median selected monthly owner costs: $1,101 with a mortgage, $455 without a mortgage; Median gross rent: $637 per month; Rental vacancy rate: 5.0%
Vital Statistics: Birth rate: 102.4 per 10,000 population; Death rate: 111.0 per 10,000 population; Age-adjusted cancer mortality rate: 158.6 deaths per 100,000 population
Health Insurance: 91.0% have insurance; 66.0% have private insurance; 40.7% have public insurance; 9.0% do not have insurance; 6.9% of children under 18 do not have insurance
Health Care: Physicians: 9.9 per 10,000 population; Dentists: 3.7 per 10,000 population; Hospital beds: 27.9 per 10,000 population; Hospital admissions: 366.8 per 10,000 population
Transportation: Commute: 88.3% car, 0.7% public transportation, 5.0% walk, 5.2% work from home; Mean travel time to work: 23.7 minutes
2016 Presidential Election: 59.7% Trump, 33.9% Clinton, 4.6% Johnson, 1.8% Stein
National and State Parks: Chenango State Forest; Hunt's Pond State Park
Additional Information Contacts
Chenango Government . . . . (607) 337-1470
  http://www.co.chenango.ny.us

Chenango County Communities

AFTON (town). Covers a land area of 45.836 square miles and a water area of 0.679 square miles. Located at 42.23° N. Lat; 75.53° W. Long. Elevation is 1,001 feet.
Population: 2,807; Growth (since 2000): -5.7%; Density: 61.2 persons per square mile; Race: 97.5% White, 0.1% Black/African American, 1.2% Asian, 0.4% American Indian/Alaska Native, 0.0% Native Hawaiian/Other Pacific Islander, 0.7% Two or more races, 1.0% Hispanic of any race; Average household size: 2.32; Median age: 49.7; Age under 18: 16.5%; Age 65 and over: 24.9%; Males per 100 females: 97.0; Marriage status: 25.7% never married, 46.3% now married, 3.1% separated, 6.5% widowed, 21.6% divorced; Foreign born: 2.1%; Speak English only: 97.0%; With disability: 16.2%; Veterans: 12.4%; Ancestry: 23.5% German, 22.0% Irish, 14.0% English, 9.3% American, 7.0% Italian
Employment: 9.7% management, business, and financial, 1.3% computer, engineering, and science, 9.4% education, legal, community service, arts, and media, 6.9% healthcare practitioners, 9.4% service, 27.5% sales and office, 2.4% natural resources, construction, and maintenance, 33.5% production, transportation, and material moving
Income: Per capita: $22,376; Median household: $46,458; Average household: $50,932; Households with income of $100,000 or more: 9.7%; Poverty rate: 11.9%
Educational Attainment: High school diploma or higher: 85.0%; Bachelor's degree or higher: 11.1%; Graduate/professional degree or higher: 5.1%

School District(s)
Afton Central SD (PK-12)
    2014-15 Enrollment: 571 . . . . (607) 639-8229
Housing: Homeownership rate: 79.4%; Median home value: $102,900; Median year structure built: 1973; Homeowner vacancy rate: 8.4%; Median selected monthly owner costs: $1,179 with a mortgage, $463 without a mortgage; Median gross rent: $625 per month; Rental vacancy rate: 0.8%
Health Insurance: 84.7% have insurance; 62.3% have private insurance; 41.5% have public insurance; 15.3% do not have insurance; 18.1% of children under 18 do not have insurance
Transportation: Commute: 82.1% car, 0.0% public transportation, 6.5% walk, 11.1% work from home; Mean travel time to work: 27.5 minutes

AFTON (village). Covers a land area of 1.527 square miles and a water area of 0.073 square miles. Located at 42.23° N. Lat; 75.52° W. Long. Elevation is 1,001 feet.
Population: 1,086; Growth (since 2000): 29.9%; Density: 711.4 persons per square mile; Race: 95.5% White, 0.2% Black/African American, 1.3% Asian, 1.0% American Indian/Alaska Native, 0.0% Native Hawaiian/Other Pacific Islander, 1.8% Two or more races, 2.5% Hispanic of any race; Average household size: 2.40; Median age: 44.5; Age under 18: 20.9%; Age 65 and over: 24.9%; Males per 100 females: 86.4; Marriage status: 29.0% never married, 45.5% now married, 4.0% separated, 9.5%

widowed, 16.0% divorced; Foreign born: 1.5%; Speak English only: 96.2%; With disability: 19.2%; Veterans: 9.3%; Ancestry: 19.0% Irish, 15.1% German, 14.0% English, 9.3% Italian, 7.0% Polish

Employment: 8.8% management, business, and financial, 3.8% computer, engineering, and science, 17.1% education, legal, community service, arts, and media, 8.0% healthcare practitioners, 17.8% service, 18.6% sales and office, 7.3% natural resources, construction, and maintenance, 18.6% production, transportation, and material moving

Income: Per capita: $21,743; Median household: $41,042; Average household: $50,635; Households with income of $100,000 or more: 10.8%; Poverty rate: 18.4%

Educational Attainment: High school diploma or higher: 85.3%; Bachelor's degree or higher: 13.6%; Graduate/professional degree or higher: 8.7%

School District(s)
Afton Central SD (PK-12)
    2014-15 Enrollment: 571 . . . . (607) 639-8229

Housing: Homeownership rate: 70.0%; Median home value: $88,300; Median year structure built: Before 1940; Homeowner vacancy rate: 1.8%; Median selected monthly owner costs: $1,074 with a mortgage, $466 without a mortgage; Median gross rent: $580 per month; Rental vacancy rate: 1.4%

Health Insurance: 90.9% have insurance; 64.7% have private insurance; 46.0% have public insurance; 9.1% do not have insurance; 7.0% of children under 18 do not have insurance

Safety: Violent crime rate: 0.0 per 10,000 population; Property crime rate: 36.8 per 10,000 population

Transportation: Commute: 90.0% car, 0.0% public transportation, 8.2% walk, 0.8% work from home; Mean travel time to work: 28.9 minutes

BAINBRIDGE (town). Covers a land area of 34.323 square miles and a water area of 0.433 square miles. Located at 42.30° N. Lat; 75.48° W. Long. Elevation is 994 feet.

History: Settled before 1790, incorporated 1829.

Population: 3,278; Growth (since 2000): -3.6%; Density: 95.5 persons per square mile; Race: 96.4% White, 0.0% Black/African American, 1.5% Asian, 0.1% American Indian/Alaska Native, 0.0% Native Hawaiian/Other Pacific Islander, 1.5% Two or more races, 2.3% Hispanic of any race; Average household size: 2.67; Median age: 38.7; Age under 18: 27.5%; Age 65 and over: 16.0%; Males per 100 females: 99.6; Marriage status: 24.0% never married, 60.8% now married, 4.0% separated, 5.9% widowed, 9.2% divorced; Foreign born: 3.8%; Speak English only: 95.2%; With disability: 16.8%; Veterans: 9.9%; Ancestry: 21.4% Irish, 19.7% German, 11.3% English, 9.6% Swedish, 9.4% Italian

Employment: 10.5% management, business, and financial, 0.6% computer, engineering, and science, 11.8% education, legal, community service, arts, and media, 4.7% healthcare practitioners, 15.4% service, 20.2% sales and office, 14.5% natural resources, construction, and maintenance, 22.3% production, transportation, and material moving

Income: Per capita: $22,489; Median household: $48,778; Average household: $59,542; Households with income of $100,000 or more: 12.4%; Poverty rate: 11.9%

Educational Attainment: High school diploma or higher: 87.8%; Bachelor's degree or higher: 20.9%; Graduate/professional degree or higher: 9.7%

School District(s)
Bainbridge-Guilford Central SD (PK-12)
    2014-15 Enrollment: 867 . . . . (607) 967-6321

Housing: Homeownership rate: 73.5%; Median home value: $95,000; Median year structure built: 1960; Homeowner vacancy rate: 6.1%; Median selected monthly owner costs: $1,135 with a mortgage, $525 without a mortgage; Median gross rent: $729 per month; Rental vacancy rate: 4.6%

Health Insurance: 80.4% have insurance; 55.3% have private insurance; 38.4% have public insurance; 19.6% do not have insurance; 27.5% of children under 18 do not have insurance

Transportation: Commute: 91.9% car, 0.2% public transportation, 4.0% walk, 3.3% work from home; Mean travel time to work: 27.0 minutes

BAINBRIDGE (village). Covers a land area of 1.239 square miles and a water area of 0.035 square miles. Located at 42.30° N. Lat; 75.48° W. Long. Elevation is 994 feet.

Population: 1,237; Growth (since 2000): -9.4%; Density: 998.5 persons per square mile; Race: 94.4% White, 0.0% Black/African American, 1.0% Asian, 0.3% American Indian/Alaska Native, 0.0% Native Hawaiian/Other Pacific Islander, 3.9% Two or more races, 3.3% Hispanic of any race;

Average household size: 2.41; Median age: 37.6; Age under 18: 26.6%; Age 65 and over: 17.5%; Males per 100 females: 93.3; Marriage status: 25.0% never married, 51.9% now married, 6.9% separated, 8.2% widowed, 15.0% divorced; Foreign born: 2.6%; Speak English only: 97.7%; With disability: 12.8%; Veterans: 11.1%; Ancestry: 25.4% German, 25.0% Irish, 12.1% English, 9.4% Italian, 8.4% American

Employment: 15.0% management, business, and financial, 1.6% computer, engineering, and science, 16.0% education, legal, community service, arts, and media, 6.1% healthcare practitioners, 12.2% service, 18.9% sales and office, 10.5% natural resources, construction, and maintenance, 19.7% production, transportation, and material moving

Income: Per capita: $22,393; Median household: $44,402; Average household: $53,239; Households with income of $100,000 or more: 12.5%; Poverty rate: 16.1%

Educational Attainment: High school diploma or higher: 88.6%; Bachelor's degree or higher: 23.2%; Graduate/professional degree or higher: 10.8%

School District(s)
Bainbridge-Guilford Central SD (PK-12)
    2014-15 Enrollment: 867 . . . . (607) 967-6321

Housing: Homeownership rate: 60.8%; Median home value: $89,100; Median year structure built: Before 1940; Homeowner vacancy rate: 6.4%; Median selected monthly owner costs: $1,137 with a mortgage, $522 without a mortgage; Median gross rent: $728 per month; Rental vacancy rate: 7.1%

Health Insurance: 91.0% have insurance; 68.7% have private insurance; 37.4% have public insurance; 9.0% do not have insurance; 4.0% of children under 18 do not have insurance

Safety: Violent crime rate: 0.0 per 10,000 population; Property crime rate: 0.0 per 10,000 population

Transportation: Commute: 89.6% car, 0.4% public transportation, 6.3% walk, 1.7% work from home; Mean travel time to work: 30.0 minutes

COLUMBUS (town). Covers a land area of 37.368 square miles and a water area of 0.124 square miles. Located at 42.69° N. Lat; 75.37° W. Long. Elevation is 1,296 feet.

Population: 904; Growth (since 2000): -2.9%; Density: 24.2 persons per square mile; Race: 100.0% White, 0.0% Black/African American, 0.0% Asian, 0.0% American Indian/Alaska Native, 0.0% Native Hawaiian/Other Pacific Islander, 0.0% Two or more races, 1.0% Hispanic of any race; Average household size: 2.55; Median age: 43.4; Age under 18: 21.8%; Age 65 and over: 15.9%; Males per 100 females: 109.7; Marriage status: 28.5% never married, 54.2% now married, 1.0% separated, 5.2% widowed, 12.0% divorced; Foreign born: 1.5%; Speak English only: 98.5%; With disability: 17.3%; Veterans: 7.5%; Ancestry: 20.0% German, 13.8% Irish, 13.5% Italian, 12.7% English, 6.0% American

Employment: 10.8% management, business, and financial, 2.3% computer, engineering, and science, 6.3% education, legal, community service, arts, and media, 7.6% healthcare practitioners, 22.2% service, 27.0% sales and office, 9.8% natural resources, construction, and maintenance, 14.1% production, transportation, and material moving

Income: Per capita: $22,602; Median household: $46,406; Average household: $56,109; Households with income of $100,000 or more: 11.9%; Poverty rate: 11.2%

Educational Attainment: High school diploma or higher: 79.3%; Bachelor's degree or higher: 14.0%; Graduate/professional degree or higher: 6.8%

Housing: Homeownership rate: 87.9%; Median home value: $91,700; Median year structure built: 1973; Homeowner vacancy rate: 1.9%; Median selected monthly owner costs: $1,182 with a mortgage, $421 without a mortgage; Median gross rent: $548 per month; Rental vacancy rate: 0.0%

Health Insurance: 83.6% have insurance; 53.8% have private insurance; 42.7% have public insurance; 16.4% do not have insurance; 9.1% of children under 18 do not have insurance

Transportation: Commute: 90.3% car, 0.5% public transportation, 2.6% walk, 6.6% work from home; Mean travel time to work: 22.4 minutes

COVENTRY (town). Covers a land area of 48.697 square miles and a water area of 0.167 square miles. Located at 42.29° N. Lat; 75.63° W. Long. Elevation is 1,660 feet.

Population: 1,581; Growth (since 2000): -0.5%; Density: 32.5 persons per square mile; Race: 97.7% White, 0.2% Black/African American, 0.7% Asian, 0.0% American Indian/Alaska Native, 0.0% Native Hawaiian/Other Pacific Islander, 1.5% Two or more races, 1.6% Hispanic of any race; Average household size: 2.66; Median age: 42.9; Age under 18: 20.3%;

Age 65 and over: 16.8%; Males per 100 females: 106.6; Marriage status: 31.1% never married, 56.6% now married, 1.1% separated, 4.2% widowed, 8.0% divorced; Foreign born: 2.1%; Speak English only: 97.9%; With disability: 20.1%; Veterans: 12.4%; Ancestry: 23.3% German, 23.0% Irish, 18.7% English, 11.7% French, 9.6% Italian

Employment: 7.2% management, business, and financial, 1.2% computer, engineering, and science, 9.1% education, legal, community service, arts, and media, 2.5% healthcare practitioners, 21.7% service, 29.6% sales and office, 10.8% natural resources, construction, and maintenance, 17.7% production, transportation, and material moving

Income: Per capita: $20,939; Median household: $44,688; Average household: $55,029; Households with income of $100,000 or more: 15.7%; Poverty rate: 12.4%

Educational Attainment: High school diploma or higher: 84.9%; Bachelor's degree or higher: 14.1%; Graduate/professional degree or higher: 3.6%

Housing: Homeownership rate: 84.9%; Median home value: $97,200; Median year structure built: 1981; Homeowner vacancy rate: 2.9%; Median selected monthly owner costs: $1,232 with a mortgage, $428 without a mortgage; Median gross rent: $519 per month; Rental vacancy rate: 0.0%

Health Insurance: 86.9% have insurance; 64.4% have private insurance; 35.4% have public insurance; 13.1% do not have insurance; 2.2% of children under 18 do not have insurance

Transportation: Commute: 95.0% car, 0.0% public transportation, 1.8% walk, 2.8% work from home; Mean travel time to work: 30.5 minutes

GERMAN (town).

Covers a land area of 28.408 square miles and a water area of 0.031 square miles. Located at 42.50° N. Lat; 75.82° W. Long.

Population: 333; Growth (since 2000): -11.9%; Density: 11.7 persons per square mile; Race: 97.3% White, 0.0% Black/African American, 0.0% Asian, 0.6% American Indian/Alaska Native, 0.0% Native Hawaiian/Other Pacific Islander, 0.9% Two or more races, 3.0% Hispanic of any race; Average household size: 2.18; Median age: 48.8; Age under 18: 14.1%; Age 65 and over: 21.3%; Males per 100 females: 105.6; Marriage status: 20.8% never married, 59.0% now married, 1.7% separated, 7.3% widowed, 12.8% divorced; Foreign born: 0.9%; Speak English only: 97.2%; With disability: 19.5%; Veterans: 12.2%; Ancestry: 19.5% English, 16.8% Irish, 15.3% German, 10.2% Italian, 9.3% Dutch

Employment: 12.8% management, business, and financial, 0.0% computer, engineering, and science, 6.8% education, legal, community service, arts, and media, 5.3% healthcare practitioners, 20.3% service, 21.1% sales and office, 10.5% natural resources, construction, and maintenance, 23.3% production, transportation, and material moving

Income: Per capita: $29,195; Median household: $40,417; Average household: $63,096; Households with income of $100,000 or more: 13.1%; Poverty rate: 12.9%

Educational Attainment: High school diploma or higher: 88.8%; Bachelor's degree or higher: 10.5%; Graduate/professional degree or higher: 5.4%

Housing: Homeownership rate: 86.9%; Median home value: $81,200; Median year structure built: 1976; Homeowner vacancy rate: 1.5%; Median selected monthly owner costs: $875 with a mortgage, $450 without a mortgage; Median gross rent: $525 per month; Rental vacancy rate: 0.0%

Health Insurance: 88.9% have insurance; 57.1% have private insurance; 47.1% have public insurance; 11.1% do not have insurance; 2.1% of children under 18 do not have insurance

Transportation: Commute: 92.1% car, 0.0% public transportation, 1.6% walk, 6.3% work from home; Mean travel time to work: 33.6 minutes

GREENE (town).

Covers a land area of 75.077 square miles and a water area of 0.542 square miles. Located at 42.31° N. Lat; 75.75° W. Long. Elevation is 919 feet.

History: Settled 1792, incorporated 1842.

Population: 5,452; Growth (since 2000): -4.8%; Density: 72.6 persons per square mile; Race: 95.1% White, 1.9% Black/African American, 0.4% Asian, 0.9% American Indian/Alaska Native, 0.0% Native Hawaiian/Other Pacific Islander, 1.5% Two or more races, 0.9% Hispanic of any race; Average household size: 2.56; Median age: 43.0; Age under 18: 22.0%; Age 65 and over: 17.1%; Males per 100 females: 98.1; Marriage status: 28.3% never married, 53.6% now married, 2.3% separated, 7.4% widowed, 10.6% divorced; Foreign born: 1.5%; Speak English only: 97.7%; With disability: 10.2%; Veterans: 8.4%; Ancestry: 24.3% English, 20.6% Irish, 15.1% German, 12.8% American, 10.0% Italian

Employment: 13.8% management, business, and financial, 5.2% computer, engineering, and science, 14.8% education, legal, community service, arts, and media, 4.2% healthcare practitioners, 17.9% service, 22.6% sales and office, 6.8% natural resources, construction, and maintenance, 14.8% production, transportation, and material moving

Income: Per capita: $26,029; Median household: $56,658; Average household: $64,944; Households with income of $100,000 or more: 18.3%; Poverty rate: 15.9%

Educational Attainment: High school diploma or higher: 93.4%; Bachelor's degree or higher: 22.4%; Graduate/professional degree or higher: 10.3%

School District(s)
Greene Central SD (PK-12)
    2014-15 Enrollment: 1,065 . . . . (607) 656-4161

Housing: Homeownership rate: 76.6%; Median home value: $125,200; Median year structure built: 1962; Homeowner vacancy rate: 1.1%; Median selected monthly owner costs: $1,275 with a mortgage, $532 without a mortgage; Median gross rent: $627 per month; Rental vacancy rate: 5.4%

Health Insurance: 94.0% have insurance; 73.1% have private insurance; 34.2% have public insurance; 6.0% do not have insurance; 0.4% of children under 18 do not have insurance

Newspapers: Paden Publishing (weekly circulation 3,500)

Transportation: Commute: 85.8% car, 0.2% public transportation, 5.9% walk, 7.8% work from home; Mean travel time to work: 23.9 minutes

Additional Information Contacts
Town of Greene. . . . . (607) 656-4191
   http://www.nygreene.com/townofgreene.htm

GREENE (village).

Covers a land area of 1.068 square miles and a water area of 0.038 square miles. Located at 42.33° N. Lat; 75.77° W. Long. Elevation is 919 feet.

Population: 1,592; Growth (since 2000): -6.4%; Density: 1,491.0 persons per square mile; Race: 95.7% White, 2.0% Black/African American, 0.3% Asian, 0.0% American Indian/Alaska Native, 0.0% Native Hawaiian/Other Pacific Islander, 2.0% Two or more races, 1.9% Hispanic of any race; Average household size: 2.32; Median age: 39.7; Age under 18: 23.6%; Age 65 and over: 18.5%; Males per 100 females: 87.4; Marriage status: 27.2% never married, 50.1% now married, 2.2% separated, 11.8% widowed, 10.9% divorced; Foreign born: 2.2%; Speak English only: 95.6%; With disability: 17.3%; Veterans: 7.4%; Ancestry: 23.3% English, 20.9% Irish, 14.6% German, 7.9% Italian, 7.8% American

Employment: 8.4% management, business, and financial, 5.9% computer, engineering, and science, 15.7% education, legal, community service, arts, and media, 6.7% healthcare practitioners, 17.9% service, 19.6% sales and office, 5.8% natural resources, construction, and maintenance, 19.9% production, transportation, and material moving

Income: Per capita: $25,494; Median household: $48,188; Average household: $57,254; Households with income of $100,000 or more: 17.7%; Poverty rate: 11.8%

Educational Attainment: High school diploma or higher: 91.5%; Bachelor's degree or higher: 24.8%; Graduate/professional degree or higher: 9.3%

School District(s)
Greene Central SD (PK-12)
    2014-15 Enrollment: 1,065 . . . . (607) 656-4161

Housing: Homeownership rate: 52.4%; Median home value: $101,900; Median year structure built: Before 1940; Homeowner vacancy rate: 4.8%; Median selected monthly owner costs: $1,143 with a mortgage, $546 without a mortgage; Median gross rent: $589 per month; Rental vacancy rate: 2.1%

Health Insurance: 93.0% have insurance; 69.8% have private insurance; 39.5% have public insurance; 7.0% do not have insurance; 1.3% of children under 18 do not have insurance

Safety: Violent crime rate: 0.0 per 10,000 population; Property crime rate: 32.9 per 10,000 population

Newspapers: Paden Publishing (weekly circulation 3,500)

Transportation: Commute: 80.4% car, 0.3% public transportation, 14.4% walk, 3.8% work from home; Mean travel time to work: 22.3 minutes

GUILFORD (CDP).

Covers a land area of 1.336 square miles and a water area of 0.118 square miles. Located at 42.41° N. Lat; 75.49° W. Long. Elevation is 1,486 feet.

Population: 339; Growth (since 2000): n/a; Density: 253.8 persons per square mile; Race: 97.9% White, 0.0% Black/African American, 0.0% Asian, 0.0% American Indian/Alaska Native, 0.0% Native Hawaiian/Other

Pacific Islander, 2.1% Two or more races, 8.8% Hispanic of any race; Average household size: 1.95; Median age: 54.3; Age under 18: 11.5%; Age 65 and over: 20.9%; Males per 100 females: 101.1; Marriage status: 18.3% never married, 63.0% now married, 2.3% separated, 5.7% widowed, 13.0% divorced; Foreign born: 2.1%; Speak English only: 95.0%; With disability: 27.1%; Veterans: 19.0%; Ancestry: 29.2% German, 24.8% Irish, 23.3% Italian, 11.5% French, 9.4% English

Employment: 0.0% management, business, and financial, 7.3% computer, engineering, and science, 0.0% education, legal, community service, arts, and media, 29.0% healthcare practitioners, 8.9% service, 0.0% sales and office, 0.0% natural resources, construction, and maintenance, 54.8% production, transportation, and material moving

Income: Per capita: $29,079; Median household: $41,364; Average household: $53,517; Households with income of $100,000 or more: 16.1%; Poverty rate: 8.8%

Educational Attainment: High school diploma or higher: 88.0%; Bachelor's degree or higher: 12.0%; Graduate/professional degree or higher: 6.0%

School District(s)

Bainbridge-Guilford Central SD (PK-12)

    2014-15 Enrollment: 867 . . . . (607) 967-6321

Housing: Homeownership rate: 75.3%; Median home value: $89,500; Median year structure built: Before 1940; Homeowner vacancy rate: 0.0%; Median selected monthly owner costs: $2,029 with a mortgage, $575 without a mortgage; Median gross rent: n/a per month; Rental vacancy rate: 0.0%

Health Insurance: 100.0% have insurance; 92.0% have private insurance; 34.2% have public insurance; 0.0% do not have insurance; 0.0% of children under 18 do not have insurance

Transportation: Commute: 91.1% car, 0.0% public transportation, 8.9% walk, 0.0% work from home; Mean travel time to work: 34.1 minutes

---

GUILFORD (town). Covers a land area of 61.716 square miles and a water area of 0.244 square miles. Located at 42.40° N. Lat; 75.45° W. Long. Elevation is 1,486 feet.

Population: 2,873; Growth (since 2000): -5.7%; Density: 46.6 persons per square mile; Race: 97.3% White, 0.5% Black/African American, 0.0% Asian, 0.0% American Indian/Alaska Native, 0.0% Native Hawaiian/Other Pacific Islander, 1.5% Two or more races, 4.1% Hispanic of any race; Average household size: 2.18; Median age: 50.4; Age under 18: 15.1%; Age 65 and over: 21.5%; Males per 100 females: 101.5; Marriage status: 25.5% never married, 52.7% now married, 0.3% separated, 10.0% widowed, 11.9% divorced; Foreign born: 1.9%; Speak English only: 97.3%; With disability: 17.7%; Veterans: 8.9%; Ancestry: 20.9% Irish, 17.6% German, 13.4% English, 12.8% American, 10.7% Italian

Employment: 20.3% management, business, and financial, 3.2% computer, engineering, and science, 12.0% education, legal, community service, arts, and media, 5.9% healthcare practitioners, 12.0% service, 14.7% sales and office, 7.5% natural resources, construction, and maintenance, 24.4% production, transportation, and material moving

Income: Per capita: $28,949; Median household: $46,667; Average household: $61,481; Households with income of $100,000 or more: 19.1%; Poverty rate: 16.6%

Educational Attainment: High school diploma or higher: 88.5%; Bachelor's degree or higher: 22.1%; Graduate/professional degree or higher: 10.5%

School District(s)

Bainbridge-Guilford Central SD (PK-12)

    2014-15 Enrollment: 867 . . . . (607) 967-6321

Housing: Homeownership rate: 83.7%; Median home value: $86,100; Median year structure built: 1970; Homeowner vacancy rate: 2.5%; Median selected monthly owner costs: $1,051 with a mortgage, $465 without a mortgage; Median gross rent: $540 per month; Rental vacancy rate: 11.5%

Health Insurance: 93.0% have insurance; 74.9% have private insurance; 35.6% have public insurance; 7.0% do not have insurance; 6.7% of children under 18 do not have insurance

Transportation: Commute: 84.7% car, 4.1% public transportation, 5.5% walk, 5.7% work from home; Mean travel time to work: 28.6 minutes

---

LINCKLAEN (town). Covers a land area of 26.263 square miles and a water area of 0.011 square miles. Located at 42.68° N. Lat; 75.84° W. Long. Elevation is 1,191 feet.

Population: 370; Growth (since 2000): -11.1%; Density: 14.1 persons per square mile; Race: 97.6% White, 0.0% Black/African American, 0.0% Asian, 0.3% American Indian/Alaska Native, 0.0% Native Hawaiian/Other

Pacific Islander, 2.2% Two or more races, 1.4% Hispanic of any race; Average household size: 2.43; Median age: 43.0; Age under 18: 17.6%; Age 65 and over: 20.3%; Males per 100 females: 106.3; Marriage status: 25.0% never married, 57.6% now married, 3.5% separated, 4.4% widowed, 13.0% divorced; Foreign born: 0.0%; Speak English only: 97.5%; With disability: 13.8%; Veterans: 12.1%; Ancestry: 13.0% German, 12.2% English, 9.7% American, 4.6% Irish, 3.2% Dutch

Employment: 10.2% management, business, and financial, 0.0% computer, engineering, and science, 14.0% education, legal, community service, arts, and media, 0.0% healthcare practitioners, 13.4% service, 8.1% sales and office, 22.0% natural resources, construction, and maintenance, 32.3% production, transportation, and material moving

Income: Per capita: $29,164; Median household: $47,500; Average household: $70,016; Households with income of $100,000 or more: 7.9%; Poverty rate: 9.7%

Educational Attainment: High school diploma or higher: 89.0%; Bachelor's degree or higher: 16.7%; Graduate/professional degree or higher: 9.3%

Housing: Homeownership rate: 84.2%; Median home value: $74,300; Median year structure built: 1970; Homeowner vacancy rate: 0.0%; Median selected monthly owner costs: $1,034 with a mortgage, $397 without a mortgage; Median gross rent: $775 per month; Rental vacancy rate: 17.2%

Health Insurance: 92.7% have insurance; 73.2% have private insurance; 33.5% have public insurance; 7.3% do not have insurance; 1.5% of children under 18 do not have insurance

Transportation: Commute: 94.0% car, 0.0% public transportation, 3.6% walk, 1.2% work from home; Mean travel time to work: 36.9 minutes

---

MCDONOUGH (town). Covers a land area of 39.038 square miles and a water area of 0.593 square miles. Located at 42.50° N. Lat; 75.73° W. Long. Elevation is 1,430 feet.

Population: 728; Growth (since 2000): -16.3%; Density: 18.6 persons per square mile; Race: 96.8% White, 0.0% Black/African American, 0.4% Asian, 0.0% American Indian/Alaska Native, 0.0% Native Hawaiian/Other Pacific Islander, 2.2% Two or more races, 4.3% Hispanic of any race; Average household size: 2.14; Median age: 52.5; Age under 18: 14.1%; Age 65 and over: 20.2%; Males per 100 females: 111.5; Marriage status: 18.4% never married, 51.0% now married, 1.6% separated, 9.6% widowed, 21.0% divorced; Foreign born: 4.4%; Speak English only: 97.6%; With disability: 19.2%; Veterans: 13.1%; Ancestry: 26.0% German, 19.5% English, 14.3% Irish, 9.8% Italian, 7.6% American

Employment: 10.8% management, business, and financial, 1.5% computer, engineering, and science, 10.8% education, legal, community service, arts, and media, 12.0% healthcare practitioners, 22.2% service, 16.0% sales and office, 9.9% natural resources, construction, and maintenance, 16.7% production, transportation, and material moving

Income: Per capita: $22,813; Median household: $38,571; Average household: $47,937; Households with income of $100,000 or more: 9.7%; Poverty rate: 12.6%

Educational Attainment: High school diploma or higher: 84.7%; Bachelor's degree or higher: 14.0%; Graduate/professional degree or higher: 6.1%

Housing: Homeownership rate: 90.0%; Median home value: $76,000; Median year structure built: 1973; Homeowner vacancy rate: 2.8%; Median selected monthly owner costs: $987 with a mortgage, $307 without a mortgage; Median gross rent: $608 per month; Rental vacancy rate: 0.0%

Health Insurance: 92.4% have insurance; 61.8% have private insurance; 47.8% have public insurance; 7.6% do not have insurance; 0.0% of children under 18 do not have insurance

Transportation: Commute: 92.2% car, 0.0% public transportation, 1.0% walk, 5.1% work from home; Mean travel time to work: 35.7 minutes

---

MOUNT UPTON (unincorporated postal area)

ZCTA: 13809

    Covers a land area of 30.076 square miles and a water area of 0 square miles. Located at 42.40° N. Lat; 75.40° W. Long. Elevation is 1,030 feet.

Population: 1,896; Growth (since 2000): 38.2%; Density: 63.0 persons per square mile; Race: 96.1% White, 0.7% Black/African American, 0.0% Asian, 0.0% American Indian/Alaska Native, 0.0% Native Hawaiian/Other Pacific Islander, 0.8% Two or more races, 4.6% Hispanic of any race; Average household size: 2.61; Median age: 36.4; Age under 18: 24.7%; Age 65 and over: 19.9%; Males per 100 females: 101.5; Marriage status: 29.5% never married, 60.6% now married, 0.0% separated, 6.6% widowed, 3.4% divorced; Foreign born: 0.0%; Speak English only: 99.1%; With disability: 14.0%; Veterans: 6.3%; Ancestry:

21.0% German, 17.8% Irish, 17.2% American, 14.3% English, 6.3% Dutch

Employment: 21.7% management, business, and financial, 0.0% computer, engineering, and science, 6.9% education, legal, community service, arts, and media, 5.0% healthcare practitioners, 16.2% service, 18.1% sales and office, 3.9% natural resources, construction, and maintenance, 28.2% production, transportation, and material moving

Income: Per capita: $22,995; Median household: $50,069; Average household: $59,199; Households with income of $100,000 or more: 10.5%; Poverty rate: 19.8%

Educational Attainment: High school diploma or higher: 86.2%; Bachelor's degree or higher: 17.1%; Graduate/professional degree or higher: 7.6%

Housing: Homeownership rate: 73.2%; Median home value: $76,400; Median year structure built: 1970; Homeowner vacancy rate: 0.0%; Median selected monthly owner costs: $1,011 with a mortgage, $457 without a mortgage; Median gross rent: $587 per month; Rental vacancy rate: 0.0%

Health Insurance: 92.5% have insurance; 74.8% have private insurance; 42.4% have public insurance; 7.5% do not have insurance; 0.0% of children under 18 do not have insurance

Transportation: Commute: 87.1% car, 6.4% public transportation, 0.5% walk, 6.0% work from home; Mean travel time to work: 23.6 minutes

NEW BERLIN (town).
Covers a land area of 46.134 square miles and a water area of 0.440 square miles. Located at 42.59° N. Lat; 75.39° W. Long. Elevation is 1,112 feet.

History: Incorporated 1819.

Population: 2,604; Growth (since 2000): -7.1%; Density: 56.4 persons per square mile; Race: 95.7% White, 0.0% Black/African American, 0.8% Asian, 0.1% American Indian/Alaska Native, 0.0% Native Hawaiian/Other Pacific Islander, 3.4% Two or more races, 1.4% Hispanic of any race; Average household size: 2.22; Median age: 52.7; Age under 18: 15.7%; Age 65 and over: 31.3%; Males per 100 females: 92.5; Marriage status: 21.1% never married, 57.0% now married, 3.9% separated, 10.3% widowed, 11.5% divorced; Foreign born: 3.0%; Speak English only: 97.3%; With disability: 25.6%; Veterans: 14.4%; Ancestry: 22.0% English, 17.0% Irish, 16.8% German, 8.6% American, 8.4% Italian

Employment: 11.8% management, business, and financial, 3.2% computer, engineering, and science, 11.8% education, legal, community service, arts, and media, 2.7% healthcare practitioners, 21.2% service, 21.8% sales and office, 8.2% natural resources, construction, and maintenance, 19.3% production, transportation, and material moving

Income: Per capita: $23,618; Median household: $38,200; Average household: $51,502; Households with income of $100,000 or more: 11.6%; Poverty rate: 15.9%

Educational Attainment: High school diploma or higher: 79.7%; Bachelor's degree or higher: 13.4%; Graduate/professional degree or higher: 5.7%

School District(s)
Unadilla Valley Central SD (PK-12)
    2014-15 Enrollment: 815 . . . . (607) 847-7500

Housing: Homeownership rate: 77.5%; Median home value: $86,800; Median year structure built: 1941; Homeowner vacancy rate: 2.5%; Median selected monthly owner costs: $1,063 with a mortgage, $415 without a mortgage; Median gross rent: $670 per month; Rental vacancy rate: 6.2%

Health Insurance: 86.9% have insurance; 57.8% have private insurance; 50.5% have public insurance; 13.1% do not have insurance; 11.2% of children under 18 do not have insurance

Safety: Violent crime rate: 0.0 per 10,000 population; Property crime rate: 94.8 per 10,000 population

Transportation: Commute: 87.7% car, 0.0% public transportation, 3.5% walk, 8.0% work from home; Mean travel time to work: 26.4 minutes

NEW BERLIN (village).
Covers a land area of 1.066 square miles and a water area of 0 square miles. Located at 42.62° N. Lat; 75.34° W. Long. Elevation is 1,112 feet.

Population: 1,170; Growth (since 2000): 3.6%; Density: 1,098.1 persons per square mile; Race: 94.5% White, 0.0% Black/African American, 0.7% Asian, 0.0% American Indian/Alaska Native, 0.0% Native Hawaiian/Other Pacific Islander, 4.8% Two or more races, 3.1% Hispanic of any race; Average household size: 2.19; Median age: 51.7; Age under 18: 19.1%; Age 65 and over: 34.0%; Males per 100 females: 85.6; Marriage status: 23.1% never married, 50.9% now married, 3.6% separated, 13.8% widowed, 12.2% divorced; Foreign born: 2.5%; Speak English only: 98.5%;

With disability: 28.9%; Veterans: 17.7%; Ancestry: 18.8% English, 18.4% German, 17.7% Irish, 11.2% American, 10.0% Italian

Employment: 6.7% management, business, and financial, 2.3% computer, engineering, and science, 15.4% education, legal, community service, arts, and media, 1.3% healthcare practitioners, 20.5% service, 25.9% sales and office, 6.7% natural resources, construction, and maintenance, 21.3% production, transportation, and material moving

Income: Per capita: $18,944; Median household: $31,563; Average household: $41,328; Households with income of $100,000 or more: 7.0%; Poverty rate: 22.4%

Educational Attainment: High school diploma or higher: 78.8%; Bachelor's degree or higher: 11.3%; Graduate/professional degree or higher: 5.2%

School District(s)
Unadilla Valley Central SD (PK-12)
    2014-15 Enrollment: 815 . . . . (607) 847-7500

Housing: Homeownership rate: 62.2%; Median home value: $78,800; Median year structure built: Before 1940; Homeowner vacancy rate: 4.9%; Median selected monthly owner costs: $1,080 with a mortgage, $566 without a mortgage; Median gross rent: $515 per month; Rental vacancy rate: 8.3%

Health Insurance: 88.9% have insurance; 53.8% have private insurance; 52.9% have public insurance; 11.1% do not have insurance; 9.4% of children under 18 do not have insurance

Transportation: Commute: 79.0% car, 0.0% public transportation, 4.5% walk, 16.4% work from home; Mean travel time to work: 21.0 minutes

NORTH NORWICH (town).
Covers a land area of 28.142 square miles and a water area of 0.102 square miles. Located at 42.59° N. Lat; 75.51° W. Long. Elevation is 1,037 feet.

Population: 1,612; Growth (since 2000): -18.0%; Density: 57.3 persons per square mile; Race: 95.0% White, 0.8% Black/African American, 0.9% Asian, 0.6% American Indian/Alaska Native, 0.0% Native Hawaiian/Other Pacific Islander, 2.5% Two or more races, 0.7% Hispanic of any race; Average household size: 2.53; Median age: 43.0; Age under 18: 22.3%; Age 65 and over: 14.8%; Males per 100 females: 99.2; Marriage status: 27.2% never married, 56.7% now married, 3.7% separated, 4.1% widowed, 12.0% divorced; Foreign born: 0.8%; Speak English only: 97.0%; With disability: 15.6%; Veterans: 6.6%; Ancestry: 14.8% Irish, 12.8% German, 12.5% English, 11.6% Italian, 8.7% American

Employment: 13.3% management, business, and financial, 5.5% computer, engineering, and science, 6.0% education, legal, community service, arts, and media, 4.5% healthcare practitioners, 14.2% service, 24.5% sales and office, 16.6% natural resources, construction, and maintenance, 15.4% production, transportation, and material moving

Income: Per capita: $25,922; Median household: $55,774; Average household: $63,387; Households with income of $100,000 or more: 17.4%; Poverty rate: 11.1%

Educational Attainment: High school diploma or higher: 89.0%; Bachelor's degree or higher: 15.6%; Graduate/professional degree or higher: 5.7%

Housing: Homeownership rate: 85.2%; Median home value: $100,200; Median year structure built: 1973; Homeowner vacancy rate: 2.7%; Median selected monthly owner costs: $1,092 with a mortgage, $482 without a mortgage; Median gross rent: $726 per month; Rental vacancy rate: 0.0%

Health Insurance: 90.4% have insurance; 69.5% have private insurance; 34.9% have public insurance; 9.6% do not have insurance; 4.7% of children under 18 do not have insurance

Transportation: Commute: 90.4% car, 0.0% public transportation, 3.1% walk, 5.9% work from home; Mean travel time to work: 20.6 minutes

NORTH PITCHER (unincorporated postal area)
ZCTA: 13124

Covers a land area of 4.685 square miles and a water area of 0.005 square miles. Located at 42.66° N. Lat; 75.82° W. Long. Elevation is 1,161 feet.

Population: 78; Growth (since 2000): -42.2%; Density: 16.6 persons per square mile; Race: 100.0% White, 0.0% Black/African American, 0.0% Asian, 0.0% American Indian/Alaska Native, 0.0% Native Hawaiian/Other Pacific Islander, 0.0% Two or more races, 6.4% Hispanic of any race; Average household size: 2.00; Median age: 42.5; Age under 18: 15.4%; Age 65 and over: 5.1%; Males per 100 females: 138.5; Marriage status: 33.8% never married, 54.9% now married, 4.2% separated, 7.0% widowed, 4.2% divorced; Foreign born: 0.0%; Speak English only: 100.0%; With disability: 17.9%; Veterans: 18.2%;

Ancestry: 16.7% American, 15.4% German, 9.0% Irish, 7.7% English, 6.4% Norwegian

Employment: 0.0% management, business, and financial, 0.0% computer, engineering, and science, 0.0% education, legal, community service, arts, and media, 4.3% healthcare practitioners, 17.4% service, 30.4% sales and office, 17.4% natural resources, construction, and maintenance, 30.4% production, transportation, and material moving

Income: Per capita: $31,176; Median household: $46,094; Average household: $59,467; Households with income of $100,000 or more: 15.4%; Poverty rate: n/a

Educational Attainment: High school diploma or higher: 100.0%; Bachelor's degree or higher: 5.1%; Graduate/professional degree or higher: n/a

Housing: Homeownership rate: 87.2%; Median home value: $83,600; Median year structure built: 1955; Homeowner vacancy rate: 0.0%; Median selected monthly owner costs: $1,042 with a mortgage, $413 without a mortgage; Median gross rent: n/a per month; Rental vacancy rate: 0.0%

Health Insurance: 79.5% have insurance; 71.8% have private insurance; 23.1% have public insurance; 20.5% do not have insurance; 16.7% of children under 18 do not have insurance

Transportation: Commute: 95.7% car, 0.0% public transportation, 0.0% walk, 0.0% work from home; Mean travel time to work: 29.2 minutes

---

NORWICH (city). County seat. Covers a land area of 2.124 square miles and a water area of 0 square miles. Located at 42.53° N. Lat; 75.52° W. Long. Elevation is 1,014 feet.

Population: 7,032; Growth (since 2000): -4.4%; Density: 3,310.1 persons per square mile; Race: 94.1% White, 1.4% Black/African American, 0.9% Asian, 0.0% American Indian/Alaska Native, 0.0% Native Hawaiian/Other Pacific Islander, 2.5% Two or more races, 3.9% Hispanic of any race; Average household size: 2.47; Median age: 35.2; Age under 18: 25.6%; Age 65 and over: 17.1%; Males per 100 females: 84.5; Marriage status: 35.0% never married, 41.8% now married, 4.3% separated, 7.3% widowed, 15.9% divorced; Foreign born: 3.4%; Speak English only: 94.5%; With disability: 17.8%; Veterans: 5.9%; Ancestry: 22.7% German, 19.0% Irish, 16.7% English, 16.1% Italian, 8.3% American

Employment: 11.4% management, business, and financial, 3.8% computer, engineering, and science, 12.5% education, legal, community service, arts, and media, 4.4% healthcare practitioners, 23.6% service, 24.4% sales and office, 6.5% natural resources, construction, and maintenance, 13.4% production, transportation, and material moving

Income: Per capita: $20,873; Median household: $38,825; Average household: $50,857; Households with income of $100,000 or more: 12.8%; Poverty rate: 25.6%

Educational Attainment: High school diploma or higher: 87.2%; Bachelor's degree or higher: 24.4%; Graduate/professional degree or higher: 11.4%

School District(s)

Delaware-Chenango-Madison-Otsego Boces

    2014-15 Enrollment: n/a . . . . (607) 335-1233

Norwich City SD (PK-12)

    2014-15 Enrollment: 1,936 . . . . (607) 334-1600

Vocational/Technical School(s)

Delaware Chenango Madison Otsego BOCES-Practical Nursing Program (Public)

    Fall 2014 Enrollment: 27 . . . . (607) 335-1216

    2015-16 Tuition: $9,700

Housing: Homeownership rate: 50.6%; Median home value: $83,600; Median year structure built: Before 1940; Homeowner vacancy rate: 0.6%; Median selected monthly owner costs: $1,083 with a mortgage, $488 without a mortgage; Median gross rent: $627 per month; Rental vacancy rate: 9.1%

Health Insurance: 92.1% have insurance; 62.3% have private insurance; 43.7% have public insurance; 7.9% do not have insurance; 6.4% of children under 18 do not have insurance

Hospitals: Chenango Memorial Hospital (139 beds)

Safety: Violent crime rate: 30.1 per 10,000 population; Property crime rate: 344.3 per 10,000 population

Newspapers: Evening Sun (daily circulation 5,000); The Gazette (weekly circulation 2,400)

Transportation: Commute: 79.4% car, 1.1% public transportation, 13.5% walk, 2.9% work from home; Mean travel time to work: 14.3 minutes

Additional Information Contacts

City of Norwich . . . . (607) 334-1230

  http://www.norwichnewyork.net

NORWICH (town). Covers a land area of 41.963 square miles and a water area of 0.075 square miles. Located at 42.51° N. Lat; 75.49° W. Long. Elevation is 1,014 feet.

History: Gail Borden born here. Settled 1788. Incorporated 1915.

Population: 3,920; Growth (since 2000): 2.2%; Density: 93.4 persons per square mile; Race: 97.6% White, 1.4% Black/African American, 0.0% Asian, 0.0% American Indian/Alaska Native, 0.0% Native Hawaiian/Other Pacific Islander, 0.7% Two or more races, 0.5% Hispanic of any race; Average household size: 2.63; Median age: 43.5; Age under 18: 19.9%; Age 65 and over: 14.8%; Males per 100 females: 103.3; Marriage status: 26.7% never married, 50.4% now married, 0.2% separated, 7.1% widowed, 15.9% divorced; Foreign born: 0.5%; Speak English only: 98.5%; With disability: 21.3%; Veterans: 7.7%; Ancestry: 20.3% English, 19.7% Irish, 15.0% Italian, 12.8% German, 12.1% American

Employment: 14.6% management, business, and financial, 2.0% computer, engineering, and science, 10.8% education, legal, community service, arts, and media, 2.2% healthcare practitioners, 20.0% service, 16.8% sales and office, 11.9% natural resources, construction, and maintenance, 21.7% production, transportation, and material moving

Income: Per capita: $22,950; Median household: $53,581; Average household: $60,084; Households with income of $100,000 or more: 16.8%; Poverty rate: 12.4%

Educational Attainment: High school diploma or higher: 85.1%; Bachelor's degree or higher: 15.6%; Graduate/professional degree or higher: 9.4%

School District(s)

Delaware-Chenango-Madison-Otsego Boces

    2014-15 Enrollment: n/a . . . . (607) 335-1233

Norwich City SD (PK-12)

    2014-15 Enrollment: 1,936 . . . . (607) 334-1600

Vocational/Technical School(s)

Delaware Chenango Madison Otsego BOCES-Practical Nursing Program (Public)

    Fall 2014 Enrollment: 27 . . . . (607) 335-1216

    2015-16 Tuition: $9,700

Housing: Homeownership rate: 82.2%; Median home value: $81,900; Median year structure built: 1972; Homeowner vacancy rate: 2.3%; Median selected monthly owner costs: $1,135 with a mortgage, $368 without a mortgage; Median gross rent: $606 per month; Rental vacancy rate: 0.0%

Health Insurance: 95.2% have insurance; 69.4% have private insurance; 40.3% have public insurance; 4.8% do not have insurance; 1.3% of children under 18 do not have insurance

Hospitals: Chenango Memorial Hospital (139 beds)

Newspapers: Evening Sun (daily circulation 5,000); The Gazette (weekly circulation 2,400)

Transportation: Commute: 95.5% car, 0.0% public transportation, 0.7% walk, 3.2% work from home; Mean travel time to work: 20.2 minutes

---

OTSELIC (town). Covers a land area of 37.977 square miles and a water area of 0.067 square miles. Located at 42.68° N. Lat; 75.74° W. Long. Elevation is 1,355 feet.

Population: 998; Growth (since 2000): -0.3%; Density: 26.3 persons per square mile; Race: 96.6% White, 0.0% Black/African American, 0.0% Asian, 1.1% American Indian/Alaska Native, 0.0% Native Hawaiian/Other Pacific Islander, 2.0% Two or more races, 3.0% Hispanic of any race; Average household size: 2.66; Median age: 39.2; Age under 18: 25.2%; Age 65 and over: 17.9%; Males per 100 females: 116.0; Marriage status: 31.3% never married, 53.5% now married, 4.0% separated, 6.5% widowed, 8.7% divorced; Foreign born: 0.5%; Speak English only: 95.9%; With disability: 18.2%; Veterans: 8.1%; Ancestry: 20.6% English, 17.8% German, 17.1% Irish, 8.1% American, 4.8% Dutch

Employment: 8.8% management, business, and financial, 2.2% computer, engineering, and science, 13.3% education, legal, community service, arts, and media, 7.1% healthcare practitioners, 16.7% service, 17.9% sales and office, 14.7% natural resources, construction, and maintenance, 19.2% production, transportation, and material moving

Income: Per capita: $21,462; Median household: $45,156; Average household: $55,762; Households with income of $100,000 or more: 13.3%; Poverty rate: 16.6%

Educational Attainment: High school diploma or higher: 85.0%; Bachelor's degree or higher: 12.2%; Graduate/professional degree or higher: 4.1%

Housing: Homeownership rate: 75.2%; Median home value: $78,600; Median year structure built: 1946; Homeowner vacancy rate: 0.7%; Median selected monthly owner costs: $900 with a mortgage, $438 without a mortgage; Median gross rent: $618 per month; Rental vacancy rate: 0.0%

Health Insurance: 92.4% have insurance; 64.9% have private insurance; 44.6% have public insurance; 7.6% do not have insurance; 4.8% of children under 18 do not have insurance

Transportation: Commute: 85.0% car, 0.5% public transportation, 10.4% walk, 4.1% work from home; Mean travel time to work: 29.9 minutes

OXFORD (town). Covers a land area of 60.063 square miles and a water area of 0.352 square miles. Located at 42.40° N. Lat; 75.60° W. Long. Elevation is 971 feet.

History: Site of N.Y. State Women's Relief Corps Home built in 1896 and now operated as the N.Y. State Veterans' Home. Settled 1788; incorporated 1808.

Population: 3,846; Growth (since 2000): -3.7%; Density: 64.0 persons per square mile; Race: 96.7% White, 0.3% Black/African American, 0.0% Asian, 0.0% American Indian/Alaska Native, 0.0% Native Hawaiian/Other Pacific Islander, 1.0% Two or more races, 3.6% Hispanic of any race; Average household size: 2.49; Median age: 50.5; Age under 18: 16.9%; Age 65 and over: 22.2%; Males per 100 females: 105.7; Marriage status: 22.7% never married, 59.3% now married, 3.2% separated, 10.0% widowed, 8.0% divorced; Foreign born: 1.2%; Speak English only: 94.8%; With disability: 22.7%; Veterans: 14.2%; Ancestry: 26.1% German, 20.8% Irish, 16.8% English, 9.6% Italian, 6.8% Dutch

Employment: 12.6% management, business, and financial, 3.0% computer, engineering, and science, 12.1% education, legal, community service, arts, and media, 4.6% healthcare practitioners, 22.8% service, 19.9% sales and office, 14.9% natural resources, construction, and maintenance, 10.1% production, transportation, and material moving

Income: Per capita: $24,554; Median household: $49,583; Average household: $59,358; Households with income of $100,000 or more: 19.1%; Poverty rate: 8.3%

Educational Attainment: High school diploma or higher: 89.3%; Bachelor's degree or higher: 16.2%; Graduate/professional degree or higher: 8.8%

School District(s)
Oxford Academy and Central SD (PK-12)
   2014-15 Enrollment: 781 . . . . (607) 843-2025

Housing: Homeownership rate: 84.3%; Median home value: $99,700; Median year structure built: 1961; Homeowner vacancy rate: 3.1%; Median selected monthly owner costs: $1,000 with a mortgage, $489 without a mortgage; Median gross rent: $651 per month; Rental vacancy rate: 5.4%

Health Insurance: 95.4% have insurance; 74.5% have private insurance; 41.7% have public insurance; 4.6% do not have insurance; 2.5% of children under 18 do not have insurance

Transportation: Commute: 87.3% car, 0.8% public transportation, 2.3% walk, 8.4% work from home; Mean travel time to work: 24.7 minutes

OXFORD (village). Covers a land area of 1.785 square miles and a water area of 0 square miles. Located at 42.44° N. Lat; 75.60° W. Long. Elevation is 971 feet.

Population: 1,370; Growth (since 2000): -13.5%; Density: 767.6 persons per square mile; Race: 97.4% White, 0.4% Black/African American, 0.0% Asian, 0.0% American Indian/Alaska Native, 0.0% Native Hawaiian/Other Pacific Islander, 1.8% Two or more races, 3.5% Hispanic of any race; Average household size: 2.50; Median age: 44.4; Age under 18: 21.1%; Age 65 and over: 17.4%; Males per 100 females: 90.0; Marriage status: 27.1% never married, 53.9% now married, 4.9% separated, 8.0% widowed, 11.0% divorced; Foreign born: 2.0%; Speak English only: 95.8%; With disability: 17.9%; Veterans: 10.7%; Ancestry: 30.4% German, 21.5% English, 21.3% Irish, 9.1% Dutch, 7.7% Italian

Employment: 12.5% management, business, and financial, 2.7% computer, engineering, and science, 11.9% education, legal, community service, arts, and media, 5.8% healthcare practitioners, 17.0% service, 27.5% sales and office, 11.2% natural resources, construction, and maintenance, 11.4% production, transportation, and material moving

Income: Per capita: $23,928; Median household: $46,287; Average household: $58,931; Households with income of $100,000 or more: 16.7%; Poverty rate: 12.5%

Educational Attainment: High school diploma or higher: 90.5%; Bachelor's degree or higher: 22.7%; Graduate/professional degree or higher: 10.6%

School District(s)
Oxford Academy and Central SD (PK-12)
   2014-15 Enrollment: 781 . . . . (607) 843-2025

Housing: Homeownership rate: 73.4%; Median home value: $91,800; Median year structure built: Before 1940; Homeowner vacancy rate: 2.0%; Median selected monthly owner costs: $1,076 with a mortgage, $529 without a mortgage; Median gross rent: $598 per month; Rental vacancy rate: 8.5%

Health Insurance: 92.0% have insurance; 70.7% have private insurance; 38.8% have public insurance; 8.0% do not have insurance; 5.5% of children under 18 do not have insurance

Transportation: Commute: 86.1% car, 1.4% public transportation, 6.2% walk, 6.4% work from home; Mean travel time to work: 24.4 minutes

PHARSALIA (town). Covers a land area of 38.816 square miles and a water area of 0.292 square miles. Located at 42.60° N. Lat; 75.73° W. Long. Elevation is 1,562 feet.

Population: 633; Growth (since 2000): 16.8%; Density: 16.3 persons per square mile; Race: 96.7% White, 0.0% Black/African American, 0.0% Asian, 0.0% American Indian/Alaska Native, 0.0% Native Hawaiian/Other Pacific Islander, 3.3% Two or more races, 0.6% Hispanic of any race; Average household size: 2.41; Median age: 48.4; Age under 18: 23.2%; Age 65 and over: 18.6%; Males per 100 females: 99.7; Marriage status: 24.7% never married, 60.0% now married, 3.1% separated, 2.9% widowed, 12.5% divorced; Foreign born: 0.0%; Speak English only: 98.2%; With disability: 18.0%; Veterans: 11.3%; Ancestry: 18.5% German, 17.7% English, 16.1% Irish, 10.3% American, 3.8% Dutch

Employment: 20.5% management, business, and financial, 2.3% computer, engineering, and science, 2.7% education, legal, community service, arts, and media, 9.5% healthcare practitioners, 14.8% service, 25.1% sales and office, 11.4% natural resources, construction, and maintenance, 13.7% production, transportation, and material moving

Income: Per capita: $20,337; Median household: $39,219; Average household: $49,249; Households with income of $100,000 or more: 7.6%; Poverty rate: 23.7%

Educational Attainment: High school diploma or higher: 84.6%; Bachelor's degree or higher: 10.6%; Graduate/professional degree or higher: 3.5%

Housing: Homeownership rate: 88.6%; Median home value: $64,200; Median year structure built: 1971; Homeowner vacancy rate: 4.4%; Median selected monthly owner costs: $900 with a mortgage, $311 without a mortgage; Median gross rent: $578 per month; Rental vacancy rate: 0.0%

Health Insurance: 92.7% have insurance; 53.7% have private insurance; 58.0% have public insurance; 7.3% do not have insurance; 7.5% of children under 18 do not have insurance

Transportation: Commute: 96.5% car, 0.8% public transportation, 0.4% walk, 2.3% work from home; Mean travel time to work: 28.4 minutes

PITCHER (town). Covers a land area of 28.465 square miles and a water area of 0.014 square miles. Located at 42.59° N. Lat; 75.83° W. Long. Elevation is 1,135 feet.

Population: 665; Growth (since 2000): -21.6%; Density: 23.4 persons per square mile; Race: 99.5% White, 0.0% Black/African American, 0.0% Asian, 0.0% American Indian/Alaska Native, 0.0% Native Hawaiian/Other Pacific Islander, 0.0% Two or more races, 2.3% Hispanic of any race; Average household size: 2.51; Median age: 43.3; Age under 18: 22.4%; Age 65 and over: 14.7%; Males per 100 females: 111.3; Marriage status: 22.7% never married, 59.2% now married, 3.0% separated, 7.2% widowed, 10.9% divorced; Foreign born: 0.8%; Speak English only: 98.6%; With disability: 16.4%; Veterans: 16.1%; Ancestry: 19.7% English, 17.3% American, 12.6% German, 9.5% Irish, 4.1% Italian

Employment: 5.0% management, business, and financial, 1.0% computer, engineering, and science, 5.3% education, legal, community service, arts, and media, 1.3% healthcare practitioners, 22.6% service, 18.6% sales and office, 13.6% natural resources, construction, and maintenance, 32.6% production, transportation, and material moving

Income: Per capita: $20,671; Median household: $46,635; Average household: $51,428; Households with income of $100,000 or more: 6.5%; Poverty rate: 19.7%

Educational Attainment: High school diploma or higher: 92.6%; Bachelor's degree or higher: 12.1%; Graduate/professional degree or higher: 4.5%

Housing: Homeownership rate: 87.9%; Median home value: $70,200; Median year structure built: 1973; Homeowner vacancy rate: 5.3%; Median selected monthly owner costs: $929 with a mortgage, $443 without a mortgage; Median gross rent: $667 per month; Rental vacancy rate: 0.0%
Health Insurance: 90.7% have insurance; 61.5% have private insurance; 46.0% have public insurance; 9.3% do not have insurance; 9.4% of children under 18 do not have insurance
Transportation: Commute: 96.2% car, 0.0% public transportation, 2.4% walk, 0.7% work from home; Mean travel time to work: 38.7 minutes

PLYMOUTH (town). Covers a land area of 42.177 square miles and a water area of 0.169 square miles. Located at 42.61° N. Lat; 75.60° W. Long. Elevation is 1,243 feet.
Population: 1,920; Growth (since 2000): -6.3%; Density: 45.5 persons per square mile; Race: 98.1% White, 0.4% Black/African American, 0.2% Asian, 1.1% American Indian/Alaska Native, 0.0% Native Hawaiian/Other Pacific Islander, 0.3% Two or more races, 2.1% Hispanic of any race; Average household size: 2.80; Median age: 45.9; Age under 18: 19.6%; Age 65 and over: 19.6%; Males per 100 females: 101.3; Marriage status: 29.6% never married, 51.8% now married, 3.6% separated, 5.2% widowed, 13.4% divorced; Foreign born: 0.2%; Speak English only: 97.6%; With disability: 22.1%; Veterans: 10.9%; Ancestry: 19.3% German, 18.3% Irish, 13.4% English, 12.9% American, 7.8% Italian
Employment: 9.9% management, business, and financial, 2.2% computer, engineering, and science, 4.8% education, legal, community service, arts, and media, 5.2% healthcare practitioners, 20.2% service, 29.9% sales and office, 12.6% natural resources, construction, and maintenance, 15.2% production, transportation, and material moving
Income: Per capita: $20,238; Median household: $41,250; Average household: $54,360; Households with income of $100,000 or more: 13.6%; Poverty rate: 22.1%
Educational Attainment: High school diploma or higher: 84.7%; Bachelor's degree or higher: 9.2%; Graduate/professional degree or higher: 2.6%
Housing: Homeownership rate: 90.2%; Median home value: $85,900; Median year structure built: 1972; Homeowner vacancy rate: 2.2%; Median selected monthly owner costs: $1,157 with a mortgage, $478 without a mortgage; Median gross rent: $672 per month; Rental vacancy rate: 0.0%
Health Insurance: 87.8% have insurance; 53.3% have private insurance; 50.6% have public insurance; 12.2% do not have insurance; 5.3% of children under 18 do not have insurance
Transportation: Commute: 93.6% car, 1.3% public transportation, 2.6% walk, 2.6% work from home; Mean travel time to work: 20.5 minutes

PRESTON (town). Covers a land area of 34.876 square miles and a water area of 0.171 square miles. Located at 42.50° N. Lat; 75.61° W. Long. Elevation is 1,470 feet.
Population: 1,081; Growth (since 2000): 16.5%; Density: 31.0 persons per square mile; Race: 98.7% White, 0.0% Black/African American, 0.4% Asian, 0.0% American Indian/Alaska Native, 0.0% Native Hawaiian/Other Pacific Islander, 0.4% Two or more races, 0.0% Hispanic of any race; Average household size: 2.52; Median age: 41.4; Age under 18: 23.4%; Age 65 and over: 11.2%; Males per 100 females: 114.4; Marriage status: 29.3% never married, 51.0% now married, 5.2% separated, 4.4% widowed, 15.4% divorced; Foreign born: 0.6%; Speak English only: 98.2%; With disability: 19.6%; Veterans: 7.4%; Ancestry: 18.9% English, 17.3% German, 11.5% Irish, 10.8% Italian, 9.7% American
Employment: 11.9% management, business, and financial, 6.4% computer, engineering, and science, 6.8% education, legal, community service, arts, and media, 6.2% healthcare practitioners, 9.5% service, 23.3% sales and office, 16.7% natural resources, construction, and maintenance, 19.3% production, transportation, and material moving
Income: Per capita: $21,903; Median household: $45,625; Average household: $54,827; Households with income of $100,000 or more: 9.8%; Poverty rate: 13.0%
Educational Attainment: High school diploma or higher: 81.3%; Bachelor's degree or higher: 12.6%; Graduate/professional degree or higher: 8.0%
Housing: Homeownership rate: 86.7%; Median home value: $78,800; Median year structure built: 1974; Homeowner vacancy rate: 5.1%; Median selected monthly owner costs: $878 with a mortgage, $358 without a mortgage; Median gross rent: $630 per month; Rental vacancy rate: 0.0%
Health Insurance: 93.8% have insurance; 77.1% have private insurance; 31.7% have public insurance; 6.2% do not have insurance; 0.8% of children under 18 do not have insurance

Transportation: Commute: 97.1% car, 0.0% public transportation, 1.6% walk, 1.2% work from home; Mean travel time to work: 25.6 minutes

SHERBURNE (town). Covers a land area of 43.554 square miles and a water area of 0.020 square miles. Located at 42.69° N. Lat; 75.48° W. Long. Elevation is 1,047 feet.
History: Former summer resort. Settled 1793, incorporated 1830.
Population: 3,983; Growth (since 2000): 0.1%; Density: 91.5 persons per square mile; Race: 97.5% White, 1.1% Black/African American, 0.1% Asian, 0.5% American Indian/Alaska Native, 0.0% Native Hawaiian/Other Pacific Islander, 0.9% Two or more races, 1.5% Hispanic of any race; Average household size: 2.39; Median age: 39.6; Age under 18: 24.9%; Age 65 and over: 14.8%; Males per 100 females: 94.0; Marriage status: 23.9% never married, 60.0% now married, 3.1% separated, 4.8% widowed, 11.3% divorced; Foreign born: 0.8%; Speak English only: 97.0%; With disability: 14.8%; Veterans: 5.9%; Ancestry: 20.6% English, 16.9% German, 14.6% Irish, 6.5% Italian, 5.9% French
Employment: 10.7% management, business, and financial, 1.2% computer, engineering, and science, 14.0% education, legal, community service, arts, and media, 9.2% healthcare practitioners, 20.1% service, 25.0% sales and office, 8.2% natural resources, construction, and maintenance, 11.8% production, transportation, and material moving
Income: Per capita: $22,608; Median household: $43,229; Average household: $54,000; Households with income of $100,000 or more: 10.1%; Poverty rate: 12.8%
Educational Attainment: High school diploma or higher: 90.8%; Bachelor's degree or higher: 18.2%; Graduate/professional degree or higher: 7.4%

School District(s)
Sherburne-Earlville Central SD (PK-12)
    2014-15 Enrollment: 1,427 . . . . (607) 674-7300
Housing: Homeownership rate: 60.4%; Median home value: $106,900; Median year structure built: 1960; Homeowner vacancy rate: 1.9%; Median selected monthly owner costs: $1,120 with a mortgage, $389 without a mortgage; Median gross rent: $619 per month; Rental vacancy rate: 2.2%
Health Insurance: 94.9% have insurance; 70.4% have private insurance; 39.6% have public insurance; 5.1% do not have insurance; 3.6% of children under 18 do not have insurance
Newspapers: Sherburne News (weekly circulation 1,900)
Transportation: Commute: 91.1% car, 0.3% public transportation, 4.0% walk, 4.6% work from home; Mean travel time to work: 21.0 minutes
Additional Information Contacts
Town of Sherburne . . . . (607) 674-4481
    http://www.sherburne.org

SHERBURNE (village). Covers a land area of 1.519 square miles and a water area of 0 square miles. Located at 42.68° N. Lat; 75.50° W. Long. Elevation is 1,047 feet.
Population: 1,359; Growth (since 2000): -6.6%; Density: 894.5 persons per square mile; Race: 96.4% White, 3.2% Black/African American, 0.2% Asian, 0.0% American Indian/Alaska Native, 0.0% Native Hawaiian/Other Pacific Islander, 0.1% Two or more races, 2.4% Hispanic of any race; Average household size: 2.10; Median age: 48.2; Age under 18: 20.9%; Age 65 and over: 19.4%; Males per 100 females: 83.7; Marriage status: 26.3% never married, 44.0% now married, 3.1% separated, 10.4% widowed, 19.4% divorced; Foreign born: 1.4%; Speak English only: 93.2%; With disability: 23.5%; Veterans: 6.4%; Ancestry: 21.8% English, 13.0% German, 10.5% Irish, 8.2% American, 8.1% Italian
Employment: 9.7% management, business, and financial, 3.4% computer, engineering, and science, 12.6% education, legal, community service, arts, and media, 4.9% healthcare practitioners, 21.3% service, 30.4% sales and office, 7.8% natural resources, construction, and maintenance, 9.7% production, transportation, and material moving
Income: Per capita: $23,416; Median household: $35,288; Average household: $48,848; Households with income of $100,000 or more: 11.2%; Poverty rate: 22.4%
Educational Attainment: High school diploma or higher: 87.5%; Bachelor's degree or higher: 20.8%; Graduate/professional degree or higher: 7.5%

School District(s)
Sherburne-Earlville Central SD (PK-12)
    2014-15 Enrollment: 1,427 . . . . (607) 674-7300
Housing: Homeownership rate: 43.4%; Median home value: $103,600; Median year structure built: Before 1940; Homeowner vacancy rate: 3.9%; Median selected monthly owner costs: $1,023 with a mortgage, $395

without a mortgage; Median gross rent: $585 per month; Rental vacancy rate: 2.4%
Health Insurance: 95.6% have insurance; 58.6% have private insurance; 51.6% have public insurance; 4.4% do not have insurance; 12.7% of children under 18 do not have insurance
Safety: Violent crime rate: 0.0 per 10,000 population; Property crime rate: 52.2 per 10,000 population
Newspapers: Sherburne News (weekly circulation 1,900)
Transportation: Commute: 77.8% car, 0.9% public transportation, 11.2% walk, 10.1% work from home; Mean travel time to work: 16.1 minutes

SMITHVILLE (town). Covers a land area of 50.445 square miles and a water area of 0.481 square miles. Located at 42.41° N. Lat; 75.76° W. Long.

Population: 1,612; Growth (since 2000): 19.7%; Density: 32.0 persons per square mile; Race: 87.7% White, 3.7% Black/African American, 2.1% Asian, 0.0% American Indian/Alaska Native, 0.9% Native Hawaiian/Other Pacific Islander, 5.6% Two or more races, 1.9% Hispanic of any race; Average household size: 2.90; Median age: 36.7; Age under 18: 27.4%; Age 65 and over: 11.5%; Males per 100 females: 115.2; Marriage status: 37.0% never married, 51.0% now married, 3.9% separated, 5.2% widowed, 6.9% divorced; Foreign born: 2.5%; Speak English only: 97.3%; With disability: 15.2%; Veterans: 9.6%; Ancestry: 19.9% Irish, 12.5% Italian, 11.7% German, 10.0% English, 7.2% American
Employment: 11.9% management, business, and financial, 3.6% computer, engineering, and science, 13.1% education, legal, community service, arts, and media, 1.1% healthcare practitioners, 23.9% service, 14.1% sales and office, 12.8% natural resources, construction, and maintenance, 19.5% production, transportation, and material moving
Income: Per capita: $18,130; Median household: $43,889; Average household: $52,129; Households with income of $100,000 or more: 9.2%; Poverty rate: 26.4%
Educational Attainment: High school diploma or higher: 85.7%; Bachelor's degree or higher: 17.1%; Graduate/professional degree or higher: 6.4%
Housing: Homeownership rate: 80.3%; Median home value: $89,400; Median year structure built: 1968; Homeowner vacancy rate: 3.3%; Median selected monthly owner costs: $1,119 with a mortgage, $468 without a mortgage; Median gross rent: $698 per month; Rental vacancy rate: 0.0%
Health Insurance: 93.9% have insurance; 68.7% have private insurance; 36.2% have public insurance; 6.1% do not have insurance; 0.2% of children under 18 do not have insurance
Transportation: Commute: 92.9% car, 2.2% public transportation, 1.3% walk, 3.6% work from home; Mean travel time to work: 29.4 minutes

SMITHVILLE FLATS (CDP). Covers a land area of 1.422 square miles and a water area of 0 square miles. Located at 42.39° N. Lat; 75.81° W. Long. Elevation is 1,024 feet.

Population: 480; Growth (since 2000): n/a; Density: 337.6 persons per square mile; Race: 83.3% White, 4.2% Black/African American, 0.0% Asian, 0.0% American Indian/Alaska Native, 2.9% Native Hawaiian/Other Pacific Islander, 9.6% Two or more races, 0.0% Hispanic of any race; Average household size: 2.79; Median age: 40.2; Age under 18: 30.8%; Age 65 and over: 7.3%; Males per 100 females: 123.6; Marriage status: 34.5% never married, 52.9% now married, 7.8% separated, 5.9% widowed, 6.7% divorced; Foreign born: 3.3%; Speak English only: 98.9%; With disability: 14.2%; Veterans: 6.0%; Ancestry: 32.9% Italian, 23.5% Irish, 21.9% German, 6.9% Dutch, 5.8% Polish
Employment: 15.6% management, business, and financial, 0.0% computer, engineering, and science, 11.9% education, legal, community service, arts, and media, 0.0% healthcare practitioners, 26.3% service, 13.8% sales and office, 9.4% natural resources, construction, and maintenance, 23.1% production, transportation, and material moving
Income: Per capita: $18,351; Median household: n/a; Average household: $52,208; Households with income of $100,000 or more: 9.3%; Poverty rate: 31.7%
Educational Attainment: High school diploma or higher: 83.6%; Bachelor's degree or higher: 10.8%; Graduate/professional degree or higher: 2.1%
Housing: Homeownership rate: 77.3%; Median home value: $98,800; Median year structure built: Before 1940; Homeowner vacancy rate: 10.1%; Median selected monthly owner costs: $965 with a mortgage, $517 without a mortgage; Median gross rent: n/a per month; Rental vacancy rate: 0.0%

Health Insurance: 91.3% have insurance; 75.0% have private insurance; 23.8% have public insurance; 8.8% do not have insurance; 0.0% of children under 18 do not have insurance
Transportation: Commute: 80.6% car, 7.7% public transportation, 2.6% walk, 9.0% work from home; Mean travel time to work: 36.0 minutes

SMYRNA (town). Covers a land area of 42.087 square miles and a water area of 0.076 square miles. Located at 42.69° N. Lat; 75.62° W. Long. Elevation is 1,204 feet.

Population: 1,317; Growth (since 2000): -7.1%; Density: 31.3 persons per square mile; Race: 98.4% White, 0.5% Black/African American, 0.0% Asian, 0.3% American Indian/Alaska Native, 0.0% Native Hawaiian/Other Pacific Islander, 0.2% Two or more races, 1.1% Hispanic of any race; Average household size: 2.64; Median age: 41.3; Age under 18: 21.9%; Age 65 and over: 17.7%; Males per 100 females: 113.0; Marriage status: 27.9% never married, 54.8% now married, 3.7% separated, 8.5% widowed, 8.8% divorced; Foreign born: 0.5%; Speak English only: 98.3%; With disability: 17.5%; Veterans: 9.2%; Ancestry: 18.3% German, 17.0% American, 16.7% English, 11.5% Irish, 7.5% Italian
Employment: 13.5% management, business, and financial, 2.1% computer, engineering, and science, 4.2% education, legal, community service, arts, and media, 2.5% healthcare practitioners, 13.2% service, 22.3% sales and office, 12.1% natural resources, construction, and maintenance, 30.1% production, transportation, and material moving
Income: Per capita: $18,860; Median household: $44,750; Average household: $48,333; Households with income of $100,000 or more: 6.6%; Poverty rate: 15.2%
Educational Attainment: High school diploma or higher: 85.5%; Bachelor's degree or higher: 14.6%; Graduate/professional degree or higher: 3.2%
Housing: Homeownership rate: 75.1%; Median home value: $89,500; Median year structure built: 1965; Homeowner vacancy rate: 0.0%; Median selected monthly owner costs: $1,092 with a mortgage, $416 without a mortgage; Median gross rent: $653 per month; Rental vacancy rate: 0.0%
Health Insurance: 88.3% have insurance; 62.0% have private insurance; 42.2% have public insurance; 11.7% do not have insurance; 13.9% of children under 18 do not have insurance
Transportation: Commute: 91.2% car, 0.0% public transportation, 2.2% walk, 4.7% work from home; Mean travel time to work: 24.1 minutes

SMYRNA (village). Covers a land area of 0.244 square miles and a water area of 0 square miles. Located at 42.69° N. Lat; 75.57° W. Long. Elevation is 1,204 feet.

Population: 236; Growth (since 2000): -2.1%; Density: 966.6 persons per square mile; Race: 100.0% White, 0.0% Black/African American, 0.0% Asian, 0.0% American Indian/Alaska Native, 0.0% Native Hawaiian/Other Pacific Islander, 0.0% Two or more races, 0.0% Hispanic of any race; Average household size: 2.99; Median age: 40.8; Age under 18: 29.7%; Age 65 and over: 16.1%; Males per 100 females: 95.4; Marriage status: 29.7% never married, 56.2% now married, 5.4% separated, 8.6% widowed, 5.4% divorced; Foreign born: 0.0%; Speak English only: 99.1%; With disability: 18.2%; Veterans: 6.6%; Ancestry: 30.9% German, 21.2% Irish, 11.0% English, 11.0% Italian, 8.1% American
Employment: 16.9% management, business, and financial, 0.0% computer, engineering, and science, 1.2% education, legal, community service, arts, and media, 2.4% healthcare practitioners, 20.5% service, 21.7% sales and office, 15.7% natural resources, construction, and maintenance, 21.7% production, transportation, and material moving
Income: Per capita: $15,600; Median household: $35,750; Average household: $43,739; Households with income of $100,000 or more: 8.9%; Poverty rate: 20.3%
Educational Attainment: High school diploma or higher: 88.8%; Bachelor's degree or higher: 13.8%; Graduate/professional degree or higher: 5.9%
Housing: Homeownership rate: 58.2%; Median home value: $74,300; Median year structure built: Before 1940; Homeowner vacancy rate: 0.0%; Median selected monthly owner costs: $992 with a mortgage, $391 without a mortgage; Median gross rent: $490 per month; Rental vacancy rate: 0.0%
Health Insurance: 86.4% have insurance; 51.3% have private insurance; 44.5% have public insurance; 13.6% do not have insurance; 20.0% of children under 18 do not have insurance
Transportation: Commute: 83.1% car, 0.0% public transportation, 10.8% walk, 6.0% work from home; Mean travel time to work: 39.2 minutes

SOUTH NEW BERLIN (unincorporated postal area)
ZCTA: 13843

Covers a land area of 54.416 square miles and a water area of 0.079 square miles. Located at 42.51° N. Lat; 75.38° W. Long. Elevation is 1,053 feet.

Population: 1,964; Growth (since 2000): 14.2%; Density: 36.1 persons per square mile; Race: 97.0% White, 0.0% Black/African American, 0.6% Asian, 0.0% American Indian/Alaska Native, 0.0% Native Hawaiian/Other Pacific Islander, 2.4% Two or more races, 0.3% Hispanic of any race; Average household size: 2.53; Median age: 43.6; Age under 18: 20.9%; Age 65 and over: 16.3%; Males per 100 females: 102.1; Marriage status: 23.9% never married, 62.1% now married, 0.0% separated, 5.2% widowed, 8.8% divorced; Foreign born: 3.0%; Speak English only: 97.9%; With disability: 14.6%; Veterans: 9.8%; Ancestry: 26.5% English, 20.4% Irish, 16.2% German, 9.0% Italian, 8.8% American

Employment: 11.7% management, business, and financial, 5.1% computer, engineering, and science, 11.6% education, legal, community service, arts, and media, 3.1% healthcare practitioners, 18.0% service, 21.1% sales and office, 12.2% natural resources, construction, and maintenance, 17.2% production, transportation, and material moving

Income: Per capita: $22,643; Median household: $44,178; Average household: $56,051; Households with income of $100,000 or more: 15.1%; Poverty rate: 16.9%

Educational Attainment: High school diploma or higher: 89.5%; Bachelor's degree or higher: 19.8%; Graduate/professional degree or higher: 7.8%

Housing: Homeownership rate: 88.2%; Median home value: $99,500; Median year structure built: 1960; Homeowner vacancy rate: 2.4%; Median selected monthly owner costs: $1,451 with a mortgage, $373 without a mortgage; Median gross rent: $731 per month; Rental vacancy rate: 0.0%

Health Insurance: 92.2% have insurance; 67.3% have private insurance; 39.6% have public insurance; 7.8% do not have insurance; 1.0% of children under 18 do not have insurance

Transportation: Commute: 92.7% car, 0.0% public transportation, 1.5% walk, 4.7% work from home; Mean travel time to work: 27.4 minutes

SOUTH OTSELIC (unincorporated postal area)
ZCTA: 13155

Covers a land area of 20.452 square miles and a water area of 0.054 square miles. Located at 42.67° N. Lat; 75.78° W. Long. Elevation is 1,227 feet.

Population: 742; Growth (since 2000): 9.6%; Density: 36.3 persons per square mile; Race: 95.6% White, 0.0% Black/African American, 0.0% Asian, 1.2% American Indian/Alaska Native, 0.0% Native Hawaiian/Other Pacific Islander, 2.8% Two or more races, 2.2% Hispanic of any race; Average household size: 2.62; Median age: 41.4; Age under 18: 24.9%; Age 65 and over: 22.1%; Males per 100 females: 110.5; Marriage status: 31.6% never married, 54.0% now married, 4.4% separated, 4.4% widowed, 9.9% divorced; Foreign born: 0.7%; Speak English only: 96.6%; With disability: 19.3%; Veterans: 10.1%; Ancestry: 22.4% English, 14.6% Irish, 13.1% German, 4.9% American, 4.3% French

Employment: 10.0% management, business, and financial, 0.6% computer, engineering, and science, 17.3% education, legal, community service, arts, and media, 9.4% healthcare practitioners, 13.0% service, 19.1% sales and office, 10.0% natural resources, construction, and maintenance, 20.6% production, transportation, and material moving

Income: Per capita: $20,727; Median household: $45,179; Average household: $54,344; Households with income of $100,000 or more: 12.4%; Poverty rate: 17.7%

Educational Attainment: High school diploma or higher: 87.8%; Bachelor's degree or higher: 18.3%; Graduate/professional degree or higher: 7.7%

School District(s)
Georgetown-South Otselic Central SD (KG-12)

    2014-15 Enrollment: 356 . . . . (315) 653-7218

Housing: Homeownership rate: 76.7%; Median home value: $75,300; Median year structure built: Before 1940; Homeowner vacancy rate: 0.0%; Median selected monthly owner costs: $903 with a mortgage, $413 without a mortgage; Median gross rent: $608 per month; Rental vacancy rate: 0.0%

Health Insurance: 95.0% have insurance; 67.5% have private insurance; 48.9% have public insurance; 5.0% do not have insurance; 0.0% of children under 18 do not have insurance

Transportation: Commute: 85.4% car, 0.0% public transportation, 13.9% walk, 0.6% work from home; Mean travel time to work: 31.3 minutes

SOUTH PLYMOUTH (unincorporated postal area)
ZCTA: 13844

Covers a land area of 23.991 square miles and a water area of 0.041 square miles. Located at 42.61° N. Lat; 75.67° W. Long. Elevation is 1,138 feet.

Population: 723; Growth (since 2000): -30.1%; Density: 30.1 persons per square mile; Race: 100.0% White, 0.0% Black/African American, 0.0% Asian, 0.0% American Indian/Alaska Native, 0.0% Native Hawaiian/Other Pacific Islander, 0.0% Two or more races, 0.6% Hispanic of any race; Average household size: 2.73; Median age: 40.6; Age under 18: 29.0%; Age 65 and over: 19.8%; Males per 100 females: 102.2; Marriage status: 26.5% never married, 54.0% now married, 5.7% separated, 6.4% widowed, 13.2% divorced; Foreign born: 0.0%; Speak English only: 98.1%; With disability: 16.5%; Veterans: 13.3%; Ancestry: 18.3% German, 16.9% English, 12.4% Irish, 10.0% American, 9.8% Italian

Employment: 13.3% management, business, and financial, 3.8% computer, engineering, and science, 0.7% education, legal, community service, arts, and media, 0.7% healthcare practitioners, 15.0% service, 30.8% sales and office, 19.6% natural resources, construction, and maintenance, 16.1% production, transportation, and material moving

Income: Per capita: $19,002; Median household: $41,750; Average household: $51,325; Households with income of $100,000 or more: 9.5%; Poverty rate: 15.1%

Educational Attainment: High school diploma or higher: 84.0%; Bachelor's degree or higher: 5.2%; Graduate/professional degree or higher: 0.2%

Housing: Homeownership rate: 81.5%; Median home value: $81,300; Median year structure built: 1972; Homeowner vacancy rate: 2.3%; Median selected monthly owner costs: $935 with a mortgage, $415 without a mortgage; Median gross rent: n/a per month; Rental vacancy rate: 0.0%

Health Insurance: 88.9% have insurance; 56.0% have private insurance; 51.3% have public insurance; 11.1% do not have insurance; 9.5% of children under 18 do not have insurance

Transportation: Commute: 93.8% car, 0.0% public transportation, 2.5% walk, 3.6% work from home; Mean travel time to work: 25.7 minutes

Clinton County

Located in northeastern New York; bounded on the north by the Canadian province of Quebec, and on the east by Lake Champlain and the Vermont border; includes the North Adirondacks. Covers a land area of 1,037.852 square miles, a water area of 79.674 square miles, and is located in the Eastern Time Zone at 44.75° N. Lat., 73.71° W. Long. The county was founded in 1788. County seat is Plattsburgh.

Clinton County is part of the Plattsburgh, NY Micropolitan Statistical Area. The entire metro area includes: Clinton County, NY

Weather Station: Chazy   Elevation: 169 feet

	Jan	Feb	Mar	Apr	May	Jun	Jul	Aug	Sep	Oct	Nov	Dec
High	27	30	40	55	68	76	80	79	70	57	45	33
Low	8	10	20	34	45	54	59	57	49	39	29	16
Precip	0.8	na	0.9	2.3	2.9	3.5	3.5	3.8	3.2	3.1	2.2	0.8
Snow	13.7	12.7	11.1	2.9	0.1	0.0	0.0	0.0	0.0	0.3	4.6	11.2

High and Low temperatures in degrees Fahrenheit; Precipitation and Snow in inches

Weather Station: Dannemora   Elevation: 1,339 feet

	Jan	Feb	Mar	Apr	May	Jun	Jul	Aug	Sep	Oct	Nov	Dec
High	26	30	38	53	65	74	78	76	68	56	43	31
Low	8	11	20	33	45	54	58	57	49	38	28	15
Precip	2.5	2.1	2.5	3.3	3.6	4.0	4.2	4.4	3.9	3.9	3.6	2.9
Snow	na	na	na	tr	0.0	0.0	0.0	0.0	0.0	tr	1.0	na

High and Low temperatures in degrees Fahrenheit; Precipitation and Snow in inches

Weather Station: Peru 2 WSW   Elevation: 509 feet

	Jan	Feb	Mar	Apr	May	Jun	Jul	Aug	Sep	Oct	Nov	Dec
High	28	32	41	56	68	77	81	79	71	58	45	33
Low	9	12	21	34	45	54	59	57	49	38	29	17
Precip	1.4	1.3	1.7	2.6	2.7	3.6	3.5	3.5	2.8	3.0	2.7	2.0
Snow	11.3	10.4	11.1	2.9	0.0	0.0	0.0	0.0	0.0	0.5	3.2	12.6

High and Low temperatures in degrees Fahrenheit; Precipitation and Snow in inches

Population: 81,685; Growth (since 2000): 2.2%; Density: 78.7 persons per square mile; Race: 91.5% White, 4.3% Black/African American, 1.3% Asian, 0.3% American Indian/Alaska Native, 0.0% Native Hawaiian/Other Pacific Islander, 1.4% two or more races, 2.7% Hispanic of any race; Average household size: 2.32; Median age: 39.4; Age under 18: 18.5%; Age 65 and over: 14.7%; Males per 100 females: 105.2; Marriage status: 35.1% never married, 49.0% now married, 2.7% separated, 6.2% widowed, 9.8% divorced; Foreign born: 4.5%; Speak English only: 94.0%; With disability: 15.0%; Veterans: 9.9%; Ancestry: 21.4% French, 16.8% Irish, 9.9% American, 8.8% English, 8.5% German
Religion: Six largest groups: 33.7% Catholicism, 2.2% Methodist/Pietist, 1.9% Muslim Estimate, 1.4% Holiness, 0.8% Presbyterian-Reformed, 0.7% Non-denominational Protestant
Economy: Unemployment rate: 4.9%; Leading industries: 19.8 % retail trade; 12.2 % health care and social assistance; 10.6 % accommodation and food services; Farms: 603 totaling 147,229 acres; Company size: 1 employs 1,000 or more persons, 1 employs 500 to 999 persons, 30 employ 100 to 499 persons, 1,831 employs less than 100 persons; Business ownership: 1,528 women-owned, 60 Black-owned, 73 Hispanic-owned, n/a Asian-owned, n/a American Indian/Alaska Native-owned
Employment: 10.0% management, business, and financial, 3.0% computer, engineering, and science, 11.9% education, legal, community service, arts, and media, 6.1% healthcare practitioners, 22.8% service, 22.9% sales and office, 8.9% natural resources, construction, and maintenance, 14.3% production, transportation, and material moving
Income: Per capita: $24,941; Median household: $49,930; Average household: $63,228; Households with income of $100,000 or more: 18.0%; Poverty rate: 16.5%
Educational Attainment: High school diploma or higher: 85.7%; Bachelor's degree or higher: 22.1%; Graduate/professional degree or higher: 10.2%
Housing: Homeownership rate: 68.1%; Median home value: $124,200; Median year structure built: 1971; Homeowner vacancy rate: 1.1%; Median selected monthly owner costs: $1,217 with a mortgage, $465 without a mortgage; Median gross rent: $744 per month; Rental vacancy rate: 4.7%
Vital Statistics: Birth rate: 90.2 per 10,000 population; Death rate: 84.8 per 10,000 population; Age-adjusted cancer mortality rate: 132.0 deaths per 100,000 population
Health Insurance: 93.9% have insurance; 72.6% have private insurance; 37.4% have public insurance; 6.1% do not have insurance; 2.3% of children under 18 do not have insurance
Health Care: Physicians: 23.7 per 10,000 population; Dentists: 5.2 per 10,000 population; Hospital beds: 35.3 per 10,000 population; Hospital admissions: 1,136.2 per 10,000 population
Transportation: Commute: 89.2% car, 0.6% public transportation, 4.7% walk, 2.8% work from home; Mean travel time to work: 20.6 minutes
2016 Presidential Election: 46.0% Trump, 47.9% Clinton, 4.2% Johnson, 2.0% Stein
National and State Parks: Ausable Marsh State Game Management Area; Clinton State Forest; Cumberland Bay State Park; King Bay State Wetland Game Management Area; Lake Alice State Game Management Area; Miner Lake State Park; New York State Game Management Area
Additional Information Contacts
Clinton Government . . . . (518) 565-4700
   http://www.clintoncountygov.com

Clinton County Communities

ALTONA (CDP). Covers a land area of 1.709 square miles and a water area of 0 square miles. Located at 44.89° N. Lat; 73.66° W. Long. Elevation is 636 feet.
Population: 789; Growth (since 2000): -25.3%; Density: 461.6 persons per square mile; Race: 61.5% White, 26.7% Black/African American, 0.5% Asian, 0.0% American Indian/Alaska Native, 0.0% Native Hawaiian/Other Pacific Islander, 1.4% Two or more races, 14.1% Hispanic of any race; Average household size: 2.23; Median age: 37.2; Age under 18: 9.0%; Age 65 and over: 11.5%; Males per 100 females: 371.0; Marriage status: 50.3% never married, 34.3% now married, 2.2% separated, 6.3% widowed, 9.2% divorced; Foreign born: 2.4%; Speak English only: 92.1%; With disability: 10.9%; Veterans: 8.4%; Ancestry: 17.4% French, 8.4% Irish, 6.3% American, 5.4% German, 5.3% Italian
Employment: 0.0% management, business, and financial, 0.0% computer, engineering, and science, 0.0% education, legal, community service, arts, and media, 0.0% healthcare practitioners, 36.1% service, 23.7% sales and office, 14.4% natural resources, construction, and maintenance, 25.8% production, transportation, and material moving
Income: Per capita: $7,192; Median household: $31,900; Average household: $34,887; Households with income of $100,000 or more: n/a; Poverty rate: 20.9%
Educational Attainment: High school diploma or higher: 69.8%; Bachelor's degree or higher: 3.9%; Graduate/professional degree or higher: 1.4%
Housing: Homeownership rate: 75.7%; Median home value: $66,600; Median year structure built: 1956; Homeowner vacancy rate: 0.0%; Median selected monthly owner costs: $650 with a mortgage, $440 without a mortgage; Median gross rent: n/a per month; Rental vacancy rate: 21.2%
Health Insurance: 96.3% have insurance; 52.6% have private insurance; 68.5% have public insurance; 3.7% do not have insurance; 0.0% of children under 18 do not have insurance
Transportation: Commute: 93.4% car, 6.6% public transportation, 0.0% walk, 0.0% work from home; Mean travel time to work: 28.6 minutes

ALTONA (town). Covers a land area of 100.983 square miles and a water area of 0.357 square miles. Located at 44.84° N. Lat; 73.67° W. Long. Elevation is 636 feet.
Population: 2,907; Growth (since 2000): -8.0%; Density: 28.8 persons per square mile; Race: 87.3% White, 7.4% Black/African American, 0.1% Asian, 0.3% American Indian/Alaska Native, 0.1% Native Hawaiian/Other Pacific Islander, 2.0% Two or more races, 4.5% Hispanic of any race; Average household size: 2.63; Median age: 37.0; Age under 18: 21.2%; Age 65 and over: 11.1%; Males per 100 females: 134.7; Marriage status: 35.3% never married, 50.0% now married, 2.0% separated, 5.9% widowed, 8.8% divorced; Foreign born: 0.9%; Speak English only: 96.5%; With disability: 18.2%; Veterans: 6.9%; Ancestry: 24.4% French, 14.4% Irish, 10.1% American, 9.9% French Canadian, 7.4% English
Employment: 8.9% management, business, and financial, 2.9% computer, engineering, and science, 4.4% education, legal, community service, arts, and media, 6.5% healthcare practitioners, 21.1% service, 25.5% sales and office, 13.1% natural resources, construction, and maintenance, 17.6% production, transportation, and material moving
Income: Per capita: $20,358; Median household: $44,889; Average household: $63,544; Households with income of $100,000 or more: 14.1%; Poverty rate: 22.6%
Educational Attainment: High school diploma or higher: 76.0%; Bachelor's degree or higher: 8.1%; Graduate/professional degree or higher: 3.6%
Housing: Homeownership rate: 83.7%; Median home value: $85,300; Median year structure built: 1980; Homeowner vacancy rate: 0.5%; Median selected monthly owner costs: $991 with a mortgage, $356 without a mortgage; Median gross rent: $664 per month; Rental vacancy rate: 7.7%
Health Insurance: 94.3% have insurance; 64.0% have private insurance; 42.0% have public insurance; 5.7% do not have insurance; 0.6% of children under 18 do not have insurance
Transportation: Commute: 96.4% car, 0.6% public transportation, 0.0% walk, 2.0% work from home; Mean travel time to work: 32.1 minutes

AU SABLE (town). Covers a land area of 39.109 square miles and a water area of 4.740 square miles. Located at 44.50° N. Lat; 73.53° W. Long.
Population: 3,136; Growth (since 2000): 4.0%; Density: 80.2 persons per square mile; Race: 95.2% White, 0.9% Black/African American, 2.1% Asian, 0.4% American Indian/Alaska Native, 0.0% Native Hawaiian/Other Pacific Islander, 1.1% Two or more races, 1.5% Hispanic of any race; Average household size: 2.38; Median age: 42.9; Age under 18: 22.1%; Age 65 and over: 16.0%; Males per 100 females: 99.9; Marriage status: 28.2% never married, 52.3% now married, 2.7% separated, 6.5% widowed, 13.0% divorced; Foreign born: 1.8%; Speak English only: 96.0%; With disability: 18.8%; Veterans: 13.4%; Ancestry: 18.4% French, 14.6% Irish, 10.7% American, 10.2% German, 8.9% English
Employment: 8.6% management, business, and financial, 2.8% computer, engineering, and science, 8.7% education, legal, community service, arts, and media, 3.6% healthcare practitioners, 23.9% service, 20.3% sales and

office, 7.4% natural resources, construction, and maintenance, 24.7% production, transportation, and material moving
Income: Per capita: $23,936; Median household: $45,917; Average household: $56,656; Households with income of $100,000 or more: 13.0%; Poverty rate: 15.6%
Educational Attainment: High school diploma or higher: 83.7%; Bachelor's degree or higher: 14.3%; Graduate/professional degree or higher: 9.5%

School District(s)
Ausable Valley Central SD (KG-12)
    2014-15 Enrollment: 1,151 . . . . (518) 834-2845
Housing: Homeownership rate: 71.3%; Median home value: $97,300; Median year structure built: 1974; Homeowner vacancy rate: 2.0%; Median selected monthly owner costs: $1,045 with a mortgage, $417 without a mortgage; Median gross rent: $633 per month; Rental vacancy rate: 7.2%
Health Insurance: 94.0% have insurance; 69.4% have private insurance; 42.2% have public insurance; 6.0% do not have insurance; 0.0% of children under 18 do not have insurance
Transportation: Commute: 94.0% car, 0.0% public transportation, 1.4% walk, 1.6% work from home; Mean travel time to work: 23.5 minutes

AU SABLE FORKS (CDP). Covers a land area of 2.520 square miles and a water area of 0.023 square miles. Located at 44.45° N. Lat; 73.67° W. Long.
Population: 472; Growth (since 2000): -29.6%; Density: 187.3 persons per square mile; Race: 100.0% White, 0.0% Black/African American, 0.0% Asian, 0.0% American Indian/Alaska Native, 0.0% Native Hawaiian/Other Pacific Islander, 0.0% Two or more races, 0.0% Hispanic of any race; Average household size: 2.20; Median age: 47.6; Age under 18: 19.5%; Age 65 and over: 20.6%; Males per 100 females: 103.3; Marriage status: 21.5% never married, 55.4% now married, 2.2% separated, 13.6% widowed, 9.4% divorced; Foreign born: 0.0%; Speak English only: 100.0%; With disability: 18.4%; Veterans: 14.5%; Ancestry: 23.9% French, 17.4% Irish, 16.5% American, 10.4% German, 9.7% English
Employment: 13.3% management, business, and financial, 2.7% computer, engineering, and science, 18.7% education, legal, community service, arts, and media, 0.0% healthcare practitioners, 22.2% service, 19.6% sales and office, 9.8% natural resources, construction, and maintenance, 13.8% production, transportation, and material moving
Income: Per capita: $24,003; Median household: $45,625; Average household: $52,272; Households with income of $100,000 or more: 10.7%; Poverty rate: 11.6%
Educational Attainment: High school diploma or higher: 81.8%; Bachelor's degree or higher: 10.7%; Graduate/professional degree or higher: 7.4%

School District(s)
Ausable Valley Central SD (KG-12)
    2014-15 Enrollment: 1,151 . . . . (518) 834-2845
Housing: Homeownership rate: 65.1%; Median home value: $111,400; Median year structure built: 1953; Homeowner vacancy rate: 0.0%; Median selected monthly owner costs: $1,091 with a mortgage, $425 without a mortgage; Median gross rent: $625 per month; Rental vacancy rate: 0.0%
Health Insurance: 94.5% have insurance; 75.0% have private insurance; 37.1% have public insurance; 5.5% do not have insurance; 0.0% of children under 18 do not have insurance
Transportation: Commute: 96.0% car, 1.3% public transportation, 0.0% walk, 2.7% work from home; Mean travel time to work: 21.7 minutes

BEEKMANTOWN (town). Covers a land area of 60.425 square miles and a water area of 9.202 square miles. Located at 44.79° N. Lat; 73.50° W. Long. Elevation is 253 feet.
Population: 5,536; Growth (since 2000): 3.9%; Density: 91.6 persons per square mile; Race: 96.3% White, 0.8% Black/African American, 0.8% Asian, 0.1% American Indian/Alaska Native, 0.0% Native Hawaiian/Other Pacific Islander, 2.0% Two or more races, 0.2% Hispanic of any race; Average household size: 2.34; Median age: 43.3; Age under 18: 20.0%; Age 65 and over: 16.0%; Males per 100 females: 99.5; Marriage status: 27.9% never married, 55.6% now married, 1.3% separated, 5.9% widowed, 10.7% divorced; Foreign born: 3.0%; Speak English only: 96.3%; With disability: 15.7%; Veterans: 15.9%; Ancestry: 23.8% French, 20.8% Irish, 16.9% American, 8.7% English, 6.8% Italian
Employment: 10.9% management, business, and financial, 1.5% computer, engineering, and science, 11.1% education, legal, community service, arts, and media, 4.6% healthcare practitioners, 27.8% service,

18.2% sales and office, 13.4% natural resources, construction, and maintenance, 12.6% production, transportation, and material moving
Income: Per capita: $27,688; Median household: $54,390; Average household: $64,866; Households with income of $100,000 or more: 17.8%; Poverty rate: 12.3%
Educational Attainment: High school diploma or higher: 91.0%; Bachelor's degree or higher: 23.7%; Graduate/professional degree or higher: 10.9%
Housing: Homeownership rate: 80.8%; Median home value: $140,500; Median year structure built: 1984; Homeowner vacancy rate: 0.0%; Median selected monthly owner costs: $1,201 with a mortgage, $472 without a mortgage; Median gross rent: $834 per month; Rental vacancy rate: 6.4%
Health Insurance: 93.7% have insurance; 74.6% have private insurance; 38.6% have public insurance; 6.3% do not have insurance; 0.0% of children under 18 do not have insurance
Transportation: Commute: 93.1% car, 0.0% public transportation, 2.2% walk, 2.8% work from home; Mean travel time to work: 23.0 minutes
Additional Information Contacts
Town of Beekmantown . . . . (518) 563-4650
  http://townofbeekmantown.com

BLACK BROOK (town). Covers a land area of 129.974 square miles and a water area of 4.361 square miles. Located at 44.52° N. Lat; 73.82° W. Long. Elevation is 974 feet.
Population: 1,431; Growth (since 2000): -13.8%; Density: 11.0 persons per square mile; Race: 98.8% White, 0.8% Black/African American, 0.0% Asian, 0.0% American Indian/Alaska Native, 0.0% Native Hawaiian/Other Pacific Islander, 0.4% Two or more races, 0.1% Hispanic of any race; Average household size: 2.26; Median age: 47.7; Age under 18: 13.8%; Age 65 and over: 21.1%; Males per 100 females: 105.1; Marriage status: 26.4% never married, 58.6% now married, 1.9% separated, 7.1% widowed, 7.9% divorced; Foreign born: 4.2%; Speak English only: 95.1%; With disability: 16.7%; Veterans: 10.9%; Ancestry: 26.4% French, 14.7% Irish, 10.4% American, 9.9% English, 9.4% German
Employment: 12.6% management, business, and financial, 1.7% computer, engineering, and science, 13.4% education, legal, community service, arts, and media, 2.5% healthcare practitioners, 19.4% service, 19.7% sales and office, 14.9% natural resources, construction, and maintenance, 15.7% production, transportation, and material moving
Income: Per capita: $26,904; Median household: $55,625; Average household: $61,091; Households with income of $100,000 or more: 15.8%; Poverty rate: 8.7%
Educational Attainment: High school diploma or higher: 83.6%; Bachelor's degree or higher: 15.4%; Graduate/professional degree or higher: 8.8%
Housing: Homeownership rate: 77.2%; Median home value: $108,200; Median year structure built: 1960; Homeowner vacancy rate: 0.6%; Median selected monthly owner costs: $1,125 with a mortgage, $469 without a mortgage; Median gross rent: $670 per month; Rental vacancy rate: 0.0%
Health Insurance: 90.5% have insurance; 74.4% have private insurance; 36.0% have public insurance; 9.5% do not have insurance; 1.5% of children under 18 do not have insurance
Transportation: Commute: 96.2% car, 0.4% public transportation, 1.2% walk, 1.9% work from home; Mean travel time to work: 26.0 minutes

CADYVILLE (unincorporated postal area)
ZCTA: 12918
  Covers a land area of 39.293 square miles and a water area of 0.415 square miles. Located at 44.70° N. Lat; 73.68° W. Long. Elevation is 745 feet.
Population: 2,145; Growth (since 2000): -22.9%; Density: 54.6 persons per square mile; Race: 95.2% White, 0.2% Black/African American, 2.3% Asian, 1.8% American Indian/Alaska Native, 0.0% Native Hawaiian/Other Pacific Islander, 0.4% Two or more races, 0.2% Hispanic of any race; Average household size: 2.42; Median age: 43.1; Age under 18: 22.4%; Age 65 and over: 18.5%; Males per 100 females: 96.8; Marriage status: 19.3% never married, 61.7% now married, 3.3% separated, 11.9% widowed, 7.0% divorced; Foreign born: 7.1%; Speak English only: 98.4%; With disability: 9.7%; Veterans: 11.4%; Ancestry: 25.9% French, 12.7% Irish, 9.2% French Canadian, 8.7% German, 5.6% American
Employment: 6.4% management, business, and financial, 0.0% computer, engineering, and science, 21.0% education, legal, community service, arts, and media, 10.0% healthcare practitioners, 22.7% service,

17.3% sales and office, 9.2% natural resources, construction, and maintenance, 13.4% production, transportation, and material moving
Income: Per capita: $28,913; Median household: $58,906; Average household: $68,877; Households with income of $100,000 or more: 30.0%; Poverty rate: 9.7%
Educational Attainment: High school diploma or higher: 91.4%; Bachelor's degree or higher: 29.4%; Graduate/professional degree or higher: 10.5%
Housing: Homeownership rate: 90.1%; Median home value: $143,100; Median year structure built: 1966; Homeowner vacancy rate: 4.7%; Median selected monthly owner costs: $1,266 with a mortgage, $515 without a mortgage; Median gross rent: $857 per month; Rental vacancy rate: 0.0%
Health Insurance: 95.7% have insurance; 79.9% have private insurance; 33.1% have public insurance; 4.3% do not have insurance; 0.0% of children under 18 do not have insurance
Transportation: Commute: 95.5% car, 0.0% public transportation, 0.0% walk, 3.0% work from home; Mean travel time to work: 22.9 minutes

CHAMPLAIN (town). Covers a land area of 51.231 square miles and a water area of 7.585 square miles. Located at 44.97° N. Lat; 73.44° W. Long. Elevation is 105 feet.
History: Settled 1789, incorporated 1873.
Population: 5,706; Growth (since 2000): -1.5%; Density: 111.4 persons per square mile; Race: 97.2% White, 0.3% Black/African American, 0.1% Asian, 0.0% American Indian/Alaska Native, 0.1% Native Hawaiian/Other Pacific Islander, 2.2% Two or more races, 0.7% Hispanic of any race; Average household size: 2.30; Median age: 43.8; Age under 18: 19.6%; Age 65 and over: 14.5%; Males per 100 females: 95.8; Marriage status: 26.2% never married, 54.2% now married, 2.9% separated, 8.6% widowed, 11.0% divorced; Foreign born: 4.6%; Speak English only: 95.5%; With disability: 13.9%; Veterans: 9.5%; Ancestry: 31.9% French, 12.6% Irish, 12.4% French Canadian, 10.4% American, 10.2% English
Employment: 14.4% management, business, and financial, 3.3% computer, engineering, and science, 8.2% education, legal, community service, arts, and media, 5.0% healthcare practitioners, 20.0% service, 19.5% sales and office, 11.4% natural resources, construction, and maintenance, 18.2% production, transportation, and material moving
Income: Per capita: $27,290; Median household: $52,128; Average household: $63,384; Households with income of $100,000 or more: 19.2%; Poverty rate: 14.1%
Educational Attainment: High school diploma or higher: 85.1%; Bachelor's degree or higher: 17.2%; Graduate/professional degree or higher: 6.5%

School District(s)
Northeastern Clinton Central SD (KG-12)
    2014-15 Enrollment: 1,358 . . . . (518) 298-8242
Housing: Homeownership rate: 70.8%; Median home value: $120,300; Median year structure built: 1963; Homeowner vacancy rate: 0.0%; Median selected monthly owner costs: $1,159 with a mortgage, $486 without a mortgage; Median gross rent: $634 per month; Rental vacancy rate: 5.7%
Health Insurance: 94.3% have insurance; 70.6% have private insurance; 40.8% have public insurance; 5.7% do not have insurance; 5.5% of children under 18 do not have insurance
Transportation: Commute: 90.5% car, 0.4% public transportation, 3.9% walk, 5.1% work from home; Mean travel time to work: 24.7 minutes
Additional Information Contacts
Town of Champlain . . . . (518) 298-8160
    http://www.townofchamplain-ny.com

CHAMPLAIN (village). Covers a land area of 1.390 square miles and a water area of 0.039 square miles. Located at 44.99° N. Lat; 73.44° W. Long. Elevation is 105 feet.
Population: 1,139; Growth (since 2000): -2.9%; Density: 819.7 persons per square mile; Race: 95.9% White, 0.7% Black/African American, 0.3% Asian, 0.0% American Indian/Alaska Native, 0.0% Native Hawaiian/Other Pacific Islander, 3.2% Two or more races, 0.7% Hispanic of any race; Average household size: 2.32; Median age: 33.3; Age under 18: 28.7%; Age 65 and over: 8.9%; Males per 100 females: 89.5; Marriage status: 29.0% never married, 42.6% now married, 1.5% separated, 9.3% widowed, 19.2% divorced; Foreign born: 0.7%; Speak English only: 98.9%; With disability: 18.5%; Veterans: 12.1%; Ancestry: 37.9% French, 21.4% Irish, 10.4% English, 8.4% French Canadian, 7.5% American
Employment: 10.5% management, business, and financial, 8.1% computer, engineering, and science, 10.7% education, legal, community

service, arts, and media, 5.5% healthcare practitioners, 16.2% service, 23.9% sales and office, 9.2% natural resources, construction, and maintenance, 16.0% production, transportation, and material moving
Income: Per capita: $22,273; Median household: $42,054; Average household: $52,299; Households with income of $100,000 or more: 14.9%; Poverty rate: 17.7%
Educational Attainment: High school diploma or higher: 86.9%; Bachelor's degree or higher: 20.6%; Graduate/professional degree or higher: 9.3%

School District(s)
Northeastern Clinton Central SD (KG-12)
    2014-15 Enrollment: 1,358 . . . . (518) 298-8242
Housing: Homeownership rate: 50.3%; Median home value: $111,300; Median year structure built: 1949; Homeowner vacancy rate: 0.0%; Median selected monthly owner costs: $1,172 with a mortgage, $545 without a mortgage; Median gross rent: $675 per month; Rental vacancy rate: 4.3%
Health Insurance: 94.3% have insurance; 64.9% have private insurance; 44.9% have public insurance; 5.7% do not have insurance; 11.9% of children under 18 do not have insurance
Transportation: Commute: 91.6% car, 2.2% public transportation, 2.0% walk, 4.2% work from home; Mean travel time to work: 23.6 minutes

CHAZY (CDP). Covers a land area of 1.696 square miles and a water area of 0.018 square miles. Located at 44.89° N. Lat; 73.43° W. Long. Elevation is 148 feet.
Population: 448; Growth (since 2000): n/a; Density: 264.2 persons per square mile; Race: 100.0% White, 0.0% Black/African American, 0.0% Asian, 0.0% American Indian/Alaska Native, 0.0% Native Hawaiian/Other Pacific Islander, 0.0% Two or more races, 0.0% Hispanic of any race; Average household size: 2.60; Median age: 43.3; Age under 18: 24.6%; Age 65 and over: 27.0%; Males per 100 females: 89.6; Marriage status: 25.7% never married, 61.6% now married, 6.6% separated, 4.0% widowed, 8.7% divorced; Foreign born: 0.0%; Speak English only: 95.9%; With disability: 10.7%; Veterans: 17.2%; Ancestry: 42.6% French, 13.2% Irish, 10.7% French Canadian, 9.8% Polish, 8.0% Welsh
Employment: 11.8% management, business, and financial, 7.8% computer, engineering, and science, 11.1% education, legal, community service, arts, and media, 11.8% healthcare practitioners, 11.1% service, 35.3% sales and office, 11.1% natural resources, construction, and maintenance, 0.0% production, transportation, and material moving
Income: Per capita: $23,577; Median household: $49,028; Average household: $60,634; Households with income of $100,000 or more: 14.0%; Poverty rate: 10.0%
Educational Attainment: High school diploma or higher: 94.1%; Bachelor's degree or higher: 10.3%; Graduate/professional degree or higher: 5.3%

School District(s)
Chazy Union Free SD (KG-12)
    2014-15 Enrollment: 466 . . . . (518) 846-7135
Housing: Homeownership rate: 84.3%; Median home value: $113,800; Median year structure built: 1956; Homeowner vacancy rate: 0.0%; Median selected monthly owner costs: $1,136 with a mortgage, $472 without a mortgage; Median gross rent: $832 per month; Rental vacancy rate: 0.0%
Health Insurance: 100.0% have insurance; 92.9% have private insurance; 34.2% have public insurance; 0.0% do not have insurance; 0.0% of children under 18 do not have insurance
Transportation: Commute: 90.2% car, 0.0% public transportation, 5.2% walk, 0.0% work from home; Mean travel time to work: 41.4 minutes

CHAZY (town). Covers a land area of 54.153 square miles and a water area of 7.163 square miles. Located at 44.86° N. Lat; 73.46° W. Long. Elevation is 148 feet.
History: Miner Institute, agricultural and environmental research center, founded by William Miner, Railroad industrialist and philanthropist, in the 19th century.
Population: 4,250; Growth (since 2000): 1.7%; Density: 78.5 persons per square mile; Race: 97.9% White, 0.6% Black/African American, 0.9% Asian, 0.0% American Indian/Alaska Native, 0.0% Native Hawaiian/Other Pacific Islander, 0.1% Two or more races, 0.5% Hispanic of any race; Average household size: 2.39; Median age: 41.7; Age under 18: 21.3%; Age 65 and over: 15.3%; Males per 100 females: 101.9; Marriage status: 28.7% never married, 58.7% now married, 5.1% separated, 4.6% widowed, 8.0% divorced; Foreign born: 3.3%; Speak English only: 96.5%; With disability: 9.2%; Veterans: 11.3%; Ancestry: 27.6% French, 13.9% Irish, 12.2% American, 9.9% English, 8.9% German

Employment: 13.1% management, business, and financial, 5.3% computer, engineering, and science, 7.0% education, legal, community service, arts, and media, 6.2% healthcare practitioners, 19.5% service, 21.9% sales and office, 11.5% natural resources, construction, and maintenance, 15.5% production, transportation, and material moving
Income: Per capita: $28,428; Median household: $60,143; Average household: $68,155; Households with income of $100,000 or more: 18.4%; Poverty rate: 12.5%
Educational Attainment: High school diploma or higher: 86.7%; Bachelor's degree or higher: 19.0%; Graduate/professional degree or higher: 8.8%

School District(s)
Chazy Union Free SD (KG-12)
    2014-15 Enrollment: 466 . . . . (518) 846-7135
Housing: Homeownership rate: 75.8%; Median home value: $124,800; Median year structure built: 1972; Homeowner vacancy rate: 0.0%; Median selected monthly owner costs: $1,205 with a mortgage, $481 without a mortgage; Median gross rent: $812 per month; Rental vacancy rate: 3.2%
Health Insurance: 93.1% have insurance; 74.9% have private insurance; 33.4% have public insurance; 6.9% do not have insurance; 4.0% of children under 18 do not have insurance
Transportation: Commute: 94.5% car, 0.0% public transportation, 2.1% walk, 2.1% work from home; Mean travel time to work: 22.3 minutes
Additional Information Contacts
Town of Chazy . . . . (518) 846-7544
    http://www.townofchazy.com

CHURUBUSCO (unincorporated postal area)
ZCTA: 12923
    Covers a land area of 52.386 square miles and a water area of 0.029 square miles. Located at 44.96° N. Lat; 73.94° W. Long. Elevation is 1,191 feet.
Population: 637; Growth (since 2000): -3.0%; Density: 12.2 persons per square mile; Race: 98.4% White, 0.0% Black/African American, 0.5% Asian, 1.1% American Indian/Alaska Native, 0.0% Native Hawaiian/Other Pacific Islander, 0.0% Two or more races, 0.2% Hispanic of any race; Average household size: 2.62; Median age: 42.3; Age under 18: 19.0%; Age 65 and over: 18.7%; Males per 100 females: 107.2; Marriage status: 32.7% never married, 56.9% now married, 2.9% separated, 6.2% widowed, 4.2% divorced; Foreign born: 2.2%; Speak English only: 95.1%; With disability: 21.0%; Veterans: 7.2%; Ancestry: 30.3% French, 12.1% Irish, 11.0% French Canadian, 10.7% American, 6.3% English
Employment: 13.8% management, business, and financial, 2.5% computer, engineering, and science, 4.6% education, legal, community service, arts, and media, 5.7% healthcare practitioners, 19.4% service, 19.1% sales and office, 15.2% natural resources, construction, and maintenance, 19.8% production, transportation, and material moving
Income: Per capita: $21,225; Median household: $40,375; Average household: $56,059; Households with income of $100,000 or more: 15.7%; Poverty rate: 17.9%
Educational Attainment: High school diploma or higher: 78.3%; Bachelor's degree or higher: 11.8%; Graduate/professional degree or higher: 4.8%
Housing: Homeownership rate: 79.0%; Median home value: $77,200; Median year structure built: 1975; Homeowner vacancy rate: 3.0%; Median selected monthly owner costs: $1,024 with a mortgage, $345 without a mortgage; Median gross rent: $625 per month; Rental vacancy rate: 20.3%
Health Insurance: 94.0% have insurance; 64.1% have private insurance; 47.4% have public insurance; 6.0% do not have insurance; 0.0% of children under 18 do not have insurance
Transportation: Commute: 85.1% car, 4.6% public transportation, 4.6% walk, 5.0% work from home; Mean travel time to work: 29.0 minutes

CLINTON (town). Covers a land area of 67.070 square miles and a water area of 0.030 square miles. Located at 44.94° N. Lat; 73.92° W. Long.
Population: 680; Growth (since 2000): -6.5%; Density: 10.1 persons per square mile; Race: 98.5% White, 0.0% Black/African American, 0.4% Asian, 1.0% American Indian/Alaska Native, 0.0% Native Hawaiian/Other Pacific Islander, 0.0% Two or more races, 0.1% Hispanic of any race; Average household size: 2.56; Median age: 42.5; Age under 18: 19.0%; Age 65 and over: 18.4%; Males per 100 females: 104.2; Marriage status: 32.0% never married, 57.0% now married, 2.7% separated, 6.2%

widowed, 4.8% divorced; Foreign born: 2.5%; Speak English only: 94.9%; With disability: 20.9%; Veterans: 7.1%; Ancestry: 29.7% French, 11.6% Irish, 10.6% American, 10.6% French Canadian, 6.5% English
Employment: 14.4% management, business, and financial, 2.3% computer, engineering, and science, 4.9% education, legal, community service, arts, and media, 5.6% healthcare practitioners, 18.6% service, 19.9% sales and office, 15.4% natural resources, construction, and maintenance, 19.0% production, transportation, and material moving
Income: Per capita: $21,911; Median household: $40,500; Average household: $57,032; Households with income of $100,000 or more: 15.0%; Poverty rate: 17.9%
Educational Attainment: High school diploma or higher: 76.9%; Bachelor's degree or higher: 10.9%; Graduate/professional degree or higher: 4.4%
Housing: Homeownership rate: 80.1%; Median home value: $78,600; Median year structure built: 1977; Homeowner vacancy rate: 2.7%; Median selected monthly owner costs: $1,058 with a mortgage, $345 without a mortgage; Median gross rent: $663 per month; Rental vacancy rate: 19.7%
Health Insurance: 93.8% have insurance; 65.1% have private insurance; 45.9% have public insurance; 6.2% do not have insurance; 0.0% of children under 18 do not have insurance
Transportation: Commute: 85.9% car, 4.3% public transportation, 4.6% walk, 4.6% work from home; Mean travel time to work: 28.5 minutes

CUMBERLAND HEAD (CDP). Covers a land area of 3.591 square miles and a water area of 0 square miles. Located at 44.72° N. Lat; 73.40° W. Long. Elevation is 144 feet.
Population: 1,564; Growth (since 2000): 2.1%; Density: 435.5 persons per square mile; Race: 98.8% White, 0.8% Black/African American, 0.0% Asian, 0.0% American Indian/Alaska Native, 0.0% Native Hawaiian/Other Pacific Islander, 0.4% Two or more races, 0.2% Hispanic of any race; Average household size: 2.16; Median age: 50.0; Age under 18: 18.7%; Age 65 and over: 21.0%; Males per 100 females: 99.9; Marriage status: 17.4% never married, 69.6% now married, 0.0% separated, 4.9% widowed, 8.1% divorced; Foreign born: 5.0%; Speak English only: 97.2%; With disability: 12.1%; Veterans: 9.1%; Ancestry: 30.2% French, 22.9% Irish, 12.7% English, 12.1% German, 8.9% American
Employment: 16.5% management, business, and financial, 3.1% computer, engineering, and science, 14.3% education, legal, community service, arts, and media, 7.9% healthcare practitioners, 15.2% service, 28.8% sales and office, 7.2% natural resources, construction, and maintenance, 7.0% production, transportation, and material moving
Income: Per capita: $39,311; Median household: $63,933; Average household: $85,400; Households with income of $100,000 or more: 22.9%; Poverty rate: 4.4%
Educational Attainment: High school diploma or higher: 90.1%; Bachelor's degree or higher: 37.6%; Graduate/professional degree or higher: 23.1%
Housing: Homeownership rate: 83.1%; Median home value: $163,000; Median year structure built: 1958; Homeowner vacancy rate: 3.7%; Median selected monthly owner costs: $1,312 with a mortgage, $490 without a mortgage; Median gross rent: $1,010 per month; Rental vacancy rate: 0.0%
Health Insurance: 96.7% have insurance; 85.5% have private insurance; 26.4% have public insurance; 3.3% do not have insurance; 0.0% of children under 18 do not have insurance
Transportation: Commute: 88.1% car, 0.4% public transportation, 0.0% walk, 10.2% work from home; Mean travel time to work: 21.5 minutes

DANNEMORA (town). Covers a land area of 59.080 square miles and a water area of 6.759 square miles. Located at 44.75° N. Lat; 73.81° W. Long. Elevation is 1,414 feet.
History: Incorporated 1881.
Population: 4,720; Growth (since 2000): -8.3%; Density: 79.9 persons per square mile; Race: 55.1% White, 34.6% Black/African American, 0.0% Asian, 0.2% American Indian/Alaska Native, 0.0% Native Hawaiian/Other Pacific Islander, 0.6% Two or more races, 16.0% Hispanic of any race; Average household size: 2.19; Median age: 39.9; Age under 18: 5.0%; Age 65 and over: 7.2%; Males per 100 females: 380.2; Marriage status: 51.5% never married, 37.7% now married, 5.5% separated, 2.3% widowed, 8.5% divorced; Foreign born: 6.9%; Speak English only: 87.7%; With disability: 18.3%; Veterans: 6.6%; Ancestry: 11.0% French, 8.2% Irish, 4.1% German, 3.7% Italian, 2.8% English
Employment: 7.1% management, business, and financial, 1.1% computer, engineering, and science, 11.8% education, legal, community service, arts,

and media, 6.1% healthcare practitioners, 26.7% service, 26.4% sales and office, 9.8% natural resources, construction, and maintenance, 10.9% production, transportation, and material moving

Income: Per capita: $9,773; Median household: $55,000; Average household: $63,466; Households with income of $100,000 or more: 18.3%; Poverty rate: 14.5%

Educational Attainment: High school diploma or higher: 73.0%; Bachelor's degree or higher: 6.9%; Graduate/professional degree or higher: 2.7%

Housing: Homeownership rate: 72.4%; Median home value: $104,100; Median year structure built: 1956; Homeowner vacancy rate: 3.2%; Median selected monthly owner costs: $1,253 with a mortgage, $477 without a mortgage; Median gross rent: $676 per month; Rental vacancy rate: 4.7%

Health Insurance: 95.8% have insurance; 70.5% have private insurance; 42.7% have public insurance; 4.2% do not have insurance; 0.0% of children under 18 do not have insurance

Transportation: Commute: 89.6% car, 0.0% public transportation, 3.2% walk, 3.8% work from home; Mean travel time to work: 25.9 minutes

Additional Information Contacts

Town of Dannemora . . . . (518) 492-7541
  http://www.townofdannemora.org

DANNEMORA (village). Covers a land area of 1.148 square miles and a water area of 0 square miles. Located at 44.72° N. Lat; 73.72° W. Long. Elevation is 1,414 feet.

Population: 3,894; Growth (since 2000): -5.7%; Density: 3,392.8 persons per square mile; Race: 48.9% White, 39.9% Black/African American, 0.0% Asian, 0.0% American Indian/Alaska Native, 0.0% Native Hawaiian/Other Pacific Islander, 0.5% Two or more races, 18.5% Hispanic of any race; Average household size: 2.21; Median age: 38.5; Age under 18: 5.2%; Age 65 and over: 3.6%; Males per 100 females: 578.6; Marriage status: 57.8% never married, 30.5% now married, 5.8% separated, 2.4% widowed, 9.3% divorced; Foreign born: 6.9%; Speak English only: 87.0%; With disability: 21.8%; Veterans: 4.6%; Ancestry: 9.6% French, 5.7% Irish, 3.7% German, 3.2% Italian, 3.0% English

Employment: 5.4% management, business, and financial, 2.6% computer, engineering, and science, 11.4% education, legal, community service, arts, and media, 4.1% healthcare practitioners, 31.5% service, 24.0% sales and office, 8.3% natural resources, construction, and maintenance, 12.7% production, transportation, and material moving

Income: Per capita: $5,685; Median household: $48,500; Average household: $53,768; Households with income of $100,000 or more: 9.2%; Poverty rate: 16.6%

Educational Attainment: High school diploma or higher: 70.6%; Bachelor's degree or higher: 4.4%; Graduate/professional degree or higher: 1.7%

Housing: Homeownership rate: 64.8%; Median home value: $101,000; Median year structure built: Before 1940; Homeowner vacancy rate: 3.4%; Median selected monthly owner costs: $1,083 with a mortgage, $485 without a mortgage; Median gross rent: $634 per month; Rental vacancy rate: 6.3%

Health Insurance: 97.0% have insurance; 64.9% have private insurance; 41.7% have public insurance; 3.0% do not have insurance; 0.0% of children under 18 do not have insurance

Transportation: Commute: 89.2% car, 0.0% public transportation, 9.2% walk, 1.6% work from home; Mean travel time to work: 23.1 minutes

ELLENBURG (town). Covers a land area of 106.567 square miles and a water area of 0.890 square miles. Located at 44.81° N. Lat; 73.86° W. Long. Elevation is 961 feet.

Population: 1,841; Growth (since 2000): 1.6%; Density: 17.3 persons per square mile; Race: 95.9% White, 0.1% Black/African American, 2.8% Asian, 0.7% American Indian/Alaska Native, 0.0% Native Hawaiian/Other Pacific Islander, 0.7% Two or more races, 1.1% Hispanic of any race; Average household size: 2.60; Median age: 41.6; Age under 18: 24.8%; Age 65 and over: 16.7%; Males per 100 females: 102.2; Marriage status: 23.2% never married, 60.3% now married, 3.3% separated, 6.7% widowed, 9.8% divorced; Foreign born: 2.0%; Speak English only: 95.7%; With disability: 18.5%; Veterans: 12.1%; Ancestry: 25.4% French, 19.1% Irish, 9.3% American, 7.9% German, 7.7% English

Employment: 12.5% management, business, and financial, 1.8% computer, engineering, and science, 7.2% education, legal, community service, arts, and media, 7.8% healthcare practitioners, 23.4% service, 16.8% sales and office, 13.2% natural resources, construction, and maintenance, 17.3% production, transportation, and material moving

Income: Per capita: $21,604; Median household: $48,026; Average household: $56,836; Households with income of $100,000 or more: 13.6%; Poverty rate: 22.5%

Educational Attainment: High school diploma or higher: 77.9%; Bachelor's degree or higher: 12.8%; Graduate/professional degree or higher: 4.6%

Housing: Homeownership rate: 79.2%; Median home value: $93,600; Median year structure built: 1969; Homeowner vacancy rate: 1.5%; Median selected monthly owner costs: $950 with a mortgage, $397 without a mortgage; Median gross rent: $728 per month; Rental vacancy rate: 6.4%

Health Insurance: 92.9% have insurance; 65.4% have private insurance; 45.9% have public insurance; 7.1% do not have insurance; 5.5% of children under 18 do not have insurance

Transportation: Commute: 83.7% car, 1.7% public transportation, 4.4% walk, 9.9% work from home; Mean travel time to work: 29.5 minutes

ELLENBURG CENTER (unincorporated postal area)
ZCTA: 12934

Covers a land area of 58.851 square miles and a water area of 0.021 square miles. Located at 44.88° N. Lat; 73.87° W. Long. Elevation is 1,220 feet.

Population: 1,077; Growth (since 2000): -4.4%; Density: 18.3 persons per square mile; Race: 97.4% White, 0.1% Black/African American, 1.6% Asian, 0.0% American Indian/Alaska Native, 0.0% Native Hawaiian/Other Pacific Islander, 0.9% Two or more races, 0.7% Hispanic of any race; Average household size: 2.67; Median age: 37.1; Age under 18: 26.8%; Age 65 and over: 16.8%; Males per 100 females: 102.6; Marriage status: 27.1% never married, 57.3% now married, 3.4% separated, 6.4% widowed, 9.2% divorced; Foreign born: 2.0%; Speak English only: 93.8%; With disability: 21.4%; Veterans: 12.6%; Ancestry: 25.8% French, 16.0% Irish, 10.9% German, 8.6% French Canadian, 7.9% American

Employment: 8.2% management, business, and financial, 2.5% computer, engineering, and science, 6.0% education, legal, community service, arts, and media, 5.5% healthcare practitioners, 27.7% service, 14.5% sales and office, 15.6% natural resources, construction, and maintenance, 20.0% production, transportation, and material moving

Income: Per capita: $19,686; Median household: $38,393; Average household: $52,931; Households with income of $100,000 or more: 12.1%; Poverty rate: 28.8%

Educational Attainment: High school diploma or higher: 71.7%; Bachelor's degree or higher: 10.6%; Graduate/professional degree or higher: 4.3%

Housing: Homeownership rate: 75.1%; Median home value: $79,600; Median year structure built: 1972; Homeowner vacancy rate: 0.0%; Median selected monthly owner costs: $942 with a mortgage, $371 without a mortgage; Median gross rent: $729 per month; Rental vacancy rate: 9.1%

Health Insurance: 90.2% have insurance; 61.1% have private insurance; 47.7% have public insurance; 9.8% do not have insurance; 8.7% of children under 18 do not have insurance

Transportation: Commute: 86.4% car, 2.7% public transportation, 0.9% walk, 10.0% work from home; Mean travel time to work: 29.4 minutes

ELLENBURG DEPOT (unincorporated postal area)
ZCTA: 12935

Covers a land area of 98.613 square miles and a water area of 3.514 square miles. Located at 44.84° N. Lat; 73.80° W. Long. Elevation is 873 feet.

Population: 1,571; Growth (since 2000): -71.4%; Density: 15.9 persons per square mile; Race: 91.8% White, 4.8% Black/African American, 0.0% Asian, 1.0% American Indian/Alaska Native, 0.0% Native Hawaiian/Other Pacific Islander, 0.1% Two or more races, 3.1% Hispanic of any race; Average household size: 2.46; Median age: 43.5; Age under 18: 16.1%; Age 65 and over: 16.4%; Males per 100 females: 109.1; Marriage status: 31.3% never married, 53.2% now married, 3.9% separated, 5.4% widowed, 10.1% divorced; Foreign born: 1.8%; Speak English only: 94.8%; With disability: 17.4%; Veterans: 10.6%; Ancestry: 25.1% French, 13.4% Irish, 9.4% English, 6.6% French Canadian, 5.2% American

Employment: 15.9% management, business, and financial, 1.4% computer, engineering, and science, 3.5% education, legal, community service, arts, and media, 7.9% healthcare practitioners, 21.2% service, 17.5% sales and office, 14.5% natural resources, construction, and maintenance, 18.2% production, transportation, and material moving

Income: Per capita: $28,140; Median household: $48,514; Average household: $76,529; Households with income of $100,000 or more: 20.3%; Poverty rate: 12.8%

Educational Attainment: High school diploma or higher: 74.7%; Bachelor's degree or higher: 14.5%; Graduate/professional degree or higher: 4.6%

School District(s)

Northern Adirondack Central SD (KG-12)

    2014-15 Enrollment: 833 . . . . (518) 594-7060

Housing: Homeownership rate: 79.1%; Median home value: $124,300; Median year structure built: 1975; Homeowner vacancy rate: 0.0%; Median selected monthly owner costs: $1,180 with a mortgage, $398 without a mortgage; Median gross rent: $746 per month; Rental vacancy rate: 0.0%

Health Insurance: 94.5% have insurance; 65.9% have private insurance; 41.8% have public insurance; 5.5% do not have insurance; 0.0% of children under 18 do not have insurance

Transportation: Commute: 91.6% car, 0.0% public transportation, 4.6% walk, 3.4% work from home; Mean travel time to work: 33.4 minutes

KEESEVILLE (village). Covers a land area of 1.173 square miles and a water area of 0.055 square miles. Located at 44.50° N. Lat; 73.48° W. Long. Elevation is 417 feet.

Population: 1,776; Growth (since 2000): -4.0%; Density: 1,513.6 persons per square mile; Race: 90.6% White, 1.9% Black/African American, 3.7% Asian, 0.0% American Indian/Alaska Native, 0.0% Native Hawaiian/Other Pacific Islander, 3.5% Two or more races, 1.7% Hispanic of any race; Average household size: 2.46; Median age: 37.9; Age under 18: 24.4%; Age 65 and over: 16.0%; Males per 100 females: 98.6; Marriage status: 33.5% never married, 47.3% now married, 3.4% separated, 9.1% widowed, 10.1% divorced; Foreign born: 3.4%; Speak English only: 93.2%; With disability: 19.5%; Veterans: 10.8%; Ancestry: 18.1% French, 17.1% Irish, 12.4% American, 9.2% German, 7.7% French Canadian

Employment: 9.7% management, business, and financial, 2.0% computer, engineering, and science, 6.2% education, legal, community service, arts, and media, 7.7% healthcare practitioners, 20.1% service, 27.2% sales and office, 10.1% natural resources, construction, and maintenance, 17.1% production, transportation, and material moving

Income: Per capita: $18,700; Median household: $37,898; Average household: $45,289; Households with income of $100,000 or more: 10.0%; Poverty rate: 27.0%

Educational Attainment: High school diploma or higher: 81.8%; Bachelor's degree or higher: 13.3%; Graduate/professional degree or higher: 6.8%

School District(s)

Ausable Valley Central SD (KG-12)

    2014-15 Enrollment: 1,151 . . . . (518) 834-2845

Housing: Homeownership rate: 63.1%; Median home value: $86,700; Median year structure built: 1951; Homeowner vacancy rate: 2.2%; Median selected monthly owner costs: $1,019 with a mortgage, $417 without a mortgage; Median gross rent: $732 per month; Rental vacancy rate: 12.5%

Health Insurance: 92.3% have insurance; 57.5% have private insurance; 51.1% have public insurance; 7.7% do not have insurance; 1.8% of children under 18 do not have insurance

Transportation: Commute: 89.3% car, 0.0% public transportation, 2.3% walk, 1.8% work from home; Mean travel time to work: 24.0 minutes

LYON MOUNTAIN (CDP). Covers a land area of 10.147 square miles and a water area of 0 square miles. Located at 44.72° N. Lat; 73.88° W. Long. Elevation is 1,798 feet.

Population: 279; Growth (since 2000): -39.1%; Density: 27.5 persons per square mile; Race: 97.8% White, 0.0% Black/African American, 0.0% Asian, 0.0% American Indian/Alaska Native, 0.0% Native Hawaiian/Other Pacific Islander, 2.2% Two or more races, 0.0% Hispanic of any race; Average household size: 1.89; Median age: 54.6; Age under 18: 11.1%; Age 65 and over: 20.8%; Males per 100 females: 88.0; Marriage status: 4.8% never married, 80.6% now married, 4.8% separated, 6.5% widowed, 8.1% divorced; Foreign born: 9.0%; Speak English only: 98.9%; With disability: 27.6%; Veterans: 16.5%; Ancestry: 39.8% Irish, 36.6% French, 9.0% Italian, 6.5% German, 6.5% Polish

Employment: 4.3% management, business, and financial, 0.0% computer, engineering, and science, 18.8% education, legal, community service, arts, and media, 5.8% healthcare practitioners, 30.4% service, 40.6% sales and office, 0.0% natural resources, construction, and maintenance, 0.0% production, transportation, and material moving

Income: Per capita: $23,609; Median household: $35,000; Average household: $44,722; Households with income of $100,000 or more: 2.7%; Poverty rate: 33.3%

Educational Attainment: High school diploma or higher: 86.3%; Bachelor's degree or higher: 5.2%; Graduate/professional degree or higher: 5.2%

Housing: Homeownership rate: 77.7%; Median home value: $46,100; Median year structure built: Before 1940; Homeowner vacancy rate: 12.9%; Median selected monthly owner costs: $1,262 with a mortgage, $440 without a mortgage; Median gross rent: $694 per month; Rental vacancy rate: 0.0%

Health Insurance: 94.3% have insurance; 63.1% have private insurance; 53.4% have public insurance; 5.7% do not have insurance; 0.0% of children under 18 do not have insurance

Transportation: Commute: 100.0% car, 0.0% public transportation, 0.0% walk, 0.0% work from home; Mean travel time to work: 33.4 minutes

MOOERS (CDP). Covers a land area of 1.193 square miles and a water area of 0.038 square miles. Located at 44.96° N. Lat; 73.60° W. Long. Elevation is 282 feet.

Population: 293; Growth (since 2000): -33.4%; Density: 245.6 persons per square mile; Race: 93.5% White, 0.0% Black/African American, 0.0% Asian, 0.0% American Indian/Alaska Native, 0.0% Native Hawaiian/Other Pacific Islander, 0.0% Two or more races, 6.5% Hispanic of any race; Average household size: 1.47; Median age: 60.1; Age under 18: 14.3%; Age 65 and over: 18.8%; Males per 100 females: 90.5; Marriage status: 52.9% never married, 19.3% now married, 6.6% separated, 19.3% widowed, 8.4% divorced; Foreign born: 0.0%; Speak English only: 100.0%; With disability: 49.1%; Veterans: 6.4%; Ancestry: 25.3% French Canadian, 17.7% English, 15.7% French, 11.9% Scottish, 7.8% American

Employment: 0.0% management, business, and financial, 0.0% computer, engineering, and science, 50.7% education, legal, community service, arts, and media, 26.1% healthcare practitioners, 0.0% service, 0.0% sales and office, 0.0% natural resources, construction, and maintenance, 23.2% production, transportation, and material moving

Income: Per capita: $24,232; Median household: $21,875; Average household: $36,271; Households with income of $100,000 or more: 9.0%; Poverty rate: 21.5%

Educational Attainment: High school diploma or higher: 82.5%; Bachelor's degree or higher: 28.3%; Graduate/professional degree or higher: 13.9%

School District(s)

Northeastern Clinton Central SD (KG-12)

    2014-15 Enrollment: 1,358 . . . . (518) 298-8242

Housing: Homeownership rate: 68.8%; Median home value: $107,000; Median year structure built: Before 1940; Homeowner vacancy rate: 0.0%; Median selected monthly owner costs: n/a with a mortgage, $450 without a mortgage; Median gross rent: n/a per month; Rental vacancy rate: 0.0%

Health Insurance: 100.0% have insurance; 62.8% have private insurance; 67.2% have public insurance; 0.0% do not have insurance; 0.0% of children under 18 do not have insurance

Transportation: Commute: 73.9% car, 0.0% public transportation, 26.1% walk, 0.0% work from home; Mean travel time to work: 0.0 minutes

MOOERS (town). Covers a land area of 87.632 square miles and a water area of 0.290 square miles. Located at 44.96° N. Lat; 73.66° W. Long. Elevation is 282 feet.

Population: 3,600; Growth (since 2000): 5.8%; Density: 41.1 persons per square mile; Race: 96.9% White, 0.8% Black/African American, 0.5% Asian, 1.3% American Indian/Alaska Native, 0.0% Native Hawaiian/Other Pacific Islander, 0.0% Two or more races, 1.0% Hispanic of any race; Average household size: 2.40; Median age: 43.3; Age under 18: 19.9%; Age 65 and over: 10.6%; Males per 100 females: 101.5; Marriage status: 26.2% never married, 57.3% now married, 1.2% separated, 5.2% widowed, 11.3% divorced; Foreign born: 0.5%; Speak English only: 98.2%; With disability: 21.1%; Veterans: 6.7%; Ancestry: 24.6% French, 17.4% American, 15.3% Irish, 13.5% English, 8.6% French Canadian

Employment: 8.4% management, business, and financial, 1.4% computer, engineering, and science, 8.6% education, legal, community service, arts, and media, 3.0% healthcare practitioners, 24.0% service, 22.8% sales and office, 15.1% natural resources, construction, and maintenance, 16.7% production, transportation, and material moving

Income: Per capita: $23,200; Median household: $41,452; Average household: $55,488; Households with income of $100,000 or more: 19.6%; Poverty rate: 16.9%

Educational Attainment: High school diploma or higher: 84.8%; Bachelor's degree or higher: 13.5%; Graduate/professional degree or higher: 5.8%

School District(s)

Northeastern Clinton Central SD (KG-12)

   2014-15 Enrollment: 1,358 . . . . (518) 298-8242

Housing: Homeownership rate: 81.2%; Median home value: $102,600; Median year structure built: 1979; Homeowner vacancy rate: 0.0%; Median selected monthly owner costs: $1,054 with a mortgage, $486 without a mortgage; Median gross rent: $495 per month; Rental vacancy rate: 0.0%

Health Insurance: 97.0% have insurance; 70.3% have private insurance; 42.4% have public insurance; 3.0% do not have insurance; 5.2% of children under 18 do not have insurance

Transportation: Commute: 94.9% car, 0.0% public transportation, 1.1% walk, 3.9% work from home; Mean travel time to work: 29.6 minutes

MOOERS FORKS (unincorporated postal area)

ZCTA: 12959

Covers a land area of 38.629 square miles and a water area of 0.101 square miles. Located at 44.95° N. Lat; 73.72° W. Long. Elevation is 374 feet.

Population: 1,370; Growth (since 2000): -6.6%; Density: 35.5 persons per square mile; Race: 94.6% White, 2.1% Black/African American, 0.0% Asian, 3.3% American Indian/Alaska Native, 0.0% Native Hawaiian/Other Pacific Islander, 0.0% Two or more races, 1.3% Hispanic of any race; Average household size: 2.30; Median age: 48.4; Age under 18: 14.2%; Age 65 and over: 11.5%; Males per 100 females: 99.9; Marriage status: 17.1% never married, 66.7% now married, 0.0% separated, 7.9% widowed, 8.2% divorced; Foreign born: 1.3%; Speak English only: 95.4%; With disability: 26.6%; Veterans: 8.5%; Ancestry: 23.8% French, 21.8% English, 20.1% American, 11.1% French Canadian, 10.6% Irish

Employment: 7.2% management, business, and financial, 0.0% computer, engineering, and science, 0.0% education, legal, community service, arts, and media, 0.0% healthcare practitioners, 26.1% service, 22.4% sales and office, 25.1% natural resources, construction, and maintenance, 19.2% production, transportation, and material moving

Income: Per capita: $26,842; Median household: $44,286; Average household: $62,228; Households with income of $100,000 or more: 27.5%; Poverty rate: 12.4%

Educational Attainment: High school diploma or higher: 87.5%; Bachelor's degree or higher: 8.9%; Graduate/professional degree or higher: 1.6%

Housing: Homeownership rate: 92.7%; Median home value: $101,200; Median year structure built: 1977; Homeowner vacancy rate: 0.0%; Median selected monthly owner costs: $1,326 with a mortgage, $501 without a mortgage; Median gross rent: n/a per month; Rental vacancy rate: 0.0%

Health Insurance: 100.0% have insurance; 82.3% have private insurance; 35.6% have public insurance; 0.0% do not have insurance; 0.0% of children under 18 do not have insurance

Transportation: Commute: 96.6% car, 0.0% public transportation, 0.0% walk, 3.4% work from home; Mean travel time to work: 30.3 minutes

MORRISONVILLE (CDP). Covers a land area of 2.611 square miles and a water area of 0.090 square miles. Located at 44.69° N. Lat; 73.55° W. Long. Elevation is 361 feet.

Population: 1,444; Growth (since 2000): -15.2%; Density: 553.0 persons per square mile; Race: 95.4% White, 1.5% Black/African American, 1.4% Asian, 0.6% American Indian/Alaska Native, 0.0% Native Hawaiian/Other Pacific Islander, 0.8% Two or more races, 1.2% Hispanic of any race; Average household size: 2.19; Median age: 36.3; Age under 18: 22.9%; Age 65 and over: 17.8%; Males per 100 females: 92.4; Marriage status: 31.4% never married, 53.0% now married, 1.9% separated, 6.7% widowed, 8.9% divorced; Foreign born: 1.9%; Speak English only: 97.1%; With disability: 21.2%; Veterans: 12.7%; Ancestry: 20.7% Irish, 15.4% French, 15.0% American, 11.8% German, 9.9% English

Employment: 7.1% management, business, and financial, 3.4% computer, engineering, and science, 20.0% education, legal, community service, arts, and media, 2.5% healthcare practitioners, 10.1% service, 33.0% sales and office, 3.2% natural resources, construction, and maintenance, 20.6% production, transportation, and material moving

Income: Per capita: $25,687; Median household: $41,336; Average household: $56,632; Households with income of $100,000 or more: 13.4%; Poverty rate: 23.9%

Educational Attainment: High school diploma or higher: 94.5%; Bachelor's degree or higher: 25.6%; Graduate/professional degree or higher: 10.9%

School District(s)

Saranac Central SD (KG-12)

   2014-15 Enrollment: 1,478 . . . . (518) 565-5600

Housing: Homeownership rate: 72.4%; Median home value: $121,100; Median year structure built: 1964; Homeowner vacancy rate: 0.0%; Median selected monthly owner costs: $1,120 with a mortgage, $474 without a mortgage; Median gross rent: $984 per month; Rental vacancy rate: 0.0%

Health Insurance: 95.6% have insurance; 70.6% have private insurance; 43.7% have public insurance; 4.4% do not have insurance; 5.7% of children under 18 do not have insurance

Transportation: Commute: 98.5% car, 0.0% public transportation, 1.5% walk, 0.0% work from home; Mean travel time to work: 13.5 minutes

PARC (CDP). Covers a land area of 1.231 square miles and a water area of 0 square miles. Located at 44.66° N. Lat; 73.45° W. Long. Elevation is 180 feet.

Population: 206; Growth (since 2000): 281.5%; Density: 167.3 persons per square mile; Race: 71.8% White, 11.7% Black/African American, 4.4% Asian, 0.0% American Indian/Alaska Native, 0.0% Native Hawaiian/Other Pacific Islander, 0.0% Two or more races, 20.4% Hispanic of any race; Average household size: 0.00; Median age: 19.7; Age under 18: 0.0%; Age 65 and over: 0.0%; Males per 100 females: 91.0; Marriage status: 100.0% never married, 0.0% now married, 0.0% separated, 0.0% widowed, 0.0% divorced; Foreign born: 4.4%; Speak English only: 80.1%; With disability: 3.9%; Veterans: 0.0%; Ancestry: 15.0% Italian, 12.6% Irish, 8.3% German, 4.9% English, 3.9% Dutch

Employment: 0.0% management, business, and financial, 0.0% computer, engineering, and science, 0.0% education, legal, community service, arts, and media, 10.0% healthcare practitioners, 16.0% service, 50.0% sales and office, 0.0% natural resources, construction, and maintenance, 24.0% production, transportation, and material moving

Income: Per capita: $4,760; Median household: n/a; Average household: n/a; Households with income of $100,000 or more: n/a; Poverty rate: n/a

Educational Attainment: High school diploma or higher: 50.0%; Bachelor's degree or higher: 50.0%; Graduate/professional degree or higher: 50.0%

Housing: Homeownership rate: 50.0%; Median home value: n/a; Median year structure built: 1955; Homeowner vacancy rate: 0.0%; Median selected monthly owner costs: n/a with a mortgage, n/a without a mortgage; Median gross rent: n/a per month; Rental vacancy rate: 0.0%

Health Insurance: 96.1% have insurance; 96.1% have private insurance; 16.0% have public insurance; 3.9% do not have insurance; 0.0% of children under 18 do not have insurance

Transportation: Commute: 54.0% car, 0.0% public transportation, 46.0% walk, 0.0% work from home; Mean travel time to work: 0.0 minutes

PERU (CDP). Covers a land area of 1.590 square miles and a water area of 0 square miles. Located at 44.58° N. Lat; 73.53° W. Long. Elevation is 335 feet.

Population: 1,300; Growth (since 2000): -14.1%; Density: 817.7 persons per square mile; Race: 100.0% White, 0.0% Black/African American, 0.0% Asian, 0.0% American Indian/Alaska Native, 0.0% Native Hawaiian/Other Pacific Islander, 0.0% Two or more races, 1.3% Hispanic of any race; Average household size: 2.41; Median age: 46.4; Age under 18: 20.9%; Age 65 and over: 24.3%; Males per 100 females: 96.9; Marriage status: 25.4% never married, 51.5% now married, 3.8% separated, 6.8% widowed, 16.3% divorced; Foreign born: 0.9%; Speak English only: 98.6%; With disability: 9.8%; Veterans: 27.3%; Ancestry: 30.8% Irish, 18.2% English, 12.7% Italian, 9.7% American, 9.7% French Canadian

Employment: 18.1% management, business, and financial, 0.0% computer, engineering, and science, 12.2% education, legal, community service, arts, and media, 10.7% healthcare practitioners, 19.3% service, 12.6% sales and office, 8.4% natural resources, construction, and maintenance, 18.7% production, transportation, and material moving

Income: Per capita: $34,936; Median household: $69,713; Average household: $85,473; Households with income of $100,000 or more: 23.6%; Poverty rate: 7.5%

Educational Attainment: High school diploma or higher: 96.2%; Bachelor's degree or higher: 45.3%; Graduate/professional degree or higher: 13.7%

School District(s)
Peru Central SD (KG-12)
   2014-15 Enrollment: 1,921 . . . . (518) 643-6002
Housing: Homeownership rate: 78.6%; Median home value: $137,100;
Median year structure built: 1956; Homeowner vacancy rate: 0.0%; Median
selected monthly owner costs: $1,218 with a mortgage, $490 without a
mortgage; Median gross rent: $924 per month; Rental vacancy rate: 35.1%
Health Insurance: 96.4% have insurance; 81.1% have private insurance;
33.8% have public insurance; 3.6% do not have insurance; 6.3% of
children under 18 do not have insurance
Transportation: Commute: 94.2% car, 0.0% public transportation, 0.0%
walk, 3.0% work from home; Mean travel time to work: 23.8 minutes

PERU (town). Covers a land area of 78.887 square miles and a water
area of 13.492 square miles. Located at 44.58° N. Lat; 73.56° W. Long.
Elevation is 335 feet.
Population: 7,013; Growth (since 2000): 10.1%; Density: 88.9 persons per
square mile; Race: 94.6% White, 2.7% Black/African American, 1.3%
Asian, 0.0% American Indian/Alaska Native, 0.0% Native Hawaiian/Other
Pacific Islander, 1.5% Two or more races, 1.6% Hispanic of any race;
Average household size: 2.54; Median age: 43.8; Age under 18: 23.2%;
Age 65 and over: 15.4%; Males per 100 females: 100.5; Marriage status:
19.9% never married, 64.7% now married, 1.4% separated, 5.2%
widowed, 10.2% divorced; Foreign born: 5.3%; Speak English only: 94.4%;
With disability: 16.5%; Veterans: 15.3%; Ancestry: 21.1% French, 18.0%
Irish, 11.6% Italian, 8.7% English, 7.3% American
Employment: 15.4% management, business, and financial, 2.1%
computer, engineering, and science, 12.2% education, legal, community
service, arts, and media, 7.6% healthcare practitioners, 18.6% service,
17.0% sales and office, 10.6% natural resources, construction, and
maintenance, 16.4% production, transportation, and material moving
Income: Per capita: $31,729; Median household: $63,580; Average
household: $81,687; Households with income of $100,000 or more: 25.8%;
Poverty rate: 12.4%
Educational Attainment: High school diploma or higher: 90.4%;
Bachelor's degree or higher: 29.7%; Graduate/professional degree or
higher: 14.8%
School District(s)
Peru Central SD (KG-12)
   2014-15 Enrollment: 1,921 . . . . (518) 643-6002
Housing: Homeownership rate: 80.9%; Median home value: $141,000;
Median year structure built: 1982; Homeowner vacancy rate: 0.5%; Median
selected monthly owner costs: $1,366 with a mortgage, $539 without a
mortgage; Median gross rent: $796 per month; Rental vacancy rate: 10.6%
Health Insurance: 94.3% have insurance; 78.4% have private insurance;
31.0% have public insurance; 5.7% do not have insurance; 2.0% of
children under 18 do not have insurance
Transportation: Commute: 91.1% car, 0.0% public transportation, 1.7%
walk, 3.3% work from home; Mean travel time to work: 22.6 minutes
Additional Information Contacts
Town of Peru . . . . (518) 643-2745
  http://www.perutown.com

PLATTSBURGH (city). County seat. Covers a land area of 5.019
square miles and a water area of 1.556 square miles. Located at 44.69° N.
Lat; 73.46° W. Long. Elevation is 138 feet.
History: Plattsburg was established at the mouth of the Saranac River,
which began to provide water power for manufacturing in 1785. The first
mills ground corn and cut lumber for the settlers.
Population: 19,845; Growth (since 2000): 5.5%; Density: 3,954.3 persons
per square mile; Race: 88.6% White, 4.3% Black/African American, 2.7%
Asian, 0.5% American Indian/Alaska Native, 0.0% Native Hawaiian/Other
Pacific Islander, 2.5% Two or more races, 3.7% Hispanic of any race;
Average household size: 2.11; Median age: 28.9; Age under 18: 14.1%;
Age 65 and over: 14.7%; Males per 100 females: 89.1; Marriage status:
53.7% never married, 30.8% now married, 2.2% separated, 6.7%
widowed, 8.9% divorced; Foreign born: 6.9%; Speak English only: 90.1%;
With disability: 13.5%; Veterans: 7.3%; Ancestry: 19.9% Irish, 16.9%
French, 12.9% German, 10.0% Italian, 8.6% English
Employment: 7.1% management, business, and financial, 3.1% computer,
engineering, and science, 15.1% education, legal, community service, arts,
and media, 6.0% healthcare practitioners, 25.5% service, 28.7% sales and
office, 3.9% natural resources, construction, and maintenance, 10.7%
production, transportation, and material moving

Income: Per capita: $21,682; Median household: $37,346; Average
household: $53,148; Households with income of $100,000 or more: 13.5%;
Poverty rate: 25.3%
Educational Attainment: High school diploma or higher: 88.7%;
Bachelor's degree or higher: 31.5%; Graduate/professional degree or
higher: 14.4%
School District(s)
Clinton-Essex-Warren-Washington Boces
   2014-15 Enrollment: n/a . . . . (518) 536-7340
Plattsburgh City SD (PK-12)
   2014-15 Enrollment: 1,873 . . . . (518) 957-6002
Four-year College(s)
SUNY College at Plattsburgh (Public)
   Fall 2014 Enrollment: 5,968 . . . . (518) 564-2000
   2015-16 Tuition: In-state $7,850; Out-of-state $17,700
Two-year College(s)
CVPH Medical Center School of Radiologic Technology (Private,
Not-for-profit)
   Fall 2014 Enrollment: 23 . . . . (518) 562-7510
Clinton Community College (Public)
   Fall 2014 Enrollment: 1,870 . . . . (518) 562-4200
   2015-16 Tuition: In-state $4,670; Out-of-state $9,670
Clinton Essex Warren Washington BOCES (Public)
   Fall 2014 Enrollment: 63 . . . . (518) 561-0100
Housing: Homeownership rate: 37.2%; Median home value: $142,900;
Median year structure built: 1960; Homeowner vacancy rate: 2.2%; Median
selected monthly owner costs: $1,308 with a mortgage, $448 without a
mortgage; Median gross rent: $747 per month; Rental vacancy rate: 5.3%
Health Insurance: 93.2% have insurance; 71.0% have private insurance;
36.9% have public insurance; 6.8% do not have insurance; 1.5% of
children under 18 do not have insurance
Hospitals: Champlain Valley Physicians Hospital Medical Center (405
beds)
Safety: Violent crime rate: 21.9 per 10,000 population; Property crime rate:
84.9 per 10,000 population
Newspapers: Press Republican (daily circulation 20,000)
Transportation: Commute: 77.2% car, 1.7% public transportation, 13.3%
walk, 1.6% work from home; Mean travel time to work: 13.7 minutes;
Amtrak: Train service available.
Airports: Plattsburgh International (primary service/non-hub)
Additional Information Contacts
City of Plattsburgh . . . . (518) 563-7702
  http://www.cityofplattsburgh.com

PLATTSBURGH (town). Covers a land area of 45.920 square miles
and a water area of 22.288 square miles. Located at 44.69° N. Lat; 73.52°
W. Long. Elevation is 138 feet.
History: During the War of 1812 a makeshift American fleet under Thomas
Macdonough defeated the British in a pitched battle on Lake Champlain
near Plattsburgh, compelling an accompanying land-invasion force under
Sir George Prevost to return to Canada. Seat of the State University of
N.Y. College at Plattsburgh. Settled 1767, Incorporated 1902.
Population: 11,847; Growth (since 2000): 5.9%; Density: 258.0 persons
per square mile; Race: 94.6% White, 2.0% Black/African American, 1.5%
Asian, 0.3% American Indian/Alaska Native, 0.0% Native Hawaiian/Other
Pacific Islander, 1.0% Two or more races, 2.0% Hispanic of any race;
Average household size: 2.32; Median age: 43.4; Age under 18: 20.2%;
Age 65 and over: 17.4%; Males per 100 females: 98.6; Marriage status:
27.5% never married, 54.0% now married, 3.5% separated, 7.1%
widowed, 11.4% divorced; Foreign born: 4.1%; Speak English only: 95.4%;
With disability: 14.5%; Veterans: 9.8%; Ancestry: 22.0% French, 19.1%
Irish, 10.1% English, 9.4% American, 9.2% German
Employment: 10.9% management, business, and financial, 3.6%
computer, engineering, and science, 12.3% education, legal, community
service, arts, and media, 6.9% healthcare practitioners, 18.7% service,
26.4% sales and office, 8.0% natural resources, construction, and
maintenance, 13.1% production, transportation, and material moving
Income: Per capita: $27,294; Median household: $53,980; Average
household: $65,880; Households with income of $100,000 or more: 17.6%;
Poverty rate: 12.8%
Educational Attainment: High school diploma or higher: 86.9%;
Bachelor's degree or higher: 25.1%; Graduate/professional degree or
higher: 12.5%

School District(s)

Clinton-Essex-Warren-Washington Boces
  2014-15 Enrollment: n/a . . . . (518) 536-7340
Plattsburgh City SD (PK-12)
  2014-15 Enrollment: 1,873 . . . . (518) 957-6002

Four-year College(s)

SUNY College at Plattsburgh (Public)
  Fall 2014 Enrollment: 5,968 . . . . (518) 564-2000
  2015-16 Tuition: In-state $7,850; Out-of-state $17,700

Two-year College(s)

CVPH Medical Center School of Radiologic Technology (Private,
Not-for-profit)
  Fall 2014 Enrollment: 23 . . . . (518) 562-7510
Clinton Community College (Public)
  Fall 2014 Enrollment: 1,870 . . . . (518) 562-4200
  2015-16 Tuition: In-state $4,670; Out-of-state $9,670
Clinton Essex Warren Washington BOCES (Public)
  Fall 2014 Enrollment: 63 . . . . (518) 561-0100

Housing: Homeownership rate: 76.8%; Median home value: $130,800; Median year structure built: 1975; Homeowner vacancy rate: 1.8%; Median selected monthly owner costs: $1,257 with a mortgage, $467 without a mortgage; Median gross rent: $821 per month; Rental vacancy rate: 0.0%
Health Insurance: 92.4% have insurance; 74.0% have private insurance; 37.2% have public insurance; 7.6% do not have insurance; 3.1% of children under 18 do not have insurance
Hospitals: Champlain Valley Physicians Hospital Medical Center (405 beds)
Newspapers: Press Republican (daily circulation 20,000)
Transportation: Commute: 94.5% car, 0.2% public transportation, 1.7% walk, 2.6% work from home; Mean travel time to work: 16.7 minutes; Amtrak: Train service available.
Airports: Plattsburgh International (primary service/non-hub)
Additional Information Contacts
Town of Plattsburgh . . . . (518) 562-6800
  http://townofplattsburgh.com

PLATTSBURGH WEST (CDP). Covers a land area of 1.774 square miles and a water area of 0.055 square miles. Located at 44.68° N. Lat; 73.50° W. Long.

Population: 1,458; Growth (since 2000): 13.1%; Density: 822.0 persons per square mile; Race: 95.1% White, 1.2% Black/African American, 0.6% Asian, 0.4% American Indian/Alaska Native, 0.0% Native Hawaiian/Other Pacific Islander, 2.0% Two or more races, 3.3% Hispanic of any race; Average household size: 2.33; Median age: 39.5; Age under 18: 22.3%; Age 65 and over: 13.8%; Males per 100 females: 92.7; Marriage status: 32.1% never married, 49.4% now married, 1.8% separated, 7.6% widowed, 10.9% divorced; Foreign born: 2.7%; Speak English only: 95.6%; With disability: 18.9%; Veterans: 10.2%; Ancestry: 21.5% Irish, 17.0% French, 10.3% American, 8.8% Dutch, 6.8% French Canadian
Employment: 3.4% management, business, and financial, 1.0% computer, engineering, and science, 3.4% education, legal, community service, arts, and media, 2.0% healthcare practitioners, 26.5% service, 36.7% sales and office, 8.8% natural resources, construction, and maintenance, 18.1% production, transportation, and material moving
Income: Per capita: $18,255; Median household: $40,363; Average household: $43,757; Households with income of $100,000 or more: 4.1%; Poverty rate: 24.7%
Educational Attainment: High school diploma or higher: 75.8%; Bachelor's degree or higher: 10.4%; Graduate/professional degree or higher: 3.1%
Housing: Homeownership rate: 72.8%; Median home value: $65,800; Median year structure built: 1989; Homeowner vacancy rate: 1.5%; Median selected monthly owner costs: $1,005 with a mortgage, $470 without a mortgage; Median gross rent: $768 per month; Rental vacancy rate: 0.0%
Health Insurance: 81.9% have insurance; 54.1% have private insurance; 45.2% have public insurance; 18.1% do not have insurance; 19.4% of children under 18 do not have insurance
Transportation: Commute: 91.1% car, 0.0% public transportation, 7.1% walk, 0.0% work from home; Mean travel time to work: 14.3 minutes

REDFORD (CDP). Covers a land area of 1.347 square miles and a water area of 0.108 square miles. Located at 44.61° N. Lat; 73.81° W. Long. Elevation is 1,171 feet.

Population: 528; Growth (since 2000): 3.1%; Density: 392.0 persons per square mile; Race: 100.0% White, 0.0% Black/African American, 0.0%

Asian, 0.0% American Indian/Alaska Native, 0.0% Native Hawaiian/Other Pacific Islander, 0.0% Two or more races, 0.0% Hispanic of any race; Average household size: 3.38; Median age: 21.3; Age under 18: 38.8%; Age 65 and over: 0.0%; Males per 100 females: 107.4; Marriage status: 41.1% never married, 53.5% now married, 14.6% separated, 0.0% widowed, 5.4% divorced; Foreign born: 0.0%; Speak English only: 100.0%; With disability: 15.3%; Veterans: 0.0%; Ancestry: 43.2% French Canadian, 18.4% American, 7.2% Russian, 3.6% Norwegian, 3.0% Canadian
Employment: 0.0% management, business, and financial, 8.3% computer, engineering, and science, 30.4% education, legal, community service, arts, and media, 0.0% healthcare practitioners, 32.2% service, 0.0% sales and office, 15.7% natural resources, construction, and maintenance, 13.5% production, transportation, and material moving
Income: Per capita: $18,072; Median household: n/a; Average household: $61,339; Households with income of $100,000 or more: 45.5%; Poverty rate: 43.4%
Educational Attainment: High school diploma or higher: 93.7%; Bachelor's degree or higher: 30.0%; Graduate/professional degree or higher: 30.0%
Housing: Homeownership rate: 45.5%; Median home value: $94,500; Median year structure built: 1992; Homeowner vacancy rate: 0.0%; Median selected monthly owner costs: $1,240 with a mortgage, n/a without a mortgage; Median gross rent: n/a per month; Rental vacancy rate: 0.0%
Health Insurance: 89.4% have insurance; 48.7% have private insurance; 44.7% have public insurance; 10.6% do not have insurance; 0.0% of children under 18 do not have insurance
Transportation: Commute: 100.0% car, 0.0% public transportation, 0.0% walk, 0.0% work from home; Mean travel time to work: 24.3 minutes

ROUSES POINT (village). Covers a land area of 1.761 square miles and a water area of 0.726 square miles. Located at 44.99° N. Lat; 73.36° W. Long. Elevation is 112 feet.

History: Incorporated 1877.
Population: 2,126; Growth (since 2000): -6.6%; Density: 1,207.4 persons per square mile; Race: 98.3% White, 0.5% Black/African American, 0.2% Asian, 0.0% American Indian/Alaska Native, 0.2% Native Hawaiian/Other Pacific Islander, 0.8% Two or more races, 0.7% Hispanic of any race; Average household size: 2.14; Median age: 44.3; Age under 18: 17.7%; Age 65 and over: 17.5%; Males per 100 females: 92.3; Marriage status: 31.3% never married, 48.6% now married, 2.2% separated, 9.7% widowed, 10.4% divorced; Foreign born: 8.4%; Speak English only: 92.5%; With disability: 11.0%; Veterans: 9.8%; Ancestry: 23.6% French, 14.3% French Canadian, 13.7% English, 11.7% American, 11.1% Irish
Employment: 11.3% management, business, and financial, 2.5% computer, engineering, and science, 9.3% education, legal, community service, arts, and media, 4.3% healthcare practitioners, 22.8% service, 23.7% sales and office, 10.0% natural resources, construction, and maintenance, 16.1% production, transportation, and material moving
Income: Per capita: $32,276; Median household: $60,556; Average household: $69,475; Households with income of $100,000 or more: 23.2%; Poverty rate: 10.9%
Educational Attainment: High school diploma or higher: 90.7%; Bachelor's degree or higher: 24.2%; Graduate/professional degree or higher: 8.3%

School District(s)

Northeastern Clinton Central SD (KG-12)
  2014-15 Enrollment: 1,358 . . . . (518) 298-8242

Housing: Homeownership rate: 57.2%; Median home value: $143,100; Median year structure built: 1961; Homeowner vacancy rate: 0.0%; Median selected monthly owner costs: $1,285 with a mortgage, $497 without a mortgage; Median gross rent: $598 per month; Rental vacancy rate: 7.2%
Health Insurance: 94.3% have insurance; 72.1% have private insurance; 36.2% have public insurance; 5.7% do not have insurance; 6.1% of children under 18 do not have insurance
Safety: Violent crime rate: 0.0 per 10,000 population; Property crime rate: 13.8 per 10,000 population
Transportation: Commute: 92.0% car, 0.0% public transportation, 6.0% walk, 1.8% work from home; Mean travel time to work: 21.9 minutes; Amtrak: Train service available.

SARANAC (town). Covers a land area of 115.286 square miles and a water area of 0.661 square miles. Located at 44.65° N. Lat; 73.81° W. Long. Elevation is 797 feet.

History: Saranac is a town in Clinton County, New York, and was first settled around 1802. The town of Saranac was established from the

western part of the town of Plattsburgh in 1824, when the iron industry was important to its economy.

Population: 4,005; Growth (since 2000): -3.8%; Density: 34.7 persons per square mile; Race: 93.0% White, 5.8% Black/African American, 0.3% Asian, 0.2% American Indian/Alaska Native, 0.0% Native Hawaiian/Other Pacific Islander, 0.2% Two or more races, 0.9% Hispanic of any race; Average household size: 2.41; Median age: 36.4; Age under 18: 25.4%; Age 65 and over: 12.1%; Males per 100 females: 100.5; Marriage status: 27.9% never married, 54.4% now married, 2.9% separated, 7.6% widowed, 10.1% divorced; Foreign born: 3.8%; Speak English only: 99.1%; With disability: 13.0%; Veterans: 9.1%; Ancestry: 21.5% French, 12.1% American, 11.2% Irish, 9.3% French Canadian, 8.7% English

Employment: 5.3% management, business, and financial, 2.5% computer, engineering, and science, 21.1% education, legal, community service, arts, and media, 7.2% healthcare practitioners, 26.0% service, 16.9% sales and office, 11.2% natural resources, construction, and maintenance, 9.9% production, transportation, and material moving

Income: Per capita: $27,856; Median household: $54,938; Average household: $66,730; Households with income of $100,000 or more: 25.6%; Poverty rate: 13.6%

Educational Attainment: High school diploma or higher: 88.6%; Bachelor's degree or higher: 26.0%; Graduate/professional degree or higher: 11.9%

School District(s)

Saranac Central SD (KG-12)

    2014-15 Enrollment: 1,478 . . . . (518) 565-5600

Housing: Homeownership rate: 82.9%; Median home value: $109,800; Median year structure built: 1974; Homeowner vacancy rate: 3.4%; Median selected monthly owner costs: $1,216 with a mortgage, $437 without a mortgage; Median gross rent: $715 per month; Rental vacancy rate: 0.0%

Health Insurance: 94.4% have insurance; 72.4% have private insurance; 33.6% have public insurance; 5.6% do not have insurance; 0.0% of children under 18 do not have insurance

Transportation: Commute: 97.8% car, 0.0% public transportation, 0.8% walk, 1.4% work from home; Mean travel time to work: 26.7 minutes

Additional Information Contacts

Town of Saranac . . . . (518) 293-6666
    http://www.townofsaranac.com

SCHUYLER FALLS (town). Covers a land area of 36.517 square miles and a water area of 0.302 square miles. Located at 44.66° N. Lat; 73.58° W. Long. Elevation is 430 feet.

Population: 5,168; Growth (since 2000): 0.8%; Density: 141.5 persons per square mile; Race: 97.7% White, 0.0% Black/African American, 1.1% Asian, 0.2% American Indian/Alaska Native, 0.0% Native Hawaiian/Other Pacific Islander, 0.8% Two or more races, 1.0% Hispanic of any race; Average household size: 2.41; Median age: 41.3; Age under 18: 21.4%; Age 65 and over: 14.9%; Males per 100 females: 99.7; Marriage status: 24.5% never married, 61.4% now married, 1.8% separated, 6.0% widowed, 8.0% divorced; Foreign born: 3.8%; Speak English only: 95.5%; With disability: 14.9%; Veterans: 11.9%; Ancestry: 21.3% French, 16.7% Irish, 14.1% American, 13.0% German, 9.9% French Canadian

Employment: 8.2% management, business, and financial, 5.1% computer, engineering, and science, 10.3% education, legal, community service, arts, and media, 9.0% healthcare practitioners, 24.8% service, 18.4% sales and office, 6.9% natural resources, construction, and maintenance, 17.3% production, transportation, and material moving

Income: Per capita: $31,480; Median household: $62,969; Average household: $74,925; Households with income of $100,000 or more: 24.3%; Poverty rate: 12.1%

Educational Attainment: High school diploma or higher: 84.8%; Bachelor's degree or higher: 21.6%; Graduate/professional degree or higher: 7.9%

Housing: Homeownership rate: 83.3%; Median home value: $130,900; Median year structure built: 1975; Homeowner vacancy rate: 0.0%; Median selected monthly owner costs: $1,189 with a mortgage, $478 without a mortgage; Median gross rent: $821 per month; Rental vacancy rate: 0.0%

Health Insurance: 97.1% have insurance; 77.6% have private insurance; 35.6% have public insurance; 2.9% do not have insurance; 3.5% of children under 18 do not have insurance

Transportation: Commute: 92.7% car, 0.1% public transportation, 0.0% walk, 3.9% work from home; Mean travel time to work: 22.1 minutes

Additional Information Contacts

Town of Schuyler Falls . . . . (518) 563-1129
    http://www.schuylerfallsny.com

WEST CHAZY (CDP). Covers a land area of 1.877 square miles and a water area of 0 square miles. Located at 44.82° N. Lat; 73.51° W. Long. Elevation is 302 feet.

Population: 986; Growth (since 2000): n/a; Density: 525.2 persons per square mile; Race: 100.0% White, 0.0% Black/African American, 0.0% Asian, 0.0% American Indian/Alaska Native, 0.0% Native Hawaiian/Other Pacific Islander, 0.0% Two or more races, 0.0% Hispanic of any race; Average household size: 2.78; Median age: 27.0; Age under 18: 35.3%; Age 65 and over: 10.8%; Males per 100 females: 101.9; Marriage status: 39.9% never married, 55.5% now married, 6.5% separated, 2.7% widowed, 1.9% divorced; Foreign born: 2.9%; Speak English only: 100.0%; With disability: 6.7%; Veterans: 16.1%; Ancestry: 23.3% American, 11.1% Polish, 10.2% Irish, 9.6% German, 9.5% French

Employment: 4.4% management, business, and financial, 0.0% computer, engineering, and science, 4.4% education, legal, community service, arts, and media, 8.5% healthcare practitioners, 20.6% service, 26.5% sales and office, 18.4% natural resources, construction, and maintenance, 17.3% production, transportation, and material moving

Income: Per capita: $19,741; Median household: $50,694; Average household: $55,772; Households with income of $100,000 or more: 11.0%; Poverty rate: 26.0%

Educational Attainment: High school diploma or higher: 76.2%; Bachelor's degree or higher: 11.3%; Graduate/professional degree or higher: 1.8%

School District(s)

Beekmantown Central SD (PK-12)

    2014-15 Enrollment: 1,900 . . . . (518) 324-2999

Housing: Homeownership rate: 64.5%; Median home value: $111,000; Median year structure built: Before 1940; Homeowner vacancy rate: 0.0%; Median selected monthly owner costs: $1,095 with a mortgage, $404 without a mortgage; Median gross rent: $771 per month; Rental vacancy rate: 0.0%

Health Insurance: 88.9% have insurance; 56.9% have private insurance; 42.4% have public insurance; 11.1% do not have insurance; 10.3% of children under 18 do not have insurance

Transportation: Commute: 100.0% car, 0.0% public transportation, 0.0% walk, 0.0% work from home; Mean travel time to work: 20.5 minutes

Columbia County

Located in southeastern New York; bounded on the east by Massachusetts, and on the west by the Hudson River. Covers a land area of 634.705 square miles, a water area of 13.560 square miles, and is located in the Eastern Time Zone at 42.25° N. Lat., 73.63° W. Long. The county was founded in 1786. County seat is Hudson.

Columbia County is part of the Hudson, NY Micropolitan Statistical Area. The entire metro area includes: Columbia County, NY

Weather Station: Hudson Correctionl Fac										Elevation: 60 feet		
	Jan	Feb	Mar	Apr	May	Jun	Jul	Aug	Sep	Oct	Nov	Dec
High	34	38	48	62	73	81	84	82	74	63	51	39
Low	16	19	27	37	47	57	61	60	53	41	33	23
Precip	2.6	2.3	3.4	3.7	3.8	4.3	3.9	3.8	4.0	4.0	3.2	3.0
Snow	11.0	7.4	4.8	1.1	0.0	0.0	0.0	0.0	0.0	0.1	1.0	6.2

High and Low temperatures in degrees Fahrenheit; Precipitation and Snow in inches

Weather Station: Valatie 1 N										Elevation: 299 feet		
	Jan	Feb	Mar	Apr	May	Jun	Jul	Aug	Sep	Oct	Nov	Dec
High	32	36	44	58	69	78	82	81	73	61	49	37
Low	13	16	24	35	46	55	59	58	50	38	31	19
Precip	2.1	1.9	2.8	3.7	4.1	4.5	4.1	4.1	4.0	3.9	3.3	2.6
Snow	10.8	8.2	6.4	2.2	0.0	0.0	0.0	0.0	0.0	0.3	2.4	11.1

High and Low temperatures in degrees Fahrenheit; Precipitation and Snow in inches

Population: 62,195; Growth (since 2000): -1.4%; Density: 98.0 persons per square mile; Race: 89.9% White, 4.4% Black/African American, 1.7% Asian, 0.1% American Indian/Alaska Native, 0.0% Native Hawaiian/Other Pacific Islander, 3.0% two or more races, 4.3% Hispanic of any race; Average household size: 2.37; Median age: 46.6; Age under 18: 19.0%; Age 65 and over: 20.1%; Males per 100 females: 101.4; Marriage status: 30.0% never married, 51.5% now married, 2.3% separated, 7.0% widowed, 11.5% divorced; Foreign born: 6.1%; Speak English only: 93.4%; With disability: 15.7%; Veterans: 9.3%; Ancestry: 22.6% German, 22.4% Irish, 16.9% Italian, 9.7% English, 7.0% Polish

Religion: Six largest groups: 24.4% Catholicism, 3.5% Methodist/Pietist, 3.1% Lutheran, 3.0% Presbyterian-Reformed, 1.3% Episcopalianism/Anglicanism, 1.2% Non-denominational Protestant

Economy: Unemployment rate: 3.5%; Leading industries: 16.1 % retail trade; 15.0 % construction; 10.3 % professional, scientific, and technical services; Farms: 494 totaling 95,378 acres; Company size: 1 employs 1,000 or more persons, 0 employ 500 to 999 persons, 17 employ 100 to 499 persons, 1,705 employ less than 100 persons; Business ownership: 2,155 women-owned, 139 Black-owned, 125 Hispanic-owned, 190 Asian-owned, n/a American Indian/Alaska Native-owned

Employment: 15.4% management, business, and financial, 2.8% computer, engineering, and science, 13.0% education, legal, community service, arts, and media, 6.1% healthcare practitioners, 20.0% service, 21.5% sales and office, 11.0% natural resources, construction, and maintenance, 10.1% production, transportation, and material moving

Income: Per capita: $32,851; Median household: $59,105; Average household: $78,720; Households with income of $100,000 or more: 24.8%; Poverty rate: 11.7%

Educational Attainment: High school diploma or higher: 88.4%; Bachelor's degree or higher: 29.3%; Graduate/professional degree or higher: 14.8%

Housing: Homeownership rate: 71.9%; Median home value: $222,100; Median year structure built: 1965; Homeowner vacancy rate: 2.9%; Median selected monthly owner costs: $1,717 with a mortgage, $644 without a mortgage; Median gross rent: $884 per month; Rental vacancy rate: 6.6%

Vital Statistics: Birth rate: 86.5 per 10,000 population; Death rate: 104.2 per 10,000 population; Age-adjusted cancer mortality rate: 165.7 deaths per 100,000 population

Health Insurance: 93.3% have insurance; 73.1% have private insurance; 36.9% have public insurance; 6.7% do not have insurance; 2.7% of children under 18 do not have insurance

Health Care: Physicians: 17.9 per 10,000 population; Dentists: 3.9 per 10,000 population; Hospital beds: 35.0 per 10,000 population; Hospital admissions: 997.3 per 10,000 population

Transportation: Commute: 86.2% car, 2.3% public transportation, 4.1% walk, 6.7% work from home; Mean travel time to work: 26.0 minutes

2016 Presidential Election: 45.0% Trump, 50.0% Clinton, 3.1% Johnson, 2.0% Stein

National and State Parks: Beebe Hill State Forest; Clermont State Historic Site; Clermont State Park; Lake Taghkanic State Park; Martin Van Buren National Historic Site; Taconic State Park

Additional Information Contacts

Columbia Government . . . . (518) 828-3339
  http://www.columbiacountyny.com

Columbia County Communities

ANCRAM (town). Covers a land area of 42.478 square miles and a water area of 0.259 square miles. Located at 42.04° N. Lat; 73.58° W. Long. Elevation is 518 feet.

Population: 1,488; Growth (since 2000): -1.7%; Density: 35.0 persons per square mile; Race: 88.9% White, 5.1% Black/African American, 2.4% Asian, 0.0% American Indian/Alaska Native, 0.0% Native Hawaiian/Other Pacific Islander, 2.4% Two or more races, 4.4% Hispanic of any race; Average household size: 2.39; Median age: 53.0; Age under 18: 18.5%; Age 65 and over: 25.3%; Males per 100 females: 105.9; Marriage status: 26.6% never married, 59.9% now married, 1.9% separated, 3.0% widowed, 10.5% divorced; Foreign born: 8.0%; Speak English only: 92.7%; With disability: 14.8%; Veterans: 9.7%; Ancestry: 28.3% Irish, 18.8% German, 8.1% Italian, 8.0% English, 7.2% American

Employment: 14.5% management, business, and financial, 7.3% computer, engineering, and science, 11.3% education, legal, community service, arts, and media, 2.0% healthcare practitioners, 13.6% service, 15.4% sales and office, 19.3% natural resources, construction, and maintenance, 16.6% production, transportation, and material moving

Income: Per capita: $37,129; Median household: $62,639; Average household: $89,472; Households with income of $100,000 or more: 28.4%; Poverty rate: 15.5%

Educational Attainment: High school diploma or higher: 88.3%; Bachelor's degree or higher: 35.1%; Graduate/professional degree or higher: 20.5%

Housing: Homeownership rate: 75.0%; Median home value: $285,500; Median year structure built: 1972; Homeowner vacancy rate: 1.9%; Median selected monthly owner costs: $1,888 with a mortgage, $732 without a

mortgage; Median gross rent: $1,231 per month; Rental vacancy rate: 9.4%

Health Insurance: 90.7% have insurance; 71.6% have private insurance; 40.9% have public insurance; 9.3% do not have insurance; 9.1% of children under 18 do not have insurance

Transportation: Commute: 72.9% car, 5.9% public transportation, 3.4% walk, 17.3% work from home; Mean travel time to work: 33.4 minutes

ANCRAMDALE (unincorporated postal area)
ZCTA: 12503

Covers a land area of 21.030 square miles and a water area of 0.158 square miles. Located at 42.04° N. Lat; 73.58° W. Long. Elevation is 548 feet.

Population: 783; Growth (since 2000): -5.7%; Density: 37.2 persons per square mile; Race: 93.2% White, 2.9% Black/African American, 1.1% Asian, 0.0% American Indian/Alaska Native, 0.0% Native Hawaiian/Other Pacific Islander, 0.4% Two or more races, 5.6% Hispanic of any race; Average household size: 2.26; Median age: 52.8; Age under 18: 17.2%; Age 65 and over: 24.9%; Males per 100 females: 107.2; Marriage status: 27.9% never married, 54.8% now married, 3.2% separated, 3.2% widowed, 14.1% divorced; Foreign born: 9.7%; Speak English only: 89.2%; With disability: 15.5%; Veterans: 11.3%; Ancestry: 21.6% German, 18.8% Irish, 10.6% English, 6.3% Italian, 5.9% American

Employment: 18.4% management, business, and financial, 7.5% computer, engineering, and science, 13.8% education, legal, community service, arts, and media, 1.9% healthcare practitioners, 15.7% service, 14.3% sales and office, 21.1% natural resources, construction, and maintenance, 7.3% production, transportation, and material moving

Income: Per capita: $40,873; Median household: $63,472; Average household: $94,641; Households with income of $100,000 or more: 31.6%; Poverty rate: 9.3%

Educational Attainment: High school diploma or higher: 87.9%; Bachelor's degree or higher: 37.7%; Graduate/professional degree or higher: 21.8%

Housing: Homeownership rate: 72.3%; Median home value: $284,400; Median year structure built: 1973; Homeowner vacancy rate: 2.4%; Median selected monthly owner costs: $1,930 with a mortgage, $680 without a mortgage; Median gross rent: $1,224 per month; Rental vacancy rate: 5.1%

Health Insurance: 89.3% have insurance; 79.1% have private insurance; 33.2% have public insurance; 10.7% do not have insurance; 14.1% of children under 18 do not have insurance

Transportation: Commute: 68.8% car, 6.5% public transportation, 4.5% walk, 20.2% work from home; Mean travel time to work: 34.8 minutes

AUSTERLITZ (town). Covers a land area of 48.722 square miles and a water area of 0.092 square miles. Located at 42.32° N. Lat; 73.52° W. Long. Elevation is 1,129 feet.

Population: 1,481; Growth (since 2000): 1.9%; Density: 30.4 persons per square mile; Race: 96.8% White, 2.4% Black/African American, 0.4% Asian, 0.0% American Indian/Alaska Native, 0.0% Native Hawaiian/Other Pacific Islander, 0.3% Two or more races, 0.5% Hispanic of any race; Average household size: 2.33; Median age: 50.5; Age under 18: 18.0%; Age 65 and over: 22.8%; Males per 100 females: 102.4; Marriage status: 24.5% never married, 55.9% now married, 0.9% separated, 5.5% widowed, 14.0% divorced; Foreign born: 3.2%; Speak English only: 97.3%; With disability: 7.2%; Veterans: 5.8%; Ancestry: 28.4% German, 24.6% Irish, 14.9% Italian, 12.8% English, 8.2% Polish

Employment: 16.8% management, business, and financial, 3.9% computer, engineering, and science, 16.9% education, legal, community service, arts, and media, 5.5% healthcare practitioners, 17.4% service, 19.3% sales and office, 15.4% natural resources, construction, and maintenance, 4.9% production, transportation, and material moving

Income: Per capita: $42,107; Median household: $64,250; Average household: $93,332; Households with income of $100,000 or more: 33.8%; Poverty rate: 14.9%

Educational Attainment: High school diploma or higher: 97.4%; Bachelor's degree or higher: 41.8%; Graduate/professional degree or higher: 26.9%

Housing: Homeownership rate: 85.5%; Median home value: $282,500; Median year structure built: 1975; Homeowner vacancy rate: 4.2%; Median selected monthly owner costs: $1,855 with a mortgage, $652 without a mortgage; Median gross rent: $750 per month; Rental vacancy rate: 10.7%

Health Insurance: 93.6% have insurance; 80.1% have private insurance; 35.6% have public insurance; 6.4% do not have insurance; 7.9% of children under 18 do not have insurance
Transportation: Commute: 84.0% car, 4.0% public transportation, 2.0% walk, 9.6% work from home; Mean travel time to work: 24.4 minutes

CANAAN (town). Covers a land area of 36.676 square miles and a water area of 0.280 square miles. Located at 42.41° N. Lat; 73.46° W. Long. Elevation is 850 feet.
Population: 1,671; Growth (since 2000): -8.2%; Density: 45.6 persons per square mile; Race: 90.5% White, 2.0% Black/African American, 2.0% Asian, 0.2% American Indian/Alaska Native, 0.0% Native Hawaiian/Other Pacific Islander, 4.1% Two or more races, 4.7% Hispanic of any race; Average household size: 2.37; Median age: 48.0; Age under 18: 22.0%; Age 65 and over: 23.5%; Males per 100 females: 110.9; Marriage status: 31.6% never married, 52.0% now married, 1.1% separated, 8.2% widowed, 8.2% divorced; Foreign born: 2.9%; Speak English only: 93.1%; With disability: 13.5%; Veterans: 7.2%; Ancestry: 24.6% German, 17.2% Irish, 10.8% Italian, 9.3% English, 8.6% Polish
Employment: 16.4% management, business, and financial, 6.4% computer, engineering, and science, 15.0% education, legal, community service, arts, and media, 5.8% healthcare practitioners, 16.6% service, 20.2% sales and office, 13.5% natural resources, construction, and maintenance, 6.1% production, transportation, and material moving
Income: Per capita: $34,741; Median household: $76,055; Average household: $87,868; Households with income of $100,000 or more: 29.6%; Poverty rate: 10.4%
Educational Attainment: High school diploma or higher: 89.6%; Bachelor's degree or higher: 38.4%; Graduate/professional degree or higher: 19.7%
School District(s)
Berkshire Union Free SD (07-12)
    2014-15 Enrollment: 78 . . . . (518) 781-3500
Housing: Homeownership rate: 82.8%; Median home value: $274,700; Median year structure built: 1961; Homeowner vacancy rate: 4.6%; Median selected monthly owner costs: $1,881 with a mortgage, $713 without a mortgage; Median gross rent: $1,291 per month; Rental vacancy rate: 0.0%
Health Insurance: 94.5% have insurance; 78.1% have private insurance; 35.9% have public insurance; 5.5% do not have insurance; 4.8% of children under 18 do not have insurance
Transportation: Commute: 83.6% car, 1.0% public transportation, 3.6% walk, 10.4% work from home; Mean travel time to work: 28.6 minutes

CHATHAM (town). Covers a land area of 53.227 square miles and a water area of 0.316 square miles. Located at 42.43° N. Lat; 73.58° W. Long. Elevation is 463 feet.
History: Incorporated 1869.
Population: 4,056; Growth (since 2000): -4.5%; Density: 76.2 persons per square mile; Race: 93.3% White, 1.1% Black/African American, 0.7% Asian, 0.0% American Indian/Alaska Native, 0.0% Native Hawaiian/Other Pacific Islander, 2.2% Two or more races, 4.4% Hispanic of any race; Average household size: 2.33; Median age: 46.3; Age under 18: 20.8%; Age 65 and over: 21.3%; Males per 100 females: 99.7; Marriage status: 26.3% never married, 60.1% now married, 1.3% separated, 4.8% widowed, 8.8% divorced; Foreign born: 5.6%; Speak English only: 95.0%; With disability: 13.6%; Veterans: 9.4%; Ancestry: 28.6% German, 23.9% Irish, 14.7% English, 14.7% Italian, 6.3% American
Employment: 18.7% management, business, and financial, 3.0% computer, engineering, and science, 16.3% education, legal, community service, arts, and media, 5.5% healthcare practitioners, 14.6% service, 17.7% sales and office, 10.1% natural resources, construction, and maintenance, 14.1% production, transportation, and material moving
Income: Per capita: $41,191; Median household: $69,598; Average household: $94,942; Households with income of $100,000 or more: 26.8%; Poverty rate: 8.3%
Educational Attainment: High school diploma or higher: 94.3%; Bachelor's degree or higher: 39.3%; Graduate/professional degree or higher: 20.4%
School District(s)
Chatham Central SD (KG-12)
    2014-15 Enrollment: 1,160 . . . . (518) 392-1501
Housing: Homeownership rate: 77.8%; Median home value: $263,300; Median year structure built: 1954; Homeowner vacancy rate: 2.6%; Median

selected monthly owner costs: $1,691 with a mortgage, $753 without a mortgage; Median gross rent: $799 per month; Rental vacancy rate: 2.8%
Health Insurance: 93.8% have insurance; 75.4% have private insurance; 37.2% have public insurance; 6.2% do not have insurance; 2.7% of children under 18 do not have insurance
Transportation: Commute: 81.1% car, 2.5% public transportation, 2.5% walk, 12.2% work from home; Mean travel time to work: 29.0 minutes
Additional Information Contacts
Town of Chatham . . . . (518) 392-1655
    http://chathamnewyork.us

CHATHAM (village). Covers a land area of 1.237 square miles and a water area of 0.004 square miles. Located at 42.36° N. Lat; 73.60° W. Long. Elevation is 463 feet.
Population: 1,381; Growth (since 2000): -21.4%; Density: 1,116.5 persons per square mile; Race: 95.0% White, 2.8% Black/African American, 1.4% Asian, 0.0% American Indian/Alaska Native, 0.0% Native Hawaiian/Other Pacific Islander, 0.8% Two or more races, 1.2% Hispanic of any race; Average household size: 2.16; Median age: 47.5; Age under 18: 15.4%; Age 65 and over: 20.1%; Males per 100 females: 96.4; Marriage status: 36.8% never married, 44.1% now married, 2.5% separated, 8.0% widowed, 11.1% divorced; Foreign born: 3.1%; Speak English only: 94.4%; With disability: 14.7%; Veterans: 6.8%; Ancestry: 28.0% Irish, 20.7% Italian, 19.1% German, 13.6% English, 10.4% French
Employment: 9.5% management, business, and financial, 1.2% computer, engineering, and science, 14.6% education, legal, community service, arts, and media, 4.1% healthcare practitioners, 13.2% service, 24.1% sales and office, 18.7% natural resources, construction, and maintenance, 14.6% production, transportation, and material moving
Income: Per capita: $27,048; Median household: $46,188; Average household: $58,651; Households with income of $100,000 or more: 18.0%; Poverty rate: 13.2%
Educational Attainment: High school diploma or higher: 88.9%; Bachelor's degree or higher: 24.6%; Graduate/professional degree or higher: 10.5%
School District(s)
Chatham Central SD (KG-12)
    2014-15 Enrollment: 1,160 . . . . (518) 392-1501
Housing: Homeownership rate: 46.6%; Median home value: $219,400; Median year structure built: Before 1940; Homeowner vacancy rate: 1.7%; Median selected monthly owner costs: $1,870 with a mortgage, $750 without a mortgage; Median gross rent: $876 per month; Rental vacancy rate: 23.0%
Health Insurance: 92.5% have insurance; 72.8% have private insurance; 36.2% have public insurance; 7.5% do not have insurance; 0.0% of children under 18 do not have insurance
Safety: Violent crime rate: 0.0 per 10,000 population; Property crime rate: 41.1 per 10,000 population
Transportation: Commute: 90.9% car, 1.3% public transportation, 2.4% walk, 5.5% work from home; Mean travel time to work: 23.0 minutes

CLAVERACK (town). Covers a land area of 47.559 square miles and a water area of 0.390 square miles. Located at 42.22° N. Lat; 73.69° W. Long. Elevation is 203 feet.
History: Fine old buildings include Van Rensselaer manor house; former county courthouse (built 1786).
Population: 5,929; Growth (since 2000): -7.4%; Density: 124.7 persons per square mile; Race: 95.6% White, 1.9% Black/African American, 0.3% Asian, 0.2% American Indian/Alaska Native, 0.0% Native Hawaiian/Other Pacific Islander, 1.7% Two or more races, 1.6% Hispanic of any race; Average household size: 2.29; Median age: 48.5; Age under 18: 18.9%; Age 65 and over: 22.0%; Males per 100 females: 99.0; Marriage status: 27.7% never married, 54.4% now married, 2.8% separated, 6.9% widowed, 10.9% divorced; Foreign born: 3.1%; Speak English only: 96.9%; With disability: 23.9%; Veterans: 11.1%; Ancestry: 39.3% German, 23.4% Irish, 14.5% Dutch, 11.5% Italian, 9.1% English
Employment: 12.2% management, business, and financial, 2.7% computer, engineering, and science, 10.7% education, legal, community service, arts, and media, 7.8% healthcare practitioners, 20.3% service, 22.2% sales and office, 10.4% natural resources, construction, and maintenance, 13.6% production, transportation, and material moving
Income: Per capita: $28,690; Median household: $50,933; Average household: $66,636; Households with income of $100,000 or more: 20.4%; Poverty rate: 12.8%

Educational Attainment: High school diploma or higher: 81.6%; Bachelor's degree or higher: 22.7%; Graduate/professional degree or higher: 10.6%

Housing: Homeownership rate: 72.9%; Median home value: $201,900; Median year structure built: 1962; Homeowner vacancy rate: 3.4%; Median selected monthly owner costs: $1,463 with a mortgage, $617 without a mortgage; Median gross rent: $872 per month; Rental vacancy rate: 8.5%

Health Insurance: 95.7% have insurance; 75.0% have private insurance; 43.4% have public insurance; 4.3% do not have insurance; 1.8% of children under 18 do not have insurance

Transportation: Commute: 92.6% car, 1.4% public transportation, 0.6% walk, 4.8% work from home; Mean travel time to work: 21.9 minutes

Additional Information Contacts

Town of Claverack. . . . . (518) 672-7911
http://www.townofclaverack.com

CLAVERACK-RED MILLS (CDP). Covers a land area of 2.978 square miles and a water area of 0.018 square miles. Located at 42.23° N. Lat; 73.72° W. Long.

Population: 735; Growth (since 2000): -30.7%; Density: 246.8 persons per square mile; Race: 100.0% White, 0.0% Black/African American, 0.0% Asian, 0.0% American Indian/Alaska Native, 0.0% Native Hawaiian/Other Pacific Islander, 0.0% Two or more races, 0.0% Hispanic of any race; Average household size: 2.04; Median age: 47.9; Age under 18: 17.8%; Age 65 and over: 24.1%; Males per 100 females: 98.5; Marriage status: 12.9% never married, 64.2% now married, 2.3% separated, 6.3% widowed, 16.6% divorced; Foreign born: 6.8%; Speak English only: 95.3%; With disability: 11.4%; Veterans: 0.0%; Ancestry: 41.6% German, 33.7% Italian, 32.8% Irish, 10.7% English, 7.9% Dutch

Employment: 16.8% management, business, and financial, 6.7% computer, engineering, and science, 25.6% education, legal, community service, arts, and media, 9.2% healthcare practitioners, 15.2% service, 14.5% sales and office, 7.8% natural resources, construction, and maintenance, 4.1% production, transportation, and material moving

Income: Per capita: $42,585; Median household: $87,404; Average household: $86,683; Households with income of $100,000 or more: 45.9%; Poverty rate: n/a

Educational Attainment: High school diploma or higher: 88.5%; Bachelor's degree or higher: 51.5%; Graduate/professional degree or higher: 23.8%

Housing: Homeownership rate: 81.1%; Median home value: $192,300; Median year structure built: 1961; Homeowner vacancy rate: 0.0%; Median selected monthly owner costs: $1,428 with a mortgage, $757 without a mortgage; Median gross rent: n/a per month; Rental vacancy rate: 0.0%

Health Insurance: 100.0% have insurance; 89.8% have private insurance; 26.0% have public insurance; 0.0% do not have insurance; 0.0% of children under 18 do not have insurance

Transportation: Commute: 96.1% car, 0.0% public transportation, 0.0% walk, 3.9% work from home; Mean travel time to work: 23.6 minutes

CLERMONT (town). Covers a land area of 17.996 square miles and a water area of 1.197 square miles. Located at 42.09° N. Lat; 73.85° W. Long. Elevation is 223 feet.

Population: 1,978; Growth (since 2000): 14.6%; Density: 109.9 persons per square mile; Race: 90.6% White, 0.4% Black/African American, 4.2% Asian, 0.1% American Indian/Alaska Native, 0.0% Native Hawaiian/Other Pacific Islander, 3.6% Two or more races, 6.8% Hispanic of any race; Average household size: 2.65; Median age: 44.8; Age under 18: 21.9%; Age 65 and over: 14.8%; Males per 100 females: 103.2; Marriage status: 27.5% never married, 57.9% now married, 3.8% separated, 5.2% widowed, 9.5% divorced; Foreign born: 5.8%; Speak English only: 94.0%; With disability: 10.1%; Veterans: 9.4%; Ancestry: 26.9% Irish, 21.0% German, 17.8% Italian, 11.3% English, 7.2% American

Employment: 14.4% management, business, and financial, 1.9% computer, engineering, and science, 12.5% education, legal, community service, arts, and media, 10.2% healthcare practitioners, 17.6% service, 15.7% sales and office, 16.8% natural resources, construction, and maintenance, 11.0% production, transportation, and material moving

Income: Per capita: $36,550; Median household: $75,288; Average household: $99,819; Households with income of $100,000 or more: 35.7%; Poverty rate: 13.9%

Educational Attainment: High school diploma or higher: 90.8%; Bachelor's degree or higher: 35.0%; Graduate/professional degree or higher: 21.7%

Housing: Homeownership rate: 80.1%; Median home value: $247,300; Median year structure built: 1974; Homeowner vacancy rate: 1.4%; Median selected monthly owner costs: $2,100 with a mortgage, $818 without a mortgage; Median gross rent: $975 per month; Rental vacancy rate: 6.5%

Health Insurance: 91.0% have insurance; 73.3% have private insurance; 30.7% have public insurance; 9.0% do not have insurance; 5.1% of children under 18 do not have insurance

Transportation: Commute: 86.1% car, 3.1% public transportation, 5.2% walk, 5.6% work from home; Mean travel time to work: 32.0 minutes

COPAKE (town). Covers a land area of 40.762 square miles and a water area of 1.280 square miles. Located at 42.13° N. Lat; 73.55° W. Long. Elevation is 545 feet.

Population: 3,574; Growth (since 2000): 9.0%; Density: 87.7 persons per square mile; Race: 96.6% White, 0.4% Black/African American, 0.2% Asian, 0.0% American Indian/Alaska Native, 0.0% Native Hawaiian/Other Pacific Islander, 2.5% Two or more races, 3.6% Hispanic of any race; Average household size: 2.43; Median age: 47.9; Age under 18: 16.7%; Age 65 and over: 21.7%; Males per 100 females: 99.2; Marriage status: 25.4% never married, 51.8% now married, 1.4% separated, 10.8% widowed, 12.0% divorced; Foreign born: 6.9%; Speak English only: 91.4%; With disability: 16.6%; Veterans: 6.0%; Ancestry: 24.3% German, 16.4% Irish, 13.7% English, 13.6% Polish, 12.1% American

Employment: 22.4% management, business, and financial, 0.8% computer, engineering, and science, 10.6% education, legal, community service, arts, and media, 3.8% healthcare practitioners, 20.8% service, 21.2% sales and office, 14.3% natural resources, construction, and maintenance, 6.0% production, transportation, and material moving

Income: Per capita: $28,521; Median household: $56,290; Average household: $72,601; Households with income of $100,000 or more: 26.5%; Poverty rate: 13.8%

Educational Attainment: High school diploma or higher: 89.0%; Bachelor's degree or higher: 27.4%; Graduate/professional degree or higher: 15.6%

Housing: Homeownership rate: 74.6%; Median home value: $240,000; Median year structure built: 1967; Homeowner vacancy rate: 11.2%; Median selected monthly owner costs: $1,449 with a mortgage, $538 without a mortgage; Median gross rent: $1,061 per month; Rental vacancy rate: 2.3%

Health Insurance: 95.0% have insurance; 76.0% have private insurance; 34.8% have public insurance; 5.0% do not have insurance; 0.0% of children under 18 do not have insurance

Transportation: Commute: 90.3% car, 2.3% public transportation, 2.8% walk, 4.6% work from home; Mean travel time to work: 29.3 minutes

COPAKE FALLS (unincorporated postal area)

ZCTA: 12517

Covers a land area of 10.459 square miles and a water area of 0.016 square miles. Located at 42.11° N. Lat; 73.51° W. Long. Elevation is 643 feet.

Population: 670; Growth (since 2000): 111.4%; Density: 64.1 persons per square mile; Race: 87.9% White, 0.0% Black/African American, 0.0% Asian, 0.0% American Indian/Alaska Native, 0.0% Native Hawaiian/Other Pacific Islander, 12.1% Two or more races, 0.0% Hispanic of any race; Average household size: 2.67; Median age: 45.5; Age under 18: 19.0%; Age 65 and over: 17.2%; Males per 100 females: 104.4; Marriage status: 21.3% never married, 52.0% now married, 1.4% separated, 18.8% widowed, 7.9% divorced; Foreign born: 1.8%; Speak English only: 96.9%; With disability: 19.1%; Veterans: 5.9%; Ancestry: 25.4% English, 25.2% German, 18.4% Irish, 15.2% Polish, 9.7% Dutch

Employment: 12.9% management, business, and financial, 0.0% computer, engineering, and science, 7.8% education, legal, community service, arts, and media, 0.0% healthcare practitioners, 26.4% service, 31.9% sales and office, 14.1% natural resources, construction, and maintenance, 6.9% production, transportation, and material moving

Income: Per capita: $29,289; Median household: $60,469; Average household: $77,647; Households with income of $100,000 or more: 30.8%; Poverty rate: 1.0%

Educational Attainment: High school diploma or higher: 87.0%; Bachelor's degree or higher: 12.6%; Graduate/professional degree or higher: 8.0%

Housing: Homeownership rate: 69.5%; Median home value: $402,300; Median year structure built: 1962; Homeowner vacancy rate: 0.0%; Median selected monthly owner costs: $1,918 with a mortgage, $0

without a mortgage; Median gross rent: $853 per month; Rental vacancy rate: 0.0%

Health Insurance: 98.8% have insurance; 80.6% have private insurance; 34.6% have public insurance; 1.2% do not have insurance; 0.0% of children under 18 do not have insurance

Transportation: Commute: 93.5% car, 6.5% public transportation, 0.0% walk, 0.0% work from home; Mean travel time to work: 24.5 minutes

COPAKE LAKE (CDP).
Covers a land area of 9.509 square miles and a water area of 0.805 square miles. Located at 42.14° N. Lat; 73.60° W. Long. Elevation is 718 feet.

Population: 518; Growth (since 2000): -32.0%; Density: 54.5 persons per square mile; Race: 100.0% White, 0.0% Black/African American, 0.0% Asian, 0.0% American Indian/Alaska Native, 0.0% Native Hawaiian/Other Pacific Islander, 0.0% Two or more races, 0.0% Hispanic of any race; Average household size: 2.50; Median age: 50.4; Age under 18: 27.0%; Age 65 and over: 25.7%; Males per 100 females: 105.2; Marriage status: 18.1% never married, 66.7% now married, 4.6% separated, 6.8% widowed, 8.3% divorced; Foreign born: 2.1%; Speak English only: 98.6%; With disability: 9.1%; Veterans: 5.8%; Ancestry: 22.8% American, 20.5% Italian, 15.4% German, 15.4% Irish, 11.2% English

Employment: 29.1% management, business, and financial, 0.0% computer, engineering, and science, 21.8% education, legal, community service, arts, and media, 15.8% healthcare practitioners, 17.9% service, 3.0% sales and office, 8.1% natural resources, construction, and maintenance, 4.3% production, transportation, and material moving

Income: Per capita: $29,391; Median household: $68,125; Average household: $73,418; Households with income of $100,000 or more: 15.4%; Poverty rate: 9.3%

Educational Attainment: High school diploma or higher: 92.7%; Bachelor's degree or higher: 32.9%; Graduate/professional degree or higher: 25.3%

Housing: Homeownership rate: 88.4%; Median home value: $255,200; Median year structure built: 1970; Homeowner vacancy rate: 30.9%; Median selected monthly owner costs: $1,344 with a mortgage, $657 without a mortgage; Median gross rent: $814 per month; Rental vacancy rate: 25.0%

Health Insurance: 95.9% have insurance; 84.9% have private insurance; 36.7% have public insurance; 4.1% do not have insurance; 0.0% of children under 18 do not have insurance

Transportation: Commute: 93.9% car, 0.0% public transportation, 3.0% walk, 3.0% work from home; Mean travel time to work: 22.2 minutes

CRARYVILLE (unincorporated postal area)
ZCTA: 12521

Covers a land area of 32.889 square miles and a water area of 0.314 square miles. Located at 42.17° N. Lat; 73.65° W. Long. Elevation is 636 feet.

Population: 1,268; Growth (since 2000): -15.4%; Density: 38.6 persons per square mile; Race: 98.8% White, 0.0% Black/African American, 0.6% Asian, 0.0% American Indian/Alaska Native, 0.0% Native Hawaiian/Other Pacific Islander, 0.6% Two or more races, 2.4% Hispanic of any race; Average household size: 2.48; Median age: 46.3; Age under 18: 23.4%; Age 65 and over: 23.4%; Males per 100 females: 104.7; Marriage status: 22.1% never married, 58.2% now married, 1.2% separated, 4.3% widowed, 15.3% divorced; Foreign born: 1.9%; Speak English only: 98.4%; With disability: 23.3%; Veterans: 15.1%; Ancestry: 29.9% German, 22.2% Irish, 21.8% Dutch, 15.1% Italian, 9.5% English

Employment: 24.3% management, business, and financial, 0.7% computer, engineering, and science, 10.9% education, legal, community service, arts, and media, 3.8% healthcare practitioners, 24.3% service, 21.5% sales and office, 9.1% natural resources, construction, and maintenance, 5.4% production, transportation, and material moving

Income: Per capita: $36,394; Median household: $68,958; Average household: $86,387; Households with income of $100,000 or more: 23.3%; Poverty rate: 12.0%

Educational Attainment: High school diploma or higher: 94.9%; Bachelor's degree or higher: 26.8%; Graduate/professional degree or higher: 19.8%

School District(s)
Taconic Hills Central SD (PK-12)
  2014-15 Enrollment: 1,452 . . . . (518) 325-2891

Housing: Homeownership rate: 86.8%; Median home value: $225,700; Median year structure built: 1973; Homeowner vacancy rate: 10.0%; Median selected monthly owner costs: $1,530 with a mortgage, $552

without a mortgage; Median gross rent: $1,076 per month; Rental vacancy rate: 10.7%

Health Insurance: 87.3% have insurance; 81.3% have private insurance; 37.5% have public insurance; 12.7% do not have insurance; 17.2% of children under 18 do not have insurance

Transportation: Commute: 84.9% car, 6.9% public transportation, 1.1% walk, 6.5% work from home; Mean travel time to work: 30.7 minutes

EAST CHATHAM (unincorporated postal area)
ZCTA: 12060

Covers a land area of 34.504 square miles and a water area of 0.132 square miles. Located at 42.41° N. Lat; 73.51° W. Long. Elevation is 702 feet.

Population: 1,373; Growth (since 2000): -1.6%; Density: 39.8 persons per square mile; Race: 92.1% White, 0.0% Black/African American, 2.5% Asian, 0.1% American Indian/Alaska Native, 0.0% Native Hawaiian/Other Pacific Islander, 5.2% Two or more races, 2.2% Hispanic of any race; Average household size: 2.35; Median age: 46.9; Age under 18: 23.6%; Age 65 and over: 20.8%; Males per 100 females: 102.0; Marriage status: 24.7% never married, 56.9% now married, 1.7% separated, 9.6% widowed, 8.8% divorced; Foreign born: 1.7%; Speak English only: 95.4%; With disability: 12.7%; Veterans: 6.3%; Ancestry: 28.6% Irish, 23.9% German, 15.8% Italian, 10.1% English, 6.8% Polish

Employment: 16.9% management, business, and financial, 5.8% computer, engineering, and science, 21.0% education, legal, community service, arts, and media, 7.2% healthcare practitioners, 16.6% service, 12.8% sales and office, 16.0% natural resources, construction, and maintenance, 3.8% production, transportation, and material moving

Income: Per capita: $40,895; Median household: $70,278; Average household: $94,257; Households with income of $100,000 or more: 28.9%; Poverty rate: 7.9%

Educational Attainment: High school diploma or higher: 97.8%; Bachelor's degree or higher: 47.6%; Graduate/professional degree or higher: 28.4%

Housing: Homeownership rate: 85.6%; Median home value: $269,000; Median year structure built: 1972; Homeowner vacancy rate: 4.4%; Median selected monthly owner costs: $1,962 with a mortgage, $734 without a mortgage; Median gross rent: n/a per month; Rental vacancy rate: 0.0%

Health Insurance: 94.7% have insurance; 79.3% have private insurance; 32.7% have public insurance; 5.3% do not have insurance; 0.6% of children under 18 do not have insurance

Transportation: Commute: 82.9% car, 2.5% public transportation, 4.0% walk, 8.7% work from home; Mean travel time to work: 31.9 minutes

ELIZAVILLE (unincorporated postal area)
ZCTA: 12523

Covers a land area of 21.889 square miles and a water area of 0.185 square miles. Located at 42.09° N. Lat; 73.76° W. Long. Elevation is 289 feet.

Population: 1,700; Growth (since 2000): -14.0%; Density: 77.7 persons per square mile; Race: 97.4% White, 0.1% Black/African American, 0.9% Asian, 0.0% American Indian/Alaska Native, 0.0% Native Hawaiian/Other Pacific Islander, 1.6% Two or more races, 4.9% Hispanic of any race; Average household size: 2.48; Median age: 45.6; Age under 18: 15.2%; Age 65 and over: 15.3%; Males per 100 females: 100.4; Marriage status: 37.1% never married, 42.5% now married, 2.3% separated, 7.1% widowed, 13.4% divorced; Foreign born: 3.8%; Speak English only: 95.6%; With disability: 18.1%; Veterans: 10.4%; Ancestry: 21.8% Italian, 20.8% German, 17.0% Irish, 9.0% English, 7.2% Dutch

Employment: 8.5% management, business, and financial, 1.7% computer, engineering, and science, 15.1% education, legal, community service, arts, and media, 12.2% healthcare practitioners, 17.6% service, 19.0% sales and office, 11.4% natural resources, construction, and maintenance, 14.5% production, transportation, and material moving

Income: Per capita: $31,299; Median household: $64,643; Average household: $76,434; Households with income of $100,000 or more: 22.9%; Poverty rate: 10.2%

Educational Attainment: High school diploma or higher: 87.8%; Bachelor's degree or higher: 27.9%; Graduate/professional degree or higher: 15.8%

Housing: Homeownership rate: 69.2%; Median home value: $255,200; Median year structure built: 1973; Homeowner vacancy rate: 1.9%; Median selected monthly owner costs: $1,717 with a mortgage, $683

without a mortgage; Median gross rent: $853 per month; Rental vacancy rate: 4.3%
Health Insurance: 84.5% have insurance; 68.5% have private insurance; 28.3% have public insurance; 15.5% do not have insurance; 3.9% of children under 18 do not have insurance
Transportation: Commute: 91.0% car, 0.9% public transportation, 0.7% walk, 5.7% work from home; Mean travel time to work: 31.8 minutes

GALLATIN (town).
Covers a land area of 39.111 square miles and a water area of 0.521 square miles. Located at 42.06° N. Lat; 73.71° W. Long.
Population: 1,812; Growth (since 2000): 20.9%; Density: 46.3 persons per square mile; Race: 95.3% White, 1.8% Black/African American, 1.0% Asian, 0.0% American Indian/Alaska Native, 0.0% Native Hawaiian/Other Pacific Islander, 1.8% Two or more races, 1.9% Hispanic of any race; Average household size: 2.46; Median age: 52.7; Age under 18: 16.6%; Age 65 and over: 22.4%; Males per 100 females: 105.7; Marriage status: 33.2% never married, 54.0% now married, 1.2% separated, 5.3% widowed, 7.5% divorced; Foreign born: 4.6%; Speak English only: 96.5%; With disability: 20.7%; Veterans: 14.7%; Ancestry: 30.7% German, 25.9% Irish, 14.1% Italian, 8.9% Polish, 6.9% Dutch
Employment: 12.7% management, business, and financial, 3.4% computer, engineering, and science, 12.0% education, legal, community service, arts, and media, 10.0% healthcare practitioners, 25.1% service, 18.2% sales and office, 13.1% natural resources, construction, and maintenance, 5.6% production, transportation, and material moving
Income: Per capita: $31,886; Median household: $69,408; Average household: $77,301; Households with income of $100,000 or more: 26.4%; Poverty rate: 6.4%
Educational Attainment: High school diploma or higher: 85.1%; Bachelor's degree or higher: 31.2%; Graduate/professional degree or higher: 17.8%
Housing: Homeownership rate: 85.4%; Median home value: $279,900; Median year structure built: 1970; Homeowner vacancy rate: 0.9%; Median selected monthly owner costs: $1,733 with a mortgage, $683 without a mortgage; Median gross rent: $1,219 per month; Rental vacancy rate: 20.7%
Health Insurance: 91.5% have insurance; 71.3% have private insurance; 37.8% have public insurance; 8.5% do not have insurance; 3.4% of children under 18 do not have insurance
Transportation: Commute: 82.3% car, 3.0% public transportation, 0.9% walk, 13.3% work from home; Mean travel time to work: 34.0 minutes

GERMANTOWN (CDP).
Covers a land area of 2.679 square miles and a water area of 0.016 square miles. Located at 42.14° N. Lat; 73.89° W. Long. Elevation is 135 feet.
Population: 860; Growth (since 2000): -0.2%; Density: 321.1 persons per square mile; Race: 87.6% White, 1.9% Black/African American, 0.9% Asian, 0.0% American Indian/Alaska Native, 0.0% Native Hawaiian/Other Pacific Islander, 8.3% Two or more races, 12.4% Hispanic of any race; Average household size: 2.52; Median age: 43.1; Age under 18: 20.8%; Age 65 and over: 15.9%; Males per 100 females: 96.1; Marriage status: 19.9% never married, 62.7% now married, 1.7% separated, 7.0% widowed, 10.4% divorced; Foreign born: 9.0%; Speak English only: 88.1%; With disability: 14.2%; Veterans: 13.4%; Ancestry: 28.5% German, 14.1% Irish, 13.5% Italian, 6.9% Dutch, 6.6% English
Employment: 10.7% management, business, and financial, 3.0% computer, engineering, and science, 9.6% education, legal, community service, arts, and media, 2.7% healthcare practitioners, 15.5% service, 28.5% sales and office, 22.3% natural resources, construction, and maintenance, 7.7% production, transportation, and material moving
Income: Per capita: $31,076; Median household: $64,792; Average household: $78,009; Households with income of $100,000 or more: 32.4%; Poverty rate: 5.2%
Educational Attainment: High school diploma or higher: 96.6%; Bachelor's degree or higher: 23.8%; Graduate/professional degree or higher: 7.4%
School District(s)
Germantown Central SD (KG-12)
    2014-15 Enrollment: 589 . . . . (518) 537-6280
Housing: Homeownership rate: 73.9%; Median home value: $231,300; Median year structure built: Before 1940; Homeowner vacancy rate: 0.0%; Median selected monthly owner costs: $1,475 with a mortgage, $719 without a mortgage; Median gross rent: $1,359 per month; Rental vacancy rate: 0.0%

Health Insurance: 94.4% have insurance; 75.5% have private insurance; 30.0% have public insurance; 5.6% do not have insurance; 0.0% of children under 18 do not have insurance
Transportation: Commute: 93.1% car, 2.5% public transportation, 2.1% walk, 2.3% work from home; Mean travel time to work: 33.4 minutes

GERMANTOWN (town).
Covers a land area of 12.103 square miles and a water area of 1.819 square miles. Located at 42.14° N. Lat; 73.87° W. Long. Elevation is 135 feet.
Population: 1,986; Growth (since 2000): -1.6%; Density: 164.1 persons per square mile; Race: 93.8% White, 1.2% Black/African American, 0.7% Asian, 0.0% American Indian/Alaska Native, 0.0% Native Hawaiian/Other Pacific Islander, 3.8% Two or more races, 7.5% Hispanic of any race; Average household size: 2.31; Median age: 47.7; Age under 18: 20.5%; Age 65 and over: 22.1%; Males per 100 females: 96.8; Marriage status: 21.7% never married, 59.6% now married, 1.3% separated, 9.3% widowed, 9.4% divorced; Foreign born: 6.3%; Speak English only: 93.0%; With disability: 15.7%; Veterans: 11.1%; Ancestry: 28.3% German, 16.4% Irish, 16.3% Italian, 9.2% English, 7.0% Russian
Employment: 14.2% management, business, and financial, 3.4% computer, engineering, and science, 15.8% education, legal, community service, arts, and media, 4.6% healthcare practitioners, 10.8% service, 24.1% sales and office, 20.5% natural resources, construction, and maintenance, 6.7% production, transportation, and material moving
Income: Per capita: $33,756; Median household: $56,591; Average household: $77,304; Households with income of $100,000 or more: 25.5%; Poverty rate: 8.5%
Educational Attainment: High school diploma or higher: 94.8%; Bachelor's degree or higher: 33.2%; Graduate/professional degree or higher: 16.1%
School District(s)
Germantown Central SD (KG-12)
    2014-15 Enrollment: 589 . . . . (518) 537-6280
Housing: Homeownership rate: 71.6%; Median home value: $260,200; Median year structure built: 1953; Homeowner vacancy rate: 1.9%; Median selected monthly owner costs: $2,027 with a mortgage, $685 without a mortgage; Median gross rent: $926 per month; Rental vacancy rate: 0.0%
Health Insurance: 95.7% have insurance; 72.3% have private insurance; 39.5% have public insurance; 4.3% do not have insurance; 0.0% of children under 18 do not have insurance
Safety: Violent crime rate: 0.0 per 10,000 population; Property crime rate: 0.0 per 10,000 population
Transportation: Commute: 84.9% car, 2.4% public transportation, 5.5% walk, 6.6% work from home; Mean travel time to work: 31.0 minutes

GHENT (CDP).
Covers a land area of 1.538 square miles and a water area of 0.011 square miles. Located at 42.33° N. Lat; 73.62° W. Long. Elevation is 407 feet.
Population: 438; Growth (since 2000): -25.3%; Density: 284.8 persons per square mile; Race: 92.2% White, 7.8% Black/African American, 0.0% Asian, 0.0% American Indian/Alaska Native, 0.0% Native Hawaiian/Other Pacific Islander, 0.0% Two or more races, 0.0% Hispanic of any race; Average household size: 4.59; Median age: 22.8; Age under 18: 38.6%; Age 65 and over: 0.0%; Males per 100 females: 105.8; Marriage status: 42.8% never married, 57.2% now married, 0.0% separated, 0.0% widowed, 0.0% divorced; Foreign born: 7.8%; Speak English only: 93.5%; With disability: 0.0%; Veterans: 9.7%; Ancestry: 41.3% Italian, 20.5% Irish, 17.6% English, 13.0% German, 7.8% Haitian
Employment: 1.2% management, business, and financial, 0.0% computer, engineering, and science, 23.8% education, legal, community service, arts, and media, 6.5% healthcare practitioners, 41.7% service, 11.3% sales and office, 0.0% natural resources, construction, and maintenance, 15.5% production, transportation, and material moving
Income: Per capita: $16,925; Median household: $53,882; Average household: $75,696; Households with income of $100,000 or more: 26.3%; Poverty rate: 29.3%
Educational Attainment: High school diploma or higher: 91.5%; Bachelor's degree or higher: 31.8%; Graduate/professional degree or higher: 12.4%
Housing: Homeownership rate: 100.0%; Median home value: $177,700; Median year structure built: Before 1940; Homeowner vacancy rate: 0.0%; Median selected monthly owner costs: $1,533 with a mortgage, n/a without a mortgage; Median gross rent: n/a per month; Rental vacancy rate: 0.0%

Health Insurance: 87.0% have insurance; 63.2% have private insurance; 26.5% have public insurance; 13.0% do not have insurance; 6.5% of children under 18 do not have insurance
Newspapers: The Columbia Paper (weekly circulation 5,000)
Transportation: Commute: 98.8% car, 0.0% public transportation, 1.2% walk, 0.0% work from home; Mean travel time to work: 24.3 minutes

GHENT (town). Covers a land area of 45.132 square miles and a water area of 0.268 square miles. Located at 42.31° N. Lat; 73.65° W. Long. Elevation is 407 feet.
History: 1818, the town of Ghent was founded from parts of the towns of Chatham, Claverack, and Kinderhook. Its name is from the Flemish city Ghent, in Flanders, Belgium. Ghent is home to the historic Van Valkenburgh-Isbister Farm, which in on the National Register of Historic Places.
Population: 5,317; Growth (since 2000): 0.8%; Density: 117.8 persons per square mile; Race: 92.9% White, 5.5% Black/African American, 0.5% Asian, 0.0% American Indian/Alaska Native, 0.0% Native Hawaiian/Other Pacific Islander, 0.5% Two or more races, 3.7% Hispanic of any race; Average household size: 2.57; Median age: 48.3; Age under 18: 16.7%; Age 65 and over: 23.4%; Males per 100 females: 99.4; Marriage status: 33.0% never married, 48.4% now married, 1.5% separated, 7.4% widowed, 11.2% divorced; Foreign born: 7.1%; Speak English only: 91.5%; With disability: 15.3%; Veterans: 10.5%; Ancestry: 27.3% Irish, 22.2% Italian, 18.1% German, 11.6% English, 7.9% French
Employment: 10.4% management, business, and financial, 3.9% computer, engineering, and science, 9.7% education, legal, community service, arts, and media, 3.0% healthcare practitioners, 27.0% service, 25.5% sales and office, 9.0% natural resources, construction, and maintenance, 11.4% production, transportation, and material moving
Income: Per capita: $34,226; Median household: $60,648; Average household: $88,739; Households with income of $100,000 or more: 27.9%; Poverty rate: 7.8%
Educational Attainment: High school diploma or higher: 88.8%; Bachelor's degree or higher: 22.4%; Graduate/professional degree or higher: 9.7%
Housing: Homeownership rate: 80.9%; Median home value: $221,000; Median year structure built: 1967; Homeowner vacancy rate: 1.4%; Median selected monthly owner costs: $1,695 with a mortgage, $601 without a mortgage; Median gross rent: $869 per month; Rental vacancy rate: 20.4%
Health Insurance: 91.4% have insurance; 77.5% have private insurance; 30.2% have public insurance; 8.6% do not have insurance; 2.1% of children under 18 do not have insurance
Newspapers: The Columbia Paper (weekly circulation 5,000)
Transportation: Commute: 89.6% car, 1.9% public transportation, 0.3% walk, 8.2% work from home; Mean travel time to work: 20.8 minutes
Additional Information Contacts
Town of Ghent. . . . . (518) 392-4644
  http://www.townofghent.org

GREENPORT (town). Covers a land area of 18.607 square miles and a water area of 1.880 square miles. Located at 42.23° N. Lat; 73.80° W. Long.
Population: 4,096; Growth (since 2000): -2.0%; Density: 220.1 persons per square mile; Race: 82.8% White, 6.8% Black/African American, 4.0% Asian, 0.0% American Indian/Alaska Native, 0.0% Native Hawaiian/Other Pacific Islander, 6.3% Two or more races, 7.7% Hispanic of any race; Average household size: 2.22; Median age: 46.8; Age under 18: 18.2%; Age 65 and over: 21.7%; Males per 100 females: 101.0; Marriage status: 32.6% never married, 45.9% now married, 2.7% separated, 9.2% widowed, 12.3% divorced; Foreign born: 6.2%; Speak English only: 90.4%; With disability: 14.6%; Veterans: 10.5%; Ancestry: 28.6% Italian, 20.4% Irish, 16.2% German, 6.9% English, 6.3% American
Employment: 14.2% management, business, and financial, 0.8% computer, engineering, and science, 12.3% education, legal, community service, arts, and media, 6.0% healthcare practitioners, 27.0% service, 22.3% sales and office, 9.1% natural resources, construction, and maintenance, 8.2% production, transportation, and material moving
Income: Per capita: $30,848; Median household: $52,230; Average household: $68,791; Households with income of $100,000 or more: 20.8%; Poverty rate: 15.8%
Educational Attainment: High school diploma or higher: 87.0%; Bachelor's degree or higher: 20.4%; Graduate/professional degree or higher: 11.9%

Housing: Homeownership rate: 67.5%; Median home value: $161,000; Median year structure built: 1971; Homeowner vacancy rate: 1.8%; Median selected monthly owner costs: $1,646 with a mortgage, $527 without a mortgage; Median gross rent: $835 per month; Rental vacancy rate: 0.0%
Health Insurance: 90.9% have insurance; 71.6% have private insurance; 41.3% have public insurance; 9.1% do not have insurance; 1.9% of children under 18 do not have insurance
Safety: Violent crime rate: 2.4 per 10,000 population; Property crime rate: 364.0 per 10,000 population
Transportation: Commute: 89.9% car, 3.7% public transportation, 4.6% walk, 1.5% work from home; Mean travel time to work: 21.8 minutes
Additional Information Contacts
Town of Greenport . . . . (518) 828-4656
  http://www.townofgreenport.com

HILLSDALE (town). Covers a land area of 47.724 square miles and a water area of 0.164 square miles. Located at 42.23° N. Lat; 73.52° W. Long. Elevation is 709 feet.
Population: 1,783; Growth (since 2000): 2.2%; Density: 37.4 persons per square mile; Race: 89.1% White, 9.0% Black/African American, 0.6% Asian, 0.0% American Indian/Alaska Native, 0.0% Native Hawaiian/Other Pacific Islander, 1.0% Two or more races, 0.3% Hispanic of any race; Average household size: 2.58; Median age: 50.0; Age under 18: 17.8%; Age 65 and over: 25.8%; Males per 100 females: 107.4; Marriage status: 25.9% never married, 62.4% now married, 2.8% separated, 3.1% widowed, 8.6% divorced; Foreign born: 15.8%; Speak English only: 94.2%; With disability: 16.5%; Veterans: 6.0%; Ancestry: 24.7% German, 20.6% Irish, 12.5% Italian, 9.4% English, 9.0% Jamaican
Employment: 11.2% management, business, and financial, 2.3% computer, engineering, and science, 16.5% education, legal, community service, arts, and media, 9.1% healthcare practitioners, 22.8% service, 23.0% sales and office, 9.2% natural resources, construction, and maintenance, 5.9% production, transportation, and material moving
Income: Per capita: $43,390; Median household: $73,250; Average household: $106,842; Households with income of $100,000 or more: 39.9%; Poverty rate: 7.3%
Educational Attainment: High school diploma or higher: 87.0%; Bachelor's degree or higher: 39.9%; Graduate/professional degree or higher: 25.2%
Housing: Homeownership rate: 77.0%; Median home value: $275,300; Median year structure built: 1960; Homeowner vacancy rate: 5.8%; Median selected monthly owner costs: $1,827 with a mortgage, $636 without a mortgage; Median gross rent: $1,021 per month; Rental vacancy rate: 8.1%
Health Insurance: 86.9% have insurance; 66.9% have private insurance; 40.9% have public insurance; 13.1% do not have insurance; 8.8% of children under 18 do not have insurance
Transportation: Commute: 79.4% car, 8.4% public transportation, 6.4% walk, 5.2% work from home; Mean travel time to work: 23.8 minutes

HOLLOWVILLE (unincorporated postal area)
ZCTA: 12530
Covers a land area of 0.348 square miles and a water area of 0 square miles. Located at 42.21° N. Lat; 73.69° W. Long. Elevation is 325 feet.
Population: 72; Growth (since 2000): n/a; Density: 207.1 persons per square mile; Race: 86.1% White, 0.0% Black/African American, 0.0% Asian, 13.9% American Indian/Alaska Native, 0.0% Native Hawaiian/Other Pacific Islander, 0.0% Two or more races, 0.0% Hispanic of any race; Average household size: 1.07; Median age: 58.8; Age under 18: 0.0%; Age 65 and over: 13.9%; Males per 100 females: 110.2; Marriage status: 86.1% never married, 13.9% now married, 0.0% separated, 0.0% widowed, 0.0% divorced; Foreign born: 13.9%; Speak English only: 100.0%; With disability: 77.8%; Veterans: 0.0%; Ancestry: 63.9% Dutch, 63.9% German, 22.2% Italian
Employment: n/a management, business, and financial, n/a computer, engineering, and science, n/a education, legal, community service, arts, and media, n/a healthcare practitioners, n/a service, n/a sales and office, n/a natural resources, construction, and maintenance, n/a production, transportation, and material moving
Income: Per capita: $18,190; Median household: $16,821; Average household: $19,548; Households with income of $100,000 or more: n/a; Poverty rate: n/a
Educational Attainment: High school diploma or higher: 22.2%; Bachelor's degree or higher: 22.2%; Graduate/professional degree or higher: 22.2%

Housing: Homeownership rate: 31.3%; Median home value: n/a; Median year structure built: Before 1940; Homeowner vacancy rate: 0.0%; Median selected monthly owner costs: $0 with a mortgage, $0 without a mortgage; Median gross rent: n/a per month; Rental vacancy rate: 0.0%

Health Insurance: 100.0% have insurance; 13.9% have private insurance; 100.0% have public insurance; 0.0% do not have insurance; 0.0% of children under 18 do not have insurance

Transportation: Commute: n/a car, n/a public transportation, n/a walk, n/a work from home; Mean travel time to work: 0.0 minutes

HUDSON (city). County seat. Covers a land area of 2.158 square miles and a water area of 0.172 square miles. Located at 42.25° N. Lat; 73.79° W. Long. Elevation is 82 feet.

History: The city was a whaling and trading port until 1812. Its industries included textiles, furniture, cement, and metal products, but these are largely gone. Many colonial and Revolutionary era homes are in the area. Olana, estate of Frederic E. Church, 2.5 miles South of city. Settled c.1622 by the Dutch and later in 1783 by English whalers; incorporated 1785.

Population: 6,572; Growth (since 2000): -12.7%; Density: 3,045.6 persons per square mile; Race: 59.9% White, 20.6% Black/African American, 7.3% Asian, 0.3% American Indian/Alaska Native, 0.3% Native Hawaiian/Other Pacific Islander, 10.3% Two or more races, 8.3% Hispanic of any race; Average household size: 2.13; Median age: 37.0; Age under 18: 21.4%; Age 65 and over: 11.9%; Males per 100 females: 106.7; Marriage status: 44.8% never married, 33.3% now married, 4.5% separated, 6.5% widowed, 15.3% divorced; Foreign born: 13.3%; Speak English only: 85.8%; With disability: 17.9%; Veterans: 5.3%; Ancestry: 15.2% Irish, 14.9% Italian, 11.4% German, 8.3% Polish, 7.2% American

Employment: 11.2% management, business, and financial, 1.0% computer, engineering, and science, 15.3% education, legal, community service, arts, and media, 4.2% healthcare practitioners, 31.2% service, 22.2% sales and office, 3.8% natural resources, construction, and maintenance, 11.1% production, transportation, and material moving

Income: Per capita: $21,969; Median household: $34,313; Average household: $48,705; Households with income of $100,000 or more: 9.7%; Poverty rate: 25.1%

Educational Attainment: High school diploma or higher: 80.7%; Bachelor's degree or higher: 22.9%; Graduate/professional degree or higher: 10.5%

School District(s)
Hudson City SD (PK-12)
    2014-15 Enrollment: 1,873 . . . . (518) 828-4360
Two-year College(s)
Columbia-Greene Community College (Public)
    Fall 2014 Enrollment: 2,047 . . . . (518) 828-4181
    2015-16 Tuition: In-state $4,552; Out-of-state $8,752

Housing: Homeownership rate: 34.0%; Median home value: $173,200; Median year structure built: Before 1940; Homeowner vacancy rate: 1.4%; Median selected monthly owner costs: $1,468 with a mortgage, $620 without a mortgage; Median gross rent: $821 per month; Rental vacancy rate: 6.0%

Health Insurance: 95.1% have insurance; 51.8% have private insurance; 52.2% have public insurance; 4.9% do not have insurance; 1.9% of children under 18 do not have insurance

Hospitals: Columbia Memorial Hospital (103 beds)

Safety: Violent crime rate: 36.7 per 10,000 population; Property crime rate: 172.7 per 10,000 population

Newspapers: Bleezarde Publishing (weekly circulation 4,200); Register-Star (daily circulation 5,200)

Transportation: Commute: 66.9% car, 3.6% public transportation, 21.0% walk, 6.5% work from home; Mean travel time to work: 21.0 minutes; Amtrak: Train service available.

Airports: Columbia County (general aviation)

Additional Information Contacts
City of Hudson. . . . . (518) 828-1030
    http://cityofhudson.org/content

KINDERHOOK (town). Covers a land area of 31.806 square miles and a water area of 0.607 square miles. Located at 42.41° N. Lat; 73.68° W. Long. Elevation is 253 feet.

History: Kinderhook (Dutch for "children's corner") was named by its Dutch settlers. President Martin Van Buren was born and buried in Kinderhook. Settled before the American Revolution. Richard Upjohn designed St. Paul's Church (1851) here. The Van Buren homestead,

"Lindenwald," is South of the village. The House of History, maintained by the county historical society, occupies an early-19th-century mansion. Incorporated 1838.

Population: 8,455; Growth (since 2000): 1.9%; Density: 265.8 persons per square mile; Race: 95.9% White, 0.6% Black/African American, 0.7% Asian, 0.0% American Indian/Alaska Native, 0.0% Native Hawaiian/Other Pacific Islander, 1.0% Two or more races, 3.9% Hispanic of any race; Average household size: 2.48; Median age: 48.1; Age under 18: 20.2%; Age 65 and over: 19.9%; Males per 100 females: 96.6; Marriage status: 23.4% never married, 57.6% now married, 2.3% separated, 7.7% widowed, 11.3% divorced; Foreign born: 4.1%; Speak English only: 94.7%; With disability: 12.2%; Veterans: 10.8%; Ancestry: 28.7% Irish, 18.8% German, 17.7% Italian, 9.7% English, 7.4% Polish

Employment: 22.4% management, business, and financial, 4.0% computer, engineering, and science, 15.0% education, legal, community service, arts, and media, 7.7% healthcare practitioners, 15.0% service, 21.3% sales and office, 7.3% natural resources, construction, and maintenance, 7.2% production, transportation, and material moving

Income: Per capita: $35,802; Median household: $81,351; Average household: $89,526; Households with income of $100,000 or more: 34.7%; Poverty rate: 4.9%

Educational Attainment: High school diploma or higher: 93.1%; Bachelor's degree or higher: 39.5%; Graduate/professional degree or higher: 18.7%

Housing: Homeownership rate: 79.7%; Median home value: $230,500; Median year structure built: 1972; Homeowner vacancy rate: 0.4%; Median selected monthly owner costs: $1,827 with a mortgage, $693 without a mortgage; Median gross rent: $992 per month; Rental vacancy rate: 7.7%

Health Insurance: 96.5% have insurance; 83.6% have private insurance; 28.9% have public insurance; 3.5% do not have insurance; 0.6% of children under 18 do not have insurance

Transportation: Commute: 90.9% car, 0.7% public transportation, 2.9% walk, 5.5% work from home; Mean travel time to work: 25.9 minutes

Additional Information Contacts
Town of Kinderhook . . . . (518) 784-2233
    http://www.kinderhook-ny.gov

KINDERHOOK (village). Covers a land area of 2.104 square miles and a water area of 0 square miles. Located at 42.39° N. Lat; 73.70° W. Long. Elevation is 253 feet.

Population: 1,389; Growth (since 2000): 8.9%; Density: 660.2 persons per square mile; Race: 98.5% White, 0.3% Black/African American, 0.0% Asian, 0.0% American Indian/Alaska Native, 0.0% Native Hawaiian/Other Pacific Islander, 1.1% Two or more races, 1.5% Hispanic of any race; Average household size: 2.10; Median age: 51.9; Age under 18: 15.6%; Age 65 and over: 22.0%; Males per 100 females: 89.5; Marriage status: 20.0% never married, 62.3% now married, 1.9% separated, 9.5% widowed, 8.2% divorced; Foreign born: 4.4%; Speak English only: 97.5%; With disability: 15.0%; Veterans: 10.6%; Ancestry: 35.5% Irish, 25.6% German, 15.8% Italian, 15.0% English, 8.1% Polish

Employment: 24.5% management, business, and financial, 1.0% computer, engineering, and science, 18.8% education, legal, community service, arts, and media, 6.8% healthcare practitioners, 5.6% service, 23.2% sales and office, 8.8% natural resources, construction, and maintenance, 11.4% production, transportation, and material moving

Income: Per capita: $50,026; Median household: $80,938; Average household: $105,613; Households with income of $100,000 or more: 35.7%; Poverty rate: 2.3%

Educational Attainment: High school diploma or higher: 97.8%; Bachelor's degree or higher: 51.6%; Graduate/professional degree or higher: 34.3%

Housing: Homeownership rate: 86.8%; Median home value: $255,600; Median year structure built: 1946; Homeowner vacancy rate: 1.9%; Median selected monthly owner costs: $1,909 with a mortgage, $713 without a mortgage; Median gross rent: $938 per month; Rental vacancy rate: 0.0%

Health Insurance: 97.5% have insurance; 91.1% have private insurance; 25.5% have public insurance; 2.5% do not have insurance; 0.0% of children under 18 do not have insurance

Transportation: Commute: 86.0% car, 2.0% public transportation, 1.6% walk, 10.5% work from home; Mean travel time to work: 28.3 minutes

LIVINGSTON (town). Covers a land area of 38.163 square miles and a water area of 0.784 square miles. Located at 42.14° N. Lat; 73.80° W. Long. Elevation is 200 feet.

Population: 3,591; Growth (since 2000): 4.9%; Density: 94.1 persons per square mile; Race: 93.7% White, 2.4% Black/African American, 0.9% Asian, 0.0% American Indian/Alaska Native, 0.0% Native Hawaiian/Other Pacific Islander, 2.6% Two or more races, 6.5% Hispanic of any race; Average household size: 2.44; Median age: 46.2; Age under 18: 17.1%; Age 65 and over: 21.1%; Males per 100 females: 97.7; Marriage status: 32.7% never married, 46.3% now married, 1.7% separated, 9.8% widowed, 11.2% divorced; Foreign born: 4.1%; Speak English only: 94.5%; With disability: 17.1%; Veterans: 9.7%; Ancestry: 21.5% German, 20.1% Italian, 18.5% Irish, 10.4% English, 9.5% French

Employment: 13.6% management, business, and financial, 1.3% computer, engineering, and science, 7.7% education, legal, community service, arts, and media, 10.2% healthcare practitioners, 15.0% service, 24.9% sales and office, 12.4% natural resources, construction, and maintenance, 15.0% production, transportation, and material moving

Income: Per capita: $31,886; Median household: $62,407; Average household: $79,809; Households with income of $100,000 or more: 21.7%; Poverty rate: 10.0%

Educational Attainment: High school diploma or higher: 83.5%; Bachelor's degree or higher: 19.3%; Graduate/professional degree or higher: 9.0%

Housing: Homeownership rate: 70.0%; Median home value: $232,400; Median year structure built: 1979; Homeowner vacancy rate: 1.2%; Median selected monthly owner costs: $1,808 with a mortgage, $717 without a mortgage; Median gross rent: $969 per month; Rental vacancy rate: 9.7%

Health Insurance: 88.5% have insurance; 69.5% have private insurance; 35.4% have public insurance; 11.5% do not have insurance; 0.0% of children under 18 do not have insurance

Transportation: Commute: 93.0% car, 1.0% public transportation, 0.4% walk, 4.8% work from home; Mean travel time to work: 28.9 minutes

LORENZ PARK (CDP). Covers a land area of 1.784 square miles and a water area of 0.163 square miles. Located at 42.27° N. Lat; 73.78° W. Long. Elevation is 180 feet.

Population: 2,265; Growth (since 2000): 14.3%; Density: 1,269.4 persons per square mile; Race: 77.7% White, 6.6% Black/African American, 4.4% Asian, 0.0% American Indian/Alaska Native, 0.0% Native Hawaiian/Other Pacific Islander, 11.3% Two or more races, 6.1% Hispanic of any race; Average household size: 2.37; Median age: 42.3; Age under 18: 24.3%; Age 65 and over: 19.2%; Males per 100 females: 93.0; Marriage status: 31.9% never married, 46.0% now married, 1.8% separated, 9.0% widowed, 13.1% divorced; Foreign born: 5.7%; Speak English only: 90.6%; With disability: 15.9%; Veterans: 12.0%; Ancestry: 34.6% Italian, 23.8% Irish, 13.0% German, 8.2% American, 7.8% Ukrainian

Employment: 15.3% management, business, and financial, 1.4% computer, engineering, and science, 7.0% education, legal, community service, arts, and media, 5.7% healthcare practitioners, 30.1% service, 20.1% sales and office, 10.1% natural resources, construction, and maintenance, 10.2% production, transportation, and material moving

Income: Per capita: $27,811; Median household: $54,583; Average household: $64,518; Households with income of $100,000 or more: 17.5%; Poverty rate: 13.1%

Educational Attainment: High school diploma or higher: 88.1%; Bachelor's degree or higher: 15.3%; Graduate/professional degree or higher: 9.4%

Housing: Homeownership rate: 67.4%; Median home value: $157,800; Median year structure built: 1973; Homeowner vacancy rate: 0.0%; Median selected monthly owner costs: $1,774 with a mortgage, $501 without a mortgage; Median gross rent: $815 per month; Rental vacancy rate: 0.0%

Health Insurance: 93.1% have insurance; 71.3% have private insurance; 39.5% have public insurance; 6.9% do not have insurance; 0.0% of children under 18 do not have insurance

Transportation: Commute: 95.4% car, 0.4% public transportation, 4.2% walk, 0.0% work from home; Mean travel time to work: 21.5 minutes

MALDEN BRIDGE (unincorporated postal area)
ZCTA: 12115

Covers a land area of 5.183 square miles and a water area of 0.034 square miles. Located at 42.48° N. Lat; 73.58° W. Long. Elevation is 387 feet.

Population: 215; Growth (since 2000): -11.2%; Density: 41.5 persons per square mile; Race: 100.0% White, 0.0% Black/African American,

0.0% Asian, 0.0% American Indian/Alaska Native, 0.0% Native Hawaiian/Other Pacific Islander, 0.0% Two or more races, 7.0% Hispanic of any race; Average household size: 2.03; Median age: 60.0; Age under 18: 4.2%; Age 65 and over: 35.8%; Males per 100 females: 90.9; Marriage status: 45.6% never married, 50.0% now married, 0.0% separated, 4.4% widowed, 0.0% divorced; Foreign born: 12.6%; Speak English only: 90.8%; With disability: 0.5%; Veterans: 0.0%; Ancestry: 29.3% German, 22.8% Italian, 19.1% English, 11.6% American, 11.2% Irish

Employment: 10.5% management, business, and financial, 7.4% computer, engineering, and science, 55.8% education, legal, community service, arts, and media, 26.3% healthcare practitioners, 0.0% service, 0.0% sales and office, 0.0% natural resources, construction, and maintenance, 0.0% production, transportation, and material moving

Income: Per capita: $79,536; Median household: $67,083; Average household: $162,483; Households with income of $100,000 or more: 24.6%; Poverty rate: n/a

Educational Attainment: High school diploma or higher: 100.0%; Bachelor's degree or higher: 64.4%; Graduate/professional degree or higher: 31.6%

Housing: Homeownership rate: 68.9%; Median home value: n/a; Median year structure built: Before 1940; Homeowner vacancy rate: 0.0%; Median selected monthly owner costs: n/a with a mortgage, n/a without a mortgage; Median gross rent: n/a per month; Rental vacancy rate: 0.0%

Health Insurance: 99.1% have insurance; 84.7% have private insurance; 35.8% have public insurance; 0.9% do not have insurance; 0.0% of children under 18 do not have insurance

Transportation: Commute: 51.6% car, 9.5% public transportation, 0.0% walk, 38.9% work from home; Mean travel time to work: 0.0 minutes

NEW LEBANON (town). Covers a land area of 35.857 square miles and a water area of 0.116 square miles. Located at 42.47° N. Lat; 73.44° W. Long. Elevation is 696 feet.

History: Samuel Tilden was born here. Site of Roman Catholic Shrine of Our Lady of Lourdes.

Population: 2,424; Growth (since 2000): -1.2%; Density: 67.6 persons per square mile; Race: 91.5% White, 1.7% Black/African American, 2.3% Asian, 0.0% American Indian/Alaska Native, 0.0% Native Hawaiian/Other Pacific Islander, 2.4% Two or more races, 2.1% Hispanic of any race; Average household size: 2.14; Median age: 46.9; Age under 18: 16.8%; Age 65 and over: 18.6%; Males per 100 females: 105.8; Marriage status: 29.4% never married, 51.5% now married, 2.0% separated, 7.5% widowed, 11.6% divorced; Foreign born: 6.1%; Speak English only: 92.7%; With disability: 10.7%; Veterans: 8.4%; Ancestry: 25.2% Irish, 17.7% German, 14.8% English, 12.7% Italian, 11.4% American

Employment: 17.6% management, business, and financial, 4.5% computer, engineering, and science, 13.0% education, legal, community service, arts, and media, 6.4% healthcare practitioners, 17.1% service, 15.8% sales and office, 16.1% natural resources, construction, and maintenance, 9.5% production, transportation, and material moving

Income: Per capita: $37,256; Median household: $55,329; Average household: $79,707; Households with income of $100,000 or more: 21.8%; Poverty rate: 7.2%

Educational Attainment: High school diploma or higher: 93.0%; Bachelor's degree or higher: 34.9%; Graduate/professional degree or higher: 20.8%

School District(s)

New Lebanon Central SD (KG-12)
    2014-15 Enrollment: 412 . . . . (518) 794-9016

Housing: Homeownership rate: 77.5%; Median home value: $198,900; Median year structure built: 1961; Homeowner vacancy rate: 4.5%; Median selected monthly owner costs: $1,855 with a mortgage, $633 without a mortgage; Median gross rent: $949 per month; Rental vacancy rate: 2.0%

Health Insurance: 90.7% have insurance; 77.2% have private insurance; 28.2% have public insurance; 9.3% do not have insurance; 5.4% of children under 18 do not have insurance

Transportation: Commute: 88.0% car, 1.8% public transportation, 3.5% walk, 5.7% work from home; Mean travel time to work: 24.2 minutes

NIVERVILLE (CDP). Covers a land area of 2.874 square miles and a water area of 0.545 square miles. Located at 42.45° N. Lat; 73.65° W. Long. Elevation is 318 feet.

Population: 1,629; Growth (since 2000): -6.2%; Density: 566.7 persons per square mile; Race: 98.7% White, 0.0% Black/African American, 1.3%

Asian, 0.0% American Indian/Alaska Native, 0.0% Native Hawaiian/Other Pacific Islander, 0.0% Two or more races, 0.6% Hispanic of any race; Average household size: 2.56; Median age: 48.8; Age under 18: 14.5%; Age 65 and over: 22.0%; Males per 100 females: 104.2; Marriage status: 20.9% never married, 61.6% now married, 3.7% separated, 4.2% widowed, 13.3% divorced; Foreign born: 2.4%; Speak English only: 97.4%; With disability: 12.0%; Veterans: 9.2%; Ancestry: 39.5% Irish, 28.8% German, 12.6% English, 10.6% Scottish, 6.6% French Canadian
Employment: 23.9% management, business, and financial, 3.5% computer, engineering, and science, 15.2% education, legal, community service, arts, and media, 7.3% healthcare practitioners, 9.8% service, 18.6% sales and office, 3.8% natural resources, construction, and maintenance, 17.8% production, transportation, and material moving
Income: Per capita: $40,251; Median household: $90,750; Average household: $101,590; Households with income of $100,000 or more: 43.6%; Poverty rate: 3.3%
Educational Attainment: High school diploma or higher: 94.0%; Bachelor's degree or higher: 32.6%; Graduate/professional degree or higher: 8.9%
Housing: Homeownership rate: 82.9%; Median home value: $228,000; Median year structure built: 1972; Homeowner vacancy rate: 0.0%; Median selected monthly owner costs: $1,864 with a mortgage, $571 without a mortgage; Median gross rent: $1,063 per month; Rental vacancy rate: 0.0%
Health Insurance: 95.9% have insurance; 80.0% have private insurance; 34.3% have public insurance; 4.1% do not have insurance; 0.0% of children under 18 do not have insurance
Transportation: Commute: 89.7% car, 0.0% public transportation, 5.1% walk, 4.1% work from home; Mean travel time to work: 30.5 minutes

NORTH CHATHAM (unincorporated postal area)
ZCTA: 12132

Covers a land area of 1.859 square miles and a water area of 0 square miles. Located at 42.47° N. Lat; 73.63° W. Long. Elevation is 351 feet.
Population: 317; Growth (since 2000): n/a; Density: 170.5 persons per square mile; Race: 65.9% White, 0.0% Black/African American, 0.0% Asian, 0.0% American Indian/Alaska Native, 0.0% Native Hawaiian/Other Pacific Islander, 0.0% Two or more races, 34.1% Hispanic of any race; Average household size: 2.71; Median age: 44.1; Age under 18: 33.4%; Age 65 and over: 43.2%; Males per 100 females: 87.8; Marriage status: 43.3% never married, 56.7% now married, 0.0% separated, 0.0% widowed, 0.0% divorced; Foreign born: 24.6%; Speak English only: 84.6%; With disability: 21.8%; Veterans: 21.3%; Ancestry: 37.5% German, 22.1% Irish, 7.3% English, 6.9% Italian, 6.6% Polish
Employment: 0.0% management, business, and financial, 0.0% computer, engineering, and science, 0.0% education, legal, community service, arts, and media, 0.0% healthcare practitioners, 50.0% service, 50.0% sales and office, 0.0% natural resources, construction, and maintenance, 0.0% production, transportation, and material moving
Income: Per capita: $19,432; Median household: $61,150; Average household: $52,694; Households with income of $100,000 or more: n/a; Poverty rate: 36.7%
Educational Attainment: High school diploma or higher: 88.2%; Bachelor's degree or higher: 10.4%; Graduate/professional degree or higher: 10.4%
Housing: Homeownership rate: 78.6%; Median home value: $149,500; Median year structure built: Before 1940; Homeowner vacancy rate: 8.0%; Median selected monthly owner costs: $1,770 with a mortgage, $0 without a mortgage; Median gross rent: n/a per month; Rental vacancy rate: 0.0%
Health Insurance: 77.3% have insurance; 42.9% have private insurance; 69.4% have public insurance; 22.7% do not have insurance; 21.7% of children under 18 do not have insurance
Transportation: Commute: 100.0% car, 0.0% public transportation, 0.0% walk, 0.0% work from home; Mean travel time to work: 0.0 minutes

OLD CHATHAM (unincorporated postal area)
ZCTA: 12136

Covers a land area of 18.151 square miles and a water area of 0.019 square miles. Located at 42.43° N. Lat; 73.56° W. Long. Elevation is 535 feet.
Population: 847; Growth (since 2000): -3.2%; Density: 46.7 persons per square mile; Race: 95.2% White, 2.8% Black/African American, 0.0% Asian, 0.0% American Indian/Alaska Native, 0.0% Native Hawaiian/Other Pacific Islander, 2.0% Two or more races, 5.7%

Hispanic of any race; Average household size: 2.23; Median age: 50.7; Age under 18: 9.8%; Age 65 and over: 21.3%; Males per 100 females: 100.0; Marriage status: 15.8% never married, 73.6% now married, 2.0% separated, 5.6% widowed, 5.0% divorced; Foreign born: 7.1%; Speak English only: 94.7%; With disability: 7.3%; Veterans: 8.5%; Ancestry: 27.6% German, 25.0% Irish, 11.1% English, 8.9% French Canadian, 7.8% Italian
Employment: 30.9% management, business, and financial, 1.4% computer, engineering, and science, 14.2% education, legal, community service, arts, and media, 5.1% healthcare practitioners, 13.0% service, 19.1% sales and office, 10.0% natural resources, construction, and maintenance, 6.3% production, transportation, and material moving
Income: Per capita: $55,817; Median household: $89,276; Average household: $123,882; Households with income of $100,000 or more: 48.5%; Poverty rate: n/a
Educational Attainment: High school diploma or higher: 98.2%; Bachelor's degree or higher: 57.2%; Graduate/professional degree or higher: 31.2%
Housing: Homeownership rate: 92.9%; Median home value: $356,400; Median year structure built: 1947; Homeowner vacancy rate: 0.0%; Median selected monthly owner costs: $1,741 with a mortgage, $1,335 without a mortgage; Median gross rent: n/a per month; Rental vacancy rate: 0.0%
Health Insurance: 95.4% have insurance; 79.1% have private insurance; 34.7% have public insurance; 4.6% do not have insurance; 0.0% of children under 18 do not have insurance
Transportation: Commute: 69.3% car, 4.1% public transportation, 7.7% walk, 16.1% work from home; Mean travel time to work: 25.1 minutes

PHILMONT (village). Covers a land area of 1.187 square miles and a water area of 0.039 square miles. Located at 42.25° N. Lat; 73.65° W. Long. Elevation is 407 feet.
Population: 1,373; Growth (since 2000): -7.2%; Density: 1,156.3 persons per square mile; Race: 90.5% White, 2.4% Black/African American, 1.2% Asian, 0.0% American Indian/Alaska Native, 0.0% Native Hawaiian/Other Pacific Islander, 6.0% Two or more races, 2.0% Hispanic of any race; Average household size: 2.50; Median age: 34.4; Age under 18: 27.3%; Age 65 and over: 11.9%; Males per 100 females: 93.4; Marriage status: 31.9% never married, 51.8% now married, 3.8% separated, 3.1% widowed, 13.2% divorced; Foreign born: 3.6%; Speak English only: 97.1%; With disability: 14.4%; Veterans: 8.9%; Ancestry: 35.6% Irish, 31.7% German, 12.5% Italian, 9.0% Dutch, 7.5% English
Employment: 9.2% management, business, and financial, 2.4% computer, engineering, and science, 9.4% education, legal, community service, arts, and media, 2.3% healthcare practitioners, 17.1% service, 34.4% sales and office, 11.3% natural resources, construction, and maintenance, 14.0% production, transportation, and material moving
Income: Per capita: $24,692; Median household: $43,188; Average household: $61,713; Households with income of $100,000 or more: 13.3%; Poverty rate: 19.9%
Educational Attainment: High school diploma or higher: 81.6%; Bachelor's degree or higher: 18.0%; Graduate/professional degree or higher: 10.1%
Housing: Homeownership rate: 47.5%; Median home value: $157,400; Median year structure built: Before 1940; Homeowner vacancy rate: 6.8%; Median selected monthly owner costs: $1,413 with a mortgage, $750 without a mortgage; Median gross rent: $753 per month; Rental vacancy rate: 17.7%
Health Insurance: 92.4% have insurance; 55.9% have private insurance; 46.7% have public insurance; 7.6% do not have insurance; 5.1% of children under 18 do not have insurance
Transportation: Commute: 93.1% car, 1.8% public transportation, 0.8% walk, 1.8% work from home; Mean travel time to work: 17.9 minutes

SPENCERTOWN (unincorporated postal area)
ZCTA: 12165

Covers a land area of 3.227 square miles and a water area of 0.002 square miles. Located at 42.31° N. Lat; 73.51° W. Long. Elevation is 686 feet.
Population: 131; Growth (since 2000): -44.5%; Density: 40.6 persons per square mile; Race: 100.0% White, 0.0% Black/African American, 0.0% Asian, 0.0% American Indian/Alaska Native, 0.0% Native Hawaiian/Other Pacific Islander, 0.0% Two or more races, 0.0% Hispanic of any race; Average household size: 1.98; Median age: 56.4; Age under 18: 3.8%; Age 65 and over: 35.1%; Males per 100 females:

110.8; Marriage status: 22.2% never married, 68.3% now married, 0.0% separated, 2.4% widowed, 7.1% divorced; Foreign born: 6.9%; Speak English only: 96.9%; With disability: 15.3%; Veterans: 11.9%; Ancestry: 23.7% Irish, 16.0% American, 13.0% English, 10.7% German, 8.4% Lithuanian

Employment: 5.3% management, business, and financial, 0.0% computer, engineering, and science, 25.3% education, legal, community service, arts, and media, 8.0% healthcare practitioners, 29.3% service, 21.3% sales and office, 4.0% natural resources, construction, and maintenance, 6.7% production, transportation, and material moving

Income: Per capita: $47,328; Median household: $105,833; Average household: $95,192; Households with income of $100,000 or more: 51.6%; Poverty rate: 20.6%

Educational Attainment: High school diploma or higher: 100.0%; Bachelor's degree or higher: 41.6%; Graduate/professional degree or higher: 27.4%

Housing: Homeownership rate: 74.2%; Median home value: $350,000; Median year structure built: 1977; Homeowner vacancy rate: 5.8%; Median selected monthly owner costs: n/a with a mortgage, n/a without a mortgage; Median gross rent: n/a per month; Rental vacancy rate: 0.0%

Health Insurance: 82.4% have insurance; 69.5% have private insurance; 45.8% have public insurance; 17.6% do not have insurance; 0.0% of children under 18 do not have insurance

Transportation: Commute: 73.3% car, 17.3% public transportation, 0.0% walk, 9.3% work from home; Mean travel time to work: 41.0 minutes

STOCKPORT (town). Covers a land area of 11.648 square miles and a water area of 1.505 square miles. Located at 42.32° N. Lat; 73.76° W. Long. Elevation is 135 feet.

Population: 2,755; Growth (since 2000): -6.1%; Density: 236.5 persons per square mile; Race: 97.4% White, 2.5% Black/African American, 0.0% Asian, 0.0% American Indian/Alaska Native, 0.0% Native Hawaiian/Other Pacific Islander, 0.0% Two or more races, 1.0% Hispanic of any race; Average household size: 2.41; Median age: 43.8; Age under 18: 18.6%; Age 65 and over: 15.9%; Males per 100 females: 106.2; Marriage status: 34.6% never married, 47.6% now married, 1.9% separated, 3.6% widowed, 14.2% divorced; Foreign born: 1.9%; Speak English only: 99.0%; With disability: 18.1%; Veterans: 9.7%; Ancestry: 27.4% Irish, 26.9% German, 21.8% Italian, 7.7% Dutch, 7.0% English

Employment: 11.6% management, business, and financial, 2.4% computer, engineering, and science, 9.5% education, legal, community service, arts, and media, 4.1% healthcare practitioners, 23.0% service, 23.1% sales and office, 15.4% natural resources, construction, and maintenance, 11.0% production, transportation, and material moving

Income: Per capita: $28,199; Median household: $51,750; Average household: $68,394; Households with income of $100,000 or more: 12.2%; Poverty rate: 9.8%

Educational Attainment: High school diploma or higher: 87.3%; Bachelor's degree or higher: 15.0%; Graduate/professional degree or higher: 3.1%

Housing: Homeownership rate: 73.7%; Median home value: $167,700; Median year structure built: 1959; Homeowner vacancy rate: 2.8%; Median selected monthly owner costs: $1,551 with a mortgage, $583 without a mortgage; Median gross rent: $910 per month; Rental vacancy rate: 0.0%

Health Insurance: 92.5% have insurance; 69.6% have private insurance; 36.2% have public insurance; 7.5% do not have insurance; 2.5% of children under 18 do not have insurance

Safety: Violent crime rate: 0.0 per 10,000 population; Property crime rate: 11.0 per 10,000 population

Transportation: Commute: 93.7% car, 0.2% public transportation, 0.6% walk, 4.3% work from home; Mean travel time to work: 27.5 minutes

STOTTVILLE (CDP). Covers a land area of 4.179 square miles and a water area of 0.030 square miles. Located at 42.29° N. Lat; 73.76° W. Long. Elevation is 115 feet.

Population: 1,355; Growth (since 2000): 0.0%; Density: 324.2 persons per square mile; Race: 94.4% White, 5.2% Black/African American, 0.0% Asian, 0.0% American Indian/Alaska Native, 0.0% Native Hawaiian/Other Pacific Islander, 0.4% Two or more races, 0.0% Hispanic of any race; Average household size: 2.35; Median age: 49.8; Age under 18: 16.9%; Age 65 and over: 20.1%; Males per 100 females: 100.4; Marriage status: 36.5% never married, 46.3% now married, 4.0% separated, 6.5% widowed, 10.7% divorced; Foreign born: 1.8%; Speak English only:

100.0%; With disability: 15.6%; Veterans: 8.8%; Ancestry: 29.0% Irish, 20.8% German, 20.6% Italian, 9.6% English, 8.1% Dutch

Employment: 15.1% management, business, and financial, 0.0% computer, engineering, and science, 12.4% education, legal, community service, arts, and media, 4.0% healthcare practitioners, 25.9% service, 13.3% sales and office, 12.7% natural resources, construction, and maintenance, 16.6% production, transportation, and material moving

Income: Per capita: $29,929; Median household: $50,083; Average household: $71,821; Households with income of $100,000 or more: 9.3%; Poverty rate: 11.4%

Educational Attainment: High school diploma or higher: 78.8%; Bachelor's degree or higher: 16.2%; Graduate/professional degree or higher: 7.0%

Housing: Homeownership rate: 60.6%; Median home value: $164,000; Median year structure built: 1953; Homeowner vacancy rate: 3.6%; Median selected monthly owner costs: $1,379 with a mortgage, $553 without a mortgage; Median gross rent: $943 per month; Rental vacancy rate: 0.0%

Health Insurance: 91.2% have insurance; 67.6% have private insurance; 41.5% have public insurance; 8.8% do not have insurance; 6.1% of children under 18 do not have insurance

Transportation: Commute: 93.2% car, 0.0% public transportation, 1.3% walk, 4.2% work from home; Mean travel time to work: 26.4 minutes

STUYVESANT (town). Covers a land area of 25.004 square miles and a water area of 1.745 square miles. Located at 42.40° N. Lat; 73.75° W. Long. Elevation is 105 feet.

Population: 2,081; Growth (since 2000): -4.9%; Density: 83.2 persons per square mile; Race: 95.8% White, 0.8% Black/African American, 0.1% Asian, 0.0% American Indian/Alaska Native, 0.0% Native Hawaiian/Other Pacific Islander, 3.0% Two or more races, 1.6% Hispanic of any race; Average household size: 2.48; Median age: 43.5; Age under 18: 20.8%; Age 65 and over: 13.9%; Males per 100 females: 101.1; Marriage status: 30.6% never married, 50.7% now married, 3.1% separated, 5.0% widowed, 13.7% divorced; Foreign born: 3.8%; Speak English only: 95.5%; With disability: 13.5%; Veterans: 12.5%; Ancestry: 24.7% Italian, 21.1% German, 16.5% Irish, 10.4% Polish, 10.0% Dutch

Employment: 14.9% management, business, and financial, 2.8% computer, engineering, and science, 16.1% education, legal, community service, arts, and media, 4.2% healthcare practitioners, 13.2% service, 25.3% sales and office, 10.4% natural resources, construction, and maintenance, 13.0% production, transportation, and material moving

Income: Per capita: $34,996; Median household: $71,711; Average household: $87,086; Households with income of $100,000 or more: 30.5%; Poverty rate: 16.3%

Educational Attainment: High school diploma or higher: 93.3%; Bachelor's degree or higher: 28.9%; Graduate/professional degree or higher: 10.7%

Housing: Homeownership rate: 77.0%; Median home value: $198,900; Median year structure built: 1971; Homeowner vacancy rate: 2.5%; Median selected monthly owner costs: $1,692 with a mortgage, $688 without a mortgage; Median gross rent: $1,019 per month; Rental vacancy rate: 9.0%

Health Insurance: 96.3% have insurance; 76.6% have private insurance; 29.6% have public insurance; 3.7% do not have insurance; 0.9% of children under 18 do not have insurance

Transportation: Commute: 91.7% car, 0.0% public transportation, 1.2% walk, 6.0% work from home; Mean travel time to work: 30.4 minutes

STUYVESANT FALLS (unincorporated postal area)
ZCTA: 12174

Covers a land area of 1.149 square miles and a water area of 0 square miles. Located at 42.35° N. Lat; 73.73° W. Long. Elevation is 210 feet.

Population: 299; Growth (since 2000): n/a; Density: 260.1 persons per square mile; Race: 99.0% White, 0.0% Black/African American, 0.0% Asian, 0.0% American Indian/Alaska Native, 0.0% Native Hawaiian/Other Pacific Islander, 1.0% Two or more races, 4.3% Hispanic of any race; Average household size: 2.62; Median age: 40.6; Age under 18: 21.1%; Age 65 and over: 9.7%; Males per 100 females: 99.4; Marriage status: 35.9% never married, 55.7% now married, 0.0% separated, 6.5% widowed, 1.9% divorced; Foreign born: 3.7%; Speak English only: 94.7%; With disability: 12.4%; Veterans: 16.1%; Ancestry: 40.1% Italian, 20.7% German, 13.0% English, 10.0% Dutch, 8.7% Irish

Employment: 7.4% management, business, and financial, 2.5% computer, engineering, and science, 16.0% education, legal, community service, arts, and media, 0.0% healthcare practitioners, 14.2% service,

40.1% sales and office, 3.1% natural resources, construction, and maintenance, 16.7% production, transportation, and material moving
Income: Per capita: $26,891; Median household: $57,917; Average household: $71,138; Households with income of $100,000 or more: 30.7%; Poverty rate: 14.0%
Educational Attainment: High school diploma or higher: 90.6%; Bachelor's degree or higher: 24.5%; Graduate/professional degree or higher: 14.6%
Housing: Homeownership rate: 60.5%; Median home value: $159,400; Median year structure built: Before 1940; Homeowner vacancy rate: 0.0%; Median selected monthly owner costs: $1,375 with a mortgage, $788 without a mortgage; Median gross rent: $1,005 per month; Rental vacancy rate: 0.0%
Health Insurance: 98.7% have insurance; 57.2% have private insurance; 45.5% have public insurance; 1.3% do not have insurance; 6.3% of children under 18 do not have insurance
Transportation: Commute: 100.0% car, 0.0% public transportation, 0.0% walk, 0.0% work from home; Mean travel time to work: 25.3 minutes

TAGHKANIC (town). Covers a land area of 39.972 square miles and a water area of 0.166 square miles. Located at 42.13° N. Lat; 73.68° W. Long. Elevation is 725 feet.
Population: 1,146; Growth (since 2000): 2.5%; Density: 28.7 persons per square mile; Race: 98.9% White, 0.0% Black/African American, 0.6% Asian, 0.0% American Indian/Alaska Native, 0.0% Native Hawaiian/Other Pacific Islander, 0.5% Two or more races, 4.6% Hispanic of any race; Average household size: 2.33; Median age: 53.0; Age under 18: 13.4%; Age 65 and over: 28.7%; Males per 100 females: 102.5; Marriage status: 22.6% never married, 60.3% now married, 0.3% separated, 4.6% widowed, 12.5% divorced; Foreign born: 4.1%; Speak English only: 97.2%; With disability: 16.4%; Veterans: 7.9%; Ancestry: 23.6% German, 16.1% Italian, 14.5% English, 13.0% Irish, 6.5% Polish
Employment: 19.0% management, business, and financial, 1.4% computer, engineering, and science, 18.0% education, legal, community service, arts, and media, 5.8% healthcare practitioners, 13.0% service, 22.2% sales and office, 13.4% natural resources, construction, and maintenance, 7.0% production, transportation, and material moving
Income: Per capita: $37,655; Median household: $62,917; Average household: $86,812; Households with income of $100,000 or more: 28.1%; Poverty rate: 16.7%
Educational Attainment: High school diploma or higher: 90.3%; Bachelor's degree or higher: 34.0%; Graduate/professional degree or higher: 18.1%
Housing: Homeownership rate: 87.0%; Median home value: $266,500; Median year structure built: 1975; Homeowner vacancy rate: 8.3%; Median selected monthly owner costs: $1,659 with a mortgage, $653 without a mortgage; Median gross rent: $893 per month; Rental vacancy rate: 9.9%
Health Insurance: 88.2% have insurance; 75.0% have private insurance; 38.2% have public insurance; 11.8% do not have insurance; 29.9% of children under 18 do not have insurance
Transportation: Commute: 77.1% car, 7.0% public transportation, 3.9% walk, 11.5% work from home; Mean travel time to work: 32.9 minutes

VALATIE (village). Covers a land area of 1.254 square miles and a water area of 0.012 square miles. Located at 42.41° N. Lat; 73.68° W. Long. Elevation is 239 feet.
History: Incorporated 1856.
Population: 1,735; Growth (since 2000): 1.3%; Density: 1,383.3 persons per square mile; Race: 90.3% White, 1.0% Black/African American, 2.8% Asian, 0.0% American Indian/Alaska Native, 0.0% Native Hawaiian/Other Pacific Islander, 1.0% Two or more races, 7.5% Hispanic of any race; Average household size: 2.58; Median age: 42.1; Age under 18: 24.6%; Age 65 and over: 23.6%; Males per 100 females: 93.1; Marriage status: 33.7% never married, 42.7% now married, 4.1% separated, 13.0% widowed, 10.6% divorced; Foreign born: 5.0%; Speak English only: 91.0%; With disability: 14.6%; Veterans: 12.5%; Ancestry: 17.5% Irish, 15.7% German, 12.9% Italian, 11.7% American, 10.6% English
Employment: 8.8% management, business, and financial, 5.4% computer, engineering, and science, 14.4% education, legal, community service, arts, and media, 9.6% healthcare practitioners, 25.1% service, 26.0% sales and office, 7.1% natural resources, construction, and maintenance, 3.7% production, transportation, and material moving

Income: Per capita: $25,968; Median household: $56,719; Average household: $68,669; Households with income of $100,000 or more: 20.8%; Poverty rate: 14.6%
Educational Attainment: High school diploma or higher: 88.3%; Bachelor's degree or higher: 29.3%; Graduate/professional degree or higher: 10.2%

School District(s)
Kinderhook Central SD (KG-12)
    2014-15 Enrollment: 1,912 . . . . (518) 758-7575
Housing: Homeownership rate: 60.5%; Median home value: $210,200; Median year structure built: 1944; Homeowner vacancy rate: 0.0%; Median selected monthly owner costs: $1,896 with a mortgage, $700 without a mortgage; Median gross rent: $763 per month; Rental vacancy rate: 7.5%
Health Insurance: 91.9% have insurance; 75.3% have private insurance; 28.2% have public insurance; 8.1% do not have insurance; 2.3% of children under 18 do not have insurance
Transportation: Commute: 89.0% car, 1.9% public transportation, 6.3% walk, 2.8% work from home; Mean travel time to work: 23.6 minutes

WEST LEBANON (unincorporated postal area)
ZCTA: 12195
    Covers a land area of 1.955 square miles and a water area of 0 square miles. Located at 42.48° N. Lat; 73.48° W. Long. Elevation is 623 feet.
Population: 157; Growth (since 2000): n/a; Density: 80.3 persons per square mile; Race: 100.0% White, 0.0% Black/African American, 0.0% Asian, 0.0% American Indian/Alaska Native, 0.0% Native Hawaiian/Other Pacific Islander, 0.0% Two or more races, 0.0% Hispanic of any race; Average household size: 1.40; Median age: 48.1; Age under 18: 0.0%; Age 65 and over: 33.1%; Males per 100 females: 97.4; Marriage status: 9.6% never married, 59.2% now married, 0.0% separated, 8.9% widowed, 22.3% divorced; Foreign born: 28.7%; Speak English only: 80.3%; With disability: 25.5%; Veterans: 14.0%; Ancestry: 20.4% Polish, 19.1% German, 16.6% Irish, 15.3% Italian, 12.1% French
Employment: 21.6% management, business, and financial, 0.0% computer, engineering, and science, 5.9% education, legal, community service, arts, and media, 18.6% healthcare practitioners, 0.0% service, 39.2% sales and office, 0.0% natural resources, construction, and maintenance, 14.7% production, transportation, and material moving
Income: Per capita: $35,806; Median household: n/a; Average household: $51,013; Households with income of $100,000 or more: 5.4%; Poverty rate: 11.5%
Educational Attainment: High school diploma or higher: 100.0%; Bachelor's degree or higher: 55.8%; Graduate/professional degree or higher: 17.4%
Housing: Homeownership rate: 53.6%; Median home value: $208,300; Median year structure built: 1967; Homeowner vacancy rate: 0.0%; Median selected monthly owner costs: n/a with a mortgage, n/a without a mortgage; Median gross rent: $861 per month; Rental vacancy rate: 0.0%
Health Insurance: 88.5% have insurance; 72.6% have private insurance; 44.6% have public insurance; 11.5% do not have insurance; 0.0% of children under 18 do not have insurance
Transportation: Commute: 85.3% car, 0.0% public transportation, 14.7% walk, 0.0% work from home; Mean travel time to work: 24.5 minutes

Cortland County

Located in central New York; drained by the Tioughnioga River. Covers a land area of 498.760 square miles, a water area of 2.758 square miles, and is located in the Eastern Time Zone at 42.59° N. Lat., 76.08° W. Long. The county was founded in 1808. County seat is Cortland.

Cortland County is part of the Cortland, NY Micropolitan Statistical Area. The entire metro area includes: Cortland County, NY

Weather Station: Tully Heiberg Forest   Elevation: 1,898 feet

	Jan	Feb	Mar	Apr	May	Jun	Jul	Aug	Sep	Oct	Nov	Dec
High	27	30	37	51	63	72	76	75	67	55	43	32
Low	12	13	20	32	43	52	57	56	48	37	28	18
Precip	2.9	2.7	3.3	4.0	4.0	4.9	4.0	4.0	4.8	4.0	4.0	3.3
Snow	26.3	23.3	21.1	7.6	0.4	tr	0.0	0.0	tr	1.8	11.9	23.4

High and Low temperatures in degrees Fahrenheit; Precipitation and Snow in inches

Population: 49,043; Growth (since 2000): 0.9%; Density: 98.3 persons per square mile; Race: 94.3% White, 1.8% Black/African American, 0.9%

Profiles of New York State

Asian, 0.1% American Indian/Alaska Native, 0.0% Native Hawaiian/Other Pacific Islander, 2.1% two or more races, 2.5% Hispanic of any race; Average household size: 2.54; Median age: 36.1; Age under 18: 20.1%; Age 65 and over: 14.7%; Males per 100 females: 95.4; Marriage status: 39.2% never married, 44.6% now married, 2.4% separated, 6.3% widowed, 9.9% divorced; Foreign born: 1.9%; Speak English only: 96.3%; With disability: 12.9%; Veterans: 8.4%; Ancestry: 18.8% English, 12.3% Irish, 10.8% German, 8.1% Italian, 7.3% American
Religion: Six largest groups: 12.9% Catholicism, 5.6% Methodist/Pietist, 2.5% Non-denominational Protestant, 2.4% Presbyterian-Reformed, 1.1% Baptist, 0.8% Latter-day Saints
Economy: Unemployment rate: 4.8%; Leading industries: 17.2 % retail trade; 13.1 % accommodation and food services; 11.9 % health care and social assistance; Farms: 518 totaling 115,024 acres; Company size: 0 employ 1,000 or more persons, 5 employ 500 to 999 persons, 21 employs 100 to 499 persons, 1,000 employ less than 100 persons; Business ownership: 821 women-owned, n/a Black-owned, 31 Hispanic-owned, 47 Asian-owned, 42 American Indian/Alaska Native-owned
Employment: 10.7% management, business, and financial, 4.5% computer, engineering, and science, 12.8% education, legal, community service, arts, and media, 5.3% healthcare practitioners, 20.3% service, 23.7% sales and office, 9.0% natural resources, construction, and maintenance, 13.7% production, transportation, and material moving
Income: Per capita: $24,228; Median household: $49,514; Average household: $63,133; Households with income of $100,000 or more: 17.9%; Poverty rate: 14.7%
Educational Attainment: High school diploma or higher: 89.9%; Bachelor's degree or higher: 23.6%; Graduate/professional degree or higher: 10.2%
Housing: Homeownership rate: 65.7%; Median home value: $108,200; Median year structure built: 1950; Homeowner vacancy rate: 1.2%; Median selected monthly owner costs: $1,228 with a mortgage, $556 without a mortgage; Median gross rent: $684 per month; Rental vacancy rate: 3.6%
Vital Statistics: Birth rate: 97.5 per 10,000 population; Death rate: 83.7 per 10,000 population; Age-adjusted cancer mortality rate: 160.3 deaths per 100,000 population
Health Insurance: 93.5% have insurance; 75.3% have private insurance; 31.6% have public insurance; 6.5% do not have insurance; 6.1% of children under 18 do not have insurance
Health Care: Physicians: 11.6 per 10,000 population; Dentists: 3.7 per 10,000 population; Hospital beds: 41.8 per 10,000 population; Hospital admissions: 861.7 per 10,000 population
Transportation: Commute: 86.7% car, 0.8% public transportation, 6.8% walk, 4.8% work from home; Mean travel time to work: 20.9 minutes
2016 Presidential Election: 49.5% Trump, 43.9% Clinton, 4.8% Johnson, 1.9% Stein
Additional Information Contacts
Cortland Government . . . . (607) 753-5021
   http://www.cortland-co.org

Cortland County Communities

BLODGETT MILLS (CDP). Covers a land area of 2.174 square miles and a water area of 0 square miles. Located at 42.57° N. Lat; 76.13° W. Long. Elevation is 1,102 feet.
Population: 321; Growth (since 2000): n/a; Density: 147.7 persons per square mile; Race: 100.0% White, 0.0% Black/African American, 0.0% Asian, 0.0% American Indian/Alaska Native, 0.0% Native Hawaiian/Other Pacific Islander, 0.0% Two or more races, 0.0% Hispanic of any race; Average household size: 2.94; Median age: 39.7; Age under 18: 22.4%; Age 65 and over: 10.0%; Males per 100 females: 104.7; Marriage status: 26.4% never married, 73.6% now married, 10.0% separated, 0.0% widowed, 0.0% divorced; Foreign born: 5.0%; Speak English only: 94.3%; With disability: 16.5%; Veterans: 0.0%; Ancestry: 19.0% Italian, 14.0% Irish, 12.1% American, 11.8% English, 1.9% Czechoslovakian
Employment: 0.0% management, business, and financial, 0.0% computer, engineering, and science, 3.7% education, legal, community service, arts, and media, 0.0% healthcare practitioners, 56.8% service, 14.8% sales and office, 7.4% natural resources, construction, and maintenance, 17.3% production, transportation, and material moving
Income: Per capita: $19,223; Median household: $51,771; Average household: $55,899; Households with income of $100,000 or more: n/a; Poverty rate: n/a

Educational Attainment: High school diploma or higher: 82.0%; Bachelor's degree or higher: 3.0%; Graduate/professional degree or higher: 3.0%
Housing: Homeownership rate: 85.3%; Median home value: $82,400; Median year structure built: 1966; Homeowner vacancy rate: 0.0%; Median selected monthly owner costs: $1,293 with a mortgage, $377 without a mortgage; Median gross rent: n/a per month; Rental vacancy rate: 0.0%
Health Insurance: 100.0% have insurance; 86.3% have private insurance; 35.8% have public insurance; 0.0% do not have insurance; 0.0% of children under 18 do not have insurance
Transportation: Commute: 86.5% car, 5.1% public transportation, 0.0% walk, 3.8% work from home; Mean travel time to work: 22.7 minutes

CINCINNATUS (town). Covers a land area of 25.356 square miles and a water area of 0.129 square miles. Located at 42.53° N. Lat; 75.91° W. Long. Elevation is 1,050 feet.
Population: 947; Growth (since 2000): -9.9%; Density: 37.3 persons per square mile; Race: 100.0% White, 0.0% Black/African American, 0.0% Asian, 0.0% American Indian/Alaska Native, 0.0% Native Hawaiian/Other Pacific Islander, 0.0% Two or more races, 0.4% Hispanic of any race; Average household size: 2.66; Median age: 40.6; Age under 18: 26.3%; Age 65 and over: 17.2%; Males per 100 females: 98.9; Marriage status: 26.2% never married, 52.7% now married, 2.6% separated, 10.4% widowed, 10.7% divorced; Foreign born: 1.0%; Speak English only: 98.8%; With disability: 19.2%; Veterans: 10.3%; Ancestry: 25.8% English, 15.8% German, 10.3% American, 9.0% Irish, 3.1% Italian
Employment: 7.2% management, business, and financial, 2.8% computer, engineering, and science, 6.7% education, legal, community service, arts, and media, 3.3% healthcare practitioners, 23.3% service, 22.3% sales and office, 24.9% natural resources, construction, and maintenance, 9.5% production, transportation, and material moving
Income: Per capita: $20,633; Median household: $43,929; Average household: $53,378; Households with income of $100,000 or more: 16.5%; Poverty rate: 21.8%
Educational Attainment: High school diploma or higher: 92.9%; Bachelor's degree or higher: 9.6%; Graduate/professional degree or higher: 6.0%
School District(s)
Cincinnatus Central SD (PK-12)
   2014-15 Enrollment: 619 . . . . (607) 863-4069
Housing: Homeownership rate: 75.6%; Median home value: $91,200; Median year structure built: 1941; Homeowner vacancy rate: 0.0%; Median selected monthly owner costs: $1,164 with a mortgage, $474 without a mortgage; Median gross rent: $662 per month; Rental vacancy rate: 6.5%
Health Insurance: 93.1% have insurance; 63.4% have private insurance; 46.6% have public insurance; 6.9% do not have insurance; 5.6% of children under 18 do not have insurance
Transportation: Commute: 87.4% car, 0.0% public transportation, 4.5% walk, 5.0% work from home; Mean travel time to work: 30.1 minutes

CORTLAND (city). County seat. Covers a land area of 3.894 square miles and a water area of 0.020 square miles. Located at 42.60° N. Lat; 76.18° W. Long. Elevation is 1,129 feet.
History: Elmer Ambrose Sperry (1860-1030), inventor, was born in Cortland. Sperry is credited with 400 patents.
Population: 19,134; Growth (since 2000): 2.1%; Density: 4,913.7 persons per square mile; Race: 92.2% White, 3.6% Black/African American, 0.7% Asian, 0.0% American Indian/Alaska Native, 0.0% Native Hawaiian/Other Pacific Islander, 2.1% Two or more races, 2.9% Hispanic of any race; Average household size: 2.40; Median age: 27.5; Age under 18: 16.3%; Age 65 and over: 12.8%; Males per 100 females: 90.7; Marriage status: 55.2% never married, 29.5% now married, 2.2% separated, 5.6% widowed, 9.7% divorced; Foreign born: 2.0%; Speak English only: 95.4%; With disability: 12.6%; Veterans: 7.2%; Ancestry: 15.6% English, 10.8% Irish, 9.7% Italian, 8.4% German, 5.7% American
Employment: 8.6% management, business, and financial, 3.2% computer, engineering, and science, 15.3% education, legal, community service, arts, and media, 5.2% healthcare practitioners, 24.5% service, 26.6% sales and office, 4.5% natural resources, construction, and maintenance, 12.1% production, transportation, and material moving
Income: Per capita: $18,999; Median household: $40,025; Average household: $49,504; Households with income of $100,000 or more: 8.8%; Poverty rate: 24.0%

Educational Attainment: High school diploma or higher: 88.7%; Bachelor's degree or higher: 23.4%; Graduate/professional degree or higher: 9.8%

School District(s)
Cortland City SD (KG-12)
    2014-15 Enrollment: 2,620 . . . . (607) 758-4100
Four-year College(s)
SUNY College at Cortland (Public)
    Fall 2014 Enrollment: 6,958 . . . . (607) 753-2011
    2015-16 Tuition: In-state $8,050; Out-of-state $17,900
Housing: Homeownership rate: 46.1%; Median home value: $94,200; Median year structure built: Before 1940; Homeowner vacancy rate: 2.9%; Median selected monthly owner costs: $1,134 with a mortgage, $537 without a mortgage; Median gross rent: $678 per month; Rental vacancy rate: 3.4%
Health Insurance: 95.1% have insurance; 75.1% have private insurance; 31.0% have public insurance; 4.9% do not have insurance; 1.9% of children under 18 do not have insurance
Hospitals: Cortland Regional Medical Center (181 beds)
Safety: Violent crime rate: 15.7 per 10,000 population; Property crime rate: 134.6 per 10,000 population
Newspapers: Cortland Standard (daily circulation 10,300)
Transportation: Commute: 78.7% car, 1.2% public transportation, 15.0% walk, 4.3% work from home; Mean travel time to work: 15.9 minutes
Additional Information Contacts
City of Cortland . . . . (607) 756-6521
    http://www.cortland.org

CORTLAND WEST (CDP). Covers a land area of 5.166 square miles and a water area of 0 square miles. Located at 42.59° N. Lat; 76.23° W. Long.
Population: 1,289; Growth (since 2000): -4.2%; Density: 249.5 persons per square mile; Race: 100.0% White, 0.0% Black/African American, 0.0% Asian, 0.0% American Indian/Alaska Native, 0.0% Native Hawaiian/Other Pacific Islander, 0.0% Two or more races, 0.0% Hispanic of any race; Average household size: 2.48; Median age: 49.0; Age under 18: 22.3%; Age 65 and over: 24.4%; Males per 100 females: 95.1; Marriage status: 14.8% never married, 74.2% now married, 0.0% separated, 3.4% widowed, 7.7% divorced; Foreign born: 0.0%; Speak English only: 100.0%; With disability: 6.2%; Veterans: 7.4%; Ancestry: 17.9% English, 17.5% Irish, 15.7% German, 11.4% Italian, 7.8% Dutch
Employment: 24.3% management, business, and financial, 5.2% computer, engineering, and science, 17.4% education, legal, community service, arts, and media, 3.7% healthcare practitioners, 13.5% service, 19.0% sales and office, 3.7% natural resources, construction, and maintenance, 13.2% production, transportation, and material moving
Income: Per capita: $35,674; Median household: $88,125; Average household: $92,577; Households with income of $100,000 or more: 42.2%; Poverty rate: 8.4%
Educational Attainment: High school diploma or higher: 86.2%; Bachelor's degree or higher: 38.3%; Graduate/professional degree or higher: 14.0%
Housing: Homeownership rate: 98.0%; Median home value: $161,100; Median year structure built: 1965; Homeowner vacancy rate: 0.0%; Median selected monthly owner costs: $1,418 with a mortgage, $682 without a mortgage; Median gross rent: n/a per month; Rental vacancy rate: 0.0%
Health Insurance: 98.4% have insurance; 91.5% have private insurance; 25.6% have public insurance; 1.6% do not have insurance; 0.0% of children under 18 do not have insurance
Transportation: Commute: 94.1% car, 0.0% public transportation, 0.0% walk, 3.9% work from home; Mean travel time to work: 18.6 minutes

CORTLANDVILLE (town). Covers a land area of 49.720 square miles and a water area of 0.180 square miles. Located at 42.60° N. Lat; 76.12° W. Long.
Population: 8,420; Growth (since 2000): 6.3%; Density: 169.3 persons per square mile; Race: 94.5% White, 0.2% Black/African American, 2.3% Asian, 0.0% American Indian/Alaska Native, 0.0% Native Hawaiian/Other Pacific Islander, 2.8% Two or more races, 4.0% Hispanic of any race; Average household size: 2.42; Median age: 44.9; Age under 18: 18.1%; Age 65 and over: 21.5%; Males per 100 females: 94.4; Marriage status: 27.4% never married, 53.7% now married, 1.3% separated, 9.5% widowed, 9.4% divorced; Foreign born: 3.4%; Speak English only: 95.4%; With disability: 14.1%; Veterans: 8.6%; Ancestry: 19.5% English, 13.2% German, 13.2% Irish, 12.6% Italian, 6.4% American

Employment: 10.3% management, business, and financial, 6.2% computer, engineering, and science, 12.8% education, legal, community service, arts, and media, 6.2% healthcare practitioners, 20.6% service, 23.5% sales and office, 9.5% natural resources, construction, and maintenance, 10.9% production, transportation, and material moving
Income: Per capita: $28,819; Median household: $59,704; Average household: $72,888; Households with income of $100,000 or more: 25.4%; Poverty rate: 6.8%
Educational Attainment: High school diploma or higher: 90.6%; Bachelor's degree or higher: 29.5%; Graduate/professional degree or higher: 12.4%
Housing: Homeownership rate: 76.6%; Median home value: $138,500; Median year structure built: 1960; Homeowner vacancy rate: 0.3%; Median selected monthly owner costs: $1,488 with a mortgage, $585 without a mortgage; Median gross rent: $695 per month; Rental vacancy rate: 6.8%
Health Insurance: 95.9% have insurance; 82.9% have private insurance; 32.7% have public insurance; 4.1% do not have insurance; 4.0% of children under 18 do not have insurance
Transportation: Commute: 91.8% car, 0.7% public transportation, 1.9% walk, 4.2% work from home; Mean travel time to work: 18.4 minutes
Additional Information Contacts
Town of Cortlandville . . . . (607) 756-5725
    http://www.cortlandville.org

CUYLER (town). Covers a land area of 43.477 square miles and a water area of 0.032 square miles. Located at 42.73° N. Lat; 75.94° W. Long. Elevation is 1,214 feet.
Population: 764; Growth (since 2000): -26.3%; Density: 17.6 persons per square mile; Race: 96.9% White, 0.0% Black/African American, 0.0% Asian, 0.5% American Indian/Alaska Native, 0.0% Native Hawaiian/Other Pacific Islander, 2.6% Two or more races, 0.0% Hispanic of any race; Average household size: 2.60; Median age: 47.4; Age under 18: 20.7%; Age 65 and over: 21.1%; Males per 100 females: 105.5; Marriage status: 28.4% never married, 51.5% now married, 4.2% separated, 10.0% widowed, 10.0% divorced; Foreign born: 0.5%; Speak English only: 98.8%; With disability: 20.9%; Veterans: 10.1%; Ancestry: 18.8% English, 13.0% Irish, 8.9% German, 5.6% American, 5.2% Italian
Employment: 6.6% management, business, and financial, 0.7% computer, engineering, and science, 5.3% education, legal, community service, arts, and media, 10.3% healthcare practitioners, 16.6% service, 19.5% sales and office, 17.5% natural resources, construction, and maintenance, 23.5% production, transportation, and material moving
Income: Per capita: $22,676; Median household: $41,364; Average household: $56,028; Households with income of $100,000 or more: 9.9%; Poverty rate: 15.2%
Educational Attainment: High school diploma or higher: 84.0%; Bachelor's degree or higher: 10.9%; Graduate/professional degree or higher: 4.0%
Housing: Homeownership rate: 72.4%; Median home value: $88,300; Median year structure built: 1978; Homeowner vacancy rate: 0.0%; Median selected monthly owner costs: $1,402 with a mortgage, $515 without a mortgage; Median gross rent: $670 per month; Rental vacancy rate: 0.0%
Health Insurance: 90.2% have insurance; 62.8% have private insurance; 43.7% have public insurance; 9.8% do not have insurance; 7.6% of children under 18 do not have insurance
Transportation: Commute: 96.5% car, 0.0% public transportation, 0.7% walk, 2.8% work from home; Mean travel time to work: 30.5 minutes

FREETOWN (town). Covers a land area of 25.486 square miles and a water area of 0.142 square miles. Located at 42.52° N. Lat; 76.02° W. Long.
Population: 674; Growth (since 2000): -14.6%; Density: 26.4 persons per square mile; Race: 98.4% White, 1.0% Black/African American, 0.0% Asian, 0.0% American Indian/Alaska Native, 0.0% Native Hawaiian/Other Pacific Islander, 0.6% Two or more races, 0.0% Hispanic of any race; Average household size: 2.64; Median age: 40.4; Age under 18: 22.7%; Age 65 and over: 10.2%; Males per 100 females: 96.1; Marriage status: 31.5% never married, 53.4% now married, 3.3% separated, 4.0% widowed, 11.1% divorced; Foreign born: 0.4%; Speak English only: 98.3%; With disability: 16.0%; Veterans: 13.1%; Ancestry: 15.3% English, 10.8% American, 10.4% German, 7.4% Irish, 5.6% Pennsylvania German
Employment: 11.0% management, business, and financial, 2.0% computer, engineering, and science, 8.4% education, legal, community service, arts, and media, 2.6% healthcare practitioners, 19.9% service,

16.4% sales and office, 17.0% natural resources, construction, and maintenance, 22.8% production, transportation, and material moving
Income: Per capita: $20,283; Median household: $47,014; Average household: $52,147; Households with income of $100,000 or more: 8.3%; Poverty rate: 12.2%
Educational Attainment: High school diploma or higher: 82.6%; Bachelor's degree or higher: 8.6%; Graduate/professional degree or higher: 2.9%
Housing: Homeownership rate: 82.0%; Median home value: $80,200; Median year structure built: 1985; Homeowner vacancy rate: 1.4%; Median selected monthly owner costs: $955 with a mortgage, $419 without a mortgage; Median gross rent: $713 per month; Rental vacancy rate: 0.0%
Health Insurance: 87.7% have insurance; 64.2% have private insurance; 33.4% have public insurance; 12.3% do not have insurance; 11.8% of children under 18 do not have insurance
Transportation: Commute: 92.4% car, 0.0% public transportation, 0.9% walk, 6.0% work from home; Mean travel time to work: 28.1 minutes

HARFORD (town). Covers a land area of 24.152 square miles and a water area of 0.023 square miles. Located at 42.44° N. Lat; 76.21° W. Long. Elevation is 1,197 feet.
Population: 810; Growth (since 2000): -12.0%; Density: 33.5 persons per square mile; Race: 94.0% White, 0.0% Black/African American, 0.0% Asian, 2.6% American Indian/Alaska Native, 0.0% Native Hawaiian/Other Pacific Islander, 3.5% Two or more races, 0.2% Hispanic of any race; Average household size: 2.52; Median age: 43.7; Age under 18: 23.6%; Age 65 and over: 17.5%; Males per 100 females: 107.7; Marriage status: 25.8% never married, 52.0% now married, 1.1% separated, 8.9% widowed, 13.3% divorced; Foreign born: 0.0%; Speak English only: 99.7%; With disability: 16.0%; Veterans: 12.9%; Ancestry: 17.3% English, 13.1% American, 6.4% German, 6.0% Irish, 4.7% Italian
Employment: 19.7% management, business, and financial, 2.6% computer, engineering, and science, 8.4% education, legal, community service, arts, and media, 7.3% healthcare practitioners, 11.8% service, 15.2% sales and office, 7.1% natural resources, construction, and maintenance, 27.8% production, transportation, and material moving
Income: Per capita: $29,416; Median household: $48,750; Average household: $72,289; Households with income of $100,000 or more: 17.7%; Poverty rate: 11.5%
Educational Attainment: High school diploma or higher: 94.1%; Bachelor's degree or higher: 12.7%; Graduate/professional degree or higher: 5.0%
Housing: Homeownership rate: 76.0%; Median home value: $102,700; Median year structure built: 1975; Homeowner vacancy rate: 0.0%; Median selected monthly owner costs: $1,250 with a mortgage, $481 without a mortgage; Median gross rent: $790 per month; Rental vacancy rate: 0.0%
Health Insurance: 92.0% have insurance; 73.8% have private insurance; 34.8% have public insurance; 8.0% do not have insurance; 3.1% of children under 18 do not have insurance
Transportation: Commute: 85.7% car, 0.5% public transportation, 2.7% walk, 10.8% work from home; Mean travel time to work: 30.6 minutes

HOMER (town). Covers a land area of 50.195 square miles and a water area of 0.461 square miles. Located at 42.66° N. Lat; 76.17° W. Long. Elevation is 1,125 feet.
History: Old Homer Village Historic District here. Settled 1791, incorporated 1835.
Population: 6,405; Growth (since 2000): 0.7%; Density: 127.6 persons per square mile; Race: 94.2% White, 0.9% Black/African American, 1.3% Asian, 0.0% American Indian/Alaska Native, 0.0% Native Hawaiian/Other Pacific Islander, 2.7% Two or more races, 2.0% Hispanic of any race; Average household size: 2.65; Median age: 40.5; Age under 18: 23.1%; Age 65 and over: 13.9%; Males per 100 females: 93.7; Marriage status: 27.2% never married, 54.9% now married, 4.2% separated, 4.8% widowed, 13.1% divorced; Foreign born: 1.7%; Speak English only: 96.5%; With disability: 13.8%; Veterans: 8.0%; Ancestry: 23.7% English, 16.6% Irish, 11.2% German, 9.5% American, 5.0% Italian
Employment: 13.2% management, business, and financial, 8.3% computer, engineering, and science, 14.6% education, legal, community service, arts, and media, 3.5% healthcare practitioners, 15.8% service, 24.8% sales and office, 7.9% natural resources, construction, and maintenance, 11.8% production, transportation, and material moving
Income: Per capita: $30,077; Median household: $60,029; Average household: $76,782; Households with income of $100,000 or more: 29.1%; Poverty rate: 9.4%

Educational Attainment: High school diploma or higher: 90.8%; Bachelor's degree or higher: 29.7%; Graduate/professional degree or higher: 14.8%

School District(s)
Homer Central SD (KG-12)
   2014-15 Enrollment: 2,083 . . . . (607) 749-7241
Housing: Homeownership rate: 71.8%; Median home value: $122,700; Median year structure built: Before 1940; Homeowner vacancy rate: 0.0%; Median selected monthly owner costs: $1,311 with a mortgage, $656 without a mortgage; Median gross rent: $703 per month; Rental vacancy rate: 5.0%
Health Insurance: 92.5% have insurance; 72.8% have private insurance; 33.9% have public insurance; 7.5% do not have insurance; 10.1% of children under 18 do not have insurance
Transportation: Commute: 92.1% car, 0.9% public transportation, 2.6% walk, 4.0% work from home; Mean travel time to work: 22.2 minutes
Additional Information Contacts
Town of Homer . . . . (607) 749-4581
   http://www.cortland-co.org/Towns/Homer.htm

HOMER (village). Covers a land area of 1.925 square miles and a water area of 0.013 square miles. Located at 42.64° N. Lat; 76.19° W. Long. Elevation is 1,125 feet.
Population: 3,224; Growth (since 2000): -4.3%; Density: 1,674.4 persons per square mile; Race: 89.2% White, 1.8% Black/African American, 2.6% Asian, 0.0% American Indian/Alaska Native, 0.0% Native Hawaiian/Other Pacific Islander, 4.6% Two or more races, 3.9% Hispanic of any race; Average household size: 2.50; Median age: 36.9; Age under 18: 24.2%; Age 65 and over: 15.2%; Males per 100 females: 86.1; Marriage status: 32.5% never married, 45.6% now married, 2.5% separated, 7.2% widowed, 14.7% divorced; Foreign born: 3.3%; Speak English only: 93.6%; With disability: 14.9%; Veterans: 6.8%; Ancestry: 21.3% English, 15.5% Irish, 14.8% German, 8.5% American, 8.0% Italian
Employment: 9.1% management, business, and financial, 4.4% computer, engineering, and science, 19.2% education, legal, community service, arts, and media, 5.0% healthcare practitioners, 18.2% service, 27.3% sales and office, 5.0% natural resources, construction, and maintenance, 11.9% production, transportation, and material moving
Income: Per capita: $25,979; Median household: $47,083; Average household: $63,063; Households with income of $100,000 or more: 21.5%; Poverty rate: 11.1%
Educational Attainment: High school diploma or higher: 92.8%; Bachelor's degree or higher: 31.8%; Graduate/professional degree or higher: 11.8%

School District(s)
Homer Central SD (KG-12)
   2014-15 Enrollment: 2,083 . . . . (607) 749-7241
Housing: Homeownership rate: 61.7%; Median home value: $114,400; Median year structure built: Before 1940; Homeowner vacancy rate: 0.0%; Median selected monthly owner costs: $1,215 with a mortgage, $591 without a mortgage; Median gross rent: $668 per month; Rental vacancy rate: 0.0%
Health Insurance: 93.3% have insurance; 71.9% have private insurance; 36.3% have public insurance; 6.7% do not have insurance; 2.6% of children under 18 do not have insurance
Transportation: Commute: 91.6% car, 0.3% public transportation, 3.3% walk, 4.0% work from home; Mean travel time to work: 21.3 minutes

LAPEER (town). Covers a land area of 25.039 square miles and a water area of 0.143 square miles. Located at 42.46° N. Lat; 76.11° W. Long. Elevation is 1,329 feet.
Population: 848; Growth (since 2000): 23.6%; Density: 33.9 persons per square mile; Race: 97.2% White, 0.0% Black/African American, 0.0% Asian, 0.0% American Indian/Alaska Native, 0.0% Native Hawaiian/Other Pacific Islander, 2.2% Two or more races, 2.6% Hispanic of any race; Average household size: 3.15; Median age: 32.3; Age under 18: 35.6%; Age 65 and over: 11.6%; Males per 100 females: 100.3; Marriage status: 22.9% never married, 67.2% now married, 1.0% separated, 4.1% widowed, 5.8% divorced; Foreign born: 0.9%; Speak English only: 91.5%; With disability: 7.4%; Veterans: 8.4%; Ancestry: 18.8% Pennsylvania German, 13.3% English, 11.9% German, 10.1% Irish, 8.4% American
Employment: 21.2% management, business, and financial, 2.7% computer, engineering, and science, 6.5% education, legal, community service, arts, and media, 1.3% healthcare practitioners, 19.4% service,

19.6% sales and office, 12.6% natural resources, construction, and maintenance, 16.7% production, transportation, and material moving
Income: Per capita: $23,405; Median household: $53,036; Average household: $73,248; Households with income of $100,000 or more: 12.2%; Poverty rate: 13.3%
Educational Attainment: High school diploma or higher: 93.1%; Bachelor's degree or higher: 14.2%; Graduate/professional degree or higher: 2.2%
Housing: Homeownership rate: 92.9%; Median home value: $100,000; Median year structure built: 1978; Homeowner vacancy rate: 5.9%; Median selected monthly owner costs: $978 with a mortgage, $538 without a mortgage; Median gross rent: $911 per month; Rental vacancy rate: 0.0%
Health Insurance: 75.5% have insurance; 62.0% have private insurance; 24.6% have public insurance; 24.5% do not have insurance; 45.7% of children under 18 do not have insurance
Transportation: Commute: 86.6% car, 0.0% public transportation, 0.0% walk, 13.1% work from home; Mean travel time to work: 22.8 minutes

LITTLE YORK (unincorporated postal area)
ZCTA: 13087
Covers a land area of 0.204 square miles and a water area of 0.169 square miles. Located at 42.71° N. Lat; 76.15° W. Long. Elevation is 1,161 feet.
Population: 203; Growth (since 2000): n/a; Density: 993.3 persons per square mile; Race: 100.0% White, 0.0% Black/African American, 0.0% Asian, 0.0% American Indian/Alaska Native, 0.0% Native Hawaiian/Other Pacific Islander, 0.0% Two or more races, 0.0% Hispanic of any race; Average household size: 2.11; Median age: 58.3; Age under 18: 10.8%; Age 65 and over: 34.0%; Males per 100 females: 90.9; Marriage status: 9.9% never married, 85.6% now married, 2.8% separated, 2.8% widowed, 1.7% divorced; Foreign born: 1.5%; Speak English only: 100.0%; With disability: 4.9%; Veterans: 6.1%; Ancestry: 41.4% English, 20.2% American, 10.8% German, 8.4% Irish, 7.4% Welsh
Employment: 4.8% management, business, and financial, 0.0% computer, engineering, and science, 37.3% education, legal, community service, arts, and media, 2.4% healthcare practitioners, 11.9% service, 38.9% sales and office, 2.4% natural resources, construction, and maintenance, 2.4% production, transportation, and material moving
Income: Per capita: $48,211; Median household: $133,750; Average household: $103,448; Households with income of $100,000 or more: 64.6%; Poverty rate: 5.4%
Educational Attainment: High school diploma or higher: 100.0%; Bachelor's degree or higher: 73.4%; Graduate/professional degree or higher: 32.0%
Housing: Homeownership rate: 100.0%; Median home value: $292,500; Median year structure built: Before 1940; Homeowner vacancy rate: 0.0%; Median selected monthly owner costs: n/a with a mortgage, n/a without a mortgage; Median gross rent: n/a per month; Rental vacancy rate: 0.0%
Health Insurance: 100.0% have insurance; 93.1% have private insurance; 38.4% have public insurance; 0.0% do not have insurance; 0.0% of children under 18 do not have insurance
Transportation: Commute: 91.7% car, 0.0% public transportation, 0.0% walk, 0.0% work from home; Mean travel time to work: 38.6 minutes

MARATHON (town). Covers a land area of 24.937 square miles and a water area of 0.133 square miles. Located at 42.43° N. Lat; 76.00° W. Long. Elevation is 1,024 feet.
Population: 2,087; Growth (since 2000): -4.7%; Density: 83.7 persons per square mile; Race: 94.3% White, 1.9% Black/African American, 1.3% Asian, 0.3% American Indian/Alaska Native, 0.0% Native Hawaiian/Other Pacific Islander, 2.2% Two or more races, 1.7% Hispanic of any race; Average household size: 2.59; Median age: 38.2; Age under 18: 26.2%; Age 65 and over: 12.7%; Males per 100 females: 102.4; Marriage status: 30.7% never married, 54.9% now married, 5.9% separated, 6.2% widowed, 8.3% divorced; Foreign born: 1.7%; Speak English only: 98.3%; With disability: 11.7%; Veterans: 13.0%; Ancestry: 26.2% English, 11.4% German, 10.3% Irish, 6.9% American, 5.2% Italian
Employment: 11.6% management, business, and financial, 2.6% computer, engineering, and science, 11.0% education, legal, community service, arts, and media, 4.5% healthcare practitioners, 20.2% service, 17.7% sales and office, 13.7% natural resources, construction, and maintenance, 18.6% production, transportation, and material moving

Income: Per capita: $26,520; Median household: $50,703; Average household: $66,648; Households with income of $100,000 or more: 22.3%; Poverty rate: 10.3%
Educational Attainment: High school diploma or higher: 93.9%; Bachelor's degree or higher: 16.6%; Graduate/professional degree or higher: 4.5%

School District(s)
Marathon Central SD (PK-12)
   2014-15 Enrollment: 750 . . . . (607) 849-3117
Housing: Homeownership rate: 78.1%; Median home value: $111,000; Median year structure built: Before 1940; Homeowner vacancy rate: 0.9%; Median selected monthly owner costs: $1,341 with a mortgage, $485 without a mortgage; Median gross rent: $519 per month; Rental vacancy rate: 3.3%
Health Insurance: 92.4% have insurance; 74.8% have private insurance; 30.8% have public insurance; 7.6% do not have insurance; 3.5% of children under 18 do not have insurance
Transportation: Commute: 92.4% car, 0.6% public transportation, 1.9% walk, 4.6% work from home; Mean travel time to work: 25.0 minutes

MARATHON (village). Covers a land area of 1.130 square miles and a water area of 0.002 square miles. Located at 42.44° N. Lat; 76.04° W. Long. Elevation is 1,024 feet.
Population: 939; Growth (since 2000): -11.7%; Density: 831.3 persons per square mile; Race: 93.3% White, 0.0% Black/African American, 2.9% Asian, 0.0% American Indian/Alaska Native, 0.0% Native Hawaiian/Other Pacific Islander, 3.8% Two or more races, 0.6% Hispanic of any race; Average household size: 2.45; Median age: 39.6; Age under 18: 23.7%; Age 65 and over: 14.8%; Males per 100 females: 90.7; Marriage status: 34.3% never married, 49.6% now married, 7.5% separated, 6.0% widowed, 10.1% divorced; Foreign born: 3.3%; Speak English only: 97.5%; With disability: 15.5%; Veterans: 12.8%; Ancestry: 24.1% English, 11.7% German, 8.2% Irish, 6.0% American, 4.5% Italian
Employment: 7.5% management, business, and financial, 3.6% computer, engineering, and science, 10.6% education, legal, community service, arts, and media, 5.6% healthcare practitioners, 17.1% service, 19.1% sales and office, 11.8% natural resources, construction, and maintenance, 24.6% production, transportation, and material moving
Income: Per capita: $22,500; Median household: $42,039; Average household: $53,073; Households with income of $100,000 or more: 14.9%; Poverty rate: 16.8%
Educational Attainment: High school diploma or higher: 93.6%; Bachelor's degree or higher: 13.5%; Graduate/professional degree or higher: 5.8%

School District(s)
Marathon Central SD (PK-12)
   2014-15 Enrollment: 750 . . . . (607) 849-3117
Housing: Homeownership rate: 61.4%; Median home value: $107,800; Median year structure built: Before 1940; Homeowner vacancy rate: 2.5%; Median selected monthly owner costs: $1,223 with a mortgage, $483 without a mortgage; Median gross rent: $502 per month; Rental vacancy rate: 3.9%
Health Insurance: 89.9% have insurance; 68.9% have private insurance; 37.7% have public insurance; 10.1% do not have insurance; 0.0% of children under 18 do not have insurance
Transportation: Commute: 89.7% car, 0.0% public transportation, 4.4% walk, 5.9% work from home; Mean travel time to work: 23.2 minutes

MCGRAW (village). Covers a land area of 0.987 square miles and a water area of 0 square miles. Located at 42.59° N. Lat; 76.10° W. Long. Elevation is 1,158 feet.
History: Incorporated 1869.
Population: 936; Growth (since 2000): -6.4%; Density: 948.3 persons per square mile; Race: 96.9% White, 0.2% Black/African American, 0.0% Asian, 0.0% American Indian/Alaska Native, 0.0% Native Hawaiian/Other Pacific Islander, 2.6% Two or more races, 4.7% Hispanic of any race; Average household size: 2.46; Median age: 43.3; Age under 18: 21.3%; Age 65 and over: 22.5%; Males per 100 females: 98.7; Marriage status: 23.8% never married, 60.8% now married, 1.4% separated, 4.7% widowed, 10.8% divorced; Foreign born: 0.0%; Speak English only: 95.9%; With disability: 16.6%; Veterans: 12.8%; Ancestry: 20.3% English, 7.9% German, 7.7% Irish, 6.2% Italian, 4.3% American
Employment: 9.3% management, business, and financial, 4.1% computer, engineering, and science, 11.5% education, legal, community service, arts, and media, 4.6% healthcare practitioners, 22.6% service, 20.2% sales and

office, 9.1% natural resources, construction, and maintenance, 18.5% production, transportation, and material moving
Income: Per capita: $24,604; Median household: $49,844; Average household: $59,964; Households with income of $100,000 or more: 12.2%; Poverty rate: 10.2%
Educational Attainment: High school diploma or higher: 84.9%; Bachelor's degree or higher: 16.3%; Graduate/professional degree or higher: 7.5%

School District(s)
Mcgraw Central SD (KG-12)
   2014-15 Enrollment: 543 . . . . (607) 836-3636
Housing: Homeownership rate: 62.7%; Median home value: $92,600; Median year structure built: Before 1940; Homeowner vacancy rate: 2.9%; Median selected monthly owner costs: $1,099 with a mortgage, $586 without a mortgage; Median gross rent: $567 per month; Rental vacancy rate: 0.0%
Health Insurance: 92.2% have insurance; 70.1% have private insurance; 36.8% have public insurance; 7.8% do not have insurance; 4.5% of children under 18 do not have insurance
Transportation: Commute: 91.5% car, 0.7% public transportation, 3.3% walk, 3.5% work from home; Mean travel time to work: 21.2 minutes

MUNSONS CORNERS (CDP). Covers a land area of 2.219 square miles and a water area of 0.010 square miles. Located at 42.57° N. Lat; 76.20° W. Long. Elevation is 1,178 feet.
Population: 2,387; Growth (since 2000): -1.6%; Density: 1,075.7 persons per square mile; Race: 96.3% White, 0.5% Black/African American, 0.2% Asian, 0.0% American Indian/Alaska Native, 0.0% Native Hawaiian/Other Pacific Islander, 2.7% Two or more races, 5.0% Hispanic of any race; Average household size: 2.04; Median age: 37.1; Age under 18: 15.8%; Age 65 and over: 24.0%; Males per 100 females: 87.0; Marriage status: 37.8% never married, 31.6% now married, 0.2% separated, 18.2% widowed, 12.3% divorced; Foreign born: 2.5%; Speak English only: 97.9%; With disability: 19.1%; Veterans: 9.7%; Ancestry: 22.9% English, 15.8% Italian, 12.4% German, 11.5% Irish, 4.7% American
Employment: 8.5% management, business, and financial, 1.9% computer, engineering, and science, 21.2% education, legal, community service, arts, and media, 5.6% healthcare practitioners, 30.5% service, 15.9% sales and office, 3.7% natural resources, construction, and maintenance, 12.7% production, transportation, and material moving
Income: Per capita: $21,188; Median household: $39,417; Average household: $50,193; Households with income of $100,000 or more: 10.5%; Poverty rate: 8.0%
Educational Attainment: High school diploma or higher: 90.9%; Bachelor's degree or higher: 29.8%; Graduate/professional degree or higher: 15.3%
Housing: Homeownership rate: 51.2%; Median home value: $120,300; Median year structure built: 1969; Homeowner vacancy rate: 0.0%; Median selected monthly owner costs: $1,302 with a mortgage, $532 without a mortgage; Median gross rent: $706 per month; Rental vacancy rate: 10.5%
Health Insurance: 95.0% have insurance; 74.4% have private insurance; 44.2% have public insurance; 5.0% do not have insurance; 2.9% of children under 18 do not have insurance
Transportation: Commute: 81.8% car, 1.6% public transportation, 6.8% walk, 8.3% work from home; Mean travel time to work: 13.3 minutes

PREBLE (town). Covers a land area of 26.845 square miles and a water area of 0.715 square miles. Located at 42.74° N. Lat; 76.13° W. Long. Elevation is 1,224 feet.
Population: 1,503; Growth (since 2000): -5.0%; Density: 56.0 persons per square mile; Race: 98.5% White, 0.8% Black/African American, 0.7% Asian, 0.0% American Indian/Alaska Native, 0.0% Native Hawaiian/Other Pacific Islander, 0.0% Two or more races, 0.8% Hispanic of any race; Average household size: 2.65; Median age: 43.0; Age under 18: 25.9%; Age 65 and over: 14.4%; Males per 100 females: 107.0; Marriage status: 32.2% never married, 53.4% now married, 2.3% separated, 4.3% widowed, 10.2% divorced; Foreign born: 0.5%; Speak English only: 98.1%; With disability: 12.4%; Veterans: 10.8%; Ancestry: 21.4% English, 17.6% Irish, 14.5% German, 6.6% Italian, 5.1% American
Employment: 13.9% management, business, and financial, 5.9% computer, engineering, and science, 9.2% education, legal, community service, arts, and media, 9.4% healthcare practitioners, 12.1% service, 19.6% sales and office, 11.3% natural resources, construction, and maintenance, 18.5% production, transportation, and material moving

Income: Per capita: $29,391; Median household: $60,714; Average household: $75,401; Households with income of $100,000 or more: 27.6%; Poverty rate: 11.9%
Educational Attainment: High school diploma or higher: 92.0%; Bachelor's degree or higher: 26.8%; Graduate/professional degree or higher: 9.2%
Housing: Homeownership rate: 84.3%; Median home value: $116,600; Median year structure built: 1967; Homeowner vacancy rate: 0.0%; Median selected monthly owner costs: $1,474 with a mortgage, $543 without a mortgage; Median gross rent: $865 per month; Rental vacancy rate: 0.0%
Health Insurance: 89.6% have insurance; 75.8% have private insurance; 27.7% have public insurance; 10.4% do not have insurance; 2.8% of children under 18 do not have insurance
Transportation: Commute: 92.6% car, 0.7% public transportation, 1.3% walk, 4.5% work from home; Mean travel time to work: 27.2 minutes
Additional Information Contacts
Town of Preble . . . . (607) 749-3199
  http://www.preble-ny.org

SCOTT (town). Covers a land area of 22.267 square miles and a water area of 0.147 square miles. Located at 42.74° N. Lat; 76.24° W. Long. Elevation is 1,411 feet.
Population: 1,022; Growth (since 2000): -14.3%; Density: 45.9 persons per square mile; Race: 100.0% White, 0.0% Black/African American, 0.0% Asian, 0.0% American Indian/Alaska Native, 0.0% Native Hawaiian/Other Pacific Islander, 0.0% Two or more races, 0.6% Hispanic of any race; Average household size: 2.95; Median age: 42.5; Age under 18: 24.7%; Age 65 and over: 15.2%; Males per 100 females: 108.1; Marriage status: 27.2% never married, 60.4% now married, 2.0% separated, 5.6% widowed, 6.7% divorced; Foreign born: 0.2%; Speak English only: 97.0%; With disability: 13.0%; Veterans: 11.6%; Ancestry: 21.0% English, 15.1% German, 13.3% Irish, 11.6% American, 4.3% Italian
Employment: 6.7% management, business, and financial, 2.6% computer, engineering, and science, 5.6% education, legal, community service, arts, and media, 5.2% healthcare practitioners, 18.5% service, 25.0% sales and office, 12.1% natural resources, construction, and maintenance, 24.4% production, transportation, and material moving
Income: Per capita: $24,653; Median household: $63,906; Average household: $70,439; Households with income of $100,000 or more: 20.5%; Poverty rate: 11.0%
Educational Attainment: High school diploma or higher: 85.6%; Bachelor's degree or higher: 18.2%; Graduate/professional degree or higher: 7.9%
Housing: Homeownership rate: 89.0%; Median home value: $101,200; Median year structure built: 1965; Homeowner vacancy rate: 1.0%; Median selected monthly owner costs: $1,261 with a mortgage, $554 without a mortgage; Median gross rent: $653 per month; Rental vacancy rate: 0.0%
Health Insurance: 94.8% have insurance; 77.1% have private insurance; 30.4% have public insurance; 5.2% do not have insurance; 2.0% of children under 18 do not have insurance
Transportation: Commute: 94.6% car, 1.7% public transportation, 0.0% walk, 3.7% work from home; Mean travel time to work: 31.6 minutes

SOLON (town). Covers a land area of 29.651 square miles and a water area of 0.076 square miles. Located at 42.61° N. Lat; 76.02° W. Long. Elevation is 1,312 feet.
Population: 1,169; Growth (since 2000): 5.5%; Density: 39.4 persons per square mile; Race: 96.5% White, 0.0% Black/African American, 0.0% Asian, 0.0% American Indian/Alaska Native, 1.8% Native Hawaiian/Other Pacific Islander, 1.7% Two or more races, 1.4% Hispanic of any race; Average household size: 2.96; Median age: 38.8; Age under 18: 23.7%; Age 65 and over: 10.7%; Males per 100 females: 100.6; Marriage status: 34.3% never married, 52.1% now married, 1.7% separated, 2.5% widowed, 11.1% divorced; Foreign born: 0.8%; Speak English only: 99.6%; With disability: 10.6%; Veterans: 10.1%; Ancestry: 17.2% Irish, 16.3% English, 11.9% American, 9.9% German, 4.5% Pennsylvania German
Employment: 10.6% management, business, and financial, 2.5% computer, engineering, and science, 3.7% education, legal, community service, arts, and media, 3.3% healthcare practitioners, 19.8% service, 23.2% sales and office, 15.6% natural resources, construction, and maintenance, 21.2% production, transportation, and material moving
Income: Per capita: $22,552; Median household: $56,442; Average household: $63,904; Households with income of $100,000 or more: 16.5%; Poverty rate: 10.6%

Educational Attainment: High school diploma or higher: 90.8%; Bachelor's degree or higher: 14.2%; Graduate/professional degree or higher: 7.3%
Housing: Homeownership rate: 81.0%; Median home value: $90,000; Median year structure built: 1980; Homeowner vacancy rate: 0.0%; Median selected monthly owner costs: $1,083 with a mortgage, $529 without a mortgage; Median gross rent: $903 per month; Rental vacancy rate: 0.0%
Health Insurance: 88.7% have insurance; 69.9% have private insurance; 27.3% have public insurance; 11.3% do not have insurance; 12.3% of children under 18 do not have insurance
Transportation: Commute: 95.0% car, 0.0% public transportation, 0.3% walk, 2.9% work from home; Mean travel time to work: 24.3 minutes

TAYLOR (town). Covers a land area of 29.995 square miles and a water area of 0.124 square miles. Located at 42.60° N. Lat; 75.92° W. Long. Elevation is 1,109 feet.
Population: 450; Growth (since 2000): -10.0%; Density: 15.0 persons per square mile; Race: 97.8% White, 0.0% Black/African American, 1.6% Asian, 0.0% American Indian/Alaska Native, 0.0% Native Hawaiian/Other Pacific Islander, 0.7% Two or more races, 2.4% Hispanic of any race; Average household size: 2.50; Median age: 45.6; Age under 18: 22.2%; Age 65 and over: 13.6%; Males per 100 females: 99.6; Marriage status: 24.3% never married, 60.0% now married, 3.0% separated, 8.4% widowed, 7.3% divorced; Foreign born: 2.7%; Speak English only: 99.8%; With disability: 12.9%; Veterans: 9.5%; Ancestry: 18.9% English, 11.1% German, 9.3% American, 4.9% Irish, 4.4% Dutch
Employment: 16.2% management, business, and financial, 1.4% computer, engineering, and science, 13.5% education, legal, community service, arts, and media, 4.5% healthcare practitioners, 18.5% service, 17.1% sales and office, 19.4% natural resources, construction, and maintenance, 9.5% production, transportation, and material moving
Income: Per capita: $25,461; Median household: $47,727; Average household: $62,114; Households with income of $100,000 or more: 14.5%; Poverty rate: 2.7%
Educational Attainment: High school diploma or higher: 92.2%; Bachelor's degree or higher: 19.7%; Graduate/professional degree or higher: 9.1%
Housing: Homeownership rate: 71.7%; Median home value: $97,500; Median year structure built: 1972; Homeowner vacancy rate: 0.0%; Median selected monthly owner costs: $982 with a mortgage, $517 without a mortgage; Median gross rent: $821 per month; Rental vacancy rate: 0.0%
Health Insurance: 96.4% have insurance; 83.1% have private insurance; 25.6% have public insurance; 3.6% do not have insurance; 0.0% of children under 18 do not have insurance
Transportation: Commute: 96.7% car, 0.0% public transportation, 0.9% walk, 2.4% work from home; Mean travel time to work: 26.0 minutes

TRUXTON (town). Covers a land area of 44.649 square miles and a water area of 0.078 square miles. Located at 42.71° N. Lat; 76.02° W. Long. Elevation is 1,152 feet.
Population: 1,029; Growth (since 2000): -16.0%; Density: 23.0 persons per square mile; Race: 98.2% White, 0.3% Black/African American, 0.0% Asian, 0.0% American Indian/Alaska Native, 0.0% Native Hawaiian/Other Pacific Islander, 1.4% Two or more races, 0.5% Hispanic of any race; Average household size: 2.50; Median age: 44.0; Age under 18: 23.1%; Age 65 and over: 14.5%; Males per 100 females: 103.4; Marriage status: 27.0% never married, 53.6% now married, 4.4% separated, 8.4% widowed, 10.9% divorced; Foreign born: 0.6%; Speak English only: 98.0%; With disability: 9.8%; Veterans: 9.6%; Ancestry: 26.9% English, 18.5% German, 16.2% Irish, 5.2% American, 5.2% Scottish
Employment: 16.4% management, business, and financial, 4.0% computer, engineering, and science, 9.1% education, legal, community service, arts, and media, 4.7% healthcare practitioners, 18.1% service, 28.7% sales and office, 9.2% natural resources, construction, and maintenance, 9.8% production, transportation, and material moving
Income: Per capita: $29,794; Median household: $62,589; Average household: $73,289; Households with income of $100,000 or more: 22.3%; Poverty rate: 7.6%
Educational Attainment: High school diploma or higher: 90.1%; Bachelor's degree or higher: 24.4%; Graduate/professional degree or higher: 9.6%
School District(s)
Homer Central SD (KG-12)
    2014-15 Enrollment: 2,083 . . . . (607) 749-7241

Housing: Homeownership rate: 77.3%; Median home value: $114,400; Median year structure built: 1975; Homeowner vacancy rate: 0.9%; Median selected monthly owner costs: $1,238 with a mortgage, $565 without a mortgage; Median gross rent: $688 per month; Rental vacancy rate: 0.0%
Health Insurance: 89.8% have insurance; 71.8% have private insurance; 30.6% have public insurance; 10.2% do not have insurance; 5.9% of children under 18 do not have insurance
Transportation: Commute: 92.3% car, 0.0% public transportation, 3.3% walk, 4.4% work from home; Mean travel time to work: 28.5 minutes

VIRGIL (town). Covers a land area of 47.363 square miles and a water area of 0.036 square miles. Located at 42.52° N. Lat; 76.16° W. Long. Elevation is 1,404 feet.
Population: 2,604; Growth (since 2000): 13.9%; Density: 55.0 persons per square mile; Race: 96.0% White, 1.7% Black/African American, 0.0% Asian, 0.3% American Indian/Alaska Native, 0.0% Native Hawaiian/Other Pacific Islander, 1.9% Two or more races, 2.4% Hispanic of any race; Average household size: 2.85; Median age: 41.5; Age under 18: 21.2%; Age 65 and over: 13.3%; Males per 100 females: 103.0; Marriage status: 29.9% never married, 55.6% now married, 0.8% separated, 5.9% widowed, 8.6% divorced; Foreign born: 2.4%; Speak English only: 96.6%; With disability: 10.6%; Veterans: 7.0%; Ancestry: 17.8% English, 12.7% German, 12.0% American, 11.6% Irish, 7.3% Italian
Employment: 12.2% management, business, and financial, 5.3% computer, engineering, and science, 11.3% education, legal, community service, arts, and media, 6.2% healthcare practitioners, 15.2% service, 17.6% sales and office, 12.1% natural resources, construction, and maintenance, 20.1% production, transportation, and material moving
Income: Per capita: $29,373; Median household: $59,716; Average household: $78,034; Households with income of $100,000 or more: 24.7%; Poverty rate: 6.8%
Educational Attainment: High school diploma or higher: 88.1%; Bachelor's degree or higher: 24.6%; Graduate/professional degree or higher: 12.9%
Housing: Homeownership rate: 81.1%; Median home value: $123,400; Median year structure built: 1975; Homeowner vacancy rate: 1.7%; Median selected monthly owner costs: $1,328 with a mortgage, $592 without a mortgage; Median gross rent: $710 per month; Rental vacancy rate: 0.0%
Health Insurance: 91.0% have insurance; 76.6% have private insurance; 26.8% have public insurance; 9.0% do not have insurance; 9.1% of children under 18 do not have insurance
Transportation: Commute: 86.9% car, 0.4% public transportation, 2.2% walk, 8.6% work from home; Mean travel time to work: 28.2 minutes

WILLET (town). Covers a land area of 25.733 square miles and a water area of 0.321 square miles. Located at 42.45° N. Lat; 75.92° W. Long. Elevation is 1,040 feet.
Population: 1,177; Growth (since 2000): 16.4%; Density: 45.7 persons per square mile; Race: 96.8% White, 0.3% Black/African American, 0.0% Asian, 0.3% American Indian/Alaska Native, 0.0% Native Hawaiian/Other Pacific Islander, 2.6% Two or more races, 2.0% Hispanic of any race; Average household size: 2.86; Median age: 34.8; Age under 18: 26.8%; Age 65 and over: 9.0%; Males per 100 females: 106.1; Marriage status: 31.9% never married, 57.0% now married, 0.7% separated, 2.8% widowed, 8.3% divorced; Foreign born: 0.5%; Speak English only: 98.7%; With disability: 9.2%; Veterans: 9.1%; Ancestry: 17.7% English, 10.7% Irish, 9.4% German, 6.0% American, 5.4% Italian
Employment: 10.4% management, business, and financial, 0.4% computer, engineering, and science, 9.9% education, legal, community service, arts, and media, 9.5% healthcare practitioners, 15.9% service, 16.5% sales and office, 30.1% natural resources, construction, and maintenance, 7.3% production, transportation, and material moving
Income: Per capita: $21,644; Median household: $52,868; Average household: $60,765; Households with income of $100,000 or more: 20.0%; Poverty rate: 13.9%
Educational Attainment: High school diploma or higher: 91.5%; Bachelor's degree or higher: 10.0%; Graduate/professional degree or higher: 4.1%
Housing: Homeownership rate: 82.5%; Median home value: $79,200; Median year structure built: 1965; Homeowner vacancy rate: 0.0%; Median selected monthly owner costs: $1,174 with a mortgage, $367 without a mortgage; Median gross rent: $525 per month; Rental vacancy rate: 0.0%
Health Insurance: 92.9% have insurance; 74.3% have private insurance; 27.7% have public insurance; 7.1% do not have insurance; 3.5% of children under 18 do not have insurance

Transportation: Commute: 90.1% car, 0.0% public transportation, 1.5% walk, 8.5% work from home; Mean travel time to work: 33.0 minutes

Delaware County

Located in southern New York, in the west Catskills; bounded on the northwest by the Susquehanna River, and on the southwest by the Delaware River and the Pennsylvania border. Covers a land area of 1,442.440 square miles, a water area of 25.006 square miles, and is located in the Eastern Time Zone at 42.19° N. Lat., 74.97° W. Long. The county was founded in 1797. County seat is Delhi.

Weather Station: Delhi 2 SE   **Elevation: 1,439 feet**

	Jan	Feb	Mar	Apr	May	Jun	Jul	Aug	Sep	Oct	Nov	Dec
High	31	34	42	55	67	75	79	78	71	59	47	36
Low	11	12	20	32	41	50	54	53	46	35	28	18
Precip	3.2	2.5	3.5	3.9	4.2	4.6	4.6	3.6	4.4	4.0	3.9	3.5
Snow	18.2	12.4	11.2	3.8	0.1	0.0	0.0	0.0	0.0	0.6	4.3	14.8

High and Low temperatures in degrees Fahrenheit; Precipitation and Snow in inches

Weather Station: Deposit   **Elevation: 1,000 feet**

	Jan	Feb	Mar	Apr	May	Jun	Jul	Aug	Sep	Oct	Nov	Dec
High	32	36	45	59	70	77	81	80	72	60	48	36
Low	14	16	23	34	44	53	57	56	50	38	30	20
Precip	2.8	2.5	3.2	3.9	3.9	4.2	4.1	3.8	4.0	3.7	3.8	3.1
Snow	na	na	na	1.7	0.0	0.0	0.0	0.0	0.0	tr	1.7	na

High and Low temperatures in degrees Fahrenheit; Precipitation and Snow in inches

Population: 46,901; Growth (since 2000): -2.4%; Density: 32.5 persons per square mile; Race: 95.1% White, 2.0% Black/African American, 0.6% Asian, 0.2% American Indian/Alaska Native, 0.0% Native Hawaiian/Other Pacific Islander, 1.5% two or more races, 3.5% Hispanic of any race; Average household size: 2.31; Median age: 46.4; Age under 18: 18.4%; Age 65 and over: 21.3%; Males per 100 females: 100.9; Marriage status: 30.1% never married, 50.9% now married, 3.1% separated, 7.5% widowed, 11.5% divorced; Foreign born: 3.7%; Speak English only: 94.5%; With disability: 16.6%; Veterans: 9.6%; Ancestry: 21.9% German, 19.3% Irish, 12.8% English, 11.4% Italian, 7.2% American

Religion: Six largest groups: 17.8% Catholicism, 8.7% Methodist/Pietist, 3.9% Presbyterian-Reformed, 3.5% Holiness, 3.2% Muslim Estimate, 1.3% Episcopalianism/Anglicanism

Economy: Unemployment rate: 4.8%; Leading industries: 18.2 % retail trade; 12.0 % construction; 11.8 % other services (except public administration); Farms: 704 totaling 145,608 acres; Company size: 0 employ 1,000 or more persons, 3 employ 500 to 999 persons, 13 employ 100 to 499 persons, 1,025 employ less than 100 persons; Business ownership: 1,302 women-owned, 26 Black-owned, 31 Hispanic-owned, 48 Asian-owned, 33 American Indian/Alaska Native-owned

Employment: 11.0% management, business, and financial, 3.0% computer, engineering, and science, 11.8% education, legal, community service, arts, and media, 5.0% healthcare practitioners, 20.9% service, 21.5% sales and office, 11.7% natural resources, construction, and maintenance, 15.1% production, transportation, and material moving

Income: Per capita: $23,835; Median household: $43,720; Average household: $55,606; Households with income of $100,000 or more: 13.9%; Poverty rate: 15.3%

Educational Attainment: High school diploma or higher: 87.0%; Bachelor's degree or higher: 20.2%; Graduate/professional degree or higher: 8.7%

Housing: Homeownership rate: 72.7%; Median home value: $132,400; Median year structure built: 1971; Homeowner vacancy rate: 2.9%; Median selected monthly owner costs: $1,156 with a mortgage, $491 without a mortgage; Median gross rent: $668 per month; Rental vacancy rate: 5.4%

Vital Statistics: Birth rate: 79.5 per 10,000 population; Death rate: 116.6 per 10,000 population; Age-adjusted cancer mortality rate: 161.8 deaths per 100,000 population

Health Insurance: 90.9% have insurance; 66.8% have private insurance; 42.4% have public insurance; 9.1% do not have insurance; 6.2% of children under 18 do not have insurance

Health Care: Physicians: 6.7 per 10,000 population; Dentists: 2.8 per 10,000 population; Hospital beds: 11.9 per 10,000 population; Hospital admissions: 265.0 per 10,000 population

Transportation: Commute: 84.6% car, 1.5% public transportation, 6.6% walk, 6.3% work from home; Mean travel time to work: 23.2 minutes

2016 Presidential Election: 60.9% Trump, 33.8% Clinton, 3.3% Johnson, 1.9% Stein

National and State Parks: Delaware State Forest

Additional Information Contacts

Delaware Government . . . . (607) 746-2123
  http://www.co.delaware.ny.us

Delaware County Communities

ANDES (CDP). Covers a land area of 1.193 square miles and a water area of <.001 square miles. Located at 42.19° N. Lat; 74.78° W. Long. Elevation is 1,598 feet.

Population: 230; Growth (since 2000): -20.4%; Density: 192.7 persons per square mile; Race: 97.0% White, 0.0% Black/African American, 1.7% Asian, 1.3% American Indian/Alaska Native, 0.0% Native Hawaiian/Other Pacific Islander, 0.0% Two or more races, 0.0% Hispanic of any race; Average household size: 2.45; Median age: 41.7; Age under 18: 27.0%; Age 65 and over: 27.4%; Males per 100 females: 96.9; Marriage status: 11.2% never married, 61.2% now married, 1.7% separated, 12.9% widowed, 14.6% divorced; Foreign born: 3.0%; Speak English only: 96.4%; With disability: 11.7%; Veterans: 14.3%; Ancestry: 37.0% German, 15.2% English, 10.9% Irish, 8.3% Italian, 4.3% American

Employment: 9.0% management, business, and financial, 0.0% computer, engineering, and science, 19.8% education, legal, community service, arts, and media, 4.5% healthcare practitioners, 25.2% service, 18.9% sales and office, 16.2% natural resources, construction, and maintenance, 6.3% production, transportation, and material moving

Income: Per capita: $24,594; Median household: $46,250; Average household: $57,129; Households with income of $100,000 or more: 10.7%; Poverty rate: 24.7%

Educational Attainment: High school diploma or higher: 90.8%; Bachelor's degree or higher: 35.0%; Graduate/professional degree or higher: 15.3%

School District(s)

Andes Central SD (PK-12)
    2014-15 Enrollment: 100 . . . . (845) 676-3167

Housing: Homeownership rate: 79.8%; Median home value: $186,800; Median year structure built: Before 1940; Homeowner vacancy rate: 10.7%; Median selected monthly owner costs: $1,433 with a mortgage, $441 without a mortgage; Median gross rent: $785 per month; Rental vacancy rate: 0.0%

Health Insurance: 95.2% have insurance; 48.3% have private insurance; 60.9% have public insurance; 4.8% do not have insurance; 0.0% of children under 18 do not have insurance

Transportation: Commute: 73.4% car, 2.8% public transportation, 11.0% walk, 12.8% work from home; Mean travel time to work: 25.9 minutes

ANDES (town). Covers a land area of 108.592 square miles and a water area of 3.694 square miles. Located at 42.13° N. Lat; 74.79° W. Long. Elevation is 1,598 feet.

Population: 1,142; Growth (since 2000): -15.8%; Density: 10.5 persons per square mile; Race: 97.0% White, 1.1% Black/African American, 1.1% Asian, 0.3% American Indian/Alaska Native, 0.0% Native Hawaiian/Other Pacific Islander, 0.4% Two or more races, 1.1% Hispanic of any race; Average household size: 2.28; Median age: 55.3; Age under 18: 16.3%; Age 65 and over: 29.8%; Males per 100 females: 107.8; Marriage status: 19.7% never married, 60.3% now married, 0.8% separated, 9.8% widowed, 10.2% divorced; Foreign born: 5.6%; Speak English only: 95.8%; With disability: 18.9%; Veterans: 12.7%; Ancestry: 22.2% English, 22.0% German, 13.0% Italian, 12.0% Irish, 9.9% American

Employment: 15.9% management, business, and financial, 1.6% computer, engineering, and science, 12.5% education, legal, community service, arts, and media, 6.2% healthcare practitioners, 19.8% service, 14.4% sales and office, 23.9% natural resources, construction, and maintenance, 5.7% production, transportation, and material moving

Income: Per capita: $27,816; Median household: $45,096; Average household: $59,922; Households with income of $100,000 or more: 15.8%; Poverty rate: 18.7%

Educational Attainment: High school diploma or higher: 88.7%; Bachelor's degree or higher: 26.6%; Graduate/professional degree or higher: 12.2%

School District(s)

Andes Central SD (PK-12)
    2014-15 Enrollment: 100 . . . . (845) 676-3167

Housing: Homeownership rate: 91.2%; Median home value: $215,400; Median year structure built: 1975; Homeowner vacancy rate: 3.2%; Median

selected monthly owner costs: $1,380 with a mortgage, $518 without a mortgage; Median gross rent: $845 per month; Rental vacancy rate: 18.5%
Health Insurance: 94.8% have insurance; 61.6% have private insurance; 54.9% have public insurance; 5.2% do not have insurance; 0.0% of children under 18 do not have insurance
Transportation: Commute: 75.1% car, 3.6% public transportation, 5.5% walk, 15.2% work from home; Mean travel time to work: 28.3 minutes

ARKVILLE (unincorporated postal area)
ZCTA: 12406

Covers a land area of 43.232 square miles and a water area of 0.080 square miles. Located at 42.08° N. Lat; 74.52° W. Long. Elevation is 1,365 feet.
Population: 789; Growth (since 2000): -11.5%; Density: 18.3 persons per square mile; Race: 92.9% White, 0.0% Black/African American, 0.0% Asian, 2.9% American Indian/Alaska Native, 0.0% Native Hawaiian/Other Pacific Islander, 4.2% Two or more races, 6.5% Hispanic of any race; Average household size: 1.80; Median age: 48.9; Age under 18: 14.8%; Age 65 and over: 12.0%; Males per 100 females: 94.6; Marriage status: 30.4% never married, 36.2% now married, 8.2% separated, 8.4% widowed, 24.9% divorced; Foreign born: 3.4%; Speak English only: 90.1%; With disability: 19.3%; Veterans: 9.1%; Ancestry: 44.1% German, 27.4% Irish, 14.8% French, 14.4% Italian, 14.3% English
Employment: 9.4% management, business, and financial, 0.6% computer, engineering, and science, 5.4% education, legal, community service, arts, and media, 7.4% healthcare practitioners, 42.2% service, 21.4% sales and office, 12.3% natural resources, construction, and maintenance, 1.4% production, transportation, and material moving
Income: Per capita: $39,341; Median household: $41,111; Average household: $70,540; Households with income of $100,000 or more: 11.1%; Poverty rate: 20.2%
Educational Attainment: High school diploma or higher: 90.0%; Bachelor's degree or higher: 24.0%; Graduate/professional degree or higher: 6.1%
Housing: Homeownership rate: 67.1%; Median home value: $173,900; Median year structure built: 1966; Homeowner vacancy rate: 2.0%; Median selected monthly owner costs: $1,114 with a mortgage, $481 without a mortgage; Median gross rent: $734 per month; Rental vacancy rate: 16.3%
Health Insurance: 90.0% have insurance; 61.7% have private insurance; 37.6% have public insurance; 10.0% do not have insurance; 0.0% of children under 18 do not have insurance
Newspapers: Catskill Mountain News (weekly circulation 4,000)
Transportation: Commute: 84.8% car, 2.6% public transportation, 11.5% walk, 1.1% work from home; Mean travel time to work: 16.5 minutes

BLOOMVILLE (CDP). Covers a land area of 1.317 square miles and a water area of 0.002 square miles. Located at 42.33° N. Lat; 74.82° W. Long. Elevation is 1,457 feet.
Population: 186; Growth (since 2000): n/a; Density: 141.3 persons per square mile; Race: 100.0% White, 0.0% Black/African American, 0.0% Asian, 0.0% American Indian/Alaska Native, 0.0% Native Hawaiian/Other Pacific Islander, 0.0% Two or more races, 0.0% Hispanic of any race; Average household size: 2.62; Median age: 46.8; Age under 18: 7.0%; Age 65 and over: 19.9%; Males per 100 females: 104.8; Marriage status: 33.0% never married, 62.5% now married, 2.3% separated, 1.7% widowed, 2.8% divorced; Foreign born: 2.2%; Speak English only: 100.0%; With disability: 23.7%; Veterans: 6.4%; Ancestry: 21.0% German, 14.0% European, 13.4% Polish, 11.3% Irish, 11.3% Scottish
Employment: 11.9% management, business, and financial, 19.5% computer, engineering, and science, 13.6% education, legal, community service, arts, and media, 2.5% healthcare practitioners, 16.1% service, 11.0% sales and office, 9.3% natural resources, construction, and maintenance, 16.1% production, transportation, and material moving
Income: Per capita: $26,997; Median household: $63,393; Average household: $67,299; Households with income of $100,000 or more: 14.1%; Poverty rate: 8.1%
Educational Attainment: High school diploma or higher: 89.0%; Bachelor's degree or higher: 15.1%; Graduate/professional degree or higher: 5.5%
Housing: Homeownership rate: 87.3%; Median home value: $102,100; Median year structure built: Before 1940; Homeowner vacancy rate: 0.0%; Median selected monthly owner costs: $883 with a mortgage, $339 without

a mortgage; Median gross rent: $569 per month; Rental vacancy rate: 0.0%
Health Insurance: 98.4% have insurance; 86.6% have private insurance; 33.9% have public insurance; 1.6% do not have insurance; 0.0% of children under 18 do not have insurance
Transportation: Commute: 90.3% car, 0.0% public transportation, 9.7% walk, 0.0% work from home; Mean travel time to work: 16.1 minutes

BOVINA (town). Covers a land area of 44.263 square miles and a water area of 0.232 square miles. Located at 42.27° N. Lat; 74.76° W. Long. Elevation is 1,844 feet.
Population: 620; Growth (since 2000): -6.6%; Density: 14.0 persons per square mile; Race: 98.2% White, 0.0% Black/African American, 0.8% Asian, 0.5% American Indian/Alaska Native, 0.0% Native Hawaiian/Other Pacific Islander, 0.5% Two or more races, 2.9% Hispanic of any race; Average household size: 2.48; Median age: 44.6; Age under 18: 21.8%; Age 65 and over: 20.0%; Males per 100 females: 109.6; Marriage status: 30.8% never married, 57.1% now married, 3.8% separated, 2.9% widowed, 9.2% divorced; Foreign born: 7.4%; Speak English only: 88.8%; With disability: 12.6%; Veterans: 14.2%; Ancestry: 23.2% German, 16.1% Irish, 14.0% English, 9.7% Dutch, 8.5% Italian
Employment: 9.5% management, business, and financial, 0.7% computer, engineering, and science, 15.5% education, legal, community service, arts, and media, 3.9% healthcare practitioners, 15.9% service, 26.5% sales and office, 16.3% natural resources, construction, and maintenance, 11.7% production, transportation, and material moving
Income: Per capita: $32,504; Median household: $53,750; Average household: $78,338; Households with income of $100,000 or more: 22.0%; Poverty rate: 15.5%
Educational Attainment: High school diploma or higher: 92.3%; Bachelor's degree or higher: 30.9%; Graduate/professional degree or higher: 15.6%
Housing: Homeownership rate: 80.0%; Median home value: $214,300; Median year structure built: 1976; Homeowner vacancy rate: 6.5%; Median selected monthly owner costs: $1,575 with a mortgage, $730 without a mortgage; Median gross rent: $933 per month; Rental vacancy rate: 0.0%
Health Insurance: 86.9% have insurance; 63.7% have private insurance; 42.9% have public insurance; 13.1% do not have insurance; 12.6% of children under 18 do not have insurance
Transportation: Commute: 71.6% car, 6.3% public transportation, 9.6% walk, 12.5% work from home; Mean travel time to work: 29.1 minutes

BOVINA CENTER (unincorporated postal area)
ZCTA: 13740

Covers a land area of 39.569 square miles and a water area of 0.050 square miles. Located at 42.27° N. Lat; 74.76° W. Long. Elevation is 1,660 feet.
Population: 489; Growth (since 2000): -13.9%; Density: 12.4 persons per square mile; Race: 97.8% White, 0.0% Black/African American, 1.0% Asian, 0.6% American Indian/Alaska Native, 0.0% Native Hawaiian/Other Pacific Islander, 0.6% Two or more races, 2.9% Hispanic of any race; Average household size: 2.36; Median age: 48.7; Age under 18: 20.4%; Age 65 and over: 23.3%; Males per 100 females: 109.8; Marriage status: 30.4% never married, 56.5% now married, 4.8% separated, 3.6% widowed, 9.4% divorced; Foreign born: 9.0%; Speak English only: 88.8%; With disability: 14.7%; Veterans: 14.9%; Ancestry: 21.5% German, 15.7% English, 15.3% Irish, 7.8% Scottish, 6.7% Italian
Employment: 10.2% management, business, and financial, 0.9% computer, engineering, and science, 19.0% education, legal, community service, arts, and media, 3.2% healthcare practitioners, 13.0% service, 25.0% sales and office, 15.7% natural resources, construction, and maintenance, 13.0% production, transportation, and material moving
Income: Per capita: $33,164; Median household: $50,938; Average household: $75,588; Households with income of $100,000 or more: 20.2%; Poverty rate: 18.2%
Educational Attainment: High school diploma or higher: 91.9%; Bachelor's degree or higher: 31.6%; Graduate/professional degree or higher: 18.0%
Housing: Homeownership rate: 77.8%; Median home value: $227,200; Median year structure built: 1979; Homeowner vacancy rate: 5.3%; Median selected monthly owner costs: $1,813 with a mortgage, $730 without a mortgage; Median gross rent: $950 per month; Rental vacancy rate: 0.0%

Health Insurance: 85.7% have insurance; 64.2% have private insurance; 43.1% have public insurance; 14.3% do not have insurance; 15.0% of children under 18 do not have insurance

Transportation: Commute: 73.5% car, 6.9% public transportation, 6.4% walk, 13.2% work from home; Mean travel time to work: 34.2 minutes

COLCHESTER (town). Covers a land area of 136.778 square miles and a water area of 5.398 square miles. Located at 42.04° N. Lat; 74.95° W. Long. Elevation is 1,280 feet.

Population: 2,089; Growth (since 2000): 2.3%; Density: 15.3 persons per square mile; Race: 97.3% White, 0.4% Black/African American, 0.0% Asian, 0.6% American Indian/Alaska Native, 0.0% Native Hawaiian/Other Pacific Islander, 1.4% Two or more races, 3.3% Hispanic of any race; Average household size: 2.32; Median age: 48.4; Age under 18: 20.2%; Age 65 and over: 24.0%; Males per 100 females: 103.6; Marriage status: 28.2% never married, 48.9% now married, 1.5% separated, 11.4% widowed, 11.5% divorced; Foreign born: 2.3%; Speak English only: 95.3%; With disability: 11.9%; Veterans: 10.3%; Ancestry: 29.9% German, 19.7% Irish, 10.7% Italian, 9.6% English, 9.2% American

Employment: 9.4% management, business, and financial, 0.0% computer, engineering, and science, 16.3% education, legal, community service, arts, and media, 5.6% healthcare practitioners, 21.9% service, 22.8% sales and office, 10.5% natural resources, construction, and maintenance, 13.5% production, transportation, and material moving

Income: Per capita: $22,051; Median household: $42,845; Average household: $50,138; Households with income of $100,000 or more: 13.5%; Poverty rate: 23.5%

Educational Attainment: High school diploma or higher: 86.0%; Bachelor's degree or higher: 22.7%; Graduate/professional degree or higher: 9.9%

Housing: Homeownership rate: 77.6%; Median home value: $121,300; Median year structure built: 1971; Homeowner vacancy rate: 5.7%; Median selected monthly owner costs: $904 with a mortgage, $299 without a mortgage; Median gross rent: $664 per month; Rental vacancy rate: 4.4%

Health Insurance: 87.2% have insurance; 62.0% have private insurance; 42.0% have public insurance; 12.8% do not have insurance; 12.6% of children under 18 do not have insurance

Safety: Violent crime rate: 9.8 per 10,000 population; Property crime rate: 58.7 per 10,000 population

Transportation: Commute: 83.7% car, 3.2% public transportation, 6.0% walk, 4.8% work from home; Mean travel time to work: 33.1 minutes

DAVENPORT (town). Covers a land area of 51.563 square miles and a water area of 0.350 square miles. Located at 42.45° N. Lat; 74.90° W. Long. Elevation is 1,306 feet.

Population: 2,893; Growth (since 2000): 4.3%; Density: 56.1 persons per square mile; Race: 97.1% White, 0.6% Black/African American, 1.7% Asian, 0.0% American Indian/Alaska Native, 0.0% Native Hawaiian/Other Pacific Islander, 0.6% Two or more races, 0.8% Hispanic of any race; Average household size: 2.46; Median age: 46.8; Age under 18: 15.7%; Age 65 and over: 21.9%; Males per 100 females: 94.7; Marriage status: 24.6% never married, 51.1% now married, 4.8% separated, 8.6% widowed, 15.7% divorced; Foreign born: 2.1%; Speak English only: 97.9%; With disability: 14.7%; Veterans: 9.4%; Ancestry: 27.8% Irish, 26.4% German, 15.3% Italian, 11.4% English, 8.2% Dutch

Employment: 11.0% management, business, and financial, 1.0% computer, engineering, and science, 13.3% education, legal, community service, arts, and media, 3.4% healthcare practitioners, 26.3% service, 23.2% sales and office, 11.7% natural resources, construction, and maintenance, 10.0% production, transportation, and material moving

Income: Per capita: $23,023; Median household: $40,855; Average household: $54,820; Households with income of $100,000 or more: 11.2%; Poverty rate: 13.8%

Educational Attainment: High school diploma or higher: 86.0%; Bachelor's degree or higher: 16.5%; Graduate/professional degree or higher: 7.5%

School District(s)
Charlotte Valley Central SD (PK-12)
    2014-15 Enrollment: 391 . . . . (607) 278-5511

Housing: Homeownership rate: 73.4%; Median home value: $113,800; Median year structure built: 1982; Homeowner vacancy rate: 5.7%; Median selected monthly owner costs: $1,166 with a mortgage, $461 without a mortgage; Median gross rent: $835 per month; Rental vacancy rate: 0.0%

Health Insurance: 91.2% have insurance; 68.1% have private insurance; 45.6% have public insurance; 8.8% do not have insurance; 7.3% of children under 18 do not have insurance

Transportation: Commute: 92.6% car, 0.0% public transportation, 2.5% walk, 4.9% work from home; Mean travel time to work: 25.3 minutes

DAVENPORT CENTER (CDP). Covers a land area of 3.102 square miles and a water area of 0.040 square miles. Located at 42.45° N. Lat; 74.90° W. Long. Elevation is 1,217 feet.

Population: 417; Growth (since 2000): n/a; Density: 134.4 persons per square mile; Race: 96.6% White, 2.2% Black/African American, 0.0% Asian, 0.0% American Indian/Alaska Native, 0.0% Native Hawaiian/Other Pacific Islander, 1.2% Two or more races, 1.2% Hispanic of any race; Average household size: 2.28; Median age: 51.4; Age under 18: 12.0%; Age 65 and over: 12.0%; Males per 100 females: 90.7; Marriage status: 15.6% never married, 48.0% now married, 12.2% separated, 6.6% widowed, 29.7% divorced; Foreign born: 0.0%; Speak English only: 100.0%; With disability: 30.0%; Veterans: 9.5%; Ancestry: 40.8% German, 35.3% Irish, 19.9% Dutch, 14.9% Italian, 12.2% English

Employment: 4.7% management, business, and financial, 4.2% computer, engineering, and science, 4.2% education, legal, community service, arts, and media, 0.0% healthcare practitioners, 42.9% service, 30.2% sales and office, 2.4% natural resources, construction, and maintenance, 11.3% production, transportation, and material moving

Income: Per capita: $25,365; Median household: $50,063; Average household: $57,750; Households with income of $100,000 or more: 6.6%; Poverty rate: 2.6%

Educational Attainment: High school diploma or higher: 85.8%; Bachelor's degree or higher: 6.9%; Graduate/professional degree or higher: n/a

Housing: Homeownership rate: 76.5%; Median home value: $82,900; Median year structure built: 1984; Homeowner vacancy rate: 0.0%; Median selected monthly owner costs: $1,150 with a mortgage, $306 without a mortgage; Median gross rent: n/a per month; Rental vacancy rate: 0.0%

Health Insurance: 77.0% have insurance; 59.2% have private insurance; 32.9% have public insurance; 23.0% do not have insurance; 46.0% of children under 18 do not have insurance

Transportation: Commute: 87.9% car, 0.0% public transportation, 0.0% walk, 12.1% work from home; Mean travel time to work: 25.5 minutes

DELANCEY (unincorporated postal area)
ZCTA: 13752

Covers a land area of 48.520 square miles and a water area of 1.402 square miles. Located at 42.19° N. Lat; 74.90° W. Long..

Population: 646; Growth (since 2000): -9.7%; Density: 13.3 persons per square mile; Race: 99.1% White, 0.0% Black/African American, 0.0% Asian, 0.0% American Indian/Alaska Native, 0.0% Native Hawaiian/Other Pacific Islander, 0.9% Two or more races, 9.1% Hispanic of any race; Average household size: 2.10; Median age: 57.8; Age under 18: 11.0%; Age 65 and over: 32.2%; Males per 100 females: 108.5; Marriage status: 26.3% never married, 48.0% now married, 1.8% separated, 10.0% widowed, 15.7% divorced; Foreign born: 9.8%; Speak English only: 89.7%; With disability: 19.5%; Veterans: 17.9%; Ancestry: 26.2% German, 24.3% Irish, 10.5% English, 9.0% Italian, 7.4% Scottish

Employment: 6.5% management, business, and financial, 0.0% computer, engineering, and science, 16.6% education, legal, community service, arts, and media, 4.7% healthcare practitioners, 18.4% service, 31.0% sales and office, 17.0% natural resources, construction, and maintenance, 5.8% production, transportation, and material moving

Income: Per capita: $43,303; Median household: $43,167; Average household: $87,411; Households with income of $100,000 or more: 15.6%; Poverty rate: 14.9%

Educational Attainment: High school diploma or higher: 90.2%; Bachelor's degree or higher: 24.7%; Graduate/professional degree or higher: 9.6%

Housing: Homeownership rate: 85.1%; Median home value: $165,000; Median year structure built: 1973; Homeowner vacancy rate: 5.4%; Median selected monthly owner costs: $1,435 with a mortgage, $445 without a mortgage; Median gross rent: $847 per month; Rental vacancy rate: 6.7%

Health Insurance: 88.5% have insurance; 64.6% have private insurance; 45.8% have public insurance; 11.5% do not have insurance; 1.4% of children under 18 do not have insurance

Transportation: Commute: 82.5% car, 0.0% public transportation, 9.5% walk, 8.0% work from home; Mean travel time to work: 21.4 minutes

DELHI (town). Covers a land area of 64.198 square miles and a water area of 0.401 square miles. Located at 42.27° N. Lat; 74.91° W. Long. Elevation is 1,371 feet.

History: Shortly after the Revolutionary War, Ebenezer Foote was so influential locally and as a member of the state legislature that he was nicknamed "the Great Mogul." At the suggestions of facetious citizens the community was named for Delhi, India, the capital city of the real Great Mogul.

Population: 4,993; Growth (since 2000): 7.9%; Density: 77.8 persons per square mile; Race: 85.8% White, 8.6% Black/African American, 0.9% Asian, 0.1% American Indian/Alaska Native, 0.0% Native Hawaiian/Other Pacific Islander, 1.8% Two or more races, 7.2% Hispanic of any race; Average household size: 2.20; Median age: 24.7; Age under 18: 10.7%; Age 65 and over: 14.4%; Males per 100 females: 109.8; Marriage status: 56.1% never married, 28.6% now married, 1.0% separated, 5.3% widowed, 10.0% divorced; Foreign born: 3.7%; Speak English only: 92.3%; With disability: 15.3%; Veterans: 5.9%; Ancestry: 22.7% German, 20.0% Irish, 10.9% Italian, 8.2% English, 4.5% American

Employment: 8.6% management, business, and financial, 5.7% computer, engineering, and science, 14.9% education, legal, community service, arts, and media, 3.8% healthcare practitioners, 29.3% service, 22.5% sales and office, 8.1% natural resources, construction, and maintenance, 7.1% production, transportation, and material moving

Income: Per capita: $22,229; Median household: $47,255; Average household: $68,922; Households with income of $100,000 or more: 20.7%; Poverty rate: 12.3%

Educational Attainment: High school diploma or higher: 91.2%; Bachelor's degree or higher: 29.9%; Graduate/professional degree or higher: 13.9%

School District(s)
Delhi Central SD (KG-12)
    2014-15 Enrollment: 766 . . . . (607) 746-1300
Four-year College(s)
SUNY College of Technology at Delhi (Public)
    Fall 2014 Enrollment: 3,598 . . . . (607) 746-4000
    2015-16 Tuition: In-state $7,855; Out-of-state $12,225
Housing: Homeownership rate: 69.8%; Median home value: $165,600; Median year structure built: 1961; Homeowner vacancy rate: 2.6%; Median selected monthly owner costs: $1,261 with a mortgage, $543 without a mortgage; Median gross rent: $763 per month; Rental vacancy rate: 12.0%
Health Insurance: 95.8% have insurance; 79.8% have private insurance; 29.2% have public insurance; 4.2% do not have insurance; 0.0% of children under 18 do not have insurance
Hospitals: O'Connor Hospital (28 beds)
Newspapers: Delaware County Times (weekly circulation 1,700)
Transportation: Commute: 76.0% car, 0.8% public transportation, 16.3% walk, 5.9% work from home; Mean travel time to work: 17.7 minutes
Additional Information Contacts
Town of Delhi . . . . (607) 746-8696
    http://townofdelhiny.com

DELHI (village). County seat. Covers a land area of 3.142 square miles and a water area of 0.050 square miles. Located at 42.28° N. Lat; 74.91° W. Long. Elevation is 1,371 feet.
Population: 3,078; Growth (since 2000): 19.2%; Density: 979.6 persons per square mile; Race: 78.4% White, 13.0% Black/African American, 0.9% Asian, 0.2% American Indian/Alaska Native, 0.0% Native Hawaiian/Other Pacific Islander, 2.9% Two or more races, 10.8% Hispanic of any race; Average household size: 2.10; Median age: 20.6; Age under 18: 9.1%; Age 65 and over: 9.4%; Males per 100 females: 119.1; Marriage status: 71.7% never married, 16.7% now married, 0.7% separated, 3.8% widowed, 7.8% divorced; Foreign born: 3.7%; Speak English only: 90.4%; With disability: 13.4%; Veterans: 3.7%; Ancestry: 18.9% German, 15.6% Irish, 13.5% Italian, 6.5% English, 5.8% Polish
Employment: 7.0% management, business, and financial, 3.4% computer, engineering, and science, 14.2% education, legal, community service, arts, and media, 4.1% healthcare practitioners, 35.8% service, 20.3% sales and office, 6.4% natural resources, construction, and maintenance, 8.7% production, transportation, and material moving
Income: Per capita: $13,174; Median household: $37,813; Average household: $51,028; Households with income of $100,000 or more: 13.1%; Poverty rate: 19.1%
Educational Attainment: High school diploma or higher: 88.0%; Bachelor's degree or higher: 31.6%; Graduate/professional degree or higher: 16.1%

School District(s)
Delhi Central SD (KG-12)
    2014-15 Enrollment: 766 . . . . (607) 746-1300
Four-year College(s)
SUNY College of Technology at Delhi (Public)
    Fall 2014 Enrollment: 3,598 . . . . (607) 746-4000
    2015-16 Tuition: In-state $7,855; Out-of-state $12,225
Housing: Homeownership rate: 55.2%; Median home value: $155,300; Median year structure built: Before 1940; Homeowner vacancy rate: 4.9%; Median selected monthly owner costs: $1,222 with a mortgage, $587 without a mortgage; Median gross rent: $741 per month; Rental vacancy rate: 9.9%
Health Insurance: 94.7% have insurance; 78.7% have private insurance; 26.1% have public insurance; 5.3% do not have insurance; 0.0% of children under 18 do not have insurance
Hospitals: O'Connor Hospital (28 beds)
Safety: Violent crime rate: 19.5 per 10,000 population; Property crime rate: 91.1 per 10,000 population
Newspapers: Delaware County Times (weekly circulation 1,700)
Transportation: Commute: 64.6% car, 1.3% public transportation, 22.7% walk, 11.0% work from home; Mean travel time to work: 13.4 minutes

DENVER (unincorporated postal area)
ZCTA: 12421
    Covers a land area of 19.606 square miles and a water area of 0.009 square miles. Located at 42.25° N. Lat; 74.55° W. Long. Elevation is 1,631 feet.
Population: 349; Growth (since 2000): -55.1%; Density: 17.8 persons per square mile; Race: 96.0% White, 0.0% Black/African American, 1.4% Asian, 0.0% American Indian/Alaska Native, 0.0% Native Hawaiian/Other Pacific Islander, 2.6% Two or more races, 1.1% Hispanic of any race; Average household size: 1.85; Median age: 58.4; Age under 18: 7.4%; Age 65 and over: 39.3%; Males per 100 females: 103.5; Marriage status: 13.6% never married, 67.7% now married, 2.7% separated, 3.0% widowed, 15.7% divorced; Foreign born: 6.9%; Speak English only: 92.9%; With disability: 10.9%; Veterans: 5.9%; Ancestry: 24.4% Irish, 19.5% Italian, 18.3% English, 12.6% German, 6.9% Russian
Employment: 5.3% management, business, and financial, 4.1% computer, engineering, and science, 16.6% education, legal, community service, arts, and media, 10.1% healthcare practitioners, 34.9% service, 12.4% sales and office, 5.3% natural resources, construction, and maintenance, 11.2% production, transportation, and material moving
Income: Per capita: $29,318; Median household: $45,313; Average household: $54,735; Households with income of $100,000 or more: 8.4%; Poverty rate: 1.7%
Educational Attainment: High school diploma or higher: 73.1%; Bachelor's degree or higher: 34.7%; Graduate/professional degree or higher: 10.2%
Housing: Homeownership rate: 91.5%; Median home value: n/a; Median year structure built: 1977; Homeowner vacancy rate: 8.9%; Median selected monthly owner costs: $1,542 with a mortgage, $738 without a mortgage; Median gross rent: n/a per month; Rental vacancy rate: 0.0%
Health Insurance: 98.3% have insurance; 78.8% have private insurance; 54.7% have public insurance; 1.7% do not have insurance; 0.0% of children under 18 do not have insurance
Transportation: Commute: 76.9% car, 5.6% public transportation, 3.1% walk, 14.4% work from home; Mean travel time to work: 47.0 minutes

DEPOSIT (town). Covers a land area of 43.015 square miles and a water area of 1.564 square miles. Located at 42.10° N. Lat; 75.37° W. Long.
Population: 1,747; Growth (since 2000): 3.6%; Density: 40.6 persons per square mile; Race: 94.4% White, 4.5% Black/African American, 0.2% Asian, 0.3% American Indian/Alaska Native, 0.0% Native Hawaiian/Other Pacific Islander, 0.5% Two or more races, 3.7% Hispanic of any race; Average household size: 2.49; Median age: 48.3; Age under 18: 19.9%; Age 65 and over: 23.2%; Males per 100 females: 91.9; Marriage status: 27.2% never married, 51.5% now married, 1.0% separated, 10.1% widowed, 11.1% divorced; Foreign born: 3.4%; Speak English only: 94.0%; With disability: 18.5%; Veterans: 12.2%; Ancestry: 21.6% German, 18.9% Irish, 16.8% English, 13.3% Italian, 6.1% Dutch
Employment: 10.2% management, business, and financial, 3.6% computer, engineering, and science, 14.0% education, legal, community

service, arts, and media, 4.5% healthcare practitioners, 14.9% service, 16.2% sales and office, 15.6% natural resources, construction, and maintenance, 21.1% production, transportation, and material moving
Income: Per capita: $22,495; Median household: $46,128; Average household: $53,358; Households with income of $100,000 or more: 14.7%; Poverty rate: 15.7%
Educational Attainment: High school diploma or higher: 88.7%; Bachelor's degree or higher: 16.2%; Graduate/professional degree or higher: 9.0%

School District(s)
Deposit Central SD (PK-12)
    2014-15 Enrollment: 563 . . . . (607) 467-5380
Housing: Homeownership rate: 69.0%; Median home value: $106,300; Median year structure built: 1963; Homeowner vacancy rate: 1.6%; Median selected monthly owner costs: $1,123 with a mortgage, $477 without a mortgage; Median gross rent: $665 per month; Rental vacancy rate: 0.9%
Health Insurance: 85.3% have insurance; 62.6% have private insurance; 42.2% have public insurance; 14.7% do not have insurance; 14.4% of children under 18 do not have insurance
Newspapers: Deposit Courier (weekly circulation 2,200)
Transportation: Commute: 87.7% car, 0.4% public transportation, 6.8% walk, 2.5% work from home; Mean travel time to work: 23.0 minutes

DEPOSIT (village).
Covers a land area of 1.263 square miles and a water area of 0.053 square miles. Located at 42.06° N. Lat; 75.42° W. Long. Elevation is 991 feet.
Population: 1,832; Growth (since 2000): 7.8%; Density: 1,450.7 persons per square mile; Race: 93.4% White, 4.1% Black/African American, 0.5% Asian, 0.0% American Indian/Alaska Native, 0.0% Native Hawaiian/Other Pacific Islander, 1.6% Two or more races, 5.2% Hispanic of any race; Average household size: 2.46; Median age: 42.9; Age under 18: 21.5%; Age 65 and over: 20.1%; Males per 100 females: 87.7; Marriage status: 27.4% never married, 52.4% now married, 1.2% separated, 9.1% widowed, 11.1% divorced; Foreign born: 3.1%; Speak English only: 93.8%; With disability: 19.2%; Veterans: 15.4%; Ancestry: 29.0% German, 22.7% Irish, 17.4% Italian, 10.6% English, 5.6% American
Employment: 4.0% management, business, and financial, 2.1% computer, engineering, and science, 7.3% education, legal, community service, arts, and media, 3.4% healthcare practitioners, 22.8% service, 22.8% sales and office, 16.7% natural resources, construction, and maintenance, 20.9% production, transportation, and material moving
Income: Per capita: $17,568; Median household: $30,357; Average household: $41,732; Households with income of $100,000 or more: 7.0%; Poverty rate: 25.5%
Educational Attainment: High school diploma or higher: 88.8%; Bachelor's degree or higher: 11.8%; Graduate/professional degree or higher: 5.0%

School District(s)
Deposit Central SD (PK-12)
    2014-15 Enrollment: 563 . . . . (607) 467-5380
Housing: Homeownership rate: 55.8%; Median home value: $95,300; Median year structure built: Before 1940; Homeowner vacancy rate: 6.1%; Median selected monthly owner costs: $1,125 with a mortgage, $515 without a mortgage; Median gross rent: $693 per month; Rental vacancy rate: 4.4%
Health Insurance: 82.8% have insurance; 50.3% have private insurance; 48.4% have public insurance; 17.2% do not have insurance; 17.5% of children under 18 do not have insurance
Newspapers: Deposit Courier (weekly circulation 2,200)
Transportation: Commute: 81.6% car, 0.0% public transportation, 12.2% walk, 3.2% work from home; Mean travel time to work: 22.0 minutes

DOWNSVILLE (CDP).
Covers a land area of 3.953 square miles and a water area of 0.079 square miles. Located at 42.08° N. Lat; 75.00° W. Long. Elevation is 1,125 feet.
Population: 648; Growth (since 2000): n/a; Density: 163.9 persons per square mile; Race: 98.5% White, 0.0% Black/African American, 0.0% Asian, 0.0% American Indian/Alaska Native, 0.0% Native Hawaiian/Other Pacific Islander, 1.5% Two or more races, 0.0% Hispanic of any race; Average household size: 2.54; Median age: 40.3; Age under 18: 29.6%; Age 65 and over: 15.1%; Males per 100 females: 91.6; Marriage status: 36.8% never married, 41.1% now married, 2.6% separated, 12.8% widowed, 9.3% divorced; Foreign born: 1.5%; Speak English only: 98.4%; With disability: 14.5%; Veterans: 5.9%; Ancestry: 34.7% German, 22.4% Irish, 18.1% American, 17.6% Dutch, 10.8% Italian

Employment: 8.4% management, business, and financial, 0.0% computer, engineering, and science, 13.0% education, legal, community service, arts, and media, 12.6% healthcare practitioners, 27.5% service, 10.3% sales and office, 14.9% natural resources, construction, and maintenance, 13.4% production, transportation, and material moving
Income: Per capita: $15,146; Median household: $27,750; Average household: $35,729; Households with income of $100,000 or more: 6.7%; Poverty rate: 45.0%
Educational Attainment: High school diploma or higher: 78.9%; Bachelor's degree or higher: 13.3%; Graduate/professional degree or higher: 3.8%

School District(s)
Downsville Central SD (PK-12)
    2014-15 Enrollment: 282 . . . . (607) 363-2101
Housing: Homeownership rate: 53.7%; Median home value: $86,700; Median year structure built: 1946; Homeowner vacancy rate: 9.3%; Median selected monthly owner costs: n/a with a mortgage, n/a without a mortgage; Median gross rent: $671 per month; Rental vacancy rate: 7.1%
Health Insurance: 79.5% have insurance; 41.7% have private insurance; 47.4% have public insurance; 20.5% do not have insurance; 24.5% of children under 18 do not have insurance
Transportation: Commute: 79.4% car, 8.0% public transportation, 3.4% walk, 9.2% work from home; Mean travel time to work: 31.0 minutes

EAST BRANCH (unincorporated postal area)
ZCTA: 13756
    Covers a land area of 45.879 square miles and a water area of 0.645 square miles. Located at 42.00° N. Lat; 75.10° W. Long. Elevation is 1,007 feet.
Population: 501; Growth (since 2000): -3.3%; Density: 10.9 persons per square mile; Race: 100.0% White, 0.0% Black/African American, 0.0% Asian, 0.0% American Indian/Alaska Native, 0.0% Native Hawaiian/Other Pacific Islander, 0.0% Two or more races, 1.6% Hispanic of any race; Average household size: 2.35; Median age: 49.4; Age under 18: 21.0%; Age 65 and over: 20.0%; Males per 100 females: 108.5; Marriage status: 27.5% never married, 55.3% now married, 1.8% separated, 10.9% widowed, 6.3% divorced; Foreign born: 3.8%; Speak English only: 97.3%; With disability: 12.8%; Veterans: 12.6%; Ancestry: 32.7% Irish, 27.9% German, 17.2% Italian, 16.4% English, 7.6% Polish
Employment: 14.1% management, business, and financial, 0.0% computer, engineering, and science, 4.5% education, legal, community service, arts, and media, 2.5% healthcare practitioners, 16.1% service, 27.1% sales and office, 2.0% natural resources, construction, and maintenance, 33.7% production, transportation, and material moving
Income: Per capita: $24,525; Median household: $46,198; Average household: $56,411; Households with income of $100,000 or more: 8.4%; Poverty rate: 13.0%
Educational Attainment: High school diploma or higher: 81.8%; Bachelor's degree or higher: 10.7%; Graduate/professional degree or higher: 5.8%
Housing: Homeownership rate: 77.5%; Median home value: $88,800; Median year structure built: 1981; Homeowner vacancy rate: 2.4%; Median selected monthly owner costs: $1,039 with a mortgage, $460 without a mortgage; Median gross rent: $699 per month; Rental vacancy rate: 0.0%
Health Insurance: 88.0% have insurance; 58.1% have private insurance; 48.5% have public insurance; 12.0% do not have insurance; 0.0% of children under 18 do not have insurance
Transportation: Commute: 85.4% car, 2.0% public transportation, 8.5% walk, 4.0% work from home; Mean travel time to work: 30.4 minutes

EAST MEREDITH (unincorporated postal area)
ZCTA: 13757
    Covers a land area of 37.199 square miles and a water area of 0.087 square miles. Located at 42.41° N. Lat; 74.89° W. Long. Elevation is 1,401 feet.
Population: 1,139; Growth (since 2000): 2.9%; Density: 30.6 persons per square mile; Race: 98.4% White, 0.3% Black/African American, 0.0% Asian, 0.0% American Indian/Alaska Native, 0.0% Native Hawaiian/Other Pacific Islander, 0.4% Two or more races, 2.4% Hispanic of any race; Average household size: 2.42; Median age: 49.7; Age under 18: 14.7%; Age 65 and over: 20.5%; Males per 100 females: 96.1; Marriage status: 22.8% never married, 57.8% now married, 3.5% separated, 6.4% widowed, 13.1% divorced; Foreign born: 2.4%; Speak

English only: 96.8%; With disability: 16.2%; Veterans: 9.0%; Ancestry: 32.6% Irish, 25.5% Italian, 17.6% German, 16.5% English, 10.6% Dutch
Employment: 14.7% management, business, and financial, 4.9% computer, engineering, and science, 7.2% education, legal, community service, arts, and media, 4.2% healthcare practitioners, 25.5% service, 12.7% sales and office, 15.8% natural resources, construction, and maintenance, 14.9% production, transportation, and material moving
Income: Per capita: $28,742; Median household: $52,056; Average household: $67,999; Households with income of $100,000 or more: 23.3%; Poverty rate: 6.9%
Educational Attainment: High school diploma or higher: 91.6%; Bachelor's degree or higher: 26.3%; Graduate/professional degree or higher: 11.8%
Housing: Homeownership rate: 88.7%; Median home value: $138,400; Median year structure built: 1986; Homeowner vacancy rate: 5.0%; Median selected monthly owner costs: $1,295 with a mortgage, $589 without a mortgage; Median gross rent: $825 per month; Rental vacancy rate: 15.9%
Health Insurance: 87.5% have insurance; 75.4% have private insurance; 43.3% have public insurance; 12.5% do not have insurance; 3.6% of children under 18 do not have insurance
Transportation: Commute: 83.1% car, 0.5% public transportation, 0.5% walk, 15.0% work from home; Mean travel time to work: 21.6 minutes

FISHS EDDY (unincorporated postal area)
ZCTA: 13774

Covers a land area of 2.844 square miles and a water area of 0.149 square miles. Located at 41.96° N. Lat; 75.15° W. Long. Elevation is 984 feet.
Population: 288; Growth (since 2000): 0.7%; Density: 101.3 persons per square mile; Race: 100.0% White, 0.0% Black/African American, 0.0% Asian, 0.0% American Indian/Alaska Native, 0.0% Native Hawaiian/Other Pacific Islander, 0.0% Two or more races, 0.0% Hispanic of any race; Average household size: 4.36; Median age: 18.8; Age under 18: 30.6%; Age 65 and over: 5.2%; Males per 100 females: 123.3; Marriage status: 46.0% never married, 54.0% now married, 0.0% separated, 0.0% widowed, 0.0% divorced; Foreign born: 0.0%; Speak English only: 100.0%; With disability: 16.0%; Veterans: 12.0%; Ancestry: 66.0% German, 10.1% American, 9.7% European, 6.9% Scottish, 4.5% English
Employment: 0.0% management, business, and financial, 4.4% computer, engineering, and science, 18.1% education, legal, community service, arts, and media, 0.0% healthcare practitioners, 21.9% service, 29.4% sales and office, 16.9% natural resources, construction, and maintenance, 9.4% production, transportation, and material moving
Income: Per capita: $14,051; Median household: $71,071; Average household: $59,394; Households with income of $100,000 or more: n/a; Poverty rate: n/a
Educational Attainment: High school diploma or higher: 80.5%; Bachelor's degree or higher: n/a; Graduate/professional degree or higher: n/a
Housing: Homeownership rate: 74.2%; Median home value: n/a; Median year structure built: 1973; Homeowner vacancy rate: 0.0%; Median selected monthly owner costs: $0 with a mortgage, $0 without a mortgage; Median gross rent: n/a per month; Rental vacancy rate: 0.0%
Health Insurance: 100.0% have insurance; 85.8% have private insurance; 19.4% have public insurance; 0.0% do not have insurance; 0.0% of children under 18 do not have insurance
Transportation: Commute: 90.6% car, 0.0% public transportation, 0.0% walk, 0.0% work from home; Mean travel time to work: 23.1 minutes

FLEISCHMANNS (village). Covers a land area of 0.655 square miles and a water area of 0.015 square miles. Located at 42.15° N. Lat; 74.53° W. Long. Elevation is 1,499 feet.
Population: 386; Growth (since 2000): 10.0%; Density: 589.2 persons per square mile; Race: 80.8% White, 1.6% Black/African American, 0.0% Asian, 0.0% American Indian/Alaska Native, 1.8% Native Hawaiian/Other Pacific Islander, 4.1% Two or more races, 31.9% Hispanic of any race; Average household size: 2.97; Median age: 38.5; Age under 18: 29.0%; Age 65 and over: 12.2%; Males per 100 females: 102.9; Marriage status: 38.0% never married, 33.9% now married, 8.1% separated, 12.5% widowed, 15.6% divorced; Foreign born: 24.4%; Speak English only: 57.9%; With disability: 17.6%; Veterans: 7.3%; Ancestry: 24.1% German, 20.5% Irish, 10.1% Italian, 8.3% Czech, 4.9% English

Employment: 3.0% management, business, and financial, 5.2% computer, engineering, and science, 9.0% education, legal, community service, arts, and media, 0.0% healthcare practitioners, 23.1% service, 24.6% sales and office, 23.9% natural resources, construction, and maintenance, 11.2% production, transportation, and material moving
Income: Per capita: $15,359; Median household: $35,938; Average household: $42,351; Households with income of $100,000 or more: 3.1%; Poverty rate: 20.2%
Educational Attainment: High school diploma or higher: 78.9%; Bachelor's degree or higher: 21.9%; Graduate/professional degree or higher: 8.9%
Housing: Homeownership rate: 70.0%; Median home value: $127,200; Median year structure built: Before 1940; Homeowner vacancy rate: 4.0%; Median selected monthly owner costs: $1,146 with a mortgage, $660 without a mortgage; Median gross rent: $696 per month; Rental vacancy rate: 18.8%
Health Insurance: 80.6% have insurance; 35.8% have private insurance; 56.0% have public insurance; 19.4% do not have insurance; 10.7% of children under 18 do not have insurance
Transportation: Commute: 91.8% car, 0.0% public transportation, 6.7% walk, 1.5% work from home; Mean travel time to work: 22.7 minutes

FRANKLIN (town). Covers a land area of 81.249 square miles and a water area of 0.278 square miles. Located at 42.33° N. Lat; 75.11° W. Long. Elevation is 1,234 feet.
Population: 2,195; Growth (since 2000): -16.3%; Density: 27.0 persons per square mile; Race: 97.4% White, 1.0% Black/African American, 0.3% Asian, 0.2% American Indian/Alaska Native, 0.0% Native Hawaiian/Other Pacific Islander, 1.0% Two or more races, 1.1% Hispanic of any race; Average household size: 2.46; Median age: 47.3; Age under 18: 22.3%; Age 65 and over: 20.6%; Males per 100 females: 102.3; Marriage status: 21.0% never married, 61.3% now married, 1.5% separated, 5.6% widowed, 12.1% divorced; Foreign born: 2.4%; Speak English only: 97.2%; With disability: 13.3%; Veterans: 13.1%; Ancestry: 23.9% German, 23.6% Irish, 20.3% English, 10.9% Scottish, 9.8% Italian
Employment: 17.0% management, business, and financial, 1.8% computer, engineering, and science, 14.5% education, legal, community service, arts, and media, 7.5% healthcare practitioners, 17.7% service, 17.2% sales and office, 12.5% natural resources, construction, and maintenance, 11.9% production, transportation, and material moving
Income: Per capita: $25,587; Median household: $57,540; Average household: $62,122; Households with income of $100,000 or more: 17.4%; Poverty rate: 6.8%
Educational Attainment: High school diploma or higher: 91.5%; Bachelor's degree or higher: 24.4%; Graduate/professional degree or higher: 10.3%

School District(s)
Franklin Central SD (PK-12)
    2014-15 Enrollment: 275 . . . . (607) 829-3551
Housing: Homeownership rate: 86.1%; Median home value: $141,600; Median year structure built: 1965; Homeowner vacancy rate: 3.6%; Median selected monthly owner costs: $1,229 with a mortgage, $519 without a mortgage; Median gross rent: $671 per month; Rental vacancy rate: 3.6%
Health Insurance: 89.7% have insurance; 74.1% have private insurance; 35.8% have public insurance; 10.3% do not have insurance; 12.4% of children under 18 do not have insurance
Transportation: Commute: 84.1% car, 0.0% public transportation, 6.4% walk, 9.0% work from home; Mean travel time to work: 23.6 minutes
Additional Information Contacts
Town of Franklin . . . . (518) 891-2189
  http://townoffranklin.com

FRANKLIN (village). Covers a land area of 0.339 square miles and a water area of 0.007 square miles. Located at 42.34° N. Lat; 75.17° W. Long. Elevation is 1,234 feet.
Population: 375; Growth (since 2000): -6.7%; Density: 1,106.6 persons per square mile; Race: 96.5% White, 3.5% Black/African American, 0.0% Asian, 0.0% American Indian/Alaska Native, 0.0% Native Hawaiian/Other Pacific Islander, 0.0% Two or more races, 0.0% Hispanic of any race; Average household size: 2.68; Median age: 31.4; Age under 18: 29.3%; Age 65 and over: 14.7%; Males per 100 females: 93.8; Marriage status: 26.1% never married, 60.6% now married, 0.0% separated, 3.1% widowed, 10.1% divorced; Foreign born: 4.3%; Speak English only: 98.6%; With disability: 17.6%; Veterans: 15.5%; Ancestry: 27.5% Irish, 27.2% German, 22.7% English, 6.7% Italian, 4.5% French Canadian

Employment: 11.9% management, business, and financial, 4.6% computer, engineering, and science, 20.5% education, legal, community service, arts, and media, 4.0% healthcare practitioners, 24.5% service, 18.5% sales and office, 10.6% natural resources, construction, and maintenance, 5.3% production, transportation, and material moving
Income: Per capita: $21,045; Median household: $46,944; Average household: $56,016; Households with income of $100,000 or more: 12.1%; Poverty rate: 12.8%
Educational Attainment: High school diploma or higher: 92.7%; Bachelor's degree or higher: 27.3%; Graduate/professional degree or higher: 16.4%

School District(s)
Franklin Central SD (PK-12)
    2014-15 Enrollment: 275 . . . . (607) 829-3551
Housing: Homeownership rate: 63.6%; Median home value: $140,100; Median year structure built: Before 1940; Homeowner vacancy rate: 11.0%; Median selected monthly owner costs: $1,146 with a mortgage, $580 without a mortgage; Median gross rent: $756 per month; Rental vacancy rate: 7.8%
Health Insurance: 92.3% have insurance; 66.9% have private insurance; 48.8% have public insurance; 7.7% do not have insurance; 7.3% of children under 18 do not have insurance
Transportation: Commute: 77.2% car, 0.0% public transportation, 11.4% walk, 8.1% work from home; Mean travel time to work: 27.1 minutes

GRAND GORGE (unincorporated postal area)
ZCTA: 12434
    Covers a land area of 13.769 square miles and a water area of 0.427 square miles. Located at 42.36° N. Lat; 74.50° W. Long. Elevation is 1,401 feet.
Population: 576; Growth (since 2000): -13.1%; Density: 41.8 persons per square mile; Race: 82.8% White, 12.8% Black/African American, 0.0% Asian, 0.0% American Indian/Alaska Native, 0.0% Native Hawaiian/Other Pacific Islander, 4.3% Two or more races, 6.1% Hispanic of any race; Average household size: 2.09; Median age: 51.0; Age under 18: 9.5%; Age 65 and over: 26.2%; Males per 100 females: 96.1; Marriage status: 34.5% never married, 44.5% now married, 5.9% separated, 14.2% widowed, 6.8% divorced; Foreign born: 0.0%; Speak English only: 94.7%; With disability: 16.3%; Veterans: 15.7%; Ancestry: 24.0% German, 21.7% Dutch, 21.2% Irish, 20.7% Italian, 12.8% American
Employment: 5.4% management, business, and financial, 4.4% computer, engineering, and science, 21.6% education, legal, community service, arts, and media, 0.0% healthcare practitioners, 19.1% service, 7.4% sales and office, 9.8% natural resources, construction, and maintenance, 32.4% production, transportation, and material moving
Income: Per capita: $20,551; Median household: $28,083; Average household: $39,537; Households with income of $100,000 or more: 13.8%; Poverty rate: 17.4%
Educational Attainment: High school diploma or higher: 83.0%; Bachelor's degree or higher: 9.5%; Graduate/professional degree or higher: 8.2%

School District(s)
Otsego-Delaware-Schoharie-Greene Boces
    2014-15 Enrollment: n/a . . . . (607) 588-6291
Housing: Homeownership rate: 66.9%; Median home value: $90,000; Median year structure built: 1955; Homeowner vacancy rate: 16.0%; Median selected monthly owner costs: $929 with a mortgage, $459 without a mortgage; Median gross rent: $575 per month; Rental vacancy rate: 13.3%
Health Insurance: 98.3% have insurance; 67.2% have private insurance; 53.8% have public insurance; 1.7% do not have insurance; 7.3% of children under 18 do not have insurance
Transportation: Commute: 83.9% car, 0.0% public transportation, 0.0% walk, 16.1% work from home; Mean travel time to work: 26.5 minutes

HALCOTTSVILLE (unincorporated postal area)
ZCTA: 12438
    Covers a land area of 0.439 square miles and a water area of 0.041 square miles. Located at 42.21° N. Lat; 74.60° W. Long. Elevation is 1,401 feet.
Population: 75; Growth (since 2000): n/a; Density: 170.8 persons per square mile; Race: 56.0% White, 0.0% Black/African American, 28.0% Asian, 0.0% American Indian/Alaska Native, 0.0% Native Hawaiian/Other Pacific Islander, 16.0% Two or more races, 0.0%

Hispanic of any race; Average household size: 2.21; Median age: 44.6; Age under 18: 16.0%; Age 65 and over: 21.3%; Males per 100 females: 84.4; Marriage status: 0.0% never married, 100.0% now married, 0.0% separated, 0.0% widowed, 0.0% divorced; Foreign born: 52.0%; Speak English only: 73.3%; With disability: 0.0%; Veterans: 0.0%; Ancestry: 21.3% German, 12.0% British, 12.0% Russian, 10.7% Dutch, 10.7% Italian
Employment: 21.1% management, business, and financial, 23.7% computer, engineering, and science, 0.0% education, legal, community service, arts, and media, 0.0% healthcare practitioners, 26.3% service, 28.9% sales and office, 0.0% natural resources, construction, and maintenance, 0.0% production, transportation, and material moving
Income: Per capita: $42,791; Median household: $101,250; Average household: $90,891; Households with income of $100,000 or more: 50.0%; Poverty rate: n/a
Educational Attainment: High school diploma or higher: 82.5%; Bachelor's degree or higher: 69.8%; Graduate/professional degree or higher: 25.4%
Housing: Homeownership rate: 100.0%; Median home value: n/a; Median year structure built: Before 1940; Homeowner vacancy rate: 0.0%; Median selected monthly owner costs: $1,611 with a mortgage, $0 without a mortgage; Median gross rent: n/a per month; Rental vacancy rate: 0.0%
Health Insurance: 88.0% have insurance; 88.0% have private insurance; 10.7% have public insurance; 12.0% do not have insurance; 0.0% of children under 18 do not have insurance
Transportation: Commute: 76.3% car, 23.7% public transportation, 0.0% walk, 0.0% work from home; Mean travel time to work: 0.0 minutes

HAMDEN (town). Covers a land area of 59.930 square miles and a water area of 0.269 square miles. Located at 42.20° N. Lat; 74.98° W. Long. Elevation is 1,286 feet.
Population: 1,258; Growth (since 2000): -1.7%; Density: 21.0 persons per square mile; Race: 94.8% White, 4.1% Black/African American, 0.0% Asian, 0.2% American Indian/Alaska Native, 0.0% Native Hawaiian/Other Pacific Islander, 0.9% Two or more races, 4.8% Hispanic of any race; Average household size: 2.39; Median age: 52.2; Age under 18: 19.2%; Age 65 and over: 25.9%; Males per 100 females: 100.2; Marriage status: 26.7% never married, 54.1% now married, 3.1% separated, 9.5% widowed, 9.7% divorced; Foreign born: 2.7%; Speak English only: 96.7%; With disability: 21.1%; Veterans: 12.5%; Ancestry: 23.1% Irish, 18.1% German, 9.6% English, 8.7% Italian, 7.4% French
Employment: 11.1% management, business, and financial, 3.8% computer, engineering, and science, 9.9% education, legal, community service, arts, and media, 10.1% healthcare practitioners, 15.8% service, 21.0% sales and office, 10.7% natural resources, construction, and maintenance, 17.6% production, transportation, and material moving
Income: Per capita: $26,967; Median household: $48,750; Average household: $62,546; Households with income of $100,000 or more: 14.7%; Poverty rate: 13.6%
Educational Attainment: High school diploma or higher: 94.1%; Bachelor's degree or higher: 25.8%; Graduate/professional degree or higher: 11.4%
Housing: Homeownership rate: 82.8%; Median home value: $175,600; Median year structure built: 1975; Homeowner vacancy rate: 1.6%; Median selected monthly owner costs: $1,261 with a mortgage, $509 without a mortgage; Median gross rent: $818 per month; Rental vacancy rate: 18.7%
Health Insurance: 92.8% have insurance; 72.3% have private insurance; 44.4% have public insurance; 7.2% do not have insurance; 3.7% of children under 18 do not have insurance
Transportation: Commute: 87.1% car, 4.4% public transportation, 3.3% walk, 5.2% work from home; Mean travel time to work: 22.8 minutes

HANCOCK (town). Covers a land area of 158.822 square miles and a water area of 2.994 square miles. Located at 41.96° N. Lat; 75.18° W. Long. Elevation is 922 feet.
Population: 3,148; Growth (since 2000): -8.7%; Density: 19.8 persons per square mile; Race: 95.9% White, 2.4% Black/African American, 0.3% Asian, 0.6% American Indian/Alaska Native, 0.0% Native Hawaiian/Other Pacific Islander, 0.3% Two or more races, 2.1% Hispanic of any race; Average household size: 2.37; Median age: 48.3; Age under 18: 18.6%; Age 65 and over: 19.9%; Males per 100 females: 110.3; Marriage status: 27.4% never married, 50.8% now married, 2.8% separated, 8.6% widowed, 13.1% divorced; Foreign born: 3.9%; Speak English only: 94.8%;

With disability: 19.5%; Veterans: 11.2%; Ancestry: 33.3% German, 20.1% Irish, 13.6% English, 12.9% Italian, 5.3% American
Employment: 10.9% management, business, and financial, 0.8% computer, engineering, and science, 10.6% education, legal, community service, arts, and media, 2.8% healthcare practitioners, 24.9% service, 23.2% sales and office, 9.0% natural resources, construction, and maintenance, 17.8% production, transportation, and material moving
Income: Per capita: $23,763; Median household: $46,250; Average household: $55,611; Households with income of $100,000 or more: 10.8%; Poverty rate: 11.5%
Educational Attainment: High school diploma or higher: 87.1%; Bachelor's degree or higher: 12.2%; Graduate/professional degree or higher: 6.6%

School District(s)
Hancock Central SD (PK-12)
    2014-15 Enrollment: 392 . . . . (607) 637-1301
Housing: Homeownership rate: 77.4%; Median home value: $115,100; Median year structure built: 1970; Homeowner vacancy rate: 1.0%; Median selected monthly owner costs: $1,132 with a mortgage, $487 without a mortgage; Median gross rent: $585 per month; Rental vacancy rate: 6.5%
Health Insurance: 90.2% have insurance; 65.2% have private insurance; 39.3% have public insurance; 9.8% do not have insurance; 2.4% of children under 18 do not have insurance
Newspapers: Hancock Herald (weekly circulation 2,400)
Transportation: Commute: 82.6% car, 1.6% public transportation, 9.3% walk, 4.2% work from home; Mean travel time to work: 25.5 minutes

HANCOCK
(village). Covers a land area of 1.502 square miles and a water area of 0.141 square miles. Located at 41.95° N. Lat; 75.28° W. Long. Elevation is 922 feet.
Population: 946; Growth (since 2000): -20.4%; Density: 629.9 persons per square mile; Race: 94.9% White, 1.5% Black/African American, 0.0% Asian, 2.1% American Indian/Alaska Native, 0.0% Native Hawaiian/Other Pacific Islander, 0.0% Two or more races, 2.3% Hispanic of any race; Average household size: 2.04; Median age: 50.9; Age under 18: 16.4%; Age 65 and over: 20.9%; Males per 100 females: 97.5; Marriage status: 28.7% never married, 45.9% now married, 4.3% separated, 10.9% widowed, 14.6% divorced; Foreign born: 5.3%; Speak English only: 95.4%; With disability: 23.2%; Veterans: 11.9%; Ancestry: 24.0% German, 19.3% Irish, 13.5% English, 11.6% Italian, 7.7% American
Employment: 7.3% management, business, and financial, 1.1% computer, engineering, and science, 5.4% education, legal, community service, arts, and media, 3.0% healthcare practitioners, 36.6% service, 24.2% sales and office, 7.8% natural resources, construction, and maintenance, 14.8% production, transportation, and material moving
Income: Per capita: $17,920; Median household: $28,333; Average household: $35,658; Households with income of $100,000 or more: 2.3%; Poverty rate: 16.6%
Educational Attainment: High school diploma or higher: 89.4%; Bachelor's degree or higher: 10.4%; Graduate/professional degree or higher: 4.8%

School District(s)
Hancock Central SD (PK-12)
    2014-15 Enrollment: 392 . . . . (607) 637-1301
Housing: Homeownership rate: 58.8%; Median home value: $100,600; Median year structure built: Before 1940; Homeowner vacancy rate: 0.0%; Median selected monthly owner costs: $1,066 with a mortgage, $484 without a mortgage; Median gross rent: $533 per month; Rental vacancy rate: 9.5%
Health Insurance: 89.5% have insurance; 50.0% have private insurance; 52.9% have public insurance; 10.5% do not have insurance; 0.0% of children under 18 do not have insurance
Safety: Violent crime rate: 10.2 per 10,000 population; Property crime rate: 213.4 per 10,000 population
Newspapers: Hancock Herald (weekly circulation 2,400)
Transportation: Commute: 79.4% car, 0.0% public transportation, 17.9% walk, 0.8% work from home; Mean travel time to work: 18.7 minutes

HARPERSFIELD
(town). Covers a land area of 42.021 square miles and a water area of 0.267 square miles. Located at 42.45° N. Lat; 74.70° W. Long. Elevation is 1,667 feet.
Population: 1,729; Growth (since 2000): 7.9%; Density: 41.1 persons per square mile; Race: 95.1% White, 0.6% Black/African American, 0.8% Asian, 0.2% American Indian/Alaska Native, 0.0% Native Hawaiian/Other Pacific Islander, 3.3% Two or more races, 3.1% Hispanic of any race;

Average household size: 2.35; Median age: 48.8; Age under 18: 18.1%; Age 65 and over: 29.4%; Males per 100 females: 96.4; Marriage status: 30.9% never married, 49.3% now married, 1.4% separated, 13.5% widowed, 6.3% divorced; Foreign born: 5.1%; Speak English only: 94.3%; With disability: 19.1%; Veterans: 12.9%; Ancestry: 31.0% German, 20.5% Irish, 17.4% Italian, 11.9% English, 9.0% Dutch
Employment: 8.1% management, business, and financial, 3.6% computer, engineering, and science, 5.9% education, legal, community service, arts, and media, 7.9% healthcare practitioners, 23.6% service, 14.0% sales and office, 17.6% natural resources, construction, and maintenance, 19.3% production, transportation, and material moving
Income: Per capita: $23,123; Median household: $46,250; Average household: $54,201; Households with income of $100,000 or more: 12.4%; Poverty rate: 12.4%
Educational Attainment: High school diploma or higher: 85.2%; Bachelor's degree or higher: 21.5%; Graduate/professional degree or higher: 8.1%
Housing: Homeownership rate: 75.6%; Median home value: $144,800; Median year structure built: 1973; Homeowner vacancy rate: 2.2%; Median selected monthly owner costs: $1,166 with a mortgage, $526 without a mortgage; Median gross rent: $723 per month; Rental vacancy rate: 0.0%
Health Insurance: 92.3% have insurance; 69.2% have private insurance; 44.0% have public insurance; 7.7% do not have insurance; 0.6% of children under 18 do not have insurance
Transportation: Commute: 90.0% car, 1.2% public transportation, 2.8% walk, 4.9% work from home; Mean travel time to work: 23.8 minutes

HOBART
(village). Covers a land area of 0.498 square miles and a water area of 0.007 square miles. Located at 42.37° N. Lat; 74.67° W. Long. Elevation is 1,650 feet.
Population: 481; Growth (since 2000): 23.3%; Density: 966.1 persons per square mile; Race: 91.9% White, 5.0% Black/African American, 1.9% Asian, 0.0% American Indian/Alaska Native, 0.0% Native Hawaiian/Other Pacific Islander, 1.2% Two or more races, 0.8% Hispanic of any race; Average household size: 2.64; Median age: 41.7; Age under 18: 21.4%; Age 65 and over: 17.3%; Males per 100 females: 106.1; Marriage status: 25.3% never married, 61.2% now married, 3.6% separated, 5.9% widowed, 7.5% divorced; Foreign born: 3.5%; Speak English only: 95.1%; With disability: 14.3%; Veterans: 11.1%; Ancestry: 28.7% Irish, 17.5% German, 14.6% English, 12.7% Italian, 8.7% Dutch
Employment: 6.1% management, business, and financial, 4.6% computer, engineering, and science, 13.2% education, legal, community service, arts, and media, 7.1% healthcare practitioners, 19.3% service, 20.8% sales and office, 5.6% natural resources, construction, and maintenance, 23.4% production, transportation, and material moving
Income: Per capita: $21,379; Median household: $46,346; Average household: $52,581; Households with income of $100,000 or more: 13.2%; Poverty rate: 19.5%
Educational Attainment: High school diploma or higher: 92.3%; Bachelor's degree or higher: 28.2%; Graduate/professional degree or higher: 8.9%
Housing: Homeownership rate: 62.1%; Median home value: $137,500; Median year structure built: Before 1940; Homeowner vacancy rate: 3.4%; Median selected monthly owner costs: $1,225 with a mortgage, $539 without a mortgage; Median gross rent: $608 per month; Rental vacancy rate: 4.2%
Health Insurance: 93.8% have insurance; 64.2% have private insurance; 43.2% have public insurance; 6.2% do not have insurance; 0.0% of children under 18 do not have insurance
Transportation: Commute: 77.7% car, 3.6% public transportation, 8.3% walk, 10.4% work from home; Mean travel time to work: 17.2 minutes

KORTRIGHT
(town). Covers a land area of 62.451 square miles and a water area of 0.182 square miles. Located at 42.40° N. Lat; 74.78° W. Long.
Population: 1,406; Growth (since 2000): -13.9%; Density: 22.5 persons per square mile; Race: 92.5% White, 1.7% Black/African American, 1.8% Asian, 0.0% American Indian/Alaska Native, 0.0% Native Hawaiian/Other Pacific Islander, 2.8% Two or more races, 3.8% Hispanic of any race; Average household size: 2.50; Median age: 46.6; Age under 18: 20.1%; Age 65 and over: 23.5%; Males per 100 females: 107.8; Marriage status: 30.9% never married, 52.1% now married, 2.6% separated, 7.3% widowed, 9.7% divorced; Foreign born: 4.7%; Speak English only: 96.6%; With disability: 18.0%; Veterans: 8.6%; Ancestry: 26.8% German, 16.4% Irish, 10.0% English, 9.2% Polish, 7.7% Italian

Employment: 18.1% management, business, and financial, 5.8% computer, engineering, and science, 8.7% education, legal, community service, arts, and media, 3.2% healthcare practitioners, 16.6% service, 18.7% sales and office, 12.4% natural resources, construction, and maintenance, 16.5% production, transportation, and material moving
Income: Per capita: $26,490; Median household: $53,661; Average household: $65,948; Households with income of $100,000 or more: 20.2%; Poverty rate: 11.4%
Educational Attainment: High school diploma or higher: 85.0%; Bachelor's degree or higher: 19.0%; Graduate/professional degree or higher: 6.5%
Housing: Homeownership rate: 89.5%; Median home value: $158,800; Median year structure built: 1980; Homeowner vacancy rate: 0.6%; Median selected monthly owner costs: $1,123 with a mortgage, $558 without a mortgage; Median gross rent: $670 per month; Rental vacancy rate: 13.8%
Health Insurance: 94.4% have insurance; 77.4% have private insurance; 41.1% have public insurance; 5.6% do not have insurance; 4.1% of children under 18 do not have insurance
Transportation: Commute: 88.2% car, 2.0% public transportation, 4.4% walk, 4.1% work from home; Mean travel time to work: 22.9 minutes

LONG EDDY (unincorporated postal area)
ZCTA: 12760
Covers a land area of 42.316 square miles and a water area of 0.403 square miles. Located at 41.90° N. Lat; 75.11° W. Long..
Population: 428; Growth (since 2000): -41.3%; Density: 10.1 persons per square mile; Race: 96.3% White, 3.7% Black/African American, 0.0% Asian, 0.0% American Indian/Alaska Native, 0.0% Native Hawaiian/Other Pacific Islander, 0.0% Two or more races, 4.9% Hispanic of any race; Average household size: 2.02; Median age: 63.3; Age under 18: 8.6%; Age 65 and over: 37.6%; Males per 100 females: 115.2; Marriage status: 17.7% never married, 43.5% now married, 0.0% separated, 13.7% widowed, 25.1% divorced; Foreign born: 3.7%; Speak English only: 96.9%; With disability: 25.7%; Veterans: 15.9%; Ancestry: 29.4% Irish, 27.1% German, 14.5% American, 8.9% Italian, 7.9% English
Employment: 16.0% management, business, and financial, 0.0% computer, engineering, and science, 9.9% education, legal, community service, arts, and media, 0.0% healthcare practitioners, 28.2% service, 29.0% sales and office, 4.6% natural resources, construction, and maintenance, 12.2% production, transportation, and material moving
Income: Per capita: $32,722; Median household: $50,962; Average household: $63,769; Households with income of $100,000 or more: 21.2%; Poverty rate: 10.7%
Educational Attainment: High school diploma or higher: 87.7%; Bachelor's degree or higher: 10.7%; Graduate/professional degree or higher: 1.9%
Housing: Homeownership rate: 87.3%; Median home value: $114,700; Median year structure built: 1970; Homeowner vacancy rate: 7.0%; Median selected monthly owner costs: $1,359 with a mortgage, $440 without a mortgage; Median gross rent: $925 per month; Rental vacancy rate: 0.0%
Health Insurance: 81.3% have insurance; 65.4% have private insurance; 48.1% have public insurance; 18.7% do not have insurance; 27.0% of children under 18 do not have insurance
Transportation: Commute: 83.5% car, 0.0% public transportation, 16.5% walk, 0.0% work from home; Mean travel time to work: 39.8 minutes

MARGARETVILLE (village). Covers a land area of 0.684 square miles and a water area of 0.018 square miles. Located at 42.15° N. Lat; 74.65° W. Long. Elevation is 1,316 feet.
Population: 566; Growth (since 2000): -12.0%; Density: 827.1 persons per square mile; Race: 97.3% White, 1.2% Black/African American, 0.0% Asian, 0.0% American Indian/Alaska Native, 0.0% Native Hawaiian/Other Pacific Islander, 1.4% Two or more races, 0.0% Hispanic of any race; Average household size: 1.75; Median age: 61.9; Age under 18: 4.6%; Age 65 and over: 42.4%; Males per 100 females: 86.8; Marriage status: 27.2% never married, 36.8% now married, 0.5% separated, 19.7% widowed, 16.3% divorced; Foreign born: 6.0%; Speak English only: 95.8%; With disability: 28.2%; Veterans: 5.2%; Ancestry: 25.1% Irish, 17.5% German, 12.0% English, 10.1% Italian, 8.3% Dutch
Employment: 15.2% management, business, and financial, 0.0% computer, engineering, and science, 13.9% education, legal, community service, arts, and media, 4.2% healthcare practitioners, 20.7% service,

20.7% sales and office, 13.5% natural resources, construction, and maintenance, 11.8% production, transportation, and material moving
Income: Per capita: $21,675; Median household: $25,673; Average household: $39,053; Households with income of $100,000 or more: 7.9%; Poverty rate: 19.4%
Educational Attainment: High school diploma or higher: 81.2%; Bachelor's degree or higher: 16.2%; Graduate/professional degree or higher: 8.1%
School District(s)
Margaretville Central SD (PK-12)
    2014-15 Enrollment: 383. . . . . (845) 586-2647
Housing: Homeownership rate: 50.9%; Median home value: $170,500; Median year structure built: Before 1940; Homeowner vacancy rate: 0.0%; Median selected monthly owner costs: $1,228 with a mortgage, $607 without a mortgage; Median gross rent: $702 per month; Rental vacancy rate: 17.1%
Health Insurance: 78.5% have insurance; 59.1% have private insurance; 50.5% have public insurance; 21.5% do not have insurance; 11.5% of children under 18 do not have insurance
Hospitals: Margaretville Memorial Hospital (15 beds)
Transportation: Commute: 82.1% car, 0.0% public transportation, 14.8% walk, 0.9% work from home; Mean travel time to work: 18.5 minutes

MASONVILLE (town). Covers a land area of 54.264 square miles and a water area of 0.179 square miles. Located at 42.23° N. Lat; 75.34° W. Long. Elevation is 1,293 feet.
Population: 1,550; Growth (since 2000): 10.3%; Density: 28.6 persons per square mile; Race: 96.1% White, 0.6% Black/African American, 1.2% Asian, 0.0% American Indian/Alaska Native, 0.0% Native Hawaiian/Other Pacific Islander, 2.1% Two or more races, 1.7% Hispanic of any race; Average household size: 2.65; Median age: 40.9; Age under 18: 24.5%; Age 65 and over: 16.5%; Males per 100 females: 107.9; Marriage status: 25.8% never married, 56.2% now married, 0.9% separated, 8.2% widowed, 9.7% divorced; Foreign born: 5.3%; Speak English only: 92.5%; With disability: 13.0%; Veterans: 9.9%; Ancestry: 22.2% German, 22.0% Irish, 11.2% English, 8.4% Italian, 7.2% Polish
Employment: 12.6% management, business, and financial, 1.3% computer, engineering, and science, 4.1% education, legal, community service, arts, and media, 3.3% healthcare practitioners, 14.9% service, 24.6% sales and office, 11.9% natural resources, construction, and maintenance, 27.4% production, transportation, and material moving
Income: Per capita: $25,905; Median household: $53,011; Average household: $66,689; Households with income of $100,000 or more: 16.0%; Poverty rate: 6.9%
Educational Attainment: High school diploma or higher: 87.0%; Bachelor's degree or higher: 12.1%; Graduate/professional degree or higher: 3.5%
Housing: Homeownership rate: 87.0%; Median home value: $116,800; Median year structure built: 1973; Homeowner vacancy rate: 4.1%; Median selected monthly owner costs: $1,195 with a mortgage, $469 without a mortgage; Median gross rent: $532 per month; Rental vacancy rate: 6.2%
Health Insurance: 94.9% have insurance; 76.3% have private insurance; 35.1% have public insurance; 5.1% do not have insurance; 0.0% of children under 18 do not have insurance
Transportation: Commute: 87.6% car, 2.3% public transportation, 3.9% walk, 5.7% work from home; Mean travel time to work: 26.3 minutes

MEREDITH (town). Covers a land area of 58.102 square miles and a water area of 0.214 square miles. Located at 42.37° N. Lat; 74.94° W. Long. Elevation is 2,169 feet.
Population: 1,437; Growth (since 2000): -9.5%; Density: 24.7 persons per square mile; Race: 97.5% White, 0.2% Black/African American, 1.3% Asian, 0.0% American Indian/Alaska Native, 0.0% Native Hawaiian/Other Pacific Islander, 0.7% Two or more races, 4.4% Hispanic of any race; Average household size: 2.31; Median age: 50.1; Age under 18: 11.2%; Age 65 and over: 21.6%; Males per 100 females: 99.6; Marriage status: 27.7% never married, 56.5% now married, 2.7% separated, 4.1% widowed, 11.7% divorced; Foreign born: 5.3%; Speak English only: 93.3%; With disability: 10.9%; Veterans: 10.4%; Ancestry: 20.7% German, 19.8% Irish, 11.6% English, 10.1% Italian, 7.4% Dutch
Employment: 15.8% management, business, and financial, 3.2% computer, engineering, and science, 16.7% education, legal, community service, arts, and media, 5.2% healthcare practitioners, 20.8% service, 15.9% sales and office, 10.1% natural resources, construction, and maintenance, 12.2% production, transportation, and material moving

Income: Per capita: $33,205; Median household: $52,378; Average household: $76,424; Households with income of $100,000 or more: 20.8%; Poverty rate: 9.0%
Educational Attainment: High school diploma or higher: 93.0%; Bachelor's degree or higher: 31.1%; Graduate/professional degree or higher: 14.2%
Housing: Homeownership rate: 79.7%; Median home value: $156,300; Median year structure built: 1976; Homeowner vacancy rate: 0.0%; Median selected monthly owner costs: $1,373 with a mortgage, $510 without a mortgage; Median gross rent: $832 per month; Rental vacancy rate: 7.5%
Health Insurance: 89.1% have insurance; 72.0% have private insurance; 36.1% have public insurance; 10.9% do not have insurance; 1.9% of children under 18 do not have insurance
Transportation: Commute: 86.8% car, 0.0% public transportation, 3.3% walk, 8.5% work from home; Mean travel time to work: 24.6 minutes

MERIDALE (unincorporated postal area)
ZCTA: 13806

Covers a land area of 3.095 square miles and a water area of 0.004 square miles. Located at 42.38° N. Lat; 74.96° W. Long. Elevation is 1,778 feet.
Population: 188; Growth (since 2000): n/a; Density: 60.7 persons per square mile; Race: 97.9% White, 0.0% Black/African American, 0.0% Asian, 0.0% American Indian/Alaska Native, 0.0% Native Hawaiian/Other Pacific Islander, 2.1% Two or more races, 1.1% Hispanic of any race; Average household size: 2.54; Median age: 47.3; Age under 18: 4.8%; Age 65 and over: 19.1%; Males per 100 females: 97.1; Marriage status: 35.9% never married, 39.1% now married, 6.5% separated, 3.8% widowed, 21.2% divorced; Foreign born: 0.0%; Speak English only: 100.0%; With disability: 6.4%; Veterans: 12.8%; Ancestry: 10.6% German, 8.5% English, 8.0% Scottish, 7.4% Irish, 4.8% American
Employment: 2.5% management, business, and financial, 0.0% computer, engineering, and science, 32.2% education, legal, community service, arts, and media, 2.5% healthcare practitioners, 22.9% service, 25.4% sales and office, 0.0% natural resources, construction, and maintenance, 14.4% production, transportation, and material moving
Income: Per capita: $29,040; Median household: $62,955; Average household: $67,485; Households with income of $100,000 or more: 21.7%; Poverty rate: 5.9%
Educational Attainment: High school diploma or higher: 92.8%; Bachelor's degree or higher: 33.1%; Graduate/professional degree or higher: 6.6%
Housing: Homeownership rate: 83.8%; Median home value: $151,900; Median year structure built: Before 1940; Homeowner vacancy rate: 0.0%; Median selected monthly owner costs: $0 with a mortgage, $517 without a mortgage; Median gross rent: n/a per month; Rental vacancy rate: 0.0%
Health Insurance: 93.6% have insurance; 80.3% have private insurance; 30.3% have public insurance; 6.4% do not have insurance; 0.0% of children under 18 do not have insurance
Transportation: Commute: 97.1% car, 0.0% public transportation, 0.0% walk, 0.0% work from home; Mean travel time to work: 19.2 minutes

MIDDLETOWN (town). Covers a land area of 96.674 square miles and a water area of 0.620 square miles. Located at 42.16° N. Lat; 74.63° W. Long.
Population: 3,671; Growth (since 2000): -9.4%; Density: 38.0 persons per square mile; Race: 93.0% White, 0.5% Black/African American, 0.9% Asian, 0.6% American Indian/Alaska Native, 0.2% Native Hawaiian/Other Pacific Islander, 2.9% Two or more races, 10.1% Hispanic of any race; Average household size: 2.04; Median age: 51.9; Age under 18: 13.8%; Age 65 and over: 23.2%; Males per 100 females: 96.7; Marriage status: 25.7% never married, 50.8% now married, 5.8% separated, 10.1% widowed, 13.4% divorced; Foreign born: 8.8%; Speak English only: 87.4%; With disability: 17.6%; Veterans: 6.4%; Ancestry: 20.9% Irish, 18.5% German, 15.4% English, 11.7% Italian, 8.3% Dutch
Employment: 12.4% management, business, and financial, 5.1% computer, engineering, and science, 9.2% education, legal, community service, arts, and media, 6.4% healthcare practitioners, 20.0% service, 21.8% sales and office, 15.6% natural resources, construction, and maintenance, 9.5% production, transportation, and material moving
Income: Per capita: $28,184; Median household: $42,103; Average household: $56,897; Households with income of $100,000 or more: 13.6%; Poverty rate: 13.7%

Educational Attainment: High school diploma or higher: 86.2%; Bachelor's degree or higher: 23.2%; Graduate/professional degree or higher: 7.1%
Housing: Homeownership rate: 71.6%; Median home value: $184,900; Median year structure built: 1975; Homeowner vacancy rate: 1.0%; Median selected monthly owner costs: $1,192 with a mortgage, $575 without a mortgage; Median gross rent: $744 per month; Rental vacancy rate: 11.0%
Health Insurance: 87.3% have insurance; 62.4% have private insurance; 42.3% have public insurance; 12.7% do not have insurance; 5.1% of children under 18 do not have insurance
Transportation: Commute: 82.1% car, 2.5% public transportation, 3.2% walk, 11.9% work from home; Mean travel time to work: 23.0 minutes

NEW KINGSTON (unincorporated postal area)
ZCTA: 12459

Covers a land area of 7.609 square miles and a water area of 0.006 square miles. Located at 42.24° N. Lat; 74.68° W. Long. Elevation is 1,686 feet.
Population: 151; Growth (since 2000): -57.3%; Density: 19.8 persons per square mile; Race: 100.0% White, 0.0% Black/African American, 0.0% Asian, 0.0% American Indian/Alaska Native, 0.0% Native Hawaiian/Other Pacific Islander, 0.0% Two or more races, 6.0% Hispanic of any race; Average household size: 1.44; Median age: 61.9; Age under 18: 0.0%; Age 65 and over: 41.1%; Males per 100 females: 103.8; Marriage status: 0.0% never married, 66.9% now married, 0.0% separated, 16.6% widowed, 16.6% divorced; Foreign born: 0.0%; Speak English only: 100.0%; With disability: 33.1%; Veterans: 7.9%; Ancestry: 41.7% Polish, 21.2% Scandinavian, 16.6% Dutch, 16.6% German, 7.9% Irish
Employment: 20.8% management, business, and financial, 0.0% computer, engineering, and science, 60.4% education, legal, community service, arts, and media, 18.9% healthcare practitioners, 0.0% service, 0.0% sales and office, 0.0% natural resources, construction, and maintenance, 0.0% production, transportation, and material moving
Income: Per capita: $40,416; Median household: $40,195; Average household: $60,026; Households with income of $100,000 or more: 10.5%; Poverty rate: n/a
Educational Attainment: High school diploma or higher: 83.4%; Bachelor's degree or higher: 27.8%; Graduate/professional degree or higher: 27.8%
Housing: Homeownership rate: 100.0%; Median home value: n/a; Median year structure built: 1975; Homeowner vacancy rate: 0.0%; Median selected monthly owner costs: $1,205 with a mortgage, $0 without a mortgage; Median gross rent: n/a per month; Rental vacancy rate: 0.0%
Health Insurance: 100.0% have insurance; 60.9% have private insurance; 80.1% have public insurance; 0.0% do not have insurance; 0.0% of children under 18 do not have insurance
Transportation: Commute: 0.0% car, 39.6% public transportation, 0.0% walk, 60.4% work from home; Mean travel time to work: 0.0 minutes

ROXBURY (town). Covers a land area of 87.114 square miles and a water area of 0.490 square miles. Located at 42.31° N. Lat; 74.53° W. Long. Elevation is 1,493 feet.
Population: 2,338; Growth (since 2000): -6.8%; Density: 26.8 persons per square mile; Race: 93.2% White, 4.0% Black/African American, 0.2% Asian, 0.5% American Indian/Alaska Native, 0.0% Native Hawaiian/Other Pacific Islander, 2.1% Two or more races, 2.2% Hispanic of any race; Average household size: 2.35; Median age: 45.6; Age under 18: 18.9%; Age 65 and over: 23.5%; Males per 100 females: 98.7; Marriage status: 28.2% never married, 54.3% now married, 2.3% separated, 8.5% widowed, 9.0% divorced; Foreign born: 4.6%; Speak English only: 93.7%; With disability: 16.6%; Veterans: 8.8%; Ancestry: 23.4% German, 23.4% Irish, 12.6% Italian, 12.4% Dutch, 10.7% English
Employment: 2.3% management, business, and financial, 3.9% computer, engineering, and science, 17.4% education, legal, community service, arts, and media, 5.0% healthcare practitioners, 28.3% service, 16.4% sales and office, 12.0% natural resources, construction, and maintenance, 14.7% production, transportation, and material moving
Income: Per capita: $21,524; Median household: $38,662; Average household: $49,528; Households with income of $100,000 or more: 10.6%; Poverty rate: 17.5%
Educational Attainment: High school diploma or higher: 85.1%; Bachelor's degree or higher: 21.0%; Graduate/professional degree or higher: 7.8%

School District(s)
Roxbury Central SD (PK-12)
    2014-15 Enrollment: 331 . . . . (607) 326-4151
Housing: Homeownership rate: 73.9%; Median home value: $153,500;
Median year structure built: 1973; Homeowner vacancy rate: 7.9%; Median
selected monthly owner costs: $1,311 with a mortgage, $530 without a
mortgage; Median gross rent: $681 per month; Rental vacancy rate: 12.5%
Health Insurance: 94.1% have insurance; 69.8% have private insurance;
51.8% have public insurance; 5.9% do not have insurance; 6.1% of
children under 18 do not have insurance
Transportation: Commute: 82.2% car, 4.5% public transportation, 3.6%
walk, 8.5% work from home; Mean travel time to work: 25.6 minutes

SIDNEY (town). Covers a land area of 49.928 square miles and a water
area of 0.675 square miles. Located at 42.31° N. Lat; 75.28° W. Long.
Elevation is 991 feet.
Population: 5,647; Growth (since 2000): -7.6%; Density: 113.1 persons
per square mile; Race: 96.7% White, 0.0% Black/African American, 0.9%
Asian, 0.0% American Indian/Alaska Native, 0.0% Native Hawaiian/Other
Pacific Islander, 2.4% Two or more races, 2.9% Hispanic of any race;
Average household size: 2.15; Median age: 48.1; Age under 18: 21.8%;
Age 65 and over: 22.5%; Males per 100 females: 94.8; Marriage status:
24.0% never married, 56.3% now married, 5.2% separated, 5.8%
widowed, 13.9% divorced; Foreign born: 2.7%; Speak English only: 95.0%;
With disability: 16.6%; Veterans: 10.7%; Ancestry: 18.7% English, 16.9%
Irish, 16.2% German, 11.8% American, 6.5% Italian
Employment: 11.9% management, business, and financial, 2.1%
computer, engineering, and science, 12.1% education, legal, community
service, arts, and media, 4.2% healthcare practitioners, 17.2% service,
29.4% sales and office, 8.8% natural resources, construction, and
maintenance, 14.3% production, transportation, and material moving
Income: Per capita: $21,910; Median household: $33,719; Average
household: $46,658; Households with income of $100,000 or more: 11.0%;
Poverty rate: 13.6%
Educational Attainment: High school diploma or higher: 89.1%;
Bachelor's degree or higher: 16.7%; Graduate/professional degree or
higher: 6.8%

School District(s)
Sidney Central SD (PK-12)
    2014-15 Enrollment: 1,088 . . . . (607) 561-7700
Housing: Homeownership rate: 65.6%; Median home value: $80,500;
Median year structure built: 1957; Homeowner vacancy rate: 2.2%; Median
selected monthly owner costs: $952 with a mortgage, $433 without a
mortgage; Median gross rent: $645 per month; Rental vacancy rate: 4.1%
Health Insurance: 91.7% have insurance; 58.6% have private insurance;
50.1% have public insurance; 8.3% do not have insurance; 6.8% of
children under 18 do not have insurance
Newspapers: Tri-Town News (weekly circulation 5,000)
Transportation: Commute: 86.4% car, 0.0% public transportation, 9.6%
walk, 4.0% work from home; Mean travel time to work: 17.9 minutes

SIDNEY (village). Covers a land area of 2.374 square miles and a water
area of 0.015 square miles. Located at 42.30° N. Lat; 75.40° W. Long.
Elevation is 991 feet.
Population: 4,146; Growth (since 2000): 1.9%; Density: 1,746.2 persons
per square mile; Race: 96.1% White, 0.0% Black/African American, 1.2%
Asian, 0.0% American Indian/Alaska Native, 0.0% Native Hawaiian/Other
Pacific Islander, 2.7% Two or more races, 3.8% Hispanic of any race;
Average household size: 2.26; Median age: 41.9; Age under 18: 26.9%;
Age 65 and over: 17.1%; Males per 100 females: 88.9; Marriage status:
26.0% never married, 51.5% now married, 6.1% separated, 6.8%
widowed, 15.7% divorced; Foreign born: 2.9%; Speak English only: 93.9%;
With disability: 13.5%; Veterans: 9.2%; Ancestry: 18.2% English, 17.6%
German, 16.3% Irish, 12.2% American, 6.3% Italian
Employment: 12.1% management, business, and financial, 2.0%
computer, engineering, and science, 14.4% education, legal, community
service, arts, and media, 3.0% healthcare practitioners, 22.1% service,
21.0% sales and office, 7.4% natural resources, construction, and
maintenance, 18.0% production, transportation, and material moving
Income: Per capita: $20,393; Median household: $31,484; Average
household: $45,512; Households with income of $100,000 or more: 12.4%;
Poverty rate: 16.8%
Educational Attainment: High school diploma or higher: 91.0%;
Bachelor's degree or higher: 20.3%; Graduate/professional degree or
higher: 9.0%

School District(s)
Sidney Central SD (PK-12)
    2014-15 Enrollment: 1,088 . . . . (607) 561-7700
Housing: Homeownership rate: 52.6%; Median home value: $81,600;
Median year structure built: 1957; Homeowner vacancy rate: 3.8%; Median
selected monthly owner costs: $982 with a mortgage, $536 without a
mortgage; Median gross rent: $638 per month; Rental vacancy rate: 4.2%
Health Insurance: 91.9% have insurance; 54.0% have private insurance;
51.1% have public insurance; 8.1% do not have insurance; 7.1% of
children under 18 do not have insurance
Safety: Violent crime rate: 18.4 per 10,000 population; Property crime rate:
434.1 per 10,000 population
Newspapers: Tri-Town News (weekly circulation 5,000)
Transportation: Commute: 86.8% car, 0.0% public transportation, 13.2%
walk, 0.0% work from home; Mean travel time to work: 17.7 minutes

SIDNEY CENTER (unincorporated postal area)
ZCTA: 13839
    Covers a land area of 39.754 square miles and a water area of 0.155
square miles. Located at 42.26° N. Lat; 75.25° W. Long. Elevation is
1,299 feet.
Population: 1,029; Growth (since 2000): -38.2%; Density: 25.9 persons
per square mile; Race: 94.6% White, 0.9% Black/African American,
1.3% Asian, 0.0% American Indian/Alaska Native, 0.0% Native
Hawaiian/Other Pacific Islander, 3.3% Two or more races, 3.5%
Hispanic of any race; Average household size: 2.07; Median age: 56.5;
Age under 18: 10.2%; Age 65 and over: 30.2%; Males per 100 females:
103.3; Marriage status: 27.5% never married, 58.6% now married, 5.6%
separated, 1.0% widowed, 12.9% divorced; Foreign born: 5.5%; Speak
English only: 92.7%; With disability: 21.7%; Veterans: 18.1%; Ancestry:
24.5% Irish, 23.7% German, 13.8% English, 10.9% Italian, 8.4%
American
Employment: 13.6% management, business, and financial, 0.0%
computer, engineering, and science, 10.3% education, legal, community
service, arts, and media, 5.2% healthcare practitioners, 10.9% service,
28.9% sales and office, 10.5% natural resources, construction, and
maintenance, 20.7% production, transportation, and material moving
Income: Per capita: $22,340; Median household: $44,000; Average
household: $45,510; Households with income of $100,000 or more:
7.6%; Poverty rate: 9.9%
Educational Attainment: High school diploma or higher: 86.7%;
Bachelor's degree or higher: 11.4%; Graduate/professional degree or
higher: 6.3%
Housing: Homeownership rate: 90.4%; Median home value: $91,400;
Median year structure built: 1968; Homeowner vacancy rate: 0.0%;
Median selected monthly owner costs: $980 with a mortgage, $358
without a mortgage; Median gross rent: $670 per month; Rental
vacancy rate: 0.0%
Health Insurance: 89.4% have insurance; 76.2% have private
insurance; 42.8% have public insurance; 10.6% do not have insurance;
0.0% of children under 18 do not have insurance
Transportation: Commute: 77.7% car, 0.6% public transportation, 3.0%
walk, 16.0% work from home; Mean travel time to work: 25.4 minutes

SOUTH KORTRIGHT (unincorporated postal area)
ZCTA: 13842
    Covers a land area of 12.491 square miles and a water area of 0.129
square miles. Located at 42.38° N. Lat; 74.72° W. Long. Elevation is
1,509 feet.
Population: 569; Growth (since 2000): 5.8%; Density: 45.6 persons per
square mile; Race: 89.8% White, 5.1% Black/African American, 0.0%
Asian, 0.0% American Indian/Alaska Native, 0.0% Native
Hawaiian/Other Pacific Islander, 4.2% Two or more races, 7.6%
Hispanic of any race; Average household size: 2.68; Median age: 45.2;
Age under 18: 13.2%; Age 65 and over: 15.3%; Males per 100 females:
155.5; Marriage status: 39.1% never married, 54.6% now married, 2.2%
separated, 4.4% widowed, 1.8% divorced; Foreign born: 2.8%; Speak
English only: 97.0%; With disability: 26.8%; Veterans: 3.4%; Ancestry:
26.9% German, 10.7% Dutch, 7.0% French, 6.9% Polish, 6.0% Italian
Employment: 23.0% management, business, and financial, 4.1%
computer, engineering, and science, 6.2% education, legal, community
service, arts, and media, 4.5% healthcare practitioners, 19.3% service,
23.9% sales and office, 1.6% natural resources, construction, and
maintenance, 17.3% production, transportation, and material moving

Income: Per capita: $21,560; Median household: $77,778; Average household: $73,491; Households with income of $100,000 or more: 15.1%; Poverty rate: 18.0%

Educational Attainment: High school diploma or higher: 83.3%; Bachelor's degree or higher: 15.9%; Graduate/professional degree or higher: 5.9%

School District(s)

South Kortright Central SD (PK-12)

2014-15 Enrollment: 408 . . . . (607) 538-9111

Housing: Homeownership rate: 90.8%; Median home value: $152,300; Median year structure built: 1982; Homeowner vacancy rate: 0.0%; Median selected monthly owner costs: $1,023 with a mortgage, $594 without a mortgage; Median gross rent: n/a per month; Rental vacancy rate: 0.0%

Health Insurance: 92.2% have insurance; 72.4% have private insurance; 35.4% have public insurance; 7.8% do not have insurance; 0.0% of children under 18 do not have insurance

Transportation: Commute: 87.1% car, 1.2% public transportation, 7.1% walk, 4.6% work from home; Mean travel time to work: 27.0 minutes

STAMFORD (town). Covers a land area of 48.505 square miles and a water area of 0.106 square miles. Located at 42.34° N. Lat; 74.67° W. Long. Elevation is 1,818 feet.

Population: 2,569; Growth (since 2000): 32.2%; Density: 53.0 persons per square mile; Race: 97.6% White, 1.4% Black/African American, 0.4% Asian, 0.0% American Indian/Alaska Native, 0.0% Native Hawaiian/Other Pacific Islander, 0.6% Two or more races, 1.3% Hispanic of any race; Average household size: 2.49; Median age: 47.1; Age under 18: 15.8%; Age 65 and over: 21.3%; Males per 100 females: 99.9; Marriage status: 30.6% never married, 54.4% now married, 2.8% separated, 5.8% widowed, 9.2% divorced; Foreign born: 3.3%; Speak English only: 93.7%; With disability: 21.1%; Veterans: 9.9%; Ancestry: 22.8% German, 20.6% Irish, 12.9% Italian, 10.9% English, 10.6% Dutch

Employment: 12.8% management, business, and financial, 3.0% computer, engineering, and science, 10.1% education, legal, community service, arts, and media, 4.1% healthcare practitioners, 26.7% service, 18.6% sales and office, 6.2% natural resources, construction, and maintenance, 18.5% production, transportation, and material moving

Income: Per capita: $21,930; Median household: $46,667; Average household: $53,013; Households with income of $100,000 or more: 12.1%; Poverty rate: 21.6%

Educational Attainment: High school diploma or higher: 86.0%; Bachelor's degree or higher: 21.8%; Graduate/professional degree or higher: 9.3%

School District(s)

Stamford Central SD (PK-12)

2014-15 Enrollment: 342 . . . . (607) 652-7301

Housing: Homeownership rate: 64.4%; Median home value: $131,200; Median year structure built: 1971; Homeowner vacancy rate: 2.4%; Median selected monthly owner costs: $1,153 with a mortgage, $492 without a mortgage; Median gross rent: $552 per month; Rental vacancy rate: 3.0%

Health Insurance: 90.5% have insurance; 58.5% have private insurance; 49.4% have public insurance; 9.5% do not have insurance; 4.2% of children under 18 do not have insurance

Newspapers: Mountain Eagle (weekly circulation 3,000)

Transportation: Commute: 87.6% car, 1.7% public transportation, 4.3% walk, 4.4% work from home; Mean travel time to work: 24.8 minutes

STAMFORD (village). Covers a land area of 1.333 square miles and a water area of 0.009 square miles. Located at 42.41° N. Lat; 74.62° W. Long. Elevation is 1,818 feet.

Population: 1,455; Growth (since 2000): 15.0%; Density: 1,091.8 persons per square mile; Race: 98.1% White, 0.7% Black/African American, 0.4% Asian, 0.0% American Indian/Alaska Native, 0.0% Native Hawaiian/Other Pacific Islander, 0.8% Two or more races, 3.0% Hispanic of any race; Average household size: 2.28; Median age: 45.8; Age under 18: 19.0%; Age 65 and over: 25.8%; Males per 100 females: 82.5; Marriage status: 33.9% never married, 36.2% now married, 1.5% separated, 14.7% widowed, 15.2% divorced; Foreign born: 6.2%; Speak English only: 92.1%; With disability: 22.4%; Veterans: 11.7%; Ancestry: 20.6% Irish, 18.8% German, 16.8% Italian, 11.8% English, 8.4% Dutch

Employment: 11.9% management, business, and financial, 4.8% computer, engineering, and science, 13.6% education, legal, community service, arts, and media, 2.4% healthcare practitioners, 30.4% service,

14.3% sales and office, 7.6% natural resources, construction, and maintenance, 14.9% production, transportation, and material moving

Income: Per capita: $20,901; Median household: $37,935; Average household: $47,648; Households with income of $100,000 or more: 13.9%; Poverty rate: 26.2%

Educational Attainment: High school diploma or higher: 86.0%; Bachelor's degree or higher: 25.6%; Graduate/professional degree or higher: 10.1%

School District(s)

Stamford Central SD (PK-12)

2014-15 Enrollment: 342 . . . . (607) 652-7301

Housing: Homeownership rate: 49.8%; Median home value: $124,300; Median year structure built: 1941; Homeowner vacancy rate: 2.5%; Median selected monthly owner costs: $1,242 with a mortgage, $563 without a mortgage; Median gross rent: $577 per month; Rental vacancy rate: 2.7%

Health Insurance: 90.5% have insurance; 57.5% have private insurance; 48.5% have public insurance; 9.5% do not have insurance; 6.2% of children under 18 do not have insurance

Newspapers: Mountain Eagle (weekly circulation 3,000)

Transportation: Commute: 81.1% car, 1.5% public transportation, 6.9% walk, 5.5% work from home; Mean travel time to work: 27.2 minutes

Additional Information Contacts

Village of Stamford . . . . (607) 652-6671
  http://www.stamfordny.com/villagewebsite

TOMPKINS (town). Covers a land area of 98.133 square miles and a water area of 6.314 square miles. Located at 42.12° N. Lat; 75.27° W. Long.

Population: 1,033; Growth (since 2000): -6.5%; Density: 10.5 persons per square mile; Race: 96.6% White, 2.9% Black/African American, 0.0% Asian, 0.0% American Indian/Alaska Native, 0.0% Native Hawaiian/Other Pacific Islander, 0.5% Two or more races, 0.5% Hispanic of any race; Average household size: 2.50; Median age: 44.8; Age under 18: 18.7%; Age 65 and over: 19.5%; Males per 100 females: 104.4; Marriage status: 32.1% never married, 55.0% now married, 5.2% separated, 2.8% widowed, 10.2% divorced; Foreign born: 2.3%; Speak English only: 95.7%; With disability: 17.3%; Veterans: 8.5%; Ancestry: 26.7% German, 13.6% Irish, 9.9% English, 9.2% French, 7.6% Polish

Employment: 4.3% management, business, and financial, 1.1% computer, engineering, and science, 4.6% education, legal, community service, arts, and media, 2.8% healthcare practitioners, 7.8% service, 28.5% sales and office, 21.3% natural resources, construction, and maintenance, 29.6% production, transportation, and material moving

Income: Per capita: $20,188; Median household: $48,229; Average household: $49,088; Households with income of $100,000 or more: 9.4%; Poverty rate: 15.8%

Educational Attainment: High school diploma or higher: 83.2%; Bachelor's degree or higher: 7.5%; Graduate/professional degree or higher: 4.6%

Housing: Homeownership rate: 79.2%; Median home value: $140,800; Median year structure built: 1977; Homeowner vacancy rate: 4.9%; Median selected monthly owner costs: $1,109 with a mortgage, $423 without a mortgage; Median gross rent: $629 per month; Rental vacancy rate: 0.0%

Health Insurance: 88.7% have insurance; 76.7% have private insurance; 33.8% have public insurance; 11.3% do not have insurance; 12.4% of children under 18 do not have insurance

Transportation: Commute: 91.1% car, 1.3% public transportation, 3.3% walk, 1.3% work from home; Mean travel time to work: 26.2 minutes

TREADWELL (unincorporated postal area)

ZCTA: 13846

Covers a land area of 8.131 square miles and a water area of 0.034 square miles. Located at 42.36° N. Lat; 75.05° W. Long. Elevation is 1,529 feet.

Population: 251; Growth (since 2000): -26.6%; Density: 30.9 persons per square mile; Race: 100.0% White, 0.0% Black/African American, 0.0% Asian, 0.0% American Indian/Alaska Native, 0.0% Native Hawaiian/Other Pacific Islander, 0.0% Two or more races, 0.0% Hispanic of any race; Average household size: 2.26; Median age: 55.3; Age under 18: 17.5%; Age 65 and over: 32.3%; Males per 100 females: 90.6; Marriage status: 10.9% never married, 72.7% now married, 0.0% separated, 8.6% widowed, 7.7% divorced; Foreign born: 0.0%; Speak English only: 94.7%; With disability: 22.7%; Veterans: 22.7%; Ancestry: 41.0% Irish, 33.5% German, 32.7% English, 11.6% Italian, 8.4% Norwegian

Employment: 28.4% management, business, and financial, 0.0% computer, engineering, and science, 21.6% education, legal, community service, arts, and media, 0.0% healthcare practitioners, 15.9% service, 4.5% sales and office, 17.0% natural resources, construction, and maintenance, 12.5% production, transportation, and material moving
Income: Per capita: $24,731; Median household: $45,625; Average household: $54,195; Households with income of $100,000 or more: 8.1%; Poverty rate: 14.7%
Educational Attainment: High school diploma or higher: 93.7%; Bachelor's degree or higher: 31.4%; Graduate/professional degree or higher: 15.9%
Housing: Homeownership rate: 100.0%; Median home value: $142,400; Median year structure built: Before 1940; Homeowner vacancy rate: 9.4%; Median selected monthly owner costs: $1,581 with a mortgage, $575 without a mortgage; Median gross rent: n/a per month; Rental vacancy rate: 0.0%
Health Insurance: 95.6% have insurance; 86.1% have private insurance; 47.0% have public insurance; 4.4% do not have insurance; 0.0% of children under 18 do not have insurance
Transportation: Commute: 87.5% car, 0.0% public transportation, 0.0% walk, 12.5% work from home; Mean travel time to work: 24.0 minutes

TROUT CREEK (unincorporated postal area)
ZCTA: 13847
Covers a land area of 3.260 square miles and a water area of 0.023 square miles. Located at 42.18° N. Lat; 75.29° W. Long. Elevation is 1,289 feet.
Population: 55; Growth (since 2000): n/a; Density: 16.9 persons per square mile; Race: 100.0% White, 0.0% Black/African American, 0.0% Asian, 0.0% American Indian/Alaska Native, 0.0% Native Hawaiian/Other Pacific Islander, 0.0% Two or more races, 0.0% Hispanic of any race; Average household size: 4.58; Median age: 21.9; Age under 18: 23.6%; Age 65 and over: 0.0%; Males per 100 females: 86.1; Marriage status: 61.8% never married, 32.7% now married, 0.0% separated, 0.0% widowed, 5.5% divorced; Foreign born: 0.0%; Speak English only: 100.0%; With disability: 40.0%; Veterans: 0.0%; Ancestry: 78.2% German, 56.4% Irish, 27.3% Polish, 5.5% English
Employment: 0.0% management, business, and financial, 15.0% computer, engineering, and science, 0.0% education, legal, community service, arts, and media, 0.0% healthcare practitioners, 0.0% service, 20.0% sales and office, 0.0% natural resources, construction, and maintenance, 65.0% production, transportation, and material moving
Income: Per capita: $9,349; Median household: n/a; Average household: n/a; Households with income of $100,000 or more: n/a; Poverty rate: n/a
Educational Attainment: High school diploma or higher: 57.1%; Bachelor's degree or higher: 14.3%; Graduate/professional degree or higher: n/a
Housing: Homeownership rate: 25.0%; Median home value: n/a; Median year structure built: 1990; Homeowner vacancy rate: 81.3%; Median selected monthly owner costs: $0 with a mortgage, $0 without a mortgage; Median gross rent: n/a per month; Rental vacancy rate: 0.0%
Health Insurance: 100.0% have insurance; 100.0% have private insurance; 72.7% have public insurance; 0.0% do not have insurance; 0.0% of children under 18 do not have insurance
Transportation: Commute: 100.0% car, 0.0% public transportation, 0.0% walk, 0.0% work from home; Mean travel time to work: 0.0 minutes

WALTON (town). Covers a land area of 96.837 square miles and a water area of 0.780 square miles. Located at 42.17° N. Lat; 75.13° W. Long. Elevation is 1,207 feet.
Population: 5,436; Growth (since 2000): -3.0%; Density: 56.1 persons per square mile; Race: 98.5% White, 0.2% Black/African American, 0.0% Asian, 0.0% American Indian/Alaska Native, 0.0% Native Hawaiian/Other Pacific Islander, 1.3% Two or more races, 2.6% Hispanic of any race; Average household size: 2.21; Median age: 44.5; Age under 18: 24.4%; Age 65 and over: 18.8%; Males per 100 females: 98.2; Marriage status: 27.5% never married, 53.8% now married, 3.9% separated, 6.4% widowed, 12.3% divorced; Foreign born: 1.2%; Speak English only: 98.4%; With disability: 17.1%; Veterans: 8.5%; Ancestry: 16.1% American, 14.3% Italian, 12.9% Irish, 11.1% German, 9.1% English
Employment: 9.5% management, business, and financial, 4.4% computer, engineering, and science, 9.5% education, legal, community service, arts, and media, 6.8% healthcare practitioners, 16.0% service, 19.8% sales and

office, 12.3% natural resources, construction, and maintenance, 21.8% production, transportation, and material moving
Income: Per capita: $21,764; Median household: $34,194; Average household: $47,146; Households with income of $100,000 or more: 12.6%; Poverty rate: 24.5%
Educational Attainment: High school diploma or higher: 79.3%; Bachelor's degree or higher: 16.3%; Graduate/professional degree or higher: 8.3%

School District(s)
Walton Central SD (PK-12)
    2014-15 Enrollment: 1,020 . . . . (607) 865-4116
Housing: Homeownership rate: 59.7%; Median home value: $117,100; Median year structure built: 1960; Homeowner vacancy rate: 1.8%; Median selected monthly owner costs: $1,143 with a mortgage, $463 without a mortgage; Median gross rent: $592 per month; Rental vacancy rate: 0.0%
Health Insurance: 88.4% have insurance; 60.4% have private insurance; 43.9% have public insurance; 11.6% do not have insurance; 8.1% of children under 18 do not have insurance
Hospitals: Delaware Valley Hospital (25 beds)
Newspapers: Walton Reporter (weekly circulation 5,100)
Transportation: Commute: 85.1% car, 1.1% public transportation, 5.4% walk, 7.4% work from home; Mean travel time to work: 21.7 minutes

WALTON (village). Covers a land area of 1.541 square miles and a water area of 0.060 square miles. Located at 42.17° N. Lat; 75.13° W. Long. Elevation is 1,207 feet.
Population: 3,026; Growth (since 2000): -1.4%; Density: 1,963.7 persons per square mile; Race: 98.9% White, 0.3% Black/African American, 0.0% Asian, 0.0% American Indian/Alaska Native, 0.0% Native Hawaiian/Other Pacific Islander, 0.8% Two or more races, 3.8% Hispanic of any race; Average household size: 2.28; Median age: 44.5; Age under 18: 26.1%; Age 65 and over: 21.1%; Males per 100 females: 92.0; Marriage status: 24.2% never married, 52.2% now married, 5.6% separated, 5.8% widowed, 17.8% divorced; Foreign born: 0.8%; Speak English only: 99.4%; With disability: 21.6%; Veterans: 10.8%; Ancestry: 20.3% Italian, 15.5% Irish, 12.0% American, 11.3% German, 6.8% Dutch
Employment: 8.2% management, business, and financial, 6.8% computer, engineering, and science, 11.0% education, legal, community service, arts, and media, 2.5% healthcare practitioners, 23.4% service, 9.6% sales and office, 11.3% natural resources, construction, and maintenance, 27.1% production, transportation, and material moving
Income: Per capita: $18,137; Median household: $28,068; Average household: $39,567; Households with income of $100,000 or more: 9.0%; Poverty rate: 30.9%
Educational Attainment: High school diploma or higher: 76.3%; Bachelor's degree or higher: 12.0%; Graduate/professional degree or higher: 5.0%

School District(s)
Walton Central SD (PK-12)
    2014-15 Enrollment: 1,020 . . . . (607) 865-4116
Housing: Homeownership rate: 46.8%; Median home value: $107,600; Median year structure built: Before 1940; Homeowner vacancy rate: 1.4%; Median selected monthly owner costs: $1,273 with a mortgage, $464 without a mortgage; Median gross rent: $569 per month; Rental vacancy rate: 0.0%
Health Insurance: 95.0% have insurance; 54.6% have private insurance; 58.8% have public insurance; 5.0% do not have insurance; 0.0% of children under 18 do not have insurance
Hospitals: Delaware Valley Hospital (25 beds)
Safety: Violent crime rate: 6.8 per 10,000 population; Property crime rate: 233.8 per 10,000 population
Newspapers: Walton Reporter (weekly circulation 5,100)
Transportation: Commute: 82.0% car, 2.7% public transportation, 6.4% walk, 6.5% work from home; Mean travel time to work: 20.2 minutes

WEST DAVENPORT (unincorporated postal area)
ZCTA: 13860
Covers a land area of 0.916 square miles and a water area of 0.002 square miles. Located at 42.45° N. Lat; 74.94° W. Long. Elevation is 1,181 feet.
Population: 56; Growth (since 2000): n/a; Density: 61.1 persons per square mile; Race: 100.0% White, 0.0% Black/African American, 0.0% Asian, 0.0% American Indian/Alaska Native, 0.0% Native Hawaiian/Other Pacific Islander, 0.0% Two or more races, 0.0% Hispanic of any race; Average household size: 2.67; Median age: 31.2;

Age under 18: 33.9%; Age 65 and over: 0.0%; Males per 100 females: 91.8; Marriage status: 59.6% never married, 40.4% now married, 0.0% separated, 0.0% widowed, 0.0% divorced; Foreign born: 0.0%; Speak English only: 100.0%; With disability: 0.0%; Veterans: 0.0%; Ancestry: 69.6% Irish, 46.4% Polish, 35.7% German, 17.9% Scottish, 12.5% Scotch-Irish

Employment: 0.0% management, business, and financial, 0.0% computer, engineering, and science, 0.0% education, legal, community service, arts, and media, 24.3% healthcare practitioners, 18.9% service, 29.7% sales and office, 0.0% natural resources, construction, and maintenance, 27.0% production, transportation, and material moving
Income: Per capita: $24,057; Median household: n/a; Average household: n/a; Households with income of $100,000 or more: n/a; Poverty rate: n/a
Educational Attainment: High school diploma or higher: 100.0%; Bachelor's degree or higher: 29.7%; Graduate/professional degree or higher: n/a
Housing: Homeownership rate: 47.6%; Median home value: n/a; Median year structure built: n/a; Homeowner vacancy rate: 0.0%; Median selected monthly owner costs: $0 with a mortgage, $0 without a mortgage; Median gross rent: n/a per month; Rental vacancy rate: 0.0%
Health Insurance: 100.0% have insurance; 100.0% have private insurance; 0.0% have public insurance; 0.0% do not have insurance; 0.0% of children under 18 do not have insurance
Transportation: Commute: 100.0% car, 0.0% public transportation, 0.0% walk, 0.0% work from home; Mean travel time to work: 0.0 minutes

Dutchess County

Located in southeastern New York; bounded on the west by the Hudson River, and on the east by Connecticut; includes part of the Taconic Mountains. Covers a land area of 795.630 square miles, a water area of 29.718 square miles, and is located in the Eastern Time Zone at 41.76° N. Lat., 73.74° W. Long. The county was founded in 1683. County seat is Poughkeepsie.

Dutchess County is part of the New York-Newark-Jersey City, NY-NJ-PA Metropolitan Statistical Area. The entire metro area includes: Dutchess County-Putnam County, NY Metropolitan Division (Dutchess County, NY; Putnam County, NY); Nassau County-Suffolk County, NY Metropolitan Division (Nassau County, NY; Suffolk County, NY); Newark, NJ-PA Metropolitan Division (Essex County, NJ; Hunterdon County, NJ; Morris County, NJ; Somerset County, NJ; Sussex County, NJ; Union County, NJ; Pike County, PA); New York-Jersey City-White Plains, NY-NJ Metropolitan Division (Bergen County, NJ; Hudson County, NJ; Middlesex County, NJ; Monmouth County, NJ; Ocean County, NJ; Passaic County, NJ; Bronx County, NY; Kings County, NY; New York County, NY; Orange County, NY; Queens County, NY; Richmond County, NY; Rockland County, NY; Westchester County, NY)

Weather Station: Poughkeepsie Dutchess Co Arpt										Elevation: 154 feet	
	Jan	Feb	Mar	Apr	May	Jun	Jul	Aug	Sep	Oct	Nov	Dec
High	35	39	48	60	71	79	84	82	74	62	51	40
Low	16	19	26	37	47	56	61	60	51	40	31	22
Precip	3.0	2.5	3.4	3.8	4.4	4.2	4.6	4.0	3.9	4.1	3.5	3.4
Snow	10.8	7.9	4.9	1.4	0.0	0.0	0.0	0.0	0.0	tr	1.8	7.4

High and Low temperatures in degrees Fahrenheit; Precipitation and Snow in inches

Population: 296,928; Growth (since 2000): 6.0%; Density: 373.2 persons per square mile; Race: 78.5% White, 10.1% Black/African American, 3.9% Asian, 0.4% American Indian/Alaska Native, 0.0% Native Hawaiian/Other Pacific Islander, 3.0% two or more races, 11.3% Hispanic of any race; Average household size: 2.61; Median age: 41.2; Age under 18: 20.6%; Age 65 and over: 15.0%; Males per 100 females: 99.2; Marriage status: 34.3% never married, 51.1% now married, 2.4% separated, 5.8% widowed, 8.9% divorced; Foreign born: 11.6%; Speak English only: 84.2%; With disability: 13.1%; Veterans: 7.2%; Ancestry: 22.2% Italian, 21.2% Irish, 14.4% German, 7.4% English, 4.6% Polish
Religion: Six largest groups: 37.4% Catholicism, 2.6% Methodist/Pietist, 2.4% Muslim Estimate, 1.9% Presbyterian-Reformed, 1.7% Episcopalianism/Anglicanism, 1.6% Non-denominational Protestant
Economy: Unemployment rate: 4.1%; Leading industries: 14.3 % retail trade; 13.1 % construction; 11.4 % health care and social assistance; Farms: 678 totaling 112,482 acres; Company size: 9 employ 1,000 or more persons, 4 employ 500 to 999 persons, 110 employ 100 to 499 persons, 7,355 employ less than 100 persons; Business ownership: 8,193

women-owned, 1,240 Black-owned, 1,424 Hispanic-owned, 1,027 Asian-owned, 183 American Indian/Alaska Native-owned
Employment: 14.5% management, business, and financial, 6.1% computer, engineering, and science, 13.4% education, legal, community service, arts, and media, 6.1% healthcare practitioners, 19.8% service, 22.9% sales and office, 8.8% natural resources, construction, and maintenance, 8.4% production, transportation, and material moving
Income: Per capita: $33,923; Median household: $71,904; Average household: $90,537; Households with income of $100,000 or more: 34.1%; Poverty rate: 9.3%
Educational Attainment: High school diploma or higher: 89.9%; Bachelor's degree or higher: 33.4%; Graduate/professional degree or higher: 15.1%
Housing: Homeownership rate: 69.1%; Median home value: $275,600; Median year structure built: 1970; Homeowner vacancy rate: 2.1%; Median selected monthly owner costs: $2,237 with a mortgage, $836 without a mortgage; Median gross rent: $1,130 per month; Rental vacancy rate: 6.6%
Vital Statistics: Birth rate: 88.4 per 10,000 population; Death rate: 84.8 per 10,000 population; Age-adjusted cancer mortality rate: 148.9 deaths per 100,000 population
Health Insurance: 92.3% have insurance; 76.3% have private insurance; 29.3% have public insurance; 7.7% do not have insurance; 3.0% of children under 18 do not have insurance
Health Care: Physicians: 26.5 per 10,000 population; Dentists: 6.8 per 10,000 population; Hospital beds: 28.8 per 10,000 population; Hospital admissions: 934.0 per 10,000 population
Air Quality Index (AQI): Percent of Days: 96.7% good, 2.7% moderate, 0.5% unhealthy for sensitive individuals, 0.0% unhealthy, 0.0% very unhealthy; Annual median: 31; Annual maximum: 111
Transportation: Commute: 83.3% car, 5.0% public transportation, 5.1% walk, 5.5% work from home; Mean travel time to work: 31.3 minutes
2016 Presidential Election: 47.7% Trump, 48.0% Clinton, 2.8% Johnson, 1.5% Stein
National and State Parks: Eleanor Roosevelt National Historic Site; Home of Franklin D Roosevelt National Historic Site; James Baird State Park; Lafayetteville State Multiple Use Area; Margaret Lewis Norrie State Park; Mills Memorial State Park; Roeliff Jansen Kill State Multiple Use Area; Taconic-Hereford State Multiple Use Area; Tivoli Bay State Unique Area; Vanderbilt Mansion National Historic Site; Walkway Over the Hudson State Historic Park; Wassaic State Multiple Use Area
Additional Information Contacts
Dutchess Government. . . . . (845) 486-2120
  http://www.dutchessny.gov

Dutchess County Communities

AMENIA (CDP). Covers a land area of 1.218 square miles and a water area of 0.027 square miles. Located at 41.85° N. Lat; 73.56° W. Long. Elevation is 568 feet.
Population: 1,060; Growth (since 2000): -4.9%; Density: 870.5 persons per square mile; Race: 81.4% White, 8.1% Black/African American, 0.0% Asian, 0.4% American Indian/Alaska Native, 0.0% Native Hawaiian/Other Pacific Islander, 0.8% Two or more races, 18.2% Hispanic of any race; Average household size: 2.43; Median age: 47.9; Age under 18: 17.7%; Age 65 and over: 11.5%; Males per 100 females: 97.3; Marriage status: 25.0% never married, 56.7% now married, 5.4% separated, 5.4% widowed, 13.0% divorced; Foreign born: 12.0%; Speak English only: 88.4%; With disability: 10.4%; Veterans: 7.1%; Ancestry: 34.2% Irish, 23.5% German, 17.8% Italian, 12.9% English, 10.8% French
Employment: 4.7% management, business, and financial, 0.0% computer, engineering, and science, 1.6% education, legal, community service, arts, and media, 6.8% healthcare practitioners, 20.1% service, 32.1% sales and office, 22.5% natural resources, construction, and maintenance, 12.3% production, transportation, and material moving
Income: Per capita: $33,711; Median household: $58,200; Average household: $78,588; Households with income of $100,000 or more: 25.3%; Poverty rate: 2.9%
Educational Attainment: High school diploma or higher: 91.2%; Bachelor's degree or higher: 27.6%; Graduate/professional degree or higher: 5.8%

School District(s)
Northeast Central SD (PK-12)
  2014-15 Enrollment: 786. . . . . (845) 373-4100

Housing: Homeownership rate: 66.7%; Median home value: $235,500; Median year structure built: 1957; Homeowner vacancy rate: 0.0%; Median selected monthly owner costs: $1,819 with a mortgage, $744 without a mortgage; Median gross rent: $787 per month; Rental vacancy rate: 0.0%

Health Insurance: 88.7% have insurance; 74.6% have private insurance; 25.0% have public insurance; 11.3% do not have insurance; 10.1% of children under 18 do not have insurance

Transportation: Commute: 94.0% car, 0.0% public transportation, 0.0% walk, 6.0% work from home; Mean travel time to work: 30.9 minutes

---

AMENIA (town). Covers a land area of 43.220 square miles and a water area of 0.396 square miles. Located at 41.83° N. Lat; 73.53° W. Long. Elevation is 568 feet.

History: Thomas L. Harris had his Brotherhood of the New Life sect here, 1863—1867.

Population: 4,351; Growth (since 2000): 7.5%; Density: 100.7 persons per square mile; Race: 89.0% White, 6.6% Black/African American, 1.1% Asian, 0.1% American Indian/Alaska Native, 0.0% Native Hawaiian/Other Pacific Islander, 0.8% Two or more races, 6.1% Hispanic of any race; Average household size: 2.30; Median age: 45.9; Age under 18: 17.8%; Age 65 and over: 19.0%; Males per 100 females: 97.9; Marriage status: 33.6% never married, 49.9% now married, 4.5% separated, 7.4% widowed, 9.1% divorced; Foreign born: 5.2%; Speak English only: 91.4%; With disability: 17.6%; Veterans: 8.4%; Ancestry: 30.7% Irish, 19.9% Italian, 18.8% German, 11.8% English, 7.7% French

Employment: 10.6% management, business, and financial, 0.6% computer, engineering, and science, 8.6% education, legal, community service, arts, and media, 3.6% healthcare practitioners, 23.5% service, 27.2% sales and office, 13.4% natural resources, construction, and maintenance, 12.7% production, transportation, and material moving

Income: Per capita: $34,074; Median household: $57,870; Average household: $79,413; Households with income of $100,000 or more: 24.0%; Poverty rate: 6.3%

Educational Attainment: High school diploma or higher: 85.4%; Bachelor's degree or higher: 27.0%; Graduate/professional degree or higher: 10.0%

School District(s)

Northeast Central SD (PK-12)

    2014-15 Enrollment: 786 . . . . (845) 373-4100

Housing: Homeownership rate: 66.7%; Median home value: $242,200; Median year structure built: 1973; Homeowner vacancy rate: 0.7%; Median selected monthly owner costs: $1,723 with a mortgage, $724 without a mortgage; Median gross rent: $939 per month; Rental vacancy rate: 0.0%

Health Insurance: 94.1% have insurance; 75.5% have private insurance; 35.4% have public insurance; 5.9% do not have insurance; 2.5% of children under 18 do not have insurance

Transportation: Commute: 87.3% car, 4.1% public transportation, 1.9% walk, 6.3% work from home; Mean travel time to work: 34.4 minutes

Additional Information Contacts

Town of Amenia . . . . (845) 373-8118
    http://ameniany.gov

ANNANDALE ON HUDSON (unincorporated postal area)
ZCTA: 12504

    Covers a land area of 1.471 square miles and a water area of 0.813 square miles. Located at 42.03° N. Lat; 73.91° W. Long..

    Population: 1,483; Growth (since 2000): n/a; Density: 1,008.2 persons per square mile; Race: 80.8% White, 4.9% Black/African American, 6.3% Asian, 0.0% American Indian/Alaska Native, 0.0% Native Hawaiian/Other Pacific Islander, 5.5% Two or more races, 9.3% Hispanic of any race; Average household size: 2.58; Median age: 20.0; Age under 18: 2.0%; Age 65 and over: 0.3%; Males per 100 females: 76.8; Marriage status: 95.7% never married, 4.3% now married, 0.0% separated, 0.0% widowed, 0.0% divorced; Foreign born: 10.7%; Speak English only: 81.3%; With disability: 7.9%; Veterans: 0.6%; Ancestry: 20.0% Italian, 14.8% Irish, 12.8% German, 5.3% English, 4.4% Polish

    Employment: 5.5% management, business, and financial, 4.3% computer, engineering, and science, 26.5% education, legal, community service, arts, and media, 0.0% healthcare practitioners, 31.3% service, 30.1% sales and office, 0.0% natural resources, construction, and maintenance, 2.2% production, transportation, and material moving

    Income: Per capita: $6,053; Median household: $68,125; Average household: $65,454; Households with income of $100,000 or more: 25.0%; Poverty rate: 40.3%

Educational Attainment: High school diploma or higher: 93.5%; Bachelor's degree or higher: 48.9%; Graduate/professional degree or higher: 37.0%

Four-year College(s)

Bard College (Private, Not-for-profit)

    Fall 2014 Enrollment: 2,469 . . . . (845) 758-6822
    2013-14 Tuition: In-state $49,906; Out-of-state $49,906

Two-year College(s)

Bard College (Private, Not-for-profit)

    Fall 2014 Enrollment: 2,469 . . . . (845) 758-6822
    2013-14 Tuition: In-state $49,906; Out-of-state $49,906

Vocational/Technical School(s)

Bard College (Private, Not-for-profit)

    Fall 2014 Enrollment: 2,469 . . . . (845) 758-6822
    2015-16 Tuition: In-state $49,906; Out-of-state $49,906

Housing: Homeownership rate: 54.2%; Median home value: n/a; Median year structure built: Before 1940; Homeowner vacancy rate: 0.0%; Median selected monthly owner costs: $0 with a mortgage, $0 without a mortgage; Median gross rent: n/a per month; Rental vacancy rate: 0.0%

Health Insurance: 92.8% have insurance; 90.3% have private insurance; 4.1% have public insurance; 7.2% do not have insurance; 0.0% of children under 18 do not have insurance

Transportation: Commute: 15.2% car, 0.0% public transportation, 62.2% walk, 16.4% work from home; Mean travel time to work: 8.5 minutes

---

ARLINGTON (CDP). Covers a land area of 0.668 square miles and a water area of 0 square miles. Located at 41.70° N. Lat; 73.90° W. Long. Elevation is 187 feet.

History: Seat of Vassar College.

Population: 3,888; Growth (since 2000): -68.8%; Density: 5,823.2 persons per square mile; Race: 58.4% White, 21.6% Black/African American, 12.0% Asian, 0.1% American Indian/Alaska Native, 0.0% Native Hawaiian/Other Pacific Islander, 1.9% Two or more races, 15.5% Hispanic of any race; Average household size: 2.17; Median age: 26.8; Age under 18: 16.5%; Age 65 and over: 13.4%; Males per 100 females: 83.3; Marriage status: 59.0% never married, 24.0% now married, 3.6% separated, 9.6% widowed, 7.4% divorced; Foreign born: 29.0%; Speak English only: 73.3%; With disability: 13.1%; Veterans: 5.9%; Ancestry: 15.8% Irish, 12.9% Italian, 8.9% Jamaican, 7.1% German, 5.2% English

Employment: 14.7% management, business, and financial, 4.4% computer, engineering, and science, 16.8% education, legal, community service, arts, and media, 8.5% healthcare practitioners, 25.1% service, 22.9% sales and office, 1.2% natural resources, construction, and maintenance, 6.4% production, transportation, and material moving

Income: Per capita: $19,380; Median household: $42,208; Average household: $53,565; Households with income of $100,000 or more: 14.8%; Poverty rate: 19.1%

Educational Attainment: High school diploma or higher: 89.7%; Bachelor's degree or higher: 38.1%; Graduate/professional degree or higher: 8.1%

Housing: Homeownership rate: 29.7%; Median home value: $216,700; Median year structure built: 1965; Homeowner vacancy rate: 0.0%; Median selected monthly owner costs: $2,352 with a mortgage, $818 without a mortgage; Median gross rent: $1,046 per month; Rental vacancy rate: 0.5%

Health Insurance: 91.1% have insurance; 65.5% have private insurance; 34.5% have public insurance; 8.9% do not have insurance; 5.6% of children under 18 do not have insurance

Transportation: Commute: 60.5% car, 4.8% public transportation, 25.6% walk, 8.4% work from home; Mean travel time to work: 22.4 minutes

---

BARRYTOWN (unincorporated postal area)
ZCTA: 12507

    Covers a land area of 1.393 square miles and a water area of 0.118 square miles. Located at 42.01° N. Lat; 73.92° W. Long. Elevation is 121 feet.

    Population: 260; Growth (since 2000): 140.7%; Density: 186.6 persons per square mile; Race: 85.4% White, 4.2% Black/African American, 5.4% Asian, 0.0% American Indian/Alaska Native, 0.0% Native Hawaiian/Other Pacific Islander, 5.0% Two or more races, 1.9% Hispanic of any race; Average household size: 2.78; Median age: 29.6; Age under 18: 10.4%; Age 65 and over: 23.8%; Males per 100 females: 111.4; Marriage status: 60.0% never married, 29.2% now married, 3.8%

separated, 5.0% widowed, 5.8% divorced; Foreign born: 6.9%; Speak English only: 92.5%; With disability: 11.2%; Veterans: 16.7%; Ancestry: 20.0% German, 18.5% English, 17.3% Scottish, 11.5% Polish, 10.8% Irish

Employment: 15.5% management, business, and financial, 10.1% computer, engineering, and science, 21.7% education, legal, community service, arts, and media, 0.0% healthcare practitioners, 23.3% service, 24.8% sales and office, 4.7% natural resources, construction, and maintenance, 0.0% production, transportation, and material moving

Income: Per capita: $31,618; Median household: $66,538; Average household: $112,085; Households with income of $100,000 or more: 29.4%; Poverty rate: 3.4%

Educational Attainment: High school diploma or higher: 87.2%; Bachelor's degree or higher: 48.9%; Graduate/professional degree or higher: 26.2%

Four-year College(s)
Unification Theological Seminary (Private, Not-for-profit, Other (none of the above))
    Fall 2014 Enrollment: 122 . . . . (845) 752-3000

Two-year College(s)
Unification Theological Seminary (Private, Not-for-profit, Other (none of the above))
    Fall 2014 Enrollment: 122 . . . . (845) 752-3000

Vocational/Technical School(s)
Unification Theological Seminary (Private, Not-for-profit, Other (none of the above))
    Fall 2014 Enrollment: 122 . . . . (845) 752-3000

Housing: Homeownership rate: 95.6%; Median home value: $497,400; Median year structure built: Before 1940; Homeowner vacancy rate: 0.0%; Median selected monthly owner costs: $2,250 with a mortgage, $1,500 without a mortgage; Median gross rent: n/a per month; Rental vacancy rate: 0.0%

Health Insurance: 85.8% have insurance; 59.6% have private insurance; 39.6% have public insurance; 14.2% do not have insurance; 51.9% of children under 18 do not have insurance

Transportation: Commute: 62.1% car, 5.2% public transportation, 27.6% walk, 5.2% work from home; Mean travel time to work: 20.1 minutes

---

BEACON (city).
Covers a land area of 4.739 square miles and a water area of 0.137 square miles. Located at 41.50° N. Lat; 73.96° W. Long. Elevation is 135 feet.

History: An incline railroad ascends Mt. Beacon, site of a towering monument to American Revolutionary soldiers who built signal fires there to warn of the coming of the British. Beacon's historic buildings include the Madam Brett homestead (1709) and the Van Wyck homestead (1732). Settled 1663, Incorporated as a city in 1913.

Population: 14,375; Growth (since 2000): 4.1%; Density: 3,033.5 persons per square mile; Race: 67.7% White, 19.7% Black/African American, 1.6% Asian, 0.9% American Indian/Alaska Native, 0.0% Native Hawaiian/Other Pacific Islander, 5.5% Two or more races, 19.7% Hispanic of any race; Average household size: 2.51; Median age: 39.6; Age under 18: 19.2%; Age 65 and over: 13.5%; Males per 100 females: 113.5; Marriage status: 43.0% never married, 41.0% now married, 3.2% separated, 6.6% widowed, 9.4% divorced; Foreign born: 12.4%; Speak English only: 80.1%; With disability: 14.1%; Veterans: 7.4%; Ancestry: 19.2% Irish, 16.0% Italian, 11.7% German, 6.2% English, 4.3% Polish

Employment: 13.0% management, business, and financial, 5.6% computer, engineering, and science, 15.2% education, legal, community service, arts, and media, 3.8% healthcare practitioners, 23.6% service, 22.8% sales and office, 7.3% natural resources, construction, and maintenance, 8.7% production, transportation, and material moving

Income: Per capita: $31,615; Median household: $65,305; Average household: $79,613; Households with income of $100,000 or more: 30.9%; Poverty rate: 11.6%

Educational Attainment: High school diploma or higher: 89.3%; Bachelor's degree or higher: 30.2%; Graduate/professional degree or higher: 12.9%

School District(s)
Beacon City SD (PK-12)
    2014-15 Enrollment: 3,172 . . . . (845) 838-6900

Housing: Homeownership rate: 53.1%; Median home value: $240,300; Median year structure built: 1954; Homeowner vacancy rate: 1.0%; Median selected monthly owner costs: $2,117 with a mortgage, $804 without a

mortgage; Median gross rent: $1,082 per month; Rental vacancy rate: 5.9%

Health Insurance: 89.4% have insurance; 66.1% have private insurance; 36.6% have public insurance; 10.6% do not have insurance; 2.3% of children under 18 do not have insurance

Safety: Violent crime rate: 38.9 per 10,000 population; Property crime rate: 173.3 per 10,000 population

Transportation: Commute: 82.6% car, 8.2% public transportation, 3.1% walk, 5.3% work from home; Mean travel time to work: 34.1 minutes

Additional Information Contacts
City of Beacon . . . . (845) 838-5000
    http://www.cityofbeacon.org

BEEKMAN (town).
Covers a land area of 29.838 square miles and a water area of 0.517 square miles. Located at 41.60° N. Lat; 73.70° W. Long. Elevation is 377 feet.

History: Beekman was named in 1697 for Kingston native Henry Beekman, who had numerous land stakes in Dutchess County. The town was also occupied by the Wappinger Indians before European settlers arrived around 1710.

Population: 14,529; Growth (since 2000): 26.9%; Density: 486.9 persons per square mile; Race: 83.0% White, 10.5% Black/African American, 1.2% Asian, 0.9% American Indian/Alaska Native, 0.0% Native Hawaiian/Other Pacific Islander, 1.7% Two or more races, 9.8% Hispanic of any race; Average household size: 2.96; Median age: 42.2; Age under 18: 21.6%; Age 65 and over: 11.5%; Males per 100 females: 131.0; Marriage status: 30.1% never married, 58.5% now married, 1.7% separated, 3.8% widowed, 7.7% divorced; Foreign born: 9.4%; Speak English only: 85.5%; With disability: 12.5%; Veterans: 7.3%; Ancestry: 32.6% Italian, 25.9% Irish, 15.0% German, 7.0% English, 4.7% American

Employment: 16.7% management, business, and financial, 5.1% computer, engineering, and science, 12.7% education, legal, community service, arts, and media, 6.8% healthcare practitioners, 14.8% service, 22.1% sales and office, 13.8% natural resources, construction, and maintenance, 7.9% production, transportation, and material moving

Income: Per capita: $36,748; Median household: $95,110; Average household: $116,945; Households with income of $100,000 or more: 47.7%; Poverty rate: 5.0%

Educational Attainment: High school diploma or higher: 90.0%; Bachelor's degree or higher: 30.2%; Graduate/professional degree or higher: 12.9%

Housing: Homeownership rate: 91.2%; Median home value: $321,800; Median year structure built: 1984; Homeowner vacancy rate: 1.4%; Median selected monthly owner costs: $2,594 with a mortgage, $839 without a mortgage; Median gross rent: $1,511 per month; Rental vacancy rate: 0.0%

Health Insurance: 96.5% have insurance; 85.0% have private insurance; 23.0% have public insurance; 3.5% do not have insurance; 2.1% of children under 18 do not have insurance

Transportation: Commute: 90.1% car, 3.2% public transportation, 0.9% walk, 5.2% work from home; Mean travel time to work: 39.4 minutes

Additional Information Contacts
Town of Beekman . . . . (845) 724-5300
    http://www.townofbeekman.com

BRINCKERHOFF (CDP).
Covers a land area of 1.120 square miles and a water area of 0.005 square miles. Located at 41.55° N. Lat; 73.87° W. Long. Elevation is 220 feet.

Population: 2,602; Growth (since 2000): -4.8%; Density: 2,323.3 persons per square mile; Race: 77.8% White, 11.8% Black/African American, 4.3% Asian, 0.0% American Indian/Alaska Native, 0.0% Native Hawaiian/Other Pacific Islander, 3.5% Two or more races, 6.9% Hispanic of any race; Average household size: 2.81; Median age: 49.0; Age under 18: 13.0%; Age 65 and over: 17.9%; Males per 100 females: 93.2; Marriage status: 32.8% never married, 53.6% now married, 1.4% separated, 5.8% widowed, 7.8% divorced; Foreign born: 7.2%; Speak English only: 87.6%; With disability: 9.0%; Veterans: 8.3%; Ancestry: 20.4% Italian, 18.0% Irish, 11.1% German, 4.4% English, 4.4% Polish

Employment: 12.0% management, business, and financial, 8.3% computer, engineering, and science, 16.5% education, legal, community service, arts, and media, 3.9% healthcare practitioners, 15.6% service, 23.3% sales and office, 12.2% natural resources, construction, and maintenance, 8.2% production, transportation, and material moving

Income: Per capita: $35,928; Median household: $95,388; Average household: $97,387; Households with income of $100,000 or more: 45.1%; Poverty rate: 6.2%
Educational Attainment: High school diploma or higher: 94.6%; Bachelor's degree or higher: 30.2%; Graduate/professional degree or higher: 14.4%
Housing: Homeownership rate: 85.9%; Median home value: $270,900; Median year structure built: 1968; Homeowner vacancy rate: 3.9%; Median selected monthly owner costs: $1,960 with a mortgage, $840 without a mortgage; Median gross rent: $1,490 per month; Rental vacancy rate: 0.0%
Health Insurance: 90.0% have insurance; 81.6% have private insurance; 23.3% have public insurance; 10.0% do not have insurance; 4.7% of children under 18 do not have insurance
Transportation: Commute: 89.6% car, 2.6% public transportation, 3.0% walk, 3.9% work from home; Mean travel time to work: 29.7 minutes

CHELSEA (unincorporated postal area)
ZCTA: 12512
Covers a land area of 0.446 square miles and a water area of <.001 square miles. Located at 41.55° N. Lat; 73.97° W. Long. Elevation is 39 feet.
Population: 69; Growth (since 2000): n/a; Density: 154.6 persons per square mile; Race: 100.0% White, 0.0% Black/African American, 0.0% Asian, 0.0% American Indian/Alaska Native, 0.0% Native Hawaiian/Other Pacific Islander, 0.0% Two or more races, 0.0% Hispanic of any race; Average household size: 1.41; Median age: 70.3; Age under 18: 0.0%; Age 65 and over: 58.0%; Males per 100 females: 104.8; Marriage status: 37.7% never married, 58.0% now married, 0.0% separated, 0.0% widowed, 4.3% divorced; Foreign born: 0.0%; Speak English only: 100.0%; With disability: 29.0%; Veterans: 37.7%; Ancestry: 71.0% Irish, 29.0% Austrian, 29.0% Hungarian
Employment: 0.0% management, business, and financial, 0.0% computer, engineering, and science, 40.8% education, legal, community service, arts, and media, 0.0% healthcare practitioners, 0.0% service, 53.1% sales and office, 0.0% natural resources, construction, and maintenance, 6.1% production, transportation, and material moving
Income: Per capita: $124,380; Median household: n/a; Average household: $175,147; Households with income of $100,000 or more: 40.8%; Poverty rate: n/a
Educational Attainment: High school diploma or higher: 100.0%; Bachelor's degree or higher: 62.3%; Graduate/professional degree or higher: 58.0%
Housing: Homeownership rate: 40.8%; Median home value: n/a; Median year structure built: Before 1940; Homeowner vacancy rate: 0.0%; Median selected monthly owner costs: $0 with a mortgage, $0 without a mortgage; Median gross rent: n/a per month; Rental vacancy rate: 0.0%
Health Insurance: 100.0% have insurance; 62.3% have private insurance; 95.7% have public insurance; 0.0% do not have insurance; 0.0% of children under 18 do not have insurance
Transportation: Commute: 100.0% car, 0.0% public transportation, 0.0% walk, 0.0% work from home; Mean travel time to work: 0.0 minutes

CLINTON (town). Covers a land area of 38.143 square miles and a water area of 0.642 square miles. Located at 41.86° N. Lat; 73.82° W. Long.
Population: 4,299; Growth (since 2000): 7.2%; Density: 112.7 persons per square mile; Race: 94.9% White, 1.1% Black/African American, 1.2% Asian, 0.0% American Indian/Alaska Native, 0.0% Native Hawaiian/Other Pacific Islander, 2.4% Two or more races, 4.0% Hispanic of any race; Average household size: 2.69; Median age: 45.6; Age under 18: 21.7%; Age 65 and over: 16.5%; Males per 100 females: 103.2; Marriage status: 28.1% never married, 59.2% now married, 1.2% separated, 3.4% widowed, 9.3% divorced; Foreign born: 4.9%; Speak English only: 95.9%; With disability: 16.8%; Veterans: 9.3%; Ancestry: 30.8% Irish, 24.4% German, 14.2% Italian, 14.1% English, 5.7% Dutch
Employment: 11.3% management, business, and financial, 4.2% computer, engineering, and science, 14.4% education, legal, community service, arts, and media, 6.8% healthcare practitioners, 16.5% service, 25.0% sales and office, 12.2% natural resources, construction, and maintenance, 9.6% production, transportation, and material moving
Income: Per capita: $44,555; Median household: $79,035; Average household: $122,202; Households with income of $100,000 or more: 40.5%; Poverty rate: 10.2%

Educational Attainment: High school diploma or higher: 91.7%; Bachelor's degree or higher: 36.7%; Graduate/professional degree or higher: 17.4%
Housing: Homeownership rate: 79.5%; Median home value: $352,400; Median year structure built: 1979; Homeowner vacancy rate: 0.7%; Median selected monthly owner costs: $2,523 with a mortgage, $973 without a mortgage; Median gross rent: $1,276 per month; Rental vacancy rate: 11.8%
Health Insurance: 91.7% have insurance; 78.2% have private insurance; 29.1% have public insurance; 8.3% do not have insurance; 10.1% of children under 18 do not have insurance
Transportation: Commute: 87.2% car, 3.5% public transportation, 1.4% walk, 7.9% work from home; Mean travel time to work: 34.5 minutes
Additional Information Contacts
Town of Clinton . . . . (845) 266-5721
http://www.townofclinton.com

CLINTON CORNERS (unincorporated postal area)
ZCTA: 12514
Covers a land area of 26.646 square miles and a water area of 0.275 square miles. Located at 41.88° N. Lat; 73.76° W. Long. Elevation is 302 feet.
Population: 3,213; Growth (since 2000): 12.6%; Density: 120.6 persons per square mile; Race: 87.9% White, 5.5% Black/African American, 0.3% Asian, 0.1% American Indian/Alaska Native, 0.0% Native Hawaiian/Other Pacific Islander, 0.9% Two or more races, 6.1% Hispanic of any race; Average household size: 2.98; Median age: 44.2; Age under 18: 18.8%; Age 65 and over: 14.2%; Males per 100 females: 101.5; Marriage status: 33.1% never married, 54.5% now married, 2.2% separated, 4.5% widowed, 7.9% divorced; Foreign born: 7.8%; Speak English only: 91.3%; With disability: 16.4%; Veterans: 7.6%; Ancestry: 33.6% Irish, 20.6% Italian, 17.2% German, 9.1% English, 6.3% Dutch
Employment: 14.2% management, business, and financial, 6.6% computer, engineering, and science, 17.8% education, legal, community service, arts, and media, 4.7% healthcare practitioners, 22.3% service, 15.5% sales and office, 11.0% natural resources, construction, and maintenance, 8.1% production, transportation, and material moving
Income: Per capita: $40,744; Median household: $89,306; Average household: $117,905; Households with income of $100,000 or more: 42.5%; Poverty rate: 5.4%
Educational Attainment: High school diploma or higher: 96.1%; Bachelor's degree or higher: 37.4%; Graduate/professional degree or higher: 16.3%
Housing: Homeownership rate: 86.1%; Median home value: $317,300; Median year structure built: 1978; Homeowner vacancy rate: 0.0%; Median selected monthly owner costs: $2,452 with a mortgage, $780 without a mortgage; Median gross rent: $956 per month; Rental vacancy rate: 0.0%
Health Insurance: 93.2% have insurance; 81.0% have private insurance; 26.2% have public insurance; 6.8% do not have insurance; 0.0% of children under 18 do not have insurance
Transportation: Commute: 86.9% car, 1.5% public transportation, 4.0% walk, 7.1% work from home; Mean travel time to work: 29.6 minutes

CROWN HEIGHTS (CDP). Covers a land area of 0.844 square miles and a water area of 0 square miles. Located at 41.64° N. Lat; 73.93° W. Long. Elevation is 112 feet.
Population: 2,830; Growth (since 2000): -5.4%; Density: 3,354.5 persons per square mile; Race: 77.0% White, 7.6% Black/African American, 4.2% Asian, 0.0% American Indian/Alaska Native, 0.0% Native Hawaiian/Other Pacific Islander, 5.9% Two or more races, 15.2% Hispanic of any race; Average household size: 2.69; Median age: 43.1; Age under 18: 23.4%; Age 65 and over: 15.8%; Males per 100 females: 91.5; Marriage status: 31.6% never married, 53.2% now married, 0.9% separated, 8.4% widowed, 6.8% divorced; Foreign born: 8.2%; Speak English only: 85.1%; With disability: 8.7%; Veterans: 7.6%; Ancestry: 20.5% Italian, 13.4% Irish, 13.0% German, 5.8% American, 4.2% Polish
Employment: 9.9% management, business, and financial, 6.9% computer, engineering, and science, 12.0% education, legal, community service, arts, and media, 4.3% healthcare practitioners, 21.0% service, 34.7% sales and office, 4.9% natural resources, construction, and maintenance, 6.3% production, transportation, and material moving
Income: Per capita: $31,506; Median household: $79,038; Average household: $82,225; Households with income of $100,000 or more: 33.2%; Poverty rate: 12.0%

Educational Attainment: High school diploma or higher: 91.5%; Bachelor's degree or higher: 27.7%; Graduate/professional degree or higher: 11.9%

Housing: Homeownership rate: 90.0%; Median home value: $239,300; Median year structure built: 1963; Homeowner vacancy rate: 0.0%; Median selected monthly owner costs: $2,123 with a mortgage, $906 without a mortgage; Median gross rent: $1,154 per month; Rental vacancy rate: 0.0%

Health Insurance: 93.0% have insurance; 83.6% have private insurance; 26.0% have public insurance; 7.0% do not have insurance; 2.9% of children under 18 do not have insurance

Transportation: Commute: 87.9% car, 6.4% public transportation, 1.6% walk, 4.1% work from home; Mean travel time to work: 25.9 minutes

DOVER (town).

DOVER (town). Covers a land area of 55.190 square miles and a water area of 1.149 square miles. Located at 41.68° N. Lat; 73.57° W. Long.

Population: 8,590; Growth (since 2000): 0.3%; Density: 155.6 persons per square mile; Race: 83.4% White, 4.9% Black/African American, 1.9% Asian, 0.0% American Indian/Alaska Native, 0.0% Native Hawaiian/Other Pacific Islander, 3.9% Two or more races, 12.1% Hispanic of any race; Average household size: 2.67; Median age: 43.0; Age under 18: 21.8%; Age 65 and over: 11.5%; Males per 100 females: 102.8; Marriage status: 33.5% never married, 52.8% now married, 2.9% separated, 3.6% widowed, 10.1% divorced; Foreign born: 10.8%; Speak English only: 87.2%; With disability: 19.9%; Veterans: 7.1%; Ancestry: 29.2% Irish, 22.1% Italian, 16.7% German, 6.8% American, 5.5% French

Employment: 11.6% management, business, and financial, 2.9% computer, engineering, and science, 9.8% education, legal, community service, arts, and media, 3.7% healthcare practitioners, 24.6% service, 19.7% sales and office, 13.8% natural resources, construction, and maintenance, 13.9% production, transportation, and material moving

Income: Per capita: $27,434; Median household: $61,858; Average household: $72,607; Households with income of $100,000 or more: 24.8%; Poverty rate: 11.1%

Educational Attainment: High school diploma or higher: 85.4%; Bachelor's degree or higher: 17.9%; Graduate/professional degree or higher: 8.5%

Housing: Homeownership rate: 72.1%; Median home value: $231,900; Median year structure built: 1978; Homeowner vacancy rate: 1.2%; Median selected monthly owner costs: $1,931 with a mortgage, $780 without a mortgage; Median gross rent: $992 per month; Rental vacancy rate: 13.9%

Health Insurance: 90.7% have insurance; 73.1% have private insurance; 31.4% have public insurance; 9.3% do not have insurance; 1.9% of children under 18 do not have insurance

Transportation: Commute: 89.3% car, 3.5% public transportation, 4.8% walk, 2.2% work from home; Mean travel time to work: 35.3 minutes

Additional Information Contacts

Town of Dover . . . . (845) 832-6111
http://townofdoverny.us

DOVER PLAINS (CDP).

DOVER PLAINS (CDP). Covers a land area of 0.677 square miles and a water area of 0.015 square miles. Located at 41.74° N. Lat; 73.57° W. Long. Elevation is 400 feet.

Population: 919; Growth (since 2000): -54.0%; Density: 1,358.0 persons per square mile; Race: 91.3% White, 0.3% Black/African American, 0.0% Asian, 0.0% American Indian/Alaska Native, 0.0% Native Hawaiian/Other Pacific Islander, 0.0% Two or more races, 16.9% Hispanic of any race; Average household size: 1.78; Median age: 49.5; Age under 18: 18.4%; Age 65 and over: 20.1%; Males per 100 females: 110.7; Marriage status: 38.3% never married, 39.8% now married, 6.3% separated, 3.5% widowed, 18.4% divorced; Foreign born: 7.8%; Speak English only: 86.8%; With disability: 21.2%; Veterans: 12.7%; Ancestry: 28.1% Irish, 14.3% German, 11.5% Italian, 10.4% French, 9.8% English

Employment: 8.8% management, business, and financial, 5.3% computer, engineering, and science, 7.3% education, legal, community service, arts, and media, 5.1% healthcare practitioners, 31.2% service, 7.7% sales and office, 3.5% natural resources, construction, and maintenance, 31.2% production, transportation, and material moving

Income: Per capita: $32,336; Median household: $41,618; Average household: $57,452; Households with income of $100,000 or more: 17.8%; Poverty rate: 9.8%

Educational Attainment: High school diploma or higher: 71.3%; Bachelor's degree or higher: 12.7%; Graduate/professional degree or higher: 5.6%

School District(s)

Dover Union Free SD (KG-12)

   2014-15 Enrollment: 1,419 . . . . (845) 877-5700

Housing: Homeownership rate: 49.6%; Median home value: n/a; Median year structure built: 1975; Homeowner vacancy rate: 8.8%; Median selected monthly owner costs: $2,477 with a mortgage, $730 without a mortgage; Median gross rent: $885 per month; Rental vacancy rate: 0.0%

Health Insurance: 94.6% have insurance; 80.8% have private insurance; 42.0% have public insurance; 5.4% do not have insurance; 0.0% of children under 18 do not have insurance

Transportation: Commute: 86.8% car, 0.0% public transportation, 5.4% walk, 7.8% work from home; Mean travel time to work: 23.5 minutes

EAST FISHKILL (town).

EAST FISHKILL (town). Covers a land area of 56.503 square miles and a water area of 0.883 square miles. Located at 41.56° N. Lat; 73.79° W. Long. Elevation is 276 feet.

History: Fishkill is famous as home to Hudson Valley Research Park (formerly known as IBM East Fishkill). While IBM produced microchips, new owner GlobalFoundries owned the automated processor facility where IBM's "Cell" processor was co-developed.

Population: 29,276; Growth (since 2000): 14.4%; Density: 518.1 persons per square mile; Race: 88.0% White, 2.7% Black/African American, 3.9% Asian, 0.1% American Indian/Alaska Native, 0.0% Native Hawaiian/Other Pacific Islander, 2.7% Two or more races, 7.2% Hispanic of any race; Average household size: 3.06; Median age: 42.6; Age under 18: 24.5%; Age 65 and over: 12.9%; Males per 100 females: 99.9; Marriage status: 26.2% never married, 62.2% now married, 1.7% separated, 4.9% widowed, 6.7% divorced; Foreign born: 10.1%; Speak English only: 85.9%; With disability: 10.9%; Veterans: 7.1%; Ancestry: 31.6% Italian, 23.4% Irish, 14.0% German, 7.3% English, 5.7% Polish

Employment: 20.6% management, business, and financial, 6.1% computer, engineering, and science, 12.3% education, legal, community service, arts, and media, 6.5% healthcare practitioners, 16.3% service, 23.2% sales and office, 8.7% natural resources, construction, and maintenance, 6.3% production, transportation, and material moving

Income: Per capita: $39,457; Median household: $101,377; Average household: $118,440; Households with income of $100,000 or more: 51.0%; Poverty rate: 3.2%

Educational Attainment: High school diploma or higher: 92.6%; Bachelor's degree or higher: 40.1%; Graduate/professional degree or higher: 17.0%

Housing: Homeownership rate: 90.8%; Median home value: $348,400; Median year structure built: 1979; Homeowner vacancy rate: 1.1%; Median selected monthly owner costs: $2,583 with a mortgage, $904 without a mortgage; Median gross rent: $1,221 per month; Rental vacancy rate: 8.5%

Health Insurance: 94.5% have insurance; 83.6% have private insurance; 21.6% have public insurance; 5.5% do not have insurance; 4.6% of children under 18 do not have insurance

Safety: Violent crime rate: 3.4 per 10,000 population; Property crime rate: 58.5 per 10,000 population

Transportation: Commute: 90.4% car, 3.7% public transportation, 0.3% walk, 5.1% work from home; Mean travel time to work: 37.4 minutes

Additional Information Contacts

Town of East Fishkill . . . . (845) 221-9191
http://www.eastfishkillny.org

FAIRVIEW (CDP).

FAIRVIEW (CDP). Covers a land area of 3.477 square miles and a water area of 0.076 square miles. Located at 41.73° N. Lat; 73.91° W. Long. Elevation is 217 feet.

Population: 5,700; Growth (since 2000): 5.1%; Density: 1,639.3 persons per square mile; Race: 75.9% White, 12.3% Black/African American, 0.5% Asian, 2.5% American Indian/Alaska Native, 0.0% Native Hawaiian/Other Pacific Islander, 3.6% Two or more races, 15.4% Hispanic of any race; Average household size: 2.77; Median age: 28.6; Age under 18: 20.4%; Age 65 and over: 9.5%; Males per 100 females: 102.4; Marriage status: 47.6% never married, 40.6% now married, 0.8% separated, 5.2% widowed, 6.6% divorced; Foreign born: 8.1%; Speak English only: 84.4%; With disability: 12.0%; Veterans: 5.4%; Ancestry: 20.1% Italian, 17.0% German, 16.9% Irish, 8.2% English, 5.0% Polish

Employment: 12.1% management, business, and financial, 2.7% computer, engineering, and science, 18.4% education, legal, community service, arts, and media, 3.1% healthcare practitioners, 24.2% service, 27.2% sales and office, 5.4% natural resources, construction, and maintenance, 6.9% production, transportation, and material moving

Income: Per capita: $24,046; Median household: $69,485; Average household: $74,001; Households with income of $100,000 or more: 29.5%; Poverty rate: 19.2%

Educational Attainment: High school diploma or higher: 86.4%; Bachelor's degree or higher: 22.6%; Graduate/professional degree or higher: 10.4%

Housing: Homeownership rate: 73.4%; Median home value: $197,000; Median year structure built: 1959; Homeowner vacancy rate: 3.1%; Median selected monthly owner costs: $2,065 with a mortgage, $868 without a mortgage; Median gross rent: $1,200 per month; Rental vacancy rate: 0.0%

Health Insurance: 92.8% have insurance; 72.3% have private insurance; 30.3% have public insurance; 7.2% do not have insurance; 1.0% of children under 18 do not have insurance

Transportation: Commute: 78.6% car, 3.0% public transportation, 10.4% walk, 5.6% work from home; Mean travel time to work: 25.8 minutes

FISHKILL (town). Covers a land area of 27.336 square miles and a water area of 4.655 square miles. Located at 41.52° N. Lat; 73.92° W. Long. Elevation is 220 feet.

History: Nearby village of Fishkill Landing joined Matteawan (1913) to form Beacon city.

Population: 23,505; Growth (since 2000): 16.0%; Density: 859.8 persons per square mile; Race: 74.3% White, 10.8% Black/African American, 7.1% Asian, 0.4% American Indian/Alaska Native, 0.1% Native Hawaiian/Other Pacific Islander, 3.7% Two or more races, 12.6% Hispanic of any race; Average household size: 2.42; Median age: 41.9; Age under 18: 18.0%; Age 65 and over: 16.5%; Males per 100 females: 103.5; Marriage status: 34.2% never married, 50.4% now married, 3.3% separated, 6.3% widowed, 9.1% divorced; Foreign born: 13.5%; Speak English only: 81.6%; With disability: 10.9%; Veterans: 8.3%; Ancestry: 23.0% Italian, 18.6% Irish, 12.8% German, 5.0% English, 4.7% Polish

Employment: 16.1% management, business, and financial, 10.4% computer, engineering, and science, 14.3% education, legal, community service, arts, and media, 5.2% healthcare practitioners, 18.1% service, 19.6% sales and office, 7.1% natural resources, construction, and maintenance, 9.2% production, transportation, and material moving

Income: Per capita: $36,195; Median household: $81,752; Average household: $91,483; Households with income of $100,000 or more: 38.0%; Poverty rate: 8.8%

Educational Attainment: High school diploma or higher: 91.9%; Bachelor's degree or higher: 34.1%; Graduate/professional degree or higher: 15.3%

School District(s)
Beacon City SD (PK-12)
    2014-15 Enrollment: 3,172 . . . . (845) 838-6900
Wappingers Central SD (KG-12)
    2014-15 Enrollment: 11,592 . . . . (845) 298-5000

Housing: Homeownership rate: 65.1%; Median home value: $275,800; Median year structure built: 1978; Homeowner vacancy rate: 1.7%; Median selected monthly owner costs: $2,225 with a mortgage, $783 without a mortgage; Median gross rent: $1,408 per month; Rental vacancy rate: 3.0%

Health Insurance: 95.1% have insurance; 81.3% have private insurance; 27.7% have public insurance; 4.9% do not have insurance; 1.2% of children under 18 do not have insurance

Safety: Violent crime rate: 3.2 per 10,000 population; Property crime rate: 73.1 per 10,000 population

Transportation: Commute: 87.3% car, 7.2% public transportation, 1.7% walk, 3.4% work from home; Mean travel time to work: 35.2 minutes

Additional Information Contacts
Town of Fishkill . . . . (845) 831-7800
    http://www.fishkill-ny.gov

FISHKILL (village). Covers a land area of 0.820 square miles and a water area of 0.004 square miles. Located at 41.53° N. Lat; 73.89° W. Long. Elevation is 220 feet.

Population: 2,001; Growth (since 2000): 15.3%; Density: 2,439.1 persons per square mile; Race: 79.8% White, 4.6% Black/African American, 12.4% Asian, 0.0% American Indian/Alaska Native, 0.0% Native Hawaiian/Other Pacific Islander, 1.9% Two or more races, 13.7% Hispanic of any race; Average household size: 2.02; Median age: 41.6; Age under 18: 22.3%; Age 65 and over: 16.5%; Males per 100 females: 87.8; Marriage status: 30.0% never married, 49.6% now married, 3.0% separated, 5.8% widowed, 14.6% divorced; Foreign born: 15.9%; Speak English only:

76.6%; With disability: 9.3%; Veterans: 7.4%; Ancestry: 30.2% Italian, 20.9% Irish, 13.2% German, 4.6% English, 4.3% French

Employment: 14.7% management, business, and financial, 13.5% computer, engineering, and science, 17.8% education, legal, community service, arts, and media, 4.9% healthcare practitioners, 16.3% service, 24.8% sales and office, 0.5% natural resources, construction, and maintenance, 7.5% production, transportation, and material moving

Income: Per capita: $33,042; Median household: $53,505; Average household: $66,682; Households with income of $100,000 or more: 23.6%; Poverty rate: 12.4%

Educational Attainment: High school diploma or higher: 91.6%; Bachelor's degree or higher: 45.6%; Graduate/professional degree or higher: 21.2%

School District(s)
Beacon City SD (PK-12)
    2014-15 Enrollment: 3,172 . . . . (845) 838-6900
Wappingers Central SD (KG-12)
    2014-15 Enrollment: 11,592 . . . . (845) 298-5000

Housing: Homeownership rate: 32.8%; Median home value: $210,900; Median year structure built: 1975; Homeowner vacancy rate: 7.9%; Median selected monthly owner costs: $1,762 with a mortgage, $594 without a mortgage; Median gross rent: $1,445 per month; Rental vacancy rate: 6.3%

Health Insurance: 91.3% have insurance; 77.1% have private insurance; 27.9% have public insurance; 8.7% do not have insurance; 5.4% of children under 18 do not have insurance

Safety: Violent crime rate: 0.0 per 10,000 population; Property crime rate: 262.2 per 10,000 population

Transportation: Commute: 87.3% car, 2.7% public transportation, 5.4% walk, 4.5% work from home; Mean travel time to work: 32.5 minutes

FREEDOM PLAINS (CDP). Covers a land area of 1.290 square miles and a water area of 0.044 square miles. Located at 41.67° N. Lat; 73.80° W. Long. Elevation is 315 feet.

Population: 472; Growth (since 2000): n/a; Density: 366.0 persons per square mile; Race: 100.0% White, 0.0% Black/African American, 0.0% Asian, 0.0% American Indian/Alaska Native, 0.0% Native Hawaiian/Other Pacific Islander, 0.0% Two or more races, 6.1% Hispanic of any race; Average household size: 1.87; Median age: 50.8; Age under 18: 15.5%; Age 65 and over: 35.6%; Males per 100 females: 72.5; Marriage status: 32.7% never married, 37.7% now married, 5.0% separated, 12.7% widowed, 16.8% divorced; Foreign born: 3.2%; Speak English only: 90.3%; With disability: 16.5%; Veterans: 8.8%; Ancestry: 37.1% Italian, 18.9% Irish, 15.3% German, 13.3% English, 11.4% French Canadian

Employment: 18.7% management, business, and financial, 6.0% computer, engineering, and science, 18.7% education, legal, community service, arts, and media, 0.0% healthcare practitioners, 9.3% service, 23.1% sales and office, 4.4% natural resources, construction, and maintenance, 19.8% production, transportation, and material moving

Income: Per capita: $41,766; Median household: $58,125; Average household: $76,659; Households with income of $100,000 or more: 36.7%; Poverty rate: 4.2%

Educational Attainment: High school diploma or higher: 95.5%; Bachelor's degree or higher: 37.6%; Graduate/professional degree or higher: 7.6%

Housing: Homeownership rate: 66.8%; Median home value: $223,300; Median year structure built: 1987; Homeowner vacancy rate: 0.0%; Median selected monthly owner costs: $1,865 with a mortgage, $843 without a mortgage; Median gross rent: $1,284 per month; Rental vacancy rate: 0.0%

Health Insurance: 100.0% have insurance; 93.9% have private insurance; 35.6% have public insurance; 0.0% do not have insurance; 0.0% of children under 18 do not have insurance

Transportation: Commute: 92.3% car, 0.0% public transportation, 0.0% walk, 7.7% work from home; Mean travel time to work: 38.8 minutes

GLENHAM (unincorporated postal area)
ZCTA: 12527
    Covers a land area of 0.156 square miles and a water area of 0 square miles. Located at 41.52° N. Lat; 73.94° W. Long. Elevation is 256 feet.
    Population: 93; Growth (since 2000): n/a; Density: 597.7 persons per square mile; Race: 32.3% White, 67.7% Black/African American, 0.0% Asian, 0.0% American Indian/Alaska Native, 0.0% Native Hawaiian/Other Pacific Islander, 0.0% Two or more races, 0.0% Hispanic of any race; Average household size: 2.51; Median age: 40.4;

Age under 18: 28.0%; Age 65 and over: 0.0%; Males per 100 females: 98.6; Marriage status: 13.4% never married, 65.7% now married, 0.0% separated, 0.0% widowed, 20.9% divorced; Foreign born: 0.0%; Speak English only: 100.0%; With disability: 0.0%; Veterans: 0.0%; Ancestry: 36.6% Greek, 29.0% African, 26.9% Italian, 19.4% European
Employment: 25.5% management, business, and financial, 0.0% computer, engineering, and science, 16.4% education, legal, community service, arts, and media, 0.0% healthcare practitioners, 16.4% service, 25.5% sales and office, 16.4% natural resources, construction, and maintenance, 0.0% production, transportation, and material moving
Income: Per capita: $35,139; Median household: n/a; Average household: $89,946; Households with income of $100,000 or more: 62.2%; Poverty rate: n/a
Educational Attainment: High school diploma or higher: 100.0%; Bachelor's degree or higher: 60.3%; Graduate/professional degree or higher: 24.1%
Housing: Homeownership rate: 62.2%; Median home value: n/a; Median year structure built: 1947; Homeowner vacancy rate: 0.0%; Median selected monthly owner costs: $0 with a mortgage, $0 without a mortgage; Median gross rent: n/a per month; Rental vacancy rate: 0.0%
Health Insurance: 100.0% have insurance; 84.9% have private insurance; 15.1% have public insurance; 0.0% do not have insurance; 0.0% of children under 18 do not have insurance
Transportation: Commute: 100.0% car, 0.0% public transportation, 0.0% walk, 0.0% work from home; Mean travel time to work: 0.0 minutes

HAVILAND (CDP).
Covers a land area of 3.863 square miles and a water area of 0.035 square miles. Located at 41.77° N. Lat; 73.90° W. Long. Elevation is 233 feet.
Population: 3,470; Growth (since 2000): -6.5%; Density: 898.2 persons per square mile; Race: 89.7% White, 5.6% Black/African American, 0.0% Asian, 0.0% American Indian/Alaska Native, 0.0% Native Hawaiian/Other Pacific Islander, 0.1% Two or more races, 7.7% Hispanic of any race; Average household size: 2.46; Median age: 47.0; Age under 18: 17.5%; Age 65 and over: 19.7%; Males per 100 females: 93.3; Marriage status: 22.6% never married, 61.6% now married, 0.5% separated, 5.1% widowed, 10.7% divorced; Foreign born: 4.6%; Speak English only: 88.9%; With disability: 16.7%; Veterans: 13.2%; Ancestry: 24.7% Irish, 21.0% Italian, 19.3% German, 11.7% English, 10.7% Polish
Employment: 10.4% management, business, and financial, 8.0% computer, engineering, and science, 18.7% education, legal, community service, arts, and media, 11.4% healthcare practitioners, 10.4% service, 24.7% sales and office, 4.3% natural resources, construction, and maintenance, 12.0% production, transportation, and material moving
Income: Per capita: $37,406; Median household: $82,885; Average household: $89,827; Households with income of $100,000 or more: 40.2%; Poverty rate: 4.1%
Educational Attainment: High school diploma or higher: 95.2%; Bachelor's degree or higher: 33.4%; Graduate/professional degree or higher: 16.3%
Housing: Homeownership rate: 88.0%; Median home value: $207,700; Median year structure built: 1964; Homeowner vacancy rate: 0.0%; Median selected monthly owner costs: $1,814 with a mortgage, $763 without a mortgage; Median gross rent: $806 per month; Rental vacancy rate: 0.0%
Health Insurance: 94.2% have insurance; 87.6% have private insurance; 27.1% have public insurance; 5.8% do not have insurance; 0.0% of children under 18 do not have insurance
Transportation: Commute: 92.7% car, 2.5% public transportation, 1.9% walk, 1.7% work from home; Mean travel time to work: 29.1 minutes

HILLSIDE LAKE (CDP).
Covers a land area of 0.523 square miles and a water area of 0.040 square miles. Located at 41.62° N. Lat; 73.80° W. Long. Elevation is 374 feet.
Population: 1,070; Growth (since 2000): -47.1%; Density: 2,046.7 persons per square mile; Race: 93.9% White, 0.0% Black/African American, 1.5% Asian, 0.0% American Indian/Alaska Native, 0.0% Native Hawaiian/Other Pacific Islander, 4.6% Two or more races, 2.8% Hispanic of any race; Average household size: 3.03; Median age: 45.2; Age under 18: 24.1%; Age 65 and over: 12.2%; Males per 100 females: 89.5; Marriage status: 30.0% never married, 55.9% now married, 1.3% separated, 11.4% widowed, 2.8% divorced; Foreign born: 7.3%; Speak English only: 93.4%; With disability: 20.7%; Veterans: 5.4%; Ancestry: 33.3% Italian, 27.2% Irish, 23.8% English, 17.9% German, 8.6% Russian
Employment: 13.3% management, business, and financial, 8.1% computer, engineering, and science, 13.5% education, legal, community

service, arts, and media, 12.8% healthcare practitioners, 15.2% service, 21.0% sales and office, 6.2% natural resources, construction, and maintenance, 9.9% production, transportation, and material moving
Income: Per capita: $26,598; Median household: $90,125; Average household: $79,406; Households with income of $100,000 or more: 36.0%; Poverty rate: 13.2%
Educational Attainment: High school diploma or higher: 87.3%; Bachelor's degree or higher: 29.9%; Graduate/professional degree or higher: 15.2%
Housing: Homeownership rate: 91.2%; Median home value: $230,100; Median year structure built: 1963; Homeowner vacancy rate: 7.7%; Median selected monthly owner costs: $2,042 with a mortgage, $457 without a mortgage; Median gross rent: n/a per month; Rental vacancy rate: 0.0%
Health Insurance: 97.4% have insurance; 83.6% have private insurance; 26.2% have public insurance; 2.6% do not have insurance; 0.0% of children under 18 do not have insurance
Transportation: Commute: 96.8% car, 1.1% public transportation, 0.0% walk, 2.1% work from home; Mean travel time to work: 36.1 minutes

HOLMES (unincorporated postal area)
ZCTA: 12531
Covers a land area of 17.495 square miles and a water area of 1.007 square miles. Located at 41.54° N. Lat; 73.67° W. Long. Elevation is 692 feet.
Population: 3,786; Growth (since 2000): 24.1%; Density: 216.4 persons per square mile; Race: 92.6% White, 2.2% Black/African American, 1.4% Asian, 0.0% American Indian/Alaska Native, 0.0% Native Hawaiian/Other Pacific Islander, 3.6% Two or more races, 1.8% Hispanic of any race; Average household size: 2.97; Median age: 44.4; Age under 18: 23.0%; Age 65 and over: 13.8%; Males per 100 females: 104.4; Marriage status: 31.7% never married, 52.5% now married, 1.2% separated, 5.7% widowed, 10.2% divorced; Foreign born: 5.8%; Speak English only: 94.6%; With disability: 8.4%; Veterans: 4.7%; Ancestry: 31.1% Italian, 20.7% Irish, 15.2% German, 6.4% Polish, 6.2% English
Employment: 18.1% management, business, and financial, 2.3% computer, engineering, and science, 10.9% education, legal, community service, arts, and media, 10.0% healthcare practitioners, 18.2% service, 19.5% sales and office, 12.0% natural resources, construction, and maintenance, 9.0% production, transportation, and material moving
Income: Per capita: $40,730; Median household: $81,686; Average household: $119,770; Households with income of $100,000 or more: 44.6%; Poverty rate: 0.3%
Educational Attainment: High school diploma or higher: 92.7%; Bachelor's degree or higher: 32.2%; Graduate/professional degree or higher: 12.1%
Housing: Homeownership rate: 82.8%; Median home value: $286,100; Median year structure built: 1970; Homeowner vacancy rate: 3.2%; Median selected monthly owner costs: $2,441 with a mortgage, $1,056 without a mortgage; Median gross rent: $1,357 per month; Rental vacancy rate: 6.6%
Health Insurance: 91.0% have insurance; 84.7% have private insurance; 15.0% have public insurance; 9.0% do not have insurance; 0.0% of children under 18 do not have insurance
Transportation: Commute: 90.8% car, 3.9% public transportation, 2.7% walk, 2.5% work from home; Mean travel time to work: 36.9 minutes

HOPEWELL JUNCTION (CDP).
Covers a land area of 0.474 square miles and a water area of <.001 square miles. Located at 41.58° N. Lat; 73.80° W. Long. Elevation is 246 feet.
Population: 362; Growth (since 2000): -86.1%; Density: 764.4 persons per square mile; Race: 84.0% White, 2.8% Black/African American, 0.0% Asian, 7.2% American Indian/Alaska Native, 0.0% Native Hawaiian/Other Pacific Islander, 6.1% Two or more races, 19.3% Hispanic of any race; Average household size: 2.35; Median age: 51.1; Age under 18: 18.8%; Age 65 and over: 21.5%; Males per 100 females: 100.0; Marriage status: 30.6% never married, 54.1% now married, 0.0% separated, 7.8% widowed, 7.5% divorced; Foreign born: 6.1%; Speak English only: 81.5%; With disability: 25.4%; Veterans: 21.1%; Ancestry: 21.3% Irish, 18.2% Italian, 17.1% American, 13.8% German, 7.7% European
Employment: 9.0% management, business, and financial, 0.0% computer, engineering, and science, 7.4% education, legal, community service, arts, and media, 10.6% healthcare practitioners, 22.9% service, 22.3% sales and office, 27.7% natural resources, construction, and maintenance, 0.0% production, transportation, and material moving

Income: Per capita: $36,500; Median household: $73,462; Average household: $80,759; Households with income of $100,000 or more: 44.8%; Poverty rate: 7.2%
Educational Attainment: High school diploma or higher: 88.3%; Bachelor's degree or higher: 26.7%; Graduate/professional degree or higher: 14.9%

School District(s)
Wappingers Central SD (KG-12)
    2014-15 Enrollment: 11,592 . . . . (845) 298-5000
Housing: Homeownership rate: 85.1%; Median home value: $265,700; Median year structure built: 1951; Homeowner vacancy rate: 0.0%; Median selected monthly owner costs: $2,643 with a mortgage, $628 without a mortgage; Median gross rent: n/a per month; Rental vacancy rate: 0.0%
Health Insurance: 95.0% have insurance; 84.0% have private insurance; 26.2% have public insurance; 5.0% do not have insurance; 0.0% of children under 18 do not have insurance
Transportation: Commute: 92.0% car, 0.0% public transportation, 0.0% walk, 0.0% work from home; Mean travel time to work: 38.8 minutes

HYDE PARK (CDP). Covers a land area of 1.206 square miles and a water area of 0.001 square miles. Located at 41.78° N. Lat; 73.93° W. Long. Elevation is 187 feet.
Population: 2,192; Growth (since 2000): n/a; Density: 1,818.1 persons per square mile; Race: 96.5% White, 0.7% Black/African American, 0.6% Asian, 0.5% American Indian/Alaska Native, 0.0% Native Hawaiian/Other Pacific Islander, 0.3% Two or more races, 4.1% Hispanic of any race; Average household size: 2.75; Median age: 36.7; Age under 18: 22.1%; Age 65 and over: 15.2%; Males per 100 females: 95.5; Marriage status: 30.9% never married, 49.9% now married, 3.7% separated, 7.8% widowed, 11.5% divorced; Foreign born: 1.7%; Speak English only: 93.6%; With disability: 8.4%; Veterans: 5.9%; Ancestry: 36.5% Irish, 31.1% Italian, 17.7% German, 16.3% English, 4.6% European
Employment: 12.0% management, business, and financial, 7.6% computer, engineering, and science, 17.2% education, legal, community service, arts, and media, 6.4% healthcare practitioners, 25.4% service, 27.1% sales and office, 1.8% natural resources, construction, and maintenance, 2.4% production, transportation, and material moving
Income: Per capita: $30,038; Median household: $75,500; Average household: $79,196; Households with income of $100,000 or more: 34.0%; Poverty rate: 12.8%
Educational Attainment: High school diploma or higher: 94.2%; Bachelor's degree or higher: 41.3%; Graduate/professional degree or higher: 18.2%

School District(s)
Hyde Park Central SD (KG-12)
    2014-15 Enrollment: 3,776 . . . . (845) 229-4005
Four-year College(s)
Culinary Institute of America (Private, Not-for-profit)
    Fall 2014 Enrollment: 2,778 . . . . (845) 452-9600
    2015-16 Tuition: In-state $29,250; Out-of-state $29,250
Housing: Homeownership rate: 72.3%; Median home value: $227,500; Median year structure built: 1956; Homeowner vacancy rate: 0.0%; Median selected monthly owner costs: $2,035 with a mortgage, $697 without a mortgage; Median gross rent: $1,306 per month; Rental vacancy rate: 13.2%
Health Insurance: 93.3% have insurance; 77.8% have private insurance; 30.2% have public insurance; 6.7% do not have insurance; 3.3% of children under 18 do not have insurance
Transportation: Commute: 84.4% car, 6.6% public transportation, 4.8% walk, 3.7% work from home; Mean travel time to work: 27.1 minutes

HYDE PARK (town). Covers a land area of 36.663 square miles and a water area of 3.195 square miles. Located at 41.81° N. Lat; 73.90° W. Long. Elevation is 187 feet.
History: Site of Roosevelt estate, part of FDR National Historic Site where President Franklin D. Roosevelt was born and is buried. Roosevelt Library contains historical material dating from 1910 until Roosevelt's death. Adjacent is the Eleanor Roosevelt National Historic Site (Val-Kill), an estate built for Mrs. Roosevelt by her husband. Frederick W. Vanderbilt mansion also here. All three homes are national historic sites. Seat of Culinary Institute of America. Settled c.1740.
Population: 21,382; Growth (since 2000): 2.5%; Density: 583.2 persons per square mile; Race: 86.3% White, 6.2% Black/African American, 3.1% Asian, 0.2% American Indian/Alaska Native, 0.0% Native Hawaiian/Other Pacific Islander, 2.4% Two or more races, 6.9% Hispanic of any race;

Average household size: 2.58; Median age: 39.6; Age under 18: 18.0%; Age 65 and over: 16.4%; Males per 100 females: 98.9; Marriage status: 36.0% never married, 48.1% now married, 2.6% separated, 5.9% widowed, 9.9% divorced; Foreign born: 6.8%; Speak English only: 88.9%; With disability: 13.5%; Veterans: 7.8%; Ancestry: 25.2% Irish, 22.9% Italian, 18.5% German, 8.9% English, 6.7% Polish
Employment: 12.4% management, business, and financial, 7.1% computer, engineering, and science, 11.9% education, legal, community service, arts, and media, 7.3% healthcare practitioners, 19.8% service, 25.1% sales and office, 8.3% natural resources, construction, and maintenance, 8.0% production, transportation, and material moving
Income: Per capita: $30,774; Median household: $73,505; Average household: $82,540; Households with income of $100,000 or more: 31.7%; Poverty rate: 10.1%
Educational Attainment: High school diploma or higher: 90.1%; Bachelor's degree or higher: 29.5%; Graduate/professional degree or higher: 14.3%

School District(s)
Hyde Park Central SD (KG-12)
    2014-15 Enrollment: 3,776 . . . . (845) 229-4005
Four-year College(s)
Culinary Institute of America (Private, Not-for-profit)
    Fall 2014 Enrollment: 2,778 . . . . (845) 452-9600
    2015-16 Tuition: In-state $29,250; Out-of-state $29,250
Housing: Homeownership rate: 71.8%; Median home value: $226,100; Median year structure built: 1966; Homeowner vacancy rate: 2.4%; Median selected monthly owner costs: $1,961 with a mortgage, $799 without a mortgage; Median gross rent: $1,062 per month; Rental vacancy rate: 6.3%
Health Insurance: 93.4% have insurance; 80.0% have private insurance; 28.7% have public insurance; 6.6% do not have insurance; 0.6% of children under 18 do not have insurance
Safety: Violent crime rate: 3.8 per 10,000 population; Property crime rate: 54.6 per 10,000 population
Transportation: Commute: 86.9% car, 3.7% public transportation, 5.0% walk, 4.0% work from home; Mean travel time to work: 29.0 minutes
Additional Information Contacts
Town of Hyde Park . . . . (845) 229-5111
    http://www.hydeparkny.us

LA GRANGE (town). Covers a land area of 39.879 square miles and a water area of 0.470 square miles. Located at 41.68° N. Lat; 73.80° W. Long.
History: The town was established in 1821 as "Freedom" from parts of the Towns of Beekman and Fishkill. Its name was changed to "LaGrange" in 1828.
Population: 15,750; Growth (since 2000): 5.5%; Density: 394.9 persons per square mile; Race: 88.3% White, 4.0% Black/African American, 4.5% Asian, 0.3% American Indian/Alaska Native, 0.0% Native Hawaiian/Other Pacific Islander, 1.6% Two or more races, 7.2% Hispanic of any race; Average household size: 2.92; Median age: 43.3; Age under 18: 24.5%; Age 65 and over: 13.7%; Males per 100 females: 98.6; Marriage status: 24.3% never married, 63.6% now married, 2.6% separated, 4.9% widowed, 7.2% divorced; Foreign born: 7.6%; Speak English only: 88.4%; With disability: 10.4%; Veterans: 8.5%; Ancestry: 24.6% Irish, 23.9% Italian, 14.7% German, 8.1% English, 5.1% Polish
Employment: 21.2% management, business, and financial, 7.0% computer, engineering, and science, 12.3% education, legal, community service, arts, and media, 6.9% healthcare practitioners, 13.8% service, 21.9% sales and office, 9.3% natural resources, construction, and maintenance, 7.5% production, transportation, and material moving
Income: Per capita: $41,051; Median household: $102,051; Average household: $118,959; Households with income of $100,000 or more: 51.0%; Poverty rate: 4.1%
Educational Attainment: High school diploma or higher: 92.9%; Bachelor's degree or higher: 40.0%; Graduate/professional degree or higher: 20.5%
Housing: Homeownership rate: 93.6%; Median home value: $291,200; Median year structure built: 1972; Homeowner vacancy rate: 0.8%; Median selected monthly owner costs: $2,419 with a mortgage, $926 without a mortgage; Median gross rent: $1,330 per month; Rental vacancy rate: 0.0%
Health Insurance: 95.4% have insurance; 86.0% have private insurance; 23.2% have public insurance; 4.6% do not have insurance; 2.1% of children under 18 do not have insurance

Transportation: Commute: 89.1% car, 2.5% public transportation, 1.2% walk, 6.9% work from home; Mean travel time to work: 34.7 minutes

Additional Information Contacts

Town of La Grange . . . . (845) 452-1830
http://www.lagrangeny.org

LAGRANGEVILLE (unincorporated postal area)

ZCTA: 12540

Covers a land area of 34.115 square miles and a water area of 0.300 square miles. Located at 41.67° N. Lat; 73.72° W. Long. Elevation is 358 feet.

Population: 7,794; Growth (since 2000): 17.5%; Density: 228.5 persons per square mile; Race: 92.5% White, 0.9% Black/African American, 4.9% Asian, 0.1% American Indian/Alaska Native, 0.0% Native Hawaiian/Other Pacific Islander, 1.4% Two or more races, 4.0% Hispanic of any race; Average household size: 2.88; Median age: 44.3; Age under 18: 24.5%; Age 65 and over: 15.9%; Males per 100 females: 101.0; Marriage status: 23.0% never married, 66.5% now married, 1.7% separated, 4.2% widowed, 6.3% divorced; Foreign born: 9.4%; Speak English only: 88.0%; With disability: 8.8%; Veterans: 7.9%; Ancestry: 27.2% Italian, 25.1% Irish, 16.7% German, 6.9% English, 5.6% American

Employment: 17.9% management, business, and financial, 8.4% computer, engineering, and science, 12.7% education, legal, community service, arts, and media, 6.2% healthcare practitioners, 14.6% service, 19.2% sales and office, 10.7% natural resources, construction, and maintenance, 10.3% production, transportation, and material moving

Income: Per capita: $40,962; Median household: $102,270; Average household: $117,222; Households with income of $100,000 or more: 51.7%; Poverty rate: 3.5%

Educational Attainment: High school diploma or higher: 94.1%; Bachelor's degree or higher: 39.7%; Graduate/professional degree or higher: 19.9%

School District(s)

Arlington Central SD (KG-12)
   2014-15 Enrollment: 8,801 . . . . (845) 486-4460

Housing: Homeownership rate: 91.5%; Median home value: $322,600; Median year structure built: 1980; Homeowner vacancy rate: 0.9%; Median selected monthly owner costs: $2,473 with a mortgage, $923 without a mortgage; Median gross rent: $1,408 per month; Rental vacancy rate: 0.0%

Health Insurance: 96.7% have insurance; 90.1% have private insurance; 20.7% have public insurance; 3.3% do not have insurance; 1.1% of children under 18 do not have insurance

Transportation: Commute: 85.9% car, 3.3% public transportation, 0.5% walk, 7.7% work from home; Mean travel time to work: 36.0 minutes

MERRITT PARK (CDP). Covers a land area of 0.444 square miles and a water area of 0 square miles. Located at 41.54° N. Lat; 73.87° W. Long. Elevation is 220 feet.

Population: 1,720; Growth (since 2000): n/a; Density: 3,872.7 persons per square mile; Race: 46.0% White, 6.2% Black/African American, 46.0% Asian, 0.0% American Indian/Alaska Native, 0.0% Native Hawaiian/Other Pacific Islander, 1.7% Two or more races, 8.3% Hispanic of any race; Average household size: 2.95; Median age: 38.7; Age under 18: 30.2%; Age 65 and over: 13.9%; Males per 100 females: 90.3; Marriage status: 19.6% never married, 71.3% now married, 0.0% separated, 2.5% widowed, 6.6% divorced; Foreign born: 40.4%; Speak English only: 54.8%; With disability: 5.2%; Veterans: 8.5%; Ancestry: 14.1% Italian, 13.3% Irish, 4.9% German, 2.1% Egyptian, 1.8% English

Employment: 18.6% management, business, and financial, 34.1% computer, engineering, and science, 10.7% education, legal, community service, arts, and media, 12.7% healthcare practitioners, 5.3% service, 11.9% sales and office, 2.1% natural resources, construction, and maintenance, 4.6% production, transportation, and material moving

Income: Per capita: $48,355; Median household: $147,808; Average household: $140,059; Households with income of $100,000 or more: 71.3%; Poverty rate: 3.0%

Educational Attainment: High school diploma or higher: 98.4%; Bachelor's degree or higher: 69.2%; Graduate/professional degree or higher: 30.4%

Housing: Homeownership rate: 84.4%; Median home value: $402,600; Median year structure built: n/a; Homeowner vacancy rate: 0.0%; Median selected monthly owner costs: $3,163 with a mortgage, $1,113 without a

mortgage; Median gross rent: $2,792 per month; Rental vacancy rate: 0.0%

Health Insurance: 96.8% have insurance; 91.4% have private insurance; 17.4% have public insurance; 3.2% do not have insurance; 4.8% of children under 18 do not have insurance

Transportation: Commute: 77.2% car, 15.8% public transportation, 1.7% walk, 5.2% work from home; Mean travel time to work: 50.2 minutes

MILAN (town). Covers a land area of 36.109 square miles and a water area of 0.468 square miles. Located at 41.98° N. Lat; 73.78° W. Long. Elevation is 433 feet.

Population: 2,268; Growth (since 2000): -50.3%; Density: 62.8 persons per square mile; Race: 84.5% White, 3.3% Black/African American, 5.2% Asian, 0.3% American Indian/Alaska Native, 0.0% Native Hawaiian/Other Pacific Islander, 2.9% Two or more races, 5.0% Hispanic of any race; Average household size: 2.36; Median age: 45.0; Age under 18: 19.3%; Age 65 and over: 17.1%; Males per 100 females: 106.4; Marriage status: 24.2% never married, 63.8% now married, 2.4% separated, 5.4% widowed, 6.7% divorced; Foreign born: 13.1%; Speak English only: 85.7%; With disability: 8.8%; Veterans: 8.4%; Ancestry: 21.1% Irish, 17.6% German, 16.6% Italian, 13.0% English, 5.3% American

Employment: 18.1% management, business, and financial, 5.8% computer, engineering, and science, 14.4% education, legal, community service, arts, and media, 5.5% healthcare practitioners, 17.0% service, 17.8% sales and office, 10.8% natural resources, construction, and maintenance, 10.7% production, transportation, and material moving

Income: Per capita: $39,688; Median household: $63,704; Average household: $93,455; Households with income of $100,000 or more: 28.3%; Poverty rate: 4.0%

Educational Attainment: High school diploma or higher: 96.1%; Bachelor's degree or higher: 42.2%; Graduate/professional degree or higher: 15.3%

Housing: Homeownership rate: 80.8%; Median home value: $325,900; Median year structure built: 1964; Homeowner vacancy rate: 0.0%; Median selected monthly owner costs: $2,216 with a mortgage, $813 without a mortgage; Median gross rent: $1,231 per month; Rental vacancy rate: 5.2%

Health Insurance: 94.5% have insurance; 80.9% have private insurance; 28.6% have public insurance; 5.5% do not have insurance; 0.9% of children under 18 do not have insurance

Transportation: Commute: 83.3% car, 3.8% public transportation, 2.4% walk, 9.9% work from home; Mean travel time to work: 32.1 minutes

MILLBROOK (village). Covers a land area of 1.931 square miles and a water area of 0.056 square miles. Located at 41.78° N. Lat; 73.69° W. Long. Elevation is 574 feet.

History: Seat of Institute of Ecosystem Studies— N.Y. Botanical Gardens; Millbrook Preparatory School. Many estates and second homes for New Yorkers. Noted for polo playing. Incorporated 1896.

Population: 1,542; Growth (since 2000): 7.9%; Density: 798.7 persons per square mile; Race: 89.5% White, 0.5% Black/African American, 4.5% Asian, 3.0% American Indian/Alaska Native, 0.0% Native Hawaiian/Other Pacific Islander, 2.5% Two or more races, 4.5% Hispanic of any race; Average household size: 2.26; Median age: 47.0; Age under 18: 20.5%; Age 65 and over: 23.5%; Males per 100 females: 87.1; Marriage status: 28.2% never married, 50.1% now married, 3.5% separated, 11.8% widowed, 9.9% divorced; Foreign born: 9.3%; Speak English only: 85.6%; With disability: 11.9%; Veterans: 11.1%; Ancestry: 34.5% Irish, 27.8% Italian, 17.6% English, 12.6% German, 5.8% Polish

Employment: 13.6% management, business, and financial, 6.4% computer, engineering, and science, 14.4% education, legal, community service, arts, and media, 7.6% healthcare practitioners, 28.0% service, 17.0% sales and office, 6.8% natural resources, construction, and maintenance, 6.3% production, transportation, and material moving

Income: Per capita: $47,469; Median household: $75,809; Average household: $105,997; Households with income of $100,000 or more: 35.1%; Poverty rate: 7.5%

Educational Attainment: High school diploma or higher: 93.5%; Bachelor's degree or higher: 43.6%; Graduate/professional degree or higher: 24.4%

School District(s)

Millbrook Central SD (KG-12)
   2014-15 Enrollment: 1,058 . . . . (845) 677-4200

Housing: Homeownership rate: 49.9%; Median home value: $368,100; Median year structure built: 1965; Homeowner vacancy rate: 6.6%; Median

selected monthly owner costs: $2,176 with a mortgage, $946 without a mortgage; Median gross rent: $1,108 per month; Rental vacancy rate: 3.1%
Health Insurance: 94.0% have insurance; 76.6% have private insurance; 34.6% have public insurance; 6.0% do not have insurance; 1.9% of children under 18 do not have insurance
Transportation: Commute: 81.3% car, 1.5% public transportation, 7.8% walk, 9.4% work from home; Mean travel time to work: 22.2 minutes

MILLERTON (village).
Covers a land area of 0.618 square miles and a water area of 0.003 square miles. Located at 41.95° N. Lat; 73.51° W. Long. Elevation is 709 feet.
Population: 866; Growth (since 2000): -6.4%; Density: 1,400.3 persons per square mile; Race: 75.9% White, 3.7% Black/African American, 5.2% Asian, 2.9% American Indian/Alaska Native, 0.0% Native Hawaiian/Other Pacific Islander, 4.6% Two or more races, 16.6% Hispanic of any race; Average household size: 2.36; Median age: 38.1; Age under 18: 17.2%; Age 65 and over: 15.6%; Males per 100 females: 100.4; Marriage status: 41.9% never married, 44.2% now married, 0.4% separated, 5.9% widowed, 8.0% divorced; Foreign born: 17.2%; Speak English only: 85.7%; With disability: 16.9%; Veterans: 5.2%; Ancestry: 32.0% Irish, 16.3% German, 11.2% Italian, 10.5% English, 5.1% American
Employment: 11.4% management, business, and financial, 0.0% computer, engineering, and science, 10.2% education, legal, community service, arts, and media, 4.4% healthcare practitioners, 35.4% service, 16.1% sales and office, 10.0% natural resources, construction, and maintenance, 12.5% production, transportation, and material moving
Income: Per capita: $26,661; Median household: $49,563; Average household: $61,637; Households with income of $100,000 or more: 20.7%; Poverty rate: 12.8%
Educational Attainment: High school diploma or higher: 83.9%; Bachelor's degree or higher: 23.2%; Graduate/professional degree or higher: 4.5%
Housing: Homeownership rate: 58.8%; Median home value: $219,800; Median year structure built: Before 1940; Homeowner vacancy rate: 0.0%; Median selected monthly owner costs: $1,833 with a mortgage, $875 without a mortgage; Median gross rent: $1,000 per month; Rental vacancy rate: 4.5%
Health Insurance: 73.8% have insurance; 44.9% have private insurance; 39.1% have public insurance; 26.2% do not have insurance; 11.4% of children under 18 do not have insurance
Safety: Violent crime rate: 0.0 per 10,000 population; Property crime rate: 13.4 per 10,000 population
Newspapers: Millerton News (weekly circulation 2,000)
Transportation: Commute: 78.5% car, 0.0% public transportation, 14.0% walk, 7.5% work from home; Mean travel time to work: 22.7 minutes

MYERS CORNER (CDP).
Covers a land area of 5.017 square miles and a water area of 0.039 square miles. Located at 41.60° N. Lat; 73.87° W. Long. Elevation is 217 feet.
Population: 6,867; Growth (since 2000): 23.8%; Density: 1,368.8 persons per square mile; Race: 82.5% White, 1.6% Black/African American, 11.2% Asian, 0.0% American Indian/Alaska Native, 0.0% Native Hawaiian/Other Pacific Islander, 2.8% Two or more races, 9.0% Hispanic of any race; Average household size: 2.88; Median age: 43.9; Age under 18: 22.0%; Age 65 and over: 14.9%; Males per 100 females: 96.8; Marriage status: 25.0% never married, 64.2% now married, 1.2% separated, 4.5% widowed, 6.3% divorced; Foreign born: 10.1%; Speak English only: 81.2%; With disability: 10.7%; Veterans: 5.2%; Ancestry: 24.0% Italian, 18.9% Irish, 11.9% German, 6.8% English, 5.8% American
Employment: 17.3% management, business, and financial, 5.3% computer, engineering, and science, 13.8% education, legal, community service, arts, and media, 5.4% healthcare practitioners, 14.6% service, 28.6% sales and office, 6.0% natural resources, construction, and maintenance, 8.9% production, transportation, and material moving
Income: Per capita: $39,062; Median household: $97,500; Average household: $111,402; Households with income of $100,000 or more: 48.9%; Poverty rate: 3.6%
Educational Attainment: High school diploma or higher: 94.4%; Bachelor's degree or higher: 41.7%; Graduate/professional degree or higher: 18.4%
Housing: Homeownership rate: 95.1%; Median home value: $309,600; Median year structure built: 1973; Homeowner vacancy rate: 2.4%; Median selected monthly owner costs: $2,244 with a mortgage, $887 without a

mortgage; Median gross rent: $1,563 per month; Rental vacancy rate: 11.4%
Health Insurance: 95.0% have insurance; 86.3% have private insurance; 22.1% have public insurance; 5.0% do not have insurance; 2.4% of children under 18 do not have insurance
Transportation: Commute: 85.9% car, 3.8% public transportation, 3.2% walk, 6.1% work from home; Mean travel time to work: 34.6 minutes

NORTH EAST (town).
Covers a land area of 43.163 square miles and a water area of 0.559 square miles. Located at 41.95° N. Lat; 73.55° W. Long.
Population: 3,011; Growth (since 2000): 0.3%; Density: 69.8 persons per square mile; Race: 86.9% White, 2.5% Black/African American, 3.8% Asian, 0.8% American Indian/Alaska Native, 0.0% Native Hawaiian/Other Pacific Islander, 1.3% Two or more races, 19.4% Hispanic of any race; Average household size: 2.57; Median age: 45.6; Age under 18: 16.4%; Age 65 and over: 16.4%; Males per 100 females: 103.3; Marriage status: 33.6% never married, 45.9% now married, 0.2% separated, 6.3% widowed, 14.2% divorced; Foreign born: 17.1%; Speak English only: 79.5%; With disability: 15.1%; Veterans: 7.4%; Ancestry: 22.3% Irish, 12.5% German, 10.1% English, 8.9% Italian, 6.0% American
Employment: 14.0% management, business, and financial, 0.8% computer, engineering, and science, 11.8% education, legal, community service, arts, and media, 3.9% healthcare practitioners, 30.7% service, 12.0% sales and office, 16.9% natural resources, construction, and maintenance, 10.0% production, transportation, and material moving
Income: Per capita: $33,244; Median household: $63,258; Average household: $82,429; Households with income of $100,000 or more: 23.9%; Poverty rate: 7.0%
Educational Attainment: High school diploma or higher: 86.4%; Bachelor's degree or higher: 27.6%; Graduate/professional degree or higher: 11.3%
Housing: Homeownership rate: 65.5%; Median home value: $289,100; Median year structure built: 1961; Homeowner vacancy rate: 0.0%; Median selected monthly owner costs: $2,114 with a mortgage, $803 without a mortgage; Median gross rent: $1,276 per month; Rental vacancy rate: 1.7%
Health Insurance: 82.9% have insurance; 59.5% have private insurance; 34.6% have public insurance; 17.1% do not have insurance; 4.5% of children under 18 do not have insurance
Transportation: Commute: 77.8% car, 4.5% public transportation, 8.4% walk, 9.3% work from home; Mean travel time to work: 28.0 minutes

PAWLING (town).
Covers a land area of 43.835 square miles and a water area of 1.187 square miles. Located at 41.57° N. Lat; 73.60° W. Long. Elevation is 463 feet.
History: In 1937, Thomas E. Dewey, three-term governor and two-time nominee for U.S. president, purchased a 486-acre farm here, although his legal address was the Roosevelt Hotel in N.Y. city. When he returned to legal practice after being governor, he resided at the World Trade Center. He and his wife are buried in Pawling Cemetery. Settled by Quakers c.1740; Incorporated 1893.
Population: 8,402; Growth (since 2000): 11.7%; Density: 191.7 persons per square mile; Race: 90.2% White, 2.1% Black/African American, 2.0% Asian, 0.1% American Indian/Alaska Native, 0.0% Native Hawaiian/Other Pacific Islander, 2.1% Two or more races, 12.6% Hispanic of any race; Average household size: 2.74; Median age: 44.4; Age under 18: 21.4%; Age 65 and over: 15.5%; Males per 100 females: 105.9; Marriage status: 30.5% never married, 52.2% now married, 0.8% separated, 6.4% widowed, 10.9% divorced; Foreign born: 11.9%; Speak English only: 83.8%; With disability: 10.8%; Veterans: 5.2%; Ancestry: 27.2% Italian, 22.1% Irish, 14.6% German, 7.4% English, 6.1% Polish
Employment: 16.3% management, business, and financial, 3.5% computer, engineering, and science, 12.5% education, legal, community service, arts, and media, 6.3% healthcare practitioners, 20.1% service, 22.3% sales and office, 11.0% natural resources, construction, and maintenance, 7.9% production, transportation, and material moving
Income: Per capita: $37,019; Median household: $78,692; Average household: $101,348; Households with income of $100,000 or more: 41.1%; Poverty rate: 5.4%
Educational Attainment: High school diploma or higher: 92.0%; Bachelor's degree or higher: 36.1%; Graduate/professional degree or higher: 14.8%

School District(s)
Pawling Central SD (KG-12)
    2014-15 Enrollment: 1,240 . . . . (845) 855-4600
Housing: Homeownership rate: 74.5%; Median home value: $305,100;
Median year structure built: 1967; Homeowner vacancy rate: 0.7%; Median
selected monthly owner costs: $2,430 with a mortgage, $1,104 without a
mortgage; Median gross rent: $1,061 per month; Rental vacancy rate:
0.0%
Health Insurance: 89.2% have insurance; 74.5% have private insurance;
26.4% have public insurance; 10.8% do not have insurance; 1.7% of
children under 18 do not have insurance
Transportation: Commute: 81.4% car, 9.4% public transportation, 4.0%
walk, 4.1% work from home; Mean travel time to work: 38.9 minutes
Additional Information Contacts
Town of Pawling . . . . (845) 855-5040
    http://www.pawling.org/Pages/index

PAWLING (village). Covers a land area of 1.997 square miles and a
water area of <.001 square miles. Located at 41.56° N. Lat; 73.60° W.
Long. Elevation is 463 feet.
Population: 2,243; Growth (since 2000): 0.4%; Density: 1,123.5 persons
per square mile; Race: 86.9% White, 3.7% Black/African American, 0.4%
Asian, 0.4% American Indian/Alaska Native, 0.0% Native Hawaiian/Other
Pacific Islander, 0.9% Two or more races, 21.3% Hispanic of any race;
Average household size: 2.44; Median age: 42.8; Age under 18: 20.8%;
Age 65 and over: 14.5%; Males per 100 females: 119.6; Marriage status:
38.8% never married, 37.4% now married, 0.4% separated, 7.7%
widowed, 16.1% divorced; Foreign born: 16.3%; Speak English only:
79.7%; With disability: 13.2%; Veterans: 4.6%; Ancestry: 30.0% Italian,
19.7% Irish, 12.4% German, 7.4% English, 5.3% American
Employment: 10.1% management, business, and financial, 2.1%
computer, engineering, and science, 10.6% education, legal, community
service, arts, and media, 8.5% healthcare practitioners, 27.4% service,
22.6% sales and office, 8.3% natural resources, construction, and
maintenance, 10.4% production, transportation, and material moving
Income: Per capita: $29,236; Median household: $56,000; Average
household: $72,213; Households with income of $100,000 or more: 27.1%;
Poverty rate: 11.2%
Educational Attainment: High school diploma or higher: 87.8%;
Bachelor's degree or higher: 31.0%; Graduate/professional degree or
higher: 13.4%

School District(s)
Pawling Central SD (KG-12)
    2014-15 Enrollment: 1,240 . . . . (845) 855-4600
Housing: Homeownership rate: 53.7%; Median home value: $280,500;
Median year structure built: 1955; Homeowner vacancy rate: 0.0%; Median
selected monthly owner costs: $2,571 with a mortgage, $1,142 without a
mortgage; Median gross rent: $883 per month; Rental vacancy rate: 0.0%
Health Insurance: 85.5% have insurance; 62.8% have private insurance;
32.7% have public insurance; 14.5% do not have insurance; 0.0% of
children under 18 do not have insurance
Transportation: Commute: 70.6% car, 14.5% public transportation, 10.7%
walk, 2.9% work from home; Mean travel time to work: 33.5 minutes

PINE PLAINS (CDP). Covers a land area of 2.078 square miles and a
water area of 0.224 square miles. Located at 41.98° N. Lat; 73.66° W.
Long. Elevation is 469 feet.
Population: 1,575; Growth (since 2000): 11.5%; Density: 757.8 persons
per square mile; Race: 95.2% White, 0.0% Black/African American, 0.0%
Asian, 0.0% American Indian/Alaska Native, 0.0% Native Hawaiian/Other
Pacific Islander, 1.1% Two or more races, 5.2% Hispanic of any race;
Average household size: 2.65; Median age: 42.2; Age under 18: 26.9%;
Age 65 and over: 17.8%; Males per 100 females: 92.2; Marriage status:
21.0% never married, 61.8% now married, 5.1% separated, 10.0%
widowed, 7.2% divorced; Foreign born: 3.0%; Speak English only: 94.5%;
With disability: 19.2%; Veterans: 6.8%; Ancestry: 26.4% German, 24.6%
Irish, 20.8% Italian, 13.7% English, 10.9% Dutch
Employment: 14.7% management, business, and financial, 3.3%
computer, engineering, and science, 11.7% education, legal, community
service, arts, and media, 4.7% healthcare practitioners, 23.2% service,
19.6% sales and office, 16.2% natural resources, construction, and
maintenance, 6.6% production, transportation, and material moving
Income: Per capita: $28,500; Median household: $60,167; Average
household: $73,627; Households with income of $100,000 or more: 20.2%;
Poverty rate: 8.4%

Educational Attainment: High school diploma or higher: 88.3%;
Bachelor's degree or higher: 18.3%; Graduate/professional degree or
higher: 10.2%
School District(s)
Pine Plains Central SD (KG-12)
    2014-15 Enrollment: 941 . . . . (518) 398-7181
Housing: Homeownership rate: 70.4%; Median home value: $223,800;
Median year structure built: 1953; Homeowner vacancy rate: 3.5%; Median
selected monthly owner costs: $1,669 with a mortgage, $606 without a
mortgage; Median gross rent: $1,131 per month; Rental vacancy rate:
0.0%
Health Insurance: 92.6% have insurance; 66.7% have private insurance;
42.7% have public insurance; 7.4% do not have insurance; 2.8% of
children under 18 do not have insurance
Transportation: Commute: 90.1% car, 1.9% public transportation, 5.5%
walk, 2.5% work from home; Mean travel time to work: 29.6 minutes

PINE PLAINS (town). Covers a land area of 30.583 square miles and
a water area of 0.589 square miles. Located at 41.97° N. Lat; 73.65° W.
Long. Elevation is 469 feet.
Population: 2,557; Growth (since 2000): -0.5%; Density: 83.6 persons per
square mile; Race: 95.3% White, 0.6% Black/African American, 0.4%
Asian, 0.0% American Indian/Alaska Native, 0.0% Native Hawaiian/Other
Pacific Islander, 0.7% Two or more races, 4.8% Hispanic of any race;
Average household size: 2.53; Median age: 45.9; Age under 18: 21.5%;
Age 65 and over: 18.5%; Males per 100 females: 94.7; Marriage status:
23.8% never married, 59.7% now married, 4.1% separated, 7.7%
widowed, 8.8% divorced; Foreign born: 4.4%; Speak English only: 94.0%;
With disability: 17.0%; Veterans: 7.9%; Ancestry: 24.4% Irish, 23.8%
German, 17.2% Italian, 13.2% English, 10.7% Dutch
Employment: 16.9% management, business, and financial, 3.6%
computer, engineering, and science, 8.2% education, legal, community
service, arts, and media, 6.7% healthcare practitioners, 19.4% service,
24.2% sales and office, 12.5% natural resources, construction, and
maintenance, 8.6% production, transportation, and material moving
Income: Per capita: $32,251; Median household: $64,732; Average
household: $80,308; Households with income of $100,000 or more: 24.7%;
Poverty rate: 8.4%
Educational Attainment: High school diploma or higher: 86.8%;
Bachelor's degree or higher: 21.7%; Graduate/professional degree or
higher: 9.8%

School District(s)
Pine Plains Central SD (KG-12)
    2014-15 Enrollment: 941 . . . . (518) 398-7181
Housing: Homeownership rate: 74.1%; Median home value: $238,900;
Median year structure built: 1961; Homeowner vacancy rate: 3.5%; Median
selected monthly owner costs: $1,754 with a mortgage, $673 without a
mortgage; Median gross rent: $1,056 per month; Rental vacancy rate:
4.0%
Health Insurance: 91.9% have insurance; 70.0% have private insurance;
37.6% have public insurance; 8.1% do not have insurance; 2.2% of
children under 18 do not have insurance
Safety: Violent crime rate: 0.0 per 10,000 population; Property crime rate:
16.3 per 10,000 population
Transportation: Commute: 84.5% car, 1.1% public transportation, 6.2%
walk, 8.2% work from home; Mean travel time to work: 27.3 minutes
Additional Information Contacts
Town of Pine Plains. . . . . (518) 398-7155
    http://pineplains-ny.gov/content

PLEASANT VALLEY (CDP). Covers a land area of 0.934 square
miles and a water area of 0.025 square miles. Located at 41.75° N. Lat;
73.83° W. Long. Elevation is 187 feet.
Population: 1,452; Growth (since 2000): -21.0%; Density: 1,553.9 persons
per square mile; Race: 87.8% White, 7.8% Black/African American, 4.4%
Asian, 0.0% American Indian/Alaska Native, 0.0% Native Hawaiian/Other
Pacific Islander, 0.0% Two or more races, 3.2% Hispanic of any race;
Average household size: 2.33; Median age: 43.4; Age under 18: 19.0%;
Age 65 and over: 17.8%; Males per 100 females: 90.2; Marriage status:
26.3% never married, 52.6% now married, 0.0% separated, 8.7%
widowed, 12.3% divorced; Foreign born: 10.6%; Speak English only:
88.6%; With disability: 20.5%; Veterans: 9.4%; Ancestry: 29.4% Italian,
24.6% German, 14.5% Irish, 9.0% English, 6.5% American
Employment: 11.5% management, business, and financial, 2.4%
computer, engineering, and science, 19.7% education, legal, community

service, arts, and media, 8.2% healthcare practitioners, 18.1% service, 24.2% sales and office, 10.6% natural resources, construction, and maintenance, 5.2% production, transportation, and material moving

Income: Per capita: $30,182; Median household: $64,423; Average household: $69,048; Households with income of $100,000 or more: 19.3%; Poverty rate: 7.8%

Educational Attainment: High school diploma or higher: 91.9%; Bachelor's degree or higher: 31.3%; Graduate/professional degree or higher: 19.1%

School District(s)
Arlington Central SD (KG-12)
   2014-15 Enrollment: 8,801 . . . . (845) 486-4460

Housing: Homeownership rate: 39.3%; Median home value: $250,900; Median year structure built: 1983; Homeowner vacancy rate: 0.0%; Median selected monthly owner costs: $1,948 with a mortgage, $671 without a mortgage; Median gross rent: $1,675 per month; Rental vacancy rate: 0.0%

Health Insurance: 91.7% have insurance; 80.4% have private insurance; 30.8% have public insurance; 8.3% do not have insurance; 10.1% of children under 18 do not have insurance

Transportation: Commute: 87.2% car, 0.0% public transportation, 0.0% walk, 12.8% work from home; Mean travel time to work: 25.8 minutes

PLEASANT VALLEY (town).
Covers a land area of 32.576 square miles and a water area of 0.564 square miles. Located at 41.77° N. Lat; 73.80° W. Long. Elevation is 187 feet.

History: Settlers arrived to the area after 1735. The town was part of the Great Nine Partners Patent of 1697, a land grant whose legality was questioned due to extortion and threats of violence.

Population: 9,730; Growth (since 2000): 7.3%; Density: 298.7 persons per square mile; Race: 91.3% White, 4.5% Black/African American, 1.7% Asian, 0.0% American Indian/Alaska Native, 0.0% Native Hawaiian/Other Pacific Islander, 1.7% Two or more races, 5.6% Hispanic of any race; Average household size: 2.45; Median age: 43.3; Age under 18: 19.8%; Age 65 and over: 14.6%; Males per 100 females: 95.6; Marriage status: 26.6% never married, 57.6% now married, 3.1% separated, 5.1% widowed, 10.7% divorced; Foreign born: 7.1%; Speak English only: 90.4%; With disability: 15.6%; Veterans: 8.7%; Ancestry: 26.6% Italian, 24.5% Irish, 18.8% German, 9.8% English, 7.4% American

Employment: 15.1% management, business, and financial, 5.1% computer, engineering, and science, 16.5% education, legal, community service, arts, and media, 4.7% healthcare practitioners, 16.6% service, 22.3% sales and office, 12.5% natural resources, construction, and maintenance, 7.3% production, transportation, and material moving

Income: Per capita: $34,424; Median household: $73,975; Average household: $83,015; Households with income of $100,000 or more: 30.4%; Poverty rate: 7.0%

Educational Attainment: High school diploma or higher: 91.4%; Bachelor's degree or higher: 28.2%; Graduate/professional degree or higher: 14.7%

School District(s)
Arlington Central SD (KG-12)
   2014-15 Enrollment: 8,801 . . . . (845) 486-4460

Housing: Homeownership rate: 70.5%; Median home value: $255,500; Median year structure built: 1973; Homeowner vacancy rate: 3.9%; Median selected monthly owner costs: $2,016 with a mortgage, $719 without a mortgage; Median gross rent: $1,430 per month; Rental vacancy rate: 6.6%

Health Insurance: 92.4% have insurance; 77.8% have private insurance; 27.8% have public insurance; 7.6% do not have insurance; 4.7% of children under 18 do not have insurance

Transportation: Commute: 91.2% car, 1.5% public transportation, 0.5% walk, 6.5% work from home; Mean travel time to work: 28.7 minutes

Additional Information Contacts
Town of Pleasant Valley . . . . (845) 635-3274
   http://pleasantvalley-ny.gov

POUGHKEEPSIE (city).
County seat. Covers a land area of 5.144 square miles and a water area of 0.575 square miles. Located at 41.69° N. Lat; 73.92° W. Long. Elevation is 200 feet.

History: It became the temporary state capital in 1777, and the U.S. Constitution was ratified (1788) here. Seat of Vassar and Marist Colleges and a community college. Several historic 18th-century buildings still stand. Hyde Park lies just north. Settled 1687 by the Dutch, Incorporated as a city 1854.

Population: 30,635; Growth (since 2000): 2.6%; Density: 5,955.6 persons per square mile; Race: 43.6% White, 36.4% Black/African American, 2.4% Asian, 0.4% American Indian/Alaska Native, 0.0% Native Hawaiian/Other Pacific Islander, 6.0% Two or more races, 21.3% Hispanic of any race; Average household size: 2.43; Median age: 36.4; Age under 18: 23.4%; Age 65 and over: 14.0%; Males per 100 females: 92.4; Marriage status: 46.4% never married, 36.1% now married, 3.2% separated, 7.1% widowed, 10.4% divorced; Foreign born: 19.6%; Speak English only: 76.6%; With disability: 15.8%; Veterans: 6.1%; Ancestry: 11.9% Italian, 11.4% Irish, 7.7% German, 7.3% Jamaican, 4.3% American

Employment: 8.9% management, business, and financial, 5.0% computer, engineering, and science, 11.0% education, legal, community service, arts, and media, 5.1% healthcare practitioners, 29.9% service, 23.1% sales and office, 7.6% natural resources, construction, and maintenance, 9.5% production, transportation, and material moving

Income: Per capita: $23,745; Median household: $38,919; Average household: $56,370; Households with income of $100,000 or more: 14.0%; Poverty rate: 24.1%

Educational Attainment: High school diploma or higher: 79.6%; Bachelor's degree or higher: 23.4%; Graduate/professional degree or higher: 9.7%

School District(s)
Arlington Central SD (KG-12)
   2014-15 Enrollment: 8,801 . . . . (845) 486-4460
Dutchess Boces
   2014-15 Enrollment: n/a . . . . (845) 486-4800
Hyde Park Central SD (KG-12)
   2014-15 Enrollment: 3,776 . . . . (845) 229-4005
Poughkeepsie City SD (PK-12)
   2014-15 Enrollment: 4,494 . . . . (845) 451-4950
Spackenkill Union Free SD (KG-12)
   2014-15 Enrollment: 1,484 . . . . (845) 463-7800
Wappingers Central SD (KG-12)
   2014-15 Enrollment: 11,592 . . . . (845) 298-5000

Four-year College(s)
Marist College (Private, Not-for-profit)
   Fall 2014 Enrollment: 6,356 . . . . (845) 575-3000
   2015-16 Tuition: In-state $33,840; Out-of-state $33,840
Vassar College (Private, Not-for-profit)
   Fall 2014 Enrollment: 2,421 . . . . (845) 437-7000
   2015-16 Tuition: In-state $51,250; Out-of-state $51,250

Two-year College(s)
Dutchess Community College (Public)
   Fall 2014 Enrollment: 9,905 . . . . (845) 431-8000
   2015-16 Tuition: In-state $3,866; Out-of-state $7,226

Vocational/Technical School(s)
Dutchess BOCES-Practical Nursing Program (Public)
   Fall 2014 Enrollment: 155 . . . . (845) 486-8001
   2015-16 Tuition: $9,950
Ridley-Lowell Business & Technical Institute-Poughkeepsie (Private, For-profit)
   Fall 2014 Enrollment: 379 . . . . (845) 471-0330
   2015-16 Tuition: $15,400

Housing: Homeownership rate: 36.2%; Median home value: $196,800; Median year structure built: 1950; Homeowner vacancy rate: 5.2%; Median selected monthly owner costs: $1,824 with a mortgage, $769 without a mortgage; Median gross rent: $1,027 per month; Rental vacancy rate: 9.0%

Health Insurance: 85.5% have insurance; 51.9% have private insurance; 46.6% have public insurance; 14.5% do not have insurance; 3.1% of children under 18 do not have insurance

Hospitals: Saint Francis Hospital (400 beds); Vassar Brothers Medical Center (365 beds)

Safety: Violent crime rate: 79.2 per 10,000 population; Property crime rate: 224.2 per 10,000 population

Newspapers: Poughkeepsie Journal (daily circulation 37,700)

Transportation: Commute: 73.1% car, 9.0% public transportation, 10.9% walk, 2.2% work from home; Mean travel time to work: 23.8 minutes; Amtrak: Train service available.

Airports: Dutchess County (general aviation)

Additional Information Contacts
City of Poughkeepsie . . . . (845) 451-4276
   http://www.cityofpoughkeepsie.com

POUGHKEEPSIE (town).
Covers a land area of 28.514 square miles and a water area of 2.630 square miles. Located at 41.67° N. Lat; 73.91° W. Long. Elevation is 200 feet.

History: The name of Poughkeepsie had its origins in a Native American name, the original probably meaning "reed-covered lodge by the little water place." The first record of European settlement dates from 1683. Growth at first was slow, but in 1777 Poughkeepsie was made the capital of the state. The chief event in the history of the town was the ratification of the Federal Constitution by the State on July 26, 1788. Early in the 19th century, Poughkeepsie became prominent as a river port. With the opening of the Erie Canal in 1825, however, competition caused a decline in the value of Dutchess County produce. Poughkeepsie turned to industry and trade. It also acquired a reputation as an educational center, with the most important advance being the founding of Vassar College in 1861.

Population: 44,786; Growth (since 2000): 4.7%; Density: 1,570.7 persons per square mile; Race: 74.6% White, 11.3% Black/African American, 6.6% Asian, 0.4% American Indian/Alaska Native, 0.1% Native Hawaiian/Other Pacific Islander, 3.1% Two or more races, 11.9% Hispanic of any race; Average household size: 2.63; Median age: 35.6; Age under 18: 20.3%; Age 65 and over: 14.5%; Males per 100 females: 91.4; Marriage status: 40.0% never married, 46.2% now married, 1.8% separated, 5.9% widowed, 7.9% divorced; Foreign born: 13.8%; Speak English only: 81.4%; With disability: 12.2%; Veterans: 5.8%; Ancestry: 21.0% Italian, 18.8% Irish, 13.1% German, 7.3% English, 4.7% Polish

Employment: 13.4% management, business, and financial, 7.2% computer, engineering, and science, 15.4% education, legal, community service, arts, and media, 5.9% healthcare practitioners, 20.1% service, 24.9% sales and office, 5.3% natural resources, construction, and maintenance, 8.0% production, transportation, and material moving

Income: Per capita: $29,308; Median household: $70,480; Average household: $84,455; Households with income of $100,000 or more: 31.9%; Poverty rate: 10.9%

Educational Attainment: High school diploma or higher: 90.5%; Bachelor's degree or higher: 36.8%; Graduate/professional degree or higher: 17.1%

School District(s)
Arlington Central SD (KG-12)
   2014-15 Enrollment: 8,801 . . . . (845) 486-4460
Dutchess Boces
   2014-15 Enrollment: n/a . . . . (845) 486-4800
Hyde Park Central SD (KG-12)
   2014-15 Enrollment: 3,776 . . . . (845) 229-4005
Poughkeepsie City SD (PK-12)
   2014-15 Enrollment: 4,494 . . . . (845) 451-4950
Spackenkill Union Free SD (KG-12)
   2014-15 Enrollment: 1,484 . . . . (845) 463-7800
Wappingers Central SD (KG-12)
   2014-15 Enrollment: 11,592 . . . . (845) 298-5000

Four-year College(s)
Marist College (Private, Not-for-profit)
   Fall 2014 Enrollment: 6,356 . . . . (845) 575-3000
   2015-16 Tuition: In-state $33,840; Out-of-state $33,840
Vassar College (Private, Not-for-profit)
   Fall 2014 Enrollment: 2,421 . . . . (845) 437-7000
   2015-16 Tuition: In-state $51,250; Out-of-state $51,250

Two-year College(s)
Dutchess Community College (Public)
   Fall 2014 Enrollment: 9,905 . . . . (845) 431-8000
   2015-16 Tuition: In-state $3,866; Out-of-state $7,226

Vocational/Technical School(s)
Dutchess BOCES-Practical Nursing Program (Public)
   Fall 2014 Enrollment: 155 . . . . (845) 486-8001
   2015-16 Tuition: $9,950
Ridley-Lowell Business & Technical Institute-Poughkeepsie (Private, For-profit)
   Fall 2014 Enrollment: 379 . . . . (845) 471-0330
   2015-16 Tuition: $15,400

Housing: Homeownership rate: 69.2%; Median home value: $240,200; Median year structure built: 1965; Homeowner vacancy rate: 2.5%; Median selected monthly owner costs: $2,188 with a mortgage, $881 without a mortgage; Median gross rent: $1,142 per month; Rental vacancy rate: 4.7%

Health Insurance: 93.9% have insurance; 77.7% have private insurance; 28.7% have public insurance; 6.1% do not have insurance; 2.6% of children under 18 do not have insurance

Hospitals: Saint Francis Hospital (400 beds); Vassar Brothers Medical Center (365 beds)

Safety: Violent crime rate: 10.3 per 10,000 population; Property crime rate: 297.6 per 10,000 population

Newspapers: Poughkeepsie Journal (daily circulation 37,700)

Transportation: Commute: 77.0% car, 4.5% public transportation, 11.4% walk, 6.1% work from home; Mean travel time to work: 25.8 minutes; Amtrak: Train service available.

Airports: Dutchess County (general aviation)

Additional Information Contacts
Town of Poughkeepsie . . . . (845) 485-3600
  http://www.townofpoughkeepsie.com

POUGHQUAG (unincorporated postal area)
ZCTA: 12570

Covers a land area of 21.510 square miles and a water area of 0.266 square miles. Located at 41.63° N. Lat; 73.68° W. Long. Elevation is 436 feet.

Population: 7,438; Growth (since 2000): 26.4%; Density: 345.8 persons per square mile; Race: 91.9% White, 4.1% Black/African American, 1.4% Asian, 0.1% American Indian/Alaska Native, 0.0% Native Hawaiian/Other Pacific Islander, 2.0% Two or more races, 7.5% Hispanic of any race; Average household size: 2.99; Median age: 42.5; Age under 18: 25.2%; Age 65 and over: 13.8%; Males per 100 females: 98.7; Marriage status: 28.3% never married, 61.6% now married, 1.4% separated, 5.0% widowed, 5.1% divorced; Foreign born: 7.4%; Speak English only: 88.3%; With disability: 13.3%; Veterans: 7.0%; Ancestry: 37.8% Italian, 26.9% Irish, 13.2% German, 9.7% English, 5.0% American

Employment: 20.8% management, business, and financial, 3.5% computer, engineering, and science, 12.6% education, legal, community service, arts, and media, 6.4% healthcare practitioners, 15.7% service, 22.6% sales and office, 11.2% natural resources, construction, and maintenance, 7.1% production, transportation, and material moving

Income: Per capita: $41,509; Median household: $100,161; Average household: $122,257; Households with income of $100,000 or more: 50.2%; Poverty rate: 3.2%

Educational Attainment: High school diploma or higher: 94.8%; Bachelor's degree or higher: 39.7%; Graduate/professional degree or higher: 18.7%

School District(s)
Arlington Central SD (KG-12)
   2014-15 Enrollment: 8,801 . . . . (845) 486-4460

Housing: Homeownership rate: 93.3%; Median home value: $350,700; Median year structure built: 1989; Homeowner vacancy rate: 1.3%; Median selected monthly owner costs: $2,744 with a mortgage, $892 without a mortgage; Median gross rent: $1,198 per month; Rental vacancy rate: 0.0%

Health Insurance: 95.7% have insurance; 86.6% have private insurance; 22.3% have public insurance; 4.3% do not have insurance; 3.6% of children under 18 do not have insurance

Transportation: Commute: 88.6% car, 4.1% public transportation, 0.7% walk, 5.4% work from home; Mean travel time to work: 39.0 minutes

RED HOOK (town).
Covers a land area of 36.169 square miles and a water area of 3.871 square miles. Located at 42.02° N. Lat; 73.89° W. Long. Elevation is 220 feet.

History: The region was settled in the late 17th century under the Schuyler Patent. Prior to 1812, Red Hook was part of the Town of Rhinebeck, but because its population was over 5,000, the Albany Legislature authorized the separation of the two precincts to encourage public attendance at town meetings via horseback or carriage.

Population: 11,274; Growth (since 2000): 8.3%; Density: 311.7 persons per square mile; Race: 91.4% White, 1.8% Black/African American, 2.1% Asian, 0.8% American Indian/Alaska Native, 0.0% Native Hawaiian/Other Pacific Islander, 1.7% Two or more races, 7.0% Hispanic of any race; Average household size: 2.49; Median age: 36.9; Age under 18: 18.4%; Age 65 and over: 14.1%; Males per 100 females: 94.5; Marriage status: 42.6% never married, 46.3% now married, 2.4% separated, 4.7% widowed, 6.4% divorced; Foreign born: 7.4%; Speak English only: 90.8%; With disability: 11.4%; Veterans: 6.6%; Ancestry: 21.6% German, 21.3% Irish, 15.4% Italian, 9.8% English, 6.7% American

Employment: 15.1% management, business, and financial, 5.6% computer, engineering, and science, 20.4% education, legal, community service, arts, and media, 6.5% healthcare practitioners, 18.6% service,

20.0% sales and office, 7.7% natural resources, construction, and maintenance, 6.2% production, transportation, and material moving
Income: Per capita: $32,692; Median household: $69,740; Average household: $92,625; Households with income of $100,000 or more: 35.1%; Poverty rate: 10.1%
Educational Attainment: High school diploma or higher: 94.1%; Bachelor's degree or higher: 46.9%; Graduate/professional degree or higher: 26.2%

School District(s)
Red Hook Central SD (KG-12)
    2014-15 Enrollment: 1,961 . . . . (845) 758-2241
Housing: Homeownership rate: 72.1%; Median home value: $281,300; Median year structure built: 1972; Homeowner vacancy rate: 1.7%; Median selected monthly owner costs: $2,282 with a mortgage, $798 without a mortgage; Median gross rent: $1,095 per month; Rental vacancy rate: 5.7%
Health Insurance: 93.8% have insurance; 84.9% have private insurance; 20.7% have public insurance; 6.2% do not have insurance; 3.1% of children under 18 do not have insurance
Transportation: Commute: 74.4% car, 4.1% public transportation, 9.7% walk, 10.7% work from home; Mean travel time to work: 24.3 minutes
Additional Information Contacts
Town of Red Hook. . . . . (845) 758-4606
    http://www.redhook.org

RED HOOK (village).
Covers a land area of 1.102 square miles and a water area of 0.012 square miles. Located at 42.00° N. Lat; 73.88° W. Long. Elevation is 220 feet.
Population: 1,715; Growth (since 2000): -5.0%; Density: 1,555.8 persons per square mile; Race: 86.7% White, 1.6% Black/African American, 4.4% Asian, 0.8% American Indian/Alaska Native, 0.0% Native Hawaiian/Other Pacific Islander, 4.1% Two or more races, 6.8% Hispanic of any race; Average household size: 2.10; Median age: 45.6; Age under 18: 18.6%; Age 65 and over: 20.3%; Males per 100 females: 87.5; Marriage status: 29.9% never married, 50.6% now married, 3.7% separated, 7.2% widowed, 12.2% divorced; Foreign born: 10.2%; Speak English only: 91.5%; With disability: 18.0%; Veterans: 9.6%; Ancestry: 26.5% German, 20.7% Irish, 12.2% Italian, 8.4% English, 6.4% French
Employment: 11.8% management, business, and financial, 3.8% computer, engineering, and science, 19.6% education, legal, community service, arts, and media, 4.7% healthcare practitioners, 23.9% service, 17.6% sales and office, 11.0% natural resources, construction, and maintenance, 7.7% production, transportation, and material moving
Income: Per capita: $34,956; Median household: $50,153; Average household: $71,851; Households with income of $100,000 or more: 22.2%; Poverty rate: 13.6%
Educational Attainment: High school diploma or higher: 90.1%; Bachelor's degree or higher: 41.9%; Graduate/professional degree or higher: 24.1%

School District(s)
Red Hook Central SD (KG-12)
    2014-15 Enrollment: 1,961 . . . . (845) 758-2241
Housing: Homeownership rate: 54.2%; Median home value: $248,100; Median year structure built: 1964; Homeowner vacancy rate: 3.5%; Median selected monthly owner costs: $2,045 with a mortgage, $800 without a mortgage; Median gross rent: $866 per month; Rental vacancy rate: 7.8%
Health Insurance: 90.3% have insurance; 77.7% have private insurance; 31.2% have public insurance; 9.7% do not have insurance; 0.0% of children under 18 do not have insurance
Safety: Violent crime rate: 25.2 per 10,000 population; Property crime rate: 222.0 per 10,000 population
Transportation: Commute: 78.4% car, 4.2% public transportation, 9.2% walk, 6.4% work from home; Mean travel time to work: 20.9 minutes

RED OAKS MILL (CDP).
Covers a land area of 2.276 square miles and a water area of 0.031 square miles. Located at 41.65° N. Lat; 73.87° W. Long. Elevation is 164 feet.
Population: 3,671; Growth (since 2000): -25.5%; Density: 1,612.8 persons per square mile; Race: 77.8% White, 11.6% Black/African American, 0.3% Asian, 0.3% American Indian/Alaska Native, 0.0% Native Hawaiian/Other Pacific Islander, 2.2% Two or more races, 13.7% Hispanic of any race; Average household size: 2.76; Median age: 42.8; Age under 18: 22.5%; Age 65 and over: 15.8%; Males per 100 females: 97.4; Marriage status: 26.5% never married, 60.8% now married, 1.5% separated, 4.1% widowed, 8.6% divorced; Foreign born: 9.2%; Speak English only: 90.2%;

With disability: 9.5%; Veterans: 10.3%; Ancestry: 22.7% Irish, 20.1% Italian, 12.8% German, 12.0% English, 4.5% Polish
Employment: 23.9% management, business, and financial, 1.8% computer, engineering, and science, 9.1% education, legal, community service, arts, and media, 6.6% healthcare practitioners, 12.5% service, 33.0% sales and office, 6.2% natural resources, construction, and maintenance, 6.8% production, transportation, and material moving
Income: Per capita: $32,772; Median household: $76,855; Average household: $87,706; Households with income of $100,000 or more: 35.5%; Poverty rate: 5.7%
Educational Attainment: High school diploma or higher: 97.2%; Bachelor's degree or higher: 36.0%; Graduate/professional degree or higher: 16.7%
Housing: Homeownership rate: 86.9%; Median home value: $260,500; Median year structure built: 1965; Homeowner vacancy rate: 0.0%; Median selected monthly owner costs: $2,284 with a mortgage, $925 without a mortgage; Median gross rent: $2,040 per month; Rental vacancy rate: 0.0%
Health Insurance: 90.0% have insurance; 76.3% have private insurance; 25.5% have public insurance; 10.0% do not have insurance; 10.7% of children under 18 do not have insurance
Transportation: Commute: 81.3% car, 3.7% public transportation, 3.0% walk, 11.5% work from home; Mean travel time to work: 37.9 minutes

RHINEBECK (town).
Covers a land area of 35.682 square miles and a water area of 4.068 square miles. Located at 41.93° N. Lat; 73.90° W. Long. Elevation is 200 feet.
History: It is the site of Beekman Arms, said to be the oldest hotel in the U.S., and of a pre-Revolutionary Dutch Reformed church and cemetery. Unique collection of aircraft from before and during World War I at Old Rhinebeck Aerodrome. Settled before 1700, incorporated 1834.
Population: 7,681; Growth (since 2000): -1.0%; Density: 215.3 persons per square mile; Race: 93.6% White, 2.8% Black/African American, 1.4% Asian, 0.0% American Indian/Alaska Native, 0.0% Native Hawaiian/Other Pacific Islander, 0.8% Two or more races, 3.6% Hispanic of any race; Average household size: 2.09; Median age: 53.5; Age under 18: 15.1%; Age 65 and over: 29.5%; Males per 100 females: 83.3; Marriage status: 25.5% never married, 54.6% now married, 2.8% separated, 9.8% widowed, 10.0% divorced; Foreign born: 9.7%; Speak English only: 89.9%; With disability: 16.4%; Veterans: 8.9%; Ancestry: 20.7% Irish, 17.5% Italian, 17.2% German, 10.6% English, 5.6% Polish
Employment: 15.9% management, business, and financial, 3.8% computer, engineering, and science, 19.0% education, legal, community service, arts, and media, 12.9% healthcare practitioners, 14.2% service, 20.6% sales and office, 6.4% natural resources, construction, and maintenance, 7.2% production, transportation, and material moving
Income: Per capita: $47,239; Median household: $66,942; Average household: $104,143; Households with income of $100,000 or more: 32.4%; Poverty rate: 6.3%
Educational Attainment: High school diploma or higher: 91.0%; Bachelor's degree or higher: 45.3%; Graduate/professional degree or higher: 22.7%

School District(s)
Rhinebeck Central SD (KG-12)
    2014-15 Enrollment: 1,122 . . . . (845) 871-5520
Housing: Homeownership rate: 67.8%; Median home value: $367,200; Median year structure built: 1964; Homeowner vacancy rate: 3.0%; Median selected monthly owner costs: $2,372 with a mortgage, $900 without a mortgage; Median gross rent: $1,019 per month; Rental vacancy rate: 5.5%
Health Insurance: 92.6% have insurance; 78.2% have private insurance; 34.5% have public insurance; 7.4% do not have insurance; 2.9% of children under 18 do not have insurance
Hospitals: Northern Dutchess Hospital (68 beds)
Transportation: Commute: 75.7% car, 3.3% public transportation, 6.8% walk, 13.7% work from home; Mean travel time to work: 25.0 minutes
Additional Information Contacts
Town of Rhinebeck . . . . (845) 876-3409
    http://www.rhinebeck-ny.gov

RHINEBECK (village).
Covers a land area of 1.523 square miles and a water area of 0.020 square miles. Located at 41.93° N. Lat; 73.91° W. Long. Elevation is 200 feet.
Population: 2,629; Growth (since 2000): -14.6%; Density: 1,725.7 persons per square mile; Race: 90.9% White, 3.7% Black/African American, 2.2%

Asian, 0.0% American Indian/Alaska Native, 0.0% Native Hawaiian/Other Pacific Islander, 1.7% Two or more races, 4.6% Hispanic of any race; Average household size: 2.04; Median age: 49.9; Age under 18: 19.0%; Age 65 and over: 27.1%; Males per 100 females: 80.5; Marriage status: 25.6% never married, 57.7% now married, 3.2% separated, 7.2% widowed, 9.5% divorced; Foreign born: 11.9%; Speak English only: 89.6%; With disability: 16.5%; Veterans: 7.7%; Ancestry: 16.2% Irish, 15.8% German, 13.7% Italian, 11.3% English, 6.1% Scottish
Employment: 16.2% management, business, and financial, 1.9% computer, engineering, and science, 22.0% education, legal, community service, arts, and media, 16.2% healthcare practitioners, 15.2% service, 17.4% sales and office, 5.0% natural resources, construction, and maintenance, 6.1% production, transportation, and material moving
Income: Per capita: $35,188; Median household: $46,944; Average household: $74,658; Households with income of $100,000 or more: 23.7%; Poverty rate: 11.2%
Educational Attainment: High school diploma or higher: 93.3%; Bachelor's degree or higher: 49.8%; Graduate/professional degree or higher: 26.6%

School District(s)
Rhinebeck Central SD (KG-12)
    2014-15 Enrollment: 1,122 . . . . (845) 871-5520
Housing: Homeownership rate: 55.7%; Median home value: $341,200; Median year structure built: 1954; Homeowner vacancy rate: 6.9%; Median selected monthly owner costs: $2,226 with a mortgage, $975 without a mortgage; Median gross rent: $1,081 per month; Rental vacancy rate: 0.0%
Health Insurance: 92.6% have insurance; 81.9% have private insurance; 35.3% have public insurance; 7.4% do not have insurance; 1.9% of children under 18 do not have insurance
Hospitals: Northern Dutchess Hospital (68 beds)
Safety: Violent crime rate: 0.0 per 10,000 population; Property crime rate: 137.3 per 10,000 population
Transportation: Commute: 73.4% car, 3.3% public transportation, 11.4% walk, 11.5% work from home; Mean travel time to work: 20.0 minutes

RHINECLIFF (CDP).
Covers a land area of 0.994 square miles and a water area of 0.014 square miles. Located at 41.92° N. Lat; 73.94° W. Long. Elevation is 46 feet.
Population: 290; Growth (since 2000): n/a; Density: 291.6 persons per square mile; Race: 94.1% White, 3.1% Black/African American, 2.1% Asian, 0.0% American Indian/Alaska Native, 0.0% Native Hawaiian/Other Pacific Islander, 0.7% Two or more races, 2.1% Hispanic of any race; Average household size: 1.95; Median age: 54.8; Age under 18: 21.4%; Age 65 and over: 36.2%; Males per 100 females: 120.2; Marriage status: 14.2% never married, 67.4% now married, 24.0% separated, 15.5% widowed, 3.0% divorced; Foreign born: 5.5%; Speak English only: 100.0%; With disability: 29.3%; Veterans: 11.8%; Ancestry: 35.9% Italian, 22.8% Irish, 20.7% German, 19.0% Scotch-Irish, 6.9% English
Employment: 4.3% management, business, and financial, 30.9% computer, engineering, and science, 39.4% education, legal, community service, arts, and media, 5.3% healthcare practitioners, 5.3% service, 5.3% sales and office, 0.0% natural resources, construction, and maintenance, 9.6% production, transportation, and material moving
Income: Per capita: $42,250; Median household: $62,331; Average household: $85,845; Households with income of $100,000 or more: 33.9%; Poverty rate: 2.1%
Educational Attainment: High school diploma or higher: 88.6%; Bachelor's degree or higher: 42.1%; Graduate/professional degree or higher: 26.8%
Housing: Homeownership rate: 96.3%; Median home value: $328,500; Median year structure built: Before 1940; Homeowner vacancy rate: 0.0%; Median selected monthly owner costs: n/a with a mortgage, n/a without a mortgage; Median gross rent: n/a per month; Rental vacancy rate: 72.2%
Health Insurance: 92.8% have insurance; 85.9% have private insurance; 42.1% have public insurance; 7.2% do not have insurance; 0.0% of children under 18 do not have insurance
Transportation: Commute: 56.7% car, 0.0% public transportation, 5.6% walk, 37.8% work from home; Mean travel time to work: 16.9 minutes; Amtrak: Train service available.

SALT POINT (CDP).
Covers a land area of 0.829 square miles and a water area of 0.004 square miles. Located at 41.81° N. Lat; 73.79° W. Long. Elevation is 236 feet.
Population: 195; Growth (since 2000): n/a; Density: 235.1 persons per square mile; Race: 99.0% White, 0.0% Black/African American, 0.0% Asian, 1.0% American Indian/Alaska Native, 0.0% Native Hawaiian/Other Pacific Islander, 0.0% Two or more races, 0.0% Hispanic of any race; Average household size: 2.53; Median age: 48.8; Age under 18: 27.7%; Age 65 and over: 16.4%; Males per 100 females: 91.9; Marriage status: 18.6% never married, 67.7% now married, 0.0% separated, 13.7% widowed, 0.0% divorced; Foreign born: 2.6%; Speak English only: 100.0%; With disability: 8.2%; Veterans: 5.7%; Ancestry: 29.2% English, 23.6% German, 12.8% Italian, 11.3% American, 9.7% Eastern European
Employment: 22.9% management, business, and financial, 9.2% computer, engineering, and science, 28.4% education, legal, community service, arts, and media, 9.2% healthcare practitioners, 9.2% service, 11.9% sales and office, 9.2% natural resources, construction, and maintenance, 0.0% production, transportation, and material moving
Income: Per capita: $48,899; Median household: $127,875; Average household: $124,169; Households with income of $100,000 or more: 58.5%; Poverty rate: 2.1%
Educational Attainment: High school diploma or higher: 88.7%; Bachelor's degree or higher: 66.0%; Graduate/professional degree or higher: 34.0%
Housing: Homeownership rate: 100.0%; Median home value: $276,700; Median year structure built: 1972; Homeowner vacancy rate: 10.5%; Median selected monthly owner costs: $1,204 with a mortgage, $488 without a mortgage; Median gross rent: n/a per month; Rental vacancy rate: 0.0%
Health Insurance: 94.9% have insurance; 88.2% have private insurance; 20.5% have public insurance; 5.1% do not have insurance; 0.0% of children under 18 do not have insurance
Transportation: Commute: 90.8% car, 0.0% public transportation, 0.0% walk, 9.2% work from home; Mean travel time to work: 25.4 minutes

SPACKENKILL (CDP).
Covers a land area of 1.775 square miles and a water area of <.001 square miles. Located at 41.65° N. Lat; 73.91° W. Long. Elevation is 151 feet.
History: Spackenkill is a hamlet Dutchess County, New York and home to an IBM plant and many of its employees. Spackenkill neighborhoods include Hagantown, Nassau, King George, Beechwood, and Crown Heights.
Population: 4,122; Growth (since 2000): -13.3%; Density: 2,322.4 persons per square mile; Race: 84.1% White, 4.6% Black/African American, 9.0% Asian, 0.0% American Indian/Alaska Native, 0.0% Native Hawaiian/Other Pacific Islander, 1.5% Two or more races, 6.5% Hispanic of any race; Average household size: 2.90; Median age: 45.9; Age under 18: 22.9%; Age 65 and over: 18.8%; Males per 100 females: 95.5; Marriage status: 24.4% never married, 65.5% now married, 1.9% separated, 4.9% widowed, 5.2% divorced; Foreign born: 13.0%; Speak English only: 80.3%; With disability: 9.4%; Veterans: 4.3%; Ancestry: 20.6% Italian, 13.2% Irish, 12.6% German, 8.7% English, 7.7% American
Employment: 22.4% management, business, and financial, 15.2% computer, engineering, and science, 15.3% education, legal, community service, arts, and media, 10.3% healthcare practitioners, 8.6% service, 18.1% sales and office, 5.8% natural resources, construction, and maintenance, 4.3% production, transportation, and material moving
Income: Per capita: $44,888; Median household: $114,297; Average household: $127,899; Households with income of $100,000 or more: 64.0%; Poverty rate: 0.9%
Educational Attainment: High school diploma or higher: 96.5%; Bachelor's degree or higher: 55.7%; Graduate/professional degree or higher: 31.6%
Housing: Homeownership rate: 94.9%; Median home value: $292,800; Median year structure built: 1964; Homeowner vacancy rate: 2.1%; Median selected monthly owner costs: $2,531 with a mortgage, $1,094 without a mortgage; Median gross rent: $1,781 per month; Rental vacancy rate: 0.0%
Health Insurance: 98.3% have insurance; 88.3% have private insurance; 25.5% have public insurance; 1.7% do not have insurance; 0.0% of children under 18 do not have insurance
Transportation: Commute: 91.2% car, 2.8% public transportation, 1.3% walk, 4.3% work from home; Mean travel time to work: 22.2 minutes

STAATSBURG (CDP). Covers a land area of 1.065 square miles and a water area of 0.001 square miles. Located at 41.85° N. Lat; 73.92° W. Long. Elevation is 30 feet.
Population: 183; Growth (since 2000): -79.9%; Density: 171.8 persons per square mile; Race: 84.7% White, 0.0% Black/African American, 4.9% Asian, 0.0% American Indian/Alaska Native, 0.0% Native Hawaiian/Other Pacific Islander, 0.0% Two or more races, 9.8% Hispanic of any race; Average household size: 1.83; Median age: 59.7; Age under 18: 4.9%; Age 65 and over: 27.3%; Males per 100 females: 99.5; Marriage status: 12.6% never married, 59.2% now married, 0.0% separated, 17.8% widowed, 10.3% divorced; Foreign born: 9.3%; Speak English only: 90.2%; With disability: 28.4%; Veterans: 9.8%; Ancestry: 38.3% German, 17.5% French, 13.1% English, 10.4% Irish, 9.3% Scottish
Employment: 43.5% management, business, and financial, 14.5% computer, engineering, and science, 27.4% education, legal, community service, arts, and media, 0.0% healthcare practitioners, 0.0% service, 14.5% sales and office, 0.0% natural resources, construction, and maintenance, 0.0% production, transportation, and material moving
Income: Per capita: $53,567; Median household: $90,313; Average household: $94,912; Households with income of $100,000 or more: 43.0%; Poverty rate: 19.1%
Educational Attainment: High school diploma or higher: 100.0%; Bachelor's degree or higher: 71.3%; Graduate/professional degree or higher: 46.3%
Housing: Homeownership rate: 77.0%; Median home value: $221,900; Median year structure built: Before 1940; Homeowner vacancy rate: 21.4%; Median selected monthly owner costs: n/a with a mortgage, n/a without a mortgage; Median gross rent: n/a per month; Rental vacancy rate: 0.0%
Health Insurance: 100.0% have insurance; 76.0% have private insurance; 42.1% have public insurance; 0.0% do not have insurance; 0.0% of children under 18 do not have insurance
Transportation: Commute: 41.9% car, 12.9% public transportation, 0.0% walk, 45.2% work from home; Mean travel time to work: 0.0 minutes

STANFORD (town). Covers a land area of 49.637 square miles and a water area of 0.649 square miles. Located at 41.90° N. Lat; 73.67° W. Long.
Population: 3,804; Growth (since 2000): 7.3%; Density: 76.6 persons per square mile; Race: 87.5% White, 6.2% Black/African American, 0.0% Asian, 0.1% American Indian/Alaska Native, 0.0% Native Hawaiian/Other Pacific Islander, 1.4% Two or more races, 10.0% Hispanic of any race; Average household size: 2.60; Median age: 44.7; Age under 18: 16.3%; Age 65 and over: 13.8%; Males per 100 females: 101.0; Marriage status: 34.5% never married, 53.3% now married, 3.5% separated, 3.1% widowed, 9.2% divorced; Foreign born: 8.3%; Speak English only: 89.2%; With disability: 15.7%; Veterans: 8.5%; Ancestry: 18.7% German, 16.9% Irish, 16.8% Italian, 10.9% English, 5.9% Dutch
Employment: 16.4% management, business, and financial, 3.2% computer, engineering, and science, 16.8% education, legal, community service, arts, and media, 6.1% healthcare practitioners, 15.7% service, 23.1% sales and office, 10.9% natural resources, construction, and maintenance, 7.8% production, transportation, and material moving
Income: Per capita: $42,746; Median household: $75,524; Average household: $113,613; Households with income of $100,000 or more: 36.9%; Poverty rate: 9.1%
Educational Attainment: High school diploma or higher: 94.9%; Bachelor's degree or higher: 32.8%; Graduate/professional degree or higher: 15.3%
Housing: Homeownership rate: 72.8%; Median home value: $278,900; Median year structure built: 1972; Homeowner vacancy rate: 3.1%; Median selected monthly owner costs: $1,939 with a mortgage, $751 without a mortgage; Median gross rent: $933 per month; Rental vacancy rate: 6.5%
Health Insurance: 91.4% have insurance; 79.1% have private insurance; 27.6% have public insurance; 8.6% do not have insurance; 0.0% of children under 18 do not have insurance
Transportation: Commute: 74.2% car, 5.4% public transportation, 10.2% walk, 9.8% work from home; Mean travel time to work: 29.9 minutes

STANFORDVILLE (unincorporated postal area)
ZCTA: 12581
Covers a land area of 40.432 square miles and a water area of 0.394 square miles. Located at 41.90° N. Lat; 73.70° W. Long. Elevation is 358 feet.

Population: 1,979; Growth (since 2000): -11.3%; Density: 48.9 persons per square mile; Race: 96.2% White, 1.9% Black/African American, 0.0% Asian, 0.0% American Indian/Alaska Native, 0.0% Native Hawaiian/Other Pacific Islander, 1.9% Two or more races, 7.3% Hispanic of any race; Average household size: 2.46; Median age: 47.4; Age under 18: 19.2%; Age 65 and over: 17.1%; Males per 100 females: 98.6; Marriage status: 26.0% never married, 61.8% now married, 3.1% separated, 1.8% widowed, 10.4% divorced; Foreign born: 8.1%; Speak English only: 91.1%; With disability: 9.9%; Veterans: 9.9%; Ancestry: 23.9% German, 16.1% Italian, 15.5% Irish, 11.9% English, 8.0% European
Employment: 20.5% management, business, and financial, 2.1% computer, engineering, and science, 12.7% education, legal, community service, arts, and media, 7.9% healthcare practitioners, 12.8% service, 25.2% sales and office, 13.8% natural resources, construction, and maintenance, 5.0% production, transportation, and material moving
Income: Per capita: $45,608; Median household: $74,688; Average household: $113,376; Households with income of $100,000 or more: 33.5%; Poverty rate: 6.4%
Educational Attainment: High school diploma or higher: 95.3%; Bachelor's degree or higher: 31.0%; Graduate/professional degree or higher: 15.9%

School District(s)
Pine Plains Central SD (KG-12)
   2014-15 Enrollment: 941 . . . . (518) 398-7181
Housing: Homeownership rate: 74.4%; Median home value: $283,700; Median year structure built: 1970; Homeowner vacancy rate: 5.2%; Median selected monthly owner costs: $1,880 with a mortgage, $682 without a mortgage; Median gross rent: $1,060 per month; Rental vacancy rate: 0.0%
Health Insurance: 94.7% have insurance; 84.2% have private insurance; 30.3% have public insurance; 5.3% do not have insurance; 0.0% of children under 18 do not have insurance
Transportation: Commute: 74.3% car, 8.4% public transportation, 5.6% walk, 11.8% work from home; Mean travel time to work: 37.2 minutes

STORMVILLE (unincorporated postal area)
ZCTA: 12582
Covers a land area of 12.782 square miles and a water area of 0.403 square miles. Located at 41.54° N. Lat; 73.74° W. Long. Elevation is 328 feet.
Population: 5,887; Growth (since 2000): 29.4%; Density: 460.6 persons per square mile; Race: 69.1% White, 20.0% Black/African American, 0.5% Asian, 0.9% American Indian/Alaska Native, 0.0% Native Hawaiian/Other Pacific Islander, 2.2% Two or more races, 13.7% Hispanic of any race; Average household size: 2.95; Median age: 43.8; Age under 18: 18.4%; Age 65 and over: 9.4%; Males per 100 females: 209.2; Marriage status: 32.9% never married, 53.4% now married, 3.4% separated, 3.3% widowed, 10.4% divorced; Foreign born: 11.2%; Speak English only: 78.7%; With disability: 12.8%; Veterans: 7.6%; Ancestry: 20.0% Italian, 18.3% Irish, 11.3% German, 6.5% English, 5.4% American
Employment: 15.8% management, business, and financial, 1.8% computer, engineering, and science, 15.3% education, legal, community service, arts, and media, 3.9% healthcare practitioners, 17.7% service, 25.5% sales and office, 8.4% natural resources, construction, and maintenance, 11.7% production, transportation, and material moving
Income: Per capita: $29,102; Median household: $94,600; Average household: $106,865; Households with income of $100,000 or more: 47.2%; Poverty rate: 4.0%
Educational Attainment: High school diploma or higher: 83.3%; Bachelor's degree or higher: 25.1%; Graduate/professional degree or higher: 9.5%
Housing: Homeownership rate: 90.2%; Median home value: $353,500; Median year structure built: 1982; Homeowner vacancy rate: 0.0%; Median selected monthly owner costs: $2,593 with a mortgage, $1,167 without a mortgage; Median gross rent: $1,313 per month; Rental vacancy rate: 0.0%
Health Insurance: 98.7% have insurance; 89.2% have private insurance; 20.8% have public insurance; 1.3% do not have insurance; 1.8% of children under 18 do not have insurance
Transportation: Commute: 87.4% car, 2.9% public transportation, 0.0% walk, 8.3% work from home; Mean travel time to work: 39.0 minutes

TITUSVILLE (CDP). Covers a land area of 0.691 square miles and a water area of <.001 square miles. Located at 41.67° N. Lat; 73.87° W. Long. Elevation is 151 feet.
Population: 561; Growth (since 2000): n/a; Density: 812.3 persons per square mile; Race: 96.3% White, 0.0% Black/African American, 2.0% Asian, 0.0% American Indian/Alaska Native, 0.0% Native Hawaiian/Other Pacific Islander, 1.8% Two or more races, 13.9% Hispanic of any race; Average household size: 2.35; Median age: 52.2; Age under 18: 19.6%; Age 65 and over: 23.5%; Males per 100 females: 96.8; Marriage status: 11.9% never married, 68.0% now married, 1.6% separated, 12.5% widowed, 7.6% divorced; Foreign born: 2.0%; Speak English only: 89.3%; With disability: 11.6%; Veterans: 12.0%; Ancestry: 30.8% Irish, 24.1% Italian, 21.2% German, 9.3% English, 7.1% Polish
Employment: 9.5% management, business, and financial, 3.7% computer, engineering, and science, 17.4% education, legal, community service, arts, and media, 12.4% healthcare practitioners, 4.5% service, 28.5% sales and office, 18.2% natural resources, construction, and maintenance, 5.8% production, transportation, and material moving
Income: Per capita: $38,812; Median household: $100,859; Average household: $88,793; Households with income of $100,000 or more: 52.3%; Poverty rate: 2.1%
Educational Attainment: High school diploma or higher: 93.6%; Bachelor's degree or higher: 46.8%; Graduate/professional degree or higher: 21.8%
Housing: Homeownership rate: 95.8%; Median home value: $236,600; Median year structure built: 1962; Homeowner vacancy rate: 0.0%; Median selected monthly owner costs: $1,852 with a mortgage, $774 without a mortgage; Median gross rent: n/a per month; Rental vacancy rate: 0.0%
Health Insurance: 100.0% have insurance; 92.0% have private insurance; 29.4% have public insurance; 0.0% do not have insurance; 0.0% of children under 18 do not have insurance
Transportation: Commute: 100.0% car, 0.0% public transportation, 0.0% walk, 0.0% work from home; Mean travel time to work: 27.0 minutes

TIVOLI (village). Covers a land area of 1.610 square miles and a water area of 0.028 square miles. Located at 42.05° N. Lat; 73.92° W. Long. Elevation is 151 feet.
Population: 1,184; Growth (since 2000): 1.8%; Density: 735.4 persons per square mile; Race: 95.4% White, 0.3% Black/African American, 0.5% Asian, 3.1% American Indian/Alaska Native, 0.0% Native Hawaiian/Other Pacific Islander, 0.0% Two or more races, 9.2% Hispanic of any race; Average household size: 2.32; Median age: 27.3; Age under 18: 10.9%; Age 65 and over: 12.9%; Males per 100 females: 89.2; Marriage status: 57.3% never married, 28.3% now married, 1.7% separated, 4.0% widowed, 10.3% divorced; Foreign born: 4.2%; Speak English only: 93.4%; With disability: 13.5%; Veterans: 6.4%; Ancestry: 19.2% German, 19.1% Italian, 18.3% Irish, 6.2% American, 5.7% French
Employment: 9.5% management, business, and financial, 4.7% computer, engineering, and science, 22.6% education, legal, community service, arts, and media, 5.4% healthcare practitioners, 22.4% service, 17.4% sales and office, 9.0% natural resources, construction, and maintenance, 9.0% production, transportation, and material moving
Income: Per capita: $26,758; Median household: $40,357; Average household: $60,741; Households with income of $100,000 or more: 18.1%; Poverty rate: 31.3%
Educational Attainment: High school diploma or higher: 87.9%; Bachelor's degree or higher: 42.7%; Graduate/professional degree or higher: 19.3%
Housing: Homeownership rate: 44.3%; Median home value: $211,500; Median year structure built: 1958; Homeowner vacancy rate: 0.0%; Median selected monthly owner costs: $1,758 with a mortgage, $686 without a mortgage; Median gross rent: $1,368 per month; Rental vacancy rate: 4.6%
Health Insurance: 89.5% have insurance; 75.7% have private insurance; 22.9% have public insurance; 10.5% do not have insurance; 14.7% of children under 18 do not have insurance
Transportation: Commute: 69.7% car, 13.6% public transportation, 9.5% walk, 7.3% work from home; Mean travel time to work: 26.4 minutes

UNION VALE (town). Covers a land area of 37.482 square miles and a water area of 0.324 square miles. Located at 41.70° N. Lat; 73.69° W. Long.
History: Union Vale is a town in Dutchess County, New York. The region was originally part of the Beekman Patent. The town was first settled

around 1716, and formed in 1827 from the towns of Beekman and LaGrange.
Population: 4,855; Growth (since 2000): 6.8%; Density: 129.5 persons per square mile; Race: 96.0% White, 0.0% Black/African American, 2.4% Asian, 0.0% American Indian/Alaska Native, 0.0% Native Hawaiian/Other Pacific Islander, 1.3% Two or more races, 3.8% Hispanic of any race; Average household size: 2.58; Median age: 48.0; Age under 18: 19.4%; Age 65 and over: 18.0%; Males per 100 females: 98.2; Marriage status: 26.3% never married, 59.8% now married, 0.0% separated, 6.5% widowed, 7.4% divorced; Foreign born: 9.3%; Speak English only: 88.3%; With disability: 13.0%; Veterans: 6.4%; Ancestry: 30.3% Italian, 23.0% Irish, 14.5% German, 4.9% Albanian, 4.2% English
Employment: 12.5% management, business, and financial, 9.0% computer, engineering, and science, 16.5% education, legal, community service, arts, and media, 7.1% healthcare practitioners, 17.4% service, 19.6% sales and office, 5.0% natural resources, construction, and maintenance, 12.9% production, transportation, and material moving
Income: Per capita: $39,970; Median household: $87,946; Average household: $102,209; Households with income of $100,000 or more: 43.3%; Poverty rate: 2.1%
Educational Attainment: High school diploma or higher: 93.5%; Bachelor's degree or higher: 41.0%; Graduate/professional degree or higher: 21.6%
Housing: Homeownership rate: 83.4%; Median home value: $322,800; Median year structure built: 1981; Homeowner vacancy rate: 1.5%; Median selected monthly owner costs: $2,265 with a mortgage, $1,015 without a mortgage; Median gross rent: $1,186 per month; Rental vacancy rate: 12.7%
Health Insurance: 97.3% have insurance; 91.2% have private insurance; 22.0% have public insurance; 2.7% do not have insurance; 0.0% of children under 18 do not have insurance
Transportation: Commute: 84.3% car, 4.6% public transportation, 0.4% walk, 6.1% work from home; Mean travel time to work: 35.5 minutes
Additional Information Contacts
Town of Union Vale . . . . (845) 724-5600
  http://www2.marist.edu/unionvale

VERBANK (unincorporated postal area)
ZCTA: 12585
Covers a land area of 4.922 square miles and a water area of 0.079 square miles. Located at 41.73° N. Lat; 73.69° W. Long. Elevation is 591 feet.
Population: 773; Growth (since 2000): -19.1%; Density: 157.0 persons per square mile; Race: 96.8% White, 0.0% Black/African American, 1.4% Asian, 0.0% American Indian/Alaska Native, 0.0% Native Hawaiian/Other Pacific Islander, 1.8% Two or more races, 2.7% Hispanic of any race; Average household size: 2.65; Median age: 45.7; Age under 18: 23.8%; Age 65 and over: 17.9%; Males per 100 females: 103.9; Marriage status: 32.9% never married, 56.0% now married, 0.0% separated, 0.0% widowed, 11.1% divorced; Foreign born: 8.3%; Speak English only: 94.4%; With disability: 9.3%; Veterans: 6.1%; Ancestry: 32.7% Italian, 25.4% Irish, 16.2% German, 9.4% French Canadian, 8.3% Lebanese
Employment: 13.8% management, business, and financial, 7.0% computer, engineering, and science, 22.1% education, legal, community service, arts, and media, 5.5% healthcare practitioners, 21.8% service, 15.8% sales and office, 0.0% natural resources, construction, and maintenance, 14.0% production, transportation, and material moving
Income: Per capita: $45,844; Median household: $115,357; Average household: $127,880; Households with income of $100,000 or more: 63.1%; Poverty rate: 6.7%
Educational Attainment: High school diploma or higher: 85.3%; Bachelor's degree or higher: 47.5%; Graduate/professional degree or higher: 32.7%
Housing: Homeownership rate: 96.4%; Median home value: $329,700; Median year structure built: 1980; Homeowner vacancy rate: 0.0%; Median selected monthly owner costs: $2,257 with a mortgage, $965 without a mortgage; Median gross rent: n/a per month; Rental vacancy rate: 66.7%
Health Insurance: 100.0% have insurance; 92.0% have private insurance; 22.5% have public insurance; 0.0% do not have insurance; 0.0% of children under 18 do not have insurance
Transportation: Commute: 85.9% car, 5.1% public transportation, 0.0% walk, 9.0% work from home; Mean travel time to work: 30.5 minutes

WAPPINGER (town).

WAPPINGER (town). Covers a land area of 27.054 square miles and a water area of 1.477 square miles. Located at 41.59° N. Lat; 73.89° W. Long.

History: Society of the Cincinnati founded here in 1783. Incorporated 1871.

Population: 27,147; Growth (since 2000): 3.3%; Density: 1,003.4 persons per square mile; Race: 75.6% White, 7.1% Black/African American, 6.8% Asian, 0.8% American Indian/Alaska Native, 0.0% Native Hawaiian/Other Pacific Islander, 2.9% Two or more races, 14.9% Hispanic of any race; Average household size: 2.65; Median age: 41.2; Age under 18: 20.1%; Age 65 and over: 14.2%; Males per 100 females: 98.0; Marriage status: 30.8% never married, 53.8% now married, 2.3% separated, 5.7% widowed, 9.6% divorced; Foreign born: 12.9%; Speak English only: 80.1%; With disability: 12.6%; Veterans: 7.0%; Ancestry: 26.1% Italian, 21.1% Irish, 13.5% German, 6.4% English, 4.8% American

Employment: 11.6% management, business, and financial, 6.2% computer, engineering, and science, 10.4% education, legal, community service, arts, and media, 6.6% healthcare practitioners, 18.9% service, 27.1% sales and office, 10.2% natural resources, construction, and maintenance, 9.0% production, transportation, and material moving

Income: Per capita: $34,564; Median household: $76,628; Average household: $89,452; Households with income of $100,000 or more: 33.9%; Poverty rate: 6.2%

Educational Attainment: High school diploma or higher: 91.4%; Bachelor's degree or higher: 31.3%; Graduate/professional degree or higher: 11.4%

Housing: Homeownership rate: 67.0%; Median home value: $282,900; Median year structure built: 1969; Homeowner vacancy rate: 2.6%; Median selected monthly owner costs: $2,223 with a mortgage, $790 without a mortgage; Median gross rent: $1,227 per month; Rental vacancy rate: 8.9%

Health Insurance: 90.4% have insurance; 77.2% have private insurance; 26.6% have public insurance; 9.6% do not have insurance; 5.9% of children under 18 do not have insurance

Transportation: Commute: 86.5% car, 6.3% public transportation, 2.3% walk, 4.3% work from home; Mean travel time to work: 33.6 minutes

Additional Information Contacts

Town of Wappinger . . . . (845) 297-4158
  http://www.townofwappinger.us

WAPPINGERS FALLS (village).

WAPPINGERS FALLS (village). Covers a land area of 1.108 square miles and a water area of 0.076 square miles. Located at 41.60° N. Lat; 73.92° W. Long. Elevation is 157 feet.

History: The Village of Wappingers Falls was named for the cascade in Wappinger Creek, which forms the boundary between Wappinger and Poughkeepsie. The Wappinger were Native Americans whose territory in the 17th century spread along the eastern bank of the Hudson River.

Population: 5,424; Growth (since 2000): 10.0%; Density: 4,894.7 persons per square mile; Race: 52.0% White, 11.7% Black/African American, 10.6% Asian, 3.2% American Indian/Alaska Native, 0.0% Native Hawaiian/Other Pacific Islander, 4.6% Two or more races, 30.5% Hispanic of any race; Average household size: 2.62; Median age: 35.7; Age under 18: 20.9%; Age 65 and over: 14.8%; Males per 100 females: 93.6; Marriage status: 34.1% never married, 45.4% now married, 3.4% separated, 10.2% widowed, 10.4% divorced; Foreign born: 23.9%; Speak English only: 61.4%; With disability: 15.2%; Veterans: 7.5%; Ancestry: 21.2% Italian, 19.8% Irish, 8.6% German, 3.6% English, 2.7% Palestinian

Employment: 7.3% management, business, and financial, 8.3% computer, engineering, and science, 8.5% education, legal, community service, arts, and media, 3.6% healthcare practitioners, 25.2% service, 28.2% sales and office, 11.6% natural resources, construction, and maintenance, 7.2% production, transportation, and material moving

Income: Per capita: $24,773; Median household: $57,536; Average household: $62,959; Households with income of $100,000 or more: 20.3%; Poverty rate: 13.1%

Educational Attainment: High school diploma or higher: 82.0%; Bachelor's degree or higher: 18.6%; Graduate/professional degree or higher: 4.6%

School District(s)

Wappingers Central SD (KG-12)
  2014-15 Enrollment: 11,592 . . . . (845) 298-5000

Housing: Homeownership rate: 32.7%; Median home value: $188,700; Median year structure built: 1963; Homeowner vacancy rate: 0.0%; Median selected monthly owner costs: $1,927 with a mortgage, $704 without a mortgage; Median gross rent: $1,224 per month; Rental vacancy rate: 15.3%

Health Insurance: 85.3% have insurance; 63.7% have private insurance; 35.6% have public insurance; 14.7% do not have insurance; 3.5% of children under 18 do not have insurance

Safety: Violent crime rate: 3.6 per 10,000 population; Property crime rate: 163.8 per 10,000 population

Newspapers: Beacon Free Press (weekly circulation 7,500); Southern Dutchess News (weekly circulation 7,500)

Transportation: Commute: 80.9% car, 9.4% public transportation, 7.2% walk, 1.4% work from home; Mean travel time to work: 32.6 minutes

Additional Information Contacts

Village of Wappingers Falls . . . . (845) 297-8773
  http://www.wappingersfallsny.gov

WASHINGTON (town).

WASHINGTON (town). Covers a land area of 58.170 square miles and a water area of 0.714 square miles. Located at 41.79° N. Lat; 73.68° W. Long.

Population: 4,721; Growth (since 2000): -0.4%; Density: 81.2 persons per square mile; Race: 92.6% White, 3.8% Black/African American, 1.6% Asian, 1.0% American Indian/Alaska Native, 0.0% Native Hawaiian/Other Pacific Islander, 1.0% Two or more races, 3.1% Hispanic of any race; Average household size: 2.35; Median age: 48.0; Age under 18: 20.3%; Age 65 and over: 21.1%; Males per 100 females: 99.4; Marriage status: 26.0% never married, 57.5% now married, 3.7% separated, 6.4% widowed, 10.1% divorced; Foreign born: 10.4%; Speak English only: 89.6%; With disability: 13.3%; Veterans: 8.2%; Ancestry: 32.3% Irish, 17.5% Italian, 16.4% German, 13.3% English, 5.3% American

Employment: 16.2% management, business, and financial, 5.2% computer, engineering, and science, 15.1% education, legal, community service, arts, and media, 5.0% healthcare practitioners, 26.1% service, 14.9% sales and office, 12.4% natural resources, construction, and maintenance, 5.1% production, transportation, and material moving

Income: Per capita: $45,197; Median household: $81,319; Average household: $108,429; Households with income of $100,000 or more: 37.7%; Poverty rate: 7.8%

Educational Attainment: High school diploma or higher: 93.2%; Bachelor's degree or higher: 39.4%; Graduate/professional degree or higher: 18.9%

Housing: Homeownership rate: 63.9%; Median home value: $428,500; Median year structure built: 1959; Homeowner vacancy rate: 6.7%; Median selected monthly owner costs: $2,529 with a mortgage, $1,064 without a mortgage; Median gross rent: $1,103 per month; Rental vacancy rate: 7.0%

Health Insurance: 92.8% have insurance; 78.8% have private insurance; 30.7% have public insurance; 7.2% do not have insurance; 2.6% of children under 18 do not have insurance

Transportation: Commute: 78.5% car, 1.4% public transportation, 9.7% walk, 8.8% work from home; Mean travel time to work: 30.3 minutes

Additional Information Contacts

Town of Washington . . . . (845) 677-3419
  http://www.washingtonny.org

WASSAIC (unincorporated postal area)

ZCTA: 12592

Covers a land area of 18.704 square miles and a water area of 0.231 square miles. Located at 41.80° N. Lat; 73.58° W. Long. Elevation is 456 feet.

Population: 1,212; Growth (since 2000): -0.2%; Density: 64.8 persons per square mile; Race: 82.5% White, 11.6% Black/African American, 3.7% Asian, 0.0% American Indian/Alaska Native, 0.0% Native Hawaiian/Other Pacific Islander, 2.1% Two or more races, 4.5% Hispanic of any race; Average household size: 2.34; Median age: 45.4; Age under 18: 15.2%; Age 65 and over: 23.3%; Males per 100 females: 96.8; Marriage status: 43.3% never married, 42.2% now married, 4.9% separated, 7.3% widowed, 7.2% divorced; Foreign born: 2.9%; Speak English only: 89.4%; With disability: 27.7%; Veterans: 4.2%; Ancestry: 21.9% Italian, 19.9% Irish, 14.1% English, 9.1% French Canadian, 8.5% French

Employment: 4.3% management, business, and financial, 0.0% computer, engineering, and science, 5.0% education, legal, community service, arts, and media, 0.0% healthcare practitioners, 35.9% service, 27.9% sales and office, 8.1% natural resources, construction, and maintenance, 18.7% production, transportation, and material moving

Income: Per capita: $29,917; Median household: $60,543; Average household: $73,013; Households with income of $100,000 or more: 22.2%; Poverty rate: 6.8%

Educational Attainment: High school diploma or higher: 84.7%; Bachelor's degree or higher: 24.5%; Graduate/professional degree or higher: 12.8%

Housing: Homeownership rate: 59.8%; Median home value: $280,600; Median year structure built: 1967; Homeowner vacancy rate: 2.8%; Median selected monthly owner costs: $1,837 with a mortgage, $698 without a mortgage; Median gross rent: $828 per month; Rental vacancy rate: 0.0%

Health Insurance: 91.0% have insurance; 62.3% have private insurance; 48.1% have public insurance; 9.0% do not have insurance; 0.0% of children under 18 do not have insurance

Transportation: Commute: 94.3% car, 5.7% public transportation, 0.0% walk, 0.0% work from home; Mean travel time to work: 38.8 minutes

WINGDALE (unincorporated postal area)

ZCTA: 12594

Covers a land area of 24.063 square miles and a water area of 0.618 square miles. Located at 41.68° N. Lat; 73.56° W. Long. Elevation is 420 feet.

Population: 4,294; Growth (since 2000): 18.7%; Density: 178.4 persons per square mile; Race: 79.4% White, 9.4% Black/African American, 0.9% Asian, 0.0% American Indian/Alaska Native, 0.0% Native Hawaiian/Other Pacific Islander, 3.9% Two or more races, 12.2% Hispanic of any race; Average household size: 2.94; Median age: 40.1; Age under 18: 21.6%; Age 65 and over: 8.6%; Males per 100 females: 99.4; Marriage status: 37.4% never married, 50.9% now married, 2.1% separated, 3.4% widowed, 8.2% divorced; Foreign born: 10.6%; Speak English only: 85.2%; With disability: 16.8%; Veterans: 4.7%; Ancestry: 27.0% Irish, 20.8% Italian, 16.3% German, 5.4% American, 4.6% Polish

Employment: 10.7% management, business, and financial, 3.1% computer, engineering, and science, 8.3% education, legal, community service, arts, and media, 2.3% healthcare practitioners, 25.6% service, 22.9% sales and office, 13.9% natural resources, construction, and maintenance, 13.2% production, transportation, and material moving

Income: Per capita: $27,180; Median household: $66,445; Average household: $78,313; Households with income of $100,000 or more: 25.6%; Poverty rate: 9.5%

Educational Attainment: High school diploma or higher: 88.1%; Bachelor's degree or higher: 20.5%; Graduate/professional degree or higher: 7.7%

School District(s)

Dover Union Free SD (KG-12)

  2014-15 Enrollment: 1,419 . . . . (845) 877-5700

Housing: Homeownership rate: 73.5%; Median home value: $236,200; Median year structure built: 1980; Homeowner vacancy rate: 0.0%; Median selected monthly owner costs: $1,929 with a mortgage, $854 without a mortgage; Median gross rent: $933 per month; Rental vacancy rate: 24.0%

Health Insurance: 87.9% have Insurance; 73.5% have private insurance; 28.6% have public insurance; 12.1% do not have insurance; 2.9% of children under 18 do not have insurance

Transportation: Commute: 85.4% car, 4.8% public transportation, 7.4% walk, 2.1% work from home; Mean travel time to work: 34.8 minutes

Erie County

Located in western New York; bounded on the west by Lake Erie; drained by the Cattaraugus and Tonawanda Creeks. Covers a land area of 1,042.693 square miles, a water area of 184.161 square miles, and is located in the Eastern Time Zone at 42.75° N. Lat., 78.78° W. Long. The county was founded in 1821. County seat is Buffalo.

Erie County is part of the Buffalo-Cheektowaga-Niagara Falls, NY Metropolitan Statistical Area. The entire metro area includes: Erie County, NY; Niagara County, NY

High and Low temperatures in degrees Fahrenheit; Precipitation and Snow in inches

Weather Station: Buffalo Greater Buffalo Int'l										Elevation: 705 feet		
	Jan	Feb	Mar	Apr	May	Jun	Jul	Aug	Sep	Oct	Nov	Dec
High	32	34	42	55	67	75	80	79	71	59	48	36
Low	19	19	26	37	47	57	62	61	54	43	34	24
Precip	3.1	2.5	2.9	3.0	3.4	3.6	3.2	3.3	4.0	3.6	4.0	3.9
Snow	24.4	17.2	13.4	2.8	0.3	tr	tr	tr	tr	0.9	8.1	26.9

High and Low temperatures in degrees Fahrenheit; Precipitation and Snow in inches

Weather Station: Wales										Elevation: 1,089 feet		
	Jan	Feb	Mar	Apr	May	Jun	Jul	Aug	Sep	Oct	Nov	Dec
High	31	32	41	55	65	74	77	76	70	58	47	35
Low	16	15	22	33	43	54	57	56	49	39	31	21
Precip	3.5	2.6	3.0	3.4	3.4	4.2	3.9	3.7	4.3	3.7	3.7	3.8
Snow	32.8	19.0	15.9	4.8	0.3	0.0	0.0	0.0	0.0	0.3	10.1	27.7

High and Low temperatures in degrees Fahrenheit; Precipitation and Snow in inches

Population: 921,584; Growth (since 2000): -3.0%; Density: 883.8 persons per square mile; Race: 78.7% White, 13.3% Black/African American, 3.2% Asian, 0.5% American Indian/Alaska Native, 0.0% Native Hawaiian/Other Pacific Islander, 2.3% two or more races, 5.0% Hispanic of any race; Average household size: 2.33; Median age: 40.4; Age under 18: 20.9%; Age 65 and over: 16.2%; Males per 100 females: 93.0; Marriage status: 36.4% never married, 46.2% now married, 2.0% separated, 7.1% widowed, 10.3% divorced; Foreign born: 6.7%; Speak English only: 89.9%; With disability: 13.1%; Veterans: 8.2%; Ancestry: 24.9% German, 17.9% Polish, 17.1% Irish, 16.6% Italian, 7.0% English

Religion: Six largest groups: 38.4% Catholicism, 3.1% Baptist, 2.7% Lutheran, 2.1% Non-denominational Protestant, 2.0% Methodist/Pietist, 2.0% Presbyterian-Reformed

Economy: Unemployment rate: 4.8%; Leading industries: 14.8 % retail trade; 11.6 % health care and social assistance; 10.4 % accommodation and food services; Farms: 1,044 totaling 142,679 acres; Company size: 27 employ 1,000 or more persons, 49 employ 500 to 999 persons, 583 employ 100 to 499 persons, 21,906 employ less than 100 persons; Business ownership: 19,041 women-owned, 4,254 Black-owned, 1,316 Hispanic-owned, 2,429 Asian-owned, 291 American Indian/Alaska Native-owned

Employment: 14.0% management, business, and financial, 4.5% computer, engineering, and science, 12.5% education, legal, community service, arts, and media, 7.1% healthcare practitioners, 18.6% service, 25.7% sales and office, 6.3% natural resources, construction, and maintenance, 11.3% production, transportation, and material moving

Income: Per capita: $28,879; Median household: $51,247; Average household: $67,940; Households with income of $100,000 or more: 20.9%; Poverty rate: 15.0%

Educational Attainment: High school diploma or higher: 90.4%; Bachelor's degree or higher: 31.6%; Graduate/professional degree or higher: 14.2%

Housing: Homeownership rate: 65.0%; Median home value: $130,000; Median year structure built: 1955; Homeowner vacancy rate: 0.7%; Median selected monthly owner costs: $1,256 with a mortgage, $501 without a mortgage; Median gross rent: $739 per month; Rental vacancy rate: 4.7%

Vital Statistics: Birth rate: 109.5 per 10,000 population; Death rate: 103.4 per 10,000 population; Age-adjusted cancer mortality rate: 179.1 deaths per 100,000 population

Health Insurance: 94.3% have insurance; 71.9% have private insurance; 36.6% have public insurance; 5.7% do not have insurance; 2.6% of children under 18 do not have insurance

Health Care: Physicians: 39.8 per 10,000 population; Dentists: 7.9 per 10,000 population; Hospital beds: 44.6 per 10,000 population; Hospital admissions: 1,344.1 per 10,000 population

Air Quality Index (AQI): Percent of Days: 66.8% good, 32.9% moderate, 0.3% unhealthy for sensitive individuals, 0.0% unhealthy, 0.0% very unhealthy; Annual median: 43; Annual maximum: 101

Transportation: Commute: 89.6% car, 3.7% public transportation, 2.9% walk, 2.6% work from home; Mean travel time to work: 21.2 minutes

2016 Presidential Election: 44.5% Trump, 51.0% Clinton, 3.0% Johnson, 1.5% Stein

National and State Parks: Beaver Island State Park; Buckhorn Island State Park; Evangola State Park; Theodore Roosevelt Inaugural National Historic Site

Additional Information Contacts

Erie Government . . . . (716) 858-8865
  http://www.erie.gov

Erie County Communities

AKRON (village). Covers a land area of 1.976 square miles and a water area of 0 square miles. Located at 43.02° N. Lat; 78.50° W. Long. Elevation is 741 feet.

History: Nearby is Tonawanda Indian Reservation. Incorporated 1849.

Population: 2,860; Growth (since 2000): -7.3%; Density: 1,447.5 persons per square mile; Race: 93.3% White, 1.0% Black/African American, 1.3% Asian, 2.2% American Indian/Alaska Native, 0.0% Native Hawaiian/Other Pacific Islander, 2.2% Two or more races, 0.8% Hispanic of any race; Average household size: 2.25; Median age: 45.1; Age under 18: 22.2%; Age 65 and over: 17.7%; Males per 100 females: 93.1; Marriage status: 30.1% never married, 46.8% now married, 0.0% separated, 7.1% widowed, 15.9% divorced; Foreign born: 5.1%; Speak English only: 93.4%; With disability: 13.4%; Veterans: 8.6%; Ancestry: 37.0% German, 19.2% Polish, 17.3% Irish, 13.3% English, 5.5% American

Employment: 8.9% management, business, and financial, 3.2% computer, engineering, and science, 10.3% education, legal, community service, arts, and media, 5.3% healthcare practitioners, 21.5% service, 24.1% sales and office, 14.8% natural resources, construction, and maintenance, 12.0% production, transportation, and material moving

Income: Per capita: $28,048; Median household: $47,311; Average household: $62,400; Households with income of $100,000 or more: 15.0%; Poverty rate: 4.9%

Educational Attainment: High school diploma or higher: 93.7%; Bachelor's degree or higher: 26.9%; Graduate/professional degree or higher: 11.8%

School District(s)
Akron Central SD (PK-12)
    2014-15 Enrollment: 1,430 . . . . (716) 542-5006
Housing: Homeownership rate: 55.2%; Median home value: $119,400; Median year structure built: 1943; Homeowner vacancy rate: 0.0%; Median selected monthly owner costs: $1,092 with a mortgage, $451 without a mortgage; Median gross rent: $654 per month; Rental vacancy rate: 0.0%
Health Insurance: 90.0% have insurance; 67.5% have private insurance; 37.8% have public insurance; 10.0% do not have insurance; 6.5% of children under 18 do not have insurance
Safety: Violent crime rate: 3.5 per 10,000 population; Property crime rate: 45.6 per 10,000 population
Newspapers: Akron Bugle (weekly circulation 1,900)
Transportation: Commute: 89.4% car, 0.0% public transportation, 6.0% walk, 4.6% work from home; Mean travel time to work: 19.6 minutes
Additional Information Contacts
Village of Akron . . . . (716) 542-9636
    http://www.erie.gov/akron

ALDEN (town). Covers a land area of 34.308 square miles and a water area of 0.201 square miles. Located at 42.91° N. Lat; 78.52° W. Long. Elevation is 863 feet.
History: Incorporated 1869.
Population: 10,382; Growth (since 2000): -0.8%; Density: 302.6 persons per square mile; Race: 85.7% White, 9.9% Black/African American, 0.1% Asian, 0.2% American Indian/Alaska Native, 0.0% Native Hawaiian/Other Pacific Islander, 2.3% Two or more races, 3.0% Hispanic of any race; Average household size: 2.50; Median age: 43.2; Age under 18: 17.8%; Age 65 and over: 14.7%; Males per 100 females: 135.8; Marriage status: 33.1% never married, 50.8% now married, 2.5% separated, 6.2% widowed, 9.9% divorced; Foreign born: 2.4%; Speak English only: 94.9%; With disability: 12.7%; Veterans: 9.2%; Ancestry: 37.7% German, 23.6% Polish, 13.8% Irish, 12.8% Italian, 7.3% English
Employment: 13.3% management, business, and financial, 4.2% computer, engineering, and science, 9.4% education, legal, community service, arts, and media, 5.7% healthcare practitioners, 17.1% service, 27.6% sales and office, 9.2% natural resources, construction, and maintenance, 13.5% production, transportation, and material moving
Income: Per capita: $24,799; Median household: $64,336; Average household: $72,993; Households with income of $100,000 or more: 24.1%; Poverty rate: 8.2%
Educational Attainment: High school diploma or higher: 89.3%; Bachelor's degree or higher: 18.9%; Graduate/professional degree or higher: 5.7%

School District(s)
Alden Central SD (KG-12)
    2014-15 Enrollment: 1,711 . . . . (716) 937-9116
Housing: Homeownership rate: 79.1%; Median home value: $153,600; Median year structure built: 1964; Homeowner vacancy rate: 0.5%; Median selected monthly owner costs: $1,342 with a mortgage, $515 without a mortgage; Median gross rent: $778 per month; Rental vacancy rate: 0.0%
Health Insurance: 95.2% have insurance; 82.1% have private insurance; 29.7% have public insurance; 4.8% do not have insurance; 5.4% of children under 18 do not have insurance

Newspapers: Alden Advertiser (weekly circulation 3,700)
Transportation: Commute: 97.5% car, 0.0% public transportation, 0.4% walk, 1.3% work from home; Mean travel time to work: 26.1 minutes
Additional Information Contacts
Town of Alden . . . . (716) 937-6969
    http://alden.erie.gov

ALDEN (village). Covers a land area of 2.718 square miles and a water area of 0 square miles. Located at 42.90° N. Lat; 78.49° W. Long. Elevation is 863 feet.
Population: 2,590; Growth (since 2000): -2.9%; Density: 952.8 persons per square mile; Race: 98.0% White, 1.0% Black/African American, 0.0% Asian, 0.2% American Indian/Alaska Native, 0.0% Native Hawaiian/Other Pacific Islander, 0.8% Two or more races, 1.2% Hispanic of any race; Average household size: 2.16; Median age: 43.5; Age under 18: 21.2%; Age 65 and over: 14.8%; Males per 100 females: 98.4; Marriage status: 29.8% never married, 47.1% now married, 1.6% separated, 9.2% widowed, 13.9% divorced; Foreign born: 1.4%; Speak English only: 98.8%; With disability: 16.8%; Veterans: 10.7%; Ancestry: 47.4% German, 23.8% Polish, 20.3% Irish, 11.3% Italian, 8.6% English
Employment: 11.4% management, business, and financial, 5.0% computer, engineering, and science, 8.1% education, legal, community service, arts, and media, 6.1% healthcare practitioners, 22.3% service, 25.4% sales and office, 5.1% natural resources, construction, and maintenance, 16.7% production, transportation, and material moving
Income: Per capita: $29,558; Median household: $52,005; Average household: $62,652; Households with income of $100,000 or more: 19.5%; Poverty rate: 11.2%
Educational Attainment: High school diploma or higher: 96.2%; Bachelor's degree or higher: 22.2%; Graduate/professional degree or higher: 8.2%

School District(s)
Alden Central SD (KG-12)
    2014-15 Enrollment: 1,711 . . . . (716) 937-9116
Housing: Homeownership rate: 65.0%; Median home value: $126,400; Median year structure built: 1962; Homeowner vacancy rate: 1.5%; Median selected monthly owner costs: $1,223 with a mortgage, $529 without a mortgage; Median gross rent: $681 per month; Rental vacancy rate: 0.0%
Health Insurance: 91.3% have insurance; 78.1% have private insurance; 31.2% have public insurance; 8.7% do not have insurance; 14.5% of children under 18 do not have insurance
Newspapers: Alden Advertiser (weekly circulation 3,700)
Transportation: Commute: 95.7% car, 0.0% public transportation, 1.5% walk, 1.9% work from home; Mean travel time to work: 27.1 minutes

AMHERST (town). Covers a land area of 53.203 square miles and a water area of 0.391 square miles. Located at 43.01° N. Lat; 78.76° W. Long. Elevation is 597 feet.
History: Amherst is home of the Amherst campus of the University at Buffalo.
Population: 124,044; Growth (since 2000): 6.5%; Density: 2,331.5 persons per square mile; Race: 82.3% White, 5.8% Black/African American, 8.4% Asian, 0.3% American Indian/Alaska Native, 0.0% Native Hawaiian/Other Pacific Islander, 2.3% Two or more races, 3.1% Hispanic of any race; Average household size: 2.34; Median age: 40.6; Age under 18: 19.5%; Age 65 and over: 18.7%; Males per 100 females: 89.9; Marriage status: 34.6% never married, 49.6% now married, 1.3% separated, 7.2% widowed, 8.6% divorced; Foreign born: 12.9%; Speak English only: 84.8%; With disability: 10.3%; Veterans: 7.0%; Ancestry: 25.3% German, 19.5% Italian, 17.0% Irish, 13.5% Polish, 8.7% English
Employment: 19.1% management, business, and financial, 6.8% computer, engineering, and science, 17.3% education, legal, community service, arts, and media, 9.0% healthcare practitioners, 13.9% service, 24.4% sales and office, 3.9% natural resources, construction, and maintenance, 5.6% production, transportation, and material moving
Income: Per capita: $37,506; Median household: $68,294; Average household: $92,050; Households with income of $100,000 or more: 33.2%; Poverty rate: 10.2%
Educational Attainment: High school diploma or higher: 95.4%; Bachelor's degree or higher: 53.4%; Graduate/professional degree or higher: 27.8%

School District(s)
Amherst Central SD (PK-12)
    2014-15 Enrollment: 2,943 . . . . (716) 362-3051

Sweet Home Central SD (KG-12)
2014-15 Enrollment: 3,254 . . . . (716) 250-1402

Four-year College(s)

Daemen College (Private, Not-for-profit)
Fall 2014 Enrollment: 2,800 . . . . (716) 839-3600
2015-16 Tuition: In-state $25,995; Out-of-state $25,995

Housing: Homeownership rate: 70.3%; Median home value: $177,400; Median year structure built: 1969; Homeowner vacancy rate: 0.7%; Median selected monthly owner costs: $1,551 with a mortgage, $627 without a mortgage; Median gross rent: $958 per month; Rental vacancy rate: 1.7%

Health Insurance: 96.6% have insurance; 84.4% have private insurance; 28.2% have public insurance; 3.4% do not have insurance; 1.5% of children under 18 do not have insurance

Safety: Violent crime rate: 9.7 per 10,000 population; Property crime rate: 159.4 per 10,000 population

Transportation: Commute: 90.4% car, 1.9% public transportation, 3.2% walk, 3.5% work from home; Mean travel time to work: 19.4 minutes

Additional Information Contacts

Town of Amherst . . . . (716) 631-7000
http://www.amherst.ny.us

ANGOLA (village). Covers a land area of 1.417 square miles and a water area of 0 square miles. Located at 42.64° N. Lat; 79.03° W. Long. Elevation is 686 feet.

History: Incorporated 1873.

Population: 1,858; Growth (since 2000): -18.0%; Density: 1,311.5 persons per square mile; Race: 92.5% White, 2.0% Black/African American, 0.2% Asian, 0.0% American Indian/Alaska Native, 0.0% Native Hawaiian/Other Pacific Islander, 5.0% Two or more races, 2.3% Hispanic of any race; Average household size: 2.30; Median age: 38.4; Age under 18: 23.4%; Age 65 and over: 16.5%; Males per 100 females: 87.7; Marriage status: 28.7% never married, 51.6% now married, 2.2% separated, 7.3% widowed, 12.4% divorced; Foreign born: 1.3%; Speak English only: 98.8%; With disability: 16.4%; Veterans: 12.1%; Ancestry: 32.0% German, 30.8% Italian, 19.7% Polish, 19.6% Irish, 7.8% American

Employment: 7.2% management, business, and financial, 3.5% computer, engineering, and science, 6.5% education, legal, community service, arts, and media, 7.7% healthcare practitioners, 14.6% service, 33.6% sales and office, 10.7% natural resources, construction, and maintenance, 16.3% production, transportation, and material moving

Income: Per capita: $26,730; Median household: $52,950; Average household: $61,173; Households with income of $100,000 or more: 17.8%; Poverty rate: 11.2%

Educational Attainment: High school diploma or higher: 90.1%; Bachelor's degree or higher: 19.9%; Graduate/professional degree or higher: 7.9%

School District(s)

Erie 2-Chautauqua-Cattaraugus Boces
2014-15 Enrollment: n/a . . . . (716) 549-4454
Evans-Brant Central SD (Lake Shore) (KG-12)
2014-15 Enrollment: 2,499 . . . . (716) 926-2201

Vocational/Technical School(s)

Erie 2 Chautauqua Cattaraugus BOCES-Practical Nursing Program (Public)
Fall 2014 Enrollment: 134 . . . . (716) 549-4454
2015-16 Tuition: $9,500

Housing: Homeownership rate: 70.3%; Median home value: $107,400; Median year structure built: 1948; Homeowner vacancy rate: 0.9%; Median selected monthly owner costs: $1,270 with a mortgage, $561 without a mortgage; Median gross rent: $601 per month; Rental vacancy rate: 14.7%

Health Insurance: 90.2% have insurance; 73.7% have private insurance; 33.2% have public insurance; 9.8% do not have insurance; 4.8% of children under 18 do not have insurance

Transportation: Commute: 92.6% car, 0.7% public transportation, 4.8% walk, 1.2% work from home; Mean travel time to work: 27.9 minutes

ANGOLA ON THE LAKE (CDP). Covers a land area of 2.546 square miles and a water area of 0 square miles. Located at 42.65° N. Lat; 79.05° W. Long. Elevation is 600 feet.

Population: 1,720; Growth (since 2000): -2.9%; Density: 675.7 persons per square mile; Race: 98.0% White, 0.2% Black/African American, 1.4% Asian, 0.0% American Indian/Alaska Native, 0.0% Native Hawaiian/Other Pacific Islander, 0.4% Two or more races, 0.3% Hispanic of any race; Average household size: 2.02; Median age: 51.3; Age under 18: 14.7%; Age 65 and over: 23.0%; Males per 100 females: 93.4; Marriage status:

30.6% never married, 49.1% now married, 0.6% separated, 9.2% widowed, 11.0% divorced; Foreign born: 3.7%; Speak English only: 98.9%; With disability: 13.8%; Veterans: 11.4%; Ancestry: 31.6% Polish, 27.7% German, 22.6% Irish, 18.9% Italian, 11.3% English

Employment: 9.2% management, business, and financial, 8.5% computer, engineering, and science, 5.9% education, legal, community service, arts, and media, 5.2% healthcare practitioners, 15.2% service, 26.8% sales and office, 8.9% natural resources, construction, and maintenance, 20.3% production, transportation, and material moving

Income: Per capita: $33,091; Median household: $40,833; Average household: $67,098; Households with income of $100,000 or more: 17.2%; Poverty rate: 7.6%

Educational Attainment: High school diploma or higher: 90.3%; Bachelor's degree or higher: 14.2%; Graduate/professional degree or higher: 6.1%

Housing: Homeownership rate: 80.5%; Median home value: $93,700; Median year structure built: 1957; Homeowner vacancy rate: 0.0%; Median selected monthly owner costs: $1,250 with a mortgage, $507 without a mortgage; Median gross rent: $832 per month; Rental vacancy rate: 0.0%

Health Insurance: 94.2% have insurance; 73.4% have private insurance; 41.4% have public insurance; 5.8% do not have insurance; 0.0% of children under 18 do not have insurance

Transportation: Commute: 97.3% car, 0.0% public transportation, 2.1% walk, 0.6% work from home; Mean travel time to work: 26.7 minutes

AURORA (town). Covers a land area of 36.393 square miles and a water area of 0.046 square miles. Located at 42.74° N. Lat; 78.64° W. Long.

History: Seat of Christ the King Seminary. Site (1895-1939) of the Roycroft Shops, founded by Elbert Hubbard. Restored home of Millard and Abigail Fillmore as a National Historic Landmark. Incorporated 1874.

Population: 13,828; Growth (since 2000): -1.2%; Density: 380.0 persons per square mile; Race: 97.2% White, 0.6% Black/African American, 0.7% Asian, 0.1% American Indian/Alaska Native, 0.0% Native Hawaiian/Other Pacific Islander, 1.1% Two or more races, 1.6% Hispanic of any race; Average household size: 2.47; Median age: 45.1; Age under 18: 21.9%; Age 65 and over: 17.4%; Males per 100 females: 92.7; Marriage status: 26.7% never married, 56.3% now married, 1.1% separated, 5.4% widowed, 11.6% divorced; Foreign born: 2.3%; Speak English only: 97.6%; With disability: 9.3%; Veterans: 6.6%; Ancestry: 35.0% German, 21.3% Irish, 15.0% Polish, 15.0% English, 13.2% Italian

Employment: 17.1% management, business, and financial, 5.2% computer, engineering, and science, 17.1% education, legal, community service, arts, and media, 9.1% healthcare practitioners, 16.0% service, 18.9% sales and office, 8.1% natural resources, construction, and maintenance, 8.4% production, transportation, and material moving

Income: Per capita: $35,879; Median household: $72,455; Average household: $88,588; Households with income of $100,000 or more: 31.3%; Poverty rate: 7.1%

Educational Attainment: High school diploma or higher: 94.2%; Bachelor's degree or higher: 47.2%; Graduate/professional degree or higher: 22.3%

Housing: Homeownership rate: 80.7%; Median home value: $190,300; Median year structure built: 1954; Homeowner vacancy rate: 0.7%; Median selected monthly owner costs: $1,675 with a mortgage, $631 without a mortgage; Median gross rent: $711 per month; Rental vacancy rate: 6.7%

Health Insurance: 95.1% have insurance; 83.2% have private insurance; 25.5% have public insurance; 4.9% do not have insurance; 4.3% of children under 18 do not have insurance

Transportation: Commute: 90.0% car, 0.4% public transportation, 2.1% walk, 6.5% work from home; Mean travel time to work: 22.2 minutes

Additional Information Contacts

Town of Aurora . . . . (716) 652-3280
http://www.townofaurora.com

BILLINGTON HEIGHTS (CDP). Covers a land area of 3.193 square miles and a water area of 0.007 square miles. Located at 42.79° N. Lat; 78.63° W. Long. Elevation is 951 feet.

Population: 1,653; Growth (since 2000): -2.2%; Density: 517.7 persons per square mile; Race: 96.6% White, 0.0% Black/African American, 0.0% Asian, 0.0% American Indian/Alaska Native, 0.0% Native Hawaiian/Other Pacific Islander, 0.0% Two or more races, 3.4% Hispanic of any race; Average household size: 2.41; Median age: 43.0; Age under 18: 19.2%; Age 65 and over: 20.2%; Males per 100 females: 95.9; Marriage status: 27.9% never married, 55.5% now married, 0.0% separated, 7.5%

widowed, 9.1% divorced; Foreign born: 2.2%; Speak English only: 93.5%; With disability: 7.9%; Veterans: 13.1%; Ancestry: 40.2% German, 20.9% Italian, 19.3% Polish, 12.5% English, 12.2% Irish

Employment: 18.1% management, business, and financial, 5.1% computer, engineering, and science, 19.8% education, legal, community service, arts, and media, 5.8% healthcare practitioners, 20.2% service, 15.3% sales and office, 12.6% natural resources, construction, and maintenance, 3.0% production, transportation, and material moving

Income: Per capita: $39,400; Median household: $84,091; Average household: $93,046; Households with income of $100,000 or more: 46.5%; Poverty rate: 2.2%

Educational Attainment: High school diploma or higher: 95.4%; Bachelor's degree or higher: 53.4%; Graduate/professional degree or higher: 23.5%

Housing: Homeownership rate: 84.5%; Median home value: $224,300; Median year structure built: 1964; Homeowner vacancy rate: 0.0%; Median selected monthly owner costs: $1,858 with a mortgage, $648 without a mortgage; Median gross rent: $619 per month; Rental vacancy rate: 0.0%

Health Insurance: 95.9% have insurance; 82.9% have private insurance; 27.7% have public insurance; 4.1% do not have insurance; 0.0% of children under 18 do not have insurance

Transportation: Commute: 96.5% car, 1.0% public transportation, 0.0% walk, 2.5% work from home; Mean travel time to work: 27.6 minutes

BLASDELL (village).
Covers a land area of 1.123 square miles and a water area of 0 square miles. Located at 42.80° N. Lat; 78.83° W. Long. Elevation is 610 feet.

History: Incorporated 1898.

Population: 2,579; Growth (since 2000): -5.1%; Density: 2,297.4 persons per square mile; Race: 94.1% White, 1.7% Black/African American, 0.0% Asian, 1.0% American Indian/Alaska Native, 0.0% Native Hawaiian/Other Pacific Islander, 1.5% Two or more races, 3.1% Hispanic of any race; Average household size: 2.32; Median age: 38.4; Age under 18: 20.8%; Age 65 and over: 12.5%; Males per 100 females: 89.4; Marriage status: 41.2% never married, 35.2% now married, 2.1% separated, 10.1% widowed, 13.5% divorced; Foreign born: 2.3%; Speak English only: 97.2%; With disability: 15.0%; Veterans: 7.9%; Ancestry: 39.9% German, 32.8% Irish, 21.1% Polish, 17.6% Italian, 6.3% English

Employment: 11.1% management, business, and financial, 2.7% computer, engineering, and science, 6.5% education, legal, community service, arts, and media, 3.9% healthcare practitioners, 27.4% service, 20.6% sales and office, 9.4% natural resources, construction, and maintenance, 18.4% production, transportation, and material moving

Income: Per capita: $22,767; Median household: $41,520; Average household: $51,881; Households with income of $100,000 or more: 9.1%; Poverty rate: 16.3%

Educational Attainment: High school diploma or higher: 92.0%; Bachelor's degree or higher: 11.5%; Graduate/professional degree or higher: 3.4%

School District(s)
Frontier Central SD (PK-12)
   2014-15 Enrollment: 5,006 . . . . (716) 926-1711

Housing: Homeownership rate: 53.1%; Median home value: $93,000; Median year structure built: 1948; Homeowner vacancy rate: 0.0%; Median selected monthly owner costs: $1,084 with a mortgage, $446 without a mortgage; Median gross rent: $673 per month; Rental vacancy rate: 3.9%

Health Insurance: 88.8% have insurance; 66.5% have private insurance; 33.7% have public insurance; 11.2% do not have insurance; 8.0% of children under 18 do not have insurance

Transportation: Commute: 90.9% car, 1.9% public transportation, 5.4% walk, 0.6% work from home; Mean travel time to work: 18.7 minutes

BOSTON (town).
Covers a land area of 35.820 square miles and a water area of 0 square miles. Located at 42.65° N. Lat; 78.76° W. Long. Elevation is 942 feet.

Population: 8,029; Growth (since 2000): 1.7%; Density: 224.1 persons per square mile; Race: 99.1% White, 0.8% Black/African American, 0.0% Asian, 0.0% American Indian/Alaska Native, 0.0% Native Hawaiian/Other Pacific Islander, 0.1% Two or more races, 0.9% Hispanic of any race; Average household size: 2.46; Median age: 45.7; Age under 18: 20.9%; Age 65 and over: 20.2%; Males per 100 females: 101.0; Marriage status: 24.8% never married, 58.6% now married, 1.3% separated, 7.0% widowed, 9.5% divorced; Foreign born: 2.0%; Speak English only: 97.6%; With disability: 10.7%; Veterans: 6.6%; Ancestry: 39.1% German, 24.1% Polish, 22.7% Irish, 19.2% Italian, 9.7% English

Employment: 11.5% management, business, and financial, 6.3% computer, engineering, and science, 11.7% education, legal, community service, arts, and media, 11.7% healthcare practitioners, 14.6% service, 22.9% sales and office, 8.3% natural resources, construction, and maintenance, 13.0% production, transportation, and material moving

Income: Per capita: $31,903; Median household: $66,959; Average household: $77,965; Households with income of $100,000 or more: 27.9%; Poverty rate: 3.6%

Educational Attainment: High school diploma or higher: 97.0%; Bachelor's degree or higher: 32.5%; Graduate/professional degree or higher: 14.5%

Housing: Homeownership rate: 82.3%; Median home value: $170,300; Median year structure built: 1969; Homeowner vacancy rate: 0.0%; Median selected monthly owner costs: $1,478 with a mortgage, $571 without a mortgage; Median gross rent: $687 per month; Rental vacancy rate: 0.0%

Health Insurance: 96.1% have insurance; 84.2% have private insurance; 30.7% have public insurance; 3.9% do not have insurance; 0.0% of children under 18 do not have insurance

Transportation: Commute: 96.3% car, 0.2% public transportation, 1.0% walk, 1.0% work from home; Mean travel time to work: 25.2 minutes

Additional Information Contacts
Town of Boston . . . . (716) 941-6113
  http://www.townofboston.com

BOWMANSVILLE (unincorporated postal area)
ZCTA: 14026

Covers a land area of 0.753 square miles and a water area of 0 square miles. Located at 42.94° N. Lat; 78.69° W. Long. Elevation is 709 feet.

Population: 597; Growth (since 2000): -17.3%; Density: 793.0 persons per square mile; Race: 98.7% White, 1.3% Black/African American, 0.0% Asian, 0.0% American Indian/Alaska Native, 0.0% Native Hawaiian/Other Pacific Islander, 0.0% Two or more races, 2.5% Hispanic of any race; Average household size: 2.05; Median age: 46.3; Age under 18: 12.4%; Age 65 and over: 17.8%; Males per 100 females: 103.0; Marriage status: 16.4% never married, 62.9% now married, 0.0% separated, 9.0% widowed, 11.7% divorced; Foreign born: 0.0%; Speak English only: 98.4%; With disability: 9.2%; Veterans: 8.0%; Ancestry: 34.2% German, 23.3% Irish, 15.9% Polish, 13.4% Italian, 11.1% English

Employment: 22.4% management, business, and financial, 7.1% computer, engineering, and science, 16.6% education, legal, community service, arts, and media, 5.5% healthcare practitioners, 2.1% service, 35.6% sales and office, 2.4% natural resources, construction, and maintenance, 8.2% production, transportation, and material moving

Income: Per capita: $55,784; Median household: $79,563; Average household: $111,963; Households with income of $100,000 or more: 38.4%; Poverty rate: 1.5%

Educational Attainment: High school diploma or higher: 96.9%; Bachelor's degree or higher: 26.3%; Graduate/professional degree or higher: 12.5%

Housing: Homeownership rate: 73.2%; Median home value: $170,800; Median year structure built: 1954; Homeowner vacancy rate: 0.0%; Median selected monthly owner costs: $1,691 with a mortgage, $596 without a mortgage; Median gross rent: $655 per month; Rental vacancy rate: 24.3%

Health Insurance: 96.8% have insurance; 83.8% have private insurance; 22.4% have public insurance; 3.2% do not have insurance; 0.0% of children under 18 do not have insurance

Transportation: Commute: 92.6% car, 0.0% public transportation, 0.0% walk, 7.4% work from home; Mean travel time to work: 17.1 minutes

BRANT (town).
Covers a land area of 24.314 square miles and a water area of 0.424 square miles. Located at 42.59° N. Lat; 79.02° W. Long. Elevation is 745 feet.

Population: 2,171; Growth (since 2000): 13.9%; Density: 89.3 persons per square mile; Race: 90.2% White, 0.5% Black/African American, 0.3% Asian, 4.1% American Indian/Alaska Native, 0.0% Native Hawaiian/Other Pacific Islander, 0.5% Two or more races, 4.7% Hispanic of any race; Average household size: 2.45; Median age: 43.8; Age under 18: 20.9%; Age 65 and over: 17.8%; Males per 100 females: 101.5; Marriage status: 31.1% never married, 53.4% now married, 2.2% separated, 4.5% widowed, 11.1% divorced; Foreign born: 3.1%; Speak English only: 92.4%; With disability: 10.0%; Veterans: 10.0%; Ancestry: 32.6% German, 28.3% Italian, 19.5% Polish, 11.7% Irish, 9.0% English

Employment: 13.1% management, business, and financial, 2.0% computer, engineering, and science, 8.9% education, legal, community

service, arts, and media, 5.0% healthcare practitioners, 17.5% service, 24.5% sales and office, 12.2% natural resources, construction, and maintenance, 16.7% production, transportation, and material moving
Income: Per capita: $30,687; Median household: $61,923; Average household: $74,713; Households with income of $100,000 or more: 25.9%; Poverty rate: 10.5%
Educational Attainment: High school diploma or higher: 92.0%; Bachelor's degree or higher: 20.2%; Graduate/professional degree or higher: 8.9%
Housing: Homeownership rate: 79.7%; Median home value: $117,000; Median year structure built: 1955; Homeowner vacancy rate: 0.0%; Median selected monthly owner costs: $1,207 with a mortgage, $485 without a mortgage; Median gross rent: $669 per month; Rental vacancy rate: 6.3%
Health Insurance: 89.6% have insurance; 66.0% have private insurance; 35.2% have public insurance; 10.4% do not have insurance; 8.6% of children under 18 do not have insurance
Safety: Violent crime rate: 4.8 per 10,000 population; Property crime rate: 125.7 per 10,000 population
Transportation: Commute: 95.6% car, 0.0% public transportation, 1.5% walk, 2.9% work from home; Mean travel time to work: 27.8 minutes

---

BUFFALO (city). County seat. Covers a land area of 40.384 square miles and a water area of 12.110 square miles. Located at 42.89° N. Lat; 78.86° W. Long. Elevation is 600 feet.
History: Although Joseph Ellicott chose and mapped the site of Buffalo for the Holland Land Company in 1799, it was not until 1804 that he divided the land into lots and offered them for sale. He modeled the city plan after that of Washington, D.C. He called the place New Amsterdam, but settlers preferred to name it after Buffalo Creek. Buffalo was incorporated as a village in 1816. The early welfare of the settlement depended on its function as a trading center. The Erie Canal, opened in 1825, brought trade and prosperity. Buffalo stood at the transportation break in the great east-west route. In 1832, Buffalo was incorporated into a city. Steam engine manufacturers and other industries sprang up. After the Civil War, Buffalo became a railroad center.
Population: 259,517; Growth (since 2000): -11.3%; Density: 6,426.2 persons per square mile; Race: 48.5% White, 37.3% Black/African American, 4.4% Asian, 0.4% American Indian/Alaska Native, 0.0% Native Hawaiian/Other Pacific Islander, 3.8% Two or more races, 10.8% Hispanic of any race; Average household size: 2.27; Median age: 33.1; Age under 18: 22.9%; Age 65 and over: 11.8%; Males per 100 females: 92.0; Marriage status: 51.2% never married, 31.5% now married, 3.3% separated, 6.5% widowed, 10.8% divorced; Foreign born: 8.8%; Speak English only: 83.4%; With disability: 16.5%; Veterans: 6.8%; Ancestry: 12.6% Irish, 12.4% German, 10.8% Italian, 9.5% Polish, 3.8% English
Employment: 10.3% management, business, and financial, 3.4% computer, engineering, and science, 13.3% education, legal, community service, arts, and media, 5.6% healthcare practitioners, 25.1% service, 24.2% sales and office, 5.3% natural resources, construction, and maintenance, 12.7% production, transportation, and material moving
Income: Per capita: $20,751; Median household: $31,918; Average household: $46,918; Households with income of $100,000 or more: 9.8%; Poverty rate: 31.4%
Educational Attainment: High school diploma or higher: 82.7%; Bachelor's degree or higher: 24.6%; Graduate/professional degree or higher: 11.2%

School District(s)

Aloma D Johnson Community Charter School (KG-04)
    2014-15 Enrollment: 296. . . . . (716) 856-4390
Buffalo Academy of Science Charter School (07-12)
    2014-15 Enrollment: 390. . . . . (716) 854-2490
Buffalo City SD (PK-12)
    2014-15 Enrollment: 35,234 . . . . (716) 816-3575
Buffalo United Charter School (KG-08)
    2014-15 Enrollment: 717. . . . . (716) 835-9862
Charter School for Applied Technologies (KG-12)
    2014-15 Enrollment: 1,935 . . . . (716) 876-7505
Cheektowaga Central SD (PK-12)
    2014-15 Enrollment: 2,166 . . . . (716) 686-3606
Community Charter School (KG-06)
    2014-15 Enrollment: n/a . . . . (716) 833-5967
Elmwood Village Charter School (KG-07)
    2014-15 Enrollment: 350. . . . . (716) 886-4581
Enterprise Charter School (KG-08)
    2014-15 Enrollment: 403. . . . . (716) 855-2114

Health Sciences Charter School
    2014-15 Enrollment: 460. . . . . (716) 888-4080
Kenmore-Tonawanda Union Free SD (PK-12)
    2014-15 Enrollment: 7,171 . . . . (716) 874-8400
King Center Charter School (KG-06)
    2014-15 Enrollment: 367. . . . . (716) 891-7912
Oracle Charter School (09-12)
    2014-15 Enrollment: 377. . . . . (716) 362-3188
Pinnacle Charter School (KG-08)
    2014-15 Enrollment: n/a . . . . (716) 842-1244
South Buffalo Charter School (KG-08)
    2014-15 Enrollment: 804. . . . . (716) 826-7213
Tapestry Charter School (KG-12)
    2014-15 Enrollment: 795. . . . . (716) 204-5883
Western New York Maritime Charter School (09-12)
    2014-15 Enrollment: 325. . . . . (716) 842-6289
Westminster Community Charter School (KG-08)
    2014-15 Enrollment: 545. . . . . (716) 816-3450

Four-year College(s)

Bryant & Stratton College-Buffalo (Private, For-profit)
    Fall 2014 Enrollment: 800 . . . . (716) 884-9120
    2015-16 Tuition: In-state $16,404; Out-of-state $16,404
Canisius College (Private, Not-for-profit, Roman Catholic)
    Fall 2014 Enrollment: 4,181 . . . . (716) 883-7000
    2015-16 Tuition: In-state $34,690; Out-of-state $34,690
D'Youville College (Private, Not-for-profit)
    Fall 2014 Enrollment: 3,067 . . . . (716) 829-8000
    2015-16 Tuition: In-state $24,370; Out-of-state $24,370
Medaille College (Private, Not-for-profit)
    Fall 2014 Enrollment: 2,479 . . . . (716) 880-2000
    2015-16 Tuition: In-state $26,252; Out-of-state $26,252
SUNY Buffalo State (Public)
    Fall 2014 Enrollment: 11,083 . . . . (716) 878-4000
    2015-16 Tuition: In-state $7,669; Out-of-state $17,519
Trocaire College (Private, Not-for-profit, Roman Catholic)
    Fall 2014 Enrollment: 1,467 . . . . (716) 826-1200
    2015-16 Tuition: In-state $16,290; Out-of-state $16,290
University at Buffalo (Public)
    Fall 2014 Enrollment: 29,995 . . . . (716) 645-2000
    2015-16 Tuition: In-state $9,381; Out-of-state $24,461
Villa Maria College (Private, Not-for-profit, Roman Catholic)
    Fall 2014 Enrollment: 477. . . . . (716) 896-0700
    2015-16 Tuition: In-state $20,260; Out-of-state $20,260

Two-year College(s)

Erie Community College (Public)
    Fall 2014 Enrollment: 12,733 . . . . (716) 851-1322
    2015-16 Tuition: In-state $5,189; Out-of-state $9,784

Vocational/Technical School(s)

Continental School of Beauty Culture-Buffalo (Private, For-profit)
    Fall 2014 Enrollment: 125 . . . . (716) 833-5016
    2015-16 Tuition: $12,440
National Tractor Trailer School Inc-Buffalo (Private, For-profit)
    Fall 2014 Enrollment: 130 . . . . (716) 849-6887
    2015-16 Tuition: $9,948

Housing: Homeownership rate: 41.5%; Median home value: $68,800; Median year structure built: Before 1940; Homeowner vacancy rate: 0.9%; Median selected monthly owner costs: $949 with a mortgage, $382 without a mortgage; Median gross rent: $699 per month; Rental vacancy rate: 5.5%
Health Insurance: 91.5% have insurance; 49.8% have private insurance; 52.0% have public insurance; 8.5% do not have insurance; 2.7% of children under 18 do not have insurance
Hospitals: Erie County Medical Center (550 beds); Kaleida Health; Mercy Hospital (349 beds); Sisters of Charity Hospital (413 beds); Upstate New York VA Healthcare System - Western NY (288 beds)
Safety: Violent crime rate: 111.9 per 10,000 population; Property crime rate: 433.0 per 10,000 population
Newspapers: Bee Publications (weekly circulation 37,000); Buffalo News (daily circulation 145,000); Riverside Review (weekly circulation 14,500); Rocket Publications (weekly circulation 34,000); Southtowns Citizen (weekly circulation 6,500)
Transportation: Commute: 77.7% car, 11.7% public transportation, 6.1% walk, 2.4% work from home; Mean travel time to work: 20.9 minutes; Amtrak: Train service available.
Airports: Buffalo Niagara International (primary service/medium hub)

Additional Information Contacts

City of Buffalo . . . . (716) 851-5431
http://www.ci.buffalo.ny.us

CATTARAUGUS RESERVATION (reservation). Covers a land area of 25.263 square miles and a water area of 0.337 square miles. Located at 42.55° N. Lat; 79.01° W. Long.

Population: 1,762; Growth (since 2000): n/a; Density: 69.7 persons per square mile; Race: 6.4% White, 0.2% Black/African American, 1.7% Asian, 83.5% American Indian/Alaska Native, 0.0% Native Hawaiian/Other Pacific Islander, 8.2% Two or more races, 4.2% Hispanic of any race; Average household size: 2.55; Median age: 38.2; Age under 18: 30.8%; Age 65 and over: 12.7%; Males per 100 females: 89.6; Marriage status: 45.5% never married, 24.7% now married, 1.3% separated, 9.0% widowed, 20.9% divorced; Foreign born: 3.7%; Speak English only: 94.4%; With disability: 15.0%; Veterans: 9.2%; Ancestry: 3.3% Irish, 1.0% Polish, 0.9% English, 0.7% American, 0.7% Italian

Employment: 14.1% management, business, and financial, 2.6% computer, engineering, and science, 16.1% education, legal, community service, arts, and media, 2.0% healthcare practitioners, 20.0% service, 27.1% sales and office, 9.1% natural resources, construction, and maintenance, 8.9% production, transportation, and material moving

Income: Per capita: $15,617; Median household: $31,223; Average household: $38,879; Households with income of $100,000 or more: 4.2%; Poverty rate: 29.5%

Educational Attainment: High school diploma or higher: 81.9%; Bachelor's degree or higher: 14.9%; Graduate/professional degree or higher: 2.0%

Housing: Homeownership rate: 78.1%; Median home value: $81,200; Median year structure built: 1984; Homeowner vacancy rate: 0.0%; Median selected monthly owner costs: $750 with a mortgage, $284 without a mortgage; Median gross rent: $343 per month; Rental vacancy rate: 0.0%

Health Insurance: 67.5% have insurance; 39.8% have private insurance; 34.5% have public insurance; 32.5% do not have insurance; 36.7% of children under 18 do not have insurance

Transportation: Commute: 93.5% car, 0.0% public transportation, 6.5% walk, 0.0% work from home; Mean travel time to work: 18.6 minutes

CHAFFEE (unincorporated postal area)
ZCTA: 14030

Covers a land area of 19.866 square miles and a water area of 0.216 square miles. Located at 42.56° N. Lat; 78.51° W. Long. Elevation is 1,460 feet.

Population: 1,595; Growth (since 2000): -1.4%; Density: 80.3 persons per square mile; Race: 99.2% White, 0.0% Black/African American, 0.0% Asian, 0.0% American Indian/Alaska Native, 0.0% Native Hawaiian/Other Pacific Islander, 0.5% Two or more races, 0.9% Hispanic of any race; Average household size: 2.55; Median age: 48.2; Age under 18: 18.6%; Age 65 and over: 18.9%; Males per 100 females: 107.0; Marriage status: 24.6% never married, 60.1% now married, 1.9% separated, 4.8% widowed, 10.5% divorced; Foreign born: 0.0%; Speak English only: 97.9%; With disability: 13.4%; Veterans: 12.5%; Ancestry: 46.6% German, 17.8% Italian, 16.7% Irish, 16.4% Polish, 10.7% English

Employment: 8.6% management, business, and financial, 1.9% computer, engineering, and science, 8.1% education, legal, community service, arts, and media, 7.2% healthcare practitioners, 18.8% service, 27.2% sales and office, 9.8% natural resources, construction, and maintenance, 18.2% production, transportation, and material moving

Income: Per capita: $25,370; Median household: $56,932; Average household: $65,821; Households with income of $100,000 or more: 21.9%; Poverty rate: 5.7%

Educational Attainment: High school diploma or higher: 92.7%; Bachelor's degree or higher: 14.6%; Graduate/professional degree or higher: 5.1%

Housing: Homeownership rate: 83.4%; Median home value: $132,200; Median year structure built: 1960; Homeowner vacancy rate: 1.6%; Median selected monthly owner costs: $1,153 with a mortgage, $351 without a mortgage; Median gross rent: $826 per month; Rental vacancy rate: 0.0%

Health Insurance: 97.9% have insurance; 83.2% have private insurance; 30.0% have public insurance; 2.1% do not have insurance; 0.0% of children under 18 do not have insurance

Transportation: Commute: 92.8% car, 0.3% public transportation, 1.0% walk, 4.6% work from home; Mean travel time to work: 26.2 minutes

CHEEKTOWAGA (CDP). Covers a land area of 25.343 square miles and a water area of 0.057 square miles. Located at 42.91° N. Lat; 78.75° W. Long. Elevation is 650 feet.

Population: 74,905; Growth (since 2000): -6.4%; Density: 2,955.6 persons per square mile; Race: 83.7% White, 11.1% Black/African American, 2.0% Asian, 0.3% American Indian/Alaska Native, 0.1% Native Hawaiian/Other Pacific Islander, 1.8% Two or more races, 3.3% Hispanic of any race; Average household size: 2.21; Median age: 43.1; Age under 18: 17.8%; Age 65 and over: 19.2%; Males per 100 females: 88.5; Marriage status: 35.2% never married, 45.0% now married, 1.2% separated, 7.7% widowed, 12.0% divorced; Foreign born: 5.3%; Speak English only: 92.4%; With disability: 13.6%; Veterans: 9.8%; Ancestry: 31.7% Polish, 25.8% German, 15.1% Italian, 13.5% Irish, 4.8% English

Employment: 11.4% management, business, and financial, 3.7% computer, engineering, and science, 8.7% education, legal, community service, arts, and media, 6.6% healthcare practitioners, 18.2% service, 30.8% sales and office, 6.9% natural resources, construction, and maintenance, 13.7% production, transportation, and material moving

Income: Per capita: $25,895; Median household: $48,508; Average household: $56,941; Households with income of $100,000 or more: 14.2%; Poverty rate: 11.4%

Educational Attainment: High school diploma or higher: 90.3%; Bachelor's degree or higher: 22.0%; Graduate/professional degree or higher: 7.9%

School District(s)

Cheektowaga Central SD (PK-12)
   2014-15 Enrollment: 2,166 . . . . (716) 686-3606
Cheektowaga-Maryvale Union Free SD (PK-12)
   2014-15 Enrollment: 2,237 . . . . (716) 631-7407
Cheektowaga-Sloan Union Free SD (PK-12)
   2014-15 Enrollment: 1,474 . . . . (716) 891-6402
Cleveland Hill Union Free SD (PK-12)
   2014-15 Enrollment: 1,341 . . . . (716) 836-7200

Vocational/Technical School(s)

Empire Beauty School-Buffalo (Private, For-profit)
   Fall 2014 Enrollment: 53 . . . . (800) 223-3271
   2015-16 Tuition: $12,000

Housing: Homeownership rate: 69.9%; Median home value: $99,400; Median year structure built: 1960; Homeowner vacancy rate: 1.3%; Median selected monthly owner costs: $1,099 with a mortgage, $471 without a mortgage; Median gross rent: $764 per month; Rental vacancy rate: 4.4%

Health Insurance: 94.0% have insurance; 75.9% have private insurance; 35.0% have public insurance; 6.0% do not have insurance; 2.7% of children under 18 do not have insurance

Newspapers: Cheektowaga Times (weekly circulation 4,000)

Transportation: Commute: 95.0% car, 1.1% public transportation, 1.6% walk, 1.2% work from home; Mean travel time to work: 19.2 minutes

CHEEKTOWAGA (town). Covers a land area of 29.423 square miles and a water area of 0.063 square miles. Located at 42.91° N. Lat; 78.74° W. Long. Elevation is 650 feet.

History: Named for the Indian translation of "place of the crab apple tree". Population grew significantly after World War II. Settled 1809. Incorporated 1834.

Population: 87,858; Growth (since 2000): -6.6%; Density: 2,986.1 persons per square mile; Race: 85.5% White, 9.7% Black/African American, 1.8% Asian, 0.2% American Indian/Alaska Native, 0.1% Native Hawaiian/Other Pacific Islander, 1.8% Two or more races, 3.1% Hispanic of any race; Average household size: 2.22; Median age: 43.0; Age under 18: 18.1%; Age 65 and over: 19.2%; Males per 100 females: 88.9; Marriage status: 34.6% never married, 45.7% now married, 1.3% separated, 7.9% widowed, 11.9% divorced; Foreign born: 5.1%; Speak English only: 92.7%; With disability: 13.5%; Veterans: 10.1%; Ancestry: 32.8% Polish, 26.2% German, 15.5% Italian, 13.7% Irish, 4.8% English

Employment: 11.4% management, business, and financial, 3.6% computer, engineering, and science, 8.6% education, legal, community service, arts, and media, 6.5% healthcare practitioners, 18.2% service, 30.6% sales and office, 6.9% natural resources, construction, and maintenance, 14.1% production, transportation, and material moving

Income: Per capita: $25,764; Median household: $48,662; Average household: $56,853; Households with income of $100,000 or more: 13.5%; Poverty rate: 10.9%

Educational Attainment: High school diploma or higher: 90.3%; Bachelor's degree or higher: 21.4%; Graduate/professional degree or higher: 7.5%

School District(s)
Cheektowaga Central SD (PK-12)
2014-15 Enrollment: 2,166 . . . . (716) 686-3606
Cheektowaga-Maryvale Union Free SD (PK-12)
2014-15 Enrollment: 2,237 . . . . (716) 631-7407
Cheektowaga-Sloan Union Free SD (PK-12)
2014-15 Enrollment: 1,474 . . . . (716) 891-6402
Cleveland Hill Union Free SD (PK-12)
2014-15 Enrollment: 1,341 . . . . (716) 836-7200

Vocational/Technical School(s)
Empire Beauty School-Buffalo (Private, For-profit)
Fall 2014 Enrollment: 53 . . . . (800) 223-3271
2015-16 Tuition: $12,000

Housing: Homeownership rate: 70.9%; Median home value: $99,400; Median year structure built: 1959; Homeowner vacancy rate: 1.4%; Median selected monthly owner costs: $1,094 with a mortgage, $471 without a mortgage; Median gross rent: $765 per month; Rental vacancy rate: 3.9%

Health Insurance: 94.3% have insurance; 76.3% have private insurance; 34.9% have public insurance; 5.7% do not have insurance; 2.6% of children under 18 do not have insurance

Safety: Violent crime rate: 24.4 per 10,000 population; Property crime rate: 302.9 per 10,000 population

Newspapers: Cheektowaga Times (weekly circulation 4,000)

Transportation: Commute: 95.1% car, 1.1% public transportation, 1.5% walk, 1.2% work from home; Mean travel time to work: 19.4 minutes

Additional Information Contacts
Town of Cheektowaga. . . . . (716) 686-3400
http://tocny.org

CLARENCE (CDP).
Covers a land area of 2.845 square miles and a water area of 0.065 square miles. Located at 42.98° N. Lat; 78.60° W. Long. Elevation is 738 feet.

Population: 3,164; Growth (since 2000): n/a; Density: 1,112.1 persons per square mile; Race: 93.7% White, 2.4% Black/African American, 2.3% Asian, 0.0% American Indian/Alaska Native, 0.0% Native Hawaiian/Other Pacific Islander, 1.4% Two or more races, 4.4% Hispanic of any race; Average household size: 2.44; Median age: 45.4; Age under 18: 20.0%; Age 65 and over: 24.4%; Males per 100 females: 79.4; Marriage status: 27.5% never married, 58.3% now married, 2.1% separated, 8.7% widowed, 5.5% divorced; Foreign born: 6.1%; Speak English only: 92.3%; With disability: 13.2%; Veterans: 7.0%; Ancestry: 37.2% German, 18.3% Italian, 16.4% Irish, 10.8% Polish, 9.6% English

Employment: 24.0% management, business, and financial, 2.7% computer, engineering, and science, 14.1% education, legal, community service, arts, and media, 14.9% healthcare practitioners, 13.0% service, 18.3% sales and office, 8.7% natural resources, construction, and maintenance, 4.3% production, transportation, and material moving

Income: Per capita: $33,954; Median household: $69,821; Average household: $87,377; Households with income of $100,000 or more: 37.8%; Poverty rate: 12.0%

Educational Attainment: High school diploma or higher: 94.2%; Bachelor's degree or higher: 43.5%; Graduate/professional degree or higher: 22.8%

School District(s)
Clarence Central SD (KG-12)
2014-15 Enrollment: 4,623 . . . . (716) 407-9102

Housing: Homeownership rate: 67.8%; Median home value: $217,000; Median year structure built: 1960; Homeowner vacancy rate: 0.0%; Median selected monthly owner costs: $1,591 with a mortgage, $897 without a mortgage; Median gross rent: $504 per month; Rental vacancy rate: 0.0%

Health Insurance: 94.7% have insurance; 87.0% have private insurance; 22.5% have public insurance; 5.3% do not have insurance; 4.9% of children under 18 do not have insurance

Transportation: Commute: 91.2% car, 0.0% public transportation, 1.0% walk, 3.9% work from home; Mean travel time to work: 20.8 minutes

---

CLARENCE (town).
Covers a land area of 53.503 square miles and a water area of 0.132 square miles. Located at 43.02° N. Lat; 78.65° W. Long. Elevation is 738 feet.

Population: 31,376; Growth (since 2000): 20.1%; Density: 586.4 persons per square mile; Race: 92.2% White, 1.3% Black/African American, 4.9% Asian, 0.0% American Indian/Alaska Native, 0.2% Native Hawaiian/Other Pacific Islander, 1.1% Two or more races, 1.8% Hispanic of any race; Average household size: 2.68; Median age: 44.4; Age under 18: 25.0%; Age 65 and over: 15.9%; Males per 100 females: 94.2; Marriage status:

24.8% never married, 62.0% now married, 1.0% separated, 6.2% widowed, 7.0% divorced; Foreign born: 7.3%; Speak English only: 91.7%; With disability: 8.5%; Veterans: 7.1%; Ancestry: 31.8% German, 24.6% Italian, 19.6% Irish, 14.8% Polish, 8.8% English

Employment: 23.0% management, business, and financial, 4.6% computer, engineering, and science, 15.4% education, legal, community service, arts, and media, 9.8% healthcare practitioners, 14.0% service, 22.3% sales and office, 5.4% natural resources, construction, and maintenance, 5.6% production, transportation, and material moving

Income: Per capita: $43,841; Median household: $90,459; Average household: $117,313; Households with income of $100,000 or more: 44.4%; Poverty rate: 4.0%

Educational Attainment: High school diploma or higher: 96.3%; Bachelor's degree or higher: 49.5%; Graduate/professional degree or higher: 25.2%

School District(s)
Clarence Central SD (KG-12)
2014-15 Enrollment: 4,623 . . . . (716) 407-9102

Housing: Homeownership rate: 83.0%; Median home value: $247,800; Median year structure built: 1981; Homeowner vacancy rate: 0.6%; Median selected monthly owner costs: $1,806 with a mortgage, $674 without a mortgage; Median gross rent: $892 per month; Rental vacancy rate: 2.1%

Health Insurance: 96.4% have insurance; 87.0% have private insurance; 22.3% have public insurance; 3.6% do not have insurance; 2.5% of children under 18 do not have insurance

Transportation: Commute: 92.8% car, 0.5% public transportation, 0.9% walk, 5.1% work from home; Mean travel time to work: 20.8 minutes

Additional Information Contacts
Town of Clarence . . . . (716) 741-4715
http://clarence.ny.us

CLARENCE CENTER (CDP).
Covers a land area of 2.258 square miles and a water area of 0 square miles. Located at 43.01° N. Lat; 78.63° W. Long. Elevation is 633 feet.

Population: 2,151; Growth (since 2000): 23.1%; Density: 952.6 persons per square mile; Race: 94.6% White, 0.0% Black/African American, 4.6% Asian, 0.0% American Indian/Alaska Native, 0.0% Native Hawaiian/Other Pacific Islander, 0.7% Two or more races, 0.0% Hispanic of any race; Average household size: 2.80; Median age: 44.3; Age under 18: 27.9%; Age 65 and over: 6.9%; Males per 100 females: 96.4; Marriage status: 21.6% never married, 68.3% now married, 0.5% separated, 2.5% widowed, 7.6% divorced; Foreign born: 5.3%; Speak English only: 89.5%; With disability: 2.8%; Veterans: 5.5%; Ancestry: 44.5% German, 27.8% Irish, 15.0% Italian, 11.9% Polish, 8.4% English

Employment: 31.4% management, business, and financial, 4.7% computer, engineering, and science, 29.3% education, legal, community service, arts, and media, 3.9% healthcare practitioners, 13.8% service, 14.5% sales and office, 1.7% natural resources, construction, and maintenance, 0.7% production, transportation, and material moving

Income: Per capita: $42,867; Median household: $111,250; Average household: $119,545; Households with income of $100,000 or more: 58.0%; Poverty rate: 0.7%

Educational Attainment: High school diploma or higher: 98.8%; Bachelor's degree or higher: 68.8%; Graduate/professional degree or higher: 35.8%

School District(s)
Clarence Central SD (KG-12)
2014-15 Enrollment: 4,623 . . . . (716) 407-9102

Housing: Homeownership rate: 92.3%; Median home value: $247,900; Median year structure built: 1980; Homeowner vacancy rate: 0.0%; Median selected monthly owner costs: $1,649 with a mortgage, $652 without a mortgage; Median gross rent: $1,125 per month; Rental vacancy rate: 0.0%

Health Insurance: 100.0% have insurance; 97.6% have private insurance; 8.3% have public insurance; 0.0% do not have insurance; 0.0% of children under 18 do not have insurance

Transportation: Commute: 86.7% car, 1.0% public transportation, 3.5% walk, 8.8% work from home; Mean travel time to work: 20.4 minutes

---

COLDEN (town).
Covers a land area of 35.633 square miles and a water area of 0.089 square miles. Located at 42.65° N. Lat; 78.65° W. Long. Elevation is 1,079 feet.

Population: 3,270; Growth (since 2000): -1.6%; Density: 91.8 persons per square mile; Race: 98.6% White, 0.1% Black/African American, 0.4% Asian, 0.0% American Indian/Alaska Native, 0.0% Native Hawaiian/Other

Pacific Islander, 0.9% Two or more races, 0.0% Hispanic of any race; Average household size: 2.50; Median age: 45.7; Age under 18: 21.4%; Age 65 and over: 15.2%; Males per 100 females: 98.2; Marriage status: 24.0% never married, 62.2% now married, 0.3% separated, 3.4% widowed, 10.4% divorced; Foreign born: 2.9%; Speak English only: 97.4%; With disability: 8.0%; Veterans: 9.5%; Ancestry: 43.1% German, 23.6% Irish, 21.3% Polish, 12.6% English, 12.0% Italian

Employment: 19.6% management, business, and financial, 6.7% computer, engineering, and science, 10.3% education, legal, community service, arts, and media, 5.7% healthcare practitioners, 18.2% service, 14.2% sales and office, 10.5% natural resources, construction, and maintenance, 14.9% production, transportation, and material moving

Income: Per capita: $33,836; Median household: $63,952; Average household: $83,618; Households with income of $100,000 or more: 31.6%; Poverty rate: 6.9%

Educational Attainment: High school diploma or higher: 94.9%; Bachelor's degree or higher: 28.5%; Graduate/professional degree or higher: 13.6%

School District(s)

Springville-Griffith Institute Central SD (KG-12)

   2014-15 Enrollment: 1,815 . . . . (716) 592-3230

Housing: Homeownership rate: 86.8%; Median home value: $189,800; Median year structure built: 1966; Homeowner vacancy rate: 0.0%; Median selected monthly owner costs: $1,496 with a mortgage, $505 without a mortgage; Median gross rent: $594 per month; Rental vacancy rate: 15.3%

Health Insurance: 94.3% have insurance; 79.6% have private insurance; 26.5% have public insurance; 5.7% do not have insurance; 5.7% of children under 18 do not have insurance

Transportation: Commute: 96.0% car, 0.0% public transportation, 0.0% walk, 2.7% work from home; Mean travel time to work: 30.0 minutes

---

COLLINS (town). Covers a land area of 47.966 square miles and a water area of 0.174 square miles. Located at 42.49° N. Lat; 78.87° W. Long. Elevation is 879 feet.

Population: 6,548; Growth (since 2000): -21.2%; Density: 136.5 persons per square mile; Race: 74.0% White, 15.3% Black/African American, 1.1% Asian, 1.2% American Indian/Alaska Native, 0.0% Native Hawaiian/Other Pacific Islander, 2.8% Two or more races, 6.9% Hispanic of any race; Average household size: 2.38; Median age: 42.1; Age under 18: 12.1%; Age 65 and over: 11.5%; Males per 100 females: 228.6; Marriage status: 43.1% never married, 38.0% now married, 3.6% separated, 5.7% widowed, 13.3% divorced; Foreign born: 3.9%; Speak English only: 88.4%; With disability: 19.7%; Veterans: 7.7%; Ancestry: 33.7% German, 10.7% English, 9.8% Irish, 8.9% Italian, 8.5% Polish

Employment: 11.3% management, business, and financial, 4.6% computer, engineering, and science, 9.5% education, legal, community service, arts, and media, 5.0% healthcare practitioners, 23.6% service, 18.5% sales and office, 11.6% natural resources, construction, and maintenance, 16.0% production, transportation, and material moving

Income: Per capita: $17,813; Median household: $53,672; Average household: $67,606; Households with income of $100,000 or more: 18.4%; Poverty rate: 14.6%

Educational Attainment: High school diploma or higher: 80.1%; Bachelor's degree or higher: 12.8%; Graduate/professional degree or higher: 4.5%

Housing: Homeownership rate: 78.5%; Median home value: $97,400; Median year structure built: 1947; Homeowner vacancy rate: 0.0%; Median selected monthly owner costs: $1,039 with a mortgage, $424 without a mortgage; Median gross rent: $587 per month; Rental vacancy rate: 7.2%

Health Insurance: 95.1% have insurance; 69.3% have private insurance; 42.4% have public insurance; 4.9% do not have insurance; 0.0% of children under 18 do not have insurance

Transportation: Commute: 91.8% car, 0.9% public transportation, 2.9% walk, 3.8% work from home; Mean travel time to work: 24.4 minutes

Additional Information Contacts

Town of Collins . . . . (716) 532-4887
  http://www.townofcollins.com

COLLINS CENTER (unincorporated postal area)

ZCTA: 14035

  Covers a land area of 0.228 square miles and a water area of 0 square miles. Located at 42.49° N. Lat; 78.85° W. Long. Elevation is 1,102 feet.

  Population: 33; Growth (since 2000): n/a; Density: 144.4 persons per square mile; Race: 100.0% White, 0.0% Black/African American, 0.0% Asian, 0.0% American Indian/Alaska Native, 0.0% Native

Hawaiian/Other Pacific Islander, 0.0% Two or more races, 0.0% Hispanic of any race; Average household size: 2.20; Median age: 52.8; Age under 18: 18.2%; Age 65 and over: 45.5%; Males per 100 females: 98.4; Marriage status: 0.0% never married, 85.2% now married, 0.0% separated, 14.8% widowed, 0.0% divorced; Foreign born: 0.0%; Speak English only: 77.8%; With disability: 18.2%; Veterans: 18.5%; Ancestry: 54.5% Polish, 36.4% Irish, 33.3% English, 12.1% French

  Employment: 0.0% management, business, and financial, 50.0% computer, engineering, and science, 50.0% education, legal, community service, arts, and media, 0.0% healthcare practitioners, 0.0% service, 0.0% sales and office, 0.0% natural resources, construction, and maintenance, 0.0% production, transportation, and material moving

  Income: Per capita: $80,721; Median household: n/a; Average household: $177,033; Households with income of $100,000 or more: 40.0%; Poverty rate: 12.1%

  Educational Attainment: High school diploma or higher: 100.0%; Bachelor's degree or higher: 44.4%; Graduate/professional degree or higher: 22.2%

  Housing: Homeownership rate: 100.0%; Median home value: n/a; Median year structure built: Before 1940; Homeowner vacancy rate: 0.0%; Median selected monthly owner costs: n/a with a mortgage, n/a without a mortgage; Median gross rent: n/a per month; Rental vacancy rate: 0.0%

  Health Insurance: 100.0% have insurance; 87.9% have private insurance; 45.5% have public insurance; 0.0% do not have insurance; 0.0% of children under 18 do not have insurance

  Transportation: Commute: 100.0% car, 0.0% public transportation, 0.0% walk, 0.0% work from home; Mean travel time to work: 0.0 minutes

---

CONCORD (town). Covers a land area of 69.934 square miles and a water area of 0.160 square miles. Located at 42.55° N. Lat; 78.70° W. Long. Elevation is 1,352 feet.

Population: 8,547; Growth (since 2000): 0.2%; Density: 122.2 persons per square mile; Race: 96.4% White, 0.9% Black/African American, 0.6% Asian, 0.8% American Indian/Alaska Native, 0.0% Native Hawaiian/Other Pacific Islander, 1.0% Two or more races, 1.3% Hispanic of any race; Average household size: 2.25; Median age: 46.5; Age under 18: 21.7%; Age 65 and over: 19.8%; Males per 100 females: 98.0; Marriage status: 23.1% never married, 55.2% now married, 2.4% separated, 7.8% widowed, 13.9% divorced; Foreign born: 2.6%; Speak English only: 96.3%; With disability: 12.3%; Veterans: 11.8%; Ancestry: 38.5% German, 19.8% Irish, 15.9% Polish, 12.0% English, 9.7% Italian

Employment: 12.6% management, business, and financial, 2.3% computer, engineering, and science, 10.0% education, legal, community service, arts, and media, 7.7% healthcare practitioners, 20.2% service, 20.8% sales and office, 12.2% natural resources, construction, and maintenance, 14.1% production, transportation, and material moving

Income: Per capita: $27,360; Median household: $50,278; Average household: $61,876; Households with income of $100,000 or more: 18.0%; Poverty rate: 9.4%

Educational Attainment: High school diploma or higher: 93.1%; Bachelor's degree or higher: 20.3%; Graduate/professional degree or higher: 9.5%

Housing: Homeownership rate: 73.5%; Median home value: $132,800; Median year structure built: 1962; Homeowner vacancy rate: 0.0%; Median selected monthly owner costs: $1,225 with a mortgage, $499 without a mortgage; Median gross rent: $583 per month; Rental vacancy rate: 0.0%

Health Insurance: 95.1% have insurance; 75.7% have private insurance; 35.7% have public insurance; 4.9% do not have insurance; 1.7% of children under 18 do not have insurance

Transportation: Commute: 93.0% car, 0.0% public transportation, 2.7% walk, 4.1% work from home; Mean travel time to work: 24.0 minutes

Additional Information Contacts

Town of Concord . . . . (716) 592-4948
  http://www.townofconcordny.com

DEPEW (village). Covers a land area of 5.074 square miles and a water area of 0 square miles. Located at 42.91° N. Lat; 78.70° W. Long. Elevation is 673 feet.

History: Founded in 1892 as a village, it was named for Chauncey M. Depew (1834-1928), a Railroad executive and later a U.S. senator. Incorporated 1894.

Population: 15,227; Growth (since 2000): -8.4%; Density: 3,001.0 persons per square mile; Race: 96.0% White, 0.9% Black/African American, 0.9% Asian, 0.1% American Indian/Alaska Native, 0.0% Native Hawaiian/Other

Pacific Islander, 1.1% Two or more races, 2.8% Hispanic of any race; Average household size: 2.33; Median age: 38.6; Age under 18: 20.3%; Age 65 and over: 17.7%; Males per 100 females: 92.8; Marriage status: 31.6% never married, 51.0% now married, 1.9% separated, 7.8% widowed, 9.6% divorced; Foreign born: 3.3%; Speak English only: 95.3%; With disability: 11.9%; Veterans: 10.0%; Ancestry: 34.5% Polish, 32.1% German, 18.3% Italian, 16.6% Irish, 5.4% English

Employment: 12.6% management, business, and financial, 2.9% computer, engineering, and science, 7.8% education, legal, community service, arts, and media, 6.3% healthcare practitioners, 19.1% service, 30.2% sales and office, 7.6% natural resources, construction, and maintenance, 13.4% production, transportation, and material moving

Income: Per capita: $24,872; Median household: $50,317; Average household: $57,275; Households with income of $100,000 or more: 11.1%; Poverty rate: 10.4%

Educational Attainment: High school diploma or higher: 93.1%; Bachelor's degree or higher: 19.8%; Graduate/professional degree or higher: 6.3%

School District(s)

Depew Union Free SD (KG-12)

    2014-15 Enrollment: 1,853 . . . . (716) 686-5105

Lancaster Central SD (KG-12)

    2014-15 Enrollment: 5,820 . . . . (716) 686-3201

Housing: Homeownership rate: 73.2%; Median home value: $109,100; Median year structure built: 1959; Homeowner vacancy rate: 1.5%; Median selected monthly owner costs: $1,130 with a mortgage, $492 without a mortgage; Median gross rent: $753 per month; Rental vacancy rate: 1.1%

Health Insurance: 94.7% have insurance; 76.4% have private insurance; 36.2% have public insurance; 5.3% do not have insurance; 1.8% of children under 18 do not have insurance

Safety: Violent crime rate: 12.5 per 10,000 population; Property crime rate: 190.3 per 10,000 population

Transportation: Commute: 95.3% car, 0.5% public transportation, 1.2% walk, 1.4% work from home; Mean travel time to work: 20.1 minutes; Amtrak: Train service available.

Additional Information Contacts

Village of Depew . . . . (716) 683-1400

    http://www.villageofdepew.org

DERBY (unincorporated postal area)

ZCTA: 14047

Covers a land area of 13.137 square miles and a water area of 1.001 square miles. Located at 42.69° N. Lat; 78.99° W. Long. Elevation is 702 feet.

Population: 6,402; Growth (since 2000): -6.3%; Density: 487.3 persons per square mile; Race: 97.8% White, 0.3% Black/African American, 0.0% Asian, 0.2% American Indian/Alaska Native, 0.0% Native Hawaiian/Other Pacific Islander, 1.2% Two or more races, 2.1% Hispanic of any race; Average household size: 2.42; Median age: 42.8; Age under 18: 20.9%; Age 65 and over: 15.5%; Males per 100 females: 98.4; Marriage status: 34.9% never married, 50.5% now married, 1.7% separated, 6.7% widowed, 7.9% divorced; Foreign born: 1.7%; Speak English only: 96.7%; With disability: 11.8%; Veterans: 10.4%; Ancestry: 32.5% German, 22.2% Irish, 21.1% Polish, 20.6% Italian, 9.6% English

Employment: 10.3% management, business, and financial, 1.3% computer, engineering, and science, 7.7% education, legal, community service, arts, and media, 7.0% healthcare practitioners, 25.3% service, 26.3% sales and office, 7.7% natural resources, construction, and maintenance, 14.4% production, transportation, and material moving

Income: Per capita: $25,153; Median household: $58,148; Average household: $61,092; Households with income of $100,000 or more: 17.6%; Poverty rate: 12.6%

Educational Attainment: High school diploma or higher: 91.3%; Bachelor's degree or higher: 21.8%; Graduate/professional degree or higher: 8.6%

School District(s)

Evans-Brant Central SD (Lake Shore) (KG-12)

    2014-15 Enrollment: 2,499 . . . . (716) 926-2201

Housing: Homeownership rate: 86.4%; Median home value: $117,900; Median year structure built: 1971; Homeowner vacancy rate: 1.7%; Median selected monthly owner costs: $1,252 with a mortgage, $509 without a mortgage; Median gross rent: $742 per month; Rental vacancy rate: 0.0%

Health Insurance: 93.2% have insurance; 77.1% have private insurance; 31.0% have public insurance; 6.8% do not have insurance; 12.1% of children under 18 do not have insurance

Transportation: Commute: 95.2% car, 0.3% public transportation, 2.0% walk, 1.3% work from home; Mean travel time to work: 25.8 minutes

EAST AMHERST (unincorporated postal area)

ZCTA: 14051

Covers a land area of 16.336 square miles and a water area of 0.070 square miles. Located at 43.04° N. Lat; 78.70° W. Long. Elevation is 594 feet.

Population: 20,654; Growth (since 2000): 14.8%; Density: 1,264.3 persons per square mile; Race: 88.8% White, 1.3% Black/African American, 7.3% Asian, 0.4% American Indian/Alaska Native, 0.3% Native Hawaiian/Other Pacific Islander, 1.5% Two or more races, 2.3% Hispanic of any race; Average household size: 2.69; Median age: 44.1; Age under 18: 24.0%; Age 65 and over: 14.9%; Males per 100 females: 95.1; Marriage status: 23.5% never married, 65.4% now married, 1.0% separated, 4.4% widowed, 6.7% divorced; Foreign born: 11.3%; Speak English only: 87.5%; With disability: 6.6%; Veterans: 7.2%; Ancestry: 25.9% German, 25.1% Italian, 15.9% Irish, 14.4% Polish, 7.2% English

Employment: 22.4% management, business, and financial, 7.2% computer, engineering, and science, 13.8% education, legal, community service, arts, and media, 9.1% healthcare practitioners, 12.0% service, 27.5% sales and office, 3.6% natural resources, construction, and maintenance, 4.3% production, transportation, and material moving

Income: Per capita: $48,432; Median household: $107,500; Average household: $129,466; Households with income of $100,000 or more: 54.5%; Poverty rate: 2.8%

Educational Attainment: High school diploma or higher: 95.8%; Bachelor's degree or higher: 60.8%; Graduate/professional degree or higher: 33.9%

School District(s)

Williamsville Central SD (KG-12)

    2014-15 Enrollment: 10,166 . . . . (716) 626-8005

Housing: Homeownership rate: 88.8%; Median home value: $246,000; Median year structure built: 1984; Homeowner vacancy rate: 0.4%; Median selected monthly owner costs: $1,875 with a mortgage, $841 without a mortgage; Median gross rent: $1,413 per month; Rental vacancy rate: 0.0%

Health Insurance: 97.6% have insurance; 90.0% have private insurance; 21.1% have public insurance; 2.4% do not have insurance; 2.1% of children under 18 do not have insurance

Transportation: Commute: 94.1% car, 0.2% public transportation, 0.3% walk, 4.7% work from home; Mean travel time to work: 22.2 minutes

EAST AURORA (village). Covers a land area of 2.512 square miles and a water area of 0.011 square miles. Located at 42.77° N. Lat; 78.62° W. Long. Elevation is 919 feet.

Population: 6,251; Growth (since 2000): -6.3%; Density: 2,488.9 persons per square mile; Race: 97.1% White, 1.3% Black/African American, 0.1% Asian, 0.1% American Indian/Alaska Native, 0.0% Native Hawaiian/Other Pacific Islander, 1.0% Two or more races, 1.8% Hispanic of any race; Average household size: 2.32; Median age: 44.7; Age under 18: 23.7%; Age 65 and over: 19.2%; Males per 100 females: 85.7; Marriage status: 27.0% never married, 52.6% now married, 1.1% separated, 6.5% widowed, 13.9% divorced; Foreign born: 1.9%; Speak English only: 97.1%; With disability: 7.6%; Veterans: 7.3%; Ancestry: 38.6% German, 21.6% Irish, 19.6% English, 13.5% Italian, 10.8% Polish

Employment: 18.1% management, business, and financial, 5.6% computer, engineering, and science, 19.7% education, legal, community service, arts, and media, 7.0% healthcare practitioners, 13.9% service, 21.5% sales and office, 8.7% natural resources, construction, and maintenance, 5.5% production, transportation, and material moving

Income: Per capita: $35,743; Median household: $66,346; Average household: $84,072; Households with income of $100,000 or more: 28.4%; Poverty rate: 8.1%

Educational Attainment: High school diploma or higher: 93.8%; Bachelor's degree or higher: 49.0%; Graduate/professional degree or higher: 25.6%

School District(s)

East Aurora Union Free SD (KG-12)

    2014-15 Enrollment: 1,818 . . . . (716) 687-2302

Iroquois Central SD (KG-12)

    2014-15 Enrollment: 2,375 . . . . (716) 652-3000

Four-year College(s)

Christ the King Seminary (Private, Not-for-profit, Roman Catholic)
Fall 2014 Enrollment: 101 . . . . (716) 652-8900

Housing: Homeownership rate: 71.7%; Median home value: $175,100; Median year structure built: Before 1940; Homeowner vacancy rate: 0.8%; Median selected monthly owner costs: $1,570 with a mortgage, $619 without a mortgage; Median gross rent: $725 per month; Rental vacancy rate: 5.0%

Health Insurance: 95.0% have insurance; 83.4% have private insurance; 26.5% have public insurance; 5.0% do not have insurance; 4.8% of children under 18 do not have insurance

Newspapers: East Aurora Advertiser (weekly circulation 4,400); Elma Review (weekly circulation 1,200)

Transportation: Commute: 88.8% car, 0.2% public transportation, 3.0% walk, 6.5% work from home; Mean travel time to work: 21.4 minutes

Additional Information Contacts

Village of East Aurora . . . . (716) 652-6000
http://www.east-aurora.ny.us

EAST CONCORD (unincorporated postal area)

ZCTA: 14055

Covers a land area of 32.337 square miles and a water area of 0.034 square miles. Located at 42.56° N. Lat; 78.60° W. Long. Elevation is 1,457 feet.

Population: 1,622; Growth (since 2000): 10.4%; Density: 50.2 persons per square mile; Race: 99.2% White, 0.0% Black/African American, 0.0% Asian, 0.0% American Indian/Alaska Native, 0.0% Native Hawaiian/Other Pacific Islander, 0.8% Two or more races, 1.2% Hispanic of any race; Average household size: 2.56; Median age: 45.5; Age under 18: 19.4%; Age 65 and over: 14.5%; Males per 100 females: 100.1; Marriage status: 31.0% never married, 58.9% now married, 0.0% separated, 5.1% widowed, 5.0% divorced; Foreign born: 2.4%; Speak English only: 98.1%; With disability: 7.3%; Veterans: 9.1%; Ancestry: 42.6% German, 25.3% Irish, 15.6% Polish, 13.7% English, 10.5% Italian

Employment: 10.9% management, business, and financial, 1.9% computer, engineering, and science, 12.6% education, legal, community service, arts, and media, 12.8% healthcare practitioners, 11.2% service, 21.7% sales and office, 10.9% natural resources, construction, and maintenance, 18.0% production, transportation, and material moving

Income: Per capita: $29,154; Median household: $63,242; Average household: $74,566; Households with income of $100,000 or more: 23.4%; Poverty rate: 5.1%

Educational Attainment: High school diploma or higher: 93.0%; Bachelor's degree or higher: 23.3%; Graduate/professional degree or higher: 11.9%

Housing: Homeownership rate: 92.7%; Median home value: $158,100; Median year structure built: 1977; Homeowner vacancy rate: 0.0%; Median selected monthly owner costs: $1,226 with a mortgage, $520 without a mortgage; Median gross rent: $496 per month; Rental vacancy rate: 0.0%

Health Insurance: 96.4% have insurance; 79.5% have private insurance; 25.8% have public insurance; 3.6% do not have insurance; 0.0% of children under 18 do not have insurance

Transportation: Commute: 92.6% car, 0.0% public transportation, 2.9% walk, 3.5% work from home; Mean travel time to work: 28.9 minutes

---

EDEN (CDP). Covers a land area of 5.594 square miles and a water area of 0 square miles. Located at 42.65° N. Lat; 78.90° W. Long. Elevation is 820 feet.

Population: 3,271; Growth (since 2000): -8.6%; Density: 584.7 persons per square mile; Race: 99.8% White, 0.1% Black/African American, 0.0% Asian, 0.0% American Indian/Alaska Native, 0.0% Native Hawaiian/Other Pacific Islander, 0.0% Two or more races, 0.7% Hispanic of any race; Average household size: 2.53; Median age: 46.5; Age under 18: 22.6%; Age 65 and over: 14.4%; Males per 100 females: 100.5; Marriage status: 26.2% never married, 56.8% now married, 1.6% separated, 5.4% widowed, 11.6% divorced; Foreign born: 2.9%; Speak English only: 97.4%; With disability: 11.0%; Veterans: 11.0%; Ancestry: 35.3% German, 23.5% Irish, 14.7% Polish, 13.6% English, 13.2% Italian

Employment: 12.2% management, business, and financial, 3.7% computer, engineering, and science, 10.1% education, legal, community service, arts, and media, 9.9% healthcare practitioners, 16.8% service, 21.6% sales and office, 11.2% natural resources, construction, and maintenance, 14.5% production, transportation, and material moving

Income: Per capita: $28,522; Median household: $64,688; Average household: $72,524; Households with income of $100,000 or more: 28.0%; Poverty rate: 4.2%

Educational Attainment: High school diploma or higher: 95.2%; Bachelor's degree or higher: 26.9%; Graduate/professional degree or higher: 8.7%

School District(s)

Eden Central SD (PK-12)
2014-15 Enrollment: 1,500 . . . . (716) 992-3629

Housing: Homeownership rate: 86.2%; Median home value: $157,300; Median year structure built: 1958; Homeowner vacancy rate: 2.3%; Median selected monthly owner costs: $1,526 with a mortgage, $616 without a mortgage; Median gross rent: $553 per month; Rental vacancy rate: 0.0%

Health Insurance: 95.8% have insurance; 86.2% have private insurance; 23.2% have public insurance; 4.2% do not have insurance; 1.4% of children under 18 do not have insurance

Transportation: Commute: 95.7% car, 0.0% public transportation, 2.4% walk, 1.3% work from home; Mean travel time to work: 25.9 minutes

---

EDEN (town). Covers a land area of 39.790 square miles and a water area of 0.069 square miles. Located at 42.66° N. Lat; 78.88° W. Long. Elevation is 820 feet.

History: The "Original American Kazoo" is still made here, and though the factory itself may no longer be toured, there is still a visitors center that explains modern production methods as well as West African origins of the instrument. Established in 1916, this is now the world's only metal kazoo factory.

Population: 7,691; Growth (since 2000): -4.8%; Density: 193.3 persons per square mile; Race: 99.8% White, 0.1% Black/African American, 0.0% Asian, 0.0% American Indian/Alaska Native, 0.0% Native Hawaiian/Other Pacific Islander, 0.0% Two or more races, 1.1% Hispanic of any race; Average household size: 2.50; Median age: 48.6; Age under 18: 19.3%; Age 65 and over: 17.7%; Males per 100 females: 100.4; Marriage status: 25.2% never married, 56.5% now married, 1.4% separated, 7.9% widowed, 10.4% divorced; Foreign born: 1.9%; Speak English only: 97.6%; With disability: 13.6%; Veterans: 11.2%; Ancestry: 38.2% German, 22.5% Irish, 18.4% Polish, 15.2% Italian, 12.3% English

Employment: 13.2% management, business, and financial, 4.9% computer, engineering, and science, 8.1% education, legal, community service, arts, and media, 8.7% healthcare practitioners, 13.7% service, 21.7% sales and office, 13.2% natural resources, construction, and maintenance, 16.5% production, transportation, and material moving

Income: Per capita: $28,442; Median household: $61,064; Average household: $70,883; Households with income of $100,000 or more: 26.5%; Poverty rate: 4.2%

Educational Attainment: High school diploma or higher: 93.3%; Bachelor's degree or higher: 24.8%; Graduate/professional degree or higher: 8.5%

School District(s)

Eden Central SD (PK-12)
2014-15 Enrollment: 1,500 . . . . (716) 992-3629

Housing: Homeownership rate: 87.5%; Median home value: $160,000; Median year structure built: 1958; Homeowner vacancy rate: 1.3%; Median selected monthly owner costs: $1,407 with a mortgage, $592 without a mortgage; Median gross rent: $564 per month; Rental vacancy rate: 0.0%

Health Insurance: 95.5% have insurance; 85.5% have private insurance; 26.5% have public insurance; 4.5% do not have insurance; 1.1% of children under 18 do not have insurance

Safety: Violent crime rate: 1.3 per 10,000 population; Property crime rate: 32.4 per 10,000 population

Transportation: Commute: 96.0% car, 0.0% public transportation, 1.4% walk, 1.8% work from home; Mean travel time to work: 30.2 minutes

Additional Information Contacts

Town of Eden . . . . (716) 992-3408
http://www.edenny.org

EGGERTSVILLE (CDP). Covers a land area of 2.851 square miles and a water area of 0.001 square miles. Located at 42.97° N. Lat; 78.81° W. Long. Elevation is 653 feet.

Population: 15,675; Growth (since 2000): n/a; Density: 5,497.4 persons per square mile; Race: 75.4% White, 15.2% Black/African American, 6.5% Asian, 0.3% American Indian/Alaska Native, 0.0% Native Hawaiian/Other Pacific Islander, 1.9% Two or more races, 1.1% Hispanic of any race; Average household size: 2.36; Median age: 40.0; Age under 18: 22.2%; Age 65 and over: 15.7%; Males per 100 females: 92.2; Marriage status:

34.1% never married, 51.2% now married, 2.4% separated, 5.3% widowed, 9.4% divorced; Foreign born: 12.7%; Speak English only: 86.8%; With disability: 9.8%; Veterans: 6.0%; Ancestry: 24.0% German, 19.4% Irish, 17.2% Italian, 9.7% Polish, 8.9% English

Employment: 15.4% management, business, and financial, 6.8% computer, engineering, and science, 19.9% education, legal, community service, arts, and media, 7.1% healthcare practitioners, 16.0% service, 22.7% sales and office, 4.6% natural resources, construction, and maintenance, 7.5% production, transportation, and material moving

Income: Per capita: $36,279; Median household: $63,964; Average household: $84,838; Households with income of $100,000 or more: 29.2%; Poverty rate: 12.9%

Educational Attainment: High school diploma or higher: 94.5%; Bachelor's degree or higher: 51.9%; Graduate/professional degree or higher: 27.9%

Housing: Homeownership rate: 72.8%; Median home value: $130,500; Median year structure built: 1952; Homeowner vacancy rate: 0.3%; Median selected monthly owner costs: $1,287 with a mortgage, $548 without a mortgage; Median gross rent: $772 per month; Rental vacancy rate: 0.0%

Health Insurance: 95.0% have insurance; 76.9% have private insurance; 32.3% have public insurance; 5.0% do not have insurance; 1.9% of children under 18 do not have insurance

Transportation: Commute: 85.2% car, 2.3% public transportation, 5.9% walk, 3.6% work from home; Mean travel time to work: 16.1 minutes

ELMA (town). Covers a land area of 34.517 square miles and a water area of 0.011 square miles. Located at 42.83° N. Lat; 78.65° W. Long. Elevation is 712 feet.

Population: 11,610; Growth (since 2000): 2.7%; Density: 336.4 persons per square mile; Race: 98.5% White, 0.0% Black/African American, 0.8% Asian, 0.0% American Indian/Alaska Native, 0.0% Native Hawaiian/Other Pacific Islander, 0.0% Two or more races, 0.7% Hispanic of any race; Average household size: 2.41; Median age: 50.6; Age under 18: 16.5%; Age 65 and over: 22.1%; Males per 100 females: 98.8; Marriage status: 22.4% never married, 62.0% now married, 0.5% separated, 6.3% widowed, 9.2% divorced; Foreign born: 3.5%; Speak English only: 95.3%; With disability: 10.7%; Veterans: 11.8%; Ancestry: 34.0% German, 29.4% Polish, 19.3% Italian, 14.9% Irish, 7.5% English

Employment: 16.1% management, business, and financial, 4.8% computer, engineering, and science, 13.5% education, legal, community service, arts, and media, 10.0% healthcare practitioners, 15.9% service, 20.4% sales and office, 9.8% natural resources, construction, and maintenance, 9.6% production, transportation, and material moving

Income: Per capita: $38,139; Median household: $78,424; Average household: $90,825; Households with income of $100,000 or more: 34.1%; Poverty rate: 2.9%

Educational Attainment: High school diploma or higher: 96.7%; Bachelor's degree or higher: 37.5%; Graduate/professional degree or higher: 17.9%

School District(s)
Iroquois Central SD (KG-12)
   2014-15 Enrollment: 2,375 . . . . (716) 652-3000

Housing: Homeownership rate: 91.6%; Median home value: $217,800; Median year structure built: 1966; Homeowner vacancy rate: 0.0%; Median selected monthly owner costs: $1,529 with a mortgage, $594 without a mortgage; Median gross rent: $689 per month; Rental vacancy rate: 0.0%

Health Insurance: 94.4% have insurance; 84.8% have private insurance; 27.8% have public insurance; 5.6% do not have insurance; 2.9% of children under 18 do not have insurance

Transportation: Commute: 93.7% car, 0.2% public transportation, 0.8% walk, 4.9% work from home; Mean travel time to work: 23.4 minutes

Additional Information Contacts
Town of Elma . . . . (716) 652-3260
  http://www.elmanewyork.com

ELMA CENTER (CDP). Covers a land area of 6.253 square miles and a water area of 0 square miles. Located at 42.83° N. Lat; 78.63° W. Long. Elevation is 804 feet.

Population: 2,639; Growth (since 2000): 5.9%; Density: 422.0 persons per square mile; Race: 99.3% White, 0.1% Black/African American, 0.6% Asian, 0.0% American Indian/Alaska Native, 0.0% Native Hawaiian/Other Pacific Islander, 0.0% Two or more races, 0.0% Hispanic of any race; Average household size: 2.44; Median age: 52.7; Age under 18: 15.0%; Age 65 and over: 28.2%; Males per 100 females: 93.9; Marriage status: 19.2% never married, 60.5% now married, 0.7% separated, 10.5%

widowed, 9.9% divorced; Foreign born: 2.4%; Speak English only: 97.1%; With disability: 11.6%; Veterans: 14.3%; Ancestry: 37.1% German, 28.1% Polish, 28.0% Italian, 11.5% Irish, 7.0% English

Employment: 21.9% management, business, and financial, 0.8% computer, engineering, and science, 14.4% education, legal, community service, arts, and media, 9.2% healthcare practitioners, 5.2% service, 22.4% sales and office, 18.3% natural resources, construction, and maintenance, 7.7% production, transportation, and material moving

Income: Per capita: $35,907; Median household: $87,708; Average household: $86,491; Households with income of $100,000 or more: 33.4%; Poverty rate: 3.3%

Educational Attainment: High school diploma or higher: 96.3%; Bachelor's degree or higher: 31.9%; Graduate/professional degree or higher: 15.7%

Housing: Homeownership rate: 95.5%; Median home value: $254,100; Median year structure built: 1970; Homeowner vacancy rate: 0.0%; Median selected monthly owner costs: $1,639 with a mortgage, $629 without a mortgage; Median gross rent: $844 per month; Rental vacancy rate: 0.0%

Health Insurance: 98.3% have insurance; 89.0% have private insurance; 32.5% have public insurance; 1.7% do not have insurance; 0.0% of children under 18 do not have insurance

Transportation: Commute: 97.9% car, 0.0% public transportation, 0.0% walk, 2.1% work from home; Mean travel time to work: 20.5 minutes

EVANS (town). Covers a land area of 41.530 square miles and a water area of 0.032 square miles. Located at 42.65° N. Lat; 79.00° W. Long.

Population: 16,318; Growth (since 2000): -7.3%; Density: 392.9 persons per square mile; Race: 96.6% White, 0.5% Black/African American, 0.3% Asian, 0.1% American Indian/Alaska Native, 0.0% Native Hawaiian/Other Pacific Islander, 2.2% Two or more races, 1.7% Hispanic of any race; Average household size: 2.36; Median age: 44.9; Age under 18: 19.5%; Age 65 and over: 17.7%; Males per 100 females: 96.6; Marriage status: 31.4% never married, 51.2% now married, 1.3% separated, 7.4% widowed, 10.0% divorced; Foreign born: 2.1%; Speak English only: 97.2%; With disability: 14.3%; Veterans: 10.3%; Ancestry: 31.3% German, 21.7% Polish, 20.8% Irish, 20.5% Italian, 8.8% English

Employment: 9.3% management, business, and financial, 2.9% computer, engineering, and science, 7.5% education, legal, community service, arts, and media, 7.6% healthcare practitioners, 20.6% service, 27.8% sales and office, 8.4% natural resources, construction, and maintenance, 15.8% production, transportation, and material moving

Income: Per capita: $27,314; Median household: $54,516; Average household: $64,167; Households with income of $100,000 or more: 18.7%; Poverty rate: 10.9%

Educational Attainment: High school diploma or higher: 93.1%; Bachelor's degree or higher: 20.7%; Graduate/professional degree or higher: 8.0%

Housing: Homeownership rate: 84.2%; Median home value: $108,400; Median year structure built: 1956; Homeowner vacancy rate: 0.8%; Median selected monthly owner costs: $1,209 with a mortgage, $520 without a mortgage; Median gross rent: $749 per month; Rental vacancy rate: 7.2%

Health Insurance: 92.0% have insurance; 75.6% have private insurance; 33.1% have public insurance; 8.0% do not have insurance; 10.7% of children under 18 do not have insurance

Safety: Violent crime rate: 12.3 per 10,000 population; Property crime rate: 140.6 per 10,000 population

Transportation: Commute: 95.9% car, 0.2% public transportation, 1.6% walk, 1.8% work from home; Mean travel time to work: 26.9 minutes

Additional Information Contacts
Town of Evans . . . . (716) 549-8787
  http://www.townofevans.org

FARNHAM (village). Covers a land area of 1.207 square miles and a water area of 0 square miles. Located at 42.60° N. Lat; 79.08° W. Long. Elevation is 640 feet.

Population: 405; Growth (since 2000): 25.8%; Density: 335.6 persons per square mile; Race: 93.1% White, 1.0% Black/African American, 0.2% Asian, 4.7% American Indian/Alaska Native, 0.0% Native Hawaiian/Other Pacific Islander, 1.0% Two or more races, 1.7% Hispanic of any race; Average household size: 2.61; Median age: 39.4; Age under 18: 18.3%; Age 65 and over: 8.1%; Males per 100 females: 94.9; Marriage status: 30.4% never married, 54.9% now married, 0.0% separated, 7.3% widowed, 7.3% divorced; Foreign born: 1.5%; Speak English only: 99.2%; With disability: 14.1%; Veterans: 4.8%; Ancestry: 31.6% Irish, 30.6% German, 25.9% Italian, 12.6% Polish, 7.7% English

Employment: 12.3% management, business, and financial, 4.7% computer, engineering, and science, 3.8% education, legal, community service, arts, and media, 9.0% healthcare practitioners, 17.0% service, 14.6% sales and office, 9.0% natural resources, construction, and maintenance, 29.7% production, transportation, and material moving
Income: Per capita: $24,949; Median household: $61,042; Average household: $64,946; Households with income of $100,000 or more: 21.6%; Poverty rate: 22.0%
Educational Attainment: High school diploma or higher: 87.5%; Bachelor's degree or higher: 9.0%; Graduate/professional degree or higher: 3.1%
Housing: Homeownership rate: 76.4%; Median home value: $86,300; Median year structure built: Before 1940; Homeowner vacancy rate: 0.0%; Median selected monthly owner costs: $1,055 with a mortgage, $543 without a mortgage; Median gross rent: $785 per month; Rental vacancy rate: 16.7%
Health Insurance: 77.3% have insurance; 62.5% have private insurance; 21.2% have public insurance; 22.7% do not have insurance; 32.4% of children under 18 do not have insurance
Transportation: Commute: 97.1% car, 0.0% public transportation, 0.0% walk, 2.9% work from home; Mean travel time to work: 30.8 minutes

---

GETZVILLE (unincorporated postal area)
ZCTA: 14068
Covers a land area of 3.460 square miles and a water area of 0 square miles. Located at 43.03° N. Lat; 78.76° W. Long. Elevation is 584 feet.
Population: 7,130; Growth (since 2000): -28.9%; Density: 2,060.9 persons per square mile; Race: 87.1% White, 3.8% Black/African American, 8.2% Asian, 0.0% American Indian/Alaska Native, 0.0% Native Hawaiian/Other Pacific Islander, 0.7% Two or more races, 2.7% Hispanic of any race; Average household size: 2.34; Median age: 49.0; Age under 18: 21.8%; Age 65 and over: 28.1%; Males per 100 females: 81.7; Marriage status: 25.0% never married, 53.1% now married, 1.3% separated, 13.2% widowed, 8.7% divorced; Foreign born: 12.4%; Speak English only: 84.0%; With disability: 15.2%; Veterans: 8.7%; Ancestry: 26.8% German, 21.4% Italian, 13.7% Polish, 10.6% Irish, 9.9% English
Employment: 25.6% management, business, and financial, 5.7% computer, engineering, and science, 15.2% education, legal, community service, arts, and media, 10.6% healthcare practitioners, 12.1% service, 25.8% sales and office, 2.0% natural resources, construction, and maintenance, 3.1% production, transportation, and material moving
Income: Per capita: $35,958; Median household: $59,262; Average household: $87,336; Households with income of $100,000 or more: 34.2%; Poverty rate: 10.0%
Educational Attainment: High school diploma or higher: 92.6%; Bachelor's degree or higher: 43.2%; Graduate/professional degree or higher: 23.7%

Four-year College(s)
Bryant & Stratton College-Amherst (Private, For-profit)
    Fall 2014 Enrollment: 356 . . . . (716) 625-6300
    2013-14 Tuition: In-state $15,678; Out-of-state $15,678
ITT Technical Institute-Getzville (Private, For-profit)
    Fall 2014 Enrollment: 326 . . . . (716) 689-2200
    2013-14 Tuition: In-state $18,048; Out-of-state $18,048
Two-year College(s)
Bryant & Stratton College-Amherst (Private, For-profit)
    Fall 2014 Enrollment: 356 . . . . (716) 625-6300
    2013-14 Tuition: In-state $15,678; Out-of-state $15,678
ITT Technical Institute-Getzville (Private, For-profit)
    Fall 2014 Enrollment: 326 . . . . (716) 689-2200
    2013-14 Tuition: In-state $18,048; Out-of-state $18,048
Vocational/Technical School(s)
Bryant & Stratton College-Amherst (Private, For-profit)
    Fall 2014 Enrollment: 356 . . . . (716) 625-6300
    2015-16 Tuition: In-state $15,678; Out-of-state $15,678
ITT Technical Institute-Getzville (Private, For-profit)
    Fall 2014 Enrollment: 326 . . . . (716) 689-2200
    2015-16 Tuition: In-state $18,048; Out-of-state $18,048
Housing: Homeownership rate: 71.5%; Median home value: $219,800; Median year structure built: 1985; Homeowner vacancy rate: 0.0%; Median selected monthly owner costs: $1,834 with a mortgage, $670 without a mortgage; Median gross rent: $1,029 per month; Rental vacancy rate: 0.0%

Health Insurance: 98.6% have insurance; 83.2% have private insurance; 35.0% have public insurance; 1.4% do not have insurance; 1.4% of children under 18 do not have insurance
Transportation: Commute: 92.8% car, 1.5% public transportation, 1.9% walk, 3.1% work from home; Mean travel time to work: 18.6 minutes

---

GLENWOOD (unincorporated postal area)
ZCTA: 14069
Covers a land area of 8.515 square miles and a water area of 0.012 square miles. Located at 42.62° N. Lat; 78.64° W. Long. Elevation is 1,191 feet.
Population: 816; Growth (since 2000): 3.9%; Density: 95.8 persons per square mile; Race: 99.8% White, 0.2% Black/African American, 0.0% Asian, 0.0% American Indian/Alaska Native, 0.0% Native Hawaiian/Other Pacific Islander, 0.0% Two or more races, 0.0% Hispanic of any race; Average household size: 2.20; Median age: 52.5; Age under 18: 22.2%; Age 65 and over: 16.8%; Males per 100 females: 105.9; Marriage status: 13.2% never married, 67.5% now married, 2.6% separated, 3.4% widowed, 15.9% divorced; Foreign born: 1.5%; Speak English only: 98.4%; With disability: 12.0%; Veterans: 12.4%; Ancestry: 39.3% German, 25.9% Irish, 19.1% Polish, 17.4% Italian, 8.5% American
Employment: 5.8% management, business, and financial, 2.3% computer, engineering, and science, 18.8% education, legal, community service, arts, and media, 5.3% healthcare practitioners, 10.2% service, 22.6% sales and office, 21.3% natural resources, construction, and maintenance, 13.7% production, transportation, and material moving
Income: Per capita: $26,718; Median household: $41,042; Average household: $58,429; Households with income of $100,000 or more: 16.0%; Poverty rate: 1.3%
Educational Attainment: High school diploma or higher: 92.7%; Bachelor's degree or higher: 28.2%; Graduate/professional degree or higher: 12.7%
Housing: Homeownership rate: 79.9%; Median home value: $185,500; Median year structure built: 1973; Homeowner vacancy rate: 0.0%; Median selected monthly owner costs: $1,415 with a mortgage, $590 without a mortgage; Median gross rent: $405 per month; Rental vacancy rate: 0.0%
Health Insurance: 99.3% have insurance; 83.3% have private insurance; 36.6% have public insurance; 0.7% do not have insurance; 0.0% of children under 18 do not have insurance
Transportation: Commute: 98.7% car, 0.0% public transportation, 0.0% walk, 0.0% work from home; Mean travel time to work: 30.5 minutes

---

GRAND ISLAND (town). Covers a land area of 28.273 square miles and a water area of 5.020 square miles. Located at 43.02° N. Lat; 78.96° W. Long.
Population: 20,679; Growth (since 2000): 11.1%; Density: 731.4 persons per square mile; Race: 93.7% White, 1.0% Black/African American, 2.2% Asian, 0.1% American Indian/Alaska Native, 0.0% Native Hawaiian/Other Pacific Islander, 1.5% Two or more races, 3.5% Hispanic of any race; Average household size: 2.61; Median age: 41.6; Age under 18: 23.1%; Age 65 and over: 15.3%; Males per 100 females: 97.3; Marriage status: 25.8% never married, 60.4% now married, 1.6% separated, 4.3% widowed, 9.5% divorced; Foreign born: 7.6%; Speak English only: 91.8%; With disability: 10.7%; Veterans: 9.2%; Ancestry: 26.6% German, 22.9% Italian, 17.6% Irish, 14.2% Polish, 11.5% English
Employment: 18.4% management, business, and financial, 6.2% computer, engineering, and science, 13.2% education, legal, community service, arts, and media, 7.0% healthcare practitioners, 13.1% service, 25.2% sales and office, 5.1% natural resources, construction, and maintenance, 11.8% production, transportation, and material moving
Income: Per capita: $34,218; Median household: $78,597; Average household: $88,725; Households with income of $100,000 or more: 37.8%; Poverty rate: 6.9%
Educational Attainment: High school diploma or higher: 95.6%; Bachelor's degree or higher: 41.8%; Graduate/professional degree or higher: 19.8%

School District(s)
Grand Island Central SD (PK-12)
    2014-15 Enrollment: 3,034 . . . . (716) 773-8801
Housing: Homeownership rate: 80.9%; Median home value: $181,900; Median year structure built: 1973; Homeowner vacancy rate: 0.9%; Median selected monthly owner costs: $1,580 with a mortgage, $674 without a mortgage; Median gross rent: $915 per month; Rental vacancy rate: 2.6%

Health Insurance: 94.4% have insurance; 83.0% have private insurance; 25.8% have public insurance; 5.6% do not have insurance; 2.4% of children under 18 do not have insurance
Newspapers: Island Dispatch (weekly circulation 1,200)
Transportation: Commute: 94.7% car, 0.4% public transportation, 0.4% walk, 3.2% work from home; Mean travel time to work: 20.6 minutes
Additional Information Contacts
Town of Grand Island . . . . (716) 773-9600
   http://www.gigov.com

GRANDYLE VILLAGE (CDP). Covers a land area of 1.883 square miles and a water area of 0 square miles. Located at 42.99° N. Lat; 78.95° W. Long. Elevation is 594 feet.
Population: 4,812; Growth (since 2000): n/a; Density: 2,555.6 persons per square mile; Race: 91.7% White, 0.3% Black/African American, 1.4% Asian, 0.0% American Indian/Alaska Native, 0.0% Native Hawaiian/Other Pacific Islander, 1.1% Two or more races, 7.6% Hispanic of any race; Average household size: 2.63; Median age: 40.3; Age under 18: 26.4%; Age 65 and over: 13.7%; Males per 100 females: 93.7; Marriage status: 25.8% never married, 56.5% now married, 0.4% separated, 4.9% widowed, 12.8% divorced; Foreign born: 8.6%; Speak English only: 90.0%; With disability: 9.0%; Veterans: 7.7%; Ancestry: 21.1% Italian, 20.7% Irish, 19.9% German, 14.0% English, 11.4% Polish
Employment: 18.4% management, business, and financial, 4.1% computer, engineering, and science, 10.0% education, legal, community service, arts, and media, 4.4% healthcare practitioners, 15.9% service, 26.2% sales and office, 4.7% natural resources, construction, and maintenance, 16.3% production, transportation, and material moving
Income: Per capita: $28,648; Median household: $67,868; Average household: $74,847; Households with income of $100,000 or more: 28.4%; Poverty rate: 10.8%
Educational Attainment: High school diploma or higher: 93.9%; Bachelor's degree or higher: 34.5%; Graduate/professional degree or higher: 12.6%
Housing: Homeownership rate: 84.5%; Median home value: $132,000; Median year structure built: 1958; Homeowner vacancy rate: 3.7%; Median selected monthly owner costs: $1,359 with a mortgage, $562 without a mortgage; Median gross rent: $963 per month; Rental vacancy rate: 0.0%
Health Insurance: 92.4% have insurance; 75.2% have private insurance; 28.6% have public insurance; 7.6% do not have insurance; 2.3% of children under 18 do not have insurance
Transportation: Commute: 95.0% car, 0.0% public transportation, 1.4% walk, 3.0% work from home; Mean travel time to work: 18.2 minutes

HAMBURG (town). Covers a land area of 41.321 square miles and a water area of 0.028 square miles. Located at 42.74° N. Lat; 78.86° W. Long. Elevation is 820 feet.
History: Seat of Hilbert College. Settled c.1808, incorporated 1874.
Population: 57,712; Growth (since 2000): 2.6%; Density: 1,396.7 persons per square mile; Race: 96.0% White, 1.3% Black/African American, 0.4% Asian, 0.2% American Indian/Alaska Native, 0.0% Native Hawaiian/Other Pacific Islander, 1.4% Two or more races, 2.4% Hispanic of any race; Average household size: 2.39; Median age: 42.5; Age under 18: 20.6%; Age 65 and over: 17.0%; Males per 100 females: 92.1; Marriage status: 29.2% never married, 52.2% now married, 1.3% separated, 7.1% widowed, 11.4% divorced; Foreign born: 2.9%; Speak English only: 96.0%; With disability: 10.8%; Veterans: 9.1%; Ancestry: 31.4% German, 24.6% Irish, 23.7% Polish, 16.4% Italian, 7.6% English
Employment: 13.7% management, business, and financial, 4.4% computer, engineering, and science, 11.5% education, legal, community service, arts, and media, 7.3% healthcare practitioners, 18.9% service, 25.3% sales and office, 7.6% natural resources, construction, and maintenance, 11.4% production, transportation, and material moving
Income: Per capita: $31,766; Median household: $62,383; Average household: $75,265; Households with income of $100,000 or more: 26.1%; Poverty rate: 7.9%
Educational Attainment: High school diploma or higher: 93.6%; Bachelor's degree or higher: 30.7%; Graduate/professional degree or higher: 12.5%

School District(s)
Frontier Central SD (PK-12)
   2014-15 Enrollment: 5,006 . . . . (716) 926-1711
Hamburg Central SD (PK-12)
   2014-15 Enrollment: 3,703 . . . . (716) 646-3220

Hopevale Union Free SD At Hamburg (09-12)
   2014-15 Enrollment: n/a . . . . (716) 648-1930
Randolph Academy Union Free SD (KG-12)
   2014-15 Enrollment: 37 . . . . (716) 358-6866
Four-year College(s)
Hilbert College (Private, Not-for-profit, Roman Catholic)
   Fall 2014 Enrollment: 1,012 . . . . (716) 649-7900
   2015-16 Tuition: In-state $20,700; Out-of-state $20,700
Housing: Homeownership rate: 73.2%; Median home value: $145,600; Median year structure built: 1968; Homeowner vacancy rate: 0.4%; Median selected monthly owner costs: $1,351 with a mortgage, $537 without a mortgage; Median gross rent: $775 per month; Rental vacancy rate: 3.5%
Health Insurance: 96.1% have insurance; 81.6% have private insurance; 28.9% have public insurance; 3.9% do not have insurance; 2.5% of children under 18 do not have insurance
Safety: Violent crime rate: 5.9 per 10,000 population; Property crime rate: 197.6 per 10,000 population
Newspapers: Sun & Erie Co. Independent (weekly circulation 10,000)
Transportation: Commute: 94.1% car, 0.8% public transportation, 1.8% walk, 2.2% work from home; Mean travel time to work: 22.4 minutes
Additional Information Contacts
Town of Hamburg . . . . (716) 649-6111
   http://www.townofhamburgny.com

HAMBURG (village). Covers a land area of 2.486 square miles and a water area of 0 square miles. Located at 42.72° N. Lat; 78.83° W. Long. Elevation is 820 feet.
Population: 9,521; Growth (since 2000): -5.9%; Density: 3,829.8 persons per square mile; Race: 95.6% White, 0.4% Black/African American, 1.0% Asian, 0.0% American Indian/Alaska Native, 0.0% Native Hawaiian/Other Pacific Islander, 2.0% Two or more races, 4.8% Hispanic of any race; Average household size: 2.32; Median age: 40.7; Age under 18: 22.7%; Age 65 and over: 18.4%; Males per 100 females: 90.1; Marriage status: 26.0% never married, 54.0% now married, 1.0% separated, 7.8% widowed, 12.3% divorced; Foreign born: 1.6%; Speak English only: 96.0%; With disability: 9.6%; Veterans: 10.3%; Ancestry: 30.6% German, 24.9% Irish, 24.2% Polish, 14.0% Italian, 7.6% English
Employment: 13.5% management, business, and financial, 6.7% computer, engineering, and science, 14.2% education, legal, community service, arts, and media, 9.2% healthcare practitioners, 16.3% service, 24.2% sales and office, 5.5% natural resources, construction, and maintenance, 10.3% production, transportation, and material moving
Income: Per capita: $32,796; Median household: $66,426; Average household: $75,475; Households with income of $100,000 or more: 27.3%; Poverty rate: 5.6%
Educational Attainment: High school diploma or higher: 95.8%; Bachelor's degree or higher: 40.0%; Graduate/professional degree or higher: 16.4%
School District(s)
Frontier Central SD (PK-12)
   2014-15 Enrollment: 5,006 . . . . (716) 926-1711
Hamburg Central SD (PK-12)
   2014-15 Enrollment: 3,703 . . . . (716) 646-3220
Hopevale Union Free SD At Hamburg (09-12)
   2014-15 Enrollment: n/a . . . . (716) 648-1930
Randolph Academy Union Free SD (KG-12)
   2014-15 Enrollment: 37 . . . . (716) 358-6866
Four-year College(s)
Hilbert College (Private, Not-for-profit, Roman Catholic)
   Fall 2014 Enrollment: 1,012 . . . . (716) 649-7900
   2015-16 Tuition: In-state $20,700; Out-of-state $20,700
Housing: Homeownership rate: 66.4%; Median home value: $149,100; Median year structure built: 1954; Homeowner vacancy rate: 0.0%; Median selected monthly owner costs: $1,367 with a mortgage, $631 without a mortgage; Median gross rent: $804 per month; Rental vacancy rate: 0.0%
Health Insurance: 96.4% have insurance; 82.5% have private insurance; 32.8% have public insurance; 3.6% do not have insurance; 0.8% of children under 18 do not have insurance
Safety: Violent crime rate: 5.2 per 10,000 population; Property crime rate: 128.1 per 10,000 population
Newspapers: Sun & Erie Co. Independent (weekly circulation 10,000)
Transportation: Commute: 92.0% car, 0.6% public transportation, 3.6% walk, 1.8% work from home; Mean travel time to work: 20.4 minutes

Additional Information Contacts

Village of Hamburg . . . . (716) 649-0200
  http://www.villagehamburg.com

HARRIS HILL (CDP). Covers a land area of 4.041 square miles and a water area of 0 square miles. Located at 42.97° N. Lat; 78.68° W. Long. Elevation is 728 feet.
Population: 5,499; Growth (since 2000): 12.7%; Density: 1,361.0 persons per square mile; Race: 90.8% White, 3.9% Black/African American, 3.3% Asian, 0.3% American Indian/Alaska Native, 0.0% Native Hawaiian/Other Pacific Islander, 1.8% Two or more races, 2.1% Hispanic of any race; Average household size: 2.52; Median age: 44.9; Age under 18: 22.9%; Age 65 and over: 18.1%; Males per 100 females: 93.2; Marriage status: 26.6% never married, 56.9% now married, 1.2% separated, 7.5% widowed, 9.1% divorced; Foreign born: 6.2%; Speak English only: 94.4%; With disability: 9.3%; Veterans: 4.5%; Ancestry: 37.8% German, 27.1% Italian, 27.0% Irish, 12.0% Polish, 7.8% English
Employment: 19.4% management, business, and financial, 6.7% computer, engineering, and science, 12.1% education, legal, community service, arts, and media, 14.7% healthcare practitioners, 18.9% service, 20.2% sales and office, 3.3% natural resources, construction, and maintenance, 4.8% production, transportation, and material moving
Income: Per capita: $38,532; Median household: $86,574; Average household: $95,787; Households with income of $100,000 or more: 37.9%; Poverty rate: 3.3%
Educational Attainment: High school diploma or higher: 97.9%; Bachelor's degree or higher: 44.8%; Graduate/professional degree or higher: 22.8%
Housing: Homeownership rate: 83.7%; Median home value: $192,500; Median year structure built: 1961; Homeowner vacancy rate: 0.0%; Median selected monthly owner costs: $1,495 with a mortgage, $561 without a mortgage; Median gross rent: $1,267 per month; Rental vacancy rate: 10.6%
Health Insurance: 97.0% have insurance; 87.9% have private insurance; 29.0% have public insurance; 3.0% do not have insurance; 1.6% of children under 18 do not have insurance
Transportation: Commute: 92.3% car, 0.0% public transportation, 0.9% walk, 6.5% work from home; Mean travel time to work: 20.2 minutes

HOLLAND (CDP). Covers a land area of 4.004 square miles and a water area of 0 square miles. Located at 42.64° N. Lat; 78.55° W. Long. Elevation is 1,106 feet.
Population: 1,236; Growth (since 2000): -2.0%; Density: 308.7 persons per square mile; Race: 98.1% White, 0.1% Black/African American, 0.0% Asian, 0.0% American Indian/Alaska Native, 0.0% Native Hawaiian/Other Pacific Islander, 1.4% Two or more races, 4.2% Hispanic of any race; Average household size: 2.51; Median age: 39.7; Age under 18: 23.5%; Age 65 and over: 16.7%; Males per 100 females: 95.1; Marriage status: 31.1% never married, 53.0% now married, 2.0% separated, 6.2% widowed, 9.7% divorced; Foreign born: 0.8%; Speak English only: 100.0%; With disability: 10.7%; Veterans: 12.8%; Ancestry: 34.6% German, 19.1% Polish, 13.6% American, 10.0% Irish, 9.0% English
Employment: 17.0% management, business, and financial, 0.0% computer, engineering, and science, 3.3% education, legal, community service, arts, and media, 1.8% healthcare practitioners, 14.5% service, 34.0% sales and office, 11.6% natural resources, construction, and maintenance, 17.9% production, transportation, and material moving
Income: Per capita: $24,003; Median household: $60,125; Average household: $60,100; Households with income of $100,000 or more: 10.4%; Poverty rate: 14.8%
Educational Attainment: High school diploma or higher: 90.3%; Bachelor's degree or higher: 17.1%; Graduate/professional degree or higher: 5.2%
School District(s)
Holland Central SD (PK-12)
  2014-15 Enrollment: 943 . . . . (716) 537-8222
Housing: Homeownership rate: 71.1%; Median home value: $122,200; Median year structure built: Before 1940; Homeowner vacancy rate: 0.0%; Median selected monthly owner costs: $1,183 with a mortgage, $477 without a mortgage; Median gross rent: $527 per month; Rental vacancy rate: 0.0%
Health Insurance: 91.0% have insurance; 70.1% have private insurance; 34.4% have public insurance; 9.0% do not have insurance; 5.5% of children under 18 do not have insurance

Transportation: Commute: 87.7% car, 0.6% public transportation, 4.6% walk, 3.7% work from home; Mean travel time to work: 22.6 minutes

HOLLAND (town). Covers a land area of 35.790 square miles and a water area of 0.036 square miles. Located at 42.67° N. Lat; 78.52° W. Long. Elevation is 1,106 feet.
Population: 3,403; Growth (since 2000): -5.6%; Density: 95.1 persons per square mile; Race: 98.2% White, 0.0% Black/African American, 0.0% Asian, 0.0% American Indian/Alaska Native, 0.0% Native Hawaiian/Other Pacific Islander, 1.6% Two or more races, 1.5% Hispanic of any race; Average household size: 2.38; Median age: 44.1; Age under 18: 21.0%; Age 65 and over: 15.1%; Males per 100 females: 101.6; Marriage status: 28.4% never married, 55.1% now married, 1.0% separated, 4.8% widowed, 11.6% divorced; Foreign born: 0.6%; Speak English only: 98.1%; With disability: 11.6%; Veterans: 10.5%; Ancestry: 38.7% German, 23.8% Polish, 14.9% Irish, 12.0% English, 9.3% American
Employment: 11.8% management, business, and financial, 4.0% computer, engineering, and science, 5.2% education, legal, community service, arts, and media, 6.0% healthcare practitioners, 11.7% service, 30.1% sales and office, 16.1% natural resources, construction, and maintenance, 15.1% production, transportation, and material moving
Income: Per capita: $28,263; Median household: $58,164; Average household: $67,213; Households with income of $100,000 or more: 17.3%; Poverty rate: 10.7%
Educational Attainment: High school diploma or higher: 91.8%; Bachelor's degree or higher: 21.8%; Graduate/professional degree or higher: 8.9%
School District(s)
Holland Central SD (PK-12)
  2014-15 Enrollment: 943 . . . . (716) 537-8222
Housing: Homeownership rate: 83.3%; Median home value: $148,400; Median year structure built: 1958; Homeowner vacancy rate: 0.0%; Median selected monthly owner costs: $1,310 with a mortgage, $560 without a mortgage; Median gross rent: $536 per month; Rental vacancy rate: 8.5%
Health Insurance: 94.2% have insurance; 77.8% have private insurance; 32.4% have public insurance; 5.8% do not have insurance; 2.2% of children under 18 do not have insurance
Transportation: Commute: 93.4% car, 0.2% public transportation, 3.0% walk, 2.4% work from home; Mean travel time to work: 29.1 minutes

IRVING (unincorporated postal area)
ZCTA: 14081
  Covers a land area of 35.169 square miles and a water area of 0.905 square miles. Located at 42.56° N. Lat; 79.07° W. Long..
  Population: 3,183; Growth (since 2000): -6.9%; Density: 90.5 persons per square mile; Race: 57.7% White, 0.8% Black/African American, 0.2% Asian, 35.3% American Indian/Alaska Native, 0.0% Native Hawaiian/Other Pacific Islander, 4.5% Two or more races, 4.3% Hispanic of any race; Average household size: 2.40; Median age: 46.3; Age under 18: 20.8%; Age 65 and over: 20.8%; Males per 100 females: 92.7; Marriage status: 31.7% never married, 45.4% now married, 3.5% separated, 7.8% widowed, 15.2% divorced; Foreign born: 1.3%; Speak English only: 96.7%; With disability: 16.9%; Veterans: 10.3%; Ancestry: 21.3% German, 13.4% Polish, 11.1% Italian, 7.1% Irish, 5.9% English
  Employment: 14.8% management, business, and financial, 2.1% computer, engineering, and science, 10.0% education, legal, community service, arts, and media, 3.3% healthcare practitioners, 23.7% service, 24.2% sales and office, 10.1% natural resources, construction, and maintenance, 11.8% production, transportation, and material moving
  Income: Per capita: $26,216; Median household: $57,019; Average household: $63,557; Households with income of $100,000 or more: 16.1%; Poverty rate: 15.8%
  Educational Attainment: High school diploma or higher: 85.4%; Bachelor's degree or higher: 16.5%; Graduate/professional degree or higher: 4.7%
  Housing: Homeownership rate: 76.4%; Median home value: $112,700; Median year structure built: 1970; Homeowner vacancy rate: 1.0%; Median selected monthly owner costs: $1,140 with a mortgage, $439 without a mortgage; Median gross rent: $686 per month; Rental vacancy rate: 1.7%
  Health Insurance: 84.4% have insurance; 63.5% have private insurance; 34.0% have public insurance; 15.6% do not have insurance; 18.7% of children under 18 do not have insurance
  Transportation: Commute: 94.8% car, 0.0% public transportation, 3.7% walk, 1.6% work from home; Mean travel time to work: 24.7 minutes

KENMORE (village). Covers a land area of 1.435 square miles and a water area of 0 square miles. Located at 42.96° N. Lat; 78.87° W. Long. Elevation is 614 feet.

History: Named for a prominent citizen. Incorporated 1899.

Population: 15,271; Growth (since 2000): -7.0%; Density: 10,639.0 persons per square mile; Race: 92.7% White, 3.8% Black/African American, 0.5% Asian, 0.1% American Indian/Alaska Native, 0.0% Native Hawaiian/Other Pacific Islander, 2.8% Two or more races, 3.2% Hispanic of any race; Average household size: 2.17; Median age: 41.4; Age under 18: 18.1%; Age 65 and over: 17.4%; Males per 100 females: 87.4; Marriage status: 35.1% never married, 46.6% now married, 1.8% separated, 7.2% widowed, 11.1% divorced; Foreign born: 2.8%; Speak English only: 96.0%; With disability: 13.4%; Veterans: 9.2%; Ancestry: 32.9% Italian, 29.3% German, 24.4% Irish, 11.7% Polish, 8.8% English

Employment: 15.1% management, business, and financial, 3.2% computer, engineering, and science, 15.6% education, legal, community service, arts, and media, 5.8% healthcare practitioners, 17.6% service, 31.2% sales and office, 4.6% natural resources, construction, and maintenance, 7.1% production, transportation, and material moving

Income: Per capita: $29,461; Median household: $51,634; Average household: $62,858; Households with income of $100,000 or more: 19.2%; Poverty rate: 8.6%

Educational Attainment: High school diploma or higher: 92.8%; Bachelor's degree or higher: 33.6%; Graduate/professional degree or higher: 16.5%

School District(s)
Kenmore-Tonawanda Union Free SD (PK-12)
    2014-15 Enrollment: 7,171 . . . . (716) 874-8400

Housing: Homeownership rate: 66.8%; Median home value: $111,200; Median year structure built: Before 1940; Homeowner vacancy rate: 0.0%; Median selected monthly owner costs: $1,197 with a mortgage, $544 without a mortgage; Median gross rent: $681 per month; Rental vacancy rate: 5.2%

Health Insurance: 96.8% have insurance; 78.1% have private insurance; 32.8% have public insurance; 3.2% do not have insurance; 0.5% of children under 18 do not have insurance

Hospitals: Kenmore Mercy Hospital (184 beds)

Safety: Violent crime rate: 10.5 per 10,000 population; Property crime rate: 210.6 per 10,000 population

Transportation: Commute: 91.3% car, 1.9% public transportation, 2.5% walk, 2.9% work from home; Mean travel time to work: 19.5 minutes

Additional Information Contacts
Village of Kenmore . . . . (716) 873-5700
    http://www.villageofkenmore.org

LACKAWANNA (city). Covers a land area of 6.571 square miles and a water area of 0.050 square miles. Located at 42.82° N. Lat; 78.83° W. Long. Elevation is 623 feet.

History: Named for the Lackawanna Steel Company. Formerly a major steel-making center, Lackawanna experienced the total decline of its foremost industry in the 1970s and 1980s. A distinguished city landmark is the elaborate Basilica of Our Lady of Victory, a Roman Catholic shrine. Incorporated 1909.

Population: 18,019; Growth (since 2000): -5.5%; Density: 2,742.2 persons per square mile; Race: 80.9% White, 10.8% Black/African American, 0.6% Asian, 0.1% American Indian/Alaska Native, 0.0% Native Hawaiian/Other Pacific Islander, 3.6% Two or more races, 9.1% Hispanic of any race; Average household size: 2.26; Median age: 39.6; Age under 18: 21.8%; Age 65 and over: 16.8%; Males per 100 females: 91.8; Marriage status: 40.3% never married, 38.3% now married, 3.4% separated, 9.2% widowed, 12.2% divorced; Foreign born: 8.5%; Speak English only: 83.1%; With disability: 18.6%; Veterans: 8.5%; Ancestry: 23.7% Polish, 17.2% German, 17.0% Irish, 15.4% Italian, 5.3% Other Arab

Employment: 9.7% management, business, and financial, 3.1% computer, engineering, and science, 7.8% education, legal, community service, arts, and media, 4.3% healthcare practitioners, 25.3% service, 25.5% sales and office, 6.8% natural resources, construction, and maintenance, 17.6% production, transportation, and material moving

Income: Per capita: $20,480; Median household: $35,352; Average household: $45,399; Households with income of $100,000 or more: 8.9%; Poverty rate: 24.4%

Educational Attainment: High school diploma or higher: 83.2%; Bachelor's degree or higher: 15.1%; Graduate/professional degree or higher: 5.2%

School District(s)
Global Concepts Charter School (KG-10)
    2014-15 Enrollment: 930 . . . . (716) 821-1903
Lackawanna City SD (PK-12)
    2014-15 Enrollment: 1,858 . . . . (716) 827-6767

Housing: Homeownership rate: 54.3%; Median home value: $82,700; Median year structure built: 1949; Homeowner vacancy rate: 1.2%; Median selected monthly owner costs: $961 with a mortgage, $425 without a mortgage; Median gross rent: $594 per month; Rental vacancy rate: 6.0%

Health Insurance: 92.0% have insurance; 58.4% have private insurance; 48.6% have public insurance; 8.0% do not have insurance; 3.9% of children under 18 do not have insurance

Safety: Violent crime rate: 55.3 per 10,000 population; Property crime rate: 227.2 per 10,000 population

Newspapers: Front Page Group (weekly circulation 15,000)

Transportation: Commute: 91.1% car, 3.9% public transportation, 1.4% walk, 0.5% work from home; Mean travel time to work: 21.8 minutes

Additional Information Contacts
City of Lackawanna . . . . (716) 827-6452
    http://www.lackawannany.gov

LAKE ERIE BEACH (CDP). Covers a land area of 3.820 square miles and a water area of 0 square miles. Located at 42.62° N. Lat; 79.08° W. Long. Elevation is 627 feet.

Population: 4,228; Growth (since 2000): -6.0%; Density: 1,106.8 persons per square mile; Race: 97.2% White, 0.0% Black/African American, 0.4% Asian, 0.2% American Indian/Alaska Native, 0.0% Native Hawaiian/Other Pacific Islander, 1.7% Two or more races, 1.5% Hispanic of any race; Average household size: 2.39; Median age: 46.2; Age under 18: 17.9%; Age 65 and over: 18.6%; Males per 100 females: 98.3; Marriage status: 29.5% never married, 53.6% now married, 1.4% separated, 6.7% widowed, 10.3% divorced; Foreign born: 2.1%; Speak English only: 97.7%; With disability: 16.5%; Veterans: 8.5%; Ancestry: 32.2% German, 19.1% Irish, 19.1% Polish, 17.0% Italian, 9.6% English

Employment: 8.3% management, business, and financial, 2.0% computer, engineering, and science, 9.3% education, legal, community service, arts, and media, 7.9% healthcare practitioners, 21.6% service, 27.3% sales and office, 5.7% natural resources, construction, and maintenance, 17.8% production, transportation, and material moving

Income: Per capita: $28,542; Median household: $60,129; Average household: $67,373; Households with income of $100,000 or more: 21.2%; Poverty rate: 8.8%

Educational Attainment: High school diploma or higher: 96.7%; Bachelor's degree or higher: 20.7%; Graduate/professional degree or higher: 9.5%

Housing: Homeownership rate: 88.3%; Median home value: $96,400; Median year structure built: 1946; Homeowner vacancy rate: 0.0%; Median selected monthly owner costs: $1,104 with a mortgage, $464 without a mortgage; Median gross rent: $921 per month; Rental vacancy rate: 0.0%

Health Insurance: 92.5% have insurance; 77.1% have private insurance; 34.2% have public insurance; 7.5% do not have insurance; 9.4% of children under 18 do not have insurance

Transportation: Commute: 98.2% car, 0.0% public transportation, 0.0% walk, 1.8% work from home; Mean travel time to work: 27.9 minutes

LAKE VIEW (unincorporated postal area)
ZCTA: 14085
    Covers a land area of 6.968 square miles and a water area of 0.345 square miles. Located at 42.72° N. Lat; 78.92° W. Long. Elevation is 718 feet.

Population: 7,040; Growth (since 2000): 26.5%; Density: 1,010.3 persons per square mile; Race: 99.0% White, 0.4% Black/African American, 0.0% Asian, 0.2% American Indian/Alaska Native, 0.2% Native Hawaiian/Other Pacific Islander, 0.0% Two or more races, 1.7% Hispanic of any race; Average household size: 2.83; Median age: 39.4; Age under 18: 25.6%; Age 65 and over: 10.0%; Males per 100 females: 101.9; Marriage status: 25.9% never married, 61.3% now married, 0.7% separated, 3.4% widowed, 9.4% divorced; Foreign born: 1.4%; Speak English only: 98.1%; With disability: 8.4%; Veterans: 10.2%; Ancestry: 33.7% Polish, 30.0% German, 29.0% Italian, 18.4% Irish, 6.6% English

Employment: 14.3% management, business, and financial, 6.1% computer, engineering, and science, 11.9% education, legal, community service, arts, and media, 10.1% healthcare practitioners, 14.3% service, 24.8% sales and office, 7.5% natural resources, construction, and maintenance, 11.0% production, transportation, and material moving

Income: Per capita: $34,374; Median household: $85,536; Average household: $96,618; Households with income of $100,000 or more: 36.3%; Poverty rate: 4.9%
Educational Attainment: High school diploma or higher: 96.4%; Bachelor's degree or higher: 36.6%; Graduate/professional degree or higher: 15.8%

School District(s)
Frontier Central SD (PK-12)
  2014-15 Enrollment: 5,006 . . . . (716) 926-1711
Housing: Homeownership rate: 96.8%; Median home value: $169,600; Median year structure built: 1980; Homeowner vacancy rate: 1.5%; Median selected monthly owner costs: $1,460 with a mortgage, $533 without a mortgage; Median gross rent: $1,058 per month; Rental vacancy rate: 29.2%
Health Insurance: 98.1% have insurance; 88.9% have private insurance; 20.8% have public insurance; 1.9% do not have insurance; 1.7% of children under 18 do not have insurance
Transportation: Commute: 95.7% car, 1.2% public transportation, 0.0% walk, 2.5% work from home; Mean travel time to work: 26.6 minutes

LANCASTER (town). Covers a land area of 37.703 square miles and a water area of 0.234 square miles. Located at 42.91° N. Lat; 78.63° W. Long. Elevation is 669 feet.
History: Incorporated 1849.
Population: 42,492; Growth (since 2000): 8.9%; Density: 1,127.0 persons per square mile; Race: 96.8% White, 0.8% Black/African American, 0.7% Asian, 0.1% American Indian/Alaska Native, 0.0% Native Hawaiian/Other Pacific Islander, 1.2% Two or more races, 2.0% Hispanic of any race; Average household size: 2.49; Median age: 41.6; Age under 18: 23.0%; Age 65 and over: 15.0%; Males per 100 females: 93.8; Marriage status: 27.9% never married, 56.8% now married, 1.6% separated, 6.8% widowed, 8.5% divorced; Foreign born: 3.3%; Speak English only: 95.1%; With disability: 9.5%; Veterans: 8.3%; Ancestry: 32.9% German, 32.2% Polish, 22.3% Italian, 16.1% Irish, 6.4% English
Employment: 16.7% management, business, and financial, 5.2% computer, engineering, and science, 10.2% education, legal, community service, arts, and media, 6.4% healthcare practitioners, 15.4% service, 27.7% sales and office, 6.5% natural resources, construction, and maintenance, 12.0% production, transportation, and material moving
Income: Per capita: $32,389; Median household: $67,223; Average household: $80,639; Households with income of $100,000 or more: 31.0%; Poverty rate: 5.8%
Educational Attainment: High school diploma or higher: 95.0%; Bachelor's degree or higher: 31.5%; Graduate/professional degree or higher: 12.1%

School District(s)
Lancaster Central SD (KG-12)
  2014-15 Enrollment: 5,820 . . . . (716) 686-3201
Housing: Homeownership rate: 77.1%; Median home value: $167,200; Median year structure built: 1972; Homeowner vacancy rate: 0.7%; Median selected monthly owner costs: $1,464 with a mortgage, $560 without a mortgage; Median gross rent: $707 per month; Rental vacancy rate: 3.2%
Health Insurance: 95.9% have insurance; 84.0% have private insurance; 26.2% have public insurance; 4.1% do not have insurance; 1.9% of children under 18 do not have insurance
Safety: Violent crime rate: 6.7 per 10,000 population; Property crime rate: 117.4 per 10,000 population
Transportation: Commute: 95.9% car, 0.4% public transportation, 0.5% walk, 2.5% work from home; Mean travel time to work: 21.9 minutes
Additional Information Contacts
Town of Lancaster. . . . . (716) 683-9028
  http://www.lancasterny.gov

LANCASTER (village). Covers a land area of 2.698 square miles and a water area of 0.034 square miles. Located at 42.90° N. Lat; 78.67° W. Long. Elevation is 669 feet.
Population: 10,300; Growth (since 2000): -7.9%; Density: 3,818.3 persons per square mile; Race: 95.0% White, 0.0% Black/African American, 1.2% Asian, 0.1% American Indian/Alaska Native, 0.0% Native Hawaiian/Other Pacific Islander, 3.5% Two or more races, 0.7% Hispanic of any race; Average household size: 2.36; Median age: 38.9; Age under 18: 21.3%; Age 65 and over: 16.1%; Males per 100 females: 91.5; Marriage status: 34.3% never married, 47.8% now married, 2.7% separated, 7.2% widowed, 10.8% divorced; Foreign born: 1.9%; Speak English only: 95.8%;

With disability: 12.8%; Veterans: 7.6%; Ancestry: 39.8% German, 30.5% Polish, 18.8% Italian, 16.0% Irish, 8.0% English
Employment: 10.7% management, business, and financial, 5.5% computer, engineering, and science, 9.7% education, legal, community service, arts, and media, 4.6% healthcare practitioners, 17.2% service, 27.2% sales and office, 8.6% natural resources, construction, and maintenance, 16.5% production, transportation, and material moving
Income: Per capita: $27,257; Median household: $49,991; Average household: $63,523; Households with income of $100,000 or more: 24.0%; Poverty rate: 7.4%
Educational Attainment: High school diploma or higher: 94.3%; Bachelor's degree or higher: 23.7%; Graduate/professional degree or higher: 8.9%

School District(s)
Lancaster Central SD (KG-12)
  2014-15 Enrollment: 5,820 . . . . (716) 686-3201
Housing: Homeownership rate: 70.8%; Median home value: $121,400; Median year structure built: 1952; Homeowner vacancy rate: 1.6%; Median selected monthly owner costs: $1,273 with a mortgage, $519 without a mortgage; Median gross rent: $674 per month; Rental vacancy rate: 3.0%
Health Insurance: 95.9% have insurance; 78.9% have private insurance; 31.9% have public insurance; 4.1% do not have insurance; 3.7% of children under 18 do not have insurance
Transportation: Commute: 97.2% car, 0.2% public transportation, 0.2% walk, 2.3% work from home; Mean travel time to work: 21.6 minutes
Additional Information Contacts
Village of Lancaster. . . . . (716) 683-2105
  http://www.lancastervillage.org

LAWTONS (unincorporated postal area)
ZCTA: 14091
  Covers a land area of 21.261 square miles and a water area of 0.008 square miles. Located at 42.54° N. Lat; 78.89° W. Long. Elevation is 850 feet.
Population: 967; Growth (since 2000): -14.8%; Density: 45.5 persons per square mile; Race: 78.7% White, 0.0% Black/African American, 0.0% Asian, 19.3% American Indian/Alaska Native, 0.0% Native Hawaiian/Other Pacific Islander, 2.0% Two or more races, 0.3% Hispanic of any race; Average household size: 2.60; Median age: 44.3; Age under 18: 22.8%; Age 65 and over: 15.0%; Males per 100 females: 105.5; Marriage status: 22.1% never married, 66.5% now married, 0.8% separated, 6.7% widowed, 4.7% divorced; Foreign born: 1.4%; Speak English only: 95.1%; With disability: 7.0%; Veterans: 10.2%; Ancestry: 36.3% German, 11.9% Irish, 9.6% Polish, 8.9% Italian, 6.6% English
Employment: 8.2% management, business, and financial, 0.0% computer, engineering, and science, 13.3% education, legal, community service, arts, and media, 8.8% healthcare practitioners, 10.3% service, 23.4% sales and office, 17.6% natural resources, construction, and maintenance, 18.3% production, transportation, and material moving
Income: Per capita: $26,905; Median household: $61,304; Average household: $68,589; Households with income of $100,000 or more: 26.8%; Poverty rate: 5.5%
Educational Attainment: High school diploma or higher: 90.1%; Bachelor's degree or higher: 19.2%; Graduate/professional degree or higher: 11.2%
Housing: Homeownership rate: 91.1%; Median home value: $99,600; Median year structure built: 1967; Homeowner vacancy rate: 0.0%; Median selected monthly owner costs: $1,168 with a mortgage, $383 without a mortgage; Median gross rent: $548 per month; Rental vacancy rate: 0.0%
Health Insurance: 88.4% have insurance; 65.6% have private insurance; 34.3% have public insurance; 11.6% do not have insurance; 17.3% of children under 18 do not have insurance
Transportation: Commute: 98.4% car, 0.0% public transportation, 1.6% walk, 0.0% work from home; Mean travel time to work: 26.8 minutes

MARILLA (town). Covers a land area of 27.505 square miles and a water area of 0.038 square miles. Located at 42.82° N. Lat; 78.53° W. Long. Elevation is 846 feet.
Population: 5,345; Growth (since 2000): -6.4%; Density: 194.3 persons per square mile; Race: 100.0% White, 0.0% Black/African American, 0.0% Asian, 0.0% American Indian/Alaska Native, 0.0% Native Hawaiian/Other Pacific Islander, 0.0% Two or more races, 1.0% Hispanic of any race; Average household size: 2.67; Median age: 47.0; Age under 18: 21.2%; Age 65 and over: 16.4%; Males per 100 females: 96.6; Marriage status:

25.2% never married, 63.6% now married, 0.4% separated, 4.3% widowed, 6.8% divorced; Foreign born: 1.5%; Speak English only: 96.4%; With disability: 8.7%; Veterans: 10.6%; Ancestry: 41.2% German, 33.8% Polish, 17.3% Irish, 13.8% Italian, 13.5% English

Employment: 11.5% management, business, and financial, 4.2% computer, engineering, and science, 9.0% education, legal, community service, arts, and media, 6.8% healthcare practitioners, 15.5% service, 30.4% sales and office, 7.9% natural resources, construction, and maintenance, 14.7% production, transportation, and material moving

Income: Per capita: $34,758; Median household: $81,432; Average household: $92,005; Households with income of $100,000 or more: 39.0%; Poverty rate: 4.1%

Educational Attainment: High school diploma or higher: 96.4%; Bachelor's degree or higher: 33.0%; Graduate/professional degree or higher: 13.0%

School District(s)

Iroquois Central SD (KG-12)

   2014-15 Enrollment: 2,375 . . . . (716) 652-3000

Housing: Homeownership rate: 93.9%; Median home value: $184,300; Median year structure built: 1973; Homeowner vacancy rate: 0.0%; Median selected monthly owner costs: $1,491 with a mortgage, $533 without a mortgage; Median gross rent: $1,044 per month; Rental vacancy rate: 21.8%

Health Insurance: 96.7% have insurance; 87.7% have private insurance; 24.2% have public insurance; 3.3% do not have insurance; 1.9% of children under 18 do not have insurance

Transportation: Commute: 96.2% car, 0.0% public transportation, 0.4% walk, 3.4% work from home; Mean travel time to work: 27.0 minutes

Additional Information Contacts

Town of Marilla . . . . (716) 652-5350
  http://townofmarilla.com

NEWSTEAD (town).
Covers a land area of 50.759 square miles and a water area of 0.286 square miles. Located at 43.02° N. Lat; 78.52° W. Long.

Population: 8,653; Growth (since 2000): 3.0%; Density: 170.5 persons per square mile; Race: 96.3% White, 1.2% Black/African American, 0.8% Asian, 0.7% American Indian/Alaska Native, 0.0% Native Hawaiian/Other Pacific Islander, 0.7% Two or more races, 0.5% Hispanic of any race; Average household size: 2.39; Median age: 46.0; Age under 18: 19.3%; Age 65 and over: 18.9%; Males per 100 females: 97.4; Marriage status: 28.0% never married, 54.2% now married, 0.5% separated, 7.1% widowed, 10.8% divorced; Foreign born: 5.0%; Speak English only: 96.6%; With disability: 12.0%; Veterans: 9.1%; Ancestry: 40.6% German, 18.2% Polish, 13.1% Irish, 10.2% English, 7.5% Italian

Employment: 11.8% management, business, and financial, 3.8% computer, engineering, and science, 8.3% education, legal, community service, arts, and media, 5.3% healthcare practitioners, 17.5% service, 23.4% sales and office, 13.4% natural resources, construction, and maintenance, 16.5% production, transportation, and material moving

Income: Per capita: $30,743; Median household: $55,409; Average household: $72,468; Households with income of $100,000 or more: 21.8%; Poverty rate: 3.9%

Educational Attainment: High school diploma or higher: 91.6%; Bachelor's degree or higher: 24.7%; Graduate/professional degree or higher: 9.4%

Housing: Homeownership rate: 78.6%; Median home value: $139,300; Median year structure built: 1965; Homeowner vacancy rate: 0.0%; Median selected monthly owner costs: $1,502 with a mortgage, $547 without a mortgage; Median gross rent: $750 per month; Rental vacancy rate: 0.0%

Health Insurance: 92.5% have insurance; 78.0% have private insurance; 29.3% have public insurance; 7.5% do not have insurance; 6.0% of children under 18 do not have insurance

Transportation: Commute: 91.6% car, 0.0% public transportation, 4.0% walk, 4.4% work from home; Mean travel time to work: 23.7 minutes

Additional Information Contacts

Town of Newstead. . . . . (716) 542-4573
  http://www.erie.gov/newstead

NORTH BOSTON (CDP).
Covers a land area of 4.074 square miles and a water area of 0 square miles. Located at 42.68° N. Lat; 78.78° W. Long. Elevation is 823 feet.

Population: 2,749; Growth (since 2000): 2.6%; Density: 674.7 persons per square mile; Race: 99.7% White, 0.0% Black/African American, 0.0% Asian, 0.0% American Indian/Alaska Native, 0.0% Native Hawaiian/Other

Pacific Islander, 0.3% Two or more races, 0.0% Hispanic of any race; Average household size: 2.41; Median age: 48.2; Age under 18: 16.2%; Age 65 and over: 26.2%; Males per 100 females: 95.7; Marriage status: 27.9% never married, 54.9% now married, 0.5% separated, 8.6% widowed, 8.7% divorced; Foreign born: 1.7%; Speak English only: 98.4%; With disability: 12.4%; Veterans: 7.2%; Ancestry: 40.4% German, 19.5% Irish, 19.2% Italian, 17.1% Polish, 14.9% English

Employment: 10.1% management, business, and financial, 4.8% computer, engineering, and science, 13.8% education, legal, community service, arts, and media, 6.5% healthcare practitioners, 21.0% service, 19.8% sales and office, 6.4% natural resources, construction, and maintenance, 17.6% production, transportation, and material moving

Income: Per capita: $27,760; Median household: $52,083; Average household: $66,411; Households with income of $100,000 or more: 20.4%; Poverty rate: 1.7%

Educational Attainment: High school diploma or higher: 99.3%; Bachelor's degree or higher: 24.3%; Graduate/professional degree or higher: 10.3%

Housing: Homeownership rate: 74.3%; Median home value: $156,500; Median year structure built: 1965; Homeowner vacancy rate: 0.0%; Median selected monthly owner costs: $1,242 with a mortgage, $519 without a mortgage; Median gross rent: $674 per month; Rental vacancy rate: 0.0%

Health Insurance: 90.5% have insurance; 70.7% have private insurance; 40.7% have public insurance; 9.5% do not have insurance; 0.0% of children under 18 do not have insurance

Transportation: Commute: 99.6% car, 0.0% public transportation, 0.0% walk, 0.0% work from home; Mean travel time to work: 21.3 minutes

NORTH COLLINS (town).
Covers a land area of 42.854 square miles and a water area of 0.173 square miles. Located at 42.57° N. Lat; 78.86° W. Long. Elevation is 827 feet.

History: Settled c.1810, incorporated 1911.

Population: 3,513; Growth (since 2000): 4.1%; Density: 82.0 persons per square mile; Race: 97.8% White, 0.4% Black/African American, 0.2% Asian, 0.8% American Indian/Alaska Native, 0.0% Native Hawaiian/Other Pacific Islander, 0.7% Two or more races, 0.3% Hispanic of any race; Average household size: 2.73; Median age: 43.6; Age under 18: 23.3%; Age 65 and over: 13.3%; Males per 100 females: 98.5; Marriage status: 23.3% never married, 63.0% now married, 1.3% separated, 4.8% widowed, 9.0% divorced; Foreign born: 1.9%; Speak English only: 97.6%; With disability: 13.7%; Veterans: 8.3%; Ancestry: 40.4% German, 20.2% Italian, 14.5% Irish, 13.9% Polish, 12.9% English

Employment: 10.2% management, business, and financial, 2.7% computer, engineering, and science, 10.4% education, legal, community service, arts, and media, 6.9% healthcare practitioners, 14.7% service, 24.7% sales and office, 15.7% natural resources, construction, and maintenance, 14.8% production, transportation, and material moving

Income: Per capita: $25,144; Median household: $64,280; Average household: $68,236; Households with income of $100,000 or more: 23.0%; Poverty rate: 5.8%

Educational Attainment: High school diploma or higher: 90.9%; Bachelor's degree or higher: 20.8%; Graduate/professional degree or higher: 10.2%

School District(s)

North Collins Central SD (PK-12)

   2014-15 Enrollment: 649. (716) 337-0101

Housing: Homeownership rate: 81.7%; Median home value: $118,400; Median year structure built: 1952; Homeowner vacancy rate: 1.7%; Median selected monthly owner costs: $1,172 with a mortgage, $550 without a mortgage; Median gross rent: $638 per month; Rental vacancy rate: 3.3%

Health Insurance: 93.2% have insurance; 74.8% have private insurance; 29.7% have public insurance; 6.8% do not have insurance; 6.0% of children under 18 do not have insurance

Transportation: Commute: 94.4% car, 0.2% public transportation, 3.8% walk, 1.2% work from home; Mean travel time to work: 27.5 minutes

NORTH COLLINS (village).
Covers a land area of 0.801 square miles and a water area of 0 square miles. Located at 42.59° N. Lat; 78.94° W. Long. Elevation is 827 feet.

Population: 1,352; Growth (since 2000): 25.3%; Density: 1,687.8 persons per square mile; Race: 96.9% White, 0.0% Black/African American, 0.6% Asian, 2.1% American Indian/Alaska Native, 0.0% Native Hawaiian/Other Pacific Islander, 0.4% Two or more races, 0.0% Hispanic of any race; Average household size: 2.80; Median age: 32.9; Age under 18: 30.7%; Age 65 and over: 11.3%; Males per 100 females: 94.6; Marriage status:

24.8% never married, 57.9% now married, 3.6% separated, 3.6% widowed, 13.6% divorced; Foreign born: 2.6%; Speak English only: 98.0%; With disability: 9.2%; Veterans: 6.8%; Ancestry: 44.5% German, 21.8% Italian, 14.8% Polish, 13.8% Irish, 11.7% English

Employment: 8.6% management, business, and financial, 1.3% computer, engineering, and science, 11.6% education, legal, community service, arts, and media, 5.6% healthcare practitioners, 22.8% service, 31.0% sales and office, 8.3% natural resources, construction, and maintenance, 10.8% production, transportation, and material moving

Income: Per capita: $20,435; Median household: $52,992; Average household: $56,445; Households with income of $100,000 or more: 12.7%; Poverty rate: 5.0%

Educational Attainment: High school diploma or higher: 88.9%; Bachelor's degree or higher: 19.4%; Graduate/professional degree or higher: 6.1%

School District(s)

North Collins Central SD (PK-12)

    2014-15 Enrollment: 649 . . . . (716) 337-0101

Housing: Homeownership rate: 64.1%; Median home value: $95,200; Median year structure built: Before 1940; Homeowner vacancy rate: 5.5%; Median selected monthly owner costs: $1,170 with a mortgage, $496 without a mortgage; Median gross rent: $638 per month; Rental vacancy rate: 0.0%

Health Insurance: 92.4% have insurance; 76.2% have private insurance; 24.3% have public insurance; 7.6% do not have insurance; 1.7% of children under 18 do not have insurance

Transportation: Commute: 89.5% car, 0.6% public transportation, 9.2% walk, 0.6% work from home; Mean travel time to work: 23.1 minutes

ORCHARD PARK (town).
Covers a land area of 38.440 square miles and a water area of 0.079 square miles. Located at 42.75° N. Lat; 78.74° W. Long. Elevation is 863 feet.

History: Until 1934, called East Hamburg. Incorporated 1921.

Population: 29,466; Growth (since 2000): 6.6%; Density: 766.5 persons per square mile; Race: 96.8% White, 0.7% Black/African American, 1.3% Asian, 0.1% American Indian/Alaska Native, 0.0% Native Hawaiian/Other Pacific Islander, 0.7% Two or more races, 1.6% Hispanic of any race; Average household size: 2.53; Median age: 45.6; Age under 18: 22.2%; Age 65 and over: 18.6%; Males per 100 females: 92.1; Marriage status: 25.3% never married, 59.7% now married, 1.4% separated, 6.6% widowed, 8.4% divorced; Foreign born: 3.8%; Speak English only: 96.0%; With disability: 8.8%; Veterans: 8.6%; Ancestry: 29.9% German, 24.3% Irish, 21.3% Polish, 19.5% Italian, 8.7% English

Employment: 20.0% management, business, and financial, 5.7% computer, engineering, and science, 14.2% education, legal, community service, arts, and media, 8.3% healthcare practitioners, 14.9% service, 23.6% sales and office, 4.3% natural resources, construction, and maintenance, 9.0% production, transportation, and material moving

Income: Per capita: $44,218; Median household: $85,660; Average household: $112,008; Households with income of $100,000 or more: 41.9%; Poverty rate: 2.4%

Educational Attainment: High school diploma or higher: 95.9%; Bachelor's degree or higher: 44.9%; Graduate/professional degree or higher: 20.7%

School District(s)

Orchard Park Central SD (KG-12)

    2014-15 Enrollment: 5,018 . . . . (716) 209-6280

Four-year College(s)

Bryant & Stratton College-Online (Private, For-profit)

    Fall 2014 Enrollment: 2,584 . . . . (800) 836-5627

    2015-16 Tuition: In-state $13,791; Out-of-state $13,791

Bryant & Stratton College-Southtowns (Private, For-profit)

    Fall 2014 Enrollment: 561 . . . . (716) 677-9500

    2015-16 Tuition: In-state $16,501; Out-of-state $16,501

Housing: Homeownership rate: 78.9%; Median home value: $209,400; Median year structure built: 1972; Homeowner vacancy rate: 0.3%; Median selected monthly owner costs: $1,704 with a mortgage, $663 without a mortgage; Median gross rent: $892 per month; Rental vacancy rate: 14.6%

Health Insurance: 98.0% have insurance; 90.3% have private insurance; 23.7% have public insurance; 2.0% do not have insurance; 1.8% of children under 18 do not have insurance

Safety: Violent crime rate: 5.4 per 10,000 population; Property crime rate: 87.6 per 10,000 population

Transportation: Commute: 94.5% car, 0.5% public transportation, 1.2% walk, 3.2% work from home; Mean travel time to work: 22.0 minutes

Additional Information Contacts

Town of Orchard Park . . . . (716) 662-6410

  http://www.orchardparkny.org

ORCHARD PARK (village).
Covers a land area of 1.346 square miles and a water area of 0.041 square miles. Located at 42.76° N. Lat; 78.74° W. Long. Elevation is 863 feet.

Population: 3,229; Growth (since 2000): -2.0%; Density: 2,398.4 persons per square mile; Race: 98.5% White, 1.2% Black/African American, 0.0% Asian, 0.0% American Indian/Alaska Native, 0.0% Native Hawaiian/Other Pacific Islander, 0.3% Two or more races, 1.6% Hispanic of any race; Average household size: 2.33; Median age: 43.5; Age under 18: 21.9%; Age 65 and over: 18.0%; Males per 100 females: 93.0; Marriage status: 25.5% never married, 58.2% now married, 2.6% separated, 4.6% widowed, 11.7% divorced; Foreign born: 2.0%; Speak English only: 99.2%; With disability: 5.8%; Veterans: 8.0%; Ancestry: 31.4% Irish, 30.3% German, 27.4% Italian, 16.4% Polish, 15.9% English

Employment: 17.8% management, business, and financial, 3.6% computer, engineering, and science, 19.2% education, legal, community service, arts, and media, 9.0% healthcare practitioners, 15.0% service, 26.7% sales and office, 3.8% natural resources, construction, and maintenance, 4.9% production, transportation, and material moving

Income: Per capita: $38,501; Median household: $75,536; Average household: $89,085; Households with income of $100,000 or more: 38.8%; Poverty rate: 2.5%

Educational Attainment: High school diploma or higher: 98.5%; Bachelor's degree or higher: 59.2%; Graduate/professional degree or higher: 32.2%

School District(s)

Orchard Park Central SD (KG-12)

    2014-15 Enrollment: 5,018 . . . . (716) 209-6280

Four-year College(s)

Bryant & Stratton College-Online (Private, For-profit)

    Fall 2014 Enrollment: 2,584 . . . . (800) 836-5627

    2015-16 Tuition: In-state $13,791; Out-of-state $13,791

Bryant & Stratton College-Southtowns (Private, For-profit)

    Fall 2014 Enrollment: 561 . . . . (716) 677-9500

    2015-16 Tuition: In-state $16,501; Out-of-state $16,501

Housing: Homeownership rate: 66.6%; Median home value: $220,100; Median year structure built: 1957; Homeowner vacancy rate: 0.0%; Median selected monthly owner costs: $1,493 with a mortgage, $765 without a mortgage; Median gross rent: $883 per month; Rental vacancy rate: 9.6%

Health Insurance: 95.6% have insurance; 88.0% have private insurance; 23.1% have public insurance; 4.4% do not have insurance; 11.3% of children under 18 do not have insurance

Transportation: Commute: 86.6% car, 0.0% public transportation, 4.9% walk, 7.5% work from home; Mean travel time to work: 18.8 minutes

SARDINIA (town).
Covers a land area of 50.175 square miles and a water area of 0.233 square miles. Located at 42.56° N. Lat; 78.53° W. Long. Elevation is 1,394 feet.

Population: 2,794; Growth (since 2000): 3.8%; Density: 55.7 persons per square mile; Race: 99.3% White, 0.0% Black/African American, 0.0% Asian, 0.0% American Indian/Alaska Native, 0.0% Native Hawaiian/Other Pacific Islander, 0.5% Two or more races, 1.3% Hispanic of any race; Average household size: 2.67; Median age: 43.6; Age under 18: 21.9%; Age 65 and over: 16.3%; Males per 100 females: 103.9; Marriage status: 26.2% never married, 60.1% now married, 1.1% separated, 4.9% widowed, 8.9% divorced; Foreign born: 0.5%; Speak English only: 97.6%; With disability: 11.2%; Veterans: 9.9%; Ancestry: 47.1% German, 19.6% Irish, 17.1% Polish, 16.4% Italian, 11.1% English

Employment: 10.9% management, business, and financial, 2.3% computer, engineering, and science, 8.1% education, legal, community service, arts, and media, 9.6% healthcare practitioners, 16.8% service, 23.4% sales and office, 13.4% natural resources, construction, and maintenance, 15.6% production, transportation, and material moving

Income: Per capita: $26,545; Median household: $60,321; Average household: $71,028; Households with income of $100,000 or more: 23.2%; Poverty rate: 5.8%

Educational Attainment: High school diploma or higher: 90.8%; Bachelor's degree or higher: 17.2%; Graduate/professional degree or higher: 7.0%

Housing: Homeownership rate: 87.7%; Median home value: $150,500; Median year structure built: 1968; Homeowner vacancy rate: 0.9%; Median

selected monthly owner costs: $1,207 with a mortgage, $468 without a mortgage; Median gross rent: $813 per month; Rental vacancy rate: 0.0%
Health Insurance: 96.9% have insurance; 81.8% have private insurance; 28.2% have public insurance; 3.1% do not have insurance; 0.0% of children under 18 do not have insurance
Transportation: Commute: 93.1% car, 0.1% public transportation, 1.9% walk, 3.2% work from home; Mean travel time to work: 29.3 minutes

SLOAN (village).
Covers a land area of 0.786 square miles and a water area of 0.006 square miles. Located at 42.89° N. Lat; 78.79° W. Long. Elevation is 614 feet.
History: Incorporated 1896.
Population: 3,624; Growth (since 2000): -4.0%; Density: 4,610.4 persons per square mile; Race: 95.2% White, 2.8% Black/African American, 0.0% Asian, 0.0% American Indian/Alaska Native, 0.0% Native Hawaiian/Other Pacific Islander, 1.7% Two or more races, 1.8% Hispanic of any race; Average household size: 2.15; Median age: 43.0; Age under 18: 19.7%; Age 65 and over: 16.0%; Males per 100 females: 92.4; Marriage status: 35.0% never married, 42.3% now married, 3.3% separated, 8.6% widowed, 14.1% divorced; Foreign born: 4.1%; Speak English only: 92.2%; With disability: 10.9%; Veterans: 13.0%; Ancestry: 49.3% Polish, 18.1% German, 14.2% Italian, 12.6% Irish, 4.6% English
Employment: 7.2% management, business, and financial, 3.1% computer, engineering, and science, 8.1% education, legal, community service, arts, and media, 3.6% healthcare practitioners, 19.1% service, 29.1% sales and office, 8.7% natural resources, construction, and maintenance, 21.2% production, transportation, and material moving
Income: Per capita: $24,001; Median household: $41,863; Average household: $50,280; Households with income of $100,000 or more: 6.3%; Poverty rate: 11.3%
Educational Attainment: High school diploma or higher: 86.0%; Bachelor's degree or higher: 9.9%; Graduate/professional degree or higher: 0.9%

School District(s)
Cheektowaga-Sloan Union Free SD (PK-12)
   2014-15 Enrollment: 1,474 . . . . (716) 891-6402
Housing: Homeownership rate: 71.8%; Median home value: $72,900; Median year structure built: 1947; Homeowner vacancy rate: 1.4%; Median selected monthly owner costs: $926 with a mortgage, $381 without a mortgage; Median gross rent: $633 per month; Rental vacancy rate: 0.0%
Health Insurance: 92.5% have insurance; 71.6% have private insurance; 33.6% have public insurance; 7.5% do not have insurance; 4.8% of children under 18 do not have insurance
Transportation: Commute: 96.7% car, 1.2% public transportation, 1.5% walk, 0.5% work from home; Mean travel time to work: 19.1 minutes

SOUTH WALES (unincorporated postal area)
ZCTA: 14139
   Covers a land area of 23.860 square miles and a water area of 0.032 square miles. Located at 42.72° N. Lat; 78.54° W. Long. Elevation is 932 feet.
Population: 2,329; Growth (since 2000): 14.7%; Density: 97.6 persons per square mile; Race: 91.2% White, 0.0% Black/African American, 8.3% Asian, 0.0% American Indian/Alaska Native, 0.0% Native Hawaiian/Other Pacific Islander, 0.0% Two or more races, 1.2% Hispanic of any race; Average household size: 2.47; Median age: 41.9; Age under 18: 22.1%; Age 65 and over: 15.9%; Males per 100 females: 99.7; Marriage status: 19.7% never married, 66.5% now married, 0.3% separated, 6.2% widowed, 7.6% divorced; Foreign born: 5.1%; Speak English only: 98.1%; With disability: 7.5%; Veterans: 6.7%; Ancestry: 34.3% German, 22.8% Polish, 15.9% Irish, 9.2% English, 7.6% Italian
Employment: 17.5% management, business, and financial, 3.0% computer, engineering, and science, 16.3% education, legal, community service, arts, and media, 8.1% healthcare practitioners, 19.9% service, 15.4% sales and office, 8.7% natural resources, construction, and maintenance, 11.1% production, transportation, and material moving
Income: Per capita: $31,189; Median household: $71,250; Average household: $75,961; Households with income of $100,000 or more: 25.0%; Poverty rate: 4.2%
Educational Attainment: High school diploma or higher: 95.0%; Bachelor's degree or higher: 40.7%; Graduate/professional degree or higher: 16.4%
Housing: Homeownership rate: 83.9%; Median home value: $178,600; Median year structure built: 1958; Homeowner vacancy rate: 0.0%; Median selected monthly owner costs: $1,468 with a mortgage, $582

without a mortgage; Median gross rent: $724 per month; Rental vacancy rate: 0.0%
Health Insurance: 95.4% have insurance; 81.8% have private insurance; 24.5% have public insurance; 4.6% do not have insurance; 4.1% of children under 18 do not have insurance
Transportation: Commute: 96.6% car, 0.0% public transportation, 1.3% walk, 2.1% work from home; Mean travel time to work: 24.3 minutes

SPRINGVILLE (village).
Covers a land area of 3.672 square miles and a water area of 0.009 square miles. Located at 42.51° N. Lat; 78.67° W. Long. Elevation is 1,329 feet.
History: Settled 1807, incorporated 1834.
Population: 4,328; Growth (since 2000): 1.8%; Density: 1,178.6 persons per square mile; Race: 94.3% White, 1.6% Black/African American, 0.0% Asian, 1.5% American Indian/Alaska Native, 0.0% Native Hawaiian/Other Pacific Islander, 1.8% Two or more races, 2.5% Hispanic of any race; Average household size: 2.18; Median age: 44.7; Age under 18: 22.0%; Age 65 and over: 19.9%; Males per 100 females: 91.6; Marriage status: 22.3% never married, 50.7% now married, 1.8% separated, 10.1% widowed, 16.9% divorced; Foreign born: 2.9%; Speak English only: 95.7%; With disability: 14.9%; Veterans: 12.0%; Ancestry: 37.2% German, 17.4% Irish, 15.4% English, 14.7% Polish, 8.5% Italian
Employment: 12.1% management, business, and financial, 4.4% computer, engineering, and science, 10.8% education, legal, community service, arts, and media, 9.0% healthcare practitioners, 24.0% service, 16.2% sales and office, 9.5% natural resources, construction, and maintenance, 14.0% production, transportation, and material moving
Income: Per capita: $26,426; Median household: $48,170; Average household: $58,297; Households with income of $100,000 or more: 17.6%; Poverty rate: 13.9%
Educational Attainment: High school diploma or higher: 92.4%; Bachelor's degree or higher: 21.5%; Graduate/professional degree or higher: 9.2%

School District(s)
Springville-Griffith Institute Central SD (KG-12)
   2014-15 Enrollment: 1,815 . . . . (716) 592-3230
Housing: Homeownership rate: 59.7%; Median home value: $116,400; Median year structure built: 1951; Homeowner vacancy rate: 0.0%; Median selected monthly owner costs: $1,130 with a mortgage, $457 without a mortgage; Median gross rent: $589 per month; Rental vacancy rate: 0.0%
Health Insurance: 94.2% have insurance; 71.4% have private insurance; 39.6% have public insurance; 5.8% do not have insurance; 2.3% of children under 18 do not have insurance
Hospitals: Bertrand Chaffee Hospital (49 beds)
Newspapers: Springville Journal (weekly circulation 10,000)
Transportation: Commute: 92.0% car, 0.0% public transportation, 4.9% walk, 2.7% work from home; Mean travel time to work: 22.3 minutes
Additional Information Contacts
Village of Springville . . . . (716) 592-4936
   http://www.villageofspringvilleny.com

TONAWANDA (CDP).
Covers a land area of 17.300 square miles and a water area of 1.336 square miles. Located at 42.99° N. Lat; 78.88° W. Long. Elevation is 574 feet.
Population: 58,149; Growth (since 2000): -5.8%; Density: 3,361.3 persons per square mile; Race: 90.5% White, 3.7% Black/African American, 3.1% Asian, 0.3% American Indian/Alaska Native, 0.0% Native Hawaiian/Other Pacific Islander, 1.7% Two or more races, 3.3% Hispanic of any race; Average household size: 2.24; Median age: 43.3; Age under 18: 19.3%; Age 65 and over: 19.4%; Males per 100 females: 89.1; Marriage status: 30.7% never married, 49.0% now married, 1.5% separated, 8.9% widowed, 11.4% divorced; Foreign born: 5.6%; Speak English only: 92.4%; With disability: 14.0%; Veterans: 8.7%; Ancestry: 29.3% German, 23.2% Italian, 21.0% Irish, 15.5% Polish, 9.0% English
Employment: 13.6% management, business, and financial, 4.9% computer, engineering, and science, 12.4% education, legal, community service, arts, and media, 6.7% healthcare practitioners, 16.7% service, 28.9% sales and office, 6.4% natural resources, construction, and maintenance, 10.3% production, transportation, and material moving
Income: Per capita: $29,084; Median household: $54,345; Average household: $64,582; Households with income of $100,000 or more: 17.5%; Poverty rate: 10.1%
Educational Attainment: High school diploma or higher: 93.0%; Bachelor's degree or higher: 32.7%; Graduate/professional degree or higher: 14.2%

School District(s)

Kenmore-Tonawanda Union Free SD (PK-12)
  2014-15 Enrollment: 7,171 . . . . (716) 874-8400
Sweet Home Central SD (KG-12)
  2014-15 Enrollment: 3,254 . . . . (716) 250-1402
Tonawanda City SD (PK-12)
  2014-15 Enrollment: 1,824 . . . . (716) 694-7784

Vocational/Technical School(s)

MarJon School of Beauty ltd-Tonawanda (Private, For-profit)
  Fall 2014 Enrollment: 64 . . . . (716) 836-6240
  2015-16 Tuition: $10,000
The Salon Professional Academy-Tonawanda (Private, For-profit)
  Fall 2014 Enrollment: 143 . . . . (716) 833-8772
  2015-16 Tuition: $18,929

Housing: Homeownership rate: 72.2%; Median home value: $118,600; Median year structure built: 1955; Homeowner vacancy rate: 0.6%; Median selected monthly owner costs: $1,156 with a mortgage, $474 without a mortgage; Median gross rent: $773 per month; Rental vacancy rate: 4.8%
Health Insurance: 96.2% have insurance; 78.3% have private insurance; 34.8% have public insurance; 3.8% do not have insurance; 0.8% of children under 18 do not have insurance
Transportation: Commute: 93.4% car, 2.1% public transportation, 1.9% walk, 1.3% work from home; Mean travel time to work: 19.6 minutes

TONAWANDA (city). Covers a land area of 3.803 square miles and a water area of 0.288 square miles. Located at 43.01° N. Lat; 78.88° W. Long. Elevation is 574 feet.
Population: 15,000; Growth (since 2000): -7.0%; Density: 3,944.0 persons per square mile; Race: 96.2% White, 0.3% Black/African American, 0.1% Asian, 0.7% American Indian/Alaska Native, 0.0% Native Hawaiian/Other Pacific Islander, 2.4% Two or more races, 2.0% Hispanic of any race; Average household size: 2.18; Median age: 43.8; Age under 18: 17.2%; Age 65 and over: 17.7%; Males per 100 females: 94.5; Marriage status: 34.9% never married, 46.9% now married, 1.7% separated, 7.7% widowed, 10.4% divorced; Foreign born: 4.0%; Speak English only: 94.2%; With disability: 15.0%; Veterans: 10.9%; Ancestry: 35.6% German, 22.1% Irish, 19.7% Italian, 16.8% Polish, 12.9% English
Employment: 10.3% management, business, and financial, 4.3% computer, engineering, and science, 8.5% education, legal, community service, arts, and media, 6.8% healthcare practitioners, 18.6% service, 31.2% sales and office, 5.7% natural resources, construction, and maintenance, 14.7% production, transportation, and material moving
Income: Per capita: $25,894; Median household: $44,805; Average household: $55,512; Households with income of $100,000 or more: 14.5%; Poverty rate: 11.5%
Educational Attainment: High school diploma or higher: 91.3%; Bachelor's degree or higher: 23.0%; Graduate/professional degree or higher: 9.2%

School District(s)

Kenmore-Tonawanda Union Free SD (PK-12)
  2014-15 Enrollment: 7,171 . . . . (716) 874-8400
Sweet Home Central SD (KG-12)
  2014-15 Enrollment: 3,254 . . . . (716) 250-1402
Tonawanda City SD (PK-12)
  2014-15 Enrollment: 1,824 . . . . (716) 694-7784

Vocational/Technical School(s)

MarJon School of Beauty ltd-Tonawanda (Private, For-profit)
  Fall 2014 Enrollment: 64 . . . . (716) 836-6240
  2015-16 Tuition: $10,000
The Salon Professional Academy-Tonawanda (Private, For-profit)
  Fall 2014 Enrollment: 143 . . . . (716) 833-8772
  2015-16 Tuition: $18,929

Housing: Homeownership rate: 72.4%; Median home value: $92,800; Median year structure built: 1950; Homeowner vacancy rate: 0.8%; Median selected monthly owner costs: $1,076 with a mortgage, $471 without a mortgage; Median gross rent: $660 per month; Rental vacancy rate: 8.2%
Health Insurance: 92.5% have insurance; 74.5% have private insurance; 35.0% have public insurance; 7.5% do not have insurance; 2.0% of children under 18 do not have insurance
Safety: Violent crime rate: 17.4 per 10,000 population; Property crime rate: 196.1 per 10,000 population
Transportation: Commute: 91.1% car, 0.8% public transportation, 4.9% walk, 1.4% work from home; Mean travel time to work: 19.7 minutes

Additional Information Contacts
City of Tonawanda . . . . (716) 695-1800
  http://www.ci.tonawanda.ny.us

TONAWANDA (town). Covers a land area of 18.735 square miles and a water area of 1.544 square miles. Located at 42.98° N. Lat; 78.88° W. Long. Elevation is 574 feet.
History: Named for the Iroquois translation of "swift water". Incorporated as a village 1854, and as a city in 1903.
Population: 73,420; Growth (since 2000): -6.1%; Density: 3,918.9 persons per square mile; Race: 90.9% White, 3.7% Black/African American, 2.5% Asian, 0.3% American Indian/Alaska Native, 0.0% Native Hawaiian/Other Pacific Islander, 1.9% Two or more races, 3.3% Hispanic of any race; Average household size: 2.23; Median age: 43.0; Age under 18: 19.0%; Age 65 and over: 19.0%; Males per 100 females: 88.8; Marriage status: 31.6% never married, 48.5% now married, 1.5% separated, 8.6% widowed, 11.3% divorced; Foreign born: 5.0%; Speak English only: 93.1%; With disability: 13.9%; Veterans: 8.8%; Ancestry: 29.3% German, 25.2% Italian, 21.7% Irish, 14.7% Polish, 9.0% English
Employment: 14.0% management, business, and financial, 4.5% computer, engineering, and science, 13.1% education, legal, community service, arts, and media, 6.5% healthcare practitioners, 16.9% service, 29.4% sales and office, 6.0% natural resources, construction, and maintenance, 9.6% production, transportation, and material moving
Income: Per capita: $29,162; Median household: $53,760; Average household: $64,211; Households with income of $100,000 or more: 17.9%; Poverty rate: 9.8%
Educational Attainment: High school diploma or higher: 93.0%; Bachelor's degree or higher: 32.9%; Graduate/professional degree or higher: 14.7%
Housing: Homeownership rate: 71.0%; Median home value: $117,000; Median year structure built: 1953; Homeowner vacancy rate: 0.5%; Median selected monthly owner costs: $1,165 with a mortgage, $488 without a mortgage; Median gross rent: $753 per month; Rental vacancy rate: 4.9%
Health Insurance: 96.3% have insurance; 78.3% have private insurance; 34.4% have public insurance; 3.7% do not have insurance; 0.8% of children under 18 do not have insurance
Safety: Violent crime rate: 24.3 per 10,000 population; Property crime rate: 190.3 per 10,000 population
Transportation: Commute: 92.9% car, 2.0% public transportation, 2.0% walk, 1.6% work from home; Mean travel time to work: 19.6 minutes
Additional Information Contacts
Town of Tonawanda . . . . (716) 877-8800
  http://www.tonawanda.ny.us

TONAWANDA RESERVATION (reservation). Covers a land area of 1.839 square miles and a water area of 0 square miles. Located at 43.08° N. Lat; 78.48° W. Long.
Population: 18; Growth (since 2000): n/a; Density: 9.8 persons per square mile; Race: 0.0% White, 0.0% Black/African American, 0.0% Asian, 100.0% American Indian/Alaska Native, 0.0% Native Hawaiian/Other Pacific Islander, 0.0% Two or more races, 0.0% Hispanic of any race; Average household size: 6.00; Median age: 18.0; Age under 18: 50.0%; Age 65 and over: 0.0%; Males per 100 females: 78.9; Marriage status: 61.5% never married, 30.8% now married, 0.0% separated, 7.7% widowed, 0.0% divorced; Foreign born: 0.0%; Speak English only: 100.0%; With disability: 0.0%; Veterans: 0.0%; Ancestry: n/a
Employment: 0.0% management, business, and financial, 0.0% computer, engineering, and science, 0.0% education, legal, community service, arts, and media, 0.0% healthcare practitioners, 0.0% service, 66.7% sales and office, 33.3% natural resources, construction, and maintenance, 0.0% production, transportation, and material moving
Income: Per capita: $17,022; Median household: n/a; Average household: n/a; Households with income of $100,000 or more: 66.7%; Poverty rate: n/a
Educational Attainment: High school diploma or higher: 20.0%; Bachelor's degree or higher: n/a; Graduate/professional degree or higher: n/a
Housing: Homeownership rate: 100.0%; Median home value: n/a; Median year structure built: n/a; Homeowner vacancy rate: 0.0%; Median selected monthly owner costs: n/a with a mortgage, n/a without a mortgage; Median gross rent: n/a per month; Rental vacancy rate: 0.0%
Health Insurance: 100.0% have insurance; 16.7% have private insurance; 83.3% have public insurance; 0.0% do not have insurance; 0.0% of children under 18 do not have insurance

Transportation: Commute: 66.7% car, 0.0% public transportation, 0.0% walk, 33.3% work from home; Mean travel time to work: 0.0 minutes

TOWN LINE (CDP).
Covers a land area of 4.622 square miles and a water area of 0.004 square miles. Located at 42.89° N. Lat; 78.57° W. Long. Elevation is 751 feet.
Population: 2,270; Growth (since 2000): -10.0%; Density: 491.2 persons per square mile; Race: 95.6% White, 1.5% Black/African American, 0.0% Asian, 0.0% American Indian/Alaska Native, 0.0% Native Hawaiian/Other Pacific Islander, 2.9% Two or more races, 0.8% Hispanic of any race; Average household size: 2.78; Median age: 45.1; Age under 18: 21.7%; Age 65 and over: 14.1%; Males per 100 females: 98.1; Marriage status: 26.6% never married, 58.3% now married, 0.4% separated, 6.9% widowed, 8.2% divorced; Foreign born: 4.5%; Speak English only: 94.6%; With disability: 16.5%; Veterans: 10.7%; Ancestry: 48.2% German, 19.9% Polish, 16.7% Irish, 11.2% Italian, 7.0% English
Employment: 10.8% management, business, and financial, 3.7% computer, engineering, and science, 13.3% education, legal, community service, arts, and media, 3.4% healthcare practitioners, 20.2% service, 27.7% sales and office, 8.0% natural resources, construction, and maintenance, 12.9% production, transportation, and material moving
Income: Per capita: $29,601; Median household: $68,750; Average household: $80,451; Households with income of $100,000 or more: 24.5%; Poverty rate: 10.9%
Educational Attainment: High school diploma or higher: 95.9%; Bachelor's degree or higher: 24.6%; Graduate/professional degree or higher: 6.9%
Housing: Homeownership rate: 88.5%; Median home value: $158,100; Median year structure built: 1964; Homeowner vacancy rate: 0.0%; Median selected monthly owner costs: $1,335 with a mortgage, $481 without a mortgage; Median gross rent: $1,087 per month; Rental vacancy rate: 0.0%
Health Insurance: 95.9% have insurance; 82.9% have private insurance; 30.5% have public insurance; 4.1% do not have insurance; 0.0% of children under 18 do not have insurance
Transportation: Commute: 98.9% car, 0.0% public transportation, 0.0% walk, 1.1% work from home; Mean travel time to work: 25.5 minutes

UNIVERSITY AT BUFFALO (CDP).
Covers a land area of 1.373 square miles and a water area of 0.089 square miles. Located at 43.00° N. Lat; 78.79° W. Long.
History: University at Buffalo, The State University of New York, is a public research university with multiple campuses located in Buffalo and Amherst, New York. The university is the largest in the SUNY system, and also the largest public university in the northeastern United States (comprising New York state and the New England region). It is also the largest one of SUNY's four comprehensive university centers.
Population: 6,174; Growth (since 2000): n/a; Density: 4,497.5 persons per square mile; Race: 56.2% White, 9.3% Black/African American, 25.7% Asian, 0.1% American Indian/Alaska Native, 0.0% Native Hawaiian/Other Pacific Islander, 3.6% Two or more races, 8.9% Hispanic of any race; Average household size: 2.06; Median age: 19.8; Age under 18: 1.3%; Age 65 and over: 0.0%; Males per 100 females: 104.1; Marriage status: 98.9% never married, 0.9% now married, 0.0% separated, 0.0% widowed, 0.1% divorced; Foreign born: 22.4%; Speak English only: 65.2%; With disability: 2.7%; Veterans: 0.1%; Ancestry: 18.1% Italian, 16.5% German, 15.9% Irish, 9.2% Polish, 5.6% English
Employment: 3.7% management, business, and financial, 6.9% computer, engineering, and science, 11.5% education, legal, community service, arts, and media, 1.7% healthcare practitioners, 28.5% service, 41.5% sales and office, 1.0% natural resources, construction, and maintenance, 5.3% production, transportation, and material moving
Income: Per capita: $3,673; Median household: n/a; Average household: $8,562; Households with income of $100,000 or more: n/a; Poverty rate: 87.1%
Educational Attainment: High school diploma or higher: 100.0%; Bachelor's degree or higher: 76.7%; Graduate/professional degree or higher: 33.7%
Housing: Homeownership rate: n/a; Median home value: n/a; Median year structure built: 1996; Homeowner vacancy rate: 0.0%; Median selected monthly owner costs: n/a with a mortgage, n/a without a mortgage; Median gross rent: $1,302 per month; Rental vacancy rate: 0.0%
Health Insurance: 99.5% have insurance; 92.2% have private insurance; 9.0% have public insurance; 0.5% do not have insurance; 0.0% of children under 18 do not have insurance

Transportation: Commute: 42.1% car, 12.3% public transportation, 37.5% walk, 6.2% work from home; Mean travel time to work: 12.3 minutes

WALES (town).
Covers a land area of 35.588 square miles and a water area of 0.051 square miles. Located at 42.74° N. Lat; 78.52° W. Long.
Population: 3,030; Growth (since 2000): 2.4%; Density: 85.1 persons per square mile; Race: 93.8% White, 0.0% Black/African American, 5.1% Asian, 0.0% American Indian/Alaska Native, 0.0% Native Hawaiian/Other Pacific Islander, 0.7% Two or more races, 1.7% Hispanic of any race; Average household size: 2.49; Median age: 45.4; Age under 18: 23.1%; Age 65 and over: 15.0%; Males per 100 females: 98.0; Marriage status: 17.2% never married, 67.3% now married, 1.5% separated, 4.4% widowed, 11.1% divorced; Foreign born: 3.7%; Speak English only: 97.0%; With disability: 7.5%; Veterans: 7.7%; Ancestry: 40.0% German, 26.1% Polish, 16.2% Irish, 9.4% English, 7.3% Italian
Employment: 21.7% management, business, and financial, 2.1% computer, engineering, and science, 8.8% education, legal, community service, arts, and media, 9.4% healthcare practitioners, 17.2% service, 18.7% sales and office, 11.2% natural resources, construction, and maintenance, 10.9% production, transportation, and material moving
Income: Per capita: $32,817; Median household: $68,250; Average household: $81,041; Households with income of $100,000 or more: 34.9%; Poverty rate: 5.0%
Educational Attainment: High school diploma or higher: 94.0%; Bachelor's degree or higher: 30.1%; Graduate/professional degree or higher: 12.9%
Housing: Homeownership rate: 92.0%; Median home value: $164,300; Median year structure built: 1969; Homeowner vacancy rate: 2.3%; Median selected monthly owner costs: $1,396 with a mortgage, $475 without a mortgage; Median gross rent: $822 per month; Rental vacancy rate: 0.0%
Health Insurance: 95.5% have insurance; 78.3% have private insurance; 27.7% have public insurance; 4.5% do not have insurance; 4.4% of children under 18 do not have insurance
Transportation: Commute: 92.9% car, 0.0% public transportation, 1.5% walk, 5.6% work from home; Mean travel time to work: 25.2 minutes

WALES CENTER (unincorporated postal area)
ZCTA: 14169
Covers a land area of 0.308 square miles and a water area of 0 square miles. Located at 42.77° N. Lat; 78.52° W. Long. Elevation is 889 feet.
Population: 217; Growth (since 2000): n/a; Density: 704.0 persons per square mile; Race: 100.0% White, 0.0% Black/African American, 0.0% Asian, 0.0% American Indian/Alaska Native, 0.0% Native Hawaiian/Other Pacific Islander, 0.0% Two or more races, 0.0% Hispanic of any race; Average household size: 1.84; Median age: 51.3; Age under 18: 24.9%; Age 65 and over: 19.8%; Males per 100 females: 86.4; Marriage status: 16.9% never married, 47.6% now married, 6.9% separated, 0.0% widowed, 35.4% divorced; Foreign born: 0.0%; Speak English only: 100.0%; With disability: 31.8%; Veterans: 15.3%; Ancestry: 40.6% German, 34.6% Polish, 18.9% Italian, 12.9% Irish, 12.4% French
Employment: 7.5% management, business, and financial, 0.0% computer, engineering, and science, 12.3% education, legal, community service, arts, and media, 0.0% healthcare practitioners, 25.5% service, 24.5% sales and office, 23.6% natural resources, construction, and maintenance, 6.6% production, transportation, and material moving
Income: Per capita: $23,797; Median household: $32,407; Average household: $43,847; Households with income of $100,000 or more: 3.4%; Poverty rate: 27.2%
Educational Attainment: High school diploma or higher: 96.3%; Bachelor's degree or higher: 5.5%; Graduate/professional degree or higher: 5.5%
Housing: Homeownership rate: 77.1%; Median home value: n/a; Median year structure built: 1992; Homeowner vacancy rate: 0.0%; Median selected monthly owner costs: n/a with a mortgage, n/a without a mortgage; Median gross rent: n/a per month; Rental vacancy rate: 0.0%
Health Insurance: 96.3% have insurance; 41.0% have private insurance; 63.6% have public insurance; 3.7% do not have insurance; 0.0% of children under 18 do not have insurance
Transportation: Commute: 92.5% car, 0.0% public transportation, 0.0% walk, 7.5% work from home; Mean travel time to work: 0.0 minutes

WANAKAH (CDP). Covers a land area of 1.204 square miles and a water area of 0 square miles. Located at 42.74° N. Lat; 78.90° W. Long. Elevation is 591 feet.
Population: 2,836; Growth (since 2000): n/a; Density: 2,354.7 persons per square mile; Race: 98.1% White, 0.0% Black/African American, 1.0% Asian, 0.9% American Indian/Alaska Native, 0.0% Native Hawaiian/Other Pacific Islander, 0.0% Two or more races, 0.0% Hispanic of any race; Average household size: 2.43; Median age: 48.3; Age under 18: 13.9%; Age 65 and over: 22.0%; Males per 100 females: 92.2; Marriage status: 21.6% never married, 63.6% now married, 1.7% separated, 8.2% widowed, 6.6% divorced; Foreign born: 1.9%; Speak English only: 96.9%; With disability: 14.4%; Veterans: 13.9%; Ancestry: 38.3% German, 33.7% Irish, 18.1% Italian, 13.1% Polish, 6.8% English
Employment: 13.1% management, business, and financial, 4.2% computer, engineering, and science, 9.4% education, legal, community service, arts, and media, 2.1% healthcare practitioners, 29.8% service, 15.7% sales and office, 12.4% natural resources, construction, and maintenance, 13.3% production, transportation, and material moving
Income: Per capita: $36,814; Median household: $72,306; Average household: $89,081; Households with income of $100,000 or more: 33.1%; Poverty rate: 0.5%
Educational Attainment: High school diploma or higher: 93.6%; Bachelor's degree or higher: 30.7%; Graduate/professional degree or higher: 9.9%
Housing: Homeownership rate: 90.8%; Median home value: $138,800; Median year structure built: 1954; Homeowner vacancy rate: 0.0%; Median selected monthly owner costs: $1,320 with a mortgage, $535 without a mortgage; Median gross rent: $871 per month; Rental vacancy rate: 0.0%
Health Insurance: 98.0% have insurance; 90.3% have private insurance; 27.8% have public insurance; 2.0% do not have insurance; 0.0% of children under 18 do not have insurance
Transportation: Commute: 100.0% car, 0.0% public transportation, 0.0% walk, 0.0% work from home; Mean travel time to work: 22.9 minutes

WEST FALLS (unincorporated postal area)
ZCTA: 14170
Covers a land area of 12.326 square miles and a water area of 0.054 square miles. Located at 42.70° N. Lat; 78.67° W. Long. Elevation is 925 feet.
Population: 2,503; Growth (since 2000): -4.9%; Density: 203.1 persons per square mile; Race: 98.0% White, 0.0% Black/African American, 0.0% Asian, 0.0% American Indian/Alaska Native, 0.0% Native Hawaiian/Other Pacific Islander, 2.0% Two or more races, 3.8% Hispanic of any race; Average household size: 2.60; Median age: 47.5; Age under 18: 20.7%; Age 65 and over: 15.3%; Males per 100 females: 102.3; Marriage status: 27.0% never married, 57.8% now married, 0.0% separated, 4.4% widowed, 10.8% divorced; Foreign born: 2.8%; Speak English only: 96.6%; With disability: 14.0%; Veterans: 9.6%; Ancestry: 41.4% German, 25.6% Irish, 16.3% Italian, 13.5% Polish, 11.7% English
Employment: 14.0% management, business, and financial, 3.4% computer, engineering, and science, 10.4% education, legal, community service, arts, and media, 11.2% healthcare practitioners, 19.1% service, 16.5% sales and office, 11.1% natural resources, construction, and maintenance, 14.2% production, transportation, and material moving
Income: Per capita: $28,966; Median household: $68,333; Average household: $73,778; Households with income of $100,000 or more: 25.5%; Poverty rate: 7.8%
Educational Attainment: High school diploma or higher: 95.6%; Bachelor's degree or higher: 21.6%; Graduate/professional degree or higher: 11.7%
Housing: Homeownership rate: 85.2%; Median home value: $164,700; Median year structure built: 1959; Homeowner vacancy rate: 0.0%; Median selected monthly owner costs: $1,483 with a mortgage, $463 without a mortgage; Median gross rent: $640 per month; Rental vacancy rate: 0.0%
Health Insurance: 90.9% have insurance; 75.0% have private insurance; 30.2% have public insurance; 9.1% do not have insurance; 7.7% of children under 18 do not have insurance
Transportation: Commute: 95.8% car, 0.0% public transportation, 0.0% walk, 3.4% work from home; Mean travel time to work: 27.5 minutes

WEST SENECA (CDP). Covers a land area of 21.357 square miles and a water area of 0.057 square miles. Located at 42.84° N. Lat; 78.75° W. Long. Elevation is 597 feet.
Population: 45,089; Growth (since 2000): -1.9%; Density: 2,111.2 persons per square mile; Race: 95.6% White, 2.1% Black/African American, 0.3% Asian, 0.1% American Indian/Alaska Native, 0.0% Native Hawaiian/Other Pacific Islander, 1.3% Two or more races, 1.9% Hispanic of any race; Average household size: 2.30; Median age: 45.1; Age under 18: 19.2%; Age 65 and over: 20.4%; Males per 100 females: 91.7; Marriage status: 28.8% never married, 52.4% now married, 1.3% separated, 9.4% widowed, 9.4% divorced; Foreign born: 2.6%; Speak English only: 95.0%; With disability: 13.4%; Veterans: 9.1%; Ancestry: 31.7% German, 27.1% Polish, 24.4% Irish, 19.1% Italian, 6.5% English
Employment: 13.3% management, business, and financial, 4.6% computer, engineering, and science, 10.1% education, legal, community service, arts, and media, 7.6% healthcare practitioners, 16.6% service, 28.5% sales and office, 6.6% natural resources, construction, and maintenance, 12.6% production, transportation, and material moving
Income: Per capita: $29,643; Median household: $59,265; Average household: $67,732; Households with income of $100,000 or more: 21.2%; Poverty rate: 6.7%
Educational Attainment: High school diploma or higher: 92.9%; Bachelor's degree or higher: 27.4%; Graduate/professional degree or higher: 10.9%
School District(s)
Erie 1 Boces
  2014-15 Enrollment: n/a . . . . (716) 821-7001
West Seneca Central SD (PK-12)
  2014-15 Enrollment: 6,958 . . . . (716) 677-3101
Vocational/Technical School(s)
Continental School of Beauty Culture-West Seneca (Private, For-profit)
  Fall 2014 Enrollment: 95 . . . . (716) 675-8205
  2015-16 Tuition: $12,440
Erie 1 BOCES (Public)
  Fall 2014 Enrollment: 369 . . . . (716) 821-7500
  2015-16 Tuition: $9,550
Housing: Homeownership rate: 76.3%; Median home value: $132,900; Median year structure built: 1964; Homeowner vacancy rate: 0.6%; Median selected monthly owner costs: $1,251 with a mortgage, $523 without a mortgage; Median gross rent: $745 per month; Rental vacancy rate: 1.7%
Health Insurance: 94.9% have insurance; 79.9% have private insurance; 32.8% have public insurance; 5.1% do not have insurance; 2.7% of children under 18 do not have insurance
Safety: Violent crime rate: 9.9 per 10,000 population; Property crime rate: 142.9 per 10,000 population
Transportation: Commute: 94.7% car, 1.1% public transportation, 1.7% walk, 2.0% work from home; Mean travel time to work: 20.8 minutes
Additional Information Contacts
Town of West Seneca . . . . (716) 674-5600
  http://www.westseneca.net

WILLIAMSVILLE (village). Covers a land area of 1.260 square miles and a water area of 0.010 square miles. Located at 42.96° N. Lat; 78.74° W. Long. Elevation is 676 feet.
History: Settled c.1800, incorporated 1869.
Population: 5,269; Growth (since 2000): -5.5%; Density: 4,181.2 persons per square mile; Race: 92.3% White, 3.4% Black/African American, 2.4% Asian, 0.2% American Indian/Alaska Native, 0.0% Native Hawaiian/Other Pacific Islander, 1.4% Two or more races, 2.5% Hispanic of any race; Average household size: 1.97; Median age: 50.7; Age under 18: 15.0%; Age 65 and over: 24.1%; Males per 100 females: 77.7; Marriage status: 29.6% never married, 44.5% now married, 1.5% separated, 8.1% widowed, 17.8% divorced; Foreign born: 8.4%; Speak English only: 90.9%; With disability: 12.2%; Veterans: 9.4%; Ancestry: 30.0% German, 19.1% Polish, 18.8% Irish, 13.6% English, 12.9% Italian
Employment: 16.5% management, business, and financial, 7.7% computer, engineering, and science, 24.5% education, legal, community service, arts, and media, 10.6% healthcare practitioners, 12.1% service, 17.3% sales and office, 3.8% natural resources, construction, and maintenance, 7.5% production, transportation, and material moving
Income: Per capita: $38,247; Median household: $59,149; Average household: $77,388; Households with income of $100,000 or more: 24.7%; Poverty rate: 7.5%

Educational Attainment: High school diploma or higher: 97.1%; Bachelor's degree or higher: 57.1%; Graduate/professional degree or higher: 28.1%

School District(s)

Clarence Central SD (KG-12)
    2014-15 Enrollment: 4,623 . . . . (716) 407-9102
Williamsville Central SD (KG-12)
    2014-15 Enrollment: 10,166 . . . . (716) 626-8005

Vocational/Technical School(s)

Leon Studio One School of Hair Design (Private, For-profit)
    Fall 2014 Enrollment: 27 . . . . (716) 631-3878
    2015-16 Tuition: $6,900
New York Institute of Massage Inc (Private, For-profit)
    Fall 2014 Enrollment: 53 . . . . (716) 633-0355
    2015-16 Tuition: $16,600

Housing: Homeownership rate: 60.2%; Median home value: $162,600; Median year structure built: 1950; Homeowner vacancy rate: 0.8%; Median selected monthly owner costs: $1,508 with a mortgage, $619 without a mortgage; Median gross rent: $861 per month; Rental vacancy rate: 0.0%

Health Insurance: 97.2% have insurance; 90.1% have private insurance; 27.1% have public insurance; 2.8% do not have insurance; 3.0% of children under 18 do not have insurance

Transportation: Commute: 89.2% car, 3.8% public transportation, 3.4% walk, 2.2% work from home; Mean travel time to work: 20.4 minutes

Additional Information Contacts
Village of Williamsville . . . . (716) 632-4120
    http://village.williamsville.ny.us

Essex County

Located in northeastern New York, in the Adirondacks; bounded on the east by Lake Champlain; drained by the Hudson and Ausable Rivers; includes Lake Placid and Saranac Lake, and Mt. Marcy, the highest point in the state (5,344 ft). Covers a land area of 1,794.228 square miles, a water area of 122.000 square miles, and is located in the Eastern Time Zone at 44.11° N. Lat., 73.78° W. Long. The county was founded in 1799. County seat is Elizabethtown.

Weather Station: Lake Placid 2 S   Elevation: 1,938 feet

	Jan	Feb	Mar	Apr	May	Jun	Jul	Aug	Sep	Oct	Nov	Dec
High	27	31	40	53	65	73	77	75	68	56	43	32
Low	6	8	16	29	39	48	53	51	44	34	24	12
Precip	2.5	2.1	2.6	2.8	3.5	4.3	4.4	4.2	3.9	3.9	3.5	3.0
Snow	na	na	18.8	7.2	0.3	0.0	0.0	0.0	tr	2.5	10.8	22.7

High and Low temperatures in degrees Fahrenheit; Precipitation and Snow in inches

Weather Station: Newcomb   Elevation: 1,620 feet

	Jan	Feb	Mar	Apr	May	Jun	Jul	Aug	Sep	Oct	Nov	Dec
High	25	28	38	51	64	72	76	74	66	55	41	29
Low	5	4	14	28	39	49	53	52	45	34	25	11
Precip	3.0	2.7	2.9	3.2	3.8	3.7	3.9	3.9	3.9	4.0	3.8	3.4
Snow	24.3	22.6	18.7	5.7	0.2	tr	0.0	0.0	tr	1.1	8.9	24.2

High and Low temperatures in degrees Fahrenheit; Precipitation and Snow in inches

Weather Station: Ray Brook   Elevation: 1,620 feet

	Jan	Feb	Mar	Apr	May	Jun	Jul	Aug	Sep	Oct	Nov	Dec
High	25	29	38	51	64	72	77	75	67	54	41	30
Low	3	5	14	28	39	48	52	51	43	33	25	12
Precip	na	na	2.5	2.7	3.1	3.8	3.7	3.8	4.1	3.4	3.4	na
Snow	23.5	19.6	19.9	9.2	0.8	tr	0.0	tr	0.1	1.6	14.6	22.4

High and Low temperatures in degrees Fahrenheit; Precipitation and Snow in inches

Population: 38,912; Growth (since 2000): 0.2%; Density: 21.7 persons per square mile; Race: 93.0% White, 3.1% Black/African American, 0.6% Asian, 0.2% American Indian/Alaska Native, 0.0% Native Hawaiian/Other Pacific Islander, 1.6% two or more races, 3.0% Hispanic of any race; Average household size: 2.37; Median age: 45.9; Age under 18: 17.6%; Age 65 and over: 20.2%; Males per 100 females: 107.4; Marriage status: 28.7% never married, 52.9% now married, 2.4% separated, 8.4% widowed, 10.0% divorced; Foreign born: 3.7%; Speak English only: 93.9%; With disability: 16.1%; Veterans: 11.4%; Ancestry: 22.6% Irish, 16.8% French, 14.2% English, 13.4% German, 8.3% Italian

Religion: Six largest groups: 21.5% Catholicism, 5.6% Methodist/Pietist, 2.0% Non-denominational Protestant, 1.3% Presbyterian-Reformed, 1.1% Episcopalianism/Anglicanism, 1.1% Baptist

Economy: Unemployment rate: 4.5%; Leading industries: 18.1 % accommodation and food services; 17.8 % retail trade; 12.6 % health care and social assistance; Farms: 261 totaling 54,837 acres; Company size: 0 employ 1,000 or more persons, 1 employs 500 to 999 persons, 13 employ 100 to 499 persons, 1,138 employ less than 100 persons; Business ownership: 1,164 women-owned, n/a Black-owned, 33 Hispanic-owned, 36 Asian-owned, n/a American Indian/Alaska Native-owned

Employment: 12.2% management, business, and financial, 2.4% computer, engineering, and science, 11.2% education, legal, community service, arts, and media, 6.5% healthcare practitioners, 24.3% service, 21.6% sales and office, 11.8% natural resources, construction, and maintenance, 9.9% production, transportation, and material moving

Income: Per capita: $26,805; Median household: $52,758; Average household: $65,324; Households with income of $100,000 or more: 17.7%; Poverty rate: 10.7%

Educational Attainment: High school diploma or higher: 88.8%; Bachelor's degree or higher: 24.2%; Graduate/professional degree or higher: 10.7%

Housing: Homeownership rate: 73.8%; Median home value: $145,100; Median year structure built: 1960; Homeowner vacancy rate: 3.9%; Median selected monthly owner costs: $1,250 with a mortgage, $519 without a mortgage; Median gross rent: $805 per month; Rental vacancy rate: 6.4%

Vital Statistics: Birth rate: 80.0 per 10,000 population; Death rate: 106.8 per 10,000 population; Age-adjusted cancer mortality rate: 177.8 deaths per 100,000 population

Health Insurance: 92.0% have insurance; 70.8% have private insurance; 39.4% have public insurance; 8.0% do not have insurance; 6.3% of children under 18 do not have insurance

Health Care: Physicians: 8.8 per 10,000 population; Dentists: 3.1 per 10,000 population; Hospital beds: 10.3 per 10,000 population; Hospital admissions: 179.9 per 10,000 population

Air Quality Index (AQI): Percent of Days: 94.8% good, 5.2% moderate, 0.0% unhealthy for sensitive individuals, 0.0% unhealthy, 0.0% very unhealthy; Annual median: 36; Annual maximum: 84

Transportation: Commute: 86.2% car, 0.7% public transportation, 4.1% walk, 5.3% work from home; Mean travel time to work: 20.8 minutes

2016 Presidential Election: 47.2% Trump, 46.0% Clinton, 4.3% Johnson, 2.5% Stein

National and State Parks: Wickham Marsh State Game Management Area

Additional Information Contacts
Essex Government . . . . (518) 873-3601
    http://www.co.essex.ny.us

Essex County Communities

BLOOMINGDALE (unincorporated postal area)

ZCTA: 12913
    Covers a land area of 27.122 square miles and a water area of 2.224 square miles. Located at 44.43° N. Lat; 74.00° W. Long. Elevation is 1,572 feet.

Population: 1,330; Growth (since 2000): 11.4%; Density: 49.0 persons per square mile; Race: 99.2% White, 0.4% Black/African American, 0.0% Asian, 0.0% American Indian/Alaska Native, 0.0% Native Hawaiian/Other Pacific Islander, 0.0% Two or more races, 1.5% Hispanic of any race; Average household size: 2.33; Median age: 47.6; Age under 18: 19.6%; Age 65 and over: 17.6%; Males per 100 females: 102.3; Marriage status: 13.8% never married, 69.3% now married, 1.6% separated, 8.1% widowed, 8.7% divorced; Foreign born: 3.3%; Speak English only: 93.4%; With disability: 19.1%; Veterans: 12.3%; Ancestry: 20.6% Irish, 18.3% French, 12.6% English, 12.1% Italian, 11.1% German

Employment: 11.9% management, business, and financial, 6.4% computer, engineering, and science, 15.2% education, legal, community service, arts, and media, 2.2% healthcare practitioners, 19.6% service, 28.9% sales and office, 9.8% natural resources, construction, and maintenance, 6.0% production, transportation, and material moving

Income: Per capita: $30,334; Median household: $55,761; Average household: $69,534; Households with income of $100,000 or more: 17.0%; Poverty rate: 8.3%

Educational Attainment: High school diploma or higher: 92.4%; Bachelor's degree or higher: 29.7%; Graduate/professional degree or higher: 15.4%

Housing: Homeownership rate: 80.7%; Median home value: $164,700; Median year structure built: 1981; Homeowner vacancy rate: 0.0%;

Median selected monthly owner costs: $1,448 with a mortgage, $523 without a mortgage; Median gross rent: $625 per month; Rental vacancy rate: 0.0%

Health Insurance: 98.4% have insurance; 83.8% have private insurance; 29.5% have public insurance; 1.6% do not have insurance; 1.5% of children under 18 do not have insurance

Transportation: Commute: 94.8% car, 0.0% public transportation, 0.7% walk, 2.5% work from home; Mean travel time to work: 17.3 minutes

CHESTERFIELD (town).
Covers a land area of 79.036 square miles and a water area of 26.336 square miles. Located at 44.45° N. Lat; 73.45° W. Long.

Population: 2,720; Growth (since 2000): 12.9%; Density: 34.4 persons per square mile; Race: 95.8% White, 0.3% Black/African American, 0.7% Asian, 0.1% American Indian/Alaska Native, 0.0% Native Hawaiian/Other Pacific Islander, 3.2% Two or more races, 2.4% Hispanic of any race; Average household size: 2.52; Median age: 47.1; Age under 18: 18.2%; Age 65 and over: 17.3%; Males per 100 females: 101.7; Marriage status: 23.3% never married, 58.3% now married, 2.5% separated, 7.6% widowed, 10.8% divorced; Foreign born: 2.6%; Speak English only: 95.3%; With disability: 14.8%; Veterans: 14.8%; Ancestry: 27.4% French, 18.2% Irish, 14.0% German, 13.5% English, 10.3% American

Employment: 15.4% management, business, and financial, 1.5% computer, engineering, and science, 13.2% education, legal, community service, arts, and media, 5.4% healthcare practitioners, 15.3% service, 23.0% sales and office, 16.8% natural resources, construction, and maintenance, 9.4% production, transportation, and material moving

Income: Per capita: $30,199; Median household: $56,548; Average household: $72,639; Households with income of $100,000 or more: 20.0%; Poverty rate: 8.3%

Educational Attainment: High school diploma or higher: 91.9%; Bachelor's degree or higher: 25.7%; Graduate/professional degree or higher: 12.2%

Housing: Homeownership rate: 82.4%; Median home value: $119,800; Median year structure built: 1968; Homeowner vacancy rate: 1.1%; Median selected monthly owner costs: $1,304 with a mortgage, $427 without a mortgage; Median gross rent: $879 per month; Rental vacancy rate: 10.0%

Health Insurance: 91.5% have insurance; 70.0% have private insurance; 37.6% have public insurance; 8.5% do not have insurance; 10.1% of children under 18 do not have insurance

Transportation: Commute: 86.2% car, 0.0% public transportation, 3.3% walk, 7.5% work from home; Mean travel time to work: 22.2 minutes

CROWN POINT (town).
Covers a land area of 76.121 square miles and a water area of 5.724 square miles. Located at 43.96° N. Lat; 73.58° W. Long. Elevation is 223 feet.

History: The French began building Fort St. Frederic in 1731. In the French and Indian Wars the fort resisted early English attacks but was demolished (1759) before the advance of Jeffrey Amherst. The British began building a new fort, Fort Amherst (renamed Crown Point), in 1759. Early in the Revolution, Crown Point was captured by Seth Warner and the Green Mt. Boys. Abandoned (1777) to Gen. John Burgoyne. Crown Point Reservation, with bathing and fishing, a Museum and ruins of colonial forts, is nearby.

Population: 1,882; Growth (since 2000): -11.2%; Density: 24.7 persons per square mile; Race: 95.9% White, 0.2% Black/African American, 2.8% Asian, 0.5% American Indian/Alaska Native, 0.0% Native Hawaiian/Other Pacific Islander, 0.6% Two or more races, 0.0% Hispanic of any race; Average household size: 2.48; Median age: 44.9; Age under 18: 19.4%; Age 65 and over: 21.6%; Males per 100 females: 104.0; Marriage status: 26.0% never married, 56.4% now married, 2.3% separated, 5.6% widowed, 12.0% divorced; Foreign born: 4.3%; Speak English only: 92.2%; With disability: 24.9%; Veterans: 13.0%; Ancestry: 22.8% French, 22.7% Irish, 12.9% English, 10.3% German, 6.9% Polish

Employment: 4.4% management, business, and financial, 5.3% computer, engineering, and science, 11.0% education, legal, community service, arts, and media, 3.5% healthcare practitioners, 28.3% service, 13.1% sales and office, 13.4% natural resources, construction, and maintenance, 21.1% production, transportation, and material moving

Income: Per capita: $22,748; Median household: $44,669; Average household: $54,040; Households with income of $100,000 or more: 9.8%; Poverty rate: 9.4%

Educational Attainment: High school diploma or higher: 86.1%; Bachelor's degree or higher: 10.3%; Graduate/professional degree or higher: 4.1%

Crown Point Central SD (PK-12)
    2014-15 Enrollment: 275 . . . . (518) 597-4200

Housing: Homeownership rate: 75.9%; Median home value: $118,000; Median year structure built: 1964; Homeowner vacancy rate: 5.4%; Median selected monthly owner costs: $1,179 with a mortgage, $340 without a mortgage; Median gross rent: $700 per month; Rental vacancy rate: 6.7%

Health Insurance: 89.4% have insurance; 65.3% have private insurance; 44.5% have public insurance; 10.6% do not have insurance; 16.4% of children under 18 do not have insurance

Transportation: Commute: 90.8% car, 0.0% public transportation, 1.3% walk, 0.0% work from home; Mean travel time to work: 29.1 minutes

ELIZABETHTOWN (CDP).
Covers a land area of 3.307 square miles and a water area of 0.004 square miles. Located at 44.23° N. Lat; 73.59° W. Long. Elevation is 564 feet.

Population: 763; Growth (since 2000): n/a; Density: 230.7 persons per square mile; Race: 94.1% White, 3.8% Black/African American, 0.8% Asian, 0.0% American Indian/Alaska Native, 0.0% Native Hawaiian/Other Pacific Islander, 1.3% Two or more races, 0.0% Hispanic of any race; Average household size: 2.17; Median age: 52.3; Age under 18: 14.5%; Age 65 and over: 29.4%; Males per 100 females: 87.1; Marriage status: 28.1% never married, 38.3% now married, 2.5% separated, 17.5% widowed, 16.1% divorced; Foreign born: 2.4%; Speak English only: 98.4%; With disability: 9.7%; Veterans: 4.6%; Ancestry: 28.6% English, 19.4% Irish, 14.9% French, 7.3% German, 6.9% Scottish

Employment: 9.1% management, business, and financial, 4.9% computer, engineering, and science, 14.3% education, legal, community service, arts, and media, 9.6% healthcare practitioners, 17.3% service, 18.4% sales and office, 11.5% natural resources, construction, and maintenance, 14.8% production, transportation, and material moving

Income: Per capita: $25,973; Median household: $50,438; Average household: $59,606; Households with income of $100,000 or more: 16.0%; Poverty rate: 12.1%

Educational Attainment: High school diploma or higher: 92.1%; Bachelor's degree or higher: 32.8%; Graduate/professional degree or higher: 16.0%

Elizabethtown-Lewis Central SD (KG-12)
    2014-15 Enrollment: 262 . . . . (518) 873-6371

Housing: Homeownership rate: 65.6%; Median home value: $139,500; Median year structure built: 1942; Homeowner vacancy rate: 8.7%; Median selected monthly owner costs: $1,188 with a mortgage, $414 without a mortgage; Median gross rent: $616 per month; Rental vacancy rate: 0.0%

Health Insurance: 96.8% have insurance; 72.9% have private insurance; 45.1% have public insurance; 3.2% do not have insurance; 0.0% of children under 18 do not have insurance

Hospitals: Elizabethtown Community Hospital (25 beds)

Newspapers: Denton Publications (weekly circulation 80,000)

Transportation: Commute: 78.4% car, 3.3% public transportation, 8.6% walk, 6.4% work from home; Mean travel time to work: 17.7 minutes

ELIZABETHTOWN (town).
County seat. Covers a land area of 81.633 square miles and a water area of 1.477 square miles. Located at 44.19° N. Lat; 73.65° W. Long. Elevation is 564 feet.

Population: 1,161; Growth (since 2000): -11.7%; Density: 14.2 persons per square mile; Race: 95.3% White, 2.5% Black/African American, 0.5% Asian, 0.0% American Indian/Alaska Native, 0.0% Native Hawaiian/Other Pacific Islander, 0.9% Two or more races, 0.8% Hispanic of any race; Average household size: 2.18; Median age: 51.3; Age under 18: 15.9%; Age 65 and over: 24.8%; Males per 100 females: 92.9; Marriage status: 24.3% never married, 46.1% now married, 1.7% separated, 16.1% widowed, 13.5% divorced; Foreign born: 2.2%; Speak English only: 97.9%; With disability: 10.7%; Veterans: 6.4%; Ancestry: 26.7% English, 21.6% Irish, 12.7% French, 9.6% German, 6.2% Italian

Employment: 9.6% management, business, and financial, 4.0% computer, engineering, and science, 17.0% education, legal, community service, arts, and media, 9.6% healthcare practitioners, 20.4% service, 16.7% sales and office, 10.7% natural resources, construction, and maintenance, 12.0% production, transportation, and material moving

Income: Per capita: $29,393; Median household: $52,000; Average household: $66,928; Households with income of $100,000 or more: 22.7%; Poverty rate: 11.1%

Educational Attainment: High school diploma or higher: 93.1%; Bachelor's degree or higher: 34.0%; Graduate/professional degree or higher: 16.9%

School District(s)
Elizabethtown-Lewis Central SD (KG-12)
   2014-15 Enrollment: 262 . . . . (518) 873-6371
Housing: Homeownership rate: 71.6%; Median home value: $157,300; Median year structure built: 1948; Homeowner vacancy rate: 7.4%; Median selected monthly owner costs: $1,142 with a mortgage, $457 without a mortgage; Median gross rent: $641 per month; Rental vacancy rate: 6.1%
Health Insurance: 92.9% have insurance; 74.2% have private insurance; 39.3% have public insurance; 7.1% do not have insurance; 4.9% of children under 18 do not have insurance
Hospitals: Elizabethtown Community Hospital (25 beds)
Newspapers: Denton Publications (weekly circulation 80,000)
Transportation: Commute: 83.2% car, 2.1% public transportation, 5.4% walk, 7.2% work from home; Mean travel time to work: 18.3 minutes

ESSEX (town). Covers a land area of 31.631 square miles and a water area of 5.969 square miles. Located at 44.28° N. Lat; 73.40° W. Long. Elevation is 125 feet.
Population: 600; Growth (since 2000): -15.8%; Density: 19.0 persons per square mile; Race: 98.0% White, 0.3% Black/African American, 0.8% Asian, 0.0% American Indian/Alaska Native, 0.0% Native Hawaiian/Other Pacific Islander, 0.8% Two or more races, 0.8% Hispanic of any race; Average household size: 2.32; Median age: 49.9; Age under 18: 10.5%; Age 65 and over: 24.5%; Males per 100 females: 104.0; Marriage status: 25.5% never married, 55.2% now married, 2.8% separated, 11.7% widowed, 7.5% divorced; Foreign born: 5.3%; Speak English only: 99.7%; With disability: 18.0%; Veterans: 11.4%; Ancestry: 19.5% English, 18.0% Irish, 11.2% German, 10.0% American, 6.7% French
Employment: 21.5% management, business, and financial, 2.3% computer, engineering, and science, 17.1% education, legal, community service, arts, and media, 6.0% healthcare practitioners, 10.4% service, 15.8% sales and office, 15.8% natural resources, construction, and maintenance, 11.1% production, transportation, and material moving
Income: Per capita: $31,662; Median household: $56,250; Average household: $70,501; Households with income of $100,000 or more: 24.0%; Poverty rate: 15.7%
Educational Attainment: High school diploma or higher: 88.9%; Bachelor's degree or higher: 36.0%; Graduate/professional degree or higher: 17.7%
Housing: Homeownership rate: 84.6%; Median home value: $159,200; Median year structure built: Before 1940; Homeowner vacancy rate: 9.2%; Median selected monthly owner costs: $1,352 with a mortgage, $469 without a mortgage; Median gross rent: n/a per month; Rental vacancy rate: 14.9%
Health Insurance: 85.2% have insurance; 64.8% have private insurance; 44.5% have public insurance; 14.8% do not have insurance; 7.9% of children under 18 do not have insurance
Transportation: Commute: 82.7% car, 3.5% public transportation, 1.8% walk, 4.6% work from home; Mean travel time to work: 22.5 minutes

JAY (town). Covers a land area of 67.688 square miles and a water area of 0.421 square miles. Located at 44.38° N. Lat; 73.70° W. Long. Elevation is 712 feet.
Population: 2,806; Growth (since 2000): 21.7%; Density: 41.5 persons per square mile; Race: 97.1% White, 0.3% Black/African American, 0.1% Asian, 0.5% American Indian/Alaska Native, 0.0% Native Hawaiian/Other Pacific Islander, 2.0% Two or more races, 0.4% Hispanic of any race; Average household size: 2.63; Median age: 44.8; Age under 18: 20.4%; Age 65 and over: 19.6%; Males per 100 females: 98.4; Marriage status: 24.6% never married, 55.4% now married, 3.3% separated, 10.7% widowed, 9.2% divorced; Foreign born: 0.4%; Speak English only: 99.4%; With disability: 15.4%; Veterans: 10.1%; Ancestry: 19.7% French, 18.1% Irish, 17.2% German, 14.0% English, 9.8% French Canadian
Employment: 9.4% management, business, and financial, 3.1% computer, engineering, and science, 11.7% education, legal, community service, arts, and media, 4.6% healthcare practitioners, 28.6% service, 20.4% sales and office, 12.7% natural resources, construction, and maintenance, 9.6% production, transportation, and material moving
Income: Per capita: $26,514; Median household: $52,390; Average household: $67,622; Households with income of $100,000 or more: 20.9%; Poverty rate: 8.1%

Educational Attainment: High school diploma or higher: 86.8%; Bachelor's degree or higher: 26.0%; Graduate/professional degree or higher: 13.8%
Housing: Homeownership rate: 78.8%; Median home value: $162,700; Median year structure built: 1974; Homeowner vacancy rate: 4.3%; Median selected monthly owner costs: $1,278 with a mortgage, $476 without a mortgage; Median gross rent: $778 per month; Rental vacancy rate: 7.8%
Health Insurance: 89.6% have insurance; 72.3% have private insurance; 35.2% have public insurance; 10.4% do not have insurance; 7.2% of children under 18 do not have insurance
Transportation: Commute: 85.3% car, 0.3% public transportation, 4.9% walk, 6.1% work from home; Mean travel time to work: 25.8 minutes

KEENE (town). Covers a land area of 155.941 square miles and a water area of 0.676 square miles. Located at 44.12° N. Lat; 73.88° W. Long. Elevation is 840 feet.
Population: 1,027; Growth (since 2000): -3.4%; Density: 6.6 persons per square mile; Race: 98.5% White, 0.0% Black/African American, 0.4% Asian, 0.0% American Indian/Alaska Native, 0.5% Native Hawaiian/Other Pacific Islander, 0.6% Two or more races, 0.0% Hispanic of any race; Average household size: 2.16; Median age: 51.4; Age under 18: 14.8%; Age 65 and over: 30.5%; Males per 100 females: 90.8; Marriage status: 21.5% never married, 61.5% now married, 4.1% separated, 7.5% widowed, 9.5% divorced; Foreign born: 3.8%; Speak English only: 95.2%; With disability: 10.9%; Veterans: 13.1%; Ancestry: 26.7% Irish, 18.9% English, 17.1% German, 14.8% Italian, 13.1% French
Employment: 12.6% management, business, and financial, 1.7% computer, engineering, and science, 15.5% education, legal, community service, arts, and media, 5.5% healthcare practitioners, 22.2% service, 21.2% sales and office, 12.4% natural resources, construction, and maintenance, 9.0% production, transportation, and material moving
Income: Per capita: $30,999; Median household: $48,542; Average household: $65,257; Households with income of $100,000 or more: 14.9%; Poverty rate: 10.2%
Educational Attainment: High school diploma or higher: 94.1%; Bachelor's degree or higher: 45.1%; Graduate/professional degree or higher: 20.3%
Housing: Homeownership rate: 74.9%; Median home value: $235,100; Median year structure built: 1967; Homeowner vacancy rate: 3.8%; Median selected monthly owner costs: $1,403 with a mortgage, $588 without a mortgage; Median gross rent: $1,289 per month; Rental vacancy rate: 2.5%
Health Insurance: 94.6% have insurance; 73.4% have private insurance; 46.2% have public insurance; 5.4% do not have insurance; 3.9% of children under 18 do not have insurance
Transportation: Commute: 87.2% car, 0.0% public transportation, 4.0% walk, 8.1% work from home; Mean travel time to work: 20.4 minutes

KEENE VALLEY (unincorporated postal area)
ZCTA: 12943
   Covers a land area of 103.005 square miles and a water area of 0.554 square miles. Located at 44.12° N. Lat; 73.88° W. Long. Elevation is 1,024 feet.
Population: 188; Growth (since 2000): -51.9%; Density: 1.8 persons per square mile; Race: 98.9% White, 0.0% Black/African American, 0.0% Asian, 0.0% American Indian/Alaska Native, 1.1% Native Hawaiian/Other Pacific Islander, 0.0% Two or more races, 0.0% Hispanic of any race; Average household size: 1.88; Median age: 50.2; Age under 18: 18.1%; Age 65 and over: 22.3%; Males per 100 females: 92.1; Marriage status: 15.2% never married, 60.1% now married, 9.5% separated, 20.9% widowed, 3.8% divorced; Foreign born: 2.7%; Speak English only: 94.1%; With disability: 26.1%; Veterans: 8.4%; Ancestry: 37.2% Irish, 21.8% German, 20.2% French, 8.5% Scottish, 6.9% Italian
Employment: 9.3% management, business, and financial, 7.5% computer, engineering, and science, 14.0% education, legal, community service, arts, and media, 0.0% healthcare practitioners, 15.9% service, 20.6% sales and office, 8.4% natural resources, construction, and maintenance, 24.3% production, transportation, and material moving
Income: Per capita: $26,731; Median household: $51,591; Average household: $51,998; Households with income of $100,000 or more: 2.0%; Poverty rate: n/a
Educational Attainment: High school diploma or higher: 94.2%; Bachelor's degree or higher: 60.4%; Graduate/professional degree or higher: 26.0%

Keene Central SD (KG-12)
   2014-15 Enrollment: 171 . . . . (518) 576-4555
Housing: Homeownership rate: 55.0%; Median home value: $251,900; Median year structure built: 1949; Homeowner vacancy rate: 14.1%; Median selected monthly owner costs: $1,750 with a mortgage, $608 without a mortgage; Median gross rent: $1,653 per month; Rental vacancy rate: 0.0%
Health Insurance: 95.7% have insurance; 70.2% have private insurance; 33.0% have public insurance; 4.3% do not have insurance; 0.0% of children under 18 do not have insurance
Transportation: Commute: 70.1% car, 0.0% public transportation, 14.0% walk, 15.9% work from home; Mean travel time to work: 21.8 minutes

LAKE PLACID (village).
Covers a land area of 1.371 square miles and a water area of 0.166 square miles. Located at 44.28° N. Lat; 73.99° W. Long. Elevation is 1,801 feet.
History: Winter Olympics (1932, 1980) and the World Bobsled Championships (1969) were held here. The farm and burial place of the abolitionist John Brown are nearby. Terminus of 133-mile Northville—Lake Placid trail connecting Adirondack foothills and High Peaks region. Settled 1850, Incorporated 1900.
Population: 2,539; Growth (since 2000): -3.8%; Density: 1,851.8 persons per square mile; Race: 90.1% White, 1.4% Black/African American, 0.7% Asian, 0.0% American Indian/Alaska Native, 0.0% Native Hawaiian/Other Pacific Islander, 4.0% Two or more races, 8.9% Hispanic of any race; Average household size: 1.95; Median age: 37.0; Age under 18: 18.6%; Age 65 and over: 17.2%; Males per 100 females: 99.6; Marriage status: 36.0% never married, 44.3% now married, 3.8% separated, 8.0% widowed, 11.7% divorced; Foreign born: 5.1%; Speak English only: 87.3%; With disability: 10.9%; Veterans: 8.7%; Ancestry: 15.8% Irish, 12.4% German, 11.0% French, 7.6% American, 7.5% Italian
Employment: 14.6% management, business, and financial, 3.6% computer, engineering, and science, 4.5% education, legal, community service, arts, and media, 7.5% healthcare practitioners, 26.6% service, 27.7% sales and office, 8.5% natural resources, construction, and maintenance, 7.1% production, transportation, and material moving
Income: Per capita: $31,414; Median household: $50,766; Average household: $62,395; Households with income of $100,000 or more: 16.4%; Poverty rate: 9.8%
Educational Attainment: High school diploma or higher: 91.1%; Bachelor's degree or higher: 32.5%; Graduate/professional degree or higher: 11.8%

Lake Placid Central SD (KG-12)
   2014-15 Enrollment: 708 . . . . (518) 523-2475
Housing: Homeownership rate: 35.8%; Median home value: $219,800; Median year structure built: 1969; Homeowner vacancy rate: 12.3%; Median selected monthly owner costs: $1,191 with a mortgage, $539 without a mortgage; Median gross rent: $744 per month; Rental vacancy rate: 7.0%
Health Insurance: 90.5% have insurance; 75.0% have private insurance; 31.4% have public insurance; 9.5% do not have insurance; 10.2% of children under 18 do not have insurance
Safety: Violent crime rate: 12.2 per 10,000 population; Property crime rate: 167.2 per 10,000 population
Newspapers: Lake Placid News (weekly circulation 4,200)
Transportation: Commute: 77.6% car, 4.5% public transportation, 11.0% walk, 6.8% work from home; Mean travel time to work: 15.4 minutes; Amtrak: Bus service available.
Airports: Lake Placid (general aviation)

LEWIS (town).
Covers a land area of 84.790 square miles and a water area of 0.210 square miles. Located at 44.32° N. Lat; 73.58° W. Long. Elevation is 666 feet.
Population: 1,495; Growth (since 2000): 24.6%; Density: 17.6 persons per square mile; Race: 93.8% White, 1.8% Black/African American, 0.1% Asian, 0.0% American Indian/Alaska Native, 0.0% Native Hawaiian/Other Pacific Islander, 1.5% Two or more races, 3.1% Hispanic of any race; Average household size: 2.59; Median age: 45.5; Age under 18: 19.1%; Age 65 and over: 19.8%; Males per 100 females: 107.2; Marriage status: 27.3% never married, 55.4% now married, 3.2% separated, 9.4% widowed, 7.8% divorced; Foreign born: 2.6%; Speak English only: 96.2%;

With disability: 13.1%; Veterans: 10.7%; Ancestry: 21.1% Irish, 18.1% French, 13.3% English, 7.6% American, 7.3% German
Employment: 7.9% management, business, and financial, 0.4% computer, engineering, and science, 5.0% education, legal, community service, arts, and media, 3.9% healthcare practitioners, 22.6% service, 22.9% sales and office, 24.5% natural resources, construction, and maintenance, 12.8% production, transportation, and material moving
Income: Per capita: $20,732; Median household: $45,871; Average household: $56,044; Households with income of $100,000 or more: 14.5%; Poverty rate: 12.1%
Educational Attainment: High school diploma or higher: 83.1%; Bachelor's degree or higher: 10.3%; Graduate/professional degree or higher: 4.5%
Housing: Homeownership rate: 82.8%; Median home value: $101,800; Median year structure built: 1975; Homeowner vacancy rate: 1.7%; Median selected monthly owner costs: $946 with a mortgage, $407 without a mortgage; Median gross rent: $744 per month; Rental vacancy rate: 0.0%
Health Insurance: 94.2% have insurance; 72.7% have private insurance; 39.9% have public insurance; 5.8% do not have insurance; 2.8% of children under 18 do not have insurance
Transportation: Commute: 89.6% car, 0.0% public transportation, 1.8% walk, 6.0% work from home; Mean travel time to work: 20.9 minutes

MINERVA (town).
Covers a land area of 156.766 square miles and a water area of 3.508 square miles. Located at 43.86° N. Lat; 74.12° W. Long. Elevation is 1,388 feet.
Population: 627; Growth (since 2000): -21.2%; Density: 4.0 persons per square mile; Race: 99.2% White, 0.0% Black/African American, 0.3% Asian, 0.2% American Indian/Alaska Native, 0.0% Native Hawaiian/Other Pacific Islander, 0.3% Two or more races, 0.3% Hispanic of any race; Average household size: 2.32; Median age: 56.2; Age under 18: 13.6%; Age 65 and over: 37.0%; Males per 100 females: 104.8; Marriage status: 17.0% never married, 68.1% now married, 0.9% separated, 8.0% widowed, 6.9% divorced; Foreign born: 2.4%; Speak English only: 94.3%; With disability: 13.1%; Veterans: 15.3%; Ancestry: 29.2% Irish, 18.3% English, 14.7% French, 9.6% German, 9.3% American
Employment: 10.0% management, business, and financial, 1.8% computer, engineering, and science, 11.5% education, legal, community service, arts, and media, 5.4% healthcare practitioners, 23.7% service, 14.3% sales and office, 21.5% natural resources, construction, and maintenance, 11.8% production, transportation, and material moving
Income: Per capita: $25,556; Median household: $49,375; Average household: $57,268; Households with income of $100,000 or more: 12.2%; Poverty rate: 15.3%
Educational Attainment: High school diploma or higher: 82.8%; Bachelor's degree or higher: 19.6%; Graduate/professional degree or higher: 10.3%
Housing: Homeownership rate: 91.8%; Median home value: $120,200; Median year structure built: 1969; Homeowner vacancy rate: 0.0%; Median selected monthly owner costs: $1,125 with a mortgage, $498 without a mortgage; Median gross rent: $850 per month; Rental vacancy rate: 0.0%
Health Insurance: 96.0% have insurance; 72.7% have private insurance; 54.9% have public insurance; 4.0% do not have insurance; 0.0% of children under 18 do not have insurance
Transportation: Commute: 91.0% car, 0.0% public transportation, 3.0% walk, 3.0% work from home; Mean travel time to work: 27.5 minutes

MINEVILLE (CDP).
Covers a land area of 3.702 square miles and a water area of 0.006 square miles. Located at 44.09° N. Lat; 73.52° W. Long. Elevation is 1,296 feet.
Population: 1,273; Growth (since 2000): n/a; Density: 343.9 persons per square mile; Race: 91.0% White, 6.0% Black/African American, 0.0% Asian, 0.5% American Indian/Alaska Native, 0.0% Native Hawaiian/Other Pacific Islander, 0.8% Two or more races, 1.7% Hispanic of any race; Average household size: 3.31; Median age: 36.5; Age under 18: 13.8%; Age 65 and over: 10.0%; Males per 100 females: 111.9; Marriage status: 38.3% never married, 45.7% now married, 0.6% separated, 1.4% widowed, 14.6% divorced; Foreign born: 0.5%; Speak English only: 96.7%; With disability: 19.1%; Veterans: 5.0%; Ancestry: 34.2% Irish, 20.6% Italian, 13.6% French, 12.2% English, 8.8% Polish
Employment: 11.5% management, business, and financial, 2.7% computer, engineering, and science, 14.4% education, legal, community service, arts, and media, 8.0% healthcare practitioners, 27.5% service, 11.8% sales and office, 10.4% natural resources, construction, and maintenance, 13.8% production, transportation, and material moving

Income: Per capita: $21,271; Median household: $57,917; Average household: $68,072; Households with income of $100,000 or more: 20.0%; Poverty rate: 12.0%

Educational Attainment: High school diploma or higher: 81.4%; Bachelor's degree or higher: 19.5%; Graduate/professional degree or higher: 7.6%

Housing: Homeownership rate: 80.8%; Median home value: $77,000; Median year structure built: 1948; Homeowner vacancy rate: 10.7%; Median selected monthly owner costs: $1,406 with a mortgage, $672 without a mortgage; Median gross rent: n/a per month; Rental vacancy rate: 0.0%

Health Insurance: 96.2% have insurance; 61.8% have private insurance; 44.3% have public insurance; 3.8% do not have insurance; 0.0% of children under 18 do not have insurance

Transportation: Commute: 77.4% car, 0.0% public transportation, 0.0% walk, 0.0% work from home; Mean travel time to work: 33.5 minutes

MORIAH (town).
Covers a land area of 64.491 square miles and a water area of 6.619 square miles. Located at 44.05° N. Lat; 73.53° W. Long. Elevation is 850 feet.

Population: 4,790; Growth (since 2000): -1.8%; Density: 74.3 persons per square mile; Race: 96.1% White, 1.8% Black/African American, 0.0% Asian, 0.3% American Indian/Alaska Native, 0.0% Native Hawaiian/Other Pacific Islander, 1.2% Two or more races, 1.0% Hispanic of any race; Average household size: 2.70; Median age: 39.6; Age under 18: 20.2%; Age 65 and over: 14.6%; Males per 100 females: 105.3; Marriage status: 29.3% never married, 54.2% now married, 1.9% separated, 5.7% widowed, 10.8% divorced; Foreign born: 0.5%; Speak English only: 97.5%; With disability: 17.8%; Veterans: 10.7%; Ancestry: 27.5% Irish, 21.6% French, 15.2% Italian, 9.7% English, 8.5% Polish

Employment: 9.7% management, business, and financial, 1.5% computer, engineering, and science, 9.8% education, legal, community service, arts, and media, 6.7% healthcare practitioners, 29.7% service, 15.2% sales and office, 12.5% natural resources, construction, and maintenance, 14.8% production, transportation, and material moving

Income: Per capita: $23,348; Median household: $55,083; Average household: $61,643; Households with income of $100,000 or more: 16.0%; Poverty rate: 9.7%

Educational Attainment: High school diploma or higher: 89.4%; Bachelor's degree or higher: 14.4%; Graduate/professional degree or higher: 4.5%

Housing: Homeownership rate: 74.0%; Median home value: $95,700; Median year structure built: 1943; Homeowner vacancy rate: 5.1%; Median selected monthly owner costs: $1,100 with a mortgage, $607 without a mortgage; Median gross rent: $848 per month; Rental vacancy rate: 6.7%

Health Insurance: 94.6% have insurance; 65.8% have private insurance; 42.8% have public insurance; 5.4% do not have insurance; 0.8% of children under 18 do not have insurance

Safety: Violent crime rate: 5.6 per 10,000 population; Property crime rate: 2.8 per 10,000 population

Transportation: Commute: 86.3% car, 0.3% public transportation, 1.4% walk, 1.8% work from home; Mean travel time to work: 30.2 minutes

MORIAH CENTER (unincorporated postal area)
ZCTA: 12961

Covers a land area of 4.001 square miles and a water area of 0 square miles. Located at 44.06° N. Lat; 73.55° W. Long. Elevation is 791 feet.

Population: 339; Growth (since 2000): 98.2%; Density: 84.7 persons per square mile; Race: 100.0% White, 0.0% Black/African American, 0.0% Asian, 0.0% American Indian/Alaska Native, 0.0% Native Hawaiian/Other Pacific Islander, 0.0% Two or more races, 0.0% Hispanic of any race; Average household size: 2.49; Median age: 58.4; Age under 18: 10.0%; Age 65 and over: 21.2%; Males per 100 females: 133.8; Marriage status: 34.5% never married, 45.1% now married, 0.0% separated, 0.0% widowed, 20.4% divorced; Foreign born: 0.0%; Speak English only: 100.0%; With disability: 27.7%; Veterans: 22.3%; Ancestry: 42.2% French, 26.8% Irish, 21.5% Italian, 20.6% English, 15.9% Polish

Employment: 18.7% management, business, and financial, 0.0% computer, engineering, and science, 5.7% education, legal, community service, arts, and media, 8.1% healthcare practitioners, 62.6% service, 0.0% sales and office, 0.0% natural resources, construction, and maintenance, 4.9% production, transportation, and material moving

Income: Per capita: $22,292; Median household: n/a; Average household: $52,857; Households with income of $100,000 or more: 5.1%; Poverty rate: n/a

Educational Attainment: High school diploma or higher: 94.9%; Bachelor's degree or higher: 7.2%; Graduate/professional degree or higher: 3.0%

Housing: Homeownership rate: 73.5%; Median home value: $84,300; Median year structure built: Before 1940; Homeowner vacancy rate: 0.0%; Median selected monthly owner costs: n/a with a mortgage, n/a without a mortgage; Median gross rent: n/a per month; Rental vacancy rate: 0.0%

Health Insurance: 95.9% have insurance; 87.6% have private insurance; 44.8% have public insurance; 4.1% do not have insurance; 0.0% of children under 18 do not have insurance

Transportation: Commute: 48.8% car, 0.0% public transportation, 0.0% walk, 18.7% work from home; Mean travel time to work: 0.0 minutes

NEW RUSSIA (unincorporated postal area)
ZCTA: 12964

Covers a land area of 34.498 square miles and a water area of 0.709 square miles. Located at 44.13° N. Lat; 73.63° W. Long. Elevation is 627 feet.

Population: 140; Growth (since 2000): -1.4%; Density: 4.1 persons per square mile; Race: 100.0% White, 0.0% Black/African American, 0.0% Asian, 0.0% American Indian/Alaska Native, 0.0% Native Hawaiian/Other Pacific Islander, 0.0% Two or more races, 0.0% Hispanic of any race; Average household size: 2.92; Median age: 35.4; Age under 18: 40.0%; Age 65 and over: 9.3%; Males per 100 females: 91.7; Marriage status: 7.1% never married, 72.6% now married, 0.0% separated, 17.9% widowed, 2.4% divorced; Foreign born: 0.0%; Speak English only: 100.0%; With disability: 0.0%; Veterans: 15.5%; Ancestry: 49.3% Irish, 17.9% German, 14.3% Italian, 6.4% Armenian, 6.4% Polish

Employment: 9.9% management, business, and financial, 2.8% computer, engineering, and science, 28.2% education, legal, community service, arts, and media, 7.0% healthcare practitioners, 32.4% service, 2.8% sales and office, 16.9% natural resources, construction, and maintenance, 0.0% production, transportation, and material moving

Income: Per capita: $43,357; Median household: n/a; Average household: $127,806; Households with income of $100,000 or more: 68.7%; Poverty rate: n/a

Educational Attainment: High school diploma or higher: 100.0%; Bachelor's degree or higher: 58.3%; Graduate/professional degree or higher: 35.7%

Housing: Homeownership rate: 52.1%; Median home value: $165,600; Median year structure built: Before 1940; Homeowner vacancy rate: 0.0%; Median selected monthly owner costs: $717 with a mortgage, $0 without a mortgage; Median gross rent: n/a per month; Rental vacancy rate: 0.0%

Health Insurance: 87.1% have insurance; 87.1% have private insurance; 9.3% have public insurance; 12.9% do not have insurance; 16.1% of children under 18 do not have insurance

Transportation: Commute: 80.6% car, 0.0% public transportation, 0.0% walk, 19.4% work from home; Mean travel time to work: 23.4 minutes

NEWCOMB (town).
Covers a land area of 226.271 square miles and a water area of 6.898 square miles. Located at 44.01° N. Lat; 74.10° W. Long. Elevation is 1,555 feet.

Population: 447; Growth (since 2000): -7.1%; Density: 2.0 persons per square mile; Race: 99.6% White, 0.0% Black/African American, 0.2% Asian, 0.0% American Indian/Alaska Native, 0.0% Native Hawaiian/Other Pacific Islander, 0.0% Two or more races, 0.9% Hispanic of any race; Average household size: 2.13; Median age: 61.3; Age under 18: 11.6%; Age 65 and over: 41.4%; Males per 100 females: 102.8; Marriage status: 22.5% never married, 52.2% now married, 2.0% separated, 15.9% widowed, 9.3% divorced; Foreign born: 3.4%; Speak English only: 95.5%; With disability: 16.1%; Veterans: 10.6%; Ancestry: 24.2% Irish, 20.4% German, 14.8% English, 13.2% French, 11.0% French Canadian

Employment: 12.7% management, business, and financial, 8.7% computer, engineering, and science, 9.2% education, legal, community service, arts, and media, 1.2% healthcare practitioners, 18.5% service, 20.8% sales and office, 14.5% natural resources, construction, and maintenance, 14.5% production, transportation, and material moving

Income: Per capita: $26,045; Median household: $46,094; Average household: $54,603; Households with income of $100,000 or more: 15.1%; Poverty rate: 10.2%

Educational Attainment: High school diploma or higher: 86.4%; Bachelor's degree or higher: 19.4%; Graduate/professional degree or higher: 12.8%

School District(s)

Newcomb Central SD (PK-12)

   2014-15 Enrollment: 96 . . . . (518) 582-3341

Housing: Homeownership rate: 92.7%; Median home value: $169,300; Median year structure built: 1963; Homeowner vacancy rate: 0.0%; Median selected monthly owner costs: $1,250 with a mortgage, $391 without a mortgage; Median gross rent: $625 per month; Rental vacancy rate: 0.0%

Health Insurance: 92.8% have insurance; 71.1% have private insurance; 56.6% have public insurance; 7.2% do not have insurance; 0.0% of children under 18 do not have insurance

Transportation: Commute: 95.7% car, 0.0% public transportation, 4.3% walk, 0.0% work from home; Mean travel time to work: 17.8 minutes

Additional Information Contacts

Town of Newcomb. . . . . (518) 582-3211
   http://www.newcombny.com/ParkitinNewcomb/Welcome.html

NORTH ELBA (town).

Covers a land area of 151.654 square miles and a water area of 4.737 square miles. Located at 44.21° N. Lat; 74.05° W. Long. Elevation is 1,965 feet.

History: Here are the farm, home (now a museum), and grave of John Brown.

Population: 8,658; Growth (since 2000): 0.0%; Density: 57.1 persons per square mile; Race: 81.0% White, 11.2% Black/African American, 0.7% Asian, 0.4% American Indian/Alaska Native, 0.0% Native Hawaiian/Other Pacific Islander, 2.4% Two or more races, 8.9% Hispanic of any race; Average household size: 2.09; Median age: 41.4; Age under 18: 13.3%; Age 65 and over: 16.9%; Males per 100 females: 139.9; Marriage status: 39.8% never married, 42.6% now married, 2.6% separated, 7.2% widowed, 10.4% divorced; Foreign born: 7.6%; Speak English only: 86.6%; With disability: 14.0%; Veterans: 7.9%; Ancestry: 21.2% Irish, 14.0% German, 10.6% English, 7.9% French, 7.0% Italian

Employment: 15.9% management, business, and financial, 2.5% computer, engineering, and science, 9.7% education, legal, community service, arts, and media, 5.8% healthcare practitioners, 29.4% service, 26.5% sales and office, 5.6% natural resources, construction, and maintenance, 4.6% production, transportation, and material moving

Income: Per capita: $27,239; Median household: $57,158; Average household: $70,424; Households with income of $100,000 or more: 24.1%; Poverty rate: 8.7%

Educational Attainment: High school diploma or higher: 89.5%; Bachelor's degree or higher: 30.2%; Graduate/professional degree or higher: 12.0%

Housing: Homeownership rate: 57.2%; Median home value: $215,200; Median year structure built: 1967; Homeowner vacancy rate: 4.1%; Median selected monthly owner costs: $1,362 with a mortgage, $593 without a mortgage; Median gross rent: $829 per month; Rental vacancy rate: 6.8%

Health Insurance: 91.8% have insurance; 77.3% have private insurance; 31.9% have public insurance; 8.2% do not have insurance; 6.3% of children under 18 do not have insurance

Transportation: Commute: 81.7% car, 2.0% public transportation, 8.6% walk, 6.2% work from home; Mean travel time to work: 15.1 minutes

Additional Information Contacts

Town of North Elba . . . . (518) 523-9516
   http://www.northelba.org

NORTH HUDSON (town).

Covers a land area of 181.452 square miles and a water area of 3.218 square miles. Located at 44.03° N. Lat; 73.76° W. Long. Elevation is 883 feet.

Population: 196; Growth (since 2000): -26.3%; Density: 1.1 persons per square mile; Race: 99.5% White, 0.0% Black/African American, 0.0% Asian, 0.5% American Indian/Alaska Native, 0.0% Native Hawaiian/Other Pacific Islander, 0.0% Two or more races, 0.5% Hispanic of any race; Average household size: 2.11; Median age: 52.8; Age under 18: 11.2%; Age 65 and over: 25.5%; Males per 100 females: 95.1; Marriage status: 24.2% never married, 58.8% now married, 0.0% separated, 9.9% widowed, 7.1% divorced; Foreign born: 1.0%; Speak English only: 96.8%; With disability: 25.0%; Veterans: 13.2%; Ancestry: 26.5% Irish, 23.0% Italian, 14.3% American, 11.7% French, 11.2% English

Employment: 12.6% management, business, and financial, 0.0% computer, engineering, and science, 5.7% education, legal, community service, arts, and media, 4.6% healthcare practitioners, 23.0% service,

21.8% sales and office, 12.6% natural resources, construction, and maintenance, 19.5% production, transportation, and material moving

Income: Per capita: $24,458; Median household: $44,583; Average household: $50,220; Households with income of $100,000 or more: 5.4%; Poverty rate: 9.2%

Educational Attainment: High school diploma or higher: 86.3%; Bachelor's degree or higher: 7.5%; Graduate/professional degree or higher: 3.1%

Housing: Homeownership rate: 84.9%; Median home value: $108,900; Median year structure built: 1972; Homeowner vacancy rate: 0.0%; Median selected monthly owner costs: $1,200 with a mortgage, $431 without a mortgage; Median gross rent: $595 per month; Rental vacancy rate: 0.0%

Health Insurance: 90.3% have insurance; 75.0% have private insurance; 42.9% have public insurance; 9.7% do not have insurance; 9.1% of children under 18 do not have insurance

Transportation: Commute: 91.5% car, 0.0% public transportation, 0.0% walk, 8.5% work from home; Mean travel time to work: 30.5 minutes

OLMSTEDVILLE (unincorporated postal area)

ZCTA: 12857

Covers a land area of 42.932 square miles and a water area of 0.551 square miles. Located at 43.82° N. Long; 73.89° W. Long. Elevation is 1,181 feet.

Population: 602; Growth (since 2000): 19.9%; Density: 14.0 persons per square mile; Race: 100.0% White, 0.0% Black/African American, 0.0% Asian, 0.0% American Indian/Alaska Native, 0.0% Native Hawaiian/Other Pacific Islander, 0.0% Two or more races, 0.0% Hispanic of any race; Average household size: 2.89; Median age: 44.6; Age under 18: 25.6%; Age 65 and over: 28.2%; Males per 100 females: 100.8; Marriage status: 13.4% never married, 72.8% now married, 0.4% separated, 8.1% widowed, 5.7% divorced; Foreign born: 4.8%; Speak English only: 89.7%; With disability: 10.1%; Veterans: 12.1%; Ancestry: 38.2% Irish, 23.6% German, 17.4% French, 15.9% English, 7.6% American

Employment: 10.4% management, business, and financial, 1.2% computer, engineering, and science, 17.6% education, legal, community service, arts, and media, 4.4% healthcare practitioners, 28.8% service, 12.0% sales and office, 19.2% natural resources, construction, and maintenance, 6.4% production, transportation, and material moving

Income: Per capita: $23,297; Median household: $49,397; Average household: $63,702; Households with income of $100,000 or more: 18.7%; Poverty rate: 8.0%

Educational Attainment: High school diploma or higher: 83.1%; Bachelor's degree or higher: 24.2%; Graduate/professional degree or higher: 10.9%

School District(s)

Minerva Central SD (PK-12)

   2014-15 Enrollment: 123 . . . . (518) 251-2000

Housing: Homeownership rate: 80.8%; Median home value: $116,300; Median year structure built: 1965; Homeowner vacancy rate: 0.0%; Median selected monthly owner costs: $1,250 with a mortgage, $481 without a mortgage; Median gross rent: $883 per month; Rental vacancy rate: 0.0%

Health Insurance: 97.8% have insurance; 66.3% have private insurance; 55.0% have public insurance; 2.2% do not have insurance; 0.0% of children under 18 do not have insurance

Transportation: Commute: 85.1% car, 0.0% public transportation, 0.8% walk, 10.8% work from home; Mean travel time to work: 27.2 minutes

PARADOX (unincorporated postal area)

ZCTA: 12858

Covers a land area of 9.785 square miles and a water area of 1.447 square miles. Located at 43.91° N. Lat; 73.68° W. Long. Elevation is 873 feet.

Population: 39; Growth (since 2000): -18.8%; Density: 4.0 persons per square mile; Race: 100.0% White, 0.0% Black/African American, 0.0% Asian, 0.0% American Indian/Alaska Native, 0.0% Native Hawaiian/Other Pacific Islander, 0.0% Two or more races, 0.0% Hispanic of any race; Average household size: 2.05; Median age: 71.7; Age under 18: 0.0%; Age 65 and over: 69.2%; Males per 100 females: 73.5; Marriage status: 0.0% never married, 89.7% now married, 0.0% separated, 5.1% widowed, 5.1% divorced; Foreign born: 0.0%; Speak English only: 100.0%; With disability: 35.9%; Veterans: 25.6%; Ancestry: 41.0% German, 38.5% Irish, 28.2% English, 15.4% French, 12.8% Italian

Employment: 40.0% management, business, and financial, 60.0% computer, engineering, and science, 0.0% education, legal, community service, arts, and media, 0.0% healthcare practitioners, 0.0% service, 0.0% sales and office, 0.0% natural resources, construction, and maintenance, 0.0% production, transportation, and material moving
Income: Per capita: $18,821; Median household: n/a; Average household: $38,579; Households with income of $100,000 or more: n/a; Poverty rate: 25.6%
Educational Attainment: High school diploma or higher: 82.1%; Bachelor's degree or higher: 43.6%; Graduate/professional degree or higher: 17.9%
Housing: Homeownership rate: 100.0%; Median home value: n/a; Median year structure built: 1952; Homeowner vacancy rate: 0.0%; Median selected monthly owner costs: $0 with a mortgage, $358 without a mortgage; Median gross rent: n/a per month; Rental vacancy rate: 100.0%
Health Insurance: 100.0% have insurance; 76.9% have private insurance; 76.9% have public insurance; 0.0% do not have insurance; 0.0% of children under 18 do not have insurance
Transportation: Commute: 60.0% car, 0.0% public transportation, 0.0% walk, 0.0% work from home; Mean travel time to work: 0.0 minutes

PORT HENRY (village). Covers a land area of 1.177 square miles and a water area of 0.300 square miles. Located at 44.05° N. Lat; 73.46° W. Long. Elevation is 243 feet.

History: Incorporated 1869.
Population: 920; Growth (since 2000): -20.1%; Density: 782.0 persons per square mile; Race: 95.5% White, 0.9% Black/African American, 0.2% Asian, 0.9% American Indian/Alaska Native, 0.0% Native Hawaiian/Other Pacific Islander, 2.3% Two or more races, 1.3% Hispanic of any race; Average household size: 2.31; Median age: 41.0; Age under 18: 22.4%; Age 65 and over: 16.5%; Males per 100 females: 98.7; Marriage status: 30.4% never married, 51.8% now married, 2.7% separated, 5.5% widowed, 12.4% divorced; Foreign born: 1.6%; Speak English only: 93.4%; With disability: 21.9%; Veterans: 10.7%; Ancestry: 17.6% Irish, 16.5% French, 15.4% Italian, 11.1% Polish, 7.3% English
Employment: 10.8% management, business, and financial, 3.6% computer, engineering, and science, 6.4% education, legal, community service, arts, and media, 4.7% healthcare practitioners, 28.2% service, 18.0% sales and office, 13.5% natural resources, construction, and maintenance, 14.9% production, transportation, and material moving
Income: Per capita: $22,290; Median household: $33,571; Average household: $50,513; Households with income of $100,000 or more: 12.9%; Poverty rate: 19.5%
Educational Attainment: High school diploma or higher: 85.7%; Bachelor's degree or higher: 14.6%; Graduate/professional degree or higher: 6.5%

School District(s)
Moriah Central SD (PK-12)
    2014-15 Enrollment: 730 . . . . (518) 546-3301
Housing: Homeownership rate: 62.9%; Median home value: $95,000; Median year structure built: Before 1940; Homeowner vacancy rate: 12.4%; Median selected monthly owner costs: $1,146 with a mortgage, $538 without a mortgage; Median gross rent: $642 per month; Rental vacancy rate: 9.3%
Health Insurance: 89.6% have insurance; 58.3% have private insurance; 44.7% have public insurance; 10.4% do not have insurance; 3.9% of children under 18 do not have insurance
Transportation: Commute: 85.0% car, 1.9% public transportation, 5.3% walk, 2.2% work from home; Mean travel time to work: 28.5 minutes; Amtrak: Train service available.

PORT KENT (unincorporated postal area)
ZCTA: 12975
    Covers a land area of 2.852 square miles and a water area of 0 square miles. Located at 44.53° N. Lat; 73.43° W. Long. Elevation is 154 feet.
Population: 355; Growth (since 2000): n/a; Density: 124.5 persons per square mile; Race: 91.3% White, 0.0% Black/African American, 5.1% Asian, 0.0% American Indian/Alaska Native, 0.0% Native Hawaiian/Other Pacific Islander, 3.7% Two or more races, 0.0% Hispanic of any race; Average household size: 2.23; Median age: 43.3; Age under 18: 20.0%; Age 65 and over: 7.3%; Males per 100 females: 86.6; Marriage status: 22.1% never married, 57.5% now married, 0.0% separated, 4.5% widowed, 15.9% divorced; Foreign born: 1.4%; Speak English only: 98.3%; With disability: 12.7%; Veterans: 12.3%; Ancestry:

19.4% Irish, 18.3% English, 18.0% French, 16.9% German, 12.1% Scottish
Employment: 17.9% management, business, and financial, 0.0% computer, engineering, and science, 26.5% education, legal, community service, arts, and media, 2.2% healthcare practitioners, 17.5% service, 15.2% sales and office, 20.6% natural resources, construction, and maintenance, 0.0% production, transportation, and material moving
Income: Per capita: $36,026; Median household: $70,509; Average household: $78,114; Households with income of $100,000 or more: 27.1%; Poverty rate: 4.5%
Educational Attainment: High school diploma or higher: 98.9%; Bachelor's degree or higher: 40.6%; Graduate/professional degree or higher: 25.8%
Housing: Homeownership rate: 71.7%; Median home value: $176,700; Median year structure built: 1959; Homeowner vacancy rate: 3.4%; Median selected monthly owner costs: $1,518 with a mortgage, $512 without a mortgage; Median gross rent: $802 per month; Rental vacancy rate: 0.0%
Health Insurance: 96.3% have insurance; 74.1% have private insurance; 33.0% have public insurance; 3.7% do not have insurance; 0.0% of children under 18 do not have insurance
Transportation: Commute: 88.8% car, 0.0% public transportation, 0.0% walk, 5.4% work from home; Mean travel time to work: 18.4 minutes; Amtrak: Train service available.

RAY BROOK (unincorporated postal area)
ZCTA: 12977
    Covers a land area of 8.945 square miles and a water area of 0.112 square miles. Located at 44.28° N. Lat; 74.07° W. Long. Elevation is 1,591 feet.
Population: 1,720; Growth (since 2000): n/a; Density: 192.3 persons per square mile; Race: 31.7% White, 45.9% Black/African American, 1.3% Asian, 1.7% American Indian/Alaska Native, 0.0% Native Hawaiian/Other Pacific Islander, 4.5% Two or more races, 27.7% Hispanic of any race; Average household size: 2.08; Median age: 35.8; Age under 18: 0.0%; Age 65 and over: 5.9%; Males per 100 females: ***.*; Marriage status: 62.0% never married, 30.9% now married, 4.2% separated, 0.0% widowed, 7.2% divorced; Foreign born: 22.0%; Speak English only: 67.3%; With disability: 48.1%; Veterans: 2.7%; Ancestry: 6.3% Irish, 5.9% French, 5.5% Italian, 3.5% West Indian, 3.4% German
Employment: 51.9% management, business, and financial, 0.0% computer, engineering, and science, 0.0% education, legal, community service, arts, and media, 0.0% healthcare practitioners, 0.0% service, 48.1% sales and office, 0.0% natural resources, construction, and maintenance, 0.0% production, transportation, and material moving
Income: Per capita: $6,306; Median household: n/a; Average household: n/a; Households with income of $100,000 or more: n/a; Poverty rate: n/a
Educational Attainment: High school diploma or higher: 80.0%; Bachelor's degree or higher: 1.5%; Graduate/professional degree or higher: 1.4%
Housing: Homeownership rate: 100.0%; Median home value: n/a; Median year structure built: n/a; Homeowner vacancy rate: 0.0%; Median selected monthly owner costs: $0 with a mortgage, $0 without a mortgage; Median gross rent: n/a per month; Rental vacancy rate: 0.0%
Health Insurance: 100.0% have insurance; 100.0% have private insurance; 100.0% have public insurance; 0.0% do not have insurance; 0.0% of children under 18 do not have insurance
Transportation: Commute: 48.1% car, 0.0% public transportation, 0.0% walk, 51.9% work from home; Mean travel time to work: 0.0 minutes

SAINT ARMAND (town). Covers a land area of 56.511 square miles and a water area of 0.934 square miles. Located at 44.37° N. Lat; 74.01° W. Long.
Population: 1,785; Growth (since 2000): 35.1%; Density: 31.6 persons per square mile; Race: 98.9% White, 0.4% Black/African American, 0.0% Asian, 0.0% American Indian/Alaska Native, 0.0% Native Hawaiian/Other Pacific Islander, 0.4% Two or more races, 1.1% Hispanic of any race; Average household size: 2.37; Median age: 49.2; Age under 18: 19.3%; Age 65 and over: 19.4%; Males per 100 females: 96.7; Marriage status: 15.9% never married, 68.7% now married, 1.4% separated, 6.0% widowed, 9.3% divorced; Foreign born: 2.8%; Speak English only: 95.1%; With disability: 17.4%; Veterans: 13.2%; Ancestry: 22.6% Irish, 18.5% French, 15.6% English, 13.5% German, 10.4% Italian

Employment: 13.7% management, business, and financial, 4.6% computer, engineering, and science, 18.0% education, legal, community service, arts, and media, 4.0% healthcare practitioners, 18.6% service, 26.9% sales and office, 9.6% natural resources, construction, and maintenance, 4.6% production, transportation, and material moving
Income: Per capita: $32,081; Median household: $57,969; Average household: $74,135; Households with income of $100,000 or more: 23.2%; Poverty rate: 9.1%
Educational Attainment: High school diploma or higher: 93.5%; Bachelor's degree or higher: 33.6%; Graduate/professional degree or higher: 17.7%
Housing: Homeownership rate: 76.4%; Median home value: $188,800; Median year structure built: 1975; Homeowner vacancy rate: 0.0%; Median selected monthly owner costs: $1,549 with a mortgage, $555 without a mortgage; Median gross rent: $742 per month; Rental vacancy rate: 0.0%
Health Insurance: 97.8% have insurance; 81.2% have private insurance; 34.2% have public insurance; 2.2% do not have insurance; 4.3% of children under 18 do not have insurance
Transportation: Commute: 95.0% car, 0.3% public transportation, 0.6% walk, 2.3% work from home; Mean travel time to work: 16.4 minutes

SCHROON (town). Covers a land area of 132.678 square miles and a water area of 8.732 square miles. Located at 43.86° N. Lat; 73.76° W. Long.

Population: 1,006; Growth (since 2000): -42.8%; Density: 7.6 persons per square mile; Race: 94.6% White, 0.6% Black/African American, 1.9% Asian, 0.2% American Indian/Alaska Native, 0.0% Native Hawaiian/Other Pacific Islander, 0.6% Two or more races, 3.6% Hispanic of any race; Average household size: 2.13; Median age: 52.0; Age under 18: 12.7%; Age 65 and over: 35.0%; Males per 100 females: 91.2; Marriage status: 22.5% never married, 57.5% now married, 0.4% separated, 12.6% widowed, 7.4% divorced; Foreign born: 6.6%; Speak English only: 95.1%; With disability: 17.5%; Veterans: 15.0%; Ancestry: 33.6% English, 18.9% Irish, 18.5% French, 16.8% German, 11.4% Italian
Employment: 9.2% management, business, and financial, 3.7% computer, engineering, and science, 15.8% education, legal, community service, arts, and media, 2.5% healthcare practitioners, 24.5% service, 19.3% sales and office, 17.3% natural resources, construction, and maintenance, 7.7% production, transportation, and material moving
Income: Per capita: $29,999; Median household: $53,452; Average household: $64,410; Households with income of $100,000 or more: 18.6%; Poverty rate: 7.3%
Educational Attainment: High school diploma or higher: 91.5%; Bachelor's degree or higher: 26.3%; Graduate/professional degree or higher: 15.8%
Housing: Homeownership rate: 79.9%; Median home value: $175,800; Median year structure built: 1964; Homeowner vacancy rate: 1.8%; Median selected monthly owner costs: $1,296 with a mortgage, $472 without a mortgage; Median gross rent: $691 per month; Rental vacancy rate: 4.1%
Health Insurance: 90.0% have insurance; 67.8% have private insurance; 49.6% have public insurance; 10.0% do not have insurance; 0.0% of children under 18 do not have insurance
Transportation: Commute: 77.1% car, 0.0% public transportation, 1.3% walk, 16.9% work from home; Mean travel time to work: 16.9 minutes

SCHROON LAKE (CDP). Covers a land area of 2.886 square miles and a water area of 0.799 square miles. Located at 43.84° N. Lat; 73.77° W. Long. Elevation is 869 feet.

Population: 474; Growth (since 2000): n/a; Density: 164.2 persons per square mile; Race: 93.2% White, 0.0% Black/African American, 1.9% Asian, 0.4% American Indian/Alaska Native, 0.0% Native Hawaiian/Other Pacific Islander, 0.0% Two or more races, 6.8% Hispanic of any race; Average household size: 1.87; Median age: 56.0; Age under 18: 9.9%; Age 65 and over: 33.3%; Males per 100 females: 86.8; Marriage status: 21.2% never married, 50.9% now married, 0.0% separated, 18.8% widowed, 9.1% divorced; Foreign born: 8.0%; Speak English only: 92.8%; With disability: 17.7%; Veterans: 12.6%; Ancestry: 34.6% English, 22.6% Irish, 20.9% French, 20.5% German, 10.5% Italian
Employment: 11.4% management, business, and financial, 4.3% computer, engineering, and science, 17.5% education, legal, community service, arts, and media, 0.0% healthcare practitioners, 26.5% service, 15.6% sales and office, 17.1% natural resources, construction, and maintenance, 7.6% production, transportation, and material moving

Income: Per capita: $37,524; Median household: $53,750; Average household: $70,658; Households with income of $100,000 or more: 27.2%; Poverty rate: 4.0%
Educational Attainment: High school diploma or higher: 97.1%; Bachelor's degree or higher: 23.5%; Graduate/professional degree or higher: 13.4%

School District(s)
Schroon Lake Central SD (PK-12)
   2014-15 Enrollment: 211 . . . . (518) 532-7164
Housing: Homeownership rate: 66.9%; Median home value: $189,800; Median year structure built: 1967; Homeowner vacancy rate: 0.0%; Median selected monthly owner costs: $1,385 with a mortgage, $509 without a mortgage; Median gross rent: $680 per month; Rental vacancy rate: 0.0%
Health Insurance: 96.0% have insurance; 76.8% have private insurance; 47.3% have public insurance; 4.0% do not have insurance; 0.0% of children under 18 do not have insurance
Transportation: Commute: 94.1% car, 0.0% public transportation, 2.0% walk, 2.5% work from home; Mean travel time to work: 15.3 minutes

SEVERANCE (unincorporated postal area)
ZCTA: 12872

Covers a land area of 0.305 square miles and a water area of 0 square miles. Located at 43.87° N. Lat; 73.73° W. Long. Elevation is 840 feet.
Population: 41; Growth (since 2000): n/a; Density: 134.4 persons per square mile; Race: 92.7% White, 0.0% Black/African American, 0.0% Asian, 0.0% American Indian/Alaska Native, 0.0% Native Hawaiian/Other Pacific Islander, 7.3% Two or more races, 7.3% Hispanic of any race; Average household size: 2.73; Median age: 49.8; Age under 18: 24.4%; Age 65 and over: 22.0%; Males per 100 females: 82.4; Marriage status: 24.4% never married, 61.0% now married, 0.0% separated, 7.3% widowed, 7.3% divorced; Foreign born: 14.6%; Speak English only: 85.4%; With disability: 0.0%; Veterans: 0.0%; Ancestry: 63.4% Dutch, 53.7% English, 31.7% German, 14.6% Romanian
Employment: 12.0% management, business, and financial, 0.0% computer, engineering, and science, 0.0% education, legal, community service, arts, and media, 0.0% healthcare practitioners, 36.0% service, 0.0% sales and office, 12.0% natural resources, construction, and maintenance, 40.0% production, transportation, and material moving
Income: Per capita: $8,980; Median household: $28,750; Average household: $22,880; Households with income of $100,000 or more: n/a; Poverty rate: 14.6%
Educational Attainment: High school diploma or higher: 100.0%; Bachelor's degree or higher: 29.0%; Graduate/professional degree or higher: 19.4%
Housing: Homeownership rate: 100.0%; Median home value: $162,500; Median year structure built: 1960; Homeowner vacancy rate: 0.0%; Median selected monthly owner costs: $0 with a mortgage, $0 without a mortgage; Median gross rent: n/a per month; Rental vacancy rate: 0.0%
Health Insurance: 100.0% have insurance; 85.4% have private insurance; 29.3% have public insurance; 0.0% do not have insurance; 0.0% of children under 18 do not have insurance
Transportation: Commute: 88.0% car, 0.0% public transportation, 0.0% walk, 12.0% work from home; Mean travel time to work: 0.0 minutes

TICONDEROGA (CDP). Covers a land area of 4.272 square miles and a water area of 0.079 square miles. Located at 43.84° N. Lat; 73.42° W. Long. Elevation is 151 feet.

Population: 3,123; Growth (since 2000): n/a; Density: 731.0 persons per square mile; Race: 97.7% White, 0.1% Black/African American, 1.2% Asian, 0.0% American Indian/Alaska Native, 0.0% Native Hawaiian/Other Pacific Islander, 0.8% Two or more races, 0.4% Hispanic of any race; Average household size: 2.51; Median age: 44.4; Age under 18: 23.2%; Age 65 and over: 16.2%; Males per 100 females: 94.4; Marriage status: 34.2% never married, 52.4% now married, 2.4% separated, 7.0% widowed, 6.4% divorced; Foreign born: 0.5%; Speak English only: 97.3%; With disability: 15.8%; Veterans: 18.9%; Ancestry: 24.5% Irish, 24.0% French, 17.8% German, 13.7% English, 9.5% Italian
Employment: 7.9% management, business, and financial, 2.1% computer, engineering, and science, 12.2% education, legal, community service, arts, and media, 13.4% healthcare practitioners, 22.5% service, 21.8% sales and office, 8.4% natural resources, construction, and maintenance, 11.7% production, transportation, and material moving

Income: Per capita: $28,679; Median household: $58,750; Average household: $72,626; Households with income of $100,000 or more: 15.3%; Poverty rate: 18.1%

Educational Attainment: High school diploma or higher: 88.9%; Bachelor's degree or higher: 19.8%; Graduate/professional degree or higher: 8.6%

School District(s)

Ticonderoga Central SD (PK-12)

    2014-15 Enrollment: 851 . . . . (518) 585-7400

Housing: Homeownership rate: 67.4%; Median home value: $114,700; Median year structure built: 1942; Homeowner vacancy rate: 9.8%; Median selected monthly owner costs: $1,292 with a mortgage, $535 without a mortgage; Median gross rent: $780 per month; Rental vacancy rate: 7.4%

Health Insurance: 88.8% have insurance; 59.6% have private insurance; 39.1% have public insurance; 11.2% do not have insurance; 17.2% of children under 18 do not have insurance

Hospitals: Moses - Ludington Hospital (99 beds)

Transportation: Commute: 87.4% car, 0.0% public transportation, 1.9% walk, 6.5% work from home; Mean travel time to work: 16.3 minutes

TICONDEROGA (town). Covers a land area of 81.433 square miles and a water area of 7.012 square miles. Located at 43.84° N. Lat; 73.55° W. Long. Elevation is 151 feet.

History: Ticonderoga is a variation of the Native American "Cheonderoga," meaning "between two waters." The French built a military road at the site and in 1755 they constructed Fort Carillon, later called Fort Ticonderoga.

Population: 5,010; Growth (since 2000): -3.0%; Density: 61.5 persons per square mile; Race: 97.7% White, 0.7% Black/African American, 0.7% Asian, 0.2% American Indian/Alaska Native, 0.0% Native Hawaiian/Other Pacific Islander, 0.5% Two or more races, 0.2% Hispanic of any race; Average household size: 2.38; Median age: 46.4; Age under 18: 22.1%; Age 65 and over: 19.8%; Males per 100 females: 97.9; Marriage status: 29.8% never married, 51.7% now married, 3.3% separated, 9.2% widowed, 9.4% divorced; Foreign born: 1.3%; Speak English only: 96.3%; With disability: 15.8%; Veterans: 17.1%; Ancestry: 25.4% Irish, 21.7% French, 16.5% German, 14.4% English, 9.2% Italian

Employment: 8.5% management, business, and financial, 1.3% computer, engineering, and science, 10.6% education, legal, community service, arts, and media, 13.1% healthcare practitioners, 22.5% service, 24.8% sales and office, 7.5% natural resources, construction, and maintenance, 11.7% production, transportation, and material moving

Income: Per capita: $27,875; Median household: $52,936; Average household: $66,062; Households with income of $100,000 or more: 13.3%; Poverty rate: 17.9%

Educational Attainment: High school diploma or higher: 87.3%; Bachelor's degree or higher: 20.8%; Graduate/professional degree or higher: 9.3%

School District(s)

Ticonderoga Central SD (PK-12)

    2014-15 Enrollment: 851 . . . . (518) 585-7400

Housing: Homeownership rate: 73.3%; Median home value: $125,000; Median year structure built: 1954; Homeowner vacancy rate: 7.0%; Median selected monthly owner costs: $1,289 with a mortgage, $528 without a mortgage; Median gross rent: $823 per month; Rental vacancy rate: 5.4%

Health Insurance: 91.5% have insurance; 63.1% have private insurance; 41.1% have public insurance; 8.5% do not have insurance; 12.1% of children under 18 do not have insurance

Hospitals: Moses - Ludington Hospital (99 beds)

Safety: Violent crime rate: 8.0 per 10,000 population; Property crime rate: 84.1 per 10,000 population

Transportation: Commute: 90.9% car, 0.0% public transportation, 1.1% walk, 4.8% work from home; Mean travel time to work: 17.6 minutes; Amtrak: Train service available.

Additional Information Contacts

Town of Ticonderoga . . . . (518) 585-6265

    http://townofticonderoga.org

UPPER JAY (unincorporated postal area)

ZCTA: 12987

    Covers a land area of 6.199 square miles and a water area of 0.015 square miles. Located at 44.32° N. Lat; 73.75° W. Long. Elevation is 673 feet.

    Population: 259; Growth (since 2000): -20.6%; Density: 41.8 persons per square mile; Race: 95.0% White, 0.0% Black/African American, 0.0% Asian, 0.0% American Indian/Alaska Native, 0.0% Native

Hawaiian/Other Pacific Islander, 5.0% Two or more races, 0.0% Hispanic of any race; Average household size: 1.66; Median age: 56.3; Age under 18: 11.6%; Age 65 and over: 36.3%; Males per 100 females: 95.1; Marriage status: 18.3% never married, 48.5% now married, 0.0% separated, 23.8% widowed, 9.4% divorced; Foreign born: 1.5%; Speak English only: 100.0%; With disability: 24.7%; Veterans: 17.0%; Ancestry: 22.0% Irish, 21.2% English, 16.2% German, 15.8% French, 12.0% Italian

Employment: 11.8% management, business, and financial, 0.0% computer, engineering, and science, 12.5% education, legal, community service, arts, and media, 9.6% healthcare practitioners, 21.3% service, 17.6% sales and office, 19.1% natural resources, construction, and maintenance, 8.1% production, transportation, and material moving

Income: Per capita: $28,363; Median household: $33,942; Average household: $47,394; Households with income of $100,000 or more: 12.2%; Poverty rate: 17.8%

Educational Attainment: High school diploma or higher: 72.6%; Bachelor's degree or higher: 21.5%; Graduate/professional degree or higher: 7.6%

Housing: Homeownership rate: 87.7%; Median home value: $150,000; Median year structure built: 1985; Homeowner vacancy rate: 0.0%; Median selected monthly owner costs: $1,458 with a mortgage, $527 without a mortgage; Median gross rent: n/a per month; Rental vacancy rate: 0.0%

Health Insurance: 83.0% have insurance; 71.8% have private insurance; 40.9% have public insurance; 17.0% do not have insurance; 0.0% of children under 18 do not have insurance

Transportation: Commute: 82.9% car, 0.0% public transportation, 4.7% walk, 12.4% work from home; Mean travel time to work: 19.6 minutes

WESTPORT (CDP). Covers a land area of 2.361 square miles and a water area of 0 square miles. Located at 44.18° N. Lat; 73.44° W. Long. Elevation is 121 feet.

Population: 427; Growth (since 2000): n/a; Density: 180.9 persons per square mile; Race: 92.5% White, 0.7% Black/African American, 0.0% Asian, 0.0% American Indian/Alaska Native, 0.0% Native Hawaiian/Other Pacific Islander, 6.1% Two or more races, 0.7% Hispanic of any race; Average household size: 2.79; Median age: 50.2; Age under 18: 20.8%; Age 65 and over: 28.3%; Males per 100 females: 81.8; Marriage status: 20.4% never married, 64.1% now married, 2.6% separated, 11.2% widowed, 4.3% divorced; Foreign born: 6.3%; Speak English only: 96.4%; With disability: 18.0%; Veterans: 12.7%; Ancestry: 20.4% English, 18.7% German, 13.3% French, 11.9% Irish, 7.5% Dutch

Employment: 21.9% management, business, and financial, 8.9% computer, engineering, and science, 6.8% education, legal, community service, arts, and media, 4.2% healthcare practitioners, 12.5% service, 12.5% sales and office, 2.6% natural resources, construction, and maintenance, 30.7% production, transportation, and material moving

Income: Per capita: $31,056; Median household: $47,639; Average household: $79,354; Households with income of $100,000 or more: 21.5%; Poverty rate: 7.3%

Educational Attainment: High school diploma or higher: 95.7%; Bachelor's degree or higher: 31.3%; Graduate/professional degree or higher: 17.8%

School District(s)

Westport Central SD (KG-12)

    2014-15 Enrollment: 224 . . . . (518) 962-8244

Housing: Homeownership rate: 85.2%; Median home value: $114,600; Median year structure built: Before 1940; Homeowner vacancy rate: 6.6%; Median selected monthly owner costs: $1,309 with a mortgage, $530 without a mortgage; Median gross rent: $929 per month; Rental vacancy rate: 56.9%

Health Insurance: 96.5% have insurance; 73.1% have private insurance; 48.2% have public insurance; 3.5% do not have insurance; 0.0% of children under 18 do not have insurance

Transportation: Commute: 82.8% car, 0.0% public transportation, 3.6% walk, 6.3% work from home; Mean travel time to work: 20.3 minutes

WESTPORT (town). Covers a land area of 58.171 square miles and a water area of 8.636 square miles. Located at 44.18° N. Lat; 73.45° W. Long. Elevation is 121 feet.

Population: 1,413; Growth (since 2000): 3.7%; Density: 24.3 persons per square mile; Race: 90.2% White, 0.2% Black/African American, 0.3% Asian, 0.1% American Indian/Alaska Native, 0.0% Native Hawaiian/Other Pacific Islander, 3.5% Two or more races, 5.8% Hispanic of any race;

Average household size: 2.53; Median age: 48.4; Age under 18: 20.9%; Age 65 and over: 24.1%; Males per 100 females: 92.4; Marriage status: 23.1% never married, 58.3% now married, 2.6% separated, 10.0% widowed, 8.6% divorced; Foreign born: 9.1%; Speak English only: 90.7%; With disability: 15.5%; Veterans: 9.3%; Ancestry: 20.8% English, 16.6% French, 12.7% Irish, 10.3% German, 7.5% Dutch
Employment: 11.0% management, business, and financial, 5.8% computer, engineering, and science, 7.0% education, legal, community service, arts, and media, 3.8% healthcare practitioners, 17.3% service, 15.6% sales and office, 20.8% natural resources, construction, and maintenance, 18.6% production, transportation, and material moving
Income: Per capita: $25,267; Median household: $44,773; Average household: $63,387; Households with income of $100,000 or more: 16.0%; Poverty rate: 11.6%
Educational Attainment: High school diploma or higher: 82.5%; Bachelor's degree or higher: 24.1%; Graduate/professional degree or higher: 13.0%

School District(s)
Westport Central SD (KG-12)
    2014-15 Enrollment: 224 . . . . (518) 962-8244
Housing: Homeownership rate: 90.1%; Median home value: $126,400; Median year structure built: 1943; Homeowner vacancy rate: 3.3%; Median selected monthly owner costs: $1,179 with a mortgage, $542 without a mortgage; Median gross rent: $892 per month; Rental vacancy rate: 34.9%
Health Insurance: 87.1% have insurance; 64.2% have private insurance; 46.6% have public insurance; 12.9% do not have insurance; 3.0% of children under 18 do not have insurance
Transportation: Commute: 76.2% car, 0.3% public transportation, 14.4% walk, 6.7% work from home; Mean travel time to work: 18.1 minutes; Amtrak: Train service available.
Additional Information Contacts
Town of Westport . . . . (518) 962-4419
    http://www.westportny.net

WILLSBORO (CDP). Covers a land area of 1.924 square miles and a water area of 0.033 square miles. Located at 44.36° N. Lat; 73.39° W. Long. Elevation is 223 feet.
Population: 891; Growth (since 2000): n/a; Density: 463.2 persons per square mile; Race: 96.7% White, 0.0% Black/African American, 0.0% Asian, 0.8% American Indian/Alaska Native, 0.0% Native Hawaiian/Other Pacific Islander, 2.5% Two or more races, 0.0% Hispanic of any race; Average household size: 2.28; Median age: 46.3; Age under 18: 18.7%; Age 65 and over: 18.6%; Males per 100 females: 98.2; Marriage status: 26.2% never married, 48.8% now married, 1.7% separated, 10.7% widowed, 14.3% divorced; Foreign born: 0.0%; Speak English only: 100.0%; With disability: 26.0%; Veterans: 11.0%; Ancestry: 29.9% German, 21.9% Irish, 19.8% French, 15.2% English, 12.0% American
Employment: 7.0% management, business, and financial, 4.0% computer, engineering, and science, 23.5% education, legal, community service, arts, and media, 1.3% healthcare practitioners, 21.3% service, 19.3% sales and office, 17.5% natural resources, construction, and maintenance, 6.3% production, transportation, and material moving
Income: Per capita: $20,531; Median household: $40,298; Average household: $45,930; Households with income of $100,000 or more: 5.1%; Poverty rate: 14.3%
Educational Attainment: High school diploma or higher: 91.0%; Bachelor's degree or higher: 13.7%; Graduate/professional degree or higher: 9.0%

School District(s)
Willsboro Central SD (PK-12)
    2014-15 Enrollment: 267 . . . . (518) 963-4456
Housing: Homeownership rate: 63.7%; Median home value: $92,800; Median year structure built: 1959; Homeowner vacancy rate: 0.0%; Median selected monthly owner costs: $876 with a mortgage, $398 without a mortgage; Median gross rent: $697 per month; Rental vacancy rate: 0.0%
Health Insurance: 93.7% have insurance; 61.8% have private insurance; 49.2% have public insurance; 6.3% do not have insurance; 0.0% of children under 18 do not have insurance
Transportation: Commute: 78.2% car, 0.0% public transportation, 8.1% walk, 5.9% work from home; Mean travel time to work: 20.0 minutes

WILLSBORO (town). Covers a land area of 42.723 square miles and a water area of 30.661 square miles. Located at 44.39° N. Lat; 73.40° W. Long. Elevation is 223 feet.
Population: 1,948; Growth (since 2000): 2.4%; Density: 45.6 persons per square mile; Race: 97.0% White, 0.1% Black/African American, 0.0% Asian, 0.4% American Indian/Alaska Native, 0.0% Native Hawaiian/Other Pacific Islander, 1.7% Two or more races, 1.0% Hispanic of any race; Average household size: 2.18; Median age: 52.7; Age under 18: 15.5%; Age 65 and over: 28.7%; Males per 100 females: 97.4; Marriage status: 23.3% never married, 54.3% now married, 1.3% separated, 10.3% widowed, 12.1% divorced; Foreign born: 2.7%; Speak English only: 95.9%; With disability: 22.8%; Veterans: 12.3%; Ancestry: 28.7% Irish, 21.4% German, 16.1% French, 16.0% English, 9.0% American
Employment: 16.7% management, business, and financial, 2.6% computer, engineering, and science, 13.0% education, legal, community service, arts, and media, 2.5% healthcare practitioners, 19.3% service, 22.1% sales and office, 15.0% natural resources, construction, and maintenance, 8.7% production, transportation, and material moving
Income: Per capita: $23,963; Median household: $45,893; Average household: $51,568; Households with income of $100,000 or more: 5.7%; Poverty rate: 10.0%
Educational Attainment: High school diploma or higher: 89.0%; Bachelor's degree or higher: 15.2%; Graduate/professional degree or higher: 6.6%

School District(s)
Willsboro Central SD (PK-12)
    2014-15 Enrollment: 267 . . . . (518) 963-4456
Housing: Homeownership rate: 77.8%; Median home value: $104,900; Median year structure built: 1956; Homeowner vacancy rate: 2.4%; Median selected monthly owner costs: $1,095 with a mortgage, $457 without a mortgage; Median gross rent: $759 per month; Rental vacancy rate: 0.0%
Health Insurance: 91.9% have insurance; 73.0% have private insurance; 44.6% have public insurance; 8.1% do not have insurance; 4.0% of children under 18 do not have insurance
Transportation: Commute: 86.0% car, 0.6% public transportation, 4.0% walk, 6.0% work from home; Mean travel time to work: 21.8 minutes

WILMINGTON (CDP). Covers a land area of 8.252 square miles and a water area of 0.088 square miles. Located at 44.39° N. Lat; 73.82° W. Long. Elevation is 1,014 feet.
Population: 1,055; Growth (since 2000): n/a; Density: 127.8 persons per square mile; Race: 98.8% White, 0.0% Black/African American, 0.0% Asian, 0.0% American Indian/Alaska Native, 0.0% Native Hawaiian/Other Pacific Islander, 1.2% Two or more races, 0.1% Hispanic of any race; Average household size: 2.56; Median age: 42.5; Age under 18: 22.2%; Age 65 and over: 12.3%; Males per 100 females: 96.0; Marriage status: 29.8% never married, 57.8% now married, 2.8% separated, 6.3% widowed, 6.1% divorced; Foreign born: 0.7%; Speak English only: 99.9%; With disability: 11.7%; Veterans: 9.6%; Ancestry: 23.2% Irish, 14.4% American, 14.0% English, 11.8% Italian, 11.7% French
Employment: 17.5% management, business, and financial, 0.3% computer, engineering, and science, 6.7% education, legal, community service, arts, and media, 9.9% healthcare practitioners, 26.9% service, 18.0% sales and office, 14.6% natural resources, construction, and maintenance, 6.1% production, transportation, and material moving
Income: Per capita: $27,971; Median household: $66,150; Average household: $71,953; Households with income of $100,000 or more: 19.2%; Poverty rate: 8.6%
Educational Attainment: High school diploma or higher: 91.5%; Bachelor's degree or higher: 32.0%; Graduate/professional degree or higher: 10.2%
Housing: Homeownership rate: 78.6%; Median home value: $223,100; Median year structure built: 1969; Homeowner vacancy rate: 2.4%; Median selected monthly owner costs: $1,295 with a mortgage, $584 without a mortgage; Median gross rent: $775 per month; Rental vacancy rate: 9.3%
Health Insurance: 90.8% have insurance; 73.8% have private insurance; 28.8% have public insurance; 9.2% do not have insurance; 0.0% of children under 18 do not have insurance
Transportation: Commute: 89.3% car, 0.5% public transportation, 1.5% walk, 3.9% work from home; Mean travel time to work: 23.1 minutes

WILMINGTON (town). Covers a land area of 65.240 square miles and a water area of 0.233 square miles. Located at 44.37° N. Lat; 73.89° W. Long. Elevation is 1,014 feet.

Population: 1,341; Growth (since 2000): 18.6%; Density: 20.6 persons per square mile; Race: 97.8% White, 0.2% Black/African American, 0.0% Asian, 0.0% American Indian/Alaska Native, 0.1% Native Hawaiian/Other Pacific Islander, 1.9% Two or more races, 2.1% Hispanic of any race; Average household size: 2.50; Median age: 43.2; Age under 18: 21.8%; Age 65 and over: 13.8%; Males per 100 females: 101.1; Marriage status: 27.8% never married, 58.2% now married, 2.2% separated, 7.2% widowed, 6.8% divorced; Foreign born: 3.4%; Speak English only: 97.0%; With disability: 11.6%; Veterans: 10.0%; Ancestry: 22.6% Irish, 13.2% English, 12.3% Italian, 11.9% German, 11.3% American

Employment: 16.0% management, business, and financial, 1.0% computer, engineering, and science, 7.8% education, legal, community service, arts, and media, 9.4% healthcare practitioners, 27.6% service, 17.7% sales and office, 15.5% natural resources, construction, and maintenance, 5.0% production, transportation, and material moving

Income: Per capita: $28,425; Median household: $65,350; Average household: $70,532; Households with income of $100,000 or more: 20.4%; Poverty rate: 8.8%

Educational Attainment: High school diploma or higher: 89.3%; Bachelor's degree or higher: 31.6%; Graduate/professional degree or higher: 10.4%

Housing: Homeownership rate: 80.7%; Median home value: $197,000; Median year structure built: 1973; Homeowner vacancy rate: 1.8%; Median selected monthly owner costs: $1,382 with a mortgage, $545 without a mortgage; Median gross rent: $888 per month; Rental vacancy rate: 7.7%

Health Insurance: 90.8% have insurance; 75.4% have private insurance; 27.5% have public insurance; 9.2% do not have insurance; 0.0% of children under 18 do not have insurance

Transportation: Commute: 89.2% car, 0.6% public transportation, 1.8% walk, 4.6% work from home; Mean travel time to work: 23.0 minutes

WITHERBEE (CDP). Covers a land area of 0.734 square miles and a water area of 0 square miles. Located at 44.08° N. Lat; 73.54° W. Long. Elevation is 1,257 feet.

Population: 333; Growth (since 2000): n/a; Density: 453.6 persons per square mile; Race: 100.0% White, 0.0% Black/African American, 0.0% Asian, 0.0% American Indian/Alaska Native, 0.0% Native Hawaiian/Other Pacific Islander, 0.0% Two or more races, 0.0% Hispanic of any race; Average household size: 2.21; Median age: 34.5; Age under 18: 35.1%; Age 65 and over: 13.8%; Males per 100 females: 94.9; Marriage status: 32.7% never married, 30.3% now married, 0.0% separated, 32.3% widowed, 4.8% divorced; Foreign born: 0.0%; Speak English only: 100.0%; With disability: 17.7%; Veterans: 5.6%; Ancestry: 40.2% Irish, 25.2% Hungarian, 24.3% American, 21.6% French Canadian, 10.2% German

Employment: 0.0% management, business, and financial, 0.0% computer, engineering, and science, 0.0% education, legal, community service, arts, and media, 28.8% healthcare practitioners, 7.7% service, 26.9% sales and office, 0.0% natural resources, construction, and maintenance, 36.5% production, transportation, and material moving

Income: Per capita: $14,207; Median household: $28,125; Average household: $30,403; Households with income of $100,000 or more: n/a; Poverty rate: 16.8%

Educational Attainment: High school diploma or higher: 100.0%; Bachelor's degree or higher: n/a; Graduate/professional degree or higher: n/a

Housing: Homeownership rate: 63.6%; Median home value: $58,300; Median year structure built: Before 1940; Homeowner vacancy rate: 0.0%; Median selected monthly owner costs: n/a with a mortgage, $515 without a mortgage; Median gross rent: $859 per month; Rental vacancy rate: 23.6%

Health Insurance: 91.0% have insurance; 38.7% have private insurance; 62.5% have public insurance; 9.0% do not have insurance; 0.0% of children under 18 do not have insurance

Transportation: Commute: 100.0% car, 0.0% public transportation, 0.0% walk, 0.0% work from home; Mean travel time to work: 0.0 minutes

Franklin County

Located in northeastern New York, partly in the Adirondacks; bounded on the north by the Canadian province of Quebec; drained by the Saranac, Saint Regis, Salmon, Little Salmon, Chateaugay, and Raquette Rivers; includes many lakes, including Saranac ke and Tupper Lake. Covers a land area of 1,629.119 square miles, a water area of 68.353 square miles, and is located in the Eastern Time Zone at 44.59° N. Lat., 74.31° W. Long. The county was founded in 1808. County seat is Malone.

Franklin County is part of the Malone, NY Micropolitan Statistical Area. The entire metro area includes: Franklin County, NY

Weather Station: Malone | | | | | | | | | Elevation: 879 feet | |

	Jan	Feb	Mar	Apr	May	Jun	Jul	Aug	Sep	Oct	Nov	Dec
High	24	26	35	51	63	72	76	75	67	54	42	30
Low	6	7	17	32	44	54	58	56	48	37	27	13
Precip	2.3	1.8	2.2	3.0	3.2	4.0	4.3	4.3	3.8	3.8	3.3	2.7
Snow	22.1	18.1	16.3	7.0	0.6	0.0	0.0	0.0	tr	2.0	9.3	20.2

High and Low temperatures in degrees Fahrenheit; Precipitation and Snow in inches

Weather Station: Tupper Lake Sunmount | | | | | | | | Elevation: 1,680 feet | |

	Jan	Feb	Mar	Apr	May	Jun	Jul	Aug	Sep	Oct	Nov	Dec
High	25	29	36	51	64	72	76	75	68	55	42	30
Low	3	5	13	29	40	49	53	52	44	34	25	11
Precip	3.1	2.6	3.0	3.3	3.7	4.0	4.6	4.6	4.1	4.0	3.9	3.3
Snow	24.6	22.7	16.8	5.1	0.2	tr	0.0	0.0	tr	1.1	7.9	22.6

High and Low temperatures in degrees Fahrenheit; Precipitation and Snow in inches

Population: 51,280; Growth (since 2000): 0.3%; Density: 31.5 persons per square mile; Race: 83.0% White, 5.6% Black/African American, 0.4% Asian, 7.2% American Indian/Alaska Native, 0.0% Native Hawaiian/Other Pacific Islander, 2.1% two or more races, 3.3% Hispanic of any race; Average household size: 2.36; Median age: 39.8; Age under 18: 20.3%; Age 65 and over: 14.5%; Males per 100 females: 121.8; Marriage status: 35.1% never married, 48.2% now married, 3.2% separated, 5.9% widowed, 10.8% divorced; Foreign born: 3.8%; Speak English only: 93.0%; With disability: 14.6%; Veterans: 9.4%; Ancestry: 18.7% French, 17.0% Irish, 9.5% English, 8.4% German, 6.3% French Canadian

Religion: Six largest groups: 35.7% Catholicism, 3.6% Methodist/Pietist, 1.0% Presbyterian-Reformed, 0.9% Baptist, 0.8% Episcopalianism/Anglicanism, 0.8% Non-denominational Protestant

Economy: Unemployment rate: 5.1%; Leading industries: 18.7 % retail trade; 17.0 % health care and social assistance; 11.6 % accommodation and food services; Farms: 688 totaling 145,023 acres; Company size: 0 employ 1,000 or more persons, 3 employ 500 to 999 persons, 7 employ 100 to 499 persons, 955 employ less than 100 persons; Business ownership: 1,084 women-owned, n/a Black-owned, n/a Hispanic-owned, 45 Asian-owned, 118 American Indian/Alaska Native-owned

Employment: 10.1% management, business, and financial, 2.6% computer, engineering, and science, 12.8% education, legal, community service, arts, and media, 6.3% healthcare practitioners, 27.0% service, 20.4% sales and office, 9.6% natural resources, construction, and maintenance, 11.2% production, transportation, and material moving

Income: Per capita: $22,488; Median household: $47,923; Average household: $58,774; Households with income of $100,000 or more: 14.9%; Poverty rate: 20.3%

Educational Attainment: High school diploma or higher: 84.9%; Bachelor's degree or higher: 17.7%; Graduate/professional degree or higher: 8.7%

Housing: Homeownership rate: 72.7%; Median home value: $101,600; Median year structure built: 1962; Homeowner vacancy rate: 1.8%; Median selected monthly owner costs: $1,106 with a mortgage, $445 without a mortgage; Median gross rent: $671 per month; Rental vacancy rate: 4.4%

Vital Statistics: Birth rate: 99.1 per 10,000 population; Death rate: 94.2 per 10,000 population; Age-adjusted cancer mortality rate: 184.8 deaths per 100,000 population

Health Insurance: 89.7% have insurance; 64.6% have private insurance; 40.5% have public insurance; 10.3% do not have insurance; 11.2% of children under 18 do not have insurance

Health Care: Physicians: 15.1 per 10,000 population; Dentists: 4.3 per 10,000 population; Hospital beds: 79.2 per 10,000 population; Hospital admissions: 983.6 per 10,000 population

Air Quality Index (AQI): Percent of Days: 97.5% good, 2.2% moderate, 0.3% unhealthy for sensitive individuals, 0.0% unhealthy, 0.0% very unhealthy; Annual median: 26; Annual maximum: 101

Transportation: Commute: 87.3% car, 0.7% public transportation, 4.3% walk, 5.8% work from home; Mean travel time to work: 20.7 minutes

2016 Presidential Election: 49.5% Trump, 44.0% Clinton, 4.3% Johnson, 2.2% Stein

National and State Parks: Franklin State Forest

Additional Information Contacts
Franklin Government.............................(518) 481-1681
http://www.franklincony.org

Franklin County Communities

BANGOR (town). Covers a land area of 43.118 square miles and a water area of 0 square miles. Located at 44.84° N. Lat; 74.43° W. Long. Elevation is 768 feet.
Population: 2,513; Growth (since 2000): 17.0%; Density: 58.3 persons per square mile; Race: 98.8% White, 0.0% Black/African American, 0.0% Asian, 0.0% American Indian/Alaska Native, 0.0% Native Hawaiian/Other Pacific Islander, 1.2% Two or more races, 0.7% Hispanic of any race; Average household size: 2.66; Median age: 34.7; Age under 18: 26.0%; Age 65 and over: 12.1%; Males per 100 females: 102.6; Marriage status: 27.3% never married, 60.9% now married, 4.4% separated, 3.1% widowed, 8.7% divorced; Foreign born: 2.8%; Speak English only: 98.3%; With disability: 16.1%; Veterans: 5.1%; Ancestry: 30.9% French, 14.8% Irish, 14.2% English, 7.8% American, 7.6% German
Employment: 8.2% management, business, and financial, 3.9% computer, engineering, and science, 18.0% education, legal, community service, arts, and media, 5.8% healthcare practitioners, 26.3% service, 16.2% sales and office, 10.9% natural resources, construction, and maintenance, 10.7% production, transportation, and material moving
Income: Per capita: $18,762; Median household: $41,971; Average household: $48,554; Households with income of $100,000 or more: 7.6%; Poverty rate: 30.5%
Educational Attainment: High school diploma or higher: 89.4%; Bachelor's degree or higher: 13.8%; Graduate/professional degree or higher: 7.4%
Housing: Homeownership rate: 75.4%; Median home value: $76,200; Median year structure built: 1976; Homeowner vacancy rate: 1.9%; Median selected monthly owner costs: $1,101 with a mortgage, $412 without a mortgage; Median gross rent: $777 per month; Rental vacancy rate: 0.0%
Health Insurance: 91.6% have insurance; 64.1% have private insurance; 48.8% have public insurance; 8.4% do not have insurance; 0.0% of children under 18 do not have insurance
Transportation: Commute: 90.9% car, 2.3% public transportation, 1.8% walk, 5.1% work from home; Mean travel time to work: 22.7 minutes

BELLMONT (town). Covers a land area of 164.141 square miles and a water area of 3.019 square miles. Located at 44.76° N. Lat; 74.13° W. Long.
Population: 1,483; Growth (since 2000): 4.2%; Density: 9.0 persons per square mile; Race: 96.9% White, 0.0% Black/African American, 0.5% Asian, 0.0% American Indian/Alaska Native, 0.0% Native Hawaiian/Other Pacific Islander, 1.9% Two or more races, 0.7% Hispanic of any race; Average household size: 2.55; Median age: 45.8; Age under 18: 21.8%; Age 65 and over: 18.5%; Males per 100 females: 109.3; Marriage status: 25.3% never married, 64.0% now married, 1.5% separated, 3.6% widowed, 7.0% divorced; Foreign born: 4.4%; Speak English only: 97.8%; With disability: 17.1%; Veterans: 9.4%; Ancestry: 32.0% French, 20.6% Irish, 10.5% American, 10.4% English, 8.0% French Canadian
Employment: 14.3% management, business, and financial, 1.6% computer, engineering, and science, 11.7% education, legal, community service, arts, and media, 4.2% healthcare practitioners, 27.3% service, 14.9% sales and office, 16.2% natural resources, construction, and maintenance, 9.7% production, transportation, and material moving
Income: Per capita: $26,980; Median household: $58,276; Average household: $66,636; Households with income of $100,000 or more: 17.5%; Poverty rate: 15.5%
Educational Attainment: High school diploma or higher: 83.8%; Bachelor's degree or higher: 15.7%; Graduate/professional degree or higher: 8.7%
Housing: Homeownership rate: 86.3%; Median home value: $87,100; Median year structure built: 1959; Homeowner vacancy rate: 1.5%; Median selected monthly owner costs: $1,052 with a mortgage, $423 without a mortgage; Median gross rent: $713 per month; Rental vacancy rate: 0.0%
Health Insurance: 91.6% have insurance; 67.0% have private insurance; 39.6% have public insurance; 8.4% do not have insurance; 9.3% of children under 18 do not have insurance
Transportation: Commute: 86.5% car, 0.8% public transportation, 1.0% walk, 11.7% work from home; Mean travel time to work: 30.9 minutes

BOMBAY (town). Covers a land area of 35.743 square miles and a water area of 0.125 square miles. Located at 44.91° N. Lat; 74.59° W. Long. Elevation is 194 feet.
Population: 1,286; Growth (since 2000): 7.9%; Density: 36.0 persons per square mile; Race: 67.2% White, 0.1% Black/African American, 1.2% Asian, 25.5% American Indian/Alaska Native, 0.0% Native Hawaiian/Other Pacific Islander, 5.8% Two or more races, 1.4% Hispanic of any race; Average household size: 2.63; Median age: 32.6; Age under 18: 29.8%; Age 65 and over: 12.9%; Males per 100 females: 99.6; Marriage status: 38.3% never married, 45.7% now married, 3.3% separated, 8.3% widowed, 7.7% divorced; Foreign born: 2.7%; Speak English only: 96.7%; With disability: 15.3%; Veterans: 9.0%; Ancestry: 16.3% French, 14.8% Irish, 11.7% German, 7.9% English, 5.4% Italian
Employment: 11.9% management, business, and financial, 0.0% computer, engineering, and science, 9.6% education, legal, community service, arts, and media, 4.3% healthcare practitioners, 33.3% service, 23.0% sales and office, 11.1% natural resources, construction, and maintenance, 6.8% production, transportation, and material moving
Income: Per capita: $22,361; Median household: $41,250; Average household: $56,612; Households with income of $100,000 or more: 15.5%; Poverty rate: 20.6%
Educational Attainment: High school diploma or higher: 88.7%; Bachelor's degree or higher: 13.2%; Graduate/professional degree or higher: 8.2%
Housing: Homeownership rate: 70.9%; Median home value: $71,300; Median year structure built: 1977; Homeowner vacancy rate: 0.0%; Median selected monthly owner costs: $1,067 with a mortgage, $423 without a mortgage; Median gross rent: $658 per month; Rental vacancy rate: 9.7%
Health Insurance: 77.8% have insurance; 50.9% have private insurance; 36.2% have public insurance; 22.2% do not have insurance; 24.5% of children under 18 do not have insurance
Transportation: Commute: 92.6% car, 0.0% public transportation, 1.6% walk, 5.1% work from home; Mean travel time to work: 21.2 minutes

BRANDON (town). Covers a land area of 41.255 square miles and a water area of 0.067 square miles. Located at 44.74° N. Lat; 74.41° W. Long.
Population: 640; Growth (since 2000): 18.1%; Density: 15.5 persons per square mile; Race: 99.4% White, 0.0% Black/African American, 0.0% Asian, 0.0% American Indian/Alaska Native, 0.0% Native Hawaiian/Other Pacific Islander, 0.6% Two or more races, 0.2% Hispanic of any race; Average household size: 2.34; Median age: 39.2; Age under 18: 18.3%; Age 65 and over: 8.1%; Males per 100 females: 113.7; Marriage status: 26.1% never married, 57.6% now married, 3.0% separated, 6.7% widowed, 9.5% divorced; Foreign born: 1.7%; Speak English only: 99.2%; With disability: 22.0%; Veterans: 13.4%; Ancestry: 23.1% French, 15.8% Irish, 8.6% American, 8.6% French Canadian, 5.8% English
Employment: 11.5% management, business, and financial, 1.5% computer, engineering, and science, 8.7% education, legal, community service, arts, and media, 1.9% healthcare practitioners, 31.6% service, 12.7% sales and office, 8.4% natural resources, construction, and maintenance, 23.8% production, transportation, and material moving
Income: Per capita: $21,337; Median household: $39,792; Average household: $46,778; Households with income of $100,000 or more: 4.1%; Poverty rate: 19.8%
Educational Attainment: High school diploma or higher: 85.5%; Bachelor's degree or higher: 9.7%; Graduate/professional degree or higher: 5.7%
Housing: Homeownership rate: 94.5%; Median home value: $57,600; Median year structure built: 1980; Homeowner vacancy rate: 0.0%; Median selected monthly owner costs: $924 with a mortgage, $381 without a mortgage; Median gross rent: $775 per month; Rental vacancy rate: 0.0%
Health Insurance: 90.2% have insurance; 59.7% have private insurance; 40.9% have public insurance; 9.8% do not have insurance; 6.0% of children under 18 do not have insurance
Transportation: Commute: 92.9% car, 0.0% public transportation, 0.6% walk, 6.4% work from home; Mean travel time to work: 21.2 minutes

BRIGHTON (town). Covers a land area of 77.896 square miles and a water area of 5.100 square miles. Located at 44.47° N. Lat; 74.25° W. Long.
Population: 1,412; Growth (since 2000): -16.1%; Density: 18.1 persons per square mile; Race: 87.8% White, 5.8% Black/African American, 2.3% Asian, 2.5% American Indian/Alaska Native, 0.0% Native Hawaiian/Other Pacific Islander, 1.5% Two or more races, 0.5% Hispanic of any race;

Average household size: 2.07; Median age: 21.9; Age under 18: 7.2%; Age 65 and over: 9.6%; Males per 100 females: 146.1; Marriage status: 68.3% never married, 23.9% now married, 0.8% separated, 2.1% widowed, 5.7% divorced; Foreign born: 3.9%; Speak English only: 91.0%; With disability: 11.9%; Veterans: 2.6%; Ancestry: 15.2% Irish, 12.0% Italian, 9.3% French, 8.7% English, 8.4% German

Employment: 11.8% management, business, and financial, 9.1% computer, engineering, and science, 13.3% education, legal, community service, arts, and media, 2.9% healthcare practitioners, 22.6% service, 25.7% sales and office, 11.1% natural resources, construction, and maintenance, 3.5% production, transportation, and material moving

Income: Per capita: $19,345; Median household: $52,000; Average household: $63,553; Households with income of $100,000 or more: 18.9%; Poverty rate: 8.5%

Educational Attainment: High school diploma or higher: 95.6%; Bachelor's degree or higher: 47.0%; Graduate/professional degree or higher: 20.0%

Housing: Homeownership rate: 79.4%; Median home value: $156,500; Median year structure built: 1946; Homeowner vacancy rate: 0.0%; Median selected monthly owner costs: $1,285 with a mortgage, $542 without a mortgage; Median gross rent: $1,313 per month; Rental vacancy rate: 0.0%

Health Insurance: 95.3% have insurance; 85.1% have private insurance; 21.1% have public insurance; 4.7% do not have insurance; 0.0% of children under 18 do not have insurance

Transportation: Commute: 64.3% car, 0.0% public transportation, 19.0% walk, 16.7% work from home; Mean travel time to work: 19.6 minutes

Additional Information Contacts

Town of Brighton . . . . (585) 784-5250
   http://www.townofbrighton.org

BRUSHTON (village).
Covers a land area of 0.276 square miles and a water area of 0 square miles. Located at 44.83° N. Lat; 74.51° W. Long. Elevation is 420 feet.

Population: 578; Growth (since 2000): 20.7%; Density: 2,091.2 persons per square mile; Race: 93.4% White, 0.7% Black/African American, 0.0% Asian, 0.5% American Indian/Alaska Native, 0.0% Native Hawaiian/Other Pacific Islander, 1.4% Two or more races, 2.2% Hispanic of any race; Average household size: 2.31; Median age: 40.0; Age under 18: 28.0%; Age 65 and over: 9.2%; Males per 100 females: 95.9; Marriage status: 25.8% never married, 57.6% now married, 3.8% separated, 4.0% widowed, 12.6% divorced; Foreign born: 2.9%; Speak English only: 94.3%; With disability: 20.4%; Veterans: 7.9%; Ancestry: 16.8% French, 15.9% Irish, 13.0% English, 10.7% French Canadian, 7.4% Pennsylvania German

Employment: 10.6% management, business, and financial, 4.8% computer, engineering, and science, 13.3% education, legal, community service, arts, and media, 5.9% healthcare practitioners, 25.0% service, 15.4% sales and office, 16.5% natural resources, construction, and maintenance, 8.5% production, transportation, and material moving

Income: Per capita: $22,151; Median household: $42,500; Average household: $51,091; Households with income of $100,000 or more: 9.6%; Poverty rate: 28.5%

Educational Attainment: High school diploma or higher: 86.7%; Bachelor's degree or higher: 18.4%; Graduate/professional degree or higher: 6.6%

School District(s)

Brushton-Moira Central SD (PK-12)
   2014-15 Enrollment: 795. . . . . (518) 529-8942

Housing: Homeownership rate: 60.4%; Median home value: $77,900; Median year structure built: Before 1940; Homeowner vacancy rate: 0.0%; Median selected monthly owner costs: $897 with a mortgage, $440 without a mortgage; Median gross rent: $591 per month; Rental vacancy rate: 5.7%

Health Insurance: 84.8% have insurance; 59.0% have private insurance; 36.3% have public insurance; 15.2% do not have insurance; 16.7% of children under 18 do not have insurance

Transportation: Commute: 98.3% car, 0.0% public transportation, 0.0% walk, 1.7% work from home; Mean travel time to work: 20.8 minutes

BURKE (town).
Covers a land area of 44.405 square miles and a water area of 0 square miles. Located at 44.93° N. Lat; 74.18° W. Long. Elevation is 863 feet.

Population: 1,207; Growth (since 2000): -11.2%; Density: 27.2 persons per square mile; Race: 96.9% White, 0.0% Black/African American, 1.3% Asian, 0.2% American Indian/Alaska Native, 0.4% Native Hawaiian/Other

Pacific Islander, 1.0% Two or more races, 1.2% Hispanic of any race; Average household size: 2.27; Median age: 44.5; Age under 18: 18.3%; Age 65 and over: 14.2%; Males per 100 females: 109.9; Marriage status: 23.4% never married, 57.7% now married, 4.1% separated, 5.7% widowed, 13.2% divorced; Foreign born: 4.2%; Speak English only: 91.8%; With disability: 8.6%; Veterans: 10.4%; Ancestry: 17.4% French, 11.2% English, 10.9% Irish, 10.4% American, 8.7% French Canadian

Employment: 12.5% management, business, and financial, 1.9% computer, engineering, and science, 9.8% education, legal, community service, arts, and media, 9.1% healthcare practitioners, 24.4% service, 14.7% sales and office, 14.9% natural resources, construction, and maintenance, 12.7% production, transportation, and material moving

Income: Per capita: $28,589; Median household: $56,667; Average household: $63,730; Households with income of $100,000 or more: 17.1%; Poverty rate: 13.1%

Educational Attainment: High school diploma or higher: 90.7%; Bachelor's degree or higher: 13.7%; Graduate/professional degree or higher: 3.7%

Housing: Homeownership rate: 85.9%; Median home value: $105,000; Median year structure built: 1979; Homeowner vacancy rate: 1.7%; Median selected monthly owner costs: $1,095 with a mortgage, $450 without a mortgage; Median gross rent: $697 per month; Rental vacancy rate: 0.0%

Health Insurance: 91.5% have insurance; 75.3% have private insurance; 30.8% have public insurance; 8.5% do not have insurance; 7.2% of children under 18 do not have insurance

Transportation: Commute: 83.5% car, 0.0% public transportation, 3.7% walk, 11.3% work from home; Mean travel time to work: 25.8 minutes

BURKE (village).
Covers a land area of 0.290 square miles and a water area of 0 square miles. Located at 44.90° N. Lat; 74.17° W. Long. Elevation is 863 feet.

Population: 169; Growth (since 2000): -20.7%; Density: 583.1 persons per square mile; Race: 99.4% White, 0.0% Black/African American, 0.0% Asian, 0.0% American Indian/Alaska Native, 0.0% Native Hawaiian/Other Pacific Islander, 0.6% Two or more races, 1.2% Hispanic of any race; Average household size: 2.33; Median age: 45.3; Age under 18: 26.6%; Age 65 and over: 20.7%; Males per 100 females: 106.9; Marriage status: 12.5% never married, 61.7% now married, 3.9% separated, 13.3% widowed, 12.5% divorced; Foreign born: 1.8%; Speak English only: 96.9%; With disability: 18.9%; Veterans: 14.5%; Ancestry: 38.5% French, 12.4% German, 11.2% English, 9.5% American, 6.5% Italian

Employment: 7.4% management, business, and financial, 0.0% computer, engineering, and science, 17.6% education, legal, community service, arts, and media, 4.4% healthcare practitioners, 35.3% service, 16.2% sales and office, 10.3% natural resources, construction, and maintenance, 8.8% production, transportation, and material moving

Income: Per capita: $21,386; Median household: $38,750; Average household: $48,207; Households with income of $100,000 or more: 11.1%; Poverty rate: 16.0%

Educational Attainment: High school diploma or higher: 89.0%; Bachelor's degree or higher: 13.6%; Graduate/professional degree or higher: 5.9%

Housing: Homeownership rate: 79.2%; Median home value: $79,200; Median year structure built: Before 1940; Homeowner vacancy rate: 0.0%; Median selected monthly owner costs: $910 with a mortgage, $338 without a mortgage; Median gross rent: $755 per month; Rental vacancy rate: 0.0%

Health Insurance: 98.8% have insurance; 81.1% have private insurance; 39.6% have public insurance; 1.2% do not have insurance; 0.0% of children under 18 do not have insurance

Transportation: Commute: 95.3% car, 0.0% public transportation, 1.6% walk, 1.6% work from home; Mean travel time to work: 21.0 minutes

CHATEAUGAY (town).
Covers a land area of 49.789 square miles and a water area of 0.012 square miles. Located at 44.93° N. Lat; 74.08° W. Long. Elevation is 945 feet.

History: Settled 1796, incorporated 1869.

Population: 1,950; Growth (since 2000): -4.2%; Density: 39.2 persons per square mile; Race: 89.8% White, 7.1% Black/African American, 0.4% Asian, 0.5% American Indian/Alaska Native, 0.0% Native Hawaiian/Other Pacific Islander, 0.5% Two or more races, 3.2% Hispanic of any race; Average household size: 2.29; Median age: 39.0; Age under 18: 17.8%; Age 65 and over: 14.3%; Males per 100 females: 116.1; Marriage status: 34.2% never married, 46.4% now married, 3.2% separated, 8.9% widowed, 10.5% divorced; Foreign born: 3.9%; Speak English only: 94.5%;

With disability: 15.6%; Veterans: 12.4%; Ancestry: 20.0% Irish, 18.8% French, 8.6% German, 7.5% French Canadian, 7.3% English
Employment: 8.1% management, business, and financial, 2.4% computer, engineering, and science, 9.1% education, legal, community service, arts, and media, 3.6% healthcare practitioners, 23.9% service, 19.9% sales and office, 14.3% natural resources, construction, and maintenance, 18.6% production, transportation, and material moving
Income: Per capita: $18,599; Median household: $36,000; Average household: $48,706; Households with income of $100,000 or more: 10.5%; Poverty rate: 27.8%
Educational Attainment: High school diploma or higher: 83.7%; Bachelor's degree or higher: 11.0%; Graduate/professional degree or higher: 6.4%

School District(s)
Chateaugay Central SD (PK-12)
    2014-15 Enrollment: 537 . . . . (518) 497-6420
Housing: Homeownership rate: 68.5%; Median home value: $86,300; Median year structure built: 1953; Homeowner vacancy rate: 4.5%; Median selected monthly owner costs: $925 with a mortgage, $438 without a mortgage; Median gross rent: $644 per month; Rental vacancy rate: 2.1%
Health Insurance: 91.8% have insurance; 61.1% have private insurance; 44.1% have public insurance; 8.2% do not have insurance; 2.1% of children under 18 do not have insurance
Transportation: Commute: 94.4% car, 0.8% public transportation, 2.6% walk, 1.5% work from home; Mean travel time to work: 23.4 minutes

CHATEAUGAY (village).
Covers a land area of 1.083 square miles and a water area of 0 square miles. Located at 44.93° N. Lat; 74.08° W. Long. Elevation is 945 feet.
Population: 626; Growth (since 2000): -21.6%; Density: 577.8 persons per square mile; Race: 97.8% White, 0.5% Black/African American, 1.1% Asian, 0.0% American Indian/Alaska Native, 0.0% Native Hawaiian/Other Pacific Islander, 0.6% Two or more races, 0.0% Hispanic of any race; Average household size: 2.09; Median age: 47.8; Age under 18: 16.9%; Age 65 and over: 21.6%; Males per 100 females: 87.2; Marriage status: 21.7% never married, 52.6% now married, 3.5% separated, 15.1% widowed, 10.7% divorced; Foreign born: 7.5%; Speak English only: 96.4%; With disability: 19.2%; Veterans: 12.1%; Ancestry: 25.1% French, 21.1% Irish, 13.4% English, 11.3% German, 6.9% Italian
Employment: 9.8% management, business, and financial, 5.1% computer, engineering, and science, 12.6% education, legal, community service, arts, and media, 1.2% healthcare practitioners, 27.2% service, 20.9% sales and office, 6.7% natural resources, construction, and maintenance, 16.5% production, transportation, and material moving
Income: Per capita: $22,680; Median household: $40,500; Average household: $47,118; Households with income of $100,000 or more: 10.5%; Poverty rate: 27.3%
Educational Attainment: High school diploma or higher: 87.1%; Bachelor's degree or higher: 16.0%; Graduate/professional degree or higher: 9.4%

School District(s)
Chateaugay Central SD (PK-12)
    2014-15 Enrollment: 537 . . . . (518) 497-6420
Housing: Homeownership rate: 59.5%; Median home value: $81,900; Median year structure built: Before 1940; Homeowner vacancy rate: 5.9%; Median selected monthly owner costs: $1,000 with a mortgage, $508 without a mortgage; Median gross rent: $556 per month; Rental vacancy rate: 3.8%
Health Insurance: 94.7% have insurance; 57.2% have private insurance; 52.7% have public insurance; 5.3% do not have insurance; 6.6% of children under 18 do not have insurance
Transportation: Commute: 88.9% car, 1.2% public transportation, 6.7% walk, 1.2% work from home; Mean travel time to work: 24.8 minutes

CONSTABLE (town).
Covers a land area of 32.806 square miles and a water area of 0.012 square miles. Located at 44.97° N. Lat; 74.28° W. Long. Elevation is 354 feet.
Population: 1,485; Growth (since 2000): 4.0%; Density: 45.3 persons per square mile; Race: 97.1% White, 1.3% Black/African American, 0.1% Asian, 0.4% American Indian/Alaska Native, 0.0% Native Hawaiian/Other Pacific Islander, 0.9% Two or more races, 1.6% Hispanic of any race; Average household size: 2.57; Median age: 43.5; Age under 18: 19.3%; Age 65 and over: 12.6%; Males per 100 females: 109.1; Marriage status: 28.8% never married, 55.3% now married, 5.2% separated, 5.2% widowed, 10.8% divorced; Foreign born: 2.6%; Speak English only: 96.6%;

With disability: 16.2%; Veterans: 13.9%; Ancestry: 26.1% French, 22.7% Irish, 8.9% American, 8.1% English, 8.0% German
Employment: 7.7% management, business, and financial, 1.5% computer, engineering, and science, 6.3% education, legal, community service, arts, and media, 6.6% healthcare practitioners, 33.5% service, 19.5% sales and office, 9.8% natural resources, construction, and maintenance, 15.1% production, transportation, and material moving
Income: Per capita: $25,388; Median household: $55,104; Average household: $65,121; Households with income of $100,000 or more: 22.1%; Poverty rate: 11.5%
Educational Attainment: High school diploma or higher: 87.7%; Bachelor's degree or higher: 11.1%; Graduate/professional degree or higher: 4.1%
Housing: Homeownership rate: 81.1%; Median home value: $93,000; Median year structure built: 1978; Homeowner vacancy rate: 0.9%; Median selected monthly owner costs: $1,130 with a mortgage, $411 without a mortgage; Median gross rent: $629 per month; Rental vacancy rate: 0.0%
Health Insurance: 92.1% have insurance; 72.3% have private insurance; 33.3% have public insurance; 7.9% do not have insurance; 0.7% of children under 18 do not have insurance
Transportation: Commute: 94.7% car, 1.1% public transportation, 1.9% walk, 2.0% work from home; Mean travel time to work: 18.7 minutes

DICKINSON (town).
Covers a land area of 44.224 square miles and a water area of 0.089 square miles. Located at 44.73° N. Lat; 74.54° W. Long. Elevation is 722 feet.
Population: 956; Growth (since 2000): 29.4%; Density: 21.6 persons per square mile; Race: 98.2% White, 0.2% Black/African American, 0.1% Asian, 0.9% American Indian/Alaska Native, 0.0% Native Hawaiian/Other Pacific Islander, 0.5% Two or more races, 1.2% Hispanic of any race; Average household size: 2.72; Median age: 40.5; Age under 18: 28.6%; Age 65 and over: 15.9%; Males per 100 females: 103.7; Marriage status: 22.9% never married, 63.3% now married, 0.7% separated, 4.3% widowed, 9.6% divorced; Foreign born: 2.0%; Speak English only: 92.4%; With disability: 13.8%; Veterans: 12.3%; Ancestry: 20.7% French, 12.3% German, 12.2% English, 8.7% Irish, 7.4% American
Employment: 12.1% management, business, and financial, 1.9% computer, engineering, and science, 10.4% education, legal, community service, arts, and media, 4.9% healthcare practitioners, 29.7% service, 21.7% sales and office, 13.7% natural resources, construction, and maintenance, 5.5% production, transportation, and material moving
Income: Per capita: $21,675; Median household: $48,125; Average household: $59,719; Households with income of $100,000 or more: 19.0%; Poverty rate: 21.5%
Educational Attainment: High school diploma or higher: 88.2%; Bachelor's degree or higher: 12.7%; Graduate/professional degree or higher: 6.6%
Housing: Homeownership rate: 91.2%; Median home value: $78,100; Median year structure built: 1968; Homeowner vacancy rate: 1.8%; Median selected monthly owner costs: $1,014 with a mortgage, $424 without a mortgage; Median gross rent: $721 per month; Rental vacancy rate: 0.0%
Health Insurance: 85.3% have insurance; 59.0% have private insurance; 42.4% have public insurance; 14.7% do not have insurance; 20.1% of children under 18 do not have insurance
Transportation: Commute: 85.5% car, 0.0% public transportation, 5.0% walk, 8.1% work from home; Mean travel time to work: 30.4 minutes

DICKINSON CENTER (unincorporated postal area)
ZCTA: 12930
Covers a land area of 36.166 square miles and a water area of 0.076 square miles. Located at 44.72° N. Lat; 74.54° W. Long. Elevation is 955 feet.
Population: 815; Growth (since 2000): 42.7%; Density: 22.5 persons per square mile; Race: 98.5% White, 0.2% Black/African American, 0.0% Asian, 0.7% American Indian/Alaska Native, 0.0% Native Hawaiian/Other Pacific Islander, 0.5% Two or more races, 1.3% Hispanic of any race; Average household size: 2.72; Median age: 37.9; Age under 18: 29.7%; Age 65 and over: 12.3%; Males per 100 females: 103.2; Marriage status: 27.7% never married, 58.0% now married, 0.8% separated, 4.5% widowed, 9.9% divorced; Foreign born: 0.7%; Speak English only: 95.8%; With disability: 12.4%; Veterans: 12.1%; Ancestry: 19.0% French, 12.6% English, 11.2% Irish, 9.9% German, 9.4% French Canadian
Employment: 12.3% management, business, and financial, 0.9% computer, engineering, and science, 11.1% education, legal, community

service, arts, and media, 3.8% healthcare practitioners, 27.8% service, 19.3% sales and office, 17.8% natural resources, construction, and maintenance, 7.0% production, transportation, and material moving
Income: Per capita: $21,700; Median household: $45,357; Average household: $59,104; Households with income of $100,000 or more: 21.7%; Poverty rate: 19.0%
Educational Attainment: High school diploma or higher: 89.6%; Bachelor's degree or higher: 14.0%; Graduate/professional degree or higher: 7.3%
Housing: Homeownership rate: 88.0%; Median home value: $76,700; Median year structure built: 1974; Homeowner vacancy rate: 2.1%; Median selected monthly owner costs: $1,092 with a mortgage, $397 without a mortgage; Median gross rent: $767 per month; Rental vacancy rate: 0.0%
Health Insurance: 90.9% have insurance; 68.1% have private insurance; 35.0% have public insurance; 9.1% do not have insurance; 1.7% of children under 18 do not have insurance
Transportation: Commute: 91.4% car, 0.0% public transportation, 2.7% walk, 4.4% work from home; Mean travel time to work: 26.1 minutes

DUANE (town). Covers a land area of 74.952 square miles and a water area of 3.032 square miles. Located at 44.60° N. Lat; 74.23° W. Long.
Population: 161; Growth (since 2000): 1.3%; Density: 2.1 persons per square mile; Race: 98.1% White, 0.0% Black/African American, 0.0% Asian, 0.0% American Indian/Alaska Native, 0.0% Native Hawaiian/Other Pacific Islander, 1.9% Two or more races, 0.0% Hispanic of any race; Average household size: 2.15; Median age: 61.6; Age under 18: 6.8%; Age 65 and over: 32.3%; Males per 100 females: 123.1; Marriage status: 14.0% never married, 66.7% now married, 0.7% separated, 6.7% widowed, 12.7% divorced; Foreign born: 1.9%; Speak English only: 97.4%; With disability: 11.2%; Veterans: 14.7%; Ancestry: 28.0% French, 24.8% English, 20.5% Irish, 11.8% Scottish, 9.9% German
Employment: 8.9% management, business, and financial, 3.6% computer, engineering, and science, 21.4% education, legal, community service, arts, and media, 1.8% healthcare practitioners, 14.3% service, 21.4% sales and office, 14.3% natural resources, construction, and maintenance, 14.3% production, transportation, and material moving
Income: Per capita: $40,234; Median household: $38,750; Average household: $65,981; Households with income of $100,000 or more: 9.3%; Poverty rate: 24.2%
Educational Attainment: High school diploma or higher: 98.0%; Bachelor's degree or higher: 20.3%; Graduate/professional degree or higher: 8.8%
Housing: Homeownership rate: 89.3%; Median home value: $151,800; Median year structure built: 1976; Homeowner vacancy rate: 2.9%; Median selected monthly owner costs: $1,083 with a mortgage, $592 without a mortgage; Median gross rent: $775 per month; Rental vacancy rate: 0.0%
Health Insurance: 96.9% have insurance; 85.7% have private insurance; 52.2% have public insurance; 3.1% do not have insurance; 0.0% of children under 18 do not have insurance
Transportation: Commute: 89.3% car, 1.8% public transportation, 3.6% walk, 5.4% work from home; Mean travel time to work: 28.1 minutes

FORT COVINGTON (town). Covers a land area of 36.734 square miles and a water area of 0 square miles. Located at 44.95° N. Lat; 74.49° W. Long. Elevation is 180 feet.
Population: 1,830; Growth (since 2000): 11.2%; Density: 49.8 persons per square mile; Race: 71.5% White, 1.7% Black/African American, 0.4% Asian, 17.0% American Indian/Alaska Native, 0.0% Native Hawaiian/Other Pacific Islander, 9.3% Two or more races, 1.1% Hispanic of any race; Average household size: 2.65; Median age: 40.7; Age under 18: 28.4%; Age 65 and over: 12.9%; Males per 100 females: 100.7; Marriage status: 36.5% never married, 47.9% now married, 3.6% separated, 7.2% widowed, 8.4% divorced; Foreign born: 3.1%; Speak English only: 93.7%; With disability: 14.2%; Veterans: 10.4%; Ancestry: 27.7% French, 11.5% Irish, 7.5% German, 6.6% English, 6.3% Italian
Employment: 8.3% management, business, and financial, 1.1% computer, engineering, and science, 12.2% education, legal, community service, arts, and media, 3.8% healthcare practitioners, 25.0% service, 21.5% sales and office, 16.0% natural resources, construction, and maintenance, 12.2% production, transportation, and material moving
Income: Per capita: $20,047; Median household: $40,000; Average household: $52,273; Households with income of $100,000 or more: 12.0%; Poverty rate: 23.0%

Educational Attainment: High school diploma or higher: 88.5%; Bachelor's degree or higher: 14.2%; Graduate/professional degree or higher: 6.7%

School District(s)
Salmon River Central SD (PK-12)
   2014-15 Enrollment: 1,595 . . . . (518) 358-6610
Housing: Homeownership rate: 78.1%; Median home value: $83,800; Median year structure built: 1966; Homeowner vacancy rate: 0.7%; Median selected monthly owner costs: $1,082 with a mortgage, $428 without a mortgage; Median gross rent: $700 per month; Rental vacancy rate: 14.2%
Health Insurance: 81.6% have insurance; 57.2% have private insurance; 38.5% have public insurance; 18.4% do not have insurance; 25.2% of children under 18 do not have insurance
Transportation: Commute: 86.0% car, 0.6% public transportation, 3.5% walk, 9.1% work from home; Mean travel time to work: 17.0 minutes

FORT COVINGTON HAMLET (CDP). Covers a land area of 19.322 square miles and a water area of 0.010 square miles. Located at 44.97° N. Lat; 74.51° W. Long.
Population: 1,481; Growth (since 2000): n/a; Density: 76.7 persons per square mile; Race: 68.9% White, 0.3% Black/African American, 0.5% Asian, 20.1% American Indian/Alaska Native, 0.0% Native Hawaiian/Other Pacific Islander, 10.2% Two or more races, 1.1% Hispanic of any race; Average household size: 2.65; Median age: 41.6; Age under 18: 28.1%; Age 65 and over: 13.6%; Males per 100 females: 99.4; Marriage status: 35.9% never married, 48.8% now married, 3.9% separated, 7.5% widowed, 7.9% divorced; Foreign born: 3.8%; Speak English only: 95.9%; With disability: 13.6%; Veterans: 10.8%; Ancestry: 26.6% French, 12.5% Irish, 8.8% German, 7.1% Italian, 5.7% English
Employment: 6.5% management, business, and financial, 1.2% computer, engineering, and science, 12.1% education, legal, community service, arts, and media, 4.0% healthcare practitioners, 24.4% service, 22.7% sales and office, 17.0% natural resources, construction, and maintenance, 12.0% production, transportation, and material moving
Income: Per capita: $21,230; Median household: $41,406; Average household: $55,370; Households with income of $100,000 or more: 12.9%; Poverty rate: 18.6%
Educational Attainment: High school diploma or higher: 88.7%; Bachelor's degree or higher: 14.1%; Graduate/professional degree or higher: 6.4%
Housing: Homeownership rate: 79.1%; Median home value: $78,900; Median year structure built: 1963; Homeowner vacancy rate: 0.9%; Median selected monthly owner costs: $1,029 with a mortgage, $441 without a mortgage; Median gross rent: $650 per month; Rental vacancy rate: 17.6%
Health Insurance: 82.4% have insurance; 61.3% have private insurance; 35.7% have public insurance; 17.6% do not have insurance; 22.1% of children under 18 do not have insurance
Transportation: Commute: 86.3% car, 0.7% public transportation, 4.1% walk, 8.3% work from home; Mean travel time to work: 16.6 minutes

FRANKLIN (town). Covers a land area of 169.827 square miles and a water area of 5.395 square miles. Located at 44.52° N. Lat; 74.07° W. Long.
Population: 1,037; Growth (since 2000): -13.4%; Density: 6.1 persons per square mile; Race: 98.6% White, 0.1% Black/African American, 0.0% Asian, 0.0% American Indian/Alaska Native, 0.0% Native Hawaiian/Other Pacific Islander, 1.3% Two or more races, 1.7% Hispanic of any race; Average household size: 2.08; Median age: 51.0; Age under 18: 15.5%; Age 65 and over: 23.4%; Males per 100 females: 102.5; Marriage status: 20.0% never married, 63.8% now married, 2.0% separated, 6.6% widowed, 9.6% divorced; Foreign born: 2.0%; Speak English only: 96.8%; With disability: 9.9%; Veterans: 17.4%; Ancestry: 30.2% Irish, 21.2% German, 12.9% English, 12.8% French, 7.9% Polish
Employment: 10.8% management, business, and financial, 4.9% computer, engineering, and science, 13.1% education, legal, community service, arts, and media, 6.6% healthcare practitioners, 23.9% service, 19.2% sales and office, 14.5% natural resources, construction, and maintenance, 7.0% production, transportation, and material moving
Income: Per capita: $32,877; Median household: $59,167; Average household: $68,681; Households with income of $100,000 or more: 19.7%; Poverty rate: 8.5%
Educational Attainment: High school diploma or higher: 93.4%; Bachelor's degree or higher: 31.1%; Graduate/professional degree or higher: 16.6%

Housing: Homeownership rate: 93.3%; Median home value: $158,900; Median year structure built: 1968; Homeowner vacancy rate: 0.0%; Median selected monthly owner costs: $1,133 with a mortgage, $568 without a mortgage; Median gross rent: $685 per month; Rental vacancy rate: 0.0%
Health Insurance: 94.3% have insurance; 76.4% have private insurance; 36.9% have public insurance; 5.7% do not have insurance; 9.0% of children under 18 do not have insurance
Transportation: Commute: 94.8% car, 0.7% public transportation, 0.7% walk, 3.8% work from home; Mean travel time to work: 30.3 minutes

GABRIELS (unincorporated postal area)
ZCTA: 12939

Covers a land area of 4.136 square miles and a water area of 0.022 square miles. Located at 44.43° N. Lat; 74.16° W. Long. Elevation is 1,699 feet.

Population: 219; Growth (since 2000): n/a; Density: 52.9 persons per square mile; Race: 100.0% White, 0.0% Black/African American, 0.0% Asian, 0.0% American Indian/Alaska Native, 0.0% Native Hawaiian/Other Pacific Islander, 0.0% Two or more races, 0.0% Hispanic of any race; Average household size: 2.03; Median age: 37.6; Age under 18: 16.9%; Age 65 and over: 4.1%; Males per 100 females: 97.1; Marriage status: 47.0% never married, 39.4% now married, 2.5% separated, 1.5% widowed, 12.1% divorced; Foreign born: 6.8%; Speak English only: 95.3%; With disability: 11.4%; Veterans: 0.0%; Ancestry: 17.4% French, 16.4% Italian, 14.6% Irish, 8.2% English, 7.8% Scottish
Employment: 19.6% management, business, and financial, 9.1% computer, engineering, and science, 0.0% education, legal, community service, arts, and media, 2.8% healthcare practitioners, 27.3% service, 16.1% sales and office, 23.1% natural resources, construction, and maintenance, 2.1% production, transportation, and material moving
Income: Per capita: $30,292; Median household: $54,688; Average household: $59,490; Households with income of $100,000 or more: 22.2%; Poverty rate: 7.8%
Educational Attainment: High school diploma or higher: 98.8%; Bachelor's degree or higher: 30.3%; Graduate/professional degree or higher: 15.2%
Housing: Homeownership rate: 80.6%; Median home value: $125,800; Median year structure built: Before 1940; Homeowner vacancy rate: 0.0%; Median selected monthly owner costs: $1,077 with a mortgage, $475 without a mortgage; Median gross rent: $1,396 per month; Rental vacancy rate: 0.0%
Health Insurance: 95.0% have insurance; 88.1% have private insurance; 12.3% have public insurance; 5.0% do not have insurance; 0.0% of children under 18 do not have insurance
Transportation: Commute: 88.8% car, 0.0% public transportation, 1.4% walk, 9.8% work from home; Mean travel time to work: 20.3 minutes

HARRIETSTOWN (town). Covers a land area of 196.866 square miles and a water area of 16.814 square miles. Located at 44.22° N. Lat; 74.21° W. Long. Elevation is 1,854 feet.

Population: 5,674; Growth (since 2000): 1.8%; Density: 28.8 persons per square mile; Race: 96.2% White, 1.3% Black/African American, 0.1% Asian, 0.1% American Indian/Alaska Native, 0.0% Native Hawaiian/Other Pacific Islander, 2.1% Two or more races, 0.5% Hispanic of any race; Average household size: 2.17; Median age: 44.4; Age under 18: 20.8%; Age 65 and over: 18.5%; Males per 100 females: 103.9; Marriage status: 32.6% never married, 50.2% now married, 3.8% separated, 6.8% widowed, 10.4% divorced; Foreign born: 3.0%; Speak English only: 96.5%; With disability: 16.3%; Veterans: 11.9%; Ancestry: 22.5% Irish, 15.3% French, 11.8% German, 11.1% English, 8.1% Italian
Employment: 12.7% management, business, and financial, 3.6% computer, engineering, and science, 11.8% education, legal, community service, arts, and media, 8.8% healthcare practitioners, 24.1% service, 22.9% sales and office, 5.9% natural resources, construction, and maintenance, 10.2% production, transportation, and material moving
Income: Per capita: $29,013; Median household: $47,848; Average household: $62,887; Households with income of $100,000 or more: 17.5%; Poverty rate: 16.5%
Educational Attainment: High school diploma or higher: 92.1%; Bachelor's degree or higher: 29.6%; Graduate/professional degree or higher: 14.7%
Housing: Homeownership rate: 56.0%; Median home value: $163,600; Median year structure built: Before 1940; Homeowner vacancy rate: 4.8%; Median selected monthly owner costs: $1,328 with a mortgage, $588

without a mortgage; Median gross rent: $651 per month; Rental vacancy rate: 8.3%
Health Insurance: 91.6% have insurance; 66.7% have private insurance; 40.9% have public insurance; 8.4% do not have insurance; 5.8% of children under 18 do not have insurance
Transportation: Commute: 78.6% car, 1.2% public transportation, 10.7% walk, 5.9% work from home; Mean travel time to work: 18.7 minutes
Additional Information Contacts
Town of Harrietstown . . . . (518) 891-1470
  http://www.harrietstown.org

HOGANSBURG (unincorporated postal area)
ZCTA: 13655

Covers a land area of 20.221 square miles and a water area of 2.252 square miles. Located at 44.98° N. Lat; 74.65° W. Long. Elevation is 171 feet.

Population: 3,394; Growth (since 2000): 32.7%; Density: 167.8 persons per square mile; Race: 5.9% White, 0.1% Black/African American, 1.9% Asian, 86.1% American Indian/Alaska Native, 0.0% Native Hawaiian/Other Pacific Islander, 5.3% Two or more races, 2.1% Hispanic of any race; Average household size: 2.55; Median age: 31.6; Age under 18: 30.9%; Age 65 and over: 12.1%; Males per 100 females: 96.4; Marriage status: 42.7% never married, 36.7% now married, 2.9% separated, 3.0% widowed, 17.5% divorced; Foreign born: 10.3%; Speak English only: 70.0%; With disability: 9.8%; Veterans: 7.7%; Ancestry: 3.2% Polish, 1.1% American, 1.1% Greek, 0.8% Italian, 0.8% German
Employment: 21.0% management, business, and financial, 8.0% computer, engineering, and science, 10.9% education, legal, community service, arts, and media, 2.4% healthcare practitioners, 15.4% service, 24.4% sales and office, 4.5% natural resources, construction, and maintenance, 13.4% production, transportation, and material moving
Income: Per capita: $17,093; Median household: $31,881; Average household: $45,781; Households with income of $100,000 or more: 9.2%; Poverty rate: 38.7%
Educational Attainment: High school diploma or higher: 84.9%; Bachelor's degree or higher: 16.5%; Graduate/professional degree or higher: 9.4%

School District(s)
Salmon River Central SD (PK-12)
  2014-15 Enrollment: 1,595 . . . . (518) 358-6610
Housing: Homeownership rate: 75.8%; Median home value: $127,800; Median year structure built: 1992; Homeowner vacancy rate: 0.0%; Median selected monthly owner costs: $789 with a mortgage, $293 without a mortgage; Median gross rent: $492 per month; Rental vacancy rate: 0.0%
Health Insurance: 62.5% have insurance; 28.6% have private insurance; 39.1% have public insurance; 37.5% do not have insurance; 49.7% of children under 18 do not have insurance
Transportation: Commute: 86.0% car, 0.0% public transportation, 0.0% walk, 0.1% work from home; Mean travel time to work: 23.2 minutes

LAKE CLEAR (unincorporated postal area)
ZCTA: 12945

Covers a land area of 33.208 square miles and a water area of 7.218 square miles. Located at 44.31° N. Lat; 74.24° W. Long. Elevation is 1,640 feet.

Population: 467; Growth (since 2000): -36.5%; Density: 14.1 persons per square mile; Race: 100.0% White, 0.0% Black/African American, 0.0% Asian, 0.0% American Indian/Alaska Native, 0.0% Native Hawaiian/Other Pacific Islander, 0.0% Two or more races, 0.0% Hispanic of any race; Average household size: 2.46; Median age: 62.4; Age under 18: 6.9%; Age 65 and over: 39.2%; Males per 100 females: 98.8; Marriage status: 12.0% never married, 72.4% now married, 2.3% separated, 12.9% widowed, 2.8% divorced; Foreign born: 5.8%; Speak English only: 90.1%; With disability: 26.1%; Veterans: 10.8%; Ancestry: 18.6% English, 16.3% Italian, 14.6% Irish, 13.5% German, 11.8% Polish
Employment: 8.8% management, business, and financial, 0.0% computer, engineering, and science, 18.8% education, legal, community service, arts, and media, 17.5% healthcare practitioners, 16.3% service, 35.8% sales and office, 1.3% natural resources, construction, and maintenance, 1.7% production, transportation, and material moving
Income: Per capita: $37,117; Median household: $71,250; Average household: $88,973; Households with income of $100,000 or more: 26.4%; Poverty rate: n/a

Educational Attainment: High school diploma or higher: 85.3%; Bachelor's degree or higher: 30.8%; Graduate/professional degree or higher: 20.9%

Housing: Homeownership rate: 100.0%; Median home value: $189,900; Median year structure built: Before 1940; Homeowner vacancy rate: 0.0%; Median selected monthly owner costs: $1,351 with a mortgage, $485 without a mortgage; Median gross rent: n/a per month; Rental vacancy rate: 100.0%

Health Insurance: 98.9% have insurance; 86.3% have private insurance; 41.8% have public insurance; 1.1% do not have insurance; 0.0% of children under 18 do not have insurance

Transportation: Commute: 100.0% car, 0.0% public transportation, 0.0% walk, 0.0% work from home; Mean travel time to work: 26.8 minutes

MALONE (town). Covers a land area of 101.519 square miles and a water area of 1.283 square miles. Located at 44.80° N. Lat; 74.29° W. Long. Elevation is 712 feet.

History: Malone was settled by Vermonters in 1802. The name was bestowed by William Constable, an early landowner, in honor of his friend, Edmund Malone, Shakespearian scholar.

Population: 14,450; Growth (since 2000): -3.5%; Density: 142.3 persons per square mile; Race: 75.3% White, 16.2% Black/African American, 0.4% Asian, 0.6% American Indian/Alaska Native, 0.0% Native Hawaiian/Other Pacific Islander, 2.7% Two or more races, 8.3% Hispanic of any race; Average household size: 2.37; Median age: 38.1; Age under 18: 16.4%; Age 65 and over: 11.5%; Males per 100 females: 175.8; Marriage status: 41.6% never married, 41.3% now married, 3.6% separated, 5.5% widowed, 11.6% divorced; Foreign born: 4.2%; Speak English only: 91.4%; With disability: 15.1%; Veterans: 9.0%; Ancestry: 16.3% French, 16.3% Irish, 8.9% English, 8.7% German, 6.0% American

Employment: 9.5% management, business, and financial, 1.6% computer, engineering, and science, 15.6% education, legal, community service, arts, and media, 8.2% healthcare practitioners, 27.2% service, 21.7% sales and office, 6.2% natural resources, construction, and maintenance, 10.0% production, transportation, and material moving

Income: Per capita: $18,040; Median household: $48,366; Average household: $59,657; Households with income of $100,000 or more: 17.6%; Poverty rate: 21.8%

Educational Attainment: High school diploma or higher: 78.0%; Bachelor's degree or higher: 15.7%; Graduate/professional degree or higher: 7.7%

School District(s)
Franklin-Essex-Hamilton Boces
    2014-15 Enrollment: n/a . . . . (518) 483-6420
Malone Central SD (PK-12)
    2014-15 Enrollment: 2,303 . . . . (518) 483-7800

Housing: Homeownership rate: 68.6%; Median home value: $102,300; Median year structure built: 1953; Homeowner vacancy rate: 1.1%; Median selected monthly owner costs: $1,201 with a mortgage, $477 without a mortgage; Median gross rent: $688 per month; Rental vacancy rate: 1.6%

Health Insurance: 94.7% have insurance; 66.5% have private insurance; 45.2% have public insurance; 5.3% do not have insurance; 3.3% of children under 18 do not have insurance

Hospitals: Alice Hyde Medical Center (151 beds)

Newspapers: Malone Telegram (daily circulation 5,600)

Transportation: Commute: 91.1% car, 0.7% public transportation, 3.0% walk, 3.0% work from home; Mean travel time to work: 17.8 minutes

Additional Information Contacts
Town of Malone . . . . (518) 483-4740
    http://www.malonetown.com

MALONE (village). County seat. Covers a land area of 3.111 square miles and a water area of 0.066 square miles. Located at 44.85° N. Lat; 74.29° W. Long. Elevation is 712 feet.

History: Was gathering point for the Fenians, who raided Canada in 1866. Settled c.1800, Incorporated 1833.

Population: 5,830; Growth (since 2000): -4.0%; Density: 1,874.2 persons per square mile; Race: 94.3% White, 1.3% Black/African American, 0.0% Asian, 0.5% American Indian/Alaska Native, 0.0% Native Hawaiian/Other Pacific Islander, 3.7% Two or more races, 2.6% Hispanic of any race; Average household size: 2.30; Median age: 41.6; Age under 18: 23.1%; Age 65 and over: 15.7%; Males per 100 females: 85.0; Marriage status: 29.7% never married, 45.0% now married, 5.3% separated, 7.9% widowed, 17.4% divorced; Foreign born: 1.3%; Speak English only: 98.2%;

With disability: 19.3%; Veterans: 10.2%; Ancestry: 15.4% French, 15.2% Irish, 14.0% English, 13.0% German, 9.0% Italian

Employment: 7.4% management, business, and financial, 1.1% computer, engineering, and science, 17.1% education, legal, community service, arts, and media, 6.4% healthcare practitioners, 29.9% service, 21.8% sales and office, 4.6% natural resources, construction, and maintenance, 11.7% production, transportation, and material moving

Income: Per capita: $21,153; Median household: $36,667; Average household: $49,145; Households with income of $100,000 or more: 12.8%; Poverty rate: 31.1%

Educational Attainment: High school diploma or higher: 81.2%; Bachelor's degree or higher: 17.7%; Graduate/professional degree or higher: 7.4%

School District(s)
Franklin-Essex-Hamilton Boces
    2014-15 Enrollment: n/a . . . . (518) 483-6420
Malone Central SD (PK-12)
    2014-15 Enrollment: 2,303 . . . . (518) 483-7800

Housing: Homeownership rate: 53.6%; Median home value: $83,400; Median year structure built: Before 1940; Homeowner vacancy rate: 1.0%; Median selected monthly owner costs: $1,190 with a mortgage, $523 without a mortgage; Median gross rent: $686 per month; Rental vacancy rate: 0.0%

Health Insurance: 93.9% have insurance; 56.7% have private insurance; 52.9% have public insurance; 6.1% do not have insurance; 0.0% of children under 18 do not have insurance

Hospitals: Alice Hyde Medical Center (151 beds)

Safety: Violent crime rate: 39.6 per 10,000 population; Property crime rate: 379.1 per 10,000 population

Newspapers: Malone Telegram (daily circulation 5,600)

Transportation: Commute: 87.2% car, 1.4% public transportation, 5.7% walk, 3.7% work from home; Mean travel time to work: 18.0 minutes

Additional Information Contacts
Village of Malone . . . . (518) 483-4570
    http://www.malonevillage.com

MOIRA (town). Covers a land area of 45.228 square miles and a water area of 0 square miles. Located at 44.83° N. Lat; 74.56° W. Long. Elevation is 420 feet.

Population: 2,894; Growth (since 2000): 1.3%; Density: 64.0 persons per square mile; Race: 96.8% White, 0.5% Black/African American, 0.0% Asian, 1.4% American Indian/Alaska Native, 0.0% Native Hawaiian/Other Pacific Islander, 0.5% Two or more races, 2.7% Hispanic of any race; Average household size: 2.28; Median age: 43.6; Age under 18: 18.2%; Age 65 and over: 17.8%; Males per 100 females: 96.5; Marriage status: 26.3% never married, 54.2% now married, 2.9% separated, 8.2% widowed, 11.3% divorced; Foreign born: 2.4%; Speak English only: 95.8%; With disability: 13.4%; Veterans: 8.3%; Ancestry: 20.1% French, 17.9% Irish, 15.3% English, 8.3% French Canadian, 7.7% American

Employment: 3.1% management, business, and financial, 0.7% computer, engineering, and science, 17.1% education, legal, community service, arts, and media, 6.7% healthcare practitioners, 29.9% service, 17.3% sales and office, 6.6% natural resources, construction, and maintenance, 18.6% production, transportation, and material moving

Income: Per capita: $28,443; Median household: $46,555; Average household: $64,858; Households with income of $100,000 or more: 14.7%; Poverty rate: 20.3%

Educational Attainment: High school diploma or higher: 86.7%; Bachelor's degree or higher: 16.6%; Graduate/professional degree or higher: 7.2%

Housing: Homeownership rate: 74.0%; Median home value: $85,800; Median year structure built: 1969; Homeowner vacancy rate: 0.5%; Median selected monthly owner costs: $989 with a mortgage, $428 without a mortgage; Median gross rent: $693 per month; Rental vacancy rate: 1.8%

Health Insurance: 92.0% have insurance; 65.7% have private insurance; 45.3% have public insurance; 8.0% do not have insurance; 7.4% of children under 18 do not have insurance

Transportation: Commute: 89.6% car, 0.0% public transportation, 0.5% walk, 10.0% work from home; Mean travel time to work: 26.8 minutes

NORTH BANGOR (unincorporated postal area)
ZCTA: 12966
    Covers a land area of 86.158 square miles and a water area of 0.067 square miles. Located at 44.80° N. Lat; 74.42° W. Long. Elevation is 666 feet.

Population: 3,189; Growth (since 2000): 12.4%; Density: 37.0 persons per square mile; Race: 99.0% White, 0.0% Black/African American, 0.0% Asian, 0.0% American Indian/Alaska Native, 0.0% Native Hawaiian/Other Pacific Islander, 1.0% Two or more races, 0.7% Hispanic of any race; Average household size: 2.56; Median age: 37.3; Age under 18: 22.7%; Age 65 and over: 11.1%; Males per 100 females: 105.1; Marriage status: 28.4% never married, 57.8% now married, 3.9% separated, 3.8% widowed, 10.0% divorced; Foreign born: 2.1%; Speak English only: 99.0%; With disability: 17.1%; Veterans: 7.1%; Ancestry: 29.5% French, 14.9% Irish, 12.2% English, 9.0% American, 7.2% German

Employment: 8.2% management, business, and financial, 3.2% computer, engineering, and science, 13.0% education, legal, community service, arts, and media, 5.3% healthcare practitioners, 29.9% service, 17.0% sales and office, 9.1% natural resources, construction, and maintenance, 14.2% production, transportation, and material moving

Income: Per capita: $19,641; Median household: $42,200; Average household: $48,479; Households with income of $100,000 or more: 7.2%; Poverty rate: 28.2%

Educational Attainment: High school diploma or higher: 88.1%; Bachelor's degree or higher: 12.6%; Graduate/professional degree or higher: 6.7%

Housing: Homeownership rate: 82.1%; Median home value: $73,000; Median year structure built: 1976; Homeowner vacancy rate: 0.0%; Median selected monthly owner costs: $1,030 with a mortgage, $409 without a mortgage; Median gross rent: $797 per month; Rental vacancy rate: 0.0%

Health Insurance: 92.5% have insurance; 65.8% have private insurance; 46.0% have public insurance; 7.5% do not have insurance; 1.0% of children under 18 do not have insurance

Transportation: Commute: 91.6% car, 1.7% public transportation, 1.4% walk, 5.3% work from home; Mean travel time to work: 22.8 minutes

OWLS HEAD (unincorporated postal area)
ZCTA: 12969

Covers a land area of 98.651 square miles and a water area of 1.857 square miles. Located at 44.71° N. Lat; 74.10° W. Long. Elevation is 1,532 feet.

Population: 421; Growth (since 2000): -24.0%; Density: 4.3 persons per square mile; Race: 100.0% White, 0.0% Black/African American, 0.0% Asian, 0.0% American Indian/Alaska Native, 0.0% Native Hawaiian/Other Pacific Islander, 0.0% Two or more races, 0.0% Hispanic of any race; Average household size: 2.28; Median age: 45.6; Age under 18: 23.0%; Age 65 and over: 26.1%; Males per 100 females: 119.2; Marriage status: 17.6% never married, 66.2% now married, 0.6% separated, 6.2% widowed, 10.0% divorced; Foreign born: 2.1%; Speak English only: 97.7%; With disability: 6.2%; Veterans: 13.0%; Ancestry: 40.4% French, 34.4% Irish, 15.0% American, 11.2% English, 6.2% French Canadian

Employment: 13.3% management, business, and financial, 2.0% computer, engineering, and science, 9.3% education, legal, community service, arts, and media, 4.0% healthcare practitioners, 26.7% service, 24.0% sales and office, 18.0% natural resources, construction, and maintenance, 2.7% production, transportation, and material moving

Income: Per capita: $23,385; Median household: $40,250; Average household: $53,083; Households with income of $100,000 or more: 10.2%; Poverty rate: 20.2%

Educational Attainment: High school diploma or higher: 87.7%; Bachelor's degree or higher: 18.4%; Graduate/professional degree or higher: 9.1%

Housing: Homeownership rate: 91.9%; Median home value: $83,700; Median year structure built: 1951; Homeowner vacancy rate: 2.2%; Median selected monthly owner costs: $988 with a mortgage, $326 without a mortgage; Median gross rent: n/a per month; Rental vacancy rate: 0.0%

Health Insurance: 92.6% have insurance; 66.5% have private insurance; 48.0% have public insurance; 7.4% do not have insurance; 5.2% of children under 18 do not have insurance

Transportation: Commute: 94.4% car, 0.0% public transportation, 0.0% walk, 5.6% work from home; Mean travel time to work: 28.0 minutes

PAUL SMITHS (CDP).
Covers a land area of 0.255 square miles and a water area of 0.135 square miles. Located at 44.43° N. Lat; 74.25° W. Long. Elevation is 1,673 feet.

Population: 667; Growth (since 2000): n/a; Density: 2,613.2 persons per square mile; Race: 80.7% White, 11.1% Black/African American, 4.2% Asian, 1.6% American Indian/Alaska Native, 0.0% Native Hawaiian/Other Pacific Islander, 2.4% Two or more races, 0.7% Hispanic of any race; Average household size: 0.00; Median age: 20.2; Age under 18: 1.0%; Age 65 and over: 0.0%; Males per 100 females: 238.9; Marriage status: 99.4% never married, 0.6% now married, 0.0% separated, 0.0% widowed, 0.0% divorced; Foreign born: 3.0%; Speak English only: 84.9%; With disability: 11.1%; Veterans: 0.0%; Ancestry: 11.5% Irish, 10.5% Italian, 6.4% German, 5.8% Polish, 4.8% American

Employment: 3.7% management, business, and financial, 11.3% computer, engineering, and science, 11.8% education, legal, community service, arts, and media, 0.0% healthcare practitioners, 28.1% service, 34.9% sales and office, 6.6% natural resources, construction, and maintenance, 3.7% production, transportation, and material moving

Income: Per capita: $6,054; Median household: n/a; Average household: n/a; Households with income of $100,000 or more: n/a; Poverty rate: n/a

Educational Attainment: High school diploma or higher: 100.0%; Bachelor's degree or higher: 100.0%; Graduate/professional degree or higher: 100.0%

Four-year College(s)
Paul Smiths College of Arts and Science (Private, Not-for-profit)
    Fall 2014 Enrollment: 892 . . . . (518) 327-6000
    2015-16 Tuition: In-state $27,130; Out-of-state $27,130

Housing: Homeownership rate: n/a; Median home value: n/a; Median year structure built: n/a; Homeowner vacancy rate: 0.0%; Median selected monthly owner costs: n/a with a mortgage, n/a without a mortgage; Median gross rent: n/a per month; Rental vacancy rate: 0.0%

Health Insurance: 98.5% have insurance; 93.1% have private insurance; 11.8% have public insurance; 1.5% do not have insurance; 0.0% of children under 18 do not have insurance

Transportation: Commute: 40.2% car, 0.0% public transportation, 39.7% walk, 20.1% work from home; Mean travel time to work: 17.6 minutes

RAINBOW LAKE (unincorporated postal area)
ZCTA: 12976

Covers a land area of 38.370 square miles and a water area of 1.198 square miles. Located at 44.52° N. Lat; 74.21° W. Long. Elevation is 1,690 feet.

Population: 179; Growth (since 2000): n/a; Density: 4.7 persons per square mile; Race: 98.3% White, 0.0% Black/African American, 0.0% Asian, 0.0% American Indian/Alaska Native, 0.0% Native Hawaiian/Other Pacific Islander, 1.7% Two or more races, 0.0% Hispanic of any race; Average household size: 1.88; Median age: 53.0; Age under 18: 6.1%; Age 65 and over: 19.0%; Males per 100 females: 100.0; Marriage status: 31.8% never married, 57.2% now married, 0.0% separated, 7.5% widowed, 3.5% divorced; Foreign born: 0.0%; Speak English only: 98.3%; With disability: 18.4%; Veterans: 3.0%; Ancestry: 25.7% English, 17.9% Italian, 13.4% German, 11.7% French, 11.2% Irish

Employment: 29.3% management, business, and financial, 0.0% computer, engineering, and science, 6.1% education, legal, community service, arts, and media, 12.2% healthcare practitioners, 9.8% service, 28.0% sales and office, 11.0% natural resources, construction, and maintenance, 3.7% production, transportation, and material moving

Income: Per capita: $39,726; Median household: $61,250; Average household: $75,605; Households with income of $100,000 or more: 26.3%; Poverty rate: 2.2%

Educational Attainment: High school diploma or higher: 100.0%; Bachelor's degree or higher: 47.1%; Graduate/professional degree or higher: 17.8%

Housing: Homeownership rate: 95.8%; Median home value: $222,900; Median year structure built: 1974; Homeowner vacancy rate: 0.0%; Median selected monthly owner costs: $1,375 with a mortgage, $641 without a mortgage; Median gross rent: n/a per month; Rental vacancy rate: 0.0%

Health Insurance: 87.2% have insurance; 79.9% have private insurance; 24.0% have public insurance; 12.8% do not have insurance; 0.0% of children under 18 do not have insurance

Transportation: Commute: 65.9% car, 0.0% public transportation, 0.0% walk, 34.1% work from home; Mean travel time to work: 23.4 minutes

SAINT REGIS FALLS (CDP). Covers a land area of 1.292 square miles and a water area of 0 square miles. Located at 44.68° N. Lat; 74.53° W. Long. Elevation is 1,266 feet.

Population: 383; Growth (since 2000): n/a; Density: 296.5 persons per square mile; Race: 100.0% White, 0.0% Black/African American, 0.0% Asian, 0.0% American Indian/Alaska Native, 0.0% Native Hawaiian/Other Pacific Islander, 0.0% Two or more races, 1.3% Hispanic of any race; Average household size: 1.90; Median age: 50.2; Age under 18: 18.0%; Age 65 and over: 18.5%; Males per 100 females: 89.4; Marriage status: 26.8% never married, 57.6% now married, 2.1% separated, 7.0% widowed, 8.5% divorced; Foreign born: 0.8%; Speak English only: 98.4%; With disability: 25.6%; Veterans: 13.1%; Ancestry: 27.7% French, 22.7% English, 20.6% Irish, 11.7% German, 8.6% Dutch

Employment: 10.4% management, business, and financial, 1.6% computer, engineering, and science, 1.6% education, legal, community service, arts, and media, 3.3% healthcare practitioners, 26.8% service, 30.6% sales and office, 21.9% natural resources, construction, and maintenance, 3.8% production, transportation, and material moving

Income: Per capita: $24,503; Median household: $40,357; Average household: $47,075; Households with income of $100,000 or more: 4.5%; Poverty rate: 20.9%

Educational Attainment: High school diploma or higher: 86.6%; Bachelor's degree or higher: 3.1%; Graduate/professional degree or higher: 1.4%

School District(s)

Saint Regis Falls Central SD (PK-12)

    2014-15 Enrollment: 278 . . . . (518) 856-9421

Housing: Homeownership rate: 79.7%; Median home value: $46,400; Median year structure built: 1954; Homeowner vacancy rate: 7.1%; Median selected monthly owner costs: $941 with a mortgage, $357 without a mortgage; Median gross rent: $759 per month; Rental vacancy rate: 0.0%

Health Insurance: 87.7% have insurance; 58.0% have private insurance; 39.9% have public insurance; 12.3% do not have insurance; 7.2% of children under 18 do not have insurance

Transportation: Commute: 92.0% car, 5.1% public transportation, 2.3% walk, 0.6% work from home; Mean travel time to work: 36.7 minutes

SAINT REGIS MOHAWK RESERVATION (reservation). Covers a land area of 18.940 square miles and a water area of 2.049 square miles. Located at 44.98° N. Lat; 74.64° W. Long.

Population: 3,247; Growth (since 2000): 20.3%; Density: 171.4 persons per square mile; Race: 6.0% White, 0.1% Black/African American, 1.9% Asian, 87.6% American Indian/Alaska Native, 0.0% Native Hawaiian/Other Pacific Islander, 3.8% Two or more races, 2.1% Hispanic of any race; Average household size: 2.62; Median age: 31.6; Age under 18: 31.1%; Age 65 and over: 11.9%; Males per 100 females: 94.8; Marriage status: 41.4% never married, 37.8% now married, 3.0% separated, 2.6% widowed, 18.2% divorced; Foreign born: 10.7%; Speak English only: 69.4%; With disability: 9.0%; Veterans: 8.0%; Ancestry: 3.3% Polish, 1.2% Greek, 0.9% Italian, 0.8% German, 0.0% French

Employment: 21.5% management, business, and financial, 8.5% computer, engineering, and science, 11.2% education, legal, community service, arts, and media, 2.5% healthcare practitioners, 14.3% service, 23.7% sales and office, 4.3% natural resources, construction, and maintenance, 14.1% production, transportation, and material moving

Income: Per capita: $17,253; Median household: $32,917; Average household: $47,432; Households with income of $100,000 or more: 9.6%; Poverty rate: 37.7%

Educational Attainment: High school diploma or higher: 85.2%; Bachelor's degree or higher: 16.4%; Graduate/professional degree or higher: 9.7%

Housing: Homeownership rate: 80.2%; Median home value: $129,000; Median year structure built: 1993; Homeowner vacancy rate: 0.0%; Median selected monthly owner costs: $783 with a mortgage, $292 without a mortgage; Median gross rent: $478 per month; Rental vacancy rate: 0.0%

Health Insurance: 61.5% have insurance; 28.9% have private insurance; 37.1% have public insurance; 38.5% do not have insurance; 51.6% of children under 18 do not have insurance

Transportation: Commute: 87.3% car, 0.0% public transportation, 0.0% walk, 0.0% work from home; Mean travel time to work: 23.8 minutes

SANTA CLARA (town). Covers a land area of 174.417 square miles and a water area of 17.292 square miles. Located at 44.50° N. Lat; 74.36° W. Long. Elevation is 1,339 feet.

Population: 455; Growth (since 2000): 15.2%; Density: 2.6 persons per square mile; Race: 94.3% White, 5.3% Black/African American, 0.0% Asian, 0.0% American Indian/Alaska Native, 0.0% Native Hawaiian/Other Pacific Islander, 0.0% Two or more races, 4.8% Hispanic of any race; Average household size: 2.13; Median age: 54.9; Age under 18: 5.7%; Age 65 and over: 27.7%; Males per 100 females: 113.0; Marriage status: 30.0% never married, 61.3% now married, 1.6% separated, 4.1% widowed, 4.6% divorced; Foreign born: 1.3%; Speak English only: 95.3%; With disability: 10.6%; Veterans: 10.7%; Ancestry: 28.8% Irish, 20.2% English, 16.5% German, 10.8% French, 7.9% Polish

Employment: 25.5% management, business, and financial, 2.8% computer, engineering, and science, 18.9% education, legal, community service, arts, and media, 8.5% healthcare practitioners, 9.4% service, 19.3% sales and office, 7.5% natural resources, construction, and maintenance, 8.0% production, transportation, and material moving

Income: Per capita: $41,379; Median household: $90,139; Average household: $109,032; Households with income of $100,000 or more: 38.9%; Poverty rate: 6.7%

Educational Attainment: High school diploma or higher: 94.7%; Bachelor's degree or higher: 52.5%; Graduate/professional degree or higher: 25.9%

Housing: Homeownership rate: 79.4%; Median home value: $298,100; Median year structure built: 1972; Homeowner vacancy rate: 7.5%; Median selected monthly owner costs: $1,828 with a mortgage, $664 without a mortgage; Median gross rent: $1,250 per month; Rental vacancy rate: 2.7%

Health Insurance: 98.2% have insurance; 90.1% have private insurance; 34.6% have public insurance; 1.8% do not have insurance; 0.0% of children under 18 do not have insurance

Transportation: Commute: 70.7% car, 0.0% public transportation, 17.8% walk, 9.6% work from home; Mean travel time to work: 22.3 minutes

SARANAC LAKE (village). Covers a land area of 2.779 square miles and a water area of 0.249 square miles. Located at 44.32° N. Lat; 74.13° W. Long. Elevation is 1,545 feet.

History: The village is named after the nearby Upper, Middle and Lower Saranac Lakes.

Population: 5,727; Growth (since 2000): 13.6%; Density: 2,060.8 persons per square mile; Race: 95.8% White, 1.3% Black/African American, 0.5% Asian, 0.1% American Indian/Alaska Native, 0.0% Native Hawaiian/Other Pacific Islander, 2.3% Two or more races, 0.1% Hispanic of any race; Average household size: 2.16; Median age: 43.4; Age under 18: 20.9%; Age 65 and over: 17.0%; Males per 100 females: 98.1; Marriage status: 35.0% never married, 46.1% now married, 3.8% separated, 6.9% widowed, 11.9% divorced; Foreign born: 2.3%; Speak English only: 97.5%; With disability: 17.4%; Veterans: 10.8%; Ancestry: 28.0% Irish, 14.1% French, 11.7% English, 10.9% German, 7.1% Italian

Employment: 11.8% management, business, and financial, 3.5% computer, engineering, and science, 11.7% education, legal, community service, arts, and media, 8.1% healthcare practitioners, 27.1% service, 25.1% sales and office, 4.7% natural resources, construction, and maintenance, 8.1% production, transportation, and material moving

Income: Per capita: $26,185; Median household: $43,795; Average household: $56,701; Households with income of $100,000 or more: 16.5%; Poverty rate: 16.7%

Educational Attainment: High school diploma or higher: 92.1%; Bachelor's degree or higher: 29.0%; Graduate/professional degree or higher: 12.4%

School District(s)

Saranac Lake Central SD (PK-12)

    2014-15 Enrollment: 1,249 . . . . (518) 891-5460

Two-year College(s)

North Country Community College (Public)

    Fall 2014 Enrollment: 1,962 . . . . (518) 891-2915

    2015-16 Tuition: In-state $5,303; Out-of-state $11,453

Housing: Homeownership rate: 48.3%; Median home value: $150,800; Median year structure built: Before 1940; Homeowner vacancy rate: 5.4%; Median selected monthly owner costs: $1,366 with a mortgage, $585 without a mortgage; Median gross rent: $675 per month; Rental vacancy rate: 7.6%

Health Insurance: 89.6% have insurance; 65.3% have private insurance; 39.1% have public insurance; 10.4% do not have insurance; 7.5% of children under 18 do not have insurance
Hospitals: Adirondack Medical Center (97 beds)
Safety: Violent crime rate: 11.3 per 10,000 population; Property crime rate: 158.6 per 10,000 population
Newspapers: Adirondack Daily Enterprise (daily circulation 4,100)
Transportation: Commute: 77.4% car, 1.3% public transportation, 13.9% walk, 5.6% work from home; Mean travel time to work: 16.8 minutes
Airports: Adirondack Regional (commercial service–non-primary)
Additional Information Contacts
Village of Saranac Lake .... (518) 891-4150
    http://www.saranaclakeny.gov

TUPPER LAKE (town). Covers a land area of 117.348 square miles and a water area of 12.754 square miles. Located at 44.24° N. Lat; 74.47° W. Long. Elevation is 1,598 feet.

Population: 5,926; Growth (since 2000): n/a; Density: 50.5 persons per square mile; Race: 96.0% White, 2.1% Black/African American, 0.1% Asian, 0.2% American Indian/Alaska Native, 0.0% Native Hawaiian/Other Pacific Islander, 1.0% Two or more races, 0.9% Hispanic of any race; Average household size: 2.27; Median age: 38.7; Age under 18: 22.0%; Age 65 and over: 16.2%; Males per 100 females: 111.2; Marriage status: 32.6% never married, 50.2% now married, 2.7% separated, 7.6% widowed, 9.6% divorced; Foreign born: 3.1%; Speak English only: 96.5%; With disability: 13.9%; Veterans: 7.4%; Ancestry: 26.3% French, 21.3% Irish, 19.6% French Canadian, 9.6% English, 8.3% German
Employment: 8.4% management, business, and financial, 1.4% computer, engineering, and science, 11.4% education, legal, community service, arts, and media, 5.3% healthcare practitioners, 33.0% service, 18.6% sales and office, 13.0% natural resources, construction, and maintenance, 8.9% production, transportation, and material moving
Income: Per capita: $24,439; Median household: $50,515; Average household: $57,788; Households with income of $100,000 or more: 11.7%; Poverty rate: 13.8%
Educational Attainment: High school diploma or higher: 85.1%; Bachelor's degree or higher: 16.9%; Graduate/professional degree or higher: 8.0%
School District(s)
Tupper Lake Central SD (PK-12)
    2014-15 Enrollment: 803......................... (518) 359-3371
Housing: Homeownership rate: 68.9%; Median home value: $122,100; Median year structure built: 1955; Homeowner vacancy rate: 2.8%; Median selected monthly owner costs: $1,099 with a mortgage, $456 without a mortgage; Median gross rent: $611 per month; Rental vacancy rate: 8.0%
Health Insurance: 93.9% have insurance; 72.3% have private insurance; 36.9% have public insurance; 6.1% do not have insurance; 3.0% of children under 18 do not have insurance
Newspapers: Free Press & Herald (weekly circulation 4,000)
Transportation: Commute: 85.9% car, 0.6% public transportation, 4.5% walk, 7.4% work from home; Mean travel time to work: 14.7 minutes

TUPPER LAKE (village). Covers a land area of 2.090 square miles and a water area of 0.044 square miles. Located at 44.23° N. Lat; 74.46° W. Long. Elevation is 1,598 feet.

History: Settled 1890, incorporated 1902.
Population: 3,566; Growth (since 2000): -9.4%; Density: 1,705.9 persons per square mile; Race: 97.9% White, 0.1% Black/African American, 0.1% Asian, 0.3% American Indian/Alaska Native, 0.0% Native Hawaiian/Other Pacific Islander, 1.6% Two or more races, 0.1% Hispanic of any race; Average household size: 2.22; Median age: 34.6; Age under 18: 25.6%; Age 65 and over: 13.9%; Males per 100 females: 97.7; Marriage status: 30.1% never married, 51.6% now married, 3.7% separated, 7.8% widowed, 10.5% divorced; Foreign born: 3.1%; Speak English only: 97.5%; With disability: 11.8%; Veterans: 8.0%; Ancestry: 27.0% French, 23.6% Irish, 22.5% French Canadian, 9.8% English, 8.3% German
Employment: 5.2% management, business, and financial, 1.4% computer, engineering, and science, 8.3% education, legal, community service, arts, and media, 3.0% healthcare practitioners, 38.6% service, 19.6% sales and office, 14.3% natural resources, construction, and maintenance, 9.6% production, transportation, and material moving
Income: Per capita: $23,131; Median household: $44,072; Average household: $49,892; Households with income of $100,000 or more: 8.6%; Poverty rate: 15.1%

Educational Attainment: High school diploma or higher: 87.5%; Bachelor's degree or higher: 12.0%; Graduate/professional degree or higher: 4.8%
School District(s)
Tupper Lake Central SD (PK-12)
    2014-15 Enrollment: 803......................... (518) 359-3371
Housing: Homeownership rate: 60.1%; Median home value: $96,100; Median year structure built: 1948; Homeowner vacancy rate: 4.7%; Median selected monthly owner costs: $961 with a mortgage, $452 without a mortgage; Median gross rent: $579 per month; Rental vacancy rate: 9.3%
Health Insurance: 92.3% have insurance; 68.6% have private insurance; 38.5% have public insurance; 7.7% do not have insurance; 3.7% of children under 18 do not have insurance
Safety: Violent crime rate: 24.9 per 10,000 population; Property crime rate: 232.8 per 10,000 population
Newspapers: Free Press & Herald (weekly circulation 4,000)
Transportation: Commute: 87.5% car, 0.9% public transportation, 5.0% walk, 6.1% work from home; Mean travel time to work: 13.6 minutes

VERMONTVILLE (unincorporated postal area)
ZCTA: 12989
    Covers a land area of 147.752 square miles and a water area of 2.814 square miles. Located at 44.52° N. Lat; 74.07° W. Long. Elevation is 1,644 feet.
Population: 923; Growth (since 2000): 8.2%; Density: 6.2 persons per square mile; Race: 98.5% White, 0.1% Black/African American, 0.0% Asian, 0.0% American Indian/Alaska Native, 0.0% Native Hawaiian/Other Pacific Islander, 1.4% Two or more races, 2.0% Hispanic of any race; Average household size: 2.16; Median age: 50.2; Age under 18: 17.2%; Age 65 and over: 23.1%; Males per 100 females: 103.6; Marriage status: 18.4% never married, 65.5% now married, 2.2% separated, 6.6% widowed, 9.5% divorced; Foreign born: 2.0%; Speak English only: 97.0%; With disability: 9.6%; Veterans: 17.0%; Ancestry: 33.2% Irish, 19.5% German, 13.4% French, 11.6% English, 8.9% Polish
Employment: 8.7% management, business, and financial, 3.4% computer, engineering, and science, 14.2% education, legal, community service, arts, and media, 7.7% healthcare practitioners, 25.7% service, 18.6% sales and office, 16.2% natural resources, construction, and maintenance, 5.5% production, transportation, and material moving
Income: Per capita: $31,172; Median household: $62,656; Average household: $67,411; Households with income of $100,000 or more: 19.6%; Poverty rate: 9.0%
Educational Attainment: High school diploma or higher: 92.5%; Bachelor's degree or higher: 28.6%; Graduate/professional degree or higher: 13.4%
Housing: Homeownership rate: 92.9%; Median home value: $149,000; Median year structure built: 1966; Homeowner vacancy rate: 0.0%; Median selected monthly owner costs: $1,130 with a mortgage, $535 without a mortgage; Median gross rent: $700 per month; Rental vacancy rate: 0.0%
Health Insurance: 94.7% have insurance; 76.4% have private insurance; 37.7% have public insurance; 5.3% do not have insurance; 9.1% of children under 18 do not have insurance
Transportation: Commute: 95.2% car, 0.8% public transportation, 0.8% walk, 3.1% work from home; Mean travel time to work: 30.8 minutes

WAVERLY (town). Covers a land area of 125.112 square miles and a water area of 1.294 square miles. Located at 44.53° N. Lat; 74.55° W. Long.

Population: 952; Growth (since 2000): -14.8%; Density: 7.6 persons per square mile; Race: 99.4% White, 0.2% Black/African American, 0.0% Asian, 0.0% American Indian/Alaska Native, 0.0% Native Hawaiian/Other Pacific Islander, 0.4% Two or more races, 0.7% Hispanic of any race; Average household size: 2.12; Median age: 45.9; Age under 18: 22.2%; Age 65 and over: 19.4%; Males per 100 females: 92.5; Marriage status: 28.2% never married, 54.4% now married, 2.6% separated, 7.6% widowed, 9.8% divorced; Foreign born: 1.5%; Speak English only: 99.2%; With disability: 25.0%; Veterans: 13.4%; Ancestry: 28.8% French, 23.8% Irish, 11.6% English, 10.8% German, 6.3% Italian
Employment: 8.1% management, business, and financial, 3.3% computer, engineering, and science, 2.5% education, legal, community service, arts, and media, 3.3% healthcare practitioners, 31.2% service, 27.4% sales and office, 16.5% natural resources, construction, and maintenance, 7.6% production, transportation, and material moving

Income: Per capita: $22,288; Median household: $40,096; Average household: $47,586; Households with income of $100,000 or more: 9.1%; Poverty rate: 24.1%

Educational Attainment: High school diploma or higher: 84.7%; Bachelor's degree or higher: 5.6%; Graduate/professional degree or higher: 3.6%

Housing: Homeownership rate: 78.4%; Median home value: $61,300; Median year structure built: 1969; Homeowner vacancy rate: 4.4%; Median selected monthly owner costs: $1,082 with a mortgage, $366 without a mortgage; Median gross rent: $672 per month; Rental vacancy rate: 0.0%

Health Insurance: 88.1% have insurance; 63.4% have private insurance; 37.8% have public insurance; 11.9% do not have insurance; 10.9% of children under 18 do not have insurance

Transportation: Commute: 94.8% car, 2.3% public transportation, 2.6% walk, 0.3% work from home; Mean travel time to work: 31.8 minutes

---

WESTVILLE (town). Covers a land area of 34.798 square miles and a water area of 0.014 square miles. Located at 44.94° N. Lat; 74.38° W. Long. Elevation is 200 feet.

Population: 1,722; Growth (since 2000): -5.5%; Density: 49.5 persons per square mile; Race: 98.5% White, 0.2% Black/African American, 0.0% Asian, 0.8% American Indian/Alaska Native, 0.0% Native Hawaiian/Other Pacific Islander, 0.5% Two or more races, 0.9% Hispanic of any race; Average household size: 2.41; Median age: 42.2; Age under 18: 21.5%; Age 65 and over: 17.1%; Males per 100 females: 106.7; Marriage status: 25.2% never married, 53.8% now married, 3.6% separated, 6.6% widowed, 14.4% divorced; Foreign born: 2.3%; Speak English only: 94.4%; With disability: 16.1%; Veterans: 9.6%; Ancestry: 19.8% French, 16.7% Irish, 8.8% German, 8.4% English, 7.6% American

Employment: 4.5% management, business, and financial, 1.6% computer, engineering, and science, 12.0% education, legal, community service, arts, and media, 6.0% healthcare practitioners, 30.6% service, 20.3% sales and office, 9.6% natural resources, construction, and maintenance, 15.4% production, transportation, and material moving

Income: Per capita: $23,997; Median household: $49,219; Average household: $56,616; Households with income of $100,000 or more: 10.6%; Poverty rate: 14.4%

Educational Attainment: High school diploma or higher: 84.7%; Bachelor's degree or higher: 10.4%; Graduate/professional degree or higher: 5.8%

Housing: Homeownership rate: 82.3%; Median home value: $81,200; Median year structure built: 1981; Homeowner vacancy rate: 0.5%; Median selected monthly owner costs: $979 with a mortgage, $374 without a mortgage; Median gross rent: $638 per month; Rental vacancy rate: 0.0%

Health Insurance: 90.4% have insurance; 64.5% have private insurance; 43.9% have public insurance; 9.6% do not have insurance; 9.2% of children under 18 do not have insurance

Transportation: Commute: 95.5% car, 0.5% public transportation, 0.4% walk, 3.6% work from home; Mean travel time to work: 21.2 minutes

---

Fulton County

Located in east central New York, in the Adirondacks; drained by East Canada Creek and the Sacandaga River; includes several lakes. Covers a land area of 495.469 square miles, a water area of 37.411 square miles, and is located in the Eastern Time Zone at 43.12° N. Lat., 74.42° W. Long. The county was founded in 1838. County seat is Johnstown.

Fulton County is part of the Gloversville, NY Micropolitan Statistical Area. The entire metro area includes: Fulton County, NY

Weather Station: Gloversville										Elevation: 898 feet	
	Jan	Feb	Mar	Apr	May	Jun	Jul	Aug	Sep	Oct	Nov	Dec
High	29	32	41	56	68	76	80	79	71	58	46	33
Low	10	12	21	33	44	54	59	57	49	36	29	17
Precip	3.1	2.7	3.5	4.1	4.3	4.3	4.2	4.5	3.9	4.1	3.4	3.4
Snow	20.9	14.2	14.6	1.6	tr	0.0	0.0	0.0	0.0	0.1	4.3	17.0

High and Low temperatures in degrees Fahrenheit; Precipitation and Snow in inches

Population: 54,606; Growth (since 2000): -0.8%; Density: 110.2 persons per square mile; Race: 95.2% White, 1.6% Black/African American, 0.6% Asian, 0.1% American Indian/Alaska Native, 0.0% Native Hawaiian/Other Pacific Islander, 1.7% two or more races, 2.7% Hispanic of any race; Average household size: 2.40; Median age: 42.8; Age under 18: 21.0%; Age 65 and over: 17.3%; Males per 100 females: 97.9; Marriage status: 28.3% never married, 52.6% now married, 3.3% separated, 7.4%

widowed, 11.8% divorced; Foreign born: 2.4%; Speak English only: 95.8%; With disability: 16.1%; Veterans: 9.4%; Ancestry: 20.2% German, 16.7% Irish, 14.7% Italian, 12.4% American, 10.9% English

Religion: Six largest groups: 14.3% Catholicism, 5.1% Methodist/Pietist, 1.9% Presbyterian-Reformed, 1.4% Non-denominational Protestant, 0.8% Latter-day Saints, 0.7% Episcopalianism/Anglicanism

Economy: Unemployment rate: 5.2%; Leading industries: 17.9 % retail trade; 15.7 % health care and social assistance; 10.9 % construction; Farms: 211 totaling 31,869 acres; Company size: 0 employ 1,000 or more persons, 3 employ 500 to 999 persons, 18 employ 100 to 499 persons, 1,155 employ less than 100 persons; Business ownership: 1,291 women-owned, n/a Black-owned, n/a Hispanic-owned, n/a Asian-owned, n/a American Indian/Alaska Native-owned

Employment: 9.6% management, business, and financial, 2.8% computer, engineering, and science, 9.8% education, legal, community service, arts, and media, 5.5% healthcare practitioners, 20.6% service, 25.0% sales and office, 9.3% natural resources, construction, and maintenance, 17.5% production, transportation, and material moving

Income: Per capita: $24,339; Median household: $46,969; Average household: $58,356; Households with income of $100,000 or more: 15.8%; Poverty rate: 17.1%

Educational Attainment: High school diploma or higher: 86.0%; Bachelor's degree or higher: 16.2%; Graduate/professional degree or higher: 7.5%

Housing: Homeownership rate: 70.4%; Median home value: $108,200; Median year structure built: 1952; Homeowner vacancy rate: 2.7%; Median selected monthly owner costs: $1,169 with a mortgage, $494 without a mortgage; Median gross rent: $711 per month; Rental vacancy rate: 5.1%

Vital Statistics: Birth rate: 94.3 per 10,000 population; Death rate: 104.5 per 10,000 population; Age-adjusted cancer mortality rate: 155.3 deaths per 100,000 population

Health Insurance: 90.6% have insurance; 64.2% have private insurance; 42.7% have public insurance; 9.4% do not have insurance; 6.5% of children under 18 do not have insurance

Health Care: Physicians: 8.7 per 10,000 population; Dentists: 3.0 per 10,000 population; Hospital beds: 29.0 per 10,000 population; Hospital admissions: 594.7 per 10,000 population

Transportation: Commute: 93.0% car, 0.6% public transportation, 1.8% walk, 3.2% work from home; Mean travel time to work: 24.1 minutes

2016 Presidential Election: 64.0% Trump, 30.9% Clinton, 3.7% Johnson, 1.5% Stein

National and State Parks: Adirondack State Park; Sir William Johnson State Park

Additional Information Contacts
Fulton Government . . . . (518) 725-0641
  http://www.fultoncountyny.gov

Fulton County Communities

BLEECKER (town). Covers a land area of 57.127 square miles and a water area of 2.285 square miles. Located at 43.17° N. Lat; 74.38° W. Long. Elevation is 1,503 feet.

Population: 679; Growth (since 2000): 18.5%; Density: 11.9 persons per square mile; Race: 97.1% White, 0.0% Black/African American, 0.4% Asian, 1.3% American Indian/Alaska Native, 0.0% Native Hawaiian/Other Pacific Islander, 1.2% Two or more races, 0.0% Hispanic of any race; Average household size: 2.39; Median age: 48.9; Age under 18: 16.5%; Age 65 and over: 22.1%; Males per 100 females: 109.8; Marriage status: 21.6% never married, 64.1% now married, 3.0% separated, 5.9% widowed, 8.4% divorced; Foreign born: 1.2%; Speak English only: 98.4%; With disability: 14.7%; Veterans: 12.0%; Ancestry: 21.6% German, 19.0% Irish, 16.3% American, 8.7% Italian, 8.5% French

Employment: 12.4% management, business, and financial, 1.9% computer, engineering, and science, 15.8% education, legal, community service, arts, and media, 6.8% healthcare practitioners, 11.7% service, 18.0% sales and office, 15.4% natural resources, construction, and maintenance, 18.0% production, transportation, and material moving

Income: Per capita: $24,437; Median household: $43,750; Average household: $58,791; Households with income of $100,000 or more: 20.4%; Poverty rate: 16.1%

Educational Attainment: High school diploma or higher: 80.6%; Bachelor's degree or higher: 25.0%; Graduate/professional degree or higher: 13.6%

Housing: Homeownership rate: 83.1%; Median home value: $140,000; Median year structure built: 1972; Homeowner vacancy rate: 5.6%; Median

selected monthly owner costs: $1,273 with a mortgage, $627 without a mortgage; Median gross rent: $782 per month; Rental vacancy rate: 0.0%
Health Insurance: 92.5% have insurance; 62.2% have private insurance; 46.5% have public insurance; 7.5% do not have insurance; 0.0% of children under 18 do not have insurance
Transportation: Commute: 100.0% car, 0.0% public transportation, 0.0% walk, 0.0% work from home; Mean travel time to work: 29.8 minutes

BROADALBIN (town).
Covers a land area of 31.722 square miles and a water area of 8.059 square miles. Located at 43.08° N. Lat; 74.15° W. Long. Elevation is 804 feet.
History: Settled 1770, incorporated 1924.
Population: 5,211; Growth (since 2000): 2.9%; Density: 164.3 persons per square mile; Race: 96.3% White, 1.5% Black/African American, 0.3% Asian, 0.0% American Indian/Alaska Native, 0.0% Native Hawaiian/Other Pacific Islander, 1.4% Two or more races, 2.1% Hispanic of any race; Average household size: 2.40; Median age: 41.6; Age under 18: 21.2%; Age 65 and over: 15.9%; Males per 100 females: 98.1; Marriage status: 25.0% never married, 55.0% now married, 1.4% separated, 6.6% widowed, 13.3% divorced; Foreign born: 0.9%; Speak English only: 98.0%; With disability: 11.3%; Veterans: 12.0%; Ancestry: 23.3% Irish, 18.8% German, 13.4% Italian, 11.3% American, 10.9% English
Employment: 10.2% management, business, and financial, 4.7% computer, engineering, and science, 5.9% education, legal, community service, arts, and media, 8.6% healthcare practitioners, 18.3% service, 28.2% sales and office, 10.3% natural resources, construction, and maintenance, 13.8% production, transportation, and material moving
Income: Per capita: $28,133; Median household: $59,024; Average household: $67,202; Households with income of $100,000 or more: 19.8%; Poverty rate: 10.3%
Educational Attainment: High school diploma or higher: 90.6%; Bachelor's degree or higher: 12.9%; Graduate/professional degree or higher: 3.7%

School District(s)
Broadalbin-Perth Central SD (02-12)
   2014-15 Enrollment: 1,846 . . . . (518) 954-2500
Housing: Homeownership rate: 82.1%; Median home value: $145,700; Median year structure built: 1965; Homeowner vacancy rate: 0.8%; Median selected monthly owner costs: $1,292 with a mortgage, $607 without a mortgage; Median gross rent: $751 per month; Rental vacancy rate: 8.1%
Health Insurance: 95.9% have insurance; 74.3% have private insurance; 33.7% have public insurance; 4.1% do not have insurance; 1.2% of children under 18 do not have insurance
Transportation: Commute: 95.1% car, 0.9% public transportation, 0.1% walk, 3.8% work from home; Mean travel time to work: 27.1 minutes
Additional Information Contacts
Town of Broadalbin . . . . (518) 883-4657
   http://www.townofbroadalbin.org

BROADALBIN (village).
Covers a land area of 1.122 square miles and a water area of 0.004 square miles. Located at 43.06° N. Lat; 74.20° W. Long. Elevation is 804 feet.
Population: 1,550; Growth (since 2000): 9.9%; Density: 1,382.0 persons per square mile; Race: 92.4% White, 2.0% Black/African American, 0.0% Asian, 0.0% American Indian/Alaska Native, 0.0% Native Hawaiian/Other Pacific Islander, 4.0% Two or more races, 4.5% Hispanic of any race; Average household size: 2.48; Median age: 34.5; Age under 18: 27.7%; Age 65 and over: 12.6%; Males per 100 females: 92.3; Marriage status: 34.2% never married, 44.6% now married, 0.0% separated, 7.0% widowed, 14.1% divorced; Foreign born: 1.0%; Speak English only: 96.0%; With disability: 8.5%; Veterans: 8.2%; Ancestry: 23.7% German, 21.7% Irish, 19.3% Italian, 11.6% English, 9.0% Polish
Employment: 12.1% management, business, and financial, 5.0% computer, engineering, and science, 6.4% education, legal, community service, arts, and media, 13.5% healthcare practitioners, 15.1% service, 26.3% sales and office, 11.2% natural resources, construction, and maintenance, 10.5% production, transportation, and material moving
Income: Per capita: $26,363; Median household: $56,439; Average household: $64,664; Households with income of $100,000 or more: 16.6%; Poverty rate: 12.2%
Educational Attainment: High school diploma or higher: 91.6%; Bachelor's degree or higher: 20.9%; Graduate/professional degree or higher: 4.8%

School District(s)
Broadalbin-Perth Central SD (02-12)
   2014-15 Enrollment: 1,846 . . . . (518) 954-2500
Housing: Homeownership rate: 56.3%; Median home value: $125,600; Median year structure built: 1940; Homeowner vacancy rate: 4.1%; Median selected monthly owner costs: $1,417 with a mortgage, $654 without a mortgage; Median gross rent: $737 per month; Rental vacancy rate: 6.8%
Health Insurance: 93.6% have insurance; 78.6% have private insurance; 26.2% have public insurance; 6.4% do not have insurance; 3.0% of children under 18 do not have insurance
Transportation: Commute: 92.9% car, 0.1% public transportation, 0.4% walk, 6.1% work from home; Mean travel time to work: 27.9 minutes

CAROGA (town).
Covers a land area of 50.627 square miles and a water area of 3.651 square miles. Located at 43.12° N. Lat; 74.53° W. Long.
Population: 1,138; Growth (since 2000): -19.1%; Density: 22.5 persons per square mile; Race: 97.9% White, 0.0% Black/African American, 0.0% Asian, 0.8% American Indian/Alaska Native, 0.0% Native Hawaiian/Other Pacific Islander, 1.3% Two or more races, 0.9% Hispanic of any race; Average household size: 2.24; Median age: 52.6; Age under 18: 12.8%; Age 65 and over: 25.7%; Males per 100 females: 113.3; Marriage status: 16.8% never married, 62.4% now married, 1.9% separated, 5.7% widowed, 15.2% divorced; Foreign born: 1.1%; Speak English only: 98.8%; With disability: 12.7%; Veterans: 12.7%; Ancestry: 18.5% German, 16.8% American, 16.6% Irish, 12.3% Italian, 10.4% English
Employment: 10.7% management, business, and financial, 6.4% computer, engineering, and science, 15.1% education, legal, community service, arts, and media, 3.4% healthcare practitioners, 16.0% service, 14.5% sales and office, 11.3% natural resources, construction, and maintenance, 22.6% production, transportation, and material moving
Income: Per capita: $28,523; Median household: $50,060; Average household: $62,913; Households with income of $100,000 or more: 17.0%; Poverty rate: 8.4%
Educational Attainment: High school diploma or higher: 92.7%; Bachelor's degree or higher: 27.4%; Graduate/professional degree or higher: 15.8%
Housing: Homeownership rate: 90.4%; Median home value: $137,500; Median year structure built: 1952; Homeowner vacancy rate: 3.3%; Median selected monthly owner costs: $1,280 with a mortgage, $479 without a mortgage; Median gross rent: $850 per month; Rental vacancy rate: 7.6%
Health Insurance: 92.3% have insurance; 77.4% have private insurance; 41.0% have public insurance; 7.7% do not have insurance; 1.4% of children under 18 do not have insurance
Transportation: Commute: 91.3% car, 0.0% public transportation, 0.0% walk, 6.7% work from home; Mean travel time to work: 26.0 minutes

CAROGA LAKE (CDP).
Covers a land area of 2.500 square miles and a water area of 0.873 square miles. Located at 43.13° N. Lat; 74.48° W. Long. Elevation is 1,480 feet.
Population: 496; Growth (since 2000): n/a; Density: 198.4 persons per square mile; Race: 99.4% White, 0.0% Black/African American, 0.0% Asian, 0.0% American Indian/Alaska Native, 0.0% Native Hawaiian/Other Pacific Islander, 0.6% Two or more races, 0.0% Hispanic of any race; Average household size: 2.13; Median age: 55.0; Age under 18: 9.3%; Age 65 and over: 27.8%; Males per 100 females: 112.3; Marriage status: 15.5% never married, 55.2% now married, 1.9% separated, 11.2% widowed, 18.1% divorced; Foreign born: 1.8%; Speak English only: 99.4%; With disability: 13.7%; Veterans: 11.6%; Ancestry: 26.2% German, 22.0% Irish, 17.9% American, 12.7% Italian, 8.5% English
Employment: 10.1% management, business, and financial, 6.7% computer, engineering, and science, 12.2% education, legal, community service, arts, and media, 7.6% healthcare practitioners, 14.3% service, 7.1% sales and office, 11.3% natural resources, construction, and maintenance, 30.7% production, transportation, and material moving
Income: Per capita: $30,351; Median household: $45,083; Average household: $62,927; Households with income of $100,000 or more: 20.2%; Poverty rate: 7.1%
Educational Attainment: High school diploma or higher: 97.5%; Bachelor's degree or higher: 33.3%; Graduate/professional degree or higher: 20.7%

School District(s)
Wheelerville Union Free SD (PK-08)
   2014-15 Enrollment: 141 . . . . (518) 835-2171

Housing: Homeownership rate: 94.8%; Median home value: $122,000; Median year structure built: 1951; Homeowner vacancy rate: 1.7%; Median selected monthly owner costs: $1,208 with a mortgage, $514 without a mortgage; Median gross rent: n/a per month; Rental vacancy rate: 25.0%
Health Insurance: 87.5% have insurance; 74.2% have private insurance; 42.7% have public insurance; 12.5% do not have insurance; 4.3% of children under 18 do not have insurance
Transportation: Commute: 88.7% car, 0.0% public transportation, 0.0% walk, 7.1% work from home; Mean travel time to work: 26.5 minutes

EPHRATAH (town).
Covers a land area of 39.170 square miles and a water area of 0.277 square miles. Located at 43.04° N. Lat; 74.56° W. Long. Elevation is 682 feet.
Population: 1,508; Growth (since 2000): -10.9%; Density: 38.5 persons per square mile; Race: 98.9% White, 0.0% Black/African American, 0.0% Asian, 0.0% American Indian/Alaska Native, 0.0% Native Hawaiian/Other Pacific Islander, 0.9% Two or more races, 0.7% Hispanic of any race; Average household size: 2.49; Median age: 47.3; Age under 18: 19.8%; Age 65 and over: 16.6%; Males per 100 females: 108.2; Marriage status: 21.2% never married, 60.2% now married, 1.0% separated, 7.7% widowed, 10.9% divorced; Foreign born: 0.2%; Speak English only: 93.8%; With disability: 16.0%; Veterans: 10.9%; Ancestry: 19.4% German, 15.3% Irish, 13.7% English, 12.9% American, 12.2% Italian
Employment: 8.3% management, business, and financial, 2.6% computer, engineering, and science, 8.1% education, legal, community service, arts, and media, 4.0% healthcare practitioners, 19.3% service, 19.9% sales and office, 17.3% natural resources, construction, and maintenance, 20.5% production, transportation, and material moving
Income: Per capita: $24,465; Median household: $46,833; Average household: $60,229; Households with income of $100,000 or more: 19.5%; Poverty rate: 11.2%
Educational Attainment: High school diploma or higher: 82.9%; Bachelor's degree or higher: 14.6%; Graduate/professional degree or higher: 4.8%
Housing: Homeownership rate: 92.2%; Median home value: $89,500; Median year structure built: 1971; Homeowner vacancy rate: 4.0%; Median selected monthly owner costs: $1,197 with a mortgage, $433 without a mortgage; Median gross rent: $725 per month; Rental vacancy rate: 0.0%
Health Insurance: 86.5% have insurance; 66.1% have private insurance; 34.6% have public insurance; 13.5% do not have insurance; 16.1% of children under 18 do not have insurance
Transportation: Commute: 93.2% car, 1.5% public transportation, 0.5% walk, 3.1% work from home; Mean travel time to work: 34.5 minutes

GLOVERSVILLE (city).
Covers a land area of 5.139 square miles and a water area of 0.009 square miles. Located at 43.05° N. Lat; 74.35° W. Long. Elevation is 820 feet.
History: Gloversville was named for its outstanding industry. The making of fine kid gloves became a Fulton County specialty. The beginnings of the industry in the county have been traced back to the 1760's when Sir William Johnson brought over as settlers a group of glovers from Perthshire, Scotland, who made gloves for local sale.
Population: 15,293; Growth (since 2000): -0.8%; Density: 2,975.7 persons per square mile; Race: 92.8% White, 2.4% Black/African American, 0.6% Asian, 0.2% American Indian/Alaska Native, 0.1% Native Hawaiian/Other Pacific Islander, 2.3% Two or more races, 4.4% Hispanic of any race; Average household size: 2.44; Median age: 37.5; Age under 18: 23.3%; Age 65 and over: 14.7%; Males per 100 females: 92.5; Marriage status: 34.7% never married, 45.9% now married, 3.2% separated, 7.2% widowed, 12.3% divorced; Foreign born: 1.8%; Speak English only: 95.6%; With disability: 18.3%; Veterans: 8.9%; Ancestry: 17.4% German, 16.0% Italian, 14.5% American, 14.4% Irish, 9.4% English
Employment: 7.4% management, business, and financial, 0.7% computer, engineering, and science, 9.3% education, legal, community service, arts, and media, 4.2% healthcare practitioners, 25.7% service, 23.3% sales and office, 7.3% natural resources, construction, and maintenance, 22.2% production, transportation, and material moving
Income: Per capita: $18,876; Median household: $35,044; Average household: $45,481; Households with income of $100,000 or more: 9.2%; Poverty rate: 29.1%
Educational Attainment: High school diploma or higher: 80.7%; Bachelor's degree or higher: 14.2%; Graduate/professional degree or higher: 7.6%

School District(s)
Gloversville City SD (PK-12)
   2014-15 Enrollment: 2,907 . . . . (518) 775-5791
Housing: Homeownership rate: 49.9%; Median home value: $76,200; Median year structure built: Before 1940; Homeowner vacancy rate: 7.7%; Median selected monthly owner costs: $1,024 with a mortgage, $485 without a mortgage; Median gross rent: $685 per month; Rental vacancy rate: 4.9%
Health Insurance: 88.2% have insurance; 50.0% have private insurance; 51.5% have public insurance; 11.8% do not have insurance; 7.2% of children under 18 do not have insurance
Hospitals: Nathan Littauer Hospital (208 beds)
Safety: Violent crime rate: 54.7 per 10,000 population; Property crime rate: 415.9 per 10,000 population
Newspapers: Leader-Herald (daily circulation 10,200)
Transportation: Commute: 91.1% car, 0.6% public transportation, 2.8% walk, 1.6% work from home; Mean travel time to work: 19.3 minutes
Additional Information Contacts
City of Gloversville. . . . . (518) 773-4542
   http://www.cityofgloversville.com

JOHNSTOWN (city).
County seat. Covers a land area of 4.875 square miles and a water area of 0.008 square miles. Located at 43.01° N. Lat; 74.38° W. Long. Elevation is 673 feet.
History: Its leather-glove industry dates back to 1800. Notable buildings include the county courthouse (1774) and Fort Johnstown (1771) and the county jail. The last American Revolutionary battle in N.Y. state was fought in Johnstown on Oct. 25, 1781. Elizabeth Cady Stanton born here. Founded 1772, Incorporated 1895.
Population: 8,500; Growth (since 2000): -0.1%; Density: 1,743.5 persons per square mile; Race: 93.5% White, 2.5% Black/African American, 1.8% Asian, 0.0% American Indian/Alaska Native, 0.0% Native Hawaiian/Other Pacific Islander, 2.2% Two or more races, 2.6% Hispanic of any race; Average household size: 2.19; Median age: 41.4; Age under 18: 20.8%; Age 65 and over: 17.1%; Males per 100 females: 89.4; Marriage status: 29.3% never married, 50.3% now married, 6.7% separated, 6.8% widowed, 13.6% divorced; Foreign born: 4.2%; Speak English only: 95.7%; With disability: 17.2%; Veterans: 7.3%; Ancestry: 24.1% German, 18.0% Irish, 15.8% Italian, 11.2% English, 6.0% American
Employment: 8.4% management, business, and financial, 3.1% computer, engineering, and science, 10.4% education, legal, community service, arts, and media, 2.7% healthcare practitioners, 18.6% service, 31.5% sales and office, 6.7% natural resources, construction, and maintenance, 18.6% production, transportation, and material moving
Income: Per capita: $26,652; Median household: $42,950; Average household: $58,673; Households with income of $100,000 or more: 16.6%; Poverty rate: 14.1%
Educational Attainment: High school diploma or higher: 89.0%; Bachelor's degree or higher: 17.1%; Graduate/professional degree or higher: 7.4%

School District(s)
Hamilton-Fulton-Montgomery Boces
   2014-15 Enrollment: n/a . . . . (518) 736-4300
Johnstown City SD (PK-12)
   2014-15 Enrollment: 1,809 . . . . (518) 762-4611
Two-year College(s)
Fulton-Montgomery Community College (Public)
   Fall 2014 Enrollment: 2,589 . . . . (518) 762-3622
   2015-16 Tuition: In-state $4,440; Out-of-state $8,340
Vocational/Technical School(s)
Hamilton Fulton Montgomery BOCES-Practical Nursing Program (Public)
   Fall 2014 Enrollment: 72 . . . . (518) 736-4305
Housing: Homeownership rate: 57.7%; Median home value: $97,100; Median year structure built: Before 1940; Homeowner vacancy rate: 0.4%; Median selected monthly owner costs: $1,106 with a mortgage, $491 without a mortgage; Median gross rent: $703 per month; Rental vacancy rate: 3.0%
Health Insurance: 89.9% have insurance; 65.7% have private insurance; 40.5% have public insurance; 10.1% do not have insurance; 4.8% of children under 18 do not have insurance
Safety: Violent crime rate: 4.8 per 10,000 population; Property crime rate: 247.4 per 10,000 population
Transportation: Commute: 97.1% car, 0.5% public transportation, 1.8% walk, 0.4% work from home; Mean travel time to work: 18.8 minutes

Additional Information Contacts
City of Johnstown . . . . (518) 736-4011
  http://www.cityofjohnstown-ny.com

JOHNSTOWN (town). Covers a land area of 70.214 square miles and
a water area of 1.082 square miles. Located at 43.04° N. Lat; 74.40° W.
Long. Elevation is 673 feet.
Population: 7,208; Growth (since 2000): 0.6%; Density: 102.7 persons per
square mile; Race: 95.4% White, 1.8% Black/African American, 0.6%
Asian, 0.0% American Indian/Alaska Native, 0.0% Native Hawaiian/Other
Pacific Islander, 0.9% Two or more races, 3.6% Hispanic of any race;
Average household size: 2.50; Median age: 45.5; Age under 18: 19.1%;
Age 65 and over: 19.5%; Males per 100 females: 111.3; Marriage status:
27.5% never married, 52.9% now married, 3.3% separated, 9.0%
widowed, 10.5% divorced; Foreign born: 4.4%; Speak English only: 92.1%;
With disability: 15.9%; Veterans: 8.7%; Ancestry: 25.7% German, 17.8%
Irish, 13.3% Italian, 13.0% English, 9.8% American
Employment: 13.4% management, business, and financial, 3.9%
computer, engineering, and science, 11.1% education, legal, community
service, arts, and media, 7.5% healthcare practitioners, 18.8% service,
21.8% sales and office, 10.2% natural resources, construction, and
maintenance, 13.1% production, transportation, and material moving
Income: Per capita: $27,085; Median household: $52,683; Average
household: $70,597; Households with income of $100,000 or more: 22.6%;
Poverty rate: 13.5%
Educational Attainment: High school diploma or higher: 86.0%;
Bachelor's degree or higher: 16.5%; Graduate/professional degree or
higher: 9.0%

School District(s)
Hamilton-Fulton-Montgomery Boces
  2014-15 Enrollment: n/a . . . . (518) 736-4300
Johnstown City SD (PK-12)
  2014-15 Enrollment: 1,809 . . . . (518) 762-4611
Two-year College(s)
Fulton-Montgomery Community College (Public)
  Fall 2014 Enrollment: 2,589 . . . . (518) 762-3622
  2015-16 Tuition: In-state $4,440; Out-of-state $8,340
Vocational/Technical School(s)
Hamilton Fulton Montgomery BOCES-Practical Nursing Program (Public)
  Fall 2014 Enrollment: 72 . . . . (518) 736-4305
Housing: Homeownership rate: 91.7%; Median home value: $117,200;
Median year structure built: 1959; Homeowner vacancy rate: 0.0%; Median
selected monthly owner costs: $1,287 with a mortgage, $451 without a
mortgage; Median gross rent: $963 per month; Rental vacancy rate: 0.0%
Health Insurance: 90.7% have insurance; 71.1% have private insurance;
41.9% have public insurance; 9.3% do not have insurance; 7.2% of
children under 18 do not have insurance
Transportation: Commute: 88.3% car, 0.3% public transportation, 0.2%
walk, 10.2% work from home; Mean travel time to work: 27.8 minutes
Additional Information Contacts
Town of Johnstown . . . . (518) 762-7070
  http://townofjohnstown.org/content

MAYFIELD (town). Covers a land area of 58.385 square miles and a
water area of 6.299 square miles. Located at 43.12° N. Lat; 74.26° W.
Long. Elevation is 850 feet.
Population: 6,390; Growth (since 2000): -0.7%; Density: 109.4 persons
per square mile; Race: 98.3% White, 0.0% Black/African American, 0.0%
Asian, 0.3% American Indian/Alaska Native, 0.0% Native Hawaiian/Other
Pacific Islander, 1.3% Two or more races, 1.5% Hispanic of any race;
Average household size: 2.41; Median age: 46.6; Age under 18: 20.1%;
Age 65 and over: 19.7%; Males per 100 females: 98.3; Marriage status:
24.2% never married, 57.6% now married, 2.9% separated, 8.2%
widowed, 9.9% divorced; Foreign born: 1.2%; Speak English only: 97.1%;
With disability: 16.0%; Veterans: 8.0%; Ancestry: 21.9% German, 16.8%
Irish, 15.9% American, 11.3% English, 11.2% Italian
Employment: 11.4% management, business, and financial, 2.3%
computer, engineering, and science, 10.3% education, legal, community
service, arts, and media, 6.8% healthcare practitioners, 21.2% service,
22.6% sales and office, 9.1% natural resources, construction, and
maintenance, 16.3% production, transportation, and material moving
Income: Per capita: $24,831; Median household: $51,737; Average
household: $59,122; Households with income of $100,000 or more: 14.5%;
Poverty rate: 13.4%

Educational Attainment: High school diploma or higher: 88.2%;
Bachelor's degree or higher: 16.3%; Graduate/professional degree or
higher: 5.9%
School District(s)
Mayfield Central SD (PK-12)
  2014-15 Enrollment: 931 . . . . (518) 661-8207
Housing: Homeownership rate: 78.1%; Median home value: $123,700;
Median year structure built: 1975; Homeowner vacancy rate: 2.5%; Median
selected monthly owner costs: $1,184 with a mortgage, $533 without a
mortgage; Median gross rent: $713 per month; Rental vacancy rate: 1.2%
Health Insurance: 91.6% have insurance; 69.2% have private insurance;
40.1% have public insurance; 8.4% do not have insurance; 3.6% of
children under 18 do not have insurance
Transportation: Commute: 95.7% car, 0.0% public transportation, 0.9%
walk, 3.3% work from home; Mean travel time to work: 23.8 minutes
Additional Information Contacts
Town of Mayfield . . . . (518) 661-5414
  http://mayfieldny.org/content

MAYFIELD (village). Covers a land area of 0.907 square miles and a
water area of 0.177 square miles. Located at 43.10° N. Lat; 74.27° W.
Long. Elevation is 850 feet.
Population: 760; Growth (since 2000): -5.0%; Density: 838.1 persons per
square mile; Race: 99.7% White, 0.0% Black/African American, 0.0%
Asian, 0.0% American Indian/Alaska Native, 0.0% Native Hawaiian/Other
Pacific Islander, 0.3% Two or more races, 2.2% Hispanic of any race;
Average household size: 2.36; Median age: 40.3; Age under 18: 18.8%;
Age 65 and over: 10.3%; Males per 100 females: 90.4; Marriage status:
34.7% never married, 53.3% now married, 0.6% separated, 4.3%
widowed, 7.7% divorced; Foreign born: 0.4%; Speak English only: 95.7%;
With disability: 8.9%; Veterans: 12.5%; Ancestry: 21.2% American, 16.2%
German, 13.7% Italian, 12.8% Irish, 11.3% English
Employment: 11.1% management, business, and financial, 2.8%
computer, engineering, and science, 9.5% education, legal, community
service, arts, and media, 6.4% healthcare practitioners, 19.4% service,
34.8% sales and office, 6.6% natural resources, construction, and
maintenance, 9.2% production, transportation, and material moving
Income: Per capita: $24,537; Median household: $54,405; Average
household: $59,613; Households with income of $100,000 or more: 11.5%;
Poverty rate: 6.9%
Educational Attainment: High school diploma or higher: 91.2%;
Bachelor's degree or higher: 19.4%; Graduate/professional degree or
higher: 9.5%
School District(s)
Mayfield Central SD (PK-12)
  2014-15 Enrollment: 931 . . . . (518) 661-8207
Housing: Homeownership rate: 78.3%; Median home value: $97,800;
Median year structure built: 1943; Homeowner vacancy rate: 0.0%; Median
selected monthly owner costs: $1,128 with a mortgage, $541 without a
mortgage; Median gross rent: $730 per month; Rental vacancy rate: 9.1%
Health Insurance: 91.6% have insurance; 77.2% have private insurance;
25.3% have public insurance; 8.4% do not have insurance; 1.4% of
children under 18 do not have insurance
Transportation: Commute: 90.1% car, 0.0% public transportation, 5.6%
walk, 3.1% work from home; Mean travel time to work: 24.5 minutes

NORTHAMPTON (town). Covers a land area of 21.116 square miles
and a water area of 13.613 square miles. Located at 43.16° N. Lat; 74.17°
W. Long.
Population: 2,626; Growth (since 2000): -4.9%; Density: 124.4 persons
per square mile; Race: 98.4% White, 0.1% Black/African American, 0.0%
Asian, 0.0% American Indian/Alaska Native, 0.2% Native Hawaiian/Other
Pacific Islander, 0.4% Two or more races, 0.8% Hispanic of any race;
Average household size: 2.40; Median age: 48.6; Age under 18: 18.1%;
Age 65 and over: 20.2%; Males per 100 females: 100.6; Marriage status:
22.3% never married, 58.9% now married, 2.2% separated, 6.8%
widowed, 12.0% divorced; Foreign born: 2.1%; Speak English only: 97.8%;
With disability: 13.7%; Veterans: 12.9%; Ancestry: 20.4% German, 17.4%
American, 16.1% Irish, 13.3% English, 10.9% Italian
Employment: 9.0% management, business, and financial, 2.1% computer,
engineering, and science, 14.7% education, legal, community service, arts,
and media, 7.9% healthcare practitioners, 21.9% service, 22.4% sales and
office, 8.4% natural resources, construction, and maintenance, 13.6%
production, transportation, and material moving

Income: Per capita: $27,419; Median household: $57,269; Average household: $65,215; Households with income of $100,000 or more: 17.6%; Poverty rate: 8.1%
Educational Attainment: High school diploma or higher: 91.2%; Bachelor's degree or higher: 19.0%; Graduate/professional degree or higher: 9.1%
Housing: Homeownership rate: 80.8%; Median home value: $163,600; Median year structure built: 1960; Homeowner vacancy rate: 4.0%; Median selected monthly owner costs: $1,209 with a mortgage, $519 without a mortgage; Median gross rent: $812 per month; Rental vacancy rate: 13.6%
Health Insurance: 93.1% have insurance; 71.6% have private insurance; 40.1% have public insurance; 6.9% do not have insurance; 10.1% of children under 18 do not have insurance
Transportation: Commute: 91.3% car, 0.0% public transportation, 4.6% walk, 2.3% work from home; Mean travel time to work: 25.4 minutes

NORTHVILLE (village).
Covers a land area of 1.039 square miles and a water area of 0.344 square miles. Located at 43.22° N. Lat; 74.17° W. Long. Elevation is 807 feet.
History: Incorporated 1873.
Population: 934; Growth (since 2000): -18.0%; Density: 899.0 persons per square mile; Race: 96.7% White, 0.2% Black/African American, 0.1% Asian, 0.0% American Indian/Alaska Native, 0.0% Native Hawaiian/Other Pacific Islander, 1.2% Two or more races, 0.0% Hispanic of any race; Average household size: 2.35; Median age: 46.0; Age under 18: 17.3%; Age 65 and over: 23.3%; Males per 100 females: 86.0; Marriage status: 27.6% never married, 59.8% now married, 3.6% separated, 8.8% widowed, 3.8% divorced; Foreign born: 3.6%; Speak English only: 97.9%; With disability: 14.5%; Veterans: 8.3%; Ancestry: 32.2% German, 19.5% English, 19.2% Irish, 16.4% American, 15.7% Italian
Employment: 7.3% management, business, and financial, 0.0% computer, engineering, and science, 10.4% education, legal, community service, arts, and media, 7.7% healthcare practitioners, 30.8% service, 29.2% sales and office, 7.7% natural resources, construction, and maintenance, 6.9% production, transportation, and material moving
Income: Per capita: $26,036; Median household: $47,875; Average household: $60,975; Households with income of $100,000 or more: 18.8%; Poverty rate: 12.3%
Educational Attainment: High school diploma or higher: 93.4%; Bachelor's degree or higher: 18.8%; Graduate/professional degree or higher: 6.8%

School District(s)
Northville Central SD (PK-12)
  2014-15 Enrollment: 481 . . . . (518) 863-7000
Housing: Homeownership rate: 73.8%; Median home value: $145,400; Median year structure built: Before 1940; Homeowner vacancy rate: 7.1%; Median selected monthly owner costs: $1,167 with a mortgage, $500 without a mortgage; Median gross rent: $842 per month; Rental vacancy rate: 24.3%
Health Insurance: 95.0% have insurance; 79.0% have private insurance; 38.0% have public insurance; 5.0% do not have insurance; 0.0% of children under 18 do not have insurance
Safety: Violent crime rate: 0.0 per 10,000 population; Property crime rate: 9.4 per 10,000 population
Transportation: Commute: 87.0% car, 0.0% public transportation, 10.1% walk, 2.0% work from home; Mean travel time to work: 23.3 minutes

OPPENHEIM (town).
Covers a land area of 56.134 square miles and a water area of 0.306 square miles. Located at 43.08° N. Lat; 74.67° W. Long. Elevation is 1,096 feet.
Population: 2,002; Growth (since 2000): 12.9%; Density: 35.7 persons per square mile; Race: 96.0% White, 1.1% Black/African American, 0.0% Asian, 0.0% American Indian/Alaska Native, 0.0% Native Hawaiian/Other Pacific Islander, 2.8% Two or more races, 0.1% Hispanic of any race; Average household size: 2.64; Median age: 40.6; Age under 18: 26.1%; Age 65 and over: 15.5%; Males per 100 females: 108.7; Marriage status: 25.6% never married, 57.6% now married, 1.8% separated, 4.4% widowed, 12.3% divorced; Foreign born: 1.2%; Speak English only: 94.2%; With disability: 17.9%; Veterans: 7.7%; Ancestry: 22.1% German, 19.1% American, 12.4% Irish, 9.2% Italian, 7.4% English
Employment: 7.2% management, business, and financial, 1.3% computer, engineering, and science, 3.1% education, legal, community service, arts, and media, 6.8% healthcare practitioners, 17.9% service, 19.8% sales and office, 17.9% natural resources, construction, and maintenance, 25.9% production, transportation, and material moving

Income: Per capita: $19,981; Median household: $42,969; Average household: $52,902; Households with income of $100,000 or more: 9.5%; Poverty rate: 19.1%
Educational Attainment: High school diploma or higher: 77.2%; Bachelor's degree or higher: 11.8%; Graduate/professional degree or higher: 5.9%
Housing: Homeownership rate: 88.6%; Median home value: $84,400; Median year structure built: 1977; Homeowner vacancy rate: 0.6%; Median selected monthly owner costs: $1,089 with a mortgage, $423 without a mortgage; Median gross rent: $725 per month; Rental vacancy rate: 14.7%
Health Insurance: 83.8% have insurance; 60.3% have private insurance; 34.5% have public insurance; 16.2% do not have insurance; 25.3% of children under 18 do not have insurance
Transportation: Commute: 93.6% car, 0.0% public transportation, 2.7% walk, 3.7% work from home; Mean travel time to work: 32.1 minutes

PERTH (town).
Covers a land area of 26.083 square miles and a water area of 0.027 square miles. Located at 43.01° N. Lat; 74.20° W. Long. Elevation is 869 feet.
Population: 3,554; Growth (since 2000): -2.3%; Density: 136.3 persons per square mile; Race: 95.7% White, 1.4% Black/African American, 1.0% Asian, 0.0% American Indian/Alaska Native, 0.0% Native Hawaiian/Other Pacific Islander, 1.1% Two or more races, 2.1% Hispanic of any race; Average household size: 2.43; Median age: 46.2; Age under 18: 21.8%; Age 65 and over: 18.4%; Males per 100 females: 98.3; Marriage status: 29.0% never married, 54.9% now married, 2.0% separated, 7.9% widowed, 8.2% divorced; Foreign born: 4.3%; Speak English only: 97.1%; With disability: 13.4%; Veterans: 12.1%; Ancestry: 27.0% Italian, 20.2% Polish, 13.9% Irish, 11.9% English, 10.6% German
Employment: 10.7% management, business, and financial, 6.5% computer, engineering, and science, 11.1% education, legal, community service, arts, and media, 4.7% healthcare practitioners, 16.3% service, 31.7% sales and office, 11.0% natural resources, construction, and maintenance, 8.0% production, transportation, and material moving
Income: Per capita: $28,965; Median household: $58,298; Average household: $71,704; Households with income of $100,000 or more: 25.7%; Poverty rate: 6.9%
Educational Attainment: High school diploma or higher: 90.6%; Bachelor's degree or higher: 21.6%; Graduate/professional degree or higher: 9.4%
Housing: Homeownership rate: 81.7%; Median home value: $155,200; Median year structure built: 1981; Homeowner vacancy rate: 0.8%; Median selected monthly owner costs: $1,535 with a mortgage, $528 without a mortgage; Median gross rent: $836 per month; Rental vacancy rate: 17.6%
Health Insurance: 95.5% have insurance; 76.7% have private insurance; 37.9% have public insurance; 4.5% do not have insurance; 1.3% of children under 18 do not have insurance
Transportation: Commute: 90.6% car, 2.9% public transportation, 3.5% walk, 2.2% work from home; Mean travel time to work: 32.8 minutes

STRATFORD (town).
Covers a land area of 74.876 square miles and a water area of 1.795 square miles. Located at 43.21° N. Lat; 74.61° W. Long. Elevation is 1,066 feet.
Population: 497; Growth (since 2000): -22.3%; Density: 6.6 persons per square mile; Race: 98.8% White, 0.0% Black/African American, 0.0% Asian, 0.4% American Indian/Alaska Native, 0.0% Native Hawaiian/Other Pacific Islander, 0.8% Two or more races, 0.0% Hispanic of any race; Average household size: 2.14; Median age: 56.3; Age under 18: 12.1%; Age 65 and over: 18.9%; Males per 100 females: 99.3; Marriage status: 15.1% never married, 61.1% now married, 2.0% separated, 9.7% widowed, 14.2% divorced; Foreign born: 1.2%; Speak English only: 96.4%; With disability: 20.3%; Veterans: 10.8%; Ancestry: 16.9% Irish, 14.3% German, 13.7% American, 11.3% English, 7.2% Italian
Employment: 11.3% management, business, and financial, 1.5% computer, engineering, and science, 6.9% education, legal, community service, arts, and media, 9.3% healthcare practitioners, 23.5% service, 17.6% sales and office, 11.8% natural resources, construction, and maintenance, 18.1% production, transportation, and material moving
Income: Per capita: $25,064; Median household: $38,214; Average household: $52,155; Households with income of $100,000 or more: 13.8%; Poverty rate: 16.7%
Educational Attainment: High school diploma or higher: 84.5%; Bachelor's degree or higher: 16.3%; Graduate/professional degree or higher: 5.2%

Housing: Homeownership rate: 92.7%; Median home value: $91,600; Median year structure built: 1974; Homeowner vacancy rate: 0.0%; Median selected monthly owner costs: $1,130 with a mortgage, $445 without a mortgage; Median gross rent: $704 per month; Rental vacancy rate: 0.0%
Health Insurance: 92.0% have insurance; 66.0% have private insurance; 50.1% have public insurance; 8.0% do not have insurance; 3.3% of children under 18 do not have insurance
Transportation: Commute: 97.5% car, 0.0% public transportation, 1.5% walk, 1.0% work from home; Mean travel time to work: 38.8 minutes

Genesee County

Located in western New York; drained by Tonawanda and Oak Orchard Creeks. Covers a land area of 492.936 square miles, a water area of 2.372 square miles, and is located in the Eastern Time Zone at 43.00° N. Lat., 78.19° W. Long. The county was founded in 1802. County seat is Batavia.

Genesee County is part of the Batavia, NY Micropolitan Statistical Area. The entire metro area includes: Genesee County, NY

Weather Station: Batavia — Elevation: 899 feet

	Jan	Feb	Mar	Apr	May	Jun	Jul	Aug	Sep	Oct	Nov	Dec
High	32	35	44	57	69	78	81	80	73	61	49	37
Low	17	18	25	37	47	57	61	60	53	42	33	22
Precip	2.0	1.8	2.2	3.0	3.3	3.7	3.3	3.2	3.8	3.2	2.8	2.4
Snow	19.6	13.2	11.9	2.2	0.3	0.0	0.0	0.0	0.0	0.4	5.0	16.2

High and Low temperatures in degrees Fahrenheit; Precipitation and Snow in inches

Population: 59,458; Growth (since 2000): -1.5%; Density: 120.6 persons per square mile; Race: 92.2% White, 2.8% Black/African American, 0.7% Asian, 1.0% American Indian/Alaska Native, 0.0% Native Hawaiian/Other Pacific Islander, 1.9% two or more races, 3.0% Hispanic of any race; Average household size: 2.45; Median age: 42.7; Age under 18: 21.0%; Age 65 and over: 16.9%; Males per 100 females: 98.1; Marriage status: 27.8% never married, 55.4% now married, 2.6% separated, 6.3% widowed, 10.6% divorced; Foreign born: 2.3%; Speak English only: 96.4%; With disability: 13.4%; Veterans: 9.4%; Ancestry: 30.6% German, 18.3% Irish, 16.3% English, 16.1% Italian, 10.8% Polish
Religion: Six largest groups: 25.7% Catholicism, 5.0% Methodist/Pietist, 2.8% Presbyterian-Reformed, 2.6% Holiness, 2.4% Non-denominational Protestant, 2.2% Baptist
Economy: Unemployment rate: 4.3%; Leading industries: 16.2 % retail trade; 12.2 % construction; 11.3 % other services (except public administration); Farms: 549 totaling 187,317 acres; Company size: 0 employ 1,000 or more persons, 0 employ 500 to 999 persons, 22 employ 100 to 499 persons, 1,326 employ less than 100 persons; Business ownership: 1,238 women-owned, n/a Black-owned, 48 Hispanic-owned, 56 Asian-owned, n/a American Indian/Alaska Native-owned
Employment: 11.0% management, business, and financial, 3.4% computer, engineering, and science, 10.2% education, legal, community service, arts, and media, 5.8% healthcare practitioners, 18.4% service, 22.5% sales and office, 11.9% natural resources, construction, and maintenance, 16.8% production, transportation, and material moving
Income: Per capita: $25,240; Median household: $50,880; Average household: $61,549; Households with income of $100,000 or more: 17.3%; Poverty rate: 13.2%
Educational Attainment: High school diploma or higher: 90.8%; Bachelor's degree or higher: 20.0%; Graduate/professional degree or higher: 8.0%
Housing: Homeownership rate: 73.0%; Median home value: $107,000; Median year structure built: 1954; Homeowner vacancy rate: 0.8%; Median selected monthly owner costs: $1,182 with a mortgage, $521 without a mortgage; Median gross rent: $724 per month; Rental vacancy rate: 2.3%
Vital Statistics: Birth rate: 98.1 per 10,000 population; Death rate: 104.3 per 10,000 population; Age-adjusted cancer mortality rate: 176.4 deaths per 100,000 population
Health Insurance: 92.3% have insurance; 73.2% have private insurance; 34.7% have public insurance; 7.7% do not have insurance; 3.9% of children under 18 do not have insurance
Health Care: Physicians: 11.2 per 10,000 population; Dentists: 3.6 per 10,000 population; Hospital beds: 43.6 per 10,000 population; Hospital admissions: 1,242.0 per 10,000 population
Transportation: Commute: 91.7% car, 0.4% public transportation, 3.4% walk, 2.9% work from home; Mean travel time to work: 21.9 minutes
2016 Presidential Election: 64.5% Trump, 29.2% Clinton, 5.0% Johnson, 1.2% Stein

National and State Parks: Oak Orchard Creek State Game Refuge; White Memorial State Game Farm
Additional Information Contacts
Genesee Government . . . . (585) 344-2550
  http://www.co.genesee.ny.us

Genesee County Communities

ALABAMA (town). Covers a land area of 42.370 square miles and a water area of 0.406 square miles. Located at 43.09° N. Lat; 78.37° W. Long. Elevation is 643 feet.
Population: 1,864; Growth (since 2000): -0.9%; Density: 44.0 persons per square mile; Race: 94.7% White, 1.6% Black/African American, 0.9% Asian, 1.1% American Indian/Alaska Native, 0.0% Native Hawaiian/Other Pacific Islander, 1.0% Two or more races, 1.7% Hispanic of any race; Average household size: 2.55; Median age: 44.6; Age under 18: 19.3%; Age 65 and over: 14.3%; Males per 100 females: 101.4; Marriage status: 27.0% never married, 60.0% now married, 2.6% separated, 6.1% widowed, 6.8% divorced; Foreign born: 2.4%; Speak English only: 96.9%; With disability: 11.7%; Veterans: 7.6%; Ancestry: 40.9% German, 15.8% English, 15.2% Irish, 13.1% Polish, 12.2% Italian
Employment: 9.0% management, business, and financial, 2.3% computer, engineering, and science, 6.6% education, legal, community service, arts, and media, 4.9% healthcare practitioners, 16.8% service, 16.4% sales and office, 17.6% natural resources, construction, and maintenance, 26.5% production, transportation, and material moving
Income: Per capita: $23,895; Median household: $54,318; Average household: $60,437; Households with income of $100,000 or more: 16.2%; Poverty rate: 11.7%
Educational Attainment: High school diploma or higher: 89.1%; Bachelor's degree or higher: 9.2%; Graduate/professional degree or higher: 3.0%
Housing: Homeownership rate: 82.7%; Median home value: $104,100; Median year structure built: 1944; Homeowner vacancy rate: 3.0%; Median selected monthly owner costs: $1,078 with a mortgage, $504 without a mortgage; Median gross rent: $625 per month; Rental vacancy rate: 0.0%
Health Insurance: 91.7% have insurance; 74.5% have private insurance; 33.9% have public insurance; 8.3% do not have insurance; 3.3% of children under 18 do not have insurance
Transportation: Commute: 92.0% car, 0.0% public transportation, 2.1% walk, 2.7% work from home; Mean travel time to work: 26.6 minutes

ALEXANDER (town). Covers a land area of 35.467 square miles and a water area of 0.096 square miles. Located at 42.92° N. Lat; 78.25° W. Long. Elevation is 932 feet.
Population: 2,597; Growth (since 2000): 6.0%; Density: 73.2 persons per square mile; Race: 99.3% White, 0.7% Black/African American, 0.1% Asian, 0.0% American Indian/Alaska Native, 0.0% Native Hawaiian/Other Pacific Islander, 0.0% Two or more races, 0.2% Hispanic of any race; Average household size: 2.74; Median age: 43.7; Age under 18: 23.0%; Age 65 and over: 13.5%; Males per 100 females: 97.2; Marriage status: 24.8% never married, 59.9% now married, 1.5% separated, 5.6% widowed, 9.8% divorced; Foreign born: 0.8%; Speak English only: 98.1%; With disability: 12.0%; Veterans: 7.2%; Ancestry: 45.1% German, 18.9% Irish, 16.8% Polish, 15.2% English, 9.7% Italian
Employment: 9.4% management, business, and financial, 3.0% computer, engineering, and science, 6.9% education, legal, community service, arts, and media, 4.5% healthcare practitioners, 20.4% service, 23.2% sales and office, 16.9% natural resources, construction, and maintenance, 15.8% production, transportation, and material moving
Income: Per capita: $25,300; Median household: $60,060; Average household: $67,369; Households with income of $100,000 or more: 18.4%; Poverty rate: 8.0%
Educational Attainment: High school diploma or higher: 89.8%; Bachelor's degree or higher: 14.1%; Graduate/professional degree or higher: 5.3%
School District(s)
Alexander Central SD (PK-12)
  2014-15 Enrollment: 889 . . . . (585) 591-1551
Housing: Homeownership rate: 85.4%; Median home value: $111,400; Median year structure built: 1953; Homeowner vacancy rate: 0.0%; Median selected monthly owner costs: $1,212 with a mortgage, $540 without a mortgage; Median gross rent: $790 per month; Rental vacancy rate: 2.8%

Health Insurance: 94.6% have insurance; 82.1% have private insurance; 29.0% have public insurance; 5.4% do not have insurance; 2.5% of children under 18 do not have insurance
Transportation: Commute: 94.6% car, 0.5% public transportation, 1.2% walk, 3.2% work from home; Mean travel time to work: 25.0 minutes

ALEXANDER (village).
Covers a land area of 0.437 square miles and a water area of 0 square miles. Located at 42.90° N. Lat; 78.26° W. Long. Elevation is 932 feet.
Population: 516; Growth (since 2000): 7.3%; Density: 1,180.1 persons per square mile; Race: 97.5% White, 2.1% Black/African American, 0.4% Asian, 0.0% American Indian/Alaska Native, 0.0% Native Hawaiian/Other Pacific Islander, 0.0% Two or more races, 0.0% Hispanic of any race; Average household size: 3.13; Median age: 37.0; Age under 18: 30.2%; Age 65 and over: 9.7%; Males per 100 females: 89.2; Marriage status: 34.9% never married, 51.9% now married, 1.5% separated, 3.0% widowed, 10.2% divorced; Foreign born: 0.6%; Speak English only: 98.0%; With disability: 10.3%; Veterans: 10.0%; Ancestry: 42.2% German, 23.1% Irish, 14.5% English, 14.5% Italian, 10.7% Polish
Employment: 8.6% management, business, and financial, 3.1% computer, engineering, and science, 6.6% education, legal, community service, arts, and media, 5.1% healthcare practitioners, 28.1% service, 21.5% sales and office, 10.2% natural resources, construction, and maintenance, 16.8% production, transportation, and material moving
Income: Per capita: $21,755; Median household: $56,250; Average household: $64,033; Households with income of $100,000 or more: 20.0%; Poverty rate: 6.7%
Educational Attainment: High school diploma or higher: 94.5%; Bachelor's degree or higher: 16.2%; Graduate/professional degree or higher: 6.8%

School District(s)
Alexander Central SD (PK-12)
    2014-15 Enrollment: 889 . . . . (585) 591-1551
Housing: Homeownership rate: 72.1%; Median home value: $106,900; Median year structure built: 1950; Homeowner vacancy rate: 0.0%; Median selected monthly owner costs: $1,080 with a mortgage, $588 without a mortgage; Median gross rent: $842 per month; Rental vacancy rate: 0.0%
Health Insurance: 96.7% have insurance; 84.5% have private insurance; 28.3% have public insurance; 3.3% do not have insurance; 3.8% of children under 18 do not have insurance
Transportation: Commute: 92.5% car, 2.4% public transportation, 1.6% walk, 2.8% work from home; Mean travel time to work: 25.9 minutes

BASOM (unincorporated postal area)
ZCTA: 14013
    Covers a land area of 40.497 square miles and a water area of 0.365 square miles. Located at 43.09° N. Lat; 78.40° W. Long. Elevation is 715 feet.
Population: 1,737; Growth (since 2000): -4.7%; Density: 42.9 persons per square mile; Race: 69.6% White, 0.5% Black/African American, 2.5% Asian, 24.7% American Indian/Alaska Native, 0.0% Native Hawaiian/Other Pacific Islander, 1.4% Two or more races, 1.6% Hispanic of any race; Average household size: 2.28; Median age: 47.9; Age under 18: 18.1%; Age 65 and over: 18.5%; Males per 100 females: 99.7; Marriage status: 30.4% never married, 55.0% now married, 2.8% separated, 5.6% widowed, 9.1% divorced; Foreign born: 2.5%; Speak English only: 93.8%; With disability: 12.5%; Veterans: 10.0%; Ancestry: 29.2% German, 11.3% Polish, 11.1% Irish, 9.8% English, 8.2% Italian
Employment: 8.9% management, business, and financial, 2.3% computer, engineering, and science, 6.0% education, legal, community service, arts, and media, 3.5% healthcare practitioners, 16.2% service, 18.3% sales and office, 13.7% natural resources, construction, and maintenance, 31.1% production, transportation, and material moving
Income: Per capita: $22,603; Median household: $48,833; Average household: $52,170; Households with income of $100,000 or more: 12.6%; Poverty rate: 12.4%
Educational Attainment: High school diploma or higher: 89.0%; Bachelor's degree or higher: 10.7%; Graduate/professional degree or higher: 3.4%
Housing: Homeownership rate: 86.2%; Median home value: $89,100; Median year structure built: 1951; Homeowner vacancy rate: 2.8%; Median selected monthly owner costs: $986 with a mortgage, $419 without a mortgage; Median gross rent: $775 per month; Rental vacancy rate: 0.0%

Health Insurance: 89.9% have insurance; 66.5% have private insurance; 41.4% have public insurance; 10.1% do not have insurance; 3.8% of children under 18 do not have insurance
Transportation: Commute: 88.7% car, 0.0% public transportation, 3.5% walk, 5.0% work from home; Mean travel time to work: 26.4 minutes

BATAVIA (city).
County seat. Covers a land area of 5.196 square miles and a water area of 0.081 square miles. Located at 43.00° N. Lat; 78.18° W. Long. Elevation is 892 feet.
History: Batavia is noteworthy as the "capital" of the Holland Land Purchase. In 1801, Joseph Ellicott, surveyor and subagent for the company, built a land office on the site. Ellicott proposed naming the place Bustia or Bustiville, for Paul Busti, the company's general agent. The latter objected and proposed Batavia, the name of the Dutch republic to which the proprietors belonged.
Population: 15,188; Growth (since 2000): -6.6%; Density: 2,923.1 persons per square mile; Race: 87.2% White, 7.1% Black/African American, 0.9% Asian, 0.4% American Indian/Alaska Native, 0.0% Native Hawaiian/Other Pacific Islander, 3.4% Two or more races, 3.7% Hispanic of any race; Average household size: 2.29; Median age: 39.0; Age under 18: 20.5%; Age 65 and over: 18.1%; Males per 100 females: 89.9; Marriage status: 31.7% never married, 48.1% now married, 2.9% separated, 8.9% widowed, 11.3% divorced; Foreign born: 2.8%; Speak English only: 96.0%; With disability: 14.9%; Veterans: 10.4%; Ancestry: 25.3% German, 22.3% Italian, 17.4% Irish, 10.4% English, 9.4% Polish
Employment: 10.2% management, business, and financial, 2.7% computer, engineering, and science, 13.5% education, legal, community service, arts, and media, 6.4% healthcare practitioners, 22.6% service, 24.1% sales and office, 6.5% natural resources, construction, and maintenance, 13.9% production, transportation, and material moving
Income: Per capita: $22,990; Median household: $41,584; Average household: $53,434; Households with income of $100,000 or more: 13.5%; Poverty rate: 22.8%
Educational Attainment: High school diploma or higher: 89.7%; Bachelor's degree or higher: 23.6%; Graduate/professional degree or higher: 10.2%

School District(s)
Batavia City SD (PK-12)
    2014-15 Enrollment: 2,370 . . . . (585) 343-2480
Two-year College(s)
Genesee Community College (Public)
    Fall 2014 Enrollment: 6,876 . . . . (585) 343-0055
    2015-16 Tuition: In-state $4,410; Out-of-state $5,010
Vocational/Technical School(s)
Continental School of Beauty Culture-Batavia (Private, For-profit)
    Fall 2014 Enrollment: 41 . . . . (585) 344-0886
    2015-16 Tuition: $12,440
Genesee Valley BOCES-Practical Nursing Program (Public)
    Fall 2014 Enrollment: 100 . . . . (585) 344-7720
    2015-16 Tuition: $11,550
Housing: Homeownership rate: 53.0%; Median home value: $94,100; Median year structure built: Before 1940; Homeowner vacancy rate: 2.6%; Median selected monthly owner costs: $1,098 with a mortgage, $477 without a mortgage; Median gross rent: $716 per month; Rental vacancy rate: 2.0%
Health Insurance: 92.7% have insurance; 65.0% have private insurance; 42.8% have public insurance; 7.3% do not have insurance; 2.9% of children under 18 do not have insurance
Hospitals: United Memorial Medical Center (126 beds)
Safety: Violent crime rate: 50.7 per 10,000 population; Property crime rate: 325.4 per 10,000 population
Newspapers: Daily News (daily circulation 12,500)
Transportation: Commute: 86.2% car, 1.0% public transportation, 6.6% walk, 1.9% work from home; Mean travel time to work: 18.2 minutes
Airports: Genesee County (general aviation)
Additional Information Contacts
City of Batavia . . . . (585) 345-6305
  http://www.batavianewyork.com

BATAVIA (town).
Covers a land area of 48.187 square miles and a water area of 0.218 square miles. Located at 43.00° N. Lat; 78.23° W. Long. Elevation is 892 feet.
History: Laid out in 1801 by Joseph Ellicott, agent for the Holland Land Company, the city was a center of the Anti-Masonic movement in the 19th century. Attica prison, site of the 1971 riots, is nearby. Incorporated 1915.

Population: 6,855; Growth (since 2000): 15.9%; Density: 142.3 persons per square mile; Race: 94.6% White, 0.4% Black/African American, 0.5% Asian, 0.5% American Indian/Alaska Native, 0.0% Native Hawaiian/Other Pacific Islander, 0.5% Two or more races, 5.7% Hispanic of any race; Average household size: 2.24; Median age: 47.2; Age under 18: 19.0%; Age 65 and over: 19.9%; Males per 100 females: 112.0; Marriage status: 22.4% never married, 60.5% now married, 4.5% separated, 3.9% widowed, 13.2% divorced; Foreign born: 2.1%; Speak English only: 94.4%; With disability: 17.5%; Veterans: 10.8%; Ancestry: 32.0% German, 24.7% English, 20.2% Italian, 15.7% Irish, 10.8% Polish
Employment: 12.9% management, business, and financial, 2.8% computer, engineering, and science, 10.3% education, legal, community service, arts, and media, 7.8% healthcare practitioners, 20.2% service, 20.7% sales and office, 9.8% natural resources, construction, and maintenance, 15.4% production, transportation, and material moving
Income: Per capita: $27,942; Median household: $47,422; Average household: $62,612; Households with income of $100,000 or more: 15.8%; Poverty rate: 8.1%
Educational Attainment: High school diploma or higher: 92.3%; Bachelor's degree or higher: 17.6%; Graduate/professional degree or higher: 7.6%

School District(s)
Batavia City SD (PK-12)
   2014-15 Enrollment: 2,370 . . . . (585) 343-2480
Two-year College(s)
Genesee Community College (Public)
   Fall 2014 Enrollment: 6,876 . . . . (585) 343-0055
   2015-16 Tuition: In-state $4,410; Out-of-state $5,010
Vocational/Technical School(s)
Continental School of Beauty Culture-Batavia (Private, For-profit)
   Fall 2014 Enrollment: 41 . . . . (585) 344-0886
   2015-16 Tuition: $12,440
Genesee Valley BOCES-Practical Nursing Program (Public)
   Fall 2014 Enrollment: 100 . . . . (585) 344-7720
   2015-16 Tuition: $11,550
Housing: Homeownership rate: 83.1%; Median home value: $108,900; Median year structure built: 1967; Homeowner vacancy rate: 0.0%; Median selected monthly owner costs: $1,294 with a mortgage, $536 without a mortgage; Median gross rent: $725 per month; Rental vacancy rate: 7.6%
Health Insurance: 88.7% have insurance; 71.3% have private insurance; 36.0% have public insurance; 11.3% do not have insurance; 11.9% of children under 18 do not have insurance
Hospitals: United Memorial Medical Center (126 beds)
Newspapers: Daily News (daily circulation 12,500)
Transportation: Commute: 93.8% car, 0.1% public transportation, 2.5% walk, 3.5% work from home; Mean travel time to work: 19.2 minutes
Airports: Genesee County (general aviation)
Additional Information Contacts
Town of Batavia. . . . . (585) 343-1729
   http://www.townofbatavia.com

BERGEN (town). Covers a land area of 27.559 square miles and a water area of 0.036 square miles. Located at 43.10° N. Lat; 77.96° W. Long. Elevation is 607 feet.
Population: 3,068; Growth (since 2000): -3.6%; Density: 111.3 persons per square mile; Race: 93.2% White, 0.0% Black/African American, 1.9% Asian, 0.3% American Indian/Alaska Native, 0.0% Native Hawaiian/Other Pacific Islander, 3.9% Two or more races, 3.1% Hispanic of any race; Average household size: 2.50; Median age: 42.6; Age under 18: 25.2%; Age 65 and over: 16.7%; Males per 100 females: 98.7; Marriage status: 28.5% never married, 53.0% now married, 1.8% separated, 8.5% widowed, 10.0% divorced; Foreign born: 3.9%; Speak English only: 96.5%; With disability: 14.9%; Veterans: 8.3%; Ancestry: 23.8% Irish, 20.7% German, 18.0% English, 8.4% Italian, 7.6% American
Employment: 7.3% management, business, and financial, 2.6% computer, engineering, and science, 10.7% education, legal, community service, arts, and media, 3.5% healthcare practitioners, 15.9% service, 26.5% sales and office, 15.7% natural resources, construction, and maintenance, 17.9% production, transportation, and material moving
Income: Per capita: $23,288; Median household: $44,625; Average household: $57,597; Households with income of $100,000 or more: 18.4%; Poverty rate: 13.5%
Educational Attainment: High school diploma or higher: 95.0%; Bachelor's degree or higher: 22.8%; Graduate/professional degree or higher: 8.1%

School District(s)
Byron-Bergen Central SD (PK-12)
   2014-15 Enrollment: 1,044 . . . . (585) 494-1220
Housing: Homeownership rate: 73.5%; Median home value: $108,000; Median year structure built: 1972; Homeowner vacancy rate: 0.0%; Median selected monthly owner costs: $1,220 with a mortgage, $632 without a mortgage; Median gross rent: $738 per month; Rental vacancy rate: 2.7%
Health Insurance: 92.8% have insurance; 76.1% have private insurance; 33.6% have public insurance; 7.2% do not have insurance; 5.4% of children under 18 do not have insurance
Transportation: Commute: 93.0% car, 1.2% public transportation, 1.7% walk, 2.2% work from home; Mean travel time to work: 22.0 minutes

BERGEN (village). Covers a land area of 0.737 square miles and a water area of 0 square miles. Located at 43.08° N. Lat; 77.94° W. Long. Elevation is 607 feet.
Population: 1,312; Growth (since 2000): 5.8%; Density: 1,781.2 persons per square mile; Race: 96.2% White, 0.1% Black/African American, 0.9% Asian, 0.6% American Indian/Alaska Native, 0.0% Native Hawaiian/Other Pacific Islander, 0.3% Two or more races, 2.5% Hispanic of any race; Average household size: 2.86; Median age: 35.1; Age under 18: 29.3%; Age 65 and over: 10.6%; Males per 100 females: 94.4; Marriage status: 34.7% never married, 53.8% now married, 0.8% separated, 3.6% widowed, 7.9% divorced; Foreign born: 2.3%; Speak English only: 95.0%; With disability: 11.6%; Veterans: 7.3%; Ancestry: 28.4% German, 25.2% Irish, 15.1% English, 11.6% Italian, 8.0% European
Employment: 13.2% management, business, and financial, 3.5% computer, engineering, and science, 15.3% education, legal, community service, arts, and media, 3.2% healthcare practitioners, 12.4% service, 25.2% sales and office, 11.8% natural resources, construction, and maintenance, 15.3% production, transportation, and material moving
Income: Per capita: $23,802; Median household: $60,313; Average household: $66,854; Households with income of $100,000 or more: 21.9%; Poverty rate: 10.6%
Educational Attainment: High school diploma or higher: 96.6%; Bachelor's degree or higher: 26.9%; Graduate/professional degree or higher: 10.7%

School District(s)
Byron-Bergen Central SD (PK-12)
   2014-15 Enrollment: 1,044 . . . . (585) 494-1220
Housing: Homeownership rate: 80.7%; Median home value: $107,200; Median year structure built: Before 1940; Homeowner vacancy rate: 0.0%; Median selected monthly owner costs: $1,192 with a mortgage, $526 without a mortgage; Median gross rent: $645 per month; Rental vacancy rate: 9.3%
Health Insurance: 89.4% have insurance; 76.2% have private insurance; 26.3% have public insurance; 10.6% do not have insurance; 10.9% of children under 18 do not have insurance
Transportation: Commute: 87.9% car, 0.0% public transportation, 3.6% walk, 4.7% work from home; Mean travel time to work: 23.1 minutes

BETHANY (town). Covers a land area of 36.035 square miles and a water area of 0.035 square miles. Located at 42.92° N. Lat; 78.13° W. Long.
Population: 1,697; Growth (since 2000): -3.6%; Density: 47.1 persons per square mile; Race: 94.6% White, 1.5% Black/African American, 0.5% Asian, 0.9% American Indian/Alaska Native, 0.0% Native Hawaiian/Other Pacific Islander, 1.5% Two or more races, 1.2% Hispanic of any race; Average household size: 2.28; Median age: 46.9; Age under 18: 18.0%; Age 65 and over: 17.9%; Males per 100 females: 103.6; Marriage status: 21.9% never married, 63.0% now married, 1.1% separated, 7.8% widowed, 7.3% divorced; Foreign born: 1.9%; Speak English only: 97.7%; With disability: 10.3%; Veterans: 8.3%; Ancestry: 29.4% German, 21.1% English, 15.9% Irish, 12.1% Italian, 6.5% American
Employment: 9.3% management, business, and financial, 5.1% computer, engineering, and science, 8.7% education, legal, community service, arts, and media, 5.3% healthcare practitioners, 16.9% service, 23.3% sales and office, 17.1% natural resources, construction, and maintenance, 14.3% production, transportation, and material moving
Income: Per capita: $26,100; Median household: $55,221; Average household: $60,210; Households with income of $100,000 or more: 14.7%; Poverty rate: 7.1%
Educational Attainment: High school diploma or higher: 93.9%; Bachelor's degree or higher: 21.5%; Graduate/professional degree or higher: 9.9%

Housing: Homeownership rate: 83.0%; Median home value: $115,000; Median year structure built: 1957; Homeowner vacancy rate: 0.0%; Median selected monthly owner costs: $1,179 with a mortgage, $473 without a mortgage; Median gross rent: $715 per month; Rental vacancy rate: 0.0%
Health Insurance: 90.5% have insurance; 80.7% have private insurance; 29.0% have public insurance; 9.5% do not have insurance; 15.4% of children under 18 do not have insurance
Transportation: Commute: 92.8% car, 0.0% public transportation, 2.7% walk, 3.5% work from home; Mean travel time to work: 25.6 minutes

BYRON (town).
Covers a land area of 32.212 square miles and a water area of 0.079 square miles. Located at 43.08° N. Lat; 78.07° W. Long. Elevation is 620 feet.
Population: 2,316; Growth (since 2000): -7.1%; Density: 71.9 persons per square mile; Race: 97.8% White, 0.3% Black/African American, 0.2% Asian, 1.2% American Indian/Alaska Native, 0.0% Native Hawaiian/Other Pacific Islander, 0.6% Two or more races, 0.3% Hispanic of any race; Average household size: 2.63; Median age: 43.5; Age under 18: 18.5%; Age 65 and over: 14.7%; Males per 100 females: 104.6; Marriage status: 30.9% never married, 55.5% now married, 2.0% separated, 4.3% widowed, 9.3% divorced; Foreign born: 0.9%; Speak English only: 98.9%; With disability: 12.5%; Veterans: 8.3%; Ancestry: 32.6% German, 27.9% English, 17.1% Irish, 9.4% Italian, 8.2% Polish
Employment: 12.0% management, business, and financial, 4.3% computer, engineering, and science, 7.9% education, legal, community service, arts, and media, 8.4% healthcare practitioners, 13.0% service, 18.8% sales and office, 18.4% natural resources, construction, and maintenance, 17.2% production, transportation, and material moving
Income: Per capita: $29,559; Median household: $65,160; Average household: $76,465; Households with income of $100,000 or more: 24.9%; Poverty rate: 11.0%
Educational Attainment: High school diploma or higher: 92.0%; Bachelor's degree or higher: 20.6%; Graduate/professional degree or higher: 8.2%
Housing: Homeownership rate: 88.0%; Median home value: $102,200; Median year structure built: 1957; Homeowner vacancy rate: 0.0%; Median selected monthly owner costs: $1,157 with a mortgage, $571 without a mortgage; Median gross rent: $788 per month; Rental vacancy rate: 0.0%
Health Insurance: 91.3% have insurance; 76.3% have private insurance; 30.0% have public insurance; 8.7% do not have insurance; 1.2% of children under 18 do not have insurance
Transportation: Commute: 96.0% car, 0.4% public transportation, 1.1% walk, 2.5% work from home; Mean travel time to work: 25.4 minutes

CORFU (village).
Covers a land area of 0.995 square miles and a water area of 0 square miles. Located at 42.96° N. Lat; 78.40° W. Long. Elevation is 863 feet.
Population: 807; Growth (since 2000): 1.5%; Density: 811.0 persons per square mile; Race: 96.8% White, 3.2% Black/African American, 0.0% Asian, 0.0% American Indian/Alaska Native, 0.0% Native Hawaiian/Other Pacific Islander, 0.0% Two or more races, 0.6% Hispanic of any race; Average household size: 2.19; Median age: 43.8; Age under 18: 17.7%; Age 65 and over: 17.6%; Males per 100 females: 92.1; Marriage status: 33.6% never married, 50.3% now married, 6.1% separated, 6.5% widowed, 9.5% divorced; Foreign born: 0.9%; Speak English only: 98.3%; With disability: 12.3%; Veterans: 10.2%; Ancestry: 43.5% German, 17.1% Polish, 16.6% English, 15.9% Irish, 14.1% Italian
Employment: 11.9% management, business, and financial, 2.3% computer, engineering, and science, 10.1% education, legal, community service, arts, and media, 6.9% healthcare practitioners, 9.6% service, 20.9% sales and office, 11.7% natural resources, construction, and maintenance, 26.6% production, transportation, and material moving
Income: Per capita: $30,349; Median household: $48,281; Average household: $65,670; Households with income of $100,000 or more: 8.2%; Poverty rate: 9.0%
Educational Attainment: High school diploma or higher: 95.6%; Bachelor's degree or higher: 17.4%; Graduate/professional degree or higher: 8.9%

School District(s)
Pembroke Central SD (PK-12)
   2014-15 Enrollment: 926 . . . . (585) 599-4525
Housing: Homeownership rate: 64.8%; Median home value: $102,300; Median year structure built: 1950; Homeowner vacancy rate: 0.0%; Median selected monthly owner costs: $1,117 with a mortgage, $521 without a mortgage; Median gross rent: $680 per month; Rental vacancy rate: 0.0%

Health Insurance: 96.0% have insurance; 79.2% have private insurance; 33.1% have public insurance; 4.0% do not have insurance; 0.0% of children under 18 do not have insurance
Transportation: Commute: 97.6% car, 0.0% public transportation, 1.0% walk, 1.5% work from home; Mean travel time to work: 22.5 minutes

DARIEN (town).
Covers a land area of 47.371 square miles and a water area of 0.219 square miles. Located at 42.91° N. Lat; 78.38° W. Long. Elevation is 1,001 feet.
Population: 3,116; Growth (since 2000): 1.8%; Density: 65.8 persons per square mile; Race: 98.3% White, 0.2% Black/African American, 0.0% Asian, 0.1% American Indian/Alaska Native, 0.0% Native Hawaiian/Other Pacific Islander, 0.4% Two or more races, 2.1% Hispanic of any race; Average household size: 2.70; Median age: 44.0; Age under 18: 24.4%; Age 65 and over: 14.7%; Males per 100 females: 105.7; Marriage status: 26.9% never married, 62.4% now married, 1.1% separated, 2.7% widowed, 8.0% divorced; Foreign born: 1.0%; Speak English only: 96.5%; With disability: 13.2%; Veterans: 7.6%; Ancestry: 38.8% German, 26.1% Polish, 18.0% Irish, 14.0% Italian, 11.1% English
Employment: 10.0% management, business, and financial, 2.6% computer, engineering, and science, 8.3% education, legal, community service, arts, and media, 4.2% healthcare practitioners, 17.0% service, 21.9% sales and office, 16.8% natural resources, construction, and maintenance, 19.2% production, transportation, and material moving
Income: Per capita: $25,955; Median household: $66,389; Average household: $68,680; Households with income of $100,000 or more: 21.7%; Poverty rate: 10.8%
Educational Attainment: High school diploma or higher: 94.3%; Bachelor's degree or higher: 18.0%; Graduate/professional degree or higher: 6.9%
Housing: Homeownership rate: 86.1%; Median home value: $139,400; Median year structure built: 1964; Homeowner vacancy rate: 0.0%; Median selected monthly owner costs: $1,336 with a mortgage, $523 without a mortgage; Median gross rent: $738 per month; Rental vacancy rate: 0.0%
Health Insurance: 92.6% have insurance; 79.0% have private insurance; 29.5% have public insurance; 7.4% do not have insurance; 2.2% of children under 18 do not have insurance
Transportation: Commute: 94.2% car, 0.1% public transportation, 1.4% walk, 1.8% work from home; Mean travel time to work: 25.8 minutes

DARIEN CENTER (unincorporated postal area)
ZCTA: 14040
   Covers a land area of 29.227 square miles and a water area of 0.191 square miles. Located at 42.89° N. Lat; 78.38° W. Long. Elevation is 1,017 feet.
Population: 2,206; Growth (since 2000): -5.4%; Density: 75.5 persons per square mile; Race: 99.2% White, 0.0% Black/African American, 0.0% Asian, 0.2% American Indian/Alaska Native, 0.0% Native Hawaiian/Other Pacific Islander, 0.6% Two or more races, 0.5% Hispanic of any race; Average household size: 2.69; Median age: 42.4; Age under 18: 24.1%; Age 65 and over: 16.1%; Males per 100 females: 108.2; Marriage status: 26.6% never married, 62.3% now married, 1.2% separated, 4.1% widowed, 7.0% divorced; Foreign born: 0.5%; Speak English only: 97.4%; With disability: 12.9%; Veterans: 7.3%; Ancestry: 37.8% German, 29.0% Polish, 17.7% Irish, 11.2% Italian, 8.9% English
Employment: 8.2% management, business, and financial, 1.5% computer, engineering, and science, 9.5% education, legal, community service, arts, and media, 2.1% healthcare practitioners, 23.0% service, 23.8% sales and office, 10.2% natural resources, construction, and maintenance, 21.7% production, transportation, and material moving
Income: Per capita: $26,443; Median household: $63,214; Average household: $69,759; Households with income of $100,000 or more: 15.9%; Poverty rate: 10.1%
Educational Attainment: High school diploma or higher: 91.9%; Bachelor's degree or higher: 16.3%; Graduate/professional degree or higher: 5.7%
Housing: Homeownership rate: 89.0%; Median home value: $141,700; Median year structure built: 1966; Homeowner vacancy rate: 0.0%; Median selected monthly owner costs: $1,329 with a mortgage, $499 without a mortgage; Median gross rent: $691 per month; Rental vacancy rate: 0.0%
Health Insurance: 94.3% have insurance; 74.8% have private insurance; 35.0% have public insurance; 5.7% do not have insurance; 3.2% of children under 18 do not have insurance

Transportation: Commute: 96.2% car, 0.1% public transportation, 1.6% walk, 1.6% work from home; Mean travel time to work: 28.5 minutes

EAST BETHANY (unincorporated postal area)

ZCTA: 14054

Covers a land area of 24.858 square miles and a water area of 0.024 square miles. Located at 42.92° N. Lat; 78.13° W. Long. Elevation is 1,001 feet.

Population: 1,253; Growth (since 2000): -7.9%; Density: 50.4 persons per square mile; Race: 93.5% White, 1.3% Black/African American, 0.7% Asian, 1.2% American Indian/Alaska Native, 0.0% Native Hawaiian/Other Pacific Islander, 1.9% Two or more races, 1.7% Hispanic of any race; Average household size: 2.23; Median age: 45.3; Age under 18: 19.3%; Age 65 and over: 14.8%; Males per 100 females: 103.3; Marriage status: 22.8% never married, 61.8% now married, 1.5% separated, 8.2% widowed, 7.3% divorced; Foreign born: 2.1%; Speak English only: 97.9%; With disability: 11.0%; Veterans: 7.8%; Ancestry: 28.5% German, 23.5% English, 17.2% Irish, 13.7% Italian, 6.8% Polish

Employment: 8.6% management, business, and financial, 5.2% computer, engineering, and science, 9.4% education, legal, community service, arts, and media, 5.8% healthcare practitioners, 18.5% service, 21.1% sales and office, 17.8% natural resources, construction, and maintenance, 13.7% production, transportation, and material moving

Income: Per capita: $26,898; Median household: $55,375; Average household: $61,058; Households with income of $100,000 or more: 15.3%; Poverty rate: 7.3%

Educational Attainment: High school diploma or higher: 93.3%; Bachelor's degree or higher: 20.4%; Graduate/professional degree or higher: 9.2%

Housing: Homeownership rate: 82.7%; Median home value: $112,600; Median year structure built: 1956; Homeowner vacancy rate: 0.0%; Median selected monthly owner costs: $1,160 with a mortgage, $459 without a mortgage; Median gross rent: $710 per month; Rental vacancy rate: 0.0%

Health Insurance: 91.0% have insurance; 81.2% have private insurance; 25.9% have public insurance; 9.0% do not have insurance; 7.9% of children under 18 do not have insurance

Transportation: Commute: 92.2% car, 0.0% public transportation, 3.0% walk, 4.0% work from home; Mean travel time to work: 25.7 minutes

ELBA (town).

Covers a land area of 35.649 square miles and a water area of 0.043 square miles. Located at 43.09° N. Lat; 78.17° W. Long. Elevation is 761 feet.

Population: 2,314; Growth (since 2000): -5.1%; Density: 64.9 persons per square mile; Race: 85.2% White, 0.5% Black/African American, 0.2% Asian, 0.5% American Indian/Alaska Native, 0.0% Native Hawaiian/Other Pacific Islander, 1.9% Two or more races, 15.6% Hispanic of any race; Average household size: 2.88; Median age: 36.2; Age under 18: 24.2%; Age 65 and over: 12.5%; Males per 100 females: 100.3; Marriage status: 26.3% never married, 61.6% now married, 1.3% separated, 4.7% widowed, 7.4% divorced; Foreign born: 9.2%; Speak English only: 85.3%; With disability: 7.8%; Veterans: 7.1%; Ancestry: 27.3% German, 15.7% Italian, 15.3% English, 15.0% Irish, 9.5% Polish

Employment: 15.2% management, business, and financial, 3.7% computer, engineering, and science, 11.5% education, legal, community service, arts, and media, 3.7% healthcare practitioners, 14.7% service, 17.4% sales and office, 22.3% natural resources, construction, and maintenance, 11.4% production, transportation, and material moving

Income: Per capita: $26,613; Median household: $69,125; Average household: $75,216; Households with income of $100,000 or more: 20.9%; Poverty rate: 7.6%

Educational Attainment: High school diploma or higher: 83.2%; Bachelor's degree or higher: 22.5%; Graduate/professional degree or higher: 7.1%

School District(s)

Elba Central SD (PK-12)

    2014-15 Enrollment: 415 . . . . (585) 757-9967

Housing: Homeownership rate: 82.1%; Median home value: $114,300; Median year structure built: 1951; Homeowner vacancy rate: 1.5%; Median selected monthly owner costs: $1,182 with a mortgage, $522 without a mortgage; Median gross rent: $702 per month; Rental vacancy rate: 4.0%

Health Insurance: 89.1% have insurance; 74.8% have private insurance; 27.0% have public insurance; 10.9% do not have insurance; 0.0% of children under 18 do not have insurance

Transportation: Commute: 81.9% car, 0.0% public transportation, 15.2% walk, 2.7% work from home; Mean travel time to work: 17.3 minutes

ELBA (village).

Covers a land area of 1.017 square miles and a water area of 0 square miles. Located at 43.08° N. Lat; 78.19° W. Long. Elevation is 761 feet.

Population: 713; Growth (since 2000): 2.4%; Density: 701.3 persons per square mile; Race: 92.1% White, 0.8% Black/African American, 0.0% Asian, 1.7% American Indian/Alaska Native, 0.0% Native Hawaiian/Other Pacific Islander, 3.1% Two or more races, 10.9% Hispanic of any race; Average household size: 2.81; Median age: 38.2; Age under 18: 26.2%; Age 65 and over: 12.6%; Males per 100 females: 104.2; Marriage status: 26.4% never married, 62.6% now married, 1.6% separated, 4.2% widowed, 6.8% divorced; Foreign born: 3.5%; Speak English only: 92.8%; With disability: 6.0%; Veterans: 10.1%; Ancestry: 29.5% German, 25.7% Irish, 18.1% Italian, 16.8% English, 14.4% Polish

Employment: 13.1% management, business, and financial, 7.2% computer, engineering, and science, 20.8% education, legal, community service, arts, and media, 3.3% healthcare practitioners, 18.8% service, 18.8% sales and office, 10.5% natural resources, construction, and maintenance, 7.5% production, transportation, and material moving

Income: Per capita: $27,241; Median household: $72,083; Average household: $75,869; Households with income of $100,000 or more: 18.9%; Poverty rate: 2.1%

Educational Attainment: High school diploma or higher: 93.1%; Bachelor's degree or higher: 29.6%; Graduate/professional degree or higher: 11.8%

School District(s)

Elba Central SD (PK-12)

    2014-15 Enrollment: 415 . . . . (585) 757-9967

Housing: Homeownership rate: 87.0%; Median home value: $113,800; Median year structure built: Before 1940; Homeowner vacancy rate: 0.9%; Median selected monthly owner costs: $1,326 with a mortgage, $539 without a mortgage; Median gross rent: $688 per month; Rental vacancy rate: 15.4%

Health Insurance: 95.5% have insurance; 89.6% have private insurance; 17.3% have public insurance; 4.5% do not have insurance; 0.0% of children under 18 do not have insurance

Transportation: Commute: 93.3% car, 0.0% public transportation, 3.2% walk, 2.9% work from home; Mean travel time to work: 18.9 minutes

LE ROY (town).

Covers a land area of 42.084 square miles and a water area of 0.090 square miles. Located at 42.99° N. Lat; 77.97° W. Long. Elevation is 896 feet.

History: In 1897, Pearl Bixby Wait, a local carpenter, perfected the formula for Jello gelatin dessert, then sold it for $450. Until 1964, General Foods had a plant that produced Jello in the village. Jello Museum is housed in the Historical Society Building. Settled 1793, Incorporated 1834.

Population: 7,559; Growth (since 2000): -3.0%; Density: 179.6 persons per square mile; Race: 92.9% White, 4.4% Black/African American, 0.2% Asian, 0.0% American Indian/Alaska Native, 0.0% Native Hawaiian/Other Pacific Islander, 2.2% Two or more races, 0.9% Hispanic of any race; Average household size: 2.44; Median age: 41.1; Age under 18: 21.7%; Age 65 and over: 18.3%; Males per 100 females: 95.6; Marriage status: 29.9% never married, 52.4% now married, 3.2% separated, 6.0% widowed, 11.7% divorced; Foreign born: 1.4%; Speak English only: 98.9%; With disability: 10.8%; Veterans: 8.1%; Ancestry: 28.8% German, 22.2% Irish, 20.5% Italian, 15.8% English, 8.3% Polish

Employment: 14.7% management, business, and financial, 4.9% computer, engineering, and science, 11.4% education, legal, community service, arts, and media, 5.2% healthcare practitioners, 17.8% service, 20.0% sales and office, 7.4% natural resources, construction, and maintenance, 18.7% production, transportation, and material moving

Income: Per capita: $26,641; Median household: $52,229; Average household: $64,540; Households with income of $100,000 or more: 21.0%; Poverty rate: 10.0%

Educational Attainment: High school diploma or higher: 91.5%; Bachelor's degree or higher: 24.1%; Graduate/professional degree or higher: 8.7%

School District(s)

Genesee Valley Boces

    2014-15 Enrollment: n/a . . . . (585) 658-7903

Le Roy Central SD (PK-12)

    2014-15 Enrollment: 1,292 . . . . (585) 768-8133

Housing: Homeownership rate: 68.1%; Median home value: $100,900; Median year structure built: 1953; Homeowner vacancy rate: 0.0%; Median selected monthly owner costs: $1,220 with a mortgage, $534 without a mortgage; Median gross rent: $774 per month; Rental vacancy rate: 0.0%
Health Insurance: 92.3% have insurance; 74.5% have private insurance; 32.5% have public insurance; 7.7% do not have insurance; 3.7% of children under 18 do not have insurance
Transportation: Commute: 93.2% car, 0.0% public transportation, 2.2% walk, 4.1% work from home; Mean travel time to work: 22.2 minutes
Additional Information Contacts
Town of Le Roy . . . . (585) 768-6910
    http://www.leroyny.org

LE ROY (village).

Covers a land area of 2.688 square miles and a water area of 0.003 square miles. Located at 42.98° N. Lat; 77.99° W. Long. Elevation is 896 feet.
Population: 4,333; Growth (since 2000): -2.9%; Density: 1,611.7 persons per square mile; Race: 92.5% White, 4.6% Black/African American, 0.0% Asian, 0.0% American Indian/Alaska Native, 0.0% Native Hawaiian/Other Pacific Islander, 2.2% Two or more races, 1.6% Hispanic of any race; Average household size: 2.45; Median age: 39.1; Age under 18: 23.8%; Age 65 and over: 16.9%; Males per 100 females: 93.5; Marriage status: 33.0% never married, 47.7% now married, 5.4% separated, 8.6% widowed, 10.6% divorced; Foreign born: 1.0%; Speak English only: 98.1%; With disability: 13.6%; Veterans: 7.4%; Ancestry: 34.5% German, 21.9% Irish, 19.9% Italian, 17.1% English, 9.7% Polish
Employment: 12.2% management, business, and financial, 4.6% computer, engineering, and science, 8.6% education, legal, community service, arts, and media, 5.0% healthcare practitioners, 24.8% service, 19.3% sales and office, 5.5% natural resources, construction, and maintenance, 19.9% production, transportation, and material moving
Income: Per capita: $25,234; Median household: $50,357; Average household: $61,532; Households with income of $100,000 or more: 14.7%; Poverty rate: 10.3%
Educational Attainment: High school diploma or higher: 88.9%; Bachelor's degree or higher: 24.0%; Graduate/professional degree or higher: 8.5%

School District(s)
Genesee Valley Boces
    2014-15 Enrollment: n/a . . . . (585) 658-7903
Le Roy Central SD (PK-12)
    2014-15 Enrollment: 1,292 . . . . (585) 768-8133
Housing: Homeownership rate: 57.6%; Median home value: $88,400; Median year structure built: Before 1940; Homeowner vacancy rate: 0.0%; Median selected monthly owner costs: $1,128 with a mortgage, $580 without a mortgage; Median gross rent: $735 per month; Rental vacancy rate: 0.0%
Health Insurance: 93.5% have insurance; 70.1% have private insurance; 35.0% have public insurance; 6.5% do not have insurance; 2.2% of children under 18 do not have insurance
Safety: Violent crime rate: 7.0 per 10,000 population; Property crime rate: 95.7 per 10,000 population
Transportation: Commute: 91.1% car, 0.0% public transportation, 4.1% walk, 4.1% work from home; Mean travel time to work: 20.7 minutes
Additional Information Contacts
Village of Le Roy . . . . (585) 768-6910
    http://www.leroyny.org

OAKFIELD (town).

Covers a land area of 23.309 square miles and a water area of 0.624 square miles. Located at 43.08° N. Lat; 78.27° W. Long. Elevation is 755 feet.
History: Settled 1850, incorporated 1858.
Population: 3,203; Growth (since 2000): 0.0%; Density: 137.4 persons per square mile; Race: 97.6% White, 1.0% Black/African American, 0.1% Asian, 0.2% American Indian/Alaska Native, 0.0% Native Hawaiian/Other Pacific Islander, 0.4% Two or more races, 1.5% Hispanic of any race; Average household size: 2.59; Median age: 41.5; Age under 18: 20.6%; Age 65 and over: 16.6%; Males per 100 females: 94.6; Marriage status: 27.7% never married, 59.1% now married, 1.1% separated, 6.6% widowed, 6.5% divorced; Foreign born: 2.5%; Speak English only: 97.7%; With disability: 13.3%; Veterans: 11.3%; Ancestry: 35.2% German, 21.9% Irish, 13.6% English, 10.9% Italian, 10.6% Polish
Employment: 13.1% management, business, and financial, 2.3% computer, engineering, and science, 7.4% education, legal, community service, arts, and media, 4.1% healthcare practitioners, 14.8% service,

28.3% sales and office, 14.5% natural resources, construction, and maintenance, 15.5% production, transportation, and material moving
Income: Per capita: $24,918; Median household: $51,188; Average household: $63,131; Households with income of $100,000 or more: 20.7%; Poverty rate: 8.7%
Educational Attainment: High school diploma or higher: 84.6%; Bachelor's degree or higher: 15.6%; Graduate/professional degree or higher: 5.6%

School District(s)
Oakfield-Alabama Central SD (PK-12)
    2014-15 Enrollment: 881 . . . . (585) 948-5211
Housing: Homeownership rate: 75.9%; Median home value: $95,900; Median year structure built: 1942; Homeowner vacancy rate: 1.3%; Median selected monthly owner costs: $1,142 with a mortgage, $543 without a mortgage; Median gross rent: $585 per month; Rental vacancy rate: 5.3%
Health Insurance: 92.6% have insurance; 73.9% have private insurance; 32.8% have public insurance; 7.4% do not have insurance; 0.9% of children under 18 do not have insurance
Transportation: Commute: 97.1% car, 0.0% public transportation, 0.8% walk, 0.9% work from home; Mean travel time to work: 24.1 minutes

OAKFIELD (village).

Covers a land area of 0.661 square miles and a water area of 0 square miles. Located at 43.06° N. Lat; 78.27° W. Long. Elevation is 755 feet.
Population: 1,767; Growth (since 2000): -2.1%; Density: 2,675.2 persons per square mile; Race: 96.3% White, 1.8% Black/African American, 0.2% Asian, 0.3% American Indian/Alaska Native, 0.0% Native Hawaiian/Other Pacific Islander, 0.8% Two or more races, 2.1% Hispanic of any race; Average household size: 2.63; Median age: 39.3; Age under 18: 21.6%; Age 65 and over: 19.1%; Males per 100 females: 90.8; Marriage status: 27.9% never married, 54.0% now married, 1.0% separated, 9.3% widowed, 8.8% divorced; Foreign born: 4.2%; Speak English only: 96.9%; With disability: 15.4%; Veterans: 12.3%; Ancestry: 32.8% German, 20.1% Irish, 15.1% Italian, 12.8% English, 10.0% Polish
Employment: 9.2% management, business, and financial, 1.8% computer, engineering, and science, 9.6% education, legal, community service, arts, and media, 5.0% healthcare practitioners, 20.7% service, 26.7% sales and office, 11.2% natural resources, construction, and maintenance, 15.8% production, transportation, and material moving
Income: Per capita: $23,258; Median household: $52,702; Average household: $59,229; Households with income of $100,000 or more: 14.6%; Poverty rate: 10.0%
Educational Attainment: High school diploma or higher: 86.6%; Bachelor's degree or higher: 12.7%; Graduate/professional degree or higher: 3.3%

School District(s)
Oakfield-Alabama Central SD (PK-12)
    2014-15 Enrollment: 881 . . . . (585) 948-5211
Housing: Homeownership rate: 71.2%; Median home value: $90,800; Median year structure built: Before 1940; Homeowner vacancy rate: 2.5%; Median selected monthly owner costs: $1,090 with a mortgage, $466 without a mortgage; Median gross rent: $594 per month; Rental vacancy rate: 7.9%
Health Insurance: 94.9% have insurance; 79.3% have private insurance; 34.6% have public insurance; 5.1% do not have insurance; 1.6% of children under 18 do not have insurance
Transportation: Commute: 95.8% car, 0.0% public transportation, 1.5% walk, 0.5% work from home; Mean travel time to work: 23.5 minutes
Additional Information Contacts
Village of Oakfield . . . . (585) 948-5862
    http://www.oakfield.govoffice.com

PAVILION (CDP).

Covers a land area of 3.312 square miles and a water area of 0 square miles. Located at 42.88° N. Lat; 78.02° W. Long. Elevation is 955 feet.
Population: 549; Growth (since 2000): n/a; Density: 165.8 persons per square mile; Race: 100.0% White, 0.0% Black/African American, 0.0% Asian, 0.0% American Indian/Alaska Native, 0.0% Native Hawaiian/Other Pacific Islander, 0.0% Two or more races, 0.0% Hispanic of any race; Average household size: 2.63; Median age: 41.3; Age under 18: 21.1%; Age 65 and over: 19.5%; Males per 100 females: 104.4; Marriage status: 28.5% never married, 46.1% now married, 1.1% separated, 10.4% widowed, 15.0% divorced; Foreign born: 1.1%; Speak English only: 100.0%; With disability: 7.8%; Veterans: 10.2%; Ancestry: 32.8% German, 21.1% English, 16.0% Irish, 9.7% American, 7.7% Italian

Employment: 10.1% management, business, and financial, 1.4% computer, engineering, and science, 1.7% education, legal, community service, arts, and media, 2.1% healthcare practitioners, 18.1% service, 33.8% sales and office, 14.3% natural resources, construction, and maintenance, 18.5% production, transportation, and material moving
Income: Per capita: $29,788; Median household: $64,250; Average household: $77,071; Households with income of $100,000 or more: 21.0%; Poverty rate: 2.9%
Educational Attainment: High school diploma or higher: 97.0%; Bachelor's degree or higher: 26.3%; Graduate/professional degree or higher: 5.2%

School District(s)
Pavilion Central SD (PK-12)
   2014-15 Enrollment: 721 . . . . (585) 584-1013
Housing: Homeownership rate: 82.3%; Median home value: $102,500; Median year structure built: 1943; Homeowner vacancy rate: 0.0%; Median selected monthly owner costs: $986 with a mortgage, $530 without a mortgage; Median gross rent: $644 per month; Rental vacancy rate: 0.0%
Health Insurance: 97.8% have insurance; 82.3% have private insurance; 38.6% have public insurance; 2.2% do not have insurance; 0.0% of children under 18 do not have insurance
Transportation: Commute: 92.3% car, 4.0% public transportation, 3.7% walk, 0.0% work from home; Mean travel time to work: 21.9 minutes

---

PAVILION (town). Covers a land area of 35.612 square miles and a water area of 0.108 square miles. Located at 42.91° N. Lat; 78.01° W. Long. Elevation is 955 feet.
Population: 2,555; Growth (since 2000): 3.6%; Density: 71.7 persons per square mile; Race: 98.6% White, 0.9% Black/African American, 0.0% Asian, 0.0% American Indian/Alaska Native, 0.0% Native Hawaiian/Other Pacific Islander, 0.5% Two or more races, 0.0% Hispanic of any race; Average household size: 2.77; Median age: 39.9; Age under 18: 23.3%; Age 65 and over: 12.1%; Males per 100 females: 108.1; Marriage status: 23.0% never married, 58.4% now married, 3.5% separated, 5.8% widowed, 12.7% divorced; Foreign born: 0.4%; Speak English only: 99.6%; With disability: 9.2%; Veterans: 6.6%; Ancestry: 27.8% German, 23.4% English, 23.1% Irish, 8.6% Italian, 7.0% American
Employment: 12.4% management, business, and financial, 4.2% computer, engineering, and science, 4.1% education, legal, community service, arts, and media, 5.6% healthcare practitioners, 13.5% service, 21.4% sales and office, 16.7% natural resources, construction, and maintenance, 22.1% production, transportation, and material moving
Income: Per capita: $24,325; Median household: $64,750; Average household: $66,328; Households with income of $100,000 or more: 17.2%; Poverty rate: 13.7%
Educational Attainment: High school diploma or higher: 93.3%; Bachelor's degree or higher: 20.1%; Graduate/professional degree or higher: 7.4%

School District(s)
Pavilion Central SD (PK-12)
   2014-15 Enrollment: 721 . . . . (585) 584-1013
Housing: Homeownership rate: 86.8%; Median home value: $113,000; Median year structure built: 1973; Homeowner vacancy rate: 0.6%; Median selected monthly owner costs: $1,242 with a mortgage, $394 without a mortgage; Median gross rent: $734 per month; Rental vacancy rate: 0.0%
Health Insurance: 95.3% have insurance; 77.9% have private insurance; 29.3% have public insurance; 4.7% do not have insurance; 2.2% of children under 18 do not have insurance
Transportation: Commute: 93.5% car, 0.9% public transportation, 1.2% walk, 4.0% work from home; Mean travel time to work: 25.1 minutes

---

PEMBROKE (town). Covers a land area of 41.627 square miles and a water area of 0.090 square miles. Located at 43.00° N. Lat; 78.39° W. Long. Elevation is 843 feet.
Population: 4,296; Growth (since 2000): -5.2%; Density: 103.2 persons per square mile; Race: 94.9% White, 1.2% Black/African American, 1.5% Asian, 0.0% American Indian/Alaska Native, 0.0% Native Hawaiian/Other Pacific Islander, 1.8% Two or more races, 1.7% Hispanic of any race; Average household size: 2.62; Median age: 45.4; Age under 18: 20.2%; Age 65 and over: 15.5%; Males per 100 females: 95.4; Marriage status: 26.5% never married, 57.5% now married, 2.4% separated, 4.1% widowed, 11.9% divorced; Foreign born: 1.2%; Speak English only: 97.8%; With disability: 12.6%; Veterans: 11.4%; Ancestry: 40.3% German, 20.6% Polish, 20.1% English, 15.7% Irish, 10.5% Italian

Employment: 6.1% management, business, and financial, 3.9% computer, engineering, and science, 7.6% education, legal, community service, arts, and media, 5.8% healthcare practitioners, 17.7% service, 24.5% sales and office, 14.3% natural resources, construction, and maintenance, 20.1% production, transportation, and material moving
Income: Per capita: $25,790; Median household: $54,828; Average household: $66,133; Households with income of $100,000 or more: 17.1%; Poverty rate: 10.9%
Educational Attainment: High school diploma or higher: 92.5%; Bachelor's degree or higher: 15.6%; Graduate/professional degree or higher: 6.7%
Housing: Homeownership rate: 84.0%; Median home value: $128,100; Median year structure built: 1961; Homeowner vacancy rate: 0.0%; Median selected monthly owner costs: $1,146 with a mortgage, $512 without a mortgage; Median gross rent: $807 per month; Rental vacancy rate: 0.0%
Health Insurance: 96.0% have insurance; 80.7% have private insurance; 29.2% have public insurance; 4.0% do not have insurance; 0.0% of children under 18 do not have insurance
Transportation: Commute: 95.4% car, 0.0% public transportation, 0.2% walk, 4.5% work from home; Mean travel time to work: 26.5 minutes
Additional Information Contacts
Town of Pembroke . . . . (585) 599-4892
  http://www.townofpembroke.org

STAFFORD (town). Covers a land area of 31.097 square miles and a water area of 0.179 square miles. Located at 42.99° N. Lat; 78.08° W. Long. Elevation is 892 feet.
Population: 2,318; Growth (since 2000): -3.8%; Density: 74.5 persons per square mile; Race: 95.8% White, 0.3% Black/African American, 1.0% Asian, 0.9% American Indian/Alaska Native, 0.0% Native Hawaiian/Other Pacific Islander, 2.0% Two or more races, 1.2% Hispanic of any race; Average household size: 2.45; Median age: 47.9; Age under 18: 20.3%; Age 65 and over: 17.9%; Males per 100 females: 101.7; Marriage status: 21.9% never married, 59.8% now married, 0.2% separated, 7.1% widowed, 11.2% divorced; Foreign born: 2.0%; Speak English only: 96.6%; With disability: 16.3%; Veterans: 9.9%; Ancestry: 31.8% German, 19.4% Irish, 16.6% English, 12.9% Italian, 9.8% American
Employment: 9.1% management, business, and financial, 4.7% computer, engineering, and science, 11.9% education, legal, community service, arts, and media, 7.6% healthcare practitioners, 17.5% service, 24.4% sales and office, 10.7% natural resources, construction, and maintenance, 14.3% production, transportation, and material moving
Income: Per capita: $25,866; Median household: $54,855; Average household: $62,342; Households with income of $100,000 or more: 18.6%; Poverty rate: 8.2%
Educational Attainment: High school diploma or higher: 90.7%; Bachelor's degree or higher: 18.7%; Graduate/professional degree or higher: 8.5%
Housing: Homeownership rate: 85.1%; Median home value: $119,200; Median year structure built: 1957; Homeowner vacancy rate: 0.0%; Median selected monthly owner costs: $1,158 with a mortgage, $589 without a mortgage; Median gross rent: $672 per month; Rental vacancy rate: 8.0%
Health Insurance: 93.4% have insurance; 78.0% have private insurance; 31.7% have public insurance; 6.6% do not have insurance; 5.3% of children under 18 do not have insurance
Transportation: Commute: 95.5% car, 0.4% public transportation, 1.1% walk, 2.0% work from home; Mean travel time to work: 22.5 minutes

---

TONAWANDA RESERVATION (reservation). Covers a land area of 9.161 square miles and a water area of 0.070 square miles. Located at 43.07° N. Lat; 78.44° W. Long.
Population: 512; Growth (since 2000): n/a; Density: 55.9 persons per square mile; Race: 5.9% White, 0.0% Black/African American, 8.4% Asian, 78.1% American Indian/Alaska Native, 0.0% Native Hawaiian/Other Pacific Islander, 3.3% Two or more races, 1.2% Hispanic of any race; Average household size: 1.95; Median age: 53.4; Age under 18: 15.4%; Age 65 and over: 24.6%; Males per 100 females: 92.4; Marriage status: 42.6% never married, 43.7% now married, 4.2% separated, 3.8% widowed, 10.0% divorced; Foreign born: 6.6%; Speak English only: 83.3%; With disability: 18.6%; Veterans: 14.3%; Ancestry: 3.9% German, 2.7% Irish, 1.0% Polish
Employment: 5.4% management, business, and financial, 0.0% computer, engineering, and science, 8.6% education, legal, community service, arts, and media, 2.2% healthcare practitioners, 17.3% service, 25.4% sales and office, 7.6% natural resources, construction, and maintenance, 33.5% production, transportation, and material moving

Income: Per capita: $17,593; Median household: $24,702; Average household: $37,017; Households with income of $100,000 or more: 5.7%; Poverty rate: 20.3%

Educational Attainment: High school diploma or higher: 88.9%; Bachelor's degree or higher: 9.9%; Graduate/professional degree or higher: 3.7%

Housing: Homeownership rate: 84.8%; Median home value: $60,800; Median year structure built: 1960; Homeowner vacancy rate: 0.0%; Median selected monthly owner costs: $864 with a mortgage, $375 without a mortgage; Median gross rent: $700 per month; Rental vacancy rate: 0.0%

Health Insurance: 86.3% have insurance; 51.8% have private insurance; 53.1% have public insurance; 13.7% do not have insurance; 0.0% of children under 18 do not have insurance

Transportation: Commute: 87.4% car, 0.0% public transportation, 4.6% walk, 8.0% work from home; Mean travel time to work: 22.7 minutes

Greene County

Located in southeastern New York, mainly in the Catskills; bounded on the east by the Hudson River; includes many small lakes. Covers a land area of 647.161 square miles, a water area of 10.888 square miles, and is located in the Eastern Time Zone at 42.29° N. Lat., 74.15° W. Long. The county was founded in 1800. County seat is Catskill.

Weather Station: Cairo 4 NW										Elevation: 490 feet		
	Jan	Feb	Mar	Apr	May	Jun	Jul	Aug	Sep	Oct	Nov	Dec
High	32	36	45	58	69	78	82	81	73	61	49	38
Low	13	15	24	35	45	54	59	57	49	38	30	20
Precip	2.8	2.4	3.6	3.8	3.4	3.9	3.3	3.0	3.9	3.8	3.8	3.1
Snow	13.3	9.8	9.9	2.0	0.0	0.0	0.0	0.0	0.0	0.1	2.2	10.7

High and Low temperatures in degrees Fahrenheit; Precipitation and Snow in inches

Population: 48,312; Growth (since 2000): 0.2%; Density: 74.7 persons per square mile; Race: 89.7% White, 6.3% Black/African American, 1.0% Asian, 0.0% American Indian/Alaska Native, 0.0% Native Hawaiian/Other Pacific Islander, 2.3% two or more races, 5.3% Hispanic of any race; Average household size: 2.55; Median age: 45.2; Age under 18: 17.8%; Age 65 and over: 19.4%; Males per 100 females: 109.1; Marriage status: 33.5% never married, 50.4% now married, 2.2% separated, 6.8% widowed, 9.3% divorced; Foreign born: 6.2%; Speak English only: 91.8%; With disability: 15.7%; Veterans: 9.6%; Ancestry: 20.6% Irish, 20.1% German, 16.8% Italian, 13.6% American, 7.1% English

Religion: Six largest groups: 20.2% Catholicism, 7.4% Methodist/Pietist, 2.3% Presbyterian-Reformed, 2.1% Non-denominational Protestant, 2.0% Lutheran, 0.8% Episcopalianism/Anglicanism

Economy: Unemployment rate: 4.6%; Leading industries: 17.6 % accommodation and food services; 17.3 % retail trade; 13.3 % construction; Farms: 273 totaling 42,986 acres; Company size: 0 employ 1,000 or more persons, 2 employ 500 to 999 persons, 13 employ 100 to 499 persons, 1,123 employ less than 100 persons; Business ownership: 1,170 women-owned, 58 Black-owned, 104 Hispanic-owned, 54 Asian-owned, 30 American Indian/Alaska Native-owned

Employment: 12.3% management, business, and financial, 3.1% computer, engineering, and science, 12.7% education, legal, community service, arts, and media, 6.0% healthcare practitioners, 19.0% service, 22.4% sales and office, 10.7% natural resources, construction, and maintenance, 13.9% production, transportation, and material moving

Income: Per capita: $26,261; Median household: $50,278; Average household: $66,557; Households with income of $100,000 or more: 20.2%; Poverty rate: 12.9%

Educational Attainment: High school diploma or higher: 86.5%; Bachelor's degree or higher: 20.6%; Graduate/professional degree or higher: 8.4%

Housing: Homeownership rate: 75.2%; Median home value: $177,700; Median year structure built: 1971; Homeowner vacancy rate: 3.3%; Median selected monthly owner costs: $1,558 with a mortgage, $583 without a mortgage; Median gross rent: $837 per month; Rental vacancy rate: 12.7%

Vital Statistics: Birth rate: 89.4 per 10,000 population; Death rate: 106.5 per 10,000 population; Age-adjusted cancer mortality rate: 198.9 deaths per 100,000 population

Health Insurance: 92.4% have insurance; 70.6% have private insurance; 37.9% have public insurance; 7.6% do not have insurance; 3.5% of children under 18 do not have insurance

Health Care: Physicians: 7.3 per 10,000 population; Dentists: 3.6 per 10,000 population; Hospital beds: 0.0 per 10,000 population; Hospital admissions: 0.0 per 10,000 population

Transportation: Commute: 89.9% car, 0.9% public transportation, 2.5% walk, 4.5% work from home; Mean travel time to work: 27.3 minutes

2016 Presidential Election: 60.6% Trump, 34.3% Clinton, 3.0% Johnson, 2.0% Stein

National and State Parks: Catskill State Park

Additional Information Contacts

Greene Government . . . . (518) 719-3270
http://www.greenegovernment.com

Greene County Communities

ACRA (unincorporated postal area)

ZCTA: 12405

Covers a land area of 7.145 square miles and a water area of 0.029 square miles. Located at 42.32° N. Lat; 74.09° W. Long. Elevation is 653 feet.

Population: 651; Growth (since 2000): 43.4%; Density: 91.1 persons per square mile; Race: 100.0% White, 0.0% Black/African American, 0.0% Asian, 0.0% American Indian/Alaska Native, 0.0% Native Hawaiian/Other Pacific Islander, 0.0% Two or more races, 0.0% Hispanic of any race; Average household size: 2.48; Median age: 65.2; Age under 18: 5.7%; Age 65 and over: 51.8%; Males per 100 females: 94.0; Marriage status: 9.4% never married, 60.4% now married, 0.0% separated, 19.1% widowed, 11.1% divorced; Foreign born: 9.2%; Speak English only: 92.5%; With disability: 31.6%; Veterans: 8.8%; Ancestry: 43.8% German, 28.4% Italian, 23.3% Irish, 7.5% American, 6.1% Scottish

Employment: 15.5% management, business, and financial, 0.0% computer, engineering, and science, 2.3% education, legal, community service, arts, and media, 30.9% healthcare practitioners, 25.0% service, 19.1% sales and office, 4.5% natural resources, construction, and maintenance, 2.7% production, transportation, and material moving

Income: Per capita: $21,743; Median household: $44,485; Average household: $50,125; Households with income of $100,000 or more: 4.9%; Poverty rate: 2.9%

Educational Attainment: High school diploma or higher: 97.7%; Bachelor's degree or higher: 16.2%; Graduate/professional degree or higher: n/a

Housing: Homeownership rate: 72.6%; Median home value: $221,100; Median year structure built: 1971; Homeowner vacancy rate: 0.0%; Median selected monthly owner costs: $1,523 with a mortgage, $706 without a mortgage; Median gross rent: $802 per month; Rental vacancy rate: 24.2%

Health Insurance: 91.1% have insurance; 61.0% have private insurance; 56.7% have public insurance; 8.9% do not have insurance; 0.0% of children under 18 do not have insurance

Transportation: Commute: 100.0% car, 0.0% public transportation, 0.0% walk, 0.0% work from home; Mean travel time to work: 31.0 minutes

ASHLAND (town). Covers a land area of 25.958 square miles and a water area of 0 square miles. Located at 42.32° N. Lat; 74.34° W. Long. Elevation is 1,421 feet.

Population: 871; Growth (since 2000): 15.8%; Density: 33.6 persons per square mile; Race: 96.2% White, 1.1% Black/African American, 0.9% Asian, 0.3% American Indian/Alaska Native, 0.0% Native Hawaiian/Other Pacific Islander, 1.4% Two or more races, 3.1% Hispanic of any race; Average household size: 2.44; Median age: 53.5; Age under 18: 17.1%; Age 65 and over: 32.0%; Males per 100 females: 99.0; Marriage status: 22.8% never married, 57.2% now married, 4.3% separated, 6.8% widowed, 13.3% divorced; Foreign born: 8.0%; Speak English only: 94.8%; With disability: 11.8%; Veterans: 18.7%; Ancestry: 20.9% Italian, 20.7% Irish, 14.8% German, 12.4% American, 8.8% English

Employment: 6.2% management, business, and financial, 4.0% computer, engineering, and science, 18.6% education, legal, community service, arts, and media, 1.2% healthcare practitioners, 14.3% service, 26.7% sales and office, 14.3% natural resources, construction, and maintenance, 14.6% production, transportation, and material moving

Income: Per capita: $33,037; Median household: $48,750; Average household: $77,252; Households with income of $100,000 or more: 24.1%; Poverty rate: 9.1%

Educational Attainment: High school diploma or higher: 92.1%; Bachelor's degree or higher: 25.7%; Graduate/professional degree or higher: 15.3%

Housing: Homeownership rate: 87.7%; Median home value: $216,500; Median year structure built: 1979; Homeowner vacancy rate: 0.0%; Median selected monthly owner costs: $1,366 with a mortgage, $472 without a mortgage; Median gross rent: $1,125 per month; Rental vacancy rate: 0.0%

Health Insurance: 94.0% have insurance; 67.2% have private insurance; 42.5% have public insurance; 6.0% do not have insurance; 2.0% of children under 18 do not have insurance

Transportation: Commute: 88.4% car, 4.5% public transportation, 0.0% walk, 4.2% work from home; Mean travel time to work: 21.3 minutes

---

ATHENS (town). Covers a land area of 26.246 square miles and a water area of 2.622 square miles. Located at 42.28° N. Lat; 73.86° W. Long. Elevation is 26 feet.

History: Settled 1686, incorporated 1805.

Population: 4,005; Growth (since 2000): 0.4%; Density: 152.6 persons per square mile; Race: 93.2% White, 0.9% Black/African American, 2.5% Asian, 0.0% American Indian/Alaska Native, 0.0% Native Hawaiian/Other Pacific Islander, 3.3% Two or more races, 7.0% Hispanic of any race; Average household size: 2.89; Median age: 47.5; Age under 18: 16.5%; Age 65 and over: 17.8%; Males per 100 females: 97.6; Marriage status: 31.2% never married, 47.9% now married, 3.8% separated, 7.9% widowed, 13.0% divorced; Foreign born: 4.3%; Speak English only: 95.7%; With disability: 19.7%; Veterans: 8.8%; Ancestry: 21.9% Irish, 21.4% Italian, 20.6% German, 11.2% American, 6.5% English

Employment: 10.4% management, business, and financial, 3.1% computer, engineering, and science, 13.2% education, legal, community service, arts, and media, 6.5% healthcare practitioners, 22.5% service, 25.7% sales and office, 9.9% natural resources, construction, and maintenance, 8.7% production, transportation, and material moving

Income: Per capita: $25,925; Median household: $51,750; Average household: $67,172; Households with income of $100,000 or more: 21.7%; Poverty rate: 15.2%

Educational Attainment: High school diploma or higher: 84.5%; Bachelor's degree or higher: 19.4%; Graduate/professional degree or higher: 8.8%

School District(s)

Coxsackie-Athens Central SD (KG-12)

    2014-15 Enrollment: 1,409 . . . . (518) 731-1710

Housing: Homeownership rate: 79.2%; Median home value: $178,700; Median year structure built: 1971; Homeowner vacancy rate: 0.7%; Median selected monthly owner costs: $1,702 with a mortgage, $623 without a mortgage; Median gross rent: $910 per month; Rental vacancy rate: 2.8%

Health Insurance: 92.3% have insurance; 66.2% have private insurance; 39.1% have public insurance; 7.7% do not have insurance; 2.0% of children under 18 do not have insurance

Transportation: Commute: 94.0% car, 0.4% public transportation, 2.1% walk, 2.8% work from home; Mean travel time to work: 26.4 minutes

Additional Information Contacts

Town of Athens . . . . (518) 945-1052
    http://www.townofathensny.com

ATHENS (village). Covers a land area of 3.420 square miles and a water area of 1.185 square miles. Located at 42.27° N. Lat; 73.82° W. Long. Elevation is 26 feet.

Population: 1,420; Growth (since 2000): -16.2%; Density: 415.3 persons per square mile; Race: 94.9% White, 1.7% Black/African American, 2.7% Asian, 0.0% American Indian/Alaska Native, 0.0% Native Hawaiian/Other Pacific Islander, 0.5% Two or more races, 6.1% Hispanic of any race; Average household size: 2.43; Median age: 48.7; Age under 18: 13.0%; Age 65 and over: 24.9%; Males per 100 females: 91.9; Marriage status: 30.9% never married, 42.3% now married, 4.3% separated, 15.1% widowed, 11.7% divorced; Foreign born: 4.2%; Speak English only: 90.7%; With disability: 14.9%; Veterans: 7.9%; Ancestry: 21.3% German, 17.8% Irish, 14.9% Italian, 11.7% American, 6.1% Dutch

Employment: 5.9% management, business, and financial, 4.4% computer, engineering, and science, 18.8% education, legal, community service, arts, and media, 8.4% healthcare practitioners, 23.5% service, 21.1% sales and office, 7.3% natural resources, construction, and maintenance, 10.6% production, transportation, and material moving

Income: Per capita: $26,547; Median household: $47,173; Average household: $59,995; Households with income of $100,000 or more: 15.3%; Poverty rate: 16.3%

Educational Attainment: High school diploma or higher: 84.6%; Bachelor's degree or higher: 20.2%; Graduate/professional degree or higher: 10.6%

School District(s)

Coxsackie-Athens Central SD (KG-12)

    2014-15 Enrollment: 1,409 . . . . (518) 731-1710

Housing: Homeownership rate: 64.5%; Median home value: $163,700; Median year structure built: Before 1940; Homeowner vacancy rate: 2.1%; Median selected monthly owner costs: $1,538 with a mortgage, $623 without a mortgage; Median gross rent: $840 per month; Rental vacancy rate: 4.2%

Health Insurance: 92.0% have insurance; 65.0% have private insurance; 44.6% have public insurance; 8.0% do not have insurance; 3.3% of children under 18 do not have insurance

Transportation: Commute: 88.3% car, 1.0% public transportation, 5.2% walk, 3.1% work from home; Mean travel time to work: 24.7 minutes

---

CAIRO (CDP). Covers a land area of 4.227 square miles and a water area of 0.006 square miles. Located at 42.31° N. Lat; 74.01° W. Long. Elevation is 374 feet.

Population: 1,325; Growth (since 2000): -4.7%; Density: 313.4 persons per square mile; Race: 99.8% White, 0.2% Black/African American, 0.0% Asian, 0.0% American Indian/Alaska Native, 0.0% Native Hawaiian/Other Pacific Islander, 0.0% Two or more races, 0.0% Hispanic of any race; Average household size: 2.19; Median age: 49.6; Age under 18: 10.3%; Age 65 and over: 12.2%; Males per 100 females: 87.9; Marriage status: 32.4% never married, 35.7% now married, 4.1% separated, 5.9% widowed, 26.0% divorced; Foreign born: 3.6%; Speak English only: 96.5%; With disability: 27.9%; Veterans: 6.5%; Ancestry: 32.5% Irish, 31.3% German, 15.5% Italian, 12.1% American, 6.4% Polish

Employment: 5.6% management, business, and financial, 0.0% computer, engineering, and science, 11.9% education, legal, community service, arts, and media, 0.0% healthcare practitioners, 30.0% service, 29.4% sales and office, 5.9% natural resources, construction, and maintenance, 17.2% production, transportation, and material moving

Income: Per capita: $18,121; Median household: $23,883; Average household: $36,471; Households with income of $100,000 or more: 5.8%; Poverty rate: 31.5%

Educational Attainment: High school diploma or higher: 69.6%; Bachelor's degree or higher: 11.1%; Graduate/professional degree or higher: 4.3%

School District(s)

Cairo-Durham Central SD (KG-12)

    2014-15 Enrollment: 1,222 . . . . (518) 622-8534

Housing: Homeownership rate: 47.6%; Median home value: $119,800; Median year structure built: 1972; Homeowner vacancy rate: 13.9%; Median selected monthly owner costs: $1,363 with a mortgage, $500 without a mortgage; Median gross rent: $925 per month; Rental vacancy rate: 7.1%

Health Insurance: 90.0% have insurance; 48.8% have private insurance; 48.5% have public insurance; 10.0% do not have insurance; 0.0% of children under 18 do not have insurance

Transportation: Commute: 100.0% car, 0.0% public transportation, 0.0% walk, 0.0% work from home; Mean travel time to work: 21.5 minutes

---

CAIRO (town). Covers a land area of 59.828 square miles and a water area of 0.254 square miles. Located at 42.30° N. Lat; 74.02° W. Long. Elevation is 374 feet.

Population: 6,543; Growth (since 2000): 3.0%; Density: 109.4 persons per square mile; Race: 95.3% White, 1.6% Black/African American, 2.7% Asian, 0.0% American Indian/Alaska Native, 0.0% Native Hawaiian/Other Pacific Islander, 0.4% Two or more races, 1.3% Hispanic of any race; Average household size: 2.47; Median age: 45.8; Age under 18: 17.8%; Age 65 and over: 17.4%; Males per 100 females: 95.0; Marriage status: 28.3% never married, 54.0% now married, 1.7% separated, 5.4% widowed, 12.3% divorced; Foreign born: 7.7%; Speak English only: 92.6%; With disability: 14.0%; Veterans: 8.2%; Ancestry: 25.1% German, 21.3% Irish, 16.4% Italian, 15.3% American, 4.5% English

Employment: 14.1% management, business, and financial, 1.3% computer, engineering, and science, 15.1% education, legal, community service, arts, and media, 6.1% healthcare practitioners, 22.8% service,

18.3% sales and office, 4.1% natural resources, construction, and maintenance, 18.2% production, transportation, and material moving

Income: Per capita: $26,634; Median household: $50,274; Average household: $62,893; Households with income of $100,000 or more: 20.6%; Poverty rate: 12.6%

Educational Attainment: High school diploma or higher: 86.3%; Bachelor's degree or higher: 17.9%; Graduate/professional degree or higher: 7.6%

School District(s)

Cairo-Durham Central SD (KG-12)

    2014-15 Enrollment: 1,222 . . . . (518) 622-8534

Housing: Homeownership rate: 71.0%; Median home value: $163,200; Median year structure built: 1974; Homeowner vacancy rate: 6.9%; Median selected monthly owner costs: $1,405 with a mortgage, $509 without a mortgage; Median gross rent: $884 per month; Rental vacancy rate: 5.8%

Health Insurance: 94.9% have insurance; 74.7% have private insurance; 33.0% have public insurance; 5.1% do not have insurance; 0.0% of children under 18 do not have insurance

Safety: Violent crime rate: 3.1 per 10,000 population; Property crime rate: 46.4 per 10,000 population

Transportation: Commute: 92.5% car, 0.8% public transportation, 1.4% walk, 2.6% work from home; Mean travel time to work: 26.3 minutes

Additional Information Contacts

Town of Cairo . . . . (518) 622-3120

    http://www.townofcairo.com/Pages/index

CATSKILL (town). Covers a land area of 60.439 square miles and a water area of 3.726 square miles. Located at 42.21° N. Lat; 73.94° W. Long. Elevation is 43 feet.

History: Originally known as Catskill Landing, the settlement of Catskill was subsidiary to the old Dutch hamlet of Kaatskill, in the hills to the west. Mountains, creeks, and village were named by the Dutch for the wildcats that occasionally came down from the hills, where they roamed in large numbers. In the heyday of turnpike and river transportation, the place bustled with prosperity. Thomas Cole lived and painted in the village. Settled 17th, incorporated in 1806.

Population: 11,558; Growth (since 2000): -2.5%; Density: 191.2 persons per square mile; Race: 82.3% White, 10.7% Black/African American, 0.7% Asian, 0.0% American Indian/Alaska Native, 0.0% Native Hawaiian/Other Pacific Islander, 5.3% Two or more races, 5.5% Hispanic of any race; Average household size: 2.61; Median age: 39.9; Age under 18: 21.3%; Age 65 and over: 18.3%; Males per 100 females: 95.5; Marriage status: 35.9% never married, 49.8% now married, 2.6% separated, 5.4% widowed, 8.9% divorced; Foreign born: 5.0%; Speak English only: 92.7%; With disability: 19.4%; Veterans: 9.6%; Ancestry: 24.8% Italian, 24.7% Irish, 19.9% German, 6.8% Polish, 6.3% American

Employment: 11.2% management, business, and financial, 1.7% computer, engineering, and science, 12.0% education, legal, community service, arts, and media, 5.7% healthcare practitioners, 17.7% service, 24.6% sales and office, 12.6% natural resources, construction, and maintenance, 14.5% production, transportation, and material moving

Income: Per capita: $25,149; Median household: $46,563; Average household: $61,259; Households with income of $100,000 or more: 15.9%; Poverty rate: 14.9%

Educational Attainment: High school diploma or higher: 88.3%; Bachelor's degree or higher: 19.4%; Graduate/professional degree or higher: 6.6%

School District(s)

Catskill Central SD (PK-12)

    2014-15 Enrollment: 1,652 . . . . (518) 943-4696

Housing: Homeownership rate: 61.7%; Median home value: $169,900; Median year structure built: 1954; Homeowner vacancy rate: 4.1%; Median selected monthly owner costs: $1,591 with a mortgage, $660 without a mortgage; Median gross rent: $824 per month; Rental vacancy rate: 18.2%

Health Insurance: 91.3% have insurance; 68.8% have private insurance; 40.5% have public insurance; 8.7% do not have insurance; 4.1% of children under 18 do not have insurance

Newspapers: Daily Mail (daily circulation 3,400)

Transportation: Commute: 89.0% car, 1.0% public transportation, 4.3% walk, 2.5% work from home; Mean travel time to work: 23.8 minutes

Additional Information Contacts

Town of Catskill . . . . (518) 943-2141

    http://www.townofcatskillny.gov/Public_Documents/index

CATSKILL (village). County seat. Covers a land area of 2.280 square miles and a water area of 0.579 square miles. Located at 42.21° N. Lat; 73.86° W. Long. Elevation is 43 feet.

Population: 3,952; Growth (since 2000): -10.0%; Density: 1,733.7 persons per square mile; Race: 73.8% White, 21.5% Black/African American, 0.0% Asian, 0.0% American Indian/Alaska Native, 0.0% Native Hawaiian/Other Pacific Islander, 4.0% Two or more races, 2.7% Hispanic of any race; Average household size: 2.59; Median age: 33.8; Age under 18: 25.2%; Age 65 and over: 13.5%; Males per 100 females: 98.9; Marriage status: 45.2% never married, 43.5% now married, 3.6% separated, 2.6% widowed, 8.8% divorced; Foreign born: 3.9%; Speak English only: 94.1%; With disability: 19.3%; Veterans: 8.7%; Ancestry: 29.8% Irish, 26.9% Italian, 15.5% German, 5.4% English, 5.3% Polish

Employment: 9.4% management, business, and financial, 1.2% computer, engineering, and science, 20.4% education, legal, community service, arts, and media, 6.0% healthcare practitioners, 16.0% service, 27.2% sales and office, 7.6% natural resources, construction, and maintenance, 12.2% production, transportation, and material moving

Income: Per capita: $23,281; Median household: $36,442; Average household: $57,815; Households with income of $100,000 or more: 12.4%; Poverty rate: 19.4%

Educational Attainment: High school diploma or higher: 96.2%; Bachelor's degree or higher: 28.3%; Graduate/professional degree or higher: 12.6%

School District(s)

Catskill Central SD (PK-12)

    2014-15 Enrollment: 1,652 . . . . (518) 943-4696

Housing: Homeownership rate: 49.8%; Median home value: $171,000; Median year structure built: Before 1940; Homeowner vacancy rate: 5.1%; Median selected monthly owner costs: $1,865 with a mortgage, $766 without a mortgage; Median gross rent: $728 per month; Rental vacancy rate: 25.1%

Health Insurance: 90.1% have insurance; 72.5% have private insurance; 35.5% have public insurance; 9.9% do not have insurance; 6.2% of children under 18 do not have insurance

Safety: Violent crime rate: 25.9 per 10,000 population; Property crime rate: 316.1 per 10,000 population

Newspapers: Daily Mail (daily circulation 3,400)

Transportation: Commute: 84.9% car, 1.9% public transportation, 4.2% walk, 1.6% work from home; Mean travel time to work: 22.5 minutes

Additional Information Contacts

Village of Catskill . . . . (518) 943-3830

    http://www.villageofcatskill.net

CLIMAX (unincorporated postal area)

ZCTA: 12042

    Covers a land area of 4.344 square miles and a water area of 0.012 square miles. Located at 42.42° N. Lat; 73.94° W. Long. Elevation is 246 feet.

Population: 179; Growth (since 2000): -78.0%; Density: 41.2 persons per square mile; Race: 100.0% White, 0.0% Black/African American, 0.0% Asian, 0.0% American Indian/Alaska Native, 0.0% Native Hawaiian/Other Pacific Islander, 0.0% Two or more races, 0.0% Hispanic of any race; Average household size: 1.95; Median age: 52.5; Age under 18: 0.0%; Age 65 and over: 26.3%; Males per 100 females: 108.5; Marriage status: 19.0% never married, 67.6% now married, 0.0% separated, 0.0% widowed, 13.4% divorced; Foreign born: 3.9%; Speak English only: 91.6%; With disability: 24.6%; Veterans: 8.4%; Ancestry: 52.5% German, 34.6% Irish, 22.3% Polish, 8.9% French, 7.3% Italian

Employment: 9.0% management, business, and financial, 16.0% computer, engineering, and science, 27.0% education, legal, community service, arts, and media, 7.0% healthcare practitioners, 12.0% service, 15.0% sales and office, 8.0% natural resources, construction, and maintenance, 6.0% production, transportation, and material moving

Income: Per capita: $29,593; Median household: n/a; Average household: $56,232; Households with income of $100,000 or more: n/a; Poverty rate: 14.5%

Educational Attainment: High school diploma or higher: 89.0%; Bachelor's degree or higher: 24.0%; Graduate/professional degree or higher: 17.5%

Housing: Homeownership rate: 64.1%; Median home value: $157,300; Median year structure built: 1955; Homeowner vacancy rate: 0.0%; Median selected monthly owner costs: $1,638 with a mortgage, $0 without a mortgage; Median gross rent: n/a per month; Rental vacancy rate: 0.0%

Health Insurance: 83.8% have insurance; 66.5% have private insurance; 30.2% have public insurance; 16.2% do not have insurance; 0.0% of children under 18 do not have insurance
Transportation: Commute: 93.6% car, 0.0% public transportation, 0.0% walk, 6.4% work from home; Mean travel time to work: 39.9 minutes

CORNWALLVILLE (unincorporated postal area)
ZCTA: 12418
Covers a land area of 13.815 square miles and a water area of 0 square miles. Located at 42.36° N. Lat; 74.16° W. Long. Elevation is 958 feet.
Population: 482; Growth (since 2000): -21.2%; Density: 34.9 persons per square mile; Race: 92.5% White, 7.5% Black/African American, 0.0% Asian, 0.0% American Indian/Alaska Native, 0.0% Native Hawaiian/Other Pacific Islander, 0.0% Two or more races, 0.0% Hispanic of any race; Average household size: 3.19; Median age: 48.0; Age under 18: 15.4%; Age 65 and over: 14.9%; Males per 100 females: 94.6; Marriage status: 39.2% never married, 55.0% now married, 1.2% separated, 2.9% widowed, 2.9% divorced; Foreign born: 5.2%; Speak English only: 97.7%; With disability: 19.5%; Veterans: 7.4%; Ancestry: 24.3% Italian, 24.1% Irish, 17.6% German, 8.5% English, 6.0% American
Employment: 3.4% management, business, and financial, 1.4% computer, engineering, and science, 9.1% education, legal, community service, arts, and media, 2.4% healthcare practitioners, 16.8% service, 26.4% sales and office, 3.4% natural resources, construction, and maintenance, 37.0% production, transportation, and material moving
Income: Per capita: $25,218; Median household: $63,393; Average household: $67,328; Households with income of $100,000 or more: 12.6%; Poverty rate: 19.9%
Educational Attainment: High school diploma or higher: 80.0%; Bachelor's degree or higher: 20.0%; Graduate/professional degree or higher: 10.4%
Housing: Homeownership rate: 96.0%; Median home value: $124,500; Median year structure built: 1964; Homeowner vacancy rate: 0.0%; Median selected monthly owner costs: $1,786 with a mortgage, $504 without a mortgage; Median gross rent: n/a per month; Rental vacancy rate: 57.1%
Health Insurance: 75.3% have insurance; 60.0% have private insurance; 28.8% have public insurance; 24.7% do not have insurance; 39.2% of children under 18 do not have insurance
Transportation: Commute: 92.8% car, 0.0% public transportation, 3.4% walk, 3.8% work from home; Mean travel time to work: 36.6 minutes

COXSACKIE (town). Covers a land area of 36.865 square miles and a water area of 1.548 square miles. Located at 42.35° N. Lat; 73.86° W. Long. Elevation is 141 feet.
History: Franklin air-cooled automobile engine invented here. Settled by the Dutch before 1700; incorporated 1867.
Population: 8,736; Growth (since 2000): -1.7%; Density: 237.0 persons per square mile; Race: 79.8% White, 18.1% Black/African American, 0.5% Asian, 0.0% American Indian/Alaska Native, 0.0% Native Hawaiian/Other Pacific Islander, 0.7% Two or more races, 12.8% Hispanic of any race; Average household size: 2.67; Median age: 37.1; Age under 18: 17.2%; Age 65 and over: 12.1%; Males per 100 females: 184.3; Marriage status: 48.9% never married, 38.1% now married, 2.5% separated, 5.6% widowed, 7.4% divorced; Foreign born: 5.2%; Speak English only: 87.3%; With disability: 12.7%; Veterans: 7.4%; Ancestry: 16.0% American, 14.2% German, 13.9% Irish, 9.8% Italian, 7.0% English
Employment: 15.0% management, business, and financial, 3.1% computer, engineering, and science, 10.4% education, legal, community service, arts, and media, 6.9% healthcare practitioners, 17.3% service, 20.0% sales and office, 9.5% natural resources, construction, and maintenance, 17.8% production, transportation, and material moving
Income: Per capita: $21,659; Median household: $64,250; Average household: $77,165; Households with income of $100,000 or more: 26.3%; Poverty rate: 10.9%
Educational Attainment: High school diploma or higher: 74.5%; Bachelor's degree or higher: 16.1%; Graduate/professional degree or higher: 6.4%
School District(s)
Coxsackie-Athens Central SD (KG-12)
    2014-15 Enrollment: 1,409 . . . . (518) 731-1710
Housing: Homeownership rate: 73.0%; Median home value: $178,600; Median year structure built: 1973; Homeowner vacancy rate: 2.5%; Median

selected monthly owner costs: $1,681 with a mortgage, $635 without a mortgage; Median gross rent: $740 per month; Rental vacancy rate: 9.7%
Health Insurance: 95.0% have insurance; 74.5% have private insurance; 33.4% have public insurance; 5.0% do not have insurance; 1.6% of children under 18 do not have insurance
Transportation: Commute: 93.0% car, 0.6% public transportation, 0.4% walk, 3.7% work from home; Mean travel time to work: 30.7 minutes
Additional Information Contacts
Town of Coxsackie . . . . (518) 731-2727
  http://www.coxsackie.org

COXSACKIE (village). Covers a land area of 2.172 square miles and a water area of 0.423 square miles. Located at 42.36° N. Lat; 73.81° W. Long. Elevation is 141 feet.
Population: 2,753; Growth (since 2000): -4.9%; Density: 1,267.7 persons per square mile; Race: 94.9% White, 3.4% Black/African American, 0.6% Asian, 0.0% American Indian/Alaska Native, 0.0% Native Hawaiian/Other Pacific Islander, 1.0% Two or more races, 2.7% Hispanic of any race; Average household size: 2.68; Median age: 40.4; Age under 18: 23.0%; Age 65 and over: 17.6%; Males per 100 females: 89.9; Marriage status: 38.8% never married, 41.9% now married, 0.8% separated, 9.1% widowed, 10.2% divorced; Foreign born: 5.3%; Speak English only: 98.5%; With disability: 16.1%; Veterans: 13.0%; Ancestry: 27.1% American, 22.2% Irish, 16.1% German, 13.7% Italian, 11.8% English
Employment: 15.5% management, business, and financial, 2.7% computer, engineering, and science, 9.3% education, legal, community service, arts, and media, 8.3% healthcare practitioners, 19.1% service, 16.8% sales and office, 9.2% natural resources, construction, and maintenance, 19.1% production, transportation, and material moving
Income: Per capita: $30,840; Median household: $55,625; Average household: $77,167; Households with income of $100,000 or more: 25.7%; Poverty rate: 9.6%
Educational Attainment: High school diploma or higher: 83.1%; Bachelor's degree or higher: 19.9%; Graduate/professional degree or higher: 7.7%
School District(s)
Coxsackie-Athens Central SD (KG-12)
    2014-15 Enrollment: 1,409 . . . . (518) 731-1710
Housing: Homeownership rate: 65.0%; Median home value: $166,000; Median year structure built: Before 1940; Homeowner vacancy rate: 4.0%; Median selected monthly owner costs: $1,802 with a mortgage, $633 without a mortgage; Median gross rent: $716 per month; Rental vacancy rate: 7.2%
Health Insurance: 96.0% have insurance; 73.3% have private insurance; 36.5% have public insurance; 4.0% do not have insurance; 0.0% of children under 18 do not have insurance
Safety: Violent crime rate: 7.4 per 10,000 population; Property crime rate: 33.3 per 10,000 population
Transportation: Commute: 93.2% car, 0.0% public transportation, 0.0% walk, 4.4% work from home; Mean travel time to work: 26.4 minutes

DURHAM (town). Covers a land area of 49.314 square miles and a water area of 0.041 square miles. Located at 42.37° N. Lat; 74.15° W. Long. Elevation is 771 feet.
Population: 2,695; Growth (since 2000): 4.0%; Density: 54.6 persons per square mile; Race: 97.9% White, 1.3% Black/African American, 0.7% Asian, 0.0% American Indian/Alaska Native, 0.0% Native Hawaiian/Other Pacific Islander, 0.0% Two or more races, 0.0% Hispanic of any race; Average household size: 2.51; Median age: 47.3; Age under 18: 17.3%; Age 65 and over: 20.9%; Males per 100 females: 101.9; Marriage status: 25.9% never married, 60.5% now married, 3.4% separated, 7.4% widowed, 6.2% divorced; Foreign born: 8.3%; Speak English only: 93.4%; With disability: 15.0%; Veterans: 11.0%; Ancestry: 25.3% Irish, 20.2% German, 11.7% Italian, 11.6% American, 8.7% English
Employment: 7.6% management, business, and financial, 5.8% computer, engineering, and science, 17.3% education, legal, community service, arts, and media, 4.7% healthcare practitioners, 19.7% service, 16.9% sales and office, 11.2% natural resources, construction, and maintenance, 16.8% production, transportation, and material moving
Income: Per capita: $27,375; Median household: $42,078; Average household: $63,588; Households with income of $100,000 or more: 17.6%; Poverty rate: 13.7%
Educational Attainment: High school diploma or higher: 89.7%; Bachelor's degree or higher: 22.6%; Graduate/professional degree or higher: 11.5%

School District(s)

Cairo-Durham Central SD (KG-12)

2014-15 Enrollment: 1,222 . . . . (518) 622-8534

Housing: Homeownership rate: 85.9%; Median home value: $176,700; Median year structure built: 1970; Homeowner vacancy rate: 5.5%; Median selected monthly owner costs: $1,442 with a mortgage, $603 without a mortgage; Median gross rent: $736 per month; Rental vacancy rate: 23.4%

Health Insurance: 91.8% have insurance; 70.9% have private insurance; 36.6% have public insurance; 8.2% do not have insurance; 7.7% of children under 18 do not have insurance

Safety: Violent crime rate: 0.0 per 10,000 population; Property crime rate: 33.7 per 10,000 population

Transportation: Commute: 90.6% car, 0.6% public transportation, 1.7% walk, 5.1% work from home; Mean travel time to work: 34.8 minutes

EARLTON (unincorporated postal area)

ZCTA: 12058

Covers a land area of 19.232 square miles and a water area of 0.306 square miles. Located at 42.35° N. Lat; 73.92° W. Long. Elevation is 417 feet.

Population: 1,956; Growth (since 2000): 39.7%; Density: 101.7 persons per square mile; Race: 93.3% White, 4.3% Black/African American, 0.4% Asian, 0.0% American Indian/Alaska Native, 0.0% Native Hawaiian/Other Pacific Islander, 1.9% Two or more races, 1.3% Hispanic of any race; Average household size: 2.72; Median age: 38.8; Age under 18: 23.6%; Age 65 and over: 9.9%; Males per 100 females: 106.7; Marriage status: 21.7% never married, 63.7% now married, 2.1% separated, 4.7% widowed, 9.9% divorced; Foreign born: 0.4%; Speak English only: 96.8%; With disability: 5.3%; Veterans: 10.3%; Ancestry: 18.9% Irish, 17.9% American, 14.2% German, 12.7% Italian, 6.9% Dutch

Employment: 12.9% management, business, and financial, 2.5% computer, engineering, and science, 6.9% education, legal, community service, arts, and media, 3.5% healthcare practitioners, 22.0% service, 19.1% sales and office, 13.5% natural resources, construction, and maintenance, 19.5% production, transportation, and material moving

Income: Per capita: $28,027; Median household: $65,000; Average household: $72,412; Households with income of $100,000 or more: 34.8%; Poverty rate: 9.5%

Educational Attainment: High school diploma or higher: 86.9%; Bachelor's degree or higher: 15.0%; Graduate/professional degree or higher: 6.8%

Housing: Homeownership rate: 80.1%; Median home value: $193,800; Median year structure built: 1983; Homeowner vacancy rate: 3.2%; Median selected monthly owner costs: $1,596 with a mortgage, $733 without a mortgage; Median gross rent: $885 per month; Rental vacancy rate: 0.0%

Health Insurance: 92.7% have insurance; 76.0% have private insurance; 24.1% have public insurance; 7.3% do not have insurance; 3.3% of children under 18 do not have insurance

Transportation: Commute: 94.8% car, 0.0% public transportation, 0.0% walk, 1.1% work from home; Mean travel time to work: 34.0 minutes

EAST DURHAM (unincorporated postal area)

ZCTA: 12423

Covers a land area of 12.716 square miles and a water area of 0 square miles. Located at 42.38° N. Lat; 74.11° W. Long. Elevation is 535 feet.

Population: 1,028; Growth (since 2000): -1.2%; Density: 80.8 persons per square mile; Race: 98.1% White, 0.0% Black/African American, 1.9% Asian, 0.0% American Indian/Alaska Native, 0.0% Native Hawaiian/Other Pacific Islander, 0.0% Two or more races, 0.0% Hispanic of any race; Average household size: 2.21; Median age: 44.5; Age under 18: 22.0%; Age 65 and over: 21.7%; Males per 100 females: 106.6; Marriage status: 24.0% never married, 53.6% now married, 6.9% separated, 11.7% widowed, 10.7% divorced; Foreign born: 10.6%; Speak English only: 95.8%; With disability: 11.2%; Veterans: 4.5%; Ancestry: 32.9% Irish, 24.3% German, 14.7% Italian, 13.7% American, 4.8% Syrian

Employment: 10.0% management, business, and financial, 9.0% computer, engineering, and science, 21.8% education, legal, community service, arts, and media, 2.8% healthcare practitioners, 22.5% service, 12.7% sales and office, 11.3% natural resources, construction, and maintenance, 10.0% production, transportation, and material moving

Income: Per capita: $29,156; Median household: $40,750; Average household: $62,718; Households with income of $100,000 or more: 20.5%; Poverty rate: 13.9%

Educational Attainment: High school diploma or higher: 92.3%; Bachelor's degree or higher: 23.0%; Graduate/professional degree or higher: 12.9%

Housing: Homeownership rate: 81.5%; Median home value: $157,700; Median year structure built: 1972; Homeowner vacancy rate: 8.4%; Median selected monthly owner costs: $1,116 with a mortgage, $610 without a mortgage; Median gross rent: $810 per month; Rental vacancy rate: 30.6%

Health Insurance: 95.1% have insurance; 67.0% have private insurance; 40.4% have public insurance; 4.9% do not have insurance; 3.1% of children under 18 do not have insurance

Transportation: Commute: 94.8% car, 0.0% public transportation, 0.0% walk, 0.0% work from home; Mean travel time to work: 34.0 minutes

EAST JEWETT (unincorporated postal area)

ZCTA: 12424

Covers a land area of 17.771 square miles and a water area of 0.115 square miles. Located at 42.25° N. Lat; 74.12° W. Long. Elevation is 1,965 feet.

Population: 280; Growth (since 2000): -7.6%; Density: 15.8 persons per square mile; Race: 100.0% White, 0.0% Black/African American, 0.0% Asian, 0.0% American Indian/Alaska Native, 0.0% Native Hawaiian/Other Pacific Islander, 0.0% Two or more races, 0.0% Hispanic of any race; Average household size: 2.01; Median age: 60.6; Age under 18: 6.4%; Age 65 and over: 40.4%; Males per 100 females: 111.9; Marriage status: 29.4% never married, 42.7% now married, 1.1% separated, 17.2% widowed, 10.7% divorced; Foreign born: 1.8%; Speak English only: 97.7%; With disability: 20.0%; Veterans: 14.5%; Ancestry: 19.3% Irish, 16.4% German, 11.8% English, 9.3% American, 7.5% Italian

Employment: 0.0% management, business, and financial, 11.8% computer, engineering, and science, 23.5% education, legal, community service, arts, and media, 20.2% healthcare practitioners, 17.6% service, 10.1% sales and office, 13.4% natural resources, construction, and maintenance, 3.4% production, transportation, and material moving

Income: Per capita: $33,998; Median household: $38,750; Average household: $55,658; Households with income of $100,000 or more: 21.6%; Poverty rate: 11.8%

Educational Attainment: High school diploma or higher: 95.3%; Bachelor's degree or higher: 37.4%; Graduate/professional degree or higher: 9.8%

Housing: Homeownership rate: 77.0%; Median home value: $200,700; Median year structure built: 1983; Homeowner vacancy rate: 0.0%; Median selected monthly owner costs: $758 with a mortgage, $540 without a mortgage; Median gross rent: $917 per month; Rental vacancy rate: 0.0%

Health Insurance: 91.4% have insurance; 53.6% have private insurance; 54.3% have public insurance; 8.6% do not have insurance; 0.0% of children under 18 do not have insurance

Transportation: Commute: 84.9% car, 0.0% public transportation, 0.0% walk, 3.4% work from home; Mean travel time to work: 37.2 minutes

ELKA PARK (unincorporated postal area)

ZCTA: 12427

Covers a land area of 41.000 square miles and a water area of 0.037 square miles. Located at 42.13° N. Lat; 74.14° W. Long. Elevation is 2,178 feet.

Population: 653; Growth (since 2000): 71.4%; Density: 15.9 persons per square mile; Race: 98.2% White, 0.0% Black/African American, 0.9% Asian, 0.0% American Indian/Alaska Native, 0.0% Native Hawaiian/Other Pacific Islander, 0.0% Two or more races, 0.9% Hispanic of any race; Average household size: 2.63; Median age: 31.0; Age under 18: 30.6%; Age 65 and over: 21.9%; Males per 100 females: 82.9; Marriage status: 41.3% never married, 49.7% now married, 0.0% separated, 7.0% widowed, 2.0% divorced; Foreign born: 9.6%; Speak English only: 86.4%; With disability: 9.0%; Veterans: 8.6%; Ancestry: 38.3% American, 20.1% Eastern European, 16.1% Irish, 14.4% German, 10.3% Italian

Employment: 40.2% management, business, and financial, 13.8% computer, engineering, and science, 13.8% education, legal, community service, arts, and media, 0.0% healthcare practitioners, 0.0% service,

0.0% sales and office, 4.2% natural resources, construction, and maintenance, 28.0% production, transportation, and material moving
Income: Per capita: $23,013; Median household: $89,044; Average household: $82,492; Households with income of $100,000 or more: 40.9%; Poverty rate: 23.3%
Educational Attainment: High school diploma or higher: 95.9%; Bachelor's degree or higher: 38.9%; Graduate/professional degree or higher: 9.2%
Housing: Homeownership rate: 92.4%; Median home value: $246,400; Median year structure built: 1976; Homeowner vacancy rate: 0.0%; Median selected monthly owner costs: n/a with a mortgage, n/a without a mortgage; Median gross rent: n/a per month; Rental vacancy rate: 0.0%
Health Insurance: 77.9% have insurance; 46.4% have private insurance; 37.7% have public insurance; 22.1% do not have insurance; 36.0% of children under 18 do not have insurance
Transportation: Commute: 60.3% car, 2.8% public transportation, 32.0% walk, 4.9% work from home; Mean travel time to work: 20.9 minutes

FREEHOLD (unincorporated postal area)
ZCTA: 12431
Covers a land area of 15.466 square miles and a water area of 0.027 square miles. Located at 42.36° N. Lat; 74.02° W. Long. Elevation is 423 feet.
Population: 1,416; Growth (since 2000): -3.2%; Density: 91.6 persons per square mile; Race: 100.0% White, 0.0% Black/African American, 0.0% Asian, 0.0% American Indian/Alaska Native, 0.0% Native Hawaiian/Other Pacific Islander, 0.0% Two or more races, 1.9% Hispanic of any race; Average household size: 2.52; Median age: 43.5; Age under 18: 20.7%; Age 65 and over: 15.0%; Males per 100 females: 105.5; Marriage status: 28.3% never married, 60.5% now married, 1.2% separated, 4.9% widowed, 6.3% divorced; Foreign born: 6.6%; Speak English only: 94.3%; With disability: 10.6%; Veterans: 8.3%; Ancestry: 36.5% American, 22.1% German, 22.0% Italian, 14.3% Irish, 8.0% Dutch
Employment: 15.1% management, business, and financial, 1.9% computer, engineering, and science, 17.7% education, legal, community service, arts, and media, 3.6% healthcare practitioners, 25.3% service, 18.1% sales and office, 11.5% natural resources, construction, and maintenance, 6.6% production, transportation, and material moving
Income: Per capita: $27,421; Median household: $39,907; Average household: $66,446; Households with income of $100,000 or more: 19.1%; Poverty rate: 18.0%
Educational Attainment: High school diploma or higher: 96.4%; Bachelor's degree or higher: 21.9%; Graduate/professional degree or higher: 12.8%
Housing: Homeownership rate: 65.2%; Median home value: $243,600; Median year structure built: 1980; Homeowner vacancy rate: 0.0%; Median selected monthly owner costs: $1,543 with a mortgage, $610 without a mortgage; Median gross rent: $1,113 per month; Rental vacancy rate: 0.0%
Health Insurance: 92.4% have insurance; 74.0% have private insurance; 32.6% have public insurance; 7.6% do not have insurance; 0.0% of children under 18 do not have insurance
Transportation: Commute: 91.8% car, 1.1% public transportation, 0.0% walk, 2.5% work from home; Mean travel time to work: 26.7 minutes

GREENVILLE (CDP). Covers a land area of 3.432 square miles and a water area of 0.020 square miles. Located at 42.41° N. Lat; 74.02° W. Long. Elevation is 709 feet.
Population: 505; Growth (since 2000): 2.4%; Density: 147.2 persons per square mile; Race: 98.2% White, 0.0% Black/African American, 1.8% Asian, 0.0% American Indian/Alaska Native, 0.0% Native Hawaiian/Other Pacific Islander, 0.0% Two or more races, 0.0% Hispanic of any race; Average household size: 2.10; Median age: 53.2; Age under 18: 11.7%; Age 65 and over: 30.1%; Males per 100 females: 89.5; Marriage status: 23.7% never married, 47.6% now married, 3.7% separated, 11.2% widowed, 17.5% divorced; Foreign born: 6.3%; Speak English only: 96.5%; With disability: 12.3%; Veterans: 16.8%; Ancestry: 35.0% Irish, 16.0% American, 15.8% German, 11.5% English, 11.3% Polish
Employment: 9.2% management, business, and financial, 0.0% computer, engineering, and science, 13.4% education, legal, community service, arts, and media, 3.8% healthcare practitioners, 15.5% service, 29.8% sales and

office, 9.2% natural resources, construction, and maintenance, 18.9% production, transportation, and material moving
Income: Per capita: $27,585; Median household: $45,333; Average household: $54,901; Households with income of $100,000 or more: 17.1%; Poverty rate: 10.5%
Educational Attainment: High school diploma or higher: 79.1%; Bachelor's degree or higher: 11.2%; Graduate/professional degree or higher: 6.6%

School District(s)
Greenville Central SD (KG-12)
   2014-15 Enrollment: 1,186 . . . . (518) 966-5070
Housing: Homeownership rate: 77.1%; Median home value: $157,900; Median year structure built: 1964; Homeowner vacancy rate: 0.0%; Median selected monthly owner costs: $1,735 with a mortgage, $579 without a mortgage; Median gross rent: $716 per month; Rental vacancy rate: 0.0%
Health Insurance: 94.1% have insurance; 77.4% have private insurance; 41.0% have public insurance; 5.9% do not have insurance; 0.0% of children under 18 do not have insurance
Transportation: Commute: 96.1% car, 0.0% public transportation, 3.9% walk, 0.0% work from home; Mean travel time to work: 25.4 minutes

GREENVILLE (town). Covers a land area of 38.788 square miles and a water area of 0.296 square miles. Located at 42.40° N. Lat; 74.01° W. Long. Elevation is 709 feet.
Population: 3,656; Growth (since 2000): 10.3%; Density: 94.3 persons per square mile; Race: 98.4% White, 0.4% Black/African American, 0.2% Asian, 0.0% American Indian/Alaska Native, 0.0% Native Hawaiian/Other Pacific Islander, 0.0% Two or more races, 1.3% Hispanic of any race; Average household size: 2.46; Median age: 47.9; Age under 18: 18.2%; Age 65 and over: 20.8%; Males per 100 females: 97.0; Marriage status: 29.0% never married, 54.6% now married, 1.2% separated, 6.9% widowed, 9.5% divorced; Foreign born: 6.6%; Speak English only: 94.4%; With disability: 15.5%; Veterans: 9.7%; Ancestry: 25.4% American, 20.5% German, 17.5% Irish, 16.1% Italian, 11.5% English
Employment: 6.6% management, business, and financial, 4.7% computer, engineering, and science, 12.3% education, legal, community service, arts, and media, 7.6% healthcare practitioners, 18.5% service, 24.6% sales and office, 12.8% natural resources, construction, and maintenance, 12.8% production, transportation, and material moving
Income: Per capita: $28,692; Median household: $50,216; Average household: $68,963; Households with income of $100,000 or more: 22.4%; Poverty rate: 11.7%
Educational Attainment: High school diploma or higher: 93.5%; Bachelor's degree or higher: 24.8%; Graduate/professional degree or higher: 11.8%

School District(s)
Greenville Central SD (KG-12)
   2014-15 Enrollment: 1,186 . . . . (518) 966-5070
Housing: Homeownership rate: 80.0%; Median home value: $163,700; Median year structure built: 1977; Homeowner vacancy rate: 0.0%; Median selected monthly owner costs: $1,648 with a mortgage, $619 without a mortgage; Median gross rent: $964 per month; Rental vacancy rate: 0.0%
Health Insurance: 95.9% have insurance; 79.5% have private insurance; 34.6% have public insurance; 4.1% do not have insurance; 0.0% of children under 18 do not have insurance
Transportation: Commute: 90.8% car, 1.1% public transportation, 1.7% walk, 4.4% work from home; Mean travel time to work: 31.5 minutes

HAINES FALLS (unincorporated postal area)
ZCTA: 12436
Covers a land area of 15.353 square miles and a water area of 0.138 square miles. Located at 42.20° N. Lat; 74.08° W. Long. Elevation is 1,903 feet.
Population: 348; Growth (since 2000): n/a; Density: 22.7 persons per square mile; Race: 100.0% White, 0.0% Black/African American, 0.0% Asian, 0.0% American Indian/Alaska Native, 0.0% Native Hawaiian/Other Pacific Islander, 0.0% Two or more races, 0.0% Hispanic of any race; Average household size: 1.96; Median age: 59.5; Age under 18: 6.3%; Age 65 and over: 22.1%; Males per 100 females: 99.5; Marriage status: 25.5% never married, 65.3% now married, 0.0% separated, 5.8% widowed, 3.4% divorced; Foreign born: 0.0%; Speak English only: 93.8%; With disability: 9.5%; Veterans: 19.3%; Ancestry: 52.6% Irish, 30.2% Polish, 27.9% Italian, 20.4% German, 6.0% French
Employment: 11.2% management, business, and financial, 0.0% computer, engineering, and science, 3.4% education, legal, community

service, arts, and media, 0.0% healthcare practitioners, 13.8% service, 39.6% sales and office, 32.1% natural resources, construction, and maintenance, 0.0% production, transportation, and material moving
Income: Per capita: $37,077; Median household: n/a; Average household: $71,579; Households with income of $100,000 or more: 46.1%; Poverty rate: 3.2%
Educational Attainment: High school diploma or higher: 97.9%; Bachelor's degree or higher: 13.1%; Graduate/professional degree or higher: 3.9%
Housing: Homeownership rate: 95.5%; Median home value: $190,400; Median year structure built: 1947; Homeowner vacancy rate: 0.0%; Median selected monthly owner costs: n/a with a mortgage, n/a without a mortgage; Median gross rent: n/a per month; Rental vacancy rate: 0.0%
Health Insurance: 100.0% have insurance; 81.0% have private insurance; 32.8% have public insurance; 0.0% do not have insurance; 0.0% of children under 18 do not have insurance
Transportation: Commute: 75.0% car, 7.5% public transportation, 0.0% walk, 17.5% work from home; Mean travel time to work: 51.0 minutes

HALCOTT (town).
Covers a land area of 23.041 square miles and a water area of 0 square miles. Located at 42.22° N. Lat; 74.48° W. Long.
Population: 266; Growth (since 2000): 37.8%; Density: 11.5 persons per square mile; Race: 85.7% White, 0.0% Black/African American, 0.0% Asian, 0.4% American Indian/Alaska Native, 0.0% Native Hawaiian/Other Pacific Islander, 13.9% Two or more races, 6.8% Hispanic of any race; Average household size: 2.24; Median age: 54.3; Age under 18: 18.4%; Age 65 and over: 23.7%; Males per 100 females: 100.0; Marriage status: 14.4% never married, 73.4% now married, 2.2% separated, 4.4% widowed, 7.9% divorced; Foreign born: 7.1%; Speak English only: 87.9%; With disability: 12.4%; Veterans: 9.7%; Ancestry: 16.5% Irish, 14.3% German, 13.5% Italian, 11.7% English, 6.0% Russian
Employment: 21.4% management, business, and financial, 3.9% computer, engineering, and science, 4.9% education, legal, community service, arts, and media, 4.9% healthcare practitioners, 34.0% service, 17.5% sales and office, 9.7% natural resources, construction, and maintenance, 3.9% production, transportation, and material moving
Income: Per capita: $30,564; Median household: $68,393; Average household: $66,287; Households with income of $100,000 or more: 14.3%; Poverty rate: 6.8%
Educational Attainment: High school diploma or higher: 92.5%; Bachelor's degree or higher: 21.6%; Graduate/professional degree or higher: 11.7%
Housing: Homeownership rate: 84.0%; Median home value: $162,500; Median year structure built: 1979; Homeowner vacancy rate: 0.0%; Median selected monthly owner costs: $1,071 with a mortgage, $410 without a mortgage; Median gross rent: $907 per month; Rental vacancy rate: 0.0%
Health Insurance: 94.4% have insurance; 77.1% have private insurance; 34.2% have public insurance; 5.6% do not have insurance; 0.0% of children under 18 do not have insurance
Transportation: Commute: 86.6% car, 2.1% public transportation, 0.0% walk, 11.3% work from home; Mean travel time to work: 50.8 minutes
Additional Information Contacts
Town of Halcott . . . . (845) 901-2625
  http://halcottcenter.wordpress.com

HANNACROIX (unincorporated postal area)
ZCTA: 12087
Covers a land area of 19.689 square miles and a water area of 0.255 square miles. Located at 42.43° N. Lat; 73.89° W. Long. Elevation is 190 feet.
Population: 1,019; Growth (since 2000): 102.2%; Density: 51.8 persons per square mile; Race: 98.3% White, 1.7% Black/African American, 0.0% Asian, 0.0% American Indian/Alaska Native, 0.0% Native Hawaiian/Other Pacific Islander, 0.0% Two or more races, 0.0% Hispanic of any race; Average household size: 2.58; Median age: 37.7; Age under 18: 16.3%; Age 65 and over: 17.6%; Males per 100 females: 105.6; Marriage status: 20.2% never married, 63.5% now married, 3.0% separated, 3.7% widowed, 12.5% divorced; Foreign born: 0.0%; Speak English only: 100.0%; With disability: 16.1%; Veterans: 12.8%; Ancestry: 33.8% German, 28.9% Irish, 10.9% Polish, 9.6% English, 7.1% American
Employment: 14.9% management, business, and financial, 6.2% computer, engineering, and science, 5.6% education, legal, community service, arts, and media, 1.4% healthcare practitioners, 12.0% service,

24.3% sales and office, 8.2% natural resources, construction, and maintenance, 27.5% production, transportation, and material moving
Income: Per capita: $26,234; Median household: $69,531; Average household: $64,559; Households with income of $100,000 or more: 8.1%; Poverty rate: 4.6%
Educational Attainment: High school diploma or higher: 95.4%; Bachelor's degree or higher: 9.9%; Graduate/professional degree or higher: 3.1%
Housing: Homeownership rate: 91.9%; Median home value: $149,600; Median year structure built: 1965; Homeowner vacancy rate: 0.0%; Median selected monthly owner costs: $1,372 with a mortgage, $527 without a mortgage; Median gross rent: n/a per month; Rental vacancy rate: 0.0%
Health Insurance: 94.1% have insurance; 86.4% have private insurance; 24.3% have public insurance; 5.9% do not have insurance; 0.0% of children under 18 do not have insurance
Transportation: Commute: 93.0% car, 3.2% public transportation, 2.6% walk, 1.2% work from home; Mean travel time to work: 33.6 minutes

HENSONVILLE (unincorporated postal area)
ZCTA: 12439
Covers a land area of 7.832 square miles and a water area of 0.023 square miles. Located at 42.28° N. Lat; 74.21° W. Long. Elevation is 1,637 feet.
Population: 345; Growth (since 2000): 222.4%; Density: 44.0 persons per square mile; Race: 97.7% White, 0.0% Black/African American, 0.0% Asian, 0.0% American Indian/Alaska Native, 0.0% Native Hawaiian/Other Pacific Islander, 0.0% Two or more races, 2.3% Hispanic of any race; Average household size: 2.18; Median age: 64.5; Age under 18: 5.5%; Age 65 and over: 49.0%; Males per 100 females: 117.9; Marriage status: 27.1% never married, 54.7% now married, 1.2% separated, 11.6% widowed, 6.7% divorced; Foreign born: 15.1%; Speak English only: 82.9%; With disability: 16.5%; Veterans: 5.8%; Ancestry: 40.3% Irish, 13.3% Italian, 12.5% Greek, 12.2% German, 9.6% American
Employment: 13.2% management, business, and financial, 2.9% computer, engineering, and science, 0.0% education, legal, community service, arts, and media, 0.0% healthcare practitioners, 64.0% service, 13.2% sales and office, 6.6% natural resources, construction, and maintenance, 0.0% production, transportation, and material moving
Income: Per capita: $25,311; Median household: $37,188; Average household: $48,320; Households with income of $100,000 or more: 12.6%; Poverty rate: 5.5%
Educational Attainment: High school diploma or higher: 86.9%; Bachelor's degree or higher: 8.4%; Graduate/professional degree or higher: 1.2%
Housing: Homeownership rate: 85.4%; Median home value: $180,500; Median year structure built: 1980; Homeowner vacancy rate: 6.9%; Median selected monthly owner costs: $1,037 with a mortgage, $466 without a mortgage; Median gross rent: $818 per month; Rental vacancy rate: 36.1%
Health Insurance: 80.9% have insurance; 62.9% have private insurance; 57.7% have public insurance; 19.1% do not have insurance; 0.0% of children under 18 do not have insurance
Transportation: Commute: 100.0% car, 0.0% public transportation, 0.0% walk, 0.0% work from home; Mean travel time to work: 23.9 minutes

HUNTER (town).
Covers a land area of 90.419 square miles and a water area of 0.322 square miles. Located at 42.17° N. Lat; 74.15° W. Long. Elevation is 1,588 feet.
Population: 2,678; Growth (since 2000): -1.6%; Density: 29.6 persons per square mile; Race: 91.9% White, 0.5% Black/African American, 0.4% Asian, 0.3% American Indian/Alaska Native, 0.0% Native Hawaiian/Other Pacific Islander, 4.1% Two or more races, 6.5% Hispanic of any race; Average household size: 2.25; Median age: 54.1; Age under 18: 18.8%; Age 65 and over: 27.6%; Males per 100 females: 102.4; Marriage status: 32.4% never married, 45.8% now married, 0.9% separated, 10.1% widowed, 11.7% divorced; Foreign born: 11.3%; Speak English only: 87.1%; With disability: 8.0%; Veterans: 9.2%; Ancestry: 23.7% Irish, 18.8% German, 17.0% American, 16.5% Italian, 7.7% Polish
Employment: 16.3% management, business, and financial, 6.1% computer, engineering, and science, 13.1% education, legal, community service, arts, and media, 2.6% healthcare practitioners, 16.1% service,

23.8% sales and office, 12.5% natural resources, construction, and maintenance, 9.4% production, transportation, and material moving
Income: Per capita: $27,522; Median household: $48,547; Average household: $63,324; Households with income of $100,000 or more: 22.6%; Poverty rate: 19.4%
Educational Attainment: High school diploma or higher: 93.8%; Bachelor's degree or higher: 33.3%; Graduate/professional degree or higher: 10.4%

School District(s)
Hunter-Tannersville Central SD (PK-12)
   2014-15 Enrollment: 354 . . . . (518) 589-5400
Housing: Homeownership rate: 76.3%; Median home value: $224,600; Median year structure built: 1970; Homeowner vacancy rate: 1.7%; Median selected monthly owner costs: $1,527 with a mortgage, $572 without a mortgage; Median gross rent: $750 per month; Rental vacancy rate: 19.8%
Health Insurance: 91.2% have insurance; 59.3% have private insurance; 46.2% have public insurance; 8.8% do not have insurance; 18.8% of children under 18 do not have insurance
Transportation: Commute: 73.0% car, 2.2% public transportation, 10.8% walk, 14.1% work from home; Mean travel time to work: 22.7 minutes

HUNTER (village).
Covers a land area of 1.735 square miles and a water area of 0.032 square miles. Located at 42.21° N. Lat; 74.22° W. Long. Elevation is 1,588 feet.
Population: 320; Growth (since 2000): -34.7%; Density: 184.4 persons per square mile; Race: 97.5% White, 1.3% Black/African American, 0.0% Asian, 0.0% American Indian/Alaska Native, 0.0% Native Hawaiian/Other Pacific Islander, 1.3% Two or more races, 0.0% Hispanic of any race; Average household size: 1.83; Median age: 57.5; Age under 18: 10.3%; Age 65 and over: 28.8%; Males per 100 females: 111.8; Marriage status: 39.9% never married, 20.9% now married, 3.3% separated, 28.9% widowed, 10.3% divorced; Foreign born: 14.1%; Speak English only: 83.1%; With disability: 11.9%; Veterans: 7.3%; Ancestry: 43.4% Italian, 18.4% Irish, 17.5% German, 9.1% Scottish, 6.6% Ukrainian
Employment: 8.9% management, business, and financial, 0.0% computer, engineering, and science, 44.5% education, legal, community service, arts, and media, 1.4% healthcare practitioners, 19.9% service, 23.3% sales and office, 0.0% natural resources, construction, and maintenance, 2.1% production, transportation, and material moving
Income: Per capita: $20,126; Median household: $27,917; Average household: $34,870; Households with income of $100,000 or more: 5.7%; Poverty rate: 43.4%
Educational Attainment: High school diploma or higher: 95.8%; Bachelor's degree or higher: 45.6%; Graduate/professional degree or higher: 9.1%

School District(s)
Hunter-Tannersville Central SD (PK-12)
   2014-15 Enrollment: 354 . . . . (518) 589-5400
Housing: Homeownership rate: 65.7%; Median home value: $159,400; Median year structure built: 1976; Homeowner vacancy rate: 5.0%; Median selected monthly owner costs: $1,554 with a mortgage, $421 without a mortgage; Median gross rent: n/a per month; Rental vacancy rate: 10.4%
Health Insurance: 93.1% have insurance; 58.1% have private insurance; 61.9% have public insurance; 6.9% do not have insurance; 0.0% of children under 18 do not have insurance
Transportation: Commute: 87.0% car, 0.0% public transportation, 4.8% walk, 8.2% work from home; Mean travel time to work: 10.6 minutes

JEFFERSON HEIGHTS (CDP).
Covers a land area of 1.476 square miles and a water area of 0.021 square miles. Located at 42.24° N. Lat; 73.88° W. Long. Elevation is 177 feet.
Population: 1,116; Growth (since 2000): 1.1%; Density: 756.1 persons per square mile; Race: 71.4% White, 4.9% Black/African American, 4.2% Asian, 0.0% American Indian/Alaska Native, 0.0% Native Hawaiian/Other Pacific Islander, 18.4% Two or more races, 9.0% Hispanic of any race; Average household size: 2.55; Median age: 51.4; Age under 18: 15.1%; Age 65 and over: 32.4%; Males per 100 females: 73.7; Marriage status: 34.3% never married, 37.8% now married, 2.9% separated, 14.1% widowed, 13.7% divorced; Foreign born: 7.3%; Speak English only: 83.4%; With disability: 9.7%; Veterans: 9.1%; Ancestry: 22.2% Irish, 14.5% German, 11.8% Polish, 11.3% Italian, 8.5% American
Employment: 8.2% management, business, and financial, 0.0% computer, engineering, and science, 7.7% education, legal, community service, arts, and media, 4.3% healthcare practitioners, 9.8% service, 36.7% sales and

office, 0.8% natural resources, construction, and maintenance, 32.4% production, transportation, and material moving
Income: Per capita: $28,224; Median household: $58,281; Average household: $73,278; Households with income of $100,000 or more: 30.3%; Poverty rate: 5.7%
Educational Attainment: High school diploma or higher: 77.1%; Bachelor's degree or higher: 19.9%; Graduate/professional degree or higher: 6.0%
Housing: Homeownership rate: 57.6%; Median home value: $186,700; Median year structure built: 1956; Homeowner vacancy rate: 0.0%; Median selected monthly owner costs: $1,951 with a mortgage, $605 without a mortgage; Median gross rent: $1,020 per month; Rental vacancy rate: 20.5%
Health Insurance: 100.0% have insurance; 90.2% have private insurance; 32.7% have public insurance; 0.0% do not have insurance; 0.0% of children under 18 do not have insurance
Transportation: Commute: 93.2% car, 0.0% public transportation, 6.8% walk, 0.0% work from home; Mean travel time to work: 16.2 minutes

JEWETT (town).
Covers a land area of 50.323 square miles and a water area of 0.199 square miles. Located at 42.24° N. Lat; 74.23° W. Long. Elevation is 1,801 feet.
Population: 828; Growth (since 2000): -14.6%; Density: 16.5 persons per square mile; Race: 99.0% White, 0.0% Black/African American, 1.0% Asian, 0.0% American Indian/Alaska Native, 0.0% Native Hawaiian/Other Pacific Islander, 0.0% Two or more races, 0.6% Hispanic of any race; Average household size: 1.85; Median age: 60.3; Age under 18: 7.4%; Age 65 and over: 38.5%; Males per 100 females: 107.6; Marriage status: 27.9% never married, 47.1% now married, 1.7% separated, 16.5% widowed, 8.5% divorced; Foreign born: 10.9%; Speak English only: 89.2%; With disability: 12.9%; Veterans: 14.0%; Ancestry: 22.1% Irish, 16.2% German, 11.7% Italian, 10.7% English, 9.5% American
Employment: 17.6% management, business, and financial, 4.3% computer, engineering, and science, 18.2% education, legal, community service, arts, and media, 11.1% healthcare practitioners, 23.5% service, 13.3% sales and office, 10.5% natural resources, construction, and maintenance, 1.5% production, transportation, and material moving
Income: Per capita: $33,730; Median household: $38,950; Average household: $56,138; Households with income of $100,000 or more: 14.4%; Poverty rate: 10.1%
Educational Attainment: High school diploma or higher: 97.2%; Bachelor's degree or higher: 29.6%; Graduate/professional degree or higher: 13.2%
Housing: Homeownership rate: 89.5%; Median home value: $211,700; Median year structure built: 1978; Homeowner vacancy rate: 0.0%; Median selected monthly owner costs: $1,362 with a mortgage, $385 without a mortgage; Median gross rent: $923 per month; Rental vacancy rate: 0.0%
Health Insurance: 89.6% have insurance; 63.2% have private insurance; 45.8% have public insurance; 10.4% do not have insurance; 3.3% of children under 18 do not have insurance
Transportation: Commute: 92.6% car, 0.0% public transportation, 0.3% walk, 2.8% work from home; Mean travel time to work: 32.8 minutes

LANESVILLE (unincorporated postal area)
ZCTA: 12450
   Covers a land area of 9.898 square miles and a water area of 0 square miles. Located at 42.13° N. Lat; 74.24° W. Long. Elevation is 1,280 feet.
Population: 121; Growth (since 2000): -71.9%; Density: 12.2 persons per square mile; Race: 100.0% White, 0.0% Black/African American, 0.0% Asian, 0.0% American Indian/Alaska Native, 0.0% Native Hawaiian/Other Pacific Islander, 0.0% Two or more races, 0.0% Hispanic of any race; Average household size: 3.10; Median age: 58.0; Age under 18: 0.0%; Age 65 and over: 48.8%; Males per 100 females: 105.6; Marriage status: 51.2% never married, 32.2% now married, 0.0% separated, 16.5% widowed, 0.0% divorced; Foreign born: 15.7%; Speak English only: 100.0%; With disability: 0.0%; Veterans: 16.5%; Ancestry: 67.8% German, 16.5% Norwegian, 15.7% English
Employment: n/a management, business, and financial, n/a computer, engineering, and science, n/a education, legal, community service, arts, and media, n/a healthcare practitioners, n/a service, n/a sales and office, n/a natural resources, construction, and maintenance, n/a production, transportation, and material moving
Income: Per capita: $10,310; Median household: n/a; Average household: n/a; Households with income of $100,000 or more: n/a; Poverty rate: 67.8%

Educational Attainment: High school diploma or higher: 100.0%; Bachelor's degree or higher: 66.9%; Graduate/professional degree or higher: n/a

Housing: Homeownership rate: 100.0%; Median home value: n/a; Median year structure built: 1981; Homeowner vacancy rate: 0.0%; Median selected monthly owner costs: $0 with a mortgage, $0 without a mortgage; Median gross rent: n/a per month; Rental vacancy rate: 0.0%

Health Insurance: 100.0% have insurance; 15.7% have private insurance; 100.0% have public insurance; 0.0% do not have insurance; 0.0% of children under 18 do not have insurance

Transportation: Commute: n/a car, n/a public transportation, n/a walk, n/a work from home; Mean travel time to work: 0.0 minutes

---

LEEDS (CDP). Covers a land area of 0.529 square miles and a water area of 0.009 square miles. Located at 42.25° N. Lat; 73.89° W. Long. Elevation is 157 feet.

Population: 480; Growth (since 2000): 30.1%; Density: 907.2 persons per square mile; Race: 93.1% White, 0.0% Black/African American, 0.0% Asian, 0.0% American Indian/Alaska Native, 0.0% Native Hawaiian/Other Pacific Islander, 6.9% Two or more races, 0.0% Hispanic of any race; Average household size: 4.95; Median age: 38.4; Age under 18: 20.8%; Age 65 and over: 0.0%; Males per 100 females: 84.8; Marriage status: 34.6% never married, 65.4% now married, 1.8% separated, 0.0% widowed, 0.0% divorced; Foreign born: 0.0%; Speak English only: 100.0%; With disability: 9.0%; Veterans: 1.8%; Ancestry: 58.1% Italian, 32.1% German, 19.2% Lithuanian, 16.9% Irish, 1.9% American

Employment: 13.2% management, business, and financial, 2.8% computer, engineering, and science, 2.2% education, legal, community service, arts, and media, 0.0% healthcare practitioners, 32.9% service, 9.7% sales and office, 39.2% natural resources, construction, and maintenance, 0.0% production, transportation, and material moving

Income: Per capita: $21,933; Median household: $82,159; Average household: $70,943; Households with income of $100,000 or more: 39.2%; Poverty rate: 20.6%

Educational Attainment: High school diploma or higher: 80.7%; Bachelor's degree or higher: 8.2%; Graduate/professional degree or higher: 2.2%

Housing: Homeownership rate: 68.0%; Median home value: $121,200; Median year structure built: 1942; Homeowner vacancy rate: 0.0%; Median selected monthly owner costs: n/a with a mortgage, n/a without a mortgage; Median gross rent: n/a per month; Rental vacancy rate: 59.7%

Health Insurance: 88.8% have insurance; 34.4% have private insurance; 54.4% have public insurance; 11.3% do not have insurance; 0.0% of children under 18 do not have insurance

Transportation: Commute: 96.6% car, 0.0% public transportation, 0.0% walk, 3.4% work from home; Mean travel time to work: 19.6 minutes

---

LEXINGTON (town). Covers a land area of 79.686 square miles and a water area of 0.037 square miles. Located at 42.21° N. Lat; 74.33° W. Long. Elevation is 1,322 feet.

Population: 968; Growth (since 2000): 16.6%; Density: 12.1 persons per square mile; Race: 100.0% White, 0.0% Black/African American, 0.0% Asian, 0.0% American Indian/Alaska Native, 0.0% Native Hawaiian/Other Pacific Islander, 0.0% Two or more races, 6.5% Hispanic of any race; Average household size: 2.40; Median age: 57.9; Age under 18: 13.1%; Age 65 and over: 28.9%; Males per 100 females: 82.1; Marriage status: 29.6% never married, 51.0% now married, 2.0% separated, 12.9% widowed, 6.5% divorced; Foreign born: 2.1%; Speak English only: 93.3%; With disability: 15.5%; Veterans: 12.6%; Ancestry: 22.5% American, 20.0% German, 17.5% Italian, 13.3% English, 11.7% Irish

Employment: 19.7% management, business, and financial, 0.0% computer, engineering, and science, 8.2% education, legal, community service, arts, and media, 6.7% healthcare practitioners, 9.7% service, 24.5% sales and office, 15.2% natural resources, construction, and maintenance, 16.1% production, transportation, and material moving

Income: Per capita: $23,954; Median household: $42,021; Average household: $52,634; Households with income of $100,000 or more: 15.1%; Poverty rate: 10.4%

Educational Attainment: High school diploma or higher: 85.0%; Bachelor's degree or higher: 17.3%; Graduate/professional degree or higher: 4.5%

Housing: Homeownership rate: 88.4%; Median home value: $216,400; Median year structure built: 1976; Homeowner vacancy rate: 3.0%; Median selected monthly owner costs: $1,611 with a mortgage, $562 without a

mortgage; Median gross rent: $1,027 per month; Rental vacancy rate: 0.0%

Health Insurance: 82.7% have insurance; 61.4% have private insurance; 40.8% have public insurance; 17.3% do not have insurance; 17.3% of children under 18 do not have insurance

Transportation: Commute: 85.5% car, 1.5% public transportation, 2.7% walk, 7.0% work from home; Mean travel time to work: 25.8 minutes

---

MAPLECREST (unincorporated postal area)
ZCTA: 12454

Covers a land area of 11.135 square miles and a water area of 0.044 square miles. Located at 42.29° N. Lat; 74.15° W. Long. Elevation is 1,762 feet.

Population: 271; Growth (since 2000): -50.9%; Density: 24.3 persons per square mile; Race: 90.0% White, 0.0% Black/African American, 0.0% Asian, 0.0% American Indian/Alaska Native, 0.0% Native Hawaiian/Other Pacific Islander, 0.0% Two or more races, 0.0% Hispanic of any race; Average household size: 2.44; Median age: 49.3; Age under 18: 18.5%; Age 65 and over: 17.0%; Males per 100 females: 106.3; Marriage status: 20.7% never married, 57.3% now married, 1.3% separated, 12.5% widowed, 9.5% divorced; Foreign born: 3.7%; Speak English only: 96.6%; With disability: 20.6%; Veterans: 11.8%; Ancestry: 41.0% German, 28.0% Irish, 20.3% English, 17.0% Italian, 10.3% American

Employment: 23.6% management, business, and financial, 5.0% computer, engineering, and science, 11.4% education, legal, community service, arts, and media, 2.1% healthcare practitioners, 14.3% service, 9.3% sales and office, 27.1% natural resources, construction, and maintenance, 7.1% production, transportation, and material moving

Income: Per capita: $29,099; Median household: $73,750; Average household: $64,234; Households with income of $100,000 or more: 13.5%; Poverty rate: 15.1%

Educational Attainment: High school diploma or higher: 86.4%; Bachelor's degree or higher: 31.8%; Graduate/professional degree or higher: 9.6%

Housing: Homeownership rate: 88.3%; Median home value: $227,400; Median year structure built: 1982; Homeowner vacancy rate: 0.0%; Median selected monthly owner costs: $1,516 with a mortgage, $575 without a mortgage; Median gross rent: n/a per month; Rental vacancy rate: 0.0%

Health Insurance: 92.0% have insurance; 74.0% have private insurance; 40.5% have public insurance; 8.0% do not have insurance; 0.0% of children under 18 do not have insurance

Transportation: Commute: 91.3% car, 0.0% public transportation, 0.0% walk, 8.7% work from home; Mean travel time to work: 25.8 minutes

---

NEW BALTIMORE (town). Covers a land area of 41.427 square miles and a water area of 1.601 square miles. Located at 42.42° N. Lat; 73.86° W. Long. Elevation is 82 feet.

Population: 3,299; Growth (since 2000): -3.5%; Density: 79.6 persons per square mile; Race: 95.6% White, 0.9% Black/African American, 0.0% Asian, 0.0% American Indian/Alaska Native, 0.0% Native Hawaiian/Other Pacific Islander, 3.0% Two or more races, 1.3% Hispanic of any race; Average household size: 2.83; Median age: 45.7; Age under 18: 16.4%; Age 65 and over: 18.8%; Males per 100 females: 99.6; Marriage status: 24.4% never married, 62.5% now married, 0.9% separated, 5.9% widowed, 7.2% divorced; Foreign born: 3.3%; Speak English only: 96.6%; With disability: 15.6%; Veterans: 10.0%; Ancestry: 27.8% German, 22.7% Irish, 16.8% American, 9.7% Italian, 9.3% English

Employment: 11.8% management, business, and financial, 5.9% computer, engineering, and science, 11.3% education, legal, community service, arts, and media, 7.9% healthcare practitioners, 17.0% service, 26.3% sales and office, 7.9% natural resources, construction, and maintenance, 11.9% production, transportation, and material moving

Income: Per capita: $33,165; Median household: $71,169; Average household: $87,730; Households with income of $100,000 or more: 26.4%; Poverty rate: 5.6%

Educational Attainment: High school diploma or higher: 91.8%; Bachelor's degree or higher: 24.2%; Graduate/professional degree or higher: 11.0%

Housing: Homeownership rate: 95.9%; Median home value: $195,900; Median year structure built: 1962; Homeowner vacancy rate: 4.3%; Median selected monthly owner costs: $1,639 with a mortgage, $540 without a mortgage; Median gross rent: n/a per month; Rental vacancy rate: 0.0%

Health Insurance: 90.7% have insurance; 77.7% have private insurance; 32.3% have public insurance; 9.3% do not have insurance; 0.0% of children under 18 do not have insurance
Transportation: Commute: 89.3% car, 1.0% public transportation, 0.0% walk, 8.7% work from home; Mean travel time to work: 29.2 minutes

OAK HILL (unincorporated postal area)
ZCTA: 12460

Covers a land area of 2.063 square miles and a water area of 0 square miles. Located at 42.42° N. Lat; 74.15° W. Long. Elevation is 643 feet.
Population: 275; Growth (since 2000): -26.9%; Density: 133.3 persons per square mile; Race: 100.0% White, 0.0% Black/African American, 0.0% Asian, 0.0% American Indian/Alaska Native, 0.0% Native Hawaiian/Other Pacific Islander, 0.0% Two or more races, 0.0% Hispanic of any race; Average household size: 3.31; Median age: 32.5; Age under 18: 30.5%; Age 65 and over: 12.0%; Males per 100 females: 97.9; Marriage status: 29.8% never married, 67.0% now married, 5.2% separated, 0.0% widowed, 3.1% divorced; Foreign born: 2.2%; Speak English only: 100.0%; With disability: 13.8%; Veterans: 11.5%; Ancestry: 46.2% American, 14.9% English, 13.5% German, 10.2% French, 10.2% Irish
Employment: 0.0% management, business, and financial, 7.6% computer, engineering, and science, 30.4% education, legal, community service, arts, and media, 0.0% healthcare practitioners, 33.7% service, 0.0% sales and office, 6.5% natural resources, construction, and maintenance, 21.7% production, transportation, and material moving
Income: Per capita: $18,833; Median household: $52,014; Average household: $62,367; Households with income of $100,000 or more: 21.7%; Poverty rate: 13.5%
Educational Attainment: High school diploma or higher: 87.9%; Bachelor's degree or higher: 28.6%; Graduate/professional degree or higher: 28.6%
Housing: Homeownership rate: 90.4%; Median home value: $185,200; Median year structure built: Before 1940; Homeowner vacancy rate: 15.7%; Median selected monthly owner costs: $1,755 with a mortgage, $567 without a mortgage; Median gross rent: n/a per month; Rental vacancy rate: 0.0%
Health Insurance: 94.5% have insurance; 77.8% have private insurance; 26.5% have public insurance; 5.5% do not have insurance; 0.0% of children under 18 do not have insurance
Transportation: Commute: 92.4% car, 0.0% public transportation, 0.0% walk, 7.6% work from home; Mean travel time to work: 37.9 minutes

PALENVILLE (CDP). Covers a land area of 3.325 square miles and a water area of 0.009 square miles. Located at 42.19° N. Lat; 74.03° W. Long. Elevation is 568 feet.
History: Legendary home of Rip Van Winkle; Sleepy Hollow, where he reputedly slept for 20 years, is nearby.
Population: 760; Growth (since 2000): -32.1%; Density: 228.5 persons per square mile; Race: 95.0% White, 3.2% Black/African American, 0.0% Asian, 0.0% American Indian/Alaska Native, 0.0% Native Hawaiian/Other Pacific Islander, 1.8% Two or more races, 0.0% Hispanic of any race; Average household size: 2.30; Median age: 46.4; Age under 18: 13.4%; Age 65 and over: 10.7%; Males per 100 females: 91.3; Marriage status: 35.3% never married, 56.1% now married, 0.0% separated, 0.0% widowed, 8.5% divorced; Foreign born: 4.2%; Speak English only: 91.8%; With disability: 11.1%; Veterans: 17.0%; Ancestry: 37.5% Italian, 26.3% Irish, 12.0% German, 10.1% Polish, 7.9% Dutch
Employment: 10.8% management, business, and financial, 0.0% computer, engineering, and science, 18.0% education, legal, community service, arts, and media, 9.3% healthcare practitioners, 23.8% service, 19.5% sales and office, 11.8% natural resources, construction, and maintenance, 6.8% production, transportation, and material moving
Income: Per capita: $27,248; Median household: $50,106; Average household: $62,799; Households with income of $100,000 or more: 19.1%; Poverty rate: 6.1%
Educational Attainment: High school diploma or higher: 97.5%; Bachelor's degree or higher: 26.2%; Graduate/professional degree or higher: 11.8%
Housing: Homeownership rate: 72.7%; Median home value: $162,500; Median year structure built: 1944; Homeowner vacancy rate: 0.0%; Median selected monthly owner costs: $1,423 with a mortgage, $772 without a mortgage; Median gross rent: $573 per month; Rental vacancy rate: 0.0%

Health Insurance: 88.3% have insurance; 75.9% have private insurance; 32.5% have public insurance; 11.7% do not have insurance; 0.0% of children under 18 do not have insurance
Transportation: Commute: 100.0% car, 0.0% public transportation, 0.0% walk, 0.0% work from home; Mean travel time to work: 27.2 minutes

PRATTSVILLE (CDP). Covers a land area of 4.038 square miles and a water area of 0 square miles. Located at 42.35° N. Lat; 74.43° W. Long. Elevation is 1,161 feet.
Population: 263; Growth (since 2000): n/a; Density: 65.1 persons per square mile; Race: 100.0% White, 0.0% Black/African American, 0.0% Asian, 0.0% American Indian/Alaska Native, 0.0% Native Hawaiian/Other Pacific Islander, 0.0% Two or more races, 0.0% Hispanic of any race; Average household size: 2.89; Median age: 44.4; Age under 18: 20.9%; Age 65 and over: 26.2%; Males per 100 females: 101.7; Marriage status: 33.3% never married, 49.3% now married, 0.0% separated, 13.7% widowed, 3.7% divorced; Foreign born: 4.9%; Speak English only: 91.7%; With disability: 8.7%; Veterans: 5.8%; Ancestry: 26.6% German, 23.6% American, 21.3% Dutch, 16.3% Italian, 11.4% Irish
Employment: 12.7% management, business, and financial, 0.0% computer, engineering, and science, 13.9% education, legal, community service, arts, and media, 3.8% healthcare practitioners, 20.3% service, 12.7% sales and office, 24.1% natural resources, construction, and maintenance, 12.7% production, transportation, and material moving
Income: Per capita: $17,168; Median household: $42,639; Average household: $45,662; Households with income of $100,000 or more: 12.1%; Poverty rate: 28.9%
Educational Attainment: High school diploma or higher: 71.2%; Bachelor's degree or higher: 8.6%; Graduate/professional degree or higher: 1.8%
Housing: Homeownership rate: 87.9%; Median home value: $131,800; Median year structure built: Before 1940; Homeowner vacancy rate: 4.8%; Median selected monthly owner costs: $1,167 with a mortgage, $317 without a mortgage; Median gross rent: n/a per month; Rental vacancy rate: 0.0%
Health Insurance: 94.3% have insurance; 51.7% have private insurance; 58.6% have public insurance; 5.7% do not have insurance; 0.0% of children under 18 do not have insurance
Transportation: Commute: 73.7% car, 0.0% public transportation, 7.9% walk, 2.6% work from home; Mean travel time to work: 20.8 minutes

PRATTSVILLE (town). Covers a land area of 19.627 square miles and a water area of 0.106 square miles. Located at 42.32° N. Lat; 74.41° W. Long. Elevation is 1,161 feet.
Population: 617; Growth (since 2000): -7.2%; Density: 31.4 persons per square mile; Race: 100.0% White, 0.0% Black/African American, 0.0% Asian, 0.0% American Indian/Alaska Native, 0.0% Native Hawaiian/Other Pacific Islander, 0.0% Two or more races, 0.0% Hispanic of any race; Average household size: 2.34; Median age: 52.8; Age under 18: 13.0%; Age 65 and over: 22.0%; Males per 100 females: 101.7; Marriage status: 24.1% never married, 57.5% now married, 0.5% separated, 11.6% widowed, 6.7% divorced; Foreign born: 8.3%; Speak English only: 90.6%; With disability: 10.4%; Veterans: 9.3%; Ancestry: 27.6% American, 18.8% German, 16.2% Dutch, 10.9% Italian, 9.9% Irish
Employment: 9.7% management, business, and financial, 1.7% computer, engineering, and science, 12.7% education, legal, community service, arts, and media, 3.8% healthcare practitioners, 16.5% service, 24.9% sales and office, 21.5% natural resources, construction, and maintenance, 9.3% production, transportation, and material moving
Income: Per capita: $24,151; Median household: $43,036; Average household: $51,889; Households with income of $100,000 or more: 10.3%; Poverty rate: 22.0%
Educational Attainment: High school diploma or higher: 85.1%; Bachelor's degree or higher: 20.0%; Graduate/professional degree or higher: 8.1%
Housing: Homeownership rate: 88.3%; Median home value: $135,300; Median year structure built: 1975; Homeowner vacancy rate: 1.7%; Median selected monthly owner costs: $1,056 with a mortgage, $402 without a mortgage; Median gross rent: $678 per month; Rental vacancy rate: 0.0%
Health Insurance: 86.5% have insurance; 60.1% have private insurance; 43.1% have public insurance; 13.5% do not have insurance; 0.0% of children under 18 do not have insurance
Transportation: Commute: 88.0% car, 0.0% public transportation, 3.8% walk, 3.0% work from home; Mean travel time to work: 29.2 minutes

PURLING (unincorporated postal area)
ZCTA: 12470

Covers a land area of 9.786 square miles and a water area of 0.039 square miles. Located at 42.30° N. Lat; 74.10° W. Long. Elevation is 482 feet.

Population: 525; Growth (since 2000): -28.0%; Density: 53.7 persons per square mile; Race: 66.1% White, 0.0% Black/African American, 33.9% Asian, 0.0% American Indian/Alaska Native, 0.0% Native Hawaiian/Other Pacific Islander, 0.0% Two or more races, 0.0% Hispanic of any race; Average household size: 2.60; Median age: 44.1; Age under 18: 17.7%; Age 65 and over: 11.4%; Males per 100 females: 92.8; Marriage status: 28.4% never married, 63.0% now married, 0.0% separated, 3.6% widowed, 5.0% divorced; Foreign born: 29.7%; Speak English only: 66.1%; With disability: 21.0%; Veterans: 6.3%; Ancestry: 18.3% American, 13.3% German, 12.0% Irish, 5.9% French, 4.4% Italian

Employment: 18.6% management, business, and financial, 0.0% computer, engineering, and science, 14.6% education, legal, community service, arts, and media, 0.0% healthcare practitioners, 34.1% service, 10.2% sales and office, 3.1% natural resources, construction, and maintenance, 19.5% production, transportation, and material moving

Income: Per capita: $20,945; Median household: $51,731; Average household: $54,173; Households with income of $100,000 or more: 19.3%; Poverty rate: 10.7%

Educational Attainment: High school diploma or higher: 98.6%; Bachelor's degree or higher: 29.9%; Graduate/professional degree or higher: 9.5%

Housing: Homeownership rate: 61.9%; Median home value: $143,400; Median year structure built: 1968; Homeowner vacancy rate: 16.1%; Median selected monthly owner costs: $880 with a mortgage, $812 without a mortgage; Median gross rent: $838 per month; Rental vacancy rate: 0.0%

Health Insurance: 92.6% have insurance; 89.3% have private insurance; 14.7% have public insurance; 7.4% do not have insurance; 0.0% of children under 18 do not have insurance

Transportation: Commute: 100.0% car, 0.0% public transportation, 0.0% walk, 0.0% work from home; Mean travel time to work: 32.2 minutes

ROUND TOP (unincorporated postal area)
ZCTA: 12473

Covers a land area of 15.016 square miles and a water area of 0 square miles. Located at 42.26° N. Lat; 74.04° W. Long. Elevation is 604 feet.

Population: 1,199; Growth (since 2000): 62.9%; Density: 79.8 persons per square mile; Race: 99.5% White, 0.5% Black/African American, 0.0% Asian, 0.0% American Indian/Alaska Native, 0.0% Native Hawaiian/Other Pacific Islander, 0.0% Two or more races, 1.8% Hispanic of any race; Average household size: 3.08; Median age: 35.9; Age under 18: 30.3%; Age 65 and over: 7.2%; Males per 100 females: 97.9; Marriage status: 41.6% never married, 50.9% now married, 0.0% separated, 3.8% widowed, 3.7% divorced; Foreign born: 5.5%; Speak English only: 98.4%; With disability: 7.1%; Veterans: 7.3%; Ancestry: 42.8% German, 25.4% American, 13.8% Irish, 8.1% Italian, 6.2% Russian

Employment: 12.1% management, business, and financial, 0.0% computer, engineering, and science, 39.8% education, legal, community service, arts, and media, 3.4% healthcare practitioners, 17.5% service, 0.6% sales and office, 0.3% natural resources, construction, and maintenance, 26.3% production, transportation, and material moving

Income: Per capita: $33,356; Median household: $73,622; Average household: $101,493; Households with income of $100,000 or more: 28.8%; Poverty rate: 13.0%

Educational Attainment: High school diploma or higher: 98.3%; Bachelor's degree or higher: 35.2%; Graduate/professional degree or higher: 16.2%

Housing: Homeownership rate: 97.3%; Median home value: $194,600; Median year structure built: 1983; Homeowner vacancy rate: 1.6%; Median selected monthly owner costs: $1,262 with a mortgage, $390 without a mortgage; Median gross rent: n/a per month; Rental vacancy rate: 0.0%

Health Insurance: 98.3% have insurance; 88.2% have private insurance; 17.0% have public insurance; 1.7% do not have insurance; 0.0% of children under 18 do not have insurance

Transportation: Commute: 86.3% car, 2.5% public transportation, 6.3% walk, 4.9% work from home; Mean travel time to work: 17.9 minutes

SOUTH CAIRO (unincorporated postal area)
ZCTA: 12482

Covers a land area of 2.211 square miles and a water area of 0 square miles. Located at 42.27° N. Lat; 73.96° W. Long. Elevation is 200 feet.

Population: 722; Growth (since 2000): 59.7%; Density: 326.5 persons per square mile; Race: 100.0% White, 0.0% Black/African American, 0.0% Asian, 0.0% American Indian/Alaska Native, 0.0% Native Hawaiian/Other Pacific Islander, 0.0% Two or more races, 2.4% Hispanic of any race; Average household size: 2.97; Median age: 38.9; Age under 18: 19.5%; Age 65 and over: 20.1%; Males per 100 females: 98.3; Marriage status: 55.1% never married, 27.2% now married, 0.0% separated, 7.9% widowed, 9.8% divorced; Foreign born: 0.0%; Speak English only: 100.0%; With disability: 43.6%; Veterans: 4.8%; Ancestry: 37.4% American, 21.2% German, 18.0% Irish, 14.4% French, 10.2% English

Employment: 13.7% management, business, and financial, 10.7% computer, engineering, and science, 12.5% education, legal, community service, arts, and media, 9.5% healthcare practitioners, 26.8% service, 16.1% sales and office, 4.2% natural resources, construction, and maintenance, 6.5% production, transportation, and material moving

Income: Per capita: $18,920; Median household: $34,222; Average household: $45,122; Households with income of $100,000 or more: 9.5%; Poverty rate: 21.5%

Educational Attainment: High school diploma or higher: 67.1%; Bachelor's degree or higher: 22.1%; Graduate/professional degree or higher: n/a

Housing: Homeownership rate: 56.8%; Median home value: $28,200; Median year structure built: 1980; Homeowner vacancy rate: 18.8%; Median selected monthly owner costs: $1,096 with a mortgage, $750 without a mortgage; Median gross rent: $622 per month; Rental vacancy rate: 0.0%

Health Insurance: 100.0% have insurance; 44.9% have private insurance; 67.2% have public insurance; 0.0% do not have insurance; 0.0% of children under 18 do not have insurance

Transportation: Commute: 100.0% car, 0.0% public transportation, 0.0% walk, 0.0% work from home; Mean travel time to work: 0.0 minutes

SURPRISE (unincorporated postal area)
ZCTA: 12176

Covers a land area of 3.326 square miles and a water area of 0.099 square miles. Located at 42.38° N. Lat; 73.98° W. Long. Elevation is 548 feet.

Population: 426; Growth (since 2000): 143.4%; Density: 128.1 persons per square mile; Race: 92.0% White, 0.0% Black/African American, 0.0% Asian, 0.0% American Indian/Alaska Native, 0.0% Native Hawaiian/Other Pacific Islander, 0.0% Two or more races, 0.0% Hispanic of any race; Average household size: 3.35; Median age: 27.1; Age under 18: 23.2%; Age 65 and over: 13.8%; Males per 100 females: 108.4; Marriage status: 47.3% never married, 45.2% now married, 0.0% separated, 1.9% widowed, 5.6% divorced; Foreign born: 4.7%; Speak English only: 92.7%; With disability: 41.5%; Veterans: 4.0%; Ancestry: 43.9% American, 21.1% German, 17.4% Dutch, 13.8% Austrian, 11.0% English

Employment: 0.0% management, business, and financial, 0.0% computer, engineering, and science, 0.0% education, legal, community service, arts, and media, 12.0% healthcare practitioners, 17.6% service, 43.5% sales and office, 16.7% natural resources, construction, and maintenance, 10.2% production, transportation, and material moving

Income: Per capita: $21,304; Median household: $75,760; Average household: $72,061; Households with income of $100,000 or more: 18.1%; Poverty rate: 14.8%

Educational Attainment: High school diploma or higher: 93.2%; Bachelor's degree or higher: 24.1%; Graduate/professional degree or higher: 8.9%

Housing: Homeownership rate: 100.0%; Median home value: $142,700; Median year structure built: 1972; Homeowner vacancy rate: 0.0%; Median selected monthly owner costs: $1,659 with a mortgage, $700 without a mortgage; Median gross rent: n/a per month; Rental vacancy rate: 0.0%

Health Insurance: 100.0% have insurance; 80.5% have private insurance; 34.0% have public insurance; 0.0% do not have insurance; 0.0% of children under 18 do not have insurance

Transportation: Commute: 96.3% car, 0.0% public transportation, 3.7% walk, 0.0% work from home; Mean travel time to work: 103.8 minutes

TANNERSVILLE (village). Covers a land area of 1.164 square miles and a water area of 0.033 square miles. Located at 42.19° N. Lat; 74.14° W. Long. Elevation is 1,900 feet.
Population: 714; Growth (since 2000): 59.4%; Density: 613.2 persons per square mile; Race: 72.4% White, 1.3% Black/African American, 0.6% Asian, 1.1% American Indian/Alaska Native, 0.0% Native Hawaiian/Other Pacific Islander, 14.7% Two or more races, 23.4% Hispanic of any race; Average household size: 2.80; Median age: 30.8; Age under 18: 31.0%; Age 65 and over: 16.0%; Males per 100 females: 117.3; Marriage status: 38.5% never married, 44.6% now married, 2.1% separated, 7.9% widowed, 9.0% divorced; Foreign born: 1.1%; Speak English only: 89.6%; With disability: 3.8%; Veterans: 5.1%; Ancestry: 26.8% Irish, 20.7% German, 16.8% American, 12.3% Italian, 7.8% Portuguese
Employment: 6.3% management, business, and financial, 0.0% computer, engineering, and science, 5.3% education, legal, community service, arts, and media, 7.2% healthcare practitioners, 18.4% service, 45.3% sales and office, 8.8% natural resources, construction, and maintenance, 8.8% production, transportation, and material moving
Income: Per capita: $19,396; Median household: $48,011; Average household: $52,756; Households with income of $100,000 or more: 6.7%; Poverty rate: 4.6%
Educational Attainment: High school diploma or higher: 87.4%; Bachelor's degree or higher: 23.7%; Graduate/professional degree or higher: 11.1%

School District(s)
Hunter-Tannersville Central SD (PK-12)
    2014-15 Enrollment: 354 . . . . (518) 589-5400
Housing: Homeownership rate: 58.0%; Median home value: $174,300; Median year structure built: 1951; Homeowner vacancy rate: 5.1%; Median selected monthly owner costs: $1,442 with a mortgage, $576 without a mortgage; Median gross rent: $918 per month; Rental vacancy rate: 21.5%
Health Insurance: 90.2% have insurance; 70.3% have private insurance; 36.6% have public insurance; 9.8% do not have insurance; 10.4% of children under 18 do not have insurance
Transportation: Commute: 90.8% car, 0.0% public transportation, 1.6% walk, 7.6% work from home; Mean travel time to work: 15.2 minutes

WEST COXSACKIE (unincorporated postal area)
ZCTA: 12192
    Covers a land area of 17.165 square miles and a water area of 0.043 square miles. Located at 42.41° N. Lat; 73.83° W. Long. Elevation is 131 feet.
Population: 1,845; Growth (since 2000): -18.7%; Density: 107.5 persons per square mile; Race: 92.6% White, 0.8% Black/African American, 0.0% Asian, 0.0% American Indian/Alaska Native, 0.0% Native Hawaiian/Other Pacific Islander, 5.3% Two or more races, 3.6% Hispanic of any race; Average household size: 3.05; Median age: 47.0; Age under 18: 20.0%; Age 65 and over: 21.7%; Males per 100 females: 95.9; Marriage status: 29.6% never married, 57.5% now married, 1.2% separated, 5.7% widowed, 7.2% divorced; Foreign born: 7.5%; Speak English only: 97.6%; With disability: 11.8%; Veterans: 10.6%; Ancestry: 24.8% American, 22.9% German, 22.0% Irish, 8.3% Italian, 7.5% French
Employment: 10.2% management, business, and financial, 3.4% computer, engineering, and science, 12.3% education, legal, community service, arts, and media, 5.1% healthcare practitioners, 20.4% service, 33.1% sales and office, 9.8% natural resources, construction, and maintenance, 5.7% production, transportation, and material moving
Income: Per capita: $29,844; Median household: $63,462; Average household: $85,863; Households with income of $100,000 or more: 27.2%; Poverty rate: 7.8%
Educational Attainment: High school diploma or higher: 92.0%; Bachelor's degree or higher: 21.8%; Graduate/professional degree or higher: 11.2%
Housing: Homeownership rate: 91.1%; Median home value: $178,700; Median year structure built: 1967; Homeowner vacancy rate: 0.0%; Median selected monthly owner costs: $1,596 with a mortgage, $509 without a mortgage; Median gross rent: $643 per month; Rental vacancy rate: 30.8%
Health Insurance: 91.3% have insurance; 70.8% have private insurance; 41.5% have public insurance; 8.7% do not have insurance; 1.9% of children under 18 do not have insurance
Transportation: Commute: 93.1% car, 0.0% public transportation, 0.0% walk, 1.8% work from home; Mean travel time to work: 31.2 minutes

WEST KILL (unincorporated postal area)
ZCTA: 12492
    Covers a land area of 38.463 square miles and a water area of 0 square miles. Located at 42.18° N. Lat; 74.34° W. Long. Elevation is 1,470 feet.
Population: 364; Growth (since 2000): 29.5%; Density: 9.5 persons per square mile; Race: 100.0% White, 0.0% Black/African American, 0.0% Asian, 0.0% American Indian/Alaska Native, 0.0% Native Hawaiian/Other Pacific Islander, 0.0% Two or more races, 15.9% Hispanic of any race; Average household size: 2.23; Median age: 58.8; Age under 18: 14.6%; Age 65 and over: 27.2%; Males per 100 females: 81.9; Marriage status: 21.2% never married, 68.5% now married, 2.6% separated, 3.9% widowed, 6.4% divorced; Foreign born: 1.1%; Speak English only: 98.6%; With disability: 12.1%; Veterans: 11.6%; Ancestry: 28.6% Italian, 24.2% English, 18.7% German, 17.9% Irish, 10.7% American
Employment: 8.2% management, business, and financial, 0.0% computer, engineering, and science, 18.2% education, legal, community service, arts, and media, 9.1% healthcare practitioners, 10.9% service, 11.8% sales and office, 23.6% natural resources, construction, and maintenance, 18.2% production, transportation, and material moving
Income: Per capita: $26,240; Median household: $50,139; Average household: $57,137; Households with income of $100,000 or more: 22.1%; Poverty rate: 14.8%
Educational Attainment: High school diploma or higher: 94.9%; Bachelor's degree or higher: 20.9%; Graduate/professional degree or higher: 6.4%
Housing: Homeownership rate: 91.4%; Median home value: $254,200; Median year structure built: 1971; Homeowner vacancy rate: 0.0%; Median selected monthly owner costs: $2,125 with a mortgage, $710 without a mortgage; Median gross rent: n/a per month; Rental vacancy rate: 0.0%
Health Insurance: 100.0% have insurance; 67.9% have private insurance; 50.8% have public insurance; 0.0% do not have insurance; 0.0% of children under 18 do not have insurance
Transportation: Commute: 78.2% car, 4.5% public transportation, 0.0% walk, 7.3% work from home; Mean travel time to work: 36.5 minutes

WINDHAM (CDP). Covers a land area of 1.877 square miles and a water area of 0 square miles. Located at 42.31° N. Lat; 74.25° W. Long. Elevation is 1,516 feet.
Population: 312; Growth (since 2000): -13.1%; Density: 166.2 persons per square mile; Race: 100.0% White, 0.0% Black/African American, 0.0% Asian, 0.0% American Indian/Alaska Native, 0.0% Native Hawaiian/Other Pacific Islander, 0.0% Two or more races, 0.0% Hispanic of any race; Average household size: 1.74; Median age: 61.8; Age under 18: 2.6%; Age 65 and over: 42.6%; Males per 100 females: 107.3; Marriage status: 19.2% never married, 54.9% now married, 0.0% separated, 9.7% widowed, 16.2% divorced; Foreign born: 6.1%; Speak English only: 93.9%; With disability: 20.5%; Veterans: 19.1%; Ancestry: 36.9% German, 21.5% Italian, 14.7% English, 11.5% American, 9.9% Irish
Employment: 3.5% management, business, and financial, 0.0% computer, engineering, and science, 16.7% education, legal, community service, arts, and media, 7.9% healthcare practitioners, 12.3% service, 21.1% sales and office, 35.1% natural resources, construction, and maintenance, 3.5% production, transportation, and material moving
Income: Per capita: $30,437; Median household: $39,135; Average household: $49,850; Households with income of $100,000 or more: 23.5%; Poverty rate: 22.4%
Educational Attainment: High school diploma or higher: 93.0%; Bachelor's degree or higher: 28.8%; Graduate/professional degree or higher: 17.4%

School District(s)
Windham-Ashland-Jewett Central SD (KG-12)
    2014-15 Enrollment: 316 . . . . (518) 734-3400
Housing: Homeownership rate: 64.2%; Median home value: $222,300; Median year structure built: 1982; Homeowner vacancy rate: 0.0%; Median selected monthly owner costs: $1,850 with a mortgage, $299 without a mortgage; Median gross rent: n/a per month; Rental vacancy rate: 12.3%
Health Insurance: 99.0% have insurance; 66.7% have private insurance; 57.4% have public insurance; 1.0% do not have insurance; 0.0% of children under 18 do not have insurance
Newspapers: Windham Journal (weekly circulation 1,700)
Transportation: Commute: 93.9% car, 0.0% public transportation, 2.6% walk, 3.5% work from home; Mean travel time to work: 18.2 minutes

WINDHAM (town). Covers a land area of 45.200 square miles and a water area of 0.137 square miles. Located at 42.32° N. Lat; 74.22° W. Long. Elevation is 1,516 feet.

Population: 1,592; Growth (since 2000): -4.1%; Density: 35.2 persons per square mile; Race: 97.5% White, 0.0% Black/African American, 0.0% Asian, 0.0% American Indian/Alaska Native, 0.0% Native Hawaiian/Other Pacific Islander, 0.3% Two or more races, 4.2% Hispanic of any race; Average household size: 2.44; Median age: 56.7; Age under 18: 9.8%; Age 65 and over: 36.8%; Males per 100 females: 104.2; Marriage status: 21.5% never married, 60.4% now married, 1.0% separated, 9.5% widowed, 8.6% divorced; Foreign born: 9.9%; Speak English only: 88.0%; With disability: 20.4%; Veterans: 16.3%; Ancestry: 23.9% German, 21.9% Irish, 15.6% Italian, 11.7% English, 11.0% American

Employment: 15.2% management, business, and financial, 1.7% computer, engineering, and science, 8.7% education, legal, community service, arts, and media, 2.3% healthcare practitioners, 25.1% service, 20.2% sales and office, 22.0% natural resources, construction, and maintenance, 4.8% production, transportation, and material moving

Income: Per capita: $28,907; Median household: $50,063; Average household: $60,750; Households with income of $100,000 or more: 17.8%; Poverty rate: 9.9%

Educational Attainment: High school diploma or higher: 87.1%; Bachelor's degree or higher: 17.2%; Graduate/professional degree or higher: 7.3%

School District(s)
Windham-Ashland-Jewett Central SD (KG-12)

   2014-15 Enrollment: 316 . . . . (518) 734-3400

Housing: Homeownership rate: 81.8%; Median home value: $229,600; Median year structure built: 1982; Homeowner vacancy rate: 2.4%; Median selected monthly owner costs: $1,435 with a mortgage, $448 without a mortgage; Median gross rent: $716 per month; Rental vacancy rate: 26.1%

Health Insurance: 88.1% have insurance; 59.9% have private insurance; 52.0% have public insurance; 11.9% do not have insurance; 1.9% of children under 18 do not have insurance

Safety: Violent crime rate: 0.0 per 10,000 population; Property crime rate: 48.1 per 10,000 population

Newspapers: Windham Journal (weekly circulation 1,700)

Transportation: Commute: 92.6% car, 0.0% public transportation, 1.3% walk, 4.4% work from home; Mean travel time to work: 23.4 minutes

Hamilton County

Located in north central New York, in the Adirondacks; drained by tributaries of the Hudson, and by the Raquette, Black, and Sacandaga Rivers; includes many lakes. Covers a land area of 1,717.373 square miles, a water area of 90.431 square miles, and is located in the Eastern Time Zone at 43.66° N. Lat., 74.50° W. Long. The county was founded in 1816. County seat is Lake Pleasant.

Weather Station: Indian Lake 2 SW   Elevation: 1,660 feet

	Jan	Feb	Mar	Apr	May	Jun	Jul	Aug	Sep	Oct	Nov	Dec
High	25	29	37	50	63	71	74	73	66	54	42	30
Low	5	6	15	28	39	49	53	52	45	34	25	13
Precip	2.8	2.3	2.9	3.2	3.6	3.7	3.9	3.6	3.7	4.2	3.3	2.9
Snow	na	na	na	3.0	0.1	0.0	0.0	0.0	0.0	0.7	na	na

High and Low temperatures in degrees Fahrenheit; Precipitation and Snow in inches

Population: 4,760; Growth (since 2000): -11.5%; Density: 2.8 persons per square mile; Race: 95.3% White, 0.5% Black/African American, 0.1% Asian, 0.1% American Indian/Alaska Native, 0.0% Native Hawaiian/Other Pacific Islander, 3.2% two or more races, 1.3% Hispanic of any race; Average household size: 3.38; Median age: 51.9; Age under 18: 15.7%; Age 65 and over: 25.8%; Males per 100 females: 102.3; Marriage status: 36.7% never married, 43.9% now married, 1.2% separated, 8.2% widowed, 11.2% divorced; Foreign born: 2.1%; Speak English only: 95.8%; With disability: 17.1%; Veterans: 15.3%; Ancestry: 21.1% German, 18.9% Irish, 16.7% English, 10.7% American, 10.1% Italian

Religion: Six largest groups: 33.7% Catholicism, 15.7% Muslim Estimate, 8.0% Methodist/Pietist, 3.3% Presbyterian-Reformed, 2.3% Holiness, 0.8% Episcopalianism/Anglicanism

Economy: Unemployment rate: 4.1%; Leading industries: 28.6 % accommodation and food services; 16.8 % construction; 16.3 % retail trade; Farms: 26 totaling 2,078 acres; Company size: 0 employ 1,000 or more persons, 0 employ 500 to 999 persons, 0 employ 100 to 499 persons, 196 employ less than 100 persons; Business ownership: 227

women-owned, n/a Black-owned, n/a Hispanic-owned, n/a Asian-owned, n/a American Indian/Alaska Native-owned

Employment: 15.7% management, business, and financial, 4.1% computer, engineering, and science, 11.0% education, legal, community service, arts, and media, 3.2% healthcare practitioners, 28.1% service, 19.0% sales and office, 11.8% natural resources, construction, and maintenance, 7.0% production, transportation, and material moving

Income: Per capita: $26,968; Median household: $48,243; Average household: $61,069; Households with income of $100,000 or more: 16.3%; Poverty rate: 12.9%

Educational Attainment: High school diploma or higher: 90.7%; Bachelor's degree or higher: 24.5%; Graduate/professional degree or higher: 10.7%

Housing: Homeownership rate: 85.5%; Median home value: $162,600; Median year structure built: 1964; Homeowner vacancy rate: 6.3%; Median selected monthly owner costs: $1,212 with a mortgage, $481 without a mortgage; Median gross rent: $622 per month; Rental vacancy rate: 14.9%

Vital Statistics: Birth rate: 65.8 per 10,000 population; Death rate: 140.1 per 10,000 population; Age-adjusted cancer mortality rate: Unreliable deaths per 100,000 population

Health Insurance: 89.7% have insurance; 73.1% have private insurance; 40.6% have public insurance; 10.3% do not have insurance; 1.2% of children under 18 do not have insurance

Health Care: Physicians: 2.1 per 10,000 population; Dentists: 0.0 per 10,000 population; Hospital beds: 0.0 per 10,000 population; Hospital admissions: 0.0 per 10,000 population

Air Quality Index (AQI): Percent of Days: 97.8% good, 2.2% moderate, 0.0% unhealthy for sensitive individuals, 0.0% unhealthy, 0.0% very unhealthy; Annual median: 31; Annual maximum: 74

Transportation: Commute: 83.4% car, 0.2% public transportation, 5.6% walk, 5.8% work from home; Mean travel time to work: 23.8 minutes

2016 Presidential Election: 65.0% Trump, 29.9% Clinton, 3.7% Johnson, 1.4% Stein

Additional Information Contacts

Hamilton Government . . . . (518) 548-3076
  http://www.hamiltoncounty.com

Hamilton County Communities

ARIETTA (town). Covers a land area of 317.178 square miles and a water area of 12.229 square miles. Located at 43.50° N. Lat; 74.58° W. Long. Elevation is 1,693 feet.

Population: 291; Growth (since 2000): -0.7%; Density: 0.9 persons per square mile; Race: 97.9% White, 0.0% Black/African American, 0.0% Asian, 0.0% American Indian/Alaska Native, 0.0% Native Hawaiian/Other Pacific Islander, 2.1% Two or more races, 2.1% Hispanic of any race; Average household size: 3.64; Median age: 55.6; Age under 18: 8.2%; Age 65 and over: 18.2%; Males per 100 females: 93.6; Marriage status: 37.4% never married, 38.9% now married, 0.4% separated, 5.9% widowed, 17.8% divorced; Foreign born: 2.1%; Speak English only: 95.8%; With disability: 11.3%; Veterans: 14.2%; Ancestry: 30.2% German, 26.1% Dutch, 21.0% Irish, 12.0% English, 8.9% American

Employment: 17.2% management, business, and financial, 1.5% computer, engineering, and science, 5.2% education, legal, community service, arts, and media, 1.5% healthcare practitioners, 22.4% service, 27.6% sales and office, 11.9% natural resources, construction, and maintenance, 12.7% production, transportation, and material moving

Income: Per capita: $35,110; Median household: $53,750; Average household: $74,305; Households with income of $100,000 or more: 22.6%; Poverty rate: 3.1%

Educational Attainment: High school diploma or higher: 90.0%; Bachelor's degree or higher: 16.4%; Graduate/professional degree or higher: 6.4%

Housing: Homeownership rate: 91.3%; Median home value: $154,700; Median year structure built: 1967; Homeowner vacancy rate: 7.1%; Median selected monthly owner costs: $1,344 with a mortgage, $417 without a mortgage; Median gross rent: n/a per month; Rental vacancy rate: 0.0%

Health Insurance: 80.4% have insurance; 65.6% have private insurance; 33.0% have public insurance; 19.6% do not have insurance; 0.0% of children under 18 do not have insurance

Transportation: Commute: 90.1% car, 0.0% public transportation, 0.0% walk, 0.8% work from home; Mean travel time to work: 19.8 minutes

BENSON (town). Covers a land area of 82.617 square miles and a water area of 0.580 square miles. Located at 43.29° N. Lat; 74.37° W. Long. Elevation is 1,165 feet.
Population: 177; Growth (since 2000): -11.9%; Density: 2.1 persons per square mile; Race: 100.0% White, 0.0% Black/African American, 0.0% Asian, 0.0% American Indian/Alaska Native, 0.0% Native Hawaiian/Other Pacific Islander, 0.0% Two or more races, 0.0% Hispanic of any race; Average household size: 2.46; Median age: 54.5; Age under 18: 16.9%; Age 65 and over: 26.0%; Males per 100 females: 102.1; Marriage status: 21.7% never married, 59.2% now married, 2.0% separated, 5.3% widowed, 13.8% divorced; Foreign born: 0.0%; Speak English only: 97.1%; With disability: 23.7%; Veterans: 22.4%; Ancestry: 41.2% German, 16.9% Irish, 15.8% English, 7.9% Scotch-Irish, 6.8% British
Employment: 13.4% management, business, and financial, 3.0% computer, engineering, and science, 6.0% education, legal, community service, arts, and media, 13.4% healthcare practitioners, 11.9% service, 40.3% sales and office, 7.5% natural resources, construction, and maintenance, 4.5% production, transportation, and material moving
Income: Per capita: $23,279; Median household: $46,875; Average household: $54,878; Households with income of $100,000 or more: 13.9%; Poverty rate: 5.6%
Educational Attainment: High school diploma or higher: 93.9%; Bachelor's degree or higher: 18.4%; Graduate/professional degree or higher: 8.8%
Housing: Homeownership rate: 94.4%; Median home value: $162,500; Median year structure built: 1966; Homeowner vacancy rate: 0.0%; Median selected monthly owner costs: $1,188 with a mortgage, $450 without a mortgage; Median gross rent: n/a per month; Rental vacancy rate: 33.3%
Health Insurance: 100.0% have insurance; 78.0% have private insurance; 42.9% have public insurance; 0.0% do not have insurance; 0.0% of children under 18 do not have insurance
Transportation: Commute: 85.7% car, 0.0% public transportation, 0.0% walk, 9.5% work from home; Mean travel time to work: 29.8 minutes

BLUE MOUNTAIN LAKE (unincorporated postal area)
ZCTA: 12812
Covers a land area of 61.949 square miles and a water area of 4.534 square miles. Located at 43.88° N. Lat; 74.39° W. Long. Elevation is 1,824 feet.
Population: 58; Growth (since 2000): -54.0%; Density: 0.9 persons per square mile; Race: 100.0% White, 0.0% Black/African American, 0.0% Asian, 0.0% American Indian/Alaska Native, 0.0% Native Hawaiian/Other Pacific Islander, 0.0% Two or more races, 0.0% Hispanic of any race; Average household size: 2.23; Median age: 64.1; Age under 18: 24.1%; Age 65 and over: 34.5%; Males per 100 females: 80.7; Marriage status: 15.4% never married, 69.2% now married, 1.9% separated, 0.0% widowed, 15.4% divorced; Foreign born: 0.0%; Speak English only: 100.0%; With disability: 12.1%; Veterans: 9.1%; Ancestry: 37.9% English, 19.0% American, 19.0% Scottish, 12.1% German, 6.9% French
Employment: 100.0% management, business, and financial, 0.0% computer, engineering, and science, 0.0% education, legal, community service, arts, and media, 0.0% healthcare practitioners, 0.0% service, 0.0% sales and office, 0.0% natural resources, construction, and maintenance, 0.0% production, transportation, and material moving
Income: Per capita: $23,600; Median household: $49,583; Average household: $55,758; Households with income of $100,000 or more: 7.7%; Poverty rate: n/a
Educational Attainment: High school diploma or higher: 84.1%; Bachelor's degree or higher: 27.3%; Graduate/professional degree or higher: 4.5%
Housing: Homeownership rate: 92.3%; Median home value: $122,500; Median year structure built: 1950; Homeowner vacancy rate: 17.2%; Median selected monthly owner costs: n/a with a mortgage, n/a without a mortgage; Median gross rent: n/a per month; Rental vacancy rate: 66.7%
Health Insurance: 100.0% have insurance; 82.8% have private insurance; 55.2% have public insurance; 0.0% do not have insurance; 0.0% of children under 18 do not have insurance
Transportation: Commute: 100.0% car, 0.0% public transportation, 0.0% walk, 0.0% work from home; Mean travel time to work: 0.0 minutes

HOFFMEISTER (unincorporated postal area)
ZCTA: 13353
Covers a land area of 197.914 square miles and a water area of 3.716 square miles. Located at 43.45° N. Lat; 74.69° W. Long. Elevation is 1,857 feet.
Population: 38; Growth (since 2000): -74.8%; Density: 0.2 persons per square mile; Race: 100.0% White, 0.0% Black/African American, 0.0% Asian, 0.0% American Indian/Alaska Native, 0.0% Native Hawaiian/Other Pacific Islander, 0.0% Two or more races, 0.0% Hispanic of any race; Average household size: 2.24; Median age: 65.0; Age under 18: 0.0%; Age 65 and over: 50.0%; Males per 100 females: 138.9; Marriage status: 5.3% never married, 50.0% now married, 0.0% separated, 15.8% widowed, 28.9% divorced; Foreign born: 0.0%; Speak English only: 100.0%; With disability: 18.4%; Veterans: 13.2%; Ancestry: 31.6% English, 28.9% German, 18.4% Irish, 13.2% Polish, 5.3% American
Employment: 22.7% management, business, and financial, 0.0% computer, engineering, and science, 9.1% education, legal, community service, arts, and media, 0.0% healthcare practitioners, 9.1% service, 45.5% sales and office, 13.6% natural resources, construction, and maintenance, 0.0% production, transportation, and material moving
Income: Per capita: $24,037; Median household: $34,375; Average household: $33,882; Households with income of $100,000 or more: n/a; Poverty rate: 5.3%
Educational Attainment: High school diploma or higher: 97.2%; Bachelor's degree or higher: n/a; Graduate/professional degree or higher: n/a
Housing: Homeownership rate: 70.6%; Median home value: $158,300; Median year structure built: 1962; Homeowner vacancy rate: 19.0%; Median selected monthly owner costs: $0 with a mortgage, $450 without a mortgage; Median gross rent: n/a per month; Rental vacancy rate: 0.0%
Health Insurance: 73.7% have insurance; 57.9% have private insurance; 65.8% have public insurance; 26.3% do not have insurance; 0.0% of children under 18 do not have insurance
Transportation: Commute: 86.4% car, 0.0% public transportation, 0.0% walk, 13.6% work from home; Mean travel time to work: 30.3 minutes

HOPE (town). Covers a land area of 40.703 square miles and a water area of 0.933 square miles. Located at 43.32° N. Lat; 74.23° W. Long. Elevation is 810 feet.
Population: 628; Growth (since 2000): 60.2%; Density: 15.4 persons per square mile; Race: 96.2% White, 0.0% Black/African American, 0.0% Asian, 0.0% American Indian/Alaska Native, 0.2% Native Hawaiian/Other Pacific Islander, 3.7% Two or more races, 1.1% Hispanic of any race; Average household size: 5.51; Median age: 39.5; Age under 18: 19.6%; Age 65 and over: 12.6%; Males per 100 females: 98.5; Marriage status: 52.2% never married, 24.9% now married, 0.9% separated, 6.4% widowed, 16.5% divorced; Foreign born: 0.2%; Speak English only: 98.8%; With disability: 12.9%; Veterans: 8.3%; Ancestry: 20.9% Irish, 18.6% German, 14.8% Italian, 8.0% American, 7.2% English
Employment: 4.5% management, business, and financial, 0.5% computer, engineering, and science, 13.6% education, legal, community service, arts, and media, 1.0% healthcare practitioners, 28.6% service, 13.1% sales and office, 28.1% natural resources, construction, and maintenance, 10.6% production, transportation, and material moving
Income: Per capita: $17,452; Median household: $58,409; Average household: $65,313; Households with income of $100,000 or more: 20.1%; Poverty rate: 14.8%
Educational Attainment: High school diploma or higher: 95.9%; Bachelor's degree or higher: 19.6%; Graduate/professional degree or higher: 5.3%
Housing: Homeownership rate: 78.9%; Median home value: $136,700; Median year structure built: 1970; Homeowner vacancy rate: 0.0%; Median selected monthly owner costs: $1,156 with a mortgage, $519 without a mortgage; Median gross rent: $767 per month; Rental vacancy rate: 0.0%
Health Insurance: 93.8% have insurance; 73.2% have private insurance; 33.5% have public insurance; 6.2% do not have insurance; 0.0% of children under 18 do not have insurance
Transportation: Commute: 94.4% car, 0.0% public transportation, 1.0% walk, 3.0% work from home; Mean travel time to work: 48.3 minutes

INDIAN LAKE (town). Covers a land area of 251.800 square miles and a water area of 14.439 square miles. Located at 43.81° N. Lat; 74.42° W. Long. Elevation is 1,742 feet.

History: Dr. Thomas Durant and William West Durant, father and son, were early promoters of the Indian Lake section of the Adirondacks. The father, financier and railroad builder, constructed a railroad from Saratoga to Blue Mountain Lake, and the son expanded his father's promotional activities by building elaborate camps and selling them to the wealthy.

Population: 825; Growth (since 2000): -43.9%; Density: 3.3 persons per square mile; Race: 93.0% White, 0.2% Black/African American, 0.0% Asian, 0.8% American Indian/Alaska Native, 0.0% Native Hawaiian/Other Pacific Islander, 5.9% Two or more races, 0.2% Hispanic of any race; Average household size: 2.43; Median age: 49.8; Age under 18: 16.4%; Age 65 and over: 33.3%; Males per 100 females: 99.7; Marriage status: 46.7% never married, 39.9% now married, 3.7% separated, 4.4% widowed, 9.1% divorced; Foreign born: 0.0%; Speak English only: 98.8%; With disability: 17.9%; Veterans: 18.6%; Ancestry: 25.2% Irish, 23.9% English, 22.9% German, 17.0% French, 14.5% American

Employment: 5.9% management, business, and financial, 5.5% computer, engineering, and science, 14.7% education, legal, community service, arts, and media, 3.3% healthcare practitioners, 42.7% service, 17.6% sales and office, 2.9% natural resources, construction, and maintenance, 7.5% production, transportation, and material moving

Income: Per capita: $32,743; Median household: $41,645; Average household: $48,829; Households with income of $100,000 or more: 7.6%; Poverty rate: 13.2%

Educational Attainment: High school diploma or higher: 88.4%; Bachelor's degree or higher: 35.9%; Graduate/professional degree or higher: 17.9%

School District(s)
Indian Lake Central SD (PK-12)

   2014-15 Enrollment: 124 . . . . (518) 648-5024

Housing: Homeownership rate: 77.1%; Median home value: $152,700; Median year structure built: 1962; Homeowner vacancy rate: 8.6%; Median selected monthly owner costs: $1,139 with a mortgage, $426 without a mortgage; Median gross rent: $520 per month; Rental vacancy rate: 14.7%

Health Insurance: 90.2% have insurance; 66.9% have private insurance; 52.2% have public insurance; 9.8% do not have insurance; 0.0% of children under 18 do not have insurance

Transportation: Commute: 90.7% car, 0.0% public transportation, 2.7% walk, 5.8% work from home; Mean travel time to work: 18.8 minutes

INLET (town). Covers a land area of 62.195 square miles and a water area of 4.176 square miles. Located at 43.72° N. Lat; 74.71° W. Long. Elevation is 1,749 feet.

Population: 458; Growth (since 2000): 12.8%; Density: 7.4 persons per square mile; Race: 100.0% White, 0.0% Black/African American, 0.0% Asian, 0.0% American Indian/Alaska Native, 0.0% Native Hawaiian/Other Pacific Islander, 0.0% Two or more races, 0.0% Hispanic of any race; Average household size: 3.61; Median age: 58.3; Age under 18: 14.4%; Age 65 and over: 28.8%; Males per 100 females: 106.8; Marriage status: 22.6% never married, 52.0% now married, 0.3% separated, 19.1% widowed, 6.3% divorced; Foreign born: 0.2%; Speak English only: 99.3%; With disability: 22.5%; Veterans: 21.2%; Ancestry: 46.5% German, 20.1% English, 17.5% French, 14.2% Irish, 12.0% American

Employment: 29.9% management, business, and financial, 0.0% computer, engineering, and science, 17.6% education, legal, community service, arts, and media, 0.0% healthcare practitioners, 24.9% service, 8.6% sales and office, 16.7% natural resources, construction, and maintenance, 2.3% production, transportation, and material moving

Income: Per capita: $27,012; Median household: $41,406; Average household: $64,812; Households with income of $100,000 or more: 18.9%; Poverty rate: 13.1%

Educational Attainment: High school diploma or higher: 97.2%; Bachelor's degree or higher: 29.9%; Graduate/professional degree or higher: 7.5%

School District(s)
Inlet Common SD (PK-06)

   2014-15 Enrollment: 28 . . . . (315) 357-3305

Housing: Homeownership rate: 92.9%; Median home value: $276,700; Median year structure built: 1955; Homeowner vacancy rate: 2.5%; Median selected monthly owner costs: $1,700 with a mortgage, $579 without a mortgage; Median gross rent: $563 per month; Rental vacancy rate: 0.0%

Health Insurance: 97.8% have insurance; 83.4% have private insurance; 41.3% have public insurance; 2.2% do not have insurance; 0.0% of children under 18 do not have insurance

Safety: Violent crime rate: 0.0 per 10,000 population; Property crime rate: 186.3 per 10,000 population

Transportation: Commute: 73.4% car, 0.0% public transportation, 5.7% walk, 7.8% work from home; Mean travel time to work: 20.4 minutes

LAKE PLEASANT (town). County seat. Covers a land area of 187.984 square miles and a water area of 10.000 square miles. Located at 43.58° N. Lat; 74.42° W. Long. Elevation is 1,785 feet.

Population: 785; Growth (since 2000): -10.4%; Density: 4.2 persons per square mile; Race: 87.6% White, 1.1% Black/African American, 0.4% Asian, 0.0% American Indian/Alaska Native, 0.0% Native Hawaiian/Other Pacific Islander, 8.9% Two or more races, 2.2% Hispanic of any race; Average household size: 3.27; Median age: 54.6; Age under 18: 14.4%; Age 65 and over: 33.1%; Males per 100 females: 98.7; Marriage status: 26.7% never married, 55.4% now married, 0.4% separated, 4.7% widowed, 13.2% divorced; Foreign born: 4.5%; Speak English only: 95.0%; With disability: 22.3%; Veterans: 10.0%; Ancestry: 23.9% English, 19.1% German, 17.5% Irish, 6.5% European, 6.1% French

Employment: 19.9% management, business, and financial, 4.2% computer, engineering, and science, 11.6% education, legal, community service, arts, and media, 1.5% healthcare practitioners, 31.5% service, 19.0% sales and office, 7.1% natural resources, construction, and maintenance, 5.3% production, transportation, and material moving

Income: Per capita: $29,444; Median household: $62,083; Average household: $71,965; Households with income of $100,000 or more: 24.1%; Poverty rate: 14.7%

Educational Attainment: High school diploma or higher: 87.9%; Bachelor's degree or higher: 27.0%; Graduate/professional degree or higher: 14.7%

Housing: Homeownership rate: 84.9%; Median home value: $213,900; Median year structure built: 1969; Homeowner vacancy rate: 6.2%; Median selected monthly owner costs: $994 with a mortgage, $580 without a mortgage; Median gross rent: $717 per month; Rental vacancy rate: 22.2%

Health Insurance: 90.1% have insurance; 76.2% have private insurance; 48.5% have public insurance; 9.9% do not have insurance; 0.0% of children under 18 do not have insurance

Transportation: Commute: 70.4% car, 0.0% public transportation, 2.1% walk, 13.4% work from home; Mean travel time to work: 16.6 minutes

LONG LAKE (CDP). Covers a land area of 11.721 square miles and a water area of 2.209 square miles. Located at 43.96° N. Lat; 74.45° W. Long. Elevation is 1,673 feet.

Population: 302; Growth (since 2000): n/a; Density: 25.8 persons per square mile; Race: 96.0% White, 3.6% Black/African American, 0.3% Asian, 0.0% American Indian/Alaska Native, 0.0% Native Hawaiian/Other Pacific Islander, 0.0% Two or more races, 0.0% Hispanic of any race; Average household size: 2.61; Median age: 53.9; Age under 18: 17.2%; Age 65 and over: 22.2%; Males per 100 females: 109.6; Marriage status: 26.8% never married, 60.9% now married, 0.0% separated, 7.2% widowed, 5.1% divorced; Foreign born: 18.5%; Speak English only: 80.3%; With disability: 15.1%; Veterans: 11.2%; Ancestry: 24.8% English, 15.9% German, 12.3% Portuguese, 11.9% American, 11.3% Irish

Employment: 6.7% management, business, and financial, 0.0% computer, engineering, and science, 8.3% education, legal, community service, arts, and media, 8.3% healthcare practitioners, 45.0% service, 22.5% sales and office, 4.2% natural resources, construction, and maintenance, 5.0% production, transportation, and material moving

Income: Per capita: $31,136; Median household: $60,000; Average household: $80,296; Households with income of $100,000 or more: 27.4%; Poverty rate: 13.7%

Educational Attainment: High school diploma or higher: 73.9%; Bachelor's degree or higher: 22.6%; Graduate/professional degree or higher: 10.2%

School District(s)
Long Lake Central SD (PK-12)

   2014-15 Enrollment: 57 . . . . (518) 624-2147

Housing: Homeownership rate: 92.2%; Median home value: $253,100; Median year structure built: 1964; Homeowner vacancy rate: 0.0%; Median selected monthly owner costs: $1,652 with a mortgage, $675 without a mortgage; Median gross rent: $550 per month; Rental vacancy rate: 28.6%

Health Insurance: 98.2% have insurance; 87.3% have private insurance; 31.0% have public insurance; 1.8% do not have insurance; 0.0% of children under 18 do not have insurance
Transportation: Commute: 89.5% car, 0.0% public transportation, 0.9% walk, 9.6% work from home; Mean travel time to work: 17.2 minutes

LONG LAKE (town).
Covers a land area of 407.033 square miles and a water area of 42.804 square miles. Located at 43.96° N. Lat; 74.65° W. Long. Elevation is 1,673 feet.
Population: 477; Growth (since 2000): -44.0%; Density: 1.2 persons per square mile; Race: 93.3% White, 2.3% Black/African American, 0.2% Asian, 0.0% American Indian/Alaska Native, 0.0% Native Hawaiian/Other Pacific Islander, 0.0% Two or more races, 4.2% Hispanic of any race; Average household size: 3.13; Median age: 53.6; Age under 18: 10.9%; Age 65 and over: 24.1%; Males per 100 females: 112.9; Marriage status: 35.3% never married, 46.6% now married, 0.0% separated, 10.9% widowed, 7.3% divorced; Foreign born: 11.7%; Speak English only: 83.2%; With disability: 11.5%; Veterans: 13.4%; Ancestry: 19.1% Irish, 18.2% English, 11.3% German, 9.9% Greek, 7.8% American
Employment: 28.6% management, business, and financial, 1.2% computer, engineering, and science, 5.8% education, legal, community service, arts, and media, 4.1% healthcare practitioners, 25.3% service, 28.2% sales and office, 4.1% natural resources, construction, and maintenance, 2.5% production, transportation, and material moving
Income: Per capita: $39,424; Median household: $56,875; Average household: $77,351; Households with income of $100,000 or more: 26.2%; Poverty rate: 8.7%
Educational Attainment: High school diploma or higher: 78.2%; Bachelor's degree or higher: 26.1%; Graduate/professional degree or higher: 9.5%

School District(s)
Long Lake Central SD (PK-12)
    2014-15 Enrollment: 57 . . . . (518) 624-2147
Housing: Homeownership rate: 89.4%; Median home value: $234,600; Median year structure built: 1963; Homeowner vacancy rate: 3.8%; Median selected monthly owner costs: $1,634 with a mortgage, $521 without a mortgage; Median gross rent: $1,025 per month; Rental vacancy rate: 35.3%
Health Insurance: 83.9% have insurance; 73.0% have private insurance; 33.6% have public insurance; 16.1% do not have insurance; 0.0% of children under 18 do not have insurance
Transportation: Commute: 64.3% car, 0.0% public transportation, 31.1% walk, 4.7% work from home; Mean travel time to work: 14.5 minutes

MOREHOUSE (town).
Covers a land area of 191.064 square miles and a water area of 3.705 square miles. Located at 43.45° N. Lat; 74.69° W. Long.
Population: 38; Growth (since 2000): -74.8%; Density: 0.2 persons per square mile; Race: 100.0% White, 0.0% Black/African American, 0.0% Asian, 0.0% American Indian/Alaska Native, 0.0% Native Hawaiian/Other Pacific Islander, 0.0% Two or more races, 0.0% Hispanic of any race; Average household size: 2.24; Median age: 65.0; Age under 18: 0.0%; Age 65 and over: 50.0%; Males per 100 females: 138.9; Marriage status: 5.3% never married, 50.0% now married, 0.0% separated, 15.8% widowed, 28.9% divorced; Foreign born: 0.0%; Speak English only: 100.0%; With disability: 18.4%; Veterans: 13.2%; Ancestry: 31.6% English, 28.9% German, 18.4% Irish, 13.2% Polish, 5.3% American
Employment: 22.7% management, business, and financial, 0.0% computer, engineering, and science, 9.1% education, legal, community service, arts, and media, 0.0% healthcare practitioners, 9.1% service, 45.5% sales and office, 13.6% natural resources, construction, and maintenance, 0.0% production, transportation, and material moving
Income: Per capita: $24,037; Median household: $34,375; Average household: $33,882; Households with income of $100,000 or more: n/a; Poverty rate: 5.3%
Educational Attainment: High school diploma or higher: 97.2%; Bachelor's degree or higher: n/a; Graduate/professional degree or higher: n/a
Housing: Homeownership rate: 70.6%; Median home value: $158,300; Median year structure built: 1962; Homeowner vacancy rate: 19.0%; Median selected monthly owner costs: n/a with a mortgage, $450 without a mortgage; Median gross rent: n/a per month; Rental vacancy rate: 0.0%
Health Insurance: 73.7% have insurance; 57.9% have private insurance; 65.8% have public insurance; 26.3% do not have insurance; 0.0% of children under 18 do not have insurance

Transportation: Commute: 86.4% car, 0.0% public transportation, 0.0% walk, 13.6% work from home; Mean travel time to work: 30.3 minutes

PISECO (unincorporated postal area)
ZCTA: 12139
Covers a land area of 239.085 square miles and a water area of 10.023 square miles. Located at 43.50° N. Lat; 74.58° W. Long. Elevation is 1,676 feet.
Population: 286; Growth (since 2000): 5.1%; Density: 1.2 persons per square mile; Race: 97.9% White, 0.0% Black/African American, 0.0% Asian, 0.0% American Indian/Alaska Native, 0.0% Native Hawaiian/Other Pacific Islander, 2.1% Two or more races, 2.1% Hispanic of any race; Average household size: 3.71; Median age: 55.0; Age under 18: 8.4%; Age 65 and over: 18.5%; Males per 100 females: 94.1; Marriage status: 36.2% never married, 39.6% now married, 0.4% separated, 6.0% widowed, 18.1% divorced; Foreign born: 2.1%; Speak English only: 95.7%; With disability: 11.5%; Veterans: 13.4%; Ancestry: 30.1% German, 24.8% Dutch, 21.3% Irish, 11.2% English, 9.1% American
Employment: 17.2% management, business, and financial, 1.5% computer, engineering, and science, 5.2% education, legal, community service, arts, and media, 1.5% healthcare practitioners, 22.4% service, 27.6% sales and office, 11.9% natural resources, construction, and maintenance, 12.7% production, transportation, and material moving
Income: Per capita: $33,555; Median household: $50,625; Average household: $69,144; Households with income of $100,000 or more: 19.5%; Poverty rate: 2.4%
Educational Attainment: High school diploma or higher: 89.8%; Bachelor's degree or higher: 15.5%; Graduate/professional degree or higher: 6.5%

School District(s)
Piseco Common SD (PK-06)
    2014-15 Enrollment: n/a . . . . (518) 548-7555
Housing: Homeownership rate: 90.9%; Median home value: $150,000; Median year structure built: 1967; Homeowner vacancy rate: 7.4%; Median selected monthly owner costs: $1,344 with a mortgage, $375 without a mortgage; Median gross rent: n/a per month; Rental vacancy rate: 0.0%
Health Insurance: 80.1% have insurance; 65.0% have private insurance; 33.6% have public insurance; 19.9% do not have insurance; 0.0% of children under 18 do not have insurance
Transportation: Commute: 90.1% car, 0.0% public transportation, 0.0% walk, 0.8% work from home; Mean travel time to work: 19.8 minutes

RAQUETTE LAKE (unincorporated postal area)
ZCTA: 13436
Covers a land area of 38.337 square miles and a water area of 9.611 square miles. Located at 43.81° N. Lat; 74.67° W. Long. Elevation is 1,765 feet.
Population: 88; Growth (since 2000): -28.5%; Density: 2.3 persons per square mile; Race: 100.0% White, 0.0% Black/African American, 0.0% Asian, 0.0% American Indian/Alaska Native, 0.0% Native Hawaiian/Other Pacific Islander, 0.0% Two or more races, 0.0% Hispanic of any race; Average household size: 3.38; Median age: 60.7; Age under 18: 0.0%; Age 65 and over: 42.0%; Males per 100 females: 129.8; Marriage status: 18.2% never married, 33.0% now married, 0.0% separated, 27.3% widowed, 21.6% divorced; Foreign born: 0.0%; Speak English only: 98.9%; With disability: 10.2%; Veterans: 30.7%; Ancestry: 27.3% Welsh, 9.1% Irish, 3.4% French, 3.4% French Canadian, 3.4% German
Employment: 31.1% management, business, and financial, 0.0% computer, engineering, and science, 0.0% education, legal, community service, arts, and media, 0.0% healthcare practitioners, 11.1% service, 46.7% sales and office, 11.1% natural resources, construction, and maintenance, 0.0% production, transportation, and material moving
Income: Per capita: $39,093; Median household: $53,750; Average household: $62,812; Households with income of $100,000 or more: 19.2%; Poverty rate: 1.1%
Educational Attainment: High school diploma or higher: 79.8%; Bachelor's degree or higher: 11.9%; Graduate/professional degree or higher: 2.4%
Housing: Homeownership rate: 80.8%; Median home value: $171,900; Median year structure built: 1966; Homeowner vacancy rate: 19.2%; Median selected monthly owner costs: $0 with a mortgage, $298 without

a mortgage; Median gross rent: n/a per month; Rental vacancy rate: 0.0%

Health Insurance: 97.7% have insurance; 76.1% have private insurance; 62.5% have public insurance; 2.3% do not have insurance; 0.0% of children under 18 do not have insurance

Transportation: Commute: 93.3% car, 0.0% public transportation, 6.7% walk, 0.0% work from home; Mean travel time to work: 25.2 minutes

SABAEL (unincorporated postal area)
ZCTA: 12864

Covers a land area of 0.209 square miles and a water area of 0 square miles. Located at 43.73° N. Lat; 74.31° W. Long. Elevation is 1,745 feet.

Population: 37; Growth (since 2000): n/a; Density: 177.3 persons per square mile; Race: 100.0% White, 0.0% Black/African American, 0.0% Asian, 0.0% American Indian/Alaska Native, 0.0% Native Hawaiian/Other Pacific Islander, 0.0% Two or more races, 0.0% Hispanic of any race; Average household size: 1.68; Median age: 65.8; Age under 18: 0.0%; Age 65 and over: 78.4%; Males per 100 females: 100.0; Marriage status: 78.4% never married, 21.6% now married, 21.6% separated, 0.0% widowed, 0.0% divorced; Foreign born: 0.0%; Speak English only: 100.0%; With disability: 37.8%; Veterans: 40.5%; Ancestry: 78.4% German, 59.5% English, 40.5% Irish, 21.6% French

Employment: 0.0% management, business, and financial, 0.0% computer, engineering, and science, 0.0% education, legal, community service, arts, and media, 0.0% healthcare practitioners, 0.0% service, 100.0% sales and office, 0.0% natural resources, construction, and maintenance, 0.0% production, transportation, and material moving

Income: Per capita: $28,395; Median household: n/a; Average household: n/a; Households with income of $100,000 or more: n/a; Poverty rate: 21.6%

Educational Attainment: High school diploma or higher: 100.0%; Bachelor's degree or higher: n/a; Graduate/professional degree or higher: n/a

Housing: Homeownership rate: 100.0%; Median home value: n/a; Median year structure built: 1965; Homeowner vacancy rate: 0.0%; Median selected monthly owner costs: $0 with a mortgage, $0 without a mortgage; Median gross rent: n/a per month; Rental vacancy rate: 0.0%

Health Insurance: 100.0% have insurance; 78.4% have private insurance; 100.0% have public insurance; 0.0% do not have insurance; 0.0% of children under 18 do not have insurance

Transportation: Commute: 100.0% car, 0.0% public transportation, 0.0% walk, 0.0% work from home; Mean travel time to work: 0.0 minutes

SPECULATOR (village).
Covers a land area of 44.571 square miles and a water area of 2.595 square miles. Located at 43.59° N. Lat; 74.36° W. Long. Elevation is 1,739 feet.

Population: 362; Growth (since 2000): 4.0%; Density: 8.1 persons per square mile; Race: 89.0% White, 2.2% Black/African American, 0.8% Asian, 0.0% American Indian/Alaska Native, 0.0% Native Hawaiian/Other Pacific Islander, 8.0% Two or more races, 0.0% Hispanic of any race; Average household size: 4.54; Median age: 56.2; Age under 18: 3.3%; Age 65 and over: 32.0%; Males per 100 females: 97.6; Marriage status: 35.3% never married, 39.3% now married, 0.0% separated, 3.4% widowed, 21.9% divorced; Foreign born: 8.8%; Speak English only: 91.3%; With disability: 28.7%; Veterans: 9.1%; Ancestry: 38.7% English, 29.0% Irish, 15.5% German, 10.8% European, 9.7% Scottish

Employment: 21.0% management, business, and financial, 0.0% computer, engineering, and science, 6.7% education, legal, community service, arts, and media, 2.6% healthcare practitioners, 42.6% service, 20.5% sales and office, 2.1% natural resources, construction, and maintenance, 4.6% production, transportation, and material moving

Income: Per capita: $35,161; Median household: $65,833; Average household: $82,870; Households with income of $100,000 or more: 22.4%; Poverty rate: 11.6%

Educational Attainment: High school diploma or higher: 83.5%; Bachelor's degree or higher: 25.6%; Graduate/professional degree or higher: 14.1%

School District(s)
Lake Pleasant Central SD (PK-09)
    2014-15 Enrollment: 102. . . . . (518) 548-7571

Housing: Homeownership rate: 89.5%; Median home value: $172,200; Median year structure built: 1968; Homeowner vacancy rate: 0.0%; Median selected monthly owner costs: $1,429 with a mortgage, $486 without a mortgage; Median gross rent: n/a per month; Rental vacancy rate: 55.6%

Health Insurance: 81.2% have insurance; 71.8% have private insurance; 47.2% have public insurance; 18.8% do not have insurance; 0.0% of children under 18 do not have insurance

Newspapers: Hamilton Co. Express (weekly circulation 3,300)

Transportation: Commute: 59.0% car, 0.0% public transportation, 1.5% walk, 19.5% work from home; Mean travel time to work: 16.1 minutes

WELLS (town).
Covers a land area of 176.800 square miles and a water area of 1.564 square miles. Located at 43.48° N. Lat; 74.29° W. Long. Elevation is 1,010 feet.

Population: 1,081; Growth (since 2000): 46.7%; Density: 6.1 persons per square mile; Race: 99.2% White, 0.2% Black/African American, 0.1% Asian, 0.0% American Indian/Alaska Native, 0.0% Native Hawaiian/Other Pacific Islander, 0.6% Two or more races, 1.0% Hispanic of any race; Average household size: 3.99; Median age: 52.3; Age under 18: 19.0%; Age 65 and over: 23.2%; Males per 100 females: 101.8; Marriage status: 37.4% never married, 43.6% now married, 1.3% separated, 10.0% widowed, 9.1% divorced; Foreign born: 0.2%; Speak English only: 96.2%; With disability: 15.5%; Veterans: 18.5%; Ancestry: 22.5% Italian, 16.0% American, 15.5% Irish, 11.9% Polish, 10.3% Slovak

Employment: 8.4% management, business, and financial, 10.9% computer, engineering, and science, 8.6% education, legal, community service, arts, and media, 6.1% healthcare practitioners, 22.3% service, 15.0% sales and office, 17.5% natural resources, construction, and maintenance, 11.1% production, transportation, and material moving

Income: Per capita: $19,292; Median household: $43,000; Average household: $53,808; Households with income of $100,000 or more: 12.1%; Poverty rate: 15.9%

Educational Attainment: High school diploma or higher: 93.6%; Bachelor's degree or higher: 17.9%; Graduate/professional degree or higher: 8.9%

School District(s)
Wells Central SD (PK-12)
    2014-15 Enrollment: 138. . . . . (518) 924-6000

Housing: Homeownership rate: 90.6%; Median home value: $147,800; Median year structure built: 1966; Homeowner vacancy rate: 9.3%; Median selected monthly owner costs: $1,162 with a mortgage, $403 without a mortgage; Median gross rent: $944 per month; Rental vacancy rate: 0.0%

Health Insurance: 86.9% have insurance; 72.9% have private insurance; 33.7% have public insurance; 13.1% do not have insurance; 4.4% of children under 18 do not have insurance

Transportation: Commute: 98.8% car, 0.9% public transportation, 0.0% walk, 0.3% work from home; Mean travel time to work: 28.0 minutes

Herkimer County

Located in central and north central New York, extending north into the Adirondacks and south into the Mohawk Valley; drained by the Mohawk, Unadilla, Black, and Moose Rivers. Covers a land area of 1,411.470 square miles, a water area of 46.487 square miles, and is located in the Eastern Time Zone at 43.46° N. Lat., 74.89° W. Long. The county was founded in 1791. County seat is Herkimer.

Herkimer County is part of the Utica-Rome, NY Metropolitan Statistical Area. The entire metro area includes: Herkimer County, NY; Oneida County, NY

Weather Station: Old Forge   Elevation: 1,720 feet

	Jan	Feb	Mar	Apr	May	Jun	Jul	Aug	Sep	Oct	Nov	Dec
High	25	29	37	50	63	71	75	74	66	54	41	30
Low	3	6	15	28	39	49	53	52	44	33	24	11
Precip	3.9	2.9	3.4	3.7	4.2	4.1	4.4	4.4	4.7	4.7	4.6	4.3
Snow	48.4	31.6	27.4	9.2	0.8	tr	0.0	0.0	tr	3.1	19.3	41.4

High and Low temperatures in degrees Fahrenheit; Precipitation and Snow in inches

Population: 64,034; Growth (since 2000): -0.6%; Density: 45.4 persons per square mile; Race: 96.0% White, 1.0% Black/African American, 0.5% Asian, 0.2% American Indian/Alaska Native, 0.3% Native Hawaiian/Other Pacific Islander, 1.5% two or more races, 1.9% Hispanic of any race; Average household size: 2.40; Median age: 42.9; Age under 18: 21.4%; Age 65 and over: 18.3%; Males per 100 females: 95.9; Marriage status: 29.1% never married, 52.2% now married, 2.2% separated, 7.2% widowed, 11.5% divorced; Foreign born: 3.1%; Speak English only: 94.8%; With disability: 13.9%; Veterans: 10.3%; Ancestry: 21.8% Irish, 21.1% German, 19.7% Italian, 11.1% English, 8.8% Polish

Religion: Six largest groups: 23.9% Catholicism, 4.5% Methodist/Pietist, 2.0% Baptist, 1.9% Presbyterian-Reformed, 1.6% Lutheran, 1.1% Episcopalianism/Anglicanism

Economy: Unemployment rate: 4.7%; Leading industries: 17.0 % retail trade; 15.0 % accommodation and food services; 13.5 % construction; Farms: 687 totaling 140,270 acres; Company size: 1 employs 1,000 or more persons, 0 employ 500 to 999 persons, 14 employ 100 to 499 persons, 1,112 employ less than 100 persons; Business ownership: 1,070 women-owned, n/a Black-owned, n/a Hispanic-owned, 38 Asian-owned, n/a American Indian/Alaska Native-owned

Employment: 11.2% management, business, and financial, 3.2% computer, engineering, and science, 10.9% education, legal, community service, arts, and media, 7.0% healthcare practitioners, 19.7% service, 24.1% sales and office, 10.1% natural resources, construction, and maintenance, 13.7% production, transportation, and material moving

Income: Per capita: $23,753; Median household: $46,229; Average household: $57,466; Households with income of $100,000 or more: 14.0%; Poverty rate: 14.6%

Educational Attainment: High school diploma or higher: 89.8%; Bachelor's degree or higher: 22.4%; Graduate/professional degree or higher: 9.3%

Housing: Homeownership rate: 71.0%; Median home value: $96,100; Median year structure built: 1955; Homeowner vacancy rate: 2.1%; Median selected monthly owner costs: $1,121 with a mortgage, $466 without a mortgage; Median gross rent: $623 per month; Rental vacancy rate: 4.2%

Vital Statistics: Birth rate: 105.2 per 10,000 population; Death rate: 105.2 per 10,000 population; Age-adjusted cancer mortality rate: 191.1 deaths per 100,000 population

Health Insurance: 91.4% have insurance; 65.8% have private insurance; 40.7% have public insurance; 8.6% do not have insurance; 4.1% of children under 18 do not have insurance

Health Care: Physicians: 6.7 per 10,000 population; Dentists: 3.3 per 10,000 population; Hospital beds: 9.2 per 10,000 population; Hospital admissions: 322.5 per 10,000 population

Air Quality Index (AQI): Percent of Days: 98.6% good, 1.4% moderate, 0.0% unhealthy for sensitive individuals, 0.0% unhealthy, 0.0% very unhealthy; Annual median: 31; Annual maximum: 67

Transportation: Commute: 88.9% car, 0.8% public transportation, 4.6% walk, 4.6% work from home; Mean travel time to work: 23.4 minutes

2016 Presidential Election: 63.8% Trump, 30.9% Clinton, 3.8% Johnson, 1.5% Stein

National and State Parks: Black Creek State Forest

Additional Information Contacts

Herkimer Government . . . . (315) 867-1129
  http://www.herkimercounty.org

Herkimer County Communities

COLD BROOK (village). Covers a land area of 0.439 square miles and a water area of 0 square miles. Located at 43.24° N. Lat; 75.04° W. Long. Elevation is 945 feet.

Population: 336; Growth (since 2000): 0.0%; Density: 765.0 persons per square mile; Race: 89.3% White, 1.5% Black/African American, 0.0% Asian, 0.0% American Indian/Alaska Native, 0.0% Native Hawaiian/Other Pacific Islander, 5.4% Two or more races, 11.3% Hispanic of any race; Average household size: 2.87; Median age: 33.7; Age under 18: 30.4%; Age 65 and over: 11.9%; Males per 100 females: 105.6; Marriage status: 38.2% never married, 46.3% now married, 6.2% separated, 6.6% widowed, 8.9% divorced; Foreign born: 0.0%; Speak English only: 94.8%; With disability: 17.3%; Veterans: 5.6%; Ancestry: 25.3% German, 25.0% Irish, 9.5% American, 9.5% English, 8.6% Italian

Employment: 13.4% management, business, and financial, 1.4% computer, engineering, and science, 4.9% education, legal, community service, arts, and media, 11.3% healthcare practitioners, 9.2% service, 27.5% sales and office, 9.2% natural resources, construction, and maintenance, 23.2% production, transportation, and material moving

Income: Per capita: $19,414; Median household: $38,125; Average household: $54,872; Households with income of $100,000 or more: 15.4%; Poverty rate: 11.9%

Educational Attainment: High school diploma or higher: 87.5%; Bachelor's degree or higher: 13.5%; Graduate/professional degree or higher: 5.5%

Housing: Homeownership rate: 74.4%; Median home value: $78,300; Median year structure built: Before 1940; Homeowner vacancy rate: 0.0%; Median selected monthly owner costs: $883 with a mortgage, $406 without

a mortgage; Median gross rent: $675 per month; Rental vacancy rate: 0.0%

Health Insurance: 90.8% have insurance; 64.0% have private insurance; 39.0% have public insurance; 9.2% do not have insurance; 0.0% of children under 18 do not have insurance

Transportation: Commute: 91.3% car, 4.3% public transportation, 0.7% walk, 3.6% work from home; Mean travel time to work: 31.5 minutes

COLUMBIA (town). Covers a land area of 35.073 square miles and a water area of 0.030 square miles. Located at 42.93° N. Lat; 75.05° W. Long.

Population: 1,544; Growth (since 2000): -5.3%; Density: 44.0 persons per square mile; Race: 98.3% White, 0.9% Black/African American, 0.0% Asian, 0.0% American Indian/Alaska Native, 0.0% Native Hawaiian/Other Pacific Islander, 0.5% Two or more races, 1.7% Hispanic of any race; Average household size: 2.56; Median age: 45.7; Age under 18: 24.3%; Age 65 and over: 18.1%; Males per 100 females: 107.1; Marriage status: 20.2% never married, 66.3% now married, 1.7% separated, 7.0% widowed, 6.5% divorced; Foreign born: 0.4%; Speak English only: 97.4%; With disability: 14.2%; Veterans: 11.5%; Ancestry: 28.4% German, 14.2% Irish, 11.5% English, 11.1% Polish, 8.3% Dutch

Employment: 12.1% management, business, and financial, 2.9% computer, engineering, and science, 10.4% education, legal, community service, arts, and media, 7.7% healthcare practitioners, 9.7% service, 20.7% sales and office, 14.1% natural resources, construction, and maintenance, 22.4% production, transportation, and material moving

Income: Per capita: $24,329; Median household: $55,667; Average household: $61,322; Households with income of $100,000 or more: 18.4%; Poverty rate: 11.9%

Educational Attainment: High school diploma or higher: 90.5%; Bachelor's degree or higher: 15.1%; Graduate/professional degree or higher: 7.5%

Housing: Homeownership rate: 92.4%; Median home value: $90,900; Median year structure built: 1973; Homeowner vacancy rate: 0.0%; Median selected monthly owner costs: $1,162 with a mortgage, $407 without a mortgage; Median gross rent: $695 per month; Rental vacancy rate: 0.0%

Health Insurance: 89.7% have insurance; 69.7% have private insurance; 34.5% have public insurance; 10.3% do not have insurance; 12.0% of children under 18 do not have insurance

Transportation: Commute: 88.1% car, 0.6% public transportation, 3.9% walk, 4.5% work from home; Mean travel time to work: 24.9 minutes

DANUBE (town). Covers a land area of 29.354 square miles and a water area of 0.259 square miles. Located at 42.98° N. Lat; 74.80° W. Long.

Population: 1,045; Growth (since 2000): -4.8%; Density: 35.6 persons per square mile; Race: 97.2% White, 0.0% Black/African American, 0.0% Asian, 2.1% American Indian/Alaska Native, 0.0% Native Hawaiian/Other Pacific Islander, 0.7% Two or more races, 0.3% Hispanic of any race; Average household size: 2.56; Median age: 43.8; Age under 18: 19.9%; Age 65 and over: 15.5%; Males per 100 females: 115.6; Marriage status: 33.5% never married, 54.1% now married, 1.2% separated, 3.7% widowed, 8.8% divorced; Foreign born: 0.6%; Speak English only: 96.9%; With disability: 12.6%; Veterans: 7.4%; Ancestry: 27.1% German, 19.5% Irish, 11.9% Italian, 8.3% American, 6.3% Dutch

Employment: 17.3% management, business, and financial, 2.9% computer, engineering, and science, 3.3% education, legal, community service, arts, and media, 5.1% healthcare practitioners, 18.9% service, 23.5% sales and office, 12.4% natural resources, construction, and maintenance, 16.6% production, transportation, and material moving

Income: Per capita: $24,080; Median household: $52,120; Average household: $61,445; Households with income of $100,000 or more: 19.6%; Poverty rate: 13.7%

Educational Attainment: High school diploma or higher: 87.2%; Bachelor's degree or higher: 17.9%; Graduate/professional degree or higher: 4.5%

Housing: Homeownership rate: 82.2%; Median home value: $87,700; Median year structure built: 1966; Homeowner vacancy rate: 0.0%; Median selected monthly owner costs: $1,189 with a mortgage, $481 without a mortgage; Median gross rent: $589 per month; Rental vacancy rate: 13.1%

Health Insurance: 83.1% have insurance; 64.5% have private insurance; 28.6% have public insurance; 16.9% do not have insurance; 14.4% of children under 18 do not have insurance

Transportation: Commute: 85.3% car, 0.0% public transportation, 5.3% walk, 8.1% work from home; Mean travel time to work: 22.6 minutes

Additional Information Contacts

Town of Danube . . . . (315) 868-6368
http://town.danube.ny.us

DOLGEVILLE (village).
Covers a land area of 1.791 square miles and a water area of 0.044 square miles. Located at 43.11° N. Lat; 74.78° W. Long. Elevation is 791 feet.

History: Incorporated 1891.

Population: 2,349; Growth (since 2000): 8.4%; Density: 1,311.9 persons per square mile; Race: 98.3% White, 0.5% Black/African American, 0.0% Asian, 0.7% American Indian/Alaska Native, 0.0% Native Hawaiian/Other Pacific Islander, 0.6% Two or more races, 2.3% Hispanic of any race; Average household size: 2.50; Median age: 37.1; Age under 18: 27.2%; Age 65 and over: 18.0%; Males per 100 females: 91.8; Marriage status: 25.1% never married, 53.9% now married, 2.8% separated, 9.7% widowed, 11.3% divorced; Foreign born: 2.7%; Speak English only: 92.9%; With disability: 12.7%; Veterans: 10.3%; Ancestry: 21.1% Italian, 20.5% German, 15.9% Irish, 10.4% English, 9.6% French

Employment: 5.4% management, business, and financial, 1.2% computer, engineering, and science, 15.8% education, legal, community service, arts, and media, 5.3% healthcare practitioners, 18.1% service, 27.3% sales and office, 13.2% natural resources, construction, and maintenance, 13.7% production, transportation, and material moving

Income: Per capita: $20,044; Median household: $43,586; Average household: $49,833; Households with income of $100,000 or more: 10.4%; Poverty rate: 18.0%

Educational Attainment: High school diploma or higher: 87.2%; Bachelor's degree or higher: 17.3%; Graduate/professional degree or higher: 11.0%

School District(s)

Dolgeville Central SD (PK-12)
   2014-15 Enrollment: 941 . . . . (315) 429-3155

Housing: Homeownership rate: 72.0%; Median home value: $78,400; Median year structure built: Before 1940; Homeowner vacancy rate: 2.0%; Median selected monthly owner costs: $1,016 with a mortgage, $474 without a mortgage; Median gross rent: $581 per month; Rental vacancy rate: 5.4%

Health Insurance: 93.8% have insurance; 56.5% have private insurance; 51.0% have public insurance; 6.2% do not have insurance; 2.5% of children under 18 do not have insurance

Safety: Violent crime rate: 23.3 per 10,000 population; Property crime rate: 46.6 per 10,000 population

Transportation: Commute: 93.0% car, 0.0% public transportation, 1.6% walk, 3.1% work from home; Mean travel time to work: 24.3 minutes

EAGLE BAY (unincorporated postal area)
ZCTA: 13331

Covers a land area of 80.667 square miles and a water area of 4.673 square miles. Located at 43.87° N. Lat; 74.88° W. Long. Elevation is 1,778 feet.

Population: 202; Growth (since 2000): -31.1%; Density: 2.5 persons per square mile; Race: 100.0% White, 0.0% Black/African American, 0.0% Asian, 0.0% American Indian/Alaska Native, 0.0% Native Hawaiian/Other Pacific Islander, 0.0% Two or more races, 0.0% Hispanic of any race; Average household size: 1.73; Median age: 70.4; Age under 18: 0.0%; Age 65 and over: 72.3%; Males per 100 females: 110.0; Marriage status: 3.5% never married, 78.2% now married, 0.0% separated, 15.3% widowed, 3.0% divorced; Foreign born: 0.0%; Speak English only: 97.0%; With disability: 5.9%; Veterans: 9.9%; Ancestry: 29.2% Polish, 27.2% English, 19.3% Irish, 14.9% Italian, 12.9% German

Employment: 6.3% management, business, and financial, 0.0% computer, engineering, and science, 0.0% education, legal, community service, arts, and media, 13.4% healthcare practitioners, 5.4% service, 61.6% sales and office, 13.4% natural resources, construction, and maintenance, 0.0% production, transportation, and material moving

Income: Per capita: $56,530; Median household: $74,063; Average household: $95,303; Households with income of $100,000 or more: 35.9%; Poverty rate: 2.5%

Educational Attainment: High school diploma or higher: 98.0%; Bachelor's degree or higher: 49.5%; Graduate/professional degree or higher: 17.8%

Housing: Homeownership rate: 100.0%; Median home value: $267,500; Median year structure built: 1960; Homeowner vacancy rate: 6.4%; Median selected monthly owner costs: $0 with a mortgage, $631

without a mortgage; Median gross rent: n/a per month; Rental vacancy rate: 0.0%

Health Insurance: 100.0% have insurance; 95.0% have private insurance; 72.3% have public insurance; 0.0% do not have insurance; 0.0% of children under 18 do not have insurance

Transportation: Commute: 48.2% car, 0.0% public transportation, 6.3% walk, 45.5% work from home; Mean travel time to work: 21.0 minutes

FAIRFIELD (town).
Covers a land area of 41.296 square miles and a water area of 0.162 square miles. Located at 43.13° N. Lat; 74.94° W. Long. Elevation is 1,266 feet.

Population: 1,493; Growth (since 2000): -7.1%; Density: 36.2 persons per square mile; Race: 96.8% White, 1.8% Black/African American, 0.3% Asian, 0.0% American Indian/Alaska Native, 0.0% Native Hawaiian/Other Pacific Islander, 1.1% Two or more races, 0.9% Hispanic of any race; Average household size: 2.65; Median age: 44.4; Age under 18: 24.1%; Age 65 and over: 15.5%; Males per 100 females: 102.6; Marriage status: 24.0% never married, 60.0% now married, 0.7% separated, 5.2% widowed, 10.8% divorced; Foreign born: 2.4%; Speak English only: 94.1%; With disability: 11.4%; Veterans: 11.0%; Ancestry: 37.8% German, 15.5% Irish, 13.0% English, 12.7% American, 9.6% Italian

Employment: 22.1% management, business, and financial, 3.8% computer, engineering, and science, 6.6% education, legal, community service, arts, and media, 5.9% healthcare practitioners, 10.3% service, 17.7% sales and office, 16.7% natural resources, construction, and maintenance, 16.8% production, transportation, and material moving

Income: Per capita: $28,937; Median household: $58,173; Average household: $76,829; Households with income of $100,000 or more: 22.7%; Poverty rate: 6.4%

Educational Attainment: High school diploma or higher: 89.4%; Bachelor's degree or higher: 19.1%; Graduate/professional degree or higher: 8.2%

Housing: Homeownership rate: 89.3%; Median home value: $111,600; Median year structure built: 1964; Homeowner vacancy rate: 1.2%; Median selected monthly owner costs: $1,230 with a mortgage, $528 without a mortgage; Median gross rent: $825 per month; Rental vacancy rate: 13.0%

Health Insurance: 89.1% have insurance; 66.7% have private insurance; 36.4% have public insurance; 10.9% do not have insurance; 1.4% of children under 18 do not have insurance

Transportation: Commute: 84.1% car, 0.3% public transportation, 6.1% walk, 9.5% work from home; Mean travel time to work: 25.0 minutes

FRANKFORT (town).
Covers a land area of 36.421 square miles and a water area of 0.106 square miles. Located at 43.04° N. Lat; 75.14° W. Long. Elevation is 407 feet.

History: Settled 1723, incorporated 1863.

Population: 7,576; Growth (since 2000): 1.3%; Density: 208.0 persons per square mile; Race: 96.5% White, 1.0% Black/African American, 0.2% Asian, 0.5% American Indian/Alaska Native, 0.0% Native Hawaiian/Other Pacific Islander, 0.7% Two or more races, 2.0% Hispanic of any race; Average household size: 2.44; Median age: 45.2; Age under 18: 18.4%; Age 65 and over: 19.4%; Males per 100 females: 94.1; Marriage status: 29.6% never married, 51.3% now married, 1.4% separated, 6.3% widowed, 12.9% divorced; Foreign born: 4.9%; Speak English only: 94.0%; With disability: 13.7%; Veterans: 10.2%; Ancestry: 36.0% Italian, 18.2% German, 17.3% Irish, 8.5% Polish, 7.5% English

Employment: 12.7% management, business, and financial, 1.9% computer, engineering, and science, 9.2% education, legal, community service, arts, and media, 8.6% healthcare practitioners, 20.7% service, 27.5% sales and office, 7.7% natural resources, construction, and maintenance, 11.7% production, transportation, and material moving

Income: Per capita: $24,407; Median household: $50,047; Average household: $59,200; Households with income of $100,000 or more: 13.3%; Poverty rate: 12.1%

Educational Attainment: High school diploma or higher: 90.3%; Bachelor's degree or higher: 22.9%; Graduate/professional degree or higher: 8.6%

School District(s)

Frankfort-Schuyler Central SD (PK-12)
   2014-15 Enrollment: 1,004 . . . . (315) 894-5083

Housing: Homeownership rate: 77.4%; Median home value: $110,600; Median year structure built: 1953; Homeowner vacancy rate: 1.6%; Median selected monthly owner costs: $1,226 with a mortgage, $478 without a mortgage; Median gross rent: $632 per month; Rental vacancy rate: 4.2%

Health Insurance: 93.5% have insurance; 75.0% have private insurance; 36.8% have public insurance; 6.5% do not have insurance; 0.0% of children under 18 do not have insurance

Safety: Violent crime rate: 4.0 per 10,000 population; Property crime rate: 36.2 per 10,000 population

Transportation: Commute: 92.3% car, 0.8% public transportation, 2.0% walk, 3.3% work from home; Mean travel time to work: 20.1 minutes

Additional Information Contacts

Town of Frankfort . . . . (315) 894-8737
   http://www.townoffrankfort.com

FRANKFORT (village).
Covers a land area of 1.014 square miles and a water area of 0.017 square miles. Located at 43.04° N. Lat; 75.07° W. Long. Elevation is 407 feet.

Population: 2,560; Growth (since 2000): 0.9%; Density: 2,525.4 persons per square mile; Race: 94.3% White, 1.8% Black/African American, 0.4% Asian, 0.7% American Indian/Alaska Native, 0.0% Native Hawaiian/Other Pacific Islander, 2.1% Two or more races, 3.0% Hispanic of any race; Average household size: 2.51; Median age: 39.3; Age under 18: 25.5%; Age 65 and over: 13.9%; Males per 100 females: 91.5; Marriage status: 36.0% never married, 42.3% now married, 1.3% separated, 4.7% widowed, 17.0% divorced; Foreign born: 2.1%; Speak English only: 95.8%; With disability: 14.3%; Veterans: 7.6%; Ancestry: 40.8% Italian, 15.5% German, 14.3% Irish, 9.3% American, 8.3% Polish

Employment: 11.3% management, business, and financial, 1.2% computer, engineering, and science, 10.4% education, legal, community service, arts, and media, 7.3% healthcare practitioners, 27.0% service, 21.6% sales and office, 4.9% natural resources, construction, and maintenance, 16.3% production, transportation, and material moving

Income: Per capita: $20,793; Median household: $43,208; Average household: $51,646; Households with income of $100,000 or more: 11.7%; Poverty rate: 21.6%

Educational Attainment: High school diploma or higher: 87.5%; Bachelor's degree or higher: 20.0%; Graduate/professional degree or higher: 8.1%

School District(s)
Frankfort-Schuyler Central SD (PK-12)
   2014-15 Enrollment: 1,004 . . . . (315) 894-5083

Housing: Homeownership rate: 62.1%; Median home value: $88,400; Median year structure built: Before 1940; Homeowner vacancy rate: 2.2%; Median selected monthly owner costs: $1,085 with a mortgage, $425 without a mortgage; Median gross rent: $557 per month; Rental vacancy rate: 7.4%

Health Insurance: 94.9% have insurance; 69.5% have private insurance; 38.6% have public insurance; 5.1% do not have insurance; 0.0% of children under 18 do not have insurance

Safety: Violent crime rate: 7.9 per 10,000 population; Property crime rate: 55.6 per 10,000 population

Transportation: Commute: 88.4% car, 0.4% public transportation, 4.0% walk, 3.4% work from home; Mean travel time to work: 19.4 minutes

---

GERMAN FLATTS (town).
Covers a land area of 33.695 square miles and a water area of 0.499 square miles. Located at 42.99° N. Lat; 74.98° W. Long.

Population: 13,078; Growth (since 2000): -4.0%; Density: 388.1 persons per square mile; Race: 94.9% White, 0.5% Black/African American, 0.7% Asian, 0.0% American Indian/Alaska Native, 1.0% Native Hawaiian/Other Pacific Islander, 2.1% Two or more races, 2.8% Hispanic of any race; Average household size: 2.37; Median age: 38.3; Age under 18: 23.6%; Age 65 and over: 16.6%; Males per 100 females: 93.2; Marriage status: 33.4% never married, 49.2% now married, 2.9% separated, 7.1% widowed, 10.4% divorced; Foreign born: 1.8%; Speak English only: 97.1%; With disability: 13.9%; Veterans: 9.1%; Ancestry: 25.2% Irish, 21.7% Italian, 19.2% German, 12.4% English, 6.2% American

Employment: 12.1% management, business, and financial, 5.0% computer, engineering, and science, 13.2% education, legal, community service, arts, and media, 8.1% healthcare practitioners, 21.4% service, 21.0% sales and office, 7.4% natural resources, construction, and maintenance, 11.8% production, transportation, and material moving

Income: Per capita: $23,003; Median household: $42,421; Average household: $54,733; Households with income of $100,000 or more: 12.9%; Poverty rate: 18.8%

Educational Attainment: High school diploma or higher: 90.6%; Bachelor's degree or higher: 24.6%; Graduate/professional degree or higher: 10.7%

Housing: Homeownership rate: 63.2%; Median home value: $85,100; Median year structure built: 1943; Homeowner vacancy rate: 2.9%; Median selected monthly owner costs: $1,028 with a mortgage, $435 without a mortgage; Median gross rent: $582 per month; Rental vacancy rate: 1.4%

Health Insurance: 90.7% have insurance; 61.4% have private insurance; 43.5% have public insurance; 9.3% do not have insurance; 4.3% of children under 18 do not have insurance

Transportation: Commute: 91.2% car, 1.2% public transportation, 3.6% walk, 2.6% work from home; Mean travel time to work: 21.0 minutes

---

HERKIMER (town).
Covers a land area of 31.662 square miles and a water area of 0.566 square miles. Located at 43.06° N. Lat; 75.00° W. Long. Elevation is 384 feet.

History: Herkimer was settled by a group of Palatines in 1725 and was long known as German Flats. In 1776 Fort Dayton, a wooden structure surrounded by a stockade, was built on a plot now at the center of town. From that fort on August 4, 1777, General Nicholas Herkimer marched to the Battle of Oriskany. The town was named for him.

Population: 10,071; Growth (since 2000): 1.1%; Density: 318.1 persons per square mile; Race: 94.9% White, 2.1% Black/African American, 1.0% Asian, 0.0% American Indian/Alaska Native, 0.0% Native Hawaiian/Other Pacific Islander, 1.4% Two or more races, 1.7% Hispanic of any race; Average household size: 2.19; Median age: 43.2; Age under 18: 16.8%; Age 65 and over: 21.1%; Males per 100 females: 90.5; Marriage status: 30.1% never married, 49.6% now married, 2.8% separated, 8.6% widowed, 11.6% divorced; Foreign born: 4.1%; Speak English only: 92.9%; With disability: 16.7%; Veterans: 12.0%; Ancestry: 22.5% German, 22.1% Italian, 21.2% Irish, 8.7% Polish, 7.9% English

Employment: 7.5% management, business, and financial, 3.6% computer, engineering, and science, 12.2% education, legal, community service, arts, and media, 4.7% healthcare practitioners, 26.0% service, 25.8% sales and office, 4.9% natural resources, construction, and maintenance, 15.3% production, transportation, and material moving

Income: Per capita: $22,302; Median household: $44,349; Average household: $51,065; Households with income of $100,000 or more: 11.2%; Poverty rate: 16.7%

Educational Attainment: High school diploma or higher: 89.8%; Bachelor's degree or higher: 21.2%; Graduate/professional degree or higher: 9.0%

School District(s)
Herkimer Central SD (PK-12)
   2014-15 Enrollment: 1,208 . . . . (315) 866-2230
Herkimer-Fulton-Hamilton-Otsego Boces
   2014-15 Enrollment: n/a . . . . (315) 867-2023

Two-year College(s)
Herkimer County Community College (Public)
   Fall 2014 Enrollment: 3,259 . . . . (315) 866-0300
   2015-16 Tuition: In-state $4,590; Out-of-state $7,650

Housing: Homeownership rate: 53.7%; Median home value: $91,200; Median year structure built: 1944; Homeowner vacancy rate: 2.8%; Median selected monthly owner costs: $1,105 with a mortgage, $484 without a mortgage; Median gross rent: $651 per month; Rental vacancy rate: 1.9%

Health Insurance: 92.3% have insurance; 62.8% have private insurance; 46.2% have public insurance; 7.7% do not have insurance; 0.5% of children under 18 do not have insurance

Newspapers: Evening Telegram (daily circulation 6,700); The Times (daily circulation 4,000)

Transportation: Commute: 85.1% car, 1.3% public transportation, 10.5% walk, 2.3% work from home; Mean travel time to work: 20.1 minutes

Additional Information Contacts

Town of Herkimer . . . . (315) 866-2690
   http://www.townofherkimer.org

HERKIMER (village).
County seat. Covers a land area of 2.588 square miles and a water area of 0.115 square miles. Located at 43.03° N. Lat; 74.99° W. Long. Elevation is 384 feet.

History: Formerly shipping, commercial and trade center for surrounding Mohawk valley Agriculture and industrial area that stretched west through village of Mohawk to Ilion and Frankfort. Herkimer County Historical Society has important documents and exhibits here. World-renowned Herkimer diamonds (actually a clear quartz) are to be found along West Canada Creek Valley north of the village. Settled c.1725, Incorporated 1807.

Population: 7,731; Growth (since 2000): 3.1%; Density: 2,986.8 persons per square mile; Race: 93.6% White, 2.6% Black/African American, 1.3%

Asian, 0.0% American Indian/Alaska Native, 0.0% Native Hawaiian/Other Pacific Islander, 1.8% Two or more races, 2.2% Hispanic of any race; Average household size: 2.11; Median age: 41.1; Age under 18: 16.5%; Age 65 and over: 21.4%; Males per 100 females: 88.6; Marriage status: 31.1% never married, 47.0% now married, 3.3% separated, 9.5% widowed, 12.3% divorced; Foreign born: 4.5%; Speak English only: 93.6%; With disability: 16.7%; Veterans: 11.0%; Ancestry: 23.6% Italian, 21.4% Irish, 21.3% German, 8.7% American, 7.9% English

Employment: 6.8% management, business, and financial, 4.3% computer, engineering, and science, 11.1% education, legal, community service, arts, and media, 4.1% healthcare practitioners, 29.9% service, 26.1% sales and office, 3.3% natural resources, construction, and maintenance, 14.5% production, transportation, and material moving

Income: Per capita: $21,159; Median household: $38,738; Average household: $47,208; Households with income of $100,000 or more: 10.3%; Poverty rate: 19.7%

Educational Attainment: High school diploma or higher: 89.3%; Bachelor's degree or higher: 21.6%; Graduate/professional degree or higher: 9.7%

School District(s)
Herkimer Central SD (PK-12)
  2014-15 Enrollment: 1,208 . . . . (315) 866-2230
Herkimer-Fulton-Hamilton-Otsego Boces
  2014-15 Enrollment: n/a . . . . (315) 867-2023

Two-year College(s)
Herkimer County Community College (Public)
  Fall 2014 Enrollment: 3,259 . . . . (315) 866-0300
  2015-16 Tuition: In-state $4,590; Out-of-state $7,650

Housing: Homeownership rate: 44.1%; Median home value: $86,500; Median year structure built: Before 1940; Homeowner vacancy rate: 2.9%; Median selected monthly owner costs: $1,107 with a mortgage, $546 without a mortgage; Median gross rent: $646 per month; Rental vacancy rate: 2.0%

Health Insurance: 90.9% have insurance; 59.7% have private insurance; 46.5% have public insurance; 9.1% do not have insurance; 0.7% of children under 18 do not have insurance

Safety: Violent crime rate: 62.2 per 10,000 population; Property crime rate: 477.6 per 10,000 population

Newspapers: Evening Telegram (daily circulation 6,700); The Times (daily circulation 4,000)

Transportation: Commute: 82.7% car, 1.7% public transportation, 12.1% walk, 2.4% work from home; Mean travel time to work: 20.5 minutes

Additional Information Contacts
Village of Herkimer . . . . (315) 866-3303
  http://village.herkimer.ny.us/content

ILION (village). Covers a land area of 2.493 square miles and a water area of 0.059 square miles. Located at 43.01° N. Lat; 75.04° W. Long. Elevation is 407 feet.

History: Part of the former Herkimer (village). Remington Arms Museum. Incorporated 1852.

Population: 8,066; Growth (since 2000): -6.3%; Density: 3,235.6 persons per square mile; Race: 93.9% White, 0.7% Black/African American, 0.2% Asian, 0.0% American Indian/Alaska Native, 1.6% Native Hawaiian/Other Pacific Islander, 2.9% Two or more races, 2.8% Hispanic of any race; Average household size: 2.29; Median age: 38.1; Age under 18: 24.6%; Age 65 and over: 15.9%; Males per 100 females: 91.8; Marriage status: 33.0% never married, 47.8% now married, 4.0% separated, 8.5% widowed, 10.7% divorced; Foreign born: 1.2%; Speak English only: 97.6%; With disability: 12.1%; Veterans: 8.5%; Ancestry: 23.9% Irish, 22.6% Italian, 17.5% German, 11.5% English, 6.3% American

Employment: 12.1% management, business, and financial, 4.9% computer, engineering, and science, 13.9% education, legal, community service, arts, and media, 7.9% healthcare practitioners, 23.1% service, 20.4% sales and office, 7.0% natural resources, construction, and maintenance, 10.7% production, transportation, and material moving

Income: Per capita: $21,718; Median household: $39,525; Average household: $50,123; Households with income of $100,000 or more: 11.3%; Poverty rate: 21.2%

Educational Attainment: High school diploma or higher: 89.7%; Bachelor's degree or higher: 25.6%; Graduate/professional degree or higher: 11.8%

School District(s)
Ilion Central SD (PK-12)
  2014-15 Enrollment: n/a . . . . (315) 894-9934

Vocational/Technical School(s)
Herkimer County BOCES-Practical Nursing Program (Public)
  Fall 2014 Enrollment: 101 . . . . (315) 895-2210
  2015-16 Tuition: $10,453

Housing: Homeownership rate: 56.9%; Median home value: $81,400; Median year structure built: 1942; Homeowner vacancy rate: 3.3%; Median selected monthly owner costs: $932 with a mortgage, $451 without a mortgage; Median gross rent: $580 per month; Rental vacancy rate: 1.8%

Health Insurance: 88.8% have insurance; 56.8% have private insurance; 45.5% have public insurance; 11.2% do not have insurance; 5.7% of children under 18 do not have insurance

Safety: Violent crime rate: 12.7 per 10,000 population; Property crime rate: 168.1 per 10,000 population

Transportation: Commute: 89.2% car, 0.9% public transportation, 4.3% walk, 3.5% work from home; Mean travel time to work: 20.6 minutes

Additional Information Contacts
Village of Ilion . . . . (315) 895-7449
  http://www.ilionny.com

JORDANVILLE (unincorporated postal area)
ZCTA: 13361

Covers a land area of 28.325 square miles and a water area of 0.003 square miles. Located at 42.90° N. Lat; 74.87° W. Long. Elevation is 1,499 feet.

Population: 969; Growth (since 2000): 33.8%; Density: 34.2 persons per square mile; Race: 97.8% White, 1.1% Black/African American, 0.7% Asian, 0.0% American Indian/Alaska Native, 0.0% Native Hawaiian/Other Pacific Islander, 0.0% Two or more races, 1.1% Hispanic of any race; Average household size: 2.59; Median age: 40.5; Age under 18: 24.5%; Age 65 and over: 13.2%; Males per 100 females: 119.1; Marriage status: 23.3% never married, 57.8% now married, 0.8% separated, 3.7% widowed, 15.2% divorced; Foreign born: 9.0%; Speak English only: 83.5%; With disability: 12.7%; Veterans: 9.0%; Ancestry: 27.0% German, 15.3% Irish, 14.2% English, 8.9% Dutch, 8.4% American

Employment: 14.5% management, business, and financial, 6.0% computer, engineering, and science, 14.5% education, legal, community service, arts, and media, 8.3% healthcare practitioners, 12.1% service, 21.9% sales and office, 15.2% natural resources, construction, and maintenance, 7.4% production, transportation, and material moving

Income: Per capita: $21,739; Median household: $51,500; Average household: $59,619; Households with income of $100,000 or more: 18.7%; Poverty rate: 6.5%

Educational Attainment: High school diploma or higher: 89.5%; Bachelor's degree or higher: 23.6%; Graduate/professional degree or higher: 8.6%

Housing: Homeownership rate: 87.0%; Median home value: $104,400; Median year structure built: 1959; Homeowner vacancy rate: 2.8%; Median selected monthly owner costs: $1,177 with a mortgage, $448 without a mortgage; Median gross rent: $725 per month; Rental vacancy rate: 0.0%

Health Insurance: 84.1% have insurance; 70.2% have private insurance; 22.7% have public insurance; 15.9% do not have insurance; 13.1% of children under 18 do not have insurance

Transportation: Commute: 76.5% car, 0.5% public transportation, 7.0% walk, 13.3% work from home; Mean travel time to work: 37.3 minutes

---

LITCHFIELD (town). Covers a land area of 29.992 square miles and a water area of 0.061 square miles. Located at 42.97° N. Lat; 75.16° W. Long. Elevation is 1,506 feet.

Population: 1,444; Growth (since 2000): -0.6%; Density: 48.1 persons per square mile; Race: 96.2% White, 0.0% Black/African American, 1.4% Asian, 0.0% American Indian/Alaska Native, 0.0% Native Hawaiian/Other Pacific Islander, 2.2% Two or more races, 0.8% Hispanic of any race; Average household size: 2.52; Median age: 45.1; Age under 18: 23.4%; Age 65 and over: 15.5%; Males per 100 females: 105.0; Marriage status: 24.7% never married, 57.8% now married, 1.6% separated, 4.2% widowed, 13.3% divorced; Foreign born: 3.7%; Speak English only: 90.9%; With disability: 8.9%; Veterans: 10.2%; Ancestry: 26.8% Irish, 19.3% German, 14.7% English, 12.3% Italian, 6.9% Welsh

Employment: 9.8% management, business, and financial, 6.8% computer, engineering, and science, 9.8% education, legal, community service, arts, and media, 12.1% healthcare practitioners, 15.3% service, 17.0% sales and office, 19.7% natural resources, construction, and maintenance, 9.5% production, transportation, and material moving

Income: Per capita: $31,593; Median household: $60,677; Average household: $79,182; Households with income of $100,000 or more: 16.9%; Poverty rate: 8.1%
Educational Attainment: High school diploma or higher: 94.2%; Bachelor's degree or higher: 26.9%; Graduate/professional degree or higher: 8.2%
Housing: Homeownership rate: 89.0%; Median home value: $122,400; Median year structure built: 1976; Homeowner vacancy rate: 0.0%; Median selected monthly owner costs: $1,170 with a mortgage, $520 without a mortgage; Median gross rent: $630 per month; Rental vacancy rate: 0.0%
Health Insurance: 93.3% have insurance; 72.1% have private insurance; 36.0% have public insurance; 6.7% do not have insurance; 2.7% of children under 18 do not have insurance
Transportation: Commute: 92.4% car, 0.0% public transportation, 1.0% walk, 6.6% work from home; Mean travel time to work: 24.1 minutes

LITTLE FALLS (city). Covers a land area of 3.838 square miles and a water area of 0.151 square miles. Located at 43.04° N. Lat; 74.86° W. Long. Elevation is 420 feet.

Population: 4,878; Growth (since 2000): -6.0%; Density: 1,270.9 persons per square mile; Race: 95.6% White, 1.4% Black/African American, 0.6% Asian, 0.3% American Indian/Alaska Native, 1.3% Native Hawaiian/Other Pacific Islander, 0.6% Two or more races, 0.9% Hispanic of any race; Average household size: 2.24; Median age: 43.6; Age under 18: 21.5%; Age 65 and over: 20.2%; Males per 100 females: 88.3; Marriage status: 28.8% never married, 43.3% now married, 2.9% separated, 10.3% widowed, 17.6% divorced; Foreign born: 3.3%; Speak English only: 95.2%; With disability: 18.7%; Veterans: 11.8%; Ancestry: 26.7% Irish, 17.9% German, 16.2% Italian, 10.4% Polish, 10.1% English
Employment: 11.2% management, business, and financial, 2.3% computer, engineering, and science, 11.5% education, legal, community service, arts, and media, 5.8% healthcare practitioners, 17.4% service, 24.5% sales and office, 8.8% natural resources, construction, and maintenance, 18.5% production, transportation, and material moving
Income: Per capita: $21,652; Median household: $38,897; Average household: $49,096; Households with income of $100,000 or more: 8.9%; Poverty rate: 20.2%
Educational Attainment: High school diploma or higher: 89.0%; Bachelor's degree or higher: 27.2%; Graduate/professional degree or higher: 10.1%

School District(s)
Little Falls City SD (KG-12)
    2014-15 Enrollment: 1,100 . . . . (315) 823-1470
Housing: Homeownership rate: 53.3%; Median home value: $79,800; Median year structure built: Before 1940; Homeowner vacancy rate: 2.9%; Median selected monthly owner costs: $1,028 with a mortgage, $473 without a mortgage; Median gross rent: $586 per month; Rental vacancy rate: 11.3%
Health Insurance: 92.9% have insurance; 59.6% have private insurance; 48.4% have public insurance; 7.1% do not have insurance; 2.6% of children under 18 do not have insurance
Hospitals: Little Falls Hospital (25 beds)
Safety: Violent crime rate: 18.7 per 10,000 population; Property crime rate: 265.4 per 10,000 population
Transportation: Commute: 85.0% car, 1.3% public transportation, 7.2% walk, 5.2% work from home; Mean travel time to work: 19.9 minutes
Additional Information Contacts
City of Little Falls . . . . (315) 823-2400
    http://www.cityoflittlefalls.net

LITTLE FALLS (town). Covers a land area of 22.340 square miles and a water area of 0.163 square miles. Located at 43.02° N. Lat; 74.89° W. Long. Elevation is 420 feet.

History: Home of Gen. Nicholas Herkimer, hero of Battle of Oriskany. Settled c.1725; incorporated as city 1895.
Population: 1,634; Growth (since 2000): 5.8%; Density: 73.1 persons per square mile; Race: 94.3% White, 1.2% Black/African American, 0.6% Asian, 0.0% American Indian/Alaska Native, 0.0% Native Hawaiian/Other Pacific Islander, 3.9% Two or more races, 0.1% Hispanic of any race; Average household size: 2.60; Median age: 43.7; Age under 18: 21.5%; Age 65 and over: 15.1%; Males per 100 females: 109.1; Marriage status: 26.8% never married, 57.0% now married, 1.1% separated, 5.4% widowed, 10.8% divorced; Foreign born: 2.5%; Speak English only: 96.3%; With disability: 8.0%; Veterans: 8.6%; Ancestry: 22.7% German, 19.5% Irish, 18.4% Italian, 11.7% American, 10.6% Polish

Employment: 13.8% management, business, and financial, 3.8% computer, engineering, and science, 11.4% education, legal, community service, arts, and media, 4.9% healthcare practitioners, 17.2% service, 19.2% sales and office, 8.2% natural resources, construction, and maintenance, 21.5% production, transportation, and material moving
Income: Per capita: $25,573; Median household: $58,487; Average household: $65,237; Households with income of $100,000 or more: 18.9%; Poverty rate: 14.0%
Educational Attainment: High school diploma or higher: 89.6%; Bachelor's degree or higher: 19.5%; Graduate/professional degree or higher: 9.4%

School District(s)
Little Falls City SD (KG-12)
    2014-15 Enrollment: 1,100 . . . . (315) 823-1470
Housing: Homeownership rate: 84.3%; Median home value: $104,200; Median year structure built: 1970; Homeowner vacancy rate: 0.0%; Median selected monthly owner costs: $1,130 with a mortgage, $443 without a mortgage; Median gross rent: $897 per month; Rental vacancy rate: 10.0%
Health Insurance: 92.8% have insurance; 73.7% have private insurance; 32.3% have public insurance; 7.2% do not have insurance; 0.0% of children under 18 do not have insurance
Hospitals: Little Falls Hospital (25 beds)
Transportation: Commute: 93.8% car, 2.4% public transportation, 1.2% walk, 2.1% work from home; Mean travel time to work: 22.1 minutes

MANHEIM (town). Covers a land area of 29.136 square miles and a water area of 0.557 square miles. Located at 43.06° N. Lat; 74.80° W. Long.

Population: 3,304; Growth (since 2000): 4.2%; Density: 113.4 persons per square mile; Race: 98.5% White, 0.4% Black/African American, 0.0% Asian, 0.5% American Indian/Alaska Native, 0.0% Native Hawaiian/Other Pacific Islander, 0.4% Two or more races, 1.8% Hispanic of any race; Average household size: 2.46; Median age: 38.8; Age under 18: 26.5%; Age 65 and over: 19.1%; Males per 100 females: 96.5; Marriage status: 26.4% never married, 54.4% now married, 2.0% separated, 8.3% widowed, 11.0% divorced; Foreign born: 1.8%; Speak English only: 93.2%; With disability: 10.9%; Veterans: 9.7%; Ancestry: 24.2% Italian, 24.0% German, 17.3% Irish, 11.0% Polish, 9.9% English
Employment: 7.9% management, business, and financial, 2.2% computer, engineering, and science, 13.3% education, legal, community service, arts, and media, 5.2% healthcare practitioners, 17.1% service, 24.3% sales and office, 16.1% natural resources, construction, and maintenance, 13.9% production, transportation, and material moving
Income: Per capita: $19,915; Median household: $41,958; Average household: $48,999; Households with income of $100,000 or more: 9.8%; Poverty rate: 16.3%
Educational Attainment: High school diploma or higher: 87.0%; Bachelor's degree or higher: 16.0%; Graduate/professional degree or higher: 9.0%
Housing: Homeownership rate: 76.4%; Median home value: $81,800; Median year structure built: Before 1940; Homeowner vacancy rate: 1.4%; Median selected monthly owner costs: $1,064 with a mortgage, $386 without a mortgage; Median gross rent: $531 per month; Rental vacancy rate: 8.7%
Health Insurance: 90.5% have insurance; 57.4% have private insurance; 45.0% have public insurance; 9.5% do not have insurance; 8.7% of children under 18 do not have insurance
Transportation: Commute: 89.7% car, 0.0% public transportation, 1.2% walk, 6.8% work from home; Mean travel time to work: 24.2 minutes

MIDDLEVILLE (village). Covers a land area of 0.765 square miles and a water area of 0.050 square miles. Located at 43.14° N. Lat; 74.97° W. Long. Elevation is 597 feet.

Population: 533; Growth (since 2000): -3.1%; Density: 696.7 persons per square mile; Race: 97.4% White, 0.0% Black/African American, 0.0% Asian, 0.0% American Indian/Alaska Native, 0.0% Native Hawaiian/Other Pacific Islander, 2.6% Two or more races, 0.0% Hispanic of any race; Average household size: 2.68; Median age: 45.1; Age under 18: 26.8%; Age 65 and over: 17.1%; Males per 100 females: 91.8; Marriage status: 28.0% never married, 47.5% now married, 0.5% separated, 6.3% widowed, 18.3% divorced; Foreign born: 0.8%; Speak English only: 100.0%; With disability: 8.6%; Veterans: 12.1%; Ancestry: 26.8% German, 24.2% Irish, 22.9% English, 10.9% American, 9.0% Italian
Employment: 12.6% management, business, and financial, 1.4% computer, engineering, and science, 7.5% education, legal, community

service, arts, and media, 9.3% healthcare practitioners, 10.3% service, 27.1% sales and office, 22.9% natural resources, construction, and maintenance, 8.9% production, transportation, and material moving

Income: Per capita: $25,901; Median household: $63,125; Average household: $69,748; Households with income of $100,000 or more: 24.1%; Poverty rate: 9.6%

Educational Attainment: High school diploma or higher: 90.5%; Bachelor's degree or higher: 16.1%; Graduate/professional degree or higher: 5.3%

Housing: Homeownership rate: 83.9%; Median home value: $95,400; Median year structure built: Before 1940; Homeowner vacancy rate: 6.7%; Median selected monthly owner costs: $1,206 with a mortgage, $619 without a mortgage; Median gross rent: $797 per month; Rental vacancy rate: 0.0%

Health Insurance: 95.5% have insurance; 69.8% have private insurance; 37.0% have public insurance; 4.5% do not have insurance; 0.0% of children under 18 do not have insurance

Transportation: Commute: 95.6% car, 1.0% public transportation, 3.4% walk, 0.0% work from home; Mean travel time to work: 33.2 minutes

---

MOHAWK (village). Covers a land area of 0.876 square miles and a water area of 0.027 square miles. Located at 43.01° N. Lat; 75.01° W. Long. Elevation is 413 feet.

History: Settled 1826, incorporated 1844.

Population: 2,571; Growth (since 2000): -3.3%; Density: 2,935.3 persons per square mile; Race: 98.2% White, 0.2% Black/African American, 0.0% Asian, 0.0% American Indian/Alaska Native, 0.0% Native Hawaiian/Other Pacific Islander, 1.6% Two or more races, 3.1% Hispanic of any race; Average household size: 2.41; Median age: 37.5; Age under 18: 20.3%; Age 65 and over: 18.6%; Males per 100 females: 91.0; Marriage status: 39.0% never married, 42.5% now married, 0.6% separated, 5.1% widowed, 13.3% divorced; Foreign born: 1.4%; Speak English only: 98.5%; With disability: 19.1%; Veterans: 9.4%; Ancestry: 30.3% Irish, 24.8% German, 23.0% Italian, 14.0% English, 8.7% Polish

Employment: 10.9% management, business, and financial, 4.9% computer, engineering, and science, 12.4% education, legal, community service, arts, and media, 9.1% healthcare practitioners, 24.6% service, 19.3% sales and office, 4.6% natural resources, construction, and maintenance, 14.2% production, transportation, and material moving

Income: Per capita: $20,704; Median household: $42,941; Average household: $50,179; Households with income of $100,000 or more: 7.6%; Poverty rate: 17.1%

Educational Attainment: High school diploma or higher: 95.5%; Bachelor's degree or higher: 21.7%; Graduate/professional degree or higher: 8.7%

School District(s)

Mohawk Central SD (PK-12)

    2014-15 Enrollment: n/a . . . . (315) 867-2904

Housing: Homeownership rate: 62.3%; Median home value: $85,300; Median year structure built: Before 1940; Homeowner vacancy rate: 2.1%; Median selected monthly owner costs: $1,037 with a mortgage, $414 without a mortgage; Median gross rent: $558 per month; Rental vacancy rate: 0.0%

Health Insurance: 92.1% have insurance; 65.8% have private insurance; 42.6% have public insurance; 7.9% do not have insurance; 0.0% of children under 18 do not have insurance

Transportation: Commute: 92.7% car, 3.1% public transportation, 2.8% walk, 1.4% work from home; Mean travel time to work: 18.7 minutes

---

NEWPORT (town). Covers a land area of 32.009 square miles and a water area of 0.443 square miles. Located at 43.18° N. Lat; 75.04° W. Long. Elevation is 663 feet.

Population: 2,176; Growth (since 2000): -0.7%; Density: 68.0 persons per square mile; Race: 94.9% White, 1.5% Black/African American, 0.0% Asian, 0.0% American Indian/Alaska Native, 0.0% Native Hawaiian/Other Pacific Islander, 3.4% Two or more races, 2.4% Hispanic of any race; Average household size: 2.71; Median age: 40.6; Age under 18: 26.2%; Age 65 and over: 15.4%; Males per 100 females: 94.6; Marriage status: 24.3% never married, 56.1% now married, 2.1% separated, 5.3% widowed, 14.3% divorced; Foreign born: 2.6%; Speak English only: 93.9%; With disability: 11.4%; Veterans: 9.7%; Ancestry: 23.0% Irish, 19.5% German, 14.2% Italian, 11.9% American, 11.2% Polish

Employment: 14.1% management, business, and financial, 3.9% computer, engineering, and science, 9.4% education, legal, community service, arts, and media, 7.3% healthcare practitioners, 12.6% service,

---

21.4% sales and office, 18.9% natural resources, construction, and maintenance, 12.3% production, transportation, and material moving

Income: Per capita: $24,120; Median household: $54,044; Average household: $64,855; Households with income of $100,000 or more: 23.8%; Poverty rate: 9.0%

Educational Attainment: High school diploma or higher: 89.8%; Bachelor's degree or higher: 17.7%; Graduate/professional degree or higher: 8.4%

School District(s)

West Canada Valley Central SD (PK-12)

    2014-15 Enrollment: 719 . . . . (315) 845-6800

Housing: Homeownership rate: 82.9%; Median home value: $112,400; Median year structure built: 1964; Homeowner vacancy rate: 0.9%; Median selected monthly owner costs: $1,261 with a mortgage, $474 without a mortgage; Median gross rent: $557 per month; Rental vacancy rate: 6.8%

Health Insurance: 91.9% have insurance; 67.0% have private insurance; 37.9% have public insurance; 8.1% do not have insurance; 9.1% of children under 18 do not have insurance

Transportation: Commute: 87.9% car, 0.4% public transportation, 4.5% walk, 6.9% work from home; Mean travel time to work: 35.6 minutes

---

NEWPORT (village). Covers a land area of 0.526 square miles and a water area of 0.064 square miles. Located at 43.19° N. Lat; 75.02° W. Long. Elevation is 663 feet.

Population: 544; Growth (since 2000): -15.0%; Density: 1,034.5 persons per square mile; Race: 92.8% White, 3.5% Black/African American, 0.0% Asian, 0.0% American Indian/Alaska Native, 0.0% Native Hawaiian/Other Pacific Islander, 3.1% Two or more races, 0.6% Hispanic of any race; Average household size: 2.30; Median age: 39.5; Age under 18: 27.4%; Age 65 and over: 16.5%; Males per 100 females: 91.6; Marriage status: 25.6% never married, 46.2% now married, 3.9% separated, 8.7% widowed, 19.5% divorced; Foreign born: 0.7%; Speak English only: 98.7%; With disability: 12.3%; Veterans: 11.4%; Ancestry: 23.2% German, 21.5% American, 16.4% Irish, 11.4% English, 10.8% Italian

Employment: 9.7% management, business, and financial, 7.4% computer, engineering, and science, 12.9% education, legal, community service, arts, and media, 0.0% healthcare practitioners, 9.7% service, 30.4% sales and office, 22.1% natural resources, construction, and maintenance, 7.8% production, transportation, and material moving

Income: Per capita: $21,381; Median household: $34,821; Average household: $48,587; Households with income of $100,000 or more: 9.7%; Poverty rate: 10.6%

Educational Attainment: High school diploma or higher: 89.4%; Bachelor's degree or higher: 18.5%; Graduate/professional degree or higher: 9.7%

School District(s)

West Canada Valley Central SD (PK-12)

    2014-15 Enrollment: 719 . . . . (315) 845-6800

Housing: Homeownership rate: 56.5%; Median home value: $98,200; Median year structure built: Before 1940; Homeowner vacancy rate: 0.0%; Median selected monthly owner costs: $1,083 with a mortgage, $520 without a mortgage; Median gross rent: $486 per month; Rental vacancy rate: 5.5%

Health Insurance: 96.5% have insurance; 70.4% have private insurance; 50.9% have public insurance; 3.5% do not have insurance; 0.0% of children under 18 do not have insurance

Transportation: Commute: 77.4% car, 0.0% public transportation, 15.4% walk, 6.3% work from home; Mean travel time to work: 32.6 minutes

---

NORWAY (town). Covers a land area of 35.560 square miles and a water area of 0.273 square miles. Located at 43.23° N. Lat; 74.95° W. Long. Elevation is 1,332 feet.

Population: 914; Growth (since 2000): 28.6%; Density: 25.7 persons per square mile; Race: 99.7% White, 0.3% Black/African American, 0.0% Asian, 0.0% American Indian/Alaska Native, 0.0% Native Hawaiian/Other Pacific Islander, 0.0% Two or more races, 1.2% Hispanic of any race; Average household size: 2.60; Median age: 45.8; Age under 18: 21.2%; Age 65 and over: 10.3%; Males per 100 females: 101.6; Marriage status: 27.3% never married, 57.1% now married, 2.2% separated, 5.3% widowed, 10.3% divorced; Foreign born: 0.7%; Speak English only: 99.3%; With disability: 11.7%; Veterans: 9.9%; Ancestry: 23.3% German, 21.0% Irish, 17.4% English, 14.6% Italian, 9.8% French

Employment: 14.5% management, business, and financial, 1.5% computer, engineering, and science, 8.7% education, legal, community service, arts, and media, 10.2% healthcare practitioners, 13.6% service,

24.0% sales and office, 11.9% natural resources, construction, and maintenance, 15.6% production, transportation, and material moving
Income: Per capita: $25,459; Median household: $54,375; Average household: $65,475; Households with income of $100,000 or more: 21.0%; Poverty rate: 10.6%
Educational Attainment: High school diploma or higher: 90.1%; Bachelor's degree or higher: 16.6%; Graduate/professional degree or higher: 5.0%
Housing: Homeownership rate: 83.0%; Median home value: $100,000; Median year structure built: 1982; Homeowner vacancy rate: 2.0%; Median selected monthly owner costs: $1,098 with a mortgage, $503 without a mortgage; Median gross rent: $598 per month; Rental vacancy rate: 0.0%
Health Insurance: 87.9% have insurance; 68.6% have private insurance; 28.8% have public insurance; 12.1% do not have insurance; 18.0% of children under 18 do not have insurance
Transportation: Commute: 91.8% car, 0.0% public transportation, 2.4% walk, 3.8% work from home; Mean travel time to work: 34.6 minutes

OHIO (town). Covers a land area of 301.344 square miles and a water area of 6.227 square miles. Located at 43.46° N. Lat; 74.89° W. Long. Elevation is 1,371 feet.
Population: 1,000; Growth (since 2000): 8.5%; Density: 3.3 persons per square mile; Race: 98.8% White, 0.0% Black/African American, 0.0% Asian, 0.2% American Indian/Alaska Native, 0.0% Native Hawaiian/Other Pacific Islander, 1.0% Two or more races, 0.4% Hispanic of any race; Average household size: 2.44; Median age: 46.9; Age under 18: 19.6%; Age 65 and over: 17.1%; Males per 100 females: 104.1; Marriage status: 27.4% never married, 58.6% now married, 2.2% separated, 5.1% widowed, 9.0% divorced; Foreign born: 1.4%; Speak English only: 96.7%; With disability: 19.0%; Veterans: 18.2%; Ancestry: 27.4% German, 22.3% Irish, 18.1% English, 15.7% Polish, 8.2% Italian
Employment: 9.7% management, business, and financial, 1.9% computer, engineering, and science, 13.6% education, legal, community service, arts, and media, 6.1% healthcare practitioners, 12.2% service, 23.6% sales and office, 20.3% natural resources, construction, and maintenance, 12.5% production, transportation, and material moving
Income: Per capita: $19,358; Median household: $35,833; Average household: $47,007; Households with income of $100,000 or more: 10.3%; Poverty rate: 22.0%
Educational Attainment: High school diploma or higher: 89.5%; Bachelor's degree or higher: 11.9%; Graduate/professional degree or higher: 4.7%
Housing: Homeownership rate: 85.6%; Median home value: $94,600; Median year structure built: 1970; Homeowner vacancy rate: 1.1%; Median selected monthly owner costs: $936 with a mortgage, $420 without a mortgage; Median gross rent: $1,016 per month; Rental vacancy rate: 0.0%
Health Insurance: 88.0% have insurance; 47.2% have private insurance; 52.8% have public insurance; 12.0% do not have insurance; 9.7% of children under 18 do not have insurance
Transportation: Commute: 91.8% car, 0.0% public transportation, 3.2% walk, 5.0% work from home; Mean travel time to work: 29.9 minutes

OLD FORGE (CDP). Covers a land area of 1.786 square miles and a water area of 0.178 square miles. Located at 43.71° N. Lat; 74.97° W. Long. Elevation is 1,736 feet.
Population: 441; Growth (since 2000): n/a; Density: 246.9 persons per square mile; Race: 98.0% White, 0.7% Black/African American, 0.0% Asian, 0.0% American Indian/Alaska Native, 0.0% Native Hawaiian/Other Pacific Islander, 0.7% Two or more races, 0.7% Hispanic of any race; Average household size: 1.60; Median age: 59.5; Age under 18: 2.3%; Age 65 and over: 28.3%; Males per 100 females: 95.3; Marriage status: 30.7% never married, 36.0% now married, 1.1% separated, 26.1% widowed, 7.1% divorced; Foreign born: 6.3%; Speak English only: 93.8%; With disability: 20.9%; Veterans: 17.2%; Ancestry: 34.2% German, 20.9% English, 20.6% Irish, 13.4% Dutch, 12.0% French Canadian
Employment: 1.9% management, business, and financial, 0.0% computer, engineering, and science, 13.4% education, legal, community service, arts, and media, 0.0% healthcare practitioners, 38.0% service, 32.9% sales and office, 12.0% natural resources, construction, and maintenance, 1.9% production, transportation, and material moving
Income: Per capita: $26,966; Median household: $24,559; Average household: $46,842; Households with income of $100,000 or more: 8.0%; Poverty rate: 14.7%

Educational Attainment: High school diploma or higher: 88.5%; Bachelor's degree or higher: 21.9%; Graduate/professional degree or higher: 7.9%
School District(s)
Town of Webb Union Free SD (KG-12)
    2014-15 Enrollment: 278. . . . . (315) 369-3222
Housing: Homeownership rate: 63.0%; Median home value: $269,600; Median year structure built: 1945; Homeowner vacancy rate: 0.0%; Median selected monthly owner costs: $767 with a mortgage, $637 without a mortgage; Median gross rent: $608 per month; Rental vacancy rate: 13.7%
Health Insurance: 89.6% have insurance; 59.9% have private insurance; 47.2% have public insurance; 10.4% do not have insurance; 0.0% of children under 18 do not have insurance
Transportation: Commute: 51.5% car, 0.0% public transportation, 29.4% walk, 18.0% work from home; Mean travel time to work: 9.2 minutes

POLAND (village). Covers a land area of 0.543 square miles and a water area of 0.006 square miles. Located at 43.23° N. Lat; 75.06° W. Long. Elevation is 709 feet.
Population: 381; Growth (since 2000): -15.5%; Density: 701.8 persons per square mile; Race: 90.6% White, 0.8% Black/African American, 0.0% Asian, 0.0% American Indian/Alaska Native, 0.0% Native Hawaiian/Other Pacific Islander, 8.1% Two or more races, 4.2% Hispanic of any race; Average household size: 2.67; Median age: 41.9; Age under 18: 24.9%; Age 65 and over: 14.2%; Males per 100 females: 89.6; Marriage status: 21.4% never married, 60.9% now married, 1.4% separated, 4.4% widowed, 13.3% divorced; Foreign born: 3.7%; Speak English only: 96.7%; With disability: 12.3%; Veterans: 10.8%; Ancestry: 18.4% German, 17.8% Irish, 12.6% Italian, 12.1% Polish, 10.5% English
Employment: 17.6% management, business, and financial, 5.3% computer, engineering, and science, 3.7% education, legal, community service, arts, and media, 7.0% healthcare practitioners, 18.2% service, 32.1% sales and office, 4.3% natural resources, construction, and maintenance, 11.8% production, transportation, and material moving
Income: Per capita: $26,006; Median household: $61,750; Average household: $69,404; Households with income of $100,000 or more: 16.7%; Poverty rate: 7.3%
Educational Attainment: High school diploma or higher: 94.4%; Bachelor's degree or higher: 29.2%; Graduate/professional degree or higher: 10.9%
School District(s)
Poland Central SD (PK-12)
    2014-15 Enrollment: 617. . . . . (315) 826-0203
Housing: Homeownership rate: 84.8%; Median home value: $108,100; Median year structure built: Before 1940; Homeowner vacancy rate: 0.0%; Median selected monthly owner costs: $1,277 with a mortgage, $467 without a mortgage; Median gross rent: $756 per month; Rental vacancy rate: 16.0%
Health Insurance: 91.6% have insurance; 72.7% have private insurance; 31.8% have public insurance; 8.4% do not have insurance; 11.6% of children under 18 do not have insurance
Transportation: Commute: 90.1% car, 2.3% public transportation, 1.2% walk, 5.8% work from home; Mean travel time to work: 23.0 minutes

RUSSIA (town). Covers a land area of 56.962 square miles and a water area of 3.456 square miles. Located at 43.30° N. Lat; 75.07° W. Long. Elevation is 1,129 feet.
Population: 2,586; Growth (since 2000): 4.0%; Density: 45.4 persons per square mile; Race: 93.3% White, 0.9% Black/African American, 0.0% Asian, 1.3% American Indian/Alaska Native, 0.0% Native Hawaiian/Other Pacific Islander, 3.8% Two or more races, 2.2% Hispanic of any race; Average household size: 2.50; Median age: 43.3; Age under 18: 24.6%; Age 65 and over: 17.6%; Males per 100 females: 103.4; Marriage status: 26.5% never married, 59.0% now married, 2.1% separated, 7.3% widowed, 7.2% divorced; Foreign born: 1.9%; Speak English only: 96.1%; With disability: 11.7%; Veterans: 9.6%; Ancestry: 22.5% German, 17.7% Irish, 12.8% English, 11.8% Italian, 9.2% Polish
Employment: 11.6% management, business, and financial, 4.6% computer, engineering, and science, 7.9% education, legal, community service, arts, and media, 12.2% healthcare practitioners, 16.6% service, 27.4% sales and office, 10.6% natural resources, construction, and maintenance, 9.0% production, transportation, and material moving
Income: Per capita: $25,106; Median household: $45,671; Average household: $63,211; Households with income of $100,000 or more: 19.9%; Poverty rate: 12.3%

Educational Attainment: High school diploma or higher: 94.4%; Bachelor's degree or higher: 34.6%; Graduate/professional degree or higher: 13.1%
Housing: Homeownership rate: 83.8%; Median home value: $123,300; Median year structure built: 1964; Homeowner vacancy rate: 1.5%; Median selected monthly owner costs: $1,298 with a mortgage, $538 without a mortgage; Median gross rent: $756 per month; Rental vacancy rate: 0.0%
Health Insurance: 93.1% have insurance; 71.3% have private insurance; 36.1% have public insurance; 6.9% do not have insurance; 1.8% of children under 18 do not have insurance
Transportation: Commute: 90.4% car, 0.7% public transportation, 0.7% walk, 8.1% work from home; Mean travel time to work: 36.8 minutes

SALISBURY (town).
Covers a land area of 107.366 square miles and a water area of 0.835 square miles. Located at 43.22° N. Lat; 74.80° W. Long. Elevation is 1,220 feet.
Population: 2,224; Growth (since 2000): 13.9%; Density: 20.7 persons per square mile; Race: 97.2% White, 0.5% Black/African American, 0.4% Asian, 0.5% American Indian/Alaska Native, 0.0% Native Hawaiian/Other Pacific Islander, 1.3% Two or more races, 1.4% Hispanic of any race; Average household size: 2.79; Median age: 37.0; Age under 18: 25.8%; Age 65 and over: 10.7%; Males per 100 females: 102.1; Marriage status: 35.1% never married, 47.0% now married, 1.2% separated, 5.2% widowed, 12.6% divorced; Foreign born: 3.5%; Speak English only: 92.9%; With disability: 15.9%; Veterans: 8.0%; Ancestry: 19.9% Irish, 18.5% German, 9.6% English, 8.7% American, 7.6% Polish
Employment: 7.7% management, business, and financial, 0.6% computer, engineering, and science, 7.0% education, legal, community service, arts, and media, 4.9% healthcare practitioners, 22.9% service, 17.6% sales and office, 17.6% natural resources, construction, and maintenance, 21.8% production, transportation, and material moving
Income: Per capita: $18,606; Median household: $45,740; Average household: $51,348; Households with income of $100,000 or more: 8.8%; Poverty rate: 11.6%
Educational Attainment: High school diploma or higher: 74.8%; Bachelor's degree or higher: 7.0%; Graduate/professional degree or higher: 1.9%
Housing: Homeownership rate: 84.6%; Median home value: $85,200; Median year structure built: 1979; Homeowner vacancy rate: 0.0%; Median selected monthly owner costs: $938 with a mortgage, $360 without a mortgage; Median gross rent: $636 per month; Rental vacancy rate: 7.0%
Health Insurance: 87.3% have insurance; 56.6% have private insurance; 40.3% have public insurance; 12.7% do not have insurance; 3.3% of children under 18 do not have insurance
Transportation: Commute: 92.5% car, 0.2% public transportation, 2.2% walk, 4.1% work from home; Mean travel time to work: 30.5 minutes

SALISBURY CENTER (unincorporated postal area)
ZCTA: 13454
Covers a land area of 43.050 square miles and a water area of 0.283 square miles. Located at 43.22° N. Lat; 74.76° W. Long. Elevation is 1,073 feet.
Population: 733; Growth (since 2000): 2.9%; Density: 17.0 persons per square mile; Race: 97.3% White, 1.6% Black/African American, 1.1% Asian, 0.0% American Indian/Alaska Native, 0.0% Native Hawaiian/Other Pacific Islander, 0.0% Two or more races, 0.0% Hispanic of any race; Average household size: 2.41; Median age: 36.2; Age under 18: 24.4%; Age 65 and over: 11.6%; Males per 100 females: 99.0; Marriage status: 36.0% never married, 49.4% now married, 0.5% separated, 7.3% widowed, 7.3% divorced; Foreign born: 3.0%; Speak English only: 94.8%; With disability: 18.7%; Veterans: 9.9%; Ancestry: 19.1% German, 17.3% Irish, 14.3% English, 10.8% American, 8.3% Italian
Employment: 3.8% management, business, and financial, 0.0% computer, engineering, and science, 8.9% education, legal, community service, arts, and media, 2.4% healthcare practitioners, 31.4% service, 14.0% sales and office, 13.7% natural resources, construction, and maintenance, 25.9% production, transportation, and material moving
Income: Per capita: $16,116; Median household: $36,125; Average household: $39,984; Households with income of $100,000 or more: 2.8%; Poverty rate: 13.8%
Educational Attainment: High school diploma or higher: 75.1%; Bachelor's degree or higher: 9.1%; Graduate/professional degree or higher: 1.7%

Housing: Homeownership rate: 83.4%; Median home value: $87,200; Median year structure built: 1981; Homeowner vacancy rate: 0.0%; Median selected monthly owner costs: $971 with a mortgage, $371 without a mortgage; Median gross rent: $664 per month; Rental vacancy rate: 16.1%
Health Insurance: 89.2% have insurance; 63.7% have private insurance; 36.2% have public insurance; 10.8% do not have insurance; 0.0% of children under 18 do not have insurance
Transportation: Commute: 86.0% car, 0.7% public transportation, 6.7% walk, 5.6% work from home; Mean travel time to work: 28.4 minutes

SCHUYLER (town).
Covers a land area of 39.874 square miles and a water area of 0.358 square miles. Located at 43.11° N. Lat; 75.10° W. Long.
Population: 3,418; Growth (since 2000): 1.0%; Density: 85.7 persons per square mile; Race: 99.6% White, 0.1% Black/African American, 0.3% Asian, 0.0% American Indian/Alaska Native, 0.0% Native Hawaiian/Other Pacific Islander, 0.0% Two or more races, 2.3% Hispanic of any race; Average household size: 2.41; Median age: 45.3; Age under 18: 20.5%; Age 65 and over: 21.5%; Males per 100 females: 94.6; Marriage status: 29.3% never married, 52.0% now married, 1.2% separated, 6.4% widowed, 12.2% divorced; Foreign born: 5.2%; Speak English only: 92.7%; With disability: 10.6%; Veterans: 8.6%; Ancestry: 30.4% Irish, 28.4% Italian, 16.8% Polish, 15.3% German, 10.3% English
Employment: 9.6% management, business, and financial, 1.8% computer, engineering, and science, 12.8% education, legal, community service, arts, and media, 8.9% healthcare practitioners, 22.2% service, 27.4% sales and office, 8.0% natural resources, construction, and maintenance, 9.2% production, transportation, and material moving
Income: Per capita: $24,639; Median household: $47,083; Average household: $59,276; Households with income of $100,000 or more: 15.1%; Poverty rate: 10.3%
Educational Attainment: High school diploma or higher: 90.5%; Bachelor's degree or higher: 22.0%; Graduate/professional degree or higher: 12.1%
Housing: Homeownership rate: 82.9%; Median home value: $87,600; Median year structure built: 1984; Homeowner vacancy rate: 2.2%; Median selected monthly owner costs: $1,123 with a mortgage, $506 without a mortgage; Median gross rent: $804 per month; Rental vacancy rate: 0.0%
Health Insurance: 94.3% have insurance; 76.9% have private insurance; 35.0% have public insurance; 5.7% do not have insurance; 0.0% of children under 18 do not have insurance
Transportation: Commute: 98.0% car, 0.0% public transportation, 0.0% walk, 2.0% work from home; Mean travel time to work: 21.8 minutes
Additional Information Contacts
Town of Schuyler . . . . (315) 733-7458
  http://townofschuyler.com

STARK (town).
Covers a land area of 31.833 square miles and a water area of 0.003 square miles. Located at 42.93° N. Lat; 74.82° W. Long.
Population: 747; Growth (since 2000): -2.6%; Density: 23.5 persons per square mile; Race: 99.2% White, 0.0% Black/African American, 0.3% Asian, 0.0% American Indian/Alaska Native, 0.0% Native Hawaiian/Other Pacific Islander, 0.5% Two or more races, 0.0% Hispanic of any race; Average household size: 2.52; Median age: 45.5; Age under 18: 22.6%; Age 65 and over: 16.7%; Males per 100 females: 112.6; Marriage status: 22.7% never married, 59.2% now married, 2.0% separated, 4.6% widowed, 13.5% divorced; Foreign born: 2.0%; Speak English only: 91.4%; With disability: 12.6%; Veterans: 9.2%; Ancestry: 33.7% German, 17.4% English, 13.7% Irish, 11.0% Dutch, 9.4% Polish
Employment: 10.2% management, business, and financial, 2.3% computer, engineering, and science, 12.0% education, legal, community service, arts, and media, 5.5% healthcare practitioners, 12.8% service, 23.9% sales and office, 17.5% natural resources, construction, and maintenance, 15.7% production, transportation, and material moving
Income: Per capita: $23,574; Median household: $52,000; Average household: $60,237; Households with income of $100,000 or more: 16.2%; Poverty rate: 4.4%
Educational Attainment: High school diploma or higher: 86.0%; Bachelor's degree or higher: 23.1%; Graduate/professional degree or higher: 8.3%
Housing: Homeownership rate: 88.5%; Median home value: $125,000; Median year structure built: Before 1940; Homeowner vacancy rate: 0.0%; Median selected monthly owner costs: $1,227 with a mortgage, $504

without a mortgage; Median gross rent: $468 per month; Rental vacancy rate: 17.1%
Health Insurance: 81.7% have insurance; 60.8% have private insurance; 31.7% have public insurance; 18.3% do not have insurance; 14.2% of children under 18 do not have insurance
Transportation: Commute: 80.5% car, 0.0% public transportation, 7.7% walk, 10.9% work from home; Mean travel time to work: 35.6 minutes

VAN HORNESVILLE (unincorporated postal area)
ZCTA: 13475
Covers a land area of 0.015 square miles and a water area of 0 square miles. Located at 42.89° N. Lat; 74.83° W. Long. Elevation is 1,152 feet.
Population: 44; Growth (since 2000): 528.6%; Density: 2,912.0 persons per square mile; Race: 100.0% White, 0.0% Black/African American, 0.0% Asian, 0.0% American Indian/Alaska Native, 0.0% Native Hawaiian/Other Pacific Islander, 0.0% Two or more races, 0.0% Hispanic of any race; Average household size: 1.91; Median age: 54.6; Age under 18: 0.0%; Age 65 and over: 13.6%; Males per 100 females: 100.0; Marriage status: 18.2% never married, 59.1% now married, 0.0% separated, 0.0% widowed, 22.7% divorced; Foreign born: 6.8%; Speak English only: 100.0%; With disability: 15.9%; Veterans: 0.0%; Ancestry: 56.8% German, 34.1% Italian, 29.5% Irish, 15.9% Swiss, 6.8% Dutch
Employment: 0.0% management, business, and financial, 10.7% computer, engineering, and science, 0.0% education, legal, community service, arts, and media, 0.0% healthcare practitioners, 0.0% service, 64.3% sales and office, 0.0% natural resources, construction, and maintenance, 25.0% production, transportation, and material moving
Income: Per capita: $30,870; Median household: n/a; Average household: $58,930; Households with income of $100,000 or more: 26.1%; Poverty rate: n/a
Educational Attainment: High school diploma or higher: 100.0%; Bachelor's degree or higher: 16.7%; Graduate/professional degree or higher: 16.7%

School District(s)
Van Hornesville-Owen D Young Central SD (KG-12)
2014-15 Enrollment: 199 . . . . (315) 858-0729
Housing: Homeownership rate: 56.5%; Median home value: $137,500; Median year structure built: Before 1940; Homeowner vacancy rate: 0.0%; Median selected monthly owner costs: $0 with a mortgage, $0 without a mortgage; Median gross rent: n/a per month; Rental vacancy rate: 41.2%
Health Insurance: 77.3% have insurance; 77.3% have private insurance; 13.6% have public insurance; 22.7% do not have insurance; 0.0% of children under 18 do not have insurance
Transportation: Commute: 75.0% car, 0.0% public transportation, 25.0% walk, 0.0% work from home; Mean travel time to work: 0.0 minutes

WARREN (town). Covers a land area of 37.791 square miles and a water area of 0.319 square miles. Located at 42.90° N. Lat; 74.94° W. Long. Elevation is 1,371 feet.
Population: 1,158; Growth (since 2000): 1.9%; Density: 30.6 persons per square mile; Race: 93.3% White, 5.9% Black/African American, 0.6% Asian, 0.0% American Indian/Alaska Native, 0.0% Native Hawaiian/Other Pacific Islander, 0.0% Two or more races, 1.4% Hispanic of any race; Average household size: 2.64; Median age: 39.2; Age under 18: 24.1%; Age 65 and over: 12.8%; Males per 100 females: 102.3; Marriage status: 28.8% never married, 54.3% now married, 3.0% separated, 4.5% widowed, 12.4% divorced; Foreign born: 11.1%; Speak English only: 88.8%; With disability: 11.1%; Veterans: 7.5%; Ancestry: 18.3% German, 18.0% English, 15.8% Irish, 10.4% Polish, 5.2% Ukrainian
Employment: 13.3% management, business, and financial, 1.2% computer, engineering, and science, 7.7% education, legal, community service, arts, and media, 7.9% healthcare practitioners, 21.4% service, 23.0% sales and office, 12.5% natural resources, construction, and maintenance, 12.9% production, transportation, and material moving
Income: Per capita: $19,678; Median household: $48,750; Average household: $54,138; Households with income of $100,000 or more: 10.5%; Poverty rate: 20.9%
Educational Attainment: High school diploma or higher: 91.9%; Bachelor's degree or higher: 22.0%; Graduate/professional degree or higher: 6.5%
Housing: Homeownership rate: 75.9%; Median home value: $97,700; Median year structure built: 1971; Homeowner vacancy rate: 5.6%; Median

selected monthly owner costs: $1,105 with a mortgage, $424 without a mortgage; Median gross rent: $810 per month; Rental vacancy rate: 4.7%
Health Insurance: 88.3% have insurance; 70.7% have private insurance; 28.7% have public insurance; 11.7% do not have insurance; 9.0% of children under 18 do not have insurance
Transportation: Commute: 82.8% car, 0.4% public transportation, 8.6% walk, 8.2% work from home; Mean travel time to work: 28.1 minutes

WEBB (town). Covers a land area of 452.284 square miles and a water area of 32.007 square miles. Located at 43.82° N. Lat; 75.04° W. Long.
Population: 1,647; Growth (since 2000): -13.9%; Density: 3.6 persons per square mile; Race: 99.5% White, 0.2% Black/African American, 0.0% Asian, 0.0% American Indian/Alaska Native, 0.0% Native Hawaiian/Other Pacific Islander, 0.2% Two or more races, 3.9% Hispanic of any race; Average household size: 1.99; Median age: 56.8; Age under 18: 10.0%; Age 65 and over: 30.8%; Males per 100 females: 101.2; Marriage status: 17.9% never married, 61.0% now married, 0.3% separated, 14.5% widowed, 6.6% divorced; Foreign born: 2.4%; Speak English only: 96.0%; With disability: 11.0%; Veterans: 11.3%; Ancestry: 26.5% German, 23.6% Irish, 19.6% English, 10.5% American, 10.1% Italian
Employment: 10.1% management, business, and financial, 0.3% computer, engineering, and science, 8.4% education, legal, community service, arts, and media, 3.3% healthcare practitioners, 17.0% service, 42.3% sales and office, 16.5% natural resources, construction, and maintenance, 2.1% production, transportation, and material moving
Income: Per capita: $40,359; Median household: $64,000; Average household: $82,013; Households with income of $100,000 or more: 23.1%; Poverty rate: 4.2%
Educational Attainment: High school diploma or higher: 95.4%; Bachelor's degree or higher: 35.0%; Graduate/professional degree or higher: 14.2%
Housing: Homeownership rate: 85.6%; Median home value: $362,000; Median year structure built: 1970; Homeowner vacancy rate: 6.9%; Median selected monthly owner costs: $1,671 with a mortgage, $660 without a mortgage; Median gross rent: $620 per month; Rental vacancy rate: 10.9%
Health Insurance: 93.4% have insurance; 77.7% have private insurance; 37.2% have public insurance; 6.6% do not have insurance; 0.0% of children under 18 do not have insurance
Safety: Violent crime rate: 0.0 per 10,000 population; Property crime rate: 93.2 per 10,000 population
Transportation: Commute: 65.2% car, 1.1% public transportation, 12.1% walk, 20.4% work from home; Mean travel time to work: 23.9 minutes

WEST WINFIELD (village). Covers a land area of 0.911 square miles and a water area of 0 square miles. Located at 42.88° N. Lat; 75.19° W. Long. Elevation is 1,191 feet.
Population: 820; Growth (since 2000): -4.9%; Density: 899.9 persons per square mile; Race: 95.5% White, 0.0% Black/African American, 0.0% Asian, 0.4% American Indian/Alaska Native, 0.0% Native Hawaiian/Other Pacific Islander, 4.1% Two or more races, 3.9% Hispanic of any race; Average household size: 2.32; Median age: 41.3; Age under 18: 21.7%; Age 65 and over: 24.4%; Males per 100 females: 84.0; Marriage status: 20.5% never married, 64.4% now married, 2.2% separated, 8.1% widowed, 7.0% divorced; Foreign born: 1.5%; Speak English only: 97.9%; With disability: 13.0%; Veterans: 9.7%; Ancestry: 22.2% Irish, 21.5% English, 19.5% German, 13.5% Welsh, 8.2% Polish
Employment: 6.8% management, business, and financial, 1.9% computer, engineering, and science, 17.2% education, legal, community service, arts, and media, 7.1% healthcare practitioners, 15.3% service, 25.7% sales and office, 13.1% natural resources, construction, and maintenance, 12.8% production, transportation, and material moving
Income: Per capita: $26,208; Median household: $55,000; Average household: $58,712; Households with income of $100,000 or more: 14.6%; Poverty rate: 11.7%
Educational Attainment: High school diploma or higher: 92.2%; Bachelor's degree or higher: 27.4%; Graduate/professional degree or higher: 12.1%

School District(s)
Mount Markham Central SD (PK-12)
2014-15 Enrollment: 1,149 . . . . (315) 822-2824
Housing: Homeownership rate: 67.5%; Median home value: $102,700; Median year structure built: 1941; Homeowner vacancy rate: 2.4%; Median selected monthly owner costs: $1,179 with a mortgage, $448 without a mortgage; Median gross rent: $478 per month; Rental vacancy rate: 0.0%

Health Insurance: 86.3% have insurance; 66.5% have private insurance; 38.8% have public insurance; 13.7% do not have insurance; 18.5% of children under 18 do not have insurance
Newspapers: West Winfield Star (weekly circulation 1,400)
Transportation: Commute: 91.3% car, 1.1% public transportation, 5.0% walk, 2.0% work from home; Mean travel time to work: 22.3 minutes

WINFIELD (town). Covers a land area of 23.639 square miles and a water area of 0.012 square miles. Located at 42.90° N. Lat; 75.17° W. Long.
Population: 2,097; Growth (since 2000): -4.8%; Density: 88.7 persons per square mile; Race: 94.2% White, 0.6% Black/African American, 0.1% Asian, 0.2% American Indian/Alaska Native, 0.0% Native Hawaiian/Other Pacific Islander, 4.3% Two or more races, 4.0% Hispanic of any race; Average household size: 2.61; Median age: 42.2; Age under 18: 22.4%; Age 65 and over: 18.7%; Males per 100 females: 96.2; Marriage status: 27.0% never married, 59.1% now married, 2.6% separated, 5.1% widowed, 8.8% divorced; Foreign born: 2.8%; Speak English only: 97.7%; With disability: 15.8%; Veterans: 11.4%; Ancestry: 23.1% Irish, 19.8% German, 19.3% English, 10.4% Welsh, 10.4% Italian
Employment: 10.1% management, business, and financial, 2.6% computer, engineering, and science, 11.6% education, legal, community service, arts, and media, 5.5% healthcare practitioners, 18.4% service, 22.5% sales and office, 13.2% natural resources, construction, and maintenance, 16.1% production, transportation, and material moving
Income: Per capita: $25,460; Median household: $61,667; Average household: $65,575; Households with income of $100,000 or more: 18.1%; Poverty rate: 11.2%
Educational Attainment: High school diploma or higher: 89.4%; Bachelor's degree or higher: 21.9%; Graduate/professional degree or higher: 8.9%
Housing: Homeownership rate: 73.6%; Median home value: $108,300; Median year structure built: 1955; Homeowner vacancy rate: 1.0%; Median selected monthly owner costs: $1,200 with a mortgage, $424 without a mortgage; Median gross rent: $619 per month; Rental vacancy rate: 0.0%
Health Insurance: 90.8% have insurance; 67.5% have private insurance; 41.8% have public insurance; 9.2% do not have insurance; 9.4% of children under 18 do not have insurance
Transportation: Commute: 91.9% car, 0.8% public transportation, 3.2% walk, 3.5% work from home; Mean travel time to work: 27.2 minutes

Jefferson County

Located in northern New York; bounded on the west by Lake Ontario, and on the northwest by the Saint Lawrence River; drained by the Black and Indian Rivers. Covers a land area of 1,268.590 square miles, a water area of 588.632 square miles, and is located in the Eastern Time Zone at 44.00° N. Lat., 76.05° W. Long. The county was founded in 1805. County seat is Watertown.

Jefferson County is part of the Watertown-Fort Drum, NY Metropolitan Statistical Area. The entire metro area includes: Jefferson County, NY

Weather Station: Watertown | | | | | | | | | | Elevation: 497 feet
	Jan	Feb	Mar	Apr	May	Jun	Jul	Aug	Sep	Oct	Nov	Dec
High	29	31	40	54	66	75	80	79	71	58	46	35
Low	10	12	22	35	47	56	61	60	52	40	31	18
Precip	3.3	2.7	2.7	3.2	3.6	3.3	3.4	4.0	4.3	4.2	4.6	3.7
Snow	31.0	25.4	13.0	3.4	tr	0.0	0.0	0.0	0.0	0.6	7.3	31.3

High and Low temperatures in degrees Fahrenheit; Precipitation and Snow in inches

Weather Station: Watertown Arpt | | | | | | | | | | Elevation: 317 feet
	Jan	Feb	Mar	Apr	May	Jun	Jul	Aug	Sep	Oct	Nov	Dec
High	29	31	40	54	66	74	79	78	70	58	47	35
Low	10	11	20	33	44	53	58	56	48	38	30	17
Precip	2.6	2.2	2.3	3.0	3.0	2.8	2.7	3.1	3.7	3.7	3.8	3.1
Snow	na	na	na	na	na	na	na	na	na	na	na	na

High and Low temperatures in degrees Fahrenheit; Precipitation and Snow in inches

Population: 118,947; Growth (since 2000): 6.5%; Density: 93.8 persons per square mile; Race: 86.4% White, 5.5% Black/African American, 1.5% Asian, 0.5% American Indian/Alaska Native, 0.2% Native Hawaiian/Other Pacific Islander, 4.2% two or more races, 6.9% Hispanic of any race; Average household size: 2.54; Median age: 31.8; Age under 18: 25.0%; Age 65 and over: 11.8%; Males per 100 females: 103.8; Marriage status: 29.2% never married, 56.6% now married, 3.0% separated, 5.1%

widowed, 9.1% divorced; Foreign born: 3.9%; Speak English only: 92.8%; With disability: 13.4%; Veterans: 14.0%; Ancestry: 20.2% Irish, 17.2% German, 10.8% English, 9.8% Italian, 9.1% French
Religion: Six largest groups: 18.2% Catholicism, 4.1% Methodist/Pietist, 2.1% Presbyterian-Reformed, 1.7% Baptist, 1.3% Muslim Estimate, 1.3% Holiness
Economy: Unemployment rate: 5.6%; Leading industries: 19.8 % retail trade; 13.6 % accommodation and food services; 11.3 % health care and social assistance; Farms: 876 totaling 290,811 acres; Company size: 1 employs 1,000 or more persons, 2 employ 500 to 999 persons, 34 employ 100 to 499 persons, 2,398 employ less than 100 persons; Business ownership: 2,027 women-owned, 62 Black-owned, 45 Hispanic-owned, 122 Asian-owned, n/a American Indian/Alaska Native-owned
Employment: 11.2% management, business, and financial, 3.1% computer, engineering, and science, 11.1% education, legal, community service, arts, and media, 6.8% healthcare practitioners, 21.5% service, 25.1% sales and office, 11.2% natural resources, construction, and maintenance, 9.8% production, transportation, and material moving
Income: Per capita: $23,659; Median household: $49,505; Average household: $60,441; Households with income of $100,000 or more: 15.2%; Poverty rate: 15.1%
Educational Attainment: High school diploma or higher: 89.4%; Bachelor's degree or higher: 20.7%; Graduate/professional degree or higher: 9.0%
Housing: Homeownership rate: 55.5%; Median home value: $141,000; Median year structure built: 1966; Homeowner vacancy rate: 2.2%; Median selected monthly owner costs: $1,238 with a mortgage, $484 without a mortgage; Median gross rent: $947 per month; Rental vacancy rate: 5.4%
Vital Statistics: Birth rate: 186.6 per 10,000 population; Death rate: 78.1 per 10,000 population; Age-adjusted cancer mortality rate: 183.4 deaths per 100,000 population
Health Insurance: 91.9% have insurance; 69.7% have private insurance; 36.4% have public insurance; 8.1% do not have insurance; 3.9% of children under 18 do not have insurance
Health Care: Physicians: 16.9 per 10,000 population; Dentists: 8.6 per 10,000 population; Hospital beds: 23.0 per 10,000 population; Hospital admissions: 902.2 per 10,000 population
Air Quality Index (AQI): Percent of Days: 97.8% good, 2.2% moderate, 0.0% unhealthy for sensitive individuals, 0.0% unhealthy, 0.0% very unhealthy; Annual median: 30; Annual maximum: 74
Transportation: Commute: 87.0% car, 0.4% public transportation, 6.8% walk, 4.0% work from home; Mean travel time to work: 17.8 minutes
2016 Presidential Election: 57.5% Trump, 36.5% Clinton, 4.4% Johnson, 1.6% Stein
National and State Parks: Brownville State Game Farm; Burnham Point State Park; Canoe Point and Picnic Point State Park; Cedar Point State Park; Grass Point State Park; Keewaydin Point State Park; Kring Point State Park; Long Point State Park; Mary Island State Park; Perch River State Game Management Area; Sackets Harbor Battlefield State Park; Southwich Beach State Park; Wellesley Island State Park; Westcott Beach State Park
Additional Information Contacts
Jefferson Government. . . . . (315) 785-3200
  http://www.co.jefferson.ny.us

Jefferson County Communities

ADAMS (town). Covers a land area of 42.270 square miles and a water area of 0.153 square miles. Located at 43.84° N. Lat; 76.05° W. Long. Elevation is 614 feet.
History: Incorporated 1851.
Population: 5,289; Growth (since 2000): 10.6%; Density: 125.1 persons per square mile; Race: 97.1% White, 0.4% Black/African American, 0.8% Asian, 0.0% American Indian/Alaska Native, 0.0% Native Hawaiian/Other Pacific Islander, 1.0% Two or more races, 1.8% Hispanic of any race; Average household size: 2.62; Median age: 36.2; Age under 18: 24.7%; Age 65 and over: 14.3%; Males per 100 females: 93.9; Marriage status: 27.8% never married, 57.9% now married, 3.8% separated, 6.8% widowed, 7.4% divorced; Foreign born: 2.1%; Speak English only: 97.1%; With disability: 14.4%; Veterans: 12.3%; Ancestry: 19.8% Irish, 14.2% German, 14.0% English, 7.8% American, 7.0% Italian
Employment: 18.0% management, business, and financial, 3.7% computer, engineering, and science, 15.0% education, legal, community service, arts, and media, 5.1% healthcare practitioners, 18.3% service,

25.6% sales and office, 8.4% natural resources, construction, and maintenance, 5.9% production, transportation, and material moving
Income: Per capita: $23,374; Median household: $46,224; Average household: $60,030; Households with income of $100,000 or more: 16.7%; Poverty rate: 15.9%
Educational Attainment: High school diploma or higher: 85.5%; Bachelor's degree or higher: 23.2%; Graduate/professional degree or higher: 12.9%

School District(s)
South Jefferson Central SD (PK-12)
   2014-15 Enrollment: 1,993 . . . . (315) 583-6104
Housing: Homeownership rate: 64.7%; Median home value: $132,500; Median year structure built: 1964; Homeowner vacancy rate: 1.1%; Median selected monthly owner costs: $1,212 with a mortgage, $499 without a mortgage; Median gross rent: $699 per month; Rental vacancy rate: 3.2%
Health Insurance: 90.3% have insurance; 66.0% have private insurance; 38.9% have public insurance; 9.7% do not have insurance; 0.5% of children under 18 do not have insurance
Newspapers: Jefferson County Journal (weekly circulation 2,800)
Transportation: Commute: 96.1% car, 0.1% public transportation, 1.6% walk, 1.8% work from home; Mean travel time to work: 19.7 minutes
Additional Information Contacts
Town of Adams . . . . (315) 232-2467
   http://www.townofadams.com

ADAMS (village).
Covers a land area of 1.447 square miles and a water area of 0 square miles. Located at 43.81° N. Lat; 76.02° W. Long. Elevation is 614 feet.
Population: 1,717; Growth (since 2000): 5.7%; Density: 1,186.6 persons per square mile; Race: 94.4% White, 0.9% Black/African American, 1.3% Asian, 0.0% American Indian/Alaska Native, 0.0% Native Hawaiian/Other Pacific Islander, 1.6% Two or more races, 5.0% Hispanic of any race; Average household size: 2.34; Median age: 34.2; Age under 18: 30.1%; Age 65 and over: 13.2%; Males per 100 females: 88.8; Marriage status: 28.6% never married, 48.7% now married, 4.2% separated, 9.4% widowed, 13.3% divorced; Foreign born: 4.0%; Speak English only: 96.6%; With disability: 16.1%; Veterans: 13.6%; Ancestry: 18.0% Irish, 14.7% English, 12.2% German, 8.8% American, 8.5% Italian
Employment: 10.3% management, business, and financial, 4.1% computer, engineering, and science, 11.6% education, legal, community service, arts, and media, 5.7% healthcare practitioners, 26.5% service, 21.4% sales and office, 9.1% natural resources, construction, and maintenance, 11.3% production, transportation, and material moving
Income: Per capita: $24,951; Median household: $40,341; Average household: $57,607; Households with income of $100,000 or more: 16.4%; Poverty rate: 18.0%
Educational Attainment: High school diploma or higher: 91.4%; Bachelor's degree or higher: 26.3%; Graduate/professional degree or higher: 11.9%

School District(s)
South Jefferson Central SD (PK-12)
   2014-15 Enrollment: 1,993 . . . . (315) 583-6104
Housing: Homeownership rate: 54.4%; Median home value: $144,300; Median year structure built: Before 1940; Homeowner vacancy rate: 3.6%; Median selected monthly owner costs: $1,300 with a mortgage, $621 without a mortgage; Median gross rent: $670 per month; Rental vacancy rate: 6.5%
Health Insurance: 92.4% have insurance; 68.5% have private insurance; 39.0% have public insurance; 7.6% do not have insurance; 1.4% of children under 18 do not have insurance
Safety: Violent crime rate: 0.0 per 10,000 population; Property crime rate: 43.2 per 10,000 population
Newspapers: Jefferson County Journal (weekly circulation 2,800)
Transportation: Commute: 92.4% car, 0.0% public transportation, 4.9% walk, 1.8% work from home; Mean travel time to work: 23.7 minutes

ADAMS CENTER (CDP).
Covers a land area of 4.855 square miles and a water area of 0.135 square miles. Located at 43.87° N. Lat; 75.99° W. Long. Elevation is 640 feet.
Population: 1,865; Growth (since 2000): 24.3%; Density: 384.1 persons per square mile; Race: 97.6% White, 0.0% Black/African American, 1.1% Asian, 0.0% American Indian/Alaska Native, 0.0% Native Hawaiian/Other Pacific Islander, 1.3% Two or more races, 0.0% Hispanic of any race; Average household size: 2.57; Median age: 36.4; Age under 18: 21.0%; Age 65 and over: 13.8%; Males per 100 females: 91.7; Marriage status:

26.4% never married, 63.7% now married, 5.2% separated, 4.4% widowed, 5.5% divorced; Foreign born: 1.9%; Speak English only: 98.9%; With disability: 17.1%; Veterans: 11.3%; Ancestry: 26.7% Irish, 18.4% German, 12.8% French Canadian, 8.8% Canadian, 7.7% American
Employment: 26.5% management, business, and financial, 3.9% computer, engineering, and science, 18.1% education, legal, community service, arts, and media, 3.9% healthcare practitioners, 15.6% service, 27.3% sales and office, 2.2% natural resources, construction, and maintenance, 2.4% production, transportation, and material moving
Income: Per capita: $21,188; Median household: $33,849; Average household: $52,799; Households with income of $100,000 or more: 8.0%; Poverty rate: 14.0%
Educational Attainment: High school diploma or higher: 88.7%; Bachelor's degree or higher: 17.4%; Graduate/professional degree or higher: 10.2%

School District(s)
South Jefferson Central SD (PK-12)
   2014-15 Enrollment: 1,993 . . . . (315) 583-6104
Housing: Homeownership rate: 66.0%; Median home value: $108,600; Median year structure built: 1974; Homeowner vacancy rate: 0.0%; Median selected monthly owner costs: $1,121 with a mortgage, $511 without a mortgage; Median gross rent: $757 per month; Rental vacancy rate: 0.0%
Health Insurance: 91.8% have insurance; 67.8% have private insurance; 37.9% have public insurance; 8.2% do not have insurance; 0.0% of children under 18 do not have insurance
Transportation: Commute: 97.8% car, 0.4% public transportation, 0.0% walk, 1.8% work from home; Mean travel time to work: 16.3 minutes

ALEXANDRIA (town).
Covers a land area of 72.657 square miles and a water area of 11.900 square miles. Located at 44.32° N. Lat; 75.88° W. Long.
History: Incorporated 1878.
Population: 4,179; Growth (since 2000): 2.0%; Density: 57.5 persons per square mile; Race: 97.9% White, 0.7% Black/African American, 0.2% Asian, 0.0% American Indian/Alaska Native, 0.0% Native Hawaiian/Other Pacific Islander, 0.9% Two or more races, 1.7% Hispanic of any race; Average household size: 2.40; Median age: 45.3; Age under 18: 19.9%; Age 65 and over: 17.4%; Males per 100 females: 100.3; Marriage status: 24.7% never married, 57.9% now married, 1.7% separated, 6.6% widowed, 10.8% divorced; Foreign born: 1.6%; Speak English only: 97.4%; With disability: 12.1%; Veterans: 9.6%; Ancestry: 26.2% German, 18.7% Irish, 15.2% French, 13.2% English, 10.0% Italian
Employment: 8.4% management, business, and financial, 1.2% computer, engineering, and science, 15.6% education, legal, community service, arts, and media, 2.9% healthcare practitioners, 21.8% service, 23.4% sales and office, 17.0% natural resources, construction, and maintenance, 9.6% production, transportation, and material moving
Income: Per capita: $26,738; Median household: $46,667; Average household: $64,410; Households with income of $100,000 or more: 15.0%; Poverty rate: 11.9%
Educational Attainment: High school diploma or higher: 87.1%; Bachelor's degree or higher: 19.4%; Graduate/professional degree or higher: 12.4%
Housing: Homeownership rate: 80.0%; Median home value: $120,700; Median year structure built: 1968; Homeowner vacancy rate: 6.3%; Median selected monthly owner costs: $1,144 with a mortgage, $505 without a mortgage; Median gross rent: $827 per month; Rental vacancy rate: 7.1%
Health Insurance: 87.5% have insurance; 65.7% have private insurance; 37.3% have public insurance; 12.5% do not have insurance; 0.0% of children under 18 do not have insurance
Transportation: Commute: 90.3% car, 0.7% public transportation, 4.7% walk, 3.1% work from home; Mean travel time to work: 20.5 minutes
Additional Information Contacts
Town of Alexandria . . . . (315) 482-9519
   http://www.townofalexandria.org

ALEXANDRIA BAY (village).
Covers a land area of 0.766 square miles and a water area of 0.759 square miles. Located at 44.34° N. Lat; 75.92° W. Long. Elevation is 269 feet.
Population: 965; Growth (since 2000): -11.3%; Density: 1,259.6 persons per square mile; Race: 95.4% White, 3.1% Black/African American, 0.8% Asian, 0.0% American Indian/Alaska Native, 0.0% Native Hawaiian/Other Pacific Islander, 0.6% Two or more races, 1.3% Hispanic of any race; Average household size: 2.08; Median age: 38.7; Age under 18: 17.2%; Age 65 and over: 17.2%; Males per 100 females: 94.6; Marriage status:

25.5% never married, 46.9% now married, 5.6% separated, 7.4% widowed, 20.2% divorced; Foreign born: 3.7%; Speak English only: 98.3%; With disability: 12.7%; Veterans: 10.2%; Ancestry: 27.3% Irish, 17.9% Italian, 17.3% German, 11.0% English, 8.1% French

Employment: 9.5% management, business, and financial, 0.7% computer, engineering, and science, 19.2% education, legal, community service, arts, and media, 5.5% healthcare practitioners, 14.5% service, 22.4% sales and office, 11.3% natural resources, construction, and maintenance, 16.9% production, transportation, and material moving

Income: Per capita: $23,829; Median household: $40,156; Average household: $49,696; Households with income of $100,000 or more: 16.3%; Poverty rate: 17.8%

Educational Attainment: High school diploma or higher: 86.6%; Bachelor's degree or higher: 21.4%; Graduate/professional degree or higher: 14.3%

School District(s)
Alexandria Central SD (PK-12)
    2014-15 Enrollment: 578 . . . . (315) 482-9971

Housing: Homeownership rate: 51.2%; Median home value: $110,700; Median year structure built: Before 1940; Homeowner vacancy rate: 6.5%; Median selected monthly owner costs: $1,166 with a mortgage, $528 without a mortgage; Median gross rent: $750 per month; Rental vacancy rate: 10.5%

Health Insurance: 89.7% have insurance; 60.4% have private insurance; 44.7% have public insurance; 10.3% do not have insurance; 0.0% of children under 18 do not have insurance

Hospitals: River Hospital (52 beds)

Newspapers: Thousand Islands Sun (weekly circulation 6,700)

Transportation: Commute: 79.8% car, 0.0% public transportation, 14.6% walk, 3.1% work from home; Mean travel time to work: 18.5 minutes

ANTWERP (town).
Covers a land area of 106.042 square miles and a water area of 2.378 square miles. Located at 44.22° N. Lat; 75.60° W. Long. Elevation is 512 feet.

Population: 1,693; Growth (since 2000): -5.6%; Density: 16.0 persons per square mile; Race: 95.6% White, 0.0% Black/African American, 1.9% Asian, 0.1% American Indian/Alaska Native, 0.0% Native Hawaiian/Other Pacific Islander, 2.4% Two or more races, 2.5% Hispanic of any race; Average household size: 2.73; Median age: 35.6; Age under 18: 25.6%; Age 65 and over: 13.1%; Males per 100 females: 101.7; Marriage status: 30.3% never married, 56.1% now married, 2.6% separated, 3.8% widowed, 9.9% divorced; Foreign born: 2.4%; Speak English only: 95.1%; With disability: 16.1%; Veterans: 14.0%; Ancestry: 15.5% American, 13.9% Irish, 12.3% English, 11.0% German, 9.7% French

Employment: 9.1% management, business, and financial, 0.0% computer, engineering, and science, 12.9% education, legal, community service, arts, and media, 8.5% healthcare practitioners, 16.7% service, 16.9% sales and office, 18.6% natural resources, construction, and maintenance, 17.3% production, transportation, and material moving

Income: Per capita: $22,934; Median household: $57,727; Average household: $62,274; Households with income of $100,000 or more: 17.4%; Poverty rate: 13.4%

Educational Attainment: High school diploma or higher: 84.2%; Bachelor's degree or higher: 10.7%; Graduate/professional degree or higher: 6.0%

School District(s)
Indian River Central SD (PK-12)
    2014-15 Enrollment: 4,140 . . . . (315) 642-3441

Housing: Homeownership rate: 78.4%; Median home value: $123,900; Median year structure built: 1944; Homeowner vacancy rate: 3.8%; Median selected monthly owner costs: $1,218 with a mortgage, $480 without a mortgage; Median gross rent: $771 per month; Rental vacancy rate: 0.0%

Health Insurance: 85.9% have insurance; 58.1% have private insurance; 43.1% have public insurance; 14.1% do not have insurance; 5.5% of children under 18 do not have insurance

Transportation: Commute: 91.2% car, 0.3% public transportation, 0.8% walk, 6.2% work from home; Mean travel time to work: 30.9 minutes

ANTWERP (village).
Covers a land area of 1.035 square miles and a water area of 0.033 square miles. Located at 44.20° N. Lat; 75.61° W. Long. Elevation is 512 feet.

Population: 511; Growth (since 2000): -28.6%; Density: 493.9 persons per square mile; Race: 93.5% White, 0.0% Black/African American, 3.1% Asian, 0.4% American Indian/Alaska Native, 0.0% Native Hawaiian/Other Pacific Islander, 2.9% Two or more races, 5.9% Hispanic of any race;

Average household size: 2.57; Median age: 35.5; Age under 18: 22.1%; Age 65 and over: 13.7%; Males per 100 females: 100.6; Marriage status: 29.7% never married, 56.8% now married, 3.9% separated, 2.7% widowed, 10.9% divorced; Foreign born: 3.7%; Speak English only: 95.4%; With disability: 19.6%; Veterans: 17.7%; Ancestry: 24.9% Irish, 17.4% English, 11.0% German, 7.6% French Canadian, 7.4% French

Employment: 5.0% management, business, and financial, 0.0% computer, engineering, and science, 14.4% education, legal, community service, arts, and media, 5.0% healthcare practitioners, 15.6% service, 27.5% sales and office, 21.3% natural resources, construction, and maintenance, 11.3% production, transportation, and material moving

Income: Per capita: $20,952; Median household: $50,139; Average household: $53,355; Households with income of $100,000 or more: 8.5%; Poverty rate: 9.1%

Educational Attainment: High school diploma or higher: 87.0%; Bachelor's degree or higher: 7.6%; Graduate/professional degree or higher: 3.7%

School District(s)
Indian River Central SD (PK-12)
    2014-15 Enrollment: 4,140 . . . . (315) 642-3441

Housing: Homeownership rate: 70.9%; Median home value: $113,300; Median year structure built: Before 1940; Homeowner vacancy rate: 11.9%; Median selected monthly owner costs: $1,363 with a mortgage, $558 without a mortgage; Median gross rent: $792 per month; Rental vacancy rate: 0.0%

Health Insurance: 85.4% have insurance; 56.9% have private insurance; 46.5% have public insurance; 14.6% do not have insurance; 5.3% of children under 18 do not have insurance

Transportation: Commute: 89.0% car, 1.0% public transportation, 1.6% walk, 7.9% work from home; Mean travel time to work: 27.8 minutes

BELLEVILLE (CDP).
Covers a land area of 0.264 square miles and a water area of 0 square miles. Located at 43.78° N. Lat; 76.12° W. Long. Elevation is 459 feet.

Population: 474; Growth (since 2000): n/a; Density: 1,792.3 persons per square mile; Race: 89.5% White, 0.0% Black/African American, 0.0% Asian, 0.0% American Indian/Alaska Native, 0.0% Native Hawaiian/Other Pacific Islander, 5.9% Two or more races, 10.5% Hispanic of any race; Average household size: 3.49; Median age: 18.1; Age under 18: 49.4%; Age 65 and over: 4.4%; Males per 100 females: 93.2; Marriage status: 20.3% never married, 50.0% now married, 0.0% separated, 8.2% widowed, 21.5% divorced; Foreign born: 0.0%; Speak English only: 88.9%; With disability: 17.7%; Veterans: 5.8%; Ancestry: 40.7% English, 18.6% German, 11.0% Polish, 10.8% Irish, 6.3% French

Employment: 11.3% management, business, and financial, 0.0% computer, engineering, and science, 0.0% education, legal, community service, arts, and media, 0.0% healthcare practitioners, 29.0% service, 11.3% sales and office, 29.0% natural resources, construction, and maintenance, 19.4% production, transportation, and material moving

Income: Per capita: $11,981; Median household: $28,784; Average household: $41,833; Households with income of $100,000 or more: 10.3%; Poverty rate: 45.6%

Educational Attainment: High school diploma or higher: 83.6%; Bachelor's degree or higher: 4.2%; Graduate/professional degree or higher: n/a

School District(s)
Belleville Henderson Central SD (PK-12)
    2014-15 Enrollment: 502 . . . . (315) 846-5826

Housing: Homeownership rate: 41.9%; Median home value: $116,800; Median year structure built: 1955; Homeowner vacancy rate: 0.0%; Median selected monthly owner costs: $1,228 with a mortgage, n/a without a mortgage; Median gross rent: $850 per month; Rental vacancy rate: 0.0%

Health Insurance: 94.7% have insurance; 37.6% have private insurance; 62.9% have public insurance; 5.3% do not have insurance; 0.0% of children under 18 do not have insurance

Transportation: Commute: 90.3% car, 0.0% public transportation, 9.7% walk, 0.0% work from home; Mean travel time to work: 25.4 minutes

BLACK RIVER (village).
Covers a land area of 1.791 square miles and a water area of 0.053 square miles. Located at 44.01° N. Lat; 75.80° W. Long. Elevation is 571 feet.

Population: 1,381; Growth (since 2000): 7.5%; Density: 771.0 persons per square mile; Race: 81.7% White, 4.6% Black/African American, 1.9% Asian, 0.0% American Indian/Alaska Native, 0.4% Native Hawaiian/Other Pacific Islander, 9.0% Two or more races, 3.8% Hispanic of any race;

Average household size: 2.64; Median age: 34.9; Age under 18: 29.3%; Age 65 and over: 14.3%; Males per 100 females: 94.5; Marriage status: 21.4% never married, 63.1% now married, 3.7% separated, 6.8% widowed, 8.7% divorced; Foreign born: 8.2%; Speak English only: 90.5%; With disability: 17.5%; Veterans: 21.2%; Ancestry: 22.4% Irish, 18.8% German, 9.7% English, 9.5% French, 7.7% Italian
Employment: 14.6% management, business, and financial, 3.1% computer, engineering, and science, 15.0% education, legal, community service, arts, and media, 8.3% healthcare practitioners, 16.1% service, 29.1% sales and office, 3.8% natural resources, construction, and maintenance, 9.9% production, transportation, and material moving
Income: Per capita: $26,017; Median household: $60,000; Average household: $67,581; Households with income of $100,000 or more: 20.2%; Poverty rate: 9.8%
Educational Attainment: High school diploma or higher: 95.1%; Bachelor's degree or higher: 26.2%; Graduate/professional degree or higher: 10.3%

School District(s)
Carthage Central SD (KG-12)
    2014-15 Enrollment: 3,385 . . . . (315) 493-5120
Housing: Homeownership rate: 61.3%; Median home value: $178,000; Median year structure built: 1958; Homeowner vacancy rate: 9.6%; Median selected monthly owner costs: $1,382 with a mortgage, $526 without a mortgage; Median gross rent: $856 per month; Rental vacancy rate: 3.7%
Health Insurance: 95.6% have insurance; 80.1% have private insurance; 32.7% have public insurance; 4.4% do not have insurance; 0.7% of children under 18 do not have insurance
Safety: Violent crime rate: 0.0 per 10,000 population; Property crime rate: 0.0 per 10,000 population
Transportation: Commute: 95.6% car, 0.0% public transportation, 0.5% walk, 1.4% work from home; Mean travel time to work: 15.2 minutes

BROWNVILLE (town). Covers a land area of 59.132 square miles and a water area of 7.320 square miles. Located at 44.03° N. Lat; 76.08° W. Long. Elevation is 348 feet.
Population: 6,444; Growth (since 2000): 10.3%; Density: 109.0 persons per square mile; Race: 96.9% White, 1.0% Black/African American, 0.9% Asian, 0.1% American Indian/Alaska Native, 0.0% Native Hawaiian/Other Pacific Islander, 1.0% Two or more races, 1.6% Hispanic of any race; Average household size: 2.69; Median age: 39.0; Age under 18: 25.1%; Age 65 and over: 12.0%; Males per 100 females: 97.3; Marriage status: 23.8% never married, 60.6% now married, 3.4% separated, 5.1% widowed, 10.5% divorced; Foreign born: 2.1%; Speak English only: 97.1%; With disability: 17.4%; Veterans: 12.1%; Ancestry: 23.8% Irish, 19.1% German, 14.2% French, 11.2% English, 6.2% American
Employment: 12.0% management, business, and financial, 0.9% computer, engineering, and science, 10.7% education, legal, community service, arts, and media, 3.9% healthcare practitioners, 23.5% service, 26.9% sales and office, 11.8% natural resources, construction, and maintenance, 10.3% production, transportation, and material moving
Income: Per capita: $24,095; Median household: $54,330; Average household: $64,594; Households with income of $100,000 or more: 19.5%; Poverty rate: 9.5%
Educational Attainment: High school diploma or higher: 88.3%; Bachelor's degree or higher: 18.4%; Graduate/professional degree or higher: 9.4%

School District(s)
General Brown Central SD (PK-12)
    2014-15 Enrollment: 1,564 . . . . (315) 779-2300
Housing: Homeownership rate: 79.5%; Median home value: $131,000; Median year structure built: 1976; Homeowner vacancy rate: 0.2%; Median selected monthly owner costs: $1,213 with a mortgage, $462 without a mortgage; Median gross rent: $749 per month; Rental vacancy rate: 2.8%
Health Insurance: 91.8% have insurance; 70.3% have private insurance; 34.6% have public insurance; 8.2% do not have insurance; 9.1% of children under 18 do not have insurance
Transportation: Commute: 94.9% car, 0.0% public transportation, 2.5% walk, 2.1% work from home; Mean travel time to work: 20.6 minutes

BROWNVILLE (village). Covers a land area of 0.673 square miles and a water area of 0.004 square miles. Located at 44.01° N. Lat; 75.98° W. Long. Elevation is 348 feet.
Population: 958; Growth (since 2000): -6.3%; Density: 1,423.5 persons per square mile; Race: 96.3% White, 2.6% Black/African American, 0.0% Asian, 0.0% American Indian/Alaska Native, 0.0% Native Hawaiian/Other

Pacific Islander, 1.0% Two or more races, 0.6% Hispanic of any race; Average household size: 2.60; Median age: 38.0; Age under 18: 27.0%; Age 65 and over: 16.0%; Males per 100 females: 89.3; Marriage status: 21.4% never married, 61.6% now married, 2.6% separated, 7.4% widowed, 9.7% divorced; Foreign born: 0.0%; Speak English only: 99.7%; With disability: 18.4%; Veterans: 17.1%; Ancestry: 26.5% German, 20.8% Irish, 10.9% French, 8.0% English, 7.4% Polish
Employment: 14.5% management, business, and financial, 0.7% computer, engineering, and science, 8.5% education, legal, community service, arts, and media, 6.9% healthcare practitioners, 19.6% service, 28.3% sales and office, 10.8% natural resources, construction, and maintenance, 10.6% production, transportation, and material moving
Income: Per capita: $23,334; Median household: $52,614; Average household: $59,893; Households with income of $100,000 or more: 16.9%; Poverty rate: 9.0%
Educational Attainment: High school diploma or higher: 89.7%; Bachelor's degree or higher: 20.2%; Graduate/professional degree or higher: 9.7%

School District(s)
General Brown Central SD (PK-12)
    2014-15 Enrollment: 1,564 . . . . (315) 779-2300
Housing: Homeownership rate: 61.2%; Median home value: $144,500; Median year structure built: Before 1940; Homeowner vacancy rate: 0.0%; Median selected monthly owner costs: $1,240 with a mortgage, $444 without a mortgage; Median gross rent: $672 per month; Rental vacancy rate: 0.0%
Health Insurance: 92.7% have insurance; 76.4% have private insurance; 29.4% have public insurance; 7.3% do not have insurance; 5.0% of children under 18 do not have insurance
Safety: Violent crime rate: 0.0 per 10,000 population; Property crime rate: 69.0 per 10,000 population
Transportation: Commute: 89.1% car, 0.2% public transportation, 5.1% walk, 4.0% work from home; Mean travel time to work: 13.1 minutes

CALCIUM (CDP). Covers a land area of 5.544 square miles and a water area of 0.002 square miles. Located at 44.05° N. Lat; 75.85° W. Long. Elevation is 469 feet.
Population: 4,102; Growth (since 2000): 22.6%; Density: 739.9 persons per square mile; Race: 57.3% White, 24.1% Black/African American, 3.1% Asian, 0.2% American Indian/Alaska Native, 0.0% Native Hawaiian/Other Pacific Islander, 11.1% Two or more races, 25.9% Hispanic of any race; Average household size: 2.46; Median age: 25.0; Age under 18: 27.5%; Age 65 and over: 3.9%; Males per 100 females: 102.5; Marriage status: 20.2% never married, 74.3% now married, 3.7% separated, 1.0% widowed, 4.5% divorced; Foreign born: 5.0%; Speak English only: 86.8%; With disability: 9.0%; Veterans: 24.1%; Ancestry: 14.5% French, 12.4% German, 9.4% English, 8.3% Italian, 5.7% Irish
Employment: 18.7% management, business, and financial, 3.4% computer, engineering, and science, 24.4% education, legal, community service, arts, and media, 0.2% healthcare practitioners, 18.3% service, 24.4% sales and office, 1.5% natural resources, construction, and maintenance, 9.1% production, transportation, and material moving
Income: Per capita: $20,638; Median household: $48,398; Average household: $49,774; Households with income of $100,000 or more: 6.8%; Poverty rate: 6.8%
Educational Attainment: High school diploma or higher: 88.9%; Bachelor's degree or higher: 27.1%; Graduate/professional degree or higher: 7.4%

School District(s)
Indian River Central SD (PK-12)
    2014-15 Enrollment: 4,140 . . . . (315) 642-3441
Housing: Homeownership rate: 14.7%; Median home value: $150,600; Median year structure built: 2000; Homeowner vacancy rate: 0.0%; Median selected monthly owner costs: $1,382 with a mortgage, $372 without a mortgage; Median gross rent: $1,207 per month; Rental vacancy rate: 6.4%
Health Insurance: 91.5% have insurance; 75.6% have private insurance; 30.4% have public insurance; 8.5% do not have insurance; 3.0% of children under 18 do not have insurance
Transportation: Commute: 91.5% car, 0.0% public transportation, 1.0% walk, 6.2% work from home; Mean travel time to work: 14.7 minutes

CAPE VINCENT (town). Covers a land area of 56.353 square miles and a water area of 33.499 square miles. Located at 44.11° N. Lat; 76.29° W. Long. Elevation is 262 feet.
Population: 2,869; Growth (since 2000): -14.2%; Density: 50.9 persons per square mile; Race: 74.6% White, 15.8% Black/African American, 0.1% Asian, 0.0% American Indian/Alaska Native, 0.0% Native Hawaiian/Other Pacific Islander, 5.2% Two or more races, 9.0% Hispanic of any race; Average household size: 2.26; Median age: 42.6; Age under 18: 13.9%; Age 65 and over: 18.5%; Males per 100 females: 177.1; Marriage status: 37.2% never married, 49.6% now married, 3.6% separated, 4.6% widowed, 8.7% divorced; Foreign born: 5.1%; Speak English only: 90.8%; With disability: 14.7%; Veterans: 8.5%; Ancestry: 21.7% Irish, 15.8% German, 10.7% French, 9.0% English, 7.8% Italian
Employment: 15.2% management, business, and financial, 3.5% computer, engineering, and science, 10.1% education, legal, community service, arts, and media, 4.4% healthcare practitioners, 20.1% service, 17.6% sales and office, 17.9% natural resources, construction, and maintenance, 11.2% production, transportation, and material moving
Income: Per capita: $20,554; Median household: $53,295; Average household: $63,351; Households with income of $100,000 or more: 18.5%; Poverty rate: 9.9%
Educational Attainment: High school diploma or higher: 84.0%; Bachelor's degree or higher: 15.2%; Graduate/professional degree or higher: 6.2%

School District(s)
Thousand Islands Central SD (KG-12)
    2014-15 Enrollment: 995 . . . . (315) 686-5594
Housing: Homeownership rate: 81.7%; Median home value: $142,600; Median year structure built: 1974; Homeowner vacancy rate: 2.9%; Median selected monthly owner costs: $1,258 with a mortgage, $434 without a mortgage; Median gross rent: $676 per month; Rental vacancy rate: 3.9%
Health Insurance: 89.0% have insurance; 72.1% have private insurance; 41.9% have public insurance; 11.0% do not have insurance; 6.3% of children under 18 do not have insurance
Transportation: Commute: 82.7% car, 0.0% public transportation, 5.0% walk, 10.2% work from home; Mean travel time to work: 27.3 minutes

CAPE VINCENT (village). Covers a land area of 0.724 square miles and a water area of 0.025 square miles. Located at 44.12° N. Lat; 76.33° W. Long. Elevation is 262 feet.
Population: 645; Growth (since 2000): -15.1%; Density: 891.5 persons per square mile; Race: 95.8% White, 0.9% Black/African American, 0.0% Asian, 0.0% American Indian/Alaska Native, 0.0% Native Hawaiian/Other Pacific Islander, 3.3% Two or more races, 4.3% Hispanic of any race; Average household size: 2.24; Median age: 46.0; Age under 18: 27.1%; Age 65 and over: 24.3%; Males per 100 females: 92.6; Marriage status: 20.6% never married, 59.8% now married, 3.9% separated, 10.9% widowed, 8.7% divorced; Foreign born: 6.4%; Speak English only: 98.2%; With disability: 19.8%; Veterans: 18.5%; Ancestry: 25.1% German, 24.0% Irish, 18.3% French, 12.4% English, 9.0% Scottish
Employment: 11.0% management, business, and financial, 5.5% computer, engineering, and science, 16.0% education, legal, community service, arts, and media, 8.4% healthcare practitioners, 20.3% service, 15.6% sales and office, 11.4% natural resources, construction, and maintenance, 11.8% production, transportation, and material moving
Income: Per capita: $25,841; Median household: $47,188; Average household: $59,333; Households with income of $100,000 or more: 12.9%; Poverty rate: 6.5%
Educational Attainment: High school diploma or higher: 95.6%; Bachelor's degree or higher: 33.8%; Graduate/professional degree or higher: 14.9%

School District(s)
Thousand Islands Central SD (KG-12)
    2014-15 Enrollment: 995 . . . . (315) 686-5594
Housing: Homeownership rate: 70.5%; Median home value: $133,500; Median year structure built: Before 1940; Homeowner vacancy rate: 3.3%; Median selected monthly owner costs: $1,223 with a mortgage, $459 without a mortgage; Median gross rent: $400 per month; Rental vacancy rate: 0.0%
Health Insurance: 89.0% have insurance; 70.9% have private insurance; 42.6% have public insurance; 11.0% do not have insurance; 12.0% of children under 18 do not have insurance
Transportation: Commute: 76.8% car, 0.0% public transportation, 8.4% walk, 14.3% work from home; Mean travel time to work: 27.2 minutes

CARTHAGE (village). Covers a land area of 2.508 square miles and a water area of 0.170 square miles. Located at 43.99° N. Lat; 75.60° W. Long. Elevation is 768 feet.
History: Settled before 1801, incorporated 1841.
Population: 3,682; Growth (since 2000): -1.0%; Density: 1,468.3 persons per square mile; Race: 96.7% White, 0.3% Black/African American, 0.7% Asian, 0.2% American Indian/Alaska Native, 0.0% Native Hawaiian/Other Pacific Islander, 2.0% Two or more races, 1.2% Hispanic of any race; Average household size: 2.64; Median age: 28.9; Age under 18: 32.1%; Age 65 and over: 12.3%; Males per 100 females: 89.3; Marriage status: 27.4% never married, 50.0% now married, 3.9% separated, 9.0% widowed, 13.6% divorced; Foreign born: 1.7%; Speak English only: 98.5%; With disability: 17.7%; Veterans: 15.3%; Ancestry: 29.2% Irish, 13.2% Italian, 12.4% English, 11.0% German, 10.8% French
Employment: 10.3% management, business, and financial, 0.0% computer, engineering, and science, 6.7% education, legal, community service, arts, and media, 10.9% healthcare practitioners, 32.3% service, 17.8% sales and office, 15.3% natural resources, construction, and maintenance, 6.6% production, transportation, and material moving
Income: Per capita: $19,773; Median household: $42,587; Average household: $52,916; Households with income of $100,000 or more: 7.8%; Poverty rate: 27.7%
Educational Attainment: High school diploma or higher: 85.3%; Bachelor's degree or higher: 8.2%; Graduate/professional degree or higher: 5.0%

School District(s)
Carthage Central SD (KG-12)
    2014-15 Enrollment: 3,385 . . . . (315) 493-5120
Housing: Homeownership rate: 45.4%; Median home value: $134,700; Median year structure built: Before 1940; Homeowner vacancy rate: 0.0%; Median selected monthly owner costs: $1,394 with a mortgage, $563 without a mortgage; Median gross rent: $916 per month; Rental vacancy rate: 6.8%
Health Insurance: 87.9% have insurance; 55.9% have private insurance; 44.5% have public insurance; 12.1% do not have insurance; 15.3% of children under 18 do not have insurance
Hospitals: Carthage Area Hospital (78 beds)
Safety: Violent crime rate: 16.4 per 10,000 population; Property crime rate: 172.5 per 10,000 population
Newspapers: Republican Tribune (weekly circulation 2,800)
Transportation: Commute: 93.6% car, 0.0% public transportation, 0.0% walk, 2.6% work from home; Mean travel time to work: 19.7 minutes

CHAMPION (town). Covers a land area of 44.184 square miles and a water area of 0.889 square miles. Located at 43.97° N. Lat; 75.71° W. Long. Elevation is 997 feet.
Population: 4,619; Growth (since 2000): 5.9%; Density: 104.5 persons per square mile; Race: 90.6% White, 2.7% Black/African American, 1.5% Asian, 0.0% American Indian/Alaska Native, 0.0% Native Hawaiian/Other Pacific Islander, 2.4% Two or more races, 7.2% Hispanic of any race; Average household size: 2.49; Median age: 38.0; Age under 18: 21.7%; Age 65 and over: 14.4%; Males per 100 females: 100.2; Marriage status: 23.5% never married, 59.2% now married, 3.5% separated, 7.2% widowed, 10.1% divorced; Foreign born: 2.7%; Speak English only: 94.0%; With disability: 16.8%; Veterans: 21.7%; Ancestry: 21.0% German, 15.1% Irish, 12.0% French, 11.8% English, 11.0% Italian
Employment: 12.2% management, business, and financial, 2.2% computer, engineering, and science, 10.8% education, legal, community service, arts, and media, 9.0% healthcare practitioners, 13.7% service, 25.3% sales and office, 13.3% natural resources, construction, and maintenance, 13.3% production, transportation, and material moving
Income: Per capita: $25,865; Median household: $61,792; Average household: $63,441; Households with income of $100,000 or more: 20.0%; Poverty rate: 12.8%
Educational Attainment: High school diploma or higher: 90.7%; Bachelor's degree or higher: 21.3%; Graduate/professional degree or higher: 6.7%
Housing: Homeownership rate: 64.0%; Median home value: $128,100; Median year structure built: 1965; Homeowner vacancy rate: 1.3%; Median selected monthly owner costs: $1,071 with a mortgage, $447 without a mortgage; Median gross rent: $1,104 per month; Rental vacancy rate: 5.9%
Health Insurance: 94.7% have insurance; 78.0% have private insurance; 31.0% have public insurance; 5.3% do not have insurance; 5.3% of children under 18 do not have insurance

Transportation: Commute: 93.6% car, 0.1% public transportation, 1.7% walk, 3.5% work from home; Mean travel time to work: 21.7 minutes
Additional Information Contacts
Town of Champion . . . . (315) 493-3240
    http://www.racog.org/Champion/Championhomepage.php

CHAUMONT (village). Covers a land area of 0.971 square miles and a water area of 0.093 square miles. Located at 44.07° N. Lat; 76.13° W. Long. Elevation is 289 feet.
Population: 796; Growth (since 2000): 34.5%; Density: 819.9 persons per square mile; Race: 95.6% White, 0.9% Black/African American, 0.9% Asian, 0.0% American Indian/Alaska Native, 0.0% Native Hawaiian/Other Pacific Islander, 2.6% Two or more races, 0.5% Hispanic of any race; Average household size: 2.71; Median age: 40.5; Age under 18: 22.7%; Age 65 and over: 18.0%; Males per 100 females: 90.8; Marriage status: 26.8% never married, 57.4% now married, 2.6% separated, 6.9% widowed, 9.0% divorced; Foreign born: 4.5%; Speak English only: 97.1%; With disability: 19.5%; Veterans: 8.8%; Ancestry: 22.6% German, 22.4% Irish, 10.1% English, 9.7% Italian, 9.2% French
Employment: 15.9% management, business, and financial, 3.6% computer, engineering, and science, 9.6% education, legal, community service, arts, and media, 8.1% healthcare practitioners, 24.6% service, 19.5% sales and office, 6.3% natural resources, construction, and maintenance, 12.6% production, transportation, and material moving
Income: Per capita: $23,641; Median household: $49,688; Average household: $64,613; Households with income of $100,000 or more: 20.3%; Poverty rate: 6.8%
Educational Attainment: High school diploma or higher: 91.2%; Bachelor's degree or higher: 21.3%; Graduate/professional degree or higher: 9.2%
School District(s)
Lyme Central SD (PK-12)
    2014-15 Enrollment: 365 . . . . (315) 649-2417
Housing: Homeownership rate: 65.7%; Median home value: $132,300; Median year structure built: Before 1940; Homeowner vacancy rate: 3.1%; Median selected monthly owner costs: $1,559 with a mortgage, $487 without a mortgage; Median gross rent: $638 per month; Rental vacancy rate: 5.7%
Health Insurance: 95.0% have insurance; 73.6% have private insurance; 37.8% have public insurance; 5.0% do not have insurance; 4.4% of children under 18 do not have insurance
Transportation: Commute: 76.3% car, 1.8% public transportation, 13.4% walk, 8.5% work from home; Mean travel time to work: 19.8 minutes

CLAYTON (town). Covers a land area of 82.360 square miles and a water area of 21.671 square miles. Located at 44.20° N. Lat; 76.08° W. Long. Elevation is 276 feet.
History: North American freshwater craft at Antique Boat Museum, similar to one at Mystic, Connecticut; Thousand Islands Museum; Clayton Historic District. Incorporated 1872.
Population: 5,236; Growth (since 2000): 8.7%; Density: 63.6 persons per square mile; Race: 99.3% White, 0.6% Black/African American, 0.0% Asian, 0.0% American Indian/Alaska Native, 0.0% Native Hawaiian/Other Pacific Islander, 0.1% Two or more races, 0.2% Hispanic of any race; Average household size: 2.58; Median age: 36.7; Age under 18: 25.6%; Age 65 and over: 15.0%; Males per 100 females: 92.7; Marriage status: 24.9% never married, 61.6% now married, 2.4% separated, 4.6% widowed, 8.9% divorced; Foreign born: 2.0%; Speak English only: 97.6%; With disability: 8.6%; Veterans: 9.7%; Ancestry: 27.9% Irish, 19.6% German, 17.5% English, 12.3% French, 8.3% French Canadian
Employment: 8.3% management, business, and financial, 5.1% computer, engineering, and science, 10.2% education, legal, community service, arts, and media, 7.1% healthcare practitioners, 20.3% service, 29.6% sales and office, 11.1% natural resources, construction, and maintenance, 8.3% production, transportation, and material moving
Income: Per capita: $26,636; Median household: $56,667; Average household: $68,742; Households with income of $100,000 or more: 22.7%; Poverty rate: 13.2%
Educational Attainment: High school diploma or higher: 93.6%; Bachelor's degree or higher: 25.0%; Graduate/professional degree or higher: 12.3%
School District(s)
Thousand Islands Central SD (KG-12)
    2014-15 Enrollment: 995 . . . . (315) 686-5594

Housing: Homeownership rate: 74.0%; Median home value: $157,700; Median year structure built: 1967; Homeowner vacancy rate: 0.0%; Median selected monthly owner costs: $1,370 with a mortgage, $553 without a mortgage; Median gross rent: $1,006 per month; Rental vacancy rate: 9.2%
Health Insurance: 91.9% have insurance; 71.5% have private insurance; 35.2% have public insurance; 8.1% do not have insurance; 1.4% of children under 18 do not have insurance
Transportation: Commute: 89.1% car, 0.0% public transportation, 5.0% walk, 4.7% work from home; Mean travel time to work: 22.8 minutes
Additional Information Contacts
Town of Clayton . . . . (315) 686-3512
    http://townofclayton.com

CLAYTON (village). Covers a land area of 1.613 square miles and a water area of 0.973 square miles. Located at 44.24° N. Lat; 76.08° W. Long. Elevation is 276 feet.
Population: 1,917; Growth (since 2000): 5.3%; Density: 1,188.5 persons per square mile; Race: 98.2% White, 1.6% Black/African American, 0.1% Asian, 0.0% American Indian/Alaska Native, 0.0% Native Hawaiian/Other Pacific Islander, 0.2% Two or more races, 0.2% Hispanic of any race; Average household size: 2.35; Median age: 37.0; Age under 18: 23.0%; Age 65 and over: 18.2%; Males per 100 females: 84.5; Marriage status: 30.2% never married, 48.6% now married, 3.4% separated, 7.5% widowed, 13.6% divorced; Foreign born: 2.1%; Speak English only: 98.4%; With disability: 14.1%; Veterans: 10.1%; Ancestry: 26.6% Irish, 20.0% English, 19.5% German, 14.0% French, 9.6% Scottish
Employment: 6.2% management, business, and financial, 2.3% computer, engineering, and science, 12.6% education, legal, community service, arts, and media, 3.9% healthcare practitioners, 34.5% service, 22.3% sales and office, 11.9% natural resources, construction, and maintenance, 6.3% production, transportation, and material moving
Income: Per capita: $26,428; Median household: $50,049; Average household: $62,156; Households with income of $100,000 or more: 19.9%; Poverty rate: 11.5%
Educational Attainment: High school diploma or higher: 92.1%; Bachelor's degree or higher: 25.3%; Graduate/professional degree or higher: 9.2%
School District(s)
Thousand Islands Central SD (KG-12)
    2014-15 Enrollment: 995 . . . . (315) 686-5594
Housing: Homeownership rate: 47.7%; Median home value: $148,400; Median year structure built: Before 1940; Homeowner vacancy rate: 0.0%; Median selected monthly owner costs: $1,344 with a mortgage, $675 without a mortgage; Median gross rent: $972 per month; Rental vacancy rate: 11.1%
Health Insurance: 90.2% have insurance; 63.6% have private insurance; 46.1% have public insurance; 9.8% do not have insurance; 0.9% of children under 18 do not have insurance
Safety: Violent crime rate: 0.0 per 10,000 population; Property crime rate: 0.0 per 10,000 population
Transportation: Commute: 85.1% car, 0.0% public transportation, 8.6% walk, 3.3% work from home; Mean travel time to work: 22.3 minutes

DEFERIET (village). Covers a land area of 0.650 square miles and a water area of 0.082 square miles. Located at 44.04° N. Lat; 75.68° W. Long. Elevation is 659 feet.
Population: 276; Growth (since 2000): -10.7%; Density: 424.7 persons per square mile; Race: 94.9% White, 0.0% Black/African American, 0.0% Asian, 0.0% American Indian/Alaska Native, 0.0% Native Hawaiian/Other Pacific Islander, 5.1% Two or more races, 1.4% Hispanic of any race; Average household size: 2.51; Median age: 32.0; Age under 18: 31.5%; Age 65 and over: 13.4%; Males per 100 females: 82.6; Marriage status: 40.7% never married, 38.3% now married, 2.9% separated, 7.7% widowed, 13.4% divorced; Foreign born: 3.6%; Speak English only: 92.1%; With disability: 13.4%; Veterans: 20.4%; Ancestry: 22.8% German, 20.7% Irish, 18.5% French, 9.4% Italian, 8.0% French Canadian
Employment: 6.1% management, business, and financial, 4.0% computer, engineering, and science, 5.1% education, legal, community service, arts, and media, 7.1% healthcare practitioners, 11.1% service, 35.4% sales and office, 18.2% natural resources, construction, and maintenance, 13.1% production, transportation, and material moving
Income: Per capita: $20,911; Median household: $50,000; Average household: $54,196; Households with income of $100,000 or more: 7.3%; Poverty rate: 20.6%

Educational Attainment: High school diploma or higher: 90.9%; Bachelor's degree or higher: 12.8%; Graduate/professional degree or higher: 2.4%

Housing: Homeownership rate: 61.8%; Median home value: $110,500; Median year structure built: Before 1940; Homeowner vacancy rate: 1.4%; Median selected monthly owner costs: $1,176 with a mortgage, $481 without a mortgage; Median gross rent: $925 per month; Rental vacancy rate: 0.0%

Health Insurance: 89.2% have insurance; 63.4% have private insurance; 43.3% have public insurance; 10.8% do not have insurance; 8.0% of children under 18 do not have insurance

Transportation: Commute: 96.3% car, 0.0% public transportation, 0.9% walk, 0.9% work from home; Mean travel time to work: 18.4 minutes

DEPAUVILLE (CDP).
Covers a land area of 9.822 square miles and a water area of 0 square miles. Located at 44.14° N. Lat; 76.05° W. Long. Elevation is 305 feet.

Population: 961; Growth (since 2000): 87.7%; Density: 97.8 persons per square mile; Race: 100.0% White, 0.0% Black/African American, 0.0% Asian, 0.0% American Indian/Alaska Native, 0.0% Native Hawaiian/Other Pacific Islander, 0.0% Two or more races, 0.8% Hispanic of any race; Average household size: 3.51; Median age: 26.1; Age under 18: 43.4%; Age 65 and over: 1.1%; Males per 100 females: 103.2; Marriage status: 22.3% never married, 72.3% now married, 1.4% separated, 0.0% widowed, 5.4% divorced; Foreign born: 0.4%; Speak English only: 96.0%; With disability: 4.9%; Veterans: 7.2%; Ancestry: 39.1% Irish, 27.1% French Canadian, 17.6% German, 10.3% Italian, 8.5% American

Employment: 12.3% management, business, and financial, 0.0% computer, engineering, and science, 7.2% education, legal, community service, arts, and media, 2.8% healthcare practitioners, 18.8% service, 38.8% sales and office, 3.1% natural resources, construction, and maintenance, 17.0% production, transportation, and material moving

Income: Per capita: $13,874; Median household: $41,176; Average household: $48,046; Households with income of $100,000 or more: 10.2%; Poverty rate: 30.3%

Educational Attainment: High school diploma or higher: 97.5%; Bachelor's degree or higher: 6.8%; Graduate/professional degree or higher: 6.8%

Housing: Homeownership rate: 86.5%; Median home value: $116,500; Median year structure built: Before 1940; Homeowner vacancy rate: 0.0%; Median selected monthly owner costs: $1,154 with a mortgage, $539 without a mortgage; Median gross rent: n/a per month; Rental vacancy rate: 0.0%

Health Insurance: 87.6% have insurance; 52.8% have private insurance; 38.9% have public insurance; 12.4% do not have insurance; 0.0% of children under 18 do not have insurance

Transportation: Commute: 73.0% car, 0.0% public transportation, 10.8% walk, 16.1% work from home; Mean travel time to work: 23.6 minutes

DEXTER (village).
Covers a land area of 0.692 square miles and a water area of 0.063 square miles. Located at 44.01° N. Lat; 76.04° W. Long. Elevation is 282 feet.

History: Incorporated 1855.

Population: 1,359; Growth (since 2000): 21.3%; Density: 1,965.1 persons per square mile; Race: 98.5% White, 1.0% Black/African American, 0.0% Asian, 0.0% American Indian/Alaska Native, 0.0% Native Hawaiian/Other Pacific Islander, 0.5% Two or more races, 3.7% Hispanic of any race; Average household size: 2.61; Median age: 33.9; Age under 18: 27.2%; Age 65 and over: 11.8%; Males per 100 females: 91.6; Marriage status: 32.7% never married, 50.3% now married, 3.8% separated, 5.9% widowed, 11.1% divorced; Foreign born: 1.2%; Speak English only: 97.4%; With disability: 21.9%; Veterans: 9.2%; Ancestry: 35.8% Irish, 19.5% German, 15.9% French, 13.7% English, 5.5% Italian

Employment: 18.0% management, business, and financial, 1.3% computer, engineering, and science, 10.1% education, legal, community service, arts, and media, 4.5% healthcare practitioners, 27.0% service, 21.8% sales and office, 9.9% natural resources, construction, and maintenance, 7.6% production, transportation, and material moving

Income: Per capita: $22,079; Median household: $47,083; Average household: $57,869; Households with income of $100,000 or more: 17.9%; Poverty rate: 18.4%

Educational Attainment: High school diploma or higher: 82.9%; Bachelor's degree or higher: 16.8%; Graduate/professional degree or higher: 7.5%

School District(s)
General Brown Central SD (PK-12)
 2014-15 Enrollment: 1,564 . . . . (315) 779-2300

Housing: Homeownership rate: 60.0%; Median home value: $123,500; Median year structure built: Before 1940; Homeowner vacancy rate: 0.0%; Median selected monthly owner costs: $1,089 with a mortgage, $416 without a mortgage; Median gross rent: $607 per month; Rental vacancy rate: 0.0%

Health Insurance: 95.0% have insurance; 64.5% have private insurance; 44.5% have public insurance; 5.0% do not have insurance; 2.4% of children under 18 do not have insurance

Safety: Violent crime rate: 0.0 per 10,000 population; Property crime rate: 35.8 per 10,000 population

Transportation: Commute: 97.5% car, 0.0% public transportation, 0.7% walk, 1.8% work from home; Mean travel time to work: 20.3 minutes

ELLISBURG (town).
Covers a land area of 85.146 square miles and a water area of 1.419 square miles. Located at 43.75° N. Lat; 76.11° W. Long. Elevation is 328 feet.

Population: 3,578; Growth (since 2000): 1.0%; Density: 42.0 persons per square mile; Race: 95.2% White, 1.1% Black/African American, 0.0% Asian, 0.6% American Indian/Alaska Native, 0.0% Native Hawaiian/Other Pacific Islander, 2.4% Two or more races, 1.6% Hispanic of any race; Average household size: 2.59; Median age: 39.5; Age under 18: 23.9%; Age 65 and over: 14.8%; Males per 100 females: 101.4; Marriage status: 21.3% never married, 64.6% now married, 0.7% separated, 3.5% widowed, 10.6% divorced; Foreign born: 1.5%; Speak English only: 95.0%; With disability: 14.1%; Veterans: 11.0%; Ancestry: 22.3% German, 20.8% English, 17.3% Irish, 6.1% Polish, 5.8% French

Employment: 11.9% management, business, and financial, 1.6% computer, engineering, and science, 9.3% education, legal, community service, arts, and media, 4.4% healthcare practitioners, 18.8% service, 21.4% sales and office, 19.6% natural resources, construction, and maintenance, 13.1% production, transportation, and material moving

Income: Per capita: $28,761; Median household: $54,303; Average household: $73,581; Households with income of $100,000 or more: 18.9%; Poverty rate: 13.5%

Educational Attainment: High school diploma or higher: 89.7%; Bachelor's degree or higher: 16.6%; Graduate/professional degree or higher: 5.5%

Housing: Homeownership rate: 78.4%; Median home value: $133,100; Median year structure built: 1968; Homeowner vacancy rate: 0.6%; Median selected monthly owner costs: $1,143 with a mortgage, $393 without a mortgage; Median gross rent: $852 per month; Rental vacancy rate: 2.9%

Health Insurance: 87.1% have insurance; 65.3% have private insurance; 32.0% have public insurance; 12.9% do not have insurance; 8.9% of children under 18 do not have insurance

Transportation: Commute: 92.3% car, 0.0% public transportation, 3.3% walk, 4.4% work from home; Mean travel time to work: 25.4 minutes

ELLISBURG (village).
Covers a land area of 1.015 square miles and a water area of 0 square miles. Located at 43.73° N. Lat; 76.13° W. Long. Elevation is 328 feet.

Population: 256; Growth (since 2000): -4.8%; Density: 252.3 persons per square mile; Race: 96.5% White, 0.4% Black/African American, 0.0% Asian, 0.0% American Indian/Alaska Native, 0.4% Native Hawaiian/Other Pacific Islander, 2.7% Two or more races, 3.1% Hispanic of any race; Average household size: 2.78; Median age: 35.5; Age under 18: 29.3%; Age 65 and over: 13.3%; Males per 100 females: 108.5; Marriage status: 29.8% never married, 52.9% now married, 2.1% separated, 4.7% widowed, 12.6% divorced; Foreign born: 0.8%; Speak English only: 95.8%; With disability: 19.9%; Veterans: 16.0%; Ancestry: 24.6% German, 19.1% English, 14.5% Irish, 7.8% Polish, 7.4% British

Employment: 11.8% management, business, and financial, 6.4% computer, engineering, and science, 9.1% education, legal, community service, arts, and media, 4.5% healthcare practitioners, 17.3% service, 29.1% sales and office, 14.5% natural resources, construction, and maintenance, 7.3% production, transportation, and material moving

Income: Per capita: $21,473; Median household: $55,500; Average household: $57,716; Households with income of $100,000 or more: 17.4%; Poverty rate: 24.2%

Educational Attainment: High school diploma or higher: 91.8%; Bachelor's degree or higher: 17.1%; Graduate/professional degree or higher: 7.6%

Housing: Homeownership rate: 72.8%; Median home value: $136,800; Median year structure built: Before 1940; Homeowner vacancy rate: 0.0%; Median selected monthly owner costs: $1,125 with a mortgage, $344 without a mortgage; Median gross rent: $665 per month; Rental vacancy rate: 0.0%
Health Insurance: 90.2% have insurance; 60.2% have private insurance; 41.0% have public insurance; 9.8% do not have insurance; 0.0% of children under 18 do not have insurance
Transportation: Commute: 99.0% car, 0.0% public transportation, 1.0% walk, 0.0% work from home; Mean travel time to work: 28.7 minutes

EVANS MILLS (village).
Covers a land area of 0.829 square miles and a water area of 0 square miles. Located at 44.09° N. Lat; 75.81° W. Long. Elevation is 423 feet.
Population: 481; Growth (since 2000): -20.5%; Density: 580.2 persons per square mile; Race: 95.0% White, 1.5% Black/African American, 0.8% Asian, 0.0% American Indian/Alaska Native, 0.0% Native Hawaiian/Other Pacific Islander, 2.1% Two or more races, 4.8% Hispanic of any race; Average household size: 2.32; Median age: 34.7; Age under 18: 21.2%; Age 65 and over: 16.4%; Males per 100 females: 103.6; Marriage status: 24.2% never married, 59.5% now married, 3.4% separated, 8.5% widowed, 7.7% divorced; Foreign born: 3.7%; Speak English only: 94.8%; With disability: 16.4%; Veterans: 16.7%; Ancestry: 21.4% Irish, 20.6% German, 12.1% Italian, 10.4% French, 8.1% American
Employment: 5.6% management, business, and financial, 2.0% computer, engineering, and science, 16.8% education, legal, community service, arts, and media, 8.1% healthcare practitioners, 12.7% service, 25.9% sales and office, 17.3% natural resources, construction, and maintenance, 11.7% production, transportation, and material moving
Income: Per capita: $25,773; Median household: $46,875; Average household: $57,904; Households with income of $100,000 or more: 12.5%; Poverty rate: 12.9%
Educational Attainment: High school diploma or higher: 91.9%; Bachelor's degree or higher: 25.1%; Graduate/professional degree or higher: 9.9%

School District(s)
Indian River Central SD (PK-12)
   2014-15 Enrollment: 4,140 . . . . (315) 642-3441
Housing: Homeownership rate: 57.2%; Median home value: $152,700; Median year structure built: 1953; Homeowner vacancy rate: 5.0%; Median selected monthly owner costs: $1,537 with a mortgage, $514 without a mortgage; Median gross rent: $779 per month; Rental vacancy rate: 0.0%
Health Insurance: 92.1% have insurance; 60.4% have private insurance; 50.2% have public insurance; 7.9% do not have insurance; 11.8% of children under 18 do not have insurance
Transportation: Commute: 93.1% car, 1.7% public transportation, 1.3% walk, 1.3% work from home; Mean travel time to work: 21.2 minutes

FELTS MILLS (CDP).
Covers a land area of 0.329 square miles and a water area of 0 square miles. Located at 44.02° N. Lat; 75.76° W. Long. Elevation is 584 feet.
Population: 257; Growth (since 2000): n/a; Density: 781.7 persons per square mile; Race: 97.3% White, 2.7% Black/African American, 0.0% Asian, 0.0% American Indian/Alaska Native, 0.0% Native Hawaiian/Other Pacific Islander, 0.0% Two or more races, 0.0% Hispanic of any race; Average household size: 2.47; Median age: 34.1; Age under 18: 26.5%; Age 65 and over: 3.5%; Males per 100 females: 95.8; Marriage status: 20.6% never married, 65.6% now married, 11.6% separated, 7.4% widowed, 6.3% divorced; Foreign born: 0.0%; Speak English only: 100.0%; With disability: 24.6%; Veterans: 30.5%; Ancestry: 29.6% Irish, 26.5% English, 22.2% German, 20.6% Scottish, 15.2% French
Employment: 6.9% management, business, and financial, 0.0% computer, engineering, and science, 0.0% education, legal, community service, arts, and media, 0.0% healthcare practitioners, 34.5% service, 41.4% sales and office, 17.2% natural resources, construction, and maintenance, 0.0% production, transportation, and material moving
Income: Per capita: $16,610; Median household: $40,227; Average household: $39,321; Households with income of $100,000 or more: n/a; Poverty rate: 12.8%
Educational Attainment: High school diploma or higher: 100.0%; Bachelor's degree or higher: 15.8%; Graduate/professional degree or higher: n/a
Housing: Homeownership rate: 51.9%; Median home value: $140,000; Median year structure built: 1942; Homeowner vacancy rate: 0.0%; Median

selected monthly owner costs: $1,306 with a mortgage, $465 without a mortgage; Median gross rent: $989 per month; Rental vacancy rate: 21.9%
Health Insurance: 81.0% have insurance; 64.2% have private insurance; 22.0% have public insurance; 19.0% do not have insurance; 0.0% of children under 18 do not have insurance
Transportation: Commute: 92.8% car, 0.0% public transportation, 7.2% walk, 0.0% work from home; Mean travel time to work: 0.0 minutes

FISHERS LANDING (CDP).
Covers a land area of 0.222 square miles and a water area of 0.002 square miles. Located at 44.28° N. Lat; 76.00° W. Long. Elevation is 262 feet.
Population: 70; Growth (since 2000): n/a; Density: 314.7 persons per square mile; Race: 100.0% White, 0.0% Black/African American, 0.0% Asian, 0.0% American Indian/Alaska Native, 0.0% Native Hawaiian/Other Pacific Islander, 0.0% Two or more races, 0.0% Hispanic of any race; Average household size: 1.59; Median age: 79.4; Age under 18: 0.0%; Age 65 and over: 82.9%; Males per 100 females: 102.3; Marriage status: 0.0% never married, 74.3% now married, 0.0% separated, 25.7% widowed, 0.0% divorced; Foreign born: 10.0%; Speak English only: 100.0%; With disability: 8.6%; Veterans: 51.4%; Ancestry: 25.7% Irish, 20.0% French, 17.1% English, 17.1% German, 10.0% Canadian
Employment: 100.0% management, business, and financial, 0.0% computer, engineering, and science, 0.0% education, legal, community service, arts, and media, 0.0% healthcare practitioners, 0.0% service, 0.0% sales and office, 0.0% natural resources, construction, and maintenance, 0.0% production, transportation, and material moving
Income: Per capita: $33,504; Median household: n/a; Average household: $54,620; Households with income of $100,000 or more: 13.6%; Poverty rate: n/a
Educational Attainment: High school diploma or higher: 90.0%; Bachelor's degree or higher: 8.6%; Graduate/professional degree or higher: n/a
Housing: Homeownership rate: 100.0%; Median home value: $187,500; Median year structure built: 1993; Homeowner vacancy rate: 0.0%; Median selected monthly owner costs: n/a with a mortgage, $473 without a mortgage; Median gross rent: n/a per month; Rental vacancy rate: 100.0%
Health Insurance: 100.0% have insurance; 90.0% have private insurance; 82.9% have public insurance; 0.0% do not have insurance; 0.0% of children under 18 do not have insurance
Transportation: Commute: 100.0% car, 0.0% public transportation, 0.0% walk, 0.0% work from home; Mean travel time to work: 0.0 minutes

FORT DRUM (CDP).
Covers a land area of 14.329 square miles and a water area of 0.093 square miles. Located at 44.04° N. Lat; 75.79° W. Long.
Population: 13,985; Growth (since 2000): 15.4%; Density: 976.0 persons per square mile; Race: 69.3% White, 13.4% Black/African American, 2.3% Asian, 1.7% American Indian/Alaska Native, 1.5% Native Hawaiian/Other Pacific Islander, 7.4% Two or more races, 19.3% Hispanic of any race; Average household size: 2.94; Median age: 22.2; Age under 18: 30.9%; Age 65 and over: 0.1%; Males per 100 females: 135.5; Marriage status: 41.1% never married, 55.0% now married, 1.3% separated, 0.4% widowed, 3.5% divorced; Foreign born: 7.3%; Speak English only: 83.2%; With disability: 6.1%; Veterans: 18.3%; Ancestry: 21.4% German, 17.7% Irish, 8.5% Italian, 3.4% French, 3.3% Polish
Employment: 9.2% management, business, and financial, 3.3% computer, engineering, and science, 8.9% education, legal, community service, arts, and media, 9.0% healthcare practitioners, 27.6% service, 29.4% sales and office, 6.4% natural resources, construction, and maintenance, 6.1% production, transportation, and material moving
Income: Per capita: $18,658; Median household: $41,966; Average household: $51,624; Households with income of $100,000 or more: 8.8%; Poverty rate: 13.7%
Educational Attainment: High school diploma or higher: 95.6%; Bachelor's degree or higher: 23.5%; Graduate/professional degree or higher: 8.3%
Housing: Homeownership rate: 0.6%; Median home value: n/a; Median year structure built: 1997; Homeowner vacancy rate: 0.0%; Median selected monthly owner costs: n/a with a mortgage, n/a without a mortgage; Median gross rent: $1,352 per month; Rental vacancy rate: 2.6%
Health Insurance: 97.5% have insurance; 90.5% have private insurance; 14.0% have public insurance; 2.5% do not have insurance; 0.6% of children under 18 do not have insurance

Transportation: Commute: 65.0% car, 0.0% public transportation, 24.8% walk, 6.4% work from home; Mean travel time to work: 9.3 minutes
Airports: Wheeler-Sack AAF (general aviation)

GLEN PARK (village).
Covers a land area of 0.708 square miles and a water area of 0.024 square miles. Located at 44.00° N. Lat; 75.96° W. Long. Elevation is 341 feet.
Population: 577; Growth (since 2000): 18.5%; Density: 814.8 persons per square mile; Race: 91.3% White, 3.3% Black/African American, 0.0% Asian, 0.0% American Indian/Alaska Native, 0.0% Native Hawaiian/Other Pacific Islander, 5.2% Two or more races, 1.0% Hispanic of any race; Average household size: 2.86; Median age: 31.6; Age under 18: 28.8%; Age 65 and over: 8.1%; Males per 100 females: 107.4; Marriage status: 30.7% never married, 56.9% now married, 3.0% separated, 5.6% widowed, 6.8% divorced; Foreign born: 1.7%; Speak English only: 97.3%; With disability: 12.2%; Veterans: 13.5%; Ancestry: 25.6% Irish, 20.8% German, 12.1% Italian, 11.3% English, 9.9% French Canadian
Employment: 11.9% management, business, and financial, 2.0% computer, engineering, and science, 10.5% education, legal, community service, arts, and media, 5.1% healthcare practitioners, 22.0% service, 28.5% sales and office, 13.6% natural resources, construction, and maintenance, 6.4% production, transportation, and material moving
Income: Per capita: $20,854; Median household: $51,500; Average household: $58,900; Households with income of $100,000 or more: 13.9%; Poverty rate: 11.3%
Educational Attainment: High school diploma or higher: 88.2%; Bachelor's degree or higher: 19.4%; Graduate/professional degree or higher: 6.2%
Housing: Homeownership rate: 77.2%; Median home value: $111,200; Median year structure built: Before 1940; Homeowner vacancy rate: 1.9%; Median selected monthly owner costs: $988 with a mortgage, $425 without a mortgage; Median gross rent: $835 per month; Rental vacancy rate: 0.0%
Health Insurance: 90.9% have insurance; 69.7% have private insurance; 33.6% have public insurance; 9.1% do not have insurance; 0.0% of children under 18 do not have insurance
Safety: Violent crime rate: 0.0 per 10,000 population; Property crime rate: 19.1 per 10,000 population
Transportation: Commute: 93.3% car, 0.0% public transportation, 1.4% walk, 2.5% work from home; Mean travel time to work: 16.4 minutes

GREAT BEND (CDP).
Covers a land area of 5.788 square miles and a water area of 0.056 square miles. Located at 44.02° N. Lat; 75.70° W. Long. Elevation is 663 feet.
Population: 854; Growth (since 2000): 6.6%; Density: 147.5 persons per square mile; Race: 92.3% White, 0.0% Black/African American, 2.6% Asian, 0.0% American Indian/Alaska Native, 0.0% Native Hawaiian/Other Pacific Islander, 0.0% Two or more races, 10.4% Hispanic of any race; Average household size: 2.68; Median age: 44.4; Age under 18: 18.6%; Age 65 and over: 21.2%; Males per 100 females: 112.3; Marriage status: 25.0% never married, 68.1% now married, 12.8% separated, 3.0% widowed, 3.9% divorced; Foreign born: 2.1%; Speak English only: 89.8%; With disability: 16.0%; Veterans: 34.1%; Ancestry: 27.4% French, 18.6% German, 8.3% American, 7.7% Italian, 5.7% English
Employment: 12.6% management, business, and financial, 0.0% computer, engineering, and science, 15.3% education, legal, community service, arts, and media, 8.3% healthcare practitioners, 8.6% service, 22.9% sales and office, 8.6% natural resources, construction, and maintenance, 23.6% production, transportation, and material moving
Income: Per capita: $26,697; Median household: $77,917; Average household: $69,578; Households with income of $100,000 or more: 25.7%; Poverty rate: 11.8%
Educational Attainment: High school diploma or higher: 92.7%; Bachelor's degree or higher: 10.3%; Graduate/professional degree or higher: 4.6%
Housing: Homeownership rate: 73.4%; Median home value: $103,300; Median year structure built: 1966; Homeowner vacancy rate: 0.0%; Median selected monthly owner costs: $783 with a mortgage, $298 without a mortgage; Median gross rent: $1,186 per month; Rental vacancy rate: 0.0%
Health Insurance: 93.7% have insurance; 59.0% have private insurance; 49.9% have public insurance; 6.3% do not have insurance; 11.9% of children under 18 do not have insurance
Transportation: Commute: 94.1% car, 0.0% public transportation, 0.0% walk, 5.9% work from home; Mean travel time to work: 21.7 minutes

HENDERSON (CDP).
Covers a land area of 0.506 square miles and a water area of 0 square miles. Located at 43.85° N. Lat; 76.19° W. Long. Elevation is 348 feet.
Population: 170; Growth (since 2000): n/a; Density: 336.0 persons per square mile; Race: 100.0% White, 0.0% Black/African American, 0.0% Asian, 0.0% American Indian/Alaska Native, 0.0% Native Hawaiian/Other Pacific Islander, 0.0% Two or more races, 0.0% Hispanic of any race; Average household size: 2.24; Median age: 48.3; Age under 18: 20.0%; Age 65 and over: 30.6%; Males per 100 females: 88.2; Marriage status: 26.4% never married, 43.8% now married, 2.1% separated, 20.8% widowed, 9.0% divorced; Foreign born: 1.8%; Speak English only: 93.8%; With disability: 15.3%; Veterans: 14.7%; Ancestry: 38.8% English, 13.5% German, 11.2% Irish, 5.9% American, 5.3% French
Employment: 4.8% management, business, and financial, 0.0% computer, engineering, and science, 15.9% education, legal, community service, arts, and media, 6.3% healthcare practitioners, 0.0% service, 34.9% sales and office, 27.0% natural resources, construction, and maintenance, 11.1% production, transportation, and material moving
Income: Per capita: $18,280; Median household: $23,333; Average household: $40,157; Households with income of $100,000 or more: 9.2%; Poverty rate: 21.8%
Educational Attainment: High school diploma or higher: 94.3%; Bachelor's degree or higher: 11.4%; Graduate/professional degree or higher: 1.6%
Housing: Homeownership rate: 60.5%; Median home value: $107,100; Median year structure built: Before 1940; Homeowner vacancy rate: 0.0%; Median selected monthly owner costs: $1,100 with a mortgage, $467 without a mortgage; Median gross rent: $367 per month; Rental vacancy rate: 0.0%
Health Insurance: 97.6% have insurance; 69.4% have private insurance; 55.3% have public insurance; 2.4% do not have insurance; 0.0% of children under 18 do not have insurance
Transportation: Commute: 96.8% car, 0.0% public transportation, 0.0% walk, 3.2% work from home; Mean travel time to work: 28.0 minutes

HENDERSON (town).
Covers a land area of 41.180 square miles and a water area of 11.756 square miles. Located at 43.86° N. Lat; 76.18° W. Long. Elevation is 348 feet.
Population: 1,526; Growth (since 2000): 10.8%; Density: 37.1 persons per square mile; Race: 97.8% White, 0.0% Black/African American, 0.1% Asian, 0.1% American Indian/Alaska Native, 0.0% Native Hawaiian/Other Pacific Islander, 1.4% Two or more races, 0.7% Hispanic of any race; Average household size: 2.34; Median age: 51.9; Age under 18: 17.5%; Age 65 and over: 30.7%; Males per 100 females: 102.4; Marriage status: 20.3% never married, 66.3% now married, 1.6% separated, 6.4% widowed, 7.0% divorced; Foreign born: 0.7%; Speak English only: 98.0%; With disability: 12.2%; Veterans: 13.2%; Ancestry: 22.4% English, 12.9% German, 12.0% Irish, 11.1% Italian, 7.9% American
Employment: 15.7% management, business, and financial, 2.2% computer, engineering, and science, 10.1% education, legal, community service, arts, and media, 3.6% healthcare practitioners, 14.4% service, 30.4% sales and office, 19.1% natural resources, construction, and maintenance, 4.6% production, transportation, and material moving
Income: Per capita: $34,531; Median household: $62,356; Average household: $80,944; Households with income of $100,000 or more: 27.9%; Poverty rate: 6.6%
Educational Attainment: High school diploma or higher: 93.8%; Bachelor's degree or higher: 23.8%; Graduate/professional degree or higher: 7.7%
Housing: Homeownership rate: 81.2%; Median home value: $171,400; Median year structure built: 1962; Homeowner vacancy rate: 4.8%; Median selected monthly owner costs: $1,375 with a mortgage, $514 without a mortgage; Median gross rent: $533 per month; Rental vacancy rate: 6.8%
Health Insurance: 96.2% have insurance; 80.9% have private insurance; 42.2% have public insurance; 3.8% do not have insurance; 0.0% of children under 18 do not have insurance
Transportation: Commute: 92.6% car, 0.0% public transportation, 2.1% walk, 4.7% work from home; Mean travel time to work: 25.9 minutes

HENDERSON HARBOR (unincorporated postal area)
ZCTA: 13651
Covers a land area of 2.449 square miles and a water area of 0.202 square miles. Located at 43.87° N. Lat; 76.18° W. Long. Elevation is 246 feet.

Population: 194; Growth (since 2000): n/a; Density: 79.2 persons per square mile; Race: 100.0% White, 0.0% Black/African American, 0.0% Asian, 0.0% American Indian/Alaska Native, 0.0% Native Hawaiian/Other Pacific Islander, 0.0% Two or more races, 0.0% Hispanic of any race; Average household size: 1.94; Median age: 67.0; Age under 18: 9.8%; Age 65 and over: 59.3%; Males per 100 females: 101.6; Marriage status: 4.5% never married, 79.7% now married, 1.1% separated, 6.2% widowed, 9.6% divorced; Foreign born: 1.5%; Speak English only: 100.0%; With disability: 10.5%; Veterans: 13.5%; Ancestry: 32.5% English, 17.0% French, 12.9% Irish, 11.3% Italian, 9.3% German

Employment: 41.3% management, business, and financial, 11.1% computer, engineering, and science, 20.6% education, legal, community service, arts, and media, 4.8% healthcare practitioners, 9.5% service, 12.7% sales and office, 0.0% natural resources, construction, and maintenance, 0.0% production, transportation, and material moving

Income: Per capita: $65,526; Median household: $79,545; Average household: $128,992; Households with income of $100,000 or more: 46.0%; Poverty rate: 1.5%

Educational Attainment: High school diploma or higher: 100.0%; Bachelor's degree or higher: 56.0%; Graduate/professional degree or higher: 25.1%

Housing: Homeownership rate: 79.0%; Median home value: $428,800; Median year structure built: 1955; Homeowner vacancy rate: 7.1%; Median selected monthly owner costs: $1,750 with a mortgage, $861 without a mortgage; Median gross rent: $1,125 per month; Rental vacancy rate: 0.0%

Health Insurance: 100.0% have insurance; 83.7% have private insurance; 65.3% have public insurance; 0.0% do not have insurance; 0.0% of children under 18 do not have insurance

Transportation: Commute: 83.6% car, 0.0% public transportation, 11.9% walk, 4.5% work from home; Mean travel time to work: 21.1 minutes

HERRINGS (village).
Covers a land area of 0.281 square miles and a water area of 0.049 square miles. Located at 44.02° N. Lat; 75.66° W. Long. Elevation is 689 feet.

Population: 78; Growth (since 2000): -39.5%; Density: 277.2 persons per square mile; Race: 97.4% White, 1.3% Black/African American, 0.0% Asian, 0.0% American Indian/Alaska Native, 0.0% Native Hawaiian/Other Pacific Islander, 0.0% Two or more races, 12.8% Hispanic of any race; Average household size: 3.25; Median age: 41.5; Age under 18: 20.5%; Age 65 and over: 14.1%; Males per 100 females: 95.7; Marriage status: 29.2% never married, 58.5% now married, 0.0% separated, 6.2% widowed, 6.2% divorced; Foreign born: 1.3%; Speak English only: 90.7%; With disability: 18.7%; Veterans: 20.3%; Ancestry: 57.7% Irish, 20.5% German, 7.7% English, 7.7% Ukrainian, 3.8% American

Employment: 5.6% management, business, and financial, 0.0% computer, engineering, and science, 8.3% education, legal, community service, arts, and media, 11.1% healthcare practitioners, 25.0% service, 13.9% sales and office, 5.6% natural resources, construction, and maintenance, 30.6% production, transportation, and material moving

Income: Per capita: $24,056; Median household: $72,500; Average household: $77,400; Households with income of $100,000 or more: 25.0%; Poverty rate: 3.8%

Educational Attainment: High school diploma or higher: 84.7%; Bachelor's degree or higher: 13.6%; Graduate/professional degree or higher: 13.6%

Housing: Homeownership rate: 95.8%; Median home value: $88,800; Median year structure built: Before 1940; Homeowner vacancy rate: 0.0%; Median selected monthly owner costs: $1,313 with a mortgage, $460 without a mortgage; Median gross rent: n/a per month; Rental vacancy rate: 0.0%

Health Insurance: 89.3% have insurance; 65.3% have private insurance; 37.3% have public insurance; 10.7% do not have insurance; 0.0% of children under 18 do not have insurance

Transportation: Commute: 97.4% car, 0.0% public transportation, 0.0% walk, 0.0% work from home; Mean travel time to work: 24.2 minutes

HOUNSFIELD (town).
Covers a land area of 48.915 square miles and a water area of 71.488 square miles. Located at 43.91° N. Lat; 76.31° W. Long.

Population: 3,568; Growth (since 2000): 7.4%; Density: 72.9 persons per square mile; Race: 94.4% White, 0.8% Black/African American, 1.3% Asian, 0.0% American Indian/Alaska Native, 0.0% Native Hawaiian/Other

Pacific Islander, 2.1% Two or more races, 2.6% Hispanic of any race; Average household size: 2.39; Median age: 35.6; Age under 18: 28.0%; Age 65 and over: 13.4%; Males per 100 females: 96.5; Marriage status: 26.3% never married, 59.7% now married, 2.1% separated, 4.2% widowed, 9.7% divorced; Foreign born: 6.4%; Speak English only: 87.9%; With disability: 13.4%; Veterans: 15.8%; Ancestry: 25.1% German, 20.0% Irish, 16.8% English, 8.3% Italian, 7.8% Polish

Employment: 11.7% management, business, and financial, 7.1% computer, engineering, and science, 10.5% education, legal, community service, arts, and media, 8.4% healthcare practitioners, 13.1% service, 27.7% sales and office, 11.7% natural resources, construction, and maintenance, 9.8% production, transportation, and material moving

Income: Per capita: $28,766; Median household: $55,152; Average household: $68,158; Households with income of $100,000 or more: 22.6%; Poverty rate: 14.9%

Educational Attainment: High school diploma or higher: 94.7%; Bachelor's degree or higher: 33.8%; Graduate/professional degree or higher: 16.8%

Housing: Homeownership rate: 61.3%; Median home value: $190,100; Median year structure built: 1980; Homeowner vacancy rate: 0.9%; Median selected monthly owner costs: $1,495 with a mortgage, $552 without a mortgage; Median gross rent: $983 per month; Rental vacancy rate: 0.0%

Health Insurance: 94.1% have insurance; 68.7% have private insurance; 40.6% have public insurance; 5.9% do not have insurance; 1.9% of children under 18 do not have insurance

Transportation: Commute: 88.7% car, 0.5% public transportation, 5.7% walk, 4.0% work from home; Mean travel time to work: 23.1 minutes

LA FARGEVILLE (CDP).
Covers a land area of 3.318 square miles and a water area of 0.055 square miles. Located at 44.20° N. Lat; 75.96° W. Long. Elevation is 377 feet.

Population: 560; Growth (since 2000): -4.8%; Density: 168.8 persons per square mile; Race: 98.9% White, 0.0% Black/African American, 0.0% Asian, 0.0% American Indian/Alaska Native, 0.0% Native Hawaiian/Other Pacific Islander, 1.1% Two or more races, 3.2% Hispanic of any race; Average household size: 2.62; Median age: 41.9; Age under 18: 27.3%; Age 65 and over: 23.0%; Males per 100 females: 91.8; Marriage status: 20.1% never married, 45.6% now married, 2.7% separated, 19.9% widowed, 14.3% divorced; Foreign born: 4.3%; Speak English only: 96.7%; With disability: 15.6%; Veterans: 9.5%; Ancestry: 35.5% Irish, 23.2% German, 16.3% English, 12.5% French, 5.7% American

Employment: 12.3% management, business, and financial, 7.1% computer, engineering, and science, 31.2% education, legal, community service, arts, and media, 7.1% healthcare practitioners, 7.8% service, 3.9% sales and office, 11.0% natural resources, construction, and maintenance, 19.5% production, transportation, and material moving

Income: Per capita: $23,147; Median household: $49,565; Average household: $60,064; Households with income of $100,000 or more: 14.0%; Poverty rate: 8.3%

Educational Attainment: High school diploma or higher: 97.2%; Bachelor's degree or higher: 29.4%; Graduate/professional degree or higher: 20.0%

School District(s)
La Fargeville Central SD (PK-12)
    2014-15 Enrollment: 556 . . . . (315) 658-2241

Housing: Homeownership rate: 80.4%; Median home value: $143,900; Median year structure built: Before 1940; Homeowner vacancy rate: 0.0%; Median selected monthly owner costs: $1,349 with a mortgage, $618 without a mortgage; Median gross rent: $713 per month; Rental vacancy rate: 0.0%

Health Insurance: 90.8% have insurance; 76.5% have private insurance; 30.9% have public insurance; 9.2% do not have insurance; 9.2% of children under 18 do not have insurance

Transportation: Commute: 91.6% car, 0.0% public transportation, 0.0% walk, 3.5% work from home; Mean travel time to work: 22.1 minutes

LE RAY (town).
Covers a land area of 73.643 square miles and a water area of 0.361 square miles. Located at 44.08° N. Lat; 75.80° W. Long.

Population: 22,385; Growth (since 2000): 12.9%; Density: 304.0 persons per square mile; Race: 69.3% White, 13.7% Black/African American, 2.6% Asian, 1.1% American Indian/Alaska Native, 1.0% Native Hawaiian/Other Pacific Islander, 8.4% Two or more races, 18.3% Hispanic of any race; Average household size: 2.77; Median age: 23.4; Age under 18: 29.0%; Age 65 and over: 2.5%; Males per 100 females: 123.5; Marriage status: 33.7% never married, 60.8% now married, 1.9% separated, 1.4%

widowed, 4.1% divorced; Foreign born: 6.7%; Speak English only: 85.1%; With disability: 8.2%; Veterans: 20.3%; Ancestry: 18.5% German, 15.3% Irish, 8.5% Italian, 6.1% French, 5.3% English

Employment: 11.8% management, business, and financial, 4.4% computer, engineering, and science, 12.8% education, legal, community service, arts, and media, 6.0% healthcare practitioners, 23.9% service, 27.4% sales and office, 7.4% natural resources, construction, and maintenance, 6.2% production, transportation, and material moving

Income: Per capita: $20,369; Median household: $45,493; Average household: $54,317; Households with income of $100,000 or more: 11.3%; Poverty rate: 11.6%

Educational Attainment: High school diploma or higher: 93.4%; Bachelor's degree or higher: 24.5%; Graduate/professional degree or higher: 8.8%

Housing: Homeownership rate: 17.9%; Median home value: $166,700; Median year structure built: 1993; Homeowner vacancy rate: 3.7%; Median selected monthly owner costs: $1,564 with a mortgage, $427 without a mortgage; Median gross rent: $1,276 per month; Rental vacancy rate: 4.9%

Health Insurance: 95.8% have insurance; 85.6% have private insurance; 20.5% have public insurance; 4.2% do not have insurance; 1.6% of children under 18 do not have insurance

Transportation: Commute: 73.6% car, 0.0% public transportation, 17.5% walk, 5.9% work from home; Mean travel time to work: 11.2 minutes

Additional Information Contacts

Town of Le Ray . . . . (315) 629-4052
   http://townofleray.org

LORRAINE (CDP).

Covers a land area of 0.483 square miles and a water area of 0 square miles. Located at 43.77° N. Lat; 75.95° W. Long. Elevation is 1,001 feet.

Population: 108; Growth (since 2000): n/a; Density: 223.7 persons per square mile; Race: 100.0% White, 0.0% Black/African American, 0.0% Asian, 0.0% American Indian/Alaska Native, 0.0% Native Hawaiian/Other Pacific Islander, 0.0% Two or more races, 0.0% Hispanic of any race; Average household size: 2.57; Median age: 54.0; Age under 18: 11.1%; Age 65 and over: 26.9%; Males per 100 females: 102.3; Marriage status: 23.5% never married, 61.2% now married, 0.0% separated, 9.2% widowed, 6.1% divorced; Foreign born: 0.0%; Speak English only: 100.0%; With disability: 23.1%; Veterans: 12.5%; Ancestry: 15.7% French, 13.0% English, 12.0% German, 8.3% Italian, 5.6% Dutch

Employment: 0.0% management, business, and financial, 4.3% computer, engineering, and science, 0.0% education, legal, community service, arts, and media, 8.7% healthcare practitioners, 39.1% service, 17.4% sales and office, 8.7% natural resources, construction, and maintenance, 21.7% production, transportation, and material moving

Income: Per capita: $23,712; Median household: $47,500; Average household: $56,219; Households with income of $100,000 or more: 9.6%; Poverty rate: 4.6%

Educational Attainment: High school diploma or higher: 88.4%; Bachelor's degree or higher: 7.0%; Graduate/professional degree or higher: 2.3%

Housing: Homeownership rate: 100.0%; Median home value: $85,000; Median year structure built: 1943; Homeowner vacancy rate: 0.0%; Median selected monthly owner costs: $880 with a mortgage, $450 without a mortgage; Median gross rent: n/a per month; Rental vacancy rate: 0.0%

Health Insurance: 89.8% have insurance; 62.0% have private insurance; 51.9% have public insurance; 10.2% do not have insurance; 0.0% of children under 18 do not have insurance

Transportation: Commute: 100.0% car, 0.0% public transportation, 0.0% walk, 0.0% work from home; Mean travel time to work: 25.2 minutes

LORRAINE (town).

Covers a land area of 38.979 square miles and a water area of 0.018 square miles. Located at 43.75° N. Lat; 75.98° W. Long. Elevation is 1,001 feet.

Population: 935; Growth (since 2000): 0.5%; Density: 24.0 persons per square mile; Race: 98.3% White, 0.3% Black/African American, 0.9% Asian, 0.2% American Indian/Alaska Native, 0.0% Native Hawaiian/Other Pacific Islander, 0.2% Two or more races, 2.8% Hispanic of any race; Average household size: 2.79; Median age: 38.9; Age under 18: 23.3%; Age 65 and over: 11.9%; Males per 100 females: 103.7; Marriage status: 26.3% never married, 57.3% now married, 2.7% separated, 5.1% widowed, 11.3% divorced; Foreign born: 0.7%; Speak English only: 93.3%; With disability: 13.3%; Veterans: 8.0%; Ancestry: 19.4% German, 15.9% English, 15.3% Irish, 12.9% French, 10.3% American

Employment: 8.0% management, business, and financial, 2.0% computer, engineering, and science, 6.2% education, legal, community service, arts, and media, 4.2% healthcare practitioners, 19.7% service, 22.4% sales and office, 19.2% natural resources, construction, and maintenance, 18.2% production, transportation, and material moving

Income: Per capita: $22,664; Median household: $43,750; Average household: $59,516; Households with income of $100,000 or more: 18.5%; Poverty rate: 15.5%

Educational Attainment: High school diploma or higher: 79.8%; Bachelor's degree or higher: 12.7%; Graduate/professional degree or higher: 2.4%

Housing: Homeownership rate: 83.9%; Median home value: $101,400; Median year structure built: 1985; Homeowner vacancy rate: 1.1%; Median selected monthly owner costs: $1,117 with a mortgage, $438 without a mortgage; Median gross rent: $1,015 per month; Rental vacancy rate: 10.0%

Health Insurance: 82.4% have insurance; 49.3% have private insurance; 42.3% have public insurance; 17.6% do not have insurance; 11.9% of children under 18 do not have insurance

Transportation: Commute: 92.9% car, 0.0% public transportation, 2.3% walk, 4.3% work from home; Mean travel time to work: 27.8 minutes

LYME (town).

Covers a land area of 55.813 square miles and a water area of 51.178 square miles. Located at 44.02° N. Lat; 76.23° W. Long.

Population: 2,456; Growth (since 2000): 21.9%; Density: 44.0 persons per square mile; Race: 95.8% White, 0.3% Black/African American, 0.5% Asian, 0.0% American Indian/Alaska Native, 0.0% Native Hawaiian/Other Pacific Islander, 3.3% Two or more races, 0.9% Hispanic of any race; Average household size: 2.61; Median age: 44.5; Age under 18: 22.8%; Age 65 and over: 19.3%; Males per 100 females: 101.9; Marriage status: 23.0% never married, 66.4% now married, 2.3% separated, 5.6% widowed, 5.0% divorced; Foreign born: 3.1%; Speak English only: 96.4%; With disability: 17.3%; Veterans: 8.9%; Ancestry: 26.5% Irish, 26.2% German, 13.9% English, 10.2% Italian, 9.1% French

Employment: 15.5% management, business, and financial, 1.2% computer, engineering, and science, 12.4% education, legal, community service, arts, and media, 5.9% healthcare practitioners, 25.2% service, 20.0% sales and office, 8.4% natural resources, construction, and maintenance, 11.4% production, transportation, and material moving

Income: Per capita: $27,238; Median household: $53,125; Average household: $71,261; Households with income of $100,000 or more: 21.5%; Poverty rate: 12.8%

Educational Attainment: High school diploma or higher: 89.7%; Bachelor's degree or higher: 22.9%; Graduate/professional degree or higher: 10.5%

Housing: Homeownership rate: 77.9%; Median home value: $161,100; Median year structure built: 1970; Homeowner vacancy rate: 3.8%; Median selected monthly owner costs: $1,561 with a mortgage, $470 without a mortgage; Median gross rent: $896 per month; Rental vacancy rate: 2.8%

Health Insurance: 95.7% have insurance; 72.7% have private insurance; 39.3% have public insurance; 4.3% do not have insurance; 1.4% of children under 18 do not have insurance

Transportation: Commute: 88.5% car, 0.6% public transportation, 4.9% walk, 5.5% work from home; Mean travel time to work: 22.5 minutes

MANNSVILLE (village).

Covers a land area of 0.897 square miles and a water area of 0.033 square miles. Located at 43.72° N. Lat; 76.07° W. Long. Elevation is 620 feet.

Population: 375; Growth (since 2000): -6.3%; Density: 418.0 persons per square mile; Race: 90.7% White, 7.2% Black/African American, 0.0% Asian, 0.0% American Indian/Alaska Native, 0.0% Native Hawaiian/Other Pacific Islander, 1.9% Two or more races, 0.0% Hispanic of any race; Average household size: 2.95; Median age: 37.6; Age under 18: 28.8%; Age 65 and over: 13.3%; Males per 100 females: 91.4; Marriage status: 23.0% never married, 58.8% now married, 0.7% separated, 6.2% widowed, 12.0% divorced; Foreign born: 0.5%; Speak English only: 99.4%; With disability: 11.0%; Veterans: 17.3%; Ancestry: 23.5% German, 22.4% Irish, 9.9% English, 6.9% French, 5.6% French Canadian

Employment: 11.7% management, business, and financial, 2.1% computer, engineering, and science, 15.9% education, legal, community service, arts, and media, 6.9% healthcare practitioners, 17.9% service, 17.9% sales and office, 13.1% natural resources, construction, and maintenance, 14.5% production, transportation, and material moving

Income: Per capita: $24,320; Median household: $67,813; Average household: $71,812; Households with income of $100,000 or more: 23.7%; Poverty rate: 4.4%
Educational Attainment: High school diploma or higher: 87.6%; Bachelor's degree or higher: 15.7%; Graduate/professional degree or higher: 8.4%

School District(s)
South Jefferson Central SD (PK-12)
    2014-15 Enrollment: 1,993 . . . . (315) 583-6104
Housing: Homeownership rate: 84.3%; Median home value: $117,800; Median year structure built: Before 1940; Homeowner vacancy rate: 6.1%; Median selected monthly owner costs: $1,150 with a mortgage, $461 without a mortgage; Median gross rent: $813 per month; Rental vacancy rate: 31.0%
Health Insurance: 84.0% have insurance; 72.5% have private insurance; 25.4% have public insurance; 16.0% do not have insurance; 4.6% of children under 18 do not have insurance
Transportation: Commute: 97.9% car, 0.0% public transportation, 1.4% walk, 0.7% work from home; Mean travel time to work: 23.6 minutes

NATURAL BRIDGE (CDP). Covers a land area of 1.389 square miles and a water area of 0 square miles. Located at 44.07° N. Lat; 75.50° W. Long. Elevation is 817 feet.
Population: 776; Growth (since 2000): 98.0%; Density: 558.5 persons per square mile; Race: 100.0% White, 0.0% Black/African American, 0.0% Asian, 0.0% American Indian/Alaska Native, 0.0% Native Hawaiian/Other Pacific Islander, 0.0% Two or more races, 0.0% Hispanic of any race; Average household size: 4.56; Median age: 25.0; Age under 18: 47.6%; Age 65 and over: 1.7%; Males per 100 females: 95.2; Marriage status: 24.7% never married, 72.4% now married, 0.0% separated, 2.9% widowed, 0.0% divorced; Foreign born: 0.0%; Speak English only: 100.0%; With disability: 14.8%; Veterans: 5.7%; Ancestry: 48.8% Irish, 44.8% Dutch, 26.2% Italian, 17.9% French, 17.5% English
Employment: 13.6% management, business, and financial, 0.0% computer, engineering, and science, 0.0% education, legal, community service, arts, and media, 8.0% healthcare practitioners, 17.6% service, 8.0% sales and office, 35.7% natural resources, construction, and maintenance, 17.1% production, transportation, and material moving
Income: Per capita: $13,130; Median household: n/a; Average household: $51,392; Households with income of $100,000 or more: 30.0%; Poverty rate: 61.6%
Educational Attainment: High school diploma or higher: 73.8%; Bachelor's degree or higher: n/a; Graduate/professional degree or higher: n/a
Housing: Homeownership rate: 60.0%; Median home value: $104,300; Median year structure built: Before 1940; Homeowner vacancy rate: 0.0%; Median selected monthly owner costs: $825 with a mortgage, n/a without a mortgage; Median gross rent: n/a per month; Rental vacancy rate: 18.1%
Health Insurance: 88.9% have insurance; 23.1% have private insurance; 70.5% have public insurance; 11.1% do not have insurance; 0.0% of children under 18 do not have insurance
Transportation: Commute: 100.0% car, 0.0% public transportation, 0.0% walk, 0.0% work from home; Mean travel time to work: 22.5 minutes

ORLEANS (town). Covers a land area of 71.423 square miles and a water area of 6.620 square miles. Located at 44.22° N. Lat; 75.95° W. Long.
Population: 2,876; Growth (since 2000): 16.7%; Density: 40.3 persons per square mile; Race: 97.7% White, 0.4% Black/African American, 0.0% Asian, 0.5% American Indian/Alaska Native, 0.0% Native Hawaiian/Other Pacific Islander, 0.9% Two or more races, 2.5% Hispanic of any race; Average household size: 2.53; Median age: 44.6; Age under 18: 19.0%; Age 65 and over: 21.8%; Males per 100 females: 101.5; Marriage status: 22.1% never married, 61.2% now married, 1.9% separated, 7.6% widowed, 9.1% divorced; Foreign born: 2.1%; Speak English only: 97.8%; With disability: 16.0%; Veterans: 15.7%; Ancestry: 24.5% Irish, 24.3% German, 13.8% English, 12.7% French, 7.9% Italian
Employment: 8.2% management, business, and financial, 1.3% computer, engineering, and science, 10.2% education, legal, community service, arts, and media, 5.2% healthcare practitioners, 22.2% service, 24.0% sales and office, 14.8% natural resources, construction, and maintenance, 14.2% production, transportation, and material moving
Income: Per capita: $25,164; Median household: $55,063; Average household: $62,830; Households with income of $100,000 or more: 16.2%; Poverty rate: 9.6%

Educational Attainment: High school diploma or higher: 89.8%; Bachelor's degree or higher: 21.3%; Graduate/professional degree or higher: 8.1%
Housing: Homeownership rate: 87.4%; Median home value: $141,500; Median year structure built: 1965; Homeowner vacancy rate: 0.0%; Median selected monthly owner costs: $1,143 with a mortgage, $453 without a mortgage; Median gross rent: $765 per month; Rental vacancy rate: 8.9%
Health Insurance: 91.0% have insurance; 75.3% have private insurance; 34.9% have public insurance; 9.0% do not have insurance; 2.6% of children under 18 do not have insurance
Transportation: Commute: 91.4% car, 0.5% public transportation, 0.8% walk, 5.1% work from home; Mean travel time to work: 24.4 minutes

OXBOW (CDP). Covers a land area of 0.202 square miles and a water area of 0 square miles. Located at 44.29° N. Lat; 75.62° W. Long. Elevation is 354 feet.
Population: 96; Growth (since 2000): n/a; Density: 474.5 persons per square mile; Race: 100.0% White, 0.0% Black/African American, 0.0% Asian, 0.0% American Indian/Alaska Native, 0.0% Native Hawaiian/Other Pacific Islander, 0.0% Two or more races, 0.0% Hispanic of any race; Average household size: 2.34; Median age: 45.3; Age under 18: 21.9%; Age 65 and over: 22.9%; Males per 100 females: 92.9; Marriage status: 15.6% never married, 63.6% now married, 0.0% separated, 10.4% widowed, 10.4% divorced; Foreign born: 0.0%; Speak English only: 100.0%; With disability: 28.1%; Veterans: 8.0%; Ancestry: 14.6% American, 14.6% Irish, 8.3% German, 7.3% Portuguese, 4.2% Italian
Employment: 0.0% management, business, and financial, 0.0% computer, engineering, and science, 0.0% education, legal, community service, arts, and media, 6.9% healthcare practitioners, 20.7% service, 17.2% sales and office, 6.9% natural resources, construction, and maintenance, 48.3% production, transportation, and material moving
Income: Per capita: $23,076; Median household: n/a; Average household: $53,449; Households with income of $100,000 or more: 17.1%; Poverty rate: 8.3%
Educational Attainment: High school diploma or higher: 88.0%; Bachelor's degree or higher: 8.0%; Graduate/professional degree or higher: 5.3%
Housing: Homeownership rate: 100.0%; Median home value: $103,900; Median year structure built: Before 1940; Homeowner vacancy rate: 0.0%; Median selected monthly owner costs: $1,107 with a mortgage, $337 without a mortgage; Median gross rent: n/a per month; Rental vacancy rate: 0.0%
Health Insurance: 85.4% have insurance; 62.5% have private insurance; 56.3% have public insurance; 14.6% do not have insurance; 0.0% of children under 18 do not have insurance
Transportation: Commute: 100.0% car, 0.0% public transportation, 0.0% walk, 0.0% work from home; Mean travel time to work: 36.6 minutes

PAMELIA (town). Covers a land area of 33.840 square miles and a water area of 1.369 square miles. Located at 44.06° N. Lat; 75.91° W. Long.
Population: 3,194; Growth (since 2000): 10.3%; Density: 94.4 persons per square mile; Race: 87.6% White, 4.1% Black/African American, 0.8% Asian, 0.3% American Indian/Alaska Native, 0.0% Native Hawaiian/Other Pacific Islander, 7.1% Two or more races, 3.4% Hispanic of any race; Average household size: 2.56; Median age: 37.5; Age under 18: 22.7%; Age 65 and over: 16.9%; Males per 100 females: 108.3; Marriage status: 27.5% never married, 58.3% now married, 2.2% separated, 2.7% widowed, 11.5% divorced; Foreign born: 1.6%; Speak English only: 95.9%; With disability: 13.9%; Veterans: 20.7%; Ancestry: 28.1% Irish, 19.7% German, 11.6% English, 9.4% Italian, 8.7% French
Employment: 19.0% management, business, and financial, 3.9% computer, engineering, and science, 11.7% education, legal, community service, arts, and media, 7.2% healthcare practitioners, 20.9% service, 15.0% sales and office, 13.9% natural resources, construction, and maintenance, 8.4% production, transportation, and material moving
Income: Per capita: $28,369; Median household: $61,058; Average household: $72,535; Households with income of $100,000 or more: 20.1%; Poverty rate: 8.0%
Educational Attainment: High school diploma or higher: 90.8%; Bachelor's degree or higher: 22.8%; Graduate/professional degree or higher: 9.0%
Housing: Homeownership rate: 71.3%; Median home value: $164,200; Median year structure built: 1979; Homeowner vacancy rate: 0.0%; Median

selected monthly owner costs: $1,388 with a mortgage, $443 without a mortgage; Median gross rent: $848 per month; Rental vacancy rate: 0.0%
Health Insurance: 83.8% have insurance; 72.7% have private insurance; 31.5% have public insurance; 16.2% do not have insurance; 24.6% of children under 18 do not have insurance
Transportation: Commute: 93.4% car, 0.0% public transportation, 5.9% walk, 0.6% work from home; Mean travel time to work: 13.8 minutes

PAMELIA CENTER (CDP). Covers a land area of 1.041 square miles and a water area of 0 square miles. Located at 44.04° N. Lat; 75.90° W. Long. Elevation is 469 feet.
Population: 404; Growth (since 2000): n/a; Density: 388.1 persons per square mile; Race: 85.9% White, 7.4% Black/African American, 1.7% Asian, 0.0% American Indian/Alaska Native, 0.0% Native Hawaiian/Other Pacific Islander, 5.0% Two or more races, 0.0% Hispanic of any race; Average household size: 2.34; Median age: 45.0; Age under 18: 12.9%; Age 65 and over: 23.3%; Males per 100 females: 107.9; Marriage status: 23.8% never married, 66.4% now married, 0.0% separated, 0.0% widowed, 9.8% divorced; Foreign born: 5.2%; Speak English only: 98.4%; With disability: 3.2%; Veterans: 42.5%; Ancestry: 31.7% English, 26.7% German, 25.2% Italian, 16.6% Irish, 7.4% American
Employment: 23.1% management, business, and financial, 0.0% computer, engineering, and science, 16.8% education, legal, community service, arts, and media, 17.3% healthcare practitioners, 13.9% service, 2.3% sales and office, 26.6% natural resources, construction, and maintenance, 0.0% production, transportation, and material moving
Income: Per capita: $43,693; Median household: $85,986; Average household: $103,232; Households with income of $100,000 or more: 31.8%; Poverty rate: 2.2%
Educational Attainment: High school diploma or higher: 100.0%; Bachelor's degree or higher: 49.4%; Graduate/professional degree or higher: 32.3%
Housing: Homeownership rate: 84.4%; Median home value: $209,800; Median year structure built: 1989; Homeowner vacancy rate: 0.0%; Median selected monthly owner costs: $1,446 with a mortgage, n/a without a mortgage; Median gross rent: $1,264 per month; Rental vacancy rate: 0.0%
Health Insurance: 96.0% have insurance; 96.0% have private insurance; 32.7% have public insurance; 4.0% do not have insurance; 0.0% of children under 18 do not have insurance
Transportation: Commute: 100.0% car, 0.0% public transportation, 0.0% walk, 0.0% work from home; Mean travel time to work: 11.7 minutes

PHILADELPHIA (town). Covers a land area of 37.593 square miles and a water area of 0.021 square miles. Located at 44.15° N. Lat; 75.71° W. Long. Elevation is 486 feet.
Population: 1,786; Growth (since 2000): -16.5%; Density: 47.5 persons per square mile; Race: 90.8% White, 2.4% Black/African American, 0.4% Asian, 0.1% American Indian/Alaska Native, 0.0% Native Hawaiian/Other Pacific Islander, 3.9% Two or more races, 5.4% Hispanic of any race; Average household size: 2.55; Median age: 33.1; Age under 18: 24.9%; Age 65 and over: 14.1%; Males per 100 females: 89.4; Marriage status: 25.8% never married, 58.4% now married, 4.2% separated, 6.0% widowed, 9.8% divorced; Foreign born: 1.8%; Speak English only: 94.1%; With disability: 11.1%; Veterans: 14.9%; Ancestry: 18.9% German, 12.4% English, 10.9% Irish, 9.0% French, 6.8% American
Employment: 8.8% management, business, and financial, 2.1% computer, engineering, and science, 13.0% education, legal, community service, arts, and media, 3.7% healthcare practitioners, 22.3% service, 29.1% sales and office, 8.9% natural resources, construction, and maintenance, 12.1% production, transportation, and material moving
Income: Per capita: $22,722; Median household: $47,031; Average household: $56,806; Households with income of $100,000 or more: 10.6%; Poverty rate: 14.4%
Educational Attainment: High school diploma or higher: 90.5%; Bachelor's degree or higher: 16.5%; Graduate/professional degree or higher: 7.1%
School District(s)
Indian River Central SD (PK-12)
   2014-15 Enrollment: 4,140 . . . . (315) 642-3441
Housing: Homeownership rate: 51.5%; Median home value: $133,600; Median year structure built: 1972; Homeowner vacancy rate: 0.0%; Median selected monthly owner costs: $1,141 with a mortgage, $410 without a mortgage; Median gross rent: $670 per month; Rental vacancy rate: 2.8%

Health Insurance: 92.0% have insurance; 72.9% have private insurance; 38.4% have public insurance; 8.0% do not have insurance; 0.7% of children under 18 do not have insurance
Transportation: Commute: 90.4% car, 0.3% public transportation, 4.9% walk, 3.3% work from home; Mean travel time to work: 20.9 minutes

PHILADELPHIA (village). Covers a land area of 0.904 square miles and a water area of 0 square miles. Located at 44.15° N. Lat; 75.71° W. Long. Elevation is 486 feet.
Population: 1,113; Growth (since 2000): -26.7%; Density: 1,230.9 persons per square mile; Race: 86.3% White, 3.3% Black/African American, 0.6% Asian, 0.0% American Indian/Alaska Native, 0.0% Native Hawaiian/Other Pacific Islander, 6.0% Two or more races, 8.4% Hispanic of any race; Average household size: 2.61; Median age: 31.8; Age under 18: 28.6%; Age 65 and over: 13.6%; Males per 100 females: 87.7; Marriage status: 26.7% never married, 59.8% now married, 5.4% separated, 5.3% widowed, 8.2% divorced; Foreign born: 1.8%; Speak English only: 91.5%; With disability: 11.1%; Veterans: 13.9%; Ancestry: 22.4% German, 12.6% Irish, 11.1% English, 7.5% American, 6.2% French
Employment: 8.7% management, business, and financial, 2.1% computer, engineering, and science, 13.6% education, legal, community service, arts, and media, 4.2% healthcare practitioners, 22.8% service, 31.3% sales and office, 7.1% natural resources, construction, and maintenance, 10.1% production, transportation, and material moving
Income: Per capita: $22,374; Median household: $46,071; Average household: $57,409; Households with income of $100,000 or more: 10.3%; Poverty rate: 17.6%
Educational Attainment: High school diploma or higher: 88.6%; Bachelor's degree or higher: 14.5%; Graduate/professional degree or higher: 5.2%
School District(s)
Indian River Central SD (PK-12)
   2014-15 Enrollment: 4,140 . . . . (315) 642-3441
Housing: Homeownership rate: 38.7%; Median home value: $129,200; Median year structure built: 1971; Homeowner vacancy rate: 0.0%; Median selected monthly owner costs: $988 with a mortgage, $387 without a mortgage; Median gross rent: $634 per month; Rental vacancy rate: 3.6%
Health Insurance: 93.2% have insurance; 75.5% have private insurance; 39.4% have public insurance; 6.8% do not have insurance; 0.9% of children under 18 do not have insurance
Transportation: Commute: 89.8% car, 0.0% public transportation, 7.5% walk, 2.7% work from home; Mean travel time to work: 19.1 minutes

PIERREPONT MANOR (CDP). Covers a land area of 0.684 square miles and a water area of 0.004 square miles. Located at 43.74° N. Lat; 76.06° W. Long. Elevation is 623 feet.
Population: 143; Growth (since 2000): n/a; Density: 208.9 persons per square mile; Race: 85.3% White, 0.0% Black/African American, 0.0% Asian, 14.7% American Indian/Alaska Native, 0.0% Native Hawaiian/Other Pacific Islander, 0.0% Two or more races, 0.0% Hispanic of any race; Average household size: 2.86; Median age: 27.4; Age under 18: 25.9%; Age 65 and over: 7.0%; Males per 100 females: 90.0; Marriage status: 0.0% never married, 100.0% now married, 4.7% separated, 0.0% widowed, 0.0% divorced; Foreign born: 14.7%; Speak English only: 87.7%; With disability: 30.1%; Veterans: 0.0%; Ancestry: 63.6% Polish, 47.6% Irish, 21.7% French Canadian, 7.0% American
Employment: 0.0% management, business, and financial, 0.0% computer, engineering, and science, 34.8% education, legal, community service, arts, and media, 0.0% healthcare practitioners, 0.0% service, 9.0% sales and office, 5.6% natural resources, construction, and maintenance, 50.6% production, transportation, and material moving
Income: Per capita: $19,383; Median household: $61,129; Average household: $55,436; Households with income of $100,000 or more: n/a; Poverty rate: n/a
Educational Attainment: High school diploma or higher: 94.9%; Bachelor's degree or higher: 37.4%; Graduate/professional degree or higher: n/a
Housing: Homeownership rate: 26.0%; Median home value: n/a; Median year structure built: 1968; Homeowner vacancy rate: 0.0%; Median selected monthly owner costs: n/a with a mortgage, n/a without a mortgage; Median gross rent: n/a per month; Rental vacancy rate: 0.0%
Health Insurance: 21.7% have insurance; 14.7% have private insurance; 7.0% have public insurance; 78.3% do not have insurance; 100.0% of children under 18 do not have insurance

Transportation: Commute: 100.0% car, 0.0% public transportation, 0.0% walk, 0.0% work from home; Mean travel time to work: 0.0 minutes

PLESSIS (CDP).
Covers a land area of 0.346 square miles and a water area of 0 square miles. Located at 44.27° N. Lat; 75.86° W. Long. Elevation is 404 feet.
Population: 115; Growth (since 2000): n/a; Density: 332.6 persons per square mile; Race: 100.0% White, 0.0% Black/African American, 0.0% Asian, 0.0% American Indian/Alaska Native, 0.0% Native Hawaiian/Other Pacific Islander, 0.0% Two or more races, 0.0% Hispanic of any race; Average household size: 2.80; Median age: 44.6; Age under 18: 0.0%; Age 65 and over: 16.5%; Males per 100 females: 113.0; Marriage status: 48.7% never married, 16.5% now married, 0.0% separated, 0.0% widowed, 34.8% divorced; Foreign born: 0.0%; Speak English only: 100.0%; With disability: 0.0%; Veterans: 7.0%; Ancestry: 59.1% Irish, 58.3% German, 29.6% American, 6.1% French
Employment: 0.0% management, business, and financial, 0.0% computer, engineering, and science, 0.0% education, legal, community service, arts, and media, 14.6% healthcare practitioners, 0.0% service, 85.4% sales and office, 0.0% natural resources, construction, and maintenance, 0.0% production, transportation, and material moving
Income: Per capita: $31,076; Median household: $83,313; Average household: $84,480; Households with income of $100,000 or more: 17.1%; Poverty rate: n/a
Educational Attainment: High school diploma or higher: 100.0%; Bachelor's degree or higher: 22.7%; Graduate/professional degree or higher: 13.3%
Housing: Homeownership rate: 100.0%; Median home value: $131,900; Median year structure built: Before 1940; Homeowner vacancy rate: 0.0%; Median selected monthly owner costs: n/a with a mortgage, n/a without a mortgage; Median gross rent: n/a per month; Rental vacancy rate: 0.0%
Health Insurance: 74.8% have insurance; 74.8% have private insurance; 16.5% have public insurance; 25.2% do not have insurance; 0.0% of children under 18 do not have insurance
Transportation: Commute: 100.0% car, 0.0% public transportation, 0.0% walk, 0.0% work from home; Mean travel time to work: 0.0 minutes

REDWOOD (CDP).
Covers a land area of 2.021 square miles and a water area of 0.534 square miles. Located at 44.30° N. Lat; 75.81° W. Long. Elevation is 367 feet.
Population: 584; Growth (since 2000): 0.0%; Density: 289.0 persons per square mile; Race: 94.0% White, 0.0% Black/African American, 0.0% Asian, 0.0% American Indian/Alaska Native, 0.0% Native Hawaiian/Other Pacific Islander, 3.9% Two or more races, 7.0% Hispanic of any race; Average household size: 3.06; Median age: 32.6; Age under 18: 28.4%; Age 65 and over: 9.6%; Males per 100 females: 100.3; Marriage status: 29.5% never married, 52.7% now married, 0.0% separated, 8.7% widowed, 9.1% divorced; Foreign born: 0.0%; Speak English only: 100.0%; With disability: 17.3%; Veterans: 12.4%; Ancestry: 18.2% German, 11.8% Italian, 9.8% Irish, 9.4% English, 7.7% American
Employment: 10.3% management, business, and financial, 0.0% computer, engineering, and science, 3.2% education, legal, community service, arts, and media, 0.0% healthcare practitioners, 51.2% service, 2.8% sales and office, 17.1% natural resources, construction, and maintenance, 15.5% production, transportation, and material moving
Income: Per capita: $14,638; Median household: $36,891; Average household: $44,184; Households with income of $100,000 or more: n/a; Poverty rate: 9.8%
Educational Attainment: High school diploma or higher: 69.4%; Bachelor's degree or higher: 6.9%; Graduate/professional degree or higher: n/a
Housing: Homeownership rate: 71.2%; Median home value: $59,200; Median year structure built: 1955; Homeowner vacancy rate: 13.9%; Median selected monthly owner costs: n/a with a mortgage, n/a without a mortgage; Median gross rent: $1,200 per month; Rental vacancy rate: 0.0%
Health Insurance: 82.7% have insurance; 58.0% have private insurance; 41.4% have public insurance; 17.3% do not have insurance; 0.0% of children under 18 do not have insurance
Transportation: Commute: 92.9% car, 4.8% public transportation, 0.0% walk, 2.4% work from home; Mean travel time to work: 25.2 minutes

RODMAN (CDP).
Covers a land area of 0.116 square miles and a water area of 0 square miles. Located at 43.85° N. Lat; 75.94° W. Long. Elevation is 725 feet.
Population: 215; Growth (since 2000): n/a; Density: 1,854.7 persons per square mile; Race: 90.2% White, 0.0% Black/African American, 1.4% Asian, 0.0% American Indian/Alaska Native, 0.0% Native Hawaiian/Other Pacific Islander, 0.0% Two or more races, 8.4% Hispanic of any race; Average household size: 4.13; Median age: 37.1; Age under 18: 33.5%; Age 65 and over: 16.7%; Males per 100 females: 112.5; Marriage status: 22.4% never married, 75.7% now married, 0.0% separated, 0.0% widowed, 2.0% divorced; Foreign born: 7.0%; Speak English only: 85.4%; With disability: 24.2%; Veterans: 5.6%; Ancestry: 30.7% Irish, 28.8% English, 23.7% German, 11.2% Polish, 7.9% Dutch
Employment: 10.0% management, business, and financial, 0.0% computer, engineering, and science, 14.3% education, legal, community service, arts, and media, 10.0% healthcare practitioners, 11.4% service, 41.4% sales and office, 0.0% natural resources, construction, and maintenance, 12.9% production, transportation, and material moving
Income: Per capita: $19,345; Median household: $61,250; Average household: $74,438; Households with income of $100,000 or more: 28.9%; Poverty rate: 2.4%
Educational Attainment: High school diploma or higher: 92.5%; Bachelor's degree or higher: 11.3%; Graduate/professional degree or higher: 7.5%
Housing: Homeownership rate: 76.9%; Median home value: $113,500; Median year structure built: Before 1940; Homeowner vacancy rate: 18.4%; Median selected monthly owner costs: $1,083 with a mortgage, $422 without a mortgage; Median gross rent: n/a per month; Rental vacancy rate: 0.0%
Health Insurance: 98.6% have insurance; 67.4% have private insurance; 47.9% have public insurance; 1.4% do not have insurance; 0.0% of children under 18 do not have insurance
Transportation: Commute: 87.1% car, 0.0% public transportation, 0.0% walk, 12.9% work from home; Mean travel time to work: 36.6 minutes

RODMAN (town).
Covers a land area of 42.227 square miles and a water area of 0.053 square miles. Located at 43.84° N. Lat; 75.90° W. Long. Elevation is 725 feet.
Population: 1,443; Growth (since 2000): 25.8%; Density: 34.2 persons per square mile; Race: 85.4% White, 0.0% Black/African American, 0.6% Asian, 8.1% American Indian/Alaska Native, 0.0% Native Hawaiian/Other Pacific Islander, 1.5% Two or more races, 4.5% Hispanic of any race; Average household size: 3.10; Median age: 32.8; Age under 18: 31.1%; Age 65 and over: 10.4%; Males per 100 females: 104.5; Marriage status: 26.4% never married, 62.7% now married, 2.0% separated, 2.4% widowed, 8.5% divorced; Foreign born: 5.2%; Speak English only: 91.7%; With disability: 10.3%; Veterans: 9.6%; Ancestry: 26.1% Irish, 19.1% English, 12.6% German, 6.4% American, 4.9% Polish
Employment: 6.7% management, business, and financial, 2.6% computer, engineering, and science, 11.9% education, legal, community service, arts, and media, 8.0% healthcare practitioners, 15.4% service, 25.5% sales and office, 14.7% natural resources, construction, and maintenance, 15.1% production, transportation, and material moving
Income: Per capita: $23,453; Median household: $63,393; Average household: $70,047; Households with income of $100,000 or more: 25.8%; Poverty rate: 4.0%
Educational Attainment: High school diploma or higher: 92.1%; Bachelor's degree or higher: 16.9%; Graduate/professional degree or higher: 10.8%
Housing: Homeownership rate: 77.6%; Median home value: $158,200; Median year structure built: 1972; Homeowner vacancy rate: 5.0%; Median selected monthly owner costs: $1,329 with a mortgage, $463 without a mortgage; Median gross rent: $2,006 per month; Rental vacancy rate: 0.0%
Health Insurance: 91.7% have insurance; 69.8% have private insurance; 32.7% have public insurance; 8.3% do not have insurance; 1.3% of children under 18 do not have insurance
Transportation: Commute: 90.4% car, 0.0% public transportation, 4.7% walk, 4.9% work from home; Mean travel time to work: 22.0 minutes

RUTLAND (town).
Covers a land area of 45.103 square miles and a water area of 0.275 square miles. Located at 43.94° N. Lat; 75.79° W. Long.
Population: 3,156; Growth (since 2000): 6.7%; Density: 70.0 persons per square mile; Race: 89.7% White, 3.8% Black/African American, 1.0%

Asian, 0.0% American Indian/Alaska Native, 0.2% Native Hawaiian/Other Pacific Islander, 4.3% Two or more races, 5.5% Hispanic of any race; Average household size: 2.67; Median age: 32.4; Age under 18: 27.9%; Age 65 and over: 10.8%; Males per 100 females: 98.8; Marriage status: 25.7% never married, 58.4% now married, 5.7% separated, 5.4% widowed, 10.5% divorced; Foreign born: 2.9%; Speak English only: 94.7%; With disability: 15.2%; Veterans: 18.0%; Ancestry: 20.3% Irish, 15.8% German, 11.7% English, 8.7% Italian, 8.4% French

Employment: 6.6% management, business, and financial, 3.5% computer, engineering, and science, 9.8% education, legal, community service, arts, and media, 10.2% healthcare practitioners, 16.8% service, 29.5% sales and office, 12.5% natural resources, construction, and maintenance, 11.0% production, transportation, and material moving

Income: Per capita: $22,864; Median household: $51,875; Average household: $59,496; Households with income of $100,000 or more: 11.7%; Poverty rate: 11.3%

Educational Attainment: High school diploma or higher: 90.8%; Bachelor's degree or higher: 19.0%; Graduate/professional degree or higher: 6.3%

Housing: Homeownership rate: 69.5%; Median home value: $138,700; Median year structure built: 1968; Homeowner vacancy rate: 2.1%; Median selected monthly owner costs: $1,309 with a mortgage, $496 without a mortgage; Median gross rent: $949 per month; Rental vacancy rate: 7.2%

Health Insurance: 89.2% have insurance; 64.6% have private insurance; 38.3% have public insurance; 10.8% do not have insurance; 4.7% of children under 18 do not have insurance

Transportation: Commute: 95.6% car, 0.0% public transportation, 1.0% walk, 2.9% work from home; Mean travel time to work: 16.9 minutes

SACKETS HARBOR (village). Covers a land area of 2.205 square miles and a water area of 0.006 square miles. Located at 43.94° N. Lat; 76.11° W. Long. Elevation is 282 feet.

History: In 1809 infantry was stationed here to enforce the Embargo Act and control smuggling. Following the outbreak of the War of 1812, it became the center of U.S. naval and military activity for Upper St. Lawrence Valley and Lake Ontario. Further expansion occurred during the 1830s and 1840s due to the Patriots War in Canada. Its growth led to the development of Pine Camp (Fort Drum) near Watertown. Zebulon Pike is buried here. Settled c.1801, Incorporated 1814.

Population: 1,495; Growth (since 2000): 7.9%; Density: 678.1 persons per square mile; Race: 89.8% White, 0.9% Black/African American, 0.9% Asian, 0.0% American Indian/Alaska Native, 0.0% Native Hawaiian/Other Pacific Islander, 4.9% Two or more races, 6.3% Hispanic of any race; Average household size: 2.13; Median age: 36.0; Age under 18: 23.2%; Age 65 and over: 15.1%; Males per 100 females: 98.4; Marriage status: 26.4% never married, 60.0% now married, 2.8% separated, 3.2% widowed, 10.4% divorced; Foreign born: 6.9%; Speak English only: 93.5%; With disability: 12.6%; Veterans: 22.3%; Ancestry: 25.4% Irish, 19.5% German, 18.6% English, 10.0% Italian, 7.5% French

Employment: 14.3% management, business, and financial, 9.6% computer, engineering, and science, 18.6% education, legal, community service, arts, and media, 5.8% healthcare practitioners, 13.5% service, 25.5% sales and office, 4.2% natural resources, construction, and maintenance, 8.7% production, transportation, and material moving

Income: Per capita: $33,814; Median household: $58,819; Average household: $71,627; Households with income of $100,000 or more: 21.1%; Poverty rate: 4.6%

Educational Attainment: High school diploma or higher: 97.1%; Bachelor's degree or higher: 48.7%; Graduate/professional degree or higher: 19.9%

School District(s)

Sackets Harbor Central SD (KG-12)
    2014-15 Enrollment: 453 . . . . (315) 646-3575

Housing: Homeownership rate: 43.9%; Median home value: $192,900; Median year structure built: 1953; Homeowner vacancy rate: 2.5%; Median selected monthly owner costs: $1,464 with a mortgage, $583 without a mortgage; Median gross rent: $1,075 per month; Rental vacancy rate: 0.0%

Health Insurance: 94.3% have insurance; 86.5% have private insurance; 27.9% have public insurance; 5.7% do not have insurance; 5.5% of children under 18 do not have insurance

Safety: Violent crime rate: 0.0 per 10,000 population; Property crime rate: 79.4 per 10,000 population

Transportation: Commute: 90.7% car, 1.1% public transportation, 3.6% walk, 4.6% work from home; Mean travel time to work: 24.0 minutes

THERESA (town). Covers a land area of 64.943 square miles and a water area of 4.789 square miles. Located at 44.26° N. Lat; 75.77° W. Long. Elevation is 407 feet.

Population: 2,973; Growth (since 2000): 23.2%; Density: 45.8 persons per square mile; Race: 94.3% White, 0.2% Black/African American, 0.4% Asian, 0.4% American Indian/Alaska Native, 0.0% Native Hawaiian/Other Pacific Islander, 4.5% Two or more races, 4.8% Hispanic of any race; Average household size: 2.77; Median age: 38.5; Age under 18: 26.1%; Age 65 and over: 11.2%; Males per 100 females: 105.9; Marriage status: 26.9% never married, 59.4% now married, 2.6% separated, 6.1% widowed, 7.6% divorced; Foreign born: 2.4%; Speak English only: 95.5%; With disability: 12.6%; Veterans: 18.7%; Ancestry: 22.2% Irish, 15.9% German, 11.9% French, 8.3% Italian, 8.0% English

Employment: 12.6% management, business, and financial, 3.6% computer, engineering, and science, 9.7% education, legal, community service, arts, and media, 2.6% healthcare practitioners, 19.9% service, 25.4% sales and office, 13.4% natural resources, construction, and maintenance, 12.8% production, transportation, and material moving

Income: Per capita: $27,044; Median household: $64,073; Average household: $73,567; Households with income of $100,000 or more: 19.7%; Poverty rate: 10.6%

Educational Attainment: High school diploma or higher: 89.3%; Bachelor's degree or higher: 16.5%; Graduate/professional degree or higher: 7.9%

School District(s)

Indian River Central SD (PK-12)
    2014-15 Enrollment: 4,140 . . . . (315) 642-3441

Housing: Homeownership rate: 74.9%; Median home value: $127,500; Median year structure built: 1978; Homeowner vacancy rate: 0.0%; Median selected monthly owner costs: $1,364 with a mortgage, $411 without a mortgage; Median gross rent: $968 per month; Rental vacancy rate: 13.5%

Health Insurance: 93.8% have insurance; 74.2% have private insurance; 35.6% have public insurance; 6.2% do not have insurance; 5.7% of children under 18 do not have insurance

Transportation: Commute: 92.0% car, 0.5% public transportation, 2.1% walk, 4.6% work from home; Mean travel time to work: 26.6 minutes

THERESA (village). Covers a land area of 1.252 square miles and a water area of 0.061 square miles. Located at 44.22° N. Lat; 75.80° W. Long. Elevation is 407 feet.

Population: 903; Growth (since 2000): 11.2%; Density: 721.3 persons per square mile; Race: 94.5% White, 0.7% Black/African American, 0.6% Asian, 1.2% American Indian/Alaska Native, 0.0% Native Hawaiian/Other Pacific Islander, 3.1% Two or more races, 7.9% Hispanic of any race; Average household size: 2.63; Median age: 36.1; Age under 18: 29.1%; Age 65 and over: 10.1%; Males per 100 females: 103.5; Marriage status: 32.2% never married, 47.9% now married, 3.4% separated, 9.2% widowed, 10.6% divorced; Foreign born: 6.2%; Speak English only: 91.6%; With disability: 17.0%; Veterans: 15.8%; Ancestry: 24.4% Irish, 22.5% German, 14.1% French, 6.8% Scottish, 5.9% American

Employment: 11.8% management, business, and financial, 2.9% computer, engineering, and science, 12.4% education, legal, community service, arts, and media, 4.7% healthcare practitioners, 24.1% service, 25.9% sales and office, 8.8% natural resources, construction, and maintenance, 9.4% production, transportation, and material moving

Income: Per capita: $23,197; Median household: $51,500; Average household: $59,080; Households with income of $100,000 or more: 14.2%; Poverty rate: 8.3%

Educational Attainment: High school diploma or higher: 88.7%; Bachelor's degree or higher: 15.4%; Graduate/professional degree or higher: 9.0%

School District(s)

Indian River Central SD (PK-12)
    2014-15 Enrollment: 4,140 . . . . (315) 642-3441

Housing: Homeownership rate: 67.7%; Median home value: $116,300; Median year structure built: Before 1940; Homeowner vacancy rate: 0.0%; Median selected monthly owner costs: $1,266 with a mortgage, $642 without a mortgage; Median gross rent: $945 per month; Rental vacancy rate: 12.6%

Health Insurance: 90.1% have insurance; 68.4% have private insurance; 39.6% have public insurance; 9.9% do not have insurance; 11.8% of children under 18 do not have insurance

Transportation: Commute: 86.3% car, 2.0% public transportation, 3.9% walk, 6.7% work from home; Mean travel time to work: 26.4 minutes

THOUSAND ISLAND PARK (CDP). Covers a land area of 0.293 square miles and a water area of 0 square miles. Located at 44.29° N. Lat; 76.03° W. Long. Elevation is 276 feet.

Population: 71; Growth (since 2000): n/a; Density: 242.3 persons per square mile; Race: 100.0% White, 0.0% Black/African American, 0.0% Asian, 0.0% American Indian/Alaska Native, 0.0% Native Hawaiian/Other Pacific Islander, 0.0% Two or more races, 0.0% Hispanic of any race; Average household size: 1.58; Median age: 72.8; Age under 18: 0.0%; Age 65 and over: 100.0%; Males per 100 females: 106.7; Marriage status: 0.0% never married, 70.4% now married, 0.0% separated, 29.6% widowed, 0.0% divorced; Foreign born: 0.0%; Speak English only: 100.0%; With disability: 9.9%; Veterans: 33.8%; Ancestry: 56.3% English, 29.6% Danish, 26.8% Lebanese, 26.8% German, 26.8% Irish

Employment: 0.0% management, business, and financial, 0.0% computer, engineering, and science, 0.0% education, legal, community service, arts, and media, 0.0% healthcare practitioners, 100.0% service, 0.0% sales and office, 0.0% natural resources, construction, and maintenance, 0.0% production, transportation, and material moving

Income: Per capita: $40,842; Median household: $59,803; Average household: $64,004; Households with income of $100,000 or more: n/a; Poverty rate: n/a

Educational Attainment: High school diploma or higher: 100.0%; Bachelor's degree or higher: 56.3%; Graduate/professional degree or higher: n/a

Housing: Homeownership rate: 100.0%; Median home value: $392,100; Median year structure built: Before 1940; Homeowner vacancy rate: 0.0%; Median selected monthly owner costs: n/a with a mortgage, n/a without a mortgage; Median gross rent: n/a per month; Rental vacancy rate: 0.0%

Health Insurance: 100.0% have insurance; 100.0% have private insurance; 100.0% have public insurance; 0.0% do not have insurance; 0.0% of children under 18 do not have insurance

Transportation: Commute: 79.2% car, 0.0% public transportation, 20.8% walk, 0.0% work from home; Mean travel time to work: 0.0 minutes

THREE MILE BAY (CDP). Covers a land area of 0.257 square miles and a water area of 0 square miles. Located at 44.08° N. Lat; 76.20° W. Long. Elevation is 259 feet.

Population: 198; Growth (since 2000): n/a; Density: 768.9 persons per square mile; Race: 72.2% White, 0.0% Black/African American, 0.0% Asian, 0.0% American Indian/Alaska Native, 0.0% Native Hawaiian/Other Pacific Islander, 27.8% Two or more races, 9.6% Hispanic of any race; Average household size: 2.61; Median age: 28.8; Age under 18: 31.3%; Age 65 and over: 23.7%; Males per 100 females: 95.7; Marriage status: 48.1% never married, 26.6% now married, 0.0% separated, 16.9% widowed, 8.4% divorced; Foreign born: 0.0%; Speak English only: 89.3%; With disability: 17.7%; Veterans: 0.0%; Ancestry: 44.4% Italian, 26.8% English, 17.7% Scottish, 17.2% Dutch, 13.6% Irish

Employment: 0.0% management, business, and financial, 0.0% computer, engineering, and science, 23.4% education, legal, community service, arts, and media, 12.5% healthcare practitioners, 64.1% service, 0.0% sales and office, 0.0% natural resources, construction, and maintenance, 0.0% production, transportation, and material moving

Income: Per capita: $15,571; Median household: $34,808; Average household: $39,221; Households with income of $100,000 or more: 5.3%; Poverty rate: 6.1%

Educational Attainment: High school diploma or higher: 96.6%; Bachelor's degree or higher: 19.8%; Graduate/professional degree or higher: 16.4%

Housing: Homeownership rate: 64.5%; Median home value: $110,400; Median year structure built: 1954; Homeowner vacancy rate: 0.0%; Median selected monthly owner costs: n/a with a mortgage, n/a without a mortgage; Median gross rent: n/a per month; Rental vacancy rate: 0.0%

Health Insurance: 92.4% have insurance; 79.8% have private insurance; 36.4% have public insurance; 7.6% do not have insurance; 0.0% of children under 18 do not have insurance

Transportation: Commute: 100.0% car, 0.0% public transportation, 0.0% walk, 0.0% work from home; Mean travel time to work: 0.0 minutes

WATERTOWN (city). County seat. Covers a land area of 9.020 square miles and a water area of 0.345 square miles. Located at 43.97° N. Lat; 75.91° W. Long. Elevation is 466 feet.

History: In 1800, five New Englanders hacked their way up from the Mohawk Valley, stopped at the rocky Black River Falls, and named the site Watertown. They built sawmills and gristmills along the river, and burned piles of lumber for potash. The five and ten cent store originated in Watertown during county fair week in 1878. Frank W. Woolworth (1852-1910), a clerk in Moore & Smith's general store, piled leftover odds and ends on a table and put up a sign: "Any Article 5 cents." The entire stock was sold out in a few hours. Inspired by this success, Woolworth opened his first store in Utica the following year.

Population: 27,250; Growth (since 2000): 2.0%; Density: 3,021.2 persons per square mile; Race: 83.7% White, 7.2% Black/African American, 1.9% Asian, 0.3% American Indian/Alaska Native, 0.2% Native Hawaiian/Other Pacific Islander, 5.1% Two or more races, 7.6% Hispanic of any race; Average household size: 2.30; Median age: 30.6; Age under 18: 23.7%; Age 65 and over: 12.4%; Males per 100 females: 91.7; Marriage status: 32.6% never married, 48.5% now married, 4.2% separated, 6.6% widowed, 12.3% divorced; Foreign born: 4.6%; Speak English only: 92.2%; With disability: 15.0%; Veterans: 12.8%; Ancestry: 21.1% Irish, 13.8% Italian, 13.6% German, 9.0% English, 8.8% French

Employment: 10.0% management, business, and financial, 3.4% computer, engineering, and science, 11.6% education, legal, community service, arts, and media, 8.3% healthcare practitioners, 24.1% service, 25.3% sales and office, 8.0% natural resources, construction, and maintenance, 9.3% production, transportation, and material moving

Income: Per capita: $21,766; Median household: $41,414; Average household: $49,879; Households with income of $100,000 or more: 9.6%; Poverty rate: 23.1%

Educational Attainment: High school diploma or higher: 88.7%; Bachelor's degree or higher: 21.0%; Graduate/professional degree or higher: 8.5%

School District(s)
Jefferson-Lewis-Hamilton-Herkimer-Oneida Boces
  2014-15 Enrollment: n/a . . . . (315) 779-7010
Watertown City SD (KG-12)
  2014-15 Enrollment: 3,976 . . . . (315) 785-3700

Two-year College(s)
Jefferson Community College (Public)
  Fall 2014 Enrollment: 3,880 . . . . (315) 786-2200
  2015-16 Tuition: In-state $4,835; Out-of-state $7,115

Vocational/Technical School(s)
Jefferson Lewis BOCES-Practical Nursing Program (Public)
  Fall 2014 Enrollment: 77 . . . . (315) 779-7200
  2015-16 Tuition: In-state $9,539; Out-of-state $9,539

Housing: Homeownership rate: 39.8%; Median home value: $125,500; Median year structure built: Before 1940; Homeowner vacancy rate: 4.6%; Median selected monthly owner costs: $1,064 with a mortgage, $492 without a mortgage; Median gross rent: $816 per month; Rental vacancy rate: 6.5%

Health Insurance: 92.2% have insurance; 60.7% have private insurance; 45.8% have public insurance; 7.8% do not have insurance; 2.7% of children under 18 do not have insurance

Hospitals: Samaritan Medical Center (287 beds)

Safety: Violent crime rate: 52.3 per 10,000 population; Property crime rate: 478.4 per 10,000 population

Newspapers: Watertown Daily Times (daily circulation 29,500)

Transportation: Commute: 88.3% car, 1.2% public transportation, 5.9% walk, 1.8% work from home; Mean travel time to work: 14.9 minutes

Airports: Watertown International (primary service/non-hub)

Additional Information Contacts
City of Watertown . . . . (315) 785-7780
  http://www.citywatertown.org

WATERTOWN (town). Covers a land area of 35.926 square miles and a water area of 0.101 square miles. Located at 43.93° N. Lat; 75.92° W. Long. Elevation is 466 feet.

History: Public Square Historic District in the city. Settled c.1800,Incorporated as a city 1869.

Population: 4,813; Growth (since 2000): 7.4%; Density: 134.0 persons per square mile; Race: 81.2% White, 6.4% Black/African American, 4.6% Asian, 0.6% American Indian/Alaska Native, 0.3% Native Hawaiian/Other Pacific Islander, 4.5% Two or more races, 4.3% Hispanic of any race; Average household size: 2.54; Median age: 39.8; Age under 18: 21.3%; Age 65 and over: 10.8%; Males per 100 females: 128.4; Marriage status: 31.7% never married, 53.3% now married, 3.9% separated, 5.5% widowed, 9.5% divorced; Foreign born: 6.6%; Speak English only: 91.2%; With disability: 11.7%; Veterans: 11.8%; Ancestry: 18.5% Irish, 15.4% Italian, 12.6% German, 8.9% English, 8.2% American

Employment: 7.6% management, business, and financial, 5.0% computer, engineering, and science, 10.6% education, legal, community service, arts,

and media, 12.1% healthcare practitioners, 20.1% service, 28.8% sales and office, 7.6% natural resources, construction, and maintenance, 8.2% production, transportation, and material moving
Income: Per capita: $30,617; Median household: $69,214; Average household: $87,574; Households with income of $100,000 or more: 26.6%; Poverty rate: 6.9%
Educational Attainment: High school diploma or higher: 87.6%; Bachelor's degree or higher: 23.4%; Graduate/professional degree or higher: 12.4%

School District(s)
Jefferson-Lewis-Hamilton-Herkimer-Oneida Boces
  2014-15 Enrollment: n/a . . . . (315) 779-7010
Watertown City SD (KG-12)
  2014-15 Enrollment: 3,976 . . . . (315) 785-3700
Two-year College(s)
Jefferson Community College (Public)
  Fall 2014 Enrollment: 3,880 . . . . (315) 786-2200
  2015-16 Tuition: In-state $4,835; Out-of-state $7,115
Vocational/Technical School(s)
Jefferson Lewis BOCES-Practical Nursing Program (Public)
  Fall 2014 Enrollment: 77 . . . . (315) 779-7200
  2015-16 Tuition: In-state $9,539; Out-of-state $9,539
Housing: Homeownership rate: 81.3%; Median home value: $171,000; Median year structure built: 1971; Homeowner vacancy rate: 0.0%; Median selected monthly owner costs: $1,372 with a mortgage, $526 without a mortgage; Median gross rent: $989 per month; Rental vacancy rate: 0.0%
Health Insurance: 93.9% have insurance; 83.9% have private insurance; 24.4% have public insurance; 6.1% do not have insurance; 1.7% of children under 18 do not have insurance
Hospitals: Samaritan Medical Center (287 beds)
Newspapers: Watertown Daily Times (daily circulation 29,500)
Transportation: Commute: 91.5% car, 0.0% public transportation, 0.6% walk, 5.2% work from home; Mean travel time to work: 17.9 minutes
Airports: Watertown International (primary service/non-hub)
Additional Information Contacts
Town of Watertown . . . . (315) 782-8248
  http://www.townofwatertownny.org

WELLESLEY ISLAND (unincorporated postal area)
ZCTA: 13640
  Covers a land area of 12.360 square miles and a water area of 0.256 square miles. Located at 44.30° N. Lat; 76.03° W. Long..
Population: 378; Growth (since 2000): 16.0%; Density: 30.6 persons per square mile; Race: 100.0% White, 0.0% Black/African American, 0.0% Asian, 0.0% American Indian/Alaska Native, 0.0% Native Hawaiian/Other Pacific Islander, 0.0% Two or more races, 0.0% Hispanic of any race; Average household size: 2.02; Median age: 62.0; Age under 18: 8.2%; Age 65 and over: 34.4%; Males per 100 females: 103.8; Marriage status: 9.2% never married, 84.1% now married, 1.4% separated, 5.2% widowed, 1.4% divorced; Foreign born: 2.9%; Speak English only: 97.1%; With disability: 7.4%; Veterans: 7.2%; Ancestry: 22.5% Italian, 16.4% Norwegian, 13.0% Irish, 12.2% Scottish, 10.1% French Canadian
Employment: 24.4% management, business, and financial, 0.0% computer, engineering, and science, 32.8% education, legal, community service, arts, and media, 0.0% healthcare practitioners, 13.4% service, 10.1% sales and office, 14.3% natural resources, construction, and maintenance, 5.0% production, transportation, and material moving
Income: Per capita: $43,465; Median household: $50,536; Average household: $86,794; Households with income of $100,000 or more: 28.9%; Poverty rate: 2.9%
Educational Attainment: High school diploma or higher: 88.5%; Bachelor's degree or higher: 46.4%; Graduate/professional degree or higher: 25.4%
Housing: Homeownership rate: 96.8%; Median home value: $247,500; Median year structure built: 1981; Homeowner vacancy rate: 7.2%; Median selected monthly owner costs: $1,286 with a mortgage, $904 without a mortgage; Median gross rent: n/a per month; Rental vacancy rate: 0.0%
Health Insurance: 88.6% have insurance; 73.8% have private insurance; 42.3% have public insurance; 11.4% do not have insurance; 0.0% of children under 18 do not have insurance
Transportation: Commute: 71.4% car, 0.0% public transportation, 0.0% walk, 16.0% work from home; Mean travel time to work: 25.3 minutes

WEST CARTHAGE (village). Covers a land area of 1.297 square miles and a water area of 0.097 square miles. Located at 43.97° N. Lat; 75.62° W. Long. Elevation is 778 feet.
History: Incorporated 1888.
Population: 2,019; Growth (since 2000): -3.9%; Density: 1,557.3 persons per square mile; Race: 84.8% White, 4.8% Black/African American, 1.4% Asian, 0.0% American Indian/Alaska Native, 0.0% Native Hawaiian/Other Pacific Islander, 5.1% Two or more races, 10.6% Hispanic of any race; Average household size: 2.31; Median age: 31.3; Age under 18: 20.1%; Age 65 and over: 12.8%; Males per 100 females: 90.2; Marriage status: 23.9% never married, 59.9% now married, 2.0% separated, 7.1% widowed, 9.1% divorced; Foreign born: 2.4%; Speak English only: 94.0%; With disability: 18.6%; Veterans: 20.2%; Ancestry: 25.2% German, 17.1% Irish, 13.2% English, 6.9% French, 6.9% Italian
Employment: 5.9% management, business, and financial, 2.4% computer, engineering, and science, 7.3% education, legal, community service, arts, and media, 10.1% healthcare practitioners, 15.1% service, 32.2% sales and office, 10.9% natural resources, construction, and maintenance, 16.1% production, transportation, and material moving
Income: Per capita: $24,949; Median household: $54,856; Average household: $57,512; Households with income of $100,000 or more: 15.1%; Poverty rate: 12.5%
Educational Attainment: High school diploma or higher: 89.8%; Bachelor's degree or higher: 27.1%; Graduate/professional degree or higher: 7.8%
Housing: Homeownership rate: 43.6%; Median home value: $136,300; Median year structure built: Before 1940; Homeowner vacancy rate: 4.1%; Median selected monthly owner costs: $1,173 with a mortgage, $460 without a mortgage; Median gross rent: $1,020 per month; Rental vacancy rate: 7.9%
Health Insurance: 94.8% have insurance; 80.3% have private insurance; 33.3% have public insurance; 5.2% do not have insurance; 5.9% of children under 18 do not have insurance
Transportation: Commute: 94.9% car, 0.2% public transportation, 4.0% walk, 0.9% work from home; Mean travel time to work: 20.0 minutes
Additional Information Contacts
Village of West Carthage . . . . (315) 493-2552
  http://villageofwestcarthage.org

WILNA (town). Covers a land area of 78.623 square miles and a water area of 0.878 square miles. Located at 44.06° N. Lat; 75.59° W. Long.
Population: 6,477; Growth (since 2000): 3.9%; Density: 82.4 persons per square mile; Race: 93.9% White, 1.9% Black/African American, 0.6% Asian, 0.1% American Indian/Alaska Native, 0.0% Native Hawaiian/Other Pacific Islander, 3.2% Two or more races, 1.5% Hispanic of any race; Average household size: 2.85; Median age: 30.3; Age under 18: 32.0%; Age 65 and over: 10.9%; Males per 100 females: 98.8; Marriage status: 31.9% never married, 51.1% now married, 3.3% separated, 7.5% widowed, 9.6% divorced; Foreign born: 1.8%; Speak English only: 98.0%; With disability: 14.7%; Veterans: 12.3%; Ancestry: 26.4% Irish, 14.1% French, 12.1% Italian, 11.0% English, 10.8% German
Employment: 12.8% management, business, and financial, 2.1% computer, engineering, and science, 3.9% education, legal, community service, arts, and media, 7.4% healthcare practitioners, 27.9% service, 20.3% sales and office, 14.4% natural resources, construction, and maintenance, 11.1% production, transportation, and material moving
Income: Per capita: $19,865; Median household: $45,208; Average household: $56,083; Households with income of $100,000 or more: 10.9%; Poverty rate: 25.5%
Educational Attainment: High school diploma or higher: 84.2%; Bachelor's degree or higher: 8.3%; Graduate/professional degree or higher: 3.3%
Housing: Homeownership rate: 53.9%; Median home value: $129,700; Median year structure built: Before 1940; Homeowner vacancy rate: 0.1%; Median selected monthly owner costs: $1,277 with a mortgage, $611 without a mortgage; Median gross rent: $906 per month; Rental vacancy rate: 6.5%
Health Insurance: 90.1% have insurance; 56.1% have private insurance; 45.8% have public insurance; 9.9% do not have insurance; 9.1% of children under 18 do not have insurance
Transportation: Commute: 86.5% car, 0.0% public transportation, 4.3% walk, 6.2% work from home; Mean travel time to work: 18.6 minutes

WORTH (town). Covers a land area of 43.218 square miles and a water area of 0.086 square miles. Located at 43.74° N. Lat; 75.84° W. Long. Elevation is 1,237 feet.

Population: 202; Growth (since 2000): -13.7%; Density: 4.7 persons per square mile; Race: 98.5% White, 0.0% Black/African American, 0.0% Asian, 0.0% American Indian/Alaska Native, 0.0% Native Hawaiian/Other Pacific Islander, 1.5% Two or more races, 0.0% Hispanic of any race; Average household size: 2.43; Median age: 40.0; Age under 18: 25.7%; Age 65 and over: 17.3%; Males per 100 females: 99.1; Marriage status: 19.5% never married, 58.5% now married, 3.1% separated, 8.8% widowed, 13.2% divorced; Foreign born: 0.5%; Speak English only: 98.9%; With disability: 12.9%; Veterans: 15.3%; Ancestry: 21.3% English, 19.8% Irish, 19.3% Italian, 13.4% French, 12.9% German

Employment: 15.5% management, business, and financial, 2.9% computer, engineering, and science, 20.4% education, legal, community service, arts, and media, 1.9% healthcare practitioners, 14.6% service, 16.5% sales and office, 15.5% natural resources, construction, and maintenance, 12.6% production, transportation, and material moving

Income: Per capita: $26,898; Median household: $60,625; Average household: $63,231; Households with income of $100,000 or more: 15.7%; Poverty rate: 23.3%

Educational Attainment: High school diploma or higher: 85.0%; Bachelor's degree or higher: 18.6%; Graduate/professional degree or higher: 10.7%

Housing: Homeownership rate: 78.3%; Median home value: $132,500; Median year structure built: 1975; Homeowner vacancy rate: 8.1%; Median selected monthly owner costs: $1,339 with a mortgage, $400 without a mortgage; Median gross rent: $844 per month; Rental vacancy rate: 0.0%

Health Insurance: 91.1% have insurance; 70.8% have private insurance; 38.6% have public insurance; 8.9% do not have insurance; 0.0% of children under 18 do not have insurance

Transportation: Commute: 93.9% car, 0.0% public transportation, 2.0% walk, 2.0% work from home; Mean travel time to work: 36.9 minutes

Kings County

See New York City

Lewis County

Located in north central New York; includes the foothills of the Adirondacks in the east; drained by the Black River. Covers a land area of 1,274.679 square miles, a water area of 15.282 square miles, and is located in the Eastern Time Zone at 43.79° N. Lat., 75.44° W. Long. The county was founded in 1805. County seat is Lowville.

Weather Station: Lowville										Elevation: 859 feet		
	Jan	Feb	Mar	Apr	May	Jun	Jul	Aug	Sep	Oct	Nov	Dec
High	26	29	37	52	65	74	78	77	69	56	44	32
Low	7	9	19	32	43	52	56	55	47	36	28	15
Precip	3.2	2.5	2.7	3.2	3.3	3.4	3.6	3.7	4.0	4.1	3.9	3.6
Snow	33.0	25.7	14.9	4.7	0.1	0.0	0.0	0.0	tr	0.8	9.3	32.9

High and Low temperatures in degrees Fahrenheit; Precipitation and Snow in inches

Population: 27,124; Growth (since 2000): 0.7%; Density: 21.3 persons per square mile; Race: 96.8% White, 0.9% Black/African American, 0.4% Asian, 0.2% American Indian/Alaska Native, 0.0% Native Hawaiian/Other Pacific Islander, 0.9% two or more races, 1.7% Hispanic of any race; Average household size: 2.54; Median age: 41.4; Age under 18: 23.5%; Age 65 and over: 16.2%; Males per 100 females: 101.1; Marriage status: 26.6% never married, 57.6% now married, 1.6% separated, 6.0% widowed, 9.8% divorced; Foreign born: 1.7%; Speak English only: 97.5%; With disability: 14.0%; Veterans: 10.9%; Ancestry: 28.3% German, 16.2% Irish, 12.4% French, 8.5% English, 5.9% American

Religion: Six largest groups: 23.8% Catholicism, 7.5% European Free-Church, 4.6% Methodist/Pietist, 1.8% Presbyterian-Reformed, 1.4% Non-denominational Protestant, 1.2% Baptist

Economy: Unemployment rate: 5.8%; Leading industries: 14.6 % retail trade; 13.6 % other services (except public administration); 12.3 % construction; Farms: 634 totaling 181,741 acres; Company size: 0 employ 1,000 or more persons, 1 employs 500 to 999 persons, 5 employ 100 to 499 persons, 522 employ less than 100 persons; Business ownership: 454 women-owned, n/a Black-owned, n/a Hispanic-owned, n/a Asian-owned, n/a American Indian/Alaska Native-owned

Employment: 10.2% management, business, and financial, 2.3% computer, engineering, and science, 10.1% education, legal, community service, arts, and media, 6.7% healthcare practitioners, 17.3% service, 18.4% sales and office, 17.9% natural resources, construction, and maintenance, 17.0% production, transportation, and material moving

Income: Per capita: $24,772; Median household: $49,819; Average household: $61,986; Households with income of $100,000 or more: 16.7%; Poverty rate: 12.1%

Educational Attainment: High school diploma or higher: 89.0%; Bachelor's degree or higher: 15.2%; Graduate/professional degree or higher: 6.5%

Housing: Homeownership rate: 76.5%; Median home value: $117,300; Median year structure built: 1966; Homeowner vacancy rate: 1.9%; Median selected monthly owner costs: $1,108 with a mortgage, $441 without a mortgage; Median gross rent: $699 per month; Rental vacancy rate: 6.4%

Vital Statistics: Birth rate: 116.9 per 10,000 population; Death rate: 97.2 per 10,000 population; Age-adjusted cancer mortality rate: 159.4 deaths per 100,000 population

Health Insurance: 90.1% have insurance; 68.3% have private insurance; 36.1% have public insurance; 9.9% do not have insurance; 7.4% of children under 18 do not have insurance

Health Care: Physicians: 9.9 per 10,000 population; Dentists: 2.2 per 10,000 population; Hospital beds: 78.8 per 10,000 population; Hospital admissions: 569.3 per 10,000 population

Transportation: Commute: 88.6% car, 0.2% public transportation, 5.9% walk, 4.2% work from home; Mean travel time to work: 24.5 minutes

2016 Presidential Election: 66.2% Trump, 28.2% Clinton, 4.4% Johnson, 1.2% Stein

National and State Parks: Sand Flats State Park; Whetstone Gulf State Park

Additional Information Contacts

Lewis Government . . . . (315) 376-5355
  http://www.lewiscountyny.org

Lewis County Communities

BEAVER FALLS (unincorporated postal area)
ZCTA: 13305

Covers a land area of 0.959 square miles and a water area of 0 square miles. Located at 43.89° N. Lat; 75.42° W. Long. Elevation is 807 feet.

Population: 469; Growth (since 2000): n/a; Density: 488.9 persons per square mile; Race: 100.0% White, 0.0% Black/African American, 0.0% Asian, 0.0% American Indian/Alaska Native, 0.0% Native Hawaiian/Other Pacific Islander, 0.0% Two or more races, 12.6% Hispanic of any race; Average household size: 4.42; Median age: 30.3; Age under 18: 39.0%; Age 65 and over: 9.2%; Males per 100 females: 99.3; Marriage status: 38.5% never married, 48.1% now married, 0.0% separated, 5.9% widowed, 7.5% divorced; Foreign born: 3.6%; Speak English only: 98.9%; With disability: 10.2%; Veterans: 20.3%; Ancestry: 35.6% German, 31.3% French, 15.1% Irish, 8.5% English, 7.0% Polish

Employment: 1.7% management, business, and financial, 0.0% computer, engineering, and science, 6.1% education, legal, community service, arts, and media, 12.2% healthcare practitioners, 28.3% service, 20.9% sales and office, 17.8% natural resources, construction, and maintenance, 13.0% production, transportation, and material moving

Income: Per capita: $25,341; Median household: $90,000; Average household: $98,075; Households with income of $100,000 or more: 30.2%; Poverty rate: 0.9%

Educational Attainment: High school diploma or higher: 100.0%; Bachelor's degree or higher: 19.2%; Graduate/professional degree or higher: 9.2%

School District(s)

Beaver River Central SD (KG-12)
    2014-15 Enrollment: 893 . . . . (315) 346-1211

Housing: Homeownership rate: 88.7%; Median home value: $159,400; Median year structure built: 1950; Homeowner vacancy rate: 11.3%; Median selected monthly owner costs: $1,419 with a mortgage, $0 without a mortgage; Median gross rent: n/a per month; Rental vacancy rate: 0.0%

Health Insurance: 92.8% have insurance; 70.8% have private insurance; 25.2% have public insurance; 7.2% do not have insurance; 15.8% of children under 18 do not have insurance

Transportation: Commute: 96.0% car, 0.0% public transportation, 2.0% walk, 0.0% work from home; Mean travel time to work: 31.3 minutes

BRANTINGHAM (unincorporated postal area)

ZCTA: 13312

Covers a land area of 63.744 square miles and a water area of 1.013 square miles. Located at 43.70° N. Lat; 75.19° W. Long. Elevation is 1,253 feet.

Population: 492; Growth (since 2000): -28.6%; Density: 7.7 persons per square mile; Race: 93.3% White, 6.7% Black/African American, 0.0% Asian, 0.0% American Indian/Alaska Native, 0.0% Native Hawaiian/Other Pacific Islander, 0.0% Two or more races, 1.0% Hispanic of any race; Average household size: 2.30; Median age: 48.3; Age under 18: 17.1%; Age 65 and over: 30.3%; Males per 100 females: 106.9; Marriage status: 25.7% never married, 64.7% now married, 3.5% separated, 4.0% widowed, 5.6% divorced; Foreign born: 1.6%; Speak English only: 100.0%; With disability: 9.3%; Veterans: 11.0%; Ancestry: 31.1% German, 23.8% Irish, 12.8% Italian, 11.4% French, 11.0% English

Employment: 14.4% management, business, and financial, 0.0% computer, engineering, and science, 4.4% education, legal, community service, arts, and media, 4.4% healthcare practitioners, 27.5% service, 15.6% sales and office, 10.0% natural resources, construction, and maintenance, 23.8% production, transportation, and material moving

Income: Per capita: $28,290; Median household: $40,882; Average household: $64,302; Households with income of $100,000 or more: 15.4%; Poverty rate: 12.3%

Educational Attainment: High school diploma or higher: 91.9%; Bachelor's degree or higher: 30.0%; Graduate/professional degree or higher: 18.4%

Housing: Homeownership rate: 72.4%; Median home value: $220,200; Median year structure built: 1957; Homeowner vacancy rate: 0.0%; Median selected monthly owner costs: $1,173 with a mortgage, $639 without a mortgage; Median gross rent: $825 per month; Rental vacancy rate: 19.2%

Health Insurance: 95.3% have insurance; 64.4% have private insurance; 54.5% have public insurance; 4.7% do not have insurance; 0.0% of children under 18 do not have insurance

Transportation: Commute: 86.3% car, 0.0% public transportation, 3.1% walk, 5.6% work from home; Mean travel time to work: 32.4 minutes

CASTORLAND (village). Covers a land area of 0.321 square miles and a water area of 0 square miles. Located at 43.89° N. Lat; 75.52° W. Long. Elevation is 741 feet.

Population: 376; Growth (since 2000): 22.9%; Density: 1,171.1 persons per square mile; Race: 100.0% White, 0.0% Black/African American, 0.0% Asian, 0.0% American Indian/Alaska Native, 0.0% Native Hawaiian/Other Pacific Islander, 0.0% Two or more races, 7.7% Hispanic of any race; Average household size: 3.03; Median age: 33.1; Age under 18: 36.7%; Age 65 and over: 16.0%; Males per 100 females: 83.8; Marriage status: 24.5% never married, 58.8% now married, 2.3% separated, 8.2% widowed, 8.6% divorced; Foreign born: 1.3%; Speak English only: 97.9%; With disability: 10.8%; Veterans: 8.2%; Ancestry: 27.7% German, 16.0% French, 13.0% Irish, 7.4% English, 7.4% Swiss

Employment: 12.8% management, business, and financial, 21.4% computer, engineering, and science, 6.0% education, legal, community service, arts, and media, 2.6% healthcare practitioners, 16.2% service, 22.2% sales and office, 7.7% natural resources, construction, and maintenance, 11.1% production, transportation, and material moving

Income: Per capita: $18,670; Median household: $45,000; Average household: $55,746; Households with income of $100,000 or more: 18.5%; Poverty rate: 15.2%

Educational Attainment: High school diploma or higher: 88.4%; Bachelor's degree or higher: 24.1%; Graduate/professional degree or higher: 8.3%

Housing: Homeownership rate: 56.5%; Median home value: $126,700; Median year structure built: Before 1940; Homeowner vacancy rate: 0.0%; Median selected monthly owner costs: $1,384 with a mortgage, $492 without a mortgage; Median gross rent: $607 per month; Rental vacancy rate: 19.4%

Health Insurance: 95.7% have insurance; 67.0% have private insurance; 47.3% have public insurance; 4.3% do not have insurance; 2.9% of children under 18 do not have insurance

Transportation: Commute: 94.9% car, 0.0% public transportation, 0.0% walk, 5.1% work from home; Mean travel time to work: 23.4 minutes

CONSTABLEVILLE (village). Covers a land area of 1.118 square miles and a water area of 0 square miles. Located at 43.56° N. Lat; 75.43° W. Long. Elevation is 1,263 feet.

Population: 239; Growth (since 2000): -21.6%; Density: 213.7 persons per square mile; Race: 91.6% White, 0.0% Black/African American, 0.0% Asian, 0.0% American Indian/Alaska Native, 0.0% Native Hawaiian/Other Pacific Islander, 8.4% Two or more races, 0.0% Hispanic of any race; Average household size: 2.04; Median age: 48.6; Age under 18: 18.8%; Age 65 and over: 13.0%; Males per 100 females: 98.4; Marriage status: 33.7% never married, 54.3% now married, 1.5% separated, 5.0% widowed, 7.0% divorced; Foreign born: 0.0%; Speak English only: 98.6%; With disability: 18.8%; Veterans: 10.8%; Ancestry: 22.2% German, 20.5% Irish, 13.8% Polish, 12.6% American, 10.5% French

Employment: 15.9% management, business, and financial, 1.8% computer, engineering, and science, 8.0% education, legal, community service, arts, and media, 6.2% healthcare practitioners, 10.6% service, 21.2% sales and office, 23.0% natural resources, construction, and maintenance, 13.3% production, transportation, and material moving

Income: Per capita: $24,089; Median household: $46,042; Average household: $54,849; Households with income of $100,000 or more: 6.8%; Poverty rate: 15.5%

Educational Attainment: High school diploma or higher: 91.7%; Bachelor's degree or higher: 14.9%; Graduate/professional degree or higher: 10.5%

School District(s)

South Lewis Central SD (PK-12)

    2014-15 Enrollment: 1,080 . . . . (315) 348-2500

Housing: Homeownership rate: 83.8%; Median home value: $74,000; Median year structure built: Before 1940; Homeowner vacancy rate: 2.0%; Median selected monthly owner costs: $1,135 with a mortgage, $513 without a mortgage; Median gross rent: n/a per month; Rental vacancy rate: 0.0%

Health Insurance: 94.6% have insurance; 66.9% have private insurance; 41.4% have public insurance; 5.4% do not have insurance; 4.4% of children under 18 do not have insurance

Transportation: Commute: 95.4% car, 0.0% public transportation, 2.8% walk, 1.8% work from home; Mean travel time to work: 29.9 minutes

COPENHAGEN (village). Covers a land area of 1.176 square miles and a water area of 0 square miles. Located at 43.89° N. Lat; 75.67° W. Long. Elevation is 1,165 feet.

Population: 716; Growth (since 2000): -17.2%; Density: 609.1 persons per square mile; Race: 97.2% White, 1.4% Black/African American, 0.3% Asian, 0.0% American Indian/Alaska Native, 0.0% Native Hawaiian/Other Pacific Islander, 1.1% Two or more races, 2.9% Hispanic of any race; Average household size: 2.29; Median age: 31.6; Age under 18: 15.6%; Age 65 and over: 17.7%; Males per 100 females: 103.8; Marriage status: 28.8% never married, 53.5% now married, 2.7% separated, 6.8% widowed, 10.8% divorced; Foreign born: 2.2%; Speak English only: 98.1%; With disability: 21.1%; Veterans: 16.3%; Ancestry: 26.1% German, 19.3% Irish, 15.6% French, 13.8% English, 5.4% American

Employment: 12.4% management, business, and financial, 2.9% computer, engineering, and science, 6.1% education, legal, community service, arts, and media, 5.1% healthcare practitioners, 27.1% service, 26.8% sales and office, 11.8% natural resources, construction, and maintenance, 8.0% production, transportation, and material moving

Income: Per capita: $26,678; Median household: $47,063; Average household: $60,904; Households with income of $100,000 or more: 19.5%; Poverty rate: 7.1%

Educational Attainment: High school diploma or higher: 83.3%; Bachelor's degree or higher: 10.4%; Graduate/professional degree or higher: 2.6%

School District(s)

Copenhagen Central SD (PK-12)

    2014-15 Enrollment: 450 . . . . (315) 688-4411

Housing: Homeownership rate: 47.3%; Median home value: $125,000; Median year structure built: 1978; Homeowner vacancy rate: 5.7%; Median selected monthly owner costs: $997 with a mortgage, $439 without a mortgage; Median gross rent: $964 per month; Rental vacancy rate: 10.8%

Health Insurance: 93.2% have insurance; 78.0% have private insurance; 36.0% have public insurance; 6.8% do not have insurance; 9.8% of children under 18 do not have insurance

Transportation: Commute: 94.9% car, 0.0% public transportation, 3.3% walk, 1.9% work from home; Mean travel time to work: 22.9 minutes

CROGHAN (town). Covers a land area of 179.182 square miles and a water area of 2.849 square miles. Located at 43.97° N. Lat; 75.36° W. Long. Elevation is 827 feet.

History: American Maple Museum.

Population: 3,123; Growth (since 2000): -1.2%; Density: 17.4 persons per square mile; Race: 98.4% White, 0.5% Black/African American, 0.0% Asian, 0.0% American Indian/Alaska Native, 0.0% Native Hawaiian/Other Pacific Islander, 0.5% Two or more races, 2.9% Hispanic of any race; Average household size: 2.58; Median age: 44.2; Age under 18: 22.4%; Age 65 and over: 17.7%; Males per 100 females: 105.4; Marriage status: 23.5% never married, 65.3% now married, 1.9% separated, 5.2% widowed, 6.1% divorced; Foreign born: 1.7%; Speak English only: 99.0%; With disability: 14.9%; Veterans: 10.4%; Ancestry: 37.5% German, 12.5% French, 9.2% Irish, 9.2% English, 5.8% Swiss

Employment: 9.0% management, business, and financial, 0.7% computer, engineering, and science, 8.9% education, legal, community service, arts, and media, 9.1% healthcare practitioners, 14.2% service, 15.0% sales and office, 21.2% natural resources, construction, and maintenance, 21.8% production, transportation, and material moving

Income: Per capita: $25,131; Median household: $51,574; Average household: $63,055; Households with income of $100,000 or more: 17.8%; Poverty rate: 7.1%

Educational Attainment: High school diploma or higher: 86.2%; Bachelor's degree or higher: 11.8%; Graduate/professional degree or higher: 6.9%

Housing: Homeownership rate: 82.8%; Median home value: $128,700; Median year structure built: 1970; Homeowner vacancy rate: 1.2%; Median selected monthly owner costs: $1,071 with a mortgage, $395 without a mortgage; Median gross rent: $584 per month; Rental vacancy rate: 8.3%

Health Insurance: 88.0% have insurance; 68.2% have private insurance; 34.2% have public insurance; 12.0% do not have insurance; 12.9% of children under 18 do not have insurance

Transportation: Commute: 90.4% car, 0.0% public transportation, 4.2% walk, 4.8% work from home; Mean travel time to work: 22.7 minutes

CROGHAN (village). Covers a land area of 0.434 square miles and a water area of 0 square miles. Located at 43.89° N. Lat; 75.39° W. Long. Elevation is 827 feet.

Population: 696; Growth (since 2000): 4.7%; Density: 1,604.2 persons per square mile; Race: 94.5% White, 0.9% Black/African American, 1.3% Asian, 0.4% American Indian/Alaska Native, 0.0% Native Hawaiian/Other Pacific Islander, 1.1% Two or more races, 2.2% Hispanic of any race; Average household size: 2.30; Median age: 41.4; Age under 18: 25.4%; Age 65 and over: 21.4%; Males per 100 females: 89.0; Marriage status: 23.1% never married, 55.5% now married, 2.9% separated, 11.3% widowed, 10.2% divorced; Foreign born: 4.2%; Speak English only: 97.7%; With disability: 23.0%; Veterans: 10.6%; Ancestry: 46.1% German, 13.9% French, 10.5% Irish, 5.5% Swiss, 4.3% English

Employment: 8.9% management, business, and financial, 1.1% computer, engineering, and science, 16.2% education, legal, community service, arts, and media, 3.3% healthcare practitioners, 11.4% service, 21.4% sales and office, 18.5% natural resources, construction, and maintenance, 19.2% production, transportation, and material moving

Income: Per capita: $20,593; Median household: $31,625; Average household: $47,157; Households with income of $100,000 or more: 12.2%; Poverty rate: 10.2%

Educational Attainment: High school diploma or higher: 87.4%; Bachelor's degree or higher: 14.8%; Graduate/professional degree or higher: 6.6%

Housing: Homeownership rate: 60.1%; Median home value: $113,300; Median year structure built: 1941; Homeowner vacancy rate: 0.0%; Median selected monthly owner costs: $1,179 with a mortgage, $447 without a mortgage; Median gross rent: $454 per month; Rental vacancy rate: 13.6%

Health Insurance: 93.7% have insurance; 68.4% have private insurance; 41.2% have public insurance; 6.3% do not have insurance; 1.1% of children under 18 do not have insurance

Transportation: Commute: 92.2% car, 0.0% public transportation, 1.9% walk, 4.7% work from home; Mean travel time to work: 20.3 minutes

DENMARK (town). Covers a land area of 50.602 square miles and a water area of 0.446 square miles. Located at 43.90° N. Lat; 75.63° W. Long. Elevation is 971 feet.

Population: 2,885; Growth (since 2000): 5.0%; Density: 57.0 persons per square mile; Race: 96.9% White, 1.8% Black/African American, 0.1% Asian, 0.0% American Indian/Alaska Native, 0.0% Native Hawaiian/Other Pacific Islander, 1.0% Two or more races, 3.3% Hispanic of any race; Average household size: 2.67; Median age: 33.4; Age under 18: 25.1%; Age 65 and over: 13.2%; Males per 100 females: 101.8; Marriage status: 26.8% never married, 60.0% now married, 1.6% separated, 4.2% widowed, 9.0% divorced; Foreign born: 0.9%; Speak English only: 98.6%; With disability: 14.4%; Veterans: 10.3%; Ancestry: 29.5% German, 16.7% Irish, 13.4% French, 7.3% English, 4.9% American

Employment: 11.2% management, business, and financial, 3.2% computer, engineering, and science, 10.9% education, legal, community service, arts, and media, 3.5% healthcare practitioners, 16.1% service, 26.2% sales and office, 17.5% natural resources, construction, and maintenance, 11.4% production, transportation, and material moving

Income: Per capita: $25,727; Median household: $54,063; Average household: $67,452; Households with income of $100,000 or more: 17.6%; Poverty rate: 10.3%

Educational Attainment: High school diploma or higher: 88.6%; Bachelor's degree or higher: 12.2%; Graduate/professional degree or higher: 3.5%

Housing: Homeownership rate: 73.6%; Median home value: $141,000; Median year structure built: 1973; Homeowner vacancy rate: 1.1%; Median selected monthly owner costs: $1,299 with a mortgage, $540 without a mortgage; Median gross rent: $945 per month; Rental vacancy rate: 14.0%

Health Insurance: 95.3% have insurance; 77.1% have private insurance; 30.7% have public insurance; 4.7% do not have insurance; 2.1% of children under 18 do not have insurance

Transportation: Commute: 89.0% car, 0.0% public transportation, 6.5% walk, 3.8% work from home; Mean travel time to work: 22.1 minutes

DIANA (town). Covers a land area of 137.094 square miles and a water area of 3.738 square miles. Located at 44.11° N. Lat; 75.37° W. Long.

Population: 1,509; Growth (since 2000): -9.2%; Density: 11.0 persons per square mile; Race: 97.6% White, 0.9% Black/African American, 0.0% Asian, 0.7% American Indian/Alaska Native, 0.0% Native Hawaiian/Other Pacific Islander, 0.9% Two or more races, 0.2% Hispanic of any race; Average household size: 2.60; Median age: 42.9; Age under 18: 22.3%; Age 65 and over: 15.4%; Males per 100 females: 95.8; Marriage status: 22.9% never married, 55.8% now married, 2.6% separated, 6.9% widowed, 14.4% divorced; Foreign born: 0.4%; Speak English only: 99.4%; With disability: 18.3%; Veterans: 15.6%; Ancestry: 18.7% German, 15.3% English, 14.0% Italian, 12.9% French, 11.8% Irish

Employment: 11.0% management, business, and financial, 2.9% computer, engineering, and science, 4.3% education, legal, community service, arts, and media, 6.8% healthcare practitioners, 24.7% service, 21.1% sales and office, 17.5% natural resources, construction, and maintenance, 11.7% production, transportation, and material moving

Income: Per capita: $21,776; Median household: $41,667; Average household: $53,495; Households with income of $100,000 or more: 14.0%; Poverty rate: 21.5%

Educational Attainment: High school diploma or higher: 85.9%; Bachelor's degree or higher: 11.3%; Graduate/professional degree or higher: 3.7%

Housing: Homeownership rate: 79.1%; Median home value: $97,400; Median year structure built: 1957; Homeowner vacancy rate: 2.8%; Median selected monthly owner costs: $1,078 with a mortgage, $398 without a mortgage; Median gross rent: $713 per month; Rental vacancy rate: 5.5%

Health Insurance: 90.9% have insurance; 66.4% have private insurance; 43.0% have public insurance; 9.1% do not have insurance; 3.9% of children under 18 do not have insurance

Transportation: Commute: 95.3% car, 0.0% public transportation, 2.6% walk, 0.0% work from home; Mean travel time to work: 31.6 minutes

GLENFIELD (unincorporated postal area)
ZCTA: 13343

Covers a land area of 56.180 square miles and a water area of 0.954 square miles. Located at 43.75° N. Lat; 75.31° W. Long. Elevation is 768 feet.

Population: 1,868; Growth (since 2000): 6.6%; Density: 33.3 persons per square mile; Race: 99.7% White, 0.0% Black/African American, 0.0% Asian, 0.0% American Indian/Alaska Native, 0.0% Native Hawaiian/Other Pacific Islander, 0.3% Two or more races, 0.7% Hispanic of any race; Average household size: 2.69; Median age: 42.0; Age under 18: 22.8%; Age 65 and over: 17.7%; Males per 100 females: 105.2; Marriage status: 21.9% never married, 59.8% now married, 1.5% separated, 4.4% widowed, 13.9% divorced; Foreign born: 0.0%; Speak

English only: 98.5%; With disability: 14.1%; Veterans: 11.7%; Ancestry: 25.4% German, 19.6% Irish, 16.1% French, 8.0% English, 5.9% Polish
Employment: 9.2% management, business, and financial, 2.0% computer, engineering, and science, 8.5% education, legal, community service, arts, and media, 6.9% healthcare practitioners, 20.3% service, 23.6% sales and office, 14.0% natural resources, construction, and maintenance, 15.5% production, transportation, and material moving
Income: Per capita: $27,362; Median household: $51,576; Average household: $71,944; Households with income of $100,000 or more: 22.3%; Poverty rate: 13.1%
Educational Attainment: High school diploma or higher: 93.0%; Bachelor's degree or higher: 17.1%; Graduate/professional degree or higher: 7.5%

School District(s)
South Lewis Central SD (PK-12)
    2014-15 Enrollment: 1,080 . . . . (315) 348-2500
Housing: Homeownership rate: 84.2%; Median home value: $109,300; Median year structure built: 1973; Homeowner vacancy rate: 3.0%; Median selected monthly owner costs: $1,046 with a mortgage, $474 without a mortgage; Median gross rent: $744 per month; Rental vacancy rate: 9.2%
Health Insurance: 90.3% have insurance; 66.9% have private insurance; 37.7% have public insurance; 9.7% do not have insurance; 8.9% of children under 18 do not have insurance
Transportation: Commute: 93.9% car, 0.0% public transportation, 1.8% walk, 4.1% work from home; Mean travel time to work: 23.2 minutes

GREIG (town). Covers a land area of 93.011 square miles and a water area of 1.354 square miles. Located at 43.70° N. Lat; 75.19° W. Long. Elevation is 807 feet.
Population: 1,384; Growth (since 2000): 1.4%; Density: 14.9 persons per square mile; Race: 96.5% White, 2.8% Black/African American, 0.0% Asian, 0.0% American Indian/Alaska Native, 0.0% Native Hawaiian/Other Pacific Islander, 0.4% Two or more races, 0.7% Hispanic of any race; Average household size: 2.52; Median age: 45.1; Age under 18: 21.4%; Age 65 and over: 23.2%; Males per 100 females: 106.4; Marriage status: 22.3% never married, 62.5% now married, 3.3% separated, 4.8% widowed, 10.4% divorced; Foreign born: 0.6%; Speak English only: 98.8%; With disability: 12.6%; Veterans: 9.6%; Ancestry: 25.0% German, 20.2% Irish, 14.0% French, 10.0% English, 6.8% American
Employment: 12.3% management, business, and financial, 1.2% computer, engineering, and science, 4.7% education, legal, community service, arts, and media, 6.5% healthcare practitioners, 19.6% service, 17.0% sales and office, 18.0% natural resources, construction, and maintenance, 20.7% production, transportation, and material moving
Income: Per capita: $28,553; Median household: $46,346; Average household: $69,652; Households with income of $100,000 or more: 20.3%; Poverty rate: 14.1%
Educational Attainment: High school diploma or higher: 92.4%; Bachelor's degree or higher: 19.4%; Graduate/professional degree or higher: 10.6%
Housing: Homeownership rate: 80.4%; Median home value: $136,400; Median year structure built: 1967; Homeowner vacancy rate: 4.1%; Median selected monthly owner costs: $1,060 with a mortgage, $519 without a mortgage; Median gross rent: $737 per month; Rental vacancy rate: 11.5%
Health Insurance: 91.5% have insurance; 64.4% have private insurance; 43.4% have public insurance; 8.5% do not have insurance; 10.8% of children under 18 do not have insurance
Transportation: Commute: 92.8% car, 0.0% public transportation, 1.3% walk, 4.1% work from home; Mean travel time to work: 28.5 minutes

HARRISBURG (town). Covers a land area of 39.882 square miles and a water area of 0.028 square miles. Located at 43.84° N. Lat; 75.67° W. Long. Elevation is 1,362 feet.
Population: 449; Growth (since 2000): 6.1%; Density: 11.3 persons per square mile; Race: 96.2% White, 0.0% Black/African American, 1.1% Asian, 0.0% American Indian/Alaska Native, 0.0% Native Hawaiian/Other Pacific Islander, 2.7% Two or more races, 0.0% Hispanic of any race; Average household size: 2.88; Median age: 33.5; Age under 18: 27.8%; Age 65 and over: 9.4%; Males per 100 females: 117.4; Marriage status: 25.9% never married, 62.2% now married, 4.0% separated, 5.2% widowed, 6.6% divorced; Foreign born: 1.1%; Speak English only: 97.0%; With disability: 10.7%; Veterans: 13.0%; Ancestry: 28.3% German, 25.2% Irish, 6.7% Scottish, 6.5% American, 5.8% French Canadian

Employment: 15.5% management, business, and financial, 0.0% computer, engineering, and science, 8.6% education, legal, community service, arts, and media, 6.4% healthcare practitioners, 19.7% service, 13.7% sales and office, 25.8% natural resources, construction, and maintenance, 10.3% production, transportation, and material moving
Income: Per capita: $26,723; Median household: $71,667; Average household: $77,246; Households with income of $100,000 or more: 23.1%; Poverty rate: 11.8%
Educational Attainment: High school diploma or higher: 81.9%; Bachelor's degree or higher: 14.3%; Graduate/professional degree or higher: 5.1%
Housing: Homeownership rate: 95.5%; Median home value: $140,600; Median year structure built: 1977; Homeowner vacancy rate: 1.3%; Median selected monthly owner costs: $1,237 with a mortgage, $477 without a mortgage; Median gross rent: n/a per month; Rental vacancy rate: 41.7%
Health Insurance: 82.4% have insurance; 62.9% have private insurance; 28.3% have public insurance; 17.6% do not have insurance; 11.2% of children under 18 do not have insurance
Transportation: Commute: 85.9% car, 0.9% public transportation, 3.1% walk, 5.7% work from home; Mean travel time to work: 27.5 minutes

HARRISVILLE (village). Covers a land area of 0.737 square miles and a water area of 0.046 square miles. Located at 44.15° N. Lat; 75.32° W. Long. Elevation is 807 feet.
Population: 590; Growth (since 2000): -9.6%; Density: 800.1 persons per square mile; Race: 99.0% White, 0.0% Black/African American, 0.0% Asian, 0.5% American Indian/Alaska Native, 0.0% Native Hawaiian/Other Pacific Islander, 0.5% Two or more races, 0.5% Hispanic of any race; Average household size: 2.74; Median age: 40.5; Age under 18: 22.5%; Age 65 and over: 13.1%; Males per 100 females: 84.7; Marriage status: 21.1% never married, 49.2% now married, 3.6% separated, 11.7% widowed, 18.0% divorced; Foreign born: 0.0%; Speak English only: 99.1%; With disability: 17.5%; Veterans: 17.5%; Ancestry: 19.7% English, 17.3% German, 16.8% Italian, 16.4% Irish, 14.6% French
Employment: 18.1% management, business, and financial, 2.1% computer, engineering, and science, 7.1% education, legal, community service, arts, and media, 4.2% healthcare practitioners, 26.5% service, 21.0% sales and office, 8.4% natural resources, construction, and maintenance, 12.6% production, transportation, and material moving
Income: Per capita: $22,217; Median household: $50,139; Average household: $57,520; Households with income of $100,000 or more: 8.4%; Poverty rate: 15.1%
Educational Attainment: High school diploma or higher: 90.3%; Bachelor's degree or higher: 17.7%; Graduate/professional degree or higher: 5.0%

School District(s)
Harrisville Central SD (PK-12)
    2014-15 Enrollment: 408 . . . . (315) 543-2707
Housing: Homeownership rate: 77.7%; Median home value: $76,600; Median year structure built: Before 1940; Homeowner vacancy rate: 3.5%; Median selected monthly owner costs: $1,111 with a mortgage, $469 without a mortgage; Median gross rent: $685 per month; Rental vacancy rate: 12.7%
Health Insurance: 93.9% have insurance; 68.5% have private insurance; 46.1% have public insurance; 6.1% do not have insurance; 0.0% of children under 18 do not have insurance
Transportation: Commute: 90.8% car, 0.0% public transportation, 6.1% walk, 0.0% work from home; Mean travel time to work: 29.0 minutes

LEWIS (town). Covers a land area of 64.607 square miles and a water area of 0.542 square miles. Located at 43.49° N. Lat; 75.56° W. Long.
Population: 784; Growth (since 2000): -8.5%; Density: 12.1 persons per square mile; Race: 96.3% White, 0.0% Black/African American, 2.9% Asian, 0.0% American Indian/Alaska Native, 0.0% Native Hawaiian/Other Pacific Islander, 0.8% Two or more races, 0.0% Hispanic of any race; Average household size: 2.60; Median age: 43.0; Age under 18: 23.1%; Age 65 and over: 9.3%; Males per 100 females: 109.3; Marriage status: 33.2% never married, 52.5% now married, 0.3% separated, 3.6% widowed, 10.6% divorced; Foreign born: 2.8%; Speak English only: 97.3%; With disability: 9.9%; Veterans: 9.2%; Ancestry: 37.0% German, 18.1% Irish, 13.1% French, 10.3% American, 10.2% Polish
Employment: 9.5% management, business, and financial, 3.5% computer, engineering, and science, 5.5% education, legal, community service, arts, and media, 4.0% healthcare practitioners, 21.1% service, 15.0% sales and

office, 24.3% natural resources, construction, and maintenance, 17.1% production, transportation, and material moving
Income: Per capita: $22,510; Median household: $42,132; Average household: $57,364; Households with income of $100,000 or more: 16.3%; Poverty rate: 15.8%
Educational Attainment: High school diploma or higher: 92.1%; Bachelor's degree or higher: 10.7%; Graduate/professional degree or higher: 3.6%
Housing: Homeownership rate: 82.4%; Median home value: $94,700; Median year structure built: 1974; Homeowner vacancy rate: 3.9%; Median selected monthly owner costs: $939 with a mortgage, $384 without a mortgage; Median gross rent: $708 per month; Rental vacancy rate: 11.7%
Health Insurance: 86.2% have insurance; 57.0% have private insurance; 36.1% have public insurance; 13.8% do not have insurance; 4.4% of children under 18 do not have insurance
Transportation: Commute: 85.2% car, 0.9% public transportation, 4.1% walk, 9.7% work from home; Mean travel time to work: 33.7 minutes

LEYDEN (town). Covers a land area of 33.330 square miles and a water area of 0.222 square miles. Located at 43.53° N. Lat; 75.38° W. Long.

History: Originally known as Kelsey's Mills, it was renamed in 1839 in anticipation of becoming a thriving port upon completion of the Black River Canal.
Population: 1,829; Growth (since 2000): 2.1%; Density: 54.9 persons per square mile; Race: 99.1% White, 0.3% Black/African American, 0.0% Asian, 0.0% American Indian/Alaska Native, 0.0% Native Hawaiian/Other Pacific Islander, 0.6% Two or more races, 0.1% Hispanic of any race; Average household size: 2.48; Median age: 40.8; Age under 18: 26.7%; Age 65 and over: 15.4%; Males per 100 females: 97.7; Marriage status: 27.3% never married, 54.3% now married, 3.5% separated, 6.3% widowed, 12.2% divorced; Foreign born: 0.7%; Speak English only: 98.1%; With disability: 13.4%; Veterans: 9.8%; Ancestry: 31.6% German, 19.1% Irish, 13.0% French, 11.6% English, 10.9% Polish
Employment: 9.0% management, business, and financial, 0.6% computer, engineering, and science, 9.7% education, legal, community service, arts, and media, 6.5% healthcare practitioners, 16.6% service, 17.2% sales and office, 19.0% natural resources, construction, and maintenance, 21.5% production, transportation, and material moving
Income: Per capita: $21,205; Median household: $42,128; Average household: $51,838; Households with income of $100,000 or more: 11.0%; Poverty rate: 17.9%
Educational Attainment: High school diploma or higher: 88.4%; Bachelor's degree or higher: 10.9%; Graduate/professional degree or higher: 2.9%
Housing: Homeownership rate: 76.4%; Median home value: $86,800; Median year structure built: 1965; Homeowner vacancy rate: 0.0%; Median selected monthly owner costs: $1,083 with a mortgage, $400 without a mortgage; Median gross rent: $726 per month; Rental vacancy rate: 14.4%
Health Insurance: 90.6% have insurance; 64.9% have private insurance; 40.3% have public insurance; 9.4% do not have insurance; 1.8% of children under 18 do not have insurance
Transportation: Commute: 92.7% car, 0.0% public transportation, 3.1% walk, 1.7% work from home; Mean travel time to work: 23.4 minutes

LOWVILLE (town). Covers a land area of 37.834 square miles and a water area of 0.291 square miles. Located at 43.81° N. Lat; 75.52° W. Long. Elevation is 883 feet.

History: Lowville was the home of Dr. Franklin B. Hough (1822-1885), called the "father of American forestry" for his conservation activities. Settled 1798, incorporated in 1854.
Population: 4,940; Growth (since 2000): 8.6%; Density: 130.6 persons per square mile; Race: 94.9% White, 1.5% Black/African American, 1.6% Asian, 0.4% American Indian/Alaska Native, 0.2% Native Hawaiian/Other Pacific Islander, 1.2% Two or more races, 0.2% Hispanic of any race; Average household size: 2.29; Median age: 44.4; Age under 18: 21.5%; Age 65 and over: 20.2%; Males per 100 females: 91.1; Marriage status: 28.6% never married, 50.2% now married, 1.0% separated, 10.2% widowed, 11.0% divorced; Foreign born: 3.1%; Speak English only: 95.6%; With disability: 16.0%; Veterans: 11.7%; Ancestry: 22.0% German, 18.9% Irish, 10.2% French, 8.8% Italian, 6.9% English
Employment: 8.8% management, business, and financial, 4.4% computer, engineering, and science, 19.5% education, legal, community service, arts, and media, 10.4% healthcare practitioners, 14.9% service, 15.8% sales

and office, 8.9% natural resources, construction, and maintenance, 17.3% production, transportation, and material moving
Income: Per capita: $27,254; Median household: $55,077; Average household: $62,949; Households with income of $100,000 or more: 19.3%; Poverty rate: 12.5%
Educational Attainment: High school diploma or higher: 90.5%; Bachelor's degree or higher: 24.8%; Graduate/professional degree or higher: 10.3%
School District(s)
Lowville Academy & Central SD (PK-12)
   2014-15 Enrollment: 1,409 . . . . (315) 376-9000
Housing: Homeownership rate: 59.6%; Median home value: $142,800; Median year structure built: Before 1940; Homeowner vacancy rate: 0.0%; Median selected monthly owner costs: $1,163 with a mortgage, $468 without a mortgage; Median gross rent: $633 per month; Rental vacancy rate: 0.0%
Health Insurance: 94.3% have insurance; 75.5% have private insurance; 34.4% have public insurance; 5.7% do not have insurance; 3.0% of children under 18 do not have insurance
Hospitals: Lewis County General Hospital (160 beds)
Newspapers: Journal & Republican (weekly circulation 5,000)
Transportation: Commute: 85.7% car, 0.0% public transportation, 12.4% walk, 1.4% work from home; Mean travel time to work: 21.1 minutes

LOWVILLE (village). County seat. Covers a land area of 1.911 square miles and a water area of 0 square miles. Located at 43.79° N. Lat; 75.49° W. Long. Elevation is 883 feet.

Population: 3,506; Growth (since 2000): 0.9%; Density: 1,834.6 persons per square mile; Race: 95.9% White, 0.3% Black/African American, 1.7% Asian, 0.0% American Indian/Alaska Native, 0.3% Native Hawaiian/Other Pacific Islander, 1.7% Two or more races, 0.0% Hispanic of any race; Average household size: 2.21; Median age: 43.9; Age under 18: 21.1%; Age 65 and over: 16.7%; Males per 100 females: 90.2; Marriage status: 31.4% never married, 50.6% now married, 1.2% separated, 6.5% widowed, 11.6% divorced; Foreign born: 3.2%; Speak English only: 95.3%; With disability: 14.8%; Veterans: 12.0%; Ancestry: 20.6% German, 20.0% Irish, 10.2% Italian, 8.1% French, 7.8% English
Employment: 11.7% management, business, and financial, 5.4% computer, engineering, and science, 20.3% education, legal, community service, arts, and media, 10.4% healthcare practitioners, 12.4% service, 15.0% sales and office, 7.7% natural resources, construction, and maintenance, 17.0% production, transportation, and material moving
Income: Per capita: $28,336; Median household: $51,641; Average household: $61,974; Households with income of $100,000 or more: 18.9%; Poverty rate: 13.6%
Educational Attainment: High school diploma or higher: 92.3%; Bachelor's degree or higher: 25.6%; Graduate/professional degree or higher: 11.0%
School District(s)
Lowville Academy & Central SD (PK-12)
   2014-15 Enrollment: 1,409 . . . . (315) 376-9000
Housing: Homeownership rate: 53.2%; Median home value: $142,400; Median year structure built: Before 1940; Homeowner vacancy rate: 0.0%; Median selected monthly owner costs: $1,159 with a mortgage, $462 without a mortgage; Median gross rent: $624 per month; Rental vacancy rate: 0.0%
Health Insurance: 92.4% have insurance; 72.6% have private insurance; 34.7% have public insurance; 7.6% do not have insurance; 4.3% of children under 18 do not have insurance
Hospitals: Lewis County General Hospital (160 beds)
Safety: Violent crime rate: 31.9 per 10,000 population; Property crime rate: 203.0 per 10,000 population
Newspapers: Journal & Republican (weekly circulation 5,000)
Transportation: Commute: 80.9% car, 0.0% public transportation, 16.9% walk, 1.4% work from home; Mean travel time to work: 19.8 minutes

LYONS FALLS (village). Covers a land area of 0.971 square miles and a water area of 0.093 square miles. Located at 43.62° N. Lat; 75.36° W. Long. Elevation is 830 feet.

History: Black River Canal, begun in 1838, completed in 1858, ceased operation in 1922. Never successfully competed with railroad. Completely abandoned in 1926 when its final function as a feeder of water to the New York State Barge Canal was assumed by Delta Lake (northeast of Rome) and Hinckley Reservoir, north of Utica.

Population: 741; Growth (since 2000): 25.4%; Density: 763.1 persons per square mile; Race: 98.9% White, 0.7% Black/African American, 0.0% Asian, 0.0% American Indian/Alaska Native, 0.0% Native Hawaiian/Other Pacific Islander, 0.4% Two or more races, 4.0% Hispanic of any race; Average household size: 2.54; Median age: 45.0; Age under 18: 24.8%; Age 65 and over: 24.6%; Males per 100 females: 102.9; Marriage status: 18.9% never married, 66.8% now married, 0.3% separated, 6.9% widowed, 7.4% divorced; Foreign born: 0.0%; Speak English only: 99.7%; With disability: 13.5%; Veterans: 16.0%; Ancestry: 27.0% German, 21.3% Irish, 9.9% English, 8.0% Italian, 8.0% Polish

Employment: 8.5% management, business, and financial, 3.1% computer, engineering, and science, 18.8% education, legal, community service, arts, and media, 0.0% healthcare practitioners, 21.5% service, 18.1% sales and office, 11.2% natural resources, construction, and maintenance, 18.8% production, transportation, and material moving

Income: Per capita: $21,428; Median household: $45,645; Average household: $53,421; Households with income of $100,000 or more: 12.0%; Poverty rate: 6.4%

Educational Attainment: High school diploma or higher: 88.6%; Bachelor's degree or higher: 14.7%; Graduate/professional degree or higher: 8.6%

Housing: Homeownership rate: 82.5%; Median home value: $93,900; Median year structure built: Before 1940; Homeowner vacancy rate: 0.0%; Median selected monthly owner costs: $1,078 with a mortgage, $465 without a mortgage; Median gross rent: $489 per month; Rental vacancy rate: 10.5%

Health Insurance: 89.6% have insurance; 73.3% have private insurance; 37.0% have public insurance; 10.4% do not have insurance; 6.0% of children under 18 do not have insurance

Transportation: Commute: 90.4% car, 0.0% public transportation, 0.8% walk, 6.4% work from home; Mean travel time to work: 27.9 minutes

LYONSDALE (town).
Covers a land area of 68.743 square miles and a water area of 1.362 square miles. Located at 43.59° N. Lat; 75.24° W. Long. Elevation is 1,066 feet.

Population: 1,240; Growth (since 2000): -2.6%; Density: 18.0 persons per square mile; Race: 97.4% White, 0.3% Black/African American, 0.0% Asian, 1.6% American Indian/Alaska Native, 0.0% Native Hawaiian/Other Pacific Islander, 0.6% Two or more races, 0.5% Hispanic of any race; Average household size: 2.52; Median age: 43.0; Age under 18: 22.6%; Age 65 and over: 15.3%; Males per 100 females: 99.5; Marriage status: 26.9% never married, 52.6% now married, 2.4% separated, 6.8% widowed, 13.7% divorced; Foreign born: 1.0%; Speak English only: 96.9%; With disability: 20.4%; Veterans: 13.3%; Ancestry: 17.6% German, 14.9% Irish, 12.5% American, 10.2% French, 8.6% English

Employment: 8.7% management, business, and financial, 1.1% computer, engineering, and science, 2.8% education, legal, community service, arts, and media, 4.8% healthcare practitioners, 23.7% service, 17.6% sales and office, 23.5% natural resources, construction, and maintenance, 17.8% production, transportation, and material moving

Income: Per capita: $17,280; Median household: $36,500; Average household: $43,028; Households with income of $100,000 or more: 6.1%; Poverty rate: 23.0%

Educational Attainment: High school diploma or higher: 82.3%; Bachelor's degree or higher: 8.5%; Graduate/professional degree or higher: 2.4%

Housing: Homeownership rate: 77.4%; Median home value: $81,100; Median year structure built: 1978; Homeowner vacancy rate: 3.8%; Median selected monthly owner costs: $937 with a mortgage, $363 without a mortgage; Median gross rent: $687 per month; Rental vacancy rate: 0.0%

Health Insurance: 85.0% have insurance; 50.7% have private insurance; 49.2% have public insurance; 15.0% do not have insurance; 16.1% of children under 18 do not have insurance

Transportation: Commute: 88.0% car, 0.0% public transportation, 3.6% walk, 7.3% work from home; Mean travel time to work: 33.5 minutes

MARTINSBURG (town).
Covers a land area of 75.684 square miles and a water area of 0.351 square miles. Located at 43.73° N. Lat; 75.54° W. Long. Elevation is 1,263 feet.

Population: 1,477; Growth (since 2000): 18.3%; Density: 19.5 persons per square mile; Race: 92.9% White, 0.1% Black/African American, 0.3% Asian, 0.4% American Indian/Alaska Native, 0.0% Native Hawaiian/Other Pacific Islander, 0.0% Two or more races, 6.9% Hispanic of any race; Average household size: 2.70; Median age: 36.8; Age under 18: 22.0%; Age 65 and over: 12.4%; Males per 100 females: 114.8; Marriage status:

35.1% never married, 50.2% now married, 0.2% separated, 4.5% widowed, 10.1% divorced; Foreign born: 5.9%; Speak English only: 89.6%; With disability: 9.2%; Veterans: 6.3%; Ancestry: 24.2% German, 17.3% Irish, 9.7% French, 9.7% Polish, 6.4% English

Employment: 14.3% management, business, and financial, 0.4% computer, engineering, and science, 8.1% education, legal, community service, arts, and media, 7.0% healthcare practitioners, 17.3% service, 21.6% sales and office, 17.5% natural resources, construction, and maintenance, 13.8% production, transportation, and material moving

Income: Per capita: $24,371; Median household: $54,750; Average household: $64,565; Households with income of $100,000 or more: 18.9%; Poverty rate: 13.8%

Educational Attainment: High school diploma or higher: 88.0%; Bachelor's degree or higher: 16.5%; Graduate/professional degree or higher: 5.4%

Housing: Homeownership rate: 73.7%; Median home value: $98,400; Median year structure built: 1948; Homeowner vacancy rate: 0.0%; Median selected monthly owner costs: $1,088 with a mortgage, $446 without a mortgage; Median gross rent: $813 per month; Rental vacancy rate: 9.8%

Health Insurance: 83.1% have insurance; 60.0% have private insurance; 32.4% have public insurance; 16.9% do not have insurance; 10.8% of children under 18 do not have insurance

Transportation: Commute: 77.2% car, 0.0% public transportation, 13.7% walk, 8.2% work from home; Mean travel time to work: 18.9 minutes

MONTAGUE (town).
Covers a land area of 65.174 square miles and a water area of 0.163 square miles. Located at 43.72° N. Lat; 75.72° W. Long.

Population: 90; Growth (since 2000): -16.7%; Density: 1.4 persons per square mile; Race: 100.0% White, 0.0% Black/African American, 0.0% Asian, 0.0% American Indian/Alaska Native, 0.0% Native Hawaiian/Other Pacific Islander, 0.0% Two or more races, 2.2% Hispanic of any race; Average household size: 2.50; Median age: 49.8; Age under 18: 30.0%; Age 65 and over: 13.3%; Males per 100 females: 85.7; Marriage status: 14.3% never married, 75.7% now married, 0.0% separated, 0.0% widowed, 10.0% divorced; Foreign born: 0.0%; Speak English only: 100.0%; With disability: 6.7%; Veterans: 6.5%; Ancestry: 32.2% Irish, 15.6% French, 15.6% Polish, 5.6% Italian, 4.4% German

Employment: 13.2% management, business, and financial, 0.0% computer, engineering, and science, 5.3% education, legal, community service, arts, and media, 2.6% healthcare practitioners, 10.5% service, 57.9% sales and office, 5.3% natural resources, construction, and maintenance, 5.3% production, transportation, and material moving

Income: Per capita: $29,592; Median household: $63,438; Average household: $75,347; Households with income of $100,000 or more: 8.4%; Poverty rate: 2.2%

Educational Attainment: High school diploma or higher: 96.8%; Bachelor's degree or higher: 17.7%; Graduate/professional degree or higher: n/a

Housing: Homeownership rate: 97.2%; Median home value: $181,300; Median year structure built: 1981; Homeowner vacancy rate: 5.4%; Median selected monthly owner costs: $2,542 with a mortgage, $388 without a mortgage; Median gross rent: n/a per month; Rental vacancy rate: 0.0%

Health Insurance: 94.4% have insurance; 65.2% have private insurance; 38.2% have public insurance; 5.6% do not have insurance; 0.0% of children under 18 do not have insurance

Transportation: Commute: 94.9% car, 0.0% public transportation, 0.0% walk, 0.0% work from home; Mean travel time to work: 40.5 minutes

NEW BREMEN (town).
Covers a land area of 55.589 square miles and a water area of 0.200 square miles. Located at 43.85° N. Lat; 75.37° W. Long. Elevation is 771 feet.

Population: 2,711; Growth (since 2000): -0.4%; Density: 48.8 persons per square mile; Race: 97.0% White, 0.9% Black/African American, 0.3% Asian, 0.1% American Indian/Alaska Native, 0.0% Native Hawaiian/Other Pacific Islander, 0.8% Two or more races, 1.4% Hispanic of any race; Average household size: 2.98; Median age: 33.0; Age under 18: 31.9%; Age 65 and over: 12.6%; Males per 100 females: 98.7; Marriage status: 28.0% never married, 57.3% now married, 0.4% separated, 4.8% widowed, 9.8% divorced; Foreign born: 0.9%; Speak English only: 98.5%; With disability: 12.9%; Veterans: 10.4%; Ancestry: 37.6% German, 21.2% French, 12.0% Irish, 7.0% English, 6.6% American

Employment: 9.6% management, business, and financial, 3.1% computer, engineering, and science, 9.2% education, legal, community service, arts, and media, 4.4% healthcare practitioners, 18.4% service, 17.6% sales and

office, 22.8% natural resources, construction, and maintenance, 15.0% production, transportation, and material moving
Income: Per capita: $21,823; Median household: $51,397; Average household: $64,355; Households with income of $100,000 or more: 18.9%; Poverty rate: 10.2%
Educational Attainment: High school diploma or higher: 89.8%; Bachelor's degree or higher: 13.4%; Graduate/professional degree or higher: 6.2%
Housing: Homeownership rate: 80.2%; Median home value: $121,500; Median year structure built: 1973; Homeowner vacancy rate: 2.7%; Median selected monthly owner costs: $1,199 with a mortgage, $454 without a mortgage; Median gross rent: $808 per month; Rental vacancy rate: 0.0%
Health Insurance: 86.6% have insurance; 64.6% have private insurance; 34.6% have public insurance; 13.4% do not have insurance; 15.9% of children under 18 do not have insurance
Transportation: Commute: 91.9% car, 0.8% public transportation, 4.3% walk, 2.6% work from home; Mean travel time to work: 25.2 minutes

OSCEOLA (town). Covers a land area of 87.007 square miles and a water area of 0.089 square miles. Located at 43.57° N. Lat; 75.69° W. Long. Elevation is 1,030 feet.
Population: 203; Growth (since 2000): -23.4%; Density: 2.3 persons per square mile; Race: 95.6% White, 0.0% Black/African American, 0.0% Asian, 0.0% American Indian/Alaska Native, 0.0% Native Hawaiian/Other Pacific Islander, 1.0% Two or more races, 4.4% Hispanic of any race; Average household size: 2.18; Median age: 52.8; Age under 18: 17.7%; Age 65 and over: 23.6%; Males per 100 females: 106.3; Marriage status: 25.4% never married, 55.4% now married, 0.0% separated, 6.2% widowed, 13.0% divorced; Foreign born: 4.4%; Speak English only: 100.0%; With disability: 7.9%; Veterans: 8.4%; Ancestry: 22.7% American, 20.7% Irish, 17.7% German, 12.8% Italian, 9.4% English
Employment: 11.8% management, business, and financial, 0.0% computer, engineering, and science, 9.2% education, legal, community service, arts, and media, 6.6% healthcare practitioners, 15.8% service, 30.3% sales and office, 7.9% natural resources, construction, and maintenance, 18.4% production, transportation, and material moving
Income: Per capita: $21,435; Median household: $38,250; Average household: $47,094; Households with income of $100,000 or more: 8.7%; Poverty rate: 18.2%
Educational Attainment: High school diploma or higher: 93.8%; Bachelor's degree or higher: 11.2%; Graduate/professional degree or higher: 8.7%
Housing: Homeownership rate: 87.1%; Median home value: $90,600; Median year structure built: 1981; Homeowner vacancy rate: 10.9%; Median selected monthly owner costs: $991 with a mortgage, $334 without a mortgage; Median gross rent: n/a per month; Rental vacancy rate: 0.0%
Health Insurance: 90.6% have insurance; 71.9% have private insurance; 41.9% have public insurance; 9.4% do not have insurance; 0.0% of children under 18 do not have insurance
Transportation: Commute: 83.6% car, 9.6% public transportation, 0.0% walk, 4.1% work from home; Mean travel time to work: 34.1 minutes

PINCKNEY (town). Covers a land area of 40.973 square miles and a water area of 0.142 square miles. Located at 43.83° N. Lat; 75.79° W. Long.
Population: 325; Growth (since 2000): 1.9%; Density: 7.9 persons per square mile; Race: 88.9% White, 0.0% Black/African American, 0.0% Asian, 1.2% American Indian/Alaska Native, 0.0% Native Hawaiian/Other Pacific Islander, 9.8% Two or more races, 0.0% Hispanic of any race; Average household size: 2.12; Median age: 36.2; Age under 18: 20.3%; Age 65 and over: 9.2%; Males per 100 females: 135.0; Marriage status: 34.7% never married, 55.5% now married, 1.9% separated, 3.0% widowed, 6.8% divorced; Foreign born: 0.0%; Speak English only: 100.0%; With disability: 7.7%; Veterans: 8.1%; Ancestry: 29.5% German, 28.6% Polish, 14.5% French, 13.8% Irish, 6.8% Dutch
Employment: 9.3% management, business, and financial, 0.0% computer, engineering, and science, 4.4% education, legal, community service, arts, and media, 2.7% healthcare practitioners, 14.2% service, 8.7% sales and office, 20.2% natural resources, construction, and maintenance, 40.4% production, transportation, and material moving
Income: Per capita: $20,216; Median household: $35,938; Average household: $44,467; Households with income of $100,000 or more: 11.8%; Poverty rate: 26.3%

Educational Attainment: High school diploma or higher: 84.9%; Bachelor's degree or higher: 7.9%; Graduate/professional degree or higher: 3.8%
Housing: Homeownership rate: 63.4%; Median home value: $118,500; Median year structure built: 1991; Homeowner vacancy rate: 2.0%; Median selected monthly owner costs: $1,162 with a mortgage, $505 without a mortgage; Median gross rent: $1,118 per month; Rental vacancy rate: 9.7%
Health Insurance: 83.6% have insurance; 69.1% have private insurance; 38.3% have public insurance; 16.4% do not have insurance; 0.0% of children under 18 do not have insurance
Transportation: Commute: 89.7% car, 0.0% public transportation, 5.2% walk, 4.0% work from home; Mean travel time to work: 25.5 minutes

PORT LEYDEN (village). Covers a land area of 0.615 square miles and a water area of 0.042 square miles. Located at 43.59° N. Lat; 75.34° W. Long. Elevation is 892 feet.
Population: 756; Growth (since 2000): 13.7%; Density: 1,229.3 persons per square mile; Race: 98.9% White, 0.8% Black/African American, 0.0% Asian, 0.0% American Indian/Alaska Native, 0.0% Native Hawaiian/Other Pacific Islander, 0.3% Two or more races, 0.3% Hispanic of any race; Average household size: 2.70; Median age: 32.9; Age under 18: 30.3%; Age 65 and over: 11.4%; Males per 100 females: 92.0; Marriage status: 35.6% never married, 48.1% now married, 6.5% separated, 6.0% widowed, 10.2% divorced; Foreign born: 1.2%; Speak English only: 99.1%; With disability: 20.9%; Veterans: 9.1%; Ancestry: 24.6% German, 22.2% Irish, 20.0% French, 18.3% Italian, 8.6% Polish
Employment: 1.4% management, business, and financial, 0.0% computer, engineering, and science, 14.4% education, legal, community service, arts, and media, 5.8% healthcare practitioners, 18.0% service, 26.6% sales and office, 19.8% natural resources, construction, and maintenance, 14.0% production, transportation, and material moving
Income: Per capita: $15,792; Median household: $30,735; Average household: $41,956; Households with income of $100,000 or more: 6.2%; Poverty rate: 26.2%
Educational Attainment: High school diploma or higher: 88.2%; Bachelor's degree or higher: 10.4%; Graduate/professional degree or higher: 0.9%

School District(s)
South Lewis Central SD (PK-12)
   2014-15 Enrollment: 1,080 . . . . (315) 348-2500
Housing: Homeownership rate: 62.0%; Median home value: $83,000; Median year structure built: Before 1940; Homeowner vacancy rate: 5.5%; Median selected monthly owner costs: $1,078 with a mortgage, $465 without a mortgage; Median gross rent: $726 per month; Rental vacancy rate: 10.3%
Health Insurance: 87.6% have insurance; 44.8% have private insurance; 53.2% have public insurance; 12.4% do not have insurance; 0.0% of children under 18 do not have insurance
Transportation: Commute: 93.4% car, 0.0% public transportation, 0.7% walk, 2.6% work from home; Mean travel time to work: 19.7 minutes

TURIN (town). Covers a land area of 31.176 square miles and a water area of 0.203 square miles. Located at 43.66° N. Lat; 75.43° W. Long. Elevation is 1,263 feet.
Population: 548; Growth (since 2000): -30.9%; Density: 17.6 persons per square mile; Race: 99.6% White, 0.4% Black/African American, 0.0% Asian, 0.0% American Indian/Alaska Native, 0.0% Native Hawaiian/Other Pacific Islander, 0.0% Two or more races, 0.0% Hispanic of any race; Average household size: 2.25; Median age: 49.1; Age under 18: 16.2%; Age 65 and over: 20.4%; Males per 100 females: 113.2; Marriage status: 23.5% never married, 62.3% now married, 1.0% separated, 5.8% widowed, 8.4% divorced; Foreign born: 0.9%; Speak English only: 97.4%; With disability: 11.9%; Veterans: 10.2%; Ancestry: 26.8% German, 20.8% Irish, 10.8% French, 10.8% Polish, 8.6% Italian
Employment: 16.9% management, business, and financial, 2.2% computer, engineering, and science, 7.2% education, legal, community service, arts, and media, 1.9% healthcare practitioners, 11.9% service, 19.7% sales and office, 19.1% natural resources, construction, and maintenance, 21.0% production, transportation, and material moving
Income: Per capita: $29,806; Median household: $56,944; Average household: $66,670; Households with income of $100,000 or more: 24.4%; Poverty rate: 2.6%

Educational Attainment: High school diploma or higher: 93.9%; Bachelor's degree or higher: 10.4%; Graduate/professional degree or higher: 3.5%

School District(s)
South Lewis Central SD (PK-12)
   2014-15 Enrollment: 1,080 . . . . (315) 348-2500
Housing: Homeownership rate: 93.4%; Median home value: $117,700; Median year structure built: Before 1940; Homeowner vacancy rate: 6.6%; Median selected monthly owner costs: $1,031 with a mortgage, $468 without a mortgage; Median gross rent: $925 per month; Rental vacancy rate: 42.9%
Health Insurance: 91.2% have insurance; 69.5% have private insurance; 38.1% have public insurance; 8.8% do not have insurance; 0.0% of children under 18 do not have insurance
Transportation: Commute: 88.6% car, 0.0% public transportation, 2.5% walk, 6.7% work from home; Mean travel time to work: 26.9 minutes

---

TURIN (village). Covers a land area of 1.026 square miles and a water area of 0 square miles. Located at 43.63° N. Lat; 75.41° W. Long. Elevation is 1,263 feet.
Population: 163; Growth (since 2000): -38.0%; Density: 158.8 persons per square mile; Race: 100.0% White, 0.0% Black/African American, 0.0% Asian, 0.0% American Indian/Alaska Native, 0.0% Native Hawaiian/Other Pacific Islander, 0.0% Two or more races, 0.0% Hispanic of any race; Average household size: 2.30; Median age: 54.1; Age under 18: 23.3%; Age 65 and over: 27.0%; Males per 100 females: 110.9; Marriage status: 21.3% never married, 63.2% now married, 2.2% separated, 4.4% widowed, 11.0% divorced; Foreign born: 0.6%; Speak English only: 100.0%; With disability: 18.4%; Veterans: 13.6%; Ancestry: 27.0% German, 11.0% French Canadian, 11.0% Polish, 10.4% Irish, 9.8% French
Employment: 2.6% management, business, and financial, 0.0% computer, engineering, and science, 11.5% education, legal, community service, arts, and media, 0.0% healthcare practitioners, 17.9% service, 26.9% sales and office, 17.9% natural resources, construction, and maintenance, 23.1% production, transportation, and material moving
Income: Per capita: $26,788; Median household: $43,438; Average household: $59,979; Households with income of $100,000 or more: 18.3%; Poverty rate: 5.5%
Educational Attainment: High school diploma or higher: 93.4%; Bachelor's degree or higher: 12.4%; Graduate/professional degree or higher: 5.8%

School District(s)
South Lewis Central SD (PK-12)
   2014-15 Enrollment: 1,080 . . . . (315) 348-2500
Housing: Homeownership rate: 95.8%; Median home value: $83,300; Median year structure built: Before 1940; Homeowner vacancy rate: 0.0%; Median selected monthly owner costs: $720 with a mortgage, $513 without a mortgage; Median gross rent: n/a per month; Rental vacancy rate: 66.7%
Health Insurance: 98.2% have insurance; 74.2% have private insurance; 46.0% have public insurance; 1.8% do not have insurance; 0.0% of children under 18 do not have insurance
Transportation: Commute: 93.5% car, 0.0% public transportation, 0.0% walk, 6.5% work from home; Mean travel time to work: 24.6 minutes

---

WATSON (town). Covers a land area of 112.737 square miles and a water area of 2.960 square miles. Located at 43.83° N. Lat; 75.24° W. Long. Elevation is 748 feet.
Population: 1,808; Growth (since 2000): -9.0%; Density: 16.0 persons per square mile; Race: 99.2% White, 0.2% Black/African American, 0.0% Asian, 0.2% American Indian/Alaska Native, 0.0% Native Hawaiian/Other Pacific Islander, 0.4% Two or more races, 2.4% Hispanic of any race; Average household size: 2.47; Median age: 45.0; Age under 18: 17.9%; Age 65 and over: 17.4%; Males per 100 females: 103.6; Marriage status: 24.4% never married, 61.0% now married, 0.5% separated, 5.6% widowed, 8.9% divorced; Foreign born: 0.9%; Speak English only: 97.5%; With disability: 15.3%; Veterans: 13.7%; Ancestry: 27.4% German, 18.9% Irish, 12.8% French, 9.7% English, 8.0% American
Employment: 6.7% management, business, and financial, 3.2% computer, engineering, and science, 7.2% education, legal, community service, arts, and media, 9.0% healthcare practitioners, 17.4% service, 21.2% sales and office, 19.4% natural resources, construction, and maintenance, 15.8% production, transportation, and material moving
Income: Per capita: $25,948; Median household: $51,319; Average household: $63,353; Households with income of $100,000 or more: 15.5%; Poverty rate: 5.9%

Educational Attainment: High school diploma or higher: 91.5%; Bachelor's degree or higher: 14.7%; Graduate/professional degree or higher: 7.8%
Housing: Homeownership rate: 88.8%; Median home value: $114,400; Median year structure built: 1981; Homeowner vacancy rate: 3.7%; Median selected monthly owner costs: $1,033 with a mortgage, $418 without a mortgage; Median gross rent: $673 per month; Rental vacancy rate: 0.0%
Health Insurance: 88.0% have insurance; 68.8% have private insurance; 35.3% have public insurance; 12.0% do not have insurance; 8.4% of children under 18 do not have insurance
Transportation: Commute: 88.6% car, 0.0% public transportation, 2.9% walk, 8.0% work from home; Mean travel time to work: 21.6 minutes

---

WEST LEYDEN (unincorporated postal area)
ZCTA: 13489
   Covers a land area of 42.699 square miles and a water area of 0.503 square miles. Located at 43.46° N. Lat; 75.55° W. Long. Elevation is 1,489 feet.
Population: 644; Growth (since 2000): -15.6%; Density: 15.1 persons per square mile; Race: 95.3% White, 0.8% Black/African American, 3.6% Asian, 0.0% American Indian/Alaska Native, 0.0% Native Hawaiian/Other Pacific Islander, 0.3% Two or more races, 0.0% Hispanic of any race; Average household size: 2.74; Median age: 44.6; Age under 18: 22.7%; Age 65 and over: 10.7%; Males per 100 females: 106.3; Marriage status: 33.0% never married, 53.0% now married, 0.4% separated, 3.4% widowed, 10.6% divorced; Foreign born: 3.7%; Speak English only: 91.2%; With disability: 10.6%; Veterans: 9.7%; Ancestry: 37.0% German, 18.2% Irish, 9.8% American, 9.5% English, 8.9% French
Employment: 10.9% management, business, and financial, 4.3% computer, engineering, and science, 6.9% education, legal, community service, arts, and media, 5.1% healthcare practitioners, 23.6% service, 13.4% sales and office, 16.3% natural resources, construction, and maintenance, 19.6% production, transportation, and material moving
Income: Per capita: $23,886; Median household: $50,750; Average household: $63,019; Households with income of $100,000 or more: 18.3%; Poverty rate: 12.9%
Educational Attainment: High school diploma or higher: 93.8%; Bachelor's degree or higher: 12.0%; Graduate/professional degree or higher: 3.6%

School District(s)
Adirondack Central SD (PK-12)
   2014-15 Enrollment: 1,322 . . . . (315) 942-9200
Housing: Homeownership rate: 85.1%; Median home value: $95,300; Median year structure built: 1975; Homeowner vacancy rate: 2.9%; Median selected monthly owner costs: $931 with a mortgage, $372 without a mortgage; Median gross rent: $675 per month; Rental vacancy rate: 0.0%
Health Insurance: 84.1% have insurance; 61.0% have private insurance; 31.2% have public insurance; 15.9% do not have insurance; 5.5% of children under 18 do not have insurance
Transportation: Commute: 82.6% car, 1.1% public transportation, 4.9% walk, 11.4% work from home; Mean travel time to work: 36.1 minutes

---

WEST TURIN (town). Covers a land area of 102.054 square miles and a water area of 0.343 square miles. Located at 43.59° N. Lat; 75.51° W. Long.
Population: 1,819; Growth (since 2000): 8.7%; Density: 17.8 persons per square mile; Race: 97.2% White, 0.5% Black/African American, 0.0% Asian, 0.0% American Indian/Alaska Native, 0.0% Native Hawaiian/Other Pacific Islander, 1.4% Two or more races, 2.2% Hispanic of any race; Average household size: 2.57; Median age: 42.7; Age under 18: 24.4%; Age 65 and over: 16.0%; Males per 100 females: 102.4; Marriage status: 22.9% never married, 67.3% now married, 2.3% separated, 3.7% widowed, 6.0% divorced; Foreign born: 0.5%; Speak English only: 99.2%; With disability: 10.5%; Veterans: 9.5%; Ancestry: 31.3% German, 15.6% Irish, 8.1% Polish, 7.4% English, 6.6% French
Employment: 11.2% management, business, and financial, 2.6% computer, engineering, and science, 10.3% education, legal, community service, arts, and media, 4.2% healthcare practitioners, 20.4% service, 15.3% sales and office, 19.3% natural resources, construction, and maintenance, 16.6% production, transportation, and material moving
Income: Per capita: $27,675; Median household: $53,750; Average household: $69,411; Households with income of $100,000 or more: 15.1%; Poverty rate: 6.2%

Educational Attainment: High school diploma or higher: 90.5%; Bachelor's degree or higher: 14.3%; Graduate/professional degree or higher: 7.4%
Housing: Homeownership rate: 86.2%; Median home value: $93,400; Median year structure built: 1941; Homeowner vacancy rate: 0.3%; Median selected monthly owner costs: $1,117 with a mortgage, $460 without a mortgage; Median gross rent: $617 per month; Rental vacancy rate: 5.8%
Health Insurance: 92.7% have insurance; 73.1% have private insurance; 34.4% have public insurance; 7.3% do not have insurance; 2.9% of children under 18 do not have insurance
Transportation: Commute: 89.7% car, 0.0% public transportation, 2.7% walk, 4.8% work from home; Mean travel time to work: 29.2 minutes

Livingston County

Located in west central New York, in the Finger Lakes area; drained by the Genesee River; includes Conesus and Hemlock Lakes. Covers a land area of 631.762 square miles, a water area of 8.496 square miles, and is located in the Eastern Time Zone at 42.73° N. Lat., 77.77° W. Long. The county was founded in 1821. County seat is Geneseo.

Livingston County is part of the Rochester, NY Metropolitan Statistical Area. The entire metro area includes: Livingston County, NY; Monroe County, NY; Ontario County, NY; Orleans County, NY; Wayne County, NY; Yates County, NY

Weather Station: Avon   Elevation: 544 feet

	Jan	Feb	Mar	Apr	May	Jun	Jul	Aug	Sep	Oct	Nov	Dec
High	32	35	43	56	68	77	81	80	73	61	49	37
Low	17	17	24	35	45	55	59	58	50	40	32	23
Precip	1.8	1.6	2.4	2.7	2.8	3.3	3.3	3.4	3.4	2.7	2.7	2.1
Snow	13.3	10.5	10.7	2.1	0.2	0.0	0.0	0.0	0.0	tr	3.7	11.4

High and Low temperatures in degrees Fahrenheit; Precipitation and Snow in inches

Weather Station: Dansville   Elevation: 660 feet

	Jan	Feb	Mar	Apr	May	Jun	Jul	Aug	Sep	Oct	Nov	Dec
High	33	36	44	58	69	78	82	81	74	62	49	38
Low	16	17	24	35	45	54	59	57	50	39	32	22
Precip	1.5	1.2	1.9	2.5	2.9	3.4	3.6	3.4	3.4	2.7	2.5	1.9
Snow	8.4	6.2	5.6	1.0	0.1	0.0	0.0	0.0	0.0	tr	1.9	6.2

High and Low temperatures in degrees Fahrenheit; Precipitation and Snow in inches

Weather Station: Hemlock   Elevation: 901 feet

	Jan	Feb	Mar	Apr	May	Jun	Jul	Aug	Sep	Oct	Nov	Dec
High	32	34	43	56	68	76	80	79	71	59	48	37
Low	16	16	23	35	45	55	59	58	52	41	32	22
Precip	1.9	1.5	2.6	3.0	3.2	3.7	3.7	3.5	3.6	3.2	3.0	2.2
Snow	na	na	na	0.0	0.0	0.0	0.0	0.0	0.0	0.0	na	na

High and Low temperatures in degrees Fahrenheit; Precipitation and Snow in inches

Population: 64,801; Growth (since 2000): 0.7%; Density: 102.6 persons per square mile; Race: 93.3% White, 2.4% Black/African American, 1.4% Asian, 0.1% American Indian/Alaska Native, 0.0% Native Hawaiian/Other Pacific Islander, 2.0% two or more races, 3.3% Hispanic of any race; Average household size: 2.42; Median age: 40.1; Age under 18: 19.1%; Age 65 and over: 15.3%; Males per 100 females: 100.7; Marriage status: 34.8% never married, 49.4% now married, 2.2% separated, 5.9% widowed, 9.9% divorced; Foreign born: 3.3%; Speak English only: 93.9%; With disability: 12.7%; Veterans: 9.0%; Ancestry: 27.6% German, 22.2% Irish, 13.9% Italian, 13.9% English, 7.1% American
Religion: Six largest groups: 22.8% Catholicism, 4.9% Methodist/Pietist, 4.6% Non-denominational Protestant, 3.1% Presbyterian-Reformed, 1.1% Holiness, 0.8% Lutheran
Economy: Unemployment rate: 4.6%; Leading industries: 17.2 % retail trade; 12.1 % accommodation and food services; 11.9 % other services (except public administration); Farms: 661 totaling 194,945 acres; Company size: 0 employ 1,000 or more persons, 1 employs 500 to 999 persons, 18 employ 100 to 499 persons, 1,220 employ less than 100 persons; Business ownership: 1,436 women-owned, n/a Black-owned, n/a Hispanic-owned, 78 Asian-owned, n/a American Indian/Alaska Native-owned
Employment: 12.7% management, business, and financial, 4.5% computer, engineering, and science, 12.7% education, legal, community service, arts, and media, 5.3% healthcare practitioners, 17.9% service, 21.9% sales and office, 11.6% natural resources, construction, and maintenance, 13.3% production, transportation, and material moving

Income: Per capita: $24,142; Median household: $51,734; Average household: $62,737; Households with income of $100,000 or more: 18.6%; Poverty rate: 14.8%
Educational Attainment: High school diploma or higher: 88.6%; Bachelor's degree or higher: 23.6%; Graduate/professional degree or higher: 10.6%
Housing: Homeownership rate: 72.7%; Median home value: $121,200; Median year structure built: 1964; Homeowner vacancy rate: 1.0%; Median selected monthly owner costs: $1,272 with a mortgage, $542 without a mortgage; Median gross rent: $721 per month; Rental vacancy rate: 5.1%
Vital Statistics: Birth rate: 82.0 per 10,000 population; Death rate: 78.8 per 10,000 population; Age-adjusted cancer mortality rate: 158.3 deaths per 100,000 population
Health Insurance: 94.2% have insurance; 76.5% have private insurance; 32.9% have public insurance; 5.8% do not have insurance; 2.9% of children under 18 do not have insurance
Health Care: Physicians: 8.2 per 10,000 population; Dentists: 4.8 per 10,000 population; Hospital beds: 8.3 per 10,000 population; Hospital admissions: 335.1 per 10,000 population
Transportation: Commute: 88.3% car, 0.5% public transportation, 6.4% walk, 3.3% work from home; Mean travel time to work: 25.2 minutes
2016 Presidential Election: 58.2% Trump, 36.0% Clinton, 4.3% Johnson, 1.5% Stein
National and State Parks: Boyd-Parker State Park; Rattlesnake Hill State Wildlife Management Area
Additional Information Contacts
Livingston Government . . . . (585) 243-7010
   http://www.co.livingston.state.ny.us

Livingston County Communities

AVON (town). Covers a land area of 41.203 square miles and a water area of 0.055 square miles. Located at 42.90° N. Lat; 77.73° W. Long. Elevation is 650 feet.
History: Incorporated 1867.
Population: 7,063; Growth (since 2000): 9.6%; Density: 171.4 persons per square mile; Race: 94.1% White, 1.3% Black/African American, 1.1% Asian, 0.0% American Indian/Alaska Native, 0.0% Native Hawaiian/Other Pacific Islander, 3.5% Two or more races, 0.9% Hispanic of any race; Average household size: 2.43; Median age: 41.2; Age under 18: 23.4%; Age 65 and over: 16.0%; Males per 100 females: 96.9; Marriage status: 29.1% never married, 55.3% now married, 3.0% separated, 5.0% widowed, 10.6% divorced; Foreign born: 2.7%; Speak English only: 96.2%; With disability: 11.0%; Veterans: 7.1%; Ancestry: 27.0% Irish, 24.5% German, 14.3% English, 13.5% Italian, 9.5% American
Employment: 16.0% management, business, and financial, 6.6% computer, engineering, and science, 11.5% education, legal, community service, arts, and media, 4.6% healthcare practitioners, 17.9% service, 20.6% sales and office, 9.2% natural resources, construction, and maintenance, 13.5% production, transportation, and material moving
Income: Per capita: $28,138; Median household: $56,380; Average household: $67,610; Households with income of $100,000 or more: 26.3%; Poverty rate: 8.4%
Educational Attainment: High school diploma or higher: 94.3%; Bachelor's degree or higher: 28.9%; Graduate/professional degree or higher: 11.9%

School District(s)
Avon Central SD (KG-12)
   2014-15 Enrollment: 1,012 . . . . (585) 226-2455
Housing: Homeownership rate: 74.6%; Median home value: $139,700; Median year structure built: 1967; Homeowner vacancy rate: 0.0%; Median selected monthly owner costs: $1,387 with a mortgage, $595 without a mortgage; Median gross rent: $789 per month; Rental vacancy rate: 3.6%
Health Insurance: 96.0% have insurance; 79.1% have private insurance; 29.2% have public insurance; 4.0% do not have insurance; 0.0% of children under 18 do not have insurance
Transportation: Commute: 94.3% car, 0.0% public transportation, 1.6% walk, 3.1% work from home; Mean travel time to work: 26.2 minutes
Additional Information Contacts
Town of Avon . . . . (585) 226-2425
   http://www.avon-ny.org/index_town.html

AVON (village). Covers a land area of 3.099 square miles and a water area of 0 square miles. Located at 42.91° N. Lat; 77.75° W. Long. Elevation is 650 feet.

Population: 3,343; Growth (since 2000): 12.3%; Density: 1,078.9 persons per square mile; Race: 94.0% White, 0.4% Black/African American, 0.5% Asian, 0.0% American Indian/Alaska Native, 0.0% Native Hawaiian/Other Pacific Islander, 5.0% Two or more races, 1.9% Hispanic of any race; Average household size: 2.43; Median age: 39.2; Age under 18: 21.7%; Age 65 and over: 17.1%; Males per 100 females: 90.7; Marriage status: 32.1% never married, 53.6% now married, 1.7% separated, 6.2% widowed, 8.0% divorced; Foreign born: 3.3%; Speak English only: 94.7%; With disability: 10.3%; Veterans: 5.5%; Ancestry: 30.9% Irish, 24.2% German, 16.9% Italian, 12.2% English, 8.0% American

Employment: 17.3% management, business, and financial, 6.8% computer, engineering, and science, 17.8% education, legal, community service, arts, and media, 4.5% healthcare practitioners, 11.4% service, 19.7% sales and office, 7.8% natural resources, construction, and maintenance, 14.8% production, transportation, and material moving

Income: Per capita: $29,073; Median household: $60,688; Average household: $70,607; Households with income of $100,000 or more: 28.8%; Poverty rate: 11.6%

Educational Attainment: High school diploma or higher: 94.7%; Bachelor's degree or higher: 34.5%; Graduate/professional degree or higher: 14.3%

School District(s)

Avon Central SD (KG-12)
    2014-15 Enrollment: 1,012 . . . . (585) 226-2455

Housing: Homeownership rate: 65.7%; Median home value: $148,000; Median year structure built: 1960; Homeowner vacancy rate: 0.0%; Median selected monthly owner costs: $1,403 with a mortgage, $599 without a mortgage; Median gross rent: $779 per month; Rental vacancy rate: 5.5%

Health Insurance: 95.6% have insurance; 81.0% have private insurance; 30.3% have public insurance; 4.4% do not have insurance; 0.0% of children under 18 do not have insurance

Safety: Violent crime rate: 6.1 per 10,000 population; Property crime rate: 45.4 per 10,000 population

Transportation: Commute: 94.0% car, 0.0% public transportation, 2.5% walk, 2.9% work from home; Mean travel time to work: 23.4 minutes

BYERSVILLE (CDP). Covers a land area of 0.510 square miles and a water area of 0 square miles. Located at 42.58° N. Lat; 77.79° W. Long. Elevation is 1,358 feet.

Population: 131; Growth (since 2000): n/a; Density: 256.8 persons per square mile; Race: 97.7% White, 0.0% Black/African American, 0.0% Asian, 0.0% American Indian/Alaska Native, 0.0% Native Hawaiian/Other Pacific Islander, 2.3% Two or more races, 0.0% Hispanic of any race; Average household size: 4.68; Median age: 33.5; Age under 18: 40.5%; Age 65 and over: 2.3%; Males per 100 females: 88.0; Marriage status: 19.3% never married, 57.8% now married, 0.0% separated, 10.8% widowed, 12.0% divorced; Foreign born: 0.0%; Speak English only: 100.0%; With disability: 17.6%; Veterans: 25.6%; Ancestry: 75.6% American, 13.0% German, 8.4% Italian, 3.8% English, 3.1% Scottish

Employment: 8.3% management, business, and financial, 0.0% computer, engineering, and science, 0.0% education, legal, community service, arts, and media, 16.7% healthcare practitioners, 19.4% service, 0.0% sales and office, 36.1% natural resources, construction, and maintenance, 19.4% production, transportation, and material moving

Income: Per capita: $12,134; Median household: $53,611; Average household: $51,496; Households with income of $100,000 or more: 10.7%; Poverty rate: 63.4%

Educational Attainment: High school diploma or higher: 87.3%; Bachelor's degree or higher: 4.2%; Graduate/professional degree or higher: 4.2%

Housing: Homeownership rate: 67.9%; Median home value: $81,700; Median year structure built: 1972; Homeowner vacancy rate: 0.0%; Median selected monthly owner costs: $850 with a mortgage, $463 without a mortgage; Median gross rent: n/a per month; Rental vacancy rate: 0.0%

Health Insurance: 96.9% have insurance; 28.2% have private insurance; 74.8% have public insurance; 3.1% do not have insurance; 0.0% of children under 18 do not have insurance

Transportation: Commute: 88.9% car, 0.0% public transportation, 0.0% walk, 11.1% work from home; Mean travel time to work: 18.4 minutes

CALEDONIA (town). Covers a land area of 43.875 square miles and a water area of 0.251 square miles. Located at 42.95° N. Lat; 77.82° W. Long. Elevation is 659 feet.

History: Incorporated 1887.

Population: 4,207; Growth (since 2000): -7.9%; Density: 95.9 persons per square mile; Race: 93.0% White, 3.6% Black/African American, 2.5% Asian, 0.0% American Indian/Alaska Native, 0.0% Native Hawaiian/Other Pacific Islander, 0.9% Two or more races, 0.8% Hispanic of any race; Average household size: 2.51; Median age: 44.9; Age under 18: 19.3%; Age 65 and over: 15.9%; Males per 100 females: 98.5; Marriage status: 28.1% never married, 56.8% now married, 1.4% separated, 6.6% widowed, 8.5% divorced; Foreign born: 3.9%; Speak English only: 97.5%; With disability: 11.9%; Veterans: 8.9%; Ancestry: 30.2% German, 24.2% Irish, 16.6% English, 15.4% Italian, 8.2% American

Employment: 10.7% management, business, and financial, 3.2% computer, engineering, and science, 10.8% education, legal, community service, arts, and media, 5.2% healthcare practitioners, 14.1% service, 24.2% sales and office, 11.6% natural resources, construction, and maintenance, 20.3% production, transportation, and material moving

Income: Per capita: $26,757; Median household: $54,469; Average household: $65,454; Households with income of $100,000 or more: 18.1%; Poverty rate: 5.8%

Educational Attainment: High school diploma or higher: 93.5%; Bachelor's degree or higher: 24.8%; Graduate/professional degree or higher: 10.3%

School District(s)

Caledonia-Mumford Central SD (PK-12)
    2014-15 Enrollment: 877 . . . . (585) 538-3400

Housing: Homeownership rate: 78.3%; Median home value: $124,200; Median year structure built: 1957; Homeowner vacancy rate: 0.0%; Median selected monthly owner costs: $1,224 with a mortgage, $576 without a mortgage; Median gross rent: $746 per month; Rental vacancy rate: 0.0%

Health Insurance: 95.7% have insurance; 81.4% have private insurance; 30.3% have public insurance; 4.3% do not have insurance; 0.0% of children under 18 do not have insurance

Transportation: Commute: 94.6% car, 0.0% public transportation, 2.6% walk, 2.2% work from home; Mean travel time to work: 22.7 minutes

Additional Information Contacts

Town of Caledonia . . . . (585) 538-4927
    http://www.townofcaledoniany.com

CALEDONIA (village). Covers a land area of 2.097 square miles and a water area of 0 square miles. Located at 42.98° N. Lat; 77.86° W. Long. Elevation is 659 feet.

Population: 2,137; Growth (since 2000): -8.2%; Density: 1,019.0 persons per square mile; Race: 92.9% White, 4.7% Black/African American, 0.9% Asian, 0.0% American Indian/Alaska Native, 0.0% Native Hawaiian/Other Pacific Islander, 1.5% Two or more races, 1.5% Hispanic of any race; Average household size: 2.32; Median age: 44.0; Age under 18: 19.3%; Age 65 and over: 16.8%; Males per 100 females: 94.6; Marriage status: 31.7% never married, 49.8% now married, 1.7% separated, 9.5% widowed, 9.0% divorced; Foreign born: 1.8%; Speak English only: 98.7%; With disability: 10.6%; Veterans: 10.5%; Ancestry: 27.3% Irish, 23.3% German, 19.2% Italian, 16.0% English, 7.7% American

Employment: 8.6% management, business, and financial, 2.7% computer, engineering, and science, 10.5% education, legal, community service, arts, and media, 4.8% healthcare practitioners, 16.0% service, 27.9% sales and office, 10.5% natural resources, construction, and maintenance, 19.0% production, transportation, and material moving

Income: Per capita: $26,482; Median household: $51,481; Average household: $60,291; Households with income of $100,000 or more: 15.8%; Poverty rate: 9.0%

Educational Attainment: High school diploma or higher: 93.7%; Bachelor's degree or higher: 21.8%; Graduate/professional degree or higher: 7.3%

School District(s)

Caledonia-Mumford Central SD (PK-12)
    2014-15 Enrollment: 877 . . . . (585) 538-3400

Housing: Homeownership rate: 66.8%; Median home value: $115,400; Median year structure built: 1948; Homeowner vacancy rate: 0.0%; Median selected monthly owner costs: $1,272 with a mortgage, $513 without a mortgage; Median gross rent: $776 per month; Rental vacancy rate: 0.0%

Health Insurance: 94.8% have insurance; 77.9% have private insurance; 34.1% have public insurance; 5.2% do not have insurance; 0.0% of children under 18 do not have insurance

Safety: Violent crime rate: 0.0 per 10,000 population; Property crime rate: 18.8 per 10,000 population
Transportation: Commute: 92.2% car, 0.0% public transportation, 4.2% walk, 2.5% work from home; Mean travel time to work: 21.1 minutes

CONESUS (town). Covers a land area of 32.891 square miles and a water area of 2.980 square miles. Located at 42.70° N. Lat; 77.64° W. Long. Elevation is 1,197 feet.
Population: 2,507; Growth (since 2000): 6.5%; Density: 76.2 persons per square mile; Race: 98.2% White, 0.0% Black/African American, 0.0% Asian, 0.9% American Indian/Alaska Native, 0.0% Native Hawaiian/Other Pacific Islander, 0.9% Two or more races, 1.6% Hispanic of any race; Average household size: 2.41; Median age: 46.6; Age under 18: 19.1%; Age 65 and over: 13.5%; Males per 100 females: 102.4; Marriage status: 24.4% never married, 63.1% now married, 1.9% separated, 3.3% widowed, 9.2% divorced; Foreign born: 4.0%; Speak English only: 96.5%; With disability: 14.1%; Veterans: 8.7%; Ancestry: 33.8% German, 24.5% Irish, 13.0% Italian, 11.3% English, 8.5% American
Employment: 5.8% management, business, and financial, 7.4% computer, engineering, and science, 13.9% education, legal, community service, arts, and media, 10.2% healthcare practitioners, 16.6% service, 22.4% sales and office, 11.9% natural resources, construction, and maintenance, 11.9% production, transportation, and material moving
Income: Per capita: $30,084; Median household: $59,926; Average household: $71,594; Households with income of $100,000 or more: 26.3%; Poverty rate: 12.7%
Educational Attainment: High school diploma or higher: 90.9%; Bachelor's degree or higher: 23.8%; Graduate/professional degree or higher: 9.1%
Housing: Homeownership rate: 89.8%; Median home value: $129,800; Median year structure built: 1980; Homeowner vacancy rate: 3.4%; Median selected monthly owner costs: $1,322 with a mortgage, $536 without a mortgage; Median gross rent: $950 per month; Rental vacancy rate: 0.0%
Health Insurance: 95.2% have insurance; 82.8% have private insurance; 25.6% have public insurance; 4.8% do not have insurance; 0.0% of children under 18 do not have insurance
Transportation: Commute: 97.0% car, 0.0% public transportation, 0.0% walk, 1.5% work from home; Mean travel time to work: 31.8 minutes

CONESUS HAMLET (CDP). Covers a land area of 1.059 square miles and a water area of 0 square miles. Located at 42.73° N. Lat; 77.67° W. Long. Elevation is 1,207 feet.
Population: 512; Growth (since 2000): n/a; Density: 483.6 persons per square mile; Race: 100.0% White, 0.0% Black/African American, 0.0% Asian, 0.0% American Indian/Alaska Native, 0.0% Native Hawaiian/Other Pacific Islander, 0.0% Two or more races, 2.9% Hispanic of any race; Average household size: 2.94; Median age: 28.1; Age under 18: 29.7%; Age 65 and over: 4.1%; Males per 100 females: 91.3; Marriage status: 33.6% never married, 57.2% now married, 4.2% separated, 1.4% widowed, 7.8% divorced; Foreign born: 0.0%; Speak English only: 98.9%; With disability: 6.1%; Veterans: 9.7%; Ancestry: 50.8% German, 48.0% Irish, 7.0% English, 6.8% Italian, 6.3% American
Employment: 0.0% management, business, and financial, 13.2% computer, engineering, and science, 14.3% education, legal, community service, arts, and media, 12.5% healthcare practitioners, 29.3% service, 23.9% sales and office, 6.8% natural resources, construction, and maintenance, 0.0% production, transportation, and material moving
Income: Per capita: $17,738; Median household: $55,521; Average household: $50,853; Households with income of $100,000 or more: 10.3%; Poverty rate: 16.2%
Educational Attainment: High school diploma or higher: 100.0%; Bachelor's degree or higher: 16.6%; Graduate/professional degree or higher: 1.7%
Housing: Homeownership rate: 64.9%; Median home value: $112,800; Median year structure built: 1944; Homeowner vacancy rate: 0.0%; Median selected monthly owner costs: $900 with a mortgage, $610 without a mortgage; Median gross rent: $1,059 per month; Rental vacancy rate: 0.0%
Health Insurance: 96.7% have insurance; 91.8% have private insurance; 12.1% have public insurance; 3.3% do not have insurance; 0.0% of children under 18 do not have insurance
Transportation: Commute: 100.0% car, 0.0% public transportation, 0.0% walk, 0.0% work from home; Mean travel time to work: 27.2 minutes

CONESUS LAKE (CDP). Covers a land area of 4.361 square miles and a water area of 5.050 square miles. Located at 42.80° N. Lat; 77.70° W. Long. Elevation is 846 feet.
Population: 2,584; Growth (since 2000): n/a; Density: 592.5 persons per square mile; Race: 97.4% White, 0.0% Black/African American, 0.5% Asian, 0.6% American Indian/Alaska Native, 0.0% Native Hawaiian/Other Pacific Islander, 1.4% Two or more races, 2.2% Hispanic of any race; Average household size: 2.09; Median age: 56.2; Age under 18: 11.7%; Age 65 and over: 27.2%; Males per 100 females: 105.2; Marriage status: 28.8% never married, 57.7% now married, 0.3% separated, 4.1% widowed, 9.4% divorced; Foreign born: 4.0%; Speak English only: 95.8%; With disability: 10.4%; Veterans: 11.2%; Ancestry: 28.0% Irish, 26.0% German, 21.9% Italian, 16.4% English, 6.6% American
Employment: 18.3% management, business, and financial, 5.7% computer, engineering, and science, 15.3% education, legal, community service, arts, and media, 4.5% healthcare practitioners, 17.5% service, 20.6% sales and office, 11.4% natural resources, construction, and maintenance, 6.7% production, transportation, and material moving
Income: Per capita: $42,437; Median household: $77,738; Average household: $86,459; Households with income of $100,000 or more: 32.3%; Poverty rate: 6.3%
Educational Attainment: High school diploma or higher: 96.8%; Bachelor's degree or higher: 38.3%; Graduate/professional degree or higher: 15.5%
Housing: Homeownership rate: 82.5%; Median home value: $215,900; Median year structure built: 1958; Homeowner vacancy rate: 0.6%; Median selected monthly owner costs: $1,601 with a mortgage, $674 without a mortgage; Median gross rent: $870 per month; Rental vacancy rate: 0.0%
Health Insurance: 96.8% have insurance; 85.4% have private insurance; 33.0% have public insurance; 3.2% do not have insurance; 0.0% of children under 18 do not have insurance
Transportation: Commute: 94.7% car, 0.0% public transportation, 0.0% walk, 5.1% work from home; Mean travel time to work: 30.0 minutes

CUMMINSVILLE (CDP). Covers a land area of 0.131 square miles and a water area of 0 square miles. Located at 42.57° N. Lat; 77.72° W. Long. Elevation is 640 feet.
Population: 146; Growth (since 2000): n/a; Density: 1,114.6 persons per square mile; Race: 100.0% White, 0.0% Black/African American, 0.0% Asian, 0.0% American Indian/Alaska Native, 0.0% Native Hawaiian/Other Pacific Islander, 0.0% Two or more races, 0.0% Hispanic of any race; Average household size: 1.74; Median age: 57.6; Age under 18: 0.0%; Age 65 and over: 25.3%; Males per 100 females: 77.7; Marriage status: 4.1% never married, 58.2% now married, 6.8% separated, 17.8% widowed, 19.9% divorced; Foreign born: 0.0%; Speak English only: 100.0%; With disability: 37.7%; Veterans: 19.9%; Ancestry: 28.1% American, 18.5% Italian, 12.3% English, 5.5% Belgian
Employment: 0.0% management, business, and financial, 0.0% computer, engineering, and science, 0.0% education, legal, community service, arts, and media, 0.0% healthcare practitioners, 0.0% service, 28.6% sales and office, 39.3% natural resources, construction, and maintenance, 32.1% production, transportation, and material moving
Income: Per capita: $21,742; Median household: $24,722; Average household: $37,882; Households with income of $100,000 or more: n/a; Poverty rate: 32.9%
Educational Attainment: High school diploma or higher: 79.3%; Bachelor's degree or higher: n/a; Graduate/professional degree or higher: n/a
Housing: Homeownership rate: 88.1%; Median home value: $41,100; Median year structure built: 1967; Homeowner vacancy rate: 0.0%; Median selected monthly owner costs: n/a with a mortgage, $423 without a mortgage; Median gross rent: n/a per month; Rental vacancy rate: 0.0%
Health Insurance: 93.8% have insurance; 65.8% have private insurance; 58.9% have public insurance; 6.2% do not have insurance; 0.0% of children under 18 do not have insurance
Transportation: Commute: 100.0% car, 0.0% public transportation, 0.0% walk, 0.0% work from home; Mean travel time to work: 0.0 minutes

CUYLERVILLE (CDP). Covers a land area of 0.421 square miles and a water area of 0 square miles. Located at 42.78° N. Lat; 77.87° W. Long. Elevation is 571 feet.
Population: 344; Growth (since 2000): n/a; Density: 816.3 persons per square mile; Race: 95.9% White, 0.0% Black/African American, 0.0% Asian, 0.0% American Indian/Alaska Native, 0.0% Native Hawaiian/Other Pacific Islander, 2.9% Two or more races, 9.9% Hispanic of any race;

Average household size: 2.16; Median age: 35.5; Age under 18: 20.1%; Age 65 and over: 17.2%; Males per 100 females: 104.8; Marriage status: 34.5% never married, 60.0% now married, 4.0% separated, 5.5% widowed, 0.0% divorced; Foreign born: 1.7%; Speak English only: 98.0%; With disability: 10.8%; Veterans: 7.3%; Ancestry: 38.7% German, 36.6% Italian, 26.5% Irish, 4.9% Pennsylvania German, 3.5% American
Employment: 14.9% management, business, and financial, 0.0% computer, engineering, and science, 13.6% education, legal, community service, arts, and media, 2.6% healthcare practitioners, 20.1% service, 37.7% sales and office, 7.1% natural resources, construction, and maintenance, 3.9% production, transportation, and material moving
Income: Per capita: $21,624; Median household: $54,250; Average household: $48,887; Households with income of $100,000 or more: 5.7%; Poverty rate: 32.3%
Educational Attainment: High school diploma or higher: 82.7%; Bachelor's degree or higher: 25.7%; Graduate/professional degree or higher: 3.8%
Housing: Homeownership rate: 56.0%; Median home value: $106,300; Median year structure built: 1970; Homeowner vacancy rate: 0.0%; Median selected monthly owner costs: $1,138 with a mortgage, $375 without a mortgage; Median gross rent: $767 per month; Rental vacancy rate: 0.0%
Health Insurance: 93.3% have insurance; 71.5% have private insurance; 34.3% have public insurance; 6.7% do not have insurance; 0.0% of children under 18 do not have insurance
Transportation: Commute: 88.6% car, 0.0% public transportation, 0.0% walk, 11.4% work from home; Mean travel time to work: 24.7 minutes

DALTON (CDP).
Covers a land area of 0.755 square miles and a water area of 0 square miles. Located at 42.54° N. Lat; 77.95° W. Long. Elevation is 1,342 feet.
Population: 306; Growth (since 2000): n/a; Density: 405.4 persons per square mile; Race: 100.0% White, 0.0% Black/African American, 0.0% Asian, 0.0% American Indian/Alaska Native, 0.0% Native Hawaiian/Other Pacific Islander, 0.0% Two or more races, 0.0% Hispanic of any race; Average household size: 2.76; Median age: 51.0; Age under 18: 21.6%; Age 65 and over: 27.1%; Males per 100 females: 102.2; Marriage status: 17.9% never married, 66.9% now married, 0.0% separated, 10.9% widowed, 4.3% divorced; Foreign born: 0.0%; Speak English only: 100.0%; With disability: 18.0%; Veterans: 15.4%; Ancestry: 45.1% English, 31.0% German, 12.4% Irish, 9.2% Dutch, 7.8% Italian
Employment: 5.9% management, business, and financial, 4.2% computer, engineering, and science, 5.0% education, legal, community service, arts, and media, 5.9% healthcare practitioners, 28.6% service, 10.9% sales and office, 21.8% natural resources, construction, and maintenance, 17.6% production, transportation, and material moving
Income: Per capita: $29,190; Median household: $72,375; Average household: $78,597; Households with income of $100,000 or more: 27.0%; Poverty rate: 5.6%
Educational Attainment: High school diploma or higher: 95.5%; Bachelor's degree or higher: 6.8%; Graduate/professional degree or higher: 2.7%
Housing: Homeownership rate: 91.9%; Median home value: $86,200; Median year structure built: Before 1940; Homeowner vacancy rate: 0.0%; Median selected monthly owner costs: $900 with a mortgage, $404 without a mortgage; Median gross rent: n/a per month; Rental vacancy rate: 0.0%
Health Insurance: 96.4% have insurance; 86.6% have private insurance; 40.5% have public insurance; 3.6% do not have insurance; 9.1% of children under 18 do not have insurance
Transportation: Commute: 97.5% car, 2.5% public transportation, 0.0% walk, 0.0% work from home; Mean travel time to work: 39.2 minutes

DANSVILLE (village).
Covers a land area of 2.608 square miles and a water area of 0 square miles. Located at 42.56° N. Lat; 77.70° W. Long. Elevation is 705 feet.
History: Clara Barton founded (1881) first local chapter of the American Red Cross here. Settled 1795, incorporated 1845.
Population: 4,537; Growth (since 2000): -6.1%; Density: 1,739.9 persons per square mile; Race: 98.4% White, 0.7% Black/African American, 0.0% Asian, 0.0% American Indian/Alaska Native, 0.0% Native Hawaiian/Other Pacific Islander, 0.6% Two or more races, 2.2% Hispanic of any race; Average household size: 2.25; Median age: 45.9; Age under 18: 22.4%; Age 65 and over: 15.7%; Males per 100 females: 89.2; Marriage status: 33.9% never married, 47.0% now married, 2.6% separated, 8.3% widowed, 10.8% divorced; Foreign born: 1.5%; Speak English only: 97.9%;

With disability: 17.6%; Veterans: 13.5%; Ancestry: 27.5% German, 23.4% Irish, 9.6% Polish, 9.0% American, 8.1% English
Employment: 13.3% management, business, and financial, 0.5% computer, engineering, and science, 17.2% education, legal, community service, arts, and media, 5.2% healthcare practitioners, 16.3% service, 21.0% sales and office, 11.7% natural resources, construction, and maintenance, 14.7% production, transportation, and material moving
Income: Per capita: $23,133; Median household: $40,841; Average household: $52,053; Households with income of $100,000 or more: 15.0%; Poverty rate: 21.3%
Educational Attainment: High school diploma or higher: 81.1%; Bachelor's degree or higher: 21.4%; Graduate/professional degree or higher: 12.5%

School District(s)
Dansville Central SD (PK-12)
   2014-15 Enrollment: 1,597 . . . . (585) 335-4000
Housing: Homeownership rate: 63.6%; Median home value: $85,700; Median year structure built: Before 1940; Homeowner vacancy rate: 1.9%; Median selected monthly owner costs: $1,071 with a mortgage, $448 without a mortgage; Median gross rent: $652 per month; Rental vacancy rate: 5.4%
Health Insurance: 92.7% have insurance; 65.3% have private insurance; 45.6% have public insurance; 7.3% do not have insurance; 7.1% of children under 18 do not have insurance
Hospitals: Nicholas H Noyes Memorial Hospital (72 beds)
Safety: Violent crime rate: 4.4 per 10,000 population; Property crime rate: 202.5 per 10,000 population
Newspapers: Genesee County Express (weekly circulation 2,800)
Transportation: Commute: 82.4% car, 0.5% public transportation, 11.8% walk, 2.8% work from home; Mean travel time to work: 28.1 minutes
Additional Information Contacts
Village of Dansville . . . . (585) 335-5330
  http://dansvilleny.us

EAST AVON (CDP).
Covers a land area of 1.310 square miles and a water area of 0 square miles. Located at 42.91° N. Lat; 77.71° W. Long. Elevation is 820 feet.
Population: 619; Growth (since 2000): n/a; Density: 472.6 persons per square mile; Race: 86.8% White, 0.0% Black/African American, 0.0% Asian, 0.0% American Indian/Alaska Native, 0.0% Native Hawaiian/Other Pacific Islander, 13.2% Two or more races, 0.0% Hispanic of any race; Average household size: 2.16; Median age: 35.2; Age under 18: 29.2%; Age 65 and over: 21.3%; Males per 100 females: 102.0; Marriage status: 31.7% never married, 39.0% now married, 3.7% separated, 2.6% widowed, 26.7% divorced; Foreign born: 0.0%; Speak English only: 100.0%; With disability: 26.3%; Veterans: 17.4%; Ancestry: 31.3% Irish, 26.0% German, 17.6% English, 16.5% American, 13.2% Jamaican
Employment: 6.6% management, business, and financial, 0.0% computer, engineering, and science, 7.0% education, legal, community service, arts, and media, 6.1% healthcare practitioners, 63.8% service, 8.3% sales and office, 8.3% natural resources, construction, and maintenance, 0.0% production, transportation, and material moving
Income: Per capita: $19,072; Median household: $32,553; Average household: $40,903; Households with income of $100,000 or more: 5.6%; Poverty rate: 12.6%
Educational Attainment: High school diploma or higher: 83.7%; Bachelor's degree or higher: 21.6%; Graduate/professional degree or higher: 9.5%
Housing: Homeownership rate: 44.1%; Median home value: $150,800; Median year structure built: 1964; Homeowner vacancy rate: 0.0%; Median selected monthly owner costs: $1,711 with a mortgage, $611 without a mortgage; Median gross rent: $1,025 per month; Rental vacancy rate: 0.0%
Health Insurance: 94.8% have insurance; 49.6% have private insurance; 55.4% have public insurance; 5.2% do not have insurance; 0.0% of children under 18 do not have insurance
Transportation: Commute: 86.9% car, 0.0% public transportation, 0.0% walk, 0.0% work from home; Mean travel time to work: 17.2 minutes

FOWLERVILLE (CDP).
Covers a land area of 0.901 square miles and a water area of 0 square miles. Located at 42.89° N. Lat; 77.85° W. Long. Elevation is 636 feet.
Population: 258; Growth (since 2000): n/a; Density: 286.2 persons per square mile; Race: 91.9% White, 8.1% Black/African American, 0.0% Asian, 0.0% American Indian/Alaska Native, 0.0% Native Hawaiian/Other

Pacific Islander, 0.0% Two or more races, 0.0% Hispanic of any race; Average household size: 2.43; Median age: 24.8; Age under 18: 23.6%; Age 65 and over: 23.6%; Males per 100 females: 110.2; Marriage status: 51.3% never married, 34.5% now married, 4.1% separated, 14.2% widowed, 0.0% divorced; Foreign born: 0.0%; Speak English only: 100.0%; With disability: 46.5%; Veterans: 10.7%; Ancestry: 48.1% Irish, 27.9% French, 26.4% Dutch, 19.0% German, 11.6% English

Employment: 13.6% management, business, and financial, 0.0% computer, engineering, and science, 0.0% education, legal, community service, arts, and media, 0.0% healthcare practitioners, 57.6% service, 15.2% sales and office, 0.0% natural resources, construction, and maintenance, 13.6% production, transportation, and material moving

Income: Per capita: $13,974; Median household: $16,719; Average household: $34,119; Households with income of $100,000 or more: 9.4%; Poverty rate: 56.6%

Educational Attainment: High school diploma or higher: 76.1%; Bachelor's degree or higher: 23.1%; Graduate/professional degree or higher: 8.5%

Housing: Homeownership rate: 45.3%; Median home value: $94,000; Median year structure built: Before 1940; Homeowner vacancy rate: 0.0%; Median selected monthly owner costs: n/a with a mortgage, $561 without a mortgage; Median gross rent: n/a per month; Rental vacancy rate: 0.0%

Health Insurance: 100.0% have insurance; 57.0% have private insurance; 86.4% have public insurance; 0.0% do not have insurance; 0.0% of children under 18 do not have insurance

Transportation: Commute: 100.0% car, 0.0% public transportation, 0.0% walk, 0.0% work from home; Mean travel time to work: 0.0 minutes

GENESEO (town).
Covers a land area of 43.944 square miles and a water area of 1.198 square miles. Located at 42.81° N. Lat; 77.78° W. Long. Elevation is 771 feet.

History: Geneseo is best known for its association with the Wadsworth family. They became the squires of the middle Genesee in 1790. Members of the family served as legislators at the state and national levels.

Population: 10,590; Growth (since 2000): 9.7%; Density: 241.0 persons per square mile; Race: 88.8% White, 2.5% Black/African American, 4.4% Asian, 0.0% American Indian/Alaska Native, 0.0% Native Hawaiian/Other Pacific Islander, 3.4% Two or more races, 4.4% Hispanic of any race; Average household size: 2.34; Median age: 21.6; Age under 18: 9.2%; Age 65 and over: 12.4%; Males per 100 females: 84.0; Marriage status: 63.5% never married, 26.4% now married, 1.3% separated, 5.3% widowed, 4.9% divorced; Foreign born: 7.2%; Speak English only: 89.3%; With disability: 11.0%; Veterans: 5.8%; Ancestry: 25.6% German, 22.3% Irish, 16.5% Italian, 13.0% English, 5.4% Polish

Employment: 10.5% management, business, and financial, 3.6% computer, engineering, and science, 22.0% education, legal, community service, arts, and media, 4.5% healthcare practitioners, 24.6% service, 21.7% sales and office, 6.3% natural resources, construction, and maintenance, 6.9% production, transportation, and material moving

Income: Per capita: $19,400; Median household: $41,952; Average household: $62,297; Households with income of $100,000 or more: 19.3%; Poverty rate: 30.2%

Educational Attainment: High school diploma or higher: 89.7%; Bachelor's degree or higher: 42.1%; Graduate/professional degree or higher: 23.6%

School District(s)
Geneseo Central SD (KG-12)
   2014-15 Enrollment: 885 . . . . (585) 243-3450

Four-year College(s)
SUNY College at Geneseo (Public)
   Fall 2014 Enrollment: 5,658 . . . . (585) 245-5000
   2015-16 Tuition: In-state $8,113; Out-of-state $17,963

Housing: Homeownership rate: 50.5%; Median home value: $157,600; Median year structure built: 1975; Homeowner vacancy rate: 0.0%; Median selected monthly owner costs: $1,541 with a mortgage, $625 without a mortgage; Median gross rent: $752 per month; Rental vacancy rate: 10.3%

Health Insurance: 97.0% have insurance; 87.5% have private insurance; 21.6% have public insurance; 3.0% do not have insurance; 1.1% of children under 18 do not have insurance

Newspapers: Livingston County News (weekly circulation 6,000)

Transportation: Commute: 66.7% car, 1.2% public transportation, 26.5% walk, 4.7% work from home; Mean travel time to work: 20.3 minutes

Additional Information Contacts
Town of Geneseo . . . . (585) 991-5000
   http://www.geneseony.org

GENESEO (village).
County seat. Covers a land area of 2.839 square miles and a water area of 0 square miles. Located at 42.80° N. Lat; 77.81° W. Long. Elevation is 771 feet.

History: Major salt mine cave-in and diversion of surface drainage into subterranean channels occurred in 1995. Estates of the Wadsworth family, northeast and south of village. English-style Genesee Valley Hunt each fall. Seat of State University of N.Y. College at Geneseo. Settled c.1790, Incorporated 1832.

Population: 8,096; Growth (since 2000): 6.8%; Density: 2,851.8 persons per square mile; Race: 85.9% White, 3.1% Black/African American, 5.8% Asian, 0.0% American Indian/Alaska Native, 0.0% Native Hawaiian/Other Pacific Islander, 4.3% Two or more races, 5.2% Hispanic of any race; Average household size: 2.53; Median age: 20.8; Age under 18: 8.1%; Age 65 and over: 7.1%; Males per 100 females: 81.5; Marriage status: 76.9% never married, 18.1% now married, 1.3% separated, 2.3% widowed, 2.7% divorced; Foreign born: 7.8%; Speak English only: 86.3%; With disability: 8.9%; Veterans: 2.6%; Ancestry: 25.7% German, 21.5% Irish, 16.0% Italian, 12.1% English, 5.5% Polish

Employment: 8.2% management, business, and financial, 3.8% computer, engineering, and science, 23.8% education, legal, community service, arts, and media, 4.1% healthcare practitioners, 28.5% service, 24.1% sales and office, 2.7% natural resources, construction, and maintenance, 4.7% production, transportation, and material moving

Income: Per capita: $13,522; Median household: $38,051; Average household: $52,668; Households with income of $100,000 or more: 16.2%; Poverty rate: 41.5%

Educational Attainment: High school diploma or higher: 88.4%; Bachelor's degree or higher: 48.0%; Graduate/professional degree or higher: 27.6%

School District(s)
Geneseo Central SD (KG-12)
   2014-15 Enrollment: 885 . . . . (585) 243-3450

Four-year College(s)
SUNY College at Geneseo (Public)
   Fall 2014 Enrollment: 5,658 . . . . (585) 245-5000
   2015-16 Tuition: In-state $8,113; Out-of-state $17,963

Housing: Homeownership rate: 42.6%; Median home value: $157,300; Median year structure built: 1974; Homeowner vacancy rate: 0.0%; Median selected monthly owner costs: $1,475 with a mortgage, $649 without a mortgage; Median gross rent: $719 per month; Rental vacancy rate: 14.0%

Health Insurance: 96.5% have insurance; 86.0% have private insurance; 18.2% have public insurance; 3.5% do not have insurance; 1.7% of children under 18 do not have insurance

Safety: Violent crime rate: 7.4 per 10,000 population; Property crime rate: 147.5 per 10,000 population

Newspapers: Livingston County News (weekly circulation 6,000)

Transportation: Commute: 55.6% car, 1.7% public transportation, 37.0% walk, 4.5% work from home; Mean travel time to work: 15.8 minutes

Additional Information Contacts
Village of Geneseo . . . . (585) 243-1177
   http://www.geneseony.org

GREIGSVILLE (CDP).
Covers a land area of 0.710 square miles and a water area of 0 square miles. Located at 42.83° N. Lat; 77.90° W. Long. Elevation is 751 feet.

Population: 296; Growth (since 2000): n/a; Density: 416.6 persons per square mile; Race: 100.0% White, 0.0% Black/African American, 0.0% Asian, 0.0% American Indian/Alaska Native, 0.0% Native Hawaiian/Other Pacific Islander, 0.0% Two or more races, 0.0% Hispanic of any race; Average household size: 2.43; Median age: 45.3; Age under 18: 13.9%; Age 65 and over: 8.8%; Males per 100 females: 104.9; Marriage status: 35.2% never married, 61.3% now married, 0.0% separated, 0.0% widowed, 3.5% divorced; Foreign born: 0.0%; Speak English only: 100.0%; With disability: 10.1%; Veterans: 9.0%; Ancestry: 45.6% Italian, 28.7% German, 25.3% Norwegian, 14.5% American, 7.8% Irish

Employment: 0.0% management, business, and financial, 10.3% computer, engineering, and science, 15.8% education, legal, community service, arts, and media, 0.0% healthcare practitioners, 17.5% service, 26.1% sales and office, 3.8% natural resources, construction, and maintenance, 26.5% production, transportation, and material moving

Income: Per capita: $36,711; Median household: $92,045; Average household: $89,479; Households with income of $100,000 or more: 48.4%; Poverty rate: n/a

Educational Attainment: High school diploma or higher: 95.9%; Bachelor's degree or higher: 10.8%; Graduate/professional degree or higher: 10.8%

Housing: Homeownership rate: 81.1%; Median home value: $97,800; Median year structure built: Before 1940; Homeowner vacancy rate: 0.0%; Median selected monthly owner costs: $1,203 with a mortgage, n/a without a mortgage; Median gross rent: n/a per month; Rental vacancy rate: 0.0%

Health Insurance: 96.6% have insurance; 93.9% have private insurance; 12.8% have public insurance; 3.4% do not have insurance; 0.0% of children under 18 do not have insurance

Transportation: Commute: 95.7% car, 0.0% public transportation, 0.0% walk, 4.3% work from home; Mean travel time to work: 13.1 minutes

GROVELAND (town). Covers a land area of 39.129 square miles and a water area of 0.725 square miles. Located at 42.71° N. Lat; 77.77° W. Long. Elevation is 614 feet.

Population: 3,334; Growth (since 2000): -13.5%; Density: 85.2 persons per square mile; Race: 70.2% White, 24.2% Black/African American, 0.1% Asian, 0.0% American Indian/Alaska Native, 0.0% Native Hawaiian/Other Pacific Islander, 1.7% Two or more races, 11.7% Hispanic of any race; Average household size: 2.48; Median age: 35.7; Age under 18: 9.1%; Age 65 and over: 7.5%; Males per 100 females: 334.9; Marriage status: 45.0% never married, 37.4% now married, 3.4% separated, 2.1% widowed, 15.6% divorced; Foreign born: 3.2%; Speak English only: 87.1%; With disability: 11.5%; Veterans: 12.8%; Ancestry: 17.8% German, 17.7% Irish, 11.5% Italian, 11.1% English, 4.8% American

Employment: 12.6% management, business, and financial, 3.8% computer, engineering, and science, 8.4% education, legal, community service, arts, and media, 7.2% healthcare practitioners, 15.0% service, 20.3% sales and office, 18.3% natural resources, construction, and maintenance, 14.3% production, transportation, and material moving

Income: Per capita: $12,356; Median household: $53,403; Average household: $67,053; Households with income of $100,000 or more: 18.7%; Poverty rate: 9.3%

Educational Attainment: High school diploma or higher: 80.1%; Bachelor's degree or higher: 12.5%; Graduate/professional degree or higher: 3.9%

Housing: Homeownership rate: 73.3%; Median home value: $134,200; Median year structure built: 1956; Homeowner vacancy rate: 0.0%; Median selected monthly owner costs: $1,360 with a mortgage, $580 without a mortgage; Median gross rent: $740 per month; Rental vacancy rate: 0.0%

Health Insurance: 92.0% have insurance; 67.0% have private insurance; 43.2% have public insurance; 8.0% do not have insurance; 3.6% of children under 18 do not have insurance

Transportation: Commute: 90.5% car, 0.2% public transportation, 4.5% walk, 3.9% work from home; Mean travel time to work: 28.6 minutes

GROVELAND STATION (CDP). Covers a land area of 0.586 square miles and a water area of 0 square miles. Located at 42.66° N. Lat; 77.77° W. Long. Elevation is 614 feet.

Population: 283; Growth (since 2000): n/a; Density: 482.6 persons per square mile; Race: 100.0% White, 0.0% Black/African American, 0.0% Asian, 0.0% American Indian/Alaska Native, 0.0% Native Hawaiian/Other Pacific Islander, 0.0% Two or more races, 0.0% Hispanic of any race; Average household size: 2.83; Median age: 34.4; Age under 18: 30.0%; Age 65 and over: 11.7%; Males per 100 females: 109.7; Marriage status: 24.3% never married, 53.7% now married, 1.4% separated, 4.1% widowed, 17.9% divorced; Foreign born: 0.0%; Speak English only: 100.0%; With disability: 8.5%; Veterans: 9.1%; Ancestry: 35.0% English, 27.2% German, 13.8% Irish, 8.8% Italian, 7.1% American

Employment: 1.8% management, business, and financial, 2.6% computer, engineering, and science, 6.1% education, legal, community service, arts, and media, 2.6% healthcare practitioners, 13.2% service, 20.2% sales and office, 25.4% natural resources, construction, and maintenance, 28.1% production, transportation, and material moving

Income: Per capita: $18,687; Median household: $46,042; Average household: $50,958; Households with income of $100,000 or more: 11.0%; Poverty rate: 15.8%

Educational Attainment: High school diploma or higher: 89.8%; Bachelor's degree or higher: 14.8%; Graduate/professional degree or higher: 2.8%

Housing: Homeownership rate: 92.0%; Median home value: $81,700; Median year structure built: Before 1940; Homeowner vacancy rate: 0.0%; Median selected monthly owner costs: $967 with a mortgage, $542 without

a mortgage; Median gross rent: $625 per month; Rental vacancy rate: 0.0%

Health Insurance: 96.8% have insurance; 54.8% have private insurance; 56.2% have public insurance; 3.2% do not have insurance; 0.0% of children under 18 do not have insurance

Transportation: Commute: 99.1% car, 0.0% public transportation, 0.0% walk, 0.9% work from home; Mean travel time to work: 30.0 minutes

HEMLOCK (CDP). Covers a land area of 1.863 square miles and a water area of 0 square miles. Located at 42.79° N. Lat; 77.61° W. Long. Elevation is 909 feet.

Population: 401; Growth (since 2000): n/a; Density: 215.3 persons per square mile; Race: 100.0% White, 0.0% Black/African American, 0.0% Asian, 0.0% American Indian/Alaska Native, 0.0% Native Hawaiian/Other Pacific Islander, 0.0% Two or more races, 0.0% Hispanic of any race; Average household size: 2.07; Median age: 36.8; Age under 18: 19.2%; Age 65 and over: 20.0%; Males per 100 females: 106.3; Marriage status: 9.6% never married, 58.6% now married, 0.0% separated, 24.0% widowed, 7.8% divorced; Foreign born: 0.0%; Speak English only: 100.0%; With disability: 5.7%; Veterans: 5.6%; Ancestry: 48.4% German, 21.9% English, 8.5% Dutch, 7.0% Italian, 4.0% Scottish

Employment: 0.0% management, business, and financial, 0.0% computer, engineering, and science, 4.9% education, legal, community service, arts, and media, 4.5% healthcare practitioners, 17.8% service, 23.1% sales and office, 26.1% natural resources, construction, and maintenance, 23.5% production, transportation, and material moving

Income: Per capita: $27,332; Median household: $54,861; Average household: $55,764; Households with income of $100,000 or more: 7.7%; Poverty rate: n/a

Educational Attainment: High school diploma or higher: 94.7%; Bachelor's degree or higher: 19.9%; Graduate/professional degree or higher: n/a

Housing: Homeownership rate: 82.5%; Median home value: $102,200; Median year structure built: Before 1940; Homeowner vacancy rate: 0.0%; Median selected monthly owner costs: $1,395 with a mortgage, $484 without a mortgage; Median gross rent: n/a per month; Rental vacancy rate: 0.0%

Health Insurance: 100.0% have insurance; 89.5% have private insurance; 26.4% have public insurance; 0.0% do not have insurance; 0.0% of children under 18 do not have insurance

Transportation: Commute: 94.3% car, 0.0% public transportation, 0.0% walk, 5.7% work from home; Mean travel time to work: 21.6 minutes

HUNT (CDP). Covers a land area of 0.119 square miles and a water area of 0 square miles. Located at 42.55° N. Lat; 77.99° W. Long. Elevation is 1,342 feet.

Population: 44; Growth (since 2000): n/a; Density: 369.5 persons per square mile; Race: 100.0% White, 0.0% Black/African American, 0.0% Asian, 0.0% American Indian/Alaska Native, 0.0% Native Hawaiian/Other Pacific Islander, 0.0% Two or more races, 0.0% Hispanic of any race; Average household size: 1.83; Median age: 56.0; Age under 18: 13.6%; Age 65 and over: 40.9%; Males per 100 females: 85.7; Marriage status: 15.8% never married, 73.7% now married, 15.8% separated, 10.5% widowed, 0.0% divorced; Foreign born: 0.0%; Speak English only: 100.0%; With disability: 38.6%; Veterans: 47.4%; Ancestry: 25.0% English, 15.9% Irish, 6.8% Dutch, 6.8% German, 6.8% Polish

Employment: 15.4% management, business, and financial, 0.0% computer, engineering, and science, 0.0% education, legal, community service, arts, and media, 15.4% healthcare practitioners, 0.0% service, 0.0% sales and office, 23.1% natural resources, construction, and maintenance, 46.2% production, transportation, and material moving

Income: Per capita: $21,661; Median household: $36,667; Average household: $39,713; Households with income of $100,000 or more: 12.5%; Poverty rate: 11.4%

Educational Attainment: High school diploma or higher: 78.9%; Bachelor's degree or higher: n/a; Graduate/professional degree or higher: n/a

Housing: Homeownership rate: 100.0%; Median home value: $55,000; Median year structure built: 1962; Homeowner vacancy rate: 0.0%; Median selected monthly owner costs: $950 with a mortgage, $300 without a mortgage; Median gross rent: n/a per month; Rental vacancy rate: 0.0%

Health Insurance: 100.0% have insurance; 88.6% have private insurance; 61.4% have public insurance; 0.0% do not have insurance; 0.0% of children under 18 do not have insurance

Transportation: Commute: 100.0% car, 0.0% public transportation, 0.0% walk, 0.0% work from home; Mean travel time to work: 0.0 minutes

KYSORVILLE (CDP). Covers a land area of 0.827 square miles and a water area of 0 square miles. Located at 42.65° N. Lat; 77.79° W. Long. Elevation is 623 feet.
Population: 156; Growth (since 2000): n/a; Density: 188.7 persons per square mile; Race: 100.0% White, 0.0% Black/African American, 0.0% Asian, 0.0% American Indian/Alaska Native, 0.0% Native Hawaiian/Other Pacific Islander, 0.0% Two or more races, 5.1% Hispanic of any race; Average household size: 2.94; Median age: 34.3; Age under 18: 32.1%; Age 65 and over: 11.5%; Males per 100 females: 96.4; Marriage status: 20.8% never married, 73.6% now married, 5.7% separated, 0.0% widowed, 5.7% divorced; Foreign born: 0.0%; Speak English only: 100.0%; With disability: 18.6%; Veterans: 17.0%; Ancestry: 23.7% English, 17.3% German, 10.3% Irish, 9.0% Italian, 6.4% American
Employment: 6.2% management, business, and financial, 0.0% computer, engineering, and science, 4.6% education, legal, community service, arts, and media, 0.0% healthcare practitioners, 43.1% service, 7.7% sales and office, 29.2% natural resources, construction, and maintenance, 9.2% production, transportation, and material moving
Income: Per capita: $21,767; Median household: $60,694; Average household: $61,594; Households with income of $100,000 or more: 11.4%; Poverty rate: 45.0%
Educational Attainment: High school diploma or higher: 64.3%; Bachelor's degree or higher: 11.2%; Graduate/professional degree or higher: 3.1%
Housing: Homeownership rate: 94.3%; Median home value: $46,700; Median year structure built: 1976; Homeowner vacancy rate: 0.0%; Median selected monthly owner costs: $850 with a mortgage, $336 without a mortgage; Median gross rent: n/a per month; Rental vacancy rate: 0.0%
Health Insurance: 98.1% have insurance; 75.0% have private insurance; 61.5% have public insurance; 1.9% do not have insurance; 0.0% of children under 18 do not have insurance
Transportation: Commute: 100.0% car, 0.0% public transportation, 0.0% walk, 0.0% work from home; Mean travel time to work: 26.7 minutes

LAKEVILLE (CDP). Covers a land area of 0.667 square miles and a water area of 0 square miles. Located at 42.84° N. Lat; 77.70° W. Long. Elevation is 823 feet.
Population: 1,055; Growth (since 2000): n/a; Density: 1,580.8 persons per square mile; Race: 95.5% White, 0.0% Black/African American, 4.5% Asian, 0.0% American Indian/Alaska Native, 0.0% Native Hawaiian/Other Pacific Islander, 0.0% Two or more races, 0.0% Hispanic of any race; Average household size: 3.80; Median age: 26.3; Age under 18: 35.5%; Age 65 and over: 3.8%; Males per 100 females: 84.8; Marriage status: 17.3% never married, 62.9% now married, 19.5% separated, 1.8% widowed, 17.9% divorced; Foreign born: 2.7%; Speak English only: 94.3%; With disability: 7.2%; Veterans: 15.1%; Ancestry: 31.6% Irish, 23.2% Dutch, 17.8% English, 16.0% German, 2.7% Italian
Employment: 19.8% management, business, and financial, 3.1% computer, engineering, and science, 2.4% education, legal, community service, arts, and media, 0.0% healthcare practitioners, 29.0% service, 17.4% sales and office, 15.9% natural resources, construction, and maintenance, 12.3% production, transportation, and material moving
Income: Per capita: $13,697; Median household: $37,500; Average household: $49,951; Households with income of $100,000 or more: 4.7%; Poverty rate: 56.8%
Educational Attainment: High school diploma or higher: 78.4%; Bachelor's degree or higher: 4.4%; Graduate/professional degree or higher: 1.8%
Housing: Homeownership rate: 45.7%; Median home value: $115,400; Median year structure built: 1977; Homeowner vacancy rate: 0.0%; Median selected monthly owner costs: $1,207 with a mortgage, n/a without a mortgage; Median gross rent: $856 per month; Rental vacancy rate: 0.0%
Health Insurance: 83.2% have insurance; 34.9% have private insurance; 56.4% have public insurance; 16.8% do not have insurance; 4.5% of children under 18 do not have insurance
Transportation: Commute: 99.5% car, 0.0% public transportation, 0.0% walk, 0.0% work from home; Mean travel time to work: 15.6 minutes

LEICESTER (town). Covers a land area of 33.929 square miles and a water area of 0.004 square miles. Located at 42.76° N. Lat; 77.90° W. Long. Elevation is 650 feet.
Population: 2,143; Growth (since 2000): -6.3%; Density: 63.2 persons per square mile; Race: 91.7% White, 0.3% Black/African American, 0.7% Asian, 0.0% American Indian/Alaska Native, 0.0% Native Hawaiian/Other Pacific Islander, 2.3% Two or more races, 6.8% Hispanic of any race; Average household size: 2.34; Median age: 44.2; Age under 18: 18.7%; Age 65 and over: 17.2%; Males per 100 females: 98.9; Marriage status: 30.9% never married, 52.4% now married, 2.2% separated, 4.7% widowed, 12.1% divorced; Foreign born: 5.8%; Speak English only: 92.0%; With disability: 10.4%; Veterans: 9.4%; Ancestry: 29.2% German, 27.6% Italian, 18.3% Irish, 11.7% Polish, 9.2% English
Employment: 9.6% management, business, and financial, 0.8% computer, engineering, and science, 9.4% education, legal, community service, arts, and media, 3.7% healthcare practitioners, 17.3% service, 22.7% sales and office, 24.2% natural resources, construction, and maintenance, 12.3% production, transportation, and material moving
Income: Per capita: $24,186; Median household: $52,006; Average household: $56,381; Households with income of $100,000 or more: 10.5%; Poverty rate: 14.0%
Educational Attainment: High school diploma or higher: 84.0%; Bachelor's degree or higher: 14.6%; Graduate/professional degree or higher: 4.4%
Housing: Homeownership rate: 70.2%; Median home value: $98,300; Median year structure built: 1970; Homeowner vacancy rate: 1.5%; Median selected monthly owner costs: $1,127 with a mortgage, $489 without a mortgage; Median gross rent: $786 per month; Rental vacancy rate: 0.0%
Health Insurance: 94.2% have insurance; 73.7% have private insurance; 37.6% have public insurance; 5.8% do not have insurance; 3.7% of children under 18 do not have insurance
Transportation: Commute: 86.1% car, 0.0% public transportation, 4.3% walk, 8.0% work from home; Mean travel time to work: 20.4 minutes

LEICESTER (village). Covers a land area of 0.367 square miles and a water area of 0 square miles. Located at 42.77° N. Lat; 77.90° W. Long. Elevation is 650 feet.
Population: 444; Growth (since 2000): -5.3%; Density: 1,209.1 persons per square mile; Race: 97.7% White, 0.0% Black/African American, 0.9% Asian, 0.0% American Indian/Alaska Native, 0.0% Native Hawaiian/Other Pacific Islander, 1.4% Two or more races, 0.2% Hispanic of any race; Average household size: 2.23; Median age: 44.9; Age under 18: 21.6%; Age 65 and over: 21.2%; Males per 100 females: 89.5; Marriage status: 26.6% never married, 53.8% now married, 1.4% separated, 5.7% widowed, 13.9% divorced; Foreign born: 0.9%; Speak English only: 96.4%; With disability: 9.2%; Veterans: 12.9%; Ancestry: 35.1% German, 30.2% Italian, 26.1% Irish, 16.0% English, 6.3% Polish
Employment: 10.1% management, business, and financial, 1.7% computer, engineering, and science, 9.7% education, legal, community service, arts, and media, 10.5% healthcare practitioners, 23.5% service, 22.3% sales and office, 11.8% natural resources, construction, and maintenance, 10.5% production, transportation, and material moving
Income: Per capita: $29,692; Median household: $60,893; Average household: $66,577; Households with income of $100,000 or more: 23.1%; Poverty rate: 1.4%
Educational Attainment: High school diploma or higher: 87.8%; Bachelor's degree or higher: 15.7%; Graduate/professional degree or higher: 7.1%
Housing: Homeownership rate: 71.4%; Median home value: $100,700; Median year structure built: 1946; Homeowner vacancy rate: 6.6%; Median selected monthly owner costs: $1,107 with a mortgage, $483 without a mortgage; Median gross rent: $763 per month; Rental vacancy rate: 0.0%
Health Insurance: 96.2% have insurance; 85.6% have private insurance; 32.0% have public insurance; 3.8% do not have insurance; 0.0% of children under 18 do not have insurance
Transportation: Commute: 100.0% car, 0.0% public transportation, 0.0% walk, 0.0% work from home; Mean travel time to work: 21.1 minutes

LIMA (town). Covers a land area of 31.891 square miles and a water area of 0.053 square miles. Located at 42.90° N. Lat; 77.61° W. Long. Elevation is 827 feet.
Population: 4,219; Growth (since 2000): -7.1%; Density: 132.3 persons per square mile; Race: 95.8% White, 0.3% Black/African American, 1.9% Asian, 0.0% American Indian/Alaska Native, 0.1% Native Hawaiian/Other Pacific Islander, 1.8% Two or more races, 1.8% Hispanic of any race;

Average household size: 2.39; Median age: 42.2; Age under 18: 19.9%; Age 65 and over: 16.5%; Males per 100 females: 97.6; Marriage status: 31.4% never married, 55.1% now married, 1.5% separated, 6.1% widowed, 7.3% divorced; Foreign born: 6.6%; Speak English only: 94.2%; With disability: 9.1%; Veterans: 8.4%; Ancestry: 28.5% German, 21.2% Irish, 17.3% English, 12.4% Italian, 8.1% American

Employment: 13.2% management, business, and financial, 6.2% computer, engineering, and science, 15.5% education, legal, community service, arts, and media, 8.6% healthcare practitioners, 18.5% service, 16.1% sales and office, 8.5% natural resources, construction, and maintenance, 13.6% production, transportation, and material moving

Income: Per capita: $25,129; Median household: $51,333; Average household: $62,319; Households with income of $100,000 or more: 18.0%; Poverty rate: 11.1%

Educational Attainment: High school diploma or higher: 93.4%; Bachelor's degree or higher: 29.5%; Graduate/professional degree or higher: 13.2%

School District(s)

Honeoye Falls-Lima Central SD (KG-12)

   2014-15 Enrollment: 2,298 . . . . (585) 624-7010

Housing: Homeownership rate: 73.1%; Median home value: $140,200; Median year structure built: 1967; Homeowner vacancy rate: 0.0%; Median selected monthly owner costs: $1,374 with a mortgage, $534 without a mortgage; Median gross rent: $664 per month; Rental vacancy rate: 2.1%

Health Insurance: 93.4% have insurance; 79.9% have private insurance; 30.1% have public insurance; 6.6% do not have insurance; 5.8% of children under 18 do not have insurance

Transportation: Commute: 87.9% car, 0.8% public transportation, 7.0% walk, 3.4% work from home; Mean travel time to work: 23.6 minutes

Additional Information Contacts

Town of Lima. . . . . (585) 582-1130
  http://www.lima-ny.org

LIMA (village). Covers a land area of 1.346 square miles and a water area of 0 square miles. Located at 42.91° N. Lat; 77.61° W. Long. Elevation is 827 feet.

Population: 2,433; Growth (since 2000): -1.1%; Density: 1,807.9 persons per square mile; Race: 93.4% White, 0.5% Black/African American, 2.6% Asian, 0.0% American Indian/Alaska Native, 0.2% Native Hawaiian/Other Pacific Islander, 3.1% Two or more races, 3.0% Hispanic of any race; Average household size: 2.40; Median age: 35.8; Age under 18: 21.3%; Age 65 and over: 13.9%; Males per 100 females: 93.1; Marriage status: 37.5% never married, 49.2% now married, 1.6% separated, 4.8% widowed, 8.5% divorced; Foreign born: 5.7%; Speak English only: 93.1%; With disability: 9.6%; Veterans: 6.1%; Ancestry: 29.2% German, 27.5% Irish, 15.0% English, 13.2% Italian, 4.8% Polish

Employment: 13.4% management, business, and financial, 5.8% computer, engineering, and science, 16.2% education, legal, community service, arts, and media, 7.2% healthcare practitioners, 19.2% service, 18.2% sales and office, 6.4% natural resources, construction, and maintenance, 13.8% production, transportation, and material moving

Income: Per capita: $23,888; Median household: $51,581; Average household: $61,493; Households with income of $100,000 or more: 19.5%; Poverty rate: 17.0%

Educational Attainment: High school diploma or higher: 91.6%; Bachelor's degree or higher: 30.9%; Graduate/professional degree or higher: 13.6%

School District(s)

Honeoye Falls-Lima Central SD (KG-12)

   2014-15 Enrollment: 2,298 . . . . (585) 624-7010

Housing: Homeownership rate: 62.4%; Median home value: $132,600; Median year structure built: 1968; Homeowner vacancy rate: 0.0%; Median selected monthly owner costs: $1,325 with a mortgage, $508 without a mortgage; Median gross rent: $658 per month; Rental vacancy rate: 2.7%

Health Insurance: 93.1% have insurance; 76.2% have private insurance; 31.6% have public insurance; 6.9% do not have insurance; 4.2% of children under 18 do not have insurance

Transportation: Commute: 86.9% car, 0.4% public transportation, 8.5% walk, 2.6% work from home; Mean travel time to work: 22.5 minutes

LINWOOD (CDP). Covers a land area of 0.929 square miles and a water area of 0 square miles. Located at 42.90° N. Lat; 77.95° W. Long. Elevation is 938 feet.

Population: 64; Growth (since 2000): n/a; Density: 68.9 persons per square mile; Race: 90.6% White, 9.4% Black/African American, 0.0%

Asian, 0.0% American Indian/Alaska Native, 0.0% Native Hawaiian/Other Pacific Islander, 0.0% Two or more races, 0.0% Hispanic of any race; Average household size: 1.88; Median age: 37.8; Age under 18: 35.9%; Age 65 and over: 32.8%; Males per 100 females: 100.0; Marriage status: 14.6% never married, 58.5% now married, 0.0% separated, 0.0% widowed, 26.8% divorced; Foreign born: 0.0%; Speak English only: 100.0%; With disability: 0.0%; Veterans: 19.5%; Ancestry: 53.1% English, 53.1% Irish, 23.4% German, 10.9% French

Employment: 100.0% management, business, and financial, 0.0% computer, engineering, and science, 0.0% education, legal, community service, arts, and media, 0.0% healthcare practitioners, 0.0% service, 0.0% sales and office, 0.0% natural resources, construction, and maintenance, 0.0% production, transportation, and material moving

Income: Per capita: $35,081; Median household: n/a; Average household: $66,459; Households with income of $100,000 or more: 23.5%; Poverty rate: n/a

Educational Attainment: High school diploma or higher: 100.0%; Bachelor's degree or higher: 36.6%; Graduate/professional degree or higher: 22.0%

Housing: Homeownership rate: 100.0%; Median home value: $152,600; Median year structure built: 1974; Homeowner vacancy rate: 0.0%; Median selected monthly owner costs: n/a with a mortgage, n/a without a mortgage; Median gross rent: n/a per month; Rental vacancy rate: 0.0%

Health Insurance: 82.8% have insurance; 46.9% have private insurance; 68.8% have public insurance; 17.2% do not have insurance; 0.0% of children under 18 do not have insurance

Transportation: Commute: 100.0% car, 0.0% public transportation, 0.0% walk, 0.0% work from home; Mean travel time to work: 0.0 minutes

LIVONIA (town). Covers a land area of 38.262 square miles and a water area of 2.812 square miles. Located at 42.81° N. Lat; 77.65° W. Long. Elevation is 1,033 feet.

Population: 7,716; Growth (since 2000): 5.9%; Density: 201.7 persons per square mile; Race: 97.2% White, 0.3% Black/African American, 0.9% Asian, 0.2% American Indian/Alaska Native, 0.0% Native Hawaiian/Other Pacific Islander, 1.4% Two or more races, 0.5% Hispanic of any race; Average household size: 2.62; Median age: 39.7; Age under 18: 25.9%; Age 65 and over: 13.8%; Males per 100 females: 95.4; Marriage status: 25.9% never married, 56.6% now married, 3.6% separated, 5.1% widowed, 12.4% divorced; Foreign born: 1.3%; Speak English only: 97.0%; With disability: 9.9%; Veterans: 10.8%; Ancestry: 32.1% German, 26.0% Irish, 15.4% English, 13.4% Italian, 9.4% Dutch

Employment: 20.9% management, business, and financial, 7.3% computer, engineering, and science, 10.0% education, legal, community service, arts, and media, 3.9% healthcare practitioners, 17.0% service, 22.1% sales and office, 10.2% natural resources, construction, and maintenance, 8.7% production, transportation, and material moving

Income: Per capita: $27,878; Median household: $62,478; Average household: $71,864; Households with income of $100,000 or more: 23.9%; Poverty rate: 12.0%

Educational Attainment: High school diploma or higher: 94.3%; Bachelor's degree or higher: 28.9%; Graduate/professional degree or higher: 10.3%

School District(s)

Livonia Central SD (PK-12)

   2014-15 Enrollment: 1,665 . . . . (585) 346-4000

Housing: Homeownership rate: 79.0%; Median home value: $150,800; Median year structure built: 1970; Homeowner vacancy rate: 1.2%; Median selected monthly owner costs: $1,523 with a mortgage, $636 without a mortgage; Median gross rent: $818 per month; Rental vacancy rate: 3.3%

Health Insurance: 93.3% have insurance; 74.4% have private insurance; 32.6% have public insurance; 6.7% do not have insurance; 1.8% of children under 18 do not have insurance

Transportation: Commute: 96.3% car, 0.2% public transportation, 0.5% walk, 2.4% work from home; Mean travel time to work: 25.9 minutes

Additional Information Contacts

Town of Livonia . . . . (585) 346-3710
  http://www.livoniany.org

LIVONIA (village). Covers a land area of 1.007 square miles and a water area of 0 square miles. Located at 42.82° N. Lat; 77.67° W. Long. Elevation is 1,033 feet.

Population: 1,196; Growth (since 2000): -12.9%; Density: 1,187.7 persons per square mile; Race: 97.1% White, 0.4% Black/African American, 0.9% Asian, 0.0% American Indian/Alaska Native, 0.0% Native Hawaiian/Other

Pacific Islander, 1.6% Two or more races, 0.0% Hispanic of any race; Average household size: 2.25; Median age: 38.8; Age under 18: 24.9%; Age 65 and over: 10.5%; Males per 100 females: 92.0; Marriage status: 29.3% never married, 46.8% now married, 3.6% separated, 6.8% widowed, 17.1% divorced; Foreign born: 1.3%; Speak English only: 93.9%; With disability: 14.0%; Veterans: 8.4%; Ancestry: 30.2% German, 20.1% Irish, 17.0% Italian, 16.3% English, 8.0% American

Employment: 17.4% management, business, and financial, 3.7% computer, engineering, and science, 11.7% education, legal, community service, arts, and media, 6.0% healthcare practitioners, 21.5% service, 23.6% sales and office, 9.0% natural resources, construction, and maintenance, 7.1% production, transportation, and material moving

Income: Per capita: $25,427; Median household: $46,250; Average household: $56,423; Households with income of $100,000 or more: 14.7%; Poverty rate: 18.8%

Educational Attainment: High school diploma or higher: 96.7%; Bachelor's degree or higher: 31.6%; Graduate/professional degree or higher: 13.4%

School District(s)

Livonia Central SD (PK-12)

   2014-15 Enrollment: 1,665 . . . . (585) 346-4000

Housing: Homeownership rate: 60.6%; Median home value: $131,600; Median year structure built: 1953; Homeowner vacancy rate: 3.0%; Median selected monthly owner costs: $1,456 with a mortgage, $665 without a mortgage; Median gross rent: $672 per month; Rental vacancy rate: 8.9%

Health Insurance: 94.0% have insurance; 76.3% have private insurance; 29.7% have public insurance; 6.0% do not have insurance; 0.0% of children under 18 do not have insurance

Transportation: Commute: 91.7% car, 0.0% public transportation, 3.2% walk, 0.7% work from home; Mean travel time to work: 25.0 minutes

LIVONIA CENTER (CDP).

Covers a land area of 0.817 square miles and a water area of 0 square miles. Located at 42.82° N. Lat; 77.64° W. Long. Elevation is 1,086 feet.

Population: 236; Growth (since 2000): n/a; Density: 289.0 persons per square mile; Race: 100.0% White, 0.0% Black/African American, 0.0% Asian, 0.0% American Indian/Alaska Native, 0.0% Native Hawaiian/Other Pacific Islander, 0.0% Two or more races, 0.0% Hispanic of any race; Average household size: 2.50; Median age: 50.0; Age under 18: 19.9%; Age 65 and over: 8.5%; Males per 100 females: 94.9; Marriage status: 25.7% never married, 67.8% now married, 13.6% separated, 6.5% widowed, 0.0% divorced; Foreign born: 0.0%; Speak English only: 100.0%; With disability: 11.0%; Veterans: 15.3%; Ancestry: 60.6% Irish, 41.5% Dutch, 14.4% English, 12.3% Italian, 6.4% French

Employment: 0.0% management, business, and financial, 22.8% computer, engineering, and science, 36.2% education, legal, community service, arts, and media, 0.0% healthcare practitioners, 0.0% service, 40.9% sales and office, 0.0% natural resources, construction, and maintenance, 0.0% production, transportation, and material moving

Income: Per capita: $31,822; Median household: $72,300; Average household: $76,391; Households with income of $100,000 or more: 32.2%; Poverty rate: 4.7%

Educational Attainment: High school diploma or higher: 93.5%; Bachelor's degree or higher: 45.3%; Graduate/professional degree or higher: 17.1%

Housing: Homeownership rate: 92.2%; Median home value: $162,500; Median year structure built: 1983; Homeowner vacancy rate: 0.0%; Median selected monthly owner costs: n/a with a mortgage, n/a without a mortgage; Median gross rent: n/a per month; Rental vacancy rate: 0.0%

Health Insurance: 100.0% have insurance; 83.1% have private insurance; 16.9% have public insurance; 0.0% do not have insurance; 0.0% of children under 18 do not have insurance

Transportation: Commute: 100.0% car, 0.0% public transportation, 0.0% walk, 0.0% work from home; Mean travel time to work: 32.1 minutes

MOUNT MORRIS (town).

Covers a land area of 50.205 square miles and a water area of 0.106 square miles. Located at 42.66° N. Lat; 77.90° W. Long. Elevation is 630 feet.

Population: 4,398; Growth (since 2000): -3.7%; Density: 87.6 persons per square mile; Race: 92.3% White, 3.0% Black/African American, 0.2% Asian, 0.0% American Indian/Alaska Native, 0.0% Native Hawaiian/Other Pacific Islander, 1.5% Two or more races, 16.3% Hispanic of any race; Average household size: 2.46; Median age: 43.6; Age under 18: 21.0%; Age 65 and over: 21.1%; Males per 100 females: 95.7; Marriage status: 32.3% never married, 46.0% now married, 2.1% separated, 9.1%

widowed, 12.6% divorced; Foreign born: 1.5%; Speak English only: 80.6%; With disability: 18.8%; Veterans: 7.8%; Ancestry: 27.1% German, 19.6% Italian, 16.4% Irish, 7.9% English, 5.5% American

Employment: 8.5% management, business, and financial, 0.9% computer, engineering, and science, 8.0% education, legal, community service, arts, and media, 4.6% healthcare practitioners, 26.1% service, 25.1% sales and office, 9.1% natural resources, construction, and maintenance, 17.7% production, transportation, and material moving

Income: Per capita: $19,094; Median household: $45,283; Average household: $47,940; Households with income of $100,000 or more: 7.5%; Poverty rate: 20.4%

Educational Attainment: High school diploma or higher: 74.6%; Bachelor's degree or higher: 9.4%; Graduate/professional degree or higher: 4.9%

School District(s)

Mount Morris Central SD (KG-12)

   2014-15 Enrollment: 550 . . . . (585) 658-2568

Housing: Homeownership rate: 61.8%; Median home value: $79,500; Median year structure built: Before 1940; Homeowner vacancy rate: 1.4%; Median selected monthly owner costs: $1,130 with a mortgage, $542 without a mortgage; Median gross rent: $662 per month; Rental vacancy rate: 5.5%

Health Insurance: 86.6% have insurance; 55.0% have private insurance; 46.2% have public insurance; 13.4% do not have insurance; 5.2% of children under 18 do not have insurance

Transportation: Commute: 89.9% car, 1.5% public transportation, 1.4% walk, 0.3% work from home; Mean travel time to work: 18.5 minutes

Additional Information Contacts

Town of Mount Morris . . . . (585) 658-2730

   http://www.mountmorrisny.com/government/town.asp

MOUNT MORRIS (village).

Covers a land area of 2.048 square miles and a water area of 0 square miles. Located at 42.72° N. Lat; 77.88° W. Long. Elevation is 630 feet.

Population: 2,505; Growth (since 2000): -23.3%; Density: 1,223.4 persons per square mile; Race: 92.1% White, 4.8% Black/African American, 0.0% Asian, 0.0% American Indian/Alaska Native, 0.0% Native Hawaiian/Other Pacific Islander, 2.2% Two or more races, 16.0% Hispanic of any race; Average household size: 2.20; Median age: 39.0; Age under 18: 22.3%; Age 65 and over: 14.0%; Males per 100 females: 98.7; Marriage status: 34.7% never married, 43.7% now married, 3.9% separated, 6.8% widowed, 14.8% divorced; Foreign born: 2.1%; Speak English only: 93.4%; With disability: 20.6%; Veterans: 9.0%; Ancestry: 27.6% Italian, 23.1% German, 17.1% Irish, 10.1% English, 5.3% American

Employment: 9.3% management, business, and financial, 1.5% computer, engineering, and science, 7.3% education, legal, community service, arts, and media, 3.2% healthcare practitioners, 32.7% service, 26.8% sales and office, 8.1% natural resources, construction, and maintenance, 11.1% production, transportation, and material moving

Income: Per capita: $20,988; Median household: $36,875; Average household: $45,516; Households with income of $100,000 or more: 7.3%; Poverty rate: 21.4%

Educational Attainment: High school diploma or higher: 84.5%; Bachelor's degree or higher: 11.5%; Graduate/professional degree or higher: 6.7%

School District(s)

Mount Morris Central SD (KG-12)

   2014-15 Enrollment: 550 . . . . (585) 658-2568

Housing: Homeownership rate: 48.5%; Median home value: $65,800; Median year structure built: Before 1940; Homeowner vacancy rate: 2.5%; Median selected monthly owner costs: $1,084 with a mortgage, $542 without a mortgage; Median gross rent: $640 per month; Rental vacancy rate: 5.9%

Health Insurance: 91.7% have insurance; 60.2% have private insurance; 47.1% have public insurance; 8.3% do not have insurance; 0.0% of children under 18 do not have insurance

Safety: Violent crime rate: 27.7 per 10,000 population; Property crime rate: 232.1 per 10,000 population

Transportation: Commute: 97.2% car, 0.2% public transportation, 2.2% walk, 0.4% work from home; Mean travel time to work: 18.0 minutes

Additional Information Contacts

Village of Mount Morris . . . . (585) 658-4160

   http://www.mountmorrisny.com/government/village.asp

NORTH DANSVILLE (town).
Covers a land area of 9.859 square miles and a water area of 0 square miles. Located at 42.56° N. Lat; 77.69° W. Long. Elevation is 705 feet.

Population: 5,450; Growth (since 2000): -5.0%; Density: 552.8 persons per square mile; Race: 98.7% White, 0.6% Black/African American, 0.0% Asian, 0.0% American Indian/Alaska Native, 0.0% Native Hawaiian/Other Pacific Islander, 0.5% Two or more races, 1.9% Hispanic of any race; Average household size: 2.21; Median age: 48.3; Age under 18: 20.3%; Age 65 and over: 17.0%; Males per 100 females: 89.5; Marriage status: 32.0% never married, 48.3% now married, 2.7% separated, 8.6% widowed, 11.1% divorced; Foreign born: 1.3%; Speak English only: 98.1%; With disability: 17.5%; Veterans: 12.7%; Ancestry: 26.7% German, 21.7% Irish, 10.4% English, 9.4% Polish, 9.2% American

Employment: 14.6% management, business, and financial, 1.0% computer, engineering, and science, 16.2% education, legal, community service, arts, and media, 5.3% healthcare practitioners, 14.7% service, 23.2% sales and office, 11.8% natural resources, construction, and maintenance, 13.2% production, transportation, and material moving

Income: Per capita: $25,327; Median household: $40,246; Average household: $55,848; Households with income of $100,000 or more: 14.5%; Poverty rate: 21.0%

Educational Attainment: High school diploma or higher: 82.6%; Bachelor's degree or higher: 20.0%; Graduate/professional degree or higher: 12.4%

Housing: Homeownership rate: 64.6%; Median home value: $85,100; Median year structure built: 1940; Homeowner vacancy rate: 1.5%; Median selected monthly owner costs: $1,077 with a mortgage, $425 without a mortgage; Median gross rent: $652 per month; Rental vacancy rate: 4.5%

Health Insurance: 91.5% have insurance; 65.4% have private insurance; 45.1% have public insurance; 8.5% do not have insurance; 6.6% of children under 18 do not have insurance

Transportation: Commute: 84.9% car, 0.4% public transportation, 9.5% walk, 3.2% work from home; Mean travel time to work: 26.0 minutes

NUNDA (town).
Covers a land area of 37.094 square miles and a water area of 0.027 square miles. Located at 42.57° N. Lat; 77.88° W. Long. Elevation is 942 feet.

History: Incorporated 1839.

Population: 3,007; Growth (since 2000): -0.3%; Density: 81.1 persons per square mile; Race: 97.8% White, 0.4% Black/African American, 0.5% Asian, 0.5% American Indian/Alaska Native, 0.0% Native Hawaiian/Other Pacific Islander, 0.8% Two or more races, 0.5% Hispanic of any race; Average household size: 2.31; Median age: 45.9; Age under 18: 22.0%; Age 65 and over: 20.2%; Males per 100 females: 96.4; Marriage status: 21.0% never married, 59.6% now married, 1.5% separated, 8.4% widowed, 11.0% divorced; Foreign born: 1.3%; Speak English only: 98.1%; With disability: 13.3%; Veterans: 14.1%; Ancestry: 28.8% German, 24.4% Irish, 23.1% English, 8.9% American, 7.1% Italian

Employment: 6.6% management, business, and financial, 4.8% computer, engineering, and science, 9.9% education, legal, community service, arts, and media, 7.2% healthcare practitioners, 13.3% service, 27.3% sales and office, 19.0% natural resources, construction, and maintenance, 11.8% production, transportation, and material moving

Income: Per capita: $23,851; Median household: $45,859; Average household: $54,512; Households with income of $100,000 or more: 14.5%; Poverty rate: 13.6%

Educational Attainment: High school diploma or higher: 91.5%; Bachelor's degree or higher: 18.5%; Graduate/professional degree or higher: 9.2%

School District(s)
Dalton-Nunda Central SD (Keshequa) (PK-12)
   2014-15 Enrollment: 749 . . . . (585) 468-2541

Housing: Homeownership rate: 74.2%; Median home value: $94,600; Median year structure built: 1942; Homeowner vacancy rate: 0.0%; Median selected monthly owner costs: $1,113 with a mortgage, $476 without a mortgage; Median gross rent: $535 per month; Rental vacancy rate: 7.4%

Health Insurance: 95.1% have insurance; 73.4% have private insurance; 40.4% have public insurance; 4.9% do not have insurance; 5.4% of children under 18 do not have insurance

Safety: Violent crime rate: 10.1 per 10,000 population; Property crime rate: 26.9 per 10,000 population

Transportation: Commute: 89.4% car, 0.9% public transportation, 2.4% walk, 2.8% work from home; Mean travel time to work: 36.6 minutes

NUNDA (village).
Covers a land area of 0.993 square miles and a water area of 0 square miles. Located at 42.58° N. Lat; 77.94° W. Long. Elevation is 942 feet.

Population: 1,422; Growth (since 2000): 6.9%; Density: 1,431.4 persons per square mile; Race: 95.8% White, 0.8% Black/African American, 1.0% Asian, 1.1% American Indian/Alaska Native, 0.0% Native Hawaiian/Other Pacific Islander, 1.3% Two or more races, 1.1% Hispanic of any race; Average household size: 2.24; Median age: 43.8; Age under 18: 22.5%; Age 65 and over: 26.7%; Males per 100 females: 85.3; Marriage status: 24.3% never married, 54.5% now married, 1.8% separated, 9.0% widowed, 12.3% divorced; Foreign born: 2.8%; Speak English only: 96.4%; With disability: 20.3%; Veterans: 14.6%; Ancestry: 25.4% German, 22.7% Irish, 17.7% English, 12.9% American, 6.7% Italian

Employment: 3.1% management, business, and financial, 2.5% computer, engineering, and science, 11.7% education, legal, community service, arts, and media, 9.8% healthcare practitioners, 19.8% service, 34.2% sales and office, 11.9% natural resources, construction, and maintenance, 6.9% production, transportation, and material moving

Income: Per capita: $20,837; Median household: $40,167; Average household: $46,561; Households with income of $100,000 or more: 8.2%; Poverty rate: 23.1%

Educational Attainment: High school diploma or higher: 89.9%; Bachelor's degree or higher: 16.7%; Graduate/professional degree or higher: 8.0%

School District(s)
Dalton-Nunda Central SD (Keshequa) (PK-12)
   2014-15 Enrollment: 749 . . . . (585) 468-2541

Housing: Homeownership rate: 60.5%; Median home value: $87,100; Median year structure built: Before 1940; Homeowner vacancy rate: 0.0%; Median selected monthly owner costs: $1,041 with a mortgage, $487 without a mortgage; Median gross rent: $559 per month; Rental vacancy rate: 9.7%

Health Insurance: 97.1% have insurance; 66.5% have private insurance; 50.1% have public insurance; 2.9% do not have insurance; 3.8% of children under 18 do not have insurance

Transportation: Commute: 89.1% car, 2.2% public transportation, 4.4% walk, 1.8% work from home; Mean travel time to work: 33.3 minutes

OSSIAN (town).
Covers a land area of 39.635 square miles and a water area of 0.028 square miles. Located at 42.51° N. Lat; 77.77° W. Long. Elevation is 1,342 feet.

Population: 690; Growth (since 2000): -8.1%; Density: 17.4 persons per square mile; Race: 98.1% White, 0.0% Black/African American, 0.0% Asian, 0.0% American Indian/Alaska Native, 0.0% Native Hawaiian/Other Pacific Islander, 1.9% Two or more races, 1.0% Hispanic of any race; Average household size: 2.32; Median age: 50.7; Age under 18: 19.9%; Age 65 and over: 22.8%; Males per 100 females: 112.1; Marriage status: 12.5% never married, 69.9% now married, 2.1% separated, 7.7% widowed, 9.9% divorced; Foreign born: 0.0%; Speak English only: 100.0%; With disability: 13.2%; Veterans: 11.8%; Ancestry: 34.6% German, 17.7% English, 11.7% Dutch, 11.2% Irish, 10.0% American

Employment: 17.1% management, business, and financial, 5.4% computer, engineering, and science, 8.5% education, legal, community service, arts, and media, 3.5% healthcare practitioners, 17.4% service, 12.3% sales and office, 21.5% natural resources, construction, and maintenance, 14.2% production, transportation, and material moving

Income: Per capita: $29,489; Median household: $65,179; Average household: $67,753; Households with income of $100,000 or more: 21.9%; Poverty rate: 9.9%

Educational Attainment: High school diploma or higher: 93.4%; Bachelor's degree or higher: 20.5%; Graduate/professional degree or higher: 9.2%

Housing: Homeownership rate: 93.3%; Median home value: $111,800; Median year structure built: 1971; Homeowner vacancy rate: 0.0%; Median selected monthly owner costs: $1,247 with a mortgage, $487 without a mortgage; Median gross rent: $565 per month; Rental vacancy rate: 18.8%

Health Insurance: 96.2% have insurance; 80.0% have private insurance; 37.8% have public insurance; 3.8% do not have insurance; 0.7% of children under 18 do not have insurance

Transportation: Commute: 95.5% car, 0.0% public transportation, 0.0% walk, 2.6% work from home; Mean travel time to work: 26.9 minutes

PIFFARD (CDP). Covers a land area of 0.934 square miles and a water area of 0 square miles. Located at 42.83° N. Lat; 77.86° W. Long. Elevation is 568 feet.

Population: 260; Growth (since 2000): n/a; Density: 278.5 persons per square mile; Race: 100.0% White, 0.0% Black/African American, 0.0% Asian, 0.0% American Indian/Alaska Native, 0.0% Native Hawaiian/Other Pacific Islander, 0.0% Two or more races, 5.0% Hispanic of any race; Average household size: 2.39; Median age: 31.8; Age under 18: 21.9%; Age 65 and over: 15.4%; Males per 100 females: 113.6; Marriage status: 14.3% never married, 52.7% now married, 0.0% separated, 0.0% widowed, 33.0% divorced; Foreign born: 0.0%; Speak English only: 95.0%; With disability: 33.1%; Veterans: 8.4%; Ancestry: 16.9% Italian, 16.5% Scottish, 14.6% English, 12.7% Polish, 8.8% German

Employment: 26.6% management, business, and financial, 0.0% computer, engineering, and science, 0.0% education, legal, community service, arts, and media, 4.9% healthcare practitioners, 6.3% service, 37.8% sales and office, 11.9% natural resources, construction, and maintenance, 12.6% production, transportation, and material moving

Income: Per capita: $25,342; Median household: $55,750; Average household: $57,920; Households with income of $100,000 or more: 6.4%; Poverty rate: 2.3%

Educational Attainment: High school diploma or higher: 91.1%; Bachelor's degree or higher: 10.3%; Graduate/professional degree or higher: n/a

Housing: Homeownership rate: 56.9%; Median home value: $108,300; Median year structure built: 1962; Homeowner vacancy rate: 0.0%; Median selected monthly owner costs: $973 with a mortgage, $488 without a mortgage; Median gross rent: n/a per month; Rental vacancy rate: 0.0%

Health Insurance: 100.0% have insurance; 69.2% have private insurance; 55.4% have public insurance; 0.0% do not have insurance; 0.0% of children under 18 do not have insurance

Transportation: Commute: 82.5% car, 0.0% public transportation, 17.5% walk, 0.0% work from home; Mean travel time to work: 19.3 minutes

PORTAGE (town). Covers a land area of 26.399 square miles and a water area of 0.236 square miles. Located at 42.56° N. Lat; 77.99° W. Long. Elevation is 1,342 feet.

Population: 756; Growth (since 2000): -12.0%; Density: 28.6 persons per square mile; Race: 100.0% White, 0.0% Black/African American, 0.0% Asian, 0.0% American Indian/Alaska Native, 0.0% Native Hawaiian/Other Pacific Islander, 0.0% Two or more races, 1.2% Hispanic of any race; Average household size: 2.20; Median age: 46.2; Age under 18: 17.6%; Age 65 and over: 18.7%; Males per 100 females: 92.2; Marriage status: 22.0% never married, 59.5% now married, 4.0% separated, 7.3% widowed, 11.2% divorced; Foreign born: 1.3%; Speak English only: 98.2%; With disability: 18.3%; Veterans: 14.6%; Ancestry: 38.6% German, 19.4% English, 15.9% Irish, 10.2% Italian, 7.7% American

Employment: 9.5% management, business, and financial, 0.0% computer, engineering, and science, 6.3% education, legal, community service, arts, and media, 6.3% healthcare practitioners, 16.3% service, 22.9% sales and office, 16.6% natural resources, construction, and maintenance, 22.1% production, transportation, and material moving

Income: Per capita: $24,583; Median household: $43,636; Average household: $54,149; Households with income of $100,000 or more: 10.5%; Poverty rate: 15.6%

Educational Attainment: High school diploma or higher: 88.9%; Bachelor's degree or higher: 9.3%; Graduate/professional degree or higher: 4.3%

Housing: Homeownership rate: 80.5%; Median home value: $78,700; Median year structure built: 1964; Homeowner vacancy rate: 3.5%; Median selected monthly owner costs: $942 with a mortgage, $487 without a mortgage; Median gross rent: $665 per month; Rental vacancy rate: 0.0%

Health Insurance: 95.2% have insurance; 74.1% have private insurance; 39.0% have public insurance; 4.8% do not have insurance; 0.8% of children under 18 do not have insurance

Transportation: Commute: 93.7% car, 0.9% public transportation, 0.0% walk, 4.8% work from home; Mean travel time to work: 30.0 minutes

RETSOF (CDP). Covers a land area of 0.451 square miles and a water area of 0 square miles. Located at 42.83° N. Lat; 77.88° W. Long. Elevation is 728 feet.

Population: 214; Growth (since 2000): n/a; Density: 474.9 persons per square mile; Race: 86.9% White, 0.0% Black/African American, 0.0% Asian, 0.0% American Indian/Alaska Native, 0.0% Native Hawaiian/Other Pacific Islander, 13.1% Two or more races, 0.0% Hispanic of any race;

Average household size: 3.01; Median age: 36.8; Age under 18: 21.5%; Age 65 and over: 7.9%; Males per 100 females: 86.8; Marriage status: 27.1% never married, 57.1% now married, 0.0% separated, 5.6% widowed, 10.2% divorced; Foreign born: 0.0%; Speak English only: 100.0%; With disability: 9.3%; Veterans: 0.0%; Ancestry: 20.6% American, 12.1% Swedish, 11.7% German, 11.2% Irish, 8.9% British

Employment: 0.0% management, business, and financial, 9.1% computer, engineering, and science, 16.7% education, legal, community service, arts, and media, 8.3% healthcare practitioners, 22.0% service, 30.3% sales and office, 0.0% natural resources, construction, and maintenance, 13.6% production, transportation, and material moving

Income: Per capita: $27,471; Median household: $70,156; Average household: $77,990; Households with income of $100,000 or more: 15.5%; Poverty rate: n/a

Educational Attainment: High school diploma or higher: 100.0%; Bachelor's degree or higher: 29.4%; Graduate/professional degree or higher: 4.9%

School District(s)

York Central SD (KG-12)
    2014-15 Enrollment: 742 . . . . (585) 243-1730

Housing: Homeownership rate: 100.0%; Median home value: $85,000; Median year structure built: 1940; Homeowner vacancy rate: 0.0%; Median selected monthly owner costs: $882 with a mortgage, n/a without a mortgage; Median gross rent: n/a per month; Rental vacancy rate: 0.0%

Health Insurance: 95.8% have insurance; 89.3% have private insurance; 14.5% have public insurance; 4.2% do not have insurance; 19.6% of children under 18 do not have insurance

Transportation: Commute: 86.4% car, 0.0% public transportation, 13.6% walk, 0.0% work from home; Mean travel time to work: 21.6 minutes

SCOTTSBURG (CDP). Covers a land area of 0.164 square miles and a water area of 0 square miles. Located at 42.66° N. Lat; 77.71° W. Long. Elevation is 925 feet.

Population: 116; Growth (since 2000): n/a; Density: 705.2 persons per square mile; Race: 100.0% White, 0.0% Black/African American, 0.0% Asian, 0.0% American Indian/Alaska Native, 0.0% Native Hawaiian/Other Pacific Islander, 0.0% Two or more races, 0.0% Hispanic of any race; Average household size: 2.23; Median age: 49.3; Age under 18: 9.5%; Age 65 and over: 14.7%; Males per 100 females: 112.7; Marriage status: 18.7% never married, 61.7% now married, 0.0% separated, 12.1% widowed, 7.5% divorced; Foreign born: 0.0%; Speak English only: 100.0%; With disability: 18.1%; Veterans: 7.6%; Ancestry: 41.4% German, 17.2% American, 15.5% Irish, 12.1% Italian, 6.0% English

Employment: 0.0% management, business, and financial, 0.0% computer, engineering, and science, 16.9% education, legal, community service, arts, and media, 0.0% healthcare practitioners, 22.0% service, 27.1% sales and office, 11.9% natural resources, construction, and maintenance, 22.0% production, transportation, and material moving

Income: Per capita: $23,891; Median household: $60,500; Average household: $54,163; Households with income of $100,000 or more: n/a; Poverty rate: 13.8%

Educational Attainment: High school diploma or higher: 97.0%; Bachelor's degree or higher: 21.2%; Graduate/professional degree or higher: 11.1%

Housing: Homeownership rate: 94.2%; Median home value: $83,800; Median year structure built: Before 1940; Homeowner vacancy rate: 0.0%; Median selected monthly owner costs: $838 with a mortgage, $490 without a mortgage; Median gross rent: n/a per month; Rental vacancy rate: 0.0%

Health Insurance: 96.6% have insurance; 89.7% have private insurance; 34.5% have public insurance; 3.4% do not have insurance; 0.0% of children under 18 do not have insurance

Transportation: Commute: 100.0% car, 0.0% public transportation, 0.0% walk, 0.0% work from home; Mean travel time to work: 35.3 minutes

SOUTH LIMA (CDP). Covers a land area of 0.883 square miles and a water area of 0 square miles. Located at 42.86° N. Lat; 77.68° W. Long. Elevation is 889 feet.

Population: 252; Growth (since 2000): n/a; Density: 285.4 persons per square mile; Race: 100.0% White, 0.0% Black/African American, 0.0% Asian, 0.0% American Indian/Alaska Native, 0.0% Native Hawaiian/Other Pacific Islander, 0.0% Two or more races, 0.0% Hispanic of any race; Average household size: 2.10; Median age: 55.3; Age under 18: 16.7%; Age 65 and over: 34.5%; Males per 100 females: 105.1; Marriage status: 26.2% never married, 54.3% now married, 0.0% separated, 19.5% widowed, 0.0% divorced; Foreign born: 4.0%; Speak English only: 100.0%;

With disability: 36.1%; Veterans: 15.7%; Ancestry: 25.4% Italian, 23.8% English, 19.8% Irish, 15.9% French, 12.7% American
Employment: 13.3% management, business, and financial, 0.0% computer, engineering, and science, 14.7% education, legal, community service, arts, and media, 10.7% healthcare practitioners, 10.7% service, 12.0% sales and office, 0.0% natural resources, construction, and maintenance, 38.7% production, transportation, and material moving
Income: Per capita: $24,202; Median household: $45,250; Average household: $49,873; Households with income of $100,000 or more: 6.7%; Poverty rate: 7.5%
Educational Attainment: High school diploma or higher: 90.5%; Bachelor's degree or higher: 13.8%; Graduate/professional degree or higher: 5.2%
Housing: Homeownership rate: 73.3%; Median home value: $111,200; Median year structure built: Before 1940; Homeowner vacancy rate: 0.0%; Median selected monthly owner costs: $1,359 with a mortgage, $688 without a mortgage; Median gross rent: n/a per month; Rental vacancy rate: 0.0%
Health Insurance: 96.0% have insurance; 86.9% have private insurance; 57.1% have public insurance; 4.0% do not have insurance; 0.0% of children under 18 do not have insurance
Transportation: Commute: 89.3% car, 0.0% public transportation, 0.0% walk, 10.7% work from home; Mean travel time to work: 23.9 minutes

SPARTA (town). Covers a land area of 27.791 square miles and a water area of 0 square miles. Located at 42.63° N. Lat; 77.70° W. Long.
Population: 1,699; Growth (since 2000): 4.4%; Density: 61.1 persons per square mile; Race: 98.4% White, 0.0% Black/African American, 0.0% Asian, 1.0% American Indian/Alaska Native, 0.0% Native Hawaiian/Other Pacific Islander, 0.6% Two or more races, 1.2% Hispanic of any race; Average household size: 2.74; Median age: 43.8; Age under 18: 25.5%; Age 65 and over: 18.6%; Males per 100 females: 101.2; Marriage status: 17.0% never married, 65.0% now married, 1.6% separated, 7.9% widowed, 10.1% divorced; Foreign born: 2.7%; Speak English only: 96.1%; With disability: 11.9%; Veterans: 8.0%; Ancestry: 34.0% German, 15.8% Irish, 13.1% American, 10.7% Italian, 10.5% English
Employment: 8.6% management, business, and financial, 3.5% computer, engineering, and science, 8.5% education, legal, community service, arts, and media, 4.9% healthcare practitioners, 19.5% service, 22.2% sales and office, 16.0% natural resources, construction, and maintenance, 16.7% production, transportation, and material moving
Income: Per capita: $26,526; Median household: $57,614; Average household: $71,453; Households with income of $100,000 or more: 18.7%; Poverty rate: 7.0%
Educational Attainment: High school diploma or higher: 87.3%; Bachelor's degree or higher: 17.5%; Graduate/professional degree or higher: 9.8%
Housing: Homeownership rate: 95.3%; Median home value: $115,100; Median year structure built: 1972; Homeowner vacancy rate: 1.5%; Median selected monthly owner costs: $1,166 with a mortgage, $501 without a mortgage; Median gross rent: $833 per month; Rental vacancy rate: 0.0%
Health Insurance: 96.1% have insurance; 76.6% have private insurance; 36.7% have public insurance; 3.9% do not have insurance; 3.5% of children under 18 do not have insurance
Transportation: Commute: 94.3% car, 0.6% public transportation, 0.8% walk, 3.8% work from home; Mean travel time to work: 30.0 minutes

SPRINGWATER (town). Covers a land area of 53.105 square miles and a water area of 0.013 square miles. Located at 42.62° N. Lat; 77.57° W. Long. Elevation is 971 feet.
Population: 2,326; Growth (since 2000): 0.2%; Density: 43.8 persons per square mile; Race: 95.8% White, 1.1% Black/African American, 0.0% Asian, 0.7% American Indian/Alaska Native, 0.2% Native Hawaiian/Other Pacific Islander, 2.1% Two or more races, 0.0% Hispanic of any race; Average household size: 2.47; Median age: 42.3; Age under 18: 21.7%; Age 65 and over: 13.1%; Males per 100 females: 105.3; Marriage status: 22.3% never married, 60.7% now married, 2.8% separated, 5.5% widowed, 11.5% divorced; Foreign born: 2.0%; Speak English only: 97.7%; With disability: 15.1%; Veterans: 8.1%; Ancestry: 30.8% German, 16.5% English, 13.6% Irish, 10.5% Italian, 6.9% American
Employment: 12.7% management, business, and financial, 7.5% computer, engineering, and science, 11.2% education, legal, community service, arts, and media, 5.5% healthcare practitioners, 9.6% service, 18.7% sales and office, 17.7% natural resources, construction, and maintenance, 17.1% production, transportation, and material moving

Income: Per capita: $24,348; Median household: $51,389; Average household: $59,370; Households with income of $100,000 or more: 16.6%; Poverty rate: 12.6%
Educational Attainment: High school diploma or higher: 86.1%; Bachelor's degree or higher: 17.2%; Graduate/professional degree or higher: 5.1%
Housing: Homeownership rate: 88.6%; Median home value: $109,000; Median year structure built: 1964; Homeowner vacancy rate: 4.3%; Median selected monthly owner costs: $1,229 with a mortgage, $412 without a mortgage; Median gross rent: $734 per month; Rental vacancy rate: 11.5%
Health Insurance: 92.2% have insurance; 72.1% have private insurance; 33.2% have public insurance; 7.8% do not have insurance; 9.5% of children under 18 do not have insurance
Transportation: Commute: 94.7% car, 0.7% public transportation, 2.0% walk, 2.2% work from home; Mean travel time to work: 35.3 minutes

SPRINGWATER HAMLET (CDP). Covers a land area of 1.331 square miles and a water area of 0 square miles. Located at 42.63° N. Lat; 77.60° W. Long.
Population: 484; Growth (since 2000): n/a; Density: 363.7 persons per square mile; Race: 99.0% White, 0.0% Black/African American, 0.0% Asian, 0.0% American Indian/Alaska Native, 1.0% Native Hawaiian/Other Pacific Islander, 0.0% Two or more races, 0.0% Hispanic of any race; Average household size: 2.50; Median age: 34.7; Age under 18: 26.9%; Age 65 and over: 9.3%; Males per 100 females: 107.2; Marriage status: 28.5% never married, 46.6% now married, 5.2% separated, 3.9% widowed, 21.0% divorced; Foreign born: 1.0%; Speak English only: 99.0%; With disability: 28.3%; Veterans: 6.8%; Ancestry: 23.3% German, 18.2% American, 11.6% English, 5.6% Irish, 1.7% Dutch
Employment: 11.5% management, business, and financial, 3.4% computer, engineering, and science, 0.0% education, legal, community service, arts, and media, 2.9% healthcare practitioners, 2.9% service, 31.0% sales and office, 9.2% natural resources, construction, and maintenance, 39.1% production, transportation, and material moving
Income: Per capita: $18,098; Median household: $35,938; Average household: $44,956; Households with income of $100,000 or more: 6.3%; Poverty rate: 26.4%
Educational Attainment: High school diploma or higher: 75.7%; Bachelor's degree or higher: 7.4%; Graduate/professional degree or higher: 3.4%
Housing: Homeownership rate: 72.1%; Median home value: $75,900; Median year structure built: 1962; Homeowner vacancy rate: 0.0%; Median selected monthly owner costs: $1,131 with a mortgage, $438 without a mortgage; Median gross rent: $739 per month; Rental vacancy rate: 23.2%
Health Insurance: 97.9% have insurance; 65.7% have private insurance; 47.7% have public insurance; 2.1% do not have insurance; 0.0% of children under 18 do not have insurance
Transportation: Commute: 97.6% car, 2.4% public transportation, 0.0% walk, 0.0% work from home; Mean travel time to work: 36.2 minutes

WADSWORTH (CDP). Covers a land area of 0.512 square miles and a water area of 0 square miles. Located at 42.82° N. Lat; 77.89° W. Long. Elevation is 741 feet.
Population: 350; Growth (since 2000): n/a; Density: 684.1 persons per square mile; Race: 100.0% White, 0.0% Black/African American, 0.0% Asian, 0.0% American Indian/Alaska Native, 0.0% Native Hawaiian/Other Pacific Islander, 0.0% Two or more races, 0.0% Hispanic of any race; Average household size: 2.94; Median age: 31.3; Age under 18: 33.4%; Age 65 and over: 7.1%; Males per 100 females: 106.5; Marriage status: 34.8% never married, 44.2% now married, 0.0% separated, 9.4% widowed, 11.6% divorced; Foreign born: 0.0%; Speak English only: 100.0%; With disability: 0.0%; Veterans: 0.0%; Ancestry: 60.3% Irish, 44.6% Italian, 23.7% German, 7.1% English, 2.6% Polish
Employment: 6.3% management, business, and financial, 12.6% computer, engineering, and science, 0.0% education, legal, community service, arts, and media, 0.0% healthcare practitioners, 25.1% service, 26.3% sales and office, 29.7% natural resources, construction, and maintenance, 0.0% production, transportation, and material moving
Income: Per capita: $24,818; Median household: n/a; Average household: $69,267; Households with income of $100,000 or more: 32.0%; Poverty rate: n/a
Educational Attainment: High school diploma or higher: 72.0%; Bachelor's degree or higher: 17.5%; Graduate/professional degree or higher: 3.7%

Housing: Homeownership rate: 83.2%; Median home value: $118,200; Median year structure built: 1950; Homeowner vacancy rate: 0.0%; Median selected monthly owner costs: n/a with a mortgage, n/a without a mortgage; Median gross rent: n/a per month; Rental vacancy rate: 0.0%
Health Insurance: 96.9% have insurance; 78.6% have private insurance; 18.3% have public insurance; 3.1% do not have insurance; 0.0% of children under 18 do not have insurance
Transportation: Commute: 92.9% car, 0.0% public transportation, 7.1% walk, 0.0% work from home; Mean travel time to work: 16.3 minutes

WEBSTERS CROSSING (CDP).
Covers a land area of 0.110 square miles and a water area of 0 square miles. Located at 42.67° N. Lat; 77.64° W. Long. Elevation is 1,339 feet.
Population: 22; Growth (since 2000): n/a; Density: 199.5 persons per square mile; Race: 100.0% White, 0.0% Black/African American, 0.0% Asian, 0.0% American Indian/Alaska Native, 0.0% Native Hawaiian/Other Pacific Islander, 0.0% Two or more races, 0.0% Hispanic of any race; Average household size: 2.00; Median age: 69.2; Age under 18: 0.0%; Age 65 and over: 54.5%; Males per 100 females: 97.1; Marriage status: 0.0% never married, 100.0% now married, 0.0% separated, 0.0% widowed, 0.0% divorced; Foreign born: 0.0%; Speak English only: 100.0%; With disability: 50.0%; Veterans: 50.0%; Ancestry: 27.3% Irish, 27.3% Italian, 22.7% German
Employment: 0.0% management, business, and financial, 0.0% computer, engineering, and science, 0.0% education, legal, community service, arts, and media, 0.0% healthcare practitioners, 0.0% service, 0.0% sales and office, 0.0% natural resources, construction, and maintenance, 100.0% production, transportation, and material moving
Income: Per capita: $25,141; Median household: n/a; Average household: n/a; Households with income of $100,000 or more: n/a; Poverty rate: n/a
Educational Attainment: High school diploma or higher: 100.0%; Bachelor's degree or higher: n/a; Graduate/professional degree or higher: n/a
Housing: Homeownership rate: 100.0%; Median home value: n/a; Median year structure built: Before 1940; Homeowner vacancy rate: 59.3%; Median selected monthly owner costs: n/a with a mortgage, n/a without a mortgage; Median gross rent: n/a per month; Rental vacancy rate: 0.0%
Health Insurance: 100.0% have insurance; 100.0% have private insurance; 77.3% have public insurance; 0.0% do not have insurance; 0.0% of children under 18 do not have insurance
Transportation: Commute: 100.0% car, 0.0% public transportation, 0.0% walk, 0.0% work from home; Mean travel time to work: 0.0 minutes

WEST SPARTA (town).
Covers a land area of 33.450 square miles and a water area of 0 square miles. Located at 42.61° N. Lat; 77.79° W. Long. Elevation is 617 feet.
Population: 1,338; Growth (since 2000): 7.6%; Density: 40.0 persons per square mile; Race: 96.0% White, 0.0% Black/African American, 1.8% Asian, 0.2% American Indian/Alaska Native, 0.0% Native Hawaiian/Other Pacific Islander, 1.8% Two or more races, 1.0% Hispanic of any race; Average household size: 2.55; Median age: 44.2; Age under 18: 22.7%; Age 65 and over: 14.0%; Males per 100 females: 101.8; Marriage status: 26.5% never married, 58.9% now married, 3.1% separated, 6.0% widowed, 8.5% divorced; Foreign born: 3.0%; Speak English only: 96.9%; With disability: 17.0%; Veterans: 10.1%; Ancestry: 21.4% German, 15.2% Irish, 15.2% American, 11.7% English, 9.9% Italian
Employment: 7.4% management, business, and financial, 0.0% computer, engineering, and science, 6.6% education, legal, community service, arts, and media, 7.6% healthcare practitioners, 18.3% service, 23.4% sales and office, 18.3% natural resources, construction, and maintenance, 18.3% production, transportation, and material moving
Income: Per capita: $21,703; Median household: $44,250; Average household: $54,699; Households with income of $100,000 or more: 9.2%; Poverty rate: 26.2%
Educational Attainment: High school diploma or higher: 83.3%; Bachelor's degree or higher: 14.9%; Graduate/professional degree or higher: 5.6%
Housing: Homeownership rate: 82.5%; Median home value: $92,500; Median year structure built: 1976; Homeowner vacancy rate: 3.9%; Median selected monthly owner costs: $1,018 with a mortgage, $465 without a mortgage; Median gross rent: $725 per month; Rental vacancy rate: 0.0%
Health Insurance: 94.3% have insurance; 67.9% have private insurance; 44.3% have public insurance; 5.7% do not have insurance; 2.6% of children under 18 do not have insurance

Transportation: Commute: 90.3% car, 0.0% public transportation, 1.1% walk, 7.6% work from home; Mean travel time to work: 25.3 minutes

WOODSVILLE (CDP).
Covers a land area of 0.317 square miles and a water area of 0 square miles. Located at 42.58° N. Lat; 77.73° W. Long. Elevation is 646 feet.
Population: 62; Growth (since 2000): n/a; Density: 195.5 persons per square mile; Race: 100.0% White, 0.0% Black/African American, 0.0% Asian, 0.0% American Indian/Alaska Native, 0.0% Native Hawaiian/Other Pacific Islander, 0.0% Two or more races, 0.0% Hispanic of any race; Average household size: 2.21; Median age: 44.2; Age under 18: 8.1%; Age 65 and over: 22.6%; Males per 100 females: 116.2; Marriage status: 40.0% never married, 50.0% now married, 6.7% separated, 0.0% widowed, 10.0% divorced; Foreign born: 0.0%; Speak English only: 100.0%; With disability: 12.9%; Veterans: 7.0%; Ancestry: 35.5% German, 30.6% Irish, 9.7% English, 4.8% French
Employment: 0.0% management, business, and financial, 0.0% computer, engineering, and science, 0.0% education, legal, community service, arts, and media, 8.8% healthcare practitioners, 26.5% service, 17.6% sales and office, 8.8% natural resources, construction, and maintenance, 38.2% production, transportation, and material moving
Income: Per capita: $21,742; Median household: $43,333; Average household: $47,200; Households with income of $100,000 or more: n/a; Poverty rate: 9.7%
Educational Attainment: High school diploma or higher: 78.7%; Bachelor's degree or higher: n/a; Graduate/professional degree or higher: n/a
Housing: Homeownership rate: 64.3%; Median home value: $54,000; Median year structure built: 1967; Homeowner vacancy rate: 33.3%; Median selected monthly owner costs: $550 with a mortgage, $433 without a mortgage; Median gross rent: n/a per month; Rental vacancy rate: 0.0%
Health Insurance: 69.4% have insurance; 64.5% have private insurance; 27.4% have public insurance; 30.6% do not have insurance; 0.0% of children under 18 do not have insurance
Transportation: Commute: 100.0% car, 0.0% public transportation, 0.0% walk, 0.0% work from home; Mean travel time to work: 19.3 minutes

YORK (town).
Covers a land area of 49.100 square miles and a water area of 0.007 square miles. Located at 42.87° N. Lat; 77.89° W. Long. Elevation is 784 feet.
Population: 3,358; Growth (since 2000): 4.3%; Density: 68.4 persons per square mile; Race: 94.7% White, 1.0% Black/African American, 0.4% Asian, 0.0% American Indian/Alaska Native, 0.0% Native Hawaiian/Other Pacific Islander, 3.9% Two or more races, 0.6% Hispanic of any race; Average household size: 2.38; Median age: 42.1; Age under 18: 20.8%; Age 65 and over: 15.1%; Males per 100 females: 107.9; Marriage status: 24.2% never married, 59.1% now married, 1.0% separated, 6.3% widowed, 10.4% divorced; Foreign born: 0.4%; Speak English only: 98.3%; With disability: 14.9%; Veterans: 7.4%; Ancestry: 29.6% Irish, 23.5% German, 17.8% Italian, 15.4% English, 6.7% American
Employment: 12.2% management, business, and financial, 5.3% computer, engineering, and science, 8.7% education, legal, community service, arts, and media, 3.9% healthcare practitioners, 13.6% service, 23.1% sales and office, 13.0% natural resources, construction, and maintenance, 20.2% production, transportation, and material moving
Income: Per capita: $28,203; Median household: $59,393; Average household: $67,226; Households with income of $100,000 or more: 20.6%; Poverty rate: 6.4%
Educational Attainment: High school diploma or higher: 91.2%; Bachelor's degree or higher: 21.5%; Graduate/professional degree or higher: 9.1%
Housing: Homeownership rate: 82.2%; Median home value: $117,100; Median year structure built: 1949; Homeowner vacancy rate: 0.0%; Median selected monthly owner costs: $1,201 with a mortgage, $545 without a mortgage; Median gross rent: $699 per month; Rental vacancy rate: 0.0%
Health Insurance: 96.2% have insurance; 84.8% have private insurance; 30.2% have public insurance; 3.8% do not have insurance; 1.3% of children under 18 do not have insurance
Transportation: Commute: 91.3% car, 0.0% public transportation, 3.8% walk, 4.2% work from home; Mean travel time to work: 23.1 minutes

YORK HAMLET (CDP). Covers a land area of 2.754 square miles and a water area of 0 square miles. Located at 42.87° N. Lat; 77.89° W. Long. Elevation is 784 feet.

Population: 459; Growth (since 2000): n/a; Density: 166.7 persons per square mile; Race: 82.8% White, 0.0% Black/African American, 0.0% Asian, 0.0% American Indian/Alaska Native, 0.0% Native Hawaiian/Other Pacific Islander, 17.2% Two or more races, 0.0% Hispanic of any race; Average household size: 1.89; Median age: 49.0; Age under 18: 16.3%; Age 65 and over: 6.1%; Males per 100 females: 103.7; Marriage status: 16.4% never married, 53.6% now married, 0.0% separated, 5.7% widowed, 24.2% divorced; Foreign born: 0.0%; Speak English only: 100.0%; With disability: 1.5%; Veterans: 7.8%; Ancestry: 36.2% English, 34.0% German, 29.4% Irish, 17.0% Italian, 11.1% American
Employment: 13.1% management, business, and financial, 8.3% computer, engineering, and science, 6.1% education, legal, community service, arts, and media, 7.3% healthcare practitioners, 5.1% service, 32.9% sales and office, 7.7% natural resources, construction, and maintenance, 19.5% production, transportation, and material moving
Income: Per capita: $36,940; Median household: $75,495; Average household: $71,379; Households with income of $100,000 or more: 16.9%; Poverty rate: 1.5%
Educational Attainment: High school diploma or higher: 100.0%; Bachelor's degree or higher: 18.2%; Graduate/professional degree or higher: 7.3%
Housing: Homeownership rate: 87.2%; Median home value: $128,900; Median year structure built: 1951; Homeowner vacancy rate: 0.0%; Median selected monthly owner costs: $1,047 with a mortgage, $448 without a mortgage; Median gross rent: n/a per month; Rental vacancy rate: 0.0%
Health Insurance: 95.4% have insurance; 95.4% have private insurance; 6.3% have public insurance; 4.6% do not have insurance; 0.0% of children under 18 do not have insurance
Transportation: Commute: 93.6% car, 0.0% public transportation, 0.0% walk, 6.4% work from home; Mean travel time to work: 31.4 minutes

Madison County

Located in central New York; drained by the Chenango and Unadilla Rivers; includes Cazenovia Lake, part of Oneida Lake, and other lakes. Covers a land area of 654.842 square miles, a water area of 6.441 square miles, and is located in the Eastern Time Zone at 42.91° N. Lat., 75.66° W. Long. The county was founded in 1806. County seat is Wampsville.

Madison County is part of the Syracuse, NY Metropolitan Statistical Area. The entire metro area includes: Madison County, NY; Onondaga County, NY; Oswego County, NY

Weather Station: Morrisville 5 SW   Elevation: 1,299 feet

	Jan	Feb	Mar	Apr	May	Jun	Jul	Aug	Sep	Oct	Nov	Dec
High	29	32	40	54	66	74	78	76	69	57	45	34
Low	11	13	20	33	43	52	56	55	49	37	29	19
Precip	3.2	3.0	3.4	3.7	4.1	4.5	4.0	3.6	4.3	4.1	3.9	3.9
Snow	30.5	25.7	21.1	5.6	0.2	0.0	0.0	0.0	tr	1.5	12.0	27.5

High and Low temperatures in degrees Fahrenheit; Precipitation and Snow in inches

Population: 72,427; Growth (since 2000): 4.3%; Density: 110.6 persons per square mile; Race: 94.8% White, 2.0% Black/African American, 0.8% Asian, 0.6% American Indian/Alaska Native, 0.0% Native Hawaiian/Other Pacific Islander, 1.5% two or more races, 2.0% Hispanic of any race; Average household size: 2.55; Median age: 40.8; Age under 18: 20.7%; Age 65 and over: 15.4%; Males per 100 females: 96.5; Marriage status: 34.6% never married, 49.3% now married, 2.6% separated, 5.4% widowed, 10.7% divorced; Foreign born: 2.3%; Speak English only: 96.4%; With disability: 11.4%; Veterans: 9.4%; Ancestry: 28.2% American, 16.3% German, 15.8% Irish, 12.9% English, 9.5% Italian
Religion: Six largest groups: 14.7% Catholicism, 5.8% Methodist/Pietist, 2.1% Baptist, 1.9% Presbyterian-Reformed, 1.3% Non-denominational Protestant, 1.3% Episcopalianism/Anglicanism
Economy: Unemployment rate: 4.6%; Leading industries: 15.7 % retail trade; 12.9 % construction; 11.8 % accommodation and food services; Farms: 838 totaling 187,496 acres; Company size: 1 employs 1,000 or more persons, 3 employ 500 to 999 persons, 17 employ 100 to 499 persons, 1,409 employ less than 100 persons; Business ownership: 1,995 women-owned, 38 Black-owned, 68 Hispanic-owned, 37 Asian-owned, n/a American Indian/Alaska Native-owned
Employment: 14.4% management, business, and financial, 4.7% computer, engineering, and science, 12.4% education, legal, community

service, arts, and media, 5.5% healthcare practitioners, 17.5% service, 22.6% sales and office, 10.3% natural resources, construction, and maintenance, 12.7% production, transportation, and material moving
Income: Per capita: $25,984; Median household: $54,145; Average household: $68,675; Households with income of $100,000 or more: 20.1%; Poverty rate: 12.2%
Educational Attainment: High school diploma or higher: 90.4%; Bachelor's degree or higher: 26.2%; Graduate/professional degree or higher: 11.5%
Housing: Homeownership rate: 75.1%; Median home value: $124,900; Median year structure built: 1962; Homeowner vacancy rate: 2.6%; Median selected monthly owner costs: $1,263 with a mortgage, $504 without a mortgage; Median gross rent: $718 per month; Rental vacancy rate: 5.1%
Vital Statistics: Birth rate: 92.7 per 10,000 population; Death rate: 80.0 per 10,000 population; Age-adjusted cancer mortality rate: 148.3 deaths per 100,000 population
Health Insurance: 94.3% have insurance; 74.1% have private insurance; 33.5% have public insurance; 5.7% do not have insurance; 2.4% of children under 18 do not have insurance
Health Care: Physicians: 14.8 per 10,000 population; Dentists: 3.5 per 10,000 population; Hospital beds: 39.6 per 10,000 population; Hospital admissions: 638.9 per 10,000 population
Transportation: Commute: 88.2% car, 0.4% public transportation, 6.1% walk, 3.9% work from home; Mean travel time to work: 22.7 minutes
2016 Presidential Election: 53.7% Trump, 39.3% Clinton, 5.3% Johnson, 1.7% Stein
National and State Parks: Chittenango Falls State Park
Additional Information Contacts
Madison Government . . . . (315) 366-2261
http://www.madisoncounty.ny.gov

Madison County Communities

BOUCKVILLE (unincorporated postal area)
ZCTA: 13310

Covers a land area of 7.576 square miles and a water area of 0.092 square miles. Located at 42.89° N. Lat; 75.57° W. Long. Elevation is 1,142 feet.
Population: 481; Growth (since 2000): -2.0%; Density: 63.5 persons per square mile; Race: 94.8% White, 0.0% Black/African American, 0.0% Asian, 0.0% American Indian/Alaska Native, 0.0% Native Hawaiian/Other Pacific Islander, 5.2% Two or more races, 5.2% Hispanic of any race; Average household size: 2.67; Median age: 43.8; Age under 18: 5.6%; Age 65 and over: 6.9%; Males per 100 females: 85.7; Marriage status: 28.2% never married, 42.8% now married, 0.0% separated, 2.7% widowed, 26.3% divorced; Foreign born: 0.0%; Speak English only: 100.0%; With disability: 16.0%; Veterans: 12.1%; Ancestry: 55.9% American, 22.2% German, 12.7% Irish, 10.6% English, 7.3% Polish
Employment: 10.0% management, business, and financial, 18.2% computer, engineering, and science, 0.0% education, legal, community service, arts, and media, 0.0% healthcare practitioners, 20.5% service, 20.0% sales and office, 5.9% natural resources, construction, and maintenance, 25.5% production, transportation, and material moving
Income: Per capita: $20,193; Median household: $48,188; Average household: $51,528; Households with income of $100,000 or more: 13.3%; Poverty rate: 7.5%
Educational Attainment: High school diploma or higher: 82.0%; Bachelor's degree or higher: 6.7%; Graduate/professional degree or higher: 1.2%
Housing: Homeownership rate: 91.1%; Median home value: $106,100; Median year structure built: 1955; Homeowner vacancy rate: 0.0%; Median selected monthly owner costs: $1,095 with a mortgage, $490 without a mortgage; Median gross rent: n/a per month; Rental vacancy rate: 0.0%
Health Insurance: 89.6% have insurance; 62.0% have private insurance; 34.5% have public insurance; 10.4% do not have insurance; 0.0% of children under 18 do not have insurance
Transportation: Commute: 93.6% car, 0.0% public transportation, 0.0% walk, 0.0% work from home; Mean travel time to work: 22.3 minutes

BROOKFIELD (town). Covers a land area of 77.822 square miles and a water area of 0.196 square miles. Located at 42.81° N. Lat; 75.34° W. Long. Elevation is 1,381 feet.
Population: 2,560; Growth (since 2000): 6.5%; Density: 32.9 persons per square mile; Race: 99.6% White, 0.0% Black/African American, 0.0% Asian, 0.0% American Indian/Alaska Native, 0.0% Native Hawaiian/Other Pacific Islander, 0.4% Two or more races, 0.0% Hispanic of any race; Average household size: 2.72; Median age: 40.2; Age under 18: 26.8%; Age 65 and over: 16.4%; Males per 100 females: 97.0; Marriage status: 28.6% never married, 54.3% now married, 2.9% separated, 4.7% widowed, 12.4% divorced; Foreign born: 0.1%; Speak English only: 96.3%; With disability: 12.1%; Veterans: 12.6%; Ancestry: 20.4% German, 17.6% Irish, 15.0% English, 13.2% American, 8.0% Polish
Employment: 9.0% management, business, and financial, 4.3% computer, engineering, and science, 6.1% education, legal, community service, arts, and media, 7.6% healthcare practitioners, 16.7% service, 18.3% sales and office, 16.1% natural resources, construction, and maintenance, 21.9% production, transportation, and material moving
Income: Per capita: $22,231; Median household: $45,278; Average household: $57,471; Households with income of $100,000 or more: 13.0%; Poverty rate: 15.7%
Educational Attainment: High school diploma or higher: 89.2%; Bachelor's degree or higher: 14.4%; Graduate/professional degree or higher: 4.2%

School District(s)
Brookfield Central SD (PK-12)
    2014-15 Enrollment: 229. . . . . (315) 899-3323
Housing: Homeownership rate: 85.5%; Median home value: $71,500; Median year structure built: 1972; Homeowner vacancy rate: 3.3%; Median selected monthly owner costs: $983 with a mortgage, $394 without a mortgage; Median gross rent: $783 per month; Rental vacancy rate: 0.0%
Health Insurance: 89.2% have insurance; 65.3% have private insurance; 36.6% have public insurance; 10.8% do not have insurance; 8.5% of children under 18 do not have insurance
Transportation: Commute: 95.1% car, 0.0% public transportation, 1.5% walk, 3.4% work from home; Mean travel time to work: 26.4 minutes

CANASTOTA (village). Covers a land area of 3.351 square miles and a water area of 0.004 square miles. Located at 43.08° N. Lat; 75.76° W. Long. Elevation is 430 feet.
History: International Boxing Hall of Fame is here. Incorporated 1835.
Population: 4,707; Growth (since 2000): 6.4%; Density: 1,404.7 persons per square mile; Race: 96.8% White, 1.5% Black/African American, 0.0% Asian, 0.0% American Indian/Alaska Native, 0.0% Native Hawaiian/Other Pacific Islander, 1.7% Two or more races, 0.0% Hispanic of any race; Average household size: 2.26; Median age: 35.5; Age under 18: 24.7%; Age 65 and over: 13.3%; Males per 100 females: 92.0; Marriage status: 30.1% never married, 49.1% now married, 2.6% separated, 6.6% widowed, 14.2% divorced; Foreign born: 0.0%; Speak English only: 97.6%; With disability: 12.3%; Veterans: 9.3%; Ancestry: 21.8% Italian, 21.0% American, 17.5% German, 17.3% Irish, 13.1% English
Employment: 17.3% management, business, and financial, 5.7% computer, engineering, and science, 11.6% education, legal, community service, arts, and media, 3.9% healthcare practitioners, 13.6% service, 28.2% sales and office, 9.2% natural resources, construction, and maintenance, 10.4% production, transportation, and material moving
Income: Per capita: $26,301; Median household: $47,431; Average household: $58,868; Households with income of $100,000 or more: 15.1%; Poverty rate: 16.2%
Educational Attainment: High school diploma or higher: 94.3%; Bachelor's degree or higher: 29.2%; Graduate/professional degree or higher: 9.4%

School District(s)
Canastota Central SD (PK-12)
    2014-15 Enrollment: 1,429 . . . . (315) 697-2025
Housing: Homeownership rate: 57.3%; Median home value: $99,300; Median year structure built: 1958; Homeowner vacancy rate: 0.0%; Median selected monthly owner costs: $1,243 with a mortgage, $439 without a mortgage; Median gross rent: $637 per month; Rental vacancy rate: 6.4%
Health Insurance: 95.8% have insurance; 75.2% have private insurance; 33.1% have public insurance; 4.2% do not have insurance; 0.0% of children under 18 do not have insurance
Safety: Violent crime rate: 12.8 per 10,000 population; Property crime rate: 102.4 per 10,000 population

Newspapers: Cazenovia Republican (weekly circulation 2,800); Madison County Eagle (weekly circulation 8,700)
Transportation: Commute: 96.1% car, 0.0% public transportation, 2.3% walk, 0.2% work from home; Mean travel time to work: 23.9 minutes
Additional Information Contacts
Village of Canastota . . . . (315) 697-7559
    http://www.canastota.com

CAZENOVIA (town). Covers a land area of 49.870 square miles and a water area of 1.844 square miles. Located at 42.92° N. Lat; 75.86° W. Long. Elevation is 1,224 feet.
History: Seat of Cazenovia College. Settled 1793, incorporated 1810.
Population: 7,053; Growth (since 2000): 8.8%; Density: 141.4 persons per square mile; Race: 94.9% White, 3.2% Black/African American, 0.9% Asian, 0.0% American Indian/Alaska Native, 0.0% Native Hawaiian/Other Pacific Islander, 0.7% Two or more races, 2.3% Hispanic of any race; Average household size: 2.54; Median age: 43.4; Age under 18: 20.2%; Age 65 and over: 17.4%; Males per 100 females: 85.9; Marriage status: 34.2% never married, 51.0% now married, 3.3% separated, 4.4% widowed, 10.4% divorced; Foreign born: 2.5%; Speak English only: 96.6%; With disability: 7.7%; Veterans: 10.2%; Ancestry: 24.1% American, 21.0% Irish, 17.7% German, 15.9% English, 9.4% Italian
Employment: 19.2% management, business, and financial, 3.9% computer, engineering, and science, 15.5% education, legal, community service, arts, and media, 6.8% healthcare practitioners, 16.0% service, 22.4% sales and office, 6.3% natural resources, construction, and maintenance, 9.9% production, transportation, and material moving
Income: Per capita: $36,255; Median household: $70,556; Average household: $101,788; Households with income of $100,000 or more: 34.3%; Poverty rate: 6.7%
Educational Attainment: High school diploma or higher: 96.8%; Bachelor's degree or higher: 48.6%; Graduate/professional degree or higher: 22.3%

School District(s)
Cazenovia Central SD (KG-12)
    2014-15 Enrollment: 1,499 . . . . (315) 655-1317
Four-year College(s)
Cazenovia College (Private, Not-for-profit)
    Fall 2014 Enrollment: 1,091 . . . . (800) 654-3210
    2015-16 Tuition: In-state $31,754; Out-of-state $31,754
Housing: Homeownership rate: 74.4%; Median home value: $253,100; Median year structure built: 1964; Homeowner vacancy rate: 4.5%; Median selected monthly owner costs: $1,862 with a mortgage, $737 without a mortgage; Median gross rent: $792 per month; Rental vacancy rate: 8.7%
Health Insurance: 96.5% have insurance; 85.0% have private insurance; 25.0% have public insurance; 3.5% do not have insurance; 1.1% of children under 18 do not have insurance
Transportation: Commute: 81.7% car, 0.5% public transportation, 7.1% walk, 10.2% work from home; Mean travel time to work: 24.5 minutes
Additional Information Contacts
Town of Cazenovia . . . . (315) 655-9213
    http://townofcazenovia.org/content

CAZENOVIA (village). Covers a land area of 1.873 square miles and a water area of 0 square miles. Located at 42.93° N. Lat; 75.85° W. Long. Elevation is 1,224 feet.
Population: 2,815; Growth (since 2000): 7.7%; Density: 1,502.7 persons per square mile; Race: 90.3% White, 8.0% Black/African American, 0.5% Asian, 0.0% American Indian/Alaska Native, 0.0% Native Hawaiian/Other Pacific Islander, 0.5% Two or more races, 4.8% Hispanic of any race; Average household size: 2.09; Median age: 38.2; Age under 18: 10.4%; Age 65 and over: 17.1%; Males per 100 females: 67.4; Marriage status: 49.7% never married, 33.2% now married, 3.1% separated, 6.1% widowed, 11.0% divorced; Foreign born: 2.3%; Speak English only: 95.2%; With disability: 8.3%; Veterans: 6.5%; Ancestry: 20.2% American, 19.9% German, 19.5% Irish, 14.4% English, 11.0% Italian
Employment: 10.9% management, business, and financial, 2.8% computer, engineering, and science, 20.6% education, legal, community service, arts, and media, 4.7% healthcare practitioners, 22.9% service, 28.5% sales and office, 5.2% natural resources, construction, and maintenance, 4.5% production, transportation, and material moving
Income: Per capita: $28,523; Median household: $56,696; Average household: $81,010; Households with income of $100,000 or more: 30.0%; Poverty rate: 11.0%

Educational Attainment: High school diploma or higher: 93.8%; Bachelor's degree or higher: 46.1%; Graduate/professional degree or higher: 22.4%

School District(s)
Cazenovia Central SD (KG-12)
  2014-15 Enrollment: 1,499 . . . . (315) 655-1317

Four-year College(s)
Cazenovia College (Private, Not-for-profit)
  Fall 2014 Enrollment: 1,091 . . . . (800) 654-3210
  2015-16 Tuition: In-state $31,754; Out-of-state $31,754

Housing: Homeownership rate: 58.1%; Median home value: $212,400; Median year structure built: Before 1940; Homeowner vacancy rate: 3.6%; Median selected monthly owner costs: $1,561 with a mortgage, $747 without a mortgage; Median gross rent: $774 per month; Rental vacancy rate: 6.1%

Health Insurance: 95.7% have insurance; 83.5% have private insurance; 27.5% have public insurance; 4.3% do not have insurance; 5.5% of children under 18 do not have insurance

Safety: Violent crime rate: 38.9 per 10,000 population; Property crime rate: 109.7 per 10,000 population

Transportation: Commute: 69.2% car, 1.4% public transportation, 19.1% walk, 10.3% work from home; Mean travel time to work: 22.3 minutes

CHITTENANGO (village).
Covers a land area of 2.441 square miles and a water area of 0 square miles. Located at 43.05° N. Lat; 75.87° W. Long. Elevation is 453 feet.

Population: 4,992; Growth (since 2000): 2.8%; Density: 2,044.9 persons per square mile; Race: 99.1% White, 0.0% Black/African American, 0.2% Asian, 0.1% American Indian/Alaska Native, 0.0% Native Hawaiian/Other Pacific Islander, 0.6% Two or more races, 1.3% Hispanic of any race; Average household size: 2.67; Median age: 38.2; Age under 18: 26.6%; Age 65 and over: 13.6%; Males per 100 females: 89.0; Marriage status: 27.4% never married, 54.1% now married, 2.3% separated, 4.7% widowed, 13.8% divorced; Foreign born: 0.7%; Speak English only: 98.8%; With disability: 10.8%; Veterans: 9.2%; Ancestry: 34.7% American, 18.9% German, 15.2% Irish, 11.8% English, 7.0% Italian

Employment: 16.4% management, business, and financial, 6.3% computer, engineering, and science, 10.9% education, legal, community service, arts, and media, 6.0% healthcare practitioners, 12.2% service, 28.5% sales and office, 6.6% natural resources, construction, and maintenance, 13.1% production, transportation, and material moving

Income: Per capita: $28,748; Median household: $62,902; Average household: $74,926; Households with income of $100,000 or more: 27.2%; Poverty rate: 5.2%

Educational Attainment: High school diploma or higher: 91.7%; Bachelor's degree or higher: 32.8%; Graduate/professional degree or higher: 11.6%

School District(s)
Chittenango Central SD (KG-12)
  2014-15 Enrollment: 1,993 . . . . (315) 687-2840

Housing: Homeownership rate: 79.2%; Median home value: $124,600; Median year structure built: 1967; Homeowner vacancy rate: 7.1%; Median selected monthly owner costs: $1,288 with a mortgage, $507 without a mortgage; Median gross rent: $674 per month; Rental vacancy rate: 10.2%

Health Insurance: 95.0% have insurance; 76.8% have private insurance; 29.0% have public insurance; 5.0% do not have insurance; 0.8% of children under 18 do not have insurance

Safety: Violent crime rate: 4.0 per 10,000 population; Property crime rate: 58.0 per 10,000 population

Transportation: Commute: 94.8% car, 0.0% public transportation, 2.6% walk, 1.5% work from home; Mean travel time to work: 24.7 minutes

Additional Information Contacts
Village of Chittenango . . . . (315) 687-3936
  http://chittenango.org

DERUYTER (town).
Covers a land area of 30.440 square miles and a water area of 0.833 square miles. Located at 42.77° N. Lat; 75.85° W. Long. Elevation is 1,286 feet.

Population: 1,610; Growth (since 2000): 5.1%; Density: 52.9 persons per square mile; Race: 95.7% White, 3.2% Black/African American, 0.7% Asian, 0.2% American Indian/Alaska Native, 0.0% Native Hawaiian/Other Pacific Islander, 0.2% Two or more races, 0.5% Hispanic of any race; Average household size: 2.56; Median age: 46.4; Age under 18: 24.0%; Age 65 and over: 19.1%; Males per 100 females: 94.0; Marriage status: 22.2% never married, 58.7% now married, 3.2% separated, 7.3%

widowed, 11.8% divorced; Foreign born: 1.6%; Speak English only: 97.9%; With disability: 11.7%; Veterans: 8.9%; Ancestry: 35.7% American, 16.0% English, 12.7% German, 8.3% Irish, 3.3% French

Employment: 12.1% management, business, and financial, 6.8% computer, engineering, and science, 9.5% education, legal, community service, arts, and media, 3.0% healthcare practitioners, 13.1% service, 27.1% sales and office, 13.8% natural resources, construction, and maintenance, 14.5% production, transportation, and material moving

Income: Per capita: $23,297; Median household: $50,000; Average household: $57,727; Households with income of $100,000 or more: 12.8%; Poverty rate: 17.2%

Educational Attainment: High school diploma or higher: 90.5%; Bachelor's degree or higher: 17.2%; Graduate/professional degree or higher: 8.1%

School District(s)
Deruyter Central SD (PK-12)
  2014-15 Enrollment: 436. . . . . (315) 852-3400

Housing: Homeownership rate: 81.1%; Median home value: $99,900; Median year structure built: 1955; Homeowner vacancy rate: 0.0%; Median selected monthly owner costs: $1,098 with a mortgage, $509 without a mortgage; Median gross rent: $548 per month; Rental vacancy rate: 5.6%

Health Insurance: 95.7% have insurance; 61.9% have private insurance; 47.0% have public insurance; 4.3% do not have insurance; 1.0% of children under 18 do not have insurance

Transportation: Commute: 84.4% car, 0.0% public transportation, 9.0% walk, 5.5% work from home; Mean travel time to work: 34.6 minutes

DERUYTER (village).
Covers a land area of 0.344 square miles and a water area of 0 square miles. Located at 42.76° N. Lat; 75.89° W. Long. Elevation is 1,286 feet.

Population: 545; Growth (since 2000): 2.6%; Density: 1,584.4 persons per square mile; Race: 97.8% White, 0.0% Black/African American, 2.2% Asian, 0.0% American Indian/Alaska Native, 0.0% Native Hawaiian/Other Pacific Islander, 0.0% Two or more races, 0.0% Hispanic of any race; Average household size: 2.38; Median age: 43.6; Age under 18: 27.2%; Age 65 and over: 17.4%; Males per 100 females: 79.4; Marriage status: 27.7% never married, 43.5% now married, 4.2% separated, 11.2% widowed, 17.7% divorced; Foreign born: 2.8%; Speak English only: 97.5%; With disability: 14.1%; Veterans: 8.3%; Ancestry: 42.6% American, 15.4% English, 10.1% German, 7.7% Irish, 5.1% Italian

Employment: 6.7% management, business, and financial, 0.8% computer, engineering, and science, 13.9% education, legal, community service, arts, and media, 4.2% healthcare practitioners, 16.4% service, 26.9% sales and office, 12.2% natural resources, construction, and maintenance, 18.9% production, transportation, and material moving

Income: Per capita: $22,893; Median household: $35,521; Average household: $53,057; Households with income of $100,000 or more: 12.3%; Poverty rate: 21.8%

Educational Attainment: High school diploma or higher: 92.2%; Bachelor's degree or higher: 20.3%; Graduate/professional degree or higher: 11.2%

School District(s)
Deruyter Central SD (PK-12)
  2014-15 Enrollment: 436. . . . . (315) 852-3400

Housing: Homeownership rate: 60.7%; Median home value: $95,600; Median year structure built: Before 1940; Homeowner vacancy rate: 0.0%; Median selected monthly owner costs: $1,169 with a mortgage, $433 without a mortgage; Median gross rent: $523 per month; Rental vacancy rate: 7.2%

Health Insurance: 96.5% have insurance; 64.0% have private insurance; 47.7% have public insurance; 3.5% do not have insurance; 0.0% of children under 18 do not have insurance

Transportation: Commute: 84.3% car, 0.0% public transportation, 11.3% walk, 4.3% work from home; Mean travel time to work: 37.7 minutes

EARLVILLE (village).
Covers a land area of 1.079 square miles and a water area of 0 square miles. Located at 42.74° N. Lat; 75.54° W. Long. Elevation is 1,099 feet.

Population: 1,102; Growth (since 2000): 39.3%; Density: 1,020.9 persons per square mile; Race: 89.4% White, 1.5% Black/African American, 0.0% Asian, 1.6% American Indian/Alaska Native, 0.0% Native Hawaiian/Other Pacific Islander, 5.8% Two or more races, 1.1% Hispanic of any race; Average household size: 3.06; Median age: 31.2; Age under 18: 31.3%; Age 65 and over: 13.7%; Males per 100 females: 98.6; Marriage status: 34.0% never married, 52.0% now married, 2.4% separated, 8.6%

widowed, 5.5% divorced; Foreign born: 0.6%; Speak English only: 97.8%; With disability: 8.5%; Veterans: 9.4%; Ancestry: 40.5% American, 15.1% Irish, 11.9% German, 10.1% English, 8.3% Italian
Employment: 11.3% management, business, and financial, 2.6% computer, engineering, and science, 10.9% education, legal, community service, arts, and media, 7.0% healthcare practitioners, 25.5% service, 26.0% sales and office, 9.8% natural resources, construction, and maintenance, 7.0% production, transportation, and material moving
Income: Per capita: $19,167; Median household: $40,313; Average household: $52,878; Households with income of $100,000 or more: 16.6%; Poverty rate: 15.0%
Educational Attainment: High school diploma or higher: 90.7%; Bachelor's degree or higher: 21.8%; Graduate/professional degree or higher: 8.7%
Housing: Homeownership rate: 61.4%; Median home value: $93,700; Median year structure built: Before 1940; Homeowner vacancy rate: 8.7%; Median selected monthly owner costs: $1,104 with a mortgage, $562 without a mortgage; Median gross rent: $833 per month; Rental vacancy rate: 6.1%
Health Insurance: 96.6% have insurance; 71.6% have private insurance; 42.1% have public insurance; 3.4% do not have insurance; 0.9% of children under 18 do not have insurance
Transportation: Commute: 95.8% car, 0.0% public transportation, 3.8% walk, 0.0% work from home; Mean travel time to work: 20.1 minutes

EATON (town). Covers a land area of 44.622 square miles and a water area of 0.949 square miles. Located at 42.89° N. Lat; 75.63° W. Long. Elevation is 1,204 feet.
Population: 4,892; Growth (since 2000): 1.4%; Density: 109.6 persons per square mile; Race: 86.0% White, 9.3% Black/African American, 1.3% Asian, 1.0% American Indian/Alaska Native, 0.1% Native Hawaiian/Other Pacific Islander, 1.8% Two or more races, 6.2% Hispanic of any race; Average household size: 2.69; Median age: 24.4; Age under 18: 14.5%; Age 65 and over: 11.5%; Males per 100 females: 102.5; Marriage status: 56.0% never married, 30.3% now married, 2.0% separated, 5.3% widowed, 8.4% divorced; Foreign born: 3.5%; Speak English only: 94.2%; With disability: 11.5%; Veterans: 5.4%; Ancestry: 45.3% American, 10.9% English, 10.0% German, 9.4% Irish, 3.9% Italian
Employment: 10.8% management, business, and financial, 8.6% computer, engineering, and science, 17.0% education, legal, community service, arts, and media, 7.2% healthcare practitioners, 20.6% service, 17.3% sales and office, 11.9% natural resources, construction, and maintenance, 6.5% production, transportation, and material moving
Income: Per capita: $17,535; Median household: $51,897; Average household: $66,133; Households with income of $100,000 or more: 17.2%; Poverty rate: 12.2%
Educational Attainment: High school diploma or higher: 85.4%; Bachelor's degree or higher: 18.5%; Graduate/professional degree or higher: 9.9%
Housing: Homeownership rate: 86.4%; Median home value: $120,000; Median year structure built: 1958; Homeowner vacancy rate: 0.9%; Median selected monthly owner costs: $1,100 with a mortgage, $479 without a mortgage; Median gross rent: $524 per month; Rental vacancy rate: 26.4%
Health Insurance: 96.0% have insurance; 78.0% have private insurance; 26.0% have public insurance; 4.0% do not have insurance; 0.6% of children under 18 do not have insurance
Transportation: Commute: 73.4% car, 0.1% public transportation, 18.6% walk, 6.1% work from home; Mean travel time to work: 18.6 minutes
Additional Information Contacts
Town of Eaton . . . . (315) 684-9111
  http://www.townofeaton.com

ERIEVILLE (unincorporated postal area)
ZCTA: 13061
  Covers a land area of 25.988 square miles and a water area of 0.976 square miles. Located at 42.87° N. Lat; 75.76° W. Long. Elevation is 1,545 feet.
  Population: 1,110; Growth (since 2000): 19.4%; Density: 42.7 persons per square mile; Race: 97.9% White, 1.4% Black/African American, 0.0% Asian, 0.7% American Indian/Alaska Native, 0.0% Native Hawaiian/Other Pacific Islander, 0.0% Two or more races, 1.4% Hispanic of any race; Average household size: 2.42; Median age: 49.8; Age under 18: 15.0%; Age 65 and over: 21.3%; Males per 100 females: 116.7; Marriage status: 27.7% never married, 53.7% now married, 4.0% separated, 4.7% widowed, 13.8% divorced; Foreign born: 0.7%; Speak

English only: 98.8%; With disability: 13.2%; Veterans: 11.0%; Ancestry: 25.1% English, 22.0% American, 19.1% German, 18.5% Irish, 8.1% Polish
Employment: 19.0% management, business, and financial, 2.8% computer, engineering, and science, 10.8% education, legal, community service, arts, and media, 5.4% healthcare practitioners, 12.8% service, 22.3% sales and office, 14.7% natural resources, construction, and maintenance, 12.3% production, transportation, and material moving
Income: Per capita: $28,983; Median household: $59,861; Average household: $68,738; Households with income of $100,000 or more: 22.7%; Poverty rate: 15.5%
Educational Attainment: High school diploma or higher: 92.6%; Bachelor's degree or higher: 29.5%; Graduate/professional degree or higher: 9.6%
Housing: Homeownership rate: 91.5%; Median home value: $164,400; Median year structure built: 1965; Homeowner vacancy rate: 3.2%; Median selected monthly owner costs: $1,276 with a mortgage, $560 without a mortgage; Median gross rent: $1,080 per month; Rental vacancy rate: 13.3%
Health Insurance: 93.4% have insurance; 70.0% have private insurance; 40.9% have public insurance; 6.6% do not have insurance; 5.4% of children under 18 do not have insurance
Transportation: Commute: 98.3% car, 0.0% public transportation, 0.0% walk, 1.7% work from home; Mean travel time to work: 26.7 minutes

FENNER (town). Covers a land area of 31.074 square miles and a water area of 0.048 square miles. Located at 42.97° N. Lat; 75.77° W. Long. Elevation is 1,552 feet.
Population: 1,766; Growth (since 2000): 5.1%; Density: 56.8 persons per square mile; Race: 96.0% White, 0.0% Black/African American, 0.0% Asian, 0.3% American Indian/Alaska Native, 0.0% Native Hawaiian/Other Pacific Islander, 3.7% Two or more races, 2.3% Hispanic of any race; Average household size: 2.59; Median age: 47.0; Age under 18: 20.3%; Age 65 and over: 16.5%; Males per 100 females: 107.2; Marriage status: 26.5% never married, 60.0% now married, 1.1% separated, 5.1% widowed, 8.3% divorced; Foreign born: 2.8%; Speak English only: 95.2%; With disability: 10.3%; Veterans: 12.1%; Ancestry: 31.3% American, 17.6% German, 15.6% Irish, 12.6% English, 6.1% Polish
Employment: 15.6% management, business, and financial, 4.8% computer, engineering, and science, 7.5% education, legal, community service, arts, and media, 5.8% healthcare practitioners, 17.0% service, 20.5% sales and office, 14.7% natural resources, construction, and maintenance, 13.9% production, transportation, and material moving
Income: Per capita: $31,943; Median household: $59,432; Average household: $81,718; Households with income of $100,000 or more: 24.0%; Poverty rate: 6.9%
Educational Attainment: High school diploma or higher: 95.1%; Bachelor's degree or higher: 25.4%; Graduate/professional degree or higher: 10.5%
Housing: Homeownership rate: 85.2%; Median home value: $109,600; Median year structure built: 1977; Homeowner vacancy rate: 1.5%; Median selected monthly owner costs: $1,222 with a mortgage, $444 without a mortgage; Median gross rent: $780 per month; Rental vacancy rate: 8.2%
Health Insurance: 87.7% have insurance; 68.8% have private insurance; 31.7% have public insurance; 12.3% do not have insurance; 14.8% of children under 18 do not have insurance
Transportation: Commute: 89.6% car, 0.8% public transportation, 6.6% walk, 3.0% work from home; Mean travel time to work: 24.0 minutes

GEORGETOWN (town). Covers a land area of 40.078 square miles and a water area of 0.099 square miles. Located at 42.79° N. Lat; 75.74° W. Long. Elevation is 1,411 feet.
Population: 535; Growth (since 2000): -43.4%; Density: 13.3 persons per square mile; Race: 95.0% White, 1.3% Black/African American, 0.0% Asian, 0.0% American Indian/Alaska Native, 0.0% Native Hawaiian/Other Pacific Islander, 1.5% Two or more races, 4.7% Hispanic of any race; Average household size: 2.32; Median age: 51.3; Age under 18: 7.7%; Age 65 and over: 21.1%; Males per 100 females: 142.3; Marriage status: 30.3% never married, 49.7% now married, 1.4% separated, 7.4% widowed, 12.5% divorced; Foreign born: 0.4%; Speak English only: 94.5%; With disability: 12.7%; Veterans: 7.1%; Ancestry: 31.2% American, 19.3% English, 12.9% German, 11.0% Irish, 4.5% Dutch
Employment: 11.3% management, business, and financial, 0.8% computer, engineering, and science, 9.0% education, legal, community service, arts, and media, 1.9% healthcare practitioners, 19.9% service,

30.1% sales and office, 12.4% natural resources, construction, and maintenance, 14.7% production, transportation, and material moving
Income: Per capita: $22,749; Median household: $50,500; Average household: $53,604; Households with income of $100,000 or more: 8.6%; Poverty rate: 8.0%
Educational Attainment: High school diploma or higher: 89.0%; Bachelor's degree or higher: 15.4%; Graduate/professional degree or higher: 5.3%

School District(s)
Georgetown-South Otselic Central SD (KG-12)
    2014-15 Enrollment: 356. . . . . (315) 653-7218
Housing: Homeownership rate: 89.5%; Median home value: $90,000; Median year structure built: 1978; Homeowner vacancy rate: 0.0%; Median selected monthly owner costs: $986 with a mortgage, $483 without a mortgage; Median gross rent: $667 per month; Rental vacancy rate: 21.4%
Health Insurance: 89.8% have insurance; 67.0% have private insurance; 39.3% have public insurance; 10.2% do not have insurance; 0.0% of children under 18 do not have insurance
Transportation: Commute: 88.1% car, 0.0% public transportation, 10.0% walk, 1.9% work from home; Mean travel time to work: 30.5 minutes

HAMILTON (town). Covers a land area of 41.339 square miles and a water area of 0.116 square miles. Located at 42.79° N. Lat; 75.49° W. Long. Elevation is 1,122 feet.
History: Seat of Colgate University. Settled 1795, incorporated 1816.
Population: 6,612; Growth (since 2000): 15.3%; Density: 159.9 persons per square mile; Race: 86.8% White, 4.8% Black/African American, 3.9% Asian, 0.2% American Indian/Alaska Native, 0.0% Native Hawaiian/Other Pacific Islander, 3.9% Two or more races, 2.6% Hispanic of any race; Average household size: 2.60; Median age: 22.2; Age under 18: 16.4%; Age 65 and over: 11.0%; Males per 100 females: 90.0; Marriage status: 59.2% never married, 31.7% now married, 1.8% separated, 4.3% widowed, 4.8% divorced; Foreign born: 4.9%; Speak English only: 91.8%; With disability: 7.5%; Veterans: 4.6%; Ancestry: 27.8% American, 14.9% German, 13.2% Irish, 9.3% English, 7.5% Italian
Employment: 12.4% management, business, and financial, 6.3% computer, engineering, and science, 26.8% education, legal, community service, arts, and media, 3.6% healthcare practitioners, 18.1% service, 17.8% sales and office, 7.3% natural resources, construction, and maintenance, 7.6% production, transportation, and material moving
Income: Per capita: $22,086; Median household: $61,080; Average household: $79,405; Households with income of $100,000 or more: 26.2%; Poverty rate: 10.2%
Educational Attainment: High school diploma or higher: 93.1%; Bachelor's degree or higher: 49.3%; Graduate/professional degree or higher: 29.1%

School District(s)
Hamilton Central SD (PK-12)
    2014-15 Enrollment: 579. . . . . (315) 824-6310
Four-year College(s)
Colgate University (Private, Not-for-profit)
    Fall 2014 Enrollment: 2,888 . . . . (315) 228-1000
    2015-16 Tuition: In-state $49,970; Out-of-state $49,970
Housing: Homeownership rate: 64.6%; Median home value: $168,300; Median year structure built: Before 1940; Homeowner vacancy rate: 1.8%; Median selected monthly owner costs: $1,288 with a mortgage, $678 without a mortgage; Median gross rent: $839 per month; Rental vacancy rate: 3.6%
Health Insurance: 96.3% have insurance; 83.3% have private insurance; 24.1% have public insurance; 3.7% do not have insurance; 0.7% of children under 18 do not have insurance
Hospitals: Community Memorial Hospital (88 beds)
Newspapers: Mid-York Weekly (weekly circulation 8,000)
Transportation: Commute: 65.0% car, 1.2% public transportation, 22.7% walk, 7.8% work from home; Mean travel time to work: 15.4 minutes
Airports: Hamilton Municipal (general aviation)
Additional Information Contacts
Town of Hamilton . . . . (315) 824-3380
    http://www.townofhamiltonny.org

HAMILTON (village). Covers a land area of 2.486 square miles and a water area of 0.192 square miles. Located at 42.83° N. Lat; 75.55° W. Long. Elevation is 1,122 feet.
Population: 4,064; Growth (since 2000): 15.8%; Density: 1,634.5 persons per square mile; Race: 80.8% White, 7.5% Black/African American, 6.3%

Asian, 0.2% American Indian/Alaska Native, 0.0% Native Hawaiian/Other Pacific Islander, 4.9% Two or more races, 3.8% Hispanic of any race; Average household size: 2.48; Median age: 21.1; Age under 18: 10.3%; Age 65 and over: 8.9%; Males per 100 females: 83.7; Marriage status: 76.3% never married, 17.6% now married, 1.2% separated, 3.7% widowed, 2.4% divorced; Foreign born: 7.6%; Speak English only: 88.4%; With disability: 7.2%; Veterans: 2.5%; Ancestry: 19.0% American, 16.3% Irish, 16.0% German, 10.9% English, 6.6% Italian
Employment: 11.8% management, business, and financial, 6.8% computer, engineering, and science, 35.5% education, legal, community service, arts, and media, 3.1% healthcare practitioners, 18.5% service, 15.3% sales and office, 4.9% natural resources, construction, and maintenance, 3.9% production, transportation, and material moving
Income: Per capita: $19,754; Median household: $71,591; Average household: $95,555; Households with income of $100,000 or more: 33.3%; Poverty rate: 16.2%
Educational Attainment: High school diploma or higher: 93.5%; Bachelor's degree or higher: 61.8%; Graduate/professional degree or higher: 41.8%

School District(s)
Hamilton Central SD (PK-12)
    2014-15 Enrollment: 579. . . . . (315) 824-6310
Four-year College(s)
Colgate University (Private, Not-for-profit)
    Fall 2014 Enrollment: 2,888 . . . . (315) 228-1000
    2015-16 Tuition: In-state $49,970; Out-of-state $49,970
Housing: Homeownership rate: 57.6%; Median home value: $233,700; Median year structure built: Before 1940; Homeowner vacancy rate: 1.6%; Median selected monthly owner costs: $1,766 with a mortgage, $873 without a mortgage; Median gross rent: $894 per month; Rental vacancy rate: 6.0%
Health Insurance: 97.0% have insurance; 88.1% have private insurance; 17.3% have public insurance; 3.0% do not have insurance; 1.2% of children under 18 do not have insurance
Hospitals: Community Memorial Hospital (88 beds)
Safety: Violent crime rate: 4.8 per 10,000 population; Property crime rate: 28.6 per 10,000 population
Newspapers: Mid-York Weekly (weekly circulation 8,000)
Transportation: Commute: 47.2% car, 2.1% public transportation, 36.0% walk, 9.0% work from home; Mean travel time to work: 11.8 minutes
Airports: Hamilton Municipal (general aviation)
Additional Information Contacts
Village of Hamilton . . . . (315) 824-0002
    http://www.hamiltonny.com

HUBBARDSVILLE (unincorporated postal area)
ZCTA: 13355
    Covers a land area of 29.107 square miles and a water area of 0.014 square miles. Located at 42.81° N. Lat; 75.43° W. Long. Elevation is 1,214 feet.
Population: 861; Growth (since 2000): 24.4%; Density: 29.6 persons per square mile; Race: 99.1% White, 0.0% Black/African American, 0.0% Asian, 0.0% American Indian/Alaska Native, 0.0% Native Hawaiian/Other Pacific Islander, 0.9% Two or more races, 12.1% Hispanic of any race; Average household size: 2.72; Median age: 30.3; Age under 18: 28.7%; Age 65 and over: 14.6%; Males per 100 females: 107.1; Marriage status: 41.0% never married, 35.3% now married, 3.8% separated, 6.9% widowed, 16.7% divorced; Foreign born: 0.3%; Speak English only: 98.4%; With disability: 16.6%; Veterans: 9.1%; Ancestry: 29.3% American, 15.2% Italian, 13.7% Irish, 7.8% Polish, 6.4% English
Employment: 1.2% management, business, and financial, 11.1% computer, engineering, and science, 6.2% education, legal, community service, arts, and media, 4.9% healthcare practitioners, 17.8% service, 26.2% sales and office, 26.5% natural resources, construction, and maintenance, 6.2% production, transportation, and material moving
Income: Per capita: $19,416; Median household: $42,672; Average household: $48,567; Households with income of $100,000 or more: 7.3%; Poverty rate: 10.0%
Educational Attainment: High school diploma or higher: 88.3%; Bachelor's degree or higher: 16.4%; Graduate/professional degree or higher: 4.9%
Housing: Homeownership rate: 63.7%; Median home value: $103,400; Median year structure built: 1973; Homeowner vacancy rate: 0.0%; Median selected monthly owner costs: $988 with a mortgage, $517

without a mortgage; Median gross rent: $783 per month; Rental vacancy rate: 0.0%
Health Insurance: 96.2% have insurance; 70.2% have private insurance; 38.8% have public insurance; 3.8% do not have insurance; 0.0% of children under 18 do not have insurance
Transportation: Commute: 79.6% car, 0.0% public transportation, 19.5% walk, 0.9% work from home; Mean travel time to work: 21.3 minutes

KIRKVILLE (unincorporated postal area)
ZCTA: 13082

Covers a land area of 23.571 square miles and a water area of 0.413 square miles. Located at 43.10° N. Lat; 75.96° W. Long..
Population: 4,511; Growth (since 2000): -10.0%; Density: 191.4 persons per square mile; Race: 96.3% White, 0.0% Black/African American, 0.7% Asian, 1.6% American Indian/Alaska Native, 0.0% Native Hawaiian/Other Pacific Islander, 1.0% Two or more races, 2.2% Hispanic of any race; Average household size: 2.56; Median age: 45.2; Age under 18: 20.3%; Age 65 and over: 19.0%; Males per 100 females: 93.8; Marriage status: 24.7% never married, 58.7% now married, 0.6% separated, 7.4% widowed, 9.1% divorced; Foreign born: 3.0%; Speak English only: 96.5%; With disability: 11.0%; Veterans: 11.8%; Ancestry: 24.5% German, 22.2% Irish, 21.0% English, 12.0% Italian, 8.4% Polish
Employment: 12.8% management, business, and financial, 5.3% computer, engineering, and science, 7.8% education, legal, community service, arts, and media, 6.1% healthcare practitioners, 17.7% service, 29.7% sales and office, 10.5% natural resources, construction, and maintenance, 10.2% production, transportation, and material moving
Income: Per capita: $28,596; Median household: $58,077; Average household: $71,181; Households with income of $100,000 or more: 21.5%; Poverty rate: 8.4%
Educational Attainment: High school diploma or higher: 92.4%; Bachelor's degree or higher: 22.7%; Graduate/professional degree or higher: 9.1%
Housing: Homeownership rate: 80.7%; Median home value: $135,300; Median year structure built: 1971; Homeowner vacancy rate: 4.1%; Median selected monthly owner costs: $1,288 with a mortgage, $530 without a mortgage; Median gross rent: $714 per month; Rental vacancy rate: 5.8%
Health Insurance: 95.1% have insurance; 74.4% have private insurance; 37.8% have public insurance; 4.9% do not have insurance; 2.3% of children under 18 do not have insurance
Transportation: Commute: 94.9% car, 0.0% public transportation, 1.2% walk, 2.8% work from home; Mean travel time to work: 19.8 minutes

LEBANON (town). Covers a land area of 43.344 square miles and a water area of 0.336 square miles. Located at 42.78° N. Lat; 75.63° W. Long. Elevation is 1,345 feet.
Population: 1,346; Growth (since 2000): 1.3%; Density: 31.1 persons per square mile; Race: 98.5% White, 0.0% Black/African American, 0.0% Asian, 0.0% American Indian/Alaska Native, 0.0% Native Hawaiian/Other Pacific Islander, 1.5% Two or more races, 0.3% Hispanic of any race; Average household size: 2.87; Median age: 42.7; Age under 18: 25.1%; Age 65 and over: 17.2%; Males per 100 females: 105.9; Marriage status: 26.7% never married, 57.5% now married, 4.3% separated, 6.5% widowed, 9.3% divorced; Foreign born: 1.4%; Speak English only: 99.0%; With disability: 13.0%; Veterans: 11.4%; Ancestry: 32.7% American, 13.5% German, 10.0% Irish, 9.3% English, 5.3% Italian
Employment: 14.2% management, business, and financial, 1.3% computer, engineering, and science, 6.9% education, legal, community service, arts, and media, 6.4% healthcare practitioners, 29.1% service, 16.8% sales and office, 17.6% natural resources, construction, and maintenance, 7.7% production, transportation, and material moving
Income: Per capita: $20,926; Median household: $48,365; Average household: $57,443; Households with income of $100,000 or more: 15.6%; Poverty rate: 13.4%
Educational Attainment: High school diploma or higher: 87.2%; Bachelor's degree or higher: 16.8%; Graduate/professional degree or higher: 9.3%
Housing: Homeownership rate: 84.4%; Median home value: $117,600; Median year structure built: 1973; Homeowner vacancy rate: 0.0%; Median selected monthly owner costs: $1,183 with a mortgage, $443 without a mortgage; Median gross rent: $850 per month; Rental vacancy rate: 0.0%

Health Insurance: 90.4% have insurance; 64.2% have private insurance; 44.4% have public insurance; 9.6% do not have insurance; 9.8% of children under 18 do not have insurance
Transportation: Commute: 86.2% car, 0.0% public transportation, 7.2% walk, 4.6% work from home; Mean travel time to work: 21.2 minutes

LENOX (town). Covers a land area of 36.243 square miles and a water area of 0.023 square miles. Located at 43.11° N. Lat; 75.76° W. Long. Elevation is 528 feet.
Population: 9,033; Growth (since 2000): 4.2%; Density: 249.2 persons per square mile; Race: 94.6% White, 1.5% Black/African American, 0.1% Asian, 0.3% American Indian/Alaska Native, 0.0% Native Hawaiian/Other Pacific Islander, 3.4% Two or more races, 0.1% Hispanic of any race; Average household size: 2.32; Median age: 42.1; Age under 18: 21.3%; Age 65 and over: 17.5%; Males per 100 females: 94.5; Marriage status: 29.4% never married, 49.2% now married, 3.1% separated, 8.7% widowed, 12.7% divorced; Foreign born: 0.3%; Speak English only: 97.2%; With disability: 13.6%; Veterans: 11.0%; Ancestry: 22.1% American, 18.0% Italian, 17.2% German, 15.1% Irish, 12.8% English
Employment: 14.2% management, business, and financial, 5.3% computer, engineering, and science, 8.5% education, legal, community service, arts, and media, 4.2% healthcare practitioners, 18.4% service, 27.0% sales and office, 10.9% natural resources, construction, and maintenance, 11.6% production, transportation, and material moving
Income: Per capita: $25,016; Median household: $46,815; Average household: $56,307; Households with income of $100,000 or more: 14.3%; Poverty rate: 17.1%
Educational Attainment: High school diploma or higher: 91.4%; Bachelor's degree or higher: 21.1%; Graduate/professional degree or higher: 6.4%
Housing: Homeownership rate: 69.5%; Median home value: $108,300; Median year structure built: 1963; Homeowner vacancy rate: 0.6%; Median selected monthly owner costs: $1,255 with a mortgage, $454 without a mortgage; Median gross rent: $685 per month; Rental vacancy rate: 4.9%
Health Insurance: 95.7% have insurance; 74.0% have private insurance; 36.7% have public insurance; 4.3% do not have insurance; 0.0% of children under 18 do not have insurance
Transportation: Commute: 95.8% car, 0.1% public transportation, 1.9% walk, 1.5% work from home; Mean travel time to work: 24.1 minutes
Additional Information Contacts
Town of Lenox . . . . (315) 697-7547
  http://www.lenoxny.com

LEONARDSVILLE (unincorporated postal area)
ZCTA: 13364

Covers a land area of 2.956 square miles and a water area of 0 square miles. Located at 42.80° N. Lat; 75.26° W. Long. Elevation is 1,168 feet.
Population: 92; Growth (since 2000): n/a; Density: 31.1 persons per square mile; Race: 100.0% White, 0.0% Black/African American, 0.0% Asian, 0.0% American Indian/Alaska Native, 0.0% Native Hawaiian/Other Pacific Islander, 0.0% Two or more races, 0.0% Hispanic of any race; Average household size: 2.04; Median age: 51.5; Age under 18: 21.7%; Age 65 and over: 12.0%; Males per 100 females: 84.1; Marriage status: 18.2% never married, 39.0% now married, 0.0% separated, 7.8% widowed, 35.1% divorced; Foreign born: 0.0%; Speak English only: 100.0%; With disability: 6.5%; Veterans: 6.9%; Ancestry: 32.6% Irish, 22.8% German, 17.4% American, 16.3% Dutch, 10.9% English
Employment: 17.7% management, business, and financial, 8.1% computer, engineering, and science, 0.0% education, legal, community service, arts, and media, 0.0% healthcare practitioners, 9.7% service, 12.9% sales and office, 41.9% natural resources, construction, and maintenance, 9.7% production, transportation, and material moving
Income: Per capita: $26,425; Median household: $40,625; Average household: $50,249; Households with income of $100,000 or more: 11.1%; Poverty rate: 5.4%
Educational Attainment: High school diploma or higher: 100.0%; Bachelor's degree or higher: 22.1%; Graduate/professional degree or higher: n/a
Housing: Homeownership rate: 100.0%; Median home value: $58,800; Median year structure built: Before 1940; Homeowner vacancy rate: 23.7%; Median selected monthly owner costs: $1,131 with a mortgage, $442 without a mortgage; Median gross rent: n/a per month; Rental vacancy rate: 0.0%

Health Insurance: 100.0% have insurance; 94.6% have private insurance; 12.0% have public insurance; 0.0% do not have insurance; 0.0% of children under 18 do not have insurance
Transportation: Commute: 100.0% car, 0.0% public transportation, 0.0% walk, 0.0% work from home; Mean travel time to work: 46.1 minutes

LINCOLN (town). Covers a land area of 24.999 square miles and a water area of 0.059 square miles. Located at 43.03° N. Lat; 75.73° W. Long. Elevation is 689 feet.
Population: 1,989; Growth (since 2000): 9.4%; Density: 79.6 persons per square mile; Race: 96.6% White, 0.4% Black/African American, 0.4% Asian, 0.0% American Indian/Alaska Native, 0.0% Native Hawaiian/Other Pacific Islander, 2.4% Two or more races, 2.3% Hispanic of any race; Average household size: 2.80; Median age: 41.9; Age under 18: 27.0%; Age 65 and over: 13.2%; Males per 100 females: 113.6; Marriage status: 24.5% never married, 64.0% now married, 1.9% separated, 5.0% widowed, 6.4% divorced; Foreign born: 3.2%; Speak English only: 94.6%; With disability: 10.3%; Veterans: 8.1%; Ancestry: 27.5% American, 16.2% Irish, 15.5% German, 11.8% Italian, 9.7% English
Employment: 15.3% management, business, and financial, 4.0% computer, engineering, and science, 11.0% education, legal, community service, arts, and media, 6.2% healthcare practitioners, 19.5% service, 17.8% sales and office, 12.3% natural resources, construction, and maintenance, 13.8% production, transportation, and material moving
Income: Per capita: $27,669; Median household: $63,750; Average household: $75,697; Households with income of $100,000 or more: 27.4%; Poverty rate: 6.2%
Educational Attainment: High school diploma or higher: 90.4%; Bachelor's degree or higher: 22.6%; Graduate/professional degree or higher: 10.0%
Housing: Homeownership rate: 89.3%; Median home value: $125,800; Median year structure built: 1973; Homeowner vacancy rate: 0.5%; Median selected monthly owner costs: $1,313 with a mortgage, $462 without a mortgage; Median gross rent: $806 per month; Rental vacancy rate: 0.0%
Health Insurance: 92.5% have insurance; 74.9% have private insurance; 30.1% have public insurance; 7.5% do not have insurance; 5.8% of children under 18 do not have insurance
Transportation: Commute: 95.7% car, 0.0% public transportation, 1.1% walk, 2.9% work from home; Mean travel time to work: 24.9 minutes

MADISON (town). Covers a land area of 40.813 square miles and a water area of 0.576 square miles. Located at 42.89° N. Lat; 75.50° W. Long. Elevation is 1,204 feet.
Population: 2,979; Growth (since 2000): 6.4%; Density: 73.0 persons per square mile; Race: 98.6% White, 0.1% Black/African American, 0.1% Asian, 0.3% American Indian/Alaska Native, 0.0% Native Hawaiian/Other Pacific Islander, 0.9% Two or more races, 3.8% Hispanic of any race; Average household size: 2.49; Median age: 51.6; Age under 18: 12.8%; Age 65 and over: 20.9%; Males per 100 females: 99.9; Marriage status: 25.2% never married, 58.3% now married, 2.5% separated, 3.6% widowed, 12.9% divorced; Foreign born: 1.8%; Speak English only: 98.2%; With disability: 13.9%; Veterans: 11.4%; Ancestry: 40.2% American, 15.6% English, 13.8% Irish, 12.4% German, 7.7% Italian
Employment: 16.4% management, business, and financial, 2.7% computer, engineering, and science, 12.6% education, legal, community service, arts, and media, 5.8% healthcare practitioners, 18.0% service, 11.9% sales and office, 13.7% natural resources, construction, and maintenance, 18.9% production, transportation, and material moving
Income: Per capita: $25,792; Median household: $49,625; Average household: $61,737; Households with income of $100,000 or more: 16.1%; Poverty rate: 17.3%
Educational Attainment: High school diploma or higher: 87.5%; Bachelor's degree or higher: 24.8%; Graduate/professional degree or higher: 10.1%

School District(s)
Madison Central SD (PK-12)
   2014-15 Enrollment: 508 . . . . (315) 893-1878
Housing: Homeownership rate: 86.5%; Median home value: $115,500; Median year structure built: 1966; Homeowner vacancy rate: 0.0%; Median selected monthly owner costs: $1,362 with a mortgage, $554 without a mortgage; Median gross rent: $602 per month; Rental vacancy rate: 0.0%
Health Insurance: 93.2% have insurance; 73.7% have private insurance; 42.0% have public insurance; 6.8% do not have insurance; 0.0% of children under 18 do not have insurance

Transportation: Commute: 96.2% car, 0.0% public transportation, 1.1% walk, 0.4% work from home; Mean travel time to work: 21.9 minutes

MADISON (village). Covers a land area of 0.502 square miles and a water area of 0 square miles. Located at 42.90° N. Lat; 75.51° W. Long. Elevation is 1,204 feet.
Population: 327; Growth (since 2000): 3.8%; Density: 651.4 persons per square mile; Race: 97.9% White, 0.0% Black/African American, 0.3% Asian, 0.0% American Indian/Alaska Native, 0.0% Native Hawaiian/Other Pacific Islander, 1.8% Two or more races, 4.0% Hispanic of any race; Average household size: 2.53; Median age: 35.5; Age under 18: 25.1%; Age 65 and over: 13.5%; Males per 100 females: 89.4; Marriage status: 31.7% never married, 55.2% now married, 6.0% separated, 4.4% widowed, 8.7% divorced; Foreign born: 0.9%; Speak English only: 98.7%; With disability: 13.8%; Veterans: 3.3%; Ancestry: 43.1% American, 17.1% German, 14.4% Irish, 14.1% English, 6.1% Welsh
Employment: 14.6% management, business, and financial, 5.6% computer, engineering, and science, 8.3% education, legal, community service, arts, and media, 10.4% healthcare practitioners, 16.7% service, 23.6% sales and office, 13.9% natural resources, construction, and maintenance, 6.9% production, transportation, and material moving
Income: Per capita: $20,749; Median household: $46,563; Average household: $52,263; Households with income of $100,000 or more: 10.1%; Poverty rate: 11.9%
Educational Attainment: High school diploma or higher: 81.2%; Bachelor's degree or higher: 13.5%; Graduate/professional degree or higher: 6.3%

School District(s)
Madison Central SD (PK-12)
   2014-15 Enrollment: 508 . . . . (315) 893-1878
Housing: Homeownership rate: 65.9%; Median home value: $92,800; Median year structure built: Before 1940; Homeowner vacancy rate: 0.0%; Median selected monthly owner costs: $1,292 with a mortgage, $458 without a mortgage; Median gross rent: $727 per month; Rental vacancy rate: 0.0%
Health Insurance: 91.4% have insurance; 52.0% have private insurance; 54.1% have public insurance; 8.6% do not have insurance; 0.0% of children under 18 do not have insurance
Transportation: Commute: 90.3% car, 0.0% public transportation, 9.7% walk, 0.0% work from home; Mean travel time to work: 18.6 minutes

MORRISVILLE (village). Covers a land area of 1.153 square miles and a water area of 0 square miles. Located at 42.90° N. Lat; 75.64° W. Long. Elevation is 1,348 feet.
Population: 1,938; Growth (since 2000): -9.8%; Density: 1,681.6 persons per square mile; Race: 76.2% White, 17.2% Black/African American, 2.4% Asian, 0.6% American Indian/Alaska Native, 0.2% Native Hawaiian/Other Pacific Islander, 2.3% Two or more races, 9.5% Hispanic of any race; Average household size: 2.60; Median age: 20.9; Age under 18: 7.3%; Age 65 and over: 11.0%; Males per 100 females: 106.1; Marriage status: 78.5% never married, 14.9% now married, 0.2% separated, 3.2% widowed, 3.4% divorced; Foreign born: 5.7%; Speak English only: 88.8%; With disability: 2.5%; Veterans: 4.3%; Ancestry: 44.5% American, 9.8% German, 9.2% Irish, 6.7% English, 3.0% Italian
Employment: 7.0% management, business, and financial, 3.4% computer, engineering, and science, 27.7% education, legal, community service, arts, and media, 0.4% healthcare practitioners, 25.2% service, 18.7% sales and office, 14.6% natural resources, construction, and maintenance, 2.9% production, transportation, and material moving
Income: Per capita: $9,610; Median household: $50,652; Average household: $58,394; Households with income of $100,000 or more: 11.8%; Poverty rate: 15.3%
Educational Attainment: High school diploma or higher: 89.5%; Bachelor's degree or higher: 25.1%; Graduate/professional degree or higher: 15.2%

School District(s)
Morrisville-Eaton Central SD (PK-12)
   2014-15 Enrollment: 751 . . . . (315) 684-9300
Four-year College(s)
Morrisville State College (Public)
   Fall 2014 Enrollment: 2,910 . . . . (315) 684-6000
   2015-16 Tuition: In-state $7,970; Out-of-state $18,020
Housing: Homeownership rate: 70.8%; Median home value: $116,000; Median year structure built: Before 1940; Homeowner vacancy rate: 5.1%; Median selected monthly owner costs: $1,278 with a mortgage, $612

without a mortgage; Median gross rent: $634 per month; Rental vacancy rate: 39.6%
Health Insurance: 97.9% have insurance; 88.0% have private insurance; 17.6% have public insurance; 2.1% do not have insurance; 2.8% of children under 18 do not have insurance
Transportation: Commute: 48.0% car, 0.2% public transportation, 40.7% walk, 8.9% work from home; Mean travel time to work: 15.4 minutes

MUNNSVILLE (village).
Covers a land area of 0.849 square miles and a water area of 0 square miles. Located at 42.98° N. Lat; 75.59° W. Long. Elevation is 659 feet.
Population: 498; Growth (since 2000): 14.0%; Density: 586.2 persons per square mile; Race: 93.0% White, 0.0% Black/African American, 0.6% Asian, 0.0% American Indian/Alaska Native, 0.0% Native Hawaiian/Other Pacific Islander, 4.6% Two or more races, 1.2% Hispanic of any race; Average household size: 2.93; Median age: 28.6; Age under 18: 28.5%; Age 65 and over: 7.0%; Males per 100 females: 95.1; Marriage status: 42.5% never married, 46.1% now married, 4.1% separated, 4.9% widowed, 6.5% divorced; Foreign born: 0.6%; Speak English only: 100.0%; With disability: 10.4%; Veterans: 6.5%; Ancestry: 54.8% American, 13.7% German, 9.2% English, 6.4% Irish, 6.0% Italian
Employment: 10.4% management, business, and financial, 3.8% computer, engineering, and science, 8.3% education, legal, community service, arts, and media, 4.6% healthcare practitioners, 21.3% service, 20.4% sales and office, 10.8% natural resources, construction, and maintenance, 20.4% production, transportation, and material moving
Income: Per capita: $21,604; Median household: $48,125; Average household: $61,024; Households with income of $100,000 or more: 11.8%; Poverty rate: 14.5%
Educational Attainment: High school diploma or higher: 91.3%; Bachelor's degree or higher: 13.9%; Graduate/professional degree or higher: 6.3%
School District(s)
Stockbridge Valley Central SD (PK-12)
    2014-15 Enrollment: 450 . . . . (315) 495-4400
Housing: Homeownership rate: 60.0%; Median home value: $95,800; Median year structure built: Before 1940; Homeowner vacancy rate: 0.0%; Median selected monthly owner costs: $1,097 with a mortgage, $430 without a mortgage; Median gross rent: $667 per month; Rental vacancy rate: 2.9%
Health Insurance: 93.8% have insurance; 70.3% have private insurance; 38.6% have public insurance; 6.2% do not have insurance; 0.0% of children under 18 do not have insurance
Transportation: Commute: 98.7% car, 0.0% public transportation, 0.0% walk, 1.3% work from home; Mean travel time to work: 19.9 minutes

NELSON (town).
Covers a land area of 43.060 square miles and a water area of 0.996 square miles. Located at 42.89° N. Lat; 75.75° W. Long. Elevation is 1,437 feet.
Population: 1,985; Growth (since 2000): 1.1%; Density: 46.1 persons per square mile; Race: 98.4% White, 0.8% Black/African American, 0.3% Asian, 0.4% American Indian/Alaska Native, 0.0% Native Hawaiian/Other Pacific Islander, 0.1% Two or more races, 1.1% Hispanic of any race; Average household size: 2.56; Median age: 44.7; Age under 18: 22.3%; Age 65 and over: 18.8%; Males per 100 females: 104.3; Marriage status: 26.8% never married, 56.8% now married, 3.3% separated, 4.6% widowed, 11.7% divorced; Foreign born: 4.0%; Speak English only: 96.5%; With disability: 9.0%; Veterans: 11.4%; Ancestry: 26.4% American, 18.5% German, 18.4% Irish, 17.4% English, 6.7% Italian
Employment: 17.8% management, business, and financial, 7.0% computer, engineering, and science, 12.4% education, legal, community service, arts, and media, 6.7% healthcare practitioners, 12.9% service, 17.8% sales and office, 14.2% natural resources, construction, and maintenance, 11.2% production, transportation, and material moving
Income: Per capita: $29,800; Median household: $69,375; Average household: $75,358; Households with income of $100,000 or more: 26.0%; Poverty rate: 10.4%
Educational Attainment: High school diploma or higher: 92.7%; Bachelor's degree or higher: 32.0%; Graduate/professional degree or higher: 14.6%
Housing: Homeownership rate: 88.8%; Median home value: $171,800; Median year structure built: 1971; Homeowner vacancy rate: 2.0%; Median selected monthly owner costs: $1,410 with a mortgage, $666 without a mortgage; Median gross rent: $1,039 per month; Rental vacancy rate: 13.0%

Health Insurance: 95.2% have insurance; 77.4% have private insurance; 34.4% have public insurance; 4.8% do not have insurance; 2.0% of children under 18 do not have insurance
Transportation: Commute: 93.9% car, 0.0% public transportation, 2.8% walk, 3.2% work from home; Mean travel time to work: 27.1 minutes

NEW WOODSTOCK (unincorporated postal area)
ZCTA: 13122
Covers a land area of 18.700 square miles and a water area of 0.015 square miles. Located at 42.84° N. Lat; 75.86° W. Long. Elevation is 1,306 feet.
Population: 1,325; Growth (since 2000): 9.6%; Density: 70.9 persons per square mile; Race: 98.6% White, 0.2% Black/African American, 0.0% Asian, 0.0% American Indian/Alaska Native, 0.0% Native Hawaiian/Other Pacific Islander, 1.1% Two or more races, 0.0% Hispanic of any race; Average household size: 3.32; Median age: 36.5; Age under 18: 38.7%; Age 65 and over: 11.2%; Males per 100 females: 93.1; Marriage status: 18.9% never married, 75.8% now married, 2.4% separated, 1.7% widowed, 3.6% divorced; Foreign born: 2.0%; Speak English only: 99.1%; With disability: 4.1%; Veterans: 24.6%; Ancestry: 37.7% American, 13.0% German, 12.9% Irish, 9.4% English, 8.1% Italian
Employment: 12.3% management, business, and financial, 6.0% computer, engineering, and science, 8.1% education, legal, community service, arts, and media, 9.0% healthcare practitioners, 13.7% service, 16.8% sales and office, 13.0% natural resources, construction, and maintenance, 21.1% production, transportation, and material moving
Income: Per capita: $22,753; Median household: $61,518; Average household: $75,934; Households with income of $100,000 or more: 18.9%; Poverty rate: 6.3%
Educational Attainment: High school diploma or higher: 95.5%; Bachelor's degree or higher: 22.0%; Graduate/professional degree or higher: 6.9%
Housing: Homeownership rate: 84.5%; Median home value: $154,200; Median year structure built: 1970; Homeowner vacancy rate: 0.0%; Median selected monthly owner costs: $1,357 with a mortgage, $470 without a mortgage; Median gross rent: $536 per month; Rental vacancy rate: 0.0%
Health Insurance: 94.4% have insurance; 73.4% have private insurance; 25.6% have public insurance; 5.6% do not have insurance; 0.0% of children under 18 do not have insurance
Transportation: Commute: 83.0% car, 0.0% public transportation, 2.9% walk, 14.1% work from home; Mean travel time to work: 26.1 minutes

NORTH BROOKFIELD (unincorporated postal area)
ZCTA: 13418
Covers a land area of 5.216 square miles and a water area of <.001 square miles. Located at 42.85° N. Lat; 75.38° W. Long. Elevation is 1,299 feet.
Population: 290; Growth (since 2000): -10.8%; Density: 55.6 persons per square mile; Race: 100.0% White, 0.0% Black/African American, 0.0% Asian, 0.0% American Indian/Alaska Native, 0.0% Native Hawaiian/Other Pacific Islander, 0.0% Two or more races, 0.0% Hispanic of any race; Average household size: 3.09; Median age: 44.8; Age under 18: 30.0%; Age 65 and over: 14.1%; Males per 100 females: 109.0; Marriage status: 37.0% never married, 51.6% now married, 0.0% separated, 8.1% widowed, 3.3% divorced; Foreign born: 0.0%; Speak English only: 100.0%; With disability: 9.0%; Veterans: 16.7%; Ancestry: 29.3% American, 17.2% German, 10.7% European, 9.3% English, 9.3% Irish
Employment: 12.9% management, business, and financial, 3.0% computer, engineering, and science, 3.0% education, legal, community service, arts, and media, 9.1% healthcare practitioners, 15.2% service, 17.4% sales and office, 19.7% natural resources, construction, and maintenance, 19.7% production, transportation, and material moving
Income: Per capita: $24,738; Median household: $53,750; Average household: $71,631; Households with income of $100,000 or more: 21.3%; Poverty rate: 14.1%
Educational Attainment: High school diploma or higher: 94.6%; Bachelor's degree or higher: 7.1%; Graduate/professional degree or higher: 2.7%
Housing: Homeownership rate: 88.3%; Median home value: $71,400; Median year structure built: Before 1940; Homeowner vacancy rate: 0.0%; Median selected monthly owner costs: $970 with a mortgage,

$396 without a mortgage; Median gross rent: n/a per month; Rental vacancy rate: 0.0%
Health Insurance: 95.2% have insurance; 63.1% have private insurance; 39.3% have public insurance; 4.8% do not have insurance; 0.0% of children under 18 do not have insurance
Transportation: Commute: 95.5% car, 0.0% public transportation, 0.0% walk, 4.5% work from home; Mean travel time to work: 27.5 minutes

ONEIDA (city).
Covers a land area of 22.047 square miles and a water area of 0.082 square miles. Located at 43.07° N. Lat; 75.67° W. Long. Elevation is 430 feet.
History: The establishment and early growth of Oneida resulted from a shrewd bargain made by Sands Higinbotham, owner of the city site, with the railroad. The railroad received free right of way across his land, plus ample ground for a station, on the condition that it stop every passenger train at the depot for ten minutes for refreshments. Higinbotham then built the Railroad House to serve meals to passengers.
Population: 11,252; Growth (since 2000): 2.4%; Density: 510.4 persons per square mile; Race: 94.5% White, 1.5% Black/African American, 0.9% Asian, 2.1% American Indian/Alaska Native, 0.0% Native Hawaiian/Other Pacific Islander, 0.7% Two or more races, 2.7% Hispanic of any race; Average household size: 2.48; Median age: 41.0; Age under 18: 22.3%; Age 65 and over: 14.2%; Males per 100 females: 93.7; Marriage status: 34.0% never married, 49.2% now married, 3.0% separated, 4.7% widowed, 12.1% divorced; Foreign born: 3.3%; Speak English only: 95.1%; With disability: 13.8%; Veterans: 11.8%; Ancestry: 28.6% American, 16.4% Irish, 15.2% German, 11.0% Italian, 10.8% English
Employment: 9.6% management, business, and financial, 2.6% computer, engineering, and science, 15.2% education, legal, community service, arts, and media, 5.2% healthcare practitioners, 22.7% service, 25.4% sales and office, 7.2% natural resources, construction, and maintenance, 12.0% production, transportation, and material moving
Income: Per capita: $23,214; Median household: $46,149; Average household: $56,941; Households with income of $100,000 or more: 14.5%; Poverty rate: 17.3%
Educational Attainment: High school diploma or higher: 87.3%; Bachelor's degree or higher: 20.6%; Graduate/professional degree or higher: 8.9%

School District(s)
Oneida City SD (PK-12)
  2014-15 Enrollment: 2,292 . . . . (315) 363-2550
Housing: Homeownership rate: 57.6%; Median home value: $106,400; Median year structure built: Before 1940; Homeowner vacancy rate: 3.1%; Median selected monthly owner costs: $1,179 with a mortgage, $479 without a mortgage; Median gross rent: $662 per month; Rental vacancy rate: 3.6%
Health Insurance: 93.1% have insurance; 65.1% have private insurance; 40.6% have public insurance; 6.9% do not have insurance; 2.8% of children under 18 do not have insurance
Hospitals: Oneida Healthcare Center (101 beds)
Safety: Violent crime rate: 18.8 per 10,000 population; Property crime rate: 353.6 per 10,000 population
Newspapers: Indian Country Today (weekly circulation 125,000); Oneida Daily Dispatch (daily circulation 6,600); Rome Observer (weekly circulation 11,000)
Transportation: Commute: 88.3% car, 1.3% public transportation, 5.9% walk, 2.0% work from home; Mean travel time to work: 18.3 minutes
Additional Information Contacts
City of Oneida . . . . (315) 363-7378
  http://www.oneidacity.com

PETERBORO (unincorporated postal area)
ZCTA: 13134
Covers a land area of 0.083 square miles and a water area of 0 square miles. Located at 42.97° N. Lat; 75.68° W. Long. Elevation is 1,296 feet.
Population: 97; Growth (since 2000): n/a; Density: 1,175.1 persons per square mile; Race: 93.8% White, 0.0% Black/African American, 0.0% Asian, 6.2% American Indian/Alaska Native, 0.0% Native Hawaiian/Other Pacific Islander, 0.0% Two or more races, 0.0% Hispanic of any race; Average household size: 2.77; Median age: 52.1; Age under 18: 14.4%; Age 65 and over: 0.0%; Males per 100 females: 70.0; Marriage status: 34.9% never married, 43.4% now married, 0.0% separated, 7.2% widowed, 14.5% divorced; Foreign born: 0.0%; Speak English only: 96.4%; With disability: 8.2%; Veterans: 0.0%; Ancestry:

63.9% American, 7.2% Scotch-Irish, 6.2% French, 6.2% German, 3.1% English
Employment: 21.2% management, business, and financial, 9.1% computer, engineering, and science, 0.0% education, legal, community service, arts, and media, 0.0% healthcare practitioners, 0.0% service, 9.1% sales and office, 9.1% natural resources, construction, and maintenance, 51.5% production, transportation, and material moving
Income: Per capita: $19,654; Median household: $44,583; Average household: $52,443; Households with income of $100,000 or more: 8.6%; Poverty rate: 15.5%
Educational Attainment: High school diploma or higher: 87.1%; Bachelor's degree or higher: 21.0%; Graduate/professional degree or higher: n/a
Housing: Homeownership rate: 74.3%; Median home value: n/a; Median year structure built: Before 1940; Homeowner vacancy rate: 0.0%; Median selected monthly owner costs: $983 with a mortgage, $0 without a mortgage; Median gross rent: n/a per month; Rental vacancy rate: 0.0%
Health Insurance: 84.5% have insurance; 38.1% have private insurance; 46.4% have public insurance; 15.5% do not have insurance; 0.0% of children under 18 do not have insurance
Transportation: Commute: 90.9% car, 0.0% public transportation, 0.0% walk, 9.1% work from home; Mean travel time to work: 0.0 minutes

SMITHFIELD (town).
Covers a land area of 24.274 square miles and a water area of 0.086 square miles. Located at 42.96° N. Lat; 75.66° W. Long.
Population: 1,243; Growth (since 2000): 3.2%; Density: 51.2 persons per square mile; Race: 96.3% White, 0.6% Black/African American, 0.0% Asian, 0.6% American Indian/Alaska Native, 0.0% Native Hawaiian/Other Pacific Islander, 2.4% Two or more races, 1.7% Hispanic of any race; Average household size: 2.66; Median age: 45.3; Age under 18: 16.0%; Age 65 and over: 15.8%; Males per 100 females: 101.6; Marriage status: 27.8% never married, 53.6% now married, 1.3% separated, 4.5% widowed, 14.1% divorced; Foreign born: 0.5%; Speak English only: 95.9%; With disability: 14.4%; Veterans: 4.4%; Ancestry: 37.7% American, 14.2% German, 10.1% English, 8.7% Irish, 5.4% Polish
Employment: 13.8% management, business, and financial, 1.5% computer, engineering, and science, 9.4% education, legal, community service, arts, and media, 4.8% healthcare practitioners, 10.8% service, 16.6% sales and office, 21.5% natural resources, construction, and maintenance, 21.5% production, transportation, and material moving
Income: Per capita: $25,219; Median household: $53,750; Average household: $65,335; Households with income of $100,000 or more: 12.1%; Poverty rate: 11.3%
Educational Attainment: High school diploma or higher: 86.9%; Bachelor's degree or higher: 14.5%; Graduate/professional degree or higher: 5.9%
Housing: Homeownership rate: 89.3%; Median home value: $104,200; Median year structure built: 1975; Homeowner vacancy rate: 0.0%; Median selected monthly owner costs: $1,204 with a mortgage, $436 without a mortgage; Median gross rent: $833 per month; Rental vacancy rate: 0.0%
Health Insurance: 88.0% have insurance; 66.1% have private insurance; 34.0% have public insurance; 12.0% do not have insurance; 18.1% of children under 18 do not have insurance
Transportation: Commute: 92.8% car, 0.9% public transportation, 0.5% walk, 4.5% work from home; Mean travel time to work: 22.9 minutes

STOCKBRIDGE (town).
Covers a land area of 31.655 square miles and a water area of 0 square miles. Located at 42.99° N. Lat; 75.59° W. Long. Elevation is 669 feet.
Population: 2,238; Growth (since 2000): 7.6%; Density: 70.7 persons per square mile; Race: 93.8% White, 0.0% Black/African American, 0.1% Asian, 3.4% American Indian/Alaska Native, 0.0% Native Hawaiian/Other Pacific Islander, 2.2% Two or more races, 0.7% Hispanic of any race; Average household size: 2.85; Median age: 38.5; Age under 18: 21.3%; Age 65 and over: 11.0%; Males per 100 females: 102.8; Marriage status: 35.2% never married, 52.2% now married, 3.8% separated, 3.8% widowed, 8.7% divorced; Foreign born: 0.9%; Speak English only: 99.5%; With disability: 10.5%; Veterans: 7.1%; Ancestry: 42.0% American, 18.8% German, 10.8% Irish, 9.8% English, 5.4% Italian
Employment: 10.3% management, business, and financial, 4.7% computer, engineering, and science, 5.7% education, legal, community service, arts, and media, 6.5% healthcare practitioners, 18.1% service,

17.5% sales and office, 13.0% natural resources, construction, and maintenance, 24.2% production, transportation, and material moving
Income: Per capita: $22,005; Median household: $49,688; Average household: $59,294; Households with income of $100,000 or more: 15.1%; Poverty rate: 12.8%
Educational Attainment: High school diploma or higher: 90.7%; Bachelor's degree or higher: 12.3%; Graduate/professional degree or higher: 4.3%
Housing: Homeownership rate: 79.2%; Median home value: $91,900; Median year structure built: 1964; Homeowner vacancy rate: 1.3%; Median selected monthly owner costs: $1,163 with a mortgage, $447 without a mortgage; Median gross rent: $714 per month; Rental vacancy rate: 1.2%
Health Insurance: 89.3% have insurance; 68.0% have private insurance; 31.4% have public insurance; 10.7% do not have insurance; 2.1% of children under 18 do not have insurance
Transportation: Commute: 95.0% car, 0.0% public transportation, 3.3% walk, 1.7% work from home; Mean travel time to work: 20.0 minutes

SULLIVAN (town).
Covers a land area of 73.163 square miles and a water area of 0.199 square miles. Located at 43.09° N. Lat; 75.88° W. Long. Elevation is 456 feet.
Population: 15,334; Growth (since 2000): 2.3%; Density: 209.6 persons per square mile; Race: 98.7% White, 0.6% Black/African American, 0.3% Asian, 0.0% American Indian/Alaska Native, 0.0% Native Hawaiian/Other Pacific Islander, 0.3% Two or more races, 1.3% Hispanic of any race; Average household size: 2.62; Median age: 44.2; Age under 18: 22.5%; Age 65 and over: 15.5%; Males per 100 females: 96.8; Marriage status: 28.2% never married, 54.2% now married, 2.1% separated, 5.6% widowed, 11.9% divorced; Foreign born: 1.8%; Speak English only: 98.6%; With disability: 11.3%; Veterans: 9.4%; Ancestry: 24.2% American, 18.8% German, 18.8% Irish, 14.6% English, 10.3% Italian
Employment: 17.6% management, business, and financial, 5.0% computer, engineering, and science, 9.0% education, legal, community service, arts, and media, 5.8% healthcare practitioners, 13.8% service, 26.0% sales and office, 9.2% natural resources, construction, and maintenance, 13.6% production, transportation, and material moving
Income: Per capita: $28,986; Median household: $63,934; Average household: $73,435; Households with income of $100,000 or more: 23.8%; Poverty rate: 7.9%
Educational Attainment: High school diploma or higher: 90.4%; Bachelor's degree or higher: 26.6%; Graduate/professional degree or higher: 11.0%
Housing: Homeownership rate: 81.0%; Median home value: $138,200; Median year structure built: 1969; Homeowner vacancy rate: 5.2%; Median selected monthly owner costs: $1,351 with a mortgage, $527 without a mortgage; Median gross rent: $762 per month; Rental vacancy rate: 3.9%
Health Insurance: 95.2% have insurance; 76.0% have private insurance; 32.7% have public insurance; 4.8% do not have insurance; 0.9% of children under 18 do not have insurance
Transportation: Commute: 93.0% car, 0.0% public transportation, 2.5% walk, 3.2% work from home; Mean travel time to work: 25.1 minutes
Additional Information Contacts
Town of Sullivan . . . . (315) 687-7221
  http://townofsullivan.org/content

WAMPSVILLE (village).
County seat. Covers a land area of 1.009 square miles and a water area of 0.007 square miles. Located at 43.08° N. Lat; 75.71° W. Long. Elevation is 482 feet.
Population: 577; Growth (since 2000): 2.9%; Density: 571.9 persons per square mile; Race: 99.7% White, 0.0% Black/African American, 0.0% Asian, 0.3% American Indian/Alaska Native, 0.0% Native Hawaiian/Other Pacific Islander, 0.0% Two or more races, 0.0% Hispanic of any race; Average household size: 2.36; Median age: 47.3; Age under 18: 17.7%; Age 65 and over: 19.8%; Males per 100 females: 93.9; Marriage status: 34.8% never married, 50.2% now married, 2.9% separated, 7.9% widowed, 7.1% divorced; Foreign born: 0.7%; Speak English only: 100.0%; With disability: 9.0%; Veterans: 14.9%; Ancestry: 60.3% American, 13.5% English, 11.1% German, 9.4% Irish, 4.7% Italian
Employment: 11.1% management, business, and financial, 4.6% computer, engineering, and science, 3.1% education, legal, community service, arts, and media, 4.6% healthcare practitioners, 18.0% service, 27.6% sales and office, 11.1% natural resources, construction, and maintenance, 19.9% production, transportation, and material moving

Income: Per capita: $22,203; Median household: $40,556; Average household: $51,870; Households with income of $100,000 or more: 16.0%; Poverty rate: 21.8%
Educational Attainment: High school diploma or higher: 91.1%; Bachelor's degree or higher: 11.3%; Graduate/professional degree or higher: 4.5%

School District(s)
Oneida City SD (PK-12)
  2014-15 Enrollment: 2,292 . . . . (315) 363-2550
Housing: Homeownership rate: 88.5%; Median home value: $132,800; Median year structure built: 1954; Homeowner vacancy rate: 6.9%; Median selected monthly owner costs: $1,160 with a mortgage, $503 without a mortgage; Median gross rent: $771 per month; Rental vacancy rate: 0.0%
Health Insurance: 96.2% have insurance; 66.0% have private insurance; 41.8% have public insurance; 3.8% do not have insurance; 0.0% of children under 18 do not have insurance
Transportation: Commute: 96.9% car, 1.2% public transportation, 0.4% walk, 1.6% work from home; Mean travel time to work: 20.1 minutes

WEST EATON (unincorporated postal area)
ZCTA: 13484
  Covers a land area of 2.550 square miles and a water area of 0 square miles. Located at 42.87° N. Lat; 75.66° W. Long. Elevation is 1,358 feet.
Population: 252; Growth (since 2000): n/a; Density: 98.8 persons per square mile; Race: 100.0% White, 0.0% Black/African American, 0.0% Asian, 0.0% American Indian/Alaska Native, 0.0% Native Hawaiian/Other Pacific Islander, 0.0% Two or more races, 0.0% Hispanic of any race; Average household size: 3.76; Median age: 15.6; Age under 18: 58.3%; Age 65 and over: 0.0%; Males per 100 females: 102.3; Marriage status: 30.9% never married, 61.2% now married, 11.2% separated, 0.0% widowed, 7.9% divorced; Foreign born: 0.0%; Speak English only: 100.0%; With disability: 6.7%; Veterans: 0.0%; Ancestry: 95.2% American
Employment: 0.0% management, business, and financial, 36.2% computer, engineering, and science, 0.0% education, legal, community service, arts, and media, 11.4% healthcare practitioners, 52.4% service, 0.0% sales and office, 0.0% natural resources, construction, and maintenance, 0.0% production, transportation, and material moving
Income: Per capita: $20,747; Median household: $92,796; Average household: $78,033; Households with income of $100,000 or more: n/a; Poverty rate: n/a
Educational Attainment: High school diploma or higher: 100.0%; Bachelor's degree or higher: 11.4%; Graduate/professional degree or higher: n/a
Housing: Homeownership rate: 100.0%; Median home value: n/a; Median year structure built: Before 1940; Homeowner vacancy rate: 0.0%; Median selected monthly owner costs: $0 with a mortgage, $0 without a mortgage; Median gross rent: n/a per month; Rental vacancy rate: 0.0%
Health Insurance: 100.0% have insurance; 77.8% have private insurance; 22.2% have public insurance; 0.0% do not have insurance; 0.0% of children under 18 do not have insurance
Transportation: Commute: 63.8% car, 0.0% public transportation, 0.0% walk, 36.2% work from home; Mean travel time to work: 0.0 minutes

WEST EDMESTON (unincorporated postal area)
ZCTA: 13485
  Covers a land area of 44.170 square miles and a water area of 0.160 square miles. Located at 42.79° N. Lat; 75.32° W. Long..
Population: 1,029; Growth (since 2000): 8.9%; Density: 23.3 persons per square mile; Race: 98.8% White, 0.3% Black/African American, 0.0% Asian, 0.0% American Indian/Alaska Native, 0.0% Native Hawaiian/Other Pacific Islander, 0.9% Two or more races, 0.0% Hispanic of any race; Average household size: 2.40; Median age: 47.9; Age under 18: 18.8%; Age 65 and over: 21.0%; Males per 100 females: 101.4; Marriage status: 20.0% never married, 65.8% now married, 3.7% separated, 4.6% widowed, 9.7% divorced; Foreign born: 1.4%; Speak English only: 98.3%; With disability: 21.3%; Veterans: 11.5%; Ancestry: 20.4% German, 14.8% American, 12.5% English, 6.3% Irish, 5.0% French
Employment: 13.8% management, business, and financial, 5.7% computer, engineering, and science, 8.8% education, legal, community service, arts, and media, 8.4% healthcare practitioners, 17.7% service, 18.8% sales and office, 8.6% natural resources, construction, and maintenance, 18.1% production, transportation, and material moving

Income: Per capita: $22,140; Median household: $40,078; Average household: $50,577; Households with income of $100,000 or more: 9.1%; Poverty rate: 16.2%

Educational Attainment: High school diploma or higher: 83.8%; Bachelor's degree or higher: 12.8%; Graduate/professional degree or higher: 5.4%

Housing: Homeownership rate: 87.4%; Median home value: $79,700; Median year structure built: 1976; Homeowner vacancy rate: 0.8%; Median selected monthly owner costs: $1,005 with a mortgage, $360 without a mortgage; Median gross rent: $803 per month; Rental vacancy rate: 0.0%

Health Insurance: 91.5% have insurance; 60.3% have private insurance; 44.4% have public insurance; 8.5% do not have insurance; 1.6% of children under 18 do not have insurance

Transportation: Commute: 89.9% car, 0.5% public transportation, 3.7% walk, 6.0% work from home; Mean travel time to work: 28.9 minutes

Manhattan Borough

See New York City

Monroe County

Located in western New York; bounded on the north by Lake Ontario; drained by the Genesee River. Covers a land area of 657.205 square miles, a water area of 709.524 square miles, and is located in the Eastern Time Zone at 43.46° N. Lat., 77.66° W. Long. The county was founded in 1821. County seat is Rochester.

Monroe County is part of the Rochester, NY Metropolitan Statistical Area. The entire metro area includes: Livingston County, NY; Monroe County, NY; Ontario County, NY; Orleans County, NY; Wayne County, NY; Yates County, NY

Weather Station: Rochester Intl Arpt   Elevation: 600 feet

	Jan	Feb	Mar	Apr	May	Jun	Jul	Aug	Sep	Oct	Nov	Dec
High	32	34	43	56	68	77	81	79	72	60	48	37
Low	18	19	26	37	47	56	61	60	52	42	33	23
Precip	2.4	1.9	2.6	2.8	2.8	3.4	3.2	3.5	3.4	2.7	2.9	2.6
Snow	27.0	21.3	17.0	3.9	0.4	tr	tr	0.0	tr	0.1	7.6	22.1

High and Low temperatures in degrees Fahrenheit; Precipitation and Snow in inches

Population: 749,356; Growth (since 2000): 1.9%; Density: 1,140.2 persons per square mile; Race: 76.0% White, 15.3% Black/African American, 3.5% Asian, 0.4% American Indian/Alaska Native, 0.0% Native Hawaiian/Other Pacific Islander, 2.7% two or more races, 7.9% Hispanic of any race; Average household size: 2.41; Median age: 38.5; Age under 18: 21.7%; Age 65 and over: 15.0%; Males per 100 females: 93.2; Marriage status: 37.3% never married, 46.4% now married, 2.3% separated, 6.3% widowed, 10.0% divorced; Foreign born: 8.3%; Speak English only: 87.1%; With disability: 12.6%; Veterans: 6.9%; Ancestry: 19.3% German, 17.8% Italian, 15.1% Irish, 10.5% English, 5.1% Polish

Religion: Six largest groups: 25.7% Catholicism, 4.8% Non-denominational Protestant, 2.8% Baptist, 2.3% Methodist/Pietist, 2.1% Lutheran, 2.0% Presbyterian-Reformed

Economy: Unemployment rate: 4.7%; Leading industries: 13.6 % retail trade; 11.5 % professional, scientific, and technical services; 11.1 % health care and social assistance; Farms: 475 totaling 98,676 acres; Company size: 22 employ 1,000 or more persons, 41 employs 500 to 999 persons, 444 employ 100 to 499 persons, 16,992 employ less than 100 persons; Business ownership: 20,290 women-owned, 5,333 Black-owned, 2,216 Hispanic-owned, 2,420 Asian-owned, 354 American Indian/Alaska Native-owned

Employment: 14.3% management, business, and financial, 7.4% computer, engineering, and science, 13.1% education, legal, community service, arts, and media, 7.1% healthcare practitioners, 17.8% service, 24.3% sales and office, 5.7% natural resources, construction, and maintenance, 10.3% production, transportation, and material moving

Income: Per capita: $29,424; Median household: $52,553; Average household: $70,955; Households with income of $100,000 or more: 22.0%; Poverty rate: 15.2%

Educational Attainment: High school diploma or higher: 90.2%; Bachelor's degree or higher: 36.2%; Graduate/professional degree or higher: 15.9%

Housing: Homeownership rate: 64.2%; Median home value: $138,600; Median year structure built: 1963; Homeowner vacancy rate: 1.1%; Median selected monthly owner costs: $1,365 with a mortgage, $576 without a mortgage; Median gross rent: $826 per month; Rental vacancy rate: 6.1%

Vital Statistics: Birth rate: 112.9 per 10,000 population; Death rate: 86.2 per 10,000 population; Age-adjusted cancer mortality rate: 161.2 deaths per 100,000 population

Health Insurance: 93.9% have insurance; 73.1% have private insurance; 34.5% have public insurance; 6.1% do not have insurance; 2.9% of children under 18 do not have insurance

Health Care: Physicians: 48.7 per 10,000 population; Dentists: 7.5 per 10,000 population; Hospital beds: 29.2 per 10,000 population; Hospital admissions: 1,330.8 per 10,000 population

Air Quality Index (AQI): Percent of Days: 81.1% good, 18.9% moderate, 0.0% unhealthy for sensitive individuals, 0.0% unhealthy, 0.0% very unhealthy; Annual median: 36; Annual maximum: 78

Transportation: Commute: 89.1% car, 2.9% public transportation, 3.2% walk, 3.5% work from home; Mean travel time to work: 19.9 minutes

2016 Presidential Election: 39.7% Trump, 54.9% Clinton, 3.8% Johnson, 1.5% Stein

National and State Parks: Hamlin Beach State Park

Additional Information Contacts

Monroe Government . . . . (585) 428-5301
  http://www.monroecounty.gov

Monroe County Communities

BRIGHTON (CDP). Covers a land area of 15.416 square miles and a water area of 0.168 square miles. Located at 43.12° N. Lat; 77.58° W. Long. Elevation is 446 feet.

Population: 36,929; Growth (since 2000): 3.8%; Density: 2,395.6 persons per square mile; Race: 79.4% White, 6.2% Black/African American, 10.8% Asian, 0.2% American Indian/Alaska Native, 0.0% Native Hawaiian/Other Pacific Islander, 2.8% Two or more races, 4.1% Hispanic of any race; Average household size: 2.16; Median age: 38.9; Age under 18: 18.0%; Age 65 and over: 18.6%; Males per 100 females: 89.3; Marriage status: 34.7% never married, 48.0% now married, 1.2% separated, 8.1% widowed, 9.2% divorced; Foreign born: 18.0%; Speak English only: 81.0%; With disability: 10.8%; Veterans: 6.2%; Ancestry: 18.2% German, 15.4% Irish, 12.8% Italian, 12.6% English, 5.9% Polish

Employment: 16.0% management, business, and financial, 12.6% computer, engineering, and science, 23.1% education, legal, community service, arts, and media, 12.1% healthcare practitioners, 11.1% service, 17.4% sales and office, 2.9% natural resources, construction, and maintenance, 4.9% production, transportation, and material moving

Income: Per capita: $41,519; Median household: $66,149; Average household: $92,493; Households with income of $100,000 or more: 30.6%; Poverty rate: 9.5%

Educational Attainment: High school diploma or higher: 94.4%; Bachelor's degree or higher: 61.9%; Graduate/professional degree or higher: 35.2%

Housing: Homeownership rate: 56.1%; Median home value: $170,300; Median year structure built: 1961; Homeowner vacancy rate: 0.4%; Median selected monthly owner costs: $1,631 with a mortgage, $757 without a mortgage; Median gross rent: $943 per month; Rental vacancy rate: 7.1%

Health Insurance: 94.5% have insurance; 84.4% have private insurance; 24.0% have public insurance; 5.5% do not have insurance; 3.8% of children under 18 do not have insurance

Safety: Violent crime rate: 5.9 per 10,000 population; Property crime rate: 209.6 per 10,000 population

Transportation: Commute: 88.7% car, 4.1% public transportation, 2.1% walk, 4.0% work from home; Mean travel time to work: 16.0 minutes

Additional Information Contacts

Town of Brighton . . . . (585) 784-5250
  http://www.townofbrighton.org

BROCKPORT (village). Covers a land area of 2.161 square miles and a water area of 0.047 square miles. Located at 43.21° N. Lat; 77.94° W. Long. Elevation is 518 feet.

History: Seat of State University of N.Y. College at Brockport. Incorporated 1829.

Population: 8,428; Growth (since 2000): 4.0%; Density: 3,899.2 persons per square mile; Race: 88.0% White, 3.5% Black/African American, 3.8% Asian, 0.5% American Indian/Alaska Native, 0.0% Native Hawaiian/Other Pacific Islander, 3.9% Two or more races, 3.7% Hispanic of any race;

Average household size: 2.38; Median age: 22.0; Age under 18: 11.2%; Age 65 and over: 11.1%; Males per 100 females: 88.3; Marriage status: 65.5% never married, 24.2% now married, 1.4% separated, 4.5% widowed, 5.8% divorced; Foreign born: 5.2%; Speak English only: 91.2%; With disability: 11.2%; Veterans: 5.2%; Ancestry: 23.0% German, 18.1% Irish, 15.1% Italian, 12.5% English, 7.7% Polish

Employment: 7.5% management, business, and financial, 4.6% computer, engineering, and science, 17.5% education, legal, community service, arts, and media, 4.7% healthcare practitioners, 24.8% service, 29.5% sales and office, 5.0% natural resources, construction, and maintenance, 6.4% production, transportation, and material moving

Income: Per capita: $17,066; Median household: $41,493; Average household: $52,236; Households with income of $100,000 or more: 15.5%; Poverty rate: 28.9%

Educational Attainment: High school diploma or higher: 92.9%; Bachelor's degree or higher: 38.6%; Graduate/professional degree or higher: 19.3%

School District(s)
Brockport Central SD (PK-12)
    2014-15 Enrollment: 3,629 . . . . (585) 637-1810

Four-year College(s)
SUNY College at Brockport (Public)
    Fall 2014 Enrollment: 8,106 . . . . (585) 395-2361
    2015-16 Tuition: In-state $7,904; Out-of-state $17,254

Housing: Homeownership rate: 44.8%; Median home value: $110,500; Median year structure built: 1957; Homeowner vacancy rate: 0.0%; Median selected monthly owner costs: $1,328 with a mortgage, $552 without a mortgage; Median gross rent: $753 per month; Rental vacancy rate: 9.6%

Health Insurance: 94.7% have insurance; 82.6% have private insurance; 22.1% have public insurance; 5.3% do not have insurance; 3.0% of children under 18 do not have insurance

Safety: Violent crime rate: 29.8 per 10,000 population; Property crime rate: 159.9 per 10,000 population

Transportation: Commute: 65.0% car, 2.0% public transportation, 28.0% walk, 2.4% work from home; Mean travel time to work: 19.1 minutes

Additional Information Contacts
Village of Brockport . . . . (585) 637-5300
    http://brockportny.org

CHILI (town). Covers a land area of 39.499 square miles and a water area of 0.369 square miles. Located at 43.09° N. Lat; 77.75° W. Long.

History: The Town of Chili was established in 1822, once the hunting ground of the Seneca Indians. The first white settler was Captain Joseph Morgan who purchased land from Peter Sheffer of neighboring Wheatland. North Chili was a stop on the Underground Railroad.

Population: 28,738; Growth (since 2000): 4.0%; Density: 727.6 persons per square mile; Race: 86.5% White, 9.2% Black/African American, 1.4% Asian, 0.3% American Indian/Alaska Native, 0.0% Native Hawaiian/Other Pacific Islander, 2.0% Two or more races, 4.3% Hispanic of any race; Average household size: 2.54; Median age: 40.2; Age under 18: 21.9%; Age 65 and over: 15.2%; Males per 100 females: 93.5; Marriage status: 31.0% never married, 53.8% now married, 1.0% separated, 5.5% widowed, 9.7% divorced; Foreign born: 5.5%; Speak English only: 91.8%; With disability: 10.1%; Veterans: 6.8%; Ancestry: 27.5% German, 20.6% Italian, 17.5% Irish, 12.7% English, 8.8% Polish

Employment: 16.2% management, business, and financial, 8.8% computer, engineering, and science, 11.8% education, legal, community service, arts, and media, 8.4% healthcare practitioners, 15.0% service, 23.0% sales and office, 6.3% natural resources, construction, and maintenance, 10.4% production, transportation, and material moving

Income: Per capita: $29,695; Median household: $63,203; Average household: $74,842; Households with income of $100,000 or more: 25.0%; Poverty rate: 6.2%

Educational Attainment: High school diploma or higher: 94.9%; Bachelor's degree or higher: 36.3%; Graduate/professional degree or higher: 14.2%

Housing: Homeownership rate: 78.0%; Median home value: $136,300; Median year structure built: 1975; Homeowner vacancy rate: 0.4%; Median selected monthly owner costs: $1,364 with a mortgage, $539 without a mortgage; Median gross rent: $898 per month; Rental vacancy rate: 3.9%

Health Insurance: 95.4% have insurance; 82.5% have private insurance; 27.8% have public insurance; 4.6% do not have insurance; 2.7% of children under 18 do not have insurance

Transportation: Commute: 93.2% car, 0.3% public transportation, 2.2% walk, 3.8% work from home; Mean travel time to work: 20.3 minutes

Additional Information Contacts
Town of Chili . . . . (585) 889-3550
    http://www.townofchili.org

CHURCHVILLE (village). Covers a land area of 1.153 square miles and a water area of 0.018 square miles. Located at 43.10° N. Lat; 77.88° W. Long. Elevation is 584 feet.

History: Frances E. Willard born here.

Population: 1,981; Growth (since 2000): 5.0%; Density: 1,717.6 persons per square mile; Race: 97.2% White, 0.4% Black/African American, 0.0% Asian, 0.0% American Indian/Alaska Native, 0.0% Native Hawaiian/Other Pacific Islander, 0.8% Two or more races, 4.5% Hispanic of any race; Average household size: 2.33; Median age: 43.2; Age under 18: 21.7%; Age 65 and over: 15.3%; Males per 100 females: 85.5; Marriage status: 27.6% never married, 56.3% now married, 3.9% separated, 8.5% widowed, 7.7% divorced; Foreign born: 0.4%; Speak English only: 97.0%; With disability: 9.5%; Veterans: 7.8%; Ancestry: 35.4% German, 22.7% Irish, 17.9% English, 17.3% Italian, 8.1% Scottish

Employment: 10.7% management, business, and financial, 8.9% computer, engineering, and science, 14.2% education, legal, community service, arts, and media, 4.5% healthcare practitioners, 18.5% service, 20.2% sales and office, 7.7% natural resources, construction, and maintenance, 15.2% production, transportation, and material moving

Income: Per capita: $30,249; Median household: $59,000; Average household: $69,556; Households with income of $100,000 or more: 22.5%; Poverty rate: 6.4%

Educational Attainment: High school diploma or higher: 96.2%; Bachelor's degree or higher: 36.5%; Graduate/professional degree or higher: 16.6%

School District(s)
Churchville-Chili Central SD (KG-12)
    2014-15 Enrollment: 3,935 . . . . (585) 293-1800

Housing: Homeownership rate: 82.3%; Median home value: $121,900; Median year structure built: 1976; Homeowner vacancy rate: 0.4%; Median selected monthly owner costs: $1,272 with a mortgage, $554 without a mortgage; Median gross rent: $689 per month; Rental vacancy rate: 0.0%

Health Insurance: 96.5% have insurance; 88.6% have private insurance; 22.6% have public insurance; 3.5% do not have insurance; 0.9% of children under 18 do not have insurance

Transportation: Commute: 98.4% car, 0.0% public transportation, 1.2% walk, 0.4% work from home; Mean travel time to work: 22.4 minutes

Additional Information Contacts
Village of Churchville . . . . (585) 293-3720
    http://www.churchville.net

CLARKSON (CDP). Covers a land area of 9.111 square miles and a water area of 0 square miles. Located at 43.24° N. Lat; 77.92° W. Long. Elevation is 427 feet.

Population: 4,325; Growth (since 2000): n/a; Density: 474.7 persons per square mile; Race: 95.2% White, 0.0% Black/African American, 0.6% Asian, 0.0% American Indian/Alaska Native, 0.0% Native Hawaiian/Other Pacific Islander, 3.6% Two or more races, 4.9% Hispanic of any race; Average household size: 2.62; Median age: 42.9; Age under 18: 26.6%; Age 65 and over: 17.5%; Males per 100 females: 93.2; Marriage status: 24.5% never married, 59.4% now married, 1.3% separated, 8.6% widowed, 7.5% divorced; Foreign born: 2.4%; Speak English only: 92.8%; With disability: 16.1%; Veterans: 8.1%; Ancestry: 29.2% German, 26.4% English, 20.3% Italian, 19.3% Irish, 8.9% Polish

Employment: 21.5% management, business, and financial, 5.8% computer, engineering, and science, 12.3% education, legal, community service, arts, and media, 3.0% healthcare practitioners, 15.2% service, 26.3% sales and office, 10.1% natural resources, construction, and maintenance, 5.7% production, transportation, and material moving

Income: Per capita: $24,977; Median household: $58,700; Average household: $64,224; Households with income of $100,000 or more: 22.0%; Poverty rate: 12.1%

Educational Attainment: High school diploma or higher: 92.5%; Bachelor's degree or higher: 33.8%; Graduate/professional degree or higher: 7.8%

Housing: Homeownership rate: 74.6%; Median home value: $136,600; Median year structure built: 1977; Homeowner vacancy rate: 0.0%; Median selected monthly owner costs: $1,275 with a mortgage, $452 without a mortgage; Median gross rent: $695 per month; Rental vacancy rate: 0.0%

Health Insurance: 98.7% have insurance; 76.1% have private insurance; 39.2% have public insurance; 1.3% do not have insurance; 0.0% of children under 18 do not have insurance
Transportation: Commute: 97.6% car, 0.0% public transportation, 0.0% walk, 1.6% work from home; Mean travel time to work: 23.8 minutes

CLARKSON (town).
Covers a land area of 33.183 square miles and a water area of 0.005 square miles. Located at 43.25° N. Lat; 77.93° W. Long. Elevation is 427 feet.
Population: 6,839; Growth (since 2000): 12.6%; Density: 206.1 persons per square mile; Race: 92.7% White, 0.3% Black/African American, 0.4% Asian, 0.0% American Indian/Alaska Native, 0.0% Native Hawaiian/Other Pacific Islander, 2.2% Two or more races, 7.9% Hispanic of any race; Average household size: 2.81; Median age: 43.7; Age under 18: 22.3%; Age 65 and over: 16.0%; Males per 100 females: 97.2; Marriage status: 28.0% never married, 56.5% now married, 0.8% separated, 8.1% widowed, 7.3% divorced; Foreign born: 6.4%; Speak English only: 90.6%; With disability: 13.7%; Veterans: 6.0%; Ancestry: 33.5% German, 22.9% English, 18.5% Irish, 17.9% Italian, 7.2% Dutch
Employment: 18.3% management, business, and financial, 4.9% computer, engineering, and science, 9.5% education, legal, community service, arts, and media, 3.7% healthcare practitioners, 15.7% service, 22.9% sales and office, 14.7% natural resources, construction, and maintenance, 10.3% production, transportation, and material moving
Income: Per capita: $25,677; Median household: $67,517; Average household: $71,145; Households with income of $100,000 or more: 26.0%; Poverty rate: 7.8%
Educational Attainment: High school diploma or higher: 87.6%; Bachelor's degree or higher: 28.8%; Graduate/professional degree or higher: 8.4%
Housing: Homeownership rate: 78.2%; Median home value: $137,200; Median year structure built: 1974; Homeowner vacancy rate: 0.0%; Median selected monthly owner costs: $1,347 with a mortgage, $475 without a mortgage; Median gross rent: $745 per month; Rental vacancy rate: 0.0%
Health Insurance: 93.4% have insurance; 75.7% have private insurance; 30.4% have public insurance; 6.6% do not have insurance; 0.0% of children under 18 do not have insurance
Transportation: Commute: 89.4% car, 7.8% public transportation, 0.4% walk, 2.0% work from home; Mean travel time to work: 23.7 minutes
Additional Information Contacts
Town of Clarkson . . . . (585) 637-1130
  http://www.clarksonny.org

EAST ROCHESTER (town/village).
Covers a land area of 1.325 square miles and a water area of 0.004 square miles. Located at 43.11° N. Lat; 77.49° W. Long. Elevation is 420 feet.
History: East Rochester was originally known as the Village of Despatch when it was incorporated in 1897. It was designed as a planned community around the New York Central Railroad mainline that ran through the center of the village.
Population: 6,678; Growth (since 2000): 0.4%; Density: 5,041.3 persons per square mile; Race: 88.9% White, 6.5% Black/African American, 1.6% Asian, 0.3% American Indian/Alaska Native, 0.0% Native Hawaiian/Other Pacific Islander, 1.7% Two or more races, 5.3% Hispanic of any race; Average household size: 2.29; Median age: 36.4; Age under 18: 22.6%; Age 65 and over: 12.6%; Males per 100 females: 96.6; Marriage status: 40.4% never married, 39.8% now married, 2.9% separated, 6.3% widowed, 13.4% divorced; Foreign born: 5.5%; Speak English only: 93.1%; With disability: 13.4%; Veterans: 7.8%; Ancestry: 26.8% Italian, 22.2% Irish, 17.3% German, 11.4% English, 6.2% American
Employment: 10.6% management, business, and financial, 4.4% computer, engineering, and science, 12.2% education, legal, community service, arts, and media, 6.5% healthcare practitioners, 20.1% service, 25.0% sales and office, 9.0% natural resources, construction, and maintenance, 12.3% production, transportation, and material moving
Income: Per capita: $24,515; Median household: $46,504; Average household: $54,809; Households with income of $100,000 or more: 13.4%; Poverty rate: 18.9%
Educational Attainment: High school diploma or higher: 91.5%; Bachelor's degree or higher: 27.0%; Graduate/professional degree or higher: 13.0%
School District(s)
East Rochester Union Free SD (PK-12)
  2014-15 Enrollment: 1,060 . . . . (585) 248-6302

Housing: Homeownership rate: 59.6%; Median home value: $94,000; Median year structure built: 1949; Homeowner vacancy rate: 3.9%; Median selected monthly owner costs: $1,217 with a mortgage, $492 without a mortgage; Median gross rent: $825 per month; Rental vacancy rate: 2.1%
Health Insurance: 90.3% have insurance; 68.0% have private insurance; 34.7% have public insurance; 9.7% do not have insurance; 0.0% of children under 18 do not have insurance
Safety: Violent crime rate: 16.4 per 10,000 population; Property crime rate: 159.2 per 10,000 population
Transportation: Commute: 92.5% car, 0.4% public transportation, 3.5% walk, 1.3% work from home; Mean travel time to work: 17.3 minutes
Additional Information Contacts
Village and Town of East Rochester . . . . (585) 586-3553
  http://eastrochester.org

FAIRPORT (village).
Covers a land area of 1.589 square miles and a water area of 0.034 square miles. Located at 43.10° N. Lat; 77.44° W. Long. Elevation is 492 feet.
History: Incorporated 1867.
Population: 5,362; Growth (since 2000): -6.6%; Density: 3,374.9 persons per square mile; Race: 94.1% White, 0.1% Black/African American, 4.0% Asian, 0.0% American Indian/Alaska Native, 0.0% Native Hawaiian/Other Pacific Islander, 1.8% Two or more races, 1.1% Hispanic of any race; Average household size: 2.10; Median age: 48.2; Age under 18: 15.1%; Age 65 and over: 21.5%; Males per 100 females: 93.0; Marriage status: 20.8% never married, 59.0% now married, 1.9% separated, 6.3% widowed, 13.8% divorced; Foreign born: 5.3%; Speak English only: 95.1%; With disability: 10.1%; Veterans: 7.8%; Ancestry: 27.3% German, 24.5% Irish, 16.2% English, 16.1% Italian, 8.6% Polish
Employment: 16.2% management, business, and financial, 11.0% computer, engineering, and science, 17.0% education, legal, community service, arts, and media, 3.5% healthcare practitioners, 13.0% service, 27.8% sales and office, 2.4% natural resources, construction, and maintenance, 9.1% production, transportation, and material moving
Income: Per capita: $37,233; Median household: $69,788; Average household: $77,626; Households with income of $100,000 or more: 24.4%; Poverty rate: 2.9%
Educational Attainment: High school diploma or higher: 95.0%; Bachelor's degree or higher: 51.1%; Graduate/professional degree or higher: 26.0%
School District(s)
Fairport Central SD (KG-12)
  2014-15 Enrollment: 6,170 . . . . (585) 421-2004
Monroe 1 Boces
  2014-15 Enrollment: n/a . . . . (585) 383-2200
Housing: Homeownership rate: 75.7%; Median home value: $167,800; Median year structure built: 1940; Homeowner vacancy rate: 2.9%; Median selected monthly owner costs: $1,446 with a mortgage, $625 without a mortgage; Median gross rent: $830 per month; Rental vacancy rate: 0.0%
Health Insurance: 96.0% have insurance; 86.6% have private insurance; 27.2% have public insurance; 4.0% do not have insurance; 0.0% of children under 18 do not have insurance
Safety: Violent crime rate: 5.6 per 10,000 population; Property crime rate: 63.2 per 10,000 population
Transportation: Commute: 89.5% car, 1.2% public transportation, 2.2% walk, 6.0% work from home; Mean travel time to work: 19.0 minutes
Additional Information Contacts
Village of Fairport . . . . (585) 223-0313
  http://www.fairport.ny.us

GATES (CDP).
Covers a land area of 1.979 square miles and a water area of 0.012 square miles. Located at 43.15° N. Lat; 77.70° W. Long.
Population: 5,034; Growth (since 2000): n/a; Density: 2,543.7 persons per square mile; Race: 81.7% White, 11.3% Black/African American, 3.8% Asian, 0.0% American Indian/Alaska Native, 0.0% Native Hawaiian/Other Pacific Islander, 0.5% Two or more races, 2.4% Hispanic of any race; Average household size: 2.47; Median age: 42.8; Age under 18: 20.2%; Age 65 and over: 20.6%; Males per 100 females: 90.9; Marriage status: 35.8% never married, 47.3% now married, 0.7% separated, 8.7% widowed, 8.3% divorced; Foreign born: 14.4%; Speak English only: 82.9%; With disability: 13.4%; Veterans: 10.0%; Ancestry: 27.9% Italian, 14.3% German, 11.3% English, 5.7% Irish, 5.6% French
Employment: 9.2% management, business, and financial, 5.6% computer, engineering, and science, 9.7% education, legal, community service, arts, and media, 6.1% healthcare practitioners, 17.4% service, 32.7% sales and

office, 11.6% natural resources, construction, and maintenance, 7.7% production, transportation, and material moving
Income: Per capita: $25,302; Median household: $50,729; Average household: $60,397; Households with income of $100,000 or more: 14.0%; Poverty rate: 8.6%
Educational Attainment: High school diploma or higher: 84.6%; Bachelor's degree or higher: 22.5%; Graduate/professional degree or higher: 5.8%
Housing: Homeownership rate: 91.6%; Median home value: $111,700; Median year structure built: 1964; Homeowner vacancy rate: 0.0%; Median selected monthly owner costs: $1,106 with a mortgage, $554 without a mortgage; Median gross rent: $682 per month; Rental vacancy rate: 0.0%
Health Insurance: 95.2% have insurance; 83.5% have private insurance; 32.4% have public insurance; 4.8% do not have insurance; 0.0% of children under 18 do not have insurance
Transportation: Commute: 96.6% car, 0.6% public transportation, 0.6% walk, 2.2% work from home; Mean travel time to work: 15.6 minutes

GATES (town).
Covers a land area of 15.200 square miles and a water area of 0.082 square miles. Located at 43.15° N. Lat; 77.71° W. Long.
Population: 28,651; Growth (since 2000): -2.1%; Density: 1,884.9 persons per square mile; Race: 82.4% White, 10.5% Black/African American, 3.6% Asian, 0.1% American Indian/Alaska Native, 0.1% Native Hawaiian/Other Pacific Islander, 2.0% Two or more races, 6.2% Hispanic of any race; Average household size: 2.37; Median age: 42.9; Age under 18: 19.5%; Age 65 and over: 19.9%; Males per 100 females: 91.1; Marriage status: 32.7% never married, 48.5% now married, 2.2% separated, 8.2% widowed, 10.7% divorced; Foreign born: 10.5%; Speak English only: 84.9%; With disability: 13.5%; Veterans: 9.0%; Ancestry: 26.2% Italian, 18.5% German, 13.3% Irish, 10.2% English, 5.7% Polish
Employment: 12.0% management, business, and financial, 5.1% computer, engineering, and science, 10.6% education, legal, community service, arts, and media, 6.3% healthcare practitioners, 17.8% service, 24.5% sales and office, 9.1% natural resources, construction, and maintenance, 14.5% production, transportation, and material moving
Income: Per capita: $25,607; Median household: $50,022; Average household: $59,191; Households with income of $100,000 or more: 15.7%; Poverty rate: 10.1%
Educational Attainment: High school diploma or higher: 87.1%; Bachelor's degree or higher: 22.7%; Graduate/professional degree or higher: 7.9%
Housing: Homeownership rate: 73.3%; Median home value: $115,200; Median year structure built: 1970; Homeowner vacancy rate: 1.2%; Median selected monthly owner costs: $1,281 with a mortgage, $514 without a mortgage; Median gross rent: $805 per month; Rental vacancy rate: 3.2%
Health Insurance: 94.2% have insurance; 74.8% have private insurance; 36.8% have public insurance; 5.8% do not have insurance; 2.4% of children under 18 do not have insurance
Safety: Violent crime rate: 29.3 per 10,000 population; Property crime rate: 340.1 per 10,000 population
Transportation: Commute: 95.1% car, 1.4% public transportation, 0.6% walk, 2.1% work from home; Mean travel time to work: 17.7 minutes
Additional Information Contacts
Town of Gates . . . . (585) 247-6100
  http://www.townofgates.org

GREECE (CDP).
Covers a land area of 4.375 square miles and a water area of 0 square miles. Located at 43.21° N. Lat; 77.70° W. Long. Elevation is 430 feet.
Population: 14,568; Growth (since 2000): -0.3%; Density: 3,330.0 persons per square mile; Race: 90.4% White, 4.2% Black/African American, 2.2% Asian, 0.1% American Indian/Alaska Native, 0.0% Native Hawaiian/Other Pacific Islander, 1.9% Two or more races, 5.0% Hispanic of any race; Average household size: 2.32; Median age: 44.0; Age under 18: 19.3%; Age 65 and over: 20.3%; Males per 100 females: 88.8; Marriage status: 28.4% never married, 49.4% now married, 1.9% separated, 9.6% widowed, 12.7% divorced; Foreign born: 8.3%; Speak English only: 89.8%; With disability: 12.6%; Veterans: 8.4%; Ancestry: 33.2% Italian, 25.1% German, 16.1% Irish, 6.4% English, 4.8% American
Employment: 12.1% management, business, and financial, 4.7% computer, engineering, and science, 12.0% education, legal, community service, arts, and media, 6.5% healthcare practitioners, 20.1% service, 25.2% sales and office, 7.5% natural resources, construction, and maintenance, 11.9% production, transportation, and material moving

Income: Per capita: $26,781; Median household: $48,028; Average household: $60,810; Households with income of $100,000 or more: 15.1%; Poverty rate: 8.4%
Educational Attainment: High school diploma or higher: 91.8%; Bachelor's degree or higher: 26.2%; Graduate/professional degree or higher: 10.8%
Housing: Homeownership rate: 74.5%; Median home value: $115,500; Median year structure built: 1964; Homeowner vacancy rate: 1.0%; Median selected monthly owner costs: $1,239 with a mortgage, $571 without a mortgage; Median gross rent: $788 per month; Rental vacancy rate: 9.0%
Health Insurance: 94.4% have insurance; 76.1% have private insurance; 37.1% have public insurance; 5.6% do not have insurance; 0.9% of children under 18 do not have insurance
Transportation: Commute: 95.2% car, 1.0% public transportation, 1.2% walk, 1.9% work from home; Mean travel time to work: 18.6 minutes

GREECE (town).
Covers a land area of 47.518 square miles and a water area of 3.875 square miles. Located at 43.25° N. Lat; 77.70° W. Long. Elevation is 430 feet.
Population: 96,674; Growth (since 2000): 2.7%; Density: 2,034.5 persons per square mile; Race: 87.9% White, 6.7% Black/African American, 2.0% Asian, 0.2% American Indian/Alaska Native, 0.0% Native Hawaiian/Other Pacific Islander, 1.3% Two or more races, 5.1% Hispanic of any race; Average household size: 2.40; Median age: 43.4; Age under 18: 19.7%; Age 65 and over: 18.1%; Males per 100 females: 90.4; Marriage status: 30.4% never married, 50.8% now married, 1.5% separated, 7.7% widowed, 11.1% divorced; Foreign born: 6.6%; Speak English only: 90.6%; With disability: 11.6%; Veterans: 7.8%; Ancestry: 26.2% Italian, 24.1% German, 18.0% Irish, 10.8% English, 4.9% Polish
Employment: 13.7% management, business, and financial, 6.1% computer, engineering, and science, 10.2% education, legal, community service, arts, and media, 6.7% healthcare practitioners, 18.2% service, 27.4% sales and office, 6.2% natural resources, construction, and maintenance, 11.6% production, transportation, and material moving
Income: Per capita: $29,061; Median household: $55,061; Average household: $68,464; Households with income of $100,000 or more: 20.6%; Poverty rate: 9.3%
Educational Attainment: High school diploma or higher: 91.9%; Bachelor's degree or higher: 28.3%; Graduate/professional degree or higher: 10.3%
Housing: Homeownership rate: 73.3%; Median home value: $128,400; Median year structure built: 1970; Homeowner vacancy rate: 1.3%; Median selected monthly owner costs: $1,323 with a mortgage, $580 without a mortgage; Median gross rent: $850 per month; Rental vacancy rate: 7.8%
Health Insurance: 93.8% have insurance; 77.6% have private insurance; 32.4% have public insurance; 6.2% do not have insurance; 2.4% of children under 18 do not have insurance
Safety: Violent crime rate: 17.4 per 10,000 population; Property crime rate: 251.0 per 10,000 population
Transportation: Commute: 94.7% car, 1.0% public transportation, 0.9% walk, 2.6% work from home; Mean travel time to work: 20.5 minutes
Additional Information Contacts
Town of Greece . . . . (585) 225-2000
  http://greeceny.gov

HAMLIN (CDP).
Covers a land area of 7.710 square miles and a water area of 0 square miles. Located at 43.30° N. Lat; 77.92° W. Long. Elevation is 312 feet.
Population: 5,587; Growth (since 2000): n/a; Density: 724.6 persons per square mile; Race: 93.1% White, 5.8% Black/African American, 0.4% Asian, 0.0% American Indian/Alaska Native, 0.0% Native Hawaiian/Other Pacific Islander, 0.6% Two or more races, 1.8% Hispanic of any race; Average household size: 2.78; Median age: 35.6; Age under 18: 26.4%; Age 65 and over: 9.5%; Males per 100 females: 97.5; Marriage status: 27.7% never married, 54.3% now married, 1.7% separated, 2.7% widowed, 15.3% divorced; Foreign born: 2.0%; Speak English only: 96.4%; With disability: 12.9%; Veterans: 11.0%; Ancestry: 36.6% German, 18.4% Irish, 18.3% Italian, 14.4% English, 8.3% Polish
Employment: 9.3% management, business, and financial, 3.2% computer, engineering, and science, 8.1% education, legal, community service, arts, and media, 6.7% healthcare practitioners, 25.4% service, 22.9% sales and office, 6.8% natural resources, construction, and maintenance, 17.7% production, transportation, and material moving

Income: Per capita: $21,510; Median household: $54,327; Average household: $58,744; Households with income of $100,000 or more: 13.6%; Poverty rate: 12.1%
Educational Attainment: High school diploma or higher: 94.2%; Bachelor's degree or higher: 19.8%; Graduate/professional degree or higher: 5.2%
Housing: Homeownership rate: 84.5%; Median home value: $95,300; Median year structure built: 1979; Homeowner vacancy rate: 1.7%; Median selected monthly owner costs: $1,157 with a mortgage, $528 without a mortgage; Median gross rent: $733 per month; Rental vacancy rate: 0.0%
Health Insurance: 96.2% have insurance; 73.6% have private insurance; 33.4% have public insurance; 3.8% do not have insurance; 2.0% of children under 18 do not have insurance
Transportation: Commute: 95.9% car, 0.3% public transportation, 0.3% walk, 3.4% work from home; Mean travel time to work: 29.0 minutes

HAMLIN (town). Covers a land area of 43.468 square miles and a water area of 1.122 square miles. Located at 43.32° N. Lat; 77.92° W. Long. Elevation is 312 feet.
Population: 9,112; Growth (since 2000): -2.6%; Density: 209.6 persons per square mile; Race: 94.1% White, 4.4% Black/African American, 0.3% Asian, 0.0% American Indian/Alaska Native, 0.0% Native Hawaiian/Other Pacific Islander, 1.2% Two or more races, 1.1% Hispanic of any race; Average household size: 2.73; Median age: 40.8; Age under 18: 23.9%; Age 65 and over: 12.3%; Males per 100 females: 98.7; Marriage status: 24.8% never married, 59.6% now married, 2.2% separated, 3.7% widowed, 11.9% divorced; Foreign born: 1.7%; Speak English only: 97.1%; With disability: 11.2%; Veterans: 10.8%; Ancestry: 35.5% German, 20.3% Irish, 15.6% Italian, 12.5% English, 9.1% Polish
Employment: 11.6% management, business, and financial, 3.9% computer, engineering, and science, 8.5% education, legal, community service, arts, and media, 5.1% healthcare practitioners, 22.3% service, 24.4% sales and office, 8.2% natural resources, construction, and maintenance, 16.1% production, transportation, and material moving
Income: Per capita: $24,406; Median household: $57,392; Average household: $65,458; Households with income of $100,000 or more: 18.1%; Poverty rate: 9.1%
Educational Attainment: High school diploma or higher: 93.3%; Bachelor's degree or higher: 22.3%; Graduate/professional degree or higher: 5.9%
Housing: Homeownership rate: 83.4%; Median home value: $108,900; Median year structure built: 1974; Homeowner vacancy rate: 1.0%; Median selected monthly owner costs: $1,282 with a mortgage, $554 without a mortgage; Median gross rent: $770 per month; Rental vacancy rate: 0.0%
Health Insurance: 95.9% have insurance; 77.0% have private insurance; 32.8% have public insurance; 4.1% do not have insurance; 1.8% of children under 18 do not have insurance
Transportation: Commute: 94.5% car, 0.2% public transportation, 0.8% walk, 4.1% work from home; Mean travel time to work: 28.9 minutes
Additional Information Contacts
Town of Hamlin . . . . (585) 964-2421
  http://www.hamlinny.org

HENRIETTA (town). Covers a land area of 35.351 square miles and a water area of 0.296 square miles. Located at 43.05° N. Lat; 77.64° W. Long. Elevation is 600 feet.
Population: 43,453; Growth (since 2000): 11.3%; Density: 1,229.2 persons per square mile; Race: 78.4% White, 9.0% Black/African American, 7.3% Asian, 0.5% American Indian/Alaska Native, 0.0% Native Hawaiian/Other Pacific Islander, 3.1% Two or more races, 4.8% Hispanic of any race; Average household size: 2.53; Median age: 33.9; Age under 18: 18.4%; Age 65 and over: 13.4%; Males per 100 females: 110.7; Marriage status: 41.4% never married, 45.5% now married, 1.7% separated, 3.9% widowed, 9.1% divorced; Foreign born: 11.4%; Speak English only: 86.1%; With disability: 11.7%; Veterans: 7.8%; Ancestry: 19.4% German, 13.8% Irish, 13.6% Italian, 9.7% English, 6.0% American
Employment: 12.3% management, business, and financial, 10.3% computer, engineering, and science, 10.8% education, legal, community service, arts, and media, 6.7% healthcare practitioners, 17.0% service, 26.7% sales and office, 5.6% natural resources, construction, and maintenance, 10.5% production, transportation, and material moving
Income: Per capita: $27,436; Median household: $61,762; Average household: $72,154; Households with income of $100,000 or more: 24.5%; Poverty rate: 12.2%

Educational Attainment: High school diploma or higher: 92.3%; Bachelor's degree or higher: 36.8%; Graduate/professional degree or higher: 14.6%
School District(s)
Rush-Henrietta Central SD (KG-12)
  2014-15 Enrollment: 5,394 . . . . (585) 359-5012
Housing: Homeownership rate: 71.0%; Median home value: $139,400; Median year structure built: 1974; Homeowner vacancy rate: 1.1%; Median selected monthly owner costs: $1,313 with a mortgage, $551 without a mortgage; Median gross rent: $944 per month; Rental vacancy rate: 4.1%
Health Insurance: 95.0% have insurance; 81.8% have private insurance; 26.4% have public insurance; 5.0% do not have insurance; 2.4% of children under 18 do not have insurance
Transportation: Commute: 90.3% car, 1.3% public transportation, 4.9% walk, 2.7% work from home; Mean travel time to work: 17.8 minutes
Additional Information Contacts
Town of Henrietta . . . . (585) 334-7700
  http://www.henrietta.org

HILTON (village). Covers a land area of 1.780 square miles and a water area of 0 square miles. Located at 43.29° N. Lat; 77.79° W. Long. Elevation is 279 feet.
Population: 5,936; Growth (since 2000): 1.4%; Density: 3,335.1 persons per square mile; Race: 94.5% White, 3.0% Black/African American, 0.6% Asian, 0.0% American Indian/Alaska Native, 0.0% Native Hawaiian/Other Pacific Islander, 1.3% Two or more races, 5.6% Hispanic of any race; Average household size: 2.65; Median age: 38.3; Age under 18: 25.3%; Age 65 and over: 13.4%; Males per 100 females: 91.2; Marriage status: 29.3% never married, 51.5% now married, 0.6% separated, 7.9% widowed, 11.2% divorced; Foreign born: 3.6%; Speak English only: 96.8%; With disability: 14.4%; Veterans: 9.3%; Ancestry: 27.4% Italian, 24.2% German, 17.5% Irish, 17.0% English, 6.1% Polish
Employment: 8.6% management, business, and financial, 4.2% computer, engineering, and science, 9.6% education, legal, community service, arts, and media, 7.6% healthcare practitioners, 13.6% service, 23.3% sales and office, 12.1% natural resources, construction, and maintenance, 20.9% production, transportation, and material moving
Income: Per capita: $25,413; Median household: $58,297; Average household: $65,452; Households with income of $100,000 or more: 24.2%; Poverty rate: 5.9%
Educational Attainment: High school diploma or higher: 94.9%; Bachelor's degree or higher: 22.6%; Graduate/professional degree or higher: 12.5%
School District(s)
Hilton Central SD (PK-12)
  2014-15 Enrollment: 4,482 . . . . (585) 392-1000
Housing: Homeownership rate: 65.8%; Median home value: $126,000; Median year structure built: 1978; Homeowner vacancy rate: 0.0%; Median selected monthly owner costs: $1,278 with a mortgage, $548 without a mortgage; Median gross rent: $887 per month; Rental vacancy rate: 9.2%
Health Insurance: 96.9% have insurance; 80.8% have private insurance; 26.0% have public insurance; 3.1% do not have insurance; 0.0% of children under 18 do not have insurance
Transportation: Commute: 94.4% car, 0.0% public transportation, 1.6% walk, 0.7% work from home; Mean travel time to work: 28.4 minutes
Additional Information Contacts
Village of Hilton . . . . (585) 392-4144
  http://www.hiltonny.org

HONEOYE FALLS (village). Covers a land area of 2.543 square miles and a water area of 0.052 square miles. Located at 42.95° N. Lat; 77.59° W. Long. Elevation is 656 feet.
History: Incorporated 1838.
Population: 2,720; Growth (since 2000): 4.8%; Density: 1,069.5 persons per square mile; Race: 97.3% White, 0.9% Black/African American, 0.0% Asian, 0.6% American Indian/Alaska Native, 0.0% Native Hawaiian/Other Pacific Islander, 1.3% Two or more races, 1.0% Hispanic of any race; Average household size: 2.15; Median age: 44.2; Age under 18: 24.9%; Age 65 and over: 18.3%; Males per 100 females: 88.6; Marriage status: 28.9% never married, 49.2% now married, 3.0% separated, 11.0% widowed, 10.9% divorced; Foreign born: 1.4%; Speak English only: 97.7%; With disability: 14.8%; Veterans: 7.4%; Ancestry: 24.7% German, 20.5% Irish, 20.1% English, 17.9% Italian, 7.4% American
Employment: 11.4% management, business, and financial, 12.3% computer, engineering, and science, 20.3% education, legal, community

service, arts, and media, 8.2% healthcare practitioners, 11.6% service, 22.0% sales and office, 8.1% natural resources, construction, and maintenance, 6.1% production, transportation, and material moving
Income: Per capita: $36,208; Median household: $61,250; Average household: $77,289; Households with income of $100,000 or more: 22.0%; Poverty rate: 6.7%
Educational Attainment: High school diploma or higher: 96.4%; Bachelor's degree or higher: 47.0%; Graduate/professional degree or higher: 24.1%

School District(s)
Honeoye Falls-Lima Central SD (KG-12)
    2014-15 Enrollment: 2,298 . . . . (585) 624-7010
Housing: Homeownership rate: 60.2%; Median home value: $166,800; Median year structure built: 1961; Homeowner vacancy rate: 3.8%; Median selected monthly owner costs: $1,582 with a mortgage, $575 without a mortgage; Median gross rent: $786 per month; Rental vacancy rate: 4.2%
Health Insurance: 95.4% have insurance; 84.0% have private insurance; 28.2% have public insurance; 4.6% do not have insurance; 0.0% of children under 18 do not have insurance
Transportation: Commute: 86.9% car, 0.0% public transportation, 4.4% walk, 8.4% work from home; Mean travel time to work: 25.8 minutes

---

IRONDEQUOIT (CDP). Covers a land area of 15.001 square miles and a water area of 1.833 square miles. Located at 43.21° N. Lat; 77.57° W. Long. Elevation is 381 feet.
History: Named for the Iroquoian translation of "bay". Settled 1791, organized 1839.
Population: 51,337; Growth (since 2000): -1.9%; Density: 3,422.2 persons per square mile; Race: 85.0% White, 9.3% Black/African American, 1.6% Asian, 0.1% American Indian/Alaska Native, 0.0% Native Hawaiian/Other Pacific Islander, 2.2% Two or more races, 7.3% Hispanic of any race; Average household size: 2.29; Median age: 43.7; Age under 18: 19.8%; Age 65 and over: 18.9%; Males per 100 females: 86.6; Marriage status: 30.5% never married, 49.6% now married, 1.8% separated, 7.8% widowed, 12.0% divorced; Foreign born: 7.5%; Speak English only: 87.5%; With disability: 12.8%; Veterans: 8.2%; Ancestry: 21.7% German, 21.5% Italian, 14.7% Irish, 11.4% English, 6.1% Polish
Employment: 16.2% management, business, and financial, 7.0% computer, engineering, and science, 12.5% education, legal, community service, arts, and media, 7.5% healthcare practitioners, 16.2% service, 24.5% sales and office, 5.7% natural resources, construction, and maintenance, 10.3% production, transportation, and material moving
Income: Per capita: $29,570; Median household: $54,275; Average household: $66,379; Households with income of $100,000 or more: 19.0%; Poverty rate: 8.5%
Educational Attainment: High school diploma or higher: 91.9%; Bachelor's degree or higher: 34.8%; Graduate/professional degree or higher: 13.1%
Housing: Homeownership rate: 78.3%; Median home value: $117,500; Median year structure built: 1955; Homeowner vacancy rate: 1.3%; Median selected monthly owner costs: $1,258 with a mortgage, $562 without a mortgage; Median gross rent: $822 per month; Rental vacancy rate: 6.4%
Health Insurance: 95.5% have insurance; 78.1% have private insurance; 33.7% have public insurance; 4.5% do not have insurance; 3.2% of children under 18 do not have insurance
Safety: Violent crime rate: 19.3 per 10,000 population; Property crime rate: 261.8 per 10,000 population
Transportation: Commute: 93.8% car, 0.9% public transportation, 0.7% walk, 3.2% work from home; Mean travel time to work: 20.0 minutes
Additional Information Contacts
Town of Irondequoit . . . . (585) 467-8840
    http://www.irondequoit.org

MENDON (town). Covers a land area of 39.472 square miles and a water area of 0.515 square miles. Located at 42.98° N. Lat; 77.56° W. Long. Elevation is 561 feet.
Population: 9,237; Growth (since 2000): 10.4%; Density: 234.0 persons per square mile; Race: 96.6% White, 0.6% Black/African American, 1.3% Asian, 0.2% American Indian/Alaska Native, 0.0% Native Hawaiian/Other Pacific Islander, 1.1% Two or more races, 1.3% Hispanic of any race; Average household size: 2.51; Median age: 45.8; Age under 18: 26.8%; Age 65 and over: 13.8%; Males per 100 females: 97.0; Marriage status: 20.4% never married, 64.6% now married, 1.5% separated, 7.2% widowed, 7.9% divorced; Foreign born: 4.0%; Speak English only: 96.8%;

With disability: 7.4%; Veterans: 5.7%; Ancestry: 23.3% German, 20.6% English, 19.9% Italian, 19.2% Irish, 4.9% American
Employment: 22.2% management, business, and financial, 13.0% computer, engineering, and science, 20.3% education, legal, community service, arts, and media, 5.6% healthcare practitioners, 10.2% service, 16.6% sales and office, 5.3% natural resources, construction, and maintenance, 6.8% production, transportation, and material moving
Income: Per capita: $55,735; Median household: $88,011; Average household: $138,401; Households with income of $100,000 or more: 45.8%; Poverty rate: 4.5%
Educational Attainment: High school diploma or higher: 97.4%; Bachelor's degree or higher: 60.5%; Graduate/professional degree or higher: 30.4%
Housing: Homeownership rate: 82.2%; Median home value: $239,700; Median year structure built: 1976; Homeowner vacancy rate: 1.0%; Median selected monthly owner costs: $2,106 with a mortgage, $846 without a mortgage; Median gross rent: $808 per month; Rental vacancy rate: 3.3%
Health Insurance: 95.1% have insurance; 90.2% have private insurance; 17.1% have public insurance; 4.9% do not have insurance; 3.8% of children under 18 do not have insurance
Transportation: Commute: 86.7% car, 0.0% public transportation, 2.1% walk, 10.9% work from home; Mean travel time to work: 23.9 minutes
Additional Information Contacts
Town of Mendon . . . . (585) 624-6060
    http://www.townofmendon.org

MUMFORD (unincorporated postal area)
ZCTA: 14511
    Covers a land area of 2.309 square miles and a water area of 0.042 square miles. Located at 43.00° N. Lat; 77.89° W. Long. Elevation is 617 feet.
    Population: 234; Growth (since 2000): n/a; Density: 101.3 persons per square mile; Race: 92.3% White, 0.0% Black/African American, 0.0% Asian, 0.0% American Indian/Alaska Native, 0.0% Native Hawaiian/Other Pacific Islander, 7.7% Two or more races, 0.0% Hispanic of any race; Average household size: 1.98; Median age: 50.7; Age under 18: 12.4%; Age 65 and over: 18.4%; Males per 100 females: 87.5; Marriage status: 16.1% never married, 59.0% now married, 6.3% separated, 12.7% widowed, 12.2% divorced; Foreign born: 0.0%; Speak English only: 100.0%; With disability: 10.7%; Veterans: 0.0%; Ancestry: 27.4% German, 25.6% Italian, 17.9% English, 16.7% Irish, 12.4% American
    Employment: 12.6% management, business, and financial, 0.0% computer, engineering, and science, 13.5% education, legal, community service, arts, and media, 11.7% healthcare practitioners, 28.8% service, 0.0% sales and office, 23.4% natural resources, construction, and maintenance, 9.9% production, transportation, and material moving
    Income: Per capita: $30,253; Median household: $45,769; Average household: $59,511; Households with income of $100,000 or more: 33.1%; Poverty rate: 5.6%
    Educational Attainment: High school diploma or higher: 92.4%; Bachelor's degree or higher: 29.7%; Graduate/professional degree or higher: 7.0%
    Housing: Homeownership rate: 88.1%; Median home value: $137,900; Median year structure built: 1942; Homeowner vacancy rate: 0.0%; Median selected monthly owner costs: $1,356 with a mortgage, $375 without a mortgage; Median gross rent: n/a per month; Rental vacancy rate: 0.0%
    Health Insurance: 87.6% have insurance; 87.6% have private insurance; 24.4% have public insurance; 12.4% do not have insurance; 51.7% of children under 18 do not have insurance
    Transportation: Commute: 100.0% car, 0.0% public transportation, 0.0% walk, 0.0% work from home; Mean travel time to work: 29.5 minutes

---

NORTH CHILI (unincorporated postal area)
ZCTA: 14514
    Covers a land area of 3.746 square miles and a water area of 0.012 square miles. Located at 43.11° N. Lat; 77.81° W. Long. Elevation is 584 feet.
    Population: 6,489; Growth (since 2000): 37.4%; Density: 1,732.0 persons per square mile; Race: 89.8% White, 3.6% Black/African American, 2.7% Asian, 0.3% American Indian/Alaska Native, 0.0% Native Hawaiian/Other Pacific Islander, 3.7% Two or more races, 7.3% Hispanic of any race; Average household size: 2.52; Median age: 41.0;

Age under 18: 23.9%; Age 65 and over: 17.6%; Males per 100 females: 89.8; Marriage status: 30.4% never married, 54.6% now married, 1.3% separated, 6.0% widowed, 9.0% divorced; Foreign born: 6.3%; Speak English only: 89.1%; With disability: 12.8%; Veterans: 7.8%; Ancestry: 29.3% German, 23.2% Italian, 18.0% Irish, 14.9% English, 8.4% Polish
Employment: 17.9% management, business, and financial, 11.6% computer, engineering, and science, 11.5% education, legal, community service, arts, and media, 7.7% healthcare practitioners, 19.5% service, 19.5% sales and office, 4.8% natural resources, construction, and maintenance, 7.4% production, transportation, and material moving
Income: Per capita: $29,741; Median household: $63,155; Average household: $75,240; Households with income of $100,000 or more: 27.7%; Poverty rate: 10.1%
Educational Attainment: High school diploma or higher: 92.7%; Bachelor's degree or higher: 35.4%; Graduate/professional degree or higher: 14.4%
Housing: Homeownership rate: 68.6%; Median home value: $152,200; Median year structure built: 1985; Homeowner vacancy rate: 0.0%; Median selected monthly owner costs: $1,424 with a mortgage, $542 without a mortgage; Median gross rent: $852 per month; Rental vacancy rate: 11.4%
Health Insurance: 92.9% have insurance; 80.5% have private insurance; 28.2% have public insurance; 7.1% do not have insurance; 3.4% of children under 18 do not have insurance
Transportation: Commute: 93.2% car, 0.0% public transportation, 2.5% walk, 2.6% work from home; Mean travel time to work: 20.2 minutes

NORTH GATES (CDP).
Covers a land area of 2.662 square miles and a water area of 0.026 square miles. Located at 43.17° N. Lat; 77.71° W. Long. Elevation is 525 feet.
Population: 9,756; Growth (since 2000): n/a; Density: 3,664.5 persons per square mile; Race: 81.2% White, 10.0% Black/African American, 4.3% Asian, 0.1% American Indian/Alaska Native, 0.2% Native Hawaiian/Other Pacific Islander, 3.3% Two or more races, 12.3% Hispanic of any race; Average household size: 2.27; Median age: 40.6; Age under 18: 19.5%; Age 65 and over: 19.3%; Males per 100 females: 90.9; Marriage status: 36.0% never married, 44.2% now married, 3.4% separated, 8.1% widowed, 11.7% divorced; Foreign born: 9.5%; Speak English only: 82.5%; With disability: 14.2%; Veterans: 8.0%; Ancestry: 28.8% Italian, 13.3% Irish, 11.1% German, 7.9% English, 6.4% Polish
Employment: 12.4% management, business, and financial, 5.3% computer, engineering, and science, 8.1% education, legal, community service, arts, and media, 3.9% healthcare practitioners, 18.4% service, 26.5% sales and office, 9.3% natural resources, construction, and maintenance, 16.2% production, transportation, and material moving
Income: Per capita: $23,563; Median household: $38,968; Average household: $51,884; Households with income of $100,000 or more: 12.6%; Poverty rate: 13.8%
Educational Attainment: High school diploma or higher: 84.7%; Bachelor's degree or higher: 17.6%; Graduate/professional degree or higher: 4.8%
Housing: Homeownership rate: 55.6%; Median home value: $110,600; Median year structure built: 1972; Homeowner vacancy rate: 4.4%; Median selected monthly owner costs: $1,291 with a mortgage, $512 without a mortgage; Median gross rent: $730 per month; Rental vacancy rate: 2.7%
Health Insurance: 93.1% have insurance; 65.1% have private insurance; 41.9% have public insurance; 6.9% do not have insurance; 3.8% of children under 18 do not have insurance
Transportation: Commute: 92.5% car, 3.6% public transportation, 0.4% walk, 2.3% work from home; Mean travel time to work: 17.6 minutes

OGDEN (town).
Covers a land area of 36.476 square miles and a water area of 0.257 square miles. Located at 43.17° N. Lat; 77.81° W. Long.
Population: 20,091; Growth (since 2000): 8.6%; Density: 550.8 persons per square mile; Race: 94.5% White, 2.1% Black/African American, 1.2% Asian, 0.3% American Indian/Alaska Native, 0.0% Native Hawaiian/Other Pacific Islander, 1.4% Two or more races, 4.3% Hispanic of any race; Average household size: 2.69; Median age: 40.8; Age under 18: 21.4%; Age 65 and over: 13.1%; Males per 100 females: 94.0; Marriage status: 28.6% never married, 55.5% now married, 1.2% separated, 5.5% widowed, 10.4% divorced; Foreign born: 6.1%; Speak English only: 90.2%; With disability: 10.5%; Veterans: 7.8%; Ancestry: 27.1% German, 24.1% Italian, 18.3% Irish, 15.3% English, 5.9% Polish
Employment: 16.6% management, business, and financial, 9.7% computer, engineering, and science, 12.7% education, legal, community

service, arts, and media, 6.7% healthcare practitioners, 14.4% service, 22.5% sales and office, 7.6% natural resources, construction, and maintenance, 9.8% production, transportation, and material moving
Income: Per capita: $31,284; Median household: $71,596; Average household: $83,571; Households with income of $100,000 or more: 32.0%; Poverty rate: 5.0%
Educational Attainment: High school diploma or higher: 95.2%; Bachelor's degree or higher: 36.6%; Graduate/professional degree or higher: 14.5%
Housing: Homeownership rate: 78.9%; Median home value: $150,700; Median year structure built: 1975; Homeowner vacancy rate: 0.2%; Median selected monthly owner costs: $1,443 with a mortgage, $633 without a mortgage; Median gross rent: $863 per month; Rental vacancy rate: 0.0%
Health Insurance: 95.3% have insurance; 85.8% have private insurance; 22.2% have public insurance; 4.7% do not have insurance; 2.3% of children under 18 do not have insurance
Safety: Violent crime rate: 9.9 per 10,000 population; Property crime rate: 93.6 per 10,000 population
Transportation: Commute: 93.6% car, 0.2% public transportation, 1.8% walk, 3.7% work from home; Mean travel time to work: 20.1 minutes
Additional Information Contacts
Town of Ogden . . . . (585) 617-6100
  http://www.ogdenny.com

PARMA (town).
Covers a land area of 42.023 square miles and a water area of 0.960 square miles. Located at 43.27° N. Lat; 77.80° W. Long.
Population: 15,823; Growth (since 2000): 6.8%; Density: 376.5 persons per square mile; Race: 95.5% White, 2.3% Black/African American, 0.9% Asian, 0.3% American Indian/Alaska Native, 0.0% Native Hawaiian/Other Pacific Islander, 0.7% Two or more races, 4.0% Hispanic of any race; Average household size: 2.69; Median age: 42.0; Age under 18: 23.3%; Age 65 and over: 15.1%; Males per 100 females: 98.7; Marriage status: 29.2% never married, 54.4% now married, 0.5% separated, 6.6% widowed, 9.8% divorced; Foreign born: 4.4%; Speak English only: 95.4%; With disability: 12.7%; Veterans: 9.5%; Ancestry: 27.4% German, 22.4% Italian, 18.3% Irish, 14.0% English, 6.6% American
Employment: 13.9% management, business, and financial, 4.5% computer, engineering, and science, 8.8% education, legal, community service, arts, and media, 7.8% healthcare practitioners, 12.8% service, 26.8% sales and office, 10.7% natural resources, construction, and maintenance, 14.6% production, transportation, and material moving
Income: Per capita: $28,160; Median household: $65,658; Average household: $74,193; Households with income of $100,000 or more: 27.5%; Poverty rate: 6.2%
Educational Attainment: High school diploma or higher: 94.4%; Bachelor's degree or higher: 26.2%; Graduate/professional degree or higher: 11.6%
Housing: Homeownership rate: 80.4%; Median home value: $137,400; Median year structure built: 1971; Homeowner vacancy rate: 0.0%; Median selected monthly owner costs: $1,352 with a mortgage, $542 without a mortgage; Median gross rent: $871 per month; Rental vacancy rate: 6.3%
Health Insurance: 96.5% have insurance; 81.9% have private insurance; 29.6% have public insurance; 3.5% do not have insurance; 1.0% of children under 18 do not have insurance
Transportation: Commute: 95.2% car, 0.0% public transportation, 1.1% walk, 2.2% work from home; Mean travel time to work: 25.8 minutes
Additional Information Contacts
Town of Parma . . . . (585) 392-9461
  http://www.parmany.org

PENFIELD (town).
Covers a land area of 37.211 square miles and a water area of 0.634 square miles. Located at 43.15° N. Lat; 77.44° W. Long. Elevation is 423 feet.
Population: 36,984; Growth (since 2000): 6.8%; Density: 993.9 persons per square mile; Race: 91.9% White, 1.8% Black/African American, 2.9% Asian, 0.1% American Indian/Alaska Native, 0.1% Native Hawaiian/Other Pacific Islander, 2.7% Two or more races, 3.6% Hispanic of any race; Average household size: 2.49; Median age: 44.8; Age under 18: 23.4%; Age 65 and over: 18.9%; Males per 100 females: 93.0; Marriage status: 24.9% never married, 59.6% now married, 1.6% separated, 6.7% widowed, 8.7% divorced; Foreign born: 7.0%; Speak English only: 91.6%; With disability: 10.1%; Veterans: 8.1%; Ancestry: 24.5% German, 23.5% Italian, 17.4% Irish, 15.0% English, 6.9% Polish
Employment: 20.4% management, business, and financial, 10.0% computer, engineering, and science, 14.1% education, legal,

service, arts, and media, 7.8% healthcare practitioners, 13.0% service, 24.7% sales and office, 3.7% natural resources, construction, and maintenance, 6.3% production, transportation, and material moving
Income: Per capita: $39,801; Median household: $78,469; Average household: $98,877; Households with income of $100,000 or more: 36.9%; Poverty rate: 4.3%
Educational Attainment: High school diploma or higher: 94.0%; Bachelor's degree or higher: 51.2%; Graduate/professional degree or higher: 24.6%

School District(s)
Penfield Central SD (KG-12)
    2014-15 Enrollment: 4,469 . . . . (585) 249-5700
Housing: Homeownership rate: 81.8%; Median home value: $179,800; Median year structure built: 1976; Homeowner vacancy rate: 1.0%; Median selected monthly owner costs: $1,721 with a mortgage, $685 without a mortgage; Median gross rent: $894 per month; Rental vacancy rate: 11.8%
Health Insurance: 97.1% have insurance; 86.2% have private insurance; 26.6% have public insurance; 2.9% do not have insurance; 1.5% of children under 18 do not have insurance
Transportation: Commute: 91.3% car, 0.6% public transportation, 1.3% walk, 6.0% work from home; Mean travel time to work: 19.4 minutes
Additional Information Contacts
Town of Penfield . . . . (585) 340-8629
    http://www.penfield.org

PERINTON (town). Covers a land area of 34.186 square miles and a water area of 0.360 square miles. Located at 43.08° N. Lat; 77.43° W. Long.
Population: 46,557; Growth (since 2000): 1.0%; Density: 1,361.9 persons per square mile; Race: 93.5% White, 1.1% Black/African American, 3.2% Asian, 0.1% American Indian/Alaska Native, 0.0% Native Hawaiian/Other Pacific Islander, 1.8% Two or more races, 2.1% Hispanic of any race; Average household size: 2.42; Median age: 45.2; Age under 18: 21.5%; Age 65 and over: 18.3%; Males per 100 females: 92.6; Marriage status: 25.2% never married, 58.8% now married, 1.4% separated, 6.0% widowed, 10.0% divorced; Foreign born: 6.4%; Speak English only: 93.8%; With disability: 8.5%; Veterans: 7.8%; Ancestry: 24.6% German, 22.6% Irish, 21.8% Italian, 14.3% English, 6.9% Polish
Employment: 20.4% management, business, and financial, 9.8% computer, engineering, and science, 15.7% education, legal, community service, arts, and media, 6.4% healthcare practitioners, 14.2% service, 22.9% sales and office, 4.6% natural resources, construction, and maintenance, 6.0% production, transportation, and material moving
Income: Per capita: $41,386; Median household: $79,105; Average household: $99,623; Households with income of $100,000 or more: 37.8%; Poverty rate: 6.1%
Educational Attainment: High school diploma or higher: 96.9%; Bachelor's degree or higher: 54.9%; Graduate/professional degree or higher: 26.0%
Housing: Homeownership rate: 77.9%; Median home value: $192,600; Median year structure built: 1975; Homeowner vacancy rate: 1.0%; Median selected monthly owner costs: $1,636 with a mortgage, $677 without a mortgage; Median gross rent: $912 per month; Rental vacancy rate: 3.2%
Health Insurance: 96.8% have insurance; 86.6% have private insurance; 25.5% have public insurance; 3.2% do not have insurance; 1.7% of children under 18 do not have insurance
Transportation: Commute: 91.5% car, 0.8% public transportation, 1.5% walk, 5.8% work from home; Mean travel time to work: 20.1 minutes
Additional Information Contacts
Town of Perinton . . . . (585) 223-0770
    http://www.perinton.org

PITTSFORD (town). Covers a land area of 23.181 square miles and a water area of 0.209 square miles. Located at 43.07° N. Lat; 77.53° W. Long. Elevation is 492 feet.
History: Incorporated 1827.
Population: 29,608; Growth (since 2000): 8.8%; Density: 1,277.3 persons per square mile; Race: 87.7% White, 2.5% Black/African American, 7.5% Asian, 0.0% American Indian/Alaska Native, 0.0% Native Hawaiian/Other Pacific Islander, 1.7% Two or more races, 2.5% Hispanic of any race; Average household size: 2.60; Median age: 43.1; Age under 18: 22.5%; Age 65 and over: 18.8%; Males per 100 females: 86.7; Marriage status: 29.4% never married, 59.7% now married, 1.0% separated, 5.4% widowed, 5.6% divorced; Foreign born: 10.3%; Speak English only: 88.0%;

With disability: 7.5%; Veterans: 6.9%; Ancestry: 19.1% Irish, 18.7% German, 16.4% Italian, 15.3% English, 6.5% Polish
Employment: 21.5% management, business, and financial, 7.6% computer, engineering, and science, 21.1% education, legal, community service, arts, and media, 10.8% healthcare practitioners, 11.6% service, 22.7% sales and office, 1.8% natural resources, construction, and maintenance, 3.0% production, transportation, and material moving
Income: Per capita: $52,317; Median household: $103,546; Average household: $147,754; Households with income of $100,000 or more: 52.3%; Poverty rate: 3.9%
Educational Attainment: High school diploma or higher: 98.0%; Bachelor's degree or higher: 73.1%; Graduate/professional degree or higher: 39.9%

School District(s)
Pittsford Central SD (KG-12)
    2014-15 Enrollment: 5,856 . . . . (585) 267-1004
Housing: Homeownership rate: 86.5%; Median home value: $262,200; Median year structure built: 1971; Homeowner vacancy rate: 1.3%; Median selected monthly owner costs: $2,208 with a mortgage, $920 without a mortgage; Median gross rent: $1,059 per month; Rental vacancy rate: 5.6%
Health Insurance: 98.5% have insurance; 92.7% have private insurance; 22.2% have public insurance; 1.5% do not have insurance; 0.6% of children under 18 do not have insurance
Transportation: Commute: 83.8% car, 0.2% public transportation, 5.8% walk, 8.5% work from home; Mean travel time to work: 17.9 minutes
Additional Information Contacts
Town of Pittsford . . . . (585) 248-6210
    http://townofpittsford.org

PITTSFORD (village). Covers a land area of 0.673 square miles and a water area of 0.019 square miles. Located at 43.09° N. Lat; 77.52° W. Long. Elevation is 492 feet.
Population: 1,516; Growth (since 2000): 6.9%; Density: 2,253.0 persons per square mile; Race: 93.1% White, 2.4% Black/African American, 2.0% Asian, 0.0% American Indian/Alaska Native, 0.0% Native Hawaiian/Other Pacific Islander, 2.5% Two or more races, 2.2% Hispanic of any race; Average household size: 2.20; Median age: 43.1; Age under 18: 21.8%; Age 65 and over: 20.3%; Males per 100 females: 86.1; Marriage status: 24.2% never married, 58.5% now married, 2.5% separated, 5.8% widowed, 11.5% divorced; Foreign born: 9.0%; Speak English only: 90.2%; With disability: 6.1%; Veterans: 8.5%; Ancestry: 23.0% Irish, 18.2% German, 17.0% English, 16.1% Italian, 6.1% Polish
Employment: 29.5% management, business, and financial, 5.8% computer, engineering, and science, 23.0% education, legal, community service, arts, and media, 8.9% healthcare practitioners, 9.3% service, 19.4% sales and office, 2.3% natural resources, construction, and maintenance, 1.7% production, transportation, and material moving
Income: Per capita: $54,348; Median household: $84,135; Average household: $123,729; Households with income of $100,000 or more: 38.9%; Poverty rate: 5.1%
Educational Attainment: High school diploma or higher: 97.1%; Bachelor's degree or higher: 74.2%; Graduate/professional degree or higher: 35.8%

School District(s)
Pittsford Central SD (KG-12)
    2014-15 Enrollment: 5,856 . . . . (585) 267-1004
Housing: Homeownership rate: 75.1%; Median home value: $234,400; Median year structure built: Before 1940; Homeowner vacancy rate: 0.0%; Median selected monthly owner costs: $1,888 with a mortgage, $850 without a mortgage; Median gross rent: $1,155 per month; Rental vacancy rate: 0.0%
Health Insurance: 98.0% have insurance; 90.1% have private insurance; 26.1% have public insurance; 2.0% do not have insurance; 2.1% of children under 18 do not have insurance
Transportation: Commute: 87.9% car, 0.0% public transportation, 1.7% walk, 10.0% work from home; Mean travel time to work: 15.8 minutes

RIGA (town). Covers a land area of 34.962 square miles and a water area of 0.266 square miles. Located at 43.08° N. Lat; 77.87° W. Long. Elevation is 636 feet.
Population: 5,628; Growth (since 2000): 3.5%; Density: 161.0 persons per square mile; Race: 96.4% White, 1.4% Black/African American, 0.3% Asian, 0.0% American Indian/Alaska Native, 0.0% Native Hawaiian/Other Pacific Islander, 1.3% Two or more races, 3.9% Hispanic of any race;

Average household size: 2.51; Median age: 47.1; Age under 18: 18.7%; Age 65 and over: 17.5%; Males per 100 females: 98.6; Marriage status: 27.4% never married, 57.1% now married, 3.0% separated, 8.6% widowed, 6.9% divorced; Foreign born: 2.1%; Speak English only: 95.5%; With disability: 12.7%; Veterans: 9.4%; Ancestry: 32.7% German, 18.9% Irish, 17.5% Italian, 16.5% English, 6.0% American

Employment: 11.2% management, business, and financial, 5.1% computer, engineering, and science, 15.1% education, legal, community service, arts, and media, 5.8% healthcare practitioners, 17.0% service, 23.7% sales and office, 9.8% natural resources, construction, and maintenance, 12.3% production, transportation, and material moving

Income: Per capita: $30,980; Median household: $58,333; Average household: $75,659; Households with income of $100,000 or more: 24.0%; Poverty rate: 8.4%

Educational Attainment: High school diploma or higher: 92.7%; Bachelor's degree or higher: 31.3%; Graduate/professional degree or higher: 15.5%

Housing: Homeownership rate: 91.7%; Median home value: $141,900; Median year structure built: 1973; Homeowner vacancy rate: 0.1%; Median selected monthly owner costs: $1,338 with a mortgage, $592 without a mortgage; Median gross rent: $762 per month; Rental vacancy rate: 0.0%

Health Insurance: 94.6% have insurance; 80.5% have private insurance; 30.8% have public insurance; 5.4% do not have insurance; 1.7% of children under 18 do not have insurance

Transportation: Commute: 95.9% car, 0.0% public transportation, 0.5% walk, 3.6% work from home; Mean travel time to work: 22.8 minutes

Additional Information Contacts

Town of Riga . . . . (585) 293-3880
  http://www.townofriga.org

ROCHESTER (city). County seat. Covers a land area of 35.781 square miles and a water area of 1.374 square miles. Located at 43.17° N. Lat; 77.62° W. Long. Elevation is 505 feet.

History: The first settler on the site of Rochester was Ebenezer "Indian" Allen, who was granted a 100-acre tract at the falls of the Genesee River on the condition that he erect a mill for use by the Native Americans. Allen built his mill in 1789. After changing hands several times, the area was finally purchased in 1803 by Colonel William Fitzhugh, Major Charles Carroll, and Colonel Nathaniel Rochester, all from Maryland. The village was incorporated as Rochesterville in 1817. The construction of the Erie Canal through Rochester assured the town supremacy over its neighbors. Rochester was the home of George Eastman, who invented and manufactured films for cameras. In 1888 the first Kodak camera was put on the market. The Eastman School of Music was later named for him. In 1840, the University of Rochester was founded by a convention of Baptists.

Population: 210,745; Growth (since 2000): -4.1%; Density: 5,889.9 persons per square mile; Race: 45.1% White, 41.1% Black/African American, 3.7% Asian, 0.9% American Indian/Alaska Native, 0.0% Native Hawaiian/Other Pacific Islander, 4.5% Two or more races, 17.4% Hispanic of any race; Average household size: 2.34; Median age: 31.0; Age under 18: 24.1%; Age 65 and over: 9.8%; Males per 100 females: 93.4; Marriage status: 55.3% never married, 28.6% now married, 4.3% separated, 5.4% widowed, 10.7% divorced; Foreign born: 9.0%; Speak English only: 80.2%; With disability: 17.3%; Veterans: 4.7%; Ancestry: 9.0% German, 8.8% Irish, 8.1% Italian, 5.1% English, 2.5% American

Employment: 9.2% management, business, and financial, 5.0% computer, engineering, and science, 12.3% education, legal, community service, arts, and media, 6.2% healthcare practitioners, 25.6% service, 24.2% sales and office, 4.5% natural resources, construction, and maintenance, 13.1% production, transportation, and material moving

Income: Per capita: $19,158; Median household: $30,960; Average household: $43,682; Households with income of $100,000 or more: 8.4%; Poverty rate: 33.5%

Educational Attainment: High school diploma or higher: 80.5%; Bachelor's degree or higher: 23.8%; Graduate/professional degree or higher: 9.7%

School District(s)

Brighton Central SD (KG-12)
  2014-15 Enrollment: 3,549 . . . . (585) 242-5200
Churchville-Chili Central SD (KG-12)
  2014-15 Enrollment: 3,935 . . . . (585) 293-1800
Discovery Charter School (KG-02)
  2014-15 Enrollment: 259 . . . . (585) 342-4032

East Irondequoit Central SD (KG-12)
  2014-15 Enrollment: 3,121 . . . . (585) 339-1210
Eugenio Maria De Hostos Charter School (KG-08)
  2014-15 Enrollment: 409 . . . . (585) 544-6170
Gates-Chili Central SD (KG-12)
  2014-15 Enrollment: 4,207 . . . . (585) 247-5050
Genesee Community Charter School (KG-06)
  2014-15 Enrollment: 216 . . . . (585) 697-1960
Greece Central SD (PK-12)
  2014-15 Enrollment: 11,312 . . . . (585) 966-2321
Penfield Central SD (KG-12)
  2014-15 Enrollment: 4,469 . . . . (585) 249-5700
Pittsford Central SD (KG-12)
  2014-15 Enrollment: 5,856 . . . . (585) 267-1004
Rochester Academy Charter School (07-12)
  2014-15 Enrollment: 361 . . . . (585) 467-9201
Rochester City SD (PK-12)
  2014-15 Enrollment: 30,014 . . . . (585) 262-8378
Rush-Henrietta Central SD (KG-12)
  2014-15 Enrollment: 5,394 . . . . (585) 359-5012
True North Rochester Prep Charter School-West Camp (05-05)
  2014-15 Enrollment: 566 . . . . (585) 368-5090
True North Rochester Preparatory Charter School (T (KG-08)
  2014-15 Enrollment: 810 . . . . (585) 436-8629
University Preparatory Charter School for Young Me (07-09)
  2014-15 Enrollment: 442 . . . . (585) 672-1280
Urban Choice Charter School (KG-08)
  2014-15 Enrollment: 404 . . . . (585) 288-5702
West Irondequoit Central SD (KG-12)
  2014-15 Enrollment: 3,619 . . . . (585) 336-2983

Four-year College(s)

Bryant & Stratton College-Greece (Private, For-profit)
  Fall 2014 Enrollment: 421 . . . . (585) 720-0660
  2015-16 Tuition: In-state $16,183; Out-of-state $16,183
Colgate Rochester Crozer Divinity School (Private, Not-for-profit)
  Fall 2014 Enrollment: 80 . . . . (585) 271-1320
Nazareth College (Private, Not-for-profit)
  Fall 2014 Enrollment: 2,818 . . . . (585) 389-2525
  2015-16 Tuition: In-state $31,745; Out-of-state $31,745
Northeastern Seminary (Private, Not-for-profit, Interdenominational)
  Fall 2014 Enrollment: 154 . . . . (585) 594-6000
Roberts Wesleyan College (Private, Not-for-profit, Free Methodist)
  Fall 2014 Enrollment: 1,762 . . . . (585) 594-6000
  2015-16 Tuition: In-state $28,630; Out-of-state $28,630
Rochester Institute of Technology (Private, Not-for-profit)
  Fall 2014 Enrollment: 16,310 . . . . (585) 475-2411
  2015-16 Tuition: In-state $37,124; Out-of-state $37,124
Saint John Fisher College (Private, Not-for-profit, Roman Catholic)
  Fall 2014 Enrollment: 3,856 . . . . (585) 385-8000
  2015-16 Tuition: In-state $30,690; Out-of-state $30,690
St Bernard's School of Theology and Ministry (Private, Not-for-profit, Roman Catholic)
  Fall 2014 Enrollment: 93 . . . . (585) 271-3657
Talmudical Institute of Upstate New York (Private, Not-for-profit)
  Fall 2014 Enrollment: 21 . . . . (716) 473-2810
  2015-16 Tuition: In-state $5,100; Out-of-state $5,100
University of Rochester (Private, Not-for-profit)
  Fall 2014 Enrollment: 11,060 . . . . (585) 275-3221
  2015-16 Tuition: In-state $48,280; Out-of-state $48,280

Two-year College(s)

Bryant & Stratton College-Henrietta (Private, For-profit)
  Fall 2014 Enrollment: 431 . . . . (585) 292-5627
  2015-16 Tuition: In-state $16,808; Out-of-state $16,808
Monroe Community College (Public)
  Fall 2014 Enrollment: 15,335 . . . . (585) 292-2000
  2015-16 Tuition: In-state $4,554; Out-of-state $8,354

Vocational/Technical School(s)

Continental School of Beauty Culture-Rochester (Private, For-profit)
  Fall 2014 Enrollment: 317 . . . . (585) 272-8060
  2015-16 Tuition: $12,440
Empire Beauty School-Rochester (Private, For-profit)
  Fall 2014 Enrollment: 127 . . . . (585) 225-4796
  2015-16 Tuition: $12,000
Isabella Graham Hart School of Practical Nursing (Private, Not-for-profit)
  Fall 2014 Enrollment: 45 . . . . (585) 922-1400

Monroe 2 Orleans BOCES-Center for Workforce Development (Public)
Fall 2014 Enrollment: 104 . . . . (585) 349-9100
2015-16 Tuition: $7,000
Onondaga School of Therapeutic Massage-Rochester (Private, For-profit)
Fall 2014 Enrollment: 82 . . . . (585) 241-0070
2015-16 Tuition: $15,575
Sharp Edgez Barber Institute (Private, For-profit)
Fall 2014 Enrollment: 61 . . . . (585) 482-2808
2015-16 Tuition: $6,956
Shear Ego International School of Hair Design (Private, For-profit)
Fall 2014 Enrollment: 111 . . . . (585) 342-0070
2015-16 Tuition: $13,740
Housing: Homeownership rate: 36.9%; Median home value: $76,200;
Median year structure built: Before 1940; Homeowner vacancy rate: 1.5%;
Median selected monthly owner costs: $1,018 with a mortgage, $456
without a mortgage; Median gross rent: $770 per month; Rental vacancy
rate: 6.7%
Health Insurance: 90.1% have insurance; 50.0% have private insurance;
50.2% have public insurance; 9.9% do not have insurance; 4.4% of
children under 18 do not have insurance
Hospitals: Highland Hospital (272 beds); Monroe Community Hospital
(566 beds); Rochester General Hospital (528 beds); Strong Memorial
Hospital (750 beds); Unity Hospital of Rochester (681 beds)
Safety: Violent crime rate: 87.6 per 10,000 population; Property crime rate:
393.8 per 10,000 population
Newspapers: City Newspaper (weekly circulation 40,000); Democrat &
Chronicle (daily circulation 156,000)
Transportation: Commute: 80.1% car, 8.8% public transportation, 6.6%
walk, 2.4% work from home; Mean travel time to work: 19.6 minutes;
Amtrak: Train service available.
Airports: Greater Rochester International (primary service/small hub)
Additional Information Contacts
City of Rochester. . . . . (585) 428-5990
http://www.cityofrochester.gov

RUSH (town). Covers a land area of 30.332 square miles and a water
area of 0.373 square miles. Located at 42.97° N. Lat; 77.67° W. Long.
Elevation is 551 feet.
Population: 3,507; Growth (since 2000): -2.7%; Density: 115.6 persons
per square mile; Race: 96.4% White, 2.1% Black/African American, 0.7%
Asian, 0.0% American Indian/Alaska Native, 0.0% Native Hawaiian/Other
Pacific Islander, 0.4% Two or more races, 2.6% Hispanic of any race;
Average household size: 2.45; Median age: 48.4; Age under 18: 20.8%;
Age 65 and over: 18.7%; Males per 100 females: 103.0; Marriage status:
19.0% never married, 67.0% now married, 1.5% separated, 3.4%
widowed, 10.6% divorced; Foreign born: 5.4%; Speak English only: 96.5%;
With disability: 9.8%; Veterans: 8.0%; Ancestry: 32.3% German, 19.6%
Irish, 19.4% Italian, 14.2% English, 5.6% American
Employment: 20.2% management, business, and financial, 9.0%
computer, engineering, and science, 13.2% education, legal, community
service, arts, and media, 9.6% healthcare practitioners, 8.6% service,
24.7% sales and office, 7.9% natural resources, construction, and
maintenance, 6.9% production, transportation, and material moving
Income: Per capita: $42,278; Median household: $89,321; Average
household: $105,188; Households with income of $100,000 or more:
39.9%; Poverty rate: 4.3%
Educational Attainment: High school diploma or higher: 97.1%;
Bachelor's degree or higher: 50.2%; Graduate/professional degree or
higher: 22.7%

School District(s)
Rush-Henrietta Central SD (KG-12)
2014-15 Enrollment: 5,394 . . . . (585) 359-5012
Housing: Homeownership rate: 91.6%; Median home value: $187,400;
Median year structure built: 1970; Homeowner vacancy rate: 0.0%; Median
selected monthly owner costs: $1,842 with a mortgage, $708 without a
mortgage; Median gross rent: $822 per month; Rental vacancy rate: 0.0%
Health Insurance: 98.3% have insurance; 88.1% have private insurance;
25.5% have public insurance; 1.7% do not have insurance; 0.0% of
children under 18 do not have insurance
Transportation: Commute: 93.9% car, 0.0% public transportation, 0.0%
walk, 5.1% work from home; Mean travel time to work: 23.3 minutes
Additional Information Contacts
Town of Rush . . . . (585) 533-1312
http://townofrush.com

SCOTTSVILLE (village). Covers a land area of 1.082 square miles
and a water area of 0.005 square miles. Located at 43.02° N. Lat; 77.75°
W. Long. Elevation is 607 feet.
Population: 2,616; Growth (since 2000): 22.9%; Density: 2,417.3 persons
per square mile; Race: 82.3% White, 12.2% Black/African American, 1.5%
Asian, 0.0% American Indian/Alaska Native, 0.0% Native Hawaiian/Other
Pacific Islander, 3.6% Two or more races, 5.4% Hispanic of any race;
Average household size: 2.80; Median age: 36.5; Age under 18: 28.9%;
Age 65 and over: 11.2%; Males per 100 females: 97.9; Marriage status:
33.6% never married, 54.2% now married, 2.0% separated, 3.6%
widowed, 8.6% divorced; Foreign born: 3.4%; Speak English only: 92.0%;
With disability: 14.7%; Veterans: 8.5%; Ancestry: 24.7% Irish, 16.3%
German, 16.2% Italian, 14.2% English, 4.4% Polish
Employment: 7.6% management, business, and financial, 5.5% computer,
engineering, and science, 14.8% education, legal, community service, arts,
and media, 5.7% healthcare practitioners, 17.5% service, 22.0% sales and
office, 9.2% natural resources, construction, and maintenance, 17.8%
production, transportation, and material moving
Income: Per capita: $25,397; Median household: $52,917; Average
household: $69,615; Households with income of $100,000 or more: 21.3%;
Poverty rate: 12.7%
Educational Attainment: High school diploma or higher: 92.3%;
Bachelor's degree or higher: 36.5%; Graduate/professional degree or
higher: 15.8%

School District(s)
Wheatland-Chili Central SD (KG-12)
2014-15 Enrollment: 679 . . . . (585) 889-6246
Housing: Homeownership rate: 69.5%; Median home value: $127,700;
Median year structure built: 1958; Homeowner vacancy rate: 0.0%; Median
selected monthly owner costs: $1,324 with a mortgage, $562 without a
mortgage; Median gross rent: $804 per month; Rental vacancy rate: 0.0%
Health Insurance: 92.2% have insurance; 71.7% have private insurance;
33.6% have public insurance; 7.8% do not have insurance; 4.2% of
children under 18 do not have insurance
Transportation: Commute: 92.8% car, 0.0% public transportation, 4.8%
walk, 2.0% work from home; Mean travel time to work: 22.7 minutes

SPENCERPORT (village). Covers a land area of 1.337 square miles
and a water area of 0.032 square miles. Located at 43.19° N. Lat; 77.81°
W. Long. Elevation is 554 feet.
History: Site of John T. Trowbridge's boyhood home. Incorporated 1867.
Population: 3,598; Growth (since 2000): 1.1%; Density: 2,690.4 persons
per square mile; Race: 94.7% White, 2.9% Black/African American, 0.2%
Asian, 0.0% American Indian/Alaska Native, 0.0% Native Hawaiian/Other
Pacific Islander, 2.3% Two or more races, 4.3% Hispanic of any race;
Average household size: 2.50; Median age: 43.8; Age under 18: 22.5%;
Age 65 and over: 13.9%; Males per 100 females: 91.0; Marriage status:
29.6% never married, 50.0% now married, 1.8% separated, 7.0%
widowed, 13.4% divorced; Foreign born: 2.4%; Speak English only: 97.1%;
With disability: 16.9%; Veterans: 9.3%; Ancestry: 29.2% German, 23.9%
Italian, 20.1% Irish, 11.7% English, 7.1% American
Employment: 17.1% management, business, and financial, 6.3%
computer, engineering, and science, 17.0% education, legal, community
service, arts, and media, 7.1% healthcare practitioners, 14.6% service,
18.1% sales and office, 9.7% natural resources, construction, and
maintenance, 10.1% production, transportation, and material moving
Income: Per capita: $31,549; Median household: $62,708; Average
household: $77,424; Households with income of $100,000 or more: 27.0%;
Poverty rate: 7.5%
Educational Attainment: High school diploma or higher: 94.5%;
Bachelor's degree or higher: 32.8%; Graduate/professional degree or
higher: 15.6%

School District(s)
Monroe 2-Orleans Boces
2014-15 Enrollment: n/a . . . . (585) 352-2411
Spencerport Central SD (KG-12)
2014-15 Enrollment: 3,715 . . . . (585) 349-5102
Housing: Homeownership rate: 67.5%; Median home value: $135,800;
Median year structure built: 1958; Homeowner vacancy rate: 0.0%; Median
selected monthly owner costs: $1,300 with a mortgage, $577 without a
mortgage; Median gross rent: $762 per month; Rental vacancy rate: 0.0%
Health Insurance: 96.9% have insurance; 86.2% have private insurance;
24.7% have public insurance; 3.1% do not have insurance; 0.0% of
children under 18 do not have insurance
Newspapers: Westside News Inc. (weekly circulation 33,000)

Transportation: Commute: 97.6% car, 0.1% public transportation, 0.0% walk, 2.3% work from home; Mean travel time to work: 19.2 minutes

SWEDEN (town). Covers a land area of 33.679 square miles and a water area of 0.152 square miles. Located at 43.18° N. Lat; 77.93° W. Long.

Population: 14,238; Growth (since 2000): 3.8%; Density: 422.8 persons per square mile; Race: 90.2% White, 3.2% Black/African American, 2.9% Asian, 0.4% American Indian/Alaska Native, 0.0% Native Hawaiian/Other Pacific Islander, 3.1% Two or more races, 3.3% Hispanic of any race; Average household size: 2.40; Median age: 26.9; Age under 18: 15.3%; Age 65 and over: 11.5%; Males per 100 females: 92.6; Marriage status: 51.6% never married, 38.0% now married, 1.7% separated, 3.7% widowed, 6.8% divorced; Foreign born: 4.7%; Speak English only: 92.5%; With disability: 10.5%; Veterans: 7.0%; Ancestry: 25.6% German, 18.3% Italian, 18.2% Irish, 13.2% English, 8.1% Polish

Employment: 9.5% management, business, and financial, 4.8% computer, engineering, and science, 17.0% education, legal, community service, arts, and media, 6.0% healthcare practitioners, 20.5% service, 28.0% sales and office, 6.3% natural resources, construction, and maintenance, 7.9% production, transportation, and material moving

Income: Per capita: $22,860; Median household: $49,876; Average household: $62,940; Households with income of $100,000 or more: 19.6%; Poverty rate: 18.8%

Educational Attainment: High school diploma or higher: 95.9%; Bachelor's degree or higher: 36.7%; Graduate/professional degree or higher: 17.8%

Housing: Homeownership rate: 58.2%; Median home value: $131,500; Median year structure built: 1971; Homeowner vacancy rate: 0.9%; Median selected monthly owner costs: $1,396 with a mortgage, $576 without a mortgage; Median gross rent: $793 per month; Rental vacancy rate: 8.0%

Health Insurance: 95.4% have insurance; 83.8% have private insurance; 24.7% have public insurance; 4.6% do not have insurance; 2.2% of children under 18 do not have insurance

Transportation: Commute: 77.9% car, 1.1% public transportation, 16.5% walk, 2.5% work from home; Mean travel time to work: 21.8 minutes

Additional Information Contacts

Town of Sweden . . . . (585) 637-2144
http://www.townofsweden.org

WEBSTER (town). Covers a land area of 33.531 square miles and a water area of 1.707 square miles. Located at 43.23° N. Lat; 77.45° W. Long. Elevation is 446 feet.

History: Incorporated 1905.

Population: 43,750; Growth (since 2000): 15.4%; Density: 1,304.8 persons per square mile; Race: 93.1% White, 1.4% Black/African American, 3.3% Asian, 0.0% American Indian/Alaska Native, 0.0% Native Hawaiian/Other Pacific Islander, 1.8% Two or more races, 2.1% Hispanic of any race; Average household size: 2.51; Median age: 42.7; Age under 18: 23.1%; Age 65 and over: 17.5%; Males per 100 females: 93.7; Marriage status: 23.7% never married, 60.7% now married, 1.5% separated, 7.0% widowed, 8.7% divorced; Foreign born: 8.9%; Speak English only: 90.2%; With disability: 9.6%; Veterans: 7.0%; Ancestry: 27.9% Italian, 23.9% German, 19.0% Irish, 11.4% English, 6.5% Polish

Employment: 17.8% management, business, and financial, 9.1% computer, engineering, and science, 11.5% education, legal, community service, arts, and media, 7.0% healthcare practitioners, 12.6% service, 25.8% sales and office, 7.2% natural resources, construction, and maintenance, 8.9% production, transportation, and material moving

Income: Per capita: $33,926; Median household: $69,987; Average household: $83,676; Households with income of $100,000 or more: 30.4%; Poverty rate: 6.9%

Educational Attainment: High school diploma or higher: 95.2%; Bachelor's degree or higher: 43.2%; Graduate/professional degree or higher: 19.4%

School District(s)

Webster Central SD (PK-12)
2014-15 Enrollment: 8,528 . . . . (585) 216-0001

Housing: Homeownership rate: 77.9%; Median home value: $175,200; Median year structure built: 1980; Homeowner vacancy rate: 1.0%; Median selected monthly owner costs: $1,570 with a mortgage, $637 without a mortgage; Median gross rent: $954 per month; Rental vacancy rate: 1.5%

Health Insurance: 96.6% have insurance; 84.1% have private insurance; 27.5% have public insurance; 3.4% do not have insurance; 2.7% of children under 18 do not have insurance

Safety: Violent crime rate: 5.4 per 10,000 population; Property crime rate: 114.0 per 10,000 population

Newspapers: Wayne County Mail (weekly circulation 2,400); Webster Herald (weekly circulation 4,200)

Transportation: Commute: 94.0% car, 0.3% public transportation, 1.1% walk, 3.6% work from home; Mean travel time to work: 20.6 minutes

Additional Information Contacts

Town of Webster . . . . (585) 872-1000
http://www.ci.webster.ny.us

WEBSTER (village). Covers a land area of 2.202 square miles and a water area of <.001 square miles. Located at 43.22° N. Lat; 77.42° W. Long. Elevation is 446 feet.

Population: 5,524; Growth (since 2000): 5.9%; Density: 2,508.4 persons per square mile; Race: 79.6% White, 2.6% Black/African American, 10.5% Asian, 0.0% American Indian/Alaska Native, 0.0% Native Hawaiian/Other Pacific Islander, 5.5% Two or more races, 6.8% Hispanic of any race; Average household size: 2.28; Median age: 34.5; Age under 18: 25.5%; Age 65 and over: 14.7%; Males per 100 females: 89.4; Marriage status: 33.5% never married, 44.1% now married, 1.9% separated, 9.9% widowed, 12.6% divorced; Foreign born: 19.1%; Speak English only: 76.9%; With disability: 12.7%; Veterans: 7.8%; Ancestry: 16.3% German, 15.7% Italian, 14.3% Irish, 8.4% English, 4.9% American

Employment: 10.1% management, business, and financial, 12.2% computer, engineering, and science, 8.7% education, legal, community service, arts, and media, 3.3% healthcare practitioners, 21.0% service, 25.3% sales and office, 9.4% natural resources, construction, and maintenance, 9.9% production, transportation, and material moving

Income: Per capita: $22,046; Median household: $35,708; Average household: $47,058; Households with income of $100,000 or more: 10.2%; Poverty rate: 29.3%

Educational Attainment: High school diploma or higher: 90.9%; Bachelor's degree or higher: 32.1%; Graduate/professional degree or higher: 12.7%

School District(s)

Webster Central SD (PK-12)
2014-15 Enrollment: 8,528 . . . . (585) 216-0001

Housing: Homeownership rate: 40.1%; Median home value: $136,500; Median year structure built: 1967; Homeowner vacancy rate: 4.7%; Median selected monthly owner costs: $1,228 with a mortgage, $476 without a mortgage; Median gross rent: $837 per month; Rental vacancy rate: 0.0%

Health Insurance: 93.4% have insurance; 57.6% have private insurance; 50.1% have public insurance; 6.6% do not have insurance; 0.0% of children under 18 do not have insurance

Newspapers: Wayne County Mail (weekly circulation 2,400); Webster Herald (weekly circulation 4,200)

Transportation: Commute: 90.8% car, 1.3% public transportation, 6.1% walk, 1.0% work from home; Mean travel time to work: 17.7 minutes

Additional Information Contacts

Village of Webster . . . . (585) 265-3770
http://www.villageofwebster.com

WEST HENRIETTA (unincorporated postal area)

ZCTA: 14586

Covers a land area of 11.146 square miles and a water area of 0.193 square miles. Located at 43.04° N. Lat; 77.69° W. Long. Elevation is 604 feet.

Population: 12,046; Growth (since 2000): 94.4%; Density: 1,080.8 persons per square mile; Race: 76.1% White, 8.9% Black/African American, 7.6% Asian, 1.1% American Indian/Alaska Native, 0.1% Native Hawaiian/Other Pacific Islander, 5.3% Two or more races, 5.0% Hispanic of any race; Average household size: 2.75; Median age: 33.0; Age under 18: 22.7%; Age 65 and over: 8.1%; Males per 100 females: 104.3; Marriage status: 38.6% never married, 49.0% now married, 1.6% separated, 3.4% widowed, 9.1% divorced; Foreign born: 12.4%; Speak English only: 86.4%; With disability: 7.7%; Veterans: 6.4%; Ancestry: 19.2% German, 13.6% Irish, 11.4% Italian, 9.7% English, 6.3% Polish

Employment: 12.1% management, business, and financial, 11.1% computer, engineering, and science, 15.3% education, legal, community service, arts, and media, 8.0% healthcare practitioners, 12.1% service, 23.8% sales and office, 4.2% natural resources, construction, and maintenance, 13.4% production, transportation, and material moving

Income: Per capita: $28,320; Median household: $77,188; Average household: $76,435; Households with income of $100,000 or more: 29.4%; Poverty rate: 12.4%

Educational Attainment: High school diploma or higher: 94.9%; Bachelor's degree or higher: 45.0%; Graduate/professional degree or higher: 18.5%

School District(s)
Rush-Henrietta Central SD (KG-12)
  2014-15 Enrollment: 5,394 . . . . (585) 359-5012
Housing: Homeownership rate: 72.6%; Median home value: $168,200; Median year structure built: 1994; Homeowner vacancy rate: 0.5%; Median selected monthly owner costs: $1,551 with a mortgage, $607 without a mortgage; Median gross rent: $1,122 per month; Rental vacancy rate: 0.0%
Health Insurance: 94.2% have insurance; 85.5% have private insurance; 17.3% have public insurance; 5.8% do not have insurance; 3.6% of children under 18 do not have insurance
Transportation: Commute: 93.3% car, 0.1% public transportation, 2.3% walk, 3.5% work from home; Mean travel time to work: 18.8 minutes

WHEATLAND (town). Covers a land area of 30.411 square miles and a water area of 0.261 square miles. Located at 43.01° N. Lat; 77.82° W. Long. Elevation is 604 feet.
Population: 4,777; Growth (since 2000): -7.2%; Density: 157.1 persons per square mile; Race: 85.3% White, 11.2% Black/African American, 0.8% Asian, 0.0% American Indian/Alaska Native, 0.0% Native Hawaiian/Other Pacific Islander, 2.4% Two or more races, 4.0% Hispanic of any race; Average household size: 2.35; Median age: 43.3; Age under 18: 21.0%; Age 65 and over: 13.6%; Males per 100 females: 100.4; Marriage status: 31.6% never married, 51.1% now married, 1.4% separated, 4.9% widowed, 12.3% divorced; Foreign born: 2.2%; Speak English only: 95.7%; With disability: 11.4%; Veterans: 7.8%; Ancestry: 22.2% German, 21.6% Irish, 16.2% Italian, 15.2% English, 4.5% American
Employment: 12.4% management, business, and financial, 5.6% computer, engineering, and science, 9.9% education, legal, community service, arts, and media, 7.7% healthcare practitioners, 19.8% service, 20.2% sales and office, 9.8% natural resources, construction, and maintenance, 14.6% production, transportation, and material moving
Income: Per capita: $29,485; Median household: $55,417; Average household: $68,052; Households with income of $100,000 or more: 21.6%; Poverty rate: 9.4%
Educational Attainment: High school diploma or higher: 94.1%; Bachelor's degree or higher: 33.1%; Graduate/professional degree or higher: 11.8%
Housing: Homeownership rate: 66.5%; Median home value: $134,700; Median year structure built: 1966; Homeowner vacancy rate: 0.0%; Median selected monthly owner costs: $1,304 with a mortgage, $566 without a mortgage; Median gross rent: $941 per month; Rental vacancy rate: 0.0%
Health Insurance: 93.7% have insurance; 79.3% have private insurance; 29.7% have public insurance; 6.3% do not have insurance; 5.9% of children under 18 do not have insurance
Transportation: Commute: 94.6% car, 0.0% public transportation, 3.8% walk, 1.4% work from home; Mean travel time to work: 22.6 minutes
Additional Information Contacts
Town of Wheatland . . . . (585) 889-1553
  http://www.townofwheatland.org

Montgomery County

Located in east central New York, in the Mohawk River Valley; crossed by the Barge Canal; drained by Schoharie Creek. Covers a land area of 403.043 square miles, a water area of 7.312 square miles, and is located in the Eastern Time Zone at 42.90° N. Lat., 74.44° W. Long. The county was founded in 1772. County seat is Fonda.

Montgomery County is part of the Amsterdam, NY Micropolitan Statistical Area. The entire metro area includes: Montgomery County, NY

Population: 49,779; Growth (since 2000): 0.1%; Density: 123.5 persons per square mile; Race: 88.9% White, 2.1% Black/African American, 0.7% Asian, 0.2% American Indian/Alaska Native, 0.0% Native Hawaiian/Other Pacific Islander, 2.7% two or more races, 12.3% Hispanic of any race; Average household size: 2.50; Median age: 41.0; Age under 18: 22.8%; Age 65 and over: 17.4%; Males per 100 females: 94.9; Marriage status: 32.6% never married, 47.6% now married, 3.1% separated, 8.4% widowed, 11.4% divorced; Foreign born: 3.2%; Speak English only: 86.4%; With disability: 15.5%; Veterans: 8.9%; Ancestry: 19.8% German, 15.4% Italian, 15.0% Irish, 11.4% Polish, 9.0% English

Religion: Six largest groups: 27.8% Catholicism, 4.4% Lutheran, 3.6% Presbyterian-Reformed, 2.6% Methodist/Pietist, 2.1% Non-denominational Protestant, 1.0% Baptist
Economy: Unemployment rate: 5.1%; Leading industries: 17.6 % health care and social assistance; 17.0 % retail trade; 10.6 % other services (except public administration); Farms: 659 totaling 131,386 acres; Company size: 1 employs 1,000 or more persons, 1 employs 500 to 999 persons, 23 employ 100 to 499 persons, 1,046 employ less than 100 persons; Business ownership: 858 women-owned, 33 Black-owned, 109 Hispanic-owned, 85 Asian-owned, n/a American Indian/Alaska Native-owned
Employment: 12.4% management, business, and financial, 2.6% computer, engineering, and science, 9.1% education, legal, community service, arts, and media, 5.6% healthcare practitioners, 19.2% service, 23.4% sales and office, 10.6% natural resources, construction, and maintenance, 17.1% production, transportation, and material moving
Income: Per capita: $23,554; Median household: $43,764; Average household: $57,536; Households with income of $100,000 or more: 14.4%; Poverty rate: 20.6%
Educational Attainment: High school diploma or higher: 84.3%; Bachelor's degree or higher: 16.2%; Graduate/professional degree or higher: 6.0%
Housing: Homeownership rate: 67.1%; Median home value: $101,600; Median year structure built: 1943; Homeowner vacancy rate: 2.3%; Median selected monthly owner costs: $1,236 with a mortgage, $537 without a mortgage; Median gross rent: $702 per month; Rental vacancy rate: 5.4%
Vital Statistics: Birth rate: 122.3 per 10,000 population; Death rate: 109.0 per 10,000 population; Age-adjusted cancer mortality rate: 171.2 deaths per 100,000 population
Health Insurance: 91.1% have insurance; 61.4% have private insurance; 44.7% have public insurance; 8.9% do not have insurance; 8.4% of children under 18 do not have insurance
Health Care: Physicians: 14.5 per 10,000 population; Dentists: 6.4 per 10,000 population; Hospital beds: 58.3 per 10,000 population; Hospital admissions: 1,246.5 per 10,000 population
Transportation: Commute: 89.3% car, 1.3% public transportation, 3.8% walk, 3.3% work from home; Mean travel time to work: 24.0 minutes
2016 Presidential Election: 59.9% Trump, 35.0% Clinton, 3.7% Johnson, 1.4% Stein
National and State Parks: Schoharie Crossing State Historic Site
Additional Information Contacts
Montgomery Government . . . . (518) 853-8111
  http://www.co.montgomery.ny.us

Montgomery County Communities

AMES (village). Covers a land area of 0.131 square miles and a water area of 0 square miles. Located at 42.84° N. Lat; 74.60° W. Long. Elevation is 705 feet.
Population: 165; Growth (since 2000): -4.6%; Density: 1,262.6 persons per square mile; Race: 99.4% White, 0.6% Black/African American, 0.0% Asian, 0.0% American Indian/Alaska Native, 0.0% Native Hawaiian/Other Pacific Islander, 0.0% Two or more races, 1.2% Hispanic of any race; Average household size: 2.50; Median age: 50.2; Age under 18: 16.4%; Age 65 and over: 29.1%; Males per 100 females: 107.1; Marriage status: 16.6% never married, 73.8% now married, 0.7% separated, 4.1% widowed, 5.5% divorced; Foreign born: 1.2%; Speak English only: 99.4%; With disability: 16.4%; Veterans: 11.6%; Ancestry: 29.1% Irish, 22.4% English, 18.2% German, 15.2% Dutch, 13.3% American
Employment: 19.7% management, business, and financial, 0.0% computer, engineering, and science, 17.1% education, legal, community service, arts, and media, 3.9% healthcare practitioners, 11.8% service, 15.8% sales and office, 19.7% natural resources, construction, and maintenance, 11.8% production, transportation, and material moving
Income: Per capita: $29,309; Median household: $61,667; Average household: $73,279; Households with income of $100,000 or more: 36.3%; Poverty rate: n/a
Educational Attainment: High school diploma or higher: 77.8%; Bachelor's degree or higher: 22.2%; Graduate/professional degree or higher: 7.9%
Housing: Homeownership rate: 72.7%; Median home value: $88,200; Median year structure built: Before 1940; Homeowner vacancy rate: 0.0%; Median selected monthly owner costs: $958 with a mortgage, $492 without a mortgage; Median gross rent: $817 per month; Rental vacancy rate: 0.0%

Health Insurance: 95.8% have insurance; 83.6% have private insurance; 38.8% have public insurance; 4.2% do not have insurance; 0.0% of children under 18 do not have insurance
Transportation: Commute: 82.9% car, 0.0% public transportation, 0.0% walk, 11.4% work from home; Mean travel time to work: 34.3 minutes

AMSTERDAM (city).
Covers a land area of 5.862 square miles and a water area of 0.391 square miles. Located at 42.94° N. Lat; 74.19° W. Long. Elevation is 361 feet.
History: Amsterdam was first settled by Albert Veeder, who came from Schenectady in 1783. The village of Amsterdam was so named in 1804. It began to grow in size and industrial importance after the Erie Canal was opened in 1825 and the Utica & Schenectady Railroad was constructed through it in 1836. The local carpet industry traces its beginnings to 1838, when William E. Greene established a carpet mill. The knitting industry was started by Greene in 1856.
Population: 18,157; Growth (since 2000): -1.1%; Density: 3,097.4 persons per square mile; Race: 76.2% White, 4.2% Black/African American, 0.5% Asian, 0.3% American Indian/Alaska Native, 0.1% Native Hawaiian/Other Pacific Islander, 5.0% Two or more races, 28.9% Hispanic of any race; Average household size: 2.47; Median age: 36.7; Age under 18: 24.2%; Age 65 and over: 16.9%; Males per 100 females: 90.0; Marriage status: 40.1% never married, 40.3% now married, 3.7% separated, 8.6% widowed, 11.1% divorced; Foreign born: 5.0%; Speak English only: 73.4%; With disability: 18.9%; Veterans: 8.1%; Ancestry: 18.8% Italian, 13.8% Irish, 12.7% Polish, 11.3% German, 5.1% English
Employment: 11.2% management, business, and financial, 1.9% computer, engineering, and science, 8.1% education, legal, community service, arts, and media, 4.5% healthcare practitioners, 21.5% service, 24.0% sales and office, 10.1% natural resources, construction, and maintenance, 18.8% production, transportation, and material moving
Income: Per capita: $20,898; Median household: $33,917; Average household: $49,751; Households with income of $100,000 or more: 12.2%; Poverty rate: 28.0%
Educational Attainment: High school diploma or higher: 80.1%; Bachelor's degree or higher: 14.4%; Graduate/professional degree or higher: 4.4%

School District(s)
Amsterdam City SD (PK-12)
    2014-15 Enrollment: 3,784 . . . . (518) 843-3180
Broadalbin-Perth Central SD (02-12)
    2014-15 Enrollment: 1,846 . . . . (518) 954-2500
Housing: Homeownership rate: 49.4%; Median home value: $91,200; Median year structure built: Before 1940; Homeowner vacancy rate: 5.1%; Median selected monthly owner costs: $1,271 with a mortgage, $561 without a mortgage; Median gross rent: $722 per month; Rental vacancy rate: 4.3%
Health Insurance: 92.5% have insurance; 52.0% have private insurance; 54.3% have public insurance; 7.5% do not have insurance; 1.3% of children under 18 do not have insurance
Hospitals: Saint Mary's Hospital at Amsterdam (143 beds)
Safety: Violent crime rate: 16.7 per 10,000 population; Property crime rate: 275.9 per 10,000 population
Newspapers: Courier-Standard-Enterprise (weekly circulation 4,000); The Recorder (daily circulation 9,200)
Transportation: Commute: 84.4% car, 1.6% public transportation, 6.0% walk, 2.8% work from home; Mean travel time to work: 20.9 minutes; Amtrak: Train service available.
Additional Information Contacts
City of Amsterdam . . . . (518) 841-4300
    http://www.amsterdamny.gov

AMSTERDAM (town).
Covers a land area of 29.701 square miles and a water area of 0.733 square miles. Located at 42.96° N. Lat; 74.17° W. Long. Elevation is 361 feet.
History: Historically famous for carpet manufacturing. The area was settled in 1783 and was named Amsterdam for its many early settlers from the Netherlands. Nearby stands Fort Johnson, home of the British colonial leader Sir William Johnson. Incorporated 1885.
Population: 5,913; Growth (since 2000): 1.6%; Density: 199.1 persons per square mile; Race: 98.0% White, 0.7% Black/African American, 0.1% Asian, 0.4% American Indian/Alaska Native, 0.0% Native Hawaiian/Other Pacific Islander, 0.4% Two or more races, 3.0% Hispanic of any race; Average household size: 2.21; Median age: 50.3; Age under 18: 15.2%; Age 65 and over: 23.9%; Males per 100 females: 92.0; Marriage status:

25.7% never married, 53.6% now married, 2.5% separated, 9.4% widowed, 11.3% divorced; Foreign born: 1.3%; Speak English only: 95.8%; With disability: 13.0%; Veterans: 8.4%; Ancestry: 24.1% German, 23.7% Polish, 18.0% Italian, 13.1% Irish, 11.1% English
Employment: 20.6% management, business, and financial, 3.3% computer, engineering, and science, 11.8% education, legal, community service, arts, and media, 6.9% healthcare practitioners, 15.0% service, 20.1% sales and office, 11.3% natural resources, construction, and maintenance, 11.0% production, transportation, and material moving
Income: Per capita: $31,015; Median household: $56,830; Average household: $68,494; Households with income of $100,000 or more: 20.5%; Poverty rate: 13.9%
Educational Attainment: High school diploma or higher: 89.9%; Bachelor's degree or higher: 21.7%; Graduate/professional degree or higher: 8.6%

School District(s)
Amsterdam City SD (PK-12)
    2014-15 Enrollment: 3,784 . . . . (518) 843-3180
Broadalbin-Perth Central SD (02-12)
    2014-15 Enrollment: 1,846 . . . . (518) 954-2500
Housing: Homeownership rate: 83.6%; Median home value: $122,300; Median year structure built: 1955; Homeowner vacancy rate: 0.4%; Median selected monthly owner costs: $1,247 with a mortgage, $564 without a mortgage; Median gross rent: $678 per month; Rental vacancy rate: 4.8%
Health Insurance: 97.6% have insurance; 79.7% have private insurance; 39.4% have public insurance; 2.4% do not have insurance; 1.8% of children under 18 do not have insurance
Hospitals: Saint Mary's Hospital at Amsterdam (143 beds)
Newspapers: Courier-Standard-Enterprise (weekly circulation 4,000); The Recorder (daily circulation 9,200)
Transportation: Commute: 96.0% car, 2.9% public transportation, 0.4% walk, 0.2% work from home; Mean travel time to work: 24.0 minutes; Amtrak: Train service available.
Additional Information Contacts
Town of Amsterdam . . . . (518) 842-7961
    http://www.townofamsterdam.org

CANAJOHARIE (town).
Covers a land area of 42.632 square miles and a water area of 0.501 square miles. Located at 42.87° N. Lat; 74.61° W. Long. Elevation is 308 feet.
History: Here are Van Alstyne House (1749), with historical collections, and a library and art gallery. Settled c.1730 by Dutch and Germans; incorporated 1829.
Population: 3,661; Growth (since 2000): -3.6%; Density: 85.9 persons per square mile; Race: 95.1% White, 1.8% Black/African American, 0.4% Asian, 0.5% American Indian/Alaska Native, 0.0% Native Hawaiian/Other Pacific Islander, 2.2% Two or more races, 3.0% Hispanic of any race; Average household size: 2.84; Median age: 42.6; Age under 18: 24.2%; Age 65 and over: 16.3%; Males per 100 females: 95.1; Marriage status: 33.8% never married, 48.1% now married, 2.0% separated, 8.1% widowed, 10.0% divorced; Foreign born: 1.9%; Speak English only: 98.0%; With disability: 14.3%; Veterans: 8.4%; Ancestry: 27.6% German, 14.0% American, 13.4% Irish, 10.6% English, 9.6% Italian
Employment: 11.9% management, business, and financial, 4.0% computer, engineering, and science, 7.7% education, legal, community service, arts, and media, 6.5% healthcare practitioners, 18.3% service, 28.2% sales and office, 6.3% natural resources, construction, and maintenance, 17.1% production, transportation, and material moving
Income: Per capita: $24,211; Median household: $50,452; Average household: $66,300; Households with income of $100,000 or more: 17.6%; Poverty rate: 16.3%
Educational Attainment: High school diploma or higher: 86.3%; Bachelor's degree or higher: 16.3%; Graduate/professional degree or higher: 7.1%

School District(s)
Canajoharie Central SD (PK-12)
    2014-15 Enrollment: 979 . . . . (518) 673-6302
Housing: Homeownership rate: 68.5%; Median home value: $107,300; Median year structure built: Before 1940; Homeowner vacancy rate: 0.0%; Median selected monthly owner costs: $1,214 with a mortgage, $574 without a mortgage; Median gross rent: $767 per month; Rental vacancy rate: 10.7%
Health Insurance: 92.8% have insurance; 64.8% have private insurance; 43.8% have public insurance; 7.2% do not have insurance; 2.7% of children under 18 do not have insurance

Transportation: Commute: 94.1% car, 0.7% public transportation, 1.7% walk, 3.3% work from home; Mean travel time to work: 25.8 minutes

CANAJOHARIE (village). Covers a land area of 1.330 square miles and a water area of 0.068 square miles. Located at 42.90° N. Lat; 74.57° W. Long. Elevation is 308 feet.

Population: 2,195; Growth (since 2000): -2.7%; Density: 1,650.4 persons per square mile; Race: 93.5% White, 2.2% Black/African American, 0.7% Asian, 0.0% American Indian/Alaska Native, 0.0% Native Hawaiian/Other Pacific Islander, 3.6% Two or more races, 2.2% Hispanic of any race; Average household size: 2.79; Median age: 41.4; Age under 18: 24.1%; Age 65 and over: 18.3%; Males per 100 females: 90.7; Marriage status: 33.6% never married, 44.5% now married, 3.0% separated, 9.8% widowed, 12.0% divorced; Foreign born: 2.1%; Speak English only: 97.9%; With disability: 17.6%; Veterans: 8.6%; Ancestry: 28.8% German, 14.4% Irish, 9.9% English, 9.7% American, 9.2% Italian

Employment: 15.0% management, business, and financial, 2.6% computer, engineering, and science, 5.9% education, legal, community service, arts, and media, 9.7% healthcare practitioners, 20.0% service, 22.1% sales and office, 5.8% natural resources, construction, and maintenance, 18.9% production, transportation, and material moving

Income: Per capita: $21,747; Median household: $45,455; Average household: $58,882; Households with income of $100,000 or more: 11.7%; Poverty rate: 20.9%

Educational Attainment: High school diploma or higher: 85.2%; Bachelor's degree or higher: 17.6%; Graduate/professional degree or higher: 7.4%

School District(s)

Canajoharie Central SD (PK-12)

    2014-15 Enrollment: 979 . . . . (518) 673-6302

Housing: Homeownership rate: 61.8%; Median home value: $95,300; Median year structure built: Before 1940; Homeowner vacancy rate: 0.0%; Median selected monthly owner costs: $1,198 with a mortgage, $565 without a mortgage; Median gross rent: $625 per month; Rental vacancy rate: 5.1%

Health Insurance: 90.8% have insurance; 56.5% have private insurance; 51.5% have public insurance; 9.2% do not have insurance; 2.6% of children under 18 do not have insurance

Safety: Violent crime rate: 13.9 per 10,000 population; Property crime rate: 83.4 per 10,000 population

Transportation: Commute: 91.7% car, 1.3% public transportation, 3.2% walk, 3.9% work from home; Mean travel time to work: 23.6 minutes

CHARLESTON (town). Covers a land area of 41.890 square miles and a water area of 0.973 square miles. Located at 42.82° N. Lat; 74.36° W. Long. Elevation is 1,138 feet.

Population: 1,313; Growth (since 2000): 1.6%; Density: 31.3 persons per square mile; Race: 97.6% White, 1.9% Black/African American, 0.0% Asian, 0.0% American Indian/Alaska Native, 0.0% Native Hawaiian/Other Pacific Islander, 0.2% Two or more races, 2.1% Hispanic of any race; Average household size: 2.49; Median age: 41.7; Age under 18: 23.5%; Age 65 and over: 13.6%; Males per 100 females: 102.8; Marriage status: 28.4% never married, 57.2% now married, 3.9% separated, 4.3% widowed, 10.1% divorced; Foreign born: 3.2%; Speak English only: 91.3%; With disability: 11.0%; Veterans: 12.1%; Ancestry: 27.6% German, 15.1% Irish, 13.1% Italian, 10.9% English, 9.0% French

Employment: 9.7% management, business, and financial, 3.3% computer, engineering, and science, 6.9% education, legal, community service, arts, and media, 8.2% healthcare practitioners, 17.2% service, 25.3% sales and office, 11.3% natural resources, construction, and maintenance, 18.1% production, transportation, and material moving

Income: Per capita: $26,047; Median household: $52,500; Average household: $63,562; Households with income of $100,000 or more: 18.4%; Poverty rate: 12.7%

Educational Attainment: High school diploma or higher: 89.9%; Bachelor's degree or higher: 14.8%; Graduate/professional degree or higher: 3.5%

Housing: Homeownership rate: 81.8%; Median home value: $133,900; Median year structure built: 1980; Homeowner vacancy rate: 3.4%; Median selected monthly owner costs: $1,427 with a mortgage, $676 without a mortgage; Median gross rent: $710 per month; Rental vacancy rate: 0.0%

Health Insurance: 83.8% have insurance; 67.8% have private insurance; 30.5% have public insurance; 16.2% do not have insurance; 29.9% of children under 18 do not have insurance

Transportation: Commute: 93.2% car, 0.9% public transportation, 0.3% walk, 4.3% work from home; Mean travel time to work: 41.4 minutes

FLORIDA (town). Covers a land area of 50.132 square miles and a water area of 1.274 square miles. Located at 42.89° N. Lat; 74.20° W. Long.

Population: 2,705; Growth (since 2000): -1.0%; Density: 54.0 persons per square mile; Race: 95.0% White, 0.7% Black/African American, 2.7% Asian, 0.0% American Indian/Alaska Native, 0.0% Native Hawaiian/Other Pacific Islander, 1.6% Two or more races, 3.5% Hispanic of any race; Average household size: 2.27; Median age: 48.0; Age under 18: 14.6%; Age 65 and over: 19.1%; Males per 100 females: 101.6; Marriage status: 25.1% never married, 56.4% now married, 1.7% separated, 6.5% widowed, 12.0% divorced; Foreign born: 3.4%; Speak English only: 95.7%; With disability: 12.6%; Veterans: 9.1%; Ancestry: 23.8% German, 21.7% Polish, 18.2% Irish, 14.2% Italian, 11.0% English

Employment: 16.6% management, business, and financial, 5.4% computer, engineering, and science, 9.0% education, legal, community service, arts, and media, 10.0% healthcare practitioners, 10.9% service, 20.1% sales and office, 13.9% natural resources, construction, and maintenance, 14.0% production, transportation, and material moving

Income: Per capita: $32,990; Median household: $52,273; Average household: $74,485; Households with income of $100,000 or more: 17.1%; Poverty rate: 5.8%

Educational Attainment: High school diploma or higher: 94.1%; Bachelor's degree or higher: 20.8%; Graduate/professional degree or higher: 8.5%

Housing: Homeownership rate: 82.0%; Median home value: $134,800; Median year structure built: 1971; Homeowner vacancy rate: 2.5%; Median selected monthly owner costs: $1,318 with a mortgage, $553 without a mortgage; Median gross rent: $850 per month; Rental vacancy rate: 6.1%

Health Insurance: 93.3% have insurance; 77.3% have private insurance; 34.3% have public insurance; 6.7% do not have insurance; 0.0% of children under 18 do not have insurance

Transportation: Commute: 90.4% car, 2.8% public transportation, 0.9% walk, 4.9% work from home; Mean travel time to work: 30.7 minutes

FONDA (village). County seat. Covers a land area of 0.539 square miles and a water area of 0.069 square miles. Located at 42.95° N. Lat; 74.37° W. Long. Elevation is 295 feet.

History: Formally a freight transfer point on the N.Y. Central railroad. Incorporated 1850.

Population: 737; Growth (since 2000): -9.0%; Density: 1,368.3 persons per square mile; Race: 93.5% White, 3.0% Black/African American, 0.9% Asian, 0.0% American Indian/Alaska Native, 0.0% Native Hawaiian/Other Pacific Islander, 0.5% Two or more races, 6.4% Hispanic of any race; Average household size: 2.43; Median age: 41.3; Age under 18: 23.2%; Age 65 and over: 13.4%; Males per 100 females: 96.3; Marriage status: 36.1% never married, 47.4% now married, 5.4% separated, 6.1% widowed, 10.5% divorced; Foreign born: 3.3%; Speak English only: 95.2%; With disability: 17.5%; Veterans: 14.0%; Ancestry: 21.2% German, 21.0% Italian, 17.9% Irish, 11.5% Dutch, 9.0% English

Employment: 10.5% management, business, and financial, 0.6% computer, engineering, and science, 6.5% education, legal, community service, arts, and media, 3.1% healthcare practitioners, 24.6% service, 21.8% sales and office, 13.0% natural resources, construction, and maintenance, 20.1% production, transportation, and material moving

Income: Per capita: $22,071; Median household: $40,208; Average household: $53,520; Households with income of $100,000 or more: 16.3%; Poverty rate: 8.8%

Educational Attainment: High school diploma or higher: 89.8%; Bachelor's degree or higher: 15.2%; Graduate/professional degree or higher: 4.2%

School District(s)

Fonda-Fultonville Central SD (PK-12)

    2014-15 Enrollment: 1,408 . . . . (518) 853-4415

Housing: Homeownership rate: 57.8%; Median home value: $79,000; Median year structure built: Before 1940; Homeowner vacancy rate: 0.0%; Median selected monthly owner costs: $1,155 with a mortgage, $405 without a mortgage; Median gross rent: $527 per month; Rental vacancy rate: 4.3%

Health Insurance: 93.6% have insurance; 63.9% have private insurance; 38.3% have public insurance; 6.4% do not have insurance; 0.0% of children under 18 do not have insurance

Transportation: Commute: 87.6% car, 0.0% public transportation, 7.9% walk, 3.1% work from home; Mean travel time to work: 19.9 minutes

FORT HUNTER (unincorporated postal area)

ZCTA: 12069

Covers a land area of 0.573 square miles and a water area of 0.118 square miles. Located at 42.95° N. Lat; 74.28° W. Long. Elevation is 292 feet.

Population: 174; Growth (since 2000): n/a; Density: 303.5 persons per square mile; Race: 100.0% White, 0.0% Black/African American, 0.0% Asian, 0.0% American Indian/Alaska Native, 0.0% Native Hawaiian/Other Pacific Islander, 0.0% Two or more races, 0.0% Hispanic of any race; Average household size: 2.90; Median age: 23.9; Age under 18: 43.1%; Age 65 and over: 14.9%; Males per 100 females: 111.6; Marriage status: 6.1% never married, 70.7% now married, 0.0% separated, 3.0% widowed, 20.2% divorced; Foreign born: 0.0%; Speak English only: 100.0%; With disability: 14.9%; Veterans: 16.2%; Ancestry: 45.4% Polish, 33.3% Irish, 31.6% German, 31.6% Scottish, 9.2% Finnish

Employment: 45.7% management, business, and financial, 0.0% computer, engineering, and science, 0.0% education, legal, community service, arts, and media, 0.0% healthcare practitioners, 0.0% service, 0.0% sales and office, 17.1% natural resources, construction, and maintenance, 37.1% production, transportation, and material moving

Income: Per capita: $18,484; Median household: n/a; Average household: $57,138; Households with income of $100,000 or more: 31.7%; Poverty rate: n/a

Educational Attainment: High school diploma or higher: 86.1%; Bachelor's degree or higher: 29.2%; Graduate/professional degree or higher: 29.2%

Housing: Homeownership rate: 68.3%; Median home value: $103,300; Median year structure built: Before 1940; Homeowner vacancy rate: 22.6%; Median selected monthly owner costs: $0 with a mortgage, $475 without a mortgage; Median gross rent: n/a per month; Rental vacancy rate: 0.0%

Health Insurance: 100.0% have insurance; 59.2% have private insurance; 55.7% have public insurance; 0.0% do not have insurance; 0.0% of children under 18 do not have insurance

Transportation: Commute: 100.0% car, 0.0% public transportation, 0.0% walk, 0.0% work from home; Mean travel time to work: 25.4 minutes

FORT JOHNSON (village). Covers a land area of 0.737 square miles and a water area of 0.109 square miles. Located at 42.96° N. Lat; 74.24° W. Long. Elevation is 308 feet.

History: Fort Johnson (1749), once home of Sir William Johnson, is now a museum.

Population: 582; Growth (since 2000): 18.5%; Density: 790.0 persons per square mile; Race: 92.3% White, 4.8% Black/African American, 0.0% Asian, 0.0% American Indian/Alaska Native, 0.0% Native Hawaiian/Other Pacific Islander, 1.7% Two or more races, 11.2% Hispanic of any race; Average household size: 2.50; Median age: 44.5; Age under 18: 15.3%; Age 65 and over: 16.8%; Males per 100 females: 86.3; Marriage status: 30.6% never married, 49.0% now married, 5.2% separated, 5.4% widowed, 15.0% divorced; Foreign born: 1.5%; Speak English only: 96.3%; With disability: 18.2%; Veterans: 11.6%; Ancestry: 17.7% German, 16.5% Polish, 15.6% Irish, 13.9% Italian, 10.1% English

Employment: 13.0% management, business, and financial, 6.3% computer, engineering, and science, 15.1% education, legal, community service, arts, and media, 6.7% healthcare practitioners, 9.2% service, 30.6% sales and office, 8.1% natural resources, construction, and maintenance, 10.9% production, transportation, and material moving

Income: Per capita: $29,719; Median household: $63,047; Average household: $71,042; Households with income of $100,000 or more: 20.2%; Poverty rate: 12.4%

Educational Attainment: High school diploma or higher: 92.1%; Bachelor's degree or higher: 26.1%; Graduate/professional degree or higher: 10.1%

Housing: Homeownership rate: 83.3%; Median home value: $96,400; Median year structure built: Before 1940; Homeowner vacancy rate: 4.0%; Median selected monthly owner costs: $1,220 with a mortgage, $540 without a mortgage; Median gross rent: $675 per month; Rental vacancy rate: 23.5%

Health Insurance: 97.1% have insurance; 83.2% have private insurance; 33.8% have public insurance; 2.9% do not have insurance; 0.0% of children under 18 do not have insurance

Transportation: Commute: 94.2% car, 1.1% public transportation, 2.2% walk, 0.7% work from home; Mean travel time to work: 25.2 minutes

FORT PLAIN (village). Covers a land area of 1.346 square miles and a water area of 0.057 square miles. Located at 42.93° N. Lat; 74.63° W. Long. Elevation is 305 feet.

History: Settled 1723, incorporated 1832.

Population: 1,949; Growth (since 2000): -14.8%; Density: 1,447.9 persons per square mile; Race: 93.5% White, 0.0% Black/African American, 3.4% Asian, 0.0% American Indian/Alaska Native, 0.0% Native Hawaiian/Other Pacific Islander, 3.1% Two or more races, 0.6% Hispanic of any race; Average household size: 2.34; Median age: 42.3; Age under 18: 22.0%; Age 65 and over: 21.5%; Males per 100 females: 89.7; Marriage status: 33.5% never married, 44.0% now married, 6.3% separated, 10.5% widowed, 11.9% divorced; Foreign born: 2.9%; Speak English only: 94.3%; With disability: 25.9%; Veterans: 8.2%; Ancestry: 27.3% German, 17.6% American, 17.1% Italian, 15.2% Irish, 10.9% English

Employment: 8.3% management, business, and financial, 2.3% computer, engineering, and science, 12.3% education, legal, community service, arts, and media, 4.7% healthcare practitioners, 23.5% service, 23.4% sales and office, 13.6% natural resources, construction, and maintenance, 11.8% production, transportation, and material moving

Income: Per capita: $18,401; Median household: $31,364; Average household: $43,136; Households with income of $100,000 or more: 6.3%; Poverty rate: 27.5%

Educational Attainment: High school diploma or higher: 83.3%; Bachelor's degree or higher: 12.7%; Graduate/professional degree or higher: 5.1%

School District(s)

Fort Plain Central SD (PK-12)

    2014-15 Enrollment: 810 . . . . (518) 993-4000

Housing: Homeownership rate: 57.5%; Median home value: $67,900; Median year structure built: Before 1940; Homeowner vacancy rate: 0.0%; Median selected monthly owner costs: $1,023 with a mortgage, $537 without a mortgage; Median gross rent: $626 per month; Rental vacancy rate: 15.4%

Health Insurance: 94.7% have insurance; 53.8% have private insurance; 60.2% have public insurance; 5.3% do not have insurance; 0.9% of children under 18 do not have insurance

Safety: Violent crime rate: 53.2 per 10,000 population; Property crime rate: 266.1 per 10,000 population

Transportation: Commute: 96.0% car, 0.0% public transportation, 2.6% walk, 1.4% work from home; Mean travel time to work: 25.3 minutes

FULTONVILLE (village). Covers a land area of 0.477 square miles and a water area of 0.043 square miles. Located at 42.95° N. Lat; 74.37° W. Long. Elevation is 289 feet.

Population: 667; Growth (since 2000): -6.1%; Density: 1,397.7 persons per square mile; Race: 92.4% White, 0.0% Black/African American, 2.5% Asian, 0.0% American Indian/Alaska Native, 0.0% Native Hawaiian/Other Pacific Islander, 5.1% Two or more races, 0.3% Hispanic of any race; Average household size: 2.59; Median age: 29.5; Age under 18: 27.3%; Age 65 and over: 8.1%; Males per 100 females: 92.6; Marriage status: 37.1% never married, 42.9% now married, 2.4% separated, 6.4% widowed, 13.7% divorced; Foreign born: 2.8%; Speak English only: 95.2%; With disability: 13.0%; Veterans: 8.2%; Ancestry: 25.8% German, 21.4% Irish, 17.5% English, 9.4% Dutch, 8.5% Italian

Employment: 3.8% management, business, and financial, 1.8% computer, engineering, and science, 15.5% education, legal, community service, arts, and media, 3.2% healthcare practitioners, 29.9% service, 26.7% sales and office, 5.3% natural resources, construction, and maintenance, 13.8% production, transportation, and material moving

Income: Per capita: $21,221; Median household: $39,758; Average household: $51,657; Households with income of $100,000 or more: 11.7%; Poverty rate: 13.3%

Educational Attainment: High school diploma or higher: 84.3%; Bachelor's degree or higher: 16.0%; Graduate/professional degree or higher: 5.0%

Housing: Homeownership rate: 68.6%; Median home value: $84,800; Median year structure built: Before 1940; Homeowner vacancy rate: 4.2%; Median selected monthly owner costs: $1,139 with a mortgage, $396

without a mortgage; Median gross rent: $742 per month; Rental vacancy rate: 12.9%
Health Insurance: 93.9% have insurance; 70.2% have private insurance; 34.5% have public insurance; 6.1% do not have insurance; 3.8% of children under 18 do not have insurance
Transportation: Commute: 92.5% car, 0.0% public transportation, 3.7% walk, 3.7% work from home; Mean travel time to work: 16.0 minutes

GLEN (town).
Covers a land area of 38.620 square miles and a water area of 0.706 square miles. Located at 42.90° N. Lat; 74.35° W. Long. Elevation is 686 feet.
Population: 2,235; Growth (since 2000): 0.6%; Density: 57.9 persons per square mile; Race: 94.4% White, 1.8% Black/African American, 1.0% Asian, 0.3% American Indian/Alaska Native, 0.0% Native Hawaiian/Other Pacific Islander, 2.2% Two or more races, 4.5% Hispanic of any race; Average household size: 2.61; Median age: 36.4; Age under 18: 21.7%; Age 65 and over: 14.9%; Males per 100 females: 110.7; Marriage status: 34.4% never married, 50.5% now married, 1.7% separated, 6.0% widowed, 9.1% divorced; Foreign born: 2.1%; Speak English only: 93.4%; With disability: 10.2%; Veterans: 7.0%; Ancestry: 25.5% German, 23.1% Irish, 10.6% Italian, 10.1% English, 9.6% Polish
Employment: 6.5% management, business, and financial, 3.1% computer, engineering, and science, 11.3% education, legal, community service, arts, and media, 1.7% healthcare practitioners, 22.0% service, 24.7% sales and office, 12.1% natural resources, construction, and maintenance, 18.7% production, transportation, and material moving
Income: Per capita: $21,989; Median household: $47,391; Average household: $57,525; Households with income of $100,000 or more: 12.3%; Poverty rate: 15.2%
Educational Attainment: High school diploma or higher: 84.6%; Bachelor's degree or higher: 17.0%; Graduate/professional degree or higher: 5.0%
Housing: Homeownership rate: 78.4%; Median home value: $103,500; Median year structure built: 1961; Homeowner vacancy rate: 1.2%; Median selected monthly owner costs: $1,244 with a mortgage, $466 without a mortgage; Median gross rent: $809 per month; Rental vacancy rate: 6.5%
Health Insurance: 92.4% have insurance; 71.3% have private insurance; 32.5% have public insurance; 7.6% do not have insurance; 11.5% of children under 18 do not have insurance
Transportation: Commute: 92.0% car, 0.0% public transportation, 2.5% walk, 4.7% work from home; Mean travel time to work: 23.6 minutes

HAGAMAN (village).
Covers a land area of 1.498 square miles and a water area of 0.046 square miles. Located at 42.97° N. Lat; 74.16° W. Long. Elevation is 718 feet.
Population: 1,414; Growth (since 2000): 4.2%; Density: 944.2 persons per square mile; Race: 96.5% White, 1.1% Black/African American, 0.2% Asian, 0.6% American Indian/Alaska Native, 0.0% Native Hawaiian/Other Pacific Islander, 0.8% Two or more races, 3.9% Hispanic of any race; Average household size: 2.38; Median age: 48.9; Age under 18: 14.7%; Age 65 and over: 20.4%; Males per 100 females: 100.6; Marriage status: 26.3% never married, 50.2% now married, 2.1% separated, 7.8% widowed, 15.8% divorced; Foreign born: 1.0%; Speak English only: 93.3%; With disability: 13.3%; Veterans: 8.0%; Ancestry: 27.7% German, 27.7% Polish, 16.4% Italian, 14.9% Irish, 12.2% English
Employment: 20.7% management, business, and financial, 2.3% computer, engineering, and science, 12.4% education, legal, community service, arts, and media, 3.1% healthcare practitioners, 18.8% service, 20.7% sales and office, 8.7% natural resources, construction, and maintenance, 13.4% production, transportation, and material moving
Income: Per capita: $28,825; Median household: $56,080; Average household: $66,109; Households with income of $100,000 or more: 19.1%; Poverty rate: 13.8%
Educational Attainment: High school diploma or higher: 93.7%; Bachelor's degree or higher: 24.3%; Graduate/professional degree or higher: 8.0%
Housing: Homeownership rate: 86.4%; Median home value: $151,800; Median year structure built: 1949; Homeowner vacancy rate: 0.0%; Median selected monthly owner costs: $1,234 with a mortgage, $653 without a mortgage; Median gross rent: $692 per month; Rental vacancy rate: 11.2%
Health Insurance: 93.1% have insurance; 75.2% have private insurance; 36.5% have public insurance; 6.9% do not have insurance; 7.7% of children under 18 do not have insurance
Transportation: Commute: 94.9% car, 2.6% public transportation, 0.6% walk, 0.4% work from home; Mean travel time to work: 23.5 minutes

MINDEN (town).
Covers a land area of 50.988 square miles and a water area of 0.449 square miles. Located at 42.93° N. Lat; 74.70° W. Long.
Population: 4,217; Growth (since 2000): 0.4%; Density: 82.7 persons per square mile; Race: 96.7% White, 0.0% Black/African American, 1.6% Asian, 0.0% American Indian/Alaska Native, 0.0% Native Hawaiian/Other Pacific Islander, 1.7% Two or more races, 0.5% Hispanic of any race; Average household size: 2.61; Median age: 41.6; Age under 18: 26.1%; Age 65 and over: 16.6%; Males per 100 females: 98.6; Marriage status: 29.6% never married, 50.7% now married, 3.8% separated, 8.6% widowed, 11.1% divorced; Foreign born: 2.2%; Speak English only: 85.2%; With disability: 17.9%; Veterans: 8.8%; Ancestry: 23.2% German, 13.7% American, 12.8% Irish, 9.9% Italian, 8.9% English
Employment: 9.4% management, business, and financial, 1.0% computer, engineering, and science, 10.1% education, legal, community service, arts, and media, 3.9% healthcare practitioners, 25.1% service, 20.4% sales and office, 9.8% natural resources, construction, and maintenance, 20.3% production, transportation, and material moving
Income: Per capita: $18,301; Median household: $36,887; Average household: $47,469; Households with income of $100,000 or more: 8.0%; Poverty rate: 25.2%
Educational Attainment: High school diploma or higher: 76.7%; Bachelor's degree or higher: 13.1%; Graduate/professional degree or higher: 5.4%
Housing: Homeownership rate: 75.1%; Median home value: $82,900; Median year structure built: Before 1940; Homeowner vacancy rate: 0.0%; Median selected monthly owner costs: $1,176 with a mortgage, $538 without a mortgage; Median gross rent: $627 per month; Rental vacancy rate: 18.5%
Health Insurance: 82.8% have insurance; 51.1% have private insurance; 48.3% have public insurance; 17.2% do not have insurance; 30.5% of children under 18 do not have insurance
Transportation: Commute: 90.2% car, 0.0% public transportation, 1.6% walk, 7.3% work from home; Mean travel time to work: 28.9 minutes
Additional Information Contacts
Town of Minden . . . . (518) 993-3443
　http://townofminden.org

MOHAWK (town).
Covers a land area of 34.681 square miles and a water area of 0.712 square miles. Located at 42.96° N. Lat; 74.40° W. Long.
Population: 3,794; Growth (since 2000): -2.8%; Density: 109.4 persons per square mile; Race: 93.1% White, 0.6% Black/African American, 1.9% Asian, 0.0% American Indian/Alaska Native, 0.0% Native Hawaiian/Other Pacific Islander, 1.1% Two or more races, 5.5% Hispanic of any race; Average household size: 2.47; Median age: 42.8; Age under 18: 23.7%; Age 65 and over: 15.1%; Males per 100 females: 97.9; Marriage status: 29.6% never married, 49.3% now married, 2.0% separated, 9.4% widowed, 11.6% divorced; Foreign born: 4.7%; Speak English only: 96.1%; With disability: 12.3%; Veterans: 7.4%; Ancestry: 24.4% German, 18.8% Irish, 16.1% Italian, 12.4% English, 11.6% Dutch
Employment: 15.7% management, business, and financial, 3.0% computer, engineering, and science, 5.6% education, legal, community service, arts, and media, 9.2% healthcare practitioners, 18.0% service, 23.9% sales and office, 9.2% natural resources, construction, and maintenance, 15.5% production, transportation, and material moving
Income: Per capita: $28,225; Median household: $56,290; Average household: $68,576; Households with income of $100,000 or more: 16.6%; Poverty rate: 7.0%
Educational Attainment: High school diploma or higher: 90.9%; Bachelor's degree or higher: 17.4%; Graduate/professional degree or higher: 6.5%
Housing: Homeownership rate: 80.0%; Median home value: $128,800; Median year structure built: 1967; Homeowner vacancy rate: 0.0%; Median selected monthly owner costs: $1,196 with a mortgage, $400 without a mortgage; Median gross rent: $635 per month; Rental vacancy rate: 1.9%
Health Insurance: 94.3% have insurance; 72.6% have private insurance; 32.1% have public insurance; 5.7% do not have insurance; 0.0% of children under 18 do not have insurance
Transportation: Commute: 92.3% car, 0.0% public transportation, 5.2% walk, 1.7% work from home; Mean travel time to work: 20.4 minutes

NELLISTON (village). Covers a land area of 1.105 square miles and a water area of 0.090 square miles. Located at 42.93° N. Lat; 74.61° W. Long. Elevation is 367 feet.
Population: 535; Growth (since 2000): -14.0%; Density: 484.3 persons per square mile; Race: 99.6% White, 0.0% Black/African American, 0.0% Asian, 0.0% American Indian/Alaska Native, 0.0% Native Hawaiian/Other Pacific Islander, 0.4% Two or more races, 2.6% Hispanic of any race; Average household size: 2.43; Median age: 47.5; Age under 18: 15.3%; Age 65 and over: 17.4%; Males per 100 females: 104.8; Marriage status: 24.9% never married, 53.8% now married, 4.2% separated, 8.6% widowed, 12.8% divorced; Foreign born: 0.7%; Speak English only: 96.8%; With disability: 22.2%; Veterans: 7.5%; Ancestry: 26.7% German, 17.9% Irish, 15.3% Dutch, 14.4% English, 11.2% Italian
Employment: 5.2% management, business, and financial, 0.8% computer, engineering, and science, 4.8% education, legal, community service, arts, and media, 4.0% healthcare practitioners, 18.8% service, 28.0% sales and office, 7.2% natural resources, construction, and maintenance, 31.2% production, transportation, and material moving
Income: Per capita: $22,823; Median household: $46,000; Average household: $51,533; Households with income of $100,000 or more: 5.5%; Poverty rate: 15.9%
Educational Attainment: High school diploma or higher: 81.3%; Bachelor's degree or higher: 9.6%; Graduate/professional degree or higher: 2.9%
Housing: Homeownership rate: 76.4%; Median home value: $76,400; Median year structure built: Before 1940; Homeowner vacancy rate: 0.0%; Median selected monthly owner costs: $1,014 with a mortgage, $471 without a mortgage; Median gross rent: $800 per month; Rental vacancy rate: 0.0%
Health Insurance: 86.9% have insurance; 61.1% have private insurance; 43.2% have public insurance; 13.1% do not have insurance; 0.0% of children under 18 do not have insurance
Transportation: Commute: 85.2% car, 0.0% public transportation, 9.2% walk, 4.4% work from home; Mean travel time to work: 26.3 minutes

PALATINE (town). Covers a land area of 41.072 square miles and a water area of 0.629 square miles. Located at 42.95° N. Lat; 74.54° W. Long. Elevation is 830 feet.
Population: 3,235; Growth (since 2000): 5.4%; Density: 78.8 persons per square mile; Race: 97.1% White, 0.6% Black/African American, 0.0% Asian, 0.0% American Indian/Alaska Native, 0.0% Native Hawaiian/Other Pacific Islander, 2.0% Two or more races, 1.6% Hispanic of any race; Average household size: 2.69; Median age: 43.1; Age under 18: 25.9%; Age 65 and over: 18.2%; Males per 100 females: 101.2; Marriage status: 21.8% never married, 55.2% now married, 2.9% separated, 9.0% widowed, 14.0% divorced; Foreign born: 1.6%; Speak English only: 93.2%; With disability: 13.1%; Veterans: 11.9%; Ancestry: 24.1% German, 17.1% English, 16.7% Irish, 13.0% Dutch, 9.7% Italian
Employment: 8.5% management, business, and financial, 2.2% computer, engineering, and science, 11.2% education, legal, community service, arts, and media, 4.1% healthcare practitioners, 21.0% service, 21.5% sales and office, 12.8% natural resources, construction, and maintenance, 18.6% production, transportation, and material moving
Income: Per capita: $22,529; Median household: $48,313; Average household: $58,981; Households with income of $100,000 or more: 15.7%; Poverty rate: 22.6%
Educational Attainment: High school diploma or higher: 83.2%; Bachelor's degree or higher: 15.8%; Graduate/professional degree or higher: 7.9%
Housing: Homeownership rate: 75.9%; Median home value: $100,600; Median year structure built: 1972; Homeowner vacancy rate: 1.0%; Median selected monthly owner costs: $1,200 with a mortgage, $548 without a mortgage; Median gross rent: $537 per month; Rental vacancy rate: 0.0%
Health Insurance: 81.4% have insurance; 59.7% have private insurance; 39.2% have public insurance; 18.6% do not have insurance; 25.7% of children under 18 do not have insurance
Transportation: Commute: 86.6% car, 0.9% public transportation, 4.1% walk, 7.4% work from home; Mean travel time to work: 21.9 minutes

PALATINE BRIDGE (village). Covers a land area of 0.883 square miles and a water area of 0.066 square miles. Located at 42.91° N. Lat; 74.58° W. Long. Elevation is 344 feet.
Population: 814; Growth (since 2000): 15.3%; Density: 921.9 persons per square mile; Race: 98.0% White, 0.4% Black/African American, 0.0% Asian, 0.0% American Indian/Alaska Native, 0.0% Native Hawaiian/Other

Pacific Islander, 0.7% Two or more races, 2.1% Hispanic of any race; Average household size: 2.38; Median age: 50.3; Age under 18: 19.7%; Age 65 and over: 28.7%; Males per 100 females: 89.0; Marriage status: 19.7% never married, 46.9% now married, 5.6% separated, 18.1% widowed, 15.4% divorced; Foreign born: 1.2%; Speak English only: 96.9%; With disability: 19.7%; Veterans: 11.5%; Ancestry: 26.8% German, 17.7% Irish, 15.4% Italian, 13.8% English, 7.2% French
Employment: 4.9% management, business, and financial, 3.4% computer, engineering, and science, 18.0% education, legal, community service, arts, and media, 4.0% healthcare practitioners, 16.9% service, 20.0% sales and office, 8.3% natural resources, construction, and maintenance, 24.6% production, transportation, and material moving
Income: Per capita: $24,045; Median household: $39,000; Average household: $57,723; Households with income of $100,000 or more: 16.8%; Poverty rate: 11.7%
Educational Attainment: High school diploma or higher: 85.5%; Bachelor's degree or higher: 16.2%; Graduate/professional degree or higher: 8.6%
Housing: Homeownership rate: 61.6%; Median home value: $96,600; Median year structure built: 1964; Homeowner vacancy rate: 4.5%; Median selected monthly owner costs: $1,164 with a mortgage, $544 without a mortgage; Median gross rent: $439 per month; Rental vacancy rate: 0.0%
Health Insurance: 94.5% have insurance; 62.9% have private insurance; 49.2% have public insurance; 5.5% do not have insurance; 1.9% of children under 18 do not have insurance
Transportation: Commute: 92.4% car, 3.5% public transportation, 0.9% walk, 3.2% work from home; Mean travel time to work: 23.1 minutes

ROOT (town). Covers a land area of 50.624 square miles and a water area of 0.426 square miles. Located at 42.84° N. Lat; 74.49° W. Long.
Population: 1,973; Growth (since 2000): 12.6%; Density: 39.0 persons per square mile; Race: 96.0% White, 2.5% Black/African American, 0.5% Asian, 0.0% American Indian/Alaska Native, 0.0% Native Hawaiian/Other Pacific Islander, 1.0% Two or more races, 0.7% Hispanic of any race; Average household size: 2.81; Median age: 40.1; Age under 18: 24.7%; Age 65 and over: 11.7%; Males per 100 females: 100.4; Marriage status: 29.4% never married, 50.4% now married, 3.7% separated, 7.7% widowed, 12.4% divorced; Foreign born: 1.0%; Speak English only: 96.6%; With disability: 13.7%; Veterans: 12.2%; Ancestry: 27.2% German, 13.6% Irish, 13.5% Italian, 11.4% English, 10.3% American
Employment: 9.9% management, business, and financial, 2.0% computer, engineering, and science, 8.2% education, legal, community service, arts, and media, 4.7% healthcare practitioners, 13.9% service, 24.8% sales and office, 15.5% natural resources, construction, and maintenance, 20.9% production, transportation, and material moving
Income: Per capita: $22,716; Median household: $52,011; Average household: $61,001; Households with income of $100,000 or more: 18.6%; Poverty rate: 18.8%
Educational Attainment: High school diploma or higher: 87.3%; Bachelor's degree or higher: 14.0%; Graduate/professional degree or higher: 5.1%
Housing: Homeownership rate: 85.1%; Median home value: $109,600; Median year structure built: 1972; Homeowner vacancy rate: 2.7%; Median selected monthly owner costs: $1,262 with a mortgage, $505 without a mortgage; Median gross rent: $827 per month; Rental vacancy rate: 7.1%
Health Insurance: 90.2% have insurance; 67.0% have private insurance; 35.2% have public insurance; 9.8% do not have insurance; 6.8% of children under 18 do not have insurance
Transportation: Commute: 93.6% car, 0.3% public transportation, 0.5% walk, 5.1% work from home; Mean travel time to work: 29.9 minutes

SAINT JOHNSVILLE (town). Covers a land area of 16.841 square miles and a water area of 0.518 square miles. Located at 43.00° N. Lat; 74.68° W. Long. Elevation is 328 feet.
Population: 2,576; Growth (since 2000): 0.4%; Density: 153.0 persons per square mile; Race: 97.6% White, 0.7% Black/African American, 0.0% Asian, 0.2% American Indian/Alaska Native, 0.0% Native Hawaiian/Other Pacific Islander, 0.6% Two or more races, 2.4% Hispanic of any race; Average household size: 2.60; Median age: 36.8; Age under 18: 26.5%; Age 65 and over: 17.5%; Males per 100 females: 89.8; Marriage status: 30.7% never married, 46.4% now married, 3.7% separated, 9.4% widowed, 13.5% divorced; Foreign born: 1.2%; Speak English only: 92.1%; With disability: 14.1%; Veterans: 11.6%; Ancestry: 21.5% German, 17.1% Italian, 16.2% Irish, 9.9% American, 9.1% Dutch

Employment: 8.3% management, business, and financial, 1.4% computer, engineering, and science, 13.0% education, legal, community service, arts, and media, 4.4% healthcare practitioners, 19.7% service, 26.7% sales and office, 9.8% natural resources, construction, and maintenance, 16.7% production, transportation, and material moving
Income: Per capita: $18,050; Median household: $36,700; Average household: $46,040; Households with income of $100,000 or more: 8.4%; Poverty rate: 26.5%
Educational Attainment: High school diploma or higher: 83.5%; Bachelor's degree or higher: 12.7%; Graduate/professional degree or higher: 6.7%

School District(s)
Oppenheim-Ephratah Central SD (PK-12)
   2014-15 Enrollment: n/a . . . . (518) 568-2014
Saint Johnsville Central SD (PK-12)
   2014-15 Enrollment: n/a . . . . (518) 568-2011
Housing: Homeownership rate: 61.0%; Median home value: $78,400; Median year structure built: Before 1940; Homeowner vacancy rate: 6.4%; Median selected monthly owner costs: $1,014 with a mortgage, $506 without a mortgage; Median gross rent: $629 per month; Rental vacancy rate: 0.0%
Health Insurance: 86.3% have insurance; 51.6% have private insurance; 45.3% have public insurance; 13.7% do not have insurance; 18.0% of children under 18 do not have insurance
Transportation: Commute: 84.7% car, 1.6% public transportation, 10.8% walk, 2.3% work from home; Mean travel time to work: 21.4 minutes

SAINT JOHNSVILLE (village). Covers a land area of 0.878 square miles and a water area of 0.001 square miles. Located at 43.00° N. Lat; 74.68° W. Long. Elevation is 328 feet.
Population: 1,789; Growth (since 2000): 6.2%; Density: 2,038.7 persons per square mile; Race: 97.0% White, 1.0% Black/African American, 0.0% Asian, 0.2% American Indian/Alaska Native, 0.0% Native Hawaiian/Other Pacific Islander, 0.4% Two or more races, 3.5% Hispanic of any race; Average household size: 2.47; Median age: 36.7; Age under 18: 24.8%; Age 65 and over: 17.3%; Males per 100 females: 85.8; Marriage status: 32.5% never married, 41.9% now married, 5.2% separated, 9.6% widowed, 16.0% divorced; Foreign born: 1.6%; Speak English only: 94.9%; With disability: 16.3%; Veterans: 12.1%; Ancestry: 24.1% German, 16.7% Irish, 12.8% Italian, 11.0% American, 10.8% Dutch
Employment: 5.9% management, business, and financial, 1.9% computer, engineering, and science, 12.4% education, legal, community service, arts, and media, 6.1% healthcare practitioners, 18.0% service, 26.4% sales and office, 9.5% natural resources, construction, and maintenance, 19.8% production, transportation, and material moving
Income: Per capita: $17,839; Median household: $34,679; Average household: $42,584; Households with income of $100,000 or more: 6.2%; Poverty rate: 25.3%
Educational Attainment: High school diploma or higher: 84.9%; Bachelor's degree or higher: 11.6%; Graduate/professional degree or higher: 5.4%

School District(s)
Oppenheim-Ephratah Central SD (PK-12)
   2014-15 Enrollment: n/a . . . . (518) 568-2014
Saint Johnsville Central SD (PK-12)
   2014-15 Enrollment: n/a . . . . (518) 568-2011
Housing: Homeownership rate: 49.7%; Median home value: $70,200; Median year structure built: Before 1940; Homeowner vacancy rate: 0.0%; Median selected monthly owner costs: $1,018 with a mortgage, $513 without a mortgage; Median gross rent: $625 per month; Rental vacancy rate: 0.0%
Health Insurance: 91.3% have insurance; 52.8% have private insurance; 48.3% have public insurance; 8.7% do not have insurance; 3.4% of children under 18 do not have insurance
Safety: Violent crime rate: 29.8 per 10,000 population; Property crime rate: 387.6 per 10,000 population
Transportation: Commute: 83.6% car, 2.2% public transportation, 10.6% walk, 2.8% work from home; Mean travel time to work: 21.4 minutes

SPRAKERS (unincorporated postal area)
ZCTA: 12166
   Covers a land area of 43.815 square miles and a water area of 0.303 square miles. Located at 42.83° N. Lat; 74.45° W. Long. Elevation is 302 feet.

Population: 1,347; Growth (since 2000): -10.3%; Density: 30.7 persons per square mile; Race: 95.6% White, 2.2% Black/African American, 0.7% Asian, 0.0% American Indian/Alaska Native, 0.0% Native Hawaiian/Other Pacific Islander, 1.5% Two or more races, 1.0% Hispanic of any race; Average household size: 2.56; Median age: 47.4; Age under 18: 20.4%; Age 65 and over: 17.7%; Males per 100 females: 107.1; Marriage status: 27.2% never married, 52.1% now married, 3.4% separated, 8.8% widowed, 11.9% divorced; Foreign born: 1.6%; Speak English only: 95.3%; With disability: 13.2%; Veterans: 13.1%; Ancestry: 27.8% German, 15.1% Irish, 14.7% Italian, 10.6% English, 9.3% American
Employment: 10.1% management, business, and financial, 1.9% computer, engineering, and science, 7.1% education, legal, community service, arts, and media, 7.3% healthcare practitioners, 10.1% service, 23.7% sales and office, 20.2% natural resources, construction, and maintenance, 19.7% production, transportation, and material moving
Income: Per capita: $24,055; Median household: $43,646; Average household: $57,910; Households with income of $100,000 or more: 16.5%; Poverty rate: 16.1%
Educational Attainment: High school diploma or higher: 87.3%; Bachelor's degree or higher: 14.0%; Graduate/professional degree or higher: 5.3%
Housing: Homeownership rate: 89.4%; Median home value: $104,200; Median year structure built: 1965; Homeowner vacancy rate: 1.6%; Median selected monthly owner costs: $1,325 with a mortgage, $502 without a mortgage; Median gross rent: $638 per month; Rental vacancy rate: 0.0%
Health Insurance: 89.0% have insurance; 68.0% have private insurance; 39.7% have public insurance; 11.0% do not have insurance; 12.4% of children under 18 do not have insurance
Transportation: Commute: 92.0% car, 1.4% public transportation, 1.1% walk, 4.6% work from home; Mean travel time to work: 36.7 minutes

TRIBES HILL (CDP). Covers a land area of 2.276 square miles and a water area of 0.135 square miles. Located at 42.95° N. Lat; 74.30° W. Long. Elevation is 420 feet.
Population: 808; Growth (since 2000): -21.1%; Density: 355.0 persons per square mile; Race: 99.4% White, 0.0% Black/African American, 0.0% Asian, 0.0% American Indian/Alaska Native, 0.0% Native Hawaiian/Other Pacific Islander, 0.6% Two or more races, 3.3% Hispanic of any race; Average household size: 2.03; Median age: 45.9; Age under 18: 20.0%; Age 65 and over: 22.9%; Males per 100 females: 93.6; Marriage status: 21.6% never married, 46.4% now married, 0.0% separated, 15.0% widowed, 17.0% divorced; Foreign born: 2.5%; Speak English only: 100.0%; With disability: 12.3%; Veterans: 8.8%; Ancestry: 30.0% Italian, 21.8% Irish, 16.2% German, 14.7% French, 13.2% English
Employment: 24.0% management, business, and financial, 14.3% computer, engineering, and science, 2.8% education, legal, community service, arts, and media, 5.1% healthcare practitioners, 11.7% service, 17.6% sales and office, 8.2% natural resources, construction, and maintenance, 16.3% production, transportation, and material moving
Income: Per capita: $39,962; Median household: $54,500; Average household: $79,938; Households with income of $100,000 or more: 22.7%; Poverty rate: 1.1%
Educational Attainment: High school diploma or higher: 88.9%; Bachelor's degree or higher: 13.7%; Graduate/professional degree or higher: 2.8%
Housing: Homeownership rate: 86.9%; Median home value: $97,600; Median year structure built: 1959; Homeowner vacancy rate: 0.0%; Median selected monthly owner costs: $1,085 with a mortgage, $323 without a mortgage; Median gross rent: $637 per month; Rental vacancy rate: 0.0%
Health Insurance: 97.2% have insurance; 90.7% have private insurance; 36.3% have public insurance; 2.8% do not have insurance; 0.0% of children under 18 do not have insurance
Transportation: Commute: 100.0% car, 0.0% public transportation, 0.0% walk, 0.0% work from home; Mean travel time to work: 22.0 minutes

Nassau County

Located in southeastern New York, on western Long Island; bounded on the west by Queens borough of New York city, on the south by the Atlantic Ocean, and on the north by Long Island Sound. Covers a land area of 284.716 square miles, a water area of 168.518 square miles, and is located in the Eastern Time Zone at 40.73° N. Lat., 73.59° W. Long. The county was founded in 1899. County seat is Mineola.

Nassau County is part of the New York-Newark-Jersey City, NY-NJ-PA Metropolitan Statistical Area. The entire metro area includes: Dutchess County-Putnam County, NY Metropolitan Division (Dutchess County, NY; Putnam County, NY); Nassau County-Suffolk County, NY Metropolitan Division (Nassau County, NY; Suffolk County, NY); Newark, NJ-PA Metropolitan Division (Essex County, NJ; Hunterdon County, NJ; Morris County, NJ; Somerset County, NJ; Sussex County, NJ; Union County, NJ; Pike County, PA); New York-Jersey City-White Plains, NY-NJ Metropolitan Division (Bergen County, NJ; Hudson County, NJ; Middlesex County, NJ; Monmouth County, NJ; Ocean County, NJ; Passaic County, NJ; Bronx County, NY; Kings County, NY; New York County, NY; Orange County, NY; Queens County, NY; Richmond County, NY; Rockland County, NY; Westchester County, NY)

Weather Station: Mineola — Elevation: 96 feet

	Jan	Feb	Mar	Apr	May	Jun	Jul	Aug	Sep	Oct	Nov	Dec
High	39	42	49	59	69	79	84	82	75	64	55	44
Low	26	27	33	42	50	60	66	65	58	47	40	31
Precip	3.5	2.7	4.3	4.4	4.0	3.9	4.4	3.7	3.8	4.0	3.8	3.7
Snow	4.9	6.4	3.6	0.6	0.0	0.0	0.0	0.0	0.0	0.0	0.1	4.2

High and Low temperatures in degrees Fahrenheit; Precipitation and Snow in inches

Weather Station: Wantagh Cedar Creek — Elevation: 9 feet

	Jan	Feb	Mar	Apr	May	Jun	Jul	Aug	Sep	Oct	Nov	Dec
High	38	40	47	56	66	76	81	81	74	64	54	43
Low	26	27	33	42	51	61	67	66	59	49	40	31
Precip	3.3	2.6	4.0	4.2	3.6	3.6	3.6	3.3	3.5	3.7	3.5	3.6
Snow	na	na	na	0.0	0.0	0.0	0.0	0.0	0.0	0.0	0.0	na

High and Low temperatures in degrees Fahrenheit; Precipitation and Snow in inches

Population: 1,354,612; Growth (since 2000): 1.5%; Density: 4,757.8 persons per square mile; Race: 70.2% White, 11.4% Black/African American, 8.5% Asian, 0.2% American Indian/Alaska Native, 0.0% Native Hawaiian/Other Pacific Islander, 3.2% two or more races, 15.8% Hispanic of any race; Average household size: 3.03; Median age: 41.3; Age under 18: 22.3%; Age 65 and over: 16.1%; Males per 100 females: 93.7; Marriage status: 31.8% never married, 54.9% now married, 1.7% separated, 6.6% widowed, 6.7% divorced; Foreign born: 21.7%; Speak English only: 72.1%; With disability: 8.4%; Veterans: 5.2%; Ancestry: 20.5% Italian, 15.2% Irish, 9.2% German, 4.8% American, 4.7% Polish
Religion: Six largest groups: 50.6% Catholicism, 6.0% Judaism, 1.4% Lutheran, 1.3% Eastern Liturgical (Orthodox), 1.3% Orthodox, 1.2% Methodist/Pietist
Economy: Unemployment rate: 4.0%; Leading industries: 14.7% professional, scientific, and technical services; 12.7% retail trade; 12.1% health care and social assistance; Farms: 55 totaling 2,682 acres; Company size: 31 employs 1,000 or more persons, 33 employ 500 to 999 persons, 708 employ 100 to 499 persons, 47,051 employs less than 100 persons; Business ownership: 48,489 women-owned, 12,370 Black-owned, 16,700 Hispanic-owned, 15,866 Asian-owned, 606 American Indian/Alaska Native-owned
Employment: 17.0% management, business, and financial, 4.1% computer, engineering, and science, 14.6% education, legal, community service, arts, and media, 7.9% healthcare practitioners, 16.3% service, 26.2% sales and office, 6.8% natural resources, construction, and maintenance, 7.1% production, transportation, and material moving
Income: Per capita: $43,206; Median household: $99,465; Average household: $129,293; Households with income of $100,000 or more: 49.7%; Poverty rate: 6.2%
Educational Attainment: High school diploma or higher: 90.8%; Bachelor's degree or higher: 42.8%; Graduate/professional degree or higher: 19.2%
Housing: Homeownership rate: 80.3%; Median home value: $446,400; Median year structure built: 1954; Homeowner vacancy rate: 1.2%; Median selected monthly owner costs: $3,069 with a mortgage, $1,286 without a mortgage; Median gross rent: $1,578 per month; Rental vacancy rate: 4.6%
Vital Statistics: Birth rate: 103.7 per 10,000 population; Death rate: 80.7 per 10,000 population; Age-adjusted cancer mortality rate: 137.9 deaths per 100,000 population
Health Insurance: 92.5% have insurance; 79.6% have private insurance; 25.3% have public insurance; 7.5% do not have insurance; 3.0% of children under 18 do not have insurance
Health Care: Physicians: 67.1 per 10,000 population; Dentists: 11.6 per 10,000 population; Hospital beds: 33.1 per 10,000 population; Hospital admissions: 1,759.2 per 10,000 population

Air Quality Index (AQI): Percent of Days: 85.2% good, 14.8% moderate, 0.0% unhealthy for sensitive individuals, 0.0% unhealthy, 0.0% very unhealthy; Annual median: 25; Annual maximum: 78
Transportation: Commute: 76.3% car, 16.3% public transportation, 2.7% walk, 3.6% work from home; Mean travel time to work: 34.9 minutes
2016 Presidential Election: 45.5% Trump, 51.7% Clinton, 1.8% Johnson, 1.0% Stein
National and State Parks: Bethpage State Park; Hempstead Lake State Park; Jones Beach State Park; Oyster Bay National Wildlife Refuge; Planting Fields Arboretum State Historic Park; Sagamore Hill National Historic Site; Valley Stream State Park
Additional Information Contacts
Nassau Government . . . . (516) 571-2664
    http://www.nassaucountyny.gov

Nassau County Communities

ALBERTSON (CDP). Covers a land area of 0.680 square miles and a water area of 0 square miles. Located at 40.77° N. Lat; 73.65° W. Long. Elevation is 138 feet.
History: Albertson is a hamlet and census-designated place (CDP) in Nassau County, New York. The first European settler was John Seren in 1644, then Townsend Albertson started a farm and gristmill and the community became known as Albertson.
Population: 5,146; Growth (since 2000): -1.0%; Density: 7,572.5 persons per square mile; Race: 76.1% White, 0.0% Black/African American, 22.7% Asian, 0.0% American Indian/Alaska Native, 0.0% Native Hawaiian/Other Pacific Islander, 0.9% Two or more races, 8.2% Hispanic of any race; Average household size: 2.93; Median age: 45.9; Age under 18: 19.0%; Age 65 and over: 20.1%; Males per 100 females: 94.6; Marriage status: 22.3% never married, 64.7% now married, 0.4% separated, 7.3% widowed, 5.7% divorced; Foreign born: 29.4%; Speak English only: 66.1%; With disability: 8.5%; Veterans: 5.1%; Ancestry: 17.9% Italian, 17.0% Irish, 8.3% Polish, 7.3% German, 4.5% English
Employment: 23.4% management, business, and financial, 7.8% computer, engineering, and science, 16.2% education, legal, community service, arts, and media, 9.1% healthcare practitioners, 9.4% service, 26.3% sales and office, 4.0% natural resources, construction, and maintenance, 3.8% production, transportation, and material moving
Income: Per capita: $41,503; Median household: $108,750; Average household: $120,031; Households with income of $100,000 or more: 52.2%; Poverty rate: 2.8%
Educational Attainment: High school diploma or higher: 93.1%; Bachelor's degree or higher: 48.9%; Graduate/professional degree or higher: 26.4%
School District(s)
Herricks Union Free SD (KG-12)
    2014-15 Enrollment: 3,923 . . . . (516) 305-8901
Mineola Union Free SD (PK-12)
    2014-15 Enrollment: 2,784 . . . . (516) 237-2001
Housing: Homeownership rate: 94.6%; Median home value: $514,000; Median year structure built: 1953; Homeowner vacancy rate: 1.7%; Median selected monthly owner costs: $3,059 with a mortgage, $1,133 without a mortgage; Median gross rent: $1,908 per month; Rental vacancy rate: 0.0%
Health Insurance: 92.6% have insurance; 82.5% have private insurance; 27.2% have public insurance; 7.4% do not have insurance; 4.4% of children under 18 do not have insurance
Transportation: Commute: 81.0% car, 12.3% public transportation, 0.2% walk, 6.5% work from home; Mean travel time to work: 32.2 minutes

ATLANTIC BEACH (village). Covers a land area of 0.439 square miles and a water area of 0.601 square miles. Located at 40.59° N. Lat; 73.73° W. Long. Elevation is 7 feet.
Population: 1,511; Growth (since 2000): -23.9%; Density: 3,443.7 persons per square mile; Race: 97.7% White, 0.0% Black/African American, 2.0% Asian, 0.0% American Indian/Alaska Native, 0.0% Native Hawaiian/Other Pacific Islander, 0.3% Two or more races, 4.7% Hispanic of any race; Average household size: 2.44; Median age: 55.3; Age under 18: 17.1%; Age 65 and over: 23.1%; Males per 100 females: 91.0; Marriage status: 20.7% never married, 64.3% now married, 1.7% separated, 7.6% widowed, 7.3% divorced; Foreign born: 10.7%; Speak English only: 92.4%; With disability: 12.2%; Veterans: 5.7%; Ancestry: 21.0% Italian, 14.4% Irish, 11.3% American, 10.6% Russian, 10.1% German

Employment: 26.4% management, business, and financial, 2.2% computer, engineering, and science, 17.1% education, legal, community service, arts, and media, 8.9% healthcare practitioners, 13.5% service, 24.8% sales and office, 3.0% natural resources, construction, and maintenance, 4.1% production, transportation, and material moving
Income: Per capita: $78,719; Median household: $110,714; Average household: $190,762; Households with income of $100,000 or more: 57.4%; Poverty rate: 3.2%
Educational Attainment: High school diploma or higher: 97.3%; Bachelor's degree or higher: 55.0%; Graduate/professional degree or higher: 25.6%
Housing: Homeownership rate: 84.1%; Median home value: $746,700; Median year structure built: 1953; Homeowner vacancy rate: 3.7%; Median selected monthly owner costs: $3,559 with a mortgage, $1,446 without a mortgage; Median gross rent: $2,429 per month; Rental vacancy rate: 0.0%
Health Insurance: 96.7% have insurance; 86.4% have private insurance; 28.2% have public insurance; 3.3% do not have insurance; 0.0% of children under 18 do not have insurance
Transportation: Commute: 71.7% car, 17.2% public transportation, 2.0% walk, 8.7% work from home; Mean travel time to work: 44.1 minutes

BALDWIN (CDP).
Covers a land area of 2.963 square miles and a water area of 0.025 square miles. Located at 40.66° N. Lat; 73.61° W. Long. Elevation is 23 feet.
History: Named for F.W. Baldwin, an early settler. Settled 1640s.
Population: 24,481; Growth (since 2000): 4.4%; Density: 8,261.8 persons per square mile; Race: 49.0% White, 31.7% Black/African American, 3.3% Asian, 0.0% American Indian/Alaska Native, 0.0% Native Hawaiian/Other Pacific Islander, 9.4% Two or more races, 25.4% Hispanic of any race; Average household size: 3.16; Median age: 38.8; Age under 18: 24.7%; Age 65 and over: 12.1%; Males per 100 females: 90.7; Marriage status: 35.9% never married, 51.7% now married, 2.3% separated, 5.5% widowed, 6.9% divorced; Foreign born: 25.0%; Speak English only: 70.1%; With disability: 6.9%; Veterans: 4.5%; Ancestry: 11.7% Irish, 11.1% Italian, 8.1% German, 5.9% Jamaican, 5.1% Haitian
Employment: 15.3% management, business, and financial, 3.9% computer, engineering, and science, 12.5% education, legal, community service, arts, and media, 9.9% healthcare practitioners, 16.5% service, 25.4% sales and office, 6.5% natural resources, construction, and maintenance, 9.9% production, transportation, and material moving
Income: Per capita: $33,532; Median household: $91,462; Average household: $104,086; Households with income of $100,000 or more: 44.4%; Poverty rate: 9.7%
Educational Attainment: High school diploma or higher: 89.5%; Bachelor's degree or higher: 38.1%; Graduate/professional degree or higher: 14.6%

School District(s)
Baldwin Union Free SD (KG-12)
    2014-15 Enrollment: 4,759 . . . . (516) 377-9271
Housing: Homeownership rate: 80.5%; Median home value: $352,300; Median year structure built: 1945; Homeowner vacancy rate: 0.4%; Median selected monthly owner costs: $2,781 with a mortgage, $1,211 without a mortgage; Median gross rent: $1,573 per month; Rental vacancy rate: 7.7%
Health Insurance: 91.4% have insurance; 79.8% have private insurance; 21.4% have public insurance; 8.6% do not have insurance; 4.7% of children under 18 do not have insurance
Transportation: Commute: 75.9% car, 18.1% public transportation, 2.4% walk, 3.0% work from home; Mean travel time to work: 37.2 minutes

BALDWIN HARBOR (CDP).
Covers a land area of 1.205 square miles and a water area of 0.522 square miles. Located at 40.63° N. Lat; 73.60° W. Long. Elevation is 13 feet.
Population: 7,724; Growth (since 2000): -5.2%; Density: 6,407.6 persons per square mile; Race: 59.2% White, 28.6% Black/African American, 3.9% Asian, 0.1% American Indian/Alaska Native, 0.0% Native Hawaiian/Other Pacific Islander, 5.1% Two or more races, 15.3% Hispanic of any race; Average household size: 3.10; Median age: 44.0; Age under 18: 21.3%; Age 65 and over: 15.4%; Males per 100 females: 93.1; Marriage status: 34.0% never married, 55.2% now married, 1.4% separated, 3.8% widowed, 7.0% divorced; Foreign born: 20.4%; Speak English only: 74.6%; With disability: 8.6%; Veterans: 5.7%; Ancestry: 15.9% Italian, 9.8% German, 9.2% Irish, 6.4% Haitian, 6.0% Jamaican

Employment: 17.0% management, business, and financial, 3.1% computer, engineering, and science, 18.8% education, legal, community service, arts, and media, 10.1% healthcare practitioners, 11.8% service, 25.5% sales and office, 7.0% natural resources, construction, and maintenance, 6.5% production, transportation, and material moving
Income: Per capita: $39,264; Median household: $102,469; Average household: $118,751; Households with income of $100,000 or more: 51.6%; Poverty rate: 4.9%
Educational Attainment: High school diploma or higher: 95.3%; Bachelor's degree or higher: 44.3%; Graduate/professional degree or higher: 21.4%
Housing: Homeownership rate: 92.0%; Median home value: $392,800; Median year structure built: 1956; Homeowner vacancy rate: 1.3%; Median selected monthly owner costs: $3,169 with a mortgage, $1,109 without a mortgage; Median gross rent: $2,170 per month; Rental vacancy rate: 6.5%
Health Insurance: 90.8% have insurance; 79.7% have private insurance; 21.4% have public insurance; 9.2% do not have insurance; 5.7% of children under 18 do not have insurance
Transportation: Commute: 75.8% car, 19.3% public transportation, 0.9% walk, 4.0% work from home; Mean travel time to work: 40.0 minutes

BARNUM ISLAND (CDP).
Covers a land area of 0.879 square miles and a water area of 0.388 square miles. Located at 40.61° N. Lat; 73.65° W. Long. Elevation is 3 feet.
Population: 2,226; Growth (since 2000): -10.5%; Density: 2,531.4 persons per square mile; Race: 85.1% White, 3.5% Black/African American, 4.7% Asian, 2.3% American Indian/Alaska Native, 0.0% Native Hawaiian/Other Pacific Islander, 1.7% Two or more races, 15.0% Hispanic of any race; Average household size: 2.79; Median age: 44.5; Age under 18: 17.9%; Age 65 and over: 20.0%; Males per 100 females: 97.5; Marriage status: 28.2% never married, 59.8% now married, 0.5% separated, 4.8% widowed, 7.2% divorced; Foreign born: 14.7%; Speak English only: 74.5%; With disability: 18.5%; Veterans: 9.3%; Ancestry: 31.9% Italian, 16.5% Irish, 9.3% German, 7.1% American, 4.9% Polish
Employment: 18.4% management, business, and financial, 1.8% computer, engineering, and science, 13.9% education, legal, community service, arts, and media, 5.1% healthcare practitioners, 14.4% service, 33.0% sales and office, 2.5% natural resources, construction, and maintenance, 10.9% production, transportation, and material moving
Income: Per capita: $41,888; Median household: $95,375; Average household: $115,521; Households with income of $100,000 or more: 44.6%; Poverty rate: 5.9%
Educational Attainment: High school diploma or higher: 80.9%; Bachelor's degree or higher: 29.4%; Graduate/professional degree or higher: 11.7%
Housing: Homeownership rate: 78.2%; Median home value: $442,000; Median year structure built: 1964; Homeowner vacancy rate: 0.0%; Median selected monthly owner costs: $3,034 with a mortgage, $1,365 without a mortgage; Median gross rent: $1,810 per month; Rental vacancy rate: 0.0%
Health Insurance: 88.0% have insurance; 70.8% have private insurance; 35.2% have public insurance; 12.0% do not have insurance; 3.8% of children under 18 do not have insurance
Transportation: Commute: 65.3% car, 23.6% public transportation, 2.9% walk, 5.4% work from home; Mean travel time to work: 41.9 minutes

BAXTER ESTATES (village).
Covers a land area of 0.182 square miles and a water area of 0 square miles. Located at 40.83° N. Lat; 73.69° W. Long. Elevation is 39 feet.
Population: 816; Growth (since 2000): -18.9%; Density: 4,471.7 persons per square mile; Race: 87.1% White, 0.0% Black/African American, 9.8% Asian, 0.0% American Indian/Alaska Native, 0.0% Native Hawaiian/Other Pacific Islander, 3.1% Two or more races, 7.8% Hispanic of any race; Average household size: 2.32; Median age: 45.4; Age under 18: 21.1%; Age 65 and over: 18.1%; Males per 100 females: 105.6; Marriage status: 24.2% never married, 59.6% now married, 1.3% separated, 8.1% widowed, 8.1% divorced; Foreign born: 21.7%; Speak English only: 78.9%; With disability: 7.8%; Veterans: 4.2%; Ancestry: 14.7% Italian, 12.7% Irish, 10.4% American, 8.1% German, 7.6% Russian
Employment: 27.1% management, business, and financial, 10.3% computer, engineering, and science, 19.1% education, legal, community service, arts, and media, 7.7% healthcare practitioners, 10.8% service, 19.8% sales and office, 3.4% natural resources, construction, and maintenance, 1.7% production, transportation, and material moving

Income: Per capita: $82,569; Median household: $114,107; Average household: $191,498; Households with income of $100,000 or more: 52.4%; Poverty rate: 2.9%
Educational Attainment: High school diploma or higher: 94.6%; Bachelor's degree or higher: 70.8%; Graduate/professional degree or higher: 35.8%
Housing: Homeownership rate: 72.1%; Median home value: $793,500; Median year structure built: 1948; Homeowner vacancy rate: 1.9%; Median selected monthly owner costs: $3,641 with a mortgage, $1,500+ without a mortgage; Median gross rent: $1,629 per month; Rental vacancy rate: 0.0%
Health Insurance: 92.5% have insurance; 84.2% have private insurance; 21.1% have public insurance; 7.5% do not have insurance; 0.0% of children under 18 do not have insurance
Transportation: Commute: 57.0% car, 27.1% public transportation, 4.3% walk, 8.0% work from home; Mean travel time to work: 41.9 minutes

BAY PARK (CDP).
Covers a land area of 0.500 square miles and a water area of 0.102 square miles. Located at 40.63° N. Lat; 73.67° W. Long. Elevation is 10 feet.
Population: 1,856; Growth (since 2000): -19.3%; Density: 3,708.6 persons per square mile; Race: 98.7% White, 0.0% Black/African American, 1.3% Asian, 0.0% American Indian/Alaska Native, 0.0% Native Hawaiian/Other Pacific Islander, 0.0% Two or more races, 3.2% Hispanic of any race; Average household size: 2.36; Median age: 47.0; Age under 18: 22.6%; Age 65 and over: 18.3%; Males per 100 females: 91.8; Marriage status: 24.8% never married, 66.4% now married, 0.6% separated, 3.5% widowed, 5.2% divorced; Foreign born: 3.2%; Speak English only: 96.5%; With disability: 9.3%; Veterans: 10.5%; Ancestry: 37.3% Irish, 30.8% Italian, 23.1% German, 12.0% American, 8.0% French
Employment: 8.4% management, business, and financial, 2.9% computer, engineering, and science, 23.3% education, legal, community service, arts, and media, 4.7% healthcare practitioners, 22.3% service, 26.0% sales and office, 8.7% natural resources, construction, and maintenance, 3.7% production, transportation, and material moving
Income: Per capita: $44,604; Median household: $78,333; Average household: $104,751; Households with income of $100,000 or more: 43.4%; Poverty rate: 1.2%
Educational Attainment: High school diploma or higher: 97.0%; Bachelor's degree or higher: 31.5%; Graduate/professional degree or higher: 12.0%
Housing: Homeownership rate: 90.5%; Median home value: $366,900; Median year structure built: 1945; Homeowner vacancy rate: 0.0%; Median selected monthly owner costs: $2,637 with a mortgage, $1,128 without a mortgage; Median gross rent: $2,288 per month; Rental vacancy rate: 0.0%
Health Insurance: 99.2% have insurance; 85.5% have private insurance; 30.2% have public insurance; 0.8% do not have insurance; 0.0% of children under 18 do not have insurance
Transportation: Commute: 84.9% car, 12.0% public transportation, 0.0% walk, 3.1% work from home; Mean travel time to work: 36.7 minutes

BAYVILLE (village).
Covers a land area of 1.450 square miles and a water area of 0.101 square miles. Located at 40.91° N. Lat; 73.56° W. Long. Elevation is 39 feet.
History: Incorporated 1919.
Population: 6,724; Growth (since 2000): -5.8%; Density: 4,637.4 persons per square mile; Race: 95.8% White, 0.3% Black/African American, 1.7% Asian, 0.0% American Indian/Alaska Native, 0.0% Native Hawaiian/Other Pacific Islander, 1.2% Two or more races, 5.3% Hispanic of any race; Average household size: 2.76; Median age: 46.4; Age under 18: 20.3%; Age 65 and over: 19.4%; Males per 100 females: 93.6; Marriage status: 29.2% never married, 57.9% now married, 1.3% separated, 6.0% widowed, 6.9% divorced; Foreign born: 7.9%; Speak English only: 88.1%; With disability: 10.5%; Veterans: 7.1%; Ancestry: 44.6% Italian, 29.8% Irish, 14.3% German, 7.1% Polish, 5.7% English
Employment: 19.4% management, business, and financial, 9.3% computer, engineering, and science, 18.4% education, legal, community service, arts, and media, 5.2% healthcare practitioners, 14.5% service, 19.7% sales and office, 6.6% natural resources, construction, and maintenance, 6.9% production, transportation, and material moving
Income: Per capita: $45,251; Median household: $101,221; Average household: $123,671; Households with income of $100,000 or more: 50.9%; Poverty rate: 5.7%

Educational Attainment: High school diploma or higher: 95.5%; Bachelor's degree or higher: 45.0%; Graduate/professional degree or higher: 20.6%

School District(s)
Locust Valley Central SD (KG-12)
 2014-15 Enrollment: 2,188 . . . . (516) 277-5001
Housing: Homeownership rate: 82.7%; Median home value: $539,600; Median year structure built: 1960; Homeowner vacancy rate: 1.1%; Median selected monthly owner costs: $3,162 with a mortgage, $1,185 without a mortgage; Median gross rent: $1,388 per month; Rental vacancy rate: 0.0%
Health Insurance: 94.8% have insurance; 82.4% have private insurance; 26.8% have public insurance; 5.2% do not have insurance; 4.4% of children under 18 do not have insurance
Transportation: Commute: 80.6% car, 10.1% public transportation, 2.5% walk, 6.5% work from home; Mean travel time to work: 36.6 minutes
Additional Information Contacts
Village of Bayville . . . . (516) 628-1439
 http://bayvilleny.gov

BELLEROSE (village).
Covers a land area of 0.125 square miles and a water area of 0 square miles. Located at 40.72° N. Lat; 73.72° W. Long. Elevation is 82 feet.
History: Settled 1908, incorporated 1924.
Population: 1,132; Growth (since 2000): -3.5%; Density: 9,038.4 persons per square mile; Race: 79.7% White, 2.4% Black/African American, 7.1% Asian, 0.0% American Indian/Alaska Native, 0.0% Native Hawaiian/Other Pacific Islander, 2.9% Two or more races, 17.4% Hispanic of any race; Average household size: 3.22; Median age: 41.9; Age under 18: 26.1%; Age 65 and over: 15.1%; Males per 100 females: 96.9; Marriage status: 28.4% never married, 61.7% now married, 0.6% separated, 4.7% widowed, 5.3% divorced; Foreign born: 9.8%; Speak English only: 78.9%; With disability: 8.3%; Veterans: 6.0%; Ancestry: 35.1% Irish, 23.7% Italian, 14.0% German, 5.9% Polish, 4.0% American
Employment: 19.9% management, business, and financial, 8.1% computer, engineering, and science, 29.4% education, legal, community service, arts, and media, 8.5% healthcare practitioners, 7.2% service, 20.4% sales and office, 2.9% natural resources, construction, and maintenance, 3.7% production, transportation, and material moving
Income: Per capita: $56,790; Median household: $177,500; Average household: $180,499; Households with income of $100,000 or more: 72.7%; Poverty rate: 2.7%
Educational Attainment: High school diploma or higher: 96.4%; Bachelor's degree or higher: 66.4%; Graduate/professional degree or higher: 36.0%

School District(s)
NYC Special Schools - District 75 (PK-12)
 2014-15 Enrollment: 22,867 . . . . (212) 802-1501
Housing: Homeownership rate: 96.3%; Median home value: $585,800; Median year structure built: Before 1940; Homeowner vacancy rate: 0.0%; Median selected monthly owner costs: $3,335 with a mortgage, $1,450 without a mortgage; Median gross rent: n/a per month; Rental vacancy rate: 38.1%
Health Insurance: 96.5% have insurance; 90.8% have private insurance; 15.8% have public insurance; 3.5% do not have insurance; 3.1% of children under 18 do not have insurance
Transportation: Commute: 66.7% car, 26.5% public transportation, 3.7% walk, 3.1% work from home; Mean travel time to work: 35.5 minutes

BELLEROSE TERRACE (CDP).
Covers a land area of 0.125 square miles and a water area of 0 square miles. Located at 40.72° N. Lat; 73.73° W. Long. Elevation is 79 feet.
Population: 2,004; Growth (since 2000): -7.1%; Density: 16,080.5 persons per square mile; Race: 54.1% White, 0.4% Black/African American, 27.2% Asian, 0.8% American Indian/Alaska Native, 0.0% Native Hawaiian/Other Pacific Islander, 5.6% Two or more races, 20.3% Hispanic of any race; Average household size: 3.37; Median age: 39.3; Age under 18: 23.5%; Age 65 and over: 10.9%; Males per 100 females: 98.2; Marriage status: 28.5% never married, 58.3% now married, 0.4% separated, 8.2% widowed, 4.9% divorced; Foreign born: 35.7%; Speak English only: 57.0%; With disability: 5.2%; Veterans: 3.7%; Ancestry: 22.1% Irish, 11.4% Italian, 7.6% German, 5.8% Polish, 4.2% American
Employment: 19.1% management, business, and financial, 2.7% computer, engineering, and science, 7.4% education, legal, community service, arts, and media, 10.0% healthcare practitioners, 19.6% service,

27.5% sales and office, 5.0% natural resources, construction, and maintenance, 8.7% production, transportation, and material moving
Income: Per capita: $35,295; Median household: $96,538; Average household: $116,506; Households with income of $100,000 or more: 49.2%; Poverty rate: 2.3%
Educational Attainment: High school diploma or higher: 93.9%; Bachelor's degree or higher: 36.8%; Graduate/professional degree or higher: 14.2%
Housing: Homeownership rate: 90.7%; Median home value: $388,400; Median year structure built: Before 1940; Homeowner vacancy rate: 5.1%; Median selected monthly owner costs: $2,747 with a mortgage, $1,124 without a mortgage; Median gross rent: n/a per month; Rental vacancy rate: 0.0%
Health Insurance: 92.1% have insurance; 74.7% have private insurance; 24.9% have public insurance; 7.9% do not have insurance; 0.0% of children under 18 do not have insurance
Transportation: Commute: 71.5% car, 23.1% public transportation, 3.7% walk, 1.7% work from home; Mean travel time to work: 37.1 minutes

BELLMORE (CDP).
Covers a land area of 2.359 square miles and a water area of 0.615 square miles. Located at 40.66° N. Lat; 73.53° W. Long. Elevation is 20 feet.
History: Bellmore was settled primarily by Englishmen who crossed Long Island Sound from Connecticut in the middle of the seventeenth century.
Population: 15,871; Growth (since 2000): -3.5%; Density: 6,729.2 persons per square mile; Race: 93.9% White, 0.8% Black/African American, 2.3% Asian, 0.0% American Indian/Alaska Native, 0.0% Native Hawaiian/Other Pacific Islander, 1.9% Two or more races, 5.7% Hispanic of any race; Average household size: 2.93; Median age: 42.6; Age under 18: 22.2%; Age 65 and over: 16.3%; Males per 100 females: 94.8; Marriage status: 24.0% never married, 63.4% now married, 1.1% separated, 7.1% widowed, 5.5% divorced; Foreign born: 7.8%; Speak English only: 90.5%; With disability: 7.6%; Veterans: 6.4%; Ancestry: 31.3% Italian, 18.7% Irish, 16.1% German, 6.3% Polish, 5.7% Russian
Employment: 18.0% management, business, and financial, 4.2% computer, engineering, and science, 18.7% education, legal, community service, arts, and media, 9.4% healthcare practitioners, 13.2% service, 24.2% sales and office, 5.3% natural resources, construction, and maintenance, 7.0% production, transportation, and material moving
Income: Per capita: $47,397; Median household: $114,474; Average household: $136,556; Households with income of $100,000 or more: 55.6%; Poverty rate: 1.9%
Educational Attainment: High school diploma or higher: 94.8%; Bachelor's degree or higher: 49.5%; Graduate/professional degree or higher: 20.8%

School District(s)
Bellmore Union Free SD (PK-06)
　　2014-15 Enrollment: 1,030 . . . . (516) 679-2909
Bellmore-Merrick Central High SD (07-12)
　　2014-15 Enrollment: 5,605 . . . . (516) 992-1001
North Bellmore Union Free SD (KG-06)
　　2014-15 Enrollment: 2,140 . . . . (516) 992-3000
Housing: Homeownership rate: 88.3%; Median home value: $457,900; Median year structure built: 1957; Homeowner vacancy rate: 1.6%; Median selected monthly owner costs: $3,181 with a mortgage, $1,336 without a mortgage; Median gross rent: $1,914 per month; Rental vacancy rate: 3.2%
Health Insurance: 97.7% have insurance; 90.5% have private insurance; 20.6% have public insurance; 2.3% do not have insurance; 0.0% of children under 18 do not have insurance
Transportation: Commute: 76.3% car, 16.7% public transportation, 0.6% walk, 6.0% work from home; Mean travel time to work: 35.9 minutes

BETHPAGE (CDP).
Covers a land area of 3.576 square miles and a water area of 0 square miles. Located at 40.75° N. Lat; 73.49° W. Long. Elevation is 105 feet.
History: Named for the biblical village of Bethpage, between Bethany and the Mount of Olives. A village restoration in Old Bethpage features 20 pre-Civil War buildings.
Population: 16,315; Growth (since 2000): -1.4%; Density: 4,562.5 persons per square mile; Race: 91.6% White, 0.5% Black/African American, 6.0% Asian, 0.0% American Indian/Alaska Native, 0.0% Native Hawaiian/Other Pacific Islander, 1.2% Two or more races, 5.4% Hispanic of any race; Average household size: 2.84; Median age: 45.9; Age under 18: 19.2%; Age 65 and over: 22.2%; Males per 100 females: 89.5; Marriage status:

27.2% never married, 58.1% now married, 0.4% separated, 8.7% widowed, 6.0% divorced; Foreign born: 11.4%; Speak English only: 84.8%; With disability: 10.2%; Veterans: 8.6%; Ancestry: 38.5% Italian, 23.5% Irish, 15.0% German, 6.5% Polish, 4.8% American
Employment: 17.9% management, business, and financial, 5.4% computer, engineering, and science, 14.7% education, legal, community service, arts, and media, 5.2% healthcare practitioners, 13.4% service, 28.8% sales and office, 7.9% natural resources, construction, and maintenance, 6.7% production, transportation, and material moving
Income: Per capita: $42,126; Median household: $99,423; Average household: $117,246; Households with income of $100,000 or more: 49.9%; Poverty rate: 2.8%
Educational Attainment: High school diploma or higher: 92.9%; Bachelor's degree or higher: 37.4%; Graduate/professional degree or higher: 13.6%

School District(s)
Bethpage Union Free SD (KG-12)
　　2014-15 Enrollment: 2,926 . . . . (516) 644-4001
Plainedge Union Free SD (KG-12)
　　2014-15 Enrollment: 3,160 . . . . (516) 992-7455

Four-year College(s)
Briarcliffe College (Private, For-profit)
　　Fall 2014 Enrollment: 1,719 . . . . (516) 918-3600
　　2015-16 Tuition: In-state $14,349; Out-of-state $14,349
Housing: Homeownership rate: 90.4%; Median home value: $412,100; Median year structure built: 1957; Homeowner vacancy rate: 0.4%; Median selected monthly owner costs: $3,037 with a mortgage, $1,080 without a mortgage; Median gross rent: $1,621 per month; Rental vacancy rate: 18.6%
Health Insurance: 96.0% have insurance; 86.1% have private insurance; 28.7% have public insurance; 4.0% do not have insurance; 3.3% of children under 18 do not have insurance
Hospitals: Saint Joseph Hospital (223 beds)
Newspapers: Bethpage Tribune (weekly circulation 2,000)
Transportation: Commute: 85.3% car, 11.0% public transportation, 0.6% walk, 2.4% work from home; Mean travel time to work: 30.8 minutes

BROOKVILLE (village).
Covers a land area of 3.937 square miles and a water area of 0.011 square miles. Located at 40.81° N. Lat; 73.57° W. Long. Elevation is 236 feet.
Population: 3,546; Growth (since 2000): 66.8%; Density: 900.7 persons per square mile; Race: 74.6% White, 8.7% Black/African American, 11.2% Asian, 0.0% American Indian/Alaska Native, 0.0% Native Hawaiian/Other Pacific Islander, 3.2% Two or more races, 8.5% Hispanic of any race; Average household size: 3.30; Median age: 21.9; Age under 18: 20.0%; Age 65 and over: 9.2%; Males per 100 females: 84.1; Marriage status: 53.4% never married, 42.5% now married, 0.8% separated, 2.7% widowed, 1.3% divorced; Foreign born: 15.4%; Speak English only: 74.3%; With disability: 5.6%; Veterans: 1.9%; Ancestry: 16.2% Italian, 9.4% Irish, 9.0% Russian, 6.2% Polish, 6.1% Eastern European
Employment: 23.6% management, business, and financial, 2.6% computer, engineering, and science, 11.1% education, legal, community service, arts, and media, 8.3% healthcare practitioners, 16.7% service, 33.4% sales and office, 1.4% natural resources, construction, and maintenance, 3.0% production, transportation, and material moving
Income: Per capita: $69,870; Median household: $214,167; Average household: $349,570; Households with income of $100,000 or more: 77.9%; Poverty rate: 2.1%
Educational Attainment: High school diploma or higher: 97.9%; Bachelor's degree or higher: 76.2%; Graduate/professional degree or higher: 40.2%

Four-year College(s)
LIU Post (Private, Not-for-profit)
　　Fall 2014 Enrollment: 9,486 . . . . (516) 299-2900
　　2015-16 Tuition: In-state $35,546; Out-of-state $35,546
Housing: Homeownership rate: 94.1%; Median home value: $1,814,700; Median year structure built: 1967; Homeowner vacancy rate: 1.2%; Median selected monthly owner costs: $4,000+ with a mortgage, $1,500+ without a mortgage; Median gross rent: $3,400 per month; Rental vacancy rate: 0.0%
Health Insurance: 96.9% have insurance; 91.3% have private insurance; 11.5% have public insurance; 3.1% do not have insurance; 0.0% of children under 18 do not have insurance
Transportation: Commute: 63.6% car, 7.0% public transportation, 17.6% walk, 10.4% work from home; Mean travel time to work: 25.9 minutes

CARLE PLACE

CARLE PLACE (CDP). Covers a land area of 0.935 square miles and a water area of 0 square miles. Located at 40.75° N. Lat; 73.61° W. Long. Elevation is 108 feet.

History: The hamlet draws its name from the Carle House, a 32-room house built by Silas Carle in Westbury in the 1800s. An early name and current nickname is Frog Hollow; the local high school's sports teams are called the Frogs and the school colors are green and white.

Population: 5,152; Growth (since 2000): -1.8%; Density: 5,510.6 persons per square mile; Race: 78.2% White, 5.4% Black/African American, 11.1% Asian, 0.4% American Indian/Alaska Native, 0.0% Native Hawaiian/Other Pacific Islander, 2.5% Two or more races, 8.5% Hispanic of any race; Average household size: 2.85; Median age: 42.5; Age under 18: 20.5%; Age 65 and over: 14.4%; Males per 100 females: 96.5; Marriage status: 32.9% never married, 52.4% now married, 1.6% separated, 7.3% widowed, 7.4% divorced; Foreign born: 24.8%; Speak English only: 67.7%; With disability: 10.6%; Veterans: 3.4%; Ancestry: 25.4% Italian, 18.8% Irish, 15.3% German, 13.8% Portuguese, 4.0% Polish

Employment: 18.3% management, business, and financial, 6.0% computer, engineering, and science, 13.0% education, legal, community service, arts, and media, 10.7% healthcare practitioners, 18.8% service, 21.3% sales and office, 7.7% natural resources, construction, and maintenance, 4.1% production, transportation, and material moving

Income: Per capita: $42,375; Median household: $98,269; Average household: $118,209; Households with income of $100,000 or more: 48.5%; Poverty rate: 9.1%

Educational Attainment: High school diploma or higher: 86.8%; Bachelor's degree or higher: 39.6%; Graduate/professional degree or higher: 15.2%

School District(s)

Carle Place Union Free SD (KG-12)

 2014-15 Enrollment: 1,359 . . . . (516) 622-6442

Housing: Homeownership rate: 69.6%; Median home value: $477,600; Median year structure built: 1954; Homeowner vacancy rate: 0.0%; Median selected monthly owner costs: $2,853 with a mortgage, $1,147 without a mortgage; Median gross rent: $1,609 per month; Rental vacancy rate: 7.8%

Health Insurance: 92.7% have insurance; 80.7% have private insurance; 21.7% have public insurance; 7.3% do not have insurance; 3.6% of children under 18 do not have insurance

Transportation: Commute: 82.9% car, 11.0% public transportation, 2.3% walk, 3.1% work from home; Mean travel time to work: 29.6 minutes

CEDARHURST

CEDARHURST (village). Covers a land area of 0.675 square miles and a water area of 0 square miles. Located at 40.63° N. Lat; 73.73° W. Long. Elevation is 30 feet.

History: Incorporated 1910.

Population: 6,655; Growth (since 2000): 8.0%; Density: 9,859.9 persons per square mile; Race: 81.2% White, 0.0% Black/African American, 2.7% Asian, 0.0% American Indian/Alaska Native, 0.0% Native Hawaiian/Other Pacific Islander, 0.4% Two or more races, 18.7% Hispanic of any race; Average household size: 3.35; Median age: 29.4; Age under 18: 28.8%; Age 65 and over: 12.3%; Males per 100 females: 93.8; Marriage status: 34.8% never married, 56.5% now married, 1.5% separated, 4.0% widowed, 4.8% divorced; Foreign born: 26.5%; Speak English only: 61.3%; With disability: 7.0%; Veterans: 2.4%; Ancestry: 10.1% Italian, 6.4% Turkish, 6.2% Russian, 6.0% Arab, 5.9% Eastern European

Employment: 16.5% management, business, and financial, 4.9% computer, engineering, and science, 12.3% education, legal, community service, arts, and media, 4.4% healthcare practitioners, 11.3% service, 27.6% sales and office, 17.2% natural resources, construction, and maintenance, 5.9% production, transportation, and material moving

Income: Per capita: $33,341; Median household: $88,913; Average household: $108,799; Households with income of $100,000 or more: 42.0%; Poverty rate: 6.3%

Educational Attainment: High school diploma or higher: 95.3%; Bachelor's degree or higher: 46.4%; Graduate/professional degree or higher: 24.4%

School District(s)

Lawrence Union Free SD (PK-12)

 2014-15 Enrollment: 2,890 . . . . (516) 295-7030

Housing: Homeownership rate: 65.6%; Median home value: $517,900; Median year structure built: 1951; Homeowner vacancy rate: 3.1%; Median selected monthly owner costs: $2,996 with a mortgage, $1,145 without a mortgage; Median gross rent: $1,607 per month; Rental vacancy rate: 15.4%

Health Insurance: 92.6% have insurance; 76.3% have private insurance; 27.2% have public insurance; 7.4% do not have insurance; 0.4% of children under 18 do not have insurance

Transportation: Commute: 75.1% car, 12.3% public transportation, 6.9% walk, 3.8% work from home; Mean travel time to work: 36.6 minutes

Additional Information Contacts

Village of Cedarhurst. . . . . (516) 295-5770
 http://www.cedarhurst.gov

CENTRE ISLAND

CENTRE ISLAND (village). Covers a land area of 1.090 square miles and a water area of 0.002 square miles. Located at 40.90° N. Lat; 73.52° W. Long. Elevation is 33 feet.

Population: 454; Growth (since 2000): 2.3%; Density: 416.5 persons per square mile; Race: 92.3% White, 0.0% Black/African American, 5.1% Asian, 0.0% American Indian/Alaska Native, 0.0% Native Hawaiian/Other Pacific Islander, 0.9% Two or more races, 4.2% Hispanic of any race; Average household size: 2.84; Median age: 50.3; Age under 18: 21.1%; Age 65 and over: 20.0%; Males per 100 females: 104.0; Marriage status: 25.0% never married, 67.3% now married, 0.0% separated, 4.0% widowed, 3.7% divorced; Foreign born: 15.0%; Speak English only: 76.6%; With disability: 4.4%; Veterans: 7.0%; Ancestry: 29.7% Italian, 21.6% German, 16.7% Irish, 11.7% English, 4.6% American

Employment: 37.7% management, business, and financial, 1.4% computer, engineering, and science, 15.8% education, legal, community service, arts, and media, 11.6% healthcare practitioners, 7.0% service, 19.1% sales and office, 6.0% natural resources, construction, and maintenance, 1.4% production, transportation, and material moving

Income: Per capita: $130,390; Median household: $144,375; Average household: $368,840; Households with income of $100,000 or more: 65.7%; Poverty rate: 3.1%

Educational Attainment: High school diploma or higher: 97.9%; Bachelor's degree or higher: 64.8%; Graduate/professional degree or higher: 34.9%

Housing: Homeownership rate: 91.3%; Median home value: $1,718,800; Median year structure built: 1956; Homeowner vacancy rate: 5.2%; Median selected monthly owner costs: $4,000+ with a mortgage, $1,500+ without a mortgage; Median gross rent: $2,375 per month; Rental vacancy rate: 0.0%

Health Insurance: 96.3% have insurance; 91.2% have private insurance; 17.0% have public insurance; 3.7% do not have insurance; 0.0% of children under 18 do not have insurance

Safety: Violent crime rate: 0.0 per 10,000 population; Property crime rate: 24.4 per 10,000 population

Transportation: Commute: 69.9% car, 9.6% public transportation, 6.7% walk, 13.4% work from home; Mean travel time to work: 39.4 minutes

COVE NECK

COVE NECK (village). Covers a land area of 1.284 square miles and a water area of 0.280 square miles. Located at 40.89° N. Lat; 73.50° W. Long. Elevation is 20 feet.

History: "Sagamore Hill," home of Theodore Roosevelt, is here.

Population: 298; Growth (since 2000): -0.7%; Density: 232.1 persons per square mile; Race: 93.6% White, 0.0% Black/African American, 4.0% Asian, 0.0% American Indian/Alaska Native, 0.0% Native Hawaiian/Other Pacific Islander, 2.3% Two or more races, 10.1% Hispanic of any race; Average household size: 3.10; Median age: 46.0; Age under 18: 29.5%; Age 65 and over: 24.5%; Males per 100 females: 115.0; Marriage status: 13.6% never married, 75.1% now married, 0.0% separated, 8.0% widowed, 3.3% divorced; Foreign born: 13.4%; Speak English only: 91.2%; With disability: 5.4%; Veterans: 9.0%; Ancestry: 18.8% Irish, 18.1% Italian, 10.7% Norwegian, 8.4% German, 7.0% English

Employment: 47.4% management, business, and financial, 0.0% computer, engineering, and science, 17.8% education, legal, community service, arts, and media, 8.9% healthcare practitioners, 6.7% service, 14.1% sales and office, 1.5% natural resources, construction, and maintenance, 3.7% production, transportation, and material moving

Income: Per capita: $162,477; Median household: $211,250; Average household: $480,301; Households with income of $100,000 or more: 85.4%; Poverty rate: 1.7%

Educational Attainment: High school diploma or higher: 98.0%; Bachelor's degree or higher: 71.3%; Graduate/professional degree or higher: 39.1%

Housing: Homeownership rate: 85.4%; Median home value: 2 million+; Median year structure built: 1959; Homeowner vacancy rate: 1.2%; Median selected monthly owner costs: $4,000+ with a mortgage, $1,500+ without a

mortgage; Median gross rent: $1,375 per month; Rental vacancy rate: 0.0%
Health Insurance: 100.0% have insurance; 92.6% have private insurance; 26.5% have public insurance; 0.0% do not have insurance; 0.0% of children under 18 do not have insurance
Transportation: Commute: 62.2% car, 17.0% public transportation, 5.2% walk, 14.8% work from home; Mean travel time to work: 37.7 minutes

EAST ATLANTIC BEACH (CDP). Covers a land area of 0.315 square miles and a water area of 0.368 square miles. Located at 40.59° N. Lat; 73.71° W. Long. Elevation is 69 feet.
Population: 2,126; Growth (since 2000): -5.8%; Density: 6,747.3 persons per square mile; Race: 95.5% White, 3.2% Black/African American, 0.4% Asian, 0.0% American Indian/Alaska Native, 0.0% Native Hawaiian/Other Pacific Islander, 0.4% Two or more races, 7.1% Hispanic of any race; Average household size: 2.42; Median age: 49.2; Age under 18: 12.5%; Age 65 and over: 21.7%; Males per 100 females: 101.1; Marriage status: 38.4% never married, 45.5% now married, 0.4% separated, 6.8% widowed, 9.4% divorced; Foreign born: 10.2%; Speak English only: 88.7%; With disability: 5.5%; Veterans: 6.5%; Ancestry: 26.7% Irish, 25.8% Italian, 8.5% German, 8.4% American, 5.6% Russian
Employment: 24.6% management, business, and financial, 1.7% computer, engineering, and science, 21.2% education, legal, community service, arts, and media, 7.9% healthcare practitioners, 8.8% service, 20.6% sales and office, 7.4% natural resources, construction, and maintenance, 7.8% production, transportation, and material moving
Income: Per capita: $74,962; Median household: $138,705; Average household: $177,891; Households with income of $100,000 or more: 65.1%; Poverty rate: 2.2%
Educational Attainment: High school diploma or higher: 98.0%; Bachelor's degree or higher: 53.4%; Graduate/professional degree or higher: 29.5%
Housing: Homeownership rate: 80.3%; Median home value: $578,300; Median year structure built: 1953; Homeowner vacancy rate: 0.0%; Median selected monthly owner costs: $3,225 with a mortgage, $1,173 without a mortgage; Median gross rent: $2,478 per month; Rental vacancy rate: 0.0%
Health Insurance: 96.6% have insurance; 92.2% have private insurance; 25.9% have public insurance; 3.4% do not have insurance; 0.0% of children under 18 do not have insurance
Transportation: Commute: 86.5% car, 11.6% public transportation, 0.0% walk, 1.8% work from home; Mean travel time to work: 39.2 minutes

EAST GARDEN CITY (CDP). Covers a land area of 2.996 square miles and a water area of 0.008 square miles. Located at 40.73° N. Lat; 73.60° W. Long. Elevation is 92 feet.
Population: 6,470; Growth (since 2000): 560.9%; Density: 2,159.6 persons per square mile; Race: 71.2% White, 16.5% Black/African American, 6.7% Asian, 0.5% American Indian/Alaska Native, 0.0% Native Hawaiian/Other Pacific Islander, 2.8% Two or more races, 9.0% Hispanic of any race; Average household size: 1.91; Median age: 22.4; Age under 18: 4.5%; Age 65 and over: 20.7%; Males per 100 females: 82.3; Marriage status: 63.6% never married, 25.9% now married, 1.1% separated, 6.4% widowed, 4.0% divorced; Foreign born: 13.7%; Speak English only: 80.1%; With disability: 7.3%; Veterans: 6.0%; Ancestry: 17.8% Italian, 14.2% Irish, 10.0% German, 7.0% Polish, 4.9% Russian
Employment: 13.7% management, business, and financial, 3.3% computer, engineering, and science, 14.0% education, legal, community service, arts, and media, 4.7% healthcare practitioners, 18.0% service, 38.1% sales and office, 3.6% natural resources, construction, and maintenance, 4.7% production, transportation, and material moving
Income: Per capita: $37,797; Median household: $104,250; Average household: $153,736; Households with income of $100,000 or more: 51.9%; Poverty rate: 5.9%
Educational Attainment: High school diploma or higher: 93.6%; Bachelor's degree or higher: 54.2%; Graduate/professional degree or higher: 27.6%
Housing: Homeownership rate: 60.1%; Median home value: $658,200; Median year structure built: 2004; Homeowner vacancy rate: 2.8%; Median selected monthly owner costs: $3,391 with a mortgage, $1,500+ without a mortgage; Median gross rent: $2,758 per month; Rental vacancy rate: 1.8%
Health Insurance: 94.3% have insurance; 84.0% have private insurance; 25.5% have public insurance; 5.7% do not have insurance; 7.2% of children under 18 do not have insurance

Transportation: Commute: 53.7% car, 8.5% public transportation, 28.8% walk, 6.6% work from home; Mean travel time to work: 21.7 minutes

EAST HILLS (village). Covers a land area of 2.273 square miles and a water area of 0 square miles. Located at 40.80° N. Lat; 73.63° W. Long. Elevation is 190 feet.
History: Incorporated 1931.
Population: 7,066; Growth (since 2000): 3.3%; Density: 3,109.2 persons per square mile; Race: 91.1% White, 0.2% Black/African American, 6.5% Asian, 0.2% American Indian/Alaska Native, 0.0% Native Hawaiian/Other Pacific Islander, 1.6% Two or more races, 3.7% Hispanic of any race; Average household size: 3.10; Median age: 42.3; Age under 18: 31.5%; Age 65 and over: 14.2%; Males per 100 females: 96.6; Marriage status: 20.7% never married, 72.3% now married, 1.1% separated, 4.0% widowed, 3.0% divorced; Foreign born: 13.3%; Speak English only: 83.8%; With disability: 7.9%; Veterans: 5.6%; Ancestry: 15.2% Russian, 12.9% Polish, 8.3% American, 8.0% Italian, 6.1% German
Employment: 23.3% management, business, and financial, 7.8% computer, engineering, and science, 16.8% education, legal, community service, arts, and media, 14.2% healthcare practitioners, 3.3% service, 28.9% sales and office, 2.9% natural resources, construction, and maintenance, 2.8% production, transportation, and material moving
Income: Per capita: $73,279; Median household: $163,710; Average household: $225,957; Households with income of $100,000 or more: 73.2%; Poverty rate: 4.3%
Educational Attainment: High school diploma or higher: 98.4%; Bachelor's degree or higher: 77.2%; Graduate/professional degree or higher: 42.4%
Housing: Homeownership rate: 98.5%; Median home value: $896,200; Median year structure built: 1956; Homeowner vacancy rate: 0.0%; Median selected monthly owner costs: $4,000+ with a mortgage, $1,500+ without a mortgage; Median gross rent: n/a per month; Rental vacancy rate: 0.0%
Health Insurance: 96.0% have insurance; 90.7% have private insurance; 15.9% have public insurance; 4.0% do not have insurance; 3.3% of children under 18 do not have insurance
Transportation: Commute: 72.0% car, 16.5% public transportation, 1.5% walk, 9.9% work from home; Mean travel time to work: 35.9 minutes
Additional Information Contacts
Village of East Hills . . . . (516) 621-5600
  http://www.villageofeasthills.org

EAST MASSAPEQUA (CDP). Covers a land area of 3.440 square miles and a water area of 0.113 square miles. Located at 40.68° N. Lat; 73.44° W. Long. Elevation is 16 feet.
History: East Massapequa is a hamlet within the Town of Oyster Bay in Nassau County, New York.
Population: 19,843; Growth (since 2000): 1.4%; Density: 5,768.7 persons per square mile; Race: 77.6% White, 10.1% Black/African American, 2.6% Asian, 0.5% American Indian/Alaska Native, 0.0% Native Hawaiian/Other Pacific Islander, 2.7% Two or more races, 18.9% Hispanic of any race; Average household size: 3.01; Median age: 41.2; Age under 18: 20.0%; Age 65 and over: 16.4%; Males per 100 females: 94.4; Marriage status: 30.2% never married, 54.0% now married, 1.9% separated, 7.2% widowed, 8.6% divorced; Foreign born: 16.2%; Speak English only: 80.1%; With disability: 11.2%; Veterans: 7.7%; Ancestry: 32.5% Italian, 20.6% Irish, 14.0% German, 4.1% English, 3.2% Polish
Employment: 16.9% management, business, and financial, 3.3% computer, engineering, and science, 13.9% education, legal, community service, arts, and media, 5.3% healthcare practitioners, 16.9% service, 27.3% sales and office, 7.6% natural resources, construction, and maintenance, 8.8% production, transportation, and material moving
Income: Per capita: $38,591; Median household: $94,589; Average household: $112,802; Households with income of $100,000 or more: 48.2%; Poverty rate: 5.8%
Educational Attainment: High school diploma or higher: 92.4%; Bachelor's degree or higher: 34.8%; Graduate/professional degree or higher: 12.8%
Housing: Homeownership rate: 84.3%; Median home value: $414,900; Median year structure built: 1957; Homeowner vacancy rate: 5.3%; Median selected monthly owner costs: $2,891 with a mortgage, $1,212 without a mortgage; Median gross rent: $1,228 per month; Rental vacancy rate: 3.6%
Health Insurance: 92.5% have insurance; 81.3% have private insurance; 25.9% have public insurance; 7.5% do not have insurance; 5.1% of children under 18 do not have insurance

Transportation: Commute: 85.2% car, 10.1% public transportation, 1.5% walk, 2.9% work from home; Mean travel time to work: 33.9 minutes

EAST MEADOW (CDP).

Covers a land area of 6.304 square miles and a water area of 0.024 square miles. Located at 40.72° N. Lat; 73.56° W. Long. Elevation is 72 feet.

History: Its name is derived from the meadow of Hempstead Plains east of the Meadow Brook (originally a brook, now replaced by a parkway of the same name).

Population: 37,836; Growth (since 2000): 1.0%; Density: 6,001.9 persons per square mile; Race: 76.3% White, 5.4% Black/African American, 11.4% Asian, 0.6% American Indian/Alaska Native, 0.0% Native Hawaiian/Other Pacific Islander, 2.0% Two or more races, 13.3% Hispanic of any race; Average household size: 2.91; Median age: 43.2; Age under 18: 18.8%; Age 65 and over: 18.2%; Males per 100 females: 98.2; Marriage status: 29.2% never married, 53.6% now married, 1.7% separated, 10.3% widowed, 7.0% divorced; Foreign born: 18.8%; Speak English only: 73.6%; With disability: 9.0%; Veterans: 6.4%; Ancestry: 22.0% Italian, 13.6% Irish, 10.6% German, 5.9% American, 5.3% Polish

Employment: 15.8% management, business, and financial, 5.4% computer, engineering, and science, 14.0% education, legal, community service, arts, and media, 8.0% healthcare practitioners, 16.3% service, 28.8% sales and office, 5.6% natural resources, construction, and maintenance, 6.2% production, transportation, and material moving

Income: Per capita: $37,369; Median household: $94,214; Average household: $110,726; Households with income of $100,000 or more: 47.7%; Poverty rate: 4.4%

Educational Attainment: High school diploma or higher: 91.1%; Bachelor's degree or higher: 36.7%; Graduate/professional degree or higher: 15.3%

School District(s)

East Meadow Union Free SD (KG-12)
   2014-15 Enrollment: 7,144 . . . . (516) 478-5776

Housing: Homeownership rate: 86.3%; Median home value: $388,000; Median year structure built: 1956; Homeowner vacancy rate: 0.4%; Median selected monthly owner costs: $2,809 with a mortgage, $1,123 without a mortgage; Median gross rent: $1,901 per month; Rental vacancy rate: 4.1%

Health Insurance: 93.4% have insurance; 82.4% have private insurance; 25.4% have public insurance; 6.6% do not have insurance; 2.8% of children under 18 do not have insurance

Hospitals: Nassau University Medical Center (1,500 beds)

Transportation: Commute: 85.0% car, 9.0% public transportation, 1.6% walk, 3.7% work from home; Mean travel time to work: 32.1 minutes

EAST NORWICH (CDP).

Covers a land area of 1.047 square miles and a water area of 0 square miles. Located at 40.85° N. Lat; 73.53° W. Long. Elevation is 207 feet.

Population: 2,751; Growth (since 2000): 2.8%; Density: 2,626.9 persons per square mile; Race: 97.1% White, 0.0% Black/African American, 1.2% Asian, 0.0% American Indian/Alaska Native, 0.0% Native Hawaiian/Other Pacific Islander, 1.5% Two or more races, 6.9% Hispanic of any race; Average household size: 2.93; Median age: 45.1; Age under 18: 24.0%; Age 65 and over: 12.9%; Males per 100 females: 91.6; Marriage status: 28.1% never married, 59.1% now married, 0.6% separated, 4.6% widowed, 8.2% divorced; Foreign born: 7.8%; Speak English only: 86.0%; With disability: 7.2%; Veterans: 5.9%; Ancestry: 41.9% Italian, 22.4% Irish, 13.9% German, 5.9% English, 5.0% Polish

Employment: 20.7% management, business, and financial, 6.8% computer, engineering, and science, 19.3% education, legal, community service, arts, and media, 11.2% healthcare practitioners, 9.9% service, 25.1% sales and office, 2.2% natural resources, construction, and maintenance, 4.7% production, transportation, and material moving

Income: Per capita: $62,052; Median household: $134,309; Average household: $178,346; Households with income of $100,000 or more: 60.9%; Poverty rate: 4.0%

Educational Attainment: High school diploma or higher: 96.4%; Bachelor's degree or higher: 58.3%; Graduate/professional degree or higher: 29.7%

School District(s)

Oyster Bay-East Norwich Central SD (PK-12)
   2014-15 Enrollment: 1,640 . . . . (516) 624-6505

Housing: Homeownership rate: 95.3%; Median home value: $622,600; Median year structure built: 1956; Homeowner vacancy rate: 3.5%; Median selected monthly owner costs: $3,422 with a mortgage, $1,065 without a

mortgage; Median gross rent: $2,821 per month; Rental vacancy rate: 0.0%

Health Insurance: 97.4% have insurance; 91.6% have private insurance; 18.1% have public insurance; 2.6% do not have insurance; 1.1% of children under 18 do not have insurance

Transportation: Commute: 81.1% car, 12.1% public transportation, 0.4% walk, 4.3% work from home; Mean travel time to work: 36.8 minutes

EAST ROCKAWAY (village).

Covers a land area of 1.017 square miles and a water area of 0.014 square miles. Located at 40.64° N. Lat; 73.67° W. Long. Elevation is 10 feet.

History: Named for the Algonquian translation of "sand place". Settled c.1688. Incorporated 1900.

Population: 9,871; Growth (since 2000): -5.2%; Density: 9,710.4 persons per square mile; Race: 96.3% White, 0.9% Black/African American, 1.0% Asian, 0.4% American Indian/Alaska Native, 0.0% Native Hawaiian/Other Pacific Islander, 0.5% Two or more races, 13.7% Hispanic of any race; Average household size: 2.67; Median age: 45.0; Age under 18: 20.6%; Age 65 and over: 14.7%; Males per 100 females: 89.3; Marriage status: 31.1% never married, 54.3% now married, 1.1% separated, 8.6% widowed, 6.0% divorced; Foreign born: 8.4%; Speak English only: 83.1%; With disability: 9.0%; Veterans: 6.0%; Ancestry: 28.1% Italian, 24.7% Irish, 8.6% German, 4.2% American, 4.0% Eastern European

Employment: 17.2% management, business, and financial, 3.1% computer, engineering, and science, 19.6% education, legal, community service, arts, and media, 4.2% healthcare practitioners, 15.5% service, 26.6% sales and office, 9.0% natural resources, construction, and maintenance, 4.8% production, transportation, and material moving

Income: Per capita: $47,223; Median household: $93,490; Average household: $125,195; Households with income of $100,000 or more: 44.9%; Poverty rate: 3.2%

Educational Attainment: High school diploma or higher: 96.2%; Bachelor's degree or higher: 44.5%; Graduate/professional degree or higher: 19.9%

School District(s)

East Rockaway Union Free SD (KG-12)
   2014-15 Enrollment: 1,213 . . . . (516) 887-8300
Lynbrook Union Free SD (KG-12)
   2014-15 Enrollment: 2,822 . . . . (516) 887-0253

Housing: Homeownership rate: 78.1%; Median home value: $444,700; Median year structure built: 1945; Homeowner vacancy rate: 2.1%; Median selected monthly owner costs: $3,176 with a mortgage, $1,109 without a mortgage; Median gross rent: $1,833 per month; Rental vacancy rate: 6.0%

Health Insurance: 95.5% have insurance; 85.6% have private insurance; 22.9% have public insurance; 4.5% do not have insurance; 0.0% of children under 18 do not have insurance

Transportation: Commute: 78.7% car, 16.2% public transportation, 1.8% walk, 2.8% work from home; Mean travel time to work: 33.1 minutes

Additional Information Contacts

Village of East Rockaway . . . . (516) 887-6300
   http://www.villageofeastrockaway.org

EAST WILLISTON (village).

Covers a land area of 0.569 square miles and a water area of 0 square miles. Located at 40.76° N. Lat; 73.63° W. Long. Elevation is 118 feet.

History: Incorporated 1926.

Population: 2,585; Growth (since 2000): 3.3%; Density: 4,545.6 persons per square mile; Race: 87.8% White, 0.5% Black/African American, 10.6% Asian, 0.0% American Indian/Alaska Native, 0.0% Native Hawaiian/Other Pacific Islander, 0.6% Two or more races, 6.3% Hispanic of any race; Average household size: 3.14; Median age: 43.7; Age under 18: 26.8%; Age 65 and over: 16.6%; Males per 100 females: 97.8; Marriage status: 27.4% never married, 61.3% now married, 0.8% separated, 5.8% widowed, 5.5% divorced; Foreign born: 10.6%; Speak English only: 86.3%; With disability: 4.6%; Veterans: 5.1%; Ancestry: 28.7% Irish, 28.6% Italian, 18.4% German, 4.1% Polish, 4.0% American

Employment: 26.4% management, business, and financial, 6.4% computer, engineering, and science, 18.7% education, legal, community service, arts, and media, 13.5% healthcare practitioners, 7.2% service, 22.5% sales and office, 3.4% natural resources, construction, and maintenance, 1.8% production, transportation, and material moving

Income: Per capita: $62,595; Median household: $136,250; Average household: $192,353; Households with income of $100,000 or more: 71.8%; Poverty rate: 2.1%

Educational Attainment: High school diploma or higher: 99.0%; Bachelor's degree or higher: 67.0%; Graduate/professional degree or higher: 37.8%

School District(s)

East Williston Union Free SD (KG-12)
   2014-15 Enrollment: 1,745 . . . . (516) 333-3758
Housing: Homeownership rate: 94.5%; Median home value: $778,100; Median year structure built: 1950; Homeowner vacancy rate: 1.9%; Median selected monthly owner costs: $3,903 with a mortgage, $1,500+ without a mortgage; Median gross rent: $3,500+ per month; Rental vacancy rate: 0.0%
Health Insurance: 97.7% have insurance; 91.2% have private insurance; 19.2% have public insurance; 2.3% do not have insurance; 0.0% of children under 18 do not have insurance
Transportation: Commute: 73.2% car, 23.0% public transportation, 1.1% walk, 2.4% work from home; Mean travel time to work: 34.7 minutes
Additional Information Contacts
Village of East Williston . . . . (516) 746-0782
   http://eastwilliston.org

ELMONT (CDP). Covers a land area of 3.369 square miles and a water area of 0.012 square miles. Located at 40.70° N. Lat; 73.71° W. Long. Elevation is 39 feet.
History: Elmont is famous as the home of Belmont Park horsracing tract, which hosts the Belmont Stakes, the third leg of the prestigious Triple Crown of thoroughbred racing.
Population: 37,388; Growth (since 2000): 14.5%; Density: 11,098.6 persons per square mile; Race: 20.7% White, 45.8% Black/African American, 14.3% Asian, 0.2% American Indian/Alaska Native, 0.0% Native Hawaiian/Other Pacific Islander, 5.4% Two or more races, 21.0% Hispanic of any race; Average household size: 3.79; Median age: 37.0; Age under 18: 20.8%; Age 65 and over: 11.7%; Males per 100 females: 92.9; Marriage status: 39.7% never married, 47.3% now married, 2.5% separated, 5.4% widowed, 7.6% divorced; Foreign born: 43.4%; Speak English only: 51.8%; With disability: 7.5%; Veterans: 2.3%; Ancestry: 15.1% Haitian, 9.7% Jamaican, 7.6% Italian, 3.7% German, 3.2% Irish
Employment: 10.9% management, business, and financial, 2.2% computer, engineering, and science, 9.5% education, legal, community service, arts, and media, 9.8% healthcare practitioners, 24.7% service, 25.4% sales and office, 8.2% natural resources, construction, and maintenance, 9.3% production, transportation, and material moving
Income: Per capita: $28,633; Median household: $89,523; Average household: $103,060; Households with income of $100,000 or more: 43.4%; Poverty rate: 8.0%
Educational Attainment: High school diploma or higher: 86.2%; Bachelor's degree or higher: 28.7%; Graduate/professional degree or higher: 10.1%

School District(s)

Elmont Union Free SD (PK-06)
   2014-15 Enrollment: 3,883 . . . . (516) 326-5500
Sewanhaka Central High SD (07-12)
   2014-15 Enrollment: 8,160 . . . . (516) 488-9800
Housing: Homeownership rate: 80.6%; Median home value: $368,700; Median year structure built: 1953; Homeowner vacancy rate: 2.3%; Median selected monthly owner costs: $2,905 with a mortgage, $1,074 without a mortgage; Median gross rent: $1,608 per month; Rental vacancy rate: 0.8%
Health Insurance: 88.2% have insurance; 68.9% have private insurance; 27.4% have public insurance; 11.8% do not have insurance; 4.8% of children under 18 do not have insurance
Newspapers: Elmont Herald (weekly circulation 3,000)
Transportation: Commute: 72.6% car, 21.5% public transportation, 2.7% walk, 1.9% work from home; Mean travel time to work: 39.5 minutes

---

FARMINGDALE (village). Covers a land area of 1.121 square miles and a water area of 0 square miles. Located at 40.73° N. Lat; 73.45° W. Long. Elevation is 72 feet.
History: Seat of State University of N.Y. at Farmingdale Settled 1695, incorporated 1904.
Population: 8,399; Growth (since 2000): 0.0%; Density: 7,494.5 persons per square mile; Race: 85.0% White, 2.0% Black/African American, 9.0% Asian, 0.0% American Indian/Alaska Native, 0.0% Native Hawaiian/Other Pacific Islander, 1.6% Two or more races, 14.9% Hispanic of any race; Average household size: 2.45; Median age: 47.2; Age under 18: 17.1%; Age 65 and over: 18.0%; Males per 100 females: 91.9; Marriage status:

29.4% never married, 52.7% now married, 1.8% separated, 7.1% widowed, 10.8% divorced; Foreign born: 17.9%; Speak English only: 79.1%; With disability: 11.5%; Veterans: 8.0%; Ancestry: 25.5% Italian, 21.1% Irish, 16.9% German, 5.9% Polish, 4.1% American
Employment: 17.6% management, business, and financial, 6.9% computer, engineering, and science, 14.4% education, legal, community service, arts, and media, 4.6% healthcare practitioners, 16.9% service, 24.3% sales and office, 9.2% natural resources, construction, and maintenance, 6.1% production, transportation, and material moving
Income: Per capita: $37,890; Median household: $73,750; Average household: $91,170; Households with income of $100,000 or more: 37.1%; Poverty rate: 5.3%
Educational Attainment: High school diploma or higher: 91.3%; Bachelor's degree or higher: 38.1%; Graduate/professional degree or higher: 15.5%

School District(s)

Farmingdale Union Free SD (KG-12)
   2014-15 Enrollment: 5,918 . . . . (516) 752-6510

Four-year College(s)

Farmingdale State College (Public)
   Fall 2014 Enrollment: 8,394 . . . . (631) 420-2000
   2015-16 Tuition: In-state $7,808; Out-of-state $17,658
Housing: Homeownership rate: 70.3%; Median home value: $358,300; Median year structure built: 1959; Homeowner vacancy rate: 1.0%; Median selected monthly owner costs: $2,663 with a mortgage, $1,105 without a mortgage; Median gross rent: $1,594 per month; Rental vacancy rate: 9.6%
Health Insurance: 95.2% have insurance; 83.9% have private insurance; 24.2% have public insurance; 4.8% do not have insurance; 3.5% of children under 18 do not have insurance
Newspapers: South Bay's Neighbor (weekly circulation 255,000)
Transportation: Commute: 78.8% car, 15.0% public transportation, 2.6% walk, 2.0% work from home; Mean travel time to work: 30.8 minutes
Additional Information Contacts
Village of Farmingdale . . . . (516) 249-0093
   http://www.farmingdalevillage.com

FLORAL PARK (village). Covers a land area of 1.417 square miles and a water area of 0.013 square miles. Located at 40.72° N. Lat; 73.70° W. Long. Elevation is 89 feet.
History: Named to promote the beauty of the town. Incorporated 1908.
Population: 16,093; Growth (since 2000): 0.8%; Density: 11,354.3 persons per square mile; Race: 87.8% White, 1.3% Black/African American, 5.5% Asian, 0.2% American Indian/Alaska Native, 0.0% Native Hawaiian/Other Pacific Islander, 2.1% Two or more races, 11.5% Hispanic of any race; Average household size: 2.82; Median age: 42.3; Age under 18: 21.2%; Age 65 and over: 17.2%; Males per 100 females: 95.1; Marriage status: 28.7% never married, 59.1% now married, 1.3% separated, 5.8% widowed, 6.3% divorced; Foreign born: 12.6%; Speak English only: 84.3%; With disability: 8.3%; Veterans: 7.7%; Ancestry: 31.6% Irish, 26.5% Italian, 17.1% German, 6.0% Polish, 3.9% English
Employment: 18.0% management, business, and financial, 4.6% computer, engineering, and science, 18.2% education, legal, community service, arts, and media, 9.0% healthcare practitioners, 13.7% service, 23.6% sales and office, 7.2% natural resources, construction, and maintenance, 5.8% production, transportation, and material moving
Income: Per capita: $45,270; Median household: $100,829; Average household: $124,467; Households with income of $100,000 or more: 50.5%; Poverty rate: 2.7%
Educational Attainment: High school diploma or higher: 95.8%; Bachelor's degree or higher: 48.5%; Graduate/professional degree or higher: 20.6%

School District(s)

Floral Park-Bellerose Union Free SD (PK-06)
   2014-15 Enrollment: 1,484 . . . . (516) 434-2725
NYC Special Schools - District 75 (PK-12)
   2014-15 Enrollment: 22,867 . . . . (212) 802-1501
Sewanhaka Central High SD (07-12)
   2014-15 Enrollment: 8,160 . . . . (516) 488-9800
Housing: Homeownership rate: 78.8%; Median home value: $492,000; Median year structure built: Before 1940; Homeowner vacancy rate: 0.0%; Median selected monthly owner costs: $3,120 with a mortgage, $1,351 without a mortgage; Median gross rent: $1,426 per month; Rental vacancy rate: 0.0%

Health Insurance: 96.5% have insurance; 89.6% have private insurance; 21.0% have public insurance; 3.5% do not have insurance; 0.6% of children under 18 do not have insurance
Safety: Violent crime rate: 1.9 per 10,000 population; Property crime rate: 36.9 per 10,000 population
Newspapers: Nassau Border Papers (weekly circulation 29,000)
Transportation: Commute: 75.6% car, 19.0% public transportation, 1.8% walk, 2.7% work from home; Mean travel time to work: 34.9 minutes
Additional Information Contacts
Village of Floral Park . . . . (516) 326-6300
    http://www.fpvillage.org

FLOWER HILL (village).
Covers a land area of 1.618 square miles and a water area of 0 square miles. Located at 40.81° N. Lat; 73.68° W. Long. Elevation is 164 feet.
History: Incorporated 1931.
Population: 4,772; Growth (since 2000): 5.9%; Density: 2,948.8 persons per square mile; Race: 83.3% White, 0.7% Black/African American, 14.3% Asian, 0.0% American Indian/Alaska Native, 0.0% Native Hawaiian/Other Pacific Islander, 1.2% Two or more races, 8.4% Hispanic of any race; Average household size: 3.29; Median age: 41.7; Age under 18: 30.9%; Age 65 and over: 15.4%; Males per 100 females: 95.7; Marriage status: 21.1% never married, 66.8% now married, 2.1% separated, 6.4% widowed, 5.8% divorced; Foreign born: 22.8%; Speak English only: 74.5%; With disability: 5.7%; Veterans: 2.8%; Ancestry: 22.1% Italian, 13.5% Irish, 11.0% American, 9.5% Polish, 7.8% German
Employment: 26.2% management, business, and financial, 9.9% computer, engineering, and science, 23.4% education, legal, community service, arts, and media, 8.8% healthcare practitioners, 5.9% service, 18.8% sales and office, 4.8% natural resources, construction, and maintenance, 2.1% production, transportation, and material moving
Income: Per capita: $83,536; Median household: $208,424; Average household: $273,321; Households with income of $100,000 or more: 69.2%; Poverty rate: 8.0%
Educational Attainment: High school diploma or higher: 93.9%; Bachelor's degree or higher: 73.7%; Graduate/professional degree or higher: 31.1%
Housing: Homeownership rate: 90.2%; Median home value: $1,068,500; Median year structure built: 1956; Homeowner vacancy rate: 0.0%; Median selected monthly owner costs: $4,000+ with a mortgage, $1,500+ without a mortgage; Median gross rent: $1,684 per month; Rental vacancy rate: 0.0%
Health Insurance: 94.9% have insurance; 87.6% have private insurance; 16.7% have public insurance; 5.1% do not have insurance; 8.8% of children under 18 do not have insurance
Transportation: Commute: 61.6% car, 23.4% public transportation, 1.2% walk, 12.5% work from home; Mean travel time to work: 38.0 minutes
Additional Information Contacts
Village of Flower Hill . . . . (516) 627-5000
    http://www.villageflowerhill.org

FRANKLIN SQUARE (CDP).
Covers a land area of 2.878 square miles and a water area of 0 square miles. Located at 40.70° N. Lat; 73.68° W. Long. Elevation is 66 feet.
History: In late 1643, Robert Fordham and John Carman purchased 100 square miles of land from the Massapequak, Mericoke, Matinecock, and Rockaway tribes. This land now occupies the towns of Hempstead and North Hempstead. It's speculated that the name "Franklin Square" honors Benjamin Franklin.
Population: 31,544; Growth (since 2000): 7.5%; Density: 10,961.6 persons per square mile; Race: 74.8% White, 3.4% Black/African American, 10.3% Asian, 0.0% American Indian/Alaska Native, 0.0% Native Hawaiian/Other Pacific Islander, 3.1% Two or more races, 16.5% Hispanic of any race; Average household size: 3.24; Median age: 40.6; Age under 18: 21.5%; Age 65 and over: 16.1%; Males per 100 females: 91.1; Marriage status: 31.9% never married, 55.2% now married, 1.0% separated, 6.9% widowed, 5.9% divorced; Foreign born: 22.7%; Speak English only: 63.7%; With disability: 8.0%; Veterans: 5.3%; Ancestry: 38.2% Italian, 15.5% Irish, 7.5% German, 3.9% Polish, 2.8% Greek
Employment: 12.9% management, business, and financial, 3.4% computer, engineering, and science, 11.2% education, legal, community service, arts, and media, 6.6% healthcare practitioners, 18.1% service, 29.6% sales and office, 10.1% natural resources, construction, and maintenance, 8.1% production, transportation, and material moving

Income: Per capita: $32,998; Median household: $96,568; Average household: $103,846; Households with income of $100,000 or more: 47.7%; Poverty rate: 5.4%
Educational Attainment: High school diploma or higher: 88.4%; Bachelor's degree or higher: 28.5%; Graduate/professional degree or higher: 9.9%

School District(s)
Franklin Square Union Free SD (KG-06)
    2014-15 Enrollment: 2,047 . . . . (516) 505-6975
Sewanhaka Central High SD (07-12)
    2014-15 Enrollment: 8,160 . . . . (516) 488-9800
Valley Stream 13 Union Free SD (KG-06)
    2014-15 Enrollment: 2,159 . . . . (516) 568-6100
Valley Stream Central High SD (07-12)
    2014-15 Enrollment: 4,558 . . . . (516) 872-5601
Housing: Homeownership rate: 82.8%; Median home value: $427,900; Median year structure built: 1953; Homeowner vacancy rate: 1.2%; Median selected monthly owner costs: $3,074 with a mortgage, $1,207 without a mortgage; Median gross rent: $1,469 per month; Rental vacancy rate: 2.9%
Health Insurance: 94.2% have insurance; 79.7% have private insurance; 26.1% have public insurance; 5.8% do not have insurance; 1.1% of children under 18 do not have insurance
Transportation: Commute: 84.3% car, 11.8% public transportation, 1.4% walk, 2.2% work from home; Mean travel time to work: 34.4 minutes

FREEPORT (village).
Covers a land area of 4.628 square miles and a water area of 0.241 square miles. Located at 40.65° N. Lat; 73.58° W. Long. Elevation is 20 feet.
History: Named for its port, used in colonial days by cargo ships to avoid British taxes. Settled as a village c.1650. Incorporated 1892.
Population: 43,251; Growth (since 2000): -1.2%; Density: 9,345.0 persons per square mile; Race: 39.3% White, 32.8% Black/African American, 1.7% Asian, 2.0% American Indian/Alaska Native, 0.0% Native Hawaiian/Other Pacific Islander, 12.0% Two or more races, 42.5% Hispanic of any race; Average household size: 3.20; Median age: 37.2; Age under 18: 23.4%; Age 65 and over: 13.7%; Males per 100 females: 94.9; Marriage status: 42.4% never married, 42.1% now married, 3.2% separated, 5.9% widowed, 9.6% divorced; Foreign born: 31.3%; Speak English only: 56.7%; With disability: 8.5%; Veterans: 4.2%; Ancestry: 6.9% Irish, 5.9% Italian, 4.0% German, 3.9% American, 3.8% Jamaican
Employment: 10.5% management, business, and financial, 2.1% computer, engineering, and science, 11.7% education, legal, community service, arts, and media, 6.0% healthcare practitioners, 22.8% service, 25.6% sales and office, 8.7% natural resources, construction, and maintenance, 12.7% production, transportation, and material moving
Income: Per capita: $28,357; Median household: $72,574; Average household: $87,631; Households with income of $100,000 or more: 33.8%; Poverty rate: 13.8%
Educational Attainment: High school diploma or higher: 81.2%; Bachelor's degree or higher: 26.4%; Graduate/professional degree or higher: 11.6%

School District(s)
Freeport Union Free SD (KG-12)
    2014-15 Enrollment: 6,867 . . . . (516) 867-5205
Housing: Homeownership rate: 67.5%; Median home value: $312,800; Median year structure built: 1952; Homeowner vacancy rate: 1.3%; Median selected monthly owner costs: $2,766 with a mortgage, $1,162 without a mortgage; Median gross rent: $1,360 per month; Rental vacancy rate: 2.6%
Health Insurance: 84.4% have insurance; 64.0% have private insurance; 31.6% have public insurance; 15.6% do not have insurance; 10.1% of children under 18 do not have insurance
Safety: Violent crime rate: 32.0 per 10,000 population; Property crime rate: 161.3 per 10,000 population
Transportation: Commute: 76.2% car, 14.2% public transportation, 5.8% walk, 2.4% work from home; Mean travel time to work: 30.7 minutes
Additional Information Contacts
Village of Freeport . . . . (516) 377-2200
    http://www.freeportny.com

GARDEN CITY (village).
Covers a land area of 5.330 square miles and a water area of 0.025 square miles. Located at 40.73° N. Lat; 73.65° W. Long. Elevation is 89 feet.

History: Named to promote the city as a beautiful place. Was founded in 1869 and planned by the merchant Alexander Stewart. In 1927, Charles Lindbergh began his historic transatlantic flight from nearby Roosevelt Field. Adelphi University is here. Incorporated 1919.

Population: 22,575; Growth (since 2000): 4.2%; Density: 4,235.5 persons per square mile; Race: 94.0% White, 0.7% Black/African American, 2.5% Asian, 0.0% American Indian/Alaska Native, 0.0% Native Hawaiian/Other Pacific Islander, 1.8% Two or more races, 4.3% Hispanic of any race; Average household size: 2.93; Median age: 42.6; Age under 18: 25.7%; Age 65 and over: 16.4%; Males per 100 females: 90.1; Marriage status: 28.9% never married, 61.7% now married, 0.7% separated, 6.1% widowed, 3.3% divorced; Foreign born: 6.3%; Speak English only: 89.4%; With disability: 6.8%; Veterans: 6.6%; Ancestry: 34.2% Irish, 33.0% Italian, 14.7% German, 5.3% English, 4.2% American

Employment: 28.6% management, business, and financial, 4.0% computer, engineering, and science, 18.6% education, legal, community service, arts, and media, 6.1% healthcare practitioners, 10.0% service, 28.6% sales and office, 2.3% natural resources, construction, and maintenance, 1.9% production, transportation, and material moving

Income: Per capita: $65,725; Median household: $153,506; Average household: $198,884; Households with income of $100,000 or more: 69.1%; Poverty rate: 3.9%

Educational Attainment: High school diploma or higher: 97.4%; Bachelor's degree or higher: 68.5%; Graduate/professional degree or higher: 32.7%

School District(s)
Garden City Union Free SD (KG-12)
    2014-15 Enrollment: 3,907 . . . . (516) 478-1010
Nassau Boces
    2014-15 Enrollment: n/a . . . . (516) 396-2200

Four-year College(s)
Adelphi University (Private, Not-for-profit)
    Fall 2014 Enrollment: 7,610 . . . . (516) 877-3000
    2015-16 Tuition: In-state $34,034; Out-of-state $34,034

Two-year College(s)
Nassau Community College (Public)
    Fall 2014 Enrollment: 22,374 . . . . (516) 572-7501
    2015-16 Tuition: In-state $4,854; Out-of-state $9,388
Sanford-Brown Institute-Garden City (Private, For-profit)
    Fall 2014 Enrollment: 717 . . . . (516) 247-2900

Vocational/Technical School(s)
Cactus Academy (Private, For-profit)
    Fall 2014 Enrollment: 123 . . . . (516) 746-0067
    2015-16 Tuition: $12,776

Housing: Homeownership rate: 93.8%; Median home value: $757,900; Median year structure built: 1948; Homeowner vacancy rate: 0.4%; Median selected monthly owner costs: $4,000+ with a mortgage, $1,500+ without a mortgage; Median gross rent: $1,959 per month; Rental vacancy rate: 0.0%

Health Insurance: 98.3% have insurance; 92.3% have private insurance; 21.0% have public insurance; 1.7% do not have insurance; 0.3% of children under 18 do not have insurance

Safety: Violent crime rate: 1.3 per 10,000 population; Property crime rate: 113.3 per 10,000 population

Newspapers: Oyster Bay Guardian (weekly circulation 6,000); Richner Communications (weekly circulation 77,400)

Transportation: Commute: 65.4% car, 25.0% public transportation, 3.1% walk, 5.9% work from home; Mean travel time to work: 36.0 minutes

Additional Information Contacts
Village of Garden City . . . . (516) 465-4000
    http://www.gardencityny.net

GARDEN CITY PARK (CDP).
Covers a land area of 0.984 square miles and a water area of 0.007 square miles. Located at 40.74° N. Lat; 73.66° W. Long. Elevation is 105 feet.

History: Garden City Park is a hamlet and census-designated place (CDP) located in the Town of North Hempstead in Nassau County on Long Island.

Population: 8,221; Growth (since 2000): 8.8%; Density: 8,350.9 persons per square mile; Race: 50.1% White, 0.8% Black/African American, 36.5% Asian, 0.0% American Indian/Alaska Native, 0.0% Native Hawaiian/Other Pacific Islander, 3.7% Two or more races, 17.3% Hispanic of any race; Average household size: 3.21; Median age: 44.5; Age under 18: 20.1%;

Age 65 and over: 19.0%; Males per 100 females: 93.8; Marriage status: 27.9% never married, 60.1% now married, 1.2% separated, 8.1% widowed, 3.9% divorced; Foreign born: 39.2%; Speak English only: 50.1%; With disability: 8.8%; Veterans: 4.8%; Ancestry: 18.1% Italian, 8.7% Irish, 8.0% German, 4.8% Polish, 2.7% Greek

Employment: 9.8% management, business, and financial, 6.0% computer, engineering, and science, 8.8% education, legal, community service, arts, and media, 15.3% healthcare practitioners, 17.0% service, 32.5% sales and office, 3.9% natural resources, construction, and maintenance, 6.8% production, transportation, and material moving

Income: Per capita: $36,777; Median household: $98,621; Average household: $115,164; Households with income of $100,000 or more: 49.3%; Poverty rate: 3.1%

Educational Attainment: High school diploma or higher: 90.3%; Bachelor's degree or higher: 39.9%; Graduate/professional degree or higher: 14.5%

School District(s)
Mineola Union Free SD (PK-12)
    2014-15 Enrollment: 2,784 . . . . (516) 237-2001
New Hyde Park-Garden City Park Union Free SD (KG-06)
    2014-15 Enrollment: 1,669 . . . . (516) 434-2305

Housing: Homeownership rate: 84.5%; Median home value: $547,800; Median year structure built: 1955; Homeowner vacancy rate: 0.0%; Median selected monthly owner costs: $3,352 with a mortgage, $1,262 without a mortgage; Median gross rent: $1,439 per month; Rental vacancy rate: 0.0%

Health Insurance: 94.3% have insurance; 76.9% have private insurance; 31.1% have public insurance; 5.7% do not have insurance; 0.0% of children under 18 do not have insurance

Transportation: Commute: 75.9% car, 18.8% public transportation, 1.8% walk, 1.7% work from home; Mean travel time to work: 34.9 minutes

GARDEN CITY SOUTH (CDP).
Covers a land area of 0.404 square miles and a water area of 0 square miles. Located at 40.71° N. Lat; 73.66° W. Long. Elevation is 72 feet.

Population: 4,265; Growth (since 2000): 7.3%; Density: 10,550.4 persons per square mile; Race: 83.0% White, 0.8% Black/African American, 10.6% Asian, 0.0% American Indian/Alaska Native, 0.0% Native Hawaiian/Other Pacific Islander, 0.2% Two or more races, 10.9% Hispanic of any race; Average household size: 3.19; Median age: 41.3; Age under 18: 19.9%; Age 65 and over: 16.2%; Males per 100 females: 91.1; Marriage status: 28.6% never married, 54.9% now married, 0.2% separated, 8.1% widowed, 8.4% divorced; Foreign born: 18.6%; Speak English only: 69.2%; With disability: 11.1%; Veterans: 6.0%; Ancestry: 33.4% Italian, 25.1% Irish, 14.0% German, 5.5% Greek, 4.5% Polish

Employment: 18.0% management, business, and financial, 3.3% computer, engineering, and science, 15.3% education, legal, community service, arts, and media, 4.6% healthcare practitioners, 15.2% service, 28.6% sales and office, 8.9% natural resources, construction, and maintenance, 6.1% production, transportation, and material moving

Income: Per capita: $43,892; Median household: $106,935; Average household: $134,315; Households with income of $100,000 or more: 51.8%; Poverty rate: 5.1%

Educational Attainment: High school diploma or higher: 88.6%; Bachelor's degree or higher: 39.6%; Graduate/professional degree or higher: 18.4%

Housing: Homeownership rate: 89.1%; Median home value: $460,500; Median year structure built: 1952; Homeowner vacancy rate: 4.0%; Median selected monthly owner costs: $2,722 with a mortgage, $1,147 without a mortgage; Median gross rent: $1,470 per month; Rental vacancy rate: 0.0%

Health Insurance: 87.6% have insurance; 77.0% have private insurance; 22.0% have public insurance; 12.4% do not have insurance; 0.0% of children under 18 do not have insurance

Transportation: Commute: 78.7% car, 15.2% public transportation, 1.9% walk, 3.5% work from home; Mean travel time to work: 32.5 minutes

GLEN COVE (city).
Covers a land area of 6.655 square miles and a water area of 12.589 square miles. Located at 40.88° N. Lat; 73.64° W. Long. Elevation is 23 feet.

History: Settled 1668, attracted affluent class after Civil War. In 1920s it became core of the Gold Coast as mansions were built, including waterfront community on East Island at north end (once known as Morgans Island when owned by J.P. Morgan). In 19th century it attracted

industry, including one of the world's largest starch factories. Incorporated as a city 1918.

Population: 27,245; Growth (since 2000): 2.3%; Density: 4,093.9 persons per square mile; Race: 62.4% White, 8.8% Black/African American, 4.1% Asian, 0.5% American Indian/Alaska Native, 0.0% Native Hawaiian/Other Pacific Islander, 2.9% Two or more races, 27.8% Hispanic of any race; Average household size: 2.79; Median age: 38.7; Age under 18: 20.7%; Age 65 and over: 18.3%; Males per 100 females: 94.9; Marriage status: 35.2% never married, 50.5% now married, 2.4% separated, 5.9% widowed, 8.4% divorced; Foreign born: 31.1%; Speak English only: 58.4%; With disability: 9.4%; Veterans: 5.1%; Ancestry: 20.1% Italian, 10.3% Irish, 7.3% German, 5.6% Polish, 3.3% English

Employment: 14.2% management, business, and financial, 2.4% computer, engineering, and science, 10.4% education, legal, community service, arts, and media, 6.3% healthcare practitioners, 27.8% service, 20.7% sales and office, 10.1% natural resources, construction, and maintenance, 8.2% production, transportation, and material moving

Income: Per capita: $37,152; Median household: $68,362; Average household: $102,443; Households with income of $100,000 or more: 33.1%; Poverty rate: 14.6%

Educational Attainment: High school diploma or higher: 80.3%; Bachelor's degree or higher: 36.0%; Graduate/professional degree or higher: 15.4%

School District(s)
Glen Cove City SD (PK-12)
   2014-15 Enrollment: 3,291 . . . . (516) 801-7010

Four-year College(s)
Webb Institute (Private, Not-for-profit)
   Fall 2014 Enrollment: 90 . . . . (516) 671-2213
   2015-16 Tuition: In-state $46,000; Out-of-state $46,000

Housing: Homeownership rate: 51.3%; Median home value: $473,200; Median year structure built: 1958; Homeowner vacancy rate: 0.0%; Median selected monthly owner costs: $2,831 with a mortgage, $1,291 without a mortgage; Median gross rent: $1,683 per month; Rental vacancy rate: 3.6%

Health Insurance: 86.4% have insurance; 68.5% have private insurance; 30.3% have public insurance; 13.6% do not have insurance; 6.0% of children under 18 do not have insurance

Hospitals: Glen Cove Hospital (265 beds)

Safety: Violent crime rate: 5.5 per 10,000 population; Property crime rate: 50.7 per 10,000 population

Newspapers: Gold Coast Gazette (weekly circulation 4,000); Record-Pilot (weekly circulation 6,000)

Transportation: Commute: 81.3% car, 7.9% public transportation, 6.0% walk, 2.9% work from home; Mean travel time to work: 27.7 minutes

Additional Information Contacts
City of Glen Cove . . . . (516) 676-2000
   http://www.glencove-li.com

GLEN HEAD (CDP). Covers a land area of 1.639 square miles and a water area of 0 square miles. Located at 40.84° N. Lat; 73.62° W. Long. Elevation is 112 feet.

History: Glen Head is consistently listed as one of the wealthiest zip codes on Long Island by a variety of sources.

Population: 4,620; Growth (since 2000): -0.1%; Density: 2,819.3 persons per square mile; Race: 89.7% White, 2.7% Black/African American, 3.3% Asian, 0.0% American Indian/Alaska Native, 0.0% Native Hawaiian/Other Pacific Islander, 1.0% Two or more races, 6.6% Hispanic of any race; Average household size: 2.78; Median age: 45.3; Age under 18: 21.5%; Age 65 and over: 16.8%; Males per 100 females: 92.1; Marriage status: 27.3% never married, 60.8% now married, 1.7% separated, 5.8% widowed, 6.1% divorced; Foreign born: 16.2%; Speak English only: 77.5%; With disability: 8.0%; Veterans: 7.5%; Ancestry: 29.7% Italian, 22.3% Irish, 14.1% German, 10.3% Polish, 6.0% English

Employment: 27.0% management, business, and financial, 2.8% computer, engineering, and science, 9.4% education, legal, community service, arts, and media, 9.6% healthcare practitioners, 17.5% service, 23.7% sales and office, 7.1% natural resources, construction, and maintenance, 2.9% production, transportation, and material moving

Income: Per capita: $49,993; Median household: $108,333; Average household: $137,377; Households with income of $100,000 or more: 54.6%; Poverty rate: 1.9%

Educational Attainment: High school diploma or higher: 94.5%; Bachelor's degree or higher: 51.5%; Graduate/professional degree or higher: 24.6%

School District(s)
North Shore Central SD (KG-12)
   2014-15 Enrollment: 2,738 . . . . (516) 277-7801

Housing: Homeownership rate: 88.2%; Median home value: $579,700; Median year structure built: 1954; Homeowner vacancy rate: 0.0%; Median selected monthly owner costs: $3,228 with a mortgage, $1,354 without a mortgage; Median gross rent: $1,588 per month; Rental vacancy rate: 0.0%

Health Insurance: 92.7% have insurance; 83.6% have private insurance; 23.1% have public insurance; 7.3% do not have insurance; 0.0% of children under 18 do not have insurance

Transportation: Commute: 80.3% car, 10.7% public transportation, 0.6% walk, 7.9% work from home; Mean travel time to work: 32.4 minutes

---

GLENWOOD LANDING (CDP). Covers a land area of 0.972 square miles and a water area of 0 square miles. Located at 40.83° N. Lat; 73.64° W. Long. Elevation is 98 feet.

Population: 3,767; Growth (since 2000): 6.4%; Density: 3,877.2 persons per square mile; Race: 92.3% White, 0.6% Black/African American, 4.9% Asian, 0.0% American Indian/Alaska Native, 0.0% Native Hawaiian/Other Pacific Islander, 1.3% Two or more races, 6.3% Hispanic of any race; Average household size: 2.74; Median age: 45.9; Age under 18: 22.9%; Age 65 and over: 14.9%; Males per 100 females: 89.1; Marriage status: 24.3% never married, 60.2% now married, 1.7% separated, 7.2% widowed, 8.3% divorced; Foreign born: 10.8%; Speak English only: 85.2%; With disability: 6.6%; Veterans: 4.1%; Ancestry: 32.2% Italian, 28.2% Irish, 15.7% German, 7.5% Polish, 5.1% English

Employment: 24.9% management, business, and financial, 5.5% computer, engineering, and science, 17.4% education, legal, community service, arts, and media, 9.8% healthcare practitioners, 5.9% service, 25.6% sales and office, 2.7% natural resources, construction, and maintenance, 8.2% production, transportation, and material moving

Income: Per capita: $53,619; Median household: $124,615; Average household: $143,857; Households with income of $100,000 or more: 63.2%; Poverty rate: 1.3%

Educational Attainment: High school diploma or higher: 98.2%; Bachelor's degree or higher: 64.8%; Graduate/professional degree or higher: 30.8%

Housing: Homeownership rate: 82.1%; Median home value: $605,100; Median year structure built: 1955; Homeowner vacancy rate: 0.0%; Median selected monthly owner costs: $3,176 with a mortgage, $1,323 without a mortgage; Median gross rent: $1,816 per month; Rental vacancy rate: 0.0%

Health Insurance: 97.9% have insurance; 91.9% have private insurance; 20.4% have public insurance; 2.1% do not have insurance; 1.0% of children under 18 do not have insurance

Transportation: Commute: 78.9% car, 17.4% public transportation, 0.4% walk, 3.3% work from home; Mean travel time to work: 41.3 minutes

---

GREAT NECK (village). Covers a land area of 1.329 square miles and a water area of 0.027 square miles. Located at 40.80° N. Lat; 73.73° W. Long. Elevation is 112 feet.

History: Great Neck, originally called "Madnan's Neck", was settled in the late 17th century, not long after settlers landed on Plymouth Rock. The area had previously been inhabited by the Mattinecock Native Americans.

Population: 10,095; Growth (since 2000): 5.8%; Density: 7,596.2 persons per square mile; Race: 86.5% White, 0.5% Black/African American, 9.1% Asian, 0.5% American Indian/Alaska Native, 0.0% Native Hawaiian/Other Pacific Islander, 1.3% Two or more races, 7.3% Hispanic of any race; Average household size: 3.15; Median age: 36.9; Age under 18: 29.6%; Age 65 and over: 16.9%; Males per 100 females: 96.5; Marriage status: 27.1% never married, 61.3% now married, 1.1% separated, 6.0% widowed, 5.6% divorced; Foreign born: 37.5%; Speak English only: 46.7%; With disability: 7.8%; Veterans: 3.5%; Ancestry: 23.8% Iranian, 12.1% American, 6.0% Russian, 5.9% Israeli, 4.6% Polish

Employment: 15.6% management, business, and financial, 7.4% computer, engineering, and science, 14.5% education, legal, community service, arts, and media, 12.5% healthcare practitioners, 7.9% service, 31.6% sales and office, 5.3% natural resources, construction, and maintenance, 5.1% production, transportation, and material moving

Income: Per capita: $38,988; Median household: $90,382; Average household: $120,477; Households with income of $100,000 or more: 43.2%; Poverty rate: 5.9%

Educational Attainment: High school diploma or higher: 90.3%; Bachelor's degree or higher: 55.0%; Graduate/professional degree or higher: 26.0%

School District(s)

Great Neck Union Free SD (PK-12)
  2014-15 Enrollment: 6,654 . . . . (516) 441-4001
Housing: Homeownership rate: 71.7%; Median home value: $692,200; Median year structure built: 1952; Homeowner vacancy rate: 1.4%; Median selected monthly owner costs: $3,601 with a mortgage, $1,500+ without a mortgage; Median gross rent: $1,843 per month; Rental vacancy rate: 8.5%
Health Insurance: 94.4% have insurance; 80.3% have private insurance; 26.6% have public insurance; 5.6% do not have insurance; 0.6% of children under 18 do not have insurance
Newspapers: Great Neck Record (weekly circulation 7,000)
Transportation: Commute: 63.3% car, 23.9% public transportation, 4.8% walk, 6.7% work from home; Mean travel time to work: 35.0 minutes
Additional Information Contacts
Village of Great Neck . . . . (516) 482-0019
  http://www.greatneckvillage.org

GREAT NECK ESTATES (village). Covers a land area of 0.757 square miles and a water area of 0.044 square miles. Located at 40.79° N. Lat; 73.74° W. Long. Elevation is 82 feet.
History: Incorporated 1911.
Population: 2,809; Growth (since 2000): 1.9%; Density: 3,711.8 persons per square mile; Race: 89.0% White, 0.0% Black/African American, 9.5% Asian, 0.0% American Indian/Alaska Native, 0.0% Native Hawaiian/Other Pacific Islander, 1.5% Two or more races, 2.3% Hispanic of any race; Average household size: 3.15; Median age: 43.2; Age under 18: 28.7%; Age 65 and over: 16.0%; Males per 100 females: 90.4; Marriage status: 25.2% never married, 65.8% now married, 1.5% separated, 3.7% widowed, 5.3% divorced; Foreign born: 26.2%; Speak English only: 63.8%; With disability: 5.5%; Veterans: 1.7%; Ancestry: 18.0% Russian, 14.2% Polish, 10.9% American, 7.7% Iranian, 4.2% Israeli
Employment: 14.6% management, business, and financial, 9.4% computer, engineering, and science, 20.4% education, legal, community service, arts, and media, 23.8% healthcare practitioners, 3.9% service, 23.2% sales and office, 3.2% natural resources, construction, and maintenance, 1.4% production, transportation, and material moving
Income: Per capita: $72,240; Median household: $176,250; Average household: $225,194; Households with income of $100,000 or more: 72.8%; Poverty rate: 0.6%
Educational Attainment: High school diploma or higher: 98.3%; Bachelor's degree or higher: 74.3%; Graduate/professional degree or higher: 47.3%
Housing: Homeownership rate: 90.6%; Median home value: $1,266,400; Median year structure built: 1942; Homeowner vacancy rate: 1.2%; Median selected monthly owner costs: $4,000+ with a mortgage, $1,500+ without a mortgage; Median gross rent: $3,500+ per month; Rental vacancy rate: 0.0%
Health Insurance: 97.2% have insurance; 90.4% have private insurance; 18.7% have public insurance; 2.8% do not have insurance; 0.0% of children under 18 do not have insurance
Safety: Violent crime rate: 0.0 per 10,000 population; Property crime rate: 17.7 per 10,000 population
Transportation: Commute: 65.1% car, 19.3% public transportation, 1.6% walk, 13.6% work from home; Mean travel time to work: 31.8 minutes

GREAT NECK GARDENS (CDP). Covers a land area of 0.171 square miles and a water area of 0 square miles. Located at 40.80° N. Lat; 73.72° W. Long. Elevation is 98 feet.
Population: 1,166; Growth (since 2000): 7.1%; Density: 6,832.5 persons per square mile; Race: 58.7% White, 0.0% Black/African American, 26.2% Asian, 0.0% American Indian/Alaska Native, 0.0% Native Hawaiian/Other Pacific Islander, 15.0% Two or more races, 0.0% Hispanic of any race; Average household size: 3.53; Median age: 43.6; Age under 18: 26.0%; Age 65 and over: 17.2%; Males per 100 females: 99.7; Marriage status: 27.1% never married, 68.6% now married, 0.0% separated, 1.7% widowed, 2.6% divorced; Foreign born: 40.5%; Speak English only: 57.3%; With disability: 3.8%; Veterans: 1.9%; Ancestry: 29.9% Iranian, 9.0% Polish, 6.3% Italian, 5.3% American, 5.3% Guyanese
Employment: 17.4% management, business, and financial, 7.6% computer, engineering, and science, 23.2% education, legal, community service, arts, and media, 14.7% healthcare practitioners, 9.3% service,

25.0% sales and office, 2.8% natural resources, construction, and maintenance, 0.0% production, transportation, and material moving
Income: Per capita: $46,823; Median household: $100,357; Average household: $158,979; Households with income of $100,000 or more: 50.9%; Poverty rate: 15.3%
Educational Attainment: High school diploma or higher: 86.1%; Bachelor's degree or higher: 72.0%; Graduate/professional degree or higher: 38.3%
Housing: Homeownership rate: 97.6%; Median home value: $809,500; Median year structure built: 1943; Homeowner vacancy rate: 0.0%; Median selected monthly owner costs: $4,000+ with a mortgage, $1,500+ without a mortgage; Median gross rent: n/a per month; Rental vacancy rate: 0.0%
Health Insurance: 89.9% have insurance; 70.8% have private insurance; 29.2% have public insurance; 10.1% do not have insurance; 9.9% of children under 18 do not have insurance
Transportation: Commute: 43.8% car, 42.3% public transportation, 4.8% walk, 5.4% work from home; Mean travel time to work: 38.9 minutes

GREAT NECK PLAZA (village). Covers a land area of 0.312 square miles and a water area of 0 square miles. Located at 40.79° N. Lat; 73.73° W. Long. Elevation is 98 feet.
Population: 6,879; Growth (since 2000): 6.9%; Density: 22,036.0 persons per square mile; Race: 78.4% White, 1.1% Black/African American, 12.0% Asian, 1.5% American Indian/Alaska Native, 0.0% Native Hawaiian/Other Pacific Islander, 4.0% Two or more races, 11.1% Hispanic of any race; Average household size: 1.83; Median age: 51.5; Age under 18: 13.8%; Age 65 and over: 31.3%; Males per 100 females: 75.4; Marriage status: 23.6% never married, 48.7% now married, 1.0% separated, 14.8% widowed, 13.0% divorced; Foreign born: 30.5%; Speak English only: 63.8%; With disability: 12.3%; Veterans: 4.3%; Ancestry: 13.1% Russian, 9.4% Iranian, 9.0% Polish, 8.6% American, 5.5% German
Employment: 21.1% management, business, and financial, 6.4% computer, engineering, and science, 19.9% education, legal, community service, arts, and media, 13.1% healthcare practitioners, 10.3% service, 24.4% sales and office, 2.5% natural resources, construction, and maintenance, 2.2% production, transportation, and material moving
Income: Per capita: $50,748; Median household: $67,138; Average household: $94,444; Households with income of $100,000 or more: 32.6%; Poverty rate: 6.7%
Educational Attainment: High school diploma or higher: 92.7%; Bachelor's degree or higher: 59.7%; Graduate/professional degree or higher: 29.9%
Housing: Homeownership rate: 50.9%; Median home value: $327,400; Median year structure built: 1959; Homeowner vacancy rate: 3.8%; Median selected monthly owner costs: $1,820 with a mortgage, $636 without a mortgage; Median gross rent: $1,756 per month; Rental vacancy rate: 5.0%
Health Insurance: 93.2% have insurance; 72.4% have private insurance; 37.2% have public insurance; 6.8% do not have insurance; 3.0% of children under 18 do not have insurance
Transportation: Commute: 52.7% car, 27.5% public transportation, 10.4% walk, 5.5% work from home; Mean travel time to work: 32.4 minutes
Additional Information Contacts
Village of Great Neck Plaza . . . . (516) 482-4500
  http://www.greatneckplaza.net

GREENVALE (CDP). Covers a land area of 0.252 square miles and a water area of 0 square miles. Located at 40.81° N. Lat; 73.63° W. Long. Elevation is 171 feet.
History: C.W. Post campus of Long Island University.
Population: 1,003; Growth (since 2000): -55.0%; Density: 3,977.7 persons per square mile; Race: 83.8% White, 0.0% Black/African American, 13.4% Asian, 0.0% American Indian/Alaska Native, 0.0% Native Hawaiian/Other Pacific Islander, 0.7% Two or more races, 5.7% Hispanic of any race; Average household size: 2.83; Median age: 53.4; Age under 18: 23.4%; Age 65 and over: 22.6%; Males per 100 females: 100.0; Marriage status: 37.5% never married, 51.2% now married, 8.1% separated, 2.9% widowed, 8.3% divorced; Foreign born: 24.6%; Speak English only: 81.0%; With disability: 8.8%; Veterans: 5.5%; Ancestry: 26.0% Irish, 19.1% Italian, 9.8% Polish, 8.6% German, 5.0% American
Employment: 16.3% management, business, and financial, 7.7% computer, engineering, and science, 23.5% education, legal, community service, arts, and media, 10.2% healthcare practitioners, 12.0% service, 24.2% sales and office, 6.1% natural resources, construction, and maintenance, 0.0% production, transportation, and material moving

Income: Per capita: $39,116; Median household: $95,417; Average household: $107,818; Households with income of $100,000 or more: 47.9%; Poverty rate: 7.9%

Educational Attainment: High school diploma or higher: 93.2%; Bachelor's degree or higher: 55.6%; Graduate/professional degree or higher: 29.0%

School District(s)

Roslyn Union Free SD (PK-12)

    2014-15 Enrollment: 3,149 . . . . (516) 801-5001

Housing: Homeownership rate: 69.0%; Median home value: $487,300; Median year structure built: 1951; Homeowner vacancy rate: 0.0%; Median selected monthly owner costs: $3,136 with a mortgage, $1,379 without a mortgage; Median gross rent: $1,451 per month; Rental vacancy rate: 0.0%

Health Insurance: 89.4% have insurance; 79.7% have private insurance; 23.6% have public insurance; 10.6% do not have insurance; 6.0% of children under 18 do not have insurance

Transportation: Commute: 73.1% car, 17.0% public transportation, 6.8% walk, 3.2% work from home; Mean travel time to work: 33.0 minutes

HARBOR HILLS (CDP). Covers a land area of 0.118 square miles and a water area of 0.059 square miles. Located at 40.79° N. Lat; 73.75° W. Long. Elevation is 69 feet.

Population: 545; Growth (since 2000): -3.2%; Density: 4,603.7 persons per square mile; Race: 80.9% White, 0.0% Black/African American, 17.6% Asian, 0.0% American Indian/Alaska Native, 0.0% Native Hawaiian/Other Pacific Islander, 1.5% Two or more races, 6.4% Hispanic of any race; Average household size: 2.82; Median age: 54.2; Age under 18: 17.2%; Age 65 and over: 28.4%; Males per 100 females: 89.1; Marriage status: 18.9% never married, 68.1% now married, 0.0% separated, 10.9% widowed, 2.1% divorced; Foreign born: 36.7%; Speak English only: 54.5%; With disability: 3.3%; Veterans: 4.2%; Ancestry: 28.6% Iranian, 14.9% Polish, 7.0% German, 6.6% American, 5.3% English

Employment: 23.2% management, business, and financial, 3.3% computer, engineering, and science, 27.6% education, legal, community service, arts, and media, 8.5% healthcare practitioners, 5.7% service, 26.4% sales and office, 5.3% natural resources, construction, and maintenance, 0.0% production, transportation, and material moving

Income: Per capita: $72,856; Median household: $141,382; Average household: $203,015; Households with income of $100,000 or more: 76.2%; Poverty rate: n/a

Educational Attainment: High school diploma or higher: 87.8%; Bachelor's degree or higher: 70.1%; Graduate/professional degree or higher: 44.5%

Housing: Homeownership rate: 100.0%; Median home value: $1,332,700; Median year structure built: 1946; Homeowner vacancy rate: 0.0%; Median selected monthly owner costs: $4,000+ with a mortgage, $1,500+ without a mortgage; Median gross rent: n/a per month; Rental vacancy rate: 0.0%

Health Insurance: 88.6% have insurance; 80.6% have private insurance; 20.9% have public insurance; 11.4% do not have insurance; 8.5% of children under 18 do not have insurance

Transportation: Commute: 65.8% car, 24.1% public transportation, 0.0% walk, 10.1% work from home; Mean travel time to work: 45.9 minutes

HARBOR ISLE (CDP). Covers a land area of 0.173 square miles and a water area of 0.055 square miles. Located at 40.60° N. Lat; 73.66° W. Long. Elevation is 10 feet.

Population: 1,529; Growth (since 2000): 14.6%; Density: 8,834.5 persons per square mile; Race: 92.7% White, 0.0% Black/African American, 1.6% Asian, 0.0% American Indian/Alaska Native, 0.0% Native Hawaiian/Other Pacific Islander, 2.4% Two or more races, 13.9% Hispanic of any race; Average household size: 2.97; Median age: 45.6; Age under 18: 25.5%; Age 65 and over: 20.9%; Males per 100 females: 96.5; Marriage status: 20.9% never married, 67.9% now married, 0.0% separated, 5.1% widowed, 6.2% divorced; Foreign born: 7.5%; Speak English only: 90.8%; With disability: 10.8%; Veterans: 9.9%; Ancestry: 24.5% Irish, 22.6% Italian, 13.7% German, 8.5% American, 5.2% Polish

Employment: 14.4% management, business, and financial, 3.6% computer, engineering, and science, 13.9% education, legal, community service, arts, and media, 5.1% healthcare practitioners, 19.5% service, 32.4% sales and office, 5.1% natural resources, construction, and maintenance, 6.0% production, transportation, and material moving

Income: Per capita: $42,649; Median household: $91,389; Average household: $125,964; Households with income of $100,000 or more: 46.7%; Poverty rate: 1.6%

Educational Attainment: High school diploma or higher: 96.6%; Bachelor's degree or higher: 43.8%; Graduate/professional degree or higher: 19.4%

Housing: Homeownership rate: 97.5%; Median home value: $452,500; Median year structure built: 1956; Homeowner vacancy rate: 5.8%; Median selected monthly owner costs: $3,101 with a mortgage, $1,163 without a mortgage; Median gross rent: n/a per month; Rental vacancy rate: 0.0%

Health Insurance: 98.8% have insurance; 90.2% have private insurance; 27.5% have public insurance; 1.2% do not have insurance; 0.0% of children under 18 do not have insurance

Transportation: Commute: 81.4% car, 17.4% public transportation, 0.0% walk, 1.2% work from home; Mean travel time to work: 35.6 minutes

HEMPSTEAD (town). Covers a land area of 118.587 square miles and a water area of 73.000 square miles. Located at 40.63° N. Lat; 73.61° W. Long. Elevation is 56 feet.

History: In 1644, the first settlers of Hempstead found a well-watered grassy plain on which their cattle grew fat. The virgin soil was excellent for timothy, rye, wheat, and maize. The score or more families who made up the settlement prospered. Not before 1801, however, did the village begin to grow appreciably.

Population: 767,916; Growth (since 2000): 1.6%; Density: 6,475.5 persons per square mile; Race: 65.2% White, 16.9% Black/African American, 5.7% Asian, 0.3% American Indian/Alaska Native, 0.0% Native Hawaiian/Other Pacific Islander, 3.9% Two or more races, 18.9% Hispanic of any race; Average household size: 3.13; Median age: 40.0; Age under 18: 22.7%; Age 65 and over: 14.9%; Males per 100 females: 93.3; Marriage status: 33.9% never married, 53.0% now married, 1.9% separated, 6.5% widowed, 6.7% divorced; Foreign born: 21.8%; Speak English only: 72.5%; With disability: 8.4%; Veterans: 5.1%; Ancestry: 19.2% Italian, 14.8% Irish, 8.6% German, 4.4% American, 4.0% Polish

Employment: 15.2% management, business, and financial, 3.6% computer, engineering, and science, 14.2% education, legal, community service, arts, and media, 7.3% healthcare practitioners, 17.9% service, 26.4% sales and office, 7.3% natural resources, construction, and maintenance, 8.1% production, transportation, and material moving

Income: Per capita: $38,126; Median household: $94,999; Average household: $117,518; Households with income of $100,000 or more: 47.6%; Poverty rate: 7.0%

Educational Attainment: High school diploma or higher: 89.6%; Bachelor's degree or higher: 38.1%; Graduate/professional degree or higher: 16.6%

School District(s)

Academy Charter School (KG-04)

    2014-15 Enrollment: 674 . . . . (516) 408-2200

Evergreen Charter School (KG-03)

    2014-15 Enrollment: 298 . . . . (516) 292-2060

Hempstead Union Free SD (PK-12)

    2014-15 Enrollment: 7,891 . . . . (516) 434-4001

Uniondale Union Free SD (KG-12)

    2014-15 Enrollment: 6,730 . . . . (516) 560-8824

Four-year College(s)

Hofstra University (Private, Not-for-profit)

    Fall 2014 Enrollment: 10,953 . . . . (516) 463-6600

    2015-16 Tuition: In-state $40,460; Out-of-state $40,460

Vocational/Technical School(s)

Access Careers (Private, For-profit)

    Fall 2014 Enrollment: 38 . . . . (516) 433-0034

    2015-16 Tuition: $1,300

Franklin Career Institute (Private, Not-for-profit)

    Fall 2014 Enrollment: 598 . . . . (516) 481-4444

    2015-16 Tuition: $19,400

Long Island Barber Institute (Private, For-profit)

    Fall 2014 Enrollment: 61 . . . . (516) 486-5424

    2015-16 Tuition: $7,500

Long Island Beauty School-Hempstead (Private, For-profit)

    Fall 2014 Enrollment: 127 . . . . (516) 483-6259

    2015-16 Tuition: $13,200

Housing: Homeownership rate: 80.5%; Median home value: $407,200; Median year structure built: 1953; Homeowner vacancy rate: 1.2%; Median selected monthly owner costs: $2,978 with a mortgage, $1,252 without a mortgage; Median gross rent: $1,484 per month; Rental vacancy rate: 4.3%

Health Insurance: 91.6% have insurance; 77.1% have private insurance; 26.0% have public insurance; 8.4% do not have insurance; 3.3% of children under 18 do not have insurance
Newspapers: Beacon Newspapers (weekly circulation 24,000)
Transportation: Commute: 76.3% car, 16.9% public transportation, 2.6% walk, 3.2% work from home; Mean travel time to work: 35.1 minutes
Additional Information Contacts
Town of Hempstead . . . . (516) 489-5000
  http://www.townofhempstead.org

HEMPSTEAD (village).
Covers a land area of 3.682 square miles and a water area of 0.005 square miles. Located at 40.70° N. Lat; 73.62° W. Long. Elevation is 56 feet.
History: The town grew significantly in the 1970s with the construction of nearby freeways, large retail outlets and the expansion of regional suburban industries. Settled in 1644 by English colonists who named it for their old home in England, Hemel-Hempstead. Seat of Hofstra University. Has many colonial houses and monuments. Founded as a village. Incorporated 1853.
Population: 55,105; Growth (since 2000): -2.6%; Density: 14,965.9 persons per square mile; Race: 16.7% White, 48.2% Black/African American, 1.7% Asian, 0.1% American Indian/Alaska Native, 0.0% Native Hawaiian/Other Pacific Islander, 4.1% Two or more races, 43.3% Hispanic of any race; Average household size: 3.42; Median age: 34.2; Age under 18: 24.9%; Age 65 and over: 10.0%; Males per 100 females: 97.1; Marriage status: 49.9% never married, 36.7% now married, 3.5% separated, 5.3% widowed, 8.1% divorced; Foreign born: 39.9%; Speak English only: 53.0%; With disability: 6.6%; Veterans: 3.2%; Ancestry: 7.0% Jamaican, 3.0% Haitian, 2.3% American, 2.0% Italian, 1.8% Irish
Employment: 8.2% management, business, and financial, 1.8% computer, engineering, and science, 6.3% education, legal, community service, arts, and media, 3.8% healthcare practitioners, 32.0% service, 23.1% sales and office, 11.3% natural resources, construction, and maintenance, 13.6% production, transportation, and material moving
Income: Per capita: $21,879; Median household: $55,417; Average household: $70,983; Households with income of $100,000 or more: 25.3%; Poverty rate: 20.7%
Educational Attainment: High school diploma or higher: 71.2%; Bachelor's degree or higher: 17.0%; Graduate/professional degree or higher: 6.6%

School District(s)
Academy Charter School (KG-04)
  2014-15 Enrollment: 674 . . . . (516) 408-2200
Evergreen Charter School (KG-03)
  2014-15 Enrollment: 298 . . . . (516) 292-2060
Hempstead Union Free SD (PK-12)
  2014-15 Enrollment: 7,891 . . . . (516) 434-4001
Uniondale Union Free SD (KG-12)
  2014-15 Enrollment: 6,730 . . . . (516) 560-8824

Four-year College(s)
Hofstra University (Private, Not-for-profit)
  Fall 2014 Enrollment: 10,953 . . . . (516) 463-6600
  2015-16 Tuition: In-state $40,460; Out-of-state $40,460

Vocational/Technical School(s)
Access Careers (Private, For-profit)
  Fall 2014 Enrollment: 38 . . . . (516) 433-0034
  2015-16 Tuition: $1,300
Franklin Career Institute (Private, Not-for-profit)
  Fall 2014 Enrollment: 598 . . . . (516) 481-4444
  2015-16 Tuition: $19,400
Long Island Barber Institute (Private, For-profit)
  Fall 2014 Enrollment: 61 . . . . (516) 486-5424
  2015-16 Tuition: $7,500
Long Island Beauty School-Hempstead (Private, For-profit)
  Fall 2014 Enrollment: 127 . . . . (516) 483-6259
  2015-16 Tuition: $13,200
Housing: Homeownership rate: 43.5%; Median home value: $308,400; Median year structure built: 1956; Homeowner vacancy rate: 2.6%; Median selected monthly owner costs: $2,855 with a mortgage, $1,260 without a mortgage; Median gross rent: $1,287 per month; Rental vacancy rate: 6.6%
Health Insurance: 77.5% have insurance; 45.0% have private insurance; 38.3% have public insurance; 22.5% do not have insurance; 5.9% of children under 18 do not have insurance

Safety: Violent crime rate: 72.1 per 10,000 population; Property crime rate: 128.2 per 10,000 population
Newspapers: Beacon Newspapers (weekly circulation 24,000)
Transportation: Commute: 66.4% car, 24.5% public transportation, 4.7% walk, 2.1% work from home; Mean travel time to work: 32.9 minutes
Additional Information Contacts
Village of Hempstead . . . . (516) 489-3400
  http://www.villageofhempstead.org

HERRICKS (CDP).
Covers a land area of 0.573 square miles and a water area of 0 square miles. Located at 40.76° N. Lat; 73.66° W. Long. Elevation is 112 feet.
History: Named for Capt. James M. Herrick,it is an unincorporated entity, governed under the jurisdiction of the Town of North Hempstead. Mail delivery is provided by the New Hyde Park Post Office utilizing the 11040 Zip Code.
Population: 4,370; Growth (since 2000): 7.2%; Density: 7,621.2 persons per square mile; Race: 52.1% White, 0.6% Black/African American, 41.8% Asian, 0.6% American Indian/Alaska Native, 0.0% Native Hawaiian/Other Pacific Islander, 2.8% Two or more races, 6.5% Hispanic of any race; Average household size: 3.36; Median age: 42.0; Age under 18: 21.6%; Age 65 and over: 16.4%; Males per 100 females: 93.1; Marriage status: 30.0% never married, 56.3% now married, 0.1% separated, 8.1% widowed, 5.6% divorced; Foreign born: 34.2%; Speak English only: 53.1%; With disability: 8.2%; Veterans: 5.7%; Ancestry: 13.1% Italian, 10.9% Irish, 8.1% German, 6.6% Polish, 5.0% Russian
Employment: 21.0% management, business, and financial, 9.9% computer, engineering, and science, 8.3% education, legal, community service, arts, and media, 18.4% healthcare practitioners, 13.1% service, 21.7% sales and office, 3.8% natural resources, construction, and maintenance, 4.0% production, transportation, and material moving
Income: Per capita: $46,327; Median household: $127,734; Average household: $151,663; Households with income of $100,000 or more: 61.2%; Poverty rate: 0.4%
Educational Attainment: High school diploma or higher: 94.1%; Bachelor's degree or higher: 54.4%; Graduate/professional degree or higher: 21.1%
Housing: Homeownership rate: 96.2%; Median home value: $587,000; Median year structure built: 1952; Homeowner vacancy rate: 1.6%; Median selected monthly owner costs: $3,117 with a mortgage, $1,394 without a mortgage; Median gross rent: $1,850 per month; Rental vacancy rate: 0.0%
Health Insurance: 95.5% have insurance; 84.6% have private insurance; 24.8% have public insurance; 4.5% do not have insurance; 0.0% of children under 18 do not have insurance
Transportation: Commute: 75.6% car, 18.8% public transportation, 2.7% walk, 2.9% work from home; Mean travel time to work: 38.8 minutes

HEWLETT (CDP).
Covers a land area of 0.881 square miles and a water area of 0.018 square miles. Located at 40.64° N. Lat; 73.69° W. Long. Elevation is 23 feet.
History: Hewlett is a hamlet and census-designated place (CDP) in Nassau County, New York on the South Shore of Long Island, and usually included as one of the Five Towns in the southwestern corner of Nassau County.
Population: 6,032; Growth (since 2000): -14.6%; Density: 6,845.7 persons per square mile; Race: 88.9% White, 1.2% Black/African American, 9.4% Asian, 0.0% American Indian/Alaska Native, 0.0% Native Hawaiian/Other Pacific Islander, 0.5% Two or more races, 3.7% Hispanic of any race; Average household size: 2.77; Median age: 45.5; Age under 18: 21.1%; Age 65 and over: 19.7%; Males per 100 females: 92.5; Marriage status: 26.0% never married, 62.0% now married, 1.5% separated, 3.8% widowed, 8.1% divorced; Foreign born: 18.5%; Speak English only: 76.5%; With disability: 7.7%; Veterans: 7.5%; Ancestry: 22.3% Italian, 14.2% American, 10.9% Russian, 10.6% Polish, 9.8% Irish
Employment: 16.6% management, business, and financial, 3.0% computer, engineering, and science, 22.0% education, legal, community service, arts, and media, 12.9% healthcare practitioners, 8.2% service, 30.0% sales and office, 0.4% natural resources, construction, and maintenance, 6.9% production, transportation, and material moving
Income: Per capita: $45,149; Median household: $106,235; Average household: $123,967; Households with income of $100,000 or more: 54.7%; Poverty rate: 4.8%

Educational Attainment: High school diploma or higher: 96.6%; Bachelor's degree or higher: 54.7%; Graduate/professional degree or higher: 28.3%

Hewlett-Woodmere Union Free SD (PK-12)
    2014-15 Enrollment: 3,079 . . . . (516) 792-4800
Housing: Homeownership rate: 85.6%; Median home value: $429,500; Median year structure built: 1953; Homeowner vacancy rate: 5.7%; Median selected monthly owner costs: $3,190 with a mortgage, $1,411 without a mortgage; Median gross rent: $1,555 per month; Rental vacancy rate: 23.0%
Health Insurance: 95.3% have insurance; 81.7% have private insurance; 28.0% have public insurance; 4.7% do not have insurance; 1.3% of children under 18 do not have insurance
Transportation: Commute: 74.8% car, 21.1% public transportation, 1.1% walk, 2.6% work from home; Mean travel time to work: 35.7 minutes

HEWLETT BAY PARK (village). Covers a land area of 0.337 square miles and a water area of 0.022 square miles. Located at 40.64° N. Lat; 73.70° W. Long. Elevation is 7 feet.
Population: 354; Growth (since 2000): -26.9%; Density: 1,050.9 persons per square mile; Race: 92.1% White, 0.8% Black/African American, 4.2% Asian, 0.0% American Indian/Alaska Native, 0.0% Native Hawaiian/Other Pacific Islander, 1.7% Two or more races, 3.4% Hispanic of any race; Average household size: 2.66; Median age: 53.3; Age under 18: 18.4%; Age 65 and over: 22.3%; Males per 100 females: 106.1; Marriage status: 20.2% never married, 69.9% now married, 0.3% separated, 5.4% widowed, 4.5% divorced; Foreign born: 16.9%; Speak English only: 78.3%; With disability: 5.1%; Veterans: 2.4%; Ancestry: 17.8% Russian, 12.4% American, 8.8% Austrian, 8.2% Polish, 5.6% Moroccan
Employment: 25.6% management, business, and financial, 1.5% computer, engineering, and science, 15.6% education, legal, community service, arts, and media, 23.1% healthcare practitioners, 1.5% service, 27.6% sales and office, 3.5% natural resources, construction, and maintenance, 1.5% production, transportation, and material moving
Income: Per capita: $163,208; Median household: $250,000+; Average household: $442,629; Households with income of $100,000 or more: 82.7%; Poverty rate: 1.4%
Educational Attainment: High school diploma or higher: 97.0%; Bachelor's degree or higher: 76.5%; Graduate/professional degree or higher: 43.3%
Housing: Homeownership rate: 98.5%; Median home value: $1,668,800; Median year structure built: 1949; Homeowner vacancy rate: 2.9%; Median selected monthly owner costs: $4,000+ with a mortgage, $1,500+ without a mortgage; Median gross rent: n/a per month; Rental vacancy rate: 0.0%
Health Insurance: 98.9% have insurance; 94.1% have private insurance; 23.2% have public insurance; 1.1% do not have insurance; 0.0% of children under 18 do not have insurance
Transportation: Commute: 74.1% car, 13.2% public transportation, 1.5% walk, 11.2% work from home; Mean travel time to work: 34.1 minutes

HEWLETT HARBOR (village). Covers a land area of 0.726 square miles and a water area of 0.104 square miles. Located at 40.63° N. Lat; 73.68° W. Long. Elevation is 7 feet.
Population: 1,229; Growth (since 2000): -3.3%; Density: 1,692.2 persons per square mile; Race: 96.7% White, 0.4% Black/African American, 2.7% Asian, 0.0% American Indian/Alaska Native, 0.0% Native Hawaiian/Other Pacific Islander, 0.2% Two or more races, 3.1% Hispanic of any race; Average household size: 2.97; Median age: 47.0; Age under 18: 26.0%; Age 65 and over: 20.3%; Males per 100 females: 97.0; Marriage status: 25.1% never married, 65.6% now married, 0.0% separated, 7.0% widowed, 2.3% divorced; Foreign born: 15.9%; Speak English only: 82.2%; With disability: 7.2%; Veterans: 6.9%; Ancestry: 27.3% Russian, 13.4% American, 9.0% Polish, 8.5% Eastern European, 6.4% Italian
Employment: 31.3% management, business, and financial, 4.8% computer, engineering, and science, 16.3% education, legal, community service, arts, and media, 10.8% healthcare practitioners, 1.7% service, 31.0% sales and office, 0.6% natural resources, construction, and maintenance, 3.5% production, transportation, and material moving
Income: Per capita: $88,295; Median household: $200,000; Average household: $260,319; Households with income of $100,000 or more: 77.8%; Poverty rate: 1.5%
Educational Attainment: High school diploma or higher: 99.2%; Bachelor's degree or higher: 75.0%; Graduate/professional degree or higher: 39.8%

Housing: Homeownership rate: 98.1%; Median home value: $1,076,400; Median year structure built: 1955; Homeowner vacancy rate: 2.4%; Median selected monthly owner costs: $4,000+ with a mortgage, $1,500+ without a mortgage; Median gross rent: n/a per month; Rental vacancy rate: 0.0%
Health Insurance: 99.1% have insurance; 91.6% have private insurance; 20.8% have public insurance; 0.9% do not have insurance; 0.0% of children under 18 do not have insurance
Transportation: Commute: 76.8% car, 14.3% public transportation, 0.6% walk, 8.3% work from home; Mean travel time to work: 37.2 minutes

HEWLETT NECK (village). Covers a land area of 0.193 square miles and a water area of 0.021 square miles. Located at 40.62° N. Lat; 73.70° W. Long. Elevation is 7 feet.
Population: 352; Growth (since 2000): -30.2%; Density: 1,827.6 persons per square mile; Race: 92.3% White, 6.5% Black/African American, 1.1% Asian, 0.0% American Indian/Alaska Native, 0.0% Native Hawaiian/Other Pacific Islander, 0.0% Two or more races, 2.3% Hispanic of any race; Average household size: 3.14; Median age: 41.0; Age under 18: 28.4%; Age 65 and over: 20.5%; Males per 100 females: 96.0; Marriage status: 18.8% never married, 77.3% now married, 0.7% separated, 3.6% widowed, 0.4% divorced; Foreign born: 13.1%; Speak English only: 77.4%; With disability: 7.7%; Veterans: 5.6%; Ancestry: 19.9% Russian, 9.9% Polish, 7.7% Israeli, 7.1% American, 4.8% European
Employment: 25.8% management, business, and financial, 0.7% computer, engineering, and science, 28.5% education, legal, community service, arts, and media, 11.9% healthcare practitioners, 3.3% service, 27.8% sales and office, 0.7% natural resources, construction, and maintenance, 1.3% production, transportation, and material moving
Income: Per capita: $97,598; Median household: $206,667; Average household: $309,791; Households with income of $100,000 or more: 86.5%; Poverty rate: 1.4%
Educational Attainment: High school diploma or higher: 99.1%; Bachelor's degree or higher: 79.0%; Graduate/professional degree or higher: 49.8%
Housing: Homeownership rate: 99.1%; Median home value: $1,090,300; Median year structure built: 1947; Homeowner vacancy rate: 0.9%; Median selected monthly owner costs: $4,000+ with a mortgage, $1,500+ without a mortgage; Median gross rent: n/a per month; Rental vacancy rate: 0.0%
Health Insurance: 98.9% have insurance; 90.9% have private insurance; 22.7% have public insurance; 1.1% do not have insurance; 1.0% of children under 18 do not have insurance
Transportation: Commute: 71.5% car, 19.2% public transportation, 0.0% walk, 9.3% work from home; Mean travel time to work: 45.5 minutes

HICKSVILLE (CDP). Covers a land area of 6.791 square miles and a water area of 0.015 square miles. Located at 40.76° N. Lat; 73.52° W. Long. Elevation is 148 feet.
History: Named for Charles Hicks, a Quaker reformer. Founded 1648.
Population: 42,333; Growth (since 2000): 2.6%; Density: 6,233.7 persons per square mile; Race: 68.8% White, 3.8% Black/African American, 21.5% Asian, 0.1% American Indian/Alaska Native, 0.0% Native Hawaiian/Other Pacific Islander, 3.3% Two or more races, 13.0% Hispanic of any race; Average household size: 3.17; Median age: 43.0; Age under 18: 18.4%; Age 65 and over: 16.2%; Males per 100 females: 96.2; Marriage status: 31.5% never married, 57.1% now married, 1.2% separated, 6.3% widowed, 5.0% divorced; Foreign born: 27.6%; Speak English only: 65.8%; With disability: 8.6%; Veterans: 6.1%; Ancestry: 19.7% Italian, 18.6% Irish, 10.6% German, 4.2% English, 3.5% Polish
Employment: 14.8% management, business, and financial, 4.1% computer, engineering, and science, 12.3% education, legal, community service, arts, and media, 7.4% healthcare practitioners, 15.9% service, 29.0% sales and office, 7.6% natural resources, construction, and maintenance, 8.9% production, transportation, and material moving
Income: Per capita: $37,215; Median household: $95,030; Average household: $113,519; Households with income of $100,000 or more: 48.7%; Poverty rate: 4.4%
Educational Attainment: High school diploma or higher: 90.8%; Bachelor's degree or higher: 36.0%; Graduate/professional degree or higher: 12.9%

Hicksville Union Free SD (KG-12)
    2014-15 Enrollment: 5,267 . . . . (516) 733-2105

Vocational/Technical School(s)

Gloria Francis School of Make-Up Artistry (Private, For-profit)
Fall 2014 Enrollment: 100 . . . . (516) 822-5546
2015-16 Tuition: $13,600

Veeb Nassau County School of Practical Nursing (Public)
Fall 2014 Enrollment: 201 . . . . (516) 572-1704
2015-16 Tuition: In-state $14,295; Out-of-state $14,295

Housing: Homeownership rate: 85.7%; Median home value: $398,100; Median year structure built: 1954; Homeowner vacancy rate: 0.8%; Median selected monthly owner costs: $2,671 with a mortgage, $989 without a mortgage; Median gross rent: $1,698 per month; Rental vacancy rate: 9.2%

Health Insurance: 93.4% have insurance; 80.6% have private insurance; 25.2% have public insurance; 6.6% do not have insurance; 2.0% of children under 18 do not have insurance

Newspapers: Litmore Publishing (weekly circulation 58,000)

Transportation: Commute: 79.5% car, 11.9% public transportation, 2.9% walk, 2.8% work from home; Mean travel time to work: 33.4 minutes

---

INWOOD (CDP).

Covers a land area of 1.581 square miles and a water area of 0.483 square miles. Located at 40.62° N. Lat; 73.75° W. Long. Elevation is 7 feet.

History: Inwood is included among the Five Towns, an informal grouping of villages and hamlets in Nassau County on the South Shore of western Long Island adjoining the border with Queens County in New York City.

Population: 10,052; Growth (since 2000): 7.8%; Density: 6,356.0 persons per square mile; Race: 30.6% White, 23.4% Black/African American, 5.6% Asian, 0.2% American Indian/Alaska Native, 0.0% Native Hawaiian/Other Pacific Islander, 5.9% Two or more races, 47.3% Hispanic of any race; Average household size: 3.36; Median age: 33.7; Age under 18: 28.8%; Age 65 and over: 12.7%; Males per 100 females: 94.2; Marriage status: 37.7% never married, 48.7% now married, 4.1% separated, 6.9% widowed, 6.7% divorced; Foreign born: 36.5%; Speak English only: 50.6%; With disability: 8.9%; Veterans: 2.9%; Ancestry: 13.8% Italian, 5.9% Irish, 4.4% American, 2.7% German, 2.2% Trinidadian and Tobagonian

Employment: 6.2% management, business, and financial, 0.6% computer, engineering, and science, 7.8% education, legal, community service, arts, and media, 6.7% healthcare practitioners, 33.8% service, 19.0% sales and office, 13.0% natural resources, construction, and maintenance, 12.9% production, transportation, and material moving

Income: Per capita: $19,647; Median household: $48,494; Average household: $62,488; Households with income of $100,000 or more: 16.4%; Poverty rate: 17.1%

Educational Attainment: High school diploma or higher: 75.4%; Bachelor's degree or higher: 16.5%; Graduate/professional degree or higher: 7.3%

School District(s)

Lawrence Union Free SD (PK-12)
2014-15 Enrollment: 2,890 . . . . (516) 295-7030

Housing: Homeownership rate: 48.3%; Median home value: $370,200; Median year structure built: 1943; Homeowner vacancy rate: 2.5%; Median selected monthly owner costs: $2,673 with a mortgage, $1,059 without a mortgage; Median gross rent: $1,340 per month; Rental vacancy rate: 1.0%

Health Insurance: 79.5% have insurance; 47.3% have private insurance; 38.9% have public insurance; 20.5% do not have insurance; 7.2% of children under 18 do not have insurance

Transportation: Commute: 64.6% car, 22.9% public transportation, 8.6% walk, 2.9% work from home; Mean travel time to work: 33.6 minutes

---

ISLAND PARK (village).

Covers a land area of 0.445 square miles and a water area of 0 square miles. Located at 40.61° N. Lat; 73.66° W. Long. Elevation is 7 feet.

History: Incorporated 1926.

Population: 4,694; Growth (since 2000): -0.8%; Density: 10,547.9 persons per square mile; Race: 80.3% White, 0.4% Black/African American, 3.0% Asian, 0.0% American Indian/Alaska Native, 0.0% Native Hawaiian/Other Pacific Islander, 3.4% Two or more races, 26.5% Hispanic of any race; Average household size: 2.51; Median age: 47.0; Age under 18: 16.2%; Age 65 and over: 18.6%; Males per 100 females: 95.6; Marriage status: 34.8% never married, 43.4% now married, 1.6% separated, 8.4% widowed, 13.5% divorced; Foreign born: 15.6%; Speak English only: 73.3%; With disability: 12.3%; Veterans: 8.2%; Ancestry: 27.1% Italian, 18.3% Irish, 9.5% German, 7.0% American, 4.8% Greek

Employment: 13.5% management, business, and financial, 1.0% computer, engineering, and science, 11.8% education, legal, community service, arts, and media, 4.0% healthcare practitioners, 16.0% service, 31.2% sales and office, 12.0% natural resources, construction, and maintenance, 10.5% production, transportation, and material moving

Income: Per capita: $31,197; Median household: $59,254; Average household: $77,075; Households with income of $100,000 or more: 31.2%; Poverty rate: 17.0%

Educational Attainment: High school diploma or higher: 91.1%; Bachelor's degree or higher: 23.7%; Graduate/professional degree or higher: 10.4%

School District(s)

Island Park Union Free SD (KG-08)
2014-15 Enrollment: 753 . . . . (516) 434-2600

Housing: Homeownership rate: 64.4%; Median home value: $350,600; Median year structure built: 1955; Homeowner vacancy rate: 2.9%; Median selected monthly owner costs: $2,873 with a mortgage, $1,075 without a mortgage; Median gross rent: $1,435 per month; Rental vacancy rate: 0.0%

Health Insurance: 91.4% have insurance; 72.7% have private insurance; 38.3% have public insurance; 8.6% do not have insurance; 2.8% of children under 18 do not have insurance

Newspapers: South Shore Tribune (weekly circulation 64,000)

Transportation: Commute: 81.6% car, 15.0% public transportation, 2.9% walk, 0.5% work from home; Mean travel time to work: 27.5 minutes

Additional Information Contacts

Village of Island Park . . . . (516) 431-0600
http://www.villageofislandpark.com

JERICHO (CDP).

Covers a land area of 3.943 square miles and a water area of 0.016 square miles. Located at 40.79° N. Lat; 73.54° W. Long. Elevation is 194 feet.

History: The English families who settled in Jericho were, or soon became, Quakers, members of the Society of Friends. Many fled from persecution in England and in the New England Colonies. They sought a peaceful existence as farmers. The name of the area was changed in 1692 from Lusum to Jericho after the town in the Middle East near the Jordan River mentioned in the Bible as part of the Promised Land.

Population: 13,746; Growth (since 2000): 5.4%; Density: 3,486.2 persons per square mile; Race: 63.6% White, 1.9% Black/African American, 31.5% Asian, 0.0% American Indian/Alaska Native, 0.1% Native Hawaiian/Other Pacific Islander, 2.1% Two or more races, 2.1% Hispanic of any race; Average household size: 2.89; Median age: 43.6; Age under 18: 24.6%; Age 65 and over: 14.8%; Males per 100 females: 93.8; Marriage status: 24.8% never married, 65.1% now married, 2.1% separated, 4.6% widowed, 5.4% divorced; Foreign born: 24.9%; Speak English only: 66.1%; With disability: 7.2%; Veterans: 4.3%; Ancestry: 12.2% Italian, 7.6% Russian, 6.6% Polish, 6.3% Eastern European, 6.0% American

Employment: 25.2% management, business, and financial, 5.7% computer, engineering, and science, 17.5% education, legal, community service, arts, and media, 11.7% healthcare practitioners, 9.2% service, 22.6% sales and office, 3.5% natural resources, construction, and maintenance, 4.6% production, transportation, and material moving

Income: Per capita: $63,075; Median household: $140,242; Average household: $183,522; Households with income of $100,000 or more: 66.9%; Poverty rate: 5.1%

Educational Attainment: High school diploma or higher: 95.5%; Bachelor's degree or higher: 67.3%; Graduate/professional degree or higher: 35.1%

School District(s)

Jericho Union Free SD (KG-12)
2014-15 Enrollment: 2,960 . . . . (516) 203-3600

Housing: Homeownership rate: 81.2%; Median home value: $673,700; Median year structure built: 1962; Homeowner vacancy rate: 0.0%; Median selected monthly owner costs: $3,925 with a mortgage, $1,500+ without a mortgage; Median gross rent: $1,843 per month; Rental vacancy rate: 0.0%

Health Insurance: 96.6% have insurance; 87.9% have private insurance; 21.2% have public insurance; 3.4% do not have insurance; 1.0% of children under 18 do not have insurance

Transportation: Commute: 77.8% car, 15.4% public transportation, 1.1% walk, 5.0% work from home; Mean travel time to work: 35.5 minutes

KENSINGTON (village). Covers a land area of 0.254 square miles and a water area of 0 square miles. Located at 40.79° N. Lat; 73.72° W. Long. Elevation is 128 feet.
Population: 1,113; Growth (since 2000): -7.9%; Density: 4,378.3 persons per square mile; Race: 85.5% White, 0.0% Black/African American, 11.1% Asian, 0.0% American Indian/Alaska Native, 0.0% Native Hawaiian/Other Pacific Islander, 3.0% Two or more races, 0.4% Hispanic of any race; Average household size: 2.74; Median age: 48.9; Age under 18: 23.9%; Age 65 and over: 24.9%; Males per 100 females: 91.3; Marriage status: 20.1% never married, 67.3% now married, 0.9% separated, 7.8% widowed, 4.8% divorced; Foreign born: 28.0%; Speak English only: 64.0%; With disability: 9.6%; Veterans: 6.0%; Ancestry: 15.9% Russian, 14.4% Iranian, 11.0% Polish, 9.8% American, 6.3% European
Employment: 27.4% management, business, and financial, 8.3% computer, engineering, and science, 20.9% education, legal, community service, arts, and media, 11.7% healthcare practitioners, 4.0% service, 25.1% sales and office, 0.6% natural resources, construction, and maintenance, 1.9% production, transportation, and material moving
Income: Per capita: $89,870; Median household: $176,667; Average household: $242,786; Households with income of $100,000 or more: 63.3%; Poverty rate: 3.2%
Educational Attainment: High school diploma or higher: 96.6%; Bachelor's degree or higher: 77.6%; Graduate/professional degree or higher: 49.2%
Housing: Homeownership rate: 96.6%; Median home value: $1,147,200; Median year structure built: Before 1940; Homeowner vacancy rate: 2.4%; Median selected monthly owner costs: $4,000+ with a mortgage, $1,500+ without a mortgage; Median gross rent: $3,500+ per month; Rental vacancy rate: 26.3%
Health Insurance: 98.1% have insurance; 85.6% have private insurance; 29.8% have public insurance; 1.9% do not have insurance; 0.0% of children under 18 do not have insurance
Safety: Violent crime rate: 0.0 per 10,000 population; Property crime rate: 0.0 per 10,000 population
Transportation: Commute: 48.8% car, 29.7% public transportation, 6.8% walk, 14.1% work from home; Mean travel time to work: 40.7 minutes

KINGS POINT (village). Covers a land area of 3.355 square miles and a water area of 0.643 square miles. Located at 40.82° N. Lat; 73.74° W. Long. Elevation is 26 feet.
History: Seat of U.S. Merchant Marine Academy (established 1942). Incorporated 1924.
Population: 5,071; Growth (since 2000): -0.1%; Density: 1,511.3 persons per square mile; Race: 93.5% White, 1.6% Black/African American, 2.7% Asian, 0.0% American Indian/Alaska Native, 0.1% Native Hawaiian/Other Pacific Islander, 1.0% Two or more races, 2.7% Hispanic of any race; Average household size: 3.35; Median age: 38.4; Age under 18: 25.7%; Age 65 and over: 17.7%; Males per 100 females: 123.9; Marriage status: 33.4% never married, 61.7% now married, 0.5% separated, 3.1% widowed, 1.8% divorced; Foreign born: 33.4%; Speak English only: 51.8%; With disability: 7.7%; Veterans: 4.2%; Ancestry: 41.1% Iranian, 14.4% American, 6.9% German, 6.0% Irish, 5.8% Italian
Employment: 23.5% management, business, and financial, 1.5% computer, engineering, and science, 10.2% education, legal, community service, arts, and media, 12.5% healthcare practitioners, 4.9% service, 38.2% sales and office, 2.1% natural resources, construction, and maintenance, 7.2% production, transportation, and material moving
Income: Per capita: $53,980; Median household: $113,160; Average household: $202,414; Households with income of $100,000 or more: 56.0%; Poverty rate: 6.5%
Educational Attainment: High school diploma or higher: 88.6%; Bachelor's degree or higher: 52.3%; Graduate/professional degree or higher: 22.2%

Four-year College(s)
United States Merchant Marine Academy (Public)
  Fall 2014 Enrollment: 961 . . . . (516) 726-5800
  2015-16 Tuition: In-state $1,107; Out-of-state $1,107
Housing: Homeownership rate: 93.9%; Median home value: $1,692,500; Median year structure built: 1957; Homeowner vacancy rate: 2.4%; Median selected monthly owner costs: $4,000+ with a mortgage, $1,500+ without a mortgage; Median gross rent: $769 per month; Rental vacancy rate: 22.1%
Health Insurance: 96.1% have insurance; 87.5% have private insurance; 23.3% have public insurance; 3.9% do not have insurance; 2.5% of children under 18 do not have insurance

Safety: Violent crime rate: 1.9 per 10,000 population; Property crime rate: 31.1 per 10,000 population
Transportation: Commute: 57.1% car, 23.8% public transportation, 5.5% walk, 12.3% work from home; Mean travel time to work: 41.8 minutes
Additional Information Contacts
Village of Kings Point . . . . (516) 504-1000
  http://www.villageofkingspoint.org

LAKE SUCCESS (village). Covers a land area of 1.845 square miles and a water area of 0.050 square miles. Located at 40.76° N. Lat; 73.71° W. Long. Elevation is 203 feet.
History: Lake Success was the temporary home of the UN from 1946 to 1950. Settled c.1730, incorporated 1926.
Population: 3,027; Growth (since 2000): 8.2%; Density: 1,640.4 persons per square mile; Race: 53.6% White, 6.4% Black/African American, 37.5% Asian, 0.1% American Indian/Alaska Native, 0.0% Native Hawaiian/Other Pacific Islander, 0.9% Two or more races, 4.2% Hispanic of any race; Average household size: 3.24; Median age: 50.9; Age under 18: 19.5%; Age 65 and over: 31.5%; Males per 100 females: 78.8; Marriage status: 22.0% never married, 57.8% now married, 1.0% separated, 15.0% widowed, 5.2% divorced; Foreign born: 29.2%; Speak English only: 59.4%; With disability: 6.2%; Veterans: 5.4%; Ancestry: 7.4% Italian, 7.3% German, 6.8% American, 4.9% Russian, 4.5% Polish
Employment: 21.9% management, business, and financial, 6.1% computer, engineering, and science, 12.5% education, legal, community service, arts, and media, 23.2% healthcare practitioners, 8.1% service, 25.3% sales and office, 0.0% natural resources, construction, and maintenance, 2.9% production, transportation, and material moving
Income: Per capita: $72,593; Median household: $173,533; Average household: $274,724; Households with income of $100,000 or more: 76.4%; Poverty rate: 5.7%
Educational Attainment: High school diploma or higher: 90.6%; Bachelor's degree or higher: 62.8%; Graduate/professional degree or higher: 32.3%
Housing: Homeownership rate: 97.6%; Median home value: $1,181,800; Median year structure built: 1955; Homeowner vacancy rate: 0.0%; Median selected monthly owner costs: $4,000+ with a mortgage, $1,500+ without a mortgage; Median gross rent: $3,500+ per month; Rental vacancy rate: 0.0%
Health Insurance: 97.5% have insurance; 90.5% have private insurance; 23.5% have public insurance; 2.5% do not have insurance; 0.7% of children under 18 do not have insurance
Safety: Violent crime rate: 0.0 per 10,000 population; Property crime rate: 111.1 per 10,000 population
Transportation: Commute: 77.3% car, 13.0% public transportation, 1.3% walk, 8.5% work from home; Mean travel time to work: 31.8 minutes

LAKEVIEW (CDP). Covers a land area of 1.000 square miles and a water area of 0.195 square miles. Located at 40.68° N. Lat; 73.65° W. Long. Elevation is 39 feet.
Population: 6,569; Growth (since 2000): 17.2%; Density: 6,569.4 persons per square mile; Race: 13.0% White, 75.4% Black/African American, 0.4% Asian, 6.2% American Indian/Alaska Native, 0.0% Native Hawaiian/Other Pacific Islander, 4.2% Two or more races, 20.9% Hispanic of any race; Average household size: 4.29; Median age: 35.0; Age under 18: 26.1%; Age 65 and over: 11.8%; Males per 100 females: 87.0; Marriage status: 45.1% never married, 43.8% now married, 6.5% separated, 6.8% widowed, 4.3% divorced; Foreign born: 28.7%; Speak English only: 70.6%; With disability: 10.2%; Veterans: 4.4%; Ancestry: 9.9% Jamaican, 6.3% Haitian, 3.8% West Indian, 3.2% Trinidadian and Tobagonian, 1.7% American
Employment: 9.2% management, business, and financial, 0.9% computer, engineering, and science, 9.1% education, legal, community service, arts, and media, 9.6% healthcare practitioners, 30.7% service, 28.2% sales and office, 4.2% natural resources, construction, and maintenance, 8.1% production, transportation, and material moving
Income: Per capita: $28,726; Median household: $111,319; Average household: $115,629; Households with income of $100,000 or more: 54.2%; Poverty rate: 9.8%
Educational Attainment: High school diploma or higher: 82.4%; Bachelor's degree or higher: 24.1%; Graduate/professional degree or higher: 11.2%
Housing: Homeownership rate: 87.8%; Median home value: $362,800; Median year structure built: 1956; Homeowner vacancy rate: 0.0%; Median selected monthly owner costs: $2,779 with a mortgage, $1,085 without a

mortgage; Median gross rent: $2,691 per month; Rental vacancy rate: 21.4%
Health Insurance: 91.5% have insurance; 77.6% have private insurance; 25.1% have public insurance; 8.5% do not have insurance; 4.0% of children under 18 do not have insurance
Transportation: Commute: 67.2% car, 27.3% public transportation, 5.1% walk, 0.4% work from home; Mean travel time to work: 37.5 minutes

LATTINGTOWN (village).
Covers a land area of 3.755 square miles and a water area of 0.077 square miles. Located at 40.89° N. Lat; 73.60° W. Long. Elevation is 66 feet.
Population: 1,542; Growth (since 2000): -17.1%; Density: 410.6 persons per square mile; Race: 91.1% White, 1.2% Black/African American, 4.6% Asian, 0.5% American Indian/Alaska Native, 0.0% Native Hawaiian/Other Pacific Islander, 0.3% Two or more races, 5.5% Hispanic of any race; Average household size: 2.68; Median age: 50.4; Age under 18: 22.6%; Age 65 and over: 27.8%; Males per 100 females: 96.3; Marriage status: 20.5% never married, 62.9% now married, 1.3% separated, 7.0% widowed, 9.7% divorced; Foreign born: 12.3%; Speak English only: 85.6%; With disability: 7.7%; Veterans: 5.9%; Ancestry: 19.3% Italian, 17.6% Irish, 14.9% German, 7.8% English, 7.8% Polish
Employment: 28.7% management, business, and financial, 2.1% computer, engineering, and science, 12.3% education, legal, community service, arts, and media, 6.4% healthcare practitioners, 13.4% service, 26.2% sales and office, 5.2% natural resources, construction, and maintenance, 5.7% production, transportation, and material moving
Income: Per capita: $93,792; Median household: $129,479; Average household: $252,253; Households with income of $100,000 or more: 60.8%; Poverty rate: 4.1%
Educational Attainment: High school diploma or higher: 91.1%; Bachelor's degree or higher: 65.0%; Graduate/professional degree or higher: 32.1%
Housing: Homeownership rate: 80.9%; Median home value: $1,110,800; Median year structure built: 1955; Homeowner vacancy rate: 3.3%; Median selected monthly owner costs: $4,000+ with a mortgage, $1,500+ without a mortgage; Median gross rent: $2,547 per month; Rental vacancy rate: 0.0%
Health Insurance: 97.5% have insurance; 88.8% have private insurance; 27.8% have public insurance; 2.5% do not have insurance; 0.9% of children under 18 do not have insurance
Transportation: Commute: 74.7% car, 10.7% public transportation, 2.8% walk, 10.7% work from home; Mean travel time to work: 34.6 minutes

LAUREL HOLLOW (village).
Covers a land area of 2.958 square miles and a water area of 0.204 square miles. Located at 40.86° N. Lat; 73.48° W. Long. Elevation is 108 feet.
History: Until 1935, called Laurelton.
Population: 1,835; Growth (since 2000): -4.9%; Density: 620.3 persons per square mile; Race: 89.8% White, 1.8% Black/African American, 7.2% Asian, 0.0% American Indian/Alaska Native, 0.0% Native Hawaiian/Other Pacific Islander, 0.7% Two or more races, 5.4% Hispanic of any race; Average household size: 3.11; Median age: 42.7; Age under 18: 28.4%; Age 65 and over: 15.5%; Males per 100 females: 93.8; Marriage status: 21.6% never married, 66.7% now married, 0.8% separated, 7.3% widowed, 4.4% divorced; Foreign born: 14.5%; Speak English only: 80.2%; With disability: 3.6%; Veterans: 4.6%; Ancestry: 19.8% Italian, 13.1% German, 11.2% Irish, 11.1% Polish, 8.8% Russian
Employment: 28.2% management, business, and financial, 5.1% computer, engineering, and science, 15.5% education, legal, community service, arts, and media, 16.3% healthcare practitioners, 5.2% service, 24.3% sales and office, 2.3% natural resources, construction, and maintenance, 3.1% production, transportation, and material moving
Income: Per capita: $96,634; Median household: $207,500; Average household: $311,514; Households with income of $100,000 or more: 76.2%; Poverty rate: 8.2%
Educational Attainment: High school diploma or higher: 97.3%; Bachelor's degree or higher: 73.9%; Graduate/professional degree or higher: 41.4%
Housing: Homeownership rate: 97.3%; Median home value: $1,434,500; Median year structure built: 1968; Homeowner vacancy rate: 1.8%; Median selected monthly owner costs: $4,000+ with a mortgage, $1,500+ without a mortgage; Median gross rent: n/a per month; Rental vacancy rate: 0.0%
Health Insurance: 98.4% have insurance; 92.1% have private insurance; 19.5% have public insurance; 1.6% do not have insurance; 2.5% of children under 18 do not have insurance

Transportation: Commute: 71.2% car, 17.0% public transportation, 2.0% walk, 8.5% work from home; Mean travel time to work: 43.4 minutes

LAWRENCE (village).
Covers a land area of 3.719 square miles and a water area of 0.912 square miles. Located at 40.60° N. Lat; 73.71° W. Long. Elevation is 23 feet.
History: Incorporated 1897.
Population: 6,529; Growth (since 2000): 0.1%; Density: 1,755.8 persons per square mile; Race: 98.3% White, 0.4% Black/African American, 1.3% Asian, 0.0% American Indian/Alaska Native, 0.0% Native Hawaiian/Other Pacific Islander, 0.0% Two or more races, 0.8% Hispanic of any race; Average household size: 2.98; Median age: 41.7; Age under 18: 27.1%; Age 65 and over: 20.5%; Males per 100 females: 92.2; Marriage status: 22.6% never married, 68.8% now married, 1.1% separated, 5.8% widowed, 2.8% divorced; Foreign born: 11.5%; Speak English only: 85.3%; With disability: 5.7%; Veterans: 4.3%; Ancestry: 16.8% Polish, 8.6% Hungarian, 7.7% European, 6.8% Russian, 5.5% Italian
Employment: 18.1% management, business, and financial, 4.3% computer, engineering, and science, 19.9% education, legal, community service, arts, and media, 16.5% healthcare practitioners, 4.1% service, 33.2% sales and office, 0.8% natural resources, construction, and maintenance, 3.2% production, transportation, and material moving
Income: Per capita: $79,693; Median household: $140,391; Average household: $235,306; Households with income of $100,000 or more: 66.2%; Poverty rate: 1.6%
Educational Attainment: High school diploma or higher: 97.6%; Bachelor's degree or higher: 77.0%; Graduate/professional degree or higher: 44.0%

School District(s)
Lawrence Union Free SD (PK-12)
    2014-15 Enrollment: 2,890 . . . . (516) 295-7030
Four-year College(s)
Sh'or Yoshuv Rabbinical College (Private, Not-for-profit, Jewish)
    Fall 2014 Enrollment: 153 . . . . (516) 239-9002
    2015-16 Tuition: In-state $9,460; Out-of-state $9,460
Housing: Homeownership rate: 85.1%; Median home value: $879,700; Median year structure built: 1959; Homeowner vacancy rate: 0.0%; Median selected monthly owner costs: $4,000+ with a mortgage, $1,500+ without a mortgage; Median gross rent: $1,612 per month; Rental vacancy rate: 9.7%
Health Insurance: 97.8% have insurance; 91.9% have private insurance; 24.4% have public insurance; 2.2% do not have insurance; 0.0% of children under 18 do not have insurance
Transportation: Commute: 72.7% car, 17.8% public transportation, 1.7% walk, 7.0% work from home; Mean travel time to work: 37.6 minutes
Additional Information Contacts
Village of Lawrence . . . . (516) 239-4600
    http://www.villageoflawrence.org

LEVITTOWN (CDP).
Covers a land area of 6.811 square miles and a water area of 0.025 square miles. Located at 40.72° N. Lat; 73.51° W. Long. Elevation is 85 feet.
History: Named for William Levitt, developer of model suburban communities. It was originally developed by Levitt and Sons, Inc. a as mass-produced area of private, low-cost housing, and became the propotoype for many postwar housing developments throughout the country. Founded 1947.
Population: 51,593; Growth (since 2000): -2.8%; Density: 7,574.9 persons per square mile; Race: 86.6% White, 0.8% Black/African American, 6.6% Asian, 0.0% American Indian/Alaska Native, 0.0% Native Hawaiian/Other Pacific Islander, 2.4% Two or more races, 12.1% Hispanic of any race; Average household size: 3.13; Median age: 41.1; Age under 18: 21.4%; Age 65 and over: 15.1%; Males per 100 females: 94.7; Marriage status: 30.2% never married, 56.6% now married, 1.9% separated, 6.6% widowed, 6.6% divorced; Foreign born: 12.7%; Speak English only: 83.7%; With disability: 10.4%; Veterans: 6.3%; Ancestry: 30.5% Italian, 22.4% Irish, 13.8% German, 5.0% Polish, 4.1% English
Employment: 14.2% management, business, and financial, 4.3% computer, engineering, and science, 13.8% education, legal, community service, arts, and media, 5.3% healthcare practitioners, 17.0% service, 29.5% sales and office, 7.6% natural resources, construction, and maintenance, 8.2% production, transportation, and material moving
Income: Per capita: $35,783; Median household: $98,810; Average household: $108,764; Households with income of $100,000 or more: 49.5%; Poverty rate: 3.0%

Educational Attainment: High school diploma or higher: 92.4%; Bachelor's degree or higher: 31.3%; Graduate/professional degree or higher: 12.3%

School District(s)
Island Trees Union Free SD (KG-12)
  2014-15 Enrollment: 2,298 . . . . (516) 520-2100
Levittown Union Free SD (KG-12)
  2014-15 Enrollment: 7,240 . . . . (516) 434-7020
Two-year College(s)
Hunter Business School (Private, For-profit)
  Fall 2014 Enrollment: 1,005 . . . . (516) 796-1000
Vocational/Technical School(s)
Brittany Beauty School (Private, For-profit)
  Fall 2014 Enrollment: 140 . . . . (516) 731-8300
  2015-16 Tuition: $13,600
Long Island Nail & Skin Care Institute (Private, For-profit)
  Fall 2014 Enrollment: 145 . . . . (516) 520-4800
  2015-16 Tuition: $8,495

Housing: Homeownership rate: 90.8%; Median home value: $357,400; Median year structure built: 1952; Homeowner vacancy rate: 0.3%; Median selected monthly owner costs: $2,775 with a mortgage, $1,112 without a mortgage; Median gross rent: $1,852 per month; Rental vacancy rate: 4.9%

Health Insurance: 95.6% have insurance; 85.6% have private insurance; 22.8% have public insurance; 4.4% do not have insurance; 1.2% of children under 18 do not have insurance

Transportation: Commute: 83.9% car, 11.5% public transportation, 1.5% walk, 1.7% work from home; Mean travel time to work: 32.2 minutes

LIDO BEACH (CDP).
Covers a land area of 1.739 square miles and a water area of 2.487 square miles. Located at 40.59° N. Lat; 73.60° W. Long. Elevation is 7 feet.

Population: 2,600; Growth (since 2000): -8.0%; Density: 1,495.2 persons per square mile; Race: 98.4% White, 0.1% Black/African American, 0.3% Asian, 0.0% American Indian/Alaska Native, 0.0% Native Hawaiian/Other Pacific Islander, 0.0% Two or more races, 8.6% Hispanic of any race; Average household size: 2.39; Median age: 52.9; Age under 18: 18.8%; Age 65 and over: 26.6%; Males per 100 females: 95.0; Marriage status: 20.7% never married, 65.7% now married, 1.0% separated, 8.4% widowed, 5.2% divorced; Foreign born: 5.1%; Speak English only: 89.3%; With disability: 10.9%; Veterans: 7.2%; Ancestry: 19.6% Irish, 14.3% Russian, 13.7% Italian, 10.4% Polish, 9.6% German

Employment: 26.4% management, business, and financial, 2.6% computer, engineering, and science, 28.9% education, legal, community service, arts, and media, 6.1% healthcare practitioners, 8.6% service, 24.7% sales and office, 0.7% natural resources, construction, and maintenance, 2.0% production, transportation, and material moving

Income: Per capita: $83,979; Median household: $143,333; Average household: $200,266; Households with income of $100,000 or more: 61.3%; Poverty rate: 2.1%

Educational Attainment: High school diploma or higher: 96.4%; Bachelor's degree or higher: 66.3%; Graduate/professional degree or higher: 36.6%

School District(s)
Long Beach City SD (PK-12)
  2014-15 Enrollment: 3,909 . . . . (516) 897-2104

Housing: Homeownership rate: 92.8%; Median home value: $670,300; Median year structure built: 1961; Homeowner vacancy rate: 5.9%; Median selected monthly owner costs: $3,545 with a mortgage, $1,500+ without a mortgage; Median gross rent: $1,984 per month; Rental vacancy rate: 0.0%

Health Insurance: 97.9% have insurance; 87.0% have private insurance; 29.6% have public insurance; 2.1% do not have insurance; 2.1% of children under 18 do not have insurance

Transportation: Commute: 67.0% car, 20.0% public transportation, 1.8% walk, 10.6% work from home; Mean travel time to work: 40.7 minutes

LOCUST VALLEY (CDP).
Covers a land area of 0.914 square miles and a water area of 0.023 square miles. Located at 40.88° N. Lat; 73.59° W. Long. Elevation is 128 feet.

Population: 3,270; Growth (since 2000): -7.1%; Density: 3,579.2 persons per square mile; Race: 87.2% White, 3.0% Black/African American, 0.4% Asian, 0.0% American Indian/Alaska Native, 0.0% Native Hawaiian/Other Pacific Islander, 0.1% Two or more races, 15.0% Hispanic of any race; Average household size: 2.67; Median age: 42.3; Age under 18: 21.8%;

Age 65 and over: 17.0%; Males per 100 females: 92.6; Marriage status: 29.6% never married, 53.5% now married, 1.9% separated, 5.7% widowed, 11.3% divorced; Foreign born: 19.1%; Speak English only: 72.7%; With disability: 9.7%; Veterans: 5.4%; Ancestry: 26.5% Irish, 25.3% Italian, 10.0% German, 5.8% English, 5.5% American

Employment: 22.6% management, business, and financial, 4.5% computer, engineering, and science, 10.0% education, legal, community service, arts, and media, 2.1% healthcare practitioners, 24.6% service, 21.1% sales and office, 9.1% natural resources, construction, and maintenance, 5.9% production, transportation, and material moving

Income: Per capita: $52,202; Median household: $85,536; Average household: $138,888; Households with income of $100,000 or more: 43.3%; Poverty rate: 3.6%

Educational Attainment: High school diploma or higher: 87.1%; Bachelor's degree or higher: 36.1%; Graduate/professional degree or higher: 13.9%

School District(s)
Locust Valley Central SD (KG-12)
  2014-15 Enrollment: 2,188 . . . . (516) 277-5001

Housing: Homeownership rate: 67.9%; Median home value: $545,300; Median year structure built: 1947; Homeowner vacancy rate: 0.0%; Median selected monthly owner costs: $3,283 with a mortgage, $1,038 without a mortgage; Median gross rent: $1,664 per month; Rental vacancy rate: 6.5%

Health Insurance: 88.6% have insurance; 78.4% have private insurance; 23.9% have public insurance; 11.4% do not have insurance; 5.3% of children under 18 do not have insurance

Newspapers: The Leader (weekly circulation 3,900)

Transportation: Commute: 78.4% car, 11.8% public transportation, 0.4% walk, 6.4% work from home; Mean travel time to work: 32.3 minutes

LONG BEACH (city).
Covers a land area of 2.215 square miles and a water area of 1.680 square miles. Located at 40.59° N. Lat; 73.67° W. Long. Elevation is 7 feet.

History: Named for its beach on the Atlantic shore of Long Island. Incorporated 1922.

Population: 33,470; Growth (since 2000): -5.6%; Density: 15,112.9 persons per square mile; Race: 81.5% White, 6.2% Black/African American, 3.8% Asian, 0.1% American Indian/Alaska Native, 0.0% Native Hawaiian/Other Pacific Islander, 2.4% Two or more races, 14.5% Hispanic of any race; Average household size: 2.23; Median age: 44.5; Age under 18: 15.5%; Age 65 and over: 17.8%; Males per 100 females: 93.3; Marriage status: 37.9% never married, 42.3% now married, 2.1% separated, 7.1% widowed, 12.7% divorced; Foreign born: 16.6%; Speak English only: 79.1%; With disability: 9.8%; Veterans: 5.4%; Ancestry: 23.1% Irish, 18.4% Italian, 8.9% German, 5.8% American, 5.5% Russian

Employment: 17.8% management, business, and financial, 3.8% computer, engineering, and science, 18.5% education, legal, community service, arts, and media, 5.0% healthcare practitioners, 17.4% service, 25.8% sales and office, 6.7% natural resources, construction, and maintenance, 4.9% production, transportation, and material moving

Income: Per capita: $46,925; Median household: $84,831; Average household: $104,685; Households with income of $100,000 or more: 42.5%; Poverty rate: 7.0%

Educational Attainment: High school diploma or higher: 93.9%; Bachelor's degree or higher: 45.9%; Graduate/professional degree or higher: 21.2%

School District(s)
Long Beach City SD (PK-12)
  2014-15 Enrollment: 3,909 . . . . (516) 897-2104
Four-year College(s)
Rabbinical College of Long Island (Private, Not-for-profit)
  Fall 2014 Enrollment: 115 . . . . (516) 431-7414
  2015-16 Tuition: In-state $8,800; Out-of-state $8,800

Housing: Homeownership rate: 56.8%; Median home value: $459,200; Median year structure built: 1956; Homeowner vacancy rate: 4.0%; Median selected monthly owner costs: $2,878 with a mortgage, $1,214 without a mortgage; Median gross rent: $1,637 per month; Rental vacancy rate: 3.7%

Health Insurance: 89.8% have insurance; 75.7% have private insurance; 27.0% have public insurance; 10.2% do not have insurance; 0.4% of children under 18 do not have insurance

Hospitals: Long Beach Medical Center (203 beds)

Safety: Violent crime rate: 13.0 per 10,000 population; Property crime rate: 93.3 per 10,000 population

Transportation: Commute: 70.1% car, 19.0% public transportation, 5.2% walk, 3.8% work from home; Mean travel time to work: 40.3 minutes
Additional Information Contacts
City of Long Beach . . . . (516) 431-1000
  http://www.longbeachny.org

LYNBROOK (village).
Covers a land area of 2.014 square miles and a water area of 0 square miles. Located at 40.66° N. Lat; 73.67° W. Long. Elevation is 20 feet.
History: Old Church dates from 1800. The area was settled in 1785 and was called Bloomfield. The name *Lynbrook*(formed by reversing the syllables in *Brooklyn*) was adopted in 1895. Incorporated 1911.
Population: 19,556; Growth (since 2000): -1.8%; Density: 9,711.0 persons per square mile; Race: 86.5% White, 3.9% Black/African American, 3.8% Asian, 0.0% American Indian/Alaska Native, 0.0% Native Hawaiian/Other Pacific Islander, 3.0% Two or more races, 15.7% Hispanic of any race; Average household size: 2.75; Median age: 43.0; Age under 18: 21.2%; Age 65 and over: 16.9%; Males per 100 females: 90.2; Marriage status: 30.2% never married, 54.2% now married, 1.3% separated, 8.0% widowed, 7.6% divorced; Foreign born: 15.0%; Speak English only: 77.3%; With disability: 11.9%; Veterans: 6.0%; Ancestry: 29.7% Italian, 20.4% Irish, 12.4% German, 6.0% American, 5.5% Polish
Employment: 18.1% management, business, and financial, 5.3% computer, engineering, and science, 17.2% education, legal, community service, arts, and media, 7.0% healthcare practitioners, 14.2% service, 26.0% sales and office, 5.9% natural resources, construction, and maintenance, 6.3% production, transportation, and material moving
Income: Per capita: $39,613; Median household: $82,189; Average household: $107,118; Households with income of $100,000 or more: 43.0%; Poverty rate: 4.9%
Educational Attainment: High school diploma or higher: 93.0%; Bachelor's degree or higher: 39.7%; Graduate/professional degree or higher: 16.6%

School District(s)
Lynbrook Union Free SD (KG-12)
  2014-15 Enrollment: 2,822 . . . . (516) 887-0253
Malverne Union Free SD (KG-12)
  2014-15 Enrollment: 1,726 . . . . (516) 887-6405
Housing: Homeownership rate: 73.9%; Median home value: $408,600; Median year structure built: 1947; Homeowner vacancy rate: 0.7%; Median selected monthly owner costs: $3,050 with a mortgage, $1,269 without a mortgage; Median gross rent: $1,650 per month; Rental vacancy rate: 3.3%
Health Insurance: 93.6% have insurance; 81.7% have private insurance; 23.6% have public insurance; 6.4% do not have insurance; 1.8% of children under 18 do not have insurance
Safety: Violent crime rate: 5.6 per 10,000 population; Property crime rate: 75.6 per 10,000 population
Transportation: Commute: 69.2% car, 22.0% public transportation, 3.5% walk, 3.2% work from home; Mean travel time to work: 39.0 minutes
Additional Information Contacts
Village of Lynbrook . . . . (516) 599-8300
  http://www.lynbrookvillage.net

MALVERNE (village).
Covers a land area of 1.058 square miles and a water area of 0 square miles. Located at 40.67° N. Lat; 73.67° W. Long. Elevation is 39 feet.
History: Settled in the early 1800s, incorporated 1921.
Population: 8,552; Growth (since 2000): -4.3%; Density: 8,084.7 persons per square mile; Race: 90.9% White, 3.0% Black/African American, 3.1% Asian, 0.2% American Indian/Alaska Native, 0.0% Native Hawaiian/Other Pacific Islander, 1.6% Two or more races, 5.1% Hispanic of any race; Average household size: 2.71; Median age: 47.2; Age under 18: 19.9%; Age 65 and over: 19.7%; Males per 100 females: 92.8; Marriage status: 28.0% never married, 55.5% now married, 1.0% separated, 9.2% widowed, 7.3% divorced; Foreign born: 9.2%; Speak English only: 90.7%; With disability: 9.2%; Veterans: 5.3%; Ancestry: 29.9% Irish, 26.8% Italian, 15.5% German, 8.1% American, 5.4% English
Employment: 21.1% management, business, and financial, 5.3% computer, engineering, and science, 18.3% education, legal, community service, arts, and media, 9.2% healthcare practitioners, 9.2% service, 24.0% sales and office, 9.3% natural resources, construction, and maintenance, 3.5% production, transportation, and material moving

Income: Per capita: $46,787; Median household: $106,795; Average household: $124,059; Households with income of $100,000 or more: 52.6%; Poverty rate: 2.2%
Educational Attainment: High school diploma or higher: 95.6%; Bachelor's degree or higher: 49.8%; Graduate/professional degree or higher: 24.3%

School District(s)
Malverne Union Free SD (KG-12)
  2014-15 Enrollment: 1,726 . . . . (516) 887-6405
Housing: Homeownership rate: 93.1%; Median home value: $437,000; Median year structure built: 1942; Homeowner vacancy rate: 0.0%; Median selected monthly owner costs: $2,983 with a mortgage, $1,320 without a mortgage; Median gross rent: $1,164 per month; Rental vacancy rate: 0.0%
Health Insurance: 95.6% have insurance; 88.6% have private insurance; 24.1% have public insurance; 4.4% do not have insurance; 0.5% of children under 18 do not have insurance
Safety: Violent crime rate: 0.0 per 10,000 population; Property crime rate: 29.1 per 10,000 population
Transportation: Commute: 76.7% car, 14.1% public transportation, 2.0% walk, 5.7% work from home; Mean travel time to work: 36.1 minutes
Additional Information Contacts
Village of Malverne . . . . (516) 599-1200
  http://www.malvernevillage.org/index.html

MALVERNE PARK OAKS (CDP).
Covers a land area of 0.130 square miles and a water area of 0 square miles. Located at 40.68° N. Lat; 73.66° W. Long. Elevation is 10 feet.
Population: 557; Growth (since 2000): 18.5%; Density: 4,277.5 persons per square mile; Race: 76.5% White, 7.5% Black/African American, 16.0% Asian, 0.0% American Indian/Alaska Native, 0.0% Native Hawaiian/Other Pacific Islander, 0.0% Two or more races, 10.6% Hispanic of any race; Average household size: 2.83; Median age: 52.6; Age under 18: 17.4%; Age 65 and over: 16.2%; Males per 100 females: 89.1; Marriage status: 21.3% never married, 75.8% now married, 0.0% separated, 2.9% widowed, 0.0% divorced; Foreign born: 29.4%; Speak English only: 77.2%; With disability: 2.5%; Veterans: 5.4%; Ancestry: 35.5% Italian, 21.9% Irish, 9.9% German, 8.3% French, 7.0% European
Employment: 30.2% management, business, and financial, 0.0% computer, engineering, and science, 19.2% education, legal, community service, arts, and media, 7.9% healthcare practitioners, 13.8% service, 28.9% sales and office, 0.0% natural resources, construction, and maintenance, 0.0% production, transportation, and material moving
Income: Per capita: $46,878; Median household: $92,292; Average household: $131,322; Households with income of $100,000 or more: 49.2%; Poverty rate: n/a
Educational Attainment: High school diploma or higher: 100.0%; Bachelor's degree or higher: 66.4%; Graduate/professional degree or higher: 37.2%
Housing: Homeownership rate: 100.0%; Median home value: $466,500; Median year structure built: 1950; Homeowner vacancy rate: 0.0%; Median selected monthly owner costs: $2,819 with a mortgage, $1,471 without a mortgage; Median gross rent: n/a per month; Rental vacancy rate: 0.0%
Health Insurance: 100.0% have insurance; 93.7% have private insurance; 21.4% have public insurance; 0.0% do not have insurance; 0.0% of children under 18 do not have insurance
Transportation: Commute: 82.1% car, 13.8% public transportation, 0.0% walk, 4.1% work from home; Mean travel time to work: 37.0 minutes

MANHASSET (CDP).
Covers a land area of 2.382 square miles and a water area of 0.034 square miles. Located at 40.78° N. Lat; 73.69° W. Long. Elevation is 98 feet.
History: Manhasset is a Native American term that translates to "the island neighborhood." In 2005, a Wall Street Journal article ranked Manhasset as the best town for raising a family in the New York metropolitan area.
Population: 8,248; Growth (since 2000): -1.4%; Density: 3,463.0 persons per square mile; Race: 73.6% White, 10.3% Black/African American, 10.1% Asian, 0.2% American Indian/Alaska Native, 0.0% Native Hawaiian/Other Pacific Islander, 1.6% Two or more races, 13.9% Hispanic of any race; Average household size: 2.96; Median age: 44.0; Age under 18: 24.2%; Age 65 and over: 19.0%; Males per 100 females: 89.0; Marriage status: 32.0% never married, 53.5% now married, 0.5% separated, 7.6% widowed, 6.9% divorced; Foreign born: 19.2%; Speak

English only: 72.3%; With disability: 7.4%; Veterans: 4.0%; Ancestry: 21.1% Italian, 13.8% Irish, 9.2% German, 6.1% American, 5.3% Greek
Employment: 23.9% management, business, and financial, 4.7% computer, engineering, and science, 13.3% education, legal, community service, arts, and media, 11.4% healthcare practitioners, 10.5% service, 27.4% sales and office, 1.9% natural resources, construction, and maintenance, 6.9% production, transportation, and material moving
Income: Per capita: $60,742; Median household: $107,283; Average household: $181,630; Households with income of $100,000 or more: 53.6%; Poverty rate: 5.1%
Educational Attainment: High school diploma or higher: 92.1%; Bachelor's degree or higher: 56.6%; Graduate/professional degree or higher: 29.9%

School District(s)
Manhasset Union Free SD (KG-12)
   2014-15 Enrollment: 3,356 . . . . (516) 267-7705
Four-year College(s)
Elmezzi Graduate School of Molecular Medicine (Private, Not-for-profit)
   Fall 2014 Enrollment: n/a . . . . (516) 562-3405
Housing: Homeownership rate: 74.3%; Median home value: $916,600; Median year structure built: 1940; Homeowner vacancy rate: 2.3%; Median selected monthly owner costs: $4,000+ with a mortgage, $1,500+ without a mortgage; Median gross rent: $1,241 per month; Rental vacancy rate: 6.4%
Health Insurance: 96.6% have insurance; 85.3% have private insurance; 25.1% have public insurance; 3.4% do not have insurance; 2.9% of children under 18 do not have insurance
Hospitals: North Shore University Hospital (900 beds)
Transportation: Commute: 59.3% car, 26.5% public transportation, 7.5% walk, 6.3% work from home; Mean travel time to work: 33.8 minutes

---

MANHASSET HILLS (CDP). Covers a land area of 0.591 square miles and a water area of 0 square miles. Located at 40.76° N. Lat; 73.68° W. Long. Elevation is 125 feet.
History: Manhasset is a Native American term that translates to "the island neighborhood. The Valley School, serving Manhasset's African American community, was closed in the 1960s by a desegregation lawsuit.
Population: 3,755; Growth (since 2000): 2.6%; Density: 6,351.3 persons per square mile; Race: 48.3% White, 0.0% Black/African American, 40.6% Asian, 0.0% American Indian/Alaska Native, 0.0% Native Hawaiian/Other Pacific Islander, 3.9% Two or more races, 16.0% Hispanic of any race; Average household size: 3.05; Median age: 46.5; Age under 18: 22.5%; Age 65 and over: 24.7%; Males per 100 females: 91.4; Marriage status: 19.1% never married, 68.9% now married, 0.2% separated, 8.9% widowed, 3.1% divorced; Foreign born: 40.5%; Speak English only: 45.4%; With disability: 9.4%; Veterans: 3.7%; Ancestry: 14.2% Italian, 5.1% Irish, 4.9% German, 4.5% Greek, 3.0% American
Employment: 25.9% management, business, and financial, 4.3% computer, engineering, and science, 11.6% education, legal, community service, arts, and media, 23.6% healthcare practitioners, 5.3% service, 24.1% sales and office, 3.8% natural resources, construction, and maintenance, 1.3% production, transportation, and material moving
Income: Per capita: $51,057; Median household: $121,759; Average household: $154,247; Households with income of $100,000 or more: 60.5%; Poverty rate: 0.9%
Educational Attainment: High school diploma or higher: 89.9%; Bachelor's degree or higher: 62.4%; Graduate/professional degree or higher: 33.3%
Housing: Homeownership rate: 92.9%; Median home value: $805,900; Median year structure built: 1964; Homeowner vacancy rate: 0.0%; Median selected monthly owner costs: $4,000+ with a mortgage, $1,500+ without a mortgage; Median gross rent: $1,280 per month; Rental vacancy rate: 0.0%
Health Insurance: 97.8% have insurance; 90.5% have private insurance; 24.9% have public insurance; 2.2% do not have insurance; 3.9% of children under 18 do not have insurance
Transportation: Commute: 75.6% car, 15.0% public transportation, 0.0% walk, 9.4% work from home; Mean travel time to work: 37.4 minutes

---

MANORHAVEN (village). Covers a land area of 0.465 square miles and a water area of 0.166 square miles. Located at 40.84° N. Lat; 73.71° W. Long. Elevation is 13 feet.
History: Incorporated 1930.
Population: 6,684; Growth (since 2000): 8.9%; Density: 14,379.1 persons per square mile; Race: 69.2% White, 0.9% Black/African American, 16.4%

Asian, 0.0% American Indian/Alaska Native, 0.3% Native Hawaiian/Other Pacific Islander, 1.5% Two or more races, 26.8% Hispanic of any race; Average household size: 2.78; Median age: 38.8; Age under 18: 21.9%; Age 65 and over: 11.4%; Males per 100 females: 96.9; Marriage status: 36.2% never married, 47.3% now married, 2.4% separated, 6.0% widowed, 10.5% divorced; Foreign born: 36.3%; Speak English only: 51.5%; With disability: 6.2%; Veterans: 2.9%; Ancestry: 13.8% Italian, 11.9% Irish, 8.4% American, 6.5% German, 3.7% Russian
Employment: 17.8% management, business, and financial, 8.4% computer, engineering, and science, 16.5% education, legal, community service, arts, and media, 7.2% healthcare practitioners, 13.6% service, 24.7% sales and office, 2.9% natural resources, construction, and maintenance, 8.8% production, transportation, and material moving
Income: Per capita: $39,267; Median household: $83,253; Average household: $107,139; Households with income of $100,000 or more: 37.9%; Poverty rate: 9.4%
Educational Attainment: High school diploma or higher: 92.7%; Bachelor's degree or higher: 48.6%; Graduate/professional degree or higher: 19.6%
Housing: Homeownership rate: 36.0%; Median home value: $514,600; Median year structure built: 1964; Homeowner vacancy rate: 4.2%; Median selected monthly owner costs: $2,745 with a mortgage, $967 without a mortgage; Median gross rent: $2,223 per month; Rental vacancy rate: 6.4%
Health Insurance: 83.3% have insurance; 69.7% have private insurance; 22.8% have public insurance; 16.7% do not have insurance; 3.6% of children under 18 do not have insurance
Transportation: Commute: 72.6% car, 20.7% public transportation, 1.6% walk, 3.5% work from home; Mean travel time to work: 44.6 minutes
Additional Information Contacts
Village of Manorhaven. . . . . (516) 883-7000
  http://www.manorhaven.org

MASSAPEQUA (CDP). Covers a land area of 3.558 square miles and a water area of 0.436 square miles. Located at 40.67° N. Lat; 73.47° W. Long. Elevation is 23 feet.
History: Named for the Massapequa Indians. It is chiefly residential. Pop. figure also includes Arlyn Oaks, Crown Village, and Nassau Shores.
Population: 22,128; Growth (since 2000): -2.3%; Density: 6,219.7 persons per square mile; Race: 95.7% White, 0.4% Black/African American, 2.7% Asian, 0.0% American Indian/Alaska Native, 0.0% Native Hawaiian/Other Pacific Islander, 0.9% Two or more races, 5.7% Hispanic of any race; Average household size: 3.13; Median age: 43.8; Age under 18: 22.8%; Age 65 and over: 16.1%; Males per 100 females: 95.3; Marriage status: 28.7% never married, 59.2% now married, 1.8% separated, 6.3% widowed, 5.7% divorced; Foreign born: 6.7%; Speak English only: 90.9%; With disability: 8.3%; Veterans: 6.8%; Ancestry: 43.9% Italian, 28.7% Irish, 17.0% German, 5.2% English, 5.0% Polish
Employment: 19.8% management, business, and financial, 4.3% computer, engineering, and science, 13.6% education, legal, community service, arts, and media, 4.1% healthcare practitioners, 15.1% service, 28.3% sales and office, 9.7% natural resources, construction, and maintenance, 5.2% production, transportation, and material moving
Income: Per capita: $46,767; Median household: $119,703; Average household: $142,563; Households with income of $100,000 or more: 58.0%; Poverty rate: 1.5%
Educational Attainment: High school diploma or higher: 95.9%; Bachelor's degree or higher: 41.5%; Graduate/professional degree or higher: 16.1%

School District(s)
Massapequa Union Free SD (KG-12)
   2014-15 Enrollment: 7,307 . . . . (516) 308-5000
Plainedge Union Free SD (KG-12)
   2014-15 Enrollment: 3,160 . . . . (516) 992-7455
Housing: Homeownership rate: 92.7%; Median home value: $485,500; Median year structure built: 1956; Homeowner vacancy rate: 2.3%; Median selected monthly owner costs: $3,166 with a mortgage, $1,423 without a mortgage; Median gross rent: $1,733 per month; Rental vacancy rate: 8.2%
Health Insurance: 97.4% have insurance; 87.5% have private insurance; 22.7% have public insurance; 2.6% do not have insurance; 0.5% of children under 18 do not have insurance
Transportation: Commute: 80.6% car, 14.7% public transportation, 0.8% walk, 3.1% work from home; Mean travel time to work: 36.4 minutes

MASSAPEQUA PARK (village).
Covers a land area of 2.210 square miles and a water area of 0.043 square miles. Located at 40.68° N. Lat; 73.45° W. Long. Elevation is 23 feet.

History: Named for the Masapequa Indians. Incorporated 1931.

Population: 17,175; Growth (since 2000): -1.9%; Density: 7,772.1 persons per square mile; Race: 97.0% White, 0.3% Black/African American, 1.2% Asian, 0.0% American Indian/Alaska Native, 0.0% Native Hawaiian/Other Pacific Islander, 1.2% Two or more races, 7.4% Hispanic of any race; Average household size: 3.09; Median age: 43.0; Age under 18: 23.3%; Age 65 and over: 16.2%; Males per 100 females: 94.1; Marriage status: 27.2% never married, 59.0% now married, 1.0% separated, 8.4% widowed, 5.4% divorced; Foreign born: 4.9%; Speak English only: 92.9%; With disability: 9.3%; Veterans: 7.5%; Ancestry: 43.1% Italian, 32.3% Irish, 17.7% German, 5.3% Polish, 4.1% English

Employment: 16.3% management, business, and financial, 3.7% computer, engineering, and science, 16.7% education, legal, community service, arts, and media, 7.0% healthcare practitioners, 15.3% service, 28.7% sales and office, 8.1% natural resources, construction, and maintenance, 4.3% production, transportation, and material moving

Income: Per capita: $40,530; Median household: $110,845; Average household: $122,755; Households with income of $100,000 or more: 54.8%; Poverty rate: 2.4%

Educational Attainment: High school diploma or higher: 96.8%; Bachelor's degree or higher: 39.0%; Graduate/professional degree or higher: 16.2%

School District(s)
Massapequa Union Free SD (KG-12)

   2014-15 Enrollment: 7,307 . . . . (516) 308-5000

Housing: Homeownership rate: 97.1%; Median home value: $444,700; Median year structure built: 1956; Homeowner vacancy rate: 0.4%; Median selected monthly owner costs: $2,943 with a mortgage, $1,166 without a mortgage; Median gross rent: $2,136 per month; Rental vacancy rate: 0.0%

Health Insurance: 96.4% have insurance; 88.7% have private insurance; 20.7% have public insurance; 3.6% do not have insurance; 1.1% of children under 18 do not have insurance

Newspapers: Massapequa Post (weekly circulation 4,500)

Transportation: Commute: 83.1% car, 12.5% public transportation, 1.0% walk, 2.7% work from home; Mean travel time to work: 36.9 minutes

Additional Information Contacts

Village of Massapequa Park . . . . (516) 798-0244
  http://www.masspk.com

MATINECOCK (village).
Covers a land area of 2.658 square miles and a water area of 0.005 square miles. Located at 40.86° N. Lat; 73.58° W. Long. Elevation is 95 feet.

Population: 813; Growth (since 2000): -2.8%; Density: 305.9 persons per square mile; Race: 92.4% White, 0.0% Black/African American, 6.8% Asian, 0.0% American Indian/Alaska Native, 0.0% Native Hawaiian/Other Pacific Islander, 0.9% Two or more races, 5.9% Hispanic of any race; Average household size: 3.09; Median age: 42.9; Age under 18: 22.3%; Age 65 and over: 19.2%; Males per 100 females: 101.0; Marriage status: 25.7% never married, 62.4% now married, 0.0% separated, 6.9% widowed, 5.1% divorced; Foreign born: 10.7%; Speak English only: 81.9%; With disability: 5.0%; Veterans: 8.4%; Ancestry: 17.8% Irish, 13.5% Italian, 13.4% English, 11.8% German, 7.9% European

Employment: 32.1% management, business, and financial, 3.0% computer, engineering, and science, 17.3% education, legal, community service, arts, and media, 2.7% healthcare practitioners, 16.7% service, 22.0% sales and office, 4.5% natural resources, construction, and maintenance, 1.8% production, transportation, and material moving

Income: Per capita: $103,252; Median household: $166,375; Average household: $310,145; Households with income of $100,000 or more: 64.6%; Poverty rate: 2.6%

Educational Attainment: High school diploma or higher: 97.9%; Bachelor's degree or higher: 75.9%; Graduate/professional degree or higher: 29.8%

Housing: Homeownership rate: 79.1%; Median home value: 2 million+; Median year structure built: 1956; Homeowner vacancy rate: 1.4%; Median selected monthly owner costs: $4,000+ with a mortgage, $1,500+ without a mortgage; Median gross rent: $1,656 per month; Rental vacancy rate: 0.0%

Health Insurance: 96.7% have insurance; 88.9% have private insurance; 20.9% have public insurance; 3.3% do not have insurance; 0.0% of children under 18 do not have insurance

Transportation: Commute: 56.7% car, 16.7% public transportation, 6.4% walk, 20.3% work from home; Mean travel time to work: 42.4 minutes

Additional Information Contacts

Village of Matinecock . . . . (516) 671-7790
  http://www.matinecockvillage.org

MERRICK (CDP).
Covers a land area of 4.019 square miles and a water area of 1.133 square miles. Located at 40.65° N. Lat; 73.55° W. Long. Elevation is 16 feet.

History: The name Merrick is taken from "Meroke", the name (meaning peaceful) of the Algonquin tribe formerly indigenous to the area. It is served by the Merrick station on the Long Island Rail Road.

Population: 20,572; Growth (since 2000): -9.6%; Density: 5,118.2 persons per square mile; Race: 92.6% White, 2.1% Black/African American, 3.0% Asian, 0.0% American Indian/Alaska Native, 0.0% Native Hawaiian/Other Pacific Islander, 0.7% Two or more races, 7.5% Hispanic of any race; Average household size: 2.97; Median age: 44.7; Age under 18: 23.0%; Age 65 and over: 14.3%; Males per 100 females: 93.3; Marriage status: 27.6% never married, 62.2% now married, 1.1% separated, 5.2% widowed, 5.0% divorced; Foreign born: 10.5%; Speak English only: 85.7%; With disability: 6.9%; Veterans: 4.6%; Ancestry: 20.1% Italian, 15.2% Irish, 9.2% German, 9.0% Russian, 7.8% Polish

Employment: 20.2% management, business, and financial, 4.5% computer, engineering, and science, 21.4% education, legal, community service, arts, and media, 6.9% healthcare practitioners, 9.2% service, 26.5% sales and office, 6.5% natural resources, construction, and maintenance, 4.9% production, transportation, and material moving

Income: Per capita: $54,831; Median household: $132,225; Average household: $160,729; Households with income of $100,000 or more: 66.1%; Poverty rate: 3.3%

Educational Attainment: High school diploma or higher: 96.8%; Bachelor's degree or higher: 57.9%; Graduate/professional degree or higher: 28.7%

School District(s)
Bellmore-Merrick Central High SD (07-12)

   2014-15 Enrollment: 5,605 . . . . (516) 992-1001

Merrick Union Free SD (KG-06)

   2014-15 Enrollment: 1,498 . . . . (516) 992-7240

North Merrick Union Free SD (KG-06)

   2014-15 Enrollment: 1,215 . . . . (516) 292-3694

Housing: Homeownership rate: 94.3%; Median home value: $527,200; Median year structure built: 1956; Homeowner vacancy rate: 0.2%; Median selected monthly owner costs: $3,430 with a mortgage, $1,500+ without a mortgage; Median gross rent: $2,113 per month; Rental vacancy rate: 13.8%

Health Insurance: 97.0% have insurance; 89.1% have private insurance; 19.6% have public insurance; 3.0% do not have insurance; 0.5% of children under 18 do not have insurance

Newspapers: L & M Publications (weekly circulation 14,000)

Transportation: Commute: 72.8% car, 20.4% public transportation, 0.7% walk, 4.0% work from home; Mean travel time to work: 38.7 minutes

MILL NECK (village).
Covers a land area of 2.609 square miles and a water area of 0.320 square miles. Located at 40.88° N. Lat; 73.56° W. Long. Elevation is 135 feet.

Population: 994; Growth (since 2000): 20.5%; Density: 381.0 persons per square mile; Race: 90.1% White, 2.7% Black/African American, 5.1% Asian, 0.0% American Indian/Alaska Native, 0.0% Native Hawaiian/Other Pacific Islander, 0.7% Two or more races, 6.2% Hispanic of any race; Average household size: 2.67; Median age: 50.9; Age under 18: 18.5%; Age 65 and over: 21.1%; Males per 100 females: 89.9; Marriage status: 27.4% never married, 62.8% now married, 0.7% separated, 5.6% widowed, 4.2% divorced; Foreign born: 12.0%; Speak English only: 83.0%; With disability: 6.4%; Veterans: 5.8%; Ancestry: 23.5% Italian, 19.0% German, 15.6% English, 15.0% Irish, 6.3% Polish

Employment: 31.5% management, business, and financial, 2.4% computer, engineering, and science, 14.4% education, legal, community service, arts, and media, 10.0% healthcare practitioners, 9.2% service, 26.3% sales and office, 4.2% natural resources, construction, and maintenance, 2.0% production, transportation, and material moving

Income: Per capita: $104,549; Median household: $140,000; Average household: $279,684; Households with income of $100,000 or more: 60.8%; Poverty rate: 3.6%

Educational Attainment: High school diploma or higher: 97.9%; Bachelor's degree or higher: 64.7%; Graduate/professional degree or higher: 29.3%

Housing: Homeownership rate: 86.3%; Median home value: $1,194,800; Median year structure built: 1954; Homeowner vacancy rate: 1.8%; Median selected monthly owner costs: $4,000+ with a mortgage, $1,500+ without a mortgage; Median gross rent: $1,813 per month; Rental vacancy rate: 10.5%

Health Insurance: 97.0% have insurance; 88.4% have private insurance; 25.4% have public insurance; 3.0% do not have insurance; 0.0% of children under 18 do not have insurance

Transportation: Commute: 79.9% car, 8.5% public transportation, 2.1% walk, 7.9% work from home; Mean travel time to work: 33.3 minutes

MINEOLA (village). County seat. Covers a land area of 1.880 square miles and a water area of 0 square miles. Located at 40.75° N. Lat; 73.64° W. Long. Elevation is 108 feet.

History: Named for the Algonquian translation of "pleasant village". Incorporated 1906.

Population: 18,980; Growth (since 2000): -1.3%; Density: 10,098.3 persons per square mile; Race: 76.1% White, 2.4% Black/African American, 11.2% Asian, 0.0% American Indian/Alaska Native, 0.0% Native Hawaiian/Other Pacific Islander, 1.0% Two or more races, 21.5% Hispanic of any race; Average household size: 2.66; Median age: 41.0; Age under 18: 20.4%; Age 65 and over: 15.9%; Males per 100 females: 96.2; Marriage status: 32.5% never married, 51.6% now married, 2.1% separated, 5.9% widowed, 10.1% divorced; Foreign born: 31.5%; Speak English only: 57.9%; With disability: 8.3%; Veterans: 4.6%; Ancestry: 19.2% Italian, 16.9% Irish, 11.7% German, 7.7% Portuguese, 3.5% Polish

Employment: 15.8% management, business, and financial, 2.7% computer, engineering, and science, 13.9% education, legal, community service, arts, and media, 10.6% healthcare practitioners, 19.3% service, 25.4% sales and office, 8.2% natural resources, construction, and maintenance, 4.0% production, transportation, and material moving

Income: Per capita: $40,189; Median household: $88,594; Average household: $103,634; Households with income of $100,000 or more: 43.3%; Poverty rate: 5.9%

Educational Attainment: High school diploma or higher: 87.5%; Bachelor's degree or higher: 40.6%; Graduate/professional degree or higher: 19.6%

School District(s)
Mineola Union Free SD (PK-12)
    2014-15 Enrollment: 2,784 . . . . (516) 237-2001

Four-year College(s)
New York College of Traditional Chinese Medicine (Private, Not-for-profit)
    Fall 2014 Enrollment: 155 . . . . (516) 739-1545

Housing: Homeownership rate: 65.3%; Median home value: $440,300; Median year structure built: 1953; Homeowner vacancy rate: 0.7%; Median selected monthly owner costs: $2,784 with a mortgage, $1,099 without a mortgage; Median gross rent: $1,524 per month; Rental vacancy rate: 3.8%

Health Insurance: 92.0% have insurance; 79.3% have private insurance; 23.8% have public insurance; 8.0% do not have insurance; 2.2% of children under 18 do not have insurance

Hospitals: Winthrop - University Hospital (591 beds)

Newspapers: Anton Newspapers (weekly circulation 52,000)

Transportation: Commute: 75.5% car, 14.3% public transportation, 7.8% walk, 1.8% work from home; Mean travel time to work: 30.5 minutes

Additional Information Contacts
Village of Mineola . . . . (516) 746-0750
    http://www.mineola-ny.gov

MUNSEY PARK (village). Covers a land area of 0.518 square miles and a water area of 0 square miles. Located at 40.80° N. Lat; 73.68° W. Long. Elevation is 161 feet.

Population: 2,715; Growth (since 2000): 3.2%; Density: 5,238.3 persons per square mile; Race: 93.4% White, 0.0% Black/African American, 4.9% Asian, 0.0% American Indian/Alaska Native, 0.0% Native Hawaiian/Other Pacific Islander, 1.6% Two or more races, 4.8% Hispanic of any race; Average household size: 3.39; Median age: 40.9; Age under 18: 30.7%; Age 65 and over: 15.7%; Males per 100 females: 102.0; Marriage status: 27.0% never married, 66.7% now married, 0.9% separated, 2.7% widowed, 3.6% divorced; Foreign born: 12.0%; Speak English only: 82.0%; With disability: 4.6%; Veterans: 5.0%; Ancestry: 28.2% Italian, 23.8% Irish, 12.9% German, 8.2% Greek, 4.7% English

Employment: 33.6% management, business, and financial, 6.4% computer, engineering, and science, 17.8% education, legal, community service, arts, and media, 8.3% healthcare practitioners, 2.9% service, 25.8% sales and office, 2.9% natural resources, construction, and maintenance, 2.3% production, transportation, and material moving

Income: Per capita: $86,287; Median household: $209,063; Average household: $289,988; Households with income of $100,000 or more: 75.7%; Poverty rate: 2.6%

Educational Attainment: High school diploma or higher: 98.0%; Bachelor's degree or higher: 81.5%; Graduate/professional degree or higher: 39.9%

Housing: Homeownership rate: 100.0%; Median home value: $1,241,000; Median year structure built: 1942; Homeowner vacancy rate: 0.6%; Median selected monthly owner costs: $4,000+ with a mortgage, $1,500+ without a mortgage; Median gross rent: n/a per month; Rental vacancy rate: 0.0%

Health Insurance: 98.5% have insurance; 91.7% have private insurance; 16.4% have public insurance; 1.5% do not have insurance; 0.7% of children under 18 do not have insurance

Transportation: Commute: 47.4% car, 48.0% public transportation, 0.0% walk, 4.7% work from home; Mean travel time to work: 44.9 minutes

MUTTONTOWN (village). Covers a land area of 6.063 square miles and a water area of 0 square miles. Located at 40.83° N. Lat; 73.54° W. Long. Elevation is 292 feet.

History: During colonial times the area was used to raise sheep for wool and meat, thus giving the town its name "mutton". The village was incorporated in 1931.

Population: 3,626; Growth (since 2000): 6.3%; Density: 598.1 persons per square mile; Race: 69.7% White, 7.2% Black/African American, 22.3% Asian, 0.0% American Indian/Alaska Native, 0.0% Native Hawaiian/Other Pacific Islander, 0.6% Two or more races, 4.4% Hispanic of any race; Average household size: 3.15; Median age: 48.8; Age under 18: 21.7%; Age 65 and over: 17.0%; Males per 100 females: 99.8; Marriage status: 26.7% never married, 64.6% now married, 0.4% separated, 5.9% widowed, 2.8% divorced; Foreign born: 23.7%; Speak English only: 67.3%; With disability: 6.3%; Veterans: 3.1%; Ancestry: 12.7% Italian, 8.2% Russian, 7.6% American, 7.4% Polish, 6.1% Irish

Employment: 22.2% management, business, and financial, 3.8% computer, engineering, and science, 17.9% education, legal, community service, arts, and media, 18.2% healthcare practitioners, 7.1% service, 24.9% sales and office, 3.8% natural resources, construction, and maintenance, 2.1% production, transportation, and material moving

Income: Per capita: $111,339; Median household: $230,179; Average household: $345,142; Households with income of $100,000 or more: 82.6%; Poverty rate: 3.4%

Educational Attainment: High school diploma or higher: 94.7%; Bachelor's degree or higher: 69.8%; Graduate/professional degree or higher: 39.7%

Housing: Homeownership rate: 96.2%; Median home value: $1,561,700; Median year structure built: 1970; Homeowner vacancy rate: 1.4%; Median selected monthly owner costs: $4,000+ with a mortgage, $1,500+ without a mortgage; Median gross rent: $2,660 per month; Rental vacancy rate: 24.1%

Health Insurance: 96.7% have insurance; 87.8% have private insurance; 18.9% have public insurance; 3.3% do not have insurance; 1.5% of children under 18 do not have insurance

Transportation: Commute: 74.5% car, 16.8% public transportation, 0.7% walk, 7.3% work from home; Mean travel time to work: 39.0 minutes

NEW CASSEL (CDP). Covers a land area of 1.479 square miles and a water area of 0 square miles. Located at 40.76° N. Lat; 73.56° W. Long. Elevation is 121 feet.

Population: 13,903; Growth (since 2000): 4.5%; Density: 9,399.4 persons per square mile; Race: 22.0% White, 38.8% Black/African American, 1.2% Asian, 0.2% American Indian/Alaska Native, 0.1% Native Hawaiian/Other Pacific Islander, 7.1% Two or more races, 48.8% Hispanic of any race; Average household size: 4.37; Median age: 32.0; Age under 18: 28.8%; Age 65 and over: 9.8%; Males per 100 females: 103.5; Marriage status: 49.4% never married, 41.0% now married, 3.3% separated, 5.0% widowed, 4.6% divorced; Foreign born: 43.5%; Speak English only: 36.7%; With disability: 4.6%; Veterans: 2.4%; Ancestry: 11.8% Haitian, 2.9% Italian, 2.8% American, 1.4% Jamaican, 1.3% Irish

Employment: 7.8% management, business, and financial, 2.1% computer, engineering, and science, 8.3% education, legal, community service, arts, and media, 2.7% healthcare practitioners, 27.3% service, 24.0% sales and

office, 9.2% natural resources, construction, and maintenance, 18.6% production, transportation, and material moving

Income: Per capita: $21,646; Median household: $73,702; Average household: $87,946; Households with income of $100,000 or more: 35.1%; Poverty rate: 13.2%

Educational Attainment: High school diploma or higher: 70.0%; Bachelor's degree or higher: 17.4%; Graduate/professional degree or higher: 6.5%

Housing: Homeownership rate: 62.5%; Median home value: $320,400; Median year structure built: 1959; Homeowner vacancy rate: 0.2%; Median selected monthly owner costs: $2,791 with a mortgage, $1,018 without a mortgage; Median gross rent: $1,222 per month; Rental vacancy rate: 3.2%

Health Insurance: 75.6% have insurance; 59.0% have private insurance; 23.4% have public insurance; 24.4% do not have insurance; 14.7% of children under 18 do not have insurance

Transportation: Commute: 86.5% car, 7.4% public transportation, 3.1% walk, 0.4% work from home; Mean travel time to work: 24.8 minutes

NEW HYDE PARK (village). Covers a land area of 0.860 square miles and a water area of 0 square miles. Located at 40.73° N. Lat; 73.69° W. Long. Elevation is 105 feet.

History: Incorporated 1927.

Population: 9,788; Growth (since 2000): 2.8%; Density: 11,386.6 persons per square mile; Race: 60.3% White, 0.9% Black/African American, 31.6% Asian, 0.0% American Indian/Alaska Native, 0.0% Native Hawaiian/Other Pacific Islander, 2.3% Two or more races, 14.6% Hispanic of any race; Average household size: 3.32; Median age: 41.1; Age under 18: 20.5%; Age 65 and over: 15.0%; Males per 100 females: 94.0; Marriage status: 28.5% never married, 59.1% now married, 1.9% separated, 7.1% widowed, 5.2% divorced; Foreign born: 34.1%; Speak English only: 57.6%; With disability: 10.4%; Veterans: 4.6%; Ancestry: 25.1% Italian, 17.1% Irish, 9.8% German, 3.9% Polish, 3.7% American

Employment: 13.0% management, business, and financial, 6.6% computer, engineering, and science, 10.7% education, legal, community service, arts, and media, 12.1% healthcare practitioners, 21.0% service, 22.5% sales and office, 7.7% natural resources, construction, and maintenance, 6.5% production, transportation, and material moving

Income: Per capita: $34,701; Median household: $103,811; Average household: $112,589; Households with income of $100,000 or more: 53.3%; Poverty rate: 3.7%

Educational Attainment: High school diploma or higher: 89.3%; Bachelor's degree or higher: 36.7%; Graduate/professional degree or higher: 14.4%

School District(s)
Great Neck Union Free SD (PK-12)
    2014-15 Enrollment: 6,654 . . . . (516) 441-4001
Herricks Union Free SD (KG-12)
    2014-15 Enrollment: 3,923 . . . . (516) 305-8901
New Hyde Park-Garden City Park Union Free SD (KG-06)
    2014-15 Enrollment: 1,669 . . . . (516) 434-2305
Sewanhaka Central High SD (07-12)
    2014-15 Enrollment: 8,160 . . . . (516) 488-9800

Housing: Homeownership rate: 83.7%; Median home value: $486,000; Median year structure built: 1952; Homeowner vacancy rate: 0.0%; Median selected monthly owner costs: $3,115 with a mortgage, $1,214 without a mortgage; Median gross rent: $1,378 per month; Rental vacancy rate: 0.0%

Health Insurance: 93.1% have insurance; 77.6% have private insurance; 25.5% have public insurance; 6.9% do not have insurance; 3.1% of children under 18 do not have insurance

Hospitals: Long Island Jewish Medical Center (452 beds)

Transportation: Commute: 75.1% car, 20.8% public transportation, 1.7% walk, 1.8% work from home; Mean travel time to work: 36.2 minutes

Additional Information Contacts
Village of New Hyde Park . . . . (516) 354-0022
    http://www.vnhp.org

NORTH BELLMORE (CDP). Covers a land area of 2.620 square miles and a water area of 0 square miles. Located at 40.69° N. Lat; 73.54° W. Long. Elevation is 46 feet.

History: Bellmore, Long Island, serves as a suburb of New York City, a 45-minute train ride. John F. Kennedy Int'l Airport is located within 15 miles (24 km) of Bellmore.

Population: 20,153; Growth (since 2000): 0.4%; Density: 7,691.3 persons per square mile; Race: 87.2% White, 1.0% Black/African American, 6.5% Asian, 0.8% American Indian/Alaska Native, 0.0% Native Hawaiian/Other Pacific Islander, 1.1% Two or more races, 8.1% Hispanic of any race; Average household size: 3.09; Median age: 43.1; Age under 18: 22.7%; Age 65 and over: 14.9%; Males per 100 females: 93.8; Marriage status: 27.4% never married, 59.3% now married, 0.9% separated, 7.1% widowed, 6.3% divorced; Foreign born: 11.1%; Speak English only: 84.3%; With disability: 7.8%; Veterans: 5.8%; Ancestry: 26.9% Italian, 17.2% Irish, 14.1% German, 6.4% Polish, 6.0% Russian

Employment: 17.7% management, business, and financial, 4.9% computer, engineering, and science, 17.7% education, legal, community service, arts, and media, 7.7% healthcare practitioners, 11.9% service, 26.9% sales and office, 6.4% natural resources, construction, and maintenance, 6.8% production, transportation, and material moving

Income: Per capita: $39,318; Median household: $104,806; Average household: $119,201; Households with income of $100,000 or more: 54.9%; Poverty rate: 4.3%

Educational Attainment: High school diploma or higher: 95.1%; Bachelor's degree or higher: 44.7%; Graduate/professional degree or higher: 20.1%

School District(s)
North Bellmore Union Free SD (KG-06)
    2014-15 Enrollment: 2,140 . . . . (516) 992-3000

Housing: Homeownership rate: 89.4%; Median home value: $433,800; Median year structure built: 1956; Homeowner vacancy rate: 0.5%; Median selected monthly owner costs: $2,907 with a mortgage, $1,319 without a mortgage; Median gross rent: $1,691 per month; Rental vacancy rate: 4.8%

Health Insurance: 94.0% have insurance; 86.3% have private insurance; 21.5% have public insurance; 6.0% do not have insurance; 4.2% of children under 18 do not have insurance

Transportation: Commute: 82.4% car, 11.5% public transportation, 1.2% walk, 4.0% work from home; Mean travel time to work: 33.7 minutes

NORTH HEMPSTEAD (town). Covers a land area of 53.512 square miles and a water area of 15.598 square miles. Located at 40.80° N. Lat; 73.68° W. Long. Elevation is 102 feet.

History: First settled around 1643 as part of the town of Hempstead. Following the Revolutionary War, the Town of North Hempstead was split off in 1784.

Population: 229,105; Growth (since 2000): 2.9%; Density: 4,281.4 persons per square mile; Race: 68.9% White, 5.7% Black/African American, 16.6% Asian, 0.2% American Indian/Alaska Native, 0.1% Native Hawaiian/Other Pacific Islander, 2.7% Two or more races, 13.7% Hispanic of any race; Average household size: 2.96; Median age: 42.5; Age under 18: 23.3%; Age 65 and over: 18.2%; Males per 100 females: 94.5; Marriage status: 28.7% never married, 58.1% now married, 1.4% separated, 6.9% widowed, 6.4% divorced; Foreign born: 29.0%; Speak English only: 61.7%; With disability: 7.9%; Veterans: 4.5%; Ancestry: 14.7% Italian, 10.3% Irish, 7.1% German, 6.7% American, 5.3% Polish

Employment: 19.7% management, business, and financial, 5.3% computer, engineering, and science, 15.1% education, legal, community service, arts, and media, 11.0% healthcare practitioners, 12.9% service, 25.4% sales and office, 4.9% natural resources, construction, and maintenance, 5.7% production, transportation, and material moving

Income: Per capita: $51,999; Median household: $104,698; Average household: $152,374; Households with income of $100,000 or more: 52.5%; Poverty rate: 5.2%

Educational Attainment: High school diploma or higher: 90.7%; Bachelor's degree or higher: 53.1%; Graduate/professional degree or higher: 25.6%

Housing: Homeownership rate: 78.3%; Median home value: $623,400; Median year structure built: 1954; Homeowner vacancy rate: 1.1%; Median selected monthly owner costs: $3,445 with a mortgage, $1,434 without a mortgage; Median gross rent: $1,692 per month; Rental vacancy rate: 5.1%

Health Insurance: 92.5% have insurance; 81.1% have private insurance; 24.5% have public insurance; 7.5% do not have insurance; 3.9% of children under 18 do not have insurance

Transportation: Commute: 71.9% car, 19.2% public transportation, 3.3% walk, 4.6% work from home; Mean travel time to work: 34.8 minutes

Additional Information Contacts
Town of North Hempstead . . . . (516) 869-7646
    http://www.northhempsteadny.gov

NORTH HILLS (village). Covers a land area of 2.759 square miles and a water area of 0 square miles. Located at 40.78° N. Lat; 73.68° W. Long. Elevation is 213 feet.

Population: 5,190; Growth (since 2000): 20.7%; Density: 1,881.0 persons per square mile; Race: 73.7% White, 0.5% Black/African American, 24.8% Asian, 0.0% American Indian/Alaska Native, 0.0% Native Hawaiian/Other Pacific Islander, 1.0% Two or more races, 0.0% Hispanic of any race; Average household size: 2.15; Median age: 61.4; Age under 18: 13.4%; Age 65 and over: 41.8%; Males per 100 females: 87.6; Marriage status: 12.1% never married, 69.9% now married, 0.0% separated, 9.2% widowed, 8.8% divorced; Foreign born: 25.0%; Speak English only: 74.4%; With disability: 12.5%; Veterans: 10.1%; Ancestry: 19.0% American, 12.1% Polish, 9.8% Russian, 9.1% Italian, 3.7% German
Employment: 31.6% management, business, and financial, 2.2% computer, engineering, and science, 14.3% education, legal, community service, arts, and media, 18.9% healthcare practitioners, 5.9% service, 24.8% sales and office, 1.6% natural resources, construction, and maintenance, 0.7% production, transportation, and material moving
Income: Per capita: $86,651; Median household: $114,716; Average household: $186,404; Households with income of $100,000 or more: 55.5%; Poverty rate: 1.5%
Educational Attainment: High school diploma or higher: 98.7%; Bachelor's degree or higher: 65.7%; Graduate/professional degree or higher: 33.9%
Housing: Homeownership rate: 90.3%; Median home value: $924,500; Median year structure built: 1986; Homeowner vacancy rate: 0.0%; Median selected monthly owner costs: $4,000+ with a mortgage, $1,500+ without a mortgage; Median gross rent: $1,548 per month; Rental vacancy rate: 0.0%
Health Insurance: 98.5% have insurance; 84.5% have private insurance; 42.1% have public insurance; 1.5% do not have insurance; 0.0% of children under 18 do not have insurance
Transportation: Commute: 80.3% car, 10.0% public transportation, 0.3% walk, 9.4% work from home; Mean travel time to work: 31.6 minutes
Additional Information Contacts
Village of North Hills . . . . (516) 627-4832
    http://www.villagenorthhills.com

NORTH LYNBROOK (CDP). Covers a land area of 0.087 square miles and a water area of 0 square miles. Located at 40.67° N. Lat; 73.67° W. Long. Elevation is 10 feet.

Population: 496; Growth (since 2000): -33.2%; Density: 5,732.4 persons per square mile; Race: 75.0% White, 0.0% Black/African American, 11.7% Asian, 0.0% American Indian/Alaska Native, 0.0% Native Hawaiian/Other Pacific Islander, 10.5% Two or more races, 18.1% Hispanic of any race; Average household size: 3.14; Median age: 46.2; Age under 18: 15.7%; Age 65 and over: 19.6%; Males per 100 females: 91.5; Marriage status: 33.7% never married, 48.6% now married, 0.0% separated, 16.0% widowed, 1.7% divorced; Foreign born: 26.4%; Speak English only: 79.7%; With disability: 6.8%; Veterans: 0.0%; Ancestry: 37.1% Italian, 31.5% German, 10.9% Irish, 6.3% Croatian, 3.8% Norwegian
Employment: 11.3% management, business, and financial, 0.0% computer, engineering, and science, 23.4% education, legal, community service, arts, and media, 4.0% healthcare practitioners, 17.7% service, 25.4% sales and office, 15.7% natural resources, construction, and maintenance, 2.4% production, transportation, and material moving
Income: Per capita: $39,503; Median household: $101,094; Average household: $123,595; Households with income of $100,000 or more: 52.3%; Poverty rate: 4.0%
Educational Attainment: High school diploma or higher: 85.1%; Bachelor's degree or higher: 30.9%; Graduate/professional degree or higher: 19.6%
Housing: Homeownership rate: 89.4%; Median home value: $406,400; Median year structure built: 1941; Homeowner vacancy rate: 0.0%; Median selected monthly owner costs: $2,450 with a mortgage, $1,418 without a mortgage; Median gross rent: n/a per month; Rental vacancy rate: 0.0%
Health Insurance: 93.7% have insurance; 86.1% have private insurance; 24.5% have public insurance; 6.3% do not have insurance; 0.0% of children under 18 do not have insurance
Transportation: Commute: 91.1% car, 3.6% public transportation, 0.0% walk, 5.2% work from home; Mean travel time to work: 46.9 minutes

NORTH MASSAPEQUA (CDP). Covers a land area of 2.995 square miles and a water area of 0.005 square miles. Located at 40.70° N. Lat; 73.47° W. Long. Elevation is 49 feet.

History: North Massapequa is a hamlet and census-designated place (CDP) located within the Town of Oyster Bay in Nassau County, New York.
Population: 18,749; Growth (since 2000): -2.1%; Density: 6,259.5 persons per square mile; Race: 95.9% White, 1.2% Black/African American, 2.1% Asian, 0.0% American Indian/Alaska Native, 0.0% Native Hawaiian/Other Pacific Islander, 0.5% Two or more races, 5.6% Hispanic of any race; Average household size: 3.02; Median age: 42.3; Age under 18: 22.7%; Age 65 and over: 16.4%; Males per 100 females: 93.1; Marriage status: 26.9% never married, 59.3% now married, 1.2% separated, 7.7% widowed, 6.0% divorced; Foreign born: 5.5%; Speak English only: 90.5%; With disability: 9.5%; Veterans: 6.8%; Ancestry: 47.5% Italian, 23.9% Irish, 16.3% German, 5.3% Polish, 3.4% Russian
Employment: 15.3% management, business, and financial, 3.6% computer, engineering, and science, 16.4% education, legal, community service, arts, and media, 4.7% healthcare practitioners, 15.4% service, 29.9% sales and office, 7.3% natural resources, construction, and maintenance, 7.4% production, transportation, and material moving
Income: Per capita: $39,241; Median household: $102,292; Average household: $115,452; Households with income of $100,000 or more: 51.2%; Poverty rate: 4.9%
Educational Attainment: High school diploma or higher: 94.5%; Bachelor's degree or higher: 33.0%; Graduate/professional degree or higher: 14.4%

School District(s)
Farmingdale Union Free SD (KG-12)
    2014-15 Enrollment: 5,918 . . . . (516) 752-6510
Plainedge Union Free SD (KG-12)
    2014-15 Enrollment: 3,160 . . . . (516) 992-7455
Housing: Homeownership rate: 92.7%; Median home value: $417,400; Median year structure built: 1956; Homeowner vacancy rate: 0.7%; Median selected monthly owner costs: $2,985 with a mortgage, $1,257 without a mortgage; Median gross rent: $1,688 per month; Rental vacancy rate: 0.0%
Health Insurance: 97.1% have insurance; 86.9% have private insurance; 23.2% have public insurance; 2.9% do not have insurance; 0.4% of children under 18 do not have insurance
Transportation: Commute: 84.4% car, 12.0% public transportation, 0.6% walk, 2.7% work from home; Mean travel time to work: 34.6 minutes

NORTH MERRICK (CDP). Covers a land area of 1.719 square miles and a water area of 0.007 square miles. Located at 40.69° N. Lat; 73.56° W. Long. Elevation is 46 feet.

History: North Merrick is located on the south shore of Long Island.
Population: 12,077; Growth (since 2000): 2.0%; Density: 7,026.2 persons per square mile; Race: 90.1% White, 1.1% Black/African American, 5.4% Asian, 0.0% American Indian/Alaska Native, 0.0% Native Hawaiian/Other Pacific Islander, 1.3% Two or more races, 7.6% Hispanic of any race; Average household size: 3.16; Median age: 41.6; Age under 18: 23.5%; Age 65 and over: 14.2%; Males per 100 females: 95.6; Marriage status: 29.2% never married, 59.2% now married, 1.0% separated, 4.9% widowed, 6.7% divorced; Foreign born: 8.5%; Speak English only: 87.0%; With disability: 6.5%; Veterans: 6.6%; Ancestry: 31.4% Italian, 28.9% Irish, 14.8% German, 5.1% Polish, 4.9% English
Employment: 17.2% management, business, and financial, 3.3% computer, engineering, and science, 17.0% education, legal, community service, arts, and media, 6.1% healthcare practitioners, 11.8% service, 29.2% sales and office, 8.3% natural resources, construction, and maintenance, 7.2% production, transportation, and material moving
Income: Per capita: $42,505; Median household: $117,150; Average household: $131,208; Households with income of $100,000 or more: 58.6%; Poverty rate: 2.4%
Educational Attainment: High school diploma or higher: 95.3%; Bachelor's degree or higher: 43.9%; Graduate/professional degree or higher: 18.7%

School District(s)
North Bellmore Union Free SD (KG-06)
    2014-15 Enrollment: 2,140 . . . . (516) 992-3000
North Merrick Union Free SD (KG-06)
    2014-15 Enrollment: 1,215 . . . . (516) 292-3694
Housing: Homeownership rate: 95.1%; Median home value: $454,300; Median year structure built: 1954; Homeowner vacancy rate: 2.1%; Median selected monthly owner costs: $3,067 with a mortgage, $1,276 without a

mortgage; Median gross rent: $2,123 per month; Rental vacancy rate: 0.0%
Health Insurance: 95.7% have insurance; 90.4% have private insurance; 18.3% have public insurance; 4.3% do not have insurance; 3.4% of children under 18 do not have insurance
Transportation: Commute: 82.2% car, 13.9% public transportation, 0.7% walk, 2.8% work from home; Mean travel time to work: 32.2 minutes

NORTH NEW HYDE PARK (CDP).
Covers a land area of 1.973 square miles and a water area of 0.022 square miles. Located at 40.75° N. Lat; 73.69° W. Long. Elevation is 115 feet.
History: North New Hyde Park is a census-designated place (CDP) in Nassau County, New York.
Population: 15,177; Growth (since 2000): 4.4%; Density: 7,693.7 persons per square mile; Race: 60.6% White, 1.7% Black/African American, 32.6% Asian, 0.4% American Indian/Alaska Native, 0.0% Native Hawaiian/Other Pacific Islander, 3.0% Two or more races, 8.5% Hispanic of any race; Average household size: 3.24; Median age: 43.9; Age under 18: 21.4%; Age 65 and over: 19.4%; Males per 100 females: 93.2; Marriage status: 28.2% never married, 61.3% now married, 1.2% separated, 7.2% widowed, 3.4% divorced; Foreign born: 29.1%; Speak English only: 56.0%; With disability: 8.4%; Veterans: 5.1%; Ancestry: 23.7% Italian, 13.5% Irish, 8.0% German, 4.0% American, 4.0% Polish
Employment: 19.0% management, business, and financial, 5.1% computer, engineering, and science, 10.3% education, legal, community service, arts, and media, 14.3% healthcare practitioners, 11.5% service, 26.8% sales and office, 7.2% natural resources, construction, and maintenance, 5.7% production, transportation, and material moving
Income: Per capita: $41,027; Median household: $109,264; Average household: $129,520; Households with income of $100,000 or more: 58.1%; Poverty rate: 3.8%
Educational Attainment: High school diploma or higher: 91.7%; Bachelor's degree or higher: 45.7%; Graduate/professional degree or higher: 20.1%
Housing: Homeownership rate: 96.0%; Median home value: $517,300; Median year structure built: 1948; Homeowner vacancy rate: 0.9%; Median selected monthly owner costs: $3,116 with a mortgage, $1,133 without a mortgage; Median gross rent: $2,013 per month; Rental vacancy rate: 0.0%
Health Insurance: 95.8% have insurance; 83.9% have private insurance; 26.3% have public insurance; 4.2% do not have insurance; 2.3% of children under 18 do not have insurance
Transportation: Commute: 79.1% car, 16.4% public transportation, 1.7% walk, 1.3% work from home; Mean travel time to work: 35.6 minutes

NORTH VALLEY STREAM (CDP).
Covers a land area of 1.864 square miles and a water area of 0.033 square miles. Located at 40.68° N. Lat; 73.71° W. Long. Elevation is 39 feet.
History: North Valley Stream is a census-designated place (CDP) in the village of Valley Stream in Nassau County, New York.
Population: 17,845; Growth (since 2000): 13.0%; Density: 9,571.4 persons per square mile; Race: 25.2% White, 54.9% Black/African American, 12.0% Asian, 0.0% American Indian/Alaska Native, 0.2% Native Hawaiian/Other Pacific Islander, 1.6% Two or more races, 12.1% Hispanic of any race; Average household size: 3.43; Median age: 41.2; Age under 18: 20.8%; Age 65 and over: 14.5%; Males per 100 females: 87.6; Marriage status: 36.7% never married, 48.7% now married, 3.1% separated, 6.4% widowed, 8.1% divorced; Foreign born: 38.0%; Speak English only: 68.7%; With disability: 8.6%; Veterans: 4.6%; Ancestry: 13.5% Haitian, 9.8% Jamaican, 9.8% Italian, 4.0% American, 3.8% Irish
Employment: 14.5% management, business, and financial, 6.5% computer, engineering, and science, 13.3% education, legal, community service, arts, and media, 11.7% healthcare practitioners, 17.7% service, 23.4% sales and office, 4.1% natural resources, construction, and maintenance, 8.8% production, transportation, and material moving
Income: Per capita: $33,970; Median household: $97,868; Average household: $109,738; Households with income of $100,000 or more: 49.1%; Poverty rate: 4.4%
Educational Attainment: High school diploma or higher: 90.7%; Bachelor's degree or higher: 36.7%; Graduate/professional degree or higher: 15.8%
Housing: Homeownership rate: 90.1%; Median home value: $375,000; Median year structure built: 1952; Homeowner vacancy rate: 1.9%; Median selected monthly owner costs: $2,860 with a mortgage, $1,046 without a

mortgage; Median gross rent: $1,921 per month; Rental vacancy rate: 0.0%
Health Insurance: 92.5% have insurance; 77.0% have private insurance; 25.5% have public insurance; 7.5% do not have insurance; 1.2% of children under 18 do not have insurance
Transportation: Commute: 74.5% car, 20.6% public transportation, 1.1% walk, 2.7% work from home; Mean travel time to work: 40.0 minutes

NORTH WANTAGH (CDP).
Covers a land area of 1.902 square miles and a water area of 0.009 square miles. Located at 40.69° N. Lat; 73.52° W. Long. Elevation is 36 feet.
Population: 11,713; Growth (since 2000): -3.6%; Density: 6,157.6 persons per square mile; Race: 94.2% White, 0.4% Black/African American, 2.1% Asian, 0.0% American Indian/Alaska Native, 0.0% Native Hawaiian/Other Pacific Islander, 1.6% Two or more races, 7.2% Hispanic of any race; Average household size: 2.86; Median age: 45.3; Age under 18: 21.3%; Age 65 and over: 20.3%; Males per 100 females: 91.5; Marriage status: 24.8% never married, 56.6% now married, 1.5% separated, 10.6% widowed, 8.0% divorced; Foreign born: 6.6%; Speak English only: 91.3%; With disability: 10.2%; Veterans: 7.0%; Ancestry: 31.4% Italian, 26.2% Irish, 16.6% German, 6.5% American, 6.5% Polish
Employment: 15.2% management, business, and financial, 4.5% computer, engineering, and science, 17.1% education, legal, community service, arts, and media, 6.4% healthcare practitioners, 18.5% service, 25.4% sales and office, 6.0% natural resources, construction, and maintenance, 6.8% production, transportation, and material moving
Income: Per capita: $40,957; Median household: $95,909; Average household: $114,283; Households with income of $100,000 or more: 48.2%; Poverty rate: 2.4%
Educational Attainment: High school diploma or higher: 93.5%; Bachelor's degree or higher: 38.5%; Graduate/professional degree or higher: 17.3%
Housing: Homeownership rate: 93.5%; Median home value: $390,400; Median year structure built: 1955; Homeowner vacancy rate: 0.0%; Median selected monthly owner costs: $3,001 with a mortgage, $1,292 without a mortgage; Median gross rent: $640 per month; Rental vacancy rate: 0.0%
Health Insurance: 97.4% have insurance; 88.6% have private insurance; 25.6% have public insurance; 2.6% do not have insurance; 0.2% of children under 18 do not have insurance
Transportation: Commute: 85.3% car, 10.2% public transportation, 0.7% walk, 3.1% work from home; Mean travel time to work: 32.8 minutes

OCEANSIDE (CDP).
Covers a land area of 4.944 square miles and a water area of 0.473 square miles. Located at 40.63° N. Lat; 73.64° W. Long. Elevation is 13 feet.
History: Originally known as South Bay, the English government first call it Christian Hook in 1674 due to predominant religious affiliation of its colonists. Land development proceeded rapidly, and oyster sales dominated the economy.
Population: 30,371; Growth (since 2000): -7.2%; Density: 6,143.4 persons per square mile; Race: 92.3% White, 0.7% Black/African American, 2.8% Asian, 0.4% American Indian/Alaska Native, 0.0% Native Hawaiian/Other Pacific Islander, 1.3% Two or more races, 9.8% Hispanic of any race; Average household size: 2.81; Median age: 44.3; Age under 18: 19.7%; Age 65 and over: 16.9%; Males per 100 females: 92.8; Marriage status: 29.6% never married, 58.7% now married, 1.1% separated, 6.6% widowed, 5.1% divorced; Foreign born: 11.9%; Speak English only: 83.7%; With disability: 8.8%; Veterans: 5.5%; Ancestry: 29.1% Italian, 18.7% Irish, 9.5% German, 6.2% Russian, 6.1% American
Employment: 17.2% management, business, and financial, 4.2% computer, engineering, and science, 17.5% education, legal, community service, arts, and media, 4.8% healthcare practitioners, 15.2% service, 29.3% sales and office, 4.9% natural resources, construction, and maintenance, 7.0% production, transportation, and material moving
Income: Per capita: $41,111; Median household: $95,690; Average household: $113,279; Households with income of $100,000 or more: 47.9%; Poverty rate: 5.5%
Educational Attainment: High school diploma or higher: 94.3%; Bachelor's degree or higher: 44.2%; Graduate/professional degree or higher: 19.8%

School District(s)
Oceanside Union Free SD (KG-12)
    2014-15 Enrollment: 5,652 . . . . (516) 678-1215
Housing: Homeownership rate: 87.7%; Median home value: $441,000; Median year structure built: 1955; Homeowner vacancy rate: 0.9%; Median

selected monthly owner costs: $2,996 with a mortgage, $1,248 without a mortgage; Median gross rent: $1,256 per month; Rental vacancy rate: 4.3%
Health Insurance: 95.7% have insurance; 85.5% have private insurance; 22.9% have public insurance; 4.3% do not have insurance; 1.2% of children under 18 do not have insurance
Hospitals: South Nassau Communities Hospital (435 beds)
Transportation: Commute: 80.0% car, 13.1% public transportation, 1.3% walk, 5.1% work from home; Mean travel time to work: 34.0 minutes

OLD BETHPAGE (CDP).
Covers a land area of 4.182 square miles and a water area of 0.003 square miles. Located at 40.75° N. Lat; 73.46° W. Long. Elevation is 174 feet.
History: In 1695, Thomas Powell bought about 10,000 acres (40 sq. km.) from local Indian tribes, including the Marsapeque, Matinecoc, and Sacatogue, for 140 English pounds. Powell called his land Bethphage, because it was situated between two other places on Long Island, Jericho and Jerusalem, just as the biblical town of Bethphage (meaning "house of figs") was situated between Jericho and Jerusalem in Israel.
Population: 5,252; Growth (since 2000): -2.7%; Density: 1,255.8 persons per square mile; Race: 93.4% White, 0.1% Black/African American, 5.4% Asian, 0.0% American Indian/Alaska Native, 0.0% Native Hawaiian/Other Pacific Islander, 1.0% Two or more races, 2.1% Hispanic of any race; Average household size: 2.89; Median age: 44.0; Age under 18: 22.6%; Age 65 and over: 17.8%; Males per 100 females: 93.2; Marriage status: 25.5% never married, 63.7% now married, 0.4% separated, 6.4% widowed, 4.3% divorced; Foreign born: 8.3%; Speak English only: 92.1%; With disability: 10.6%; Veterans: 5.0%; Ancestry: 26.2% Italian, 18.4% Irish, 12.6% Russian, 12.4% German, 6.0% Polish
Employment: 25.9% management, business, and financial, 5.2% computer, engineering, and science, 23.6% education, legal, community service, arts, and media, 7.2% healthcare practitioners, 7.5% service, 25.2% sales and office, 2.5% natural resources, construction, and maintenance, 2.9% production, transportation, and material moving
Income: Per capita: $50,304; Median household: $117,600; Average household: $143,122; Households with income of $100,000 or more: 57.3%; Poverty rate: 2.8%
Educational Attainment: High school diploma or higher: 96.2%; Bachelor's degree or higher: 59.6%; Graduate/professional degree or higher: 29.3%

School District(s)
Plainview-Old Bethpage Central SD (KG-12)
  2014-15 Enrollment: 4,938 . . . . (516) 434-3001
Housing: Homeownership rate: 90.9%; Median home value: $544,600; Median year structure built: 1960; Homeowner vacancy rate: 1.0%; Median selected monthly owner costs: $3,727 with a mortgage, $1,500+ without a mortgage; Median gross rent: $298 per month; Rental vacancy rate: 0.0%
Health Insurance: 95.9% have insurance; 85.9% have private insurance; 24.6% have public insurance; 4.1% do not have insurance; 4.4% of children under 18 do not have insurance
Transportation: Commute: 79.4% car, 12.6% public transportation, 2.4% walk, 5.5% work from home; Mean travel time to work: 31.8 minutes

OLD BROOKVILLE (village).
Covers a land area of 3.999 square miles and a water area of 0.001 square miles. Located at 40.84° N. Lat; 73.61° W. Long. Elevation is 92 feet.
Population: 2,307; Growth (since 2000): 6.5%; Density: 577.0 persons per square mile; Race: 78.0% White, 0.8% Black/African American, 16.6% Asian, 0.0% American Indian/Alaska Native, 0.0% Native Hawaiian/Other Pacific Islander, 2.3% Two or more races, 3.8% Hispanic of any race; Average household size: 3.20; Median age: 43.8; Age under 18: 26.2%; Age 65 and over: 17.4%; Males per 100 females: 102.5; Marriage status: 27.3% never married, 62.9% now married, 0.0% separated, 6.4% widowed, 3.4% divorced; Foreign born: 18.3%; Speak English only: 71.4%; With disability: 8.7%; Veterans: 5.0%; Ancestry: 30.8% Italian, 15.7% Irish, 9.3% German, 4.1% American, 4.1% Russian
Employment: 32.4% management, business, and financial, 0.0% computer, engineering, and science, 11.8% education, legal, community service, arts, and media, 16.3% healthcare practitioners, 6.0% service, 28.4% sales and office, 3.7% natural resources, construction, and maintenance, 1.4% production, transportation, and material moving
Income: Per capita: $97,226; Median household: $194,205; Average household: $309,353; Households with income of $100,000 or more: 80.3%; Poverty rate: 3.8%

Educational Attainment: High school diploma or higher: 95.5%; Bachelor's degree or higher: 71.2%; Graduate/professional degree or higher: 36.7%
Housing: Homeownership rate: 90.3%; Median home value: $1,781,300; Median year structure built: 1965; Homeowner vacancy rate: 0.5%; Median selected monthly owner costs: $4,000+ with a mortgage, $1,500+ without a mortgage; Median gross rent: $2,375 per month; Rental vacancy rate: 0.0%
Health Insurance: 96.6% have insurance; 92.5% have private insurance; 18.0% have public insurance; 3.4% do not have insurance; 1.8% of children under 18 do not have insurance
Safety: Violent crime rate: 0.0 per 10,000 population; Property crime rate: 126.6 per 10,000 population
Transportation: Commute: 80.7% car, 11.7% public transportation, 0.0% walk, 7.6% work from home; Mean travel time to work: 40.3 minutes

OLD WESTBURY (village).
Covers a land area of 8.573 square miles and a water area of 0 square miles. Located at 40.79° N. Lat; 73.60° W. Long. Elevation is 161 feet.
History: Westbury was named by Henry Willis, one of the first English settlers after a town in his home county of Wiltshire, England. Westbury had been a Quaker community of isolated farms until the railroad came in 1836.
Population: 4,418; Growth (since 2000): 4.5%; Density: 515.4 persons per square mile; Race: 66.0% White, 8.6% Black/African American, 18.2% Asian, 0.6% American Indian/Alaska Native, 0.0% Native Hawaiian/Other Pacific Islander, 3.8% Two or more races, 7.7% Hispanic of any race; Average household size: 3.26; Median age: 22.9; Age under 18: 17.7%; Age 65 and over: 11.0%; Males per 100 females: 94.5; Marriage status: 52.4% never married, 41.9% now married, 0.1% separated, 3.3% widowed, 2.5% divorced; Foreign born: 22.5%; Speak English only: 69.4%; With disability: 4.3%; Veterans: 1.9%; Ancestry: 12.8% Italian, 6.9% Russian, 6.7% Polish, 6.1% German, 5.9% Irish
Employment: 19.6% management, business, and financial, 3.2% computer, engineering, and science, 9.6% education, legal, community service, arts, and media, 16.8% healthcare practitioners, 15.6% service, 30.7% sales and office, 1.4% natural resources, construction, and maintenance, 3.1% production, transportation, and material moving
Income: Per capita: $72,907; Median household: $168,750; Average household: $330,208; Households with income of $100,000 or more: 72.3%; Poverty rate: 3.2%
Educational Attainment: High school diploma or higher: 97.4%; Bachelor's degree or higher: 72.1%; Graduate/professional degree or higher: 41.5%

School District(s)
East Williston Union Free SD (KG-12)
  2014-15 Enrollment: 1,745 . . . . (516) 333-3758
Westbury Union Free SD (PK-12)
  2014-15 Enrollment: 4,975 . . . . (516) 876-5016
Four-year College(s)
New York Institute of Technology (Private, Not-for-profit)
  Fall 2014 Enrollment: 7,872 . . . . (516) 686-7516
  2015-16 Tuition: In-state $33,480; Out-of-state $33,480
SUNY College at Old Westbury (Public)
  Fall 2014 Enrollment: 4,504 . . . . (516) 876-3000
  2015-16 Tuition: In-state $7,643; Out-of-state $17,493
Housing: Homeownership rate: 91.8%; Median home value: $1,687,500; Median year structure built: 1975; Homeowner vacancy rate: 1.8%; Median selected monthly owner costs: $4,000+ with a mortgage, $1,500+ without a mortgage; Median gross rent: $1,574 per month; Rental vacancy rate: 16.3%
Health Insurance: 94.6% have insurance; 85.8% have private insurance; 15.7% have public insurance; 5.4% do not have insurance; 0.9% of children under 18 do not have insurance
Safety: Violent crime rate: 6.5 per 10,000 population; Property crime rate: 71.8 per 10,000 population
Transportation: Commute: 65.7% car, 10.9% public transportation, 14.9% walk, 6.0% work from home; Mean travel time to work: 29.7 minutes
Additional Information Contacts
Village of Old Westbury. . . . . (516) 626-0800
  http://www.villageofoldwestbury.org

OYSTER BAY (CDP).

Covers a land area of 1.233 square miles and a water area of 0.370 square miles. Located at 40.87° N. Lat; 73.53° W. Long. Elevation is 49 feet.
Population: 6,562; Growth (since 2000): -3.9%; Density: 5,320.1 persons per square mile; Race: 88.2% White, 4.5% Black/African American, 2.3% Asian, 0.0% American Indian/Alaska Native, 0.0% Native Hawaiian/Other Pacific Islander, 0.7% Two or more races, 9.3% Hispanic of any race; Average household size: 2.46; Median age: 42.8; Age under 18: 23.2%; Age 65 and over: 19.5%; Males per 100 females: 93.4; Marriage status: 27.3% never married, 52.0% now married, 0.9% separated, 9.9% widowed, 10.7% divorced; Foreign born: 11.5%; Speak English only: 84.7%; With disability: 11.6%; Veterans: 8.1%; Ancestry: 37.2% Italian, 27.9% Irish, 8.2% Polish, 6.6% German, 4.0% French
Employment: 20.6% management, business, and financial, 5.9% computer, engineering, and science, 12.9% education, legal, community service, arts, and media, 9.1% healthcare practitioners, 22.3% service, 18.7% sales and office, 5.1% natural resources, construction, and maintenance, 5.4% production, transportation, and material moving
Income: Per capita: $51,485; Median household: $91,453; Average household: $124,505; Households with income of $100,000 or more: 44.0%; Poverty rate: 3.6%
Educational Attainment: High school diploma or higher: 91.5%; Bachelor's degree or higher: 49.5%; Graduate/professional degree or higher: 17.7%

School District(s)
Oyster Bay-East Norwich Central SD (PK-12)
    2014-15 Enrollment: 1,640 . . . . (516) 624-6505
Housing: Homeownership rate: 63.2%; Median home value: $562,300; Median year structure built: 1957; Homeowner vacancy rate: 0.0%; Median selected monthly owner costs: $2,866 with a mortgage, $1,259 without a mortgage; Median gross rent: $1,830 per month; Rental vacancy rate: 3.4%
Health Insurance: 94.7% have insurance; 83.2% have private insurance; 28.6% have public insurance; 5.3% do not have insurance; 0.0% of children under 18 do not have insurance
Transportation: Commute: 82.4% car, 8.2% public transportation, 4.8% walk, 3.1% work from home; Mean travel time to work: 27.7 minutes

OYSTER BAY (town).

Covers a land area of 103.747 square miles and a water area of 65.652 square miles. Located at 40.80° N. Lat; 73.51° W. Long. Elevation is 49 feet.
History: Nearby is Theodore Roosevelt's estate, Sagamore Hill, which was made a national shrine in 1953 and a National Historic Site in 1963. Also of interest in Oyster Bay are several 18th-century houses, the Theodore Roosevelt Memorial Bird Sanctuary, a 12-acre wildlife sanctuary owned by the National Audubon Society, which adjoins Roosevelt's grave and the Oyster Bay National Wildlife Refuge. Settled 1653.
Population: 296,876; Growth (since 2000): 1.0%; Density: 2,861.5 persons per square mile; Race: 83.7% White, 2.5% Black/African American, 10.3% Asian, 0.1% American Indian/Alaska Native, 0.0% Native Hawaiian/Other Pacific Islander, 1.7% Two or more races, 8.1% Hispanic of any race; Average household size: 2.96; Median age: 43.7; Age under 18: 21.6%; Age 65 and over: 17.1%; Males per 100 females: 94.0; Marriage status: 27.9% never married, 59.3% now married, 1.3% separated, 6.9% widowed, 6.0% divorced; Foreign born: 15.4%; Speak English only: 79.5%; With disability: 8.7%; Veterans: 6.2%; Ancestry: 28.8% Italian, 19.6% Irish, 12.6% German, 5.9% Polish, 4.4% Russian
Employment: 19.7% management, business, and financial, 4.8% computer, engineering, and science, 15.2% education, legal, community service, arts, and media, 7.5% healthcare practitioners, 13.5% service, 26.9% sales and office, 6.4% natural resources, construction, and maintenance, 5.9% production, transportation, and material moving
Income: Per capita: $49,697; Median household: $112,162; Average household: $146,462; Households with income of $100,000 or more: 55.9%; Poverty rate: 3.7%
Educational Attainment: High school diploma or higher: 94.1%; Bachelor's degree or higher: 47.0%; Graduate/professional degree or higher: 20.9%

School District(s)
Oyster Bay-East Norwich Central SD (PK-12)
    2014-15 Enrollment: 1,640 . . . . (516) 624-6505
Housing: Homeownership rate: 87.5%; Median home value: $470,800; Median year structure built: 1957; Homeowner vacancy rate: 1.1%; Median selected monthly owner costs: $3,125 with a mortgage, $1,284 without a

mortgage; Median gross rent: $1,722 per month; Rental vacancy rate: 5.4%
Health Insurance: 95.7% have insurance; 86.0% have private insurance; 23.3% have public insurance; 4.3% do not have insurance; 1.6% of children under 18 do not have insurance
Transportation: Commute: 80.1% car, 12.9% public transportation, 1.9% walk, 4.0% work from home; Mean travel time to work: 34.4 minutes
Additional Information Contacts
Town of Oyster Bay. . . . . (516) 624-6332
    http://www.oysterbaytown.com

OYSTER BAY COVE (village).

Covers a land area of 4.187 square miles and a water area of 0.069 square miles. Located at 40.86° N. Lat; 73.51° W. Long. Elevation is 72 feet.
Population: 2,190; Growth (since 2000): -3.2%; Density: 523.1 persons per square mile; Race: 88.9% White, 1.4% Black/African American, 8.4% Asian, 0.0% American Indian/Alaska Native, 0.0% Native Hawaiian/Other Pacific Islander, 0.5% Two or more races, 1.6% Hispanic of any race; Average household size: 3.05; Median age: 47.0; Age under 18: 23.4%; Age 65 and over: 17.6%; Males per 100 females: 94.6; Marriage status: 22.6% never married, 70.8% now married, 1.1% separated, 4.3% widowed, 2.3% divorced; Foreign born: 12.6%; Speak English only: 83.0%; With disability: 5.3%; Veterans: 4.3%; Ancestry: 15.7% Italian, 13.3% Irish, 9.3% Russian, 8.2% German, 7.8% American
Employment: 28.2% management, business, and financial, 2.9% computer, engineering, and science, 15.5% education, legal, community service, arts, and media, 14.9% healthcare practitioners, 8.2% service, 24.2% sales and office, 4.5% natural resources, construction, and maintenance, 1.7% production, transportation, and material moving
Income: Per capita: $102,983; Median household: $210,288; Average household: $308,861; Households with income of $100,000 or more: 81.2%; Poverty rate: 0.5%
Educational Attainment: High school diploma or higher: 97.6%; Bachelor's degree or higher: 72.4%; Graduate/professional degree or higher: 36.3%
Housing: Homeownership rate: 93.6%; Median home value: $1,506,300; Median year structure built: 1974; Homeowner vacancy rate: 1.2%; Median selected monthly owner costs: $4,000+ with a mortgage, $1,500+ without a mortgage; Median gross rent: $1,500 per month; Rental vacancy rate: 0.0%
Health Insurance: 96.7% have insurance; 92.4% have private insurance; 18.6% have public insurance; 3.3% do not have insurance; 1.4% of children under 18 do not have insurance
Safety: Violent crime rate: 4.7 per 10,000 population; Property crime rate: 37.4 per 10,000 population
Transportation: Commute: 76.9% car, 11.2% public transportation, 0.3% walk, 11.2% work from home; Mean travel time to work: 34.6 minutes

PLAINEDGE (CDP).

Covers a land area of 1.404 square miles and a water area of 0 square miles. Located at 40.72° N. Lat; 73.48° W. Long. Elevation is 66 feet.
Population: 9,343; Growth (since 2000): 1.6%; Density: 6,654.2 persons per square mile; Race: 92.6% White, 0.2% Black/African American, 2.9% Asian, 0.0% American Indian/Alaska Native, 0.0% Native Hawaiian/Other Pacific Islander, 1.7% Two or more races, 9.1% Hispanic of any race; Average household size: 3.18; Median age: 43.5; Age under 18: 21.6%; Age 65 and over: 14.9%; Males per 100 females: 94.2; Marriage status: 29.3% never married, 57.1% now married, 2.0% separated, 7.0% widowed, 6.6% divorced; Foreign born: 9.9%; Speak English only: 86.3%; With disability: 9.2%; Veterans: 4.7%; Ancestry: 39.5% Italian, 28.7% Irish, 17.3% German, 5.2% Polish, 4.0% English
Employment: 16.0% management, business, and financial, 4.7% computer, engineering, and science, 14.3% education, legal, community service, arts, and media, 6.6% healthcare practitioners, 10.0% service, 33.2% sales and office, 7.9% natural resources, construction, and maintenance, 7.3% production, transportation, and material moving
Income: Per capita: $36,896; Median household: $108,287; Average household: $113,920; Households with income of $100,000 or more: 53.8%; Poverty rate: 2.7%
Educational Attainment: High school diploma or higher: 93.2%; Bachelor's degree or higher: 36.1%; Graduate/professional degree or higher: 12.5%
Housing: Homeownership rate: 90.0%; Median home value: $398,100; Median year structure built: 1956; Homeowner vacancy rate: 0.0%; Median selected monthly owner costs: $2,816 with a mortgage, $1,267 without a

mortgage; Median gross rent: $1,978 per month; Rental vacancy rate: 0.0%

Health Insurance: 96.7% have insurance; 90.1% have private insurance; 20.5% have public insurance; 3.3% do not have insurance; 0.4% of children under 18 do not have insurance

Transportation: Commute: 87.3% car, 8.6% public transportation, 0.3% walk, 1.8% work from home; Mean travel time to work: 31.3 minutes

PLAINVIEW (CDP). Covers a land area of 5.733 square miles and a water area of 0.011 square miles. Located at 40.78° N. Lat; 73.47° W. Long. Elevation is 148 feet.

History: Plainview was settled in 1648, when Welsh settler Robert Williams bought land that included a small pond named the Moscopas, meaning "hole of dirt and water." Neighboring land was purchased by Thomas Powell in 1695 as part of the Bethpage Purchase, and the area was called "Mannatto Hill." Manitou was the Native American word for "god" or "spirit."

Population: 26,199; Growth (since 2000): 2.2%; Density: 4,570.0 persons per square mile; Race: 82.8% White, 1.0% Black/African American, 13.9% Asian, 0.2% American Indian/Alaska Native, 0.0% Native Hawaiian/Other Pacific Islander, 1.2% Two or more races, 4.9% Hispanic of any race; Average household size: 2.92; Median age: 44.3; Age under 18: 23.5%; Age 65 and over: 18.3%; Males per 100 females: 93.3; Marriage status: 21.9% never married, 65.9% now married, 1.0% separated, 7.5% widowed, 4.7% divorced; Foreign born: 16.7%; Speak English only: 78.6%; With disability: 8.0%; Veterans: 5.4%; Ancestry: 15.8% Italian, 10.0% Russian, 9.8% Polish, 8.2% Irish, 7.6% American

Employment: 21.6% management, business, and financial, 5.2% computer, engineering, and science, 21.0% education, legal, community service, arts, and media, 8.6% healthcare practitioners, 9.5% service, 26.0% sales and office, 3.8% natural resources, construction, and maintenance, 4.3% production, transportation, and material moving

Income: Per capita: $50,293; Median household: $123,856; Average household: $146,173; Households with income of $100,000 or more: 60.3%; Poverty rate: 2.8%

Educational Attainment: High school diploma or higher: 95.7%; Bachelor's degree or higher: 61.0%; Graduate/professional degree or higher: 30.9%

School District(s)

Bethpage Union Free SD (KG-12)

2014-15 Enrollment: 2,926 . . . . (516) 644-4001

Plainview-Old Bethpage Central SD (KG-12)

2014-15 Enrollment: 4,938 . . . . (516) 434-3001

Syosset Central SD (KG-12)

2014-15 Enrollment: 6,336 . . . . (516) 364-5605

Housing: Homeownership rate: 92.9%; Median home value: $492,300; Median year structure built: 1957; Homeowner vacancy rate: 0.5%; Median selected monthly owner costs: $3,186 with a mortgage, $1,430 without a mortgage; Median gross rent: $2,000 per month; Rental vacancy rate: 6.1%

Health Insurance: 97.3% have insurance; 87.5% have private insurance; 24.4% have public insurance; 2.7% do not have insurance; 1.0% of children under 18 do not have insurance

Hospitals: Plainview Hospital (239 beds)

Transportation: Commute: 79.3% car, 15.0% public transportation, 0.8% walk, 4.7% work from home; Mean travel time to work: 36.2 minutes

PLANDOME (village). Covers a land area of 0.495 square miles and a water area of 0.009 square miles. Located at 40.81° N. Lat; 73.70° W. Long. Elevation is 72 feet.

Population: 1,278; Growth (since 2000): 0.5%; Density: 2,583.1 persons per square mile; Race: 92.7% White, 0.0% Black/African American, 5.7% Asian, 0.0% American Indian/Alaska Native, 0.0% Native Hawaiian/Other Pacific Islander, 1.6% Two or more races, 2.3% Hispanic of any race; Average household size: 3.27; Median age: 42.8; Age under 18: 30.8%; Age 65 and over: 13.0%; Males per 100 females: 94.1; Marriage status: 24.8% never married, 69.3% now married, 0.7% separated, 3.3% widowed, 2.6% divorced; Foreign born: 8.2%; Speak English only: 87.8%; With disability: 2.9%; Veterans: 4.4%; Ancestry: 26.4% Irish, 26.3% Italian, 9.1% German, 7.2% American, 7.1% English

Employment: 36.6% management, business, and financial, 1.5% computer, engineering, and science, 16.4% education, legal, community service, arts, and media, 6.5% healthcare practitioners, 3.4% service, 31.3% sales and office, 2.9% natural resources, construction, and maintenance, 1.4% production, transportation, and material moving

Income: Per capita: $122,361; Median household: $250,000+; Average household: $384,841; Households with income of $100,000 or more: 78.6%; Poverty rate: 3.8%

Educational Attainment: High school diploma or higher: 99.4%; Bachelor's degree or higher: 80.7%; Graduate/professional degree or higher: 44.3%

Housing: Homeownership rate: 93.6%; Median home value: $1,650,800; Median year structure built: Before 1940; Homeowner vacancy rate: 1.8%; Median selected monthly owner costs: $4,000+ with a mortgage, $1,500+ without a mortgage; Median gross rent: $3,500+ per month; Rental vacancy rate: 0.0%

Health Insurance: 97.9% have insurance; 94.6% have private insurance; 13.1% have public insurance; 2.1% do not have insurance; 0.0% of children under 18 do not have insurance

Transportation: Commute: 52.6% car, 39.4% public transportation, 0.5% walk, 6.3% work from home; Mean travel time to work: 41.2 minutes

PLANDOME HEIGHTS (village). Covers a land area of 0.181 square miles and a water area of 0.007 square miles. Located at 40.80° N. Lat; 73.71° W. Long. Elevation is 89 feet.

Population: 988; Growth (since 2000): 1.8%; Density: 5,462.3 persons per square mile; Race: 81.4% White, 0.0% Black/African American, 16.9% Asian, 0.0% American Indian/Alaska Native, 0.0% Native Hawaiian/Other Pacific Islander, 0.8% Two or more races, 4.4% Hispanic of any race; Average household size: 3.19; Median age: 41.8; Age under 18: 30.7%; Age 65 and over: 15.0%; Males per 100 females: 92.5; Marriage status: 25.8% never married, 63.6% now married, 1.2% separated, 6.8% widowed, 3.8% divorced; Foreign born: 16.8%; Speak English only: 79.6%; With disability: 6.0%; Veterans: 2.9%; Ancestry: 20.5% Italian, 15.9% Irish, 11.8% American, 11.4% German, 5.3% English

Employment: 29.8% management, business, and financial, 7.1% computer, engineering, and science, 22.7% education, legal, community service, arts, and media, 10.8% healthcare practitioners, 4.8% service, 21.0% sales and office, 1.9% natural resources, construction, and maintenance, 1.9% production, transportation, and material moving

Income: Per capita: $82,041; Median household: $213,000; Average household: $256,767; Households with income of $100,000 or more: 81.3%; Poverty rate: 2.7%

Educational Attainment: High school diploma or higher: 98.1%; Bachelor's degree or higher: 78.8%; Graduate/professional degree or higher: 44.7%

Housing: Homeownership rate: 95.2%; Median home value: $1,005,500; Median year structure built: 1943; Homeowner vacancy rate: 0.0%; Median selected monthly owner costs: $4,000+ with a mortgage, $1,500+ without a mortgage; Median gross rent: $3,500+ per month; Rental vacancy rate: 0.0%

Health Insurance: 98.5% have insurance; 92.8% have private insurance; 16.8% have public insurance; 1.5% do not have insurance; 0.7% of children under 18 do not have insurance

Transportation: Commute: 54.2% car, 36.7% public transportation, 2.6% walk, 6.5% work from home; Mean travel time to work: 39.8 minutes

PLANDOME MANOR (village). Covers a land area of 0.484 square miles and a water area of 0.022 square miles. Located at 40.81° N. Lat; 73.70° W. Long. Elevation is 30 feet.

Population: 813; Growth (since 2000): -3.0%; Density: 1,678.4 persons per square mile; Race: 90.7% White, 0.0% Black/African American, 9.3% Asian, 0.0% American Indian/Alaska Native, 0.0% Native Hawaiian/Other Pacific Islander, 0.0% Two or more races, 6.3% Hispanic of any race; Average household size: 2.79; Median age: 46.1; Age under 18: 28.0%; Age 65 and over: 19.6%; Males per 100 females: 92.1; Marriage status: 20.0% never married, 66.9% now married, 0.2% separated, 8.2% widowed, 5.0% divorced; Foreign born: 11.6%; Speak English only: 79.6%; With disability: 8.1%; Veterans: 5.6%; Ancestry: 27.6% Italian, 21.3% Irish, 11.2% Greek, 8.2% German, 7.7% American

Employment: 29.5% management, business, and financial, 3.7% computer, engineering, and science, 22.8% education, legal, community service, arts, and media, 11.0% healthcare practitioners, 2.5% service, 23.9% sales and office, 4.2% natural resources, construction, and maintenance, 2.5% production, transportation, and material moving

Income: Per capita: $122,882; Median household: $170,625; Average household: $347,350; Households with income of $100,000 or more: 70.4%; Poverty rate: 1.7%

Educational Attainment: High school diploma or higher: 96.0%; Bachelor's degree or higher: 72.0%; Graduate/professional degree or higher: 35.3%
Housing: Homeownership rate: 94.5%; Median home value: $1,526,800; Median year structure built: 1956; Homeowner vacancy rate: 0.0%; Median selected monthly owner costs: $4,000+ with a mortgage, $1,500+ without a mortgage; Median gross rent: $3,500+ per month; Rental vacancy rate: 0.0%
Health Insurance: 98.3% have insurance; 93.5% have private insurance; 19.6% have public insurance; 1.7% do not have insurance; 0.0% of children under 18 do not have insurance
Transportation: Commute: 65.2% car, 28.2% public transportation, 0.0% walk, 6.0% work from home; Mean travel time to work: 40.4 minutes

POINT LOOKOUT (CDP). Covers a land area of 0.226 square miles and a water area of 0 square miles. Located at 40.59° N. Lat; 73.58° W. Long. Elevation is 7 feet.
Population: 1,267; Growth (since 2000): -13.9%; Density: 5,605.8 persons per square mile; Race: 100.0% White, 0.0% Black/African American, 0.0% Asian, 0.0% American Indian/Alaska Native, 0.0% Native Hawaiian/Other Pacific Islander, 0.0% Two or more races, 3.9% Hispanic of any race; Average household size: 2.55; Median age: 46.0; Age under 18: 21.5%; Age 65 and over: 27.2%; Males per 100 females: 93.2; Marriage status: 20.6% never married, 63.4% now married, 3.1% separated, 12.3% widowed, 3.8% divorced; Foreign born: 6.5%; Speak English only: 93.6%; With disability: 8.3%; Veterans: 11.1%; Ancestry: 70.6% Irish, 18.2% Italian, 15.0% German, 7.6% American, 6.4% English
Employment: 23.2% management, business, and financial, 3.9% computer, engineering, and science, 23.4% education, legal, community service, arts, and media, 8.3% healthcare practitioners, 8.5% service, 27.7% sales and office, 2.9% natural resources, construction, and maintenance, 2.0% production, transportation, and material moving
Income: Per capita: $58,333; Median household: $111,534; Average household: $146,390; Households with income of $100,000 or more: 67.4%; Poverty rate: n/a
Educational Attainment: High school diploma or higher: 97.7%; Bachelor's degree or higher: 56.7%; Graduate/professional degree or higher: 23.3%
Housing: Homeownership rate: 80.8%; Median home value: $825,000; Median year structure built: Before 1940; Homeowner vacancy rate: 0.0%; Median selected monthly owner costs: $3,571 with a mortgage, $1,500+ without a mortgage; Median gross rent: $1,927 per month; Rental vacancy rate: 28.6%
Health Insurance: 93.1% have insurance; 87.8% have private insurance; 28.6% have public insurance; 6.9% do not have insurance; 0.0% of children under 18 do not have insurance
Transportation: Commute: 68.5% car, 13.7% public transportation, 7.5% walk, 10.4% work from home; Mean travel time to work: 36.1 minutes

PORT WASHINGTON (CDP). Covers a land area of 4.185 square miles and a water area of 1.429 square miles. Located at 40.83° N. Lat; 73.68° W. Long. Elevation is 102 feet.
History: Named for George Washington, first President of the U.S. Initially important for extensive sand pits; center for seaplanes 1900-1920; early College of Long Island, 1920-1930s.
Population: 16,233; Growth (since 2000): 6.7%; Density: 3,878.9 persons per square mile; Race: 84.3% White, 3.1% Black/African American, 6.4% Asian, 0.0% American Indian/Alaska Native, 0.0% Native Hawaiian/Other Pacific Islander, 2.0% Two or more races, 13.4% Hispanic of any race; Average household size: 2.80; Median age: 42.5; Age under 18: 25.2%; Age 65 and over: 19.5%; Males per 100 females: 92.0; Marriage status: 22.6% never married, 63.4% now married, 1.0% separated, 6.6% widowed, 7.5% divorced; Foreign born: 19.1%; Speak English only: 76.6%; With disability: 6.5%; Veterans: 5.0%; Ancestry: 18.1% Italian, 13.2% Irish, 9.1% German, 8.6% American, 7.2% Russian
Employment: 25.6% management, business, and financial, 5.4% computer, engineering, and science, 23.1% education, legal, community service, arts, and media, 5.0% healthcare practitioners, 11.4% service, 21.3% sales and office, 4.6% natural resources, construction, and maintenance, 3.6% production, transportation, and material moving
Income: Per capita: $59,483; Median household: $106,005; Average household: $165,789; Households with income of $100,000 or more: 53.9%; Poverty rate: 3.5%

Educational Attainment: High school diploma or higher: 93.0%; Bachelor's degree or higher: 64.1%; Graduate/professional degree or higher: 29.1%
School District(s)
Port Washington Union Free SD (PK-12)
    2014-15 Enrollment: 5,301 . . . . (516) 767-5005
Housing: Homeownership rate: 70.4%; Median home value: $721,200; Median year structure built: 1950; Homeowner vacancy rate: 0.7%; Median selected monthly owner costs: $3,745 with a mortgage, $1,500+ without a mortgage; Median gross rent: $1,787 per month; Rental vacancy rate: 7.4%
Health Insurance: 93.2% have insurance; 83.6% have private insurance; 25.5% have public insurance; 6.8% do not have insurance; 2.3% of children under 18 do not have insurance
Safety: Violent crime rate: 6.2 per 10,000 population; Property crime rate: 57.8 per 10,000 population
Newspapers: Port Washington News (weekly circulation 8,000)
Transportation: Commute: 54.1% car, 29.4% public transportation, 7.2% walk, 7.8% work from home; Mean travel time to work: 40.0 minutes

PORT WASHINGTON NORTH (village). Covers a land area of 0.478 square miles and a water area of 0.018 square miles. Located at 40.84° N. Lat; 73.70° W. Long. Elevation is 30 feet.
Population: 3,190; Growth (since 2000): 18.1%; Density: 6,679.7 persons per square mile; Race: 85.7% White, 4.9% Black/African American, 8.3% Asian, 0.0% American Indian/Alaska Native, 0.0% Native Hawaiian/Other Pacific Islander, 1.2% Two or more races, 4.2% Hispanic of any race; Average household size: 2.44; Median age: 45.8; Age under 18: 22.5%; Age 65 and over: 25.9%; Males per 100 females: 91.0; Marriage status: 23.9% never married, 61.1% now married, 0.3% separated, 9.5% widowed, 5.4% divorced; Foreign born: 17.3%; Speak English only: 82.6%; With disability: 6.2%; Veterans: 4.8%; Ancestry: 15.1% Italian, 13.1% American, 10.0% Irish, 9.2% Russian, 6.3% German
Employment: 21.6% management, business, and financial, 6.0% computer, engineering, and science, 27.3% education, legal, community service, arts, and media, 8.3% healthcare practitioners, 6.3% service, 26.2% sales and office, 0.6% natural resources, construction, and maintenance, 3.6% production, transportation, and material moving
Income: Per capita: $63,899; Median household: $106,902; Average household: $155,611; Households with income of $100,000 or more: 52.6%; Poverty rate: 2.4%
Educational Attainment: High school diploma or higher: 96.8%; Bachelor's degree or higher: 67.0%; Graduate/professional degree or higher: 32.4%
Housing: Homeownership rate: 70.2%; Median home value: $760,700; Median year structure built: 1968; Homeowner vacancy rate: 0.0%; Median selected monthly owner costs: $3,706 with a mortgage, $1,500+ without a mortgage; Median gross rent: $1,946 per month; Rental vacancy rate: 0.0%
Health Insurance: 98.6% have insurance; 85.1% have private insurance; 31.0% have public insurance; 1.4% do not have insurance; 0.0% of children under 18 do not have insurance
Transportation: Commute: 64.3% car, 29.8% public transportation, 0.0% walk, 5.8% work from home; Mean travel time to work: 39.6 minutes

ROCKVILLE CENTRE (village). Covers a land area of 3.247 square miles and a water area of 0.085 square miles. Located at 40.66° N. Lat; 73.64° W. Long. Elevation is 26 feet.
History: Named for Reverend Mordecai "Rock" Smith. Seat of Molloy Catholic College for Women. Incorporated 1893.
Population: 24,155; Growth (since 2000): -1.7%; Density: 7,438.7 persons per square mile; Race: 87.1% White, 4.1% Black/African American, 1.9% Asian, 0.3% American Indian/Alaska Native, 0.0% Native Hawaiian/Other Pacific Islander, 3.3% Two or more races, 10.8% Hispanic of any race; Average household size: 2.63; Median age: 43.1; Age under 18: 24.2%; Age 65 and over: 18.4%; Males per 100 females: 88.2; Marriage status: 31.2% never married, 55.2% now married, 1.3% separated, 6.2% widowed, 7.4% divorced; Foreign born: 9.4%; Speak English only: 86.3%; With disability: 9.2%; Veterans: 5.0%; Ancestry: 34.7% Irish, 24.7% Italian, 11.2% German, 4.6% Polish, 4.3% English
Employment: 23.8% management, business, and financial, 3.3% computer, engineering, and science, 20.6% education, legal, community service, arts, and media, 7.7% healthcare practitioners, 13.4% service, 23.6% sales and office, 4.4% natural resources, construction, and maintenance, 3.2% production, transportation, and material moving

Income: Per capita: $55,282; Median household: $106,415; Average household: $145,097; Households with income of $100,000 or more: 52.2%; Poverty rate: 4.9%

Educational Attainment: High school diploma or higher: 96.1%; Bachelor's degree or higher: 59.5%; Graduate/professional degree or higher: 30.0%

School District(s)

Rockville Centre Union Free SD (KG-12)

    2014-15 Enrollment: 3,583 . . . . (516) 255-8920

Four-year College(s)

Molloy College (Private, Not-for-profit, Roman Catholic)

    Fall 2014 Enrollment: 4,497 . . . . (516) 323-3000

    2015-16 Tuition: In-state $28,030; Out-of-state $28,030

Housing: Homeownership rate: 69.5%; Median home value: $600,600; Median year structure built: 1944; Homeowner vacancy rate: 2.0%; Median selected monthly owner costs: $3,518 with a mortgage, $1,496 without a mortgage; Median gross rent: $1,394 per month; Rental vacancy rate: 1.0%

Health Insurance: 97.5% have insurance; 87.3% have private insurance; 24.2% have public insurance; 2.5% do not have insurance; 0.0% of children under 18 do not have insurance

Hospitals: Mercy Medical Center (375 beds)

Safety: Violent crime rate: 5.0 per 10,000 population; Property crime rate: 80.1 per 10,000 population

Transportation: Commute: 64.0% car, 26.0% public transportation, 3.1% walk, 5.5% work from home; Mean travel time to work: 38.1 minutes

Additional Information Contacts

Village of Rockville Centre . . . . (516) 678-9300
    http://www.rvcny.us

ROOSEVELT (CDP). Covers a land area of 1.770 square miles and a water area of 0.010 square miles. Located at 40.68° N. Lat; 73.58° W. Long. Elevation is 39 feet.

History: Named for Franklin Delano Roosevelt, 32nd President of the U.S. Troubled school district was taken over by the State Department of Education in mid-1990s for restructuring and improvement.

Population: 16,645; Growth (since 2000): 5.0%; Density: 9,401.9 persons per square mile; Race: 15.7% White, 60.5% Black/African American, 1.0% Asian, 0.4% American Indian/Alaska Native, 0.0% Native Hawaiian/Other Pacific Islander, 11.9% Two or more races, 35.1% Hispanic of any race; Average household size: 3.83; Median age: 33.4; Age under 18: 26.5%; Age 65 and over: 10.1%; Males per 100 females: 93.0; Marriage status: 45.1% never married, 43.3% now married, 3.7% separated, 5.0% widowed, 6.5% divorced; Foreign born: 32.2%; Speak English only: 64.6%; With disability: 9.2%; Veterans: 2.1%; Ancestry: 5.6% Jamaican, 2.9% American, 2.3% Haitian, 1.3% African, 1.1% Guyanese

Employment: 6.3% management, business, and financial, 0.7% computer, engineering, and science, 8.0% education, legal, community service, arts, and media, 3.9% healthcare practitioners, 28.9% service, 27.1% sales and office, 6.6% natural resources, construction, and maintenance, 18.5% production, transportation, and material moving

Income: Per capita: $21,818; Median household: $65,469; Average household: $78,736; Households with income of $100,000 or more: 33.8%; Poverty rate: 13.3%

Educational Attainment: High school diploma or higher: 76.0%; Bachelor's degree or higher: 12.7%; Graduate/professional degree or higher: 4.1%

School District(s)

Roosevelt Children's Academy Charter School (KG-08)

    2014-15 Enrollment: 636 . . . . (516) 867-6202

Roosevelt Union Free SD (PK-12)

    2014-15 Enrollment: 3,363 . . . . (516) 345-7001

Housing: Homeownership rate: 66.7%; Median home value: $288,600; Median year structure built: 1951; Homeowner vacancy rate: 3.9%; Median selected monthly owner costs: $2,597 with a mortgage, $1,067 without a mortgage; Median gross rent: $1,458 per month; Rental vacancy rate: 4.1%

Health Insurance: 82.8% have insurance; 57.3% have private insurance; 34.2% have public insurance; 17.2% do not have insurance; 7.3% of children under 18 do not have insurance

Transportation: Commute: 77.8% car, 15.4% public transportation, 2.5% walk, 2.5% work from home; Mean travel time to work: 30.1 minutes

ROSLYN (village). Covers a land area of 0.645 square miles and a water area of 0.012 square miles. Located at 40.80° N. Lat; 73.65° W. Long. Elevation is 39 feet.

History: Cedarmere, home of William Cullen Bryant, is here. Incorporated 1932.

Population: 2,779; Growth (since 2000): 8.1%; Density: 4,308.0 persons per square mile; Race: 85.2% White, 0.9% Black/African American, 9.7% Asian, 0.0% American Indian/Alaska Native, 0.0% Native Hawaiian/Other Pacific Islander, 3.8% Two or more races, 5.0% Hispanic of any race; Average household size: 2.22; Median age: 43.7; Age under 18: 16.7%; Age 65 and over: 27.4%; Males per 100 females: 82.7; Marriage status: 32.2% never married, 44.1% now married, 0.5% separated, 13.4% widowed, 10.3% divorced; Foreign born: 18.6%; Speak English only: 73.2%; With disability: 10.3%; Veterans: 5.4%; Ancestry: 20.5% American, 13.8% Italian, 12.1% Russian, 8.8% Polish, 6.0% Iranian

Employment: 20.0% management, business, and financial, 6.6% computer, engineering, and science, 22.5% education, legal, community service, arts, and media, 10.7% healthcare practitioners, 10.5% service, 24.6% sales and office, 4.3% natural resources, construction, and maintenance, 0.8% production, transportation, and material moving

Income: Per capita: $67,545; Median household: $87,019; Average household: $161,684; Households with income of $100,000 or more: 45.3%; Poverty rate: 7.9%

Educational Attainment: High school diploma or higher: 96.6%; Bachelor's degree or higher: 67.9%; Graduate/professional degree or higher: 28.1%

Housing: Homeownership rate: 66.5%; Median home value: $511,300; Median year structure built: 1958; Homeowner vacancy rate: 1.6%; Median selected monthly owner costs: $3,127 with a mortgage, $1,296 without a mortgage; Median gross rent: $2,056 per month; Rental vacancy rate: 3.1%

Health Insurance: 94.2% have insurance; 86.0% have private insurance; 24.7% have public insurance; 5.8% do not have insurance; 6.2% of children under 18 do not have insurance

Hospitals: Saint Francis Hospital - Roslyn (279 beds)

Transportation: Commute: 76.8% car, 15.1% public transportation, 1.7% walk, 6.4% work from home; Mean travel time to work: 36.8 minutes

ROSLYN ESTATES (village). Covers a land area of 0.438 square miles and a water area of 0 square miles. Located at 40.79° N. Lat; 73.66° W. Long. Elevation is 233 feet.

Population: 1,159; Growth (since 2000): -4.2%; Density: 2,648.6 persons per square mile; Race: 88.4% White, 1.3% Black/African American, 10.0% Asian, 0.0% American Indian/Alaska Native, 0.0% Native Hawaiian/Other Pacific Islander, 0.3% Two or more races, 0.3% Hispanic of any race; Average household size: 2.98; Median age: 45.6; Age under 18: 29.7%; Age 65 and over: 19.1%; Males per 100 females: 96.7; Marriage status: 15.7% never married, 74.5% now married, 0.3% separated, 5.4% widowed, 4.5% divorced; Foreign born: 17.2%; Speak English only: 76.5%; With disability: 5.8%; Veterans: 3.4%; Ancestry: 23.5% American, 9.0% Russian, 7.2% Polish, 7.1% German, 5.6% European

Employment: 26.9% management, business, and financial, 1.2% computer, engineering, and science, 22.4% education, legal, community service, arts, and media, 18.3% healthcare practitioners, 2.3% service, 26.1% sales and office, 1.4% natural resources, construction, and maintenance, 1.4% production, transportation, and material moving

Income: Per capita: $101,605; Median household: $206,719; Average household: $301,387; Households with income of $100,000 or more: 73.8%; Poverty rate: 3.7%

Educational Attainment: High school diploma or higher: 98.7%; Bachelor's degree or higher: 80.3%; Graduate/professional degree or higher: 49.0%

Housing: Homeownership rate: 94.9%; Median home value: $1,032,000; Median year structure built: 1955; Homeowner vacancy rate: 0.0%; Median selected monthly owner costs: $4,000+ with a mortgage, $1,500+ without a mortgage; Median gross rent: $2,361 per month; Rental vacancy rate: 9.1%

Health Insurance: 97.2% have insurance; 89.6% have private insurance; 21.8% have public insurance; 2.8% do not have insurance; 2.3% of children under 18 do not have insurance

Transportation: Commute: 77.1% car, 15.9% public transportation, 0.4% walk, 6.6% work from home; Mean travel time to work: 33.3 minutes

ROSLYN HARBOR (village). Covers a land area of 1.186 square miles and a water area of 0.002 square miles. Located at 40.81° N. Lat; 73.64° W. Long. Elevation is 108 feet.

Population: 952; Growth (since 2000): -6.9%; Density: 802.9 persons per square mile; Race: 81.6% White, 2.5% Black/African American, 13.3% Asian, 0.0% American Indian/Alaska Native, 0.0% Native Hawaiian/Other Pacific Islander, 2.5% Two or more races, 3.2% Hispanic of any race; Average household size: 2.77; Median age: 51.1; Age under 18: 23.0%; Age 65 and over: 22.0%; Males per 100 females: 90.4; Marriage status: 22.2% never married, 67.1% now married, 0.5% separated, 6.7% widowed, 4.1% divorced; Foreign born: 18.9%; Speak English only: 73.3%; With disability: 6.9%; Veterans: 4.2%; Ancestry: 13.3% American, 10.9% Polish, 8.7% Russian, 7.8% Italian, 6.0% Greek
Employment: 20.5% management, business, and financial, 4.2% computer, engineering, and science, 21.4% education, legal, community service, arts, and media, 13.7% healthcare practitioners, 4.7% service, 33.0% sales and office, 1.9% natural resources, construction, and maintenance, 0.7% production, transportation, and material moving
Income: Per capita: $90,504; Median household: $160,250; Average household: $250,437; Households with income of $100,000 or more: 68.3%; Poverty rate: 2.9%
Educational Attainment: High school diploma or higher: 98.1%; Bachelor's degree or higher: 74.5%; Graduate/professional degree or higher: 39.1%
Housing: Homeownership rate: 90.4%; Median home value: $1,049,600; Median year structure built: 1959; Homeowner vacancy rate: 0.6%; Median selected monthly owner costs: $4,000+ with a mortgage, $1,500+ without a mortgage; Median gross rent: $2,327 per month; Rental vacancy rate: 0.0%
Health Insurance: 95.5% have insurance; 87.6% have private insurance; 22.3% have public insurance; 4.5% do not have insurance; 6.4% of children under 18 do not have insurance
Transportation: Commute: 80.6% car, 12.7% public transportation, 0.0% walk, 6.7% work from home; Mean travel time to work: 33.4 minutes

ROSLYN HEIGHTS (CDP). Covers a land area of 1.476 square miles and a water area of 0 square miles. Located at 40.78° N. Lat; 73.64° W. Long. Elevation is 177 feet.

History: Ebenezer Close, stated that the rules [of the Post Office in setting up new names] specified a short, pleasant-sounding name which had not been chosen for any Post Office in the United States. Of the names proposed, only ten fitted the rules. Of these ten, the name Roslyn, said to have been proposed by Mr. Cairns because our valley reminded him of Roslin, Scotland, received the most votes and was subsequently approved by all.
Population: 6,969; Growth (since 2000): 10.7%; Density: 4,722.2 persons per square mile; Race: 64.6% White, 5.1% Black/African American, 22.7% Asian, 0.0% American Indian/Alaska Native, 0.0% Native Hawaiian/Other Pacific Islander, 4.1% Two or more races, 10.1% Hispanic of any race; Average household size: 3.30; Median age: 40.4; Age under 18: 25.7%; Age 65 and over: 15.3%; Males per 100 females: 94.4; Marriage status: 29.7% never married, 56.6% now married, 2.9% separated, 7.5% widowed, 6.2% divorced; Foreign born: 28.6%; Speak English only: 62.8%; With disability: 9.4%; Veterans: 3.6%; Ancestry: 11.5% Italian, 9.8% American, 6.6% Russian, 6.3% Iranian, 4.2% Irish
Employment: 23.0% management, business, and financial, 3.4% computer, engineering, and science, 15.6% education, legal, community service, arts, and media, 12.1% healthcare practitioners, 14.2% service, 22.7% sales and office, 2.7% natural resources, construction, and maintenance, 6.2% production, transportation, and material moving
Income: Per capita: $49,790; Median household: $103,105; Average household: $160,551; Households with income of $100,000 or more: 53.4%; Poverty rate: 5.8%
Educational Attainment: High school diploma or higher: 93.6%; Bachelor's degree or higher: 61.8%; Graduate/professional degree or higher: 28.0%
School District(s)
East Williston Union Free SD (KG-12)
   2014-15 Enrollment: 1,745 . . . . (516) 333-3758
Roslyn Union Free SD (PK-12)
   2014-15 Enrollment: 3,149 . . . . (516) 801-5001
Housing: Homeownership rate: 84.1%; Median home value: $692,100; Median year structure built: 1956; Homeowner vacancy rate: 1.2%; Median selected monthly owner costs: $3,780 with a mortgage, $1,500+ without a

mortgage; Median gross rent: $1,180 per month; Rental vacancy rate: 12.7%
Health Insurance: 91.0% have insurance; 79.8% have private insurance; 23.8% have public insurance; 9.0% do not have insurance; 1.8% of children under 18 do not have insurance
Transportation: Commute: 70.1% car, 22.0% public transportation, 2.7% walk, 4.9% work from home; Mean travel time to work: 40.2 minutes

RUSSELL GARDENS (village). Covers a land area of 0.174 square miles and a water area of 0 square miles. Located at 40.78° N. Lat; 73.73° W. Long. Elevation is 131 feet.

Population: 878; Growth (since 2000): -18.2%; Density: 5,056.8 persons per square mile; Race: 72.1% White, 1.1% Black/African American, 24.5% Asian, 0.0% American Indian/Alaska Native, 0.0% Native Hawaiian/Other Pacific Islander, 1.5% Two or more races, 4.2% Hispanic of any race; Average household size: 2.77; Median age: 46.5; Age under 18: 23.2%; Age 65 and over: 18.5%; Males per 100 females: 94.0; Marriage status: 23.9% never married, 68.2% now married, 1.4% separated, 4.3% widowed, 3.6% divorced; Foreign born: 27.7%; Speak English only: 63.9%; With disability: 9.7%; Veterans: 5.8%; Ancestry: 15.1% Russian, 10.6% Polish, 9.2% American, 6.0% Italian, 4.0% Eastern European
Employment: 37.8% management, business, and financial, 7.9% computer, engineering, and science, 16.0% education, legal, community service, arts, and media, 18.0% healthcare practitioners, 4.0% service, 14.6% sales and office, 1.1% natural resources, construction, and maintenance, 0.7% production, transportation, and material moving
Income: Per capita: $83,332; Median household: $158,750; Average household: $234,603; Households with income of $100,000 or more: 62.9%; Poverty rate: 3.3%
Educational Attainment: High school diploma or higher: 96.1%; Bachelor's degree or higher: 78.7%; Graduate/professional degree or higher: 45.8%
Housing: Homeownership rate: 75.3%; Median home value: $1,049,000; Median year structure built: 1944; Homeowner vacancy rate: 0.0%; Median selected monthly owner costs: $4,000+ with a mortgage, $1,500+ without a mortgage; Median gross rent: $1,458 per month; Rental vacancy rate: 20.6%
Health Insurance: 98.4% have insurance; 87.2% have private insurance; 21.1% have public insurance; 1.6% do not have insurance; 0.0% of children under 18 do not have insurance
Transportation: Commute: 60.1% car, 34.0% public transportation, 2.0% walk, 3.9% work from home; Mean travel time to work: 40.2 minutes

SADDLE ROCK (village). Covers a land area of 0.246 square miles and a water area of 0.022 square miles. Located at 40.79° N. Lat; 73.75° W. Long. Elevation is 82 feet.

Population: 904; Growth (since 2000): 14.3%; Density: 3,672.9 persons per square mile; Race: 90.2% White, 1.0% Black/African American, 8.0% Asian, 0.0% American Indian/Alaska Native, 0.0% Native Hawaiian/Other Pacific Islander, 0.9% Two or more races, 0.4% Hispanic of any race; Average household size: 3.66; Median age: 40.9; Age under 18: 25.7%; Age 65 and over: 18.3%; Males per 100 females: 103.9; Marriage status: 30.1% never married, 59.9% now married, 0.4% separated, 5.4% widowed, 4.6% divorced; Foreign born: 45.2%; Speak English only: 36.5%; With disability: 10.2%; Veterans: 2.2%; Ancestry: 30.2% Iranian, 9.3% American, 6.0% Polish, 3.3% European, 3.2% Russian
Employment: 24.7% management, business, and financial, 1.1% computer, engineering, and science, 18.2% education, legal, community service, arts, and media, 11.4% healthcare practitioners, 8.2% service, 29.5% sales and office, 4.3% natural resources, construction, and maintenance, 2.6% production, transportation, and material moving
Income: Per capita: $71,651; Median household: $124,375; Average household: $253,273; Households with income of $100,000 or more: 62.4%; Poverty rate: 3.9%
Educational Attainment: High school diploma or higher: 94.4%; Bachelor's degree or higher: 57.7%; Graduate/professional degree or higher: 33.7%
Housing: Homeownership rate: 92.3%; Median home value: $1,330,000; Median year structure built: 1956; Homeowner vacancy rate: 0.0%; Median selected monthly owner costs: $4,000+ with a mortgage, $1,500+ without a mortgage; Median gross rent: n/a per month; Rental vacancy rate: 0.0%
Health Insurance: 92.8% have insurance; 82.3% have private insurance; 21.5% have public insurance; 7.2% do not have insurance; 6.0% of children under 18 do not have insurance

Transportation: Commute: 63.6% car, 28.4% public transportation, 0.0% walk, 7.9% work from home; Mean travel time to work: 42.0 minutes

Additional Information Contacts

Village of Saddle Rock . . . . (516) 482-9400
http://www.saddlerock.org

SADDLE ROCK ESTATES (CDP). Covers a land area of 0.078 square miles and a water area of 0 square miles. Located at 40.79° N. Lat; 73.74° W. Long. Elevation is 26 feet.

Population: 343; Growth (since 2000): -19.1%; Density: 4,424.3 persons per square mile; Race: 87.8% White, 0.0% Black/African American, 12.2% Asian, 0.0% American Indian/Alaska Native, 0.0% Native Hawaiian/Other Pacific Islander, 0.0% Two or more races, 0.0% Hispanic of any race; Average household size: 2.88; Median age: 52.1; Age under 18: 17.5%; Age 65 and over: 25.1%; Males per 100 females: 99.1; Marriage status: 27.6% never married, 58.1% now married, 0.0% separated, 8.3% widowed, 6.0% divorced; Foreign born: 21.6%; Speak English only: 78.6%; With disability: 8.5%; Veterans: 6.0%; Ancestry: 23.6% Polish, 11.1% Russian, 7.3% American, 5.2% Finnish, 4.7% German

Employment: 27.1% management, business, and financial, 12.4% computer, engineering, and science, 18.2% education, legal, community service, arts, and media, 11.8% healthcare practitioners, 10.6% service, 20.0% sales and office, 0.0% natural resources, construction, and maintenance, 0.0% production, transportation, and material moving

Income: Per capita: $58,382; Median household: $147,969; Average household: $161,980; Households with income of $100,000 or more: 64.8%; Poverty rate: n/a

Educational Attainment: High school diploma or higher: 100.0%; Bachelor's degree or higher: 91.5%; Graduate/professional degree or higher: 53.5%

Housing: Homeownership rate: 100.0%; Median home value: $944,200; Median year structure built: Before 1940; Homeowner vacancy rate: 0.0%; Median selected monthly owner costs: $3,368 with a mortgage, $1,500+ without a mortgage; Median gross rent: n/a per month; Rental vacancy rate: 0.0%

Health Insurance: 94.8% have insurance; 84.3% have private insurance; 39.4% have public insurance; 5.2% do not have insurance; 0.0% of children under 18 do not have insurance

Transportation: Commute: 67.1% car, 32.9% public transportation, 0.0% walk, 0.0% work from home; Mean travel time to work: 34.0 minutes

SALISBURY (CDP). Covers a land area of 1.737 square miles and a water area of 0.024 square miles. Located at 40.75° N. Lat; 73.56° W. Long. Elevation is 108 feet.

Population: 12,467; Growth (since 2000): 1.0%; Density: 7,177.8 persons per square mile; Race: 74.9% White, 1.7% Black/African American, 15.7% Asian, 0.2% American Indian/Alaska Native, 0.0% Native Hawaiian/Other Pacific Islander, 2.8% Two or more races, 15.1% Hispanic of any race; Average household size: 3.17; Median age: 42.0; Age under 18: 21.0%; Age 65 and over: 15.8%; Males per 100 females: 92.3; Marriage status: 28.6% never married, 59.2% now married, 0.9% separated, 7.6% widowed, 4.6% divorced; Foreign born: 23.4%; Speak English only: 66.1%; With disability: 8.7%; Veterans: 3.7%; Ancestry: 22.7% Italian, 12.8% Irish, 8.8% German, 4.6% Polish, 3.8% Russian

Employment: 16.9% management, business, and financial, 5.6% computer, engineering, and science, 14.3% education, legal, community service, arts, and media, 9.1% healthcare practitioners, 16.2% service, 23.0% sales and office, 7.9% natural resources, construction, and maintenance, 7.1% production, transportation, and material moving

Income: Per capita: $38,652; Median household: $99,015; Average household: $119,102; Households with income of $100,000 or more: 49.0%; Poverty rate: 4.6%

Educational Attainment: High school diploma or higher: 90.7%; Bachelor's degree or higher: 40.8%; Graduate/professional degree or higher: 16.9%

Housing: Homeownership rate: 92.2%; Median home value: $414,200; Median year structure built: 1955; Homeowner vacancy rate: 0.3%; Median selected monthly owner costs: $2,950 with a mortgage, $1,252 without a mortgage; Median gross rent: $1,508 per month; Rental vacancy rate: 0.0%

Health Insurance: 94.8% have insurance; 83.8% have private insurance; 22.0% have public insurance; 5.2% do not have insurance; 0.7% of children under 18 do not have insurance

Transportation: Commute: 86.1% car, 9.6% public transportation, 0.4% walk, 3.4% work from home; Mean travel time to work: 33.5 minutes

SANDS POINT (village). Covers a land area of 4.230 square miles and a water area of 1.379 square miles. Located at 40.85° N. Lat; 73.70° W. Long. Elevation is 43 feet.

History: Sands Point promontory (lighthouse) is at tip of Manhasset Neck, Northwest of village.

Population: 2,715; Growth (since 2000): -2.5%; Density: 641.8 persons per square mile; Race: 87.0% White, 0.9% Black/African American, 9.8% Asian, 0.0% American Indian/Alaska Native, 0.0% Native Hawaiian/Other Pacific Islander, 1.7% Two or more races, 5.1% Hispanic of any race; Average household size: 2.89; Median age: 49.1; Age under 18: 23.1%; Age 65 and over: 22.3%; Males per 100 females: 95.7; Marriage status: 23.4% never married, 65.3% now married, 0.9% separated, 5.3% widowed, 6.1% divorced; Foreign born: 16.8%; Speak English only: 81.5%; With disability: 7.1%; Veterans: 4.2%; Ancestry: 15.1% American, 13.9% Italian, 11.7% Russian, 8.4% Polish, 8.3% Eastern European

Employment: 33.9% management, business, and financial, 4.6% computer, engineering, and science, 14.4% education, legal, community service, arts, and media, 7.8% healthcare practitioners, 6.4% service, 28.3% sales and office, 3.2% natural resources, construction, and maintenance, 1.3% production, transportation, and material moving

Income: Per capita: $116,486; Median household: $185,119; Average household: $335,953; Households with income of $100,000 or more: 76.2%; Poverty rate: 0.9%

Educational Attainment: High school diploma or higher: 95.3%; Bachelor's degree or higher: 76.0%; Graduate/professional degree or higher: 41.8%

Housing: Homeownership rate: 94.2%; Median home value: 2 million+; Median year structure built: 1960; Homeowner vacancy rate: 0.0%; Median selected monthly owner costs: $4,000+ with a mortgage, $1,500+ without a mortgage; Median gross rent: $2,031 per month; Rental vacancy rate: 0.0%

Health Insurance: 98.5% have insurance; 92.9% have private insurance; 21.0% have public insurance; 1.5% do not have insurance; 0.0% of children under 18 do not have insurance

Safety: Violent crime rate: 0.0 per 10,000 population; Property crime rate: 47.2 per 10,000 population

Transportation: Commute: 61.4% car, 22.9% public transportation, 2.6% walk, 10.2% work from home; Mean travel time to work: 41.6 minutes

Additional Information Contacts

Village of Sands Point . . . . (516) 883-3044
http://www.sandspoint.org

SEA CLIFF (village). Covers a land area of 1.115 square miles and a water area of 0.847 square miles. Located at 40.85° N. Lat; 73.65° W. Long. Elevation is 184 feet.

History: Incorporated 1883.

Population: 5,025; Growth (since 2000): -0.8%; Density: 4,507.4 persons per square mile; Race: 91.2% White, 3.1% Black/African American, 1.6% Asian, 0.0% American Indian/Alaska Native, 0.0% Native Hawaiian/Other Pacific Islander, 2.0% Two or more races, 4.7% Hispanic of any race; Average household size: 2.56; Median age: 46.9; Age under 18: 21.6%; Age 65 and over: 15.4%; Males per 100 females: 94.0; Marriage status: 26.7% never married, 60.3% now married, 0.8% separated, 5.1% widowed, 7.9% divorced; Foreign born: 10.4%; Speak English only: 81.5%; With disability: 7.0%; Veterans: 4.2%; Ancestry: 24.8% Irish, 22.7% Italian, 18.3% German, 9.0% English, 7.6% Russian

Employment: 19.1% management, business, and financial, 5.8% computer, engineering, and science, 26.7% education, legal, community service, arts, and media, 7.7% healthcare practitioners, 11.7% service, 20.8% sales and office, 5.7% natural resources, construction, and maintenance, 2.5% production, transportation, and material moving

Income: Per capita: $57,344; Median household: $110,997; Average household: $148,492; Households with income of $100,000 or more: 58.7%; Poverty rate: 4.8%

Educational Attainment: High school diploma or higher: 97.1%; Bachelor's degree or higher: 66.5%; Graduate/professional degree or higher: 35.1%

School District(s)

North Shore Central SD (KG-12)
    2014-15 Enrollment: 2,738 . . . . (516) 277-7801

Housing: Homeownership rate: 71.9%; Median home value: $649,200; Median year structure built: Before 1940; Homeowner vacancy rate: 0.0%; Median selected monthly owner costs: $3,510 with a mortgage, $1,500+ without a mortgage; Median gross rent: $1,645 per month; Rental vacancy rate: 0.0%

Health Insurance: 94.9% have insurance; 88.3% have private insurance; 21.2% have public insurance; 5.1% do not have insurance; 1.2% of children under 18 do not have insurance
Transportation: Commute: 73.5% car, 16.2% public transportation, 4.7% walk, 4.7% work from home; Mean travel time to work: 33.7 minutes
Additional Information Contacts
Village of Sea Cliff . . . . (516) 671-0080
  http://www.seacliff-ny.gov

SEAFORD (CDP).
Covers a land area of 2.611 square miles and a water area of 0.054 square miles. Located at 40.67° N. Lat; 73.49° W. Long. Elevation is 10 feet.
History: The county Museum of Natural History is here. Settled 1643.
Population: 15,656; Growth (since 2000): -0.9%; Density: 5,997.2 persons per square mile; Race: 97.2% White, 0.0% Black/African American, 1.1% Asian, 0.1% American Indian/Alaska Native, 0.0% Native Hawaiian/Other Pacific Islander, 1.5% Two or more races, 5.7% Hispanic of any race; Average household size: 3.01; Median age: 42.6; Age under 18: 21.9%; Age 65 and over: 15.0%; Males per 100 females: 94.9; Marriage status: 29.5% never married, 58.3% now married, 1.5% separated, 6.5% widowed, 5.7% divorced; Foreign born: 7.4%; Speak English only: 91.8%; With disability: 9.8%; Veterans: 6.3%; Ancestry: 38.5% Italian, 30.5% Irish, 20.8% German, 5.3% Polish, 4.6% English
Employment: 14.9% management, business, and financial, 3.0% computer, engineering, and science, 16.1% education, legal, community service, arts, and media, 6.6% healthcare practitioners, 13.3% service, 29.3% sales and office, 10.2% natural resources, construction, and maintenance, 6.6% production, transportation, and material moving
Income: Per capita: $42,110; Median household: $106,795; Average household: $123,649; Households with income of $100,000 or more: 54.9%; Poverty rate: 2.9%
Educational Attainment: High school diploma or higher: 94.9%; Bachelor's degree or higher: 38.0%; Graduate/professional degree or higher: 14.8%

School District(s)
Levittown Union Free SD (KG-12)
  2014-15 Enrollment: 7,240 . . . . (516) 434-7020
Seaford Union Free SD (KG-12)
  2014-15 Enrollment: 2,372 . . . . (516) 592-4002
Housing: Homeownership rate: 87.9%; Median home value: $428,000; Median year structure built: 1957; Homeowner vacancy rate: 0.6%; Median selected monthly owner costs: $3,040 with a mortgage, $1,265 without a mortgage; Median gross rent: $1,820 per month; Rental vacancy rate: 0.0%
Health Insurance: 96.7% have insurance; 89.6% have private insurance; 20.2% have public insurance; 3.3% do not have insurance; 0.3% of children under 18 do not have insurance
Transportation: Commute: 82.8% car, 11.5% public transportation, 1.3% walk, 4.4% work from home; Mean travel time to work: 32.4 minutes

SEARINGTOWN (CDP).
Covers a land area of 0.929 square miles and a water area of 0 square miles. Located at 40.77° N. Lat; 73.66° W. Long. Elevation is 125 feet.
History: The hamlet derives its name from the Searing family, once numerous in the area and among the first parishioners at the Methodist church that was erected in 1788.
Population: 4,765; Growth (since 2000): -5.3%; Density: 5,131.4 persons per square mile; Race: 51.6% White, 1.2% Black/African American, 44.0% Asian, 0.2% American Indian/Alaska Native, 0.0% Native Hawaiian/Other Pacific Islander, 2.0% Two or more races, 1.6% Hispanic of any race; Average household size: 3.27; Median age: 47.3; Age under 18: 22.5%; Age 65 and over: 18.5%; Males per 100 females: 95.4; Marriage status: 23.2% never married, 65.1% now married, 0.0% separated, 7.3% widowed, 4.3% divorced; Foreign born: 36.4%; Speak English only: 44.9%; With disability: 8.4%; Veterans: 4.7%; Ancestry: 7.8% Italian, 6.5% Greek, 6.3% Iranian, 6.2% German, 5.4% Polish
Employment: 28.4% management, business, and financial, 7.7% computer, engineering, and science, 12.3% education, legal, community service, arts, and media, 14.4% healthcare practitioners, 7.0% service, 24.8% sales and office, 3.2% natural resources, construction, and maintenance, 2.2% production, transportation, and material moving
Income: Per capita: $55,194; Median household: $156,875; Average household: $177,796; Households with income of $100,000 or more: 66.5%; Poverty rate: 0.8%

Educational Attainment: High school diploma or higher: 93.6%; Bachelor's degree or higher: 61.0%; Graduate/professional degree or higher: 32.8%
Housing: Homeownership rate: 98.4%; Median home value: $751,400; Median year structure built: 1961; Homeowner vacancy rate: 5.1%; Median selected monthly owner costs: $4,000+ with a mortgage, $1,500+ without a mortgage; Median gross rent: n/a per month; Rental vacancy rate: 0.0%
Health Insurance: 97.2% have insurance; 86.6% have private insurance; 23.8% have public insurance; 2.8% do not have insurance; 0.8% of children under 18 do not have insurance
Transportation: Commute: 77.0% car, 16.9% public transportation, 1.3% walk, 3.1% work from home; Mean travel time to work: 39.5 minutes

SOUTH FARMINGDALE (CDP).
Covers a land area of 2.218 square miles and a water area of 0.004 square miles. Located at 40.72° N. Lat; 73.45° W. Long. Elevation is 59 feet.
History: South Farmingdale is a hamlet and census-designated place (CDP) in the Town of Oyster Bay in Nassau County, New York.
Population: 15,130; Growth (since 2000): 0.5%; Density: 6,822.6 persons per square mile; Race: 88.5% White, 3.0% Black/African American, 5.1% Asian, 0.0% American Indian/Alaska Native, 0.0% Native Hawaiian/Other Pacific Islander, 1.7% Two or more races, 11.7% Hispanic of any race; Average household size: 3.15; Median age: 42.2; Age under 18: 22.6%; Age 65 and over: 15.0%; Males per 100 females: 95.7; Marriage status: 28.7% never married, 59.4% now married, 1.5% separated, 7.1% widowed, 4.8% divorced; Foreign born: 10.2%; Speak English only: 85.3%; With disability: 7.9%; Veterans: 6.8%; Ancestry: 38.9% Italian, 24.5% Irish, 18.3% German, 4.8% Polish, 4.4% English
Employment: 13.7% management, business, and financial, 4.7% computer, engineering, and science, 10.2% education, legal, community service, arts, and media, 6.1% healthcare practitioners, 19.1% service, 29.1% sales and office, 8.8% natural resources, construction, and maintenance, 8.4% production, transportation, and material moving
Income: Per capita: $37,159; Median household: $106,954; Average household: $114,303; Households with income of $100,000 or more: 54.9%; Poverty rate: 3.5%
Educational Attainment: High school diploma or higher: 94.3%; Bachelor's degree or higher: 33.9%; Graduate/professional degree or higher: 13.0%
Housing: Homeownership rate: 91.3%; Median home value: $376,200; Median year structure built: 1956; Homeowner vacancy rate: 0.4%; Median selected monthly owner costs: $2,729 with a mortgage, $1,219 without a mortgage; Median gross rent: $2,021 per month; Rental vacancy rate: 14.3%
Health Insurance: 95.5% have insurance; 85.3% have private insurance; 21.8% have public insurance; 4.5% do not have insurance; 0.3% of children under 18 do not have insurance
Transportation: Commute: 84.0% car, 9.8% public transportation, 2.0% walk, 3.8% work from home; Mean travel time to work: 30.4 minutes

SOUTH FLORAL PARK (village).
Covers a land area of 0.096 square miles and a water area of 0 square miles. Located at 40.71° N. Lat; 73.70° W. Long. Elevation is 72 feet.
History: Until 1931 called Jamaica Square.
Population: 2,058; Growth (since 2000): 30.4%; Density: 21,442.6 persons per square mile; Race: 11.0% White, 59.7% Black/African American, 7.0% Asian, 0.2% American Indian/Alaska Native, 0.0% Native Hawaiian/Other Pacific Islander, 9.6% Two or more races, 23.7% Hispanic of any race; Average household size: 3.57; Median age: 35.9; Age under 18: 24.7%; Age 65 and over: 10.3%; Males per 100 females: 87.1; Marriage status: 34.1% never married, 53.0% now married, 1.3% separated, 4.1% widowed, 8.8% divorced; Foreign born: 39.7%; Speak English only: 70.4%; With disability: 10.5%; Veterans: 4.8%; Ancestry: 14.1% Jamaican, 6.4% Haitian, 4.6% Guyanese, 3.4% Trinidadian and Tobagonian, 3.3% West Indian
Employment: 13.7% management, business, and financial, 1.5% computer, engineering, and science, 12.1% education, legal, community service, arts, and media, 9.3% healthcare practitioners, 19.4% service, 22.4% sales and office, 10.7% natural resources, construction, and maintenance, 11.0% production, transportation, and material moving
Income: Per capita: $30,080; Median household: $91,250; Average household: $102,230; Households with income of $100,000 or more: 46.9%; Poverty rate: 3.5%

Educational Attainment: High school diploma or higher: 92.5%; Bachelor's degree or higher: 28.5%; Graduate/professional degree or higher: 10.2%
Housing: Homeownership rate: 74.5%; Median home value: $377,400; Median year structure built: 1955; Homeowner vacancy rate: 2.1%; Median selected monthly owner costs: $2,995 with a mortgage, $1,031 without a mortgage; Median gross rent: $1,509 per month; Rental vacancy rate: 5.2%
Health Insurance: 87.5% have insurance; 71.6% have private insurance; 22.8% have public insurance; 12.5% do not have insurance; 2.6% of children under 18 do not have insurance
Transportation: Commute: 72.1% car, 20.2% public transportation, 5.3% walk, 0.9% work from home; Mean travel time to work: 40.7 minutes

SOUTH HEMPSTEAD (CDP).
Covers a land area of 0.578 square miles and a water area of 0 square miles. Located at 40.68° N. Lat; 73.62° W. Long. Elevation is 43 feet.
Population: 3,152; Growth (since 2000): -1.1%; Density: 5,449.9 persons per square mile; Race: 72.7% White, 14.4% Black/African American, 2.7% Asian, 0.0% American Indian/Alaska Native, 0.0% Native Hawaiian/Other Pacific Islander, 1.5% Two or more races, 20.6% Hispanic of any race; Average household size: 3.06; Median age: 40.6; Age under 18: 26.1%; Age 65 and over: 16.6%; Males per 100 females: 93.3; Marriage status: 31.2% never married, 54.8% now married, 2.8% separated, 4.8% widowed, 9.2% divorced; Foreign born: 17.1%; Speak English only: 80.2%; With disability: 5.7%; Veterans: 6.7%; Ancestry: 27.4% Irish, 16.8% Italian, 12.3% German, 5.1% English, 4.6% Polish
Employment: 15.6% management, business, and financial, 4.4% computer, engineering, and science, 16.4% education, legal, community service, arts, and media, 9.2% healthcare practitioners, 18.2% service, 26.5% sales and office, 5.8% natural resources, construction, and maintenance, 3.9% production, transportation, and material moving
Income: Per capita: $41,171; Median household: $112,250; Average household: $123,972; Households with income of $100,000 or more: 55.4%; Poverty rate: 2.4%
Educational Attainment: High school diploma or higher: 95.5%; Bachelor's degree or higher: 49.6%; Graduate/professional degree or higher: 23.3%

School District(s)
Rockville Centre Union Free SD (KG-12)
    2014-15 Enrollment: 3,583 . . . . (516) 255-8920
Housing: Homeownership rate: 84.8%; Median home value: $384,200; Median year structure built: 1951; Homeowner vacancy rate: 1.1%; Median selected monthly owner costs: $2,879 with a mortgage, $1,322 without a mortgage; Median gross rent: $1,560 per month; Rental vacancy rate: 0.0%
Health Insurance: 89.3% have insurance; 76.7% have private insurance; 24.8% have public insurance; 10.7% do not have insurance; 2.8% of children under 18 do not have insurance
Transportation: Commute: 80.0% car, 14.4% public transportation, 2.4% walk, 2.7% work from home; Mean travel time to work: 32.7 minutes

SOUTH VALLEY STREAM (CDP).
Covers a land area of 0.873 square miles and a water area of 0 square miles. Located at 40.66° N. Lat; 73.72° W. Long. Elevation is 10 feet.
History: South Valley Stream is a hamlet in Nassau County, New York, located in the southern part of the Town of Hempstead.
Population: 6,588; Growth (since 2000): 16.8%; Density: 7,547.8 persons per square mile; Race: 42.5% White, 33.2% Black/African American, 15.3% Asian, 0.0% American Indian/Alaska Native, 0.0% Native Hawaiian/Other Pacific Islander, 2.9% Two or more races, 12.2% Hispanic of any race; Average household size: 3.23; Median age: 37.6; Age under 18: 21.4%; Age 65 and over: 14.6%; Males per 100 females: 92.1; Marriage status: 31.4% never married, 54.1% now married, 0.7% separated, 6.1% widowed, 8.4% divorced; Foreign born: 33.9%; Speak English only: 65.5%; With disability: 6.5%; Veterans: 4.5%; Ancestry: 6.2% Irish, 5.6% Russian, 5.5% Italian, 5.2% American, 4.2% Haitian
Employment: 21.4% management, business, and financial, 3.0% computer, engineering, and science, 10.3% education, legal, community service, arts, and media, 9.4% healthcare practitioners, 17.5% service, 26.3% sales and office, 6.0% natural resources, construction, and maintenance, 6.1% production, transportation, and material moving
Income: Per capita: $40,000; Median household: $111,189; Average household: $124,176; Households with income of $100,000 or more: 52.5%; Poverty rate: 6.4%

Educational Attainment: High school diploma or higher: 92.7%; Bachelor's degree or higher: 50.3%; Graduate/professional degree or higher: 23.9%
Housing: Homeownership rate: 80.2%; Median home value: $436,000; Median year structure built: 1955; Homeowner vacancy rate: 0.0%; Median selected monthly owner costs: $3,181 with a mortgage, $1,477 without a mortgage; Median gross rent: $1,266 per month; Rental vacancy rate: 0.0%
Health Insurance: 91.1% have insurance; 75.2% have private insurance; 25.8% have public insurance; 8.9% do not have insurance; 4.2% of children under 18 do not have insurance
Transportation: Commute: 67.7% car, 24.3% public transportation, 3.9% walk, 3.2% work from home; Mean travel time to work: 42.2 minutes

STEWART MANOR (village).
Covers a land area of 0.210 square miles and a water area of 0 square miles. Located at 40.72° N. Lat; 73.69° W. Long. Elevation is 85 feet.
History: Laid out 1926, incorporated 1927.
Population: 2,113; Growth (since 2000): 9.2%; Density: 10,076.7 persons per square mile; Race: 87.0% White, 1.4% Black/African American, 4.9% Asian, 0.0% American Indian/Alaska Native, 0.0% Native Hawaiian/Other Pacific Islander, 1.9% Two or more races, 11.3% Hispanic of any race; Average household size: 2.83; Median age: 42.9; Age under 18: 24.6%; Age 65 and over: 20.1%; Males per 100 females: 88.3; Marriage status: 23.9% never married, 63.7% now married, 0.3% separated, 7.7% widowed, 4.7% divorced; Foreign born: 11.3%; Speak English only: 83.5%; With disability: 7.2%; Veterans: 8.1%; Ancestry: 38.8% Irish, 30.8% Italian, 17.9% German, 5.1% English, 4.4% Polish
Employment: 27.6% management, business, and financial, 4.9% computer, engineering, and science, 16.0% education, legal, community service, arts, and media, 8.9% healthcare practitioners, 9.7% service, 25.3% sales and office, 4.8% natural resources, construction, and maintenance, 2.8% production, transportation, and material moving
Income: Per capita: $47,770; Median household: $112,917; Average household: $134,073; Households with income of $100,000 or more: 60.6%; Poverty rate: 1.0%
Educational Attainment: High school diploma or higher: 97.1%; Bachelor's degree or higher: 53.8%; Graduate/professional degree or higher: 23.2%

School District(s)
Elmont Union Free SD (PK-06)
    2014-15 Enrollment: 3,883 . . . . (516) 326-5500
Housing: Homeownership rate: 91.3%; Median home value: $497,000; Median year structure built: Before 1940; Homeowner vacancy rate: 1.9%; Median selected monthly owner costs: $2,917 with a mortgage, $1,278 without a mortgage; Median gross rent: $1,746 per month; Rental vacancy rate: 0.0%
Health Insurance: 93.3% have insurance; 86.5% have private insurance; 23.7% have public insurance; 6.7% do not have insurance; 2.7% of children under 18 do not have insurance
Transportation: Commute: 73.6% car, 20.7% public transportation, 2.0% walk, 2.7% work from home; Mean travel time to work: 39.7 minutes

SYOSSET (CDP).
Covers a land area of 4.974 square miles and a water area of 0 square miles. Located at 40.82° N. Lat; 73.50° W. Long. Elevation is 210 feet.
History: Syosset was established in 1846. Booming businesses in the area during this era included horse and livestock sales, cider milling, a pickle factory, and entrepreneur enterprises such as DV Horton's "Medicinal Root Beer".
Population: 19,157; Growth (since 2000): 3.3%; Density: 3,851.7 persons per square mile; Race: 72.1% White, 1.0% Black/African American, 24.4% Asian, 0.2% American Indian/Alaska Native, 0.0% Native Hawaiian/Other Pacific Islander, 2.0% Two or more races, 4.7% Hispanic of any race; Average household size: 3.04; Median age: 42.8; Age under 18: 25.7%; Age 65 and over: 15.5%; Males per 100 females: 98.3; Marriage status: 23.7% never married, 66.5% now married, 1.2% separated, 4.7% widowed, 5.1% divorced; Foreign born: 22.6%; Speak English only: 68.5%; With disability: 7.9%; Veterans: 4.9%; Ancestry: 16.3% Italian, 11.4% Irish, 9.3% German, 6.9% Russian, 6.5% Polish
Employment: 27.6% management, business, and financial, 7.2% computer, engineering, and science, 15.4% education, legal, community service, arts, and media, 10.5% healthcare practitioners, 6.4% service, 25.2% sales and office, 3.7% natural resources, construction, and maintenance, 4.0% production, transportation, and material moving

Income: Per capita: $60,654; Median household: $145,879; Average household: $183,728; Households with income of $100,000 or more: 67.1%; Poverty rate: 4.4%

Educational Attainment: High school diploma or higher: 95.3%; Bachelor's degree or higher: 63.7%; Graduate/professional degree or higher: 29.9%

School District(s)
Cold Spring Harbor Central SD (KG-12)
    2014-15 Enrollment: 1,814 . . . . (631) 367-5931
NYC Special Schools - District 75 (PK-12)
    2014-15 Enrollment: 22,867 . . . . (212) 802-1501
Syosset Central SD (KG-12)
    2014-15 Enrollment: 6,336 . . . . (516) 364-5605

Four-year College(s)
New York College of Health Professions (Private, Not-for-profit)
    Fall 2014 Enrollment: 732 . . . . (516) 364-0808
    2015-16 Tuition: In-state $14,226; Out-of-state $14,226

Vocational/Technical School(s)
Star Career Academy-Syosset (Private, For-profit)
    Fall 2014 Enrollment: 277 . . . . (516) 364-4344
    2015-16 Tuition: $13,733

Housing: Homeownership rate: 90.6%; Median home value: $611,400; Median year structure built: 1957; Homeowner vacancy rate: 1.1%; Median selected monthly owner costs: $3,692 with a mortgage, $1,500+ without a mortgage; Median gross rent: $1,679 per month; Rental vacancy rate: 0.0%

Health Insurance: 96.2% have insurance; 88.4% have private insurance; 20.0% have public insurance; 3.8% do not have insurance; 1.6% of children under 18 do not have insurance

Newspapers: Long Island Press (weekly circulation 65,000)

Transportation: Commute: 72.9% car, 18.3% public transportation, 1.6% walk, 5.9% work from home; Mean travel time to work: 38.6 minutes

THOMASTON (village). Covers a land area of 0.408 square miles and a water area of 0 square miles. Located at 40.79° N. Lat; 73.72° W. Long. Elevation is 200 feet.

Population: 2,624; Growth (since 2000): 0.7%; Density: 6,438.6 persons per square mile; Race: 74.8% White, 0.3% Black/African American, 24.4% Asian, 0.2% American Indian/Alaska Native, 0.0% Native Hawaiian/Other Pacific Islander, 0.3% Two or more races, 7.6% Hispanic of any race; Average household size: 2.86; Median age: 41.7; Age under 18: 27.6%; Age 65 and over: 16.0%; Males per 100 females: 89.9; Marriage status: 23.4% never married, 65.3% now married, 2.5% separated, 4.5% widowed, 6.8% divorced; Foreign born: 30.0%; Speak English only: 61.7%; With disability: 6.4%; Veterans: 3.8%; Ancestry: 11.9% Russian, 5.7% Eastern European, 5.7% Polish, 4.6% American, 3.8% Italian

Employment: 19.3% management, business, and financial, 6.2% computer, engineering, and science, 22.4% education, legal, community service, arts, and media, 9.5% healthcare practitioners, 11.3% service, 26.8% sales and office, 0.4% natural resources, construction, and maintenance, 4.1% production, transportation, and material moving

Income: Per capita: $61,089; Median household: $115,625; Average household: $173,385; Households with income of $100,000 or more: 60.2%; Poverty rate: 6.3%

Educational Attainment: High school diploma or higher: 95.9%; Bachelor's degree or higher: 67.2%; Graduate/professional degree or higher: 40.8%

Housing: Homeownership rate: 84.7%; Median home value: $753,700; Median year structure built: 1950; Homeowner vacancy rate: 0.0%; Median selected monthly owner costs: $3,280 with a mortgage, $1,426 without a mortgage; Median gross rent: $2,344 per month; Rental vacancy rate: 9.7%

Health Insurance: 93.2% have insurance; 84.0% have private insurance; 20.0% have public insurance; 6.8% do not have insurance; 3.3% of children under 18 do not have insurance

Transportation: Commute: 58.1% car, 34.4% public transportation, 0.6% walk, 6.4% work from home; Mean travel time to work: 38.8 minutes

UNIONDALE (CDP). Covers a land area of 2.707 square miles and a water area of 0 square miles. Located at 40.70° N. Lat; 73.59° W. Long. Elevation is 52 feet.

History: Named for the American union of states. Downtown suburban growth since the 1970s.

Population: 25,092; Growth (since 2000): 9.0%; Density: 9,270.8 persons per square mile; Race: 22.7% White, 46.3% Black/African American, 2.0%

Asian, 0.4% American Indian/Alaska Native, 0.0% Native Hawaiian/Other Pacific Islander, 13.4% Two or more races, 39.8% Hispanic of any race; Average household size: 4.11; Median age: 34.4; Age under 18: 24.4%; Age 65 and over: 12.2%; Males per 100 females: 93.6; Marriage status: 43.3% never married, 42.2% now married, 3.3% separated, 6.0% widowed, 8.6% divorced; Foreign born: 41.1%; Speak English only: 50.8%; With disability: 7.5%; Veterans: 3.1%; Ancestry: 8.4% Haitian, 6.5% Jamaican, 3.2% American, 2.6% Irish, 2.0% German

Employment: 7.8% management, business, and financial, 3.0% computer, engineering, and science, 10.2% education, legal, community service, arts, and media, 6.5% healthcare practitioners, 25.3% service, 23.1% sales and office, 9.6% natural resources, construction, and maintenance, 14.5% production, transportation, and material moving

Income: Per capita: $22,700; Median household: $69,655; Average household: $88,238; Households with income of $100,000 or more: 34.7%; Poverty rate: 12.6%

Educational Attainment: High school diploma or higher: 78.6%; Bachelor's degree or higher: 21.0%; Graduate/professional degree or higher: 6.8%

School District(s)
Uniondale Union Free SD (KG-12)
    2014-15 Enrollment: 6,730 . . . . (516) 560-8824

Housing: Homeownership rate: 73.9%; Median home value: $301,800; Median year structure built: 1952; Homeowner vacancy rate: 2.4%; Median selected monthly owner costs: $2,599 with a mortgage, $948 without a mortgage; Median gross rent: $1,326 per month; Rental vacancy rate: 8.2%

Health Insurance: 81.2% have insurance; 57.9% have private insurance; 30.0% have public insurance; 18.8% do not have insurance; 11.6% of children under 18 do not have insurance

Transportation: Commute: 84.3% car, 11.5% public transportation, 2.0% walk, 1.1% work from home; Mean travel time to work: 30.6 minutes

UNIVERSITY GARDENS (CDP). Covers a land area of 0.533 square miles and a water area of 0 square miles. Located at 40.78° N. Lat; 73.73° W. Long. Elevation is 144 feet.

History: Occupying the northern portion of Lake Success, this area was the temporary headquarters of the United Nations while its headquarters building in New York City was built. It borders the New York City borough of Queens.

Population: 4,122; Growth (since 2000): -0.4%; Density: 7,730.7 persons per square mile; Race: 52.6% White, 6.0% Black/African American, 37.2% Asian, 0.0% American Indian/Alaska Native, 0.0% Native Hawaiian/Other Pacific Islander, 2.4% Two or more races, 3.8% Hispanic of any race; Average household size: 2.61; Median age: 45.7; Age under 18: 21.6%; Age 65 and over: 16.6%; Males per 100 females: 92.6; Marriage status: 29.5% never married, 60.8% now married, 1.6% separated, 4.2% widowed, 5.6% divorced; Foreign born: 40.6%; Speak English only: 56.8%; With disability: 7.9%; Veterans: 3.3%; Ancestry: 9.7% American, 5.6% Russian, 5.0% Polish, 4.5% Italian, 4.3% Jamaican

Employment: 27.4% management, business, and financial, 9.8% computer, engineering, and science, 20.2% education, legal, community service, arts, and media, 5.6% healthcare practitioners, 5.7% service, 26.0% sales and office, 0.8% natural resources, construction, and maintenance, 4.5% production, transportation, and material moving

Income: Per capita: $60,675; Median household: $105,078; Average household: $157,244; Households with income of $100,000 or more: 54.1%; Poverty rate: 5.2%

Educational Attainment: High school diploma or higher: 94.7%; Bachelor's degree or higher: 69.8%; Graduate/professional degree or higher: 33.9%

Housing: Homeownership rate: 86.0%; Median home value: $608,200; Median year structure built: 1948; Homeowner vacancy rate: 3.0%; Median selected monthly owner costs: $2,753 with a mortgage, $1,307 without a mortgage; Median gross rent: $1,527 per month; Rental vacancy rate: 0.0%

Health Insurance: 95.1% have insurance; 86.4% have private insurance; 19.8% have public insurance; 4.9% do not have insurance; 1.9% of children under 18 do not have insurance

Transportation: Commute: 67.2% car, 29.0% public transportation, 2.6% walk, 1.2% work from home; Mean travel time to work: 40.8 minutes

UPPER BROOKVILLE (village). Covers a land area of 4.319 square miles and a water area of 0 square miles. Located at 40.85° N. Lat; 73.56° W. Long. Elevation is 157 feet.
Population: 1,528; Growth (since 2000): -15.2%; Density: 353.8 persons per square mile; Race: 78.1% White, 0.9% Black/African American, 17.3% Asian, 0.0% American Indian/Alaska Native, 0.0% Native Hawaiian/Other Pacific Islander, 3.5% Two or more races, 3.9% Hispanic of any race; Average household size: 3.30; Median age: 50.5; Age under 18: 15.4%; Age 65 and over: 24.0%; Males per 100 females: 94.3; Marriage status: 29.3% never married, 60.4% now married, 0.9% separated, 7.1% widowed, 3.2% divorced; Foreign born: 22.6%; Speak English only: 65.6%; With disability: 7.5%; Veterans: 5.0%; Ancestry: 23.0% Italian, 14.6% Irish, 9.3% German, 6.7% Greek, 5.6% English
Employment: 28.7% management, business, and financial, 5.4% computer, engineering, and science, 12.9% education, legal, community service, arts, and media, 12.7% healthcare practitioners, 2.9% service, 33.1% sales and office, 2.9% natural resources, construction, and maintenance, 1.4% production, transportation, and material moving
Income: Per capita: $116,562; Median household: $250,000+; Average household: $379,468; Households with income of $100,000 or more: 78.4%; Poverty rate: 1.5%
Educational Attainment: High school diploma or higher: 96.6%; Bachelor's degree or higher: 63.0%; Graduate/professional degree or higher: 36.2%
Housing: Homeownership rate: 94.8%; Median home value: $1,960,200; Median year structure built: 1969; Homeowner vacancy rate: 0.0%; Median selected monthly owner costs: $4,000+ with a mortgage, $1,500+ without a mortgage; Median gross rent: $3,250 per month; Rental vacancy rate: 0.0%
Health Insurance: 98.2% have insurance; 86.6% have private insurance; 25.2% have public insurance; 1.8% do not have insurance; 0.8% of children under 18 do not have insurance
Transportation: Commute: 80.2% car, 11.8% public transportation, 1.2% walk, 6.8% work from home; Mean travel time to work: 35.8 minutes

VALLEY STREAM (village). Covers a land area of 3.482 square miles and a water area of 0.017 square miles. Located at 40.66° N. Lat; 73.70° W. Long. Elevation is 16 feet.
History: Valley Stream was originally referred to as "the land between Near Rockaway and Jamaica." The northeast section received the name Tigertown, and in the mid 1880s, Rum Junction. The northern section of the Village was known as Cookie Hill, because of its racy reputation.
Population: 37,838; Growth (since 2000): 4.0%; Density: 10,866.3 persons per square mile; Race: 46.1% White, 20.6% Black/African American, 14.3% Asian, 0.1% American Indian/Alaska Native, 0.0% Native Hawaiian/Other Pacific Islander, 3.6% Two or more races, 29.3% Hispanic of any race; Average household size: 3.28; Median age: 38.4; Age under 18: 23.6%; Age 65 and over: 13.5%; Males per 100 females: 92.6; Marriage status: 33.6% never married, 53.3% now married, 1.9% separated, 6.1% widowed, 7.1% divorced; Foreign born: 34.2%; Speak English only: 58.0%; With disability: 9.6%; Veterans: 5.1%; Ancestry: 14.9% Italian, 8.9% Irish, 4.9% German, 4.2% American, 2.4% Haitian
Employment: 12.4% management, business, and financial, 3.9% computer, engineering, and science, 11.0% education, legal, community service, arts, and media, 9.0% healthcare practitioners, 19.4% service, 27.2% sales and office, 8.8% natural resources, construction, and maintenance, 8.2% production, transportation, and material moving
Income: Per capita: $33,303; Median household: $90,018; Average household: $105,515; Households with income of $100,000 or more: 44.6%; Poverty rate: 7.5%
Educational Attainment: High school diploma or higher: 89.8%; Bachelor's degree or higher: 34.0%; Graduate/professional degree or higher: 10.5%
School District(s)
Elmont Union Free SD (PK-06)
    2014-15 Enrollment: 3,883 . . . . (516) 326-5500
Hewlett-Woodmere Union Free SD (PK-12)
    2014-15 Enrollment: 3,079 . . . . (516) 792-4800
Valley Stream 13 Union Free SD (KG-06)
    2014-15 Enrollment: 2,159 . . . . (516) 568-6100
Valley Stream 24 Union Free SD (KG-06)
    2014-15 Enrollment: 1,105 . . . . (516) 434-2830
Valley Stream 30 Union Free SD (KG-06)
    2014-15 Enrollment: 1,567 . . . . (516) 434-3600

Valley Stream Central High SD (07-12)
    2014-15 Enrollment: 4,558 . . . . (516) 872-5601
Housing: Homeownership rate: 80.1%; Median home value: $371,000; Median year structure built: 1950; Homeowner vacancy rate: 1.4%; Median selected monthly owner costs: $2,941 with a mortgage, $1,158 without a mortgage; Median gross rent: $1,581 per month; Rental vacancy rate: 1.0%
Health Insurance: 90.4% have insurance; 70.3% have private insurance; 29.7% have public insurance; 9.6% do not have insurance; 4.0% of children under 18 do not have insurance
Hospitals: Franklin Hospital (305 beds)
Transportation: Commute: 74.0% car, 21.2% public transportation, 2.0% walk, 1.6% work from home; Mean travel time to work: 40.3 minutes
Additional Information Contacts
Village of Valley Stream . . . . (516) 825-4200
    http://www.vsvny.org

WANTAGH (CDP). Covers a land area of 3.830 square miles and a water area of 0.297 square miles. Located at 40.67° N. Lat; 73.51° W. Long. Elevation is 26 feet.
History: Wantagh was inhabited by the Merokee (or Merikoke) tribe of the Metoac Indians prior to European settlement in the mid-17th century. The Merokee were part of the greater Montauk tribe that loosely ruled Long Island's Native Americans. Wantagh was the chief of the Merokee tribe in 1647, and then the grand chief of the Montauk tribe from 1651-1658.
Population: 18,939; Growth (since 2000): -0.2%; Density: 4,944.5 persons per square mile; Race: 95.6% White, 0.3% Black/African American, 2.9% Asian, 0.0% American Indian/Alaska Native, 0.1% Native Hawaiian/Other Pacific Islander, 1.0% Two or more races, 5.9% Hispanic of any race; Average household size: 3.20; Median age: 42.2; Age under 18: 24.1%; Age 65 and over: 15.2%; Males per 100 females: 93.5; Marriage status: 29.1% never married, 61.1% now married, 0.9% separated, 5.1% widowed, 4.7% divorced; Foreign born: 6.4%; Speak English only: 92.4%; With disability: 7.1%; Veterans: 6.6%; Ancestry: 30.1% Italian, 28.9% Irish, 17.8% German, 6.2% Polish, 5.3% English
Employment: 21.0% management, business, and financial, 6.0% computer, engineering, and science, 16.4% education, legal, community service, arts, and media, 6.6% healthcare practitioners, 13.5% service, 24.6% sales and office, 6.0% natural resources, construction, and maintenance, 5.8% production, transportation, and material moving
Income: Per capita: $49,793; Median household: $127,407; Average household: $156,983; Households with income of $100,000 or more: 61.1%; Poverty rate: 2.5%
Educational Attainment: High school diploma or higher: 96.0%; Bachelor's degree or higher: 46.2%; Graduate/professional degree or higher: 19.1%
School District(s)
Levittown Union Free SD (KG-12)
    2014-15 Enrollment: 7,240 . . . . (516) 434-7020
Wantagh Union Free SD (KG-12)
    2014-15 Enrollment: 3,142 . . . . (516) 679-6300
Housing: Homeownership rate: 94.9%; Median home value: $467,400; Median year structure built: 1955; Homeowner vacancy rate: 0.5%; Median selected monthly owner costs: $3,226 with a mortgage, $1,293 without a mortgage; Median gross rent: $1,637 per month; Rental vacancy rate: 0.0%
Health Insurance: 97.4% have insurance; 91.2% have private insurance; 19.4% have public insurance; 2.6% do not have insurance; 0.7% of children under 18 do not have insurance
Transportation: Commute: 82.4% car, 14.3% public transportation, 0.5% walk, 2.5% work from home; Mean travel time to work: 34.4 minutes

WEST HEMPSTEAD (CDP). Covers a land area of 2.656 square miles and a water area of 0.071 square miles. Located at 40.70° N. Lat; 73.65° W. Long. Elevation is 69 feet.
History: West Hempstead was home to the first international automobile race in the United States, running through farms and village streets, known as the Vanderbilt Cup.
Population: 19,012; Growth (since 2000): 1.6%; Density: 7,159.4 persons per square mile; Race: 72.8% White, 7.9% Black/African American, 7.6% Asian, 0.0% American Indian/Alaska Native, 0.0% Native Hawaiian/Other Pacific Islander, 5.6% Two or more races, 19.8% Hispanic of any race; Average household size: 3.22; Median age: 41.1; Age under 18: 23.7%; Age 65 and over: 14.8%; Males per 100 females: 96.4; Marriage status: 32.2% never married, 55.5% now married, 1.5% separated, 5.6%

widowed, 6.7% divorced; Foreign born: 20.8%; Speak English only: 70.6%; With disability: 7.8%; Veterans: 4.8%; Ancestry: 20.9% Italian, 12.1% Irish, 9.1% German, 6.0% American, 4.2% Polish

Employment: 15.3% management, business, and financial, 3.7% computer, engineering, and science, 14.0% education, legal, community service, arts, and media, 9.1% healthcare practitioners, 16.9% service, 27.4% sales and office, 8.1% natural resources, construction, and maintenance, 5.5% production, transportation, and material moving

Income: Per capita: $37,244; Median household: $96,870; Average household: $117,567; Households with income of $100,000 or more: 48.9%; Poverty rate: 5.9%

Educational Attainment: High school diploma or higher: 90.2%; Bachelor's degree or higher: 38.5%; Graduate/professional degree or higher: 17.1%

School District(s)

West Hempstead Union Free SD (KG-12)

2014-15 Enrollment: 2,169 . . . . (516) 390-3107

Housing: Homeownership rate: 84.2%; Median home value: $395,100; Median year structure built: 1951; Homeowner vacancy rate: 0.7%; Median selected monthly owner costs: $2,862 with a mortgage, $1,211 without a mortgage; Median gross rent: $1,626 per month; Rental vacancy rate: 7.3%

Health Insurance: 91.6% have insurance; 78.7% have private insurance; 24.7% have public insurance; 8.4% do not have insurance; 0.9% of children under 18 do not have insurance

Transportation: Commute: 79.2% car, 13.3% public transportation, 1.9% walk, 4.0% work from home; Mean travel time to work: 36.1 minutes

WESTBURY (village). Covers a land area of 2.374 square miles and a water area of 0 square miles. Located at 40.76° N. Lat; 73.59° W. Long. Elevation is 105 feet.

History: Named for Westbury, England. Old Westbury Gardens and manor of former Phipps estate rivals formal gardens of Europe. Seat of N.Y. Institute of Technology's central campus; State University of N.Y. College at Old Westbury. Incorporated 1924.

Population: 15,273; Growth (since 2000): 7.1%; Density: 6,433.7 persons per square mile; Race: 47.4% White, 22.9% Black/African American, 7.7% Asian, 0.2% American Indian/Alaska Native, 0.5% Native Hawaiian/Other Pacific Islander, 6.4% Two or more races, 27.6% Hispanic of any race; Average household size: 3.14; Median age: 39.1; Age under 18: 21.4%; Age 65 and over: 15.3%; Males per 100 females: 96.2; Marriage status: 33.0% never married, 52.2% now married, 2.1% separated, 7.2% widowed, 7.5% divorced; Foreign born: 33.3%; Speak English only: 56.6%; With disability: 8.7%; Veterans: 4.1%; Ancestry: 15.9% Italian, 8.3% Irish, 4.8% Haitian, 4.6% German, 4.5% Jamaican

Employment: 14.3% management, business, and financial, 3.2% computer, engineering, and science, 12.3% education, legal, community service, arts, and media, 6.0% healthcare practitioners, 20.8% service, 24.1% sales and office, 7.0% natural resources, construction, and maintenance, 12.3% production, transportation, and material moving

Income: Per capita: $35,949; Median household: $85,510; Average household: $108,338; Households with income of $100,000 or more: 41.8%; Poverty rate: 7.1%

Educational Attainment: High school diploma or higher: 85.3%; Bachelor's degree or higher: 34.3%; Graduate/professional degree or higher: 15.0%

School District(s)

East Meadow Union Free SD (KG-12)

2014-15 Enrollment: 7,144 . . . . (516) 478-5776

Westbury Union Free SD (PK-12)

2014-15 Enrollment: 4,975 . . . . (516) 876-5016

Housing: Homeownership rate: 74.9%; Median home value: $413,300; Median year structure built: 1954; Homeowner vacancy rate: 1.9%; Median selected monthly owner costs: $3,092 with a mortgage, $1,244 without a mortgage; Median gross rent: $1,560 per month; Rental vacancy rate: 3.5%

Health Insurance: 83.2% have insurance; 72.2% have private insurance; 23.4% have public insurance; 16.8% do not have insurance; 12.9% of children under 18 do not have insurance

Transportation: Commute: 81.4% car, 13.7% public transportation, 1.5% walk, 3.0% work from home; Mean travel time to work: 30.9 minutes

Additional Information Contacts

Village of Westbury . . . . (516) 334-1700
  http://www.villageofwestbury.org

WILLISTON PARK (village). Covers a land area of 0.626 square miles and a water area of 0 square miles. Located at 40.76° N. Lat; 73.65° W. Long. Elevation is 125 feet.

History: Incorporated 1926.

Population: 7,322; Growth (since 2000): 0.8%; Density: 11,704.7 persons per square mile; Race: 79.3% White, 0.5% Black/African American, 11.5% Asian, 2.2% American Indian/Alaska Native, 0.0% Native Hawaiian/Other Pacific Islander, 2.8% Two or more races, 11.7% Hispanic of any race; Average household size: 2.92; Median age: 40.8; Age under 18: 23.4%; Age 65 and over: 14.9%; Males per 100 females: 92.4; Marriage status: 31.1% never married, 56.4% now married, 0.7% separated, 5.5% widowed, 7.0% divorced; Foreign born: 18.8%; Speak English only: 72.3%; With disability: 7.3%; Veterans: 6.7%; Ancestry: 32.1% Irish, 26.6% Italian, 15.0% German, 7.6% Polish, 4.3% American

Employment: 16.4% management, business, and financial, 4.5% computer, engineering, and science, 15.8% education, legal, community service, arts, and media, 8.2% healthcare practitioners, 13.8% service, 28.5% sales and office, 7.9% natural resources, construction, and maintenance, 4.9% production, transportation, and material moving

Income: Per capita: $40,089; Median household: $101,105; Average household: $114,788; Households with income of $100,000 or more: 51.6%; Poverty rate: 3.9%

Educational Attainment: High school diploma or higher: 92.6%; Bachelor's degree or higher: 50.3%; Graduate/professional degree or higher: 22.9%

School District(s)

Herricks Union Free SD (KG-12)

2014-15 Enrollment: 3,923 . . . . (516) 305-8901

Housing: Homeownership rate: 79.4%; Median home value: $471,400; Median year structure built: Before 1940; Homeowner vacancy rate: 0.0%; Median selected monthly owner costs: $2,644 with a mortgage, $1,232 without a mortgage; Median gross rent: $1,679 per month; Rental vacancy rate: 11.2%

Health Insurance: 96.3% have insurance; 87.0% have private insurance; 22.4% have public insurance; 3.7% do not have insurance; 2.6% of children under 18 do not have insurance

Transportation: Commute: 83.9% car, 14.0% public transportation, 0.6% walk, 1.2% work from home; Mean travel time to work: 32.0 minutes

Additional Information Contacts

Village of Williston Park . . . . (516) 746-2193
  http://www.villageofwillistonpark.org

WOODBURY (CDP). Covers a land area of 5.009 square miles and a water area of 0.016 square miles. Located at 40.82° N. Lat; 73.47° W. Long. Elevation is 164 feet.

History: Woodbury was originally a part of New Amsterdam. It was a Dutch colony until taken over by the British in the mid 1600s. According to records, one of the early names of this community was East Woods. Poet Walt Whitman and industrialist Andrew Mellon each once resided in Woodbury Hills.

Population: 8,473; Growth (since 2000): -6.0%; Density: 1,691.7 persons per square mile; Race: 86.9% White, 1.8% Black/African American, 9.6% Asian, 0.0% American Indian/Alaska Native, 0.0% Native Hawaiian/Other Pacific Islander, 1.0% Two or more races, 2.7% Hispanic of any race; Average household size: 2.57; Median age: 51.1; Age under 18: 18.8%; Age 65 and over: 27.6%; Males per 100 females: 87.4; Marriage status: 17.3% never married, 61.4% now married, 0.9% separated, 13.9% widowed, 7.3% divorced; Foreign born: 17.6%; Speak English only: 79.0%; With disability: 8.9%; Veterans: 4.8%; Ancestry: 15.8% Italian, 10.9% Russian, 9.5% Polish, 7.4% American, 7.4% German

Employment: 31.4% management, business, and financial, 6.4% computer, engineering, and science, 14.2% education, legal, community service, arts, and media, 16.2% healthcare practitioners, 6.2% service, 23.3% sales and office, 1.2% natural resources, construction, and maintenance, 1.0% production, transportation, and material moving

Income: Per capita: $84,066; Median household: $158,679; Average household: $235,064; Households with income of $100,000 or more: 66.4%; Poverty rate: 3.9%

Educational Attainment: High school diploma or higher: 94.8%; Bachelor's degree or higher: 63.5%; Graduate/professional degree or higher: 32.5%

School District(s)

Syosset Central SD (KG-12)

2014-15 Enrollment: 6,336 . . . . (516) 364-5605

Housing: Homeownership rate: 87.0%; Median home value: $862,200; Median year structure built: 1980; Homeowner vacancy rate: 1.4%; Median selected monthly owner costs: $4,000+ with a mortgage, $1,500+ without a mortgage; Median gross rent: $2,209 per month; Rental vacancy rate: 0.0%

Health Insurance: 98.7% have insurance; 91.9% have private insurance; 23.7% have public insurance; 1.3% do not have insurance; 0.0% of children under 18 do not have insurance

Transportation: Commute: 75.4% car, 19.4% public transportation, 0.2% walk, 4.4% work from home; Mean travel time to work: 39.1 minutes

WOODMERE (CDP).

Covers a land area of 2.551 square miles and a water area of 0.267 square miles. Located at 40.64° N. Lat; 73.72° W. Long. Elevation is 23 feet.

History: Woodmere is one of the Long Island communities known as the "Five Towns", which is usually said to comprise the villages of Lawrence and Cedarhurst, the hamlets of Woodmere and Inwood, and "The Hewletts." It gets its name from Samuel Wood, who opened a hotel there that flopped.

Population: 17,217; Growth (since 2000): 4.7%; Density: 6,750.3 persons per square mile; Race: 89.1% White, 4.3% Black/African American, 1.9% Asian, 0.0% American Indian/Alaska Native, 0.0% Native Hawaiian/Other Pacific Islander, 1.5% Two or more races, 7.1% Hispanic of any race; Average household size: 3.31; Median age: 37.4; Age under 18: 31.6%; Age 65 and over: 14.7%; Males per 100 females: 96.0; Marriage status: 27.4% never married, 61.6% now married, 0.7% separated, 7.4% widowed, 3.7% divorced; Foreign born: 14.2%; Speak English only: 77.2%; With disability: 6.9%; Veterans: 3.3%; Ancestry: 12.9% American, 11.9% Polish, 10.4% Russian, 7.3% Italian, 7.1% Eastern European

Employment: 21.8% management, business, and financial, 3.9% computer, engineering, and science, 23.8% education, legal, community service, arts, and media, 12.1% healthcare practitioners, 6.4% service, 23.9% sales and office, 4.2% natural resources, construction, and maintenance, 3.9% production, transportation, and material moving

Income: Per capita: $48,827; Median household: $126,968; Average household: $162,277; Households with income of $100,000 or more: 61.9%; Poverty rate: 4.4%

Educational Attainment: High school diploma or higher: 95.5%; Bachelor's degree or higher: 63.7%; Graduate/professional degree or higher: 35.8%

Housing: Homeownership rate: 89.2%; Median home value: $572,700; Median year structure built: 1957; Homeowner vacancy rate: 2.1%; Median selected monthly owner costs: $3,643 with a mortgage, $1,500+ without a mortgage; Median gross rent: $1,871 per month; Rental vacancy rate: 5.3%

Health Insurance: 97.1% have insurance; 84.7% have private insurance; 22.4% have public insurance; 2.9% do not have insurance; 2.6% of children under 18 do not have insurance

Transportation: Commute: 66.9% car, 23.3% public transportation, 2.3% walk, 5.6% work from home; Mean travel time to work: 43.1 minutes

WOODSBURGH (village).

Covers a land area of 0.340 square miles and a water area of 0.044 square miles. Located at 40.62° N. Lat; 73.71° W. Long. Elevation is 7 feet.

Population: 740; Growth (since 2000): -11.0%; Density: 2,173.6 persons per square mile; Race: 97.0% White, 0.8% Black/African American, 1.5% Asian, 0.0% American Indian/Alaska Native, 0.0% Native Hawaiian/Other Pacific Islander, 0.7% Two or more races, 2.0% Hispanic of any race; Average household size: 2.87; Median age: 44.7; Age under 18: 25.3%; Age 65 and over: 18.1%; Males per 100 females: 95.0; Marriage status: 19.2% never married, 72.9% now married, 2.6% separated, 4.5% widowed, 3.4% divorced; Foreign born: 10.3%; Speak English only: 76.5%; With disability: 6.9%; Veterans: 2.9%; Ancestry: 24.3% Polish, 17.4% Russian, 13.9% American, 6.5% Hungarian, 5.9% German

Employment: 16.4% management, business, and financial, 2.3% computer, engineering, and science, 20.6% education, legal, community service, arts, and media, 25.5% healthcare practitioners, 5.2% service, 26.3% sales and office, 0.5% natural resources, construction, and maintenance, 3.1% production, transportation, and material moving

Income: Per capita: $88,357; Median household: $168,750; Average household: $251,577; Households with income of $100,000 or more: 72.9%; Poverty rate: 4.5%

Educational Attainment: High school diploma or higher: 98.8%; Bachelor's degree or higher: 73.5%; Graduate/professional degree or higher: 44.1%

Housing: Homeownership rate: 94.2%; Median home value: $959,000; Median year structure built: 1950; Homeowner vacancy rate: 2.0%; Median selected monthly owner costs: $4,000+ with a mortgage, $1,500+ without a mortgage; Median gross rent: $2,179 per month; Rental vacancy rate: 0.0%

Health Insurance: 99.5% have insurance; 91.4% have private insurance; 18.1% have public insurance; 0.5% do not have insurance; 0.0% of children under 18 do not have insurance

Transportation: Commute: 79.9% car, 10.3% public transportation, 1.1% walk, 8.7% work from home; Mean travel time to work: 34.2 minutes

New York City

Covers a land area of 302.643 square miles and a water area of 165.841 square miles. Located at 40.66° N. Lat; 73.93° W. Long. Elevation is 33 feet.

History: Adrien Block erected four trading houses in New York in 1613, prompting permanent settlement. In 1633, the first church was built, and that was soon followed by the establishment of Fort Amsterdam. After the battle of Long Island in 1776, when Sir William Howe's British forces defeated the forces of General George Washington, the city passed into English hands and remained in their control until 1783. Congress met in New York from 1785-1790, and it was here that George Washington was inaugurated as president.

Population: 8,426,743; Growth (since 2000): 5.2%; Density: 27,843.8 persons per square mile; Race: 43.3% White, 24.5% Black/African American, 13.5% Asian, 0.4% American Indian/Alaska Native, 0.0% Native Hawaiian/Other Pacific Islander, 3.2% Two or more races, 28.9% Hispanic of any race; Average household size: 2.65; Median age: 35.8; Age under 18: 21.3%; Age 65 and over: 12.7%; Males per 100 females: 90.4; Marriage status: 44.0% never married, 42.5% now married, 3.3% separated, 5.6% widowed, 8.0% divorced; Foreign born: 37.2%; Speak English only: 50.9%; With disability: 10.4%; Veterans: 2.7%; Ancestry: 6.7% Italian, 4.6% American, 4.5% Irish, 3.0% German, 2.7% Jamaican

Employment: 15.1% management, business, and financial, 4.2% computer, engineering, and science, 15.1% education, legal, community service, arts, and media, 5.0% healthcare practitioners, 23.1% service, 22.8% sales and office, 6.1% natural resources, construction, and maintenance, 8.6% production, transportation, and material moving

Income: Per capita: $33,078; Median household: $53,373; Average household: $85,704; Households with income of $100,000 or more: 26.3%; Poverty rate: 20.6%

Educational Attainment: High school diploma or higher: 80.3%; Bachelor's degree or higher: 35.7%; Graduate/professional degree or higher: 14.6%

Housing: Homeownership rate: 31.8%; Median home value: $494,800; Median year structure built: 1949; Homeowner vacancy rate: 2.1%; Median selected monthly owner costs: $2,526 with a mortgage, $811 without a mortgage; Median gross rent: $1,255 per month; Rental vacancy rate: 3.5%

Health Insurance: 87.6% have insurance; 55.0% have private insurance; 40.3% have public insurance; 12.4% do not have insurance; 3.6% of children under 18 do not have insurance

Safety: Violent crime rate: 58.6 per 10,000 population; Property crime rate: 151.9 per 10,000 population

Transportation: Commute: 26.7% car, 56.5% public transportation, 10.2% walk, 4.0% work from home; Mean travel time to work: 39.9 minutes; Amtrak: Train and bus service available.

Additional Information Contacts

Bronx Chamber of Commerce . . . . (718) 828-3900
    http://www.bronxchamber.org
Brooklyn Chamber of Commerce . . . . (718) 875-1000
    http://www.ibrooklyn.com
City of New York . . . . (212) 669-2400
    http://nyc.gov
Greater Harlem Chamber of Commerce . . . . (212) 862-7200
    http://greaterharlemchamber.com
Greater New York Chamber of Commerce . . . . (212) 686-7220
    http://www.ny-chamber.com
Greenwich Village-Chelsea Chamber of Commerce . . . . . . (646) 470-1773
    http://www.villagechelsea.com
Manhattan Chamber of Commerce . . . . (212) 479-7772
    http://www.manhattancc.org
New York Women's Chamber of Commerce . . . . (212) 491-9640
    http://www.nywcc.org

Queens Chamber of Commerce . . . . (718) 898-8500
    http://www.queenschamber.org
Rockaway Chamber of Commerce . . . . (718) 979-7030
    http://www.rockawaychamberofcommerce.com
Staten Island Chamber of Commerce . . . . (718) 727-1900
    http://www.sichamber.com

Five Boroughs of New York City

BRONX (borough). Aka Bronx County. Located in southeastern New York State; the northernmost borough of New York city, situated between Manhattan and the Westchester County line; bounded on the west by the Hudson River, on the southwest by Spuyten Duyvil Creek and the Harlem River, on the south by the East River, and on the east by Long Island Sound. Covers a land area of 42.096 square miles, a water area of 15.382 square miles, and is located in the Eastern Time Zone at 40.85° N. Lat., 73.85° W. Long. The county was founded in 1914.

Bronx County is part of the New York-Newark-Jersey City, NY-NJ-PA Metropolitan Statistical Area. The entire metro area includes: Dutchess County-Putnam County, NY Metropolitan Division (Dutchess County, NY; Putnam County, NY); Nassau County-Suffolk County, NY Metropolitan Division (Nassau County, NY; Suffolk County, NY); Newark, NJ-PA Metropolitan Division (Essex County, NJ; Hunterdon County, NJ; Morris County, NJ; Somerset County, NJ; Sussex County, NJ; Union County, NJ; Pike County, PA); New York-Jersey City-White Plains, NY-NJ Metropolitan Division (Bergen County, NJ; Hudson County, NJ; Middlesex County, NJ; Monmouth County, NJ; Ocean County, NJ; Passaic County, NJ; Bronx County, NY; Kings County, NY; New York County, NY; Orange County, NY; Queens County, NY; Richmond County, NY; Rockland County, NY; Westchester County, NY)

Population: 1,428,357; Growth (since 2000): 7.2%; Density: 33,930.7 persons per square mile; Race: 21.0% White, 33.3% Black/African American, 3.7% Asian, 0.6% American Indian/Alaska Native, 0.0% Native Hawaiian/Other Pacific Islander, 3.6% two or more races, 54.6% Hispanic of any race; Average household size: 2.86; Median age: 33.2; Age under 18: 25.7%; Age 65 and over: 11.1%; Males per 100 females: 88.3; Marriage status: 48.8% never married, 36.4% now married, 5.5% separated, 5.5% widowed, 9.2% divorced; Foreign born: 34.4%; Speak English only: 41.7%; With disability: 13.6%; Veterans: 2.9%; Ancestry: 4.6% Jamaican, 3.3% Italian, 2.7% American, 2.3% African, 2.2% Irish
Religion: Six largest groups: 25.5% Catholicism, 2.8% Muslim Estimate, 1.8% Non-denominational Protestant, 1.7% Baptist, 1.2% Pentecostal, 1.0% Judaism
Economy: Unemployment rate: 7.7%; Leading industries: 23.8 % retail trade; 13.0 % real estate and rental and leasing; 12.9 % health care and social assistance; Farms: 1 totaling n/a acres; Company size: 21 employs 1,000 or more persons, 23 employ 500 to 999 persons, 272 employ 100 to 499 persons, 17,150 employ less than 100 persons; Business ownership: 68,705 women-owned, 42,720 Black-owned, 67,559 Hispanic-owned, 9,668 Asian-owned, 2,331 American Indian/Alaska Native-owned
Employment: 8.1% management, business, and financial, 2.0% computer, engineering, and science, 10.0% education, legal, community service, arts, and media, 4.2% healthcare practitioners, 33.3% service, 24.2% sales and office, 7.1% natural resources, construction, and maintenance, 11.0% production, transportation, and material moving
Income: Per capita: $18,456; Median household: $34,299; Average household: $50,191; Households with income of $100,000 or more: 12.4%; Poverty rate: 30.7%
Educational Attainment: High school diploma or higher: 70.6%; Bachelor's degree or higher: 18.9%; Graduate/professional degree or higher: 6.6%
Housing: Homeownership rate: 19.0%; Median home value: $363,400; Median year structure built: 1949; Homeowner vacancy rate: 2.7%; Median selected monthly owner costs: $2,362 with a mortgage, $725 without a mortgage; Median gross rent: $1,074 per month; Rental vacancy rate: 2.8%
Vital Statistics: Birth rate: 148.8 per 10,000 population; Death rate: 69.9 per 10,000 population; Age-adjusted cancer mortality rate: 151.7 deaths per 100,000 population
Health Insurance: 86.3% have insurance; 43.1% have private insurance; 52.0% have public insurance; 13.7% do not have insurance; 3.8% of children under 18 do not have insurance

Health Care: Physicians: 28.8 per 10,000 population; Dentists: 4.7 per 10,000 population; Hospital beds: 36.0 per 10,000 population; Hospital admissions: 1,296.2 per 10,000 population
Air Quality Index (AQI): Percent of Days: 63.0% good, 36.4% moderate, 0.5% unhealthy for sensitive individuals, 0.0% unhealthy, 0.0% very unhealthy; Annual median: 45; Annual maximum: 114
Transportation: Commute: 27.3% car, 59.7% public transportation, 8.0% walk, 3.3% work from home; Mean travel time to work: 43.0 minutes
2016 Presidential Election: 9.5% Trump, 88.8% Clinton, 0.6% Johnson, 1.1% Stein
National and State Parks: Roberto Clemente State Park

School District(s)
Academic Leadership Charter School (KG-03)
    2014-15 Enrollment: 376 . . . . (718) 585-4215
Bronx Academy of Promise Charter School (KG-05)
    2014-15 Enrollment: 581 . . . . (718) 293-6950
Bronx Charter School for Better Learning (KG-05)
    2014-15 Enrollment: 470 . . . . (718) 655-6660
Bronx Charter School for Children (KG-05)
    2014-15 Enrollment: 424 . . . . (718) 402-3300
Bronx Charter School for Excellence (PK-07)
    2014-15 Enrollment: 636 . . . . (718) 828-7301
Bronx Charter School for the Arts (KG-05)
    2014-15 Enrollment: 315 . . . . (718) 893-1042
Bronx Community Charter School (KG-04)
    2014-15 Enrollment: 352 . . . . (718) 944-1400
Bronx Global Learning Institute for Girls Charter (KG-04)
    2014-15 Enrollment: 375 . . . . (718) 993-1740
Bronx Lighthouse Charter School (KG-09)
    2014-15 Enrollment: 665 . . . . (646) 915-0025
Bronx Preparatory Charter School (05-12)
    2014-15 Enrollment: 764 . . . . (718) 294-0841
Bronx Success Academy Charter School 1 (KG-02)
    2014-15 Enrollment: 535 . . . . (347) 286-7951
Bronx Success Academy Charter School 2 (KG-02)
    2014-15 Enrollment: 546 . . . . (347) 286-7966
Dr Richard Izquierdo Health and Science Charter Sc
    2014-15 Enrollment: 523 . . . . (718) 378-0490
Equality Charter School (06-08)
    2014-15 Enrollment: 355 . . . . (718) 320-3032
Family Life Academy Charter School (KG-08)
    2014-15 Enrollment: 467 . . . . (718) 410-8100
Girls Preparatory Charter School of the Bronx (KG-03)
    2014-15 Enrollment: 551 . . . . (718) 292-2113
Grand Concourse Academy Charter School (KG-05)
    2014-15 Enrollment: 389 . . . . (718) 590-1300
Green Dot Ny Charter School (09-12)
    2014-15 Enrollment: 376 . . . . (718) 585-0560
Harriet Tubman Charter School (KG-08)
    2014-15 Enrollment: 653 . . . . (718) 537-9912
Hyde Leadership Charter School (KG-11)
    2014-15 Enrollment: 970 . . . . (718) 991-5500
Icahn Charter School 1 (KG-08)
    2014-15 Enrollment: 326 . . . . (718) 716-8105
Icahn Charter School 2
    2014-15 Enrollment: 324 . . . . (718) 828-6107
Icahn Charter School 3
    2014-15 Enrollment: 318 . . . . (718) 828-0034
Icahn Charter School 5
    2014-15 Enrollment: 217 . . . . (718) 828-0034
International Leadership Charter School (09-12)
    2014-15 Enrollment: 306 . . . . (718) 562-2300
Kipp Academy Charter School (KG-11)
    2014-15 Enrollment: 985 . . . . (718) 665-3555
Metropolitan Lighthouse Charter School
    2014-15 Enrollment: 370 . . . . (646) 241-7005
Mott Haven Academy Charter School (KG-04)
    2014-15 Enrollment: 292 . . . . (718) 292-7015
New Visions Charter High School for Advanced Math (09-09)
    2014-15 Enrollment: 466 . . . . (718) 817-7683
New Visions Charter High School for the Humanities (09-09)
    2014-15 Enrollment: 422 . . . . (718) 817-7686
New York City Geographic District # 7 (PK-12)
    2014-15 Enrollment: 19,916 . . . . (718) 742-6500

New York City Geographic District # 8 (PK-12)
2014-15 Enrollment: 28,669 . . . . (718) 828-6653
New York City Geographic District # 9 (PK-12)
2014-15 Enrollment: 36,061 . . . . (718) 579-7143
New York City Geographic District #10 (PK-12)
2014-15 Enrollment: 55,177 . . . . (718) 741-5852
New York City Geographic District #11 (PK-12)
2014-15 Enrollment: 39,484 . . . . (718) 519-2620
New York City Geographic District #12 (PK-12)
2014-15 Enrollment: 23,956 . . . . (718) 328-2310
New York City Montessori Charter School (KG-01)
2014-15 Enrollment: 250. . . . . (347) 226-9094
NYC Charter HS-Architecture Engineering Construction (09-12)
2014-15 Enrollment: 438. . . . . (646) 400-5566
NYC Special Schools - District 75 (PK-12)
2014-15 Enrollment: 22,867 . . . . (212) 802-1501
South Bronx Charter School-Inter Cultures and Arts (KG-05)
2014-15 Enrollment: 434. . . . . (718) 292-5737
South Bronx Classical Charter School (KG-05)
2014-15 Enrollment: 373. . . . . (718) 860-4340

Four-year College(s)
College of Mount Saint Vincent (Private, Not-for-profit, Roman Catholic)
Fall 2014 Enrollment: 1,915 . . . . (718) 405-3200
2015-16 Tuition: In-state $22,490; Out-of-state $22,490
CUNY Lehman College (Public)
Fall 2014 Enrollment: 12,398 . . . . (718) 960-8000
2015-16 Tuition: In-state $6,760; Out-of-state $13,870
Fordham University (Private, Not-for-profit, Roman Catholic)
Fall 2014 Enrollment: 15,231 . . . . (718) 817-1000
2015-16 Tuition: In-state $47,317; Out-of-state $47,317
Manhattan College (Riverdale) (Private, Not-for-profit, Roman Catholic)
Fall 2014 Enrollment: 3,970 . . . . (718) 862-8000
2015-16 Tuition: In-state $38,580; Out-of-state $38,580
Monroe College (Private, For-profit)
Fall 2014 Enrollment: 7,002 . . . . (718) 933-6700
2015-16 Tuition: In-state $14,148; Out-of-state $14,148
SUNY Maritime College (Throggs Neck) (Public)
Fall 2014 Enrollment: 1,799 . . . . (718) 409-7200
2015-16 Tuition: In-state $7,809; Out-of-state $17,659
Yeshiva of the Telshe Alumni (Riverdale) (Private, Not-for-profit)
Fall 2014 Enrollment: 116 . . . . (718) 601-3523
2015-16 Tuition: In-state $9,100; Out-of-state $9,100

Two-year College(s)
CUNY Bronx Community College (Public)
Fall 2014 Enrollment: 11,506 . . . . (718) 289-5100
2015-16 Tuition: In-state $5,206; Out-of-state $8,086
CUNY Hostos Community College (Public)
Fall 2014 Enrollment: 6,985 . . . . (718) 518-4444
2015-16 Tuition: In-state $5,208; Out-of-state $8,088
School of Professional Horticulture New York Botanical Garden (Private, Not-for-profit)
Fall 2014 Enrollment: 6. . . . . (718) 817-8797
2015-16 Tuition: In-state $7,500; Out-of-state $7,500

Vocational/Technical School(s)
American Beauty School (Private, For-profit)
Fall 2014 Enrollment: 201. . . . . (718) 931-7400
2015-16 Tuition: $8,190
Brittany Beauty School (Private, For-profit)
Fall 2014 Enrollment: 166. . . . . (718) 220-0400
2015-16 Tuition: $13,600

Hospitals: Bronx Childrens Psychiatric Center (78 beds); Bronx Psychiatric Center (360 beds); Bronx-Lebanon Hospital Center (847 beds); Calvary Hospital (225 beds); Hebrew Hospital Home (480 beds); Jacobi Medical Center (527 beds); Lincoln Medical and Mental Health Center (595 beds); Montefiore Medical Center (1062 beds); North Central Bronx Hospital (202 beds); Our Lady of Mercy Medical Center (345 beds); St. Barnabas Hospital (461 beds); Union Community Health Center (201 beds); Veterans Affairs Medical Center (459 beds); Weiler Hospital; Westchester Square Medical Center (205 beds)

Newspapers: Bronx Times Reporter (weekly circulation 57000); Co-Op City Times (weekly circulation 50000); Hagedorn Communications (weekly circulation 39300); Metro North Media (weekly circulation 53000); Norwood News (weekly circulation 15000); Riverdale Press (weekly circulation 14000)

Additional Information Contacts
Bronx County Government . . . . (718) 590-3557
  http://bronxboropres.nyc.gov
Bronx Chamber of Commerce. (718) 828-3900
  http://www.bronxchamber.org

BROOKLYN (borough). Aka Kings County. Located in southeastern New York State. One of the five counties/boroughs of New York City. Covers a land area of 70.816 square miles, a water area of 26.102 square miles, and is located in the Eastern Time Zone at 40.64° N. Lat., 73.95° W. Long. The county was founded in 1683.

Kings County is part of the New York-Newark-Jersey City, NY-NJ-PA Metropolitan Statistical Area. The entire metro area includes: Dutchess County-Putnam County, NY Metropolitan Division (Dutchess County, NY; Putnam County, NY); Nassau County-Suffolk County, NY Metropolitan Division (Nassau County, NY; Suffolk County, NY); Newark, NJ-PA Metropolitan Division (Essex County, NJ; Hunterdon County, NJ; Morris County, NJ; Somerset County, NJ; Sussex County, NJ; Union County, NJ; Pike County, PA); New York-Jersey City-White Plains, NY-NJ Metropolitan Division (Bergen County, NJ; Hudson County, NJ; Middlesex County, NJ; Monmouth County, NJ; Ocean County, NJ; Passaic County, NJ; Bronx County, NY; Kings County, NY; New York County, NY; Orange County, NY; Queens County, NY; Richmond County, NY; Rockland County, NY; Westchester County, NY)

Weather Station: New York Ave V Brooklyn										Elevation: 20 feet		
	Jan	Feb	Mar	Apr	May	Jun	Jul	Aug	Sep	Oct	Nov	Dec
High	39	42	50	60	70	79	84	83	76	65	55	44
Low	27	29	35	45	54	64	70	69	62	50	42	32
Precip	3.5	2.7	4.2	4.4	4.2	3.9	4.8	3.7	3.7	3.7	3.8	3.3
Snow	6.6	7.3	3.9	0.7	0.0	0.0	0.0	0.0	0.0	tr	0.3	3.5

High and Low temperatures in degrees Fahrenheit; Precipitation and Snow in inches

Population: 2,595,259; Growth (since 2000): 5.3%; Density: 36,648.0 persons per square mile; Race: 43.4% White, 33.5% Black/African American, 11.5% Asian, 0.3% American Indian/Alaska Native, 0.0% Native Hawaiian/Other Pacific Islander, 2.4% two or more races, 19.6% Hispanic of any race; Average household size: 2.74; Median age: 34.4; Age under 18: 23.4%; Age 65 and over: 11.9%; Males per 100 females: 89.3; Marriage status: 43.9% never married, 43.3% now married, 3.2% separated, 5.6% widowed, 7.3% divorced; Foreign born: 37.5%; Speak English only: 53.4%; With disability: 9.9%; Veterans: 2.3%; Ancestry: 5.7% American, 5.2% Italian, 3.3% Jamaican, 3.2% Irish, 3.1% Russian

Religion: Six largest groups: 24.9% Catholicism, 11.5% Judaism, 3.8% Muslim Estimate, 3.2% Baptist, 2.4% Non-denominational Protestant, 1.1% Pentecostal

Economy: Unemployment rate: 5.8%; Leading industries: 19.1 % retail trade; 11.9 % health care and social assistance; 10.8 % other services (except public administration); Farms: 10 totaling n/a acres; Company size: 39 employ 1,000 or more persons, 68 employ 500 to 999 persons, 553 employ 100 to 499 persons, 54,063 employ less than 100 persons; Business ownership: 118,489 women-owned, 63,209 Black-owned, 36,081 Hispanic-owned, 47,982 Asian-owned, 1,920 American Indian/Alaska Native-owned

Employment: 13.1% management, business, and financial, 4.2% computer, engineering, and science, 16.5% education, legal, community service, arts, and media, 4.8% healthcare practitioners, 24.1% service, 22.3% sales and office, 6.3% natural resources, construction, and maintenance, 8.8% production, transportation, and material moving

Income: Per capita: $26,774; Median household: $48,201; Average household: $71,957; Households with income of $100,000 or more: 22.2%; Poverty rate: 23.2%

Educational Attainment: High school diploma or higher: 79.3%; Bachelor's degree or higher: 32.8%; Graduate/professional degree or higher: 12.8%

Housing: Homeownership rate: 29.3%; Median home value: $570,200; Median year structure built: Before 1940; Homeowner vacancy rate: 2.3%; Median selected monthly owner costs: $2,635 with a mortgage, $815 without a mortgage; Median gross rent: $1,215 per month; Rental vacancy rate: 3.7%

Vital Statistics: Birth rate: 158.2 per 10,000 population; Death rate: 64.0 per 10,000 population; Age-adjusted cancer mortality rate: 143.1 deaths per 100,000 population

Health Insurance: 88.0% have insurance; 51.4% have private insurance; 43.4% have public insurance; 12.0% do not have insurance; 3.2% of children under 18 do not have insurance
Health Care: Physicians: 31.7 per 10,000 population; Dentists: 6.0 per 10,000 population; Hospital beds: 26.2 per 10,000 population; Hospital admissions: 987.5 per 10,000 population
Air Quality Index (AQI): Percent of Days: 79.2% good, 20.8% moderate, 0.0% unhealthy for sensitive individuals, 0.0% unhealthy, 0.0% very unhealthy; Annual median: 32; Annual maximum: 86
Transportation: Commute: 23.0% car, 61.7% public transportation, 8.8% walk, 3.9% work from home; Mean travel time to work: 41.7 minutes
2016 Presidential Election: 17.6% Trump, 80.0% Clinton, 0.9% Johnson, 1.5% Stein
National and State Parks: Empire - Fulton Ferry State Park; Gateway National Recreation Area

School District(s)

Achievement First Apollo Charter School
2014-15 Enrollment: 580 . . . . (347) 471-2620
Achievement First Brownsville Charter School (KG-04)
2014-15 Enrollment: 727 . . . . (347) 471-2600
Achievement First Bushwick Charter School (KG-09)
2014-15 Enrollment: 1,030 . . . . (718) 443-1213
Achievement First Crown Heights Charter School (KG-11)
2014-15 Enrollment: 980 . . . . (718) 774-0762
Achievement First East New York Charter School (KG-07)
2014-15 Enrollment: 837 . . . . (718) 485-4924
Achievement First Endeavor Charter School (KG-10)
2014-15 Enrollment: 972 . . . . (718) 622-4786
Bedford Stuyvesant Collegiate Charter School (05-08)
2014-15 Enrollment: 402 . . . . (718) 669-7460
Bedford Stuyvesant New Beginnings Charter School
2014-15 Enrollment: 523 . . . . (718) 453-1001
Beginning With Children Charter School (KG-08)
2014-15 Enrollment: 403 . . . . (718) 388-8847
Believe Northside Charter High School (09-11)
2014-15 Enrollment: 381 . . . . (347) 390-1273
Believe Southside Charter High School (09-11)
2014-15 Enrollment: n/a . . . . (718) 390-1275
Brooklyn Ascend Charter School (KG-05)
2014-15 Enrollment: 974 . . . . (718) 907-9150
Brooklyn Charter School (The) (KG-05)
2014-15 Enrollment: 235 . . . . (718) 302-2085
Brooklyn Dreams Charter School
2014-15 Enrollment: 580 . . . . (718) 859-8400
Brooklyn East Collegiate Charter School
2014-15 Enrollment: 327 . . . . (718) 250-5760
Brooklyn Excelsior Charter School (KG-08)
2014-15 Enrollment: 710 . . . . (718) 246-5681
Brooklyn Prospect Charter School (06-08)
2014-15 Enrollment: 769 . . . . (347) 889-7041
Brooklyn Scholars Charter School (KG-06)
2014-15 Enrollment: 631 . . . . (718) 348-9360
Brownsville Ascend Charter School
2014-15 Enrollment: 785 . . . . (347) 294-2600
Brownsville Collegiate Charter School (05-08)
2014-15 Enrollment: 396 . . . . (718) 636-0370
Bushwick Ascend Charter School (KG-02)
2014-15 Enrollment: 630 . . . . (718) 240-9162
Community Partnership Charter School (KG-07)
2014-15 Enrollment: 403 . . . . (718) 399-1495
Community Roots Charter School (KG-05)
2014-15 Enrollment: 454 . . . . (718) 858-1629
Coney Island Preparatory Public Charter School (05-07)
2014-15 Enrollment: 652 . . . . (718) 513-6951
Cultural Arts Academy Charter School At Spring Cre (KG-02)
2014-15 Enrollment: 298 . . . . (718) 683-3300
Excellence Boys Charter School of Bedford Stuyvesa (KG-08)
2014-15 Enrollment: 727 . . . . (718) 638-1830
Excellence Girls Charter School (KG-03)
2014-15 Enrollment: 590 . . . . (718) 638-1875
Explore Charter School (KG-08)
2014-15 Enrollment: 521 . . . . (718) 703-4484
Explore Empower Charter School (KG-04)
2014-15 Enrollment: 466 . . . . (718) 771-2090

Explore Excel Charter School (KG-03)
2014-15 Enrollment: 415 . . . . (718) 303-3245
Fahari Academy Charter School (05-07)
2014-15 Enrollment: 385 . . . . (718) 218-3185
Hebrew Language Academy Charter School (KG-03)
2014-15 Enrollment: 467 . . . . (718) 377-7200
Hellenic Classical Charter School (KG-08)
2014-15 Enrollment: 477 . . . . (718) 499-0957
Hyde Leadership Charter School-Brooklyn
2014-15 Enrollment: 390 . . . . (718) 495-5620
Imagine Me Leadership Charter School
2014-15 Enrollment: 225 . . . . (347) 985-2140
Invictus Preparatory Charter School (05-05)
2014-15 Enrollment: 304 . . . . (718) 235-1682
Kings Collegiate Charter School (05-09)
2014-15 Enrollment: 489 . . . . (718) 342-6047
Kipp Amp Charter School (05-11)
2014-15 Enrollment: 842 . . . . (718) 943-3710
La Cima Charter School (KG-04)
2014-15 Enrollment: 429 . . . . (718) 443-2136
Leadership Preparatory Bedford Stuyvesant Charter (KG-06)
2014-15 Enrollment: 707 . . . . (718) 636-0360
Leadership Preparatory Brownsville Charter School (KG-03)
2014-15 Enrollment: 571 . . . . (718) 669-7461
Leadership Preparatory Ocean Hill Charter School (KG-02)
2014-15 Enrollment: 607 . . . . (718) 250-5767
Lefferts Gardens Charter School
2014-15 Enrollment: 442 . . . . (718) 284-1480
New Hope Academy Charter School (KG-03)
2014-15 Enrollment: 387 . . . . (718) 337-8303
New York City Geographic District #13 (PK-12)
2014-15 Enrollment: 21,600 . . . . (718) 636-3284
New York City Geographic District #14 (PK-12)
2014-15 Enrollment: 19,814 . . . . (718) 302-7600
New York City Geographic District #15 (PK-12)
2014-15 Enrollment: 30,644 . . . . (718) 935-4317
New York City Geographic District #16 (PK-12)
2014-15 Enrollment: 7,647 . . . . (718) 574-2834
New York City Geographic District #17 (PK-12)
2014-15 Enrollment: 24,056 . . . . (718) 221-4372
New York City Geographic District #18 (PK-12)
2014-15 Enrollment: 16,838 . . . . (718) 566-6008
New York City Geographic District #19 (PK-12)
2014-15 Enrollment: 22,690 . . . . (718) 240-2700
New York City Geographic District #20 (PK-12)
2014-15 Enrollment: 49,171 . . . . (718) 759-4908
New York City Geographic District #21 (PK-12)
2014-15 Enrollment: 34,428 . . . . (718) 648-0209
New York City Geographic District #22 (PK-12)
2014-15 Enrollment: 34,798 . . . . (718) 968-6115
New York City Geographic District #23 (PK-12)
2014-15 Enrollment: 10,087 . . . . (718) 240-3677
New York City Geographic District #32 (PK-12)
2014-15 Enrollment: 13,120 . . . . (718) 574-1100
NYC Special Schools - District 75 (PK-12)
2014-15 Enrollment: 22,867 . . . . (212) 802-1501
Ocean Hill Collegiate Charter School
2014-15 Enrollment: 305 . . . . (718) 250-5765
Pave Academy Charter School (KG-04)
2014-15 Enrollment: 414 . . . . (718) 858-7813
Success Academy Charter School-Bedford Stuyvesant 1
2014-15 Enrollment: 433 . . . . (718) 635-3295
Summit Academy Charter School (06-08)
2014-15 Enrollment: 329 . . . . (718) 875-1403
Teaching Firms of America Professional Prep Charte
2014-15 Enrollment: 323 . . . . (718) 285-3787
UFT Charter School (KG-11)
2014-15 Enrollment: 957 . . . . (718) 922-0438
Williamsburg Charter High School (09-12)
2014-15 Enrollment: 960 . . . . (718) 782-9830
Williamsburg Collegiate Charter School (05-11)
2014-15 Enrollment: 520 . . . . (718) 302-4018

Four-year College(s)

Bais Medrash Elyon (Private, Not-for-profit)
Fall 2014 Enrollment: 97 . . . . (718) 253-1664

Bet Medrash Gadol Ateret Torah (Private, Not-for-profit)
Fall 2014 Enrollment: n/a . . . . (718) 375-7100
2015-16 Tuition: In-state $9,200; Out-of-state $9,200
Beth Hamedrash Shaarei Yosher Institute (Private, Not-for-profit)
Fall 2014 Enrollment: 48 . . . . (718) 854-2290
2015-16 Tuition: In-state $8,250; Out-of-state $8,250
Beth Hatalmud Rabbinical College (Private, Not-for-profit)
Fall 2014 Enrollment: 29 . . . . (718) 259-2525
2015-16 Tuition: In-state $7,700; Out-of-state $7,700
Brooklyn Law School (Private, Not-for-profit)
Fall 2014 Enrollment: 1,141 . . . . (718) 625-2200
Central Yeshiva Tomchei Tmimim Lubavitz (Private, Not-for-profit)
Fall 2014 Enrollment: 726 . . . . (718) 774-3430
2015-16 Tuition: In-state $6,700; Out-of-state $6,700
CUNY Brooklyn College (Public)
Fall 2014 Enrollment: 17,390 . . . . (718) 951-5000
2015-16 Tuition: In-state $6,838; Out-of-state $13,948
CUNY Medgar Evers College (Public)
Fall 2014 Enrollment: 6,701 . . . . (718) 270-4900
2015-16 Tuition: In-state $6,680; Out-of-state $13,790
CUNY New York City College of Technology (Public)
Fall 2014 Enrollment: 17,374 . . . . (718) 260-5500
2015-16 Tuition: In-state $6,669; Out-of-state $13,779
LIU Brooklyn (Private, Not-for-profit)
Fall 2014 Enrollment: 8,354 . . . . (718) 488-1011
2015-16 Tuition: In-state $35,546; Out-of-state $35,546
Machzikei Hadath Rabbinical College (Private, Not-for-profit)
Fall 2014 Enrollment: 147 . . . . (718) 854-8791
2015-16 Tuition: In-state $11,050; Out-of-state $11,050
Mesivta Torah Vodaath Rabbinical Seminary (Private, Not-for-profit, Jewish)
Fall 2014 Enrollment: 344 . . . . (718) 621-3651
2015-16 Tuition: In-state $11,010; Out-of-state $11,010
Mesivta of Eastern Parkway-Yeshiva Zichron Meilech (Private, Not-for-profit)
Fall 2014 Enrollment: 35 . . . . (718) 438-1002
2015-16 Tuition: In-state $8,600; Out-of-state $8,600
Mirrer Yeshiva Cent Institute (Private, Not-for-profit, Jewish)
Fall 2014 Enrollment: 197 . . . . (718) 645-0536
2015-16 Tuition: In-state $6,650; Out-of-state $6,650
Pratt Institute-Main (Private, Not-for-profit)
Fall 2014 Enrollment: 4,690 . . . . (718) 636-3600
2015-16 Tuition: In-state $46,586; Out-of-state $46,586
Rabbinical Academy Mesivta Rabbi Chaim Berlin (Private, Not-for-profit)
Fall 2014 Enrollment: 249 . . . . (718) 377-0777
2015-16 Tuition: In-state $12,250; Out-of-state $12,250
Rabbinical College Bobover Yeshiva Bnei Zion (Private, Not-for-profit, Jewish)
Fall 2014 Enrollment: 321 . . . . (718) 438-2018
2015-16 Tuition: In-state $7,750; Out-of-state $7,750
Rabbinical College Ohr Yisroel (Private, Not-for-profit, Jewish)
Fall 2014 Enrollment: 104 . . . . (718) 633-4715
2015-16 Tuition: In-state $9,000; Out-of-state $9,000
Rabbinical College of Ch'san Sofer New York (Private, Not-for-profit, Jewish)
Fall 2014 Enrollment: 45 . . . . (718) 236-1171
2015-16 Tuition: In-state $8,000; Out-of-state $8,000
Rabbinical College of Ohr Shimon Yisroel (Private, Not-for-profit, Jewish)
Fall 2014 Enrollment: 164 . . . . (718) 855-4092
2015-16 Tuition: In-state $11,600; Out-of-state $11,600
Saint Joseph's College-New York (Private, Not-for-profit)
Fall 2014 Enrollment: 4,979 . . . . (718) 940-5300
2015-16 Tuition: In-state $24,113; Out-of-state $24,113
St Francis College (Private, Not-for-profit)
Fall 2014 Enrollment: 2,749 . . . . (718) 522-2300
2015-16 Tuition: In-state $23,800; Out-of-state $23,800
SUNY Downstate Medical Center (Public)
Fall 2014 Enrollment: 1,865 . . . . (718) 270-1000
Talmudical Seminary Oholei Torah (Private, Not-for-profit)
Fall 2014 Enrollment: 330 . . . . (718) 774-5050
2015-16 Tuition: In-state $9,300; Out-of-state $9,300
Talmudical Seminary of Bobov (Private, Not-for-profit, Jewish)
Fall 2014 Enrollment: 327 . . . . (718) 854-8700
2015-16 Tuition: In-state $7,500; Out-of-state $7,500

Torah Temimah Talmudical Seminary (Private, Not-for-profit)
Fall 2014 Enrollment: 102 . . . . (718) 853-8500
2015-16 Tuition: In-state $10,750; Out-of-state $10,750
United Talmudical Seminary (Private, Not-for-profit, Jewish)
Fall 2014 Enrollment: 2,421 . . . . (718) 963-9770
2015-16 Tuition: In-state $13,575; Out-of-state $13,575
Yeshiva Derech Chaim (Private, Not-for-profit)
Fall 2014 Enrollment: 151 . . . . (718) 438-5476
2015-16 Tuition: In-state $11,300; Out-of-state $11,300
Yeshiva Gedola Ohr Yisrael (Private, Not-for-profit)
Fall 2014 Enrollment: n/a . . . . (718) 382-8702
2015-16 Tuition: In-state $6,750; Out-of-state $6,750
Yeshiva Gedolah Imrei Yosef D'spinka (Private, Not-for-profit, Jewish)
Fall 2014 Enrollment: 122 . . . . (718) 851-8721
2015-16 Tuition: In-state $8,000; Out-of-state $8,000
Yeshiva Karlin Stolin (Private, Not-for-profit)
Fall 2014 Enrollment: 113 . . . . (718) 232-7800
2015-16 Tuition: In-state $9,650; Out-of-state $9,650
Yeshiva Sholom Shachna (Private, Not-for-profit)
Fall 2014 Enrollment: n/a . . . . (718) 253-1664
2015-16 Tuition: In-state $9,550; Out-of-state $9,550
Yeshiva and Kollel Harbotzas Torah (Private, Not-for-profit)
Fall 2014 Enrollment: 52 . . . . (718) 692-0208
Yeshiva of Machzikai Hadas (Private, Not-for-profit)
Fall 2014 Enrollment: 373 . . . . (718) 853-2442
2015-16 Tuition: In-state $8,000; Out-of-state $8,000
Yeshivas Novominsk (Private, Not-for-profit)
Fall 2014 Enrollment: 129 . . . . (718) 438-2727
2015-16 Tuition: In-state $9,700; Out-of-state $9,700
Yeshivat Mikdash Melech (Private, Not-for-profit)
Fall 2014 Enrollment: 140 . . . . (718) 339-1090
2015-16 Tuition: In-state $8,100; Out-of-state $8,100

Two-year College(s)

ASA College (Private, For-profit)
Fall 2014 Enrollment: 4,624 . . . . (718) 522-9073
2015-16 Tuition: In-state $12,898; Out-of-state $12,898
Associated Beth Rivkah Schools (Private, Not-for-profit)
Fall 2014 Enrollment: 147 . . . . (718) 735-0400
2015-16 Tuition: In-state $7,500; Out-of-state $7,500
CUNY Kingsborough Community College (Public)
Fall 2014 Enrollment: 17,758 . . . . (718) 368-5000
2015-16 Tuition: In-state $5,202; Out-of-state $8,082
Merkaz Bnos-Business School (Private, Not-for-profit, Jewish)
Fall 2014 Enrollment: 109 . . . . (718) 234-4000
New York Methodist Hospital Center for Allied Health Education (Private, Not-for-profit)
Fall 2014 Enrollment: 227 . . . . (718) 645-3500
2015-16 Tuition: In-state $28,825; Out-of-state $28,825

Vocational/Technical School(s)

AMG School of Licensed Practical Nursing (Private, For-profit)
Fall 2014 Enrollment: n/a . . . . (718) 596-5300
2015-16 Tuition: $30,000
Access Careers (Private, For-profit)
Fall 2014 Enrollment: 286 . . . . (718) 643-9060
2015-16 Tuition: $819
Allen School-Brooklyn (Private, For-profit)
Fall 2014 Enrollment: 476 . . . . (718) 243-1700
2015-16 Tuition: $16,080
Charles Stuart School of Diamond Setting (Private, For-profit)
Fall 2014 Enrollment: 27 . . . . (718) 339-2640
2015-16 Tuition: $11,950
EDP School of Computer Programming (Private, Not-for-profit)
Fall 2014 Enrollment: 105 . . . . (718) 332-6469
2015-16 Tuition: $4,200
Empire Beauty School-Brooklyn (Private, For-profit)
Fall 2014 Enrollment: 125 . . . . (800) 920-4593
2015-16 Tuition: $12,000
Hair Design Institute at Fifth Avenue-Brooklyn (Private, For-profit)
Fall 2014 Enrollment: 129 . . . . (718) 745-1000
2015-16 Tuition: $13,200
Manhattan School of Computer Technology (Private, Not-for-profit)
Fall 2014 Enrollment: 519 . . . . (212) 349-9768
2015-16 Tuition: $3,800

Seminar L'moros Bais Yaakov (Private, Not-for-profit)
Fall 2014 Enrollment: 281 . . . . (718) 851-2900
2015-16 Tuition: In-state $8,470; Out-of-state $8,470
Hospitals: Beth Israel Medical Center-Kings Highway Division (212 beds); Brookdale University Hospital and Medical Center (529 beds); Brooklyn Hospital Center (416 beds); Caledonian Hospital; Coney Island Hospital (387 beds); Interfaith Medical Center (277 beds); Kings County Hospital Center (627 beds); Kingsboro Psychiatric Center (305 beds); Kingsbrook Jewish Medical Center (864 beds); Long Island College Hospital (506 beds); Lutheran Medical Center (476 beds); Maimonides Medical Center (705 beds); NY Community Hospital of Brooklyn (134 beds); New York Methodist Hospital (576 beds); SUNY Downstate Medical Center (376 beds); St. Mary's Hospital (285 beds); VA New York Harbor Healthcare System (942 beds); Victory Memorial Hospital (346 beds); Woodhull Medical & Mental Health Center; Wyckoff Heights Medical Center (305 beds)
Newspapers: Brooklyn Daily Eagle (daily circulation 10100); Brooklyn Spectator (weekly circulation 9000); Brooklyn View (weekly circulation 135000); Canarsie Courier (weekly circulation 5000); Courier-Life Inc. (weekly circulation 390000); EWA Publications (weekly circulation 588000); Greenpoint Gazette (weekly circulation 5500); Home Reporter (weekly circulation 11000); Spring Creek Sun (weekly circulation 10500); The Brooklyn Paper (weekly circulation 259000)
Additional Information Contacts
Brooklyn Chamber of Commerce . . . . (718) 875-1000
http://www.ibrooklyn.com
Kings County Government . . . . (718) 802-3700
http://www.brooklyn-usa.org

MANHATTAN (borough). Aka New York County. Located in southeastern New York State. One of the five counties/boroughs New York City. Covers a land area of 22.829 square miles, a water area of 10.762 square miles, and is located in the Eastern Time Zone at 40.78° N. Lat., 73.97° W. Long. The county was founded in 1683.

New York County is part of the New York-Newark-Jersey City, NY-NJ-PA Metropolitan Statistical Area. The entire metro area includes: Dutchess County-Putnam County, NY Metropolitan Division (Dutchess County, NY; Putnam County, NY); Nassau County-Suffolk County, NY Metropolitan Division (Nassau County, NY; Suffolk County, NY); Newark, NJ-PA Metropolitan Division (Essex County, NJ; Hunterdon County, NJ; Morris County, NJ; Somerset County, NJ; Sussex County, NJ; Union County, NJ; Pike County, PA); New York-Jersey City-White Plains, NY-NJ Metropolitan Division (Bergen County, NJ; Hudson County, NJ; Middlesex County, NJ; Monmouth County, NJ; Ocean County, NJ; Passaic County, NJ; Bronx County, NY; Kings County, NY; New York County, NY; Orange County, NY; Queens County, NY; Richmond County, NY; Rockland County, NY; Westchester County, NY)

Weather Station: New York Central Park Observ   Elevation: 131 feet

	Jan	Feb	Mar	Apr	May	Jun	Jul	Aug	Sep	Oct	Nov	Dec
High	39	42	50	62	72	80	85	84	76	65	55	44
Low	27	29	35	45	54	63	69	68	61	50	41	32
Precip	3.6	2.9	4.1	4.4	4.2	4.5	4.7	4.2	4.2	4.4	4.0	3.9
Snow	7.0	7.6	3.8	0.6	tr	0.0	tr	0.0	0.0	tr	0.3	4.3

High and Low temperatures in degrees Fahrenheit; Precipitation and Snow in inches

Population: 1,629,507; Growth (since 2000): 6.0%; Density: 71,379.8 persons per square mile; Race: 56.4% White, 15.0% Black/African American, 11.7% Asian, 0.4% American Indian/Alaska Native, 0.1% Native Hawaiian/Other Pacific Islander, 4.1% two or more races, 25.8% Hispanic of any race; Average household size: 2.09; Median age: 36.6; Age under 18: 14.6%; Age 65 and over: 14.1%; Males per 100 females: 88.5; Marriage status: 50.7% never married, 35.8% now married, 2.9% separated, 4.8% widowed, 8.8% divorced; Foreign born: 28.9%; Speak English only: 59.7%; With disability: 9.8%; Veterans: 2.5%; Ancestry: 7.1% Irish, 6.3% German, 6.2% Italian, 5.6% American, 4.4% Russian
Religion: Six largest groups: 20.4% Catholicism, 6.2% Judaism, 2.7% Muslim Estimate, 2.7% Non-denominational Protestant, 2.4% Baptist, 1.7% Presbyterian-Reformed
Economy: Unemployment rate: 5.0%; Leading industries: 17.0 % professional, scientific, and technical services; 11.0 % retail trade; 10.5 % other services (except public administration); Farms: 6 totaling n/a acres; Company size: 204 employ 1,000 or more persons, 296 employ 500 to 999 persons, 2,793 employ 100 to 499 persons, 102,705 employ less than 100 persons; Business ownership: 114,896 women-owned, 24,859

Black-owned, 38,504 Hispanic-owned, 40,216 Asian-owned, 1,910 American Indian/Alaska Native-owned
Employment: 26.2% management, business, and financial, 6.0% computer, engineering, and science, 22.0% education, legal, community service, arts, and media, 5.0% healthcare practitioners, 13.8% service, 20.7% sales and office, 2.1% natural resources, construction, and maintenance, 4.1% production, transportation, and material moving
Income: Per capita: $64,993; Median household: $72,871; Average household: $135,687; Households with income of $100,000 or more: 39.6%; Poverty rate: 17.9%
Educational Attainment: High school diploma or higher: 86.6%; Bachelor's degree or higher: 59.9%; Graduate/professional degree or higher: 28.4%
Housing: Homeownership rate: 22.9%; Median home value: $848,700; Median year structure built: 1949; Homeowner vacancy rate: 2.6%; Median selected monthly owner costs: $3,010 with a mortgage, $967 without a mortgage; Median gross rent: $1,519 per month; Rental vacancy rate: 4.0%
Vital Statistics: Birth rate: 113.5 per 10,000 population; Death rate: 66.4 per 10,000 population; Age-adjusted cancer mortality rate: 140.1 deaths per 100,000 population
Health Insurance: 91.1% have insurance; 67.3% have private insurance; 31.8% have public insurance; 8.9% do not have insurance; 3.2% of children under 18 do not have insurance
Health Care: Physicians: 124.1 per 10,000 population; Dentists: 17.3 per 10,000 population; Hospital beds: 71.8 per 10,000 population; Hospital admissions: 2,550.0 per 10,000 population
Air Quality Index (AQI): Percent of Days: 60.0% good, 39.7% moderate, 0.3% unhealthy for sensitive individuals, 0.0% unhealthy, 0.0% very unhealthy; Annual median: 45; Annual maximum: 104
Transportation: Commute: 8.0% car, 59.2% public transportation, 20.7% walk, 6.8% work from home; Mean travel time to work: 31.1 minutes
2016 Presidential Election: 9.8% Trump, 87.4% Clinton, 1.4% Johnson, 1.4% Stein
National and State Parks: African Burial Ground National Monument; Castle Clinton National Monument; Federal Hall National Memorial; General Grant National Memorial; Governors Island National Monument; Hamilton Grange National Memorial; Riverbank State Park; Theodore Roosevelt Birthplace National Historic Site
Airports: Downtown Manhattan/Wall St (general aviation); East 34th Street (general aviation); West 30th St. (general aviation)

School District(s)
Amber Charter School (KG-05)
2014-15 Enrollment: 497 . . . . (212) 534-9667
Broome Street Academy Charter High School (09-09)
2014-15 Enrollment: 349 . . . . (212) 453-0295
Democracy Prep Harlem Charter School (06-07)
2014-15 Enrollment: 787 . . . . (212) 281-1248
Democracy Preparatory Charter School (06-11)
2014-15 Enrollment: 747 . . . . (212) 281-3061
Dream Charter School (KG-04)
2014-15 Enrollment: 395 . . . . (212) 722-0232
East Harlem Scholars Academy Charter School (KG-01)
2014-15 Enrollment: 277 . . . . (212) 348-2518
Future Leaders Institute Charter School (KG-08)
2014-15 Enrollment: 399 . . . . (212) 678-2868
Girls Preparatory Charter School of New York (KG-07)
2014-15 Enrollment: 577 . . . . (212) 388-0241
Harbor Science and Arts Charter School (KG-08)
2014-15 Enrollment: 266 . . . . (917) 261-2700
Harlem Children's Zone Promise Academy Charter Sch (KG-12)
2014-15 Enrollment: 1,036 . . . . (646) 556-6275
Harlem Children's Zone Promise Academy II Charter (KG-07)
2014-15 Enrollment: 801 . . . . (212) 360-3255
Harlem Day Charter School (KG-05)
2014-15 Enrollment: 692 . . . . (212) 876-9953
Harlem Link Charter School (KG-05)
2014-15 Enrollment: 301 . . . . (212) 289-3249
Harlem Success Academy Charter School (KG-06)
2014-15 Enrollment: 931 . . . . (646) 277-7170
Harlem Success Academy Charter School 2 (KG-04)
2014-15 Enrollment: 739 . . . . (646) 747-1300
Harlem Success Academy Charter School 3 (KG-04)
2014-15 Enrollment: 803 . . . . (646) 747-2305

Harlem Success Academy Charter School 4 (KG-04)
  2014-15 Enrollment: 618 . . . . (646) 747-1310
Harlem Success Academy Charter School 5
  2014-15 Enrollment: 523 . . . . (646) 380-2590
Harlem Village Academy Charter School Ehvacs (05-12)
  2014-15 Enrollment: 818 . . . . (646) 812-9298
Harlem Village Academy Leadership Charter School (05-11)
  2014-15 Enrollment: 799 . . . . (646) 812-9400
Icahn Charter School 4
  2014-15 Enrollment: 288 . . . . (718) 828-0034
Innovate Manhattan Charter School (06-07)
  2014-15 Enrollment: 149 . . . . (212) 432-4310
Inwood Academy for Leadership Charter School
  2014-15 Enrollment: 585 . . . . (646) 665-5570
John V Lindsay Wildcat Academy Charter School (09-12)
  2014-15 Enrollment: 468 . . . . (212) 209-6036
Kipp Infinity Charter School (KG-11)
  2014-15 Enrollment: 1,085 . . . . (212) 991-2600
Kipp Success Through Teamwork Achieve & Respon Col (05-11)
  2014-15 Enrollment: 669 . . . . (212) 991-2650
Manhattan Charter School (KG-05)
  2014-15 Enrollment: 262 . . . . (212) 533-2743
New Heights Academy Charter School (05-12)
  2014-15 Enrollment: 735 . . . . (212) 283-5400
New York Center for Autism Charter School (03-06)
  2014-15 Enrollment: 32 . . . . (212) 860-2580
New York City Geographic District # 1 (PK-12)
  2014-15 Enrollment: 11,676 . . . . (212) 353-2948
New York City Geographic District # 2 (PK-12)
  2014-15 Enrollment: 62,392 . . . . (212) 356-3739
New York City Geographic District # 3 (PK-12)
  2014-15 Enrollment: 22,548 . . . . (212) 678-5857
New York City Geographic District # 4 (PK-12)
  2014-15 Enrollment: 13,794 . . . . (212) 348-2873
New York City Geographic District # 5 (PK-12)
  2014-15 Enrollment: 12,215 . . . . (212) 769-7500
New York City Geographic District # 6 (PK-12)
  2014-15 Enrollment: 23,767 . . . . (212) 521-3757
New York French-American Charter School
  2014-15 Enrollment: 251 . . . . (212) 666-4134
NYC Special Schools - District 75 (PK-12)
  2014-15 Enrollment: 22,867 . . . . (212) 802-1501
Opportunity Charter School (06-12)
  2014-15 Enrollment: 474 . . . . (212) 866-6137
Rensaissance Charter High School for Innovation
  2014-15 Enrollment: 441 . . . . (212) 722-5871
Saint Hope Leadership Academy Charter School (05-08)
  2014-15 Enrollment: 278 . . . . (212) 283-1204
Sisulu-Walker Charter School of Harlem (KG-05)
  2014-15 Enrollment: 241 . . . . (212) 663-8216
The Equity Project Charter School (05-07)
  2014-15 Enrollment: 480 . . . . (646) 254-6451
Upper West Success Academy Charter School (KG-01)
  2014-15 Enrollment: 473 . . . . (646) 274-1581
Voice Charter School of New York (KG-04)
  2014-15 Enrollment: 593 . . . . (718) 361-1694

Four-year College(s)

American Musical and Dramatic Academy (Private, Not-for-profit)
  Fall 2014 Enrollment: 1,735 . . . . (212) 787-5300
  2015-16 Tuition: In-state $33,920; Out-of-state $33,920
Bank Street College of Education (Private, Not-for-profit)
  Fall 2014 Enrollment: 747 . . . . (212) 875-4400
Barnard College (Private, Not-for-profit)
  Fall 2014 Enrollment: 2,573 . . . . (212) 854-5262
  2015-16 Tuition: In-state $47,631; Out-of-state $47,631
Berkeley College-New York (Private, For-profit)
  Fall 2014 Enrollment: 4,479 . . . . (212) 986-4343
  2015-16 Tuition: In-state $24,300; Out-of-state $24,300
Boricua College (Private, Not-for-profit)
  Fall 2014 Enrollment: 1,163 . . . . (212) 694-1000
  2015-16 Tuition: In-state $10,625; Out-of-state $10,625
CUNY Bernard M Baruch College (Public)
  Fall 2014 Enrollment: 18,090 . . . . (646) 312-1000
  2015-16 Tuition: In-state $6,810; Out-of-state $13,920

CUNY City College (Public)
  Fall 2014 Enrollment: 15,579 . . . . (212) 650-7000
  2015-16 Tuition: In-state $6,689; Out-of-state $13,799
CUNY Graduate School and University Center (Public)
  Fall 2014 Enrollment: 7,013 . . . . (212) 817-7000
CUNY Hunter College (Public)
  Fall 2014 Enrollment: 23,112 . . . . (212) 772-4000
  2015-16 Tuition: In-state $6,782; Out-of-state $13,892
CUNY John Jay College of Criminal Justice (Public)
  Fall 2014 Enrollment: 15,045 . . . . (212) 237-8000
  2015-16 Tuition: In-state $6,810; Out-of-state $13,920
Christie's Education (Private, For-profit)
  Fall 2014 Enrollment: 65 . . . . (212) 355-1501
Columbia University in the City of New York (Private, Not-for-profit)
  Fall 2014 Enrollment: 27,589 . . . . (212) 854-1754
  2015-16 Tuition: In-state $53,000; Out-of-state $53,000
Cooper Union for the Advancement of Science and Art (Private, Not-for-profit)
  Fall 2014 Enrollment: 966 . . . . (212) 353-4100
  2015-16 Tuition: In-state $42,650; Out-of-state $42,650
DeVry College of New York (Private, For-profit)
  Fall 2014 Enrollment: 2,026 . . . . (212) 312-4300
  2015-16 Tuition: In-state $19,568; Out-of-state $19,568
Fashion Institute of Technology (Public)
  Fall 2014 Enrollment: 9,764 . . . . (212) 217-7999
  2015-16 Tuition: In-state $5,230; Out-of-state $14,230
Globe Institute of Technology (Private, For-profit)
  Fall 2014 Enrollment: 490 . . . . (212) 349-4330
  2015-16 Tuition: In-state $11,120; Out-of-state $11,120
Hebrew Union College-Jewish Institute of Religion (Private, Not-for-profit, Jewish)
  Fall 2014 Enrollment: 346 . . . . (212) 674-5300
Helene Fuld College of Nursing (Private, Not-for-profit)
  Fall 2014 Enrollment: 444 . . . . (212) 616-7200
  2015-16 Tuition: In-state $18,764; Out-of-state $18,764
Icahn School of Medicine at Mount Sinai (Private, Not-for-profit)
  Fall 2014 Enrollment: 1,074 . . . . (212) 241-6500
Jewish Theological Seminary of America (Private, Not-for-profit, Jewish)
  Fall 2014 Enrollment: 405 . . . . (212) 678-8000
  2015-16 Tuition: In-state $20,340; Out-of-state $20,340
LIM College (Private, For-profit)
  Fall 2014 Enrollment: 1,737 . . . . (212) 752-1530
  2015-16 Tuition: In-state $24,825; Out-of-state $24,825
Manhattan School of Music (Private, Not-for-profit)
  Fall 2014 Enrollment: 957 . . . . (212) 749-2802
  2015-16 Tuition: In-state $42,600; Out-of-state $42,600
Marymount Manhattan College (Private, Not-for-profit)
  Fall 2014 Enrollment: 1,858 . . . . (212) 517-0400
  2015-16 Tuition: In-state $28,700; Out-of-state $28,700
Mesivtha Tifereth Jerusalem of America (Private, Not-for-profit, Jewish)
  Fall 2014 Enrollment: 72 . . . . (212) 964-2830
  2015-16 Tuition: In-state $10,250; Out-of-state $10,250
Metropolitan College of New York (Private, Not-for-profit)
  Fall 2014 Enrollment: 1,228 . . . . (800) 338-4465
  2015-16 Tuition: In-state $18,030; Out-of-state $18,030
New York Academy of Art (Private, Not-for-profit)
  Fall 2014 Enrollment: 108 . . . . (212) 966-0300
New York College of Podiatric Medicine (Private, Not-for-profit)
  Fall 2014 Enrollment: 381 . . . . (212) 410-8000
New York Law School (Private, Not-for-profit)
  Fall 2014 Enrollment: 1,029 . . . . (212) 431-2100
New York School of Interior Design (Private, Not-for-profit)
  Fall 2014 Enrollment: 539 . . . . (212) 472-1500
  2015-16 Tuition: In-state $22,670; Out-of-state $22,670
New York Theological Seminary (Private, Not-for-profit, Interdenominational)
  Fall 2014 Enrollment: 396 . . . . (212) 870-1211
New York University (Private, Not-for-profit)
  Fall 2014 Enrollment: 49,274 . . . . (212) 998-1212
  2015-16 Tuition: In-state $47,750; Out-of-state $47,750
Pace University-New York (Private, Not-for-profit)
  Fall 2014 Enrollment: 12,857 . . . . (212) 346-1200
  2015-16 Tuition: In-state $41,333; Out-of-state $41,333
Pacific College of Oriental Medicine-New York (Private, For-profit)
  Fall 2014 Enrollment: 560 . . . . (212) 982-3456
  2015-16 Tuition: In-state $12,205; Out-of-state $12,205

Phillips Beth Israel School of Nursing (Private, Not-for-profit)
Fall 2014 Enrollment: 278 . . . . (212) 614-6114
2015-16 Tuition: In-state $22,545; Out-of-state $22,545
Relay Graduate School of Education (Private, Not-for-profit)
Fall 2014 Enrollment: 958 . . . . (212) 228-1888
Rockefeller University (Private, Not-for-profit)
Fall 2014 Enrollment: 209 . . . . (212) 327-8000
SUNY College of Optometry (Public)
Fall 2014 Enrollment: 363 . . . . (212) 938-4000
School of Visual Arts (Private, For-profit)
Fall 2014 Enrollment: 4,397 . . . . (212) 592-2000
2015-16 Tuition: In-state $35,000; Out-of-state $35,000
Sotheby's Institute of Art-NY (Private, For-profit)
Fall 2014 Enrollment: 153 . . . . (212) 517-3929
Teachers College at Columbia University (Private, Not-for-profit)
Fall 2014 Enrollment: 5,011 . . . . (212) 678-3000
The General Theological Seminary (Private, Not-for-profit, Protestant
Episcopal)
Fall 2014 Enrollment: 76 . . . . (212) 243-5150
The Juilliard School (Private, Not-for-profit)
Fall 2014 Enrollment: 926 . . . . (212) 799-5000
2015-16 Tuition: In-state $39,720; Out-of-state $39,720
The King's College (Private, Not-for-profit, Interdenominational)
Fall 2014 Enrollment: 487 . . . . (212) 659-7200
2015-16 Tuition: In-state $33,270; Out-of-state $33,270
The New School (Private, Not-for-profit)
Fall 2014 Enrollment: 10,477 . . . . (212) 229-5600
2015-16 Tuition: In-state $43,813; Out-of-state $43,813
Touro College (Private, Not-for-profit)
Fall 2014 Enrollment: 12,381 . . . . (646) 565-6000
2015-16 Tuition: In-state $16,700; Out-of-state $16,700
Tri-State College of Acupuncture (Private, For-profit)
Fall 2014 Enrollment: 110 . . . . (212) 242-2255
Union Theological Seminary in the City of New York (Private, Not-for-profit)
Fall 2014 Enrollment: 233 . . . . (212) 662-7100
Weill Cornell Medical College (Private, Not-for-profit)
Fall 2014 Enrollment: 1,023 . . . . (212) 746-1050
Yeshiva University (Private, Not-for-profit)
Fall 2014 Enrollment: 6,348 . . . . (212) 960-5400
2015-16 Tuition: In-state $39,530; Out-of-state $39,530

Two-year College(s)

American Academy McAllister Institute of Funeral Service (Private,
Not-for-profit)
Fall 2014 Enrollment: 424 . . . . (212) 757-1190
2015-16 Tuition: In-state $15,878; Out-of-state $15,878
American Academy of Dramatic Arts-New York (Private, Not-for-profit)
Fall 2014 Enrollment: 253 . . . . (212) 686-9244
2015-16 Tuition: In-state $30,650; Out-of-state $30,650
CUNY Borough of Manhattan Community College (Public)
Fall 2014 Enrollment: 26,606 . . . . (212) 220-8000
2015-16 Tuition: In-state $5,170; Out-of-state $8,050
Circle in the Square Theater School (Private, Not-for-profit)
Fall 2014 Enrollment: 69 . . . . (212) 307-0388
2015-16 Tuition: In-state $16,040; Out-of-state $16,040
Dance Theatre of Harlem Inc (Private, Not-for-profit)
Fall 2014 Enrollment: 3 . . . . (212) 690-2800
2015-16 Tuition: In-state $6,300; Out-of-state $6,300
Joffrey Ballet School (Private, For-profit)
Fall 2014 Enrollment: 262 . . . . (888) 438-3808
2015-16 Tuition: In-state $15,099; Out-of-state $15,099
Mandl School-The College of Allied Health (Private, For-profit)
Fall 2014 Enrollment: 707 . . . . (212) 247-3434
2015-16 Tuition: In-state $13,095; Out-of-state $13,095
Memorial Hospital School of Radiation Therapy Technology (Private,
Not-for-profit)
Fall 2014 Enrollment: 15 . . . . (212) 639-6835
Mildred Elley-New York Campus (Private, For-profit)
Fall 2014 Enrollment: 590 . . . . (212) 380-9004
2015-16 Tuition: In-state $12,165; Out-of-state $12,165
Neighborhood Playhouse School of the Theater (Private, Not-for-profit)
Fall 2014 Enrollment: 80 . . . . (212) 688-3770
2015-16 Tuition: In-state $15,800; Out-of-state $15,800
New York Career Institute (Private, For-profit)
Fall 2014 Enrollment: 545 . . . . (212) 962-0002
2015-16 Tuition: In-state $13,650; Out-of-state $13,650

New York Conservatory for Dramatic Arts (Private, For-profit)
Fall 2014 Enrollment: 237 . . . . (212) 645-0030
2015-16 Tuition: In-state $31,200; Out-of-state $31,200
Professional Business College (Private, Not-for-profit)
Fall 2014 Enrollment: n/a . . . . (212) 226-7300
Sanford-Brown Institute-New York (Private, For-profit)
Fall 2014 Enrollment: 1,226 . . . . (646) 313-4510
Stella and Charles Guttman Community College (Public)
Fall 2014 Enrollment: 691 . . . . (646) 313-8000
2015-16 Tuition: In-state $5,194; Out-of-state $8,074
Swedish Institute a College of Health Sciences (Private, For-profit)
Fall 2014 Enrollment: 792 . . . . (212) 924-5900
2015-16 Tuition: In-state $13,750; Out-of-state $13,750
Technical Career Institutes (Private, For-profit)
Fall 2014 Enrollment: 2,762 . . . . (212) 594-4000
2015-16 Tuition: In-state $13,700; Out-of-state $13,700
The Ailey School (Private, Not-for-profit)
Fall 2014 Enrollment: 96 . . . . (212) 405-9008
2015-16 Tuition: In-state $11,865; Out-of-state $11,865
The Art Institute of New York City (Private, For-profit)
Fall 2014 Enrollment: 898 . . . . (212) 226-5500
2015-16 Tuition: In-state $19,752; Out-of-state $19,752
The Collective School Of Music (Private, For-profit)
Fall 2014 Enrollment: 52 . . . . (212) 741-0091
2015-16 Tuition: In-state $30,250; Out-of-state $30,250
Wood Tobe-Coburn School (Private, For-profit)
Fall 2014 Enrollment: 411 . . . . (212) 686-9040
2015-16 Tuition: In-state $16,860; Out-of-state $16,860

Vocational/Technical School(s)

American Academy of Personal Training (Private, For-profit)
Fall 2014 Enrollment: 187 . . . . (212) 242-2278
2015-16 Tuition: $5,025
Arrojo Cosmetology School (Private, For-profit)
Fall 2014 Enrollment: 29 . . . . (212) 242-7786
2015-16 Tuition: $14,700
Atelier Esthetique Institute of Esthetics (Private, For-profit)
Fall 2014 Enrollment: 127 . . . . (212) 725-6130
2015-16 Tuition: $9,000
Aveda Institute-New York (Private, For-profit)
Fall 2014 Enrollment: 229 . . . . (212) 807-1492
2015-16 Tuition: $16,995
Carsten Institute of Cosmetology (Private, For-profit)
Fall 2014 Enrollment: 115 . . . . (212) 675-4884
2015-16 Tuition: $14,416
Christine Valmy International School for Esthetics Skin Care & Makeup
(Private, For-profit)
Fall 2014 Enrollment: 278 . . . . (212) 779-7800
2015-16 Tuition: $8,000
Culinary Tech Center (Private, For-profit)
Fall 2014 Enrollment: n/a . . . . (646) 559-8551
2015-16 Tuition: $12,195
Dermalogica Academy (Private, For-profit)
Fall 2014 Enrollment: n/a . . . . (212) 243-3000
2015-16 Tuition: $10,100
Digital Film Academy (Private, For-profit)
Fall 2014 Enrollment: 88 . . . . (212) 333-4013
2015-16 Tuition: $17,520
Empire Beauty School-Manhattan (Private, For-profit)
Fall 2014 Enrollment: 585 . . . . (800) 920-4593
2015-16 Tuition: $12,000
Gemological Institute of America-New York (Private, Not-for-profit)
Fall 2014 Enrollment: 202 . . . . (212) 944-5900
2015-16 Tuition: $21,000
Hair Design Institute at Fifth Avenue-New York (Private, For-profit)
Fall 2014 Enrollment: 182 . . . . (212) 868-7171
2015-16 Tuition: $13,200
Institute of Audio Research (Private, For-profit)
Fall 2014 Enrollment: 473 . . . . (212) 777-8550
2015-16 Tuition: $16,530
Institute of Culinary Education (Private, For-profit)
Fall 2014 Enrollment: 664 . . . . (212) 847-0700
2015-16 Tuition: $37,160
Lia Schorr Institute of Cosmetic Skin Care Training (Private, For-profit)
Fall 2014 Enrollment: 35 . . . . (212) 486-9541
2015-16 Tuition: $7,500

Manhattan Institute (Private, For-profit)
  Fall 2014 Enrollment: 1,221 . . . . (212) 564-1234
  2015-16 Tuition: $760
New Age Training (Private, For-profit)
  Fall 2014 Enrollment: 136 . . . . (212) 947-7940
  2015-16 Tuition: $9,200
SAE Institute of Technology-New York (Private, For-profit)
  Fall 2014 Enrollment: 121 . . . . (212) 944-9121
  2015-16 Tuition: $22,400
Spanish-American Institute (Private, Not-for-profit)
  Fall 2014 Enrollment: n/a . . . . (212) 840-7111
  2015-16 Tuition: $9,700
Star Career Academy-New York (Private, For-profit)
  Fall 2014 Enrollment: 723 . . . . (212) 675-6655
  2015-16 Tuition: $14,915
Studio Jewelers (Private, For-profit)
  Fall 2014 Enrollment: 55 . . . . (212) 686-1944
  2015-16 Tuition: $9,000
The International Culinary Center (Private, For-profit)
  Fall 2014 Enrollment: 452 . . . . (212) 219-8890
  2015-16 Tuition: $47,900

Hospitals: Bellevue Hospital Center (809 beds); Beth Israel Medical Center (1368 beds); Cabrini Medical Center (493 beds); Cornerstone of Medical Arts Center Hospital (100 beds); Department of Veteran Affairs NY Harbor Health System (350 beds); Gracie Square Hospital (157 beds); Harlem Hospital Center (272 beds); Hospital for Special Surgery (160 beds); Lenox Hill Hospital (652 beds); Manhattan Eye, Ear & Throat Hospital (150 beds); Manhattan Psychiatric Center; Memorial Sloan-Kettering Cancer Center (437 beds); Metropolitan Hospital Center (341 beds); Mount Sinai Medical Center (1171 beds); NYU Hospital for Joint Diseases (216 beds); NYU Langone Medical Center (724 beds); New York - Presbyterian Hospital (2344 beds); New York Downtown Hospital (155 beds); New York Eye and Ear Infirmary (103 beds); New York State Psychiatric Institute (70 beds); North General Hospital (152 beds); Rockefeller University Hospital (20 beds); SVCMC-Saint Vincent's Centers NY & West Branches (756 beds); St. Luke's Roosevelt Hospital Center (1046 beds); St. Vincent's Hospital & Medical Center of NY (727 beds); St. Vincent's Midtown Hospital (150 beds)

Newspapers: AM New York (daily circulation 267000); Daily News (daily circulation 603000); Downtown Express (weekly circulation 50000); Manhattan Media (weekly circulation 57000); Metro New York (daily circulation 327000); NY Town & Village (weekly circulation 8500); New York Post (daily circulation 704000); New York Times (daily circulation 1040000); Resident Publications (weekly circulation 160000); The New York Observer (weekly circulation 50000); The Villager (weekly circulation 26000); Village Voice (weekly circulation 253000); Wall Street Journal (daily circulation 2100000)

Additional Information Contacts

City of New York . . . . (212) 669-2400
  http://nyc.gov
Greater Harlem Chamber of Commerce . . . . (212) 862-7200
  http://greaterharlemchamber.com
Greater New York Chamber of Commerce . . . . (212) 686-7220
  http://www.ny-chamber.com
Greenwich Village-Chelsea Chamber of Commerce . . . . . . (646) 470-1773
  http://www.villagechelsea.com
Manhattan Chamber of Commerce . . . . (212) 479-7772
  http://www.manhattancc.org
New York Women's Chamber of Commerce . . . . (212) 491-9640
  http://www.nywcc.org

QUEENS (borough).

Aka Queens County. Located in southeastern New York State, on Long Island; one of the five counties/boroughs New York City; bounded on the west and north by the East River. Covers a land area of 108.532 square miles, a water area of 69.675 square miles, and is located in the Eastern Time Zone at 40.66° N. Lat., 73.84° W. Long. The county was founded in 1683. County seat is Jamaica.

Queens County is part of the New York-Newark-Jersey City, NY-NJ-PA Metropolitan Statistical Area. The entire metro area includes: Dutchess County-Putnam County, NY Metropolitan Division (Dutchess County, NY; Putnam County, NY); Nassau County-Suffolk County, NY Metropolitan Division (Nassau County, NY; Suffolk County, NY); Newark, NJ-PA Metropolitan Division (Essex County, NJ; Hunterdon County, NJ; Morris County, NJ; Somerset County, NJ; Sussex County, NJ; Union County, NJ; Pike County, PA); New York-Jersey City-White Plains, NY-NJ Metropolitan

Division (Bergen County, NJ; Hudson County, NJ; Middlesex County, NJ; Monmouth County, NJ; Ocean County, NJ; Passaic County, NJ; Bronx County, NY; Kings County, NY; New York County, NY; Orange County, NY; Queens County, NY; Richmond County, NY; Rockland County, NY; Westchester County, NY)

Weather Station: New York J F Kennedy Int'l Arpt   Elevation: 16 feet

	Jan	Feb	Mar	Apr	May	Jun	Jul	Aug	Sep	Oct	Nov	Dec
High	39	42	49	59	68	78	83	82	75	64	54	44
Low	26	28	34	44	53	63	69	68	61	50	41	32
Precip	3.2	2.4	3.8	4.0	4.0	3.9	4.1	3.6	3.4	3.6	3.4	3.3
Snow	6.4	7.4	3.6	0.8	tr	0.0	tr	0.0	0.0	tr	0.3	4.2

High and Low temperatures in degrees Fahrenheit; Precipitation and Snow in inches

Weather Station: New York Laguardia Arpt   Elevation: 11 feet

	Jan	Feb	Mar	Apr	May	Jun	Jul	Aug	Sep	Oct	Nov	Dec
High	39	42	49	61	71	80	85	84	76	65	54	44
Low	27	29	35	45	55	64	70	70	63	52	42	33
Precip	3.2	2.6	3.9	4.1	3.8	4.0	4.6	4.1	3.7	3.7	3.5	3.5
Snow	7.5	8.2	4.5	0.6	tr	0.0	tr	tr	0.0	tr	0.3	4.8

High and Low temperatures in degrees Fahrenheit; Precipitation and Snow in inches

Population: 2,301,139; Growth (since 2000): 3.2%; Density: 21,202.4 persons per square mile; Race: 41.1% White, 18.5% Black/African American, 24.4% Asian, 0.4% American Indian/Alaska Native, 0.0% Native Hawaiian/Other Pacific Islander, 3.4% two or more races, 27.9% Hispanic of any race; Average household size: 2.91; Median age: 37.7; Age under 18: 20.5%; Age 65 and over: 13.4%; Males per 100 females: 93.8; Marriage status: 38.3% never married, 48.1% now married, 2.8% separated, 5.9% widowed, 7.7% divorced; Foreign born: 47.8%; Speak English only: 43.7%; With disability: 9.5%; Veterans: 2.7%; Ancestry: 5.7% Italian, 4.0% Irish, 3.8% American, 2.8% Guyanese, 2.8% Jamaican
Religion: Six largest groups: 30.4% Catholicism, 3.9% Judaism, 3.7% Muslim Estimate, 1.7% Methodist/Pietist, 1.6% Eastern Liturgical (Orthodox), 1.6% Orthodox
Economy: Unemployment rate: 4.9%; Leading industries: 16.2 % retail trade; 12.1 % other services (except public administration); 11.3 % construction; Farms: 6 totaling 442 acres; Company size: 46 employ 1,000 or more persons, 44 employ 500 to 999 persons, 580 employ 100 to 499 persons, 46,840 employ less than 100 persons; Business ownership: 97,982 women-owned, 30,783 Black-owned, 52,719 Hispanic-owned, 91,714 Asian-owned, 1,930 American Indian/Alaska Native-owned
Employment: 12.4% management, business, and financial, 3.8% computer, engineering, and science, 11.0% education, legal, community service, arts, and media, 5.1% healthcare practitioners, 24.8% service, 24.0% sales and office, 8.2% natural resources, construction, and maintenance, 10.7% production, transportation, and material moving
Income: Per capita: $26,876; Median household: $57,720; Average household: $75,162; Households with income of $100,000 or more: 25.5%; Poverty rate: 15.1%
Educational Attainment: High school diploma or higher: 80.4%; Bachelor's degree or higher: 30.4%; Graduate/professional degree or higher: 11.1%
Housing: Homeownership rate: 43.6%; Median home value: $450,300; Median year structure built: 1951; Homeowner vacancy rate: 1.7%; Median selected monthly owner costs: $2,425 with a mortgage, $791 without a mortgage; Median gross rent: $1,367 per month; Rental vacancy rate: 3.0%
Vital Statistics: Birth rate: 130.1 per 10,000 population; Death rate: 64.7 per 10,000 population; Age-adjusted cancer mortality rate: 132.1 deaths per 100,000 population
Health Insurance: 84.4% have insurance; 54.5% have private insurance; 37.4% have public insurance; 15.6% do not have insurance; 4.4% of children under 18 do not have insurance
Health Care: Physicians: 26.3 per 10,000 population; Dentists: 7.1 per 10,000 population; Hospital beds: 15.1 per 10,000 population; Hospital admissions: 629.4 per 10,000 population
Air Quality Index (AQI): Percent of Days: 71.8% good, 27.4% moderate, 0.8% unhealthy for sensitive individuals, 0.0% unhealthy, 0.0% very unhealthy; Annual median: 41; Annual maximum: 114
Transportation: Commute: 38.0% car, 52.3% public transportation, 5.8% walk, 2.4% work from home; Mean travel time to work: 42.6 minutes
2016 Presidential Election: 21.9% Trump, 75.7% Clinton, 1.0% Johnson, 1.4% Stein
National and State Parks: Gateway National Recreation Area; Bayswater Point State Park; Gantry Plaza State Park

Airports: John F Kennedy International (primary service/large hub); La Guardia (primary service/large hub)

School District(s)

Academy of the City Charter School (KG-01)
2014-15 Enrollment: 359 . . . . (718) 487-9857
Challenge Preparatory Charter School (KG-02)
2014-15 Enrollment: 494 . . . . (718) 327-1352
Growing Up Green Charter School (KG-03)
2014-15 Enrollment: 600 . . . . (347) 642-4306
Merrick Academy-Queens Public Charter School (KG-06)
2014-15 Enrollment: 494 . . . . (718) 479-3753
New York City Geographic District #24 (PK-12)
2014-15 Enrollment: 57,598 . . . . (718) 592-3357
New York City Geographic District #25 (PK-12)
2014-15 Enrollment: 36,693 . . . . (718) 281-7605
New York City Geographic District #26 (PK-12)
2014-15 Enrollment: 31,744 . . . . (718) 631-6943
New York City Geographic District #27 (PK-12)
2014-15 Enrollment: 44,520 . . . . (718) 642-5800
New York City Geographic District #28 (PK-12)
2014-15 Enrollment: 39,925 . . . . (718) 557-2618
New York City Geographic District #29 (PK-12)
2014-15 Enrollment: 27,037 . . . . (718) 264-3146
New York City Geographic District #30 (PK-12)
2014-15 Enrollment: 40,008 . . . . (718) 391-8323
NYC Special Schools - District 75 (PK-12)
2014-15 Enrollment: 22,867 . . . . (212) 802-1501
Our World Neighborhood Charter School (KG-08)
2014-15 Enrollment: 699 . . . . (718) 392-3405
Peninsula Preparatory Academy Charter School (KG-05)
2014-15 Enrollment: 324 . . . . (646) 403-9231
Renaissance Charter School (The) (KG-12)
2014-15 Enrollment: 544 . . . . (718) 803-0060
Riverton Street Charter School
2014-15 Enrollment: 728 . . . . (718) 481-8200
Rochdale Early Advantage Charter School
2014-15 Enrollment: 229 . . . . (718) 978-0041

Four-year College(s)

Beis Medrash Heichal Dovid (Private, Not-for-profit, Jewish)
Fall 2014 Enrollment: 111 . . . . (718) 868-2300
2015-16 Tuition: In-state $9,200; Out-of-state $9,200
CUNY Queens College (Public)
Fall 2014 Enrollment: 19,310 . . . . (718) 997-5000
2015-16 Tuition: In-state $6,938; Out-of-state $14,048
CUNY School of Law (Public)
Fall 2014 Enrollment: 325 . . . . (718) 340-4200
CUNY York College (Public)
Fall 2014 Enrollment: 8,493 . . . . (718) 262-2000
2015-16 Tuition: In-state $6,748; Out-of-state $13,858
Plaza College (Private, For-profit)
Fall 2014 Enrollment: 716 . . . . (718) 779-1430
2015-16 Tuition: In-state $11,350; Out-of-state $11,350
Rabbinical Seminary of America (Private, Not-for-profit, Jewish)
Fall 2014 Enrollment: 500 . . . . (718) 268-4700
2015-16 Tuition: In-state $9,600; Out-of-state $9,600
St John's University-New York (Private, Not-for-profit, Roman Catholic)
Fall 2014 Enrollment: 20,445 . . . . (718) 990-6161
2015-16 Tuition: In-state $38,680; Out-of-state $38,680
Vaughn College of Aeronautics and Technology (Private, Not-for-profit)
Fall 2014 Enrollment: 1,614 . . . . (718) 429-6600
2015-16 Tuition: In-state $22,680; Out-of-state $22,680
Yeshiva of Far Rockaway Derech Ayson Rabbinical Seminary (Private, Not-for-profit)
Fall 2014 Enrollment: 38 . . . . (718) 327-7600
2015-16 Tuition: In-state $10,500; Out-of-state $10,500
Yeshiva Shaar Hatorah (Private, Not-for-profit, Jewish)
Fall 2014 Enrollment: 76 . . . . (718) 846-1940
2015-16 Tuition: In-state $14,960; Out-of-state $14,960

Two-year College(s)

Bramson ORT College (Private, Not-for-profit)
Fall 2014 Enrollment: 641 . . . . (718) 261-5800
2015-16 Tuition: In-state $11,330; Out-of-state $11,330

CUNY LaGuardia Community College (Public)
Fall 2014 Enrollment: 20,231 . . . . (718) 482-7200
2015-16 Tuition: In-state $5,218; Out-of-state $8,098
CUNY Queensborough Community College (Public)
Fall 2014 Enrollment: 16,182 . . . . (718) 631-6262
2015-16 Tuition: In-state $5,210; Out-of-state $8,090
Long Island Business Institute (Private, For-profit)
Fall 2014 Enrollment: 397 . . . . (718) 939-5100
2015-16 Tuition: In-state $14,279; Out-of-state $14,279
Miami Ad School-New York (Private, For-profit)
Fall 2014 Enrollment: 99 . . . . (305) 538-3193
2015-16 Tuition: In-state $19,400; Out-of-state $19,400
New York Automotive and Diesel Institute (Private, For-profit)
Fall 2014 Enrollment: 346 . . . . (718) 658-0006
New York Medical Career Training Center (Private, For-profit)
Fall 2014 Enrollment: 284 . . . . (718) 460-1717
St Paul's School of Nursing-Queens (Private, For-profit)
Fall 2014 Enrollment: 504 . . . . (718) 357-0500
2015-16 Tuition: In-state $21,946; Out-of-state $21,946

Vocational/Technical School(s)

Ace Computer Training Center (Private, For-profit)
Fall 2014 Enrollment: 162 . . . . (718) 575-3223
Allen School-Jamaica (Private, For-profit)
Fall 2014 Enrollment: 322 . . . . (718) 291-2200
2015-16 Tuition: $16,080
Alliance Computing Solutions (Private, For-profit)
Fall 2014 Enrollment: 36 . . . . (718) 661-9771
2015-16 Tuition: $9,100
Apex Technical School (Private, For-profit)
Fall 2014 Enrollment: 1,259 . . . . (212) 645-3300
2015-16 Tuition: $18,200
Berk Trade and Business School (Private, For-profit)
Fall 2014 Enrollment: 243 . . . . (718) 729-0909
2015-16 Tuition: $11,225
Empire Beauty School-Queens (Private, For-profit)
Fall 2014 Enrollment: 131 . . . . (800) 920-4593
2015-16 Tuition: $12,000
Grace International Beauty School (Private, For-profit)
Fall 2014 Enrollment: 12 . . . . (718) 886-6660
2015-16 Tuition: $7,800
Lincoln Technical Institute-Whitestone (Private, For-profit)
Fall 2014 Enrollment: 733 . . . . (718) 640-9800
2015-16 Tuition: $31,980
Metropolitan Learning Institute (Private, Not-for-profit)
Fall 2014 Enrollment: 717 . . . . (718) 897-0482
2015-16 Tuition: $16,500
Midway Paris Beauty School (Private, For-profit)
Fall 2014 Enrollment: 108 . . . . (718) 418-2790
2015-16 Tuition: $12,600
New Life Business Institute (Private, For-profit)
Fall 2014 Enrollment: 86 . . . . (718) 523-6530
2015-16 Tuition: $15,612
New York School for Medical and Dental Assistants (Private, For-profit)
Fall 2014 Enrollment: 264 . . . . (718) 793-2330
2015-16 Tuition: $14,300

Hospitals: Coler-Goldwater Specialty Hospital and Nursing Facility (2014 beds); Creedmoor Psychiatric Center (452 beds); Elmhurst Hospital Center (525 beds); Flushing Hospital Medical Center (293 beds); Forest Hills Hospital (222 beds); Forest Hills Hospital (312 beds); Hillside Hospital (223 beds); Holliswood Hospital (110 beds); Jamaica Hospital Medical Center (387 beds); New York Hospital Queens (439 beds); Peninsula Hospital Center (272 beds); Queens Childrens Psychiatric Center (86 beds); Queens Hospital Center (408 beds); St. John's Episcopal Hospital, South Shore (332 beds); St. Mary's Hospital for Children (95 beds)

Newspapers: Forum South (weekly circulation 60000); Queens Chronicle (weekly circulation 160000); Queens Gazette (weekly circulation 90000); Queens Ledger (weekly circulation 150000); Queens Times (weekly circulation 75000); Queens Tribune (weekly circulation 171000); Schneps Publications (weekly circulation 80000); The Wave (weekly circulation 13000); Times Newsweekly (weekly circulation 27000); Times/Ledger Newspapers (weekly circulation 45000); Woodside Herald (weekly circulation 16000)

Additional Information Contacts
Queens County Government . . . . (718) 286-3000
http://www.queensbp.org

Queens Chamber of Commerce . . . . (718) 898-8500
http://www.queenschamber.org
Rockaway Chamber of Commerce . . . . (718) 979-7030
http://www.rockawaychamberofcommerce.com

Neighborhoods in Queens

ARVERNE (unincorporated postal area)
ZCTA: 11692

Covers a land area of 0.999 square miles and a water area of 0.070 square miles. Located at 40.59° N. Lat; 73.79° W. Long. Elevation is 7 feet.

Population: 18,955; Growth (since 2000): 19.3%; Density: 18,981.1 persons per square mile; Race: 28.6% White, 58.1% Black/African American, 3.9% Asian, 0.5% American Indian/Alaska Native, 0.0% Native Hawaiian/Other Pacific Islander, 2.7% Two or more races, 24.3% Hispanic of any race; Average household size: 2.89; Median age: 35.6; Age under 18: 27.6%; Age 65 and over: 11.2%; Males per 100 females: 84.0; Marriage status: 46.1% never married, 37.0% now married, 5.2% separated, 7.3% widowed, 9.6% divorced; Foreign born: 30.2%; Speak English only: 66.3%; With disability: 17.5%; Veterans: 4.1%; Ancestry: 6.2% American, 5.5% Jamaican, 3.8% Irish, 3.2% Nigerian, 2.6% Polish

Employment: 9.7% management, business, and financial, 2.7% computer, engineering, and science, 11.0% education, legal, community service, arts, and media, 4.6% healthcare practitioners, 30.5% service, 22.0% sales and office, 10.5% natural resources, construction, and maintenance, 8.9% production, transportation, and material moving

Income: Per capita: $20,644; Median household: $42,127; Average household: $58,512; Households with income of $100,000 or more: 14.9%; Poverty rate: 21.5%

Educational Attainment: High school diploma or higher: 73.6%; Bachelor's degree or higher: 20.0%; Graduate/professional degree or higher: 7.1%

Housing: Homeownership rate: 34.9%; Median home value: $349,200; Median year structure built: 1965; Homeowner vacancy rate: 1.4%; Median selected monthly owner costs: $2,574 with a mortgage, $626 without a mortgage; Median gross rent: $847 per month; Rental vacancy rate: 7.5%

Health Insurance: 89.0% have insurance; 51.4% have private insurance; 43.1% have public insurance; 11.0% do not have insurance; 2.4% of children under 18 do not have insurance

Transportation: Commute: 46.2% car, 46.9% public transportation, 3.5% walk, 1.9% work from home; Mean travel time to work: 53.7 minutes

ASTORIA (unincorporated postal area)
ZCTA: 11102

Covers a land area of 0.808 square miles and a water area of 0.003 square miles. Located at 40.77° N. Lat; 73.93° W. Long. Elevation is 23 feet.

Population: 35,271; Growth (since 2000): -2.8%; Density: 43,663.7 persons per square mile; Race: 58.3% White, 11.2% Black/African American, 12.6% Asian, 0.5% American Indian/Alaska Native, 0.3% Native Hawaiian/Other Pacific Islander, 3.3% Two or more races, 32.6% Hispanic of any race; Average household size: 2.49; Median age: 33.4; Age under 18: 15.7%; Age 65 and over: 10.3%; Males per 100 females: 99.7; Marriage status: 49.1% never married, 40.1% now married, 3.1% separated, 3.7% widowed, 7.1% divorced; Foreign born: 42.8%; Speak English only: 41.1%; With disability: 9.1%; Veterans: 1.9%; Ancestry: 6.7% Italian, 5.9% Greek, 4.9% Irish, 4.8% American, 3.4% German

Employment: 14.7% management, business, and financial, 5.1% computer, engineering, and science, 18.1% education, legal, community service, arts, and media, 2.9% healthcare practitioners, 25.1% service, 19.8% sales and office, 6.0% natural resources, construction, and maintenance, 8.4% production, transportation, and material moving

Income: Per capita: $29,517; Median household: $51,123; Average household: $71,031; Households with income of $100,000 or more: 23.9%; Poverty rate: 18.6%

Educational Attainment: High school diploma or higher: 80.1%; Bachelor's degree or higher: 41.9%; Graduate/professional degree or higher: 12.9%

Housing: Homeownership rate: 14.0%; Median home value: $602,400; Median year structure built: 1954; Homeowner vacancy rate: 2.1%; Median selected monthly owner costs: $2,689 with a mortgage, $847

without a mortgage; Median gross rent: $1,490 per month; Rental vacancy rate: 3.4%

Health Insurance: 82.0% have insurance; 54.1% have private insurance; 35.5% have public insurance; 18.0% do not have insurance; 2.1% of children under 18 do not have insurance

Transportation: Commute: 16.9% car, 69.7% public transportation, 7.2% walk, 4.1% work from home; Mean travel time to work: 37.6 minutes

ZCTA: 11103

Covers a land area of 0.711 square miles and a water area of 0 square miles. Located at 40.76° N. Lat; 73.91° W. Long. Elevation is 23 feet.

Population: 39,231; Growth (since 2000): -11.5%; Density: 55,171.4 persons per square mile; Race: 71.3% White, 3.4% Black/African American, 15.7% Asian, 0.2% American Indian/Alaska Native, 0.1% Native Hawaiian/Other Pacific Islander, 3.0% Two or more races, 23.6% Hispanic of any race; Average household size: 2.36; Median age: 34.1; Age under 18: 14.0%; Age 65 and over: 11.0%; Males per 100 females: 99.8; Marriage status: 48.3% never married, 41.3% now married, 2.4% separated, 4.1% widowed, 6.4% divorced; Foreign born: 43.9%; Speak English only: 41.5%; With disability: 7.7%; Veterans: 1.9%; Ancestry: 10.4% Italian, 7.3% Irish, 6.1% German, 5.7% Greek, 4.1% American

Employment: 16.6% management, business, and financial, 6.0% computer, engineering, and science, 17.8% education, legal, community service, arts, and media, 4.1% healthcare practitioners, 21.6% service, 19.9% sales and office, 7.2% natural resources, construction, and maintenance, 6.8% production, transportation, and material moving

Income: Per capita: $33,013; Median household: $59,243; Average household: $74,020; Households with income of $100,000 or more: 23.7%; Poverty rate: 15.3%

Educational Attainment: High school diploma or higher: 85.8%; Bachelor's degree or higher: 46.6%; Graduate/professional degree or higher: 16.2%

Housing: Homeownership rate: 14.9%; Median home value: $654,700; Median year structure built: 1941; Homeowner vacancy rate: 0.0%; Median selected monthly owner costs: $2,746 with a mortgage, $953 without a mortgage; Median gross rent: $1,465 per month; Rental vacancy rate: 3.7%

Health Insurance: 82.1% have insurance; 56.7% have private insurance; 30.8% have public insurance; 17.9% do not have insurance; 4.3% of children under 18 do not have insurance

Transportation: Commute: 15.7% car, 72.5% public transportation, 6.3% walk, 2.9% work from home; Mean travel time to work: 38.2 minutes

ZCTA: 11105

Covers a land area of 1.632 square miles and a water area of 0 square miles. Located at 40.78° N. Lat; 73.91° W. Long. Elevation is 23 feet.

Population: 37,194; Growth (since 2000): -11.7%; Density: 22,791.1 persons per square mile; Race: 76.1% White, 2.3% Black/African American, 12.2% Asian, 0.3% American Indian/Alaska Native, 0.0% Native Hawaiian/Other Pacific Islander, 2.1% Two or more races, 20.3% Hispanic of any race; Average household size: 2.39; Median age: 34.3; Age under 18: 15.5%; Age 65 and over: 11.2%; Males per 100 females: 95.1; Marriage status: 45.0% never married, 42.5% now married, 2.0% separated, 4.2% widowed, 8.3% divorced; Foreign born: 35.4%; Speak English only: 46.0%; With disability: 8.5%; Veterans: 2.3%; Ancestry: 13.3% Italian, 12.5% Greek, 7.4% Irish, 6.1% German, 5.4% American

Employment: 17.9% management, business, and financial, 4.9% computer, engineering, and science, 18.8% education, legal, community service, arts, and media, 4.1% healthcare practitioners, 17.7% service, 22.8% sales and office, 5.9% natural resources, construction, and maintenance, 7.8% production, transportation, and material moving

Income: Per capita: $35,004; Median household: $61,646; Average household: $79,957; Households with income of $100,000 or more: 29.4%; Poverty rate: 12.3%

Educational Attainment: High school diploma or higher: 85.6%; Bachelor's degree or higher: 48.2%; Graduate/professional degree or higher: 16.0%

Housing: Homeownership rate: 25.8%; Median home value: $679,900; Median year structure built: 1944; Homeowner vacancy rate: 0.0%; Median selected monthly owner costs: $2,644 with a mortgage, $961 without a mortgage; Median gross rent: $1,538 per month; Rental vacancy rate: 3.2%

Health Insurance: 87.1% have insurance; 65.9% have private insurance; 28.3% have public insurance; 12.9% do not have insurance; 3.1% of children under 18 do not have insurance

Transportation: Commute: 23.0% car, 64.8% public transportation, 6.9% walk, 3.8% work from home; Mean travel time to work: 38.6 minutes

ZCTA: 11106

Covers a land area of 0.857 square miles and a water area of 0.014 square miles. Located at 40.76° N. Lat; 73.93° W. Long. Elevation is 23 feet.

Population: 38,812; Growth (since 2000): -10.0%; Density: 45,285.0 persons per square mile; Race: 57.1% White, 7.0% Black/African American, 19.4% Asian, 0.2% American Indian/Alaska Native, 0.0% Native Hawaiian/Other Pacific Islander, 3.8% Two or more races, 29.7% Hispanic of any race; Average household size: 2.27; Median age: 36.4; Age under 18: 14.2%; Age 65 and over: 13.6%; Males per 100 females: 94.7; Marriage status: 45.8% never married, 40.2% now married, 2.9% separated, 5.9% widowed, 8.1% divorced; Foreign born: 41.7%; Speak English only: 41.7%; With disability: 11.1%; Veterans: 2.7%; Ancestry: 7.3% Italian, 6.0% Irish, 4.5% American, 3.9% Greek, 3.6% German

Employment: 16.1% management, business, and financial, 4.7% computer, engineering, and science, 17.8% education, legal, community service, arts, and media, 3.7% healthcare practitioners, 25.0% service, 20.9% sales and office, 5.1% natural resources, construction, and maintenance, 6.7% production, transportation, and material moving

Income: Per capita: $32,723; Median household: $54,109; Average household: $71,621; Households with income of $100,000 or more: 24.7%; Poverty rate: 19.8%

Educational Attainment: High school diploma or higher: 84.5%; Bachelor's degree or higher: 44.5%; Graduate/professional degree or higher: 15.9%

Housing: Homeownership rate: 17.9%; Median home value: $434,200; Median year structure built: 1949; Homeowner vacancy rate: 1.6%; Median selected monthly owner costs: $2,331 with a mortgage, $798 without a mortgage; Median gross rent: $1,380 per month; Rental vacancy rate: 2.6%

Health Insurance: 85.4% have insurance; 59.2% have private insurance; 34.1% have public insurance; 14.6% do not have insurance; 3.5% of children under 18 do not have insurance

Transportation: Commute: 13.6% car, 73.8% public transportation, 6.9% walk, 3.2% work from home; Mean travel time to work: 37.4 minutes

BAYSIDE (unincorporated postal area)

ZCTA: 11360

Covers a land area of 1.425 square miles and a water area of 0 square miles. Located at 40.78° N. Lat; 73.78° W. Long. Elevation is 79 feet.

Population: 19,605; Growth (since 2000): 1.3%; Density: 13,756.6 persons per square mile; Race: 67.1% White, 1.0% Black/African American, 24.4% Asian, 0.2% American Indian/Alaska Native, 0.0% Native Hawaiian/Other Pacific Islander, 3.5% Two or more races, 10.0% Hispanic of any race; Average household size: 2.29; Median age: 49.1; Age under 18: 16.4%; Age 65 and over: 25.9%; Males per 100 females: 83.3; Marriage status: 23.6% never married, 58.6% now married, 0.8% separated, 10.2% widowed, 7.6% divorced; Foreign born: 34.1%; Speak English only: 55.4%; With disability: 13.9%; Veterans: 6.6%; Ancestry: 13.1% Italian, 7.3% Polish, 7.1% Russian, 6.2% Greek, 5.5% Irish

Employment: 23.0% management, business, and financial, 3.7% computer, engineering, and science, 15.7% education, legal, community service, arts, and media, 7.8% healthcare practitioners, 13.4% service, 25.7% sales and office, 7.1% natural resources, construction, and maintenance, 3.6% production, transportation, and material moving

Income: Per capita: $43,302; Median household: $80,235; Average household: $97,078; Households with income of $100,000 or more: 38.8%; Poverty rate: 6.2%

Educational Attainment: High school diploma or higher: 93.6%; Bachelor's degree or higher: 49.0%; Graduate/professional degree or higher: 23.3%

Housing: Homeownership rate: 68.5%; Median home value: $503,000; Median year structure built: 1966; Homeowner vacancy rate: 0.9%; Median selected monthly owner costs: $2,407 with a mortgage, $968 without a mortgage; Median gross rent: $1,880 per month; Rental vacancy rate: 2.1%

Health Insurance: 95.6% have insurance; 79.1% have private insurance; 34.8% have public insurance; 4.4% do not have insurance; 0.0% of children under 18 do not have insurance

Transportation: Commute: 64.8% car, 27.4% public transportation, 2.3% walk, 4.8% work from home; Mean travel time to work: 40.9 minutes

ZCTA: 11361

Covers a land area of 1.758 square miles and a water area of 0.019 square miles. Located at 40.76° N. Lat; 73.77° W. Long. Elevation is 79 feet.

Population: 30,207; Growth (since 2000): 3.4%; Density: 17,179.7 persons per square mile; Race: 51.2% White, 2.4% Black/African American, 36.0% Asian, 0.6% American Indian/Alaska Native, 0.0% Native Hawaiian/Other Pacific Islander, 3.1% Two or more races, 16.4% Hispanic of any race; Average household size: 2.80; Median age: 41.3; Age under 18: 18.7%; Age 65 and over: 15.7%; Males per 100 females: 91.7; Marriage status: 31.0% never married, 55.4% now married, 2.4% separated, 6.7% widowed, 6.9% divorced; Foreign born: 41.3%; Speak English only: 43.9%; With disability: 8.6%; Veterans: 3.3%; Ancestry: 12.9% Italian, 10.1% Irish, 5.4% Greek, 4.7% German, 3.6% American

Employment: 19.9% management, business, and financial, 5.1% computer, engineering, and science, 13.7% education, legal, community service, arts, and media, 5.6% healthcare practitioners, 15.9% service, 25.8% sales and office, 6.8% natural resources, construction, and maintenance, 7.3% production, transportation, and material moving

Income: Per capita: $34,071; Median household: $79,158; Average household: $93,310; Households with income of $100,000 or more: 38.0%; Poverty rate: 9.4%

Educational Attainment: High school diploma or higher: 88.7%; Bachelor's degree or higher: 43.4%; Graduate/professional degree or higher: 17.9%

Housing: Homeownership rate: 57.8%; Median home value: $588,600; Median year structure built: 1954; Homeowner vacancy rate: 1.0%; Median selected monthly owner costs: $2,593 with a mortgage, $806 without a mortgage; Median gross rent: $1,659 per month; Rental vacancy rate: 3.6%

Health Insurance: 89.1% have insurance; 72.2% have private insurance; 27.6% have public insurance; 10.9% do not have insurance; 4.9% of children under 18 do not have insurance

Transportation: Commute: 63.6% car, 29.0% public transportation, 3.1% walk, 2.8% work from home; Mean travel time to work: 39.0 minutes

BREEZY POINT (unincorporated postal area)

ZCTA: 11697

Covers a land area of 2.220 square miles and a water area of <.001 square miles. Located at 40.56° N. Lat; 73.92° W. Long. Elevation is 7 feet.

Population: 4,006; Growth (since 2000): -5.2%; Density: 1,804.7 persons per square mile; Race: 98.9% White, 0.1% Black/African American, 0.0% Asian, 0.0% American Indian/Alaska Native, 0.0% Native Hawaiian/Other Pacific Islander, 1.0% Two or more races, 1.5% Hispanic of any race; Average household size: 2.63; Median age: 44.7; Age under 18: 26.3%; Age 65 and over: 20.3%; Males per 100 females: 86.0; Marriage status: 30.7% never married, 55.1% now married, 1.7% separated, 9.1% widowed, 5.2% divorced; Foreign born: 2.9%; Speak English only: 97.6%; With disability: 14.4%; Veterans: 9.5%; Ancestry: 58.9% Irish, 19.1% Italian, 11.6% German, 5.7% American, 3.5% English

Employment: 18.6% management, business, and financial, 3.5% computer, engineering, and science, 21.5% education, legal, community service, arts, and media, 7.7% healthcare practitioners, 21.8% service, 16.7% sales and office, 6.1% natural resources, construction, and maintenance, 4.1% production, transportation, and material moving

Income: Per capita: $42,135; Median household: $93,333; Average household: $109,500; Households with income of $100,000 or more: 47.9%; Poverty rate: 3.5%

Educational Attainment: High school diploma or higher: 97.1%; Bachelor's degree or higher: 48.8%; Graduate/professional degree or higher: 22.0%

Housing: Homeownership rate: 96.6%; Median home value: $530,400; Median year structure built: 1966; Homeowner vacancy rate: 0.0%; Median selected monthly owner costs: $2,100 with a mortgage, $589 without a mortgage; Median gross rent: n/a per month; Rental vacancy rate: 0.0%

Health Insurance: 97.0% have insurance; 90.0% have private insurance; 26.8% have public insurance; 3.0% do not have insurance; 3.1% of children under 18 do not have insurance

Transportation: Commute: 81.2% car, 14.8% public transportation, 2.3% walk, 1.2% work from home; Mean travel time to work: 42.4 minutes

CAMBRIA HEIGHTS (unincorporated postal area)
ZCTA: 11411

Covers a land area of 1.169 square miles and a water area of 0 square miles. Located at 40.69° N. Lat; 73.74° W. Long. Elevation is 49 feet.

Population: 19,208; Growth (since 2000): -9.7%; Density: 16,432.6 persons per square mile; Race: 3.1% White, 91.3% Black/African American, 0.8% Asian, 0.3% American Indian/Alaska Native, 0.0% Native Hawaiian/Other Pacific Islander, 2.3% Two or more races, 5.6% Hispanic of any race; Average household size: 3.19; Median age: 44.1; Age under 18: 17.5%; Age 65 and over: 19.8%; Males per 100 females: 81.1; Marriage status: 38.2% never married, 44.3% now married, 3.9% separated, 7.8% widowed, 9.8% divorced; Foreign born: 38.2%; Speak English only: 80.7%; With disability: 9.6%; Veterans: 5.4%; Ancestry: 21.2% Jamaican, 11.2% Haitian, 5.9% American, 3.9% Guyanese, 2.8% West Indian

Employment: 10.6% management, business, and financial, 2.0% computer, engineering, and science, 13.0% education, legal, community service, arts, and media, 9.0% healthcare practitioners, 23.3% service, 26.6% sales and office, 4.7% natural resources, construction, and maintenance, 10.7% production, transportation, and material moving

Income: Per capita: $31,421; Median household: $81,149; Average household: $93,447; Households with income of $100,000 or more: 39.7%; Poverty rate: 3.9%

Educational Attainment: High school diploma or higher: 90.3%; Bachelor's degree or higher: 31.3%; Graduate/professional degree or higher: 13.2%

Housing: Homeownership rate: 83.7%; Median home value: $389,000; Median year structure built: 1947; Homeowner vacancy rate: 0.9%; Median selected monthly owner costs: $2,364 with a mortgage, $742 without a mortgage; Median gross rent: $1,377 per month; Rental vacancy rate: 5.5%

Health Insurance: 91.1% have insurance; 72.3% have private insurance; 32.5% have public insurance; 8.9% do not have insurance; 5.9% of children under 18 do not have insurance

Transportation: Commute: 60.8% car, 35.6% public transportation, 1.0% walk, 1.9% work from home; Mean travel time to work: 48.5 minutes

COLLEGE POINT (unincorporated postal area)
ZCTA: 11356

Covers a land area of 1.571 square miles and a water area of 0 square miles. Located at 40.78° N. Lat; 73.84° W. Long. Elevation is 69 feet.

Population: 24,631; Growth (since 2000): 20.5%; Density: 15,674.7 persons per square mile; Race: 35.9% White, 1.8% Black/African American, 32.1% Asian, 0.6% American Indian/Alaska Native, 0.0% Native Hawaiian/Other Pacific Islander, 2.9% Two or more races, 38.3% Hispanic of any race; Average household size: 3.19; Median age: 35.6; Age under 18: 23.0%; Age 65 and over: 11.0%; Males per 100 females: 95.1; Marriage status: 32.4% never married, 54.1% now married, 2.3% separated, 5.2% widowed, 8.3% divorced; Foreign born: 47.0%; Speak English only: 28.7%; With disability: 7.7%; Veterans: 2.7%; Ancestry: 7.8% Italian, 6.1% American, 4.2% Irish, 3.2% German, 1.5% Afghan

Employment: 13.9% management, business, and financial, 1.7% computer, engineering, and science, 6.5% education, legal, community service, arts, and media, 3.0% healthcare practitioners, 22.1% service, 32.2% sales and office, 9.5% natural resources, construction, and maintenance, 11.1% production, transportation, and material moving

Income: Per capita: $24,718; Median household: $57,194; Average household: $75,112; Households with income of $100,000 or more: 22.3%; Poverty rate: 12.3%

Educational Attainment: High school diploma or higher: 80.4%; Bachelor's degree or higher: 21.8%; Graduate/professional degree or higher: 5.9%

Housing: Homeownership rate: 45.5%; Median home value: $555,500; Median year structure built: 1959; Homeowner vacancy rate: 3.5%; Median selected monthly owner costs: $2,716 with a mortgage, $853 without a mortgage; Median gross rent: $1,475 per month; Rental vacancy rate: 2.7%

Health Insurance: 80.9% have insurance; 51.3% have private insurance; 35.4% have public insurance; 19.1% do not have insurance; 6.1% of children under 18 do not have insurance

Transportation: Commute: 53.0% car, 37.1% public transportation, 5.7% walk, 3.8% work from home; Mean travel time to work: 41.9 minutes

CORONA (unincorporated postal area)
ZCTA: 11368

Covers a land area of 2.632 square miles and a water area of 0.036 square miles. Located at 40.75° N. Lat; 73.85° W. Long. Elevation is 43 feet.

Population: 112,709; Growth (since 2000): 14.0%; Density: 42,823.5 persons per square mile; Race: 41.4% White, 13.1% Black/African American, 10.7% Asian, 0.8% American Indian/Alaska Native, 0.0% Native Hawaiian/Other Pacific Islander, 2.5% Two or more races, 73.9% Hispanic of any race; Average household size: 3.85; Median age: 31.5; Age under 18: 25.8%; Age 65 and over: 8.1%; Males per 100 females: 113.4; Marriage status: 45.6% never married, 42.5% now married, 4.3% separated, 4.2% widowed, 7.6% divorced; Foreign born: 61.2%; Speak English only: 14.0%; With disability: 9.1%; Veterans: 0.8%; Ancestry: 3.2% American, 1.5% African, 0.7% Jamaican, 0.7% Italian, 0.6% Haitian

Employment: 4.5% management, business, and financial, 1.0% computer, engineering, and science, 3.8% education, legal, community service, arts, and media, 2.4% healthcare practitioners, 38.5% service, 18.8% sales and office, 16.3% natural resources, construction, and maintenance, 14.6% production, transportation, and material moving

Income: Per capita: $15,834; Median household: $45,004; Average household: $55,919; Households with income of $100,000 or more: 13.4%; Poverty rate: 23.9%

Educational Attainment: High school diploma or higher: 60.0%; Bachelor's degree or higher: 10.9%; Graduate/professional degree or higher: 3.4%

Housing: Homeownership rate: 21.2%; Median home value: $465,300; Median year structure built: 1958; Homeowner vacancy rate: 2.5%; Median selected monthly owner costs: $2,805 with a mortgage, $759 without a mortgage; Median gross rent: $1,423 per month; Rental vacancy rate: 2.0%

Health Insurance: 67.5% have insurance; 30.4% have private insurance; 43.3% have public insurance; 32.5% do not have insurance; 4.2% of children under 18 do not have insurance

Transportation: Commute: 20.6% car, 67.6% public transportation, 8.6% walk, 1.2% work from home; Mean travel time to work: 42.8 minutes

EAST ELMHURST (unincorporated postal area)
ZCTA: 11369

Covers a land area of 1.068 square miles and a water area of 0 square miles. Located at 40.76° N. Lat; 73.87° W. Long. Elevation is 75 feet.

Population: 39,001; Growth (since 2000): 8.0%; Density: 36,531.2 persons per square mile; Race: 26.1% White, 16.6% Black/African American, 13.1% Asian, 0.1% American Indian/Alaska Native, 0.0% Native Hawaiian/Other Pacific Islander, 4.5% Two or more races, 63.0% Hispanic of any race; Average household size: 3.31; Median age: 35.2; Age under 18: 21.2%; Age 65 and over: 11.0%; Males per 100 females: 99.8; Marriage status: 44.6% never married, 42.8% now married, 3.7% separated, 5.1% widowed, 7.5% divorced; Foreign born: 55.9%; Speak English only: 24.0%; With disability: 7.4%; Veterans: 2.0%; Ancestry: 6.6% American, 1.5% Italian, 1.3% Jamaican, 1.0% Haitian, 0.8% Irish

Employment: 8.9% management, business, and financial, 2.7% computer, engineering, and science, 6.6% education, legal, community service, arts, and media, 3.6% healthcare practitioners, 31.3% service, 22.2% sales and office, 11.6% natural resources, construction, and maintenance, 13.1% production, transportation, and material moving

Income: Per capita: $21,184; Median household: $52,310; Average household: $67,171; Households with income of $100,000 or more: 19.1%; Poverty rate: 17.3%

Educational Attainment: High school diploma or higher: 76.2%; Bachelor's degree or higher: 18.9%; Graduate/professional degree or higher: 6.3%

Housing: Homeownership rate: 47.5%; Median home value: $471,700; Median year structure built: 1950; Homeowner vacancy rate: 3.6%; Median selected monthly owner costs: $2,763 with a mortgage, $826 without a mortgage; Median gross rent: $1,336 per month; Rental vacancy rate: 3.0%

Health Insurance: 77.4% have insurance; 42.4% have private insurance; 41.7% have public insurance; 22.6% do not have insurance; 7.7% of children under 18 do not have insurance
Transportation: Commute: 32.5% car, 55.5% public transportation, 6.8% walk, 2.2% work from home; Mean travel time to work: 41.7 minutes

ZCTA: 11370
Covers a land area of 1.423 square miles and a water area of 0 square miles. Located at 40.77° N. Lat; 73.89° W. Long. Elevation is 75 feet.
Population: 35,507; Growth (since 2000): -17.7%; Density: 24,960.2 persons per square mile; Race: 38.7% White, 14.6% Black/African American, 20.2% Asian, 0.6% American Indian/Alaska Native, 0.0% Native Hawaiian/Other Pacific Islander, 3.5% Two or more races, 38.8% Hispanic of any race; Average household size: 3.15; Median age: 36.8; Age under 18: 16.1%; Age 65 and over: 10.9%; Males per 100 females: 162.0; Marriage status: 48.4% never married, 41.8% now married, 1.8% separated, 4.9% widowed, 4.9% divorced; Foreign born: 47.4%; Speak English only: 31.6%; With disability: 9.1%; Veterans: 1.8%; Ancestry: 6.0% American, 4.6% Greek, 4.3% Italian, 1.9% Irish, 1.1% Egyptian
Employment: 11.4% management, business, and financial, 2.6% computer, engineering, and science, 9.3% education, legal, community service, arts, and media, 4.6% healthcare practitioners, 25.5% service, 22.6% sales and office, 8.6% natural resources, construction, and maintenance, 15.4% production, transportation, and material moving
Income: Per capita: $20,057; Median household: $53,427; Average household: $75,046; Households with income of $100,000 or more: 25.6%; Poverty rate: 17.2%
Educational Attainment: High school diploma or higher: 71.1%; Bachelor's degree or higher: 20.4%; Graduate/professional degree or higher: 7.6%
Housing: Homeownership rate: 45.4%; Median home value: $540,500; Median year structure built: 1954; Homeowner vacancy rate: 2.4%; Median selected monthly owner costs: $2,681 with a mortgage, $796 without a mortgage; Median gross rent: $1,539 per month; Rental vacancy rate: 5.5%
Health Insurance: 83.6% have insurance; 49.4% have private insurance; 42.5% have public insurance; 16.4% do not have insurance; 2.7% of children under 18 do not have insurance
Transportation: Commute: 35.9% car, 55.0% public transportation, 5.6% walk, 1.7% work from home; Mean travel time to work: 37.4 minutes

ELMHURST (unincorporated postal area)
ZCTA: 11373
Covers a land area of 1.527 square miles and a water area of 0 square miles. Located at 40.74° N. Lat; 73.88° W. Long. Elevation is 26 feet.
Population: 98,554; Growth (since 2000): -6.8%; Density: 64,523.0 persons per square mile; Race: 34.1% White, 1.8% Black/African American, 49.4% Asian, 0.5% American Indian/Alaska Native, 0.0% Native Hawaiian/Other Pacific Islander, 2.4% Two or more races, 40.3% Hispanic of any race; Average household size: 3.14; Median age: 37.2; Age under 18: 18.9%; Age 65 and over: 11.9%; Males per 100 females: 103.1; Marriage status: 39.2% never married, 48.8% now married, 2.8% separated, 5.0% widowed, 7.0% divorced; Foreign born: 68.9%; Speak English only: 12.8%; With disability: 8.3%; Veterans: 1.2%; Ancestry: 1.8% American, 1.2% Irish, 0.8% Italian, 0.7% German, 0.5% Polish
Employment: 9.6% management, business, and financial, 3.6% computer, engineering, and science, 6.6% education, legal, community service, arts, and media, 4.0% healthcare practitioners, 33.6% service, 21.3% sales and office, 7.9% natural resources, construction, and maintenance, 13.5% production, transportation, and material moving
Income: Per capita: $21,324; Median household: $47,588; Average household: $62,616; Households with income of $100,000 or more: 17.8%; Poverty rate: 20.6%
Educational Attainment: High school diploma or higher: 71.6%; Bachelor's degree or higher: 27.0%; Graduate/professional degree or higher: 8.1%
Housing: Homeownership rate: 26.9%; Median home value: $473,900; Median year structure built: 1952; Homeowner vacancy rate: 1.4%; Median selected monthly owner costs: $2,305 with a mortgage, $754 without a mortgage; Median gross rent: $1,373 per month; Rental vacancy rate: 1.7%
Health Insurance: 76.5% have insurance; 39.9% have private insurance; 43.9% have public insurance; 23.5% do not have insurance; 3.7% of children under 18 do not have insurance

Transportation: Commute: 17.8% car, 71.6% public transportation, 7.2% walk, 1.5% work from home; Mean travel time to work: 42.2 minutes

FAR ROCKAWAY (unincorporated postal area)
ZCTA: 11691
Covers a land area of 2.834 square miles and a water area of 0.033 square miles. Located at 40.60° N. Lat; 73.76° W. Long. Elevation is 16 feet.
Population: 63,989; Growth (since 2000): 13.9%; Density: 22,580.8 persons per square mile; Race: 39.0% White, 46.7% Black/African American, 3.4% Asian, 0.2% American Indian/Alaska Native, 0.1% Native Hawaiian/Other Pacific Islander, 2.5% Two or more races, 29.0% Hispanic of any race; Average household size: 3.12; Median age: 32.4; Age under 18: 29.8%; Age 65 and over: 12.3%; Males per 100 females: 88.3; Marriage status: 42.8% never married, 40.6% now married, 5.1% separated, 7.1% widowed, 9.5% divorced; Foreign born: 32.4%; Speak English only: 63.2%; With disability: 16.1%; Veterans: 3.1%; Ancestry: 6.5% American, 5.1% Jamaican, 2.6% Guyanese, 2.1% Russian, 1.9% Polish
Employment: 10.0% management, business, and financial, 1.5% computer, engineering, and science, 11.2% education, legal, community service, arts, and media, 4.7% healthcare practitioners, 31.7% service, 21.4% sales and office, 9.0% natural resources, construction, and maintenance, 10.6% production, transportation, and material moving
Income: Per capita: $18,571; Median household: $42,023; Average household: $55,708; Households with income of $100,000 or more: 15.6%; Poverty rate: 23.3%
Educational Attainment: High school diploma or higher: 70.9%; Bachelor's degree or higher: 21.6%; Graduate/professional degree or higher: 8.3%
Housing: Homeownership rate: 24.7%; Median home value: $431,300; Median year structure built: 1962; Homeowner vacancy rate: 2.5%; Median selected monthly owner costs: $2,843 with a mortgage, $969 without a mortgage; Median gross rent: $1,074 per month; Rental vacancy rate: 2.9%
Health Insurance: 88.3% have insurance; 48.2% have private insurance; 46.3% have public insurance; 11.7% do not have insurance; 3.0% of children under 18 do not have insurance
Transportation: Commute: 44.5% car, 39.8% public transportation, 9.7% walk, 2.6% work from home; Mean travel time to work: 47.0 minutes

ZCTA: 11693
Covers a land area of 0.997 square miles and a water area of 0 square miles. Located at 40.59° N. Lat; 73.81° W. Long. Elevation is 16 feet.
Population: 11,194; Growth (since 2000): 0.3%; Density: 11,226.0 persons per square mile; Race: 56.3% White, 27.3% Black/African American, 6.2% Asian, 0.0% American Indian/Alaska Native, 0.0% Native Hawaiian/Other Pacific Islander, 3.1% Two or more races, 20.5% Hispanic of any race; Average household size: 2.42; Median age: 40.6; Age under 18: 21.6%; Age 65 and over: 12.6%; Males per 100 females: 86.9; Marriage status: 43.9% never married, 38.0% now married, 3.2% separated, 5.3% widowed, 12.9% divorced; Foreign born: 21.7%; Speak English only: 65.8%; With disability: 19.4%; Veterans: 4.6%; Ancestry: 19.3% Irish, 8.4% Italian, 7.1% German, 6.1% Polish, 6.0% American
Employment: 11.5% management, business, and financial, 3.5% computer, engineering, and science, 14.8% education, legal, community service, arts, and media, 7.2% healthcare practitioners, 23.5% service, 19.8% sales and office, 11.6% natural resources, construction, and maintenance, 8.1% production, transportation, and material moving
Income: Per capita: $27,294; Median household: $53,281; Average household: $64,300; Households with income of $100,000 or more: 24.5%; Poverty rate: 19.9%
Educational Attainment: High school diploma or higher: 83.2%; Bachelor's degree or higher: 24.3%; Graduate/professional degree or higher: 6.3%
Housing: Homeownership rate: 47.5%; Median home value: $313,100; Median year structure built: 1958; Homeowner vacancy rate: 4.7%; Median selected monthly owner costs: $2,153 with a mortgage, $767 without a mortgage; Median gross rent: $935 per month; Rental vacancy rate: 4.7%
Health Insurance: 89.4% have insurance; 56.6% have private insurance; 41.5% have public insurance; 10.6% do not have insurance; 4.3% of children under 18 do not have insurance

Transportation: Commute: 50.0% car, 43.4% public transportation, 2.9% walk, 3.1% work from home; Mean travel time to work: 55.2 minutes

FLUSHING (unincorporated postal area)
ZCTA: 11354

Covers a land area of 2.167 square miles and a water area of 0.032 square miles. Located at 40.77° N. Lat; 73.83° W. Long. Elevation is 85 feet.
Population: 56,908; Growth (since 2000): 4.7%; Density: 26,260.5 persons per square mile; Race: 23.6% White, 3.7% Black/African American, 60.8% Asian, 0.3% American Indian/Alaska Native, 0.0% Native Hawaiian/Other Pacific Islander, 2.6% Two or more races, 16.3% Hispanic of any race; Average household size: 2.75; Median age: 44.2; Age under 18: 14.9%; Age 65 and over: 18.0%; Males per 100 females: 87.8; Marriage status: 31.6% never married, 53.3% now married, 3.3% separated, 7.7% widowed, 7.4% divorced; Foreign born: 63.9%; Speak English only: 21.1%; With disability: 9.1%; Veterans: 2.3%; Ancestry: 4.2% Italian, 4.1% American, 2.1% Irish, 1.5% Greek, 1.4% German
Employment: 11.5% management, business, and financial, 3.6% computer, engineering, and science, 8.0% education, legal, community service, arts, and media, 5.5% healthcare practitioners, 29.9% service, 26.0% sales and office, 6.2% natural resources, construction, and maintenance, 9.4% production, transportation, and material moving
Income: Per capita: $23,633; Median household: $44,741; Average household: $62,568; Households with income of $100,000 or more: 17.2%; Poverty rate: 21.0%
Educational Attainment: High school diploma or higher: 77.3%; Bachelor's degree or higher: 23.5%; Graduate/professional degree or higher: 7.5%
Housing: Homeownership rate: 38.8%; Median home value: $421,000; Median year structure built: 1959; Homeowner vacancy rate: 4.6%; Median selected monthly owner costs: $2,298 with a mortgage, $719 without a mortgage; Median gross rent: $1,344 per month; Rental vacancy rate: 3.5%
Health Insurance: 77.6% have insurance; 46.2% have private insurance; 37.5% have public insurance; 22.4% do not have insurance; 6.4% of children under 18 do not have insurance
Transportation: Commute: 41.9% car, 41.1% public transportation, 13.4% walk, 2.4% work from home; Mean travel time to work: 39.8 minutes
ZCTA: 11355

Covers a land area of 1.735 square miles and a water area of 0 square miles. Located at 40.75° N. Lat; 73.82° W. Long. Elevation is 85 feet.
Population: 82,790; Growth (since 2000): -0.6%; Density: 47,716.6 persons per square mile; Race: 13.9% White, 2.8% Black/African American, 73.3% Asian, 0.6% American Indian/Alaska Native, 0.0% Native Hawaiian/Other Pacific Islander, 2.4% Two or more races, 13.8% Hispanic of any race; Average household size: 3.01; Median age: 41.4; Age under 18: 17.0%; Age 65 and over: 15.1%; Males per 100 females: 93.2; Marriage status: 30.6% never married, 57.2% now married, 2.4% separated, 6.2% widowed, 6.0% divorced; Foreign born: 72.5%; Speak English only: 14.3%; With disability: 6.9%; Veterans: 1.2%; Ancestry: 1.7% Italian, 1.5% American, 0.9% Irish, 0.8% Russian, 0.5% Haitian
Employment: 10.0% management, business, and financial, 4.4% computer, engineering, and science, 6.1% education, legal, community service, arts, and media, 4.7% healthcare practitioners, 32.3% service, 23.4% sales and office, 6.8% natural resources, construction, and maintenance, 12.3% production, transportation, and material moving
Income: Per capita: $19,180; Median household: $39,168; Average household: $54,472; Households with income of $100,000 or more: 14.9%; Poverty rate: 21.5%
Educational Attainment: High school diploma or higher: 70.9%; Bachelor's degree or higher: 23.8%; Graduate/professional degree or higher: 8.3%
Housing: Homeownership rate: 31.7%; Median home value: $500,500; Median year structure built: 1959; Homeowner vacancy rate: 3.3%; Median selected monthly owner costs: $2,453 with a mortgage, $786 without a mortgage; Median gross rent: $1,287 per month; Rental vacancy rate: 2.9%
Health Insurance: 74.0% have insurance; 36.2% have private insurance; 42.5% have public insurance; 26.0% do not have insurance; 14.3% of children under 18 do not have insurance

Transportation: Commute: 36.8% car, 44.8% public transportation, 14.3% walk, 1.9% work from home; Mean travel time to work: 41.3 minutes
ZCTA: 11358

Covers a land area of 1.949 square miles and a water area of 0 square miles. Located at 40.76° N. Lat; 73.80° W. Long. Elevation is 85 feet.
Population: 37,486; Growth (since 2000): -3.0%; Density: 19,229.4 persons per square mile; Race: 46.1% White, 1.4% Black/African American, 42.7% Asian, 0.1% American Indian/Alaska Native, 0.1% Native Hawaiian/Other Pacific Islander, 3.1% Two or more races, 16.4% Hispanic of any race; Average household size: 2.85; Median age: 42.9; Age under 18: 17.6%; Age 65 and over: 17.0%; Males per 100 females: 94.3; Marriage status: 30.5% never married, 56.8% now married, 1.5% separated, 6.0% widowed, 6.6% divorced; Foreign born: 50.1%; Speak English only: 33.1%; With disability: 7.3%; Veterans: 3.4%; Ancestry: 12.5% Italian, 7.2% Greek, 6.5% Irish, 3.1% German, 2.9% American
Employment: 14.4% management, business, and financial, 4.3% computer, engineering, and science, 13.2% education, legal, community service, arts, and media, 6.3% healthcare practitioners, 20.2% service, 26.4% sales and office, 6.5% natural resources, construction, and maintenance, 8.8% production, transportation, and material moving
Income: Per capita: $30,752; Median household: $65,258; Average household: $83,944; Households with income of $100,000 or more: 30.1%; Poverty rate: 10.4%
Educational Attainment: High school diploma or higher: 85.0%; Bachelor's degree or higher: 35.2%; Graduate/professional degree or higher: 12.8%
Housing: Homeownership rate: 56.1%; Median home value: $643,300; Median year structure built: 1948; Homeowner vacancy rate: 0.7%; Median selected monthly owner costs: $2,721 with a mortgage, $913 without a mortgage; Median gross rent: $1,514 per month; Rental vacancy rate: 5.2%
Health Insurance: 80.6% have insurance; 56.7% have private insurance; 32.0% have public insurance; 19.4% do not have insurance; 10.3% of children under 18 do not have insurance
Transportation: Commute: 55.4% car, 36.4% public transportation, 4.1% walk, 2.5% work from home; Mean travel time to work: 40.8 minutes
ZCTA: 11367

Covers a land area of 2.379 square miles and a water area of 0.186 square miles. Located at 40.73° N. Lat; 73.83° W. Long. Elevation is 85 feet.
Population: 42,667; Growth (since 2000): 11.6%; Density: 17,933.2 persons per square mile; Race: 57.3% White, 9.5% Black/African American, 24.7% Asian, 0.2% American Indian/Alaska Native, 0.0% Native Hawaiian/Other Pacific Islander, 3.5% Two or more races, 14.1% Hispanic of any race; Average household size: 2.84; Median age: 35.2; Age under 18: 24.1%; Age 65 and over: 13.7%; Males per 100 females: 91.0; Marriage status: 33.3% never married, 54.3% now married, 1.6% separated, 5.9% widowed, 6.5% divorced; Foreign born: 40.3%; Speak English only: 41.1%; With disability: 7.9%; Veterans: 2.4%; Ancestry: 8.2% American, 6.1% Russian, 3.3% Polish, 3.3% Italian, 2.9% Israeli
Employment: 15.4% management, business, and financial, 5.9% computer, engineering, and science, 14.1% education, legal, community service, arts, and media, 8.7% healthcare practitioners, 17.5% service, 25.6% sales and office, 5.1% natural resources, construction, and maintenance, 7.8% production, transportation, and material moving
Income: Per capita: $26,129; Median household: $56,557; Average household: $73,718; Households with income of $100,000 or more: 26.2%; Poverty rate: 13.6%
Educational Attainment: High school diploma or higher: 85.3%; Bachelor's degree or higher: 38.7%; Graduate/professional degree or higher: 16.2%
Housing: Homeownership rate: 47.4%; Median home value: $378,000; Median year structure built: 1954; Homeowner vacancy rate: 1.7%; Median selected monthly owner costs: $1,887 with a mortgage, $698 without a mortgage; Median gross rent: $1,238 per month; Rental vacancy rate: 1.4%
Health Insurance: 91.1% have insurance; 63.9% have private insurance; 35.0% have public insurance; 8.9% do not have insurance; 2.9% of children under 18 do not have insurance
Transportation: Commute: 47.0% car, 43.7% public transportation, 5.8% walk, 2.5% work from home; Mean travel time to work: 41.4 minutes

FOREST HILLS (unincorporated postal area)
ZCTA: 11375

Covers a land area of 1.980 square miles and a water area of 0 square miles. Located at 40.72° N. Lat; 73.85° W. Long. Elevation is 59 feet.
Population: 70,723; Growth (since 2000): 0.7%; Density: 35,711.8 persons per square mile; Race: 62.8% White, 3.4% Black/African American, 26.4% Asian, 0.3% American Indian/Alaska Native, 0.1% Native Hawaiian/Other Pacific Islander, 3.2% Two or more races, 13.1% Hispanic of any race; Average household size: 2.18; Median age: 41.9; Age under 18: 18.2%; Age 65 and over: 18.7%; Males per 100 females: 85.7; Marriage status: 30.2% never married, 54.2% now married, 1.8% separated, 7.4% widowed, 8.2% divorced; Foreign born: 45.5%; Speak English only: 43.7%; With disability: 10.6%; Veterans: 2.7%; Ancestry: 9.5% Russian, 6.2% Italian, 5.5% American, 5.3% Polish, 5.0% Irish
Employment: 21.1% management, business, and financial, 9.5% computer, engineering, and science, 19.9% education, legal, community service, arts, and media, 7.3% healthcare practitioners, 11.1% service, 21.8% sales and office, 3.8% natural resources, construction, and maintenance, 5.6% production, transportation, and material moving
Income: Per capita: $44,879; Median household: $72,414; Average household: $95,909; Households with income of $100,000 or more: 35.3%; Poverty rate: 8.5%
Educational Attainment: High school diploma or higher: 93.3%; Bachelor's degree or higher: 57.9%; Graduate/professional degree or higher: 27.7%
Housing: Homeownership rate: 49.8%; Median home value: $360,100; Median year structure built: 1951; Homeowner vacancy rate: 1.3%; Median selected monthly owner costs: $1,760 with a mortgage, $664 without a mortgage; Median gross rent: $1,566 per month; Rental vacancy rate: 2.2%
Health Insurance: 93.3% have insurance; 74.3% have private insurance; 29.3% have public insurance; 6.7% do not have insurance; 3.4% of children under 18 do not have insurance
Transportation: Commute: 27.1% car, 61.5% public transportation, 6.1% walk, 4.2% work from home; Mean travel time to work: 41.7 minutes

FRESH MEADOWS (unincorporated postal area)
ZCTA: 11365

Covers a land area of 2.497 square miles and a water area of 0.018 square miles. Located at 40.74° N. Lat; 73.79° W. Long. Elevation is 36 feet.
Population: 45,041; Growth (since 2000): 8.4%; Density: 18,040.5 persons per square mile; Race: 34.8% White, 6.7% Black/African American, 44.7% Asian, 0.3% American Indian/Alaska Native, 0.1% Native Hawaiian/Other Pacific Islander, 3.0% Two or more races, 19.9% Hispanic of any race; Average household size: 2.85; Median age: 41.4; Age under 18: 21.6%; Age 65 and over: 14.8%; Males per 100 females: 89.2; Marriage status: 28.8% never married, 57.4% now married, 1.6% separated, 6.9% widowed, 6.9% divorced; Foreign born: 46.7%; Speak English only: 36.6%; With disability: 8.8%; Veterans: 4.1%; Ancestry: 5.7% Italian, 3.9% Irish, 3.8% Russian, 3.0% Polish, 2.1% German
Employment: 13.9% management, business, and financial, 5.1% computer, engineering, and science, 12.1% education, legal, community service, arts, and media, 6.8% healthcare practitioners, 18.0% service, 29.0% sales and office, 7.5% natural resources, construction, and maintenance, 7.6% production, transportation, and material moving
Income: Per capita: $28,720; Median household: $59,520; Average household: $79,166; Households with income of $100,000 or more: 26.8%; Poverty rate: 14.0%
Educational Attainment: High school diploma or higher: 85.9%; Bachelor's degree or higher: 35.5%; Graduate/professional degree or higher: 14.4%
Housing: Homeownership rate: 47.2%; Median home value: $596,300; Median year structure built: 1955; Homeowner vacancy rate: 0.6%; Median selected monthly owner costs: $2,859 with a mortgage, $830 without a mortgage; Median gross rent: $1,390 per month; Rental vacancy rate: 2.0%
Health Insurance: 88.5% have insurance; 60.1% have private insurance; 36.9% have public insurance; 11.5% do not have insurance; 2.5% of children under 18 do not have insurance
Transportation: Commute: 58.9% car, 35.7% public transportation, 2.3% walk, 2.2% work from home; Mean travel time to work: 42.8 minutes

ZCTA: 11366

Covers a land area of 1.095 square miles and a water area of 0 square miles. Located at 40.73° N. Lat; 73.79° W. Long. Elevation is 36 feet.
Population: 13,192; Growth (since 2000): -1.3%; Density: 12,051.8 persons per square mile; Race: 45.8% White, 5.6% Black/African American, 43.6% Asian, 0.0% American Indian/Alaska Native, 0.0% Native Hawaiian/Other Pacific Islander, 2.5% Two or more races, 8.8% Hispanic of any race; Average household size: 3.10; Median age: 40.2; Age under 18: 20.8%; Age 65 and over: 15.1%; Males per 100 females: 93.1; Marriage status: 31.9% never married, 57.4% now married, 1.5% separated, 6.8% widowed, 4.0% divorced; Foreign born: 49.8%; Speak English only: 36.1%; With disability: 8.4%; Veterans: 2.3%; Ancestry: 10.5% Russian, 3.3% Polish, 3.1% Irish, 3.1% American, 2.6% Italian
Employment: 15.3% management, business, and financial, 7.4% computer, engineering, and science, 14.0% education, legal, community service, arts, and media, 8.4% healthcare practitioners, 15.1% service, 25.0% sales and office, 6.6% natural resources, construction, and maintenance, 8.2% production, transportation, and material moving
Income: Per capita: $30,870; Median household: $72,486; Average household: $93,774; Households with income of $100,000 or more: 36.5%; Poverty rate: 13.3%
Educational Attainment: High school diploma or higher: 88.6%; Bachelor's degree or higher: 47.8%; Graduate/professional degree or higher: 19.1%
Housing: Homeownership rate: 71.7%; Median home value: $647,900; Median year structure built: 1951; Homeowner vacancy rate: 2.5%; Median selected monthly owner costs: $2,736 with a mortgage, $982 without a mortgage; Median gross rent: $1,574 per month; Rental vacancy rate: 3.6%
Health Insurance: 92.2% have insurance; 71.3% have private insurance; 31.6% have public insurance; 7.8% do not have insurance; 1.5% of children under 18 do not have insurance
Transportation: Commute: 55.0% car, 35.9% public transportation, 4.9% walk, 3.5% work from home; Mean travel time to work: 41.5 minutes

GLEN OAKS (unincorporated postal area)
ZCTA: 11004

Covers a land area of 0.950 square miles and a water area of 0 square miles. Located at 40.75° N. Lat; 73.71° W. Long. Elevation is 118 feet.
Population: 13,778; Growth (since 2000): -6.2%; Density: 14,501.4 persons per square mile; Race: 49.8% White, 7.8% Black/African American, 35.3% Asian, 0.3% American Indian/Alaska Native, 0.0% Native Hawaiian/Other Pacific Islander, 4.0% Two or more races, 11.8% Hispanic of any race; Average household size: 2.66; Median age: 45.6; Age under 18: 16.1%; Age 65 and over: 18.5%; Males per 100 females: 87.4; Marriage status: 32.6% never married, 49.9% now married, 1.1% separated, 8.6% widowed, 8.8% divorced; Foreign born: 33.9%; Speak English only: 57.9%; With disability: 11.0%; Veterans: 4.5%; Ancestry: 14.9% Italian, 8.2% Irish, 6.7% German, 4.8% American, 3.5% Polish
Employment: 12.9% management, business, and financial, 6.9% computer, engineering, and science, 11.7% education, legal, community service, arts, and media, 10.8% healthcare practitioners, 10.9% service, 32.5% sales and office, 5.9% natural resources, construction, and maintenance, 8.5% production, transportation, and material moving
Income: Per capita: $37,119; Median household: $85,968; Average household: $99,830; Households with income of $100,000 or more: 40.1%; Poverty rate: 7.6%
Educational Attainment: High school diploma or higher: 90.1%; Bachelor's degree or higher: 39.7%; Graduate/professional degree or higher: 18.4%
Housing: Homeownership rate: 76.8%; Median home value: $457,600; Median year structure built: 1954; Homeowner vacancy rate: 1.2%; Median selected monthly owner costs: $2,288 with a mortgage, $878 without a mortgage; Median gross rent: $1,248 per month; Rental vacancy rate: 0.0%
Health Insurance: 93.4% have insurance; 80.1% have private insurance; 25.7% have public insurance; 6.6% do not have insurance; 3.4% of children under 18 do not have insurance
Transportation: Commute: 70.4% car, 24.0% public transportation, 2.3% walk, 2.3% work from home; Mean travel time to work: 39.1 minutes

HOLLIS (unincorporated postal area)
ZCTA: 11423

Covers a land area of 1.411 square miles and a water area of 0 square miles. Located at 40.72° N. Lat; 73.77° W. Long. Elevation is 59 feet.
Population: 31,982; Growth (since 2000): 2.4%; Density: 22,667.7 persons per square mile; Race: 15.8% White, 37.3% Black/African American, 26.2% Asian, 1.7% American Indian/Alaska Native, 0.3% Native Hawaiian/Other Pacific Islander, 7.0% Two or more races, 15.4% Hispanic of any race; Average household size: 3.22; Median age: 40.3; Age under 18: 20.1%; Age 65 and over: 14.2%; Males per 100 females: 89.5; Marriage status: 37.8% never married, 47.9% now married, 2.4% separated, 6.1% widowed, 8.1% divorced; Foreign born: 51.9%; Speak English only: 63.5%; With disability: 11.4%; Veterans: 2.8%; Ancestry: 15.3% Guyanese, 6.4% Haitian, 6.1% American, 6.0% Jamaican, 3.6% West Indian
Employment: 10.9% management, business, and financial, 2.8% computer, engineering, and science, 8.0% education, legal, community service, arts, and media, 6.8% healthcare practitioners, 26.6% service, 25.4% sales and office, 9.1% natural resources, construction, and maintenance, 10.6% production, transportation, and material moving
Income: Per capita: $26,278; Median household: $62,179; Average household: $80,672; Households with income of $100,000 or more: 27.5%; Poverty rate: 9.9%
Educational Attainment: High school diploma or higher: 80.0%; Bachelor's degree or higher: 26.9%; Graduate/professional degree or higher: 8.5%
Housing: Homeownership rate: 59.7%; Median home value: $430,100; Median year structure built: 1948; Homeowner vacancy rate: 1.7%; Median selected monthly owner costs: $2,451 with a mortgage, $917 without a mortgage; Median gross rent: $1,237 per month; Rental vacancy rate: 4.3%
Health Insurance: 87.4% have insurance; 56.9% have private insurance; 38.7% have public insurance; 12.6% do not have insurance; 3.8% of children under 18 do not have insurance
Transportation: Commute: 47.3% car, 46.7% public transportation, 2.4% walk, 2.1% work from home; Mean travel time to work: 46.4 minutes

HOWARD BEACH (unincorporated postal area)
ZCTA: 11414

Covers a land area of 2.300 square miles and a water area of 0.087 square miles. Located at 40.66° N. Lat; 73.84° W. Long. Elevation is 3 feet.
Population: 28,700; Growth (since 2000): 2.1%; Density: 12,480.1 persons per square mile; Race: 82.4% White, 2.3% Black/African American, 4.3% Asian, 0.0% American Indian/Alaska Native, 0.0% Native Hawaiian/Other Pacific Islander, 2.3% Two or more races, 21.1% Hispanic of any race; Average household size: 2.69; Median age: 45.5; Age under 18: 18.9%; Age 65 and over: 21.3%; Males per 100 females: 88.8; Marriage status: 31.2% never married, 53.5% now married, 1.2% separated, 7.4% widowed, 7.9% divorced; Foreign born: 19.4%; Speak English only: 65.2%; With disability: 13.3%; Veterans: 6.4%; Ancestry: 33.1% Italian, 11.5% Irish, 6.7% German, 5.4% Polish, 3.3% American
Employment: 14.6% management, business, and financial, 3.0% computer, engineering, and science, 14.2% education, legal, community service, arts, and media, 5.4% healthcare practitioners, 16.9% service, 29.0% sales and office, 7.0% natural resources, construction, and maintenance, 9.9% production, transportation, and material moving
Income: Per capita: $34,333; Median household: $68,374; Average household: $88,917; Households with income of $100,000 or more: 31.4%; Poverty rate: 9.2%
Educational Attainment: High school diploma or higher: 85.2%; Bachelor's degree or higher: 27.3%; Graduate/professional degree or higher: 9.2%
Housing: Homeownership rate: 71.2%; Median home value: $503,100; Median year structure built: 1963; Homeowner vacancy rate: 2.1%; Median selected monthly owner costs: $2,024 with a mortgage, $868 without a mortgage; Median gross rent: $1,514 per month; Rental vacancy rate: 0.0%
Health Insurance: 93.6% have insurance; 72.0% have private insurance; 36.2% have public insurance; 6.4% do not have insurance; 2.4% of children under 18 do not have insurance
Transportation: Commute: 69.4% car, 27.3% public transportation, 2.0% walk, 0.9% work from home; Mean travel time to work: 38.9 minutes

JACKSON HEIGHTS (unincorporated postal area)
ZCTA: 11372

Covers a land area of 0.737 square miles and a water area of 0 square miles. Located at 40.75° N. Lat; 73.88° W. Long. Elevation is 79 feet.
Population: 64,754; Growth (since 2000): -9.2%; Density: 87,807.6 persons per square mile; Race: 60.8% White, 2.7% Black/African American, 19.9% Asian, 0.3% American Indian/Alaska Native, 0.1% Native Hawaiian/Other Pacific Islander, 2.9% Two or more races, 59.1% Hispanic of any race; Average household size: 2.60; Median age: 39.0; Age under 18: 17.5%; Age 65 and over: 13.6%; Males per 100 females: 102.2; Marriage status: 44.0% never married, 40.5% now married, 3.3% separated, 5.2% widowed, 10.2% divorced; Foreign born: 61.6%; Speak English only: 18.6%; With disability: 7.7%; Veterans: 1.6%; Ancestry: 2.6% Italian, 2.5% Irish, 2.3% German, 2.1% American, 1.8% Russian
Employment: 11.1% management, business, and financial, 3.9% computer, engineering, and science, 11.2% education, legal, community service, arts, and media, 2.5% healthcare practitioners, 28.4% service, 20.6% sales and office, 8.0% natural resources, construction, and maintenance, 14.4% production, transportation, and material moving
Income: Per capita: $25,805; Median household: $50,485; Average household: $63,963; Households with income of $100,000 or more: 16.9%; Poverty rate: 18.3%
Educational Attainment: High school diploma or higher: 74.8%; Bachelor's degree or higher: 29.9%; Graduate/professional degree or higher: 10.6%
Housing: Homeownership rate: 29.8%; Median home value: $263,800; Median year structure built: 1946; Homeowner vacancy rate: 1.2%; Median selected monthly owner costs: $1,481 with a mortgage, $481 without a mortgage; Median gross rent: $1,316 per month; Rental vacancy rate: 1.9%
Health Insurance: 77.3% have insurance; 43.0% have private insurance; 41.8% have public insurance; 22.7% do not have insurance; 3.8% of children under 18 do not have insurance
Transportation: Commute: 20.3% car, 69.9% public transportation, 7.0% walk, 1.5% work from home; Mean travel time to work: 39.3 minutes

JAMAICA (unincorporated postal area)
ZCTA: 11430

Covers a land area of 7.118 square miles and a water area of 0.256 square miles. Located at 40.65° N. Lat; 73.79° W. Long. Elevation is 43 feet.
Population: 186; Growth (since 2000): -18.8%; Density: 26.1 persons per square mile; Race: 8.6% White, 68.8% Black/African American, 0.0% Asian, 0.0% American Indian/Alaska Native, 0.0% Native Hawaiian/Other Pacific Islander, 2.7% Two or more races, 33.3% Hispanic of any race; Average household size: 0.00; Median age: 42.3; Age under 18: 0.0%; Age 65 and over: 3.2%; Males per 100 females: 58.6; Marriage status: 82.8% never married, 12.4% now married, 7.5% separated, 0.0% widowed, 4.8% divorced; Foreign born: 13.4%; Speak English only: 69.9%; With disability: 26.3%; Veterans: 5.4%; Ancestry: 5.4% Haitian, 3.2% Jamaican, 2.7% Italian, 2.7% Polish
Employment: 0.0% management, business, and financial, 0.0% computer, engineering, and science, 0.0% education, legal, community service, arts, and media, 0.0% healthcare practitioners, 34.1% service, 32.9% sales and office, 6.1% natural resources, construction, and maintenance, 26.8% production, transportation, and material moving
Income: Per capita: $7,581; Median household: n/a; Average household: n/a; Households with income of $100,000 or more: n/a; Poverty rate: 83.3%
Educational Attainment: High school diploma or higher: 70.4%; Bachelor's degree or higher: 8.6%; Graduate/professional degree or higher: 3.1%
Housing: Homeownership rate: n/a; Median home value: n/a; Median year structure built: n/a; Homeowner vacancy rate: 0.0%; Median selected monthly owner costs: $0 with a mortgage, $0 without a mortgage; Median gross rent: n/a per month; Rental vacancy rate: 0.0%
Health Insurance: 92.5% have insurance; 0.0% have private insurance; 92.5% have public insurance; 7.5% do not have insurance; 0.0% of children under 18 do not have insurance
Transportation: Commute: 0.0% car, 89.0% public transportation, 11.0% walk, 0.0% work from home; Mean travel time to work: 60.3 minutes

ZCTA: 11432

Covers a land area of 2.149 square miles and a water area of 0 square miles. Located at 40.72° N. Lat; 73.79° W. Long. Elevation is 43 feet.
Population: 63,533; Growth (since 2000): 11.4%; Density: 29,562.2 persons per square mile; Race: 22.6% White, 15.5% Black/African American, 41.8% Asian, 0.5% American Indian/Alaska Native, 0.0% Native Hawaiian/Other Pacific Islander, 4.4% Two or more races, 25.5% Hispanic of any race; Average household size: 3.21; Median age: 34.8; Age under 18: 21.4%; Age 65 and over: 13.0%; Males per 100 females: 97.3; Marriage status: 40.4% never married, 47.4% now married, 2.3% separated, 5.8% widowed, 6.4% divorced; Foreign born: 58.0%; Speak English only: 32.2%; With disability: 8.2%; Veterans: 1.6%; Ancestry: 4.8% Guyanese, 2.7% Haitian, 2.4% Italian, 2.2% American, 2.0% Irish
Employment: 11.1% management, business, and financial, 3.5% computer, engineering, and science, 9.5% education, legal, community service, arts, and media, 5.6% healthcare practitioners, 26.3% service, 26.4% sales and office, 6.2% natural resources, construction, and maintenance, 11.4% production, transportation, and material moving
Income: Per capita: $21,903; Median household: $50,702; Average household: $70,442; Households with income of $100,000 or more: 22.0%; Poverty rate: 19.9%
Educational Attainment: High school diploma or higher: 77.5%; Bachelor's degree or higher: 34.7%; Graduate/professional degree or higher: 12.5%
Housing: Homeownership rate: 36.1%; Median home value: $509,100; Median year structure built: 1952; Homeowner vacancy rate: 1.7%; Median selected monthly owner costs: $2,475 with a mortgage, $857 without a mortgage; Median gross rent: $1,317 per month; Rental vacancy rate: 3.0%
Health Insurance: 85.4% have insurance; 47.0% have private insurance; 44.9% have public insurance; 14.6% do not have insurance; 5.0% of children under 18 do not have insurance
Transportation: Commute: 29.4% car, 58.0% public transportation, 8.4% walk, 2.5% work from home; Mean travel time to work: 45.2 minutes

ZCTA: 11433

Covers a land area of 1.552 square miles and a water area of 0 square miles. Located at 40.70° N. Lat; 73.79° W. Long. Elevation is 43 feet.
Population: 34,111; Growth (since 2000): 20.0%; Density: 21,979.3 persons per square mile; Race: 3.7% White, 69.8% Black/African American, 6.2% Asian, 0.6% American Indian/Alaska Native, 0.0% Native Hawaiian/Other Pacific Islander, 3.2% Two or more races, 19.3% Hispanic of any race; Average household size: 3.27; Median age: 33.6; Age under 18: 27.1%; Age 65 and over: 11.3%; Males per 100 females: 82.9; Marriage status: 50.3% never married, 36.2% now married, 4.6% separated, 5.9% widowed, 7.6% divorced; Foreign born: 37.5%; Speak English only: 75.1%; With disability: 11.0%; Veterans: 3.7%; Ancestry: 11.5% Jamaican, 7.8% Guyanese, 2.6% Trinidadian and Tobagonian, 2.1% American, 1.9% West Indian
Employment: 6.6% management, business, and financial, 1.8% computer, engineering, and science, 8.7% education, legal, community service, arts, and media, 3.6% healthcare practitioners, 35.9% service, 23.2% sales and office, 7.8% natural resources, construction, and maintenance, 12.3% production, transportation, and material moving
Income: Per capita: $19,200; Median household: $42,964; Average household: $59,055; Households with income of $100,000 or more: 18.1%; Poverty rate: 21.8%
Educational Attainment: High school diploma or higher: 76.8%; Bachelor's degree or higher: 16.7%; Graduate/professional degree or higher: 5.2%
Housing: Homeownership rate: 42.1%; Median home value: $371,100; Median year structure built: 1957; Homeowner vacancy rate: 5.9%; Median selected monthly owner costs: $2,413 with a mortgage, $597 without a mortgage; Median gross rent: $1,071 per month; Rental vacancy rate: 1.8%
Health Insurance: 85.8% have insurance; 45.8% have private insurance; 45.4% have public insurance; 14.2% do not have insurance; 4.3% of children under 18 do not have insurance
Transportation: Commute: 38.8% car, 53.2% public transportation, 5.8% walk, 1.4% work from home; Mean travel time to work: 46.5 minutes

ZCTA: 11434

Covers a land area of 3.239 square miles and a water area of 0.066 square miles. Located at 40.68° N. Lat; 73.78° W. Long. Elevation is 43 feet.

Population: 65,892; Growth (since 2000): 11.4%; Density: 20,344.6 persons per square mile; Race: 2.8% White, 89.1% Black/African American, 1.3% Asian, 0.0% American Indian/Alaska Native, 0.0% Native Hawaiian/Other Pacific Islander, 1.7% Two or more races, 9.0% Hispanic of any race; Average household size: 3.08; Median age: 36.6; Age under 18: 23.7%; Age 65 and over: 13.1%; Males per 100 females: 77.6; Marriage status: 47.9% never married, 36.1% now married, 4.5% separated, 6.3% widowed, 9.6% divorced; Foreign born: 29.4%; Speak English only: 87.2%; With disability: 12.1%; Veterans: 4.9%; Ancestry: 14.6% Jamaican, 3.8% Haitian, 3.7% Guyanese, 3.3% Trinidadian and Tobagonian, 2.8% West Indian
Employment: 9.0% management, business, and financial, 2.0% computer, engineering, and science, 12.0% education, legal, community service, arts, and media, 5.1% healthcare practitioners, 26.8% service, 26.8% sales and office, 6.7% natural resources, construction, and maintenance, 11.6% production, transportation, and material moving
Income: Per capita: $23,804; Median household: $58,076; Average household: $70,071; Households with income of $100,000 or more: 25.0%; Poverty rate: 12.5%
Educational Attainment: High school diploma or higher: 85.6%; Bachelor's degree or higher: 22.1%; Graduate/professional degree or higher: 7.3%
Housing: Homeownership rate: 49.3%; Median home value: $371,200; Median year structure built: 1961; Homeowner vacancy rate: 3.4%; Median selected monthly owner costs: $2,460 with a mortgage, $685 without a mortgage; Median gross rent: $1,135 per month; Rental vacancy rate: 1.1%
Health Insurance: 89.5% have insurance; 62.5% have private insurance; 36.1% have public insurance; 10.5% do not have insurance; 4.2% of children under 18 do not have insurance
Transportation: Commute: 47.4% car, 45.4% public transportation, 3.5% walk, 3.0% work from home; Mean travel time to work: 48.3 minutes

ZCTA: 11435

Covers a land area of 1.515 square miles and a water area of 0 square miles. Located at 40.70° N. Lat; 73.81° W. Long. Elevation is 43 feet.
Population: 55,323; Growth (since 2000): 2.7%; Density: 36,526.9 persons per square mile; Race: 22.0% White, 23.1% Black/African American, 22.2% Asian, 0.2% American Indian/Alaska Native, 0.0% Native Hawaiian/Other Pacific Islander, 5.7% Two or more races, 31.6% Hispanic of any race; Average household size: 2.93; Median age: 35.3; Age under 18: 21.8%; Age 65 and over: 10.7%; Males per 100 females: 96.4; Marriage status: 40.9% never married, 47.2% now married, 2.6% separated, 5.2% widowed, 6.7% divorced; Foreign born: 53.4%; Speak English only: 45.2%; With disability: 10.0%; Veterans: 1.9%; Ancestry: 9.4% Guyanese, 3.3% Jamaican, 2.8% American, 2.3% Russian, 2.3% Trinidadian and Tobagonian
Employment: 13.3% management, business, and financial, 4.2% computer, engineering, and science, 8.6% education, legal, community service, arts, and media, 4.9% healthcare practitioners, 24.4% service, 23.5% sales and office, 9.8% natural resources, construction, and maintenance, 11.4% production, transportation, and material moving
Income: Per capita: $23,672; Median household: $52,686; Average household: $66,645; Households with income of $100,000 or more: 21.2%; Poverty rate: 18.6%
Educational Attainment: High school diploma or higher: 76.7%; Bachelor's degree or higher: 28.1%; Graduate/professional degree or higher: 10.1%
Housing: Homeownership rate: 34.8%; Median home value: $336,700; Median year structure built: 1953; Homeowner vacancy rate: 1.9%; Median selected monthly owner costs: $2,261 with a mortgage, $752 without a mortgage; Median gross rent: $1,327 per month; Rental vacancy rate: 2.9%
Health Insurance: 82.2% have insurance; 44.1% have private insurance; 43.3% have public insurance; 17.8% do not have insurance; 4.2% of children under 18 do not have insurance
Transportation: Commute: 30.7% car, 62.4% public transportation, 3.9% walk, 1.7% work from home; Mean travel time to work: 46.6 minutes

ZCTA: 11436

Covers a land area of 0.788 square miles and a water area of 0 square miles. Located at 40.68° N. Lat; 73.80° W. Long. Elevation is 43 feet.
Population: 19,425; Growth (since 2000): 7.0%; Density: 24,656.2 persons per square mile; Race: 6.2% White, 70.2% Black/African American, 6.9% Asian, 0.7% American Indian/Alaska Native, 0.0%

Native Hawaiian/Other Pacific Islander, 3.4% Two or more races, 14.5% Hispanic of any race; Average household size: 3.52; Median age: 35.1; Age under 18: 23.1%; Age 65 and over: 11.4%; Males per 100 females: 87.6; Marriage status: 44.6% never married, 41.0% now married, 3.5% separated, 7.1% widowed, 7.3% divorced; Foreign born: 37.9%; Speak English only: 80.6%; With disability: 12.3%; Veterans: 3.0%; Ancestry: 11.6% Guyanese, 7.3% Jamaican, 6.9% Trinidadian and Tobagonian, 2.2% West Indian, 2.0% American

Employment: 7.7% management, business, and financial, 2.0% computer, engineering, and science, 8.3% education, legal, community service, arts, and media, 5.0% healthcare practitioners, 25.4% service, 28.9% sales and office, 10.3% natural resources, construction, and maintenance, 12.3% production, transportation, and material moving

Income: Per capita: $23,910; Median household: $64,005; Average household: $78,107; Households with income of $100,000 or more: 26.8%; Poverty rate: 13.7%

Educational Attainment: High school diploma or higher: 81.6%; Bachelor's degree or higher: 17.7%; Graduate/professional degree or higher: 6.2%

Housing: Homeownership rate: 68.0%; Median home value: $362,400; Median year structure built: 1950; Homeowner vacancy rate: 1.8%; Median selected monthly owner costs: $2,279 with a mortgage, $716 without a mortgage; Median gross rent: $1,420 per month; Rental vacancy rate: 3.8%

Health Insurance: 88.8% have insurance; 56.1% have private insurance; 40.6% have public insurance; 11.2% do not have insurance; 4.5% of children under 18 do not have insurance

Transportation: Commute: 48.4% car, 45.3% public transportation, 2.6% walk, 1.9% work from home; Mean travel time to work: 48.2 minutes

KEW GARDENS (unincorporated postal area)
ZCTA: 11415

Covers a land area of 0.568 square miles and a water area of 0 square miles. Located at 40.71° N. Lat; 73.83° W. Long. Elevation is 92 feet.

Population: 19,403; Growth (since 2000): -7.4%; Density: 34,151.3 persons per square mile; Race: 60.6% White, 7.6% Black/African American, 18.3% Asian, 0.2% American Indian/Alaska Native, 0.0% Native Hawaiian/Other Pacific Islander, 3.3% Two or more races, 21.7% Hispanic of any race; Average household size: 2.35; Median age: 36.8; Age under 18: 21.0%; Age 65 and over: 14.4%; Males per 100 females: 91.8; Marriage status: 37.0% never married, 48.5% now married, 2.0% separated, 6.9% widowed, 7.7% divorced; Foreign born: 39.1%; Speak English only: 46.2%; With disability: 8.5%; Veterans: 2.3%; Ancestry: 8.8% American, 4.7% Russian, 4.3% Irish, 4.1% Italian, 4.0% Polish

Employment: 16.8% management, business, and financial, 6.0% computer, engineering, and science, 19.0% education, legal, community service, arts, and media, 5.9% healthcare practitioners, 18.6% service, 22.2% sales and office, 3.9% natural resources, construction, and maintenance, 7.7% production, transportation, and material moving

Income: Per capita: $35,221; Median household: $63,756; Average household: $80,334; Households with income of $100,000 or more: 28.1%; Poverty rate: 10.4%

Educational Attainment: High school diploma or higher: 89.7%; Bachelor's degree or higher: 46.2%; Graduate/professional degree or higher: 20.8%

Housing: Homeownership rate: 36.9%; Median home value: $305,500; Median year structure built: 1949; Homeowner vacancy rate: 0.8%; Median selected monthly owner costs: $1,953 with a mortgage, $700 without a mortgage; Median gross rent: $1,397 per month; Rental vacancy rate: 6.3%

Health Insurance: 92.3% have insurance; 70.3% have private insurance; 28.3% have public insurance; 7.7% do not have insurance; 2.9% of children under 18 do not have insurance

Transportation: Commute: 32.6% car, 54.7% public transportation, 5.2% walk, 5.1% work from home; Mean travel time to work: 42.7 minutes

LITTLE NECK (unincorporated postal area)
ZCTA: 11362

Covers a land area of 2.517 square miles and a water area of 0.042 square miles. Located at 40.76° N. Lat; 73.74° W. Long. Elevation is 98 feet.

Population: 18,139; Growth (since 2000): 3.6%; Density: 7,207.0 persons per square mile; Race: 51.5% White, 2.7% Black/African

American, 42.5% Asian, 0.0% American Indian/Alaska Native, 0.1% Native Hawaiian/Other Pacific Islander, 1.6% Two or more races, 8.4% Hispanic of any race; Average household size: 2.53; Median age: 45.3; Age under 18: 17.3%; Age 65 and over: 20.2%; Males per 100 females: 90.2; Marriage status: 28.4% never married, 57.4% now married, 1.5% separated, 7.3% widowed, 7.0% divorced; Foreign born: 39.7%; Speak English only: 48.4%; With disability: 10.0%; Veterans: 4.2%; Ancestry: 11.6% Italian, 7.5% Irish, 5.9% German, 5.3% Greek, 4.3% Russian

Employment: 20.1% management, business, and financial, 6.0% computer, engineering, and science, 13.2% education, legal, community service, arts, and media, 10.6% healthcare practitioners, 15.3% service, 24.8% sales and office, 4.1% natural resources, construction, and maintenance, 5.9% production, transportation, and material moving

Income: Per capita: $40,211; Median household: $86,758; Average household: $99,502; Households with income of $100,000 or more: 39.8%; Poverty rate: 7.6%

Educational Attainment: High school diploma or higher: 91.4%; Bachelor's degree or higher: 49.0%; Graduate/professional degree or higher: 21.3%

Housing: Homeownership rate: 79.4%; Median home value: $529,500; Median year structure built: 1957; Homeowner vacancy rate: 0.5%; Median selected monthly owner costs: $2,240 with a mortgage, $880 without a mortgage; Median gross rent: $1,757 per month; Rental vacancy rate: 4.6%

Health Insurance: 92.5% have insurance; 78.0% have private insurance; 27.9% have public insurance; 7.5% do not have insurance; 2.9% of children under 18 do not have insurance

Transportation: Commute: 69.4% car, 21.7% public transportation, 3.2% walk, 4.6% work from home; Mean travel time to work: 40.2 minutes
ZCTA: 11363

Covers a land area of 0.869 square miles and a water area of 0 square miles. Located at 40.77° N. Lat; 73.75° W. Long. Elevation is 98 feet.

Population: 7,662; Growth (since 2000): 10.8%; Density: 8,821.4 persons per square mile; Race: 60.5% White, 0.8% Black/African American, 31.1% Asian, 0.0% American Indian/Alaska Native, 0.0% Native Hawaiian/Other Pacific Islander, 3.6% Two or more races, 15.3% Hispanic of any race; Average household size: 2.89; Median age: 43.8; Age under 18: 21.7%; Age 65 and over: 17.0%; Males per 100 females: 90.6; Marriage status: 26.7% never married, 60.7% now married, 0.8% separated, 5.1% widowed, 7.5% divorced; Foreign born: 33.2%; Speak English only: 49.4%; With disability: 8.1%; Veterans: 4.4%; Ancestry: 18.4% Italian, 12.5% Irish, 9.0% German, 4.3% American, 3.7% Greek

Employment: 22.6% management, business, and financial, 4.3% computer, engineering, and science, 14.7% education, legal, community service, arts, and media, 5.7% healthcare practitioners, 13.4% service, 26.3% sales and office, 6.3% natural resources, construction, and maintenance, 6.8% production, transportation, and material moving

Income: Per capita: $42,925; Median household: $89,219; Average household: $121,953; Households with income of $100,000 or more: 41.3%; Poverty rate: 7.2%

Educational Attainment: High school diploma or higher: 94.6%; Bachelor's degree or higher: 49.0%; Graduate/professional degree or higher: 20.4%

Housing: Homeownership rate: 69.1%; Median home value: $798,000; Median year structure built: 1950; Homeowner vacancy rate: 0.5%; Median selected monthly owner costs: $3,434 with a mortgage, $1,105 without a mortgage; Median gross rent: $1,748 per month; Rental vacancy rate: 2.7%

Health Insurance: 92.7% have insurance; 81.5% have private insurance; 24.9% have public insurance; 7.3% do not have insurance; 1.1% of children under 18 do not have insurance

Transportation: Commute: 60.4% car, 31.8% public transportation, 2.8% walk, 4.3% work from home; Mean travel time to work: 38.3 minutes

LONG ISLAND CITY (unincorporated postal area)
ZCTA: 11101

Covers a land area of 2.615 square miles and a water area of 0.116 square miles. Located at 40.75° N. Lat; 73.94° W. Long. Elevation is 13 feet.

Population: 25,880; Growth (since 2000): 1.1%; Density: 9,895.2 persons per square mile; Race: 47.5% White, 16.1% Black/African American, 18.6% Asian, 1.0% American Indian/Alaska Native, 0.1% Native Hawaiian/Other Pacific Islander, 3.8% Two or more races, 32.7%

Hispanic of any race; Average household size: 2.14; Median age: 36.1; Age under 18: 15.6%; Age 65 and over: 9.8%; Males per 100 females: 100.0; Marriage status: 47.2% never married, 38.5% now married, 4.1% separated, 3.9% widowed, 10.4% divorced; Foreign born: 39.5%; Speak English only: 46.6%; With disability: 8.6%; Veterans: 2.4%; Ancestry: 6.2% Italian, 6.1% American, 4.5% Irish, 3.1% German, 2.2% English
Employment: 18.4% management, business, and financial, 5.3% computer, engineering, and science, 15.9% education, legal, community service, arts, and media, 2.7% healthcare practitioners, 21.8% service, 21.8% sales and office, 4.7% natural resources, construction, and maintenance, 9.4% production, transportation, and material moving
Income: Per capita: $36,573; Median household: $48,013; Average household: $77,677; Households with income of $100,000 or more: 26.9%; Poverty rate: 21.9%
Educational Attainment: High school diploma or higher: 80.5%; Bachelor's degree or higher: 41.4%; Graduate/professional degree or higher: 16.4%
Housing: Homeownership rate: 17.1%; Median home value: $755,100; Median year structure built: 1945; Homeowner vacancy rate: 1.8%; Median selected monthly owner costs: $3,330 with a mortgage, $827 without a mortgage; Median gross rent: $1,271 per month; Rental vacancy rate: 2.0%
Health Insurance: 85.0% have insurance; 54.5% have private insurance; 36.8% have public insurance; 15.0% do not have insurance; 2.4% of children under 18 do not have insurance
Transportation: Commute: 13.6% car, 74.7% public transportation, 7.0% walk, 2.3% work from home; Mean travel time to work: 34.2 minutes

ZCTA: 11109
Covers a land area of 0.040 square miles and a water area of 0.010 square miles. Located at 40.75° N. Lat; 73.96° W. Long. Elevation is 13 feet.
Population: 4,702; Growth (since 2000): n/a; Density: 117,183.8 persons per square mile; Race: 67.1% White, 5.1% Black/African American, 21.6% Asian, 0.0% American Indian/Alaska Native, 0.0% Native Hawaiian/Other Pacific Islander, 4.8% Two or more races, 5.1% Hispanic of any race; Average household size: 1.84; Median age: 31.9; Age under 18: 12.3%; Age 65 and over: 3.4%; Males per 100 females: 122.4; Marriage status: 40.4% never married, 50.1% now married, 1.0% separated, 2.8% widowed, 6.6% divorced; Foreign born: 37.3%; Speak English only: 56.5%; With disability: 3.4%; Veterans: 2.2%; Ancestry: 11.1% Irish, 9.6% Italian, 8.6% German, 6.3% American, 5.3% Russian
Employment: 32.8% management, business, and financial, 12.5% computer, engineering, and science, 20.2% education, legal, community service, arts, and media, 11.9% healthcare practitioners, 4.1% service, 17.0% sales and office, 0.7% natural resources, construction, and maintenance, 0.9% production, transportation, and material moving
Income: Per capita: $84,846; Median household: $129,505; Average household: $155,054; Households with income of $100,000 or more: 61.1%; Poverty rate: 9.3%
Educational Attainment: High school diploma or higher: 99.6%; Bachelor's degree or higher: 82.3%; Graduate/professional degree or higher: 44.3%
Housing: Homeownership rate: 15.2%; Median home value: $473,600; Median year structure built: 2005; Homeowner vacancy rate: 0.0%; Median selected monthly owner costs: $2,190 with a mortgage, $438 without a mortgage; Median gross rent: $2,875 per month; Rental vacancy rate: 8.0%
Health Insurance: 87.2% have insurance; 86.7% have private insurance; 6.5% have public insurance; 12.8% do not have insurance; 14.8% of children under 18 do not have insurance
Transportation: Commute: 15.5% car, 77.1% public transportation, 3.2% walk, 3.2% work from home; Mean travel time to work: 30.5 minutes

MASPETH (unincorporated postal area)
ZCTA: 11378
Covers a land area of 2.554 square miles and a water area of 0.056 square miles. Located at 40.72° N. Lat; 73.91° W. Long. Elevation is 30 feet.
Population: 31,756; Growth (since 2000): -6.7%; Density: 12,434.3 persons per square mile; Race: 77.6% White, 1.8% Black/African American, 9.5% Asian, 0.2% American Indian/Alaska Native, 0.0% Native Hawaiian/Other Pacific Islander, 1.8% Two or more races, 31.0% Hispanic of any race; Average household size: 2.54; Median age: 39.2;

Age under 18: 20.7%; Age 65 and over: 13.3%; Males per 100 females: 95.9; Marriage status: 33.9% never married, 51.6% now married, 2.3% separated, 5.9% widowed, 8.6% divorced; Foreign born: 38.3%; Speak English only: 46.4%; With disability: 7.6%; Veterans: 3.1%; Ancestry: 16.1% Polish, 15.6% Italian, 12.6% Irish, 6.3% German, 3.1% American
Employment: 12.7% management, business, and financial, 3.3% computer, engineering, and science, 8.6% education, legal, community service, arts, and media, 4.8% healthcare practitioners, 22.7% service, 24.2% sales and office, 13.9% natural resources, construction, and maintenance, 9.8% production, transportation, and material moving
Income: Per capita: $30,288; Median household: $57,127; Average household: $74,249; Households with income of $100,000 or more: 22.8%; Poverty rate: 12.2%
Educational Attainment: High school diploma or higher: 85.3%; Bachelor's degree or higher: 26.5%; Graduate/professional degree or higher: 8.7%
Housing: Homeownership rate: 51.7%; Median home value: $544,700; Median year structure built: 1943; Homeowner vacancy rate: 0.3%; Median selected monthly owner costs: $2,599 with a mortgage, $782 without a mortgage; Median gross rent: $1,402 per month; Rental vacancy rate: 3.8%
Health Insurance: 84.5% have insurance; 63.8% have private insurance; 28.5% have public insurance; 15.5% do not have insurance; 4.6% of children under 18 do not have insurance
Transportation: Commute: 46.7% car, 45.8% public transportation, 4.3% walk, 2.0% work from home; Mean travel time to work: 39.6 minutes

MIDDLE VILLAGE (unincorporated postal area)
ZCTA: 11379
Covers a land area of 2.075 square miles and a water area of 0 square miles. Located at 40.72° N. Lat; 73.88° W. Long. Elevation is 98 feet.
Population: 35,476; Growth (since 2000): 22.4%; Density: 17,100.9 persons per square mile; Race: 84.5% White, 1.5% Black/African American, 8.0% Asian, 0.0% American Indian/Alaska Native, 0.0% Native Hawaiian/Other Pacific Islander, 1.7% Two or more races, 18.8% Hispanic of any race; Average household size: 2.59; Median age: 43.3; Age under 18: 18.8%; Age 65 and over: 18.7%; Males per 100 females: 90.4; Marriage status: 30.1% never married, 53.7% now married, 1.6% separated, 8.1% widowed, 8.2% divorced; Foreign born: 32.5%; Speak English only: 57.6%; With disability: 9.1%; Veterans: 4.4%; Ancestry: 22.7% Italian, 12.4% Irish, 9.6% German, 7.8% Polish, 6.4% American
Employment: 16.3% management, business, and financial, 4.3% computer, engineering, and science, 13.0% education, legal, community service, arts, and media, 5.5% healthcare practitioners, 16.8% service, 25.8% sales and office, 9.7% natural resources, construction, and maintenance, 8.6% production, transportation, and material moving
Income: Per capita: $33,256; Median household: $71,551; Average household: $83,602; Households with income of $100,000 or more: 33.5%; Poverty rate: 9.8%
Educational Attainment: High school diploma or higher: 86.0%; Bachelor's degree or higher: 31.4%; Graduate/professional degree or higher: 11.3%
Housing: Homeownership rate: 59.4%; Median home value: $563,100; Median year structure built: 1950; Homeowner vacancy rate: 0.2%; Median selected monthly owner costs: $2,630 with a mortgage, $753 without a mortgage; Median gross rent: $1,353 per month; Rental vacancy rate: 3.2%
Health Insurance: 90.5% have insurance; 69.9% have private insurance; 29.9% have public insurance; 9.5% do not have insurance; 3.9% of children under 18 do not have insurance
Transportation: Commute: 50.6% car, 41.8% public transportation, 4.5% walk, 2.1% work from home; Mean travel time to work: 39.0 minutes

OAKLAND GARDENS (unincorporated postal area)
ZCTA: 11364
Covers a land area of 2.466 square miles and a water area of 0 square miles. Located at 40.75° N. Lat; 73.76° W. Long. Elevation is 79 feet.
Population: 34,949; Growth (since 2000): 1.2%; Density: 14,172.3 persons per square mile; Race: 41.9% White, 2.7% Black/African American, 49.8% Asian, 0.2% American Indian/Alaska Native, 0.2% Native Hawaiian/Other Pacific Islander, 2.9% Two or more races, 7.7% Hispanic of any race; Average household size: 2.64; Median age: 43.7; Age under 18: 19.9%; Age 65 and over: 17.1%; Males per 100 females:

89.6; Marriage status: 27.5% never married, 58.0% now married, 1.6% separated, 6.1% widowed, 8.4% divorced; Foreign born: 45.1%; Speak English only: 39.3%; With disability: 8.2%; Veterans: 3.3%; Ancestry: 8.4% Italian, 6.1% Irish, 3.7% American, 3.7% Greek, 3.6% Russian

Employment: 18.3% management, business, and financial, 6.0% computer, engineering, and science, 13.6% education, legal, community service, arts, and media, 10.0% healthcare practitioners, 14.9% service, 24.4% sales and office, 5.7% natural resources, construction, and maintenance, 6.9% production, transportation, and material moving

Income: Per capita: $34,465; Median household: $72,477; Average household: $88,789; Households with income of $100,000 or more: 34.6%; Poverty rate: 8.1%

Educational Attainment: High school diploma or higher: 90.0%; Bachelor's degree or higher: 45.2%; Graduate/professional degree or higher: 18.5%

Housing: Homeownership rate: 72.7%; Median home value: $506,900; Median year structure built: 1954; Homeowner vacancy rate: 0.8%; Median selected monthly owner costs: $2,401 with a mortgage, $785 without a mortgage; Median gross rent: $1,582 per month; Rental vacancy rate: 2.8%

Health Insurance: 90.4% have insurance; 69.8% have private insurance; 28.8% have public insurance; 9.6% do not have insurance; 5.7% of children under 18 do not have insurance

Transportation: Commute: 64.7% car, 28.8% public transportation, 1.9% walk, 3.9% work from home; Mean travel time to work: 42.7 minutes

OZONE PARK (unincorporated postal area)

ZCTA: 11416

Covers a land area of 0.666 square miles and a water area of 0 square miles. Located at 40.68° N. Lat; 73.85° W. Long. Elevation is 33 feet.

Population: 26,625; Growth (since 2000): 12.5%; Density: 39,997.4 persons per square mile; Race: 26.5% White, 6.5% Black/African American, 35.0% Asian, 0.1% American Indian/Alaska Native, 0.0% Native Hawaiian/Other Pacific Islander, 6.4% Two or more races, 43.1% Hispanic of any race; Average household size: 3.72; Median age: 33.6; Age under 18: 25.5%; Age 65 and over: 7.8%; Males per 100 females: 99.0; Marriage status: 37.6% never married, 49.8% now married, 2.7% separated, 4.7% widowed, 7.9% divorced; Foreign born: 51.8%; Speak English only: 39.1%; With disability: 10.8%; Veterans: 1.3%; Ancestry: 8.8% Guyanese, 5.5% Italian, 2.2% Irish, 1.7% Polish, 1.5% German

Employment: 10.8% management, business, and financial, 2.3% computer, engineering, and science, 7.9% education, legal, community service, arts, and media, 5.0% healthcare practitioners, 27.1% service, 23.9% sales and office, 10.1% natural resources, construction, and maintenance, 12.8% production, transportation, and material moving

Income: Per capita: $20,849; Median household: $58,392; Average household: $72,849; Households with income of $100,000 or more: 23.3%; Poverty rate: 17.6%

Educational Attainment: High school diploma or higher: 75.4%; Bachelor's degree or higher: 22.0%; Graduate/professional degree or higher: 5.8%

Housing: Homeownership rate: 42.0%; Median home value: $442,900; Median year structure built: Before 1940; Homeowner vacancy rate: 1.9%; Median selected monthly owner costs: $2,532 with a mortgage, $755 without a mortgage; Median gross rent: $1,355 per month; Rental vacancy rate: 1.7%

Health Insurance: 86.1% have insurance; 47.1% have private insurance; 43.1% have public insurance; 13.9% do not have insurance; 2.6% of children under 18 do not have insurance

Transportation: Commute: 37.6% car, 53.0% public transportation, 5.3% walk, 3.1% work from home; Mean travel time to work: 46.3 minutes

ZCTA: 11417

Covers a land area of 1.119 square miles and a water area of 0 square miles. Located at 40.68° N. Lat; 73.84° W. Long. Elevation is 33 feet.

Population: 32,415; Growth (since 2000): 13.3%; Density: 28,966.9 persons per square mile; Race: 38.0% White, 7.2% Black/African American, 28.2% Asian, 0.3% American Indian/Alaska Native, 0.0% Native Hawaiian/Other Pacific Islander, 6.8% Two or more races, 38.8% Hispanic of any race; Average household size: 3.43; Median age: 36.7; Age under 18: 22.2%; Age 65 and over: 10.5%; Males per 100 females: 93.6; Marriage status: 35.8% never married, 51.1% now married, 2.2% separated, 5.1% widowed, 7.9% divorced; Foreign born: 45.8%; Speak English only: 48.0%; With disability: 11.6%; Veterans: 2.9%; Ancestry:

12.5% Italian, 8.9% Guyanese, 3.3% Irish, 2.5% Trinidadian and Tobagonian, 2.2% Polish

Employment: 9.0% management, business, and financial, 2.4% computer, engineering, and science, 8.9% education, legal, community service, arts, and media, 4.6% healthcare practitioners, 25.6% service, 28.2% sales and office, 9.5% natural resources, construction, and maintenance, 11.8% production, transportation, and material moving

Income: Per capita: $24,249; Median household: $62,057; Average household: $79,020; Households with income of $100,000 or more: 27.7%; Poverty rate: 16.3%

Educational Attainment: High school diploma or higher: 78.1%; Bachelor's degree or higher: 21.7%; Graduate/professional degree or higher: 7.4%

Housing: Homeownership rate: 56.7%; Median home value: $437,100; Median year structure built: 1943; Homeowner vacancy rate: 1.6%; Median selected monthly owner costs: $2,473 with a mortgage, $762 without a mortgage; Median gross rent: $1,334 per month; Rental vacancy rate: 3.2%

Health Insurance: 86.9% have insurance; 54.2% have private insurance; 39.4% have public insurance; 13.1% do not have insurance; 2.4% of children under 18 do not have insurance

Transportation: Commute: 43.7% car, 47.3% public transportation, 5.2% walk, 2.5% work from home; Mean travel time to work: 44.2 minutes

QUEENS (borough).

Covers a land area of 108.532 square miles and a water area of 69.675 square miles. Located at 40.66° N. Lat; 73.84° W. Long. Elevation is 43 feet.

Population: 2,301,139; Growth (since 2000): 3.2%; Density: 21,202.4 persons per square mile; Race: 41.1% White, 18.5% Black/African American, 24.4% Asian, 0.4% American Indian/Alaska Native, 0.0% Native Hawaiian/Other Pacific Islander, 3.4% Two or more races, 27.9% Hispanic of any race; Average household size: 2.91; Median age: 37.7; Age under 18: 20.5%; Age 65 and over: 13.4%; Males per 100 females: 93.8; Marriage status: 38.3% never married, 48.1% now married, 2.8% separated, 5.9% widowed, 7.7% divorced; Foreign born: 47.8%; Speak English only: 43.7%; With disability: 9.5%; Veterans: 2.7%; Ancestry: 5.7% Italian, 4.0% Irish, 3.8% American, 2.8% Guyanese, 2.8% Jamaican

Employment: 12.4% management, business, and financial, 3.8% computer, engineering, and science, 11.0% education, legal, community service, arts, and media, 5.1% healthcare practitioners, 24.8% service, 24.0% sales and office, 8.2% natural resources, construction, and maintenance, 10.7% production, transportation, and material moving

Income: Per capita: $26,876; Median household: $57,720; Average household: $75,162; Households with income of $100,000 or more: 25.5%; Poverty rate: 15.1%

Educational Attainment: High school diploma or higher: 80.4%; Bachelor's degree or higher: 30.4%; Graduate/professional degree or higher: 11.1%

Housing: Homeownership rate: 43.6%; Median home value: $450,300; Median year structure built: 1951; Homeowner vacancy rate: 1.7%; Median selected monthly owner costs: $2,425 with a mortgage, $791 without a mortgage; Median gross rent: $1,367 per month; Rental vacancy rate: 3.0%

Health Insurance: 84.4% have insurance; 54.5% have private insurance; 37.4% have public insurance; 15.6% do not have insurance; 4.4% of children under 18 do not have insurance

Hospitals:

Newspapers: Forum South (weekly circulation 60,000); Queens Chronicle (weekly circulation 160,000); Queens Gazette (weekly circulation 90,000); Queens Ledger (weekly circulation 150,000); Queens Times (weekly circulation 75,000); Queens Tribune (weekly circulation 171,000); Schneps Publications (weekly circulation 80,000); The Wave (weekly circulation 13,000); Times Newsweekly (weekly circulation 27,000); Times/Ledger Newspapers (weekly circulation 45,000); Woodside Herald (weekly circulation 16,000)

Transportation: Commute: 38.0% car, 52.3% public transportation, 5.8% walk, 2.4% work from home; Mean travel time to work: 42.6 minutes

Additional Information Contacts

Borough of Queens . . . . (718) 286-3000
   http://www.queensbp.org

QUEENS VILLAGE (unincorporated postal area)
ZCTA: 11427

Covers a land area of 1.576 square miles and a water area of 0 square miles. Located at 40.73° N. Lat; 73.75° W. Long. Elevation is 89 feet.
Population: 23,568; Growth (since 2000): 2.4%; Density: 14,951.5 persons per square mile; Race: 27.6% White, 25.7% Black/African American, 31.9% Asian, 0.3% American Indian/Alaska Native, 0.0% Native Hawaiian/Other Pacific Islander, 6.3% Two or more races, 14.5% Hispanic of any race; Average household size: 2.94; Median age: 41.6; Age under 18: 18.2%; Age 65 and over: 14.7%; Males per 100 females: 93.8; Marriage status: 33.7% never married, 53.4% now married, 2.2% separated, 6.6% widowed, 6.3% divorced; Foreign born: 47.8%; Speak English only: 51.4%; With disability: 9.8%; Veterans: 3.2%; Ancestry: 9.0% Guyanese, 6.1% Haitian, 4.1% Irish, 3.9% American, 3.5% Italian
Employment: 14.0% management, business, and financial, 4.7% computer, engineering, and science, 11.3% education, legal, community service, arts, and media, 9.3% healthcare practitioners, 18.0% service, 25.6% sales and office, 6.5% natural resources, construction, and maintenance, 10.6% production, transportation, and material moving
Income: Per capita: $28,860; Median household: $66,007; Average household: $83,020; Households with income of $100,000 or more: 30.2%; Poverty rate: 8.7%
Educational Attainment: High school diploma or higher: 84.8%; Bachelor's degree or higher: 31.9%; Graduate/professional degree or higher: 11.5%
Housing: Homeownership rate: 58.2%; Median home value: $455,700; Median year structure built: 1950; Homeowner vacancy rate: 1.0%; Median selected monthly owner costs: $2,342 with a mortgage, $790 without a mortgage; Median gross rent: $1,275 per month; Rental vacancy rate: 3.0%
Health Insurance: 88.0% have insurance; 65.4% have private insurance; 30.5% have public insurance; 12.0% do not have insurance; 5.9% of children under 18 do not have insurance
Transportation: Commute: 56.8% car, 37.9% public transportation, 2.6% walk, 2.1% work from home; Mean travel time to work: 45.4 minutes

ZCTA: 11428

Covers a land area of 0.833 square miles and a water area of 0 square miles. Located at 40.72° N. Lat; 73.74° W. Long. Elevation is 89 feet.
Population: 19,744; Growth (since 2000): -6.1%; Density: 23,713.1 persons per square mile; Race: 22.2% White, 18.4% Black/African American, 29.6% Asian, 0.4% American Indian/Alaska Native, 0.7% Native Hawaiian/Other Pacific Islander, 11.8% Two or more races, 23.8% Hispanic of any race; Average household size: 3.51; Median age: 40.2; Age under 18: 19.0%; Age 65 and over: 12.2%; Males per 100 females: 94.0; Marriage status: 33.3% never married, 55.9% now married, 2.7% separated, 4.7% widowed, 6.0% divorced; Foreign born: 55.1%; Speak English only: 52.5%; With disability: 7.9%; Veterans: 2.4%; Ancestry: 18.1% Guyanese, 7.2% Haitian, 3.1% American, 2.7% Italian, 2.3% Irish
Employment: 10.8% management, business, and financial, 2.4% computer, engineering, and science, 8.7% education, legal, community service, arts, and media, 5.1% healthcare practitioners, 20.6% service, 29.3% sales and office, 9.1% natural resources, construction, and maintenance, 14.0% production, transportation, and material moving
Income: Per capita: $22,940; Median household: $67,151; Average household: $75,806; Households with income of $100,000 or more: 28.7%; Poverty rate: 12.4%
Educational Attainment: High school diploma or higher: 81.3%; Bachelor's degree or higher: 20.0%; Graduate/professional degree or higher: 5.6%
Housing: Homeownership rate: 65.5%; Median home value: $424,200; Median year structure built: Before 1940; Homeowner vacancy rate: 0.9%; Median selected monthly owner costs: $2,476 with a mortgage, $800 without a mortgage; Median gross rent: $1,377 per month; Rental vacancy rate: 4.4%
Health Insurance: 87.5% have insurance; 60.8% have private insurance; 32.5% have public insurance; 12.5% do not have insurance; 5.0% of children under 18 do not have insurance
Transportation: Commute: 55.4% car, 39.3% public transportation, 2.0% walk, 2.2% work from home; Mean travel time to work: 45.8 minutes

ZCTA: 11429

Covers a land area of 1.301 square miles and a water area of 0 square miles. Located at 40.71° N. Lat; 73.74° W. Long. Elevation is 89 feet.

Population: 26,362; Growth (since 2000): -4.6%; Density: 20,261.7 persons per square mile; Race: 4.7% White, 79.9% Black/African American, 3.0% Asian, 0.4% American Indian/Alaska Native, 0.0% Native Hawaiian/Other Pacific Islander, 3.6% Two or more races, 12.3% Hispanic of any race; Average household size: 3.58; Median age: 39.6; Age under 18: 20.1%; Age 65 and over: 12.9%; Males per 100 females: 85.2; Marriage status: 46.8% never married, 40.1% now married, 3.6% separated, 5.6% widowed, 7.5% divorced; Foreign born: 45.0%; Speak English only: 65.6%; With disability: 10.4%; Veterans: 3.3%; Ancestry: 21.2% Haitian, 13.0% Jamaican, 5.4% Guyanese, 3.7% West Indian, 2.4% Trinidadian and Tobagonian
Employment: 10.8% management, business, and financial, 1.3% computer, engineering, and science, 8.9% education, legal, community service, arts, and media, 6.0% healthcare practitioners, 26.9% service, 27.4% sales and office, 7.7% natural resources, construction, and maintenance, 10.9% production, transportation, and material moving
Income: Per capita: $25,051; Median household: $68,684; Average household: $82,902; Households with income of $100,000 or more: 31.1%; Poverty rate: 11.7%
Educational Attainment: High school diploma or higher: 83.9%; Bachelor's degree or higher: 20.2%; Graduate/professional degree or higher: 6.1%
Housing: Homeownership rate: 70.9%; Median home value: $379,300; Median year structure built: 1945; Homeowner vacancy rate: 1.9%; Median selected monthly owner costs: $2,394 with a mortgage, $752 without a mortgage; Median gross rent: $1,331 per month; Rental vacancy rate: 1.7%
Health Insurance: 87.5% have insurance; 58.5% have private insurance; 36.0% have public insurance; 12.5% do not have insurance; 5.0% of children under 18 do not have insurance
Transportation: Commute: 52.6% car, 42.1% public transportation, 1.9% walk, 1.8% work from home; Mean travel time to work: 47.9 minutes

REGO PARK (unincorporated postal area)
ZCTA: 11374

Covers a land area of 0.934 square miles and a water area of 0 square miles. Located at 40.73° N. Lat; 73.86° W. Long. Elevation is 92 feet.
Population: 43,399; Growth (since 2000): -1.8%; Density: 46,448.8 persons per square mile; Race: 59.7% White, 3.4% Black/African American, 27.2% Asian, 0.2% American Indian/Alaska Native, 0.0% Native Hawaiian/Other Pacific Islander, 3.8% Two or more races, 17.8% Hispanic of any race; Average household size: 2.23; Median age: 42.2; Age under 18: 16.0%; Age 65 and over: 18.6%; Males per 100 females: 88.5; Marriage status: 33.6% never married, 50.7% now married, 2.2% separated, 8.0% widowed, 7.7% divorced; Foreign born: 58.1%; Speak English only: 31.7%; With disability: 12.2%; Veterans: 2.3%; Ancestry: 13.5% Russian, 3.8% Italian, 3.3% Irish, 2.9% Polish, 2.5% German
Employment: 17.9% management, business, and financial, 7.2% computer, engineering, and science, 11.8% education, legal, community service, arts, and media, 7.9% healthcare practitioners, 19.8% service, 22.4% sales and office, 3.3% natural resources, construction, and maintenance, 9.7% production, transportation, and material moving
Income: Per capita: $32,731; Median household: $52,132; Average household: $70,852; Households with income of $100,000 or more: 24.4%; Poverty rate: 15.0%
Educational Attainment: High school diploma or higher: 90.4%; Bachelor's degree or higher: 48.0%; Graduate/professional degree or higher: 19.2%
Housing: Homeownership rate: 35.0%; Median home value: $288,900; Median year structure built: 1953; Homeowner vacancy rate: 0.7%; Median selected monthly owner costs: $1,705 with a mortgage, $668 without a mortgage; Median gross rent: $1,349 per month; Rental vacancy rate: 2.6%
Health Insurance: 88.7% have insurance; 60.9% have private insurance; 34.9% have public insurance; 11.3% do not have insurance; 4.0% of children under 18 do not have insurance
Transportation: Commute: 27.7% car, 58.5% public transportation, 9.6% walk, 3.2% work from home; Mean travel time to work: 41.7 minutes

RICHMOND HILL (unincorporated postal area)
ZCTA: 11418

Covers a land area of 1.633 square miles and a water area of 0 square miles. Located at 40.70° N. Lat; 73.84° W. Long. Elevation is 59 feet.

Population: 39,308; Growth (since 2000): 7.5%; Density: 24,070.3 persons per square mile; Race: 36.0% White, 8.1% Black/African American, 25.6% Asian, 0.8% American Indian/Alaska Native, 0.0% Native Hawaiian/Other Pacific Islander, 6.8% Two or more races, 43.5% Hispanic of any race; Average household size: 3.42; Median age: 34.5; Age under 18: 24.1%; Age 65 and over: 9.6%; Males per 100 females: 100.5; Marriage status: 37.6% never married, 51.5% now married, 2.6% separated, 4.3% widowed, 6.6% divorced; Foreign born: 51.6%; Speak English only: 39.4%; With disability: 9.9%; Veterans: 2.3%; Ancestry: 7.5% Guyanese, 3.7% Italian, 3.6% Irish, 2.3% German, 2.2% Trinidadian and Tobagonian

Employment: 10.9% management, business, and financial, 3.5% computer, engineering, and science, 8.6% education, legal, community service, arts, and media, 4.0% healthcare practitioners, 26.1% service, 23.9% sales and office, 10.6% natural resources, construction, and maintenance, 12.4% production, transportation, and material moving

Income: Per capita: $22,529; Median household: $61,480; Average household: $73,486; Households with income of $100,000 or more: 25.2%; Poverty rate: 16.5%

Educational Attainment: High school diploma or higher: 74.9%; Bachelor's degree or higher: 25.7%; Graduate/professional degree or higher: 8.8%

Housing: Homeownership rate: 42.2%; Median home value: $446,900; Median year structure built: Before 1940; Homeowner vacancy rate: 3.1%; Median selected monthly owner costs: $2,651 with a mortgage, $793 without a mortgage; Median gross rent: $1,357 per month; Rental vacancy rate: 3.4%

Health Insurance: 82.7% have insurance; 45.7% have private insurance; 41.5% have public insurance; 17.3% do not have insurance; 2.7% of children under 18 do not have insurance

Transportation: Commute: 35.0% car, 53.6% public transportation, 6.4% walk, 3.6% work from home; Mean travel time to work: 44.1 minutes

RIDGEWOOD (unincorporated postal area)
ZCTA: 11385

Covers a land area of 3.613 square miles and a water area of 0.032 square miles. Located at 40.70° N. Lat; 73.89° W. Long. Elevation is 75 feet.

Population: 102,209; Growth (since 2000): 4.8%; Density: 28,291.1 persons per square mile; Race: 82.8% White, 2.1% Black/African American, 6.7% Asian, 0.3% American Indian/Alaska Native, 0.0% Native Hawaiian/Other Pacific Islander, 1.7% Two or more races, 43.9% Hispanic of any race; Average household size: 2.92; Median age: 35.2; Age under 18: 22.5%; Age 65 and over: 10.2%; Males per 100 females: 96.9; Marriage status: 39.4% never married, 47.3% now married, 2.8% separated, 5.7% widowed, 7.6% divorced; Foreign born: 41.0%; Speak English only: 44.3%; With disability: 6.2%; Veterans: 2.1%; Ancestry: 10.9% Polish, 8.5% Italian, 6.0% American, 5.1% Irish, 5.0% German

Employment: 9.4% management, business, and financial, 2.9% computer, engineering, and science, 10.1% education, legal, community service, arts, and media, 3.6% healthcare practitioners, 26.7% service, 22.4% sales and office, 12.4% natural resources, construction, and maintenance, 12.4% production, transportation, and material moving

Income: Per capita: $25,100; Median household: $55,331; Average household: $69,571; Households with income of $100,000 or more: 22.6%; Poverty rate: 15.6%

Educational Attainment: High school diploma or higher: 80.4%; Bachelor's degree or higher: 22.2%; Graduate/professional degree or higher: 7.2%

Housing: Homeownership rate: 30.7%; Median home value: $487,400; Median year structure built: Before 1940; Homeowner vacancy rate: 0.5%; Median selected monthly owner costs: $2,625 with a mortgage, $758 without a mortgage; Median gross rent: $1,294 per month; Rental vacancy rate: 4.1%

Health Insurance: 82.9% have insurance; 49.9% have private insurance; 38.2% have public insurance; 17.1% do not have insurance; 4.0% of children under 18 do not have insurance

Transportation: Commute: 28.2% car, 61.3% public transportation, 6.7% walk, 2.3% work from home; Mean travel time to work: 37.9 minutes

ROCKAWAY PARK (unincorporated postal area)
ZCTA: 11694

Covers a land area of 1.366 square miles and a water area of <.001 square miles. Located at 40.58° N. Lat; 73.84° W. Long. Elevation is 7 feet.

Population: 20,773; Growth (since 2000): 7.8%; Density: 15,211.1 persons per square mile; Race: 81.9% White, 7.8% Black/African American, 3.7% Asian, 0.1% American Indian/Alaska Native, 0.0% Native Hawaiian/Other Pacific Islander, 1.6% Two or more races, 13.9% Hispanic of any race; Average household size: 2.44; Median age: 45.1; Age under 18: 21.6%; Age 65 and over: 20.3%; Males per 100 females: 95.4; Marriage status: 32.6% never married, 51.4% now married, 4.6% separated, 7.4% widowed, 8.5% divorced; Foreign born: 14.7%; Speak English only: 77.7%; With disability: 17.9%; Veterans: 5.9%; Ancestry: 30.0% Irish, 17.0% Italian, 8.2% German, 5.7% American, 5.0% Polish

Employment: 16.9% management, business, and financial, 2.4% computer, engineering, and science, 16.6% education, legal, community service, arts, and media, 8.3% healthcare practitioners, 17.7% service, 21.4% sales and office, 9.7% natural resources, construction, and maintenance, 6.9% production, transportation, and material moving

Income: Per capita: $39,931; Median household: $75,094; Average household: $100,077; Households with income of $100,000 or more: 34.0%; Poverty rate: 5.9%

Educational Attainment: High school diploma or higher: 87.9%; Bachelor's degree or higher: 38.4%; Graduate/professional degree or higher: 16.8%

Housing: Homeownership rate: 50.4%; Median home value: $622,700; Median year structure built: 1954; Homeowner vacancy rate: 1.4%; Median selected monthly owner costs: $2,713 with a mortgage, $995 without a mortgage; Median gross rent: $1,212 per month; Rental vacancy rate: 8.7%

Health Insurance: 93.7% have insurance; 73.5% have private insurance; 34.9% have public insurance; 6.3% do not have insurance; 2.8% of children under 18 do not have insurance

Transportation: Commute: 59.0% car, 32.5% public transportation, 3.3% walk, 2.1% work from home; Mean travel time to work: 48.6 minutes

ROSEDALE (unincorporated postal area)
ZCTA: 11422

Covers a land area of 1.969 square miles and a water area of 0.079 square miles. Located at 40.66° N. Lat; 73.74° W. Long. Elevation is 16 feet.

Population: 33,245; Growth (since 2000): 9.2%; Density: 16,888.4 persons per square mile; Race: 7.7% White, 85.6% Black/African American, 2.3% Asian, 0.1% American Indian/Alaska Native, 0.0% Native Hawaiian/Other Pacific Islander, 2.0% Two or more races, 8.4% Hispanic of any race; Average household size: 3.45; Median age: 35.1; Age under 18: 24.3%; Age 65 and over: 10.6%; Males per 100 females: 83.2; Marriage status: 43.6% never married, 41.0% now married, 3.7% separated, 5.2% widowed, 10.2% divorced; Foreign born: 41.3%; Speak English only: 72.7%; With disability: 7.0%; Veterans: 2.9%; Ancestry: 19.9% Jamaican, 12.1% Haitian, 5.6% American, 3.6% Guyanese, 3.4% West Indian

Employment: 10.1% management, business, and financial, 3.0% computer, engineering, and science, 11.6% education, legal, community service, arts, and media, 7.9% healthcare practitioners, 26.4% service, 25.2% sales and office, 6.8% natural resources, construction, and maintenance, 9.0% production, transportation, and material moving

Income: Per capita: $28,435; Median household: $84,955; Average household: $92,702; Households with income of $100,000 or more: 39.9%; Poverty rate: 8.6%

Educational Attainment: High school diploma or higher: 89.0%; Bachelor's degree or higher: 29.8%; Graduate/professional degree or higher: 10.0%

Housing: Homeownership rate: 65.5%; Median home value: $410,200; Median year structure built: 1956; Homeowner vacancy rate: 1.2%; Median selected monthly owner costs: $2,586 with a mortgage, $803 without a mortgage; Median gross rent: $1,593 per month; Rental vacancy rate: 2.7%

Health Insurance: 91.0% have insurance; 69.5% have private insurance; 28.9% have public insurance; 9.0% do not have insurance; 3.8% of children under 18 do not have insurance

Transportation: Commute: 59.0% car, 36.5% public transportation, 0.9% walk, 3.0% work from home; Mean travel time to work: 50.4 minutes

SAINT ALBANS (unincorporated postal area)
ZCTA: 11412

Covers a land area of 1.646 square miles and a water area of 0 square miles. Located at 40.70° N. Lat; 73.76° W. Long. Elevation is 49 feet.
Population: 37,832; Growth (since 2000): 1.0%; Density: 22,977.7 persons per square mile; Race: 1.9% White, 88.9% Black/African American, 2.5% Asian, 0.2% American Indian/Alaska Native, 0.0% Native Hawaiian/Other Pacific Islander, 3.3% Two or more races, 6.5% Hispanic of any race; Average household size: 3.47; Median age: 40.1; Age under 18: 22.0%; Age 65 and over: 13.7%; Males per 100 females: 80.8; Marriage status: 45.0% never married, 38.5% now married, 4.5% separated, 6.3% widowed, 10.1% divorced; Foreign born: 36.1%; Speak English only: 85.6%; With disability: 10.9%; Veterans: 3.9%; Ancestry: 22.0% Jamaican, 13.9% American, 6.9% Haitian, 6.6% Guyanese, 4.4% Trinidadian and Tobagonian
Employment: 9.9% management, business, and financial, 1.8% computer, engineering, and science, 8.7% education, legal, community service, arts, and media, 5.5% healthcare practitioners, 30.0% service, 26.3% sales and office, 6.4% natural resources, construction, and maintenance, 11.4% production, transportation, and material moving
Income: Per capita: $25,833; Median household: $72,458; Average household: $82,631; Households with income of $100,000 or more: 31.5%; Poverty rate: 9.1%
Educational Attainment: High school diploma or higher: 87.3%; Bachelor's degree or higher: 22.2%; Graduate/professional degree or higher: 8.3%
Housing: Homeownership rate: 73.9%; Median home value: $380,200; Median year structure built: 1946; Homeowner vacancy rate: 1.4%; Median selected monthly owner costs: $2,469 with a mortgage, $792 without a mortgage; Median gross rent: $1,278 per month; Rental vacancy rate: 5.0%
Health Insurance: 87.5% have insurance; 62.1% have private insurance; 32.8% have public insurance; 12.5% do not have insurance; 7.1% of children under 18 do not have insurance
Transportation: Commute: 49.9% car, 44.9% public transportation, 2.3% walk, 2.2% work from home; Mean travel time to work: 50.8 minutes

SOUTH OZONE PARK (unincorporated postal area)
ZCTA: 11420

Covers a land area of 2.078 square miles and a water area of 0 square miles. Located at 40.67° N. Lat; 73.82° W. Long. Elevation is 26 feet.
Population: 50,820; Growth (since 2000): 11.7%; Density: 24,456.1 persons per square mile; Race: 16.1% White, 25.8% Black/African American, 23.3% Asian, 1.4% American Indian/Alaska Native, 0.2% Native Hawaiian/Other Pacific Islander, 6.1% Two or more races, 24.1% Hispanic of any race; Average household size: 3.76; Median age: 37.0; Age under 18: 22.6%; Age 65 and over: 10.7%; Males per 100 females: 93.7; Marriage status: 37.7% never married, 49.2% now married, 3.6% separated, 5.7% widowed, 7.5% divorced; Foreign born: 52.2%; Speak English only: 68.5%; With disability: 9.6%; Veterans: 2.5%; Ancestry: 13.2% Guyanese, 10.4% West Indian, 3.3% Trinidadian and Tobagonian, 2.8% Italian, 2.0% Jamaican
Employment: 9.2% management, business, and financial, 3.0% computer, engineering, and science, 7.3% education, legal, community service, arts, and media, 4.2% healthcare practitioners, 23.4% service, 29.9% sales and office, 10.5% natural resources, construction, and maintenance, 12.5% production, transportation, and material moving
Income: Per capita: $22,502; Median household: $59,660; Average household: $79,434; Households with income of $100,000 or more: 26.7%; Poverty rate: 13.1%
Educational Attainment: High school diploma or higher: 74.6%; Bachelor's degree or higher: 17.6%; Graduate/professional degree or higher: 4.3%
Housing: Homeownership rate: 66.4%; Median home value: $420,800; Median year structure built: 1946; Homeowner vacancy rate: 0.8%; Median selected monthly owner costs: $2,492 with a mortgage, $765 without a mortgage; Median gross rent: $1,395 per month; Rental vacancy rate: 2.7%

Health Insurance: 86.3% have insurance; 51.8% have private insurance; 40.8% have public insurance; 13.7% do not have insurance; 5.1% of children under 18 do not have insurance
Transportation: Commute: 48.3% car, 45.3% public transportation, 2.2% walk, 2.0% work from home; Mean travel time to work: 47.7 minutes

SOUTH RICHMOND HILL (unincorporated postal area)
ZCTA: 11419

Covers a land area of 1.129 square miles and a water area of 0 square miles. Located at 40.69° N. Lat; 73.82° W. Long..
Population: 49,306; Growth (since 2000): 0.9%; Density: 43,660.3 persons per square mile; Race: 11.0% White, 18.5% Black/African American, 29.2% Asian, 0.7% American Indian/Alaska Native, 0.1% Native Hawaiian/Other Pacific Islander, 7.1% Two or more races, 18.8% Hispanic of any race; Average household size: 3.99; Median age: 35.9; Age under 18: 20.8%; Age 65 and over: 9.2%; Males per 100 females: 99.6; Marriage status: 38.4% never married, 51.6% now married, 2.4% separated, 4.4% widowed, 5.6% divorced; Foreign born: 63.3%; Speak English only: 62.1%; With disability: 7.6%; Veterans: 1.6%; Ancestry: 15.1% Guyanese, 4.4% Trinidadian and Tobagonian, 2.3% West Indian, 1.3% Italian, 1.3% Jamaican
Employment: 8.1% management, business, and financial, 2.3% computer, engineering, and science, 4.7% education, legal, community service, arts, and media, 3.4% healthcare practitioners, 26.0% service, 27.1% sales and office, 13.3% natural resources, construction, and maintenance, 15.0% production, transportation, and material moving
Income: Per capita: $20,109; Median household: $58,266; Average household: $73,064; Households with income of $100,000 or more: 23.6%; Poverty rate: 17.2%
Educational Attainment: High school diploma or higher: 73.4%; Bachelor's degree or higher: 17.8%; Graduate/professional degree or higher: 4.4%
Housing: Homeownership rate: 55.3%; Median home value: $426,500; Median year structure built: Before 1940; Homeowner vacancy rate: 1.5%; Median selected monthly owner costs: $2,556 with a mortgage, $809 without a mortgage; Median gross rent: $1,366 per month; Rental vacancy rate: 2.9%
Health Insurance: 81.6% have insurance; 39.9% have private insurance; 45.7% have public insurance; 18.4% do not have insurance; 3.5% of children under 18 do not have insurance
Transportation: Commute: 39.4% car, 51.4% public transportation, 6.0% walk, 1.4% work from home; Mean travel time to work: 46.2 minutes

SPRINGFIELD GARDENS (unincorporated postal area)
ZCTA: 11413

Covers a land area of 3.100 square miles and a water area of 0.033 square miles. Located at 40.67° N. Lat; 73.75° W. Long. Elevation is 30 feet.
Population: 42,560; Growth (since 2000): 6.9%; Density: 13,730.2 persons per square mile; Race: 2.8% White, 91.1% Black/African American, 1.3% Asian, 0.1% American Indian/Alaska Native, 0.2% Native Hawaiian/Other Pacific Islander, 1.9% Two or more races, 5.5% Hispanic of any race; Average household size: 3.44; Median age: 38.4; Age under 18: 22.2%; Age 65 and over: 14.0%; Males per 100 females: 83.2; Marriage status: 44.2% never married, 39.8% now married, 3.3% separated, 6.5% widowed, 9.5% divorced; Foreign born: 35.3%; Speak English only: 85.4%; With disability: 10.1%; Veterans: 4.4%; Ancestry: 22.7% Jamaican, 7.5% Haitian, 3.9% American, 3.5% West Indian, 3.4% Guyanese
Employment: 11.2% management, business, and financial, 2.6% computer, engineering, and science, 11.2% education, legal, community service, arts, and media, 8.1% healthcare practitioners, 27.4% service, 23.7% sales and office, 6.8% natural resources, construction, and maintenance, 9.0% production, transportation, and material moving
Income: Per capita: $28,943; Median household: $81,287; Average household: $92,538; Households with income of $100,000 or more: 38.1%; Poverty rate: 7.3%
Educational Attainment: High school diploma or higher: 87.7%; Bachelor's degree or higher: 26.5%; Graduate/professional degree or higher: 9.8%
Housing: Homeownership rate: 73.1%; Median home value: $405,500; Median year structure built: 1951; Homeowner vacancy rate: 1.1%; Median selected monthly owner costs: $2,507 with a mortgage, $799

without a mortgage; Median gross rent: $1,502 per month; Rental vacancy rate: 1.2%
Health Insurance: 91.6% have insurance; 68.9% have private insurance; 33.6% have public insurance; 8.4% do not have insurance; 3.2% of children under 18 do not have insurance
Transportation: Commute: 53.8% car, 41.4% public transportation, 1.7% walk, 2.1% work from home; Mean travel time to work: 52.0 minutes

SUNNYSIDE (unincorporated postal area)
ZCTA: 11104

Covers a land area of 0.390 square miles and a water area of 0 square miles. Located at 40.74° N. Lat; 73.92° W. Long. Elevation is 16 feet.
Population: 26,718; Growth (since 2000): -9.4%; Density: 68,507.9 persons per square mile; Race: 65.8% White, 1.3% Black/African American, 24.5% Asian, 0.1% American Indian/Alaska Native, 0.0% Native Hawaiian/Other Pacific Islander, 3.2% Two or more races, 28.9% Hispanic of any race; Average household size: 2.31; Median age: 37.7; Age under 18: 16.2%; Age 65 and over: 12.2%; Males per 100 females: 94.7; Marriage status: 41.3% never married, 47.8% now married, 3.0% separated, 4.0% widowed, 6.9% divorced; Foreign born: 51.9%; Speak English only: 35.0%; With disability: 7.6%; Veterans: 2.1%; Ancestry: 7.5% Irish, 5.0% Italian, 3.6% German, 3.6% Romanian, 3.5% American
Employment: 13.8% management, business, and financial, 4.6% computer, engineering, and science, 17.9% education, legal, community service, arts, and media, 4.1% healthcare practitioners, 24.3% service, 20.3% sales and office, 4.5% natural resources, construction, and maintenance, 10.4% production, transportation, and material moving
Income: Per capita: $31,756; Median household: $55,294; Average household: $70,828; Households with income of $100,000 or more: 22.0%; Poverty rate: 14.8%
Educational Attainment: High school diploma or higher: 85.6%; Bachelor's degree or higher: 42.0%; Graduate/professional degree or higher: 13.0%
Housing: Homeownership rate: 15.8%; Median home value: $396,800; Median year structure built: Before 1940; Homeowner vacancy rate: 0.5%; Median selected monthly owner costs: $1,954 with a mortgage, $720 without a mortgage; Median gross rent: $1,421 per month; Rental vacancy rate: 1.6%
Health Insurance: 78.8% have insurance; 49.8% have private insurance; 33.8% have public insurance; 21.2% do not have insurance; 4.9% of children under 18 do not have insurance
Transportation: Commute: 13.5% car, 72.2% public transportation, 6.8% walk, 4.0% work from home; Mean travel time to work: 39.1 minutes

WHITESTONE (unincorporated postal area)
ZCTA: 11357

Covers a land area of 2.802 square miles and a water area of 0 square miles. Located at 40.79° N. Lat; 73.81° W. Long. Elevation is 49 feet.
Population: 39,737; Growth (since 2000): 0.6%; Density: 14,182.4 persons per square mile; Race: 75.1% White, 0.5% Black/African American, 19.2% Asian, 0.3% American Indian/Alaska Native, 0.0% Native Hawaiian/Other Pacific Islander, 2.5% Two or more races, 12.9% Hispanic of any race; Average household size: 2.66; Median age: 44.6; Age under 18: 19.3%; Age 65 and over: 21.5%; Males per 100 females: 90.3; Marriage status: 27.1% never married, 57.3% now married, 1.3% separated, 8.0% widowed, 7.6% divorced; Foreign born: 33.0%; Speak English only: 48.1%; With disability: 10.4%; Veterans: 5.2%; Ancestry: 28.9% Italian, 9.4% Greek, 9.3% Irish, 4.5% German, 3.5% American
Employment: 19.0% management, business, and financial, 4.6% computer, engineering, and science, 14.9% education, legal, community service, arts, and media, 3.8% healthcare practitioners, 13.3% service, 29.0% sales and office, 9.0% natural resources, construction, and maintenance, 6.4% production, transportation, and material moving
Income: Per capita: $35,216; Median household: $73,750; Average household: $91,915; Households with income of $100,000 or more: 34.8%; Poverty rate: 6.0%
Educational Attainment: High school diploma or higher: 85.9%; Bachelor's degree or higher: 36.7%; Graduate/professional degree or higher: 13.6%
Housing: Homeownership rate: 74.7%; Median home value: $599,000; Median year structure built: 1956; Homeowner vacancy rate: 1.7%; Median selected monthly owner costs: $2,480 with a mortgage, $919

without a mortgage; Median gross rent: $1,610 per month; Rental vacancy rate: 5.7%
Health Insurance: 92.2% have insurance; 74.7% have private insurance; 30.2% have public insurance; 7.8% do not have insurance; 4.4% of children under 18 do not have insurance
Transportation: Commute: 70.7% car, 23.9% public transportation, 2.8% walk, 2.0% work from home; Mean travel time to work: 38.0 minutes

WOODHAVEN (unincorporated postal area)
ZCTA: 11421

Covers a land area of 1.288 square miles and a water area of 0 square miles. Located at 40.69° N. Lat; 73.86° W. Long. Elevation is 43 feet.
Population: 43,024; Growth (since 2000): 14.2%; Density: 33,401.9 persons per square mile; Race: 48.3% White, 5.5% Black/African American, 19.1% Asian, 0.6% American Indian/Alaska Native, 0.0% Native Hawaiian/Other Pacific Islander, 5.6% Two or more races, 56.8% Hispanic of any race; Average household size: 3.52; Median age: 35.8; Age under 18: 23.1%; Age 65 and over: 10.1%; Males per 100 females: 97.5; Marriage status: 37.4% never married, 49.3% now married, 2.8% separated, 4.9% widowed, 8.3% divorced; Foreign born: 45.9%; Speak English only: 34.0%; With disability: 10.3%; Veterans: 2.5%; Ancestry: 4.3% Italian, 4.3% Guyanese, 3.0% Polish, 2.8% Irish, 2.5% German
Employment: 9.1% management, business, and financial, 2.8% computer, engineering, and science, 8.8% education, legal, community service, arts, and media, 3.7% healthcare practitioners, 28.2% service, 26.4% sales and office, 8.5% natural resources, construction, and maintenance, 12.4% production, transportation, and material moving
Income: Per capita: $23,538; Median household: $60,996; Average household: $78,211; Households with income of $100,000 or more: 27.1%; Poverty rate: 14.4%
Educational Attainment: High school diploma or higher: 75.6%; Bachelor's degree or higher: 21.6%; Graduate/professional degree or higher: 6.6%
Housing: Homeownership rate: 55.5%; Median home value: $406,300; Median year structure built: Before 1940; Homeowner vacancy rate: 2.0%; Median selected monthly owner costs: $2,431 with a mortgage, $699 without a mortgage; Median gross rent: $1,396 per month; Rental vacancy rate: 3.6%
Health Insurance: 85.7% have insurance; 51.0% have private insurance; 39.7% have public insurance; 14.3% do not have insurance; 4.2% of children under 18 do not have insurance
Transportation: Commute: 33.7% car, 58.7% public transportation, 5.0% walk, 1.8% work from home; Mean travel time to work: 46.8 minutes

WOODSIDE (unincorporated postal area)
ZCTA: 11377

Covers a land area of 2.547 square miles and a water area of 0 square miles. Located at 40.74° N. Lat; 73.91° W. Long. Elevation is 59 feet.
Population: 90,615; Growth (since 2000): 2.6%; Density: 35,582.6 persons per square mile; Race: 47.9% White, 2.7% Black/African American, 37.3% Asian, 0.4% American Indian/Alaska Native, 0.0% Native Hawaiian/Other Pacific Islander, 2.6% Two or more races, 38.8% Hispanic of any race; Average household size: 2.87; Median age: 36.7; Age under 18: 19.0%; Age 65 and over: 11.5%; Males per 100 females: 101.4; Marriage status: 41.9% never married, 46.1% now married, 2.3% separated, 5.2% widowed, 6.8% divorced; Foreign born: 58.0%; Speak English only: 22.6%; With disability: 6.8%; Veterans: 2.4%; Ancestry: 4.2% Irish, 2.8% Italian, 2.4% American, 1.7% German, 1.6% Greek
Employment: 11.4% management, business, and financial, 4.1% computer, engineering, and science, 9.1% education, legal, community service, arts, and media, 3.4% healthcare practitioners, 26.3% service, 22.8% sales and office, 7.6% natural resources, construction, and maintenance, 15.3% production, transportation, and material moving
Income: Per capita: $23,745; Median household: $50,436; Average household: $64,842; Households with income of $100,000 or more: 18.8%; Poverty rate: 15.9%
Educational Attainment: High school diploma or higher: 74.3%; Bachelor's degree or higher: 28.6%; Graduate/professional degree or higher: 8.8%
Housing: Homeownership rate: 28.9%; Median home value: $428,200; Median year structure built: 1948; Homeowner vacancy rate: 2.3%; Median selected monthly owner costs: $2,057 with a mortgage, $719

without a mortgage; Median gross rent: $1,380 per month; Rental vacancy rate: 2.3%
Health Insurance: 78.5% have insurance; 44.3% have private insurance; 39.7% have public insurance; 21.5% do not have insurance; 2.7% of children under 18 do not have insurance
Transportation: Commute: 21.7% car, 68.9% public transportation, 6.1% walk, 1.5% work from home; Mean travel time to work: 37.9 minutes

End of Neighborhoods in Queens

STATEN ISLAND (borough). Aka Richmond County. Located in southeastern New York State. One of the five counties/boroughs of New York City. Covers a land area of 58.370 square miles, a water area of 43.921 square miles, and is located in the Eastern Time Zone at 40.56° N. Lat., 74.14° W. Long. The county was founded in 1683. County seat is Saint George.

Richmond County is part of the New York-Newark-Jersey City, NY-NJ-PA Metropolitan Statistical Area. The entire metro area includes: Dutchess County-Putnam County, NY Metropolitan Division (Dutchess County, NY; Putnam County, NY); Nassau County-Suffolk County, NY Metropolitan Division (Nassau County, NY; Suffolk County, NY); Newark, NJ-PA Metropolitan Division (Essex County, NJ; Hunterdon County, NJ; Morris County, NJ; Somerset County, NJ; Sussex County, NJ; Union County, NJ; Pike County, PA); New York-Jersey City-White Plains, NY-NJ Metropolitan Division (Bergen County, NJ; Hudson County, NJ; Middlesex County, NJ; Monmouth County, NJ; Ocean County, NJ; Passaic County, NJ; Bronx County, NY; Kings County, NY; New York County, NY; Orange County, NY; Queens County, NY; Richmond County, NY; Rockland County, NY; Westchester County, NY)

Population: 472,481; Growth (since 2000): 6.5%; Density: 8,094.5 persons per square mile; Race: 75.3% White, 10.5% Black/African American, 8.0% Asian, 0.2% American Indian/Alaska Native, 0.0% Native Hawaiian/Other Pacific Islander, 2.2% two or more races, 17.8% Hispanic of any race; Average household size: 2.81; Median age: 39.3; Age under 18: 22.5%; Age 65 and over: 14.1%; Males per 100 females: 94.1; Marriage status: 33.5% never married, 53.0% now married, 1.8% separated, 6.7% widowed, 6.8% divorced; Foreign born: 21.6%; Speak English only: 69.6%; With disability: 9.9%; Veterans: 5.0%; Ancestry: 31.4% Italian, 12.5% Irish, 4.4% German, 4.4% American, 3.9% Polish
Religion: Six largest groups: 54.2% Catholicism, 1.7% Muslim Estimate, 1.6% Eastern Liturgical (Orthodox), 1.6% Orthodox, 1.5% Judaism, 1.3% Non-denominational Protestant
Economy: Unemployment rate: 5.6%; Leading industries: 14.8 % retail trade; 14.5 % health care and social assistance; 13.2 % construction; Farms: 8 totaling n/a acres; Company size: 5 employ 1,000 or more persons, 9 employ 500 to 999 persons, 108 employ 100 to 499 persons, 8,922 employ less than 100 persons; Business ownership: 13,921 women-owned, 3,953 Black-owned, 4,241 Hispanic-owned, 4,242 Asian-owned, 179 American Indian/Alaska Native-owned
Employment: 13.5% management, business, and financial, 4.4% computer, engineering, and science, 14.1% education, legal, community service, arts, and media, 7.3% healthcare practitioners, 19.5% service, 24.3% sales and office, 9.0% natural resources, construction, and maintenance, 8.0% production, transportation, and material moving
Income: Per capita: $32,041; Median household: $73,197; Average household: $90,236; Households with income of $100,000 or more: 35.2%; Poverty rate: 12.5%
Educational Attainment: High school diploma or higher: 88.7%; Bachelor's degree or higher: 30.8%; Graduate/professional degree or higher: 12.4%
Housing: Homeownership rate: 68.8%; Median home value: $439,500; Median year structure built: 1972; Homeowner vacancy rate: 1.8%; Median selected monthly owner costs: $2,390 with a mortgage, $815 without a mortgage; Median gross rent: $1,169 per month; Rental vacancy rate: 6.9%
Vital Statistics: Birth rate: 113.5 per 10,000 population; Death rate: 80.5 per 10,000 population; Age-adjusted cancer mortality rate: 159.2 deaths per 100,000 population
Health Insurance: 92.8% have insurance; 70.3% have private insurance; 31.6% have public insurance; 7.2% do not have insurance; 2.9% of children under 18 do not have insurance

Health Care: Physicians: 40.9 per 10,000 population; Dentists: 6.4 per 10,000 population; Hospital beds: 29.4 per 10,000 population; Hospital admissions: 1,211.7 per 10,000 population
Air Quality Index (AQI): Percent of Days: 68.5% good, 30.4% moderate, 1.1% unhealthy for sensitive individuals, 0.0% unhealthy, 0.0% very unhealthy; Annual median: 41; Annual maximum: 124
Transportation: Commute: 64.5% car, 29.8% public transportation, 2.5% walk, 2.3% work from home; Mean travel time to work: 42.6 minutes
2016 Presidential Election: 56.4% Trump, 41.2% Clinton, 1.4% Johnson, 1.0% Stein
National and State Parks: Clay Pit Ponds State Park Preserve; Gateway National Recreation Area

School District(s)
Hawthorne-Cedar Knolls Union Free SD (KG-12)
  2014-15 Enrollment: 261 . . . . (914) 749-2903
John W Lavelle Preparatory Charter School (06-08)
  2014-15 Enrollment: 442 . . . . (347) 855-2238
New World Preparatory Charter School (06-08)
  2014-15 Enrollment: 355 . . . . (718) 705-8972
New York City Geographic District #31 (PK-12)
  2014-15 Enrollment: 60,252 . . . . (718) 420-5667
NYC Special Schools - District 75 (PK-12)
  2014-15 Enrollment: 22,867 . . . . (212) 802-1501
Staten Island Community Charter School
  2014-15 Enrollment: 299 . . . . (347) 857-6981
Four-year College(s)
College of Staten Island CUNY (Public)
  Fall 2014 Enrollment: 14,346 . . . . (718) 982-2000
  2015-16 Tuition: In-state $6,890; Out-of-state $14,000
Wagner College (Private, Not-for-profit, Lutheran Church in America)
  Fall 2014 Enrollment: 2,231 . . . . (718) 390-3100
  2015-16 Tuition: In-state $42,480; Out-of-state $42,480
Two-year College(s)
St Paul's School of Nursing-Staten Island (Private, For-profit)
  Fall 2014 Enrollment: 694 . . . . (718) 517-7700
  2015-16 Tuition: In-state $21,769; Out-of-state $21,769
Vocational/Technical School(s)
Academy of Cosmetology and Esthetics NYC (Private, For-profit)
  Fall 2014 Enrollment: 107 . . . . (718) 979-9001
  2015-16 Tuition: $14,500
Career School of NY (Private, Not-for-profit)
  Fall 2014 Enrollment: 67 . . . . (718) 420-6440
  2015-16 Tuition: $12,345
Hospitals: Richmond University Medical Center; South Beach Psychiatric Center (322 beds); St. Vincent's Staten Island/Bayley Seton Campuses (198 beds); Staten Island University Hospital (813 beds)
Newspapers: Staten Island Advance (daily circulation 58000)
Additional Information Contacts
Richmond County Government . . . . (718) 816-8200
  http://statenislandusa.com
Staten Island Chamber of Commerce . . . . (718) 727-1900
  http://www.sichamber.com

New York County

See New York City

Niagara County

Located in western New York; bounded on the west by the Niagara River and Lake Erie, and on the north by Lake Ontario; drained by Tonawanda Creek; includes Niagara Falls. Covers a land area of 522.359 square miles, a water area of 617.310 square miles, and is located in the Eastern Time Zone at 43.46° N. Lat., 78.79° W. Long. The county was founded in 1808. County seat is Lockport.

Niagara County is part of the Buffalo-Cheektowaga-Niagara Falls, NY Metropolitan Statistical Area. The entire metro area includes: Erie County, NY; Niagara County, NY

Population: 214,150; Growth (since 2000): -2.6%; Density: 410.0 persons per square mile; Race: 88.0% White, 7.4% Black/African American, 1.2% Asian, 1.0% American Indian/Alaska Native, 0.0% Native Hawaiian/Other Pacific Islander, 2.0% two or more races, 2.5% Hispanic of any race; Average household size: 2.39; Median age: 42.6; Age under 18: 20.6%;

Age 65 and over: 16.9%; Males per 100 females: 94.2; Marriage status: 32.3% never married, 49.0% now married, 1.9% separated, 7.4% widowed, 11.3% divorced; Foreign born: 4.0%; Speak English only: 95.9%; With disability: 13.4%; Veterans: 9.0%; Ancestry: 25.3% German, 17.6% Italian, 16.0% Irish, 11.6% Polish, 10.7% American

Religion: Six largest groups: 24.0% Catholicism, 5.9% Lutheran, 4.1% Methodist/Pietist, 2.0% Presbyterian-Reformed, 1.9% Non-denominational Protestant, 1.3% Baptist

Economy: Unemployment rate: 5.4%; Leading industries: 16.4 % retail trade; 11.6 % accommodation and food services; 11.2 % other services (except public administration); Farms: 760 totaling 142,818 acres; Company size: 2 employ 1,000 or more persons, 4 employ 500 to 999 persons, 74 employ 100 to 499 persons, 4,432 employ less than 100 persons; Business ownership: 4,337 women-owned, 304 Black-owned, 171 Hispanic-owned, 187 Asian-owned, 123 American Indian/Alaska Native-owned

Employment: 11.9% management, business, and financial, 4.1% computer, engineering, and science, 9.6% education, legal, community service, arts, and media, 6.1% healthcare practitioners, 18.8% service, 26.4% sales and office, 8.8% natural resources, construction, and maintenance, 14.3% production, transportation, and material moving

Income: Per capita: $26,891; Median household: $49,449; Average household: $63,419; Households with income of $100,000 or more: 18.2%; Poverty rate: 13.7%

Educational Attainment: High school diploma or higher: 90.5%; Bachelor's degree or higher: 23.2%; Graduate/professional degree or higher: 9.7%

Housing: Homeownership rate: 70.9%; Median home value: $108,000; Median year structure built: 1954; Homeowner vacancy rate: 4.7%; Median selected monthly owner costs: $1,198 with a mortgage, $522 without a mortgage; Median gross rent: $654 per month; Rental vacancy rate: 13.8%

Vital Statistics: Birth rate: 103.0 per 10,000 population; Death rate: 108.6 per 10,000 population; Age-adjusted cancer mortality rate: 170.3 deaths per 100,000 population

Health Insurance: 93.7% have insurance; 72.9% have private insurance; 37.1% have public insurance; 6.3% do not have insurance; 2.6% of children under 18 do not have insurance

Health Care: Physicians: 11.8 per 10,000 population; Dentists: 5.1 per 10,000 population; Hospital beds: 37.6 per 10,000 population; Hospital admissions: 961.0 per 10,000 population

Air Quality Index (AQI): Percent of Days: 96.1% good, 3.9% moderate, 0.0% unhealthy for sensitive individuals, 0.0% unhealthy, 0.0% very unhealthy; Annual median: 33; Annual maximum: 87

Transportation: Commute: 93.0% car, 1.2% public transportation, 2.2% walk, 2.4% work from home; Mean travel time to work: 21.2 minutes

2016 Presidential Election: 56.7% Trump, 38.8% Clinton, 3.1% Johnson, 1.4% Stein

National and State Parks: Brydges State Park; Devils Hole State Park; Fort Niagara State Park; Fourmile Creek State Park; Joseph Davis State Park; Lower Niagara River State Park; New York State Reservation; Whirlpool State Park

Additional Information Contacts

Niagara Government . . . . (716) 439-7025
   http://www.niagaracounty.com

Niagara County Communities

APPLETON (unincorporated postal area)
ZCTA: 14008

Covers a land area of 24.452 square miles and a water area of 0.858 square miles. Located at 43.31° N. Lat; 78.62° W. Long. Elevation is 338 feet.

Population: 1,459; Growth (since 2000): -2.0%; Density: 59.7 persons per square mile; Race: 96.0% White, 0.3% Black/African American, 0.0% Asian, 3.5% American Indian/Alaska Native, 0.0% Native Hawaiian/Other Pacific Islander, 0.2% Two or more races, 0.8% Hispanic of any race; Average household size: 2.79; Median age: 43.0; Age under 18: 24.1%; Age 65 and over: 12.6%; Males per 100 females: 102.1; Marriage status: 27.0% never married, 46.3% now married, 2.0% separated, 7.2% widowed, 19.5% divorced; Foreign born: 1.0%; Speak English only: 99.0%; With disability: 8.2%; Veterans: 7.7%; Ancestry: 29.5% American, 21.4% German, 15.1% English, 14.7% Italian, 8.4% Irish

Employment: 8.5% management, business, and financial, 2.0% computer, engineering, and science, 2.5% education, legal, community

service, arts, and media, 9.3% healthcare practitioners, 16.1% service, 31.8% sales and office, 6.0% natural resources, construction, and maintenance, 23.9% production, transportation, and material moving

Income: Per capita: $23,839; Median household: $55,625; Average household: $65,206; Households with income of $100,000 or more: 17.6%; Poverty rate: 12.5%

Educational Attainment: High school diploma or higher: 91.0%; Bachelor's degree or higher: 13.1%; Graduate/professional degree or higher: 3.2%

Housing: Homeownership rate: 81.5%; Median home value: $105,400; Median year structure built: Before 1940; Homeowner vacancy rate: 7.9%; Median selected monthly owner costs: $1,186 with a mortgage, $450 without a mortgage; Median gross rent: n/a per month; Rental vacancy rate: 23.8%

Health Insurance: 96.3% have insurance; 73.5% have private insurance; 35.0% have public insurance; 3.7% do not have insurance; 0.0% of children under 18 do not have insurance

Transportation: Commute: 87.9% car, 0.3% public transportation, 2.9% walk, 3.3% work from home; Mean travel time to work: 28.9 minutes

BARKER (village).
Covers a land area of 0.420 square miles and a water area of 0 square miles. Located at 43.33° N. Lat; 78.55° W. Long. Elevation is 328 feet.

Population: 738; Growth (since 2000): 27.9%; Density: 1,757.8 persons per square mile; Race: 100.0% White, 0.0% Black/African American, 0.0% Asian, 0.0% American Indian/Alaska Native, 0.0% Native Hawaiian/Other Pacific Islander, 0.0% Two or more races, 22.2% Hispanic of any race; Average household size: 3.34; Median age: 30.2; Age 65 and over: 7.7%; Males per 100 females: 88.3; Marriage status: 28.7% never married, 57.2% now married, 2.4% separated, 3.9% widowed, 10.2% divorced; Foreign born: 3.7%; Speak English only: 86.8%; With disability: 7.0%; Veterans: 13.6%; Ancestry: 23.4% German, 16.4% American, 11.9% English, 10.8% Irish, 9.9% Polish

Employment: 15.6% management, business, and financial, 2.0% computer, engineering, and science, 8.3% education, legal, community service, arts, and media, 6.6% healthcare practitioners, 15.0% service, 16.3% sales and office, 13.6% natural resources, construction, and maintenance, 22.6% production, transportation, and material moving

Income: Per capita: $15,206; Median household: $41,458; Average household: $50,438; Households with income of $100,000 or more: 9.0%; Poverty rate: 13.1%

Educational Attainment: High school diploma or higher: 91.4%; Bachelor's degree or higher: 8.9%; Graduate/professional degree or higher: 3.6%

School District(s)

Barker Central SD (PK-12)
   2014-15 Enrollment: 838 . . . . (716) 795-3832

Housing: Homeownership rate: 65.2%; Median home value: $90,000; Median year structure built: Before 1940; Homeowner vacancy rate: 0.0%; Median selected monthly owner costs: $996 with a mortgage, $524 without a mortgage; Median gross rent: $612 per month; Rental vacancy rate: 19.8%

Health Insurance: 81.7% have insurance; 49.1% have private insurance; 42.5% have public insurance; 18.3% do not have insurance; 12.4% of children under 18 do not have insurance

Transportation: Commute: 86.3% car, 0.0% public transportation, 8.0% walk, 5.7% work from home; Mean travel time to work: 23.8 minutes

BURT (unincorporated postal area)
ZCTA: 14028

Covers a land area of 13.537 square miles and a water area of 0.512 square miles. Located at 43.32° N. Lat; 78.72° W. Long. Elevation is 315 feet.

Population: 1,423; Growth (since 2000): -18.1%; Density: 105.1 persons per square mile; Race: 93.5% White, 0.3% Black/African American, 0.1% Asian, 2.8% American Indian/Alaska Native, 0.0% Native Hawaiian/Other Pacific Islander, 1.3% Two or more races, 3.7% Hispanic of any race; Average household size: 2.50; Median age: 43.0; Age under 18: 19.7%; Age 65 and over: 10.8%; Males per 100 females: 104.7; Marriage status: 33.1% never married, 58.9% now married, 0.6% separated, 4.6% widowed, 3.4% divorced; Foreign born: 1.8%; Speak English only: 98.0%; With disability: 11.8%; Veterans: 7.9%; Ancestry: 38.4% German, 21.8% Irish, 17.8% Italian, 15.2% Polish, 12.3% English

Employment: 20.5% management, business, and financial, 3.5% computer, engineering, and science, 5.9% education, legal, community

service, arts, and media, 7.7% healthcare practitioners, 21.0% service, 21.0% sales and office, 10.5% natural resources, construction, and maintenance, 9.8% production, transportation, and material moving
Income: Per capita: $28,537; Median household: $60,625; Average household: $70,780; Households with income of $100,000 or more: 28.7%; Poverty rate: 14.3%
Educational Attainment: High school diploma or higher: 91.8%; Bachelor's degree or higher: 25.6%; Graduate/professional degree or higher: 7.9%

School District(s)
Newfane Central SD (PK-12)
   2014-15 Enrollment: 1,652 . . . . (716) 778-6854
Housing: Homeownership rate: 87.9%; Median home value: $101,600; Median year structure built: 1951; Homeowner vacancy rate: 12.2%; Median selected monthly owner costs: $1,108 with a mortgage, $425 without a mortgage; Median gross rent: $833 per month; Rental vacancy rate: 36.4%
Health Insurance: 92.0% have insurance; 79.4% have private insurance; 22.9% have public insurance; 8.0% do not have insurance; 0.0% of children under 18 do not have insurance
Transportation: Commute: 92.6% car, 0.0% public transportation, 0.1% walk, 6.0% work from home; Mean travel time to work: 27.1 minutes

---

CAMBRIA (town).
Covers a land area of 39.710 square miles and a water area of 0 square miles. Located at 43.18° N. Lat; 78.82° W. Long. Elevation is 476 feet.
Population: 5,832; Growth (since 2000): 8.1%; Density: 146.9 persons per square mile; Race: 94.7% White, 2.5% Black/African American, 0.0% Asian, 0.5% American Indian/Alaska Native, 0.0% Native Hawaiian/Other Pacific Islander, 2.3% Two or more races, 0.2% Hispanic of any race; Average household size: 2.56; Median age: 42.6; Age under 18: 18.9%; Age 65 and over: 15.8%; Males per 100 females: 101.3; Marriage status: 32.3% never married, 54.5% now married, 1.8% separated, 7.6% widowed, 5.5% divorced; Foreign born: 2.2%; Speak English only: 99.3%; With disability: 7.4%; Veterans: 8.6%; Ancestry: 31.4% German, 22.6% Irish, 17.1% American, 13.0% Italian, 12.9% Polish
Employment: 10.4% management, business, and financial, 3.9% computer, engineering, and science, 5.7% education, legal, community service, arts, and media, 12.3% healthcare practitioners, 17.2% service, 22.6% sales and office, 14.5% natural resources, construction, and maintenance, 13.4% production, transportation, and material moving
Income: Per capita: $31,937; Median household: $66,080; Average household: $80,138; Households with income of $100,000 or more: 29.5%; Poverty rate: 3.5%
Educational Attainment: High school diploma or higher: 96.5%; Bachelor's degree or higher: 21.9%; Graduate/professional degree or higher: 5.5%
Housing: Homeownership rate: 92.1%; Median home value: $158,900; Median year structure built: 1970; Homeowner vacancy rate: 3.5%; Median selected monthly owner costs: $1,479 with a mortgage, $596 without a mortgage; Median gross rent: $625 per month; Rental vacancy rate: 0.0%
Health Insurance: 96.4% have insurance; 87.1% have private insurance; 23.9% have public insurance; 3.6% do not have insurance; 4.3% of children under 18 do not have insurance
Transportation: Commute: 94.7% car, 0.1% public transportation, 1.1% walk, 3.7% work from home; Mean travel time to work: 23.2 minutes
Additional Information Contacts
Town of Cambria . . . . (716) 433-7664
  http://www.townofcambria.com

GASPORT (CDP).
Covers a land area of 2.869 square miles and a water area of 0.051 square miles. Located at 43.20° N. Lat; 78.58° W. Long. Elevation is 515 feet.
Population: 1,103; Growth (since 2000): -11.6%; Density: 384.4 persons per square mile; Race: 98.4% White, 0.9% Black/African American, 0.0% Asian, 0.7% American Indian/Alaska Native, 0.0% Native Hawaiian/Other Pacific Islander, 0.0% Two or more races, 0.0% Hispanic of any race; Average household size: 2.15; Median age: 37.9; Age under 18: 21.3%; Age 65 and over: 15.1%; Males per 100 females: 89.7; Marriage status: 27.7% never married, 43.4% now married, 5.1% separated, 5.5% widowed, 23.4% divorced; Foreign born: 1.3%; Speak English only: 98.4%; With disability: 11.7%; Veterans: 8.6%; Ancestry: 27.9% German, 23.5% Irish, 19.9% American, 14.9% English, 9.0% Italian
Employment: 12.0% management, business, and financial, 0.0% computer, engineering, and science, 0.0% education, legal, community

service, arts, and media, 6.5% healthcare practitioners, 7.1% service, 11.2% sales and office, 5.2% natural resources, construction, and maintenance, 57.9% production, transportation, and material moving
Income: Per capita: $21,068; Median household: $46,347; Average household: $45,228; Households with income of $100,000 or more: 1.1%; Poverty rate: 11.7%
Educational Attainment: High school diploma or higher: 91.6%; Bachelor's degree or higher: 9.9%; Graduate/professional degree or higher: 2.1%

School District(s)
Royalton-Hartland Central SD (PK-12)
   2014-15 Enrollment: 1,437 . . . . (716) 735-2000
Housing: Homeownership rate: 68.4%; Median home value: $82,900; Median year structure built: Before 1940; Homeowner vacancy rate: 0.0%; Median selected monthly owner costs: $1,082 with a mortgage, $706 without a mortgage; Median gross rent: $625 per month; Rental vacancy rate: 25.7%
Health Insurance: 98.3% have insurance; 89.4% have private insurance; 19.4% have public insurance; 1.7% do not have insurance; 0.0% of children under 18 do not have insurance
Transportation: Commute: 100.0% car, 0.0% public transportation, 0.0% walk, 0.0% work from home; Mean travel time to work: 24.1 minutes

---

HARTLAND (town).
Covers a land area of 52.378 square miles and a water area of 0.037 square miles. Located at 43.26° N. Lat; 78.55° W. Long. Elevation is 404 feet.
Population: 4,061; Growth (since 2000): -2.5%; Density: 77.5 persons per square mile; Race: 96.5% White, 0.0% Black/African American, 0.3% Asian, 1.6% American Indian/Alaska Native, 0.0% Native Hawaiian/Other Pacific Islander, 1.3% Two or more races, 0.9% Hispanic of any race; Average household size: 2.49; Median age: 48.3; Age under 18: 20.5%; Age 65 and over: 15.9%; Males per 100 females: 103.7; Marriage status: 21.6% never married, 66.2% now married, 1.2% separated, 6.9% widowed, 5.3% divorced; Foreign born: 2.1%; Speak English only: 98.3%; With disability: 11.7%; Veterans: 11.7%; Ancestry: 36.5% German, 17.7% Irish, 17.5% English, 15.2% Italian, 11.7% Polish
Employment: 10.8% management, business, and financial, 5.0% computer, engineering, and science, 7.7% education, legal, community service, arts, and media, 5.5% healthcare practitioners, 14.1% service, 25.2% sales and office, 15.0% natural resources, construction, and maintenance, 16.8% production, transportation, and material moving
Income: Per capita: $25,212; Median household: $56,546; Average household: $61,487; Households with income of $100,000 or more: 15.6%; Poverty rate: 9.2%
Educational Attainment: High school diploma or higher: 90.9%; Bachelor's degree or higher: 13.3%; Graduate/professional degree or higher: 7.1%
Housing: Homeownership rate: 82.7%; Median home value: $99,500; Median year structure built: 1955; Homeowner vacancy rate: 3.5%; Median selected monthly owner costs: $1,335 with a mortgage, $459 without a mortgage; Median gross rent: $602 per month; Rental vacancy rate: 14.0%
Health Insurance: 94.8% have insurance; 75.7% have private insurance; 40.7% have public insurance; 5.2% do not have insurance; 2.6% of children under 18 do not have insurance
Transportation: Commute: 94.0% car, 0.0% public transportation, 0.2% walk, 5.1% work from home; Mean travel time to work: 30.2 minutes
Additional Information Contacts
Town of Hartland . . . . (716) 735-7179
  http://townofhartland.org/content

LEWISTON (town).
Covers a land area of 37.121 square miles and a water area of 4.010 square miles. Located at 43.18° N. Lat; 78.95° W. Long. Elevation is 381 feet.
History: As with Lewis county, named after Governor Morgan Lewis. Settled c.1796, incorporated 1822.
Population: 16,072; Growth (since 2000): -1.1%; Density: 433.0 persons per square mile; Race: 95.2% White, 0.9% Black/African American, 1.8% Asian, 0.3% American Indian/Alaska Native, 0.0% Native Hawaiian/Other Pacific Islander, 0.9% Two or more races, 2.6% Hispanic of any race; Average household size: 2.33; Median age: 44.6; Age under 18: 17.0%; Age 65 and over: 21.8%; Males per 100 females: 88.7; Marriage status: 31.6% never married, 52.3% now married, 1.3% separated, 8.2% widowed, 7.9% divorced; Foreign born: 6.5%; Speak English only: 93.4%; With disability: 9.5%; Veterans: 8.9%; Ancestry: 26.2% Italian, 20.9% German, 17.1% Irish, 11.6% Polish, 11.2% English

Employment: 16.0% management, business, and financial, 3.7% computer, engineering, and science, 11.4% education, legal, community service, arts, and media, 8.2% healthcare practitioners, 18.3% service, 27.6% sales and office, 6.2% natural resources, construction, and maintenance, 8.7% production, transportation, and material moving
Income: Per capita: $33,225; Median household: $68,200; Average household: $83,839; Households with income of $100,000 or more: 28.8%; Poverty rate: 4.9%
Educational Attainment: High school diploma or higher: 95.1%; Bachelor's degree or higher: 40.4%; Graduate/professional degree or higher: 19.5%

School District(s)
Niagara-Wheatfield Central SD (PK-12)
   2014-15 Enrollment: 3,761 . . . . (716) 215-3003
Housing: Homeownership rate: 80.9%; Median home value: $161,400; Median year structure built: 1960; Homeowner vacancy rate: 3.7%; Median selected monthly owner costs: $1,378 with a mortgage, $576 without a mortgage; Median gross rent: $804 per month; Rental vacancy rate: 3.3%
Health Insurance: 96.2% have insurance; 88.2% have private insurance; 25.6% have public insurance; 3.8% do not have insurance; 1.9% of children under 18 do not have insurance
Hospitals: Mount Saint Mary's Hospital & Health Center (179 beds)
Safety: Violent crime rate: 3.1 per 10,000 population; Property crime rate: 80.3 per 10,000 population
Transportation: Commute: 93.0% car, 0.5% public transportation, 3.1% walk, 2.7% work from home; Mean travel time to work: 19.7 minutes
Additional Information Contacts
Town of Lewiston . . . . (716) 754-8213
  http://www.townoflewiston.us

LEWISTON (village). Covers a land area of 1.097 square miles and a water area of 0.139 square miles. Located at 43.17° N. Lat; 79.04° W. Long. Elevation is 381 feet.
Population: 2,598; Growth (since 2000): -6.6%; Density: 2,369.1 persons per square mile; Race: 94.1% White, 0.0% Black/African American, 4.8% Asian, 1.1% American Indian/Alaska Native, 0.0% Native Hawaiian/Other Pacific Islander, 0.0% Two or more races, 0.9% Hispanic of any race; Average household size: 2.21; Median age: 44.9; Age under 18: 21.3%; Age 65 and over: 21.2%; Males per 100 females: 80.5; Marriage status: 27.7% never married, 46.6% now married, 1.6% separated, 11.8% widowed, 13.9% divorced; Foreign born: 6.0%; Speak English only: 96.3%; With disability: 7.7%; Veterans: 7.0%; Ancestry: 21.9% Italian, 19.3% Irish, 19.2% German, 18.7% American, 11.1% Polish
Employment: 18.5% management, business, and financial, 4.8% computer, engineering, and science, 7.3% education, legal, community service, arts, and media, 9.8% healthcare practitioners, 14.0% service, 30.3% sales and office, 4.1% natural resources, construction, and maintenance, 11.2% production, transportation, and material moving
Income: Per capita: $33,205; Median household: $53,704; Average household: $73,365; Households with income of $100,000 or more: 21.1%; Poverty rate: 6.8%
Educational Attainment: High school diploma or higher: 96.8%; Bachelor's degree or higher: 47.3%; Graduate/professional degree or higher: 18.3%

School District(s)
Niagara-Wheatfield Central SD (PK-12)
   2014-15 Enrollment: 3,761 . . . . (716) 215-3003
Housing: Homeownership rate: 71.2%; Median home value: $140,000; Median year structure built: 1956; Homeowner vacancy rate: 4.6%; Median selected monthly owner costs: $1,330 with a mortgage, $526 without a mortgage; Median gross rent: $858 per month; Rental vacancy rate: 6.9%
Health Insurance: 98.5% have insurance; 86.6% have private insurance; 27.2% have public insurance; 1.5% do not have insurance; 0.0% of children under 18 do not have insurance
Hospitals: Mount Saint Mary's Hospital & Health Center (179 beds)
Transportation: Commute: 91.7% car, 0.0% public transportation, 2.5% walk, 4.9% work from home; Mean travel time to work: 21.3 minutes

---

LOCKPORT (city). County seat. Covers a land area of 8.400 square miles and a water area of 0.046 square miles. Located at 43.17° N. Lat; 78.70° W. Long. Elevation is 614 feet.
Population: 20,857; Growth (since 2000): -6.4%; Density: 2,483.0 persons per square mile; Race: 88.0% White, 7.2% Black/African American, 0.9% Asian, 0.2% American Indian/Alaska Native, 0.0% Native Hawaiian/Other Pacific Islander, 2.9% Two or more races, 4.6% Hispanic of any race;

Average household size: 2.31; Median age: 40.4; Age under 18: 22.0%; Age 65 and over: 15.4%; Males per 100 females: 91.3; Marriage status: 35.2% never married, 43.5% now married, 2.2% separated, 7.1% widowed, 14.1% divorced; Foreign born: 3.7%; Speak English only: 96.9%; With disability: 13.8%; Veterans: 9.3%; Ancestry: 27.7% German, 15.5% Irish, 13.2% American, 13.1% Italian, 11.5% English
Employment: 10.4% management, business, and financial, 3.7% computer, engineering, and science, 10.7% education, legal, community service, arts, and media, 5.0% healthcare practitioners, 18.6% service, 23.5% sales and office, 8.3% natural resources, construction, and maintenance, 19.7% production, transportation, and material moving
Income: Per capita: $24,910; Median household: $41,298; Average household: $56,191; Households with income of $100,000 or more: 13.0%; Poverty rate: 16.2%
Educational Attainment: High school diploma or higher: 88.8%; Bachelor's degree or higher: 21.0%; Graduate/professional degree or higher: 9.4%

School District(s)
Lockport City SD (PK-12)
   2014-15 Enrollment: 4,830 . . . . (716) 478-4835
Starpoint Central SD (KG-12)
   2014-15 Enrollment: 2,670 . . . . (716) 210-2352
Vocational/Technical School(s)
MarJon School of Beauty ltd-Lockport (Private, For-profit)
   Fall 2014 Enrollment: 25 . . . . (716) 433-1028
   2015-16 Tuition: $10,000
Housing: Homeownership rate: 57.4%; Median home value: $83,900; Median year structure built: Before 1940; Homeowner vacancy rate: 8.3%; Median selected monthly owner costs: $1,077 with a mortgage, $493 without a mortgage; Median gross rent: $663 per month; Rental vacancy rate: 16.2%
Health Insurance: 91.8% have insurance; 66.3% have private insurance; 40.8% have public insurance; 8.2% do not have insurance; 5.3% of children under 18 do not have insurance
Hospitals: Eastern Niagara Hospital (134 beds)
Safety: Violent crime rate: 34.9 per 10,000 population; Property crime rate: 254.8 per 10,000 population
Newspapers: Journal-Register (weekly circulation 1,900); Lockport Union-Sun & Journal (daily circulation 2,700); Union-Sun & Journal (daily circulation 11,500)
Transportation: Commute: 93.2% car, 0.2% public transportation, 3.0% walk, 1.9% work from home; Mean travel time to work: 20.7 minutes
Additional Information Contacts
City of Lockport . . . . (716) 439-6676
  http://www.elockport.com

LOCKPORT (town). Covers a land area of 44.843 square miles and a water area of 0.052 square miles. Located at 43.15° N. Lat; 78.69° W. Long. Elevation is 614 feet.
History: Built around a series of locks on the old Erie Canal. Settled 1821, incorporated 1865.
Population: 20,304; Growth (since 2000): 3.3%; Density: 452.8 persons per square mile; Race: 90.4% White, 4.9% Black/African American, 1.7% Asian, 0.1% American Indian/Alaska Native, 0.0% Native Hawaiian/Other Pacific Islander, 1.6% Two or more races, 3.8% Hispanic of any race; Average household size: 2.39; Median age: 42.1; Age under 18: 20.8%; Age 65 and over: 17.3%; Males per 100 females: 98.9; Marriage status: 28.4% never married, 53.7% now married, 1.3% separated, 5.4% widowed, 12.5% divorced; Foreign born: 3.5%; Speak English only: 95.5%; With disability: 10.8%; Veterans: 8.7%; Ancestry: 28.8% German, 16.7% Irish, 15.5% Italian, 14.7% American, 11.2% English
Employment: 11.0% management, business, and financial, 5.2% computer, engineering, and science, 10.4% education, legal, community service, arts, and media, 7.0% healthcare practitioners, 15.0% service, 28.0% sales and office, 10.0% natural resources, construction, and maintenance, 13.4% production, transportation, and material moving
Income: Per capita: $28,999; Median household: $62,030; Average household: $69,349; Households with income of $100,000 or more: 21.7%; Poverty rate: 8.9%
Educational Attainment: High school diploma or higher: 92.9%; Bachelor's degree or higher: 27.3%; Graduate/professional degree or higher: 9.7%

School District(s)
Lockport City SD (PK-12)
   2014-15 Enrollment: 4,830 . . . . (716) 478-4835

Starpoint Central SD (KG-12)
  2014-15 Enrollment: 2,670 . . . . (716) 210-2352
Vocational/Technical School(s)
MarJon School of Beauty ltd-Lockport (Private, For-profit)
  Fall 2014 Enrollment: 25 . . . . (716) 433-1028
  2015-16 Tuition: $10,000
Housing: Homeownership rate: 78.5%; Median home value: $121,400;
Median year structure built: 1981; Homeowner vacancy rate: 2.0%; Median
selected monthly owner costs: $1,406 with a mortgage, $603 without a
mortgage; Median gross rent: $552 per month; Rental vacancy rate: 15.9%
Health Insurance: 94.9% have insurance; 78.8% have private insurance;
32.9% have public insurance; 5.1% do not have insurance; 1.9% of
children under 18 do not have insurance
Hospitals: Eastern Niagara Hospital (134 beds)
Newspapers: Journal-Register (weekly circulation 1,900); Lockport
Union-Sun & Journal (daily circulation 2,700); Union-Sun & Journal (daily
circulation 11,500)
Transportation: Commute: 94.6% car, 0.6% public transportation, 0.7%
walk, 2.8% work from home; Mean travel time to work: 23.3 minutes
Additional Information Contacts
Town of Lockport . . . . (716) 439-9524
  http://www.elockport.com

MIDDLEPORT (village). Covers a land area of 0.872 square miles
and a water area of 0 square miles. Located at 43.21° N. Lat; 78.48° W.
Long. Elevation is 515 feet.
History: Grew after completion of Erie Canal (1825). Settled 1812,
incorporated 1859.
Population: 1,788; Growth (since 2000): -6.7%; Density: 2,050.7 persons
per square mile; Race: 98.2% White, 0.0% Black/African American, 0.4%
Asian, 0.0% American Indian/Alaska Native, 0.0% Native Hawaiian/Other
Pacific Islander, 1.0% Two or more races, 0.5% Hispanic of any race;
Average household size: 2.50; Median age: 38.4; Age under 18: 25.6%;
Age 65 and over: 15.2%; Males per 100 females: 91.1; Marriage status:
29.4% never married, 49.7% now married, 3.7% separated, 9.1%
widowed, 11.9% divorced; Foreign born: 1.7%; Speak English only: 98.6%;
With disability: 15.3%; Veterans: 10.2%; Ancestry: 30.3% American, 28.3%
German, 15.7% English, 13.5% Irish, 8.9% Polish
Employment: 7.4% management, business, and financial, 2.8% computer,
engineering, and science, 9.3% education, legal, community service, arts,
and media, 4.1% healthcare practitioners, 19.4% service, 25.1% sales and
office, 7.4% natural resources, construction, and maintenance, 24.7%
production, transportation, and material moving
Income: Per capita: $24,055; Median household: $47,174; Average
household: $59,437; Households with income of $100,000 or more: 15.8%;
Poverty rate: 12.1%
Educational Attainment: High school diploma or higher: 89.8%;
Bachelor's degree or higher: 15.6%; Graduate/professional degree or
higher: 5.9%
School District(s)
Royalton-Hartland Central SD (PK-12)
  2014-15 Enrollment: 1,437 . . . . (716) 735-2000
Housing: Homeownership rate: 65.6%; Median home value: $87,100;
Median year structure built: Before 1940; Homeowner vacancy rate: 6.0%;
Median selected monthly owner costs: $1,090 with a mortgage, $575
without a mortgage; Median gross rent: $588 per month; Rental vacancy
rate: 8.7%
Health Insurance: 93.9% have insurance; 74.0% have private insurance;
34.1% have public insurance; 6.1% do not have insurance; 1.3% of
children under 18 do not have insurance
Safety: Violent crime rate: 0.0 per 10,000 population; Property crime rate:
123.0 per 10,000 population
Transportation: Commute: 96.4% car, 0.0% public transportation, 2.4%
walk, 0.8% work from home; Mean travel time to work: 22.7 minutes

---

NEWFANE (CDP). Covers a land area of 5.303 square miles and a
water area of 0 square miles. Located at 43.29° N. Lat; 78.69° W. Long.
Elevation is 344 feet.
Population: 3,769; Growth (since 2000): 20.5%; Density: 710.7 persons
per square mile; Race: 98.9% White, 0.4% Black/African American, 0.0%
Asian, 0.2% American Indian/Alaska Native, 0.0% Native Hawaiian/Other
Pacific Islander, 0.5% Two or more races, 0.0% Hispanic of any race;
Average household size: 2.39; Median age: 41.7; Age under 18: 22.4%;
Age 65 and over: 22.6%; Males per 100 females: 89.6; Marriage status:
20.4% never married, 53.6% now married, 0.6% separated, 12.5%

widowed, 13.5% divorced; Foreign born: 2.4%; Speak English only: 99.7%;
With disability: 7.0%; Veterans: 8.0%; Ancestry: 31.9% German, 25.2%
American, 12.9% English, 12.1% Irish, 8.3% Italian
Employment: 14.2% management, business, and financial, 6.5%
computer, engineering, and science, 8.0% education, legal, community
service, arts, and media, 8.0% healthcare practitioners, 18.5% service,
18.6% sales and office, 6.4% natural resources, construction, and
maintenance, 19.9% production, transportation, and material moving
Income: Per capita: $23,270; Median household: $47,127; Average
household: $55,712; Households with income of $100,000 or more: 15.5%;
Poverty rate: 13.1%
Educational Attainment: High school diploma or higher: 90.6%;
Bachelor's degree or higher: 17.4%; Graduate/professional degree or
higher: 4.8%
School District(s)
Newfane Central SD (PK-12)
  2014-15 Enrollment: 1,652 . . . . (716) 778-6854
Housing: Homeownership rate: 78.4%; Median home value: $86,400;
Median year structure built: 1957; Homeowner vacancy rate: 2.8%; Median
selected monthly owner costs: $1,057 with a mortgage, $456 without a
mortgage; Median gross rent: $573 per month; Rental vacancy rate: 9.8%
Health Insurance: 88.0% have insurance; 67.0% have private insurance;
33.6% have public insurance; 12.0% do not have insurance; 6.5% of
children under 18 do not have insurance
Transportation: Commute: 98.7% car, 0.0% public transportation, 0.6%
walk, 0.7% work from home; Mean travel time to work: 20.7 minutes

---

NEWFANE (town). Covers a land area of 51.823 square miles and a
water area of 1.657 square miles. Located at 43.29° N. Lat; 78.69° W.
Long. Elevation is 344 feet.
History: The Town of Newfane, in Niagara County, New York, was
established in 1824 by James VanHorn and others. It is comprised of parts
of the Towns of Hartland, Somerset, and Wilson.
Population: 9,511; Growth (since 2000): -1.5%; Density: 183.5 persons
per square mile; Race: 97.8% White, 0.2% Black/African American, 0.0%
Asian, 0.5% American Indian/Alaska Native, 0.0% Native Hawaiian/Other
Pacific Islander, 1.1% Two or more races, 0.6% Hispanic of any race;
Average household size: 2.50; Median age: 43.2; Age under 18: 19.8%;
Age 65 and over: 18.4%; Males per 100 females: 96.4; Marriage status:
25.5% never married, 53.7% now married, 1.2% separated, 8.4%
widowed, 12.3% divorced; Foreign born: 1.5%; Speak English only: 99.0%;
With disability: 9.5%; Veterans: 6.8%; Ancestry: 30.6% German, 22.9%
American, 16.3% Irish, 14.0% English, 12.3% Italian
Employment: 11.4% management, business, and financial, 3.2%
computer, engineering, and science, 6.1% education, legal, community
service, arts, and media, 9.0% healthcare practitioners, 19.4% service,
21.1% sales and office, 11.3% natural resources, construction, and
maintenance, 18.6% production, transportation, and material moving
Income: Per capita: $25,143; Median household: $52,428; Average
household: $61,644; Households with income of $100,000 or more: 17.3%;
Poverty rate: 10.8%
Educational Attainment: High school diploma or higher: 90.3%;
Bachelor's degree or higher: 17.0%; Graduate/professional degree or
higher: 4.9%
School District(s)
Newfane Central SD (PK-12)
  2014-15 Enrollment: 1,652 . . . . (716) 778-6854
Housing: Homeownership rate: 82.3%; Median home value: $108,700;
Median year structure built: 1955; Homeowner vacancy rate: 3.6%; Median
selected monthly owner costs: $1,132 with a mortgage, $481 without a
mortgage; Median gross rent: $628 per month; Rental vacancy rate: 16.5%
Health Insurance: 91.1% have insurance; 73.8% have private insurance;
30.0% have public insurance; 8.9% do not have insurance; 3.6% of
children under 18 do not have insurance
Transportation: Commute: 95.9% car, 0.1% public transportation, 1.2%
walk, 2.0% work from home; Mean travel time to work: 23.9 minutes
Additional Information Contacts
Town of Newfane . . . . (716) 778-8531
  http://www.townofnewfane.com

NIAGARA (town). Covers a land area of 9.484 square miles and a
water area of 0 square miles. Located at 43.12° N. Lat; 78.98° W. Long.
History: Niagara was founded in 1812 as the "Town of Schlosser" after the
local Fort Schlosser and British Army Captain Joseph Schlosser. In 1836
western parts of the town became the Town of Wheatfield, New York.

Population: 8,227; Growth (since 2000): -8.4%; Density: 867.5 persons per square mile; Race: 93.1% White, 4.6% Black/African American, 0.0% Asian, 1.6% American Indian/Alaska Native, 0.0% Native Hawaiian/Other Pacific Islander, 0.6% Two or more races, 1.6% Hispanic of any race; Average household size: 2.33; Median age: 47.9; Age under 18: 16.1%; Age 65 and over: 17.0%; Males per 100 females: 92.1; Marriage status: 30.8% never married, 44.7% now married, 2.6% separated, 9.1% widowed, 15.4% divorced; Foreign born: 2.9%; Speak English only: 96.9%; With disability: 15.2%; Veterans: 9.6%; Ancestry: 19.8% German, 18.8% Italian, 18.1% American, 11.3% Irish, 10.8% Polish
Employment: 11.0% management, business, and financial, 3.3% computer, engineering, and science, 2.6% education, legal, community service, arts, and media, 4.3% healthcare practitioners, 27.2% service, 27.7% sales and office, 9.5% natural resources, construction, and maintenance, 14.3% production, transportation, and material moving
Income: Per capita: $25,007; Median household: $45,826; Average household: $55,609; Households with income of $100,000 or more: 12.6%; Poverty rate: 14.8%
Educational Attainment: High school diploma or higher: 90.4%; Bachelor's degree or higher: 12.2%; Graduate/professional degree or higher: 4.1%
Housing: Homeownership rate: 73.2%; Median home value: $82,600; Median year structure built: 1965; Homeowner vacancy rate: 3.6%; Median selected monthly owner costs: $995 with a mortgage, $463 without a mortgage; Median gross rent: $697 per month; Rental vacancy rate: 10.2%
Health Insurance: 90.5% have insurance; 68.9% have private insurance; 39.0% have public insurance; 9.5% do not have insurance; 2.0% of children under 18 do not have insurance
Safety: Violent crime rate: 16.0 per 10,000 population; Property crime rate: 583.2 per 10,000 population
Transportation: Commute: 93.3% car, 1.3% public transportation, 2.1% walk, 3.2% work from home; Mean travel time to work: 18.7 minutes
Additional Information Contacts
Town of Niagara . . . . (716) 297-2150
http://www.townofniagara.com

NIAGARA FALLS (city). Covers a land area of 14.086 square miles and a water area of 2.742 square miles. Located at 43.09° N. Lat; 79.01° W. Long. Elevation is 614 feet.

History: Named for the Iroquois Indian translation of "at the neck". The first published view of Niagara Falls, reproduced in a volume in 1697, was a sketch made by Father Louis Hennepin, who visited the falls in 1678. In 1745 and 1750 the French built two forts near the falls to supplement Fort Niagara at the mouth of the river and to guard the upper end of the portage. Before the approach of the British in 1759, Chabert Joncaire, French master of the portage, burned the forts and retreated across the river. Under British occupation, Fort Schlosser was erected. Augustus Porter purchased the land immediately surrounding the falls in 1805 or 1806, and became master of the portage. Visioning a manufacturing center that would rival the English city, Porter named the settlement Manchester. The settlement and fort were burned in the War of 1812. The Niagara water power turned the first generator in 1881, and the falls continued to be a source of power for the surrounding area. The falls have been a tourist attraction since at least the early 19th century.
Population: 49,435; Growth (since 2000): -11.1%; Density: 3,509.5 persons per square mile; Race: 70.0% White, 23.0% Black/African American, 1.0% Asian, 1.3% American Indian/Alaska Native, 0.0% Native Hawaiian/Other Pacific Islander, 4.0% Two or more races, 2.7% Hispanic of any race; Average household size: 2.31; Median age: 39.2; Age under 18: 22.1%; Age 65 and over: 14.9%; Males per 100 females: 91.2; Marriage status: 40.7% never married, 39.1% now married, 2.9% separated, 7.8% widowed, 12.4% divorced; Foreign born: 5.0%; Speak English only: 95.1%; With disability: 16.8%; Veterans: 8.8%; Ancestry: 20.5% Italian, 13.5% German, 12.7% Irish, 8.8% American, 7.9% Polish
Employment: 8.6% management, business, and financial, 2.8% computer, engineering, and science, 9.8% education, legal, community service, arts, and media, 4.4% healthcare practitioners, 25.2% service, 29.2% sales and office, 7.2% natural resources, construction, and maintenance, 12.8% production, transportation, and material moving
Income: Per capita: $19,964; Median household: $31,560; Average household: $44,388; Households with income of $100,000 or more: 8.2%; Poverty rate: 26.7%
Educational Attainment: High school diploma or higher: 85.6%; Bachelor's degree or higher: 17.4%; Graduate/professional degree or higher: 7.5%

School District(s)
Niagara Charter School (KG-06)
    2014-15 Enrollment: 349 . . . . (716) 297-4520
Niagara Falls City SD (PK-12)
    2014-15 Enrollment: 6,901 . . . . (716) 286-4205
Niagara-Wheatfield Central SD (PK-12)
    2014-15 Enrollment: 3,761 . . . . (716) 215-3003
Vocational/Technical School(s)
Cheryl Fells School of Business (Private, For-profit)
    Fall 2014 Enrollment: 72 . . . . (716) 297-2750
    2015-16 Tuition: $12,600
Housing: Homeownership rate: 56.6%; Median home value: $67,400; Median year structure built: 1941; Homeowner vacancy rate: 10.7%; Median selected monthly owner costs: $944 with a mortgage, $431 without a mortgage; Median gross rent: $638 per month; Rental vacancy rate: 18.2%
Health Insurance: 92.6% have insurance; 58.1% have private insurance; 51.3% have public insurance; 7.4% do not have insurance; 2.1% of children under 18 do not have insurance
Hospitals: Niagara Falls Memorial Medical Center
Safety: Violent crime rate: 113.3 per 10,000 population; Property crime rate: 515.6 per 10,000 population
Newspapers: Niagara Gazette (daily circulation 18,900)
Transportation: Commute: 88.7% car, 4.0% public transportation, 4.0% walk, 1.3% work from home; Mean travel time to work: 17.8 minutes; Amtrak: Train service available.
Airports: Niagara Falls International (primary service/non-hub)
Additional Information Contacts
City of Niagara Falls . . . . (716) 286-4393
http://www.niagarafallsusa.org

NIAGARA UNIVERSITY (unincorporated postal area)
ZCTA: 14109
    Covers a land area of 0.474 square miles and a water area of 0 square miles. Located at 43.14° N. Lat; 79.03° W. Long..
    Population: 1,153; Growth (since 2000): n/a; Density: 2,434.7 persons per square mile; Race: 86.6% White, 5.9% Black/African American, 1.3% Asian, 0.0% American Indian/Alaska Native, 0.0% Native Hawaiian/Other Pacific Islander, 0.5% Two or more races, 9.4% Hispanic of any race; Average household size: 0.00; Median age: 19.3; Age under 18: 0.8%; Age 65 and over: 0.0%; Males per 100 females: 76.2; Marriage status: 99.3% never married, 0.0% now married, 0.0% separated, 0.0% widowed, 0.7% divorced; Foreign born: 2.4%; Speak English only: 92.8%; With disability: 3.8%; Veterans: 1.0%; Ancestry: 33.5% German, 26.9% Italian, 25.2% Irish, 10.1% Polish, 7.0% English
    Employment: 0.0% management, business, and financial, 0.0% computer, engineering, and science, 20.6% education, legal, community service, arts, and media, 0.0% healthcare practitioners, 38.9% service, 35.2% sales and office, 0.0% natural resources, construction, and maintenance, 5.3% production, transportation, and material moving
    Income: Per capita: $3,786; Median household: n/a; Average household: n/a; Households with income of $100,000 or more: n/a; Poverty rate: n/a
    Educational Attainment: High school diploma or higher: 100.0%; Bachelor's degree or higher: 40.0%; Graduate/professional degree or higher: n/a

Four-year College(s)
Niagara University (Private, Not-for-profit, Roman Catholic)
    Fall 2014 Enrollment: 4,015 . . . . (716) 285-1212
    2013-14 Tuition: In-state $29,900; Out-of-state $29,900
Two-year College(s)
Niagara University (Private, Not-for-profit, Roman Catholic)
    Fall 2014 Enrollment: 4,015 . . . . (716) 285-1212
    2013-14 Tuition: In-state $29,900; Out-of-state $29,900
Vocational/Technical School(s)
Niagara University (Private, Not-for-profit, Roman Catholic)
    Fall 2014 Enrollment: 4,015 . . . . (716) 285-1212
    2015-16 Tuition: In-state $29,900; Out-of-state $29,900
Housing: Homeownership rate: n/a; Median home value: n/a; Median year structure built: n/a; Homeowner vacancy rate: 0.0%; Median selected monthly owner costs: $0 with a mortgage, $0 without a mortgage; Median gross rent: n/a per month; Rental vacancy rate: 0.0%
Health Insurance: 97.7% have insurance; 97.7% have private insurance; 0.0% have public insurance; 2.3% do not have insurance; 0.0% of children under 18 do not have insurance

Transportation: Commute: 47.0% car, 0.0% public transportation, 45.5% walk, 5.0% work from home; Mean travel time to work: 10.5 minutes

NORTH TONAWANDA (city). Covers a land area of 10.100 square miles and a water area of 0.802 square miles. Located at 43.05° N. Lat; 78.87° W. Long. Elevation is 574 feet.
History: Named for its location north of Tonawanda. Settled c.1802. Incorporated as a city 1897.
Population: 31,077; Growth (since 2000): -6.6%; Density: 3,076.8 persons per square mile; Race: 95.6% White, 1.4% Black/African American, 0.9% Asian, 0.3% American Indian/Alaska Native, 0.0% Native Hawaiian/Other Pacific Islander, 1.5% Two or more races, 1.9% Hispanic of any race; Average household size: 2.25; Median age: 42.8; Age under 18: 18.5%; Age 65 and over: 16.9%; Males per 100 females: 95.3; Marriage status: 32.6% never married, 47.8% now married, 1.8% separated, 7.8% widowed, 11.7% divorced; Foreign born: 3.4%; Speak English only: 95.5%; With disability: 14.7%; Veterans: 10.1%; Ancestry: 32.9% German, 21.5% Polish, 19.5% Irish, 17.9% Italian, 10.4% English
Employment: 11.8% management, business, and financial, 4.5% computer, engineering, and science, 9.8% education, legal, community service, arts, and media, 6.3% healthcare practitioners, 18.5% service, 27.6% sales and office, 7.1% natural resources, construction, and maintenance, 14.3% production, transportation, and material moving
Income: Per capita: $29,140; Median household: $48,235; Average household: $64,256; Households with income of $100,000 or more: 18.2%; Poverty rate: 10.1%
Educational Attainment: High school diploma or higher: 92.1%; Bachelor's degree or higher: 25.1%; Graduate/professional degree or higher: 9.0%

School District(s)
Niagara-Wheatfield Central SD (PK-12)
   2014-15 Enrollment: 3,761 . . . . (716) 215-3003
North Tonawanda City SD (KG-12)
   2014-15 Enrollment: 3,735 . . . . (716) 807-3500
Vocational/Technical School(s)
Leon Studio One School of Hair Design & Career Training Center (Private, For-profit)
   Fall 2014 Enrollment: 18 . . . . (716) 260-1652
   2015-16 Tuition: $6,900
Housing: Homeownership rate: 67.7%; Median home value: $107,500; Median year structure built: 1954; Homeowner vacancy rate: 0.0%; Median selected monthly owner costs: $1,171 with a mortgage, $541 without a mortgage; Median gross rent: $666 per month; Rental vacancy rate: 4.4%
Health Insurance: 93.7% have insurance; 76.0% have private insurance; 34.3% have public insurance; 6.3% do not have insurance; 1.7% of children under 18 do not have insurance
Safety: Violent crime rate: 13.6 per 10,000 population; Property crime rate: 150.8 per 10,000 population
Newspapers: Tonawanda News (daily circulation 8,000)
Transportation: Commute: 94.6% car, 0.6% public transportation, 1.5% walk, 1.7% work from home; Mean travel time to work: 20.3 minutes
Additional Information Contacts
City of North Tonawanda. . . . . (716) 695-8555
   http://www.northtonawanda.org

OLCOTT (CDP). Covers a land area of 4.547 square miles and a water area of 0.744 square miles. Located at 43.33° N. Lat; 78.70° W. Long. Elevation is 272 feet.
Population: 1,096; Growth (since 2000): -5.2%; Density: 241.1 persons per square mile; Race: 92.6% White, 0.3% Black/African American, 0.1% Asian, 2.7% American Indian/Alaska Native, 0.0% Native Hawaiian/Other Pacific Islander, 1.6% Two or more races, 2.6% Hispanic of any race; Average household size: 2.23; Median age: 44.3; Age under 18: 16.1%; Age 65 and over: 10.6%; Males per 100 females: 100.2; Marriage status: 37.2% never married, 41.7% now married, 1.9% separated, 7.0% widowed, 14.1% divorced; Foreign born: 2.3%; Speak English only: 99.6%; With disability: 12.6%; Veterans: 4.5%; Ancestry: 34.3% American, 21.6% German, 15.3% Irish, 9.2% English, 7.8% Italian
Employment: 12.2% management, business, and financial, 2.3% computer, engineering, and science, 5.2% education, legal, community service, arts, and media, 13.2% healthcare practitioners, 32.4% service, 7.0% sales and office, 22.3% natural resources, construction, and maintenance, 5.6% production, transportation, and material moving

Income: Per capita: $27,107; Median household: $57,775; Average household: $58,888; Households with income of $100,000 or more: 13.0%; Poverty rate: 16.9%
Educational Attainment: High school diploma or higher: 92.9%; Bachelor's degree or higher: 22.8%; Graduate/professional degree or higher: 4.9%
Housing: Homeownership rate: 74.6%; Median home value: $97,700; Median year structure built: 1952; Homeowner vacancy rate: 3.7%; Median selected monthly owner costs: $1,148 with a mortgage, $428 without a mortgage; Median gross rent: $793 per month; Rental vacancy rate: 45.6%
Health Insurance: 98.1% have insurance; 79.2% have private insurance; 26.3% have public insurance; 1.9% do not have insurance; 0.0% of children under 18 do not have insurance
Transportation: Commute: 97.3% car, 0.0% public transportation, 2.1% walk, 0.2% work from home; Mean travel time to work: 27.0 minutes

PENDLETON (town). Covers a land area of 27.086 square miles and a water area of 0.270 square miles. Located at 43.10° N. Lat; 78.76° W. Long. Elevation is 581 feet.
Population: 6,521; Growth (since 2000): 7.8%; Density: 240.7 persons per square mile; Race: 99.7% White, 0.0% Black/African American, 0.0% Asian, 0.0% American Indian/Alaska Native, 0.0% Native Hawaiian/Other Pacific Islander, 0.2% Two or more races, 0.0% Hispanic of any race; Average household size: 2.84; Median age: 43.9; Age under 18: 23.0%; Age 65 and over: 15.3%; Males per 100 females: 98.7; Marriage status: 25.5% never married, 61.5% now married, 0.5% separated, 4.5% widowed, 8.5% divorced; Foreign born: 2.4%; Speak English only: 99.1%; With disability: 10.2%; Veterans: 7.3%; Ancestry: 35.4% German, 20.7% Italian, 18.4% Irish, 15.3% Polish, 13.6% English
Employment: 12.4% management, business, and financial, 4.6% computer, engineering, and science, 7.8% education, legal, community service, arts, and media, 8.6% healthcare practitioners, 13.5% service, 29.8% sales and office, 8.3% natural resources, construction, and maintenance, 15.0% production, transportation, and material moving
Income: Per capita: $32,129; Median household: $72,243; Average household: $89,350; Households with income of $100,000 or more: 32.3%; Poverty rate: 3.3%
Educational Attainment: High school diploma or higher: 95.1%; Bachelor's degree or higher: 25.9%; Graduate/professional degree or higher: 11.7%
Housing: Homeownership rate: 94.1%; Median home value: $173,000; Median year structure built: 1972; Homeowner vacancy rate: 0.0%; Median selected monthly owner costs: $1,583 with a mortgage, $640 without a mortgage; Median gross rent: $914 per month; Rental vacancy rate: 0.0%
Health Insurance: 96.8% have insurance; 83.3% have private insurance; 25.4% have public insurance; 3.2% do not have insurance; 1.9% of children under 18 do not have insurance
Transportation: Commute: 94.3% car, 0.1% public transportation, 0.8% walk, 4.0% work from home; Mean travel time to work: 23.2 minutes
Additional Information Contacts
Town of Pendleton . . . . (716) 625-8833
   http://pendletonny.us

PORTER (town). Covers a land area of 33.055 square miles and a water area of 4.659 square miles. Located at 43.26° N. Lat; 78.97° W. Long.
Population: 6,685; Growth (since 2000): -3.4%; Density: 202.2 persons per square mile; Race: 96.9% White, 1.1% Black/African American, 0.0% Asian, 1.2% American Indian/Alaska Native, 0.0% Native Hawaiian/Other Pacific Islander, 0.8% Two or more races, 3.2% Hispanic of any race; Average household size: 2.52; Median age: 47.7; Age under 18: 20.4%; Age 65 and over: 19.0%; Males per 100 females: 100.3; Marriage status: 26.5% never married, 55.3% now married, 2.1% separated, 7.2% widowed, 11.0% divorced; Foreign born: 5.1%; Speak English only: 97.5%; With disability: 13.0%; Veterans: 10.6%; Ancestry: 26.7% German, 20.7% Irish, 15.7% Italian, 13.9% English, 10.8% Polish
Employment: 12.5% management, business, and financial, 5.2% computer, engineering, and science, 10.1% education, legal, community service, arts, and media, 7.2% healthcare practitioners, 17.2% service, 27.5% sales and office, 10.7% natural resources, construction, and maintenance, 9.6% production, transportation, and material moving
Income: Per capita: $32,998; Median household: $67,169; Average household: $81,787; Households with income of $100,000 or more: 27.4%; Poverty rate: 8.3%

Educational Attainment: High school diploma or higher: 92.6%; Bachelor's degree or higher: 28.7%; Graduate/professional degree or higher: 13.5%
Housing: Homeownership rate: 85.2%; Median home value: $140,500; Median year structure built: 1958; Homeowner vacancy rate: 3.6%; Median selected monthly owner costs: $1,304 with a mortgage, $567 without a mortgage; Median gross rent: $776 per month; Rental vacancy rate: 6.5%
Health Insurance: 95.5% have insurance; 82.0% have private insurance; 32.9% have public insurance; 4.5% do not have insurance; 1.0% of children under 18 do not have insurance
Transportation: Commute: 92.7% car, 0.0% public transportation, 2.8% walk, 3.6% work from home; Mean travel time to work: 24.4 minutes
Additional Information Contacts
Town of Porter . . . . (716) 745-3730
  http://www.townofporter.net

RANSOMVILLE (CDP). Covers a land area of 6.243 square miles and a water area of 0 square miles. Located at 43.24° N. Lat; 78.91° W. Long. Elevation is 325 feet.

Population: 1,668; Growth (since 2000): 12.1%; Density: 267.2 persons per square mile; Race: 92.9% White, 0.0% Black/African American, 0.0% Asian, 3.5% American Indian/Alaska Native, 0.0% Native Hawaiian/Other Pacific Islander, 2.4% Two or more races, 6.1% Hispanic of any race; Average household size: 2.72; Median age: 44.0; Age under 18: 22.7%; Age 65 and over: 13.8%; Males per 100 females: 103.3; Marriage status: 30.4% never married, 55.5% now married, 1.9% separated, 5.2% widowed, 8.9% divorced; Foreign born: 3.6%; Speak English only: 99.2%; With disability: 10.9%; Veterans: 9.2%; Ancestry: 33.9% German, 22.2% American, 17.4% Irish, 10.9% English, 7.1% Polish
Employment: 15.2% management, business, and financial, 3.0% computer, engineering, and science, 6.9% education, legal, community service, arts, and media, 4.2% healthcare practitioners, 16.6% service, 27.5% sales and office, 14.6% natural resources, construction, and maintenance, 11.8% production, transportation, and material moving
Income: Per capita: $29,393; Median household: $69,875; Average household: $78,762; Households with income of $100,000 or more: 29.5%; Poverty rate: 12.8%
Educational Attainment: High school diploma or higher: 91.7%; Bachelor's degree or higher: 10.9%; Graduate/professional degree or higher: 3.5%

School District(s)
Wilson Central SD (PK-12)
  2014-15 Enrollment: 1,225 . . . . (716) 751-9341
Housing: Homeownership rate: 85.2%; Median home value: $124,200; Median year structure built: 1950; Homeowner vacancy rate: 0.0%; Median selected monthly owner costs: $1,083 with a mortgage, $567 without a mortgage; Median gross rent: $966 per month; Rental vacancy rate: 0.0%
Health Insurance: 98.4% have insurance; 79.5% have private insurance; 35.2% have public insurance; 1.6% do not have insurance; 3.7% of children under 18 do not have insurance
Transportation: Commute: 92.7% car, 0.0% public transportation, 3.8% walk, 2.7% work from home; Mean travel time to work: 24.7 minutes

RAPIDS (CDP). Covers a land area of 3.644 square miles and a water area of 0 square miles. Located at 43.10° N. Lat; 78.64° W. Long. Elevation is 591 feet.

Population: 1,653; Growth (since 2000): 21.9%; Density: 453.6 persons per square mile; Race: 98.2% White, 0.0% Black/African American, 0.0% Asian, 0.0% American Indian/Alaska Native, 0.0% Native Hawaiian/Other Pacific Islander, 0.5% Two or more races, 2.1% Hispanic of any race; Average household size: 2.54; Median age: 35.1; Age under 18: 24.4%; Age 65 and over: 13.4%; Males per 100 females: 99.3; Marriage status: 24.1% never married, 58.9% now married, 1.7% separated, 2.3% widowed, 14.6% divorced; Foreign born: 0.4%; Speak English only: 100.0%; With disability: 9.1%; Veterans: 5.4%; Ancestry: 28.4% American, 23.0% German, 22.5% Italian, 13.4% Irish, 7.7% Polish
Employment: 17.6% management, business, and financial, 0.4% computer, engineering, and science, 7.4% education, legal, community service, arts, and media, 14.1% healthcare practitioners, 22.5% service, 19.1% sales and office, 3.3% natural resources, construction, and maintenance, 15.6% production, transportation, and material moving
Income: Per capita: $32,795; Median household: $65,357; Average household: $81,461; Households with income of $100,000 or more: 39.8%; Poverty rate: 2.0%

Educational Attainment: High school diploma or higher: 91.7%; Bachelor's degree or higher: 28.6%; Graduate/professional degree or higher: 7.6%
Housing: Homeownership rate: 91.0%; Median home value: $106,900; Median year structure built: 1983; Homeowner vacancy rate: 0.0%; Median selected monthly owner costs: $1,682 with a mortgage, $558 without a mortgage; Median gross rent: n/a per month; Rental vacancy rate: 0.0%
Health Insurance: 97.7% have insurance; 88.9% have private insurance; 18.2% have public insurance; 2.3% do not have insurance; 0.0% of children under 18 do not have insurance
Transportation: Commute: 95.6% car, 0.0% public transportation, 0.0% walk, 4.4% work from home; Mean travel time to work: 24.5 minutes

ROYALTON (town). Covers a land area of 69.966 square miles and a water area of 0.311 square miles. Located at 43.15° N. Lat; 78.55° W. Long.

Population: 7,599; Growth (since 2000): -1.4%; Density: 108.6 persons per square mile; Race: 97.6% White, 0.4% Black/African American, 0.5% Asian, 0.1% American Indian/Alaska Native, 0.9% Native Hawaiian/Other Pacific Islander, 0.4% Two or more races, 0.1% Hispanic of any race; Average household size: 2.73; Median age: 41.5; Age under 18: 23.6%; Age 65 and over: 15.3%; Males per 100 females: 96.6; Marriage status: 27.6% never married, 56.6% now married, 3.3% separated, 6.5% widowed, 9.3% divorced; Foreign born: 2.2%; Speak English only: 97.8%; With disability: 13.2%; Veterans: 7.3%; Ancestry: 34.5% German, 17.8% Irish, 16.2% American, 13.5% English, 9.8% Italian
Employment: 13.7% management, business, and financial, 2.6% computer, engineering, and science, 9.8% education, legal, community service, arts, and media, 5.7% healthcare practitioners, 14.6% service, 16.3% sales and office, 11.1% natural resources, construction, and maintenance, 26.2% production, transportation, and material moving
Income: Per capita: $24,561; Median household: $52,068; Average household: $65,474; Households with income of $100,000 or more: 20.3%; Poverty rate: 11.7%
Educational Attainment: High school diploma or higher: 90.4%; Bachelor's degree or higher: 17.3%; Graduate/professional degree or higher: 8.0%
Housing: Homeownership rate: 81.4%; Median home value: $108,800; Median year structure built: 1945; Homeowner vacancy rate: 1.3%; Median selected monthly owner costs: $1,196 with a mortgage, $603 without a mortgage; Median gross rent: $668 per month; Rental vacancy rate: 12.7%
Health Insurance: 95.9% have insurance; 77.5% have private insurance; 32.3% have public insurance; 4.1% do not have insurance; 2.0% of children under 18 do not have insurance
Transportation: Commute: 95.1% car, 0.6% public transportation, 1.4% walk, 2.6% work from home; Mean travel time to work: 24.1 minutes
Additional Information Contacts
Town of Royalton . . . . (716) 772-2431
  http://townofroyalton.org/content

SANBORN (CDP). Covers a land area of 2.633 square miles and a water area of 0 square miles. Located at 43.15° N. Lat; 78.88° W. Long. Elevation is 633 feet.

Population: 1,361; Growth (since 2000): n/a; Density: 516.9 persons per square mile; Race: 88.0% White, 9.0% Black/African American, 3.0% Asian, 0.0% American Indian/Alaska Native, 0.0% Native Hawaiian/Other Pacific Islander, 0.0% Two or more races, 0.0% Hispanic of any race; Average household size: 2.27; Median age: 39.1; Age under 18: 20.6%; Age 65 and over: 13.8%; Males per 100 females: 92.6; Marriage status: 28.1% never married, 43.0% now married, 0.0% separated, 11.9% widowed, 17.0% divorced; Foreign born: 2.1%; Speak English only: 97.4%; With disability: 10.6%; Veterans: 9.6%; Ancestry: 27.7% German, 16.5% English, 14.5% American, 12.0% Irish, 11.2% Polish
Employment: 6.3% management, business, and financial, 0.5% computer, engineering, and science, 3.6% education, legal, community service, arts, and media, 7.9% healthcare practitioners, 34.4% service, 24.3% sales and office, 8.5% natural resources, construction, and maintenance, 14.5% production, transportation, and material moving
Income: Per capita: $23,698; Median household: $53,598; Average household: $53,923; Households with income of $100,000 or more: 11.3%; Poverty rate: 5.3%
Educational Attainment: High school diploma or higher: 89.4%; Bachelor's degree or higher: 17.9%; Graduate/professional degree or higher: 5.9%

Housing: Homeownership rate: 79.7%; Median home value: $117,200;
Median year structure built: 1955; Homeowner vacancy rate: 9.5%; Median
selected monthly owner costs: $1,076 with a mortgage, $572 without a
mortgage; Median gross rent: $781 per month; Rental vacancy rate: 10.1%
Health Insurance: 93.8% have insurance; 81.6% have private insurance;
30.0% have public insurance; 6.2% do not have insurance; 10.4% of
children under 18 do not have insurance
Transportation: Commute: 81.6% car, 0.8% public transportation, 5.6%
walk, 12.0% work from home; Mean travel time to work: 19.1 minutes

SOMERSET (town).
Covers a land area of 37.108 square miles and a
water area of 0.063 square miles. Located at 43.34° N. Lat; 78.55° W.
Long. Elevation is 305 feet.
Population: 2,747; Growth (since 2000): -4.1%; Density: 74.0 persons per
square mile; Race: 97.2% White, 0.2% Black/African American, 0.0%
Asian, 1.0% American Indian/Alaska Native, 0.0% Native Hawaiian/Other
Pacific Islander, 1.5% Two or more races, 6.1% Hispanic of any race;
Average household size: 2.83; Median age: 40.7; Age under 18: 25.7%;
Age 65 and over: 11.7%; Males per 100 females: 101.1; Marriage status:
29.4% never married, 55.1% now married, 1.7% separated, 4.2%
widowed, 11.4% divorced; Foreign born: 2.1%; Speak English only: 95.2%;
With disability: 12.3%; Veterans: 12.2%; Ancestry: 25.0% German, 22.9%
American, 16.5% English, 11.1% Irish, 9.2% Italian
Employment: 16.7% management, business, and financial, 3.4%
computer, engineering, and science, 8.3% education, legal, community
service, arts, and media, 2.3% healthcare practitioners, 16.7% service,
18.1% sales and office, 14.0% natural resources, construction, and
maintenance, 20.6% production, transportation, and material moving
Income: Per capita: $23,507; Median household: $52,131; Average
household: $65,211; Households with income of $100,000 or more: 20.5%;
Poverty rate: 11.1%
Educational Attainment: High school diploma or higher: 91.7%;
Bachelor's degree or higher: 15.3%; Graduate/professional degree or
higher: 4.7%
Housing: Homeownership rate: 81.3%; Median home value: $104,400;
Median year structure built: Before 1940; Homeowner vacancy rate: 6.7%;
Median selected monthly owner costs: $1,053 with a mortgage, $529
without a mortgage; Median gross rent: $633 per month; Rental vacancy
rate: 14.3%
Health Insurance: 91.5% have insurance; 69.8% have private insurance;
34.6% have public insurance; 8.5% do not have insurance; 4.7% of
children under 18 do not have insurance
Transportation: Commute: 88.1% car, 0.2% public transportation, 3.0%
walk, 5.7% work from home; Mean travel time to work: 27.0 minutes

SOUTH LOCKPORT (CDP).
Covers a land area of 5.714 square
miles and a water area of 0.014 square miles. Located at 43.14° N. Lat;
78.68° W. Long. Elevation is 633 feet.
Population: 7,788; Growth (since 2000): -8.9%; Density: 1,363.0 persons
per square mile; Race: 85.8% White, 7.0% Black/African American, 3.3%
Asian, 0.0% American Indian/Alaska Native, 0.0% Native Hawaiian/Other
Pacific Islander, 2.2% Two or more races, 5.6% Hispanic of any race;
Average household size: 2.24; Median age: 42.0; Age under 18: 21.9%;
Age 65 and over: 19.4%; Males per 100 females: 90.7; Marriage status:
31.9% never married, 45.4% now married, 1.8% separated, 7.5%
widowed, 15.2% divorced; Foreign born: 4.6%; Speak English only: 93.8%;
With disability: 16.1%; Veterans: 10.6%; Ancestry: 27.1% German, 17.3%
Italian, 14.6% Irish, 12.0% Polish, 11.4% American
Employment: 8.9% management, business, and financial, 4.7% computer,
engineering, and science, 7.4% education, legal, community service, arts,
and media, 7.3% healthcare practitioners, 17.2% service, 31.5% sales and
office, 11.1% natural resources, construction, and maintenance, 12.0%
production, transportation, and material moving

Income: Per capita: $24,595; Median household: $43,441; Average
household: $53,902; Households with income of $100,000 or more: 12.2%;
Poverty rate: 15.4%
Educational Attainment: High school diploma or higher: 90.2%;
Bachelor's degree or higher: 19.0%; Graduate/professional degree or
higher: 7.8%
Housing: Homeownership rate: 65.8%; Median home value: $93,300;
Median year structure built: 1986; Homeowner vacancy rate: 3.5%; Median
selected monthly owner costs: $1,229 with a mortgage, $637 without a
mortgage; Median gross rent: $569 per month; Rental vacancy rate: 17.1%
Health Insurance: 90.5% have insurance; 67.0% have private insurance;
42.6% have public insurance; 9.5% do not have insurance; 4.7% of
children under 18 do not have insurance
Transportation: Commute: 94.1% car, 1.0% public transportation, 1.4%
walk, 2.2% work from home; Mean travel time to work: 23.4 minutes

TUSCARORA NATION RESERVATION (reservation).
Covers a land area of 9.083 square miles and a water area of 0 square
miles. Located at 43.16° N. Lat; 78.95° W. Long.
Population: 1,023; Growth (since 2000): -10.1%; Density: 112.6 persons
per square mile; Race: 9.0% White, 0.0% Black/African American, 7.8%
Asian, 79.9% American Indian/Alaska Native, 0.1% Native Hawaiian/Other
Pacific Islander, 2.4% Two or more races, 2.6% Hispanic of any race;
Average household size: 2.65; Median age: 36.5; Age under 18: 27.2%;
Age 65 and over: 13.9%; Males per 100 females: 100.0; Marriage status:
37.5% never married, 41.3% now married, 2.2% separated, 11.1%
widowed, 10.1% divorced; Foreign born: 4.6%; Speak English only: 88.8%;
With disability: 11.4%; Veterans: 4.4%; Ancestry: 2.5% Italian, 2.3%
American, 2.3% Greek, 2.1% German, 0.9% Irish
Employment: 4.4% management, business, and financial, 6.2% computer,
engineering, and science, 16.5% education, legal, community service, arts,
and media, 3.4% healthcare practitioners, 15.0% service, 35.8% sales and
office, 11.5% natural resources, construction, and maintenance, 7.2%
production, transportation, and material moving
Income: Per capita: $19,254; Median household: $34,891; Average
household: $51,969; Households with income of $100,000 or more: 14.6%;
Poverty rate: 31.1%
Educational Attainment: High school diploma or higher: 89.2%;
Bachelor's degree or higher: 15.5%; Graduate/professional degree or
higher: 5.1%
Housing: Homeownership rate: 92.0%; Median home value: $73,900;
Median year structure built: 1951; Homeowner vacancy rate: 10.9%;
Median selected monthly owner costs: $2,639 with a mortgage, $315
without a mortgage; Median gross rent: $721 per month; Rental vacancy
rate: 19.0%
Health Insurance: 72.5% have insurance; 44.4% have private insurance;
34.5% have public insurance; 27.5% do not have insurance; 25.9% of
children under 18 do not have insurance
Transportation: Commute: 91.1% car, 0.0% public transportation, 0.6%
walk, 8.3% work from home; Mean travel time to work: 18.0 minutes

WHEATFIELD (town).
Covers a land area of 27.911 square miles and
a water area of 0.680 square miles. Located at 43.10° N. Lat; 78.89° W.
Long.
Population: 18,270; Growth (since 2000): 29.7%; Density: 654.6 persons
per square mile; Race: 91.3% White, 3.5% Black/African American, 3.8%
Asian, 0.3% American Indian/Alaska Native, 0.0% Native Hawaiian/Other
Pacific Islander, 0.7% Two or more races, 3.3% Hispanic of any race;
Average household size: 2.52; Median age: 45.4; Age under 18: 21.7%;
Age 65 and over: 20.1%; Males per 100 females: 92.0; Marriage status:
25.4% never married, 58.4% now married, 1.0% separated, 7.8%
widowed, 8.3% divorced; Foreign born: 5.6%; Speak English only: 94.0%;
With disability: 13.1%; Veterans: 8.6%; Ancestry: 30.0% German, 20.6%
Italian, 16.5% Polish, 15.5% Irish, 10.3% English
Employment: 17.9% management, business, and financial, 6.0%
computer, engineering, and science, 11.6% education, legal, community
service, arts, and media, 5.4% healthcare practitioners, 12.8% service,
25.1% sales and office, 9.6% natural resources, construction, and
maintenance, 11.7% production, transportation, and material moving
Income: Per capita: $32,454; Median household: $70,547; Average
household: $81,791; Households with income of $100,000 or more: 32.3%;
Poverty rate: 6.2%
Educational Attainment: High school diploma or higher: 91.7%;
Bachelor's degree or higher: 31.7%; Graduate/professional degree or
higher: 15.1%

Housing: Homeownership rate: 79.0%; Median home value: $178,800; Median year structure built: 1988; Homeowner vacancy rate: 1.7%; Median selected monthly owner costs: $1,488 with a mortgage, $594 without a mortgage; Median gross rent: $600 per month; Rental vacancy rate: 12.9%
Health Insurance: 95.9% have insurance; 84.0% have private insurance; 29.0% have public insurance; 4.1% do not have insurance; 2.1% of children under 18 do not have insurance
Transportation: Commute: 94.8% car, 0.6% public transportation, 0.9% walk, 3.3% work from home; Mean travel time to work: 22.1 minutes
Additional Information Contacts
Town of Wheatfield . . . . (716) 694-6440
    http://wheatfield.ny.us

WILSON (town).
Covers a land area of 49.405 square miles and a water area of 2.057 square miles. Located at 43.27° N. Lat; 78.81° W. Long. Elevation is 279 feet.
History: Incorporated 1858.
Population: 5,929; Growth (since 2000): 1.5%; Density: 120.0 persons per square mile; Race: 97.0% White, 0.7% Black/African American, 0.8% Asian, 0.2% American Indian/Alaska Native, 0.0% Native Hawaiian/Other Pacific Islander, 0.7% Two or more races, 1.3% Hispanic of any race; Average household size: 2.56; Median age: 45.0; Age under 18: 21.3%; Age 65 and over: 16.2%; Males per 100 females: 99.1; Marriage status: 29.0% never married, 50.9% now married, 1.2% separated, 5.5% widowed, 14.6% divorced; Foreign born: 1.6%; Speak English only: 98.3%; With disability: 13.5%; Veterans: 8.4%; Ancestry: 26.7% German, 17.3% American, 16.2% Irish, 12.3% English, 10.9% Italian
Employment: 13.5% management, business, and financial, 4.8% computer, engineering, and science, 11.3% education, legal, community service, arts, and media, 5.4% healthcare practitioners, 15.1% service, 25.5% sales and office, 9.3% natural resources, construction, and maintenance, 15.1% production, transportation, and material moving
Income: Per capita: $33,113; Median household: $58,438; Average household: $82,203; Households with income of $100,000 or more: 22.2%; Poverty rate: 10.7%
Educational Attainment: High school diploma or higher: 88.4%; Bachelor's degree or higher: 21.8%; Graduate/professional degree or higher: 9.3%

School District(s)
Wilson Central SD (PK-12)
    2014-15 Enrollment: 1,225 . . . . (716) 751-9341
Housing: Homeownership rate: 86.6%; Median home value: $118,800; Median year structure built: 1954; Homeowner vacancy rate: 9.3%; Median selected monthly owner costs: $1,389 with a mortgage, $551 without a mortgage; Median gross rent: $720 per month; Rental vacancy rate: 22.4%
Health Insurance: 95.1% have insurance; 75.2% have private insurance; 36.2% have public insurance; 4.9% do not have insurance; 0.2% of children under 18 do not have insurance
Transportation: Commute: 94.7% car, 0.6% public transportation, 2.5% walk, 2.2% work from home; Mean travel time to work: 27.0 minutes
Additional Information Contacts
Town of Wilson . . . . (716) 751-6704
    http://www.wilsonnewyork.com

WILSON (village).
Covers a land area of 0.813 square miles and a water area of 0.190 square miles. Located at 43.31° N. Lat; 78.83° W. Long. Elevation is 279 feet.
Population: 1,163; Growth (since 2000): -4.1%; Density: 1,430.3 persons per square mile; Race: 98.9% White, 0.3% Black/African American, 0.0% Asian, 0.6% American Indian/Alaska Native, 0.0% Native Hawaiian/Other Pacific Islander, 0.0% Two or more races, 0.0% Hispanic of any race; Average household size: 2.22; Median age: 46.0; Age under 18: 19.9%; Age 65 and over: 22.2%; Males per 100 females: 92.7; Marriage status: 23.2% never married, 52.6% now married, 0.3% separated, 8.5% widowed, 15.6% divorced; Foreign born: 0.9%; Speak English only: 98.4%; With disability: 15.7%; Veterans: 11.1%; Ancestry: 29.7% German, 21.8% English, 16.6% Irish, 13.9% American, 10.8% Polish
Employment: 17.8% management, business, and financial, 4.5% computer, engineering, and science, 8.0% education, legal, community service, arts, and media, 9.0% healthcare practitioners, 7.4% service, 24.5% sales and office, 16.4% natural resources, construction, and maintenance, 12.5% production, transportation, and material moving
Income: Per capita: $28,886; Median household: $52,115; Average household: $62,426; Households with income of $100,000 or more: 20.2%; Poverty rate: 10.3%

Educational Attainment: High school diploma or higher: 95.8%; Bachelor's degree or higher: 24.7%; Graduate/professional degree or higher: 11.9%

School District(s)
Wilson Central SD (PK-12)
    2014-15 Enrollment: 1,225 . . . . (716) 751-9341
Housing: Homeownership rate: 70.4%; Median home value: $94,000; Median year structure built: Before 1940; Homeowner vacancy rate: 4.8%; Median selected monthly owner costs: $1,256 with a mortgage, $502 without a mortgage; Median gross rent: $521 per month; Rental vacancy rate: 14.9%
Health Insurance: 96.0% have insurance; 73.3% have private insurance; 41.4% have public insurance; 4.0% do not have insurance; 1.3% of children under 18 do not have insurance
Transportation: Commute: 94.4% car, 0.0% public transportation, 2.3% walk, 3.3% work from home; Mean travel time to work: 27.4 minutes
Additional Information Contacts
Village of Wilson . . . . (716) 751-6764
    http://villageofwilson.org/content

YOUNGSTOWN (village).
Covers a land area of 1.097 square miles and a water area of 0.266 square miles. Located at 43.25° N. Lat; 79.04° W. Long. Elevation is 295 feet.
History: Just North is Fort Niagara, which has been restored.
Population: 1,967; Growth (since 2000): 0.5%; Density: 1,793.1 persons per square mile; Race: 98.6% White, 0.8% Black/African American, 0.0% Asian, 0.1% American Indian/Alaska Native, 0.0% Native Hawaiian/Other Pacific Islander, 0.6% Two or more races, 2.4% Hispanic of any race; Average household size: 2.46; Median age: 47.1; Age under 18: 22.5%; Age 65 and over: 23.8%; Males per 100 females: 96.2; Marriage status: 25.6% never married, 56.2% now married, 2.7% separated, 7.5% widowed, 10.8% divorced; Foreign born: 4.8%; Speak English only: 96.6%; With disability: 15.4%; Veterans: 10.8%; Ancestry: 21.9% German, 20.3% Irish, 19.4% English, 14.8% Italian, 12.7% American
Employment: 8.9% management, business, and financial, 4.5% computer, engineering, and science, 10.5% education, legal, community service, arts, and media, 8.1% healthcare practitioners, 19.6% service, 29.2% sales and office, 9.6% natural resources, construction, and maintenance, 9.7% production, transportation, and material moving
Income: Per capita: $33,340; Median household: $56,875; Average household: $80,452; Households with income of $100,000 or more: 22.3%; Poverty rate: 8.3%
Educational Attainment: High school diploma or higher: 94.0%; Bachelor's degree or higher: 31.0%; Graduate/professional degree or higher: 15.3%

School District(s)
Lewiston-Porter Central SD (PK-12)
    2014-15 Enrollment: 2,112 . . . . (716) 286-7266
Housing: Homeownership rate: 80.1%; Median home value: $124,500; Median year structure built: 1957; Homeowner vacancy rate: 3.2%; Median selected monthly owner costs: $1,265 with a mortgage, $494 without a mortgage; Median gross rent: $744 per month; Rental vacancy rate: 0.0%
Health Insurance: 96.5% have insurance; 83.6% have private insurance; 38.3% have public insurance; 3.5% do not have insurance; 0.0% of children under 18 do not have insurance
Safety: Violent crime rate: 0.0 per 10,000 population; Property crime rate: 21.2 per 10,000 population
Transportation: Commute: 94.8% car, 0.0% public transportation, 1.9% walk, 1.7% work from home; Mean travel time to work: 24.4 minutes

Oneida County

Located in central New York; bounded partly on the west by Oneida Lake, rising to the Adirondacks in the east and northeast; drained by the Mohawk and Black Rivers; includes several lakes. Covers a land area of 1,212.429 square miles, a water area of 45.227 square miles, and is located in the Eastern Time Zone at 43.24° N. Lat., 75.43° W. Long. The county was founded in 1798. County seat is Utica.

Oneida County is part of the Utica-Rome, NY Metropolitan Statistical Area. The entire metro area includes: Herkimer County, NY; Oneida County, NY

Weather Station: Boonville 2 SSW | Elevation: 1,580 feet

	Jan	Feb	Mar	Apr	May	Jun	Jul	Aug	Sep	Oct	Nov	Dec
High	25	28	36	51	63	71	75	74	66	54	41	30
Low	8	10	19	32	43	52	57	55	48	37	27	15
Precip	5.0	4.0	4.5	4.5	4.5	4.7	4.4	4.7	5.5	5.6	5.4	5.5
Snow	52.9	39.8	31.4	8.6	0.2	tr	0.0	0.0	tr	2.2	17.8	44.7

High and Low temperatures in degrees Fahrenheit; Precipitation and Snow in inches

Weather Station: Utica Oneida County Arpt | Elevation: 711 feet

	Jan	Feb	Mar	Apr	May	Jun	Jul	Aug	Sep	Oct	Nov	Dec
High	29	32	41	55	68	76	80	79	71	58	46	34
Low	14	16	24	36	46	55	60	58	51	40	31	20
Precip	2.9	2.4	3.2	3.5	3.9	4.3	3.9	3.9	4.1	3.7	3.9	3.4
Snow	na	na	na	na	na	na	na	na	na	na	na	na

High and Low temperatures in degrees Fahrenheit; Precipitation and Snow in inches

Population: 233,558; Growth (since 2000): -0.8%; Density: 192.6 persons per square mile; Race: 86.0% White, 6.0% Black/African American, 3.6% Asian, 0.2% American Indian/Alaska Native, 0.0% Native Hawaiian/Other Pacific Islander, 2.5% two or more races, 5.1% Hispanic of any race; Average household size: 2.43; Median age: 41.2; Age under 18: 21.5%; Age 65 and over: 17.1%; Males per 100 females: 99.3; Marriage status: 34.3% never married, 46.2% now married, 2.2% separated, 8.0% widowed, 11.5% divorced; Foreign born: 7.7%; Speak English only: 88.1%; With disability: 15.6%; Veterans: 9.9%; Ancestry: 17.3% Italian, 15.3% German, 15.2% Irish, 13.6% American, 9.2% Polish

Religion: Six largest groups: 36.9% Catholicism, 3.6% Methodist/Pietist, 1.9% Non-denominational Protestant, 1.6% Presbyterian-Reformed, 1.4% Baptist, 1.3% Lutheran

Economy: Unemployment rate: 4.6%; Leading industries: 16.9 % retail trade; 12.2 % health care and social assistance; 12.0 % accommodation and food services; Farms: 1,066 totaling 205,106 acres; Company size: 8 employ 1,000 or more persons, 11 employs 500 to 999 persons, 106 employ 100 to 499 persons, 4,783 employ less than 100 persons; Business ownership: 4,803 women-owned, 528 Black-owned, 484 Hispanic-owned, 583 Asian-owned, 90 American Indian/Alaska Native-owned

Employment: 12.3% management, business, and financial, 3.9% computer, engineering, and science, 12.1% education, legal, community service, arts, and media, 6.7% healthcare practitioners, 20.7% service, 23.6% sales and office, 8.1% natural resources, construction, and maintenance, 12.7% production, transportation, and material moving

Income: Per capita: $25,982; Median household: $48,246; Average household: $63,857; Households with income of $100,000 or more: 17.4%; Poverty rate: 17.1%

Educational Attainment: High school diploma or higher: 87.8%; Bachelor's degree or higher: 23.2%; Graduate/professional degree or higher: 9.4%

Housing: Homeownership rate: 65.7%; Median home value: $114,000; Median year structure built: 1955; Homeowner vacancy rate: 1.9%; Median selected monthly owner costs: $1,231 with a mortgage, $503 without a mortgage; Median gross rent: $706 per month; Rental vacancy rate: 5.8%

Vital Statistics: Birth rate: 113.3 per 10,000 population; Death rate: 104.5 per 10,000 population; Age-adjusted cancer mortality rate: 173.8 deaths per 100,000 population

Health Insurance: 93.4% have insurance; 66.4% have private insurance; 42.2% have public insurance; 6.6% do not have insurance; 2.9% of children under 18 do not have insurance

Health Care: Physicians: 22.9 per 10,000 population; Dentists: 5.5 per 10,000 population; Hospital beds: 66.0 per 10,000 population; Hospital admissions: 1,324.1 per 10,000 population

Air Quality Index (AQI): Percent of Days: 86.6% good, 13.4% moderate, 0.0% unhealthy for sensitive individuals, 0.0% unhealthy, 0.0% very unhealthy; Annual median: 27; Annual maximum: 71

Transportation: Commute: 90.4% car, 1.1% public transportation, 3.8% walk, 3.7% work from home; Mean travel time to work: 19.9 minutes

2016 Presidential Election: 57.0% Trump, 37.4% Clinton, 4.2% Johnson, 1.4% Stein

National and State Parks: Boonville Gorge State Park; Fort Stanwix National Monument; Verona Beach State Park

Additional Information Contacts

Oneida Government . . . . (315) 798-5794
http://www.ocgov.net

Oneida County Communities

ALDER CREEK (unincorporated postal area)
ZCTA: 13301

Covers a land area of 2.443 square miles and a water area of 0.163 square miles. Located at 43.42° N. Lat; 75.22° W. Long. Elevation is 1,194 feet.

Population: 84; Growth (since 2000): -61.6%; Density: 34.4 persons per square mile; Race: 100.0% White, 0.0% Black/African American, 0.0% Asian, 0.0% American Indian/Alaska Native, 0.0% Native Hawaiian/Other Pacific Islander, 0.0% Two or more races, 0.0% Hispanic of any race; Average household size: 1.95; Median age: 54.7; Age under 18: 17.9%; Age 65 and over: 10.7%; Males per 100 females: 139.0; Marriage status: 0.0% never married, 75.4% now married, 0.0% separated, 13.0% widowed, 11.6% divorced; Foreign born: 0.0%; Speak English only: 100.0%; With disability: 20.2%; Veterans: 24.6%; Ancestry: 27.4% German, 23.8% English, 13.1% Scottish, 9.5% Irish, 2.4% Italian

Employment: 0.0% management, business, and financial, 0.0% computer, engineering, and science, 3.8% education, legal, community service, arts, and media, 17.3% healthcare practitioners, 13.5% service, 36.5% sales and office, 28.8% natural resources, construction, and maintenance, 0.0% production, transportation, and material moving

Income: Per capita: $41,857; Median household: $74,107; Average household: $81,067; Households with income of $100,000 or more: 25.6%; Poverty rate: n/a

Educational Attainment: High school diploma or higher: 100.0%; Bachelor's degree or higher: 30.4%; Graduate/professional degree or higher: 15.9%

Housing: Homeownership rate: 100.0%; Median home value: $234,400; Median year structure built: 1982; Homeowner vacancy rate: 24.6%; Median selected monthly owner costs: $1,375 with a mortgage, $450 without a mortgage; Median gross rent: n/a per month; Rental vacancy rate: 0.0%

Health Insurance: 100.0% have insurance; 90.5% have private insurance; 20.2% have public insurance; 0.0% do not have insurance; 0.0% of children under 18 do not have insurance

Transportation: Commute: 100.0% car, 0.0% public transportation, 0.0% walk, 0.0% work from home; Mean travel time to work: 33.2 minutes

ANNSVILLE (town). Covers a land area of 60.167 square miles and a water area of 0.308 square miles. Located at 43.35° N. Lat; 75.61° W. Long.

Population: 2,994; Growth (since 2000): 1.3%; Density: 49.8 persons per square mile; Race: 96.7% White, 0.9% Black/African American, 0.3% Asian, 0.0% American Indian/Alaska Native, 0.0% Native Hawaiian/Other Pacific Islander, 1.8% Two or more races, 2.0% Hispanic of any race; Average household size: 2.77; Median age: 37.9; Age under 18: 26.6%; Age 65 and over: 11.3%; Males per 100 females: 102.4; Marriage status: 31.3% never married, 52.7% now married, 3.0% separated, 5.2% widowed, 10.8% divorced; Foreign born: 2.6%; Speak English only: 95.7%; With disability: 17.9%; Veterans: 12.8%; Ancestry: 22.4% American, 19.1% Irish, 17.4% German, 8.4% French, 8.2% English

Employment: 12.7% management, business, and financial, 2.9% computer, engineering, and science, 6.9% education, legal, community service, arts, and media, 3.1% healthcare practitioners, 21.9% service, 23.8% sales and office, 9.7% natural resources, construction, and maintenance, 19.0% production, transportation, and material moving

Income: Per capita: $21,062; Median household: $43,542; Average household: $56,089; Households with income of $100,000 or more: 15.5%; Poverty rate: 20.8%

Educational Attainment: High school diploma or higher: 82.1%; Bachelor's degree or higher: 11.4%; Graduate/professional degree or higher: 5.5%

Housing: Homeownership rate: 74.4%; Median home value: $89,800; Median year structure built: 1981; Homeowner vacancy rate: 0.0%; Median selected monthly owner costs: $1,156 with a mortgage, $445 without a mortgage; Median gross rent: $821 per month; Rental vacancy rate: 5.1%

Health Insurance: 92.1% have insurance; 60.0% have private insurance; 45.2% have public insurance; 7.9% do not have insurance; 6.6% of children under 18 do not have insurance

Transportation: Commute: 90.6% car, 0.2% public transportation, 1.7% walk, 7.0% work from home; Mean travel time to work: 27.2 minutes

AUGUSTA (town). Covers a land area of 27.728 square miles and a water area of 0 square miles. Located at 42.98° N. Lat; 75.50° W. Long. Elevation is 955 feet.
Population: 2,370; Growth (since 2000): 20.5%; Density: 85.5 persons per square mile; Race: 97.4% White, 0.8% Black/African American, 0.0% Asian, 0.0% American Indian/Alaska Native, 0.0% Native Hawaiian/Other Pacific Islander, 0.5% Two or more races, 1.8% Hispanic of any race; Average household size: 2.53; Median age: 36.3; Age under 18: 24.8%; Age 65 and over: 13.3%; Males per 100 females: 100.0; Marriage status: 26.1% never married, 52.5% now married, 4.3% separated, 4.5% widowed, 16.9% divorced; Foreign born: 1.6%; Speak English only: 90.2%; With disability: 9.8%; Veterans: 8.5%; Ancestry: 19.1% Irish, 17.8% American, 16.8% German, 16.6% English, 8.5% Polish
Employment: 15.4% management, business, and financial, 3.3% computer, engineering, and science, 8.8% education, legal, community service, arts, and media, 6.2% healthcare practitioners, 18.5% service, 17.4% sales and office, 19.0% natural resources, construction, and maintenance, 11.2% production, transportation, and material moving
Income: Per capita: $26,383; Median household: $51,250; Average household: $65,371; Households with income of $100,000 or more: 15.9%; Poverty rate: 16.7%
Educational Attainment: High school diploma or higher: 91.6%; Bachelor's degree or higher: 21.5%; Graduate/professional degree or higher: 5.9%
Housing: Homeownership rate: 78.3%; Median home value: $95,500; Median year structure built: Before 1940; Homeowner vacancy rate: 1.2%; Median selected monthly owner costs: $1,088 with a mortgage, $462 without a mortgage; Median gross rent: $753 per month; Rental vacancy rate: 2.9%
Health Insurance: 89.2% have insurance; 68.2% have private insurance; 31.8% have public insurance; 10.8% do not have insurance; 8.5% of children under 18 do not have insurance
Transportation: Commute: 88.0% car, 0.3% public transportation, 4.0% walk, 6.1% work from home; Mean travel time to work: 28.5 minutes

AVA (town). Covers a land area of 37.667 square miles and a water area of 0.038 square miles. Located at 43.41° N. Lat; 75.44° W. Long. Elevation is 1,371 feet.
Population: 626; Growth (since 2000): -13.7%; Density: 16.6 persons per square mile; Race: 88.3% White, 3.2% Black/African American, 2.2% Asian, 0.0% American Indian/Alaska Native, 0.3% Native Hawaiian/Other Pacific Islander, 5.9% Two or more races, 0.5% Hispanic of any race; Average household size: 2.56; Median age: 43.7; Age under 18: 21.4%; Age 65 and over: 14.7%; Males per 100 females: 104.2; Marriage status: 29.9% never married, 54.8% now married, 4.5% separated, 4.7% widowed, 10.6% divorced; Foreign born: 3.8%; Speak English only: 93.8%; With disability: 10.1%; Veterans: 17.7%; Ancestry: 22.8% American, 18.8% German, 15.0% Irish, 13.9% English, 12.6% Polish
Employment: 8.0% management, business, and financial, 2.0% computer, engineering, and science, 5.6% education, legal, community service, arts, and media, 2.0% healthcare practitioners, 27.2% service, 15.9% sales and office, 18.6% natural resources, construction, and maintenance, 20.6% production, transportation, and material moving
Income: Per capita: $21,319; Median household: $48,750; Average household: $53,207; Households with income of $100,000 or more: 11.0%; Poverty rate: 7.6%
Educational Attainment: High school diploma or higher: 89.2%; Bachelor's degree or higher: 9.2%; Graduate/professional degree or higher: 3.7%
Housing: Homeownership rate: 90.2%; Median home value: $86,300; Median year structure built: 1974; Homeowner vacancy rate: 4.7%; Median selected monthly owner costs: $1,075 with a mortgage, $347 without a mortgage; Median gross rent: $622 per month; Rental vacancy rate: 0.0%
Health Insurance: 93.0% have insurance; 62.5% have private insurance; 42.5% have public insurance; 7.0% do not have insurance; 0.0% of children under 18 do not have insurance
Transportation: Commute: 91.5% car, 0.0% public transportation, 1.1% walk, 6.0% work from home; Mean travel time to work: 34.8 minutes

BARNEVELD (village). Covers a land area of 0.192 square miles and a water area of 0 square miles. Located at 43.27° N. Lat; 75.19° W. Long. Elevation is 801 feet.
History: Nearby, in Steuben Memorial Park, is the reconstructed log cabin and the grave of Baron von Steuben.

Population: 221; Growth (since 2000): -33.4%; Density: 1,150.0 persons per square mile; Race: 90.0% White, 0.0% Black/African American, 0.0% Asian, 0.0% American Indian/Alaska Native, 0.0% Native Hawaiian/Other Pacific Islander, 10.0% Two or more races, 2.7% Hispanic of any race; Average household size: 2.23; Median age: 51.2; Age under 18: 19.0%; Age 65 and over: 29.4%; Males per 100 females: 104.3; Marriage status: 29.5% never married, 60.7% now married, 1.1% separated, 6.0% widowed, 3.8% divorced; Foreign born: 3.2%; Speak English only: 97.1%; With disability: 9.0%; Veterans: 11.7%; Ancestry: 20.4% Irish, 18.1% German, 17.2% American, 12.2% English, 10.9% Polish
Employment: 8.9% management, business, and financial, 3.6% computer, engineering, and science, 2.7% education, legal, community service, arts, and media, 15.2% healthcare practitioners, 20.5% service, 33.0% sales and office, 9.8% natural resources, construction, and maintenance, 6.3% production, transportation, and material moving
Income: Per capita: $37,272; Median household: $57,292; Average household: $80,479; Households with income of $100,000 or more: 24.2%; Poverty rate: 10.9%
Educational Attainment: High school diploma or higher: 97.7%; Bachelor's degree or higher: 37.0%; Graduate/professional degree or higher: 13.3%
Housing: Homeownership rate: 65.7%; Median home value: $111,800; Median year structure built: Before 1940; Homeowner vacancy rate: 5.8%; Median selected monthly owner costs: $1,188 with a mortgage, $617 without a mortgage; Median gross rent: $700 per month; Rental vacancy rate: 10.5%
Health Insurance: 95.0% have insurance; 66.1% have private insurance; 51.6% have public insurance; 5.0% do not have insurance; 9.5% of children under 18 do not have insurance
Transportation: Commute: 79.2% car, 0.0% public transportation, 0.0% walk, 9.9% work from home; Mean travel time to work: 20.5 minutes

BLOSSVALE (unincorporated postal area)
ZCTA: 13308
Covers a land area of 38.655 square miles and a water area of 0.663 square miles. Located at 43.25° N. Lat; 75.66° W. Long. Elevation is 420 feet.
Population: 2,695; Growth (since 2000): -44.6%; Density: 69.7 persons per square mile; Race: 99.6% White, 0.4% Black/African American, 0.0% Asian, 0.0% American Indian/Alaska Native, 0.0% Native Hawaiian/Other Pacific Islander, 0.0% Two or more races, 0.3% Hispanic of any race; Average household size: 1.99; Median age: 49.1; Age under 18: 17.0%; Age 65 and over: 22.8%; Males per 100 females: 99.1; Marriage status: 18.6% never married, 51.7% now married, 2.9% separated, 9.5% widowed, 20.2% divorced; Foreign born: 1.2%; Speak English only: 97.5%; With disability: 20.0%; Veterans: 16.5%; Ancestry: 22.8% German, 21.3% American, 20.8% English, 17.2% Irish, 11.8% Italian
Employment: 8.3% management, business, and financial, 2.1% computer, engineering, and science, 4.1% education, legal, community service, arts, and media, 5.7% healthcare practitioners, 8.7% service, 29.5% sales and office, 24.2% natural resources, construction, and maintenance, 17.3% production, transportation, and material moving
Income: Per capita: $25,290; Median household: $40,585; Average household: $49,304; Households with income of $100,000 or more: 9.0%; Poverty rate: 18.9%
Educational Attainment: High school diploma or higher: 84.2%; Bachelor's degree or higher: 9.9%; Graduate/professional degree or higher: 1.8%
School District(s)
Camden Central SD (PK-12)
    2014-15 Enrollment: 2,316 . . . . (315) 245-4075
Housing: Homeownership rate: 80.8%; Median home value: $102,800; Median year structure built: 1978; Homeowner vacancy rate: 0.0%; Median selected monthly owner costs: $1,443 with a mortgage, $435 without a mortgage; Median gross rent: $819 per month; Rental vacancy rate: 0.0%
Health Insurance: 93.5% have insurance; 63.3% have private insurance; 48.9% have public insurance; 6.5% do not have insurance; 3.5% of children under 18 do not have insurance
Transportation: Commute: 93.1% car, 0.0% public transportation, 1.7% walk, 1.3% work from home; Mean travel time to work: 33.5 minutes

BOONVILLE (town). Covers a land area of 71.878 square miles and a water area of 0.698 square miles. Located at 43.46° N. Lat; 75.29° W. Long. Elevation is 1,148 feet.
History: Author and critic Walter D. Edmonds born here and lived in nearby Talcottville. Settled c.1791, incorporated 1855.
Population: 4,551; Growth (since 2000): -0.5%; Density: 63.3 persons per square mile; Race: 98.2% White, 0.1% Black/African American, 1.2% Asian, 0.0% American Indian/Alaska Native, 0.0% Native Hawaiian/Other Pacific Islander, 0.5% Two or more races, 0.9% Hispanic of any race; Average household size: 2.54; Median age: 42.9; Age under 18: 21.6%; Age 65 and over: 18.0%; Males per 100 females: 96.3; Marriage status: 32.0% never married, 48.9% now married, 2.2% separated, 8.2% widowed, 11.0% divorced; Foreign born: 1.5%; Speak English only: 95.8%; With disability: 14.9%; Veterans: 12.7%; Ancestry: 22.6% German, 16.6% American, 15.4% Irish, 9.9% French, 8.5% Polish
Employment: 13.7% management, business, and financial, 1.5% computer, engineering, and science, 7.8% education, legal, community service, arts, and media, 9.7% healthcare practitioners, 16.2% service, 20.2% sales and office, 10.7% natural resources, construction, and maintenance, 20.0% production, transportation, and material moving
Income: Per capita: $26,563; Median household: $57,473; Average household: $67,293; Households with income of $100,000 or more: 20.4%; Poverty rate: 14.7%
Educational Attainment: High school diploma or higher: 91.5%; Bachelor's degree or higher: 22.3%; Graduate/professional degree or higher: 11.0%

School District(s)
Adirondack Central SD (PK-12)
   2014-15 Enrollment: 1,322 . . . . (315) 942-9200
Housing: Homeownership rate: 72.6%; Median home value: $99,600; Median year structure built: 1958; Homeowner vacancy rate: 1.8%; Median selected monthly owner costs: $966 with a mortgage, $399 without a mortgage; Median gross rent: $558 per month; Rental vacancy rate: 0.0%
Health Insurance: 91.3% have insurance; 72.1% have private insurance; 36.5% have public insurance; 8.7% do not have insurance; 6.3% of children under 18 do not have insurance
Newspapers: Boonville Herald (weekly circulation 4,400)
Transportation: Commute: 85.2% car, 0.1% public transportation, 7.5% walk, 6.5% work from home; Mean travel time to work: 24.5 minutes
Additional Information Contacts
Town of Boonville . . . . (315) 943-2064
   http://townofboonville.org/content

BOONVILLE (village). Covers a land area of 1.729 square miles and a water area of 0.004 square miles. Located at 43.48° N. Lat; 75.33° W. Long. Elevation is 1,148 feet.
Population: 2,067; Growth (since 2000): -3.3%; Density: 1,195.2 persons per square mile; Race: 97.3% White, 0.2% Black/African American, 1.4% Asian, 0.0% American Indian/Alaska Native, 0.0% Native Hawaiian/Other Pacific Islander, 1.1% Two or more races, 1.5% Hispanic of any race; Average household size: 2.28; Median age: 43.6; Age under 18: 21.2%; Age 65 and over: 23.0%; Males per 100 females: 91.0; Marriage status: 36.6% never married, 34.6% now married, 2.9% separated, 11.8% widowed, 17.0% divorced; Foreign born: 1.6%; Speak English only: 95.8%; With disability: 20.1%; Veterans: 11.6%; Ancestry: 24.0% German, 18.0% American, 16.2% Irish, 12.3% French, 11.9% Polish
Employment: 11.3% management, business, and financial, 1.0% computer, engineering, and science, 6.4% education, legal, community service, arts, and media, 9.3% healthcare practitioners, 18.4% service, 25.2% sales and office, 15.1% natural resources, construction, and maintenance, 13.3% production, transportation, and material moving
Income: Per capita: $21,593; Median household: $32,500; Average household: $50,540; Households with income of $100,000 or more: 12.5%; Poverty rate: 19.4%
Educational Attainment: High school diploma or higher: 87.9%; Bachelor's degree or higher: 16.1%; Graduate/professional degree or higher: 7.6%

School District(s)
Adirondack Central SD (PK-12)
   2014-15 Enrollment: 1,322 . . . . (315) 942-9200
Housing: Homeownership rate: 51.5%; Median home value: $82,000; Median year structure built: Before 1940; Homeowner vacancy rate: 0.0%; Median selected monthly owner costs: $912 with a mortgage, $348 without a mortgage; Median gross rent: $539 per month; Rental vacancy rate: 0.0%

Health Insurance: 91.3% have insurance; 60.8% have private insurance; 49.7% have public insurance; 8.7% do not have insurance; 8.2% of children under 18 do not have insurance
Safety: Violent crime rate: 0.0 per 10,000 population; Property crime rate: 19.5 per 10,000 population
Newspapers: Boonville Herald (weekly circulation 4,400)
Transportation: Commute: 89.8% car, 0.0% public transportation, 8.3% walk, 1.4% work from home; Mean travel time to work: 24.1 minutes
Additional Information Contacts
Village of Boonville . . . . (315) 943-2052
   http://village.boonville.ny.us/content

BRIDGEWATER (town). Covers a land area of 23.845 square miles and a water area of 0.012 square miles. Located at 42.90° N. Lat; 75.27° W. Long. Elevation is 1,211 feet.
Population: 1,395; Growth (since 2000): -16.5%; Density: 58.5 persons per square mile; Race: 98.0% White, 0.7% Black/African American, 0.0% Asian, 0.1% American Indian/Alaska Native, 0.0% Native Hawaiian/Other Pacific Islander, 1.2% Two or more races, 2.5% Hispanic of any race; Average household size: 2.67; Median age: 38.4; Age under 18: 23.6%; Age 65 and over: 11.8%; Males per 100 females: 104.6; Marriage status: 30.9% never married, 54.1% now married, 2.2% separated, 5.0% widowed, 10.1% divorced; Foreign born: 1.7%; Speak English only: 92.0%; With disability: 13.7%; Veterans: 8.8%; Ancestry: 21.6% American, 18.5% German, 17.8% Irish, 12.1% English, 8.3% Italian
Employment: 9.6% management, business, and financial, 3.3% computer, engineering, and science, 9.3% education, legal, community service, arts, and media, 8.0% healthcare practitioners, 18.0% service, 26.8% sales and office, 10.2% natural resources, construction, and maintenance, 14.7% production, transportation, and material moving
Income: Per capita: $22,586; Median household: $44,667; Average household: $57,557; Households with income of $100,000 or more: 13.6%; Poverty rate: 16.3%
Educational Attainment: High school diploma or higher: 88.6%; Bachelor's degree or higher: 12.9%; Graduate/professional degree or higher: 5.5%
Housing: Homeownership rate: 79.7%; Median home value: $83,000; Median year structure built: 1979; Homeowner vacancy rate: 2.1%; Median selected monthly owner costs: $1,074 with a mortgage, $438 without a mortgage; Median gross rent: $650 per month; Rental vacancy rate: 9.4%
Health Insurance: 89.9% have insurance; 63.5% have private insurance; 39.4% have public insurance; 10.1% do not have insurance; 4.3% of children under 18 do not have insurance
Transportation: Commute: 90.2% car, 0.0% public transportation, 3.8% walk, 6.0% work from home; Mean travel time to work: 23.8 minutes

BRIDGEWATER (village). Covers a land area of 0.607 square miles and a water area of 0 square miles. Located at 42.88° N. Lat; 75.25° W. Long. Elevation is 1,211 feet.
Population: 612; Growth (since 2000): 5.7%; Density: 1,008.9 persons per square mile; Race: 99.0% White, 0.0% Black/African American, 0.0% Asian, 0.0% American Indian/Alaska Native, 0.0% Native Hawaiian/Other Pacific Islander, 1.0% Two or more races, 5.2% Hispanic of any race; Average household size: 2.90; Median age: 29.5; Age under 18: 35.0%; Age 65 and over: 11.8%; Males per 100 females: 99.2; Marriage status: 36.2% never married, 48.1% now married, 2.3% separated, 3.7% widowed, 12.1% divorced; Foreign born: 2.9%; Speak English only: 91.0%; With disability: 10.3%; Veterans: 7.8%; Ancestry: 34.6% American, 23.9% Irish, 14.5% German, 10.8% Dutch, 9.6% English
Employment: 11.0% management, business, and financial, 8.5% computer, engineering, and science, 6.3% education, legal, community service, arts, and media, 8.1% healthcare practitioners, 20.2% service, 17.6% sales and office, 8.8% natural resources, construction, and maintenance, 19.5% production, transportation, and material moving
Income: Per capita: $16,344; Median household: $41,250; Average household: $46,171; Households with income of $100,000 or more: 4.7%; Poverty rate: 20.7%
Educational Attainment: High school diploma or higher: 86.4%; Bachelor's degree or higher: 9.3%; Graduate/professional degree or higher: 2.8%
Housing: Homeownership rate: 68.7%; Median home value: $66,300; Median year structure built: 1972; Homeowner vacancy rate: 5.7%; Median selected monthly owner costs: $825 with a mortgage, $469 without a mortgage; Median gross rent: $611 per month; Rental vacancy rate: 14.3%

Health Insurance: 92.6% have insurance; 60.6% have private insurance; 48.0% have public insurance; 7.4% do not have insurance; 5.6% of children under 18 do not have insurance
Transportation: Commute: 86.3% car, 0.0% public transportation, 9.8% walk, 3.9% work from home; Mean travel time to work: 21.2 minutes

CAMDEN (town).
Covers a land area of 54.013 square miles and a water area of 0.141 square miles. Located at 43.35° N. Lat; 75.77° W. Long. Elevation is 502 feet.
History: Incorporated 1834.
Population: 4,925; Growth (since 2000): -2.0%; Density: 91.2 persons per square mile; Race: 96.6% White, 0.5% Black/African American, 0.6% Asian, 0.0% American Indian/Alaska Native, 0.0% Native Hawaiian/Other Pacific Islander, 1.8% Two or more races, 1.7% Hispanic of any race; Average household size: 2.57; Median age: 41.4; Age under 18: 25.8%; Age 65 and over: 15.2%; Males per 100 females: 97.8; Marriage status: 25.1% never married, 55.4% now married, 2.3% separated, 7.0% widowed, 12.5% divorced; Foreign born: 1.2%; Speak English only: 97.8%; With disability: 17.0%; Veterans: 11.8%; Ancestry: 25.6% American, 20.5% Irish, 13.8% German, 11.6% English, 6.5% Polish
Employment: 12.4% management, business, and financial, 0.5% computer, engineering, and science, 12.9% education, legal, community service, arts, and media, 2.3% healthcare practitioners, 21.1% service, 21.6% sales and office, 11.2% natural resources, construction, and maintenance, 18.0% production, transportation, and material moving
Income: Per capita: $22,393; Median household: $45,645; Average household: $55,722; Households with income of $100,000 or more: 14.5%; Poverty rate: 16.1%
Educational Attainment: High school diploma or higher: 87.9%; Bachelor's degree or higher: 19.3%; Graduate/professional degree or higher: 8.3%

School District(s)
Camden Central SD (PK-12)
    2014-15 Enrollment: 2,316 . . . . (315) 245-4075
Housing: Homeownership rate: 70.5%; Median home value: $111,800; Median year structure built: 1963; Homeowner vacancy rate: 0.4%; Median selected monthly owner costs: $1,125 with a mortgage, $501 without a mortgage; Median gross rent: $646 per month; Rental vacancy rate: 11.3%
Health Insurance: 92.9% have insurance; 67.4% have private insurance; 41.0% have public insurance; 7.1% do not have insurance; 1.3% of children under 18 do not have insurance
Newspapers: Queen Central News (weekly circulation 7,600)
Transportation: Commute: 90.5% car, 0.0% public transportation, 6.1% walk, 2.7% work from home; Mean travel time to work: 26.7 minutes

CAMDEN (village).
Covers a land area of 2.436 square miles and a water area of 0 square miles. Located at 43.34° N. Lat; 75.75° W. Long. Elevation is 502 feet.
Population: 2,491; Growth (since 2000): 6.9%; Density: 1,022.5 persons per square mile; Race: 93.3% White, 1.1% Black/African American, 1.2% Asian, 0.1% American Indian/Alaska Native, 0.0% Native Hawaiian/Other Pacific Islander, 3.5% Two or more races, 1.7% Hispanic of any race; Average household size: 2.42; Median age: 40.1; Age under 18: 26.7%; Age 65 and over: 17.6%; Males per 100 females: 93.8; Marriage status: 29.4% never married, 44.6% now married, 2.8% separated, 10.9% widowed, 15.1% divorced; Foreign born: 2.1%; Speak English only: 97.4%; With disability: 18.0%; Veterans: 11.9%; Ancestry: 27.9% American, 21.0% Irish, 17.1% German, 13.0% English, 6.9% French
Employment: 10.3% management, business, and financial, 1.2% computer, engineering, and science, 14.4% education, legal, community service, arts, and media, 2.8% healthcare practitioners, 24.6% service, 22.8% sales and office, 9.3% natural resources, construction, and maintenance, 14.6% production, transportation, and material moving
Income: Per capita: $20,558; Median household: $35,926; Average household: $47,916; Households with income of $100,000 or more: 11.1%; Poverty rate: 20.6%
Educational Attainment: High school diploma or higher: 88.1%; Bachelor's degree or higher: 17.9%; Graduate/professional degree or higher: 8.4%

School District(s)
Camden Central SD (PK-12)
    2014-15 Enrollment: 2,316 . . . . (315) 245-4075
Housing: Homeownership rate: 52.8%; Median home value: $92,600; Median year structure built: Before 1940; Homeowner vacancy rate: 0.9%; Median selected monthly owner costs: $1,125 with a mortgage, $527

without a mortgage; Median gross rent: $647 per month; Rental vacancy rate: 12.9%
Health Insurance: 90.8% have insurance; 59.7% have private insurance; 49.6% have public insurance; 9.2% do not have insurance; 1.4% of children under 18 do not have insurance
Safety: Violent crime rate: 9.1 per 10,000 population; Property crime rate: 172.6 per 10,000 population
Newspapers: Queen Central News (weekly circulation 7,600)
Transportation: Commute: 84.3% car, 0.0% public transportation, 11.5% walk, 3.6% work from home; Mean travel time to work: 23.4 minutes

CASSVILLE (unincorporated postal area)
ZCTA: 13318
    Covers a land area of 25.383 square miles and a water area of 0.012 square miles. Located at 42.92° N. Lat; 75.26° W. Long. Elevation is 1,240 feet.
Population: 1,175; Growth (since 2000): -17.8%; Density: 46.3 persons per square mile; Race: 98.1% White, 0.9% Black/African American, 0.0% Asian, 0.1% American Indian/Alaska Native, 0.0% Native Hawaiian/Other Pacific Islander, 0.9% Two or more races, 0.3% Hispanic of any race; Average household size: 2.68; Median age: 41.6; Age under 18: 19.1%; Age 65 and over: 10.5%; Males per 100 females: 104.8; Marriage status: 35.7% never married, 51.4% now married, 0.9% separated, 5.1% widowed, 7.8% divorced; Foreign born: 1.2%; Speak English only: 95.1%; With disability: 12.3%; Veterans: 6.9%; Ancestry: 17.4% Irish, 12.2% Italian, 11.9% German, 11.4% Polish, 10.6% English
Employment: 8.3% management, business, and financial, 2.9% computer, engineering, and science, 8.1% education, legal, community service, arts, and media, 6.0% healthcare practitioners, 19.6% service, 31.8% sales and office, 12.0% natural resources, construction, and maintenance, 11.2% production, transportation, and material moving
Income: Per capita: $26,192; Median household: $58,864; Average household: $67,448; Households with income of $100,000 or more: 20.3%; Poverty rate: 6.6%
Educational Attainment: High school diploma or higher: 92.7%; Bachelor's degree or higher: 12.6%; Graduate/professional degree or higher: 6.6%
Housing: Homeownership rate: 91.6%; Median home value: $120,100; Median year structure built: 1985; Homeowner vacancy rate: 0.0%; Median selected monthly owner costs: $1,296 with a mortgage, $431 without a mortgage; Median gross rent: $725 per month; Rental vacancy rate: 0.0%
Health Insurance: 90.2% have insurance; 74.6% have private insurance; 27.6% have public insurance; 9.8% do not have insurance; 0.9% of children under 18 do not have insurance
Transportation: Commute: 93.9% car, 0.0% public transportation, 0.0% walk, 6.1% work from home; Mean travel time to work: 26.0 minutes

CHADWICKS (CDP).
Covers a land area of 1.327 square miles and a water area of 0 square miles. Located at 43.03° N. Lat; 75.27° W. Long. Elevation is 709 feet.
Population: 1,757; Growth (since 2000): n/a; Density: 1,323.8 persons per square mile; Race: 100.0% White, 0.0% Black/African American, 0.0% Asian, 0.0% American Indian/Alaska Native, 0.0% Native Hawaiian/Other Pacific Islander, 0.0% Two or more races, 3.0% Hispanic of any race; Average household size: 2.93; Median age: 30.0; Age under 18: 28.7%; Age 65 and over: 19.4%; Males per 100 females: 92.8; Marriage status: 28.9% never married, 54.2% now married, 1.3% separated, 2.8% widowed, 14.2% divorced; Foreign born: 2.2%; Speak English only: 96.2%; With disability: 21.1%; Veterans: 16.6%; Ancestry: 29.9% German, 27.1% Irish, 14.1% American, 13.9% Italian, 11.6% Welsh
Employment: 11.2% management, business, and financial, 2.1% computer, engineering, and science, 0.0% education, legal, community service, arts, and media, 2.3% healthcare practitioners, 31.0% service, 40.8% sales and office, 1.8% natural resources, construction, and maintenance, 10.8% production, transportation, and material moving
Income: Per capita: $15,933; Median household: $37,833; Average household: $44,286; Households with income of $100,000 or more: 2.3%; Poverty rate: 8.6%
Educational Attainment: High school diploma or higher: 87.4%; Bachelor's degree or higher: 14.9%; Graduate/professional degree or higher: 3.9%
Housing: Homeownership rate: 40.0%; Median home value: $84,400; Median year structure built: 1965; Homeowner vacancy rate: 0.0%; Median

selected monthly owner costs: $1,295 with a mortgage, $443 without a mortgage; Median gross rent: $750 per month; Rental vacancy rate: 10.9%
Health Insurance: 98.7% have insurance; 60.8% have private insurance; 63.4% have public insurance; 1.3% do not have insurance; 0.0% of children under 18 do not have insurance
Transportation: Commute: 91.8% car, 0.0% public transportation, 0.0% walk, 8.2% work from home; Mean travel time to work: 17.3 minutes

CLARK MILLS (CDP).

Covers a land area of 1.492 square miles and a water area of 0.019 square miles. Located at 43.09° N. Lat; 75.38° W. Long. Elevation is 515 feet.
Population: 2,139; Growth (since 2000): 50.2%; Density: 1,433.4 persons per square mile; Race: 99.3% White, 0.0% Black/African American, 0.7% Asian, 0.0% American Indian/Alaska Native, 0.0% Native Hawaiian/Other Pacific Islander, 0.0% Two or more races, 1.1% Hispanic of any race; Average household size: 2.05; Median age: 45.4; Age under 18: 20.3%; Age 65 and over: 18.4%; Males per 100 females: 95.0; Marriage status: 22.4% never married, 54.2% now married, 0.9% separated, 8.5% widowed, 14.9% divorced; Foreign born: 1.7%; Speak English only: 95.7%; With disability: 11.8%; Veterans: 13.3%; Ancestry: 32.3% American, 22.3% German, 15.6% Irish, 14.4% Polish, 12.1% Italian
Employment: 14.8% management, business, and financial, 2.5% computer, engineering, and science, 13.5% education, legal, community service, arts, and media, 9.8% healthcare practitioners, 15.7% service, 23.5% sales and office, 8.6% natural resources, construction, and maintenance, 11.6% production, transportation, and material moving
Income: Per capita: $27,765; Median household: $52,222; Average household: $56,321; Households with income of $100,000 or more: 9.9%; Poverty rate: 19.0%
Educational Attainment: High school diploma or higher: 93.1%; Bachelor's degree or higher: 27.7%; Graduate/professional degree or higher: 8.2%
Housing: Homeownership rate: 54.7%; Median home value: $87,100; Median year structure built: 1973; Homeowner vacancy rate: 0.0%; Median selected monthly owner costs: $1,125 with a mortgage, $547 without a mortgage; Median gross rent: $812 per month; Rental vacancy rate: 4.4%
Health Insurance: 98.8% have insurance; 72.4% have private insurance; 45.2% have public insurance; 1.2% do not have insurance; 0.0% of children under 18 do not have insurance
Transportation: Commute: 98.3% car, 0.0% public transportation, 1.7% walk, 0.0% work from home; Mean travel time to work: 16.4 minutes

CLAYVILLE (village).

Covers a land area of 0.439 square miles and a water area of 0.004 square miles. Located at 42.98° N. Lat; 75.25° W. Long. Elevation is 961 feet.
Population: 328; Growth (since 2000): -26.3%; Density: 746.9 persons per square mile; Race: 96.3% White, 0.3% Black/African American, 0.0% Asian, 0.0% American Indian/Alaska Native, 0.0% Native Hawaiian/Other Pacific Islander, 3.4% Two or more races, 0.0% Hispanic of any race; Average household size: 2.34; Median age: 37.0; Age under 18: 20.4%; Age 65 and over: 9.5%; Males per 100 females: 113.4; Marriage status: 37.7% never married, 50.7% now married, 3.0% separated, 6.0% widowed, 5.6% divorced; Foreign born: 0.6%; Speak English only: 99.7%; With disability: 13.7%; Veterans: 10.3%; Ancestry: 27.4% American, 18.3% Irish, 16.8% Italian, 16.5% German, 12.2% English
Employment: 12.3% management, business, and financial, 3.7% computer, engineering, and science, 11.2% education, legal, community service, arts, and media, 1.1% healthcare practitioners, 26.2% service, 15.0% sales and office, 12.3% natural resources, construction, and maintenance, 18.2% production, transportation, and material moving
Income: Per capita: $23,338; Median household: $44,167; Average household: $52,976; Households with income of $100,000 or more: 9.3%; Poverty rate: 11.3%
Educational Attainment: High school diploma or higher: 85.7%; Bachelor's degree or higher: 13.4%; Graduate/professional degree or higher: 8.5%
Housing: Homeownership rate: 65.7%; Median home value: $77,800; Median year structure built: Before 1940; Homeowner vacancy rate: 0.0%; Median selected monthly owner costs: $1,083 with a mortgage, $458 without a mortgage; Median gross rent: $700 per month; Rental vacancy rate: 8.8%
Health Insurance: 89.3% have insurance; 75.6% have private insurance; 29.0% have public insurance; 10.7% do not have insurance; 10.4% of children under 18 do not have insurance

Transportation: Commute: 98.9% car, 0.0% public transportation, 0.0% walk, 1.1% work from home; Mean travel time to work: 20.5 minutes

CLINTON (village).

Covers a land area of 0.626 square miles and a water area of 0 square miles. Located at 43.05° N. Lat; 75.38° W. Long. Elevation is 604 feet.
History: Seat of Hamilton College. Elihu Root was born here. Clinton Village Historic District. Incorporated 1843.
Population: 1,850; Growth (since 2000): -5.2%; Density: 2,955.9 persons per square mile; Race: 93.8% White, 1.1% Black/African American, 2.3% Asian, 0.0% American Indian/Alaska Native, 0.0% Native Hawaiian/Other Pacific Islander, 2.2% Two or more races, 4.1% Hispanic of any race; Average household size: 2.14; Median age: 46.9; Age under 18: 19.2%; Age 65 and over: 19.7%; Males per 100 females: 90.2; Marriage status: 29.7% never married, 49.6% now married, 3.0% separated, 6.9% widowed, 13.8% divorced; Foreign born: 5.1%; Speak English only: 93.4%; With disability: 13.1%; Veterans: 7.8%; Ancestry: 26.1% German, 23.8% Irish, 18.8% English, 12.7% Italian, 6.6% American
Employment: 16.9% management, business, and financial, 5.0% computer, engineering, and science, 22.0% education, legal, community service, arts, and media, 11.9% healthcare practitioners, 15.5% service, 16.1% sales and office, 4.7% natural resources, construction, and maintenance, 7.8% production, transportation, and material moving
Income: Per capita: $37,824; Median household: $54,813; Average household: $76,328; Households with income of $100,000 or more: 21.3%; Poverty rate: 11.0%
Educational Attainment: High school diploma or higher: 97.5%; Bachelor's degree or higher: 54.8%; Graduate/professional degree or higher: 30.0%
School District(s)
Clinton Central SD (KG-12)
    2014-15 Enrollment: 1,305 . . . . (315) 557-2253
Four-year College(s)
Hamilton College (Private, Not-for-profit)
    Fall 2014 Enrollment: 1,904 . . . . (315) 859-4011
    2015-16 Tuition: In-state $49,500; Out-of-state $49,500
Housing: Homeownership rate: 56.6%; Median home value: $171,900; Median year structure built: Before 1940; Homeowner vacancy rate: 0.0%; Median selected monthly owner costs: $1,688 with a mortgage, $608 without a mortgage; Median gross rent: $849 per month; Rental vacancy rate: 0.0%
Health Insurance: 96.3% have insurance; 84.0% have private insurance; 28.4% have public insurance; 3.7% do not have insurance; 0.0% of children under 18 do not have insurance
Newspapers: Clinton Courier (weekly circulation 1,800)
Transportation: Commute: 86.4% car, 1.1% public transportation, 7.4% walk, 2.6% work from home; Mean travel time to work: 17.5 minutes

DEANSBORO (unincorporated postal area)
ZCTA: 13328

Covers a land area of 15.864 square miles and a water area of 0 square miles. Located at 42.99° N. Lat; 75.43° W. Long. Elevation is 817 feet.
Population: 1,389; Growth (since 2000): 9.7%; Density: 87.6 persons per square mile; Race: 99.4% White, 0.0% Black/African American, 0.4% Asian, 0.1% American Indian/Alaska Native, 0.0% Native Hawaiian/Other Pacific Islander, 0.0% Two or more races, 0.0% Hispanic of any race; Average household size: 2.49; Median age: 42.6; Age under 18: 22.0%; Age 65 and over: 13.0%; Males per 100 females: 107.0; Marriage status: 25.7% never married, 63.1% now married, 1.1% separated, 1.2% widowed, 10.0% divorced; Foreign born: 0.4%; Speak English only: 96.4%; With disability: 6.9%; Veterans: 5.3%; Ancestry: 28.2% American, 21.2% German, 13.5% Irish, 13.2% English, 8.9% Polish
Employment: 14.3% management, business, and financial, 2.1% computer, engineering, and science, 17.3% education, legal, community service, arts, and media, 6.4% healthcare practitioners, 21.9% service, 14.7% sales and office, 11.3% natural resources, construction, and maintenance, 12.2% production, transportation, and material moving
Income: Per capita: $28,415; Median household: $55,313; Average household: $69,322; Households with income of $100,000 or more: 19.2%; Poverty rate: 11.9%
Educational Attainment: High school diploma or higher: 92.0%; Bachelor's degree or higher: 33.3%; Graduate/professional degree or higher: 8.9%

Housing: Homeownership rate: 78.1%; Median home value: $129,100; Median year structure built: 1953; Homeowner vacancy rate: 0.0%; Median selected monthly owner costs: $1,243 with a mortgage, $458 without a mortgage; Median gross rent: $681 per month; Rental vacancy rate: 0.0%

Health Insurance: 93.2% have insurance; 77.6% have private insurance; 24.9% have public insurance; 6.8% do not have insurance; 5.6% of children under 18 do not have insurance

Transportation: Commute: 92.6% car, 0.0% public transportation, 0.7% walk, 6.3% work from home; Mean travel time to work: 25.6 minutes

DEERFIELD (town).
Covers a land area of 32.941 square miles and a water area of 0.107 square miles. Located at 43.19° N. Lat; 75.15° W. Long. Elevation is 443 feet.

Population: 4,281; Growth (since 2000): 9.6%; Density: 130.0 persons per square mile; Race: 97.2% White, 1.1% Black/African American, 0.7% Asian, 0.0% American Indian/Alaska Native, 0.0% Native Hawaiian/Other Pacific Islander, 0.8% Two or more races, 0.6% Hispanic of any race; Average household size: 2.69; Median age: 42.7; Age under 18: 20.0%; Age 65 and over: 14.8%; Males per 100 females: 98.7; Marriage status: 29.0% never married, 58.6% now married, 0.5% separated, 5.4% widowed, 7.0% divorced; Foreign born: 6.5%; Speak English only: 92.1%; With disability: 9.2%; Veterans: 8.0%; Ancestry: 26.2% Italian, 18.1% Irish, 17.9% German, 17.0% Polish, 10.9% American

Employment: 14.9% management, business, and financial, 5.9% computer, engineering, and science, 12.6% education, legal, community service, arts, and media, 9.4% healthcare practitioners, 16.6% service, 24.3% sales and office, 7.1% natural resources, construction, and maintenance, 9.2% production, transportation, and material moving

Income: Per capita: $30,432; Median household: $70,707; Average household: $80,350; Households with income of $100,000 or more: 31.9%; Poverty rate: 7.3%

Educational Attainment: High school diploma or higher: 93.5%; Bachelor's degree or higher: 31.3%; Graduate/professional degree or higher: 12.5%

Housing: Homeownership rate: 89.3%; Median home value: $142,000; Median year structure built: 1963; Homeowner vacancy rate: 0.0%; Median selected monthly owner costs: $1,404 with a mortgage, $508 without a mortgage; Median gross rent: $873 per month; Rental vacancy rate: 7.1%

Health Insurance: 91.7% have insurance; 81.0% have private insurance; 23.2% have public insurance; 8.3% do not have insurance; 4.9% of children under 18 do not have insurance

Transportation: Commute: 94.7% car, 0.2% public transportation, 0.8% walk, 4.2% work from home; Mean travel time to work: 19.2 minutes

Additional Information Contacts

Town of Deerfield . . . . (315) 724-0413
   http://townofdeerfield.org/content

DURHAMVILLE (CDP).
Covers a land area of 1.372 square miles and a water area of 0 square miles. Located at 43.12° N. Lat; 75.67° W. Long. Elevation is 433 feet.

Population: 806; Growth (since 2000): n/a; Density: 587.4 persons per square mile; Race: 100.0% White, 0.0% Black/African American, 0.0% Asian, 0.0% American Indian/Alaska Native, 0.0% Native Hawaiian/Other Pacific Islander, 0.0% Two or more races, 0.0% Hispanic of any race; Average household size: 3.05; Median age: 28.8; Age under 18: 42.7%; Age 65 and over: 16.0%; Males per 100 females: 115.5; Marriage status: 20.0% never married, 62.0% now married, 12.9% separated, 14.9% widowed, 3.1% divorced; Foreign born: 0.0%; Speak English only: 98.1%; With disability: 25.9%; Veterans: 6.1%; Ancestry: 43.5% American, 17.9% Scottish, 16.7% German, 10.4% Russian, 6.2% Welsh

Employment: 10.7% management, business, and financial, 0.0% computer, engineering, and science, 0.0% education, legal, community service, arts, and media, 0.0% healthcare practitioners, 12.1% service, 0.0% sales and office, 0.0% natural resources, construction, and maintenance, 77.1% production, transportation, and material moving

Income: Per capita: $12,982; Median household: $35,852; Average household: $36,181; Households with income of $100,000 or more: n/a; Poverty rate: 53.0%

Educational Attainment: High school diploma or higher: 87.0%; Bachelor's degree or higher: n/a; Graduate/professional degree or higher: n/a

School District(s)

Oneida City SD (PK-12)
   2014-15 Enrollment: 2,292 . . . . (315) 363-2550

Housing: Homeownership rate: 36.4%; Median home value: $94,900; Median year structure built: Before 1940; Homeowner vacancy rate: 0.0%; Median selected monthly owner costs: n/a with a mortgage, n/a without a mortgage; Median gross rent: $722 per month; Rental vacancy rate: 0.0%

Health Insurance: 100.0% have insurance; 31.0% have private insurance; 80.6% have public insurance; 0.0% do not have insurance; 0.0% of children under 18 do not have insurance

Transportation: Commute: 100.0% car, 0.0% public transportation, 0.0% walk, 0.0% work from home; Mean travel time to work: 0.0 minutes

FLORENCE (town).
Covers a land area of 54.922 square miles and a water area of 0.094 square miles. Located at 43.42° N. Lat; 75.74° W. Long. Elevation is 978 feet.

Population: 1,011; Growth (since 2000): -6.9%; Density: 18.4 persons per square mile; Race: 96.8% White, 0.6% Black/African American, 0.7% Asian, 0.0% American Indian/Alaska Native, 0.0% Native Hawaiian/Other Pacific Islander, 1.0% Two or more races, 2.0% Hispanic of any race; Average household size: 2.57; Median age: 43.4; Age under 18: 19.6%; Age 65 and over: 13.2%; Males per 100 females: 102.2; Marriage status: 33.4% never married, 54.1% now married, 2.5% separated, 4.5% widowed, 8.0% divorced; Foreign born: 0.7%; Speak English only: 96.9%; With disability: 17.0%; Veterans: 10.8%; Ancestry: 21.8% American, 18.7% German, 16.7% Irish, 13.6% English, 9.5% French

Employment: 5.7% management, business, and financial, 1.9% computer, engineering, and science, 7.8% education, legal, community service, arts, and media, 5.7% healthcare practitioners, 12.3% service, 20.7% sales and office, 14.4% natural resources, construction, and maintenance, 31.5% production, transportation, and material moving

Income: Per capita: $19,306; Median household: $42,543; Average household: $47,700; Households with income of $100,000 or more: 7.9%; Poverty rate: 8.7%

Educational Attainment: High school diploma or higher: 82.9%; Bachelor's degree or higher: 10.7%; Graduate/professional degree or higher: 2.5%

Housing: Homeownership rate: 77.6%; Median home value: $84,400; Median year structure built: 1982; Homeowner vacancy rate: 0.0%; Median selected monthly owner costs: $952 with a mortgage, $422 without a mortgage; Median gross rent: $715 per month; Rental vacancy rate: 7.4%

Health Insurance: 92.4% have insurance; 63.7% have private insurance; 41.6% have public insurance; 7.6% do not have insurance; 1.5% of children under 18 do not have insurance

Transportation: Commute: 91.4% car, 0.0% public transportation, 0.0% walk, 4.7% work from home; Mean travel time to work: 32.1 minutes

FLOYD (town).
Covers a land area of 34.616 square miles and a water area of 0.175 square miles. Located at 43.24° N. Lat; 75.32° W. Long. Elevation is 561 feet.

Population: 3,803; Growth (since 2000): -1.7%; Density: 109.9 persons per square mile; Race: 96.0% White, 0.5% Black/African American, 0.3% Asian, 1.9% American Indian/Alaska Native, 0.0% Native Hawaiian/Other Pacific Islander, 1.3% Two or more races, 1.7% Hispanic of any race; Average household size: 2.64; Median age: 43.3; Age under 18: 23.6%; Age 65 and over: 15.9%; Males per 100 females: 102.6; Marriage status: 25.4% never married, 53.5% now married, 2.8% separated, 6.9% widowed, 14.2% divorced; Foreign born: 0.9%; Speak English only: 97.8%; With disability: 17.7%; Veterans: 11.4%; Ancestry: 22.4% Italian, 21.2% German, 17.7% American, 14.9% Irish, 9.6% English

Employment: 9.0% management, business, and financial, 6.3% computer, engineering, and science, 17.2% education, legal, community service, arts, and media, 11.7% healthcare practitioners, 14.5% service, 22.1% sales and office, 10.7% natural resources, construction, and maintenance, 8.5% production, transportation, and material moving

Income: Per capita: $31,707; Median household: $60,139; Average household: $81,339; Households with income of $100,000 or more: 28.8%; Poverty rate: 11.4%

Educational Attainment: High school diploma or higher: 95.5%; Bachelor's degree or higher: 21.0%; Graduate/professional degree or higher: 6.0%

Housing: Homeownership rate: 91.3%; Median home value: $103,900; Median year structure built: 1977; Homeowner vacancy rate: 1.7%; Median selected monthly owner costs: $1,540 with a mortgage, $526 without a mortgage; Median gross rent: $516 per month; Rental vacancy rate: 15.0%

Health Insurance: 89.9% have insurance; 65.6% have private insurance; 37.7% have public insurance; 10.1% do not have insurance; 8.5% of children under 18 do not have insurance

Transportation: Commute: 95.7% car, 0.0% public transportation, 0.7% walk, 1.9% work from home; Mean travel time to work: 21.8 minutes
Additional Information Contacts
Town of Floyd . . . . (315) 865-4256
　http://town.floyd.ny.us

FORESTPORT (town). Covers a land area of 76.915 square miles and a water area of 1.985 square miles. Located at 43.50° N. Lat; 75.15° W. Long. Elevation is 1,122 feet.
Population: 1,509; Growth (since 2000): -10.8%; Density: 19.6 persons per square mile; Race: 99.5% White, 0.0% Black/African American, 0.0% Asian, 0.1% American Indian/Alaska Native, 0.0% Native Hawaiian/Other Pacific Islander, 0.3% Two or more races, 0.0% Hispanic of any race; Average household size: 2.13; Median age: 54.4; Age under 18: 11.6%; Age 65 and over: 24.7%; Males per 100 females: 105.8; Marriage status: 21.7% never married, 53.6% now married, 1.2% separated, 8.3% widowed, 16.4% divorced; Foreign born: 0.5%; Speak English only: 99.3%; With disability: 18.5%; Veterans: 13.9%; Ancestry: 22.9% German, 20.3% Irish, 16.9% English, 13.7% American, 10.5% Italian
Employment: 12.3% management, business, and financial, 0.0% computer, engineering, and science, 8.5% education, legal, community service, arts, and media, 5.8% healthcare practitioners, 20.5% service, 28.9% sales and office, 18.8% natural resources, construction, and maintenance, 5.2% production, transportation, and material moving
Income: Per capita: $28,200; Median household: $47,663; Average household: $58,678; Households with income of $100,000 or more: 17.6%; Poverty rate: 14.2%
Educational Attainment: High school diploma or higher: 90.5%; Bachelor's degree or higher: 19.2%; Graduate/professional degree or higher: 7.4%

School District(s)
Adirondack Central SD (PK-12)
　2014-15 Enrollment: 1,322 . . . . (315) 942-9200
Housing: Homeownership rate: 80.7%; Median home value: $134,000; Median year structure built: 1970; Homeowner vacancy rate: 13.1%; Median selected monthly owner costs: $1,047 with a mortgage, $421 without a mortgage; Median gross rent: $696 per month; Rental vacancy rate: 6.2%
Health Insurance: 94.2% have insurance; 69.0% have private insurance; 46.1% have public insurance; 5.8% do not have insurance; 1.7% of children under 18 do not have insurance
Transportation: Commute: 88.7% car, 0.0% public transportation, 5.6% walk, 5.6% work from home; Mean travel time to work: 33.7 minutes

FRANKLIN SPRINGS (unincorporated postal area)
ZCTA: 13341
　Covers a land area of 0.184 square miles and a water area of 0 square miles. Located at 43.04° N. Lat; 75.40° W. Long. Elevation is 630 feet.
Population: 142; Growth (since 2000): 163.0%; Density: 771.1 persons per square mile; Race: 100.0% White, 0.0% Black/African American, 0.0% Asian, 0.0% American Indian/Alaska Native, 0.0% Native Hawaiian/Other Pacific Islander, 0.0% Two or more races, 0.0% Hispanic of any race; Average household size: 2.33; Median age: 36.2; Age under 18: 21.8%; Age 65 and over: 26.8%; Males per 100 females: 82.1; Marriage status: 15.3% never married, 80.2% now married, 0.0% separated, 0.0% widowed, 4.5% divorced; Foreign born: 0.0%; Speak English only: 100.0%; With disability: 7.0%; Veterans: 17.1%; Ancestry: 41.5% Italian, 28.2% Turkish, 27.5% Irish, 26.1% English, 9.9% Swedish
Employment: 0.0% management, business, and financial, 7.3% computer, engineering, and science, 17.1% education, legal, community service, arts, and media, 6.1% healthcare practitioners, 31.7% service, 31.7% sales and office, 6.1% natural resources, construction, and maintenance, 0.0% production, transportation, and material moving
Income: Per capita: $37,724; Median household: $107,938; Average household: $87,925; Households with income of $100,000 or more: 55.7%; Poverty rate: 11.3%
Educational Attainment: High school diploma or higher: 95.3%; Bachelor's degree or higher: 50.9%; Graduate/professional degree or higher: 26.4%
Housing: Homeownership rate: 100.0%; Median home value: n/a; Median year structure built: 1952; Homeowner vacancy rate: 0.0%; Median selected monthly owner costs: n/a with a mortgage, n/a without a mortgage; Median gross rent: n/a per month; Rental vacancy rate: 0.0%

Health Insurance: 96.5% have insurance; 96.5% have private insurance; 16.9% have public insurance; 3.5% do not have insurance; 0.0% of children under 18 do not have insurance
Transportation: Commute: 100.0% car, 0.0% public transportation, 0.0% walk, 0.0% work from home; Mean travel time to work: 18.5 minutes

HINCKLEY (unincorporated postal area)
ZCTA: 13352
　Covers a land area of 0.168 square miles and a water area of 0.017 square miles. Located at 43.31° N. Lat; 75.12° W. Long. Elevation is 1,197 feet.
Population: 146; Growth (since 2000): n/a; Density: 870.3 persons per square mile; Race: 100.0% White, 0.0% Black/African American, 0.0% Asian, 0.0% American Indian/Alaska Native, 0.0% Native Hawaiian/Other Pacific Islander, 0.0% Two or more races, 0.0% Hispanic of any race; Average household size: 2.98; Median age: 38.4; Age under 18: 27.4%; Age 65 and over: 8.2%; Males per 100 females: 71.1; Marriage status: 22.6% never married, 39.6% now married, 0.0% separated, 0.0% widowed, 37.7% divorced; Foreign born: 0.0%; Speak English only: 87.0%; With disability: 13.0%; Veterans: 0.0%; Ancestry: 58.9% Welsh, 58.2% Irish, 42.5% French, 14.4% Dutch, 13.0% Italian
Employment: 0.0% management, business, and financial, 0.0% computer, engineering, and science, 0.0% education, legal, community service, arts, and media, 0.0% healthcare practitioners, 38.9% service, 16.7% sales and office, 0.0% natural resources, construction, and maintenance, 44.4% production, transportation, and material moving
Income: Per capita: $10,708; Median household: n/a; Average household: $30,398; Households with income of $100,000 or more: n/a; Poverty rate: 13.0%
Educational Attainment: High school diploma or higher: 48.8%; Bachelor's degree or higher: n/a; Graduate/professional degree or higher: n/a
Housing: Homeownership rate: 100.0%; Median home value: n/a; Median year structure built: Before 1940; Homeowner vacancy rate: 0.0%; Median selected monthly owner costs: n/a with a mortgage, n/a without a mortgage; Median gross rent: n/a per month; Rental vacancy rate: 0.0%
Health Insurance: 100.0% have insurance; 87.0% have private insurance; 21.2% have public insurance; 0.0% do not have insurance; 0.0% of children under 18 do not have insurance
Transportation: Commute: 100.0% car, 0.0% public transportation, 0.0% walk, 0.0% work from home; Mean travel time to work: 0.0 minutes

HOLLAND PATENT (village). Covers a land area of 0.506 square miles and a water area of 0.002 square miles. Located at 43.24° N. Lat; 75.26° W. Long. Elevation is 640 feet.
Population: 373; Growth (since 2000): -19.1%; Density: 737.8 persons per square mile; Race: 99.2% White, 0.0% Black/African American, 0.0% Asian, 0.0% American Indian/Alaska Native, 0.0% Native Hawaiian/Other Pacific Islander, 0.8% Two or more races, 0.0% Hispanic of any race; Average household size: 2.35; Median age: 42.3; Age under 18: 18.8%; Age 65 and over: 19.6%; Males per 100 females: 96.6; Marriage status: 32.4% never married, 48.6% now married, 2.1% separated, 4.6% widowed, 14.4% divorced; Foreign born: 0.8%; Speak English only: 97.3%; With disability: 7.3%; Veterans: 16.6%; Ancestry: 26.0% American, 19.8% German, 18.0% Irish, 9.1% English, 8.8% Welsh
Employment: 8.1% management, business, and financial, 0.9% computer, engineering, and science, 12.3% education, legal, community service, arts, and media, 14.2% healthcare practitioners, 24.2% service, 18.5% sales and office, 10.0% natural resources, construction, and maintenance, 11.8% production, transportation, and material moving
Income: Per capita: $29,638; Median household: $67,708; Average household: $70,121; Households with income of $100,000 or more: 19.5%; Poverty rate: 9.4%
Educational Attainment: High school diploma or higher: 95.7%; Bachelor's degree or higher: 24.5%; Graduate/professional degree or higher: 11.9%

School District(s)
Holland Patent Central SD (PK-12)
　2014-15 Enrollment: 1,512 . . . . (315) 865-7221
Housing: Homeownership rate: 79.2%; Median home value: $140,600; Median year structure built: Before 1940; Homeowner vacancy rate: 6.7%; Median selected monthly owner costs: $1,296 with a mortgage, $591

without a mortgage; Median gross rent: $683 per month; Rental vacancy rate: 41.1%

Health Insurance: 96.5% have insurance; 85.4% have private insurance; 37.7% have public insurance; 3.5% do not have insurance; 0.0% of children under 18 do not have insurance

Transportation: Commute: 91.1% car, 0.0% public transportation, 6.1% walk, 2.8% work from home; Mean travel time to work: 17.7 minutes

Additional Information Contacts

Village of Holland Patent . . . . (315) 865-4853
  http://village.holland-patent.ny.us/content

KIRKLAND (town). Covers a land area of 33.783 square miles and a water area of 0.051 square miles. Located at 43.04° N. Lat; 75.38° W. Long. Elevation is 528 feet.

Population: 10,231; Growth (since 2000): 0.9%; Density: 302.8 persons per square mile; Race: 92.1% White, 2.7% Black/African American, 3.0% Asian, 0.0% American Indian/Alaska Native, 0.0% Native Hawaiian/Other Pacific Islander, 1.2% Two or more races, 2.8% Hispanic of any race; Average household size: 2.26; Median age: 38.0; Age under 18: 15.0%; Age 65 and over: 18.0%; Males per 100 females: 90.5; Marriage status: 41.9% never married, 41.5% now married, 1.4% separated, 7.5% widowed, 9.2% divorced; Foreign born: 7.4%; Speak English only: 90.9%; With disability: 9.8%; Veterans: 7.2%; Ancestry: 20.9% German, 18.1% American, 16.7% Irish, 13.5% English, 12.7% Italian

Employment: 15.8% management, business, and financial, 5.8% computer, engineering, and science, 17.6% education, legal, community service, arts, and media, 8.5% healthcare practitioners, 16.0% service, 23.7% sales and office, 5.1% natural resources, construction, and maintenance, 7.4% production, transportation, and material moving

Income: Per capita: $31,880; Median household: $63,031; Average household: $86,215; Households with income of $100,000 or more: 24.6%; Poverty rate: 7.3%

Educational Attainment: High school diploma or higher: 95.0%; Bachelor's degree or higher: 43.8%; Graduate/professional degree or higher: 20.5%

Housing: Homeownership rate: 61.7%; Median home value: $168,300; Median year structure built: 1960; Homeowner vacancy rate: 2.2%; Median selected monthly owner costs: $1,526 with a mortgage, $594 without a mortgage; Median gross rent: $861 per month; Rental vacancy rate: 2.8%

Health Insurance: 96.0% have insurance; 81.8% have private insurance; 28.4% have public insurance; 4.0% do not have insurance; 0.5% of children under 18 do not have insurance

Safety: Violent crime rate: 0.0 per 10,000 population; Property crime rate: 25.1 per 10,000 population

Transportation: Commute: 82.4% car, 0.2% public transportation, 10.7% walk, 5.8% work from home; Mean travel time to work: 16.0 minutes

Additional Information Contacts

Town of Kirkland . . . . (315) 853-5401
  http://townofkirkland.org/content

KNOXBORO (unincorporated postal area)
ZCTA: 13362

Covers a land area of 0.276 square miles and a water area of 0 square miles. Located at 42.98° N. Lat; 75.52° W. Long. Elevation is 1,096 feet.

Population: 102; Growth (since 2000): n/a; Density: 369.5 persons per square mile; Race: 100.0% White, 0.0% Black/African American, 0.0% Asian, 0.0% American Indian/Alaska Native, 0.0% Native Hawaiian/Other Pacific Islander, 0.0% Two or more races, 0.0% Hispanic of any race; Average household size: 2.13; Median age: 38.8; Age under 18: 9.8%; Age 65 and over: 11.8%; Males per 100 females: 93.5; Marriage status: 30.4% never married, 34.8% now married, 0.0% separated, 0.0% widowed, 34.8% divorced; Foreign born: 0.0%; Speak English only: 100.0%; With disability: 0.0%; Veterans: 18.6%; Ancestry: 39.2% Italian, 25.5% German, 15.7% American, 15.7% Irish, 5.9% Welsh

Employment: 14.5% management, business, and financial, 0.0% computer, engineering, and science, 0.0% education, legal, community service, arts, and media, 8.1% healthcare practitioners, 8.1% service, 61.3% sales and office, 0.0% natural resources, construction, and maintenance, 8.1% production, transportation, and material moving

Income: Per capita: $37,878; Median household: n/a; Average household: $74,048; Households with income of $100,000 or more: 35.4%; Poverty rate: 11.8%

Educational Attainment: High school diploma or higher: 100.0%; Bachelor's degree or higher: 25.0%; Graduate/professional degree or higher: 13.0%

Housing: Homeownership rate: 66.7%; Median home value: n/a; Median year structure built: Before 1940; Homeowner vacancy rate: 0.0%; Median selected monthly owner costs: $1,573 with a mortgage, $0 without a mortgage; Median gross rent: n/a per month; Rental vacancy rate: 0.0%

Health Insurance: 100.0% have insurance; 87.5% have private insurance; 25.0% have public insurance; 0.0% do not have insurance; 0.0% of children under 18 do not have insurance

Transportation: Commute: 76.5% car, 0.0% public transportation, 0.0% walk, 23.5% work from home; Mean travel time to work: 31.8 minutes

LEE (town). Covers a land area of 45.106 square miles and a water area of 0.447 square miles. Located at 43.33° N. Lat; 75.52° W. Long. Elevation is 505 feet.

Population: 6,488; Growth (since 2000): -5.6%; Density: 143.8 persons per square mile; Race: 95.1% White, 2.3% Black/African American, 0.8% Asian, 0.0% American Indian/Alaska Native, 0.0% Native Hawaiian/Other Pacific Islander, 1.1% Two or more races, 3.3% Hispanic of any race; Average household size: 2.51; Median age: 46.3; Age under 18: 20.1%; Age 65 and over: 20.6%; Males per 100 females: 97.7; Marriage status: 23.1% never married, 60.3% now married, 0.9% separated, 7.0% widowed, 9.6% divorced; Foreign born: 2.2%; Speak English only: 97.2%; With disability: 15.4%; Veterans: 11.9%; Ancestry: 21.8% Italian, 18.6% German, 15.8% American, 15.1% Irish, 10.2% Polish

Employment: 14.3% management, business, and financial, 2.9% computer, engineering, and science, 12.8% education, legal, community service, arts, and media, 5.1% healthcare practitioners, 20.2% service, 22.2% sales and office, 12.0% natural resources, construction, and maintenance, 10.5% production, transportation, and material moving

Income: Per capita: $31,459; Median household: $65,283; Average household: $77,228; Households with income of $100,000 or more: 25.8%; Poverty rate: 5.4%

Educational Attainment: High school diploma or higher: 92.2%; Bachelor's degree or higher: 22.6%; Graduate/professional degree or higher: 8.4%

Housing: Homeownership rate: 86.2%; Median home value: $123,400; Median year structure built: 1968; Homeowner vacancy rate: 3.0%; Median selected monthly owner costs: $1,160 with a mortgage, $488 without a mortgage; Median gross rent: $936 per month; Rental vacancy rate: 0.0%

Health Insurance: 94.9% have insurance; 77.7% have private insurance; 36.1% have public insurance; 5.1% do not have insurance; 4.4% of children under 18 do not have insurance

Transportation: Commute: 91.8% car, 0.6% public transportation, 0.6% walk, 5.1% work from home; Mean travel time to work: 23.8 minutes

Additional Information Contacts

Town of Lee . . . . (315) 336-3438
  http://townofleeny.org/content

LEE CENTER (unincorporated postal area)
ZCTA: 13363

Covers a land area of 21.188 square miles and a water area of 0.045 square miles. Located at 43.32° N. Lat; 75.51° W. Long. Elevation is 617 feet.

Population: 2,244; Growth (since 2000): -6.4%; Density: 105.9 persons per square mile; Race: 98.1% White, 0.4% Black/African American, 0.0% Asian, 0.0% American Indian/Alaska Native, 0.0% Native Hawaiian/Other Pacific Islander, 0.0% Two or more races, 4.3% Hispanic of any race; Average household size: 2.60; Median age: 40.9; Age under 18: 19.6%; Age 65 and over: 16.4%; Males per 100 females: 98.7; Marriage status: 23.2% never married, 55.7% now married, 1.0% separated, 7.4% widowed, 13.7% divorced; Foreign born: 1.4%; Speak English only: 97.1%; With disability: 17.3%; Veterans: 14.0%; Ancestry: 19.8% German, 17.7% American, 14.9% Italian, 14.7% Irish, 8.6% English

Employment: 13.3% management, business, and financial, 3.4% computer, engineering, and science, 11.5% education, legal, community service, arts, and media, 6.1% healthcare practitioners, 22.4% service, 18.5% sales and office, 12.7% natural resources, construction, and maintenance, 12.0% production, transportation, and material moving

Income: Per capita: $27,474; Median household: $58,947; Average household: $69,241; Households with income of $100,000 or more: 23.3%; Poverty rate: 10.6%

Educational Attainment: High school diploma or higher: 94.3%; Bachelor's degree or higher: 17.3%; Graduate/professional degree or higher: 5.1%
Housing: Homeownership rate: 80.0%; Median home value: $109,000; Median year structure built: 1977; Homeowner vacancy rate: 9.0%; Median selected monthly owner costs: $1,139 with a mortgage, $504 without a mortgage; Median gross rent: $954 per month; Rental vacancy rate: 0.0%
Health Insurance: 95.9% have insurance; 74.5% have private insurance; 40.1% have public insurance; 4.1% do not have insurance; 0.0% of children under 18 do not have insurance
Transportation: Commute: 93.8% car, 0.0% public transportation, 0.9% walk, 2.6% work from home; Mean travel time to work: 25.2 minutes

MARCY (town). Covers a land area of 32.890 square miles and a water area of 0.428 square miles. Located at 43.17° N. Lat; 75.27° W. Long. Elevation is 604 feet.
Population: 9,258; Growth (since 2000): -2.2%; Density: 281.5 persons per square mile; Race: 75.2% White, 12.7% Black/African American, 3.0% Asian, 0.5% American Indian/Alaska Native, 0.0% Native Hawaiian/Other Pacific Islander, 5.3% Two or more races, 9.2% Hispanic of any race; Average household size: 2.84; Median age: 39.9; Age under 18: 16.6%; Age 65 and over: 10.2%; Males per 100 females: 208.9; Marriage status: 42.9% never married, 42.5% now married, 2.8% separated, 4.6% widowed, 9.9% divorced; Foreign born: 8.3%; Speak English only: 83.9%; With disability: 13.6%; Veterans: 7.7%; Ancestry: 16.1% American, 15.4% German, 12.3% Italian, 11.8% Irish, 11.3% Polish
Employment: 9.6% management, business, and financial, 2.0% computer, engineering, and science, 16.3% education, legal, community service, arts, and media, 5.9% healthcare practitioners, 17.1% service, 28.9% sales and office, 9.5% natural resources, construction, and maintenance, 10.7% production, transportation, and material moving
Income: Per capita: $25,208; Median household: $76,060; Average household: $96,952; Households with income of $100,000 or more: 29.8%; Poverty rate: 6.7%
Educational Attainment: High school diploma or higher: 82.7%; Bachelor's degree or higher: 24.6%; Graduate/professional degree or higher: 8.2%

School District(s)
Whitesboro Central SD (KG-12)
    2014-15 Enrollment: 3,298 . . . . (315) 266-3303
Housing: Homeownership rate: 86.9%; Median home value: $162,400; Median year structure built: 1966; Homeowner vacancy rate: 1.9%; Median selected monthly owner costs: $1,524 with a mortgage, $559 without a mortgage; Median gross rent: $805 per month; Rental vacancy rate: 0.0%
Health Insurance: 95.4% have insurance; 81.5% have private insurance; 29.2% have public insurance; 4.6% do not have insurance; 2.0% of children under 18 do not have insurance
Transportation: Commute: 88.9% car, 1.5% public transportation, 0.5% walk, 8.2% work from home; Mean travel time to work: 19.0 minutes
Additional Information Contacts
Town of Marcy . . . . (315) 768-4800
   http://townofmarcy.org/content

MARSHALL (town). Covers a land area of 32.802 square miles and a water area of 0 square miles. Located at 42.97° N. Lat; 75.39° W. Long. Elevation is 1,365 feet.
Population: 2,073; Growth (since 2000): -2.5%; Density: 63.2 persons per square mile; Race: 98.9% White, 0.0% Black/African American, 0.3% Asian, 0.1% American Indian/Alaska Native, 0.0% Native Hawaiian/Other Pacific Islander, 0.6% Two or more races, 0.7% Hispanic of any race; Average household size: 2.52; Median age: 40.0; Age under 18: 22.3%; Age 65 and over: 16.1%; Males per 100 females: 105.5; Marriage status: 26.8% never married, 59.3% now married, 2.1% separated, 4.1% widowed, 9.8% divorced; Foreign born: 0.9%; Speak English only: 95.5%; With disability: 9.8%; Veterans: 9.8%; Ancestry: 23.9% American, 18.9% Irish, 16.2% German, 14.4% English, 8.5% Italian
Employment: 15.0% management, business, and financial, 1.6% computer, engineering, and science, 13.2% education, legal, community service, arts, and media, 3.9% healthcare practitioners, 23.8% service, 16.1% sales and office, 10.9% natural resources, construction, and maintenance, 15.6% production, transportation, and material moving
Income: Per capita: $26,280; Median household: $50,329; Average household: $64,395; Households with income of $100,000 or more: 21.7%; Poverty rate: 13.4%

Educational Attainment: High school diploma or higher: 89.0%; Bachelor's degree or higher: 25.5%; Graduate/professional degree or higher: 9.2%
Housing: Homeownership rate: 79.5%; Median home value: $111,700; Median year structure built: 1956; Homeowner vacancy rate: 0.0%; Median selected monthly owner costs: $1,158 with a mortgage, $462 without a mortgage; Median gross rent: $664 per month; Rental vacancy rate: 0.0%
Health Insurance: 91.3% have insurance; 69.6% have private insurance; 32.7% have public insurance; 8.7% do not have insurance; 6.3% of children under 18 do not have insurance
Transportation: Commute: 92.1% car, 0.3% public transportation, 3.5% walk, 3.8% work from home; Mean travel time to work: 24.9 minutes

NEW HARTFORD (town). Covers a land area of 25.357 square miles and a water area of 0.118 square miles. Located at 43.06° N. Lat; 75.28° W. Long. Elevation is 541 feet.
History: Settled c.1787, incorporated 1870.
Population: 22,090; Growth (since 2000): 4.3%; Density: 871.2 persons per square mile; Race: 93.4% White, 1.9% Black/African American, 3.2% Asian, 0.4% American Indian/Alaska Native, 0.0% Native Hawaiian/Other Pacific Islander, 1.0% Two or more races, 1.4% Hispanic of any race; Average household size: 2.27; Median age: 47.3; Age under 18: 18.9%; Age 65 and over: 25.1%; Males per 100 females: 86.6; Marriage status: 25.7% never married, 53.7% now married, 1.3% separated, 11.3% widowed, 9.3% divorced; Foreign born: 7.0%; Speak English only: 91.3%; With disability: 13.1%; Veterans: 10.6%; Ancestry: 24.1% Italian, 19.2% Irish, 17.0% German, 13.8% American, 9.6% Polish
Employment: 16.3% management, business, and financial, 5.3% computer, engineering, and science, 15.2% education, legal, community service, arts, and media, 8.7% healthcare practitioners, 15.8% service, 25.7% sales and office, 5.8% natural resources, construction, and maintenance, 7.3% production, transportation, and material moving
Income: Per capita: $38,676; Median household: $60,603; Average household: $88,880; Households with income of $100,000 or more: 27.4%; Poverty rate: 6.0%
Educational Attainment: High school diploma or higher: 93.4%; Bachelor's degree or higher: 40.3%; Graduate/professional degree or higher: 19.9%

School District(s)
New Hartford Central SD (KG-12)
    2014-15 Enrollment: 2,644 . . . . (315) 624-1218
Oneida-Herkimer-Madison Boces
    2014-15 Enrollment: n/a . . . . (315) 793-8561
Housing: Homeownership rate: 72.4%; Median home value: $154,000; Median year structure built: 1964; Homeowner vacancy rate: 1.7%; Median selected monthly owner costs: $1,379 with a mortgage, $573 without a mortgage; Median gross rent: $804 per month; Rental vacancy rate: 11.3%
Health Insurance: 97.0% have insurance; 83.0% have private insurance; 33.5% have public insurance; 3.0% do not have insurance; 1.1% of children under 18 do not have insurance
Safety: Violent crime rate: 5.9 per 10,000 population; Property crime rate: 406.2 per 10,000 population
Transportation: Commute: 94.3% car, 0.1% public transportation, 1.3% walk, 4.1% work from home; Mean travel time to work: 16.7 minutes
Additional Information Contacts
Town of New Hartford . . . . (315) 733-7500
   http://www.newhartfordtown.com

NEW HARTFORD (village). Covers a land area of 0.617 square miles and a water area of 0 square miles. Located at 43.07° N. Lat; 75.29° W. Long. Elevation is 541 feet.
Population: 1,813; Growth (since 2000): -3.9%; Density: 2,939.6 persons per square mile; Race: 96.4% White, 2.6% Black/African American, 0.0% Asian, 0.4% American Indian/Alaska Native, 0.0% Native Hawaiian/Other Pacific Islander, 0.5% Two or more races, 3.1% Hispanic of any race; Average household size: 2.17; Median age: 46.2; Age under 18: 21.7%; Age 65 and over: 20.7%; Males per 100 females: 82.5; Marriage status: 27.3% never married, 50.4% now married, 3.1% separated, 12.2% widowed, 10.1% divorced; Foreign born: 2.1%; Speak English only: 98.7%; With disability: 15.3%; Veterans: 10.1%; Ancestry: 25.0% Irish, 22.6% Italian, 20.2% German, 12.9% English, 11.3% American
Employment: 17.4% management, business, and financial, 4.2% computer, engineering, and science, 19.8% education, legal, community service, arts, and media, 6.7% healthcare practitioners, 10.8% service,

26.2% sales and office, 6.0% natural resources, construction, and maintenance, 8.8% production, transportation, and material moving
Income: Per capita: $37,160; Median household: $54,961; Average household: $78,064; Households with income of $100,000 or more: 30.0%; Poverty rate: 10.8%
Educational Attainment: High school diploma or higher: 95.1%; Bachelor's degree or higher: 44.9%; Graduate/professional degree or higher: 20.5%

School District(s)
New Hartford Central SD (KG-12)
    2014-15 Enrollment: 2,644 . . . . (315) 624-1218
Oneida-Herkimer-Madison Boces
    2014-15 Enrollment: n/a . . . . (315) 793-8561
Housing: Homeownership rate: 65.9%; Median home value: $158,700; Median year structure built: 1941; Homeowner vacancy rate: 3.3%; Median selected monthly owner costs: $1,497 with a mortgage, $619 without a mortgage; Median gross rent: $961 per month; Rental vacancy rate: 0.0%
Health Insurance: 96.5% have insurance; 86.2% have private insurance; 26.5% have public insurance; 3.5% do not have insurance; 0.0% of children under 18 do not have insurance
Transportation: Commute: 87.1% car, 0.1% public transportation, 8.6% walk, 2.0% work from home; Mean travel time to work: 15.5 minutes

NEW YORK MILLS (village).
Covers a land area of 1.180 square miles and a water area of 0 square miles. Located at 43.10° N. Lat; 75.29° W. Long. Elevation is 466 feet.
History: Incorporated 1922.
Population: 3,243; Growth (since 2000): 1.6%; Density: 2,748.4 persons per square mile; Race: 96.9% White, 1.0% Black/African American, 0.7% Asian, 0.0% American Indian/Alaska Native, 0.0% Native Hawaiian/Other Pacific Islander, 1.3% Two or more races, 0.0% Hispanic of any race; Average household size: 2.03; Median age: 43.3; Age under 18: 26.7%; Age 65 and over: 24.3%; Males per 100 females: 92.1; Marriage status: 31.7% never married, 37.1% now married, 2.3% separated, 11.7% widowed, 19.6% divorced; Foreign born: 3.3%; Speak English only: 89.1%; With disability: 16.5%; Veterans: 15.8%; Ancestry: 25.9% Polish, 21.5% American, 20.2% Italian, 11.3% Irish, 10.7% German
Employment: 10.0% management, business, and financial, 1.4% computer, engineering, and science, 9.2% education, legal, community service, arts, and media, 5.3% healthcare practitioners, 20.1% service, 27.7% sales and office, 9.0% natural resources, construction, and maintenance, 17.4% production, transportation, and material moving
Income: Per capita: $21,532; Median household: $32,383; Average household: $42,405; Households with income of $100,000 or more: 8.4%; Poverty rate: 18.2%
Educational Attainment: High school diploma or higher: 95.2%; Bachelor's degree or higher: 14.1%; Graduate/professional degree or higher: 3.4%

School District(s)
New York Mills Union Free SD (KG-12)
    2014-15 Enrollment: 589 . . . . (315) 768-8127
Housing: Homeownership rate: 42.2%; Median home value: $109,500; Median year structure built: 1948; Homeowner vacancy rate: 5.7%; Median selected monthly owner costs: $1,068 with a mortgage, $391 without a mortgage; Median gross rent: $743 per month; Rental vacancy rate: 8.9%
Health Insurance: 99.0% have insurance; 63.7% have private insurance; 56.8% have public insurance; 1.0% do not have insurance; 0.0% of children under 18 do not have insurance
Transportation: Commute: 96.6% car, 0.0% public transportation, 3.4% walk, 0.0% work from home; Mean travel time to work: 13.9 minutes

NORTH BAY (unincorporated postal area)
ZCTA: 13123
    Covers a land area of 2.366 square miles and a water area of 0 square miles. Located at 43.23° N. Lat; 75.77° W. Long. Elevation is 476 feet.
Population: 229; Growth (since 2000): n/a; Density: 96.8 persons per square mile; Race: 100.0% White, 0.0% Black/African American, 0.0% Asian, 0.0% American Indian/Alaska Native, 0.0% Native Hawaiian/Other Pacific Islander, 0.0% Two or more races, 0.0% Hispanic of any race; Average household size: 2.79; Median age: 58.1; Age under 18: 0.0%; Age 65 and over: 20.1%; Males per 100 females: 101.3; Marriage status: 31.0% never married, 45.4% now married, 0.0% separated, 6.1% widowed, 17.5% divorced; Foreign born: 0.0%; Speak English only: 100.0%; With disability: 14.8%; Veterans: 6.1%; Ancestry:

47.6% English, 36.7% German, 17.5% Norwegian, 14.8% Polish, 14.0% Irish
Employment: 0.0% management, business, and financial, 0.0% computer, engineering, and science, 20.4% education, legal, community service, arts, and media, 0.0% healthcare practitioners, 0.0% service, 19.5% sales and office, 0.0% natural resources, construction, and maintenance, 60.2% production, transportation, and material moving
Income: Per capita: $29,783; Median household: $66,875; Average household: $78,355; Households with income of $100,000 or more: 26.8%; Poverty rate: n/a
Educational Attainment: High school diploma or higher: 86.9%; Bachelor's degree or higher: n/a; Graduate/professional degree or higher: n/a

School District(s)
Camden Central SD (PK-12)
    2014-15 Enrollment: 2,316 . . . . (315) 245-4075
Housing: Homeownership rate: 100.0%; Median home value: $106,300; Median year structure built: 1945; Homeowner vacancy rate: 0.0%; Median selected monthly owner costs: $1,226 with a mortgage, $0 without a mortgage; Median gross rent: n/a per month; Rental vacancy rate: 100.0%
Health Insurance: 100.0% have insurance; 76.4% have private insurance; 50.7% have public insurance; 0.0% do not have insurance; 0.0% of children under 18 do not have insurance
Transportation: Commute: 79.6% car, 0.0% public transportation, 20.4% walk, 0.0% work from home; Mean travel time to work: 0.0 minutes

ONEIDA CASTLE (village).
Covers a land area of 0.514 square miles and a water area of 0 square miles. Located at 43.08° N. Lat; 75.63° W. Long. Elevation is 449 feet.
History: Center of Oneida Territory, site of chief settlement of Oneida people.
Population: 689; Growth (since 2000): 9.9%; Density: 1,340.6 persons per square mile; Race: 96.1% White, 0.0% Black/African American, 0.7% Asian, 1.6% American Indian/Alaska Native, 0.0% Native Hawaiian/Other Pacific Islander, 1.6% Two or more races, 1.2% Hispanic of any race; Average household size: 2.38; Median age: 35.6; Age under 18: 23.2%; Age 65 and over: 16.7%; Males per 100 females: 88.3; Marriage status: 27.1% never married, 49.7% now married, 2.8% separated, 6.7% widowed, 16.5% divorced; Foreign born: 1.6%; Speak English only: 96.5%; With disability: 7.3%; Veterans: 15.9%; Ancestry: 26.0% American, 17.6% German, 16.0% Irish, 15.1% Italian, 12.3% English
Employment: 9.0% management, business, and financial, 3.7% computer, engineering, and science, 9.8% education, legal, community service, arts, and media, 8.2% healthcare practitioners, 22.2% service, 21.4% sales and office, 9.0% natural resources, construction, and maintenance, 16.9% production, transportation, and material moving
Income: Per capita: $26,748; Median household: $51,406; Average household: $64,261; Households with income of $100,000 or more: 17.6%; Poverty rate: 10.1%
Educational Attainment: High school diploma or higher: 95.3%; Bachelor's degree or higher: 23.5%; Graduate/professional degree or higher: 7.4%
Housing: Homeownership rate: 70.2%; Median home value: $119,900; Median year structure built: Before 1940; Homeowner vacancy rate: 0.0%; Median selected monthly owner costs: $1,250 with a mortgage, $405 without a mortgage; Median gross rent: $810 per month; Rental vacancy rate: 0.0%
Health Insurance: 95.1% have insurance; 77.3% have private insurance; 30.7% have public insurance; 4.9% do not have insurance; 1.3% of children under 18 do not have insurance
Transportation: Commute: 93.1% car, 0.0% public transportation, 4.3% walk, 2.7% work from home; Mean travel time to work: 22.9 minutes

ORISKANY (village).
Covers a land area of 0.792 square miles and a water area of 0 square miles. Located at 43.16° N. Lat; 75.33° W. Long. Elevation is 430 feet.
History: Obelisk at Oriskany Battlefield (Northwest) marks site of an engagement (Aug. 6, 1777) of the Saratoga campaign, one of the bloodiest battles of the American Revolution. Incorporated 1914.
Population: 1,280; Growth (since 2000): -12.3%; Density: 1,617.0 persons per square mile; Race: 99.5% White, 0.5% Black/African American, 0.0% Asian, 0.0% American Indian/Alaska Native, 0.0% Native Hawaiian/Other Pacific Islander, 0.0% Two or more races, 0.7% Hispanic of any race;

Average household size: 2.14; Median age: 48.7; Age under 18: 19.6%; Age 65 and over: 27.0%; Males per 100 females: 85.4; Marriage status: 27.2% never married, 45.6% now married, 1.7% separated, 12.2% widowed, 15.0% divorced; Foreign born: 1.5%; Speak English only: 98.0%; With disability: 17.1%; Veterans: 14.4%; Ancestry: 20.1% Italian, 19.5% German, 19.2% American, 18.9% English, 18.1% Irish
Employment: 9.2% management, business, and financial, 5.2% computer, engineering, and science, 13.7% education, legal, community service, arts, and media, 8.8% healthcare practitioners, 20.8% service, 29.7% sales and office, 1.3% natural resources, construction, and maintenance, 11.3% production, transportation, and material moving
Income: Per capita: $25,818; Median household: $46,394; Average household: $55,029; Households with income of $100,000 or more: 14.5%; Poverty rate: 6.6%
Educational Attainment: High school diploma or higher: 95.1%; Bachelor's degree or higher: 20.3%; Graduate/professional degree or higher: 5.5%

School District(s)
Oriskany Central SD (PK-12)
    2014-15 Enrollment: 634 . . . . (315) 768-2058
Housing: Homeownership rate: 63.9%; Median home value: $115,600; Median year structure built: 1951; Homeowner vacancy rate: 4.8%; Median selected monthly owner costs: $1,187 with a mortgage, $540 without a mortgage; Median gross rent: $719 per month; Rental vacancy rate: 5.6%
Health Insurance: 95.9% have insurance; 78.0% have private insurance; 39.5% have public insurance; 4.1% do not have insurance; 0.0% of children under 18 do not have insurance
Safety: Violent crime rate: 0.0 per 10,000 population; Property crime rate: 72.8 per 10,000 population
Transportation: Commute: 94.5% car, 0.5% public transportation, 3.2% walk, 1.8% work from home; Mean travel time to work: 14.3 minutes

ORISKANY FALLS (village). Covers a land area of 0.506 square miles and a water area of 0 square miles. Located at 42.94° N. Lat; 75.46° W. Long. Elevation is 974 feet.
Population: 857; Growth (since 2000): 22.8%; Density: 1,692.9 persons per square mile; Race: 98.7% White, 0.4% Black/African American, 0.0% Asian, 0.0% American Indian/Alaska Native, 0.0% Native Hawaiian/Other Pacific Islander, 0.7% Two or more races, 0.2% Hispanic of any race; Average household size: 2.60; Median age: 33.1; Age under 18: 28.7%; Age 65 and over: 14.9%; Males per 100 females: 99.5; Marriage status: 22.3% never married, 57.5% now married, 7.5% separated, 6.9% widowed, 13.3% divorced; Foreign born: 0.2%; Speak English only: 97.1%; With disability: 11.1%; Veterans: 10.0%; Ancestry: 26.3% American, 25.4% Irish, 20.2% German, 14.6% English, 8.3% French
Employment: 14.6% management, business, and financial, 2.2% computer, engineering, and science, 8.0% education, legal, community service, arts, and media, 3.8% healthcare practitioners, 23.1% service, 19.8% sales and office, 13.2% natural resources, construction, and maintenance, 15.4% production, transportation, and material moving
Income: Per capita: $24,347; Median household: $54,063; Average household: $61,424; Households with income of $100,000 or more: 11.0%; Poverty rate: 8.7%
Educational Attainment: High school diploma or higher: 89.8%; Bachelor's degree or higher: 15.2%; Graduate/professional degree or higher: 3.8%
Housing: Homeownership rate: 59.5%; Median home value: $76,000; Median year structure built: Before 1940; Homeowner vacancy rate: 0.0%; Median selected monthly owner costs: $1,034 with a mortgage, $482 without a mortgage; Median gross rent: $663 per month; Rental vacancy rate: 4.3%
Health Insurance: 92.8% have insurance; 63.9% have private insurance; 37.3% have public insurance; 7.2% do not have insurance; 9.8% of children under 18 do not have insurance
Transportation: Commute: 94.1% car, 0.8% public transportation, 2.8% walk, 2.2% work from home; Mean travel time to work: 26.7 minutes

PARIS (town). Covers a land area of 31.476 square miles and a water area of 0.015 square miles. Located at 42.97° N. Lat; 75.27° W. Long. Elevation is 1,489 feet.
Population: 4,387; Growth (since 2000): -4.8%; Density: 139.4 persons per square mile; Race: 95.2% White, 1.8% Black/African American, 1.1% Asian, 0.2% American Indian/Alaska Native, 0.0% Native Hawaiian/Other Pacific Islander, 1.7% Two or more races, 2.4% Hispanic of any race; Average household size: 2.51; Median age: 45.5; Age under 18: 17.8%;

Age 65 and over: 16.3%; Males per 100 females: 97.7; Marriage status: 32.9% never married, 56.0% now married, 2.0% separated, 5.9% widowed, 5.2% divorced; Foreign born: 3.2%; Speak English only: 96.5%; With disability: 13.1%; Veterans: 10.0%; Ancestry: 17.1% German, 15.5% American, 12.9% Irish, 12.4% Italian, 12.2% English
Employment: 14.6% management, business, and financial, 5.9% computer, engineering, and science, 9.4% education, legal, community service, arts, and media, 8.3% healthcare practitioners, 23.0% service, 20.3% sales and office, 11.5% natural resources, construction, and maintenance, 7.0% production, transportation, and material moving
Income: Per capita: $30,776; Median household: $63,271; Average household: $75,216; Households with income of $100,000 or more: 24.6%; Poverty rate: 6.1%
Educational Attainment: High school diploma or higher: 93.7%; Bachelor's degree or higher: 28.3%; Graduate/professional degree or higher: 11.5%
Housing: Homeownership rate: 84.5%; Median home value: $139,000; Median year structure built: 1957; Homeowner vacancy rate: 0.5%; Median selected monthly owner costs: $1,348 with a mortgage, $583 without a mortgage; Median gross rent: $711 per month; Rental vacancy rate: 9.9%
Health Insurance: 92.2% have insurance; 80.1% have private insurance; 27.0% have public insurance; 7.8% do not have insurance; 0.9% of children under 18 do not have insurance
Transportation: Commute: 97.5% car, 0.0% public transportation, 0.3% walk, 1.4% work from home; Mean travel time to work: 21.6 minutes
Additional Information Contacts
Town of Paris . . . . (315) 839-5400
    http://town.paris.ny.us/content

PROSPECT (village). Covers a land area of 0.208 square miles and a water area of 0 square miles. Located at 43.30° N. Lat; 75.15° W. Long. Elevation is 1,184 feet.
Population: 214; Growth (since 2000): -35.2%; Density: 1,029.5 persons per square mile; Race: 95.3% White, 0.0% Black/African American, 0.5% Asian, 0.0% American Indian/Alaska Native, 0.0% Native Hawaiian/Other Pacific Islander, 4.2% Two or more races, 0.5% Hispanic of any race; Average household size: 2.43; Median age: 38.9; Age under 18: 22.4%; Age 65 and over: 16.8%; Males per 100 females: 99.3; Marriage status: 28.1% never married, 45.0% now married, 2.9% separated, 13.5% widowed, 13.5% divorced; Foreign born: 0.5%; Speak English only: 99.5%; With disability: 9.4%; Veterans: 11.6%; Ancestry: 21.0% German, 19.2% Irish, 15.0% Polish, 14.0% American, 12.6% Italian
Employment: 5.7% management, business, and financial, 1.6% computer, engineering, and science, 10.7% education, legal, community service, arts, and media, 10.7% healthcare practitioners, 25.4% service, 22.1% sales and office, 10.7% natural resources, construction, and maintenance, 13.1% production, transportation, and material moving
Income: Per capita: $29,036; Median household: $47,143; Average household: $65,507; Households with income of $100,000 or more: 21.6%; Poverty rate: 6.1%
Educational Attainment: High school diploma or higher: 92.9%; Bachelor's degree or higher: 16.2%; Graduate/professional degree or higher: 6.5%
Housing: Homeownership rate: 84.1%; Median home value: $97,100; Median year structure built: Before 1940; Homeowner vacancy rate: 11.9%; Median selected monthly owner costs: $1,104 with a mortgage, $408 without a mortgage; Median gross rent: $625 per month; Rental vacancy rate: 36.4%
Health Insurance: 94.3% have insurance; 78.8% have private insurance; 24.1% have public insurance; 5.7% do not have insurance; 4.2% of children under 18 do not have insurance
Transportation: Commute: 92.5% car, 0.0% public transportation, 4.2% walk, 3.3% work from home; Mean travel time to work: 21.3 minutes

REMSEN (town). Covers a land area of 35.465 square miles and a water area of 1.490 square miles. Located at 43.37° N. Lat; 75.15° W. Long. Elevation is 1,184 feet.
History: Reconstructed log cabin of Baron von Steuben, drillmaster to Continental Army, state historic site, 2 miles West.
Population: 1,869; Growth (since 2000): -4.5%; Density: 52.7 persons per square mile; Race: 97.2% White, 0.5% Black/African American, 0.6% Asian, 0.0% American Indian/Alaska Native, 0.0% Native Hawaiian/Other Pacific Islander, 1.7% Two or more races, 2.1% Hispanic of any race; Average household size: 2.31; Median age: 44.3; Age under 18: 17.3%; Age 65 and over: 13.8%; Males per 100 females: 99.7; Marriage status:

24.0% never married, 58.4% now married, 2.0% separated, 6.3% widowed, 11.3% divorced; Foreign born: 1.0%; Speak English only: 97.4%; With disability: 15.2%; Veterans: 9.7%; Ancestry: 20.0% Irish, 16.5% German, 15.0% Welsh, 13.9% American, 13.0% Italian

Employment: 9.0% management, business, and financial, 2.6% computer, engineering, and science, 11.8% education, legal, community service, arts, and media, 3.0% healthcare practitioners, 20.3% service, 29.8% sales and office, 9.5% natural resources, construction, and maintenance, 13.9% production, transportation, and material moving

Income: Per capita: $28,574; Median household: $53,964; Average household: $63,998; Households with income of $100,000 or more: 16.5%; Poverty rate: 11.9%

Educational Attainment: High school diploma or higher: 91.5%; Bachelor's degree or higher: 18.6%; Graduate/professional degree or higher: 7.5%

School District(s)

Remsen Central SD (PK-12)

    2014-15 Enrollment: 437 . . . . (315) 831-3797

Housing: Homeownership rate: 86.3%; Median home value: $103,300; Median year structure built: 1969; Homeowner vacancy rate: 3.6%; Median selected monthly owner costs: $1,208 with a mortgage, $461 without a mortgage; Median gross rent: $754 per month; Rental vacancy rate: 10.6%

Health Insurance: 93.0% have insurance; 76.8% have private insurance; 33.5% have public insurance; 7.0% do not have insurance; 0.0% of children under 18 do not have insurance

Transportation: Commute: 93.8% car, 0.0% public transportation, 0.6% walk, 4.3% work from home; Mean travel time to work: 30.1 minutes

---

REMSEN (village). Covers a land area of 0.372 square miles and a water area of 0 square miles. Located at 43.33° N. Lat; 75.19° W. Long. Elevation is 1,184 feet.

Population: 506; Growth (since 2000): -4.7%; Density: 1,359.1 persons per square mile; Race: 93.3% White, 0.2% Black/African American, 1.4% Asian, 0.0% American Indian/Alaska Native, 0.0% Native Hawaiian/Other Pacific Islander, 5.1% Two or more races, 5.9% Hispanic of any race; Average household size: 2.46; Median age: 36.0; Age under 18: 22.9%; Age 65 and over: 13.6%; Males per 100 females: 85.4; Marriage status: 42.1% never married, 41.8% now married, 3.7% separated, 3.2% widowed, 13.0% divorced; Foreign born: 2.0%; Speak English only: 93.7%; With disability: 21.5%; Veterans: 9.0%; Ancestry: 21.3% Irish, 18.2% American, 14.8% Italian, 13.6% Welsh, 11.3% German

Employment: 12.4% management, business, and financial, 0.0% computer, engineering, and science, 2.7% education, legal, community service, arts, and media, 4.3% healthcare practitioners, 21.1% service, 36.8% sales and office, 6.5% natural resources, construction, and maintenance, 16.2% production, transportation, and material moving

Income: Per capita: $20,314; Median household: $40,769; Average household: $48,015; Households with income of $100,000 or more: 6.4%; Poverty rate: 25.5%

Educational Attainment: High school diploma or higher: 88.8%; Bachelor's degree or higher: 9.7%; Graduate/professional degree or higher: 1.1%

School District(s)

Remsen Central SD (PK-12)

    2014-15 Enrollment: 437 . . . . (315) 831-3797

Housing: Homeownership rate: 67.0%; Median home value: $73,500; Median year structure built: Before 1940; Homeowner vacancy rate: 5.5%; Median selected monthly owner costs: $1,089 with a mortgage, $467 without a mortgage; Median gross rent: $695 per month; Rental vacancy rate: 16.0%

Health Insurance: 89.5% have insurance; 56.7% have private insurance; 47.8% have public insurance; 10.5% do not have insurance; 0.0% of children under 18 do not have insurance

Transportation: Commute: 93.4% car, 0.0% public transportation, 1.1% walk, 1.1% work from home; Mean travel time to work: 38.6 minutes

---

ROME (city). Covers a land area of 74.791 square miles and a water area of 0.811 square miles. Located at 43.23° N. Lat; 75.49° W. Long. Elevation is 456 feet.

History: Laid out c.1786 on the site of Fort Stanwix. The city was a busy portage point, and had great strategic importance during the French and Indian War and in the American Revolution. The Six Nation Treaty of 1768 was concluded here. Site of the Battle of Oriskany, one of the Revolution's bloodiest battles. Construction on the Erie Canal began (1817) in Rome. Incorporated as a city 1870.

Population: 32,916; Growth (since 2000): -5.8%; Density: 440.1 persons per square mile; Race: 88.1% White, 5.3% Black/African American, 1.2% Asian, 0.2% American Indian/Alaska Native, 0.0% Native Hawaiian/Other Pacific Islander, 2.8% Two or more races, 6.4% Hispanic of any race; Average household size: 2.30; Median age: 40.1; Age under 18: 20.6%; Age 65 and over: 17.5%; Males per 100 females: 105.6; Marriage status: 36.4% never married, 40.7% now married, 2.9% separated, 9.0% widowed, 13.9% divorced; Foreign born: 3.3%; Speak English only: 92.2%; With disability: 17.6%; Veterans: 12.2%; Ancestry: 22.2% Italian, 16.9% Irish, 16.4% American, 15.5% German, 8.5% English

Employment: 13.1% management, business, and financial, 4.8% computer, engineering, and science, 11.8% education, legal, community service, arts, and media, 6.9% healthcare practitioners, 20.0% service, 24.1% sales and office, 6.5% natural resources, construction, and maintenance, 12.8% production, transportation, and material moving

Income: Per capita: $24,391; Median household: $43,323; Average household: $57,459; Households with income of $100,000 or more: 14.7%; Poverty rate: 18.6%

Educational Attainment: High school diploma or higher: 87.8%; Bachelor's degree or higher: 19.3%; Graduate/professional degree or higher: 8.0%

School District(s)

Rome City SD (PK-12)

    2014-15 Enrollment: 5,541 . . . . (315) 338-6521

Housing: Homeownership rate: 54.4%; Median home value: $90,500; Median year structure built: 1951; Homeowner vacancy rate: 2.1%; Median selected monthly owner costs: $1,164 with a mortgage, $521 without a mortgage; Median gross rent: $713 per month; Rental vacancy rate: 4.9%

Health Insurance: 93.2% have insurance; 66.7% have private insurance; 44.7% have public insurance; 6.8% do not have insurance; 2.3% of children under 18 do not have insurance

Hospitals: Rome Memorial Hospital (129 beds)

Safety: Violent crime rate: 12.4 per 10,000 population; Property crime rate: 190.9 per 10,000 population

Newspapers: Daily Sentinel (daily circulation 13,700)

Transportation: Commute: 89.3% car, 0.8% public transportation, 5.3% walk, 3.0% work from home; Mean travel time to work: 17.8 minutes; Amtrak: Train service available.

Airports: Griffiss International (general aviation)

Additional Information Contacts

City of Rome . . . . (315) 339-7658

    http://www.romenewyork.com

SANGERFIELD (town). Covers a land area of 30.802 square miles and a water area of 0.179 square miles. Located at 42.89° N. Lat; 75.38° W. Long. Elevation is 1,247 feet.

Population: 2,529; Growth (since 2000): -3.1%; Density: 82.1 persons per square mile; Race: 99.2% White, 0.4% Black/African American, 0.0% Asian, 0.0% American Indian/Alaska Native, 0.0% Native Hawaiian/Other Pacific Islander, 0.5% Two or more races, 0.7% Hispanic of any race; Average household size: 2.32; Median age: 48.8; Age under 18: 17.7%; Age 65 and over: 19.5%; Males per 100 females: 96.2; Marriage status: 26.2% never married, 50.8% now married, 3.2% separated, 11.3% widowed, 11.6% divorced; Foreign born: 0.4%; Speak English only: 98.7%; With disability: 14.2%; Veterans: 10.6%; Ancestry: 28.5% American, 17.4% Irish, 15.8% German, 14.2% English, 6.7% Italian

Employment: 9.9% management, business, and financial, 4.8% computer, engineering, and science, 9.7% education, legal, community service, arts, and media, 9.1% healthcare practitioners, 13.5% service, 23.3% sales and office, 11.7% natural resources, construction, and maintenance, 17.9% production, transportation, and material moving

Income: Per capita: $22,757; Median household: $44,420; Average household: $52,043; Households with income of $100,000 or more: 11.7%; Poverty rate: 15.2%

Educational Attainment: High school diploma or higher: 87.7%; Bachelor's degree or higher: 18.1%; Graduate/professional degree or higher: 7.1%

Housing: Homeownership rate: 64.0%; Median home value: $100,100; Median year structure built: Before 1940; Homeowner vacancy rate: 4.3%; Median selected monthly owner costs: $1,170 with a mortgage, $454 without a mortgage; Median gross rent: $585 per month; Rental vacancy rate: 5.8%

Health Insurance: 92.5% have insurance; 73.8% have private insurance; 34.1% have public insurance; 7.5% do not have insurance; 3.3% of children under 18 do not have insurance

Transportation: Commute: 92.0% car, 0.0% public transportation, 3.0% walk, 3.7% work from home; Mean travel time to work: 25.4 minutes

SAUQUOIT (unincorporated postal area)
ZCTA: 13456

Covers a land area of 28.072 square miles and a water area of 0 square miles. Located at 43.00° N. Lat; 75.26° W. Long. Elevation is 866 feet.
Population: 4,341; Growth (since 2000): 1.5%; Density: 154.6 persons per square mile; Race: 95.4% White, 1.8% Black/African American, 1.1% Asian, 0.2% American Indian/Alaska Native, 0.0% Native Hawaiian/Other Pacific Islander, 1.4% Two or more races, 2.4% Hispanic of any race; Average household size: 2.59; Median age: 44.6; Age under 18: 18.0%; Age 65 and over: 16.2%; Males per 100 females: 94.2; Marriage status: 32.6% never married, 54.7% now married, 2.1% separated, 6.2% widowed, 6.5% divorced; Foreign born: 3.5%; Speak English only: 95.1%; With disability: 12.3%; Veterans: 10.5%; Ancestry: 17.9% German, 16.8% Italian, 15.4% Irish, 12.8% Polish, 12.4% American
Employment: 14.1% management, business, and financial, 5.5% computer, engineering, and science, 10.7% education, legal, community service, arts, and media, 9.0% healthcare practitioners, 22.6% service, 20.5% sales and office, 9.3% natural resources, construction, and maintenance, 8.3% production, transportation, and material moving
Income: Per capita: $33,394; Median household: $63,922; Average household: $84,481; Households with income of $100,000 or more: 26.6%; Poverty rate: 5.6%
Educational Attainment: High school diploma or higher: 93.8%; Bachelor's degree or higher: 31.7%; Graduate/professional degree or higher: 13.7%

School District(s)
Sauquoit Valley Central SD (PK-12)
　　2014-15 Enrollment: 1,050 . . . . (315) 839-6311
Housing: Homeownership rate: 85.0%; Median home value: $135,600; Median year structure built: 1963; Homeowner vacancy rate: 0.6%; Median selected monthly owner costs: $1,296 with a mortgage, $567 without a mortgage; Median gross rent: $734 per month; Rental vacancy rate: 9.1%
Health Insurance: 92.8% have insurance; 78.7% have private insurance; 27.9% have public insurance; 7.2% do not have insurance; 0.0% of children under 18 do not have insurance
Transportation: Commute: 96.8% car, 0.0% public transportation, 0.3% walk, 1.6% work from home; Mean travel time to work: 20.7 minutes

SHERRILL (city). Covers a land area of 2.311 square miles and a water area of 0 square miles. Located at 43.07° N. Lat; 75.60° W. Long. Elevation is 495 feet.
History: Incorporated 1916.
Population: 3,073; Growth (since 2000): -2.4%; Density: 1,329.5 persons per square mile; Race: 95.9% White, 3.5% Black/African American, 0.3% Asian, 0.0% American Indian/Alaska Native, 0.0% Native Hawaiian/Other Pacific Islander, 0.0% Two or more races, 3.8% Hispanic of any race; Average household size: 2.36; Median age: 46.0; Age under 18: 19.9%; Age 65 and over: 20.4%; Males per 100 females: 93.5; Marriage status: 26.1% never married, 54.8% now married, 1.2% separated, 7.6% widowed, 11.4% divorced; Foreign born: 4.8%; Speak English only: 93.1%; With disability: 12.4%; Veterans: 7.7%; Ancestry: 22.7% German, 20.0% Irish, 17.5% Italian, 11.9% English, 6.9% Polish
Employment: 10.2% management, business, and financial, 5.5% computer, engineering, and science, 11.3% education, legal, community service, arts, and media, 11.5% healthcare practitioners, 18.6% service, 22.1% sales and office, 9.6% natural resources, construction, and maintenance, 11.1% production, transportation, and material moving
Income: Per capita: $31,038; Median household: $55,943; Average household: $71,142; Households with income of $100,000 or more: 19.9%; Poverty rate: 7.9%
Educational Attainment: High school diploma or higher: 90.6%; Bachelor's degree or higher: 28.8%; Graduate/professional degree or higher: 10.9%

School District(s)
Sherrill City SD (PK-12)
　　2014-15 Enrollment: 2,003 . . . . (315) 829-7425
Housing: Homeownership rate: 73.1%; Median home value: $133,100; Median year structure built: 1952; Homeowner vacancy rate: 0.0%; Median selected monthly owner costs: $1,247 with a mortgage, $461 without a mortgage; Median gross rent: $601 per month; Rental vacancy rate: 0.0%

Health Insurance: 96.1% have insurance; 81.4% have private insurance; 32.4% have public insurance; 3.9% do not have insurance; 4.9% of children under 18 do not have insurance
Safety: Violent crime rate: 13.0 per 10,000 population; Property crime rate: 45.5 per 10,000 population
Transportation: Commute: 93.5% car, 0.0% public transportation, 0.8% walk, 5.6% work from home; Mean travel time to work: 24.6 minutes
Additional Information Contacts
City of Sherrill . . . . (315) 363-2440
　　http://www.sherrillny.org

STEUBEN (town). Covers a land area of 42.653 square miles and a water area of 0.048 square miles. Located at 43.35° N. Lat; 75.26° W. Long. Elevation is 928 feet.
Population: 1,103; Growth (since 2000): -5.9%; Density: 25.9 persons per square mile; Race: 100.0% White, 0.0% Black/African American, 0.0% Asian, 0.0% American Indian/Alaska Native, 0.0% Native Hawaiian/Other Pacific Islander, 0.0% Two or more races, 0.0% Hispanic of any race; Average household size: 2.45; Median age: 47.1; Age under 18: 18.9%; Age 65 and over: 17.6%; Males per 100 females: 107.9; Marriage status: 30.1% never married, 53.0% now married, 0.7% separated, 3.3% widowed, 13.6% divorced; Foreign born: 0.7%; Speak English only: 96.4%; With disability: 10.2%; Veterans: 10.2%; Ancestry: 23.8% German, 18.0% American, 14.1% Irish, 11.5% Polish, 11.2% Welsh
Employment: 11.4% management, business, and financial, 2.7% computer, engineering, and science, 6.6% education, legal, community service, arts, and media, 5.7% healthcare practitioners, 23.3% service, 19.5% sales and office, 10.8% natural resources, construction, and maintenance, 19.9% production, transportation, and material moving
Income: Per capita: $26,446; Median household: $50,938; Average household: $63,520; Households with income of $100,000 or more: 15.4%; Poverty rate: 8.1%
Educational Attainment: High school diploma or higher: 92.8%; Bachelor's degree or higher: 14.8%; Graduate/professional degree or higher: 4.9%
Housing: Homeownership rate: 90.2%; Median home value: $120,400; Median year structure built: 1983; Homeowner vacancy rate: 2.2%; Median selected monthly owner costs: $1,196 with a mortgage, $547 without a mortgage; Median gross rent: $639 per month; Rental vacancy rate: 0.0%
Health Insurance: 93.8% have insurance; 77.7% have private insurance; 31.1% have public insurance; 6.2% do not have insurance; 3.4% of children under 18 do not have insurance
Transportation: Commute: 96.1% car, 0.0% public transportation, 0.4% walk, 3.5% work from home; Mean travel time to work: 27.5 minutes

STITTVILLE (unincorporated postal area)
ZCTA: 13469

Covers a land area of 4.017 square miles and a water area of 0.073 square miles. Located at 43.21° N. Lat; 75.30° W. Long. Elevation is 538 feet.
Population: 1,095; Growth (since 2000): 35.7%; Density: 272.6 persons per square mile; Race: 87.3% White, 1.3% Black/African American, 0.0% Asian, 1.8% American Indian/Alaska Native, 0.0% Native Hawaiian/Other Pacific Islander, 9.6% Two or more races, 0.0% Hispanic of any race; Average household size: 2.92; Median age: 35.7; Age under 18: 33.7%; Age 65 and over: 12.0%; Males per 100 females: 101.2; Marriage status: 32.2% never married, 51.4% now married, 0.0% separated, 10.8% widowed, 5.7% divorced; Foreign born: 0.0%; Speak English only: 95.2%; With disability: 10.0%; Veterans: 11.0%; Ancestry: 34.0% American, 14.4% German, 11.7% Irish, 8.5% Italian, 8.3% French Canadian
Employment: 2.1% management, business, and financial, 11.5% computer, engineering, and science, 31.0% education, legal, community service, arts, and media, 9.4% healthcare practitioners, 7.7% service, 22.6% sales and office, 4.7% natural resources, construction, and maintenance, 10.9% production, transportation, and material moving
Income: Per capita: $26,851; Median household: $70,000; Average household: $78,786; Households with income of $100,000 or more: 28.2%; Poverty rate: 1.8%
Educational Attainment: High school diploma or higher: 94.4%; Bachelor's degree or higher: 34.8%; Graduate/professional degree or higher: 10.0%
Housing: Homeownership rate: 84.7%; Median home value: $124,400; Median year structure built: 1950; Homeowner vacancy rate: 0.0%; Median selected monthly owner costs: $1,453 with a mortgage, $485

without a mortgage; Median gross rent: n/a per month; Rental vacancy rate: 0.0%

Health Insurance: 95.0% have insurance; 75.3% have private insurance; 24.8% have public insurance; 5.0% do not have insurance; 4.9% of children under 18 do not have insurance

Transportation: Commute: 95.3% car, 0.0% public transportation, 0.0% walk, 4.7% work from home; Mean travel time to work: 19.1 minutes

SYLVAN BEACH (village). Covers a land area of 0.687 square miles and a water area of 0.021 square miles. Located at 43.21° N. Lat; 75.72° W. Long. Elevation is 374 feet.

Population: 856; Growth (since 2000): -20.1%; Density: 1,246.9 persons per square mile; Race: 97.8% White, 0.0% Black/African American, 0.0% Asian, 0.4% American Indian/Alaska Native, 0.0% Native Hawaiian/Other Pacific Islander, 1.9% Two or more races, 0.0% Hispanic of any race; Average household size: 1.99; Median age: 52.1; Age under 18: 12.3%; Age 65 and over: 28.5%; Males per 100 females: 98.0; Marriage status: 13.0% never married, 55.9% now married, 2.0% separated, 13.9% widowed, 17.2% divorced; Foreign born: 0.0%; Speak English only: 100.0%; With disability: 24.4%; Veterans: 16.0%; Ancestry: 35.7% American, 18.9% Irish, 17.3% German, 16.4% English, 13.8% Italian

Employment: 19.4% management, business, and financial, 0.0% computer, engineering, and science, 8.8% education, legal, community service, arts, and media, 4.4% healthcare practitioners, 13.3% service, 18.0% sales and office, 13.3% natural resources, construction, and maintenance, 22.8% production, transportation, and material moving

Income: Per capita: $24,006; Median household: $40,147; Average household: $46,728; Households with income of $100,000 or more: 7.0%; Poverty rate: 12.3%

Educational Attainment: High school diploma or higher: 86.1%; Bachelor's degree or higher: 14.2%; Graduate/professional degree or higher: 3.6%

Housing: Homeownership rate: 74.7%; Median home value: $97,800; Median year structure built: 1967; Homeowner vacancy rate: 7.3%; Median selected monthly owner costs: $1,119 with a mortgage, $470 without a mortgage; Median gross rent: $909 per month; Rental vacancy rate: 4.4%

Health Insurance: 96.4% have insurance; 59.0% have private insurance; 56.5% have public insurance; 3.6% do not have insurance; 0.0% of children under 18 do not have insurance

Transportation: Commute: 89.5% car, 0.0% public transportation, 3.7% walk, 6.8% work from home; Mean travel time to work: 26.7 minutes

TABERG (unincorporated postal area)
ZCTA: 13471

Covers a land area of 93.842 square miles and a water area of 0.368 square miles. Located at 43.36° N. Lat; 75.58° W. Long. Elevation is 518 feet.

Population: 3,545; Growth (since 2000): 2.3%; Density: 37.8 persons per square mile; Race: 96.2% White, 0.8% Black/African American, 0.3% Asian, 0.0% American Indian/Alaska Native, 0.0% Native Hawaiian/Other Pacific Islander, 2.6% Two or more races, 1.7% Hispanic of any race; Average household size: 2.82; Median age: 40.6; Age under 18: 26.5%; Age 65 and over: 12.7%; Males per 100 females: 101.7; Marriage status: 29.1% never married, 57.4% now married, 2.8% separated, 3.9% widowed, 9.6% divorced; Foreign born: 2.2%; Speak English only: 96.1%; With disability: 18.2%; Veterans: 11.5%; Ancestry: 24.0% American, 18.1% Irish, 17.3% German, 8.8% English, 8.3% French

Employment: 10.4% management, business, and financial, 2.4% computer, engineering, and science, 7.4% education, legal, community service, arts, and media, 4.3% healthcare practitioners, 24.9% service, 21.9% sales and office, 9.8% natural resources, construction, and maintenance, 19.0% production, transportation, and material moving

Income: Per capita: $20,545; Median household: $50,402; Average household: $55,837; Households with income of $100,000 or more: 14.5%; Poverty rate: 19.6%

Educational Attainment: High school diploma or higher: 82.0%; Bachelor's degree or higher: 12.6%; Graduate/professional degree or higher: 5.9%

School District(s)
Camden Central SD (PK-12)

    2014-15 Enrollment: 2,316 . . . . (315) 245-4075

Housing: Homeownership rate: 79.2%; Median home value: $95,500; Median year structure built: 1976; Homeowner vacancy rate: 0.0%; Median selected monthly owner costs: $1,082 with a mortgage, $451

without a mortgage; Median gross rent: $832 per month; Rental vacancy rate: 5.4%

Health Insurance: 93.4% have insurance; 58.9% have private insurance; 47.5% have public insurance; 6.6% do not have insurance; 5.6% of children under 18 do not have insurance

Transportation: Commute: 92.5% car, 0.1% public transportation, 1.4% walk, 5.5% work from home; Mean travel time to work: 27.5 minutes

TRENTON (town). Covers a land area of 43.376 square miles and a water area of 0.341 square miles. Located at 43.26° N. Lat; 75.21° W. Long.

Population: 4,466; Growth (since 2000): -4.4%; Density: 103.0 persons per square mile; Race: 97.4% White, 0.0% Black/African American, 0.6% Asian, 0.0% American Indian/Alaska Native, 0.0% Native Hawaiian/Other Pacific Islander, 1.9% Two or more races, 0.5% Hispanic of any race; Average household size: 2.56; Median age: 43.7; Age under 18: 21.3%; Age 65 and over: 17.0%; Males per 100 females: 100.3; Marriage status: 28.0% never married, 56.0% now married, 0.8% separated, 5.1% widowed, 10.9% divorced; Foreign born: 3.6%; Speak English only: 94.4%; With disability: 12.1%; Veterans: 9.9%; Ancestry: 21.2% Irish, 18.2% German, 16.3% American, 14.3% Polish, 12.0% English

Employment: 12.0% management, business, and financial, 2.6% computer, engineering, and science, 14.9% education, legal, community service, arts, and media, 6.8% healthcare practitioners, 15.0% service, 26.8% sales and office, 7.5% natural resources, construction, and maintenance, 14.5% production, transportation, and material moving

Income: Per capita: $31,219; Median household: $68,528; Average household: $78,432; Households with income of $100,000 or more: 28.7%; Poverty rate: 8.6%

Educational Attainment: High school diploma or higher: 92.7%; Bachelor's degree or higher: 34.4%; Graduate/professional degree or higher: 16.0%

Housing: Homeownership rate: 83.6%; Median home value: $148,200; Median year structure built: 1954; Homeowner vacancy rate: 3.4%; Median selected monthly owner costs: $1,423 with a mortgage, $559 without a mortgage; Median gross rent: $716 per month; Rental vacancy rate: 10.9%

Health Insurance: 96.2% have insurance; 79.3% have private insurance; 34.0% have public insurance; 3.8% do not have insurance; 2.4% of children under 18 do not have insurance

Transportation: Commute: 94.5% car, 0.1% public transportation, 1.7% walk, 2.7% work from home; Mean travel time to work: 25.5 minutes

Additional Information Contacts

Town of Trenton . . . . (315) 896-2664
  http://town.trenton.ny.us/content

UTICA (city). County seat. Covers a land area of 16.759 square miles and a water area of 0.256 square miles. Located at 43.10° N. Lat; 75.23° W. Long. Elevation is 456 feet.

History: The area around Utica was called "Yah-nun-da-da-sis," meaning "around the hill," by the Oneida people, in reference to the way their trails circled the nearby hills. The site was included in Cosby's Manor, a grant of 22,000 acres made by George II to William Cosby, governor of the Province of New York, and others in 1734. In 1758 the British erected Fort Schuyler. It was abandoned in the early 1760's. In 1798 the settlement was incorporated as a village, and the present name was determined by a chance selection from a hatful of paper slips. The Erie Canal brought new prosperity and the city was chartered in 1832. The textile industry, the backbone of Utica's economic structure, began with the opening of the woolen and cotton mills in the mid-1840's.

Population: 61,628; Growth (since 2000): 1.6%; Density: 3,677.3 persons per square mile; Race: 65.4% White, 15.6% Black/African American, 9.9% Asian, 0.3% American Indian/Alaska Native, 0.1% Native Hawaiian/Other Pacific Islander, 5.0% Two or more races, 11.4% Hispanic of any race; Average household size: 2.48; Median age: 34.0; Age under 18: 25.5%; Age 65 and over: 14.8%; Males per 100 females: 92.6; Marriage status: 44.2% never married, 35.8% now married, 2.6% separated, 8.1% widowed, 11.9% divorced; Foreign born: 18.9%; Speak English only: 72.3%; With disability: 19.8%; Veterans: 6.8%; Ancestry: 18.5% Italian, 9.7% Irish, 9.0% German, 7.1% Polish, 5.8% Yugoslavian

Employment: 8.4% management, business, and financial, 3.1% computer, engineering, and science, 12.0% education, legal, community service, arts, and media, 5.8% healthcare practitioners, 27.4% service, 23.7% sales and office, 5.1% natural resources, construction, and maintenance, 14.7% production, transportation, and material moving

Income: Per capita: $17,879; Median household: $30,504; Average household: $44,062; Households with income of $100,000 or more: 8.4%; Poverty rate: 32.2%
Educational Attainment: High school diploma or higher: 79.1%; Bachelor's degree or higher: 16.4%; Graduate/professional degree or higher: 5.7%

School District(s)
Utica City SD (PK-12)
    2014-15 Enrollment: 9,998 . . . . (315) 792-2222
Whitesboro Central SD (KG-12)
    2014-15 Enrollment: 3,298 . . . . (315) 266-3303
Four-year College(s)
SUNY Polytechnic Institute (Public)
    Fall 2014 Enrollment: 2,740 . . . . (315) 792-7100
    2015-16 Tuition: In-state $7,759; Out-of-state $17,609
Utica College (Private, Not-for-profit)
    Fall 2014 Enrollment: 4,249 . . . . (315) 792-3111
    2015-16 Tuition: In-state $34,466; Out-of-state $34,466
Two-year College(s)
Mohawk Valley Community College (Public)
    Fall 2014 Enrollment: 7,149 . . . . (315) 792-5400
    2015-16 Tuition: In-state $4,616; Out-of-state $8,576
Saint Elizabeth College of Nursing (Private, Not-for-profit, Roman Catholic)
    Fall 2014 Enrollment: 209 . . . . (315) 801-8144
    2015-16 Tuition: In-state $14,864; Out-of-state $21,264
Utica School of Commerce (Private, For-profit)
    Fall 2014 Enrollment: 282 . . . . (315) 733-2307
    2015-16 Tuition: In-state $13,500; Out-of-state $13,500
Housing: Homeownership rate: 46.4%; Median home value: $89,200; Median year structure built: Before 1940; Homeowner vacancy rate: 2.4%; Median selected monthly owner costs: $1,101 with a mortgage, $472 without a mortgage; Median gross rent: $666 per month; Rental vacancy rate: 5.3%
Health Insurance: 91.8% have insurance; 45.5% have private insurance; 57.7% have public insurance; 8.2% do not have insurance; 3.1% of children under 18 do not have insurance
Hospitals: Faxton - Saint Luke's Healthcare; Saint Elizabeth Medical Center (201 beds)
Safety: Violent crime rate: 57.1 per 10,000 population; Property crime rate: 359.4 per 10,000 population
Newspapers: Observer-Dispatch (daily circulation 41,000)
Transportation: Commute: 86.6% car, 3.7% public transportation, 5.9% walk, 2.3% work from home; Mean travel time to work: 17.5 minutes; Amtrak: Train service available.
Additional Information Contacts
City of Utica . . . . (315) 792-0113
    http://www.cityofutica.com

VERNON (town). Covers a land area of 37.827 square miles and a water area of 0.011 square miles. Located at 43.07° N. Lat; 75.53° W. Long. Elevation is 633 feet.
Population: 5,412; Growth (since 2000): 1.4%; Density: 143.1 persons per square mile; Race: 97.4% White, 1.0% Black/African American, 0.2% Asian, 0.8% American Indian/Alaska Native, 0.0% Native Hawaiian/Other Pacific Islander, 0.5% Two or more races, 2.4% Hispanic of any race; Average household size: 2.52; Median age: 40.6; Age under 18: 19.5%; Age 65 and over: 15.7%; Males per 100 females: 98.0; Marriage status: 31.9% never married, 46.0% now married, 2.5% separated, 7.8% widowed, 14.3% divorced; Foreign born: 0.9%; Speak English only: 97.2%; With disability: 15.5%; Veterans: 10.1%; Ancestry: 29.0% American, 17.7% German, 16.4% Irish, 11.0% Polish, 10.0% English
Employment: 11.3% management, business, and financial, 2.6% computer, engineering, and science, 11.1% education, legal, community service, arts, and media, 8.0% healthcare practitioners, 21.5% service, 18.6% sales and office, 7.3% natural resources, construction, and maintenance, 19.7% production, transportation, and material moving
Income: Per capita: $26,538; Median household: $51,875; Average household: $64,778; Households with income of $100,000 or more: 18.5%; Poverty rate: 7.6%
Educational Attainment: High school diploma or higher: 90.4%; Bachelor's degree or higher: 19.6%; Graduate/professional degree or higher: 4.9%

School District(s)
Sherrill City SD (PK-12)
    2014-15 Enrollment: 2,003 . . . . (315) 829-7425

Housing: Homeownership rate: 75.0%; Median home value: $122,700; Median year structure built: 1957; Homeowner vacancy rate: 2.7%; Median selected monthly owner costs: $1,403 with a mortgage, $494 without a mortgage; Median gross rent: $735 per month; Rental vacancy rate: 15.9%
Health Insurance: 92.6% have insurance; 72.5% have private insurance; 34.3% have public insurance; 7.4% do not have insurance; 0.2% of children under 18 do not have insurance
Transportation: Commute: 94.5% car, 0.0% public transportation, 2.7% walk, 2.1% work from home; Mean travel time to work: 20.8 minutes
Additional Information Contacts
Town of Vernon . . . . (315) 829-2422
    http://www.townofvernon.com

VERNON (village). Covers a land area of 0.946 square miles and a water area of 0.003 square miles. Located at 43.08° N. Lat; 75.54° W. Long. Elevation is 633 feet.
Population: 1,198; Growth (since 2000): 3.7%; Density: 1,266.5 persons per square mile; Race: 96.8% White, 0.6% Black/African American, 0.7% Asian, 0.5% American Indian/Alaska Native, 0.0% Native Hawaiian/Other Pacific Islander, 1.4% Two or more races, 1.1% Hispanic of any race; Average household size: 2.24; Median age: 40.4; Age under 18: 16.4%; Age 65 and over: 16.6%; Males per 100 females: 99.7; Marriage status: 33.6% never married, 44.8% now married, 4.8% separated, 7.5% widowed, 14.1% divorced; Foreign born: 2.0%; Speak English only: 98.0%; With disability: 17.1%; Veterans: 10.2%; Ancestry: 24.2% American, 19.6% German, 18.7% Irish, 15.6% Italian, 14.6% English
Employment: 12.0% management, business, and financial, 1.6% computer, engineering, and science, 18.4% education, legal, community service, arts, and media, 2.4% healthcare practitioners, 19.9% service, 21.6% sales and office, 12.3% natural resources, construction, and maintenance, 11.8% production, transportation, and material moving
Income: Per capita: $26,578; Median household: $55,952; Average household: $58,398; Households with income of $100,000 or more: 11.7%; Poverty rate: 11.4%
Educational Attainment: High school diploma or higher: 93.3%; Bachelor's degree or higher: 22.6%; Graduate/professional degree or higher: 9.6%

School District(s)
Sherrill City SD (PK-12)
    2014-15 Enrollment: 2,003 . . . . (315) 829-7425
Housing: Homeownership rate: 46.6%; Median home value: $113,300; Median year structure built: 1948; Homeowner vacancy rate: 1.2%; Median selected monthly owner costs: $1,362 with a mortgage, $505 without a mortgage; Median gross rent: $643 per month; Rental vacancy rate: 4.4%
Health Insurance: 96.1% have insurance; 73.4% have private insurance; 38.0% have public insurance; 3.9% do not have insurance; 0.0% of children under 18 do not have insurance
Safety: Violent crime rate: 0.0 per 10,000 population; Property crime rate: 172.9 per 10,000 population
Transportation: Commute: 87.5% car, 0.0% public transportation, 9.3% walk, 3.2% work from home; Mean travel time to work: 19.0 minutes

---

VERNON CENTER (unincorporated postal area)
ZCTA: 13477
    Covers a land area of 20.250 square miles and a water area of 0 square miles. Located at 43.03° N. Lat; 75.51° W. Long. Elevation is 801 feet.
Population: 1,505; Growth (since 2000): 7.7%; Density: 74.3 persons per square mile; Race: 97.2% White, 1.0% Black/African American, 0.0% Asian, 1.8% American Indian/Alaska Native, 0.0% Native Hawaiian/Other Pacific Islander, 0.0% Two or more races, 0.0% Hispanic of any race; Average household size: 2.70; Median age: 38.0; Age under 18: 21.3%; Age 65 and over: 11.8%; Males per 100 females: 98.9; Marriage status: 43.3% never married, 39.1% now married, 3.4% separated, 7.7% widowed, 9.8% divorced; Foreign born: 1.0%; Speak English only: 99.0%; With disability: 11.8%; Veterans: 6.8%; Ancestry: 42.3% American, 24.5% German, 14.6% Irish, 10.3% English, 7.6% Polish
Employment: 7.0% management, business, and financial, 4.8% computer, engineering, and science, 11.9% education, legal, community service, arts, and media, 6.6% healthcare practitioners, 25.5% service, 13.6% sales and office, 13.7% natural resources, construction, and maintenance, 17.0% production, transportation, and material moving
Income: Per capita: $22,453; Median household: $46,375; Average household: $57,520; Households with income of $100,000 or more: 16.8%; Poverty rate: 9.9%

Educational Attainment: High school diploma or higher: 96.6%; Bachelor's degree or higher: 13.0%; Graduate/professional degree or higher: 1.0%

Housing: Homeownership rate: 88.2%; Median home value: $138,800; Median year structure built: 1992; Homeowner vacancy rate: 0.0%; Median selected monthly owner costs: $1,437 with a mortgage, $496 without a mortgage; Median gross rent: $688 per month; Rental vacancy rate: 0.0%

Health Insurance: 84.9% have insurance; 64.4% have private insurance; 30.2% have public insurance; 15.1% do not have insurance; 0.0% of children under 18 do not have insurance

Transportation: Commute: 100.0% car, 0.0% public transportation, 0.0% walk, 0.0% work from home; Mean travel time to work: 20.9 minutes

VERONA (CDP).

Covers a land area of 1.878 square miles and a water area of 0 square miles. Located at 43.14° N. Lat; 75.57° W. Long. Elevation is 495 feet.

Population: 735; Growth (since 2000): n/a; Density: 391.4 persons per square mile; Race: 100.0% White, 0.0% Black/African American, 0.0% Asian, 0.0% American Indian/Alaska Native, 0.0% Native Hawaiian/Other Pacific Islander, 0.0% Two or more races, 0.0% Hispanic of any race; Average household size: 2.55; Median age: 46.1; Age under 18: 22.6%; Age 65 and over: 24.8%; Males per 100 females: 95.0; Marriage status: 20.0% never married, 59.2% now married, 0.0% separated, 12.2% widowed, 8.6% divorced; Foreign born: 0.0%; Speak English only: 93.7%; With disability: 8.2%; Veterans: 14.8%; Ancestry: 21.9% German, 17.6% English, 13.2% Irish, 6.9% Italian, 6.5% French Canadian

Employment: 5.5% management, business, and financial, 9.0% computer, engineering, and science, 11.7% education, legal, community service, arts, and media, 0.0% healthcare practitioners, 24.1% service, 21.4% sales and office, 9.7% natural resources, construction, and maintenance, 18.6% production, transportation, and material moving

Income: Per capita: $20,736; Median household: $53,804; Average household: $52,332; Households with income of $100,000 or more: n/a; Poverty rate: 22.4%

Educational Attainment: High school diploma or higher: 75.2%; Bachelor's degree or higher: 6.1%; Graduate/professional degree or higher: n/a

School District(s)

Madison-Oneida Boces
  2014-15 Enrollment: n/a . . . . (315) 361-5510
Sherrill City SD (PK-12)
  2014-15 Enrollment: 2,003 . . . . (315) 829-7425

Vocational/Technical School(s)

Madison Oneida BOCES-Practical Nursing Program (Public)
  Fall 2014 Enrollment: 51 . . . . (315) 361-5800
  2015-16 Tuition: $9,140

Housing: Homeownership rate: 94.8%; Median home value: $97,300; Median year structure built: 1957; Homeowner vacancy rate: 0.0%; Median selected monthly owner costs: $919 with a mortgage, $445 without a mortgage; Median gross rent: n/a per month; Rental vacancy rate: 0.0%

Health Insurance: 100.0% have insurance; 69.0% have private insurance; 53.2% have public insurance; 0.0% do not have insurance; 0.0% of children under 18 do not have insurance

Transportation: Commute: 98.3% car, 1.7% public transportation, 0.0% walk, 0.0% work from home; Mean travel time to work: 18.6 minutes

VERONA (town).

Covers a land area of 69.230 square miles and a water area of 0.365 square miles. Located at 43.16° N. Lat; 75.63° W. Long. Elevation is 495 feet.

History: Site of Oneida Nation's Turning Stone Casino (68,000 square foot ; opened in 1990), first legal gambling casino in N.Y. state in over a century. Costing $10 million, it is one of the largest table game operations in the U.S. Owned and operated by the Oneida, one of 70 tribes across the U.S. who are allowed to offer gambling under the Indian Gaming Act of 1988, which was designed to generate wealth on impoverished reservations.

Population: 6,299; Growth (since 2000): -2.0%; Density: 91.0 persons per square mile; Race: 98.1% White, 0.3% Black/African American, 0.0% Asian, 0.0% American Indian/Alaska Native, 0.0% Native Hawaiian/Other Pacific Islander, 1.2% Two or more races, 0.4% Hispanic of any race; Average household size: 2.64; Median age: 40.7; Age under 18: 26.0%; Age 65 and over: 14.5%; Males per 100 females: 102.4; Marriage status: 26.8% never married, 56.4% now married, 2.9% separated, 5.7%

widowed, 11.1% divorced; Foreign born: 0.2%; Speak English only: 97.0%; With disability: 13.5%; Veterans: 13.0%; Ancestry: 21.1% American, 17.2% German, 16.2% Irish, 13.1% Italian, 10.7% English

Employment: 11.1% management, business, and financial, 1.7% computer, engineering, and science, 7.4% education, legal, community service, arts, and media, 5.3% healthcare practitioners, 21.9% service, 16.6% sales and office, 13.0% natural resources, construction, and maintenance, 23.1% production, transportation, and material moving

Income: Per capita: $25,963; Median household: $56,105; Average household: $66,831; Households with income of $100,000 or more: 12.3%; Poverty rate: 16.7%

Educational Attainment: High school diploma or higher: 90.6%; Bachelor's degree or higher: 13.3%; Graduate/professional degree or higher: 4.8%

School District(s)

Madison-Oneida Boces
  2014-15 Enrollment: n/a . . . . (315) 361-5510
Sherrill City SD (PK-12)
  2014-15 Enrollment: 2,003 . . . . (315) 829-7425

Vocational/Technical School(s)

Madison Oneida BOCES-Practical Nursing Program (Public)
  Fall 2014 Enrollment: 51 . . . . (315) 361-5800
  2015-16 Tuition: $9,140

Housing: Homeownership rate: 74.8%; Median home value: $110,900; Median year structure built: 1959; Homeowner vacancy rate: 0.0%; Median selected monthly owner costs: $1,174 with a mortgage, $465 without a mortgage; Median gross rent: $647 per month; Rental vacancy rate: 0.0%

Health Insurance: 93.7% have insurance; 61.5% have private insurance; 45.4% have public insurance; 6.3% do not have insurance; 4.4% of children under 18 do not have insurance

Transportation: Commute: 94.3% car, 0.2% public transportation, 3.7% walk, 1.5% work from home; Mean travel time to work: 20.1 minutes

Additional Information Contacts

Town of Verona . . . . (315) 363-6799
  http://townverona.org/content

VERONA BEACH (unincorporated postal area)

ZCTA: 13162

Covers a land area of 1.758 square miles and a water area of 0.022 square miles. Located at 43.19° N. Lat; 75.71° W. Long. Elevation is 374 feet.

Population: 519; Growth (since 2000): n/a; Density: 295.3 persons per square mile; Race: 100.0% White, 0.0% Black/African American, 0.0% Asian, 0.0% American Indian/Alaska Native, 0.0% Native Hawaiian/Other Pacific Islander, 0.0% Two or more races, 0.0% Hispanic of any race; Average household size: 2.43; Median age: 42.3; Age under 18: 26.8%; Age 65 and over: 9.6%; Males per 100 females: 98.5; Marriage status: 35.2% never married, 49.2% now married, 0.0% separated, 0.0% widowed, 15.6% divorced; Foreign born: 0.0%; Speak English only: 100.0%; With disability: 2.5%; Veterans: 22.9%; Ancestry: 34.3% American, 17.3% Italian, 17.3% Polish, 13.5% Dutch, 12.1% Scotch-Irish

Employment: 13.5% management, business, and financial, 0.0% computer, engineering, and science, 5.1% education, legal, community service, arts, and media, 0.0% healthcare practitioners, 0.0% service, 13.8% sales and office, 42.5% natural resources, construction, and maintenance, 25.1% production, transportation, and material moving

Income: Per capita: $59,887; Median household: $81,571; Average household: $143,545; Households with income of $100,000 or more: 20.5%; Poverty rate: n/a

Educational Attainment: High school diploma or higher: 100.0%; Bachelor's degree or higher: 23.0%; Graduate/professional degree or higher: 13.8%

Housing: Homeownership rate: 78.5%; Median home value: $133,500; Median year structure built: 1964; Homeowner vacancy rate: 0.0%; Median selected monthly owner costs: $1,512 with a mortgage, $0 without a mortgage; Median gross rent: n/a per month; Rental vacancy rate: 0.0%

Health Insurance: 89.8% have insurance; 70.9% have private insurance; 28.5% have public insurance; 10.2% do not have insurance; 12.9% of children under 18 do not have insurance

Transportation: Commute: 82.9% car, 0.0% public transportation, 13.1% walk, 4.0% work from home; Mean travel time to work: 17.2 minutes

VIENNA (town). Covers a land area of 61.448 square miles and a water area of 33.628 square miles. Located at 43.23° N. Lat; 75.77° W. Long. Elevation is 463 feet.

Population: 5,470; Growth (since 2000): -6.0%; Density: 89.0 persons per square mile; Race: 98.6% White, 0.0% Black/African American, 0.0% Asian, 0.1% American Indian/Alaska Native, 0.0% Native Hawaiian/Other Pacific Islander, 1.4% Two or more races, 0.0% Hispanic of any race; Average household size: 2.25; Median age: 45.8; Age under 18: 19.9%; Age 65 and over: 18.6%; Males per 100 females: 102.0; Marriage status: 18.7% never married, 57.1% now married, 3.0% separated, 8.7% widowed, 15.5% divorced; Foreign born: 1.2%; Speak English only: 99.0%; With disability: 14.1%; Veterans: 13.9%; Ancestry: 24.4% American, 18.4% German, 16.9% English, 14.7% Irish, 10.6% Italian

Employment: 9.7% management, business, and financial, 2.5% computer, engineering, and science, 7.7% education, legal, community service, arts, and media, 4.1% healthcare practitioners, 20.4% service, 20.4% sales and office, 16.1% natural resources, construction, and maintenance, 19.3% production, transportation, and material moving

Income: Per capita: $23,325; Median household: $42,338; Average household: $51,399; Households with income of $100,000 or more: 9.0%; Poverty rate: 16.4%

Educational Attainment: High school diploma or higher: 84.9%; Bachelor's degree or higher: 10.3%; Graduate/professional degree or higher: 3.3%

Housing: Homeownership rate: 81.9%; Median home value: $104,600; Median year structure built: 1974; Homeowner vacancy rate: 3.2%; Median selected monthly owner costs: $1,248 with a mortgage, $425 without a mortgage; Median gross rent: $895 per month; Rental vacancy rate: 10.4%

Health Insurance: 92.8% have insurance; 63.0% have private insurance; 44.1% have public insurance; 7.2% do not have insurance; 4.4% of children under 18 do not have insurance

Transportation: Commute: 92.3% car, 0.0% public transportation, 5.0% walk, 0.8% work from home; Mean travel time to work: 33.2 minutes

Additional Information Contacts

Town of Vienna . . . . (315) 245-2191
  http://townofvienna.ny.gov

WASHINGTON MILLS (CDP). Covers a land area of 0.670 square miles and a water area of 0 square miles. Located at 43.05° N. Lat; 75.28° W. Long. Elevation is 620 feet.

Population: 1,360; Growth (since 2000): n/a; Density: 2,030.5 persons per square mile; Race: 91.4% White, 1.0% Black/African American, 2.6% Asian, 0.0% American Indian/Alaska Native, 0.0% Native Hawaiian/Other Pacific Islander, 4.9% Two or more races, 5.1% Hispanic of any race; Average household size: 2.55; Median age: 34.3; Age under 18: 10.1%; Age 65 and over: 17.2%; Males per 100 females: 92.7; Marriage status: 43.5% never married, 46.5% now married, 3.9% separated, 5.9% widowed, 4.0% divorced; Foreign born: 15.1%; Speak English only: 91.4%; With disability: 6.5%; Veterans: 6.0%; Ancestry: 36.1% American, 23.8% Irish, 19.9% Italian, 5.7% English, 5.1% German

Employment: 2.0% management, business, and financial, 7.5% computer, engineering, and science, 22.0% education, legal, community service, arts, and media, 17.5% healthcare practitioners, 28.3% service, 15.1% sales and office, 2.6% natural resources, construction, and maintenance, 5.0% production, transportation, and material moving

Income: Per capita: $29,128; Median household: $54,265; Average household: $71,580; Households with income of $100,000 or more: 18.9%; Poverty rate: 17.9%

Educational Attainment: High school diploma or higher: 96.9%; Bachelor's degree or higher: 44.4%; Graduate/professional degree or higher: 22.8%

Housing: Homeownership rate: 45.5%; Median home value: $166,200; Median year structure built: 1971; Homeowner vacancy rate: 0.0%; Median selected monthly owner costs: $1,034 with a mortgage, $664 without a mortgage; Median gross rent: $938 per month; Rental vacancy rate: 13.0%

Health Insurance: 95.1% have insurance; 78.7% have private insurance; 29.8% have public insurance; 4.9% do not have insurance; 0.0% of children under 18 do not have insurance

Transportation: Commute: 99.7% car, 0.3% public transportation, 0.0% walk, 0.0% work from home; Mean travel time to work: 16.0 minutes

WATERVILLE (village). Covers a land area of 1.416 square miles and a water area of 0 square miles. Located at 42.93° N. Lat; 75.38° W. Long. Elevation is 1,201 feet.

History: George Eastman born here. Incorporated 1871.

Population: 1,574; Growth (since 2000): -8.5%; Density: 1,111.7 persons per square mile; Race: 98.3% White, 0.6% Black/African American, 0.0% Asian, 0.0% American Indian/Alaska Native, 0.0% Native Hawaiian/Other Pacific Islander, 1.0% Two or more races, 0.8% Hispanic of any race; Average household size: 2.33; Median age: 44.5; Age under 18: 16.4%; Age 65 and over: 21.3%; Males per 100 females: 91.2; Marriage status: 31.9% never married, 43.5% now married, 4.4% separated, 13.6% widowed, 10.9% divorced; Foreign born: 0.6%; Speak English only: 98.3%; With disability: 19.4%; Veterans: 10.6%; Ancestry: 28.7% American, 22.8% Irish, 18.6% German, 14.7% English, 7.2% Italian

Employment: 9.7% management, business, and financial, 3.1% computer, engineering, and science, 10.0% education, legal, community service, arts, and media, 10.6% healthcare practitioners, 18.2% service, 24.7% sales and office, 7.2% natural resources, construction, and maintenance, 16.4% production, transportation, and material moving

Income: Per capita: $22,025; Median household: $39,375; Average household: $51,261; Households with income of $100,000 or more: 13.3%; Poverty rate: 15.1%

Educational Attainment: High school diploma or higher: 90.9%; Bachelor's degree or higher: 20.1%; Graduate/professional degree or higher: 8.0%

School District(s)

Waterville Central SD (PK-12)
  2014-15 Enrollment: 801 . . . . (315) 841-3910

Housing: Homeownership rate: 54.6%; Median home value: $97,900; Median year structure built: Before 1940; Homeowner vacancy rate: 8.0%; Median selected monthly owner costs: $1,188 with a mortgage, $514 without a mortgage; Median gross rent: $603 per month; Rental vacancy rate: 0.7%

Health Insurance: 92.8% have insurance; 75.4% have private insurance; 35.7% have public insurance; 7.2% do not have insurance; 3.9% of children under 18 do not have insurance

Newspapers: Waterville Times (weekly circulation 2,600)

Transportation: Commute: 92.8% car, 0.4% public transportation, 6.5% walk, 0.3% work from home; Mean travel time to work: 25.8 minutes

WESTDALE (unincorporated postal area)
ZCTA: 13483

  Covers a land area of 6.920 square miles and a water area of 0.082 square miles. Located at 43.40° N. Lat; 75.83° W. Long. Elevation is 551 feet.

Population: 219; Growth (since 2000): 36.9%; Density: 31.6 persons per square mile; Race: 95.9% White, 0.0% Black/African American, 0.0% Asian, 0.0% American Indian/Alaska Native, 0.0% Native Hawaiian/Other Pacific Islander, 0.0% Two or more races, 4.1% Hispanic of any race; Average household size: 2.23; Median age: 43.1; Age under 18: 17.8%; Age 65 and over: 14.2%; Males per 100 females: 82.9; Marriage status: 35.0% never married, 37.8% now married, 6.1% separated, 8.9% widowed, 18.3% divorced; Foreign born: 0.0%; Speak English only: 95.4%; With disability: 16.9%; Veterans: 7.8%; Ancestry: 28.3% American, 15.5% Italian, 9.6% Ukrainian, 8.2% French, 6.4% German

Employment: 19.1% management, business, and financial, 0.0% computer, engineering, and science, 6.4% education, legal, community service, arts, and media, 5.5% healthcare practitioners, 20.9% service, 5.5% sales and office, 14.5% natural resources, construction, and maintenance, 28.2% production, transportation, and material moving

Income: Per capita: $27,440; Median household: $42,188; Average household: $60,900; Households with income of $100,000 or more: 19.4%; Poverty rate: 5.5%

Educational Attainment: High school diploma or higher: 60.1%; Bachelor's degree or higher: 10.8%; Graduate/professional degree or higher: 10.8%

Housing: Homeownership rate: 54.1%; Median home value: $87,600; Median year structure built: 1972; Homeowner vacancy rate: 0.0%; Median selected monthly owner costs: $980 with a mortgage, $503 without a mortgage; Median gross rent: $713 per month; Rental vacancy rate: 0.0%

Health Insurance: 88.6% have insurance; 36.1% have private insurance; 55.7% have public insurance; 11.4% do not have insurance; 0.0% of children under 18 do not have insurance

Transportation: Commute: 100.0% car, 0.0% public transportation, 0.0% walk, 0.0% work from home; Mean travel time to work: 31.4 minutes

WESTERN (town). Covers a land area of 51.206 square miles and a water area of 3.465 square miles. Located at 43.35° N. Lat; 75.41° W. Long.

Population: 2,007; Growth (since 2000): -1.1%; Density: 39.2 persons per square mile; Race: 98.2% White, 1.2% Black/African American, 0.0% Asian, 0.0% American Indian/Alaska Native, 0.0% Native Hawaiian/Other Pacific Islander, 0.5% Two or more races, 1.9% Hispanic of any race; Average household size: 2.42; Median age: 46.3; Age under 18: 17.7%; Age 65 and over: 17.3%; Males per 100 females: 104.9; Marriage status: 24.7% never married, 56.1% now married, 0.3% separated, 9.7% widowed, 9.6% divorced; Foreign born: 1.3%; Speak English only: 96.9%; With disability: 14.3%; Veterans: 8.8%; Ancestry: 20.8% German, 19.2% Irish, 16.4% Italian, 15.1% American, 12.7% English

Employment: 11.3% management, business, and financial, 9.0% computer, engineering, and science, 4.5% education, legal, community service, arts, and media, 9.7% healthcare practitioners, 19.7% service, 24.7% sales and office, 17.5% natural resources, construction, and maintenance, 3.7% production, transportation, and material moving

Income: Per capita: $33,704; Median household: $62,371; Average household: $78,709; Households with income of $100,000 or more: 22.0%; Poverty rate: 9.1%

Educational Attainment: High school diploma or higher: 94.3%; Bachelor's degree or higher: 22.4%; Graduate/professional degree or higher: 10.9%

Housing: Homeownership rate: 80.5%; Median home value: $133,400; Median year structure built: 1961; Homeowner vacancy rate: 2.1%; Median selected monthly owner costs: $1,435 with a mortgage, $487 without a mortgage; Median gross rent: $735 per month; Rental vacancy rate: 0.0%

Health Insurance: 93.2% have insurance; 79.1% have private insurance; 31.3% have public insurance; 6.8% do not have insurance; 8.2% of children under 18 do not have insurance

Transportation: Commute: 90.1% car, 0.0% public transportation, 4.2% walk, 5.7% work from home; Mean travel time to work: 22.9 minutes

WESTERNVILLE (unincorporated postal area)
ZCTA: 13486

Covers a land area of 29.450 square miles and a water area of 3.465 square miles. Located at 43.35° N. Lat; 75.34° W. Long. Elevation is 561 feet.

Population: 729; Growth (since 2000): -12.4%; Density: 24.8 persons per square mile; Race: 100.0% White, 0.0% Black/African American, 0.0% Asian, 0.0% American Indian/Alaska Native, 0.0% Native Hawaiian/Other Pacific Islander, 0.0% Two or more races, 0.4% Hispanic of any race; Average household size: 2.26; Median age: 42.5; Age under 18: 20.0%; Age 65 and over: 15.6%; Males per 100 females: 99.3; Marriage status: 41.8% never married, 42.0% now married, 0.8% separated, 8.8% widowed, 7.4% divorced; Foreign born: 1.2%; Speak English only: 94.2%; With disability: 15.0%; Veterans: 7.4%; Ancestry: 18.7% German, 18.0% Polish, 17.3% Irish, 16.2% American, 13.7% English

Employment: 14.5% management, business, and financial, 8.6% computer, engineering, and science, 0.8% education, legal, community service, arts, and media, 9.7% healthcare practitioners, 18.3% service, 28.8% sales and office, 9.4% natural resources, construction, and maintenance, 9.9% production, transportation, and material moving

Income: Per capita: $29,064; Median household: $55,583; Average household: $62,969; Households with income of $100,000 or more: 14.9%; Poverty rate: 12.4%

Educational Attainment: High school diploma or higher: 93.0%; Bachelor's degree or higher: 18.7%; Graduate/professional degree or higher: 9.6%

Housing: Homeownership rate: 73.7%; Median home value: $104,900; Median year structure built: 1954; Homeowner vacancy rate: 0.0%; Median selected monthly owner costs: $1,375 with a mortgage, $405 without a mortgage; Median gross rent: $730 per month; Rental vacancy rate: 0.0%

Health Insurance: 91.2% have insurance; 73.4% have private insurance; 39.4% have public insurance; 8.8% do not have insurance; 3.4% of children under 18 do not have insurance

Transportation: Commute: 88.3% car, 0.0% public transportation, 4.6% walk, 7.1% work from home; Mean travel time to work: 23.0 minutes

WESTMORELAND (CDP). Covers a land area of 0.687 square miles and a water area of 0 square miles. Located at 43.12° N. Lat; 75.40° W. Long. Elevation is 522 feet.

Population: 584; Growth (since 2000): n/a; Density: 850.3 persons per square mile; Race: 72.4% White, 0.0% Black/African American, 12.0% Asian, 0.0% American Indian/Alaska Native, 0.0% Native Hawaiian/Other Pacific Islander, 15.6% Two or more races, 0.0% Hispanic of any race; Average household size: 2.67; Median age: 41.1; Age under 18: 32.4%; Age 65 and over: 9.9%; Males per 100 females: 95.9; Marriage status: 28.4% never married, 49.3% now married, 0.0% separated, 0.0% widowed, 22.4% divorced; Foreign born: 12.0%; Speak English only: 90.8%; With disability: 0.0%; Veterans: 13.2%; Ancestry: 40.1% American, 17.5% Greek, 15.8% English, 15.8% German, 9.2% Irish

Employment: 5.2% management, business, and financial, 0.0% computer, engineering, and science, 0.0% education, legal, community service, arts, and media, 0.0% healthcare practitioners, 51.5% service, 13.4% sales and office, 13.4% natural resources, construction, and maintenance, 16.4% production, transportation, and material moving

Income: Per capita: $26,652; Median household: $81,797; Average household: $70,536; Households with income of $100,000 or more: 25.1%; Poverty rate: n/a

Educational Attainment: High school diploma or higher: 93.9%; Bachelor's degree or higher: 4.6%; Graduate/professional degree or higher: n/a

School District(s)
Westmoreland Central SD (KG-12)
   2014-15 Enrollment: 987 . . . . (315) 557-2614

Housing: Homeownership rate: 55.7%; Median home value: n/a; Median year structure built: 1981; Homeowner vacancy rate: 0.0%; Median selected monthly owner costs: n/a with a mortgage, $649 without a mortgage; Median gross rent: n/a per month; Rental vacancy rate: 0.0%

Health Insurance: 93.7% have insurance; 81.7% have private insurance; 27.4% have public insurance; 6.3% do not have insurance; 0.0% of children under 18 do not have insurance

Transportation: Commute: 84.3% car, 0.0% public transportation, 0.0% walk, 15.7% work from home; Mean travel time to work: 0.0 minutes

WESTMORELAND (town). Covers a land area of 43.136 square miles and a water area of 0.015 square miles. Located at 43.12° N. Lat; 75.45° W. Long. Elevation is 522 feet.

Population: 6,135; Growth (since 2000): -1.2%; Density: 142.2 persons per square mile; Race: 93.0% White, 0.2% Black/African American, 3.4% Asian, 0.0% American Indian/Alaska Native, 0.1% Native Hawaiian/Other Pacific Islander, 3.1% Two or more races, 2.2% Hispanic of any race; Average household size: 2.47; Median age: 46.8; Age under 18: 20.7%; Age 65 and over: 17.2%; Males per 100 females: 100.4; Marriage status: 26.1% never married, 58.0% now married, 2.9% separated, 7.4% widowed, 8.5% divorced; Foreign born: 3.9%; Speak English only: 93.7%; With disability: 10.0%; Veterans: 11.6%; Ancestry: 17.1% German, 16.3% English, 14.1% Irish, 13.6% Italian, 12.4% American

Employment: 15.2% management, business, and financial, 6.7% computer, engineering, and science, 7.2% education, legal, community service, arts, and media, 4.9% healthcare practitioners, 22.3% service, 20.9% sales and office, 12.2% natural resources, construction, and maintenance, 10.6% production, transportation, and material moving

Income: Per capita: $32,373; Median household: $71,875; Average household: $78,489; Households with income of $100,000 or more: 29.3%; Poverty rate: 8.8%

Educational Attainment: High school diploma or higher: 93.0%; Bachelor's degree or higher: 24.9%; Graduate/professional degree or higher: 9.6%

School District(s)
Westmoreland Central SD (KG-12)
   2014-15 Enrollment: 987 . . . . (315) 557-2614

Housing: Homeownership rate: 86.7%; Median home value: $140,600; Median year structure built: 1975; Homeowner vacancy rate: 0.0%; Median selected monthly owner costs: $1,370 with a mortgage, $558 without a mortgage; Median gross rent: $916 per month; Rental vacancy rate: 0.0%

Health Insurance: 94.1% have insurance; 82.1% have private insurance; 28.6% have public insurance; 5.9% do not have insurance; 1.8% of children under 18 do not have insurance

Transportation: Commute: 91.4% car, 0.0% public transportation, 1.8% walk, 6.9% work from home; Mean travel time to work: 23.6 minutes

Additional Information Contacts
Town of Westmoreland . . . . (315) 853-8001
http://town.westmoreland.ny.us/content

WHITESBORO (village). Covers a land area of 1.050 square miles and a water area of 0 square miles. Located at 43.12° N. Lat; 75.30° W. Long. Elevation is 423 feet.
History: Settled 1784, incorporated 1813.
Population: 3,731; Growth (since 2000): -5.4%; Density: 3,554.6 persons per square mile; Race: 99.3% White, 0.5% Black/African American, 0.0% Asian, 0.2% American Indian/Alaska Native, 0.0% Native Hawaiian/Other Pacific Islander, 0.0% Two or more races, 0.1% Hispanic of any race; Average household size: 2.15; Median age: 43.0; Age under 18: 22.3%; Age 65 and over: 18.7%; Males per 100 females: 86.7; Marriage status: 36.7% never married, 35.7% now married, 4.4% separated, 8.1% widowed, 19.5% divorced; Foreign born: 0.2%; Speak English only: 99.5%; With disability: 9.4%; Veterans: 16.1%; Ancestry: 23.9% Irish, 22.3% Italian, 19.4% Polish, 16.7% German, 12.8% English
Employment: 7.8% management, business, and financial, 2.6% computer, engineering, and science, 6.7% education, legal, community service, arts, and media, 6.4% healthcare practitioners, 24.2% service, 30.4% sales and office, 10.1% natural resources, construction, and maintenance, 11.8% production, transportation, and material moving
Income: Per capita: $27,555; Median household: $46,439; Average household: $56,911; Households with income of $100,000 or more: 9.5%; Poverty rate: 15.3%
Educational Attainment: High school diploma or higher: 95.6%; Bachelor's degree or higher: 20.5%; Graduate/professional degree or higher: 4.1%
School District(s)
Whitesboro Central SD (KG-12)
    2014-15 Enrollment: 3,298 . . . . (315) 266-3303
Housing: Homeownership rate: 53.8%; Median home value: $93,600; Median year structure built: 1953; Homeowner vacancy rate: 0.0%; Median selected monthly owner costs: $1,119 with a mortgage, $526 without a mortgage; Median gross rent: $597 per month; Rental vacancy rate: 12.3%
Health Insurance: 95.0% have insurance; 67.3% have private insurance; 40.7% have public insurance; 5.0% do not have insurance; 0.0% of children under 18 do not have insurance
Safety: Violent crime rate: 8.1 per 10,000 population; Property crime rate: 75.7 per 10,000 population
Transportation: Commute: 92.5% car, 0.0% public transportation, 0.8% walk, 6.7% work from home; Mean travel time to work: 13.4 minutes
Additional Information Contacts
Village of Whitesboro . . . . (315) 736-1613
http://village.whitesboro.ny.us/content

WHITESTOWN (town). Covers a land area of 27.318 square miles and a water area of 0.002 square miles. Located at 43.14° N. Lat; 75.34° W. Long.
Population: 18,659; Growth (since 2000): 0.1%; Density: 683.0 persons per square mile; Race: 97.5% White, 1.2% Black/African American, 0.6% Asian, 0.1% American Indian/Alaska Native, 0.0% Native Hawaiian/Other Pacific Islander, 0.4% Two or more races, 1.0% Hispanic of any race; Average household size: 2.33; Median age: 43.6; Age under 18: 19.8%; Age 65 and over: 18.7%; Males per 100 females: 96.0; Marriage status: 31.9% never married, 46.9% now married, 1.5% separated, 9.1% widowed, 12.1% divorced; Foreign born: 2.5%; Speak English only: 95.0%; With disability: 12.7%; Veterans: 12.5%; Ancestry: 21.0% Italian, 19.9% Polish, 19.6% Irish, 18.0% German, 13.3% American
Employment: 15.4% management, business, and financial, 4.0% computer, engineering, and science, 12.0% education, legal, community service, arts, and media, 5.9% healthcare practitioners, 18.7% service, 26.9% sales and office, 7.4% natural resources, construction, and maintenance, 9.7% production, transportation, and material moving
Income: Per capita: $30,311; Median household: $53,934; Average household: $69,819; Households with income of $100,000 or more: 21.0%; Poverty rate: 9.6%
Educational Attainment: High school diploma or higher: 93.3%; Bachelor's degree or higher: 27.0%; Graduate/professional degree or higher: 9.7%
Housing: Homeownership rate: 72.9%; Median home value: $118,700; Median year structure built: 1956; Homeowner vacancy rate: 1.0%; Median selected monthly owner costs: $1,195 with a mortgage, $526 without a mortgage; Median gross rent: $665 per month; Rental vacancy rate: 6.7%

Health Insurance: 95.1% have insurance; 75.6% have private insurance; 36.1% have public insurance; 4.9% do not have insurance; 1.6% of children under 18 do not have insurance
Safety: Violent crime rate: 0.0 per 10,000 population; Property crime rate: 89.7 per 10,000 population
Transportation: Commute: 93.9% car, 0.7% public transportation, 1.4% walk, 3.7% work from home; Mean travel time to work: 16.3 minutes
Additional Information Contacts
Town of Whitestown . . . . (315) 736-4224
http://town.whitestown.ny.us/content

WOODGATE (unincorporated postal area)
ZCTA: 13494
    Covers a land area of 17.509 square miles and a water area of 0.408 square miles. Located at 43.53° N. Lat; 75.14° W. Long. Elevation is 1,480 feet.
Population: 268; Growth (since 2000): n/a; Density: 15.3 persons per square mile; Race: 99.3% White, 0.0% Black/African American, 0.0% Asian, 0.7% American Indian/Alaska Native, 0.0% Native Hawaiian/Other Pacific Islander, 0.0% Two or more races, 0.0% Hispanic of any race; Average household size: 2.18; Median age: 55.2; Age under 18: 11.6%; Age 65 and over: 26.9%; Males per 100 females: 107.9; Marriage status: 20.7% never married, 49.6% now married, 2.4% separated, 5.3% widowed, 24.4% divorced; Foreign born: 0.0%; Speak English only: 98.8%; With disability: 18.7%; Veterans: 14.3%; Ancestry: 20.5% Irish, 18.7% English, 17.5% German, 16.8% American, 12.7% Italian
Employment: 10.2% management, business, and financial, 0.0% computer, engineering, and science, 6.1% education, legal, community service, arts, and media, 10.2% healthcare practitioners, 14.3% service, 34.7% sales and office, 17.3% natural resources, construction, and maintenance, 7.1% production, transportation, and material moving
Income: Per capita: $28,197; Median household: $45,250; Average household: $60,394; Households with income of $100,000 or more: 16.2%; Poverty rate: 8.6%
Educational Attainment: High school diploma or higher: 77.6%; Bachelor's degree or higher: 26.7%; Graduate/professional degree or higher: 11.4%
Housing: Homeownership rate: 89.4%; Median home value: $147,900; Median year structure built: 1962; Homeowner vacancy rate: 13.4%; Median selected monthly owner costs: n/a with a mortgage, n/a without a mortgage; Median gross rent: n/a per month; Rental vacancy rate: 0.0%
Health Insurance: 92.5% have insurance; 64.2% have private insurance; 47.0% have public insurance; 7.5% do not have insurance; 0.0% of children under 18 do not have insurance
Transportation: Commute: 92.4% car, 0.0% public transportation, 4.3% walk, 3.3% work from home; Mean travel time to work: 32.5 minutes

YORKVILLE (village). Covers a land area of 0.671 square miles and a water area of 0 square miles. Located at 43.11° N. Lat; 75.27° W. Long. Elevation is 433 feet.
History: Henry Inman, one of the most prominent and versatile of the first generation of American-trained artists, was born here in 1801.
Population: 2,642; Growth (since 2000): -1.2%; Density: 3,935.4 persons per square mile; Race: 97.5% White, 0.0% Black/African American, 0.9% Asian, 0.0% American Indian/Alaska Native, 0.0% Native Hawaiian/Other Pacific Islander, 0.2% Two or more races, 2.0% Hispanic of any race; Average household size: 2.37; Median age: 35.3; Age under 18: 17.4%; Age 65 and over: 15.9%; Males per 100 females: 95.4; Marriage status: 46.5% never married, 35.9% now married, 0.1% separated, 6.2% widowed, 11.4% divorced; Foreign born: 7.0%; Speak English only: 89.8%; With disability: 13.9%; Veterans: 7.7%; Ancestry: 20.3% Polish, 17.9% Irish, 15.6% German, 13.6% Italian, 12.8% American
Employment: 13.2% management, business, and financial, 2.3% computer, engineering, and science, 13.5% education, legal, community service, arts, and media, 5.6% healthcare practitioners, 19.2% service, 30.0% sales and office, 9.5% natural resources, construction, and maintenance, 6.7% production, transportation, and material moving
Income: Per capita: $26,456; Median household: $52,438; Average household: $60,196; Households with income of $100,000 or more: 9.3%; Poverty rate: 12.0%
Educational Attainment: High school diploma or higher: 90.0%; Bachelor's degree or higher: 23.6%; Graduate/professional degree or higher: 7.6%

Housing: Homeownership rate: 70.2%; Median home value: $87,200; Median year structure built: 1943; Homeowner vacancy rate: 0.0%; Median selected monthly owner costs: $1,019 with a mortgage, $453 without a mortgage; Median gross rent: $668 per month; Rental vacancy rate: 2.9%
Health Insurance: 91.4% have insurance; 67.2% have private insurance; 36.9% have public insurance; 8.6% do not have insurance; 0.0% of children under 18 do not have insurance
Transportation: Commute: 94.8% car, 2.6% public transportation, 0.0% walk, 1.7% work from home; Mean travel time to work: 17.4 minutes

Onondaga County

Located in central New York, in the Finger Lakes area; drained by the Seneca and Oswego Rivers; includes Oneida and Skaneateles Lakes. Covers a land area of 778.390 square miles, a water area of 27.228 square miles, and is located in the Eastern Time Zone at 43.01° N. Lat., 76.20° W. Long. The county was founded in 1794. County seat is Syracuse.

Onondaga County is part of the Syracuse, NY Metropolitan Statistical Area. The entire metro area includes: Madison County, NY; Onondaga County, NY; Oswego County, NY

Weather Station: Syracuse Hancock Int'l Arpt   Elevation: 410 feet

	Jan	Feb	Mar	Apr	May	Jun	Jul	Aug	Sep	Oct	Nov	Dec
High	32	34	43	57	69	77	82	80	72	60	48	37
Low	16	17	25	36	46	56	61	60	52	41	33	22
Precip	2.5	2.0	3.0	3.3	3.2	3.2	3.7	3.4	3.6	3.4	3.5	3.1
Snow	34.9	26.2	18.7	3.8	0.1	tr	tr	tr	tr	0.4	9.7	30.7

High and Low temperatures in degrees Fahrenheit; Precipitation and Snow in inches

Population: 468,304; Growth (since 2000): 2.2%; Density: 601.6 persons per square mile; Race: 80.4% White, 11.1% Black/African American, 3.6% Asian, 0.7% American Indian/Alaska Native, 0.0% Native Hawaiian/Other Pacific Islander, 3.3% two or more races, 4.5% Hispanic of any race; Average household size: 2.43; Median age: 38.8; Age under 18: 22.1%; Age 65 and over: 14.9%; Males per 100 females: 92.9; Marriage status: 36.8% never married, 46.8% now married, 2.2% separated, 6.2% widowed, 10.2% divorced; Foreign born: 7.4%; Speak English only: 89.5%; With disability: 12.1%; Veterans: 7.7%; Ancestry: 22.0% Irish, 17.7% Italian, 17.4% German, 10.8% English, 6.4% Polish
Religion: Six largest groups: 35.0% Catholicism, 4.4% Methodist/Pietist, 2.4% Baptist, 2.1% Non-denominational Protestant, 1.7% Lutheran, 1.5% Pentecostal
Economy: Unemployment rate: 4.3%; Leading industries: 14.4 % retail trade; 10.9 % health care and social assistance; 10.3 % other services (except public administration); Farms: 681 totaling 150,269 acres; Company size: 11 employs 1,000 or more persons, 30 employ 500 to 999 persons, 288 employ 100 to 499 persons, 11,480 employ less than 100 persons; Business ownership: 11,094 women-owned, 2,442 Black-owned, 834 Hispanic-owned, 1,222 Asian-owned, 223 American Indian/Alaska Native-owned
Employment: 14.4% management, business, and financial, 5.2% computer, engineering, and science, 13.7% education, legal, community service, arts, and media, 7.5% healthcare practitioners, 17.1% service, 25.8% sales and office, 6.8% natural resources, construction, and maintenance, 9.4% production, transportation, and material moving
Income: Per capita: $29,444; Median household: $55,092; Average household: $72,139; Households with income of $100,000 or more: 23.1%; Poverty rate: 15.4%
Educational Attainment: High school diploma or higher: 90.2%; Bachelor's degree or higher: 34.1%; Graduate/professional degree or higher: 15.1%
Housing: Homeownership rate: 65.3%; Median home value: $135,900; Median year structure built: 1961; Homeowner vacancy rate: 1.7%; Median selected monthly owner costs: $1,350 with a mortgage, $545 without a mortgage; Median gross rent: $787 per month; Rental vacancy rate: 5.9%
Vital Statistics: Birth rate: 112.5 per 10,000 population; Death rate: 87.1 per 10,000 population; Age-adjusted cancer mortality rate: 169.9 deaths per 100,000 population
Health Insurance: 93.3% have insurance; 73.1% have private insurance; 34.4% have public insurance; 6.7% do not have insurance; 3.4% of children under 18 do not have insurance
Health Care: Physicians: 50.0 per 10,000 population; Dentists: 7.3 per 10,000 population; Hospital beds: 38.8 per 10,000 population; Hospital admissions: 1,688.8 per 10,000 population

Air Quality Index (AQI): Percent of Days: 86.3% good, 13.7% moderate, 0.0% unhealthy for sensitive individuals, 0.0% unhealthy, 0.0% very unhealthy; Annual median: 33; Annual maximum: 77
Transportation: Commute: 87.6% car, 3.2% public transportation, 4.4% walk, 3.6% work from home; Mean travel time to work: 20.1 minutes
2016 Presidential Election: 40.3% Trump, 54.1% Clinton, 4.1% Johnson, 1.5% Stein
National and State Parks: Cicero Swamp State Wildlife Management Area; Clark Reservation State Park; Erie Canal State Park; Green Lakes State Park; Three Rivers State Wildlife Management Area
Additional Information Contacts
Onondaga Government . . . . (315) 435-2229
http://www.ongov.net

Onondaga County Communities

APULIA STATION (unincorporated postal area)
ZCTA: 13020
Covers a land area of 0.468 square miles and a water area of 0 square miles. Located at 42.82° N. Lat; 76.07° W. Long. Elevation is 1,243 feet.
Population: 132; Growth (since 2000): n/a; Density: 282.3 persons per square mile; Race: 80.3% White, 12.1% Black/African American, 0.0% Asian, 0.0% American Indian/Alaska Native, 0.0% Native Hawaiian/Other Pacific Islander, 7.6% Two or more races, 15.2% Hispanic of any race; Average household size: 2.93; Median age: 44.7; Age under 18: 23.5%; Age 65 and over: 8.3%; Males per 100 females: 120.6; Marriage status: 39.8% never married, 54.4% now married, 3.9% separated, 2.9% widowed, 2.9% divorced; Foreign born: 4.5%; Speak English only: 95.5%; With disability: 12.9%; Veterans: 13.9%; Ancestry: 30.3% Italian, 22.0% French, 20.5% English, 11.4% Dutch, 8.3% Irish
Employment: 42.2% management, business, and financial, 6.7% computer, engineering, and science, 0.0% education, legal, community service, arts, and media, 0.0% healthcare practitioners, 0.0% service, 11.1% sales and office, 33.3% natural resources, construction, and maintenance, 6.7% production, transportation, and material moving
Income: Per capita: $17,452; Median household: $45,750; Average household: $51,549; Households with income of $100,000 or more: 13.3%; Poverty rate: 31.1%
Educational Attainment: High school diploma or higher: 88.0%; Bachelor's degree or higher: n/a; Graduate/professional degree or higher: n/a
Housing: Homeownership rate: 91.1%; Median home value: $126,000; Median year structure built: Before 1940; Homeowner vacancy rate: 0.0%; Median selected monthly owner costs: n/a with a mortgage, n/a without a mortgage; Median gross rent: n/a per month; Rental vacancy rate: 0.0%
Health Insurance: 75.0% have insurance; 30.3% have private insurance; 50.0% have public insurance; 25.0% do not have insurance; 32.3% of children under 18 do not have insurance
Transportation: Commute: 100.0% car, 0.0% public transportation, 0.0% walk, 0.0% work from home; Mean travel time to work: 24.9 minutes

BALDWINSVILLE (village). Covers a land area of 3.092 square miles and a water area of 0.180 square miles. Located at 43.16° N. Lat; 76.33° W. Long. Elevation is 381 feet.
History: Settled 1796, incorporated 1847.
Population: 7,692; Growth (since 2000): 9.1%; Density: 2,487.3 persons per square mile; Race: 93.7% White, 0.9% Black/African American, 0.4% Asian, 0.4% American Indian/Alaska Native, 0.0% Native Hawaiian/Other Pacific Islander, 4.6% Two or more races, 3.3% Hispanic of any race; Average household size: 2.41; Median age: 43.7; Age under 18: 23.1%; Age 65 and over: 21.8%; Males per 100 females: 89.8; Marriage status: 25.2% never married, 50.2% now married, 1.4% separated, 9.5% widowed, 15.2% divorced; Foreign born: 1.7%; Speak English only: 97.8%; With disability: 13.1%; Veterans: 9.4%; Ancestry: 25.7% German, 25.0% Irish, 16.6% Italian, 16.4% English, 7.9% Polish
Employment: 11.0% management, business, and financial, 4.4% computer, engineering, and science, 14.2% education, legal, community service, arts, and media, 7.2% healthcare practitioners, 20.3% service, 23.8% sales and office, 9.9% natural resources, construction, and maintenance, 9.2% production, transportation, and material moving
Income: Per capita: $25,065; Median household: $47,431; Average household: $59,542; Households with income of $100,000 or more: 18.8%; Poverty rate: 9.0%

Educational Attainment: High school diploma or higher: 92.0%; Bachelor's degree or higher: 30.0%; Graduate/professional degree or higher: 12.8%

School District(s)
Baldwinsville Central SD (KG-12)
   2014-15 Enrollment: 5,646 . . . . (315) 638-6043
Housing: Homeownership rate: 62.5%; Median home value: $120,000; Median year structure built: 1964; Homeowner vacancy rate: 0.4%; Median selected monthly owner costs: $1,258 with a mortgage, $492 without a mortgage; Median gross rent: $734 per month; Rental vacancy rate: 5.6%
Health Insurance: 93.9% have insurance; 75.5% have private insurance; 36.3% have public insurance; 6.1% do not have insurance; 1.4% of children under 18 do not have insurance
Safety: Violent crime rate: 1.3 per 10,000 population; Property crime rate: 88.3 per 10,000 population
Transportation: Commute: 91.0% car, 0.1% public transportation, 4.1% walk, 4.0% work from home; Mean travel time to work: 23.1 minutes
Additional Information Contacts
Village of Baldwinsville . . . . (315) 635-3521
   http://www.baldwinsville.org

BREWERTON (CDP). Covers a land area of 3.166 square miles and a water area of 0.172 square miles. Located at 43.23° N. Lat; 76.14° W. Long. Elevation is 384 feet.
History: Here are remains of Fort Brewerton (1759), now in state reservation.
Population: 4,414; Growth (since 2000): 27.8%; Density: 1,394.0 persons per square mile; Race: 95.7% White, 0.0% Black/African American, 2.5% Asian, 0.0% American Indian/Alaska Native, 0.0% Native Hawaiian/Other Pacific Islander, 1.7% Two or more races, 0.4% Hispanic of any race; Average household size: 2.60; Median age: 33.0; Age under 18: 27.7%; Age 65 and over: 9.5%; Males per 100 females: 96.6; Marriage status: 26.0% never married, 52.8% now married, 2.4% separated, 7.4% widowed, 13.7% divorced; Foreign born: 3.1%; Speak English only: 92.6%; With disability: 10.4%; Veterans: 4.9%; Ancestry: 22.4% German, 22.3% Italian, 19.3% Irish, 18.9% English, 11.9% Polish
Employment: 10.9% management, business, and financial, 8.5% computer, engineering, and science, 5.9% education, legal, community service, arts, and media, 2.4% healthcare practitioners, 21.2% service, 28.9% sales and office, 6.6% natural resources, construction, and maintenance, 15.6% production, transportation, and material moving
Income: Per capita: $25,870; Median household: $57,708; Average household: $66,155; Households with income of $100,000 or more: 15.8%; Poverty rate: 21.0%
Educational Attainment: High school diploma or higher: 92.1%; Bachelor's degree or higher: 21.2%; Graduate/professional degree or higher: 8.7%

School District(s)
Central Square Central SD (PK-12)
   2014-15 Enrollment: 4,051 . . . . (315) 668-4220
Housing: Homeownership rate: 61.0%; Median home value: $134,500; Median year structure built: 1988; Homeowner vacancy rate: 0.0%; Median selected monthly owner costs: $1,349 with a mortgage, $571 without a mortgage; Median gross rent: $961 per month; Rental vacancy rate: 11.6%
Health Insurance: 94.9% have insurance; 64.2% have private insurance; 42.4% have public insurance; 5.1% do not have insurance; 0.9% of children under 18 do not have insurance
Transportation: Commute: 85.9% car, 2.8% public transportation, 3.8% walk, 6.6% work from home; Mean travel time to work: 25.2 minutes

---

BRIDGEPORT (CDP). Covers a land area of 1.724 square miles and a water area of 0.015 square miles. Located at 43.15° N. Lat; 75.99° W. Long.
Population: 1,668; Growth (since 2000): 0.2%; Density: 967.7 persons per square mile; Race: 98.3% White, 0.1% Black/African American, 0.0% Asian, 1.6% American Indian/Alaska Native, 0.0% Native Hawaiian/Other Pacific Islander, 0.0% Two or more races, 6.0% Hispanic of any race; Average household size: 2.37; Median age: 45.1; Age under 18: 21.5%; Age 65 and over: 13.2%; Males per 100 females: 93.8; Marriage status: 30.1% never married, 36.6% now married, 1.1% separated, 5.0% widowed, 28.2% divorced; Foreign born: 1.0%; Speak English only: 99.0%; With disability: 16.2%; Veterans: 10.2%; Ancestry: 23.6% American, 17.2% German, 15.3% Irish, 15.1% English, 12.1% French Canadian
Employment: 8.8% management, business, and financial, 1.0% computer, engineering, and science, 1.9% education, legal, community service, arts,

and media, 0.9% healthcare practitioners, 30.1% service, 32.7% sales and office, 15.3% natural resources, construction, and maintenance, 9.4% production, transportation, and material moving
Income: Per capita: $22,925; Median household: $47,038; Average household: $52,318; Households with income of $100,000 or more: 14.9%; Poverty rate: 16.4%
Educational Attainment: High school diploma or higher: 83.4%; Bachelor's degree or higher: 5.6%; Graduate/professional degree or higher: 0.2%

School District(s)
Chittenango Central SD (KG-12)
   2014-15 Enrollment: 1,993 . . . . (315) 687-2840
Housing: Homeownership rate: 67.8%; Median home value: $86,500; Median year structure built: 1964; Homeowner vacancy rate: 0.0%; Median selected monthly owner costs: $971 with a mortgage, $386 without a mortgage; Median gross rent: $563 per month; Rental vacancy rate: 0.0%
Health Insurance: 92.0% have insurance; 59.7% have private insurance; 41.4% have public insurance; 8.0% do not have insurance; 0.0% of children under 18 do not have insurance
Transportation: Commute: 93.6% car, 0.0% public transportation, 6.4% walk, 0.0% work from home; Mean travel time to work: 20.8 minutes

---

CAMILLUS (town). Covers a land area of 34.424 square miles and a water area of 0.017 square miles. Located at 43.07° N. Lat; 76.31° W. Long. Elevation is 433 feet.
History: Once a major cutlery manufacturing center. Incorporated 1852.
Population: 24,333; Growth (since 2000): 5.1%; Density: 706.9 persons per square mile; Race: 94.6% White, 0.9% Black/African American, 2.8% Asian, 0.4% American Indian/Alaska Native, 0.1% Native Hawaiian/Other Pacific Islander, 1.1% Two or more races, 2.7% Hispanic of any race; Average household size: 2.48; Median age: 42.0; Age under 18: 21.6%; Age 65 and over: 17.4%; Males per 100 females: 91.6; Marriage status: 29.0% never married, 54.0% now married, 1.6% separated, 6.5% widowed, 10.4% divorced; Foreign born: 7.2%; Speak English only: 90.9%; With disability: 9.0%; Veterans: 8.2%; Ancestry: 26.9% Irish, 21.9% Italian, 19.1% German, 13.6% English, 10.2% Polish
Employment: 13.5% management, business, and financial, 6.0% computer, engineering, and science, 14.3% education, legal, community service, arts, and media, 10.0% healthcare practitioners, 14.5% service, 26.2% sales and office, 6.7% natural resources, construction, and maintenance, 8.8% production, transportation, and material moving
Income: Per capita: $31,712; Median household: $65,172; Average household: $77,358; Households with income of $100,000 or more: 27.1%; Poverty rate: 6.3%
Educational Attainment: High school diploma or higher: 95.0%; Bachelor's degree or higher: 38.4%; Graduate/professional degree or higher: 16.6%

School District(s)
West Genesee Central SD (KG-12)
   2014-15 Enrollment: 4,816 . . . . (315) 487-4562
Housing: Homeownership rate: 80.5%; Median home value: $139,000; Median year structure built: 1965; Homeowner vacancy rate: 1.2%; Median selected monthly owner costs: $1,361 with a mortgage, $549 without a mortgage; Median gross rent: $885 per month; Rental vacancy rate: 5.3%
Health Insurance: 93.6% have insurance; 82.7% have private insurance; 26.4% have public insurance; 6.4% do not have insurance; 4.3% of children under 18 do not have insurance
Safety: Violent crime rate: 11.1 per 10,000 population; Property crime rate: 168.7 per 10,000 population
Transportation: Commute: 93.7% car, 0.9% public transportation, 1.8% walk, 3.1% work from home; Mean travel time to work: 21.3 minutes
Additional Information Contacts
Town of Camillus . . . . (315) 488-1335
   http://www.townofcamillus.com

CAMILLUS (village). Covers a land area of 0.390 square miles and a water area of 0 square miles. Located at 43.04° N. Lat; 76.31° W. Long. Elevation is 433 feet.
Population: 1,242; Growth (since 2000): -0.6%; Density: 3,182.1 persons per square mile; Race: 92.8% White, 4.9% Black/African American, 0.2% Asian, 0.0% American Indian/Alaska Native, 0.0% Native Hawaiian/Other Pacific Islander, 2.0% Two or more races, 2.3% Hispanic of any race; Average household size: 2.16; Median age: 40.7; Age under 18: 21.7%; Age 65 and over: 19.0%; Males per 100 females: 93.2; Marriage status: 33.3% never married, 46.2% now married, 3.9% separated, 9.2%

widowed, 11.3% divorced; Foreign born: 3.3%; Speak English only: 97.6%; With disability: 11.6%; Veterans: 9.2%; Ancestry: 27.0% Irish, 23.2% English, 22.0% German, 16.4% Italian, 8.1% Polish
Employment: 12.9% management, business, and financial, 6.2% computer, engineering, and science, 12.0% education, legal, community service, arts, and media, 6.7% healthcare practitioners, 16.1% service, 28.4% sales and office, 7.1% natural resources, construction, and maintenance, 10.6% production, transportation, and material moving
Income: Per capita: $27,165; Median household: $49,688; Average household: $57,967; Households with income of $100,000 or more: 18.4%; Poverty rate: 10.1%
Educational Attainment: High school diploma or higher: 96.9%; Bachelor's degree or higher: 27.6%; Graduate/professional degree or higher: 9.5%

School District(s)
West Genesee Central SD (KG-12)
    2014-15 Enrollment: 4,816 . . . . (315) 487-4562
Housing: Homeownership rate: 53.2%; Median home value: $105,300; Median year structure built: 1956; Homeowner vacancy rate: 1.9%; Median selected monthly owner costs: $1,209 with a mortgage, $487 without a mortgage; Median gross rent: $687 per month; Rental vacancy rate: 5.7%
Health Insurance: 91.4% have insurance; 72.4% have private insurance; 37.0% have public insurance; 8.6% do not have insurance; 2.2% of children under 18 do not have insurance
Transportation: Commute: 91.7% car, 1.2% public transportation, 1.2% walk, 3.9% work from home; Mean travel time to work: 21.3 minutes

CICERO (town). Covers a land area of 48.274 square miles and a water area of 0.191 square miles. Located at 43.17° N. Lat; 76.06° W. Long. Elevation is 394 feet.
Population: 31,648; Growth (since 2000): 13.1%; Density: 655.6 persons per square mile; Race: 95.3% White, 1.4% Black/African American, 0.9% Asian, 0.4% American Indian/Alaska Native, 0.0% Native Hawaiian/Other Pacific Islander, 1.8% Two or more races, 1.7% Hispanic of any race; Average household size: 2.58; Median age: 40.1; Age under 18: 24.1%; Age 65 and over: 12.8%; Males per 100 females: 96.1; Marriage status: 27.5% never married, 57.4% now married, 2.0% separated, 5.3% widowed, 9.9% divorced; Foreign born: 2.9%; Speak English only: 95.9%; With disability: 9.8%; Veterans: 7.8%; Ancestry: 25.5% Irish, 23.5% Italian, 21.7% German, 11.1% English, 8.5% Polish
Employment: 14.2% management, business, and financial, 5.3% computer, engineering, and science, 10.3% education, legal, community service, arts, and media, 7.0% healthcare practitioners, 15.8% service, 28.1% sales and office, 7.3% natural resources, construction, and maintenance, 11.9% production, transportation, and material moving
Income: Per capita: $32,092; Median household: $68,409; Average household: $81,482; Households with income of $100,000 or more: 28.5%; Poverty rate: 7.8%
Educational Attainment: High school diploma or higher: 94.3%; Bachelor's degree or higher: 29.7%; Graduate/professional degree or higher: 12.0%

School District(s)
North Syracuse Central SD (PK-12)
    2014-15 Enrollment: 9,119 . . . . (315) 218-2151
Housing: Homeownership rate: 79.4%; Median home value: $147,200; Median year structure built: 1979; Homeowner vacancy rate: 0.9%; Median selected monthly owner costs: $1,442 with a mortgage, $592 without a mortgage; Median gross rent: $825 per month; Rental vacancy rate: 3.7%
Health Insurance: 96.1% have insurance; 81.5% have private insurance; 26.4% have public insurance; 3.9% do not have insurance; 1.4% of children under 18 do not have insurance
Safety: Violent crime rate: 5.1 per 10,000 population; Property crime rate: 109.9 per 10,000 population
Transportation: Commute: 94.3% car, 0.5% public transportation, 1.3% walk, 2.7% work from home; Mean travel time to work: 19.4 minutes
Additional Information Contacts
Town of Cicero . . . . (315) 699-8109
    http://ciceronewyork.net

CLAY (town). Covers a land area of 47.958 square miles and a water area of 0.901 square miles. Located at 43.18° N. Lat; 76.19° W. Long. Elevation is 394 feet.
Population: 59,294; Growth (since 2000): 0.8%; Density: 1,236.4 persons per square mile; Race: 90.0% White, 4.9% Black/African American, 1.9% Asian, 0.4% American Indian/Alaska Native, 0.0% Native Hawaiian/Other

Pacific Islander, 2.5% Two or more races, 3.4% Hispanic of any race; Average household size: 2.52; Median age: 39.3; Age under 18: 22.8%; Age 65 and over: 13.6%; Males per 100 females: 93.9; Marriage status: 30.9% never married, 53.1% now married, 1.7% separated, 5.2% widowed, 10.8% divorced; Foreign born: 5.2%; Speak English only: 92.9%; With disability: 9.6%; Veterans: 8.9%; Ancestry: 24.6% Irish, 22.2% Italian, 20.2% German, 11.3% English, 6.9% Polish
Employment: 14.5% management, business, and financial, 5.9% computer, engineering, and science, 10.7% education, legal, community service, arts, and media, 8.0% healthcare practitioners, 15.9% service, 28.8% sales and office, 6.4% natural resources, construction, and maintenance, 9.8% production, transportation, and material moving
Income: Per capita: $30,355; Median household: $64,717; Average household: $75,117; Households with income of $100,000 or more: 25.0%; Poverty rate: 8.9%
Educational Attainment: High school diploma or higher: 93.9%; Bachelor's degree or higher: 32.2%; Graduate/professional degree or higher: 11.8%
Housing: Homeownership rate: 73.6%; Median home value: $139,500; Median year structure built: 1975; Homeowner vacancy rate: 1.0%; Median selected monthly owner costs: $1,374 with a mortgage, $525 without a mortgage; Median gross rent: $862 per month; Rental vacancy rate: 5.5%
Health Insurance: 94.7% have insurance; 80.8% have private insurance; 28.3% have public insurance; 5.3% do not have insurance; 2.5% of children under 18 do not have insurance
Transportation: Commute: 93.7% car, 0.9% public transportation, 1.7% walk, 3.0% work from home; Mean travel time to work: 20.0 minutes
Additional Information Contacts
Town of Clay . . . . (315) 652-3800
    http://www.townofclay.org

DE WITT (town). Covers a land area of 33.774 square miles and a water area of 0.092 square miles. Located at 43.05° N. Lat; 76.07° W. Long.
Population: 25,738; Growth (since 2000): 6.9%; Density: 762.1 persons per square mile; Race: 83.8% White, 6.6% Black/African American, 5.5% Asian, 0.2% American Indian/Alaska Native, 0.0% Native Hawaiian/Other Pacific Islander, 2.9% Two or more races, 3.0% Hispanic of any race; Average household size: 2.36; Median age: 42.8; Age under 18: 20.5%; Age 65 and over: 17.0%; Males per 100 females: 94.5; Marriage status: 35.1% never married, 49.3% now married, 1.5% separated, 5.7% widowed, 10.0% divorced; Foreign born: 10.4%; Speak English only: 86.9%; With disability: 14.2%; Veterans: 7.4%; Ancestry: 21.4% Irish, 17.2% Italian, 17.2% German, 12.6% English, 6.6% Polish
Employment: 17.4% management, business, and financial, 5.8% computer, engineering, and science, 17.1% education, legal, community service, arts, and media, 6.7% healthcare practitioners, 16.1% service, 24.9% sales and office, 4.1% natural resources, construction, and maintenance, 7.7% production, transportation, and material moving
Income: Per capita: $35,986; Median household: $63,734; Average household: $88,111; Households with income of $100,000 or more: 27.9%; Poverty rate: 7.9%
Educational Attainment: High school diploma or higher: 92.0%; Bachelor's degree or higher: 44.3%; Graduate/professional degree or higher: 23.2%

School District(s)
Jamesville-Dewitt Central SD (KG-12)
    2014-15 Enrollment: 2,951 . . . . (315) 445-8304
Housing: Homeownership rate: 72.5%; Median home value: $150,200; Median year structure built: 1961; Homeowner vacancy rate: 0.3%; Median selected monthly owner costs: $1,433 with a mortgage, $575 without a mortgage; Median gross rent: $785 per month; Rental vacancy rate: 4.4%
Health Insurance: 93.0% have insurance; 78.2% have private insurance; 30.7% have public insurance; 7.0% do not have insurance; 4.6% of children under 18 do not have insurance
Transportation: Commute: 87.6% car, 2.2% public transportation, 3.4% walk, 4.7% work from home; Mean travel time to work: 16.7 minutes
Additional Information Contacts
Town of De Witt . . . . (315) 446-3910
    http://www.townofdewitt.com

DELPHI FALLS (unincorporated postal area)
ZCTA: 13051
    Covers a land area of 0.236 square miles and a water area of 0 square miles. Located at 42.88° N. Lat; 75.91° W. Long. Elevation is 948 feet.

Population: 173; Growth (since 2000): n/a; Density: 734.0 persons per square mile; Race: 100.0% White, 0.0% Black/African American, 0.0% Asian, 0.0% American Indian/Alaska Native, 0.0% Native Hawaiian/Other Pacific Islander, 0.0% Two or more races, 0.0% Hispanic of any race; Average household size: 2.37; Median age: 13.9; Age under 18: 51.4%; Age 65 and over: 6.4%; Males per 100 females: 112.5; Marriage status: 19.0% never married, 81.0% now married, 0.0% separated, 0.0% widowed, 0.0% divorced; Foreign born: 0.0%; Speak English only: 100.0%; With disability: 0.0%; Veterans: 0.0%; Ancestry: 78.0% English, 78.0% German, 12.7% Irish, 9.2% Eastern European, 6.4% Danish
Employment: 0.0% management, business, and financial, 0.0% computer, engineering, and science, 0.0% education, legal, community service, arts, and media, 0.0% healthcare practitioners, 0.0% service, 80.7% sales and office, 0.0% natural resources, construction, and maintenance, 19.3% production, transportation, and material moving
Income: Per capita: $7,754; Median household: n/a; Average household: $18,377; Households with income of $100,000 or more: n/a; Poverty rate: 78.0%
Educational Attainment: High school diploma or higher: 100.0%; Bachelor's degree or higher: 19.0%; Graduate/professional degree or higher: 19.0%
Housing: Homeownership rate: n/a; Median home value: n/a; Median year structure built: Before 1940; Homeowner vacancy rate: 0.0%; Median selected monthly owner costs: $0 with a mortgage, $0 without a mortgage; Median gross rent: $740 per month; Rental vacancy rate: 0.0%
Health Insurance: 64.2% have insurance; 12.7% have private insurance; 57.8% have public insurance; 35.8% do not have insurance; 0.0% of children under 18 do not have insurance
Transportation: Commute: 100.0% car, 0.0% public transportation, 0.0% walk, 0.0% work from home; Mean travel time to work: 0.0 minutes

EAST SYRACUSE (village). Covers a land area of 1.622 square miles and a water area of 0 square miles. Located at 43.06° N. Lat; 76.07° W. Long. Elevation is 433 feet.
Population: 3,043; Growth (since 2000): -4.2%; Density: 1,875.9 persons per square mile; Race: 94.2% White, 1.8% Black/African American, 0.0% Asian, 0.0% American Indian/Alaska Native, 0.0% Native Hawaiian/Other Pacific Islander, 1.8% Two or more races, 2.5% Hispanic of any race; Average household size: 2.24; Median age: 35.0; Age under 18: 23.7%; Age 65 and over: 10.5%; Males per 100 females: 99.7; Marriage status: 38.9% never married, 39.9% now married, 3.8% separated, 6.4% widowed, 14.7% divorced; Foreign born: 8.6%; Speak English only: 92.5%; With disability: 16.6%; Veterans: 4.6%; Ancestry: 25.6% Irish, 17.0% Italian, 15.7% German, 12.2% English, 9.5% American
Employment: 16.0% management, business, and financial, 5.1% computer, engineering, and science, 6.1% education, legal, community service, arts, and media, 2.9% healthcare practitioners, 24.0% service, 29.6% sales and office, 4.7% natural resources, construction, and maintenance, 11.7% production, transportation, and material moving
Income: Per capita: $21,560; Median household: $35,566; Average household: $46,924; Households with income of $100,000 or more: 7.5%; Poverty rate: 17.4%
Educational Attainment: High school diploma or higher: 87.0%; Bachelor's degree or higher: 19.5%; Graduate/professional degree or higher: 4.8%
School District(s)
East Syracuse-Minoa Central SD (PK-12)
    2014-15 Enrollment: 3,546 . . . . (315) 434-3012
Housing: Homeownership rate: 46.5%; Median home value: $89,700; Median year structure built: Before 1940; Homeowner vacancy rate: 3.5%; Median selected monthly owner costs: $1,156 with a mortgage, $441 without a mortgage; Median gross rent: $701 per month; Rental vacancy rate: 6.0%
Health Insurance: 91.7% have insurance; 66.7% have private insurance; 38.5% have public insurance; 8.3% do not have insurance; 3.0% of children under 18 do not have insurance
Transportation: Commute: 80.8% car, 4.8% public transportation, 3.3% walk, 10.2% work from home; Mean travel time to work: 15.9 minutes

ELBRIDGE (town). Covers a land area of 37.539 square miles and a water area of 0.756 square miles. Located at 43.05° N. Lat; 76.44° W. Long. Elevation is 545 feet.
Population: 5,860; Growth (since 2000): -3.8%; Density: 156.1 persons per square mile; Race: 97.8% White, 0.0% Black/African American, 0.1% Asian, 0.9% American Indian/Alaska Native, 0.0% Native Hawaiian/Other Pacific Islander, 1.0% Two or more races, 0.4% Hispanic of any race; Average household size: 2.54; Median age: 45.2; Age under 18: 18.9%; Age 65 and over: 16.3%; Males per 100 females: 100.9; Marriage status: 26.9% never married, 53.1% now married, 4.5% separated, 5.6% widowed, 14.4% divorced; Foreign born: 2.1%; Speak English only: 98.6%; With disability: 12.5%; Veterans: 8.8%; Ancestry: 27.4% Irish, 22.2% English, 16.7% German, 10.3% Italian, 10.2% Polish
Employment: 11.8% management, business, and financial, 5.0% computer, engineering, and science, 11.9% education, legal, community service, arts, and media, 5.1% healthcare practitioners, 13.0% service, 27.7% sales and office, 12.4% natural resources, construction, and maintenance, 13.1% production, transportation, and material moving
Income: Per capita: $28,113; Median household: $57,481; Average household: $69,521; Households with income of $100,000 or more: 24.0%; Poverty rate: 8.3%
Educational Attainment: High school diploma or higher: 88.0%; Bachelor's degree or higher: 23.3%; Graduate/professional degree or higher: 8.1%
School District(s)
Jordan-Elbridge Central SD (PK-12)
    2014-15 Enrollment: 1,382 . . . . (315) 689-8500
Housing: Homeownership rate: 82.8%; Median home value: $115,500; Median year structure built: 1964; Homeowner vacancy rate: 3.2%; Median selected monthly owner costs: $1,155 with a mortgage, $485 without a mortgage; Median gross rent: $692 per month; Rental vacancy rate: 3.9%
Health Insurance: 90.8% have insurance; 73.4% have private insurance; 29.6% have public insurance; 9.2% do not have insurance; 1.6% of children under 18 do not have insurance
Transportation: Commute: 94.5% car, 0.4% public transportation, 2.5% walk, 2.6% work from home; Mean travel time to work: 21.2 minutes
Additional Information Contacts
Town of Elbridge . . . . (315) 689-9031
    http://www.townofelbridge.com

ELBRIDGE (village). Covers a land area of 1.126 square miles and a water area of 0 square miles. Located at 43.04° N. Lat; 76.44° W. Long. Elevation is 545 feet.
Population: 1,080; Growth (since 2000): -2.1%; Density: 959.4 persons per square mile; Race: 94.4% White, 0.0% Black/African American, 0.2% Asian, 2.5% American Indian/Alaska Native, 0.0% Native Hawaiian/Other Pacific Islander, 1.5% Two or more races, 2.2% Hispanic of any race; Average household size: 2.56; Median age: 42.7; Age under 18: 18.4%; Age 65 and over: 14.8%; Males per 100 females: 94.8; Marriage status: 33.1% never married, 49.6% now married, 1.0% separated, 4.2% widowed, 13.1% divorced; Foreign born: 3.8%; Speak English only: 96.8%; With disability: 9.7%; Veterans: 10.1%; Ancestry: 26.1% Irish, 18.7% German, 14.0% English, 12.5% Italian, 10.5% Polish
Employment: 9.1% management, business, and financial, 6.8% computer, engineering, and science, 14.6% education, legal, community service, arts, and media, 7.9% healthcare practitioners, 6.2% service, 28.9% sales and office, 14.4% natural resources, construction, and maintenance, 12.2% production, transportation, and material moving
Income: Per capita: $32,726; Median household: $68,438; Average household: $82,230; Households with income of $100,000 or more: 33.6%; Poverty rate: 2.4%
Educational Attainment: High school diploma or higher: 96.9%; Bachelor's degree or higher: 21.4%; Graduate/professional degree or higher: 5.5%
School District(s)
Jordan-Elbridge Central SD (PK-12)
    2014-15 Enrollment: 1,382 . . . . (315) 689-8500
Housing: Homeownership rate: 72.0%; Median home value: $140,500; Median year structure built: 1961; Homeowner vacancy rate: 0.7%; Median selected monthly owner costs: $1,386 with a mortgage, $510 without a mortgage; Median gross rent: $815 per month; Rental vacancy rate: 6.3%
Health Insurance: 90.5% have insurance; 81.1% have private insurance; 26.4% have public insurance; 9.5% do not have insurance; 4.5% of children under 18 do not have insurance

Transportation: Commute: 92.4% car, 0.0% public transportation, 1.9% walk, 5.7% work from home; Mean travel time to work: 22.0 minutes

FABIUS (town).
Covers a land area of 46.497 square miles and a water area of 0.275 square miles. Located at 42.82° N. Lat; 75.99° W. Long. Elevation is 1,266 feet.

Population: 2,282; Growth (since 2000): 15.6%; Density: 49.1 persons per square mile; Race: 91.8% White, 1.1% Black/African American, 0.6% Asian, 0.0% American Indian/Alaska Native, 0.0% Native Hawaiian/Other Pacific Islander, 1.6% Two or more races, 8.7% Hispanic of any race; Average household size: 2.98; Median age: 38.9; Age under 18: 23.8%; Age 65 and over: 11.6%; Males per 100 females: 104.2; Marriage status: 31.9% never married, 55.8% now married, 1.5% separated, 3.7% widowed, 8.6% divorced; Foreign born: 7.6%; Speak English only: 90.6%; With disability: 11.2%; Veterans: 7.7%; Ancestry: 22.9% English, 21.7% German, 16.8% Irish, 11.4% Italian, 10.5% French

Employment: 16.4% management, business, and financial, 4.2% computer, engineering, and science, 10.7% education, legal, community service, arts, and media, 6.9% healthcare practitioners, 12.5% service, 15.0% sales and office, 26.3% natural resources, construction, and maintenance, 8.1% production, transportation, and material moving

Income: Per capita: $30,168; Median household: $74,091; Average household: $86,851; Households with income of $100,000 or more: 32.3%; Poverty rate: 5.8%

Educational Attainment: High school diploma or higher: 93.1%; Bachelor's degree or higher: 24.6%; Graduate/professional degree or higher: 9.5%

School District(s)
Fabius-Pompey Central SD (KG-12)
   2014-15 Enrollment: 695. . . . . (315) 683-5301

Housing: Homeownership rate: 86.6%; Median home value: $139,100; Median year structure built: 1956; Homeowner vacancy rate: 1.6%; Median selected monthly owner costs: $1,435 with a mortgage, $496 without a mortgage; Median gross rent: $763 per month; Rental vacancy rate: 2.9%

Health Insurance: 87.9% have insurance; 74.7% have private insurance; 24.0% have public insurance; 12.1% do not have insurance; 5.6% of children under 18 do not have insurance

Transportation: Commute: 77.1% car, 0.6% public transportation, 16.3% walk, 5.3% work from home; Mean travel time to work: 25.3 minutes

FABIUS (village).
Covers a land area of 0.398 square miles and a water area of 0 square miles. Located at 42.83° N. Lat; 75.98° W. Long. Elevation is 1,266 feet.

Population: 310; Growth (since 2000): -12.7%; Density: 779.1 persons per square mile; Race: 98.7% White, 0.0% Black/African American, 0.0% Asian, 0.0% American Indian/Alaska Native, 0.0% Native Hawaiian/Other Pacific Islander, 0.6% Two or more races, 1.0% Hispanic of any race; Average household size: 2.54; Median age: 42.3; Age under 18: 28.1%; Age 65 and over: 13.2%; Males per 100 females: 89.2; Marriage status: 29.8% never married, 53.2% now married, 0.4% separated, 5.2% widowed, 11.7% divorced; Foreign born: 1.3%; Speak English only: 95.9%; With disability: 8.1%; Veterans: 9.4%; Ancestry: 27.1% Irish, 18.7% English, 16.1% Italian, 15.8% German, 5.5% Swiss

Employment: 15.3% management, business, and financial, 3.7% computer, engineering, and science, 12.3% education, legal, community service, arts, and media, 4.3% healthcare practitioners, 14.7% service, 28.8% sales and office, 12.9% natural resources, construction, and maintenance, 8.0% production, transportation, and material moving

Income: Per capita: $29,029; Median household: $59,286; Average household: $72,528; Households with income of $100,000 or more: 22.2%; Poverty rate: 5.5%

Educational Attainment: High school diploma or higher: 94.9%; Bachelor's degree or higher: 32.0%; Graduate/professional degree or higher: 15.7%

School District(s)
Fabius-Pompey Central SD (KG-12)
   2014-15 Enrollment: 695. . . . . (315) 683-5301

Housing: Homeownership rate: 75.4%; Median home value: $114,700; Median year structure built: Before 1940; Homeowner vacancy rate: 4.2%; Median selected monthly owner costs: $1,325 with a mortgage, $550 without a mortgage; Median gross rent: $630 per month; Rental vacancy rate: 9.1%

Health Insurance: 92.6% have insurance; 84.5% have private insurance; 22.9% have public insurance; 7.4% do not have insurance; 0.0% of children under 18 do not have insurance

Transportation: Commute: 93.2% car, 0.0% public transportation, 2.5% walk, 4.3% work from home; Mean travel time to work: 29.2 minutes

FAIRMOUNT (CDP).
Covers a land area of 3.334 square miles and a water area of 0 square miles. Located at 43.04° N. Lat; 76.25° W. Long. Elevation is 492 feet.

Population: 10,106; Growth (since 2000): -6.4%; Density: 3,031.4 persons per square mile; Race: 95.0% White, 0.9% Black/African American, 2.8% Asian, 0.2% American Indian/Alaska Native, 0.0% Native Hawaiian/Other Pacific Islander, 0.9% Two or more races, 2.9% Hispanic of any race; Average household size: 2.44; Median age: 42.3; Age under 18: 20.3%; Age 65 and over: 18.8%; Males per 100 females: 88.5; Marriage status: 32.3% never married, 49.5% now married, 1.9% separated, 7.4% widowed, 10.8% divorced; Foreign born: 7.4%; Speak English only: 90.1%; With disability: 8.5%; Veterans: 8.0%; Ancestry: 29.1% Irish, 22.0% Italian, 18.2% German, 11.4% English, 9.4% Polish

Employment: 9.6% management, business, and financial, 3.8% computer, engineering, and science, 14.4% education, legal, community service, arts, and media, 11.4% healthcare practitioners, 15.8% service, 25.8% sales and office, 8.9% natural resources, construction, and maintenance, 10.3% production, transportation, and material moving

Income: Per capita: $28,979; Median household: $62,396; Average household: $69,072; Households with income of $100,000 or more: 22.3%; Poverty rate: 4.5%

Educational Attainment: High school diploma or higher: 94.3%; Bachelor's degree or higher: 31.8%; Graduate/professional degree or higher: 14.9%

Housing: Homeownership rate: 80.5%; Median home value: $122,300; Median year structure built: 1958; Homeowner vacancy rate: 2.5%; Median selected monthly owner costs: $1,228 with a mortgage, $510 without a mortgage; Median gross rent: $987 per month; Rental vacancy rate: 2.4%

Health Insurance: 93.2% have insurance; 81.2% have private insurance; 29.6% have public insurance; 6.8% do not have insurance; 5.8% of children under 18 do not have insurance

Transportation: Commute: 93.8% car, 1.4% public transportation, 2.7% walk, 2.0% work from home; Mean travel time to work: 20.8 minutes

FAYETTEVILLE (village).
Covers a land area of 1.746 square miles and a water area of 0 square miles. Located at 43.03° N. Lat; 76.00° W. Long. Elevation is 535 feet.

History: Incorporated 1844.

Population: 4,203; Growth (since 2000): 0.3%; Density: 2,406.8 persons per square mile; Race: 97.0% White, 1.4% Black/African American, 1.3% Asian, 0.0% American Indian/Alaska Native, 0.0% Native Hawaiian/Other Pacific Islander, 0.2% Two or more races, 2.7% Hispanic of any race; Average household size: 2.25; Median age: 42.9; Age under 18: 21.2%; Age 65 and over: 19.1%; Males per 100 females: 91.2; Marriage status: 28.9% never married, 53.4% now married, 0.4% separated, 6.5% widowed, 11.1% divorced; Foreign born: 4.9%; Speak English only: 95.8%; With disability: 9.4%; Veterans: 7.7%; Ancestry: 34.5% Irish, 19.1% German, 18.8% Italian, 11.3% English, 7.5% French

Employment: 14.4% management, business, and financial, 5.9% computer, engineering, and science, 22.5% education, legal, community service, arts, and media, 11.3% healthcare practitioners, 10.3% service, 26.5% sales and office, 6.2% natural resources, construction, and maintenance, 2.9% production, transportation, and material moving

Income: Per capita: $43,126; Median household: $71,930; Average household: $95,959; Households with income of $100,000 or more: 34.8%; Poverty rate: 4.8%

Educational Attainment: High school diploma or higher: 97.1%; Bachelor's degree or higher: 56.3%; Graduate/professional degree or higher: 31.3%

School District(s)
Fayetteville-Manlius Central SD (KG-12)
   2014-15 Enrollment: 4,191 . . . . (315) 692-1200

Housing: Homeownership rate: 71.7%; Median home value: $167,200; Median year structure built: 1955; Homeowner vacancy rate: 0.0%; Median selected monthly owner costs: $1,622 with a mortgage, $669 without a mortgage; Median gross rent: $1,007 per month; Rental vacancy rate: 6.2%

Health Insurance: 95.0% have insurance; 79.7% have private insurance; 31.6% have public insurance; 5.0% do not have insurance; 4.7% of children under 18 do not have insurance

Transportation: Commute: 94.2% car, 0.2% public transportation, 2.2% walk, 3.0% work from home; Mean travel time to work: 21.1 minutes

Additional Information Contacts
Village of Fayetteville . . . . (315) 637-9864
  http://www.fayettevilleny.gov

GALEVILLE (CDP). Covers a land area of 1.152 square miles and a water area of 0.006 square miles. Located at 43.09° N. Lat; 76.18° W. Long. Elevation is 423 feet.
Population: 4,821; Growth (since 2000): 7.7%; Density: 4,184.9 persons per square mile; Race: 79.0% White, 10.1% Black/African American, 8.5% Asian, 0.3% American Indian/Alaska Native, 0.0% Native Hawaiian/Other Pacific Islander, 2.0% Two or more races, 1.0% Hispanic of any race; Average household size: 2.25; Median age: 46.0; Age under 18: 20.9%; Age 65 and over: 24.3%; Males per 100 females: 82.4; Marriage status: 30.8% never married, 47.9% now married, 2.0% separated, 11.7% widowed, 9.6% divorced; Foreign born: 12.6%; Speak English only: 87.0%; With disability: 17.0%; Veterans: 9.7%; Ancestry: 25.2% Italian, 20.2% Irish, 19.1% German, 10.0% English, 6.1% Polish
Employment: 3.8% management, business, and financial, 6.1% computer, engineering, and science, 8.1% education, legal, community service, arts, and media, 7.1% healthcare practitioners, 22.5% service, 37.7% sales and office, 5.2% natural resources, construction, and maintenance, 9.6% production, transportation, and material moving
Income: Per capita: $22,542; Median household: $42,097; Average household: $49,391; Households with income of $100,000 or more: 8.6%; Poverty rate: 11.9%
Educational Attainment: High school diploma or higher: 82.6%; Bachelor's degree or higher: 14.4%; Graduate/professional degree or higher: 6.5%
Housing: Homeownership rate: 68.6%; Median home value: $98,100; Median year structure built: 1957; Homeowner vacancy rate: 0.0%; Median selected monthly owner costs: $1,019 with a mortgage, $371 without a mortgage; Median gross rent: $808 per month; Rental vacancy rate: 0.0%
Health Insurance: 94.6% have insurance; 67.7% have private insurance; 45.7% have public insurance; 5.4% do not have insurance; 4.7% of children under 18 do not have insurance
Transportation: Commute: 91.7% car, 4.1% public transportation, 1.4% walk, 1.9% work from home; Mean travel time to work: 15.5 minutes

GEDDES (town). Covers a land area of 9.156 square miles and a water area of 3.104 square miles. Located at 43.08° N. Lat; 76.22° W. Long.
Population: 16,951; Growth (since 2000): -4.4%; Density: 1,851.3 persons per square mile; Race: 95.2% White, 0.7% Black/African American, 0.7% Asian, 0.6% American Indian/Alaska Native, 0.0% Native Hawaiian/Other Pacific Islander, 2.2% Two or more races, 4.5% Hispanic of any race; Average household size: 2.39; Median age: 43.4; Age under 18: 19.2%; Age 65 and over: 19.8%; Males per 100 females: 87.4; Marriage status: 30.5% never married, 50.6% now married, 1.9% separated, 8.9% widowed, 10.0% divorced; Foreign born: 5.9%; Speak English only: 91.0%; With disability: 11.7%; Veterans: 8.4%; Ancestry: 28.1% Italian, 27.0% Irish, 13.7% German, 10.5% Polish, 7.3% English
Employment: 13.8% management, business, and financial, 3.7% computer, engineering, and science, 11.0% education, legal, community service, arts, and media, 6.4% healthcare practitioners, 20.0% service, 26.5% sales and office, 8.3% natural resources, construction, and maintenance, 10.3% production, transportation, and material moving
Income: Per capita: $29,795; Median household: $55,904; Average household: $69,849; Households with income of $100,000 or more: 21.3%; Poverty rate: 8.2%
Educational Attainment: High school diploma or higher: 91.3%; Bachelor's degree or higher: 31.1%; Graduate/professional degree or higher: 12.9%
Housing: Homeownership rate: 75.7%; Median home value: $127,700; Median year structure built: 1954; Homeowner vacancy rate: 2.0%; Median selected monthly owner costs: $1,222 with a mortgage, $525 without a mortgage; Median gross rent: $674 per month; Rental vacancy rate: 5.9%
Health Insurance: 94.2% have insurance; 79.2% have private insurance; 34.0% have public insurance; 5.8% do not have insurance; 3.8% of children under 18 do not have insurance
Safety: Violent crime rate: 6.7 per 10,000 population; Property crime rate: 231.0 per 10,000 population
Transportation: Commute: 93.1% car, 1.2% public transportation, 2.6% walk, 2.2% work from home; Mean travel time to work: 19.3 minutes
Additional Information Contacts
Town of Geddes . . . . (315) 468-3600
  http://www.townofgeddes.com

JAMESVILLE (unincorporated postal area)
ZCTA: 13078
Covers a land area of 38.921 square miles and a water area of 0.463 square miles. Located at 42.96° N. Lat; 76.06° W. Long. Elevation is 607 feet.
Population: 10,397; Growth (since 2000): 20.5%; Density: 267.1 persons per square mile; Race: 84.9% White, 5.0% Black/African American, 5.3% Asian, 0.8% American Indian/Alaska Native, 0.0% Native Hawaiian/Other Pacific Islander, 3.7% Two or more races, 2.5% Hispanic of any race; Average household size: 2.53; Median age: 46.6; Age under 18: 19.7%; Age 65 and over: 19.7%; Males per 100 females: 101.8; Marriage status: 31.0% never married, 56.4% now married, 1.4% separated, 7.0% widowed, 5.5% divorced; Foreign born: 8.3%; Speak English only: 89.9%; With disability: 12.5%; Veterans: 9.6%; Ancestry: 26.3% Irish, 18.6% German, 17.7% Italian, 14.8% English, 7.0% Polish
Employment: 21.9% management, business, and financial, 8.2% computer, engineering, and science, 15.0% education, legal, community service, arts, and media, 9.1% healthcare practitioners, 9.7% service, 20.1% sales and office, 9.4% natural resources, construction, and maintenance, 6.5% production, transportation, and material moving
Income: Per capita: $47,202; Median household: $83,558; Average household: $124,175; Households with income of $100,000 or more: 44.4%; Poverty rate: 4.9%
Educational Attainment: High school diploma or higher: 94.0%; Bachelor's degree or higher: 47.0%; Graduate/professional degree or higher: 23.0%

School District(s)
Jamesville-Dewitt Central SD (KG-12)
  2014-15 Enrollment: 2,951 . . . . (315) 445-8304
Housing: Homeownership rate: 81.5%; Median home value: $179,100; Median year structure built: 1974; Homeowner vacancy rate: 0.0%; Median selected monthly owner costs: $1,644 with a mortgage, $742 without a mortgage; Median gross rent: $936 per month; Rental vacancy rate: 2.4%
Health Insurance: 92.1% have insurance; 81.5% have private insurance; 25.0% have public insurance; 7.9% do not have insurance; 6.6% of children under 18 do not have insurance
Transportation: Commute: 88.7% car, 0.8% public transportation, 1.1% walk, 8.0% work from home; Mean travel time to work: 22.7 minutes

JORDAN (village). Covers a land area of 1.146 square miles and a water area of 0 square miles. Located at 43.07° N. Lat; 76.47° W. Long. Elevation is 413 feet.
History: Incorporated 1835.
Population: 1,495; Growth (since 2000): 13.8%; Density: 1,305.0 persons per square mile; Race: 98.5% White, 0.0% Black/African American, 0.2% Asian, 0.2% American Indian/Alaska Native, 0.0% Native Hawaiian/Other Pacific Islander, 1.1% Two or more races, 0.0% Hispanic of any race; Average household size: 2.63; Median age: 40.3; Age under 18: 22.8%; Age 65 and over: 11.6%; Males per 100 females: 102.1; Marriage status: 30.9% never married, 52.6% now married, 4.4% separated, 5.3% widowed, 11.1% divorced; Foreign born: 2.2%; Speak English only: 98.0%; With disability: 13.8%; Veterans: 8.3%; Ancestry: 33.6% Irish, 23.7% English, 22.0% German, 10.0% Polish, 8.0% Italian
Employment: 15.9% management, business, and financial, 4.3% computer, engineering, and science, 13.4% education, legal, community service, arts, and media, 7.9% healthcare practitioners, 10.5% service, 28.6% sales and office, 8.6% natural resources, construction, and maintenance, 10.9% production, transportation, and material moving
Income: Per capita: $26,603; Median household: $50,313; Average household: $67,537; Households with income of $100,000 or more: 23.9%; Poverty rate: 6.5%
Educational Attainment: High school diploma or higher: 94.1%; Bachelor's degree or higher: 28.1%; Graduate/professional degree or higher: 9.3%

School District(s)
Jordan-Elbridge Central SD (PK-12)
  2014-15 Enrollment: 1,382 . . . . (315) 689-8500
Housing: Homeownership rate: 65.8%; Median home value: $98,100; Median year structure built: 1940; Homeowner vacancy rate: 4.6%; Median selected monthly owner costs: $1,153 with a mortgage, $538 without a mortgage; Median gross rent: $594 per month; Rental vacancy rate: 4.0%
Health Insurance: 91.8% have insurance; 75.0% have private insurance; 27.0% have public insurance; 8.2% do not have insurance; 2.6% of children under 18 do not have insurance

Safety: Violent crime rate: 0.0 per 10,000 population; Property crime rate: 15.0 per 10,000 population
Transportation: Commute: 93.7% car, 0.0% public transportation, 3.9% walk, 2.4% work from home; Mean travel time to work: 22.8 minutes

LAFAYETTE (town). Covers a land area of 39.233 square miles and a water area of 0.413 square miles. Located at 42.91° N. Lat; 76.10° W. Long. Elevation is 1,132 feet.

Population: 4,943; Growth (since 2000): 2.3%; Density: 126.0 persons per square mile; Race: 92.6% White, 2.9% Black/African American, 1.3% Asian, 1.8% American Indian/Alaska Native, 0.0% Native Hawaiian/Other Pacific Islander, 1.4% Two or more races, 0.0% Hispanic of any race; Average household size: 2.52; Median age: 39.3; Age under 18: 24.6%; Age 65 and over: 14.5%; Males per 100 females: 99.4; Marriage status: 33.7% never married, 50.2% now married, 1.4% separated, 7.5% widowed, 8.7% divorced; Foreign born: 2.1%; Speak English only: 97.4%; With disability: 6.4%; Veterans: 6.6%; Ancestry: 31.0% Irish, 20.7% Italian, 19.4% German, 18.6% English, 7.7% American
Employment: 22.2% management, business, and financial, 5.6% computer, engineering, and science, 10.0% education, legal, community service, arts, and media, 4.0% healthcare practitioners, 16.4% service, 25.0% sales and office, 10.2% natural resources, construction, and maintenance, 6.7% production, transportation, and material moving
Income: Per capita: $30,487; Median household: $63,776; Average household: $75,757; Households with income of $100,000 or more: 30.4%; Poverty rate: 11.0%
Educational Attainment: High school diploma or higher: 96.2%; Bachelor's degree or higher: 35.4%; Graduate/professional degree or higher: 18.4%

School District(s)
Lafayette Central SD (PK-12)
    2014-15 Enrollment: 895 . . . . (315) 677-9728
Housing: Homeownership rate: 78.1%; Median home value: $154,500; Median year structure built: 1972; Homeowner vacancy rate: 0.0%; Median selected monthly owner costs: $1,431 with a mortgage, $550 without a mortgage; Median gross rent: $995 per month; Rental vacancy rate: 8.9%
Health Insurance: 89.5% have insurance; 76.8% have private insurance; 23.5% have public insurance; 10.5% do not have insurance; 11.2% of children under 18 do not have insurance
Transportation: Commute: 93.4% car, 0.0% public transportation, 1.1% walk, 4.5% work from home; Mean travel time to work: 27.5 minutes
Additional Information Contacts
Town of La Fayette . . . . (315) 677-3674
    http://www.townoflafayette.com

LAKELAND (CDP). Covers a land area of 1.483 square miles and a water area of 0 square miles. Located at 43.09° N. Lat; 76.24° W. Long. Elevation is 479 feet.

Population: 2,747; Growth (since 2000): -3.7%; Density: 1,851.8 persons per square mile; Race: 99.1% White, 0.0% Black/African American, 0.4% Asian, 0.3% American Indian/Alaska Native, 0.0% Native Hawaiian/Other Pacific Islander, 0.2% Two or more races, 3.6% Hispanic of any race; Average household size: 2.49; Median age: 48.2; Age under 18: 16.2%; Age 65 and over: 20.5%; Males per 100 females: 92.1; Marriage status: 23.9% never married, 59.7% now married, 1.7% separated, 6.1% widowed, 10.3% divorced; Foreign born: 7.5%; Speak English only: 89.5%; With disability: 10.4%; Veterans: 7.5%; Ancestry: 25.1% Italian, 16.6% Irish, 14.8% Polish, 12.5% German, 8.3% English
Employment: 11.4% management, business, and financial, 2.8% computer, engineering, and science, 8.4% education, legal, community service, arts, and media, 10.0% healthcare practitioners, 17.4% service, 28.2% sales and office, 9.2% natural resources, construction, and maintenance, 12.7% production, transportation, and material moving
Income: Per capita: $27,802; Median household: $61,250; Average household: $66,739; Households with income of $100,000 or more: 17.5%; Poverty rate: 3.2%
Educational Attainment: High school diploma or higher: 94.2%; Bachelor's degree or higher: 24.1%; Graduate/professional degree or higher: 9.1%
Housing: Homeownership rate: 85.1%; Median home value: $130,400; Median year structure built: 1970; Homeowner vacancy rate: 2.6%; Median selected monthly owner costs: $1,105 with a mortgage, $520 without a mortgage; Median gross rent: $1,000 per month; Rental vacancy rate: 12.3%

Health Insurance: 91.1% have insurance; 80.6% have private insurance; 32.2% have public insurance; 8.9% do not have insurance; 27.5% of children under 18 do not have insurance
Transportation: Commute: 98.9% car, 0.0% public transportation, 0.0% walk, 1.1% work from home; Mean travel time to work: 17.1 minutes

LIVERPOOL (village). Covers a land area of 0.757 square miles and a water area of 0 square miles. Located at 43.11° N. Lat; 76.21° W. Long. Elevation is 420 feet.

History: Incorporated 1830.
Population: 2,230; Growth (since 2000): -11.0%; Density: 2,945.4 persons per square mile; Race: 95.2% White, 2.7% Black/African American, 0.6% Asian, 0.2% American Indian/Alaska Native, 0.0% Native Hawaiian/Other Pacific Islander, 1.3% Two or more races, 3.3% Hispanic of any race; Average household size: 1.94; Median age: 48.1; Age under 18: 13.3%; Age 65 and over: 21.2%; Males per 100 females: 88.5; Marriage status: 40.2% never married, 41.0% now married, 1.7% separated, 7.3% widowed, 11.4% divorced; Foreign born: 3.1%; Speak English only: 97.6%; With disability: 9.2%; Veterans: 10.0%; Ancestry: 29.1% Irish, 24.1% Italian, 22.5% German, 19.1% English, 7.8% Polish
Employment: 12.5% management, business, and financial, 7.7% computer, engineering, and science, 17.1% education, legal, community service, arts, and media, 5.2% healthcare practitioners, 16.9% service, 26.9% sales and office, 6.3% natural resources, construction, and maintenance, 7.4% production, transportation, and material moving
Income: Per capita: $33,133; Median household: $56,033; Average household: $63,963; Households with income of $100,000 or more: 17.1%; Poverty rate: 6.6%
Educational Attainment: High school diploma or higher: 96.0%; Bachelor's degree or higher: 37.3%; Graduate/professional degree or higher: 14.8%

School District(s)
Liverpool Central SD (KG-12)
    2014-15 Enrollment: 7,323 . . . . (315) 622-7125
Four-year College(s)
Bryant & Stratton College-Syracuse North (Private, For-profit)
    Fall 2014 Enrollment: 472 . . . . (315) 652-6500
    2015-16 Tuition: In-state $16,243; Out-of-state $16,243
Two-year College(s)
ITT Technical Institute-Liverpool (Private, For-profit)
    Fall 2014 Enrollment: 215 . . . . (315) 461-8000
    2015-16 Tuition: In-state $18,048; Out-of-state $18,048
Vocational/Technical School(s)
National Tractor Trailer School Inc-Liverpool (Private, For-profit)
    Fall 2014 Enrollment: 146 . . . . (315) 451-2430
    2015-16 Tuition: $9,948
Onondaga Cortland Madison BOCES (Public)
    Fall 2014 Enrollment: 511 . . . . (315) 453-4455
    2015-16 Tuition: $11,800
Housing: Homeownership rate: 63.9%; Median home value: $122,300; Median year structure built: 1952; Homeowner vacancy rate: 0.0%; Median selected monthly owner costs: $1,310 with a mortgage, $572 without a mortgage; Median gross rent: $835 per month; Rental vacancy rate: 3.8%
Health Insurance: 93.9% have insurance; 78.3% have private insurance; 33.9% have public insurance; 6.1% do not have insurance; 1.4% of children under 18 do not have insurance
Safety: Violent crime rate: 8.7 per 10,000 population; Property crime rate: 139.4 per 10,000 population
Transportation: Commute: 85.5% car, 3.7% public transportation, 4.3% walk, 5.9% work from home; Mean travel time to work: 17.4 minutes
Additional Information Contacts
Village of Liverpool . . . . (315) 457-3441
    http://www.villageofliverpool.org

LYNCOURT (CDP). Covers a land area of 1.243 square miles and a water area of 0 square miles. Located at 43.08° N. Lat; 76.13° W. Long. Elevation is 446 feet.

Population: 4,098; Growth (since 2000): -4.0%; Density: 3,296.7 persons per square mile; Race: 85.4% White, 5.1% Black/African American, 3.0% Asian, 0.0% American Indian/Alaska Native, 0.0% Native Hawaiian/Other Pacific Islander, 5.7% Two or more races, 4.2% Hispanic of any race; Average household size: 2.25; Median age: 43.9; Age under 18: 19.5%; Age 65 and over: 17.8%; Males per 100 females: 90.6; Marriage status: 35.7% never married, 40.4% now married, 0.6% separated, 10.9% widowed, 13.0% divorced; Foreign born: 5.7%; Speak English only: 90.3%;

With disability: 13.4%; Veterans: 10.1%; Ancestry: 32.8% Italian, 20.6% Irish, 18.3% German, 8.2% Polish, 7.2% English
Employment: 14.5% management, business, and financial, 6.5% computer, engineering, and science, 4.4% education, legal, community service, arts, and media, 6.1% healthcare practitioners, 20.9% service, 25.3% sales and office, 7.7% natural resources, construction, and maintenance, 14.5% production, transportation, and material moving
Income: Per capita: $22,869; Median household: $44,709; Average household: $49,856; Households with income of $100,000 or more: 10.3%; Poverty rate: 19.7%
Educational Attainment: High school diploma or higher: 86.9%; Bachelor's degree or higher: 17.0%; Graduate/professional degree or higher: 3.0%
Housing: Homeownership rate: 76.9%; Median home value: $91,300; Median year structure built: 1954; Homeowner vacancy rate: 1.3%; Median selected monthly owner costs: $1,117 with a mortgage, $425 without a mortgage; Median gross rent: $813 per month; Rental vacancy rate: 5.2%
Health Insurance: 90.1% have insurance; 71.8% have private insurance; 40.6% have public insurance; 9.9% do not have insurance; 14.8% of children under 18 do not have insurance
Transportation: Commute: 91.1% car, 0.8% public transportation, 2.9% walk, 2.6% work from home; Mean travel time to work: 14.8 minutes

LYSANDER (town). Covers a land area of 61.715 square miles and a water area of 2.894 square miles. Located at 43.18° N. Lat; 76.37° W. Long. Elevation is 413 feet.
Population: 22,369; Growth (since 2000): 16.0%; Density: 362.5 persons per square mile; Race: 94.2% White, 0.8% Black/African American, 1.5% Asian, 0.2% American Indian/Alaska Native, 0.1% Native Hawaiian/Other Pacific Islander, 3.2% Two or more races, 2.9% Hispanic of any race; Average household size: 2.55; Median age: 44.6; Age under 18: 23.4%; Age 65 and over: 15.8%; Males per 100 females: 95.4; Marriage status: 23.1% never married, 61.6% now married, 1.3% separated, 5.4% widowed, 9.8% divorced; Foreign born: 2.9%; Speak English only: 95.1%; With disability: 8.8%; Veterans: 9.6%; Ancestry: 25.7% Irish, 23.5% German, 18.7% Italian, 14.8% English, 6.7% American
Employment: 16.5% management, business, and financial, 4.9% computer, engineering, and science, 14.4% education, legal, community service, arts, and media, 10.5% healthcare practitioners, 11.7% service, 27.2% sales and office, 7.4% natural resources, construction, and maintenance, 7.5% production, transportation, and material moving
Income: Per capita: $36,033; Median household: $78,489; Average household: $90,670; Households with income of $100,000 or more: 36.6%; Poverty rate: 7.7%
Educational Attainment: High school diploma or higher: 95.4%; Bachelor's degree or higher: 44.0%; Graduate/professional degree or higher: 20.1%
Housing: Homeownership rate: 80.0%; Median home value: $180,000; Median year structure built: 1980; Homeowner vacancy rate: 1.6%; Median selected monthly owner costs: $1,573 with a mortgage, $623 without a mortgage; Median gross rent: $790 per month; Rental vacancy rate: 7.5%
Health Insurance: 95.9% have insurance; 84.0% have private insurance; 27.8% have public insurance; 4.1% do not have insurance; 1.6% of children under 18 do not have insurance
Transportation: Commute: 92.8% car, 0.4% public transportation, 2.3% walk, 3.9% work from home; Mean travel time to work: 23.9 minutes
Additional Information Contacts
Town of Lysander . . . . (315) 638-0224
  http://www.townoflysander.org

MANLIUS (town). Covers a land area of 49.218 square miles and a water area of 0.735 square miles. Located at 43.05° N. Lat; 75.98° W. Long. Elevation is 591 feet.
History: Settled 1789 incorporated 1842,
Population: 32,400; Growth (since 2000): 1.7%; Density: 658.3 persons per square mile; Race: 89.7% White, 2.8% Black/African American, 3.8% Asian, 0.3% American Indian/Alaska Native, 0.0% Native Hawaiian/Other Pacific Islander, 2.6% Two or more races, 1.8% Hispanic of any race; Average household size: 2.42; Median age: 45.3; Age under 18: 23.5%; Age 65 and over: 18.3%; Males per 100 females: 91.2; Marriage status: 23.6% never married, 59.4% now married, 1.4% separated, 6.8% widowed, 10.2% divorced; Foreign born: 7.4%; Speak English only: 91.4%; With disability: 9.7%; Veterans: 8.8%; Ancestry: 25.3% Irish, 19.1% German, 16.2% Italian, 13.2% English, 5.3% Polish

Employment: 18.2% management, business, and financial, 5.7% computer, engineering, and science, 20.9% education, legal, community service, arts, and media, 10.4% healthcare practitioners, 11.4% service, 22.6% sales and office, 4.8% natural resources, construction, and maintenance, 5.9% production, transportation, and material moving
Income: Per capita: $41,620; Median household: $75,316; Average household: $100,151; Households with income of $100,000 or more: 37.2%; Poverty rate: 5.7%
Educational Attainment: High school diploma or higher: 96.9%; Bachelor's degree or higher: 52.7%; Graduate/professional degree or higher: 27.4%

School District(s)
Fayetteville-Manlius Central SD (KG-12)
  2014-15 Enrollment: 4,191 . . . . (315) 692-1200
Housing: Homeownership rate: 79.5%; Median home value: $171,700; Median year structure built: 1969; Homeowner vacancy rate: 0.1%; Median selected monthly owner costs: $1,660 with a mortgage, $700 without a mortgage; Median gross rent: $878 per month; Rental vacancy rate: 4.2%
Health Insurance: 96.5% have insurance; 83.1% have private insurance; 29.4% have public insurance; 3.5% do not have insurance; 2.0% of children under 18 do not have insurance
Safety: Violent crime rate: 4.5 per 10,000 population; Property crime rate: 165.4 per 10,000 population
Transportation: Commute: 92.7% car, 0.5% public transportation, 1.6% walk, 4.7% work from home; Mean travel time to work: 21.6 minutes
Additional Information Contacts
Town of Manlius . . . . (315) 637-3521
  http://www.townofmanlius.org

MANLIUS (village). Covers a land area of 1.785 square miles and a water area of 0.002 square miles. Located at 43.00° N. Lat; 75.98° W. Long. Elevation is 591 feet.
Population: 4,670; Growth (since 2000): -3.1%; Density: 2,615.8 persons per square mile; Race: 90.0% White, 2.8% Black/African American, 3.5% Asian, 0.9% American Indian/Alaska Native, 0.0% Native Hawaiian/Other Pacific Islander, 2.9% Two or more races, 2.0% Hispanic of any race; Average household size: 2.46; Median age: 41.3; Age under 18: 25.8%; Age 65 and over: 17.2%; Males per 100 females: 87.4; Marriage status: 24.7% never married, 56.3% now married, 1.3% separated, 6.9% widowed, 12.1% divorced; Foreign born: 7.0%; Speak English only: 90.2%; With disability: 12.3%; Veterans: 6.1%; Ancestry: 27.1% Irish, 15.3% German, 14.1% Italian, 10.3% English, 10.2% American
Employment: 19.5% management, business, and financial, 3.2% computer, engineering, and science, 24.4% education, legal, community service, arts, and media, 10.8% healthcare practitioners, 12.0% service, 21.0% sales and office, 3.0% natural resources, construction, and maintenance, 6.1% production, transportation, and material moving
Income: Per capita: $38,489; Median household: $71,667; Average household: $94,478; Households with income of $100,000 or more: 36.2%; Poverty rate: 6.0%
Educational Attainment: High school diploma or higher: 96.7%; Bachelor's degree or higher: 59.7%; Graduate/professional degree or higher: 25.0%

School District(s)
Fayetteville-Manlius Central SD (KG-12)
  2014-15 Enrollment: 4,191 . . . . (315) 692-1200
Housing: Homeownership rate: 65.9%; Median home value: $188,900; Median year structure built: 1970; Homeowner vacancy rate: 0.0%; Median selected monthly owner costs: $1,873 with a mortgage, $869 without a mortgage; Median gross rent: $763 per month; Rental vacancy rate: 3.4%
Health Insurance: 98.0% have insurance; 82.3% have private insurance; 29.8% have public insurance; 2.0% do not have insurance; 0.0% of children under 18 do not have insurance
Transportation: Commute: 92.0% car, 1.0% public transportation, 2.7% walk, 4.1% work from home; Mean travel time to work: 23.7 minutes
Additional Information Contacts
Village of Manlius . . . . (315) 637-3521
  http://www.townofmanlius.org

MARCELLUS (town). Covers a land area of 32.445 square miles and a water area of 0.140 square miles. Located at 42.94° N. Lat; 76.32° W. Long. Elevation is 682 feet.
History: Incorporated 1846.
Population: 6,196; Growth (since 2000): -1.9%; Density: 191.0 persons per square mile; Race: 95.8% White, 0.5% Black/African American, 1.1%

Asian, 1.2% American Indian/Alaska Native, 0.0% Native Hawaiian/Other Pacific Islander, 1.5% Two or more races, 1.2% Hispanic of any race; Average household size: 2.50; Median age: 46.5; Age under 18: 23.1%; Age 65 and over: 17.1%; Males per 100 females: 97.7; Marriage status: 25.8% never married, 57.9% now married, 1.2% separated, 7.1% widowed, 9.2% divorced; Foreign born: 1.9%; Speak English only: 96.9%; With disability: 10.8%; Veterans: 8.8%; Ancestry: 35.5% Irish, 25.7% English, 19.5% German, 11.5% Italian, 7.3% Polish

Employment: 24.4% management, business, and financial, 5.4% computer, engineering, and science, 11.5% education, legal, community service, arts, and media, 7.4% healthcare practitioners, 15.4% service, 21.2% sales and office, 9.4% natural resources, construction, and maintenance, 5.3% production, transportation, and material moving

Income: Per capita: $36,382; Median household: $70,889; Average household: $86,931; Households with income of $100,000 or more: 31.3%; Poverty rate: 4.1%

Educational Attainment: High school diploma or higher: 97.8%; Bachelor's degree or higher: 44.3%; Graduate/professional degree or higher: 17.7%

School District(s)

Marcellus Central SD (KG-12)

   2014-15 Enrollment: 1,770 . . . . (315) 673-6000

Housing: Homeownership rate: 85.2%; Median home value: $174,000; Median year structure built: 1964; Homeowner vacancy rate: 0.6%; Median selected monthly owner costs: $1,639 with a mortgage, $604 without a mortgage; Median gross rent: $758 per month; Rental vacancy rate: 3.2%

Health Insurance: 93.1% have insurance; 83.8% have private insurance; 25.9% have public insurance; 6.9% do not have insurance; 8.3% of children under 18 do not have insurance

Transportation: Commute: 88.0% car, 0.4% public transportation, 1.5% walk, 9.6% work from home; Mean travel time to work: 22.9 minutes

MARCELLUS (village).
Covers a land area of 0.622 square miles and a water area of 0 square miles. Located at 42.98° N. Lat; 76.34° W. Long. Elevation is 682 feet.

Population: 1,655; Growth (since 2000): -9.4%; Density: 2,661.4 persons per square mile; Race: 95.0% White, 0.7% Black/African American, 3.6% Asian, 0.4% American Indian/Alaska Native, 0.0% Native Hawaiian/Other Pacific Islander, 0.3% Two or more races, 0.3% Hispanic of any race; Average household size: 2.17; Median age: 48.2; Age under 18: 19.6%; Age 65 and over: 23.7%; Males per 100 females: 86.5; Marriage status: 34.8% never married, 44.7% now married, 2.0% separated, 9.2% widowed, 11.3% divorced; Foreign born: 3.3%; Speak English only: 97.1%; With disability: 14.4%; Veterans: 8.2%; Ancestry: 39.0% Irish, 23.6% English, 17.6% German, 13.4% Italian, 8.7% Polish

Employment: 16.1% management, business, and financial, 2.3% computer, engineering, and science, 17.2% education, legal, community service, arts, and media, 6.2% healthcare practitioners, 18.2% service, 24.2% sales and office, 9.3% natural resources, construction, and maintenance, 6.4% production, transportation, and material moving

Income: Per capita: $42,969; Median household: $50,455; Average household: $85,536; Households with income of $100,000 or more: 24.0%; Poverty rate: 5.6%

Educational Attainment: High school diploma or higher: 98.0%; Bachelor's degree or higher: 45.8%; Graduate/professional degree or higher: 18.7%

School District(s)

Marcellus Central SD (KG-12)

   2014-15 Enrollment: 1,770 . . . . (315) 673-6000

Housing: Homeownership rate: 58.8%; Median home value: $150,700; Median year structure built: 1958; Homeowner vacancy rate: 0.0%; Median selected monthly owner costs: $1,389 with a mortgage, $572 without a mortgage; Median gross rent: $743 per month; Rental vacancy rate: 3.7%

Health Insurance: 92.1% have insurance; 80.9% have private insurance; 33.2% have public insurance; 7.9% do not have insurance; 2.5% of children under 18 do not have insurance

Safety: Violent crime rate: 0.0 per 10,000 population; Property crime rate: 50.8 per 10,000 population

Transportation: Commute: 89.7% car, 0.6% public transportation, 3.9% walk, 5.8% work from home; Mean travel time to work: 22.1 minutes

Additional Information Contacts

Village of Marcellus . . . . (315) 673-3112

   http://villageofmarcellus.com

MARIETTA (unincorporated postal area)
ZCTA: 13110

Covers a land area of 24.574 square miles and a water area of 0.010 square miles. Located at 42.90° N. Lat; 76.28° W. Long. Elevation is 797 feet.

Population: 2,257; Growth (since 2000): -8.7%; Density: 91.8 persons per square mile; Race: 99.1% White, 0.0% Black/African American, 0.3% Asian, 0.0% American Indian/Alaska Native, 0.0% Native Hawaiian/Other Pacific Islander, 0.6% Two or more races, 3.1% Hispanic of any race; Average household size: 2.42; Median age: 49.8; Age under 18: 19.8%; Age 65 and over: 20.0%; Males per 100 females: 106.9; Marriage status: 21.4% never married, 59.6% now married, 2.4% separated, 9.5% widowed, 9.5% divorced; Foreign born: 1.8%; Speak English only: 96.1%; With disability: 11.1%; Veterans: 10.0%; Ancestry: 24.7% Irish, 23.3% English, 23.1% German, 8.3% American, 5.5% Polish

Employment: 11.9% management, business, and financial, 6.5% computer, engineering, and science, 12.4% education, legal, community service, arts, and media, 8.6% healthcare practitioners, 13.5% service, 25.6% sales and office, 14.6% natural resources, construction, and maintenance, 7.0% production, transportation, and material moving

Income: Per capita: $34,629; Median household: $70,769; Average household: $82,592; Households with income of $100,000 or more: 28.7%; Poverty rate: 5.3%

Educational Attainment: High school diploma or higher: 93.1%; Bachelor's degree or higher: 30.4%; Graduate/professional degree or higher: 12.0%

Housing: Homeownership rate: 92.2%; Median home value: $163,000; Median year structure built: 1969; Homeowner vacancy rate: 2.3%; Median selected monthly owner costs: $1,367 with a mortgage, $575 without a mortgage; Median gross rent: $683 per month; Rental vacancy rate: 0.0%

Health Insurance: 96.1% have insurance; 79.1% have private insurance; 33.9% have public insurance; 3.9% do not have insurance; 0.0% of children under 18 do not have insurance

Transportation: Commute: 88.7% car, 0.0% public transportation, 0.6% walk, 10.3% work from home; Mean travel time to work: 28.7 minutes

MATTYDALE (CDP).
Covers a land area of 1.920 square miles and a water area of 0 square miles. Located at 43.10° N. Lat; 76.14° W. Long. Elevation is 404 feet.

Population: 6,434; Growth (since 2000): 1.1%; Density: 3,350.2 persons per square mile; Race: 86.0% White, 7.1% Black/African American, 1.3% Asian, 1.0% American Indian/Alaska Native, 0.0% Native Hawaiian/Other Pacific Islander, 4.0% Two or more races, 5.8% Hispanic of any race; Average household size: 2.49; Median age: 36.5; Age under 18: 26.2%; Age 65 and over: 13.0%; Males per 100 females: 91.5; Marriage status: 40.3% never married, 37.6% now married, 2.1% separated, 7.9% widowed, 14.2% divorced; Foreign born: 2.1%; Speak English only: 96.6%; With disability: 12.0%; Veterans: 9.8%; Ancestry: 24.3% Irish, 20.3% Italian, 19.3% German, 9.8% English, 8.2% French

Employment: 10.1% management, business, and financial, 2.3% computer, engineering, and science, 4.7% education, legal, community service, arts, and media, 3.2% healthcare practitioners, 19.5% service, 32.7% sales and office, 7.0% natural resources, construction, and maintenance, 20.5% production, transportation, and material moving

Income: Per capita: $20,969; Median household: $44,882; Average household: $50,915; Households with income of $100,000 or more: 9.2%; Poverty rate: 16.6%

Educational Attainment: High school diploma or higher: 91.1%; Bachelor's degree or higher: 11.4%; Graduate/professional degree or higher: 3.8%

Vocational/Technical School(s)

Continental School of Beauty Culture-Mattydale (Private, For-profit)

   Fall 2014 Enrollment: 242 . . . . (585) 272-8060

   2015-16 Tuition: $12,440

Housing: Homeownership rate: 62.4%; Median home value: $84,400; Median year structure built: 1952; Homeowner vacancy rate: 3.4%; Median selected monthly owner costs: $989 with a mortgage, $376 without a mortgage; Median gross rent: $855 per month; Rental vacancy rate: 4.5%

Health Insurance: 89.7% have insurance; 64.2% have private insurance; 39.9% have public insurance; 10.3% do not have insurance; 2.1% of children under 18 do not have insurance

Transportation: Commute: 90.6% car, 1.9% public transportation, 5.8% walk, 0.6% work from home; Mean travel time to work: 16.5 minutes

MEMPHIS (unincorporated postal area)
ZCTA: 13112

Covers a land area of 20.254 square miles and a water area of 1.328 square miles. Located at 43.11° N. Lat; 76.42° W. Long. Elevation is 433 feet.

Population: 1,950; Growth (since 2000): 1.5%; Density: 96.3 persons per square mile; Race: 93.6% White, 0.3% Black/African American, 0.0% Asian, 1.1% American Indian/Alaska Native, 0.0% Native Hawaiian/Other Pacific Islander, 0.6% Two or more races, 3.1% Hispanic of any race; Average household size: 2.70; Median age: 39.4; Age under 18: 27.3%; Age 65 and over: 17.6%; Males per 100 females: 106.2; Marriage status: 24.7% never married, 58.6% now married, 0.9% separated, 6.3% widowed, 10.4% divorced; Foreign born: 2.4%; Speak English only: 94.2%; With disability: 16.1%; Veterans: 5.8%; Ancestry: 13.9% Irish, 13.0% English, 12.8% German, 11.9% American, 10.4% Italian

Employment: 7.3% management, business, and financial, 6.8% computer, engineering, and science, 15.7% education, legal, community service, arts, and media, 11.8% healthcare practitioners, 17.1% service, 21.3% sales and office, 10.2% natural resources, construction, and maintenance, 9.8% production, transportation, and material moving

Income: Per capita: $26,402; Median household: $55,000; Average household: $70,372; Households with income of $100,000 or more: 20.2%; Poverty rate: 20.1%

Educational Attainment: High school diploma or higher: 92.6%; Bachelor's degree or higher: 25.1%; Graduate/professional degree or higher: 12.9%

Housing: Homeownership rate: 94.3%; Median home value: $133,700; Median year structure built: 1956; Homeowner vacancy rate: 0.0%; Median selected monthly owner costs: $1,273 with a mortgage, $471 without a mortgage; Median gross rent: n/a per month; Rental vacancy rate: 0.0%

Health Insurance: 95.2% have insurance; 76.0% have private insurance; 40.2% have public insurance; 4.8% do not have insurance; 2.4% of children under 18 do not have insurance

Transportation: Commute: 92.2% car, 0.0% public transportation, 3.7% walk, 3.1% work from home; Mean travel time to work: 27.3 minutes

MINOA (village).
Covers a land area of 1.273 square miles and a water area of 0 square miles. Located at 43.07° N. Lat; 76.01° W. Long. Elevation is 413 feet.

Population: 3,514; Growth (since 2000): 5.0%; Density: 2,760.0 persons per square mile; Race: 96.6% White, 1.2% Black/African American, 0.0% Asian, 0.0% American Indian/Alaska Native, 0.0% Native Hawaiian/Other Pacific Islander, 2.2% Two or more races, 1.8% Hispanic of any race; Average household size: 2.44; Median age: 33.9; Age under 18: 24.0%; Age 65 and over: 15.6%; Males per 100 females: 88.0; Marriage status: 26.4% never married, 53.2% now married, 1.3% separated, 9.3% widowed, 11.1% divorced; Foreign born: 1.5%; Speak English only: 97.4%; With disability: 10.6%; Veterans: 6.6%; Ancestry: 28.2% Irish, 17.6% German, 16.4% English, 15.7% Italian, 5.9% French

Employment: 11.8% management, business, and financial, 4.1% computer, engineering, and science, 25.2% education, legal, community service, arts, and media, 4.8% healthcare practitioners, 17.1% service, 27.7% sales and office, 4.3% natural resources, construction, and maintenance, 5.1% production, transportation, and material moving

Income: Per capita: $30,814; Median household: $59,209; Average household: $74,012; Households with income of $100,000 or more: 26.8%; Poverty rate: 2.7%

Educational Attainment: High school diploma or higher: 98.3%; Bachelor's degree or higher: 37.7%; Graduate/professional degree or higher: 20.0%

School District(s)
East Syracuse-Minoa Central SD (PK-12)
    2014-15 Enrollment: 3,546 . . . . (315) 434-3012

Housing: Homeownership rate: 83.3%; Median home value: $137,000; Median year structure built: 1972; Homeowner vacancy rate: 0.0%; Median selected monthly owner costs: $1,271 with a mortgage, $577 without a mortgage; Median gross rent: $758 per month; Rental vacancy rate: 0.0%

Health Insurance: 99.7% have insurance; 91.2% have private insurance; 24.6% have public insurance; 0.3% do not have insurance; 0.0% of children under 18 do not have insurance

Transportation: Commute: 95.5% car, 1.8% public transportation, 1.8% walk, 0.9% work from home; Mean travel time to work: 17.8 minutes

NEDROW (CDP).
Covers a land area of 0.959 square miles and a water area of 0 square miles. Located at 42.98° N. Lat; 76.14° W. Long. Elevation is 472 feet.

Population: 2,176; Growth (since 2000): -3.9%; Density: 2,268.1 persons per square mile; Race: 71.7% White, 12.7% Black/African American, 1.4% Asian, 8.1% American Indian/Alaska Native, 0.0% Native Hawaiian/Other Pacific Islander, 6.0% Two or more races, 3.9% Hispanic of any race; Average household size: 2.42; Median age: 41.1; Age under 18: 18.0%; Age 65 and over: 13.2%; Males per 100 females: 91.6; Marriage status: 40.6% never married, 42.6% now married, 2.1% separated, 6.9% widowed, 9.9% divorced; Foreign born: 4.5%; Speak English only: 94.8%; With disability: 14.9%; Veterans: 7.8%; Ancestry: 21.6% Irish, 18.2% German, 13.3% English, 11.8% Italian, 5.0% Polish

Employment: 11.1% management, business, and financial, 6.4% computer, engineering, and science, 8.5% education, legal, community service, arts, and media, 5.5% healthcare practitioners, 15.3% service, 33.6% sales and office, 11.8% natural resources, construction, and maintenance, 7.7% production, transportation, and material moving

Income: Per capita: $27,754; Median household: $51,944; Average household: $65,409; Households with income of $100,000 or more: 12.9%; Poverty rate: 12.0%

Educational Attainment: High school diploma or higher: 89.4%; Bachelor's degree or higher: 17.8%; Graduate/professional degree or higher: 9.9%

School District(s)
Lafayette Central SD (PK-12)
    2014-15 Enrollment: 895 . . . . (315) 677-9728
Onondaga Central SD (PK-12)
    2014-15 Enrollment: 904 . . . . (315) 552-5000

Housing: Homeownership rate: 89.6%; Median home value: $84,500; Median year structure built: 1951; Homeowner vacancy rate: 2.2%; Median selected monthly owner costs: $989 with a mortgage, $472 without a mortgage; Median gross rent: $685 per month; Rental vacancy rate: 0.0%

Health Insurance: 93.8% have insurance; 67.1% have private insurance; 38.5% have public insurance; 6.2% do not have insurance; 4.6% of children under 18 do not have insurance

Transportation: Commute: 93.0% car, 3.2% public transportation, 1.7% walk, 2.1% work from home; Mean travel time to work: 19.5 minutes

NORTH SYRACUSE (village).
Covers a land area of 1.958 square miles and a water area of 0 square miles. Located at 43.13° N. Lat; 76.13° W. Long. Elevation is 420 feet.

History: Incorporated 1925.

Population: 6,641; Growth (since 2000): -3.2%; Density: 3,392.2 persons per square mile; Race: 93.0% White, 0.9% Black/African American, 0.0% Asian, 1.3% American Indian/Alaska Native, 0.0% Native Hawaiian/Other Pacific Islander, 4.8% Two or more races, 3.3% Hispanic of any race; Average household size: 2.08; Median age: 41.5; Age under 18: 19.0%; Age 65 and over: 21.9%; Males per 100 females: 93.3; Marriage status: 32.3% never married, 43.2% now married, 1.6% separated, 10.8% widowed, 13.8% divorced; Foreign born: 2.3%; Speak English only: 96.6%; With disability: 14.9%; Veterans: 10.6%; Ancestry: 27.0% Irish, 19.4% German, 17.9% Italian, 11.9% English, 8.7% French

Employment: 10.1% management, business, and financial, 3.6% computer, engineering, and science, 13.3% education, legal, community service, arts, and media, 6.3% healthcare practitioners, 16.4% service, 38.0% sales and office, 5.1% natural resources, construction, and maintenance, 7.2% production, transportation, and material moving

Income: Per capita: $26,722; Median household: $43,411; Average household: $54,220; Households with income of $100,000 or more: 13.2%; Poverty rate: 8.6%

Educational Attainment: High school diploma or higher: 92.6%; Bachelor's degree or higher: 23.5%; Graduate/professional degree or higher: 8.8%

School District(s)
North Syracuse Central SD (PK-12)
    2014-15 Enrollment: 9,119 . . . . (315) 218-2151

Housing: Homeownership rate: 60.3%; Median home value: $101,300; Median year structure built: 1959; Homeowner vacancy rate: 1.0%; Median selected monthly owner costs: $1,128 with a mortgage, $472 without a mortgage; Median gross rent: $783 per month; Rental vacancy rate: 5.4%

Health Insurance: 93.5% have insurance; 76.6% have private insurance; 34.2% have public insurance; 6.5% do not have insurance; 2.8% of children under 18 do not have insurance

Safety: Violent crime rate: 10.1 per 10,000 population; Property crime rate: 105.8 per 10,000 population

Transportation: Commute: 91.9% car, 0.7% public transportation, 2.2% walk, 3.5% work from home; Mean travel time to work: 18.3 minutes

Additional Information Contacts

Village of North Syracuse . . . . (315) 458-0900
http://northsyracuseny.org

ONONDAGA (town). Covers a land area of 57.741 square miles and a water area of 0.096 square miles. Located at 42.98° N. Lat; 76.22° W. Long.

History: The town is named after the native Onondaga tribe, part of the Iroquois Confederacy. As early as 1600, Onondaga served as the capital of the Iroquois League and the primary settlement of the Onondaga people.

Population: 23,145; Growth (since 2000): 9.9%; Density: 400.8 persons per square mile; Race: 89.6% White, 4.0% Black/African American, 2.7% Asian, 1.0% American Indian/Alaska Native, 0.0% Native Hawaiian/Other Pacific Islander, 2.3% Two or more races, 3.6% Hispanic of any race; Average household size: 2.51; Median age: 44.3; Age under 18: 20.9%; Age 65 and over: 17.3%; Males per 100 females: 92.8; Marriage status: 29.9% never married, 55.5% now married, 1.7% separated, 7.6% widowed, 7.0% divorced; Foreign born: 5.6%; Speak English only: 91.0%; With disability: 10.4%; Veterans: 8.0%; Ancestry: 26.6% Irish, 19.7% German, 18.9% Italian, 13.9% English, 7.2% Polish

Employment: 16.9% management, business, and financial, 6.7% computer, engineering, and science, 13.6% education, legal, community service, arts, and media, 9.9% healthcare practitioners, 13.2% service, 25.3% sales and office, 6.6% natural resources, construction, and maintenance, 7.9% production, transportation, and material moving

Income: Per capita: $36,926; Median household: $73,815; Average household: $96,135; Households with income of $100,000 or more: 37.2%; Poverty rate: 4.3%

Educational Attainment: High school diploma or higher: 92.9%; Bachelor's degree or higher: 40.0%; Graduate/professional degree or higher: 19.1%

Housing: Homeownership rate: 81.2%; Median home value: $172,200; Median year structure built: 1973; Homeowner vacancy rate: 1.8%; Median selected monthly owner costs: $1,585 with a mortgage, $610 without a mortgage; Median gross rent: $885 per month; Rental vacancy rate: 8.0%

Health Insurance: 96.7% have insurance; 86.4% have private insurance; 24.2% have public insurance; 3.3% do not have insurance; 2.0% of children under 18 do not have insurance

Transportation: Commute: 93.1% car, 1.6% public transportation, 1.8% walk, 3.1% work from home; Mean travel time to work: 20.9 minutes

Additional Information Contacts

Town of Onondaga . . . . (315) 469-1583
http://www.townofonondagany.com

ONONDAGA NATION RESERVATION (reservation). Covers a land area of 9.247 square miles and a water area of 0.046 square miles. Located at 42.93° N. Lat; 76.15° W. Long.

Population: 161; Growth (since 2000): -89.1%; Density: 17.4 persons per square mile; Race: 0.0% White, 0.0% Black/African American, 0.0% Asian, 0.0% American Indian/Alaska Native, 0.0% Native Hawaiian/Other Pacific Islander, 42.2% Two or more races, 100.0% Hispanic of any race; Average household size: 3.58; Median age: 71.3; Age under 18: 0.0%; Age 65 and over: 57.8%; Males per 100 females: 87.2; Marriage status: 42.2% never married, 0.0% now married, 0.0% separated, 57.8% widowed, 0.0% divorced; Foreign born: 57.8%; Speak English only: 42.2%; With disability: 0.0%; Veterans: 0.0%; Ancestry: 42.2% American

Employment: 100.0% management, business, and financial, 0.0% computer, engineering, and science, 0.0% education, legal, community service, arts, and media, 0.0% healthcare practitioners, 0.0% service, 0.0% sales and office, 0.0% natural resources, construction, and maintenance, 0.0% production, transportation, and material moving

Income: Per capita: $30,648; Median household: n/a; Average household: n/a; Households with income of $100,000 or more: n/a; Poverty rate: n/a

Educational Attainment: High school diploma or higher: 100.0%; Bachelor's degree or higher: 29.8%; Graduate/professional degree or higher: n/a

Housing: Homeownership rate: 100.0%; Median home value: n/a; Median year structure built: n/a; Homeowner vacancy rate: 0.0%; Median selected monthly owner costs: n/a with a mortgage, n/a without a mortgage; Median gross rent: n/a per month; Rental vacancy rate: 0.0%

Health Insurance: 57.8% have insurance; 0.0% have private insurance; 57.8% have public insurance; 42.2% do not have insurance; 0.0% of children under 18 do not have insurance

Transportation: Commute: 0.0% car, 100.0% public transportation, 0.0% walk, 0.0% work from home; Mean travel time to work: 0.0 minutes

OTISCO (town). Covers a land area of 29.532 square miles and a water area of 1.629 square miles. Located at 42.86° N. Lat; 76.23° W. Long. Elevation is 1,480 feet.

Population: 2,560; Growth (since 2000): 0.0%; Density: 86.7 persons per square mile; Race: 98.9% White, 0.0% Black/African American, 0.0% Asian, 0.0% American Indian/Alaska Native, 0.0% Native Hawaiian/Other Pacific Islander, 1.1% Two or more races, 1.1% Hispanic of any race; Average household size: 2.56; Median age: 45.5; Age under 18: 22.7%; Age 65 and over: 13.9%; Males per 100 females: 105.7; Marriage status: 26.1% never married, 61.0% now married, 3.1% separated, 5.2% widowed, 7.6% divorced; Foreign born: 0.0%; Speak English only: 99.5%; With disability: 11.0%; Veterans: 8.2%; Ancestry: 31.6% German, 22.1% Irish, 20.2% English, 7.1% Italian, 6.7% Polish

Employment: 17.7% management, business, and financial, 4.4% computer, engineering, and science, 14.3% education, legal, community service, arts, and media, 4.4% healthcare practitioners, 11.5% service, 24.9% sales and office, 14.9% natural resources, construction, and maintenance, 7.9% production, transportation, and material moving

Income: Per capita: $31,853; Median household: $70,045; Average household: $80,637; Households with income of $100,000 or more: 24.4%; Poverty rate: 9.1%

Educational Attainment: High school diploma or higher: 94.8%; Bachelor's degree or higher: 27.9%; Graduate/professional degree or higher: 12.7%

Housing: Homeownership rate: 87.3%; Median home value: $160,700; Median year structure built: 1978; Homeowner vacancy rate: 0.0%; Median selected monthly owner costs: $1,416 with a mortgage, $583 without a mortgage; Median gross rent: $730 per month; Rental vacancy rate: 0.0%

Health Insurance: 91.5% have insurance; 78.2% have private insurance; 25.1% have public insurance; 8.5% do not have insurance; 3.8% of children under 18 do not have insurance

Transportation: Commute: 89.2% car, 0.0% public transportation, 0.3% walk, 9.5% work from home; Mean travel time to work: 27.1 minutes

POMPEY (town). Covers a land area of 66.378 square miles and a water area of 0.097 square miles. Located at 42.92° N. Lat; 75.99° W. Long. Elevation is 1,673 feet.

Population: 7,286; Growth (since 2000): 18.3%; Density: 109.8 persons per square mile; Race: 94.0% White, 0.9% Black/African American, 3.4% Asian, 0.4% American Indian/Alaska Native, 0.0% Native Hawaiian/Other Pacific Islander, 1.3% Two or more races, 0.8% Hispanic of any race; Average household size: 2.79; Median age: 45.5; Age under 18: 23.9%; Age 65 and over: 13.9%; Males per 100 females: 101.9; Marriage status: 27.8% never married, 61.6% now married, 1.2% separated, 3.1% widowed, 7.5% divorced; Foreign born: 4.4%; Speak English only: 93.4%; With disability: 7.2%; Veterans: 7.0%; Ancestry: 25.3% German, 23.7% Irish, 16.3% English, 9.6% Italian, 7.1% Polish

Employment: 20.3% management, business, and financial, 7.7% computer, engineering, and science, 15.3% education, legal, community service, arts, and media, 5.7% healthcare practitioners, 8.4% service, 20.6% sales and office, 15.9% natural resources, construction, and maintenance, 5.9% production, transportation, and material moving

Income: Per capita: $49,293; Median household: $98,849; Average household: $133,319; Households with income of $100,000 or more: 48.9%; Poverty rate: 3.1%

Educational Attainment: High school diploma or higher: 97.0%; Bachelor's degree or higher: 47.4%; Graduate/professional degree or higher: 17.3%

Housing: Homeownership rate: 88.5%; Median home value: $224,700; Median year structure built: 1980; Homeowner vacancy rate: 2.2%; Median selected monthly owner costs: $1,914 with a mortgage, $759 without a mortgage; Median gross rent: $733 per month; Rental vacancy rate: 0.0%

Health Insurance: 94.6% have insurance; 83.4% have private insurance; 20.1% have public insurance; 5.4% do not have insurance; 0.0% of children under 18 do not have insurance

Transportation: Commute: 88.9% car, 0.0% public transportation, 1.9% walk, 8.7% work from home; Mean travel time to work: 24.6 minutes

Additional Information Contacts
Town of Pompey . . . . (315) 682-9877
    http://www.townofpompey.com

SALINA (town). Covers a land area of 13.750 square miles and a water area of 1.311 square miles. Located at 43.10° N. Lat; 76.17° W. Long.
Population: 33,598; Growth (since 2000): 0.9%; Density: 2,443.5 persons per square mile; Race: 88.7% White, 4.9% Black/African American, 2.0% Asian, 0.2% American Indian/Alaska Native, 0.0% Native Hawaiian/Other Pacific Islander, 3.5% Two or more races, 3.2% Hispanic of any race; Average household size: 2.24; Median age: 43.5; Age under 18: 19.2%; Age 65 and over: 19.4%; Males per 100 females: 90.4; Marriage status: 33.2% never married, 46.9% now married, 2.4% separated, 7.9% widowed, 12.0% divorced; Foreign born: 5.8%; Speak English only: 92.7%; With disability: 13.3%; Veterans: 10.5%; Ancestry: 26.7% Italian, 22.6% Irish, 20.7% German, 12.1% English, 7.3% Polish
Employment: 14.5% management, business, and financial, 5.5% computer, engineering, and science, 11.7% education, legal, community service, arts, and media, 6.1% healthcare practitioners, 16.2% service, 28.5% sales and office, 6.2% natural resources, construction, and maintenance, 11.3% production, transportation, and material moving
Income: Per capita: $28,213; Median household: $52,259; Average household: $62,010; Households with income of $100,000 or more: 15.5%; Poverty rate: 11.1%
Educational Attainment: High school diploma or higher: 91.1%; Bachelor's degree or higher: 26.1%; Graduate/professional degree or higher: 9.9%
Housing: Homeownership rate: 66.6%; Median home value: $108,800; Median year structure built: 1959; Homeowner vacancy rate: 2.6%; Median selected monthly owner costs: $1,186 with a mortgage, $471 without a mortgage; Median gross rent: $848 per month; Rental vacancy rate: 3.1%
Health Insurance: 93.1% have insurance; 74.7% have private insurance; 35.9% have public insurance; 6.9% do not have insurance; 2.4% of children under 18 do not have insurance
Transportation: Commute: 92.2% car, 1.8% public transportation, 2.1% walk, 2.9% work from home; Mean travel time to work: 18.0 minutes
Additional Information Contacts
Town of Salina . . . . (315) 457-2710
    http://www.salina.ny.us

SENECA KNOLLS (CDP). Covers a land area of 1.248 square miles and a water area of 0 square miles. Located at 43.12° N. Lat; 76.29° W. Long. Elevation is 407 feet.
Population: 2,393; Growth (since 2000): 11.9%; Density: 1,916.8 persons per square mile; Race: 97.3% White, 1.0% Black/African American, 0.0% Asian, 0.0% American Indian/Alaska Native, 0.0% Native Hawaiian/Other Pacific Islander, 1.8% Two or more races, 3.8% Hispanic of any race; Average household size: 2.45; Median age: 42.4; Age under 18: 19.9%; Age 65 and over: 14.7%; Males per 100 females: 94.5; Marriage status: 32.0% never married, 51.1% now married, 0.0% separated, 6.5% widowed, 10.3% divorced; Foreign born: 5.1%; Speak English only: 100.0%; With disability: 9.6%; Veterans: 9.3%; Ancestry: 35.1% Irish, 22.9% German, 22.3% English, 11.7% Italian, 11.5% American
Employment: 8.4% management, business, and financial, 0.0% computer, engineering, and science, 5.5% education, legal, community service, arts, and media, 13.0% healthcare practitioners, 18.2% service, 28.5% sales and office, 14.0% natural resources, construction, and maintenance, 12.6% production, transportation, and material moving
Income: Per capita: $25,209; Median household: $53,611; Average household: $60,323; Households with income of $100,000 or more: 13.9%; Poverty rate: 5.8%
Educational Attainment: High school diploma or higher: 94.8%; Bachelor's degree or higher: 15.7%; Graduate/professional degree or higher: 8.6%
Housing: Homeownership rate: 98.3%; Median home value: $92,300; Median year structure built: 1959; Homeowner vacancy rate: 0.0%; Median selected monthly owner costs: $1,124 with a mortgage, $473 without a mortgage; Median gross rent: n/a per month; Rental vacancy rate: 0.0%
Health Insurance: 97.0% have insurance; 80.4% have private insurance; 31.6% have public insurance; 3.0% do not have insurance; 0.0% of children under 18 do not have insurance
Transportation: Commute: 90.4% car, 1.2% public transportation, 5.7% walk, 2.7% work from home; Mean travel time to work: 20.6 minutes

SKANEATELES (town). Covers a land area of 42.606 square miles and a water area of 6.220 square miles. Located at 42.89° N. Lat; 76.41° W. Long. Elevation is 873 feet.
History: Village in a Historic District. Settled before 1800, incorporated 1833.
Population: 7,235; Growth (since 2000): -1.2%; Density: 169.8 persons per square mile; Race: 98.1% White, 0.0% Black/African American, 0.7% Asian, 0.5% American Indian/Alaska Native, 0.0% Native Hawaiian/Other Pacific Islander, 0.6% Two or more races, 1.3% Hispanic of any race; Average household size: 2.38; Median age: 49.4; Age under 18: 21.7%; Age 65 and over: 23.2%; Males per 100 females: 94.2; Marriage status: 20.8% never married, 63.1% now married, 0.9% separated, 6.8% widowed, 9.3% divorced; Foreign born: 2.0%; Speak English only: 96.6%; With disability: 9.7%; Veterans: 8.6%; Ancestry: 30.8% Irish, 22.9% German, 19.5% English, 16.3% Italian, 7.6% Polish
Employment: 21.6% management, business, and financial, 6.2% computer, engineering, and science, 20.7% education, legal, community service, arts, and media, 8.9% healthcare practitioners, 8.8% service, 20.8% sales and office, 6.6% natural resources, construction, and maintenance, 6.4% production, transportation, and material moving
Income: Per capita: $53,131; Median household: $89,420; Average household: $125,733; Households with income of $100,000 or more: 42.8%; Poverty rate: 3.6%
Educational Attainment: High school diploma or higher: 98.3%; Bachelor's degree or higher: 56.3%; Graduate/professional degree or higher: 27.2%

School District(s)
Skaneateles Central SD (KG-12)
    2014-15 Enrollment: 1,422 . . . . (315) 291-2221
Housing: Homeownership rate: 80.0%; Median home value: $268,100; Median year structure built: 1955; Homeowner vacancy rate: 3.2%; Median selected monthly owner costs: $1,981 with a mortgage, $796 without a mortgage; Median gross rent: $764 per month; Rental vacancy rate: 8.3%
Health Insurance: 96.2% have insurance; 87.4% have private insurance; 27.5% have public insurance; 3.8% do not have insurance; 2.0% of children under 18 do not have insurance
Transportation: Commute: 90.5% car, 0.5% public transportation, 4.5% walk, 3.9% work from home; Mean travel time to work: 23.1 minutes
Airports: Skaneateles Aero Drome (general aviation)
Additional Information Contacts
Town of Skaneateles . . . . (315) 685-3473
    http://www.townofskaneateles.com

SKANEATELES (village). Covers a land area of 1.414 square miles and a water area of 0.307 square miles. Located at 42.95° N. Lat; 76.43° W. Long. Elevation is 873 feet.
Population: 2,553; Growth (since 2000): -2.4%; Density: 1,806.0 persons per square mile; Race: 98.0% White, 0.1% Black/African American, 1.4% Asian, 0.0% American Indian/Alaska Native, 0.0% Native Hawaiian/Other Pacific Islander, 0.4% Two or more races, 2.4% Hispanic of any race; Average household size: 2.19; Median age: 52.5; Age under 18: 22.7%; Age 65 and over: 28.3%; Males per 100 females: 81.9; Marriage status: 18.0% never married, 58.1% now married, 1.1% separated, 10.4% widowed, 13.5% divorced; Foreign born: 2.4%; Speak English only: 95.8%; With disability: 11.1%; Veterans: 12.1%; Ancestry: 35.8% Irish, 18.8% German, 17.8% English, 15.9% Italian, 6.6% Polish
Employment: 27.7% management, business, and financial, 1.3% computer, engineering, and science, 25.0% education, legal, community service, arts, and media, 13.0% healthcare practitioners, 7.3% service, 15.7% sales and office, 4.9% natural resources, construction, and maintenance, 5.1% production, transportation, and material moving
Income: Per capita: $56,048; Median household: $79,871; Average household: $121,819; Households with income of $100,000 or more: 41.5%; Poverty rate: 4.9%
Educational Attainment: High school diploma or higher: 98.5%; Bachelor's degree or higher: 67.1%; Graduate/professional degree or higher: 31.9%

School District(s)
Skaneateles Central SD (KG-12)
    2014-15 Enrollment: 1,422 . . . . (315) 291-2221
Housing: Homeownership rate: 67.8%; Median home value: $323,700; Median year structure built: Before 1940; Homeowner vacancy rate: 3.7%; Median selected monthly owner costs: $2,197 with a mortgage, $719 without a mortgage; Median gross rent: $713 per month; Rental vacancy rate: 7.0%

Health Insurance: 97.1% have insurance; 89.9% have private insurance; 31.3% have public insurance; 2.9% do not have insurance; 0.9% of children under 18 do not have insurance
Safety: Violent crime rate: 0.0 per 10,000 population; Property crime rate: 142.2 per 10,000 population
Transportation: Commute: 84.8% car, 1.7% public transportation, 5.3% walk, 7.9% work from home; Mean travel time to work: 25.2 minutes
Airports: Skaneateles Aero Drome (general aviation)

SKANEATELES FALLS (unincorporated postal area)
ZCTA: 13153

Covers a land area of 0.894 square miles and a water area of 0 square miles. Located at 43.00° N. Lat; 76.45° W. Long. Elevation is 705 feet.
Population: 201; Growth (since 2000): n/a; Density: 224.8 persons per square mile; Race: 100.0% White, 0.0% Black/African American, 0.0% Asian, 0.0% American Indian/Alaska Native, 0.0% Native Hawaiian/Other Pacific Islander, 0.0% Two or more races, 0.0% Hispanic of any race; Average household size: 2.42; Median age: 50.2; Age under 18: 9.0%; Age 65 and over: 23.9%; Males per 100 females: 111.1; Marriage status: 25.1% never married, 66.7% now married, 0.0% separated, 4.9% widowed, 3.3% divorced; Foreign born: 0.0%; Speak English only: 94.0%; With disability: 14.9%; Veterans: 3.3%; Ancestry: 40.8% German, 22.4% English, 22.4% French, 13.9% Irish, 5.0% Scottish
Employment: 9.4% management, business, and financial, 10.4% computer, engineering, and science, 16.7% education, legal, community service, arts, and media, 0.0% healthcare practitioners, 6.3% service, 41.7% sales and office, 0.0% natural resources, construction, and maintenance, 15.6% production, transportation, and material moving
Income: Per capita: $30,528; Median household: $47,250; Average household: $71,412; Households with income of $100,000 or more: 18.0%; Poverty rate: 10.0%
Educational Attainment: High school diploma or higher: 87.8%; Bachelor's degree or higher: 27.9%; Graduate/professional degree or higher: 14.5%
Housing: Homeownership rate: 75.9%; Median home value: $168,800; Median year structure built: Before 1940; Homeowner vacancy rate: 27.6%; Median selected monthly owner costs: $1,714 with a mortgage, $475 without a mortgage; Median gross rent: n/a per month; Rental vacancy rate: 0.0%
Health Insurance: 100.0% have insurance; 74.6% have private insurance; 38.8% have public insurance; 0.0% do not have insurance; 0.0% of children under 18 do not have insurance
Transportation: Commute: 100.0% car, 0.0% public transportation, 0.0% walk, 0.0% work from home; Mean travel time to work: 13.9 minutes

SOLVAY (village). Covers a land area of 1.654 square miles and a water area of 0 square miles. Located at 43.06° N. Lat; 76.21° W. Long. Elevation is 499 feet.
History: In the 20th century, after earlier exploited salt springs had lost their deposits, brine wells provided basis for manufacturing of chlorines, caustic soda, and bicarbonate of soda. Former heavy-manufacturing and chemical-manufacturing have disappeared, mainly due to stricter environmental-quality standards. Incorporated 1894.
Population: 6,490; Growth (since 2000): -5.2%; Density: 3,925.0 persons per square mile; Race: 92.2% White, 0.5% Black/African American, 1.5% Asian, 0.9% American Indian/Alaska Native, 0.0% Native Hawaiian/Other Pacific Islander, 4.6% Two or more races, 7.8% Hispanic of any race; Average household size: 2.23; Median age: 38.5; Age under 18: 19.2%; Age 65 and over: 16.4%; Males per 100 females: 92.0; Marriage status: 35.0% never married, 44.5% now married, 3.2% separated, 9.0% widowed, 11.6% divorced; Foreign born: 7.1%; Speak English only: 89.0%; With disability: 13.9%; Veterans: 7.7%; Ancestry: 32.6% Italian, 22.6% Irish, 13.4% German, 9.5% Polish, 9.0% French
Employment: 10.5% management, business, and financial, 4.0% computer, engineering, and science, 8.7% education, legal, community service, arts, and media, 4.8% healthcare practitioners, 22.1% service, 27.0% sales and office, 9.8% natural resources, construction, and maintenance, 13.0% production, transportation, and material moving
Income: Per capita: $25,736; Median household: $41,944; Average household: $55,123; Households with income of $100,000 or more: 12.8%; Poverty rate: 12.7%

Educational Attainment: High school diploma or higher: 86.4%; Bachelor's degree or higher: 22.4%; Graduate/professional degree or higher: 8.1%

School District(s)
Solvay Union Free SD (PK-12)
    2014-15 Enrollment: 1,523 . . . . (315) 468-1111
Housing: Homeownership rate: 55.1%; Median home value: $109,500; Median year structure built: 1951; Homeowner vacancy rate: 2.2%; Median selected monthly owner costs: $1,109 with a mortgage, $495 without a mortgage; Median gross rent: $620 per month; Rental vacancy rate: 4.3%
Health Insurance: 91.8% have insurance; 71.7% have private insurance; 37.7% have public insurance; 8.2% do not have insurance; 0.0% of children under 18 do not have insurance
Safety: Violent crime rate: 28.0 per 10,000 population; Property crime rate: 174.4 per 10,000 population
Transportation: Commute: 91.7% car, 2.1% public transportation, 3.6% walk, 1.2% work from home; Mean travel time to work: 20.1 minutes
Additional Information Contacts
Village of Solvay . . . . (315) 468-1670
    http://villageofsolvay.com

SPAFFORD (town). Covers a land area of 32.698 square miles and a water area of 6.518 square miles. Located at 42.83° N. Lat; 76.29° W. Long. Elevation is 1,686 feet.
Population: 1,663; Growth (since 2000): 0.1%; Density: 50.9 persons per square mile; Race: 98.4% White, 0.0% Black/African American, 0.7% Asian, 0.5% American Indian/Alaska Native, 0.0% Native Hawaiian/Other Pacific Islander, 0.1% Two or more races, 2.8% Hispanic of any race; Average household size: 2.55; Median age: 50.5; Age under 18: 20.9%; Age 65 and over: 18.8%; Males per 100 females: 98.6; Marriage status: 20.0% never married, 64.7% now married, 1.5% separated, 5.8% widowed, 9.5% divorced; Foreign born: 1.4%; Speak English only: 97.0%; With disability: 10.6%; Veterans: 7.1%; Ancestry: 21.3% English, 21.3% Irish, 21.1% German, 11.0% Italian, 7.7% American
Employment: 14.4% management, business, and financial, 8.8% computer, engineering, and science, 13.5% education, legal, community service, arts, and media, 7.2% healthcare practitioners, 10.7% service, 25.1% sales and office, 15.4% natural resources, construction, and maintenance, 4.9% production, transportation, and material moving
Income: Per capita: $41,679; Median household: $75,357; Average household: $104,124; Households with income of $100,000 or more: 39.1%; Poverty rate: 7.2%
Educational Attainment: High school diploma or higher: 95.6%; Bachelor's degree or higher: 45.5%; Graduate/professional degree or higher: 20.4%
Housing: Homeownership rate: 89.1%; Median home value: $209,200; Median year structure built: 1976; Homeowner vacancy rate: 5.1%; Median selected monthly owner costs: $1,657 with a mortgage, $672 without a mortgage; Median gross rent: $645 per month; Rental vacancy rate: 0.0%
Health Insurance: 95.2% have insurance; 88.4% have private insurance; 23.5% have public insurance; 4.8% do not have insurance; 1.4% of children under 18 do not have insurance
Transportation: Commute: 93.0% car, 0.5% public transportation, 0.5% walk, 6.0% work from home; Mean travel time to work: 34.1 minutes

SYRACUSE (city). County seat. Covers a land area of 25.043 square miles and a water area of 0.565 square miles. Located at 43.04° N. Lat; 76.14° W. Long. Elevation is 397 feet.
History: The beginnings and early growth of Syracuse are identified with salt. What the French soldiers and Jesuits saw in 1654 was a swamp. The salt springs were discovered by Father Simon LeMoyne. The first settler was Ephraim Webster, who arrived in 1786 and opened a trading station. Syracuse was incorporated as a village in 1825. The name was suggested by John Wilkinson, the first postmaster, who had read a poem describing the ancient Greek city in Sicily, which had also grown around a marsh and salt springs. In 1848, the villages of Syracuse and Salina, together with Lodi, were joined and incorporated as the city of Syracuse in 1881.
Population: 144,564; Growth (since 2000): -1.9%; Density: 5,772.5 persons per square mile; Race: 55.2% White, 29.3% Black/African American, 6.6% Asian, 1.1% American Indian/Alaska Native, 0.0% Native Hawaiian/Other Pacific Islander, 5.4% Two or more races, 8.4% Hispanic of any race; Average household size: 2.38; Median age: 29.9; Age under 18: 22.6%; Age 65 and over: 11.3%; Males per 100 females: 91.0; Marriage status: 54.4% never married, 29.7% now married, 3.4% separated, 5.8% widowed, 10.0% divorced; Foreign born: 11.9%; Speak

English only: 81.9%; With disability: 15.4%; Veterans: 5.5%; Ancestry: 14.4% Irish, 12.6% Italian, 11.2% German, 5.0% English, 4.2% Polish
Employment: 10.3% management, business, and financial, 4.1% computer, engineering, and science, 14.7% education, legal, community service, arts, and media, 5.8% healthcare practitioners, 24.4% service, 24.8% sales and office, 5.6% natural resources, construction, and maintenance, 10.3% production, transportation, and material moving
Income: Per capita: $19,558; Median household: $31,881; Average household: $47,578; Households with income of $100,000 or more: 11.0%; Poverty rate: 34.8%
Educational Attainment: High school diploma or higher: 80.2%; Bachelor's degree or higher: 26.4%; Graduate/professional degree or higher: 12.2%

School District(s)

Lyncourt Union Free SD (PK-08)
    2014-15 Enrollment: 360 . . . . (315) 455-7571
North Syracuse Central SD (PK-12)
    2014-15 Enrollment: 9,119 . . . . (315) 218-2151
Onondaga-Cortland-Madison Boces
    2014-15 Enrollment: n/a . . . . (315) 433-2602
Solvay Union Free SD (PK-12)
    2014-15 Enrollment: 1,523 . . . . (315) 468-1111
Southside Academy Charter School (KG-08)
    2014-15 Enrollment: 688 . . . . (315) 476-3019
Syracuse Academy of Science Charter School (KG-12)
    2014-15 Enrollment: 853 . . . . (315) 428-8997
Syracuse City SD (PK-12)
    2014-15 Enrollment: 21,110 . . . . (315) 435-4161
West Genesee Central SD (KG-12)
    2014-15 Enrollment: 4,816 . . . . (315) 487-4562
Westhill Central SD (KG-12)
    2014-15 Enrollment: 1,814 . . . . (315) 426-3218

Four-year College(s)

Le Moyne College (Private, Not-for-profit, Roman Catholic)
    Fall 2014 Enrollment: 3,381 . . . . (315) 445-4100
    2015-16 Tuition: In-state $32,250; Out-of-state $32,250
SUNY College of Environmental Science and Forestry (Public)
    Fall 2014 Enrollment: 2,200 . . . . (315) 470-6500
    2015-16 Tuition: In-state $7,848; Out-of-state $17,698
Syracuse University (Private, Not-for-profit)
    Fall 2014 Enrollment: 21,492 . . . . (315) 443-1870
    2015-16 Tuition: In-state $43,318; Out-of-state $43,318
Upstate Medical University (Public)
    Fall 2014 Enrollment: 1,516 . . . . (315) 464-5540

Two-year College(s)

Bryant & Stratton College-Syracuse (Private, For-profit)
    Fall 2014 Enrollment: 516 . . . . (315) 472-6603
    2015-16 Tuition: In-state $16,763; Out-of-state $16,763
Onondaga Community College (Public)
    Fall 2014 Enrollment: 12,271 . . . . (315) 498-2622
    2015-16 Tuition: In-state $5,014; Out-of-state $9,184
Pomeroy College of Nursing at Crouse Hospital (Private, Not-for-profit)
    Fall 2014 Enrollment: 345 . . . . (315) 470-7481
    2015-16 Tuition: In-state $11,078; Out-of-state $11,078
St Joseph's College of Nursing at St Joseph's Hospital Health Center (Private, Not-for-profit, Roman Catholic)
    Fall 2014 Enrollment: 317 . . . . (315) 448-5040
    2015-16 Tuition: In-state $18,600; Out-of-state $18,600

Vocational/Technical School(s)

Onondaga School of Therapeutic Massage-Syracuse (Private, For-profit)
    Fall 2014 Enrollment: 60 . . . . (315) 424-1159
    2015-16 Tuition: $15,575
Syracuse City Schools Practical Nursing Program (Public)
    Fall 2014 Enrollment: 33 . . . . (315) 435-4150
    2015-16 Tuition: $12,600

Housing: Homeownership rate: 38.6%; Median home value: $88,800; Median year structure built: 1945; Homeowner vacancy rate: 3.3%; Median selected monthly owner costs: $1,076 with a mortgage, $470 without a mortgage; Median gross rent: $730 per month; Rental vacancy rate: 6.9%
Health Insurance: 90.3% have insurance; 55.4% have private insurance; 46.9% have public insurance; 9.7% do not have insurance; 5.0% of children under 18 do not have insurance
Hospitals: Crouse Hospital (566 beds); Saint Joseph's Hospital Health Center (431 beds); Syracuse VA Medical Center (164 beds); University Hospital SUNY Health Science Center (356 beds)

Safety: Violent crime rate: 79.3 per 10,000 population; Property crime rate: 353.2 per 10,000 population
Newspapers: Eagle Newspapers (weekly circulation 51,000); Post-Standard (daily circulation 114,000); Syracuse New Times (weekly circulation 40,000)
Transportation: Commute: 73.8% car, 9.4% public transportation, 11.1% walk, 3.1% work from home; Mean travel time to work: 18.3 minutes; Amtrak: Train service available.
Airports: Syracuse Hancock International (primary service/small hub)
Additional Information Contacts
City of Syracuse . . . . (315) 448-8005
  http://www.syrgov.net/home.aspx

TULLY (town). Covers a land area of 25.754 square miles and a water area of 0.525 square miles. Located at 42.81° N. Lat; 76.14° W. Long. Elevation is 1,250 feet.
History: One of many former Finger Lake valleys, with rich agricultural soils.
Population: 2,734; Growth (since 2000): 0.9%; Density: 106.2 persons per square mile; Race: 95.2% White, 0.8% Black/African American, 1.5% Asian, 1.0% American Indian/Alaska Native, 0.0% Native Hawaiian/Other Pacific Islander, 0.8% Two or more races, 2.3% Hispanic of any race; Average household size: 2.60; Median age: 44.9; Age under 18: 25.0%; Age 65 and over: 16.1%; Males per 100 females: 95.6; Marriage status: 31.8% never married, 52.6% now married, 1.1% separated, 6.0% widowed, 9.6% divorced; Foreign born: 2.1%; Speak English only: 98.4%; With disability: 12.0%; Veterans: 10.3%; Ancestry: 28.9% Irish, 25.1% German, 15.7% English, 11.6% Italian, 4.8% Polish
Employment: 14.6% management, business, and financial, 4.2% computer, engineering, and science, 18.1% education, legal, community service, arts, and media, 6.3% healthcare practitioners, 16.2% service, 19.7% sales and office, 10.0% natural resources, construction, and maintenance, 10.9% production, transportation, and material moving
Income: Per capita: $33,450; Median household: $65,588; Average household: $85,460; Households with income of $100,000 or more: 30.2%; Poverty rate: 7.0%
Educational Attainment: High school diploma or higher: 94.7%; Bachelor's degree or higher: 42.2%; Graduate/professional degree or higher: 19.0%

School District(s)

Tully Central SD (KG-12)
    2014-15 Enrollment: 936 . . . . (315) 696-6204
Housing: Homeownership rate: 75.2%; Median home value: $171,500; Median year structure built: 1972; Homeowner vacancy rate: 0.0%; Median selected monthly owner costs: $1,654 with a mortgage, $662 without a mortgage; Median gross rent: $789 per month; Rental vacancy rate: 6.7%
Health Insurance: 93.0% have insurance; 75.9% have private insurance; 32.3% have public insurance; 7.0% do not have insurance; 1.8% of children under 18 do not have insurance
Transportation: Commute: 87.6% car, 0.0% public transportation, 1.3% walk, 10.8% work from home; Mean travel time to work: 22.4 minutes

TULLY (village). Covers a land area of 0.717 square miles and a water area of 0 square miles. Located at 42.80° N. Lat; 76.11° W. Long. Elevation is 1,250 feet.
Population: 1,082; Growth (since 2000): 17.1%; Density: 1,508.1 persons per square mile; Race: 93.1% White, 0.2% Black/African American, 1.7% Asian, 2.6% American Indian/Alaska Native, 0.0% Native Hawaiian/Other Pacific Islander, 1.1% Two or more races, 4.6% Hispanic of any race; Average household size: 2.46; Median age: 33.8; Age under 18: 24.2%; Age 65 and over: 15.9%; Males per 100 females: 87.3; Marriage status: 42.0% never married, 33.7% now married, 0.7% separated, 9.6% widowed, 14.7% divorced; Foreign born: 0.9%; Speak English only: 97.9%; With disability: 14.7%; Veterans: 8.9%; Ancestry: 28.5% German, 21.2% Irish, 18.3% English, 10.5% Italian, 7.0% Polish
Employment: 8.8% management, business, and financial, 3.6% computer, engineering, and science, 14.8% education, legal, community service, arts, and media, 7.9% healthcare practitioners, 23.2% service, 13.9% sales and office, 11.6% natural resources, construction, and maintenance, 16.3% production, transportation, and material moving
Income: Per capita: $26,543; Median household: $45,887; Average household: $62,194; Households with income of $100,000 or more: 15.1%; Poverty rate: 13.6%

Educational Attainment: High school diploma or higher: 90.7%; Bachelor's degree or higher: 26.0%; Graduate/professional degree or higher: 14.1%

School District(s)

Tully Central SD (KG-12)

    2014-15 Enrollment: 936 . . . . (315) 696-6204

Housing: Homeownership rate: 53.4%; Median home value: $120,300; Median year structure built: Before 1940; Homeowner vacancy rate: 0.0%; Median selected monthly owner costs: $1,247 with a mortgage, $562 without a mortgage; Median gross rent: $769 per month; Rental vacancy rate: 0.0%

Health Insurance: 90.6% have insurance; 65.0% have private insurance; 39.4% have public insurance; 9.4% do not have insurance; 0.8% of children under 18 do not have insurance

Transportation: Commute: 85.4% car, 0.0% public transportation, 0.7% walk, 13.3% work from home; Mean travel time to work: 23.1 minutes

VAN BUREN (town). Covers a land area of 35.408 square miles and a water area of 0.704 square miles. Located at 43.12° N. Lat; 76.35° W. Long. Elevation is 499 feet.

Population: 13,344; Growth (since 2000): 5.3%; Density: 376.9 persons per square mile; Race: 95.1% White, 0.7% Black/African American, 1.0% Asian, 0.5% American Indian/Alaska Native, 0.0% Native Hawaiian/Other Pacific Islander, 1.6% Two or more races, 2.7% Hispanic of any race; Average household size: 2.29; Median age: 45.0; Age under 18: 20.1%; Age 65 and over: 20.1%; Males per 100 females: 94.9; Marriage status: 26.6% never married, 51.3% now married, 0.8% separated, 8.4% widowed, 13.7% divorced; Foreign born: 3.8%; Speak English only: 97.0%; With disability: 12.8%; Veterans: 9.2%; Ancestry: 28.5% Irish, 22.8% German, 15.9% English, 13.8% Italian, 7.7% Polish

Employment: 12.6% management, business, and financial, 6.2% computer, engineering, and science, 9.8% education, legal, community service, arts, and media, 9.2% healthcare practitioners, 15.3% service, 24.8% sales and office, 10.4% natural resources, construction, and maintenance, 11.7% production, transportation, and material moving

Income: Per capita: $28,877; Median household: $54,622; Average household: $65,220; Households with income of $100,000 or more: 19.3%; Poverty rate: 5.9%

Educational Attainment: High school diploma or higher: 93.4%; Bachelor's degree or higher: 26.4%; Graduate/professional degree or higher: 9.4%

Housing: Homeownership rate: 72.3%; Median home value: $113,600; Median year structure built: 1969; Homeowner vacancy rate: 1.7%; Median selected monthly owner costs: $1,184 with a mortgage, $484 without a mortgage; Median gross rent: $819 per month; Rental vacancy rate: 3.1%

Health Insurance: 95.0% have insurance; 79.2% have private insurance; 33.4% have public insurance; 5.0% do not have insurance; 2.2% of children under 18 do not have insurance

Transportation: Commute: 93.4% car, 0.9% public transportation, 2.3% walk, 3.3% work from home; Mean travel time to work: 23.2 minutes

Additional Information Contacts

Town of Van Buren . . . . (315) 635-3010

    http://www.townofvanburen.com

VILLAGE GREEN (CDP). Covers a land area of 1.154 square miles and a water area of 0.008 square miles. Located at 43.13° N. Lat; 76.31° W. Long. Elevation is 440 feet.

Population: 3,527; Growth (since 2000): -10.6%; Density: 3,056.5 persons per square mile; Race: 95.6% White, 0.0% Black/African American, 2.0% Asian, 0.6% American Indian/Alaska Native, 0.0% Native Hawaiian/Other Pacific Islander, 1.8% Two or more races, 0.0% Hispanic of any race; Average household size: 1.92; Median age: 46.9; Age under 18: 15.0%; Age 65 and over: 22.8%; Males per 100 females: 91.4; Marriage status: 25.6% never married, 48.5% now married, 0.0% separated, 8.4% widowed, 17.4% divorced; Foreign born: 4.6%; Speak English only: 95.5%; With disability: 11.7%; Veterans: 9.7%; Ancestry: 29.5% Irish, 27.5% German, 17.1% English, 14.8% Italian, 9.8% Polish

Employment: 16.2% management, business, and financial, 9.0% computer, engineering, and science, 12.9% education, legal, community service, arts, and media, 9.8% healthcare practitioners, 7.8% service, 26.1% sales and office, 7.5% natural resources, construction, and maintenance, 10.8% production, transportation, and material moving

Income: Per capita: $32,935; Median household: $51,824; Average household: $62,351; Households with income of $100,000 or more: 16.4%; Poverty rate: 3.9%

Educational Attainment: High school diploma or higher: 93.9%; Bachelor's degree or higher: 30.3%; Graduate/professional degree or higher: 8.6%

Housing: Homeownership rate: 58.8%; Median home value: $95,100; Median year structure built: 1976; Homeowner vacancy rate: 1.3%; Median selected monthly owner costs: $974 with a mortgage, $477 without a mortgage; Median gross rent: $840 per month; Rental vacancy rate: 0.0%

Health Insurance: 95.4% have insurance; 79.3% have private insurance; 35.7% have public insurance; 4.6% do not have insurance; 0.0% of children under 18 do not have insurance

Transportation: Commute: 94.3% car, 2.3% public transportation, 0.0% walk, 3.4% work from home; Mean travel time to work: 25.3 minutes

WARNERS (unincorporated postal area)

ZCTA: 13164

Covers a land area of 10.726 square miles and a water area of 0.009 square miles. Located at 43.10° N. Lat; 76.31° W. Long. Elevation is 430 feet.

Population: 2,494; Growth (since 2000): 41.8%; Density: 232.5 persons per square mile; Race: 94.1% White, 0.7% Black/African American, 3.6% Asian, 0.0% American Indian/Alaska Native, 0.0% Native Hawaiian/Other Pacific Islander, 1.2% Two or more races, 3.6% Hispanic of any race; Average household size: 2.80; Median age: 38.1; Age under 18: 27.1%; Age 65 and over: 8.6%; Males per 100 females: 105.6; Marriage status: 23.8% never married, 61.8% now married, 1.6% separated, 4.3% widowed, 10.1% divorced; Foreign born: 8.1%; Speak English only: 90.9%; With disability: 8.6%; Veterans: 8.4%; Ancestry: 28.9% Irish, 20.3% German, 18.0% Polish, 17.4% Italian, 16.6% English

Employment: 12.1% management, business, and financial, 7.2% computer, engineering, and science, 14.9% education, legal, community service, arts, and media, 11.6% healthcare practitioners, 16.0% service, 12.1% sales and office, 9.0% natural resources, construction, and maintenance, 17.2% production, transportation, and material moving

Income: Per capita: $29,708; Median household: $72,750; Average household: $81,199; Households with income of $100,000 or more: 33.7%; Poverty rate: 4.3%

Educational Attainment: High school diploma or higher: 92.3%; Bachelor's degree or higher: 31.7%; Graduate/professional degree or higher: 14.2%

Housing: Homeownership rate: 93.2%; Median home value: $156,500; Median year structure built: 1965; Homeowner vacancy rate: 0.0%; Median selected monthly owner costs: $1,623 with a mortgage, $417 without a mortgage; Median gross rent: $739 per month; Rental vacancy rate: 0.0%

Health Insurance: 91.8% have insurance; 79.1% have private insurance; 19.9% have public insurance; 8.2% do not have insurance; 7.5% of children under 18 do not have insurance

Transportation: Commute: 96.1% car, 0.0% public transportation, 0.5% walk, 3.4% work from home; Mean travel time to work: 24.4 minutes

WESTVALE (CDP). Covers a land area of 1.364 square miles and a water area of 0 square miles. Located at 43.04° N. Lat; 76.22° W. Long. Elevation is 505 feet.

Population: 5,210; Growth (since 2000): 0.9%; Density: 3,818.7 persons per square mile; Race: 96.1% White, 1.1% Black/African American, 0.1% Asian, 0.6% American Indian/Alaska Native, 0.0% Native Hawaiian/Other Pacific Islander, 0.8% Two or more races, 1.7% Hispanic of any race; Average household size: 2.59; Median age: 42.9; Age under 18: 21.8%; Age 65 and over: 18.6%; Males per 100 females: 85.8; Marriage status: 29.9% never married, 55.9% now married, 0.8% separated, 6.3% widowed, 7.8% divorced; Foreign born: 4.8%; Speak English only: 93.5%; With disability: 9.5%; Veterans: 7.7%; Ancestry: 38.1% Irish, 26.7% Italian, 17.3% German, 10.1% Polish, 8.3% English

Employment: 18.2% management, business, and financial, 3.9% computer, engineering, and science, 15.2% education, legal, community service, arts, and media, 6.6% healthcare practitioners, 18.6% service, 26.5% sales and office, 5.5% natural resources, construction, and maintenance, 5.5% production, transportation, and material moving

Income: Per capita: $35,119; Median household: $75,609; Average household: $89,518; Households with income of $100,000 or more: 34.3%; Poverty rate: 6.8%

Educational Attainment: High school diploma or higher: 97.0%; Bachelor's degree or higher: 47.1%; Graduate/professional degree or higher: 22.0%

Housing: Homeownership rate: 94.3%; Median home value: $142,900; Median year structure built: 1954; Homeowner vacancy rate: 2.3%; Median selected monthly owner costs: $1,391 with a mortgage, $607 without a mortgage; Median gross rent: $739 per month; Rental vacancy rate: 0.0%
Health Insurance: 98.3% have insurance; 86.3% have private insurance; 30.1% have public insurance; 1.7% do not have insurance; 0.0% of children under 18 do not have insurance
Transportation: Commute: 93.0% car, 1.0% public transportation, 2.2% walk, 3.1% work from home; Mean travel time to work: 20.2 minutes

Ontario County

Located in west central New York, in the Finger Lakes area; bounded partly on the east by Seneca Lake; drained by Honeoye, Mud, and Flint Creeks; includes Canandaigua, Honeoye, and Canadice Lakes. Covers a land area of 644.065 square miles, a water area of 18.461 square miles, and is located in the Eastern Time Zone at 42.86° N. Lat., 77.30° W. Long. The county was founded in 1789. County seat is Canandaigua.

Ontario County is part of the Rochester, NY Metropolitan Statistical Area. The entire metro area includes: Livingston County, NY; Monroe County, NY; Ontario County, NY; Orleans County, NY; Wayne County, NY; Yates County, NY

Weather Station: Canandaigua 3 S   Elevation: 720 feet

	Jan	Feb	Mar	Apr	May	Jun	Jul	Aug	Sep	Oct	Nov	Dec
High	33	35	42	55	67	77	81	79	72	60	49	38
Low	18	19	25	36	46	57	62	60	54	42	34	24
Precip	1.8	1.6	2.6	3.2	3.0	3.6	3.6	3.2	3.5	2.9	2.9	2.2
Snow	na	na	na	0.0	0.0	0.0	0.0	0.0	0.0	tr	tr	na

High and Low temperatures in degrees Fahrenheit; Precipitation and Snow in inches

Weather Station: Geneva Research Farm   Elevation: 717 feet

	Jan	Feb	Mar	Apr	May	Jun	Jul	Aug	Sep	Oct	Nov	Dec
High	31	33	41	55	67	76	80	79	71	59	47	36
Low	16	17	25	36	47	56	61	59	52	41	33	22
Precip	1.7	1.5	2.4	2.9	3.0	3.6	3.4	3.0	3.6	3.2	2.8	2.2
Snow	13.7	11.6	11.3	2.3	tr	0.0	0.0	0.0	0.0	0.1	4.1	11.3

High and Low temperatures in degrees Fahrenheit; Precipitation and Snow in inches

Population: 109,192; Growth (since 2000): 8.9%; Density: 169.5 persons per square mile; Race: 93.4% White, 2.5% Black/African American, 1.2% Asian, 0.3% American Indian/Alaska Native, 0.0% Native Hawaiian/Other Pacific Islander, 1.7% two or more races, 4.1% Hispanic of any race; Average household size: 2.38; Median age: 43.1; Age under 18: 21.3%; Age 65 and over: 17.1%; Males per 100 females: 95.6; Marriage status: 29.1% never married, 53.0% now married, 2.2% separated, 6.8% widowed, 11.1% divorced; Foreign born: 3.7%; Speak English only: 93.0%; With disability: 11.9%; Veterans: 9.5%; Ancestry: 23.1% German, 19.7% Irish, 17.3% English, 14.3% Italian, 7.0% American
Religion: Six largest groups: 23.6% Catholicism, 5.8% Methodist/Pietist, 3.4% Presbyterian-Reformed, 2.0% Holiness, 1.9% Baptist, 1.4% Lutheran
Economy: Unemployment rate: 4.0%; Leading industries: 18.8 % retail trade; 11.3 % construction; 10.8 % accommodation and food services; Farms: 853 totaling 192,616 acres; Company size: 3 employ 1,000 or more persons, 3 employ 500 to 999 persons, 65 employ 100 to 499 persons, 2,807 employ less than 100 persons; Business ownership: 3,189 women-owned, 128 Black-owned, 103 Hispanic-owned, 78 Asian-owned, 73 American Indian/Alaska Native-owned
Employment: 14.4% management, business, and financial, 4.9% computer, engineering, and science, 12.2% education, legal, community service, arts, and media, 7.3% healthcare practitioners, 17.0% service, 23.7% sales and office, 8.8% natural resources, construction, and maintenance, 11.6% production, transportation, and material moving
Income: Per capita: $30,934; Median household: $57,416; Average household: $75,308; Households with income of $100,000 or more: 23.8%; Poverty rate: 10.4%
Educational Attainment: High school diploma or higher: 92.3%; Bachelor's degree or higher: 31.7%; Graduate/professional degree or higher: 14.5%
Housing: Homeownership rate: 72.8%; Median home value: $145,700; Median year structure built: 1972; Homeowner vacancy rate: 0.9%; Median selected monthly owner costs: $1,323 with a mortgage, $574 without a mortgage; Median gross rent: $809 per month; Rental vacancy rate: 4.1%

Vital Statistics: Birth rate: 95.0 per 10,000 population; Death rate: 93.2 per 10,000 population; Age-adjusted cancer mortality rate: 165.5 deaths per 100,000 population
Health Insurance: 93.2% have insurance; 75.4% have private insurance; 33.3% have public insurance; 6.8% do not have insurance; 5.1% of children under 18 do not have insurance
Health Care: Physicians: 24.9 per 10,000 population; Dentists: 5.2 per 10,000 population; Hospital beds: 72.6 per 10,000 population; Hospital admissions: 1,210.9 per 10,000 population
Transportation: Commute: 90.4% car, 0.9% public transportation, 3.9% walk, 3.7% work from home; Mean travel time to work: 23.0 minutes
2016 Presidential Election: 50.4% Trump, 43.1% Clinton, 4.8% Johnson, 1.7% Stein
National and State Parks: Ganondagan State Historic Site
Additional Information Contacts
Ontario Government . . . . (585) 396-4447
  http://www.co.ontario.ny.us

Ontario County Communities

BLOOMFIELD (village). Covers a land area of 1.397 square miles and a water area of 0 square miles. Located at 42.90° N. Lat; 77.42° W. Long. Elevation is 876 feet.
Population: 1,550; Growth (since 2000): 22.3%; Density: 1,109.6 persons per square mile; Race: 97.7% White, 1.7% Black/African American, 0.0% Asian, 0.0% American Indian/Alaska Native, 0.0% Native Hawaiian/Other Pacific Islander, 0.5% Two or more races, 2.1% Hispanic of any race; Average household size: 2.42; Median age: 41.4; Age under 18: 25.5%; Age 65 and over: 13.0%; Males per 100 females: 89.0; Marriage status: 30.7% never married, 52.2% now married, 2.8% separated, 5.3% widowed, 11.8% divorced; Foreign born: 0.0%; Speak English only: 98.9%; With disability: 12.2%; Veterans: 5.7%; Ancestry: 32.6% German, 27.9% Irish, 24.1% English, 6.8% Polish, 6.2% Italian
Employment: 19.9% management, business, and financial, 3.3% computer, engineering, and science, 9.6% education, legal, community service, arts, and media, 3.1% healthcare practitioners, 18.9% service, 21.6% sales and office, 10.6% natural resources, construction, and maintenance, 12.9% production, transportation, and material moving
Income: Per capita: $27,483; Median household: $55,298; Average household: $67,214; Households with income of $100,000 or more: 22.0%; Poverty rate: 16.9%
Educational Attainment: High school diploma or higher: 96.0%; Bachelor's degree or higher: 34.9%; Graduate/professional degree or higher: 10.9%

School District(s)
East Bloomfield Central SD (PK-12)
  2014-15 Enrollment: 963 . . . . (585) 657-6121
Housing: Homeownership rate: 69.9%; Median home value: $133,800; Median year structure built: 1952; Homeowner vacancy rate: 1.8%; Median selected monthly owner costs: $1,175 with a mortgage, $572 without a mortgage; Median gross rent: $731 per month; Rental vacancy rate: 8.2%
Health Insurance: 96.2% have insurance; 75.4% have private insurance; 32.2% have public insurance; 3.8% do not have insurance; 0.0% of children under 18 do not have insurance
Transportation: Commute: 91.6% car, 0.3% public transportation, 1.0% walk, 5.2% work from home; Mean travel time to work: 23.6 minutes
Additional Information Contacts
Village of Bloomfield . . . . (585) 657-7554
  http://www.bloomfieldny.org

BRISTOL (town). Covers a land area of 36.694 square miles and a water area of 0.015 square miles. Located at 42.81° N. Lat; 77.43° W. Long. Elevation is 1,165 feet.
Population: 2,175; Growth (since 2000): -10.2%; Density: 59.3 persons per square mile; Race: 98.8% White, 0.0% Black/African American, 0.0% Asian, 0.3% American Indian/Alaska Native, 0.0% Native Hawaiian/Other Pacific Islander, 1.0% Two or more races, 0.8% Hispanic of any race; Average household size: 2.57; Median age: 46.6; Age under 18: 21.4%; Age 65 and over: 11.8%; Males per 100 females: 102.4; Marriage status: 24.5% never married, 58.2% now married, 2.3% separated, 6.1% widowed, 11.3% divorced; Foreign born: 2.5%; Speak English only: 99.1%; With disability: 8.1%; Veterans: 9.4%; Ancestry: 23.8% Irish, 23.6% German, 20.4% English, 7.5% Italian, 6.9% American
Employment: 12.7% management, business, and financial, 6.1% computer, engineering, and science, 8.3% education, legal, community

service, arts, and media, 3.9% healthcare practitioners, 16.8% service, 19.8% sales and office, 16.5% natural resources, construction, and maintenance, 15.8% production, transportation, and material moving
Income: Per capita: $28,323; Median household: $66,458; Average household: $72,115; Households with income of $100,000 or more: 24.4%; Poverty rate: 6.3%
Educational Attainment: High school diploma or higher: 93.0%; Bachelor's degree or higher: 24.0%; Graduate/professional degree or higher: 11.6%
Housing: Homeownership rate: 92.7%; Median home value: $152,000; Median year structure built: 1974; Homeowner vacancy rate: 0.0%; Median selected monthly owner costs: $1,355 with a mortgage, $552 without a mortgage; Median gross rent: $494 per month; Rental vacancy rate: 7.5%
Health Insurance: 94.4% have insurance; 82.9% have private insurance; 21.8% have public insurance; 5.6% do not have insurance; 8.2% of children under 18 do not have insurance
Transportation: Commute: 93.5% car, 1.0% public transportation, 1.1% walk, 4.4% work from home; Mean travel time to work: 31.3 minutes
Additional Information Contacts
Town of Bristol. . . . . (585) 229-2400
   http://www.townofbristol.org

CANADICE (town). Covers a land area of 29.851 square miles and a water area of 2.585 square miles. Located at 42.72° N. Lat; 77.56° W. Long.
Population: 1,825; Growth (since 2000): -1.1%; Density: 61.1 persons per square mile; Race: 99.2% White, 0.0% Black/African American, 0.0% Asian, 0.0% American Indian/Alaska Native, 0.0% Native Hawaiian/Other Pacific Islander, 0.0% Two or more races, 1.8% Hispanic of any race; Average household size: 2.21; Median age: 50.3; Age under 18: 15.2%; Age 65 and over: 18.0%; Males per 100 females: 103.7; Marriage status: 26.5% never married, 51.8% now married, 2.0% separated, 2.7% widowed, 19.0% divorced; Foreign born: 0.4%; Speak English only: 99.0%; With disability: 9.5%; Veterans: 8.8%; Ancestry: 32.4% German, 19.5% Irish, 15.3% English, 11.2% Italian, 5.9% American
Employment: 12.7% management, business, and financial, 7.1% computer, engineering, and science, 9.0% education, legal, community service, arts, and media, 5.2% healthcare practitioners, 10.9% service, 18.4% sales and office, 8.7% natural resources, construction, and maintenance, 28.0% production, transportation, and material moving
Income: Per capita: $31,474; Median household: $53,469; Average household: $70,265; Households with income of $100,000 or more: 21.7%; Poverty rate: 11.0%
Educational Attainment: High school diploma or higher: 89.6%; Bachelor's degree or higher: 29.5%; Graduate/professional degree or higher: 13.6%
Housing: Homeownership rate: 83.8%; Median home value: $132,300; Median year structure built: 1971; Homeowner vacancy rate: 0.0%; Median selected monthly owner costs: $1,065 with a mortgage, $549 without a mortgage; Median gross rent: $746 per month; Rental vacancy rate: 0.0%
Health Insurance: 91.6% have insurance; 77.3% have private insurance; 32.8% have public insurance; 8.4% do not have insurance; 1.1% of children under 18 do not have insurance
Transportation: Commute: 96.6% car, 0.0% public transportation, 0.9% walk, 1.4% work from home; Mean travel time to work: 37.6 minutes

---

CANANDAIGUA (city). County seat. Covers a land area of 4.594 square miles and a water area of 0.253 square miles. Located at 42.89° N. Lat; 77.28° W. Long. Elevation is 787 feet.
History: Built on the site of a Seneca Iroquois village, Canandaigua was an important railroad junction and home port for several steamboats by the mid-19th century. After the Civil War, local industries included brick works, several mills, and the regionally prominent McKechnie Brewery. Canandaigua was the site of the Susan B. Anthony trial in 1873.
Population: 10,499; Growth (since 2000): -6.8%; Density: 2,285.2 persons per square mile; Race: 95.8% White, 0.9% Black/African American, 1.3% Asian, 0.0% American Indian/Alaska Native, 0.2% Native Hawaiian/Other Pacific Islander, 1.2% Two or more races, 1.4% Hispanic of any race; Average household size: 2.13; Median age: 40.5; Age under 18: 19.5%; Age 65 and over: 19.3%; Males per 100 females: 88.8; Marriage status: 33.1% never married, 43.8% now married, 3.6% separated, 8.2% widowed, 14.9% divorced; Foreign born: 2.9%; Speak English only: 95.0%; With disability: 12.5%; Veterans: 10.3%; Ancestry: 23.6% German, 22.3% Irish, 18.0% English, 15.2% Italian, 4.7% Polish

Employment: 13.2% management, business, and financial, 2.6% computer, engineering, and science, 16.5% education, legal, community service, arts, and media, 9.8% healthcare practitioners, 20.8% service, 20.1% sales and office, 8.3% natural resources, construction, and maintenance, 8.7% production, transportation, and material moving
Income: Per capita: $30,452; Median household: $43,185; Average household: $65,505; Households with income of $100,000 or more: 17.2%; Poverty rate: 15.4%
Educational Attainment: High school diploma or higher: 93.8%; Bachelor's degree or higher: 35.0%; Graduate/professional degree or higher: 17.1%

School District(s)
Canandaigua City SD (PK-12)
   2014-15 Enrollment: 3,683 . . . . (585) 396-3700
Two-year College(s)
Finger Lakes Community College (Public)
   Fall 2014 Enrollment: 6,793 . . . . (585) 394-3500
   2015-16 Tuition: In-state $4,704; Out-of-state $8,884
Housing: Homeownership rate: 53.6%; Median home value: $155,800; Median year structure built: 1954; Homeowner vacancy rate: 1.3%; Median selected monthly owner costs: $1,370 with a mortgage, $534 without a mortgage; Median gross rent: $785 per month; Rental vacancy rate: 4.3%
Health Insurance: 93.5% have insurance; 72.7% have private insurance; 39.2% have public insurance; 6.5% do not have insurance; 3.7% of children under 18 do not have insurance
Hospitals: Canandaigua VA Medical Center (251 beds); F F Thompson Hospital (113 beds)
Safety: Violent crime rate: 34.4 per 10,000 population; Property crime rate: 202.4 per 10,000 population
Newspapers: Daily Messenger (daily circulation 11,700); Messenger Post Media (weekly circulation 86,000)
Transportation: Commute: 84.8% car, 3.6% public transportation, 4.8% walk, 4.1% work from home; Mean travel time to work: 21.7 minutes
Additional Information Contacts
City of Canandaigua . . . . (585) 396-5000
   http://canandaigua.govoffice.com

CANANDAIGUA (town). Covers a land area of 56.796 square miles and a water area of 5.735 square miles. Located at 42.86° N. Lat; 77.31° W. Long. Elevation is 787 feet.
History: It is named from native word "Kah-nan-dah-kwe" meaning "the chosen spot" or "the chosen place."
Population: 10,390; Growth (since 2000): 35.8%; Density: 182.9 persons per square mile; Race: 95.1% White, 1.3% Black/African American, 0.6% Asian, 0.0% American Indian/Alaska Native, 0.1% Native Hawaiian/Other Pacific Islander, 1.8% Two or more races, 2.3% Hispanic of any race; Average household size: 2.29; Median age: 47.9; Age under 18: 19.6%; Age 65 and over: 21.3%; Males per 100 females: 95.6; Marriage status: 21.9% never married, 55.5% now married, 2.7% separated, 9.6% widowed, 13.0% divorced; Foreign born: 3.3%; Speak English only: 94.9%; With disability: 16.9%; Veterans: 11.3%; Ancestry: 25.6% German, 22.8% Irish, 17.0% English, 12.9% Italian, 6.7% American
Employment: 16.4% management, business, and financial, 6.4% computer, engineering, and science, 12.7% education, legal, community service, arts, and media, 5.8% healthcare practitioners, 13.1% service, 29.5% sales and office, 6.7% natural resources, construction, and maintenance, 9.4% production, transportation, and material moving
Income: Per capita: $33,752; Median household: $59,443; Average household: $78,763; Households with income of $100,000 or more: 27.1%; Poverty rate: 9.5%
Educational Attainment: High school diploma or higher: 94.6%; Bachelor's degree or higher: 38.4%; Graduate/professional degree or higher: 21.9%

School District(s)
Canandaigua City SD (PK-12)
   2014-15 Enrollment: 3,683 . . . . (585) 396-3700
Two-year College(s)
Finger Lakes Community College (Public)
   Fall 2014 Enrollment: 6,793 . . . . (585) 394-3500
   2015-16 Tuition: In-state $4,704; Out-of-state $8,884
Housing: Homeownership rate: 69.2%; Median home value: $215,400; Median year structure built: 1989; Homeowner vacancy rate: 0.0%; Median selected monthly owner costs: $1,561 with a mortgage, $721 without a mortgage; Median gross rent: $984 per month; Rental vacancy rate: 11.2%

Health Insurance: 96.6% have insurance; 78.6% have private insurance; 35.9% have public insurance; 3.4% do not have insurance; 0.0% of children under 18 do not have insurance
Hospitals: Canandaigua VA Medical Center (251 beds); F F Thompson Hospital (113 beds)
Newspapers: Daily Messenger (daily circulation 11,700); Messenger Post Media (weekly circulation 86,000)
Transportation: Commute: 94.9% car, 0.7% public transportation, 0.9% walk, 3.4% work from home; Mean travel time to work: 24.0 minutes
Additional Information Contacts
Town of Canandaigua . . . . (585) 394-1120
   http://www.townofcanandaigua.org

CLIFTON SPRINGS (village). Covers a land area of 1.519 square miles and a water area of 0 square miles. Located at 42.96° N. Lat; 77.14° W. Long. Elevation is 577 feet.
Population: 2,180; Growth (since 2000): -1.9%; Density: 1,435.1 persons per square mile; Race: 91.5% White, 5.3% Black/African American, 0.2% Asian, 0.0% American Indian/Alaska Native, 0.0% Native Hawaiian/Other Pacific Islander, 1.8% Two or more races, 3.0% Hispanic of any race; Average household size: 2.35; Median age: 44.0; Age under 18: 22.8%; Age 65 and over: 21.5%; Males per 100 females: 80.7; Marriage status: 24.9% never married, 47.5% now married, 0.0% separated, 12.2% widowed, 15.4% divorced; Foreign born: 1.6%; Speak English only: 94.7%; With disability: 17.2%; Veterans: 9.1%; Ancestry: 22.8% Irish, 19.6% German, 15.8% English, 12.8% Italian, 8.6% Dutch
Employment: 10.2% management, business, and financial, 3.7% computer, engineering, and science, 10.2% education, legal, community service, arts, and media, 9.0% healthcare practitioners, 16.2% service, 23.9% sales and office, 6.0% natural resources, construction, and maintenance, 20.8% production, transportation, and material moving
Income: Per capita: $24,932; Median household: $47,868; Average household: $61,861; Households with income of $100,000 or more: 23.2%; Poverty rate: 11.7%
Educational Attainment: High school diploma or higher: 88.8%; Bachelor's degree or higher: 18.3%; Graduate/professional degree or higher: 8.3%

School District(s)
Phelps-Clifton Springs Central SD (KG-12)
   2014-15 Enrollment: 1,649 . . . . (315) 548-6420
Housing: Homeownership rate: 59.7%; Median home value: $112,500; Median year structure built: Before 1940; Homeowner vacancy rate: 0.0%; Median selected monthly owner costs: $1,094 with a mortgage, $543 without a mortgage; Median gross rent: $669 per month; Rental vacancy rate: 4.2%
Health Insurance: 95.9% have insurance; 72.7% have private insurance; 41.1% have public insurance; 4.1% do not have insurance; 0.0% of children under 18 do not have insurance
Hospitals: Clifton Springs Hospital & Clinic (262 beds)
Transportation: Commute: 87.8% car, 0.4% public transportation, 9.2% walk, 1.0% work from home; Mean travel time to work: 19.5 minutes

CRYSTAL BEACH (CDP). Covers a land area of 0.682 square miles and a water area of 0.203 square miles. Located at 42.81° N. Lat; 77.26° W. Long. Elevation is 699 feet.
Population: 727; Growth (since 2000): n/a; Density: 1,066.7 persons per square mile; Race: 92.2% White, 0.0% Black/African American, 7.8% Asian, 0.0% American Indian/Alaska Native, 0.0% Native Hawaiian/Other Pacific Islander, 0.0% Two or more races, 0.0% Hispanic of any race; Average household size: 1.98; Median age: 50.8; Age under 18: 15.3%; Age 65 and over: 30.4%; Males per 100 females: 100.0; Marriage status: 21.3% never married, 64.0% now married, 4.8% separated, 1.8% widowed, 12.8% divorced; Foreign born: 10.5%; Speak English only: 92.2%; With disability: 9.8%; Veterans: 17.5%; Ancestry: 24.6% American, 12.7% Italian, 12.1% Irish, 11.4% German, 9.4% English
Employment: 0.0% management, business, and financial, 2.1% computer, engineering, and science, 8.9% education, legal, community service, arts, and media, 0.0% healthcare practitioners, 22.0% service, 17.1% sales and office, 30.0% natural resources, construction, and maintenance, 19.9% production, transportation, and material moving
Income: Per capita: $30,030; Median household: $45,433; Average household: $60,274; Households with income of $100,000 or more: 17.7%; Poverty rate: 29.6%

Educational Attainment: High school diploma or higher: 80.2%; Bachelor's degree or higher: 19.1%; Graduate/professional degree or higher: 10.3%
Housing: Homeownership rate: 65.4%; Median home value: $162,500; Median year structure built: 1975; Homeowner vacancy rate: 0.0%; Median selected monthly owner costs: $764 with a mortgage, $448 without a mortgage; Median gross rent: $763 per month; Rental vacancy rate: 0.0%
Health Insurance: 86.2% have insurance; 51.2% have private insurance; 51.6% have public insurance; 13.8% do not have insurance; 0.0% of children under 18 do not have insurance
Transportation: Commute: 100.0% car, 0.0% public transportation, 0.0% walk, 0.0% work from home; Mean travel time to work: 25.3 minutes

EAST BLOOMFIELD (town). Covers a land area of 33.195 square miles and a water area of 0.139 square miles. Located at 42.90° N. Lat; 77.42° W. Long. Elevation is 1,070 feet.
Population: 3,608; Growth (since 2000): 7.3%; Density: 108.7 persons per square mile; Race: 99.0% White, 0.7% Black/African American, 0.0% Asian, 0.0% American Indian/Alaska Native, 0.0% Native Hawaiian/Other Pacific Islander, 0.2% Two or more races, 0.9% Hispanic of any race; Average household size: 2.48; Median age: 45.6; Age under 18: 22.5%; Age 65 and over: 16.0%; Males per 100 females: 99.1; Marriage status: 31.0% never married, 55.1% now married, 1.1% separated, 3.4% widowed, 10.5% divorced; Foreign born: 1.7%; Speak English only: 97.8%; With disability: 13.3%; Veterans: 9.4%; Ancestry: 31.7% German, 29.5% English, 28.3% Irish, 9.9% Italian, 6.5% French
Employment: 16.8% management, business, and financial, 6.1% computer, engineering, and science, 6.2% education, legal, community service, arts, and media, 5.2% healthcare practitioners, 18.6% service, 25.4% sales and office, 11.1% natural resources, construction, and maintenance, 10.6% production, transportation, and material moving
Income: Per capita: $32,385; Median household: $62,772; Average household: $79,750; Households with income of $100,000 or more: 25.5%; Poverty rate: 8.4%
Educational Attainment: High school diploma or higher: 93.2%; Bachelor's degree or higher: 30.2%; Graduate/professional degree or higher: 11.0%
Housing: Homeownership rate: 80.8%; Median home value: $156,900; Median year structure built: 1966; Homeowner vacancy rate: 0.7%; Median selected monthly owner costs: $1,310 with a mortgage, $583 without a mortgage; Median gross rent: $719 per month; Rental vacancy rate: 5.8%
Health Insurance: 89.5% have insurance; 69.4% have private insurance; 34.0% have public insurance; 10.5% do not have insurance; 9.0% of children under 18 do not have insurance
Transportation: Commute: 91.8% car, 0.1% public transportation, 2.7% walk, 4.6% work from home; Mean travel time to work: 23.2 minutes

FARMINGTON (town). Covers a land area of 39.430 square miles and a water area of 0 square miles. Located at 42.99° N. Lat; 77.31° W. Long. Elevation is 561 feet.
Population: 12,653; Growth (since 2000): 19.5%; Density: 320.9 persons per square mile; Race: 91.4% White, 2.5% Black/African American, 1.8% Asian, 0.5% American Indian/Alaska Native, 0.0% Native Hawaiian/Other Pacific Islander, 3.2% Two or more races, 6.2% Hispanic of any race; Average household size: 2.57; Median age: 37.5; Age under 18: 28.6%; Age 65 and over: 11.7%; Males per 100 females: 95.8; Marriage status: 25.2% never married, 57.4% now married, 2.8% separated, 5.2% widowed, 12.2% divorced; Foreign born: 5.6%; Speak English only: 91.8%; With disability: 9.3%; Veterans: 10.4%; Ancestry: 27.0% German, 19.3% Irish, 17.1% Italian, 16.5% English, 8.1% American
Employment: 15.9% management, business, and financial, 8.9% computer, engineering, and science, 11.4% education, legal, community service, arts, and media, 9.6% healthcare practitioners, 11.8% service, 25.4% sales and office, 8.0% natural resources, construction, and maintenance, 8.9% production, transportation, and material moving
Income: Per capita: $28,757; Median household: $64,889; Average household: $73,029; Households with income of $100,000 or more: 24.5%; Poverty rate: 10.6%
Educational Attainment: High school diploma or higher: 93.6%; Bachelor's degree or higher: 36.4%; Graduate/professional degree or higher: 11.5%
Housing: Homeownership rate: 72.7%; Median home value: $145,900; Median year structure built: 1980; Homeowner vacancy rate: 1.0%; Median selected monthly owner costs: $1,373 with a mortgage, $531 without a mortgage; Median gross rent: $991 per month; Rental vacancy rate: 0.0%

Health Insurance: 91.8% have insurance; 74.2% have private insurance; 28.5% have public insurance; 8.2% do not have insurance; 6.2% of children under 18 do not have insurance
Transportation: Commute: 93.6% car, 0.8% public transportation, 0.8% walk, 3.8% work from home; Mean travel time to work: 26.6 minutes
Additional Information Contacts
Town of Farmington . . . . (315) 986-8100
  http://www.townoffarmingtonny.com

GENEVA (city).
Covers a land area of 4.210 square miles and a water area of 1.632 square miles. Located at 42.86° N. Lat; 76.98° W. Long. Elevation is 443 feet.
History: Named for Geneva, Switzerland, by Swiss settlers. The area of the city of Geneva includes the site of the Native American settlement of Kanadesaga. After the Revolution, other settlers began to arrive. Captain Charles Williamson, agent for the Pulteney Estate, recognized the superb advantages of the site and laid out Main Street on the terrace overlooking the lake.
Population: 13,157; Growth (since 2000): -3.4%; Density: 3,125.1 persons per square mile; Race: 78.0% White, 11.7% Black/African American, 2.9% Asian, 0.9% American Indian/Alaska Native, 0.0% Native Hawaiian/Other Pacific Islander, 2.9% Two or more races, 13.8% Hispanic of any race; Average household size: 2.30; Median age: 27.7; Age under 18: 18.8%; Age 65 and over: 13.1%; Males per 100 females: 87.8; Marriage status: 53.6% never married, 32.1% now married, 2.1% separated, 5.4% widowed, 8.9% divorced; Foreign born: 6.3%; Speak English only: 83.5%; With disability: 13.3%; Veterans: 6.0%; Ancestry: 19.3% Irish, 16.4% Italian, 14.0% German, 10.8% English, 4.4% American
Employment: 8.7% management, business, and financial, 2.7% computer, engineering, and science, 17.2% education, legal, community service, arts, and media, 7.0% healthcare practitioners, 24.5% service, 23.3% sales and office, 5.3% natural resources, construction, and maintenance, 11.2% production, transportation, and material moving
Income: Per capita: $19,839; Median household: $40,000; Average household: $53,023; Households with income of $100,000 or more: 12.6%; Poverty rate: 24.1%
Educational Attainment: High school diploma or higher: 87.1%; Bachelor's degree or higher: 26.5%; Graduate/professional degree or higher: 14.0%
School District(s)
Geneva City SD (PK-12)
  2014-15 Enrollment: 2,243 . . . . (315) 781-0400
Four-year College(s)
Hobart William Smith Colleges (Private, Not-for-profit)
  Fall 2014 Enrollment: 2,425 . . . . (315) 781-3000
  2015-16 Tuition: In-state $49,677; Out-of-state $49,677
Two-year College(s)
Finger Lakes Health College of Nursing (Private, Not-for-profit)
  Fall 2014 Enrollment: 135 . . . . (315) 787-4005
  2015-16 Tuition: In-state $11,540; Out-of-state $11,540
Vocational/Technical School(s)
Marion S Whelan School of Nursing of Geneva General Hospital (Private, Not-for-profit)
  Fall 2014 Enrollment: 29 . . . . (315) 787-4005
  2015-16 Tuition: In-state $9,150; Out-of-state $9,150
Housing: Homeownership rate: 50.1%; Median home value: $90,700; Median year structure built: Before 1940; Homeowner vacancy rate: 0.0%; Median selected monthly owner costs: $1,039 with a mortgage, $513 without a mortgage; Median gross rent: $708 per month; Rental vacancy rate: 5.4%
Health Insurance: 91.9% have insurance; 65.8% have private insurance; 37.8% have public insurance; 8.1% do not have insurance; 2.9% of children under 18 do not have insurance
Hospitals: Geneva General Hospital (136 beds)
Safety: Violent crime rate: 22.1 per 10,000 population; Property crime rate: 292.1 per 10,000 population
Newspapers: Finger Lakes Times (daily circulation 15,600)
Transportation: Commute: 75.0% car, 0.9% public transportation, 17.8% walk, 3.6% work from home; Mean travel time to work: 16.9 minutes
Additional Information Contacts
City of Geneva. . . . . (315) 828-6550
  http://www.geneva.ny.us

GENEVA (town).
Covers a land area of 19.091 square miles and a water area of 0.007 square miles. Located at 42.83° N. Lat; 77.01° W. Long. Elevation is 443 feet.
History: Hobart College and William Smith College are in the city. Settled 1788; Incorporated as village in 1812, as city in 1897.
Population: 3,255; Growth (since 2000): -1.0%; Density: 170.5 persons per square mile; Race: 92.4% White, 3.5% Black/African American, 0.3% Asian, 0.0% American Indian/Alaska Native, 0.0% Native Hawaiian/Other Pacific Islander, 1.0% Two or more races, 11.8% Hispanic of any race; Average household size: 2.10; Median age: 50.7; Age under 18: 16.4%; Age 65 and over: 26.1%; Males per 100 females: 91.7; Marriage status: 24.3% never married, 56.4% now married, 3.5% separated, 11.4% widowed, 7.9% divorced; Foreign born: 2.1%; Speak English only: 90.2%; With disability: 13.1%; Veterans: 11.7%; Ancestry: 22.9% Italian, 17.8% English, 16.0% Irish, 14.9% German, 10.4% American
Employment: 10.9% management, business, and financial, 6.6% computer, engineering, and science, 17.4% education, legal, community service, arts, and media, 12.1% healthcare practitioners, 14.3% service, 23.1% sales and office, 6.8% natural resources, construction, and maintenance, 8.9% production, transportation, and material moving
Income: Per capita: $32,904; Median household: $55,133; Average household: $69,663; Households with income of $100,000 or more: 20.4%; Poverty rate: 9.3%
Educational Attainment: High school diploma or higher: 93.5%; Bachelor's degree or higher: 35.3%; Graduate/professional degree or higher: 13.2%
School District(s)
Geneva City SD (PK-12)
  2014-15 Enrollment: 2,243 . . . . (315) 781-0400
Four-year College(s)
Hobart William Smith Colleges (Private, Not-for-profit)
  Fall 2014 Enrollment: 2,425 . . . . (315) 781-3000
  2015-16 Tuition: In-state $49,677; Out-of-state $49,677
Two-year College(s)
Finger Lakes Health College of Nursing (Private, Not-for-profit)
  Fall 2014 Enrollment: 135 . . . . (315) 787-4005
  2015-16 Tuition: In-state $11,540; Out-of-state $11,540
Vocational/Technical School(s)
Marion S Whelan School of Nursing of Geneva General Hospital (Private, Not-for-profit)
  Fall 2014 Enrollment: 29 . . . . (315) 787-4005
  2015-16 Tuition: In-state $9,150; Out-of-state $9,150
Housing: Homeownership rate: 64.6%; Median home value: $170,000; Median year structure built: 1967; Homeowner vacancy rate: 0.0%; Median selected monthly owner costs: $1,393 with a mortgage, $547 without a mortgage; Median gross rent: $817 per month; Rental vacancy rate: 0.0%
Health Insurance: 96.8% have insurance; 81.5% have private insurance; 40.9% have public insurance; 3.2% do not have insurance; 0.0% of children under 18 do not have insurance
Hospitals: Geneva General Hospital (136 beds)
Newspapers: Finger Lakes Times (daily circulation 15,600)
Transportation: Commute: 91.0% car, 0.6% public transportation, 3.0% walk, 2.2% work from home; Mean travel time to work: 16.3 minutes

GORHAM (CDP).
Covers a land area of 1.897 square miles and a water area of 0 square miles. Located at 42.80° N. Lat; 77.13° W. Long. Elevation is 889 feet.
Population: 601; Growth (since 2000): n/a; Density: 316.8 persons per square mile; Race: 100.0% White, 0.0% Black/African American, 0.0% Asian, 0.0% American Indian/Alaska Native, 0.0% Native Hawaiian/Other Pacific Islander, 0.0% Two or more races, 0.0% Hispanic of any race; Average household size: 2.80; Median age: 47.3; Age under 18: 23.3%; Age 65 and over: 5.7%; Males per 100 females: 86.4; Marriage status: 25.6% never married, 66.3% now married, 0.0% separated, 1.7% widowed, 6.4% divorced; Foreign born: 0.0%; Speak English only: 98.4%; With disability: 6.7%; Veterans: 18.0%; Ancestry: 37.1% Irish, 13.8% German, 11.5% English, 7.2% Italian, 5.0% French
Employment: 19.6% management, business, and financial, 13.4% computer, engineering, and science, 17.9% education, legal, community service, arts, and media, 0.0% healthcare practitioners, 29.2% service, 9.2% sales and office, 0.0% natural resources, construction, and maintenance, 10.7% production, transportation, and material moving
Income: Per capita: $24,426; Median household: $61,036; Average household: $68,087; Households with income of $100,000 or more: 17.7%; Poverty rate: n/a

Educational Attainment: High school diploma or higher: 100.0%; Bachelor's degree or higher: 31.3%; Graduate/professional degree or higher: 6.5%

School District(s)
Gorham-Middlesex Central SD (Marcus Whitman) (PK-12)
    2014-15 Enrollment: 1,286 . . . . (585) 554-4848
Housing: Homeownership rate: 90.2%; Median home value: $100,600; Median year structure built: Before 1940; Homeowner vacancy rate: 0.0%; Median selected monthly owner costs: n/a with a mortgage, n/a without a mortgage; Median gross rent: n/a per month; Rental vacancy rate: 0.0%
Health Insurance: 95.8% have insurance; 87.7% have private insurance; 21.3% have public insurance; 4.2% do not have insurance; 0.0% of children under 18 do not have insurance
Transportation: Commute: 88.4% car, 0.0% public transportation, 8.3% walk, 3.3% work from home; Mean travel time to work: 23.2 minutes

GORHAM (town). Covers a land area of 48.854 square miles and a water area of 4.315 square miles. Located at 42.80° N. Lat; 77.20° W. Long. Elevation is 889 feet.
Population: 4,262; Growth (since 2000): 12.9%; Density: 87.2 persons per square mile; Race: 97.3% White, 0.4% Black/African American, 1.3% Asian, 0.0% American Indian/Alaska Native, 0.0% Native Hawaiian/Other Pacific Islander, 0.9% Two or more races, 1.0% Hispanic of any race; Average household size: 2.31; Median age: 49.9; Age under 18: 17.0%; Age 65 and over: 20.6%; Males per 100 females: 96.9; Marriage status: 23.2% never married, 60.0% now married, 1.5% separated, 5.8% widowed, 11.0% divorced; Foreign born: 3.0%; Speak English only: 92.0%; With disability: 12.2%; Veterans: 9.9%; Ancestry: 24.5% German, 17.0% Irish, 16.6% English, 10.7% American, 9.0% Italian
Employment: 13.0% management, business, and financial, 4.8% computer, engineering, and science, 11.2% education, legal, community service, arts, and media, 2.7% healthcare practitioners, 16.9% service, 22.4% sales and office, 14.6% natural resources, construction, and maintenance, 14.4% production, transportation, and material moving
Income: Per capita: $31,964; Median household: $63,113; Average household: $73,588; Households with income of $100,000 or more: 23.8%; Poverty rate: 6.9%
Educational Attainment: High school diploma or higher: 90.6%; Bachelor's degree or higher: 29.3%; Graduate/professional degree or higher: 15.0%

School District(s)
Gorham-Middlesex Central SD (Marcus Whitman) (PK-12)
    2014-15 Enrollment: 1,286 . . . . (585) 554-4848
Housing: Homeownership rate: 87.5%; Median home value: $180,900; Median year structure built: 1965; Homeowner vacancy rate: 0.6%; Median selected monthly owner costs: $1,373 with a mortgage, $540 without a mortgage; Median gross rent: $588 per month; Rental vacancy rate: 0.0%
Health Insurance: 88.8% have insurance; 74.0% have private insurance; 32.0% have public insurance; 11.2% do not have insurance; 22.4% of children under 18 do not have insurance
Transportation: Commute: 92.8% car, 0.4% public transportation, 3.6% walk, 3.0% work from home; Mean travel time to work: 24.9 minutes
Additional Information Contacts
Town of Gorham . . . . (585) 526-6317
    http://www.gorham-ny.com

HALL (CDP). Covers a land area of 1.023 square miles and a water area of 0 square miles. Located at 42.80° N. Lat; 77.07° W. Long. Elevation is 935 feet.
Population: 152; Growth (since 2000): n/a; Density: 148.6 persons per square mile; Race: 100.0% White, 0.0% Black/African American, 0.0% Asian, 0.0% American Indian/Alaska Native, 0.0% Native Hawaiian/Other Pacific Islander, 0.0% Two or more races, 0.0% Hispanic of any race; Average household size: 2.30; Median age: 49.3; Age under 18: 11.2%; Age 65 and over: 17.8%; Males per 100 females: 101.9; Marriage status: 14.1% never married, 82.2% now married, 0.0% separated, 0.0% widowed, 3.7% divorced; Foreign born: 0.0%; Speak English only: 100.0%; With disability: 11.2%; Veterans: 10.4%; Ancestry: 32.9% Irish, 26.3% English, 20.4% Italian, 17.8% German, 13.2% Danish
Employment: 29.5% management, business, and financial, 0.0% computer, engineering, and science, 0.0% education, legal, community service, arts, and media, 0.0% healthcare practitioners, 4.8% service, 52.4% sales and office, 8.6% natural resources, construction, and maintenance, 4.8% production, transportation, and material moving

Income: Per capita: $39,501; Median household: $103,654; Average household: $89,717; Households with income of $100,000 or more: 59.1%; Poverty rate: n/a
Educational Attainment: High school diploma or higher: 93.3%; Bachelor's degree or higher: 22.2%; Graduate/professional degree or higher: 9.6%
Housing: Homeownership rate: 92.4%; Median home value: $158,200; Median year structure built: Before 1940; Homeowner vacancy rate: 0.0%; Median selected monthly owner costs: $1,171 with a mortgage, n/a without a mortgage; Median gross rent: n/a per month; Rental vacancy rate: 72.2%
Health Insurance: 84.2% have insurance; 84.2% have private insurance; 17.8% have public insurance; 15.8% do not have insurance; 0.0% of children under 18 do not have insurance
Transportation: Commute: 100.0% car, 0.0% public transportation, 0.0% walk, 0.0% work from home; Mean travel time to work: 23.6 minutes

HONEOYE (CDP). Covers a land area of 0.921 square miles and a water area of 0 square miles. Located at 42.79° N. Lat; 77.51° W. Long. Elevation is 814 feet.
Population: 655; Growth (since 2000): n/a; Density: 711.3 persons per square mile; Race: 96.5% White, 0.0% Black/African American, 0.0% Asian, 3.5% American Indian/Alaska Native, 0.0% Native Hawaiian/Other Pacific Islander, 0.0% Two or more races, 15.1% Hispanic of any race; Average household size: 2.36; Median age: 46.0; Age under 18: 11.5%; Age 65 and over: 21.4%; Males per 100 females: 107.5; Marriage status: 23.6% never married, 50.3% now married, 2.1% separated, 22.8% widowed, 3.3% divorced; Foreign born: 6.6%; Speak English only: 96.1%; With disability: 2.9%; Veterans: 7.4%; Ancestry: 44.0% Italian, 43.1% German, 19.7% English, 18.6% Irish, 10.1% French
Employment: 14.7% management, business, and financial, 0.0% computer, engineering, and science, 6.7% education, legal, community service, arts, and media, 0.0% healthcare practitioners, 13.3% service, 40.7% sales and office, 6.0% natural resources, construction, and maintenance, 18.6% production, transportation, and material moving
Income: Per capita: $21,759; Median household: $43,026; Average household: $48,756; Households with income of $100,000 or more: 15.5%; Poverty rate: n/a
Educational Attainment: High school diploma or higher: 97.3%; Bachelor's degree or higher: 17.2%; Graduate/professional degree or higher: 4.3%

School District(s)
Honeoye Central SD (KG-12)
    2014-15 Enrollment: 628 . . . . (585) 229-4125
Housing: Homeownership rate: 80.6%; Median home value: $118,000; Median year structure built: Before 1940; Homeowner vacancy rate: 16.4%; Median selected monthly owner costs: $824 with a mortgage, n/a without a mortgage; Median gross rent: $1,025 per month; Rental vacancy rate: 0.0%
Health Insurance: 95.3% have insurance; 55.3% have private insurance; 44.6% have public insurance; 4.7% do not have insurance; 0.0% of children under 18 do not have insurance
Transportation: Commute: 73.0% car, 0.0% public transportation, 27.0% walk, 0.0% work from home; Mean travel time to work: 24.9 minutes

HOPEWELL (town). Covers a land area of 35.676 square miles and a water area of 0.020 square miles. Located at 42.89° N. Lat; 77.20° W. Long.
Population: 3,739; Growth (since 2000): 11.7%; Density: 104.8 persons per square mile; Race: 91.3% White, 4.0% Black/African American, 0.0% Asian, 0.3% American Indian/Alaska Native, 0.0% Native Hawaiian/Other Pacific Islander, 1.8% Two or more races, 3.8% Hispanic of any race; Average household size: 2.60; Median age: 42.3; Age under 18: 20.2%; Age 65 and over: 17.8%; Males per 100 females: 112.8; Marriage status: 33.5% never married, 45.9% now married, 1.7% separated, 7.4% widowed, 13.2% divorced; Foreign born: 2.6%; Speak English only: 95.9%; With disability: 13.3%; Veterans: 8.6%; Ancestry: 22.5% English, 21.7% German, 18.0% Irish, 12.9% American, 6.3% Italian
Employment: 6.9% management, business, and financial, 5.7% computer, engineering, and science, 8.4% education, legal, community service, arts, and media, 7.4% healthcare practitioners, 24.7% service, 21.6% sales and office, 12.0% natural resources, construction, and maintenance, 13.4% production, transportation, and material moving
Income: Per capita: $23,993; Median household: $56,354; Average household: $67,410; Households with income of $100,000 or more: 20.7%; Poverty rate: 8.7%

Educational Attainment: High school diploma or higher: 88.0%; Bachelor's degree or higher: 14.9%; Graduate/professional degree or higher: 4.0%
Housing: Homeownership rate: 90.3%; Median home value: $117,600; Median year structure built: 1982; Homeowner vacancy rate: 0.0%; Median selected monthly owner costs: $1,168 with a mortgage, $542 without a mortgage; Median gross rent: $966 per month; Rental vacancy rate: 0.0%
Health Insurance: 92.2% have insurance; 67.1% have private insurance; 40.6% have public insurance; 7.8% do not have insurance; 3.9% of children under 18 do not have insurance
Transportation: Commute: 93.9% car, 2.1% public transportation, 1.6% walk, 1.9% work from home; Mean travel time to work: 23.8 minutes

IONIA (unincorporated postal area)
ZCTA: 14475
Covers a land area of 1.526 square miles and a water area of 0 square miles. Located at 42.94° N. Lat; 77.50° W. Long. Elevation is 889 feet.
Population: 243; Growth (since 2000): 9.0%; Density: 159.3 persons per square mile; Race: 100.0% White, 0.0% Black/African American, 0.0% Asian, 0.0% American Indian/Alaska Native, 0.0% Native Hawaiian/Other Pacific Islander, 0.0% Two or more races, 0.0% Hispanic of any race; Average household size: 2.76; Median age: 44.3; Age under 18: 27.6%; Age 65 and over: 16.5%; Males per 100 females: 93.4; Marriage status: 28.3% never married, 59.9% now married, 0.0% separated, 0.0% widowed, 11.8% divorced; Foreign born: 0.0%; Speak English only: 96.3%; With disability: 7.8%; Veterans: 1.7%; Ancestry: 30.5% Irish, 23.5% English, 21.4% German, 14.0% Scotch-Irish, 9.5% Scottish
Employment: 10.9% management, business, and financial, 4.2% computer, engineering, and science, 9.2% education, legal, community service, arts, and media, 3.4% healthcare practitioners, 18.5% service, 22.7% sales and office, 9.2% natural resources, construction, and maintenance, 21.8% production, transportation, and material moving
Income: Per capita: $30,101; Median household: $84,167; Average household: $81,815; Households with income of $100,000 or more: 28.4%; Poverty rate: 8.6%
Educational Attainment: High school diploma or higher: 97.0%; Bachelor's degree or higher: 49.4%; Graduate/professional degree or higher: 20.2%
Housing: Homeownership rate: 84.1%; Median home value: $272,200; Median year structure built: 1976; Homeowner vacancy rate: 0.0%; Median selected monthly owner costs: $1,550 with a mortgage, $1,014 without a mortgage; Median gross rent: n/a per month; Rental vacancy rate: 0.0%
Health Insurance: 96.3% have insurance; 92.6% have private insurance; 21.8% have public insurance; 3.7% do not have insurance; 6.0% of children under 18 do not have insurance
Transportation: Commute: 94.6% car, 5.4% public transportation, 0.0% walk, 0.0% work from home; Mean travel time to work: 25.2 minutes

MANCHESTER (town). Covers a land area of 37.818 square miles and a water area of 0.032 square miles. Located at 42.99° N. Lat; 77.19° W. Long. Elevation is 591 feet.
History: Incorporated 1892.
Population: 9,421; Growth (since 2000): 1.8%; Density: 249.1 persons per square mile; Race: 96.2% White, 1.6% Black/African American, 0.0% Asian, 0.4% American Indian/Alaska Native, 0.0% Native Hawaiian/Other Pacific Islander, 1.3% Two or more races, 1.8% Hispanic of any race; Average household size: 2.43; Median age: 44.6; Age under 18: 22.5%; Age 65 and over: 18.7%; Males per 100 females: 94.2; Marriage status: 24.1% never married, 53.6% now married, 2.8% separated, 8.6% widowed, 13.7% divorced; Foreign born: 1.8%; Speak English only: 96.8%; With disability: 15.6%; Veterans: 9.7%; Ancestry: 24.0% German, 21.1% Irish, 19.8% English, 11.6% Italian, 9.4% Dutch
Employment: 9.0% management, business, and financial, 3.4% computer, engineering, and science, 7.6% education, legal, community service, arts, and media, 6.6% healthcare practitioners, 20.6% service, 24.8% sales and office, 11.7% natural resources, construction, and maintenance, 16.3% production, transportation, and material moving
Income: Per capita: $24,408; Median household: $51,074; Average household: $59,742; Households with income of $100,000 or more: 15.8%; Poverty rate: 9.2%
Educational Attainment: High school diploma or higher: 84.7%; Bachelor's degree or higher: 14.0%; Graduate/professional degree or higher: 5.4%

Housing: Homeownership rate: 79.2%; Median home value: $92,900; Median year structure built: 1963; Homeowner vacancy rate: 2.0%; Median selected monthly owner costs: $1,079 with a mortgage, $537 without a mortgage; Median gross rent: $724 per month; Rental vacancy rate: 6.1%
Health Insurance: 91.6% have insurance; 70.3% have private insurance; 39.6% have public insurance; 8.4% do not have insurance; 9.3% of children under 18 do not have insurance
Transportation: Commute: 94.2% car, 0.8% public transportation, 1.8% walk, 2.3% work from home; Mean travel time to work: 20.8 minutes
Additional Information Contacts
Town of Manchester . . . . (315) 462-6224
  http://manchesterny.org

MANCHESTER (village). Covers a land area of 1.176 square miles and a water area of 0 square miles. Located at 42.97° N. Lat; 77.23° W. Long. Elevation is 591 feet.
Population: 1,712; Growth (since 2000): 16.1%; Density: 1,455.5 persons per square mile; Race: 95.3% White, 1.2% Black/African American, 0.0% Asian, 1.9% American Indian/Alaska Native, 0.0% Native Hawaiian/Other Pacific Islander, 1.5% Two or more races, 1.9% Hispanic of any race; Average household size: 2.22; Median age: 40.8; Age under 18: 21.0%; Age 65 and over: 15.6%; Males per 100 females: 91.4; Marriage status: 21.6% never married, 55.0% now married, 5.0% separated, 10.6% widowed, 12.9% divorced; Foreign born: 2.8%; Speak English only: 96.5%; With disability: 13.6%; Veterans: 10.0%; Ancestry: 26.3% German, 20.5% English, 20.4% Irish, 18.0% Italian, 9.6% Dutch
Employment: 10.3% management, business, and financial, 4.2% computer, engineering, and science, 2.6% education, legal, community service, arts, and media, 6.1% healthcare practitioners, 22.9% service, 22.7% sales and office, 12.1% natural resources, construction, and maintenance, 19.0% production, transportation, and material moving
Income: Per capita: $25,073; Median household: $52,500; Average household: $55,087; Households with income of $100,000 or more: 10.9%; Poverty rate: 11.2%
Educational Attainment: High school diploma or higher: 92.3%; Bachelor's degree or higher: 16.1%; Graduate/professional degree or higher: 4.8%
Housing: Homeownership rate: 76.8%; Median home value: $84,200; Median year structure built: 1972; Homeowner vacancy rate: 3.9%; Median selected monthly owner costs: $1,111 with a mortgage, $539 without a mortgage; Median gross rent: $865 per month; Rental vacancy rate: 0.0%
Health Insurance: 93.1% have insurance; 76.8% have private insurance; 32.4% have public insurance; 6.9% do not have insurance; 0.0% of children under 18 do not have insurance
Safety: Violent crime rate: 0.0 per 10,000 population; Property crime rate: 0.0 per 10,000 population
Transportation: Commute: 97.0% car, 0.4% public transportation, 1.1% walk, 0.4% work from home; Mean travel time to work: 20.4 minutes

NAPLES (town). Covers a land area of 39.685 square miles and a water area of <.001 square miles. Located at 42.62° N. Lat; 77.43° W. Long. Elevation is 804 feet.
History: Incorporated 1894.
Population: 2,388; Growth (since 2000): -2.2%; Density: 60.2 persons per square mile; Race: 98.7% White, 0.3% Black/African American, 0.0% Asian, 0.0% American Indian/Alaska Native, 0.0% Native Hawaiian/Other Pacific Islander, 0.6% Two or more races, 1.3% Hispanic of any race; Average household size: 2.37; Median age: 48.7; Age under 18: 16.2%; Age 65 and over: 21.8%; Males per 100 females: 93.5; Marriage status: 28.9% never married, 52.3% now married, 2.2% separated, 7.9% widowed, 10.9% divorced; Foreign born: 2.0%; Speak English only: 96.0%; With disability: 10.6%; Veterans: 13.0%; Ancestry: 28.5% German, 17.4% Irish, 15.9% English, 8.4% Italian, 6.5% Dutch
Employment: 12.0% management, business, and financial, 4.2% computer, engineering, and science, 12.3% education, legal, community service, arts, and media, 10.2% healthcare practitioners, 24.2% service, 13.3% sales and office, 12.6% natural resources, construction, and maintenance, 11.2% production, transportation, and material moving
Income: Per capita: $23,855; Median household: $47,039; Average household: $56,300; Households with income of $100,000 or more: 16.3%; Poverty rate: 14.5%
Educational Attainment: High school diploma or higher: 91.8%; Bachelor's degree or higher: 24.3%; Graduate/professional degree or higher: 12.6%

School District(s)
Naples Central SD (PK-12)
    2014-15 Enrollment: 754 . . . . (585) 374-7901

School District(s)
Naples Central SD (PK-12)
    2014-15 Enrollment: 754 . . . . (585) 374-7901
Housing: Homeownership rate: 77.0%; Median home value: $141,300; Median year structure built: 1963; Homeowner vacancy rate: 2.9%; Median selected monthly owner costs: $1,135 with a mortgage, $540 without a mortgage; Median gross rent: $703 per month; Rental vacancy rate: 4.2%
Health Insurance: 93.0% have insurance; 68.0% have private insurance; 42.5% have public insurance; 7.0% do not have insurance; 0.0% of children under 18 do not have insurance
Transportation: Commute: 88.8% car, 0.0% public transportation, 5.5% walk, 5.2% work from home; Mean travel time to work: 29.4 minutes

NAPLES (village). Covers a land area of 0.985 square miles and a water area of 0 square miles. Located at 42.62° N. Lat; 77.40° W. Long. Elevation is 804 feet.
Population: 990; Growth (since 2000): -7.6%; Density: 1,005.6 persons per square mile; Race: 98.8% White, 0.0% Black/African American, 0.0% Asian, 0.0% American Indian/Alaska Native, 0.0% Native Hawaiian/Other Pacific Islander, 1.2% Two or more races, 2.7% Hispanic of any race; Average household size: 2.44; Median age: 46.1; Age under 18: 16.8%; Age 65 and over: 18.6%; Males per 100 females: 86.6; Marriage status: 36.1% never married, 45.5% now married, 3.2% separated, 5.1% widowed, 13.3% divorced; Foreign born: 1.9%; Speak English only: 98.3%; With disability: 9.3%; Veterans: 14.4%; Ancestry: 32.2% German, 20.0% Irish, 16.6% English, 14.4% Italian, 5.8% Polish
Employment: 7.2% management, business, and financial, 1.7% computer, engineering, and science, 21.1% education, legal, community service, arts, and media, 7.4% healthcare practitioners, 27.7% service, 17.9% sales and office, 8.3% natural resources, construction, and maintenance, 8.7% production, transportation, and material moving
Income: Per capita: $23,340; Median household: $47,917; Average household: $56,686; Households with income of $100,000 or more: 15.9%; Poverty rate: 16.9%
Educational Attainment: High school diploma or higher: 93.9%; Bachelor's degree or higher: 26.2%; Graduate/professional degree or higher: 14.0%

School District(s)
Naples Central SD (PK-12)
    2014-15 Enrollment: 754 . . . . (585) 374-7901
Housing: Homeownership rate: 61.2%; Median home value: $113,500; Median year structure built: Before 1940; Homeowner vacancy rate: 2.4%; Median selected monthly owner costs: $1,204 with a mortgage, $539 without a mortgage; Median gross rent: $663 per month; Rental vacancy rate: 6.0%
Health Insurance: 93.4% have insurance; 62.4% have private insurance; 46.5% have public insurance; 6.6% do not have insurance; 0.0% of children under 18 do not have insurance
Transportation: Commute: 86.3% car, 0.0% public transportation, 10.0% walk, 3.6% work from home; Mean travel time to work: 22.9 minutes

PHELPS (town). Covers a land area of 64.951 square miles and a water area of 0.293 square miles. Located at 42.96° N. Lat; 77.05° W. Long. Elevation is 522 feet.
Population: 7,000; Growth (since 2000): -0.2%; Density: 107.8 persons per square mile; Race: 96.4% White, 1.2% Black/African American, 0.2% Asian, 0.0% American Indian/Alaska Native, 0.0% Native Hawaiian/Other Pacific Islander, 2.1% Two or more races, 0.6% Hispanic of any race; Average household size: 2.43; Median age: 44.5; Age under 18: 20.3%; Age 65 and over: 16.8%; Males per 100 females: 98.1; Marriage status: 25.8% never married, 55.8% now married, 1.6% separated, 6.1% widowed, 12.3% divorced; Foreign born: 0.9%; Speak English only: 97.3%; With disability: 10.9%; Veterans: 14.8%; Ancestry: 23.3% German, 19.2% English, 17.5% Irish, 11.9% American, 11.8% Dutch
Employment: 14.7% management, business, and financial, 4.3% computer, engineering, and science, 10.9% education, legal, community service, arts, and media, 6.7% healthcare practitioners, 15.5% service, 16.2% sales and office, 7.9% natural resources, construction, and maintenance, 23.9% production, transportation, and material moving
Income: Per capita: $29,351; Median household: $58,482; Average household: $70,958; Households with income of $100,000 or more: 22.1%; Poverty rate: 10.6%
Educational Attainment: High school diploma or higher: 92.5%; Bachelor's degree or higher: 17.4%; Graduate/professional degree or higher: 8.8%

Housing: Homeownership rate: 77.8%; Median home value: $118,900; Median year structure built: 1957; Homeowner vacancy rate: 0.0%; Median selected monthly owner costs: $1,130 with a mortgage, $528 without a mortgage; Median gross rent: $736 per month; Rental vacancy rate: 0.0%
Health Insurance: 91.9% have insurance; 77.3% have private insurance; 29.6% have public insurance; 8.1% do not have insurance; 7.9% of children under 18 do not have insurance
Transportation: Commute: 92.1% car, 0.3% public transportation, 4.2% walk, 3.3% work from home; Mean travel time to work: 19.4 minutes
Additional Information Contacts
Town of Phelps . . . . (315) 548-5691
    http://www.phelpsny.com/residents/town

PHELPS (village). Covers a land area of 1.172 square miles and a water area of 0 square miles. Located at 42.96° N. Lat; 77.06° W. Long. Elevation is 522 feet.
Population: 1,983; Growth (since 2000): 0.7%; Density: 1,691.4 persons per square mile; Race: 97.7% White, 0.3% Black/African American, 0.4% Asian, 0.0% American Indian/Alaska Native, 0.0% Native Hawaiian/Other Pacific Islander, 1.3% Two or more races, 1.8% Hispanic of any race; Average household size: 2.23; Median age: 42.1; Age under 18: 21.2%; Age 65 and over: 17.3%; Males per 100 females: 93.5; Marriage status: 32.0% never married, 46.2% now married, 3.3% separated, 9.8% widowed, 12.0% divorced; Foreign born: 0.4%; Speak English only: 99.4%; With disability: 15.0%; Veterans: 14.8%; Ancestry: 26.5% German, 25.0% Irish, 24.0% English, 14.9% Dutch, 7.8% Italian
Employment: 19.0% management, business, and financial, 7.5% computer, engineering, and science, 8.3% education, legal, community service, arts, and media, 7.1% healthcare practitioners, 13.4% service, 18.4% sales and office, 6.3% natural resources, construction, and maintenance, 20.0% production, transportation, and material moving
Income: Per capita: $28,379; Median household: $51,992; Average household: $62,355; Households with income of $100,000 or more: 12.4%; Poverty rate: 11.4%
Educational Attainment: High school diploma or higher: 94.1%; Bachelor's degree or higher: 19.8%; Graduate/professional degree or higher: 8.7%
Housing: Homeownership rate: 64.1%; Median home value: $109,800; Median year structure built: Before 1940; Homeowner vacancy rate: 0.0%; Median selected monthly owner costs: $1,198 with a mortgage, $496 without a mortgage; Median gross rent: $703 per month; Rental vacancy rate: 0.0%
Health Insurance: 94.7% have insurance; 73.4% have private insurance; 34.8% have public insurance; 5.3% do not have insurance; 0.0% of children under 18 do not have insurance
Transportation: Commute: 89.2% car, 1.1% public transportation, 7.7% walk, 1.5% work from home; Mean travel time to work: 18.1 minutes
Additional Information Contacts
Village of Phelps . . . . (315) 548-3861
    http://www.phelpsny.com/village

PORT GIBSON (CDP). Covers a land area of 1.171 square miles and a water area of 0.032 square miles. Located at 43.03° N. Lat; 77.16° W. Long. Elevation is 476 feet.
Population: 495; Growth (since 2000): n/a; Density: 422.6 persons per square mile; Race: 98.0% White, 1.0% Black/African American, 0.0% Asian, 0.0% American Indian/Alaska Native, 0.0% Native Hawaiian/Other Pacific Islander, 1.0% Two or more races, 0.0% Hispanic of any race; Average household size: 2.39; Median age: 48.4; Age under 18: 17.0%; Age 65 and over: 39.4%; Males per 100 females: 106.8; Marriage status: 24.3% never married, 61.1% now married, 0.0% separated, 0.0% widowed, 14.6% divorced; Foreign born: 0.0%; Speak English only: 100.0%; With disability: 12.5%; Veterans: 1.7%; Ancestry: 32.3% English, 21.0% German, 21.0% Irish, 12.3% Dutch, 7.9% American
Employment: 2.5% management, business, and financial, 6.7% computer, engineering, and science, 7.4% education, legal, community service, arts, and media, 5.0% healthcare practitioners, 34.4% service, 14.2% sales and office, 22.7% natural resources, construction, and maintenance, 7.1% production, transportation, and material moving
Income: Per capita: $25,771; Median household: $58,854; Average household: $61,785; Households with income of $100,000 or more: 8.8%; Poverty rate: 8.9%
Educational Attainment: High school diploma or higher: 64.6%; Bachelor's degree or higher: 8.8%; Graduate/professional degree or higher: 7.1%

Housing: Homeownership rate: 87.7%; Median home value: $87,800; Median year structure built: 1949; Homeowner vacancy rate: 0.0%; Median selected monthly owner costs: n/a with a mortgage, n/a without a mortgage; Median gross rent: $715 per month; Rental vacancy rate: 0.0%
Health Insurance: 99.2% have insurance; 87.7% have private insurance; 46.9% have public insurance; 0.8% do not have insurance; 0.0% of children under 18 do not have insurance
Transportation: Commute: 96.1% car, 0.0% public transportation, 0.0% walk, 3.9% work from home; Mean travel time to work: 28.3 minutes

RICHMOND (town).

Covers a land area of 42.432 square miles and a water area of 1.960 square miles. Located at 42.79° N. Lat; 77.52° W. Long. Elevation is 814 feet.
Population: 3,326; Growth (since 2000): -3.7%; Density: 78.4 persons per square mile; Race: 94.7% White, 0.0% Black/African American, 0.0% Asian, 1.3% American Indian/Alaska Native, 0.0% Native Hawaiian/Other Pacific Islander, 3.5% Two or more races, 5.4% Hispanic of any race; Average household size: 2.36; Median age: 51.0; Age under 18: 11.8%; Age 65 and over: 17.7%; Males per 100 females: 105.1; Marriage status: 17.8% never married, 64.4% now married, 0.9% separated, 7.3% widowed, 10.5% divorced; Foreign born: 4.4%; Speak English only: 90.5%; With disability: 9.5%; Veterans: 7.0%; Ancestry: 26.0% German, 20.4% Italian, 14.6% English, 13.0% Irish, 11.5% American
Employment: 14.5% management, business, and financial, 2.7% computer, engineering, and science, 11.8% education, legal, community service, arts, and media, 0.9% healthcare practitioners, 17.3% service, 31.7% sales and office, 12.8% natural resources, construction, and maintenance, 8.2% production, transportation, and material moving
Income: Per capita: $29,819; Median household: $62,586; Average household: $69,629; Households with income of $100,000 or more: 23.1%; Poverty rate: 2.3%
Educational Attainment: High school diploma or higher: 94.3%; Bachelor's degree or higher: 25.5%; Graduate/professional degree or higher: 14.0%
Housing: Homeownership rate: 93.8%; Median home value: $138,600; Median year structure built: 1966; Homeowner vacancy rate: 6.2%; Median selected monthly owner costs: $1,151 with a mortgage, $734 without a mortgage; Median gross rent: $904 per month; Rental vacancy rate: 0.0%
Health Insurance: 97.3% have insurance; 80.5% have private insurance; 33.0% have public insurance; 2.7% do not have insurance; 0.0% of children under 18 do not have insurance
Transportation: Commute: 91.7% car, 0.0% public transportation, 6.3% walk, 2.0% work from home; Mean travel time to work: 30.4 minutes

SENECA (town).

Covers a land area of 50.450 square miles and a water area of 0 square miles. Located at 42.83° N. Lat; 77.07° W. Long.
Population: 2,742; Growth (since 2000): 0.4%; Density: 54.4 persons per square mile; Race: 98.5% White, 0.2% Black/African American, 0.3% Asian, 0.0% American Indian/Alaska Native, 0.0% Native Hawaiian/Other Pacific Islander, 1.0% Two or more races, 1.7% Hispanic of any race; Average household size: 2.67; Median age: 45.1; Age under 18: 20.5%; Age 65 and over: 15.2%; Males per 100 females: 110.1; Marriage status: 26.3% never married, 61.7% now married, 0.6% separated, 4.8% widowed, 7.3% divorced; Foreign born: 0.7%; Speak English only: 96.5%; With disability: 11.1%; Veterans: 7.6%; Ancestry: 21.2% Irish, 20.5% German, 18.5% English, 13.7% Italian, 7.9% Dutch
Employment: 18.7% management, business, and financial, 1.8% computer, engineering, and science, 8.5% education, legal, community service, arts, and media, 6.0% healthcare practitioners, 17.0% service, 23.7% sales and office, 14.3% natural resources, construction, and maintenance, 9.9% production, transportation, and material moving
Income: Per capita: $30,233; Median household: $64,461; Average household: $79,558; Households with income of $100,000 or more: 26.2%; Poverty rate: 5.6%
Educational Attainment: High school diploma or higher: 91.7%; Bachelor's degree or higher: 23.9%; Graduate/professional degree or higher: 10.1%
Housing: Homeownership rate: 83.3%; Median home value: $132,100; Median year structure built: 1941; Homeowner vacancy rate: 2.6%; Median selected monthly owner costs: $1,285 with a mortgage, $459 without a mortgage; Median gross rent: $708 per month; Rental vacancy rate: 7.1%
Health Insurance: 90.1% have insurance; 75.7% have private insurance; 30.5% have public insurance; 9.9% do not have insurance; 15.0% of children under 18 do not have insurance

Transportation: Commute: 96.3% car, 0.9% public transportation, 0.3% walk, 2.5% work from home; Mean travel time to work: 22.6 minutes

SHORTSVILLE (village).

Covers a land area of 0.668 square miles and a water area of 0 square miles. Located at 42.96° N. Lat; 77.22° W. Long. Elevation is 620 feet.
Population: 1,385; Growth (since 2000): 4.9%; Density: 2,074.6 persons per square mile; Race: 95.2% White, 0.7% Black/African American, 0.0% Asian, 0.1% American Indian/Alaska Native, 0.0% Native Hawaiian/Other Pacific Islander, 4.0% Two or more races, 1.2% Hispanic of any race; Average household size: 2.24; Median age: 48.0; Age under 18: 17.4%; Age 65 and over: 16.6%; Males per 100 females: 96.3; Marriage status: 29.1% never married, 50.9% now married, 3.9% separated, 6.7% widowed, 13.3% divorced; Foreign born: 0.9%; Speak English only: 96.9%; With disability: 14.7%; Veterans: 13.5%; Ancestry: 23.4% Irish, 20.9% English, 20.0% German, 13.8% Italian, 6.9% Dutch
Employment: 9.4% management, business, and financial, 5.0% computer, engineering, and science, 12.8% education, legal, community service, arts, and media, 7.7% healthcare practitioners, 21.4% service, 22.1% sales and office, 5.8% natural resources, construction, and maintenance, 15.7% production, transportation, and material moving
Income: Per capita: $29,017; Median household: $50,329; Average household: $65,122; Households with income of $100,000 or more: 18.9%; Poverty rate: 13.1%
Educational Attainment: High school diploma or higher: 89.4%; Bachelor's degree or higher: 13.3%; Graduate/professional degree or higher: 3.8%

School District(s)

Manchester-Shortsville Central SD (Red Jacket) (PK-12)
   2014-15 Enrollment: 850. . . . . (585) 289-3964
Housing: Homeownership rate: 76.5%; Median home value: $102,000; Median year structure built: Before 1940; Homeowner vacancy rate: 0.0%; Median selected monthly owner costs: $1,169 with a mortgage, $557 without a mortgage; Median gross rent: $558 per month; Rental vacancy rate: 19.9%
Health Insurance: 93.8% have insurance; 73.5% have private insurance; 36.8% have public insurance; 6.2% do not have insurance; 3.3% of children under 18 do not have insurance
Safety: Violent crime rate: 0.0 per 10,000 population; Property crime rate: 0.0 per 10,000 population
Transportation: Commute: 95.5% car, 0.0% public transportation, 0.4% walk, 3.4% work from home; Mean travel time to work: 22.7 minutes

SOUTH BRISTOL (town).

Covers a land area of 38.973 square miles and a water area of 3.051 square miles. Located at 42.70° N. Lat; 77.41° W. Long. Elevation is 1,086 feet.
Population: 1,725; Growth (since 2000): 4.9%; Density: 44.3 persons per square mile; Race: 97.3% White, 0.0% Black/African American, 0.2% Asian, 0.1% American Indian/Alaska Native, 0.0% Native Hawaiian/Other Pacific Islander, 2.3% Two or more races, 0.9% Hispanic of any race; Average household size: 2.20; Median age: 52.5; Age under 18: 17.6%; Age 65 and over: 24.3%; Males per 100 females: 100.3; Marriage status: 20.8% never married, 63.2% now married, 0.6% separated, 7.4% widowed, 8.6% divorced; Foreign born: 3.7%; Speak English only: 98.9%; With disability: 9.2%; Veterans: 8.7%; Ancestry: 29.0% German, 20.9% English, 17.9% Irish, 12.3% Italian, 9.0% Dutch
Employment: 20.2% management, business, and financial, 3.2% computer, engineering, and science, 13.0% education, legal, community service, arts, and media, 9.7% healthcare practitioners, 18.1% service, 18.1% sales and office, 7.6% natural resources, construction, and maintenance, 10.1% production, transportation, and material moving
Income: Per capita: $41,658; Median household: $74,231; Average household: $91,837; Households with income of $100,000 or more: 31.9%; Poverty rate: 10.0%
Educational Attainment: High school diploma or higher: 95.9%; Bachelor's degree or higher: 45.9%; Graduate/professional degree or higher: 22.5%
Housing: Homeownership rate: 89.4%; Median home value: $218,100; Median year structure built: 1979; Homeowner vacancy rate: 0.6%; Median selected monthly owner costs: $1,523 with a mortgage, $822 without a mortgage; Median gross rent: $781 per month; Rental vacancy rate: 9.8%
Health Insurance: 98.5% have insurance; 83.7% have private insurance; 33.5% have public insurance; 1.5% do not have insurance; 0.0% of children under 18 do not have insurance

Transportation: Commute: 89.6% car, 0.0% public transportation, 0.7% walk, 8.8% work from home; Mean travel time to work: 29.8 minutes

STANLEY (unincorporated postal area)
ZCTA: 14561

Covers a land area of 51.876 square miles and a water area of 0 square miles. Located at 42.82° N. Lat; 77.13° W. Long. Elevation is 889 feet.
Population: 3,057; Growth (since 2000): 6.3%; Density: 58.9 persons per square mile; Race: 98.6% White, 0.2% Black/African American, 0.2% Asian, 0.0% American Indian/Alaska Native, 0.0% Native Hawaiian/Other Pacific Islander, 1.0% Two or more races, 1.1% Hispanic of any race; Average household size: 2.79; Median age: 41.3; Age under 18: 24.4%; Age 65 and over: 9.9%; Males per 100 females: 104.6; Marriage status: 29.8% never married, 53.9% now married, 1.3% separated, 4.7% widowed, 11.5% divorced; Foreign born: 0.2%; Speak English only: 90.6%; With disability: 9.2%; Veterans: 9.4%; Ancestry: 27.0% German, 21.3% Irish, 19.5% English, 9.2% Italian, 6.7% Dutch
Employment: 15.8% management, business, and financial, 3.9% computer, engineering, and science, 11.3% education, legal, community service, arts, and media, 5.1% healthcare practitioners, 18.6% service, 19.4% sales and office, 13.4% natural resources, construction, and maintenance, 12.5% production, transportation, and material moving
Income: Per capita: $29,482; Median household: $64,535; Average household: $81,197; Households with income of $100,000 or more: 24.7%; Poverty rate: 4.9%
Educational Attainment: High school diploma or higher: 92.5%; Bachelor's degree or higher: 22.9%; Graduate/professional degree or higher: 6.9%
Housing: Homeownership rate: 87.1%; Median home value: $127,900; Median year structure built: Before 1940; Homeowner vacancy rate: 2.4%; Median selected monthly owner costs: $1,313 with a mortgage, $435 without a mortgage; Median gross rent: $710 per month; Rental vacancy rate: 0.0%
Health Insurance: 85.1% have insurance; 72.6% have private insurance; 25.8% have public insurance; 14.9% do not have insurance; 26.8% of children under 18 do not have insurance
Transportation: Commute: 91.5% car, 0.1% public transportation, 3.9% walk, 4.3% work from home; Mean travel time to work: 21.7 minutes

VICTOR (town). Covers a land area of 35.918 square miles and a water area of 0.013 square miles. Located at 42.99° N. Lat; 77.43° W. Long. Elevation is 577 feet.
History: Incorporated 1879.
Population: 14,496; Growth (since 2000): 45.3%; Density: 403.6 persons per square mile; Race: 95.8% White, 0.7% Black/African American, 2.7% Asian, 0.1% American Indian/Alaska Native, 0.0% Native Hawaiian/Other Pacific Islander, 0.5% Two or more races, 2.0% Hispanic of any race; Average household size: 2.52; Median age: 43.1; Age under 18: 26.0%; Age 65 and over: 16.3%; Males per 100 females: 95.5; Marriage status: 23.2% never married, 64.3% now married, 1.7% separated, 6.8% widowed, 5.7% divorced; Foreign born: 5.5%; Speak English only: 91.0%; With disability: 8.2%; Veterans: 6.8%; Ancestry: 21.4% German, 20.0% Italian, 17.7% Irish, 15.9% English, 5.7% American
Employment: 22.4% management, business, and financial, 5.9% computer, engineering, and science, 13.6% education, legal, community service, arts, and media, 9.5% healthcare practitioners, 11.2% service, 28.0% sales and office, 4.1% natural resources, construction, and maintenance, 5.3% production, transportation, and material moving
Income: Per capita: $48,259; Median household: $86,589; Average household: $121,398; Households with income of $100,000 or more: 43.2%; Poverty rate: 2.3%
Educational Attainment: High school diploma or higher: 96.9%; Bachelor's degree or higher: 52.6%; Graduate/professional degree or higher: 24.7%

School District(s)
Victor Central SD (PK-12)
    2014-15 Enrollment: 4,459 . . . . (585) 924-3252
Housing: Homeownership rate: 78.3%; Median home value: $241,800; Median year structure built: 1992; Homeowner vacancy rate: 0.2%; Median selected monthly owner costs: $1,984 with a mortgage, $740 without a mortgage; Median gross rent: $1,322 per month; Rental vacancy rate: 0.4%
Health Insurance: 96.2% have insurance; 88.2% have private insurance; 22.4% have public insurance; 3.8% do not have insurance; 2.3% of children under 18 do not have insurance

Transportation: Commute: 93.2% car, 0.5% public transportation, 0.4% walk, 5.2% work from home; Mean travel time to work: 22.5 minutes
Additional Information Contacts
Town of Victor . . . . (585) 742-5080
  http://www.victorny.org

VICTOR (village). Covers a land area of 1.373 square miles and a water area of 0 square miles. Located at 42.98° N. Lat; 77.41° W. Long. Elevation is 577 feet.
Population: 2,768; Growth (since 2000): 13.8%; Density: 2,016.4 persons per square mile; Race: 97.1% White, 0.0% Black/African American, 1.2% Asian, 0.0% American Indian/Alaska Native, 0.0% Native Hawaiian/Other Pacific Islander, 0.7% Two or more races, 2.2% Hispanic of any race; Average household size: 2.86; Median age: 35.6; Age under 18: 31.0%; Age 65 and over: 12.5%; Males per 100 females: 96.4; Marriage status: 29.9% never married, 57.1% now married, 2.4% separated, 6.5% widowed, 6.5% divorced; Foreign born: 2.1%; Speak English only: 97.0%; With disability: 7.5%; Veterans: 7.5%; Ancestry: 25.8% German, 23.2% Irish, 22.2% Italian, 14.4% English, 7.4% Polish
Employment: 16.7% management, business, and financial, 6.8% computer, engineering, and science, 19.2% education, legal, community service, arts, and media, 9.4% healthcare practitioners, 14.7% service, 24.4% sales and office, 2.2% natural resources, construction, and maintenance, 6.5% production, transportation, and material moving
Income: Per capita: $30,854; Median household: $72,900; Average household: $87,788; Households with income of $100,000 or more: 29.6%; Poverty rate: 5.1%
Educational Attainment: High school diploma or higher: 95.9%; Bachelor's degree or higher: 47.5%; Graduate/professional degree or higher: 21.5%

School District(s)
Victor Central SD (PK-12)
    2014-15 Enrollment: 4,459 . . . . (585) 924-3252
Housing: Homeownership rate: 75.7%; Median home value: $184,200; Median year structure built: 1971; Homeowner vacancy rate: 1.5%; Median selected monthly owner costs: $1,381 with a mortgage, $671 without a mortgage; Median gross rent: $791 per month; Rental vacancy rate: 2.1%
Health Insurance: 94.9% have insurance; 83.3% have private insurance; 24.6% have public insurance; 5.1% do not have insurance; 0.0% of children under 18 do not have insurance
Transportation: Commute: 94.9% car, 0.6% public transportation, 1.1% walk, 3.1% work from home; Mean travel time to work: 20.5 minutes

WEST BLOOMFIELD (town). Covers a land area of 25.461 square miles and a water area of 0.039 square miles. Located at 42.89° N. Lat; 77.50° W. Long. Elevation is 948 feet.
Population: 2,531; Growth (since 2000): -0.7%; Density: 99.4 persons per square mile; Race: 98.3% White, 0.0% Black/African American, 0.8% Asian, 0.1% American Indian/Alaska Native, 0.0% Native Hawaiian/Other Pacific Islander, 0.5% Two or more races, 0.7% Hispanic of any race; Average household size: 2.37; Median age: 46.1; Age under 18: 19.9%; Age 65 and over: 18.8%; Males per 100 females: 100.8; Marriage status: 26.9% never married, 55.7% now married, 1.8% separated, 5.0% widowed, 12.4% divorced; Foreign born: 4.3%; Speak English only: 95.7%; With disability: 12.2%; Veterans: 14.2%; Ancestry: 26.1% German, 23.7% English, 21.0% Irish, 10.2% Italian, 6.8% French
Employment: 16.1% management, business, and financial, 3.9% computer, engineering, and science, 6.0% education, legal, community service, arts, and media, 3.9% healthcare practitioners, 15.1% service, 19.7% sales and office, 18.1% natural resources, construction, and maintenance, 17.1% production, transportation, and material moving
Income: Per capita: $26,725; Median household: $51,705; Average household: $62,952; Households with income of $100,000 or more: 18.6%; Poverty rate: 11.1%
Educational Attainment: High school diploma or higher: 93.7%; Bachelor's degree or higher: 22.8%; Graduate/professional degree or higher: 6.5%
Housing: Homeownership rate: 86.2%; Median home value: $105,100; Median year structure built: 1974; Homeowner vacancy rate: 1.3%; Median selected monthly owner costs: $1,186 with a mortgage, $568 without a mortgage; Median gross rent: $704 per month; Rental vacancy rate: 0.0%
Health Insurance: 87.7% have insurance; 70.3% have private insurance; 36.0% have public insurance; 12.3% do not have insurance; 4.0% of children under 18 do not have insurance

Transportation: Commute: 94.6% car, 0.5% public transportation, 0.7% walk, 4.2% work from home; Mean travel time to work: 22.7 minutes

Orange County

Located in southeastern New York; bounded on the east by the Hudson River, and on the southwest by the Delaware River and the New Jersey and Pennsylvania borders; includes parts of the Hudson highlands, the Ramapos, and the Shawangunk Range. Covers a land area of 811.686 square miles, a water area of 26.959 square miles, and is located in the Eastern Time Zone at 41.40° N. Lat., 74.31° W. Long. The county was founded in 1683. County seat is Goshen.

Orange County is part of the New York-Newark-Jersey City, NY-NJ-PA Metropolitan Statistical Area. The entire metro area includes: Dutchess County-Putnam County, NY Metropolitan Division (Dutchess County, NY; Putnam County, NY); Nassau County-Suffolk County, NY Metropolitan Division (Nassau County, NY; Suffolk County, NY); Newark, NJ-PA Metropolitan Division (Essex County, NJ; Hunterdon County, NJ; Morris County, NJ; Somerset County, NJ; Sussex County, NJ; Union County, NJ; Pike County, PA); New York-Jersey City-White Plains, NY-NJ Metropolitan Division (Bergen County, NJ; Hudson County, NJ; Middlesex County, NJ; Monmouth County, NJ; Ocean County, NJ; Passaic County, NJ; Bronx County, NY; Kings County, NY; New York County, NY; Orange County, NY; Queens County, NY; Richmond County, NY; Rockland County, NY; Westchester County, NY)

Weather Station: Middletown 2 NW — Elevation: 700 feet

	Jan	Feb	Mar	Apr	May	Jun	Jul	Aug	Sep	Oct	Nov	Dec
High	35	39	48	61	72	79	83	82	75	63	51	40
Low	19	20	28	39	49	58	63	62	54	43	34	25
Precip	2.7	2.3	3.1	4.0	4.1	4.5	4.0	4.0	4.2	3.8	3.6	3.1
Snow	na	na	na	tr	0.0	0.0	0.0	0.0	0.0	0.0	0.2	na

High and Low temperatures in degrees Fahrenheit; Precipitation and Snow in inches

Weather Station: Port Jervis — Elevation: 470 feet

	Jan	Feb	Mar	Apr	May	Jun	Jul	Aug	Sep	Oct	Nov	Dec
High	35	39	48	62	73	80	84	82	74	62	51	39
Low	17	19	26	37	47	56	61	60	52	40	32	22
Precip	3.0	2.7	3.7	4.0	4.0	4.3	4.0	3.8	4.5	4.2	3.6	3.6
Snow	12.2	9.4	7.1	1.7	0.0	0.0	0.0	0.0	0.0	tr	2.0	9.3

High and Low temperatures in degrees Fahrenheit; Precipitation and Snow in inches

Weather Station: Walden 1 ESE — Elevation: 379 feet

	Jan	Feb	Mar	Apr	May	Jun	Jul	Aug	Sep	Oct	Nov	Dec
High	34	38	46	59	70	78	83	81	74	62	51	39
Low	14	17	25	36	46	55	60	58	50	38	30	21
Precip	2.9	2.5	3.6	3.9	4.1	4.5	4.0	3.8	4.1	4.0	3.6	3.4
Snow	12.6	9.0	8.2	1.3	0.0	0.0	0.0	0.0	0.0	tr	1.5	8.6

High and Low temperatures in degrees Fahrenheit; Precipitation and Snow in inches

Weather Station: West Point — Elevation: 319 feet

	Jan	Feb	Mar	Apr	May	Jun	Jul	Aug	Sep	Oct	Nov	Dec
High	36	39	48	61	72	80	85	83	75	63	52	40
Low	21	23	30	40	50	59	64	63	55	45	36	26
Precip	3.6	2.8	3.9	4.2	4.1	4.6	4.5	4.4	4.5	4.8	4.4	4.1
Snow	11.5	9.4	5.8	0.2	0.0	0.0	0.0	0.0	0.0	tr	0.8	5.7

High and Low temperatures in degrees Fahrenheit; Precipitation and Snow in inches

Population: 375,384; Growth (since 2000): 10.0%; Density: 462.5 persons per square mile; Race: 75.1% White, 10.1% Black/African American, 2.6% Asian, 0.3% American Indian/Alaska Native, 0.0% Native Hawaiian/Other Pacific Islander, 3.4% two or more races, 19.1% Hispanic of any race; Average household size: 2.90; Median age: 36.8; Age under 18: 26.3%; Age 65 and over: 12.1%; Males per 100 females: 99.9; Marriage status: 34.0% never married, 52.1% now married, 2.2% separated, 5.3% widowed, 8.6% divorced; Foreign born: 11.0%; Speak English only: 75.7%; With disability: 11.9%; Veterans: 7.9%; Ancestry: 18.2% Irish, 16.4% Italian, 13.6% American, 11.1% German, 5.2% English

Religion: Six largest groups: 35.2% Catholicism, 6.5% Judaism, 2.1% Methodist/Pietist, 1.9% Presbyterian-Reformed, 1.2% Lutheran, 1.1% Pentecostal

Economy: Unemployment rate: 4.3%; Leading industries: 16.8 % retail trade; 11.0 % construction; 10.7 % other services (except public administration); Farms: 658 totaling 88,030 acres; Company size: 3 employ 1,000 or more persons, 9 employ 500 to 999 persons, 168 employ 100 to 499 persons, 9,009 employ less than 100 persons; Business

ownership: 9,576 women-owned, 1,742 Black-owned, 2,678 Hispanic-owned, 1,630 Asian-owned, 130 American Indian/Alaska Native-owned

Employment: 13.1% management, business, and financial, 4.0% computer, engineering, and science, 12.3% education, legal, community service, arts, and media, 5.8% healthcare practitioners, 19.0% service, 26.2% sales and office, 8.4% natural resources, construction, and maintenance, 11.3% production, transportation, and material moving

Income: Per capita: $31,023; Median household: $70,848; Average household: $89,479; Households with income of $100,000 or more: 34.5%; Poverty rate: 12.8%

Educational Attainment: High school diploma or higher: 89.1%; Bachelor's degree or higher: 29.2%; Graduate/professional degree or higher: 11.9%

Housing: Homeownership rate: 68.8%; Median home value: $262,500; Median year structure built: 1970; Homeowner vacancy rate: 2.4%; Median selected monthly owner costs: $2,274 with a mortgage, $856 without a mortgage; Median gross rent: $1,155 per month; Rental vacancy rate: 5.0%

Vital Statistics: Birth rate: 132.0 per 10,000 population; Death rate: 70.2 per 10,000 population; Age-adjusted cancer mortality rate: 160.7 deaths per 100,000 population

Health Insurance: 92.1% have insurance; 71.9% have private insurance; 31.1% have public insurance; 7.9% do not have insurance; 2.8% of children under 18 do not have insurance

Health Care: Physicians: 23.3 per 10,000 population; Dentists: 6.7 per 10,000 population; Hospital beds: 26.0 per 10,000 population; Hospital admissions: 1,008.9 per 10,000 population

Air Quality Index (AQI): Percent of Days: 85.5% good, 14.2% moderate, 0.3% unhealthy for sensitive individuals, 0.0% unhealthy, 0.0% very unhealthy; Annual median: 34; Annual maximum: 122

Transportation: Commute: 84.2% car, 5.1% public transportation, 3.9% walk, 4.9% work from home; Mean travel time to work: 33.2 minutes

2016 Presidential Election: 50.8% Trump, 45.2% Clinton, 2.6% Johnson, 1.4% Stein

National and State Parks: Cherry Island State Wildlife Management Area; Hudson Highlands State Park; Sloop Hill State Unique Area; Storm King State Park

Additional Information Contacts

Orange Government . . . . (845) 291-2690
http://www.co.orange.ny.us

Orange County Communities

ARDEN (unincorporated postal area)
ZCTA: 10910

Covers a land area of 2.080 square miles and a water area of 0.042 square miles. Located at 41.28° N. Lat; 74.14° W. Long. Elevation is 512 feet.

Population: 23; Growth (since 2000): n/a; Density: 11.1 persons per square mile; Race: 100.0% White, 0.0% Black/African American, 0.0% Asian, 0.0% American Indian/Alaska Native, 0.0% Native Hawaiian/Other Pacific Islander, 0.0% Two or more races, 0.0% Hispanic of any race; Average household size: 0.00; Median age: n/a; Age under 18: 0.0%; Age 65 and over: 0.0%; Males per 100 females: 133.3; Marriage status: 0.0% never married, 0.0% now married, 0.0% separated, 100.0% widowed, 0.0% divorced; Foreign born: 0.0%; Speak English only: 100.0%; With disability: 0.0%; Veterans: 0.0%; Ancestry: 100.0% English, 100.0% Italian

Employment: 0.0% management, business, and financial, 100.0% computer, engineering, and science, 0.0% education, legal, community service, arts, and media, 0.0% healthcare practitioners, 0.0% service, 0.0% sales and office, 0.0% natural resources, construction, and maintenance, 0.0% production, transportation, and material moving

Income: Per capita: n/a; Median household: n/a; Average household: n/a; Households with income of $100,000 or more: 100.0%; Poverty rate: n/a

Educational Attainment: High school diploma or higher: 100.0%; Bachelor's degree or higher: 100.0%; Graduate/professional degree or higher: n/a

Housing: Homeownership rate: n/a; Median home value: n/a; Median year structure built: n/a; Homeowner vacancy rate: 0.0%; Median selected monthly owner costs: $0 with a mortgage, $0 without a mortgage; Median gross rent: n/a per month; Rental vacancy rate: 0.0%

Health Insurance: 100.0% have insurance; 100.0% have private insurance; 0.0% have public insurance; 0.0% do not have insurance; 0.0% of children under 18 do not have insurance
Transportation: Commute: 100.0% car, 0.0% public transportation, 0.0% walk, 0.0% work from home; Mean travel time to work: 0.0 minutes

BALMVILLE (CDP).
Covers a land area of 2.117 square miles and a water area of 0.004 square miles. Located at 41.53° N. Lat; 74.02° W. Long. Elevation is 217 feet.
Population: 2,741; Growth (since 2000): -17.9%; Density: 1,294.5 persons per square mile; Race: 67.9% White, 10.7% Black/African American, 2.4% Asian, 0.0% American Indian/Alaska Native, 0.0% Native Hawaiian/Other Pacific Islander, 8.4% Two or more races, 28.2% Hispanic of any race; Average household size: 2.62; Median age: 43.4; Age under 18: 20.8%; Age 65 and over: 17.8%; Males per 100 females: 96.5; Marriage status: 26.2% never married, 53.7% now married, 2.3% separated, 9.0% widowed, 11.2% divorced; Foreign born: 13.1%; Speak English only: 70.1%; With disability: 16.2%; Veterans: 7.0%; Ancestry: 16.3% American, 14.2% Irish, 13.5% German, 12.2% Italian, 5.1% English
Employment: 20.4% management, business, and financial, 4.3% computer, engineering, and science, 13.8% education, legal, community service, arts, and media, 6.9% healthcare practitioners, 12.4% service, 30.3% sales and office, 5.6% natural resources, construction, and maintenance, 6.4% production, transportation, and material moving
Income: Per capita: $35,288; Median household: $63,750; Average household: $89,482; Households with income of $100,000 or more: 29.3%; Poverty rate: 7.5%
Educational Attainment: High school diploma or higher: 95.2%; Bachelor's degree or higher: 33.7%; Graduate/professional degree or higher: 16.1%
Housing: Homeownership rate: 73.0%; Median home value: $265,000; Median year structure built: 1961; Homeowner vacancy rate: 0.0%; Median selected monthly owner costs: $2,360 with a mortgage, $739 without a mortgage; Median gross rent: $1,206 per month; Rental vacancy rate: 0.0%
Health Insurance: 92.6% have insurance; 74.7% have private insurance; 34.2% have public insurance; 7.4% do not have insurance; 3.0% of children under 18 do not have insurance
Transportation: Commute: 88.1% car, 3.7% public transportation, 1.8% walk, 6.3% work from home; Mean travel time to work: 36.7 minutes

BEAVER DAM LAKE (CDP).
Note: Statistics that would complete this profile are not available because the CDP was created after the 2010 Census was released.

BLOOMING GROVE (town).
Covers a land area of 34.736 square miles and a water area of 0.616 square miles. Located at 41.40° N. Lat; 74.18° W. Long. Elevation is 358 feet.
Population: 17,826; Growth (since 2000): 2.7%; Density: 513.2 persons per square mile; Race: 84.1% White, 3.8% Black/African American, 1.3% Asian, 0.0% American Indian/Alaska Native, 0.0% Native Hawaiian/Other Pacific Islander, 2.0% Two or more races, 17.6% Hispanic of any race; Average household size: 2.93; Median age: 42.3; Age under 18: 22.9%; Age 65 and over: 13.3%; Males per 100 females: 97.1; Marriage status: 30.8% never married, 56.5% now married, 2.2% separated, 5.0% widowed, 7.7% divorced; Foreign born: 8.3%; Speak English only: 84.8%; With disability: 10.7%; Veterans: 7.3%; Ancestry: 29.6% Irish, 22.1% Italian, 14.9% German, 12.8% American, 4.6% English
Employment: 12.8% management, business, and financial, 6.2% computer, engineering, and science, 9.6% education, legal, community service, arts, and media, 5.5% healthcare practitioners, 21.6% service, 26.0% sales and office, 8.1% natural resources, construction, and maintenance, 10.2% production, transportation, and material moving
Income: Per capita: $35,693; Median household: $89,221; Average household: $102,323; Households with income of $100,000 or more: 44.2%; Poverty rate: 6.6%
Educational Attainment: High school diploma or higher: 93.5%; Bachelor's degree or higher: 29.1%; Graduate/professional degree or higher: 11.7%
Housing: Homeownership rate: 83.2%; Median home value: $272,600; Median year structure built: 1969; Homeowner vacancy rate: 2.0%; Median selected monthly owner costs: $2,419 with a mortgage, $1,028 without a mortgage; Median gross rent: $1,013 per month; Rental vacancy rate: 9.8%

Health Insurance: 94.7% have insurance; 82.3% have private insurance; 24.0% have public insurance; 5.3% do not have insurance; 2.2% of children under 18 do not have insurance
Safety: Violent crime rate: 3.4 per 10,000 population; Property crime rate: 61.3 per 10,000 population
Transportation: Commute: 90.4% car, 6.0% public transportation, 0.4% walk, 2.5% work from home; Mean travel time to work: 39.3 minutes
Additional Information Contacts
Town of Blooming Grove. . . . . (845) 496-3895
  http://www.townofbloominggroveny.com

BULLVILLE (unincorporated postal area)
ZCTA: 10915
Covers a land area of 0.144 square miles and a water area of 0 square miles. Located at 41.55° N. Lat; 74.36° W. Long. Elevation is 515 feet.
Population: 104; Growth (since 2000): n/a; Density: 720.4 persons per square mile; Race: 100.0% White, 0.0% Black/African American, 0.0% Asian, 0.0% American Indian/Alaska Native, 0.0% Native Hawaiian/Other Pacific Islander, 0.0% Two or more races, 0.0% Hispanic of any race; Average household size: 2.05; Median age: 43.7; Age under 18: 0.0%; Age 65 and over: 0.0%; Males per 100 females: 124.5; Marriage status: 100.0% never married, 0.0% now married, 0.0% separated, 0.0% widowed, 0.0% divorced; Foreign born: 0.0%; Speak English only: 100.0%; With disability: 39.4%; Veterans: 0.0%; Ancestry: 100.0% American
Employment: 0.0% management, business, and financial, 0.0% computer, engineering, and science, 0.0% education, legal, community service, arts, and media, 0.0% healthcare practitioners, 0.0% service, 19.0% sales and office, 81.0% natural resources, construction, and maintenance, 0.0% production, transportation, and material moving
Income: Per capita: $24,250; Median household: n/a; Average household: n/a; Households with income of $100,000 or more: n/a; Poverty rate: 39.4%
Educational Attainment: High school diploma or higher: 57.6%; Bachelor's degree or higher: n/a; Graduate/professional degree or higher: n/a
Housing: Homeownership rate: 100.0%; Median home value: n/a; Median year structure built: n/a; Homeowner vacancy rate: 0.0%; Median selected monthly owner costs: $0 with a mortgage, $0 without a mortgage; Median gross rent: n/a per month; Rental vacancy rate: 0.0%
Health Insurance: 39.4% have insurance; 0.0% have private insurance; 39.4% have public insurance; 60.6% do not have insurance; 0.0% of children under 18 do not have insurance
Transportation: Commute: 61.9% car, 0.0% public transportation, 38.1% walk, 0.0% work from home; Mean travel time to work: 0.0 minutes

CAMPBELL HALL (unincorporated postal area)
ZCTA: 10916
Covers a land area of 20.201 square miles and a water area of 0.091 square miles. Located at 41.44° N. Lat; 74.25° W. Long. Elevation is 400 feet.
Population: 4,238; Growth (since 2000): 4.1%; Density: 209.8 persons per square mile; Race: 90.7% White, 2.4% Black/African American, 4.6% Asian, 0.0% American Indian/Alaska Native, 0.0% Native Hawaiian/Other Pacific Islander, 1.7% Two or more races, 6.2% Hispanic of any race; Average household size: 3.23; Median age: 41.7; Age under 18: 25.7%; Age 65 and over: 13.5%; Males per 100 females: 97.8; Marriage status: 30.0% never married, 60.5% now married, 0.7% separated, 5.7% widowed, 3.8% divorced; Foreign born: 8.9%; Speak English only: 87.4%; With disability: 11.0%; Veterans: 9.7%; Ancestry: 26.6% Italian, 25.3% Irish, 12.2% German, 7.1% Polish, 6.4% American
Employment: 15.7% management, business, and financial, 2.8% computer, engineering, and science, 13.5% education, legal, community service, arts, and media, 9.0% healthcare practitioners, 14.2% service, 25.2% sales and office, 9.4% natural resources, construction, and maintenance, 10.2% production, transportation, and material moving
Income: Per capita: $37,572; Median household: $105,104; Average household: $119,872; Households with income of $100,000 or more: 54.9%; Poverty rate: 4.7%
Educational Attainment: High school diploma or higher: 94.3%; Bachelor's degree or higher: 33.4%; Graduate/professional degree or higher: 12.0%
Housing: Homeownership rate: 91.0%; Median home value: $346,200; Median year structure built: 1983; Homeowner vacancy rate: 0.0%;

Median selected monthly owner costs: $2,704 with a mortgage, $1,123 without a mortgage; Median gross rent: $2,047 per month; Rental vacancy rate: 0.0%

Health Insurance: 96.4% have insurance; 81.3% have private insurance; 24.9% have public insurance; 3.6% do not have insurance; 0.0% of children under 18 do not have insurance

Transportation: Commute: 93.6% car, 3.5% public transportation, 0.0% walk, 2.8% work from home; Mean travel time to work: 33.7 minutes

CENTRAL VALLEY (unincorporated postal area)
ZCTA: 10917

Covers a land area of 3.716 square miles and a water area of 0.031 square miles. Located at 41.32° N. Lat; 74.12° W. Long. Elevation is 522 feet.

Population: 2,030; Growth (since 2000): 23.0%; Density: 546.3 persons per square mile; Race: 85.2% White, 0.0% Black/African American, 3.9% Asian, 0.0% American Indian/Alaska Native, 0.0% Native Hawaiian/Other Pacific Islander, 4.4% Two or more races, 28.7% Hispanic of any race; Average household size: 3.25; Median age: 41.8; Age under 18: 23.1%; Age 65 and over: 13.7%; Males per 100 females: 102.5; Marriage status: 29.3% never married, 54.7% now married, 0.0% separated, 6.7% widowed, 9.2% divorced; Foreign born: 21.7%; Speak English only: 72.7%; With disability: 8.4%; Veterans: 5.8%; Ancestry: 21.1% Irish, 17.0% American, 12.0% German, 10.2% Italian, 7.6% English

Employment: 20.5% management, business, and financial, 0.0% computer, engineering, and science, 10.3% education, legal, community service, arts, and media, 15.8% healthcare practitioners, 13.8% service, 20.5% sales and office, 10.0% natural resources, construction, and maintenance, 9.0% production, transportation, and material moving

Income: Per capita: $40,658; Median household: $96,077; Average household: $129,050; Households with income of $100,000 or more: 44.1%; Poverty rate: 7.3%

Educational Attainment: High school diploma or higher: 96.3%; Bachelor's degree or higher: 33.6%; Graduate/professional degree or higher: 21.9%

School District(s)
Monroe-Woodbury Central SD (KG-12)

2014-15 Enrollment: 6,986 . . . . (845) 460-6200

Housing: Homeownership rate: 75.6%; Median home value: $333,300; Median year structure built: 1964; Homeowner vacancy rate: 0.0%; Median selected monthly owner costs: $2,840 with a mortgage, $1,000 without a mortgage; Median gross rent: $1,454 per month; Rental vacancy rate: 0.0%

Health Insurance: 94.3% have insurance; 81.2% have private insurance; 25.9% have public insurance; 5.7% do not have insurance; 3.6% of children under 18 do not have insurance

Transportation: Commute: 93.0% car, 3.9% public transportation, 0.0% walk, 0.7% work from home; Mean travel time to work: 33.4 minutes

CHESTER (town). Covers a land area of 25.049 square miles and a water area of 0.151 square miles. Located at 41.33° N. Lat; 74.28° W. Long. Elevation is 479 feet.

History: Hambletonian, famous trotter, foaled and buried here. Incorporated 1892.

Population: 11,902; Growth (since 2000): -2.0%; Density: 475.1 persons per square mile; Race: 76.3% White, 9.8% Black/African American, 4.7% Asian, 0.0% American Indian/Alaska Native, 0.0% Native Hawaiian/Other Pacific Islander, 2.7% Two or more races, 18.0% Hispanic of any race; Average household size: 2.86; Median age: 41.6; Age under 18: 20.4%; Age 65 and over: 14.5%; Males per 100 females: 94.7; Marriage status: 31.8% never married, 53.3% now married, 2.6% separated, 3.8% widowed, 11.1% divorced; Foreign born: 14.5%; Speak English only: 80.7%; With disability: 14.0%; Veterans: 6.4%; Ancestry: 24.0% Italian, 19.3% Irish, 11.4% American, 9.1% German, 4.7% Polish

Employment: 14.3% management, business, and financial, 5.4% computer, engineering, and science, 16.5% education, legal, community service, arts, and media, 7.2% healthcare practitioners, 15.9% service, 26.7% sales and office, 6.1% natural resources, construction, and maintenance, 8.0% production, transportation, and material moving

Income: Per capita: $36,864; Median household: $89,089; Average household: $104,484; Households with income of $100,000 or more: 41.9%; Poverty rate: 4.7%

Educational Attainment: High school diploma or higher: 94.6%; Bachelor's degree or higher: 35.6%; Graduate/professional degree or higher: 14.0%

School District(s)
Chester Union Free SD (KG-12)

2014-15 Enrollment: 1,062 . . . . (845) 469-5052

Housing: Homeownership rate: 82.0%; Median home value: $295,400; Median year structure built: 1981; Homeowner vacancy rate: 0.7%; Median selected monthly owner costs: $2,334 with a mortgage, $971 without a mortgage; Median gross rent: $1,377 per month; Rental vacancy rate: 0.0%

Health Insurance: 93.9% have insurance; 82.4% have private insurance; 23.2% have public insurance; 6.1% do not have insurance; 3.6% of children under 18 do not have insurance

Safety: Violent crime rate: 10.1 per 10,000 population; Property crime rate: 20.2 per 10,000 population

Newspapers: Straus Newspapers (weekly circulation 27,000)

Transportation: Commute: 85.4% car, 6.2% public transportation, 1.2% walk, 7.0% work from home; Mean travel time to work: 36.6 minutes

CHESTER (village). Covers a land area of 2.148 square miles and a water area of 0 square miles. Located at 41.36° N. Lat; 74.28° W. Long. Elevation is 479 feet.

Population: 3,928; Growth (since 2000): 14.0%; Density: 1,828.6 persons per square mile; Race: 65.9% White, 18.5% Black/African American, 6.8% Asian, 0.0% American Indian/Alaska Native, 0.0% Native Hawaiian/Other Pacific Islander, 4.4% Two or more races, 22.6% Hispanic of any race; Average household size: 2.52; Median age: 40.4; Age under 18: 18.4%; Age 65 and over: 11.5%; Males per 100 females: 94.6; Marriage status: 37.5% never married, 47.4% now married, 5.8% separated, 3.4% widowed, 11.7% divorced; Foreign born: 19.7%; Speak English only: 78.7%; With disability: 17.9%; Veterans: 7.4%; Ancestry: 22.6% Italian, 17.5% Irish, 12.1% American, 8.4% German, 3.6% Polish

Employment: 11.4% management, business, and financial, 4.6% computer, engineering, and science, 11.0% education, legal, community service, arts, and media, 3.1% healthcare practitioners, 20.6% service, 29.0% sales and office, 5.4% natural resources, construction, and maintenance, 14.9% production, transportation, and material moving

Income: Per capita: $31,135; Median household: $62,929; Average household: $76,066; Households with income of $100,000 or more: 25.8%; Poverty rate: 8.8%

Educational Attainment: High school diploma or higher: 92.1%; Bachelor's degree or higher: 26.6%; Graduate/professional degree or higher: 8.6%

School District(s)
Chester Union Free SD (KG-12)

2014-15 Enrollment: 1,062 . . . . (845) 469-5052

Housing: Homeownership rate: 67.5%; Median home value: $198,200; Median year structure built: 1982; Homeowner vacancy rate: 2.1%; Median selected monthly owner costs: $2,114 with a mortgage, $860 without a mortgage; Median gross rent: $1,282 per month; Rental vacancy rate: 0.0%

Health Insurance: 90.5% have insurance; 72.7% have private insurance; 28.1% have public insurance; 9.5% do not have insurance; 1.4% of children under 18 do not have insurance

Safety: Violent crime rate: 17.9 per 10,000 population; Property crime rate: 189.7 per 10,000 population

Newspapers: Straus Newspapers (weekly circulation 27,000)

Transportation: Commute: 86.8% car, 6.8% public transportation, 1.3% walk, 5.1% work from home; Mean travel time to work: 31.9 minutes

CIRCLEVILLE (unincorporated postal area)
ZCTA: 10919

Covers a land area of 4.116 square miles and a water area of 0.019 square miles. Located at 41.53° N. Lat; 74.39° W. Long. Elevation is 617 feet.

Population: 1,405; Growth (since 2000): 150.0%; Density: 341.3 persons per square mile; Race: 98.1% White, 1.1% Black/African American, 0.8% Asian, 0.0% American Indian/Alaska Native, 0.0% Native Hawaiian/Other Pacific Islander, 0.0% Two or more races, 9.0% Hispanic of any race; Average household size: 2.75; Median age: 47.2; Age under 18: 16.4%; Age 65 and over: 13.5%; Males per 100 females: 103.1; Marriage status: 38.6% never married, 47.6% now married, 0.5% separated, 4.2% widowed, 9.6% divorced; Foreign born: 5.3%; Speak English only: 94.0%; With disability: 9.4%; Veterans: 9.2%; Ancestry:

29.8% American, 24.5% Irish, 20.6% German, 13.8% Italian, 3.6% Polish

Employment: 11.5% management, business, and financial, 1.6% computer, engineering, and science, 5.4% education, legal, community service, arts, and media, 3.4% healthcare practitioners, 12.5% service, 35.7% sales and office, 9.6% natural resources, construction, and maintenance, 20.3% production, transportation, and material moving

Income: Per capita: $36,149; Median household: $97,703; Average household: $98,073; Households with income of $100,000 or more: 43.3%; Poverty rate: 5.6%

Educational Attainment: High school diploma or higher: 82.7%; Bachelor's degree or higher: 22.6%; Graduate/professional degree or higher: 13.5%

School District(s)

Pine Bush Central SD (PK-12)

    2014-15 Enrollment: 5,487 . . . . (845) 744-2031

Housing: Homeownership rate: 88.2%; Median home value: $244,800; Median year structure built: 1964; Homeowner vacancy rate: 0.0%; Median selected monthly owner costs: $2,442 with a mortgage, $736 without a mortgage; Median gross rent: n/a per month; Rental vacancy rate: 0.0%

Health Insurance: 88.2% have insurance; 79.2% have private insurance; 19.8% have public insurance; 11.8% do not have insurance; 0.0% of children under 18 do not have insurance

Transportation: Commute: 91.1% car, 0.7% public transportation, 0.0% walk, 4.7% work from home; Mean travel time to work: 39.4 minutes

CORNWALL (town).

Covers a land area of 26.653 square miles and a water area of 1.479 square miles. Located at 41.41° N. Lat; 74.06° W. Long.

History: Seat of N.Y. Military Academy and private schools. Incorporated 1884.

Population: 12,548; Growth (since 2000): 2.0%; Density: 470.8 persons per square mile; Race: 91.4% White, 0.3% Black/African American, 2.4% Asian, 0.0% American Indian/Alaska Native, 0.0% Native Hawaiian/Other Pacific Islander, 4.1% Two or more races, 11.9% Hispanic of any race; Average household size: 2.67; Median age: 40.8; Age under 18: 26.1%; Age 65 and over: 14.1%; Males per 100 females: 95.2; Marriage status: 27.9% never married, 55.8% now married, 1.0% separated, 4.9% widowed, 11.5% divorced; Foreign born: 5.3%; Speak English only: 90.0%; With disability: 11.9%; Veterans: 11.4%; Ancestry: 27.9% Irish, 20.2% Italian, 17.3% German, 14.4% American, 8.1% English

Employment: 19.1% management, business, and financial, 4.8% computer, engineering, and science, 18.8% education, legal, community service, arts, and media, 6.1% healthcare practitioners, 14.4% service, 24.3% sales and office, 6.0% natural resources, construction, and maintenance, 6.3% production, transportation, and material moving

Income: Per capita: $40,997; Median household: $86,019; Average household: $108,272; Households with income of $100,000 or more: 41.6%; Poverty rate: 5.5%

Educational Attainment: High school diploma or higher: 96.5%; Bachelor's degree or higher: 47.3%; Graduate/professional degree or higher: 24.9%

School District(s)

Cornwall Central SD (KG-12)

    2014-15 Enrollment: 3,259 . . . . (845) 534-8009

Housing: Homeownership rate: 70.5%; Median home value: $324,400; Median year structure built: 1961; Homeowner vacancy rate: 2.5%; Median selected monthly owner costs: $2,600 with a mortgage, $1,056 without a mortgage; Median gross rent: $1,315 per month; Rental vacancy rate: 9.7%

Health Insurance: 95.5% have insurance; 85.8% have private insurance; 21.5% have public insurance; 4.5% do not have insurance; 2.8% of children under 18 do not have insurance

Safety: Violent crime rate: 5.3 per 10,000 population; Property crime rate: 36.8 per 10,000 population

Newspapers: Cornwall Local (weekly circulation 3,300)

Transportation: Commute: 87.2% car, 3.6% public transportation, 2.9% walk, 5.6% work from home; Mean travel time to work: 33.1 minutes

Additional Information Contacts

Town of Cornwall. . . . . (845) 534-9100

    http://www.cornwallny.com

CORNWALL-ON-HUDSON (village).

Covers a land area of 1.987 square miles and a water area of 0.105 square miles. Located at 41.43° N. Lat; 74.02° W. Long. Elevation is 161 feet.

Population: 2,984; Growth (since 2000): -2.4%; Density: 1,501.8 persons per square mile; Race: 93.7% White, 0.2% Black/African American, 1.3% Asian, 0.0% American Indian/Alaska Native, 0.0% Native Hawaiian/Other Pacific Islander, 3.8% Two or more races, 5.8% Hispanic of any race; Average household size: 2.59; Median age: 41.7; Age under 18: 25.1%; Age 65 and over: 15.5%; Males per 100 females: 97.0; Marriage status: 28.3% never married, 57.4% now married, 1.3% separated, 3.6% widowed, 10.7% divorced; Foreign born: 3.5%; Speak English only: 90.7%; With disability: 8.1%; Veterans: 14.0%; Ancestry: 24.1% Irish, 22.4% Italian, 17.1% German, 13.0% American, 9.5% English

Employment: 20.3% management, business, and financial, 3.4% computer, engineering, and science, 21.8% education, legal, community service, arts, and media, 6.0% healthcare practitioners, 12.8% service, 24.1% sales and office, 4.9% natural resources, construction, and maintenance, 6.7% production, transportation, and material moving

Income: Per capita: $45,863; Median household: $93,077; Average household: $118,567; Households with income of $100,000 or more: 45.7%; Poverty rate: 3.5%

Educational Attainment: High school diploma or higher: 94.7%; Bachelor's degree or higher: 51.1%; Graduate/professional degree or higher: 30.5%

School District(s)

Cornwall Central SD (KG-12)

    2014-15 Enrollment: 3,259 . . . . (845) 534-8009

Housing: Homeownership rate: 70.8%; Median home value: $323,500; Median year structure built: 1947; Homeowner vacancy rate: 1.4%; Median selected monthly owner costs: $2,810 with a mortgage, $1,050 without a mortgage; Median gross rent: $1,294 per month; Rental vacancy rate: 3.5%

Health Insurance: 92.4% have insurance; 83.1% have private insurance; 23.8% have public insurance; 7.6% do not have insurance; 10.6% of children under 18 do not have insurance

Safety: Violent crime rate: 3.4 per 10,000 population; Property crime rate: 27.0 per 10,000 population

Transportation: Commute: 83.4% car, 4.1% public transportation, 5.5% walk, 5.6% work from home; Mean travel time to work: 32.6 minutes

CRAWFORD (town).

Covers a land area of 40.031 square miles and a water area of 0.084 square miles. Located at 41.57° N. Lat; 74.32° W. Long.

Population: 9,265; Growth (since 2000): 17.7%; Density: 231.4 persons per square mile; Race: 90.4% White, 3.3% Black/African American, 0.6% Asian, 0.5% American Indian/Alaska Native, 0.0% Native Hawaiian/Other Pacific Islander, 0.8% Two or more races, 10.1% Hispanic of any race; Average household size: 2.85; Median age: 40.2; Age under 18: 24.6%; Age 65 and over: 12.9%; Males per 100 females: 99.3; Marriage status: 33.7% never married, 53.8% now married, 1.2% separated, 3.8% widowed, 8.7% divorced; Foreign born: 3.8%; Speak English only: 89.8%; With disability: 14.3%; Veterans: 8.8%; Ancestry: 21.7% Italian, 21.6% Irish, 16.1% American, 15.8% German, 9.1% English

Employment: 9.2% management, business, and financial, 4.2% computer, engineering, and science, 14.9% education, legal, community service, arts, and media, 4.4% healthcare practitioners, 16.0% service, 25.6% sales and office, 14.3% natural resources, construction, and maintenance, 11.4% production, transportation, and material moving

Income: Per capita: $35,357; Median household: $76,932; Average household: $98,135; Households with income of $100,000 or more: 40.2%; Poverty rate: 8.5%

Educational Attainment: High school diploma or higher: 88.4%; Bachelor's degree or higher: 27.3%; Graduate/professional degree or higher: 10.3%

Housing: Homeownership rate: 80.8%; Median home value: $264,500; Median year structure built: 1979; Homeowner vacancy rate: 2.1%; Median selected monthly owner costs: $2,114 with a mortgage, $897 without a mortgage; Median gross rent: $943 per month; Rental vacancy rate: 3.4%

Health Insurance: 96.0% have insurance; 84.0% have private insurance; 23.3% have public insurance; 4.0% do not have insurance; 2.1% of children under 18 do not have insurance

Safety: Violent crime rate: 7.6 per 10,000 population; Property crime rate: 96.6 per 10,000 population

Transportation: Commute: 93.3% car, 0.9% public transportation, 1.9% walk, 3.0% work from home; Mean travel time to work: 34.4 minutes

Additional Information Contacts
Town of Crawford . . . . (845) 744-2029
http://townofcrawford.org

CUDDEBACKVILLE (unincorporated postal area)

ZCTA: 12729

Covers a land area of 22.195 square miles and a water area of 0.346 square miles. Located at 41.48° N. Lat; 74.62° W. Long. Elevation is 535 feet.

Population: 2,143; Growth (since 2000): 64.6%; Density: 96.6 persons per square mile; Race: 94.4% White, 0.2% Black/African American, 0.0% Asian, 0.0% American Indian/Alaska Native, 0.0% Native Hawaiian/Other Pacific Islander, 4.9% Two or more races, 3.3% Hispanic of any race; Average household size: 2.79; Median age: 45.4; Age under 18: 26.8%; Age 65 and over: 16.0%; Males per 100 females: 108.2; Marriage status: 32.6% never married, 54.5% now married, 5.1% separated, 5.5% widowed, 7.3% divorced; Foreign born: 1.2%; Speak English only: 95.0%; With disability: 21.6%; Veterans: 9.4%; Ancestry: 41.6% American, 18.8% Irish, 15.6% German, 13.4% Italian, 7.7% English

Employment: 7.4% management, business, and financial, 2.6% computer, engineering, and science, 5.4% education, legal, community service, arts, and media, 6.7% healthcare practitioners, 13.5% service, 36.5% sales and office, 16.8% natural resources, construction, and maintenance, 11.1% production, transportation, and material moving

Income: Per capita: $30,494; Median household: $51,542; Average household: $81,062; Households with income of $100,000 or more: 25.8%; Poverty rate: 19.3%

Educational Attainment: High school diploma or higher: 85.6%; Bachelor's degree or higher: 18.9%; Graduate/professional degree or higher: 5.2%

School District(s)

Port Jervis City SD (KG-12)

    2014-15 Enrollment: 2,832 . . . . (845) 858-3100

Housing: Homeownership rate: 62.8%; Median home value: $172,300; Median year structure built: 1967; Homeowner vacancy rate: 4.0%; Median selected monthly owner costs: $1,737 with a mortgage, $728 without a mortgage; Median gross rent: $1,020 per month; Rental vacancy rate: 5.9%

Health Insurance: 93.7% have insurance; 54.9% have private insurance; 50.5% have public insurance; 6.3% do not have insurance; 0.0% of children under 18 do not have insurance

Transportation: Commute: 93.2% car, 0.0% public transportation, 0.0% walk, 1.4% work from home; Mean travel time to work: 27.1 minutes

DEERPARK (town).

Covers a land area of 66.502 square miles and a water area of 1.452 square miles. Located at 41.44° N. Lat; 74.66° W. Long.

History: Deer Park, a hamlet and census-designated place (CDP), is a residential hamlet located in the pine barrens in the northeast corner of the town of Babylon. It grew out of Jacob Conklin's 1610 settlement of the Half Way Hollow Hills, later Wheatley Heights. Charles Wilson started what is now Deer Park in 1853 about eleven years after the Long Island Rail Road arrived in 1842.

Population: 7,826; Growth (since 2000): -0.4%; Density: 117.7 persons per square mile; Race: 91.2% White, 2.6% Black/African American, 0.2% Asian, 0.0% American Indian/Alaska Native, 0.0% Native Hawaiian/Other Pacific Islander, 4.0% Two or more races, 7.6% Hispanic of any race; Average household size: 2.47; Median age: 44.6; Age under 18: 22.3%; Age 65 and over: 18.8%; Males per 100 females: 100.1; Marriage status: 28.8% never married, 53.5% now married, 3.0% separated, 8.1% widowed, 9.7% divorced; Foreign born: 1.5%; Speak English only: 94.5%; With disability: 19.8%; Veterans: 10.0%; Ancestry: 27.4% American, 21.9% Irish, 15.6% German, 13.5% Italian, 7.1% English

Employment: 8.3% management, business, and financial, 1.3% computer, engineering, and science, 10.1% education, legal, community service, arts, and media, 3.3% healthcare practitioners, 24.1% service, 24.1% sales and office, 11.9% natural resources, construction, and maintenance, 16.8% production, transportation, and material moving

Income: Per capita: $25,316; Median household: $45,930; Average household: $60,467; Households with income of $100,000 or more: 18.1%; Poverty rate: 13.0%

Educational Attainment: High school diploma or higher: 86.4%; Bachelor's degree or higher: 13.7%; Graduate/professional degree or higher: 4.8%

Housing: Homeownership rate: 78.2%; Median home value: $174,200; Median year structure built: 1968; Homeowner vacancy rate: 4.2%; Median selected monthly owner costs: $1,762 with a mortgage, $672 without a mortgage; Median gross rent: $1,085 per month; Rental vacancy rate: 9.4%

Health Insurance: 92.8% have insurance; 65.6% have private insurance; 41.8% have public insurance; 7.2% do not have insurance; 4.3% of children under 18 do not have insurance

Safety: Violent crime rate: 10.3 per 10,000 population; Property crime rate: 125.0 per 10,000 population

Transportation: Commute: 94.3% car, 0.8% public transportation, 0.7% walk, 3.0% work from home; Mean travel time to work: 29.5 minutes

Additional Information Contacts
Town of Deerpark . . . . (845) 856-2210
http://townofdeerpark.org

FIRTHCLIFFE (CDP).

Covers a land area of 2.965 square miles and a water area of 0.035 square miles. Located at 41.44° N. Lat; 74.03° W. Long. Elevation is 299 feet.

Population: 4,681; Growth (since 2000): -5.8%; Density: 1,578.8 persons per square mile; Race: 92.6% White, 0.0% Black/African American, 1.8% Asian, 0.0% American Indian/Alaska Native, 0.0% Native Hawaiian/Other Pacific Islander, 2.5% Two or more races, 16.2% Hispanic of any race; Average household size: 2.42; Median age: 41.2; Age under 18: 24.8%; Age 65 and over: 16.6%; Males per 100 females: 87.4; Marriage status: 28.1% never married, 47.2% now married, 0.8% separated, 6.5% widowed, 18.2% divorced; Foreign born: 6.3%; Speak English only: 87.7%; With disability: 13.4%; Veterans: 10.9%; Ancestry: 27.2% Irish, 22.3% Italian, 19.3% German, 15.0% American, 9.0% English

Employment: 19.8% management, business, and financial, 2.0% computer, engineering, and science, 15.3% education, legal, community service, arts, and media, 5.9% healthcare practitioners, 16.0% service, 29.3% sales and office, 4.8% natural resources, construction, and maintenance, 7.0% production, transportation, and material moving

Income: Per capita: $36,369; Median household: $70,985; Average household: $87,328; Households with income of $100,000 or more: 24.2%; Poverty rate: 4.4%

Educational Attainment: High school diploma or higher: 95.9%; Bachelor's degree or higher: 40.1%; Graduate/professional degree or higher: 20.5%

Housing: Homeownership rate: 55.9%; Median home value: $275,300; Median year structure built: 1962; Homeowner vacancy rate: 4.6%; Median selected monthly owner costs: $2,515 with a mortgage, $866 without a mortgage; Median gross rent: $1,272 per month; Rental vacancy rate: 12.0%

Health Insurance: 95.2% have insurance; 85.1% have private insurance; 24.7% have public insurance; 4.8% do not have insurance; 1.2% of children under 18 do not have insurance

Transportation: Commute: 90.8% car, 1.9% public transportation, 1.8% walk, 5.0% work from home; Mean travel time to work: 30.0 minutes

FLORIDA (village).

Covers a land area of 2.251 square miles and a water area of 0.004 square miles. Located at 41.33° N. Lat; 74.35° W. Long. Elevation is 446 feet.

History: William H. Seward was born here.

Population: 2,865; Growth (since 2000): 11.4%; Density: 1,272.5 persons per square mile; Race: 80.6% White, 8.2% Black/African American, 1.6% Asian, 0.0% American Indian/Alaska Native, 0.0% Native Hawaiian/Other Pacific Islander, 5.2% Two or more races, 15.2% Hispanic of any race; Average household size: 2.80; Median age: 40.8; Age under 18: 24.9%; Age 65 and over: 13.2%; Males per 100 females: 91.0; Marriage status: 26.7% never married, 55.9% now married, 3.7% separated, 7.1% widowed, 10.2% divorced; Foreign born: 8.1%; Speak English only: 84.6%; With disability: 11.5%; Veterans: 8.8%; Ancestry: 19.7% Irish, 19.5% Italian, 15.2% Polish, 13.7% German, 7.9% American

Employment: 19.1% management, business, and financial, 5.2% computer, engineering, and science, 13.4% education, legal, community service, arts, and media, 3.9% healthcare practitioners, 14.5% service, 24.5% sales and office, 11.3% natural resources, construction, and maintenance, 8.1% production, transportation, and material moving

Income: Per capita: $34,617; Median household: $87,845; Average household: $94,856; Households with income of $100,000 or more: 44.1%; Poverty rate: 2.6%

Educational Attainment: High school diploma or higher: 94.4%; Bachelor's degree or higher: 32.8%; Graduate/professional degree or higher: 10.6%

School District(s)
Florida Union Free SD (KG-12)
    2014-15 Enrollment: 866 . . . . (845) 651-3095
Housing: Homeownership rate: 75.3%; Median home value: $260,800; Median year structure built: 1966; Homeowner vacancy rate: 0.0%; Median selected monthly owner costs: $2,343 with a mortgage, $863 without a mortgage; Median gross rent: $1,064 per month; Rental vacancy rate: 0.0%
Health Insurance: 95.9% have insurance; 83.9% have private insurance; 24.2% have public insurance; 4.1% do not have insurance; 0.0% of children under 18 do not have insurance
Safety: Violent crime rate: 3.4 per 10,000 population; Property crime rate: 110.3 per 10,000 population
Transportation: Commute: 90.4% car, 3.7% public transportation, 1.5% walk, 3.7% work from home; Mean travel time to work: 40.6 minutes

FORT MONTGOMERY (CDP).
Covers a land area of 1.484 square miles and a water area of 0.031 square miles. Located at 41.34° N. Lat; 73.99° W. Long. Elevation is 161 feet.
Population: 1,421; Growth (since 2000): 0.2%; Density: 957.8 persons per square mile; Race: 82.6% White, 6.5% Black/African American, 1.3% Asian, 1.2% American Indian/Alaska Native, 0.0% Native Hawaiian/Other Pacific Islander, 3.2% Two or more races, 8.2% Hispanic of any race; Average household size: 2.51; Median age: 41.5; Age under 18: 13.4%; Age 65 and over: 16.1%; Males per 100 females: 104.6; Marriage status: 31.9% never married, 57.2% now married, 0.0% separated, 0.9% widowed, 10.0% divorced; Foreign born: 5.6%; Speak English only: 89.3%; With disability: 14.5%; Veterans: 8.3%; Ancestry: 30.9% Irish, 21.3% Italian, 16.3% American, 15.8% German, 8.8% English
Employment: 19.6% management, business, and financial, 10.2% computer, engineering, and science, 16.7% education, legal, community service, arts, and media, 6.1% healthcare practitioners, 11.4% service, 21.4% sales and office, 7.7% natural resources, construction, and maintenance, 6.8% production, transportation, and material moving
Income: Per capita: $41,160; Median household: $92,250; Average household: $102,050; Households with income of $100,000 or more: 44.5%; Poverty rate: 9.0%
Educational Attainment: High school diploma or higher: 91.2%; Bachelor's degree or higher: 42.6%; Graduate/professional degree or higher: 16.3%

School District(s)
Highland Falls Central SD (KG-12)
    2014-15 Enrollment: 1,000 . . . . (845) 446-9575
Housing: Homeownership rate: 72.3%; Median home value: $244,800; Median year structure built: 1968; Homeowner vacancy rate: 6.0%; Median selected monthly owner costs: $1,981 with a mortgage, $983 without a mortgage; Median gross rent: $1,560 per month; Rental vacancy rate: 0.0%
Health Insurance: 93.4% have insurance; 84.7% have private insurance; 20.5% have public insurance; 6.6% do not have insurance; 8.4% of children under 18 do not have insurance
Transportation: Commute: 88.4% car, 4.0% public transportation, 3.4% walk, 4.2% work from home; Mean travel time to work: 29.4 minutes

GARDNERTOWN (CDP).
Covers a land area of 4.826 square miles and a water area of 0.017 square miles. Located at 41.54° N. Lat; 74.06° W. Long. Elevation is 410 feet.
Population: 5,033; Growth (since 2000): 11.0%; Density: 1,042.9 persons per square mile; Race: 74.0% White, 14.9% Black/African American, 1.4% Asian, 0.0% American Indian/Alaska Native, 0.0% Native Hawaiian/Other Pacific Islander, 4.7% Two or more races, 15.0% Hispanic of any race; Average household size: 2.94; Median age: 37.7; Age under 18: 23.3%; Age 65 and over: 13.3%; Males per 100 females: 96.9; Marriage status: 32.9% never married, 48.7% now married, 3.9% separated, 6.8% widowed, 11.6% divorced; Foreign born: 10.7%; Speak English only: 80.8%; With disability: 11.9%; Veterans: 7.5%; Ancestry: 22.6% Italian, 15.2% Irish, 12.3% American, 8.5% English, 7.7% German
Employment: 12.4% management, business, and financial, 4.8% computer, engineering, and science, 14.4% education, legal, community service, arts, and media, 0.7% healthcare practitioners, 25.0% service, 22.6% sales and office, 8.3% natural resources, construction, and maintenance, 11.8% production, transportation, and material moving

Income: Per capita: $29,440; Median household: $69,594; Average household: $83,714; Households with income of $100,000 or more: 26.9%; Poverty rate: 2.4%
Educational Attainment: High school diploma or higher: 90.9%; Bachelor's degree or higher: 23.5%; Graduate/professional degree or higher: 8.0%
Housing: Homeownership rate: 82.5%; Median home value: $226,700; Median year structure built: 1955; Homeowner vacancy rate: 1.7%; Median selected monthly owner costs: $2,220 with a mortgage, $689 without a mortgage; Median gross rent: $1,181 per month; Rental vacancy rate: 7.4%
Health Insurance: 90.6% have insurance; 77.9% have private insurance; 24.1% have public insurance; 9.4% do not have insurance; 2.8% of children under 18 do not have insurance
Transportation: Commute: 91.7% car, 2.5% public transportation, 0.0% walk, 4.5% work from home; Mean travel time to work: 25.4 minutes

GOSHEN (town).
Covers a land area of 43.642 square miles and a water area of 0.290 square miles. Located at 41.38° N. Lat; 74.35° W. Long. Elevation is 436 feet.
History: Good Time and Historic (or Harriman) harness-racing tracks are here; and the Hambletonian race is held here. Settled during 18th century; incorporated 1809.
Population: 13,700; Growth (since 2000): 6.1%; Density: 313.9 persons per square mile; Race: 81.6% White, 6.6% Black/African American, 4.6% Asian, 0.0% American Indian/Alaska Native, 0.0% Native Hawaiian/Other Pacific Islander, 3.0% Two or more races, 12.6% Hispanic of any race; Average household size: 2.61; Median age: 43.8; Age under 18: 21.2%; Age 65 and over: 17.6%; Males per 100 females: 102.2; Marriage status: 29.8% never married, 53.2% now married, 1.5% separated, 8.6% widowed, 8.4% divorced; Foreign born: 8.4%; Speak English only: 87.6%; With disability: 13.2%; Veterans: 8.7%; Ancestry: 21.8% Irish, 21.0% Italian, 14.3% American, 10.6% German, 8.1% English
Employment: 18.8% management, business, and financial, 4.2% computer, engineering, and science, 16.5% education, legal, community service, arts, and media, 7.7% healthcare practitioners, 12.9% service, 26.5% sales and office, 6.6% natural resources, construction, and maintenance, 6.7% production, transportation, and material moving
Income: Per capita: $39,360; Median household: $87,762; Average household: $110,702; Households with income of $100,000 or more: 41.5%; Poverty rate: 5.4%
Educational Attainment: High school diploma or higher: 91.2%; Bachelor's degree or higher: 37.1%; Graduate/professional degree or higher: 13.7%

School District(s)
Goshen Central SD (KG-12)
    2014-15 Enrollment: 2,949 . . . . (845) 615-6720
Orange-Ulster Boces
    2014-15 Enrollment: n/a . . . . (845) 291-0100
Vocational/Technical School(s)
Orange Ulster BOCES-Practical Nursing Program (Public)
    Fall 2014 Enrollment: 50 . . . . (845) 291-0100
    2015-16 Tuition: $12,896
Housing: Homeownership rate: 66.9%; Median home value: $319,500; Median year structure built: 1969; Homeowner vacancy rate: 3.0%; Median selected monthly owner costs: $2,696 with a mortgage, $896 without a mortgage; Median gross rent: $1,174 per month; Rental vacancy rate: 8.2%
Health Insurance: 94.1% have insurance; 84.0% have private insurance; 24.5% have public insurance; 5.9% do not have insurance; 2.3% of children under 18 do not have insurance
Newspapers: Goshen Independent (weekly circulation 2,300)
Transportation: Commute: 85.5% car, 4.0% public transportation, 1.1% walk, 8.4% work from home; Mean travel time to work: 33.9 minutes
Additional Information Contacts
Town of Goshen . . . . (845) 294-6250
    http://www.townofgoshen.org

GOSHEN (village).
County seat. Covers a land area of 3.330 square miles and a water area of 0 square miles. Located at 41.40° N. Lat; 74.33° W. Long. Elevation is 436 feet.
Population: 5,394; Growth (since 2000): -5.0%; Density: 1,619.9 persons per square mile; Race: 84.1% White, 2.9% Black/African American, 2.8% Asian, 0.0% American Indian/Alaska Native, 0.0% Native Hawaiian/Other Pacific Islander, 4.8% Two or more races, 16.3% Hispanic of any race;

Average household size: 2.39; Median age: 43.3; Age under 18: 23.6%; Age 65 and over: 18.7%; Males per 100 females: 87.6; Marriage status: 31.6% never married, 47.5% now married, 2.1% separated, 10.1% widowed, 10.8% divorced; Foreign born: 7.2%; Speak English only: 87.4%; With disability: 11.1%; Veterans: 8.2%; Ancestry: 24.3% Irish, 16.5% Italian, 15.4% American, 12.7% English, 11.6% German

Employment: 21.2% management, business, and financial, 3.8% computer, engineering, and science, 17.1% education, legal, community service, arts, and media, 7.2% healthcare practitioners, 11.1% service, 26.4% sales and office, 3.8% natural resources, construction, and maintenance, 9.3% production, transportation, and material moving

Income: Per capita: $37,724; Median household: $73,750; Average household: $90,719; Households with income of $100,000 or more: 35.1%; Poverty rate: 6.1%

Educational Attainment: High school diploma or higher: 92.8%; Bachelor's degree or higher: 43.6%; Graduate/professional degree or higher: 16.3%

School District(s)
Goshen Central SD (KG-12)
  2014-15 Enrollment: 2,949 . . . . (845) 615-6720
Orange-Ulster Boces
  2014-15 Enrollment: n/a . . . . (845) 291-0100

Vocational/Technical School(s)
Orange Ulster BOCES-Practical Nursing Program (Public)
  Fall 2014 Enrollment: 50 . . . . (845) 291-0100
  2015-16 Tuition: $12,896

Housing: Homeownership rate: 51.7%; Median home value: $324,100; Median year structure built: 1963; Homeowner vacancy rate: 2.5%; Median selected monthly owner costs: $2,388 with a mortgage, $996 without a mortgage; Median gross rent: $1,227 per month; Rental vacancy rate: 9.4%

Health Insurance: 95.4% have insurance; 86.3% have private insurance; 23.8% have public insurance; 4.6% do not have insurance; 3.1% of children under 18 do not have insurance

Safety: Violent crime rate: 5.6 per 10,000 population; Property crime rate: 104.4 per 10,000 population

Newspapers: Goshen Independent (weekly circulation 2,300)

Transportation: Commute: 84.4% car, 5.5% public transportation, 0.8% walk, 7.0% work from home; Mean travel time to work: 32.4 minutes

Additional Information Contacts
Village of Goshen . . . . (845) 294-6750
  http://www.villageofgoshen-ny.gov

GREENVILLE (town).
Covers a land area of 30.015 square miles and a water area of 0.484 square miles. Located at 41.37° N. Lat; 74.60° W. Long. Elevation is 1,037 feet.

Population: 4,650; Growth (since 2000): 22.4%; Density: 154.9 persons per square mile; Race: 90.0% White, 0.3% Black/African American, 4.6% Asian, 0.0% American Indian/Alaska Native, 0.0% Native Hawaiian/Other Pacific Islander, 3.1% Two or more races, 7.9% Hispanic of any race; Average household size: 3.08; Median age: 40.6; Age under 18: 24.4%; Age 65 and over: 11.4%; Males per 100 females: 103.1; Marriage status: 31.9% never married, 57.9% now married, 2.1% separated, 2.3% widowed, 8.0% divorced; Foreign born: 6.7%; Speak English only: 89.7%; With disability: 10.2%; Veterans: 9.7%; Ancestry: 35.2% Irish, 21.1% Italian, 14.6% German, 10.6% American, 8.6% English

Employment: 8.2% management, business, and financial, 2.9% computer, engineering, and science, 11.6% education, legal, community service, arts, and media, 6.9% healthcare practitioners, 25.3% service, 22.2% sales and office, 9.2% natural resources, construction, and maintenance, 13.6% production, transportation, and material moving

Income: Per capita: $34,319; Median household: $80,625; Average household: $104,079; Households with income of $100,000 or more: 43.6%; Poverty rate: 5.4%

Educational Attainment: High school diploma or higher: 94.6%; Bachelor's degree or higher: 25.3%; Graduate/professional degree or higher: 9.7%

Housing: Homeownership rate: 92.3%; Median home value: $280,500; Median year structure built: 1987; Homeowner vacancy rate: 2.1%; Median selected monthly owner costs: $2,163 with a mortgage, $845 without a mortgage; Median gross rent: $1,092 per month; Rental vacancy rate: 0.0%

Health Insurance: 92.9% have insurance; 82.9% have private insurance; 22.0% have public insurance; 7.1% do not have insurance; 2.5% of children under 18 do not have insurance

Transportation: Commute: 93.1% car, 0.5% public transportation, 0.0% walk, 6.4% work from home; Mean travel time to work: 36.1 minutes

Additional Information Contacts
Town of Greenville . . . . (518) 966-5055
  http://www.townofgreenvilleny.com

GREENWOOD LAKE (village).
Covers a land area of 2.048 square miles and a water area of 0.424 square miles. Located at 41.22° N. Lat; 74.29° W. Long. Elevation is 630 feet.

Population: 3,118; Growth (since 2000): -8.6%; Density: 1,522.4 persons per square mile; Race: 87.7% White, 1.9% Black/African American, 0.0% Asian, 0.0% American Indian/Alaska Native, 0.0% Native Hawaiian/Other Pacific Islander, 8.1% Two or more races, 12.0% Hispanic of any race; Average household size: 2.55; Median age: 43.5; Age under 18: 21.9%; Age 65 and over: 8.9%; Males per 100 females: 98.4; Marriage status: 25.6% never married, 48.9% now married, 0.5% separated, 5.5% widowed, 19.9% divorced; Foreign born: 2.9%; Speak English only: 90.5%; With disability: 15.7%; Veterans: 12.0%; Ancestry: 29.0% German, 24.6% Irish, 20.4% Italian, 18.7% American, 8.5% English

Employment: 15.3% management, business, and financial, 10.2% computer, engineering, and science, 12.8% education, legal, community service, arts, and media, 2.2% healthcare practitioners, 16.5% service, 18.4% sales and office, 12.4% natural resources, construction, and maintenance, 12.3% production, transportation, and material moving

Income: Per capita: $39,848; Median household: $78,611; Average household: $99,917; Households with income of $100,000 or more: 37.3%; Poverty rate: 2.9%

Educational Attainment: High school diploma or higher: 95.1%; Bachelor's degree or higher: 23.8%; Graduate/professional degree or higher: 12.5%

School District(s)
Greenwood Lake Union Free SD (KG-08)
  2014-15 Enrollment: 555 . . . . (845) 782-8678

Housing: Homeownership rate: 80.0%; Median home value: $266,900; Median year structure built: 1953; Homeowner vacancy rate: 4.5%; Median selected monthly owner costs: $1,966 with a mortgage, $1,210 without a mortgage; Median gross rent: $999 per month; Rental vacancy rate: 0.0%

Health Insurance: 91.2% have insurance; 75.0% have private insurance; 22.6% have public insurance; 8.8% do not have insurance; 0.0% of children under 18 do not have insurance

Safety: Violent crime rate: 9.7 per 10,000 population; Property crime rate: 90.3 per 10,000 population

Newspapers: Greenwood Lake News (weekly circulation 5,000)

Transportation: Commute: 84.7% car, 7.0% public transportation, 2.2% walk, 6.1% work from home; Mean travel time to work: 49.7 minutes

HAMPTONBURGH (town).
Covers a land area of 26.758 square miles and a water area of 0.211 square miles. Located at 41.45° N. Lat; 74.24° W. Long. Elevation is 446 feet.

Population: 5,543; Growth (since 2000): 18.3%; Density: 207.2 persons per square mile; Race: 85.1% White, 3.8% Black/African American, 6.4% Asian, 0.0% American Indian/Alaska Native, 0.0% Native Hawaiian/Other Pacific Islander, 1.5% Two or more races, 8.1% Hispanic of any race; Average household size: 3.31; Median age: 41.8; Age under 18: 23.1%; Age 65 and over: 12.1%; Males per 100 females: 97.5; Marriage status: 31.0% never married, 59.5% now married, 0.6% separated, 4.9% widowed, 4.7% divorced; Foreign born: 12.8%; Speak English only: 85.2%; With disability: 11.5%; Veterans: 9.4%; Ancestry: 23.0% Italian, 21.4% Irish, 11.1% German, 8.1% American, 6.1% English

Employment: 15.2% management, business, and financial, 1.8% computer, engineering, and science, 16.1% education, legal, community service, arts, and media, 7.3% healthcare practitioners, 14.9% service, 28.9% sales and office, 7.6% natural resources, construction, and maintenance, 8.3% production, transportation, and material moving

Income: Per capita: $34,704; Median household: $102,321; Average household: $112,727; Households with income of $100,000 or more: 51.2%; Poverty rate: 5.9%

Educational Attainment: High school diploma or higher: 94.2%; Bachelor's degree or higher: 30.3%; Graduate/professional degree or higher: 12.1%

Housing: Homeownership rate: 91.6%; Median home value: $352,600; Median year structure built: 1981; Homeowner vacancy rate: 0.0%; Median selected monthly owner costs: $2,663 with a mortgage, $1,134 without a mortgage; Median gross rent: $1,969 per month; Rental vacancy rate: 0.0%

Health Insurance: 95.6% have insurance; 82.0% have private insurance; 24.4% have public insurance; 4.4% do not have insurance; 0.0% of children under 18 do not have insurance
Transportation: Commute: 92.5% car, 2.6% public transportation, 0.7% walk, 3.9% work from home; Mean travel time to work: 31.0 minutes
Additional Information Contacts
Town of Hamptonburgh . . . . (845) 427-2424
  http://townofhamptonburgh.org/content

HARRIMAN (village).
Covers a land area of 1.004 square miles and a water area of 0.018 square miles. Located at 41.31° N. Lat; 74.14° W. Long. Elevation is 538 feet.
Population: 2,704; Growth (since 2000): 20.1%; Density: 2,692.6 persons per square mile; Race: 53.3% White, 19.6% Black/African American, 1.4% Asian, 0.0% American Indian/Alaska Native, 0.0% Native Hawaiian/Other Pacific Islander, 3.1% Two or more races, 28.8% Hispanic of any race; Average household size: 2.49; Median age: 36.2; Age under 18: 21.3%; Age 65 and over: 9.5%; Males per 100 females: 94.4; Marriage status: 35.4% never married, 51.8% now married, 3.3% separated, 3.9% widowed, 8.9% divorced; Foreign born: 20.9%; Speak English only: 62.1%; With disability: 13.9%; Veterans: 6.4%; Ancestry: 11.8% Irish, 10.5% Italian, 9.4% American, 6.8% German, 6.0% Jamaican
Employment: 8.8% management, business, and financial, 6.0% computer, engineering, and science, 7.6% education, legal, community service, arts, and media, 3.6% healthcare practitioners, 31.3% service, 25.4% sales and office, 8.1% natural resources, construction, and maintenance, 9.3% production, transportation, and material moving
Income: Per capita: $30,172; Median household: $61,688; Average household: $72,622; Households with income of $100,000 or more: 22.0%; Poverty rate: 8.8%
Educational Attainment: High school diploma or higher: 85.8%; Bachelor's degree or higher: 31.8%; Graduate/professional degree or higher: 12.9%
School District(s)
Monroe-Woodbury Central SD (KG-12)
  2014-15 Enrollment: 6,986 . . . . (845) 460-6200
Housing: Homeownership rate: 51.2%; Median home value: $168,500; Median year structure built: 1983; Homeowner vacancy rate: 0.0%; Median selected monthly owner costs: $2,056 with a mortgage, $915 without a mortgage; Median gross rent: $1,297 per month; Rental vacancy rate: 2.8%
Health Insurance: 88.1% have insurance; 75.3% have private insurance; 20.8% have public insurance; 11.9% do not have insurance; 9.9% of children under 18 do not have insurance
Safety: Violent crime rate: 16.1 per 10,000 population; Property crime rate: 145.3 per 10,000 population
Transportation: Commute: 77.9% car, 11.9% public transportation, 4.4% walk, 4.6% work from home; Mean travel time to work: 34.1 minutes

HIGHLAND FALLS (village).
Covers a land area of 1.090 square miles and a water area of 0.009 square miles. Located at 41.36° N. Lat; 73.97° W. Long. Elevation is 141 feet.
Population: 3,856; Growth (since 2000): 4.8%; Density: 3,536.4 persons per square mile; Race: 67.7% White, 13.8% Black/African American, 7.3% Asian, 0.4% American Indian/Alaska Native, 0.0% Native Hawaiian/Other Pacific Islander, 5.6% Two or more races, 13.4% Hispanic of any race; Average household size: 2.17; Median age: 41.6; Age under 18: 15.6%; Age 65 and over: 13.9%; Males per 100 females: 97.1; Marriage status: 33.4% never married, 53.4% now married, 2.7% separated, 4.3% widowed, 8.9% divorced; Foreign born: 12.6%; Speak English only: 79.9%; With disability: 12.5%; Veterans: 14.9%; Ancestry: 17.5% Irish, 15.4% Italian, 14.5% German, 14.1% American, 6.3% English
Employment: 15.1% management, business, and financial, 3.8% computer, engineering, and science, 15.9% education, legal, community service, arts, and media, 6.5% healthcare practitioners, 15.9% service, 24.9% sales and office, 8.8% natural resources, construction, and maintenance, 9.1% production, transportation, and material moving
Income: Per capita: $40,669; Median household: $80,475; Average household: $85,908; Households with income of $100,000 or more: 35.7%; Poverty rate: 5.1%
Educational Attainment: High school diploma or higher: 93.4%; Bachelor's degree or higher: 36.6%; Graduate/professional degree or higher: 14.9%

School District(s)
Highland Falls Central SD (KG-12)
  2014-15 Enrollment: 1,000 . . . . (845) 446-9575
Housing: Homeownership rate: 44.6%; Median home value: $231,000; Median year structure built: Before 1940; Homeowner vacancy rate: 1.9%; Median selected monthly owner costs: $2,216 with a mortgage, $1,010 without a mortgage; Median gross rent: $1,100 per month; Rental vacancy rate: 0.0%
Health Insurance: 94.3% have insurance; 83.6% have private insurance; 27.0% have public insurance; 5.7% do not have insurance; 4.8% of children under 18 do not have insurance
Newspapers: News Of The Highlands (weekly circulation 2,700)
Transportation: Commute: 85.2% car, 4.9% public transportation, 6.6% walk, 3.2% work from home; Mean travel time to work: 20.3 minutes

HIGHLAND MILLS (unincorporated postal area)
ZCTA: 10930
Covers a land area of 13.876 square miles and a water area of 0.171 square miles. Located at 41.36° N. Lat; 74.11° W. Long. Elevation is 509 feet.
Population: 9,021; Growth (since 2000): 21.9%; Density: 650.1 persons per square mile; Race: 88.3% White, 3.7% Black/African American, 4.1% Asian, 0.0% American Indian/Alaska Native, 0.0% Native Hawaiian/Other Pacific Islander, 1.3% Two or more races, 13.0% Hispanic of any race; Average household size: 3.22; Median age: 39.7; Age under 18: 27.1%; Age 65 and over: 12.0%; Males per 100 females: 98.1; Marriage status: 29.8% never married, 59.6% now married, 1.5% separated, 4.7% widowed, 5.9% divorced; Foreign born: 17.4%; Speak English only: 77.9%; With disability: 8.6%; Veterans: 7.5%; Ancestry: 24.5% Irish, 16.0% Italian, 12.2% American, 12.1% German, 6.9% Polish
Employment: 13.8% management, business, and financial, 7.2% computer, engineering, and science, 10.7% education, legal, community service, arts, and media, 9.0% healthcare practitioners, 10.9% service, 32.9% sales and office, 5.8% natural resources, construction, and maintenance, 9.6% production, transportation, and material moving
Income: Per capita: $41,471; Median household: $129,477; Average household: $130,746; Households with income of $100,000 or more: 65.0%; Poverty rate: 4.9%
Educational Attainment: High school diploma or higher: 94.5%; Bachelor's degree or higher: 45.8%; Graduate/professional degree or higher: 21.8%
Housing: Homeownership rate: 91.6%; Median home value: $321,000; Median year structure built: 1979; Homeowner vacancy rate: 0.0%; Median selected monthly owner costs: $2,726 with a mortgage, $1,061 without a mortgage; Median gross rent: n/a per month; Rental vacancy rate: 10.0%
Health Insurance: 94.8% have insurance; 89.1% have private insurance; 15.5% have public insurance; 5.2% do not have insurance; 0.4% of children under 18 do not have insurance
Transportation: Commute: 86.9% car, 5.9% public transportation, 0.3% walk, 6.1% work from home; Mean travel time to work: 37.7 minutes

HIGHLANDS (town).
Covers a land area of 30.410 square miles and a water area of 3.060 square miles. Located at 41.37° N. Lat; 74.01° W. Long.
Population: 12,243; Growth (since 2000): -1.9%; Density: 402.6 persons per square mile; Race: 77.6% White, 7.4% Black/African American, 4.6% Asian, 0.5% American Indian/Alaska Native, 0.0% Native Hawaiian/Other Pacific Islander, 5.9% Two or more races, 12.9% Hispanic of any race; Average household size: 2.66; Median age: 23.1; Age under 18: 18.9%; Age 65 and over: 6.7%; Males per 100 females: 163.2; Marriage status: 53.7% never married, 38.8% now married, 0.9% separated, 2.0% widowed, 5.6% divorced; Foreign born: 7.3%; Speak English only: 83.7%; With disability: 11.0%; Veterans: 22.5%; Ancestry: 20.1% Irish, 18.3% German, 13.1% American, 12.8% Italian, 9.1% English
Employment: 14.1% management, business, and financial, 5.7% computer, engineering, and science, 18.0% education, legal, community service, arts, and media, 7.1% healthcare practitioners, 16.5% service, 22.4% sales and office, 7.3% natural resources, construction, and maintenance, 8.9% production, transportation, and material moving
Income: Per capita: $29,087; Median household: $87,394; Average household: $95,929; Households with income of $100,000 or more: 40.5%; Poverty rate: 5.2%

Educational Attainment: High school diploma or higher: 94.7%; Bachelor's degree or higher: 46.4%; Graduate/professional degree or higher: 22.0%

Housing: Homeownership rate: 39.6%; Median home value: $233,000; Median year structure built: 1951; Homeowner vacancy rate: 3.1%; Median selected monthly owner costs: $2,168 with a mortgage, $970 without a mortgage; Median gross rent: $1,505 per month; Rental vacancy rate: 0.0%

Health Insurance: 95.9% have insurance; 87.1% have private insurance; 20.0% have public insurance; 4.1% do not have insurance; 2.1% of children under 18 do not have insurance

Safety: Violent crime rate: 3.6 per 10,000 population; Property crime rate: 14.5 per 10,000 population

Transportation: Commute: 52.7% car, 2.4% public transportation, 22.1% walk, 21.9% work from home; Mean travel time to work: 16.9 minutes

Additional Information Contacts

Town of Highlands. . . . . (845) 446-4280
    http://townofhighlands.com

HOWELLS (unincorporated postal area)
ZCTA: 10932

Covers a land area of 0.149 square miles and a water area of <.001 square miles. Located at 41.48° N. Lat; 74.46° W. Long. Elevation is 679 feet.

Population: 100; Growth (since 2000): n/a; Density: 670.1 persons per square mile; Race: 100.0% White, 0.0% Black/African American, 0.0% Asian, 0.0% American Indian/Alaska Native, 0.0% Native Hawaiian/Other Pacific Islander, 0.0% Two or more races, 0.0% Hispanic of any race; Average household size: 4.17; Median age: 57.4; Age under 18: 8.0%; Age 65 and over: 36.0%; Males per 100 females: 71.4; Marriage status: 50.0% never married, 50.0% now married, 0.0% separated, 0.0% widowed, 0.0% divorced; Foreign born: 19.0%; Speak English only: 91.0%; With disability: 19.0%; Veterans: 20.7%; Ancestry: 93.0% Irish, 33.0% Polish

Employment: 0.0% management, business, and financial, 0.0% computer, engineering, and science, 0.0% education, legal, community service, arts, and media, 0.0% healthcare practitioners, 0.0% service, 100.0% sales and office, 0.0% natural resources, construction, and maintenance, 0.0% production, transportation, and material moving

Income: Per capita: $16,965; Median household: n/a; Average household: n/a; Households with income of $100,000 or more: n/a; Poverty rate: n/a

Educational Attainment: High school diploma or higher: 100.0%; Bachelor's degree or higher: 67.6%; Graduate/professional degree or higher: 32.4%

Housing: Homeownership rate: 100.0%; Median home value: n/a; Median year structure built: n/a; Homeowner vacancy rate: 0.0%; Median selected monthly owner costs: $0 with a mortgage, $0 without a mortgage; Median gross rent: n/a per month; Rental vacancy rate: 0.0%

Health Insurance: 100.0% have insurance; 100.0% have private insurance; 58.0% have public insurance; 0.0% do not have insurance; 0.0% of children under 18 do not have insurance

Transportation: Commute: 100.0% car, 0.0% public transportation, 0.0% walk, 0.0% work from home; Mean travel time to work: 0.0 minutes

HUGUENOT (unincorporated postal area)
ZCTA: 12746

Covers a land area of 14.181 square miles and a water area of 0.323 square miles. Located at 41.44° N. Lat; 74.66° W. Long. Elevation is 469 feet.

Population: 1,388; Growth (since 2000): 21.3%; Density: 97.9 persons per square mile; Race: 91.7% White, 3.4% Black/African American, 0.0% Asian, 0.0% American Indian/Alaska Native, 0.0% Native Hawaiian/Other Pacific Islander, 4.9% Two or more races, 8.9% Hispanic of any race; Average household size: 3.30; Median age: 35.2; Age under 18: 22.7%; Age 65 and over: 9.5%; Males per 100 females: 97.7; Marriage status: 34.0% never married, 59.8% now married, 0.0% separated, 0.0% widowed, 6.2% divorced; Foreign born: 0.9%; Speak English only: 90.8%; With disability: 14.8%; Veterans: 7.5%; Ancestry: 29.0% Irish, 17.3% American, 16.6% German, 13.3% Italian, 7.4% European

Employment: 10.4% management, business, and financial, 1.4% computer, engineering, and science, 10.1% education, legal, community service, arts, and media, 0.9% healthcare practitioners, 18.0% service,

18.2% sales and office, 16.3% natural resources, construction, and maintenance, 24.5% production, transportation, and material moving

Income: Per capita: $28,479; Median household: $83,221; Average household: $89,112; Households with income of $100,000 or more: 31.7%; Poverty rate: 0.4%

Educational Attainment: High school diploma or higher: 90.9%; Bachelor's degree or higher: 15.4%; Graduate/professional degree or higher: 6.3%

Housing: Homeownership rate: 76.0%; Median home value: $207,900; Median year structure built: 1970; Homeowner vacancy rate: 0.0%; Median selected monthly owner costs: $1,844 with a mortgage, $576 without a mortgage; Median gross rent: $1,109 per month; Rental vacancy rate: 28.8%

Health Insurance: 86.5% have insurance; 73.0% have private insurance; 18.4% have public insurance; 13.5% do not have insurance; 17.8% of children under 18 do not have insurance

Transportation: Commute: 83.2% car, 3.9% public transportation, 2.2% walk, 10.7% work from home; Mean travel time to work: 33.3 minutes

JOHNSON (unincorporated postal area)
ZCTA: 10933

Covers a land area of 1.092 square miles and a water area of 0.005 square miles. Located at 41.37° N. Lat; 74.51° W. Long. Elevation is 509 feet.

Population: 809; Growth (since 2000): n/a; Density: 740.7 persons per square mile; Race: 92.8% White, 0.0% Black/African American, 0.0% Asian, 0.0% American Indian/Alaska Native, 0.0% Native Hawaiian/Other Pacific Islander, 0.0% Two or more races, 0.0% Hispanic of any race; Average household size: 3.61; Median age: 30.5; Age under 18: 31.0%; Age 65 and over: 0.0%; Males per 100 females: 98.7; Marriage status: 35.1% never married, 51.5% now married, 0.0% separated, 4.5% widowed, 8.9% divorced; Foreign born: 2.2%; Speak English only: 96.2%; With disability: 15.9%; Veterans: 11.6%; Ancestry: 35.2% American, 30.0% Italian, 21.5% German, 14.8% Irish, 5.6% English

Employment: 7.2% management, business, and financial, 18.8% computer, engineering, and science, 2.9% education, legal, community service, arts, and media, 0.0% healthcare practitioners, 26.7% service, 33.3% sales and office, 11.0% natural resources, construction, and maintenance, 0.0% production, transportation, and material moving

Income: Per capita: $25,400; Median household: $97,845; Average household: $90,375; Households with income of $100,000 or more: 38.8%; Poverty rate: 7.2%

Educational Attainment: High school diploma or higher: 100.0%; Bachelor's degree or higher: 23.7%; Graduate/professional degree or higher: 6.4%

Housing: Homeownership rate: 100.0%; Median home value: $277,800; Median year structure built: 1978; Homeowner vacancy rate: 0.0%; Median selected monthly owner costs: n/a with a mortgage, n/a without a mortgage; Median gross rent: n/a per month; Rental vacancy rate: 0.0%

Health Insurance: 91.1% have insurance; 85.2% have private insurance; 12.0% have public insurance; 8.9% do not have insurance; 0.0% of children under 18 do not have insurance

Transportation: Commute: 100.0% car, 0.0% public transportation, 0.0% walk, 0.0% work from home; Mean travel time to work: 21.6 minutes

KIRYAS JOEL (village). Covers a land area of 1.109 square miles and a water area of 0.006 square miles. Located at 41.34° N. Lat; 74.17° W. Long. Elevation is 686 feet.

History: Founded in 1974 by the Satmar sect of Hasidic Jews to accommodate, in part, their burgeoning population in the Williamsburg section of Brooklyn.

Population: 21,749; Growth (since 2000): 65.5%; Density: 19,618.5 persons per square mile; Race: 99.7% White, 0.0% Black/African American, 0.1% Asian, 0.2% American Indian/Alaska Native, 0.0% Native Hawaiian/Other Pacific Islander, 0.0% Two or more races, 2.1% Hispanic of any race; Average household size: 5.62; Median age: 12.9; Age under 18: 61.2%; Age 65 and over: 1.4%; Males per 100 females: 107.3; Marriage status: 23.5% never married, 75.0% now married, 0.4% separated, 1.1% widowed, 0.3% divorced; Foreign born: 6.9%; Speak English only: 5.5%; With disability: 2.9%; Veterans: 0.5%; Ancestry: 20.5% American, 17.3% Hungarian, 4.5% Romanian, 3.6% European, 1.8% Israeli

Employment: 10.6% management, business, and financial, 2.5% computer, engineering, and science, 23.7% education, legal, community service, arts, and media, 0.5% healthcare practitioners, 13.8% service, 33.1% sales and office, 4.8% natural resources, construction, and maintenance, 11.1% production, transportation, and material moving
Income: Per capita: $7,658; Median household: $26,099; Average household: $42,880; Households with income of $100,000 or more: 10.7%; Poverty rate: 56.6%
Educational Attainment: High school diploma or higher: 64.0%; Bachelor's degree or higher: 7.9%; Graduate/professional degree or higher: 1.5%
Housing: Homeownership rate: 30.6%; Median home value: $349,200; Median year structure built: 1997; Homeowner vacancy rate: 2.2%; Median selected monthly owner costs: $1,830 with a mortgage, $963 without a mortgage; Median gross rent: $1,127 per month; Rental vacancy rate: 0.0%
Health Insurance: 98.8% have insurance; 24.0% have private insurance; 80.8% have public insurance; 1.2% do not have insurance; 0.8% of children under 18 do not have insurance
Transportation: Commute: 44.2% car, 19.6% public transportation, 28.8% walk, 5.5% work from home; Mean travel time to work: 26.6 minutes

MAYBROOK (village). Covers a land area of 1.354 square miles and a water area of 0.006 square miles. Located at 41.49° N. Lat; 74.21° W. Long. Elevation is 420 feet.
History: Incorporated 1925.
Population: 3,093; Growth (since 2000): 0.3%; Density: 2,283.9 persons per square mile; Race: 74.7% White, 16.1% Black/African American, 1.6% Asian, 0.1% American Indian/Alaska Native, 0.1% Native Hawaiian/Other Pacific Islander, 5.9% Two or more races, 16.5% Hispanic of any race; Average household size: 2.54; Median age: 38.2; Age under 18: 17.9%; Age 65 and over: 9.8%; Males per 100 females: 86.0; Marriage status: 39.8% never married, 41.8% now married, 2.1% separated, 6.0% widowed, 12.3% divorced; Foreign born: 11.3%; Speak English only: 76.2%; With disability: 11.9%; Veterans: 8.2%; Ancestry: 18.1% Irish, 17.4% Italian, 15.7% German, 9.7% American, 4.7% Albanian
Employment: 9.1% management, business, and financial, 2.8% computer, engineering, and science, 5.0% education, legal, community service, arts, and media, 9.3% healthcare practitioners, 21.7% service, 28.6% sales and office, 10.5% natural resources, construction, and maintenance, 13.0% production, transportation, and material moving
Income: Per capita: $30,068; Median household: $58,621; Average household: $74,767; Households with income of $100,000 or more: 28.2%; Poverty rate: 10.9%
Educational Attainment: High school diploma or higher: 90.6%; Bachelor's degree or higher: 24.9%; Graduate/professional degree or higher: 8.8%

School District(s)
Valley Central SD (Montgomery) (KG-12)
    2014-15 Enrollment: 4,464 . . . . (845) 457-2400
Housing: Homeownership rate: 59.1%; Median home value: $172,800; Median year structure built: 1972; Homeowner vacancy rate: 3.7%; Median selected monthly owner costs: $1,840 with a mortgage, $665 without a mortgage; Median gross rent: $1,103 per month; Rental vacancy rate: 5.2%
Health Insurance: 89.8% have insurance; 72.2% have private insurance; 26.3% have public insurance; 10.2% do not have insurance; 3.3% of children under 18 do not have insurance
Safety: Violent crime rate: 3.2 per 10,000 population; Property crime rate: 3.2 per 10,000 population
Transportation: Commute: 88.7% car, 7.1% public transportation, 1.1% walk, 2.8% work from home; Mean travel time to work: 33.6 minutes
Additional Information Contacts
Village of Maybrook. . . . . (845) 427-2717
    http://www.villageofmaybrook.com

MECHANICSTOWN (CDP). Covers a land area of 3.345 square miles and a water area of 0.056 square miles. Located at 41.45° N. Lat; 74.39° W. Long. Elevation is 531 feet.
Population: 7,130; Growth (since 2000): 17.6%; Density: 2,131.8 persons per square mile; Race: 54.8% White, 25.9% Black/African American, 3.0% Asian, 0.2% American Indian/Alaska Native, 0.3% Native Hawaiian/Other Pacific Islander, 6.1% Two or more races, 25.9% Hispanic of any race; Average household size: 2.49; Median age: 43.3; Age under 18: 19.7%; Age 65 and over: 20.2%; Males per 100 females: 84.7; Marriage status:

34.2% never married, 45.6% now married, 3.7% separated, 9.6% widowed, 10.6% divorced; Foreign born: 16.0%; Speak English only: 71.2%; With disability: 16.5%; Veterans: 7.5%; Ancestry: 16.4% American, 15.7% Italian, 12.0% Irish, 9.5% German, 3.3% English
Employment: 14.0% management, business, and financial, 2.2% computer, engineering, and science, 10.6% education, legal, community service, arts, and media, 4.2% healthcare practitioners, 17.4% service, 30.6% sales and office, 5.6% natural resources, construction, and maintenance, 15.3% production, transportation, and material moving
Income: Per capita: $28,882; Median household: $50,804; Average household: $71,360; Households with income of $100,000 or more: 25.1%; Poverty rate: 10.6%
Educational Attainment: High school diploma or higher: 86.2%; Bachelor's degree or higher: 19.0%; Graduate/professional degree or higher: 7.6%
Housing: Homeownership rate: 43.7%; Median home value: $205,300; Median year structure built: 1979; Homeowner vacancy rate: 0.0%; Median selected monthly owner costs: $1,838 with a mortgage, $764 without a mortgage; Median gross rent: $1,103 per month; Rental vacancy rate: 0.0%
Health Insurance: 89.5% have insurance; 70.3% have private insurance; 32.0% have public insurance; 10.5% do not have insurance; 0.0% of children under 18 do not have insurance
Transportation: Commute: 85.9% car, 5.2% public transportation, 2.8% walk, 0.9% work from home; Mean travel time to work: 34.9 minutes

MIDDLETOWN (city). Covers a land area of 5.076 square miles and a water area of 0.026 square miles. Located at 41.44° N. Lat; 74.42° W. Long. Elevation is 558 feet.
History: Settled 1756, Incorporated as a city 1888.
Population: 27,828; Growth (since 2000): 9.6%; Density: 5,482.4 persons per square mile; Race: 46.2% White, 22.6% Black/African American, 3.4% Asian, 0.6% American Indian/Alaska Native, 0.0% Native Hawaiian/Other Pacific Islander, 4.0% Two or more races, 38.4% Hispanic of any race; Average household size: 2.74; Median age: 33.9; Age under 18: 24.9%; Age 65 and over: 11.5%; Males per 100 females: 95.6; Marriage status: 43.0% never married, 43.4% now married, 4.1% separated, 5.2% widowed, 8.4% divorced; Foreign born: 18.4%; Speak English only: 64.2%; With disability: 14.0%; Veterans: 5.5%; Ancestry: 15.7% American, 8.7% Irish, 7.8% Italian, 5.8% German, 4.1% Polish
Employment: 12.2% management, business, and financial, 1.9% computer, engineering, and science, 8.3% education, legal, community service, arts, and media, 4.6% healthcare practitioners, 24.8% service, 25.7% sales and office, 7.0% natural resources, construction, and maintenance, 15.5% production, transportation, and material moving
Income: Per capita: $23,320; Median household: $50,441; Average household: $61,374; Households with income of $100,000 or more: 19.6%; Poverty rate: 19.6%
Educational Attainment: High school diploma or higher: 83.0%; Bachelor's degree or higher: 19.3%; Graduate/professional degree or higher: 7.2%

School District(s)
Middletown City SD (PK-12)
    2014-15 Enrollment: 7,318 . . . . (845) 326-1158
Minisink Valley Central SD (KG-12)
    2014-15 Enrollment: 3,992 . . . . (845) 355-5100
Two-year College(s)
Orange County Community College (Public)
    Fall 2014 Enrollment: 6,951 . . . . (845) 344-6222
    2015-16 Tuition: In-state $5,128; Out-of-state $9,614
Vocational/Technical School(s)
Beauty School of Middletown (Private, For-profit)
    Fall 2014 Enrollment: 73 . . . . (845) 343-2171
    2015-16 Tuition: $13,100
Housing: Homeownership rate: 52.4%; Median home value: $191,000; Median year structure built: 1949; Homeowner vacancy rate: 1.7%; Median selected monthly owner costs: $1,973 with a mortgage, $696 without a mortgage; Median gross rent: $1,102 per month; Rental vacancy rate: 4.0%
Health Insurance: 86.8% have insurance; 62.0% have private insurance; 35.6% have public insurance; 13.2% do not have insurance; 3.3% of children under 18 do not have insurance
Hospitals: Orange Regional Medical Center (174 beds)
Safety: Violent crime rate: 40.9 per 10,000 population; Property crime rate: 247.2 per 10,000 population

Newspapers: The Gazette (weekly circulation 9,000); Times Herald Record (daily circulation 79,100)
Transportation: Commute: 84.8% car, 4.5% public transportation, 3.4% walk, 3.3% work from home; Mean travel time to work: 31.3 minutes
Additional Information Contacts
City of Middletown . . . . (845) 346-4101
http://www.middletown-ny.com

MINISINK (town).
Covers a land area of 23.029 square miles and a water area of 0.144 square miles. Located at 41.32° N. Lat; 74.54° W. Long.
Population: 4,515; Growth (since 2000): 25.9%; Density: 196.1 persons per square mile; Race: 89.9% White, 2.4% Black/African American, 0.1% Asian, 1.5% American Indian/Alaska Native, 0.0% Native Hawaiian/Other Pacific Islander, 1.5% Two or more races, 7.4% Hispanic of any race; Average household size: 3.13; Median age: 36.9; Age under 18: 29.5%; Age 65 and over: 8.0%; Males per 100 females: 99.6; Marriage status: 33.2% never married, 52.1% now married, 1.1% separated, 5.7% widowed, 9.0% divorced; Foreign born: 4.2%; Speak English only: 91.2%; With disability: 13.2%; Veterans: 9.6%; Ancestry: 26.7% Italian, 19.9% American, 15.9% Irish, 15.1% German, 8.8% Polish
Employment: 13.5% management, business, and financial, 4.2% computer, engineering, and science, 10.9% education, legal, community service, arts, and media, 4.4% healthcare practitioners, 19.5% service, 29.9% sales and office, 9.5% natural resources, construction, and maintenance, 8.1% production, transportation, and material moving
Income: Per capita: $32,361; Median household: $93,833; Average household: $99,699; Households with income of $100,000 or more: 44.5%; Poverty rate: 6.2%
Educational Attainment: High school diploma or higher: 93.6%; Bachelor's degree or higher: 25.6%; Graduate/professional degree or higher: 12.3%
Housing: Homeownership rate: 88.0%; Median home value: $271,200; Median year structure built: 1977; Homeowner vacancy rate: 0.0%; Median selected monthly owner costs: $2,179 with a mortgage, $854 without a mortgage; Median gross rent: $1,188 per month; Rental vacancy rate: 3.7%
Health Insurance: 90.9% have insurance; 81.5% have private insurance; 17.2% have public insurance; 9.1% do not have insurance; 6.7% of children under 18 do not have insurance
Transportation: Commute: 91.9% car, 3.0% public transportation, 0.0% walk, 4.8% work from home; Mean travel time to work: 39.8 minutes
Additional Information Contacts
Town of Minisink . . . . (845) 726-3700
http://www.townofminisink.com

MONROE (town).
Covers a land area of 19.976 square miles and a water area of 1.280 square miles. Located at 41.30° N. Lat; 74.20° W. Long. Elevation is 643 feet.
History: Incorporated 1894.
Population: 41,756; Growth (since 2000): 33.0%; Density: 2,090.3 persons per square mile; Race: 89.4% White, 2.4% Black/African American, 2.6% Asian, 0.4% American Indian/Alaska Native, 0.0% Native Hawaiian/Other Pacific Islander, 1.7% Two or more races, 9.6% Hispanic of any race; Average household size: 3.99; Median age: 21.7; Age under 18: 44.1%; Age 65 and over: 5.8%; Males per 100 females: 103.2; Marriage status: 29.4% never married, 63.1% now married, 1.0% separated, 3.0% widowed, 4.4% divorced; Foreign born: 9.9%; Speak English only: 42.6%; With disability: 6.4%; Veterans: 4.4%; Ancestry: 15.2% American, 11.7% Italian, 10.8% Irish, 9.6% Hungarian, 5.7% German
Employment: 14.1% management, business, and financial, 4.5% computer, engineering, and science, 16.6% education, legal, community service, arts, and media, 6.0% healthcare practitioners, 15.8% service, 28.9% sales and office, 5.2% natural resources, construction, and maintenance, 8.9% production, transportation, and material moving
Income: Per capita: $22,531; Median household: $65,523; Average household: $87,705; Households with income of $100,000 or more: 35.2%; Poverty rate: 32.7%
Educational Attainment: High school diploma or higher: 83.9%; Bachelor's degree or higher: 33.1%; Graduate/professional degree or higher: 11.6%
School District(s)
Greenwood Lake Union Free SD (KG-08)
    2014-15 Enrollment: 555 . . . . (845) 782-8678

Kiryas Joel Village Union Free SD (PK-KG)
    2014-15 Enrollment: 156 . . . . (845) 782-2300
Monroe-Woodbury Central SD (KG-12)
    2014-15 Enrollment: 6,986 . . . . (845) 460-6200
Four-year College(s)
Uta Mesivta of Kiryas Joel (Private, Not-for-profit, Jewish)
    Fall 2014 Enrollment: 1,634 . . . . (845) 783-9901
    2015-16 Tuition: In-state $9,800; Out-of-state $9,800
Housing: Homeownership rate: 61.6%; Median home value: $324,400; Median year structure built: 1984; Homeowner vacancy rate: 2.4%; Median selected monthly owner costs: $2,355 with a mortgage, $1,035 without a mortgage; Median gross rent: $1,198 per month; Rental vacancy rate: 0.9%
Health Insurance: 96.3% have insurance; 51.4% have private insurance; 52.5% have public insurance; 3.7% do not have insurance; 1.1% of children under 18 do not have insurance
Transportation: Commute: 70.3% car, 12.7% public transportation, 9.7% walk, 5.0% work from home; Mean travel time to work: 33.3 minutes
Additional Information Contacts
Town of Monroe . . . . (845) 783-1900
http://www.monroeny.org

MONROE (village).
Covers a land area of 3.453 square miles and a water area of 0.064 square miles. Located at 41.32° N. Lat; 74.18° W. Long. Elevation is 643 feet.
Population: 8,532; Growth (since 2000): 9.7%; Density: 2,470.6 persons per square mile; Race: 77.8% White, 2.5% Black/African American, 6.2% Asian, 1.1% American Indian/Alaska Native, 0.0% Native Hawaiian/Other Pacific Islander, 3.0% Two or more races, 19.3% Hispanic of any race; Average household size: 3.21; Median age: 35.6; Age under 18: 26.7%; Age 65 and over: 10.4%; Males per 100 females: 102.1; Marriage status: 33.9% never married, 55.7% now married, 0.6% separated, 4.2% widowed, 6.2% divorced; Foreign born: 15.8%; Speak English only: 75.2%; With disability: 9.9%; Veterans: 7.7%; Ancestry: 29.5% Italian, 26.4% Irish, 8.1% German, 7.0% American, 3.8% Polish
Employment: 13.5% management, business, and financial, 4.4% computer, engineering, and science, 14.3% education, legal, community service, arts, and media, 9.6% healthcare practitioners, 16.7% service, 28.0% sales and office, 4.4% natural resources, construction, and maintenance, 8.9% production, transportation, and material moving
Income: Per capita: $42,582; Median household: $106,000; Average household: $130,432; Households with income of $100,000 or more: 54.6%; Poverty rate: 8.9%
Educational Attainment: High school diploma or higher: 92.5%; Bachelor's degree or higher: 43.5%; Graduate/professional degree or higher: 16.7%
School District(s)
Greenwood Lake Union Free SD (KG-08)
    2014-15 Enrollment: 555 . . . . (845) 782-8678
Kiryas Joel Village Union Free SD (PK-KG)
    2014-15 Enrollment: 156 . . . . (845) 782-2300
Monroe-Woodbury Central SD (KG-12)
    2014-15 Enrollment: 6,986 . . . . (845) 460-6200
Four-year College(s)
Uta Mesivta of Kiryas Joel (Private, Not-for-profit, Jewish)
    Fall 2014 Enrollment: 1,634 . . . . (845) 783-9901
    2015-16 Tuition: In-state $9,800; Out-of-state $9,800
Housing: Homeownership rate: 79.7%; Median home value: $308,100; Median year structure built: 1975; Homeowner vacancy rate: 1.5%; Median selected monthly owner costs: $2,489 with a mortgage, $1,156 without a mortgage; Median gross rent: $1,481 per month; Rental vacancy rate: 3.9%
Health Insurance: 93.3% have insurance; 79.7% have private insurance; 23.3% have public insurance; 6.7% do not have insurance; 1.6% of children under 18 do not have insurance
Safety: Violent crime rate: 4.6 per 10,000 population; Property crime rate: 183.6 per 10,000 population
Transportation: Commute: 79.6% car, 8.6% public transportation, 2.3% walk, 4.2% work from home; Mean travel time to work: 34.9 minutes
Additional Information Contacts
Village of Monroe . . . . (845) 782-8341
http://www.villageofmonroe.org

MONTGOMERY (town). Covers a land area of 50.256 square miles and a water area of 0.933 square miles. Located at 41.54° N. Lat; 74.21° W. Long. Elevation is 358 feet.
Population: 23,194; Growth (since 2000): 11.0%; Density: 461.5 persons per square mile; Race: 84.0% White, 4.8% Black/African American, 1.3% Asian, 0.0% American Indian/Alaska Native, 0.1% Native Hawaiian/Other Pacific Islander, 2.3% Two or more races, 14.5% Hispanic of any race; Average household size: 2.82; Median age: 38.7; Age under 18: 23.4%; Age 65 and over: 12.7%; Males per 100 females: 94.9; Marriage status: 31.5% never married, 52.6% now married, 1.6% separated, 5.9% widowed, 10.0% divorced; Foreign born: 7.4%; Speak English only: 85.5%; With disability: 11.4%; Veterans: 7.7%; Ancestry: 21.7% Irish, 18.9% Italian, 14.8% German, 13.3% American, 6.6% English
Employment: 11.3% management, business, and financial, 4.7% computer, engineering, and science, 15.3% education, legal, community service, arts, and media, 5.0% healthcare practitioners, 16.5% service, 25.3% sales and office, 9.4% natural resources, construction, and maintenance, 12.4% production, transportation, and material moving
Income: Per capita: $32,173; Median household: $71,655; Average household: $88,737; Households with income of $100,000 or more: 34.8%; Poverty rate: 8.1%
Educational Attainment: High school diploma or higher: 90.8%; Bachelor's degree or higher: 27.4%; Graduate/professional degree or higher: 11.9%
School District(s)
Valley Central SD (Montgomery) (KG-12)
    2014-15 Enrollment: 4,464 . . . . (845) 457-2400
Housing: Homeownership rate: 70.2%; Median home value: $228,700; Median year structure built: 1974; Homeowner vacancy rate: 3.0%; Median selected monthly owner costs: $2,110 with a mortgage, $766 without a mortgage; Median gross rent: $1,103 per month; Rental vacancy rate: 4.8%
Health Insurance: 92.9% have insurance; 77.5% have private insurance; 28.0% have public insurance; 7.1% do not have insurance; 2.2% of children under 18 do not have insurance
Safety: Violent crime rate: 11.1 per 10,000 population; Property crime rate: 61.3 per 10,000 population
Transportation: Commute: 89.5% car, 3.9% public transportation, 3.3% walk, 2.4% work from home; Mean travel time to work: 32.8 minutes
Airports: Orange County (general aviation)
Additional Information Contacts
Town of Montgomery. . . . . (845) 457-2660
   http://www.townofmontgomery.com

MONTGOMERY (village). Covers a land area of 1.406 square miles and a water area of 0.042 square miles. Located at 41.52° N. Lat; 74.24° W. Long. Elevation is 358 feet.
Population: 4,311; Growth (since 2000): 18.6%; Density: 3,066.9 persons per square mile; Race: 93.1% White, 1.2% Black/African American, 0.8% Asian, 0.0% American Indian/Alaska Native, 0.5% Native Hawaiian/Other Pacific Islander, 0.7% Two or more races, 18.4% Hispanic of any race; Average household size: 2.74; Median age: 42.0; Age under 18: 25.0%; Age 65 and over: 16.8%; Males per 100 females: 91.9; Marriage status: 20.9% never married, 62.9% now married, 1.2% separated, 6.5% widowed, 9.8% divorced; Foreign born: 3.8%; Speak English only: 86.5%; With disability: 12.8%; Veterans: 8.6%; Ancestry: 27.4% Irish, 21.6% Italian, 15.9% German, 15.8% American, 7.6% English
Employment: 12.7% management, business, and financial, 5.9% computer, engineering, and science, 17.5% education, legal, community service, arts, and media, 8.1% healthcare practitioners, 15.6% service, 18.7% sales and office, 12.5% natural resources, construction, and maintenance, 9.1% production, transportation, and material moving
Income: Per capita: $33,586; Median household: $77,907; Average household: $89,466; Households with income of $100,000 or more: 38.7%; Poverty rate: 4.3%
Educational Attainment: High school diploma or higher: 90.0%; Bachelor's degree or higher: 29.2%; Graduate/professional degree or higher: 12.5%
School District(s)
Valley Central SD (Montgomery) (KG-12)
    2014-15 Enrollment: 4,464 . . . . (845) 457-2400
Housing: Homeownership rate: 64.4%; Median home value: $234,900; Median year structure built: 1983; Homeowner vacancy rate: 0.0%; Median selected monthly owner costs: $1,948 with a mortgage, $909 without a

mortgage; Median gross rent: $1,102 per month; Rental vacancy rate: 9.4%
Health Insurance: 95.9% have insurance; 83.3% have private insurance; 28.6% have public insurance; 4.1% do not have insurance; 0.0% of children under 18 do not have insurance
Safety: Violent crime rate: 6.2 per 10,000 population; Property crime rate: 43.4 per 10,000 population
Transportation: Commute: 92.8% car, 2.2% public transportation, 0.7% walk, 1.7% work from home; Mean travel time to work: 35.8 minutes
Airports: Orange County (general aviation)

MOUNT HOPE (town). Covers a land area of 25.134 square miles and a water area of 0.362 square miles. Located at 41.46° N. Lat; 74.53° W. Long. Elevation is 823 feet.
Population: 7,000; Growth (since 2000): 5.4%; Density: 278.5 persons per square mile; Race: 71.2% White, 18.7% Black/African American, 1.5% Asian, 0.1% American Indian/Alaska Native, 0.0% Native Hawaiian/Other Pacific Islander, 3.2% Two or more races, 16.0% Hispanic of any race; Average household size: 3.01; Median age: 41.4; Age under 18: 17.4%; Age 65 and over: 8.9%; Males per 100 females: 165.2; Marriage status: 37.2% never married, 49.5% now married, 3.6% separated, 2.8% widowed, 10.5% divorced; Foreign born: 7.3%; Speak English only: 84.4%; With disability: 12.4%; Veterans: 6.6%; Ancestry: 20.5% Irish, 16.3% Italian, 10.9% American, 9.8% German, 8.0% English
Employment: 9.6% management, business, and financial, 3.3% computer, engineering, and science, 11.5% education, legal, community service, arts, and media, 5.7% healthcare practitioners, 26.1% service, 21.1% sales and office, 13.4% natural resources, construction, and maintenance, 9.3% production, transportation, and material moving
Income: Per capita: $22,936; Median household: $77,845; Average household: $85,894; Households with income of $100,000 or more: 37.6%; Poverty rate: 11.0%
Educational Attainment: High school diploma or higher: 89.7%; Bachelor's degree or higher: 19.9%; Graduate/professional degree or higher: 7.1%
Housing: Homeownership rate: 86.4%; Median home value: $250,200; Median year structure built: 1974; Homeowner vacancy rate: 2.9%; Median selected monthly owner costs: $2,138 with a mortgage, $888 without a mortgage; Median gross rent: $1,578 per month; Rental vacancy rate: 6.0%
Health Insurance: 93.7% have insurance; 79.9% have private insurance; 27.0% have public insurance; 6.3% do not have insurance; 4.8% of children under 18 do not have insurance
Safety: Violent crime rate: 1.4 per 10,000 population; Property crime rate: 62.0 per 10,000 population
Transportation: Commute: 93.2% car, 2.5% public transportation, 0.1% walk, 3.2% work from home; Mean travel time to work: 40.9 minutes
Additional Information Contacts
Town of Mount Hope . . . . (845) 386-1460
   http://townofmounthope.org/content

MOUNTAIN LODGE PARK (CDP). Covers a land area of 1.185 square miles and a water area of <.001 square miles. Located at 41.39° N. Lat; 74.14° W. Long. Elevation is 784 feet.
Population: 1,639; Growth (since 2000): n/a; Density: 1,383.0 persons per square mile; Race: 88.0% White, 3.5% Black/African American, 0.0% Asian, 0.0% American Indian/Alaska Native, 0.0% Native Hawaiian/Other Pacific Islander, 4.8% Two or more races, 13.6% Hispanic of any race; Average household size: 2.67; Median age: 43.0; Age under 18: 22.0%; Age 65 and over: 9.2%; Males per 100 females: 100.3; Marriage status: 35.5% never married, 49.8% now married, 0.6% separated, 2.8% widowed, 11.8% divorced; Foreign born: 0.7%; Speak English only: 94.1%; With disability: 19.2%; Veterans: 7.4%; Ancestry: 32.6% Irish, 25.8% German, 23.9% Italian, 18.4% American, 8.1% English
Employment: 9.3% management, business, and financial, 9.2% computer, engineering, and science, 7.0% education, legal, community service, arts, and media, 5.8% healthcare practitioners, 24.7% service, 19.8% sales and office, 10.4% natural resources, construction, and maintenance, 13.7% production, transportation, and material moving
Income: Per capita: $35,992; Median household: $86,902; Average household: $93,627; Households with income of $100,000 or more: 38.5%; Poverty rate: 1.1%
Educational Attainment: High school diploma or higher: 86.1%; Bachelor's degree or higher: 16.0%; Graduate/professional degree or higher: 4.1%

Housing: Homeownership rate: 93.3%; Median home value: $200,000; Median year structure built: 1950; Homeowner vacancy rate: 7.2%; Median selected monthly owner costs: n/a with a mortgage, n/a without a mortgage; Median gross rent: n/a per month; Rental vacancy rate: 53.9%
Health Insurance: 91.0% have insurance; 72.9% have private insurance; 28.1% have public insurance; 9.0% do not have insurance; 8.9% of children under 18 do not have insurance
Transportation: Commute: 94.5% car, 4.4% public transportation, 0.0% walk, 1.1% work from home; Mean travel time to work: 40.1 minutes

MOUNTAINVILLE (unincorporated postal area)
ZCTA: 10953

Covers a land area of 1.102 square miles and a water area of 0.013 square miles. Located at 41.40° N. Lat; 74.08° W. Long. Elevation is 299 feet.
Population: 102; Growth (since 2000): n/a; Density: 92.6 persons per square mile; Race: 92.2% White, 0.0% Black/African American, 0.0% Asian, 0.0% American Indian/Alaska Native, 0.0% Native Hawaiian/Other Pacific Islander, 0.0% Two or more races, 7.8% Hispanic of any race; Average household size: 2.04; Median age: 61.7; Age under 18: 7.8%; Age 65 and over: 48.0%; Males per 100 females: 121.1; Marriage status: 7.4% never married, 92.6% now married, 0.0% separated, 0.0% widowed, 0.0% divorced; Foreign born: 0.0%; Speak English only: 92.2%; With disability: 30.4%; Veterans: 25.5%; Ancestry: 34.3% English, 34.3% Italian, 25.5% Irish, 24.5% Swedish, 23.5% Dutch
Employment: 0.0% management, business, and financial, 0.0% computer, engineering, and science, 20.6% education, legal, community service, arts, and media, 0.0% healthcare practitioners, 23.5% service, 35.3% sales and office, 0.0% natural resources, construction, and maintenance, 20.6% production, transportation, and material moving
Income: Per capita: $56,896; Median household: $123,600; Average household: $114,150; Households with income of $100,000 or more: 72.0%; Poverty rate: n/a
Educational Attainment: High school diploma or higher: 100.0%; Bachelor's degree or higher: 41.5%; Graduate/professional degree or higher: 34.0%
Housing: Homeownership rate: 100.0%; Median home value: n/a; Median year structure built: 1975; Homeowner vacancy rate: 0.0%; Median selected monthly owner costs: $3,250 with a mortgage, $0 without a mortgage; Median gross rent: n/a per month; Rental vacancy rate: 0.0%
Health Insurance: 100.0% have insurance; 100.0% have private insurance; 48.0% have public insurance; 0.0% do not have insurance; 0.0% of children under 18 do not have insurance
Transportation: Commute: 100.0% car, 0.0% public transportation, 0.0% walk, 0.0% work from home; Mean travel time to work: 0.0 minutes

NEW HAMPTON (unincorporated postal area)
ZCTA: 10958

Covers a land area of 22.866 square miles and a water area of 0.139 square miles. Located at 41.37° N. Lat; 74.43° W. Long. Elevation is 538 feet.
Population: 2,899; Growth (since 2000): -2.3%; Density: 126.8 persons per square mile; Race: 86.3% White, 9.1% Black/African American, 1.5% Asian, 0.0% American Indian/Alaska Native, 0.0% Native Hawaiian/Other Pacific Islander, 0.3% Two or more races, 10.0% Hispanic of any race; Average household size: 2.78; Median age: 44.8; Age under 18: 15.9%; Age 65 and over: 13.0%; Males per 100 females: 112.5; Marriage status: 33.8% never married, 51.7% now married, 0.8% separated, 4.6% widowed, 9.9% divorced; Foreign born: 8.4%; Speak English only: 92.7%; With disability: 14.8%; Veterans: 11.6%; Ancestry: 21.4% American, 20.5% Irish, 15.4% German, 13.9% Italian, 9.1% Polish
Employment: 13.4% management, business, and financial, 1.8% computer, engineering, and science, 12.8% education, legal, community service, arts, and media, 3.3% healthcare practitioners, 16.9% service, 23.6% sales and office, 12.0% natural resources, construction, and maintenance, 16.1% production, transportation, and material moving
Income: Per capita: $30,996; Median household: $103,203; Average household: $98,481; Households with income of $100,000 or more: 50.6%; Poverty rate: 5.1%
Educational Attainment: High school diploma or higher: 87.5%; Bachelor's degree or higher: 27.0%; Graduate/professional degree or higher: 11.2%

Housing: Homeownership rate: 84.6%; Median home value: $286,300; Median year structure built: 1967; Homeowner vacancy rate: 0.0%; Median selected monthly owner costs: $2,248 with a mortgage, $864 without a mortgage; Median gross rent: $1,008 per month; Rental vacancy rate: 10.1%
Health Insurance: 95.0% have insurance; 81.4% have private insurance; 23.6% have public insurance; 5.0% do not have insurance; 0.0% of children under 18 do not have insurance
Transportation: Commute: 96.1% car, 0.6% public transportation, 1.2% walk, 1.5% work from home; Mean travel time to work: 29.1 minutes

NEW WINDSOR (CDP). Covers a land area of 3.762 square miles and a water area of 0.042 square miles. Located at 41.47° N. Lat; 74.03° W. Long. Elevation is 161 feet.
Population: 8,691; Growth (since 2000): -4.3%; Density: 2,310.5 persons per square mile; Race: 70.1% White, 11.7% Black/African American, 1.1% Asian, 0.0% American Indian/Alaska Native, 0.0% Native Hawaiian/Other Pacific Islander, 6.1% Two or more races, 28.7% Hispanic of any race; Average household size: 2.51; Median age: 42.4; Age under 18: 19.6%; Age 65 and over: 16.1%; Males per 100 females: 95.3; Marriage status: 34.1% never married, 51.2% now married, 2.9% separated, 4.5% widowed, 10.2% divorced; Foreign born: 11.5%; Speak English only: 73.8%; With disability: 11.3%; Veterans: 9.9%; Ancestry: 15.7% Italian, 15.5% Irish, 9.0% German, 8.1% American, 4.3% English
Employment: 9.6% management, business, and financial, 1.8% computer, engineering, and science, 11.3% education, legal, community service, arts, and media, 6.8% healthcare practitioners, 19.9% service, 28.1% sales and office, 8.0% natural resources, construction, and maintenance, 14.5% production, transportation, and material moving
Income: Per capita: $32,180; Median household: $66,443; Average household: $78,899; Households with income of $100,000 or more: 25.9%; Poverty rate: 5.3%
Educational Attainment: High school diploma or higher: 86.7%; Bachelor's degree or higher: 22.9%; Graduate/professional degree or higher: 8.5%

School District(s)
Cornwall Central SD (KG-12)
 2014-15 Enrollment: 3,259 . . . . (845) 534-8009
Newburgh City SD (PK-12)
 2014-15 Enrollment: 11,648 . . . . (845) 563-3510
Washingtonville Central SD (PK-12)
 2014-15 Enrollment: 4,286 . . . . (845) 497-4000
Housing: Homeownership rate: 70.4%; Median home value: $227,000; Median year structure built: 1963; Homeowner vacancy rate: 4.8%; Median selected monthly owner costs: $2,191 with a mortgage, $797 without a mortgage; Median gross rent: $1,097 per month; Rental vacancy rate: 3.3%
Health Insurance: 90.6% have insurance; 70.8% have private insurance; 32.3% have public insurance; 9.4% do not have insurance; 0.0% of children under 18 do not have insurance
Newspapers: The Sentinel (weekly circulation 6,000)
Transportation: Commute: 92.2% car, 4.7% public transportation, 0.5% walk, 1.8% work from home; Mean travel time to work: 34.5 minutes

NEW WINDSOR (town). Covers a land area of 34.070 square miles and a water area of 2.994 square miles. Located at 41.47° N. Lat; 74.11° W. Long. Elevation is 161 feet.
History: Was home of George Clinton. De Witt Clinton was born here.
Population: 25,959; Growth (since 2000): 13.5%; Density: 761.9 persons per square mile; Race: 68.8% White, 13.9% Black/African American, 4.8% Asian, 0.0% American Indian/Alaska Native, 0.0% Native Hawaiian/Other Pacific Islander, 4.8% Two or more races, 21.5% Hispanic of any race; Average household size: 2.74; Median age: 39.6; Age under 18: 22.6%; Age 65 and over: 13.3%; Males per 100 females: 95.4; Marriage status: 33.3% never married, 52.3% now married, 2.2% separated, 5.2% widowed, 9.2% divorced; Foreign born: 12.4%; Speak English only: 75.4%; With disability: 12.1%; Veterans: 9.1%; Ancestry: 19.8% Irish, 16.9% Italian, 9.8% German, 9.0% American, 3.5% Polish
Employment: 12.5% management, business, and financial, 3.2% computer, engineering, and science, 11.6% education, legal, community service, arts, and media, 7.4% healthcare practitioners, 18.9% service, 27.5% sales and office, 7.9% natural resources, construction, and maintenance, 11.0% production, transportation, and material moving

Income: Per capita: $32,888; Median household: $69,916; Average household: $88,326; Households with income of $100,000 or more: 33.6%; Poverty rate: 4.4%

Educational Attainment: High school diploma or higher: 91.1%; Bachelor's degree or higher: 29.9%; Graduate/professional degree or higher: 11.7%

School District(s)

Cornwall Central SD (KG-12)

   2014-15 Enrollment: 3,259 . . . . (845) 534-8009

Newburgh City SD (PK-12)

   2014-15 Enrollment: 11,648 . . . . (845) 563-3510

Washingtonville Central SD (PK-12)

   2014-15 Enrollment: 4,286 . . . . (845) 497-4000

Housing: Homeownership rate: 73.3%; Median home value: $250,200; Median year structure built: 1974; Homeowner vacancy rate: 3.9%; Median selected monthly owner costs: $2,354 with a mortgage, $830 without a mortgage; Median gross rent: $1,167 per month; Rental vacancy rate: 2.1%

Health Insurance: 91.5% have insurance; 73.6% have private insurance; 28.6% have public insurance; 8.5% do not have insurance; 1.3% of children under 18 do not have insurance

Safety: Violent crime rate: 13.2 per 10,000 population; Property crime rate: 166.4 per 10,000 population

Newspapers: The Sentinel (weekly circulation 6,000)

Transportation: Commute: 86.3% car, 6.6% public transportation, 2.6% walk, 3.3% work from home; Mean travel time to work: 36.6 minutes

Additional Information Contacts

Town of New Windsor . . . . (845) 563-4611
   http://town.new-windsor.ny.us

NEWBURGH (city).

Covers a land area of 3.804 square miles and a water area of 0.980 square miles. Located at 41.50° N. Lat; 74.02° W. Long. Elevation is 131 feet.

History: Has many old houses, and the streets run sharply to the river. At Hasbrouck House (1750; now a Museum), Washington made his headquarters from April 1782 to Aug. 1783. It was in Newburgh that the Continental Army was disbanded. Mt. St. Mary College is in the city. West Point is located a few miles to the south. Settled 1709 by Palatines; Incorporated 1800.

Population: 28,495; Growth (since 2000): 0.8%; Density: 7,490.2 persons per square mile; Race: 37.3% White, 29.2% Black/African American, 0.6% Asian, 1.0% American Indian/Alaska Native, 0.0% Native Hawaiian/Other Pacific Islander, 3.8% Two or more races, 51.7% Hispanic of any race; Average household size: 3.18; Median age: 27.3; Age under 18: 33.7%; Age 65 and over: 7.8%; Males per 100 females: 94.6; Marriage status: 49.7% never married, 37.7% now married, 4.7% separated, 5.3% widowed, 7.3% divorced; Foreign born: 24.8%; Speak English only: 52.4%; With disability: 13.0%; Veterans: 4.3%; Ancestry: 11.3% American, 6.7% Italian, 5.8% Irish, 3.5% German, 3.3% Jamaican

Employment: 8.9% management, business, and financial, 2.1% computer, engineering, and science, 6.4% education, legal, community service, arts, and media, 2.6% healthcare practitioners, 26.3% service, 22.8% sales and office, 10.7% natural resources, construction, and maintenance, 20.2% production, transportation, and material moving

Income: Per capita: $16,126; Median household: $34,348; Average household: $49,899; Households with income of $100,000 or more: 13.5%; Poverty rate: 34.2%

Educational Attainment: High school diploma or higher: 70.1%; Bachelor's degree or higher: 11.7%; Graduate/professional degree or higher: 4.7%

School District(s)

Marlboro Central SD (KG-12)

   2014-15 Enrollment: 1,972 . . . . (845) 236-5802

Newburgh City SD (PK-12)

   2014-15 Enrollment: 11,648 . . . . (845) 563-3510

Valley Central SD (Montgomery) (KG-12)

   2014-15 Enrollment: 4,464 . . . . (845) 457-2400

Four-year College(s)

Mount Saint Mary College (Private, Not-for-profit, Roman Catholic)

   Fall 2014 Enrollment: 2,479 . . . . (845) 561-0800

   2015-16 Tuition: In-state $28,233; Out-of-state $28,233

Housing: Homeownership rate: 32.3%; Median home value: $165,800; Median year structure built: Before 1940; Homeowner vacancy rate: 7.7%; Median selected monthly owner costs: $1,960 with a mortgage, $756

without a mortgage; Median gross rent: $1,081 per month; Rental vacancy rate: 8.4%

Health Insurance: 79.9% have insurance; 42.8% have private insurance; 44.4% have public insurance; 20.1% do not have insurance; 7.3% of children under 18 do not have insurance

Hospitals: Saint Luke's Cornwall Hospital (259 beds)

Safety: Violent crime rate: 146.7 per 10,000 population; Property crime rate: 282.0 per 10,000 population

Newspapers: Times Community Newspapers (weekly circulation 8,000)

Transportation: Commute: 71.1% car, 6.5% public transportation, 9.6% walk, 2.8% work from home; Mean travel time to work: 24.0 minutes

Airports: Stewart International (primary service/non-hub)

Additional Information Contacts

City of Newburgh . . . . (845) 569-7311
   http://www.cityofnewburgh-ny.gov

NEWBURGH (town).

Covers a land area of 42.678 square miles and a water area of 4.265 square miles. Located at 41.56° N. Lat; 74.06° W. Long. Elevation is 131 feet.

Population: 30,664; Growth (since 2000): 11.2%; Density: 718.5 persons per square mile; Race: 76.9% White, 10.1% Black/African American, 2.3% Asian, 0.0% American Indian/Alaska Native, 0.0% Native Hawaiian/Other Pacific Islander, 4.0% Two or more races, 18.6% Hispanic of any race; Average household size: 2.82; Median age: 41.2; Age under 18: 22.5%; Age 65 and over: 14.7%; Males per 100 females: 95.7; Marriage status: 30.0% never married, 54.4% now married, 1.9% separated, 5.8% widowed, 9.8% divorced; Foreign born: 9.3%; Speak English only: 80.0%; With disability: 11.3%; Veterans: 8.4%; Ancestry: 25.4% Italian, 19.4% Irish, 11.3% German, 9.8% American, 7.2% English

Employment: 13.9% management, business, and financial, 4.5% computer, engineering, and science, 11.7% education, legal, community service, arts, and media, 5.4% healthcare practitioners, 20.1% service, 26.0% sales and office, 9.7% natural resources, construction, and maintenance, 8.7% production, transportation, and material moving

Income: Per capita: $34,628; Median household: $79,654; Average household: $95,188; Households with income of $100,000 or more: 37.7%; Poverty rate: 6.4%

Educational Attainment: High school diploma or higher: 91.1%; Bachelor's degree or higher: 29.2%; Graduate/professional degree or higher: 12.1%

School District(s)

Marlboro Central SD (KG-12)

   2014-15 Enrollment: 1,972 . . . . (845) 236-5802

Newburgh City SD (PK-12)

   2014-15 Enrollment: 11,648 . . . . (845) 563-3510

Valley Central SD (Montgomery) (KG-12)

   2014-15 Enrollment: 4,464 . . . . (845) 457-2400

Four-year College(s)

Mount Saint Mary College (Private, Not-for-profit, Roman Catholic)

   Fall 2014 Enrollment: 2,479 . . . . (845) 561-0800

   2015-16 Tuition: In-state $28,233; Out-of-state $28,233

Housing: Homeownership rate: 81.4%; Median home value: $252,500; Median year structure built: 1969; Homeowner vacancy rate: 1.6%; Median selected monthly owner costs: $2,273 with a mortgage, $783 without a mortgage; Median gross rent: $1,296 per month; Rental vacancy rate: 8.9%

Health Insurance: 92.4% have insurance; 77.8% have private insurance; 27.4% have public insurance; 7.6% do not have insurance; 3.6% of children under 18 do not have insurance

Hospitals: Saint Luke's Cornwall Hospital (259 beds)

Safety: Violent crime rate: 9.7 per 10,000 population; Property crime rate: 337.0 per 10,000 population

Newspapers: Times Community Newspapers (weekly circulation 8,000)

Transportation: Commute: 90.7% car, 5.0% public transportation, 0.5% walk, 3.4% work from home; Mean travel time to work: 30.7 minutes

Airports: Stewart International (primary service/non-hub)

Additional Information Contacts

Town of Newburgh . . . . (845) 564-4554
   http://www.townofnewburgh.org

ORANGE LAKE (CDP).

Covers a land area of 6.044 square miles and a water area of 0.656 square miles. Located at 41.54° N. Lat; 74.09° W. Long. Elevation is 492 feet.

Population: 6,718; Growth (since 2000): 10.4%; Density: 1,111.5 persons per square mile; Race: 71.5% White, 11.0% Black/African American, 4.9%

Asian, 0.2% American Indian/Alaska Native, 0.0% Native Hawaiian/Other Pacific Islander, 3.5% Two or more races, 22.2% Hispanic of any race; Average household size: 2.73; Median age: 43.3; Age under 18: 18.8%; Age 65 and over: 19.8%; Males per 100 females: 93.4; Marriage status: 29.5% never married, 54.4% now married, 1.5% separated, 7.6% widowed, 8.5% divorced; Foreign born: 10.7%; Speak English only: 75.0%; With disability: 10.8%; Veterans: 7.3%; Ancestry: 29.1% Italian, 21.3% Irish, 9.0% German, 5.7% American, 3.8% English

Employment: 16.4% management, business, and financial, 1.3% computer, engineering, and science, 13.6% education, legal, community service, arts, and media, 7.3% healthcare practitioners, 23.4% service, 23.7% sales and office, 7.6% natural resources, construction, and maintenance, 6.7% production, transportation, and material moving

Income: Per capita: $38,915; Median household: $93,590; Average household: $104,704; Households with income of $100,000 or more: 46.7%; Poverty rate: 8.3%

Educational Attainment: High school diploma or higher: 90.0%; Bachelor's degree or higher: 28.8%; Graduate/professional degree or higher: 11.4%

Housing: Homeownership rate: 84.7%; Median home value: $256,300; Median year structure built: 1972; Homeowner vacancy rate: 2.2%; Median selected monthly owner costs: $2,241 with a mortgage, $671 without a mortgage; Median gross rent: $1,497 per month; Rental vacancy rate: 11.8%

Health Insurance: 95.0% have insurance; 79.8% have private insurance; 29.6% have public insurance; 5.0% do not have insurance; 0.0% of children under 18 do not have insurance

Transportation: Commute: 87.7% car, 6.9% public transportation, 0.0% walk, 5.2% work from home; Mean travel time to work: 34.5 minutes

OTISVILLE (village).

Covers a land area of 0.764 square miles and a water area of 0 square miles. Located at 41.47° N. Lat; 74.54° W. Long. Elevation is 853 feet.

Population: 1,110; Growth (since 2000): 12.2%; Density: 1,452.6 persons per square mile; Race: 77.7% White, 5.5% Black/African American, 4.0% Asian, 0.0% American Indian/Alaska Native, 0.0% Native Hawaiian/Other Pacific Islander, 4.4% Two or more races, 18.6% Hispanic of any race; Average household size: 2.87; Median age: 41.1; Age under 18: 24.0%; Age 65 and over: 10.5%; Males per 100 females: 106.6; Marriage status: 26.6% never married, 60.5% now married, 2.8% separated, 2.4% widowed, 10.5% divorced; Foreign born: 5.0%; Speak English only: 84.4%; With disability: 14.6%; Veterans: 9.2%; Ancestry: 26.4% Irish, 15.4% American, 14.1% Italian, 8.5% English, 7.6% Polish

Employment: 10.8% management, business, and financial, 5.1% computer, engineering, and science, 11.7% education, legal, community service, arts, and media, 5.6% healthcare practitioners, 16.1% service, 25.9% sales and office, 12.4% natural resources, construction, and maintenance, 12.4% production, transportation, and material moving

Income: Per capita: $34,144; Median household: $83,162; Average household: $94,296; Households with income of $100,000 or more: 40.8%; Poverty rate: 6.7%

Educational Attainment: High school diploma or higher: 89.2%; Bachelor's degree or higher: 22.7%; Graduate/professional degree or higher: 11.6%

School District(s)

Minisink Valley Central SD (KG-12)
    2014-15 Enrollment: 3,992 . . . . (845) 355-5100

Housing: Homeownership rate: 80.4%; Median home value: $203,700; Median year structure built: Before 1940; Homeowner vacancy rate: 0.0%; Median selected monthly owner costs: $2,033 with a mortgage, $697 without a mortgage; Median gross rent: $1,260 per month; Rental vacancy rate: 9.5%

Health Insurance: 90.4% have insurance; 83.7% have private insurance; 20.4% have public insurance; 9.6% do not have insurance; 10.9% of children under 18 do not have insurance

Transportation: Commute: 92.0% car, 2.4% public transportation, 0.6% walk, 5.0% work from home; Mean travel time to work: 34.8 minutes

Additional Information Contacts

Village of Otisville . . . . (845) 386-5172
    http://villageofotisville.com

PINE BUSH (CDP).

Covers a land area of 2.106 square miles and a water area of 0.003 square miles. Located at 41.61° N. Lat; 74.30° W. Long. Elevation is 387 feet.

Population: 1,514; Growth (since 2000): -1.6%; Density: 718.8 persons per square mile; Race: 89.4% White, 5.4% Black/African American, 0.0% Asian, 0.0% American Indian/Alaska Native, 0.0% Native Hawaiian/Other Pacific Islander, 1.3% Two or more races, 6.7% Hispanic of any race; Average household size: 1.98; Median age: 53.6; Age under 18: 12.8%; Age 65 and over: 30.6%; Males per 100 females: 81.8; Marriage status: 30.8% never married, 45.6% now married, 2.1% separated, 8.8% widowed, 14.8% divorced; Foreign born: 2.7%; Speak English only: 88.8%; With disability: 25.1%; Veterans: 10.0%; Ancestry: 25.3% Italian, 24.6% Irish, 18.0% American, 14.3% German, 8.7% English

Employment: 7.0% management, business, and financial, 0.0% computer, engineering, and science, 34.3% education, legal, community service, arts, and media, 5.6% healthcare practitioners, 13.7% service, 23.7% sales and office, 4.6% natural resources, construction, and maintenance, 11.0% production, transportation, and material moving

Income: Per capita: $27,293; Median household: $38,405; Average household: $53,763; Households with income of $100,000 or more: 19.1%; Poverty rate: 11.3%

Educational Attainment: High school diploma or higher: 89.8%; Bachelor's degree or higher: 30.8%; Graduate/professional degree or higher: 14.0%

School District(s)

Pine Bush Central SD (PK-12)
    2014-15 Enrollment: 5,487 . . . . (845) 744-2031

Housing: Homeownership rate: 52.5%; Median home value: $211,400; Median year structure built: 1976; Homeowner vacancy rate: 0.0%; Median selected monthly owner costs: $1,592 with a mortgage, $725 without a mortgage; Median gross rent: $719 per month; Rental vacancy rate: 5.8%

Health Insurance: 98.1% have insurance; 77.0% have private insurance; 39.8% have public insurance; 1.9% do not have insurance; 5.2% of children under 18 do not have insurance

Transportation: Commute: 86.0% car, 2.6% public transportation, 5.6% walk, 5.9% work from home; Mean travel time to work: 24.3 minutes

PINE ISLAND (unincorporated postal area)

ZCTA: 10969

Covers a land area of 11.221 square miles and a water area of 0.008 square miles. Located at 41.29° N. Lat; 74.49° W. Long. Elevation is 410 feet.

Population: 1,717; Growth (since 2000): 58.4%; Density: 153.0 persons per square mile; Race: 76.0% White, 0.0% Black/African American, 0.0% Asian, 0.0% American Indian/Alaska Native, 0.0% Native Hawaiian/Other Pacific Islander, 2.3% Two or more races, 25.9% Hispanic of any race; Average household size: 3.19; Median age: 41.8; Age under 18: 18.8%; Age 65 and over: 8.0%; Males per 100 females: 106.4; Marriage status: 41.4% never married, 51.6% now married, 2.4% separated, 2.3% widowed, 4.7% divorced; Foreign born: 18.8%; Speak English only: 77.3%; With disability: 8.9%; Veterans: 3.0%; Ancestry: 16.5% Polish, 15.0% American, 13.6% German, 13.5% Italian, 12.2% Irish

Employment: 7.0% management, business, and financial, 5.0% computer, engineering, and science, 6.2% education, legal, community service, arts, and media, 4.8% healthcare practitioners, 32.7% service, 27.2% sales and office, 8.5% natural resources, construction, and maintenance, 8.6% production, transportation, and material moving

Income: Per capita: $41,786; Median household: $92,500; Average household: $124,710; Households with income of $100,000 or more: 48.5%; Poverty rate: 0.5%

Educational Attainment: High school diploma or higher: 90.3%; Bachelor's degree or higher: 19.4%; Graduate/professional degree or higher: 5.7%

Housing: Homeownership rate: 63.0%; Median home value: $306,500; Median year structure built: 1960; Homeowner vacancy rate: 0.0%; Median selected monthly owner costs: $2,380 with a mortgage, $747 without a mortgage; Median gross rent: $2,092 per month; Rental vacancy rate: 0.0%

Health Insurance: 74.6% have insurance; 64.4% have private insurance; 14.0% have public insurance; 25.4% do not have insurance; 17.0% of children under 18 do not have insurance

Transportation: Commute: 65.2% car, 5.9% public transportation, 22.2% walk, 6.8% work from home; Mean travel time to work: 36.6 minutes

PORT JERVIS (city).
Covers a land area of 2.529 square miles and a water area of 0.180 square miles. Located at 41.38° N. Lat; 74.69° W. Long. Elevation is 440 feet.

History: Grew after opening (1828) of Delaware and Hudson Canal. It is one of the largest equestrian centers in nation. Settled before 1700, Incorporated 1907.

Population: 8,681; Growth (since 2000): -2.0%; Density: 3,432.6 persons per square mile; Race: 74.9% White, 11.1% Black/African American, 2.6% Asian, 0.2% American Indian/Alaska Native, 0.0% Native Hawaiian/Other Pacific Islander, 8.5% Two or more races, 9.2% Hispanic of any race; Average household size: 2.51; Median age: 39.5; Age under 18: 25.1%; Age 65 and over: 14.8%; Males per 100 females: 92.9; Marriage status: 34.8% never married, 42.8% now married, 3.2% separated, 11.3% widowed, 11.2% divorced; Foreign born: 6.2%; Speak English only: 91.6%; With disability: 18.4%; Veterans: 9.7%; Ancestry: 20.2% American, 15.2% Irish, 14.0% German, 11.6% Italian, 6.3% Polish

Employment: 8.2% management, business, and financial, 2.7% computer, engineering, and science, 6.1% education, legal, community service, arts, and media, 5.8% healthcare practitioners, 26.2% service, 26.4% sales and office, 6.7% natural resources, construction, and maintenance, 17.8% production, transportation, and material moving

Income: Per capita: $23,004; Median household: $41,682; Average household: $56,464; Households with income of $100,000 or more: 15.3%; Poverty rate: 17.2%

Educational Attainment: High school diploma or higher: 83.2%; Bachelor's degree or higher: 17.6%; Graduate/professional degree or higher: 5.1%

School District(s)
Port Jervis City SD (KG-12)
    2014-15 Enrollment: 2,832 . . . . (845) 858-3100

Housing: Homeownership rate: 50.7%; Median home value: $162,600; Median year structure built: Before 1940; Homeowner vacancy rate: 2.5%; Median selected monthly owner costs: $1,517 with a mortgage, $767 without a mortgage; Median gross rent: $932 per month; Rental vacancy rate: 4.1%

Health Insurance: 89.1% have insurance; 59.3% have private insurance; 40.5% have public insurance; 10.9% do not have insurance; 4.7% of children under 18 do not have insurance

Hospitals: Bon Secours Community Hospital (183 beds)

Safety: Violent crime rate: 39.6 per 10,000 population; Property crime rate: 294.5 per 10,000 population

Transportation: Commute: 77.7% car, 1.5% public transportation, 8.6% walk, 7.4% work from home; Mean travel time to work: 24.3 minutes

Additional Information Contacts
City of Port Jervis . . . . (845) 858-4000
    http://portjervisny.org

ROCK TAVERN (unincorporated postal area)
ZCTA: 12575

Covers a land area of 9.893 square miles and a water area of 0.254 square miles. Located at 41.47° N. Lat; 74.18° W. Long. Elevation is 417 feet.

Population: 1,995; Growth (since 2000): -4.5%; Density: 201.7 persons per square mile; Race: 81.3% White, 10.9% Black/African American, 4.7% Asian, 0.0% American Indian/Alaska Native, 0.0% Native Hawaiian/Other Pacific Islander, 2.2% Two or more races, 16.0% Hispanic of any race; Average household size: 3.05; Median age: 43.2; Age under 18: 26.0%; Age 65 and over: 4.8%; Males per 100 females: 94.7; Marriage status: 27.2% never married, 65.5% now married, 0.0% separated, 2.5% widowed, 4.8% divorced; Foreign born: 12.6%; Speak English only: 85.8%; With disability: 3.6%; Veterans: 9.7%; Ancestry: 25.6% Irish, 14.3% Italian, 13.9% American, 12.3% German, 10.9% West Indian

Employment: 17.7% management, business, and financial, 3.8% computer, engineering, and science, 6.1% education, legal, community service, arts, and media, 8.3% healthcare practitioners, 10.8% service, 32.7% sales and office, 7.7% natural resources, construction, and maintenance, 13.0% production, transportation, and material moving

Income: Per capita: $41,883; Median household: $120,833; Average household: $125,675; Households with income of $100,000 or more: 51.8%; Poverty rate: 2.1%

Educational Attainment: High school diploma or higher: 100.0%; Bachelor's degree or higher: 43.8%; Graduate/professional degree or higher: 16.8%

Housing: Homeownership rate: 94.2%; Median home value: $343,900; Median year structure built: 1992; Homeowner vacancy rate: 0.0%; Median selected monthly owner costs: $2,463 with a mortgage, $967 without a mortgage; Median gross rent: n/a per month; Rental vacancy rate: 0.0%

Health Insurance: 96.7% have insurance; 95.6% have private insurance; 8.0% have public insurance; 3.3% do not have insurance; 0.0% of children under 18 do not have insurance

Transportation: Commute: 82.2% car, 11.0% public transportation, 2.6% walk, 4.3% work from home; Mean travel time to work: 54.9 minutes

SALISBURY MILLS (CDP).
Covers a land area of 0.499 square miles and a water area of 0.005 square miles. Located at 41.43° N. Lat; 74.11° W. Long. Elevation is 305 feet.

Population: 308; Growth (since 2000): n/a; Density: 617.5 persons per square mile; Race: 91.6% White, 0.0% Black/African American, 0.0% Asian, 0.0% American Indian/Alaska Native, 0.0% Native Hawaiian/Other Pacific Islander, 8.4% Two or more races, 0.0% Hispanic of any race; Average household size: 3.62; Median age: 43.4; Age under 18: 16.9%; Age 65 and over: 9.7%; Males per 100 females: 103.8; Marriage status: 49.1% never married, 27.0% now married, 0.0% separated, 6.6% widowed, 17.3% divorced; Foreign born: 6.8%; Speak English only: 100.0%; With disability: 13.3%; Veterans: 2.3%; Ancestry: 35.4% Italian, 31.2% Irish, 24.4% English, 24.0% German, 15.3% Polish

Employment: 4.3% management, business, and financial, 18.4% computer, engineering, and science, 6.4% education, legal, community service, arts, and media, 0.0% healthcare practitioners, 23.4% service, 34.8% sales and office, 12.8% natural resources, construction, and maintenance, 0.0% production, transportation, and material moving

Income: Per capita: $39,205; Median household: $106,607; Average household: $140,228; Households with income of $100,000 or more: 55.3%; Poverty rate: 8.4%

Educational Attainment: High school diploma or higher: 96.4%; Bachelor's degree or higher: 28.5%; Graduate/professional degree or higher: 15.5%

Housing: Homeownership rate: 77.6%; Median home value: $341,200; Median year structure built: 1966; Homeowner vacancy rate: 0.0%; Median selected monthly owner costs: $2,206 with a mortgage, n/a without a mortgage; Median gross rent: n/a per month; Rental vacancy rate: 0.0%

Health Insurance: 96.1% have insurance; 60.1% have private insurance; 45.5% have public insurance; 3.9% do not have insurance; 0.0% of children under 18 do not have insurance

Transportation: Commute: 75.2% car, 12.8% public transportation, 0.0% walk, 12.1% work from home; Mean travel time to work: 32.9 minutes

SCOTCHTOWN (CDP).
Covers a land area of 4.226 square miles and a water area of 0.012 square miles. Located at 41.47° N. Lat; 74.37° W. Long. Elevation is 722 feet.

Population: 9,061; Growth (since 2000): 1.2%; Density: 2,144.3 persons per square mile; Race: 55.0% White, 25.2% Black/African American, 6.0% Asian, 2.3% American Indian/Alaska Native, 0.0% Native Hawaiian/Other Pacific Islander, 4.1% Two or more races, 23.5% Hispanic of any race; Average household size: 2.83; Median age: 38.5; Age under 18: 23.8%; Age 65 and over: 12.3%; Males per 100 females: 94.5; Marriage status: 36.4% never married, 51.1% now married, 1.9% separated, 5.2% widowed, 7.3% divorced; Foreign born: 12.4%; Speak English only: 75.5%; With disability: 12.9%; Veterans: 6.8%; Ancestry: 13.7% Italian, 12.3% Irish, 11.4% American, 7.0% German, 3.1% English

Employment: 11.5% management, business, and financial, 4.5% computer, engineering, and science, 10.6% education, legal, community service, arts, and media, 7.3% healthcare practitioners, 20.8% service, 26.9% sales and office, 5.0% natural resources, construction, and maintenance, 13.4% production, transportation, and material moving

Income: Per capita: $27,861; Median household: $65,991; Average household: $76,679; Households with income of $100,000 or more: 26.1%; Poverty rate: 4.3%

Educational Attainment: High school diploma or higher: 91.5%; Bachelor's degree or higher: 26.4%; Graduate/professional degree or higher: 9.3%

Housing: Homeownership rate: 63.0%; Median home value: $258,000; Median year structure built: 1976; Homeowner vacancy rate: 2.5%; Median selected monthly owner costs: $2,153 with a mortgage, $791 without a mortgage; Median gross rent: $1,209 per month; Rental vacancy rate: 4.4%

Health Insurance: 92.5% have insurance; 78.0% have private insurance; 24.1% have public insurance; 7.5% do not have insurance; 2.6% of children under 18 do not have insurance
Transportation: Commute: 93.0% car, 4.0% public transportation, 0.2% walk, 1.4% work from home; Mean travel time to work: 33.8 minutes

SLATE HILL (unincorporated postal area)
ZCTA: 10973

Covers a land area of 8.395 square miles and a water area of 0.129 square miles. Located at 41.38° N. Lat; 74.48° W. Long. Elevation is 499 feet.

Population: 2,603; Growth (since 2000): 37.9%; Density: 310.1 persons per square mile; Race: 86.3% White, 7.0% Black/African American, 1.5% Asian, 0.6% American Indian/Alaska Native, 0.0% Native Hawaiian/Other Pacific Islander, 0.0% Two or more races, 9.6% Hispanic of any race; Average household size: 3.15; Median age: 42.0; Age under 18: 22.6%; Age 65 and over: 7.5%; Males per 100 females: 100.9; Marriage status: 39.2% never married, 52.6% now married, 1.5% separated, 3.3% widowed, 4.9% divorced; Foreign born: 10.1%; Speak English only: 86.6%; With disability: 11.9%; Veterans: 5.6%; Ancestry: 30.1% American, 26.0% Italian, 20.5% Irish, 16.4% German, 3.2% English

Employment: 10.3% management, business, and financial, 3.1% computer, engineering, and science, 15.3% education, legal, community service, arts, and media, 11.3% healthcare practitioners, 11.3% service, 22.6% sales and office, 11.1% natural resources, construction, and maintenance, 14.8% production, transportation, and material moving
Income: Per capita: $33,310; Median household: $91,250; Average household: $100,620; Households with income of $100,000 or more: 44.6%; Poverty rate: 5.7%
Educational Attainment: High school diploma or higher: 90.1%; Bachelor's degree or higher: 27.5%; Graduate/professional degree or higher: 10.5%
Housing: Homeownership rate: 70.6%; Median home value: $260,600; Median year structure built: 1970; Homeowner vacancy rate: 0.0%; Median selected monthly owner costs: $2,137 with a mortgage, $906 without a mortgage; Median gross rent: $1,113 per month; Rental vacancy rate: 11.8%
Health Insurance: 92.8% have insurance; 78.1% have private insurance; 19.4% have public insurance; 7.2% do not have insurance; 0.0% of children under 18 do not have insurance
Transportation: Commute: 97.6% car, 1.1% public transportation, 0.4% walk, 0.9% work from home; Mean travel time to work: 27.6 minutes

SOUTH BLOOMING GROVE (village). Covers a land area of
4.674 square miles and a water area of 0.033 square miles. Located at 41.37° N. Lat; 74.17° W. Long. Elevation is 535 feet.
Population: 3,214; Growth (since 2000): n/a; Density: 687.7 persons per square mile; Race: 79.0% White, 5.3% Black/African American, 4.0% Asian, 0.2% American Indian/Alaska Native, 0.0% Native Hawaiian/Other Pacific Islander, 4.4% Two or more races, 18.0% Hispanic of any race; Average household size: 2.83; Median age: 39.8; Age under 18: 23.2%; Age 65 and over: 14.4%; Males per 100 females: 97.8; Marriage status: 31.9% never married, 54.4% now married, 3.3% separated, 5.6% widowed, 8.1% divorced; Foreign born: 13.5%; Speak English only: 77.3%; With disability: 11.8%; Veterans: 7.1%; Ancestry: 20.3% Irish, 19.9% Italian, 13.6% American, 13.1% German, 4.0% Polish
Employment: 10.0% management, business, and financial, 3.9% computer, engineering, and science, 8.1% education, legal, community service, arts, and media, 6.9% healthcare practitioners, 26.0% service, 24.4% sales and office, 9.6% natural resources, construction, and maintenance, 11.2% production, transportation, and material moving
Income: Per capita: $32,833; Median household: $77,946; Average household: $90,386; Households with income of $100,000 or more: 36.0%; Poverty rate: 7.3%
Educational Attainment: High school diploma or higher: 94.1%; Bachelor's degree or higher: 24.4%; Graduate/professional degree or higher: 10.4%
Housing: Homeownership rate: 80.0%; Median home value: $265,800; Median year structure built: 1967; Homeowner vacancy rate: 0.0%; Median selected monthly owner costs: $2,217 with a mortgage, $993 without a mortgage; Median gross rent: $1,194 per month; Rental vacancy rate: 0.0%

Health Insurance: 95.2% have insurance; 78.3% have private insurance; 32.4% have public insurance; 4.8% do not have insurance; 1.6% of children under 18 do not have insurance
Transportation: Commute: 91.7% car, 5.2% public transportation, 0.0% walk, 1.4% work from home; Mean travel time to work: 40.2 minutes

SOUTHFIELDS (unincorporated postal area)
ZCTA: 10975

Covers a land area of 5.883 square miles and a water area of 0.121 square miles. Located at 41.27° N. Lat; 74.17° W. Long. Elevation is 505 feet.

Population: 297; Growth (since 2000): -3.3%; Density: 50.5 persons per square mile; Race: 100.0% White, 0.0% Black/African American, 0.0% Asian, 0.0% American Indian/Alaska Native, 0.0% Native Hawaiian/Other Pacific Islander, 0.0% Two or more races, 18.9% Hispanic of any race; Average household size: 1.78; Median age: 44.8; Age under 18: 16.5%; Age 65 and over: 31.0%; Males per 100 females: 124.8; Marriage status: 10.7% never married, 57.3% now married, 0.0% separated, 7.5% widowed, 24.5% divorced; Foreign born: 0.0%; Speak English only: 92.6%; With disability: 25.6%; Veterans: 10.1%; Ancestry: 37.0% Irish, 27.9% Italian, 25.6% American, 10.1% Czech, 9.1% German

Employment: 9.3% management, business, and financial, 17.4% computer, engineering, and science, 3.5% education, legal, community service, arts, and media, 16.3% healthcare practitioners, 2.9% service, 50.6% sales and office, 0.0% natural resources, construction, and maintenance, 0.0% production, transportation, and material moving
Income: Per capita: $67,730; Median household: n/a; Average household: $125,612; Households with income of $100,000 or more: 29.4%; Poverty rate: n/a
Educational Attainment: High school diploma or higher: 92.1%; Bachelor's degree or higher: 26.1%; Graduate/professional degree or higher: 7.5%
Housing: Homeownership rate: 74.9%; Median home value: $184,600; Median year structure built: 1971; Homeowner vacancy rate: 0.0%; Median selected monthly owner costs: $1,865 with a mortgage, $0 without a mortgage; Median gross rent: $1,489 per month; Rental vacancy rate: 0.0%
Health Insurance: 92.6% have insurance; 70.0% have private insurance; 31.0% have public insurance; 7.4% do not have insurance; 0.0% of children under 18 do not have insurance
Transportation: Commute: 96.9% car, 3.1% public transportation, 0.0% walk, 0.0% work from home; Mean travel time to work: 59.4 minutes

SPARROW BUSH (unincorporated postal area)
ZCTA: 12780

Covers a land area of 23.825 square miles and a water area of 0.716 square miles. Located at 41.44° N. Lat; 74.73° W. Long. Elevation is 502 feet.

Population: 2,068; Growth (since 2000): -2.3%; Density: 86.8 persons per square mile; Race: 87.2% White, 5.6% Black/African American, 0.0% Asian, 0.0% American Indian/Alaska Native, 0.0% Native Hawaiian/Other Pacific Islander, 1.6% Two or more races, 9.4% Hispanic of any race; Average household size: 2.24; Median age: 43.5; Age under 18: 26.1%; Age 65 and over: 16.9%; Males per 100 females: 105.9; Marriage status: 26.4% never married, 49.7% now married, 2.8% separated, 11.2% widowed, 12.7% divorced; Foreign born: 1.1%; Speak English only: 95.9%; With disability: 17.6%; Veterans: 8.5%; Ancestry: 35.2% American, 18.6% Irish, 13.0% German, 7.2% English, 6.0% Italian

Employment: 9.9% management, business, and financial, 1.6% computer, engineering, and science, 11.5% education, legal, community service, arts, and media, 2.4% healthcare practitioners, 28.2% service, 21.4% sales and office, 10.0% natural resources, construction, and maintenance, 14.9% production, transportation, and material moving
Income: Per capita: $20,692; Median household: $36,490; Average household: $45,075; Households with income of $100,000 or more: 12.0%; Poverty rate: 21.8%
Educational Attainment: High school diploma or higher: 85.5%; Bachelor's degree or higher: 12.0%; Graduate/professional degree or higher: 8.3%
Housing: Homeownership rate: 81.6%; Median home value: $164,600; Median year structure built: 1971; Homeowner vacancy rate: 5.1%; Median selected monthly owner costs: $1,760 with a mortgage, $632

without a mortgage; Median gross rent: $1,178 per month; Rental vacancy rate: 10.5%

Health Insurance: 92.7% have insurance; 74.4% have private insurance; 32.5% have public insurance; 7.3% do not have insurance; 3.5% of children under 18 do not have insurance

Transportation: Commute: 98.9% car, 0.0% public transportation, 0.0% walk, 1.1% work from home; Mean travel time to work: 30.7 minutes

STERLING FOREST (unincorporated postal area)
ZCTA: 10979

Covers a land area of 0.146 square miles and a water area of 0 square miles. Located at 41.18° N. Lat; 74.31° W. Long. Elevation is 656 feet.

Population: 301; Growth (since 2000): n/a; Density: 2,065.6 persons per square mile; Race: 71.1% White, 0.0% Black/African American, 0.0% Asian, 0.0% American Indian/Alaska Native, 0.0% Native Hawaiian/Other Pacific Islander, 28.9% Two or more races, 0.0% Hispanic of any race; Average household size: 2.41; Median age: 45.8; Age under 18: 22.3%; Age 65 and over: 0.0%; Males per 100 females: 107.1; Marriage status: 26.5% never married, 62.4% now married, 0.0% separated, 11.1% widowed, 0.0% divorced; Foreign born: 15.3%; Speak English only: 100.0%; With disability: 44.5%; Veterans: 0.0%; Ancestry: 37.9% Irish, 31.2% German, 19.6% French, 19.3% Russian, 18.6% Italian

Employment: 0.0% management, business, and financial, 0.0% computer, engineering, and science, 0.0% education, legal, community service, arts, and media, 0.0% healthcare practitioners, 44.6% service, 0.0% sales and office, 26.8% natural resources, construction, and maintenance, 28.6% production, transportation, and material moving

Income: Per capita: $26,761; Median household: $68,125; Average household: $59,260; Households with income of $100,000 or more: n/a; Poverty rate: n/a

Educational Attainment: High school diploma or higher: 80.3%; Bachelor's degree or higher: n/a; Graduate/professional degree or higher: n/a

Housing: Homeownership rate: 100.0%; Median home value: $266,800; Median year structure built: 1965; Homeowner vacancy rate: 0.0%; Median selected monthly owner costs: $2,005 with a mortgage, $0 without a mortgage; Median gross rent: n/a per month; Rental vacancy rate: 0.0%

Health Insurance: 90.0% have insurance; 72.4% have private insurance; 17.6% have public insurance; 10.0% do not have insurance; 0.0% of children under 18 do not have insurance

Transportation: Commute: 100.0% car, 0.0% public transportation, 0.0% walk, 0.0% work from home; Mean travel time to work: 0.0 minutes

THOMPSON RIDGE (unincorporated postal area)
ZCTA: 10985

Covers a land area of 0.257 square miles and a water area of 0 square miles. Located at 41.58° N. Lat; 74.37° W. Long. Elevation is 456 feet.

Population: 34; Growth (since 2000): -40.4%; Density: 132.3 persons per square mile; Race: 100.0% White, 0.0% Black/African American, 0.0% Asian, 0.0% American Indian/Alaska Native, 0.0% Native Hawaiian/Other Pacific Islander, 0.0% Two or more races, 0.0% Hispanic of any race; Average household size: 2.13; Median age: 35.9; Age under 18: 0.0%; Age 65 and over: 20.6%; Males per 100 females: 81.3; Marriage status: 52.9% never married, 47.1% now married, 0.0% separated, 0.0% widowed, 0.0% divorced; Foreign born: 0.0%; Speak English only: 100.0%; With disability: 0.0%; Veterans: 0.0%; Ancestry: 52.9% German, 26.5% English, 26.5% Irish, 26.5% Italian, 20.6% Polish

Employment: 28.0% management, business, and financial, 0.0% computer, engineering, and science, 0.0% education, legal, community service, arts, and media, 0.0% healthcare practitioners, 0.0% service, 36.0% sales and office, 36.0% natural resources, construction, and maintenance, 0.0% production, transportation, and material moving

Income: Per capita: $66,988; Median household: n/a; Average household: n/a; Households with income of $100,000 or more: 56.3%; Poverty rate: 26.5%

Educational Attainment: High school diploma or higher: 100.0%; Bachelor's degree or higher: 52.9%; Graduate/professional degree or higher: n/a

Housing: Homeownership rate: 100.0%; Median home value: n/a; Median year structure built: n/a; Homeowner vacancy rate: 0.0%; Median selected monthly owner costs: $0 with a mortgage, $0 without a mortgage; Median gross rent: n/a per month; Rental vacancy rate: 0.0%

Health Insurance: 100.0% have insurance; 73.5% have private insurance; 47.1% have public insurance; 0.0% do not have insurance; 0.0% of children under 18 do not have insurance

Transportation: Commute: 100.0% car, 0.0% public transportation, 0.0% walk, 0.0% work from home; Mean travel time to work: 0.0 minutes

TUXEDO (town). Covers a land area of 47.047 square miles and a water area of 2.299 square miles. Located at 41.24° N. Lat; 74.17° W. Long.

History: Tuxedo Park colony here, a private residential development begun (1886) by Pierre Lorillard, became known for its sports and social functions. King's College relocated here from Briarcliff Manor.

Population: 3,596; Growth (since 2000): 7.9%; Density: 76.4 persons per square mile; Race: 88.0% White, 1.9% Black/African American, 4.9% Asian, 0.0% American Indian/Alaska Native, 0.0% Native Hawaiian/Other Pacific Islander, 1.7% Two or more races, 8.1% Hispanic of any race; Average household size: 2.29; Median age: 46.6; Age under 18: 21.5%; Age 65 and over: 21.8%; Males per 100 females: 99.8; Marriage status: 23.8% never married, 54.1% now married, 1.4% separated, 11.1% widowed, 11.0% divorced; Foreign born: 10.8%; Speak English only: 84.6%; With disability: 14.1%; Veterans: 9.6%; Ancestry: 22.3% Irish, 18.7% Italian, 15.6% German, 11.2% American, 7.9% English

Employment: 23.3% management, business, and financial, 7.9% computer, engineering, and science, 13.0% education, legal, community service, arts, and media, 5.4% healthcare practitioners, 9.6% service, 30.5% sales and office, 5.8% natural resources, construction, and maintenance, 4.5% production, transportation, and material moving

Income: Per capita: $53,892; Median household: $94,111; Average household: $122,821; Households with income of $100,000 or more: 46.6%; Poverty rate: 1.6%

Educational Attainment: High school diploma or higher: 94.4%; Bachelor's degree or higher: 53.0%; Graduate/professional degree or higher: 24.4%

Housing: Homeownership rate: 78.8%; Median home value: $418,100; Median year structure built: 1962; Homeowner vacancy rate: 1.1%; Median selected monthly owner costs: $2,830 with a mortgage, $1,328 without a mortgage; Median gross rent: $1,425 per month; Rental vacancy rate: 9.9%

Health Insurance: 95.9% have insurance; 86.0% have private insurance; 24.8% have public insurance; 4.1% do not have insurance; 1.0% of children under 18 do not have insurance

Safety: Violent crime rate: 0.0 per 10,000 population; Property crime rate: 3.4 per 10,000 population

Transportation: Commute: 81.7% car, 10.5% public transportation, 0.5% walk, 6.8% work from home; Mean travel time to work: 39.1 minutes

Additional Information Contacts

Town of Tuxedo . . . . (845) 351-4411
    http://www.tuxedogov.org

TUXEDO PARK (village). Covers a land area of 2.655 square miles and a water area of 0.566 square miles. Located at 41.20° N. Lat; 74.21° W. Long. Elevation is 407 feet.

Population: 590; Growth (since 2000): -19.3%; Density: 222.2 persons per square mile; Race: 79.5% White, 0.0% Black/African American, 14.1% Asian, 0.0% American Indian/Alaska Native, 0.0% Native Hawaiian/Other Pacific Islander, 6.4% Two or more races, 2.9% Hispanic of any race; Average household size: 2.55; Median age: 48.6; Age under 18: 24.9%; Age 65 and over: 24.9%; Males per 100 females: 104.3; Marriage status: 16.6% never married, 73.3% now married, 4.5% separated, 5.8% widowed, 4.3% divorced; Foreign born: 9.8%; Speak English only: 86.8%; With disability: 11.5%; Veterans: 9.5%; Ancestry: 24.1% Irish, 12.4% German, 11.9% English, 11.5% Italian, 9.8% American

Employment: 24.7% management, business, and financial, 7.6% computer, engineering, and science, 20.0% education, legal, community service, arts, and media, 4.0% healthcare practitioners, 14.5% service, 23.3% sales and office, 2.9% natural resources, construction, and maintenance, 2.9% production, transportation, and material moving

Income: Per capita: $68,966; Median household: $120,521; Average household: $179,798; Households with income of $100,000 or more: 58.0%; Poverty rate: 2.4%

Educational Attainment: High school diploma or higher: 98.6%; Bachelor's degree or higher: 69.5%; Graduate/professional degree or higher: 32.1%

School District(s)

Tuxedo Union Free SD (KG-12)

2014-15 Enrollment: 496 . . . . (845) 351-4799

Housing: Homeownership rate: 89.6%; Median home value: $1,031,300; Median year structure built: Before 1940; Homeowner vacancy rate: 6.2%; Median selected monthly owner costs: $4,000+ with a mortgage, $1,500+ without a mortgage; Median gross rent: $1,354 per month; Rental vacancy rate: 33.3%

Health Insurance: 97.8% have insurance; 83.1% have private insurance; 26.8% have public insurance; 2.2% do not have insurance; 5.4% of children under 18 do not have insurance

Transportation: Commute: 61.3% car, 22.6% public transportation, 3.9% walk, 11.7% work from home; Mean travel time to work: 52.9 minutes

UNIONVILLE (village).

Covers a land area of 0.310 square miles and a water area of 0 square miles. Located at 41.30° N. Lat; 74.56° W. Long. Elevation is 535 feet.

Population: 596; Growth (since 2000): 11.2%; Density: 1,920.1 persons per square mile; Race: 83.1% White, 6.4% Black/African American, 0.0% Asian, 0.0% American Indian/Alaska Native, 0.0% Native Hawaiian/Other Pacific Islander, 4.0% Two or more races, 14.3% Hispanic of any race; Average household size: 2.58; Median age: 39.8; Age under 18: 28.5%; Age 65 and over: 16.6%; Males per 100 females: 90.1; Marriage status: 24.8% never married, 48.5% now married, 5.2% separated, 12.0% widowed, 14.7% divorced; Foreign born: 5.4%; Speak English only: 94.3%; With disability: 14.6%; Veterans: 11.5%; Ancestry: 29.7% American, 26.7% Irish, 14.9% German, 13.3% Italian, 6.4% English

Employment: 12.2% management, business, and financial, 4.1% computer, engineering, and science, 10.2% education, legal, community service, arts, and media, 4.4% healthcare practitioners, 23.5% service, 12.6% sales and office, 16.0% natural resources, construction, and maintenance, 17.0% production, transportation, and material moving

Income: Per capita: $26,852; Median household: $67,857; Average household: $68,542; Households with income of $100,000 or more: 15.3%; Poverty rate: 5.4%

Educational Attainment: High school diploma or higher: 89.1%; Bachelor's degree or higher: 23.1%; Graduate/professional degree or higher: 8.8%

Housing: Homeownership rate: 86.0%; Median home value: $197,300; Median year structure built: Before 1940; Homeowner vacancy rate: 0.0%; Median selected monthly owner costs: $1,698 with a mortgage, $855 without a mortgage; Median gross rent: $1,039 per month; Rental vacancy rate: 14.9%

Health Insurance: 84.6% have insurance; 65.8% have private insurance; 27.7% have public insurance; 15.4% do not have insurance; 18.2% of children under 18 do not have insurance

Transportation: Commute: 90.4% car, 3.6% public transportation, 0.0% walk, 3.6% work from home; Mean travel time to work: 37.9 minutes

VAILS GATE (CDP).

Covers a land area of 1.061 square miles and a water area of 0 square miles. Located at 41.46° N. Lat; 74.05° W. Long. Elevation is 282 feet.

Population: 3,509; Growth (since 2000): 5.7%; Density: 3,306.8 persons per square mile; Race: 54.9% White, 21.1% Black/African American, 11.0% Asian, 0.0% American Indian/Alaska Native, 0.0% Native Hawaiian/Other Pacific Islander, 3.9% Two or more races, 22.4% Hispanic of any race; Average household size: 2.32; Median age: 40.0; Age under 18: 15.9%; Age 65 and over: 16.7%; Males per 100 females: 87.0; Marriage status: 36.3% never married, 42.5% now married, 2.0% separated, 9.6% widowed, 11.7% divorced; Foreign born: 24.5%; Speak English only: 66.3%; With disability: 15.9%; Veterans: 5.9%; Ancestry: 14.8% Italian, 14.1% American, 11.1% Irish, 5.0% Haitian, 4.9% German

Employment: 5.0% management, business, and financial, 3.8% computer, engineering, and science, 4.6% education, legal, community service, arts, and media, 8.2% healthcare practitioners, 29.6% service, 34.7% sales and office, 5.3% natural resources, construction, and maintenance, 8.7% production, transportation, and material moving

Income: Per capita: $24,665; Median household: $40,467; Average household: $55,431; Households with income of $100,000 or more: 14.9%; Poverty rate: 11.1%

Educational Attainment: High school diploma or higher: 86.7%; Bachelor's degree or higher: 18.4%; Graduate/professional degree or higher: 5.8%

Housing: Homeownership rate: 44.3%; Median home value: $203,300; Median year structure built: 1970; Homeowner vacancy rate: 0.0%; Median

selected monthly owner costs: $2,190 with a mortgage, $634 without a mortgage; Median gross rent: $1,116 per month; Rental vacancy rate: 2.2%

Health Insurance: 85.0% have insurance; 56.5% have private insurance; 39.8% have public insurance; 15.0% do not have insurance; 3.8% of children under 18 do not have insurance

Transportation: Commute: 80.8% car, 3.4% public transportation, 14.6% walk, 0.7% work from home; Mean travel time to work: 26.9 minutes

WALDEN (village).

Covers a land area of 1.968 square miles and a water area of 0.082 square miles. Located at 41.56° N. Lat; 74.19° W. Long. Elevation is 374 feet.

History: Former factory town. Incorporated 1855.

Population: 6,886; Growth (since 2000): 11.7%; Density: 3,498.8 persons per square mile; Race: 75.3% White, 4.6% Black/African American, 0.9% Asian, 0.0% American Indian/Alaska Native, 0.0% Native Hawaiian/Other Pacific Islander, 3.7% Two or more races, 21.5% Hispanic of any race; Average household size: 3.08; Median age: 34.1; Age under 18: 25.5%; Age 65 and over: 9.0%; Males per 100 females: 93.2; Marriage status: 41.4% never married, 44.7% now married, 2.3% separated, 6.0% widowed, 8.0% divorced; Foreign born: 7.2%; Speak English only: 81.5%; With disability: 14.6%; Veterans: 7.0%; Ancestry: 17.5% Irish, 16.2% Italian, 15.2% German, 11.6% American, 6.6% English

Employment: 10.2% management, business, and financial, 2.4% computer, engineering, and science, 17.5% education, legal, community service, arts, and media, 2.6% healthcare practitioners, 14.7% service, 29.5% sales and office, 8.8% natural resources, construction, and maintenance, 14.3% production, transportation, and material moving

Income: Per capita: $26,028; Median household: $66,989; Average household: $76,806; Households with income of $100,000 or more: 28.8%; Poverty rate: 12.9%

Educational Attainment: High school diploma or higher: 88.8%; Bachelor's degree or higher: 22.6%; Graduate/professional degree or higher: 9.0%

School District(s)

Valley Central SD (Montgomery) (KG-12)

2014-15 Enrollment: 4,464 . . . . (845) 457-2400

Housing: Homeownership rate: 64.1%; Median home value: $214,300; Median year structure built: 1956; Homeowner vacancy rate: 5.0%; Median selected monthly owner costs: $2,061 with a mortgage, $677 without a mortgage; Median gross rent: $994 per month; Rental vacancy rate: 4.3%

Health Insurance: 94.0% have insurance; 74.2% have private insurance; 31.6% have public insurance; 6.0% do not have insurance; 1.4% of children under 18 do not have insurance

Safety: Violent crime rate: 14.7 per 10,000 population; Property crime rate: 121.6 per 10,000 population

Transportation: Commute: 89.2% car, 3.8% public transportation, 4.9% walk, 1.2% work from home; Mean travel time to work: 31.7 minutes

Additional Information Contacts

Village of Walden . . . . (845) 778-2177
http://www.villageofwalden.org

WALLKILL (town).

Covers a land area of 62.107 square miles and a water area of 0.736 square miles. Located at 41.49° N. Lat; 74.40° W. Long.

History: The original land patent for the town was dated 1724, but the town wasn't established until 1772. Wallkill's claim to fame during the American Revolution was the production of gunpowder in factories in Phillipsburgh and Craigville.

Population: 28,023; Growth (since 2000): 13.6%; Density: 451.2 persons per square mile; Race: 64.0% White, 17.9% Black/African American, 3.5% Asian, 0.9% American Indian/Alaska Native, 0.1% Native Hawaiian/Other Pacific Islander, 4.5% Two or more races, 21.5% Hispanic of any race; Average household size: 2.75; Median age: 40.7; Age under 18: 22.6%; Age 65 and over: 13.9%; Males per 100 females: 92.5; Marriage status: 34.4% never married, 50.4% now married, 2.6% separated, 6.3% widowed, 8.9% divorced; Foreign born: 11.6%; Speak English only: 77.7%; With disability: 12.8%; Veterans: 7.2%; Ancestry: 16.4% American, 14.9% Irish, 14.7% Italian, 10.2% German, 4.2% English

Employment: 12.0% management, business, and financial, 3.3% computer, engineering, and science, 10.0% education, legal, community service, arts, and media, 6.0% healthcare practitioners, 19.6% service, 29.1% sales and office, 6.8% natural resources, construction, and maintenance, 13.2% production, transportation, and material moving

Income: Per capita: $29,585; Median household: $64,650; Average household: $79,772; Households with income of $100,000 or more: 28.2%; Poverty rate: 8.1%
Educational Attainment: High school diploma or higher: 88.2%; Bachelor's degree or higher: 24.4%; Graduate/professional degree or higher: 9.4%

School District(s)
Wallkill Central SD (KG-12)
   2014-15 Enrollment: 3,102 . . . . (845) 895-7101
Housing: Homeownership rate: 66.4%; Median home value: $242,800; Median year structure built: 1977; Homeowner vacancy rate: 2.5%; Median selected monthly owner costs: $2,116 with a mortgage, $762 without a mortgage; Median gross rent: $1,193 per month; Rental vacancy rate: 3.1%
Health Insurance: 91.6% have insurance; 76.0% have private insurance; 26.1% have public insurance; 8.4% do not have insurance; 1.6% of children under 18 do not have insurance
Safety: Violent crime rate: 14.8 per 10,000 population; Property crime rate: 195.4 per 10,000 population
Transportation: Commute: 90.4% car, 3.8% public transportation, 1.4% walk, 2.1% work from home; Mean travel time to work: 34.2 minutes
Additional Information Contacts
Town of Wallkill . . . . (845) 692-7800
   http://www.townofwallkill.com

WALTON PARK (CDP).
Covers a land area of 2.329 square miles and a water area of 0.348 square miles. Located at 41.31° N. Lat; 74.23° W. Long. Elevation is 843 feet.
Population: 2,281; Growth (since 2000): -2.1%; Density: 979.4 persons per square mile; Race: 80.9% White, 4.3% Black/African American, 7.0% Asian, 0.0% American Indian/Alaska Native, 0.0% Native Hawaiian/Other Pacific Islander, 0.0% Two or more races, 14.1% Hispanic of any race; Average household size: 3.39; Median age: 36.0; Age under 18: 26.4%; Age 65 and over: 8.4%; Males per 100 females: 98.7; Marriage status: 33.6% never married, 55.0% now married, 0.0% separated, 2.6% widowed, 8.8% divorced; Foreign born: 9.1%; Speak English only: 82.5%; With disability: 5.2%; Veterans: 6.5%; Ancestry: 19.7% Irish, 19.5% Italian, 15.1% German, 10.4% American, 5.8% Polish
Employment: 6.4% management, business, and financial, 8.8% computer, engineering, and science, 7.5% education, legal, community service, arts, and media, 9.5% healthcare practitioners, 21.4% service, 28.5% sales and office, 9.2% natural resources, construction, and maintenance, 8.8% production, transportation, and material moving
Income: Per capita: $32,954; Median household: $106,406; Average household: $109,776; Households with income of $100,000 or more: 55.9%; Poverty rate: 3.0%
Educational Attainment: High school diploma or higher: 95.6%; Bachelor's degree or higher: 42.4%; Graduate/professional degree or higher: 13.3%
Housing: Homeownership rate: 95.5%; Median home value: $320,900; Median year structure built: 1969; Homeowner vacancy rate: 0.0%; Median selected monthly owner costs: $2,385 with a mortgage, $913 without a mortgage; Median gross rent: n/a per month; Rental vacancy rate: 0.0%
Health Insurance: 97.2% have insurance; 89.3% have private insurance; 14.6% have public insurance; 2.8% do not have insurance; 0.0% of children under 18 do not have insurance
Transportation: Commute: 87.2% car, 9.8% public transportation, 0.0% walk, 1.7% work from home; Mean travel time to work: 41.2 minutes

WARWICK (town).
Covers a land area of 101.340 square miles and a water area of 3.546 square miles. Located at 41.26° N. Lat; 74.36° W. Long. Elevation is 518 feet.
History: Warwick was settled in 1746 by English immigrants from Warwickshire. Warwick Village Historic District. Incorporated in 1867.
Population: 31,446; Growth (since 2000): 2.2%; Density: 310.3 persons per square mile; Race: 85.8% White, 5.7% Black/African American, 0.9% Asian, 0.1% American Indian/Alaska Native, 0.0% Native Hawaiian/Other Pacific Islander, 4.2% Two or more races, 11.0% Hispanic of any race; Average household size: 2.64; Median age: 43.7; Age under 18: 23.6%; Age 65 and over: 15.1%; Males per 100 females: 100.0; Marriage status: 26.8% never married, 56.6% now married, 2.2% separated, 5.8% widowed, 10.8% divorced; Foreign born: 6.8%; Speak English only: 89.0%; With disability: 12.6%; Veterans: 9.6%; Ancestry: 25.8% Irish, 18.3% Italian, 16.3% German, 11.9% American, 8.4% English

Employment: 15.2% management, business, and financial, 5.0% computer, engineering, and science, 12.7% education, legal, community service, arts, and media, 5.3% healthcare practitioners, 16.5% service, 24.7% sales and office, 11.0% natural resources, construction, and maintenance, 9.6% production, transportation, and material moving
Income: Per capita: $42,407; Median household: $84,807; Average household: $110,976; Households with income of $100,000 or more: 41.2%; Poverty rate: 5.3%
Educational Attainment: High school diploma or higher: 94.4%; Bachelor's degree or higher: 35.6%; Graduate/professional degree or higher: 14.7%

School District(s)
Warwick Valley Central SD (KG-12)
   2014-15 Enrollment: 3,723 . . . . (845) 987-3000
Housing: Homeownership rate: 79.1%; Median home value: $305,900; Median year structure built: 1970; Homeowner vacancy rate: 2.5%; Median selected monthly owner costs: $2,421 with a mortgage, $1,026 without a mortgage; Median gross rent: $1,144 per month; Rental vacancy rate: 3.8%
Health Insurance: 94.0% have insurance; 82.2% have private insurance; 24.8% have public insurance; 6.0% do not have insurance; 2.8% of children under 18 do not have insurance
Hospitals: Saint Anthony Community Hospital (73 beds)
Safety: Violent crime rate: 5.5 per 10,000 population; Property crime rate: 80.8 per 10,000 population
Newspapers: Warwick Valley Dispatch (weekly circulation 3,000)
Transportation: Commute: 84.6% car, 4.8% public transportation, 3.4% walk, 6.8% work from home; Mean travel time to work: 40.4 minutes
Additional Information Contacts
Town of Warwick . . . . (845) 986-1124
   http://www.townofwarwick.org/index.shtml

WARWICK (village).
Covers a land area of 2.417 square miles and a water area of 0.004 square miles. Located at 41.26° N. Lat; 74.35° W. Long. Elevation is 518 feet.
Population: 6,797; Growth (since 2000): 6.0%; Density: 2,812.5 persons per square mile; Race: 92.7% White, 4.0% Black/African American, 0.0% Asian, 0.0% American Indian/Alaska Native, 0.0% Native Hawaiian/Other Pacific Islander, 2.1% Two or more races, 8.0% Hispanic of any race; Average household size: 2.32; Median age: 46.2; Age under 18: 21.9%; Age 65 and over: 25.0%; Males per 100 females: 82.8; Marriage status: 23.0% never married, 54.0% now married, 4.0% separated, 9.5% widowed, 13.5% divorced; Foreign born: 5.3%; Speak English only: 89.2%; With disability: 17.0%; Veterans: 13.9%; Ancestry: 28.4% Irish, 16.9% Italian, 15.3% German, 11.7% American, 10.2% Polish
Employment: 13.9% management, business, and financial, 2.3% computer, engineering, and science, 11.4% education, legal, community service, arts, and media, 6.9% healthcare practitioners, 15.9% service, 29.7% sales and office, 9.1% natural resources, construction, and maintenance, 10.8% production, transportation, and material moving
Income: Per capita: $35,710; Median household: $66,987; Average household: $82,003; Households with income of $100,000 or more: 33.0%; Poverty rate: 6.7%
Educational Attainment: High school diploma or higher: 93.4%; Bachelor's degree or higher: 36.8%; Graduate/professional degree or higher: 13.9%

School District(s)
Warwick Valley Central SD (KG-12)
   2014-15 Enrollment: 3,723 . . . . (845) 987-3000
Housing: Homeownership rate: 63.4%; Median home value: $295,600; Median year structure built: 1980; Homeowner vacancy rate: 0.0%; Median selected monthly owner costs: $2,360 with a mortgage, $884 without a mortgage; Median gross rent: $968 per month; Rental vacancy rate: 8.5%
Health Insurance: 96.0% have insurance; 82.0% have private insurance; 32.6% have public insurance; 4.0% do not have insurance; 3.6% of children under 18 do not have insurance
Hospitals: Saint Anthony Community Hospital (73 beds)
Newspapers: Warwick Valley Dispatch (weekly circulation 3,000)
Transportation: Commute: 84.8% car, 3.2% public transportation, 5.9% walk, 5.2% work from home; Mean travel time to work: 35.4 minutes
Additional Information Contacts
Village of Warwick . . . . (845) 986-2031
   http://www.villageofwarwick.org

WASHINGTON HEIGHTS (CDP).
Covers a land area of 1.486 square miles and a water area of 0.005 square miles. Located at 41.47° N. Lat; 74.42° W. Long. Elevation is 666 feet.

Population: 2,149; Growth (since 2000): 63.1%; Density: 1,445.8 persons per square mile; Race: 44.8% White, 20.4% Black/African American, 0.0% Asian, 0.0% American Indian/Alaska Native, 0.0% Native Hawaiian/Other Pacific Islander, 6.7% Two or more races, 35.0% Hispanic of any race; Average household size: 2.91; Median age: 36.4; Age under 18: 24.1%; Age 65 and over: 7.7%; Males per 100 females: 93.0; Marriage status: 34.0% never married, 47.8% now married, 4.1% separated, 4.0% widowed, 14.2% divorced; Foreign born: 12.1%; Speak English only: 65.2%; With disability: 9.9%; Veterans: 5.0%; Ancestry: 16.7% American, 13.8% Irish, 9.3% Italian, 8.4% German, 7.7% Bahamian

Employment: 17.9% management, business, and financial, 1.6% computer, engineering, and science, 10.1% education, legal, community service, arts, and media, 7.5% healthcare practitioners, 16.1% service, 18.8% sales and office, 8.0% natural resources, construction, and maintenance, 20.0% production, transportation, and material moving

Income: Per capita: $28,400; Median household: $71,226; Average household: $80,171; Households with income of $100,000 or more: 26.1%; Poverty rate: 7.2%

Educational Attainment: High school diploma or higher: 83.3%; Bachelor's degree or higher: 27.1%; Graduate/professional degree or higher: 12.7%

Housing: Homeownership rate: 79.7%; Median home value: $226,200; Median year structure built: 1965; Homeowner vacancy rate: 9.4%; Median selected monthly owner costs: $2,311 with a mortgage, $633 without a mortgage; Median gross rent: $1,562 per month; Rental vacancy rate: 0.0%

Health Insurance: 91.0% have insurance; 68.9% have private insurance; 26.6% have public insurance; 9.0% do not have insurance; 0.0% of children under 18 do not have insurance

Transportation: Commute: 92.3% car, 2.7% public transportation, 1.3% walk, 0.0% work from home; Mean travel time to work: 51.4 minutes

WASHINGTONVILLE (village).
Covers a land area of 2.538 square miles and a water area of 0.014 square miles. Located at 41.43° N. Lat; 74.16° W. Long. Elevation is 305 feet.

Population: 5,814; Growth (since 2000): -0.6%; Density: 2,290.6 persons per square mile; Race: 75.7% White, 5.4% Black/African American, 1.8% Asian, 0.0% American Indian/Alaska Native, 0.0% Native Hawaiian/Other Pacific Islander, 2.2% Two or more races, 25.2% Hispanic of any race; Average household size: 2.73; Median age: 42.9; Age under 18: 20.7%; Age 65 and over: 14.7%; Males per 100 females: 93.9; Marriage status: 32.5% never married, 53.9% now married, 2.4% separated, 6.0% widowed, 7.6% divorced; Foreign born: 7.8%; Speak English only: 83.3%; With disability: 11.8%; Veterans: 7.1%; Ancestry: 26.1% Irish, 21.9% Italian, 13.0% German, 10.4% American, 6.2% English

Employment: 11.1% management, business, and financial, 8.6% computer, engineering, and science, 11.5% education, legal, community service, arts, and media, 5.6% healthcare practitioners, 19.7% service, 28.3% sales and office, 6.1% natural resources, construction, and maintenance, 9.2% production, transportation, and material moving

Income: Per capita: $34,594; Median household: $72,690; Average household: $91,432; Households with income of $100,000 or more: 34.9%; Poverty rate: 7.1%

Educational Attainment: High school diploma or higher: 94.6%; Bachelor's degree or higher: 29.7%; Graduate/professional degree or higher: 13.7%

School District(s)
Washingtonville Central SD (PK-12)
   2014-15 Enrollment: 4,286 . . . . (845) 497-4000

Housing: Homeownership rate: 76.4%; Median home value: $248,400; Median year structure built: 1982; Homeowner vacancy rate: 2.1%; Median selected monthly owner costs: $2,388 with a mortgage, $888 without a mortgage; Median gross rent: $864 per month; Rental vacancy rate: 8.6%

Health Insurance: 95.1% have insurance; 84.5% have private insurance; 21.8% have public insurance; 4.9% do not have insurance; 1.7% of children under 18 do not have insurance

Safety: Violent crime rate: 5.2 per 10,000 population; Property crime rate: 64.2 per 10,000 population

Newspapers: Orange County Post (weekly circulation 2,600)

Transportation: Commute: 88.1% car, 6.5% public transportation, 1.1% walk, 3.4% work from home; Mean travel time to work: 39.2 minutes

Additional Information Contacts
Village of Washingtonville . . . . (845) 496-3221

WAWAYANDA (town).
Covers a land area of 34.720 square miles and a water area of 0.309 square miles. Located at 41.38° N. Lat; 74.47° W. Long.

Population: 7,272; Growth (since 2000): 15.9%; Density: 209.4 persons per square mile; Race: 84.6% White, 3.5% Black/African American, 1.7% Asian, 0.2% American Indian/Alaska Native, 0.0% Native Hawaiian/Other Pacific Islander, 1.6% Two or more races, 15.6% Hispanic of any race; Average household size: 3.01; Median age: 41.4; Age under 18: 23.4%; Age 65 and over: 9.0%; Males per 100 females: 98.2; Marriage status: 36.8% never married, 52.9% now married, 2.7% separated, 3.3% widowed, 7.0% divorced; Foreign born: 10.4%; Speak English only: 82.8%; With disability: 11.1%; Veterans: 7.2%; Ancestry: 22.7% American, 20.2% Italian, 19.1% Irish, 15.4% German, 9.7% Polish

Employment: 11.0% management, business, and financial, 2.3% computer, engineering, and science, 13.6% education, legal, community service, arts, and media, 8.2% healthcare practitioners, 19.4% service, 23.7% sales and office, 10.0% natural resources, construction, and maintenance, 11.9% production, transportation, and material moving

Income: Per capita: $33,530; Median household: $92,695; Average household: $97,485; Households with income of $100,000 or more: 47.9%; Poverty rate: 7.1%

Educational Attainment: High school diploma or higher: 91.8%; Bachelor's degree or higher: 30.8%; Graduate/professional degree or higher: 12.0%

Housing: Homeownership rate: 72.6%; Median home value: $275,000; Median year structure built: 1974; Homeowner vacancy rate: 1.2%; Median selected monthly owner costs: $2,229 with a mortgage, $835 without a mortgage; Median gross rent: $1,202 per month; Rental vacancy rate: 6.9%

Health Insurance: 93.4% have insurance; 75.8% have private insurance; 26.2% have public insurance; 6.6% do not have insurance; 1.8% of children under 18 do not have insurance

Transportation: Commute: 96.4% car, 1.0% public transportation, 0.8% walk, 1.1% work from home; Mean travel time to work: 28.8 minutes

Additional Information Contacts
Town of Wawayanda . . . . (845) 355-5700
  http://www.townofwawayanda.com

WEST POINT (CDP).
Covers a land area of 19.749 square miles and a water area of 0.901 square miles. Located at 41.36° N. Lat; 74.02° W. Long. Elevation is 157 feet.

History: The site of the United States Military Reservation has been known as West Point since Revolutionary times. In 1802, Congress authorized the establishment of the military academy here. It became a military school of the first order under Major Sylvanus Thayer, superintendent from 1817 to 1833. Many Civil War leaders on both sides were graduates of West Point.

Population: 6,830; Growth (since 2000): -4.3%; Density: 345.8 persons per square mile; Race: 81.8% White, 4.1% Black/African American, 3.9% Asian, 0.4% American Indian/Alaska Native, 0.0% Native Hawaiian/Other Pacific Islander, 6.7% Two or more races, 13.9% Hispanic of any race; Average household size: 3.91; Median age: 20.8; Age under 18: 22.3%; Age 65 and over: 0.4%; Males per 100 females: 261.1; Marriage status: 71.7% never married, 25.7% now married, 0.1% separated, 0.4% widowed, 2.3% divorced; Foreign born: 4.5%; Speak English only: 84.5%; With disability: 6.8%; Veterans: 45.8%; Ancestry: 20.8% German, 18.6% Irish, 11.8% American, 10.8% English, 9.6% Italian

Employment: 6.6% management, business, and financial, 4.6% computer, engineering, and science, 23.7% education, legal, community service, arts, and media, 8.9% healthcare practitioners, 22.8% service, 17.5% sales and office, 4.0% natural resources, construction, and maintenance, 11.9% production, transportation, and material moving

Income: Per capita: $19,763; Median household: $100,385; Average household: $114,831; Households with income of $100,000 or more: 50.3%; Poverty rate: 3.9%

Educational Attainment: High school diploma or higher: 98.9%; Bachelor's degree or higher: 68.6%; Graduate/professional degree or higher: 39.0%

Four-year College(s)
United States Military Academy (Public)
   Fall 2014 Enrollment: 4,414 . . . . (845) 938-4011

Housing: Homeownership rate: 0.5%; Median home value: n/a; Median year structure built: 1973; Homeowner vacancy rate: 0.0%; Median selected monthly owner costs: n/a with a mortgage, n/a without a mortgage; Median gross rent: $3,119 per month; Rental vacancy rate: 0.0%

Health Insurance: 99.9% have insurance; 94.1% have private insurance; 9.2% have public insurance; 0.1% do not have insurance; 0.2% of children under 18 do not have insurance

Transportation: Commute: 24.1% car, 0.5% public transportation, 36.2% walk, 37.6% work from home; Mean travel time to work: 9.0 minutes

WESTTOWN (unincorporated postal area)

ZCTA: 10998

Covers a land area of 18.653 square miles and a water area of 0.141 square miles. Located at 41.32° N. Lat; 74.54° W. Long. Elevation is 502 feet.

Population: 2,736; Growth (since 2000): -25.0%; Density: 146.7 persons per square mile; Race: 89.9% White, 2.6% Black/African American, 0.1% Asian, 2.4% American Indian/Alaska Native, 0.0% Native Hawaiian/Other Pacific Islander, 0.8% Two or more races, 9.1% Hispanic of any race; Average household size: 3.16; Median age: 40.6; Age under 18: 27.6%; Age 65 and over: 8.8%; Males per 100 females: 100.0; Marriage status: 35.8% never married, 53.5% now married, 0.8% separated, 4.4% widowed, 6.3% divorced; Foreign born: 5.1%; Speak English only: 87.9%; With disability: 13.2%; Veterans: 9.3%; Ancestry: 25.3% Italian, 15.3% American, 14.5% Irish, 13.2% German, 11.5% Polish

Employment: 13.2% management, business, and financial, 0.6% computer, engineering, and science, 13.9% education, legal, community service, arts, and media, 4.2% healthcare practitioners, 18.9% service, 35.2% sales and office, 6.8% natural resources, construction, and maintenance, 7.2% production, transportation, and material moving

Income: Per capita: $32,292; Median household: $98,036; Average household: $100,366; Households with income of $100,000 or more: 47.4%; Poverty rate: 6.9%

Educational Attainment: High school diploma or higher: 91.7%; Bachelor's degree or higher: 27.6%; Graduate/professional degree or higher: 16.0%

Housing: Homeownership rate: 87.1%; Median home value: $300,300; Median year structure built: 1985; Homeowner vacancy rate: 0.0%; Median selected monthly owner costs: $2,369 with a mortgage, $921 without a mortgage; Median gross rent: $1,236 per month; Rental vacancy rate: 0.0%

Health Insurance: 91.7% have insurance; 82.9% have private insurance; 17.2% have public insurance; 8.3% do not have insurance; 7.7% of children under 18 do not have insurance

Transportation: Commute: 92.9% car, 3.9% public transportation, 0.0% walk, 3.3% work from home; Mean travel time to work: 43.2 minutes

WOODBURY (town).

Covers a land area of 36.124 square miles and a water area of 1.076 square miles. Located at 41.33° N. Lat; 74.10° W. Long. Elevation is 482 feet.

Population: 11,452; Growth (since 2000): 21.1%; Density: 317.0 persons per square mile; Race: 85.2% White, 3.3% Black/African American, 3.9% Asian, 0.0% American Indian/Alaska Native, 0.0% Native Hawaiian/Other Pacific Islander, 2.1% Two or more races, 17.9% Hispanic of any race; Average household size: 3.20; Median age: 40.4; Age under 18: 26.1%; Age 65 and over: 12.2%; Males per 100 females: 98.7; Marriage status: 29.3% never married, 59.1% now married, 1.3% separated, 4.8% widowed, 6.8% divorced; Foreign born: 18.9%; Speak English only: 73.2%; With disability: 8.8%; Veterans: 6.9%; Ancestry: 21.6% Irish, 14.5% Italian, 12.8% American, 10.8% German, 6.4% Polish

Employment: 15.0% management, business, and financial, 5.6% computer, engineering, and science, 10.3% education, legal, community service, arts, and media, 9.4% healthcare practitioners, 12.6% service, 31.0% sales and office, 6.4% natural resources, construction, and maintenance, 9.9% production, transportation, and material moving

Income: Per capita: $40,638; Median household: $122,232; Average household: $127,109; Households with income of $100,000 or more: 58.9%; Poverty rate: 5.6%

Educational Attainment: High school diploma or higher: 94.6%; Bachelor's degree or higher: 42.9%; Graduate/professional degree or higher: 21.6%

Housing: Homeownership rate: 86.4%; Median home value: $318,400; Median year structure built: 1978; Homeowner vacancy rate: 0.0%; Median

selected monthly owner costs: $2,751 with a mortgage, $1,053 without a mortgage; Median gross rent: $1,521 per month; Rental vacancy rate: 5.1%

Health Insurance: 94.9% have insurance; 88.0% have private insurance; 17.0% have public insurance; 5.1% do not have insurance; 0.9% of children under 18 do not have insurance

Safety: Violent crime rate: 5.5 per 10,000 population; Property crime rate: 450.0 per 10,000 population

Transportation: Commute: 86.6% car, 6.5% public transportation, 0.6% walk, 5.1% work from home; Mean travel time to work: 37.3 minutes

Additional Information Contacts

Town of Woodbury . . . . (845) 928-6829
http://www.townofwoodbury.com/home.shtml

WOODBURY (village).

Covers a land area of 35.602 square miles and a water area of 1.061 square miles. Located at 41.33° N. Lat; 74.10° W. Long. Elevation is 482 feet.

Population: 10,873; Growth (since 2000): n/a; Density: 305.4 persons per square mile; Race: 86.9% White, 3.1% Black/African American, 4.1% Asian, 0.0% American Indian/Alaska Native, 0.0% Native Hawaiian/Other Pacific Islander, 1.9% Two or more races, 16.9% Hispanic of any race; Average household size: 3.20; Median age: 40.3; Age under 18: 25.9%; Age 65 and over: 12.5%; Males per 100 females: 98.2; Marriage status: 29.8% never married, 58.3% now married, 1.3% separated, 5.0% widowed, 6.9% divorced; Foreign born: 18.5%; Speak English only: 74.6%; With disability: 8.8%; Veterans: 6.8%; Ancestry: 22.7% Irish, 14.8% Italian, 12.6% American, 11.0% German, 6.1% Polish

Employment: 15.0% management, business, and financial, 5.8% computer, engineering, and science, 10.5% education, legal, community service, arts, and media, 9.8% healthcare practitioners, 11.6% service, 31.5% sales and office, 6.6% natural resources, construction, and maintenance, 9.2% production, transportation, and material moving

Income: Per capita: $41,204; Median household: $127,660; Average household: $129,095; Households with income of $100,000 or more: 60.5%; Poverty rate: 5.3%

Educational Attainment: High school diploma or higher: 94.6%; Bachelor's degree or higher: 43.1%; Graduate/professional degree or higher: 21.4%

Housing: Homeownership rate: 87.7%; Median home value: $321,100; Median year structure built: 1976; Homeowner vacancy rate: 0.0%; Median selected monthly owner costs: $2,756 with a mortgage, $1,053 without a mortgage; Median gross rent: $1,574 per month; Rental vacancy rate: 5.9%

Health Insurance: 94.8% have insurance; 87.7% have private insurance; 17.5% have public insurance; 5.2% do not have insurance; 0.9% of children under 18 do not have insurance

Transportation: Commute: 86.7% car, 6.1% public transportation, 0.6% walk, 5.4% work from home; Mean travel time to work: 37.0 minutes

Orleans County

Located in western New York; bounded on the north by Lake Ontario; drained by Oak Orchard Creek. Covers a land area of 391.259 square miles, a water area of 426.163 square miles, and is located in the Eastern Time Zone at 43.50° N. Lat., 78.23° W. Long. The county was founded in 1824. County seat is Albion.

Orleans County is part of the Rochester, NY Metropolitan Statistical Area. The entire metro area includes: Livingston County, NY; Monroe County, NY; Ontario County, NY; Orleans County, NY; Wayne County, NY; Yates County, NY

Weather Station: Albion 2 NE   Elevation: 439 feet

	Jan	Feb	Mar	Apr	May	Jun	Jul	Aug	Sep	Oct	Nov	Dec
High	32	35	44	57	69	78	82	80	73	61	49	37
Low	18	19	26	37	47	57	62	61	54	43	34	24
Precip	2.7	2.0	2.8	3.0	3.0	3.1	3.0	3.0	3.6	3.1	3.2	3.0
Snow	19.5	13.6	11.1	2.1	0.3	0.0	0.0	0.0	0.0	0.2	4.5	15.1

High and Low temperatures in degrees Fahrenheit; Precipitation and Snow in inches

Population: 42,204; Growth (since 2000): -4.5%; Density: 107.9 persons per square mile; Race: 89.5% White, 6.1% Black/African American, 0.6% Asian, 0.6% American Indian/Alaska Native, 0.1% Native Hawaiian/Other Pacific Islander, 1.8% two or more races, 4.5% Hispanic of any race; Average household size: 2.43; Median age: 42.2; Age under 18: 20.6%; Age 65 and over: 15.7%; Males per 100 females: 98.1; Marriage status:

30.1% never married, 51.1% now married, 2.7% separated, 6.4% widowed, 12.4% divorced; Foreign born: 3.4%; Speak English only: 93.8%; With disability: 17.1%; Veterans: 9.4%; Ancestry: 27.4% German, 16.7% English, 16.2% Irish, 13.1% Italian, 8.4% Polish

Religion: Six largest groups: 15.9% Catholicism, 8.4% Baptist, 5.5% Methodist/Pietist, 2.3% Lutheran, 1.8% Non-denominational Protestant, 1.8% Presbyterian-Reformed

Economy: Unemployment rate: 5.1%; Leading industries: 14.4 % retail trade; 14.2 % construction; 13.9 % other services (except public administration); Farms: 487 totaling 135,090 acres; Company size: 0 employ 1,000 or more persons, 2 employ 500 to 999 persons, 10 employ 100 to 499 persons, 643 employ less than 100 persons; Business ownership: 667 women-owned, 50 Black-owned, 41 Hispanic-owned, n/a Asian-owned, n/a American Indian/Alaska Native-owned

Employment: 10.5% management, business, and financial, 3.1% computer, engineering, and science, 8.7% education, legal, community service, arts, and media, 4.3% healthcare practitioners, 17.5% service, 22.5% sales and office, 14.9% natural resources, construction, and maintenance, 18.4% production, transportation, and material moving

Income: Per capita: $22,070; Median household: $46,359; Average household: $56,908; Households with income of $100,000 or more: 13.9%; Poverty rate: 15.7%

Educational Attainment: High school diploma or higher: 85.4%; Bachelor's degree or higher: 15.4%; Graduate/professional degree or higher: 5.8%

Housing: Homeownership rate: 75.6%; Median home value: $91,300; Median year structure built: 1946; Homeowner vacancy rate: 1.4%; Median selected monthly owner costs: $1,203 with a mortgage, $554 without a mortgage; Median gross rent: $639 per month; Rental vacancy rate: 1.4%

Vital Statistics: Birth rate: 98.4 per 10,000 population; Death rate: 95.7 per 10,000 population; Age-adjusted cancer mortality rate: 174.8 deaths per 100,000 population

Health Insurance: 91.5% have insurance; 67.8% have private insurance; 41.4% have public insurance; 8.5% do not have insurance; 5.7% of children under 18 do not have insurance

Health Care: Physicians: 4.8 per 10,000 population; Dentists: 2.2 per 10,000 population; Hospital beds: 23.9 per 10,000 population; Hospital admissions: 595.4 per 10,000 population

Transportation: Commute: 93.1% car, 0.9% public transportation, 1.3% walk, 2.8% work from home; Mean travel time to work: 24.6 minutes

2016 Presidential Election: 67.2% Trump, 27.5% Clinton, 4.2% Johnson, 1.1% Stein

National and State Parks: Golden Hill State Park; Iroquois National Wildlife Refuge; Lakeside Beach State Park

Additional Information Contacts
Orleans Government . . . . (585) 589-5334
   http://www.orleansny.com

Orleans County Communities

ALBION (town). Covers a land area of 25.257 square miles and a water area of 0.093 square miles. Located at 43.23° N. Lat; 78.21° W. Long. Elevation is 538 feet.

History: Albion was the home of George M. Pullman (1831-1897), originator of the Pullman railroad cars. Pullman was a cabinetmaker here from 1848 to 1855. Disgusted with the dirt, discomfort, and inconvenience of early railroad passenger cars, he conceived the idea of a car with the luxuries of beds and upholstered seats. Incorporated in 1828.

Population: 8,403; Growth (since 2000): 4.5%; Density: 332.7 persons per square mile; Race: 72.4% White, 19.7% Black/African American, 0.5% Asian, 0.5% American Indian/Alaska Native, 0.0% Native Hawaiian/Other Pacific Islander, 1.3% Two or more races, 11.1% Hispanic of any race; Average household size: 2.36; Median age: 36.8; Age under 18: 16.8%; Age 65 and over: 12.3%; Males per 100 females: 99.0; Marriage status: 41.7% never married, 39.5% now married, 2.8% separated, 6.8% widowed, 12.1% divorced; Foreign born: 6.6%; Speak English only: 89.9%; With disability: 20.4%; Veterans: 6.1%; Ancestry: 22.2% German, 15.3% Irish, 13.3% Italian, 11.3% English, 4.2% Polish

Employment: 6.5% management, business, and financial, 0.6% computer, engineering, and science, 11.4% education, legal, community service, arts, and media, 5.2% healthcare practitioners, 20.5% service, 23.2% sales and office, 15.9% natural resources, construction, and maintenance, 16.6% production, transportation, and material moving

Income: Per capita: $14,264; Median household: $26,520; Average household: $46,614; Households with income of $100,000 or more: 11.3%; Poverty rate: 27.8%

Educational Attainment: High school diploma or higher: 74.8%; Bachelor's degree or higher: 10.3%; Graduate/professional degree or higher: 3.9%

School District(s)
Albion Central SD (PK-12)
   2014-15 Enrollment: 1,991 . . . . (585) 589-2056
Housing: Homeownership rate: 56.2%; Median home value: $89,400; Median year structure built: Before 1940; Homeowner vacancy rate: 2.8%; Median selected monthly owner costs: $1,233 with a mortgage, $549 without a mortgage; Median gross rent: $611 per month; Rental vacancy rate: 3.7%

Health Insurance: 87.7% have insurance; 53.1% have private insurance; 49.1% have public insurance; 12.3% do not have insurance; 2.6% of children under 18 do not have insurance

Transportation: Commute: 91.4% car, 0.7% public transportation, 2.9% walk, 1.2% work from home; Mean travel time to work: 20.5 minutes

Additional Information Contacts
Town of Albion . . . . (585) 589-7048
   http://www.townofalbion.com

ALBION (village). County seat. Covers a land area of 2.920 square miles and a water area of 0 square miles. Located at 43.25° N. Lat; 78.19° W. Long. Elevation is 538 feet.

Population: 5,631; Growth (since 2000): -24.3%; Density: 1,928.7 persons per square mile; Race: 80.2% White, 12.8% Black/African American, 0.6% Asian, 0.1% American Indian/Alaska Native, 0.0% Native Hawaiian/Other Pacific Islander, 0.3% Two or more races, 10.3% Hispanic of any race; Average household size: 2.27; Median age: 38.1; Age under 18: 21.8%; Age 65 and over: 16.7%; Males per 100 females: 90.7; Marriage status: 30.9% never married, 49.7% now married, 2.9% separated, 9.1% widowed, 10.4% divorced; Foreign born: 7.6%; Speak English only: 90.6%; With disability: 23.9%; Veterans: 8.1%; Ancestry: 27.4% German, 16.1% Irish, 13.7% English, 11.5% Italian, 4.4% Polish

Employment: 6.2% management, business, and financial, 1.1% computer, engineering, and science, 9.3% education, legal, community service, arts, and media, 3.0% healthcare practitioners, 24.2% service, 20.5% sales and office, 19.5% natural resources, construction, and maintenance, 16.3% production, transportation, and material moving

Income: Per capita: $17,975; Median household: $24,205; Average household: $41,452; Households with income of $100,000 or more: 8.1%; Poverty rate: 29.7%

Educational Attainment: High school diploma or higher: 75.2%; Bachelor's degree or higher: 9.1%; Graduate/professional degree or higher: 2.9%

School District(s)
Albion Central SD (PK-12)
   2014-15 Enrollment: 1,991 . . . . (585) 589-2056
Housing: Homeownership rate: 53.8%; Median home value: $71,600; Median year structure built: Before 1940; Homeowner vacancy rate: 3.0%; Median selected monthly owner costs: $1,111 with a mortgage, $504 without a mortgage; Median gross rent: $599 per month; Rental vacancy rate: 3.5%

Health Insurance: 87.7% have insurance; 51.8% have private insurance; 52.5% have public insurance; 12.3% do not have insurance; 3.0% of children under 18 do not have insurance

Safety: Violent crime rate: 23.4 per 10,000 population; Property crime rate: 278.6 per 10,000 population

Transportation: Commute: 89.8% car, 0.8% public transportation, 3.2% walk, 2.1% work from home; Mean travel time to work: 17.9 minutes

Additional Information Contacts
Village of Albion . . . . (585) 589-9176
   http://vil.albion.ny.us/content

BARRE (town). Covers a land area of 55.040 square miles and a water area of 0.011 square miles. Located at 43.18° N. Lat; 78.21° W. Long.
Population: 1,935; Growth (since 2000): -8.9%; Density: 35.2 persons per square mile; Race: 97.5% White, 0.0% Black/African American, 0.2% Asian, 0.0% American Indian/Alaska Native, 0.0% Native Hawaiian/Other Pacific Islander, 1.2% Two or more races, 4.1% Hispanic of any race; Average household size: 2.59; Median age: 46.4; Age under 18: 19.6%; Age 65 and over: 16.7%; Males per 100 females: 105.6; Marriage status: 24.4% never married, 60.0% now married, 2.7% separated, 5.9%

widowed, 9.7% divorced; Foreign born: 2.8%; Speak English only: 95.4%; With disability: 15.0%; Veterans: 9.3%; Ancestry: 29.0% English, 22.1% German, 16.1% Irish, 10.3% American, 7.8% Polish

Employment: 11.0% management, business, and financial, 4.2% computer, engineering, and science, 5.9% education, legal, community service, arts, and media, 6.3% healthcare practitioners, 18.3% service, 22.3% sales and office, 12.6% natural resources, construction, and maintenance, 19.3% production, transportation, and material moving

Income: Per capita: $24,776; Median household: $55,078; Average household: $63,142; Households with income of $100,000 or more: 14.8%; Poverty rate: 11.4%

Educational Attainment: High school diploma or higher: 85.0%; Bachelor's degree or higher: 14.5%; Graduate/professional degree or higher: 4.1%

Housing: Homeownership rate: 88.5%; Median home value: $90,700; Median year structure built: Before 1940; Homeowner vacancy rate: 0.0%; Median selected monthly owner costs: $1,194 with a mortgage, $539 without a mortgage; Median gross rent: $825 per month; Rental vacancy rate: 3.4%

Health Insurance: 89.3% have insurance; 66.9% have private insurance; 39.3% have public insurance; 10.7% do not have insurance; 10.5% of children under 18 do not have insurance

Transportation: Commute: 93.8% car, 0.4% public transportation, 2.0% walk, 1.7% work from home; Mean travel time to work: 26.2 minutes

CARLTON (town). Covers a land area of 43.607 square miles and a water area of 0.801 square miles. Located at 43.34° N. Lat; 78.21° W. Long. Elevation is 344 feet.

Population: 2,957; Growth (since 2000): -0.1%; Density: 67.8 persons per square mile; Race: 90.6% White, 3.6% Black/African American, 0.1% Asian, 1.0% American Indian/Alaska Native, 0.0% Native Hawaiian/Other Pacific Islander, 3.7% Two or more races, 1.8% Hispanic of any race; Average household size: 2.25; Median age: 49.8; Age under 18: 17.2%; Age 65 and over: 19.7%; Males per 100 females: 102.3; Marriage status: 24.1% never married, 58.2% now married, 1.7% separated, 6.1% widowed, 11.6% divorced; Foreign born: 4.4%; Speak English only: 94.1%; With disability: 14.0%; Veterans: 8.9%; Ancestry: 36.1% German, 16.8% Irish, 13.9% English, 13.3% Italian, 11.9% Polish

Employment: 8.6% management, business, and financial, 4.4% computer, engineering, and science, 6.8% education, legal, community service, arts, and media, 1.5% healthcare practitioners, 16.4% service, 22.6% sales and office, 22.8% natural resources, construction, and maintenance, 16.8% production, transportation, and material moving

Income: Per capita: $27,193; Median household: $52,546; Average household: $61,203; Households with income of $100,000 or more: 15.0%; Poverty rate: 7.3%

Educational Attainment: High school diploma or higher: 89.6%; Bachelor's degree or higher: 20.2%; Graduate/professional degree or higher: 6.7%

Housing: Homeownership rate: 91.4%; Median home value: $102,000; Median year structure built: 1953; Homeowner vacancy rate: 0.0%; Median selected monthly owner costs: $1,365 with a mortgage, $654 without a mortgage; Median gross rent: n/a per month; Rental vacancy rate: 0.0%

Health Insurance: 91.3% have insurance; 66.3% have private insurance; 42.9% have public insurance; 8.7% do not have insurance; 2.8% of children under 18 do not have insurance

Transportation: Commute: 91.4% car, 0.0% public transportation, 0.5% walk, 2.2% work from home; Mean travel time to work: 30.0 minutes

CLARENDON (town). Covers a land area of 35.219 square miles and a water area of 0 square miles. Located at 43.17° N. Lat; 78.06° W. Long. Elevation is 607 feet.

Population: 3,612; Growth (since 2000): 6.5%; Density: 102.6 persons per square mile; Race: 95.2% White, 1.3% Black/African American, 0.0% Asian, 1.4% American Indian/Alaska Native, 0.0% Native Hawaiian/Other Pacific Islander, 2.1% Two or more races, 2.2% Hispanic of any race; Average household size: 2.43; Median age: 45.9; Age under 18: 16.4%; Age 65 and over: 16.7%; Males per 100 females: 95.4; Marriage status: 23.6% never married, 58.0% now married, 2.1% separated, 3.2% widowed, 15.2% divorced; Foreign born: 0.9%; Speak English only: 97.4%; With disability: 16.0%; Veterans: 11.9%; Ancestry: 29.0% German, 20.1% English, 18.3% Irish, 16.7% Italian, 6.5% Polish

Employment: 11.0% management, business, and financial, 5.3% computer, engineering, and science, 5.6% education, legal, community service, arts, and media, 3.7% healthcare practitioners, 19.2% service,

25.9% sales and office, 9.3% natural resources, construction, and maintenance, 20.0% production, transportation, and material moving

Income: Per capita: $26,181; Median household: $50,189; Average household: $61,876; Households with income of $100,000 or more: 18.5%; Poverty rate: 12.5%

Educational Attainment: High school diploma or higher: 85.9%; Bachelor's degree or higher: 15.2%; Graduate/professional degree or higher: 5.1%

Housing: Homeownership rate: 88.3%; Median home value: $97,900; Median year structure built: 1978; Homeowner vacancy rate: 3.4%; Median selected monthly owner costs: $1,288 with a mortgage, $668 without a mortgage; Median gross rent: $697 per month; Rental vacancy rate: 0.0%

Health Insurance: 93.8% have insurance; 77.2% have private insurance; 37.8% have public insurance; 6.2% do not have insurance; 10.8% of children under 18 do not have insurance

Transportation: Commute: 95.9% car, 1.8% public transportation, 0.0% walk, 1.1% work from home; Mean travel time to work: 33.9 minutes

GAINES (town). Covers a land area of 34.419 square miles and a water area of 0.040 square miles. Located at 43.28° N. Lat; 78.20° W. Long. Elevation is 423 feet.

Population: 3,306; Growth (since 2000): -11.6%; Density: 96.1 persons per square mile; Race: 94.2% White, 4.2% Black/African American, 0.8% Asian, 0.1% American Indian/Alaska Native, 0.0% Native Hawaiian/Other Pacific Islander, 0.8% Two or more races, 0.0% Hispanic of any race; Average household size: 2.61; Median age: 43.1; Age under 18: 19.4%; Age 65 and over: 17.0%; Males per 100 females: 94.9; Marriage status: 28.2% never married, 53.4% now married, 4.2% separated, 5.2% widowed, 13.2% divorced; Foreign born: 1.3%; Speak English only: 98.7%; With disability: 21.1%; Veterans: 11.7%; Ancestry: 23.0% German, 22.9% Irish, 18.9% English, 18.1% Italian, 11.7% Polish

Employment: 12.4% management, business, and financial, 5.5% computer, engineering, and science, 11.6% education, legal, community service, arts, and media, 3.3% healthcare practitioners, 13.1% service, 28.2% sales and office, 13.9% natural resources, construction, and maintenance, 12.0% production, transportation, and material moving

Income: Per capita: $22,481; Median household: $48,293; Average household: $58,494; Households with income of $100,000 or more: 14.3%; Poverty rate: 11.7%

Educational Attainment: High school diploma or higher: 86.4%; Bachelor's degree or higher: 17.8%; Graduate/professional degree or higher: 5.8%

Housing: Homeownership rate: 83.2%; Median home value: $87,200; Median year structure built: 1979; Homeowner vacancy rate: 0.0%; Median selected monthly owner costs: $1,217 with a mortgage, $492 without a mortgage; Median gross rent: $536 per month; Rental vacancy rate: 0.0%

Health Insurance: 96.9% have insurance; 75.0% have private insurance; 39.9% have public insurance; 3.1% do not have insurance; 0.0% of children under 18 do not have insurance

Transportation: Commute: 96.0% car, 0.0% public transportation, 0.3% walk, 3.7% work from home; Mean travel time to work: 17.2 minutes

HOLLEY (village). Covers a land area of 1.268 square miles and a water area of 0 square miles. Located at 43.22° N. Lat; 78.03° W. Long. Elevation is 541 feet.

History: Incorporated 1867.

Population: 2,032; Growth (since 2000): 12.8%; Density: 1,602.4 persons per square mile; Race: 96.4% White, 0.6% Black/African American, 0.5% Asian, 0.2% American Indian/Alaska Native, 0.1% Native Hawaiian/Other Pacific Islander, 1.9% Two or more races, 1.1% Hispanic of any race; Average household size: 2.37; Median age: 36.2; Age under 18: 25.7%; Age 65 and over: 11.6%; Males per 100 females: 94.7; Marriage status: 32.9% never married, 40.0% now married, 3.7% separated, 9.0% widowed, 18.1% divorced; Foreign born: 1.5%; Speak English only: 96.4%; With disability: 13.2%; Veterans: 9.7%; Ancestry: 25.9% German, 21.8% Italian, 19.9% Irish, 13.0% English, 9.8% American

Employment: 8.8% management, business, and financial, 2.3% computer, engineering, and science, 7.7% education, legal, community service, arts, and media, 2.9% healthcare practitioners, 22.9% service, 26.3% sales and office, 9.4% natural resources, construction, and maintenance, 19.8% production, transportation, and material moving

Income: Per capita: $18,334; Median household: $35,034; Average household: $43,240; Households with income of $100,000 or more: 9.1%; Poverty rate: 26.3%

Educational Attainment: High school diploma or higher: 88.4%; Bachelor's degree or higher: 11.5%; Graduate/professional degree or higher: 3.8%

School District(s)

Holley Central SD (PK-12)

2014-15 Enrollment: 1,115 . . . . (585) 638-6316

Housing: Homeownership rate: 55.2%; Median home value: $82,700; Median year structure built: Before 1940; Homeowner vacancy rate: 0.0%; Median selected monthly owner costs: $957 with a mortgage, $461 without a mortgage; Median gross rent: $638 per month; Rental vacancy rate: 3.0%

Health Insurance: 92.1% have insurance; 64.6% have private insurance; 46.3% have public insurance; 7.9% do not have insurance; 2.7% of children under 18 do not have insurance

Safety: Violent crime rate: 34.4 per 10,000 population; Property crime rate: 309.8 per 10,000 population

Transportation: Commute: 94.5% car, 1.1% public transportation, 1.5% walk, 1.6% work from home; Mean travel time to work: 25.4 minutes

KENDALL (town). Covers a land area of 32.857 square miles and a water area of 0.061 square miles. Located at 43.33° N. Lat; 78.05° W. Long. Elevation is 338 feet.

Population: 2,693; Growth (since 2000): -5.1%; Density: 82.0 persons per square mile; Race: 96.1% White, 0.2% Black/African American, 0.0% Asian, 1.1% American Indian/Alaska Native, 0.0% Native Hawaiian/Other Pacific Islander, 2.0% Two or more races, 2.3% Hispanic of any race; Average household size: 2.60; Median age: 45.0; Age under 18: 24.4%; Age 65 and over: 15.5%; Males per 100 females: 101.9; Marriage status: 22.5% never married, 62.6% now married, 2.2% separated, 5.7% widowed, 9.3% divorced; Foreign born: 1.4%; Speak English only: 98.4%; With disability: 17.8%; Veterans: 10.8%; Ancestry: 34.7% German, 20.5% Irish, 14.8% English, 9.9% Italian, 9.5% Polish

Employment: 15.8% management, business, and financial, 3.7% computer, engineering, and science, 8.8% education, legal, community service, arts, and media, 3.7% healthcare practitioners, 14.5% service, 20.8% sales and office, 15.7% natural resources, construction, and maintenance, 17.2% production, transportation, and material moving

Income: Per capita: $24,029; Median household: $53,272; Average household: $62,828; Households with income of $100,000 or more: 15.3%; Poverty rate: 14.6%

Educational Attainment: High school diploma or higher: 88.7%; Bachelor's degree or higher: 15.9%; Graduate/professional degree or higher: 7.2%

School District(s)

Kendall Central SD (PK-12)

2014-15 Enrollment: 737 . . . . (585) 659-2741

Housing: Homeownership rate: 80.9%; Median home value: $116,700; Median year structure built: 1954; Homeowner vacancy rate: 1.9%; Median selected monthly owner costs: $1,229 with a mortgage, $558 without a mortgage; Median gross rent: $738 per month; Rental vacancy rate: 0.0%

Health Insurance: 95.9% have insurance; 75.6% have private insurance; 38.5% have public insurance; 4.1% do not have insurance; 0.9% of children under 18 do not have insurance

Transportation: Commute: 94.4% car, 0.3% public transportation, 0.9% walk, 4.3% work from home; Mean travel time to work: 29.8 minutes

KNOWLESVILLE (unincorporated postal area)

ZCTA: 14479

Covers a land area of 1.480 square miles and a water area of 0 square miles. Located at 43.24° N. Lat; 78.31° W. Long. Elevation is 512 feet.

Population: 282; Growth (since 2000): n/a; Density: 190.5 persons per square mile; Race: 100.0% White, 0.0% Black/African American, 0.0% Asian, 0.0% American Indian/Alaska Native, 0.0% Native Hawaiian/Other Pacific Islander, 0.0% Two or more races, 0.0% Hispanic of any race; Average household size: 2.29; Median age: 29.5; Age under 18: 22.7%; Age 65 and over: 3.2%; Males per 100 females: 97.8; Marriage status: 37.6% never married, 54.1% now married, 10.6% separated, 4.1% widowed, 4.1% divorced; Foreign born: 3.2%; Speak English only: 96.0%; With disability: 17.0%; Veterans: 15.1%; Ancestry: 25.9% Italian, 12.1% German, 11.3% Polish, 10.6% English, 7.1% French Canadian

Employment: 7.2% management, business, and financial, 0.0% computer, engineering, and science, 5.1% education, legal, community service, arts, and media, 0.0% healthcare practitioners, 5.1% service,

37.0% sales and office, 8.7% natural resources, construction, and maintenance, 37.0% production, transportation, and material moving

Income: Per capita: $22,046; Median household: n/a; Average household: $52,266; Households with income of $100,000 or more: 16.2%; Poverty rate: 20.2%

Educational Attainment: High school diploma or higher: 58.5%; Bachelor's degree or higher: n/a; Graduate/professional degree or higher: n/a

Housing: Homeownership rate: 69.1%; Median home value: $76,500; Median year structure built: Before 1940; Homeowner vacancy rate: 0.0%; Median selected monthly owner costs: $1,347 with a mortgage, $0 without a mortgage; Median gross rent: $626 per month; Rental vacancy rate: 0.0%

Health Insurance: 80.1% have insurance; 56.7% have private insurance; 26.6% have public insurance; 19.9% do not have insurance; 37.5% of children under 18 do not have insurance

Transportation: Commute: 100.0% car, 0.0% public transportation, 0.0% walk, 0.0% work from home; Mean travel time to work: 23.2 minutes

LYNDONVILLE (village). Covers a land area of 1.024 square miles and a water area of 0 square miles. Located at 43.32° N. Lat; 78.39° W. Long. Elevation is 322 feet.

History: Incorporated 1903.

Population: 789; Growth (since 2000): -8.5%; Density: 770.1 persons per square mile; Race: 95.9% White, 0.8% Black/African American, 0.9% Asian, 0.3% American Indian/Alaska Native, 0.4% Native Hawaiian/Other Pacific Islander, 1.8% Two or more races, 0.6% Hispanic of any race; Average household size: 2.39; Median age: 38.9; Age under 18: 22.8%; Age 65 and over: 14.3%; Males per 100 females: 98.6; Marriage status: 23.0% never married, 56.9% now married, 3.1% separated, 4.2% widowed, 15.9% divorced; Foreign born: 1.0%; Speak English only: 97.4%; With disability: 10.6%; Veterans: 10.5%; Ancestry: 28.1% English, 27.2% German, 11.3% Irish, 8.4% American, 7.5% Italian

Employment: 14.1% management, business, and financial, 1.7% computer, engineering, and science, 10.3% education, legal, community service, arts, and media, 1.4% healthcare practitioners, 8.3% service, 25.3% sales and office, 12.4% natural resources, construction, and maintenance, 26.4% production, transportation, and material moving

Income: Per capita: $25,826; Median household: $50,441; Average household: $62,455; Households with income of $100,000 or more: 14.2%; Poverty rate: 6.7%

Educational Attainment: High school diploma or higher: 92.4%; Bachelor's degree or higher: 18.7%; Graduate/professional degree or higher: 6.0%

School District(s)

Lyndonville Central SD (PK-12)

2014-15 Enrollment: 642 . . . . (585) 765-3101

Housing: Homeownership rate: 81.8%; Median home value: $82,100; Median year structure built: Before 1940; Homeowner vacancy rate: 0.0%; Median selected monthly owner costs: $1,017 with a mortgage, $498 without a mortgage; Median gross rent: $650 per month; Rental vacancy rate: 0.0%

Health Insurance: 92.5% have insurance; 69.3% have private insurance; 35.4% have public insurance; 7.5% do not have insurance; 0.0% of children under 18 do not have insurance

Transportation: Commute: 93.4% car, 0.6% public transportation, 4.8% walk, 0.6% work from home; Mean travel time to work: 27.3 minutes

MEDINA (village). Covers a land area of 3.299 square miles and a water area of 0.078 square miles. Located at 43.22° N. Lat; 78.39° W. Long. Elevation is 531 feet.

History: Incorporated 1832.

Population: 5,936; Growth (since 2000): -7.5%; Density: 1,799.5 persons per square mile; Race: 90.2% White, 5.5% Black/African American, 1.1% Asian, 0.5% American Indian/Alaska Native, 0.0% Native Hawaiian/Other Pacific Islander, 2.6% Two or more races, 7.1% Hispanic of any race; Average household size: 2.20; Median age: 39.1; Age under 18: 24.0%; Age 65 and over: 19.4%; Males per 100 females: 87.8; Marriage status: 30.0% never married, 46.5% now married, 2.7% separated, 9.3% widowed, 14.3% divorced; Foreign born: 2.2%; Speak English only: 93.9%; With disability: 22.3%; Veterans: 10.5%; Ancestry: 26.9% German, 18.3% Irish, 16.2% English, 12.2% Polish, 9.7% Italian

Employment: 10.6% management, business, and financial, 2.9% computer, engineering, and science, 13.4% education, legal, community

service, arts, and media, 6.1% healthcare practitioners, 15.4% service, 16.7% sales and office, 14.7% natural resources, construction, and maintenance, 20.3% production, transportation, and material moving
Income: Per capita: $21,750; Median household: $41,538; Average household: $48,624; Households with income of $100,000 or more: 8.0%; Poverty rate: 17.4%
Educational Attainment: High school diploma or higher: 90.8%; Bachelor's degree or higher: 21.9%; Graduate/professional degree or higher: 10.1%

School District(s)
Medina Central SD (PK-12)
   2014-15 Enrollment: 1,719 . . . . (585) 798-2700
Orleans-Niagara Boces
   2014-15 Enrollment: n/a . . . . (716) 731-6800
Housing: Homeownership rate: 59.0%; Median home value: $69,300; Median year structure built: Before 1940; Homeowner vacancy rate: 1.6%; Median selected monthly owner costs: $1,032 with a mortgage, $540 without a mortgage; Median gross rent: $630 per month; Rental vacancy rate: 0.0%
Health Insurance: 93.2% have insurance; 65.4% have private insurance; 52.4% have public insurance; 6.8% do not have insurance; 0.0% of children under 18 do not have insurance
Hospitals: Medina Memorial Hospital (101 beds)
Safety: Violent crime rate: 13.7 per 10,000 population; Property crime rate: 220.0 per 10,000 population
Transportation: Commute: 88.8% car, 3.2% public transportation, 2.0% walk, 3.5% work from home; Mean travel time to work: 19.2 minutes
Additional Information Contacts
Village of Medina. . . . . (585) 798-1790
   http://villagemedina.org/content

MURRAY (town).
Covers a land area of 31.059 square miles and a water area of 0.040 square miles. Located at 43.26° N. Lat; 78.06° W. Long. Elevation is 410 feet.
Population: 4,877; Growth (since 2000): -22.1%; Density: 157.0 persons per square mile; Race: 96.8% White, 1.0% Black/African American, 0.2% Asian, 0.8% American Indian/Alaska Native, 0.1% Native Hawaiian/Other Pacific Islander, 0.8% Two or more races, 1.3% Hispanic of any race; Average household size: 2.43; Median age: 40.7; Age under 18: 22.1%; Age 65 and over: 15.0%; Males per 100 females: 97.0; Marriage status: 30.9% never married, 45.0% now married, 2.5% separated, 7.6% widowed, 16.4% divorced; Foreign born: 1.9%; Speak English only: 94.7%; With disability: 14.8%; Veterans: 7.4%; Ancestry: 22.1% Italian, 20.5% German, 15.8% English, 15.3% Irish, 7.5% American
Employment: 9.9% management, business, and financial, 2.9% computer, engineering, and science, 6.0% education, legal, community service, arts, and media, 4.9% healthcare practitioners, 19.5% service, 23.6% sales and office, 14.6% natural resources, construction, and maintenance, 18.5% production, transportation, and material moving
Income: Per capita: $24,741; Median household: $43,280; Average household: $60,082; Households with income of $100,000 or more: 16.2%; Poverty rate: 16.4%
Educational Attainment: High school diploma or higher: 91.0%; Bachelor's degree or higher: 13.7%; Graduate/professional degree or higher: 3.3%
Housing: Homeownership rate: 73.7%; Median home value: $89,700; Median year structure built: 1942; Homeowner vacancy rate: 0.0%; Median selected monthly owner costs: $1,094 with a mortgage, $499 without a mortgage; Median gross rent: $645 per month; Rental vacancy rate: 2.2%
Health Insurance: 93.2% have insurance; 71.4% have private insurance; 39.2% have public insurance; 6.8% do not have insurance; 1.3% of children under 18 do not have insurance
Transportation: Commute: 96.4% car, 0.4% public transportation, 0.6% walk, 2.1% work from home; Mean travel time to work: 26.1 minutes
Additional Information Contacts
Town of Murray. . . . . (585) 638-6570
   http://www.townofmurray.org

RIDGEWAY (town).
Covers a land area of 50.026 square miles and a water area of 0.216 square miles. Located at 43.26° N. Lat; 78.38° W. Long. Elevation is 417 feet.
Population: 6,647; Growth (since 2000): -3.5%; Density: 132.9 persons per square mile; Race: 93.1% White, 2.7% Black/African American, 0.7% Asian, 0.5% American Indian/Alaska Native, 0.0% Native Hawaiian/Other Pacific Islander, 2.9% Two or more races, 4.3% Hispanic of any race;

Average household size: 2.50; Median age: 36.2; Age under 18: 26.1%; Age 65 and over: 14.4%; Males per 100 females: 97.2; Marriage status: 29.6% never married, 52.5% now married, 2.5% separated, 6.4% widowed, 11.5% divorced; Foreign born: 3.2%; Speak English only: 92.0%; With disability: 17.2%; Veterans: 12.6%; Ancestry: 30.6% German, 16.0% English, 13.5% Irish, 11.7% Italian, 11.4% Polish
Employment: 10.7% management, business, and financial, 2.1% computer, engineering, and science, 10.9% education, legal, community service, arts, and media, 5.6% healthcare practitioners, 17.9% service, 19.1% sales and office, 14.2% natural resources, construction, and maintenance, 19.6% production, transportation, and material moving
Income: Per capita: $23,216; Median household: $50,666; Average household: $58,160; Households with income of $100,000 or more: 13.9%; Poverty rate: 11.3%
Educational Attainment: High school diploma or higher: 87.8%; Bachelor's degree or higher: 19.4%; Graduate/professional degree or higher: 9.1%
Housing: Homeownership rate: 71.4%; Median home value: $87,800; Median year structure built: Before 1940; Homeowner vacancy rate: 1.4%; Median selected monthly owner costs: $1,158 with a mortgage, $533 without a mortgage; Median gross rent: $684 per month; Rental vacancy rate: 0.0%
Health Insurance: 92.3% have insurance; 69.1% have private insurance; 40.0% have public insurance; 7.7% do not have insurance; 7.4% of children under 18 do not have insurance
Transportation: Commute: 89.7% car, 2.0% public transportation, 1.6% walk, 4.7% work from home; Mean travel time to work: 19.8 minutes

SHELBY (town).
Covers a land area of 46.390 square miles and a water area of 0.339 square miles. Located at 43.17° N. Lat; 78.39° W. Long. Elevation is 600 feet.
Population: 5,242; Growth (since 2000): -3.3%; Density: 113.0 persons per square mile; Race: 88.3% White, 6.3% Black/African American, 1.8% Asian, 0.2% American Indian/Alaska Native, 0.4% Native Hawaiian/Other Pacific Islander, 2.3% Two or more races, 6.0% Hispanic of any race; Average household size: 2.26; Median age: 43.7; Age under 18: 20.7%; Age 65 and over: 20.6%; Males per 100 females: 93.1; Marriage status: 30.8% never married, 49.9% now married, 3.2% separated, 8.7% widowed, 10.7% divorced; Foreign born: 4.4%; Speak English only: 92.7%; With disability: 18.9%; Veterans: 9.6%; Ancestry: 27.4% German, 18.6% English, 15.4% Irish, 11.2% Polish, 9.4% Italian
Employment: 12.3% management, business, and financial, 2.4% computer, engineering, and science, 9.3% education, legal, community service, arts, and media, 3.9% healthcare practitioners, 19.0% service, 18.4% sales and office, 12.8% natural resources, construction, and maintenance, 21.9% production, transportation, and material moving
Income: Per capita: $20,855; Median household: $40,464; Average household: $48,005; Households with income of $100,000 or more: 9.5%; Poverty rate: 21.8%
Educational Attainment: High school diploma or higher: 90.1%; Bachelor's degree or higher: 17.4%; Graduate/professional degree or higher: 7.6%
Housing: Homeownership rate: 68.8%; Median home value: $80,700; Median year structure built: Before 1940; Homeowner vacancy rate: 1.7%; Median selected monthly owner costs: $1,153 with a mortgage, $538 without a mortgage; Median gross rent: $629 per month; Rental vacancy rate: 0.0%
Health Insurance: 90.0% have insurance; 66.2% have private insurance; 47.4% have public insurance; 10.0% do not have insurance; 8.2% of children under 18 do not have insurance
Transportation: Commute: 91.9% car, 1.4% public transportation, 2.0% walk, 3.9% work from home; Mean travel time to work: 20.7 minutes
Additional Information Contacts
Town of Shelby . . . . (585) 798-3120
   http://www.townofshelbyny.org

WATERPORT (unincorporated postal area)
ZCTA: 14571
   Covers a land area of 18.355 square miles and a water area of 0.505 square miles. Located at 43.34° N. Lat; 78.25° W. Long. Elevation is 351 feet.
   Population: 1,004; Growth (since 2000): -10.3%; Density: 54.7 persons per square mile; Race: 88.2% White, 6.7% Black/African American, 0.4% Asian, 3.1% American Indian/Alaska Native, 0.0% Native Hawaiian/Other Pacific Islander, 1.1% Two or more races, 0.5%

Hispanic of any race; Average household size: 1.90; Median age: 51.7; Age under 18: 10.7%; Age 65 and over: 25.2%; Males per 100 females: 103.5; Marriage status: 24.3% never married, 62.5% now married, 3.4% separated, 4.2% widowed, 9.0% divorced; Foreign born: 6.1%; Speak English only: 95.1%; With disability: 11.8%; Veterans: 6.1%; Ancestry: 28.2% German, 21.6% Irish, 20.7% Italian, 12.7% English, 10.7% Hungarian

Employment: 2.3% management, business, and financial, 2.7% computer, engineering, and science, 9.6% education, legal, community service, arts, and media, 0.0% healthcare practitioners, 19.1% service, 16.9% sales and office, 21.6% natural resources, construction, and maintenance, 27.8% production, transportation, and material moving

Income: Per capita: $31,220; Median household: $46,900; Average household: $61,655; Households with income of $100,000 or more: 17.5%; Poverty rate: 7.0%

Educational Attainment: High school diploma or higher: 86.1%; Bachelor's degree or higher: 17.6%; Graduate/professional degree or higher: 5.4%

Housing: Homeownership rate: 95.2%; Median home value: $84,900; Median year structure built: 1954; Homeowner vacancy rate: 0.0%; Median selected monthly owner costs: $1,259 with a mortgage, $685 without a mortgage; Median gross rent: n/a per month; Rental vacancy rate: 0.0%

Health Insurance: 85.9% have insurance; 70.4% have private insurance; 35.1% have public insurance; 14.1% do not have insurance; 0.0% of children under 18 do not have insurance

Transportation: Commute: 83.4% car, 0.0% public transportation, 1.5% walk, 4.4% work from home; Mean travel time to work: 27.1 minutes

YATES (town). Covers a land area of 37.387 square miles and a water area of 0 square miles. Located at 43.34° N. Lat; 78.39° W. Long. Elevation is 325 feet.

Population: 2,532; Growth (since 2000): 0.9%; Density: 67.7 persons per square mile; Race: 96.8% White, 2.1% Black/African American, 0.4% Asian, 0.1% American Indian/Alaska Native, 0.1% Native Hawaiian/Other Pacific Islander, 0.6% Two or more races, 0.9% Hispanic of any race; Average household size: 2.57; Median age: 44.0; Age under 18: 23.5%; Age 65 and over: 12.5%; Males per 100 females: 103.9; Marriage status: 20.8% never married, 61.0% now married, 2.3% separated, 5.0% widowed, 13.1% divorced; Foreign born: 1.6%; Speak English only: 93.4%; With disability: 10.9%; Veterans: 8.7%; Ancestry: 39.6% German, 22.6% English, 13.3% Irish, 8.6% Polish, 6.3% American

Employment: 9.0% management, business, and financial, 2.4% computer, engineering, and science, 9.6% education, legal, community service, arts, and media, 3.8% healthcare practitioners, 11.6% service, 23.5% sales and office, 20.8% natural resources, construction, and maintenance, 19.3% production, transportation, and material moving

Income: Per capita: $25,799; Median household: $54,801; Average household: $66,026; Households with income of $100,000 or more: 14.4%; Poverty rate: 9.9%

Educational Attainment: High school diploma or higher: 84.3%; Bachelor's degree or higher: 13.7%; Graduate/professional degree or higher: 5.1%

Housing: Homeownership rate: 89.2%; Median home value: $92,100; Median year structure built: 1947; Homeowner vacancy rate: 2.3%; Median selected monthly owner costs: $1,137 with a mortgage, $613 without a mortgage; Median gross rent: $706 per month; Rental vacancy rate: 0.0%

Health Insurance: 85.2% have insurance; 66.6% have private insurance; 30.1% have public insurance; 14.8% do not have insurance; 16.7% of children under 18 do not have insurance

Transportation: Commute: 92.9% car, 0.2% public transportation, 2.1% walk, 2.6% work from home; Mean travel time to work: 26.1 minutes

Oswego County

Located in north central New York; bounded on the northwest by Lake Ontario, and on the south by Oneida Lake and the Oneida River; drained by the Oswego and Salmon Rivers. Covers a land area of 951.650 square miles, a water area of 360.433 square miles, and is located in the Eastern Time Zone at 43.46° N. Lat., 76.21° W. Long. The county was founded in 1816. County seat is Oswego.

Oswego County is part of the Syracuse, NY Metropolitan Statistical Area. The entire metro area includes: Madison County, NY; Onondaga County, NY; Oswego County, NY

Weather Station: Oswego East										Elevation: 350 feet		
	Jan	Feb	Mar	Apr	May	Jun	Jul	Aug	Sep	Oct	Nov	Dec
High	31	33	41	54	65	75	80	79	71	59	47	36
Low	18	19	26	37	47	56	62	61	54	44	35	24
Precip	3.6	2.8	3.2	3.5	3.3	3.0	3.1	3.4	3.9	4.1	4.5	3.8
Snow	45.0	32.8	17.1	3.8	tr	0.0	0.0	0.0	tr	0.2	8.5	34.6

High and Low temperatures in degrees Fahrenheit; Precipitation and Snow in inches

Population: 121,183; Growth (since 2000): -1.0%; Density: 127.3 persons per square mile; Race: 95.6% White, 0.9% Black/African American, 0.6% Asian, 0.2% American Indian/Alaska Native, 0.0% Native Hawaiian/Other Pacific Islander, 1.7% two or more races, 2.3% Hispanic of any race; Average household size: 2.57; Median age: 39.2; Age under 18: 22.0%; Age 65 and over: 13.7%; Males per 100 females: 99.4; Marriage status: 32.8% never married, 49.7% now married, 2.9% separated, 5.8% widowed, 11.7% divorced; Foreign born: 1.9%; Speak English only: 95.7%; With disability: 14.5%; Veterans: 9.2%; Ancestry: 20.8% Irish, 18.7% German, 14.0% English, 13.6% Italian, 8.1% French

Religion: Six largest groups: 20.8% Catholicism, 6.3% Methodist/Pietist, 1.8% Holiness, 1.7% Non-denominational Protestant, 0.9% Baptist, 0.7% Presbyterian-Reformed

Economy: Unemployment rate: 5.8%; Leading industries: 16.9 % retail trade; 14.4 % construction; 13.9 % accommodation and food services; Farms: 657 totaling 94,209 acres; Company size: 1 employs 1,000 or more persons, 5 employ 500 to 999 persons, 23 employ 100 to 499 persons, 2,124 employ less than 100 persons; Business ownership: 2,150 women-owned, 43 Black-owned, 69 Hispanic-owned, 152 Asian-owned, n/a American Indian/Alaska Native-owned

Employment: 10.0% management, business, and financial, 3.5% computer, engineering, and science, 10.3% education, legal, community service, arts, and media, 5.0% healthcare practitioners, 20.4% service, 22.6% sales and office, 12.0% natural resources, construction, and maintenance, 16.3% production, transportation, and material moving

Income: Per capita: $23,466; Median household: $47,860; Average household: $60,560; Households with income of $100,000 or more: 16.2%; Poverty rate: 18.6%

Educational Attainment: High school diploma or higher: 86.4%; Bachelor's degree or higher: 17.6%; Graduate/professional degree or higher: 7.3%

Housing: Homeownership rate: 72.1%; Median home value: $94,800; Median year structure built: 1968; Homeowner vacancy rate: 2.3%; Median selected monthly owner costs: $1,182 with a mortgage, $483 without a mortgage; Median gross rent: $721 per month; Rental vacancy rate: 6.6%

Vital Statistics: Birth rate: 110.4 per 10,000 population; Death rate: 86.3 per 10,000 population; Age-adjusted cancer mortality rate: 179.3 deaths per 100,000 population

Health Insurance: 92.2% have insurance; 64.8% have private insurance; 40.9% have public insurance; 7.8% do not have insurance; 4.9% of children under 18 do not have insurance

Health Care: Physicians: 7.9 per 10,000 population; Dentists: 4.4 per 10,000 population; Hospital beds: 10.4 per 10,000 population; Hospital admissions: 423.8 per 10,000 population

Air Quality Index (AQI): Percent of Days: 98.4% good, 1.6% moderate, 0.0% unhealthy for sensitive individuals, 0.0% unhealthy, 0.0% very unhealthy; Annual median: 30; Annual maximum: 100

Transportation: Commute: 90.5% car, 0.8% public transportation, 4.0% walk, 3.7% work from home; Mean travel time to work: 23.8 minutes

2016 Presidential Election: 58.1% Trump, 35.9% Clinton, 4.5% Johnson, 1.5% Stein

National and State Parks: Battle Island State Park; Fort Brewerton State Park; Happy Valley State Wildlife Management Area; Littlejohn State Game Management Area; Selkirk Shores State Park; Threemile Bay State Game Management Area

Additional Information Contacts
Oswego Government . . . . (315) 349-8385
  http://www.co.oswego.ny.us

Oswego County Communities

ALBION (town). Covers a land area of 47.286 square miles and a water area of 0.532 square miles. Located at 43.49° N. Lat; 76.03° W. Long.
Population: 2,461; Growth (since 2000): 18.1%; Density: 52.0 persons per square mile; Race: 97.2% White, 0.1% Black/African American, 0.4% Asian, 0.0% American Indian/Alaska Native, 0.0% Native Hawaiian/Other Pacific Islander, 2.2% Two or more races, 0.7% Hispanic of any race;

Average household size: 3.00; Median age: 36.1; Age under 18: 30.5%; Age 65 and over: 10.2%; Males per 100 females: 106.1; Marriage status: 25.4% never married, 54.9% now married, 3.5% separated, 4.7% widowed, 15.0% divorced; Foreign born: 0.6%; Speak English only: 96.6%; With disability: 14.1%; Veterans: 11.8%; Ancestry: 19.2% Irish, 17.6% English, 16.9% German, 11.3% French, 10.6% American

Employment: 10.3% management, business, and financial, 2.0% computer, engineering, and science, 6.7% education, legal, community service, arts, and media, 10.0% healthcare practitioners, 18.5% service, 17.4% sales and office, 13.8% natural resources, construction, and maintenance, 21.2% production, transportation, and material moving

Income: Per capita: $18,132; Median household: $44,607; Average household: $53,397; Households with income of $100,000 or more: 11.4%; Poverty rate: 28.1%

Educational Attainment: High school diploma or higher: 81.2%; Bachelor's degree or higher: 10.0%; Graduate/professional degree or higher: 5.0%

Housing: Homeownership rate: 85.2%; Median home value: $76,400; Median year structure built: 1981; Homeowner vacancy rate: 0.0%; Median selected monthly owner costs: $1,065 with a mortgage, $404 without a mortgage; Median gross rent: $900 per month; Rental vacancy rate: 0.0%

Health Insurance: 85.0% have insurance; 51.7% have private insurance; 43.6% have public insurance; 15.0% do not have insurance; 9.7% of children under 18 do not have insurance

Transportation: Commute: 91.8% car, 3.4% public transportation, 0.7% walk, 3.8% work from home; Mean travel time to work: 29.6 minutes

ALTMAR (village). Covers a land area of 2.069 square miles and a water area of 0.010 square miles. Located at 43.51° N. Lat; 76.01° W. Long. Elevation is 574 feet.

Population: 412; Growth (since 2000): 17.4%; Density: 199.1 persons per square mile; Race: 97.1% White, 0.0% Black/African American, 1.2% Asian, 0.0% American Indian/Alaska Native, 0.0% Native Hawaiian/Other Pacific Islander, 1.5% Two or more races, 0.2% Hispanic of any race; Average household size: 2.84; Median age: 30.8; Age under 18: 37.1%; Age 65 and over: 8.0%; Males per 100 females: 116.5; Marriage status: 31.0% never married, 42.2% now married, 7.3% separated, 4.2% widowed, 22.6% divorced; Foreign born: 1.9%; Speak English only: 97.0%; With disability: 18.9%; Veterans: 7.7%; Ancestry: 21.1% Irish, 20.6% English, 16.7% German, 12.9% French, 7.3% Polish

Employment: 6.1% management, business, and financial, 4.3% computer, engineering, and science, 5.2% education, legal, community service, arts, and media, 0.9% healthcare practitioners, 20.9% service, 24.3% sales and office, 10.4% natural resources, construction, and maintenance, 27.8% production, transportation, and material moving

Income: Per capita: $13,778; Median household: $27,386; Average household: $38,554; Households with income of $100,000 or more: 6.9%; Poverty rate: 44.9%

Educational Attainment: High school diploma or higher: 75.5%; Bachelor's degree or higher: 4.6%; Graduate/professional degree or higher: 3.0%

School District(s)
Altmar Parish-Williamstown Central SD (PK-12)
    2014-15 Enrollment: 1,297 . . . . (315) 625-5251

Housing: Homeownership rate: 58.6%; Median home value: $51,700; Median year structure built: 1979; Homeowner vacancy rate: 0.0%; Median selected monthly owner costs: $875 with a mortgage, $557 without a mortgage; Median gross rent: $783 per month; Rental vacancy rate: 0.0%

Health Insurance: 85.7% have insurance; 30.6% have private insurance; 62.9% have public insurance; 14.3% do not have insurance; 8.5% of children under 18 do not have insurance

Transportation: Commute: 91.2% car, 4.4% public transportation, 0.0% walk, 1.8% work from home; Mean travel time to work: 25.8 minutes

AMBOY (town). Covers a land area of 37.049 square miles and a water area of 0.692 square miles. Located at 43.38° N. Lat; 75.92° W. Long.

Population: 1,269; Growth (since 2000): -3.3%; Density: 34.3 persons per square mile; Race: 97.6% White, 0.2% Black/African American, 0.0% Asian, 0.1% American Indian/Alaska Native, 0.0% Native Hawaiian/Other Pacific Islander, 1.1% Two or more races, 1.1% Hispanic of any race; Average household size: 2.79; Median age: 41.5; Age under 18: 24.1%; Age 65 and over: 12.5%; Males per 100 females: 108.1; Marriage status: 30.9% never married, 54.7% now married, 4.2% separated, 4.2% widowed, 10.2% divorced; Foreign born: 0.7%; Speak English only: 96.5%;

With disability: 14.7%; Veterans: 12.8%; Ancestry: 19.6% German, 19.3% Irish, 11.5% English, 11.3% Italian, 8.4% Polish

Employment: 10.9% management, business, and financial, 2.0% computer, engineering, and science, 5.8% education, legal, community service, arts, and media, 1.1% healthcare practitioners, 18.1% service, 28.6% sales and office, 9.9% natural resources, construction, and maintenance, 23.5% production, transportation, and material moving

Income: Per capita: $21,704; Median household: $50,089; Average household: $58,437; Households with income of $100,000 or more: 16.3%; Poverty rate: 12.0%

Educational Attainment: High school diploma or higher: 75.5%; Bachelor's degree or higher: 8.5%; Graduate/professional degree or higher: 1.5%

Housing: Homeownership rate: 89.2%; Median home value: $85,200; Median year structure built: 1984; Homeowner vacancy rate: 4.9%; Median selected monthly owner costs: $1,089 with a mortgage, $423 without a mortgage; Median gross rent: $888 per month; Rental vacancy rate: 0.0%

Health Insurance: 83.0% have insurance; 51.9% have private insurance; 42.6% have public insurance; 17.0% do not have insurance; 10.5% of children under 18 do not have insurance

Transportation: Commute: 95.3% car, 0.0% public transportation, 0.0% walk, 3.2% work from home; Mean travel time to work: 39.6 minutes

BERNHARDS BAY (unincorporated postal area)
ZCTA: 13028
    Covers a land area of 18.688 square miles and a water area of 0.302 square miles. Located at 43.30° N. Lat; 75.93° W. Long. Elevation is 390 feet.

Population: 1,426; Growth (since 2000): 3.3%; Density: 76.3 persons per square mile; Race: 91.4% White, 0.0% Black/African American, 0.0% Asian, 0.0% American Indian/Alaska Native, 0.0% Native Hawaiian/Other Pacific Islander, 0.7% Two or more races, 7.9% Hispanic of any race; Average household size: 2.56; Median age: 47.1; Age under 18: 22.2%; Age 65 and over: 17.5%; Males per 100 females: 113.3; Marriage status: 28.9% never married, 59.6% now married, 2.7% separated, 2.6% widowed, 8.9% divorced; Foreign born: 0.0%; Speak English only: 92.4%; With disability: 9.2%; Veterans: 16.9%; Ancestry: 31.1% Irish, 30.6% German, 8.1% French, 7.3% English, 7.2% American

Employment: 15.5% management, business, and financial, 1.9% computer, engineering, and science, 2.7% education, legal, community service, arts, and media, 0.0% healthcare practitioners, 18.7% service, 28.1% sales and office, 22.0% natural resources, construction, and maintenance, 11.1% production, transportation, and material moving

Income: Per capita: $27,951; Median household: $40,000; Average household: $72,031; Households with income of $100,000 or more: 18.9%; Poverty rate: 9.6%

Educational Attainment: High school diploma or higher: 84.4%; Bachelor's degree or higher: 11.8%; Graduate/professional degree or higher: 6.0%

Housing: Homeownership rate: 71.0%; Median home value: $159,900; Median year structure built: 1969; Homeowner vacancy rate: 2.7%; Median selected monthly owner costs: $1,337 with a mortgage, $571 without a mortgage; Median gross rent: $932 per month; Rental vacancy rate: 0.0%

Health Insurance: 83.9% have insurance; 55.3% have private insurance; 43.6% have public insurance; 16.1% do not have insurance; 21.5% of children under 18 do not have insurance

Transportation: Commute: 94.3% car, 0.0% public transportation, 2.2% walk, 3.5% work from home; Mean travel time to work: 39.5 minutes

BOYLSTON (town). Covers a land area of 39.152 square miles and a water area of 0.021 square miles. Located at 43.66° N. Lat; 75.95° W. Long.

Population: 513; Growth (since 2000): 1.6%; Density: 13.1 persons per square mile; Race: 95.7% White, 0.0% Black/African American, 0.0% Asian, 1.4% American Indian/Alaska Native, 0.0% Native Hawaiian/Other Pacific Islander, 2.9% Two or more races, 4.3% Hispanic of any race; Average household size: 2.63; Median age: 40.7; Age under 18: 25.3%; Age 65 and over: 15.6%; Males per 100 females: 115.3; Marriage status: 30.9% never married, 58.1% now married, 2.4% separated, 4.1% widowed, 6.9% divorced; Foreign born: 1.0%; Speak English only: 97.8%; With disability: 12.8%; Veterans: 15.6%; Ancestry: 18.5% English, 13.1% French, 12.9% German, 11.1% Irish, 9.0% Polish

Employment: 6.6% management, business, and financial, 2.6% computer, engineering, and science, 7.9% education, legal, community service, arts, and media, 5.3% healthcare practitioners, 20.2% service, 14.9% sales and office, 23.2% natural resources, construction, and maintenance, 19.3% production, transportation, and material moving
Income: Per capita: $23,722; Median household: $56,250; Average household: $59,972; Households with income of $100,000 or more: 14.4%; Poverty rate: 13.1%
Educational Attainment: High school diploma or higher: 93.1%; Bachelor's degree or higher: 20.0%; Graduate/professional degree or higher: 8.6%
Housing: Homeownership rate: 87.7%; Median home value: $116,500; Median year structure built: 1974; Homeowner vacancy rate: 0.0%; Median selected monthly owner costs: $1,287 with a mortgage, $450 without a mortgage; Median gross rent: $650 per month; Rental vacancy rate: 0.0%
Health Insurance: 85.1% have insurance; 65.4% have private insurance; 36.0% have public insurance; 14.9% do not have insurance; 1.5% of children under 18 do not have insurance
Transportation: Commute: 91.3% car, 0.0% public transportation, 1.3% walk, 6.5% work from home; Mean travel time to work: 33.3 minutes

CENTRAL SQUARE (village). Covers a land area of 1.906 square miles and a water area of 0 square miles. Located at 43.29° N. Lat; 76.14° W. Long. Elevation is 449 feet.
Population: 1,945; Growth (since 2000): 18.2%; Density: 1,020.3 persons per square mile; Race: 98.9% White, 0.1% Black/African American, 0.0% Asian, 0.0% American Indian/Alaska Native, 0.0% Native Hawaiian/Other Pacific Islander, 1.0% Two or more races, 0.1% Hispanic of any race; Average household size: 2.32; Median age: 41.5; Age under 18: 22.3%; Age 65 and over: 17.1%; Males per 100 females: 83.5; Marriage status: 27.6% never married, 54.2% now married, 2.0% separated, 7.7% widowed, 10.5% divorced; Foreign born: 1.6%; Speak English only: 94.4%; With disability: 16.5%; Veterans: 11.3%; Ancestry: 21.3% Irish, 21.0% German, 16.0% English, 15.6% Italian, 8.0% French
Employment: 12.5% management, business, and financial, 4.5% computer, engineering, and science, 10.6% education, legal, community service, arts, and media, 6.1% healthcare practitioners, 13.2% service, 35.0% sales and office, 9.9% natural resources, construction, and maintenance, 8.2% production, transportation, and material moving
Income: Per capita: $25,974; Median household: $45,240; Average household: $59,123; Households with income of $100,000 or more: 18.7%; Poverty rate: 14.7%
Educational Attainment: High school diploma or higher: 89.0%; Bachelor's degree or higher: 19.9%; Graduate/professional degree or higher: 6.4%

School District(s)
Central Square Central SD (PK-12)
    2014-15 Enrollment: 4,051 . . . . (315) 668-4220
Housing: Homeownership rate: 61.8%; Median home value: $141,700; Median year structure built: 1973; Homeowner vacancy rate: 3.2%; Median selected monthly owner costs: $1,397 with a mortgage, $607 without a mortgage; Median gross rent: $724 per month; Rental vacancy rate: 5.6%
Health Insurance: 98.5% have insurance; 76.3% have private insurance; 38.3% have public insurance; 1.5% do not have insurance; 0.7% of children under 18 do not have insurance
Safety: Violent crime rate: 11.0 per 10,000 population; Property crime rate: 308.2 per 10,000 population
Transportation: Commute: 99.2% car, 0.0% public transportation, 0.0% walk, 0.8% work from home; Mean travel time to work: 29.1 minutes

CLEVELAND (village). Covers a land area of 1.131 square miles and a water area of 0.093 square miles. Located at 43.24° N. Lat; 75.88° W. Long. Elevation is 436 feet.
Population: 776; Growth (since 2000): 2.4%; Density: 685.9 persons per square mile; Race: 99.0% White, 0.0% Black/African American, 0.0% Asian, 0.0% American Indian/Alaska Native, 0.0% Native Hawaiian/Other Pacific Islander, 1.0% Two or more races, 0.8% Hispanic of any race; Average household size: 2.84; Median age: 35.9; Age under 18: 25.8%; Age 65 and over: 14.4%; Males per 100 females: 106.0; Marriage status: 34.1% never married, 44.3% now married, 2.9% separated, 10.7% widowed, 10.9% divorced; Foreign born: 0.5%; Speak English only: 100.0%; With disability: 12.5%; Veterans: 5.4%; Ancestry: 19.3% English, 18.9% German, 16.5% Irish, 9.8% Polish, 8.0% Italian
Employment: 10.8% management, business, and financial, 0.9% computer, engineering, and science, 3.4% education, legal, community

service, arts, and media, 3.7% healthcare practitioners, 23.7% service, 30.8% sales and office, 8.6% natural resources, construction, and maintenance, 18.2% production, transportation, and material moving
Income: Per capita: $22,062; Median household: $43,438; Average household: $60,364; Households with income of $100,000 or more: 17.2%; Poverty rate: 22.3%
Educational Attainment: High school diploma or higher: 87.8%; Bachelor's degree or higher: 7.3%; Graduate/professional degree or higher: 3.0%

School District(s)
Central Square Central SD (PK-12)
    2014-15 Enrollment: 4,051 . . . . (315) 668-4220
Housing: Homeownership rate: 82.1%; Median home value: $79,700; Median year structure built: 1954; Homeowner vacancy rate: 0.0%; Median selected monthly owner costs: $1,194 with a mortgage, $428 without a mortgage; Median gross rent: $1,068 per month; Rental vacancy rate: 0.0%
Health Insurance: 91.0% have insurance; 53.6% have private insurance; 46.3% have public insurance; 9.0% do not have insurance; 3.0% of children under 18 do not have insurance
Transportation: Commute: 97.8% car, 0.0% public transportation, 0.0% walk, 2.2% work from home; Mean travel time to work: 40.0 minutes

CONSTANTIA (CDP). Covers a land area of 3.009 square miles and a water area of 0.007 square miles. Located at 43.26° N. Lat; 76.01° W. Long. Elevation is 384 feet.
Population: 837; Growth (since 2000): -24.4%; Density: 278.2 persons per square mile; Race: 100.0% White, 0.0% Black/African American, 0.0% Asian, 0.0% American Indian/Alaska Native, 0.0% Native Hawaiian/Other Pacific Islander, 0.0% Two or more races, 0.0% Hispanic of any race; Average household size: 1.92; Median age: 55.0; Age under 18: 6.0%; Age 65 and over: 20.9%; Males per 100 females: 106.3; Marriage status: 25.9% never married, 56.3% now married, 5.0% separated, 7.1% widowed, 10.7% divorced; Foreign born: 3.2%; Speak English only: 100.0%; With disability: 12.9%; Veterans: 9.8%; Ancestry: 21.1% English, 20.7% German, 20.2% Irish, 13.6% Italian, 11.2% Polish
Employment: 7.2% management, business, and financial, 6.0% computer, engineering, and science, 15.6% education, legal, community service, arts, and media, 8.0% healthcare practitioners, 7.2% service, 23.8% sales and office, 14.0% natural resources, construction, and maintenance, 18.3% production, transportation, and material moving
Income: Per capita: $37,307; Median household: $54,261; Average household: $70,077; Households with income of $100,000 or more: 19.0%; Poverty rate: 3.2%
Educational Attainment: High school diploma or higher: 88.2%; Bachelor's degree or higher: 23.7%; Graduate/professional degree or higher: 10.2%

School District(s)
Central Square Central SD (PK-12)
    2014-15 Enrollment: 4,051 . . . . (315) 668-4220
Housing: Homeownership rate: 90.3%; Median home value: $101,900; Median year structure built: 1966; Homeowner vacancy rate: 0.0%; Median selected monthly owner costs: $1,065 with a mortgage, $481 without a mortgage; Median gross rent: $566 per month; Rental vacancy rate: 58.4%
Health Insurance: 86.5% have insurance; 76.5% have private insurance; 27.5% have public insurance; 13.5% do not have insurance; 0.0% of children under 18 do not have insurance
Transportation: Commute: 92.4% car, 0.0% public transportation, 5.7% walk, 1.8% work from home; Mean travel time to work: 26.9 minutes

CONSTANTIA (town). Covers a land area of 56.765 square miles and a water area of 42.915 square miles. Located at 43.26° N. Lat; 75.96° W. Long. Elevation is 384 feet.
Population: 4,943; Growth (since 2000): -3.9%; Density: 87.1 persons per square mile; Race: 96.2% White, 0.0% Black/African American, 0.2% Asian, 0.0% American Indian/Alaska Native, 0.0% Native Hawaiian/Other Pacific Islander, 1.3% Two or more races, 2.4% Hispanic of any race; Average household size: 2.60; Median age: 42.3; Age under 18: 21.6%; Age 65 and over: 14.3%; Males per 100 females: 109.3; Marriage status: 28.0% never married, 57.0% now married, 4.3% separated, 5.6% widowed, 9.4% divorced; Foreign born: 0.9%; Speak English only: 97.7%; With disability: 12.4%; Veterans: 10.0%; Ancestry: 23.0% German, 22.8% Irish, 13.8% English, 10.5% Italian, 9.8% American
Employment: 12.3% management, business, and financial, 3.9% computer, engineering, and science, 6.6% education, legal, community

service, arts, and media, 5.9% healthcare practitioners, 17.1% service, 23.4% sales and office, 16.8% natural resources, construction, and maintenance, 14.0% production, transportation, and material moving
Income: Per capita: $26,362; Median household: $51,917; Average household: $67,629; Households with income of $100,000 or more: 17.3%; Poverty rate: 10.8%
Educational Attainment: High school diploma or higher: 86.0%; Bachelor's degree or higher: 14.7%; Graduate/professional degree or higher: 6.5%

School District(s)
Central Square Central SD (PK-12)
    2014-15 Enrollment: 4,051 . . . . (315) 668-4220
Housing: Homeownership rate: 83.4%; Median home value: $108,700; Median year structure built: 1973; Homeowner vacancy rate: 1.6%; Median selected monthly owner costs: $1,243 with a mortgage, $509 without a mortgage; Median gross rent: $915 per month; Rental vacancy rate: 15.8%
Health Insurance: 90.4% have insurance; 65.5% have private insurance; 37.1% have public insurance; 9.6% do not have insurance; 6.9% of children under 18 do not have insurance
Transportation: Commute: 93.2% car, 0.4% public transportation, 3.2% walk, 3.2% work from home; Mean travel time to work: 35.1 minutes
Additional Information Contacts
Town of Constantia . . . . (315) 623-7771
    http://townconstantia.org

FULTON (city).
Covers a land area of 3.755 square miles and a water area of 1.001 square miles. Located at 43.30° N. Lat; 76.40° W. Long. Elevation is 361 feet.
History: Incorporated as village in 1835, as city in 1902.
Population: 11,713; Growth (since 2000): -1.2%; Density: 3,119.7 persons per square mile; Race: 94.8% White, 0.3% Black/African American, 0.5% Asian, 0.2% American Indian/Alaska Native, 0.0% Native Hawaiian/Other Pacific Islander, 1.2% Two or more races, 5.3% Hispanic of any race; Average household size: 2.59; Median age: 36.8; Age under 18: 25.6%; Age 65 and over: 12.4%; Males per 100 females: 91.9; Marriage status: 32.5% never married, 45.8% now married, 3.2% separated, 7.5% widowed, 14.1% divorced; Foreign born: 2.7%; Speak English only: 94.2%; With disability: 15.8%; Veterans: 9.1%; Ancestry: 18.0% Irish, 16.8% German, 15.9% Italian, 11.9% English, 7.6% French
Employment: 9.1% management, business, and financial, 2.9% computer, engineering, and science, 10.1% education, legal, community service, arts, and media, 4.4% healthcare practitioners, 20.4% service, 23.2% sales and office, 10.5% natural resources, construction, and maintenance, 19.3% production, transportation, and material moving
Income: Per capita: $18,315; Median household: $36,126; Average household: $46,595; Households with income of $100,000 or more: 8.7%; Poverty rate: 31.1%
Educational Attainment: High school diploma or higher: 83.8%; Bachelor's degree or higher: 14.6%; Graduate/professional degree or higher: 6.0%

School District(s)
Fulton City SD (PK-12)
    2014-15 Enrollment: 3,558 . . . . (315) 593-5510
Mexico Central SD (PK-12)
    2014-15 Enrollment: 2,155 . . . . (315) 963-8400
Housing: Homeownership rate: 53.2%; Median home value: $76,600; Median year structure built: 1941; Homeowner vacancy rate: 2.8%; Median selected monthly owner costs: $1,056 with a mortgage, $491 without a mortgage; Median gross rent: $686 per month; Rental vacancy rate: 9.6%
Health Insurance: 91.6% have insurance; 52.5% have private insurance; 51.6% have public insurance; 8.4% do not have insurance; 5.2% of children under 18 do not have insurance
Safety: Violent crime rate: 19.0 per 10,000 population; Property crime rate: 368.5 per 10,000 population
Newspapers: Fulton Patriot Advertiser (weekly circulation 5,700); The Valley News (weekly circulation 8,100)
Transportation: Commute: 90.1% car, 0.5% public transportation, 5.6% walk, 2.1% work from home; Mean travel time to work: 21.6 minutes
Additional Information Contacts
City of Fulton . . . . (315) 592-5390
    http://www.cityoffulton.com

GRANBY (town).
Covers a land area of 44.713 square miles and a water area of 1.730 square miles. Located at 43.29° N. Lat; 76.44° W. Long.
Population: 6,725; Growth (since 2000): -4.1%; Density: 150.4 persons per square mile; Race: 97.4% White, 0.7% Black/African American, 0.0% Asian, 0.2% American Indian/Alaska Native, 0.0% Native Hawaiian/Other Pacific Islander, 1.4% Two or more races, 0.9% Hispanic of any race; Average household size: 2.75; Median age: 39.1; Age under 18: 21.7%; Age 65 and over: 14.7%; Males per 100 females: 104.7; Marriage status: 31.3% never married, 56.4% now married, 2.9% separated, 5.1% widowed, 7.2% divorced; Foreign born: 1.5%; Speak English only: 96.1%; With disability: 14.0%; Veterans: 5.8%; Ancestry: 16.4% Irish, 12.9% German, 12.5% English, 11.7% French, 8.5% Italian
Employment: 7.9% management, business, and financial, 6.4% computer, engineering, and science, 5.1% education, legal, community service, arts, and media, 10.8% healthcare practitioners, 18.3% service, 20.4% sales and office, 11.2% natural resources, construction, and maintenance, 20.0% production, transportation, and material moving
Income: Per capita: $26,720; Median household: $49,700; Average household: $71,908; Households with income of $100,000 or more: 17.8%; Poverty rate: 13.9%
Educational Attainment: High school diploma or higher: 83.7%; Bachelor's degree or higher: 18.4%; Graduate/professional degree or higher: 6.5%
Housing: Homeownership rate: 80.4%; Median home value: $88,800; Median year structure built: 1970; Homeowner vacancy rate: 4.7%; Median selected monthly owner costs: $1,129 with a mortgage, $457 without a mortgage; Median gross rent: $671 per month; Rental vacancy rate: 0.0%
Health Insurance: 92.6% have insurance; 62.8% have private insurance; 42.9% have public insurance; 7.4% do not have insurance; 9.9% of children under 18 do not have insurance
Transportation: Commute: 88.8% car, 0.0% public transportation, 3.8% walk, 6.1% work from home; Mean travel time to work: 23.4 minutes
Additional Information Contacts
Town of Granby . . . . (315) 598-6500
    http://towngranby.org/content

HANNIBAL (town).
Covers a land area of 44.655 square miles and a water area of 0.171 square miles. Located at 43.31° N. Lat; 76.55° W. Long. Elevation is 328 feet.
Population: 4,763; Growth (since 2000): -3.9%; Density: 106.7 persons per square mile; Race: 95.8% White, 0.9% Black/African American, 0.4% Asian, 0.0% American Indian/Alaska Native, 0.0% Native Hawaiian/Other Pacific Islander, 2.9% Two or more races, 1.7% Hispanic of any race; Average household size: 2.52; Median age: 40.6; Age under 18: 22.8%; Age 65 and over: 11.4%; Males per 100 females: 102.5; Marriage status: 29.2% never married, 49.8% now married, 3.3% separated, 5.7% widowed, 15.3% divorced; Foreign born: 1.2%; Speak English only: 98.1%; With disability: 15.6%; Veterans: 9.9%; Ancestry: 21.6% German, 19.5% Irish, 16.9% Italian, 15.0% English, 7.9% American
Employment: 7.2% management, business, and financial, 2.8% computer, engineering, and science, 6.6% education, legal, community service, arts, and media, 6.6% healthcare practitioners, 21.8% service, 22.3% sales and office, 12.2% natural resources, construction, and maintenance, 20.5% production, transportation, and material moving
Income: Per capita: $22,265; Median household: $49,345; Average household: $55,169; Households with income of $100,000 or more: 8.5%; Poverty rate: 18.3%
Educational Attainment: High school diploma or higher: 86.5%; Bachelor's degree or higher: 8.6%; Graduate/professional degree or higher: 2.8%

School District(s)
Hannibal Central SD (PK-12)
    2014-15 Enrollment: 1,407 . . . . (315) 564-7900
Housing: Homeownership rate: 82.5%; Median home value: $84,200; Median year structure built: 1980; Homeowner vacancy rate: 3.2%; Median selected monthly owner costs: $1,158 with a mortgage, $416 without a mortgage; Median gross rent: $775 per month; Rental vacancy rate: 2.9%
Health Insurance: 91.2% have insurance; 59.0% have private insurance; 46.8% have public insurance; 8.8% do not have insurance; 2.0% of children under 18 do not have insurance
Transportation: Commute: 92.9% car, 2.5% public transportation, 1.7% walk, 2.9% work from home; Mean travel time to work: 23.2 minutes

Additional Information Contacts
Town of Hannibal . . . . (315) 564-6037
  http://hannibalny.org

HANNIBAL (village).
Covers a land area of 1.152 square miles and a water area of 0 square miles. Located at 43.32° N. Lat; 76.58° W. Long. Elevation is 328 feet.

Population: 604; Growth (since 2000): 11.4%; Density: 524.1 persons per square mile; Race: 100.0% White, 0.0% Black/African American, 0.0% Asian, 0.0% American Indian/Alaska Native, 0.0% Native Hawaiian/Other Pacific Islander, 0.0% Two or more races, 3.3% Hispanic of any race; Average household size: 2.54; Median age: 43.0; Age under 18: 21.5%; Age 65 and over: 21.5%; Males per 100 females: 89.4; Marriage status: 29.0% never married, 50.7% now married, 4.1% separated, 4.9% widowed, 15.4% divorced; Foreign born: 2.2%; Speak English only: 96.4%; With disability: 17.1%; Veterans: 12.2%; Ancestry: 31.3% Irish, 19.7% German, 17.9% English, 12.3% Italian, 8.8% Dutch

Employment: 7.0% management, business, and financial, 4.1% computer, engineering, and science, 4.9% education, legal, community service, arts, and media, 4.9% healthcare practitioners, 17.3% service, 32.1% sales and office, 5.3% natural resources, construction, and maintenance, 24.3% production, transportation, and material moving

Income: Per capita: $23,309; Median household: $53,542; Average household: $58,185; Households with income of $100,000 or more: 14.2%; Poverty rate: 13.1%

Educational Attainment: High school diploma or higher: 88.5%; Bachelor's degree or higher: 13.3%; Graduate/professional degree or higher: 4.5%

School District(s)
Hannibal Central SD (PK-12)
  2014-15 Enrollment: 1,407 . . . . (315) 564-7900

Housing: Homeownership rate: 72.3%; Median home value: $90,400; Median year structure built: Before 1940; Homeowner vacancy rate: 3.9%; Median selected monthly owner costs: $1,051 with a mortgage, $445 without a mortgage; Median gross rent: $797 per month; Rental vacancy rate: 0.0%

Health Insurance: 98.0% have insurance; 70.5% have private insurance; 51.0% have public insurance; 2.0% do not have insurance; 0.0% of children under 18 do not have insurance

Transportation: Commute: 86.4% car, 0.0% public transportation, 8.9% walk, 4.2% work from home; Mean travel time to work: 22.9 minutes

HASTINGS (town).
Covers a land area of 45.645 square miles and a water area of 0.352 square miles. Located at 43.32° N. Lat; 76.16° W. Long. Elevation is 476 feet.

History: Hastings was the first town settled in Oswego County when Oliver Stevens built a building near the abandoned Fort Brewerton in 1789, where he traded with Indians and operated a tavern for the boatmen who frequented the nearby river and lake

Population: 9,416; Growth (since 2000): 7.0%; Density: 206.3 persons per square mile; Race: 96.5% White, 0.0% Black/African American, 0.9% Asian, 0.9% American Indian/Alaska Native, 0.0% Native Hawaiian/Other Pacific Islander, 1.7% Two or more races, 0.5% Hispanic of any race; Average household size: 2.75; Median age: 42.7; Age under 18: 22.4%; Age 65 and over: 14.2%; Males per 100 females: 97.3; Marriage status: 26.5% never married, 56.3% now married, 2.0% separated, 5.6% widowed, 11.6% divorced; Foreign born: 1.8%; Speak English only: 97.1%; With disability: 15.7%; Veterans: 9.2%; Ancestry: 19.4% German, 17.7% Irish, 16.0% English, 14.6% Italian, 9.8% French

Employment: 13.2% management, business, and financial, 3.0% computer, engineering, and science, 7.2% education, legal, community service, arts, and media, 3.0% healthcare practitioners, 18.0% service, 25.5% sales and office, 11.0% natural resources, construction, and maintenance, 19.1% production, transportation, and material moving

Income: Per capita: $24,264; Median household: $51,309; Average household: $63,888; Households with income of $100,000 or more: 19.0%; Poverty rate: 13.4%

Educational Attainment: High school diploma or higher: 87.5%; Bachelor's degree or higher: 11.4%; Graduate/professional degree or higher: 4.8%

Housing: Homeownership rate: 81.7%; Median home value: $124,000; Median year structure built: 1982; Homeowner vacancy rate: 1.0%; Median selected monthly owner costs: $1,302 with a mortgage, $486 without a mortgage; Median gross rent: $736 per month; Rental vacancy rate: 5.4%

Health Insurance: 95.3% have insurance; 65.9% have private insurance; 41.9% have public insurance; 4.7% do not have insurance; 1.4% of children under 18 do not have insurance

Transportation: Commute: 94.2% car, 1.4% public transportation, 0.9% walk, 3.0% work from home; Mean travel time to work: 26.1 minutes

Additional Information Contacts
Town of Hastings . . . . (315) 668-2456
  http://www.hastingsny.org

LACONA (village).
Covers a land area of 1.110 square miles and a water area of 0.003 square miles. Located at 43.64° N. Lat; 76.07° W. Long. Elevation is 558 feet.

Population: 682; Growth (since 2000): 15.6%; Density: 614.5 persons per square mile; Race: 96.6% White, 0.1% Black/African American, 0.3% Asian, 0.0% American Indian/Alaska Native, 0.0% Native Hawaiian/Other Pacific Islander, 2.8% Two or more races, 0.3% Hispanic of any race; Average household size: 2.69; Median age: 36.6; Age under 18: 27.7%; Age 65 and over: 11.1%; Males per 100 females: 110.1; Marriage status: 37.9% never married, 43.7% now married, 3.7% separated, 5.4% widowed, 12.9% divorced; Foreign born: 0.6%; Speak English only: 98.1%; With disability: 17.2%; Veterans: 10.8%; Ancestry: 21.1% German, 16.0% English, 15.2% Irish, 10.9% Italian, 7.9% French

Employment: 14.4% management, business, and financial, 3.3% computer, engineering, and science, 6.3% education, legal, community service, arts, and media, 1.9% healthcare practitioners, 23.7% service, 20.7% sales and office, 15.2% natural resources, construction, and maintenance, 14.4% production, transportation, and material moving

Income: Per capita: $21,648; Median household: $52,500; Average household: $58,195; Households with income of $100,000 or more: 23.2%; Poverty rate: 19.9%

Educational Attainment: High school diploma or higher: 88.4%; Bachelor's degree or higher: 15.2%; Graduate/professional degree or higher: 8.2%

Housing: Homeownership rate: 60.8%; Median home value: $102,800; Median year structure built: Before 1940; Homeowner vacancy rate: 0.0%; Median selected monthly owner costs: $1,083 with a mortgage, $485 without a mortgage; Median gross rent: $593 per month; Rental vacancy rate: 0.0%

Health Insurance: 95.3% have insurance; 62.0% have private insurance; 42.7% have public insurance; 4.7% do not have insurance; 0.0% of children under 18 do not have insurance

Transportation: Commute: 91.5% car, 2.6% public transportation, 0.4% walk, 3.7% work from home; Mean travel time to work: 32.5 minutes

MALLORY (unincorporated postal area)
ZCTA: 13103

Covers a land area of 0.342 square miles and a water area of 0.015 square miles. Located at 43.33° N. Lat; 76.11° W. Long. Elevation is 413 feet.

Population: 489; Growth (since 2000): n/a; Density: 1,429.8 persons per square mile; Race: 97.8% White, 2.2% Black/African American, 0.0% Asian, 0.0% American Indian/Alaska Native, 0.0% Native Hawaiian/Other Pacific Islander, 0.0% Two or more races, 0.0% Hispanic of any race; Average household size: 3.02; Median age: 36.5; Age under 18: 36.0%; Age 65 and over: 3.9%; Males per 100 females: 109.0; Marriage status: 38.1% never married, 32.6% now married, 2.7% separated, 0.0% widowed, 29.3% divorced; Foreign born: 0.0%; Speak English only: 100.0%; With disability: 28.2%; Veterans: 0.0%; Ancestry: 50.7% German, 30.5% Italian, 14.7% Irish, 13.9% American, 5.5% English

Employment: 24.4% management, business, and financial, 0.0% computer, engineering, and science, 0.0% education, legal, community service, arts, and media, 0.0% healthcare practitioners, 22.0% service, 8.1% sales and office, 22.8% natural resources, construction, and maintenance, 22.8% production, transportation, and material moving

Income: Per capita: $12,776; Median household: n/a; Average household: $38,601; Households with income of $100,000 or more: 18.5%; Poverty rate: 79.8%

Educational Attainment: High school diploma or higher: 71.7%; Bachelor's degree or higher: 10.8%; Graduate/professional degree or higher: n/a

Housing: Homeownership rate: 86.4%; Median home value: n/a; Median year structure built: 1978; Homeowner vacancy rate: 0.0%; Median selected monthly owner costs: $1,300 with a mortgage, $606

without a mortgage; Median gross rent: n/a per month; Rental vacancy rate: 0.0%

Health Insurance: 90.6% have insurance; 17.0% have private insurance; 81.4% have public insurance; 9.4% do not have insurance; 0.0% of children under 18 do not have insurance

Transportation: Commute: 77.2% car, 0.0% public transportation, 0.0% walk, 22.8% work from home; Mean travel time to work: 0.0 minutes

---

MEXICO (town). Covers a land area of 46.272 square miles and a water area of 0.717 square miles. Located at 43.46° N. Lat; 76.20° W. Long. Elevation is 410 feet.

Population: 5,190; Growth (since 2000): 0.2%; Density: 112.2 persons per square mile; Race: 95.0% White, 0.6% Black/African American, 0.2% Asian, 0.0% American Indian/Alaska Native, 0.0% Native Hawaiian/Other Pacific Islander, 3.5% Two or more races, 0.8% Hispanic of any race; Average household size: 2.64; Median age: 40.9; Age under 18: 24.3%; Age 65 and over: 14.0%; Males per 100 females: 98.4; Marriage status: 27.9% never married, 54.1% now married, 2.3% separated, 6.3% widowed, 11.7% divorced; Foreign born: 1.5%; Speak English only: 98.3%; With disability: 17.8%; Veterans: 10.0%; Ancestry: 20.9% Irish, 20.4% German, 16.7% English, 12.1% American, 9.0% Italian

Employment: 11.2% management, business, and financial, 2.3% computer, engineering, and science, 10.8% education, legal, community service, arts, and media, 5.2% healthcare practitioners, 21.5% service, 24.8% sales and office, 8.9% natural resources, construction, and maintenance, 15.4% production, transportation, and material moving

Income: Per capita: $25,406; Median household: $54,778; Average household: $65,676; Households with income of $100,000 or more: 20.9%; Poverty rate: 18.0%

Educational Attainment: High school diploma or higher: 89.0%; Bachelor's degree or higher: 15.6%; Graduate/professional degree or higher: 7.7%

School District(s)

Mexico Central SD (PK-12)
    2014-15 Enrollment: 2,155 . . . . (315) 963-8400
Oswego Boces
    2014-15 Enrollment: n/a . . . . (315) 963-4222

Vocational/Technical School(s)

Center for Instruction Technology & Innovation (CiTi) (Public)
    Fall 2014 Enrollment: 95 . . . . (315) 963-4256
    2015-16 Tuition: $9,995

Housing: Homeownership rate: 77.1%; Median home value: $105,000; Median year structure built: 1976; Homeowner vacancy rate: 4.4%; Median selected monthly owner costs: $1,246 with a mortgage, $531 without a mortgage; Median gross rent: $630 per month; Rental vacancy rate: 2.0%

Health Insurance: 95.7% have insurance; 66.5% have private insurance; 42.8% have public insurance; 4.3% do not have insurance; 1.7% of children under 18 do not have insurance

Newspapers: Oswego Co. Weeklies (weekly circulation 33,000)

Transportation: Commute: 92.3% car, 0.8% public transportation, 2.1% walk, 4.8% work from home; Mean travel time to work: 23.5 minutes

Additional Information Contacts

Town of Mexico . . . . (315) 963-7633
    http://town.mexicony.net

MEXICO (village). Covers a land area of 2.145 square miles and a water area of 0 square miles. Located at 43.47° N. Lat; 76.23° W. Long. Elevation is 410 feet.

Population: 1,702; Growth (since 2000): 8.3%; Density: 793.6 persons per square mile; Race: 95.2% White, 0.3% Black/African American, 0.2% Asian, 0.0% American Indian/Alaska Native, 0.0% Native Hawaiian/Other Pacific Islander, 2.4% Two or more races, 1.5% Hispanic of any race; Average household size: 2.49; Median age: 37.1; Age under 18: 30.1%; Age 65 and over: 10.5%; Males per 100 females: 84.1; Marriage status: 26.6% never married, 53.2% now married, 2.5% separated, 3.8% widowed, 16.4% divorced; Foreign born: 1.6%; Speak English only: 96.9%; With disability: 12.2%; Veterans: 9.8%; Ancestry: 21.2% Irish, 18.6% English, 14.3% German, 12.6% Italian, 10.5% American

Employment: 18.5% management, business, and financial, 5.1% computer, engineering, and science, 14.0% education, legal, community service, arts, and media, 3.2% healthcare practitioners, 20.1% service, 16.9% sales and office, 7.7% natural resources, construction, and maintenance, 14.6% production, transportation, and material moving

Income: Per capita: $26,520; Median household: $51,111; Average household: $64,428; Households with income of $100,000 or more: 19.6%; Poverty rate: 21.2%

Educational Attainment: High school diploma or higher: 93.7%; Bachelor's degree or higher: 22.7%; Graduate/professional degree or higher: 12.2%

School District(s)

Mexico Central SD (PK-12)
    2014-15 Enrollment: 2,155 . . . . (315) 963-8400
Oswego Boces
    2014-15 Enrollment: n/a . . . . (315) 963-4222

Vocational/Technical School(s)

Center for Instruction Technology & Innovation (CiTi) (Public)
    Fall 2014 Enrollment: 95 . . . . (315) 963-4256
    2015-16 Tuition: $9,995

Housing: Homeownership rate: 55.4%; Median home value: $112,300; Median year structure built: 1950; Homeowner vacancy rate: 0.0%; Median selected monthly owner costs: $1,313 with a mortgage, $555 without a mortgage; Median gross rent: $634 per month; Rental vacancy rate: 2.9%

Health Insurance: 94.2% have insurance; 63.9% have private insurance; 40.0% have public insurance; 5.8% do not have insurance; 2.0% of children under 18 do not have insurance

Newspapers: Oswego Co. Weeklies (weekly circulation 33,000)

Transportation: Commute: 87.2% car, 0.3% public transportation, 4.1% walk, 8.4% work from home; Mean travel time to work: 21.6 minutes

---

MINETTO (CDP). Covers a land area of 3.323 square miles and a water area of 0.263 square miles. Located at 43.40° N. Lat; 76.48° W. Long. Elevation is 325 feet.

Population: 933; Growth (since 2000): -14.1%; Density: 280.8 persons per square mile; Race: 97.3% White, 0.2% Black/African American, 2.0% Asian, 0.3% American Indian/Alaska Native, 0.0% Native Hawaiian/Other Pacific Islander, 0.0% Two or more races, 1.2% Hispanic of any race; Average household size: 2.22; Median age: 45.2; Age under 18: 22.4%; Age 65 and over: 20.8%; Males per 100 females: 100.9; Marriage status: 26.2% never married, 55.6% now married, 3.8% separated, 8.0% widowed, 10.2% divorced; Foreign born: 1.5%; Speak English only: 96.3%; With disability: 10.1%; Veterans: 11.9%; Ancestry: 30.4% German, 23.8% Irish, 14.8% Italian, 12.6% English, 10.3% Polish

Employment: 16.8% management, business, and financial, 3.0% computer, engineering, and science, 22.1% education, legal, community service, arts, and media, 7.8% healthcare practitioners, 10.1% service, 14.3% sales and office, 5.1% natural resources, construction, and maintenance, 20.7% production, transportation, and material moving

Income: Per capita: $30,996; Median household: $65,170; Average household: $68,190; Households with income of $100,000 or more: 24.6%; Poverty rate: 13.7%

Educational Attainment: High school diploma or higher: 93.9%; Bachelor's degree or higher: 35.9%; Graduate/professional degree or higher: 14.0%

School District(s)

Oswego City SD (PK-12)
    2014-15 Enrollment: 3,912 . . . . (315) 341-2001

Housing: Homeownership rate: 81.2%; Median home value: $112,900; Median year structure built: 1957; Homeowner vacancy rate: 3.7%; Median selected monthly owner costs: $1,214 with a mortgage, $464 without a mortgage; Median gross rent: $536 per month; Rental vacancy rate: 0.0%

Health Insurance: 95.0% have insurance; 75.0% have private insurance; 38.0% have public insurance; 5.0% do not have insurance; 0.0% of children under 18 do not have insurance

Transportation: Commute: 96.6% car, 0.2% public transportation, 0.7% walk, 2.4% work from home; Mean travel time to work: 21.8 minutes

---

MINETTO (town). Covers a land area of 5.762 square miles and a water area of 0.279 square miles. Located at 43.40° N. Lat; 76.48° W. Long. Elevation is 325 feet.

Population: 1,500; Growth (since 2000): -9.8%; Density: 260.3 persons per square mile; Race: 96.5% White, 0.9% Black/African American, 1.5% Asian, 0.2% American Indian/Alaska Native, 0.0% Native Hawaiian/Other Pacific Islander, 0.8% Two or more races, 1.0% Hispanic of any race; Average household size: 2.30; Median age: 44.5; Age under 18: 22.7%; Age 65 and over: 18.5%; Males per 100 females: 98.2; Marriage status: 26.8% never married, 56.8% now married, 2.8% separated, 6.9% widowed, 9.5% divorced; Foreign born: 2.1%; Speak English only: 96.1%;

With disability: 8.5%; Veterans: 10.7%; Ancestry: 24.6% German, 24.2% Irish, 15.0% Italian, 11.1% English, 10.2% Polish
Employment: 14.9% management, business, and financial, 3.0% computer, engineering, and science, 20.2% education, legal, community service, arts, and media, 5.9% healthcare practitioners, 11.7% service, 17.0% sales and office, 9.3% natural resources, construction, and maintenance, 18.0% production, transportation, and material moving
Income: Per capita: $31,062; Median household: $59,583; Average household: $70,996; Households with income of $100,000 or more: 24.9%; Poverty rate: 11.2%
Educational Attainment: High school diploma or higher: 93.6%; Bachelor's degree or higher: 35.4%; Graduate/professional degree or higher: 14.3%

School District(s)
Oswego City SD (PK-12)
    2014-15 Enrollment: 3,912 . . . . (315) 341-2001
Housing: Homeownership rate: 80.8%; Median home value: $115,000; Median year structure built: 1965; Homeowner vacancy rate: 2.4%; Median selected monthly owner costs: $1,221 with a mortgage, $477 without a mortgage; Median gross rent: $625 per month; Rental vacancy rate: 0.0%
Health Insurance: 94.0% have insurance; 73.0% have private insurance; 35.9% have public insurance; 6.0% do not have insurance; 0.0% of children under 18 do not have insurance
Transportation: Commute: 96.5% car, 0.1% public transportation, 0.4% walk, 3.0% work from home; Mean travel time to work: 22.6 minutes

NEW HAVEN (town). Covers a land area of 31.099 square miles and a water area of 2.315 square miles. Located at 43.47° N. Lat; 76.32° W. Long. Elevation is 423 feet.
Population: 2,886; Growth (since 2000): -1.5%; Density: 92.8 persons per square mile; Race: 97.5% White, 0.1% Black/African American, 0.9% Asian, 0.0% American Indian/Alaska Native, 0.0% Native Hawaiian/Other Pacific Islander, 1.4% Two or more races, 0.0% Hispanic of any race; Average household size: 2.73; Median age: 42.4; Age under 18: 21.1%; Age 65 and over: 11.4%; Males per 100 females: 102.1; Marriage status: 26.2% never married, 54.5% now married, 4.2% separated, 4.2% widowed, 15.2% divorced; Foreign born: 0.5%; Speak English only: 94.3%; With disability: 13.9%; Veterans: 10.1%; Ancestry: 20.3% Irish, 18.9% German, 15.3% English, 10.8% Italian, 8.0% American
Employment: 9.0% management, business, and financial, 2.5% computer, engineering, and science, 8.6% education, legal, community service, arts, and media, 2.5% healthcare practitioners, 21.4% service, 22.6% sales and office, 21.3% natural resources, construction, and maintenance, 12.0% production, transportation, and material moving
Income: Per capita: $24,968; Median household: $51,875; Average household: $65,242; Households with income of $100,000 or more: 17.9%; Poverty rate: 12.8%
Educational Attainment: High school diploma or higher: 88.6%; Bachelor's degree or higher: 15.3%; Graduate/professional degree or higher: 6.2%

School District(s)
Mexico Central SD (PK-12)
    2014-15 Enrollment: 2,155 . . . . (315) 963-8400
Housing: Homeownership rate: 80.5%; Median home value: $86,300; Median year structure built: 1977; Homeowner vacancy rate: 1.0%; Median selected monthly owner costs: $1,211 with a mortgage, $503 without a mortgage; Median gross rent: $774 per month; Rental vacancy rate: 12.3%
Health Insurance: 93.6% have insurance; 70.5% have private insurance; 34.1% have public insurance; 6.4% do not have insurance; 0.8% of children under 18 do not have insurance
Transportation: Commute: 90.6% car, 0.0% public transportation, 6.0% walk, 2.9% work from home; Mean travel time to work: 24.4 minutes

ORWELL (town). Covers a land area of 39.582 square miles and a water area of 1.684 square miles. Located at 43.56° N. Lat; 75.95° W. Long. Elevation is 801 feet.
Population: 1,372; Growth (since 2000): 9.4%; Density: 34.7 persons per square mile; Race: 92.6% White, 2.4% Black/African American, 0.0% Asian, 0.0% American Indian/Alaska Native, 0.0% Native Hawaiian/Other Pacific Islander, 2.3% Two or more races, 4.7% Hispanic of any race; Average household size: 2.94; Median age: 35.0; Age under 18: 28.1%; Age 65 and over: 11.8%; Males per 100 females: 117.3; Marriage status: 33.7% never married, 46.3% now married, 2.9% separated, 5.9% widowed, 14.1% divorced; Foreign born: 2.0%; Speak English only: 87.2%;

With disability: 12.9%; Veterans: 9.7%; Ancestry: 18.6% English, 17.6% German, 14.6% Irish, 8.2% Italian, 6.5% French Canadian
Employment: 5.4% management, business, and financial, 5.8% computer, engineering, and science, 4.6% education, legal, community service, arts, and media, 3.9% healthcare practitioners, 19.7% service, 14.9% sales and office, 20.9% natural resources, construction, and maintenance, 24.8% production, transportation, and material moving
Income: Per capita: $20,334; Median household: $52,313; Average household: $61,738; Households with income of $100,000 or more: 13.6%; Poverty rate: 24.5%
Educational Attainment: High school diploma or higher: 75.6%; Bachelor's degree or higher: 12.3%; Graduate/professional degree or higher: 4.3%
Housing: Homeownership rate: 87.8%; Median home value: $85,700; Median year structure built: 1978; Homeowner vacancy rate: 0.0%; Median selected monthly owner costs: $1,115 with a mortgage, $363 without a mortgage; Median gross rent: $781 per month; Rental vacancy rate: 0.0%
Health Insurance: 86.7% have insurance; 57.7% have private insurance; 38.6% have public insurance; 13.3% do not have insurance; 16.9% of children under 18 do not have insurance
Transportation: Commute: 92.1% car, 0.0% public transportation, 2.1% walk, 4.8% work from home; Mean travel time to work: 35.7 minutes

OSWEGO (city). County seat. Covers a land area of 7.614 square miles and a water area of 3.614 square miles. Located at 43.46° N. Lat; 76.50° W. Long. Elevation is 285 feet.
History: The name of Oswego is of Indian origin, meaning "pouring out of waters." The strategic importance of the place led to the erection of a fort in 1722. Soon after military occupation ceased, settlement began. Its commanding position at the terminus of the inland water route made Oswego a busy port.
Population: 17,988; Growth (since 2000): 0.2%; Density: 2,362.5 persons per square mile; Race: 92.8% White, 2.1% Black/African American, 0.8% Asian, 0.1% American Indian/Alaska Native, 0.1% Native Hawaiian/Other Pacific Islander, 2.2% Two or more races, 4.0% Hispanic of any race; Average household size: 2.27; Median age: 33.8; Age under 18: 19.9%; Age 65 and over: 14.7%; Males per 100 females: 93.4; Marriage status: 40.1% never married, 41.2% now married, 3.5% separated, 6.8% widowed, 11.9% divorced; Foreign born: 2.7%; Speak English only: 93.8%; With disability: 12.1%; Veterans: 8.0%; Ancestry: 27.2% Irish, 18.3% Italian, 17.8% German, 8.2% English, 7.5% French
Employment: 9.8% management, business, and financial, 3.9% computer, engineering, and science, 13.7% education, legal, community service, arts, and media, 6.4% healthcare practitioners, 24.0% service, 22.1% sales and office, 9.1% natural resources, construction, and maintenance, 11.0% production, transportation, and material moving
Income: Per capita: $23,078; Median household: $38,113; Average household: $53,022; Households with income of $100,000 or more: 13.2%; Poverty rate: 29.1%
Educational Attainment: High school diploma or higher: 87.3%; Bachelor's degree or higher: 26.3%; Graduate/professional degree or higher: 12.2%

School District(s)
Oswego City SD (PK-12)
    2014-15 Enrollment: 3,912 . . . . (315) 341-2001
Four-year College(s)
SUNY College at Oswego (Public)
    Fall 2014 Enrollment: 8,034 . . . . (315) 312-2500
    2015-16 Tuition: In-state $7,934; Out-of-state $17,784
Housing: Homeownership rate: 51.2%; Median home value: $80,700; Median year structure built: Before 1940; Homeowner vacancy rate: 3.1%; Median selected monthly owner costs: $1,035 with a mortgage, $477 without a mortgage; Median gross rent: $714 per month; Rental vacancy rate: 7.2%
Health Insurance: 92.2% have insurance; 66.7% have private insurance; 41.7% have public insurance; 7.8% do not have insurance; 2.9% of children under 18 do not have insurance
Hospitals: Oswego Hospital (74 beds)
Safety: Violent crime rate: 34.0 per 10,000 population; Property crime rate: 272.0 per 10,000 population
Newspapers: Oswego Palladium-Times (daily circulation 7,300)
Transportation: Commute: 88.8% car, 1.5% public transportation, 7.5% walk, 0.7% work from home; Mean travel time to work: 17.0 minutes

Additional Information Contacts
City of Oswego . . . . (315) 342-8116
   http://www.oswegony.org

OSWEGO (town). Covers a land area of 27.333 square miles and a water area of 2.016 square miles. Located at 43.40° N. Lat; 76.56° W. Long. Elevation is 285 feet.
History: Trading post established here after the English founded Oswego (1722) became vital to the Albany fur trade. Its strategic location prompted the building of Fort Oswego (1727), Fort George (1755) and Fort Ontario (1755), which were much contested in the colonial wars. Importance as a lake port came with the completion of the Barge Canal (1917) and the St. Lawrence Seaway (1959). Seat of State University College of Arts and Science at Oswego. Founded 1722, Incorporated as a city 1848.
Population: 7,913; Growth (since 2000): 8.6%; Density: 289.5 persons per square mile; Race: 89.1% White, 5.1% Black/African American, 1.8% Asian, 0.0% American Indian/Alaska Native, 0.0% Native Hawaiian/Other Pacific Islander, 1.9% Two or more races, 5.3% Hispanic of any race; Average household size: 2.75; Median age: 20.8; Age under 18: 12.7%; Age 65 and over: 8.6%; Males per 100 females: 101.2; Marriage status: 60.7% never married, 31.4% now married, 0.7% separated, 2.3% widowed, 5.6% divorced; Foreign born: 4.1%; Speak English only: 91.1%; With disability: 8.6%; Veterans: 3.9%; Ancestry: 26.8% Irish, 23.9% Italian, 19.3% German, 12.6% Polish, 11.5% English
Employment: 8.4% management, business, and financial, 4.4% computer, engineering, and science, 14.8% education, legal, community service, arts, and media, 2.7% healthcare practitioners, 33.3% service, 20.5% sales and office, 6.9% natural resources, construction, and maintenance, 8.9% production, transportation, and material moving
Income: Per capita: $19,920; Median household: $75,200; Average household: $82,617; Households with income of $100,000 or more: 31.5%; Poverty rate: 15.0%
Educational Attainment: High school diploma or higher: 90.3%; Bachelor's degree or higher: 35.2%; Graduate/professional degree or higher: 17.5%

School District(s)
Oswego City SD (PK-12)
   2014-15 Enrollment: 3,912 . . . . (315) 341-2001

Four-year College(s)
SUNY College at Oswego (Public)
   Fall 2014 Enrollment: 8,034 . . . . (315) 312-2500
   2015-16 Tuition: In-state $7,934; Out-of-state $17,784
Housing: Homeownership rate: 88.6%; Median home value: $139,800; Median year structure built: 1973; Homeowner vacancy rate: 1.6%; Median selected monthly owner costs: $1,380 with a mortgage, $551 without a mortgage; Median gross rent: $831 per month; Rental vacancy rate: 19.9%
Health Insurance: 96.5% have insurance; 80.9% have private insurance; 24.4% have public insurance; 3.5% do not have insurance; 0.6% of children under 18 do not have insurance
Hospitals: Oswego Hospital (74 beds)
Newspapers: Oswego Palladium-Times (daily circulation 7,300)
Transportation: Commute: 72.7% car, 1.4% public transportation, 20.5% walk, 3.4% work from home; Mean travel time to work: 18.9 minutes
Additional Information Contacts
Town of Oswego . . . . (315) 343-2586
   http://www.townofoswego.com

PALERMO (town). Covers a land area of 40.464 square miles and a water area of 0.279 square miles. Located at 43.37° N. Lat; 76.26° W. Long. Elevation is 469 feet.
Population: 3,648; Growth (since 2000): -1.0%; Density: 90.2 persons per square mile; Race: 97.8% White, 0.0% Black/African American, 1.7% Asian, 0.0% American Indian/Alaska Native, 0.0% Native Hawaiian/Other Pacific Islander, 0.4% Two or more races, 0.2% Hispanic of any race; Average household size: 2.74; Median age: 41.4; Age under 18: 22.3%; Age 65 and over: 13.5%; Males per 100 females: 101.5; Marriage status: 33.3% never married, 52.9% now married, 2.2% separated, 4.4% widowed, 9.5% divorced; Foreign born: 1.7%; Speak English only: 96.3%; With disability: 15.8%; Veterans: 11.0%; Ancestry: 24.6% Irish, 18.6% German, 16.6% English, 14.0% French, 10.0% Italian
Employment: 12.1% management, business, and financial, 2.5% computer, engineering, and science, 6.2% education, legal, community service, arts, and media, 1.6% healthcare practitioners, 24.2% service, 18.8% sales and office, 17.5% natural resources, construction, and maintenance, 17.0% production, transportation, and material moving

Income: Per capita: $21,219; Median household: $47,670; Average household: $56,585; Households with income of $100,000 or more: 10.7%; Poverty rate: 12.3%
Educational Attainment: High school diploma or higher: 87.3%; Bachelor's degree or higher: 8.9%; Graduate/professional degree or higher: 2.9%
Housing: Homeownership rate: 78.0%; Median home value: $90,600; Median year structure built: 1976; Homeowner vacancy rate: 0.0%; Median selected monthly owner costs: $1,207 with a mortgage, $492 without a mortgage; Median gross rent: $718 per month; Rental vacancy rate: 0.0%
Health Insurance: 88.9% have insurance; 58.3% have private insurance; 42.3% have public insurance; 11.1% do not have insurance; 3.1% of children under 18 do not have insurance
Transportation: Commute: 95.1% car, 0.0% public transportation, 2.7% walk, 2.1% work from home; Mean travel time to work: 27.1 minutes

PARISH (town). Covers a land area of 41.725 square miles and a water area of 0.225 square miles. Located at 43.40° N. Lat; 76.06° W. Long. Elevation is 495 feet.
Population: 2,240; Growth (since 2000): -16.9%; Density: 53.7 persons per square mile; Race: 98.6% White, 0.0% Black/African American, 0.0% Asian, 0.0% American Indian/Alaska Native, 0.0% Native Hawaiian/Other Pacific Islander, 1.3% Two or more races, 0.9% Hispanic of any race; Average household size: 2.70; Median age: 43.7; Age under 18: 21.5%; Age 65 and over: 13.5%; Males per 100 females: 98.0; Marriage status: 28.0% never married, 53.5% now married, 3.7% separated, 6.6% widowed, 11.9% divorced; Foreign born: 1.3%; Speak English only: 97.3%; With disability: 14.5%; Veterans: 10.8%; Ancestry: 20.6% German, 18.8% Irish, 11.2% French, 10.3% American, 10.3% Polish
Employment: 7.8% management, business, and financial, 2.5% computer, engineering, and science, 9.6% education, legal, community service, arts, and media, 7.8% healthcare practitioners, 14.8% service, 24.7% sales and office, 10.8% natural resources, construction, and maintenance, 22.0% production, transportation, and material moving
Income: Per capita: $26,347; Median household: $53,808; Average household: $68,443; Households with income of $100,000 or more: 20.1%; Poverty rate: 10.0%
Educational Attainment: High school diploma or higher: 85.2%; Bachelor's degree or higher: 13.6%; Graduate/professional degree or higher: 5.8%

School District(s)
Altmar Parish-Williamstown Central SD (PK-12)
   2014-15 Enrollment: 1,297 . . . . (315) 625-5251
Housing: Homeownership rate: 85.7%; Median home value: $109,600; Median year structure built: 1973; Homeowner vacancy rate: 3.8%; Median selected monthly owner costs: $1,172 with a mortgage, $504 without a mortgage; Median gross rent: $710 per month; Rental vacancy rate: 3.1%
Health Insurance: 91.4% have insurance; 68.5% have private insurance; 35.1% have public insurance; 8.6% do not have insurance; 0.2% of children under 18 do not have insurance
Transportation: Commute: 94.7% car, 0.0% public transportation, 1.0% walk, 2.7% work from home; Mean travel time to work: 34.0 minutes

PARISH (village). Covers a land area of 1.605 square miles and a water area of 0 square miles. Located at 43.41° N. Lat; 76.13° W. Long. Elevation is 495 feet.
Population: 489; Growth (since 2000): -4.5%; Density: 304.6 persons per square mile; Race: 98.0% White, 0.0% Black/African American, 0.0% Asian, 0.2% American Indian/Alaska Native, 0.0% Native Hawaiian/Other Pacific Islander, 1.8% Two or more races, 3.1% Hispanic of any race; Average household size: 2.84; Median age: 34.2; Age under 18: 25.2%; Age 65 and over: 12.5%; Males per 100 females: 99.1; Marriage status: 30.6% never married, 52.5% now married, 2.4% separated, 4.6% widowed, 12.3% divorced; Foreign born: 3.1%; Speak English only: 97.5%; With disability: 12.3%; Veterans: 10.1%; Ancestry: 23.5% Irish, 22.1% German, 15.3% English, 12.3% French, 8.8% Polish
Employment: 10.2% management, business, and financial, 1.3% computer, engineering, and science, 7.6% education, legal, community service, arts, and media, 3.4% healthcare practitioners, 14.0% service, 22.5% sales and office, 16.9% natural resources, construction, and maintenance, 24.2% production, transportation, and material moving
Income: Per capita: $25,035; Median household: $54,444; Average household: $66,835; Households with income of $100,000 or more: 15.8%; Poverty rate: 13.4%

Educational Attainment: High school diploma or higher: 93.1%; Bachelor's degree or higher: 22.2%; Graduate/professional degree or higher: 11.4%

School District(s)

Altmar Parish-Williamstown Central SD (PK-12)

2014-15 Enrollment: 1,297 . . . . (315) 625-5251

Housing: Homeownership rate: 65.7%; Median home value: $95,000; Median year structure built: Before 1940; Homeowner vacancy rate: 4.1%; Median selected monthly owner costs: $1,231 with a mortgage, $606 without a mortgage; Median gross rent: $655 per month; Rental vacancy rate: 5.9%

Health Insurance: 93.5% have insurance; 65.6% have private insurance; 40.1% have public insurance; 6.5% do not have insurance; 0.8% of children under 18 do not have insurance

Transportation: Commute: 87.8% car, 0.0% public transportation, 3.0% walk, 4.8% work from home; Mean travel time to work: 28.6 minutes

PENNELLVILLE (unincorporated postal area)

ZCTA: 13132

Covers a land area of 23.726 square miles and a water area of 0.407 square miles. Located at 43.27° N. Lat; 76.25° W. Long. Elevation is 413 feet.

Population: 3,347; Growth (since 2000): -22.3%; Density: 141.1 persons per square mile; Race: 93.7% White, 0.8% Black/African American, 1.9% Asian, 0.8% American Indian/Alaska Native, 0.0% Native Hawaiian/Other Pacific Islander, 2.8% Two or more races, 0.9% Hispanic of any race; Average household size: 2.35; Median age: 47.6; Age under 18: 12.5%; Age 65 and over: 19.3%; Males per 100 females: 104.7; Marriage status: 27.9% never married, 51.6% now married, 7.1% separated, 9.0% widowed, 11.5% divorced; Foreign born: 3.2%; Speak English only: 94.9%; With disability: 16.0%; Veterans: 8.2%; Ancestry: 23.8% German, 22.1% Irish, 12.7% Italian, 12.7% English, 7.3% French

Employment: 13.8% management, business, and financial, 4.4% computer, engineering, and science, 6.8% education, legal, community service, arts, and media, 2.2% healthcare practitioners, 13.6% service, 30.3% sales and office, 19.8% natural resources, construction, and maintenance, 9.2% production, transportation, and material moving

Income: Per capita: $28,287; Median household: $57,688; Average household: $66,555; Households with income of $100,000 or more: 21.3%; Poverty rate: 10.2%

Educational Attainment: High school diploma or higher: 89.5%; Bachelor's degree or higher: 21.0%; Graduate/professional degree or higher: 8.8%

Housing: Homeownership rate: 85.4%; Median home value: $102,800; Median year structure built: 1976; Homeowner vacancy rate: 0.0%; Median selected monthly owner costs: $1,418 with a mortgage, $487 without a mortgage; Median gross rent: $868 per month; Rental vacancy rate: 0.0%

Health Insurance: 93.9% have insurance; 70.9% have private insurance; 38.5% have public insurance; 6.1% do not have insurance; 0.0% of children under 18 do not have insurance

Transportation: Commute: 91.5% car, 0.0% public transportation, 0.8% walk, 7.7% work from home; Mean travel time to work: 20.6 minutes

PHOENIX (village). Covers a land area of 1.171 square miles and a water area of 0.119 square miles. Located at 43.23° N. Lat; 76.30° W. Long. Elevation is 371 feet.

History: Incorporated 1849.

Population: 2,496; Growth (since 2000): 10.9%; Density: 2,132.3 persons per square mile; Race: 92.1% White, 0.5% Black/African American, 2.4% Asian, 0.0% American Indian/Alaska Native, 0.0% Native Hawaiian/Other Pacific Islander, 5.0% Two or more races, 4.6% Hispanic of any race; Average household size: 2.43; Median age: 32.9; Age under 18: 27.4%; Age 65 and over: 9.7%; Males per 100 females: 90.7; Marriage status: 37.0% never married, 43.1% now married, 4.9% separated, 7.3% widowed, 12.7% divorced; Foreign born: 1.6%; Speak English only: 94.7%; With disability: 12.5%; Veterans: 9.4%; Ancestry: 16.9% Irish, 16.8% German, 15.6% Italian, 11.4% American, 11.0% English

Employment: 7.9% management, business, and financial, 4.4% computer, engineering, and science, 10.9% education, legal, community service, arts, and media, 2.4% healthcare practitioners, 20.0% service, 29.7% sales and office, 9.2% natural resources, construction, and maintenance, 15.5% production, transportation, and material moving

Income: Per capita: $21,992; Median household: $34,476; Average household: $53,479; Households with income of $100,000 or more: 6.3%; Poverty rate: 24.1%

Educational Attainment: High school diploma or higher: 89.7%; Bachelor's degree or higher: 14.5%; Graduate/professional degree or higher: 3.8%

School District(s)

Phoenix Central SD (PK-12)

2014-15 Enrollment: 1,890 . . . . (315) 695-1555

Housing: Homeownership rate: 41.6%; Median home value: $89,000; Median year structure built: 1942; Homeowner vacancy rate: 0.0%; Median selected monthly owner costs: $1,142 with a mortgage, $520 without a mortgage; Median gross rent: $650 per month; Rental vacancy rate: 0.0%

Health Insurance: 92.0% have insurance; 54.1% have private insurance; 49.6% have public insurance; 8.0% do not have insurance; 0.0% of children under 18 do not have insurance

Transportation: Commute: 90.3% car, 1.5% public transportation, 3.9% walk, 4.2% work from home; Mean travel time to work: 22.9 minutes

PULASKI (village). Covers a land area of 3.484 square miles and a water area of 0.106 square miles. Located at 43.57° N. Lat; 76.12° W. Long. Elevation is 371 feet.

History: Incorporated 1832.

Population: 2,214; Growth (since 2000): -7.7%; Density: 635.5 persons per square mile; Race: 97.7% White, 0.0% Black/African American, 0.5% Asian, 0.0% American Indian/Alaska Native, 0.0% Native Hawaiian/Other Pacific Islander, 1.8% Two or more races, 0.9% Hispanic of any race; Average household size: 2.34; Median age: 36.9; Age under 18: 27.4%; Age 65 and over: 15.6%; Males per 100 females: 93.9; Marriage status: 29.1% never married, 46.9% now married, 6.7% separated, 7.5% widowed, 16.6% divorced; Foreign born: 1.8%; Speak English only: 98.7%; With disability: 17.2%; Veterans: 9.2%; Ancestry: 27.3% German, 24.1% Irish, 20.2% English, 11.7% French, 7.1% Italian

Employment: 8.6% management, business, and financial, 3.6% computer, engineering, and science, 14.9% education, legal, community service, arts, and media, 4.1% healthcare practitioners, 21.0% service, 18.8% sales and office, 12.1% natural resources, construction, and maintenance, 16.8% production, transportation, and material moving

Income: Per capita: $23,143; Median household: $45,000; Average household: $53,144; Households with income of $100,000 or more: 17.1%; Poverty rate: 20.0%

Educational Attainment: High school diploma or higher: 92.6%; Bachelor's degree or higher: 19.2%; Graduate/professional degree or higher: 8.3%

School District(s)

Pulaski Central SD (PK-12)

2014-15 Enrollment: 1,159 . . . . (315) 298-5188

Housing: Homeownership rate: 47.5%; Median home value: $96,000; Median year structure built: 1949; Homeowner vacancy rate: 4.1%; Median selected monthly owner costs: $1,217 with a mortgage, $479 without a mortgage; Median gross rent: $617 per month; Rental vacancy rate: 5.0%

Health Insurance: 93.9% have insurance; 66.1% have private insurance; 42.7% have public insurance; 6.1% do not have insurance; 3.3% of children under 18 do not have insurance

Safety: Violent crime rate: 0.0 per 10,000 population; Property crime rate: 129.3 per 10,000 population

Transportation: Commute: 93.3% car, 0.0% public transportation, 4.2% walk, 2.4% work from home; Mean travel time to work: 25.6 minutes

REDFIELD (town). Covers a land area of 89.817 square miles and a water area of 3.606 square miles. Located at 43.59° N. Lat; 75.83° W. Long. Elevation is 948 feet.

Population: 555; Growth (since 2000): -8.6%; Density: 6.2 persons per square mile; Race: 100.0% White, 0.0% Black/African American, 0.0% Asian, 0.0% American Indian/Alaska Native, 0.0% Native Hawaiian/Other Pacific Islander, 0.0% Two or more races, 1.3% Hispanic of any race; Average household size: 2.58; Median age: 45.4; Age under 18: 19.6%; Age 65 and over: 23.4%; Males per 100 females: 103.7; Marriage status: 24.6% never married, 53.8% now married, 1.1% separated, 6.9% widowed, 14.7% divorced; Foreign born: 0.7%; Speak English only: 98.1%; With disability: 15.9%; Veterans: 9.9%; Ancestry: 24.5% German, 15.9% Irish, 12.8% Italian, 12.4% English, 11.2% American

Employment: 11.5% management, business, and financial, 8.8% computer, engineering, and science, 7.4% education, legal, community service, arts, and media, 3.2% healthcare practitioners, 23.5% service,

17.5% sales and office, 12.0% natural resources, construction, and maintenance, 16.1% production, transportation, and material moving
Income: Per capita: $21,721; Median household: $49,625; Average household: $54,113; Households with income of $100,000 or more: 9.7%; Poverty rate: 19.1%
Educational Attainment: High school diploma or higher: 87.8%; Bachelor's degree or higher: 13.8%; Graduate/professional degree or higher: 6.0%
Housing: Homeownership rate: 94.9%; Median home value: $83,800; Median year structure built: 1979; Homeowner vacancy rate: 3.3%; Median selected monthly owner costs: $959 with a mortgage, $383 without a mortgage; Median gross rent: n/a per month; Rental vacancy rate: 38.9%
Health Insurance: 90.3% have insurance; 60.5% have private insurance; 48.8% have public insurance; 9.7% do not have insurance; 2.8% of children under 18 do not have insurance
Transportation: Commute: 91.9% car, 0.0% public transportation, 0.0% walk, 4.8% work from home; Mean travel time to work: 40.6 minutes

RICHLAND (town). Covers a land area of 57.248 square miles and a water area of 2.801 square miles. Located at 43.55° N. Lat; 76.15° W. Long. Elevation is 545 feet.
Population: 5,708; Growth (since 2000): -2.0%; Density: 99.7 persons per square mile; Race: 98.8% White, 0.3% Black/African American, 0.2% Asian, 0.0% American Indian/Alaska Native, 0.0% Native Hawaiian/Other Pacific Islander, 0.8% Two or more races, 1.1% Hispanic of any race; Average household size: 2.63; Median age: 37.8; Age under 18: 29.0%; Age 65 and over: 14.7%; Males per 100 females: 99.2; Marriage status: 22.9% never married, 55.3% now married, 3.9% separated, 7.6% widowed, 14.3% divorced; Foreign born: 1.6%; Speak English only: 91.6%; With disability: 15.7%; Veterans: 9.5%; Ancestry: 23.3% German, 19.4% Irish, 18.1% English, 9.1% French, 8.0% Italian
Employment: 9.4% management, business, and financial, 2.4% computer, engineering, and science, 14.8% education, legal, community service, arts, and media, 4.0% healthcare practitioners, 17.7% service, 21.5% sales and office, 12.9% natural resources, construction, and maintenance, 17.4% production, transportation, and material moving
Income: Per capita: $21,426; Median household: $41,875; Average household: $55,493; Households with income of $100,000 or more: 16.5%; Poverty rate: 20.6%
Educational Attainment: High school diploma or higher: 84.4%; Bachelor's degree or higher: 15.3%; Graduate/professional degree or higher: 6.7%
Housing: Homeownership rate: 65.6%; Median home value: $101,700; Median year structure built: 1962; Homeowner vacancy rate: 6.7%; Median selected monthly owner costs: $1,210 with a mortgage, $490 without a mortgage; Median gross rent: $715 per month; Rental vacancy rate: 3.4%
Health Insurance: 86.2% have insurance; 61.2% have private insurance; 41.8% have public insurance; 13.8% do not have insurance; 24.9% of children under 18 do not have insurance
Transportation: Commute: 90.1% car, 0.0% public transportation, 3.5% walk, 5.3% work from home; Mean travel time to work: 25.0 minutes

SAND RIDGE (CDP). Covers a land area of 2.399 square miles and a water area of 0.036 square miles. Located at 43.26° N. Lat; 76.24° W. Long. Elevation is 433 feet.
Population: 663; Growth (since 2000): -26.8%; Density: 276.4 persons per square mile; Race: 95.9% White, 0.0% Black/African American, 0.0% Asian, 4.1% American Indian/Alaska Native, 0.0% Native Hawaiian/Other Pacific Islander, 0.0% Two or more races, 0.0% Hispanic of any race; Average household size: 1.97; Median age: 53.6; Age under 18: 5.6%; Age 65 and over: 25.2%; Males per 100 females: 105.6; Marriage status: 24.5% never married, 48.8% now married, 14.4% separated, 16.6% widowed, 10.2% divorced; Foreign born: 0.0%; Speak English only: 100.0%; With disability: 36.3%; Veterans: 13.6%; Ancestry: 16.6% English, 15.5% French, 13.6% German, 13.6% Irish, 8.0% Italian
Employment: 4.2% management, business, and financial, 6.6% computer, engineering, and science, 8.0% education, legal, community service, arts, and media, 6.6% healthcare practitioners, 11.9% service, 21.0% sales and office, 27.3% natural resources, construction, and maintenance, 14.3% production, transportation, and material moving
Income: Per capita: $21,086; Median household: $34,015; Average household: $40,451; Households with income of $100,000 or more: 6.8%; Poverty rate: 17.3%

Educational Attainment: High school diploma or higher: 70.9%; Bachelor's degree or higher: 4.3%; Graduate/professional degree or higher: 4.3%
Housing: Homeownership rate: 82.4%; Median home value: n/a; Median year structure built: 1976; Homeowner vacancy rate: 0.0%; Median selected monthly owner costs: $1,271 with a mortgage, $492 without a mortgage; Median gross rent: n/a per month; Rental vacancy rate: 0.0%
Health Insurance: 84.3% have insurance; 51.3% have private insurance; 53.7% have public insurance; 15.7% do not have insurance; 0.0% of children under 18 do not have insurance
Transportation: Commute: 100.0% car, 0.0% public transportation, 0.0% walk, 0.0% work from home; Mean travel time to work: 19.6 minutes

SANDY CREEK (town). Covers a land area of 42.284 square miles and a water area of 4.157 square miles. Located at 43.63° N. Lat; 76.12° W. Long. Elevation is 499 feet.
Population: 3,878; Growth (since 2000): 0.4%; Density: 91.7 persons per square mile; Race: 98.5% White, 0.2% Black/African American, 0.3% Asian, 0.0% American Indian/Alaska Native, 0.0% Native Hawaiian/Other Pacific Islander, 1.0% Two or more races, 0.6% Hispanic of any race; Average household size: 2.40; Median age: 43.1; Age under 18: 21.1%; Age 65 and over: 19.8%; Males per 100 females: 102.9; Marriage status: 25.6% never married, 59.2% now married, 1.6% separated, 5.1% widowed, 10.0% divorced; Foreign born: 1.0%; Speak English only: 98.5%; With disability: 18.9%; Veterans: 13.7%; Ancestry: 22.7% German, 22.4% English, 16.9% Irish, 7.3% Dutch, 5.8% Italian
Employment: 17.2% management, business, and financial, 3.6% computer, engineering, and science, 8.7% education, legal, community service, arts, and media, 3.9% healthcare practitioners, 19.7% service, 20.1% sales and office, 13.6% natural resources, construction, and maintenance, 13.2% production, transportation, and material moving
Income: Per capita: $23,527; Median household: $44,853; Average household: $55,538; Households with income of $100,000 or more: 14.8%; Poverty rate: 17.4%
Educational Attainment: High school diploma or higher: 89.5%; Bachelor's degree or higher: 15.2%; Graduate/professional degree or higher: 6.6%

School District(s)
Sandy Creek Central SD (PK-12)
    2014-15 Enrollment: 835 . . . . (315) 387-3445
Housing: Homeownership rate: 73.2%; Median home value: $97,000; Median year structure built: 1967; Homeowner vacancy rate: 0.0%; Median selected monthly owner costs: $1,158 with a mortgage, $469 without a mortgage; Median gross rent: $724 per month; Rental vacancy rate: 11.3%
Health Insurance: 92.1% have insurance; 61.7% have private insurance; 47.1% have public insurance; 7.9% do not have insurance; 3.8% of children under 18 do not have insurance
Transportation: Commute: 95.6% car, 0.6% public transportation, 1.0% walk, 2.2% work from home; Mean travel time to work: 29.4 minutes

SANDY CREEK (village). Covers a land area of 1.351 square miles and a water area of 0 square miles. Located at 43.64° N. Lat; 76.09° W. Long. Elevation is 499 feet.
Population: 875; Growth (since 2000): 10.9%; Density: 647.5 persons per square mile; Race: 99.2% White, 0.6% Black/African American, 0.0% Asian, 0.0% American Indian/Alaska Native, 0.0% Native Hawaiian/Other Pacific Islander, 0.2% Two or more races, 1.6% Hispanic of any race; Average household size: 2.74; Median age: 33.1; Age under 18: 29.9%; Age 65 and over: 12.8%; Males per 100 females: 95.7; Marriage status: 26.6% never married, 61.4% now married, 0.2% separated, 3.4% widowed, 8.7% divorced; Foreign born: 1.6%; Speak English only: 98.6%; With disability: 20.7%; Veterans: 15.8%; Ancestry: 28.0% English, 21.4% German, 19.4% Irish, 12.6% Dutch, 7.2% French
Employment: 14.2% management, business, and financial, 5.6% computer, engineering, and science, 2.2% education, legal, community service, arts, and media, 6.7% healthcare practitioners, 20.6% service, 15.8% sales and office, 15.0% natural resources, construction, and maintenance, 20.0% production, transportation, and material moving
Income: Per capita: $20,526; Median household: $47,679; Average household: $55,524; Households with income of $100,000 or more: 15.0%; Poverty rate: 20.7%
Educational Attainment: High school diploma or higher: 93.4%; Bachelor's degree or higher: 15.5%; Graduate/professional degree or higher: 2.5%

Sandy Creek Central SD (PK-12)
  2014-15 Enrollment: 835 . . . . (315) 387-3445
Housing: Homeownership rate: 65.2%; Median home value: $85,600; Median year structure built: Before 1940; Homeowner vacancy rate: 0.0%; Median selected monthly owner costs: $980 with a mortgage, $483 without a mortgage; Median gross rent: $622 per month; Rental vacancy rate: 0.0%
Health Insurance: 94.2% have insurance; 62.4% have private insurance; 43.1% have public insurance; 5.8% do not have insurance; 0.0% of children under 18 do not have insurance
Transportation: Commute: 94.0% car, 0.6% public transportation, 2.6% walk, 1.4% work from home; Mean travel time to work: 25.8 minutes

SCHROEPPEL (town). Covers a land area of 42.201 square miles and a water area of 0.996 square miles. Located at 43.26° N. Lat; 76.28° W. Long.
Population: 8,404; Growth (since 2000): -1.9%; Density: 199.1 persons per square mile; Race: 95.8% White, 0.5% Black/African American, 0.7% Asian, 0.3% American Indian/Alaska Native, 0.0% Native Hawaiian/Other Pacific Islander, 2.7% Two or more races, 2.1% Hispanic of any race; Average household size: 2.51; Median age: 41.8; Age under 18: 22.0%; Age 65 and over: 14.3%; Males per 100 females: 99.8; Marriage status: 28.9% never married, 50.5% now married, 4.7% separated, 7.3% widowed, 13.4% divorced; Foreign born: 1.0%; Speak English only: 97.2%; With disability: 17.3%; Veterans: 9.3%; Ancestry: 18.5% German, 16.0% Irish, 13.5% Italian, 13.1% English, 8.9% American
Employment: 9.3% management, business, and financial, 3.9% computer, engineering, and science, 10.6% education, legal, community service, arts, and media, 3.0% healthcare practitioners, 16.2% service, 26.5% sales and office, 16.1% natural resources, construction, and maintenance, 14.4% production, transportation, and material moving
Income: Per capita: $24,467; Median household: $52,978; Average household: $61,291; Households with income of $100,000 or more: 15.1%; Poverty rate: 15.8%
Educational Attainment: High school diploma or higher: 88.2%; Bachelor's degree or higher: 17.2%; Graduate/professional degree or higher: 7.0%
Housing: Homeownership rate: 75.4%; Median home value: $98,600; Median year structure built: 1969; Homeowner vacancy rate: 0.0%; Median selected monthly owner costs: $1,269 with a mortgage, $516 without a mortgage; Median gross rent: $700 per month; Rental vacancy rate: 0.0%
Health Insurance: 93.3% have insurance; 65.8% have private insurance; 39.6% have public insurance; 6.7% do not have insurance; 0.0% of children under 18 do not have insurance
Transportation: Commute: 87.2% car, 0.4% public transportation, 1.4% walk, 10.5% work from home; Mean travel time to work: 22.1 minutes
Additional Information Contacts
Town of Schroeppel . . . . (315) 695-2778
  http://townofschroeppel.com/content

SCRIBA (town). Covers a land area of 40.571 square miles and a water area of 3.342 square miles. Located at 43.46° N. Lat; 76.42° W. Long. Elevation is 367 feet.
Population: 6,746; Growth (since 2000): -8.0%; Density: 166.3 persons per square mile; Race: 97.0% White, 0.5% Black/African American, 1.6% Asian, 0.0% American Indian/Alaska Native, 0.0% Native Hawaiian/Other Pacific Islander, 0.9% Two or more races, 2.6% Hispanic of any race; Average household size: 2.35; Median age: 44.7; Age under 18: 19.6%; Age 65 and over: 14.3%; Males per 100 females: 98.0; Marriage status: 28.9% never married, 52.4% now married, 3.1% separated, 3.3% widowed, 15.3% divorced; Foreign born: 2.2%; Speak English only: 96.7%; With disability: 16.5%; Veterans: 11.5%; Ancestry: 22.4% Irish, 19.4% English, 14.8% Italian, 12.7% German, 11.7% American
Employment: 7.9% management, business, and financial, 2.9% computer, engineering, and science, 11.2% education, legal, community service, arts, and media, 5.0% healthcare practitioners, 19.9% service, 26.8% sales and office, 7.7% natural resources, construction, and maintenance, 18.6% production, transportation, and material moving
Income: Per capita: $29,406; Median household: $53,398; Average household: $67,812; Households with income of $100,000 or more: 23.1%; Poverty rate: 10.9%
Educational Attainment: High school diploma or higher: 82.8%; Bachelor's degree or higher: 19.1%; Graduate/professional degree or higher: 7.1%

Housing: Homeownership rate: 71.7%; Median home value: $104,300; Median year structure built: 1982; Homeowner vacancy rate: 2.7%; Median selected monthly owner costs: $1,474 with a mortgage, $465 without a mortgage; Median gross rent: $707 per month; Rental vacancy rate: 5.7%
Health Insurance: 95.1% have insurance; 76.4% have private insurance; 34.1% have public insurance; 4.9% do not have insurance; 0.0% of children under 18 do not have insurance
Transportation: Commute: 93.7% car, 0.9% public transportation, 0.3% walk, 2.4% work from home; Mean travel time to work: 21.3 minutes
Additional Information Contacts
Town of Scriba . . . . (315) 343-3375
  http://scribany.org

SUNY OSWEGO (CDP). Covers a land area of 0.324 square miles and a water area of 0.302 square miles. Located at 43.46° N. Lat; 76.54° W. Long.
Population: 3,559; Growth (since 2000): n/a; Density: 10,969.5 persons per square mile; Race: 78.3% White, 10.6% Black/African American, 3.8% Asian, 0.0% American Indian/Alaska Native, 0.0% Native Hawaiian/Other Pacific Islander, 4.2% Two or more races, 9.9% Hispanic of any race; Average household size: 0.00; Median age: 19.6; Age under 18: 1.4%; Age 65 and over: 0.0%; Males per 100 females: 95.7; Marriage status: 99.7% never married, 0.0% now married, 0.0% separated, 0.0% widowed, 0.3% divorced; Foreign born: 6.3%; Speak English only: 85.0%; With disability: 2.7%; Veterans: 0.0%; Ancestry: 29.6% Italian, 28.7% Irish, 24.2% German, 11.6% Polish, 6.7% English
Employment: 2.3% management, business, and financial, 5.0% computer, engineering, and science, 9.6% education, legal, community service, arts, and media, 0.0% healthcare practitioners, 46.1% service, 33.3% sales and office, 1.9% natural resources, construction, and maintenance, 1.8% production, transportation, and material moving
Income: Per capita: $6,510; Median household: n/a; Average household: n/a; Households with income of $100,000 or more: n/a; Poverty rate: 41.2%
Educational Attainment: High school diploma or higher: 41.2%; Bachelor's degree or higher: 41.2%; Graduate/professional degree or higher: n/a
Housing: Homeownership rate: n/a; Median home value: n/a; Median year structure built: n/a; Homeowner vacancy rate: 0.0%; Median selected monthly owner costs: n/a with a mortgage, n/a without a mortgage; Median gross rent: n/a per month; Rental vacancy rate: 0.0%
Health Insurance: 97.8% have insurance; 89.0% have private insurance; 11.1% have public insurance; 2.2% do not have insurance; 12.0% of children under 18 do not have insurance
Transportation: Commute: 30.5% car, 4.1% public transportation, 58.3% walk, 5.4% work from home; Mean travel time to work: 9.2 minutes

VOLNEY (town). Covers a land area of 48.240 square miles and a water area of 0.916 square miles. Located at 43.36° N. Lat; 76.37° W. Long. Elevation is 443 feet.
Population: 5,868; Growth (since 2000): -3.7%; Density: 121.6 persons per square mile; Race: 98.3% White, 0.1% Black/African American, 0.0% Asian, 1.0% American Indian/Alaska Native, 0.0% Native Hawaiian/Other Pacific Islander, 0.7% Two or more races, 1.6% Hispanic of any race; Average household size: 2.73; Median age: 41.2; Age under 18: 20.4%; Age 65 and over: 16.0%; Males per 100 females: 101.5; Marriage status: 26.6% never married, 56.3% now married, 3.1% separated, 6.6% widowed, 10.5% divorced; Foreign born: 2.0%; Speak English only: 98.6%; With disability: 14.9%; Veterans: 12.8%; Ancestry: 20.9% Irish, 19.0% German, 16.3% English, 11.0% Italian, 8.7% American
Employment: 11.3% management, business, and financial, 3.0% computer, engineering, and science, 13.4% education, legal, community service, arts, and media, 5.2% healthcare practitioners, 16.6% service, 18.4% sales and office, 14.2% natural resources, construction, and maintenance, 17.8% production, transportation, and material moving
Income: Per capita: $26,622; Median household: $61,633; Average household: $70,561; Households with income of $100,000 or more: 20.5%; Poverty rate: 8.7%
Educational Attainment: High school diploma or higher: 88.7%; Bachelor's degree or higher: 22.8%; Graduate/professional degree or higher: 6.2%
Housing: Homeownership rate: 80.2%; Median home value: $95,200; Median year structure built: 1978; Homeowner vacancy rate: 2.2%; Median selected monthly owner costs: $1,062 with a mortgage, $576 without a mortgage; Median gross rent: $934 per month; Rental vacancy rate: 8.5%

Health Insurance: 90.4% have insurance; 64.1% have private insurance; 39.4% have public insurance; 9.6% do not have insurance; 6.1% of children under 18 do not have insurance
Transportation: Commute: 94.2% car, 0.0% public transportation, 0.0% walk, 5.3% work from home; Mean travel time to work: 21.4 minutes
Additional Information Contacts
Town of Volney . . . . (315) 593-8288
   http://www.townofvolney.com

WEST MONROE (town). Covers a land area of 33.746 square miles and a water area of 4.841 square miles. Located at 43.31° N. Lat; 76.09° W. Long. Elevation is 397 feet.
Population: 4,240; Growth (since 2000): -4.2%; Density: 125.6 persons per square mile; Race: 97.6% White, 0.3% Black/African American, 0.0% Asian, 0.2% American Indian/Alaska Native, 0.0% Native Hawaiian/Other Pacific Islander, 1.8% Two or more races, 0.2% Hispanic of any race; Average household size: 2.69; Median age: 41.7; Age under 18: 22.7%; Age 65 and over: 12.4%; Males per 100 females: 106.4; Marriage status: 32.3% never married, 48.0% now married, 0.5% separated, 6.5% widowed, 13.3% divorced; Foreign born: 1.3%; Speak English only: 97.4%; With disability: 14.1%; Veterans: 8.0%; Ancestry: 22.6% German, 17.1% Irish, 15.5% English, 14.9% Italian, 9.3% American
Employment: 9.3% management, business, and financial, 5.0% computer, engineering, and science, 8.3% education, legal, community service, arts, and media, 5.5% healthcare practitioners, 16.7% service, 19.8% sales and office, 16.7% natural resources, construction, and maintenance, 18.6% production, transportation, and material moving
Income: Per capita: $24,107; Median household: $53,480; Average household: $62,510; Households with income of $100,000 or more: 21.0%; Poverty rate: 17.9%
Educational Attainment: High school diploma or higher: 87.6%; Bachelor's degree or higher: 13.1%; Graduate/professional degree or higher: 4.4%
Housing: Homeownership rate: 88.1%; Median home value: $104,800; Median year structure built: 1983; Homeowner vacancy rate: 0.0%; Median selected monthly owner costs: $1,326 with a mortgage, $527 without a mortgage; Median gross rent: $963 per month; Rental vacancy rate: 0.0%
Health Insurance: 93.8% have insurance; 66.1% have private insurance; 43.2% have public insurance; 6.2% do not have insurance; 1.1% of children under 18 do not have insurance
Transportation: Commute: 95.2% car, 0.0% public transportation, 0.0% walk, 4.8% work from home; Mean travel time to work: 29.9 minutes
Additional Information Contacts
Town of West Monroe . . . . (315) 668-8314
   http://www.townofwestmonroe-ny.us

WILLIAMSTOWN (town). Covers a land area of 38.672 square miles and a water area of 0.491 square miles. Located at 43.46° N. Lat; 75.89° W. Long. Elevation is 600 feet.
Population: 1,244; Growth (since 2000): -7.9%; Density: 32.2 persons per square mile; Race: 95.8% White, 0.0% Black/African American, 0.0% Asian, 0.0% American Indian/Alaska Native, 0.0% Native Hawaiian/Other Pacific Islander, 3.5% Two or more races, 0.4% Hispanic of any race; Average household size: 3.12; Median age: 37.6; Age under 18: 26.8%; Age 65 and over: 12.6%; Males per 100 females: 102.1; Marriage status: 30.7% never married, 54.5% now married, 2.5% separated, 4.5% widowed, 10.4% divorced; Foreign born: 1.3%; Speak English only: 97.9%; With disability: 14.6%; Veterans: 13.8%; Ancestry: 19.2% Irish, 16.1% German, 13.0% English, 12.9% American, 6.4% Polish
Employment: 7.7% management, business, and financial, 2.4% computer, engineering, and science, 4.4% education, legal, community service, arts, and media, 2.0% healthcare practitioners, 21.5% service, 25.9% sales and office, 9.6% natural resources, construction, and maintenance, 26.5% production, transportation, and material moving
Income: Per capita: $19,842; Median household: $53,359; Average household: $58,158; Households with income of $100,000 or more: 12.5%; Poverty rate: 13.8%
Educational Attainment: High school diploma or higher: 82.6%; Bachelor's degree or higher: 5.3%; Graduate/professional degree or higher: 0.4%
Housing: Homeownership rate: 90.2%; Median home value: $77,000; Median year structure built: 1976; Homeowner vacancy rate: 3.2%; Median selected monthly owner costs: $1,052 with a mortgage, $407 without a mortgage; Median gross rent: $944 per month; Rental vacancy rate: 25.0%

Health Insurance: 91.4% have insurance; 61.4% have private insurance; 41.9% have public insurance; 8.6% do not have insurance; 3.3% of children under 18 do not have insurance
Transportation: Commute: 93.0% car, 1.7% public transportation, 2.8% walk, 1.7% work from home; Mean travel time to work: 28.3 minutes

Otsego County

Located in central New York; bounded on the west by the Unadilla River; drained by the Susquehanna River; includes Canadarago Lake and other lakes. Covers a land area of 1,001.700 square miles, a water area of 14.052 square miles, and is located in the Eastern Time Zone at 42.63° N. Lat., 75.03° W. Long. The county was founded in 1791. County seat is Cooperstown.

Otsego County is part of the Oneonta, NY Micropolitan Statistical Area. The entire metro area includes: Otsego County, NY

Weather Station: Cherry Valley 2 NNE										Elevation: 1,359 feet		
	Jan	Feb	Mar	Apr	May	Jun	Jul	Aug	Sep	Oct	Nov	Dec
High	28	32	40	54	66	74	78	76	69	57	46	33
Low	12	14	22	34	44	53	58	57	49	38	30	18
Precip	3.3	2.8	3.9	4.1	4.4	4.5	4.5	4.2	4.0	3.9	3.8	3.3
Snow	32.8	21.1	22.1	5.9	0.4	0.0	0.0	0.0	tr	1.1	9.2	24.5

High and Low temperatures in degrees Fahrenheit; Precipitation and Snow in inches

Weather Station: Cooperstown										Elevation: 1,200 feet		
	Jan	Feb	Mar	Apr	May	Jun	Jul	Aug	Sep	Oct	Nov	Dec
High	31	34	42	56	68	76	80	78	71	59	47	35
Low	12	13	21	33	43	52	57	56	48	37	29	19
Precip	2.9	2.4	3.4	3.7	3.9	4.5	4.3	4.0	3.8	3.8	3.3	3.1
Snow	21.7	16.4	15.3	4.0	0.1	0.0	0.0	0.0	tr	0.5	6.1	18.0

High and Low temperatures in degrees Fahrenheit; Precipitation and Snow in inches

Weather Station: Maryland 6 SW										Elevation: 3,911 feet		
	Jan	Feb	Mar	Apr	May	Jun	Jul	Aug	Sep	Oct	Nov	Dec
High	31	33	42	56	67	75	79	78	70	59	47	35
Low	12	12	20	32	41	51	55	54	47	36	29	19
Precip	3.2	2.5	3.4	3.5	3.6	4.3	4.4	3.5	3.6	3.5	3.4	3.2
Snow	21.2	16.0	13.3	3.3	0.2	0.0	0.0	0.0	0.0	0.8	6.0	16.0

High and Low temperatures in degrees Fahrenheit; Precipitation and Snow in inches

Population: 61,399; Growth (since 2000): -0.4%; Density: 61.3 persons per square mile; Race: 94.0% White, 1.9% Black/African American, 1.2% Asian, 0.2% American Indian/Alaska Native, 0.0% Native Hawaiian/Other Pacific Islander, 1.8% two or more races, 3.4% Hispanic of any race; Average household size: 2.36; Median age: 41.6; Age under 18: 17.2%; Age 65 and over: 18.0%; Males per 100 females: 93.7; Marriage status: 35.6% never married, 48.0% now married, 2.0% separated, 6.5% widowed, 9.8% divorced; Foreign born: 3.6%; Speak English only: 93.8%; With disability: 12.7%; Veterans: 9.5%; Ancestry: 21.6% German, 18.5% Irish, 14.8% English, 12.5% Italian, 7.8% American
Religion: Six largest groups: 18.6% Catholicism, 8.5% Methodist/Pietist, 2.1% Episcopalianism/Anglicanism, 1.8% Presbyterian-Reformed, 1.7% Baptist, 1.6% Non-denominational Protestant
Economy: Unemployment rate: 4.2%; Leading industries: 19.9 % retail trade; 15.1 % accommodation and food services; 11.5 % health care and social assistance; Farms: 995 totaling 180,750 acres; Company size: 1 employs 1,000 or more persons, 3 employ 500 to 999 persons, 21 employs 100 to 499 persons, 1,390 employ less than 100 persons; Business ownership: 1,400 women-owned, 27 Black-owned, 143 Hispanic-owned, 53 Asian-owned, n/a American Indian/Alaska Native-owned
Employment: 12.7% management, business, and financial, 3.2% computer, engineering, and science, 13.6% education, legal, community service, arts, and media, 7.3% healthcare practitioners, 20.2% service, 22.4% sales and office, 9.5% natural resources, construction, and maintenance, 11.1% production, transportation, and material moving
Income: Per capita: $24,625; Median household: $48,588; Average household: $62,240; Households with income of $100,000 or more: 16.7%; Poverty rate: 16.5%
Educational Attainment: High school diploma or higher: 89.9%; Bachelor's degree or higher: 27.7%; Graduate/professional degree or higher: 13.5%
Housing: Homeownership rate: 73.4%; Median home value: $142,800; Median year structure built: 1956; Homeowner vacancy rate: 1.7%; Median selected monthly owner costs: $1,249 with a mortgage, $476 without a mortgage; Median gross rent: $776 per month; Rental vacancy rate: 8.4%

Vital Statistics: Birth rate: 86.4 per 10,000 population; Death rate: 101.3 per 10,000 population; Age-adjusted cancer mortality rate: 140.4 deaths per 100,000 population

Health Insurance: 92.6% have insurance; 71.5% have private insurance; 36.3% have public insurance; 7.4% do not have insurance; 3.7% of children under 18 do not have insurance

Health Care: Physicians: 58.4 per 10,000 population; Dentists: 4.9 per 10,000 population; Hospital beds: 59.9 per 10,000 population; Hospital admissions: 1,893.9 per 10,000 population

Transportation: Commute: 81.7% car, 1.8% public transportation, 9.0% walk, 6.2% work from home; Mean travel time to work: 21.7 minutes

2016 Presidential Election: 52.5% Trump, 41.2% Clinton, 4.2% Johnson, 2.1% Stein

National and State Parks: Gilbert Lake State Park

Additional Information Contacts

Otsego Government . . . . (607) 547-4276
   http://www.otsegocounty.com

Otsego County Communities

BURLINGTON (town). Covers a land area of 44.891 square miles and a water area of 0.122 square miles. Located at 42.72° N. Lat; 75.14° W. Long. Elevation is 1,535 feet.

Population: 1,094; Growth (since 2000): 0.8%; Density: 24.4 persons per square mile; Race: 99.3% White, 0.3% Black/African American, 0.0% Asian, 0.3% American Indian/Alaska Native, 0.0% Native Hawaiian/Other Pacific Islander, 0.2% Two or more races, 1.1% Hispanic of any race; Average household size: 2.59; Median age: 44.1; Age under 18: 20.7%; Age 65 and over: 16.5%; Males per 100 females: 108.4; Marriage status: 27.6% never married, 58.9% now married, 1.6% separated, 4.0% widowed, 9.6% divorced; Foreign born: 0.8%; Speak English only: 96.1%; With disability: 13.0%; Veterans: 6.7%; Ancestry: 26.8% German, 16.2% American, 14.5% Irish, 11.1% English, 5.1% Dutch

Employment: 13.2% management, business, and financial, 1.2% computer, engineering, and science, 8.3% education, legal, community service, arts, and media, 5.0% healthcare practitioners, 15.5% service, 29.5% sales and office, 13.6% natural resources, construction, and maintenance, 13.8% production, transportation, and material moving

Income: Per capita: $22,983; Median household: $48,194; Average household: $56,949; Households with income of $100,000 or more: 12.0%; Poverty rate: 15.2%

Educational Attainment: High school diploma or higher: 92.1%; Bachelor's degree or higher: 10.0%; Graduate/professional degree or higher: 3.0%

Housing: Homeownership rate: 89.6%; Median home value: $107,300; Median year structure built: 1970; Homeowner vacancy rate: 2.1%; Median selected monthly owner costs: $917 with a mortgage, $411 without a mortgage; Median gross rent: $875 per month; Rental vacancy rate: 0.0%

Health Insurance: 84.8% have insurance; 55.9% have private insurance; 40.9% have public insurance; 15.2% do not have insurance; 24.3% of children under 18 do not have insurance

Transportation: Commute: 93.6% car, 0.8% public transportation, 2.6% walk, 2.6% work from home; Mean travel time to work: 21.6 minutes

BURLINGTON FLATS (unincorporated postal area)
ZCTA: 13315

Covers a land area of 49.097 square miles and a water area of 0.170 square miles. Located at 42.74° N. Lat; 75.14° W. Long. Elevation is 1,289 feet.

Population: 1,400; Growth (since 2000): 0.2%; Density: 28.5 persons per square mile; Race: 99.2% White, 0.4% Black/African American, 0.0% Asian, 0.2% American Indian/Alaska Native, 0.0% Native Hawaiian/Other Pacific Islander, 0.1% Two or more races, 0.7% Hispanic of any race; Average household size: 2.69; Median age: 44.6; Age under 18: 22.4%; Age 65 and over: 15.4%; Males per 100 females: 109.0; Marriage status: 25.7% never married, 61.9% now married, 1.2% separated, 4.9% widowed, 7.5% divorced; Foreign born: 0.9%; Speak English only: 96.3%; With disability: 13.2%; Veterans: 9.4%; Ancestry: 23.7% German, 17.6% Irish, 17.1% American, 10.1% English, 6.3% Dutch

Employment: 12.0% management, business, and financial, 1.7% computer, engineering, and science, 9.0% education, legal, community service, arts, and media, 6.8% healthcare practitioners, 16.2% service, 23.2% sales and office, 17.0% natural resources, construction, and maintenance, 14.2% production, transportation, and material moving

Income: Per capita: $21,807; Median household: $49,861; Average household: $56,729; Households with income of $100,000 or more: 12.9%; Poverty rate: 14.2%

Educational Attainment: High school diploma or higher: 92.0%; Bachelor's degree or higher: 11.3%; Graduate/professional degree or higher: 3.9%

Housing: Homeownership rate: 92.1%; Median home value: $112,500; Median year structure built: 1972; Homeowner vacancy rate: 1.6%; Median selected monthly owner costs: $1,030 with a mortgage, $432 without a mortgage; Median gross rent: $1,088 per month; Rental vacancy rate: 0.0%

Health Insurance: 87.0% have insurance; 60.0% have private insurance; 39.1% have public insurance; 13.0% do not have insurance; 16.6% of children under 18 do not have insurance

Transportation: Commute: 93.6% car, 0.6% public transportation, 1.8% walk, 3.7% work from home; Mean travel time to work: 23.5 minutes

BUTTERNUTS (town). Covers a land area of 53.829 square miles and a water area of 0.040 square miles. Located at 42.47° N. Lat; 75.32° W. Long.

Population: 1,966; Growth (since 2000): 9.7%; Density: 36.5 persons per square mile; Race: 96.5% White, 0.2% Black/African American, 1.6% Asian, 0.0% American Indian/Alaska Native, 0.0% Native Hawaiian/Other Pacific Islander, 1.7% Two or more races, 2.2% Hispanic of any race; Average household size: 2.37; Median age: 47.6; Age under 18: 16.9%; Age 65 and over: 18.6%; Males per 100 females: 97.6; Marriage status: 23.6% never married, 56.5% now married, 1.2% separated, 8.8% widowed, 11.1% divorced; Foreign born: 3.7%; Speak English only: 95.6%; With disability: 12.8%; Veterans: 10.0%; Ancestry: 22.1% German, 19.8% English, 17.9% Irish, 13.7% American, 7.3% Italian

Employment: 17.9% management, business, and financial, 2.8% computer, engineering, and science, 14.6% education, legal, community service, arts, and media, 3.5% healthcare practitioners, 11.1% service, 18.7% sales and office, 14.2% natural resources, construction, and maintenance, 17.2% production, transportation, and material moving

Income: Per capita: $25,862; Median household: $52,563; Average household: $61,321; Households with income of $100,000 or more: 17.0%; Poverty rate: 15.3%

Educational Attainment: High school diploma or higher: 91.3%; Bachelor's degree or higher: 23.3%; Graduate/professional degree or higher: 10.9%

Housing: Homeownership rate: 83.6%; Median home value: $149,800; Median year structure built: 1970; Homeowner vacancy rate: 3.3%; Median selected monthly owner costs: $1,275 with a mortgage, $424 without a mortgage; Median gross rent: $876 per month; Rental vacancy rate: 0.0%

Health Insurance: 91.6% have insurance; 66.9% have private insurance; 40.3% have public insurance; 8.4% do not have insurance; 2.4% of children under 18 do not have insurance

Transportation: Commute: 89.2% car, 0.2% public transportation, 4.6% walk, 5.5% work from home; Mean travel time to work: 26.2 minutes

CHERRY VALLEY (town). Covers a land area of 40.375 square miles and a water area of 0.007 square miles. Located at 42.81° N. Lat; 74.72° W. Long. Elevation is 1,345 feet.

History: Burned (Nov. 11, 1778) during American Revolution by Native American and Tory forces; over 40 people killed. Settled c.1740.

Population: 1,299; Growth (since 2000): 2.6%; Density: 32.2 persons per square mile; Race: 94.8% White, 0.6% Black/African American, 2.2% Asian, 0.0% American Indian/Alaska Native, 0.0% Native Hawaiian/Other Pacific Islander, 2.5% Two or more races, 3.2% Hispanic of any race; Average household size: 2.27; Median age: 48.5; Age under 18: 16.2%; Age 65 and over: 20.3%; Males per 100 females: 92.9; Marriage status: 26.8% never married, 58.8% now married, 1.2% separated, 4.9% widowed, 9.6% divorced; Foreign born: 2.2%; Speak English only: 96.3%; With disability: 12.3%; Veterans: 7.9%; Ancestry: 22.0% German, 16.0% Irish, 15.5% English, 9.7% Italian, 6.4% American

Employment: 13.4% management, business, and financial, 2.3% computer, engineering, and science, 10.2% education, legal, community service, arts, and media, 4.6% healthcare practitioners, 17.6% service, 30.9% sales and office, 12.1% natural resources, construction, and maintenance, 9.0% production, transportation, and material moving

Income: Per capita: $28,871; Median household: $58,162; Average household: $65,854; Households with income of $100,000 or more: 18.8%; Poverty rate: 14.9%

Educational Attainment: High school diploma or higher: 91.4%; Bachelor's degree or higher: 25.5%; Graduate/professional degree or higher: 11.8%

School District(s)
Cherry Valley-Springfield Central SD (PK-12)
    2014-15 Enrollment: 501 . . . . (607) 264-9332
Housing: Homeownership rate: 79.5%; Median home value: $164,200; Median year structure built: Before 1940; Homeowner vacancy rate: 1.5%; Median selected monthly owner costs: $1,331 with a mortgage, $583 without a mortgage; Median gross rent: $867 per month; Rental vacancy rate: 0.0%
Health Insurance: 90.3% have insurance; 74.9% have private insurance; 36.2% have public insurance; 9.7% do not have insurance; 14.2% of children under 18 do not have insurance
Transportation: Commute: 80.3% car, 2.2% public transportation, 7.9% walk, 9.6% work from home; Mean travel time to work: 27.1 minutes

CHERRY VALLEY (village). Covers a land area of 0.510 square
miles and a water area of <.001 square miles. Located at 42.80° N. Lat; 74.75° W. Long. Elevation is 1,345 feet.
Population: 562; Growth (since 2000): -5.1%; Density: 1,102.8 persons per square mile; Race: 93.6% White, 1.4% Black/African American, 2.8% Asian, 0.0% American Indian/Alaska Native, 0.0% Native Hawaiian/Other Pacific Islander, 2.1% Two or more races, 4.4% Hispanic of any race; Average household size: 2.24; Median age: 49.7; Age under 18: 16.9%; Age 65 and over: 22.6%; Males per 100 females: 81.2; Marriage status: 27.7% never married, 57.7% now married, 2.3% separated, 6.4% widowed, 8.2% divorced; Foreign born: 3.9%; Speak English only: 96.3%; With disability: 16.0%; Veterans: 10.9%; Ancestry: 16.9% Irish, 14.8% German, 13.7% English, 7.5% Italian, 4.6% Scottish
Employment: 10.5% management, business, and financial, 1.4% computer, engineering, and science, 8.5% education, legal, community service, arts, and media, 3.4% healthcare practitioners, 21.4% service, 33.3% sales and office, 9.5% natural resources, construction, and maintenance, 11.9% production, transportation, and material moving
Income: Per capita: $26,070; Median household: $55,556; Average household: $58,079; Households with income of $100,000 or more: 15.2%; Poverty rate: 15.1%
Educational Attainment: High school diploma or higher: 90.6%; Bachelor's degree or higher: 22.3%; Graduate/professional degree or higher: 12.9%

School District(s)
Cherry Valley-Springfield Central SD (PK-12)
    2014-15 Enrollment: 501 . . . . (607) 264-9332
Housing: Homeownership rate: 73.2%; Median home value: $124,300; Median year structure built: Before 1940; Homeowner vacancy rate: 1.1%; Median selected monthly owner costs: $1,213 with a mortgage, $485 without a mortgage; Median gross rent: $765 per month; Rental vacancy rate: 0.0%
Health Insurance: 94.1% have insurance; 74.4% have private insurance; 42.7% have public insurance; 5.9% do not have insurance; 10.5% of children under 18 do not have insurance
Transportation: Commute: 68.8% car, 3.9% public transportation, 14.9% walk, 12.4% work from home; Mean travel time to work: 23.4 minutes

COOPERSTOWN (village). County seat. Covers a land area of
1.635 square miles and a water area of 0.210 square miles. Located at 42.70° N. Lat; 74.93° W. Long. Elevation is 1,227 feet.
History: Founded by William Cooper, who brought his family here in 1787. His son, James Fenimore Cooper, made his home here after returning from abroad in 1833, and the region is described in his Leatherstocking Tales. Fenimore House is the headquarters of N.Y. State Historical Association. Other attractions include Farmers' Museum and the famous National Baseball Hall of Fame and Museum, which commemorates the founding (1839) of baseball here by Abner Doubleday. Incorporated 1807.
Population: 2,185; Growth (since 2000): 7.5%; Density: 1,336.7 persons per square mile; Race: 89.6% White, 0.9% Black/African American, 8.0% Asian, 0.7% American Indian/Alaska Native, 0.0% Native Hawaiian/Other Pacific Islander, 0.5% Two or more races, 1.9% Hispanic of any race; Average household size: 2.06; Median age: 51.1; Age under 18: 14.1%; Age 65 and over: 20.5%; Males per 100 females: 81.4; Marriage status: 26.0% never married, 57.9% now married, 1.8% separated, 8.0% widowed, 8.1% divorced; Foreign born: 7.1%; Speak English only: 89.3%; With disability: 7.0%; Veterans: 9.4%; Ancestry: 22.6% German, 22.5% Irish, 21.8% English, 12.1% Italian, 6.4% Scottish

Employment: 12.0% management, business, and financial, 5.0% computer, engineering, and science, 20.7% education, legal, community service, arts, and media, 22.4% healthcare practitioners, 15.9% service, 17.7% sales and office, 0.9% natural resources, construction, and maintenance, 5.3% production, transportation, and material moving
Income: Per capita: $45,288; Median household: $62,222; Average household: $97,305; Households with income of $100,000 or more: 31.0%; Poverty rate: 11.3%
Educational Attainment: High school diploma or higher: 94.9%; Bachelor's degree or higher: 53.8%; Graduate/professional degree or higher: 33.1%

School District(s)
Cooperstown Central SD (KG-12)
    2014-15 Enrollment: 885 . . . . (607) 547-5364
Housing: Homeownership rate: 58.8%; Median home value: $286,600; Median year structure built: Before 1940; Homeowner vacancy rate: 2.1%; Median selected monthly owner costs: $1,981 with a mortgage, $767 without a mortgage; Median gross rent: $829 per month; Rental vacancy rate: 11.1%
Health Insurance: 95.3% have insurance; 81.4% have private insurance; 33.6% have public insurance; 4.7% do not have insurance; 3.9% of children under 18 do not have insurance
Hospitals: Mary Imogene Bassett Hospital (180 beds)
Safety: Violent crime rate: 5.5 per 10,000 population; Property crime rate: 77.7 per 10,000 population
Newspapers: Cooperstown Crier (weekly circulation 2,500); Freeman's Journal (weekly circulation 2,500); Hometown Oneonta (weekly circulation 9,700)
Transportation: Commute: 53.9% car, 0.9% public transportation, 36.0% walk, 6.0% work from home; Mean travel time to work: 15.1 minutes

DECATUR (town). Covers a land area of 20.562 square miles and a
water area of 0.197 square miles. Located at 42.66° N. Lat; 74.71° W. Long. Elevation is 1,617 feet.
Population: 312; Growth (since 2000): -23.9%; Density: 15.2 persons per square mile; Race: 86.9% White, 0.0% Black/African American, 6.4% Asian, 0.0% American Indian/Alaska Native, 0.0% Native Hawaiian/Other Pacific Islander, 6.7% Two or more races, 2.2% Hispanic of any race; Average household size: 2.54; Median age: 45.7; Age under 18: 22.4%; Age 65 and over: 19.2%; Males per 100 females: 105.2; Marriage status: 22.9% never married, 51.8% now married, 1.6% separated, 13.3% widowed, 12.0% divorced; Foreign born: 7.7%; Speak English only: 94.0%; With disability: 16.7%; Veterans: 9.9%; Ancestry: 22.1% German, 19.2% Irish, 15.1% English, 9.3% American, 8.0% Slovene
Employment: 11.3% management, business, and financial, 1.6% computer, engineering, and science, 6.5% education, legal, community service, arts, and media, 5.6% healthcare practitioners, 25.8% service, 21.0% sales and office, 11.3% natural resources, construction, and maintenance, 16.9% production, transportation, and material moving
Income: Per capita: $20,776; Median household: $37,656; Average household: $51,890; Households with income of $100,000 or more: 12.2%; Poverty rate: 19.4%
Educational Attainment: High school diploma or higher: 88.0%; Bachelor's degree or higher: 18.0%; Graduate/professional degree or higher: 8.3%
Housing: Homeownership rate: 89.4%; Median home value: $137,500; Median year structure built: 1954; Homeowner vacancy rate: 3.5%; Median selected monthly owner costs: $1,281 with a mortgage, $525 without a mortgage; Median gross rent: $430 per month; Rental vacancy rate: 0.0%
Health Insurance: 92.6% have insurance; 60.3% have private insurance; 44.2% have public insurance; 7.4% do not have insurance; 0.0% of children under 18 do not have insurance
Transportation: Commute: 89.9% car, 0.0% public transportation, 5.0% walk, 5.0% work from home; Mean travel time to work: 33.9 minutes

EAST SPRINGFIELD (unincorporated postal area)
ZCTA: 13333
    Covers a land area of 1.701 square miles and a water area of 0.003 square miles. Located at 42.84° N. Lat; 74.82° W. Long. Elevation is 1,322 feet.
    Population: 61; Growth (since 2000): -57.0%; Density: 35.9 persons per square mile; Race: 100.0% White, 0.0% Black/African American, 0.0% Asian, 0.0% American Indian/Alaska Native, 0.0% Native Hawaiian/Other Pacific Islander, 0.0% Two or more races, 0.0% Hispanic of any race; Average household size: 2.26; Median age: 50.9;

Age under 18: 0.0%; Age 65 and over: 41.0%; Males per 100 females: 106.7; Marriage status: 19.7% never married, 80.3% now married, 0.0% separated, 0.0% widowed, 0.0% divorced; Foreign born: 0.0%; Speak English only: 100.0%; With disability: 6.6%; Veterans: 4.9%; Ancestry: 31.1% German, 19.7% Scottish, 16.4% American, 9.8% European, 6.6% Dutch

Employment: 0.0% management, business, and financial, 0.0% computer, engineering, and science, 39.3% education, legal, community service, arts, and media, 10.7% healthcare practitioners, 0.0% service, 14.3% sales and office, 0.0% natural resources, construction, and maintenance, 35.7% production, transportation, and material moving

Income: Per capita: $19,777; Median household: $60,125; Average household: $43,519; Households with income of $100,000 or more: n/a; Poverty rate: 27.9%

Educational Attainment: High school diploma or higher: 100.0%; Bachelor's degree or higher: 29.6%; Graduate/professional degree or higher: 22.2%

Housing: Homeownership rate: 100.0%; Median home value: $123,800; Median year structure built: Before 1940; Homeowner vacancy rate: 0.0%; Median selected monthly owner costs: $0 with a mortgage, $640 without a mortgage; Median gross rent: n/a per month; Rental vacancy rate: 0.0%

Health Insurance: 100.0% have insurance; 78.7% have private insurance; 49.2% have public insurance; 0.0% do not have insurance; 0.0% of children under 18 do not have insurance

Transportation: Commute: 100.0% car, 0.0% public transportation, 0.0% walk, 0.0% work from home; Mean travel time to work: 0.0 minutes

EAST WORCESTER (unincorporated postal area)
ZCTA: 12064

Covers a land area of 11.429 square miles and a water area of 0.014 square miles. Located at 42.61° N. Lat; 74.66° W. Long. Elevation is 1,463 feet.

Population: 339; Growth (since 2000): -29.4%; Density: 29.7 persons per square mile; Race: 95.0% White, 5.0% Black/African American, 0.0% Asian, 0.0% American Indian/Alaska Native, 0.0% Native Hawaiian/Other Pacific Islander, 0.0% Two or more races, 0.9% Hispanic of any race; Average household size: 1.75; Median age: 50.3; Age under 18: 17.7%; Age 65 and over: 21.8%; Males per 100 females: 121.7; Marriage status: 36.9% never married, 37.3% now married, 8.0% separated, 5.9% widowed, 19.9% divorced; Foreign born: 1.2%; Speak English only: 94.7%; With disability: 14.7%; Veterans: 18.3%; Ancestry: 38.6% German, 32.4% Irish, 12.4% Italian, 8.3% Dutch, 6.2% English

Employment: 6.5% management, business, and financial, 0.0% computer, engineering, and science, 12.9% education, legal, community service, arts, and media, 12.3% healthcare practitioners, 5.2% service, 23.9% sales and office, 3.2% natural resources, construction, and maintenance, 36.1% production, transportation, and material moving

Income: Per capita: $27,860; Median household: $60,119; Average household: $49,910; Households with income of $100,000 or more: 2.1%; Poverty rate: 24.8%

Educational Attainment: High school diploma or higher: 87.1%; Bachelor's degree or higher: 18.8%; Graduate/professional degree or higher: 9.4%

Housing: Homeownership rate: 64.4%; Median home value: $116,300; Median year structure built: 1950; Homeowner vacancy rate: 0.0%; Median selected monthly owner costs: $1,151 with a mortgage, $419 without a mortgage; Median gross rent: $680 per month; Rental vacancy rate: 16.9%

Health Insurance: 95.6% have insurance; 61.1% have private insurance; 52.5% have public insurance; 4.4% do not have insurance; 0.0% of children under 18 do not have insurance

Transportation: Commute: 94.8% car, 3.2% public transportation, 1.9% walk, 0.0% work from home; Mean travel time to work: 38.2 minutes

EDMESTON (CDP). Covers a land area of 4.345 square miles and a water area of 0 square miles. Located at 42.70° N. Lat; 75.25° W. Long. Elevation is 1,204 feet.

Population: 794; Growth (since 2000): n/a; Density: 182.7 persons per square mile; Race: 97.0% White, 0.0% Black/African American, 1.4% Asian, 0.0% American Indian/Alaska Native, 0.0% Native Hawaiian/Other Pacific Islander, 1.3% Two or more races, 0.9% Hispanic of any race; Average household size: 2.66; Median age: 35.8; Age under 18: 26.8%; Age 65 and over: 9.9%; Males per 100 females: 93.8; Marriage status: 30.1% never married, 59.9% now married, 3.0% separated, 3.0%

widowed, 6.9% divorced; Foreign born: 2.5%; Speak English only: 100.0%; With disability: 12.3%; Veterans: 7.9%; Ancestry: 24.2% English, 16.1% American, 13.6% Irish, 9.9% French, 7.9% German

Employment: 7.2% management, business, and financial, 2.3% computer, engineering, and science, 9.7% education, legal, community service, arts, and media, 10.4% healthcare practitioners, 27.5% service, 16.4% sales and office, 18.0% natural resources, construction, and maintenance, 8.5% production, transportation, and material moving

Income: Per capita: $24,997; Median household: $53,611; Average household: $65,251; Households with income of $100,000 or more: 14.4%; Poverty rate: 8.7%

Educational Attainment: High school diploma or higher: 89.9%; Bachelor's degree or higher: 15.4%; Graduate/professional degree or higher: 8.7%

School District(s)
Edmeston Central SD (PK-12)
    2014-15 Enrollment: 438 . . . . (607) 965-8931

Housing: Homeownership rate: 78.5%; Median home value: $105,800; Median year structure built: Before 1940; Homeowner vacancy rate: 0.0%; Median selected monthly owner costs: $1,098 with a mortgage, $446 without a mortgage; Median gross rent: $586 per month; Rental vacancy rate: 12.3%

Health Insurance: 95.2% have insurance; 76.3% have private insurance; 29.6% have public insurance; 4.8% do not have insurance; 0.0% of children under 18 do not have insurance

Transportation: Commute: 89.4% car, 3.4% public transportation, 3.1% walk, 1.4% work from home; Mean travel time to work: 16.9 minutes

EDMESTON (town). Covers a land area of 44.297 square miles and a water area of 0.084 square miles. Located at 42.72° N. Lat; 75.26° W. Long. Elevation is 1,204 feet.

Population: 1,897; Growth (since 2000): 4.0%; Density: 42.8 persons per square mile; Race: 95.2% White, 3.4% Black/African American, 0.6% Asian, 0.0% American Indian/Alaska Native, 0.0% Native Hawaiian/Other Pacific Islander, 0.6% Two or more races, 0.6% Hispanic of any race; Average household size: 2.59; Median age: 41.5; Age under 18: 24.0%; Age 65 and over: 15.3%; Males per 100 females: 97.2; Marriage status: 32.7% never married, 54.3% now married, 2.1% separated, 3.9% widowed, 9.2% divorced; Foreign born: 2.4%; Speak English only: 99.4%; With disability: 12.2%; Veterans: 7.6%; Ancestry: 22.9% English, 14.1% American, 14.1% Irish, 13.3% German, 6.2% French

Employment: 12.6% management, business, and financial, 4.4% computer, engineering, and science, 8.2% education, legal, community service, arts, and media, 7.1% healthcare practitioners, 20.9% service, 17.8% sales and office, 16.8% natural resources, construction, and maintenance, 12.4% production, transportation, and material moving

Income: Per capita: $23,715; Median household: $55,117; Average household: $63,069; Households with income of $100,000 or more: 14.2%; Poverty rate: 11.4%

Educational Attainment: High school diploma or higher: 93.9%; Bachelor's degree or higher: 15.5%; Graduate/professional degree or higher: 6.1%

School District(s)
Edmeston Central SD (PK-12)
    2014-15 Enrollment: 438 . . . . (607) 965-8931

Housing: Homeownership rate: 81.5%; Median home value: $108,500; Median year structure built: 1950; Homeowner vacancy rate: 0.0%; Median selected monthly owner costs: $1,106 with a mortgage, $451 without a mortgage; Median gross rent: $627 per month; Rental vacancy rate: 6.5%

Health Insurance: 93.3% have insurance; 69.6% have private insurance; 37.3% have public insurance; 6.7% do not have insurance; 2.5% of children under 18 do not have insurance

Transportation: Commute: 92.1% car, 1.9% public transportation, 2.4% walk, 2.3% work from home; Mean travel time to work: 21.7 minutes

EXETER (town). Covers a land area of 32.078 square miles and a water area of 0.615 square miles. Located at 42.80° N. Lat; 75.08° W. Long.

Population: 892; Growth (since 2000): -6.5%; Density: 27.8 persons per square mile; Race: 94.5% White, 0.3% Black/African American, 1.2% Asian, 0.9% American Indian/Alaska Native, 0.0% Native Hawaiian/Other Pacific Islander, 1.3% Two or more races, 0.8% Hispanic of any race; Average household size: 2.37; Median age: 47.7; Age under 18: 18.6%; Age 65 and over: 17.7%; Males per 100 females: 90.9; Marriage status: 19.8% never married, 60.1% now married, 2.2% separated, 8.9%

widowed, 11.3% divorced; Foreign born: 3.7%; Speak English only: 98.3%; With disability: 16.0%; Veterans: 9.8%; Ancestry: 16.3% Irish, 15.8% German, 12.2% American, 10.9% English, 5.2% Dutch
Employment: 9.9% management, business, and financial, 1.9% computer, engineering, and science, 6.1% education, legal, community service, arts, and media, 6.5% healthcare practitioners, 14.0% service, 28.6% sales and office, 17.4% natural resources, construction, and maintenance, 15.5% production, transportation, and material moving
Income: Per capita: $25,607; Median household: $50,938; Average household: $58,933; Households with income of $100,000 or more: 20.0%; Poverty rate: 15.6%
Educational Attainment: High school diploma or higher: 84.8%; Bachelor's degree or higher: 15.0%; Graduate/professional degree or higher: 5.1%
Housing: Homeownership rate: 89.4%; Median home value: $108,700; Median year structure built: 1961; Homeowner vacancy rate: 0.0%; Median selected monthly owner costs: $1,026 with a mortgage, $357 without a mortgage; Median gross rent: $1,077 per month; Rental vacancy rate: 18.4%
Health Insurance: 93.6% have insurance; 61.3% have private insurance; 48.2% have public insurance; 6.4% do not have insurance; 0.6% of children under 18 do not have insurance
Transportation: Commute: 93.2% car, 0.0% public transportation, 0.7% walk, 6.1% work from home; Mean travel time to work: 25.1 minutes

FLY CREEK (unincorporated postal area)
ZCTA: 13337
Covers a land area of 18.498 square miles and a water area of 0.116 square miles. Located at 42.76° N. Lat; 75.00° W. Long. Elevation is 1,302 feet.
Population: 602; Growth (since 2000): -30.6%; Density: 32.5 persons per square mile; Race: 93.4% White, 0.0% Black/African American, 3.7% Asian, 0.0% American Indian/Alaska Native, 0.0% Native Hawaiian/Other Pacific Islander, 3.0% Two or more races, 4.3% Hispanic of any race; Average household size: 2.27; Median age: 55.0; Age under 18: 14.8%; Age 65 and over: 30.7%; Males per 100 females: 101.5; Marriage status: 16.4% never married, 75.7% now married, 3.8% separated, 4.6% widowed, 3.3% divorced; Foreign born: 7.3%; Speak English only: 93.3%; With disability: 7.8%; Veterans: 11.9%; Ancestry: 27.9% English, 19.4% Irish, 13.8% Polish, 11.1% German, 7.1% Austrian
Employment: 21.1% management, business, and financial, 9.0% computer, engineering, and science, 13.5% education, legal, community service, arts, and media, 22.9% healthcare practitioners, 17.3% service, 7.9% sales and office, 1.5% natural resources, construction, and maintenance, 6.8% production, transportation, and material moving
Income: Per capita: $42,705; Median household: $51,932; Average household: $94,309; Households with income of $100,000 or more: 22.2%; Poverty rate: 6.6%
Educational Attainment: High school diploma or higher: 98.2%; Bachelor's degree or higher: 54.8%; Graduate/professional degree or higher: 42.1%
Housing: Homeownership rate: 82.3%; Median home value: $320,000; Median year structure built: 1970; Homeowner vacancy rate: 0.0%; Median selected monthly owner costs: $1,691 with a mortgage, $394 without a mortgage; Median gross rent: n/a per month; Rental vacancy rate: 0.0%
Health Insurance: 97.5% have insurance; 79.6% have private insurance; 40.7% have public insurance; 2.5% do not have insurance; 0.0% of children under 18 do not have insurance
Transportation: Commute: 83.1% car, 0.0% public transportation, 4.1% walk, 12.8% work from home; Mean travel time to work: 12.4 minutes

GARRATTSVILLE (unincorporated postal area)
ZCTA: 13342
Covers a land area of 7.941 square miles and a water area of 0.056 square miles. Located at 42.65° N. Lat; 75.20° W. Long. Elevation is 1,302 feet.
Population: 188; Growth (since 2000): -19.0%; Density: 23.7 persons per square mile; Race: 100.0% White, 0.0% Black/African American, 0.0% Asian, 0.0% American Indian/Alaska Native, 0.0% Native Hawaiian/Other Pacific Islander, 0.0% Two or more races, 0.0% Hispanic of any race; Average household size: 2.19; Median age: 53.6; Age under 18: 9.0%; Age 65 and over: 17.0%; Males per 100 females: 79.3; Marriage status: 25.3% never married, 63.8% now married, 2.3%

separated, 1.7% widowed, 9.2% divorced; Foreign born: 0.0%; Speak English only: 97.2%; With disability: 13.8%; Veterans: 8.2%; Ancestry: 31.9% Irish, 24.5% English, 22.9% German, 16.5% French, 10.6% Italian
Employment: 24.3% management, business, and financial, 3.7% computer, engineering, and science, 17.8% education, legal, community service, arts, and media, 0.0% healthcare practitioners, 4.7% service, 25.2% sales and office, 9.3% natural resources, construction, and maintenance, 15.0% production, transportation, and material moving
Income: Per capita: $33,555; Median household: $56,667; Average household: $72,737; Households with income of $100,000 or more: 19.7%; Poverty rate: 3.7%
Educational Attainment: High school diploma or higher: 95.7%; Bachelor's degree or higher: 14.9%; Graduate/professional degree or higher: 11.8%
Housing: Homeownership rate: 95.3%; Median home value: $121,400; Median year structure built: Before 1940; Homeowner vacancy rate: 9.9%; Median selected monthly owner costs: $863 with a mortgage, $425 without a mortgage; Median gross rent: n/a per month; Rental vacancy rate: 0.0%
Health Insurance: 93.6% have insurance; 72.3% have private insurance; 38.8% have public insurance; 6.4% do not have insurance; 17.6% of children under 18 do not have insurance
Transportation: Commute: 81.4% car, 0.0% public transportation, 8.2% walk, 10.3% work from home; Mean travel time to work: 20.5 minutes

GILBERTSVILLE (village).
Covers a land area of 1.003 square miles and a water area of 0 square miles. Located at 42.47° N. Lat; 75.32° W. Long. Elevation is 1,093 feet.
Population: 361; Growth (since 2000): -3.7%; Density: 360.0 persons per square mile; Race: 92.5% White, 0.0% Black/African American, 4.2% Asian, 0.0% American Indian/Alaska Native, 0.0% Native Hawaiian/Other Pacific Islander, 3.3% Two or more races, 0.8% Hispanic of any race; Average household size: 2.33; Median age: 52.4; Age under 18: 21.1%; Age 65 and over: 28.3%; Males per 100 females: 70.5; Marriage status: 25.2% never married, 47.1% now married, 3.2% separated, 13.9% widowed, 13.9% divorced; Foreign born: 10.5%; Speak English only: 93.9%; With disability: 17.5%; Veterans: 13.3%; Ancestry: 28.8% English, 22.4% German, 22.4% Irish, 11.6% Italian, 6.4% American
Employment: 16.9% management, business, and financial, 3.9% computer, engineering, and science, 21.4% education, legal, community service, arts, and media, 6.5% healthcare practitioners, 11.0% service, 24.7% sales and office, 3.2% natural resources, construction, and maintenance, 12.3% production, transportation, and material moving
Income: Per capita: $27,209; Median household: $43,281; Average household: $66,010; Households with income of $100,000 or more: 19.4%; Poverty rate: 17.5%
Educational Attainment: High school diploma or higher: 87.8%; Bachelor's degree or higher: 23.6%; Graduate/professional degree or higher: 10.3%
School District(s)
Gilbertsville-Mount Upton Central SD (PK-12)
    2014-15 Enrollment: 396. . . . . (607) 783-2207
Housing: Homeownership rate: 73.5%; Median home value: $129,700; Median year structure built: Before 1940; Homeowner vacancy rate: 5.6%; Median selected monthly owner costs: $1,131 with a mortgage, $506 without a mortgage; Median gross rent: $555 per month; Rental vacancy rate: 0.0%
Health Insurance: 94.7% have insurance; 67.0% have private insurance; 49.0% have public insurance; 5.3% do not have insurance; 5.3% of children under 18 do not have insurance
Transportation: Commute: 82.4% car, 1.4% public transportation, 2.0% walk, 12.8% work from home; Mean travel time to work: 25.9 minutes

HARTWICK (CDP).
Covers a land area of 3.457 square miles and a water area of 0 square miles. Located at 42.66° N. Lat; 75.06° W. Long. Elevation is 1,329 feet.
Population: 577; Growth (since 2000): n/a; Density: 166.9 persons per square mile; Race: 99.7% White, 0.0% Black/African American, 0.0% Asian, 0.0% American Indian/Alaska Native, 0.0% Native Hawaiian/Other Pacific Islander, 0.3% Two or more races, 0.0% Hispanic of any race; Average household size: 2.28; Median age: 36.7; Age under 18: 20.6%; Age 65 and over: 8.0%; Males per 100 females: 96.6; Marriage status: 31.0% never married, 49.0% now married, 0.8% separated, 8.9% widowed, 11.2% divorced; Foreign born: 0.9%; Speak English only: 99.1%;

With disability: 7.5%; Veterans: 7.2%; Ancestry: 35.9% German, 18.2% Irish, 12.7% Italian, 9.2% American, 7.5% English
Employment: 12.4% management, business, and financial, 0.0% computer, engineering, and science, 9.6% education, legal, community service, arts, and media, 14.0% healthcare practitioners, 16.5% service, 25.8% sales and office, 5.3% natural resources, construction, and maintenance, 16.5% production, transportation, and material moving
Income: Per capita: $24,402; Median household: $37,083; Average household: $56,613; Households with income of $100,000 or more: 16.6%; Poverty rate: 18.7%
Educational Attainment: High school diploma or higher: 90.1%; Bachelor's degree or higher: 31.3%; Graduate/professional degree or higher: 9.9%
Housing: Homeownership rate: 74.7%; Median home value: $131,300; Median year structure built: Before 1940; Homeowner vacancy rate: 0.0%; Median selected monthly owner costs: $1,130 with a mortgage, $459 without a mortgage; Median gross rent: $563 per month; Rental vacancy rate: 20.0%
Health Insurance: 91.7% have insurance; 75.7% have private insurance; 28.2% have public insurance; 8.3% do not have insurance; 0.0% of children under 18 do not have insurance
Transportation: Commute: 90.2% car, 3.2% public transportation, 1.9% walk, 4.7% work from home; Mean travel time to work: 22.3 minutes

HARTWICK (town). Covers a land area of 40.082 square miles and a water area of 0.342 square miles. Located at 42.64° N. Lat; 75.02° W. Long. Elevation is 1,329 feet.

Population: 1,915; Growth (since 2000): -13.1%; Density: 47.8 persons per square mile; Race: 96.6% White, 0.1% Black/African American, 1.8% Asian, 0.0% American Indian/Alaska Native, 0.0% Native Hawaiian/Other Pacific Islander, 0.6% Two or more races, 0.8% Hispanic of any race; Average household size: 2.40; Median age: 44.6; Age under 18: 21.5%; Age 65 and over: 16.2%; Males per 100 females: 100.4; Marriage status: 26.4% never married, 54.7% now married, 3.8% separated, 6.2% widowed, 12.6% divorced; Foreign born: 2.5%; Speak English only: 96.2%; With disability: 12.0%; Veterans: 11.2%; Ancestry: 31.4% German, 22.0% Irish, 18.4% English, 10.5% Italian, 6.3% American
Employment: 11.7% management, business, and financial, 2.5% computer, engineering, and science, 9.6% education, legal, community service, arts, and media, 15.1% healthcare practitioners, 21.4% service, 22.0% sales and office, 7.3% natural resources, construction, and maintenance, 10.2% production, transportation, and material moving
Income: Per capita: $25,952; Median household: $43,125; Average household: $62,361; Households with income of $100,000 or more: 20.2%; Poverty rate: 14.5%
Educational Attainment: High school diploma or higher: 93.2%; Bachelor's degree or higher: 28.8%; Graduate/professional degree or higher: 12.6%
Housing: Homeownership rate: 82.3%; Median home value: $172,100; Median year structure built: 1971; Homeowner vacancy rate: 2.2%; Median selected monthly owner costs: $1,244 with a mortgage, $463 without a mortgage; Median gross rent: $713 per month; Rental vacancy rate: 10.2%
Health Insurance: 91.8% have insurance; 69.9% have private insurance; 38.9% have public insurance; 8.2% do not have insurance; 7.8% of children under 18 do not have insurance
Transportation: Commute: 87.7% car, 2.9% public transportation, 2.6% walk, 5.9% work from home; Mean travel time to work: 20.2 minutes
Additional Information Contacts
Town of Hartwick . . . . (607) 293-8123
  http://townofhartwick.org

LAURENS (town). Covers a land area of 42.049 square miles and a water area of 0.119 square miles. Located at 42.54° N. Lat; 75.12° W. Long. Elevation is 1,112 feet.

Population: 2,740; Growth (since 2000): 14.1%; Density: 65.2 persons per square mile; Race: 99.0% White, 0.3% Black/African American, 0.5% Asian, 0.0% American Indian/Alaska Native, 0.0% Native Hawaiian/Other Pacific Islander, 0.2% Two or more races, 7.1% Hispanic of any race; Average household size: 2.44; Median age: 47.2; Age under 18: 20.9%; Age 65 and over: 21.5%; Males per 100 females: 91.2; Marriage status: 26.4% never married, 52.8% now married, 2.5% separated, 6.6% widowed, 14.2% divorced; Foreign born: 6.5%; Speak English only: 91.4%; With disability: 14.9%; Veterans: 9.8%; Ancestry: 25.8% German, 19.2% Irish, 18.1% English, 11.0% American, 7.4% Italian

Employment: 11.9% management, business, and financial, 4.2% computer, engineering, and science, 13.1% education, legal, community service, arts, and media, 5.5% healthcare practitioners, 26.1% service, 21.9% sales and office, 9.7% natural resources, construction, and maintenance, 7.6% production, transportation, and material moving
Income: Per capita: $21,385; Median household: $41,322; Average household: $51,073; Households with income of $100,000 or more: 11.0%; Poverty rate: 25.8%
Educational Attainment: High school diploma or higher: 91.3%; Bachelor's degree or higher: 23.2%; Graduate/professional degree or higher: 10.9%
School District(s)
Laurens Central SD (KG-12)
  2014-15 Enrollment: 344 . . . . (607) 432-2050
Housing: Homeownership rate: 80.3%; Median home value: $146,400; Median year structure built: 1971; Homeowner vacancy rate: 0.0%; Median selected monthly owner costs: $1,339 with a mortgage, $487 without a mortgage; Median gross rent: $773 per month; Rental vacancy rate: 1.8%
Health Insurance: 90.3% have insurance; 58.6% have private insurance; 50.4% have public insurance; 9.7% do not have insurance; 0.7% of children under 18 do not have insurance
Transportation: Commute: 93.5% car, 0.2% public transportation, 1.6% walk, 4.8% work from home; Mean travel time to work: 21.9 minutes

LAURENS (village). Covers a land area of 0.128 square miles and a water area of 0 square miles. Located at 42.53° N. Lat; 75.09° W. Long. Elevation is 1,112 feet.

Population: 233; Growth (since 2000): -15.9%; Density: 1,814.5 persons per square mile; Race: 98.7% White, 0.9% Black/African American, 0.0% Asian, 0.0% American Indian/Alaska Native, 0.0% Native Hawaiian/Other Pacific Islander, 0.4% Two or more races, 9.0% Hispanic of any race; Average household size: 2.24; Median age: 44.4; Age under 18: 15.0%; Age 65 and over: 11.6%; Males per 100 females: 67.5; Marriage status: 39.6% never married, 38.1% now married, 4.0% separated, 6.4% widowed, 15.8% divorced; Foreign born: 3.4%; Speak English only: 89.0%; With disability: 21.5%; Veterans: 11.1%; Ancestry: 31.3% Irish, 24.0% German, 20.6% Italian, 15.0% English, 10.3% French
Employment: 13.6% management, business, and financial, 0.0% computer, engineering, and science, 7.6% education, legal, community service, arts, and media, 4.2% healthcare practitioners, 17.8% service, 33.1% sales and office, 7.6% natural resources, construction, and maintenance, 16.1% production, transportation, and material moving
Income: Per capita: $21,585; Median household: $42,500; Average household: $49,065; Households with income of $100,000 or more: 7.7%; Poverty rate: 15.5%
Educational Attainment: High school diploma or higher: 92.4%; Bachelor's degree or higher: 19.6%; Graduate/professional degree or higher: 4.4%
School District(s)
Laurens Central SD (KG-12)
  2014-15 Enrollment: 344 . . . . (607) 432-2050
Housing: Homeownership rate: 66.3%; Median home value: $108,900; Median year structure built: Before 1940; Homeowner vacancy rate: 0.0%; Median selected monthly owner costs: $1,264 with a mortgage, $400 without a mortgage; Median gross rent: $675 per month; Rental vacancy rate: 0.0%
Health Insurance: 84.1% have insurance; 57.9% have private insurance; 42.5% have public insurance; 15.9% do not have insurance; 0.0% of children under 18 do not have insurance
Transportation: Commute: 89.0% car, 1.7% public transportation, 5.1% walk, 4.2% work from home; Mean travel time to work: 23.9 minutes

MARYLAND (town). Covers a land area of 52.406 square miles and a water area of 0.135 square miles. Located at 42.55° N. Lat; 74.87° W. Long. Elevation is 1,230 feet.

Population: 1,934; Growth (since 2000): 0.7%; Density: 36.9 persons per square mile; Race: 98.3% White, 0.4% Black/African American, 0.0% Asian, 0.0% American Indian/Alaska Native, 0.0% Native Hawaiian/Other Pacific Islander, 1.3% Two or more races, 0.5% Hispanic of any race; Average household size: 2.51; Median age: 46.4; Age under 18: 17.3%; Age 65 and over: 16.2%; Males per 100 females: 97.6; Marriage status: 27.5% never married, 53.2% now married, 1.1% separated, 8.5% widowed, 10.7% divorced; Foreign born: 2.4%; Speak English only: 98.7%; With disability: 14.2%; Veterans: 7.4%; Ancestry: 27.2% German, 22.6% Irish, 19.2% English, 9.6% Italian, 5.2% Polish

Employment: 8.2% management, business, and financial, 0.5% computer, engineering, and science, 8.2% education, legal, community service, arts, and media, 3.0% healthcare practitioners, 31.4% service, 24.1% sales and office, 8.0% natural resources, construction, and maintenance, 16.7% production, transportation, and material moving
Income: Per capita: $20,865; Median household: $49,911; Average household: $52,050; Households with income of $100,000 or more: 7.8%; Poverty rate: 16.6%
Educational Attainment: High school diploma or higher: 88.9%; Bachelor's degree or higher: 15.5%; Graduate/professional degree or higher: 4.2%
Housing: Homeownership rate: 74.6%; Median home value: $122,400; Median year structure built: 1954; Homeowner vacancy rate: 4.8%; Median selected monthly owner costs: $1,221 with a mortgage, $556 without a mortgage; Median gross rent: $751 per month; Rental vacancy rate: 0.0%
Health Insurance: 93.3% have insurance; 69.4% have private insurance; 40.3% have public insurance; 6.7% do not have insurance; 0.9% of children under 18 do not have insurance
Transportation: Commute: 92.2% car, 0.0% public transportation, 4.8% walk, 2.1% work from home; Mean travel time to work: 25.1 minutes

MIDDLEFIELD (town). Covers a land area of 63.334 square miles and a water area of 0.371 square miles. Located at 42.70° N. Lat; 74.86° W. Long. Elevation is 1,250 feet.
Population: 1,993; Growth (since 2000): -11.4%; Density: 31.5 persons per square mile; Race: 93.9% White, 1.6% Black/African American, 3.4% Asian, 0.3% American Indian/Alaska Native, 0.0% Native Hawaiian/Other Pacific Islander, 0.5% Two or more races, 2.7% Hispanic of any race; Average household size: 2.22; Median age: 52.6; Age under 18: 15.4%; Age 65 and over: 23.4%; Males per 100 females: 100.4; Marriage status: 26.1% never married, 56.5% now married, 1.9% separated, 7.0% widowed, 10.4% divorced; Foreign born: 3.8%; Speak English only: 92.9%; With disability: 8.8%; Veterans: 13.0%; Ancestry: 27.5% German, 13.8% English, 13.5% Irish, 10.5% Italian, 4.9% Polish
Employment: 15.3% management, business, and financial, 2.8% computer, engineering, and science, 10.8% education, legal, community service, arts, and media, 12.0% healthcare practitioners, 19.8% service, 18.9% sales and office, 13.7% natural resources, construction, and maintenance, 6.8% production, transportation, and material moving
Income: Per capita: $35,309; Median household: $63,500; Average household: $81,216; Households with income of $100,000 or more: 26.0%; Poverty rate: 8.2%
Educational Attainment: High school diploma or higher: 93.6%; Bachelor's degree or higher: 39.1%; Graduate/professional degree or higher: 28.4%
Housing: Homeownership rate: 79.8%; Median home value: $253,800; Median year structure built: 1970; Homeowner vacancy rate: 0.0%; Median selected monthly owner costs: $1,590 with a mortgage, $543 without a mortgage; Median gross rent: $824 per month; Rental vacancy rate: 0.0%
Health Insurance: 91.3% have insurance; 73.5% have private insurance; 40.0% have public insurance; 8.7% do not have insurance; 6.8% of children under 18 do not have insurance
Transportation: Commute: 81.1% car, 0.6% public transportation, 9.5% walk, 7.5% work from home; Mean travel time to work: 19.7 minutes

MILFORD (town). Covers a land area of 46.117 square miles and a water area of 1.030 square miles. Located at 42.55° N. Lat; 74.98° W. Long. Elevation is 1,207 feet.
Population: 2,982; Growth (since 2000): 1.5%; Density: 64.7 persons per square mile; Race: 98.0% White, 0.5% Black/African American, 0.7% Asian, 0.0% American Indian/Alaska Native, 0.0% Native Hawaiian/Other Pacific Islander, 0.5% Two or more races, 0.5% Hispanic of any race; Average household size: 2.22; Median age: 46.2; Age under 18: 18.2%; Age 65 and over: 21.9%; Males per 100 females: 99.9; Marriage status: 22.8% never married, 56.2% now married, 3.5% separated, 6.0% widowed, 14.9% divorced; Foreign born: 2.5%; Speak English only: 94.9%; With disability: 16.8%; Veterans: 15.9%; Ancestry: 22.6% German, 20.9% English, 16.6% Italian, 15.4% Irish, 12.9% American
Employment: 12.7% management, business, and financial, 3.1% computer, engineering, and science, 5.4% education, legal, community service, arts, and media, 6.7% healthcare practitioners, 26.5% service, 31.2% sales and office, 3.6% natural resources, construction, and maintenance, 10.8% production, transportation, and material moving

Income: Per capita: $27,930; Median household: $46,027; Average household: $62,570; Households with income of $100,000 or more: 15.0%; Poverty rate: 13.1%
Educational Attainment: High school diploma or higher: 87.7%; Bachelor's degree or higher: 24.2%; Graduate/professional degree or higher: 10.9%

School District(s)
Milford Central SD (PK-12)
   2014-15 Enrollment: 422 . . . . (607) 286-3341
Housing: Homeownership rate: 76.5%; Median home value: $121,600; Median year structure built: 1960; Homeowner vacancy rate: 0.5%; Median selected monthly owner costs: $1,328 with a mortgage, $466 without a mortgage; Median gross rent: $913 per month; Rental vacancy rate: 8.8%
Health Insurance: 96.0% have insurance; 73.6% have private insurance; 41.3% have public insurance; 4.0% do not have insurance; 0.6% of children under 18 do not have insurance
Transportation: Commute: 86.9% car, 1.0% public transportation, 2.5% walk, 8.5% work from home; Mean travel time to work: 25.5 minutes

MILFORD (village). Covers a land area of 0.424 square miles and a water area of 0 square miles. Located at 42.59° N. Lat; 74.95° W. Long. Elevation is 1,207 feet.
Population: 396; Growth (since 2000): -22.5%; Density: 933.4 persons per square mile; Race: 92.7% White, 0.5% Black/African American, 4.8% Asian, 0.0% American Indian/Alaska Native, 0.0% Native Hawaiian/Other Pacific Islander, 1.5% Two or more races, 2.3% Hispanic of any race; Average household size: 2.10; Median age: 48.8; Age under 18: 14.9%; Age 65 and over: 19.4%; Males per 100 females: 91.2; Marriage status: 24.3% never married, 52.5% now married, 1.4% separated, 5.5% widowed, 17.7% divorced; Foreign born: 4.5%; Speak English only: 92.7%; With disability: 17.2%; Veterans: 11.9%; Ancestry: 21.2% German, 14.6% Irish, 12.6% Italian, 11.1% English, 5.1% American
Employment: 9.7% management, business, and financial, 3.6% computer, engineering, and science, 11.3% education, legal, community service, arts, and media, 11.8% healthcare practitioners, 19.5% service, 26.7% sales and office, 5.1% natural resources, construction, and maintenance, 12.3% production, transportation, and material moving
Income: Per capita: $31,714; Median household: $37,917; Average household: $66,286; Households with income of $100,000 or more: 17.5%; Poverty rate: 11.4%
Educational Attainment: High school diploma or higher: 89.1%; Bachelor's degree or higher: 26.5%; Graduate/professional degree or higher: 14.3%

School District(s)
Milford Central SD (PK-12)
   2014-15 Enrollment: 422 . . . . (607) 286-3341
Housing: Homeownership rate: 67.2%; Median home value: $118,400; Median year structure built: Before 1940; Homeowner vacancy rate: 3.8%; Median selected monthly owner costs: $1,383 with a mortgage, $536 without a mortgage; Median gross rent: $540 per month; Rental vacancy rate: 0.0%
Health Insurance: 95.7% have insurance; 74.2% have private insurance; 38.6% have public insurance; 4.3% do not have insurance; 5.1% of children under 18 do not have insurance
Transportation: Commute: 87.4% car, 2.1% public transportation, 3.7% walk, 5.8% work from home; Mean travel time to work: 28.4 minutes

MORRIS (town). Covers a land area of 39.067 square miles and a water area of 0.126 square miles. Located at 42.54° N. Lat; 75.26° W. Long. Elevation is 1,145 feet.
Population: 1,616; Growth (since 2000): -13.4%; Density: 41.4 persons per square mile; Race: 97.0% White, 0.0% Black/African American, 1.2% Asian, 0.0% American Indian/Alaska Native, 0.0% Native Hawaiian/Other Pacific Islander, 1.8% Two or more races, 0.7% Hispanic of any race; Average household size: 2.43; Median age: 44.8; Age under 18: 18.5%; Age 65 and over: 20.9%; Males per 100 females: 97.9; Marriage status: 25.7% never married, 55.7% now married, 2.0% separated, 6.9% widowed, 11.7% divorced; Foreign born: 3.3%; Speak English only: 97.7%; With disability: 12.6%; Veterans: 13.0%; Ancestry: 22.1% German, 20.9% Irish, 20.4% English, 12.6% Italian, 10.1% American
Employment: 17.5% management, business, and financial, 6.7% computer, engineering, and science, 7.4% education, legal, community service, arts, and media, 7.1% healthcare practitioners, 17.8% service, 19.1% sales and office, 10.9% natural resources, construction, and maintenance, 13.5% production, transportation, and material moving

Income: Per capita: $24,149; Median household: $46,076; Average household: $57,507; Households with income of $100,000 or more: 13.1%; Poverty rate: 13.8%

Educational Attainment: High school diploma or higher: 91.6%; Bachelor's degree or higher: 24.6%; Graduate/professional degree or higher: 7.5%

School District(s)

Morris Central SD (PK-12)

    2014-15 Enrollment: 400 . . . . (607) 263-6102

Housing: Homeownership rate: 76.5%; Median home value: $129,100; Median year structure built: Before 1940; Homeowner vacancy rate: 2.7%; Median selected monthly owner costs: $1,182 with a mortgage, $445 without a mortgage; Median gross rent: $649 per month; Rental vacancy rate: 8.8%

Health Insurance: 97.0% have insurance; 68.7% have private insurance; 47.6% have public insurance; 3.0% do not have insurance; 0.0% of children under 18 do not have insurance

Transportation: Commute: 81.0% car, 1.7% public transportation, 3.8% walk, 12.2% work from home; Mean travel time to work: 25.0 minutes

MORRIS (village).

Covers a land area of 0.746 square miles and a water area of 0.008 square miles. Located at 42.55° N. Lat; 75.25° W. Long. Elevation is 1,145 feet.

Population: 396; Growth (since 2000): -33.0%; Density: 531.1 persons per square mile; Race: 96.5% White, 0.0% Black/African American, 0.0% Asian, 0.0% American Indian/Alaska Native, 0.0% Native Hawaiian/Other Pacific Islander, 3.5% Two or more races, 2.5% Hispanic of any race; Average household size: 2.01; Median age: 45.7; Age under 18: 13.4%; Age 65 and over: 24.5%; Males per 100 females: 95.6; Marriage status: 27.0% never married, 47.7% now married, 3.3% separated, 9.6% widowed, 15.7% divorced; Foreign born: 3.3%; Speak English only: 98.5%; With disability: 13.1%; Veterans: 13.7%; Ancestry: 27.5% English, 22.0% Irish, 17.4% German, 15.4% Italian, 13.9% American

Employment: 29.1% management, business, and financial, 1.0% computer, engineering, and science, 8.2% education, legal, community service, arts, and media, 12.8% healthcare practitioners, 17.9% service, 18.9% sales and office, 4.1% natural resources, construction, and maintenance, 8.2% production, transportation, and material moving

Income: Per capita: $26,291; Median household: $40,000; Average household: $52,512; Households with income of $100,000 or more: 15.4%; Poverty rate: 10.1%

Educational Attainment: High school diploma or higher: 95.3%; Bachelor's degree or higher: 28.7%; Graduate/professional degree or higher: 7.7%

School District(s)

Morris Central SD (PK-12)

    2014-15 Enrollment: 400 . . . . (607) 263-6102

Housing: Homeownership rate: 66.5%; Median home value: $124,300; Median year structure built: Before 1940; Homeowner vacancy rate: 0.0%; Median selected monthly owner costs: $1,125 with a mortgage, $429 without a mortgage; Median gross rent: $623 per month; Rental vacancy rate: 8.5%

Health Insurance: 94.7% have insurance; 74.5% have private insurance; 43.9% have public insurance; 5.3% do not have insurance; 0.0% of children under 18 do not have insurance

Transportation: Commute: 84.7% car, 0.0% public transportation, 11.2% walk, 3.1% work from home; Mean travel time to work: 23.6 minutes

MOUNT VISION (unincorporated postal area)

ZCTA: 13810

Covers a land area of 40.028 square miles and a water area of 0.183 square miles. Located at 42.61° N. Lat; 75.11° W. Long. Elevation is 1,171 feet.

Population: 1,105; Growth (since 2000): -14.7%; Density: 27.6 persons per square mile; Race: 97.5% White, 0.5% Black/African American, 1.6% Asian, 0.0% American Indian/Alaska Native, 0.0% Native Hawaiian/Other Pacific Islander, 0.5% Two or more races, 0.0% Hispanic of any race; Average household size: 2.13; Median age: 49.8; Age under 18: 18.1%; Age 65 and over: 23.2%; Males per 100 females: 93.4; Marriage status: 24.7% never married, 51.1% now married, 0.6% separated, 6.6% widowed, 17.6% divorced; Foreign born: 3.8%; Speak English only: 98.7%; With disability: 11.0%; Veterans: 12.3%; Ancestry: 23.3% German, 20.3% Irish, 13.9% English, 11.2% American, 10.0% Italian

Employment: 10.2% management, business, and financial, 4.5% computer, engineering, and science, 5.8% education, legal, community service, arts, and media, 5.1% healthcare practitioners, 16.0% service, 33.6% sales and office, 15.4% natural resources, construction, and maintenance, 9.4% production, transportation, and material moving

Income: Per capita: $22,395; Median household: $34,688; Average household: $47,557; Households with income of $100,000 or more: 8.3%; Poverty rate: 17.5%

Educational Attainment: High school diploma or higher: 91.8%; Bachelor's degree or higher: 17.1%; Graduate/professional degree or higher: 7.1%

Housing: Homeownership rate: 81.7%; Median home value: $129,500; Median year structure built: 1974; Homeowner vacancy rate: 2.3%; Median selected monthly owner costs: $1,163 with a mortgage, $501 without a mortgage; Median gross rent: $647 per month; Rental vacancy rate: 4.0%

Health Insurance: 94.7% have insurance; 73.6% have private insurance; 43.1% have public insurance; 5.3% do not have insurance; 0.0% of children under 18 do not have insurance

Transportation: Commute: 93.7% car, 0.0% public transportation, 3.3% walk, 2.3% work from home; Mean travel time to work: 21.2 minutes

NEW LISBON (town).

Covers a land area of 44.355 square miles and a water area of 0.301 square miles. Located at 42.62° N. Lat; 75.13° W. Long. Elevation is 1,247 feet.

Population: 1,013; Growth (since 2000): -9.2%; Density: 22.8 persons per square mile; Race: 99.1% White, 0.0% Black/African American, 0.4% Asian, 0.0% American Indian/Alaska Native, 0.0% Native Hawaiian/Other Pacific Islander, 0.5% Two or more races, 0.5% Hispanic of any race; Average household size: 2.24; Median age: 48.9; Age under 18: 17.2%; Age 65 and over: 18.5%; Males per 100 females: 90.8; Marriage status: 22.1% never married, 59.0% now married, 1.5% separated, 6.6% widowed, 12.4% divorced; Foreign born: 2.3%; Speak English only: 97.2%; With disability: 12.5%; Veterans: 13.6%; Ancestry: 18.6% Irish, 18.2% English, 17.2% German, 14.9% American, 12.0% Italian

Employment: 12.6% management, business, and financial, 4.4% computer, engineering, and science, 11.2% education, legal, community service, arts, and media, 6.4% healthcare practitioners, 10.6% service, 23.6% sales and office, 14.8% natural resources, construction, and maintenance, 16.6% production, transportation, and material moving

Income: Per capita: $26,794; Median household: $50,000; Average household: $59,678; Households with income of $100,000 or more: 13.7%; Poverty rate: 9.4%

Educational Attainment: High school diploma or higher: 92.8%; Bachelor's degree or higher: 17.0%; Graduate/professional degree or higher: 7.8%

Housing: Homeownership rate: 86.7%; Median home value: $116,100; Median year structure built: 1976; Homeowner vacancy rate: 4.5%; Median selected monthly owner costs: $1,117 with a mortgage, $454 without a mortgage; Median gross rent: $821 per month; Rental vacancy rate: 0.0%

Health Insurance: 95.0% have insurance; 75.5% have private insurance; 35.1% have public insurance; 5.0% do not have insurance; 0.0% of children under 18 do not have insurance

Transportation: Commute: 84.8% car, 0.0% public transportation, 6.0% walk, 8.6% work from home; Mean travel time to work: 22.0 minutes

ONEONTA (city).

Covers a land area of 4.361 square miles and a water area of 0.004 square miles. Located at 42.45° N. Lat; 75.07° W. Long. Elevation is 1,112 feet.

History: Oneonta grew after the coming of the railroad in 1865; however, no vestiges of importance as a railroad center exist today. Brotherhood of Railroad Brakemen founded here in 1883), which was renamed Brotherhood of Railroad Trainmen in 1889. Seat of the State University of N.Y. College at Oneonta and Hartwick College. National Soccer Hall of Fame. Settled c.1780, Incorporated as a city 1909.

Population: 13,862; Growth (since 2000): 4.3%; Density: 3,178.4 persons per square mile; Race: 89.1% White, 3.6% Black/African American, 2.2% Asian, 0.4% American Indian/Alaska Native, 0.0% Native Hawaiian/Other Pacific Islander, 3.0% Two or more races, 6.9% Hispanic of any race; Average household size: 2.26; Median age: 21.8; Age under 18: 10.8%; Age 65 and over: 10.6%; Males per 100 females: 83.9; Marriage status: 66.2% never married, 23.9% now married, 1.3% separated, 4.3% widowed, 5.6% divorced; Foreign born: 3.9%; Speak English only: 90.9%; With disability: 9.9%; Veterans: 5.9%; Ancestry: 22.8% Irish, 21.3% Italian, 19.6% German, 8.5% English, 6.5% Polish

Employment: 13.7% management, business, and financial, 4.3% computer, engineering, and science, 21.2% education, legal, community service, arts, and media, 5.0% healthcare practitioners, 24.2% service, 22.5% sales and office, 4.6% natural resources, construction, and maintenance, 4.5% production, transportation, and material moving
Income: Per capita: $18,435; Median household: $40,186; Average household: $56,185; Households with income of $100,000 or more: 15.0%; Poverty rate: 29.5%
Educational Attainment: High school diploma or higher: 93.3%; Bachelor's degree or higher: 45.1%; Graduate/professional degree or higher: 21.9%

School District(s)
Oneonta City SD (PK-12)
    2014-15 Enrollment: 1,756 . . . . (607) 433-8232
Four-year College(s)
Hartwick College (Private, Not-for-profit)
    Fall 2014 Enrollment: 1,540 . . . . (607) 431-4000
    2015-16 Tuition: In-state $41,440; Out-of-state $41,440
SUNY Oneonta (Public)
    Fall 2014 Enrollment: 6,101 . . . . (607) 436-3500
    2015-16 Tuition: In-state $7,870; Out-of-state $17,720
Vocational/Technical School(s)
Otsego Area BOCES-Practical Nursing Program (Public)
    Fall 2014 Enrollment: 39 . . . . (607) 431-2562
    2015-16 Tuition: $9,840
Housing: Homeownership rate: 46.4%; Median home value: $147,000; Median year structure built: Before 1940; Homeowner vacancy rate: 1.2%; Median selected monthly owner costs: $1,248 with a mortgage, $480 without a mortgage; Median gross rent: $802 per month; Rental vacancy rate: 9.1%
Health Insurance: 93.5% have insurance; 78.7% have private insurance; 23.6% have public insurance; 6.5% do not have insurance; 2.9% of children under 18 do not have insurance
Hospitals: Aurelia Osborn Fox Memorial Hospital (128 beds)
Safety: Violent crime rate: 17.4 per 10,000 population; Property crime rate: 190.2 per 10,000 population
Newspapers: Daily Star (daily circulation 15,900)
Transportation: Commute: 62.3% car, 5.8% public transportation, 26.1% walk, 3.0% work from home; Mean travel time to work: 15.4 minutes
Airports: Oneonta Municipal (general aviation)
Additional Information Contacts
City of Oneonta . . . . (607) 432-6450
    http://www.oneonta.ny.us

ONEONTA (town). Covers a land area of 32.911 square miles and a water area of 0.252 square miles. Located at 42.43° N. Lat; 75.10° W. Long. Elevation is 1,112 feet.
Population: 5,147; Growth (since 2000): 3.1%; Density: 156.4 persons per square mile; Race: 86.3% White, 7.8% Black/African American, 0.0% Asian, 0.1% American Indian/Alaska Native, 0.0% Native Hawaiian/Other Pacific Islander, 3.0% Two or more races, 6.7% Hispanic of any race; Average household size: 2.45; Median age: 42.2; Age under 18: 18.4%; Age 65 and over: 18.7%; Males per 100 females: 97.1; Marriage status: 34.4% never married, 48.4% now married, 2.7% separated, 5.9% widowed, 11.4% divorced; Foreign born: 6.0%; Speak English only: 87.8%; With disability: 13.2%; Veterans: 12.4%; Ancestry: 23.6% German, 14.0% Italian, 13.5% English, 9.3% Irish, 6.6% American
Employment: 13.7% management, business, and financial, 0.8% computer, engineering, and science, 17.9% education, legal, community service, arts, and media, 10.3% healthcare practitioners, 20.0% service, 21.0% sales and office, 8.4% natural resources, construction, and maintenance, 8.0% production, transportation, and material moving
Income: Per capita: $26,701; Median household: $57,925; Average household: $70,425; Households with income of $100,000 or more: 22.4%; Poverty rate: 21.0%
Educational Attainment: High school diploma or higher: 91.0%; Bachelor's degree or higher: 33.7%; Graduate/professional degree or higher: 18.7%

School District(s)
Oneonta City SD (PK-12)
    2014-15 Enrollment: 1,756 . . . . (607) 433-8232
Four-year College(s)
Hartwick College (Private, Not-for-profit)
    Fall 2014 Enrollment: 1,540 . . . . (607) 431-4000
    2015-16 Tuition: In-state $41,440; Out-of-state $41,440

SUNY Oneonta (Public)
    Fall 2014 Enrollment: 6,101 . . . . (607) 436-3500
    2015-16 Tuition: In-state $7,870; Out-of-state $17,720
Vocational/Technical School(s)
Otsego Area BOCES-Practical Nursing Program (Public)
    Fall 2014 Enrollment: 39 . . . . (607) 431-2562
    2015-16 Tuition: $9,840
Housing: Homeownership rate: 83.5%; Median home value: $157,900; Median year structure built: 1971; Homeowner vacancy rate: 0.0%; Median selected monthly owner costs: $1,243 with a mortgage, $511 without a mortgage; Median gross rent: $867 per month; Rental vacancy rate: 24.6%
Health Insurance: 89.8% have insurance; 68.6% have private insurance; 35.1% have public insurance; 10.2% do not have insurance; 0.9% of children under 18 do not have insurance
Hospitals: Aurelia Osborn Fox Memorial Hospital (128 beds)
Newspapers: Daily Star (daily circulation 15,900)
Transportation: Commute: 87.1% car, 1.0% public transportation, 2.5% walk, 9.2% work from home; Mean travel time to work: 20.2 minutes
Airports: Oneonta Municipal (general aviation)
Additional Information Contacts
Town of Oneonta . . . . (607) 432-2900
    http://www.townofoneonta.org

OTEGO (town). Covers a land area of 45.633 square miles and a water area of 0.076 square miles. Located at 42.46° N. Lat; 75.19° W. Long. Elevation is 1,070 feet.
Population: 3,049; Growth (since 2000): -4.2%; Density: 66.8 persons per square mile; Race: 95.0% White, 0.5% Black/African American, 0.4% Asian, 0.2% American Indian/Alaska Native, 0.0% Native Hawaiian/Other Pacific Islander, 3.9% Two or more races, 0.2% Hispanic of any race; Average household size: 2.46; Median age: 48.2; Age under 18: 16.3%; Age 65 and over: 23.2%; Males per 100 females: 94.1; Marriage status: 24.5% never married, 56.5% now married, 1.1% separated, 7.0% widowed, 12.0% divorced; Foreign born: 3.3%; Speak English only: 98.0%; With disability: 14.4%; Veterans: 8.0%; Ancestry: 20.9% German, 15.4% Irish, 14.5% English, 14.0% Italian, 9.7% American
Employment: 6.6% management, business, and financial, 2.5% computer, engineering, and science, 17.2% education, legal, community service, arts, and media, 2.7% healthcare practitioners, 17.6% service, 27.1% sales and office, 10.5% natural resources, construction, and maintenance, 15.7% production, transportation, and material moving
Income: Per capita: $24,565; Median household: $47,900; Average household: $59,644; Households with income of $100,000 or more: 18.1%; Poverty rate: 13.0%
Educational Attainment: High school diploma or higher: 85.2%; Bachelor's degree or higher: 23.8%; Graduate/professional degree or higher: 10.2%

School District(s)
Otego-Unadilla Central SD (KG-12)
    2014-15 Enrollment: 942 . . . . (607) 988-5038
Housing: Homeownership rate: 77.1%; Median home value: $134,400; Median year structure built: 1973; Homeowner vacancy rate: 1.1%; Median selected monthly owner costs: $1,250 with a mortgage, $507 without a mortgage; Median gross rent: $717 per month; Rental vacancy rate: 9.9%
Health Insurance: 92.8% have insurance; 66.6% have private insurance; 39.0% have public insurance; 7.2% do not have insurance; 0.0% of children under 18 do not have insurance
Transportation: Commute: 92.4% car, 0.0% public transportation, 1.9% walk, 3.8% work from home; Mean travel time to work: 20.8 minutes

---

OTEGO (village). Covers a land area of 1.159 square miles and a water area of 0 square miles. Located at 42.39° N. Lat; 75.18° W. Long. Elevation is 1,070 feet.
Population: 1,152; Growth (since 2000): 9.5%; Density: 993.6 persons per square mile; Race: 89.1% White, 0.3% Black/African American, 1.1% Asian, 0.0% American Indian/Alaska Native, 0.0% Native Hawaiian/Other Pacific Islander, 9.4% Two or more races, 0.5% Hispanic of any race; Average household size: 2.46; Median age: 41.8; Age under 18: 21.3%; Age 65 and over: 17.4%; Males per 100 females: 90.2; Marriage status: 27.0% never married, 60.4% now married, 1.2% separated, 2.2% widowed, 10.4% divorced; Foreign born: 5.0%; Speak English only: 97.4%; With disability: 15.5%; Veterans: 8.5%; Ancestry: 18.7% Irish, 18.1% German, 14.7% English, 11.0% French, 10.3% Italian
Employment: 11.8% management, business, and financial, 2.2% computer, engineering, and science, 15.7% education, legal, community

service, arts, and media, 7.3% healthcare practitioners, 22.2% service, 23.7% sales and office, 5.0% natural resources, construction, and maintenance, 12.1% production, transportation, and material moving
Income: Per capita: $26,975; Median household: $55,202; Average household: $65,282; Households with income of $100,000 or more: 16.2%; Poverty rate: 9.8%
Educational Attainment: High school diploma or higher: 92.9%; Bachelor's degree or higher: 29.4%; Graduate/professional degree or higher: 15.3%

School District(s)
Otego-Unadilla Central SD (KG-12)
   2014-15 Enrollment: 942 . . . . (607) 988-5038
Housing: Homeownership rate: 69.3%; Median home value: $133,800; Median year structure built: 1953; Homeowner vacancy rate: 3.3%; Median selected monthly owner costs: $1,293 with a mortgage, $495 without a mortgage; Median gross rent: $729 per month; Rental vacancy rate: 17.9%
Health Insurance: 89.3% have insurance; 65.5% have private insurance; 36.1% have public insurance; 10.7% do not have insurance; 0.0% of children under 18 do not have insurance
Transportation: Commute: 87.8% car, 0.0% public transportation, 5.1% walk, 1.8% work from home; Mean travel time to work: 20.6 minutes

OTSEGO (town).
Covers a land area of 53.890 square miles and a water area of 5.162 square miles. Located at 42.76° N. Lat; 74.96° W. Long.
Population: 3,832; Growth (since 2000): -1.8%; Density: 71.1 persons per square mile; Race: 94.2% White, 0.9% Black/African American, 3.5% Asian, 0.5% American Indian/Alaska Native, 0.0% Native Hawaiian/Other Pacific Islander, 0.7% Two or more races, 1.7% Hispanic of any race; Average household size: 2.20; Median age: 51.9; Age under 18: 15.0%; Age 65 and over: 24.5%; Males per 100 females: 85.6; Marriage status: 20.7% never married, 58.7% now married, 1.8% separated, 12.4% widowed, 8.3% divorced; Foreign born: 5.5%; Speak English only: 93.2%; With disability: 8.3%; Veterans: 10.7%; Ancestry: 25.2% English, 19.8% Irish, 15.1% German, 9.1% Italian, 7.0% American
Employment: 14.1% management, business, and financial, 5.2% computer, engineering, and science, 19.7% education, legal, community service, arts, and media, 17.8% healthcare practitioners, 16.3% service, 17.3% sales and office, 3.6% natural resources, construction, and maintenance, 6.1% production, transportation, and material moving
Income: Per capita: $40,711; Median household: $63,900; Average household: $93,892; Households with income of $100,000 or more: 27.4%; Poverty rate: 8.8%
Educational Attainment: High school diploma or higher: 92.8%; Bachelor's degree or higher: 48.3%; Graduate/professional degree or higher: 28.1%
Housing: Homeownership rate: 70.5%; Median home value: $283,400; Median year structure built: Before 1940; Homeowner vacancy rate: 1.9%; Median selected monthly owner costs: $1,844 with a mortgage, $626 without a mortgage; Median gross rent: $810 per month; Rental vacancy rate: 9.9%
Health Insurance: 96.0% have insurance; 83.0% have private insurance; 31.6% have public insurance; 4.0% do not have insurance; 0.5% of children under 18 do not have insurance
Transportation: Commute: 71.0% car, 0.6% public transportation, 19.0% walk, 7.4% work from home; Mean travel time to work: 15.8 minutes

PITTSFIELD (town).
Covers a land area of 37.986 square miles and a water area of 0.116 square miles. Located at 42.61° N. Lat; 75.27° W. Long. Elevation is 1,155 feet.
Population: 1,267; Growth (since 2000): -2.2%; Density: 33.4 persons per square mile; Race: 98.5% White, 0.2% Black/African American, 0.2% Asian, 0.0% American Indian/Alaska Native, 0.0% Native Hawaiian/Other Pacific Islander, 1.0% Two or more races, 2.7% Hispanic of any race; Average household size: 2.58; Median age: 47.4; Age under 18: 19.9%; Age 65 and over: 19.1%; Males per 100 females: 103.0; Marriage status: 28.2% never married, 58.7% now married, 3.7% separated, 6.4% widowed, 6.7% divorced; Foreign born: 2.3%; Speak English only: 96.4%; With disability: 20.3%; Veterans: 5.9%; Ancestry: 17.5% German, 17.2% Irish, 13.1% English, 9.6% Italian, 9.6% American
Employment: 11.2% management, business, and financial, 2.5% computer, engineering, and science, 4.8% education, legal, community service, arts, and media, 7.9% healthcare practitioners, 16.8% service, 21.6% sales and office, 11.6% natural resources, construction, and maintenance, 23.6% production, transportation, and material moving

Income: Per capita: $22,819; Median household: $44,767; Average household: $58,958; Households with income of $100,000 or more: 19.1%; Poverty rate: 10.4%
Educational Attainment: High school diploma or higher: 79.5%; Bachelor's degree or higher: 10.6%; Graduate/professional degree or higher: 3.1%
Housing: Homeownership rate: 86.2%; Median home value: $97,000; Median year structure built: 1977; Homeowner vacancy rate: 0.0%; Median selected monthly owner costs: $1,160 with a mortgage, $409 without a mortgage; Median gross rent: $700 per month; Rental vacancy rate: 5.6%
Health Insurance: 92.8% have insurance; 68.0% have private insurance; 34.8% have public insurance; 7.2% do not have insurance; 2.0% of children under 18 do not have insurance
Transportation: Commute: 89.5% car, 3.0% public transportation, 3.8% walk, 3.0% work from home; Mean travel time to work: 29.5 minutes

PLAINFIELD (town).
Covers a land area of 29.500 square miles and a water area of 0 square miles. Located at 42.83° N. Lat; 75.19° W. Long.
Population: 893; Growth (since 2000): -9.4%; Density: 30.3 persons per square mile; Race: 96.3% White, 0.1% Black/African American, 0.6% Asian, 0.6% American Indian/Alaska Native, 0.0% Native Hawaiian/Other Pacific Islander, 2.5% Two or more races, 0.8% Hispanic of any race; Average household size: 2.45; Median age: 45.0; Age under 18: 22.3%; Age 65 and over: 21.2%; Males per 100 females: 102.4; Marriage status: 22.8% never married, 61.1% now married, 1.9% separated, 6.6% widowed, 9.5% divorced; Foreign born: 2.9%; Speak English only: 94.1%; With disability: 17.7%; Veterans: 9.8%; Ancestry: 19.5% German, 16.6% English, 14.8% Irish, 12.4% American, 8.6% Welsh
Employment: 14.3% management, business, and financial, 5.4% computer, engineering, and science, 9.2% education, legal, community service, arts, and media, 3.2% healthcare practitioners, 5.9% service, 21.3% sales and office, 22.1% natural resources, construction, and maintenance, 18.6% production, transportation, and material moving
Income: Per capita: $24,130; Median household: $46,979; Average household: $58,738; Households with income of $100,000 or more: 15.4%; Poverty rate: 9.8%
Educational Attainment: High school diploma or higher: 84.9%; Bachelor's degree or higher: 19.4%; Graduate/professional degree or higher: 7.7%
Housing: Homeownership rate: 83.6%; Median home value: $96,100; Median year structure built: 1975; Homeowner vacancy rate: 0.0%; Median selected monthly owner costs: $1,163 with a mortgage, $406 without a mortgage; Median gross rent: $648 per month; Rental vacancy rate: 0.0%
Health Insurance: 92.4% have insurance; 64.4% have private insurance; 44.7% have public insurance; 7.6% do not have insurance; 9.0% of children under 18 do not have insurance
Transportation: Commute: 93.7% car, 0.5% public transportation, 1.1% walk, 4.7% work from home; Mean travel time to work: 28.9 minutes

PORTLANDVILLE (unincorporated postal area)
ZCTA: 13834
   Covers a land area of 0.348 square miles and a water area of 0.041 square miles. Located at 42.53° N. Lat; 74.97° W. Long. Elevation is 1,152 feet.
Population: 44; Growth (since 2000): -74.1%; Density: 126.5 persons per square mile; Race: 100.0% White, 0.0% Black/African American, 0.0% Asian, 0.0% American Indian/Alaska Native, 0.0% Native Hawaiian/Other Pacific Islander, 0.0% Two or more races, 0.0% Hispanic of any race; Average household size: 0.00; Median age: n/a; Age under 18: 0.0%; Age 65 and over: 22.7%; Males per 100 females: 114.5; Marriage status: 22.7% never married, 0.0% now married, 0.0% separated, 0.0% widowed, 77.3% divorced; Foreign born: 0.0%; Speak English only: 100.0%; With disability: 22.7%; Veterans: 100.0%; Ancestry: 77.3% American, 22.7% German
Employment: 22.7% management, business, and financial, 0.0% computer, engineering, and science, 0.0% education, legal, community service, arts, and media, 0.0% healthcare practitioners, 0.0% service, 77.3% sales and office, 0.0% natural resources, construction, and maintenance, 0.0% production, transportation, and material moving
Income: Per capita: n/a; Median household: n/a; Average household: n/a; Households with income of $100,000 or more: n/a; Poverty rate: 77.3%
Educational Attainment: High school diploma or higher: 100.0%; Bachelor's degree or higher: 22.7%; Graduate/professional degree or higher: 22.7%

Housing: Homeownership rate: 100.0%; Median home value: n/a; Median year structure built: Before 1940; Homeowner vacancy rate: 0.0%; Median selected monthly owner costs: $0 with a mortgage, $0 without a mortgage; Median gross rent: n/a per month; Rental vacancy rate: 0.0%

Health Insurance: 22.7% have insurance; 22.7% have private insurance; 22.7% have public insurance; 77.3% do not have insurance; 0.0% of children under 18 do not have insurance

Transportation: Commute: 77.3% car, 0.0% public transportation, 22.7% walk, 0.0% work from home; Mean travel time to work: 0.0 minutes

RICHFIELD (town).
Covers a land area of 30.858 square miles and a water area of 1.598 square miles. Located at 42.85° N. Lat; 75.05° W. Long. Elevation is 1,476 feet.

History: Health resort until mid-20th century; sulphur springs. Incorporated 1934.

Population: 2,368; Growth (since 2000): -2.3%; Density: 76.7 persons per square mile; Race: 95.5% White, 0.8% Black/African American, 1.9% Asian, 0.9% American Indian/Alaska Native, 0.0% Native Hawaiian/Other Pacific Islander, 0.7% Two or more races, 0.6% Hispanic of any race; Average household size: 2.30; Median age: 47.6; Age under 18: 16.4%; Age 65 and over: 20.7%; Males per 100 females: 95.6; Marriage status: 27.6% never married, 51.9% now married, 2.7% separated, 6.4% widowed, 14.1% divorced; Foreign born: 2.6%; Speak English only: 96.3%; With disability: 17.2%; Veterans: 14.8%; Ancestry: 22.5% Irish, 18.8% German, 10.1% English, 8.5% American, 7.3% Dutch

Employment: 10.3% management, business, and financial, 1.6% computer, engineering, and science, 9.6% education, legal, community service, arts, and media, 9.1% healthcare practitioners, 18.8% service, 24.1% sales and office, 14.0% natural resources, construction, and maintenance, 12.5% production, transportation, and material moving

Income: Per capita: $24,141; Median household: $45,960; Average household: $54,262; Households with income of $100,000 or more: 7.9%; Poverty rate: 11.6%

Educational Attainment: High school diploma or higher: 85.9%; Bachelor's degree or higher: 15.4%; Graduate/professional degree or higher: 6.8%

Housing: Homeownership rate: 70.1%; Median home value: $115,100; Median year structure built: Before 1940; Homeowner vacancy rate: 4.5%; Median selected monthly owner costs: $1,104 with a mortgage, $435 without a mortgage; Median gross rent: $624 per month; Rental vacancy rate: 5.3%

Health Insurance: 88.5% have insurance; 62.5% have private insurance; 45.0% have public insurance; 11.5% do not have insurance; 4.4% of children under 18 do not have insurance

Transportation: Commute: 81.1% car, 1.1% public transportation, 7.4% walk, 8.8% work from home; Mean travel time to work: 24.2 minutes

RICHFIELD SPRINGS (village).
Covers a land area of 1.007 square miles and a water area of 0 square miles. Located at 42.85° N. Lat; 74.99° W. Long. Elevation is 1,312 feet.

Population: 1,229; Growth (since 2000): -2.1%; Density: 1,221.0 persons per square mile; Race: 93.5% White, 1.3% Black/African American, 2.8% Asian, 1.5% American Indian/Alaska Native, 0.0% Native Hawaiian/Other Pacific Islander, 0.7% Two or more races, 1.2% Hispanic of any race; Average household size: 2.11; Median age: 46.2; Age under 18: 16.7%; Age 65 and over: 16.9%; Males per 100 females: 89.5; Marriage status: 28.8% never married, 50.1% now married, 3.6% separated, 5.7% widowed, 15.4% divorced; Foreign born: 3.6%; Speak English only: 95.5%; With disability: 19.7%; Veterans: 11.4%; Ancestry: 26.2% Irish, 17.2% German, 9.8% English, 9.4% American, 5.0% Polish

Employment: 7.2% management, business, and financial, 2.8% computer, engineering, and science, 15.0% education, legal, community service, arts, and media, 4.4% healthcare practitioners, 18.7% service, 26.9% sales and office, 11.9% natural resources, construction, and maintenance, 13.1% production, transportation, and material moving

Income: Per capita: $20,852; Median household: $34,393; Average household: $43,992; Households with income of $100,000 or more: 6.7%; Poverty rate: 16.4%

Educational Attainment: High school diploma or higher: 82.6%; Bachelor's degree or higher: 19.2%; Graduate/professional degree or higher: 8.0%

Richfield Springs Central SD (PK-12)
    2014-15 Enrollment: 506. . . . . (315) 858-0610

Housing: Homeownership rate: 55.7%; Median home value: $97,900; Median year structure built: Before 1940; Homeowner vacancy rate: 5.0%; Median selected monthly owner costs: $1,173 with a mortgage, $446 without a mortgage; Median gross rent: $592 per month; Rental vacancy rate: 6.3%

Health Insurance: 86.6% have insurance; 54.5% have private insurance; 48.4% have public insurance; 13.4% do not have insurance; 2.4% of children under 18 do not have insurance

Transportation: Commute: 75.1% car, 2.3% public transportation, 15.2% walk, 5.9% work from home; Mean travel time to work: 23.6 minutes

ROSEBOOM (town).
Covers a land area of 33.407 square miles and a water area of 0.104 square miles. Located at 42.73° N. Lat; 74.71° W. Long. Elevation is 1,289 feet.

Population: 669; Growth (since 2000): -2.2%; Density: 20.0 persons per square mile; Race: 98.4% White, 0.3% Black/African American, 0.3% Asian, 0.0% American Indian/Alaska Native, 0.0% Native Hawaiian/Other Pacific Islander, 1.0% Two or more races, 0.3% Hispanic of any race; Average household size: 2.21; Median age: 46.1; Age under 18: 21.1%; Age 65 and over: 18.4%; Males per 100 females: 102.6; Marriage status: 27.5% never married, 52.9% now married, 1.1% separated, 8.2% widowed, 11.4% divorced; Foreign born: 1.3%; Speak English only: 97.2%; With disability: 14.2%; Veterans: 11.2%; Ancestry: 22.3% German, 19.6% Irish, 12.6% English, 8.1% Dutch, 7.6% Italian

Employment: 7.0% management, business, and financial, 2.3% computer, engineering, and science, 16.9% education, legal, community service, arts, and media, 4.1% healthcare practitioners, 11.6% service, 31.4% sales and office, 13.1% natural resources, construction, and maintenance, 13.7% production, transportation, and material moving

Income: Per capita: $24,594; Median household: $50,673; Average household: $54,060; Households with income of $100,000 or more: 10.9%; Poverty rate: 8.8%

Educational Attainment: High school diploma or higher: 90.1%; Bachelor's degree or higher: 25.9%; Graduate/professional degree or higher: 13.9%

Housing: Homeownership rate: 81.5%; Median home value: $119,300; Median year structure built: 1966; Homeowner vacancy rate: 0.0%; Median selected monthly owner costs: $1,045 with a mortgage, $436 without a mortgage; Median gross rent: $921 per month; Rental vacancy rate: 0.0%

Health Insurance: 96.7% have insurance; 77.0% have private insurance; 34.5% have public insurance; 3.3% do not have insurance; 0.7% of children under 18 do not have insurance

Transportation: Commute: 92.6% car, 0.9% public transportation, 0.6% walk, 5.3% work from home; Mean travel time to work: 27.4 minutes

SCHENEVUS (CDP).
Covers a land area of 1.029 square miles and a water area of 0 square miles. Located at 42.55° N. Lat; 74.83° W. Long. Elevation is 1,302 feet.

Population: 537; Growth (since 2000): n/a; Density: 522.1 persons per square mile; Race: 100.0% White, 0.0% Black/African American, 0.0% Asian, 0.0% American Indian/Alaska Native, 0.0% Native Hawaiian/Other Pacific Islander, 0.0% Two or more races, 0.0% Hispanic of any race; Average household size: 2.81; Median age: 45.1; Age under 18: 12.7%; Age 65 and over: 8.4%; Males per 100 females: 88.7; Marriage status: 30.0% never married, 50.7% now married, 0.0% separated, 7.1% widowed, 12.2% divorced; Foreign born: 0.0%; Speak English only: 98.6%; With disability: 13.0%; Veterans: 4.3%; Ancestry: 28.5% English, 16.4% German, 11.4% Irish, 8.6% French, 7.6% Italian

Employment: 2.5% management, business, and financial, 1.6% computer, engineering, and science, 9.4% education, legal, community service, arts, and media, 0.0% healthcare practitioners, 40.9% service, 18.8% sales and office, 9.1% natural resources, construction, and maintenance, 17.8% production, transportation, and material moving

Income: Per capita: $17,901; Median household: n/a; Average household: $48,820; Households with income of $100,000 or more: 7.3%; Poverty rate: 15.1%

Educational Attainment: High school diploma or higher: 88.9%; Bachelor's degree or higher: 10.8%; Graduate/professional degree or higher: 0.9%

Schenevus Central SD (PK-12)
    2014-15 Enrollment: 373. . . . . (607) 638-5530

Housing: Homeownership rate: 55.0%; Median home value: $110,700; Median year structure built: Before 1940; Homeowner vacancy rate: 12.5%; Median selected monthly owner costs: $1,266 with a mortgage, $575 without a mortgage; Median gross rent: $618 per month; Rental vacancy rate: 0.0%
Health Insurance: 97.4% have insurance; 74.9% have private insurance; 33.3% have public insurance; 2.6% do not have insurance; 0.0% of children under 18 do not have insurance
Transportation: Commute: 95.6% car, 0.0% public transportation, 1.0% walk, 0.6% work from home; Mean travel time to work: 25.9 minutes

SPRINGFIELD (town). Covers a land area of 42.894 square miles and a water area of 2.614 square miles. Located at 42.83° N. Lat; 74.87° W. Long. Elevation is 1,355 feet.
Population: 1,342; Growth (since 2000): -0.6%; Density: 31.3 persons per square mile; Race: 98.8% White, 0.0% Black/African American, 0.0% Asian, 0.0% American Indian/Alaska Native, 0.0% Native Hawaiian/Other Pacific Islander, 1.2% Two or more races, 0.4% Hispanic of any race; Average household size: 2.46; Median age: 47.4; Age under 18: 22.7%; Age 65 and over: 21.2%; Males per 100 females: 105.8; Marriage status: 18.8% never married, 65.3% now married, 1.9% separated, 6.5% widowed, 9.4% divorced; Foreign born: 0.7%; Speak English only: 91.5%; With disability: 14.7%; Veterans: 8.8%; Ancestry: 22.7% German, 16.3% English, 15.3% Irish, 13.2% American, 7.4% Dutch
Employment: 20.9% management, business, and financial, 3.5% computer, engineering, and science, 8.2% education, legal, community service, arts, and media, 4.4% healthcare practitioners, 16.4% service, 17.4% sales and office, 19.4% natural resources, construction, and maintenance, 9.8% production, transportation, and material moving
Income: Per capita: $24,972; Median household: $49,875; Average household: $61,556; Households with income of $100,000 or more: 18.2%; Poverty rate: 11.8%
Educational Attainment: High school diploma or higher: 87.6%; Bachelor's degree or higher: 22.0%; Graduate/professional degree or higher: 10.7%
Housing: Homeownership rate: 73.0%; Median home value: $156,800; Median year structure built: 1959; Homeowner vacancy rate: 2.9%; Median selected monthly owner costs: $1,161 with a mortgage, $373 without a mortgage; Median gross rent: $679 per month; Rental vacancy rate: 0.0%
Health Insurance: 81.1% have insurance; 52.5% have private insurance; 43.0% have public insurance; 18.9% do not have insurance; 26.6% of children under 18 do not have insurance
Transportation: Commute: 72.8% car, 0.5% public transportation, 3.5% walk, 22.1% work from home; Mean travel time to work: 24.1 minutes

SPRINGFIELD CENTER (unincorporated postal area)
ZCTA: 13468
Covers a land area of 9.726 square miles and a water area of 0.108 square miles. Located at 42.85° N. Lat; 74.85° W. Long. Elevation is 1,260 feet.
Population: 416; Growth (since 2000): -9.4%; Density: 42.8 persons per square mile; Race: 100.0% White, 0.0% Black/African American, 0.0% Asian, 0.0% American Indian/Alaska Native, 0.0% Native Hawaiian/Other Pacific Islander, 0.0% Two or more races, 1.2% Hispanic of any race; Average household size: 2.81; Median age: 38.5; Age under 18: 31.5%; Age 65 and over: 11.8%; Males per 100 females: 93.6; Marriage status: 23.0% never married, 63.5% now married, 3.0% separated, 3.6% widowed, 9.9% divorced; Foreign born: 0.0%; Speak English only: 94.3%; With disability: 12.7%; Veterans: 9.1%; Ancestry: 24.5% Irish, 17.8% English, 16.1% American, 15.1% German, 11.8% Welsh
Employment: 19.8% management, business, and financial, 1.6% computer, engineering, and science, 3.1% education, legal, community service, arts, and media, 7.8% healthcare practitioners, 28.1% service, 16.1% sales and office, 16.1% natural resources, construction, and maintenance, 7.3% production, transportation, and material moving
Income: Per capita: $23,831; Median household: $46,000; Average household: $66,780; Households with income of $100,000 or more: 19.6%; Poverty rate: 16.5%
Educational Attainment: High school diploma or higher: 84.8%; Bachelor's degree or higher: 18.7%; Graduate/professional degree or higher: 10.1%
Housing: Homeownership rate: 72.3%; Median home value: $168,800; Median year structure built: 1973; Homeowner vacancy rate: 0.0%; Median selected monthly owner costs: $1,250 with a mortgage, $310

without a mortgage; Median gross rent: $767 per month; Rental vacancy rate: 0.0%
Health Insurance: 76.0% have insurance; 47.4% have private insurance; 41.3% have public insurance; 24.0% do not have insurance; 36.6% of children under 18 do not have insurance
Transportation: Commute: 75.1% car, 1.7% public transportation, 0.0% walk, 23.2% work from home; Mean travel time to work: 26.7 minutes

UNADILLA (town). Covers a land area of 46.254 square miles and a water area of 0.419 square miles. Located at 42.37° N. Lat; 75.33° W. Long. Elevation is 1,010 feet.
History: During the early years of the Revolution, Native American villages in the vicinity of Unadilla were gathering places for Tories bent on destruction of frontier patriot settlements. In 1778, an American force destroyed the villages. The place began to grow with construction of the Catskill Turnpike soon after 1800. Settled in 1790, incorporated in 1827.
Population: 4,312; Growth (since 2000): -5.2%; Density: 93.2 persons per square mile; Race: 97.6% White, 0.4% Black/African American, 0.0% Asian, 0.1% American Indian/Alaska Native, 0.0% Native Hawaiian/Other Pacific Islander, 1.3% Two or more races, 1.3% Hispanic of any race; Average household size: 2.51; Median age: 43.3; Age under 18: 23.2%; Age 65 and over: 19.3%; Males per 100 females: 98.0; Marriage status: 24.6% never married, 58.2% now married, 2.7% separated, 8.1% widowed, 9.1% divorced; Foreign born: 2.0%; Speak English only: 97.7%; With disability: 13.1%; Veterans: 8.2%; Ancestry: 25.4% German, 18.7% Irish, 17.9% English, 9.0% Dutch, 8.2% Italian
Employment: 9.8% management, business, and financial, 3.2% computer, engineering, and science, 8.3% education, legal, community service, arts, and media, 6.3% healthcare practitioners, 17.8% service, 19.2% sales and office, 11.9% natural resources, construction, and maintenance, 23.5% production, transportation, and material moving
Income: Per capita: $23,199; Median household: $50,938; Average household: $57,013; Households with income of $100,000 or more: 15.9%; Poverty rate: 9.0%
Educational Attainment: High school diploma or higher: 88.2%; Bachelor's degree or higher: 15.1%; Graduate/professional degree or higher: 5.8%
School District(s)
Otego-Unadilla Central SD (KG-12)
    2014-15 Enrollment: 942 . . . . (607) 988-5038
Housing: Homeownership rate: 79.2%; Median home value: $103,600; Median year structure built: 1967; Homeowner vacancy rate: 3.1%; Median selected monthly owner costs: $1,147 with a mortgage, $417 without a mortgage; Median gross rent: $619 per month; Rental vacancy rate: 4.5%
Health Insurance: 93.9% have insurance; 73.6% have private insurance; 40.6% have public insurance; 6.1% do not have insurance; 1.4% of children under 18 do not have insurance
Transportation: Commute: 91.0% car, 0.3% public transportation, 0.9% walk, 7.1% work from home; Mean travel time to work: 25.0 minutes

UNADILLA (village). Covers a land area of 1.037 square miles and a water area of 0.049 square miles. Located at 42.33° N. Lat; 75.31° W. Long. Elevation is 1,010 feet.
Population: 831; Growth (since 2000): -26.3%; Density: 801.7 persons per square mile; Race: 96.4% White, 0.0% Black/African American, 0.0% Asian, 0.6% American Indian/Alaska Native, 0.0% Native Hawaiian/Other Pacific Islander, 3.0% Two or more races, 3.0% Hispanic of any race; Average household size: 2.22; Median age: 42.7; Age under 18: 23.5%; Age 65 and over: 19.4%; Males per 100 females: 90.9; Marriage status: 27.0% never married, 56.0% now married, 1.7% separated, 9.6% widowed, 7.4% divorced; Foreign born: 1.0%; Speak English only: 96.3%; With disability: 18.1%; Veterans: 10.1%; Ancestry: 36.1% Irish, 27.4% German, 17.1% English, 12.8% Italian, 8.9% Dutch
Employment: 5.8% management, business, and financial, 5.0% computer, engineering, and science, 9.7% education, legal, community service, arts, and media, 10.3% healthcare practitioners, 10.6% service, 29.5% sales and office, 12.0% natural resources, construction, and maintenance, 17.0% production, transportation, and material moving
Income: Per capita: $22,773; Median household: $39,375; Average household: $50,025; Households with income of $100,000 or more: 14.7%; Poverty rate: 9.9%
Educational Attainment: High school diploma or higher: 82.2%; Bachelor's degree or higher: 19.6%; Graduate/professional degree or higher: 5.7%

Otego-Unadilla Central SD (KG-12)

2014-15 Enrollment: 942 . . . . (607) 988-5038

Housing: Homeownership rate: 68.8%; Median home value: $107,700; Median year structure built: Before 1940; Homeowner vacancy rate: 3.4%; Median selected monthly owner costs: $1,118 with a mortgage, $552 without a mortgage; Median gross rent: $584 per month; Rental vacancy rate: 7.1%

Health Insurance: 91.9% have insurance; 61.9% have private insurance; 46.7% have public insurance; 8.1% do not have insurance; 7.2% of children under 18 do not have insurance

Transportation: Commute: 95.2% car, 1.4% public transportation, 0.6% walk, 2.5% work from home; Mean travel time to work: 28.0 minutes

WELLS BRIDGE (unincorporated postal area)

ZCTA: 13859

Covers a land area of 0.480 square miles and a water area of 0.030 square miles. Located at 42.37° N. Lat; 75.25° W. Long. Elevation is 1,043 feet.

Population: 277; Growth (since 2000): 30.0%; Density: 577.3 persons per square mile; Race: 93.5% White, 2.9% Black/African American, 0.0% Asian, 0.0% American Indian/Alaska Native, 0.0% Native Hawaiian/Other Pacific Islander, 3.6% Two or more races, 0.0% Hispanic of any race; Average household size: 2.61; Median age: 34.1; Age under 18: 31.8%; Age 65 and over: 17.0%; Males per 100 females: 104.5; Marriage status: 29.9% never married, 59.2% now married, 4.0% separated, 7.0% widowed, 4.0% divorced; Foreign born: 2.2%; Speak English only: 100.0%; With disability: 22.0%; Veterans: 0.0%; Ancestry: 32.1% Norwegian, 29.6% German, 27.1% English, 23.8% Australian, 12.3% Irish

Employment: 0.0% management, business, and financial, 5.0% computer, engineering, and science, 0.0% education, legal, community service, arts, and media, 4.2% healthcare practitioners, 25.0% service, 25.8% sales and office, 0.0% natural resources, construction, and maintenance, 40.0% production, transportation, and material moving

Income: Per capita: $21,227; Median household: $63,021; Average household: $50,718; Households with income of $100,000 or more: n/a; Poverty rate: 6.5%

Educational Attainment: High school diploma or higher: 77.9%; Bachelor's degree or higher: 4.0%; Graduate/professional degree or higher: n/a

Housing: Homeownership rate: 75.5%; Median home value: $96,500; Median year structure built: 1962; Homeowner vacancy rate: 0.0%; Median selected monthly owner costs: n/a with a mortgage, n/a without a mortgage; Median gross rent: $1,047 per month; Rental vacancy rate: 0.0%

Health Insurance: 97.1% have insurance; 88.1% have private insurance; 17.0% have public insurance; 2.9% do not have insurance; 0.0% of children under 18 do not have insurance

Transportation: Commute: 100.0% car, 0.0% public transportation, 0.0% walk, 0.0% work from home; Mean travel time to work: 0.0 minutes

WEST END (CDP). Covers a land area of 3.652 square miles and a water area of 0.075 square miles. Located at 42.48° N. Lat; 75.09° W. Long. Elevation is 1,280 feet.

Population: 1,482; Growth (since 2000): -18.3%; Density: 405.8 persons per square mile; Race: 95.5% White, 1.6% Black/African American, 0.0% Asian, 0.0% American Indian/Alaska Native, 0.0% Native Hawaiian/Other Pacific Islander, 0.3% Two or more races, 5.1% Hispanic of any race; Average household size: 2.02; Median age: 55.4; Age under 18: 11.2%; Age 65 and over: 31.0%; Males per 100 females: 92.8; Marriage status: 24.3% never married, 58.7% now married, 2.8% separated, 10.7% widowed, 6.4% divorced; Foreign born: 10.5%; Speak English only: 86.4%; With disability: 19.0%; Veterans: 14.1%; Ancestry: 21.1% English, 18.2% German, 13.0% Irish, 9.4% Italian, 7.3% American

Employment: 10.7% management, business, and financial, 0.0% computer, engineering, and science, 20.4% education, legal, community service, arts, and media, 15.3% healthcare practitioners, 18.0% service, 28.9% sales and office, 6.4% natural resources, construction, and maintenance, 0.3% production, transportation, and material moving

Income: Per capita: $28,990; Median household: $50,030; Average household: $58,955; Households with income of $100,000 or more: 16.1%; Poverty rate: 16.9%

Educational Attainment: High school diploma or higher: 89.1%; Bachelor's degree or higher: 36.1%; Graduate/professional degree or higher: 24.3%

Housing: Homeownership rate: 83.5%; Median home value: $133,800; Median year structure built: 1957; Homeowner vacancy rate: 0.0%; Median selected monthly owner costs: $1,016 with a mortgage, $490 without a mortgage; Median gross rent: $918 per month; Rental vacancy rate: 15.0%

Health Insurance: 93.0% have insurance; 73.0% have private insurance; 39.5% have public insurance; 7.0% do not have insurance; 0.0% of children under 18 do not have insurance

Transportation: Commute: 94.4% car, 0.0% public transportation, 2.7% walk, 2.7% work from home; Mean travel time to work: 17.9 minutes

WEST ONEONTA (unincorporated postal area)

ZCTA: 13861

Covers a land area of 4.410 square miles and a water area of 0.017 square miles. Located at 42.51° N. Lat; 75.15° W. Long. Elevation is 1,138 feet.

Population: 429; Growth (since 2000): -34.2%; Density: 97.3 persons per square mile; Race: 85.8% White, 3.5% Black/African American, 0.0% Asian, 0.0% American Indian/Alaska Native, 0.0% Native Hawaiian/Other Pacific Islander, 10.7% Two or more races, 6.5% Hispanic of any race; Average household size: 3.23; Median age: 37.1; Age under 18: 33.8%; Age 65 and over: 10.0%; Males per 100 females: 100.0; Marriage status: 32.4% never married, 43.2% now married, 0.0% separated, 1.2% widowed, 23.1% divorced; Foreign born: 4.4%; Speak English only: 95.7%; With disability: 24.0%; Veterans: 12.0%; Ancestry: 29.4% German, 19.6% American, 16.1% Irish, 15.6% English, 7.9% French

Employment: 5.1% management, business, and financial, 0.0% computer, engineering, and science, 29.4% education, legal, community service, arts, and media, 0.0% healthcare practitioners, 42.9% service, 9.6% sales and office, 11.3% natural resources, construction, and maintenance, 1.7% production, transportation, and material moving

Income: Per capita: $26,472; Median household: n/a; Average household: $92,300; Households with income of $100,000 or more: 51.9%; Poverty rate: 10.5%

Educational Attainment: High school diploma or higher: 91.6%; Bachelor's degree or higher: 22.1%; Graduate/professional degree or higher: n/a

Housing: Homeownership rate: 86.5%; Median home value: $153,100; Median year structure built: 1965; Homeowner vacancy rate: 0.0%; Median selected monthly owner costs: $1,656 with a mortgage, $0 without a mortgage; Median gross rent: n/a per month; Rental vacancy rate: 0.0%

Health Insurance: 93.7% have insurance; 66.4% have private insurance; 37.8% have public insurance; 6.3% do not have insurance; 0.0% of children under 18 do not have insurance

Transportation: Commute: 100.0% car, 0.0% public transportation, 0.0% walk, 0.0% work from home; Mean travel time to work: 31.4 minutes

WESTFORD (town). Covers a land area of 33.853 square miles and a water area of 0.056 square miles. Located at 42.64° N. Lat; 74.82° W. Long. Elevation is 1,562 feet.

Population: 906; Growth (since 2000): 15.6%; Density: 26.8 persons per square mile; Race: 96.8% White, 1.0% Black/African American, 0.4% Asian, 0.0% American Indian/Alaska Native, 0.0% Native Hawaiian/Other Pacific Islander, 1.7% Two or more races, 1.1% Hispanic of any race; Average household size: 2.57; Median age: 41.6; Age under 18: 25.5%; Age 65 and over: 13.6%; Males per 100 females: 99.5; Marriage status: 22.3% never married, 57.6% now married, 0.4% separated, 2.8% widowed, 17.4% divorced; Foreign born: 2.2%; Speak English only: 98.0%; With disability: 13.1%; Veterans: 11.6%; Ancestry: 24.9% German, 19.5% Irish, 12.0% English, 10.0% Italian, 9.8% Dutch

Employment: 10.1% management, business, and financial, 8.5% computer, engineering, and science, 9.2% education, legal, community service, arts, and media, 2.5% healthcare practitioners, 19.9% service, 22.0% sales and office, 16.5% natural resources, construction, and maintenance, 11.4% production, transportation, and material moving

Income: Per capita: $24,343; Median household: $51,927; Average household: $63,002; Households with income of $100,000 or more: 15.2%; Poverty rate: 6.4%

Educational Attainment: High school diploma or higher: 90.4%; Bachelor's degree or higher: 28.7%; Graduate/professional degree or higher: 9.6%
Housing: Homeownership rate: 83.2%; Median home value: $134,000; Median year structure built: 1972; Homeowner vacancy rate: 3.0%; Median selected monthly owner costs: $1,215 with a mortgage, $541 without a mortgage; Median gross rent: $788 per month; Rental vacancy rate: 0.0%
Health Insurance: 94.8% have insurance; 73.5% have private insurance; 35.9% have public insurance; 5.2% do not have insurance; 1.3% of children under 18 do not have insurance
Transportation: Commute: 91.0% car, 0.0% public transportation, 0.5% walk, 8.0% work from home; Mean travel time to work: 32.5 minutes

WORCESTER (CDP). Covers a land area of 8.563 square miles and a water area of 0.046 square miles. Located at 42.61° N. Lat; 74.74° W. Long. Elevation is 1,335 feet.
Population: 973; Growth (since 2000): n/a; Density: 113.6 persons per square mile; Race: 97.5% White, 1.3% Black/African American, 0.0% Asian, 0.0% American Indian/Alaska Native, 0.0% Native Hawaiian/Other Pacific Islander, 0.0% Two or more races, 3.4% Hispanic of any race; Average household size: 2.27; Median age: 52.5; Age under 18: 16.8%; Age 65 and over: 32.6%; Males per 100 females: 90.9; Marriage status: 20.8% never married, 61.1% now married, 1.9% separated, 10.9% widowed, 7.2% divorced; Foreign born: 1.0%; Speak English only: 94.7%; With disability: 12.0%; Veterans: 8.1%; Ancestry: 25.1% Irish, 16.2% Italian, 15.8% German, 8.5% American, 8.3% English
Employment: 7.3% management, business, and financial, 1.5% computer, engineering, and science, 8.1% education, legal, community service, arts, and media, 7.3% healthcare practitioners, 26.0% service, 26.5% sales and office, 17.7% natural resources, construction, and maintenance, 5.6% production, transportation, and material moving
Income: Per capita: $24,257; Median household: $39,900; Average household: $55,453; Households with income of $100,000 or more: 17.1%; Poverty rate: 15.1%
Educational Attainment: High school diploma or higher: 83.7%; Bachelor's degree or higher: 23.7%; Graduate/professional degree or higher: 13.0%

School District(s)
Worcester Central SD (PK-12)
    2014-15 Enrollment: 364 . . . . (607) 397-8785
Housing: Homeownership rate: 80.0%; Median home value: $106,200; Median year structure built: Before 1940; Homeowner vacancy rate: 0.0%; Median selected monthly owner costs: $1,214 with a mortgage, $420 without a mortgage; Median gross rent: $795 per month; Rental vacancy rate: 28.8%
Health Insurance: 92.1% have insurance; 70.1% have private insurance; 49.6% have public insurance; 7.9% do not have insurance; 16.0% of children under 18 do not have insurance
Transportation: Commute: 89.4% car, 0.0% public transportation, 3.8% walk, 6.8% work from home; Mean travel time to work: 29.2 minutes

WORCESTER (town). Covers a land area of 46.710 square miles and a water area of 0.163 square miles. Located at 42.58° N. Lat; 74.72° W. Long. Elevation is 1,335 feet.
Population: 2,099; Growth (since 2000): -4.9%; Density: 44.9 persons per square mile; Race: 96.7% White, 1.4% Black/African American, 0.0% Asian, 0.7% American Indian/Alaska Native, 0.0% Native Hawaiian/Other Pacific Islander, 0.4% Two or more races, 8.1% Hispanic of any race; Average household size: 2.24; Median age: 50.5; Age under 18: 19.1%; Age 65 and over: 25.0%; Males per 100 females: 97.9; Marriage status: 25.7% never married, 54.6% now married, 2.2% separated, 8.6% widowed, 11.1% divorced; Foreign born: 4.6%; Speak English only: 89.7%; With disability: 14.2%; Veterans: 12.6%; Ancestry: 22.7% Irish, 20.5% German, 13.3% Italian, 9.1% French, 7.1% English
Employment: 12.7% management, business, and financial, 1.2% computer, engineering, and science, 9.1% education, legal, community service, arts, and media, 10.3% healthcare practitioners, 18.9% service, 20.6% sales and office, 11.2% natural resources, construction, and maintenance, 16.1% production, transportation, and material moving
Income: Per capita: $24,814; Median household: $45,833; Average household: $56,482; Households with income of $100,000 or more: 14.0%; Poverty rate: 16.3%
Educational Attainment: High school diploma or higher: 83.1%; Bachelor's degree or higher: 21.8%; Graduate/professional degree or higher: 10.4%

School District(s)
Worcester Central SD (PK-12)
    2014-15 Enrollment: 364 . . . . (607) 397-8785
Housing: Homeownership rate: 79.1%; Median home value: $118,400; Median year structure built: 1956; Homeowner vacancy rate: 1.9%; Median selected monthly owner costs: $1,232 with a mortgage, $459 without a mortgage; Median gross rent: $694 per month; Rental vacancy rate: 19.8%
Health Insurance: 94.3% have insurance; 71.8% have private insurance; 44.5% have public insurance; 5.7% do not have insurance; 6.5% of children under 18 do not have insurance
Transportation: Commute: 92.4% car, 0.6% public transportation, 2.4% walk, 4.7% work from home; Mean travel time to work: 32.4 minutes

Putnam County

Located in southeastern New York; bounded on the west by the Hudson River, and on the east by Connecticut; includes part of the Taconic Mountains. Covers a land area of 230.312 square miles, a water area of 15.939 square miles, and is located in the Eastern Time Zone at 41.43° N. Lat., 73.74° W. Long. The county was founded in 1812. County seat is Carmel.

Putnam County is part of the New York-Newark-Jersey City, NY-NJ-PA Metropolitan Statistical Area. The entire metro area includes: Dutchess County-Putnam County, NY Metropolitan Division (Dutchess County, NY; Putnam County, NY); Nassau County-Suffolk County, NY Metropolitan Division (Nassau County, NY; Suffolk County, NY); Newark, NJ-PA Metropolitan Division (Essex County, NJ; Hunterdon County, NJ; Morris County, NJ; Somerset County, NJ; Sussex County, NJ; Union County, NJ; Pike County, PA); New York-Jersey City-White Plains, NY-NJ Metropolitan Division (Bergen County, NJ; Hudson County, NJ; Middlesex County, NJ; Monmouth County, NJ; Ocean County, NJ; Passaic County, NJ; Bronx County, NY; Kings County, NY; New York County, NY; Orange County, NY; Queens County, NY; Richmond County, NY; Rockland County, NY; Westchester County, NY)

Population: 99,488; Growth (since 2000): 3.9%; Density: 432.0 persons per square mile; Race: 90.1% White, 2.3% Black/African American, 2.3% Asian, 0.5% American Indian/Alaska Native, 0.0% Native Hawaiian/Other Pacific Islander, 2.2% two or more races, 12.7% Hispanic of any race; Average household size: 2.84; Median age: 42.8; Age under 18: 22.0%; Age 65 and over: 14.1%; Males per 100 females: 99.7; Marriage status: 28.2% never married, 58.8% now married, 1.4% separated, 5.0% widowed, 7.9% divorced; Foreign born: 12.7%; Speak English only: 81.0%; With disability: 10.3%; Veterans: 6.1%; Ancestry: 29.1% Italian, 24.8% Irish, 13.0% German, 6.2% English, 5.1% American
Religion: Six largest groups: 41.5% Catholicism, 1.2% Methodist/Pietist, 1.2% Lutheran, 1.2% Judaism, 1.0% Episcopalianism/Anglicanism, 0.8% Presbyterian-Reformed
Economy: Unemployment rate: 4.0%; Leading industries: 20.6 % construction; 11.0 % retail trade; 11.0 % professional, scientific, and technical services; Farms: 72 totaling 5,908 acres; Company size: 0 employ 1,000 or more persons, 2 employ 500 to 999 persons, 15 employ 100 to 499 persons, 2,857 employ less than 100 persons; Business ownership: 3,373 women-owned, 266 Black-owned, 709 Hispanic-owned, 357 Asian-owned, 26 American Indian/Alaska Native-owned
Employment: 14.5% management, business, and financial, 4.9% computer, engineering, and science, 14.8% education, legal, community service, arts, and media, 6.5% healthcare practitioners, 17.1% service, 25.5% sales and office, 10.7% natural resources, construction, and maintenance, 5.9% production, transportation, and material moving
Income: Per capita: $41,173; Median household: $96,148; Average household: $117,519; Households with income of $100,000 or more: 48.3%; Poverty rate: 5.3%
Educational Attainment: High school diploma or higher: 92.4%; Bachelor's degree or higher: 37.9%; Graduate/professional degree or higher: 16.1%
Housing: Homeownership rate: 82.0%; Median home value: $354,900; Median year structure built: 1968; Homeowner vacancy rate: 1.1%; Median selected monthly owner costs: $2,697 with a mortgage, $1,065 without a mortgage; Median gross rent: $1,234 per month; Rental vacancy rate: 3.2%
Vital Statistics: Birth rate: 83.4 per 10,000 population; Death rate: 69.7 per 10,000 population; Age-adjusted cancer mortality rate: 166.0 deaths per 100,000 population

Health Insurance: 92.3% have insurance; 81.9% have private insurance; 22.5% have public insurance; 7.7% do not have insurance; 2.8% of children under 18 do not have insurance
Health Care: Physicians: 19.5 per 10,000 population; Dentists: 5.5 per 10,000 population; Hospital beds: 31.1 per 10,000 population; Hospital admissions: 1,053.6 per 10,000 population
Air Quality Index (AQI): Percent of Days: 94.8% good, 4.7% moderate, 0.5% unhealthy for sensitive individuals, 0.0% unhealthy, 0.0% very unhealthy; Annual median: 31; Annual maximum: 116
Transportation: Commute: 85.1% car, 8.3% public transportation, 1.2% walk, 4.5% work from home; Mean travel time to work: 38.8 minutes
2016 Presidential Election: 56.1% Trump, 40.2% Clinton, 2.4% Johnson, 1.2% Stein
National and State Parks: Clarence Fahnestock Memorial State Park
Additional Information Contacts
Putnam Government . . . . (845) 225-3641
  http://www.putnamcountyny.com

Putnam County Communities

BREWSTER (village). Covers a land area of 0.467 square miles and a water area of 0.004 square miles. Located at 41.40° N. Lat; 73.61° W. Long. Elevation is 466 feet.
History: Jurist James Kent born nearby, 1763. Settled 1850, incorporated 1894.
Population: 2,212; Growth (since 2000): 2.3%; Density: 4,734.4 persons per square mile; Race: 68.3% White, 1.9% Black/African American, 1.9% Asian, 4.5% American Indian/Alaska Native, 0.0% Native Hawaiian/Other Pacific Islander, 8.5% Two or more races, 60.2% Hispanic of any race; Average household size: 2.70; Median age: 33.1; Age under 18: 19.3%; Age 65 and over: 8.4%; Males per 100 females: 161.2; Marriage status: 43.5% never married, 47.3% now married, 2.1% separated, 2.7% widowed, 6.5% divorced; Foreign born: 48.4%; Speak English only: 41.2%; With disability: 10.1%; Veterans: 3.8%; Ancestry: 10.8% Irish, 5.7% German, 5.2% Italian, 4.9% American, 4.2% English
Employment: 5.4% management, business, and financial, 3.1% computer, engineering, and science, 3.9% education, legal, community service, arts, and media, 0.3% healthcare practitioners, 35.2% service, 23.1% sales and office, 19.9% natural resources, construction, and maintenance, 9.2% production, transportation, and material moving
Income: Per capita: $22,011; Median household: $49,917; Average household: $57,741; Households with income of $100,000 or more: 16.7%; Poverty rate: 19.7%
Educational Attainment: High school diploma or higher: 63.6%; Bachelor's degree or higher: 16.5%; Graduate/professional degree or higher: 5.4%
School District(s)
Brewster Central SD (KG-12)
  2014-15 Enrollment: 3,283 . . . . (845) 279-8000
Housing: Homeownership rate: 17.6%; Median home value: $267,700; Median year structure built: Before 1940; Homeowner vacancy rate: 0.0%; Median selected monthly owner costs: $2,245 with a mortgage, $1,011 without a mortgage; Median gross rent: $1,174 per month; Rental vacancy rate: 2.1%
Health Insurance: 62.2% have insurance; 40.4% have private insurance; 28.8% have public insurance; 37.8% do not have insurance; 0.0% of children under 18 do not have insurance
Safety: Violent crime rate: 30.0 per 10,000 population; Property crime rate: 42.8 per 10,000 population
Transportation: Commute: 78.3% car, 12.6% public transportation, 3.2% walk, 1.3% work from home; Mean travel time to work: 30.0 minutes

BREWSTER HILL (CDP). Covers a land area of 0.870 square miles and a water area of 0.110 square miles. Located at 41.42° N. Lat; 73.61° W. Long. Elevation is 617 feet.
Population: 1,378; Growth (since 2000): -38.1%; Density: 1,583.5 persons per square mile; Race: 91.6% White, 0.0% Black/African American, 2.3% Asian, 0.0% American Indian/Alaska Native, 0.0% Native Hawaiian/Other Pacific Islander, 6.1% Two or more races, 10.1% Hispanic of any race; Average household size: 2.68; Median age: 47.1; Age under 18: 20.8%; Age 65 and over: 14.2%; Males per 100 females: 98.0; Marriage status: 9.1% never married, 70.9% now married, 0.0% separated, 3.9% widowed, 16.1% divorced; Foreign born: 8.1%; Speak English only: 87.4%; With disability: 7.8%; Veterans: 15.1%; Ancestry: 31.3% Italian, 30.3% Irish, 16.5% German, 11.3% American, 9.2% Polish

Employment: 8.8% management, business, and financial, 13.0% computer, engineering, and science, 18.5% education, legal, community service, arts, and media, 4.6% healthcare practitioners, 12.3% service, 33.6% sales and office, 7.6% natural resources, construction, and maintenance, 1.5% production, transportation, and material moving
Income: Per capita: $37,790; Median household: $90,909; Average household: $98,935; Households with income of $100,000 or more: 42.5%; Poverty rate: 1.2%
Educational Attainment: High school diploma or higher: 92.1%; Bachelor's degree or higher: 29.3%; Graduate/professional degree or higher: 12.4%
Housing: Homeownership rate: 100.0%; Median home value: $331,100; Median year structure built: 1957; Homeowner vacancy rate: 0.0%; Median selected monthly owner costs: $1,977 with a mortgage, $964 without a mortgage; Median gross rent: n/a per month; Rental vacancy rate: 100.0%
Health Insurance: 86.2% have insurance; 78.7% have private insurance; 25.5% have public insurance; 13.8% do not have insurance; 22.0% of children under 18 do not have insurance
Transportation: Commute: 89.5% car, 5.9% public transportation, 0.0% walk, 4.7% work from home; Mean travel time to work: 33.9 minutes

CARMEL (town). County seat. Covers a land area of 35.907 square miles and a water area of 4.786 square miles. Located at 41.39° N. Lat; 73.72° W. Long. Elevation is 561 feet.
Population: 34,376; Growth (since 2000): 4.2%; Density: 957.4 persons per square mile; Race: 90.7% White, 1.3% Black/African American, 2.8% Asian, 0.8% American Indian/Alaska Native, 0.0% Native Hawaiian/Other Pacific Islander, 1.7% Two or more races, 11.3% Hispanic of any race; Average household size: 2.94; Median age: 42.5; Age under 18: 22.7%; Age 65 and over: 13.6%; Males per 100 females: 98.4; Marriage status: 27.8% never married, 59.4% now married, 0.8% separated, 5.2% widowed, 7.6% divorced; Foreign born: 12.7%; Speak English only: 81.2%; With disability: 9.8%; Veterans: 5.7%; Ancestry: 33.3% Italian, 26.2% Irish, 11.8% German, 5.3% American, 5.2% Polish
Employment: 14.6% management, business, and financial, 3.9% computer, engineering, and science, 15.1% education, legal, community service, arts, and media, 6.6% healthcare practitioners, 16.5% service, 25.0% sales and office, 12.1% natural resources, construction, and maintenance, 6.2% production, transportation, and material moving
Income: Per capita: $41,585; Median household: $103,438; Average household: $120,711; Households with income of $100,000 or more: 51.4%; Poverty rate: 3.2%
Educational Attainment: High school diploma or higher: 93.3%; Bachelor's degree or higher: 38.5%; Graduate/professional degree or higher: 17.2%
School District(s)
Carmel Central SD (KG-12)
  2014-15 Enrollment: 4,277 . . . . (845) 878-2094
Housing: Homeownership rate: 83.5%; Median home value: $379,300; Median year structure built: 1969; Homeowner vacancy rate: 0.4%; Median selected monthly owner costs: $2,864 with a mortgage, $1,105 without a mortgage; Median gross rent: $1,177 per month; Rental vacancy rate: 3.2%
Health Insurance: 92.5% have insurance; 83.1% have private insurance; 21.0% have public insurance; 7.5% do not have insurance; 3.6% of children under 18 do not have insurance
Hospitals: Putnam Hospital Center (164 beds)
Safety: Violent crime rate: 2.0 per 10,000 population; Property crime rate: 45.6 per 10,000 population
Newspapers: Putnam County Courier (weekly circulation 4,800)
Transportation: Commute: 88.4% car, 6.8% public transportation, 0.9% walk, 3.5% work from home; Mean travel time to work: 36.9 minutes
Additional Information Contacts
Town of Carmel . . . . (845) 628-1500
  http://www.ci.carmel.ny.us

CARMEL HAMLET (CDP). Covers a land area of 8.335 square miles and a water area of 2.055 square miles. Located at 41.42° N. Lat; 73.69° W. Long.
Population: 6,542; Growth (since 2000): 15.8%; Density: 784.8 persons per square mile; Race: 86.9% White, 2.2% Black/African American, 5.8% Asian, 0.0% American Indian/Alaska Native, 0.0% Native Hawaiian/Other Pacific Islander, 2.7% Two or more races, 11.8% Hispanic of any race; Average household size: 2.79; Median age: 45.0; Age under 18: 23.1%; Age 65 and over: 16.8%; Males per 100 females: 98.6; Marriage status:

29.1% never married, 54.1% now married, 0.5% separated, 8.3% widowed, 8.5% divorced; Foreign born: 11.8%; Speak English only: 83.5%; With disability: 12.2%; Veterans: 4.7%; Ancestry: 25.7% Italian, 24.0% Irish, 13.4% German, 8.6% Polish, 6.2% English

Employment: 13.3% management, business, and financial, 2.6% computer, engineering, and science, 14.2% education, legal, community service, arts, and media, 5.6% healthcare practitioners, 11.4% service, 34.1% sales and office, 11.8% natural resources, construction, and maintenance, 7.0% production, transportation, and material moving

Income: Per capita: $38,573; Median household: $83,636; Average household: $109,548; Households with income of $100,000 or more: 41.8%; Poverty rate: 5.6%

Educational Attainment: High school diploma or higher: 86.1%; Bachelor's degree or higher: 35.9%; Graduate/professional degree or higher: 17.5%

Housing: Homeownership rate: 71.6%; Median home value: $340,000; Median year structure built: 1969; Homeowner vacancy rate: 0.0%; Median selected monthly owner costs: $3,131 with a mortgage, $983 without a mortgage; Median gross rent: $1,084 per month; Rental vacancy rate: 0.0%

Health Insurance: 90.6% have insurance; 75.3% have private insurance; 28.3% have public insurance; 9.4% do not have insurance; 12.7% of children under 18 do not have insurance

Transportation: Commute: 87.5% car, 8.9% public transportation, 0.4% walk, 3.2% work from home; Mean travel time to work: 37.7 minutes

COLD SPRING (village). Covers a land area of 0.594 square miles and a water area of 0.005 square miles. Located at 41.42° N. Lat; 73.95° W. Long. Elevation is 115 feet.

History: Settled before the American Revolution; incorporated 1846.

Population: 1,790; Growth (since 2000): -9.7%; Density: 3,014.9 persons per square mile; Race: 92.2% White, 0.6% Black/African American, 1.2% Asian, 1.6% American Indian/Alaska Native, 0.0% Native Hawaiian/Other Pacific Islander, 1.8% Two or more races, 7.9% Hispanic of any race; Average household size: 2.19; Median age: 45.6; Age under 18: 19.2%; Age 65 and over: 18.3%; Males per 100 females: 90.6; Marriage status: 29.2% never married, 57.5% now married, 2.6% separated, 6.9% widowed, 6.5% divorced; Foreign born: 7.9%; Speak English only: 84.9%; With disability: 12.2%; Veterans: 8.1%; Ancestry: 28.0% Italian, 27.8% Irish, 14.4% German, 10.1% English, 5.0% Russian

Employment: 17.0% management, business, and financial, 4.3% computer, engineering, and science, 21.1% education, legal, community service, arts, and media, 4.4% healthcare practitioners, 17.3% service, 24.0% sales and office, 5.3% natural resources, construction, and maintenance, 6.6% production, transportation, and material moving

Income: Per capita: $46,196; Median household: $83,125; Average household: $99,588; Households with income of $100,000 or more: 37.7%; Poverty rate: 7.5%

Educational Attainment: High school diploma or higher: 97.1%; Bachelor's degree or higher: 48.3%; Graduate/professional degree or higher: 21.8%

School District(s)
Haldane Central SD (KG-12)
   2014-15 Enrollment: 859 . . . . (845) 265-9254

Housing: Homeownership rate: 60.0%; Median home value: $367,900; Median year structure built: 1943; Homeowner vacancy rate: 3.5%; Median selected monthly owner costs: $2,500 with a mortgage, $1,192 without a mortgage; Median gross rent: $1,305 per month; Rental vacancy rate: 8.9%

Health Insurance: 94.8% have insurance; 85.7% have private insurance; 23.2% have public insurance; 5.2% do not have insurance; 2.3% of children under 18 do not have insurance

Newspapers: Putnam County News & Recorder (weekly circulation 4,200)

Transportation: Commute: 55.3% car, 30.3% public transportation, 9.0% walk, 4.9% work from home; Mean travel time to work: 48.0 minutes

GARRISON (unincorporated postal area)
ZCTA: 10524

Covers a land area of 20.802 square miles and a water area of 0.324 square miles. Located at 41.38° N. Lat; 73.93° W. Long. Elevation is 49 feet.

Population: 4,252; Growth (since 2000): 0.5%; Density: 204.4 persons per square mile; Race: 86.3% White, 3.1% Black/African American, 4.2% Asian, 0.0% American Indian/Alaska Native, 0.0% Native Hawaiian/Other Pacific Islander, 4.7% Two or more races, 7.2%

Hispanic of any race; Average household size: 2.71; Median age: 47.8; Age under 18: 18.4%; Age 65 and over: 18.5%; Males per 100 females: 95.4; Marriage status: 25.2% never married, 65.2% now married, 2.4% separated, 4.3% widowed, 5.4% divorced; Foreign born: 10.6%; Speak English only: 86.8%; With disability: 11.4%; Veterans: 7.7%; Ancestry: 28.7% Irish, 24.3% Italian, 11.6% German, 9.4% English, 6.2% American

Employment: 17.4% management, business, and financial, 3.9% computer, engineering, and science, 19.6% education, legal, community service, arts, and media, 8.5% healthcare practitioners, 16.0% service, 20.6% sales and office, 6.9% natural resources, construction, and maintenance, 7.1% production, transportation, and material moving

Income: Per capita: $55,343; Median household: $119,583; Average household: $159,108; Households with income of $100,000 or more: 58.0%; Poverty rate: 8.0%

Educational Attainment: High school diploma or higher: 95.7%; Bachelor's degree or higher: 51.4%; Graduate/professional degree or higher: 23.8%

School District(s)
Garrison Union Free SD (KG-08)
   2014-15 Enrollment: 226 . . . . (845) 424-3689

Housing: Homeownership rate: 86.5%; Median home value: $450,000; Median year structure built: 1970; Homeowner vacancy rate: 0.4%; Median selected monthly owner costs: $2,868 with a mortgage, $1,211 without a mortgage; Median gross rent: $1,775 per month; Rental vacancy rate: 6.7%

Health Insurance: 95.3% have insurance; 82.5% have private insurance; 27.1% have public insurance; 4.7% do not have insurance; 1.8% of children under 18 do not have insurance

Transportation: Commute: 69.8% car, 16.4% public transportation, 1.2% walk, 11.5% work from home; Mean travel time to work: 40.1 minutes

KENT (town). Covers a land area of 40.504 square miles and a water area of 2.822 square miles. Located at 41.46° N. Lat; 73.73° W. Long.

History: Kent was part of the Philipse Patent of 1679, when it was populated by the Wappinger tribe. Daniel Nimham (1724-1778) was the last chief of the Wappingers and was the most prominent Native American of his time in the Hudson Valley.

Population: 13,416; Growth (since 2000): -4.2%; Density: 331.2 persons per square mile; Race: 87.3% White, 5.2% Black/African American, 0.7% Asian, 0.4% American Indian/Alaska Native, 0.0% Native Hawaiian/Other Pacific Islander, 2.1% Two or more races, 15.0% Hispanic of any race; Average household size: 2.82; Median age: 44.1; Age under 18: 21.3%; Age 65 and over: 15.9%; Males per 100 females: 98.9; Marriage status: 26.6% never married, 58.8% now married, 2.4% separated, 5.7% widowed, 8.9% divorced; Foreign born: 12.4%; Speak English only: 82.0%; With disability: 12.7%; Veterans: 7.4%; Ancestry: 23.7% Italian, 20.4% Irish, 13.2% German, 6.5% American, 5.1% English

Employment: 12.9% management, business, and financial, 4.5% computer, engineering, and science, 11.5% education, legal, community service, arts, and media, 5.9% healthcare practitioners, 18.5% service, 28.1% sales and office, 11.8% natural resources, construction, and maintenance, 6.7% production, transportation, and material moving

Income: Per capita: $40,308; Median household: $88,877; Average household: $114,646; Households with income of $100,000 or more: 43.2%; Poverty rate: 5.1%

Educational Attainment: High school diploma or higher: 93.6%; Bachelor's degree or higher: 32.1%; Graduate/professional degree or higher: 14.5%

Housing: Homeownership rate: 86.9%; Median home value: $287,600; Median year structure built: 1962; Homeowner vacancy rate: 1.9%; Median selected monthly owner costs: $2,436 with a mortgage, $1,023 without a mortgage; Median gross rent: $1,370 per month; Rental vacancy rate: 0.0%

Health Insurance: 93.7% have insurance; 83.6% have private insurance; 24.7% have public insurance; 6.3% do not have insurance; 1.8% of children under 18 do not have insurance

Safety: Violent crime rate: 1.5 per 10,000 population; Property crime rate: 34.4 per 10,000 population

Transportation: Commute: 88.3% car, 6.9% public transportation, 0.8% walk, 3.1% work from home; Mean travel time to work: 41.2 minutes

Additional Information Contacts
Town of Kent . . . . (845) 225-3943
   http://www.townofkentny.com

LAKE CARMEL (CDP). Covers a land area of 5.161 square miles and a water area of 0.333 square miles. Located at 41.46° N. Lat; 73.67° W. Long. Elevation is 801 feet.
Population: 8,294; Growth (since 2000): -4.3%; Density: 1,607.0 persons per square mile; Race: 84.0% White, 6.6% Black/African American, 0.6% Asian, 0.7% American Indian/Alaska Native, 0.0% Native Hawaiian/Other Pacific Islander, 1.8% Two or more races, 18.2% Hispanic of any race; Average household size: 2.84; Median age: 42.3; Age under 18: 21.8%; Age 65 and over: 14.3%; Males per 100 females: 99.9; Marriage status: 26.7% never married, 59.4% now married, 2.8% separated, 6.2% widowed, 7.7% divorced; Foreign born: 15.1%; Speak English only: 78.0%; With disability: 11.8%; Veterans: 7.6%; Ancestry: 25.2% Italian, 20.5% Irish, 11.5% German, 6.0% American, 5.0% Polish
Employment: 10.4% management, business, and financial, 4.4% computer, engineering, and science, 12.1% education, legal, community service, arts, and media, 4.2% healthcare practitioners, 20.9% service, 30.2% sales and office, 11.2% natural resources, construction, and maintenance, 6.7% production, transportation, and material moving
Income: Per capita: $35,493; Median household: $86,705; Average household: $97,789; Households with income of $100,000 or more: 41.3%; Poverty rate: 5.6%
Educational Attainment: High school diploma or higher: 93.4%; Bachelor's degree or higher: 28.1%; Graduate/professional degree or higher: 12.2%
Housing: Homeownership rate: 87.6%; Median home value: $263,900; Median year structure built: 1957; Homeowner vacancy rate: 2.0%; Median selected monthly owner costs: $2,279 with a mortgage, $984 without a mortgage; Median gross rent: $1,438 per month; Rental vacancy rate: 0.0%
Health Insurance: 92.5% have insurance; 83.1% have private insurance; 22.5% have public insurance; 7.5% do not have insurance; 2.9% of children under 18 do not have insurance
Transportation: Commute: 89.7% car, 7.9% public transportation, 0.0% walk, 2.1% work from home; Mean travel time to work: 40.9 minutes

LAKE PEEKSKILL (unincorporated postal area)
ZCTA: 10537
Covers a land area of 1.077 square miles and a water area of 0.095 square miles. Located at 41.34° N. Lat; 73.88° W. Long. Elevation is 315 feet.
Population: 1,842; Growth (since 2000): -9.4%; Density: 1,710.4 persons per square mile; Race: 83.2% White, 7.3% Black/African American, 7.3% Asian, 0.0% American Indian/Alaska Native, 0.0% Native Hawaiian/Other Pacific Islander, 2.1% Two or more races, 7.0% Hispanic of any race; Average household size: 2.53; Median age: 46.2; Age under 18: 20.8%; Age 65 and over: 11.8%; Males per 100 females: 101.0; Marriage status: 30.4% never married, 43.7% now married, 2.7% separated, 6.5% widowed, 19.4% divorced; Foreign born: 11.7%; Speak English only: 74.8%; With disability: 8.4%; Veterans: 10.9%; Ancestry: 33.1% Italian, 21.8% Irish, 19.2% German, 7.7% Greek, 5.6% American
Employment: 14.8% management, business, and financial, 6.4% computer, engineering, and science, 19.1% education, legal, community service, arts, and media, 6.8% healthcare practitioners, 17.4% service, 27.2% sales and office, 8.3% natural resources, construction, and maintenance, 0.0% production, transportation, and material moving
Income: Per capita: $39,700; Median household: $77,396; Average household: $99,556; Households with income of $100,000 or more: 43.2%; Poverty rate: 6.2%
Educational Attainment: High school diploma or higher: 92.0%; Bachelor's degree or higher: 47.7%; Graduate/professional degree or higher: 16.1%
Housing: Homeownership rate: 91.9%; Median home value: $274,100; Median year structure built: 1947; Homeowner vacancy rate: 13.4%; Median selected monthly owner costs: $2,514 with a mortgage, $750 without a mortgage; Median gross rent: n/a per month; Rental vacancy rate: 0.0%
Health Insurance: 94.2% have insurance; 77.1% have private insurance; 29.2% have public insurance; 5.8% do not have insurance; 0.0% of children under 18 do not have insurance
Transportation: Commute: 80.1% car, 12.2% public transportation, 0.0% walk, 5.8% work from home; Mean travel time to work: 44.7 minutes

MAHOPAC (CDP). Covers a land area of 5.279 square miles and a water area of 1.171 square miles. Located at 41.37° N. Lat; 73.74° W. Long. Elevation is 666 feet.
History: Mahopac was originally inhabited by the Wappinger Native Americans, an Algonquian tribe. The land was patented in 1697 by Adolphus Philipse, son of a wealthy Anglo-Dutch gentryman.
Population: 8,083; Growth (since 2000): -4.7%; Density: 1,531.0 persons per square mile; Race: 89.9% White, 0.2% Black/African American, 1.9% Asian, 0.0% American Indian/Alaska Native, 0.0% Native Hawaiian/Other Pacific Islander, 2.5% Two or more races, 13.4% Hispanic of any race; Average household size: 2.76; Median age: 41.3; Age under 18: 19.9%; Age 65 and over: 13.9%; Males per 100 females: 101.2; Marriage status: 28.9% never married, 58.7% now married, 1.7% separated, 4.1% widowed, 8.2% divorced; Foreign born: 19.7%; Speak English only: 74.0%; With disability: 9.0%; Veterans: 5.0%; Ancestry: 30.3% Italian, 25.0% Irish, 11.0% German, 6.6% Albanian, 5.7% American
Employment: 12.9% management, business, and financial, 4.2% computer, engineering, and science, 17.5% education, legal, community service, arts, and media, 4.7% healthcare practitioners, 18.1% service, 24.8% sales and office, 12.6% natural resources, construction, and maintenance, 5.2% production, transportation, and material moving
Income: Per capita: $43,282; Median household: $95,619; Average household: $117,406; Households with income of $100,000 or more: 46.5%; Poverty rate: 6.2%
Educational Attainment: High school diploma or higher: 93.7%; Bachelor's degree or higher: 41.5%; Graduate/professional degree or higher: 21.0%
School District(s)
Mahopac Central SD (KG-12)
2014-15 Enrollment: 4,538 . . . . (845) 628-3415
Housing: Homeownership rate: 74.5%; Median home value: $370,800; Median year structure built: 1965; Homeowner vacancy rate: 0.3%; Median selected monthly owner costs: $2,645 with a mortgage, $1,065 without a mortgage; Median gross rent: $1,214 per month; Rental vacancy rate: 4.1%
Health Insurance: 90.7% have insurance; 78.7% have private insurance; 22.2% have public insurance; 9.3% do not have insurance; 4.7% of children under 18 do not have insurance
Newspapers: Putnam County Press (weekly circulation 12,000)
Transportation: Commute: 82.5% car, 6.8% public transportation, 3.5% walk, 6.1% work from home; Mean travel time to work: 36.7 minutes

NELSONVILLE (village). Covers a land area of 1.034 square miles and a water area of 0.001 square miles. Located at 41.43° N. Lat; 73.95° W. Long. Elevation is 187 feet.
Population: 805; Growth (since 2000): 42.5%; Density: 778.7 persons per square mile; Race: 95.9% White, 0.7% Black/African American, 1.7% Asian, 0.0% American Indian/Alaska Native, 0.0% Native Hawaiian/Other Pacific Islander, 1.0% Two or more races, 7.7% Hispanic of any race; Average household size: 3.18; Median age: 38.1; Age under 18: 29.1%; Age 65 and over: 6.3%; Males per 100 females: 97.5; Marriage status: 28.3% never married, 61.0% now married, 1.0% separated, 5.0% widowed, 5.8% divorced; Foreign born: 6.3%; Speak English only: 95.2%; With disability: 7.9%; Veterans: 4.2%; Ancestry: 35.0% Italian, 34.3% Irish, 14.5% German, 9.3% English, 6.3% American
Employment: 13.0% management, business, and financial, 5.1% computer, engineering, and science, 21.4% education, legal, community service, arts, and media, 7.1% healthcare practitioners, 20.1% service, 16.3% sales and office, 8.4% natural resources, construction, and maintenance, 8.7% production, transportation, and material moving
Income: Per capita: $40,681; Median household: $107,500; Average household: $135,147; Households with income of $100,000 or more: 52.4%; Poverty rate: 1.9%
Educational Attainment: High school diploma or higher: 94.1%; Bachelor's degree or higher: 46.9%; Graduate/professional degree or higher: 20.8%
Housing: Homeownership rate: 74.0%; Median home value: $382,300; Median year structure built: 1960; Homeowner vacancy rate: 0.0%; Median selected monthly owner costs: $2,960 with a mortgage, $1,167 without a mortgage; Median gross rent: $1,656 per month; Rental vacancy rate: 0.0%
Health Insurance: 95.8% have insurance; 88.3% have private insurance; 15.9% have public insurance; 4.3% do not have insurance; 0.0% of children under 18 do not have insurance

Transportation: Commute: 70.4% car, 20.8% public transportation, 4.7% walk, 4.2% work from home; Mean travel time to work: 40.2 minutes

---

PATTERSON (town). Covers a land area of 32.208 square miles and a water area of 0.696 square miles. Located at 41.48° N. Lat; 73.59° W. Long. Elevation is 443 feet.

History: Patterson is located in a valley which was formerly part of the Patterson Great Swamp. The village, originally named Franklin, was settled about 1770 by Scots discharged from the British army after service in the French and Indian War. The present name was adopted in 1808 when the legislature passed a law abolishing the numerous "Franklins" in the state. The town was then named after Matthew Patterson, an early settler.

Population: 12,025; Growth (since 2000): 6.4%; Density: 373.4 persons per square mile; Race: 85.5% White, 3.9% Black/African American, 4.6% Asian, 0.0% American Indian/Alaska Native, 0.0% Native Hawaiian/Other Pacific Islander, 3.1% Two or more races, 16.5% Hispanic of any race; Average household size: 2.88; Median age: 39.4; Age under 18: 20.6%; Age 65 and over: 11.3%; Males per 100 females: 102.4; Marriage status: 33.8% never married, 53.4% now married, 0.8% separated, 4.7% widowed, 8.1% divorced; Foreign born: 12.3%; Speak English only: 78.5%; With disability: 13.1%; Veterans: 5.3%; Ancestry: 23.8% Irish, 21.1% Italian, 12.5% German, 8.2% English, 4.8% American

Employment: 12.8% management, business, and financial, 4.5% computer, engineering, and science, 12.8% education, legal, community service, arts, and media, 7.9% healthcare practitioners, 19.9% service, 25.4% sales and office, 8.1% natural resources, construction, and maintenance, 8.5% production, transportation, and material moving

Income: Per capita: $31,364; Median household: $87,143; Average household: $96,970; Households with income of $100,000 or more: 42.6%; Poverty rate: 8.9%

Educational Attainment: High school diploma or higher: 91.4%; Bachelor's degree or higher: 27.3%; Graduate/professional degree or higher: 10.5%

School District(s)

Carmel Central SD (KG-12)
    2014-15 Enrollment: 4,277 . . . . (845) 878-2094
Housing: Homeownership rate: 80.6%; Median home value: $301,700; Median year structure built: 1972; Homeowner vacancy rate: 2.6%; Median selected monthly owner costs: $2,636 with a mortgage, $839 without a mortgage; Median gross rent: $1,195 per month; Rental vacancy rate: 0.0%
Health Insurance: 89.6% have insurance; 77.6% have private insurance; 22.7% have public insurance; 10.4% do not have insurance; 3.4% of children under 18 do not have insurance
Transportation: Commute: 86.5% car, 5.7% public transportation, 2.8% walk, 4.0% work from home; Mean travel time to work: 39.4 minutes
Additional Information Contacts
Town of Patterson . . . . (845) 878-6500
    http://www.pattersonny.org

PEACH LAKE (CDP). Covers a land area of 2.664 square miles and a water area of 0.380 square miles. Located at 41.37° N. Lat; 73.58° W. Long. Elevation is 561 feet.

Population: 1,428; Growth (since 2000): -14.5%; Density: 536.0 persons per square mile; Race: 98.7% White, 0.8% Black/African American, 0.6% Asian, 0.0% American Indian/Alaska Native, 0.0% Native Hawaiian/Other Pacific Islander, 0.0% Two or more races, 5.3% Hispanic of any race; Average household size: 2.61; Median age: 47.2; Age under 18: 23.1%; Age 65 and over: 16.8%; Males per 100 females: 95.8; Marriage status: 23.2% never married, 61.1% now married, 0.0% separated, 4.8% widowed, 10.8% divorced; Foreign born: 2.9%; Speak English only: 95.8%; With disability: 9.1%; Veterans: 7.0%; Ancestry: 35.3% Irish, 33.8% Italian, 17.6% German, 9.0% English, 3.6% American

Employment: 12.6% management, business, and financial, 4.5% computer, engineering, and science, 24.4% education, legal, community service, arts, and media, 9.8% healthcare practitioners, 16.0% service, 23.4% sales and office, 5.0% natural resources, construction, and maintenance, 4.3% production, transportation, and material moving

Income: Per capita: $48,114; Median household: $113,375; Average household: $122,853; Households with income of $100,000 or more: 56.3%; Poverty rate: 6.1%

Educational Attainment: High school diploma or higher: 97.4%; Bachelor's degree or higher: 59.7%; Graduate/professional degree or higher: 19.0%

Housing: Homeownership rate: 91.2%; Median home value: $368,300; Median year structure built: 1963; Homeowner vacancy rate: 12.3%; Median selected monthly owner costs: $2,324 with a mortgage, $769 without a mortgage; Median gross rent: $2,342 per month; Rental vacancy rate: 0.0%
Health Insurance: 94.1% have insurance; 90.3% have private insurance; 20.5% have public insurance; 5.9% do not have insurance; 6.1% of children under 18 do not have insurance
Transportation: Commute: 85.2% car, 6.3% public transportation, 0.0% walk, 6.9% work from home; Mean travel time to work: 33.7 minutes

---

PHILIPSTOWN (town). Covers a land area of 48.785 square miles and a water area of 2.785 square miles. Located at 41.41° N. Lat; 73.92° W. Long.

Population: 9,699; Growth (since 2000): 2.9%; Density: 198.8 persons per square mile; Race: 90.7% White, 1.8% Black/African American, 2.5% Asian, 0.3% American Indian/Alaska Native, 0.0% Native Hawaiian/Other Pacific Islander, 3.5% Two or more races, 6.8% Hispanic of any race; Average household size: 2.65; Median age: 45.7; Age under 18: 21.6%; Age 65 and over: 17.1%; Males per 100 females: 95.8; Marriage status: 26.0% never married, 62.9% now married, 2.1% separated, 5.1% widowed, 6.0% divorced; Foreign born: 8.8%; Speak English only: 88.4%; With disability: 11.5%; Veterans: 7.2%; Ancestry: 27.8% Irish, 26.0% Italian, 14.4% German, 10.9% English, 4.4% Polish

Employment: 17.2% management, business, and financial, 5.1% computer, engineering, and science, 19.4% education, legal, community service, arts, and media, 6.4% healthcare practitioners, 16.0% service, 22.7% sales and office, 7.2% natural resources, construction, and maintenance, 6.0% production, transportation, and material moving

Income: Per capita: $50,497; Median household: $102,670; Average household: $136,146; Households with income of $100,000 or more: 50.9%; Poverty rate: 5.7%

Educational Attainment: High school diploma or higher: 96.4%; Bachelor's degree or higher: 50.1%; Graduate/professional degree or higher: 21.5%

Housing: Homeownership rate: 77.4%; Median home value: $433,300; Median year structure built: 1966; Homeowner vacancy rate: 0.8%; Median selected monthly owner costs: $2,829 with a mortgage, $1,153 without a mortgage; Median gross rent: $1,487 per month; Rental vacancy rate: 5.3%
Health Insurance: 94.5% have insurance; 82.4% have private insurance; 25.8% have public insurance; 5.5% do not have insurance; 1.5% of children under 18 do not have insurance
Transportation: Commute: 67.8% car, 17.7% public transportation, 2.9% walk, 11.0% work from home; Mean travel time to work: 42.8 minutes
Additional Information Contacts
Town of Philipstown . . . . (845) 265-3329
    http://philipstown.com

PUTNAM LAKE (CDP). Covers a land area of 3.841 square miles and a water area of 0.419 square miles. Located at 41.47° N. Lat; 73.55° W. Long. Elevation is 512 feet.

Population: 3,877; Growth (since 2000): 0.6%; Density: 1,009.3 persons per square mile; Race: 88.9% White, 5.0% Black/African American, 1.4% Asian, 0.0% American Indian/Alaska Native, 0.0% Native Hawaiian/Other Pacific Islander, 4.4% Two or more races, 16.1% Hispanic of any race; Average household size: 2.69; Median age: 44.5; Age under 18: 20.2%; Age 65 and over: 12.7%; Males per 100 females: 102.4; Marriage status: 33.1% never married, 51.7% now married, 0.9% separated, 5.8% widowed, 9.4% divorced; Foreign born: 9.3%; Speak English only: 80.2%; With disability: 19.3%; Veterans: 6.8%; Ancestry: 27.8% Irish, 21.4% Italian, 14.6% German, 9.2% English, 5.2% American

Employment: 12.2% management, business, and financial, 3.5% computer, engineering, and science, 10.3% education, legal, community service, arts, and media, 6.9% healthcare practitioners, 21.9% service, 24.7% sales and office, 9.4% natural resources, construction, and maintenance, 11.1% production, transportation, and material moving

Income: Per capita: $33,700; Median household: $82,083; Average household: $89,608; Households with income of $100,000 or more: 40.2%; Poverty rate: 2.9%

Educational Attainment: High school diploma or higher: 88.3%; Bachelor's degree or higher: 24.3%; Graduate/professional degree or higher: 8.5%

Housing: Homeownership rate: 86.1%; Median home value: $226,300; Median year structure built: 1952; Homeowner vacancy rate: 0.0%; Median

selected monthly owner costs: $1,900 with a mortgage, $669 without a mortgage; Median gross rent: $1,400 per month; Rental vacancy rate: 0.0%
Health Insurance: 94.1% have insurance; 82.5% have private insurance; 25.1% have public insurance; 5.9% do not have insurance; 1.2% of children under 18 do not have insurance
Transportation: Commute: 94.4% car, 4.3% public transportation, 0.4% walk, 0.3% work from home; Mean travel time to work: 41.1 minutes

PUTNAM VALLEY (town). Covers a land area of 41.175 square miles and a water area of 1.605 square miles. Located at 41.40° N. Lat; 73.84° W. Long. Elevation is 161 feet.
Population: 11,738; Growth (since 2000): 9.8%; Density: 285.1 persons per square mile; Race: 94.7% White, 1.4% Black/African American, 1.4% Asian, 0.5% American Indian/Alaska Native, 0.0% Native Hawaiian/Other Pacific Islander, 1.5% Two or more races, 9.6% Hispanic of any race; Average household size: 2.83; Median age: 45.1; Age under 18: 21.5%; Age 65 and over: 16.9%; Males per 100 females: 101.1; Marriage status: 24.4% never married, 62.4% now married, 1.6% separated, 4.6% widowed, 8.6% divorced; Foreign born: 12.5%; Speak English only: 76.9%; With disability: 8.5%; Veterans: 6.4%; Ancestry: 31.7% Italian, 22.4% Irish, 14.2% German, 7.0% English, 5.4% American
Employment: 15.6% management, business, and financial, 9.5% computer, engineering, and science, 14.6% education, legal, community service, arts, and media, 7.1% healthcare practitioners, 16.3% service, 22.7% sales and office, 10.4% natural resources, construction, and maintenance, 3.7% production, transportation, and material moving
Income: Per capita: $43,102; Median household: $101,277; Average household: $119,050; Households with income of $100,000 or more: 50.7%; Poverty rate: 6.1%
Educational Attainment: High school diploma or higher: 89.9%; Bachelor's degree or higher: 40.4%; Graduate/professional degree or higher: 14.3%

School District(s)
Putnam Valley Central SD (KG-12)
    2014-15 Enrollment: 1,741 . . . . (845) 528-8143
Housing: Homeownership rate: 88.6%; Median home value: $376,800; Median year structure built: 1961; Homeowner vacancy rate: 2.7%; Median selected monthly owner costs: $2,880 with a mortgage, $1,169 without a mortgage; Median gross rent: $1,155 per month; Rental vacancy rate: 0.0%
Health Insurance: 95.8% have insurance; 85.7% have private insurance; 23.6% have public insurance; 4.2% do not have insurance; 0.5% of children under 18 do not have insurance
Transportation: Commute: 84.6% car, 10.3% public transportation, 0.4% walk, 3.9% work from home; Mean travel time to work: 44.5 minutes
Additional Information Contacts
Town of Putnam Valley . . . . (845) 526-2121
  http://www.putnamvalley.com

SOUTHEAST (town). Covers a land area of 31.734 square miles and a water area of 3.245 square miles. Located at 41.41° N. Lat; 73.60° W. Long.
History: The Tilly Foster Iron Mine (established 1790), located on a 128-acre farm owned by Tilly Foster, was the largest of a number of mines in the area. The town was named after this mine. For a time high-grade iron ore was shipped from here to Pennsylvania. Became open-pit mine in 1889, closed in 1897 after an avalanche.
Population: 18,234; Growth (since 2000): 5.3%; Density: 574.6 persons per square mile; Race: 90.8% White, 1.9% Black/African American, 1.6% Asian, 0.5% American Indian/Alaska Native, 0.0% Native Hawaiian/Other Pacific Islander, 2.6% Two or more races, 16.2% Hispanic of any race; Average household size: 2.79; Median age: 41.1; Age under 18: 22.6%; Age 65 and over: 12.0%; Males per 100 females: 102.5; Marriage status: 30.1% never married, 56.9% now married, 1.6% separated, 4.6% widowed, 8.4% divorced; Foreign born: 15.2%; Speak English only: 80.6%; With disability: 8.0%; Veterans: 5.9%; Ancestry: 30.5% Italian, 26.2% Irish, 13.9% German, 5.3% English, 4.6% American
Employment: 14.2% management, business, and financial, 4.5% computer, engineering, and science, 15.6% education, legal, community service, arts, and media, 5.5% healthcare practitioners, 16.8% service, 28.0% sales and office, 10.9% natural resources, construction, and maintenance, 4.4% production, transportation, and material moving

Income: Per capita: $41,300; Median household: $91,786; Average household: $114,665; Households with income of $100,000 or more: 46.8%; Poverty rate: 6.5%
Educational Attainment: High school diploma or higher: 89.9%; Bachelor's degree or higher: 39.5%; Graduate/professional degree or higher: 17.1%
Housing: Homeownership rate: 74.7%; Median home value: $343,200; Median year structure built: 1977; Homeowner vacancy rate: 0.0%; Median selected monthly owner costs: $2,435 with a mortgage, $1,054 without a mortgage; Median gross rent: $1,279 per month; Rental vacancy rate: 5.6%
Health Insurance: 89.3% have insurance; 78.4% have private insurance; 21.3% have public insurance; 10.7% do not have insurance; 3.9% of children under 18 do not have insurance
Transportation: Commute: 85.3% car, 7.7% public transportation, 0.6% walk, 4.8% work from home; Mean travel time to work: 35.1 minutes
Additional Information Contacts
Town of Southeast . . . . (845) 279-4313
  http://www.townofsoutheast-ny.com/Home

Queens County and Borough
See New York City

Rensselaer County
Located in eastern New York; bounded on the west by the Hudson River, and on the east by Massachusetts and Vermont; includes part of the Taconic Mountains; drained by the Hoosic River. Covers a land area of 652.431 square miles, a water area of 12.962 square miles, and is located in the Eastern Time Zone at 42.71° N. Lat., 73.51° W. Long. The county was founded in 1791. County seat is Troy.

Rensselaer County is part of the Albany-Schenectady-Troy, NY Metropolitan Statistical Area. The entire metro area includes: Albany County, NY; Rensselaer County, NY; Saratoga County, NY; Schenectady County, NY; Schoharie County, NY

Weather Station: Grafton												Elevation: 1,560 feet
	Jan	Feb	Mar	Apr	May	Jun	Jul	Aug	Sep	Oct	Nov	Dec
High	28	32	41	54	66	74	78	76	68	57	45	33
Low	12	15	23	34	45	53	58	57	50	39	29	18
Precip	2.9	2.6	3.6	3.9	4.5	4.2	4.5	4.5	4.2	4.0	4.0	3.2
Snow	20.6	14.9	15.4	5.9	0.2	0.0	0.0	0.0	tr	1.3	7.2	17.8

High and Low temperatures in degrees Fahrenheit; Precipitation and Snow in inches

Weather Station: Troy Lock and Dam												Elevation: 23 feet
	Jan	Feb	Mar	Apr	May	Jun	Jul	Aug	Sep	Oct	Nov	Dec
High	32	35	44	59	70	79	84	82	74	62	49	37
Low	15	17	25	37	48	58	63	61	53	41	32	22
Precip	2.2	1.9	3.0	3.3	3.7	4.2	4.4	4.1	3.3	3.7	3.1	2.6
Snow	12.7	8.0	7.5	1.3	0.0	0.0	0.0	0.0	0.0	0.1	1.8	7.2

High and Low temperatures in degrees Fahrenheit; Precipitation and Snow in inches

Population: 159,900; Growth (since 2000): 4.8%; Density: 245.1 persons per square mile; Race: 87.3% White, 6.1% Black/African American, 2.3% Asian, 0.1% American Indian/Alaska Native, 0.0% Native Hawaiian/Other Pacific Islander, 3.5% two or more races, 4.3% Hispanic of any race; Average household size: 2.43; Median age: 39.8; Age under 18: 20.5%; Age 65 and over: 14.7%; Males per 100 females: 97.5; Marriage status: 36.3% never married, 48.2% now married, 2.2% separated, 6.1% widowed, 9.4% divorced; Foreign born: 4.7%; Speak English only: 93.1%; With disability: 12.5%; Veterans: 8.2%; Ancestry: 26.2% Irish, 17.4% German, 16.5% Italian, 10.5% English, 8.6% French
Religion: Six largest groups: 28.1% Catholicism, 3.4% Methodist/Pietist, 1.9% Presbyterian-Reformed, 1.5% Lutheran, 1.3% Baptist, 1.3% Non-denominational Protestant
Economy: Unemployment rate: 4.1%; Leading industries: 14.4 % construction; 14.0 % retail trade; 12.1 % health care and social assistance; Farms: 495 totaling 88,763 acres; Company size: 3 employ 1,000 or more persons, 3 employ 500 to 999 persons, 58 employ 100 to 499 persons, 2,898 employ less than 100 persons; Business ownership: 3,632 women-owned, 560 Black-owned, 256 Hispanic-owned, 197 Asian-owned, 99 American Indian/Alaska Native-owned
Employment: 14.5% management, business, and financial, 6.5% computer, engineering, and science, 11.9% education, legal, community

service, arts, and media, 6.1% healthcare practitioners, 16.7% service, 25.4% sales and office, 8.6% natural resources, construction, and maintenance, 10.3% production, transportation, and material moving
Income: Per capita: $30,803; Median household: $60,709; Average household: $75,645; Households with income of $100,000 or more: 26.1%; Poverty rate: 12.4%
Educational Attainment: High school diploma or higher: 90.8%; Bachelor's degree or higher: 28.6%; Graduate/professional degree or higher: 12.4%
Housing: Homeownership rate: 65.0%; Median home value: $179,100; Median year structure built: 1957; Homeowner vacancy rate: 1.5%; Median selected monthly owner costs: $1,579 with a mortgage, $624 without a mortgage; Median gross rent: $875 per month; Rental vacancy rate: 3.3%
Vital Statistics: Birth rate: 111.1 per 10,000 population; Death rate: 94.5 per 10,000 population; Age-adjusted cancer mortality rate: 173.0 deaths per 100,000 population
Health Insurance: 94.3% have insurance; 76.4% have private insurance; 31.9% have public insurance; 5.7% do not have insurance; 1.4% of children under 18 do not have insurance
Health Care: Physicians: 18.0 per 10,000 population; Dentists: 4.4 per 10,000 population; Hospital beds: 25.7 per 10,000 population; Hospital admissions: 761.9 per 10,000 population
Transportation: Commute: 89.5% car, 2.2% public transportation, 4.2% walk, 3.2% work from home; Mean travel time to work: 23.1 minutes
2016 Presidential Election: 47.7% Trump, 46.2% Clinton, 4.2% Johnson, 1.9% Stein
National and State Parks: Crailo State Historic Site; State Forest Rensselaer Number 3
Additional Information Contacts
Rensselaer Government . . . . (518) 270-4080
    http://www.rensco.com

Rensselaer County Communities

AVERILL PARK (CDP).
Covers a land area of 2.933 square miles and a water area of 0.118 square miles. Located at 42.64° N. Lat; 73.55° W. Long. Elevation is 784 feet.
Population: 1,413; Growth (since 2000): -6.9%; Density: 481.8 persons per square mile; Race: 100.0% White, 0.0% Black/African American, 0.0% Asian, 0.0% American Indian/Alaska Native, 0.0% Native Hawaiian/Other Pacific Islander, 0.0% Two or more races, 2.7% Hispanic of any race; Average household size: 2.53; Median age: 40.2; Age under 18: 26.9%; Age 65 and over: 9.3%; Males per 100 females: 99.9; Marriage status: 16.3% never married, 62.5% now married, 6.1% separated, 8.0% widowed, 13.3% divorced; Foreign born: 0.0%; Speak English only: 95.9%; With disability: 8.3%; Veterans: 5.9%; Ancestry: 21.6% Irish, 15.9% English, 15.2% German, 13.2% Italian, 12.7% Polish
Employment: 13.4% management, business, and financial, 12.6% computer, engineering, and science, 11.8% education, legal, community service, arts, and media, 2.7% healthcare practitioners, 13.0% service, 24.2% sales and office, 13.6% natural resources, construction, and maintenance, 8.8% production, transportation, and material moving
Income: Per capita: $32,904; Median household: $73,261; Average household: $81,499; Households with income of $100,000 or more: 33.5%; Poverty rate: 1.6%
Educational Attainment: High school diploma or higher: 97.8%; Bachelor's degree or higher: 27.2%; Graduate/professional degree or higher: 9.1%

School District(s)
Averill Park Central SD (KG-12)
    2014-15 Enrollment: 2,964 . . . . (518) 674-7055
Housing: Homeownership rate: 79.7%; Median home value: $189,600; Median year structure built: 1957; Homeowner vacancy rate: 3.5%; Median selected monthly owner costs: n/a with a mortgage, n/a without a mortgage; Median gross rent: $636 per month; Rental vacancy rate: 0.0%
Health Insurance: 100.0% have insurance; 98.1% have private insurance; 12.8% have public insurance; 0.0% do not have insurance; 0.0% of children under 18 do not have insurance
Newspapers: The Advertiser (weekly circulation 48,000)
Transportation: Commute: 100.0% car, 0.0% public transportation, 0.0% walk, 0.0% work from home; Mean travel time to work: 28.9 minutes

BERLIN (town).
Covers a land area of 59.603 square miles and a water area of 0.319 square miles. Located at 42.66° N. Lat; 73.38° W. Long. Elevation is 840 feet.
Population: 1,727; Growth (since 2000): -9.2%; Density: 29.0 persons per square mile; Race: 99.2% White, 0.0% Black/African American, 0.0% Asian, 0.0% American Indian/Alaska Native, 0.0% Native Hawaiian/Other Pacific Islander, 0.8% Two or more races, 0.2% Hispanic of any race; Average household size: 2.43; Median age: 44.9; Age under 18: 19.2%; Age 65 and over: 21.0%; Males per 100 females: 96.9; Marriage status: 22.4% never married, 60.9% now married, 2.0% separated, 11.3% widowed, 5.5% divorced; Foreign born: 0.2%; Speak English only: 98.7%; With disability: 18.1%; Veterans: 10.0%; Ancestry: 37.4% German, 23.1% Irish, 17.3% English, 11.8% Italian, 8.6% Polish
Employment: 10.0% management, business, and financial, 4.0% computer, engineering, and science, 11.4% education, legal, community service, arts, and media, 5.1% healthcare practitioners, 13.2% service, 22.9% sales and office, 21.2% natural resources, construction, and maintenance, 12.1% production, transportation, and material moving
Income: Per capita: $27,501; Median household: $58,167; Average household: $65,417; Households with income of $100,000 or more: 15.0%; Poverty rate: 3.3%
Educational Attainment: High school diploma or higher: 89.4%; Bachelor's degree or higher: 22.5%; Graduate/professional degree or higher: 12.3%

School District(s)
Berlin Central SD (PK-12)
    2014-15 Enrollment: 736 . . . . (518) 658-2690
Housing: Homeownership rate: 85.5%; Median home value: $130,700; Median year structure built: 1961; Homeowner vacancy rate: 1.1%; Median selected monthly owner costs: $1,262 with a mortgage, $510 without a mortgage; Median gross rent: $1,125 per month; Rental vacancy rate: 8.8%
Health Insurance: 91.0% have insurance; 80.0% have private insurance; 31.2% have public insurance; 9.0% do not have insurance; 10.5% of children under 18 do not have insurance
Transportation: Commute: 93.5% car, 0.5% public transportation, 3.3% walk, 2.7% work from home; Mean travel time to work: 33.7 minutes

BRAINARD (unincorporated postal area)
ZCTA: 12024
    Covers a land area of 1.042 square miles and a water area of 0 square miles. Located at 42.48° N. Lat; 73.53° W. Long. Elevation is 679 feet.
Population: 92; Growth (since 2000): n/a; Density: 88.3 persons per square mile; Race: 100.0% White, 0.0% Black/African American, 0.0% Asian, 0.0% American Indian/Alaska Native, 0.0% Native Hawaiian/Other Pacific Islander, 0.0% Two or more races, 0.0% Hispanic of any race; Average household size: 3.54; Median age: 42.3; Age under 18: 45.7%; Age 65 and over: 0.0%; Males per 100 females: 93.8; Marriage status: 0.0% never married, 74.0% now married, 26.0% separated, 0.0% widowed, 26.0% divorced; Foreign born: 0.0%; Speak English only: 100.0%; With disability: 12.0%; Veterans: 22.0%; Ancestry: 45.7% American, 28.3% Irish, 26.1% Polish, 14.1% Italian
Employment: 0.0% management, business, and financial, 0.0% computer, engineering, and science, 0.0% education, legal, community service, arts, and media, 0.0% healthcare practitioners, 0.0% service, 50.0% sales and office, 50.0% natural resources, construction, and maintenance, 0.0% production, transportation, and material moving
Income: Per capita: $13,707; Median household: n/a; Average household: n/a; Households with income of $100,000 or more: n/a; Poverty rate: n/a
Educational Attainment: High school diploma or higher: 100.0%; Bachelor's degree or higher: n/a; Graduate/professional degree or higher: n/a
Housing: Homeownership rate: 100.0%; Median home value: n/a; Median year structure built: n/a; Homeowner vacancy rate: 0.0%; Median selected monthly owner costs: $0 with a mortgage, $0 without a mortgage; Median gross rent: n/a per month; Rental vacancy rate: 0.0%
Health Insurance: 85.9% have insurance; 28.3% have private insurance; 71.7% have public insurance; 14.1% do not have insurance; 0.0% of children under 18 do not have insurance
Transportation: Commute: 100.0% car, 0.0% public transportation, 0.0% walk, 0.0% work from home; Mean travel time to work: 0.0 minutes

BRUNSWICK (town). Covers a land area of 44.347 square miles and a water area of 0.280 square miles. Located at 42.75° N. Lat; 73.58° W. Long. Elevation is 518 feet.

Population: 12,244; Growth (since 2000): 5.0%; Density: 276.1 persons per square mile; Race: 93.4% White, 1.2% Black/African American, 3.4% Asian, 0.0% American Indian/Alaska Native, 0.0% Native Hawaiian/Other Pacific Islander, 1.7% Two or more races, 0.9% Hispanic of any race; Average household size: 2.36; Median age: 48.8; Age under 18: 15.5%; Age 65 and over: 18.2%; Males per 100 females: 97.5; Marriage status: 23.9% never married, 59.5% now married, 1.5% separated, 5.4% widowed, 11.3% divorced; Foreign born: 4.5%; Speak English only: 94.9%; With disability: 9.3%; Veterans: 8.1%; Ancestry: 31.3% Irish, 19.4% Italian, 18.9% German, 11.5% English, 10.0% French

Employment: 12.8% management, business, and financial, 7.8% computer, engineering, and science, 12.3% education, legal, community service, arts, and media, 6.3% healthcare practitioners, 11.8% service, 29.8% sales and office, 9.4% natural resources, construction, and maintenance, 9.8% production, transportation, and material moving

Income: Per capita: $42,968; Median household: $86,469; Average household: $100,139; Households with income of $100,000 or more: 39.8%; Poverty rate: 2.1%

Educational Attainment: High school diploma or higher: 94.6%; Bachelor's degree or higher: 35.8%; Graduate/professional degree or higher: 17.0%

Housing: Homeownership rate: 80.3%; Median home value: $197,800; Median year structure built: 1964; Homeowner vacancy rate: 2.7%; Median selected monthly owner costs: $1,652 with a mortgage, $709 without a mortgage; Median gross rent: $989 per month; Rental vacancy rate: 9.7%

Health Insurance: 95.1% have insurance; 87.3% have private insurance; 26.2% have public insurance; 4.9% do not have insurance; 0.0% of children under 18 do not have insurance

Transportation: Commute: 94.1% car, 0.5% public transportation, 1.8% walk, 3.4% work from home; Mean travel time to work: 22.1 minutes

Additional Information Contacts

Town of Brunswick . . . . (518) 279-3461
    http://www.townofbrunswick.org

BUSKIRK (unincorporated postal area)

ZCTA: 12028

Covers a land area of 22.573 square miles and a water area of 0.274 square miles. Located at 42.93° N. Lat; 73.44° W. Long. Elevation is 364 feet.

Population: 951; Growth (since 2000): -13.5%; Density: 42.1 persons per square mile; Race: 92.8% White, 0.0% Black/African American, 1.5% Asian, 0.0% American Indian/Alaska Native, 0.0% Native Hawaiian/Other Pacific Islander, 5.7% Two or more races, 2.6% Hispanic of any race; Average household size: 2.78; Median age: 40.4; Age under 18: 22.3%; Age 65 and over: 11.5%; Males per 100 females: 102.8; Marriage status: 18.8% never married, 70.1% now married, 0.8% separated, 4.7% widowed, 6.5% divorced; Foreign born: 7.4%; Speak English only: 91.7%; With disability: 7.6%; Veterans: 11.5%; Ancestry: 25.2% German, 19.1% Irish, 14.9% Polish, 8.7% Italian, 6.8% English

Employment: 18.1% management, business, and financial, 0.0% computer, engineering, and science, 12.7% education, legal, community service, arts, and media, 11.3% healthcare practitioners, 13.2% service, 20.6% sales and office, 7.6% natural resources, construction, and maintenance, 16.4% production, transportation, and material moving

Income: Per capita: $37,102; Median household: $81,923; Average household: $100,295; Households with income of $100,000 or more: 44.7%; Poverty rate: 3.6%

Educational Attainment: High school diploma or higher: 95.3%; Bachelor's degree or higher: 27.3%; Graduate/professional degree or higher: 11.4%

Housing: Homeownership rate: 92.7%; Median home value: $195,100; Median year structure built: 1965; Homeowner vacancy rate: 0.0%; Median selected monthly owner costs: $1,490 with a mortgage, $715 without a mortgage; Median gross rent: n/a per month; Rental vacancy rate: 0.0%

Health Insurance: 99.1% have insurance; 88.9% have private insurance; 17.4% have public insurance; 0.9% do not have insurance; 0.0% of children under 18 do not have insurance

Transportation: Commute: 94.7% car, 1.7% public transportation, 0.0% walk, 3.6% work from home; Mean travel time to work: 35.5 minutes

CASTLETON-ON-HUDSON (village). Covers a land area of 0.714 square miles and a water area of <.001 square miles. Located at 42.53° N. Lat; 73.75° W. Long. Elevation is 151 feet.

History: Settled by the Dutch c.1630; incorporated 1827.

Population: 1,322; Growth (since 2000): -18.3%; Density: 1,851.4 persons per square mile; Race: 95.3% White, 1.6% Black/African American, 0.4% Asian, 0.2% American Indian/Alaska Native, 0.0% Native Hawaiian/Other Pacific Islander, 2.5% Two or more races, 1.9% Hispanic of any race; Average household size: 2.43; Median age: 44.6; Age under 18: 21.5%; Age 65 and over: 16.9%; Males per 100 females: 88.4; Marriage status: 22.5% never married, 59.4% now married, 3.1% separated, 8.7% widowed, 9.4% divorced; Foreign born: 1.4%; Speak English only: 97.9%; With disability: 11.6%; Veterans: 12.6%; Ancestry: 26.0% German, 21.9% Irish, 17.6% Italian, 12.4% English, 7.9% Dutch

Employment: 18.0% management, business, and financial, 7.2% computer, engineering, and science, 8.9% education, legal, community service, arts, and media, 8.3% healthcare practitioners, 13.5% service, 25.3% sales and office, 7.1% natural resources, construction, and maintenance, 11.7% production, transportation, and material moving

Income: Per capita: $32,925; Median household: $68,375; Average household: $81,334; Households with income of $100,000 or more: 25.2%; Poverty rate: 4.3%

Educational Attainment: High school diploma or higher: 91.4%; Bachelor's degree or higher: 34.1%; Graduate/professional degree or higher: 15.0%

School District(s)

East Greenbush Central SD (KG-12)
    2014-15 Enrollment: 4,106 . . . . (518) 207-2531
Questar III Boces (R-C-G) (09-12)
    2014-15 Enrollment: n/a . . . . (518) 479-6882
Schodack Central SD (KG-12)
    2014-15 Enrollment: 908 . . . . (518) 732-2297

Housing: Homeownership rate: 79.0%; Median home value: $163,200; Median year structure built: Before 1940; Homeowner vacancy rate: 2.7%; Median selected monthly owner costs: $1,625 with a mortgage, $663 without a mortgage; Median gross rent: $819 per month; Rental vacancy rate: 0.0%

Health Insurance: 93.7% have insurance; 79.2% have private insurance; 26.6% have public insurance; 6.3% do not have insurance; 2.8% of children under 18 do not have insurance

Transportation: Commute: 96.4% car, 0.3% public transportation, 0.8% walk, 2.5% work from home; Mean travel time to work: 28.0 minutes

CHERRY PLAIN (unincorporated postal area)

ZCTA: 12040

Covers a land area of 1.307 square miles and a water area of 0 square miles. Located at 42.64° N. Lat; 73.35° W. Long..

Population: 146; Growth (since 2000): n/a; Density: 111.7 persons per square mile; Race: 100.0% White, 0.0% Black/African American, 0.0% Asian, 0.0% American Indian/Alaska Native, 0.0% Native Hawaiian/Other Pacific Islander, 0.0% Two or more races, 2.7% Hispanic of any race; Average household size: 2.75; Median age: 31.1; Age under 18: 20.5%; Age 65 and over: 12.3%; Males per 100 females: 105.5; Marriage status: 9.5% never married, 75.0% now married, 0.0% separated, 5.2% widowed, 10.3% divorced; Foreign born: 0.0%; Speak English only: 100.0%; With disability: 29.5%; Veterans: 6.0%; Ancestry: 50.0% Italian, 43.2% Irish, 15.8% German, 8.2% French, 7.5% English

Employment: 7.7% management, business, and financial, 0.0% computer, engineering, and science, 15.4% education, legal, community service, arts, and media, 0.0% healthcare practitioners, 14.3% service, 9.9% sales and office, 38.5% natural resources, construction, and maintenance, 14.3% production, transportation, and material moving

Income: Per capita: $18,333; Median household: $39,063; Average household: $48,940; Households with income of $100,000 or more: 7.5%; Poverty rate: n/a

Educational Attainment: High school diploma or higher: 91.9%; Bachelor's degree or higher: 9.5%; Graduate/professional degree or higher: 4.1%

School District(s)

Berlin Central SD (PK-12)
    2014-15 Enrollment: 736 . . . . (518) 658-2690

Housing: Homeownership rate: 100.0%; Median home value: $93,700; Median year structure built: Before 1940; Homeowner vacancy rate: 0.0%; Median selected monthly owner costs: n/a with a mortgage, n/a

without a mortgage; Median gross rent: n/a per month; Rental vacancy rate: 0.0%
Health Insurance: 58.9% have insurance; 50.0% have private insurance; 17.1% have public insurance; 41.1% do not have insurance; 100.0% of children under 18 do not have insurance
Transportation: Commute: 100.0% car, 0.0% public transportation, 0.0% walk, 0.0% work from home; Mean travel time to work: 22.5 minutes

CROPSEYVILLE (unincorporated postal area)
ZCTA: 12052

Covers a land area of 30.302 square miles and a water area of 1.047 square miles. Located at 42.75° N. Lat; 73.48° W. Long. Elevation is 558 feet.
Population: 1,524; Growth (since 2000): 52.4%; Density: 50.3 persons per square mile; Race: 92.7% White, 2.8% Black/African American, 0.8% Asian, 0.0% American Indian/Alaska Native, 0.0% Native Hawaiian/Other Pacific Islander, 3.8% Two or more races, 0.1% Hispanic of any race; Average household size: 2.48; Median age: 44.4; Age under 18: 18.0%; Age 65 and over: 12.6%; Males per 100 females: 105.8; Marriage status: 31.7% never married, 53.3% now married, 1.8% separated, 3.5% widowed, 11.5% divorced; Foreign born: 3.1%; Speak English only: 98.2%; With disability: 10.0%; Veterans: 7.0%; Ancestry: 33.4% Irish, 18.8% German, 15.4% French, 12.8% Italian, 12.2% English
Employment: 12.5% management, business, and financial, 9.3% computer, engineering, and science, 11.9% education, legal, community service, arts, and media, 5.5% healthcare practitioners, 18.9% service, 25.4% sales and office, 9.6% natural resources, construction, and maintenance, 6.9% production, transportation, and material moving
Income: Per capita: $32,880; Median household: $66,012; Average household: $80,915; Households with income of $100,000 or more: 31.5%; Poverty rate: 9.9%
Educational Attainment: High school diploma or higher: 95.3%; Bachelor's degree or higher: 30.1%; Graduate/professional degree or higher: 12.4%
Housing: Homeownership rate: 79.3%; Median home value: $174,700; Median year structure built: 1967; Homeowner vacancy rate: 0.0%; Median selected monthly owner costs: $1,455 with a mortgage, $596 without a mortgage; Median gross rent: $679 per month; Rental vacancy rate: 0.0%
Health Insurance: 90.9% have insurance; 79.5% have private insurance; 22.0% have public insurance; 9.1% do not have insurance; 0.0% of children under 18 do not have insurance
Transportation: Commute: 96.1% car, 0.0% public transportation, 0.0% walk, 3.7% work from home; Mean travel time to work: 35.6 minutes

EAGLE BRIDGE (unincorporated postal area)
ZCTA: 12057

Covers a land area of 35.163 square miles and a water area of 0.012 square miles. Located at 42.97° N. Lat; 73.35° W. Long. Elevation is 404 feet.
Population: 2,056; Growth (since 2000): 20.0%; Density: 58.5 persons per square mile; Race: 97.3% White, 0.0% Black/African American, 2.7% Asian, 0.0% American Indian/Alaska Native, 0.0% Native Hawaiian/Other Pacific Islander, 0.0% Two or more races, 0.0% Hispanic of any race; Average household size: 2.39; Median age: 43.6; Age under 18: 25.0%; Age 65 and over: 18.7%; Males per 100 females: 99.5; Marriage status: 18.6% never married, 61.7% now married, 3.2% separated, 4.5% widowed, 15.3% divorced; Foreign born: 1.8%; Speak English only: 97.8%; With disability: 14.7%; Veterans: 12.8%; Ancestry: 22.8% American, 22.1% Irish, 14.5% English, 8.2% German, 7.1% French
Employment: 15.5% management, business, and financial, 0.8% computer, engineering, and science, 7.6% education, legal, community service, arts, and media, 4.6% healthcare practitioners, 15.5% service, 18.3% sales and office, 13.6% natural resources, construction, and maintenance, 24.1% production, transportation, and material moving
Income: Per capita: $24,640; Median household: $46,797; Average household: $59,070; Households with income of $100,000 or more: 15.9%; Poverty rate: 6.5%
Educational Attainment: High school diploma or higher: 93.2%; Bachelor's degree or higher: 15.4%; Graduate/professional degree or higher: 5.8%

Housing: Homeownership rate: 87.9%; Median home value: $173,100; Median year structure built: 1974; Homeowner vacancy rate: 1.6%; Median selected monthly owner costs: $1,185 with a mortgage, $771 without a mortgage; Median gross rent: $723 per month; Rental vacancy rate: 0.0%
Health Insurance: 98.1% have insurance; 79.7% have private insurance; 35.3% have public insurance; 1.9% do not have insurance; 0.0% of children under 18 do not have insurance
Transportation: Commute: 82.5% car, 1.7% public transportation, 8.8% walk, 7.0% work from home; Mean travel time to work: 25.6 minutes

EAST GREENBUSH (CDP).
Covers a land area of 2.664 square miles and a water area of 0.006 square miles. Located at 42.59° N. Lat; 73.70° W. Long. Elevation is 341 feet.
Population: 4,752; Growth (since 2000): 16.3%; Density: 1,783.7 persons per square mile; Race: 88.2% White, 2.3% Black/African American, 2.8% Asian, 0.0% American Indian/Alaska Native, 0.0% Native Hawaiian/Other Pacific Islander, 6.1% Two or more races, 6.2% Hispanic of any race; Average household size: 2.56; Median age: 42.3; Age under 18: 23.7%; Age 65 and over: 13.4%; Males per 100 females: 95.3; Marriage status: 29.4% never married, 59.6% now married, 0.9% separated, 4.1% widowed, 6.9% divorced; Foreign born: 5.2%; Speak English only: 92.4%; With disability: 9.8%; Veterans: 12.6%; Ancestry: 29.7% Irish, 17.5% German, 15.6% Italian, 14.2% English, 7.9% Polish
Employment: 21.4% management, business, and financial, 10.8% computer, engineering, and science, 18.6% education, legal, community service, arts, and media, 5.8% healthcare practitioners, 9.2% service, 21.8% sales and office, 7.6% natural resources, construction, and maintenance, 4.9% production, transportation, and material moving
Income: Per capita: $40,256; Median household: $88,583; Average household: $100,889; Households with income of $100,000 or more: 41.7%; Poverty rate: 2.7%
Educational Attainment: High school diploma or higher: 97.0%; Bachelor's degree or higher: 49.1%; Graduate/professional degree or higher: 25.4%

School District(s)
East Greenbush Central SD (KG-12)
   2014-15 Enrollment: 4,106 . . . . (518) 207-2531
Housing: Homeownership rate: 63.9%; Median home value: $250,700; Median year structure built: 1978; Homeowner vacancy rate: 0.0%; Median selected monthly owner costs: $1,870 with a mortgage, $742 without a mortgage; Median gross rent: $1,041 per month; Rental vacancy rate: 0.0%
Health Insurance: 98.9% have insurance; 89.9% have private insurance; 19.6% have public insurance; 1.1% do not have insurance; 0.0% of children under 18 do not have insurance
Transportation: Commute: 95.9% car, 0.8% public transportation, 0.1% walk, 2.0% work from home; Mean travel time to work: 18.9 minutes

EAST GREENBUSH (town).
Covers a land area of 24.020 square miles and a water area of 0.274 square miles. Located at 42.61° N. Lat; 73.70° W. Long. Elevation is 341 feet.
Population: 16,463; Growth (since 2000): 5.8%; Density: 685.4 persons per square mile; Race: 91.6% White, 1.8% Black/African American, 3.7% Asian, 0.1% American Indian/Alaska Native, 0.0% Native Hawaiian/Other Pacific Islander, 2.2% Two or more races, 4.2% Hispanic of any race; Average household size: 2.45; Median age: 44.2; Age under 18: 21.8%; Age 65 and over: 15.4%; Males per 100 females: 91.2; Marriage status: 27.6% never married, 57.5% now married, 2.0% separated, 6.0% widowed, 8.9% divorced; Foreign born: 5.2%; Speak English only: 92.7%; With disability: 9.3%; Veterans: 11.1%; Ancestry: 30.3% Irish, 19.2% German, 18.8% Italian, 11.8% English, 8.8% Polish
Employment: 18.4% management, business, and financial, 7.7% computer, engineering, and science, 14.4% education, legal, community service, arts, and media, 6.1% healthcare practitioners, 11.9% service, 27.3% sales and office, 7.5% natural resources, construction, and maintenance, 6.7% production, transportation, and material moving
Income: Per capita: $37,848; Median household: $70,258; Average household: $92,046; Households with income of $100,000 or more: 33.5%; Poverty rate: 4.9%
Educational Attainment: High school diploma or higher: 96.0%; Bachelor's degree or higher: 39.6%; Graduate/professional degree or higher: 20.6%

School District(s)

East Greenbush Central SD (KG-12)

2014-15 Enrollment: 4,106 . . . . (518) 207-2531

Housing: Homeownership rate: 76.9%; Median home value: $199,800; Median year structure built: 1974; Homeowner vacancy rate: 2.0%; Median selected monthly owner costs: $1,721 with a mortgage, $642 without a mortgage; Median gross rent: $1,060 per month; Rental vacancy rate: 1.0%

Health Insurance: 96.9% have insurance; 88.7% have private insurance; 22.7% have public insurance; 3.1% do not have insurance; 0.4% of children under 18 do not have insurance

Safety: Violent crime rate: 11.6 per 10,000 population; Property crime rate: 225.9 per 10,000 population

Transportation: Commute: 93.7% car, 1.4% public transportation, 1.4% walk, 2.8% work from home; Mean travel time to work: 19.4 minutes

Additional Information Contacts

Town of East Greenbush. . . . . (518) 477-4775

http://eastgreenbush.org

EAST NASSAU (village). Covers a land area of 4.863 square miles and a water area of 0.009 square miles. Located at 42.54° N. Lat; 73.50° W. Long. Elevation is 571 feet.

Population: 624; Growth (since 2000): 9.3%; Density: 128.3 persons per square mile; Race: 90.2% White, 1.6% Black/African American, 0.8% Asian, 0.8% American Indian/Alaska Native, 0.0% Native Hawaiian/Other Pacific Islander, 5.3% Two or more races, 6.3% Hispanic of any race; Average household size: 2.58; Median age: 40.2; Age under 18: 27.2%; Age 65 and over: 15.1%; Males per 100 females: 105.2; Marriage status: 26.0% never married, 53.9% now married, 2.8% separated, 4.9% widowed, 15.2% divorced; Foreign born: 2.6%; Speak English only: 95.3%; With disability: 9.3%; Veterans: 11.7%; Ancestry: 22.9% German, 22.0% Irish, 12.8% American, 11.4% Italian, 10.4% English

Employment: 18.8% management, business, and financial, 6.6% computer, engineering, and science, 9.6% education, legal, community service, arts, and media, 8.6% healthcare practitioners, 18.2% service, 19.1% sales and office, 8.9% natural resources, construction, and maintenance, 10.2% production, transportation, and material moving

Income: Per capita: $28,531; Median household: $68,438; Average household: $71,308; Households with income of $100,000 or more: 20.3%; Poverty rate: 4.4%

Educational Attainment: High school diploma or higher: 97.0%; Bachelor's degree or higher: 31.8%; Graduate/professional degree or higher: 11.0%

Housing: Homeownership rate: 76.4%; Median home value: $184,500; Median year structure built: 1948; Homeowner vacancy rate: 6.6%; Median selected monthly owner costs: $1,563 with a mortgage, $695 without a mortgage; Median gross rent: $997 per month; Rental vacancy rate: 9.5%

Health Insurance: 93.8% have insurance; 77.7% have private insurance; 31.7% have public insurance; 6.3% do not have insurance; 0.0% of children under 18 do not have insurance

Transportation: Commute: 87.4% car, 0.3% public transportation, 2.7% walk, 7.6% work from home; Mean travel time to work: 33.5 minutes

EAST SCHODACK (unincorporated postal area)

ZCTA: 12063

Covers a land area of 1.425 square miles and a water area of 0.004 square miles. Located at 42.57° N. Lat; 73.64° W. Long. Elevation is 456 feet.

Population: 334; Growth (since 2000): 74.0%; Density: 234.4 persons per square mile; Race: 97.3% White, 0.0% Black/African American, 2.7% Asian, 0.0% American Indian/Alaska Native, 0.0% Native Hawaiian/Other Pacific Islander, 0.0% Two or more races, 0.0% Hispanic of any race; Average household size: 2.78; Median age: 49.1; Age under 18: 9.6%; Age 65 and over: 7.5%; Males per 100 females: 93.0; Marriage status: 24.8% never married, 62.1% now married, 6.0% separated, 0.0% widowed, 13.2% divorced; Foreign born: 2.7%; Speak English only: 97.3%; With disability: 13.2%; Veterans: 6.3%; Ancestry: 24.9% German, 23.4% English, 17.7% American, 5.4% Danish, 5.1% French Canadian

Employment: 24.1% management, business, and financial, 5.3% computer, engineering, and science, 7.3% education, legal, community service, arts, and media, 14.3% healthcare practitioners, 13.9% service, 20.4% sales and office, 14.7% natural resources, construction, and maintenance, 0.0% production, transportation, and material moving

Income: Per capita: $66,342; Median household: $155,658; Average household: $184,174; Households with income of $100,000 or more: 64.1%; Poverty rate: n/a

Educational Attainment: High school diploma or higher: 100.0%; Bachelor's degree or higher: 47.9%; Graduate/professional degree or higher: 18.6%

Housing: Homeownership rate: 100.0%; Median home value: $267,800; Median year structure built: 1959; Homeowner vacancy rate: 0.0%; Median selected monthly owner costs: $2,342 with a mortgage, $829 without a mortgage; Median gross rent: n/a per month; Rental vacancy rate: 0.0%

Health Insurance: 100.0% have insurance; 100.0% have private insurance; 12.0% have public insurance; 0.0% do not have insurance; 0.0% of children under 18 do not have insurance

Transportation: Commute: 100.0% car, 0.0% public transportation, 0.0% walk, 0.0% work from home; Mean travel time to work: 19.5 minutes

GRAFTON (town). Covers a land area of 44.721 square miles and a water area of 1.241 square miles. Located at 42.76° N. Lat; 73.46° W. Long. Elevation is 1,473 feet.

Population: 2,145; Growth (since 2000): 8.0%; Density: 48.0 persons per square mile; Race: 95.1% White, 2.0% Black/African American, 0.8% Asian, 0.0% American Indian/Alaska Native, 0.0% Native Hawaiian/Other Pacific Islander, 2.1% Two or more races, 2.1% Hispanic of any race; Average household size: 2.42; Median age: 47.2; Age under 18: 17.6%; Age 65 and over: 14.4%; Males per 100 females: 102.5; Marriage status: 29.5% never married, 57.6% now married, 0.9% separated, 3.7% widowed, 9.2% divorced; Foreign born: 1.5%; Speak English only: 97.6%; With disability: 8.0%; Veterans: 9.0%; Ancestry: 31.8% Irish, 20.8% German, 17.3% French, 12.3% English, 8.9% Italian

Employment: 17.0% management, business, and financial, 6.1% computer, engineering, and science, 12.1% education, legal, community service, arts, and media, 5.6% healthcare practitioners, 15.3% service, 20.6% sales and office, 10.6% natural resources, construction, and maintenance, 12.7% production, transportation, and material moving

Income: Per capita: $33,053; Median household: $65,592; Average household: $78,866; Households with income of $100,000 or more: 29.9%; Poverty rate: 8.2%

Educational Attainment: High school diploma or higher: 95.7%; Bachelor's degree or higher: 28.1%; Graduate/professional degree or higher: 11.4%

Housing: Homeownership rate: 83.8%; Median home value: $182,200; Median year structure built: 1971; Homeowner vacancy rate: 0.0%; Median selected monthly owner costs: $1,476 with a mortgage, $574 without a mortgage; Median gross rent: $848 per month; Rental vacancy rate: 0.0%

Health Insurance: 94.2% have insurance; 82.8% have private insurance; 24.5% have public insurance; 5.8% do not have insurance; 0.0% of children under 18 do not have insurance

Transportation: Commute: 94.8% car, 0.0% public transportation, 0.5% walk, 4.1% work from home; Mean travel time to work: 34.5 minutes

HAMPTON MANOR (CDP). Covers a land area of 0.624 square miles and a water area of 0.023 square miles. Located at 42.62° N. Lat; 73.72° W. Long. Elevation is 207 feet.

Population: 2,104; Growth (since 2000): -16.7%; Density: 3,371.2 persons per square mile; Race: 93.2% White, 0.5% Black/African American, 1.8% Asian, 0.0% American Indian/Alaska Native, 0.0% Native Hawaiian/Other Pacific Islander, 1.6% Two or more races, 3.6% Hispanic of any race; Average household size: 2.06; Median age: 44.9; Age under 18: 20.4%; Age 65 and over: 13.2%; Males per 100 females: 90.9; Marriage status: 30.8% never married, 53.4% now married, 2.4% separated, 9.4% widowed, 6.5% divorced; Foreign born: 3.4%; Speak English only: 93.4%; With disability: 9.2%; Veterans: 8.5%; Ancestry: 30.4% Irish, 25.6% German, 18.8% Italian, 10.6% French, 10.1% Polish

Employment: 12.3% management, business, and financial, 4.1% computer, engineering, and science, 11.1% education, legal, community service, arts, and media, 3.3% healthcare practitioners, 25.1% service, 27.6% sales and office, 5.9% natural resources, construction, and maintenance, 10.5% production, transportation, and material moving

Income: Per capita: $30,156; Median household: $62,745; Average household: $62,424; Households with income of $100,000 or more: 19.4%; Poverty rate: 13.5%

Educational Attainment: High school diploma or higher: 97.6%; Bachelor's degree or higher: 19.2%; Graduate/professional degree or higher: 13.4%
Housing: Homeownership rate: 85.9%; Median home value: $154,700; Median year structure built: 1948; Homeowner vacancy rate: 0.0%; Median selected monthly owner costs: $1,471 with a mortgage, $524 without a mortgage; Median gross rent: $782 per month; Rental vacancy rate: 0.0%
Health Insurance: 96.8% have insurance; 84.7% have private insurance; 26.0% have public insurance; 3.2% do not have insurance; 0.0% of children under 18 do not have insurance
Transportation: Commute: 91.8% car, 2.5% public transportation, 4.3% walk, 0.0% work from home; Mean travel time to work: 16.5 minutes

HOOSICK (town).
Covers a land area of 63.032 square miles and a water area of 0.113 square miles. Located at 42.88° N. Lat; 73.35° W. Long. Elevation is 482 feet.
History: Bennington Battlefield Park is Northeast. Hoosick Falls Historic District. Incorporated 1827.
Population: 6,858; Growth (since 2000): 1.5%; Density: 108.8 persons per square mile; Race: 97.7% White, 0.5% Black/African American, 0.0% Asian, 0.1% American Indian/Alaska Native, 0.0% Native Hawaiian/Other Pacific Islander, 1.6% Two or more races, 2.1% Hispanic of any race; Average household size: 2.60; Median age: 40.7; Age under 18: 22.9%; Age 65 and over: 15.4%; Males per 100 females: 90.7; Marriage status: 35.1% never married, 49.2% now married, 4.2% separated, 6.5% widowed, 9.3% divorced; Foreign born: 1.7%; Speak English only: 96.0%; With disability: 14.6%; Veterans: 9.2%; Ancestry: 25.0% Irish, 13.4% German, 10.5% French, 9.6% English, 9.6% Italian
Employment: 12.5% management, business, and financial, 2.8% computer, engineering, and science, 9.3% education, legal, community service, arts, and media, 10.4% healthcare practitioners, 18.5% service, 18.9% sales and office, 10.0% natural resources, construction, and maintenance, 17.5% production, transportation, and material moving
Income: Per capita: $24,356; Median household: $58,147; Average household: $61,936; Households with income of $100,000 or more: 19.6%; Poverty rate: 11.4%
Educational Attainment: High school diploma or higher: 91.0%; Bachelor's degree or higher: 19.0%; Graduate/professional degree or higher: 4.7%
Housing: Homeownership rate: 70.2%; Median home value: $151,500; Median year structure built: Before 1940; Homeowner vacancy rate: 0.0%; Median selected monthly owner costs: $1,394 with a mortgage, $634 without a mortgage; Median gross rent: $805 per month; Rental vacancy rate: 6.1%
Health Insurance: 93.0% have insurance; 69.4% have private insurance; 38.4% have public insurance; 7.0% do not have insurance; 1.1% of children under 18 do not have insurance
Transportation: Commute: 91.0% car, 0.8% public transportation, 2.3% walk, 3.1% work from home; Mean travel time to work: 26.0 minutes
Additional Information Contacts
Town of Hoosick . . . . (518) 686-4571
http://townofhoosick.org

HOOSICK FALLS (village).
Covers a land area of 1.598 square miles and a water area of 0 square miles. Located at 42.90° N. Lat; 73.35° W. Long. Elevation is 446 feet.
Population: 3,453; Growth (since 2000): 0.5%; Density: 2,160.8 persons per square mile; Race: 97.5% White, 1.0% Black/African American, 0.0% Asian, 0.0% American Indian/Alaska Native, 0.0% Native Hawaiian/Other Pacific Islander, 1.6% Two or more races, 1.6% Hispanic of any race; Average household size: 2.48; Median age: 41.4; Age under 18: 22.1%; Age 65 and over: 17.7%; Males per 100 females: 87.5; Marriage status: 37.1% never married, 44.0% now married, 6.1% separated, 8.0% widowed, 10.8% divorced; Foreign born: 1.7%; Speak English only: 96.0%; With disability: 16.7%; Veterans: 8.7%; Ancestry: 24.6% Irish, 13.2% American, 12.5% Italian, 10.7% Polish, 9.5% German
Employment: 8.4% management, business, and financial, 0.5% computer, engineering, and science, 11.6% education, legal, community service, arts, and media, 11.2% healthcare practitioners, 15.1% service, 24.0% sales and office, 7.7% natural resources, construction, and maintenance, 21.4% production, transportation, and material moving
Income: Per capita: $24,215; Median household: $52,045; Average household: $59,097; Households with income of $100,000 or more: 17.2%; Poverty rate: 10.9%

Educational Attainment: High school diploma or higher: 92.3%; Bachelor's degree or higher: 21.3%; Graduate/professional degree or higher: 6.1%
School District(s)
Hoosick Falls Central SD (PK-12)
  2014-15 Enrollment: 1,145 . . . . (518) 686-7012
Housing: Homeownership rate: 62.1%; Median home value: $118,700; Median year structure built: Before 1940; Homeowner vacancy rate: 0.0%; Median selected monthly owner costs: $1,304 with a mortgage, $617 without a mortgage; Median gross rent: $810 per month; Rental vacancy rate: 9.0%
Health Insurance: 92.8% have insurance; 63.8% have private insurance; 46.5% have public insurance; 7.2% do not have insurance; 0.0% of children under 18 do not have insurance
Safety: Violent crime rate: 26.4 per 10,000 population; Property crime rate: 102.6 per 10,000 population
Transportation: Commute: 92.8% car, 0.0% public transportation, 3.5% walk, 3.8% work from home; Mean travel time to work: 27.5 minutes

JOHNSONVILLE (unincorporated postal area)
ZCTA: 12094
Covers a land area of 28.234 square miles and a water area of 0.582 square miles. Located at 42.90° N. Lat; 73.49° W. Long. Elevation is 377 feet.
Population: 2,656; Growth (since 2000): 22.8%; Density: 94.1 persons per square mile; Race: 100.0% White, 0.0% Black/African American, 0.0% Asian, 0.0% American Indian/Alaska Native, 0.0% Native Hawaiian/Other Pacific Islander, 0.0% Two or more races, 0.3% Hispanic of any race; Average household size: 2.95; Median age: 35.1; Age under 18: 32.5%; Age 65 and over: 11.0%; Males per 100 females: 100.4; Marriage status: 16.2% never married, 73.6% now married, 5.6% separated, 6.3% widowed, 3.9% divorced; Foreign born: 0.4%; Speak English only: 99.4%; With disability: 6.4%; Veterans: 10.3%; Ancestry: 31.2% Irish, 25.9% German, 17.1% Italian, 12.8% French, 10.2% English
Employment: 18.1% management, business, and financial, 4.5% computer, engineering, and science, 3.6% education, legal, community service, arts, and media, 17.2% healthcare practitioners, 12.5% service, 15.4% sales and office, 15.5% natural resources, construction, and maintenance, 13.2% production, transportation, and material moving
Income: Per capita: $25,986; Median household: $74,625; Average household: $76,107; Households with income of $100,000 or more: 31.2%; Poverty rate: 6.0%
Educational Attainment: High school diploma or higher: 93.1%; Bachelor's degree or higher: 18.4%; Graduate/professional degree or higher: 9.6%
Housing: Homeownership rate: 92.2%; Median home value: $185,200; Median year structure built: 1978; Homeowner vacancy rate: 4.7%; Median selected monthly owner costs: $1,570 with a mortgage, $528 without a mortgage; Median gross rent: $713 per month; Rental vacancy rate: 0.0%
Health Insurance: 92.6% have insurance; 77.8% have private insurance; 24.8% have public insurance; 7.4% do not have insurance; 0.0% of children under 18 do not have insurance
Transportation: Commute: 97.5% car, 0.0% public transportation, 2.2% walk, 0.3% work from home; Mean travel time to work: 37.4 minutes

MELROSE (unincorporated postal area)
ZCTA: 12121
Covers a land area of 20.614 square miles and a water area of 2.959 square miles. Located at 42.84° N. Lat; 73.61° W. Long. Elevation is 390 feet.
Population: 1,781; Growth (since 2000): -1.4%; Density: 86.4 persons per square mile; Race: 97.1% White, 0.7% Black/African American, 0.8% Asian, 0.2% American Indian/Alaska Native, 0.0% Native Hawaiian/Other Pacific Islander, 1.2% Two or more races, 0.0% Hispanic of any race; Average household size: 2.46; Median age: 48.5; Age under 18: 15.9%; Age 65 and over: 20.6%; Males per 100 females: 97.3; Marriage status: 21.1% never married, 62.9% now married, 0.4% separated, 5.7% widowed, 10.3% divorced; Foreign born: 2.6%; Speak English only: 98.2%; With disability: 12.0%; Veterans: 9.9%; Ancestry: 27.7% Irish, 14.9% English, 12.4% Polish, 9.8% German, 9.5% Italian
Employment: 18.0% management, business, and financial, 7.7% computer, engineering, and science, 3.5% education, legal, community service, arts, and media, 4.4% healthcare practitioners, 9.3% service,

31.7% sales and office, 9.9% natural resources, construction, and maintenance, 15.5% production, transportation, and material moving
Income: Per capita: $30,830; Median household: $67,243; Average household: $73,432; Households with income of $100,000 or more: 21.6%; Poverty rate: 3.3%
Educational Attainment: High school diploma or higher: 98.0%; Bachelor's degree or higher: 18.7%; Graduate/professional degree or higher: 4.8%
Housing: Homeownership rate: 92.8%; Median home value: $203,300; Median year structure built: 1969; Homeowner vacancy rate: 0.0%; Median selected monthly owner costs: $1,626 with a mortgage, $657 without a mortgage; Median gross rent: n/a per month; Rental vacancy rate: 0.0%
Health Insurance: 97.6% have insurance; 85.4% have private insurance; 30.9% have public insurance; 2.4% do not have insurance; 0.0% of children under 18 do not have insurance
Transportation: Commute: 96.5% car, 0.0% public transportation, 0.0% walk, 2.5% work from home; Mean travel time to work: 27.6 minutes

NASSAU (town). Covers a land area of 44.444 square miles and a water area of 0.792 square miles. Located at 42.55° N. Lat; 73.54° W. Long. Elevation is 404 feet.
Population: 4,811; Growth (since 2000): -0.1%; Density: 108.2 persons per square mile; Race: 92.0% White, 2.4% Black/African American, 1.4% Asian, 0.1% American Indian/Alaska Native, 0.0% Native Hawaiian/Other Pacific Islander, 3.0% Two or more races, 4.0% Hispanic of any race; Average household size: 2.48; Median age: 42.6; Age under 18: 23.4%; Age 65 and over: 15.2%; Males per 100 females: 102.0; Marriage status: 24.3% never married, 56.3% now married, 2.4% separated, 6.6% widowed, 12.8% divorced; Foreign born: 2.7%; Speak English only: 97.4%; With disability: 15.2%; Veterans: 6.8%; Ancestry: 27.5% Irish, 24.3% German, 15.5% Italian, 11.2% American, 10.8% English
Employment: 14.9% management, business, and financial, 6.4% computer, engineering, and science, 8.7% education, legal, community service, arts, and media, 8.0% healthcare practitioners, 15.0% service, 21.8% sales and office, 11.1% natural resources, construction, and maintenance, 14.0% production, transportation, and material moving
Income: Per capita: $31,883; Median household: $62,860; Average household: $77,410; Households with income of $100,000 or more: 28.9%; Poverty rate: 5.7%
Educational Attainment: High school diploma or higher: 92.7%; Bachelor's degree or higher: 23.4%; Graduate/professional degree or higher: 11.3%

School District(s)
East Greenbush Central SD (KG-12)
    2014-15 Enrollment: 4,106 . . . . (518) 207-2531
Housing: Homeownership rate: 80.4%; Median home value: $173,500; Median year structure built: 1954; Homeowner vacancy rate: 3.0%; Median selected monthly owner costs: $1,624 with a mortgage, $651 without a mortgage; Median gross rent: $922 per month; Rental vacancy rate: 10.5%
Health Insurance: 96.3% have insurance; 81.6% have private insurance; 33.7% have public insurance; 3.7% do not have insurance; 0.9% of children under 18 do not have insurance
Transportation: Commute: 94.5% car, 1.0% public transportation, 0.6% walk, 3.0% work from home; Mean travel time to work: 28.6 minutes
Additional Information Contacts
Town of Nassau . . . . (518) 766-2343
    http://townofnassau.org/content

NASSAU (village). Covers a land area of 0.699 square miles and a water area of 0 square miles. Located at 42.51° N. Lat; 73.61° W. Long. Elevation is 404 feet.
Population: 1,077; Growth (since 2000): -7.2%; Density: 1,541.3 persons per square mile; Race: 94.2% White, 1.6% Black/African American, 0.0% Asian, 0.1% American Indian/Alaska Native, 0.0% Native Hawaiian/Other Pacific Islander, 3.3% Two or more races, 4.2% Hispanic of any race; Average household size: 2.34; Median age: 40.2; Age under 18: 22.0%; Age 65 and over: 17.7%; Males per 100 females: 94.0; Marriage status: 25.6% never married, 61.3% now married, 2.1% separated, 5.3% widowed, 7.8% divorced; Foreign born: 1.0%; Speak English only: 97.9%; With disability: 16.5%; Veterans: 6.8%; Ancestry: 37.0% Irish, 32.8% German, 14.0% English, 13.9% Italian, 7.8% American
Employment: 13.9% management, business, and financial, 4.1% computer, engineering, and science, 7.4% education, legal, community service, arts, and media, 8.5% healthcare practitioners, 13.5% service,

29.9% sales and office, 11.9% natural resources, construction, and maintenance, 10.8% production, transportation, and material moving
Income: Per capita: $29,855; Median household: $67,188; Average household: $69,348; Households with income of $100,000 or more: 20.1%; Poverty rate: 5.8%
Educational Attainment: High school diploma or higher: 95.8%; Bachelor's degree or higher: 24.5%; Graduate/professional degree or higher: 10.6%
School District(s)
East Greenbush Central SD (KG-12)
    2014-15 Enrollment: 4,106 . . . . (518) 207-2531
Housing: Homeownership rate: 69.6%; Median home value: $162,000; Median year structure built: 1942; Homeowner vacancy rate: 2.1%; Median selected monthly owner costs: $1,527 with a mortgage, $688 without a mortgage; Median gross rent: $704 per month; Rental vacancy rate: 12.1%
Health Insurance: 97.1% have insurance; 84.2% have private insurance; 33.0% have public insurance; 2.9% do not have insurance; 4.2% of children under 18 do not have insurance
Safety: Violent crime rate: 17.8 per 10,000 population; Property crime rate: 26.8 per 10,000 population
Transportation: Commute: 92.6% car, 1.5% public transportation, 1.3% walk, 4.6% work from home; Mean travel time to work: 27.9 minutes

NORTH GREENBUSH (town). Covers a land area of 18.545 square miles and a water area of 0.363 square miles. Located at 42.67° N. Lat; 73.67° W. Long.
Population: 12,131; Growth (since 2000): 12.3%; Density: 654.1 persons per square mile; Race: 94.5% White, 2.4% Black/African American, 1.2% Asian, 0.0% American Indian/Alaska Native, 0.0% Native Hawaiian/Other Pacific Islander, 1.7% Two or more races, 3.2% Hispanic of any race; Average household size: 2.49; Median age: 43.4; Age under 18: 21.3%; Age 65 and over: 19.3%; Males per 100 females: 88.8; Marriage status: 28.1% never married, 54.4% now married, 1.4% separated, 8.4% widowed, 9.1% divorced; Foreign born: 5.5%; Speak English only: 92.5%; With disability: 12.8%; Veterans: 10.0%; Ancestry: 29.1% Irish, 23.4% Italian, 21.7% German, 9.4% English, 7.3% French
Employment: 21.6% management, business, and financial, 5.3% computer, engineering, and science, 13.0% education, legal, community service, arts, and media, 5.8% healthcare practitioners, 14.6% service, 26.0% sales and office, 7.1% natural resources, construction, and maintenance, 6.7% production, transportation, and material moving
Income: Per capita: $38,119; Median household: $80,845; Average household: $94,803; Households with income of $100,000 or more: 36.6%; Poverty rate: 5.1%
Educational Attainment: High school diploma or higher: 93.5%; Bachelor's degree or higher: 34.4%; Graduate/professional degree or higher: 15.0%
Housing: Homeownership rate: 74.5%; Median home value: $201,900; Median year structure built: 1965; Homeowner vacancy rate: 0.3%; Median selected monthly owner costs: $1,622 with a mortgage, $654 without a mortgage; Median gross rent: $1,142 per month; Rental vacancy rate: 3.8%
Health Insurance: 95.5% have insurance; 83.5% have private insurance; 26.5% have public insurance; 4.5% do not have insurance; 2.2% of children under 18 do not have insurance
Safety: Violent crime rate: 8.2 per 10,000 population; Property crime rate: 185.5 per 10,000 population
Transportation: Commute: 91.4% car, 0.4% public transportation, 1.2% walk, 6.8% work from home; Mean travel time to work: 20.8 minutes
Additional Information Contacts
Town of North Greenbush . . . . (518) 283-4306
    http://www.townofng.com

PETERSBURGH (town). Aka Petersburg. Covers a land area of 41.605 square miles and a water area of 0.003 square miles. Located at 42.78° N. Lat; 73.33° W. Long.
Population: 1,661; Growth (since 2000): 6.3%; Density: 39.9 persons per square mile; Race: 98.4% White, 0.0% Black/African American, 0.0% Asian, 0.0% American Indian/Alaska Native, 0.0% Native Hawaiian/Other Pacific Islander, 1.6% Two or more races, 1.1% Hispanic of any race; Average household size: 2.53; Median age: 45.5; Age under 18: 19.6%; Age 65 and over: 20.1%; Males per 100 females: 110.9; Marriage status: 22.9% never married, 55.7% now married, 1.4% separated, 8.2% widowed, 13.2% divorced; Foreign born: 3.9%; Speak English only: 95.6%;

With disability: 14.9%; Veterans: 11.5%; Ancestry: 30.0% German, 24.4% Irish, 15.8% English, 12.2% Italian, 9.9% French

Employment: 15.7% management, business, and financial, 2.3% computer, engineering, and science, 9.4% education, legal, community service, arts, and media, 3.2% healthcare practitioners, 14.0% service, 19.5% sales and office, 14.8% natural resources, construction, and maintenance, 21.2% production, transportation, and material moving

Income: Per capita: $27,188; Median household: $53,429; Average household: $66,369; Households with income of $100,000 or more: 16.0%; Poverty rate: 9.4%

Educational Attainment: High school diploma or higher: 87.1%; Bachelor's degree or higher: 20.2%; Graduate/professional degree or higher: 10.9%

Housing: Homeownership rate: 88.6%; Median home value: $150,900; Median year structure built: 1976; Homeowner vacancy rate: 0.0%; Median selected monthly owner costs: $1,358 with a mortgage, $459 without a mortgage; Median gross rent: $756 per month; Rental vacancy rate: 10.7%

Health Insurance: 92.7% have insurance; 73.4% have private insurance; 36.7% have public insurance; 7.3% do not have insurance; 3.7% of children under 18 do not have insurance

Transportation: Commute: 92.8% car, 0.0% public transportation, 2.3% walk, 4.9% work from home; Mean travel time to work: 29.4 minutes

PITTSTOWN (town).
Covers a land area of 61.628 square miles and a water area of 3.216 square miles. Located at 42.87° N. Lat; 73.52° W. Long. Elevation is 568 feet.

Population: 5,728; Growth (since 2000): 1.5%; Density: 92.9 persons per square mile; Race: 100.0% White, 0.0% Black/African American, 0.0% Asian, 0.0% American Indian/Alaska Native, 0.0% Native Hawaiian/Other Pacific Islander, 0.0% Two or more races, 0.4% Hispanic of any race; Average household size: 2.63; Median age: 43.1; Age under 18: 22.2%; Age 65 and over: 14.5%; Males per 100 females: 99.5; Marriage status: 21.6% never married, 61.8% now married, 2.6% separated, 8.3% widowed, 8.3% divorced; Foreign born: 1.5%; Speak English only: 97.9%; With disability: 12.8%; Veterans: 10.5%; Ancestry: 28.0% Irish, 26.9% German, 14.2% Italian, 11.2% French, 11.1% English

Employment: 14.2% management, business, and financial, 6.7% computer, engineering, and science, 6.9% education, legal, community service, arts, and media, 12.6% healthcare practitioners, 13.8% service, 19.3% sales and office, 12.6% natural resources, construction, and maintenance, 14.0% production, transportation, and material moving

Income: Per capita: $29,507; Median household: $72,444; Average household: $76,490; Households with income of $100,000 or more: 30.5%; Poverty rate: 8.6%

Educational Attainment: High school diploma or higher: 92.6%; Bachelor's degree or higher: 19.6%; Graduate/professional degree or higher: 7.7%

Housing: Homeownership rate: 88.3%; Median home value: $186,400; Median year structure built: 1974; Homeowner vacancy rate: 2.1%; Median selected monthly owner costs: $1,743 with a mortgage, $611 without a mortgage; Median gross rent: $866 per month; Rental vacancy rate: 0.0%

Health Insurance: 93.4% have Insurance; 79.7% have private insurance; 26.8% have public insurance; 6.6% do not have insurance; 0.2% of children under 18 do not have insurance

Transportation: Commute: 95.3% car, 0.2% public transportation, 0.1% walk, 3.7% work from home; Mean travel time to work: 34.3 minutes

Additional Information Contacts

Town of Pittstown . . . . (518) 753-4222
  http://pittstown.us

POESTENKILL (CDP).
Covers a land area of 5.876 square miles and a water area of 0.066 square miles. Located at 42.70° N. Lat; 73.54° W. Long. Elevation is 479 feet.

Population: 1,010; Growth (since 2000): -1.4%; Density: 171.9 persons per square mile; Race: 99.3% White, 0.0% Black/African American, 0.0% Asian, 0.7% American Indian/Alaska Native, 0.0% Native Hawaiian/Other Pacific Islander, 0.0% Two or more races, 0.0% Hispanic of any race; Average household size: 2.29; Median age: 46.4; Age under 18: 22.0%; Age 65 and over: 20.9%; Males per 100 females: 90.8; Marriage status: 25.6% never married, 51.0% now married, 1.1% separated, 11.0% widowed, 12.3% divorced; Foreign born: 1.1%; Speak English only: 98.1%; With disability: 26.5%; Veterans: 8.9%; Ancestry: 28.7% Irish, 24.7% German, 18.4% French, 15.6% Italian, 11.6% American

Employment: 15.9% management, business, and financial, 2.6% computer, engineering, and science, 6.8% education, legal, community

service, arts, and media, 12.7% healthcare practitioners, 12.0% service, 29.9% sales and office, 13.1% natural resources, construction, and maintenance, 7.0% production, transportation, and material moving

Income: Per capita: $33,096; Median household: $71,932; Average household: $75,254; Households with income of $100,000 or more: 25.9%; Poverty rate: 0.3%

Educational Attainment: High school diploma or higher: 85.8%; Bachelor's degree or higher: 24.2%; Graduate/professional degree or higher: 12.9%

School District(s)
Averill Park Central SD (KG-12)
  2014-15 Enrollment: 2,964 . . . . (518) 674-7055

Housing: Homeownership rate: 85.3%; Median home value: $205,500; Median year structure built: 1962; Homeowner vacancy rate: 0.0%; Median selected monthly owner costs: $1,492 with a mortgage, $589 without a mortgage; Median gross rent: $918 per month; Rental vacancy rate: 0.0%

Health Insurance: 100.0% have insurance; 78.1% have private insurance; 46.2% have public insurance; 0.0% do not have insurance; 0.0% of children under 18 do not have insurance

Transportation: Commute: 95.8% car, 0.0% public transportation, 0.0% walk, 4.2% work from home; Mean travel time to work: 30.1 minutes

POESTENKILL (town).
Covers a land area of 32.355 square miles and a water area of 0.220 square miles. Located at 42.70° N. Lat; 73.52° W. Long. Elevation is 479 feet.

Population: 4,533; Growth (since 2000): 11.8%; Density: 140.1 persons per square mile; Race: 99.3% White, 0.0% Black/African American, 0.0% Asian, 0.2% American Indian/Alaska Native, 0.0% Native Hawaiian/Other Pacific Islander, 0.4% Two or more races, 0.5% Hispanic of any race; Average household size: 2.68; Median age: 41.5; Age under 18: 23.8%; Age 65 and over: 13.0%; Males per 100 females: 98.4; Marriage status: 25.6% never married, 59.5% now married, 0.2% separated, 5.4% widowed, 9.5% divorced; Foreign born: 0.9%; Speak English only: 97.9%; With disability: 12.7%; Veterans: 8.1%; Ancestry: 26.1% Irish, 21.4% Italian, 19.4% German, 16.0% English, 13.0% French

Employment: 17.8% management, business, and financial, 7.4% computer, engineering, and science, 8.6% education, legal, community service, arts, and media, 6.2% healthcare practitioners, 15.7% service, 26.3% sales and office, 10.5% natural resources, construction, and maintenance, 7.6% production, transportation, and material moving

Income: Per capita: $35,737; Median household: $85,682; Average household: $94,151; Households with income of $100,000 or more: 32.0%; Poverty rate: 1.9%

Educational Attainment: High school diploma or higher: 92.6%; Bachelor's degree or higher: 35.0%; Graduate/professional degree or higher: 14.9%

School District(s)
Averill Park Central SD (KG-12)
  2014-15 Enrollment: 2,964 . . . . (518) 674-7055

Housing: Homeownership rate: 81.5%; Median home value: $207,100; Median year structure built: 1970; Homeowner vacancy rate: 2.0%; Median selected monthly owner costs: $1,719 with a mortgage, $600 without a mortgage; Median gross rent: $900 per month; Rental vacancy rate: 0.0%

Health Insurance: 98.2% have insurance; 88.5% have private insurance; 24.8% have public insurance; 1.8% do not have insurance; 0.0% of children under 18 do not have insurance

Transportation: Commute: 96.3% car, 0.0% public transportation, 0.4% walk, 2.1% work from home; Mean travel time to work: 26.1 minutes

Additional Information Contacts

Town of Poestenkill . . . . (518) 283-5100
  http://poestenkillny.com/content

RENSSELAER (city).
Covers a land area of 3.171 square miles and a water area of 0.334 square miles. Located at 42.65° N. Lat; 73.73° W. Long. Elevation is 16 feet.

History: The city was formed by the union of several villages within the tract granted to Kiliaen Van Rensselaer by the chartered Dutch West Indies Company. At the 17th-century Fort Crailo, now a museum, the British surgeon Richard Shuckburg is said to have written "Yankee Doodle." Settled 1630 by Dutch, incorporated 1897.

Population: 9,502; Growth (since 2000): 22.4%; Density: 2,997.0 persons per square mile; Race: 82.5% White, 4.8% Black/African American, 2.5% Asian, 0.0% American Indian/Alaska Native, 0.0% Native Hawaiian/Other Pacific Islander, 8.1% Two or more races, 5.6% Hispanic of any race; Average household size: 2.24; Median age: 36.8; Age under 18: 21.8%;

Age 65 and over: 12.8%; Males per 100 females: 92.7; Marriage status: 39.3% never married, 39.7% now married, 2.7% separated, 9.1% widowed, 11.9% divorced; Foreign born: 4.1%; Speak English only: 97.3%; With disability: 16.4%; Veterans: 9.6%; Ancestry: 30.7% Irish, 18.2% German, 15.7% Italian, 7.7% English, 6.9% Dutch

Employment: 14.9% management, business, and financial, 3.3% computer, engineering, and science, 9.9% education, legal, community service, arts, and media, 7.8% healthcare practitioners, 23.0% service, 21.7% sales and office, 8.5% natural resources, construction, and maintenance, 10.9% production, transportation, and material moving

Income: Per capita: $28,181; Median household: $47,114; Average household: $62,399; Households with income of $100,000 or more: 18.6%; Poverty rate: 19.6%

Educational Attainment: High school diploma or higher: 89.6%; Bachelor's degree or higher: 23.2%; Graduate/professional degree or higher: 9.5%

School District(s)
East Greenbush Central SD (KG-12)
   2014-15 Enrollment: 4,106 . . . . (518) 207-2531
Nys Office of Children and Family Services (06-12)
   2014-15 Enrollment: 367 . . . . (518) 473-7793
Rensselaer City SD (PK-12)
   2014-15 Enrollment: 1,121 . . . . (518) 465-7509

Housing: Homeownership rate: 44.1%; Median home value: $141,700; Median year structure built: Before 1940; Homeowner vacancy rate: 0.6%; Median selected monthly owner costs: $1,339 with a mortgage, $557 without a mortgage; Median gross rent: $870 per month; Rental vacancy rate: 2.6%

Health Insurance: 92.5% have insurance; 64.1% have private insurance; 43.0% have public insurance; 7.5% do not have insurance; 2.0% of children under 18 do not have insurance

Safety: Violent crime rate: 21.1 per 10,000 population; Property crime rate: 141.1 per 10,000 population

Transportation: Commute: 90.6% car, 4.1% public transportation, 1.7% walk, 2.5% work from home; Mean travel time to work: 18.6 minutes; Amtrak: Train service available.

Additional Information Contacts
City of Rensselaer . . . . (518) 462-4266
   http://www.rensselaerny.gov/Home.aspx

SAND LAKE (town). Covers a land area of 35.049 square miles and a water area of 1.120 square miles. Located at 42.63° N. Lat; 73.54° W. Long. Elevation is 781 feet.

Population: 8,536; Growth (since 2000): 6.9%; Density: 243.5 persons per square mile; Race: 98.0% White, 0.5% Black/African American, 0.7% Asian, 0.0% American Indian/Alaska Native, 0.0% Native Hawaiian/Other Pacific Islander, 0.5% Two or more races, 1.0% Hispanic of any race; Average household size: 2.60; Median age: 45.1; Age under 18: 20.6%; Age 65 and over: 15.9%; Males per 100 females: 98.3; Marriage status: 22.5% never married, 63.0% now married, 1.4% separated, 5.5% widowed, 9.0% divorced; Foreign born: 2.4%; Speak English only: 96.3%; With disability: 6.7%; Veterans: 6.4%; Ancestry: 26.6% Irish, 25.7% German, 13.8% Italian, 13.5% English, 8.8% French

Employment: 13.6% management, business, and financial, 10.7% computer, engineering, and science, 11.1% education, legal, community service, arts, and media, 4.5% healthcare practitioners, 13.4% service, 23.6% sales and office, 10.9% natural resources, construction, and maintenance, 12.1% production, transportation, and material moving

Income: Per capita: $40,069; Median household: $83,904; Average household: $102,553; Households with income of $100,000 or more: 39.1%; Poverty rate: 2.4%

Educational Attainment: High school diploma or higher: 95.3%; Bachelor's degree or higher: 34.6%; Graduate/professional degree or higher: 14.0%

Housing: Homeownership rate: 87.8%; Median home value: $227,800; Median year structure built: 1966; Homeowner vacancy rate: 2.7%; Median selected monthly owner costs: $1,661 with a mortgage, $734 without a mortgage; Median gross rent: $763 per month; Rental vacancy rate: 0.0%

Health Insurance: 97.1% have insurance; 90.2% have private insurance; 21.5% have public insurance; 2.9% do not have insurance; 1.3% of children under 18 do not have insurance

Transportation: Commute: 95.9% car, 0.4% public transportation, 1.0% walk, 2.0% work from home; Mean travel time to work: 25.9 minutes

Additional Information Contacts
Town of Sand Lake . . . . (518) 674-2026
   http://townofsandlake.us/content

SCHAGHTICOKE (town). Covers a land area of 49.747 square miles and a water area of 2.114 square miles. Located at 42.88° N. Lat; 73.61° W. Long. Elevation is 358 feet.

History: On the northern border of the county, north of Troy, the town contains a village, also called Schaghticoke, and part of the village of Valley Falls. It was named for the Native American tribe formed in the seventeenth century from remnant peoples of eastern New York and New England, which has one of the oldest reservations in the United States.

Population: 7,668; Growth (since 2000): 2.8%; Density: 154.1 persons per square mile; Race: 94.4% White, 2.8% Black/African American, 0.4% Asian, 0.2% American Indian/Alaska Native, 0.0% Native Hawaiian/Other Pacific Islander, 1.9% Two or more races, 1.5% Hispanic of any race; Average household size: 2.68; Median age: 42.4; Age under 18: 22.6%; Age 65 and over: 16.7%; Males per 100 females: 98.8; Marriage status: 29.1% never married, 54.4% now married, 1.5% separated, 7.5% widowed, 9.1% divorced; Foreign born: 2.2%; Speak English only: 97.7%; With disability: 10.6%; Veterans: 9.6%; Ancestry: 35.4% Irish, 18.7% Italian, 12.8% French, 11.5% English, 10.9% German

Employment: 15.1% management, business, and financial, 3.5% computer, engineering, and science, 7.6% education, legal, community service, arts, and media, 4.4% healthcare practitioners, 16.0% service, 27.9% sales and office, 12.8% natural resources, construction, and maintenance, 12.8% production, transportation, and material moving

Income: Per capita: $29,275; Median household: $65,964; Average household: $76,973; Households with income of $100,000 or more: 29.3%; Poverty rate: 9.4%

Educational Attainment: High school diploma or higher: 90.6%; Bachelor's degree or higher: 20.2%; Graduate/professional degree or higher: 6.7%

School District(s)
Hoosic Valley Central SD (PK-12)
   2014-15 Enrollment: 1,002 . . . . (518) 753-4450

Housing: Homeownership rate: 87.9%; Median home value: $174,000; Median year structure built: 1964; Homeowner vacancy rate: 0.1%; Median selected monthly owner costs: $1,573 with a mortgage, $602 without a mortgage; Median gross rent: $740 per month; Rental vacancy rate: 0.0%

Health Insurance: 94.7% have insurance; 79.8% have private insurance; 29.6% have public insurance; 5.3% do not have insurance; 1.8% of children under 18 do not have insurance

Transportation: Commute: 96.9% car, 0.3% public transportation, 0.4% walk, 1.9% work from home; Mean travel time to work: 30.7 minutes

Additional Information Contacts
Town of Schaghticoke . . . . (518) 753-6915
   http://townofschaghticoke.org/content

SCHAGHTICOKE (village). Covers a land area of 0.758 square miles and a water area of 0.235 square miles. Located at 42.90° N. Lat; 73.59° W. Long. Elevation is 358 feet.

Population: 564; Growth (since 2000): -16.6%; Density: 744.0 persons per square mile; Race: 98.4% White, 0.0% Black/African American, 0.0% Asian, 1.1% American Indian/Alaska Native, 0.0% Native Hawaiian/Other Pacific Islander, 0.0% Two or more races, 1.8% Hispanic of any race; Average household size: 2.53; Median age: 34.8; Age under 18: 24.6%; Age 65 and over: 11.5%; Males per 100 females: 110.7; Marriage status: 27.9% never married, 52.4% now married, 0.0% separated, 8.6% widowed, 11.1% divorced; Foreign born: 0.5%; Speak English only: 96.9%; With disability: 17.7%; Veterans: 12.0%; Ancestry: 30.1% Irish, 21.1% Italian, 18.3% German, 13.5% French, 8.3% English

Employment: 2.7% management, business, and financial, 5.1% computer, engineering, and science, 6.5% education, legal, community service, arts, and media, 4.4% healthcare practitioners, 10.6% service, 27.3% sales and office, 26.6% natural resources, construction, and maintenance, 16.7% production, transportation, and material moving

Income: Per capita: $24,320; Median household: $50,625; Average household: $59,317; Households with income of $100,000 or more: 17.0%; Poverty rate: 11.1%

Educational Attainment: High school diploma or higher: 93.8%; Bachelor's degree or higher: 11.1%; Graduate/professional degree or higher: 3.3%

School District(s)

Hoosic Valley Central SD (PK-12)
   2014-15 Enrollment: 1,002 . . . . (518) 753-4450
Housing: Homeownership rate: 66.8%; Median home value: $155,700; Median year structure built: Before 1940; Homeowner vacancy rate: 0.0%; Median selected monthly owner costs: $1,425 with a mortgage, $546 without a mortgage; Median gross rent: $696 per month; Rental vacancy rate: 0.0%
Health Insurance: 92.7% have insurance; 78.4% have private insurance; 28.4% have public insurance; 7.3% do not have insurance; 0.0% of children under 18 do not have insurance
Transportation: Commute: 95.9% car, 0.0% public transportation, 3.4% walk, 0.0% work from home; Mean travel time to work: 32.6 minutes

SCHODACK (town). Covers a land area of 61.927 square miles and a water area of 1.676 square miles. Located at 42.53° N. Lat; 73.68° W. Long.

Population: 13,069; Growth (since 2000): 4.3%; Density: 211.0 persons per square mile; Race: 96.4% White, 1.1% Black/African American, 1.1% Asian, 0.0% American Indian/Alaska Native, 0.0% Native Hawaiian/Other Pacific Islander, 0.9% Two or more races, 0.9% Hispanic of any race; Average household size: 2.59; Median age: 45.0; Age under 18: 20.9%; Age 65 and over: 16.8%; Males per 100 females: 97.2; Marriage status: 26.9% never married, 60.3% now married, 3.6% separated, 5.1% widowed, 7.8% divorced; Foreign born: 2.0%; Speak English only: 97.2%; With disability: 10.1%; Veterans: 10.9%; Ancestry: 23.9% Irish, 21.0% German, 17.0% English, 16.3% Italian, 9.8% Polish
Employment: 19.0% management, business, and financial, 6.9% computer, engineering, and science, 8.6% education, legal, community service, arts, and media, 8.1% healthcare practitioners, 16.1% service, 21.0% sales and office, 10.0% natural resources, construction, and maintenance, 10.2% production, transportation, and material moving
Income: Per capita: $38,718; Median household: $78,573; Average household: $101,457; Households with income of $100,000 or more: 38.8%; Poverty rate: 4.2%
Educational Attainment: High school diploma or higher: 92.6%; Bachelor's degree or higher: 30.3%; Graduate/professional degree or higher: 13.8%
Housing: Homeownership rate: 82.6%; Median home value: $222,300; Median year structure built: 1968; Homeowner vacancy rate: 0.9%; Median selected monthly owner costs: $1,750 with a mortgage, $751 without a mortgage; Median gross rent: $844 per month; Rental vacancy rate: 3.1%
Health Insurance: 94.4% have insurance; 84.7% have private insurance; 25.4% have public insurance; 5.6% do not have insurance; 2.4% of children under 18 do not have Insurance
Safety: Violent crime rate: 7.7 per 10,000 population; Property crime rate: 69.3 per 10,000 population
Transportation: Commute: 95.4% car, 0.3% public transportation, 0.2% walk, 3.7% work from home; Mean travel time to work: 22.4 minutes
Additional Information Contacts
Town of Schodack. . . . . (518) 477-7918
   http://www.schodack.org

SCHODACK LANDING (unincorporated postal area)

ZCTA: 12156
   Covers a land area of 14.344 square miles and a water area of 0.682 square miles. Located at 42.48° N. Lat; 73.75° W. Long. Elevation is 59 feet.
   Population: 1,175; Growth (since 2000): 27.3%; Density: 81.9 persons per square mile; Race: 99.8% White, 0.2% Black/African American, 0.0% Asian, 0.0% American Indian/Alaska Native, 0.0% Native Hawaiian/Other Pacific Islander, 0.0% Two or more races, 0.0% Hispanic of any race; Average household size: 2.92; Median age: 36.3; Age under 18: 34.6%; Age 65 and over: 12.8%; Males per 100 females: 103.4; Marriage status: 30.3% never married, 60.9% now married, 0.0% separated, 4.4% widowed, 4.5% divorced; Foreign born: 0.5%; Speak English only: 100.0%; With disability: 5.7%; Veterans: 4.3%; Ancestry: 28.1% English, 21.0% Syrian, 17.7% Irish, 16.2% American, 10.4% German
   Employment: 29.4% management, business, and financial, 0.6% computer, engineering, and science, 6.2% education, legal, community service, arts, and media, 14.2% healthcare practitioners, 1.8% service, 22.4% sales and office, 13.1% natural resources, construction, and maintenance, 12.3% production, transportation, and material moving

Income: Per capita: $30,856; Median household: $78,170; Average household: $89,337; Households with income of $100,000 or more: 38.7%; Poverty rate: 5.3%
Educational Attainment: High school diploma or higher: 88.9%; Bachelor's degree or higher: 24.6%; Graduate/professional degree or higher: 12.7%
Housing: Homeownership rate: 83.1%; Median home value: $284,200; Median year structure built: 1959; Homeowner vacancy rate: 0.0%; Median selected monthly owner costs: $2,117 with a mortgage, $748 without a mortgage; Median gross rent: $685 per month; Rental vacancy rate: 0.0%
Health Insurance: 94.0% have insurance; 90.4% have private insurance; 13.9% have public insurance; 6.0% do not have insurance; 0.0% of children under 18 do not have insurance
Transportation: Commute: 93.8% car, 0.0% public transportation, 0.0% walk, 4.9% work from home; Mean travel time to work: 23.3 minutes

STEPHENTOWN (town). Covers a land area of 57.880 square miles and a water area of 0.196 square miles. Located at 42.55° N. Lat; 73.41° W. Long. Elevation is 876 feet.

Population: 2,891; Growth (since 2000): 0.6%; Density: 49.9 persons per square mile; Race: 99.0% White, 0.0% Black/African American, 0.6% Asian, 0.0% American Indian/Alaska Native, 0.0% Native Hawaiian/Other Pacific Islander, 0.4% Two or more races, 2.0% Hispanic of any race; Average household size: 2.45; Median age: 45.6; Age under 18: 21.8%; Age 65 and over: 15.4%; Males per 100 females: 100.5; Marriage status: 29.4% never married, 57.4% now married, 1.2% separated, 4.4% widowed, 8.7% divorced; Foreign born: 1.2%; Speak English only: 95.2%; With disability: 15.7%; Veterans: 10.5%; Ancestry: 24.0% Irish, 21.7% German, 17.8% English, 16.4% Italian, 11.6% American
Employment: 13.2% management, business, and financial, 5.0% computer, engineering, and science, 12.7% education, legal, community service, arts, and media, 4.5% healthcare practitioners, 20.8% service, 22.6% sales and office, 8.9% natural resources, construction, and maintenance, 12.4% production, transportation, and material moving
Income: Per capita: $30,340; Median household: $61,202; Average household: $73,496; Households with income of $100,000 or more: 24.1%; Poverty rate: 12.0%
Educational Attainment: High school diploma or higher: 93.9%; Bachelor's degree or higher: 18.7%; Graduate/professional degree or higher: 9.0%
Housing: Homeownership rate: 82.5%; Median home value: $177,300; Median year structure built: 1980; Homeowner vacancy rate: 2.9%; Median selected monthly owner costs: $1,193 with a mortgage, $560 without a mortgage; Median gross rent: $957 per month; Rental vacancy rate: 3.5%
Health Insurance: 93.9% have insurance; 81.3% have private insurance; 27.3% have public insurance; 6.1% do not have insurance; 0.0% of children under 18 do not have insurance
Transportation: Commute: 91.3% car, 0.0% public transportation, 1.2% walk, 6.5% work from home; Mean travel time to work: 34.1 minutes

TROY (city). County seat. Covers a land area of 10.357 square miles and a water area of 0.700 square miles. Located at 42.74° N. Lat; 73.68° W. Long. Elevation is 33 feet.

History: The early name of Troy was Pa-an-pa-ack, "field of standing corn." The site was part of the patroonship granted to Kiliaen Van Rensselaer by the Dutch West India Company. For 120 years, it was occupied by Dutch farmers. Some argument took place about the name, but "Troy" was selected in 1789 at a public meeting.
Population: 49,933; Growth (since 2000): 1.6%; Density: 4,821.1 persons per square mile; Race: 71.9% White, 16.0% Black/African American, 4.0% Asian, 0.2% American Indian/Alaska Native, 0.0% Native Hawaiian/Other Pacific Islander, 6.7% Two or more races, 8.8% Hispanic of any race; Average household size: 2.28; Median age: 30.6; Age under 18: 19.3%; Age 65 and over: 11.3%; Males per 100 females: 102.1; Marriage status: 55.2% never married, 30.6% now married, 2.6% separated, 5.1% widowed, 9.1% divorced; Foreign born: 7.8%; Speak English only: 87.5%; With disability: 14.6%; Veterans: 5.6%; Ancestry: 20.9% Irish, 15.3% Italian, 10.9% German, 7.9% French, 6.9% English
Employment: 10.3% management, business, and financial, 6.9% computer, engineering, and science, 14.5% education, legal, community service, arts, and media, 4.2% healthcare practitioners, 20.8% service, 27.9% sales and office, 5.7% natural resources, construction, and maintenance, 9.7% production, transportation, and material moving

Income: Per capita: $21,445; Median household: $38,954; Average household: $51,553; Households with income of $100,000 or more: 13.5%; Poverty rate: 26.1%

Educational Attainment: High school diploma or higher: 84.7%; Bachelor's degree or higher: 25.2%; Graduate/professional degree or higher: 10.1%

School District(s)

Ark Community Charter School (KG-06)
  2014-15 Enrollment: n/a . . . . (518) 274-6312
Brunswick Central SD (Brittonkill) (PK-12)
  2014-15 Enrollment: 1,194 . . . . (518) 279-4600
East Greenbush Central SD (KG-12)
  2014-15 Enrollment: 4,106 . . . . (518) 207-2531
Lansingburgh Central SD (KG-12)
  2014-15 Enrollment: 2,428 . . . . (518) 233-6850
North Greenbush Common SD (Williams) (KG-01)
  2014-15 Enrollment: 21 . . . . (518) 283-6748
Troy City SD (PK-12)
  2014-15 Enrollment: 4,167 . . . . (518) 328-5085
True North Troy Preparatory Charter School (05-07)
  2014-15 Enrollment: 450 . . . . (518) 445-3100

Four-year College(s)

Rensselaer Polytechnic Institute (Private, Not-for-profit)
  Fall 2014 Enrollment: 6,835 . . . . (518) 276-6000
  2015-16 Tuition: In-state $49,341; Out-of-state $49,341
The Sage Colleges (Private, Not-for-profit)
  Fall 2014 Enrollment: 2,878 . . . . (518) 244-2000
  2015-16 Tuition: In-state $28,400; Out-of-state $28,400

Two-year College(s)

Hudson Valley Community College (Public)
  Fall 2014 Enrollment: 12,177 . . . . (518) 629-4822
  2015-16 Tuition: In-state $5,188; Out-of-state $13,388
Samaritan Hospital School of Nursing (Private, Not-for-profit)
  Fall 2014 Enrollment: 164 . . . . (518) 268-5130
  2015-16 Tuition: In-state $12,142; Out-of-state $12,142

Vocational/Technical School(s)

Rensselaer BOCES-Practical Nursing Program (Public)
  Fall 2014 Enrollment: 50 . . . . (518) 479-6913

Housing: Homeownership rate: 38.2%; Median home value: $143,800; Median year structure built: Before 1940; Homeowner vacancy rate: 1.5%; Median selected monthly owner costs: $1,444 with a mortgage, $563 without a mortgage; Median gross rent: $842 per month; Rental vacancy rate: 3.0%

Health Insurance: 92.8% have insurance; 63.5% have private insurance; 40.0% have public insurance; 7.2% do not have insurance; 1.5% of children under 18 do not have insurance

Hospitals: Saint Mary's Hospital - Troy (201 beds); Samaritan Hospital (238 beds)

Safety: Violent crime rate: 85.8 per 10,000 population; Property crime rate: 403.6 per 10,000 population

Newspapers: The Record (daily circulation 15,200)

Transportation: Commute: 78.4% car, 5.8% public transportation, 11.9% walk, 2.6% work from home; Mean travel time to work: 20.3 minutes

Additional Information Contacts

City of Troy . . . . (518) 279-7134
  http://www.troyny.gov

VALLEY FALLS (village).

Covers a land area of 0.463 square miles and a water area of 0.025 square miles. Located at 42.90° N. Lat; 73.56° W. Long. Elevation is 335 feet.

Population: 531; Growth (since 2000): 8.1%; Density: 1,145.8 persons per square mile; Race: 98.7% White, 0.0% Black/African American, 1.1% Asian, 0.0% American Indian/Alaska Native, 0.0% Native Hawaiian/Other Pacific Islander, 0.2% Two or more races, 0.8% Hispanic of any race; Average household size: 2.57; Median age: 41.4; Age under 18: 24.5%; Age 65 and over: 15.1%; Males per 100 females: 86.4; Marriage status: 30.7% never married, 59.9% now married, 2.4% separated, 2.9% widowed, 6.5% divorced; Foreign born: 1.1%; Speak English only: 98.0%; With disability: 14.7%; Veterans: 10.8%; Ancestry: 36.3% Irish, 20.2% English, 17.9% German, 16.4% Italian, 9.0% Polish

Employment: 10.8% management, business, and financial, 7.4% computer, engineering, and science, 14.9% education, legal, community service, arts, and media, 5.2% healthcare practitioners, 23.0% service, 15.6% sales and office, 8.6% natural resources, construction, and maintenance, 14.5% production, transportation, and material moving

Income: Per capita: $38,277; Median household: $80,179; Average household: $98,857; Households with income of $100,000 or more: 39.2%; Poverty rate: 6.3%

Educational Attainment: High school diploma or higher: 98.6%; Bachelor's degree or higher: 35.4%; Graduate/professional degree or higher: 18.0%

Housing: Homeownership rate: 75.4%; Median home value: $159,400; Median year structure built: Before 1940; Homeowner vacancy rate: 1.9%; Median selected monthly owner costs: $1,600 with a mortgage, $610 without a mortgage; Median gross rent: $886 per month; Rental vacancy rate: 0.0%

Health Insurance: 95.8% have insurance; 87.1% have private insurance; 25.3% have public insurance; 4.2% do not have insurance; 2.3% of children under 18 do not have insurance

Transportation: Commute: 92.3% car, 2.2% public transportation, 0.7% walk, 3.3% work from home; Mean travel time to work: 30.6 minutes

WEST SAND LAKE (CDP).

Covers a land area of 4.704 square miles and a water area of 0.088 square miles. Located at 42.64° N. Lat; 73.59° W. Long. Elevation is 525 feet.

Population: 2,845; Growth (since 2000): 16.6%; Density: 604.8 persons per square mile; Race: 94.5% White, 1.5% Black/African American, 2.0% Asian, 0.1% American Indian/Alaska Native, 0.0% Native Hawaiian/Other Pacific Islander, 1.1% Two or more races, 0.4% Hispanic of any race; Average household size: 2.66; Median age: 44.7; Age under 18: 21.6%; Age 65 and over: 11.6%; Males per 100 females: 94.7; Marriage status: 25.1% never married, 64.2% now married, 0.2% separated, 5.9% widowed, 4.7% divorced; Foreign born: 4.9%; Speak English only: 95.0%; With disability: 3.2%; Veterans: 4.4%; Ancestry: 26.3% German, 24.3% Irish, 11.9% French, 9.9% English, 9.0% Ukrainian

Employment: 8.0% management, business, and financial, 11.7% computer, engineering, and science, 10.6% education, legal, community service, arts, and media, 6.4% healthcare practitioners, 8.0% service, 29.0% sales and office, 11.9% natural resources, construction, and maintenance, 14.4% production, transportation, and material moving

Income: Per capita: $38,133; Median household: $86,523; Average household: $99,196; Households with income of $100,000 or more: 30.8%; Poverty rate: 2.4%

Educational Attainment: High school diploma or higher: 93.7%; Bachelor's degree or higher: 42.7%; Graduate/professional degree or higher: 16.4%

School District(s)

Averill Park Central SD (KG-12)
  2014-15 Enrollment: 2,964 . . . . (518) 674-7055

Housing: Homeownership rate: 88.4%; Median home value: $223,400; Median year structure built: 1963; Homeowner vacancy rate: 6.4%; Median selected monthly owner costs: $1,738 with a mortgage, $785 without a mortgage; Median gross rent: $750 per month; Rental vacancy rate: 0.0%

Health Insurance: 97.1% have insurance; 91.1% have private insurance; 16.0% have public insurance; 2.9% do not have insurance; 0.0% of children under 18 do not have insurance

Transportation: Commute: 97.2% car, 0.0% public transportation, 1.6% walk, 0.6% work from home; Mean travel time to work: 23.8 minutes

WYNANTSKILL (CDP).

Covers a land area of 2.360 square miles and a water area of 0.003 square miles. Located at 42.69° N. Lat; 73.64° W. Long. Elevation is 335 feet.

Population: 3,036; Growth (since 2000): 0.6%; Density: 1,286.6 persons per square mile; Race: 93.9% White, 3.5% Black/African American, 0.2% Asian, 0.0% American Indian/Alaska Native, 0.0% Native Hawaiian/Other Pacific Islander, 2.4% Two or more races, 2.4% Hispanic of any race; Average household size: 2.45; Median age: 39.6; Age under 18: 20.6%; Age 65 and over: 15.1%; Males per 100 females: 90.2; Marriage status: 25.2% never married, 61.2% now married, 1.7% separated, 6.5% widowed, 7.1% divorced; Foreign born: 3.1%; Speak English only: 92.5%; With disability: 13.8%; Veterans: 9.8%; Ancestry: 41.4% Irish, 28.2% Italian, 17.9% German, 11.9% French, 9.6% English

Employment: 19.7% management, business, and financial, 4.4% computer, engineering, and science, 10.7% education, legal, community service, arts, and media, 6.1% healthcare practitioners, 13.2% service, 26.5% sales and office, 10.9% natural resources, construction, and maintenance, 8.4% production, transportation, and material moving

Income: Per capita: $34,657; Median household: $81,360; Average household: $83,599; Households with income of $100,000 or more: 38.0%; Poverty rate: 3.1%

Educational Attainment: High school diploma or higher: 91.1%; Bachelor's degree or higher: 29.2%; Graduate/professional degree or higher: 12.9%

School District(s)

Wynantskill Union Free SD (KG-08)

    2014-15 Enrollment: 321. . . . . (518) 283-4679

Housing: Homeownership rate: 90.0%; Median home value: $174,100; Median year structure built: 1955; Homeowner vacancy rate: 0.0%; Median selected monthly owner costs: $1,538 with a mortgage, $638 without a mortgage; Median gross rent: $891 per month; Rental vacancy rate: 0.0%

Health Insurance: 96.8% have insurance; 81.9% have private insurance; 25.4% have public insurance; 3.2% do not have insurance; 0.0% of children under 18 do not have insurance

Transportation: Commute: 93.0% car, 0.0% public transportation, 1.7% walk, 4.5% work from home; Mean travel time to work: 21.7 minutes

Richmond County

See New York City

Rockland County

Located in southeastern New York; bounded on the east by the Hudson River, and on the southwest and south by New Jersey; includes part of the Ramapo Mountains; drained by the Hackensack and Ramapo Rivers. Covers a land area of 173.550 square miles, a water area of 25.792 square miles, and is located in the Eastern Time Zone at 41.15° N. Lat., 74.02° W. Long. The county was founded in 1798. County seat is New City.

Rockland County is part of the New York-Newark-Jersey City, NY-NJ-PA Metropolitan Statistical Area. The entire metro area includes: Dutchess County-Putnam County, NY Metropolitan Division (Dutchess County, NY; Putnam County, NY); Nassau County-Suffolk County, NY Metropolitan Division (Nassau County, NY; Suffolk County, NY); Newark, NJ-PA Metropolitan Division (Essex County, NJ; Hunterdon County, NJ; Morris County, NJ; Somerset County, NJ; Sussex County, NJ; Union County, NJ; Pike County, PA); New York-Jersey City-White Plains, NY-NJ Metropolitan Division (Bergen County, NJ; Hudson County, NJ; Middlesex County, NJ; Monmouth County, NJ; Ocean County, NJ; Passaic County, NJ; Bronx County, NY; Kings County, NY; New York County, NY; Orange County, NY; Queens County, NY; Richmond County, NY; Rockland County, NY; Westchester County, NY)

Population: 320,688; Growth (since 2000): 11.8%; Density: 1,847.8 persons per square mile; Race: 70.8% White, 12.5% Black/African American, 6.2% Asian, 0.2% American Indian/Alaska Native, 0.0% Native Hawaiian/Other Pacific Islander, 2.4% two or more races, 16.8% Hispanic of any race; Average household size: 3.17; Median age: 36.3; Age under 18: 27.7%; Age 65 and over: 14.5%; Males per 100 females: 96.3; Marriage status: 32.6% never married, 55.1% now married, 1.9% separated, 5.8% widowed, 6.6% divorced; Foreign born: 21.2%; Speak English only: 62.3%; With disability: 9.0%; Veterans: 4.6%; Ancestry: 14.3% Irish, 14.1% Italian, 6.8% German, 5.9% American, 5.1% Polish

Religion: Six largest groups: 35.1% Catholicism, 22.0% Judaism, 2.8% Non-denominational Protestant, 1.5% Muslim Estimate, 1.3% Baptist, 0.9% Eastern Liturgical (Orthodox)

Economy: Unemployment rate: 4.2%; Leading industries: 13.5 % professional, scientific, and technical services; 13.0 % retail trade; 11.9 % health care and social assistance; Farms: 23 totaling 526 acres; Company size: 3 employ 1,000 or more persons, 19 employ 500 to 999 persons, 134 employ 100 to 499 persons, 9,390 employ less than 100 persons; Business ownership: 9,433 women-owned, 2,180 Black-owned, 3,221 Hispanic-owned, 2,376 Asian-owned, 119 American Indian/Alaska Native-owned

Employment: 15.5% management, business, and financial, 4.8% computer, engineering, and science, 15.8% education, legal, community service, arts, and media, 7.8% healthcare practitioners, 18.5% service, 23.5% sales and office, 7.0% natural resources, construction, and maintenance, 7.0% production, transportation, and material moving

Income: Per capita: $34,647; Median household: $84,855; Average household: $108,859; Households with income of $100,000 or more: 42.5%; Poverty rate: 14.6%

Educational Attainment: High school diploma or higher: 87.3%; Bachelor's degree or higher: 40.3%; Graduate/professional degree or higher: 18.1%

Housing: Homeownership rate: 68.9%; Median home value: $419,100; Median year structure built: 1969; Homeowner vacancy rate: 1.4%; Median selected monthly owner costs: $2,973 with a mortgage, $1,209 without a mortgage; Median gross rent: $1,335 per month; Rental vacancy rate: 4.7%

Vital Statistics: Birth rate: 159.6 per 10,000 population; Death rate: 70.1 per 10,000 population; Age-adjusted cancer mortality rate: 130.2 deaths per 100,000 population

Health Insurance: 91.3% have insurance; 66.6% have private insurance; 36.0% have public insurance; 8.7% do not have insurance; 3.9% of children under 18 do not have insurance

Health Care: Physicians: 36.4 per 10,000 population; Dentists: 10.2 per 10,000 population; Hospital beds: 56.9 per 10,000 population; Hospital admissions: 1,098.7 per 10,000 population

Air Quality Index (AQI): Percent of Days: 82.5% good, 16.4% moderate, 1.1% unhealthy for sensitive individuals, 0.0% unhealthy, 0.0% very unhealthy; Annual median: 36; Annual maximum: 119

Transportation: Commute: 81.7% car, 8.6% public transportation, 3.5% walk, 4.7% work from home; Mean travel time to work: 30.6 minutes

2016 Presidential Election: 45.5% Trump, 51.8% Clinton, 1.7% Johnson, 1.0% Stein

National and State Parks: Bear Mountain State Park; Blauvelt State Park; High Tor State Park; Hook Mountain State Park; Iona Island Component Hudson River National Estuarine Research Reserve; Palisades State Park; Piermont Marsh Component Hudson River National Estuarine Research Reserve; Rockland Lake State Park; Stony Point State Park; Tallman Mountain State Park

Additional Information Contacts

Rockland Government. . . . . (845) 638-5070
   http://www.co.rockland.ny.us

Rockland County Communities

AIRMONT (village). Covers a land area of 4.643 square miles and a water area of 0.002 square miles. Located at 41.10° N. Lat; 74.10° W. Long. Elevation is 587 feet.

Population: 8,808; Growth (since 2000): 12.9%; Density: 1,897.0 persons per square mile; Race: 88.6% White, 2.0% Black/African American, 4.0% Asian, 0.3% American Indian/Alaska Native, 0.0% Native Hawaiian/Other Pacific Islander, 3.7% Two or more races, 9.6% Hispanic of any race; Average household size: 3.11; Median age: 39.9; Age under 18: 25.4%; Age 65 and over: 19.3%; Males per 100 females: 90.6; Marriage status: 26.0% never married, 59.0% now married, 1.5% separated, 8.8% widowed, 6.2% divorced; Foreign born: 16.1%; Speak English only: 64.5%; With disability: 9.0%; Veterans: 5.8%; Ancestry: 16.8% Italian, 12.9% Irish, 9.2% American, 6.0% Russian, 5.6% German

Employment: 21.7% management, business, and financial, 6.1% computer, engineering, and science, 16.8% education, legal, community service, arts, and media, 7.4% healthcare practitioners, 9.3% service, 27.0% sales and office, 9.1% natural resources, construction, and maintenance, 2.6% production, transportation, and material moving

Income: Per capita: $37,503; Median household: $91,458; Average household: $116,623; Households with income of $100,000 or more: 45.5%; Poverty rate: 8.4%

Educational Attainment: High school diploma or higher: 89.0%; Bachelor's degree or higher: 45.0%; Graduate/professional degree or higher: 24.2%

Housing: Homeownership rate: 75.4%; Median home value: $454,900; Median year structure built: 1970; Homeowner vacancy rate: 2.1%; Median selected monthly owner costs: $3,170 with a mortgage, $1,305 without a mortgage; Median gross rent: $1,184 per month; Rental vacancy rate: 2.5%

Health Insurance: 96.9% have insurance; 74.7% have private insurance; 37.6% have public insurance; 3.1% do not have insurance; 0.2% of children under 18 do not have insurance

Transportation: Commute: 83.4% car, 8.3% public transportation, 0.3% walk, 6.2% work from home; Mean travel time to work: 30.6 minutes

Additional Information Contacts

Village of Airmont . . . . (845) 357-8111
   http://www.airmont.org

BARDONIA (CDP). Covers a land area of 2.574 square miles and a water area of 0.355 square miles. Located at 41.11° N. Lat; 73.98° W. Long. Elevation is 295 feet.

History: Bardonia is named for the Bardon Brothers - John and the twins Phillip and Conrad - who came from Bavaria in the 1849 and opened several businesses.

Population: 3,551; Growth (since 2000): -18.7%; Density: 1,379.6 persons per square mile; Race: 84.7% White, 1.3% Black/African American, 10.2% Asian, 0.0% American Indian/Alaska Native, 0.0% Native Hawaiian/Other Pacific Islander, 3.0% Two or more races, 2.6% Hispanic of any race; Average household size: 2.70; Median age: 50.6; Age under 18: 17.3%; Age 65 and over: 25.1%; Males per 100 females: 93.0; Marriage status: 28.0% never married, 59.4% now married, 1.0% separated, 6.4% widowed, 6.2% divorced; Foreign born: 16.2%; Speak English only: 78.5%; With disability: 5.9%; Veterans: 4.6%; Ancestry: 30.6% Italian, 26.2% Irish, 8.3% German, 7.5% Russian, 7.4% American

Employment: 19.2% management, business, and financial, 10.2% computer, engineering, and science, 11.4% education, legal, community service, arts, and media, 11.1% healthcare practitioners, 13.4% service, 25.3% sales and office, 4.0% natural resources, construction, and maintenance, 5.5% production, transportation, and material moving

Income: Per capita: $53,152; Median household: $115,927; Average household: $140,420; Households with income of $100,000 or more: 57.8%; Poverty rate: 2.1%

Educational Attainment: High school diploma or higher: 95.6%; Bachelor's degree or higher: 57.5%; Graduate/professional degree or higher: 26.2%

School District(s)

Clarkstown Central SD (KG-12)
   2014-15 Enrollment: 8,478 . . . . (845) 639-6418

Housing: Homeownership rate: 86.4%; Median home value: $505,000; Median year structure built: 1973; Homeowner vacancy rate: 0.0%; Median selected monthly owner costs: $3,310 with a mortgage, $1,350 without a mortgage; Median gross rent: n/a per month; Rental vacancy rate: 0.0%

Health Insurance: 96.2% have insurance; 89.8% have private insurance; 27.1% have public insurance; 3.8% do not have insurance; 6.0% of children under 18 do not have insurance

Transportation: Commute: 87.4% car, 4.5% public transportation, 0.8% walk, 6.8% work from home; Mean travel time to work: 32.4 minutes

BLAUVELT (CDP). Covers a land area of 4.502 square miles and a water area of 0.105 square miles. Located at 41.07° N. Lat; 73.95° W. Long. Elevation is 197 feet.

History: Blauvelt section of Palisades Interstate Park is here.

Population: 5,394; Growth (since 2000): 3.6%; Density: 1,198.1 persons per square mile; Race: 87.3% White, 2.9% Black/African American, 5.5% Asian, 0.0% American Indian/Alaska Native, 0.0% Native Hawaiian/Other Pacific Islander, 1.3% Two or more races, 9.6% Hispanic of any race; Average household size: 3.04; Median age: 41.4; Age under 18: 25.1%; Age 65 and over: 17.9%; Males per 100 females: 95.0; Marriage status: 31.8% never married, 58.9% now married, 0.5% separated, 6.4% widowed, 2.9% divorced; Foreign born: 12.5%; Speak English only: 83.1%; With disability: 7.7%; Veterans: 7.3%; Ancestry: 35.8% Irish, 20.6% Italian, 10.2% German, 7.3% English, 6.1% American

Employment: 18.5% management, business, and financial, 4.9% computer, engineering, and science, 21.5% education, legal, community service, arts, and media, 5.3% healthcare practitioners, 15.2% service, 22.3% sales and office, 8.5% natural resources, construction, and maintenance, 3.8% production, transportation, and material moving

Income: Per capita: $45,190; Median household: $118,929; Average household: $146,251; Households with income of $100,000 or more: 57.9%; Poverty rate: 4.0%

Educational Attainment: High school diploma or higher: 93.4%; Bachelor's degree or higher: 53.3%; Graduate/professional degree or higher: 25.0%

School District(s)

South Orangetown Central SD (PK-12)
   2014-15 Enrollment: 3,272 . . . . (845) 680-1050

Housing: Homeownership rate: 97.0%; Median home value: $500,400; Median year structure built: 1962; Homeowner vacancy rate: 1.6%; Median selected monthly owner costs: $3,093 with a mortgage, $1,244 without a mortgage; Median gross rent: n/a per month; Rental vacancy rate: 0.0%

Health Insurance: 91.4% have insurance; 83.3% have private insurance; 21.6% have public insurance; 8.6% do not have insurance; 13.5% of children under 18 do not have insurance

Transportation: Commute: 88.1% car, 5.2% public transportation, 2.6% walk, 4.1% work from home; Mean travel time to work: 31.3 minutes

CHESTNUT RIDGE (village). Covers a land area of 4.968 square miles and a water area of 0.003 square miles. Located at 41.08° N. Lat; 74.05° W. Long. Elevation is 417 feet.

Population: 8,090; Growth (since 2000): 3.3%; Density: 1,628.4 persons per square mile; Race: 60.3% White, 23.9% Black/African American, 5.1% Asian, 0.1% American Indian/Alaska Native, 0.0% Native Hawaiian/Other Pacific Islander, 3.3% Two or more races, 13.4% Hispanic of any race; Average household size: 3.15; Median age: 42.4; Age under 18: 25.0%; Age 65 and over: 18.0%; Males per 100 females: 94.6; Marriage status: 30.0% never married, 56.8% now married, 1.5% separated, 6.5% widowed, 6.7% divorced; Foreign born: 20.6%; Speak English only: 72.8%; With disability: 10.1%; Veterans: 6.5%; Ancestry: 10.6% Italian, 7.0% Polish, 6.8% Irish, 6.4% American, 6.0% German

Employment: 16.0% management, business, and financial, 6.3% computer, engineering, and science, 16.6% education, legal, community service, arts, and media, 9.8% healthcare practitioners, 15.6% service, 22.4% sales and office, 4.9% natural resources, construction, and maintenance, 8.4% production, transportation, and material moving

Income: Per capita: $35,120; Median household: $89,813; Average household: $108,478; Households with income of $100,000 or more: 45.7%; Poverty rate: 8.5%

Educational Attainment: High school diploma or higher: 92.1%; Bachelor's degree or higher: 42.4%; Graduate/professional degree or higher: 18.9%

School District(s)

East Ramapo Central SD (Spring Valley) (PK-12)
   2014-15 Enrollment: 8,881 . . . . (845) 577-6011

Housing: Homeownership rate: 80.5%; Median home value: $424,400; Median year structure built: 1966; Homeowner vacancy rate: 1.5%; Median selected monthly owner costs: $3,101 with a mortgage, $1,225 without a mortgage; Median gross rent: $1,441 per month; Rental vacancy rate: 4.1%

Health Insurance: 93.3% have insurance; 71.6% have private insurance; 34.9% have public insurance; 6.7% do not have insurance; 2.4% of children under 18 do not have insurance

Transportation: Commute: 83.5% car, 7.9% public transportation, 2.2% walk, 6.0% work from home; Mean travel time to work: 32.1 minutes

Additional Information Contacts

Village of Chestnut Ridge . . . . (845) 425-2805
   http://www.chestnutridgevillage.org

CLARKSTOWN (town). Covers a land area of 38.475 square miles and a water area of 8.593 square miles. Located at 41.13° N. Lat; 73.97° W. Long.

History: The town of Clarkstown was created in 1791 in Orange County, before Rockland County was formed. In 2008 Clarkstown became one of 600 municipalities nationwide to sign the United States Mayor's Climate Protection Agreement to reduce carbon dioxide emissions to seven percent below the 1990 levels by 2012.

Population: 86,334; Growth (since 2000): 5.2%; Density: 2,243.9 persons per square mile; Race: 71.3% White, 9.6% Black/African American, 11.3% Asian, 0.2% American Indian/Alaska Native, 0.0% Native Hawaiian/Other Pacific Islander, 3.2% Two or more races, 13.2% Hispanic of any race; Average household size: 2.88; Median age: 44.3; Age under 18: 21.8%; Age 65 and over: 18.2%; Males per 100 females: 94.1; Marriage status: 28.7% never married, 58.1% now married, 1.7% separated, 6.3% widowed, 6.9% divorced; Foreign born: 22.1%; Speak English only: 70.6%; With disability: 9.0%; Veterans: 5.1%; Ancestry: 21.0% Italian, 17.7% Irish, 7.4% German, 5.6% American, 4.8% Polish

Employment: 18.1% management, business, and financial, 6.1% computer, engineering, and science, 15.9% education, legal, community service, arts, and media, 9.9% healthcare practitioners, 14.5% service, 23.9% sales and office, 5.8% natural resources, construction, and maintenance, 5.8% production, transportation, and material moving

Income: Per capita: $44,842; Median household: $104,050; Average household: $127,739; Households with income of $100,000 or more: 52.6%; Poverty rate: 5.6%

Educational Attainment: High school diploma or higher: 91.3%; Bachelor's degree or higher: 49.6%; Graduate/professional degree or higher: 22.5%

Housing: Homeownership rate: 79.6%; Median home value: $444,800; Median year structure built: 1971; Homeowner vacancy rate: 0.7%; Median

selected monthly owner costs: $3,082 with a mortgage, $1,243 without a mortgage; Median gross rent: $1,423 per month; Rental vacancy rate: 4.7%

Health Insurance: 93.8% have insurance; 80.9% have private insurance; 27.0% have public insurance; 6.2% do not have insurance; 2.5% of children under 18 do not have insurance

Safety: Violent crime rate: 13.3 per 10,000 population; Property crime rate: 172.5 per 10,000 population

Transportation: Commute: 86.1% car, 7.1% public transportation, 1.4% walk, 4.6% work from home; Mean travel time to work: 31.9 minutes

Additional Information Contacts

Town of Clarkstown . . . . (845) 639-2000
http://www.town.clarkstown.ny.us

CONGERS (CDP). Covers a land area of 3.068 square miles and a water area of 0.744 square miles. Located at 41.15° N. Lat; 73.94° W. Long. Elevation is 177 feet.

History: Congers, named after Abraham B. Conger, was settled in the late 17th century by Dutch, German and English settlers. It was originally known as Cedar Grove Corner and then Waldberg, which is German for "forest mountain."

Population: 8,698; Growth (since 2000): 4.8%; Density: 2,835.1 persons per square mile; Race: 78.9% White, 3.3% Black/African American, 10.9% Asian, 0.0% American Indian/Alaska Native, 0.0% Native Hawaiian/Other Pacific Islander, 2.7% Two or more races, 14.6% Hispanic of any race; Average household size: 3.01; Median age: 43.2; Age under 18: 22.7%; Age 65 and over: 15.5%; Males per 100 females: 93.6; Marriage status: 29.7% never married, 55.3% now married, 1.5% separated, 6.5% widowed, 8.5% divorced; Foreign born: 18.5%; Speak English only: 74.8%; With disability: 9.1%; Veterans: 5.2%; Ancestry: 31.1% Italian, 24.7% Irish, 10.5% German, 4.2% American, 3.6% Polish

Employment: 16.0% management, business, and financial, 4.6% computer, engineering, and science, 15.7% education, legal, community service, arts, and media, 8.5% healthcare practitioners, 14.3% service, 26.7% sales and office, 8.8% natural resources, construction, and maintenance, 5.4% production, transportation, and material moving

Income: Per capita: $43,134; Median household: $109,935; Average household: $127,752; Households with income of $100,000 or more: 56.8%; Poverty rate: 4.1%

Educational Attainment: High school diploma or higher: 90.3%; Bachelor's degree or higher: 46.1%; Graduate/professional degree or higher: 22.2%

School District(s)

Clarkstown Central SD (KG-12)
    2014-15 Enrollment: 8,478 . . . . (845) 639-6418

Housing: Homeownership rate: 85.9%; Median home value: $445,400; Median year structure built: 1969; Homeowner vacancy rate: 0.0%; Median selected monthly owner costs: $3,232 with a mortgage, $1,212 without a mortgage; Median gross rent: $1,460 per month; Rental vacancy rate: 6.9%

Health Insurance: 94.1% have insurance; 84.7% have private insurance; 22.4% have public insurance; 5.9% do not have insurance; 3.2% of children under 18 do not have insurance

Transportation: Commute: 91.0% car, 3.7% public transportation, 0.4% walk, 4.8% work from home; Mean travel time to work: 30.9 minutes

---

GARNERVILLE (unincorporated postal area)
ZCTA: 10923

Covers a land area of 1.967 square miles and a water area of 0.036 square miles. Located at 41.20° N. Lat; 74.00° W. Long. Elevation is 210 feet.

Population: 8,473; Growth (since 2000): -8.6%; Density: 4,308.2 persons per square mile; Race: 70.6% White, 11.7% Black/African American, 4.0% Asian, 0.0% American Indian/Alaska Native, 0.0% Native Hawaiian/Other Pacific Islander, 2.2% Two or more races, 37.7% Hispanic of any race; Average household size: 3.19; Median age: 39.6; Age under 18: 23.3%; Age 65 and over: 11.2%; Males per 100 females: 94.2; Marriage status: 38.8% never married, 52.0% now married, 2.3% separated, 5.2% widowed, 4.0% divorced; Foreign born: 21.9%; Speak English only: 63.0%; With disability: 10.6%; Veterans: 5.3%; Ancestry: 16.2% Irish, 16.2% Italian, 7.7% German, 5.1% Haitian, 4.9% Polish

Employment: 10.0% management, business, and financial, 4.1% computer, engineering, and science, 11.5% education, legal, community service, arts, and media, 7.4% healthcare practitioners, 23.8% service,

25.4% sales and office, 6.6% natural resources, construction, and maintenance, 11.2% production, transportation, and material moving

Income: Per capita: $31,463; Median household: $83,734; Average household: $97,805; Households with income of $100,000 or more: 41.4%; Poverty rate: 11.0%

Educational Attainment: High school diploma or higher: 87.9%; Bachelor's degree or higher: 30.7%; Graduate/professional degree or higher: 13.2%

School District(s)

Haverstraw-Stony Point CSD (North Rockland) (KG-12)
    2014-15 Enrollment: 8,010 . . . . (845) 942-3002

Housing: Homeownership rate: 63.6%; Median home value: $348,400; Median year structure built: 1971; Homeowner vacancy rate: 0.0%; Median selected monthly owner costs: $3,063 with a mortgage, $1,135 without a mortgage; Median gross rent: $1,363 per month; Rental vacancy rate: 1.9%

Health Insurance: 89.3% have insurance; 68.1% have private insurance; 32.1% have public insurance; 10.7% do not have insurance; 1.9% of children under 18 do not have insurance

Transportation: Commute: 87.2% car, 8.2% public transportation, 0.5% walk, 1.6% work from home; Mean travel time to work: 33.7 minutes

---

GRAND VIEW-ON-HUDSON (village). Covers a land area of 0.176 square miles and a water area of <.001 square miles. Located at 41.07° N. Lat; 73.92° W. Long. Elevation is -3 feet.

Population: 295; Growth (since 2000): 3.9%; Density: 1,679.8 persons per square mile; Race: 97.3% White, 0.0% Black/African American, 1.4% Asian, 0.0% American Indian/Alaska Native, 0.0% Native Hawaiian/Other Pacific Islander, 1.4% Two or more races, 6.4% Hispanic of any race; Average household size: 2.40; Median age: 49.3; Age under 18: 19.0%; Age 65 and over: 22.0%; Males per 100 females: 80.4; Marriage status: 28.2% never married, 58.8% now married, 1.2% separated, 5.9% widowed, 7.1% divorced; Foreign born: 9.8%; Speak English only: 88.4%; With disability: 4.4%; Veterans: 8.8%; Ancestry: 19.0% German, 16.3% Irish, 11.2% Russian, 9.8% Italian, 8.8% English

Employment: 30.9% management, business, and financial, 5.1% computer, engineering, and science, 33.1% education, legal, community service, arts, and media, 7.3% healthcare practitioners, 3.9% service, 14.0% sales and office, 3.4% natural resources, construction, and maintenance, 2.2% production, transportation, and material moving

Income: Per capita: $62,766; Median household: $126,250; Average household: $150,381; Households with income of $100,000 or more: 64.3%; Poverty rate: 1.7%

Educational Attainment: High school diploma or higher: 99.6%; Bachelor's degree or higher: 79.2%; Graduate/professional degree or higher: 34.1%

Housing: Homeownership rate: 78.9%; Median home value: $902,800; Median year structure built: Before 1940; Homeowner vacancy rate: 4.0%; Median selected monthly owner costs: $4,000+ with a mortgage, $1,500+ without a mortgage; Median gross rent: $3,023 per month; Rental vacancy rate: 16.1%

Health Insurance: 98.6% have insurance; 89.8% have private insurance; 23.4% have public insurance; 1.4% do not have insurance; 0.0% of children under 18 do not have insurance

Transportation: Commute: 85.1% car, 2.3% public transportation, 0.6% walk, 12.0% work from home; Mean travel time to work: 36.0 minutes

---

HAVERSTRAW (town). Covers a land area of 22.155 square miles and a water area of 5.260 square miles. Located at 41.20° N. Lat; 74.04° W. Long. Elevation is 33 feet.

History: In Haverstraw, James Wood discovered the modern system of burning brick, and set up brickyards in the town. At its peak, the industry included 40 brickyards.

Population: 37,261; Growth (since 2000): 10.2%; Density: 1,681.8 persons per square mile; Race: 56.9% White, 16.0% Black/African American, 4.1% Asian, 0.2% American Indian/Alaska Native, 0.0% Native Hawaiian/Other Pacific Islander, 3.3% Two or more races, 44.8% Hispanic of any race; Average household size: 3.13; Median age: 36.0; Age under 18: 23.9%; Age 65 and over: 12.0%; Males per 100 females: 94.0; Marriage status: 39.3% never married, 48.5% now married, 3.7% separated, 4.7% widowed, 7.4% divorced; Foreign born: 27.8%; Speak English only: 54.3%; With disability: 11.5%; Veterans: 5.0%; Ancestry: 13.5% Italian, 11.9% Irish, 6.2% German, 4.8% Haitian, 4.0% American

Employment: 8.8% management, business, and financial, 3.5% computer, engineering, and science, 10.0% education, legal, community service, arts,

and media, 6.7% healthcare practitioners, 27.2% service, 23.2% sales and office, 8.4% natural resources, construction, and maintenance, 12.2% production, transportation, and material moving

Income: Per capita: $29,883; Median household: $73,117; Average household: $91,530; Households with income of $100,000 or more: 34.6%; Poverty rate: 11.7%

Educational Attainment: High school diploma or higher: 82.6%; Bachelor's degree or higher: 28.1%; Graduate/professional degree or higher: 11.6%

School District(s)
Haverstraw-Stony Point CSD (North Rockland) (KG-12)

   2014-15 Enrollment: 8,010 . . . . (845) 942-3002

Housing: Homeownership rate: 60.8%; Median home value: $309,300; Median year structure built: 1971; Homeowner vacancy rate: 1.5%; Median selected monthly owner costs: $2,662 with a mortgage, $1,158 without a mortgage; Median gross rent: $1,357 per month; Rental vacancy rate: 2.4%

Health Insurance: 87.5% have insurance; 62.1% have private insurance; 35.4% have public insurance; 12.5% do not have insurance; 4.5% of children under 18 do not have insurance

Safety: Violent crime rate: 13.0 per 10,000 population; Property crime rate: 91.2 per 10,000 population

Transportation: Commute: 83.2% car, 8.5% public transportation, 2.5% walk, 3.7% work from home; Mean travel time to work: 30.5 minutes

Additional Information Contacts

Town of Haverstraw . . . . (845) 942-3727
   http://townofhaverstraw.us

HAVERSTRAW (village). Covers a land area of 1.980 square miles and a water area of 3.057 square miles. Located at 41.18° N. Lat; 73.94° W. Long. Elevation is 33 feet.

Population: 12,094; Growth (since 2000): 19.5%; Density: 6,107.8 persons per square mile; Race: 46.4% White, 16.6% Black/African American, 1.3% Asian, 0.6% American Indian/Alaska Native, 0.0% Native Hawaiian/Other Pacific Islander, 2.8% Two or more races, 64.6% Hispanic of any race; Average household size: 3.24; Median age: 33.2; Age under 18: 24.6%; Age 65 and over: 12.0%; Males per 100 females: 94.4; Marriage status: 41.0% never married, 44.8% now married, 5.9% separated, 5.3% widowed, 8.9% divorced; Foreign born: 37.5%; Speak English only: 37.7%; With disability: 13.5%; Veterans: 4.8%; Ancestry: 7.1% Irish, 6.2% Italian, 2.9% American, 2.7% German, 2.4% Haitian

Employment: 5.6% management, business, and financial, 2.7% computer, engineering, and science, 7.6% education, legal, community service, arts, and media, 6.1% healthcare practitioners, 29.0% service, 21.7% sales and office, 8.7% natural resources, construction, and maintenance, 18.5% production, transportation, and material moving

Income: Per capita: $25,193; Median household: $56,061; Average household: $80,163; Households with income of $100,000 or more: 28.1%; Poverty rate: 17.3%

Educational Attainment: High school diploma or higher: 74.0%; Bachelor's degree or higher: 23.2%; Graduate/professional degree or higher: 9.2%

School District(s)
Haverstraw-Stony Point CSD (North Rockland) (KG-12)

   2014-15 Enrollment: 8,010 . . . . (845) 942-3002

Housing: Homeownership rate: 43.6%; Median home value: $261,000; Median year structure built: 1958; Homeowner vacancy rate: 0.8%; Median selected monthly owner costs: $2,559 with a mortgage, $970 without a mortgage; Median gross rent: $1,296 per month; Rental vacancy rate: 2.7%

Health Insurance: 84.8% have insurance; 47.0% have private insurance; 45.3% have public insurance; 15.2% do not have insurance; 1.4% of children under 18 do not have insurance

Transportation: Commute: 77.3% car, 13.6% public transportation, 3.5% walk, 2.5% work from home; Mean travel time to work: 28.2 minutes

Additional Information Contacts

Village of Haverstraw . . . . (845) 429-0300
   http://www.voh-ny.com/index.htm

HILLBURN (village). Covers a land area of 2.251 square miles and a water area of 0.018 square miles. Located at 41.13° N. Lat; 74.17° W. Long. Elevation is 308 feet.

History: Incorporated 1893.

Population: 872; Growth (since 2000): -1.0%; Density: 387.4 persons per square mile; Race: 47.1% White, 19.4% Black/African American, 1.8%

Asian, 8.4% American Indian/Alaska Native, 0.0% Native Hawaiian/Other Pacific Islander, 14.3% Two or more races, 15.3% Hispanic of any race; Average household size: 2.92; Median age: 43.5; Age under 18: 24.2%; Age 65 and over: 13.5%; Males per 100 females: 108.6; Marriage status: 29.1% never married, 52.7% now married, 4.9% separated, 5.6% widowed, 12.6% divorced; Foreign born: 14.1%; Speak English only: 78.0%; With disability: 9.6%; Veterans: 8.2%; Ancestry: 13.4% Italian, 12.8% Irish, 11.5% Haitian, 8.6% German, 8.5% English

Employment: 14.0% management, business, and financial, 6.6% computer, engineering, and science, 8.5% education, legal, community service, arts, and media, 3.1% healthcare practitioners, 22.7% service, 20.4% sales and office, 9.7% natural resources, construction, and maintenance, 14.9% production, transportation, and material moving

Income: Per capita: $32,374; Median household: $77,321; Average household: $87,271; Households with income of $100,000 or more: 38.9%; Poverty rate: 9.6%

Educational Attainment: High school diploma or higher: 89.9%; Bachelor's degree or higher: 24.5%; Graduate/professional degree or higher: 9.2%

Housing: Homeownership rate: 75.6%; Median home value: $317,700; Median year structure built: Before 1940; Homeowner vacancy rate: 5.0%; Median selected monthly owner costs: $2,308 with a mortgage, $1,050 without a mortgage; Median gross rent: $1,361 per month; Rental vacancy rate: 6.1%

Health Insurance: 88.9% have insurance; 74.2% have private insurance; 24.7% have public insurance; 11.1% do not have insurance; 3.3% of children under 18 do not have insurance

Transportation: Commute: 85.6% car, 7.1% public transportation, 2.2% walk, 5.1% work from home; Mean travel time to work: 27.5 minutes

Additional Information Contacts

Village of Hillburn . . . . (845) 357-2036
   http://www.hillburn.org

HILLCREST (CDP). Covers a land area of 1.297 square miles and a water area of 0 square miles. Located at 41.13° N. Lat; 74.04° W. Long. Elevation is 512 feet.

Population: 7,317; Growth (since 2000): 3.0%; Density: 5,639.7 persons per square mile; Race: 22.2% White, 56.9% Black/African American, 9.4% Asian, 0.0% American Indian/Alaska Native, 0.0% Native Hawaiian/Other Pacific Islander, 2.8% Two or more races, 17.7% Hispanic of any race; Average household size: 3.71; Median age: 41.6; Age under 18: 19.7%; Age 65 and over: 16.6%; Males per 100 females: 96.1; Marriage status: 33.7% never married, 52.4% now married, 1.9% separated, 6.9% widowed, 7.1% divorced; Foreign born: 42.9%; Speak English only: 50.5%; With disability: 9.3%; Veterans: 3.5%; Ancestry: 24.8% Haitian, 8.9% Jamaican, 6.4% American, 2.4% Italian, 2.2% Irish

Employment: 6.0% management, business, and financial, 3.1% computer, engineering, and science, 12.2% education, legal, community service, arts, and media, 12.7% healthcare practitioners, 27.9% service, 15.4% sales and office, 9.9% natural resources, construction, and maintenance, 12.8% production, transportation, and material moving

Income: Per capita: $28,345; Median household: $94,156; Average household: $99,576; Households with income of $100,000 or more: 46.4%; Poverty rate: 4.2%

Educational Attainment: High school diploma or higher: 84.2%; Bachelor's degree or higher: 26.7%; Graduate/professional degree or higher: 9.1%

Housing: Homeownership rate: 85.4%; Median home value: $357,500; Median year structure built: 1963; Homeowner vacancy rate: 2.3%; Median selected monthly owner costs: $2,784 with a mortgage, $1,203 without a mortgage; Median gross rent: $1,159 per month; Rental vacancy rate: 0.0%

Health Insurance: 86.6% have insurance; 68.5% have private insurance; 28.6% have public insurance; 13.4% do not have insurance; 11.4% of children under 18 do not have insurance

Transportation: Commute: 89.3% car, 7.0% public transportation, 0.7% walk, 1.0% work from home; Mean travel time to work: 28.8 minutes

KASER (village). Covers a land area of 0.172 square miles and a water area of 0 square miles. Located at 41.12° N. Lat; 74.07° W. Long. Elevation is 538 feet.

Population: 4,998; Growth (since 2000): 50.7%; Density: 29,010.4 persons per square mile; Race: 99.4% White, 0.0% Black/African American, 0.4% Asian, 0.0% American Indian/Alaska Native, 0.0% Native Hawaiian/Other Pacific Islander, 0.2% Two or more races, 0.2% Hispanic

of any race; Average household size: 5.20; Median age: 14.2; Age under 18: 57.8%; Age 65 and over: 1.0%; Males per 100 females: 105.5; Marriage status: 22.0% never married, 76.7% now married, 0.5% separated, 0.5% widowed, 0.8% divorced; Foreign born: 5.6%; Speak English only: 7.3%; With disability: 4.0%; Veterans: 0.0%; Ancestry: 29.1% European, 22.7% Hungarian, 14.4% American, 12.6% Israeli, 3.3% Polish

Employment: 5.7% management, business, and financial, 7.3% computer, engineering, and science, 46.8% education, legal, community service, arts, and media, 0.0% healthcare practitioners, 4.6% service, 30.1% sales and office, 2.6% natural resources, construction, and maintenance, 2.9% production, transportation, and material moving

Income: Per capita: $5,912; Median household: $20,048; Average household: $30,675; Households with income of $100,000 or more: 4.4%; Poverty rate: 73.7%

Educational Attainment: High school diploma or higher: 76.4%; Bachelor's degree or higher: 2.5%; Graduate/professional degree or higher: 1.6%

Housing: Homeownership rate: 3.8%; Median home value: $376,700; Median year structure built: 1996; Homeowner vacancy rate: 0.0%; Median selected monthly owner costs: $3,700 with a mortgage, $538 without a mortgage; Median gross rent: $1,028 per month; Rental vacancy rate: 1.2%

Health Insurance: 97.1% have insurance; 8.6% have private insurance; 90.9% have public insurance; 2.9% do not have insurance; 0.2% of children under 18 do not have insurance

Transportation: Commute: 37.6% car, 13.2% public transportation, 40.0% walk, 3.5% work from home; Mean travel time to work: 15.1 minutes

MONSEY (CDP).
Covers a land area of 2.273 square miles and a water area of 0.014 square miles. Located at 41.11° N. Lat; 74.08° W. Long. Elevation is 545 feet.

History: Rockland County was inhabited by the Munsee band of Lenape Native Americans, or Delaware Indians, of the Algonquian tribe. Monsey Glen, an Indian encampment, is located west of the intersection of NY 59 and NY 306, where rock shelters are still visible. The Monsey railroad station is named for Munsee, a Lenape chief, and was built in 1841.

Population: 21,001; Growth (since 2000): 44.8%; Density: 9,240.4 persons per square mile; Race: 94.6% White, 2.3% Black/African American, 0.2% Asian, 0.2% American Indian/Alaska Native, 0.0% Native Hawaiian/Other Pacific Islander, 0.4% Two or more races, 3.0% Hispanic of any race; Average household size: 5.36; Median age: 16.7; Age under 18: 53.1%; Age 65 and over: 5.6%; Males per 100 females: 106.0; Marriage status: 34.0% never married, 62.5% now married, 0.5% separated, 1.8% widowed, 1.7% divorced; Foreign born: 12.0%; Speak English only: 22.6%; With disability: 5.7%; Veterans: 1.0%; Ancestry: 29.9% European, 16.5% Hungarian, 8.2% Polish, 7.2% American, 4.6% Russian

Employment: 15.0% management, business, and financial, 2.9% computer, engineering, and science, 32.7% education, legal, community service, arts, and media, 1.6% healthcare practitioners, 8.9% service, 29.7% sales and office, 5.0% natural resources, construction, and maintenance, 4.3% production, transportation, and material moving

Income: Per capita: $11,552; Median household: $37,426; Average household: $60,572; Households with income of $100,000 or more: 16.3%; Poverty rate: 46.9%

Educational Attainment: High school diploma or higher: 78.5%; Bachelor's degree or higher: 16.7%; Graduate/professional degree or higher: 6.9%

School District(s)
East Ramapo Central SD (Spring Valley) (PK-12)
   2014-15 Enrollment: 8,881 . . . . (845) 577-6011

Four-year College(s)
Beth Medrash Meor Yitzchok (Private, Not-for-profit)
   Fall 2014 Enrollment: n/a . . . . (845) 426-3488
   2015-16 Tuition: In-state $8,200; Out-of-state $8,200
Rabbinical College Beth Shraga (Private, Not-for-profit)
   Fall 2014 Enrollment: 41 . . . . (845) 356-1980
   2015-16 Tuition: In-state $12,050; Out-of-state $12,050
Yeshiva D'monsey Rabbinical College (Private, Not-for-profit)
   Fall 2014 Enrollment: 60 . . . . (845) 352-5852
   2015-16 Tuition: In-state $6,000; Out-of-state $6,000
Yeshiva Gedolah Kesser Torah (Private, Not-for-profit)
   Fall 2014 Enrollment: 67 . . . . (845) 406-4308
   2015-16 Tuition: In-state $10,200; Out-of-state $10,200

Yeshivath Viznitz (Private, Not-for-profit)
   Fall 2014 Enrollment: 631 . . . . (845) 731-3700
   2015-16 Tuition: In-state $8,600; Out-of-state $8,600

Housing: Homeownership rate: 39.5%; Median home value: $569,300; Median year structure built: 1987; Homeowner vacancy rate: 1.9%; Median selected monthly owner costs: $3,313 with a mortgage, $1,455 without a mortgage; Median gross rent: $1,333 per month; Rental vacancy rate: 1.8%

Health Insurance: 94.7% have insurance; 32.6% have private insurance; 68.9% have public insurance; 5.3% do not have insurance; 2.4% of children under 18 do not have insurance

Transportation: Commute: 62.6% car, 11.4% public transportation, 15.2% walk, 7.4% work from home; Mean travel time to work: 21.5 minutes

MONTEBELLO (village).
Covers a land area of 4.346 square miles and a water area of 0.010 square miles. Located at 41.13° N. Lat; 74.11° W. Long. Elevation is 318 feet.

History: Montebello was incorporated in 1986.

Population: 4,616; Growth (since 2000): 25.2%; Density: 1,062.1 persons per square mile; Race: 77.6% White, 13.8% Black/African American, 4.2% Asian, 0.0% American Indian/Alaska Native, 0.0% Native Hawaiian/Other Pacific Islander, 0.6% Two or more races, 4.9% Hispanic of any race; Average household size: 3.02; Median age: 46.2; Age under 18: 24.8%; Age 65 and over: 18.3%; Males per 100 females: 93.1; Marriage status: 25.3% never married, 58.7% now married, 0.3% separated, 8.3% widowed, 7.6% divorced; Foreign born: 14.6%; Speak English only: 89.5%; With disability: 9.6%; Veterans: 4.8%; Ancestry: 22.6% Italian, 11.6% German, 9.9% Irish, 8.9% English, 4.6% American

Employment: 29.9% management, business, and financial, 4.2% computer, engineering, and science, 16.2% education, legal, community service, arts, and media, 14.7% healthcare practitioners, 7.1% service, 22.1% sales and office, 1.8% natural resources, construction, and maintenance, 3.9% production, transportation, and material moving

Income: Per capita: $68,771; Median household: $132,614; Average household: $203,664; Households with income of $100,000 or more: 61.4%; Poverty rate: 1.7%

Educational Attainment: High school diploma or higher: 95.2%; Bachelor's degree or higher: 62.2%; Graduate/professional degree or higher: 32.4%

Housing: Homeownership rate: 90.2%; Median home value: $630,400; Median year structure built: 1976; Homeowner vacancy rate: 0.0%; Median selected monthly owner costs: $4,000+ with a mortgage, $1,500+ without a mortgage; Median gross rent: $1,590 per month; Rental vacancy rate: 0.0%

Health Insurance: 97.4% have insurance; 90.5% have private insurance; 20.6% have public insurance; 2.6% do not have insurance; 2.8% of children under 18 do not have insurance

Transportation: Commute: 81.1% car, 11.7% public transportation, 0.3% walk, 6.8% work from home; Mean travel time to work: 36.6 minutes

Additional Information Contacts
Village of Montebello . . . . (845) 368-2211
   http://www.villageofmontebello.com

MOUNT IVY (CDP).
Covers a land area of 1.467 square miles and a water area of 0 square miles. Located at 41.19° N. Lat; 74.03° W. Long. Elevation is 463 feet.

Population: 7,090; Growth (since 2000): 8.5%; Density: 4,833.3 persons per square mile; Race: 57.3% White, 17.1% Black/African American, 6.0% Asian, 0.0% American Indian/Alaska Native, 0.0% Native Hawaiian/Other Pacific Islander, 5.7% Two or more races, 29.6% Hispanic of any race; Average household size: 2.64; Median age: 33.4; Age under 18: 24.7%; Age 65 and over: 9.7%; Males per 100 females: 90.2; Marriage status: 40.2% never married, 47.4% now married, 2.3% separated, 3.8% widowed, 8.6% divorced; Foreign born: 23.1%; Speak English only: 67.3%; With disability: 7.5%; Veterans: 3.2%; Ancestry: 20.0% Italian, 14.9% Irish, 9.9% German, 5.6% Russian, 5.0% Polish

Employment: 10.1% management, business, and financial, 3.6% computer, engineering, and science, 14.3% education, legal, community service, arts, and media, 6.7% healthcare practitioners, 26.7% service, 20.9% sales and office, 8.9% natural resources, construction, and maintenance, 8.7% production, transportation, and material moving

Income: Per capita: $31,461; Median household: $70,226; Average household: $80,528; Households with income of $100,000 or more: 26.3%; Poverty rate: 9.1%

Educational Attainment: High school diploma or higher: 87.7%; Bachelor's degree or higher: 32.6%; Graduate/professional degree or higher: 13.2%
Housing: Homeownership rate: 61.2%; Median home value: $229,900; Median year structure built: 1978; Homeowner vacancy rate: 4.8%; Median selected monthly owner costs: $2,273 with a mortgage, $1,216 without a mortgage; Median gross rent: $1,627 per month; Rental vacancy rate: 3.4%
Health Insurance: 84.5% have insurance; 65.2% have private insurance; 28.1% have public insurance; 15.5% do not have insurance; 14.4% of children under 18 do not have insurance
Transportation: Commute: 86.8% car, 3.5% public transportation, 0.8% walk, 8.7% work from home; Mean travel time to work: 31.4 minutes

NANUET (CDP). Covers a land area of 5.433 square miles and a water area of 0.005 square miles. Located at 41.10° N. Lat; 74.02° W. Long. Elevation is 299 feet.
History: Named for a local Indian chief. International Shrine of St. Anthony is here.
Population: 18,678; Growth (since 2000): 11.8%; Density: 3,438.0 persons per square mile; Race: 62.5% White, 14.0% Black/African American, 14.3% Asian, 0.6% American Indian/Alaska Native, 0.0% Native Hawaiian/Other Pacific Islander, 2.9% Two or more races, 15.9% Hispanic of any race; Average household size: 2.71; Median age: 44.4; Age under 18: 20.3%; Age 65 and over: 18.4%; Males per 100 females: 89.4; Marriage status: 29.3% never married, 54.4% now married, 1.8% separated, 8.0% widowed, 8.2% divorced; Foreign born: 29.1%; Speak English only: 63.2%; With disability: 10.3%; Veterans: 4.6%; Ancestry: 18.7% Italian, 18.5% Irish, 7.2% German, 6.2% Haitian, 4.4% Polish
Employment: 16.4% management, business, and financial, 6.2% computer, engineering, and science, 12.6% education, legal, community service, arts, and media, 8.3% healthcare practitioners, 17.5% service, 25.7% sales and office, 5.4% natural resources, construction, and maintenance, 7.9% production, transportation, and material moving
Income: Per capita: $39,183; Median household: $89,650; Average household: $104,547; Households with income of $100,000 or more: 42.9%; Poverty rate: 5.1%
Educational Attainment: High school diploma or higher: 88.4%; Bachelor's degree or higher: 40.5%; Graduate/professional degree or higher: 15.6%
School District(s)
Nanuet Union Free SD (PK-12)
    2014-15 Enrollment: 2,262 . . . . (845) 627-9888
Vocational/Technical School(s)
Capri Cosmetology Learning Centers (Private, For-profit)
    Fall 2014 Enrollment: 223 . . . . (845) 623-6339
    2015-16 Tuition: $13,100
Housing: Homeownership rate: 66.5%; Median home value: $394,800; Median year structure built: 1975; Homeowner vacancy rate: 1.0%; Median selected monthly owner costs: $3,065 with a mortgage, $1,105 without a mortgage; Median gross rent: $1,585 per month; Rental vacancy rate: 3.7%
Health Insurance: 93.8% have insurance; 76.4% have private insurance; 30.8% have public insurance; 6.2% do not have insurance; 0.4% of children under 18 do not have insurance
Newspapers: Rockland County Times (weekly circulation 12,000)
Transportation: Commute: 84.8% car, 8.7% public transportation, 1.7% walk, 3.6% work from home; Mean travel time to work: 31.1 minutes

NEW CITY (CDP). County seat. Covers a land area of 15.582 square miles and a water area of 0.793 square miles. Located at 41.15° N. Lat; 73.99° W. Long. Elevation is 157 feet.
History: New City is the county seat, and most populous community of Rockland County. Its downtown is one of the main business districts in the county.
Population: 33,722; Growth (since 2000): -0.9%; Density: 2,164.1 persons per square mile; Race: 75.6% White, 8.0% Black/African American, 11.3% Asian, 0.0% American Indian/Alaska Native, 0.0% Native Hawaiian/Other Pacific Islander, 3.8% Two or more races, 7.9% Hispanic of any race; Average household size: 3.02; Median age: 44.9; Age under 18: 21.7%; Age 65 and over: 18.5%; Males per 100 females: 96.4; Marriage status: 26.6% never married, 63.4% now married, 1.1% separated, 4.9% widowed, 5.1% divorced; Foreign born: 19.2%; Speak English only: 74.5%; With disability: 8.7%; Veterans: 5.7%; Ancestry: 19.5% Italian, 15.0% Irish, 7.5% German, 6.9% Russian, 6.4% American

Employment: 20.4% management, business, and financial, 6.0% computer, engineering, and science, 17.2% education, legal, community service, arts, and media, 11.7% healthcare practitioners, 12.0% service, 22.6% sales and office, 4.8% natural resources, construction, and maintenance, 5.4% production, transportation, and material moving
Income: Per capita: $48,389; Median household: $119,528; Average household: $145,336; Households with income of $100,000 or more: 60.7%; Poverty rate: 4.5%
Educational Attainment: High school diploma or higher: 93.7%; Bachelor's degree or higher: 57.7%; Graduate/professional degree or higher: 27.6%
School District(s)
Clarkstown Central SD (KG-12)
    2014-15 Enrollment: 8,478 . . . . (845) 639-6418
East Ramapo Central SD (Spring Valley) (PK-12)
    2014-15 Enrollment: 8,881 . . . . (845) 577-6011
Housing: Homeownership rate: 90.1%; Median home value: $473,100; Median year structure built: 1970; Homeowner vacancy rate: 0.6%; Median selected monthly owner costs: $3,088 with a mortgage, $1,340 without a mortgage; Median gross rent: $1,237 per month; Rental vacancy rate: 6.9%
Health Insurance: 96.0% have insurance; 85.8% have private insurance; 25.2% have public insurance; 4.0% do not have insurance; 1.4% of children under 18 do not have insurance
Transportation: Commute: 87.1% car, 6.8% public transportation, 0.6% walk, 4.4% work from home; Mean travel time to work: 33.1 minutes

NEW HEMPSTEAD (village). Covers a land area of 2.853 square miles and a water area of 0.010 square miles. Located at 41.15° N. Lat; 74.05° W. Long. Elevation is 581 feet.
History: New Hempstead, formally known as Kakiat, is a village in the Town of Ramapo. Joseph Berger of The New York Times said in a 1997 article that New Hempstead was one of several Town of Ramapo villages formed by non-Jewish people and more secular Jewish people "to preserve the sparse Better Homes and Gardens ambiance that attracted them to Rockland County.
Population: 5,265; Growth (since 2000): 10.4%; Density: 1,845.3 persons per square mile; Race: 65.8% White, 14.2% Black/African American, 7.0% Asian, 0.0% American Indian/Alaska Native, 0.0% Native Hawaiian/Other Pacific Islander, 1.8% Two or more races, 17.2% Hispanic of any race; Average household size: 4.40; Median age: 30.9; Age under 18: 32.1%; Age 65 and over: 9.2%; Males per 100 females: 99.6; Marriage status: 39.3% never married, 51.7% now married, 2.0% separated, 5.4% widowed, 3.6% divorced; Foreign born: 20.2%; Speak English only: 69.0%; With disability: 6.6%; Veterans: 2.9%; Ancestry: 13.8% European, 11.4% Polish, 9.9% American, 9.6% Russian, 4.7% Italian
Employment: 12.1% management, business, and financial, 4.2% computer, engineering, and science, 12.9% education, legal, community service, arts, and media, 8.4% healthcare practitioners, 21.9% service, 24.7% sales and office, 7.9% natural resources, construction, and maintenance, 7.8% production, transportation, and material moving
Income: Per capita: $29,319; Median household: $107,875; Average household: $126,439; Households with income of $100,000 or more: 53.7%; Poverty rate: 3.2%
Educational Attainment: High school diploma or higher: 89.8%; Bachelor's degree or higher: 41.1%; Graduate/professional degree or higher: 15.8%
Housing: Homeownership rate: 94.4%; Median home value: $454,600; Median year structure built: 1966; Homeowner vacancy rate: 0.0%; Median selected monthly owner costs: $2,985 with a mortgage, $1,214 without a mortgage; Median gross rent: $1,934 per month; Rental vacancy rate: 0.0%
Health Insurance: 86.9% have insurance; 64.5% have private insurance; 27.9% have public insurance; 13.1% do not have insurance; 7.4% of children under 18 do not have insurance
Transportation: Commute: 85.1% car, 8.3% public transportation, 0.0% walk, 5.5% work from home; Mean travel time to work: 35.3 minutes

NEW SQUARE (village). Covers a land area of 0.356 square miles and a water area of 0 square miles. Located at 41.14° N. Lat; 74.03° W. Long. Elevation is 489 feet.
History: A community of Orthodox Hasidic Jews of the Skvirer sect lives here.
Population: 7,540; Growth (since 2000): 63.1%; Density: 21,161.6 persons per square mile; Race: 99.0% White, 0.1% Black/African

American, 0.0% Asian, 0.2% American Indian/Alaska Native, 0.0% Native Hawaiian/Other Pacific Islander, 0.7% Two or more races, 0.3% Hispanic of any race; Average household size: 5.90; Median age: 14.1; Age under 18: 60.9%; Age 65 and over: 0.5%; Males per 100 females: 107.5; Marriage status: 29.2% never married, 69.6% now married, 0.3% separated, 0.8% widowed, 0.3% divorced; Foreign born: 3.3%; Speak English only: 5.7%; With disability: 2.7%; Veterans: 0.4%; Ancestry: 32.8% Hungarian, 19.5% European, 11.9% Polish, 7.4% American, 4.8% Russian

Employment: 11.6% management, business, and financial, 2.2% computer, engineering, and science, 37.5% education, legal, community service, arts, and media, 0.5% healthcare practitioners, 11.0% service, 26.4% sales and office, 4.4% natural resources, construction, and maintenance, 6.4% production, transportation, and material moving

Income: Per capita: $5,514; Median household: $22,470; Average household: $32,432; Households with income of $100,000 or more: 3.7%; Poverty rate: 70.5%

Educational Attainment: High school diploma or higher: 70.6%; Bachelor's degree or higher: 4.1%; Graduate/professional degree or higher: 1.1%

Housing: Homeownership rate: 14.1%; Median home value: $328,800; Median year structure built: 1996; Homeowner vacancy rate: 0.0%; Median selected monthly owner costs: $2,724 with a mortgage, $414 without a mortgage; Median gross rent: $1,280 per month; Rental vacancy rate: 0.0%

Health Insurance: 98.5% have insurance; 15.4% have private insurance; 87.2% have public insurance; 1.5% do not have insurance; 1.4% of children under 18 do not have insurance

Transportation: Commute: 33.1% car, 7.7% public transportation, 48.2% walk, 7.7% work from home; Mean travel time to work: 17.5 minutes

---

NYACK (village). Covers a land area of 0.770 square miles and a water area of 0.838 square miles. Located at 41.09° N. Lat; 73.91° W. Long. Elevation is 72 feet.

History: Was a 19th-century health resort, port, and boat-building center. Birthplace of artist Edward Hopper. Settled 1684, incorporated 1833.

Population: 6,769; Growth (since 2000): 0.5%; Density: 8,794.6 persons per square mile; Race: 73.3% White, 17.3% Black/African American, 2.4% Asian, 0.3% American Indian/Alaska Native, 0.0% Native Hawaiian/Other Pacific Islander, 4.0% Two or more races, 16.9% Hispanic of any race; Average household size: 2.14; Median age: 40.4; Age under 18: 21.3%; Age 65 and over: 15.7%; Males per 100 females: 86.3; Marriage status: 36.2% never married, 46.7% now married, 5.3% separated, 5.3% widowed, 11.9% divorced; Foreign born: 17.8%; Speak English only: 80.5%; With disability: 12.4%; Veterans: 4.9%; Ancestry: 21.0% Irish, 11.0% English, 10.1% German, 8.5% Italian, 6.4% Welsh

Employment: 19.9% management, business, and financial, 8.4% computer, engineering, and science, 22.2% education, legal, community service, arts, and media, 7.8% healthcare practitioners, 18.4% service, 15.3% sales and office, 6.1% natural resources, construction, and maintenance, 1.7% production, transportation, and material moving

Income: Per capita: $40,316; Median household: $64,464; Average household: $83,986; Households with income of $100,000 or more: 26.6%; Poverty rate: 17.6%

Educational Attainment: High school diploma or higher: 87.7%; Bachelor's degree or higher: 50.4%; Graduate/professional degree or higher: 24.9%

School District(s)

Nyack Union Free SD (KG-12)
 2014-15 Enrollment: 3,040 . . . . (845) 353-7015

Four-year College(s)

Nyack College (Private, Not-for-profit, Christ and Missionary Alliance Church)
 Fall 2014 Enrollment: 2,896 . . . . (845) 675-4400
 2015-16 Tuition: In-state $24,300; Out-of-state $24,300

Housing: Homeownership rate: 31.4%; Median home value: $426,000; Median year structure built: 1955; Homeowner vacancy rate: 6.0%; Median selected monthly owner costs: $2,720 with a mortgage, $1,367 without a mortgage; Median gross rent: $1,442 per month; Rental vacancy rate: 5.2%

Health Insurance: 90.9% have insurance; 66.2% have private insurance; 35.1% have public insurance; 9.1% do not have insurance; 6.0% of children under 18 do not have insurance

Hospitals: Nyack Hospital (375 beds)

Transportation: Commute: 79.4% car, 7.9% public transportation, 6.7% walk, 5.1% work from home; Mean travel time to work: 29.4 minutes

Additional Information Contacts

Village of Nyack. . . . . (845) 358-0548
 http://nyack-ny.gov

ORANGEBURG (CDP). Covers a land area of 3.073 square miles and a water area of 0 square miles. Located at 41.05° N. Lat; 73.94° W. Long. Elevation is 118 feet.

Population: 4,442; Growth (since 2000): 31.1%; Density: 1,445.7 persons per square mile; Race: 75.3% White, 3.4% Black/African American, 15.2% Asian, 0.1% American Indian/Alaska Native, 0.0% Native Hawaiian/Other Pacific Islander, 1.7% Two or more races, 11.1% Hispanic of any race; Average household size: 2.43; Median age: 45.9; Age under 18: 16.9%; Age 65 and over: 26.8%; Males per 100 females: 73.8; Marriage status: 42.6% never married, 41.3% now married, 0.7% separated, 10.0% widowed, 6.1% divorced; Foreign born: 18.8%; Speak English only: 73.9%; With disability: 16.0%; Veterans: 5.1%; Ancestry: 29.4% Irish, 18.5% Italian, 10.1% German, 6.6% American, 4.2% English

Employment: 14.7% management, business, and financial, 4.8% computer, engineering, and science, 17.3% education, legal, community service, arts, and media, 8.6% healthcare practitioners, 16.1% service, 25.0% sales and office, 4.8% natural resources, construction, and maintenance, 8.8% production, transportation, and material moving

Income: Per capita: $32,445; Median household: $80,814; Average household: $90,839; Households with income of $100,000 or more: 38.6%; Poverty rate: 13.7%

Educational Attainment: High school diploma or higher: 89.7%; Bachelor's degree or higher: 49.7%; Graduate/professional degree or higher: 21.8%

School District(s)

South Orangetown Central SD (PK-12)
 2014-15 Enrollment: 3,272 . . . . (845) 680-1050

Four-year College(s)

Dominican College of Blauvelt (Private, Not-for-profit)
 Fall 2014 Enrollment: 1,980 . . . . (845) 359-7800
 2015-16 Tuition: In-state $26,450; Out-of-state $26,450

LIU Hudson at Rockland (Private, Not-for-profit)
 Fall 2014 Enrollment: 239 . . . . (845) 359-7200

Housing: Homeownership rate: 67.6%; Median home value: $459,300; Median year structure built: 1966; Homeowner vacancy rate: 1.7%; Median selected monthly owner costs: $2,971 with a mortgage, $1,215 without a mortgage; Median gross rent: $823 per month; Rental vacancy rate: 6.4%

Health Insurance: 94.9% have insurance; 76.1% have private insurance; 35.9% have public insurance; 5.1% do not have insurance; 0.4% of children under 18 do not have insurance

Transportation: Commute: 81.4% car, 4.9% public transportation, 8.7% walk, 5.0% work from home; Mean travel time to work: 31.4 minutes

---

ORANGETOWN (town). Covers a land area of 24.098 square miles and a water area of 7.268 square miles. Located at 41.05° N. Lat; 73.95° W. Long. Elevation is 200 feet.

History: Orangetown was first settled around 1680, the first town formed in Rockland County. Its Dutch settlers purchased land from the Tappan Indians in 1686.

Population: 50,095; Growth (since 2000): 5.0%; Density: 2,078.8 persons per square mile; Race: 82.1% White, 5.5% Black/African American, 8.5% Asian, 0.5% American Indian/Alaska Native, 0.0% Native Hawaiian/Other Pacific Islander, 1.7% Two or more races, 9.6% Hispanic of any race; Average household size: 2.64; Median age: 42.8; Age under 18: 21.7%; Age 65 and over: 18.3%; Males per 100 females: 92.3; Marriage status: 33.7% never married, 52.2% now married, 1.5% separated, 6.8% widowed, 7.3% divorced; Foreign born: 15.3%; Speak English only: 81.1%; With disability: 10.7%; Veterans: 5.5%; Ancestry: 30.9% Irish, 17.8% Italian, 11.0% German, 5.8% English, 5.6% American

Employment: 19.2% management, business, and financial, 5.9% computer, engineering, and science, 18.8% education, legal, community service, arts, and media, 7.0% healthcare practitioners, 16.7% service, 21.2% sales and office, 7.0% natural resources, construction, and maintenance, 4.3% production, transportation, and material moving

Income: Per capita: $44,117; Median household: $92,257; Average household: $120,135; Households with income of $100,000 or more: 47.1%; Poverty rate: 8.1%

Educational Attainment: High school diploma or higher: 91.0%; Bachelor's degree or higher: 50.6%; Graduate/professional degree or higher: 23.4%

Housing: Homeownership rate: 72.3%; Median home value: $464,100; Median year structure built: 1961; Homeowner vacancy rate: 2.1%; Median selected monthly owner costs: $3,107 with a mortgage, $1,194 without a mortgage; Median gross rent: $1,384 per month; Rental vacancy rate: 6.4%

Health Insurance: 93.8% have insurance; 80.9% have private insurance; 26.5% have public insurance; 6.2% do not have insurance; 6.3% of children under 18 do not have insurance

Safety: Violent crime rate: 7.9 per 10,000 population; Property crime rate: 78.3 per 10,000 population

Transportation: Commute: 83.1% car, 7.2% public transportation, 3.2% walk, 5.8% work from home; Mean travel time to work: 31.3 minutes

Additional Information Contacts
Town of Orangetown . . . . (845) 359-5100
   http://www.orangetown.com

PALISADES (unincorporated postal area)
ZCTA: 10964

Covers a land area of 2.466 square miles and a water area of 0 square miles. Located at 41.02° N. Lat; 73.91° W. Long. Elevation is 194 feet.

Population: 1,557; Growth (since 2000): 21.5%; Density: 631.3 persons per square mile; Race: 88.9% White, 1.7% Black/African American, 8.1% Asian, 0.8% American Indian/Alaska Native, 0.0% Native Hawaiian/Other Pacific Islander, 0.6% Two or more races, 5.3% Hispanic of any race; Average household size: 2.64; Median age: 54.7; Age under 18: 13.8%; Age 65 and over: 34.1%; Males per 100 females: 95.2; Marriage status: 28.8% never married, 58.0% now married, 0.0% separated, 8.8% widowed, 4.4% divorced; Foreign born: 18.6%; Speak English only: 73.0%; With disability: 12.1%; Veterans: 1.9%; Ancestry: 24.1% Irish, 20.6% Italian, 16.9% German, 11.6% Polish, 8.3% Russian

Employment: 26.7% management, business, and financial, 5.7% computer, engineering, and science, 13.8% education, legal, community service, arts, and media, 7.1% healthcare practitioners, 12.6% service, 24.2% sales and office, 2.9% natural resources, construction, and maintenance, 6.9% production, transportation, and material moving

Income: Per capita: $52,050; Median household: $83,257; Average household: $138,846; Households with income of $100,000 or more: 43.5%; Poverty rate: 5.7%

Educational Attainment: High school diploma or higher: 92.6%; Bachelor's degree or higher: 50.0%; Graduate/professional degree or higher: 29.8%

Housing: Homeownership rate: 64.7%; Median home value: $533,900; Median year structure built: 1968; Homeowner vacancy rate: 0.0%; Median selected monthly owner costs: $3,724 with a mortgage, $1,263 without a mortgage; Median gross rent: n/a per month; Rental vacancy rate: 20.5%

Health Insurance: 95.1% have insurance; 73.5% have private insurance; 35.3% have public insurance; 4.9% do not have insurance; 0.0% of children under 18 do not have insurance

Transportation: Commute: 75.6% car, 0.0% public transportation, 0.7% walk, 23.7% work from home; Mean travel time to work: 33.1 minutes

PEARL RIVER (CDP).
Covers a land area of 6.799 square miles and a water area of 0.400 square miles. Located at 41.06° N. Lat; 74.01° W. Long. Elevation is 243 feet.

History: In 1696, Pearl River was originally part of a larger portion of land known as the Kakiat Patent that was granted to Daniel Honan and Michael Hawdon. In 1713, the land was split into north and south plots. After the Revolutionary War, the land was further divided and sold. In the early 1870s, the town was divided into five different parts: Middletown, Sickletown, Pascack, Muddy Brook, and Naurashaun.

Population: 16,383; Growth (since 2000): 5.3%; Density: 2,409.7 persons per square mile; Race: 89.3% White, 2.1% Black/African American, 6.3% Asian, 0.9% American Indian/Alaska Native, 0.0% Native Hawaiian/Other Pacific Islander, 0.7% Two or more races, 6.9% Hispanic of any race; Average household size: 2.83; Median age: 40.3; Age under 18: 23.6%; Age 65 and over: 15.6%; Males per 100 females: 95.8; Marriage status: 31.0% never married, 54.7% now married, 1.3% separated, 6.8% widowed, 7.5% divorced; Foreign born: 12.6%; Speak English only: 86.7%; With disability: 8.8%; Veterans: 5.8%; Ancestry: 45.1% Irish, 21.9% Italian, 11.2% German, 6.3% American, 3.8% English

Employment: 19.6% management, business, and financial, 5.1% computer, engineering, and science, 18.3% education, legal, community service, arts, and media, 5.3% healthcare practitioners, 18.2% service,

19.9% sales and office, 9.9% natural resources, construction, and maintenance, 3.6% production, transportation, and material moving

Income: Per capita: $41,934; Median household: $96,233; Average household: $117,165; Households with income of $100,000 or more: 48.7%; Poverty rate: 7.2%

Educational Attainment: High school diploma or higher: 91.9%; Bachelor's degree or higher: 44.9%; Graduate/professional degree or higher: 19.2%

School District(s)
Pearl River Union Free SD (KG-12)
   2014-15 Enrollment: 2,605 . . . . (845) 620-3922

Housing: Homeownership rate: 79.0%; Median home value: $440,100; Median year structure built: 1960; Homeowner vacancy rate: 1.4%; Median selected monthly owner costs: $3,098 with a mortgage, $1,080 without a mortgage; Median gross rent: $1,351 per month; Rental vacancy rate: 2.5%

Health Insurance: 93.7% have insurance; 86.2% have private insurance; 21.9% have public insurance; 6.3% do not have insurance; 7.7% of children under 18 do not have insurance

Transportation: Commute: 84.1% car, 7.8% public transportation, 2.1% walk, 4.8% work from home; Mean travel time to work: 32.1 minutes

PIERMONT (village).
Covers a land area of 0.679 square miles and a water area of 0.473 square miles. Located at 41.04° N. Lat; 73.91° W. Long. Elevation is 92 feet.

History: Until the 1980s, manufacturing (paperboard, silk ribbons). Site of Camp Shanks, which was operational during World Wars I and II. Pier (1 mile long) from which village takes its name was used for embarkation of troops. Site where 1983 Woody Allen movie *The Purple Rose of Cairo* was filmed. Incorporated 1847.

Population: 2,557; Growth (since 2000): -1.9%; Density: 3,763.1 persons per square mile; Race: 84.2% White, 3.1% Black/African American, 8.5% Asian, 0.0% American Indian/Alaska Native, 0.0% Native Hawaiian/Other Pacific Islander, 1.9% Two or more races, 6.5% Hispanic of any race; Average household size: 2.02; Median age: 50.7; Age under 18: 16.2%; Age 65 and over: 24.0%; Males per 100 females: 89.9; Marriage status: 32.4% never married, 53.0% now married, 0.6% separated, 5.1% widowed, 9.5% divorced; Foreign born: 14.5%; Speak English only: 82.5%; With disability: 10.6%; Veterans: 6.3%; Ancestry: 25.7% Irish, 16.3% Italian, 12.5% German, 9.0% English, 7.9% American

Employment: 13.4% management, business, and financial, 9.6% computer, engineering, and science, 20.7% education, legal, community service, arts, and media, 9.0% healthcare practitioners, 16.9% service, 24.6% sales and office, 4.6% natural resources, construction, and maintenance, 1.2% production, transportation, and material moving

Income: Per capita: $73,400; Median household: $92,445; Average household: $149,158; Households with income of $100,000 or more: 47.2%; Poverty rate: 5.6%

Educational Attainment: High school diploma or higher: 94.9%; Bachelor's degree or higher: 67.6%; Graduate/professional degree or higher: 34.5%

School District(s)
South Orangetown Central SD (PK-12)
   2014-15 Enrollment: 3,272 . . . . (845) 680-1050

Housing: Homeownership rate: 67.8%; Median home value: $626,300; Median year structure built: 1963; Homeowner vacancy rate: 0.0%; Median selected monthly owner costs: $3,542 with a mortgage, $1,500+ without a mortgage; Median gross rent: $1,413 per month; Rental vacancy rate: 9.8%

Health Insurance: 94.7% have insurance; 81.4% have private insurance; 27.3% have public insurance; 5.3% do not have insurance; 0.0% of children under 18 do not have insurance

Safety: Violent crime rate: 3.9 per 10,000 population; Property crime rate: 65.8 per 10,000 population

Transportation: Commute: 85.0% car, 4.1% public transportation, 2.2% walk, 5.8% work from home; Mean travel time to work: 33.5 minutes

POMONA (village).
Covers a land area of 2.397 square miles and a water area of 0 square miles. Located at 41.19° N. Lat; 74.05° W. Long. Elevation is 456 feet.

Population: 3,286; Growth (since 2000): 20.5%; Density: 1,370.7 persons per square mile; Race: 68.0% White, 15.4% Black/African American, 6.6% Asian, 0.0% American Indian/Alaska Native, 0.0% Native Hawaiian/Other Pacific Islander, 2.3% Two or more races, 16.0% Hispanic of any race; Average household size: 3.32; Median age: 38.3; Age under 18: 24.5%;

Age 65 and over: 13.6%; Males per 100 females: 99.2; Marriage status: 37.8% never married, 55.7% now married, 0.4% separated, 3.5% widowed, 3.1% divorced; Foreign born: 22.0%; Speak English only: 70.1%; With disability: 9.0%; Veterans: 3.9%; Ancestry: 8.6% Italian, 8.2% Polish, 7.8% Russian, 7.5% German, 6.0% Irish

Employment: 20.5% management, business, and financial, 6.7% computer, engineering, and science, 13.2% education, legal, community service, arts, and media, 10.5% healthcare practitioners, 14.1% service, 22.5% sales and office, 8.3% natural resources, construction, and maintenance, 4.2% production, transportation, and material moving

Income: Per capita: $46,228; Median household: $128,661; Average household: $150,564; Households with income of $100,000 or more: 65.4%; Poverty rate: 8.0%

Educational Attainment: High school diploma or higher: 91.7%; Bachelor's degree or higher: 52.1%; Graduate/professional degree or higher: 25.8%

Housing: Homeownership rate: 89.8%; Median home value: $472,500; Median year structure built: 1978; Homeowner vacancy rate: 0.0%; Median selected monthly owner costs: $3,381 with a mortgage, $1,258 without a mortgage; Median gross rent: $2,641 per month; Rental vacancy rate: 0.0%

Health Insurance: 90.3% have insurance; 68.5% have private insurance; 30.4% have public insurance; 9.7% do not have insurance; 2.6% of children under 18 do not have insurance

Transportation: Commute: 79.6% car, 8.7% public transportation, 0.5% walk, 9.3% work from home; Mean travel time to work: 37.3 minutes

RAMAPO (town). Covers a land area of 61.198 square miles and a water area of 0.696 square miles. Located at 41.14° N. Lat; 74.10° W. Long. Elevation is 331 feet.

History: Ramapo was formerly known as New Hempstead then later Hampstead. The city name, recorded variously as Ramopuck, Ramapock, or Ramapough, is Native American for either "sweet water" or "sloping/slanting rocks."

Population: 131,648; Growth (since 2000): 20.9%; Density: 2,151.2 persons per square mile; Race: 68.9% White, 16.6% Black/African American, 3.1% Asian, 0.2% American Indian/Alaska Native, 0.0% Native Hawaiian/Other Pacific Islander, 1.8% Two or more races, 13.9% Hispanic of any race; Average household size: 3.74; Median age: 28.4; Age under 18: 35.8%; Age 65 and over: 11.1%; Males per 100 females: 100.0; Marriage status: 33.4% never married, 55.6% now married, 1.8% separated, 5.2% widowed, 5.9% divorced; Foreign born: 22.2%; Speak English only: 48.8%; With disability: 7.4%; Veterans: 3.3%; Ancestry: 11.1% European, 7.4% Hungarian, 7.3% Haitian, 6.9% American, 6.8% Italian

Employment: 13.7% management, business, and financial, 3.9% computer, engineering, and science, 16.7% education, legal, community service, arts, and media, 7.2% healthcare practitioners, 20.1% service, 24.4% sales and office, 7.0% natural resources, construction, and maintenance, 7.1% production, transportation, and material moving

Income: Per capita: $25,046; Median household: $66,911; Average household: $91,351; Households with income of $100,000 or more: 33.1%; Poverty rate: 24.9%

Educational Attainment: High school diploma or higher: 83.1%; Bachelor's degree or higher: 32.5%; Graduate/professional degree or higher: 14.6%

Housing: Homeownership rate: 58.5%; Median home value: $400,500; Median year structure built: 1970; Homeowner vacancy rate: 1.7%; Median selected monthly owner costs: $2,920 with a mortgage, $1,219 without a mortgage; Median gross rent: $1,264 per month; Rental vacancy rate: 4.3%

Health Insurance: 89.4% have insurance; 51.1% have private insurance; 46.9% have public insurance; 10.6% do not have insurance; 3.8% of children under 18 do not have insurance

Safety: Violent crime rate: 8.6 per 10,000 population; Property crime rate: 68.4 per 10,000 population

Transportation: Commute: 75.7% car, 11.1% public transportation, 6.1% walk, 4.9% work from home; Mean travel time to work: 28.7 minutes

Additional Information Contacts

Town of Ramapo . . . . (845) 357-5100
　http://www.ramapo.org

SLOATSBURG (village). Covers a land area of 2.467 square miles and a water area of 0.038 square miles. Located at 41.16° N. Lat; 74.19° W. Long. Elevation is 341 feet.

History: Settled before 1775, incorporated 1929.

Population: 3,106; Growth (since 2000): -0.4%; Density: 1,259.0 persons per square mile; Race: 87.7% White, 6.5% Black/African American, 2.5% Asian, 0.5% American Indian/Alaska Native, 0.0% Native Hawaiian/Other Pacific Islander, 0.9% Two or more races, 13.2% Hispanic of any race; Average household size: 2.91; Median age: 38.5; Age under 18: 23.9%; Age 65 and over: 12.0%; Males per 100 females: 104.2; Marriage status: 36.0% never married, 50.2% now married, 1.5% separated, 5.5% widowed, 8.3% divorced; Foreign born: 9.0%; Speak English only: 87.3%; With disability: 9.5%; Veterans: 5.1%; Ancestry: 30.6% Italian, 24.0% Irish, 18.3% German, 6.5% Polish, 4.9% American

Employment: 12.8% management, business, and financial, 2.4% computer, engineering, and science, 18.5% education, legal, community service, arts, and media, 8.0% healthcare practitioners, 19.4% service, 23.9% sales and office, 9.7% natural resources, construction, and maintenance, 5.2% production, transportation, and material moving

Income: Per capita: $33,733; Median household: $86,189; Average household: $97,341; Households with income of $100,000 or more: 42.9%; Poverty rate: 4.7%

Educational Attainment: High school diploma or higher: 92.5%; Bachelor's degree or higher: 38.8%; Graduate/professional degree or higher: 14.9%

School District(s)

Ramapo Central SD (Suffern) (KG-12)
　2014-15 Enrollment: 4,518 . . . . (845) 357-7783

Housing: Homeownership rate: 76.2%; Median home value: $321,100; Median year structure built: 1955; Homeowner vacancy rate: 2.0%; Median selected monthly owner costs: $2,722 with a mortgage, $1,213 without a mortgage; Median gross rent: $1,453 per month; Rental vacancy rate: 0.0%

Health Insurance: 91.9% have insurance; 82.6% have private insurance; 20.7% have public insurance; 8.1% do not have insurance; 5.4% of children under 18 do not have insurance

Transportation: Commute: 88.1% car, 4.5% public transportation, 3.0% walk, 4.4% work from home; Mean travel time to work: 30.8 minutes

SOUTH NYACK (village). Covers a land area of 0.605 square miles and a water area of 1.079 square miles. Located at 41.08° N. Lat; 73.92° W. Long. Elevation is 72 feet.

History: Incorporated 1878.

Population: 3,549; Growth (since 2000): 2.2%; Density: 5,866.1 persons per square mile; Race: 74.0% White, 11.9% Black/African American, 6.4% Asian, 1.3% American Indian/Alaska Native, 0.3% Native Hawaiian/Other Pacific Islander, 4.5% Two or more races, 10.1% Hispanic of any race; Average household size: 2.29; Median age: 36.2; Age under 18: 16.7%; Age 65 and over: 13.7%; Males per 100 females: 87.1; Marriage status: 45.3% never married, 40.4% now married, 0.7% separated, 5.9% widowed, 8.4% divorced; Foreign born: 11.9%; Speak English only: 80.1%; With disability: 13.1%; Veterans: 3.2%; Ancestry: 18.2% Irish, 12.9% Italian, 11.6% German, 8.1% English, 7.2% Haitian

Employment: 22.8% management, business, and financial, 8.9% computer, engineering, and science, 24.8% education, legal, community service, arts, and media, 6.8% healthcare practitioners, 10.8% service, 19.2% sales and office, 2.5% natural resources, construction, and maintenance, 4.3% production, transportation, and material moving

Income: Per capita: $45,356; Median household: $100,231; Average household: $121,456; Households with income of $100,000 or more: 50.2%; Poverty rate: 5.7%

Educational Attainment: High school diploma or higher: 96.9%; Bachelor's degree or higher: 60.0%; Graduate/professional degree or higher: 32.4%

Housing: Homeownership rate: 57.0%; Median home value: $452,200; Median year structure built: Before 1940; Homeowner vacancy rate: 3.5%; Median selected monthly owner costs: $3,374 with a mortgage, $1,500+ without a mortgage; Median gross rent: $1,616 per month; Rental vacancy rate: 9.0%

Health Insurance: 95.1% have insurance; 81.3% have private insurance; 23.4% have public insurance; 4.9% do not have insurance; 1.0% of children under 18 do not have insurance

Safety: Violent crime rate: 13.9 per 10,000 population; Property crime rate: 61.2 per 10,000 population

Transportation: Commute: 74.4% car, 12.7% public transportation, 5.4% walk, 6.8% work from home; Mean travel time to work: 30.5 minutes

SPARKILL (CDP). Covers a land area of 0.529 square miles and a water area of 0 square miles. Located at 41.03° N. Lat; 73.93° W. Long. Elevation is 52 feet.

Population: 1,523; Growth (since 2000): n/a; Density: 2,876.7 persons per square mile; Race: 70.7% White, 7.9% Black/African American, 13.5% Asian, 0.0% American Indian/Alaska Native, 0.0% Native Hawaiian/Other Pacific Islander, 6.3% Two or more races, 16.5% Hispanic of any race; Average household size: 2.93; Median age: 41.0; Age under 18: 28.8%; Age 65 and over: 12.2%; Males per 100 females: 96.9; Marriage status: 34.1% never married, 52.2% now married, 0.0% separated, 4.9% widowed, 8.8% divorced; Foreign born: 22.5%; Speak English only: 72.5%; With disability: 7.6%; Veterans: 1.1%; Ancestry: 12.6% Irish, 11.2% Italian, 9.4% Russian, 8.5% German, 6.1% American

Employment: 19.5% management, business, and financial, 6.6% computer, engineering, and science, 9.3% education, legal, community service, arts, and media, 10.2% healthcare practitioners, 15.8% service, 28.4% sales and office, 5.7% natural resources, construction, and maintenance, 4.4% production, transportation, and material moving

Income: Per capita: $40,937; Median household: $100,481; Average household: $116,099; Households with income of $100,000 or more: 50.5%; Poverty rate: 9.7%

Educational Attainment: High school diploma or higher: 91.5%; Bachelor's degree or higher: 50.9%; Graduate/professional degree or higher: 18.3%

Four-year College(s)

St. Thomas Aquinas College (Private, Not-for-profit)
Fall 2014 Enrollment: 1,942 . . . . (845) 398-4000
2015-16 Tuition: In-state $28,740; Out-of-state $28,740

Housing: Homeownership rate: 90.2%; Median home value: $456,500; Median year structure built: 1965; Homeowner vacancy rate: 0.0%; Median selected monthly owner costs: $3,005 with a mortgage, $1,210 without a mortgage; Median gross rent: n/a per month; Rental vacancy rate: 0.0%

Health Insurance: 97.4% have insurance; 85.5% have private insurance; 21.7% have public insurance; 2.6% do not have insurance; 0.0% of children under 18 do not have insurance

Transportation: Commute: 86.3% car, 13.7% public transportation, 0.0% walk, 0.0% work from home; Mean travel time to work: 35.1 minutes

SPRING VALLEY (village). Covers a land area of 2.016 square miles and a water area of 0.002 square miles. Located at 41.11° N. Lat; 74.05° W. Long. Elevation is 446 feet.

History: Named for a spring in the area. Incorporated 1902.

Population: 32,221; Growth (since 2000): 26.5%; Density: 15,984.8 persons per square mile; Race: 30.0% White, 39.9% Black/African American, 2.9% Asian, 0.0% American Indian/Alaska Native, 0.0% Native Hawaiian/Other Pacific Islander, 2.2% Two or more races, 29.3% Hispanic of any race; Average household size: 3.72; Median age: 28.8; Age under 18: 33.3%; Age 65 and over: 7.8%; Males per 100 females: 103.1; Marriage status: 41.8% never married, 46.7% now married, 3.9% separated, 4.2% widowed, 7.3% divorced; Foreign born: 41.9%; Speak English only: 34.7%; With disability: 6.6%; Veterans: 2.2%; Ancestry: 20.2% Haitian, 5.5% American, 5.3% European, 3.6% Jamaican, 2.8% Hungarian

Employment: 7.9% management, business, and financial, 1.7% computer, engineering, and science, 8.9% education, legal, community service, arts, and media, 4.8% healthcare practitioners, 34.6% service, 22.1% sales and office, 9.3% natural resources, construction, and maintenance, 10.7% production, transportation, and material moving

Income: Per capita: $19,103; Median household: $45,326; Average household: $65,658; Households with income of $100,000 or more: 16.5%; Poverty rate: 25.7%

Educational Attainment: High school diploma or higher: 69.3%; Bachelor's degree or higher: 17.1%; Graduate/professional degree or higher: 5.6%

School District(s)

East Ramapo Central SD (Spring Valley) (PK-12)
2014-15 Enrollment: 8,881 . . . . (845) 577-6011

Four-year College(s)

Be'er Yaakov Talmudic Seminary (Private, Not-for-profit)
Fall 2014 Enrollment: 382 . . . . (845) 406-9699
2015-16 Tuition: In-state $8,750; Out-of-state $8,750

Housing: Homeownership rate: 31.0%; Median home value: $253,400; Median year structure built: 1970; Homeowner vacancy rate: 2.0%; Median selected monthly owner costs: $2,169 with a mortgage, $921 without a mortgage; Median gross rent: $1,204 per month; Rental vacancy rate: 7.3%

Health Insurance: 76.9% have insurance; 35.5% have private insurance; 46.9% have public insurance; 23.1% do not have insurance; 6.1% of children under 18 do not have insurance

Safety: Violent crime rate: 47.3 per 10,000 population; Property crime rate: 112.2 per 10,000 population

Transportation: Commute: 72.1% car, 16.8% public transportation, 5.5% walk, 2.3% work from home; Mean travel time to work: 27.3 minutes

Additional Information Contacts

Village of Spring Valley . . . . (845) 352-1100
http://www.villagespringvalley.org

STONY POINT (CDP). Covers a land area of 5.442 square miles and a water area of 1.293 square miles. Located at 41.23° N. Lat; 74.00° W. Long. Elevation is 118 feet.

Population: 12,882; Growth (since 2000): 9.7%; Density: 2,367.3 persons per square mile; Race: 79.3% White, 8.1% Black/African American, 2.3% Asian, 0.0% American Indian/Alaska Native, 0.0% Native Hawaiian/Other Pacific Islander, 2.7% Two or more races, 18.5% Hispanic of any race; Average household size: 3.01; Median age: 42.8; Age under 18: 21.1%; Age 65 and over: 16.3%; Males per 100 females: 96.5; Marriage status: 30.8% never married, 57.9% now married, 1.4% separated, 6.3% widowed, 4.9% divorced; Foreign born: 12.0%; Speak English only: 80.3%; With disability: 11.2%; Veterans: 7.1%; Ancestry: 28.1% Italian, 25.3% Irish, 12.7% German, 4.6% American, 4.5% English

Employment: 17.4% management, business, and financial, 4.0% computer, engineering, and science, 14.7% education, legal, community service, arts, and media, 5.3% healthcare practitioners, 15.5% service, 23.0% sales and office, 10.8% natural resources, construction, and maintenance, 9.3% production, transportation, and material moving

Income: Per capita: $38,453; Median household: $93,688; Average household: $113,373; Households with income of $100,000 or more: 46.5%; Poverty rate: 5.0%

Educational Attainment: High school diploma or higher: 91.9%; Bachelor's degree or higher: 32.8%; Graduate/professional degree or higher: 13.0%

School District(s)

Haverstraw-Stony Point CSD (North Rockland) (KG-12)
2014-15 Enrollment: 8,010 . . . . (845) 942-3002

Housing: Homeownership rate: 83.4%; Median home value: $361,900; Median year structure built: 1968; Homeowner vacancy rate: 1.9%; Median selected monthly owner costs: $2,809 with a mortgage, $1,079 without a mortgage; Median gross rent: $1,401 per month; Rental vacancy rate: 15.3%

Health Insurance: 93.7% have insurance; 82.9% have private insurance; 25.2% have public insurance; 6.3% do not have insurance; 2.0% of children under 18 do not have insurance

Transportation: Commute: 90.4% car, 4.4% public transportation, 0.5% walk, 3.2% work from home; Mean travel time to work: 33.7 minutes

STONY POINT (town). Covers a land area of 27.624 square miles and a water area of 3.975 square miles. Located at 41.25° N. Lat; 74.00° W. Long. Elevation is 118 feet.

History: Named for a local rocky bluff that projects into the Hudson River. Nearby is Stony Point Museum (1936) in battlefield reservation (part of Palisades Interstate Park), commemorating storming of Stony Point by "Mad" Anthony Wayne's Continental forces in July 1779.

Population: 15,350; Growth (since 2000): 7.8%; Density: 555.7 persons per square mile; Race: 81.8% White, 7.3% Black/African American, 2.1% Asian, 0.0% American Indian/Alaska Native, 0.0% Native Hawaiian/Other Pacific Islander, 2.4% Two or more races, 16.8% Hispanic of any race; Average household size: 2.99; Median age: 43.1; Age under 18: 21.5%; Age 65 and over: 16.2%; Males per 100 females: 97.1; Marriage status: 29.5% never married, 59.1% now married, 1.4% separated, 6.1% widowed, 5.4% divorced; Foreign born: 11.0%; Speak English only: 81.8%; With disability: 10.7%; Veterans: 7.1%; Ancestry: 27.3% Italian, 26.2% Irish, 14.1% German, 5.7% English, 5.3% American

Employment: 18.7% management, business, and financial, 3.8% computer, engineering, and science, 14.7% education, legal, community service, arts, and media, 5.1% healthcare practitioners, 15.0% service,

22.6% sales and office, 11.3% natural resources, construction, and maintenance, 8.7% production, transportation, and material moving
Income: Per capita: $40,313; Median household: $97,083; Average household: $118,361; Households with income of $100,000 or more: 48.7%; Poverty rate: 4.7%
Educational Attainment: High school diploma or higher: 91.8%; Bachelor's degree or higher: 34.7%; Graduate/professional degree or higher: 13.6%

School District(s)
Haverstraw-Stony Point CSD (North Rockland) (KG-12)
   2014-15 Enrollment: 8,010 . . . . (845) 942-3002
Housing: Homeownership rate: 84.5%; Median home value: $371,500; Median year structure built: 1970; Homeowner vacancy rate: 1.6%; Median selected monthly owner costs: $2,839 with a mortgage, $1,109 without a mortgage; Median gross rent: $1,378 per month; Rental vacancy rate: 13.9%
Health Insurance: 94.0% have insurance; 83.8% have private insurance; 24.4% have public insurance; 6.0% do not have insurance; 2.4% of children under 18 do not have insurance
Safety: Violent crime rate: 4.5 per 10,000 population; Property crime rate: 49.5 per 10,000 population
Transportation: Commute: 90.2% car, 4.7% public transportation, 0.5% walk, 3.2% work from home; Mean travel time to work: 33.5 minutes
Additional Information Contacts
Town of Stony Point . . . . (845) 786-2716
   http://www.townofstonypoint.org

SUFFERN (village). Covers a land area of 2.089 square miles and a water area of 0.028 square miles. Located at 41.11° N. Lat; 74.14° W. Long. Elevation is 312 feet.
History: Named for John Suffern, original member of the first state legislature. Incorporated 1896.
Population: 10,914; Growth (since 2000): -0.8%; Density: 5,225.4 persons per square mile; Race: 74.6% White, 6.6% Black/African American, 4.1% Asian, 0.0% American Indian/Alaska Native, 0.0% Native Hawaiian/Other Pacific Islander, 3.7% Two or more races, 18.8% Hispanic of any race; Average household size: 2.46; Median age: 41.3; Age under 18: 20.2%; Age 65 and over: 18.2%; Males per 100 females: 94.6; Marriage status: 31.8% never married, 50.4% now married, 2.2% separated, 7.7% widowed, 10.1% divorced; Foreign born: 18.2%; Speak English only: 74.3%; With disability: 11.4%; Veterans: 4.8%; Ancestry: 19.7% Italian, 14.9% Irish, 7.3% Polish, 7.1% American, 6.4% Russian
Employment: 16.5% management, business, and financial, 5.8% computer, engineering, and science, 16.0% education, legal, community service, arts, and media, 6.5% healthcare practitioners, 18.5% service, 26.6% sales and office, 5.3% natural resources, construction, and maintenance, 4.9% production, transportation, and material moving
Income: Per capita: $37,787; Median household: $81,661; Average household: $92,320; Households with income of $100,000 or more: 37.6%; Poverty rate: 7.6%
Educational Attainment: High school diploma or higher: 92.3%; Bachelor's degree or higher: 44.8%; Graduate/professional degree or higher: 21.7%

School District(s)
East Ramapo Central SD (Spring Valley) (PK-12)
   2014-15 Enrollment: 8,881 . . . . (845) 577-6011
Ramapo Central SD (Suffern) (KG-12)
   2014-15 Enrollment: 4,518 . . . . (845) 357-7783

Four-year College(s)
Yeshiva Shaarei Torah of Rockland (Private, Not-for-profit, Jewish)
   Fall 2014 Enrollment: 98 . . . . (845) 352-3431
   2015-16 Tuition: In-state $11,600; Out-of-state $11,600

Two-year College(s)
Rockland Community College (Public)
   Fall 2014 Enrollment: 7,520 . . . . (845) 574-4000
   2015-16 Tuition: In-state $4,654; Out-of-state $8,953
Housing: Homeownership rate: 69.9%; Median home value: $305,400; Median year structure built: 1970; Homeowner vacancy rate: 2.2%; Median selected monthly owner costs: $2,405 with a mortgage, $1,013 without a mortgage; Median gross rent: $1,421 per month; Rental vacancy rate: 4.2%
Health Insurance: 92.7% have insurance; 75.8% have private insurance; 31.6% have public insurance; 7.3% do not have insurance; 0.5% of children under 18 do not have insurance
Hospitals: Good Samaritan Hospital of Suffern (370 beds)

Safety: Violent crime rate: 9.0 per 10,000 population; Property crime rate: 59.7 per 10,000 population
Transportation: Commute: 81.6% car, 9.9% public transportation, 3.7% walk, 4.0% work from home; Mean travel time to work: 30.4 minutes
Additional Information Contacts
Village of Suffern . . . . (845) 357-2600
   http://www.suffernvillage.com

TAPPAN (CDP). Covers a land area of 2.771 square miles and a water area of 0.006 square miles. Located at 41.03° N. Lat; 73.95° W. Long. Elevation is 43 feet.
History: De Wint Mansion was Washington's headquarters in 1780 and 1783. John Andre, British spy in the American Revolution, was tried and hanged here.
Population: 6,873; Growth (since 2000): 1.7%; Density: 2,480.5 persons per square mile; Race: 78.0% White, 1.8% Black/African American, 18.8% Asian, 0.1% American Indian/Alaska Native, 0.0% Native Hawaiian/Other Pacific Islander, 0.3% Two or more races, 9.1% Hispanic of any race; Average household size: 2.99; Median age: 45.0; Age under 18: 22.9%; Age 65 and over: 21.1%; Males per 100 females: 95.4; Marriage status: 26.2% never married, 60.1% now married, 0.7% separated, 8.1% widowed, 5.6% divorced; Foreign born: 22.1%; Speak English only: 73.6%; With disability: 9.9%; Veterans: 7.1%; Ancestry: 22.5% Irish, 17.5% Italian, 11.3% German, 6.9% American, 4.8% Polish
Employment: 19.1% management, business, and financial, 4.4% computer, engineering, and science, 13.2% education, legal, community service, arts, and media, 10.7% healthcare practitioners, 15.6% service, 26.2% sales and office, 3.1% natural resources, construction, and maintenance, 7.8% production, transportation, and material moving
Income: Per capita: $49,420; Median household: $117,059; Average household: $145,586; Households with income of $100,000 or more: 59.9%; Poverty rate: 1.4%
Educational Attainment: High school diploma or higher: 91.3%; Bachelor's degree or higher: 54.0%; Graduate/professional degree or higher: 24.4%

School District(s)
South Orangetown Central SD (PK-12)
   2014-15 Enrollment: 3,272 . . . . (845) 680-1050
Housing: Homeownership rate: 94.3%; Median home value: $470,100; Median year structure built: 1965; Homeowner vacancy rate: 2.2%; Median selected monthly owner costs: $3,055 with a mortgage, $1,188 without a mortgage; Median gross rent: $2,160 per month; Rental vacancy rate: 19.8%
Health Insurance: 96.9% have insurance; 86.7% have private insurance; 25.3% have public insurance; 3.1% do not have insurance; 3.5% of children under 18 do not have insurance
Transportation: Commute: 88.1% car, 4.3% public transportation, 0.0% walk, 7.6% work from home; Mean travel time to work: 31.0 minutes

THIELLS (CDP). Covers a land area of 1.827 square miles and a water area of 0.031 square miles. Located at 41.20° N. Lat; 74.01° W. Long. Elevation is 272 feet.
Population: 5,173; Growth (since 2000): 8.7%; Density: 2,831.7 persons per square mile; Race: 81.0% White, 7.2% Black/African American, 4.4% Asian, 0.0% American Indian/Alaska Native, 0.0% Native Hawaiian/Other Pacific Islander, 1.9% Two or more races, 22.7% Hispanic of any race; Average household size: 3.35; Median age: 42.9; Age under 18: 20.5%; Age 65 and over: 16.2%; Males per 100 females: 94.9; Marriage status: 34.1% never married, 54.6% now married, 1.3% separated, 6.0% widowed, 5.3% divorced; Foreign born: 13.2%; Speak English only: 75.7%; With disability: 10.6%; Veterans: 5.2%; Ancestry: 27.8% Italian, 24.6% Irish, 8.4% German, 5.2% Haitian, 4.1% American
Employment: 10.7% management, business, and financial, 3.9% computer, engineering, and science, 14.6% education, legal, community service, arts, and media, 8.1% healthcare practitioners, 22.0% service, 29.7% sales and office, 5.3% natural resources, construction, and maintenance, 5.7% production, transportation, and material moving
Income: Per capita: $35,931; Median household: $110,435; Average household: $116,612; Households with income of $100,000 or more: 58.9%; Poverty rate: 5.5%
Educational Attainment: High school diploma or higher: 95.5%; Bachelor's degree or higher: 39.0%; Graduate/professional degree or higher: 13.8%

School District(s)
Haverstraw-Stony Point CSD (North Rockland) (KG-12)
  2014-15 Enrollment: 8,010 . . . . (845) 942-3002
Housing: Homeownership rate: 88.9%; Median home value: $368,000;
Median year structure built: 1973; Homeowner vacancy rate: 0.0%; Median
selected monthly owner costs: $2,998 with a mortgage, $1,255 without a
mortgage; Median gross rent: $1,558 per month; Rental vacancy rate:
0.0%
Health Insurance: 95.1% have insurance; 82.3% have private insurance;
26.3% have public insurance; 4.9% do not have insurance; 0.5% of
children under 18 do not have insurance
Transportation: Commute: 90.0% car, 7.0% public transportation, 1.2%
walk, 1.8% work from home; Mean travel time to work: 33.1 minutes

TOMKINS COVE (unincorporated postal area)
ZCTA: 10986
  Covers a land area of 10.801 square miles and a water area of 0.173
  square miles. Located at 41.29° N. Lat; 74.00° W. Long. Elevation is
  144 feet.
Population: 1,836; Growth (since 2000): 5.6%; Density: 170.0 persons
per square mile; Race: 95.8% White, 1.6% Black/African American,
1.3% Asian, 0.0% American Indian/Alaska Native, 0.0% Native
Hawaiian/Other Pacific Islander, 1.3% Two or more races, 7.5%
Hispanic of any race; Average household size: 3.07; Median age: 40.3;
Age under 18: 26.9%; Age 65 and over: 9.0%; Males per 100 females:
100.6; Marriage status: 25.8% never married, 65.1% now married, 0.7%
separated, 3.2% widowed, 5.9% divorced; Foreign born: 5.5%; Speak
English only: 89.5%; With disability: 7.0%; Veterans: 7.6%; Ancestry:
34.9% Irish, 23.9% German, 23.4% Italian, 12.7% English, 8.5%
Norwegian
Employment: 25.5% management, business, and financial, 2.3%
computer, engineering, and science, 13.1% education, legal, community
service, arts, and media, 5.0% healthcare practitioners, 13.7% service,
19.5% sales and office, 17.2% natural resources, construction, and
maintenance, 3.7% production, transportation, and material moving
Income: Per capita: $48,474; Median household: $119,671; Average
household: $148,517; Households with income of $100,000 or more:
61.9%; Poverty rate: 2.3%
Educational Attainment: High school diploma or higher: 96.9%;
Bachelor's degree or higher: 47.9%; Graduate/professional degree or
higher: 16.3%
Housing: Homeownership rate: 90.5%; Median home value: $459,400;
Median year structure built: 1982; Homeowner vacancy rate: 0.0%;
Median selected monthly owner costs: $2,926 with a mortgage, $1,324
without a mortgage; Median gross rent: $1,350 per month; Rental
vacancy rate: 0.0%
Health Insurance: 98.5% have insurance; 94.3% have private
insurance; 14.4% have public insurance; 1.5% do not have insurance;
1.8% of children under 18 do not have insurance
Transportation: Commute: 91.2% car, 4.6% public transportation, 0.8%
walk, 3.3% work from home; Mean travel time to work: 34.0 minutes

UPPER NYACK (village). Covers a land area of 1.222 square miles
and a water area of 3.143 square miles. Located at 41.12° N. Lat; 73.91°
W. Long. Elevation is 187 feet.
Population: 2,050; Growth (since 2000): 10.0%; Density: 1,677.9 persons
per square mile; Race: 89.3% White, 6.4% Black/African American, 2.8%
Asian, 0.4% American Indian/Alaska Native, 0.0% Native Hawaiian/Other
Pacific Islander, 0.6% Two or more races, 5.7% Hispanic of any race;
Average household size: 2.51; Median age: 49.4; Age under 18: 22.4%;
Age 65 and over: 19.8%; Males per 100 females: 100.1; Marriage status:
29.5% never married, 56.8% now married, 0.9% separated, 5.5%
widowed, 8.2% divorced; Foreign born: 9.2%; Speak English only: 86.5%;
With disability: 9.6%; Veterans: 5.8%; Ancestry: 20.2% Irish, 17.6% Italian,
12.9% German, 8.6% American, 7.9% English
Employment: 21.3% management, business, and financial, 8.0%
computer, engineering, and science, 31.2% education, legal, community
service, arts, and media, 4.1% healthcare practitioners, 11.0% service,
16.5% sales and office, 5.4% natural resources, construction, and
maintenance, 2.5% production, transportation, and material moving
Income: Per capita: $63,733; Median household: $117,917; Average
household: $167,909; Households with income of $100,000 or more:
58.9%; Poverty rate: 3.7%

Educational Attainment: High school diploma or higher: 97.6%;
Bachelor's degree or higher: 65.3%; Graduate/professional degree or
higher: 37.0%
School District(s)
Nyack Union Free SD (KG-12)
  2014-15 Enrollment: 3,040 . . . . (845) 353-7015
Housing: Homeownership rate: 90.1%; Median home value: $530,700;
Median year structure built: 1953; Homeowner vacancy rate: 1.9%; Median
selected monthly owner costs: $3,310 with a mortgage, $1,500+ without a
mortgage; Median gross rent: $1,917 per month; Rental vacancy rate:
0.0%
Health Insurance: 96.8% have insurance; 89.7% have private insurance;
22.4% have public insurance; 3.2% do not have insurance; 0.0% of
children under 18 do not have insurance
Transportation: Commute: 75.0% car, 9.8% public transportation, 1.0%
walk, 13.6% work from home; Mean travel time to work: 33.9 minutes

VALLEY COTTAGE (CDP). Covers a land area of 4.309 square
miles and a water area of 0.023 square miles. Located at 41.12° N. Lat;
73.94° W. Long. Elevation is 177 feet.
History: Valley Cottage is a hamlet and census-designated place in the
town of Clarkstown, Rockland County, New York.
Population: 10,191; Growth (since 2000): 9.9%; Density: 2,365.3 persons
per square mile; Race: 75.4% White, 5.9% Black/African American, 13.2%
Asian, 0.3% American Indian/Alaska Native, 0.0% Native Hawaiian/Other
Pacific Islander, 2.6% Two or more races, 14.5% Hispanic of any race;
Average household size: 2.86; Median age: 47.6; Age under 18: 20.5%;
Age 65 and over: 20.0%; Males per 100 females: 92.1; Marriage status:
27.4% never married, 55.8% now married, 2.7% separated, 8.3%
widowed, 8.5% divorced; Foreign born: 21.3%; Speak English only: 72.3%;
With disability: 7.7%; Veterans: 5.3%; Ancestry: 25.1% Italian, 18.3% Irish,
6.1% German, 4.2% English, 3.4% American
Employment: 16.3% management, business, and financial, 5.5%
computer, engineering, and science, 17.3% education, legal, community
service, arts, and media, 9.9% healthcare practitioners, 18.4% service,
24.2% sales and office, 6.6% natural resources, construction, and
maintenance, 1.9% production, transportation, and material moving
Income: Per capita: $38,618; Median household: $102,500; Average
household: $109,227; Households with income of $100,000 or more:
52.0%; Poverty rate: 8.0%
Educational Attainment: High school diploma or higher: 92.2%;
Bachelor's degree or higher: 46.3%; Graduate/professional degree or
higher: 19.0%
School District(s)
Nyack Union Free SD (KG-12)
  2014-15 Enrollment: 3,040 . . . . (845) 353-7015
Housing: Homeownership rate: 82.1%; Median home value: $387,900;
Median year structure built: 1971; Homeowner vacancy rate: 1.2%; Median
selected monthly owner costs: $2,761 with a mortgage, $1,091 without a
mortgage; Median gross rent: $1,627 per month; Rental vacancy rate:
0.0%
Health Insurance: 92.1% have insurance; 80.0% have private insurance;
26.1% have public insurance; 7.9% do not have insurance; 6.3% of
children under 18 do not have insurance
Transportation: Commute: 87.5% car, 5.3% public transportation, 2.0%
walk, 4.6% work from home; Mean travel time to work: 29.1 minutes

VIOLA (CDP). Covers a land area of 2.678 square miles and a water
area of <.001 square miles. Located at 41.13° N. Lat; 74.08° W. Long.
Elevation is 571 feet.
History: Viola was originally known as Mechanicsville. The well known
Alms House (or "County Poor House") was established in 1837, at Viola, in
the Town of Ramapo, for the poor and destitute (debtors). The inmates
contributed to their upkeep by tending the farm.
Population: 6,282; Growth (since 2000): 5.9%; Density: 2,345.6 persons
per square mile; Race: 94.7% White, 0.5% Black/African American, 1.2%
Asian, 0.0% American Indian/Alaska Native, 0.0% Native Hawaiian/Other
Pacific Islander, 0.3% Two or more races, 4.9% Hispanic of any race;
Average household size: 3.78; Median age: 26.7; Age under 18: 36.5%;
Age 65 and over: 16.1%; Males per 100 females: 96.0; Marriage status:
32.9% never married, 54.0% now married, 1.3% separated, 8.9%
widowed, 4.3% divorced; Foreign born: 14.8%; Speak English only: 59.1%;
With disability: 10.1%; Veterans: 1.8%; Ancestry: 12.9% Polish, 11.1%
European, 9.7% Russian, 8.2% Hungarian, 6.5% German

Employment: 19.7% management, business, and financial, 4.6% computer, engineering, and science, 14.4% education, legal, community service, arts, and media, 12.1% healthcare practitioners, 5.9% service, 30.9% sales and office, 2.7% natural resources, construction, and maintenance, 9.5% production, transportation, and material moving

Income: Per capita: $26,314; Median household: $63,977; Average household: $96,641; Households with income of $100,000 or more: 41.1%; Poverty rate: 19.8%

Educational Attainment: High school diploma or higher: 93.0%; Bachelor's degree or higher: 41.6%; Graduate/professional degree or higher: 20.2%

Housing: Homeownership rate: 63.2%; Median home value: $550,400; Median year structure built: 1976; Homeowner vacancy rate: 2.5%; Median selected monthly owner costs: $3,543 with a mortgage, $1,500+ without a mortgage; Median gross rent: $1,044 per month; Rental vacancy rate: 7.7%

Health Insurance: 89.8% have insurance; 54.2% have private insurance; 45.1% have public insurance; 10.2% do not have insurance; 13.9% of children under 18 do not have insurance

Transportation: Commute: 70.7% car, 17.0% public transportation, 2.4% walk, 8.7% work from home; Mean travel time to work: 38.0 minutes

WESLEY HILLS (village).

Covers a land area of 3.353 square miles and a water area of 0.023 square miles. Located at 41.16° N. Lat; 74.08° W. Long. Elevation is 531 feet.

History: Wesley Hills, originally named Wesley Chapel, named after a chapel built in 1829 by a circuit-riding preacher named James Sherwood. The northeast corner of Grandview Avenue and Route 202 was the Kakiat Airstrip. Early air-mail delivery was flown from there.

Population: 5,820; Growth (since 2000): 20.0%; Density: 1,736.0 persons per square mile; Race: 96.3% White, 0.9% Black/African American, 1.1% Asian, 0.0% American Indian/Alaska Native, 0.0% Native Hawaiian/Other Pacific Islander, 0.6% Two or more races, 2.8% Hispanic of any race; Average household size: 3.72; Median age: 28.6; Age under 18: 41.1%; Age 65 and over: 14.0%; Males per 100 females: 101.0; Marriage status: 26.1% never married, 67.3% now married, 0.2% separated, 1.2% widowed, 5.4% divorced; Foreign born: 9.7%; Speak English only: 82.2%; With disability: 5.9%; Veterans: 3.1%; Ancestry: 17.0% Polish, 14.1% American, 12.6% European, 11.7% Russian, 7.6% Italian

Employment: 18.6% management, business, and financial, 6.4% computer, engineering, and science, 15.0% education, legal, community service, arts, and media, 13.5% healthcare practitioners, 8.9% service, 30.5% sales and office, 5.4% natural resources, construction, and maintenance, 1.6% production, transportation, and material moving

Income: Per capita: $39,559; Median household: $107,660; Average household: $146,554; Households with income of $100,000 or more: 54.9%; Poverty rate: 5.5%

Educational Attainment: High school diploma or higher: 94.5%; Bachelor's degree or higher: 58.9%; Graduate/professional degree or higher: 35.0%

Housing: Homeownership rate: 92.8%; Median home value: $560,900; Median year structure built: 1967; Homeowner vacancy rate: 1.5%; Median selected monthly owner costs: $3,296 with a mortgage, $1,445 without a mortgage; Median gross rent: n/a per month; Rental vacancy rate: 0.0%

Health Insurance: 94.4% have insurance; 78.7% have private insurance; 26.7% have public insurance; 5.6% do not have insurance; 2.7% of children under 18 do not have insurance

Transportation: Commute: 81.4% car, 3.5% public transportation, 0.5% walk, 14.6% work from home; Mean travel time to work: 32.7 minutes

Additional Information Contacts
Village of Wesley Hills . . . . (845) 354-0400
  http://www.wesleyhills.org

WEST HAVERSTRAW (village).

Covers a land area of 1.519 square miles and a water area of 0.024 square miles. Located at 41.21° N. Lat; 73.99° W. Long. Elevation is 108 feet.

History: Named, probably, for a variation of the Dutch translation of "oat-straw," or for a Dutch name. Incorporated 1883.

Population: 10,347; Growth (since 2000): 0.5%; Density: 6,809.7 persons per square mile; Race: 55.6% White, 17.1% Black/African American, 4.2% Asian, 0.0% American Indian/Alaska Native, 0.0% Native Hawaiian/Other Pacific Islander, 3.2% Two or more races, 52.2% Hispanic of any race; Average household size: 3.43; Median age: 33.9; Age under 18: 25.7%; Age 65 and over: 9.0%; Males per 100 females: 94.8; Marriage status: 40.9% never married, 49.2% now married, 3.9% separated, 3.3%

widowed, 6.6% divorced; Foreign born: 26.6%; Speak English only: 50.4%; With disability: 12.0%; Veterans: 6.6%; Ancestry: 10.7% Italian, 9.9% Irish, 7.6% Haitian, 6.9% German, 4.9% American

Employment: 7.5% management, business, and financial, 3.8% computer, engineering, and science, 6.5% education, legal, community service, arts, and media, 4.6% healthcare practitioners, 31.9% service, 22.6% sales and office, 10.4% natural resources, construction, and maintenance, 12.7% production, transportation, and material moving

Income: Per capita: $25,760; Median household: $75,455; Average household: $86,038; Households with income of $100,000 or more: 30.9%; Poverty rate: 11.7%

Educational Attainment: High school diploma or higher: 80.0%; Bachelor's degree or higher: 19.1%; Graduate/professional degree or higher: 8.8%

School District(s)
Haverstraw-Stony Point CSD (North Rockland) (KG-12)
  2014-15 Enrollment: 8,010 . . . . (845) 942-3002

Housing: Homeownership rate: 61.0%; Median home value: $278,900; Median year structure built: 1965; Homeowner vacancy rate: 0.8%; Median selected monthly owner costs: $2,725 with a mortgage, $899 without a mortgage; Median gross rent: $1,325 per month; Rental vacancy rate: 1.6%

Health Insurance: 87.5% have insurance; 64.0% have private insurance; 34.6% have public insurance; 12.5% do not have insurance; 3.7% of children under 18 do not have insurance

Hospitals: Helen Hayes Hospital (155 beds)

Transportation: Commute: 84.0% car, 7.1% public transportation, 3.7% walk, 1.7% work from home; Mean travel time to work: 29.4 minutes

Additional Information Contacts
Village of West Haverstraw . . . . (845) 947-2800
  http://westhaverstraw.wordpress.com

WEST NYACK (CDP).

Covers a land area of 2.940 square miles and a water area of 0.021 square miles. Located at 41.09° N. Lat; 73.97° W. Long. Elevation is 75 feet.

Population: 3,939; Growth (since 2000): 20.0%; Density: 1,339.9 persons per square mile; Race: 84.9% White, 3.0% Black/African American, 10.0% Asian, 0.0% American Indian/Alaska Native, 0.0% Native Hawaiian/Other Pacific Islander, 1.7% Two or more races, 7.6% Hispanic of any race; Average household size: 2.73; Median age: 43.9; Age under 18: 26.9%; Age 65 and over: 18.7%; Males per 100 females: 96.0; Marriage status: 23.9% never married, 61.0% now married, 2.8% separated, 8.2% widowed, 6.9% divorced; Foreign born: 11.9%; Speak English only: 81.2%; With disability: 10.0%; Veterans: 6.2%; Ancestry: 29.3% Irish, 28.3% Italian, 10.7% American, 9.3% English, 9.0% German

Employment: 20.0% management, business, and financial, 6.6% computer, engineering, and science, 18.4% education, legal, community service, arts, and media, 14.5% healthcare practitioners, 10.2% service, 20.0% sales and office, 3.3% natural resources, construction, and maintenance, 7.1% production, transportation, and material moving

Income: Per capita: $52,710; Median household: $120,114; Average household: $144,070; Households with income of $100,000 or more: 59.3%; Poverty rate: 2.8%

Educational Attainment: High school diploma or higher: 96.7%; Bachelor's degree or higher: 51.3%; Graduate/professional degree or higher: 24.4%

School District(s)
Clarkstown Central SD (KG-12)
  2014-15 Enrollment: 8,478 . . . . (845) 639-6418
Rockland Boces
  2014-15 Enrollment: n/a . . . . (845) 627-4701

Vocational/Technical School(s)
Rockland County BOCES-Practical Nursing Program (Public)
  Fall 2014 Enrollment: 96 . . . . (845) 627-4770
  2015-16 Tuition: $12,836

Housing: Homeownership rate: 93.6%; Median home value: $473,700; Median year structure built: 1963; Homeowner vacancy rate: 0.0%; Median selected monthly owner costs: $3,252 with a mortgage, $1,097 without a mortgage; Median gross rent: $1,178 per month; Rental vacancy rate: 0.0%

Health Insurance: 98.3% have insurance; 89.4% have private insurance; 23.5% have public insurance; 1.7% do not have insurance; 0.0% of children under 18 do not have insurance

Newspapers: Rockland Review (weekly circulation 20,000)

Transportation: Commute: 86.3% car, 9.0% public transportation, 0.0% walk, 4.7% work from home; Mean travel time to work: 33.8 minutes

Saint Lawrence County

Located in northern New York; bounded on the northwest by the Saint Lawrence River; drained by the Saint Regis, Indian, Grass, Oswegatchie, and Raquette Rivers; plains area, rising to the Adirondacks in the southeast; includes Black and Cranberry Lak Covers a land area of 2,680.377 square miles, a water area of 141.062 square miles, and is located in the Eastern Time Zone at 44.49° N. Lat., 75.07° W. Long. The county was founded in 1802. County seat is Canton.

Saint Lawrence County is part of the Ogdensburg-Massena, NY Micropolitan Statistical Area. The entire metro area includes: Saint Lawrence County, NY

Weather Station: Canton 4 SE   Elevation: 399 feet

	Jan	Feb	Mar	Apr	May	Jun	Jul	Aug	Sep	Oct	Nov	Dec
High	26	29	39	53	66	74	79	77	69	57	45	32
Low	5	8	18	33	44	54	58	56	48	37	28	14
Precip	2.1	1.8	2.1	2.9	3.1	3.3	3.9	3.7	4.0	3.9	3.4	2.6
Snow	20.1	16.9	12.4	3.7	tr	0.0	0.0	0.0	tr	0.6	5.8	18.5

High and Low temperatures in degrees Fahrenheit; Precipitation and Snow in inches

Weather Station: Gouverneur 3 NW   Elevation: 419 feet

	Jan	Feb	Mar	Apr	May	Jun	Jul	Aug	Sep	Oct	Nov	Dec
High	27	31	40	55	67	76	80	79	71	58	45	33
Low	6	8	18	32	42	52	56	55	46	36	28	14
Precip	2.3	2.0	2.2	3.0	3.1	3.3	3.6	3.4	3.9	4.0	3.7	2.7
Snow	21.9	18.2	13.6	3.9	tr	0.0	0.0	0.0	tr	1.0	6.8	19.2

High and Low temperatures in degrees Fahrenheit; Precipitation and Snow in inches

Weather Station: Lawrenceville 3 SW   Elevation: 500 feet

	Jan	Feb	Mar	Apr	May	Jun	Jul	Aug	Sep	Oct	Nov	Dec
High	27	30	40	55	68	76	80	79	71	58	45	32
Low	8	10	20	33	45	54	59	57	49	39	29	15
Precip	2.2	1.9	2.3	3.0	3.0	3.9	4.1	3.9	4.1	3.7	3.5	2.7
Snow	15.7	14.0	13.3	4.1	0.2	0.0	0.0	0.0	0.0	0.5	6.3	14.3

High and Low temperatures in degrees Fahrenheit; Precipitation and Snow in inches

Weather Station: Massena Arpt   Elevation: 213 feet

	Jan	Feb	Mar	Apr	May	Jun	Jul	Aug	Sep	Oct	Nov	Dec
High	24	28	39	54	67	76	81	78	70	57	44	31
Low	5	8	19	33	45	53	58	56	48	37	28	14
Precip	2.2	1.9	2.3	2.8	3.1	3.4	3.6	3.5	3.6	3.2	3.1	2.6
Snow	na	na	na	na	na	na	na	na	na	na	na	na

High and Low temperatures in degrees Fahrenheit; Precipitation and Snow in inches

Weather Station: Wanakena Ranger School   Elevation: 1,509 feet

	Jan	Feb	Mar	Apr	May	Jun	Jul	Aug	Sep	Oct	Nov	Dec
High	27	30	38	52	66	74	78	76	68	55	43	31
Low	4	5	14	30	41	50	54	53	45	35	25	12
Precip	2.8	2.3	2.7	3.0	3.8	4.0	4.7	4.2	4.6	4.1	3.9	3.1
Snow	29.6	25.3	17.3	6.0	0.3	0.0	0.0	0.0	tr	1.6	11.2	25.8

High and Low temperatures in degrees Fahrenheit; Precipitation and Snow in inches

Population: 112,011; Growth (since 2000): 0.1%; Density: 41.8 persons per square mile; Race: 93.1% White, 2.2% Black/African American, 1.0% Asian, 0.8% American Indian/Alaska Native, 0.1% Native Hawaiian/Other Pacific Islander, 1.9% two or more races, 2.2% Hispanic of any race; Average household size: 2.42; Median age: 37.8; Age under 18: 20.7%; Age 65 and over: 14.9%; Males per 100 females: 103.2; Marriage status: 36.5% never married, 46.6% now married, 2.3% separated, 6.9% widowed, 10.1% divorced; Foreign born: 4.4%; Speak English only: 91.9%; With disability: 15.5%; Veterans: 9.0%; Ancestry: 18.1% Irish, 14.4% French, 12.4% English, 10.3% German, 7.2% Italian

Religion: Six largest groups: 21.9% Catholicism, 3.8% Methodist/Pietist, 2.3% Presbyterian-Reformed, 1.7% European Free-Church, 1.2% Non-denominational Protestant, 1.1% Episcopalianism/Anglicanism

Economy: Unemployment rate: 5.3%; Leading industries: 20.3 % retail trade; 12.8 % health care and social assistance; 12.4 % other services (except public administration); Farms: 1,303 totaling 356,909 acres; Company size: 2 employ 1,000 or more persons, 3 employ 500 to 999 persons, 31 employs 100 to 499 persons, 1,923 employ less than 100 persons; Business ownership: 1,744 women-owned, n/a Black-owned, n/a Hispanic-owned, 75 Asian-owned, 81 American Indian/Alaska Native-owned

Employment: 10.5% management, business, and financial, 2.5% computer, engineering, and science, 14.1% education, legal, community service, arts, and media, 6.1% healthcare practitioners, 22.7% service, 22.6% sales and office, 10.6% natural resources, construction, and maintenance, 10.8% production, transportation, and material moving

Income: Per capita: $22,562; Median household: $44,705; Average household: $58,676; Households with income of $100,000 or more: 13.9%; Poverty rate: 19.4%

Educational Attainment: High school diploma or higher: 88.0%; Bachelor's degree or higher: 22.3%; Graduate/professional degree or higher: 11.3%

Housing: Homeownership rate: 71.4%; Median home value: $87,600; Median year structure built: 1960; Homeowner vacancy rate: 1.7%; Median selected monthly owner costs: $1,078 with a mortgage, $450 without a mortgage; Median gross rent: $700 per month; Rental vacancy rate: 3.6%

Vital Statistics: Birth rate: 107.6 per 10,000 population; Death rate: 91.8 per 10,000 population; Age-adjusted cancer mortality rate: 165.9 deaths per 100,000 population

Health Insurance: 90.4% have insurance; 66.9% have private insurance; 37.8% have public insurance; 9.6% do not have insurance; 8.8% of children under 18 do not have insurance

Health Care: Physicians: 15.9 per 10,000 population; Dentists: 3.6 per 10,000 population; Hospital beds: 45.0 per 10,000 population; Hospital admissions: 1,011.4 per 10,000 population

Transportation: Commute: 86.3% car, 0.4% public transportation, 6.7% walk, 4.7% work from home; Mean travel time to work: 20.9 minutes

2016 Presidential Election: 51.6% Trump, 42.6% Clinton, 3.7% Johnson, 2.1% Stein

National and State Parks: Adirondack State Park; Cedar Island State Park; Cold Spring Brook State Forest; Coles Creek State Park; Degrasse State Forest; Donnerville State Forest; Greenwood Creek State Forest; Higley Flow State Park; Jacques Cartier State Park; Orebed Creek State Forest; Saint Lawrence State Forest; Silver Hill State Forest; Stammer Creek State Forest; Taylor Creek State Forest; Trout Lake State Forest; Whippoorwill Corners State Forest; Wilson Hill State Fish and Game Managemen

Additional Information Contacts

Saint Lawrence Government . . . . (315) 379-2276
  http://www.co.st-lawrence.ny.us

Saint Lawrence County Communities

BRASHER (town). Covers a land area of 91.103 square miles and a water area of 0.967 square miles. Located at 44.89° N. Lat; 74.72° W. Long.

Population: 2,074; Growth (since 2000): -11.3%; Density: 22.8 persons per square mile; Race: 91.2% White, 0.8% Black/African American, 1.1% Asian, 1.4% American Indian/Alaska Native, 0.0% Native Hawaiian/Other Pacific Islander, 5.3% Two or more races, 1.9% Hispanic of any race; Average household size: 2.43; Median age: 43.9; Age under 18: 21.7%; Age 65 and over: 12.4%; Males per 100 females: 96.4; Marriage status: 25.2% never married, 59.4% now married, 2.2% separated, 4.8% widowed, 10.6% divorced; Foreign born: 4.7%; Speak English only: 92.8%; With disability: 20.8%; Veterans: 11.5%; Ancestry: 24.0% French, 22.3% Irish, 11.6% English, 7.5% Italian, 7.4% German

Employment: 9.4% management, business, and financial, 0.7% computer, engineering, and science, 12.3% education, legal, community service, arts, and media, 4.4% healthcare practitioners, 22.2% service, 16.3% sales and office, 21.4% natural resources, construction, and maintenance, 13.3% production, transportation, and material moving

Income: Per capita: $21,056; Median household: $46,875; Average household: $51,095; Households with income of $100,000 or more: 10.4%; Poverty rate: 17.2%

Educational Attainment: High school diploma or higher: 88.4%; Bachelor's degree or higher: 16.4%; Graduate/professional degree or higher: 6.7%

Housing: Homeownership rate: 77.5%; Median home value: $88,200; Median year structure built: 1971; Homeowner vacancy rate: 3.9%; Median selected monthly owner costs: $1,018 with a mortgage, $462 without a mortgage; Median gross rent: $705 per month; Rental vacancy rate: 0.0%

Health Insurance: 90.3% have insurance; 59.3% have private insurance; 44.5% have public insurance; 9.7% do not have insurance; 5.3% of children under 18 do not have insurance

Transportation: Commute: 92.9% car, 0.0% public transportation, 3.4% walk, 3.7% work from home; Mean travel time to work: 24.4 minutes

BRASHER FALLS (CDP).
Covers a land area of 1.638 square miles and a water area of 0.101 square miles. Located at 44.81° N. Lat; 74.79° W. Long. Elevation is 289 feet.
Population: 452; Growth (since 2000): n/a; Density: 275.9 persons per square mile; Race: 99.6% White, 0.0% Black/African American, 0.0% Asian, 0.0% American Indian/Alaska Native, 0.0% Native Hawaiian/Other Pacific Islander, 0.4% Two or more races, 0.4% Hispanic of any race; Average household size: 2.03; Median age: 53.2; Age under 18: 23.7%; Age 65 and over: 25.0%; Males per 100 females: 89.5; Marriage status: 19.4% never married, 61.2% now married, 3.1% separated, 10.7% widowed, 8.7% divorced; Foreign born: 5.3%; Speak English only: 93.5%; With disability: 26.1%; Veterans: 15.9%; Ancestry: 32.5% Irish, 22.6% French, 14.6% Italian, 11.3% English, 10.6% Dutch
Employment: 9.7% management, business, and financial, 2.9% computer, engineering, and science, 25.7% education, legal, community service, arts, and media, 5.3% healthcare practitioners, 10.7% service, 16.5% sales and office, 17.5% natural resources, construction, and maintenance, 11.7% production, transportation, and material moving
Income: Per capita: $26,800; Median household: $54,120; Average household: $54,741; Households with income of $100,000 or more: 11.6%; Poverty rate: 12.2%
Educational Attainment: High school diploma or higher: 95.3%; Bachelor's degree or higher: 31.5%; Graduate/professional degree or higher: 13.1%

School District(s)
Brasher Falls Central SD (PK-12)
    2014-15 Enrollment: 1,033 . . . . (315) 389-5131
Housing: Homeownership rate: 68.6%; Median home value: $101,400; Median year structure built: 1954; Homeowner vacancy rate: 0.0%; Median selected monthly owner costs: $1,227 with a mortgage, $496 without a mortgage; Median gross rent: $525 per month; Rental vacancy rate: 0.0%
Health Insurance: 96.5% have insurance; 71.9% have private insurance; 45.1% have public insurance; 3.5% do not have insurance; 0.0% of children under 18 do not have insurance
Transportation: Commute: 91.8% car, 0.0% public transportation, 8.2% walk, 0.0% work from home; Mean travel time to work: 25.5 minutes

BRIER HILL (unincorporated postal area)
ZCTA: 13614
    Covers a land area of 8.966 square miles and a water area of 0 square miles. Located at 44.53° N. Lat; 75.69° W. Long. Elevation is 341 feet.
Population: 250; Growth (since 2000): -13.5%; Density: 27.9 persons per square mile; Race: 94.0% White, 0.0% Black/African American, 0.0% Asian, 4.4% American Indian/Alaska Native, 0.0% Native Hawaiian/Other Pacific Islander, 1.6% Two or more races, 0.0% Hispanic of any race; Average household size: 2.31; Median age: 56.7; Age under 18: 7.6%; Age 65 and over: 34.8%; Males per 100 females: 85.9; Marriage status: 10.8% never married, 71.9% now married, 1.3% separated, 7.4% widowed, 10.0% divorced; Foreign born: 1.6%; Speak English only: 81.6%; With disability: 23.6%; Veterans: 16.0%; Ancestry: 24.4% English, 23.2% Irish, 17.2% French, 3.6% German, 3.6% Scottish
Employment: 3.7% management, business, and financial, 10.2% computer, engineering, and science, 23.1% education, legal, community service, arts, and media, 14.8% healthcare practitioners, 17.6% service, 6.5% sales and office, 10.2% natural resources, construction, and maintenance, 13.9% production, transportation, and material moving
Income: Per capita: $25,314; Median household: $35,625; Average household: $56,245; Households with income of $100,000 or more: 25.0%; Poverty rate: 8.4%
Educational Attainment: High school diploma or higher: 94.2%; Bachelor's degree or higher: 16.1%; Graduate/professional degree or higher: n/a
Housing: Homeownership rate: 80.6%; Median home value: $56,800; Median year structure built: 1991; Homeowner vacancy rate: 19.4%; Median selected monthly owner costs: $690 with a mortgage, $418 without a mortgage; Median gross rent: n/a per month; Rental vacancy rate: 0.0%
Health Insurance: 95.6% have insurance; 62.4% have private insurance; 59.6% have public insurance; 4.4% do not have insurance; 0.0% of children under 18 do not have insurance

Transportation: Commute: 79.6% car, 0.0% public transportation, 0.0% walk, 20.4% work from home; Mean travel time to work: 26.5 minutes

CANTON (town).
Covers a land area of 104.765 square miles and a water area of 1.098 square miles. Located at 44.57° N. Lat; 75.21° W. Long. Elevation is 377 feet.
History: Seat of Saint Lawrence University and the State University of N.Y. College of Technology. Frederic Remington born here. Irving Bacheller born in nearby Pierrepont. Settled 1799, incorporated 1845.
Population: 11,339; Growth (since 2000): 9.7%; Density: 108.2 persons per square mile; Race: 90.6% White, 3.5% Black/African American, 0.7% Asian, 0.4% American Indian/Alaska Native, 0.3% Native Hawaiian/Other Pacific Islander, 3.2% Two or more races, 3.7% Hispanic of any race; Average household size: 2.33; Median age: 27.6; Age under 18: 14.8%; Age 65 and over: 14.2%; Males per 100 females: 96.2; Marriage status: 53.6% never married, 32.3% now married, 0.7% separated, 6.6% widowed, 7.6% divorced; Foreign born: 6.3%; Speak English only: 91.1%; With disability: 12.8%; Veterans: 6.5%; Ancestry: 17.5% Irish, 12.9% English, 11.0% German, 10.3% French, 7.4% Italian
Employment: 8.4% management, business, and financial, 4.2% computer, engineering, and science, 26.2% education, legal, community service, arts, and media, 5.0% healthcare practitioners, 19.5% service, 20.6% sales and office, 7.2% natural resources, construction, and maintenance, 9.0% production, transportation, and material moving
Income: Per capita: $20,961; Median household: $50,456; Average household: $64,492; Households with income of $100,000 or more: 18.0%; Poverty rate: 18.9%
Educational Attainment: High school diploma or higher: 89.6%; Bachelor's degree or higher: 34.4%; Graduate/professional degree or higher: 21.1%

School District(s)
Canton Central SD (PK-12)
    2014-15 Enrollment: 1,313 . . . . (315) 386-8561
Saint Lawrence-Lewis Boces
    2014-15 Enrollment: n/a . . . . (315) 386-4504

Four-year College(s)
SUNY College of Technology at Canton (Public)
    Fall 2014 Enrollment: 3,278 . . . . (315) 386-7011
    2015-16 Tuition: In-state $7,855; Out-of-state $12,245
St Lawrence University (Private, Not-for-profit)
    Fall 2014 Enrollment: 2,419 . . . . (315) 229-5011
    2015-16 Tuition: In-state $49,420; Out-of-state $49,420
Housing: Homeownership rate: 68.1%; Median home value: $119,700; Median year structure built: 1961; Homeowner vacancy rate: 1.0%; Median selected monthly owner costs: $1,242 with a mortgage, $537 without a mortgage; Median gross rent: $780 per month; Rental vacancy rate: 8.0%
Health Insurance: 92.8% have insurance; 74.5% have private insurance; 29.1% have public insurance; 7.2% do not have insurance; 3.9% of children under 18 do not have insurance
Newspapers: St. Lawrence Plaindealer (weekly circulation 3,500)
Transportation: Commute: 70.0% car, 1.8% public transportation, 17.0% walk, 7.5% work from home; Mean travel time to work: 17.8 minutes
Additional Information Contacts
Town of Canton . . . . (315) 386-2871
    http://www.cantonnewyork.us

CANTON (village).
County seat. Covers a land area of 3.576 square miles and a water area of 0.100 square miles. Located at 44.60° N. Lat; 75.17° W. Long. Elevation is 377 feet.
Population: 6,665; Growth (since 2000): 13.3%; Density: 1,863.6 persons per square mile; Race: 87.6% White, 5.4% Black/African American, 1.2% Asian, 0.8% American Indian/Alaska Native, 0.5% Native Hawaiian/Other Pacific Islander, 2.9% Two or more races, 5.5% Hispanic of any race; Average household size: 2.14; Median age: 21.7; Age under 18: 10.4%; Age 65 and over: 10.7%; Males per 100 females: 97.7; Marriage status: 69.0% never married, 21.4% now married, 0.3% separated, 3.0% widowed, 6.6% divorced; Foreign born: 8.1%; Speak English only: 88.5%; With disability: 7.4%; Veterans: 4.5%; Ancestry: 16.4% Irish, 9.0% Italian, 9.0% German, 8.9% English, 5.7% French
Employment: 8.3% management, business, and financial, 4.3% computer, engineering, and science, 35.3% education, legal, community service, arts, and media, 4.5% healthcare practitioners, 16.2% service, 22.0% sales and office, 3.4% natural resources, construction, and maintenance, 6.0% production, transportation, and material moving

Income: Per capita: $18,732; Median household: $48,988; Average household: $70,547; Households with income of $100,000 or more: 19.5%; Poverty rate: 19.6%
Educational Attainment: High school diploma or higher: 90.6%; Bachelor's degree or higher: 46.7%; Graduate/professional degree or higher: 30.9%

School District(s)
Canton Central SD (PK-12)
    2014-15 Enrollment: 1,313 . . . . (315) 386-8561
Saint Lawrence-Lewis Boces
    2014-15 Enrollment: n/a . . . . (315) 386-4504
Four-year College(s)
SUNY College of Technology at Canton (Public)
    Fall 2014 Enrollment: 3,278 . . . . (315) 386-7011
    2015-16 Tuition: In-state $7,855; Out-of-state $12,245
St Lawrence University (Private, Not-for-profit)
    Fall 2014 Enrollment: 2,419 . . . . (315) 229-5011
    2015-16 Tuition: In-state $49,420; Out-of-state $49,420
Housing: Homeownership rate: 45.8%; Median home value: $162,800; Median year structure built: 1958; Homeowner vacancy rate: 0.0%; Median selected monthly owner costs: $1,522 with a mortgage, $832 without a mortgage; Median gross rent: $782 per month; Rental vacancy rate: 5.4%
Health Insurance: 93.9% have insurance; 80.9% have private insurance; 21.3% have public insurance; 6.1% do not have insurance; 3.7% of children under 18 do not have insurance
Safety: Violent crime rate: 3.0 per 10,000 population; Property crime rate: 47.9 per 10,000 population
Newspapers: St. Lawrence Plaindealer (weekly circulation 3,500)
Transportation: Commute: 53.4% car, 3.3% public transportation, 30.9% walk, 6.9% work from home; Mean travel time to work: 15.8 minutes
Additional Information Contacts
Village of Canton . . . . (315) 386-2871
http://www.cantonnewyork.us

CHASE MILLS (unincorporated postal area)
ZCTA: 13621

Covers a land area of 27.207 square miles and a water area of 0.825 square miles. Located at 44.83° N. Lat; 75.08° W. Long. Elevation is 269 feet.
Population: 447; Growth (since 2000): -36.1%; Density: 16.4 persons per square mile; Race: 100.0% White, 0.0% Black/African American, 0.0% Asian, 0.0% American Indian/Alaska Native, 0.0% Native Hawaiian/Other Pacific Islander, 0.0% Two or more races, 0.0% Hispanic of any race; Average household size: 2.27; Median age: 43.0; Age under 18: 21.5%; Age 65 and over: 5.6%; Males per 100 females: 101.2; Marriage status: 43.2% never married, 36.6% now married, 2.7% separated, 5.5% widowed, 14.8% divorced; Foreign born: 0.7%; Speak English only: 100.0%; With disability: 20.8%; Veterans: 12.0%; Ancestry: 35.1% French, 23.7% Irish, 13.6% English, 6.7% German, 6.0% French Canadian
Employment: 3.8% management, business, and financial, 0.0% computer, engineering, and science, 0.0% education, legal, community service, arts, and media, 14.4% healthcare practitioners, 52.5% service, 18.8% sales and office, 8.8% natural resources, construction, and maintenance, 1.9% production, transportation, and material moving
Income: Per capita: $20,122; Median household: $37,188; Average household: $44,285; Households with income of $100,000 or more: 4.0%; Poverty rate: 37.1%
Educational Attainment: High school diploma or higher: 84.1%; Bachelor's degree or higher: 16.3%; Graduate/professional degree or higher: 8.1%
Housing: Homeownership rate: 81.7%; Median home value: $55,700; Median year structure built: 1970; Homeowner vacancy rate: 4.7%; Median selected monthly owner costs: $769 with a mortgage, $290 without a mortgage; Median gross rent: $1,018 per month; Rental vacancy rate: 0.0%
Health Insurance: 89.7% have insurance; 46.1% have private insurance; 62.0% have public insurance; 10.3% do not have insurance; 0.0% of children under 18 do not have insurance
Transportation: Commute: 91.6% car, 0.0% public transportation, 0.0% walk, 8.4% work from home; Mean travel time to work: 24.1 minutes

CHILDWOLD (unincorporated postal area)
ZCTA: 12922

Covers a land area of 43.968 square miles and a water area of 1.404 square miles. Located at 44.29° N. Lat; 74.70° W. Long. Elevation is 1,627 feet.
Population: 37; Growth (since 2000): -36.2%; Density: 0.8 persons per square mile; Race: 81.1% White, 2.7% Black/African American, 16.2% Asian, 0.0% American Indian/Alaska Native, 0.0% Native Hawaiian/Other Pacific Islander, 0.0% Two or more races, 0.0% Hispanic of any race; Average household size: 1.68; Median age: 56.9; Age under 18: 10.8%; Age 65 and over: 32.4%; Males per 100 females: 103.1; Marriage status: 42.9% never married, 25.7% now married, 0.0% separated, 11.4% widowed, 20.0% divorced; Foreign born: 0.0%; Speak English only: 100.0%; With disability: 24.3%; Veterans: 0.0%; Ancestry: 32.4% German, 24.3% Italian, 16.2% Guyanese, 16.2% Irish, 16.2% Scottish
Employment: 27.8% management, business, and financial, 0.0% computer, engineering, and science, 33.3% education, legal, community service, arts, and media, 0.0% healthcare practitioners, 0.0% service, 38.9% sales and office, 0.0% natural resources, construction, and maintenance, 0.0% production, transportation, and material moving
Income: Per capita: $28,581; Median household: $53,125; Average household: $48,900; Households with income of $100,000 or more: 9.1%; Poverty rate: 10.8%
Educational Attainment: High school diploma or higher: 93.9%; Bachelor's degree or higher: 15.2%; Graduate/professional degree or higher: 3.0%
Housing: Homeownership rate: 100.0%; Median home value: n/a; Median year structure built: 1950; Homeowner vacancy rate: 0.0%; Median selected monthly owner costs: n/a with a mortgage, n/a without a mortgage; Median gross rent: n/a per month; Rental vacancy rate: 0.0%
Health Insurance: 83.8% have insurance; 64.9% have private insurance; 48.6% have public insurance; 16.2% do not have insurance; 0.0% of children under 18 do not have insurance
Transportation: Commute: 100.0% car, 0.0% public transportation, 0.0% walk, 0.0% work from home; Mean travel time to work: 0.0 minutes

CHIPPEWA BAY (unincorporated postal area)
ZCTA: 13623

Covers a land area of 0.396 square miles and a water area of 0 square miles. Located at 44.45° N. Lat; 75.75° W. Long. Elevation is 289 feet.
Population: 43; Growth (since 2000): n/a; Density: 108.5 persons per square mile; Race: 100.0% White, 0.0% Black/African American, 0.0% Asian, 0.0% American Indian/Alaska Native, 0.0% Native Hawaiian/Other Pacific Islander, 0.0% Two or more races, 0.0% Hispanic of any race; Average household size: 2.39; Median age: 34.4; Age under 18: 7.0%; Age 65 and over: 14.0%; Males per 100 females: 104.2; Marriage status: 40.0% never married, 35.0% now married, 0.0% separated, 0.0% widowed, 25.0% divorced; Foreign born: 0.0%; Speak English only: 100.0%; With disability: 14.0%; Veterans: 17.5%; Ancestry: 46.5% German, 30.2% English, 20.9% Italian, 18.6% Scottish, 14.0% European
Employment: 0.0% management, business, and financial, 0.0% computer, engineering, and science, 0.0% education, legal, community service, arts, and media, 25.9% healthcare practitioners, 29.6% service, 14.8% sales and office, 0.0% natural resources, construction, and maintenance, 29.6% production, transportation, and material moving
Income: Per capita: $29,709; Median household: $78,750; Average household: $70,972; Households with income of $100,000 or more: 22.2%; Poverty rate: 14.0%
Educational Attainment: High school diploma or higher: 83.8%; Bachelor's degree or higher: 29.7%; Graduate/professional degree or higher: 21.6%
Housing: Homeownership rate: 83.3%; Median home value: n/a; Median year structure built: 1988; Homeowner vacancy rate: 0.0%; Median selected monthly owner costs: $1,425 with a mortgage, $0 without a mortgage; Median gross rent: n/a per month; Rental vacancy rate: 0.0%
Health Insurance: 100.0% have insurance; 46.5% have private insurance; 53.5% have public insurance; 0.0% do not have insurance; 0.0% of children under 18 do not have insurance
Transportation: Commute: 88.9% car, 11.1% public transportation, 0.0% walk, 0.0% work from home; Mean travel time to work: 28.7 minutes

CLARE (town). Covers a land area of 96.556 square miles and a water area of 0.698 square miles. Located at 44.36° N. Lat; 75.01° W. Long. Elevation is 820 feet.
Population: 128; Growth (since 2000): 14.3%; Density: 1.3 persons per square mile; Race: 97.7% White, 0.0% Black/African American, 0.0% Asian, 1.6% American Indian/Alaska Native, 0.0% Native Hawaiian/Other Pacific Islander, 0.8% Two or more races, 0.0% Hispanic of any race; Average household size: 3.05; Median age: 36.1; Age under 18: 32.0%; Age 65 and over: 16.4%; Males per 100 females: 98.1; Marriage status: 44.7% never married, 38.8% now married, 0.0% separated, 8.7% widowed, 7.8% divorced; Foreign born: 0.0%; Speak English only: 97.6%; With disability: 18.0%; Veterans: 12.6%; Ancestry: 21.9% Irish, 17.2% English, 16.4% Italian, 10.2% American, 9.4% French
Employment: 4.8% management, business, and financial, 0.0% computer, engineering, and science, 2.4% education, legal, community service, arts, and media, 7.1% healthcare practitioners, 21.4% service, 31.0% sales and office, 19.0% natural resources, construction, and maintenance, 14.3% production, transportation, and material moving
Income: Per capita: $15,485; Median household: $48,333; Average household: $46,412; Households with income of $100,000 or more: 2.4%; Poverty rate: 35.2%
Educational Attainment: High school diploma or higher: 80.6%; Bachelor's degree or higher: 9.7%; Graduate/professional degree or higher: 1.4%
Housing: Homeownership rate: 76.2%; Median home value: $64,000; Median year structure built: 1974; Homeowner vacancy rate: 0.0%; Median selected monthly owner costs: $1,083 with a mortgage, $338 without a mortgage; Median gross rent: $575 per month; Rental vacancy rate: 0.0%
Health Insurance: 72.7% have insurance; 43.8% have private insurance; 39.1% have public insurance; 27.3% do not have insurance; 39.0% of children under 18 do not have insurance
Transportation: Commute: 95.1% car, 0.0% public transportation, 0.0% walk, 0.0% work from home; Mean travel time to work: 28.8 minutes

CLIFTON (town). Covers a land area of 134.360 square miles and a water area of 15.985 square miles. Located at 44.20° N. Lat; 74.89° W. Long.
Population: 785; Growth (since 2000): -0.8%; Density: 5.8 persons per square mile; Race: 94.0% White, 0.0% Black/African American, 0.8% Asian, 1.4% American Indian/Alaska Native, 0.0% Native Hawaiian/Other Pacific Islander, 3.3% Two or more races, 0.9% Hispanic of any race; Average household size: 2.51; Median age: 46.6; Age under 18: 16.6%; Age 65 and over: 26.0%; Males per 100 females: 109.2; Marriage status: 25.4% never married, 57.0% now married, 0.7% separated, 11.1% widowed, 6.4% divorced; Foreign born: 1.7%; Speak English only: 95.1%; With disability: 26.6%; Veterans: 12.2%; Ancestry: 19.9% English, 19.1% Irish, 13.8% French, 6.8% Scottish, 6.0% German
Employment: 10.4% management, business, and financial, 1.0% computer, engineering, and science, 8.5% education, legal, community service, arts, and media, 0.0% healthcare practitioners, 31.3% service, 24.4% sales and office, 6.5% natural resources, construction, and maintenance, 17.9% production, transportation, and material moving
Income: Per capita: $22,023; Median household: $31,932; Average household: $51,536; Households with income of $100,000 or more: 11.1%; Poverty rate: 25.9%
Educational Attainment: High school diploma or higher: 80.2%; Bachelor's degree or higher: 15.9%; Graduate/professional degree or higher: 7.8%
Housing: Homeownership rate: 80.8%; Median home value: $84,000; Median year structure built: 1959; Homeowner vacancy rate: 3.8%; Median selected monthly owner costs: $1,221 with a mortgage, $402 without a mortgage; Median gross rent: $845 per month; Rental vacancy rate: 0.0%
Health Insurance: 93.1% have insurance; 51.3% have private insurance; 60.6% have public insurance; 6.9% do not have insurance; 3.8% of children under 18 do not have insurance
Transportation: Commute: 87.4% car, 0.0% public transportation, 3.5% walk, 9.0% work from home; Mean travel time to work: 34.4 minutes

COLTON (CDP). Covers a land area of 1.688 square miles and a water area of 0.073 square miles. Located at 44.57° N. Lat; 74.95° W. Long. Elevation is 873 feet.
Population: 428; Growth (since 2000): n/a; Density: 253.5 persons per square mile; Race: 97.2% White, 0.0% Black/African American, 0.9% Asian, 0.0% American Indian/Alaska Native, 0.0% Native Hawaiian/Other Pacific Islander, 1.9% Two or more races, 0.9% Hispanic of any race;

Average household size: 2.21; Median age: 43.9; Age under 18: 22.2%; Age 65 and over: 13.1%; Males per 100 females: 93.8; Marriage status: 16.2% never married, 58.1% now married, 0.0% separated, 12.4% widowed, 13.3% divorced; Foreign born: 2.6%; Speak English only: 99.2%; With disability: 22.4%; Veterans: 4.8%; Ancestry: 34.8% Irish, 25.9% French, 20.8% German, 17.1% English, 8.6% American
Employment: 13.9% management, business, and financial, 7.2% computer, engineering, and science, 21.2% education, legal, community service, arts, and media, 0.0% healthcare practitioners, 20.2% service, 21.6% sales and office, 10.1% natural resources, construction, and maintenance, 5.8% production, transportation, and material moving
Income: Per capita: $24,564; Median household: $44,559; Average household: $53,564; Households with income of $100,000 or more: 14.4%; Poverty rate: 14.3%
Educational Attainment: High school diploma or higher: 92.4%; Bachelor's degree or higher: 25.2%; Graduate/professional degree or higher: 16.4%
School District(s)
Colton-Pierrepont Central SD (PK-12)
 2014-15 Enrollment: 321 . . . . (315) 262-2100
Housing: Homeownership rate: 72.2%; Median home value: $97,100; Median year structure built: Before 1940; Homeowner vacancy rate: 5.4%; Median selected monthly owner costs: $1,053 with a mortgage, $388 without a mortgage; Median gross rent: $838 per month; Rental vacancy rate: 0.0%
Health Insurance: 87.6% have insurance; 65.7% have private insurance; 37.6% have public insurance; 12.4% do not have insurance; 5.3% of children under 18 do not have insurance
Transportation: Commute: 92.2% car, 0.0% public transportation, 1.5% walk, 2.4% work from home; Mean travel time to work: 21.5 minutes

COLTON (town). Covers a land area of 241.702 square miles and a water area of 13.252 square miles. Located at 44.37° N. Lat; 74.81° W. Long. Elevation is 873 feet.
Population: 1,717; Growth (since 2000): 18.2%; Density: 7.1 persons per square mile; Race: 95.5% White, 1.8% Black/African American, 0.8% Asian, 0.0% American Indian/Alaska Native, 0.0% Native Hawaiian/Other Pacific Islander, 1.1% Two or more races, 1.6% Hispanic of any race; Average household size: 2.17; Median age: 50.0; Age under 18: 17.4%; Age 65 and over: 26.6%; Males per 100 females: 104.9; Marriage status: 20.4% never married, 56.6% now married, 1.2% separated, 11.8% widowed, 11.2% divorced; Foreign born: 3.7%; Speak English only: 96.5%; With disability: 23.1%; Veterans: 8.4%; Ancestry: 24.8% English, 21.5% Irish, 17.6% French, 13.9% German, 7.0% American
Employment: 15.1% management, business, and financial, 4.0% computer, engineering, and science, 19.6% education, legal, community service, arts, and media, 2.0% healthcare practitioners, 18.8% service, 22.2% sales and office, 11.2% natural resources, construction, and maintenance, 7.2% production, transportation, and material moving
Income: Per capita: $26,252; Median household: $45,278; Average household: $56,077; Households with income of $100,000 or more: 16.0%; Poverty rate: 14.6%
Educational Attainment: High school diploma or higher: 94.1%; Bachelor's degree or higher: 30.2%; Graduate/professional degree or higher: 19.1%
School District(s)
Colton-Pierrepont Central SD (PK-12)
 2014-15 Enrollment: 321 . . . . (315) 262-2100
Housing: Homeownership rate: 78.9%; Median home value: $130,100; Median year structure built: 1968; Homeowner vacancy rate: 1.2%; Median selected monthly owner costs: $1,161 with a mortgage, $442 without a mortgage; Median gross rent: $815 per month; Rental vacancy rate: 0.0%
Health Insurance: 91.4% have insurance; 71.3% have private insurance; 45.8% have public insurance; 8.6% do not have insurance; 4.3% of children under 18 do not have insurance
Transportation: Commute: 93.1% car, 0.0% public transportation, 2.4% walk, 2.9% work from home; Mean travel time to work: 22.0 minutes

CRANBERRY LAKE (CDP). Covers a land area of 19.437 square miles and a water area of 0.276 square miles. Located at 44.18° N. Lat; 74.87° W. Long. Elevation is 1,489 feet.
Population: 187; Growth (since 2000): n/a; Density: 9.6 persons per square mile; Race: 100.0% White, 0.0% Black/African American, 0.0% Asian, 0.0% American Indian/Alaska Native, 0.0% Native Hawaiian/Other Pacific Islander, 0.0% Two or more races, 0.0% Hispanic of any race;

Average household size: 2.28; Median age: 65.8; Age under 18: 9.1%; Age 65 and over: 50.8%; Males per 100 females: 115.1; Marriage status: 22.4% never married, 64.1% now married, 0.0% separated, 11.2% widowed, 2.4% divorced; Foreign born: 3.7%; Speak English only: 90.4%; With disability: 18.2%; Veterans: 16.5%; Ancestry: 32.1% English, 27.3% Irish, 13.9% German, 6.4% Swedish, 5.9% French
Employment: 35.7% management, business, and financial, 0.0% computer, engineering, and science, 7.1% education, legal, community service, arts, and media, 0.0% healthcare practitioners, 35.7% service, 14.3% sales and office, 7.1% natural resources, construction, and maintenance, 0.0% production, transportation, and material moving
Income: Per capita: $30,837; Median household: $51,500; Average household: $65,820; Households with income of $100,000 or more: 15.8%; Poverty rate: 11.8%
Educational Attainment: High school diploma or higher: 94.2%; Bachelor's degree or higher: 35.9%; Graduate/professional degree or higher: 13.5%
Housing: Homeownership rate: 96.3%; Median home value: $239,300; Median year structure built: 1959; Homeowner vacancy rate: 3.7%; Median selected monthly owner costs: $1,625 with a mortgage, $705 without a mortgage; Median gross rent: n/a per month; Rental vacancy rate: 0.0%
Health Insurance: 95.2% have insurance; 70.1% have private insurance; 69.0% have public insurance; 4.8% do not have insurance; 0.0% of children under 18 do not have insurance
Transportation: Commute: 100.0% car, 0.0% public transportation, 0.0% walk, 0.0% work from home; Mean travel time to work: 42.0 minutes

DE KALB (town). Covers a land area of 82.523 square miles and a water area of 0.684 square miles. Located at 44.48° N. Lat; 75.37° W. Long. Elevation is 331 feet.
Population: 2,291; Growth (since 2000): 3.5%; Density: 27.8 persons per square mile; Race: 97.6% White, 0.5% Black/African American, 0.2% Asian, 0.0% American Indian/Alaska Native, 0.0% Native Hawaiian/Other Pacific Islander, 0.9% Two or more races, 1.7% Hispanic of any race; Average household size: 2.88; Median age: 33.4; Age under 18: 29.7%; Age 65 and over: 12.6%; Males per 100 females: 103.9; Marriage status: 25.6% never married, 56.7% now married, 5.5% separated, 6.5% widowed, 11.2% divorced; Foreign born: 2.6%; Speak English only: 90.2%; With disability: 15.4%; Veterans: 10.9%; Ancestry: 17.7% Irish, 10.6% American, 9.3% English, 7.4% German, 6.7% French
Employment: 8.5% management, business, and financial, 2.5% computer, engineering, and science, 4.0% education, legal, community service, arts, and media, 5.7% healthcare practitioners, 30.4% service, 18.3% sales and office, 18.3% natural resources, construction, and maintenance, 12.2% production, transportation, and material moving
Income: Per capita: $21,090; Median household: $50,560; Average household: $59,220; Households with income of $100,000 or more: 12.6%; Poverty rate: 20.6%
Educational Attainment: High school diploma or higher: 83.5%; Bachelor's degree or higher: 13.8%; Graduate/professional degree or higher: 6.2%
Housing: Homeownership rate: 84.2%; Median home value: $87,100; Median year structure built: 1953; Homeowner vacancy rate: 0.0%; Median selected monthly owner costs: $1,044 with a mortgage, $381 without a mortgage; Median gross rent: $638 per month; Rental vacancy rate: 0.8%
Health Insurance: 83.3% have insurance; 62.8% have private insurance; 34.0% have public insurance; 16.7% do not have insurance; 24.8% of children under 18 do not have insurance
Transportation: Commute: 89.8% car, 0.0% public transportation, 2.3% walk, 3.6% work from home; Mean travel time to work: 25.8 minutes

DE PEYSTER (town). Covers a land area of 42.927 square miles and a water area of 2.169 square miles. Located at 44.54° N. Lat; 75.46° W. Long. Elevation is 374 feet.
Population: 1,166; Growth (since 2000): 24.6%; Density: 27.2 persons per square mile; Race: 97.9% White, 0.2% Black/African American, 0.2% Asian, 0.5% American Indian/Alaska Native, 0.4% Native Hawaiian/Other Pacific Islander, 0.8% Two or more races, 1.2% Hispanic of any race; Average household size: 3.91; Median age: 25.1; Age under 18: 37.2%; Age 65 and over: 9.4%; Males per 100 females: 102.0; Marriage status: 35.1% never married, 54.5% now married, 2.4% separated, 4.8% widowed, 5.6% divorced; Foreign born: 1.9%; Speak English only: 61.3%; With disability: 14.8%; Veterans: 5.1%; Ancestry: 17.7% Dutch, 10.5% Pennsylvania German, 9.4% Irish, 8.5% English, 8.5% French

Employment: 18.7% management, business, and financial, 0.8% computer, engineering, and science, 9.1% education, legal, community service, arts, and media, 5.6% healthcare practitioners, 15.5% service, 10.9% sales and office, 18.9% natural resources, construction, and maintenance, 20.5% production, transportation, and material moving
Income: Per capita: $13,238; Median household: $41,818; Average household: $49,661; Households with income of $100,000 or more: 12.4%; Poverty rate: 36.8%
Educational Attainment: High school diploma or higher: 64.4%; Bachelor's degree or higher: 12.8%; Graduate/professional degree or higher: 2.7%
Housing: Homeownership rate: 83.6%; Median home value: $73,000; Median year structure built: 1976; Homeowner vacancy rate: 2.7%; Median selected monthly owner costs: $1,018 with a mortgage, $319 without a mortgage; Median gross rent: $708 per month; Rental vacancy rate: 0.0%
Health Insurance: 59.0% have insurance; 36.4% have private insurance; 31.2% have public insurance; 41.0% do not have insurance; 45.2% of children under 18 do not have insurance
Transportation: Commute: 69.5% car, 0.0% public transportation, 6.0% walk, 17.0% work from home; Mean travel time to work: 24.3 minutes

DEKALB JUNCTION (CDP). Covers a land area of 3.883 square miles and a water area of 0.062 square miles. Located at 44.51° N. Lat; 75.29° W. Long.
Population: 576; Growth (since 2000): n/a; Density: 148.3 persons per square mile; Race: 100.0% White, 0.0% Black/African American, 0.0% Asian, 0.0% American Indian/Alaska Native, 0.0% Native Hawaiian/Other Pacific Islander, 0.0% Two or more races, 2.1% Hispanic of any race; Average household size: 3.56; Median age: 30.3; Age under 18: 31.4%; Age 65 and over: 5.4%; Males per 100 females: 107.6; Marriage status: 31.4% never married, 61.5% now married, 11.6% separated, 0.9% widowed, 6.1% divorced; Foreign born: 2.3%; Speak English only: 93.3%; With disability: 15.6%; Veterans: 14.2%; Ancestry: 23.4% Irish, 15.6% English, 10.6% Dutch, 6.8% French, 5.4% American
Employment: 1.9% management, business, and financial, 4.9% computer, engineering, and science, 5.3% education, legal, community service, arts, and media, 8.3% healthcare practitioners, 31.6% service, 19.9% sales and office, 21.1% natural resources, construction, and maintenance, 7.1% production, transportation, and material moving
Income: Per capita: $23,212; Median household: $70,500; Average household: $80,081; Households with income of $100,000 or more: 27.1%; Poverty rate: 6.4%
Educational Attainment: High school diploma or higher: 84.7%; Bachelor's degree or higher: 22.8%; Graduate/professional degree or higher: 2.6%

School District(s)
Hermon-Dekalb Central SD (PK-12)
　　2014-15 Enrollment: 421 . . . . (315) 347-3442
Housing: Homeownership rate: 87.7%; Median home value: $96,300; Median year structure built: 1958; Homeowner vacancy rate: 0.0%; Median selected monthly owner costs: $1,263 with a mortgage, $280 without a mortgage; Median gross rent: $442 per month; Rental vacancy rate: 0.0%
Health Insurance: 86.3% have insurance; 75.2% have private insurance; 18.9% have public insurance; 13.7% do not have insurance; 9.4% of children under 18 do not have insurance
Transportation: Commute: 92.7% car, 0.0% public transportation, 0.0% walk, 0.0% work from home; Mean travel time to work: 15.4 minutes

EDWARDS (town). Covers a land area of 50.471 square miles and a water area of 0.831 square miles. Located at 44.29° N. Lat; 75.28° W. Long. Elevation is 669 feet.
Population: 947; Growth (since 2000): -17.5%; Density: 18.8 persons per square mile; Race: 94.2% White, 0.3% Black/African American, 0.8% Asian, 0.3% American Indian/Alaska Native, 0.0% Native Hawaiian/Other Pacific Islander, 4.1% Two or more races, 1.8% Hispanic of any race; Average household size: 2.35; Median age: 42.1; Age under 18: 18.2%; Age 65 and over: 16.4%; Males per 100 females: 94.9; Marriage status: 36.8% never married, 46.7% now married, 1.3% separated, 8.3% widowed, 8.1% divorced; Foreign born: 5.5%; Speak English only: 91.7%; With disability: 15.3%; Veterans: 10.3%; Ancestry: 14.3% English, 13.6% French, 12.5% Irish, 10.7% French Canadian, 8.2% American
Employment: 5.9% management, business, and financial, 3.7% computer, engineering, and science, 6.4% education, legal, community service, arts, and media, 5.4% healthcare practitioners, 24.7% service, 20.2% sales and

office, 14.6% natural resources, construction, and maintenance, 19.0% production, transportation, and material moving

Income: Per capita: $18,849; Median household: $38,958; Average household: $43,682; Households with income of $100,000 or more: 4.4%; Poverty rate: 16.1%

Educational Attainment: High school diploma or higher: 88.8%; Bachelor's degree or higher: 11.4%; Graduate/professional degree or higher: 3.8%

Housing: Homeownership rate: 65.2%; Median home value: $75,500; Median year structure built: 1965; Homeowner vacancy rate: 1.5%; Median selected monthly owner costs: $983 with a mortgage, $444 without a mortgage; Median gross rent: $760 per month; Rental vacancy rate: 0.0%

Health Insurance: 90.2% have insurance; 59.3% have private insurance; 46.4% have public insurance; 9.8% do not have insurance; 2.3% of children under 18 do not have insurance

Transportation: Commute: 85.5% car, 1.3% public transportation, 4.3% walk, 6.3% work from home; Mean travel time to work: 37.1 minutes

FINE (town). Covers a land area of 166.799 square miles and a water area of 2.618 square miles. Located at 44.15° N. Lat; 75.09° W. Long. Elevation is 965 feet.

Population: 1,398; Growth (since 2000): -13.8%; Density: 8.4 persons per square mile; Race: 97.1% White, 1.3% Black/African American, 0.1% Asian, 0.5% American Indian/Alaska Native, 0.0% Native Hawaiian/Other Pacific Islander, 0.7% Two or more races, 2.4% Hispanic of any race; Average household size: 2.27; Median age: 48.3; Age under 18: 17.8%; Age 65 and over: 24.0%; Males per 100 females: 108.6; Marriage status: 22.7% never married, 59.8% now married, 4.6% separated, 8.1% widowed, 9.3% divorced; Foreign born: 1.1%; Speak English only: 96.7%; With disability: 19.3%; Veterans: 15.7%; Ancestry: 21.5% French, 20.9% English, 18.2% Irish, 12.4% German, 7.2% American

Employment: 12.8% management, business, and financial, 2.2% computer, engineering, and science, 8.7% education, legal, community service, arts, and media, 7.5% healthcare practitioners, 24.8% service, 22.0% sales and office, 14.8% natural resources, construction, and maintenance, 7.3% production, transportation, and material moving

Income: Per capita: $22,967; Median household: $44,074; Average household: $53,094; Households with income of $100,000 or more: 9.7%; Poverty rate: 18.3%

Educational Attainment: High school diploma or higher: 82.3%; Bachelor's degree or higher: 11.9%; Graduate/professional degree or higher: 6.7%

Housing: Homeownership rate: 84.7%; Median home value: $69,200; Median year structure built: 1956; Homeowner vacancy rate: 2.0%; Median selected monthly owner costs: $845 with a mortgage, $441 without a mortgage; Median gross rent: $582 per month; Rental vacancy rate: 12.6%

Health Insurance: 95.7% have insurance; 67.9% have private insurance; 49.6% have public insurance; 4.3% do not have insurance; 0.8% of children under 18 do not have insurance

Transportation: Commute: 85.9% car, 0.0% public transportation, 2.9% walk, 9.7% work from home; Mean travel time to work: 33.5 minutes

FOWLER (town). Covers a land area of 59.325 square miles and a water area of 1.368 square miles. Located at 44.28° N. Lat; 75.40° W. Long. Elevation is 591 feet.

Population: 2,206; Growth (since 2000): 1.2%; Density: 37.2 persons per square mile; Race: 97.8% White, 0.9% Black/African American, 0.8% Asian, 0.0% American Indian/Alaska Native, 0.0% Native Hawaiian/Other Pacific Islander, 0.5% Two or more races, 0.7% Hispanic of any race; Average household size: 2.50; Median age: 42.2; Age under 18: 20.1%; Age 65 and over: 13.6%; Males per 100 females: 102.0; Marriage status: 27.9% never married, 61.0% now married, 0.9% separated, 5.4% widowed, 5.7% divorced; Foreign born: 1.0%; Speak English only: 97.8%; With disability: 14.3%; Veterans: 9.6%; Ancestry: 17.6% Irish, 14.7% French, 11.7% English, 11.3% American, 7.8% German

Employment: 8.0% management, business, and financial, 2.1% computer, engineering, and science, 6.1% education, legal, community service, arts, and media, 5.0% healthcare practitioners, 25.6% service, 23.8% sales and office, 15.2% natural resources, construction, and maintenance, 14.3% production, transportation, and material moving

Income: Per capita: $24,461; Median household: $46,923; Average household: $59,444; Households with income of $100,000 or more: 13.0%; Poverty rate: 12.8%

Educational Attainment: High school diploma or higher: 89.6%; Bachelor's degree or higher: 13.6%; Graduate/professional degree or higher: 4.0%

Housing: Homeownership rate: 84.9%; Median home value: $104,400; Median year structure built: 1982; Homeowner vacancy rate: 1.8%; Median selected monthly owner costs: $1,011 with a mortgage, $385 without a mortgage; Median gross rent: $957 per month; Rental vacancy rate: 0.0%

Health Insurance: 93.8% have insurance; 64.7% have private insurance; 40.7% have public insurance; 6.2% do not have insurance; 0.0% of children under 18 do not have insurance

Transportation: Commute: 97.1% car, 0.0% public transportation, 0.0% walk, 2.9% work from home; Mean travel time to work: 27.4 minutes

GOUVERNEUR (town). Covers a land area of 71.217 square miles and a water area of 1.074 square miles. Located at 44.36° N. Lat; 75.49° W. Long. Elevation is 440 feet.

History: Named for Gouverneur Morris, whose mansion still stands. Laid out 1787, Incorporated 1850.

Population: 7,027; Growth (since 2000): -5.3%; Density: 98.7 persons per square mile; Race: 89.3% White, 6.3% Black/African American, 0.0% Asian, 0.3% American Indian/Alaska Native, 0.0% Native Hawaiian/Other Pacific Islander, 1.8% Two or more races, 4.0% Hispanic of any race; Average household size: 2.54; Median age: 39.4; Age under 18: 20.2%; Age 65 and over: 10.8%; Males per 100 females: 127.8; Marriage status: 37.5% never married, 42.6% now married, 2.2% separated, 7.2% widowed, 12.6% divorced; Foreign born: 3.1%; Speak English only: 92.5%; With disability: 17.7%; Veterans: 8.3%; Ancestry: 15.4% Irish, 14.5% German, 11.0% English, 8.4% French, 8.1% American

Employment: 9.7% management, business, and financial, 1.3% computer, engineering, and science, 11.2% education, legal, community service, arts, and media, 9.2% healthcare practitioners, 17.6% service, 20.1% sales and office, 17.3% natural resources, construction, and maintenance, 13.5% production, transportation, and material moving

Income: Per capita: $18,602; Median household: $33,503; Average household: $51,451; Households with income of $100,000 or more: 9.4%; Poverty rate: 25.8%

Educational Attainment: High school diploma or higher: 81.7%; Bachelor's degree or higher: 11.0%; Graduate/professional degree or higher: 5.2%

School District(s)

Gouverneur Central SD (PK-12)
    2014-15 Enrollment: 1,679 . . . . (315) 287-4870

Housing: Homeownership rate: 58.8%; Median home value: $87,000; Median year structure built: 1953; Homeowner vacancy rate: 2.9%; Median selected monthly owner costs: $1,035 with a mortgage, $531 without a mortgage; Median gross rent: $692 per month; Rental vacancy rate: 10.1%

Health Insurance: 87.6% have insurance; 52.2% have private insurance; 45.6% have public insurance; 12.4% do not have insurance; 9.4% of children under 18 do not have insurance

Hospitals: Gouverneur Hospital

Newspapers: Gouverneur Tribune-Press (weekly circulation 4,000)

Transportation: Commute: 92.6% car, 0.0% public transportation, 1.0% walk, 3.2% work from home; Mean travel time to work: 23.0 minutes

Additional Information Contacts

Town of Gouverneur . . . . (315) 287-2340
    http://www.gouverneurny.com

GOUVERNEUR (village). Covers a land area of 2.191 square miles and a water area of 0.087 square miles. Located at 44.34° N. Lat; 75.47° W. Long. Elevation is 440 feet.

Population: 3,882; Growth (since 2000): -8.9%; Density: 1,772.0 persons per square mile; Race: 96.8% White, 2.4% Black/African American, 0.1% Asian, 0.5% American Indian/Alaska Native, 0.0% Native Hawaiian/Other Pacific Islander, 0.2% Two or more races, 0.5% Hispanic of any race; Average household size: 2.44; Median age: 41.4; Age under 18: 20.8%; Age 65 and over: 12.9%; Males per 100 females: 93.8; Marriage status: 35.2% never married, 42.4% now married, 1.7% separated, 8.7% widowed, 13.7% divorced; Foreign born: 3.1%; Speak English only: 97.4%; With disability: 19.5%; Veterans: 11.1%; Ancestry: 16.3% Irish, 14.3% German, 13.1% English, 12.7% French, 8.8% American

Employment: 10.4% management, business, and financial, 0.9% computer, engineering, and science, 9.5% education, legal, community service, arts, and media, 4.4% healthcare practitioners, 19.4% service, 22.1% sales and office, 20.2% natural resources, construction, and maintenance, 13.2% production, transportation, and material moving

Income: Per capita: $18,886; Median household: $35,175; Average household: $45,332; Households with income of $100,000 or more: 9.3%; Poverty rate: 27.7%

Educational Attainment: High school diploma or higher: 86.7%; Bachelor's degree or higher: 12.3%; Graduate/professional degree or higher: 6.3%

School District(s)

Gouverneur Central SD (PK-12)

    2014-15 Enrollment: 1,679 . . . . (315) 287-4870

Housing: Homeownership rate: 47.6%; Median home value: $92,000; Median year structure built: Before 1940; Homeowner vacancy rate: 5.3%; Median selected monthly owner costs: $975 with a mortgage, $604 without a mortgage; Median gross rent: $681 per month; Rental vacancy rate: 12.0%

Health Insurance: 87.0% have insurance; 50.3% have private insurance; 49.1% have public insurance; 13.0% do not have insurance; 2.1% of children under 18 do not have insurance

Hospitals: Gouverneur Hospital

Newspapers: Gouverneur Tribune-Press (weekly circulation 4,000)

Transportation: Commute: 95.1% car, 0.0% public transportation, 0.7% walk, 1.1% work from home; Mean travel time to work: 24.3 minutes

HAILESBORO (CDP).
Covers a land area of 4.727 square miles and a water area of 0.080 square miles. Located at 44.31° N. Lat; 75.43° W. Long. Elevation is 492 feet.

Population: 686; Growth (since 2000): n/a; Density: 145.1 persons per square mile; Race: 99.4% White, 0.6% Black/African American, 0.0% Asian, 0.0% American Indian/Alaska Native, 0.0% Native Hawaiian/Other Pacific Islander, 0.0% Two or more races, 0.0% Hispanic of any race; Average household size: 2.41; Median age: 35.7; Age under 18: 16.6%; Age 65 and over: 12.4%; Males per 100 females: 89.1; Marriage status: 34.8% never married, 57.7% now married, 1.8% separated, 5.7% widowed, 1.8% divorced; Foreign born: 0.7%; Speak English only: 99.3%; With disability: 10.8%; Veterans: 8.6%; Ancestry: 24.3% Irish, 16.6% French, 15.2% American, 9.5% German, 7.9% English

Employment: 5.9% management, business, and financial, 2.2% computer, engineering, and science, 3.3% education, legal, community service, arts, and media, 3.7% healthcare practitioners, 14.4% service, 31.1% sales and office, 18.9% natural resources, construction, and maintenance, 20.4% production, transportation, and material moving

Income: Per capita: $21,627; Median household: $44,519; Average household: $48,434; Households with income of $100,000 or more: 6.3%; Poverty rate: 20.0%

Educational Attainment: High school diploma or higher: 93.7%; Bachelor's degree or higher: 12.1%; Graduate/professional degree or higher: 4.2%

Housing: Homeownership rate: 72.1%; Median home value: $125,000; Median year structure built: 1969; Homeowner vacancy rate: 0.0%; Median selected monthly owner costs: $763 with a mortgage, $377 without a mortgage; Median gross rent: $1,225 per month; Rental vacancy rate: 0.0%

Health Insurance: 90.2% have insurance; 65.5% have private insurance; 33.3% have public insurance; 9.8% do not have insurance; 0.0% of children under 18 do not have insurance

Transportation: Commute: 100.0% car, 0.0% public transportation, 0.0% walk, 0.0% work from home; Mean travel time to work: 28.0 minutes

HAMMOND (town).
Covers a land area of 62.197 square miles and a water area of 15.709 square miles. Located at 44.44° N. Lat; 75.73° W. Long. Elevation is 358 feet.

Population: 1,411; Growth (since 2000): 16.9%; Density: 22.7 persons per square mile; Race: 96.0% White, 0.5% Black/African American, 0.5% Asian, 0.1% American Indian/Alaska Native, 0.0% Native Hawaiian/Other Pacific Islander, 2.7% Two or more races, 0.9% Hispanic of any race; Average household size: 2.44; Median age: 36.9; Age under 18: 26.4%; Age 65 and over: 17.1%; Males per 100 females: 97.2; Marriage status: 28.7% never married, 54.8% now married, 1.9% separated, 6.9% widowed, 9.6% divorced; Foreign born: 2.7%; Speak English only: 95.5%; With disability: 10.8%; Veterans: 10.0%; Ancestry: 20.1% Irish, 15.7% English, 15.4% German, 12.6% Italian, 9.0% French

Employment: 13.4% management, business, and financial, 1.2% computer, engineering, and science, 7.5% education, legal, community service, arts, and media, 7.5% healthcare practitioners, 18.3% service, 21.9% sales and office, 20.7% natural resources, construction, and maintenance, 9.4% production, transportation, and material moving

Income: Per capita: $23,031; Median household: $46,509; Average household: $55,496; Households with income of $100,000 or more: 10.2%; Poverty rate: 22.6%

Educational Attainment: High school diploma or higher: 90.3%; Bachelor's degree or higher: 24.8%; Graduate/professional degree or higher: 13.6%

School District(s)

Hammond Central SD (PK-12)

    2014-15 Enrollment: 310 . . . . (315) 324-5931

Housing: Homeownership rate: 74.3%; Median home value: $83,700; Median year structure built: 1964; Homeowner vacancy rate: 3.6%; Median selected monthly owner costs: $1,095 with a mortgage, $420 without a mortgage; Median gross rent: $643 per month; Rental vacancy rate: 0.0%

Health Insurance: 89.3% have insurance; 60.4% have private insurance; 43.7% have public insurance; 10.7% do not have insurance; 7.8% of children under 18 do not have insurance

Transportation: Commute: 78.4% car, 1.9% public transportation, 3.4% walk, 13.5% work from home; Mean travel time to work: 30.9 minutes

HAMMOND (village).
Covers a land area of 0.586 square miles and a water area of 0 square miles. Located at 44.45° N. Lat; 75.69° W. Long. Elevation is 358 feet.

Population: 342; Growth (since 2000): 13.2%; Density: 584.0 persons per square mile; Race: 97.1% White, 0.0% Black/African American, 0.6% Asian, 0.0% American Indian/Alaska Native, 0.0% Native Hawaiian/Other Pacific Islander, 1.8% Two or more races, 2.6% Hispanic of any race; Average household size: 2.61; Median age: 32.6; Age under 18: 31.3%; Age 65 and over: 13.2%; Males per 100 females: 78.3; Marriage status: 27.9% never married, 54.9% now married, 0.8% separated, 11.1% widowed, 6.1% divorced; Foreign born: 2.3%; Speak English only: 98.1%; With disability: 13.1%; Veterans: 9.2%; Ancestry: 22.5% German, 16.1% Italian, 14.6% French, 12.9% Irish, 12.0% English

Employment: 7.3% management, business, and financial, 2.9% computer, engineering, and science, 9.5% education, legal, community service, arts, and media, 3.6% healthcare practitioners, 21.9% service, 44.5% sales and office, 5.8% natural resources, construction, and maintenance, 4.4% production, transportation, and material moving

Income: Per capita: $16,690; Median household: $35,938; Average household: $42,129; Households with income of $100,000 or more: 7.7%; Poverty rate: 27.8%

Educational Attainment: High school diploma or higher: 93.9%; Bachelor's degree or higher: 17.0%; Graduate/professional degree or higher: 9.4%

School District(s)

Hammond Central SD (PK-12)

    2014-15 Enrollment: 310 . . . . (315) 324-5931

Housing: Homeownership rate: 64.9%; Median home value: $61,500; Median year structure built: Before 1940; Homeowner vacancy rate: 0.0%; Median selected monthly owner costs: $850 with a mortgage, $360 without a mortgage; Median gross rent: $616 per month; Rental vacancy rate: 0.0%

Health Insurance: 88.1% have insurance; 56.3% have private insurance; 45.8% have public insurance; 11.9% do not have insurance; 3.7% of children under 18 do not have insurance

Transportation: Commute: 78.6% car, 0.0% public transportation, 6.3% walk, 11.1% work from home; Mean travel time to work: 32.9 minutes

HANNAWA FALLS (CDP).
Covers a land area of 5.110 square miles and a water area of 0.302 square miles. Located at 44.60° N. Lat; 74.97° W. Long. Elevation is 558 feet.

Population: 925; Growth (since 2000): n/a; Density: 181.0 persons per square mile; Race: 96.3% White, 0.4% Black/African American, 2.9% Asian, 0.0% American Indian/Alaska Native, 0.0% Native Hawaiian/Other Pacific Islander, 0.3% Two or more races, 3.7% Hispanic of any race; Average household size: 2.21; Median age: 49.2; Age under 18: 18.9%; Age 65 and over: 29.1%; Males per 100 females: 107.6; Marriage status: 19.0% never married, 61.0% now married, 0.7% separated, 11.5% widowed, 8.5% divorced; Foreign born: 4.3%; Speak English only: 98.8%; With disability: 15.1%; Veterans: 12.1%; Ancestry: 21.5% French, 17.9% Irish, 14.1% English, 13.2% German, 6.3% Canadian

Employment: 12.3% management, business, and financial, 5.3% computer, engineering, and science, 20.8% education, legal, community service, arts, and media, 7.3% healthcare practitioners, 19.3% service, 20.3% sales and office, 5.8% natural resources, construction, and maintenance, 9.3% production, transportation, and material moving

Income: Per capita: $31,213; Median household: $55,735; Average household: $70,241; Households with income of $100,000 or more: 23.4%; Poverty rate: 10.1%

Educational Attainment: High school diploma or higher: 96.6%; Bachelor's degree or higher: 43.3%; Graduate/professional degree or higher: 19.3%

Housing: Homeownership rate: 85.9%; Median home value: $124,700; Median year structure built: 1970; Homeowner vacancy rate: 0.0%; Median selected monthly owner costs: $991 with a mortgage, $511 without a mortgage; Median gross rent: $1,005 per month; Rental vacancy rate: 0.0%

Health Insurance: 99.5% have insurance; 83.5% have private insurance; 40.4% have public insurance; 0.5% do not have insurance; 0.0% of children under 18 do not have insurance

Transportation: Commute: 93.3% car, 4.8% public transportation, 0.0% walk, 1.9% work from home; Mean travel time to work: 15.1 minutes

HERMON (town).
Covers a land area of 53.146 square miles and a water area of 1.080 square miles. Located at 44.40° N. Lat; 75.29° W. Long. Elevation is 499 feet.

Population: 1,058; Growth (since 2000): -1.0%; Density: 19.9 persons per square mile; Race: 98.2% White, 0.7% Black/African American, 0.0% Asian, 0.0% American Indian/Alaska Native, 0.1% Native Hawaiian/Other Pacific Islander, 1.0% Two or more races, 1.0% Hispanic of any race; Average household size: 2.45; Median age: 41.3; Age under 18: 21.3%; Age 65 and over: 18.8%; Males per 100 females: 97.5; Marriage status: 30.4% never married, 49.6% now married, 2.5% separated, 8.9% widowed, 11.1% divorced; Foreign born: 1.4%; Speak English only: 96.6%; With disability: 14.6%; Veterans: 11.5%; Ancestry: 15.5% English, 14.1% Irish, 13.0% French, 9.6% Italian, 8.0% German

Employment: 9.4% management, business, and financial, 1.7% computer, engineering, and science, 11.0% education, legal, community service, arts, and media, 4.2% healthcare practitioners, 34.2% service, 18.8% sales and office, 15.2% natural resources, construction, and maintenance, 5.6% production, transportation, and material moving

Income: Per capita: $21,612; Median household: $41,667; Average household: $50,838; Households with income of $100,000 or more: 8.6%; Poverty rate: 17.0%

Educational Attainment: High school diploma or higher: 86.9%; Bachelor's degree or higher: 17.5%; Graduate/professional degree or higher: 5.1%

Housing: Homeownership rate: 79.8%; Median home value: $76,700; Median year structure built: 1958; Homeowner vacancy rate: 0.0%; Median selected monthly owner costs: $961 with a mortgage, $555 without a mortgage; Median gross rent: $575 per month; Rental vacancy rate: 10.3%

Health Insurance: 87.4% have insurance; 64.7% have private insurance; 43.9% have public insurance; 12.6% do not have insurance; 16.4% of children under 18 do not have insurance

Transportation: Commute: 98.7% car, 0.0% public transportation, 0.9% walk, 0.4% work from home; Mean travel time to work: 29.3 minutes

HERMON (village).
Covers a land area of 0.380 square miles and a water area of 0 square miles. Located at 44.47° N. Lat; 75.23° W. Long. Elevation is 499 feet.

Population: 404; Growth (since 2000): 0.5%; Density: 1,063.5 persons per square mile; Race: 95.3% White, 1.7% Black/African American, 0.0% Asian, 0.0% American Indian/Alaska Native, 0.2% Native Hawaiian/Other Pacific Islander, 2.7% Two or more races, 2.7% Hispanic of any race; Average household size: 2.14; Median age: 33.9; Age under 18: 25.7%; Age 65 and over: 18.6%; Males per 100 females: 84.3; Marriage status: 39.2% never married, 34.1% now married, 4.1% separated, 10.5% widowed, 16.2% divorced; Foreign born: 2.2%; Speak English only: 98.7%; With disability: 17.3%; Veterans: 11.3%; Ancestry: 22.8% Irish, 17.8% English, 17.1% German, 15.6% Italian, 11.9% French

Employment: 7.0% management, business, and financial, 5.1% computer, engineering, and science, 6.4% education, legal, community service, arts, and media, 7.6% healthcare practitioners, 34.4% service, 22.3% sales and office, 5.1% natural resources, construction, and maintenance, 12.1% production, transportation, and material moving

Income: Per capita: $19,639; Median household: $33,750; Average household: $41,317; Households with income of $100,000 or more: 7.0%; Poverty rate: 26.8%

Educational Attainment: High school diploma or higher: 80.6%; Bachelor's degree or higher: 18.3%; Graduate/professional degree or higher: 2.7%

Housing: Homeownership rate: 68.3%; Median home value: $71,400; Median year structure built: Before 1940; Homeowner vacancy rate: 0.0%; Median selected monthly owner costs: $963 with a mortgage, $533 without a mortgage; Median gross rent: $420 per month; Rental vacancy rate: 14.5%

Health Insurance: 91.3% have insurance; 64.9% have private insurance; 51.5% have public insurance; 8.7% do not have insurance; 0.0% of children under 18 do not have insurance

Transportation: Commute: 97.4% car, 0.0% public transportation, 2.6% walk, 0.0% work from home; Mean travel time to work: 25.4 minutes

HEUVELTON (village).
Covers a land area of 0.761 square miles and a water area of 0.107 square miles. Located at 44.62° N. Lat; 75.40° W. Long. Elevation is 315 feet.

Population: 798; Growth (since 2000): -0.7%; Density: 1,049.0 persons per square mile; Race: 97.4% White, 1.1% Black/African American, 0.0% Asian, 0.6% American Indian/Alaska Native, 0.0% Native Hawaiian/Other Pacific Islander, 0.6% Two or more races, 1.5% Hispanic of any race; Average household size: 2.51; Median age: 41.5; Age under 18: 23.9%; Age 65 and over: 12.3%; Males per 100 females: 84.0; Marriage status: 28.9% never married, 54.2% now married, 3.5% separated, 8.8% widowed, 8.0% divorced; Foreign born: 3.4%; Speak English only: 95.8%; With disability: 13.0%; Veterans: 10.0%; Ancestry: 20.2% Irish, 14.3% French, 13.9% English, 9.6% German, 8.1% American

Employment: 5.7% management, business, and financial, 2.3% computer, engineering, and science, 7.0% education, legal, community service, arts, and media, 13.1% healthcare practitioners, 25.8% service, 23.5% sales and office, 12.4% natural resources, construction, and maintenance, 10.3% production, transportation, and material moving

Income: Per capita: $25,093; Median household: $54,500; Average household: $60,543; Households with income of $100,000 or more: 15.7%; Poverty rate: 5.0%

Educational Attainment: High school diploma or higher: 91.0%; Bachelor's degree or higher: 19.4%; Graduate/professional degree or higher: 9.5%

School District(s)
Heuvelton Central SD (PK-12)
    2014-15 Enrollment: 524 . . . . (315) 344-2414

Housing: Homeownership rate: 77.7%; Median home value: $78,900; Median year structure built: Before 1940; Homeowner vacancy rate: 0.8%; Median selected monthly owner costs: $1,089 with a mortgage, $480 without a mortgage; Median gross rent: $588 per month; Rental vacancy rate: 0.0%

Health Insurance: 93.6% have insurance; 75.1% have private insurance; 33.7% have public insurance; 6.4% do not have insurance; 0.0% of children under 18 do not have insurance

Transportation: Commute: 93.3% car, 0.0% public transportation, 4.6% walk, 1.3% work from home; Mean travel time to work: 25.5 minutes

HOPKINTON (town).
Covers a land area of 185.340 square miles and a water area of 1.704 square miles. Located at 44.54° N. Lat; 74.66° W. Long. Elevation is 794 feet.

Population: 1,108; Growth (since 2000): 8.6%; Density: 6.0 persons per square mile; Race: 97.8% White, 0.0% Black/African American, 0.5% Asian, 0.8% American Indian/Alaska Native, 0.0% Native Hawaiian/Other Pacific Islander, 0.5% Two or more races, 0.4% Hispanic of any race; Average household size: 2.49; Median age: 41.1; Age under 18: 26.4%; Age 65 and over: 17.5%; Males per 100 females: 104.8; Marriage status: 27.7% never married, 58.9% now married, 2.1% separated, 5.4% widowed, 8.1% divorced; Foreign born: 2.4%; Speak English only: 97.5%; With disability: 13.4%; Veterans: 10.8%; Ancestry: 24.5% Irish, 22.3% German, 13.8% French, 11.8% English, 6.9% Italian

Employment: 12.4% management, business, and financial, 10.0% computer, engineering, and science, 15.1% education, legal, community service, arts, and media, 3.9% healthcare practitioners, 20.0% service, 17.1% sales and office, 10.5% natural resources, construction, and maintenance, 11.0% production, transportation, and material moving

Income: Per capita: $21,085; Median household: $39,792; Average household: $51,470; Households with income of $100,000 or more: 11.5%; Poverty rate: 13.5%

Educational Attainment: High school diploma or higher: 90.7%; Bachelor's degree or higher: 24.2%; Graduate/professional degree or higher: 9.3%

Housing: Homeownership rate: 84.9%; Median home value: $102,600; Median year structure built: 1970; Homeowner vacancy rate: 1.3%; Median

selected monthly owner costs: $1,201 with a mortgage, $466 without a mortgage; Median gross rent: $606 per month; Rental vacancy rate: 0.0%
Health Insurance: 89.5% have insurance; 67.5% have private insurance; 34.6% have public insurance; 10.5% do not have insurance; 0.0% of children under 18 do not have insurance
Transportation: Commute: 96.8% car, 0.0% public transportation, 2.2% walk, 1.0% work from home; Mean travel time to work: 30.0 minutes

LAWRENCE (town). Covers a land area of 47.610 square miles and a water area of 0.058 square miles. Located at 44.75° N. Lat; 74.68° W. Long.
Population: 1,780; Growth (since 2000): 15.2%; Density: 37.4 persons per square mile; Race: 95.2% White, 0.4% Black/African American, 1.8% Asian, 0.7% American Indian/Alaska Native, 0.0% Native Hawaiian/Other Pacific Islander, 1.5% Two or more races, 1.3% Hispanic of any race; Average household size: 2.85; Median age: 39.2; Age under 18: 28.5%; Age 65 and over: 13.7%; Males per 100 females: 102.9; Marriage status: 31.5% never married, 56.8% now married, 2.1% separated, 2.5% widowed, 9.2% divorced; Foreign born: 2.6%; Speak English only: 86.8%; With disability: 18.5%; Veterans: 12.3%; Ancestry: 19.0% French, 15.7% German, 15.5% English, 11.9% Irish, 8.1% American
Employment: 10.9% management, business, and financial, 2.3% computer, engineering, and science, 8.1% education, legal, community service, arts, and media, 6.9% healthcare practitioners, 29.5% service, 16.4% sales and office, 10.5% natural resources, construction, and maintenance, 15.4% production, transportation, and material moving
Income: Per capita: $18,167; Median household: $44,476; Average household: $50,762; Households with income of $100,000 or more: 9.3%; Poverty rate: 23.2%
Educational Attainment: High school diploma or higher: 85.0%; Bachelor's degree or higher: 14.6%; Graduate/professional degree or higher: 6.7%
Housing: Homeownership rate: 81.8%; Median home value: $74,100; Median year structure built: 1972; Homeowner vacancy rate: 3.9%; Median selected monthly owner costs: $957 with a mortgage, $430 without a mortgage; Median gross rent: $700 per month; Rental vacancy rate: 0.0%
Health Insurance: 85.7% have insurance; 57.8% have private insurance; 39.4% have public insurance; 14.3% do not have insurance; 25.0% of children under 18 do not have insurance
Transportation: Commute: 94.4% car, 0.0% public transportation, 2.4% walk, 1.8% work from home; Mean travel time to work: 22.7 minutes

LISBON (town). Covers a land area of 108.280 square miles and a water area of 5.636 square miles. Located at 44.70° N. Lat; 75.31° W. Long. Elevation is 338 feet.
Population: 4,100; Growth (since 2000): 1.3%; Density: 37.9 persons per square mile; Race: 98.0% White, 0.0% Black/African American, 0.5% Asian, 0.7% American Indian/Alaska Native, 0.0% Native Hawaiian/Other Pacific Islander, 0.8% Two or more races, 0.3% Hispanic of any race; Average household size: 2.54; Median age: 44.4; Age under 18: 25.3%; Age 65 and over: 16.4%; Males per 100 females: 101.3; Marriage status: 23.7% never married, 56.9% now married, 0.6% separated, 8.2% widowed, 11.3% divorced; Foreign born: 1.7%; Speak English only: 94.4%; With disability: 13.7%; Veterans: 9.6%; Ancestry: 21.6% Irish, 13.3% French, 11.1% English, 10.8% Italian, 9.4% German
Employment: 12.1% management, business, and financial, 2.0% computer, engineering, and science, 14.6% education, legal, community service, arts, and media, 5.4% healthcare practitioners, 28.7% service, 18.7% sales and office, 7.3% natural resources, construction, and maintenance, 11.1% production, transportation, and material moving
Income: Per capita: $32,260; Median household: $57,314; Average household: $81,185; Households with income of $100,000 or more: 24.9%; Poverty rate: 10.3%
Educational Attainment: High school diploma or higher: 88.1%; Bachelor's degree or higher: 22.4%; Graduate/professional degree or higher: 12.7%

School District(s)
Lisbon Central SD (PK-12)
    2014-15 Enrollment: 594 . . . . (315) 393-4951
Housing: Homeownership rate: 87.0%; Median home value: $95,800; Median year structure built: 1973; Homeowner vacancy rate: 0.0%; Median selected monthly owner costs: $1,165 with a mortgage, $395 without a mortgage; Median gross rent: $683 per month; Rental vacancy rate: 6.3%

Health Insurance: 89.2% have insurance; 67.7% have private insurance; 34.3% have public insurance; 10.8% do not have insurance; 15.5% of children under 18 do not have insurance
Transportation: Commute: 92.0% car, 0.0% public transportation, 2.0% walk, 4.5% work from home; Mean travel time to work: 20.6 minutes
Additional Information Contacts
Town of Lisbon . . . . (315) 393-5988
    http://www.lisbonny.net

LOUISVILLE (town). Covers a land area of 48.525 square miles and a water area of 15.342 square miles. Located at 44.91° N. Lat; 75.01° W. Long. Elevation is 217 feet.
Population: 3,155; Growth (since 2000): -1.3%; Density: 65.0 persons per square mile; Race: 91.3% White, 0.0% Black/African American, 1.3% Asian, 5.3% American Indian/Alaska Native, 0.0% Native Hawaiian/Other Pacific Islander, 2.2% Two or more races, 2.7% Hispanic of any race; Average household size: 2.29; Median age: 47.3; Age under 18: 20.0%; Age 65 and over: 17.8%; Males per 100 females: 93.2; Marriage status: 20.0% never married, 65.1% now married, 5.3% separated, 5.5% widowed, 9.4% divorced; Foreign born: 3.8%; Speak English only: 94.2%; With disability: 19.6%; Veterans: 9.9%; Ancestry: 27.4% French, 19.7% Irish, 14.5% German, 12.1% English, 5.9% Italian
Employment: 18.0% management, business, and financial, 0.9% computer, engineering, and science, 9.9% education, legal, community service, arts, and media, 4.8% healthcare practitioners, 25.1% service, 23.9% sales and office, 10.9% natural resources, construction, and maintenance, 6.5% production, transportation, and material moving
Income: Per capita: $26,069; Median household: $48,182; Average household: $58,779; Households with income of $100,000 or more: 14.2%; Poverty rate: 11.8%
Educational Attainment: High school diploma or higher: 87.0%; Bachelor's degree or higher: 23.6%; Graduate/professional degree or higher: 10.0%
Housing: Homeownership rate: 76.9%; Median home value: $108,200; Median year structure built: 1978; Homeowner vacancy rate: 0.0%; Median selected monthly owner costs: $1,099 with a mortgage, $389 without a mortgage; Median gross rent: $718 per month; Rental vacancy rate: 0.0%
Health Insurance: 94.0% have insurance; 77.0% have private insurance; 38.0% have public insurance; 6.0% do not have insurance; 0.0% of children under 18 do not have insurance
Transportation: Commute: 93.4% car, 0.0% public transportation, 0.0% walk, 5.5% work from home; Mean travel time to work: 16.9 minutes

MACOMB (town). Covers a land area of 60.717 square miles and a water area of 2.428 square miles. Located at 44.44° N. Lat; 75.57° W. Long.
Population: 1,040; Growth (since 2000): 22.9%; Density: 17.1 persons per square mile; Race: 96.3% White, 1.0% Black/African American, 0.9% Asian, 0.3% American Indian/Alaska Native, 0.0% Native Hawaiian/Other Pacific Islander, 0.5% Two or more races, 0.0% Hispanic of any race; Average household size: 2.78; Median age: 38.7; Age under 18: 24.9%; Age 65 and over: 13.2%; Males per 100 females: 116.7; Marriage status: 27.1% never married, 56.2% now married, 1.6% separated, 7.2% widowed, 9.5% divorced; Foreign born: 5.1%; Speak English only: 92.6%; With disability: 14.9%; Veterans: 9.6%; Ancestry: 13.6% English, 12.7% Irish, 9.7% American, 7.7% French, 6.9% Polish
Employment: 11.4% management, business, and financial, 1.4% computer, engineering, and science, 6.7% education, legal, community service, arts, and media, 10.4% healthcare practitioners, 27.4% service, 16.5% sales and office, 18.1% natural resources, construction, and maintenance, 8.1% production, transportation, and material moving
Income: Per capita: $21,109; Median household: $52,000; Average household: $57,134; Households with income of $100,000 or more: 11.0%; Poverty rate: 19.7%
Educational Attainment: High school diploma or higher: 88.5%; Bachelor's degree or higher: 10.7%; Graduate/professional degree or higher: 6.3%
Housing: Homeownership rate: 87.4%; Median home value: $85,100; Median year structure built: 1958; Homeowner vacancy rate: 2.1%; Median selected monthly owner costs: $1,071 with a mortgage, $352 without a mortgage; Median gross rent: $575 per month; Rental vacancy rate: 13.0%
Health Insurance: 91.5% have insurance; 66.9% have private insurance; 37.9% have public insurance; 8.5% do not have insurance; 0.8% of children under 18 do not have insurance

Transportation: Commute: 90.7% car, 0.2% public transportation, 1.9% walk, 7.2% work from home; Mean travel time to work: 33.6 minutes

MADRID (CDP).
Covers a land area of 3.727 square miles and a water area of 0.133 square miles. Located at 44.75° N. Lat; 75.13° W. Long. Elevation is 325 feet.

Population: 659; Growth (since 2000): n/a; Density: 176.8 persons per square mile; Race: 94.5% White, 1.2% Black/African American, 0.0% Asian, 1.4% American Indian/Alaska Native, 0.0% Native Hawaiian/Other Pacific Islander, 2.4% Two or more races, 2.0% Hispanic of any race; Average household size: 2.47; Median age: 53.3; Age under 18: 21.2%; Age 65 and over: 32.3%; Males per 100 females: 102.4; Marriage status: 26.3% never married, 52.5% now married, 5.8% separated, 13.4% widowed, 7.8% divorced; Foreign born: 0.5%; Speak English only: 98.3%; With disability: 30.9%; Veterans: 7.0%; Ancestry: 17.6% English, 17.6% French, 9.9% Italian, 9.7% Irish, 9.6% German

Employment: 9.2% management, business, and financial, 1.9% computer, engineering, and science, 9.2% education, legal, community service, arts, and media, 4.3% healthcare practitioners, 31.4% service, 17.4% sales and office, 20.8% natural resources, construction, and maintenance, 5.8% production, transportation, and material moving

Income: Per capita: $17,164; Median household: $33,625; Average household: $43,781; Households with income of $100,000 or more: 7.6%; Poverty rate: 25.0%

Educational Attainment: High school diploma or higher: 73.3%; Bachelor's degree or higher: 16.4%; Graduate/professional degree or higher: 8.0%

School District(s)
Madrid-Waddington Central SD (PK-12)

 2014-15 Enrollment: 693 . . . . (315) 322-5746

Housing: Homeownership rate: 67.9%; Median home value: $79,700; Median year structure built: Before 1940; Homeowner vacancy rate: 0.0%; Median selected monthly owner costs: $1,188 with a mortgage, $522 without a mortgage; Median gross rent: $594 per month; Rental vacancy rate: 0.0%

Health Insurance: 95.4% have insurance; 58.6% have private insurance; 58.3% have public insurance; 4.6% do not have insurance; 0.0% of children under 18 do not have insurance

Transportation: Commute: 77.3% car, 0.0% public transportation, 7.4% walk, 13.3% work from home; Mean travel time to work: 24.9 minutes

MADRID (town).
Covers a land area of 52.984 square miles and a water area of 0.598 square miles. Located at 44.77° N. Lat; 75.13° W. Long. Elevation is 325 feet.

Population: 1,721; Growth (since 2000): -5.9%; Density: 32.5 persons per square mile; Race: 95.4% White, 0.5% Black/African American, 1.9% Asian, 0.5% American Indian/Alaska Native, 0.0% Native Hawaiian/Other Pacific Islander, 1.6% Two or more races, 1.5% Hispanic of any race; Average household size: 2.56; Median age: 42.1; Age under 18: 24.3%; Age 65 and over: 20.3%; Males per 100 females: 101.7; Marriage status: 27.6% never married, 52.5% now married, 2.8% separated, 9.4% widowed, 10.5% divorced; Foreign born: 3.2%; Speak English only: 90.1%; With disability: 19.3%; Veterans: 9.5%; Ancestry: 17.1% Irish, 16.4% French, 15.7% English, 12.0% German, 8.8% Italian

Employment: 11.9% management, business, and financial, 2.9% computer, engineering, and science, 9.0% education, legal, community service, arts, and media, 7.5% healthcare practitioners, 27.8% service, 17.4% sales and office, 14.8% natural resources, construction, and maintenance, 8.7% production, transportation, and material moving

Income: Per capita: $24,292; Median household: $38,750; Average household: $61,274; Households with income of $100,000 or more: 16.8%; Poverty rate: 27.5%

Educational Attainment: High school diploma or higher: 81.2%; Bachelor's degree or higher: 19.3%; Graduate/professional degree or higher: 8.2%

School District(s)
Madrid-Waddington Central SD (PK-12)

 2014-15 Enrollment: 693 . . . . (315) 322-5746

Housing: Homeownership rate: 78.4%; Median home value: $81,400; Median year structure built: 1956; Homeowner vacancy rate: 3.0%; Median selected monthly owner costs: $1,267 with a mortgage, $478 without a mortgage; Median gross rent: $646 per month; Rental vacancy rate: 0.0%

Health Insurance: 89.7% have insurance; 60.6% have private insurance; 46.0% have public insurance; 10.3% do not have insurance; 14.8% of children under 18 do not have insurance

Transportation: Commute: 86.6% car, 0.6% public transportation, 5.0% walk, 7.2% work from home; Mean travel time to work: 22.7 minutes

MASSENA (town).
Covers a land area of 44.369 square miles and a water area of 11.774 square miles. Located at 44.96° N. Lat; 74.83° W. Long. Elevation is 230 feet.

History: Settled 1792, incorporated 1886.

Population: 12,721; Growth (since 2000): -3.0%; Density: 286.7 persons per square mile; Race: 93.8% White, 0.2% Black/African American, 1.9% Asian, 1.5% American Indian/Alaska Native, 0.0% Native Hawaiian/Other Pacific Islander, 2.3% Two or more races, 0.8% Hispanic of any race; Average household size: 2.23; Median age: 40.8; Age under 18: 23.1%; Age 65 and over: 16.5%; Males per 100 females: 91.9; Marriage status: 31.7% never married, 46.5% now married, 2.9% separated, 9.5% widowed, 12.3% divorced; Foreign born: 5.0%; Speak English only: 93.8%; With disability: 20.2%; Veterans: 9.3%; Ancestry: 22.0% French, 20.7% Irish, 10.2% French Canadian, 9.0% English, 8.6% Italian

Employment: 12.7% management, business, and financial, 2.3% computer, engineering, and science, 13.0% education, legal, community service, arts, and media, 4.0% healthcare practitioners, 18.9% service, 29.1% sales and office, 8.0% natural resources, construction, and maintenance, 11.9% production, transportation, and material moving

Income: Per capita: $21,173; Median household: $37,830; Average household: $47,262; Households with income of $100,000 or more: 8.9%; Poverty rate: 22.0%

Educational Attainment: High school diploma or higher: 89.2%; Bachelor's degree or higher: 21.1%; Graduate/professional degree or higher: 11.4%

School District(s)
Massena Central SD (PK-12)

 2014-15 Enrollment: 2,821 . . . . (315) 764-3700

Housing: Homeownership rate: 61.0%; Median home value: $77,500; Median year structure built: 1953; Homeowner vacancy rate: 0.8%; Median selected monthly owner costs: $970 with a mortgage, $441 without a mortgage; Median gross rent: $709 per month; Rental vacancy rate: 2.2%

Health Insurance: 90.0% have insurance; 63.4% have private insurance; 43.4% have public insurance; 10.0% do not have insurance; 6.3% of children under 18 do not have insurance

Hospitals: Massena Memorial Hospital (50 beds)

Newspapers: Daily Courier-Observer (daily circulation 4,900)

Transportation: Commute: 91.9% car, 0.2% public transportation, 4.5% walk, 2.1% work from home; Mean travel time to work: 17.6 minutes

Airports: Massena International-Richards Field (commercial service–non-primary)

Additional Information Contacts

Town of Massena . . . . (315) 769-5228
 http://www.massena.ny.us

MASSENA (village).
Covers a land area of 4.524 square miles and a water area of 0.200 square miles. Located at 44.93° N. Lat; 74.89° W. Long. Elevation is 230 feet.

Population: 11,086; Growth (since 2000): -1.1%; Density: 2,450.3 persons per square mile; Race: 95.3% White, 0.2% Black/African American, 2.3% Asian, 1.0% American Indian/Alaska Native, 0.0% Native Hawaiian/Other Pacific Islander, 1.0% Two or more races, 0.7% Hispanic of any race; Average household size: 2.27; Median age: 37.5; Age under 18: 23.7%; Age 65 and over: 14.6%; Males per 100 females: 90.6; Marriage status: 32.2% never married, 46.8% now married, 3.4% separated, 8.8% widowed, 12.2% divorced; Foreign born: 4.6%; Speak English only: 94.5%; With disability: 18.3%; Veterans: 8.8%; Ancestry: 22.5% French, 21.5% Irish, 10.2% French Canadian, 9.1% Italian, 8.6% English

Employment: 12.9% management, business, and financial, 2.3% computer, engineering, and science, 14.0% education, legal, community service, arts, and media, 4.9% healthcare practitioners, 17.6% service, 29.5% sales and office, 6.7% natural resources, construction, and maintenance, 12.1% production, transportation, and material moving

Income: Per capita: $21,299; Median household: $37,967; Average household: $48,280; Households with income of $100,000 or more: 9.4%; Poverty rate: 21.6%

Educational Attainment: High school diploma or higher: 89.3%; Bachelor's degree or higher: 21.9%; Graduate/professional degree or higher: 12.4%

School District(s)
Massena Central SD (PK-12)

 2014-15 Enrollment: 2,821 . . . . (315) 764-3700

Housing: Homeownership rate: 60.1%; Median home value: $77,900; Median year structure built: 1952; Homeowner vacancy rate: 0.9%; Median selected monthly owner costs: $980 with a mortgage, $474 without a mortgage; Median gross rent: $711 per month; Rental vacancy rate: 2.5%
Health Insurance: 89.9% have insurance; 64.1% have private insurance; 41.6% have public insurance; 10.1% do not have insurance; 7.1% of children under 18 do not have insurance
Hospitals: Massena Memorial Hospital (50 beds)
Safety: Violent crime rate: 16.9 per 10,000 population; Property crime rate: 379.5 per 10,000 population
Newspapers: Daily Courier-Observer (daily circulation 4,900)
Transportation: Commute: 93.4% car, 0.3% public transportation, 4.0% walk, 1.8% work from home; Mean travel time to work: 17.3 minutes
Airports: Massena International-Richards Field (commercial service–non-primary)
Additional Information Contacts
Village of Massena . . . . (315) 769-8625
    http://www.massenaworks.com

MORRISTOWN (town). Covers a land area of 45.721 square miles and a water area of 13.724 square miles. Located at 44.53° N. Lat; 75.63° W. Long. Elevation is 289 feet.
Population: 1,943; Growth (since 2000): -5.2%; Density: 42.5 persons per square mile; Race: 97.4% White, 0.4% Black/African American, 0.2% Asian, 1.0% American Indian/Alaska Native, 0.0% Native Hawaiian/Other Pacific Islander, 1.1% Two or more races, 0.2% Hispanic of any race; Average household size: 2.43; Median age: 48.7; Age under 18: 17.1%; Age 65 and over: 25.0%; Males per 100 females: 96.4; Marriage status: 22.1% never married, 59.7% now married, 1.1% separated, 7.2% widowed, 11.0% divorced; Foreign born: 2.7%; Speak English only: 86.0%; With disability: 14.3%; Veterans: 11.6%; Ancestry: 15.8% Irish, 12.8% English, 11.9% German, 8.3% American, 7.1% French
Employment: 17.8% management, business, and financial, 1.6% computer, engineering, and science, 11.8% education, legal, community service, arts, and media, 5.9% healthcare practitioners, 19.4% service, 23.0% sales and office, 10.0% natural resources, construction, and maintenance, 10.4% production, transportation, and material moving
Income: Per capita: $31,485; Median household: $50,500; Average household: $75,670; Households with income of $100,000 or more: 20.7%; Poverty rate: 16.9%
Educational Attainment: High school diploma or higher: 84.9%; Bachelor's degree or higher: 20.3%; Graduate/professional degree or higher: 4.6%
School District(s)
Morristown Central SD (PK-12)
    2014-15 Enrollment: 350 . . . . (315) 375-8814
Housing: Homeownership rate: 80.2%; Median home value: $88,700; Median year structure built: 1967; Homeowner vacancy rate: 9.2%; Median selected monthly owner costs: $1,202 with a mortgage, $472 without a mortgage; Median gross rent: $742 per month; Rental vacancy rate: 21.1%
Health Insurance: 86.1% have insurance; 59.4% have private insurance; 45.6% have public insurance; 13.9% do not have insurance; 17.5% of children under 18 do not have insurance
Transportation: Commute: 81.8% car, 1.8% public transportation, 6.4% walk, 10.0% work from home; Mean travel time to work: 27.2 minutes

MORRISTOWN (village). Covers a land area of 0.980 square miles and a water area of 0.042 square miles. Located at 44.58° N. Lat; 75.65° W. Long. Elevation is 289 feet.
Population: 431; Growth (since 2000): -5.5%; Density: 439.7 persons per square mile; Race: 97.4% White, 1.6% Black/African American, 0.2% Asian, 0.5% American Indian/Alaska Native, 0.0% Native Hawaiian/Other Pacific Islander, 0.2% Two or more races, 0.2% Hispanic of any race; Average household size: 2.39; Median age: 42.0; Age under 18: 15.5%; Age 65 and over: 21.3%; Males per 100 females: 85.4; Marriage status: 36.6% never married, 49.2% now married, 0.5% separated, 6.4% widowed, 7.7% divorced; Foreign born: 3.9%; Speak English only: 95.9%; With disability: 14.6%; Veterans: 11.5%; Ancestry: 24.4% Irish, 16.2% German, 12.1% French Canadian, 10.0% Italian, 9.0% English
Employment: 10.1% management, business, and financial, 0.9% computer, engineering, and science, 8.3% education, legal, community service, arts, and media, 6.9% healthcare practitioners, 17.4% service, 34.9% sales and office, 8.7% natural resources, construction, and maintenance, 12.8% production, transportation, and material moving

Income: Per capita: $27,349; Median household: $58,750; Average household: $64,646; Households with income of $100,000 or more: 18.9%; Poverty rate: 6.7%
Educational Attainment: High school diploma or higher: 90.4%; Bachelor's degree or higher: 20.8%; Graduate/professional degree or higher: 6.1%
School District(s)
Morristown Central SD (PK-12)
    2014-15 Enrollment: 350 . . . . (315) 375-8814
Housing: Homeownership rate: 80.0%; Median home value: $93,300; Median year structure built: 1946; Homeowner vacancy rate: 11.7%; Median selected monthly owner costs: $1,231 with a mortgage, $375 without a mortgage; Median gross rent: $956 per month; Rental vacancy rate: 22.2%
Health Insurance: 93.7% have insurance; 68.4% have private insurance; 48.0% have public insurance; 6.3% do not have insurance; 1.5% of children under 18 do not have insurance
Transportation: Commute: 89.4% car, 3.7% public transportation, 2.8% walk, 4.1% work from home; Mean travel time to work: 22.9 minutes

NEWTON FALLS (unincorporated postal area)
ZCTA: 13666
    Covers a land area of 39.110 square miles and a water area of 3.442 square miles. Located at 44.22° N. Lat; 74.93° W. Long. Elevation is 1,496 feet.
Population: 288; Growth (since 2000): n/a; Density: 7.4 persons per square mile; Race: 95.5% White, 0.0% Black/African American, 0.0% Asian, 0.7% American Indian/Alaska Native, 0.0% Native Hawaiian/Other Pacific Islander, 3.1% Two or more races, 1.7% Hispanic of any race; Average household size: 2.74; Median age: 37.9; Age under 18: 16.7%; Age 65 and over: 21.2%; Males per 100 females: 101.5; Marriage status: 28.9% never married, 53.8% now married, 0.8% separated, 11.9% widowed, 5.5% divorced; Foreign born: 0.0%; Speak English only: 93.9%; With disability: 34.0%; Veterans: 8.8%; Ancestry: 22.9% English, 18.4% French, 12.5% Irish, 10.1% Scottish, 4.2% Polish
Employment: 7.4% management, business, and financial, 0.0% computer, engineering, and science, 16.2% education, legal, community service, arts, and media, 0.0% healthcare practitioners, 23.5% service, 41.2% sales and office, 4.4% natural resources, construction, and maintenance, 7.4% production, transportation, and material moving
Income: Per capita: $20,642; Median household: $24,844; Average household: $52,430; Households with income of $100,000 or more: 11.5%; Poverty rate: 41.7%
Educational Attainment: High school diploma or higher: 65.3%; Bachelor's degree or higher: 13.1%; Graduate/professional degree or higher: 7.7%
Housing: Homeownership rate: 72.4%; Median home value: n/a; Median year structure built: 1955; Homeowner vacancy rate: 8.4%; Median selected monthly owner costs: $1,125 with a mortgage, $357 without a mortgage; Median gross rent: $1,538 per month; Rental vacancy rate: 0.0%
Health Insurance: 91.0% have insurance; 30.6% have private insurance; 71.5% have public insurance; 9.0% do not have insurance; 0.0% of children under 18 do not have insurance
Transportation: Commute: 97.1% car, 0.0% public transportation, 0.0% walk, 2.9% work from home; Mean travel time to work: 24.9 minutes

NICHOLVILLE (unincorporated postal area)
ZCTA: 12965
    Covers a land area of 9.535 square miles and a water area of 0.025 square miles. Located at 44.70° N. Lat; 74.69° W. Long. Elevation is 791 feet.
Population: 500; Growth (since 2000): 2.2%; Density: 52.4 persons per square mile; Race: 98.8% White, 0.0% Black/African American, 1.2% Asian, 0.0% American Indian/Alaska Native, 0.0% Native Hawaiian/Other Pacific Islander, 0.0% Two or more races, 0.0% Hispanic of any race; Average household size: 2.39; Median age: 44.9; Age under 18: 19.8%; Age 65 and over: 16.4%; Males per 100 females: 91.8; Marriage status: 28.9% never married, 59.5% now married, 0.7% separated, 3.8% widowed, 7.8% divorced; Foreign born: 3.6%; Speak English only: 96.9%; With disability: 13.8%; Veterans: 12.2%; Ancestry: 22.6% English, 14.0% French Canadian, 13.8% Italian, 11.2% German, 10.4% Irish
Employment: 6.1% management, business, and financial, 11.1% computer, engineering, and science, 5.1% education, legal, community

service, arts, and media, 3.5% healthcare practitioners, 24.7% service, 32.8% sales and office, 12.1% natural resources, construction, and maintenance, 4.5% production, transportation, and material moving
Income: Per capita: $19,406; Median household: $38,542; Average household: $44,804; Households with income of $100,000 or more: 9.6%; Poverty rate: 15.2%
Educational Attainment: High school diploma or higher: 90.9%; Bachelor's degree or higher: 17.9%; Graduate/professional degree or higher: 7.7%
Housing: Homeownership rate: 84.2%; Median home value: $86,100; Median year structure built: Before 1940; Homeowner vacancy rate: 0.0%; Median selected monthly owner costs: $1,131 with a mortgage, $466 without a mortgage; Median gross rent: $629 per month; Rental vacancy rate: 0.0%
Health Insurance: 93.0% have insurance; 59.4% have private insurance; 42.8% have public insurance; 7.0% do not have insurance; 0.0% of children under 18 do not have insurance
Transportation: Commute: 89.9% car, 0.0% public transportation, 5.1% walk, 2.0% work from home; Mean travel time to work: 24.2 minutes

NORFOLK (CDP).
Covers a land area of 2.702 square miles and a water area of 0.112 square miles. Located at 44.79° N. Lat; 74.99° W. Long. Elevation is 259 feet.
Population: 1,387; Growth (since 2000): 4.0%; Density: 513.3 persons per square mile; Race: 95.2% White, 1.6% Black/African American, 0.0% Asian, 1.7% American Indian/Alaska Native, 0.0% Native Hawaiian/Other Pacific Islander, 1.5% Two or more races, 1.5% Hispanic of any race; Average household size: 2.42; Median age: 32.4; Age under 18: 27.8%; Age 65 and over: 9.6%; Males per 100 females: 98.1; Marriage status: 44.4% never married, 43.9% now married, 4.1% separated, 8.9% widowed, 2.8% divorced; Foreign born: 2.7%; Speak English only: 97.6%; With disability: 15.8%; Veterans: 6.9%; Ancestry: 24.0% Irish, 17.5% German, 14.4% English, 13.9% French, 6.2% Italian
Employment: 13.6% management, business, and financial, 0.0% computer, engineering, and science, 5.1% education, legal, community service, arts, and media, 0.0% healthcare practitioners, 39.2% service, 27.4% sales and office, 8.5% natural resources, construction, and maintenance, 6.1% production, transportation, and material moving
Income: Per capita: $17,771; Median household: $31,406; Average household: $43,123; Households with income of $100,000 or more: 7.1%; Poverty rate: 24.2%
Educational Attainment: High school diploma or higher: 96.4%; Bachelor's degree or higher: 12.8%; Graduate/professional degree or higher: 7.3%
Housing: Homeownership rate: 56.8%; Median home value: $70,600; Median year structure built: Before 1940; Homeowner vacancy rate: 0.0%; Median selected monthly owner costs: $1,112 with a mortgage, $426 without a mortgage; Median gross rent: $646 per month; Rental vacancy rate: 0.0%
Health Insurance: 96.5% have insurance; 73.3% have private insurance; 34.1% have public insurance; 3.5% do not have insurance; 0.0% of children under 18 do not have insurance
Transportation: Commute: 96.7% car, 2.1% public transportation, 0.0% walk, 1.1% work from home; Mean travel time to work: 23.2 minutes

NORFOLK (town).
Covers a land area of 56.740 square miles and a water area of 1.004 square miles. Located at 44.84° N. Lat; 74.93° W. Long. Elevation is 259 feet.
History: Settled in 1809. Amish people moved into the area in the mid-1970s and opened a cheese mill, cheese factories, sawmills, and gristmills; they are no longer here. William P. Rogers, who grew up here, was appointed U.S. Attorney General in 1958.
Population: 4,636; Growth (since 2000): 1.6%; Density: 81.7 persons per square mile; Race: 97.2% White, 0.7% Black/African American, 0.2% Asian, 1.2% American Indian/Alaska Native, 0.0% Native Hawaiian/Other Pacific Islander, 0.8% Two or more races, 0.5% Hispanic of any race; Average household size: 2.56; Median age: 35.2; Age under 18: 26.0%; Age 65 and over: 12.3%; Males per 100 females: 99.0; Marriage status: 29.8% never married, 56.8% now married, 2.6% separated, 4.8% widowed, 8.6% divorced; Foreign born: 2.0%; Speak English only: 97.6%; With disability: 14.3%; Veterans: 10.7%; Ancestry: 20.6% French, 18.8% Irish, 13.4% English, 9.6% German, 7.6% French Canadian
Employment: 5.4% management, business, and financial, 0.5% computer, engineering, and science, 9.9% education, legal, community service, arts, and media, 1.8% healthcare practitioners, 32.4% service, 28.1% sales and

office, 12.4% natural resources, construction, and maintenance, 9.6% production, transportation, and material moving
Income: Per capita: $21,285; Median household: $44,074; Average household: $53,516; Households with income of $100,000 or more: 9.5%; Poverty rate: 18.7%
Educational Attainment: High school diploma or higher: 91.4%; Bachelor's degree or higher: 14.8%; Graduate/professional degree or higher: 9.2%
Housing: Homeownership rate: 72.6%; Median home value: $75,400; Median year structure built: 1964; Homeowner vacancy rate: 1.9%; Median selected monthly owner costs: $1,076 with a mortgage, $419 without a mortgage; Median gross rent: $731 per month; Rental vacancy rate: 0.0%
Health Insurance: 93.2% have insurance; 66.0% have private insurance; 39.8% have public insurance; 6.8% do not have insurance; 1.5% of children under 18 do not have insurance
Safety: Violent crime rate: 6.6 per 10,000 population; Property crime rate: 6.6 per 10,000 population
Transportation: Commute: 96.7% car, 0.7% public transportation, 0.7% walk, 2.0% work from home; Mean travel time to work: 22.0 minutes
Additional Information Contacts
Town of Norfolk . . . . (315) 384-4821
http://www.norfolkny.us

NORTH LAWRENCE (unincorporated postal area)
ZCTA: 12967
Covers a land area of 37.607 square miles and a water area of 0.032 square miles. Located at 44.77° N. Lat; 74.66° W. Long. Elevation is 338 feet.
Population: 1,191; Growth (since 2000): 8.4%; Density: 31.7 persons per square mile; Race: 96.6% White, 0.6% Black/African American, 0.0% Asian, 0.2% American Indian/Alaska Native, 0.0% Native Hawaiian/Other Pacific Islander, 2.1% Two or more races, 2.9% Hispanic of any race; Average household size: 2.86; Median age: 38.3; Age under 18: 30.4%; Age 65 and over: 12.7%; Males per 100 females: 106.6; Marriage status: 29.1% never married, 56.6% now married, 2.0% separated, 3.6% widowed, 10.7% divorced; Foreign born: 1.4%; Speak English only: 82.8%; With disability: 21.1%; Veterans: 10.3%; Ancestry: 21.4% German, 19.1% French, 12.8% English, 11.8% Irish, 10.2% American
Employment: 14.2% management, business, and financial, 0.0% computer, engineering, and science, 7.5% education, legal, community service, arts, and media, 9.4% healthcare practitioners, 33.4% service, 11.3% sales and office, 7.0% natural resources, construction, and maintenance, 17.3% production, transportation, and material moving
Income: Per capita: $16,948; Median household: $44,145; Average household: $47,763; Households with income of $100,000 or more: 6.2%; Poverty rate: 25.5%
Educational Attainment: High school diploma or higher: 85.8%; Bachelor's degree or higher: 10.8%; Graduate/professional degree or higher: 5.0%
Housing: Homeownership rate: 85.1%; Median home value: $68,300; Median year structure built: 1974; Homeowner vacancy rate: 3.3%; Median selected monthly owner costs: $899 with a mortgage, $427 without a mortgage; Median gross rent: $494 per month; Rental vacancy rate: 0.0%
Health Insurance: 82.0% have insurance; 55.1% have private insurance; 40.1% have public insurance; 18.0% do not have insurance; 34.3% of children under 18 do not have insurance
Transportation: Commute: 94.5% car, 0.0% public transportation, 2.2% walk, 2.2% work from home; Mean travel time to work: 23.3 minutes

NORWOOD (village).
Covers a land area of 2.095 square miles and a water area of 0.169 square miles. Located at 44.75° N. Lat; 75.00° W. Long. Elevation is 331 feet.
History: Originally an Adirondack-Saint Lawrence Valley railroad center and industrial village, but now purely a residential community. Incorporated 1871.
Population: 1,644; Growth (since 2000): -2.4%; Density: 784.8 persons per square mile; Race: 97.7% White, 0.1% Black/African American, 0.2% Asian, 1.2% American Indian/Alaska Native, 0.0% Native Hawaiian/Other Pacific Islander, 0.7% Two or more races, 2.6% Hispanic of any race; Average household size: 2.31; Median age: 37.6; Age under 18: 23.5%; Age 65 and over: 17.2%; Males per 100 females: 97.0; Marriage status: 34.5% never married, 45.1% now married, 2.5% separated, 7.1% widowed, 13.3% divorced; Foreign born: 2.9%; Speak English only: 95.7%;

With disability: 17.1%; Veterans: 9.7%; Ancestry: 15.5% Irish, 15.4% French, 14.4% English, 11.4% Italian, 9.3% French Canadian
Employment: 12.4% management, business, and financial, 1.5% computer, engineering, and science, 18.7% education, legal, community service, arts, and media, 7.3% healthcare practitioners, 24.3% service, 20.3% sales and office, 3.6% natural resources, construction, and maintenance, 11.8% production, transportation, and material moving
Income: Per capita: $21,824; Median household: $41,734; Average household: $49,617; Households with income of $100,000 or more: 9.4%; Poverty rate: 19.5%
Educational Attainment: High school diploma or higher: 89.1%; Bachelor's degree or higher: 26.3%; Graduate/professional degree or higher: 11.4%

School District(s)
Norwood-Norfolk Central SD (PK-12)
  2014-15 Enrollment: 1,063 . . . . (315) 353-6631
Housing: Homeownership rate: 65.0%; Median home value: $77,200; Median year structure built: Before 1940; Homeowner vacancy rate: 2.2%; Median selected monthly owner costs: $997 with a mortgage, $497 without a mortgage; Median gross rent: $671 per month; Rental vacancy rate: 0.0%
Health Insurance: 88.4% have insurance; 64.2% have private insurance; 38.7% have public insurance; 11.6% do not have insurance; 10.3% of children under 18 do not have insurance
Transportation: Commute: 95.9% car, 0.0% public transportation, 2.1% walk, 1.7% work from home; Mean travel time to work: 19.8 minutes

OGDENSBURG (city). Covers a land area of 4.956 square miles and a water area of 3.181 square miles. Located at 44.71° N. Lat; 75.46° W. Long. Elevation is 295 feet.
History: Settled by French missionaries and trappers 1749; was strategically important in the War of 1812. Seat of Mater Dei, and Wadhams Hall Seminary and College and a Museum with works of Frederic Remington, who lived here. Rhoda Fox Graves was the first woman to serve the state's Assembly and Senate. Incorporated as a city 1868.
Population: 10,996; Growth (since 2000): -11.1%; Density: 2,218.9 persons per square mile; Race: 86.6% White, 7.1% Black/African American, 0.7% Asian, 0.4% American Indian/Alaska Native, 0.0% Native Hawaiian/Other Pacific Islander, 2.7% Two or more races, 4.4% Hispanic of any race; Average household size: 2.26; Median age: 38.1; Age under 18: 19.7%; Age 65 and over: 14.0%; Males per 100 females: 120.6; Marriage status: 38.8% never married, 41.8% now married, 4.7% separated, 6.6% widowed, 12.8% divorced; Foreign born: 4.7%; Speak English only: 90.5%; With disability: 16.0%; Veterans: 8.3%; Ancestry: 17.6% Irish, 16.4% French, 11.3% English, 10.0% German, 7.3% French Canadian
Employment: 9.6% management, business, and financial, 0.6% computer, engineering, and science, 11.2% education, legal, community service, arts, and media, 10.5% healthcare practitioners, 22.3% service, 27.5% sales and office, 6.9% natural resources, construction, and maintenance, 11.3% production, transportation, and material moving
Income: Per capita: $22,272; Median household: $36,135; Average household: $58,207; Households with income of $100,000 or more: 12.4%; Poverty rate: 23.5%
Educational Attainment: High school diploma or higher: 84.0%; Bachelor's degree or higher: 15.9%; Graduate/professional degree or higher: 7.5%

School District(s)
Ogdensburg City SD (PK-12)
  2014-15 Enrollment: 1,698 . . . . (315) 393-0900
Housing: Homeownership rate: 60.1%; Median home value: $67,900; Median year structure built: Before 1940; Homeowner vacancy rate: 1.0%; Median selected monthly owner costs: $977 with a mortgage, $455 without a mortgage; Median gross rent: $603 per month; Rental vacancy rate: 2.7%
Health Insurance: 91.9% have insurance; 64.8% have private insurance; 45.0% have public insurance; 8.1% do not have insurance; 2.3% of children under 18 do not have insurance
Hospitals: Claxton - Hepburn Medical Center (159 beds)
Safety: Violent crime rate: 31.4 per 10,000 population; Property crime rate: 301.5 per 10,000 population
Newspapers: Canton Rural News (weekly circulation 13,000); Ogdensburg Journal (daily circulation 5,800); The Advance News (weekly circulation 11,000)

Transportation: Commute: 88.2% car, 0.2% public transportation, 5.3% walk, 3.0% work from home; Mean travel time to work: 13.9 minutes
Airports: Ogdensburg International (commercial service–non-primary)
Additional Information Contacts
City of Ogdensburg . . . . (315) 393-3540
  http://www.ogdensburg.org

OSWEGATCHIE (town). Covers a land area of 65.498 square miles and a water area of 5.705 square miles. Located at 44.63° N. Lat; 75.49° W. Long. Elevation is 1,355 feet.
Population: 4,418; Growth (since 2000): 1.1%; Density: 67.5 persons per square mile; Race: 97.1% White, 0.9% Black/African American, 1.0% Asian, 0.3% American Indian/Alaska Native, 0.4% Native Hawaiian/Other Pacific Islander, 0.1% Two or more races, 0.3% Hispanic of any race; Average household size: 2.73; Median age: 43.9; Age under 18: 25.4%; Age 65 and over: 18.4%; Males per 100 females: 91.7; Marriage status: 28.1% never married, 50.8% now married, 1.0% separated, 12.7% widowed, 8.3% divorced; Foreign born: 4.3%; Speak English only: 78.4%; With disability: 13.7%; Veterans: 12.4%; Ancestry: 14.4% Irish, 10.0% French, 8.9% Pennsylvania German, 8.5% American, 8.3% Dutch
Employment: 14.1% management, business, and financial, 1.1% computer, engineering, and science, 5.8% education, legal, community service, arts, and media, 9.6% healthcare practitioners, 20.6% service, 29.4% sales and office, 12.6% natural resources, construction, and maintenance, 6.9% production, transportation, and material moving
Income: Per capita: $23,237; Median household: $49,615; Average household: $62,573; Households with income of $100,000 or more: 14.7%; Poverty rate: 27.0%
Educational Attainment: High school diploma or higher: 84.1%; Bachelor's degree or higher: 17.6%; Graduate/professional degree or higher: 8.4%
Housing: Homeownership rate: 91.1%; Median home value: $89,800; Median year structure built: 1973; Homeowner vacancy rate: 0.8%; Median selected monthly owner costs: $1,089 with a mortgage, $431 without a mortgage; Median gross rent: $514 per month; Rental vacancy rate: 0.0%
Health Insurance: 76.6% have insurance; 58.1% have private insurance; 33.3% have public insurance; 23.4% do not have insurance; 42.2% of children under 18 do not have insurance
Transportation: Commute: 92.6% car, 0.0% public transportation, 3.3% walk, 3.4% work from home; Mean travel time to work: 18.0 minutes

PARISHVILLE (CDP). Covers a land area of 3.292 square miles and a water area of 0.067 square miles. Located at 44.63° N. Lat; 74.79° W. Long. Elevation is 892 feet.
Population: 832; Growth (since 2000): n/a; Density: 252.7 persons per square mile; Race: 98.2% White, 0.0% Black/African American, 0.5% Asian, 0.0% American Indian/Alaska Native, 0.0% Native Hawaiian/Other Pacific Islander, 1.3% Two or more races, 0.8% Hispanic of any race; Average household size: 2.62; Median age: 29.0; Age under 18: 25.4%; Age 65 and over: 11.3%; Males per 100 females: 93.7; Marriage status: 28.8% never married, 49.9% now married, 2.1% separated, 7.1% widowed, 14.1% divorced; Foreign born: 1.9%; Speak English only: 97.3%; With disability: 17.1%; Veterans: 17.4%; Ancestry: 32.7% English, 23.1% Irish, 18.9% French Canadian, 13.0% French, 6.4% German
Employment: 4.0% management, business, and financial, 3.7% computer, engineering, and science, 8.0% education, legal, community service, arts, and media, 6.1% healthcare practitioners, 18.3% service, 30.0% sales and office, 12.2% natural resources, construction, and maintenance, 17.8% production, transportation, and material moving
Income: Per capita: $20,932; Median household: $50,036; Average household: $54,371; Households with income of $100,000 or more: 12.3%; Poverty rate: 17.6%
Educational Attainment: High school diploma or higher: 92.7%; Bachelor's degree or higher: 20.0%; Graduate/professional degree or higher: 6.9%

School District(s)
Parishville-Hopkinton Central SD (PK-12)
  2014-15 Enrollment: 447 . . . . (315) 265-4642
Housing: Homeownership rate: 72.6%; Median home value: $107,900; Median year structure built: 1956; Homeowner vacancy rate: 0.0%; Median selected monthly owner costs: $905 with a mortgage, $385 without a mortgage; Median gross rent: $710 per month; Rental vacancy rate: 0.0%
Health Insurance: 96.4% have insurance; 65.5% have private insurance; 53.2% have public insurance; 3.6% do not have insurance; 7.1% of children under 18 do not have insurance

Transportation: Commute: 93.4% car, 0.0% public transportation, 4.1% walk, 2.5% work from home; Mean travel time to work: 33.5 minutes

PARISHVILLE (town). Covers a land area of 98.159 square miles and a water area of 3.270 square miles. Located at 44.55° N. Lat; 74.78° W. Long. Elevation is 892 feet.
Population: 2,289; Growth (since 2000): 11.7%; Density: 23.3 persons per square mile; Race: 97.1% White, 0.0% Black/African American, 1.4% Asian, 0.0% American Indian/Alaska Native, 0.0% Native Hawaiian/Other Pacific Islander, 1.6% Two or more races, 0.3% Hispanic of any race; Average household size: 2.49; Median age: 36.8; Age under 18: 22.6%; Age 65 and over: 15.7%; Males per 100 females: 103.3; Marriage status: 29.1% never married, 54.0% now married, 1.3% separated, 4.4% widowed, 12.5% divorced; Foreign born: 2.8%; Speak English only: 94.4%; With disability: 12.7%; Veterans: 12.6%; Ancestry: 24.2% Irish, 18.9% English, 14.5% French, 12.0% French Canadian, 8.6% German
Employment: 9.1% management, business, and financial, 1.4% computer, engineering, and science, 10.3% education, legal, community service, arts, and media, 6.6% healthcare practitioners, 22.8% service, 24.2% sales and office, 12.3% natural resources, construction, and maintenance, 13.3% production, transportation, and material moving
Income: Per capita: $22,192; Median household: $47,500; Average household: $54,380; Households with income of $100,000 or more: 12.0%; Poverty rate: 14.8%
Educational Attainment: High school diploma or higher: 93.0%; Bachelor's degree or higher: 24.9%; Graduate/professional degree or higher: 11.4%

School District(s)
Parishville-Hopkinton Central SD (PK-12)
    2014-15 Enrollment: 447 . . . . (315) 265-4642
Housing: Homeownership rate: 72.5%; Median home value: $104,800; Median year structure built: 1972; Homeowner vacancy rate: 0.0%; Median selected monthly owner costs: $973 with a mortgage, $406 without a mortgage; Median gross rent: $864 per month; Rental vacancy rate: 0.0%
Health Insurance: 89.3% have insurance; 64.8% have private insurance; 41.6% have public insurance; 10.7% do not have insurance; 9.1% of children under 18 do not have insurance
Transportation: Commute: 92.6% car, 0.0% public transportation, 1.5% walk, 5.9% work from home; Mean travel time to work: 27.6 minutes

PIERCEFIELD (town). Covers a land area of 104.155 square miles and a water area of 6.910 square miles. Located at 44.22° N. Lat; 74.60° W. Long. Elevation is 1,572 feet.
Population: 308; Growth (since 2000): 1.0%; Density: 3.0 persons per square mile; Race: 97.1% White, 0.3% Black/African American, 0.0% Asian, 0.0% American Indian/Alaska Native, 0.0% Native Hawaiian/Other Pacific Islander, 1.3% Two or more races, 2.6% Hispanic of any race; Average household size: 2.41; Median age: 51.2; Age under 18: 17.5%; Age 65 and over: 22.7%; Males per 100 females: 93.8; Marriage status: 17.6% never married, 65.1% now married, 1.5% separated, 2.7% widowed, 14.6% divorced; Foreign born: 4.2%; Speak English only: 97.9%; With disability: 19.2%; Veterans: 12.6%; Ancestry: 22.1% German, 21.4% French, 15.3% English, 13.0% Irish, 11.4% Italian
Employment: 10.6% management, business, and financial, 2.1% computer, engineering, and science, 12.0% education, legal, community service, arts, and media, 9.9% healthcare practitioners, 27.5% service, 20.4% sales and office, 13.4% natural resources, construction, and maintenance, 4.2% production, transportation, and material moving
Income: Per capita: $24,810; Median household: $58,333; Average household: $63,351; Households with income of $100,000 or more: 14.8%; Poverty rate: 8.3%
Educational Attainment: High school diploma or higher: 89.9%; Bachelor's degree or higher: 28.7%; Graduate/professional degree or higher: 12.2%
Housing: Homeownership rate: 93.8%; Median home value: $104,700; Median year structure built: 1954; Homeowner vacancy rate: 3.1%; Median selected monthly owner costs: $1,163 with a mortgage, $394 without a mortgage; Median gross rent: n/a per month; Rental vacancy rate: 0.0%
Health Insurance: 89.3% have insurance; 74.7% have private insurance; 30.2% have public insurance; 10.7% do not have insurance; 0.0% of children under 18 do not have insurance
Transportation: Commute: 99.2% car, 0.0% public transportation, 0.0% walk, 0.8% work from home; Mean travel time to work: 21.6 minutes

PIERREPONT (town). Covers a land area of 60.252 square miles and a water area of 0.468 square miles. Located at 44.53° N. Lat; 75.01° W. Long. Elevation is 741 feet.
Population: 2,585; Growth (since 2000): -3.3%; Density: 42.9 persons per square mile; Race: 97.8% White, 0.2% Black/African American, 1.4% Asian, 0.5% American Indian/Alaska Native, 0.0% Native Hawaiian/Other Pacific Islander, 0.2% Two or more races, 1.3% Hispanic of any race; Average household size: 2.51; Median age: 45.2; Age under 18: 19.9%; Age 65 and over: 19.1%; Males per 100 females: 103.2; Marriage status: 23.0% never married, 61.3% now married, 3.6% separated, 6.3% widowed, 9.4% divorced; Foreign born: 2.2%; Speak English only: 99.2%; With disability: 14.7%; Veterans: 11.9%; Ancestry: 24.5% English, 18.5% Irish, 14.1% French, 10.9% German, 6.1% Dutch
Employment: 7.6% management, business, and financial, 4.6% computer, engineering, and science, 17.6% education, legal, community service, arts, and media, 7.7% healthcare practitioners, 22.8% service, 17.8% sales and office, 13.8% natural resources, construction, and maintenance, 8.0% production, transportation, and material moving
Income: Per capita: $26,811; Median household: $54,063; Average household: $66,180; Households with income of $100,000 or more: 17.5%; Poverty rate: 11.4%
Educational Attainment: High school diploma or higher: 92.0%; Bachelor's degree or higher: 29.9%; Graduate/professional degree or higher: 13.2%
Housing: Homeownership rate: 87.4%; Median home value: $107,600; Median year structure built: 1971; Homeowner vacancy rate: 0.0%; Median selected monthly owner costs: $1,138 with a mortgage, $428 without a mortgage; Median gross rent: $747 per month; Rental vacancy rate: 0.0%
Health Insurance: 94.6% have insurance; 77.0% have private insurance; 37.9% have public insurance; 5.4% do not have insurance; 0.0% of children under 18 do not have insurance
Transportation: Commute: 94.0% car, 1.6% public transportation, 0.0% walk, 4.4% work from home; Mean travel time to work: 22.8 minutes

PITCAIRN (town). Covers a land area of 58.518 square miles and a water area of 0.937 square miles. Located at 44.22° N. Lat; 75.27° W. Long. Elevation is 781 feet.
Population: 733; Growth (since 2000): -6.4%; Density: 12.5 persons per square mile; Race: 98.0% White, 0.0% Black/African American, 0.8% Asian, 0.1% American Indian/Alaska Native, 0.5% Native Hawaiian/Other Pacific Islander, 0.5% Two or more races, 1.4% Hispanic of any race; Average household size: 2.68; Median age: 39.0; Age under 18: 27.1%; Age 65 and over: 16.1%; Males per 100 females: 105.8; Marriage status: 25.7% never married, 59.9% now married, 2.7% separated, 3.2% widowed, 11.2% divorced; Foreign born: 1.9%; Speak English only: 98.2%; With disability: 18.4%; Veterans: 12.2%; Ancestry: 16.0% American, 15.6% French, 14.2% German, 13.6% Irish, 10.4% English
Employment: 6.4% management, business, and financial, 0.7% computer, engineering, and science, 12.8% education, legal, community service, arts, and media, 3.9% healthcare practitioners, 22.1% service, 19.2% sales and office, 18.5% natural resources, construction, and maintenance, 16.4% production, transportation, and material moving
Income: Per capita: $21,030; Median household: $50,083; Average household: $55,427; Households with income of $100,000 or more: 9.9%; Poverty rate: 15.5%
Educational Attainment: High school diploma or higher: 84.3%; Bachelor's degree or higher: 11.0%; Graduate/professional degree or higher: 7.5%
Housing: Homeownership rate: 87.9%; Median home value: $92,300; Median year structure built: 1975; Homeowner vacancy rate: 2.8%; Median selected monthly owner costs: $1,144 with a mortgage, $363 without a mortgage; Median gross rent: $615 per month; Rental vacancy rate: 0.0%
Health Insurance: 91.1% have insurance; 66.0% have private insurance; 40.2% have public insurance; 8.9% do not have insurance; 1.0% of children under 18 do not have insurance
Transportation: Commute: 96.4% car, 0.0% public transportation, 0.0% walk, 1.4% work from home; Mean travel time to work: 31.5 minutes

POTSDAM (town). Covers a land area of 101.403 square miles and a water area of 2.049 square miles. Located at 44.68° N. Lat; 75.04° W. Long. Elevation is 433 feet.
History: In 1804, William Bullard and others came to Potsdam from Massachusetts, pooled their resources, and purchased a tract of land on which they established the "Union." Property was held in common, an accurate account of labor and materials contributed by each member was

kept, and all proceeds were divided pro rata annually. The group prospered for a few years but dissolved in 1810, when the land was evenly divided among the members. In the 19th century, sandstone quarries near Potsdam employed hundreds of workers. Seat of State University of New York College at Potsdam and Clarkson University. Incorporated in 1831.

Population: 16,263; Growth (since 2000): 1.9%; Density: 160.4 persons per square mile; Race: 89.8% White, 3.4% Black/African American, 2.3% Asian, 0.7% American Indian/Alaska Native, 0.2% Native Hawaiian/Other Pacific Islander, 2.3% Two or more races, 3.6% Hispanic of any race; Average household size: 2.32; Median age: 24.0; Age under 18: 14.4%; Age 65 and over: 9.7%; Males per 100 females: 107.9; Marriage status: 56.9% never married, 31.0% now married, 1.3% separated, 4.3% widowed, 7.9% divorced; Foreign born: 8.4%; Speak English only: 89.6%; With disability: 10.6%; Veterans: 5.2%; Ancestry: 17.2% Irish, 12.2% German, 11.4% English, 10.8% Italian, 8.8% French

Employment: 10.2% management, business, and financial, 3.3% computer, engineering, and science, 23.2% education, legal, community service, arts, and media, 4.6% healthcare practitioners, 21.0% service, 22.8% sales and office, 5.5% natural resources, construction, and maintenance, 9.4% production, transportation, and material moving

Income: Per capita: $21,200; Median household: $48,626; Average household: $65,181; Households with income of $100,000 or more: 18.8%; Poverty rate: 19.7%

Educational Attainment: High school diploma or higher: 92.8%; Bachelor's degree or higher: 41.4%; Graduate/professional degree or higher: 22.4%

School District(s)
Potsdam Central SD (PK-12)
    2014-15 Enrollment: 1,315 . . . . (315) 265-2000
Four-year College(s)
Clarkson University (Private, Not-for-profit)
    Fall 2014 Enrollment: 3,873 . . . . (315) 268-6400
    2015-16 Tuition: In-state $44,630; Out-of-state $44,630
SUNY College at Potsdam (Public)
    Fall 2014 Enrollment: 3,979 . . . . (315) 267-2000
    2015-16 Tuition: In-state $7,923; Out-of-state $17,773

Housing: Homeownership rate: 58.6%; Median home value: $106,600; Median year structure built: 1961; Homeowner vacancy rate: 1.9%; Median selected monthly owner costs: $1,230 with a mortgage, $547 without a mortgage; Median gross rent: $708 per month; Rental vacancy rate: 2.7%

Health Insurance: 94.3% have insurance; 76.9% have private insurance; 26.1% have public insurance; 5.7% do not have insurance; 2.9% of children under 18 do not have insurance

Hospitals: Canton - Potsdam Hospital (94 beds)

Newspapers: North Country This Week (weekly circulation 10,500)

Transportation: Commute: 70.3% car, 0.4% public transportation, 20.3% walk, 6.4% work from home; Mean travel time to work: 15.9 minutes

Airports: Potsdam Municipal/Damon Field (general aviation)

Additional Information Contacts
Town of Potsdam . . . . (315) 265-3430
    http://www.potsdamny.us

POTSDAM (village).
Covers a land area of 4.447 square miles and a water area of 0.495 square miles. Located at 44.67° N. Lat; 74.99° W. Long. Elevation is 433 feet.

Population: 9,656; Growth (since 2000): 2.5%; Density: 2,171.3 persons per square mile; Race: 87.5% White, 5.4% Black/African American, 2.0% Asian, 0.7% American Indian/Alaska Native, 0.2% Native Hawaiian/Other Pacific Islander, 1.9% Two or more races, 5.1% Hispanic of any race; Average household size: 2.05; Median age: 21.3; Age under 18: 7.9%; Age 65 and over: 8.2%; Males per 100 females: 113.9; Marriage status: 72.9% never married, 18.1% now married, 1.2% separated, 4.1% widowed, 5.0% divorced; Foreign born: 10.9%; Speak English only: 87.4%; With disability: 9.4%; Veterans: 3.1%; Ancestry: 15.6% Irish, 14.2% German, 11.7% Italian, 10.1% English, 5.6% French

Employment: 9.5% management, business, and financial, 3.0% computer, engineering, and science, 29.3% education, legal, community service, arts, and media, 1.4% healthcare practitioners, 19.3% service, 24.7% sales and office, 3.0% natural resources, construction, and maintenance, 9.8% production, transportation, and material moving

Income: Per capita: $16,171; Median household: $36,300; Average household: $57,228; Households with income of $100,000 or more: 13.5%; Poverty rate: 28.8%

Educational Attainment: High school diploma or higher: 92.5%; Bachelor's degree or higher: 54.6%; Graduate/professional degree or higher: 31.8%

School District(s)
Potsdam Central SD (PK-12)
    2014-15 Enrollment: 1,315 . . . . (315) 265-2000
Four-year College(s)
Clarkson University (Private, Not-for-profit)
    Fall 2014 Enrollment: 3,873 . . . . (315) 268-6400
    2015-16 Tuition: In-state $44,630; Out-of-state $44,630
SUNY College at Potsdam (Public)
    Fall 2014 Enrollment: 3,979 . . . . (315) 267-2000
    2015-16 Tuition: In-state $7,923; Out-of-state $17,773

Housing: Homeownership rate: 38.4%; Median home value: $107,800; Median year structure built: 1958; Homeowner vacancy rate: 2.1%; Median selected monthly owner costs: $1,300 with a mortgage, $608 without a mortgage; Median gross rent: $701 per month; Rental vacancy rate: 3.7%

Health Insurance: 94.0% have insurance; 77.6% have private insurance; 23.3% have public insurance; 6.0% do not have insurance; 4.8% of children under 18 do not have insurance

Hospitals: Canton - Potsdam Hospital (94 beds)

Safety: Violent crime rate: 3.1 per 10,000 population; Property crime rate: 150.0 per 10,000 population

Newspapers: North Country This Week (weekly circulation 10,500)

Transportation: Commute: 48.7% car, 0.8% public transportation, 38.0% walk, 9.5% work from home; Mean travel time to work: 12.2 minutes

Airports: Potsdam Municipal/Damon Field (general aviation)

Additional Information Contacts
Village of Potsdam . . . . (315) 265-7480
    http://www.vi.potsdam.ny.us

PYRITES (unincorporated postal area)
ZCTA: 13677

Covers a land area of 0.196 square miles and a water area of 0.031 square miles. Located at 44.51° N. Lat; 75.18° W. Long. Elevation is 502 feet.

Population: 273; Growth (since 2000): n/a; Density: 1,389.4 persons per square mile; Race: 100.0% White, 0.0% Black/African American, 0.0% Asian, 0.0% American Indian/Alaska Native, 0.0% Native Hawaiian/Other Pacific Islander, 0.0% Two or more races, 0.0% Hispanic of any race; Average household size: 3.90; Median age: 35.2; Age under 18: 44.7%; Age 65 and over: 4.0%; Males per 100 females: 78.8; Marriage status: 17.9% never married, 82.1% now married, 0.0% separated, 0.0% widowed, 0.0% divorced; Foreign born: 0.0%; Speak English only: 100.0%; With disability: 23.8%; Veterans: 7.3%; Ancestry: 66.3% French, 66.3% German, 23.8% Czechoslovakian

Employment: 0.0% management, business, and financial, 0.0% computer, engineering, and science, 47.6% education, legal, community service, arts, and media, 0.0% healthcare practitioners, 52.4% service, 0.0% sales and office, 0.0% natural resources, construction, and maintenance, 0.0% production, transportation, and material moving

Income: Per capita: $15,110; Median household: n/a; Average household: n/a; Households with income of $100,000 or more: n/a; Poverty rate: 5.9%

Educational Attainment: High school diploma or higher: 89.4%; Bachelor's degree or higher: n/a; Graduate/professional degree or higher: n/a

Housing: Homeownership rate: 84.3%; Median home value: n/a; Median year structure built: n/a; Homeowner vacancy rate: 0.0%; Median selected monthly owner costs: $0 with a mortgage, $0 without a mortgage; Median gross rent: n/a per month; Rental vacancy rate: 0.0%

Health Insurance: 100.0% have insurance; 94.1% have private insurance; 9.9% have public insurance; 0.0% do not have insurance; 0.0% of children under 18 do not have insurance

Transportation: Commute: 100.0% car, 0.0% public transportation, 0.0% walk, 0.0% work from home; Mean travel time to work: 0.0 minutes

RAYMONDVILLE (unincorporated postal area)
ZCTA: 13678

Covers a land area of 0.785 square miles and a water area of 0.039 square miles. Located at 44.81° N. Lat; 74.99° W. Long. Elevation is 253 feet.

Population: 262; Growth (since 2000): n/a; Density: 333.6 persons per square mile; Race: 100.0% White, 0.0% Black/African American, 0.0% Asian, 0.0% American Indian/Alaska Native, 0.0% Native

Hawaiian/Other Pacific Islander, 0.0% Two or more races, 0.0% Hispanic of any race; Average household size: 2.26; Median age: 33.6; Age under 18: 19.1%; Age 65 and over: 5.7%; Males per 100 females: 93.6; Marriage status: 47.2% never married, 49.1% now married, 0.0% separated, 0.0% widowed, 3.8% divorced; Foreign born: 5.3%; Speak English only: 100.0%; With disability: 3.4%; Veterans: 6.6%; Ancestry: 29.0% English, 29.0% Scottish, 13.7% French, 12.2% Irish, 12.2% Norwegian

Employment: 0.0% management, business, and financial, 0.0% computer, engineering, and science, 25.0% education, legal, community service, arts, and media, 36.4% healthcare practitioners, 9.1% service, 0.0% sales and office, 0.0% natural resources, construction, and maintenance, 29.5% production, transportation, and material moving

Income: Per capita: $18,622; Median household: n/a; Average household: $42,242; Households with income of $100,000 or more: n/a; Poverty rate: 14.1%

Educational Attainment: High school diploma or higher: 86.3%; Bachelor's degree or higher: 16.0%; Graduate/professional degree or higher: 16.0%

Housing: Homeownership rate: 39.7%; Median home value: n/a; Median year structure built: 1974; Homeowner vacancy rate: 0.0%; Median selected monthly owner costs: $0 with a mortgage, $0 without a mortgage; Median gross rent: $469 per month; Rental vacancy rate: 0.0%

Health Insurance: 100.0% have insurance; 82.8% have private insurance; 19.8% have public insurance; 0.0% do not have insurance; 0.0% of children under 18 do not have insurance

Transportation: Commute: 100.0% car, 0.0% public transportation, 0.0% walk, 0.0% work from home; Mean travel time to work: 0.0 minutes

RENSSELAER FALLS (village). Covers a land area of 0.291 square miles and a water area of 0.027 square miles. Located at 44.59° N. Lat; 75.32° W. Long. Elevation is 328 feet.
Population: 403; Growth (since 2000): 19.6%; Density: 1,386.9 persons per square mile; Race: 98.8% White, 0.0% Black/African American, 0.0% Asian, 0.0% American Indian/Alaska Native, 0.0% Native Hawaiian/Other Pacific Islander, 0.2% Two or more races, 1.5% Hispanic of any race; Average household size: 2.70; Median age: 33.1; Age under 18: 32.5%; Age 65 and over: 10.2%; Males per 100 females: 91.9; Marriage status: 30.5% never married, 51.3% now married, 0.7% separated, 8.2% widowed, 10.0% divorced; Foreign born: 0.0%; Speak English only: 99.1%; With disability: 14.1%; Veterans: 6.6%; Ancestry: 22.6% French, 21.8% Irish, 16.4% English, 6.0% French Canadian, 5.2% American
Employment: 3.1% management, business, and financial, 3.1% computer, engineering, and science, 18.6% education, legal, community service, arts, and media, 10.6% healthcare practitioners, 34.2% service, 18.6% sales and office, 7.5% natural resources, construction, and maintenance, 4.3% production, transportation, and material moving
Income: Per capita: $19,405; Median household: $31,691; Average household: $49,838; Households with income of $100,000 or more: 18.8%; Poverty rate: 22.1%
Educational Attainment: High school diploma or higher: 89.2%; Bachelor's degree or higher: 26.5%; Graduate/professional degree or higher: 14.5%
Housing: Homeownership rate: 71.8%; Median home value: $73,200; Median year structure built: Before 1940; Homeowner vacancy rate: 0.0%; Median selected monthly owner costs: $1,007 with a mortgage, $360 without a mortgage; Median gross rent: $750 per month; Rental vacancy rate: 0.0%
Health Insurance: 88.6% have insurance; 54.1% have private insurance; 52.4% have public insurance; 11.4% do not have insurance; 3.8% of children under 18 do not have insurance
Transportation: Commute: 93.0% car, 1.3% public transportation, 0.0% walk, 5.7% work from home; Mean travel time to work: 30.0 minutes

RICHVILLE (village). Covers a land area of 0.738 square miles and a water area of 0 square miles. Located at 44.42° N. Lat; 75.39° W. Long. Elevation is 407 feet.
Population: 363; Growth (since 2000): 32.5%; Density: 491.7 persons per square mile; Race: 96.7% White, 0.6% Black/African American, 1.1% Asian, 0.0% American Indian/Alaska Native, 0.0% Native Hawaiian/Other Pacific Islander, 1.7% Two or more races, 1.9% Hispanic of any race; Average household size: 2.95; Median age: 31.9; Age under 18: 32.0%; Age 65 and over: 8.3%; Males per 100 females: 105.7; Marriage status: 33.2% never married, 50.8% now married, 0.0% separated, 7.0%

widowed, 9.0% divorced; Foreign born: 2.5%; Speak English only: 97.1%; With disability: 14.4%; Veterans: 13.5%; Ancestry: 22.0% Irish, 20.4% English, 14.6% French, 9.4% American, 7.2% German
Employment: 7.8% management, business, and financial, 0.0% computer, engineering, and science, 7.8% education, legal, community service, arts, and media, 2.3% healthcare practitioners, 28.9% service, 23.4% sales and office, 13.3% natural resources, construction, and maintenance, 16.4% production, transportation, and material moving
Income: Per capita: $21,560; Median household: $47,250; Average household: $62,193; Households with income of $100,000 or more: 11.3%; Poverty rate: 16.8%
Educational Attainment: High school diploma or higher: 89.0%; Bachelor's degree or higher: 14.2%; Graduate/professional degree or higher: 8.3%
Housing: Homeownership rate: 80.5%; Median home value: $76,300; Median year structure built: Before 1940; Homeowner vacancy rate: 0.0%; Median selected monthly owner costs: $892 with a mortgage, $453 without a mortgage; Median gross rent: $675 per month; Rental vacancy rate: 4.0%
Health Insurance: 96.4% have insurance; 63.1% have private insurance; 46.9% have public insurance; 3.6% do not have insurance; 0.0% of children under 18 do not have insurance
Transportation: Commute: 93.8% car, 0.0% public transportation, 3.9% walk, 1.6% work from home; Mean travel time to work: 27.0 minutes

ROSSIE (town). Covers a land area of 37.880 square miles and a water area of 1.363 square miles. Located at 44.33° N. Lat; 75.62° W. Long. Elevation is 276 feet.
Population: 777; Growth (since 2000): -1.3%; Density: 20.5 persons per square mile; Race: 99.5% White, 0.1% Black/African American, 0.0% Asian, 0.0% American Indian/Alaska Native, 0.0% Native Hawaiian/Other Pacific Islander, 0.4% Two or more races, 1.2% Hispanic of any race; Average household size: 2.45; Median age: 40.7; Age under 18: 23.6%; Age 65 and over: 18.3%; Males per 100 females: 99.3; Marriage status: 29.1% never married, 56.6% now married, 1.3% separated, 5.9% widowed, 8.3% divorced; Foreign born: 2.1%; Speak English only: 97.8%; With disability: 12.5%; Veterans: 9.7%; Ancestry: 14.9% Irish, 10.0% French, 9.8% English, 8.8% American, 8.6% German
Employment: 13.3% management, business, and financial, 1.0% computer, engineering, and science, 8.1% education, legal, community service, arts, and media, 8.4% healthcare practitioners, 16.2% service, 12.3% sales and office, 19.8% natural resources, construction, and maintenance, 20.8% production, transportation, and material moving
Income: Per capita: $20,608; Median household: $41,563; Average household: $49,887; Households with income of $100,000 or more: 11.3%; Poverty rate: 18.8%
Educational Attainment: High school diploma or higher: 87.3%; Bachelor's degree or higher: 19.7%; Graduate/professional degree or higher: 8.7%
Housing: Homeownership rate: 85.5%; Median home value: $77,100; Median year structure built: 1972; Homeowner vacancy rate: 4.9%; Median selected monthly owner costs: $1,262 with a mortgage, $479 without a mortgage; Median gross rent: $598 per month; Rental vacancy rate: 0.0%
Health Insurance: 88.7% have insurance; 55.1% have private insurance; 50.2% have public insurance; 11.3% do not have insurance; 4.4% of children under 18 do not have insurance
Transportation: Commute: 91.3% car, 0.6% public transportation, 0.6% walk, 7.4% work from home; Mean travel time to work: 31.6 minutes

RUSSELL (town). Covers a land area of 96.675 square miles and a water area of 0.618 square miles. Located at 44.40° N. Lat; 75.14° W. Long. Elevation is 617 feet.
Population: 1,947; Growth (since 2000): 8.1%; Density: 20.1 persons per square mile; Race: 97.6% White, 0.3% Black/African American, 0.1% Asian, 0.2% American Indian/Alaska Native, 0.0% Native Hawaiian/Other Pacific Islander, 1.8% Two or more races, 0.0% Hispanic of any race; Average household size: 2.54; Median age: 40.5; Age under 18: 23.8%; Age 65 and over: 15.4%; Males per 100 females: 103.7; Marriage status: 24.2% never married, 57.9% now married, 3.2% separated, 7.3% widowed, 10.5% divorced; Foreign born: 2.3%; Speak English only: 97.1%; With disability: 13.9%; Veterans: 10.4%; Ancestry: 17.6% French, 16.7% Irish, 16.3% English, 7.2% American, 6.3% Italian
Employment: 4.2% management, business, and financial, 2.5% computer, engineering, and science, 6.4% education, legal, community service, arts, and media, 10.1% healthcare practitioners, 25.4% service, 23.7% sales

and office, 12.8% natural resources, construction, and maintenance, 14.9% production, transportation, and material moving

Income: Per capita: $22,726; Median household: $42,938; Average household: $56,594; Households with income of $100,000 or more: 11.8%; Poverty rate: 11.5%

Educational Attainment: High school diploma or higher: 90.4%; Bachelor's degree or higher: 19.6%; Graduate/professional degree or higher: 7.2%

School District(s)
Edwards-Knox Central SD (PK-12)

    2014-15 Enrollment: 584 . . . . (315) 562-8141

Housing: Homeownership rate: 83.1%; Median home value: $79,500; Median year structure built: 1980; Homeowner vacancy rate: 1.7%; Median selected monthly owner costs: $1,073 with a mortgage, $421 without a mortgage; Median gross rent: $626 per month; Rental vacancy rate: 0.0%

Health Insurance: 93.6% have insurance; 71.1% have private insurance; 38.4% have public insurance; 6.4% do not have insurance; 2.2% of children under 18 do not have insurance

Transportation: Commute: 91.6% car, 0.0% public transportation, 2.1% walk, 6.0% work from home; Mean travel time to work: 33.9 minutes

SOUTH COLTON (unincorporated postal area)
ZCTA: 13687

Covers a land area of 134.416 square miles and a water area of 9.784 square miles. Located at 44.43° N. Lat; 74.84° W. Long. Elevation is 935 feet.

Population: 582; Growth (since 2000): 74.8%; Density: 4.3 persons per square mile; Race: 96.0% White, 1.7% Black/African American, 0.0% Asian, 0.0% American Indian/Alaska Native, 0.0% Native Hawaiian/Other Pacific Islander, 0.0% Two or more races, 2.2% Hispanic of any race; Average household size: 2.32; Median age: 49.0; Age under 18: 17.4%; Age 65 and over: 24.1%; Males per 100 females: 108.3; Marriage status: 27.9% never married, 46.0% now married, 1.1% separated, 11.3% widowed, 14.9% divorced; Foreign born: 5.2%; Speak English only: 92.6%; With disability: 23.7%; Veterans: 7.3%; Ancestry: 31.3% English, 15.3% French, 10.3% Irish, 9.5% German, 7.6% American

Employment: 14.4% management, business, and financial, 2.5% computer, engineering, and science, 16.4% education, legal, community service, arts, and media, 5.0% healthcare practitioners, 13.9% service, 27.4% sales and office, 16.4% natural resources, construction, and maintenance, 4.0% production, transportation, and material moving

Income: Per capita: $23,609; Median household: $43,693; Average household: $52,766; Households with income of $100,000 or more: 11.6%; Poverty rate: 16.7%

Educational Attainment: High school diploma or higher: 93.1%; Bachelor's degree or higher: 20.3%; Graduate/professional degree or higher: 11.1%

Housing: Homeownership rate: 71.3%; Median home value: $115,800; Median year structure built: 1977; Homeowner vacancy rate: 0.0%; Median selected monthly owner costs: $964 with a mortgage, $417 without a mortgage; Median gross rent: $1,150 per month; Rental vacancy rate: 0.0%

Health Insurance: 86.6% have insurance; 66.8% have private insurance; 39.5% have public insurance; 13.4% do not have insurance; 7.9% of children under 18 do not have insurance

Transportation: Commute: 91.2% car, 0.0% public transportation, 7.1% walk, 1.8% work from home; Mean travel time to work: 24.2 minutes

STAR LAKE (CDP)
Covers a land area of 4.338 square miles and a water area of 0.426 square miles. Located at 44.17° N. Lat; 75.04° W. Long. Elevation is 1,486 feet.

Population: 719; Growth (since 2000): -16.4%; Density: 165.8 persons per square mile; Race: 94.2% White, 0.8% Black/African American, 1.1% Asian, 1.3% American Indian/Alaska Native, 0.0% Native Hawaiian/Other Pacific Islander, 2.4% Two or more races, 1.5% Hispanic of any race; Average household size: 2.28; Median age: 47.8; Age under 18: 22.5%; Age 65 and over: 24.9%; Males per 100 females: 105.3; Marriage status: 20.0% never married, 57.6% now married, 6.4% separated, 11.2% widowed, 11.2% divorced; Foreign born: 1.5%; Speak English only: 97.5%; With disability: 22.4%; Veterans: 11.7%; Ancestry: 24.5% French, 17.7% Irish, 16.3% English, 7.8% Italian, 5.6% German

Employment: 9.6% management, business, and financial, 1.6% computer, engineering, and science, 10.4% education, legal, community service, arts, and media, 4.4% healthcare practitioners, 21.3% service, 24.1% sales and

office, 14.5% natural resources, construction, and maintenance, 14.1% production, transportation, and material moving

Income: Per capita: $22,472; Median household: $41,750; Average household: $50,397; Households with income of $100,000 or more: 8.4%; Poverty rate: 18.4%

Educational Attainment: High school diploma or higher: 80.6%; Bachelor's degree or higher: 13.6%; Graduate/professional degree or higher: 8.7%

School District(s)
Clifton-Fine Central SD (PK-12)

    2014-15 Enrollment: 304 . . . . (315) 848-3333

Housing: Homeownership rate: 76.6%; Median home value: $68,400; Median year structure built: 1955; Homeowner vacancy rate: 0.0%; Median selected monthly owner costs: $873 with a mortgage, $466 without a mortgage; Median gross rent: $461 per month; Rental vacancy rate: 3.9%

Health Insurance: 96.5% have insurance; 69.8% have private insurance; 47.0% have public insurance; 3.5% do not have insurance; 4.3% of children under 18 do not have insurance

Hospitals: Clifton Fine Hospital

Transportation: Commute: 87.0% car, 0.0% public transportation, 0.0% walk, 9.7% work from home; Mean travel time to work: 34.1 minutes

STOCKHOLM (town).
Covers a land area of 93.897 square miles and a water area of 0.392 square miles. Located at 44.75° N. Lat; 74.86° W. Long.

Population: 3,681; Growth (since 2000): 2.5%; Density: 39.2 persons per square mile; Race: 98.1% White, 0.8% Black/African American, 0.0% Asian, 0.0% American Indian/Alaska Native, 0.0% Native Hawaiian/Other Pacific Islander, 1.1% Two or more races, 0.9% Hispanic of any race; Average household size: 2.39; Median age: 42.1; Age under 18: 25.1%; Age 65 and over: 18.1%; Males per 100 females: 104.9; Marriage status: 21.6% never married, 54.8% now married, 1.5% separated, 9.1% widowed, 14.5% divorced; Foreign born: 4.3%; Speak English only: 90.6%; With disability: 19.8%; Veterans: 12.8%; Ancestry: 18.5% Irish, 17.3% French, 16.7% French Canadian, 12.8% English, 8.8% German

Employment: 8.0% management, business, and financial, 6.8% computer, engineering, and science, 14.5% education, legal, community service, arts, and media, 7.7% healthcare practitioners, 26.8% service, 15.3% sales and office, 9.1% natural resources, construction, and maintenance, 11.7% production, transportation, and material moving

Income: Per capita: $28,886; Median household: $44,632; Average household: $66,864; Households with income of $100,000 or more: 15.4%; Poverty rate: 14.1%

Educational Attainment: High school diploma or higher: 91.6%; Bachelor's degree or higher: 18.8%; Graduate/professional degree or higher: 11.7%

Housing: Homeownership rate: 87.2%; Median home value: $76,000; Median year structure built: 1972; Homeowner vacancy rate: 3.4%; Median selected monthly owner costs: $878 with a mortgage, $395 without a mortgage; Median gross rent: $574 per month; Rental vacancy rate: 0.0%

Health Insurance: 94.3% have insurance; 73.0% have private insurance; 40.2% have public insurance; 5.7% do not have insurance; 0.0% of children under 18 do not have insurance

Transportation: Commute: 91.2% car, 0.0% public transportation, 1.8% walk, 5.5% work from home; Mean travel time to work: 23.4 minutes

WADDINGTON (town).
Covers a land area of 51.606 square miles and a water area of 6.367 square miles. Located at 44.83° N. Lat; 75.19° W. Long. Elevation is 272 feet.

Population: 2,263; Growth (since 2000): 2.3%; Density: 43.9 persons per square mile; Race: 91.4% White, 1.5% Black/African American, 0.0% Asian, 5.0% American Indian/Alaska Native, 0.0% Native Hawaiian/Other Pacific Islander, 1.9% Two or more races, 1.6% Hispanic of any race; Average household size: 2.49; Median age: 43.7; Age under 18: 21.8%; Age 65 and over: 15.6%; Males per 100 females: 91.9; Marriage status: 31.6% never married, 51.6% now married, 4.5% separated, 7.1% widowed, 9.8% divorced; Foreign born: 1.7%; Speak English only: 99.3%; With disability: 16.4%; Veterans: 13.9%; Ancestry: 24.2% Irish, 18.9% French, 11.5% German, 11.4% English, 7.1% Italian

Employment: 11.6% management, business, and financial, 3.8% computer, engineering, and science, 7.0% education, legal, community service, arts, and media, 6.3% healthcare practitioners, 26.5% service, 15.6% sales and office, 16.6% natural resources, construction, and maintenance, 12.7% production, transportation, and material moving

Income: Per capita: $27,623; Median household: $62,432; Average household: $66,762; Households with income of $100,000 or more: 21.0%; Poverty rate: 14.9%

Educational Attainment: High school diploma or higher: 93.9%; Bachelor's degree or higher: 21.4%; Graduate/professional degree or higher: 5.8%

Housing: Homeownership rate: 72.7%; Median home value: $115,200; Median year structure built: 1972; Homeowner vacancy rate: 1.2%; Median selected monthly owner costs: $1,190 with a mortgage, $464 without a mortgage; Median gross rent: $808 per month; Rental vacancy rate: 0.0%

Health Insurance: 88.0% have insurance; 68.0% have private insurance; 35.6% have public insurance; 12.0% do not have insurance; 16.6% of children under 18 do not have insurance

Transportation: Commute: 93.7% car, 0.0% public transportation, 4.7% walk, 1.5% work from home; Mean travel time to work: 23.3 minutes

WADDINGTON (village).
Covers a land area of 2.180 square miles and a water area of 0.187 square miles. Located at 44.86° N. Lat; 75.20° W. Long. Elevation is 272 feet.

Population: 953; Growth (since 2000): 3.3%; Density: 437.2 persons per square mile; Race: 89.7% White, 3.5% Black/African American, 0.0% Asian, 3.3% American Indian/Alaska Native, 0.0% Native Hawaiian/Other Pacific Islander, 3.6% Two or more races, 3.9% Hispanic of any race; Average household size: 2.19; Median age: 47.9; Age under 18: 19.3%; Age 65 and over: 19.8%; Males per 100 females: 82.0; Marriage status: 22.2% never married, 59.6% now married, 4.5% separated, 8.6% widowed, 9.7% divorced; Foreign born: 2.0%; Speak English only: 99.4%; With disability: 21.6%; Veterans: 11.6%; Ancestry: 30.5% Irish, 24.1% French, 17.2% English, 8.4% German, 8.1% Italian

Employment: 12.1% management, business, and financial, 5.8% computer, engineering, and science, 8.4% education, legal, community service, arts, and media, 6.9% healthcare practitioners, 31.4% service, 14.8% sales and office, 12.1% natural resources, construction, and maintenance, 8.4% production, transportation, and material moving

Income: Per capita: $29,623; Median household: $49,844; Average household: $63,038; Households with income of $100,000 or more: 20.7%; Poverty rate: 12.5%

Educational Attainment: High school diploma or higher: 89.4%; Bachelor's degree or higher: 30.2%; Graduate/professional degree or higher: 5.7%

Housing: Homeownership rate: 66.7%; Median home value: $109,100; Median year structure built: 1966; Homeowner vacancy rate: 2.7%; Median selected monthly owner costs: $1,128 with a mortgage, $482 without a mortgage; Median gross rent: $786 per month; Rental vacancy rate: 0.0%

Health Insurance: 95.7% have insurance; 75.7% have private insurance; 38.5% have public insurance; 4.3% do not have insurance; 0.0% of children under 18 do not have insurance

Transportation: Commute: 92.4% car, 0.0% public transportation, 4.9% walk, 2.2% work from home; Mean travel time to work: 22.3 minutes

WANAKENA (unincorporated postal area)
ZCTA: 13695

Covers a land area of 17.001 square miles and a water area of 0.334 square miles. Located at 44.10° N. Lat; 74.92° W. Long. Elevation is 1,503 feet.

Population: 134; Growth (since 2000): n/a; Density: 7.9 persons per square mile; Race: 85.8% White, 3.0% Black/African American, 0.0% Asian, 5.2% American Indian/Alaska Native, 0.0% Native Hawaiian/Other Pacific Islander, 3.0% Two or more races, 0.0% Hispanic of any race; Average household size: 1.78; Median age: 56.6; Age under 18: 0.0%; Age 65 and over: 35.8%; Males per 100 females: 179.2; Marriage status: 44.8% never married, 52.2% now married, 0.0% separated, 3.0% widowed, 0.0% divorced; Foreign born: 0.0%; Speak English only: 97.0%; With disability: 23.9%; Veterans: 14.9%; Ancestry: 32.8% English, 32.8% Irish, 14.9% Scottish, 12.7% German, 9.0% French Canadian

Employment: 44.7% management, business, and financial, 0.0% computer, engineering, and science, 0.0% education, legal, community service, arts, and media, 3.9% healthcare practitioners, 21.1% service, 15.8% sales and office, 5.3% natural resources, construction, and maintenance, 9.2% production, transportation, and material moving

Income: Per capita: $29,513; Median household: $95,156; Average household: $77,142; Households with income of $100,000 or more: 33.3%; Poverty rate: 3.8%

Educational Attainment: High school diploma or higher: 100.0%; Bachelor's degree or higher: 31.3%; Graduate/professional degree or higher: 8.8%

Housing: Homeownership rate: 100.0%; Median home value: $243,200; Median year structure built: 1950; Homeowner vacancy rate: 0.0%; Median selected monthly owner costs: n/a with a mortgage, n/a without a mortgage; Median gross rent: n/a per month; Rental vacancy rate: 100.0%

Health Insurance: 100.0% have insurance; 93.3% have private insurance; 35.8% have public insurance; 0.0% do not have insurance; 0.0% of children under 18 do not have insurance

Transportation: Commute: 43.8% car, 0.0% public transportation, 12.5% walk, 43.8% work from home; Mean travel time to work: 14.0 minutes

WEST STOCKHOLM (unincorporated postal area)
ZCTA: 13696

Covers a land area of 1.862 square miles and a water area of 0 square miles. Located at 44.69° N. Lat; 74.89° W. Long. Elevation is 384 feet.

Population: 71; Growth (since 2000): n/a; Density: 38.1 persons per square mile; Race: 100.0% White, 0.0% Black/African American, 0.0% Asian, 0.0% American Indian/Alaska Native, 0.0% Native Hawaiian/Other Pacific Islander, 0.0% Two or more races, 0.0% Hispanic of any race; Average household size: 1.29; Median age: 59.5; Age under 18: 0.0%; Age 65 and over: 0.0%; Males per 100 females: 102.3; Marriage status: 0.0% never married, 42.3% now married, 0.0% separated, 0.0% widowed, 57.7% divorced; Foreign born: 0.0%; Speak English only: 100.0%; With disability: 0.0%; Veterans: 0.0%; Ancestry: 77.5% Irish

Employment: 0.0% management, business, and financial, 0.0% computer, engineering, and science, 0.0% education, legal, community service, arts, and media, 0.0% healthcare practitioners, 0.0% service, 0.0% sales and office, 0.0% natural resources, construction, and maintenance, 100.0% production, transportation, and material moving

Income: Per capita: $43,625; Median household: n/a; Average household: n/a; Households with income of $100,000 or more: 25.5%; Poverty rate: n/a

Educational Attainment: High school diploma or higher: 100.0%; Bachelor's degree or higher: 57.7%; Graduate/professional degree or higher: 57.7%

Housing: Homeownership rate: 100.0%; Median home value: n/a; Median year structure built: Before 1940; Homeowner vacancy rate: 46.1%; Median selected monthly owner costs: $0 with a mortgage, $0 without a mortgage; Median gross rent: n/a per month; Rental vacancy rate: 0.0%

Health Insurance: 100.0% have insurance; 100.0% have private insurance; 0.0% have public insurance; 0.0% do not have insurance; 0.0% of children under 18 do not have insurance

Transportation: Commute: 100.0% car, 0.0% public transportation, 0.0% walk, 0.0% work from home; Mean travel time to work: 0.0 minutes

WINTHROP (CDP).
Covers a land area of 2.777 square miles and a water area of 0.023 square miles. Located at 44.80° N. Lat; 74.81° W. Long. Elevation is 325 feet.

Population: 371; Growth (since 2000): n/a; Density: 133.6 persons per square mile; Race: 100.0% White, 0.0% Black/African American, 0.0% Asian, 0.0% American Indian/Alaska Native, 0.0% Native Hawaiian/Other Pacific Islander, 0.0% Two or more races, 0.0% Hispanic of any race; Average household size: 1.93; Median age: 55.5; Age under 18: 13.5%; Age 65 and over: 22.6%; Males per 100 females: 96.9; Marriage status: 10.0% never married, 34.0% now married, 4.7% separated, 30.2% widowed, 25.9% divorced; Foreign born: 5.4%; Speak English only: 94.1%; With disability: 40.2%; Veterans: 8.7%; Ancestry: 31.0% Welsh, 17.5% French, 12.4% Irish, 4.6% Scottish, 4.0% American

Employment: 0.0% management, business, and financial, 0.0% computer, engineering, and science, 9.5% education, legal, community service, arts, and media, 28.4% healthcare practitioners, 30.2% service, 0.0% sales and office, 17.2% natural resources, construction, and maintenance, 14.7% production, transportation, and material moving

Income: Per capita: $36,423; Median household: $48,750; Average household: $66,112; Households with income of $100,000 or more: 18.2%; Poverty rate: 12.7%

Educational Attainment: High school diploma or higher: 89.4%; Bachelor's degree or higher: 15.0%; Graduate/professional degree or higher: 15.0%

Housing: Homeownership rate: 92.2%; Median home value: $53,700; Median year structure built: Before 1940; Homeowner vacancy rate: 0.0%; Median selected monthly owner costs: n/a with a mortgage, n/a without a mortgage; Median gross rent: n/a per month; Rental vacancy rate: 0.0%
Health Insurance: 77.4% have insurance; 59.8% have private insurance; 40.2% have public insurance; 22.6% do not have insurance; 0.0% of children under 18 do not have insurance
Transportation: Commute: 100.0% car, 0.0% public transportation, 0.0% walk, 0.0% work from home; Mean travel time to work: 23.4 minutes

Saratoga County

Located in eastern New York, partly in the Adirondacks; bounded on the east by the Hudson River, and on the south by the Mohawk River; includes Saratoga Lake. Covers a land area of 809.984 square miles, a water area of 33.824 square miles, and is located in the Eastern Time Zone at 43.11° N. Lat., 73.86° W. Long. The county was founded in 1791. County seat is Ballston Spa.

Saratoga County is part of the Albany-Schenectady-Troy, NY Metropolitan Statistical Area. The entire metro area includes: Albany County, NY; Rensselaer County, NY; Saratoga County, NY; Schenectady County, NY; Schoharie County, NY

Weather Station: Conklingville Dam											Elevation: 808 feet	
	Jan	Feb	Mar	Apr	May	Jun	Jul	Aug	Sep	Oct	Nov	Dec
High	29	33	41	54	66	74	78	77	69	58	46	33
Low	9	12	21	33	45	54	58	57	49	38	30	17
Precip	3.4	2.8	4.0	3.7	4.1	4.1	4.2	4.0	3.8	3.7	3.8	3.8
Snow	19.9	13.8	13.8	2.6	tr	0.0	0.0	0.0	0.0	0.1	3.7	16.5

High and Low temperatures in degrees Fahrenheit; Precipitation and Snow in inches

Weather Station: Saratoga Springs 4 SW											Elevation: 310 feet	
	Jan	Feb	Mar	Apr	May	Jun	Jul	Aug	Sep	Oct	Nov	Dec
High	31	35	45	60	72	80	83	82	74	61	48	36
Low	12	15	24	35	46	55	60	58	50	39	30	19
Precip	3.2	2.5	3.5	3.7	4.1	4.3	4.3	4.1	3.7	3.8	3.8	3.6
Snow	19.1	12.6	11.6	2.3	tr	0.0	0.0	0.0	tr	0.1	3.1	14.2

High and Low temperatures in degrees Fahrenheit; Precipitation and Snow in inches

Population: 223,774; Growth (since 2000): 11.5%; Density: 276.3 persons per square mile; Race: 93.8% White, 1.6% Black/African American, 2.4% Asian, 0.1% American Indian/Alaska Native, 0.0% Native Hawaiian/Other Pacific Islander, 1.6% two or more races, 2.8% Hispanic of any race; Average household size: 2.44; Median age: 41.8; Age under 18: 21.5%; Age 65 and over: 15.2%; Males per 100 females: 96.9; Marriage status: 28.5% never married, 55.9% now married, 1.9% separated, 5.3% widowed, 10.3% divorced; Foreign born: 4.9%; Speak English only: 93.2%; With disability: 11.1%; Veterans: 9.7%; Ancestry: 24.4% Irish, 18.8% Italian, 15.9% German, 12.2% English, 8.4% French
Religion: Six largest groups: 23.9% Catholicism, 4.1% Methodist/Pietist, 3.1% Non-denominational Protestant, 1.9% Episcopalianism/Anglicanism, 1.2% Lutheran, 1.2% Presbyterian-Reformed
Economy: Unemployment rate: 3.7%; Leading industries: 14.5 % retail trade; 12.5 % construction; 12.0 % professional, scientific, and technical services; Farms: 583 totaling 78,849 acres; Company size: 4 employ 1,000 or more persons, 7 employ 500 to 999 persons, 71 employs 100 to 499 persons, 5,116 employ less than 100 persons; Business ownership: 5,863 women-owned, 190 Black-owned, 268 Hispanic-owned, 636 Asian-owned, 43 American Indian/Alaska Native-owned
Employment: 17.0% management, business, and financial, 8.5% computer, engineering, and science, 12.0% education, legal, community service, arts, and media, 6.6% healthcare practitioners, 15.4% service, 24.1% sales and office, 7.9% natural resources, construction, and maintenance, 8.6% production, transportation, and material moving
Income: Per capita: $35,922; Median household: $71,496; Average household: $87,951; Households with income of $100,000 or more: 33.0%; Poverty rate: 6.6%
Educational Attainment: High school diploma or higher: 94.1%; Bachelor's degree or higher: 39.0%; Graduate/professional degree or higher: 16.0%
Housing: Homeownership rate: 71.6%; Median home value: $232,900; Median year structure built: 1980; Homeowner vacancy rate: 1.3%; Median selected monthly owner costs: $1,691 with a mortgage, $591 without a mortgage; Median gross rent: $993 per month; Rental vacancy rate: 4.8%

Vital Statistics: Birth rate: 100.1 per 10,000 population; Death rate: 81.8 per 10,000 population; Age-adjusted cancer mortality rate: 169.7 deaths per 100,000 population
Health Insurance: 95.1% have insurance; 82.6% have private insurance; 27.1% have public insurance; 4.9% do not have insurance; 2.7% of children under 18 do not have insurance
Health Care: Physicians: 22.6 per 10,000 population; Dentists: 6.1 per 10,000 population; Hospital beds: 12.9 per 10,000 population; Hospital admissions: 481.7 per 10,000 population
Air Quality Index (AQI): Percent of Days: 98.6% good, 1.4% moderate, 0.0% unhealthy for sensitive individuals, 0.0% unhealthy, 0.0% very unhealthy; Annual median: 30; Annual maximum: 90
Transportation: Commute: 90.7% car, 0.9% public transportation, 2.0% walk, 5.4% work from home; Mean travel time to work: 25.1 minutes
2016 Presidential Election: 48.5% Trump, 45.3% Clinton, 4.6% Johnson, 1.6% Stein
National and State Parks: Moreau Lake State Park; New York State Game Management Area; Peebles Island State Park; Saratoga National Historical Park; Saratoga Spa State Park; Wilkinson National Recreation Trail
Additional Information Contacts
Saratoga Government . . . . (518) 885-2213
http://www.saratogacountyny.gov

Saratoga County Communities

BALLSTON (town). Covers a land area of 29.576 square miles and a water area of 0.462 square miles. Located at 42.95° N. Lat; 73.89° W. Long.
History: Founded in 1785, the town was purchased by Eliphalet Ball from the Mcdonald brothers, and he paid the brothers one barrel of rum for the right to name the town after himself. Over time the name was shortened to Ballston.
Population: 10,203; Growth (since 2000): 16.9%; Density: 345.0 persons per square mile; Race: 95.4% White, 0.8% Black/African American, 1.9% Asian, 0.0% American Indian/Alaska Native, 0.1% Native Hawaiian/Other Pacific Islander, 1.3% Two or more races, 2.1% Hispanic of any race; Average household size: 2.66; Median age: 43.8; Age under 18: 23.4%; Age 65 and over: 16.9%; Males per 100 females: 91.5; Marriage status: 27.6% never married, 58.8% now married, 2.4% separated, 4.6% widowed, 9.0% divorced; Foreign born: 2.8%; Speak English only: 95.3%; With disability: 8.7%; Veterans: 8.3%; Ancestry: 26.7% Irish, 23.6% German, 18.5% English, 16.8% Italian, 9.0% Polish
Employment: 14.2% management, business, and financial, 9.3% computer, engineering, and science, 14.3% education, legal, community service, arts, and media, 5.5% healthcare practitioners, 14.9% service, 25.2% sales and office, 8.9% natural resources, construction, and maintenance, 7.7% production, transportation, and material moving
Income: Per capita: $35,923; Median household: $82,860; Average household: $95,836; Households with income of $100,000 or more: 39.7%; Poverty rate: 6.2%
Educational Attainment: High school diploma or higher: 96.3%; Bachelor's degree or higher: 44.3%; Graduate/professional degree or higher: 20.6%
Housing: Homeownership rate: 77.3%; Median home value: $263,300; Median year structure built: 1973; Homeowner vacancy rate: 2.1%; Median selected monthly owner costs: $1,769 with a mortgage, $607 without a mortgage; Median gross rent: $970 per month; Rental vacancy rate: 0.0%
Health Insurance: 97.9% have insurance; 83.3% have private insurance; 30.1% have public insurance; 2.1% do not have insurance; 0.0% of children under 18 do not have insurance
Transportation: Commute: 92.0% car, 1.3% public transportation, 2.0% walk, 3.8% work from home; Mean travel time to work: 26.4 minutes
Additional Information Contacts
Town of Ballston . . . . (518) 885-8502
http://www.townofballstonny.org

BALLSTON LAKE (unincorporated postal area)
ZCTA: 12019
Covers a land area of 29.500 square miles and a water area of 0.493 square miles. Located at 42.93° N. Lat; 73.88° W. Long. Elevation is 266 feet.
Population: 14,584; Growth (since 2000): 9.5%; Density: 494.4 persons per square mile; Race: 93.4% White, 1.4% Black/African American, 2.2% Asian, 0.0% American Indian/Alaska Native, 0.1% Native

Hawaiian/Other Pacific Islander, 3.0% Two or more races, 1.2% Hispanic of any race; Average household size: 2.57; Median age: 44.4; Age under 18: 21.4%; Age 65 and over: 17.6%; Males per 100 females: 98.9; Marriage status: 24.1% never married, 62.2% now married, 1.1% separated, 4.6% widowed, 9.1% divorced; Foreign born: 4.7%; Speak English only: 95.4%; With disability: 7.2%; Veterans: 10.8%; Ancestry: 24.3% Irish, 21.3% Italian, 18.6% German, 12.3% English, 8.7% Polish
Employment: 17.2% management, business, and financial, 10.7% computer, engineering, and science, 10.4% education, legal, community service, arts, and media, 8.0% healthcare practitioners, 11.7% service, 25.9% sales and office, 9.2% natural resources, construction, and maintenance, 6.8% production, transportation, and material moving
Income: Per capita: $41,113; Median household: $88,059; Average household: $103,850; Households with income of $100,000 or more: 42.9%; Poverty rate: 3.0%
Educational Attainment: High school diploma or higher: 96.6%; Bachelor's degree or higher: 44.9%; Graduate/professional degree or higher: 20.7%

School District(s)
Burnt Hills-Ballston Lake Central SD (KG-12)
    2014-15 Enrollment: 3,100 . . . . (518) 399-9141
Shenendehowa Central SD (KG-12)
    2014-15 Enrollment: 9,842 . . . . (518) 881-0610
Housing: Homeownership rate: 78.3%; Median home value: $270,400; Median year structure built: 1976; Homeowner vacancy rate: 2.1%; Median selected monthly owner costs: $1,836 with a mortgage, $674 without a mortgage; Median gross rent: $957 per month; Rental vacancy rate: 0.0%
Health Insurance: 97.0% have insurance; 89.2% have private insurance; 25.3% have public insurance; 3.0% do not have insurance; 3.1% of children under 18 do not have insurance
Transportation: Commute: 91.1% car, 1.4% public transportation, 0.6% walk, 6.2% work from home; Mean travel time to work: 25.9 minutes

BALLSTON SPA (village). County seat. Covers a land area of 1.599 square miles and a water area of 0.009 square miles. Located at 43.01° N. Lat; 73.85° W. Long. Elevation is 315 feet.
History: Formerly a popular resort. Settled 1771, incorporated 1807.
Population: 5,256; Growth (since 2000): -5.4%; Density: 3,288.1 persons per square mile; Race: 93.9% White, 1.8% Black/African American, 0.7% Asian, 0.9% American Indian/Alaska Native, 0.0% Native Hawaiian/Other Pacific Islander, 2.5% Two or more races, 4.8% Hispanic of any race; Average household size: 2.21; Median age: 38.5; Age under 18: 20.0%; Age 65 and over: 17.5%; Males per 100 females: 94.2; Marriage status: 37.2% never married, 43.5% now married, 0.5% separated, 10.4% widowed, 8.9% divorced; Foreign born: 2.6%; Speak English only: 94.3%; With disability: 9.0%; Veterans: 11.8%; Ancestry: 21.5% Irish, 19.3% German, 11.5% English, 11.1% Italian, 9.2% Polish
Employment: 12.7% management, business, and financial, 11.0% computer, engineering, and science, 13.4% education, legal, community service, arts, and media, 6.1% healthcare practitioners, 15.4% service, 22.2% sales and office, 7.6% natural resources, construction, and maintenance, 11.6% production, transportation, and material moving
Income: Per capita: $30,465; Median household: $60,989; Average household: $68,343; Households with income of $100,000 or more: 19.0%; Poverty rate: 7.7%
Educational Attainment: High school diploma or higher: 96.2%; Bachelor's degree or higher: 36.2%; Graduate/professional degree or higher: 14.6%

School District(s)
Ballston Spa Central SD (KG-12)
    2014-15 Enrollment: 4,202 . . . . (518) 884-7195
Vocational/Technical School(s)
John Paolo's Xtreme Beauty Institute-Goldwell Product Artistry (Private, For-profit)
    Fall 2014 Enrollment: 101 . . . . (518) 583-3700
    2015-16 Tuition: $13,500
Housing: Homeownership rate: 49.9%; Median home value: $201,600; Median year structure built: Before 1940; Homeowner vacancy rate: 0.0%; Median selected monthly owner costs: $1,671 with a mortgage, $512 without a mortgage; Median gross rent: $924 per month; Rental vacancy rate: 7.6%
Health Insurance: 95.7% have insurance; 70.7% have private insurance; 42.9% have public insurance; 4.3% do not have insurance; 1.9% of children under 18 do not have insurance

Safety: Violent crime rate: 9.3 per 10,000 population; Property crime rate: 154.1 per 10,000 population
Newspapers: Ballston Journal (weekly circulation 2,200)
Transportation: Commute: 87.2% car, 1.3% public transportation, 1.5% walk, 8.1% work from home; Mean travel time to work: 26.7 minutes

BURNT HILLS (unincorporated postal area)
ZCTA: 12027
Covers a land area of 7.172 square miles and a water area of 0.022 square miles. Located at 42.94° N. Lat; 73.91° W. Long. Elevation is 407 feet.
Population: 3,762; Growth (since 2000): 2.8%; Density: 524.5 persons per square mile; Race: 97.7% White, 1.0% Black/African American, 1.1% Asian, 0.0% American Indian/Alaska Native, 0.0% Native Hawaiian/Other Pacific Islander, 0.2% Two or more races, 0.6% Hispanic of any race; Average household size: 2.59; Median age: 46.1; Age under 18: 22.6%; Age 65 and over: 18.8%; Males per 100 females: 91.4; Marriage status: 22.3% never married, 66.4% now married, 2.5% separated, 2.7% widowed, 8.6% divorced; Foreign born: 1.9%; Speak English only: 98.9%; With disability: 9.4%; Veterans: 7.9%; Ancestry: 25.3% Irish, 23.8% German, 20.0% English, 19.1% Italian, 8.4% Polish
Employment: 20.7% management, business, and financial, 11.9% computer, engineering, and science, 15.7% education, legal, community service, arts, and media, 5.9% healthcare practitioners, 7.6% service, 22.6% sales and office, 9.6% natural resources, construction, and maintenance, 6.0% production, transportation, and material moving
Income: Per capita: $40,456; Median household: $86,656; Average household: $102,797; Households with income of $100,000 or more: 44.4%; Poverty rate: 0.6%
Educational Attainment: High school diploma or higher: 98.7%; Bachelor's degree or higher: 57.6%; Graduate/professional degree or higher: 23.8%

School District(s)
Burnt Hills-Ballston Lake Central SD (KG-12)
    2014-15 Enrollment: 3,100 . . . . (518) 399-9141
Housing: Homeownership rate: 85.1%; Median home value: $254,400; Median year structure built: 1967; Homeowner vacancy rate: 0.0%; Median selected monthly owner costs: $1,677 with a mortgage, $626 without a mortgage; Median gross rent: $1,048 per month; Rental vacancy rate: 3.6%
Health Insurance: 98.2% have insurance; 87.3% have private insurance; 26.1% have public insurance; 1.8% do not have insurance; 0.0% of children under 18 do not have insurance
Transportation: Commute: 93.5% car, 1.0% public transportation, 1.5% walk, 2.6% work from home; Mean travel time to work: 28.3 minutes

CHARLTON (town). Covers a land area of 32.774 square miles and a water area of 0.188 square miles. Located at 42.96° N. Lat; 73.99° W. Long. Elevation is 495 feet.
Population: 4,183; Growth (since 2000): 5.8%; Density: 127.6 persons per square mile; Race: 97.6% White, 0.8% Black/African American, 0.0% Asian, 0.0% American Indian/Alaska Native, 0.0% Native Hawaiian/Other Pacific Islander, 1.6% Two or more races, 0.6% Hispanic of any race; Average household size: 2.58; Median age: 46.7; Age under 18: 20.0%; Age 65 and over: 20.3%; Males per 100 females: 96.5; Marriage status: 22.8% never married, 61.8% now married, 2.0% separated, 5.7% widowed, 9.7% divorced; Foreign born: 4.0%; Speak English only: 96.2%; With disability: 8.4%; Veterans: 11.2%; Ancestry: 23.0% German, 19.7% Irish, 19.2% English, 16.0% Italian, 15.9% Polish
Employment: 14.2% management, business, and financial, 7.9% computer, engineering, and science, 9.1% education, legal, community service, arts, and media, 5.9% healthcare practitioners, 17.8% service, 25.0% sales and office, 15.1% natural resources, construction, and maintenance, 4.9% production, transportation, and material moving
Income: Per capita: $38,448; Median household: $79,252; Average household: $97,504; Households with income of $100,000 or more: 32.4%; Poverty rate: 2.9%
Educational Attainment: High school diploma or higher: 95.5%; Bachelor's degree or higher: 30.3%; Graduate/professional degree or higher: 13.0%
Housing: Homeownership rate: 94.4%; Median home value: $249,300; Median year structure built: 1968; Homeowner vacancy rate: 0.5%; Median selected monthly owner costs: $1,800 with a mortgage, $698 without a mortgage; Median gross rent: $693 per month; Rental vacancy rate: 0.0%

Health Insurance: 96.8% have insurance; 90.0% have private insurance; 26.0% have public insurance; 3.2% do not have insurance; 0.0% of children under 18 do not have insurance
Transportation: Commute: 95.1% car, 0.1% public transportation, 0.0% walk, 3.8% work from home; Mean travel time to work: 26.2 minutes
Additional Information Contacts
Town of Charlton . . . . (518) 384-0152
   http://www.townofcharlton.org

CLIFTON PARK (town). Covers a land area of 48.202 square miles and a water area of 2.004 square miles. Located at 42.86° N. Lat; 73.82° W. Long. Elevation is 344 feet.

History: Clifton Park was first settled in the 17th century. It was named in 1707 by Nanning Harmansen, who wrote to Lord Cornbury requesting a Patent for Land he bought from the Native Americans known as Shenendehowa, and that the patent to be known by "Your name of Cliftons Park."
Population: 37,046; Growth (since 2000): 12.3%; Density: 768.6 persons per square mile; Race: 90.6% White, 2.3% Black/African American, 4.6% Asian, 0.0% American Indian/Alaska Native, 0.1% Native Hawaiian/Other Pacific Islander, 1.6% Two or more races, 3.4% Hispanic of any race; Average household size: 2.55; Median age: 42.7; Age under 18: 24.0%; Age 65 and over: 15.8%; Males per 100 females: 95.2; Marriage status: 23.3% never married, 63.1% now married, 1.2% separated, 4.8% widowed, 8.7% divorced; Foreign born: 7.0%; Speak English only: 90.2%; With disability: 7.5%; Veterans: 9.0%; Ancestry: 24.4% Irish, 20.5% Italian, 16.8% German, 10.9% English, 7.2% Polish
Employment: 22.0% management, business, and financial, 12.8% computer, engineering, and science, 14.8% education, legal, community service, arts, and media, 8.3% healthcare practitioners, 9.4% service, 22.0% sales and office, 5.2% natural resources, construction, and maintenance, 5.4% production, transportation, and material moving
Income: Per capita: $43,401; Median household: $95,100; Average household: $109,802; Households with income of $100,000 or more: 48.5%; Poverty rate: 2.5%
Educational Attainment: High school diploma or higher: 96.8%; Bachelor's degree or higher: 56.6%; Graduate/professional degree or higher: 25.7%

School District(s)
Shenendehowa Central SD (KG-12)
   2014-15 Enrollment: 9,842 . . . . (518) 881-0610
Housing: Homeownership rate: 80.7%; Median home value: $276,800; Median year structure built: 1982; Homeowner vacancy rate: 0.5%; Median selected monthly owner costs: $1,903 with a mortgage, $651 without a mortgage; Median gross rent: $1,125 per month; Rental vacancy rate: 5.0%
Health Insurance: 97.6% have insurance; 90.8% have private insurance; 20.6% have public insurance; 2.4% do not have insurance; 1.3% of children under 18 do not have insurance
Transportation: Commute: 92.3% car, 0.8% public transportation, 0.5% walk, 5.8% work from home; Mean travel time to work: 25.1 minutes
Additional Information Contacts
Town of Clifton Park . . . . (518) 371-6651
   http://www.cliftonpark.org

CORINTH (town). Covers a land area of 56.763 square miles and a water area of 1.372 square miles. Located at 43.23° N. Lat; 73.92° W. Long. Elevation is 610 feet.

History: Incorporated 1886.
Population: 6,503; Growth (since 2000): 8.7%; Density: 114.6 persons per square mile; Race: 95.8% White, 2.1% Black/African American, 0.2% Asian, 0.0% American Indian/Alaska Native, 0.0% Native Hawaiian/Other Pacific Islander, 1.6% Two or more races, 2.8% Hispanic of any race; Average household size: 2.70; Median age: 40.3; Age under 18: 23.3%; Age 65 and over: 15.3%; Males per 100 females: 96.5; Marriage status: 27.3% never married, 56.5% now married, 2.7% separated, 6.1% widowed, 10.2% divorced; Foreign born: 2.4%; Speak English only: 96.9%; With disability: 16.6%; Veterans: 12.7%; Ancestry: 21.1% American, 12.7% Irish, 10.2% French, 9.7% German, 9.2% English
Employment: 6.6% management, business, and financial, 4.7% computer, engineering, and science, 10.7% education, legal, community service, arts, and media, 4.2% healthcare practitioners, 25.3% service, 20.4% sales and office, 12.7% natural resources, construction, and maintenance, 15.4% production, transportation, and material moving

Income: Per capita: $23,517; Median household: $51,352; Average household: $62,205; Households with income of $100,000 or more: 18.4%; Poverty rate: 15.0%
Educational Attainment: High school diploma or higher: 89.6%; Bachelor's degree or higher: 18.0%; Graduate/professional degree or higher: 6.1%

School District(s)
Corinth Central SD (KG-12)
   2014-15 Enrollment: 1,201 . . . . (518) 654-2601
Housing: Homeownership rate: 78.4%; Median home value: $136,000; Median year structure built: 1960; Homeowner vacancy rate: 1.1%; Median selected monthly owner costs: $1,253 with a mortgage, $454 without a mortgage; Median gross rent: $808 per month; Rental vacancy rate: 5.5%
Health Insurance: 94.4% have insurance; 71.9% have private insurance; 37.9% have public insurance; 5.6% do not have insurance; 1.1% of children under 18 do not have insurance
Transportation: Commute: 92.7% car, 0.2% public transportation, 1.6% walk, 5.3% work from home; Mean travel time to work: 24.6 minutes
Additional Information Contacts
Town of Corinth . . . . (518) 654-9232
   http://townofcorinthny.com

CORINTH (village). Covers a land area of 1.067 square miles and a water area of 0.039 square miles. Located at 43.25° N. Lat; 73.83° W. Long. Elevation is 610 feet.

Population: 2,545; Growth (since 2000): 2.9%; Density: 2,386.0 persons per square mile; Race: 95.7% White, 0.4% Black/African American, 0.4% Asian, 0.0% American Indian/Alaska Native, 0.0% Native Hawaiian/Other Pacific Islander, 2.9% Two or more races, 2.1% Hispanic of any race; Average household size: 2.59; Median age: 37.1; Age under 18: 26.4%; Age 65 and over: 13.6%; Males per 100 females: 93.3; Marriage status: 28.3% never married, 50.2% now married, 3.5% separated, 8.2% widowed, 13.4% divorced; Foreign born: 2.1%; Speak English only: 96.3%; With disability: 18.7%; Veterans: 11.9%; Ancestry: 18.2% Irish, 16.2% American, 13.4% German, 12.4% Italian, 10.7% English
Employment: 8.4% management, business, and financial, 3.9% computer, engineering, and science, 7.1% education, legal, community service, arts, and media, 5.5% healthcare practitioners, 26.8% service, 20.7% sales and office, 11.9% natural resources, construction, and maintenance, 15.7% production, transportation, and material moving
Income: Per capita: $20,697; Median household: $42,183; Average household: $52,847; Households with income of $100,000 or more: 7.6%; Poverty rate: 19.6%
Educational Attainment: High school diploma or higher: 86.9%; Bachelor's degree or higher: 14.7%; Graduate/professional degree or higher: 5.0%

School District(s)
Corinth Central SD (KG-12)
   2014-15 Enrollment: 1,201 . . . . (518) 654-2601
Housing: Homeownership rate: 62.2%; Median home value: $135,400; Median year structure built: Before 1940; Homeowner vacancy rate: 0.0%; Median selected monthly owner costs: $1,199 with a mortgage, $489 without a mortgage; Median gross rent: $801 per month; Rental vacancy rate: 7.5%
Health Insurance: 91.4% have insurance; 65.7% have private insurance; 40.4% have public insurance; 8.6% do not have insurance; 2.4% of children under 18 do not have insurance
Transportation: Commute: 90.9% car, 0.4% public transportation, 4.4% walk, 4.0% work from home; Mean travel time to work: 25.2 minutes

COUNTRY KNOLLS (CDP). Covers a land area of 1.582 square miles and a water area of <.001 square miles. Located at 42.91° N. Lat; 73.81° W. Long. Elevation is 282 feet.

Population: 2,102; Growth (since 2000): -2.5%; Density: 1,328.7 persons per square mile; Race: 91.2% White, 3.2% Black/African American, 5.0% Asian, 0.0% American Indian/Alaska Native, 0.0% Native Hawaiian/Other Pacific Islander, 0.6% Two or more races, 2.9% Hispanic of any race; Average household size: 2.82; Median age: 43.6; Age under 18: 25.7%; Age 65 and over: 23.1%; Males per 100 females: 100.0; Marriage status: 15.9% never married, 73.9% now married, 0.4% separated, 5.4% widowed, 4.8% divorced; Foreign born: 6.5%; Speak English only: 94.0%; With disability: 8.2%; Veterans: 12.0%; Ancestry: 28.4% Irish, 20.0% Italian, 15.2% German, 12.3% English, 9.4% American
Employment: 26.7% management, business, and financial, 15.6% computer, engineering, and science, 13.1% education, legal, community

service, arts, and media, 6.4% healthcare practitioners, 8.9% service, 16.3% sales and office, 7.9% natural resources, construction, and maintenance, 5.1% production, transportation, and material moving
Income: Per capita: $40,951; Median household: $104,764; Average household: $112,022; Households with income of $100,000 or more: 55.5%; Poverty rate: n/a
Educational Attainment: High school diploma or higher: 99.1%; Bachelor's degree or higher: 66.1%; Graduate/professional degree or higher: 25.1%
Housing: Homeownership rate: 96.0%; Median home value: $264,600; Median year structure built: 1970; Homeowner vacancy rate: 0.0%; Median selected monthly owner costs: $1,855 with a mortgage, $663 without a mortgage; Median gross rent: n/a per month; Rental vacancy rate: 0.0%
Health Insurance: 99.0% have insurance; 91.7% have private insurance; 26.7% have public insurance; 1.0% do not have insurance; 0.0% of children under 18 do not have insurance
Transportation: Commute: 94.9% car, 1.6% public transportation, 0.0% walk, 1.7% work from home; Mean travel time to work: 29.8 minutes

---

DAY (town). Covers a land area of 64.112 square miles and a water area of 5.420 square miles. Located at 43.32° N. Lat; 74.03° W. Long.
Population: 805; Growth (since 2000): -12.5%; Density: 12.6 persons per square mile; Race: 97.1% White, 1.0% Black/African American, 0.0% Asian, 0.0% American Indian/Alaska Native, 0.0% Native Hawaiian/Other Pacific Islander, 1.6% Two or more races, 0.5% Hispanic of any race; Average household size: 2.13; Median age: 55.4; Age under 18: 12.5%; Age 65 and over: 27.8%; Males per 100 females: 110.8; Marriage status: 17.9% never married, 62.0% now married, 2.1% separated, 6.3% widowed, 13.8% divorced; Foreign born: 2.2%; Speak English only: 96.3%; With disability: 22.4%; Veterans: 15.4%; Ancestry: 16.0% Irish, 14.9% German, 12.9% English, 10.9% American, 10.1% French
Employment: 13.2% management, business, and financial, 2.6% computer, engineering, and science, 5.3% education, legal, community service, arts, and media, 5.3% healthcare practitioners, 19.4% service, 20.4% sales and office, 23.7% natural resources, construction, and maintenance, 10.2% production, transportation, and material moving
Income: Per capita: $29,752; Median household: $49,583; Average household: $62,097; Households with income of $100,000 or more: 16.7%; Poverty rate: 15.5%
Educational Attainment: High school diploma or higher: 85.5%; Bachelor's degree or higher: 15.7%; Graduate/professional degree or higher: 6.1%
Housing: Homeownership rate: 86.8%; Median home value: $159,500; Median year structure built: 1971; Homeowner vacancy rate: 7.1%; Median selected monthly owner costs: $1,538 with a mortgage, $400 without a mortgage; Median gross rent: $800 per month; Rental vacancy rate: 15.3%
Health Insurance: 90.2% have insurance; 65.6% have private insurance; 48.4% have public insurance; 9.8% do not have insurance; 11.9% of children under 18 do not have insurance
Transportation: Commute: 89.0% car, 0.0% public transportation, 2.7% walk, 8.2% work from home; Mean travel time to work: 43.9 minutes

---

EDINBURG (town). Covers a land area of 60.169 square miles and a water area of 6.925 square miles. Located at 43.22° N. Lat; 74.07° W. Long. Elevation is 889 feet.
Population: 1,402; Growth (since 2000): 1.3%; Density: 23.3 persons per square mile; Race: 99.8% White, 0.2% Black/African American, 0.0% Asian, 0.0% American Indian/Alaska Native, 0.0% Native Hawaiian/Other Pacific Islander, 0.0% Two or more races, 1.0% Hispanic of any race; Average household size: 2.20; Median age: 53.1; Age under 18: 13.6%; Age 65 and over: 29.7%; Males per 100 females: 106.5; Marriage status: 20.1% never married, 58.9% now married, 2.6% separated, 6.9% widowed, 14.1% divorced; Foreign born: 0.0%; Speak English only: 99.2%; With disability: 16.2%; Veterans: 15.5%; Ancestry: 15.8% Irish, 15.3% American, 14.9% English, 14.3% German, 8.8% Dutch
Employment: 5.8% management, business, and financial, 3.2% computer, engineering, and science, 8.3% education, legal, community service, arts, and media, 7.7% healthcare practitioners, 21.2% service, 21.0% sales and office, 22.7% natural resources, construction, and maintenance, 10.0% production, transportation, and material moving
Income: Per capita: $29,053; Median household: $51,774; Average household: $63,030; Households with income of $100,000 or more: 17.2%; Poverty rate: 7.1%

Educational Attainment: High school diploma or higher: 88.1%; Bachelor's degree or higher: 17.6%; Graduate/professional degree or higher: 7.9%

School District(s)
Edinburg Common SD (PK-06)
   2014-15 Enrollment: 89 . . . . (518) 863-8412
Housing: Homeownership rate: 93.1%; Median home value: $219,800; Median year structure built: 1971; Homeowner vacancy rate: 0.0%; Median selected monthly owner costs: $1,259 with a mortgage, $375 without a mortgage; Median gross rent: $713 per month; Rental vacancy rate: 0.0%
Health Insurance: 91.2% have insurance; 79.0% have private insurance; 39.6% have public insurance; 8.8% do not have insurance; 11.1% of children under 18 do not have insurance
Transportation: Commute: 96.6% car, 0.7% public transportation, 0.0% walk, 2.2% work from home; Mean travel time to work: 41.3 minutes
Additional Information Contacts
Town of Edinburg . . . . (518) 863-2034
  http://www.edinburgny.com

GALWAY (town). Covers a land area of 43.824 square miles and a water area of 1.180 square miles. Located at 43.03° N. Lat; 74.03° W. Long. Elevation is 830 feet.
Population: 3,541; Growth (since 2000): -1.3%; Density: 80.8 persons per square mile; Race: 96.2% White, 0.0% Black/African American, 0.0% Asian, 1.2% American Indian/Alaska Native, 0.0% Native Hawaiian/Other Pacific Islander, 2.5% Two or more races, 2.5% Hispanic of any race; Average household size: 2.28; Median age: 49.9; Age under 18: 20.4%; Age 65 and over: 22.3%; Males per 100 females: 105.3; Marriage status: 23.7% never married, 58.9% now married, 1.5% separated, 5.7% widowed, 11.6% divorced; Foreign born: 2.5%; Speak English only: 92.7%; With disability: 12.4%; Veterans: 14.8%; Ancestry: 28.0% Irish, 18.8% German, 17.7% English, 15.4% Italian, 12.3% Polish
Employment: 16.7% management, business, and financial, 2.5% computer, engineering, and science, 10.7% education, legal, community service, arts, and media, 9.6% healthcare practitioners, 21.4% service, 16.3% sales and office, 11.5% natural resources, construction, and maintenance, 11.2% production, transportation, and material moving
Income: Per capita: $33,372; Median household: $61,765; Average household: $75,397; Households with income of $100,000 or more: 26.4%; Poverty rate: 5.5%
Educational Attainment: High school diploma or higher: 93.6%; Bachelor's degree or higher: 30.9%; Graduate/professional degree or higher: 14.3%

School District(s)
Galway Central SD (KG-12)
   2014-15 Enrollment: 884 . . . . (518) 882-1033
Housing: Homeownership rate: 89.9%; Median home value: $220,500; Median year structure built: 1975; Homeowner vacancy rate: 0.6%; Median selected monthly owner costs: $1,440 with a mortgage, $494 without a mortgage; Median gross rent: $852 per month; Rental vacancy rate: 0.0%
Health Insurance: 95.8% have insurance; 82.8% have private insurance; 39.3% have public insurance; 4.2% do not have insurance; 4.1% of children under 18 do not have insurance
Transportation: Commute: 90.0% car, 0.1% public transportation, 4.4% walk, 4.1% work from home; Mean travel time to work: 27.3 minutes

---

GALWAY (village). Covers a land area of 0.256 square miles and a water area of 0 square miles. Located at 43.02° N. Lat; 74.03° W. Long. Elevation is 830 feet.
Population: 320; Growth (since 2000): 49.5%; Density: 1,250.1 persons per square mile; Race: 97.8% White, 0.0% Black/African American, 0.0% Asian, 0.0% American Indian/Alaska Native, 0.0% Native Hawaiian/Other Pacific Islander, 2.2% Two or more races, 3.8% Hispanic of any race; Average household size: 2.96; Median age: 36.8; Age under 18: 24.7%; Age 65 and over: 14.7%; Males per 100 females: 92.3; Marriage status: 19.4% never married, 60.9% now married, 0.4% separated, 4.8% widowed, 14.9% divorced; Foreign born: 0.6%; Speak English only: 98.9%; With disability: 16.6%; Veterans: 7.7%; Ancestry: 34.7% German, 27.2% Irish, 23.4% English, 12.2% French, 9.7% Italian
Employment: 14.5% management, business, and financial, 3.5% computer, engineering, and science, 20.8% education, legal, community service, arts, and media, 2.3% healthcare practitioners, 34.7% service, 7.5% sales and office, 2.9% natural resources, construction, and maintenance, 13.9% production, transportation, and material moving

Income: Per capita: $25,685; Median household: $59,615; Average household: $72,996; Households with income of $100,000 or more: 27.8%; Poverty rate: 5.7%
Educational Attainment: High school diploma or higher: 88.3%; Bachelor's degree or higher: 35.0%; Graduate/professional degree or higher: 16.8%

School District(s)
Galway Central SD (KG-12)
    2014-15 Enrollment: 884. . . . . (518) 882-1033
Housing: Homeownership rate: 75.9%; Median home value: $185,000; Median year structure built: Before 1940; Homeowner vacancy rate: 8.9%; Median selected monthly owner costs: $1,450 with a mortgage, $708 without a mortgage; Median gross rent: $1,021 per month; Rental vacancy rate: 0.0%
Health Insurance: 92.7% have insurance; 67.7% have private insurance; 51.4% have public insurance; 7.3% do not have insurance; 7.6% of children under 18 do not have insurance
Transportation: Commute: 78.9% car, 0.0% public transportation, 12.2% walk, 5.0% work from home; Mean travel time to work: 28.9 minutes

GANSEVOORT (unincorporated postal area)
ZCTA: 12831
    Covers a land area of 67.169 square miles and a water area of 0.992 square miles. Located at 43.20° N. Lat; 73.69° W. Long. Elevation is 239 feet.
Population: 17,727; Growth (since 2000): 24.8%; Density: 263.9 persons per square mile; Race: 95.0% White, 2.4% Black/African American, 0.9% Asian, 0.0% American Indian/Alaska Native, 0.0% Native Hawaiian/Other Pacific Islander, 0.8% Two or more races, 2.6% Hispanic of any race; Average household size: 2.66; Median age: 40.7; Age under 18: 25.8%; Age 65 and over: 10.7%; Males per 100 females: 102.5; Marriage status: 23.8% never married, 62.0% now married, 2.2% separated, 4.9% widowed, 9.3% divorced; Foreign born: 3.0%; Speak English only: 96.3%; With disability: 8.8%; Veterans: 7.9%; Ancestry: 26.8% Irish, 18.6% Italian, 13.7% German, 13.0% English, 11.6% American
Employment: 18.0% management, business, and financial, 8.1% computer, engineering, and science, 13.5% education, legal, community service, arts, and media, 6.1% healthcare practitioners, 14.2% service, 24.9% sales and office, 6.5% natural resources, construction, and maintenance, 8.7% production, transportation, and material moving
Income: Per capita: $32,984; Median household: $78,505; Average household: $88,922; Households with income of $100,000 or more: 37.6%; Poverty rate: 4.2%
Educational Attainment: High school diploma or higher: 94.9%; Bachelor's degree or higher: 34.0%; Graduate/professional degree or higher: 14.4%
Housing: Homeownership rate: 76.3%; Median home value: $229,600; Median year structure built: 1989; Homeowner vacancy rate: 0.4%; Median selected monthly owner costs: $1,682 with a mortgage, $537 without a mortgage; Median gross rent: $1,125 per month; Rental vacancy rate: 1.2%
Health Insurance: 96.7% have insurance; 86.3% have private insurance; 21.7% have public insurance; 3.3% do not have insurance; 0.7% of children under 18 do not have insurance
Transportation: Commute: 93.3% car, 0.3% public transportation, 0.4% walk, 5.5% work from home; Mean travel time to work: 25.7 minutes

GREENFIELD (town). Covers a land area of 67.388 square miles and a water area of 0.299 square miles. Located at 43.14° N. Lat; 73.87° W. Long. Elevation is 591 feet.
Population: 7,791; Growth (since 2000): 5.8%; Density: 115.6 persons per square mile; Race: 96.0% White, 0.6% Black/African American, 1.0% Asian, 0.0% American Indian/Alaska Native, 0.0% Native Hawaiian/Other Pacific Islander, 1.9% Two or more races, 0.4% Hispanic of any race; Average household size: 2.39; Median age: 46.6; Age under 18: 21.9%; Age 65 and over: 18.6%; Males per 100 females: 98.0; Marriage status: 20.4% never married, 64.2% now married, 2.8% separated, 6.5% widowed, 8.8% divorced; Foreign born: 1.8%; Speak English only: 95.6%; With disability: 12.5%; Veterans: 10.4%; Ancestry: 25.7% Irish, 22.0% German, 14.2% English, 11.1% Italian, 8.6% American
Employment: 15.0% management, business, and financial, 4.9% computer, engineering, and science, 14.3% education, legal, community service, arts, and media, 7.9% healthcare practitioners, 21.2% service,

21.4% sales and office, 9.4% natural resources, construction, and maintenance, 5.9% production, transportation, and material moving
Income: Per capita: $33,757; Median household: $66,317; Average household: $80,502; Households with income of $100,000 or more: 26.6%; Poverty rate: 10.2%
Educational Attainment: High school diploma or higher: 92.4%; Bachelor's degree or higher: 39.6%; Graduate/professional degree or higher: 15.5%
Housing: Homeownership rate: 81.1%; Median home value: $219,000; Median year structure built: 1984; Homeowner vacancy rate: 1.1%; Median selected monthly owner costs: $1,644 with a mortgage, $564 without a mortgage; Median gross rent: $1,259 per month; Rental vacancy rate: 13.4%
Health Insurance: 93.8% have insurance; 81.4% have private insurance; 28.8% have public insurance; 6.2% do not have insurance; 1.3% of children under 18 do not have insurance
Transportation: Commute: 89.2% car, 1.0% public transportation, 0.0% walk, 7.4% work from home; Mean travel time to work: 27.6 minutes
Additional Information Contacts
Town of Greenfield . . . . (518) 893-7432
  http://www.townofgreenfield.com

GREENFIELD CENTER (unincorporated postal area)
ZCTA: 12833
    Covers a land area of 35.246 square miles and a water area of 0.152 square miles. Located at 43.15° N. Lat; 73.84° W. Long. Elevation is 686 feet.
Population: 4,183; Growth (since 2000): -6.9%; Density: 118.7 persons per square mile; Race: 94.0% White, 1.0% Black/African American, 1.6% Asian, 0.0% American Indian/Alaska Native, 0.0% Native Hawaiian/Other Pacific Islander, 3.4% Two or more races, 0.9% Hispanic of any race; Average household size: 2.44; Median age: 47.9; Age under 18: 21.3%; Age 65 and over: 15.9%; Males per 100 females: 100.0; Marriage status: 20.6% never married, 64.5% now married, 3.2% separated, 6.0% widowed, 9.0% divorced; Foreign born: 1.7%; Speak English only: 93.8%; With disability: 8.2%; Veterans: 9.7%; Ancestry: 25.9% German, 21.8% Irish, 15.1% English, 11.8% Italian, 8.1% French
Employment: 11.1% management, business, and financial, 3.6% computer, engineering, and science, 11.5% education, legal, community service, arts, and media, 8.2% healthcare practitioners, 21.8% service, 25.9% sales and office, 10.7% natural resources, construction, and maintenance, 7.1% production, transportation, and material moving
Income: Per capita: $32,373; Median household: $65,898; Average household: $78,690; Households with income of $100,000 or more: 25.4%; Poverty rate: 8.8%
Educational Attainment: High school diploma or higher: 88.5%; Bachelor's degree or higher: 34.3%; Graduate/professional degree or higher: 12.0%

School District(s)
Saratoga Springs City SD (KG-12)
    2014-15 Enrollment: 6,481 . . . . (518) 583-4708
Housing: Homeownership rate: 84.4%; Median home value: $213,700; Median year structure built: 1982; Homeowner vacancy rate: 0.0%; Median selected monthly owner costs: $1,611 with a mortgage, $565 without a mortgage; Median gross rent: $928 per month; Rental vacancy rate: 7.3%
Health Insurance: 93.6% have insurance; 78.8% have private insurance; 28.4% have public insurance; 6.4% do not have insurance; 2.5% of children under 18 do not have insurance
Transportation: Commute: 92.8% car, 1.0% public transportation, 0.0% walk, 4.8% work from home; Mean travel time to work: 27.1 minutes

HADLEY (CDP). Covers a land area of 1.117 square miles and a water area of 0.199 square miles. Located at 43.30° N. Lat; 73.83° W. Long. Elevation is 630 feet.
Population: 846; Growth (since 2000): n/a; Density: 757.1 persons per square mile; Race: 98.3% White, 0.0% Black/African American, 0.0% Asian, 0.0% American Indian/Alaska Native, 0.0% Native Hawaiian/Other Pacific Islander, 1.7% Two or more races, 0.6% Hispanic of any race; Average household size: 2.07; Median age: 46.2; Age under 18: 15.1%; Age 65 and over: 20.6%; Males per 100 females: 94.4; Marriage status: 20.2% never married, 61.4% now married, 3.9% separated, 3.8% widowed, 14.6% divorced; Foreign born: 2.5%; Speak English only: 95.9%; With disability: 17.1%; Veterans: 20.5%; Ancestry: 17.4% American, 12.8% English, 12.5% Italian, 10.6% Irish, 8.0% German

Employment: 3.9% management, business, and financial, 1.7% computer, engineering, and science, 16.1% education, legal, community service, arts, and media, 0.8% healthcare practitioners, 22.8% service, 21.1% sales and office, 14.4% natural resources, construction, and maintenance, 19.2% production, transportation, and material moving
Income: Per capita: $23,004; Median household: $48,000; Average household: $47,664; Households with income of $100,000 or more: 8.6%; Poverty rate: 9.8%
Educational Attainment: High school diploma or higher: 86.1%; Bachelor's degree or higher: 13.5%; Graduate/professional degree or higher: 4.9%
Housing: Homeownership rate: 74.5%; Median home value: $138,200; Median year structure built: 1966; Homeowner vacancy rate: 4.4%; Median selected monthly owner costs: $1,264 with a mortgage, $418 without a mortgage; Median gross rent: $834 per month; Rental vacancy rate: 0.0%
Health Insurance: 88.7% have insurance; 63.8% have private insurance; 48.2% have public insurance; 11.3% do not have insurance; 0.0% of children under 18 do not have insurance
Transportation: Commute: 87.9% car, 0.0% public transportation, 0.0% walk, 12.1% work from home; Mean travel time to work: 29.8 minutes

HADLEY (town).
Covers a land area of 39.705 square miles and a water area of 1.380 square miles. Located at 43.34° N. Lat; 73.91° W. Long. Elevation is 630 feet.
Population: 1,745; Growth (since 2000): -11.5%; Density: 43.9 persons per square mile; Race: 96.9% White, 0.0% Black/African American, 0.0% Asian, 0.0% American Indian/Alaska Native, 0.0% Native Hawaiian/Other Pacific Islander, 2.8% Two or more races, 0.6% Hispanic of any race; Average household size: 2.36; Median age: 46.2; Age under 18: 19.0%; Age 65 and over: 16.2%; Males per 100 females: 99.6; Marriage status: 22.6% never married, 63.1% now married, 2.2% separated, 3.4% widowed, 10.9% divorced; Foreign born: 2.0%; Speak English only: 97.6%; With disability: 17.0%; Veterans: 14.6%; Ancestry: 16.8% American, 15.3% Irish, 13.9% Italian, 10.5% English, 9.4% French
Employment: 8.8% management, business, and financial, 3.4% computer, engineering, and science, 10.7% education, legal, community service, arts, and media, 2.8% healthcare practitioners, 22.0% service, 21.9% sales and office, 13.6% natural resources, construction, and maintenance, 16.8% production, transportation, and material moving
Income: Per capita: $26,190; Median household: $53,663; Average household: $61,664; Households with income of $100,000 or more: 13.2%; Poverty rate: 10.4%
Educational Attainment: High school diploma or higher: 86.4%; Bachelor's degree or higher: 17.0%; Graduate/professional degree or higher: 3.9%
Housing: Homeownership rate: 81.1%; Median home value: $154,500; Median year structure built: 1973; Homeowner vacancy rate: 2.3%; Median selected monthly owner costs: $1,348 with a mortgage, $450 without a mortgage; Median gross rent: $847 per month; Rental vacancy rate: 0.0%
Health Insurance: 90.9% have insurance; 68.4% have private insurance; 38.2% have public insurance; 9.1% do not have insurance; 2.1% of children under 18 do not have insurance
Transportation: Commute: 88.8% car, 0.7% public transportation, 1.1% walk, 9.4% work from home; Mean travel time to work: 29.7 minutes
Additional Information Contacts
Town of Hadley . . . . (518) 696-3112
  http://www.townofhadley.org

HALFMOON (town).
Covers a land area of 32.580 square miles and a water area of 1.050 square miles. Located at 42.86° N. Lat; 73.73° W. Long. Elevation is 276 feet.
Population: 22,847; Growth (since 2000): 23.7%; Density: 701.3 persons per square mile; Race: 89.3% White, 1.8% Black/African American, 6.9% Asian, 0.2% American Indian/Alaska Native, 0.0% Native Hawaiian/Other Pacific Islander, 1.3% Two or more races, 3.8% Hispanic of any race; Average household size: 2.39; Median age: 41.3; Age under 18: 20.7%; Age 65 and over: 14.4%; Males per 100 females: 95.6; Marriage status: 29.9% never married, 53.8% now married, 2.9% separated, 4.9% widowed, 11.4% divorced; Foreign born: 10.4%; Speak English only: 88.1%; With disability: 10.4%; Veterans: 7.3%; Ancestry: 23.6% Irish, 18.9% Italian, 14.6% German, 10.6% English, 8.7% Polish
Employment: 19.4% management, business, and financial, 10.3% computer, engineering, and science, 8.7% education, legal, community service, arts, and media, 8.2% healthcare practitioners, 16.0% service,

22.9% sales and office, 6.9% natural resources, construction, and maintenance, 7.7% production, transportation, and material moving
Income: Per capita: $38,891; Median household: $68,218; Average household: $91,739; Households with income of $100,000 or more: 32.3%; Poverty rate: 9.1%
Educational Attainment: High school diploma or higher: 93.5%; Bachelor's degree or higher: 42.7%; Graduate/professional degree or higher: 16.0%
Housing: Homeownership rate: 62.9%; Median home value: $232,600; Median year structure built: 1988; Homeowner vacancy rate: 1.2%; Median selected monthly owner costs: $1,730 with a mortgage, $631 without a mortgage; Median gross rent: $1,044 per month; Rental vacancy rate: 2.7%
Health Insurance: 93.1% have insurance; 80.8% have private insurance; 26.5% have public insurance; 6.9% do not have insurance; 2.7% of children under 18 do not have insurance
Transportation: Commute: 91.9% car, 0.8% public transportation, 1.3% walk, 4.7% work from home; Mean travel time to work: 23.3 minutes
Additional Information Contacts
Town of Halfmoon . . . . (518) 371-2592
  http://www.townofhalfmoon.org

MALTA (town).
Covers a land area of 27.922 square miles and a water area of 3.532 square miles. Located at 42.98° N. Lat; 73.79° W. Long. Elevation is 341 feet.
Population: 14,919; Growth (since 2000): 14.7%; Density: 534.3 persons per square mile; Race: 95.6% White, 1.0% Black/African American, 1.3% Asian, 0.0% American Indian/Alaska Native, 0.0% Native Hawaiian/Other Pacific Islander, 1.7% Two or more races, 2.7% Hispanic of any race; Average household size: 2.30; Median age: 43.4; Age under 18: 19.4%; Age 65 and over: 15.0%; Males per 100 females: 98.6; Marriage status: 23.7% never married, 59.1% now married, 0.9% separated, 4.4% widowed, 12.7% divorced; Foreign born: 5.3%; Speak English only: 93.7%; With disability: 9.3%; Veterans: 9.4%; Ancestry: 25.3% Irish, 22.1% Italian, 17.6% German, 11.8% English, 8.3% French
Employment: 18.4% management, business, and financial, 12.2% computer, engineering, and science, 11.3% education, legal, community service, arts, and media, 4.9% healthcare practitioners, 10.1% service, 28.2% sales and office, 8.5% natural resources, construction, and maintenance, 6.5% production, transportation, and material moving
Income: Per capita: $40,177; Median household: $82,080; Average household: $92,074; Households with income of $100,000 or more: 38.3%; Poverty rate: 3.3%
Educational Attainment: High school diploma or higher: 96.9%; Bachelor's degree or higher: 44.1%; Graduate/professional degree or higher: 17.2%
Housing: Homeownership rate: 69.1%; Median home value: $249,000; Median year structure built: 1985; Homeowner vacancy rate: 2.1%; Median selected monthly owner costs: $1,752 with a mortgage, $728 without a mortgage; Median gross rent: $1,027 per month; Rental vacancy rate: 7.3%
Health Insurance: 96.7% have insurance; 88.8% have private insurance; 21.2% have public insurance; 3.3% do not have insurance; 2.4% of children under 18 do not have insurance
Transportation: Commute: 92.4% car, 1.0% public transportation, 0.5% walk, 5.4% work from home; Mean travel time to work: 26.1 minutes
Additional Information Contacts
Town of Malta . . . . (518) 899-2552
  http://www.malta-town.org

MECHANICVILLE (city).
Covers a land area of 0.841 square miles and a water area of 0.079 square miles. Located at 42.90° N. Lat; 73.69° W. Long. Elevation is 89 feet.
History: Settled before 1700; incorporated as village in 1859, as city in 1915.
Population: 5,205; Growth (since 2000): 3.7%; Density: 6,191.7 persons per square mile; Race: 95.8% White, 1.7% Black/African American, 0.9% Asian, 0.0% American Indian/Alaska Native, 0.0% Native Hawaiian/Other Pacific Islander, 1.4% Two or more races, 2.3% Hispanic of any race; Average household size: 2.29; Median age: 39.5; Age under 18: 20.8%; Age 65 and over: 15.7%; Males per 100 females: 87.0; Marriage status: 38.9% never married, 39.8% now married, 3.9% separated, 7.5% widowed, 13.9% divorced; Foreign born: 2.2%; Speak English only: 97.4%; With disability: 18.1%; Veterans: 11.0%; Ancestry: 32.2% Italian, 28.4% Irish, 14.8% French, 11.6% German, 11.4% English

Employment: 8.1% management, business, and financial, 4.3% computer, engineering, and science, 9.9% education, legal, community service, arts, and media, 3.1% healthcare practitioners, 20.9% service, 29.9% sales and office, 10.4% natural resources, construction, and maintenance, 13.3% production, transportation, and material moving
Income: Per capita: $23,447; Median household: $41,042; Average household: $52,646; Households with income of $100,000 or more: 15.8%; Poverty rate: 16.3%
Educational Attainment: High school diploma or higher: 90.4%; Bachelor's degree or higher: 17.2%; Graduate/professional degree or higher: 4.5%

School District(s)
Mechanicville City SD (KG-12)
    2014-15 Enrollment: 1,392 . . . . (518) 664-5727
Housing: Homeownership rate: 39.1%; Median home value: $150,100; Median year structure built: Before 1940; Homeowner vacancy rate: 0.7%; Median selected monthly owner costs: $1,540 with a mortgage, $472 without a mortgage; Median gross rent: $771 per month; Rental vacancy rate: 6.4%
Health Insurance: 91.2% have insurance; 75.7% have private insurance; 32.0% have public insurance; 8.8% do not have insurance; 5.2% of children under 18 do not have insurance
Safety: Violent crime rate: 19.4 per 10,000 population; Property crime rate: 131.7 per 10,000 population
Newspapers: The Express (weekly circulation 2,800)
Transportation: Commute: 93.5% car, 0.5% public transportation, 2.9% walk, 2.3% work from home; Mean travel time to work: 25.2 minutes
Additional Information Contacts
City of Mechanicville . . . . (518) 664-9884
  http://www.mechanicville.com

MIDDLE GROVE (unincorporated postal area)
ZCTA: 12850
    Covers a land area of 46.763 square miles and a water area of 0.883 square miles. Located at 43.10° N. Lat; 73.98° W. Long. Elevation is 551 feet.
Population: 3,143; Growth (since 2000): 40.2%; Density: 67.2 persons per square mile; Race: 96.4% White, 0.2% Black/African American, 0.2% Asian, 0.0% American Indian/Alaska Native, 0.0% Native Hawaiian/Other Pacific Islander, 2.0% Two or more races, 1.5% Hispanic of any race; Average household size: 2.75; Median age: 41.1; Age under 18: 24.6%; Age 65 and over: 14.4%; Males per 100 females: 109.2; Marriage status: 28.1% never married, 60.9% now married, 0.2% separated, 1.9% widowed, 9.1% divorced; Foreign born: 3.6%; Speak English only: 96.6%; With disability: 8.0%; Veterans: 15.0%; Ancestry: 20.1% German, 19.0% Irish, 15.5% Italian, 12.4% English, 9.1% Polish
Employment: 15.2% management, business, and financial, 17.6% computer, engineering, and science, 12.9% education, legal, community service, arts, and media, 7.7% healthcare practitioners, 17.4% service, 15.2% sales and office, 9.8% natural resources, construction, and maintenance, 4.3% production, transportation, and material moving
Income: Per capita: $33,741; Median household: $74,622; Average household: $91,358; Households with income of $100,000 or more: 36.1%; Poverty rate: 8.5%
Educational Attainment: High school diploma or higher: 92.2%; Bachelor's degree or higher: 39.2%; Graduate/professional degree or higher: 17.9%
Housing: Homeownership rate: 87.4%; Median home value: $232,600; Median year structure built: 1983; Homeowner vacancy rate: 0.0%; Median selected monthly owner costs: $1,715 with a mortgage, $492 without a mortgage; Median gross rent: $1,442 per month; Rental vacancy rate: 0.0%
Health Insurance: 95.5% have insurance; 85.9% have private insurance; 21.6% have public insurance; 4.5% do not have insurance; 0.0% of children under 18 do not have insurance
Transportation: Commute: 86.9% car, 0.4% public transportation, 3.1% walk, 9.1% work from home; Mean travel time to work: 26.9 minutes

MILTON (CDP). Covers a land area of 1.487 square miles and a water area of 0.005 square miles. Located at 43.04° N. Lat; 73.85° W. Long. Elevation is 420 feet.
Population: 3,536; Growth (since 2000): 31.4%; Density: 2,378.6 persons per square mile; Race: 98.6% White, 0.0% Black/African American, 1.4% Asian, 0.0% American Indian/Alaska Native, 0.0% Native Hawaiian/Other Pacific Islander, 0.0% Two or more races, 1.8% Hispanic of any race;

Average household size: 2.88; Median age: 36.1; Age under 18: 22.4%; Age 65 and over: 12.9%; Males per 100 females: 91.4; Marriage status: 31.7% never married, 59.1% now married, 1.0% separated, 3.9% widowed, 5.3% divorced; Foreign born: 2.9%; Speak English only: 94.4%; With disability: 9.1%; Veterans: 11.9%; Ancestry: 33.5% Irish, 23.5% Italian, 20.1% German, 15.9% English, 10.5% French
Employment: 16.4% management, business, and financial, 4.2% computer, engineering, and science, 10.1% education, legal, community service, arts, and media, 9.0% healthcare practitioners, 10.2% service, 32.6% sales and office, 8.6% natural resources, construction, and maintenance, 8.9% production, transportation, and material moving
Income: Per capita: $33,090; Median household: $90,417; Average household: $94,611; Households with income of $100,000 or more: 42.1%; Poverty rate: 3.1%
Educational Attainment: High school diploma or higher: 99.2%; Bachelor's degree or higher: 43.0%; Graduate/professional degree or higher: 16.5%
Housing: Homeownership rate: 85.0%; Median home value: $214,200; Median year structure built: 1992; Homeowner vacancy rate: 5.0%; Median selected monthly owner costs: $1,786 with a mortgage, $570 without a mortgage; Median gross rent: $1,544 per month; Rental vacancy rate: 17.9%
Health Insurance: 94.7% have insurance; 85.3% have private insurance; 21.5% have public insurance; 5.3% do not have insurance; 6.7% of children under 18 do not have insurance
Transportation: Commute: 97.3% car, 0.0% public transportation, 0.0% walk, 2.7% work from home; Mean travel time to work: 23.0 minutes

MILTON (town). Covers a land area of 35.690 square miles and a water area of 0.064 square miles. Located at 43.05° N. Lat; 73.90° W. Long. Elevation is 420 feet.
History: In 1959, the film, The Fugitive Kid, based on a play by Tennessee Williams, starring Marlon Brando and Anna Magnani, was filmed in Milton. The main street was reconstructed to resemble an old town in the deep south.
Population: 18,873; Growth (since 2000): 10.3%; Density: 528.8 persons per square mile; Race: 95.9% White, 1.0% Black/African American, 0.6% Asian, 0.7% American Indian/Alaska Native, 0.0% Native Hawaiian/Other Pacific Islander, 1.8% Two or more races, 2.0% Hispanic of any race; Average household size: 2.58; Median age: 37.0; Age under 18: 23.7%; Age 65 and over: 11.5%; Males per 100 females: 100.9; Marriage status: 33.1% never married, 53.0% now married, 1.3% separated, 4.6% widowed, 9.3% divorced; Foreign born: 1.9%; Speak English only: 96.0%; With disability: 13.1%; Veterans: 11.0%; Ancestry: 23.8% Irish, 18.3% German, 17.8% Italian, 13.1% English, 9.5% French
Employment: 13.3% management, business, and financial, 6.5% computer, engineering, and science, 10.4% education, legal, community service, arts, and media, 6.6% healthcare practitioners, 16.3% service, 24.1% sales and office, 9.9% natural resources, construction, and maintenance, 13.0% production, transportation, and material moving
Income: Per capita: $29,830; Median household: $66,147; Average household: $76,853; Households with income of $100,000 or more: 28.7%; Poverty rate: 8.1%
Educational Attainment: High school diploma or higher: 94.3%; Bachelor's degree or higher: 32.5%; Graduate/professional degree or higher: 10.5%
Housing: Homeownership rate: 73.7%; Median home value: $188,400; Median year structure built: 1983; Homeowner vacancy rate: 1.3%; Median selected monthly owner costs: $1,575 with a mortgage, $578 without a mortgage; Median gross rent: $991 per month; Rental vacancy rate: 9.0%
Health Insurance: 94.0% have insurance; 75.0% have private insurance; 32.4% have public insurance; 6.0% do not have insurance; 3.9% of children under 18 do not have insurance
Transportation: Commute: 92.2% car, 0.6% public transportation, 0.8% walk, 4.7% work from home; Mean travel time to work: 25.8 minutes
Additional Information Contacts
Town of Milton . . . . (518) 885-9220
  http://www.townofmiltonny.org

MOREAU (town). Covers a land area of 41.924 square miles and a water area of 1.657 square miles. Located at 43.25° N. Lat; 73.67° W. Long. Elevation is 341 feet.
Population: 15,058; Growth (since 2000): 8.9%; Density: 359.2 persons per square mile; Race: 96.2% White, 2.3% Black/African American, 0.5% Asian, 0.0% American Indian/Alaska Native, 0.0% Native Hawaiian/Other

Pacific Islander, 0.5% Two or more races, 2.7% Hispanic of any race; Average household size: 2.45; Median age: 42.6; Age under 18: 20.5%; Age 65 and over: 12.8%; Males per 100 females: 100.2; Marriage status: 31.7% never married, 49.0% now married, 2.5% separated, 6.5% widowed, 12.7% divorced; Foreign born: 1.8%; Speak English only: 96.4%; With disability: 12.0%; Veterans: 8.1%; Ancestry: 22.0% Irish, 13.6% French, 13.5% Italian, 11.2% American, 10.4% English

Employment: 12.8% management, business, and financial, 4.8% computer, engineering, and science, 8.1% education, legal, community service, arts, and media, 7.3% healthcare practitioners, 15.9% service, 27.5% sales and office, 8.2% natural resources, construction, and maintenance, 15.3% production, transportation, and material moving

Income: Per capita: $28,436; Median household: $59,761; Average household: $70,561; Households with income of $100,000 or more: 23.6%; Poverty rate: 6.9%

Educational Attainment: High school diploma or higher: 92.9%; Bachelor's degree or higher: 19.8%; Graduate/professional degree or higher: 7.2%

Housing: Homeownership rate: 73.5%; Median home value: $170,800; Median year structure built: 1974; Homeowner vacancy rate: 0.2%; Median selected monthly owner costs: $1,375 with a mortgage, $519 without a mortgage; Median gross rent: $907 per month; Rental vacancy rate: 3.4%

Health Insurance: 92.8% have insurance; 78.6% have private insurance; 27.5% have public insurance; 7.2% do not have insurance; 3.5% of children under 18 do not have insurance

Transportation: Commute: 96.3% car, 0.5% public transportation, 0.5% walk, 2.0% work from home; Mean travel time to work: 22.7 minutes

Additional Information Contacts
Town of Moreau . . . . (518) 792-1030
  http://www.townofmoreau.org

NORTH BALLSTON SPA (CDP). Covers a land area of 0.824 square miles and a water area of 0.004 square miles. Located at 43.02° N. Lat; 73.85° W. Long.

Population: 1,569; Growth (since 2000): 26.8%; Density: 1,904.2 persons per square mile; Race: 89.2% White, 2.5% Black/African American, 0.0% Asian, 5.2% American Indian/Alaska Native, 0.0% Native Hawaiian/Other Pacific Islander, 3.1% Two or more races, 0.4% Hispanic of any race; Average household size: 2.50; Median age: 34.8; Age under 18: 22.6%; Age 65 and over: 14.7%; Males per 100 females: 96.8; Marriage status: 35.6% never married, 45.2% now married, 0.0% separated, 6.5% widowed, 12.8% divorced; Foreign born: 1.2%; Speak English only: 91.7%; With disability: 21.0%; Veterans: 12.5%; Ancestry: 33.1% German, 23.5% Irish, 15.8% Italian, 15.7% English, 8.6% American

Employment: 4.6% management, business, and financial, 3.0% computer, engineering, and science, 23.9% education, legal, community service, arts, and media, 1.9% healthcare practitioners, 12.1% service, 25.8% sales and office, 21.1% natural resources, construction, and maintenance, 7.7% production, transportation, and material moving

Income: Per capita: $29,341; Median household: $62,778; Average household: $71,410; Households with income of $100,000 or more: 35.3%; Poverty rate: 3.9%

Educational Attainment: High school diploma or higher: 88.1%; Bachelor's degree or higher: 26.5%; Graduate/professional degree or higher: 3.4%

Housing: Homeownership rate: 81.9%; Median home value: $183,500; Median year structure built: 1959; Homeowner vacancy rate: 0.0%; Median selected monthly owner costs: $1,275 with a mortgage, $545 without a mortgage; Median gross rent: n/a per month; Rental vacancy rate: 0.0%

Health Insurance: 93.1% have insurance; 74.4% have private insurance; 34.8% have public insurance; 6.9% do not have insurance; 0.0% of children under 18 do not have insurance

Transportation: Commute: 92.4% car, 0.3% public transportation, 0.0% walk, 0.0% work from home; Mean travel time to work: 21.3 minutes

NORTHUMBERLAND (town). Covers a land area of 32.299 square miles and a water area of 0.619 square miles. Located at 43.16° N. Lat; 73.63° W. Long. Elevation is 112 feet.

Population: 5,150; Growth (since 2000): 11.9%; Density: 159.4 persons per square mile; Race: 97.0% White, 1.4% Black/African American, 0.0% Asian, 0.1% American Indian/Alaska Native, 0.0% Native Hawaiian/Other Pacific Islander, 1.0% Two or more races, 3.0% Hispanic of any race; Average household size: 2.80; Median age: 40.5; Age under 18: 24.6%; Age 65 and over: 10.3%; Males per 100 females: 103.5; Marriage status: 22.8% never married, 65.6% now married, 2.0% separated, 4.8%

widowed, 6.9% divorced; Foreign born: 0.7%; Speak English only: 96.7%; With disability: 12.4%; Veterans: 10.5%; Ancestry: 24.5% Irish, 14.9% German, 14.0% American, 14.0% English, 11.2% Italian

Employment: 15.3% management, business, and financial, 7.6% computer, engineering, and science, 11.4% education, legal, community service, arts, and media, 5.1% healthcare practitioners, 17.2% service, 23.9% sales and office, 9.5% natural resources, construction, and maintenance, 10.1% production, transportation, and material moving

Income: Per capita: $29,724; Median household: $72,174; Average household: $82,212; Households with income of $100,000 or more: 32.6%; Poverty rate: 7.4%

Educational Attainment: High school diploma or higher: 92.9%; Bachelor's degree or higher: 24.7%; Graduate/professional degree or higher: 9.0%

Housing: Homeownership rate: 87.9%; Median home value: $190,900; Median year structure built: 1985; Homeowner vacancy rate: 2.6%; Median selected monthly owner costs: $1,469 with a mortgage, $513 without a mortgage; Median gross rent: $1,038 per month; Rental vacancy rate: 0.0%

Health Insurance: 96.9% have insurance; 85.4% have private insurance; 24.0% have public insurance; 3.1% do not have insurance; 0.6% of children under 18 do not have insurance

Transportation: Commute: 92.4% car, 0.3% public transportation, 1.5% walk, 4.9% work from home; Mean travel time to work: 26.3 minutes

Additional Information Contacts
Town of Northumberland . . . . (518) 792-9179
  http://www.townofnorthumberland.org

PORTER CORNERS (unincorporated postal area)
ZCTA: 12859

Covers a land area of 22.017 square miles and a water area of 0.058 square miles. Located at 43.17° N. Lat; 73.92° W. Long. Elevation is 663 feet.

Population: 2,297; Growth (since 2000): 15.8%; Density: 104.3 persons per square mile; Race: 98.3% White, 0.0% Black/African American, 0.0% Asian, 0.0% American Indian/Alaska Native, 0.0% Native Hawaiian/Other Pacific Islander, 1.7% Two or more races, 0.1% Hispanic of any race; Average household size: 2.40; Median age: 37.6; Age under 18: 23.6%; Age 65 and over: 14.2%; Males per 100 females: 101.1; Marriage status: 27.1% never married, 62.1% now married, 3.7% separated, 4.1% widowed, 6.8% divorced; Foreign born: 0.8%; Speak English only: 97.0%; With disability: 15.1%; Veterans: 11.0%; Ancestry: 23.9% Irish, 15.0% American, 14.9% English, 13.3% German, 10.0% French

Employment: 16.4% management, business, and financial, 3.7% computer, engineering, and science, 17.1% education, legal, community service, arts, and media, 7.0% healthcare practitioners, 17.8% service, 14.1% sales and office, 11.6% natural resources, construction, and maintenance, 12.4% production, transportation, and material moving

Income: Per capita: $28,881; Median household: $55,776; Average household: $68,518; Households with income of $100,000 or more: 23.3%; Poverty rate: 13.8%

Educational Attainment: High school diploma or higher: 93.0%; Bachelor's degree or higher: 29.9%; Graduate/professional degree or higher: 12.7%

Housing: Homeownership rate: 86.6%; Median home value: $175,800; Median year structure built: 1984; Homeowner vacancy rate: 0.0%; Median selected monthly owner costs: $1,574 with a mortgage, $498 without a mortgage; Median gross rent: $1,302 per month; Rental vacancy rate: 0.0%

Health Insurance: 93.3% have insurance; 81.3% have private insurance; 25.0% have public insurance; 6.7% do not have insurance; 0.0% of children under 18 do not have insurance

Transportation: Commute: 88.5% car, 1.7% public transportation, 0.0% walk, 5.8% work from home; Mean travel time to work: 30.5 minutes

PROVIDENCE (town). Covers a land area of 43.996 square miles and a water area of 1.098 square miles. Located at 43.12° N. Lat; 74.04° W. Long.

Population: 2,207; Growth (since 2000): 19.9%; Density: 50.2 persons per square mile; Race: 97.1% White, 0.2% Black/African American, 0.0% Asian, 0.0% American Indian/Alaska Native, 0.0% Native Hawaiian/Other Pacific Islander, 2.7% Two or more races, 2.9% Hispanic of any race; Average household size: 2.69; Median age: 43.0; Age under 18: 20.2%; Age 65 and over: 11.9%; Males per 100 females: 111.1; Marriage status:

30.4% never married, 57.1% now married, 0.7% separated, 3.5% widowed, 9.0% divorced; Foreign born: 2.7%; Speak English only: 94.9%; With disability: 7.5%; Veterans: 17.7%; Ancestry: 23.8% German, 18.4% Italian, 14.9% Irish, 12.5% English, 10.4% Polish

Employment: 15.3% management, business, and financial, 16.2% computer, engineering, and science, 8.1% education, legal, community service, arts, and media, 6.1% healthcare practitioners, 12.0% service, 17.1% sales and office, 14.8% natural resources, construction, and maintenance, 10.4% production, transportation, and material moving

Income: Per capita: $30,051; Median household: $73,043; Average household: $78,952; Households with income of $100,000 or more: 29.1%; Poverty rate: 6.3%

Educational Attainment: High school diploma or higher: 86.4%; Bachelor's degree or higher: 19.3%; Graduate/professional degree or higher: 5.5%

Housing: Homeownership rate: 86.0%; Median home value: $183,100; Median year structure built: 1982; Homeowner vacancy rate: 1.1%; Median selected monthly owner costs: $1,606 with a mortgage, $477 without a mortgage; Median gross rent: $1,113 per month; Rental vacancy rate: 0.0%

Health Insurance: 93.7% have insurance; 82.8% have private insurance; 22.7% have public insurance; 6.3% do not have insurance; 0.9% of children under 18 do not have insurance

Transportation: Commute: 94.5% car, 0.4% public transportation, 0.3% walk, 4.3% work from home; Mean travel time to work: 30.6 minutes

REXFORD (unincorporated postal area)

ZCTA: 12148

Covers a land area of 15.649 square miles and a water area of 1.280 square miles. Located at 42.83° N. Lat; 73.85° W. Long. Elevation is 249 feet.

Population: 4,629; Growth (since 2000): 58.0%; Density: 295.8 persons per square mile; Race: 94.3% White, 0.0% Black/African American, 4.3% Asian, 0.0% American Indian/Alaska Native, 0.0% Native Hawaiian/Other Pacific Islander, 0.8% Two or more races, 6.3% Hispanic of any race; Average household size: 2.55; Median age: 43.4; Age under 18: 25.9%; Age 65 and over: 16.8%; Males per 100 females: 93.2; Marriage status: 16.6% never married, 67.5% now married, 0.7% separated, 6.0% widowed, 9.9% divorced; Foreign born: 10.1%; Speak English only: 87.5%; With disability: 8.2%; Veterans: 10.4%; Ancestry: 23.8% Italian, 15.3% German, 14.8% Irish, 13.5% English, 7.4% French

Employment: 20.7% management, business, and financial, 12.9% computer, engineering, and science, 13.1% education, legal, community service, arts, and media, 11.9% healthcare practitioners, 8.6% service, 22.8% sales and office, 5.9% natural resources, construction, and maintenance, 4.2% production, transportation, and material moving

Income: Per capita: $45,043; Median household: $101,307; Average household: $113,825; Households with income of $100,000 or more: 51.3%; Poverty rate: 1.5%

Educational Attainment: High school diploma or higher: 97.9%; Bachelor's degree or higher: 51.1%; Graduate/professional degree or higher: 29.3%

School District(s)

Niskayuna Central SD (KG-12)

    2014-15 Enrollment: 4,114 . . . . (518) 377-4666

Housing: Homeownership rate: 84.8%; Median home value: $299,600; Median year structure built: 1991; Homeowner vacancy rate: 0.0%; Median selected monthly owner costs: $2,138 with a mortgage, $666 without a mortgage; Median gross rent: $2,625 per month; Rental vacancy rate: 14.6%

Health Insurance: 96.9% have insurance; 87.2% have private insurance; 24.2% have public insurance; 3.1% do not have insurance; 3.1% of children under 18 do not have insurance

Transportation: Commute: 86.8% car, 0.0% public transportation, 0.6% walk, 12.6% work from home; Mean travel time to work: 24.8 minutes

ROCK CITY FALLS (unincorporated postal area)

ZCTA: 12863

Covers a land area of 3.594 square miles and a water area of 0 square miles. Located at 43.06° N. Lat; 73.93° W. Long. Elevation is 453 feet.

Population: 690; Growth (since 2000): 15.8%; Density: 192.0 persons per square mile; Race: 100.0% White, 0.0% Black/African American, 0.0% Asian, 0.0% American Indian/Alaska Native, 0.0% Native Hawaiian/Other Pacific Islander, 0.0% Two or more races, 7.7% Hispanic of any race; Average household size: 2.62; Median age: 44.6;

Age under 18: 15.2%; Age 65 and over: 16.5%; Males per 100 females: 98.1; Marriage status: 31.2% never married, 55.0% now married, 0.0% separated, 1.0% widowed, 12.8% divorced; Foreign born: 0.0%; Speak English only: 98.7%; With disability: 8.9%; Veterans: 6.7%; Ancestry: 46.5% American, 14.5% Italian, 8.3% English, 7.8% Irish, 4.6% German

Employment: 9.8% management, business, and financial, 7.7% computer, engineering, and science, 7.4% education, legal, community service, arts, and media, 2.2% healthcare practitioners, 14.2% service, 18.2% sales and office, 11.4% natural resources, construction, and maintenance, 29.2% production, transportation, and material moving

Income: Per capita: $32,134; Median household: $69,125; Average household: $81,800; Households with income of $100,000 or more: 25.5%; Poverty rate: 1.9%

Educational Attainment: High school diploma or higher: 93.5%; Bachelor's degree or higher: 28.7%; Graduate/professional degree or higher: 9.4%

Housing: Homeownership rate: 82.1%; Median home value: $188,600; Median year structure built: 1977; Homeowner vacancy rate: 0.0%; Median selected monthly owner costs: n/a with a mortgage, n/a without a mortgage; Median gross rent: $873 per month; Rental vacancy rate: 0.0%

Health Insurance: 94.6% have insurance; 75.7% have private insurance; 29.5% have public insurance; 5.4% do not have insurance; 0.0% of children under 18 do not have insurance

Transportation: Commute: 77.9% car, 0.0% public transportation, 0.0% walk, 8.6% work from home; Mean travel time to work: 39.8 minutes

ROUND LAKE (village). Covers a land area of 1.123 square miles and a water area of 0.107 square miles. Located at 42.94° N. Lat; 73.80° W. Long. Elevation is 164 feet.

Population: 693; Growth (since 2000): 14.7%; Density: 617.0 persons per square mile; Race: 94.7% White, 0.0% Black/African American, 1.2% Asian, 0.4% American Indian/Alaska Native, 0.0% Native Hawaiian/Other Pacific Islander, 2.6% Two or more races, 5.6% Hispanic of any race; Average household size: 2.17; Median age: 46.0; Age under 18: 14.7%; Age 65 and over: 16.3%; Males per 100 females: 89.4; Marriage status: 23.8% never married, 54.8% now married, 1.2% separated, 5.4% widowed, 16.1% divorced; Foreign born: 3.3%; Speak English only: 92.8%; With disability: 14.6%; Veterans: 10.8%; Ancestry: 24.7% Irish, 16.6% German, 16.3% Italian, 13.7% English, 9.1% French

Employment: 15.6% management, business, and financial, 21.8% computer, engineering, and science, 14.1% education, legal, community service, arts, and media, 9.0% healthcare practitioners, 10.5% service, 15.9% sales and office, 6.4% natural resources, construction, and maintenance, 6.7% production, transportation, and material moving

Income: Per capita: $38,833; Median household: $77,813; Average household: $83,663; Households with income of $100,000 or more: 34.3%; Poverty rate: 4.6%

Educational Attainment: High school diploma or higher: 98.6%; Bachelor's degree or higher: 59.8%; Graduate/professional degree or higher: 21.9%

Housing: Homeownership rate: 76.8%; Median home value: $198,500; Median year structure built: Before 1940; Homeowner vacancy rate: 0.0%; Median selected monthly owner costs: $1,713 with a mortgage, $613 without a mortgage; Median gross rent: $1,053 per month; Rental vacancy rate: 8.6%

Health Insurance: 95.8% have insurance; 81.8% have private insurance; 26.7% have public insurance; 4.2% do not have insurance; 0.0% of children under 18 do not have insurance

Transportation: Commute: 90.2% car, 0.0% public transportation, 1.8% walk, 7.9% work from home; Mean travel time to work: 22.3 minutes

Additional Information Contacts

Village of Round Lake . . . . (518) 899-2800
    http://www.roundlakevillage.org

SARATOGA (town). Covers a land area of 40.562 square miles and a water area of 2.339 square miles. Located at 43.05° N. Lat; 73.65° W. Long.

History: Saratoga was named for a Mohawk Indian word that described the Indian hunting grounds located along both sides of the Hudson River. Thought to derive from either 'Se-rach-ta-gue' meaning 'the hillside country of the quiet river" or 'sharató:ken,' meaning "where you get a blister on your heels."

Population: 5,687; Growth (since 2000): 10.6%; Density: 140.2 persons per square mile; Race: 93.7% White, 3.7% Black/African American, 0.6%

Asian, 0.2% American Indian/Alaska Native, 0.0% Native Hawaiian/Other Pacific Islander, 1.8% Two or more races, 3.1% Hispanic of any race; Average household size: 2.50; Median age: 40.9; Age under 18: 24.0%; Age 65 and over: 14.5%; Males per 100 females: 98.5; Marriage status: 28.4% never married, 52.5% now married, 3.3% separated, 5.0% widowed, 14.0% divorced; Foreign born: 3.9%; Speak English only: 94.6%; With disability: 12.2%; Veterans: 9.7%; Ancestry: 25.9% Irish, 17.3% German, 11.4% Italian, 10.9% English, 10.1% American

Employment: 18.3% management, business, and financial, 7.0% computer, engineering, and science, 8.1% education, legal, community service, arts, and media, 4.8% healthcare practitioners, 19.3% service, 21.6% sales and office, 12.4% natural resources, construction, and maintenance, 8.4% production, transportation, and material moving
Income: Per capita: $37,627; Median household: $67,628; Average household: $94,093; Households with income of $100,000 or more: 29.8%; Poverty rate: 7.3%
Educational Attainment: High school diploma or higher: 91.7%; Bachelor's degree or higher: 34.8%; Graduate/professional degree or higher: 12.8%
Housing: Homeownership rate: 78.2%; Median home value: $219,600; Median year structure built: 1974; Homeowner vacancy rate: 3.6%; Median selected monthly owner costs: $1,692 with a mortgage, $613 without a mortgage; Median gross rent: $896 per month; Rental vacancy rate: 3.1%
Health Insurance: 94.5% have insurance; 76.3% have private insurance; 32.3% have public insurance; 5.5% do not have insurance; 7.4% of children under 18 do not have insurance
Transportation: Commute: 91.6% car, 1.0% public transportation, 1.8% walk, 5.0% work from home; Mean travel time to work: 26.0 minutes
Additional Information Contacts
Town of Saratoga . . . . (518) 695-3644
   http://www.townofsaratoga.com

SARATOGA SPRINGS (city). Covers a land area of 28.065 square miles and a water area of 0.807 square miles. Located at 43.07° N. Lat; 73.78° W. Long. Elevation is 299 feet.
History: The growth and development of Saratoga Springs has been closely associated with its mineral springs, the waters of which began to be used in 1774. Rumors of the healing powers of the water circulated. In 1789, Gideon Putnam arrived and in 1802 he erected the three-story Union Hall, a hotel for visitors. People were attracted to the spot, and Putnam was ready to sell them lots around his hotel.
Population: 27,244; Growth (since 2000): 4.0%; Density: 970.8 persons per square mile; Race: 92.1% White, 1.9% Black/African American, 3.1% Asian, 0.0% American Indian/Alaska Native, 0.0% Native Hawaiian/Other Pacific Islander, 2.5% Two or more races, 4.2% Hispanic of any race; Average household size: 2.11; Median age: 39.1; Age under 18: 15.9%; Age 65 and over: 17.7%; Males per 100 females: 93.4; Marriage status: 39.1% never married, 46.4% now married, 2.1% separated, 5.4% widowed, 9.1% divorced; Foreign born: 6.6%; Speak English only: 89.4%; With disability: 11.7%; Veterans: 10.5%; Ancestry: 24.0% Irish, 19.0% Italian, 16.5% German, 12.3% English, 6.6% French
Employment: 20.7% management, business, and financial, 8.5% computer, engineering, and science, 16.3% education, legal, community service, arts, and media, 6.1% healthcare practitioners, 17.0% service, 22.9% sales and office, 3.5% natural resources, construction, and maintenance, 5.2% production, transportation, and material moving
Income: Per capita: $40,673; Median household: $70,187; Average household: $93,144; Households with income of $100,000 or more: 32.4%; Poverty rate: 6.8%
Educational Attainment: High school diploma or higher: 94.6%; Bachelor's degree or higher: 50.3%; Graduate/professional degree or higher: 23.3%
School District(s)
Saratoga Springs City SD (KG-12)
   2014-15 Enrollment: 6,481 . . . . (518) 583-4708
Four-year College(s)
SUNY Empire State College (Public)
   Fall 2014 Enrollment: 11,952 . . . . (518) 587-2100
   2015-16 Tuition: In-state $6,985; Out-of-state $16,835
Skidmore College (Private, Not-for-profit)
   Fall 2014 Enrollment: 2,646 . . . . (518) 580-5000
   2015-16 Tuition: In-state $49,120; Out-of-state $49,120
Housing: Homeownership rate: 54.5%; Median home value: $311,400; Median year structure built: 1971; Homeowner vacancy rate: 2.8%; Median selected monthly owner costs: $1,881 with a mortgage, $733 without a

mortgage; Median gross rent: $1,008 per month; Rental vacancy rate: 4.3%
Health Insurance: 94.6% have insurance; 83.2% have private insurance; 27.1% have public insurance; 5.4% do not have insurance; 3.2% of children under 18 do not have insurance
Hospitals: Saratoga Hospital (243 beds)
Safety: Violent crime rate: 21.0 per 10,000 population; Property crime rate: 197.8 per 10,000 population
Newspapers: Community News (weekly circulation 28,000); The Saratogian (daily circulation 10,300)
Transportation: Commute: 78.4% car, 1.6% public transportation, 9.4% walk, 8.8% work from home; Mean travel time to work: 22.6 minutes; Amtrak: Train and bus service available.
Airports: Saratoga County (general aviation)
Additional Information Contacts
City of Saratoga Springs . . . . (518) 587-3550
   http://www.saratoga-springs.org

SCHUYLERVILLE (village). Covers a land area of 0.533 square miles and a water area of 0.054 square miles. Located at 43.10° N. Lat; 73.58° W. Long. Elevation is 128 feet.
Population: 1,621; Growth (since 2000): 35.4%; Density: 3,041.2 persons per square mile; Race: 91.7% White, 5.8% Black/African American, 0.3% Asian, 0.2% American Indian/Alaska Native, 0.0% Native Hawaiian/Other Pacific Islander, 2.0% Two or more races, 1.9% Hispanic of any race; Average household size: 2.46; Median age: 33.8; Age under 18: 26.9%; Age 65 and over: 11.7%; Males per 100 females: 89.3; Marriage status: 30.3% never married, 45.8% now married, 4.0% separated, 7.3% widowed, 16.7% divorced; Foreign born: 4.1%; Speak English only: 94.7%; With disability: 13.4%; Veterans: 9.2%; Ancestry: 19.2% Irish, 16.3% Italian, 14.9% German, 13.4% American, 12.5% English
Employment: 15.7% management, business, and financial, 5.0% computer, engineering, and science, 9.4% education, legal, community service, arts, and media, 2.4% healthcare practitioners, 22.4% service, 21.6% sales and office, 13.1% natural resources, construction, and maintenance, 10.4% production, transportation, and material moving
Income: Per capita: $24,771; Median household: $54,766; Average household: $59,272; Households with income of $100,000 or more: 14.7%; Poverty rate: 11.0%
Educational Attainment: High school diploma or higher: 89.2%; Bachelor's degree or higher: 24.8%; Graduate/professional degree or higher: 10.0%
School District(s)
Schuylerville Central SD (KG-12)
   2014-15 Enrollment: 1,696 . . . . (518) 695-3255
Housing: Homeownership rate: 55.0%; Median home value: $144,200; Median year structure built: Before 1940; Homeowner vacancy rate: 0.0%; Median selected monthly owner costs: $1,322 with a mortgage, $561 without a mortgage; Median gross rent: $809 per month; Rental vacancy rate: 5.2%
Health Insurance: 96.1% have insurance; 72.4% have private insurance; 35.5% have public insurance; 3.9% do not have insurance; 3.2% of children under 18 do not have insurance
Transportation: Commute: 92.7% car, 1.3% public transportation, 3.1% walk, 2.0% work from home; Mean travel time to work: 26.4 minutes

SOUTH GLENS FALLS (village). Covers a land area of 1.358 square miles and a water area of 0.132 square miles. Located at 43.29° N. Lat; 73.63° W. Long. Elevation is 344 feet.
History: Incorporated 1895.
Population: 3,586; Growth (since 2000): 6.5%; Density: 2,639.8 persons per square mile; Race: 96.8% White, 2.4% Black/African American, 0.7% Asian, 0.0% American Indian/Alaska Native, 0.0% Native Hawaiian/Other Pacific Islander, 0.0% Two or more races, 4.6% Hispanic of any race; Average household size: 2.05; Median age: 41.1; Age under 18: 18.1%; Age 65 and over: 14.6%; Males per 100 females: 90.2; Marriage status: 37.4% never married, 37.5% now married, 2.3% separated, 7.0% widowed, 18.0% divorced; Foreign born: 0.7%; Speak English only: 98.6%; With disability: 16.5%; Veterans: 9.5%; Ancestry: 23.6% Irish, 15.7% Italian, 14.4% American, 12.8% French, 11.5% English
Employment: 11.4% management, business, and financial, 3.2% computer, engineering, and science, 8.0% education, legal, community service, arts, and media, 2.9% healthcare practitioners, 20.5% service, 25.1% sales and office, 8.5% natural resources, construction, and maintenance, 20.4% production, transportation, and material moving

Income: Per capita: $24,273; Median household: $44,418; Average household: $49,937; Households with income of $100,000 or more: 8.8%; Poverty rate: 10.0%

Educational Attainment: High school diploma or higher: 91.0%; Bachelor's degree or higher: 14.4%; Graduate/professional degree or higher: 6.4%

School District(s)
South Glens Falls Central SD (KG-12)

    2014-15 Enrollment: 3,189 . . . . (518) 793-9617

Housing: Homeownership rate: 51.5%; Median home value: $153,500; Median year structure built: 1946; Homeowner vacancy rate: 0.0%; Median selected monthly owner costs: $1,268 with a mortgage, $489 without a mortgage; Median gross rent: $787 per month; Rental vacancy rate: 5.3%

Health Insurance: 93.2% have insurance; 67.6% have private insurance; 40.6% have public insurance; 6.8% do not have insurance; 1.5% of children under 18 do not have insurance

Safety: Violent crime rate: 38.9 per 10,000 population; Property crime rate: 141.8 per 10,000 population

Transportation: Commute: 95.3% car, 0.4% public transportation, 0.6% walk, 2.2% work from home; Mean travel time to work: 21.6 minutes

STILLWATER (town). Covers a land area of 41.191 square miles and a water area of 2.383 square miles. Located at 42.97° N. Lat; 73.69° W. Long. Elevation is 92 feet.

History: The American Revolutionary battles (Sept. 19, 1777, and Oct. 7, 1777) fought near here are commemorated by Saratoga National Historical Park, 9 miles Southeast of Saratoga Springs.

Population: 8,392; Growth (since 2000): 11.6%; Density: 203.7 persons per square mile; Race: 98.7% White, 0.9% Black/African American, 0.2% Asian, 0.0% American Indian/Alaska Native, 0.0% Native Hawaiian/Other Pacific Islander, 0.1% Two or more races, 2.0% Hispanic of any race; Average household size: 2.75; Median age: 42.0; Age under 18: 26.2%; Age 65 and over: 14.6%; Males per 100 females: 100.8; Marriage status: 23.8% never married, 60.7% now married, 0.9% separated, 6.6% widowed, 8.9% divorced; Foreign born: 2.5%; Speak English only: 97.0%; With disability: 13.4%; Veterans: 9.4%; Ancestry: 34.1% Italian, 28.7% Irish, 12.6% English, 11.0% French, 10.6% Polish

Employment: 14.5% management, business, and financial, 5.5% computer, engineering, and science, 9.8% education, legal, community service, arts, and media, 5.8% healthcare practitioners, 15.3% service, 29.2% sales and office, 10.4% natural resources, construction, and maintenance, 9.5% production, transportation, and material moving

Income: Per capita: $31,303; Median household: $73,179; Average household: $84,201; Households with income of $100,000 or more: 28.7%; Poverty rate: 5.9%

Educational Attainment: High school diploma or higher: 91.8%; Bachelor's degree or higher: 23.7%; Graduate/professional degree or higher: 6.3%

School District(s)
Stillwater Central SD (PK-12)

    2014-15 Enrollment: 1,197 . . . . (518) 373-6100

Housing: Homeownership rate: 83.2%; Median home value: $229,000; Median year structure built: 1979; Homeowner vacancy rate: 0.0%; Median selected monthly owner costs: $1,752 with a mortgage, $563 without a mortgage; Median gross rent: $973 per month; Rental vacancy rate: 4.1%

Health Insurance: 96.2% have insurance; 75.3% have private insurance; 32.1% have public insurance; 3.8% do not have insurance; 2.0% of children under 18 do not have insurance

Safety: Violent crime rate: 0.0 per 10,000 population; Property crime rate: 25.4 per 10,000 population

Transportation: Commute: 91.1% car, 1.4% public transportation, 0.5% walk, 6.5% work from home; Mean travel time to work: 31.0 minutes

Additional Information Contacts

Town of Stillwater . . . . (518) 664-6148
    http://www.stillwaterny.org

STILLWATER (village). Covers a land area of 1.258 square miles and a water area of 0.204 square miles. Located at 42.94° N. Lat; 73.64° W. Long. Elevation is 92 feet.

Population: 1,812; Growth (since 2000): 10.2%; Density: 1,440.4 persons per square mile; Race: 97.5% White, 1.0% Black/African American, 0.9% Asian, 0.0% American Indian/Alaska Native, 0.0% Native Hawaiian/Other Pacific Islander, 0.6% Two or more races, 1.8% Hispanic of any race; Average household size: 2.79; Median age: 35.5; Age under 18: 29.2%; Age 65 and over: 12.4%; Males per 100 females: 93.8; Marriage status:

28.7% never married, 52.7% now married, 2.0% separated, 6.7% widowed, 12.0% divorced; Foreign born: 2.5%; Speak English only: 96.8%; With disability: 15.9%; Veterans: 10.5%; Ancestry: 36.1% Irish, 23.7% Italian, 16.2% English, 16.1% German, 10.7% French

Employment: 9.5% management, business, and financial, 3.1% computer, engineering, and science, 8.1% education, legal, community service, arts, and media, 6.1% healthcare practitioners, 15.1% service, 33.2% sales and office, 11.1% natural resources, construction, and maintenance, 13.8% production, transportation, and material moving

Income: Per capita: $26,541; Median household: $64,722; Average household: $72,234; Households with income of $100,000 or more: 26.0%; Poverty rate: 13.4%

Educational Attainment: High school diploma or higher: 96.1%; Bachelor's degree or higher: 21.7%; Graduate/professional degree or higher: 6.0%

School District(s)
Stillwater Central SD (PK-12)

    2014-15 Enrollment: 1,197 . . . . (518) 373-6100

Housing: Homeownership rate: 72.2%; Median home value: $193,400; Median year structure built: 1959; Homeowner vacancy rate: 0.0%; Median selected monthly owner costs: $1,475 with a mortgage, $560 without a mortgage; Median gross rent: $894 per month; Rental vacancy rate: 10.4%

Health Insurance: 95.6% have insurance; 69.9% have private insurance; 36.7% have public insurance; 4.4% do not have insurance; 1.1% of children under 18 do not have insurance

Transportation: Commute: 97.3% car, 0.0% public transportation, 0.8% walk, 1.2% work from home; Mean travel time to work: 29.0 minutes

VICTORY (village). Covers a land area of 0.525 square miles and a water area of 0 square miles. Located at 43.09° N. Lat; 73.59° W. Long. Elevation is 203 feet.

Population: 471; Growth (since 2000): -13.4%; Density: 896.3 persons per square mile; Race: 97.2% White, 1.7% Black/African American, 0.0% Asian, 1.1% American Indian/Alaska Native, 0.0% Native Hawaiian/Other Pacific Islander, 0.0% Two or more races, 0.0% Hispanic of any race; Average household size: 2.59; Median age: 35.5; Age under 18: 23.8%; Age 65 and over: 11.3%; Males per 100 females: 101.0; Marriage status: 31.6% never married, 51.7% now married, 3.5% separated, 4.0% widowed, 12.6% divorced; Foreign born: 0.4%; Speak English only: 97.6%; With disability: 14.4%; Veterans: 11.4%; Ancestry: 33.1% American, 25.1% Irish, 18.7% French, 14.2% German, 8.1% Italian

Employment: 6.5% management, business, and financial, 3.3% computer, engineering, and science, 18.2% education, legal, community service, arts, and media, 2.3% healthcare practitioners, 26.6% service, 22.0% sales and office, 15.9% natural resources, construction, and maintenance, 5.1% production, transportation, and material moving

Income: Per capita: $22,783; Median household: $51,250; Average household: $57,948; Households with income of $100,000 or more: 13.7%; Poverty rate: 12.5%

Educational Attainment: High school diploma or higher: 85.5%; Bachelor's degree or higher: 22.1%; Graduate/professional degree or higher: 11.0%

Housing: Homeownership rate: 74.7%; Median home value: $125,000; Median year structure built: 1942; Homeowner vacancy rate: 8.2%; Median selected monthly owner costs: $1,490 with a mortgage, $496 without a mortgage; Median gross rent: $900 per month; Rental vacancy rate: 0.0%

Health Insurance: 88.7% have insurance; 63.5% have private insurance; 35.2% have public insurance; 11.3% do not have insurance; 13.4% of children under 18 do not have insurance

Transportation: Commute: 93.2% car, 0.0% public transportation, 0.0% walk, 6.8% work from home; Mean travel time to work: 27.0 minutes

VICTORY MILLS (unincorporated postal area)
ZCTA: 12884

    Covers a land area of 0.498 square miles and a water area of 0 square miles. Located at 43.09° N. Lat; 73.59° W. Long. Elevation is 203 feet.

    Population: 293; Growth (since 2000): n/a; Density: 588.2 persons per square mile; Race: 97.3% White, 2.7% Black/African American, 0.0% Asian, 0.0% American Indian/Alaska Native, 0.0% Native Hawaiian/Other Pacific Islander, 0.0% Two or more races, 0.0% Hispanic of any race; Average household size: 2.33; Median age: 47.5; Age under 18: 15.7%; Age 65 and over: 10.2%; Males per 100 females: 98.4; Marriage status: 24.7% never married, 48.6% now married, 4.5% separated, 5.3% widowed, 21.5% divorced; Foreign born: 0.0%; Speak English only: 100.0%; With disability: 22.9%; Veterans: 8.1%; Ancestry:

27.0% French, 25.3% Irish, 22.5% American, 18.8% German, 9.6% Italian

Employment: 6.6% management, business, and financial, 1.5% computer, engineering, and science, 8.1% education, legal, community service, arts, and media, 2.2% healthcare practitioners, 50.0% service, 7.4% sales and office, 9.6% natural resources, construction, and maintenance, 14.7% production, transportation, and material moving

Income: Per capita: $23,802; Median household: $46,250; Average household: $53,794; Households with income of $100,000 or more: 14.3%; Poverty rate: 15.0%

Educational Attainment: High school diploma or higher: 80.5%; Bachelor's degree or higher: 12.6%; Graduate/professional degree or higher: 6.0%

Housing: Homeownership rate: 77.0%; Median home value: $105,500; Median year structure built: Before 1940; Homeowner vacancy rate: 5.3%; Median selected monthly owner costs: $1,148 with a mortgage, $422 without a mortgage; Median gross rent: $944 per month; Rental vacancy rate: 0.0%

Health Insurance: 82.3% have insurance; 53.6% have private insurance; 36.5% have public insurance; 17.7% do not have insurance; 32.6% of children under 18 do not have insurance

Transportation: Commute: 100.0% car, 0.0% public transportation, 0.0% walk, 0.0% work from home; Mean travel time to work: 25.6 minutes

---

WATERFORD (town). Covers a land area of 6.567 square miles and a water area of 0.845 square miles. Located at 42.80° N. Lat; 73.69° W. Long. Elevation is 69 feet.

History: Incorporated 1794.

Population: 8,412; Growth (since 2000): -1.2%; Density: 1,281.0 persons per square mile; Race: 91.9% White, 1.7% Black/African American, 2.1% Asian, 0.0% American Indian/Alaska Native, 0.0% Native Hawaiian/Other Pacific Islander, 3.5% Two or more races, 1.6% Hispanic of any race; Average household size: 2.26; Median age: 40.1; Age under 18: 18.2%; Age 65 and over: 13.3%; Males per 100 females: 96.0; Marriage status: 36.6% never married, 48.8% now married, 1.9% separated, 5.7% widowed, 8.9% divorced; Foreign born: 5.4%; Speak English only: 93.1%; With disability: 13.9%; Veterans: 9.1%; Ancestry: 26.6% Irish, 19.3% Italian, 12.1% French, 11.4% English, 11.1% German

Employment: 12.7% management, business, and financial, 5.0% computer, engineering, and science, 8.9% education, legal, community service, arts, and media, 5.6% healthcare practitioners, 19.1% service, 27.6% sales and office, 8.7% natural resources, construction, and maintenance, 12.6% production, transportation, and material moving

Income: Per capita: $30,761; Median household: $60,387; Average household: $68,109; Households with income of $100,000 or more: 20.1%; Poverty rate: 8.0%

Educational Attainment: High school diploma or higher: 92.7%; Bachelor's degree or higher: 25.6%; Graduate/professional degree or higher: 9.1%

School District(s)
Waterford-Halfmoon Union Free SD (KG-12)
    2014-15 Enrollment: 818 . . . . (518) 237-0800

Housing: Homeownership rate: 57.2%; Median home value: $203,700; Median year structure built: 1958; Homeowner vacancy rate: 1.8%; Median selected monthly owner costs: $1,492 with a mortgage, $532 without a mortgage; Median gross rent: $854 per month; Rental vacancy rate: 2.5%

Health Insurance: 93.0% have insurance; 81.5% have private insurance; 26.0% have public insurance; 7.0% do not have insurance; 9.1% of children under 18 do not have insurance

Safety: Violent crime rate: 3.6 per 10,000 population; Property crime rate: 36.0 per 10,000 population

Transportation: Commute: 88.7% car, 1.3% public transportation, 2.9% walk, 6.8% work from home; Mean travel time to work: 21.6 minutes

Additional Information Contacts
Town of Waterford . . . . (518) 235-8282
    http://www.town.waterford.ny.us

WATERFORD (village). Covers a land area of 0.283 square miles and a water area of 0.075 square miles. Located at 42.79° N. Lat; 73.68° W. Long. Elevation is 69 feet.

Population: 2,233; Growth (since 2000): 1.3%; Density: 7,894.9 persons per square mile; Race: 88.4% White, 3.4% Black/African American, 5.1% Asian, 0.0% American Indian/Alaska Native, 0.0% Native Hawaiian/Other Pacific Islander, 2.9% Two or more races, 4.6% Hispanic of any race;

Average household size: 2.18; Median age: 38.6; Age under 18: 15.3%; Age 65 and over: 15.2%; Males per 100 females: 97.2; Marriage status: 41.5% never married, 43.4% now married, 3.3% separated, 3.5% widowed, 11.6% divorced; Foreign born: 3.5%; Speak English only: 93.9%; With disability: 18.8%; Veterans: 8.5%; Ancestry: 34.6% Irish, 20.2% Italian, 12.6% French, 12.0% English, 9.6% German

Employment: 14.6% management, business, and financial, 4.4% computer, engineering, and science, 9.8% education, legal, community service, arts, and media, 1.8% healthcare practitioners, 24.0% service, 24.5% sales and office, 10.4% natural resources, construction, and maintenance, 10.5% production, transportation, and material moving

Income: Per capita: $25,608; Median household: $47,386; Average household: $54,552; Households with income of $100,000 or more: 11.5%; Poverty rate: 13.5%

Educational Attainment: High school diploma or higher: 89.4%; Bachelor's degree or higher: 23.4%; Graduate/professional degree or higher: 8.5%

School District(s)
Waterford-Halfmoon Union Free SD (KG-12)
    2014-15 Enrollment: 818 . . . . (518) 237-0800

Housing: Homeownership rate: 46.2%; Median home value: $173,200; Median year structure built: Before 1940; Homeowner vacancy rate: 2.7%; Median selected monthly owner costs: $1,441 with a mortgage, $490 without a mortgage; Median gross rent: $769 per month; Rental vacancy rate: 0.0%

Health Insurance: 89.0% have insurance; 72.5% have private insurance; 32.6% have public insurance; 11.0% do not have insurance; 2.6% of children under 18 do not have insurance

Transportation: Commute: 80.4% car, 3.4% public transportation, 9.2% walk, 5.7% work from home; Mean travel time to work: 21.3 minutes

Additional Information Contacts
Village of Waterford . . . . (518) 235-9898
    http://www.waterfordny.org

WILTON (town). Covers a land area of 35.834 square miles and a water area of 0.118 square miles. Located at 43.15° N. Lat; 73.73° W. Long. Elevation is 348 feet.

Population: 16,561; Growth (since 2000): 32.4%; Density: 462.2 persons per square mile; Race: 95.5% White, 1.6% Black/African American, 1.2% Asian, 0.0% American Indian/Alaska Native, 0.0% Native Hawaiian/Other Pacific Islander, 1.3% Two or more races, 2.5% Hispanic of any race; Average household size: 2.54; Median age: 42.4; Age under 18: 24.8%; Age 65 and over: 13.2%; Males per 100 females: 96.3; Marriage status: 20.5% never married, 62.2% now married, 1.7% separated, 5.6% widowed, 11.7% divorced; Foreign born: 4.8%; Speak English only: 95.9%; With disability: 10.5%; Veterans: 8.3%; Ancestry: 29.3% Irish, 22.2% Italian, 15.7% German, 11.5% English, 9.2% American

Employment: 19.2% management, business, and financial, 7.9% computer, engineering, and science, 15.4% education, legal, community service, arts, and media, 5.9% healthcare practitioners, 14.8% service, 24.4% sales and office, 5.3% natural resources, construction, and maintenance, 7.0% production, transportation, and material moving

Income: Per capita: $35,903; Median household: $75,885; Average household: $91,106; Households with income of $100,000 or more: 36.9%; Poverty rate: 5.3%

Educational Attainment: High school diploma or higher: 94.8%; Bachelor's degree or higher: 40.5%; Graduate/professional degree or higher: 17.7%

School District(s)
South Glens Falls Central SD (KG-12)
    2014-15 Enrollment: 3,189 . . . . (518) 793-9617

Housing: Homeownership rate: 74.8%; Median home value: $248,300; Median year structure built: 1992; Homeowner vacancy rate: 0.7%; Median selected monthly owner costs: $1,720 with a mortgage, $565 without a mortgage; Median gross rent: $1,239 per month; Rental vacancy rate: 4.9%

Health Insurance: 96.5% have insurance; 84.7% have private insurance; 24.7% have public insurance; 3.5% do not have insurance; 2.3% of children under 18 do not have insurance

Transportation: Commute: 93.7% car, 0.6% public transportation, 0.0% walk, 5.1% work from home; Mean travel time to work: 25.1 minutes

Additional Information Contacts
Town of Wilton . . . . (518) 587-1939
    http://www.townofwilton.com

Schenectady County

Located in eastern New York; bounded on the north by Schoharie Creek; crossed by the Mohawk River. Covers a land area of 204.516 square miles, a water area of 4.870 square miles, and is located in the Eastern Time Zone at 42.82° N. Lat., 74.04° W. Long. The county was founded in 1809. County seat is Schenectady.

Schenectady County is part of the Albany-Schenectady-Troy, NY Metropolitan Statistical Area. The entire metro area includes: Albany County, NY; Rensselaer County, NY; Saratoga County, NY; Schenectady County, NY; Schoharie County, NY

Population: 154,796; Growth (since 2000): 5.6%; Density: 756.9 persons per square mile; Race: 78.4% White, 10.2% Black/African American, 4.3% Asian, 0.2% American Indian/Alaska Native, 0.0% Native Hawaiian/Other Pacific Islander, 3.6% two or more races, 6.4% Hispanic of any race; Average household size: 2.65; Median age: 39.9; Age under 18: 22.1%; Age 65 and over: 15.3%; Males per 100 females: 93.7; Marriage status: 35.6% never married, 46.9% now married, 2.1% separated, 7.6% widowed, 9.9% divorced; Foreign born: 9.7%; Speak English only: 89.7%; With disability: 13.1%; Veterans: 7.8%; Ancestry: 19.8% Italian, 17.3% Irish, 14.8% German, 8.3% English, 8.0% Polish
Religion: Six largest groups: 28.6% Catholicism, 3.9% Muslim Estimate, 3.7% Presbyterian-Reformed, 2.1% Lutheran, 2.1% Methodist/Pietist, 1.5% Judaism
Economy: Unemployment rate: 4.3%; Leading industries: 15.6 % retail trade; 13.7 % health care and social assistance; 12.6 % construction; Farms: 169 totaling 19,868 acres; Company size: 4 employ 1,000 or more persons, 5 employ 500 to 999 persons, 63 employ 100 to 499 persons, 3,001 employs less than 100 persons; Business ownership: 3,414 women-owned, 817 Black-owned, 348 Hispanic-owned, 465 Asian-owned, 64 American Indian/Alaska Native-owned
Employment: 13.7% management, business, and financial, 6.1% computer, engineering, and science, 12.2% education, legal, community service, arts, and media, 6.3% healthcare practitioners, 19.4% service, 25.4% sales and office, 7.0% natural resources, construction, and maintenance, 10.0% production, transportation, and material moving
Income: Per capita: $28,902; Median household: $58,114; Average household: $72,662; Households with income of $100,000 or more: 23.5%; Poverty rate: 12.6%
Educational Attainment: High school diploma or higher: 90.5%; Bachelor's degree or higher: 30.5%; Graduate/professional degree or higher: 14.1%
Housing: Homeownership rate: 66.5%; Median home value: $165,800; Median year structure built: 1951; Homeowner vacancy rate: 2.2%; Median selected monthly owner costs: $1,522 with a mortgage, $639 without a mortgage; Median gross rent: $845 per month; Rental vacancy rate: 6.8%
Vital Statistics: Birth rate: 112.1 per 10,000 population; Death rate: 94.5 per 10,000 population; Age-adjusted cancer mortality rate: 161.9 deaths per 100,000 population
Health Insurance: 93.1% have insurance; 71.5% have private insurance; 35.1% have public insurance; 6.9% do not have insurance; 2.6% of children under 18 do not have insurance
Health Care: Physicians: 27.7 per 10,000 population; Dentists: 7.9 per 10,000 population; Hospital beds: 49.0 per 10,000 population; Hospital admissions: 1,834.8 per 10,000 population
Transportation: Commute: 87.9% car, 4.0% public transportation, 3.3% walk, 3.4% work from home; Mean travel time to work: 22.6 minutes
2016 Presidential Election: 43.6% Trump, 50.8% Clinton, 3.9% Johnson, 1.7% Stein
Additional Information Contacts
Schenectady Government . . . . (518) 388-4282
  http://www.schenectadycounty.com

Schenectady County Communities

ALPLAUS (unincorporated postal area)
ZCTA: 12008
  Covers a land area of 0.831 square miles and a water area of 0.175 square miles. Located at 42.85° N. Lat; 73.91° W. Long. Elevation is 259 feet.
  Population: 606; Growth (since 2000): 40.6%; Density: 728.9 persons per square mile; Race: 90.4% White, 0.0% Black/African American, 9.6% Asian, 0.0% American Indian/Alaska Native, 0.0% Native

Hawaiian/Other Pacific Islander, 0.0% Two or more races, 8.6% Hispanic of any race; Average household size: 2.97; Median age: 40.1; Age under 18: 23.4%; Age 65 and over: 13.5%; Males per 100 females: 103.7; Marriage status: 27.6% never married, 58.3% now married, 1.2% separated, 4.3% widowed, 9.8% divorced; Foreign born: 6.6%; Speak English only: 82.8%; With disability: 5.1%; Veterans: 11.4%; Ancestry: 16.8% German, 13.9% Italian, 12.9% Irish, 12.5% Portuguese, 10.4% Dutch
Employment: 3.8% management, business, and financial, 18.8% computer, engineering, and science, 13.2% education, legal, community service, arts, and media, 7.7% healthcare practitioners, 6.4% service, 30.8% sales and office, 5.1% natural resources, construction, and maintenance, 14.1% production, transportation, and material moving
Income: Per capita: $34,215; Median household: $93,250; Average household: $98,016; Households with income of $100,000 or more: 48.3%; Poverty rate: 1.0%
Educational Attainment: High school diploma or higher: 94.4%; Bachelor's degree or higher: 47.2%; Graduate/professional degree or higher: 18.9%
Housing: Homeownership rate: 96.5%; Median home value: $234,400; Median year structure built: Before 1940; Homeowner vacancy rate: 0.0%; Median selected monthly owner costs: $2,188 with a mortgage, $771 without a mortgage; Median gross rent: n/a per month; Rental vacancy rate: 0.0%
Health Insurance: 99.8% have insurance; 89.9% have private insurance; 24.3% have public insurance; 0.2% do not have insurance; 0.0% of children under 18 do not have insurance
Transportation: Commute: 79.5% car, 0.0% public transportation, 0.0% walk, 20.5% work from home; Mean travel time to work: 17.8 minutes

DELANSON (village). Covers a land area of 0.644 square miles and a water area of 0.003 square miles. Located at 42.75° N. Lat; 74.18° W. Long. Elevation is 817 feet.
Population: 390; Growth (since 2000): 1.3%; Density: 605.7 persons per square mile; Race: 99.2% White, 0.0% Black/African American, 0.3% Asian, 0.0% American Indian/Alaska Native, 0.0% Native Hawaiian/Other Pacific Islander, 0.5% Two or more races, 0.5% Hispanic of any race; Average household size: 2.98; Median age: 34.9; Age under 18: 29.7%; Age 65 and over: 12.8%; Males per 100 females: 96.4; Marriage status: 30.1% never married, 59.8% now married, 0.3% separated, 4.9% widowed, 5.2% divorced; Foreign born: 1.5%; Speak English only: 100.0%; With disability: 6.9%; Veterans: 7.3%; Ancestry: 26.2% German, 21.5% Irish, 18.7% American, 17.9% Italian, 11.8% English
Employment: 14.2% management, business, and financial, 8.4% computer, engineering, and science, 9.5% education, legal, community service, arts, and media, 4.2% healthcare practitioners, 21.1% service, 24.7% sales and office, 9.5% natural resources, construction, and maintenance, 8.4% production, transportation, and material moving
Income: Per capita: $27,184; Median household: $70,417; Average household: $78,027; Households with income of $100,000 or more: 30.6%; Poverty rate: 3.8%
Educational Attainment: High school diploma or higher: 98.4%; Bachelor's degree or higher: 24.4%; Graduate/professional degree or higher: 8.7%

School District(s)
Duanesburg Central SD (KG-12)
  2014-15 Enrollment: 763 . . . . (518) 895-2279
Housing: Homeownership rate: 80.2%; Median home value: $158,100; Median year structure built: Before 1940; Homeowner vacancy rate: 0.0%; Median selected monthly owner costs: $1,633 with a mortgage, $655 without a mortgage; Median gross rent: $1,143 per month; Rental vacancy rate: 0.0%
Health Insurance: 97.9% have insurance; 83.6% have private insurance; 23.6% have public insurance; 2.1% do not have insurance; 0.0% of children under 18 do not have insurance
Transportation: Commute: 92.6% car, 2.1% public transportation, 2.7% walk, 2.7% work from home; Mean travel time to work: 28.8 minutes

DUANE LAKE (CDP). Covers a land area of 2.401 square miles and a water area of 0.194 square miles. Located at 42.75° N. Lat; 74.11° W. Long. Elevation is 922 feet.
Population: 361; Growth (since 2000): 1.1%; Density: 150.3 persons per square mile; Race: 85.9% White, 3.3% Black/African American, 0.0% Asian, 0.0% American Indian/Alaska Native, 0.0% Native Hawaiian/Other Pacific Islander, 6.1% Two or more races, 10.8% Hispanic of any race;

Average household size: 2.28; Median age: 48.3; Age under 18: 17.2%; Age 65 and over: 20.5%; Males per 100 females: 97.0; Marriage status: 17.4% never married, 72.6% now married, 0.0% separated, 0.0% widowed, 10.0% divorced; Foreign born: 0.0%; Speak English only: 100.0%; With disability: 4.2%; Veterans: 9.7%; Ancestry: 34.6% German, 18.6% Dutch, 14.1% Polish, 12.7% English, 12.5% French

Employment: 14.2% management, business, and financial, 8.1% computer, engineering, and science, 14.2% education, legal, community service, arts, and media, 7.6% healthcare practitioners, 12.8% service, 28.0% sales and office, 15.2% natural resources, construction, and maintenance, 0.0% production, transportation, and material moving

Income: Per capita: $43,930; Median household: $115,441; Average household: $105,180; Households with income of $100,000 or more: 60.8%; Poverty rate: n/a

Educational Attainment: High school diploma or higher: 100.0%; Bachelor's degree or higher: 56.5%; Graduate/professional degree or higher: 31.3%

Housing: Homeownership rate: 100.0%; Median home value: $269,100; Median year structure built: 1965; Homeowner vacancy rate: 0.0%; Median selected monthly owner costs: $1,823 with a mortgage, n/a without a mortgage; Median gross rent: n/a per month; Rental vacancy rate: 0.0%

Health Insurance: 80.6% have insurance; 80.6% have private insurance; 24.7% have public insurance; 19.4% do not have insurance; 0.0% of children under 18 do not have insurance

Transportation: Commute: 83.4% car, 0.0% public transportation, 9.0% walk, 7.6% work from home; Mean travel time to work: 26.9 minutes

DUANESBURG (CDP).
Covers a land area of 2.449 square miles and a water area of 0.096 square miles. Located at 42.76° N. Lat; 74.13° W. Long. Elevation is 718 feet.

Population: 359; Growth (since 2000): 5.9%; Density: 146.6 persons per square mile; Race: 100.0% White, 0.0% Black/African American, 0.0% Asian, 0.0% American Indian/Alaska Native, 0.0% Native Hawaiian/Other Pacific Islander, 0.0% Two or more races, 13.4% Hispanic of any race; Average household size: 3.59; Median age: 40.8; Age under 18: 22.3%; Age 65 and over: 0.0%; Males per 100 females: 89.8; Marriage status: 29.4% never married, 70.6% now married, 0.0% separated, 0.0% widowed, 0.0% divorced; Foreign born: 0.0%; Speak English only: 84.1%; With disability: 4.5%; Veterans: 19.4%; Ancestry: 40.4% Italian, 37.0% Irish, 15.0% English, 15.0% Polish, 12.3% American

Employment: 11.8% management, business, and financial, 9.0% computer, engineering, and science, 8.4% education, legal, community service, arts, and media, 0.0% healthcare practitioners, 9.0% service, 30.9% sales and office, 21.3% natural resources, construction, and maintenance, 9.6% production, transportation, and material moving

Income: Per capita: $24,947; Median household: n/a; Average household: $71,859; Households with income of $100,000 or more: 32.0%; Poverty rate: 10.0%

Educational Attainment: High school diploma or higher: 100.0%; Bachelor's degree or higher: 22.4%; Graduate/professional degree or higher: 6.5%

Housing: Homeownership rate: 64.0%; Median home value: $162,100; Median year structure built: 1950; Homeowner vacancy rate: 0.0%; Median selected monthly owner costs: $2,015 with a mortgage, n/a without a mortgage; Median gross rent: n/a per month; Rental vacancy rate: 0.0%

Health Insurance: 100.0% have insurance; 100.0% have private insurance; 0.0% have public insurance; 0.0% do not have insurance; 0.0% of children under 18 do not have insurance

Transportation: Commute: 100.0% car, 0.0% public transportation, 0.0% walk, 0.0% work from home; Mean travel time to work: 28.3 minutes

DUANESBURG (town).
Covers a land area of 70.782 square miles and a water area of 1.250 square miles. Located at 42.78° N. Lat; 74.17° W. Long. Elevation is 718 feet.

Population: 6,280; Growth (since 2000): 8.1%; Density: 88.7 persons per square mile; Race: 95.2% White, 0.2% Black/African American, 2.0% Asian, 0.0% American Indian/Alaska Native, 0.0% Native Hawaiian/Other Pacific Islander, 2.3% Two or more races, 2.6% Hispanic of any race; Average household size: 3.18; Median age: 41.9; Age under 18: 20.5%; Age 65 and over: 9.8%; Males per 100 females: 100.5; Marriage status: 33.8% never married, 57.3% now married, 0.6% separated, 3.3% widowed, 5.6% divorced; Foreign born: 3.5%; Speak English only: 96.6%; With disability: 9.9%; Veterans: 10.4%; Ancestry: 26.2% Irish, 23.5% German, 11.5% English, 10.9% Italian, 9.3% French

Employment: 12.0% management, business, and financial, 8.2% computer, engineering, and science, 9.2% education, legal, community service, arts, and media, 5.7% healthcare practitioners, 16.3% service, 27.2% sales and office, 13.3% natural resources, construction, and maintenance, 8.2% production, transportation, and material moving

Income: Per capita: $29,867; Median household: $81,777; Average household: $87,863; Households with income of $100,000 or more: 38.5%; Poverty rate: 5.3%

Educational Attainment: High school diploma or higher: 93.4%; Bachelor's degree or higher: 27.1%; Graduate/professional degree or higher: 13.2%

Housing: Homeownership rate: 87.7%; Median home value: $209,000; Median year structure built: 1974; Homeowner vacancy rate: 0.0%; Median selected monthly owner costs: $1,778 with a mortgage, $704 without a mortgage; Median gross rent: $1,248 per month; Rental vacancy rate: 0.0%

Health Insurance: 93.4% have insurance; 82.0% have private insurance; 21.0% have public insurance; 6.6% do not have insurance; 2.1% of children under 18 do not have insurance

Transportation: Commute: 88.6% car, 0.1% public transportation, 1.1% walk, 9.5% work from home; Mean travel time to work: 27.0 minutes

Additional Information Contacts

Town of Duanesburg . . . . (518) 895-8920
  http://www.duanesburg.net

EAST GLENVILLE (CDP).
Covers a land area of 7.165 square miles and a water area of 0.287 square miles. Located at 42.86° N. Lat; 73.92° W. Long. Elevation is 361 feet.

Population: 6,621; Growth (since 2000): 9.2%; Density: 924.0 persons per square mile; Race: 92.7% White, 0.9% Black/African American, 2.4% Asian, 0.0% American Indian/Alaska Native, 0.0% Native Hawaiian/Other Pacific Islander, 2.3% Two or more races, 3.7% Hispanic of any race; Average household size: 2.60; Median age: 44.2; Age under 18: 22.3%; Age 65 and over: 19.7%; Males per 100 females: 92.5; Marriage status: 26.6% never married, 55.7% now married, 1.7% separated, 10.2% widowed, 7.5% divorced; Foreign born: 4.5%; Speak English only: 93.9%; With disability: 9.8%; Veterans: 10.4%; Ancestry: 24.1% Irish, 18.1% Italian, 17.9% German, 12.3% Polish, 9.3% English

Employment: 12.1% management, business, and financial, 11.5% computer, engineering, and science, 15.4% education, legal, community service, arts, and media, 8.1% healthcare practitioners, 18.6% service, 21.2% sales and office, 6.2% natural resources, construction, and maintenance, 7.0% production, transportation, and material moving

Income: Per capita: $31,590; Median household: $72,295; Average household: $80,617; Households with income of $100,000 or more: 30.4%; Poverty rate: 4.4%

Educational Attainment: High school diploma or higher: 96.4%; Bachelor's degree or higher: 37.2%; Graduate/professional degree or higher: 17.2%

Housing: Homeownership rate: 76.6%; Median home value: $199,200; Median year structure built: 1967; Homeowner vacancy rate: 0.0%; Median selected monthly owner costs: $1,743 with a mortgage, $643 without a mortgage; Median gross rent: $914 per month; Rental vacancy rate: 4.5%

Health Insurance: 95.3% have insurance; 86.5% have private insurance; 24.8% have public insurance; 4.7% do not have insurance; 3.8% of children under 18 do not have insurance

Transportation: Commute: 89.6% car, 0.3% public transportation, 4.9% walk, 4.5% work from home; Mean travel time to work: 21.8 minutes

GLENVILLE (town).
Covers a land area of 49.186 square miles and a water area of 1.490 square miles. Located at 42.89° N. Lat; 73.99° W. Long. Elevation is 705 feet.

Population: 29,489; Growth (since 2000): 4.6%; Density: 599.5 persons per square mile; Race: 94.5% White, 1.7% Black/African American, 1.1% Asian, 0.0% American Indian/Alaska Native, 0.0% Native Hawaiian/Other Pacific Islander, 2.1% Two or more races, 3.1% Hispanic of any race; Average household size: 2.59; Median age: 44.1; Age under 18: 21.6%; Age 65 and over: 18.7%; Males per 100 females: 94.0; Marriage status: 28.4% never married, 53.8% now married, 1.2% separated, 8.1% widowed, 9.6% divorced; Foreign born: 3.4%; Speak English only: 95.1%; With disability: 12.1%; Veterans: 9.6%; Ancestry: 23.5% Irish, 21.6% Italian, 19.8% German, 12.3% English, 9.0% Polish

Employment: 14.9% management, business, and financial, 6.8% computer, engineering, and science, 13.1% education, legal, community service, arts, and media, 8.3% healthcare practitioners, 14.9% service,

27.1% sales and office, 6.4% natural resources, construction, and maintenance, 8.6% production, transportation, and material moving
Income: Per capita: $31,712; Median household: $67,308; Average household: $78,321; Households with income of $100,000 or more: 28.2%; Poverty rate: 4.9%
Educational Attainment: High school diploma or higher: 95.0%; Bachelor's degree or higher: 34.8%; Graduate/professional degree or higher: 16.6%
Housing: Homeownership rate: 76.3%; Median home value: $183,000; Median year structure built: 1958; Homeowner vacancy rate: 1.2%; Median selected monthly owner costs: $1,612 with a mortgage, $645 without a mortgage; Median gross rent: $945 per month; Rental vacancy rate: 7.9%
Health Insurance: 96.0% have insurance; 82.7% have private insurance; 29.0% have public insurance; 4.0% do not have insurance; 2.5% of children under 18 do not have insurance
Safety: Violent crime rate: 5.0 per 10,000 population; Property crime rate: 200.7 per 10,000 population
Transportation: Commute: 92.5% car, 1.0% public transportation, 2.8% walk, 2.8% work from home; Mean travel time to work: 23.0 minutes
Additional Information Contacts
Town of Glenville . . . . (518) 688-1200
http://www.townofglenville.org

MARIAVILLE LAKE (CDP). Covers a land area of 5.623 square miles and a water area of 0.380 square miles. Located at 42.82° N. Lat; 74.13° W. Long. Elevation is 1,289 feet.
Population: 609; Growth (since 2000): -14.2%; Density: 108.3 persons per square mile; Race: 95.1% White, 0.0% Black/African American, 2.5% Asian, 0.0% American Indian/Alaska Native, 0.0% Native Hawaiian/Other Pacific Islander, 2.5% Two or more races, 0.0% Hispanic of any race; Average household size: 3.17; Median age: 43.3; Age under 18: 19.5%; Age 65 and over: 5.4%; Males per 100 females: 109.9; Marriage status: 40.7% never married, 52.8% now married, 0.0% separated, 0.9% widowed, 5.7% divorced; Foreign born: 3.1%; Speak English only: 85.7%; With disability: 11.2%; Veterans: 7.6%; Ancestry: 28.7% Irish, 20.2% English, 19.5% French, 15.9% German, 7.4% American
Employment: 8.0% management, business, and financial, 20.8% computer, engineering, and science, 10.1% education, legal, community service, arts, and media, 0.0% healthcare practitioners, 13.1% service, 30.0% sales and office, 4.3% natural resources, construction, and maintenance, 13.8% production, transportation, and material moving
Income: Per capita: $27,801; Median household: $80,417; Average household: $83,271; Households with income of $100,000 or more: 36.9%; Poverty rate: 13.1%
Educational Attainment: High school diploma or higher: 96.2%; Bachelor's degree or higher: 39.9%; Graduate/professional degree or higher: 13.1%
Housing: Homeownership rate: 100.0%; Median home value: $203,100; Median year structure built: 1975; Homeowner vacancy rate: 0.0%; Median selected monthly owner costs: $1,799 with a mortgage, $904 without a mortgage; Median gross rent: n/a per month; Rental vacancy rate: 0.0%
Health Insurance: 92.2% have insurance; 83.5% have private insurance; 17.4% have public insurance; 7.8% do not have insurance; 0.0% of children under 18 do not have insurance
Transportation: Commute: 94.8% car, 0.0% public transportation, 0.0% walk, 5.2% work from home; Mean travel time to work: 32.8 minutes

NISKAYUNA (town). Covers a land area of 14.152 square miles and a water area of 0.890 square miles. Located at 42.80° N. Lat; 73.87° W. Long. Elevation is 292 feet.
Population: 22,050; Growth (since 2000): 8.6%; Density: 1,558.1 persons per square mile; Race: 86.2% White, 3.2% Black/African American, 7.6% Asian, 0.1% American Indian/Alaska Native, 0.0% Native Hawaiian/Other Pacific Islander, 2.5% Two or more races, 3.2% Hispanic of any race; Average household size: 2.76; Median age: 43.6; Age under 18: 24.5%; Age 65 and over: 18.0%; Males per 100 females: 93.0; Marriage status: 24.1% never married, 61.0% now married, 1.1% separated, 7.2% widowed, 7.7% divorced; Foreign born: 14.3%; Speak English only: 84.7%; With disability: 11.8%; Veterans: 6.4%; Ancestry: 21.3% Italian, 19.1% German, 16.6% Irish, 9.8% English, 9.0% Polish
Employment: 22.7% management, business, and financial, 13.1% computer, engineering, and science, 16.8% education, legal, community service, arts, and media, 8.1% healthcare practitioners, 8.0% service, 20.7% sales and office, 5.8% natural resources, construction, and maintenance, 4.7% production, transportation, and material moving

Income: Per capita: $44,950; Median household: $98,063; Average household: $122,567; Households with income of $100,000 or more: 49.1%; Poverty rate: 5.2%
Educational Attainment: High school diploma or higher: 96.1%; Bachelor's degree or higher: 58.7%; Graduate/professional degree or higher: 33.3%
Housing: Homeownership rate: 83.1%; Median home value: $255,100; Median year structure built: 1961; Homeowner vacancy rate: 0.2%; Median selected monthly owner costs: $1,935 with a mortgage, $839 without a mortgage; Median gross rent: $1,054 per month; Rental vacancy rate: 9.1%
Health Insurance: 96.7% have insurance; 86.4% have private insurance; 24.6% have public insurance; 3.3% do not have insurance; 0.9% of children under 18 do not have insurance
Safety: Violent crime rate: 4.9 per 10,000 population; Property crime rate: 140.7 per 10,000 population
Transportation: Commute: 93.1% car, 0.6% public transportation, 1.4% walk, 3.7% work from home; Mean travel time to work: 20.9 minutes
Additional Information Contacts
Town of Niskayuna . . . . (518) 386-4500
http://www.niskayuna.org

PATTERSONVILLE (unincorporated postal area)
ZCTA: 12137
Covers a land area of 23.978 square miles and a water area of 0.396 square miles. Located at 42.86° N. Lat; 74.13° W. Long. Elevation is 269 feet.
Population: 1,825; Growth (since 2000): 18.2%; Density: 76.1 persons per square mile; Race: 92.0% White, 0.0% Black/African American, 3.6% Asian, 0.0% American Indian/Alaska Native, 0.0% Native Hawaiian/Other Pacific Islander, 4.4% Two or more races, 1.8% Hispanic of any race; Average household size: 2.97; Median age: 41.0; Age under 18: 18.7%; Age 65 and over: 11.9%; Males per 100 females: 98.7; Marriage status: 36.5% never married, 52.9% now married, 0.4% separated, 4.3% widowed, 6.3% divorced; Foreign born: 4.1%; Speak English only: 93.5%; With disability: 11.0%; Veterans: 9.6%; Ancestry: 25.3% Irish, 19.2% German, 16.2% French, 15.4% Polish, 11.7% Italian
Employment: 12.6% management, business, and financial, 6.7% computer, engineering, and science, 12.1% education, legal, community service, arts, and media, 4.5% healthcare practitioners, 15.1% service, 20.7% sales and office, 9.1% natural resources, construction, and maintenance, 19.1% production, transportation, and material moving
Income: Per capita: $25,611; Median household: $61,563; Average household: $69,064; Households with income of $100,000 or more: 25.8%; Poverty rate: 9.2%
Educational Attainment: High school diploma or higher: 92.3%; Bachelor's degree or higher: 17.2%; Graduate/professional degree or higher: 4.8%
Housing: Homeownership rate: 85.0%; Median home value: $190,800; Median year structure built: 1965; Homeowner vacancy rate: 0.0%; Median selected monthly owner costs: $1,599 with a mortgage, $596 without a mortgage; Median gross rent: $1,064 per month; Rental vacancy rate: 13.2%
Health Insurance: 93.0% have insurance; 72.7% have private insurance; 31.6% have public insurance; 7.0% do not have insurance; 3.8% of children under 18 do not have insurance
Transportation: Commute: 93.8% car, 0.0% public transportation, 1.3% walk, 2.0% work from home; Mean travel time to work: 28.7 minutes

PRINCETOWN (town). Covers a land area of 23.924 square miles and a water area of 0.287 square miles. Located at 42.81° N. Lat; 74.08° W. Long. Elevation is 420 feet.
Population: 2,068; Growth (since 2000): -3.0%; Density: 86.4 persons per square mile; Race: 99.7% White, 0.3% Black/African American, 0.0% Asian, 0.0% American Indian/Alaska Native, 0.0% Native Hawaiian/Other Pacific Islander, 0.0% Two or more races, 1.5% Hispanic of any race; Average household size: 2.76; Median age: 47.9; Age under 18: 16.4%; Age 65 and over: 19.8%; Males per 100 females: 100.5; Marriage status: 30.6% never married, 55.8% now married, 0.6% separated, 5.7% widowed, 7.8% divorced; Foreign born: 1.9%; Speak English only: 94.8%; With disability: 9.1%; Veterans: 9.7%; Ancestry: 19.2% Italian, 19.0% Irish, 17.7% German, 15.1% Polish, 11.7% English
Employment: 13.0% management, business, and financial, 7.5% computer, engineering, and science, 14.7% education, legal, community service, arts, and media, 3.9% healthcare practitioners, 14.9% service,

21.5% sales and office, 15.5% natural resources, construction, and maintenance, 9.1% production, transportation, and material moving
Income: Per capita: $37,188; Median household: $81,050; Average household: $90,905; Households with income of $100,000 or more: 34.9%; Poverty rate: 5.0%
Educational Attainment: High school diploma or higher: 93.9%; Bachelor's degree or higher: 35.0%; Graduate/professional degree or higher: 14.8%
Housing: Homeownership rate: 86.7%; Median home value: $219,000; Median year structure built: 1974; Homeowner vacancy rate: 0.6%; Median selected monthly owner costs: $1,703 with a mortgage, $596 without a mortgage; Median gross rent: $824 per month; Rental vacancy rate: 13.2%
Health Insurance: 93.9% have insurance; 82.8% have private insurance; 30.5% have public insurance; 6.1% do not have insurance; 7.6% of children under 18 do not have insurance
Transportation: Commute: 93.2% car, 0.5% public transportation, 1.7% walk, 4.1% work from home; Mean travel time to work: 26.2 minutes

ROTTERDAM (CDP).
Covers a land area of 6.933 square miles and a water area of 0.006 square miles. Located at 42.78° N. Lat; 73.95° W. Long. Elevation is 338 feet.
Population: 20,949; Growth (since 2000): 2.0%; Density: 3,021.4 persons per square mile; Race: 91.3% White, 2.8% Black/African American, 2.0% Asian, 0.1% American Indian/Alaska Native, 0.0% Native Hawaiian/Other Pacific Islander, 2.9% Two or more races, 3.5% Hispanic of any race; Average household size: 2.67; Median age: 41.7; Age under 18: 21.5%; Age 65 and over: 18.0%; Males per 100 females: 90.9; Marriage status: 31.0% never married, 48.5% now married, 2.0% separated, 9.4% widowed, 11.1% divorced; Foreign born: 4.3%; Speak English only: 93.5%; With disability: 12.2%; Veterans: 9.1%; Ancestry: 33.7% Italian, 21.6% Irish, 16.3% German, 10.2% Polish, 8.5% English
Employment: 13.6% management, business, and financial, 4.0% computer, engineering, and science, 9.4% education, legal, community service, arts, and media, 5.4% healthcare practitioners, 22.2% service, 27.1% sales and office, 7.4% natural resources, construction, and maintenance, 10.9% production, transportation, and material moving
Income: Per capita: $28,778; Median household: $60,269; Average household: $71,480; Households with income of $100,000 or more: 20.9%; Poverty rate: 7.0%
Educational Attainment: High school diploma or higher: 93.2%; Bachelor's degree or higher: 22.2%; Graduate/professional degree or higher: 7.9%
Housing: Homeownership rate: 80.6%; Median home value: $158,500; Median year structure built: 1955; Homeowner vacancy rate: 4.4%; Median selected monthly owner costs: $1,397 with a mortgage, $516 without a mortgage; Median gross rent: $875 per month; Rental vacancy rate: 3.3%
Health Insurance: 94.9% have insurance; 78.9% have private insurance; 31.4% have public insurance; 5.1% do not have insurance; 1.2% of children under 18 do not have insurance
Transportation: Commute: 94.3% car, 0.8% public transportation, 1.1% walk, 3.1% work from home; Mean travel time to work: 21.4 minutes

ROTTERDAM (town).
Covers a land area of 35.692 square miles and a water area of 0.768 square miles. Located at 42.81° N. Lat; 74.01° W. Long. Elevation is 338 feet.
History: Settled c.1670, incorporated 1821.
Population: 29,174; Growth (since 2000): 3.0%; Density: 817.4 persons per square mile; Race: 92.9% White, 2.1% Black/African American, 1.9% Asian, 0.1% American Indian/Alaska Native, 0.0% Native Hawaiian/Other Pacific Islander, 2.2% Two or more races, 2.9% Hispanic of any race; Average household size: 2.66; Median age: 42.0; Age under 18: 21.9%; Age 65 and over: 17.3%; Males per 100 females: 92.2; Marriage status: 31.2% never married, 49.6% now married, 1.9% separated, 8.6% widowed, 10.7% divorced; Foreign born: 3.9%; Speak English only: 94.4%; With disability: 11.6%; Veterans: 9.3%; Ancestry: 32.0% Italian, 23.3% Irish, 16.8% German, 11.0% Polish, 8.8% English
Employment: 14.3% management, business, and financial, 4.0% computer, engineering, and science, 10.1% education, legal, community service, arts, and media, 5.8% healthcare practitioners, 21.2% service, 26.0% sales and office, 7.4% natural resources, construction, and maintenance, 11.3% production, transportation, and material moving
Income: Per capita: $30,366; Median household: $65,106; Average household: $75,273; Households with income of $100,000 or more: 24.1%; Poverty rate: 6.0%

Educational Attainment: High school diploma or higher: 93.9%; Bachelor's degree or higher: 25.0%; Graduate/professional degree or higher: 9.6%
Housing: Homeownership rate: 79.3%; Median home value: $166,500; Median year structure built: 1958; Homeowner vacancy rate: 3.7%; Median selected monthly owner costs: $1,469 with a mortgage, $554 without a mortgage; Median gross rent: $919 per month; Rental vacancy rate: 3.6%
Health Insurance: 95.3% have insurance; 81.5% have private insurance; 29.1% have public insurance; 4.7% do not have insurance; 1.0% of children under 18 do not have insurance
Safety: Violent crime rate: 9.5 per 10,000 population; Property crime rate: 310.3 per 10,000 population
Transportation: Commute: 93.9% car, 0.7% public transportation, 1.4% walk, 3.3% work from home; Mean travel time to work: 21.9 minutes
Additional Information Contacts
Town of Rotterdam . . . . (518) 355-7575
  http://rotterdamny.org

ROTTERDAM JUNCTION (unincorporated postal area)
ZCTA: 12150
  Covers a land area of 1.096 square miles and a water area of 0.094 square miles. Located at 42.88° N. Lat; 74.05° W. Long. Elevation is 249 feet.
Population: 774; Growth (since 2000): -7.4%; Density: 706.0 persons per square mile; Race: 98.7% White, 0.0% Black/African American, 1.3% Asian, 0.0% American Indian/Alaska Native, 0.0% Native Hawaiian/Other Pacific Islander, 0.0% Two or more races, 0.0% Hispanic of any race; Average household size: 2.55; Median age: 47.0; Age under 18: 23.1%; Age 65 and over: 22.0%; Males per 100 females: 91.2; Marriage status: 33.3% never married, 43.2% now married, 0.0% separated, 7.7% widowed, 15.8% divorced; Foreign born: 5.7%; Speak English only: 96.4%; With disability: 14.0%; Veterans: 9.4%; Ancestry: 25.2% Italian, 24.9% Irish, 12.7% American, 11.9% English, 9.7% German
Employment: 11.5% management, business, and financial, 2.7% computer, engineering, and science, 16.1% education, legal, community service, arts, and media, 18.0% healthcare practitioners, 4.0% service, 23.3% sales and office, 10.7% natural resources, construction, and maintenance, 13.7% production, transportation, and material moving
Income: Per capita: $27,631; Median household: $64,286; Average household: $68,392; Households with income of $100,000 or more: 22.4%; Poverty rate: 1.9%
Educational Attainment: High school diploma or higher: 97.3%; Bachelor's degree or higher: 32.1%; Graduate/professional degree or higher: 10.4%
Housing: Homeownership rate: 95.7%; Median home value: $174,300; Median year structure built: 1966; Homeowner vacancy rate: 0.0%; Median selected monthly owner costs: $1,510 with a mortgage, $650 without a mortgage; Median gross rent: n/a per month; Rental vacancy rate: 0.0%
Health Insurance: 91.5% have insurance; 84.0% have private insurance; 31.7% have public insurance; 8.5% do not have insurance; 0.0% of children under 18 do not have insurance
Transportation: Commute: 84.7% car, 0.0% public transportation, 0.0% walk, 15.3% work from home; Mean travel time to work: 24.2 minutes

SCHENECTADY (city).
County seat. Covers a land area of 10.779 square miles and a water area of 0.185 square miles. Located at 42.80° N. Lat; 73.93° W. Long. Elevation is 243 feet.
History: The site of Schenectady was called "Schonowe" meaning "big flats" by the Mohawk people. In 1662, Arent Van Curler, with a small group of Dutchmen, emigrated from Albany to the "Groote Vlachte" ("big flats") and purchased land. The first major migration of English into Schenectady began about 1700. In 1848, a locomotive factory was organized that was Schenectady's largest industry for a half century. In 1886, Thomas A. Edison bought two abandoned factory buildings for the Edison Company. In 1892 it was consolidated with the Thompson-Huston Company of Lynn, Massachusetts, to form the General Electric Company. Schenectady became the city that "lights and hauls the world."
Population: 65,735; Growth (since 2000): 6.3%; Density: 6,098.2 persons per square mile; Race: 59.9% White, 21.2% Black/African American, 6.0% Asian, 0.5% American Indian/Alaska Native, 0.0% Native Hawaiian/Other Pacific Islander, 5.4% Two or more races, 10.9% Hispanic of any race; Average household size: 2.59; Median age: 35.1; Age under 18: 22.0%; Age 65 and over: 12.5%; Males per 100 females: 93.7; Marriage status:

45.0% never married, 36.7% now married, 3.1% separated, 7.5% widowed, 10.9% divorced; Foreign born: 14.5%; Speak English only: 86.0%; With disability: 15.0%; Veterans: 6.3%; Ancestry: 13.9% Italian, 11.1% Irish, 9.2% German, 5.7% Polish, 5.4% English

Employment: 9.8% management, business, and financial, 4.0% computer, engineering, and science, 11.4% education, legal, community service, arts, and media, 5.2% healthcare practitioners, 25.2% service, 25.8% sales and office, 6.5% natural resources, construction, and maintenance, 12.1% production, transportation, and material moving

Income: Per capita: $21,257; Median household: $40,755; Average household: $50,740; Households with income of $100,000 or more: 11.1%; Poverty rate: 22.8%

Educational Attainment: High school diploma or higher: 84.3%; Bachelor's degree or higher: 21.1%; Graduate/professional degree or higher: 8.3%

School District(s)
Guilderland Central SD (KG-12)
   2014-15 Enrollment: 4,984 . . . . (518) 456-6200
Niskayuna Central SD (KG-12)
   2014-15 Enrollment: 4,114 . . . . (518) 377-4666
Rotterdam-Mohonasen Central SD (KG-12)
   2014-15 Enrollment: 2,818 . . . . (518) 356-8200
Schalmont Central SD (KG-12)
   2014-15 Enrollment: 1,822 . . . . (518) 355-9200
Schenectady City SD (PK-12)
   2014-15 Enrollment: 10,066 . . . . (518) 370-8100

Four-year College(s)
Union College (Private, Not-for-profit)
   Fall 2014 Enrollment: 2,242 . . . . (518) 388-6000
   2015-16 Tuition: In-state $50,013; Out-of-state $50,013
Union Graduate College (Private, Not-for-profit)
   Fall 2014 Enrollment: 431 . . . . (518) 631-9900

Two-year College(s)
Belanger School of Nursing (Private, Not-for-profit)
   Fall 2014 Enrollment: 127 . . . . (518) 243-4471
   2015-16 Tuition: In-state $9,632; Out-of-state $9,632
Schenectady County Community College (Public)
   Fall 2014 Enrollment: 6,497 . . . . (518) 381-1200
   2015-16 Tuition: In-state $4,054; Out-of-state $7,582

Vocational/Technical School(s)
Modern Welding School (Private, For-profit)
   Fall 2014 Enrollment: 88 . . . . (518) 374-1216
   2015-16 Tuition: $13,600
Paul Mitchell the School-Schenectady (Private, For-profit)
   Fall 2014 Enrollment: 93 . . . . (518) 370-4590
   2015-16 Tuition: $11,000

Housing: Homeownership rate: 48.4%; Median home value: $114,400; Median year structure built: Before 1940; Homeowner vacancy rate: 3.2%; Median selected monthly owner costs: $1,304 with a mortgage, $611 without a mortgage; Median gross rent: $811 per month; Rental vacancy rate: 6.9%

Health Insurance: 89.6% have insurance; 55.7% have private insurance; 45.6% have public insurance; 10.4% do not have insurance; 4.0% of children under 18 do not have insurance

Hospitals: Ellis Hospital (368 beds); Sunnyview Hospital & Rehabilitation Center (104 beds)

Newspapers: Daily Gazette (daily circulation 52,000)

Transportation: Commute: 80.5% car, 9.0% public transportation, 5.5% walk, 2.9% work from home; Mean travel time to work: 22.7 minutes; Amtrak: Train service available.

Airports: Schenectady County (general aviation)

Additional Information Contacts
City of Schenectady . . . . (518) 382-5199
   http://www.cityofschenectady.com

SCOTIA (village). Covers a land area of 1.685 square miles and a water area of 0.104 square miles. Located at 42.83° N. Lat; 73.96° W. Long. Elevation is 243 feet.

History: Scotia Naval Supply Depot closed. Settled before 1660, incorporated 1904.

Population: 7,744; Growth (since 2000): -2.7%; Density: 4,594.7 persons per square mile; Race: 93.1% White, 3.3% Black/African American, 0.5% Asian, 0.0% American Indian/Alaska Native, 0.0% Native Hawaiian/Other Pacific Islander, 2.8% Two or more races, 2.8% Hispanic of any race; Average household size: 2.53; Median age: 38.1; Age under 18: 24.1%;

Age 65 and over: 15.1%; Males per 100 females: 93.9; Marriage status: 31.2% never married, 49.1% now married, 0.9% separated, 6.0% widowed, 13.7% divorced; Foreign born: 2.0%; Speak English only: 96.8%; With disability: 12.6%; Veterans: 8.6%; Ancestry: 26.7% Irish, 20.9% Italian, 18.7% German, 11.8% English, 9.6% French

Employment: 12.4% management, business, and financial, 4.2% computer, engineering, and science, 9.6% education, legal, community service, arts, and media, 7.7% healthcare practitioners, 17.1% service, 33.0% sales and office, 5.7% natural resources, construction, and maintenance, 10.2% production, transportation, and material moving

Income: Per capita: $26,853; Median household: $54,607; Average household: $63,509; Households with income of $100,000 or more: 17.9%; Poverty rate: 6.1%

Educational Attainment: High school diploma or higher: 95.6%; Bachelor's degree or higher: 30.4%; Graduate/professional degree or higher: 15.4%

School District(s)
Burnt Hills-Ballston Lake Central SD (KG-12)
   2014-15 Enrollment: 3,100 . . . . (518) 399-9141
Scotia-Glenville Central SD (KG-12)
   2014-15 Enrollment: 2,571 . . . . (518) 382-1215

Housing: Homeownership rate: 68.9%; Median home value: $138,000; Median year structure built: 1941; Homeowner vacancy rate: 4.3%; Median selected monthly owner costs: $1,445 with a mortgage, $542 without a mortgage; Median gross rent: $827 per month; Rental vacancy rate: 6.9%

Health Insurance: 96.8% have insurance; 78.5% have private insurance; 31.3% have public insurance; 3.2% do not have insurance; 0.7% of children under 18 do not have insurance

Safety: Violent crime rate: 16.6 per 10,000 population; Property crime rate: 217.3 per 10,000 population

Transportation: Commute: 89.9% car, 1.0% public transportation, 5.5% walk, 2.1% work from home; Mean travel time to work: 20.4 minutes

Additional Information Contacts
Village of Scotia . . . . (518) 374-1071
   http://www.villageofscotia.org

Schoharie County

Located in east central New York, partly in the Catskills; crossed by The Helderbergs; drained by Schoharie and Catskill Creeks. Covers a land area of 621.819 square miles, a water area of 4.508 square miles, and is located in the Eastern Time Zone at 42.59° N. Lat., 74.44° W. Long. The county was founded in 1795. County seat is Schoharie.

Schoharie County is part of the Albany-Schenectady-Troy, NY Metropolitan Statistical Area. The entire metro area includes: Albany County, NY; Rensselaer County, NY; Saratoga County, NY; Schenectady County, NY; Schoharie County, NY

Weather Station: Lansing Manor								Elevation: 1,100 feet			
	Jan	Feb	Mar	Apr	May	Jun	Jul	Aug	Sep	Oct	Nov	Dec
High	34	35	44	57	68	77	81	80	72	60	49	38
Low	13	13	22	33	43	53	57	56	49	37	30	19
Precip	2.5	2.0	3.0	3.4	3.7	4.2	4.7	3.5	3.6	4.3	2.9	2.4
Snow	17.0	9.8	10.9	2.2	tr	0.0	0.0	0.0	0.0	0.6	3.7	11.2

High and Low temperatures in degrees Fahrenheit; Precipitation and Snow in inches

Population: 31,913; Growth (since 2000): 1.0%; Density: 51.3 persons per square mile; Race: 96.0% White, 1.4% Black/African American, 0.8% Asian, 0.1% American Indian/Alaska Native, 0.0% Native Hawaiian/Other Pacific Islander, 1.3% two or more races, 3.0% Hispanic of any race; Average household size: 2.46; Median age: 43.3; Age under 18: 18.9%; Age 65 and over: 17.7%; Males per 100 females: 100.0; Marriage status: 30.9% never married, 51.0% now married, 2.4% separated, 7.6% widowed, 10.5% divorced; Foreign born: 2.7%; Speak English only: 95.6%; With disability: 15.8%; Veterans: 10.7%; Ancestry: 25.9% German, 22.7% Irish, 12.9% Italian, 10.3% English, 8.4% Dutch

Religion: Six largest groups: 20.7% Catholicism, 6.3% Methodist/Pietist, 4.6% Lutheran, 2.4% Presbyterian-Reformed, 1.6% Non-denominational Protestant, 1.2% Latter-day Saints

Economy: Unemployment rate: 4.7%; Leading industries: 17.5 % retail trade; 14.0 % construction; 10.9 % health care and social assistance; Farms: 532 totaling 98,369 acres; Company size: 0 employ 1,000 or more persons, 1 employs 500 to 999 persons, 5 employ 100 to 499 persons, 564 employ less than 100 persons; Business ownership: 590

women-owned, n/a Black-owned, n/a Hispanic-owned, n/a Asian-owned, n/a American Indian/Alaska Native-owned

Employment: 14.2% management, business, and financial, 3.5% computer, engineering, and science, 11.3% education, legal, community service, arts, and media, 4.5% healthcare practitioners, 18.1% service, 22.9% sales and office, 12.5% natural resources, construction, and maintenance, 13.1% production, transportation, and material moving

Income: Per capita: $25,498; Median household: $51,195; Average household: $62,802; Households with income of $100,000 or more: 16.7%; Poverty rate: 12.9%

Educational Attainment: High school diploma or higher: 88.2%; Bachelor's degree or higher: 19.6%; Graduate/professional degree or higher: 8.4%

Housing: Homeownership rate: 76.7%; Median home value: $147,000; Median year structure built: 1972; Homeowner vacancy rate: 1.5%; Median selected monthly owner costs: $1,339 with a mortgage, $541 without a mortgage; Median gross rent: $733 per month; Rental vacancy rate: 3.9%

Vital Statistics: Birth rate: 80.1 per 10,000 population; Death rate: 89.4 per 10,000 population; Age-adjusted cancer mortality rate: 161.9 deaths per 100,000 population

Health Insurance: 93.0% have insurance; 71.1% have private insurance; 38.4% have public insurance; 7.0% do not have insurance; 1.9% of children under 18 do not have insurance

Health Care: Physicians: 6.3 per 10,000 population; Dentists: 2.9 per 10,000 population; Hospital beds: 12.6 per 10,000 population; Hospital admissions: 236.4 per 10,000 population

Transportation: Commute: 88.0% car, 1.5% public transportation, 5.5% walk, 4.2% work from home; Mean travel time to work: 29.7 minutes

2016 Presidential Election: 63.6% Trump, 30.6% Clinton, 3.8% Johnson, 2.0% Stein

National and State Parks: Max V Shaul State Park; Mine Kill State Park

Additional Information Contacts

Schoharie Government . . . . (518) 295-8114
  http://www.schohariecounty-ny.gov

Schoharie County Communities

BLENHEIM (town). Covers a land area of 33.933 square miles and a water area of 0.461 square miles. Located at 42.49° N. Lat; 74.52° W. Long.

Population: 328; Growth (since 2000): -0.6%; Density: 9.7 persons per square mile; Race: 98.2% White, 1.8% Black/African American, 0.0% Asian, 0.0% American Indian/Alaska Native, 0.0% Native Hawaiian/Other Pacific Islander, 0.0% Two or more races, 2.1% Hispanic of any race; Average household size: 2.56; Median age: 47.1; Age under 18: 15.9%; Age 65 and over: 25.3%; Males per 100 females: 96.4; Marriage status: 25.6% never married, 56.1% now married, 5.2% separated, 7.3% widowed, 11.1% divorced; Foreign born: 5.2%; Speak English only: 94.4%; With disability: 28.7%; Veterans: 18.1%; Ancestry: 44.5% German, 22.3% Irish, 20.1% Polish, 10.1% Dutch, 7.3% English

Employment: 14.2% management, business, and financial, 1.7% computer, engineering, and science, 8.3% education, legal, community service, arts, and media, 5.0% healthcare practitioners, 26.7% service, 28.3% sales and office, 5.0% natural resources, construction, and maintenance, 10.8% production, transportation, and material moving

Income: Per capita: $24,326; Median household: $51,750; Average household: $60,751; Households with income of $100,000 or more: 10.2%; Poverty rate: 11.6%

Educational Attainment: High school diploma or higher: 89.5%; Bachelor's degree or higher: 13.4%; Graduate/professional degree or higher: 5.9%

Housing: Homeownership rate: 86.7%; Median home value: $147,300; Median year structure built: 1977; Homeowner vacancy rate: 3.5%; Median selected monthly owner costs: $1,161 with a mortgage, $590 without a mortgage; Median gross rent: $950 per month; Rental vacancy rate: 0.0%

Health Insurance: 97.0% have insurance; 71.6% have private insurance; 48.5% have public insurance; 3.0% do not have insurance; 0.0% of children under 18 do not have insurance

Transportation: Commute: 95.0% car, 0.0% public transportation, 1.7% walk, 3.3% work from home; Mean travel time to work: 39.2 minutes

BROOME (town). Covers a land area of 47.741 square miles and a water area of 0.250 square miles. Located at 42.50° N. Lat; 74.29° W. Long.

Population: 870; Growth (since 2000): -8.1%; Density: 18.2 persons per square mile; Race: 98.0% White, 0.5% Black/African American, 0.9% Asian, 0.0% American Indian/Alaska Native, 0.0% Native Hawaiian/Other Pacific Islander, 0.0% Two or more races, 2.2% Hispanic of any race; Average household size: 2.16; Median age: 51.5; Age under 18: 14.9%; Age 65 and over: 27.5%; Males per 100 females: 107.9; Marriage status: 23.0% never married, 58.5% now married, 3.8% separated, 6.4% widowed, 12.1% divorced; Foreign born: 4.6%; Speak English only: 97.3%; With disability: 14.4%; Veterans: 11.5%; Ancestry: 26.8% Irish, 20.7% German, 16.2% Italian, 9.7% English, 7.5% Dutch

Employment: 17.9% management, business, and financial, 1.1% computer, engineering, and science, 10.7% education, legal, community service, arts, and media, 0.8% healthcare practitioners, 12.4% service, 18.1% sales and office, 19.8% natural resources, construction, and maintenance, 19.2% production, transportation, and material moving

Income: Per capita: $27,923; Median household: $46,987; Average household: $58,371; Households with income of $100,000 or more: 10.7%; Poverty rate: 10.5%

Educational Attainment: High school diploma or higher: 87.1%; Bachelor's degree or higher: 13.9%; Graduate/professional degree or higher: 6.0%

Housing: Homeownership rate: 88.8%; Median home value: $140,700; Median year structure built: 1973; Homeowner vacancy rate: 0.6%; Median selected monthly owner costs: $1,340 with a mortgage, $591 without a mortgage; Median gross rent: $598 per month; Rental vacancy rate: 0.0%

Health Insurance: 92.8% have insurance; 78.2% have private insurance; 40.3% have public insurance; 7.2% do not have insurance; 1.5% of children under 18 do not have insurance

Transportation: Commute: 89.8% car, 4.2% public transportation, 0.0% walk, 5.3% work from home; Mean travel time to work: 39.4 minutes

CARLISLE (town). Covers a land area of 34.124 square miles and a water area of 0.128 square miles. Located at 42.74° N. Lat; 74.44° W. Long. Elevation is 1,283 feet.

Population: 1,846; Growth (since 2000): 5.0%; Density: 54.1 persons per square mile; Race: 93.3% White, 1.5% Black/African American, 3.6% Asian, 0.0% American Indian/Alaska Native, 0.0% Native Hawaiian/Other Pacific Islander, 0.8% Two or more races, 2.5% Hispanic of any race; Average household size: 2.71; Median age: 39.5; Age under 18: 20.2%; Age 65 and over: 11.6%; Males per 100 females: 100.0; Marriage status: 29.0% never married, 56.4% now married, 1.7% separated, 4.8% widowed, 9.9% divorced; Foreign born: 2.9%; Speak English only: 95.1%; With disability: 8.6%; Veterans: 9.5%; Ancestry: 27.5% German, 20.3% Irish, 12.0% English, 7.4% American, 7.4% Italian

Employment: 20.5% management, business, and financial, 3.7% computer, engineering, and science, 10.9% education, legal, community service, arts, and media, 4.0% healthcare practitioners, 16.5% service, 14.7% sales and office, 17.2% natural resources, construction, and maintenance, 12.4% production, transportation, and material moving

Income: Per capita: $26,060; Median household: $60,774; Average household: $69,079; Households with income of $100,000 or more: 17.4%; Poverty rate: 9.8%

Educational Attainment: High school diploma or higher: 89.3%; Bachelor's degree or higher: 24.2%; Graduate/professional degree or higher: 9.0%

Housing: Homeownership rate: 77.1%; Median home value: $143,900; Median year structure built: 1975; Homeowner vacancy rate: 1.5%; Median selected monthly owner costs: $1,404 with a mortgage, $595 without a mortgage; Median gross rent: $802 per month; Rental vacancy rate: 0.0%

Health Insurance: 90.7% have insurance; 75.5% have private insurance; 25.3% have public insurance; 9.3% do not have insurance; 0.0% of children under 18 do not have insurance

Transportation: Commute: 89.7% car, 0.0% public transportation, 3.8% walk, 6.0% work from home; Mean travel time to work: 29.8 minutes

CENTRAL BRIDGE (CDP). Covers a land area of 1.843 square miles and a water area of 0.014 square miles. Located at 42.71° N. Lat; 74.35° W. Long. Elevation is 620 feet.

Population: 282; Growth (since 2000): n/a; Density: 153.0 persons per square mile; Race: 89.7% White, 0.0% Black/African American, 0.0% Asian, 0.0% American Indian/Alaska Native, 0.0% Native Hawaiian/Other Pacific Islander, 10.3% Two or more races, 0.0% Hispanic of any race;

Average household size: 2.39; Median age: 41.9; Age under 18: 15.6%; Age 65 and over: 37.2%; Males per 100 females: 97.7; Marriage status: 22.1% never married, 69.6% now married, 5.9% separated, 4.3% widowed, 4.0% divorced; Foreign born: 0.0%; Speak English only: 100.0%; With disability: 11.0%; Veterans: 22.3%; Ancestry: 42.6% German, 14.5% American, 13.5% Norwegian, 13.1% French, 5.3% Canadian
Employment: 9.4% management, business, and financial, 13.2% computer, engineering, and science, 14.2% education, legal, community service, arts, and media, 0.0% healthcare practitioners, 25.5% service, 28.3% sales and office, 0.0% natural resources, construction, and maintenance, 9.4% production, transportation, and material moving
Income: Per capita: $15,631; Median household: $31,346; Average household: $34,469; Households with income of $100,000 or more: n/a; Poverty rate: 27.0%
Educational Attainment: High school diploma or higher: 83.2%; Bachelor's degree or higher: 10.1%; Graduate/professional degree or higher: 5.9%
Housing: Homeownership rate: 78.8%; Median home value: $79,600; Median year structure built: 1944; Homeowner vacancy rate: 0.0%; Median selected monthly owner costs: n/a with a mortgage, $546 without a mortgage; Median gross rent: n/a per month; Rental vacancy rate: 0.0%
Health Insurance: 100.0% have insurance; 90.4% have private insurance; 52.1% have public insurance; 0.0% do not have insurance; 0.0% of children under 18 do not have insurance
Transportation: Commute: 85.4% car, 0.0% public transportation, 0.0% walk, 14.6% work from home; Mean travel time to work: 0.0 minutes

CHARLOTTEVILLE (unincorporated postal area)
ZCTA: 12036

Covers a land area of 7.406 square miles and a water area of 0.008 square miles. Located at 42.54° N. Lat; 74.67° W. Long. Elevation is 1,604 feet.
Population: 196; Growth (since 2000): -26.0%; Density: 26.5 persons per square mile; Race: 97.4% White, 0.0% Black/African American, 2.6% Asian, 0.0% American Indian/Alaska Native, 0.0% Native Hawaiian/Other Pacific Islander, 0.0% Two or more races, 18.4% Hispanic of any race; Average household size: 2.13; Median age: 47.5; Age under 18: 21.9%; Age 65 and over: 23.0%; Males per 100 females: 103.6; Marriage status: 32.1% never married, 50.0% now married, 0.0% separated, 8.9% widowed, 8.9% divorced; Foreign born: 6.1%; Speak English only: 89.9%; With disability: 18.9%; Veterans: 9.8%; Ancestry: 22.4% German, 21.9% Irish, 18.9% Dutch, 16.8% Italian, 11.2% English
Employment: 8.7% management, business, and financial, 0.0% computer, engineering, and science, 4.3% education, legal, community service, arts, and media, 0.0% healthcare practitioners, 24.6% service, 21.7% sales and office, 14.5% natural resources, construction, and maintenance, 26.1% production, transportation, and material moving
Income: Per capita: $19,771; Median household: $36,875; Average household: $41,922; Households with income of $100,000 or more: 4.3%; Poverty rate: 14.3%
Educational Attainment: High school diploma or higher: 77.0%; Bachelor's degree or higher: 14.2%; Graduate/professional degree or higher: 6.1%
Housing: Homeownership rate: 88.0%; Median home value: $142,000; Median year structure built: 1962; Homeowner vacancy rate: 0.0%; Median selected monthly owner costs: $1,250 with a mortgage, $421 without a mortgage; Median gross rent: n/a per month; Rental vacancy rate: 0.0%
Health Insurance: 84.2% have insurance; 55.6% have private insurance; 41.3% have public insurance; 15.8% do not have insurance; 7.0% of children under 18 do not have insurance
Transportation: Commute: 90.9% car, 0.0% public transportation, 0.0% walk, 4.5% work from home; Mean travel time to work: 32.9 minutes

COBLESKILL (town). Covers a land area of 30.599 square miles and
a water area of 0.179 square miles. Located at 42.69° N. Lat; 74.44° W. Long. Elevation is 922 feet.
History: The Borst & Burnhans Plant began in Cobleskill in 1800 as a feed, flour, and grist mill, and became famous for its pancake flour in 1890. The Harder Refrigerator Plant, established in 1859, made threshing machines, silos, manure spreaders, and refrigerators. Seat of State University of N.Y. College. of Agriculture and Technology at Cobleskill. Cobleskill Historic District. Settled in 1752, incorporated in 1868.
Population: 6,502; Growth (since 2000): 1.5%; Density: 212.5 persons per square mile; Race: 90.7% White, 4.8% Black/African American, 0.5%

Asian, 0.0% American Indian/Alaska Native, 0.2% Native Hawaiian/Other Pacific Islander, 2.8% Two or more races, 5.2% Hispanic of any race; Average household size: 2.34; Median age: 32.2; Age under 18: 16.5%; Age 65 and over: 16.3%; Males per 100 females: 94.9; Marriage status: 45.8% never married, 35.7% now married, 1.4% separated, 9.5% widowed, 9.0% divorced; Foreign born: 3.1%; Speak English only: 93.2%; With disability: 14.4%; Veterans: 8.9%; Ancestry: 24.5% Irish, 19.6% German, 14.9% Italian, 8.4% English, 7.4% Dutch
Employment: 10.7% management, business, and financial, 3.0% computer, engineering, and science, 15.3% education, legal, community service, arts, and media, 4.3% healthcare practitioners, 27.7% service, 22.5% sales and office, 6.7% natural resources, construction, and maintenance, 9.8% production, transportation, and material moving
Income: Per capita: $22,825; Median household: $46,204; Average household: $60,835; Households with income of $100,000 or more: 15.3%; Poverty rate: 16.2%
Educational Attainment: High school diploma or higher: 90.2%; Bachelor's degree or higher: 22.9%; Graduate/professional degree or higher: 12.6%

School District(s)
Cobleskill-Richmondville Central SD (PK-12)
    2014-15 Enrollment: 1,842 . . . . (518) 234-4032

Four-year College(s)
SUNY College of Agriculture and Technology at Cobleskill (Public)
    Fall 2014 Enrollment: 2,535 . . . . (518) 255-5525
    2015-16 Tuition: In-state $7,719; Out-of-state $17,569
Housing: Homeownership rate: 54.1%; Median home value: $154,000; Median year structure built: 1968; Homeowner vacancy rate: 2.2%; Median selected monthly owner costs: $1,461 with a mortgage, $556 without a mortgage; Median gross rent: $740 per month; Rental vacancy rate: 7.4%
Health Insurance: 94.9% have insurance; 73.9% have private insurance; 36.4% have public insurance; 5.1% do not have insurance; 0.0% of children under 18 do not have insurance
Hospitals: Cobleskill Regional Hospital (40 beds)
Newspapers: Cobleskill Times-Journal (weekly circulation 6,000)
Transportation: Commute: 76.1% car, 2.1% public transportation, 17.0% walk, 4.6% work from home; Mean travel time to work: 23.4 minutes
Additional Information Contacts
Town of Cobleskill . . . . (518) 234-1719
    http://www.townofcobleskill.com

COBLESKILL (village). Covers a land area of 3.572 square miles and
a water area of 0.004 square miles. Located at 42.68° N. Lat; 74.49° W. Long. Elevation is 922 feet.
Population: 4,602; Growth (since 2000): 1.5%; Density: 1,288.4 persons per square mile; Race: 89.0% White, 6.7% Black/African American, 0.7% Asian, 0.0% American Indian/Alaska Native, 0.3% Native Hawaiian/Other Pacific Islander, 2.2% Two or more races, 6.2% Hispanic of any race; Average household size: 2.24; Median age: 25.3; Age under 18: 14.9%; Age 65 and over: 14.6%; Males per 100 females: 93.0; Marriage status: 56.0% never married, 29.1% now married, 1.3% separated, 8.5% widowed, 6.4% divorced; Foreign born: 3.5%; Speak English only: 92.3%; With disability: 15.0%; Veterans: 8.3%; Ancestry: 26.0% Irish, 19.3% German, 13.3% Italian, 7.3% English, 5.4% American
Employment: 10.0% management, business, and financial, 2.9% computer, engineering, and science, 12.3% education, legal, community service, arts, and media, 2.7% healthcare practitioners, 33.7% service, 23.3% sales and office, 7.4% natural resources, construction, and maintenance, 7.7% production, transportation, and material moving
Income: Per capita: $20,586; Median household: $36,824; Average household: $56,721; Households with income of $100,000 or more: 13.7%; Poverty rate: 21.2%
Educational Attainment: High school diploma or higher: 87.2%; Bachelor's degree or higher: 27.3%; Graduate/professional degree or higher: 13.7%

School District(s)
Cobleskill-Richmondville Central SD (PK-12)
    2014-15 Enrollment: 1,842 . . . . (518) 234-4032

Four-year College(s)
SUNY College of Agriculture and Technology at Cobleskill (Public)
    Fall 2014 Enrollment: 2,535 . . . . (518) 255-5525
    2015-16 Tuition: In-state $7,719; Out-of-state $17,569
Housing: Homeownership rate: 41.8%; Median home value: $147,900; Median year structure built: 1963; Homeowner vacancy rate: 0.0%; Median

selected monthly owner costs: $1,665 with a mortgage, $624 without a mortgage; Median gross rent: $726 per month; Rental vacancy rate: 8.7%
Health Insurance: 94.5% have insurance; 73.7% have private insurance; 36.0% have public insurance; 5.5% do not have insurance; 0.0% of children under 18 do not have insurance
Hospitals: Cobleskill Regional Hospital (40 beds)
Safety: Violent crime rate: 6.7 per 10,000 population; Property crime rate: 391.2 per 10,000 population
Newspapers: Cobleskill Times-Journal (weekly circulation 6,000)
Transportation: Commute: 67.8% car, 3.0% public transportation, 24.7% walk, 4.3% work from home; Mean travel time to work: 23.4 minutes
Additional Information Contacts
Village of Cobleskill . . . . (518) 234-3891
    http://www.schohariecounty-ny.gov/CountyWebSite/villcob

CONESVILLE (town). Covers a land area of 39.466 square miles and a water area of 0.404 square miles. Located at 42.40° N. Lat; 74.34° W. Long. Elevation is 1,381 feet.

Population: 741; Growth (since 2000): 2.1%; Density: 18.8 persons per square mile; Race: 98.2% White, 0.0% Black/African American, 0.0% Asian, 0.0% American Indian/Alaska Native, 0.0% Native Hawaiian/Other Pacific Islander, 0.9% Two or more races, 5.5% Hispanic of any race; Average household size: 2.32; Median age: 52.3; Age under 18: 14.2%; Age 65 and over: 26.9%; Males per 100 females: 96.3; Marriage status: 25.2% never married, 57.8% now married, 3.1% separated, 6.4% widowed, 10.6% divorced; Foreign born: 8.2%; Speak English only: 91.3%; With disability: 19.0%; Veterans: 12.9%; Ancestry: 24.0% Irish, 21.6% German, 18.2% Italian, 14.2% English, 8.6% Dutch
Employment: 12.2% management, business, and financial, 0.0% computer, engineering, and science, 9.6% education, legal, community service, arts, and media, 3.3% healthcare practitioners, 20.9% service, 15.5% sales and office, 18.2% natural resources, construction, and maintenance, 20.3% production, transportation, and material moving
Income: Per capita: $27,479; Median household: $51,250; Average household: $62,737; Households with income of $100,000 or more: 13.8%; Poverty rate: 10.8%
Educational Attainment: High school diploma or higher: 82.6%; Bachelor's degree or higher: 14.1%; Graduate/professional degree or higher: 7.2%
Housing: Homeownership rate: 92.8%; Median home value: $122,100; Median year structure built: 1982; Homeowner vacancy rate: 0.0%; Median selected monthly owner costs: $1,197 with a mortgage, $489 without a mortgage; Median gross rent: $750 per month; Rental vacancy rate: 0.0%
Health Insurance: 90.7% have insurance; 73.3% have private insurance; 37.4% have public insurance; 9.3% do not have insurance; 0.0% of children under 18 do not have insurance
Transportation: Commute: 83.7% car, 1.3% public transportation, 1.3% walk, 13.1% work from home; Mean travel time to work: 36.0 minutes

ESPERANCE (town). Covers a land area of 19.666 square miles and a water area of 0.371 square miles. Located at 42.75° N. Lat; 74.32° W. Long. Elevation is 581 feet.

Population: 1,840; Growth (since 2000): -9.9%; Density: 93.6 persons per square mile; Race: 97.9% White, 0.1% Black/African American, 0.3% Asian, 0.0% American Indian/Alaska Native, 0.0% Native Hawaiian/Other Pacific Islander, 1.4% Two or more races, 2.4% Hispanic of any race; Average household size: 2.56; Median age: 42.5; Age under 18: 21.8%; Age 65 and over: 15.8%; Males per 100 females: 101.6; Marriage status: 28.1% never married, 51.8% now married, 0.9% separated, 6.3% widowed, 13.9% divorced; Foreign born: 1.6%; Speak English only: 99.4%; With disability: 15.6%; Veterans: 12.7%; Ancestry: 30.2% German, 16.7% Irish, 12.3% English, 10.3% Dutch, 7.7% Italian
Employment: 8.5% management, business, and financial, 2.5% computer, engineering, and science, 8.3% education, legal, community service, arts, and media, 4.6% healthcare practitioners, 11.2% service, 32.3% sales and office, 8.8% natural resources, construction, and maintenance, 23.8% production, transportation, and material moving
Income: Per capita: $26,316; Median household: $58,059; Average household: $64,442; Households with income of $100,000 or more: 18.4%; Poverty rate: 10.1%
Educational Attainment: High school diploma or higher: 93.1%; Bachelor's degree or higher: 15.6%; Graduate/professional degree or higher: 4.0%
Housing: Homeownership rate: 87.1%; Median home value: $120,400; Median year structure built: 1971; Homeowner vacancy rate: 0.0%; Median

selected monthly owner costs: $1,318 with a mortgage, $515 without a mortgage; Median gross rent: $808 per month; Rental vacancy rate: 0.0%
Health Insurance: 92.2% have insurance; 78.3% have private insurance; 32.8% have public insurance; 7.8% do not have insurance; 0.7% of children under 18 do not have insurance
Transportation: Commute: 97.0% car, 0.0% public transportation, 1.0% walk, 1.5% work from home; Mean travel time to work: 28.9 minutes
Additional Information Contacts
Town of Esperance . . . . (518) 875-6109
    http://townofesperance.org

ESPERANCE (village). Covers a land area of 0.491 square miles and a water area of 0.030 square miles. Located at 42.76° N. Lat; 74.26° W. Long. Elevation is 581 feet.

Population: 357; Growth (since 2000): -6.1%; Density: 726.9 persons per square mile; Race: 98.3% White, 0.0% Black/African American, 1.7% Asian, 0.0% American Indian/Alaska Native, 0.0% Native Hawaiian/Other Pacific Islander, 0.0% Two or more races, 3.1% Hispanic of any race; Average household size: 2.73; Median age: 33.7; Age under 18: 30.5%; Age 65 and over: 11.2%; Males per 100 females: 106.6; Marriage status: 29.9% never married, 50.8% now married, 0.4% separated, 8.0% widowed, 11.4% divorced; Foreign born: 1.7%; Speak English only: 98.2%; With disability: 17.3%; Veterans: 5.8%; Ancestry: 37.5% German, 26.3% Irish, 21.3% Italian, 10.4% English, 9.0% Scottish
Employment: 9.7% management, business, and financial, 3.9% computer, engineering, and science, 15.6% education, legal, community service, arts, and media, 1.9% healthcare practitioners, 15.6% service, 24.0% sales and office, 13.0% natural resources, construction, and maintenance, 16.2% production, transportation, and material moving
Income: Per capita: $21,221; Median household: $54,063; Average household: $53,669; Households with income of $100,000 or more: 10.7%; Poverty rate: 6.2%
Educational Attainment: High school diploma or higher: 96.4%; Bachelor's degree or higher: 13.8%; Graduate/professional degree or higher: 2.7%
Housing: Homeownership rate: 80.9%; Median home value: $139,100; Median year structure built: 1948; Homeowner vacancy rate: 0.0%; Median selected monthly owner costs: $1,326 with a mortgage, $663 without a mortgage; Median gross rent: $950 per month; Rental vacancy rate: 0.0%
Health Insurance: 92.3% have insurance; 73.6% have private insurance; 26.7% have public insurance; 7.7% do not have insurance; 2.8% of children under 18 do not have insurance
Transportation: Commute: 93.1% car, 0.0% public transportation, 5.0% walk, 1.9% work from home; Mean travel time to work: 30.5 minutes

FULTON (town). Covers a land area of 64.978 square miles and a water area of 0.027 square miles. Located at 42.59° N. Lat; 74.45° W. Long.

Population: 1,145; Growth (since 2000): -23.4%; Density: 17.6 persons per square mile; Race: 96.5% White, 1.6% Black/African American, 0.0% Asian, 0.3% American Indian/Alaska Native, 0.0% Native Hawaiian/Other Pacific Islander, 1.7% Two or more races, 0.5% Hispanic of any race; Average household size: 2.20; Median age: 44.5; Age under 18: 20.5%; Age 65 and over: 17.2%; Males per 100 females: 127.8; Marriage status: 17.1% never married, 66.4% now married, 3.2% separated, 8.8% widowed, 7.7% divorced; Foreign born: 3.1%; Speak English only: 97.3%; With disability: 16.4%; Veterans: 11.5%; Ancestry: 28.6% German, 18.3% Irish, 14.1% Dutch, 13.9% English, 13.9% Italian
Employment: 11.4% management, business, and financial, 2.4% computer, engineering, and science, 13.1% education, legal, community service, arts, and media, 7.1% healthcare practitioners, 14.0% service, 21.2% sales and office, 20.7% natural resources, construction, and maintenance, 10.0% production, transportation, and material moving
Income: Per capita: $26,544; Median household: $43,661; Average household: $59,353; Households with income of $100,000 or more: 15.9%; Poverty rate: 10.5%
Educational Attainment: High school diploma or higher: 85.0%; Bachelor's degree or higher: 19.5%; Graduate/professional degree or higher: 10.0%
Housing: Homeownership rate: 87.4%; Median home value: $131,900; Median year structure built: 1972; Homeowner vacancy rate: 4.7%; Median selected monthly owner costs: $1,314 with a mortgage, $490 without a mortgage; Median gross rent: $700 per month; Rental vacancy rate: 0.0%

Health Insurance: 94.2% have insurance; 70.3% have private insurance; 40.8% have public insurance; 5.8% do not have insurance; 0.0% of children under 18 do not have insurance
Transportation: Commute: 92.7% car, 0.0% public transportation, 2.7% walk, 2.7% work from home; Mean travel time to work: 27.8 minutes

FULTONHAM (unincorporated postal area)
ZCTA: 12071

Covers a land area of 9.231 square miles and a water area of 0 square miles. Located at 42.55° N. Lat; 74.42° W. Long. Elevation is 702 feet.
Population: 247; Growth (since 2000): -11.5%; Density: 26.8 persons per square mile; Race: 97.6% White, 1.2% Black/African American, 0.0% Asian, 1.2% American Indian/Alaska Native, 0.0% Native Hawaiian/Other Pacific Islander, 0.0% Two or more races, 0.0% Hispanic of any race; Average household size: 2.09; Median age: 47.3; Age under 18: 20.6%; Age 65 and over: 18.2%; Males per 100 females: 104.5; Marriage status: 19.2% never married, 58.1% now married, 1.5% separated, 17.2% widowed, 5.4% divorced; Foreign born: 12.6%; Speak English only: 100.0%; With disability: 17.4%; Veterans: 3.6%; Ancestry: 30.4% German, 25.1% English, 18.6% Dutch, 13.0% Italian, 10.9% Polish
Employment: 22.2% management, business, and financial, 0.0% computer, engineering, and science, 8.7% education, legal, community service, arts, and media, 11.1% healthcare practitioners, 4.8% service, 24.6% sales and office, 11.9% natural resources, construction, and maintenance, 16.7% production, transportation, and material moving
Income: Per capita: $34,336; Median household: $51,563; Average household: $70,327; Households with income of $100,000 or more: 21.2%; Poverty rate: 4.5%
Educational Attainment: High school diploma or higher: 97.3%; Bachelor's degree or higher: 24.3%; Graduate/professional degree or higher: 4.3%
Housing: Homeownership rate: 83.9%; Median home value: $152,500; Median year structure built: Before 1940; Homeowner vacancy rate: 0.0%; Median selected monthly owner costs: $1,192 with a mortgage, $700 without a mortgage; Median gross rent: n/a per month; Rental vacancy rate: 0.0%
Health Insurance: 93.9% have insurance; 80.2% have private insurance; 25.9% have public insurance; 6.1% do not have insurance; 0.0% of children under 18 do not have insurance
Transportation: Commute: 100.0% car, 0.0% public transportation, 0.0% walk, 0.0% work from home; Mean travel time to work: 18.5 minutes

GILBOA (town). Covers a land area of 57.800 square miles and a water area of 1.576 square miles. Located at 42.43° N. Lat; 74.45° W. Long. Elevation is 1,027 feet.
Population: 1,430; Growth (since 2000): 17.7%; Density: 24.7 persons per square mile; Race: 98.0% White, 0.1% Black/African American, 0.4% Asian, 0.0% American Indian/Alaska Native, 0.0% Native Hawaiian/Other Pacific Islander, 1.1% Two or more races, 1.8% Hispanic of any race; Average household size: 2.80; Median age: 43.5; Age under 18: 22.5%; Age 65 and over: 15.8%; Males per 100 females: 104.9; Marriage status: 27.1% never married, 57.2% now married, 3.4% separated, 3.5% widowed, 12.3% divorced; Foreign born: 2.8%; Speak English only: 96.7%; With disability: 16.5%; Veterans: 13.1%; Ancestry: 34.4% German, 29.1% Irish, 15.1% Italian, 8.9% Dutch, 7.7% English
Employment: 16.1% management, business, and financial, 0.3% computer, engineering, and science, 10.4% education, legal, community service, arts, and media, 7.0% healthcare practitioners, 16.9% service, 19.2% sales and office, 10.4% natural resources, construction, and maintenance, 19.7% production, transportation, and material moving
Income: Per capita: $29,722; Median household: $67,279; Average household: $81,548; Households with income of $100,000 or more: 20.9%; Poverty rate: 9.7%
Educational Attainment: High school diploma or higher: 89.3%; Bachelor's degree or higher: 14.9%; Graduate/professional degree or higher: 5.9%

School District(s)
Gilboa-Conesville Central SD (PK-12)
    2014-15 Enrollment: 342. . . . . (607) 588-7541
Housing: Homeownership rate: 83.4%; Median home value: $162,500; Median year structure built: 1978; Homeowner vacancy rate: 0.0%; Median selected monthly owner costs: $1,315 with a mortgage, $363 without a mortgage; Median gross rent: $804 per month; Rental vacancy rate: 0.0%

Health Insurance: 88.6% have insurance; 69.3% have private insurance; 36.9% have public insurance; 11.4% do not have insurance; 14.3% of children under 18 do not have insurance
Transportation: Commute: 93.0% car, 0.5% public transportation, 5.3% walk, 1.2% work from home; Mean travel time to work: 26.5 minutes

HOWES CAVE (unincorporated postal area)
ZCTA: 12092

Covers a land area of 14.957 square miles and a water area of 0.172 square miles. Located at 42.70° N. Lat; 74.38° W. Long. Elevation is 781 feet.
Population: 735; Growth (since 2000): -14.6%; Density: 49.1 persons per square mile; Race: 96.1% White, 0.0% Black/African American, 0.0% Asian, 0.0% American Indian/Alaska Native, 0.0% Native Hawaiian/Other Pacific Islander, 3.9% Two or more races, 0.0% Hispanic of any race; Average household size: 2.25; Median age: 51.6; Age under 18: 18.9%; Age 65 and over: 24.4%; Males per 100 females: 97.0; Marriage status: 19.0% never married, 48.2% now married, 2.5% separated, 20.4% widowed, 12.4% divorced; Foreign born: 2.3%; Speak English only: 98.1%; With disability: 20.5%; Veterans: 7.4%; Ancestry: 32.8% German, 19.0% Dutch, 15.4% American, 12.2% Italian, 11.2% Irish
Employment: 6.6% management, business, and financial, 13.0% computer, engineering, and science, 14.8% education, legal, community service, arts, and media, 5.7% healthcare practitioners, 13.0% service, 10.9% sales and office, 14.8% natural resources, construction, and maintenance, 21.1% production, transportation, and material moving
Income: Per capita: $26,621; Median household: $41,500; Average household: $56,805; Households with income of $100,000 or more: 21.1%; Poverty rate: 8.3%
Educational Attainment: High school diploma or higher: 90.3%; Bachelor's degree or higher: 16.9%; Graduate/professional degree or higher: 4.4%
Housing: Homeownership rate: 78.2%; Median home value: $106,700; Median year structure built: 1973; Homeowner vacancy rate: 0.0%; Median selected monthly owner costs: $1,268 with a mortgage, $439 without a mortgage; Median gross rent: $644 per month; Rental vacancy rate: 0.0%
Health Insurance: 96.6% have insurance; 69.7% have private insurance; 48.7% have public insurance; 3.4% do not have insurance; 0.0% of children under 18 do not have insurance
Transportation: Commute: 87.2% car, 0.0% public transportation, 3.7% walk, 9.0% work from home; Mean travel time to work: 29.6 minutes

JEFFERSON (town). Covers a land area of 43.251 square miles and a water area of 0.163 square miles. Located at 42.49° N. Lat; 74.61° W. Long. Elevation is 1,867 feet.
Population: 1,483; Growth (since 2000): 15.4%; Density: 34.3 persons per square mile; Race: 97.5% White, 0.3% Black/African American, 0.5% Asian, 0.2% American Indian/Alaska Native, 0.0% Native Hawaiian/Other Pacific Islander, 1.6% Two or more races, 2.6% Hispanic of any race; Average household size: 2.41; Median age: 46.1; Age under 18: 20.2%; Age 65 and over: 18.3%; Males per 100 females: 105.8; Marriage status: 27.4% never married, 52.8% now married, 2.6% separated, 7.1% widowed, 12.7% divorced; Foreign born: 3.2%; Speak English only: 97.2%; With disability: 17.3%; Veterans: 9.7%; Ancestry: 30.7% German, 20.9% Irish, 20.3% Italian, 9.2% English, 8.2% French
Employment: 10.7% management, business, and financial, 2.6% computer, engineering, and science, 12.9% education, legal, community service, arts, and media, 3.6% healthcare practitioners, 12.8% service, 21.9% sales and office, 12.9% natural resources, construction, and maintenance, 22.7% production, transportation, and material moving
Income: Per capita: $25,936; Median household: $51,193; Average household: $60,460; Households with income of $100,000 or more: 11.4%; Poverty rate: 12.4%
Educational Attainment: High school diploma or higher: 83.4%; Bachelor's degree or higher: 22.6%; Graduate/professional degree or higher: 8.7%

School District(s)
Jefferson Central SD (KG-12)
    2014-15 Enrollment: 296. . . . . (607) 652-7821
Housing: Homeownership rate: 83.9%; Median home value: $161,300; Median year structure built: 1978; Homeowner vacancy rate: 0.0%; Median selected monthly owner costs: $1,269 with a mortgage, $572 without a mortgage; Median gross rent: $541 per month; Rental vacancy rate: 0.0%

Health Insurance: 89.1% have insurance; 69.2% have private insurance; 37.9% have public insurance; 10.9% do not have insurance; 7.0% of children under 18 do not have insurance
Transportation: Commute: 91.3% car, 2.2% public transportation, 2.5% walk, 3.1% work from home; Mean travel time to work: 29.1 minutes

MIDDLEBURGH (town). Covers a land area of 49.111 square miles and a water area of 0.098 square miles. Located at 42.62° N. Lat; 74.31° W. Long. Elevation is 640 feet.

Population: 3,643; Growth (since 2000): 3.6%; Density: 74.2 persons per square mile; Race: 99.6% White, 0.3% Black/African American, 0.0% Asian, 0.0% American Indian/Alaska Native, 0.0% Native Hawaiian/Other Pacific Islander, 0.1% Two or more races, 3.7% Hispanic of any race; Average household size: 2.29; Median age: 47.8; Age under 18: 14.5%; Age 65 and over: 20.5%; Males per 100 females: 94.6; Marriage status: 32.6% never married, 46.1% now married, 2.1% separated, 10.5% widowed, 10.8% divorced; Foreign born: 0.8%; Speak English only: 95.8%; With disability: 26.3%; Veterans: 12.2%; Ancestry: 29.8% German, 24.7% Irish, 12.5% Dutch, 11.7% English, 11.6% Italian
Employment: 13.3% management, business, and financial, 4.8% computer, engineering, and science, 12.3% education, legal, community service, arts, and media, 4.7% healthcare practitioners, 15.0% service, 25.1% sales and office, 13.9% natural resources, construction, and maintenance, 11.0% production, transportation, and material moving
Income: Per capita: $26,775; Median household: $42,679; Average household: $59,215; Households with income of $100,000 or more: 14.3%; Poverty rate: 14.9%
Educational Attainment: High school diploma or higher: 85.0%; Bachelor's degree or higher: 16.2%; Graduate/professional degree or higher: 6.6%

School District(s)
Middleburgh Central SD (PK-12)
    2014-15 Enrollment: 805. . . . . (518) 827-3625
Housing: Homeownership rate: 80.9%; Median home value: $121,900; Median year structure built: 1969; Homeowner vacancy rate: 4.1%; Median selected monthly owner costs: $1,158 with a mortgage, $551 without a mortgage; Median gross rent: $735 per month; Rental vacancy rate: 5.3%
Health Insurance: 93.4% have insurance; 64.5% have private insurance; 48.8% have public insurance; 6.6% do not have insurance; 1.7% of children under 18 do not have insurance
Transportation: Commute: 87.3% car, 4.1% public transportation, 4.3% walk, 2.3% work from home; Mean travel time to work: 35.3 minutes

MIDDLEBURGH (village). Covers a land area of 1.247 square miles and a water area of 0 square miles. Located at 42.60° N. Lat; 74.33° W. Long. Elevation is 640 feet.

Population: 1,448; Growth (since 2000): 3.6%; Density: 1,160.9 persons per square mile; Race: 99.3% White, 0.4% Black/African American, 0.0% Asian, 0.0% American Indian/Alaska Native, 0.0% Native Hawaiian/Other Pacific Islander, 0.3% Two or more races, 1.5% Hispanic of any race; Average household size: 2.32; Median age: 47.8; Age under 18: 16.0%; Age 65 and over: 19.1%; Males per 100 females: 85.9; Marriage status: 37.0% never married, 42.4% now married, 2.9% separated, 5.8% widowed, 14.8% divorced; Foreign born: 2.0%; Speak English only: 96.1%; With disability: 22.3%; Veterans: 9.3%; Ancestry: 31.0% Irish, 27.4% German, 15.6% English, 14.5% Italian, 9.7% Dutch
Employment: 12.0% management, business, and financial, 2.3% computer, engineering, and science, 15.4% education, legal, community service, arts, and media, 3.8% healthcare practitioners, 28.7% service, 23.1% sales and office, 5.9% natural resources, construction, and maintenance, 8.8% production, transportation, and material moving
Income: Per capita: $23,728; Median household: $43,482; Average household: $52,820; Households with income of $100,000 or more: 10.2%; Poverty rate: 14.2%
Educational Attainment: High school diploma or higher: 88.3%; Bachelor's degree or higher: 18.3%; Graduate/professional degree or higher: 8.0%

School District(s)
Middleburgh Central SD (PK-12)
    2014-15 Enrollment: 805. . . . . (518) 827-3625
Housing: Homeownership rate: 68.0%; Median home value: $129,100; Median year structure built: 1962; Homeowner vacancy rate: 1.4%; Median selected monthly owner costs: $1,224 with a mortgage, $593 without a mortgage; Median gross rent: $720 per month; Rental vacancy rate: 7.9%

Health Insurance: 90.3% have insurance; 72.9% have private insurance; 38.7% have public insurance; 9.7% do not have insurance; 3.9% of children under 18 do not have insurance
Transportation: Commute: 87.4% car, 1.0% public transportation, 6.1% walk, 5.5% work from home; Mean travel time to work: 24.3 minutes

NORTH BLENHEIM (unincorporated postal area)
ZCTA: 12131
    Covers a land area of 7.065 square miles and a water area of 0.405 square miles. Located at 42.46° N. Lat; 74.46° W. Long. Elevation is 791 feet.
Population: 141; Growth (since 2000): -35.0%; Density: 20.0 persons per square mile; Race: 100.0% White, 0.0% Black/African American, 0.0% Asian, 0.0% American Indian/Alaska Native, 0.0% Native Hawaiian/Other Pacific Islander, 0.0% Two or more races, 0.0% Hispanic of any race; Average household size: 2.94; Median age: 46.6; Age under 18: 15.6%; Age 65 and over: 24.1%; Males per 100 females: 117.0; Marriage status: 26.8% never married, 57.7% now married, 6.5% separated, 4.1% widowed, 11.4% divorced; Foreign born: 5.0%; Speak English only: 94.9%; With disability: 38.3%; Veterans: 24.4%; Ancestry: 56.0% German, 24.8% Polish, 17.7% Irish, 7.8% English, 7.8% Italian
Employment: 0.0% management, business, and financial, 4.1% computer, engineering, and science, 4.1% education, legal, community service, arts, and media, 6.1% healthcare practitioners, 40.8% service, 20.4% sales and office, 4.1% natural resources, construction, and maintenance, 20.4% production, transportation, and material moving
Income: Per capita: $21,732; Median household: $58,750; Average household: $60,896; Households with income of $100,000 or more: 10.5%; Poverty rate: 14.2%
Educational Attainment: High school diploma or higher: 87.0%; Bachelor's degree or higher: 9.3%; Graduate/professional degree or higher: 5.6%
Housing: Homeownership rate: 87.5%; Median home value: $125,000; Median year structure built: 1985; Homeowner vacancy rate: 8.7%; Median selected monthly owner costs: n/a with a mortgage, n/a without a mortgage; Median gross rent: n/a per month; Rental vacancy rate: 0.0%
Health Insurance: 100.0% have insurance; 62.4% have private insurance; 55.3% have public insurance; 0.0% do not have insurance; 0.0% of children under 18 do not have insurance
Transportation: Commute: 91.8% car, 0.0% public transportation, 4.1% walk, 4.1% work from home; Mean travel time to work: 27.7 minutes

RICHMONDVILLE (town). Covers a land area of 30.160 square miles and a water area of 0.065 square miles. Located at 42.64° N. Lat; 74.55° W. Long. Elevation is 1,096 feet.

Population: 2,573; Growth (since 2000): 6.7%; Density: 85.3 persons per square mile; Race: 96.0% White, 0.9% Black/African American, 1.5% Asian, 0.5% American Indian/Alaska Native, 0.0% Native Hawaiian/Other Pacific Islander, 1.1% Two or more races, 1.6% Hispanic of any race; Average household size: 2.47; Median age: 39.1; Age under 18: 21.8%; Age 65 and over: 16.1%; Males per 100 females: 94.5; Marriage status: 28.9% never married, 50.7% now married, 1.7% separated, 9.0% widowed, 11.4% divorced; Foreign born: 2.1%; Speak English only: 97.0%; With disability: 12.6%; Veterans: 10.7%; Ancestry: 29.0% Irish, 27.9% German, 13.3% Italian, 7.7% Dutch, 7.4% English
Employment: 17.2% management, business, and financial, 4.1% computer, engineering, and science, 8.0% education, legal, community service, arts, and media, 4.6% healthcare practitioners, 21.7% service, 22.2% sales and office, 13.7% natural resources, construction, and maintenance, 8.5% production, transportation, and material moving
Income: Per capita: $23,892; Median household: $43,182; Average household: $57,233; Households with income of $100,000 or more: 14.3%; Poverty rate: 13.6%
Educational Attainment: High school diploma or higher: 86.1%; Bachelor's degree or higher: 24.0%; Graduate/professional degree or higher: 10.4%

School District(s)
Cobleskill-Richmondville Central SD (PK-12)
    2014-15 Enrollment: 1,842 . . . . (518) 234-4032
Housing: Homeownership rate: 70.4%; Median home value: $156,500; Median year structure built: 1970; Homeowner vacancy rate: 1.5%; Median selected monthly owner costs: $1,476 with a mortgage, $474 without a mortgage; Median gross rent: $702 per month; Rental vacancy rate: 4.0%

Health Insurance: 93.6% have insurance; 63.2% have private insurance; 42.3% have public insurance; 6.4% do not have insurance; 0.0% of children under 18 do not have insurance
Transportation: Commute: 91.0% car, 1.7% public transportation, 4.1% walk, 2.0% work from home; Mean travel time to work: 28.2 minutes

RICHMONDVILLE (village). Covers a land area of 1.846 square miles and a water area of 0 square miles. Located at 42.63° N. Lat; 74.56° W. Long. Elevation is 1,096 feet.
Population: 918; Growth (since 2000): 16.8%; Density: 497.2 persons per square mile; Race: 93.7% White, 0.2% Black/African American, 1.5% Asian, 1.5% American Indian/Alaska Native, 0.0% Native Hawaiian/Other Pacific Islander, 3.1% Two or more races, 1.0% Hispanic of any race; Average household size: 2.79; Median age: 36.4; Age under 18: 26.8%; Age 65 and over: 16.8%; Males per 100 females: 82.5; Marriage status: 32.8% never married, 51.8% now married, 4.3% separated, 6.4% widowed, 8.9% divorced; Foreign born: 2.0%; Speak English only: 98.1%; With disability: 17.1%; Veterans: 11.2%; Ancestry: 31.3% Irish, 24.3% German, 16.1% Italian, 6.6% American, 6.3% Dutch
Employment: 10.5% management, business, and financial, 0.0% computer, engineering, and science, 9.6% education, legal, community service, arts, and media, 6.4% healthcare practitioners, 24.5% service, 18.1% sales and office, 14.3% natural resources, construction, and maintenance, 16.6% production, transportation, and material moving
Income: Per capita: $21,007; Median household: $43,214; Average household: $54,555; Households with income of $100,000 or more: 9.5%; Poverty rate: 12.5%
Educational Attainment: High school diploma or higher: 78.6%; Bachelor's degree or higher: 11.2%; Graduate/professional degree or higher: 7.0%

School District(s)
Cobleskill-Richmondville Central SD (PK-12)
    2014-15 Enrollment: 1,842 . . . . (518) 234-4032
Housing: Homeownership rate: 53.7%; Median home value: $121,200; Median year structure built: 1954; Homeowner vacancy rate: 3.2%; Median selected monthly owner costs: $1,380 with a mortgage, $470 without a mortgage; Median gross rent: $648 per month; Rental vacancy rate: 0.0%
Health Insurance: 92.3% have insurance; 56.0% have private insurance; 50.7% have public insurance; 7.7% do not have insurance; 0.0% of children under 18 do not have insurance
Transportation: Commute: 86.5% car, 5.6% public transportation, 5.0% walk, 0.6% work from home; Mean travel time to work: 30.8 minutes

SCHOHARIE (town). Covers a land area of 29.830 square miles and a water area of 0.129 square miles. Located at 42.68° N. Lat; 74.31° W. Long. Elevation is 600 feet.
History: Has 18th-century buildings including Old Stone Fort; 1772, now a museum. Incorporated 1867.
Population: 3,094; Growth (since 2000): -6.2%; Density: 103.7 persons per square mile; Race: 97.4% White, 1.3% Black/African American, 0.0% Asian, 0.0% American Indian/Alaska Native, 0.0% Native Hawaiian/Other Pacific Islander, 0.9% Two or more races, 1.0% Hispanic of any race; Average household size: 2.37; Median age: 50.7; Age under 18: 17.8%; Age 65 and over: 25.5%; Males per 100 females: 93.5; Marriage status: 23.0% never married, 60.1% now married, 2.8% separated, 6.5% widowed, 10.4% divorced; Foreign born: 3.1%; Speak English only: 96.9%; With disability: 17.7%; Veterans: 11.4%; Ancestry: 23.2% German, 14.9% Irish, 14.0% American, 13.6% English, 10.5% Italian
Employment: 17.1% management, business, and financial, 7.1% computer, engineering, and science, 8.3% education, legal, community service, arts, and media, 6.5% healthcare practitioners, 11.2% service, 27.6% sales and office, 11.1% natural resources, construction, and maintenance, 11.1% production, transportation, and material moving
Income: Per capita: $27,333; Median household: $51,821; Average household: $63,299; Households with income of $100,000 or more: 21.5%; Poverty rate: 9.6%
Educational Attainment: High school diploma or higher: 87.3%; Bachelor's degree or higher: 15.8%; Graduate/professional degree or higher: 6.2%

School District(s)
Schoharie Central SD (KG-12)
    2014-15 Enrollment: 867 . . . . (518) 295-6679
Housing: Homeownership rate: 79.5%; Median home value: $167,300; Median year structure built: 1972; Homeowner vacancy rate: 1.7%; Median

selected monthly owner costs: $1,262 with a mortgage, $612 without a mortgage; Median gross rent: $644 per month; Rental vacancy rate: 1.1%
Health Insurance: 96.6% have insurance; 75.8% have private insurance; 42.7% have public insurance; 3.4% do not have insurance; 2.7% of children under 18 do not have insurance
Transportation: Commute: 93.0% car, 0.4% public transportation, 2.3% walk, 3.5% work from home; Mean travel time to work: 31.9 minutes

SCHOHARIE (village). County seat. Covers a land area of 1.658 square miles and a water area of <.001 square miles. Located at 42.67° N. Lat; 74.31° W. Long. Elevation is 600 feet.
Population: 859; Growth (since 2000): -16.6%; Density: 518.0 persons per square mile; Race: 94.1% White, 4.7% Black/African American, 0.0% Asian, 0.0% American Indian/Alaska Native, 0.0% Native Hawaiian/Other Pacific Islander, 0.0% Two or more races, 3.5% Hispanic of any race; Average household size: 2.04; Median age: 50.3; Age under 18: 14.0%; Age 65 and over: 26.5%; Males per 100 females: 91.7; Marriage status: 32.7% never married, 38.3% now married, 0.3% separated, 11.2% widowed, 17.9% divorced; Foreign born: 2.2%; Speak English only: 97.8%; With disability: 26.3%; Veterans: 12.0%; Ancestry: 17.3% German, 16.5% Irish, 11.2% European, 11.1% Dutch, 7.6% English
Employment: 14.1% management, business, and financial, 4.3% computer, engineering, and science, 8.4% education, legal, community service, arts, and media, 7.1% healthcare practitioners, 7.9% service, 28.5% sales and office, 12.8% natural resources, construction, and maintenance, 16.8% production, transportation, and material moving
Income: Per capita: $27,779; Median household: $45,417; Average household: $56,491; Households with income of $100,000 or more: 15.0%; Poverty rate: 17.4%
Educational Attainment: High school diploma or higher: 85.4%; Bachelor's degree or higher: 14.4%; Graduate/professional degree or higher: 6.1%

School District(s)
Schoharie Central SD (KG-12)
    2014-15 Enrollment: 867 . . . . (518) 295-6679
Housing: Homeownership rate: 52.4%; Median home value: $149,000; Median year structure built: 1948; Homeowner vacancy rate: 7.7%; Median selected monthly owner costs: $1,760 with a mortgage, $651 without a mortgage; Median gross rent: $790 per month; Rental vacancy rate: 1.6%
Health Insurance: 96.5% have insurance; 71.1% have private insurance; 48.0% have public insurance; 3.5% do not have insurance; 0.0% of children under 18 do not have insurance
Safety: Violent crime rate: 0.0 per 10,000 population; Property crime rate: 12.0 per 10,000 population
Transportation: Commute: 91.2% car, 1.2% public transportation, 4.1% walk, 0.9% work from home; Mean travel time to work: 24.3 minutes

SEWARD (town). Covers a land area of 36.377 square miles and a water area of 0.079 square miles. Located at 42.71° N. Lat; 74.58° W. Long. Elevation is 1,184 feet.
Population: 1,518; Growth (since 2000): -7.3%; Density: 41.7 persons per square mile; Race: 98.7% White, 0.1% Black/African American, 0.0% Asian, 0.3% American Indian/Alaska Native, 0.0% Native Hawaiian/Other Pacific Islander, 0.4% Two or more races, 2.0% Hispanic of any race; Average household size: 2.48; Median age: 45.7; Age under 18: 19.2%; Age 65 and over: 15.9%; Males per 100 females: 100.8; Marriage status: 25.1% never married, 60.5% now married, 4.8% separated, 5.7% widowed, 8.7% divorced; Foreign born: 3.3%; Speak English only: 95.8%; With disability: 11.3%; Veterans: 9.4%; Ancestry: 28.9% German, 20.0% Irish, 14.0% Italian, 9.3% English, 7.6% American
Employment: 17.2% management, business, and financial, 2.4% computer, engineering, and science, 13.2% education, legal, community service, arts, and media, 2.9% healthcare practitioners, 11.6% service, 21.7% sales and office, 16.5% natural resources, construction, and maintenance, 14.4% production, transportation, and material moving
Income: Per capita: $28,120; Median household: $57,188; Average household: $68,596; Households with income of $100,000 or more: 21.8%; Poverty rate: 7.5%
Educational Attainment: High school diploma or higher: 89.3%; Bachelor's degree or higher: 24.6%; Graduate/professional degree or higher: 6.8%
Housing: Homeownership rate: 90.7%; Median home value: $157,800; Median year structure built: 1965; Homeowner vacancy rate: 0.0%; Median selected monthly owner costs: $1,497 with a mortgage, $535 without a mortgage; Median gross rent: $950 per month; Rental vacancy rate: 0.0%

Health Insurance: 93.5% have insurance; 76.6% have private insurance; 31.1% have public insurance; 6.5% do not have insurance; 0.0% of children under 18 do not have insurance

Transportation: Commute: 91.3% car, 2.0% public transportation, 1.1% walk, 4.4% work from home; Mean travel time to work: 31.1 minutes

---

SHARON (town). Covers a land area of 39.062 square miles and a water area of 0.098 square miles. Located at 42.78° N. Lat; 74.61° W. Long. Elevation is 1,184 feet.

History: Former health resort, with sulphur springs.

Population: 2,036; Growth (since 2000): 10.5%; Density: 52.1 persons per square mile; Race: 96.9% White, 0.1% Black/African American, 2.3% Asian, 0.0% American Indian/Alaska Native, 0.0% Native Hawaiian/Other Pacific Islander, 0.8% Two or more races, 2.0% Hispanic of any race; Average household size: 2.66; Median age: 42.8; Age under 18: 20.0%; Age 65 and over: 14.1%; Males per 100 females: 105.6; Marriage status: 27.4% never married, 56.1% now married, 5.1% separated, 6.4% widowed, 10.0% divorced; Foreign born: 3.3%; Speak English only: 93.8%; With disability: 12.3%; Veterans: 9.8%; Ancestry: 20.2% Irish, 19.1% German, 11.1% Italian, 10.1% English, 8.3% Dutch

Employment: 13.2% management, business, and financial, 3.5% computer, engineering, and science, 5.9% education, legal, community service, arts, and media, 3.2% healthcare practitioners, 16.2% service, 26.7% sales and office, 16.3% natural resources, construction, and maintenance, 15.0% production, transportation, and material moving

Income: Per capita: $22,045; Median household: $47,697; Average household: $57,068; Households with income of $100,000 or more: 15.1%; Poverty rate: 21.8%

Educational Attainment: High school diploma or higher: 90.1%; Bachelor's degree or higher: 16.3%; Graduate/professional degree or higher: 5.2%

Housing: Homeownership rate: 66.2%; Median home value: $140,800; Median year structure built: 1952; Homeowner vacancy rate: 0.0%; Median selected monthly owner costs: $1,230 with a mortgage, $628 without a mortgage; Median gross rent: $734 per month; Rental vacancy rate: 0.0%

Health Insurance: 88.9% have insurance; 63.7% have private insurance; 38.0% have public insurance; 11.1% do not have insurance; 1.7% of children under 18 do not have insurance

Transportation: Commute: 89.7% car, 0.2% public transportation, 1.6% walk, 7.9% work from home; Mean travel time to work: 27.9 minutes

---

SHARON SPRINGS (village). Covers a land area of 1.827 square miles and a water area of 0 square miles. Located at 42.79° N. Lat; 74.61° W. Long. Elevation is 1,102 feet.

Population: 614; Growth (since 2000): 12.2%; Density: 336.1 persons per square mile; Race: 91.7% White, 0.0% Black/African American, 6.2% Asian, 0.0% American Indian/Alaska Native, 0.0% Native Hawaiian/Other Pacific Islander, 2.1% Two or more races, 0.5% Hispanic of any race; Average household size: 2.49; Median age: 45.3; Age under 18: 16.1%; Age 65 and over: 13.7%; Males per 100 females: 100.7; Marriage status: 31.0% never married, 45.7% now married, 2.6% separated, 7.3% widowed, 16.0% divorced; Foreign born: 6.5%; Speak English only: 90.9%; With disability: 17.8%; Veterans: 11.3%; Ancestry: 22.1% Irish, 17.8% German, 15.0% English, 14.7% Italian, 9.8% European

Employment: 13.9% management, business, and financial, 3.2% computer, engineering, and science, 7.8% education, legal, community service, arts, and media, 4.6% healthcare practitioners, 18.5% service, 21.7% sales and office, 17.8% natural resources, construction, and maintenance, 12.5% production, transportation, and material moving

Income: Per capita: $23,104; Median household: $46,875; Average household: $54,819; Households with income of $100,000 or more: 14.3%; Poverty rate: 15.6%

Educational Attainment: High school diploma or higher: 85.0%; Bachelor's degree or higher: 18.8%; Graduate/professional degree or higher: 4.3%

School District(s)

Sharon Springs Central SD (KG-12)

    2014-15 Enrollment: 284 . . . . (518) 284-2266

Housing: Homeownership rate: 53.8%; Median home value: $113,800; Median year structure built: 1945; Homeowner vacancy rate: 0.0%; Median selected monthly owner costs: $1,125 with a mortgage, $646 without a mortgage; Median gross rent: $677 per month; Rental vacancy rate: 0.0%

Health Insurance: 91.7% have insurance; 54.1% have private insurance; 51.5% have public insurance; 8.3% do not have insurance; 0.0% of children under 18 do not have insurance

Transportation: Commute: 91.4% car, 0.7% public transportation, 0.7% walk, 7.1% work from home; Mean travel time to work: 32.4 minutes

---

SLOANSVILLE (unincorporated postal area)

ZCTA: 12160

    Covers a land area of 17.720 square miles and a water area of 0.139 square miles. Located at 42.76° N. Lat; 74.38° W. Long. Elevation is 679 feet.

Population: 907; Growth (since 2000): -22.9%; Density: 51.2 persons per square mile; Race: 99.0% White, 0.0% Black/African American, 0.0% Asian, 0.0% American Indian/Alaska Native, 0.0% Native Hawaiian/Other Pacific Islander, 0.4% Two or more races, 5.4% Hispanic of any race; Average household size: 2.65; Median age: 48.7; Age under 18: 19.6%; Age 65 and over: 9.6%; Males per 100 females: 104.8; Marriage status: 20.2% never married, 65.1% now married, 1.1% separated, 4.8% widowed, 9.9% divorced; Foreign born: 1.3%; Speak English only: 97.3%; With disability: 12.8%; Veterans: 12.2%; Ancestry: 32.5% German, 18.2% Irish, 9.8% English, 5.1% Italian, 4.2% European

Employment: 9.5% management, business, and financial, 1.9% computer, engineering, and science, 7.7% education, legal, community service, arts, and media, 2.1% healthcare practitioners, 16.7% service, 25.5% sales and office, 16.9% natural resources, construction, and maintenance, 19.7% production, transportation, and material moving

Income: Per capita: $25,012; Median household: $58,333; Average household: $64,751; Households with income of $100,000 or more: 14.9%; Poverty rate: 15.9%

Educational Attainment: High school diploma or higher: 89.3%; Bachelor's degree or higher: 14.9%; Graduate/professional degree or higher: 5.0%

Housing: Homeownership rate: 91.2%; Median home value: $131,000; Median year structure built: 1978; Homeowner vacancy rate: 2.5%; Median selected monthly owner costs: $1,316 with a mortgage, $533 without a mortgage; Median gross rent: $540 per month; Rental vacancy rate: 0.0%

Health Insurance: 87.1% have insurance; 67.4% have private insurance; 28.2% have public insurance; 12.9% do not have insurance; 0.0% of children under 18 do not have insurance

Transportation: Commute: 92.1% car, 0.0% public transportation, 0.9% walk, 6.1% work from home; Mean travel time to work: 31.5 minutes

---

SUMMIT (town). Covers a land area of 37.085 square miles and a water area of 0.399 square miles. Located at 42.57° N. Lat; 74.60° W. Long. Elevation is 2,116 feet.

Population: 1,070; Growth (since 2000): -4.7%; Density: 28.9 persons per square mile; Race: 96.0% White, 0.0% Black/African American, 0.5% Asian, 0.0% American Indian/Alaska Native, 0.0% Native Hawaiian/Other Pacific Islander, 3.6% Two or more races, 3.4% Hispanic of any race; Average household size: 2.48; Median age: 42.5; Age under 18: 23.1%; Age 65 and over: 15.0%; Males per 100 females: 115.4; Marriage status: 26.5% never married, 57.1% now married, 2.0% separated, 7.9% widowed, 8.5% divorced; Foreign born: 2.7%; Speak English only: 97.4%; With disability: 12.9%; Veterans: 12.3%; Ancestry: 26.4% German, 25.1% Irish, 16.5% Italian, 14.5% English, 10.4% Dutch

Employment: 25.1% management, business, and financial, 2.1% computer, engineering, and science, 9.6% education, legal, community service, arts, and media, 2.1% healthcare practitioners, 24.8% service, 20.5% sales and office, 6.6% natural resources, construction, and maintenance, 9.3% production, transportation, and material moving

Income: Per capita: $25,063; Median household: $53,654; Average household: $61,056; Households with income of $100,000 or more: 18.7%; Poverty rate: 12.9%

Educational Attainment: High school diploma or higher: 90.8%; Bachelor's degree or higher: 19.0%; Graduate/professional degree or higher: 7.0%

Housing: Homeownership rate: 92.8%; Median home value: $153,100; Median year structure built: 1973; Homeowner vacancy rate: 0.0%; Median selected monthly owner costs: $1,206 with a mortgage, $453 without a mortgage; Median gross rent: $913 per month; Rental vacancy rate: 8.8%

Health Insurance: 90.9% have insurance; 63.7% have private insurance; 37.2% have public insurance; 9.1% do not have insurance; 5.7% of children under 18 do not have insurance

Transportation: Commute: 92.7% car, 0.0% public transportation, 2.8% walk, 3.9% work from home; Mean travel time to work: 32.5 minutes

WARNERVILLE (unincorporated postal area)
ZCTA: 12187

Covers a land area of 23.019 square miles and a water area of 0.023 square miles. Located at 42.62° N. Lat; 74.46° W. Long. Elevation is 925 feet.

Population: 432; Growth (since 2000): -36.8%; Density: 18.8 persons per square mile; Race: 99.3% White, 0.0% Black/African American, 0.0% Asian, 0.0% American Indian/Alaska Native, 0.0% Native Hawaiian/Other Pacific Islander, 0.7% Two or more races, 3.9% Hispanic of any race; Average household size: 2.17; Median age: 46.7; Age under 18: 16.7%; Age 65 and over: 18.5%; Males per 100 females: 108.1; Marriage status: 17.5% never married, 56.3% now married, 3.7% separated, 11.0% widowed, 15.2% divorced; Foreign born: 1.4%; Speak English only: 92.9%; With disability: 20.4%; Veterans: 13.6%; Ancestry: 29.9% German, 20.8% Irish, 20.1% English, 19.0% Italian, 6.3% American

Employment: 33.8% management, business, and financial, 2.4% computer, engineering, and science, 8.7% education, legal, community service, arts, and media, 2.9% healthcare practitioners, 21.7% service, 15.0% sales and office, 6.8% natural resources, construction, and maintenance, 8.7% production, transportation, and material moving

Income: Per capita: $29,012; Median household: $49,464; Average household: $60,619; Households with income of $100,000 or more: 14.0%; Poverty rate: 12.3%

Educational Attainment: High school diploma or higher: 91.7%; Bachelor's degree or higher: 34.5%; Graduate/professional degree or higher: 16.4%

Housing: Homeownership rate: 100.0%; Median home value: $159,100; Median year structure built: 1968; Homeowner vacancy rate: 0.0%; Median selected monthly owner costs: $1,326 with a mortgage, $489 without a mortgage; Median gross rent: n/a per month; Rental vacancy rate: 0.0%

Health Insurance: 95.1% have insurance; 72.9% have private insurance; 33.1% have public insurance; 4.9% do not have insurance; 0.0% of children under 18 do not have insurance

Transportation: Commute: 78.9% car, 0.0% public transportation, 14.4% walk, 5.2% work from home; Mean travel time to work: 31.1 minutes

WEST FULTON (unincorporated postal area)
ZCTA: 12194

Covers a land area of 15.429 square miles and a water area of 0.009 square miles. Located at 42.53° N. Lat; 74.45° W. Long. Elevation is 1,158 feet.

Population: 156; Growth (since 2000): -27.4%; Density: 10.1 persons per square mile; Race: 100.0% White, 0.0% Black/African American, 0.0% Asian, 0.0% American Indian/Alaska Native, 0.0% Native Hawaiian/Other Pacific Islander, 0.0% Two or more races, 0.0% Hispanic of any race; Average household size: 2.36; Median age: 51.0; Age under 18: 23.7%; Age 65 and over: 23.1%; Males per 100 females: 99.0; Marriage status: 5.7% never married, 80.5% now married, 4.1% separated, 3.3% widowed, 10.6% divorced; Foreign born: 1.3%; Speak English only: 93.9%; With disability: 17.9%; Veterans: 8.4%; Ancestry: 38.5% German, 17.3% Irish, 11.5% American, 11.5% English, 10.3% Italian

Employment: 24.1% management, business, and financial, 5.6% computer, engineering, and science, 5.6% education, legal, community service, arts, and media, 3.7% healthcare practitioners, 0.0% service, 22.2% sales and office, 33.3% natural resources, construction, and maintenance, 5.6% production, transportation, and material moving

Income: Per capita: $25,112; Median household: $61,250; Average household: $58,779; Households with income of $100,000 or more: 9.0%; Poverty rate: 16.7%

Educational Attainment: High school diploma or higher: 91.4%; Bachelor's degree or higher: 9.5%; Graduate/professional degree or higher: 6.0%

Housing: Homeownership rate: 100.0%; Median home value: n/a; Median year structure built: 1970; Homeowner vacancy rate: 12.0%; Median selected monthly owner costs: $1,304 with a mortgage, $570 without a mortgage; Median gross rent: n/a per month; Rental vacancy rate: 0.0%

Health Insurance: 92.3% have insurance; 72.4% have private insurance; 38.5% have public insurance; 7.7% do not have insurance; 0.0% of children under 18 do not have insurance

Transportation: Commute: 72.2% car, 0.0% public transportation, 16.7% walk, 11.1% work from home; Mean travel time to work: 29.7 minutes

WRIGHT (town). Covers a land area of 28.636 square miles and a water area of 0.082 square miles. Located at 42.67° N. Lat; 74.21° W. Long.

Population: 1,794; Growth (since 2000): 16.0%; Density: 62.6 persons per square mile; Race: 97.3% White, 0.2% Black/African American, 1.6% Asian, 0.0% American Indian/Alaska Native, 0.0% Native Hawaiian/Other Pacific Islander, 0.9% Two or more races, 4.5% Hispanic of any race; Average household size: 2.97; Median age: 38.7; Age under 18: 25.1%; Age 65 and over: 12.7%; Males per 100 females: 105.5; Marriage status: 26.9% never married, 55.5% now married, 2.0% separated, 5.7% widowed, 12.0% divorced; Foreign born: 1.4%; Speak English only: 95.4%; With disability: 12.9%; Veterans: 9.4%; Ancestry: 29.7% German, 24.9% Irish, 11.3% Italian, 8.4% English, 8.1% American

Employment: 12.1% management, business, and financial, 5.7% computer, engineering, and science, 13.1% education, legal, community service, arts, and media, 6.1% healthcare practitioners, 17.6% service, 20.3% sales and office, 15.3% natural resources, construction, and maintenance, 9.8% production, transportation, and material moving

Income: Per capita: $26,094; Median household: $63,375; Average household: $74,307; Households with income of $100,000 or more: 23.6%; Poverty rate: 11.1%

Educational Attainment: High school diploma or higher: 91.4%; Bachelor's degree or higher: 25.1%; Graduate/professional degree or higher: 13.9%

Housing: Homeownership rate: 86.8%; Median home value: $159,700; Median year structure built: 1977; Homeowner vacancy rate: 0.0%; Median selected monthly owner costs: $1,498 with a mortgage, $549 without a mortgage; Median gross rent: $827 per month; Rental vacancy rate: 0.0%

Health Insurance: 93.2% have insurance; 73.4% have private insurance; 35.9% have public insurance; 6.8% do not have insurance; 0.0% of children under 18 do not have insurance

Transportation: Commute: 90.4% car, 0.0% public transportation, 1.3% walk, 7.6% work from home; Mean travel time to work: 34.5 minutes

Schuyler County

Located in west central New York, in the Finger Lakes region; drained by Cayuta and Catherine Creeks; includes Lamoka and Cayuta Lakes and part of Seneca Lake. Covers a land area of 328.333 square miles, a water area of 13.995 square miles, and is located in the Eastern Time Zone at 42.42° N. Lat., 76.94° W. Long. The county was founded in 1854. County seat is Watkins Glen.

Population: 18,410; Growth (since 2000): -4.2%; Density: 56.1 persons per square mile; Race: 96.6% White, 1.1% Black/African American, 0.5% Asian, 0.2% American Indian/Alaska Native, 0.0% Native Hawaiian/Other Pacific Islander, 1.4% two or more races, 1.7% Hispanic of any race; Average household size: 2.35; Median age: 45.5; Age under 18: 19.9%; Age 65 and over: 18.8%; Males per 100 females: 98.9; Marriage status: 26.9% never married, 51.8% now married, 2.6% separated, 7.6% widowed, 13.8% divorced; Foreign born: 1.6%; Speak English only: 97.1%; With disability: 14.9%; Veterans: 11.4%; Ancestry: 20.4% American, 18.1% Irish, 15.0% German, 14.5% English, 8.6% Italian

Religion: Six largest groups: 12.9% Catholicism, 6.1% Methodist/Pietist, 3.2% Baptist, 2.7% Presbyterian-Reformed, 0.8% Episcopalianism/Anglicanism, 0.8% Non-denominational Protestant

Economy: Unemployment rate: 4.8%; Leading industries: 18.3 % accommodation and food services; 16.5 % retail trade; 12.0 % other services (except public administration); Farms: 393 totaling 69,222 acres; Company size: 0 employ 1,000 or more persons, 0 employ 500 to 999 persons, 9 employ 100 to 499 persons, 373 employ less than 100 persons; Business ownership: 440 women-owned, n/a Black-owned, n/a Hispanic-owned, n/a Asian-owned, n/a American Indian/Alaska Native-owned

Employment: 12.8% management, business, and financial, 3.4% computer, engineering, and science, 10.3% education, legal, community service, arts, and media, 6.3% healthcare practitioners, 20.6% service, 20.2% sales and office, 12.1% natural resources, construction, and maintenance, 14.3% production, transportation, and material moving

Income: Per capita: $25,189; Median household: $47,680; Average household: $59,578; Households with income of $100,000 or more: 15.8%; Poverty rate: 14.5%

Educational Attainment: High school diploma or higher: 89.9%; Bachelor's degree or higher: 19.5%; Graduate/professional degree or higher: 9.4%

Housing: Homeownership rate: 77.2%; Median home value: $108,500; Median year structure built: 1961; Homeowner vacancy rate: 0.6%; Median selected monthly owner costs: $1,135 with a mortgage, $444 without a mortgage; Median gross rent: $640 per month; Rental vacancy rate: 9.3%

Vital Statistics: Birth rate: 86.9 per 10,000 population; Death rate: 99.0 per 10,000 population; Age-adjusted cancer mortality rate: 148.2 deaths per 100,000 population

Health Insurance: 90.1% have insurance; 64.5% have private insurance; 39.7% have public insurance; 9.9% do not have insurance; 3.8% of children under 18 do not have insurance

Health Care: Physicians: 13.7 per 10,000 population; Dentists: 2.2 per 10,000 population; Hospital beds: 75.2 per 10,000 population; Hospital admissions: 593.8 per 10,000 population

Transportation: Commute: 90.5% car, 0.8% public transportation, 3.9% walk, 3.5% work from home; Mean travel time to work: 25.6 minutes

2016 Presidential Election: 58.3% Trump, 35.7% Clinton, 3.6% Johnson, 2.5% Stein

National and State Parks: Cliffside State Forest; Connecticut Hill State Game Management Area; Finger Lakes National Forest; Green Mountain National Forest-Hector Ranger District; Watkins Glen State Park

Additional Information Contacts

Schuyler Government . . . . (607) 535-8133
http://www.schuylercounty.us

Schuyler County Communities

ALPINE (unincorporated postal area)

ZCTA: 14805

Covers a land area of 27.655 square miles and a water area of 0.599 square miles. Located at 42.35° N. Lat; 76.72° W. Long. Elevation is 1,165 feet.

Population: 1,023; Growth (since 2000): -15.2%; Density: 37.0 persons per square mile; Race: 94.3% White, 2.3% Black/African American, 0.0% Asian, 1.0% American Indian/Alaska Native, 0.0% Native Hawaiian/Other Pacific Islander, 2.3% Two or more races, 2.8% Hispanic of any race; Average household size: 2.49; Median age: 43.8; Age under 18: 22.4%; Age 65 and over: 18.4%; Males per 100 females: 100.0; Marriage status: 25.8% never married, 63.1% now married, 0.5% separated, 4.7% widowed, 6.4% divorced; Foreign born: 2.5%; Speak English only: 97.9%; With disability: 11.8%; Veterans: 12.0%; Ancestry: 16.5% Irish, 14.7% American, 13.3% German, 13.1% English, 12.8% Italian

Employment: 12.0% management, business, and financial, 2.2% computer, engineering, and science, 16.2% education, legal, community service, arts, and media, 4.4% healthcare practitioners, 14.0% service, 23.2% sales and office, 10.1% natural resources, construction, and maintenance, 17.9% production, transportation, and material moving

Income: Per capita: $25,791; Median household: $55,655; Average household: $63,718; Households with income of $100,000 or more: 15.6%; Poverty rate: 13.7%

Educational Attainment: High school diploma or higher: 93.3%; Bachelor's degree or higher: 28.0%; Graduate/professional degree or higher: 12.3%

Housing: Homeownership rate: 84.4%; Median home value: $111,300; Median year structure built: 1965; Homeowner vacancy rate: 0.0%; Median selected monthly owner costs: $1,308 with a mortgage, $407 without a mortgage; Median gross rent: $788 per month; Rental vacancy rate: 0.0%

Health Insurance: 95.3% have insurance; 73.2% have private insurance; 36.4% have public insurance; 4.7% do not have insurance; 1.7% of children under 18 do not have insurance

Transportation: Commute: 93.3% car, 2.0% public transportation, 0.7% walk, 2.0% work from home; Mean travel time to work: 31.9 minutes

BEAVER DAMS (unincorporated postal area)

ZCTA: 14812

Covers a land area of 77.543 square miles and a water area of 0.085 square miles. Located at 42.30° N. Lat; 77.01° W. Long. Elevation is 1,263 feet.

Population: 3,332; Growth (since 2000): -15.3%; Density: 43.0 persons per square mile; Race: 95.6% White, 2.6% Black/African American, 0.3% Asian, 0.0% American Indian/Alaska Native, 0.0% Native

Hawaiian/Other Pacific Islander, 0.5% Two or more races, 2.0% Hispanic of any race; Average household size: 2.68; Median age: 37.5; Age under 18: 25.4%; Age 65 and over: 11.1%; Males per 100 females: 111.6; Marriage status: 26.8% never married, 59.2% now married, 2.7% separated, 4.9% widowed, 9.2% divorced; Foreign born: 1.1%; Speak English only: 96.6%; With disability: 13.5%; Veterans: 9.9%; Ancestry: 23.8% American, 17.4% Irish, 13.2% English, 11.9% German, 10.3% Italian

Employment: 5.9% management, business, and financial, 6.5% computer, engineering, and science, 7.8% education, legal, community service, arts, and media, 5.0% healthcare practitioners, 17.3% service, 21.5% sales and office, 16.9% natural resources, construction, and maintenance, 19.1% production, transportation, and material moving

Income: Per capita: $22,661; Median household: $58,889; Average household: $63,405; Households with income of $100,000 or more: 16.9%; Poverty rate: 12.7%

Educational Attainment: High school diploma or higher: 87.5%; Bachelor's degree or higher: 15.5%; Graduate/professional degree or higher: 6.6%

Housing: Homeownership rate: 88.6%; Median home value: $87,400; Median year structure built: 1972; Homeowner vacancy rate: 0.0%; Median selected monthly owner costs: $1,104 with a mortgage, $438 without a mortgage; Median gross rent: $609 per month; Rental vacancy rate: 25.4%

Health Insurance: 95.4% have insurance; 72.7% have private insurance; 34.0% have public insurance; 4.6% do not have insurance; 0.4% of children under 18 do not have insurance

Transportation: Commute: 96.2% car, 0.0% public transportation, 1.1% walk, 1.5% work from home; Mean travel time to work: 26.0 minutes

BURDETT (village). Covers a land area of 0.962 square miles and a water area of 0 square miles. Located at 42.42° N. Lat; 76.84° W. Long. Elevation is 978 feet.

Population: 364; Growth (since 2000): 2.0%; Density: 378.2 persons per square mile; Race: 98.9% White, 0.0% Black/African American, 0.0% Asian, 1.1% American Indian/Alaska Native, 0.0% Native Hawaiian/Other Pacific Islander, 0.0% Two or more races, 0.0% Hispanic of any race; Average household size: 2.17; Median age: 45.9; Age under 18: 15.7%; Age 65 and over: 23.6%; Males per 100 females: 87.8; Marriage status: 32.3% never married, 44.9% now married, 3.4% separated, 9.2% widowed, 13.5% divorced; Foreign born: 0.0%; Speak English only: 99.1%; With disability: 13.2%; Veterans: 5.9%; Ancestry: 25.8% German, 19.5% American, 19.5% Italian, 14.6% English, 6.9% Irish

Employment: 12.8% management, business, and financial, 4.1% computer, engineering, and science, 13.8% education, legal, community service, arts, and media, 8.7% healthcare practitioners, 19.5% service, 15.9% sales and office, 11.8% natural resources, construction, and maintenance, 13.3% production, transportation, and material moving

Income: Per capita: $25,671; Median household: $47,500; Average household: $52,951; Households with income of $100,000 or more: 8.4%; Poverty rate: 13.1%

Educational Attainment: High school diploma or higher: 91.9%; Bachelor's degree or higher: 26.6%; Graduate/professional degree or higher: 9.6%

Housing: Homeownership rate: 79.2%; Median home value: $116,500; Median year structure built: Before 1940; Homeowner vacancy rate: 4.3%; Median selected monthly owner costs: $1,375 with a mortgage, $489 without a mortgage; Median gross rent: $708 per month; Rental vacancy rate: 0.0%

Health Insurance: 92.3% have insurance; 72.0% have private insurance; 39.6% have public insurance; 7.7% do not have insurance; 0.0% of children under 18 do not have insurance

Transportation: Commute: 84.9% car, 4.2% public transportation, 2.6% walk, 7.8% work from home; Mean travel time to work: 24.9 minutes

CATHARINE (town). Covers a land area of 32.295 square miles and a water area of 0.605 square miles. Located at 42.34° N. Lat; 76.73° W. Long. Elevation is 1,178 feet.

Population: 1,769; Growth (since 2000): -8.3%; Density: 54.8 persons per square mile; Race: 97.6% White, 0.5% Black/African American, 0.0% Asian, 0.7% American Indian/Alaska Native, 0.0% Native Hawaiian/Other Pacific Islander, 1.1% Two or more races, 1.9% Hispanic of any race; Average household size: 2.46; Median age: 41.1; Age under 18: 25.6%; Age 65 and over: 18.0%; Males per 100 females: 96.2; Marriage status: 26.0% never married, 52.7% now married, 2.2% separated, 8.4%

widowed, 12.9% divorced; Foreign born: 0.7%; Speak English only: 97.9%; With disability: 12.8%; Veterans: 11.1%; Ancestry: 17.3% Irish, 16.8% English, 15.3% American, 14.0% German, 8.0% Italian
Employment: 9.6% management, business, and financial, 1.4% computer, engineering, and science, 11.7% education, legal, community service, arts, and media, 2.9% healthcare practitioners, 18.9% service, 23.4% sales and office, 10.1% natural resources, construction, and maintenance, 22.0% production, transportation, and material moving
Income: Per capita: $22,219; Median household: $46,950; Average household: $54,700; Households with income of $100,000 or more: 9.5%; Poverty rate: 15.4%
Educational Attainment: High school diploma or higher: 90.2%; Bachelor's degree or higher: 18.0%; Graduate/professional degree or higher: 9.1%
Housing: Homeownership rate: 79.2%; Median home value: $105,500; Median year structure built: 1949; Homeowner vacancy rate: 0.4%; Median selected monthly owner costs: $1,144 with a mortgage, $468 without a mortgage; Median gross rent: $590 per month; Rental vacancy rate: 14.5%
Health Insurance: 91.9% have insurance; 69.4% have private insurance; 37.1% have public insurance; 8.1% do not have insurance; 4.4% of children under 18 do not have insurance
Transportation: Commute: 90.6% car, 1.9% public transportation, 3.8% walk, 2.3% work from home; Mean travel time to work: 30.1 minutes

CAYUTA (town). Covers a land area of 20.319 square miles and a water area of <.001 square miles. Located at 42.27° N. Lat; 76.68° W. Long. Elevation is 1,102 feet.
Population: 425; Growth (since 2000): -22.0%; Density: 20.9 persons per square mile; Race: 90.4% White, 7.1% Black/African American, 0.0% Asian, 0.5% American Indian/Alaska Native, 0.0% Native Hawaiian/Other Pacific Islander, 2.1% Two or more races, 2.1% Hispanic of any race; Average household size: 2.37; Median age: 43.7; Age under 18: 17.4%; Age 65 and over: 14.8%; Males per 100 females: 100.7; Marriage status: 23.4% never married, 61.3% now married, 1.1% separated, 4.7% widowed, 10.6% divorced; Foreign born: 6.4%; Speak English only: 99.0%; With disability: 16.7%; Veterans: 10.5%; Ancestry: 20.7% American, 18.1% Irish, 12.7% German, 8.5% Italian, 5.9% English
Employment: 13.2% management, business, and financial, 2.1% computer, engineering, and science, 11.1% education, legal, community service, arts, and media, 0.0% healthcare practitioners, 32.1% service, 20.5% sales and office, 9.5% natural resources, construction, and maintenance, 11.6% production, transportation, and material moving
Income: Per capita: $19,744; Median household: $36,875; Average household: $46,562; Households with income of $100,000 or more: 10.0%; Poverty rate: 24.7%
Educational Attainment: High school diploma or higher: 89.5%; Bachelor's degree or higher: 11.7%; Graduate/professional degree or higher: 4.9%
Housing: Homeownership rate: 77.7%; Median home value: $85,600; Median year structure built: 1974; Homeowner vacancy rate: 0.0%; Median selected monthly owner costs: $1,033 with a mortgage, $330 without a mortgage; Median gross rent: $832 per month; Rental vacancy rate: 14.3%
Health Insurance: 95.1% have insurance; 52.2% have private insurance; 52.5% have public insurance; 4.9% do not have insurance; 0.0% of children under 18 do not have insurance
Transportation: Commute: 97.8% car, 0.0% public transportation, 0.0% walk, 2.2% work from home; Mean travel time to work: 28.1 minutes

DIX (town). Covers a land area of 36.258 square miles and a water area of 0.454 square miles. Located at 42.33° N. Lat; 76.90° W. Long.
Population: 3,905; Growth (since 2000): -7.0%; Density: 107.7 persons per square mile; Race: 96.8% White, 1.3% Black/African American, 0.7% Asian, 0.0% American Indian/Alaska Native, 0.0% Native Hawaiian/Other Pacific Islander, 1.1% Two or more races, 2.6% Hispanic of any race; Average household size: 2.35; Median age: 44.1; Age under 18: 21.2%; Age 65 and over: 19.9%; Males per 100 females: 93.0; Marriage status: 26.0% never married, 49.5% now married, 3.8% separated, 7.5% widowed, 16.9% divorced; Foreign born: 1.8%; Speak English only: 97.2%; With disability: 15.7%; Veterans: 14.4%; Ancestry: 22.5% American, 18.7% Irish, 13.9% German, 12.6% English, 8.3% Italian
Employment: 5.8% management, business, and financial, 2.4% computer, engineering, and science, 8.0% education, legal, community service, arts, and media, 9.8% healthcare practitioners, 28.9% service, 19.4% sales and office, 9.0% natural resources, construction, and maintenance, 16.5% production, transportation, and material moving

Income: Per capita: $23,158; Median household: $42,318; Average household: $55,723; Households with income of $100,000 or more: 13.2%; Poverty rate: 16.8%
Educational Attainment: High school diploma or higher: 87.6%; Bachelor's degree or higher: 14.0%; Graduate/professional degree or higher: 6.2%
Housing: Homeownership rate: 70.5%; Median home value: $96,700; Median year structure built: 1948; Homeowner vacancy rate: 1.5%; Median selected monthly owner costs: $1,079 with a mortgage, $437 without a mortgage; Median gross rent: $613 per month; Rental vacancy rate: 8.9%
Health Insurance: 89.5% have insurance; 59.9% have private insurance; 41.6% have public insurance; 10.5% do not have insurance; 3.5% of children under 18 do not have insurance
Transportation: Commute: 84.0% car, 0.3% public transportation, 11.6% walk, 1.8% work from home; Mean travel time to work: 19.7 minutes

HECTOR (town). Covers a land area of 102.369 square miles and a water area of 10.214 square miles. Located at 42.46° N. Lat; 76.78° W. Long. Elevation is 853 feet.
History: The town is named after Hector Ely, who was the firstborn son of the town founders. The area was originally under the dominion of the Iroquois and became part of the Central New York Military Tract, used to pay soldiers of the American Revolution. The area's first permanent settler arrived in 1791.
Population: 4,995; Growth (since 2000): 2.9%; Density: 48.8 persons per square mile; Race: 97.7% White, 0.0% Black/African American, 0.4% Asian, 0.1% American Indian/Alaska Native, 0.0% Native Hawaiian/Other Pacific Islander, 1.9% Two or more races, 1.8% Hispanic of any race; Average household size: 2.22; Median age: 48.4; Age under 18: 13.5%; Age 65 and over: 17.5%; Males per 100 females: 102.2; Marriage status: 31.8% never married, 48.5% now married, 2.1% separated, 6.5% widowed, 13.2% divorced; Foreign born: 2.1%; Speak English only: 97.6%; With disability: 10.6%; Veterans: 8.6%; Ancestry: 21.3% American, 20.6% Irish, 16.8% German, 14.6% English, 6.6% Italian
Employment: 16.3% management, business, and financial, 3.9% computer, engineering, and science, 12.9% education, legal, community service, arts, and media, 6.0% healthcare practitioners, 17.0% service, 19.0% sales and office, 16.4% natural resources, construction, and maintenance, 8.4% production, transportation, and material moving
Income: Per capita: $31,026; Median household: $56,203; Average household: $68,298; Households with income of $100,000 or more: 21.2%; Poverty rate: 7.6%
Educational Attainment: High school diploma or higher: 94.5%; Bachelor's degree or higher: 29.4%; Graduate/professional degree or higher: 18.2%
Housing: Homeownership rate: 85.0%; Median home value: $125,400; Median year structure built: 1971; Homeowner vacancy rate: 0.3%; Median selected monthly owner costs: $1,199 with a mortgage, $453 without a mortgage; Median gross rent: $790 per month; Rental vacancy rate: 11.5%
Health Insurance: 85.8% have insurance; 67.1% have private insurance; 32.8% have public insurance; 14.2% do not have insurance; 2.2% of children under 18 do not have insurance
Transportation: Commute: 93.7% car, 1.3% public transportation, 0.2% walk, 4.0% work from home; Mean travel time to work: 29.5 minutes
Additional Information Contacts
Town of Hector . . . . (607) 546-5286
    http://home.htva.net/~townofhector

MONTOUR (town). Covers a land area of 18.579 square miles and a water area of 0.005 square miles. Located at 42.34° N. Lat; 76.83° W. Long. Elevation is 482 feet.
History: Chequaga (or Shequaga) Falls here attract tourists, especially when snowmelt in the spring enhances the awesome spectacle.
Population: 2,406; Growth (since 2000): -1.6%; Density: 129.5 persons per square mile; Race: 98.4% White, 0.0% Black/African American, 0.2% Asian, 0.4% American Indian/Alaska Native, 0.0% Native Hawaiian/Other Pacific Islander, 0.7% Two or more races, 0.9% Hispanic of any race; Average household size: 2.23; Median age: 47.5; Age under 18: 22.8%; Age 65 and over: 20.3%; Males per 100 females: 92.5; Marriage status: 24.0% never married, 46.4% now married, 2.6% separated, 11.2% widowed, 18.4% divorced; Foreign born: 0.7%; Speak English only: 98.4%; With disability: 20.4%; Veterans: 9.8%; Ancestry: 19.5% American, 16.7% English, 16.6% Irish, 12.4% German, 10.8% Italian
Employment: 14.0% management, business, and financial, 4.3% computer, engineering, and science, 7.8% education, legal, community

service, arts, and media, 6.5% healthcare practitioners, 22.8% service, 21.0% sales and office, 6.9% natural resources, construction, and maintenance, 16.7% production, transportation, and material moving
Income: Per capita: $20,691; Median household: $36,842; Average household: $47,208; Households with income of $100,000 or more: 11.2%; Poverty rate: 20.6%
Educational Attainment: High school diploma or higher: 87.4%; Bachelor's degree or higher: 14.0%; Graduate/professional degree or higher: 3.7%
Housing: Homeownership rate: 59.5%; Median home value: $97,100; Median year structure built: 1950; Homeowner vacancy rate: 0.0%; Median selected monthly owner costs: $1,094 with a mortgage, $457 without a mortgage; Median gross rent: $562 per month; Rental vacancy rate: 7.4%
Health Insurance: 94.2% have insurance; 60.7% have private insurance; 45.6% have public insurance; 5.8% do not have insurance; 0.4% of children under 18 do not have insurance
Transportation: Commute: 91.6% car, 1.2% public transportation, 3.1% walk, 3.2% work from home; Mean travel time to work: 20.0 minutes

MONTOUR FALLS (village).
Covers a land area of 3.008 square miles and a water area of 0.024 square miles. Located at 42.35° N. Lat; 76.85° W. Long. Elevation is 449 feet.
Population: 1,821; Growth (since 2000): 1.3%; Density: 605.3 persons per square mile; Race: 97.0% White, 1.0% Black/African American, 0.8% Asian, 0.5% American Indian/Alaska Native, 0.0% Native Hawaiian/Other Pacific Islander, 0.2% Two or more races, 1.3% Hispanic of any race; Average household size: 2.17; Median age: 50.8; Age under 18: 21.1%; Age 65 and over: 27.0%; Males per 100 females: 81.6; Marriage status: 23.3% never married, 40.9% now married, 2.8% separated, 13.9% widowed, 21.9% divorced; Foreign born: 3.0%; Speak English only: 96.5%; With disability: 22.4%; Veterans: 8.5%; Ancestry: 21.6% American, 16.1% Irish, 12.2% German, 11.7% English, 10.4% Italian
Employment: 12.9% management, business, and financial, 2.7% computer, engineering, and science, 6.7% education, legal, community service, arts, and media, 7.7% healthcare practitioners, 24.6% service, 18.7% sales and office, 7.9% natural resources, construction, and maintenance, 18.9% production, transportation, and material moving
Income: Per capita: $18,397; Median household: $32,702; Average household: $42,480; Households with income of $100,000 or more: 8.7%; Poverty rate: 24.9%
Educational Attainment: High school diploma or higher: 83.6%; Bachelor's degree or higher: 10.8%; Graduate/professional degree or higher: 3.1%
School District(s)
Odessa-Montour Central SD (PK-12)
 2014-15 Enrollment: 778 . . . . (607) 594-3341
Housing: Homeownership rate: 49.2%; Median home value: $84,700; Median year structure built: Before 1940; Homeowner vacancy rate: 0.0%; Median selected monthly owner costs: $998 with a mortgage, $440 without a mortgage; Median gross rent: $531 per month; Rental vacancy rate: 8.1%
Health Insurance: 94.0% have insurance; 46.6% have private insurance; 55.8% have public insurance; 6.0% do not have insurance; 0.5% of children under 18 do not have insurance
Hospitals: Schuyler Hospital (169 beds)
Transportation: Commute: 93.7% car, 0.0% public transportation, 4.1% walk, 1.2% work from home; Mean travel time to work: 18.3 minutes

ODESSA (village).
Covers a land area of 1.137 square miles and a water area of 0 square miles. Located at 42.33° N. Lat; 76.79° W. Long. Elevation is 1,043 feet.
Population: 661; Growth (since 2000): 7.1%; Density: 581.6 persons per square mile; Race: 97.9% White, 1.4% Black/African American, 0.0% Asian, 0.5% American Indian/Alaska Native, 0.0% Native Hawaiian/Other Pacific Islander, 0.3% Two or more races, 1.5% Hispanic of any race; Average household size: 2.34; Median age: 41.4; Age under 18: 23.6%; Age 65 and over: 17.2%; Males per 100 females: 94.4; Marriage status: 27.3% never married, 45.4% now married, 4.0% separated, 12.0% widowed, 15.4% divorced; Foreign born: 0.0%; Speak English only: 98.0%; With disability: 10.3%; Veterans: 10.5%; Ancestry: 19.1% English, 18.5% Irish, 16.2% American, 12.6% German, 12.1% Polish
Employment: 9.0% management, business, and financial, 1.5% computer, engineering, and science, 8.0% education, legal, community service, arts, and media, 9.3% healthcare practitioners, 23.5% service, 22.0% sales and

office, 5.6% natural resources, construction, and maintenance, 21.1% production, transportation, and material moving
Income: Per capita: $21,546; Median household: $45,278; Average household: $51,694; Households with income of $100,000 or more: 10.7%; Poverty rate: 18.5%
Educational Attainment: High school diploma or higher: 91.6%; Bachelor's degree or higher: 20.0%; Graduate/professional degree or higher: 10.2%
School District(s)
Odessa-Montour Central SD (PK-12)
 2014-15 Enrollment: 778 . . . . (607) 594-3341
Housing: Homeownership rate: 67.0%; Median home value: $106,100; Median year structure built: 1946; Homeowner vacancy rate: 1.1%; Median selected monthly owner costs: $1,180 with a mortgage, $519 without a mortgage; Median gross rent: $570 per month; Rental vacancy rate: 7.3%
Health Insurance: 90.0% have insurance; 62.9% have private insurance; 38.9% have public insurance; 10.0% do not have insurance; 10.3% of children under 18 do not have insurance
Transportation: Commute: 89.7% car, 1.9% public transportation, 6.9% walk, 1.6% work from home; Mean travel time to work: 27.1 minutes

ORANGE (town).
Covers a land area of 54.069 square miles and a water area of 0.385 square miles. Located at 42.34° N. Lat; 77.04° W. Long.
Population: 1,710; Growth (since 2000): -2.4%; Density: 31.6 persons per square mile; Race: 91.6% White, 4.9% Black/African American, 1.2% Asian, 0.0% American Indian/Alaska Native, 0.0% Native Hawaiian/Other Pacific Islander, 1.8% Two or more races, 1.5% Hispanic of any race; Average household size: 2.51; Median age: 38.6; Age under 18: 19.8%; Age 65 and over: 13.5%; Males per 100 females: 126.0; Marriage status: 28.6% never married, 56.2% now married, 2.5% separated, 5.3% widowed, 9.9% divorced; Foreign born: 2.2%; Speak English only: 96.6%; With disability: 17.0%; Veterans: 11.2%; Ancestry: 16.8% Irish, 16.7% American, 15.6% English, 15.4% German, 12.2% Italian
Employment: 10.6% management, business, and financial, 5.2% computer, engineering, and science, 9.9% education, legal, community service, arts, and media, 4.4% healthcare practitioners, 18.1% service, 24.4% sales and office, 16.1% natural resources, construction, and maintenance, 11.2% production, transportation, and material moving
Income: Per capita: $24,019; Median household: $48,042; Average household: $64,868; Households with income of $100,000 or more: 14.6%; Poverty rate: 18.8%
Educational Attainment: High school diploma or higher: 85.5%; Bachelor's degree or higher: 16.2%; Graduate/professional degree or higher: 2.5%
Housing: Homeownership rate: 87.7%; Median home value: $86,200; Median year structure built: 1977; Homeowner vacancy rate: 0.0%; Median selected monthly owner costs: $1,179 with a mortgage, $447 without a mortgage; Median gross rent: $584 per month; Rental vacancy rate: 10.6%
Health Insurance: 95.2% have insurance; 71.4% have private insurance; 37.6% have public insurance; 4.8% do not have insurance; 4.1% of children under 18 do not have insurance
Transportation: Commute: 91.4% car, 0.0% public transportation, 4.1% walk, 2.2% work from home; Mean travel time to work: 28.2 minutes

READING (town).
Covers a land area of 27.149 square miles and a water area of 0 square miles. Located at 42.42° N. Lat; 76.94° W. Long.
Population: 1,547; Growth (since 2000): -13.4%; Density: 57.0 persons per square mile; Race: 93.6% White, 1.4% Black/African American, 1.0% Asian, 0.6% American Indian/Alaska Native, 0.0% Native Hawaiian/Other Pacific Islander, 3.3% Two or more races, 2.1% Hispanic of any race; Average household size: 2.49; Median age: 48.6; Age under 18: 22.0%; Age 65 and over: 20.4%; Males per 100 females: 95.3; Marriage status: 19.6% never married, 61.2% now married, 2.0% separated, 7.9% widowed, 11.3% divorced; Foreign born: 1.6%; Speak English only: 95.0%; With disability: 14.9%; Veterans: 16.6%; Ancestry: 22.1% German, 20.7% Irish, 18.9% English, 12.3% Italian, 11.2% American
Employment: 16.7% management, business, and financial, 4.0% computer, engineering, and science, 8.1% education, legal, community service, arts, and media, 3.6% healthcare practitioners, 17.7% service, 19.6% sales and office, 13.2% natural resources, construction, and maintenance, 17.1% production, transportation, and material moving
Income: Per capita: $27,753; Median household: $60,350; Average household: $67,235; Households with income of $100,000 or more: 23.2%; Poverty rate: 5.8%

Educational Attainment: High school diploma or higher: 92.9%; Bachelor's degree or higher: 21.3%; Graduate/professional degree or higher: 9.2%

Housing: Homeownership rate: 87.9%; Median home value: $137,900; Median year structure built: 1964; Homeowner vacancy rate: 0.0%; Median selected monthly owner costs: $1,028 with a mortgage, $415 without a mortgage; Median gross rent: $750 per month; Rental vacancy rate: 8.5%

Health Insurance: 91.2% have insurance; 70.4% have private insurance; 37.9% have public insurance; 8.8% do not have insurance; 9.4% of children under 18 do not have insurance

Transportation: Commute: 92.3% car, 0.0% public transportation, 4.3% walk, 3.4% work from home; Mean travel time to work: 21.4 minutes

ROCK STREAM (unincorporated postal area)

ZCTA: 14878

Covers a land area of 16.039 square miles and a water area of 0 square miles. Located at 42.45° N. Lat; 76.94° W. Long..

Population: 623; Growth (since 2000): -16.6%; Density: 38.8 persons per square mile; Race: 98.7% White, 0.0% Black/African American, 0.6% Asian, 0.0% American Indian/Alaska Native, 0.0% Native Hawaiian/Other Pacific Islander, 0.6% Two or more races, 1.1% Hispanic of any race; Average household size: 2.47; Median age: 42.4; Age under 18: 23.1%; Age 65 and over: 27.8%; Males per 100 females: 100.8; Marriage status: 10.8% never married, 72.4% now married, 1.4% separated, 7.2% widowed, 9.6% divorced; Foreign born: 1.3%; Speak English only: 92.3%; With disability: 11.6%; Veterans: 15.2%; Ancestry: 28.4% Irish, 22.5% English, 22.3% German, 9.0% American, 6.3% Dutch

Employment: 19.2% management, business, and financial, 3.1% computer, engineering, and science, 16.8% education, legal, community service, arts, and media, 3.1% healthcare practitioners, 20.3% service, 12.0% sales and office, 18.2% natural resources, construction, and maintenance, 7.2% production, transportation, and material moving

Income: Per capita: $35,026; Median household: $69,318; Average household: $85,291; Households with income of $100,000 or more: 40.9%; Poverty rate: 2.1%

Educational Attainment: High school diploma or higher: 93.2%; Bachelor's degree or higher: 31.4%; Graduate/professional degree or higher: 25.9%

Housing: Homeownership rate: 88.9%; Median home value: $121,000; Median year structure built: 1962; Homeowner vacancy rate: 0.0%; Median selected monthly owner costs: n/a with a mortgage, n/a without a mortgage; Median gross rent: $734 per month; Rental vacancy rate: 0.0%

Health Insurance: 91.5% have insurance; 53.1% have private insurance; 54.3% have public insurance; 8.5% do not have insurance; 0.0% of children under 18 do not have insurance

Transportation: Commute: 89.7% car, 0.0% public transportation, 9.3% walk, 1.0% work from home; Mean travel time to work: 20.4 minutes

TYRONE (town). Covers a land area of 37.296 square miles and a water area of 2.332 square miles. Located at 42.44° N. Lat; 77.04° W. Long. Elevation is 1,171 feet.

Population: 1,653; Growth (since 2000): -3.6%; Density: 44.3 persons per square mile; Race: 99.2% White, 0.5% Black/African American, 0.2% Asian, 0.2% American Indian/Alaska Native, 0.0% Native Hawaiian/Other Pacific Islander, 0.0% Two or more races, 0.2% Hispanic of any race; Average household size: 2.52; Median age: 46.1; Age under 18: 24.2%; Age 65 and over: 23.1%; Males per 100 females: 95.7; Marriage status: 23.8% never married, 58.6% now married, 3.3% separated, 7.8% widowed, 9.7% divorced; Foreign born: 0.5%; Speak English only: 94.6%; With disability: 17.6%; Veterans: 12.4%; Ancestry: 31.6% American, 10.8% Irish, 10.6% German, 9.6% English, 7.1% Polish

Employment: 17.3% management, business, and financial, 3.2% computer, engineering, and science, 10.6% education, legal, community service, arts, and media, 8.9% healthcare practitioners, 13.6% service, 17.8% sales and office, 8.6% natural resources, construction, and maintenance, 19.9% production, transportation, and material moving

Income: Per capita: $22,285; Median household: $43,833; Average household: $55,610; Households with income of $100,000 or more: 14.2%; Poverty rate: 21.8%

Educational Attainment: High school diploma or higher: 85.4%; Bachelor's degree or higher: 13.9%; Graduate/professional degree or higher: 6.0%

Housing: Homeownership rate: 72.7%; Median home value: $118,700; Median year structure built: 1959; Homeowner vacancy rate: 1.6%; Median selected monthly owner costs: $1,061 with a mortgage, $441 without a mortgage; Median gross rent: $713 per month; Rental vacancy rate: 4.8%

Health Insurance: 90.1% have insurance; 58.4% have private insurance; 50.8% have public insurance; 9.9% do not have insurance; 6.3% of children under 18 do not have insurance

Transportation: Commute: 87.2% car, 0.0% public transportation, 0.0% walk, 10.3% work from home; Mean travel time to work: 30.0 minutes

WATKINS GLEN (village). County seat. Covers a land area of 1.559 square miles and a water area of 0.383 square miles. Located at 42.38° N. Lat; 76.87° W. Long. Elevation is 463 feet.

History: The resort hotel here is famed for its mineral spring water. An international Grand Prix sports-car race was held here annually until 1981. Incorporated 1842.

Population: 1,912; Growth (since 2000): -11.0%; Density: 1,226.4 persons per square mile; Race: 95.3% White, 0.8% Black/African American, 0.9% Asian, 0.0% American Indian/Alaska Native, 0.0% Native Hawaiian/Other Pacific Islander, 3.0% Two or more races, 4.0% Hispanic of any race; Average household size: 2.21; Median age: 40.2; Age under 18: 22.1%; Age 65 and over: 21.2%; Males per 100 females: 87.2; Marriage status: 37.3% never married, 39.3% now married, 1.5% separated, 5.9% widowed, 17.5% divorced; Foreign born: 1.5%; Speak English only: 97.6%; With disability: 17.9%; Veterans: 13.6%; Ancestry: 18.7% Irish, 18.3% German, 16.9% American, 14.6% Italian, 11.2% English

Employment: 9.7% management, business, and financial, 1.3% computer, engineering, and science, 11.0% education, legal, community service, arts, and media, 6.5% healthcare practitioners, 33.0% service, 19.1% sales and office, 5.3% natural resources, construction, and maintenance, 14.1% production, transportation, and material moving

Income: Per capita: $22,986; Median household: $35,556; Average household: $51,948; Households with income of $100,000 or more: 9.2%; Poverty rate: 20.8%

Educational Attainment: High school diploma or higher: 87.3%; Bachelor's degree or higher: 24.0%; Graduate/professional degree or higher: 10.0%

School District(s)

Watkins Glen Central SD (PK-12)

2014-15 Enrollment: 1,119 . . . . (607) 535-3220

Housing: Homeownership rate: 58.8%; Median home value: $113,200; Median year structure built: Before 1940; Homeowner vacancy rate: 0.0%; Median selected monthly owner costs: $955 with a mortgage, $461 without a mortgage; Median gross rent: $620 per month; Rental vacancy rate: 0.0%

Health Insurance: 90.1% have insurance; 58.8% have private insurance; 45.9% have public insurance; 9.9% do not have insurance; 4.3% of children under 18 do not have insurance

Safety: Violent crime rate: 15.9 per 10,000 population; Property crime rate: 386.0 per 10,000 population

Transportation: Commute: 71.2% car, 0.6% public transportation, 22.0% walk, 4.1% work from home; Mean travel time to work: 17.0 minutes

Seneca County

Located in west central New York, in the Finger Lakes region; bounded on the east by Cayuga Lake and the Seneca River, and partly on the west by Seneca Lake. Covers a land area of 323.705 square miles, a water area of 66.734 square miles, and is located in the Eastern Time Zone at 42.78° N. Lat., 76.83° W. Long. The county was founded in 1804. County seat is Waterloo.

Seneca County is part of the Seneca Falls, NY Micropolitan Statistical Area. The entire metro area includes: Seneca County, NY

Population: 35,144; Growth (since 2000): 5.4%; Density: 108.6 persons per square mile; Race: 92.1% White, 4.5% Black/African American, 0.7% Asian, 0.3% American Indian/Alaska Native, 0.0% Native Hawaiian/Other Pacific Islander, 2.1% two or more races, 3.1% Hispanic of any race; Average household size: 2.37; Median age: 42.3; Age under 18: 20.4%; Age 65 and over: 16.7%; Males per 100 females: 109.9; Marriage status: 31.1% never married, 49.6% now married, 2.2% separated, 6.7% widowed, 12.6% divorced; Foreign born: 2.1%; Speak English only: 94.1%; With disability: 15.8%; Veterans: 10.0%; Ancestry: 19.7% German, 18.1% Irish, 16.0% Italian, 14.2% English, 8.2% American

Religion: Six largest groups: 3.1% Methodist/Pietist, 2.7% Catholicism, 2.1% European Free-Church, 1.9% Presbyterian-Reformed, 1.7% Non-denominational Protestant, 1.4% Latter-day Saints

Economy: Unemployment rate: 4.3%; Leading industries: 25.8 % retail trade; 10.9 % accommodation and food services; 10.9 % other services (except public administration); Farms: 584 totaling 130,206 acres; Company size: 0 employ 1,000 or more persons, 2 employ 500 to 999 persons, 10 employ 100 to 499 persons, 704 employ less than 100 persons; Business ownership: 561 women-owned, n/a Black-owned, n/a Hispanic-owned, 46 Asian-owned, n/a American Indian/Alaska Native-owned

Employment: 12.7% management, business, and financial, 2.8% computer, engineering, and science, 11.1% education, legal, community service, arts, and media, 5.0% healthcare practitioners, 18.3% service, 23.5% sales and office, 11.0% natural resources, construction, and maintenance, 15.6% production, transportation, and material moving

Income: Per capita: $24,666; Median household: $49,292; Average household: $62,828; Households with income of $100,000 or more: 16.9%; Poverty rate: 12.7%

Educational Attainment: High school diploma or higher: 85.3%; Bachelor's degree or higher: 20.2%; Graduate/professional degree or higher: 8.3%

Housing: Homeownership rate: 72.3%; Median home value: $97,000; Median year structure built: 1959; Homeowner vacancy rate: 1.4%; Median selected monthly owner costs: $1,141 with a mortgage, $491 without a mortgage; Median gross rent: $716 per month; Rental vacancy rate: 7.5%

Vital Statistics: Birth rate: 108.5 per 10,000 population; Death rate: 89.9 per 10,000 population; Age-adjusted cancer mortality rate: 195.2 deaths per 100,000 population

Health Insurance: 89.7% have insurance; 70.1% have private insurance; 35.9% have public insurance; 10.3% do not have insurance; 10.7% of children under 18 do not have insurance

Health Care: Physicians: 3.7 per 10,000 population; Dentists: 2.3 per 10,000 population; Hospital beds: 0.0 per 10,000 population; Hospital admissions: 0.0 per 10,000 population

Transportation: Commute: 90.8% car, 0.5% public transportation, 3.3% walk, 3.9% work from home; Mean travel time to work: 23.3 minutes

2016 Presidential Election: 52.3% Trump, 41.2% Clinton, 4.6% Johnson, 1.9% Stein

National and State Parks: Cayuga Lake State Park; Lodi Point State Marine Park; Montezuma National Wildlife Refuge; Sampson State Park; Seneca Lake State Park; Women's Rights National Historical Park

Additional Information Contacts
Seneca Government . . . . (315) 539-1771
  http://www.co.seneca.ny.us

Seneca County Communities

COVERT (town). Covers a land area of 31.385 square miles and a water area of 6.195 square miles. Located at 42.58° N. Lat; 76.70° W. Long. Elevation is 906 feet.

Population: 2,328; Growth (since 2000): 4.5%; Density: 74.2 persons per square mile; Race: 96.6% White, 0.0% Black/African American, 1.3% Asian, 0.5% American Indian/Alaska Native, 0.0% Native Hawaiian/Other Pacific Islander, 0.3% Two or more races, 1.7% Hispanic of any race; Average household size: 2.32; Median age: 47.2; Age under 18: 19.2%; Age 65 and over: 22.8%; Males per 100 females: 105.9; Marriage status: 28.2% never married, 55.2% now married, 1.3% separated, 7.0% widowed, 9.7% divorced; Foreign born: 3.8%; Speak English only: 95.3%; With disability: 12.7%; Veterans: 9.9%; Ancestry: 20.0% English, 18.9% Irish, 15.1% Italian, 14.8% German, 7.2% American

Employment: 19.0% management, business, and financial, 2.5% computer, engineering, and science, 15.7% education, legal, community service, arts, and media, 8.3% healthcare practitioners, 16.3% service, 19.4% sales and office, 10.5% natural resources, construction, and maintenance, 8.2% production, transportation, and material moving

Income: Per capita: $28,699; Median household: $51,544; Average household: $66,712; Households with income of $100,000 or more: 18.5%; Poverty rate: 9.5%

Educational Attainment: High school diploma or higher: 90.8%; Bachelor's degree or higher: 30.6%; Graduate/professional degree or higher: 15.0%

Housing: Homeownership rate: 81.6%; Median home value: $113,200; Median year structure built: 1952; Homeowner vacancy rate: 0.7%; Median

selected monthly owner costs: $1,164 with a mortgage, $522 without a mortgage; Median gross rent: $876 per month; Rental vacancy rate: 13.0%

Health Insurance: 90.2% have insurance; 74.0% have private insurance; 34.3% have public insurance; 9.8% do not have insurance; 8.7% of children under 18 do not have insurance

Transportation: Commute: 85.9% car, 2.5% public transportation, 7.6% walk, 4.0% work from home; Mean travel time to work: 26.6 minutes

FAYETTE (town). Covers a land area of 54.819 square miles and a water area of 11.583 square miles. Located at 42.84° N. Lat; 76.86° W. Long. Elevation is 607 feet.

Population: 3,918; Growth (since 2000): 7.5%; Density: 71.5 persons per square mile; Race: 96.2% White, 0.4% Black/African American, 0.7% Asian, 0.0% American Indian/Alaska Native, 0.0% Native Hawaiian/Other Pacific Islander, 2.7% Two or more races, 0.3% Hispanic of any race; Average household size: 2.55; Median age: 46.0; Age under 18: 23.5%; Age 65 and over: 16.3%; Males per 100 females: 97.2; Marriage status: 22.1% never married, 61.5% now married, 2.0% separated, 5.9% widowed, 10.5% divorced; Foreign born: 2.1%; Speak English only: 96.4%; With disability: 13.5%; Veterans: 11.2%; Ancestry: 28.3% German, 18.4% Irish, 15.3% English, 15.3% Italian, 6.5% Dutch

Employment: 21.7% management, business, and financial, 2.9% computer, engineering, and science, 8.4% education, legal, community service, arts, and media, 3.4% healthcare practitioners, 13.4% service, 23.2% sales and office, 9.3% natural resources, construction, and maintenance, 17.8% production, transportation, and material moving

Income: Per capita: $31,254; Median household: $65,531; Average household: $79,647; Households with income of $100,000 or more: 20.1%; Poverty rate: 9.0%

Educational Attainment: High school diploma or higher: 88.4%; Bachelor's degree or higher: 22.9%; Graduate/professional degree or higher: 8.0%

Housing: Homeownership rate: 81.1%; Median home value: $125,900; Median year structure built: 1970; Homeowner vacancy rate: 3.0%; Median selected monthly owner costs: $1,336 with a mortgage, $530 without a mortgage; Median gross rent: $728 per month; Rental vacancy rate: 2.0%

Health Insurance: 86.9% have insurance; 74.3% have private insurance; 27.6% have public insurance; 13.1% do not have insurance; 16.7% of children under 18 do not have insurance

Transportation: Commute: 92.8% car, 0.0% public transportation, 1.4% walk, 3.6% work from home; Mean travel time to work: 18.3 minutes

INTERLAKEN (village). Covers a land area of 0.267 square miles and a water area of 0 square miles. Located at 42.62° N. Lat; 76.72° W. Long. Elevation is 906 feet.

Population: 703; Growth (since 2000): 4.3%; Density: 2,629.0 persons per square mile; Race: 97.7% White, 0.0% Black/African American, 1.4% Asian, 0.0% American Indian/Alaska Native, 0.0% Native Hawaiian/Other Pacific Islander, 0.9% Two or more races, 0.0% Hispanic of any race; Average household size: 2.43; Median age: 37.8; Age under 18: 18.6%; Age 65 and over: 14.4%; Males per 100 females: 99.3; Marriage status: 38.9% never married, 41.6% now married, 2.2% separated, 10.0% widowed, 9.5% divorced; Foreign born: 5.7%; Speak English only: 94.1%; With disability: 14.9%; Veterans: 7.7%; Ancestry: 24.0% English, 21.2% Irish, 15.5% German, 10.7% Italian, 8.3% American

Employment: 13.4% management, business, and financial, 1.5% computer, engineering, and science, 22.0% education, legal, community service, arts, and media, 4.7% healthcare practitioners, 16.6% service, 22.3% sales and office, 9.4% natural resources, construction, and maintenance, 10.1% production, transportation, and material moving

Income: Per capita: $23,103; Median household: $48,958; Average household: $57,418; Households with income of $100,000 or more: 15.0%; Poverty rate: 19.8%

Educational Attainment: High school diploma or higher: 89.0%; Bachelor's degree or higher: 32.0%; Graduate/professional degree or higher: 13.1%

School District(s)
South Seneca Central SD (PK-12)
  2014-15 Enrollment: 735. . . . . (607) 869-9636

Housing: Homeownership rate: 75.1%; Median home value: $76,600; Median year structure built: Before 1940; Homeowner vacancy rate: 0.0%; Median selected monthly owner costs: $1,061 with a mortgage, $477 without a mortgage; Median gross rent: $717 per month; Rental vacancy rate: 0.0%

Health Insurance: 92.5% have insurance; 65.3% have private insurance; 39.5% have public insurance; 7.5% do not have insurance; 3.8% of children under 18 do not have insurance
Safety: Violent crime rate: 0.0 per 10,000 population; Property crime rate: 16.0 per 10,000 population
Transportation: Commute: 89.3% car, 2.0% public transportation, 7.9% walk, 0.8% work from home; Mean travel time to work: 25.2 minutes

JUNIUS (town). Covers a land area of 26.709 square miles and a water area of 0.145 square miles. Located at 42.97° N. Lat; 76.91° W. Long. Elevation is 443 feet.
Population: 1,401; Growth (since 2000): 2.9%; Density: 52.5 persons per square mile; Race: 98.7% White, 0.0% Black/African American, 0.0% Asian, 0.0% American Indian/Alaska Native, 0.0% Native Hawaiian/Other Pacific Islander, 1.3% Two or more races, 5.3% Hispanic of any race; Average household size: 2.66; Median age: 38.5; Age under 18: 29.1%; Age 65 and over: 14.1%; Males per 100 females: 103.5; Marriage status: 24.1% never married, 53.7% now married, 2.1% separated, 8.8% widowed, 13.5% divorced; Foreign born: 1.3%; Speak English only: 93.2%; With disability: 12.7%; Veterans: 10.2%; Ancestry: 28.3% German, 14.8% Italian, 14.3% American, 10.3% Irish, 8.4% English
Employment: 11.9% management, business, and financial, 5.2% computer, engineering, and science, 9.6% education, legal, community service, arts, and media, 4.1% healthcare practitioners, 16.0% service, 18.6% sales and office, 13.1% natural resources, construction, and maintenance, 21.4% production, transportation, and material moving
Income: Per capita: $23,545; Median household: $53,690; Average household: $62,910; Households with income of $100,000 or more: 12.8%; Poverty rate: 12.6%
Educational Attainment: High school diploma or higher: 86.8%; Bachelor's degree or higher: 15.4%; Graduate/professional degree or higher: 5.1%
Housing: Homeownership rate: 83.5%; Median home value: $97,100; Median year structure built: 1973; Homeowner vacancy rate: 0.9%; Median selected monthly owner costs: $985 with a mortgage, $439 without a mortgage; Median gross rent: $692 per month; Rental vacancy rate: 0.0%
Health Insurance: 85.1% have insurance; 67.7% have private insurance; 31.5% have public insurance; 14.9% do not have insurance; 21.6% of children under 18 do not have insurance
Transportation: Commute: 91.1% car, 0.8% public transportation, 4.2% walk, 2.8% work from home; Mean travel time to work: 21.5 minutes

LODI (town). Covers a land area of 34.190 square miles and a water area of 5.574 square miles. Located at 42.59° N. Lat; 76.83° W. Long. Elevation is 1,106 feet.
Population: 1,636; Growth (since 2000): 10.8%; Density: 47.8 persons per square mile; Race: 96.8% White, 0.1% Black/African American, 0.0% Asian, 1.1% American Indian/Alaska Native, 0.0% Native Hawaiian/Other Pacific Islander, 1.7% Two or more races, 0.9% Hispanic of any race; Average household size: 2.32; Median age: 44.6; Age under 18: 19.6%; Age 65 and over: 18.3%; Males per 100 females: 104.2; Marriage status: 24.0% never married, 62.1% now married, 2.6% separated, 4.3% widowed, 9.5% divorced; Foreign born: 0.7%; Speak English only: 97.2%; With disability: 16.6%; Veterans: 10.6%; Ancestry: 21.0% English, 20.4% Irish, 16.9% German, 15.6% American, 10.9% Dutch
Employment: 9.8% management, business, and financial, 6.4% computer, engineering, and science, 14.6% education, legal, community service, arts, and media, 5.1% healthcare practitioners, 27.3% service, 15.6% sales and office, 12.9% natural resources, construction, and maintenance, 8.3% production, transportation, and material moving
Income: Per capita: $26,923; Median household: $56,042; Average household: $63,422; Households with income of $100,000 or more: 19.6%; Poverty rate: 9.5%
Educational Attainment: High school diploma or higher: 88.6%; Bachelor's degree or higher: 21.7%; Graduate/professional degree or higher: 13.6%
Housing: Homeownership rate: 82.3%; Median home value: $97,900; Median year structure built: 1971; Homeowner vacancy rate: 0.0%; Median selected monthly owner costs: $1,192 with a mortgage, $473 without a mortgage; Median gross rent: $550 per month; Rental vacancy rate: 3.1%
Health Insurance: 93.5% have insurance; 76.0% have private insurance; 32.8% have public insurance; 6.5% do not have insurance; 0.6% of children under 18 do not have insurance
Transportation: Commute: 92.7% car, 0.3% public transportation, 3.4% walk, 3.3% work from home; Mean travel time to work: 30.2 minutes

LODI (village). Covers a land area of 0.551 square miles and a water area of 0.002 square miles. Located at 42.61° N. Lat; 76.82° W. Long. Elevation is 1,106 feet.
Population: 404; Growth (since 2000): 19.5%; Density: 733.0 persons per square mile; Race: 99.5% White, 0.0% Black/African American, 0.0% Asian, 0.2% American Indian/Alaska Native, 0.0% Native Hawaiian/Other Pacific Islander, 0.0% Two or more races, 0.5% Hispanic of any race; Average household size: 2.30; Median age: 39.6; Age under 18: 15.8%; Age 65 and over: 10.4%; Males per 100 females: 122.1; Marriage status: 19.5% never married, 65.6% now married, 3.2% separated, 2.3% widowed, 12.6% divorced; Foreign born: 0.2%; Speak English only: 99.2%; With disability: 14.4%; Veterans: 7.6%; Ancestry: 24.0% English, 18.8% German, 12.4% American, 10.9% Irish, 7.4% Dutch
Employment: 5.7% management, business, and financial, 13.7% computer, engineering, and science, 14.6% education, legal, community service, arts, and media, 4.2% healthcare practitioners, 32.1% service, 8.5% sales and office, 12.7% natural resources, construction, and maintenance, 8.5% production, transportation, and material moving
Income: Per capita: $26,157; Median household: $45,781; Average household: $59,325; Households with income of $100,000 or more: 19.9%; Poverty rate: 10.4%
Educational Attainment: High school diploma or higher: 90.8%; Bachelor's degree or higher: 23.8%; Graduate/professional degree or higher: 17.5%
Housing: Homeownership rate: 79.5%; Median home value: $59,300; Median year structure built: Before 1940; Homeowner vacancy rate: 0.0%; Median selected monthly owner costs: $1,152 with a mortgage, $394 without a mortgage; Median gross rent: $700 per month; Rental vacancy rate: 10.0%
Health Insurance: 90.8% have insurance; 61.9% have private insurance; 39.9% have public insurance; 9.2% do not have insurance; 3.1% of children under 18 do not have insurance
Transportation: Commute: 92.9% car, 0.9% public transportation, 5.2% walk, 0.0% work from home; Mean travel time to work: 24.3 minutes

OVID (town). Covers a land area of 30.861 square miles and a water area of 7.893 square miles. Located at 42.65° N. Lat; 76.80° W. Long. Elevation is 968 feet.
Population: 2,166; Growth (since 2000): -21.4%; Density: 70.2 persons per square mile; Race: 94.5% White, 2.0% Black/African American, 1.5% Asian, 0.8% American Indian/Alaska Native, 0.0% Native Hawaiian/Other Pacific Islander, 0.9% Two or more races, 1.0% Hispanic of any race; Average household size: 2.31; Median age: 43.6; Age under 18: 22.5%; Age 65 and over: 18.3%; Males per 100 females: 101.1; Marriage status: 25.7% never married, 53.4% now married, 3.0% separated, 8.1% widowed, 12.9% divorced; Foreign born: 1.8%; Speak English only: 94.1%; With disability: 15.5%; Veterans: 9.5%; Ancestry: 20.7% German, 20.5% English, 15.3% Irish, 12.5% American, 7.2% Dutch
Employment: 14.0% management, business, and financial, 1.6% computer, engineering, and science, 15.6% education, legal, community service, arts, and media, 7.0% healthcare practitioners, 24.6% service, 19.3% sales and office, 12.5% natural resources, construction, and maintenance, 5.3% production, transportation, and material moving
Income: Per capita: $25,895; Median household: $43,884; Average household: $60,499; Households with income of $100,000 or more: 15.1%; Poverty rate: 15.7%
Educational Attainment: High school diploma or higher: 86.3%; Bachelor's degree or higher: 23.5%; Graduate/professional degree or higher: 10.9%

School District(s)
South Seneca Central SD (PK-12)
   2014-15 Enrollment: 735. . . . . (607) 869-9636
Housing: Homeownership rate: 75.8%; Median home value: $100,800; Median year structure built: 1960; Homeowner vacancy rate: 1.1%; Median selected monthly owner costs: $1,099 with a mortgage, $471 without a mortgage; Median gross rent: $682 per month; Rental vacancy rate: 11.2%
Health Insurance: 84.2% have insurance; 64.6% have private insurance; 34.6% have public insurance; 15.8% do not have insurance; 18.1% of children under 18 do not have insurance
Transportation: Commute: 90.1% car, 0.1% public transportation, 4.2% walk, 3.9% work from home; Mean travel time to work: 31.1 minutes

OVID (village). Covers a land area of 0.398 square miles and a water area of 0 square miles. Located at 42.68° N. Lat; 76.82° W. Long. Elevation is 968 feet.

Population: 602; Growth (since 2000): -1.6%; Density: 1,514.3 persons per square mile; Race: 84.2% White, 6.1% Black/African American, 4.3% Asian, 3.0% American Indian/Alaska Native, 0.0% Native Hawaiian/Other Pacific Islander, 1.2% Two or more races, 3.3% Hispanic of any race; Average household size: 2.25; Median age: 35.2; Age under 18: 25.2%; Age 65 and over: 14.3%; Males per 100 females: 93.6; Marriage status: 33.0% never married, 35.1% now married, 1.3% separated, 13.7% widowed, 18.2% divorced; Foreign born: 4.8%; Speak English only: 96.5%; With disability: 16.3%; Veterans: 11.3%; Ancestry: 30.9% German, 26.2% Irish, 12.8% English, 5.6% American, 5.6% Dutch

Employment: 10.6% management, business, and financial, 2.6% computer, engineering, and science, 18.1% education, legal, community service, arts, and media, 5.3% healthcare practitioners, 23.4% service, 20.8% sales and office, 13.2% natural resources, construction, and maintenance, 6.0% production, transportation, and material moving

Income: Per capita: $28,720; Median household: $43,393; Average household: $64,236; Households with income of $100,000 or more: 12.3%; Poverty rate: 11.8%

Educational Attainment: High school diploma or higher: 82.7%; Bachelor's degree or higher: 17.3%; Graduate/professional degree or higher: 7.8%

School District(s)
South Seneca Central SD (PK-12)

    2014-15 Enrollment: 735 . . . . (607) 869-9636

Housing: Homeownership rate: 63.7%; Median home value: $96,000; Median year structure built: Before 1940; Homeowner vacancy rate: 4.5%; Median selected monthly owner costs: $943 with a mortgage, $447 without a mortgage; Median gross rent: $700 per month; Rental vacancy rate: 16.4%

Health Insurance: 86.0% have insurance; 59.3% have private insurance; 39.4% have public insurance; 14.0% do not have insurance; 0.0% of children under 18 do not have insurance

Transportation: Commute: 89.4% car, 0.0% public transportation, 6.8% walk, 3.8% work from home; Mean travel time to work: 26.2 minutes

ROMULUS (CDP). Covers a land area of 0.609 square miles and a water area of 0 square miles. Located at 42.75° N. Lat; 76.84° W. Long. Elevation is 718 feet.

Population: 524; Growth (since 2000): n/a; Density: 861.0 persons per square mile; Race: 99.6% White, 0.0% Black/African American, 0.0% Asian, 0.0% American Indian/Alaska Native, 0.0% Native Hawaiian/Other Pacific Islander, 0.4% Two or more races, 8.8% Hispanic of any race; Average household size: 3.08; Median age: 38.6; Age under 18: 26.9%; Age 65 and over: 13.5%; Males per 100 females: 96.6; Marriage status: 28.3% never married, 61.3% now married, 1.0% separated, 4.6% widowed, 5.8% divorced; Foreign born: 0.0%; Speak English only: 99.2%; With disability: 8.6%; Veterans: 11.7%; Ancestry: 26.7% American, 18.3% German, 18.3% Irish, 13.4% English, 11.3% Italian

Employment: 5.6% management, business, and financial, 0.0% computer, engineering, and science, 6.4% education, legal, community service, arts, and media, 7.3% healthcare practitioners, 22.3% service, 30.5% sales and office, 9.9% natural resources, construction, and maintenance, 18.0% production, transportation, and material moving

Income: Per capita: $19,068; Median household: $55,227; Average household: $57,642; Households with income of $100,000 or more: 8.3%; Poverty rate: 11.6%

Educational Attainment: High school diploma or higher: 83.5%; Bachelor's degree or higher: 7.0%; Graduate/professional degree or higher: 4.6%

School District(s)
Romulus Central SD (PK-12)

    2014-15 Enrollment: 402 . . . . (866) 810-0345

Housing: Homeownership rate: 76.2%; Median home value: $70,000; Median year structure built: 1951; Homeowner vacancy rate: 0.0%; Median selected monthly owner costs: $826 with a mortgage, $446 without a mortgage; Median gross rent: $783 per month; Rental vacancy rate: 0.0%

Health Insurance: 87.0% have insurance; 65.3% have private insurance; 34.7% have public insurance; 13.0% do not have insurance; 17.0% of children under 18 do not have insurance

Transportation: Commute: 87.1% car, 0.0% public transportation, 11.6% walk, 1.3% work from home; Mean travel time to work: 19.2 minutes

ROMULUS (town). Covers a land area of 37.792 square miles and a water area of 13.591 square miles. Located at 42.71° N. Lat; 76.83° W. Long. Elevation is 718 feet.

History: The town is named after the mythical founder of Rome, Romulus, a name assigned by a clerk with an interest in the classics. Before the American Revolution, this area was controlled by both the Cayuga tribe and the Seneca tribe. Jesuit missionaries visited the area in the 17th Century. A punitive action in 1779 destroyed native villages and drove many of the Native Americans away. Romulus contains the area of Kendaia (Apple Town), a former Iroquois (Cayuga) village destroyed by the residents in anticipation of the arrival of the Sullivan Expedition on September 5, 1779.

Population: 4,359; Growth (since 2000): 114.1%; Density: 115.3 persons per square mile; Race: 66.5% White, 30.2% Black/African American, 0.1% Asian, 1.2% American Indian/Alaska Native, 0.0% Native Hawaiian/Other Pacific Islander, 1.6% Two or more races, 11.3% Hispanic of any race; Average household size: 2.50; Median age: 35.8; Age under 18: 11.4%; Age 65 and over: 10.0%; Males per 100 females: 264.2; Marriage status: 50.7% never married, 36.8% now married, 3.0% separated, 3.2% widowed, 9.4% divorced; Foreign born: 3.9%; Speak English only: 86.4%; With disability: 13.5%; Veterans: 6.7%; Ancestry: 12.8% German, 12.2% Irish, 7.5% English, 6.7% American, 6.1% Italian

Employment: 13.0% management, business, and financial, 1.6% computer, engineering, and science, 12.0% education, legal, community service, arts, and media, 3.6% healthcare practitioners, 20.6% service, 25.8% sales and office, 11.9% natural resources, construction, and maintenance, 11.3% production, transportation, and material moving

Income: Per capita: $13,722; Median household: $55,288; Average household: $64,214; Households with income of $100,000 or more: 18.3%; Poverty rate: 8.8%

Educational Attainment: High school diploma or higher: 65.7%; Bachelor's degree or higher: 9.4%; Graduate/professional degree or higher: 4.2%

School District(s)
Romulus Central SD (PK-12)

    2014-15 Enrollment: 402 . . . . (866) 810-0345

Housing: Homeownership rate: 71.7%; Median home value: $106,800; Median year structure built: 1964; Homeowner vacancy rate: 0.0%; Median selected monthly owner costs: $1,230 with a mortgage, $445 without a mortgage; Median gross rent: $832 per month; Rental vacancy rate: 2.1%

Health Insurance: 79.4% have insurance; 64.9% have private insurance; 32.8% have public insurance; 20.6% do not have insurance; 23.7% of children under 18 do not have insurance

Transportation: Commute: 83.3% car, 0.5% public transportation, 7.2% walk, 7.9% work from home; Mean travel time to work: 25.3 minutes

Additional Information Contacts

Town of Romulus . . . . (607) 869-9326

    http://www.romulustown.com

SENECA FALLS (town). Covers a land area of 24.217 square miles and a water area of 3.242 square miles. Located at 42.91° N. Lat; 76.79° W. Long. Elevation is 449 feet.

History: Seneca Falls owes its early industrial development to the 50-foot waterfall which provided power, and its fame to great women who mothered the causes of woman's suffrage, anti-slavery, and temperance. Amelia Jenks Bloomer (1818-1894), wife of the local postmaster, did not invent the bloomers but she introduced them and advocated them as a uniform for women fighting for suffrage. Elizabeth Cady Stanton (1815-1902) moved to Seneca Falls in 1847, and the two called together the first convention of women fighting for suffrage. Susan B. Anthony (1820-1906) also joined the group and was president of the American Women's Suffrage Association until 1900.

Population: 8,950; Growth (since 2000): -4.2%; Density: 369.6 persons per square mile; Race: 94.6% White, 1.0% Black/African American, 1.7% Asian, 0.0% American Indian/Alaska Native, 0.1% Native Hawaiian/Other Pacific Islander, 2.5% Two or more races, 2.6% Hispanic of any race; Average household size: 2.25; Median age: 42.2; Age under 18: 19.3%; Age 65 and over: 17.1%; Males per 100 females: 97.5; Marriage status: 32.0% never married, 47.4% now married, 1.5% separated, 7.4% widowed, 13.2% divorced; Foreign born: 2.6%; Speak English only: 93.4%; With disability: 16.7%; Veterans: 10.3%; Ancestry: 24.7% Italian, 21.1% Irish, 18.2% German, 13.8% English, 7.2% American

Employment: 12.1% management, business, and financial, 3.3% computer, engineering, and science, 11.6% education, legal, community service, arts, and media, 4.9% healthcare practitioners, 17.2% service,

24.9% sales and office, 9.0% natural resources, construction, and maintenance, 16.9% production, transportation, and material moving
Income: Per capita: $26,000; Median household: $46,588; Average household: $59,855; Households with income of $100,000 or more: 18.4%; Poverty rate: 15.0%
Educational Attainment: High school diploma or higher: 90.4%; Bachelor's degree or higher: 27.4%; Graduate/professional degree or higher: 10.5%

School District(s)
Seneca Falls Central SD (KG-12)
    2014-15 Enrollment: 1,301 . . . . (315) 568-5818

Four-year College(s)
New York Chiropractic College (Private, Not-for-profit)
    Fall 2014 Enrollment: 965 . . . . (315) 568-3000
Housing: Homeownership rate: 63.7%; Median home value: $96,600; Median year structure built: 1953; Homeowner vacancy rate: 2.1%; Median selected monthly owner costs: $1,124 with a mortgage, $513 without a mortgage; Median gross rent: $722 per month; Rental vacancy rate: 10.1%
Health Insurance: 93.7% have insurance; 72.9% have private insurance; 37.3% have public insurance; 6.3% do not have insurance; 4.9% of children under 18 do not have insurance
Safety: Violent crime rate: 20.4 per 10,000 population; Property crime rate: 352.9 per 10,000 population
Transportation: Commute: 90.2% car, 0.2% public transportation, 3.5% walk, 4.0% work from home; Mean travel time to work: 22.3 minutes
Additional Information Contacts
Town of Seneca Falls . . . . (315) 568-8013
    http://www.senecafalls.com

SENECA FALLS (CDP).
Covers a land area of 4.414 square miles and a water area of 0.157 square miles. Located at 42.91° N. Lat; 76.80° W. Long. Elevation is 449 feet.
History: Elizabeth Cady Stanton lived here and helped organize first women's rights convention in U.S., held here in 1848. Women's Rights National Historic Park and Museum, located in the restored Elizabeth Cady Stanton House, and the National Women's Hall of Fame are here. Settled 1787, Incorporated 1831.
Population: 6,493; Growth (since 2000): -5.4%; Density: 1,471.1 persons per square mile; Race: 94.6% White, 1.2% Black/African American, 1.3% Asian, 0.0% American Indian/Alaska Native, 0.2% Native Hawaiian/Other Pacific Islander, 2.6% Two or more races, 1.8% Hispanic of any race; Average household size: 2.29; Median age: 41.6; Age under 18: 20.3%; Age 65 and over: 17.2%; Males per 100 females: 95.5; Marriage status: 31.3% never married, 46.8% now married, 1.1% separated, 8.5% widowed, 13.4% divorced; Foreign born: 2.3%; Speak English only: 94.3%; With disability: 17.0%; Veterans: 11.7%; Ancestry: 26.3% Italian, 21.3% Irish, 16.9% German, 14.0% English, 8.2% American
Employment: 12.0% management, business, and financial, 3.6% computer, engineering, and science, 11.7% education, legal, community service, arts, and media, 5.9% healthcare practitioners, 16.5% service, 25.4% sales and office, 8.9% natural resources, construction, and maintenance, 15.9% production, transportation, and material moving
Income: Per capita: $25,132; Median household: $46,518; Average household: $57,738; Households with income of $100,000 or more: 18.1%; Poverty rate: 16.1%
Educational Attainment: High school diploma or higher: 91.5%; Bachelor's degree or higher: 28.9%; Graduate/professional degree or higher: 9.8%

School District(s)
Seneca Falls Central SD (KG-12)
    2014-15 Enrollment: 1,301 . . . . (315) 568-5818

Four-year College(s)
New York Chiropractic College (Private, Not-for-profit)
    Fall 2014 Enrollment: 965 . . . . (315) 568-3000
Housing: Homeownership rate: 63.8%; Median home value: $86,900; Median year structure built: Before 1940; Homeowner vacancy rate: 2.8%; Median selected monthly owner costs: $1,033 with a mortgage, $506 without a mortgage; Median gross rent: $725 per month; Rental vacancy rate: 11.7%
Health Insurance: 94.3% have insurance; 74.0% have private insurance; 38.5% have public insurance; 5.7% do not have insurance; 1.9% of children under 18 do not have insurance
Transportation: Commute: 90.4% car, 0.1% public transportation, 3.0% walk, 3.8% work from home; Mean travel time to work: 21.9 minutes

Additional Information Contacts
Village of Seneca Falls . . . . (315) 568-8107
    http://www.senecafalls.com/village-listings.php

TYRE (town).
Covers a land area of 30.054 square miles and a water area of 3.060 square miles. Located at 42.99° N. Lat; 76.79° W. Long. Elevation is 410 feet.
Population: 1,023; Growth (since 2000): 13.8%; Density: 34.0 persons per square mile; Race: 99.7% White, 0.0% Black/African American, 0.0% Asian, 0.3% American Indian/Alaska Native, 0.0% Native Hawaiian/Other Pacific Islander, 0.0% Two or more races, 0.0% Hispanic of any race; Average household size: 2.59; Median age: 40.7; Age under 18: 27.9%; Age 65 and over: 11.8%; Males per 100 females: 101.9; Marriage status: 24.9% never married, 55.8% now married, 1.4% separated, 4.7% widowed, 14.6% divorced; Foreign born: 0.4%; Speak English only: 94.4%; With disability: 13.1%; Veterans: 11.1%; Ancestry: 27.5% German, 18.5% Irish, 16.3% English, 16.0% Italian, 9.7% American
Employment: 14.4% management, business, and financial, 4.3% computer, engineering, and science, 7.8% education, legal, community service, arts, and media, 3.3% healthcare practitioners, 12.1% service, 16.5% sales and office, 22.2% natural resources, construction, and maintenance, 19.3% production, transportation, and material moving
Income: Per capita: $24,451; Median household: $47,356; Average household: $63,076; Households with income of $100,000 or more: 17.8%; Poverty rate: 11.7%
Educational Attainment: High school diploma or higher: 83.7%; Bachelor's degree or higher: 18.3%; Graduate/professional degree or higher: 5.3%
Housing: Homeownership rate: 88.6%; Median home value: $91,300; Median year structure built: 1963; Homeowner vacancy rate: 0.8%; Median selected monthly owner costs: $1,160 with a mortgage, $432 without a mortgage; Median gross rent: n/a per month; Rental vacancy rate: 0.0%
Health Insurance: 82.6% have insurance; 65.0% have private insurance; 31.4% have public insurance; 17.4% do not have insurance; 24.9% of children under 18 do not have insurance
Transportation: Commute: 89.1% car, 3.1% public transportation, 2.7% walk, 5.0% work from home; Mean travel time to work: 23.6 minutes

VARICK (town).
Covers a land area of 31.994 square miles and a water area of 13.676 square miles. Located at 42.78° N. Lat; 76.85° W. Long.
Population: 1,795; Growth (since 2000): 3.8%; Density: 56.1 persons per square mile; Race: 94.5% White, 2.1% Black/African American, 0.2% Asian, 0.0% American Indian/Alaska Native, 0.0% Native Hawaiian/Other Pacific Islander, 2.3% Two or more races, 3.8% Hispanic of any race; Average household size: 2.59; Median age: 43.5; Age under 18: 24.9%; Age 65 and over: 21.0%; Males per 100 females: 105.4; Marriage status: 24.6% never married, 62.2% now married, 1.7% separated, 5.4% widowed, 7.9% divorced; Foreign born: 1.3%; Speak English only: 94.2%; With disability: 14.3%; Veterans: 10.1%; Ancestry: 22.3% German, 16.1% English, 16.1% Irish, 12.8% American, 11.6% Italian
Employment: 11.2% management, business, and financial, 3.9% computer, engineering, and science, 6.6% education, legal, community service, arts, and media, 9.3% healthcare practitioners, 16.9% service, 21.9% sales and office, 12.0% natural resources, construction, and maintenance, 18.2% production, transportation, and material moving
Income: Per capita: $27,200; Median household: $57,222; Average household: $73,845; Households with income of $100,000 or more: 23.5%; Poverty rate: 9.0%
Educational Attainment: High school diploma or higher: 86.2%; Bachelor's degree or higher: 25.3%; Graduate/professional degree or higher: 11.7%
Housing: Homeownership rate: 82.6%; Median home value: $140,500; Median year structure built: 1966; Homeowner vacancy rate: 4.6%; Median selected monthly owner costs: $1,294 with a mortgage, $613 without a mortgage; Median gross rent: $902 per month; Rental vacancy rate: 0.0%
Health Insurance: 83.7% have insurance; 64.3% have private insurance; 37.0% have public insurance; 16.3% do not have insurance; 21.9% of children under 18 do not have insurance
Transportation: Commute: 89.6% car, 0.0% public transportation, 3.6% walk, 6.8% work from home; Mean travel time to work: 24.9 minutes

WATERLOO (town). Covers a land area of 21.668 square miles and a water area of 0.147 square miles. Located at 42.92° N. Lat; 76.91° W. Long. Elevation is 453 feet.

History: Official birthplace of the Memorial Day celebration, May 5, 1866 (celebrated on May 30). Incorporated 1824.

Population: 7,568; Growth (since 2000): -3.8%; Density: 349.3 persons per square mile; Race: 95.7% White, 1.0% Black/African American, 0.0% Asian, 0.1% American Indian/Alaska Native, 0.0% Native Hawaiian/Other Pacific Islander, 3.0% Two or more races, 1.8% Hispanic of any race; Average household size: 2.31; Median age: 43.9; Age under 18: 21.6%; Age 65 and over: 17.9%; Males per 100 females: 92.3; Marriage status: 29.6% never married, 44.2% now married, 3.0% separated, 9.0% widowed, 17.2% divorced; Foreign born: 1.2%; Speak English only: 97.3%; With disability: 19.0%; Veterans: 11.2%; Ancestry: 19.8% Irish, 19.8% German, 18.1% Italian, 13.4% English, 6.6% American

Employment: 6.9% management, business, and financial, 1.3% computer, engineering, and science, 9.6% education, legal, community service, arts, and media, 4.3% healthcare practitioners, 20.1% service, 27.7% sales and office, 11.4% natural resources, construction, and maintenance, 18.6% production, transportation, and material moving

Income: Per capita: $23,535; Median household: $44,892; Average household: $54,906; Households with income of $100,000 or more: 11.9%; Poverty rate: 14.9%

Educational Attainment: High school diploma or higher: 87.1%; Bachelor's degree or higher: 12.3%; Graduate/professional degree or higher: 4.5%

School District(s)

Waterloo Central SD (PK-12)
2014-15 Enrollment: 1,709 . . . . (315) 539-1500

Housing: Homeownership rate: 66.6%; Median home value: $78,500; Median year structure built: 1956; Homeowner vacancy rate: 0.0%; Median selected monthly owner costs: $1,069 with a mortgage, $475 without a mortgage; Median gross rent: $680 per month; Rental vacancy rate: 6.7%

Health Insurance: 93.1% have insurance; 67.7% have private insurance; 42.5% have public insurance; 6.9% do not have insurance; 1.7% of children under 18 do not have insurance

Transportation: Commute: 94.0% car, 0.4% public transportation, 1.3% walk, 2.7% work from home; Mean travel time to work: 21.9 minutes

WATERLOO (village). County seat. Covers a land area of 2.157 square miles and a water area of 0.047 square miles. Located at 42.90° N. Lat; 76.86° W. Long. Elevation is 453 feet.

Population: 5,048; Growth (since 2000): -1.2%; Density: 2,340.3 persons per square mile; Race: 94.4% White, 0.4% Black/African American, 0.0% Asian, 0.0% American Indian/Alaska Native, 0.0% Native Hawaiian/Other Pacific Islander, 5.1% Two or more races, 0.9% Hispanic of any race; Average household size: 2.42; Median age: 41.1; Age under 18: 24.4%; Age 65 and over: 18.2%; Males per 100 females: 86.5; Marriage status: 32.0% never married, 40.2% now married, 2.9% separated, 10.7% widowed, 17.0% divorced; Foreign born: 0.6%; Speak English only: 98.5%; With disability: 13.1%; Veterans: 10.9%; Ancestry: 23.9% Irish, 21.0% Italian, 20.2% German, 15.9% English, 5.2% American

Employment: 10.4% management, business, and financial, 2.1% computer, engineering, and science, 9.9% education, legal, community service, arts, and media, 4.4% healthcare practitioners, 21.1% service, 26.1% sales and office, 9.9% natural resources, construction, and maintenance, 16.1% production, transportation, and material moving

Income: Per capita: $24,558; Median household: $45,919; Average household: $60,748; Households with income of $100,000 or more: 18.1%; Poverty rate: 15.9%

Educational Attainment: High school diploma or higher: 90.8%; Bachelor's degree or higher: 19.5%; Graduate/professional degree or higher: 5.6%

School District(s)

Waterloo Central SD (PK-12)
2014-15 Enrollment: 1,709 . . . . (315) 539-1500

Housing: Homeownership rate: 65.7%; Median home value: $82,800; Median year structure built: 1949; Homeowner vacancy rate: 0.0%; Median selected monthly owner costs: $1,086 with a mortgage, $548 without a mortgage; Median gross rent: $629 per month; Rental vacancy rate: 5.8%

Health Insurance: 93.8% have insurance; 70.4% have private insurance; 40.7% have public insurance; 6.2% do not have insurance; 2.3% of children under 18 do not have insurance

Safety: Violent crime rate: 21.9 per 10,000 population; Property crime rate: 310.5 per 10,000 population

Transportation: Commute: 94.2% car, 0.0% public transportation, 1.6% walk, 1.9% work from home; Mean travel time to work: 20.8 minutes

Additional Information Contacts

Village of Waterloo . . . . (315) 539-9131
http://www.waterloony.com

WILLARD (unincorporated postal area)

ZCTA: 14588

Covers a land area of 0.241 square miles and a water area of 0 square miles. Located at 42.68° N. Lat; 76.87° W. Long. Elevation is 600 feet.

Population: 741; Growth (since 2000): n/a; Density: 3,077.3 persons per square mile; Race: 50.2% White, 45.1% Black/African American, 0.8% Asian, 1.2% American Indian/Alaska Native, 0.0% Native Hawaiian/Other Pacific Islander, 2.7% Two or more races, 16.3% Hispanic of any race; Average household size: 2.00; Median age: 33.9; Age under 18: 1.9%; Age 65 and over: 3.5%; Males per 100 females: 813.4; Marriage status: 64.8% never married, 24.4% now married, 2.0% separated, 0.0% widowed, 10.8% divorced; Foreign born: 4.3%; Speak English only: 86.4%; With disability: 20.6%; Veterans: 1.7%; Ancestry: 9.9% Irish, 9.3% English, 7.4% German, 4.5% Italian, 3.2% Polish

Employment: 0.0% management, business, and financial, 0.0% computer, engineering, and science, 0.0% education, legal, community service, arts, and media, 0.0% healthcare practitioners, 21.4% service, 55.7% sales and office, 22.9% natural resources, construction, and maintenance, 0.0% production, transportation, and material moving

Income: Per capita: $7,959; Median household: $83,583; Average household: $75,296; Households with income of $100,000 or more: 33.3%; Poverty rate: n/a

Educational Attainment: High school diploma or higher: 63.2%; Bachelor's degree or higher: n/a; Graduate/professional degree or higher: n/a

Housing: Homeownership rate: 84.3%; Median home value: $91,000; Median year structure built: 1986; Homeowner vacancy rate: 0.0%; Median selected monthly owner costs: $767 with a mortgage, $0 without a mortgage; Median gross rent: n/a per month; Rental vacancy rate: 0.0%

Health Insurance: 100.0% have insurance; 100.0% have private insurance; 25.5% have public insurance; 0.0% do not have insurance; 0.0% of children under 18 do not have insurance

Transportation: Commute: 100.0% car, 0.0% public transportation, 0.0% walk, 0.0% work from home; Mean travel time to work: 0.0 minutes

Staten Island Borough

See New York City

Steuben County

Located in southern New York, partly in the Finger Lakes region; bounded on the south by Pennsylvania; drained by the Canisteo, Cohocton, Tioga, and Chemung Rivers; includes part of Keuka Lake. Covers a land area of 1,390.559 square miles, a water area of 13.524 square miles, and is located in the Eastern Time Zone at 42.27° N. Lat., 77.39° W. Long. The county was founded in 1796. County seat is Bath.

Steuben County is part of the Corning, NY Micropolitan Statistical Area. The entire metro area includes: Steuben County, NY

Weather Station: Bath   Elevation: 1,120 feet

	Jan	Feb	Mar	Apr	May	Jun	Jul	Aug	Sep	Oct	Nov	Dec
High	32	35	43	56	68	77	81	79	72	60	47	36
Low	13	14	21	32	41	50	55	54	46	35	29	19
Precip	1.7	1.5	2.1	2.8	2.9	3.8	3.2	2.8	3.4	2.5	2.7	2.1
Snow	11.1	9.1	10.3	1.5	tr	tr	0.0	0.0	0.0	tr	3.6	9.2

High and Low temperatures in degrees Fahrenheit; Precipitation and Snow in inches

Population: 98,665; Growth (since 2000): -0.1%; Density: 71.0 persons per square mile; Race: 95.0% White, 1.6% Black/African American, 1.5% Asian, 0.2% American Indian/Alaska Native, 0.0% Native Hawaiian/Other Pacific Islander, 1.4% two or more races, 1.5% Hispanic of any race; Average household size: 2.36; Median age: 42.0; Age under 18: 22.5%; Age 65 and over: 17.0%; Males per 100 females: 98.5; Marriage status: 26.8% never married, 53.6% now married, 3.1% separated, 7.2% widowed, 12.4% divorced; Foreign born: 2.4%; Speak English only: 95.0%;

With disability: 15.7%; Veterans: 11.7%; Ancestry: 21.3% German, 17.8% Irish, 14.3% English, 12.8% American, 9.0% Italian
Religion: Six largest groups: 14.1% Catholicism, 6.4% Methodist/Pietist, 3.9% Holiness, 2.5% Non-denominational Protestant, 1.9% Presbyterian-Reformed, 1.8% Baptist
Economy: Unemployment rate: 5.4%; Leading industries: 18.2 % retail trade; 12.9 % health care and social assistance; 12.2 % accommodation and food services; Farms: 1,667 totaling 405,727 acres; Company size: 0 employ 1,000 or more persons, 7 employ 500 to 999 persons, 32 employ 100 to 499 persons, 1,761 employs less than 100 persons; Business ownership: 1,741 women-owned, n/a Black-owned, 34 Hispanic-owned, 166 Asian-owned, n/a American Indian/Alaska Native-owned
Employment: 11.9% management, business, and financial, 5.7% computer, engineering, and science, 10.5% education, legal, community service, arts, and media, 5.4% healthcare practitioners, 18.5% service, 20.9% sales and office, 11.5% natural resources, construction, and maintenance, 15.6% production, transportation, and material moving
Income: Per capita: $25,800; Median household: $47,280; Average household: $61,543; Households with income of $100,000 or more: 15.6%; Poverty rate: 16.3%
Educational Attainment: High school diploma or higher: 89.3%; Bachelor's degree or higher: 21.3%; Graduate/professional degree or higher: 10.2%
Housing: Homeownership rate: 70.0%; Median home value: $91,000; Median year structure built: 1960; Homeowner vacancy rate: 1.2%; Median selected monthly owner costs: $1,090 with a mortgage, $453 without a mortgage; Median gross rent: $658 per month; Rental vacancy rate: 4.5%
Vital Statistics: Birth rate: 110.4 per 10,000 population; Death rate: 100.2 per 10,000 population; Age-adjusted cancer mortality rate: 169.2 deaths per 100,000 population
Health Insurance: 90.7% have insurance; 66.4% have private insurance; 39.9% have public insurance; 9.3% do not have insurance; 8.1% of children under 18 do not have insurance
Health Care: Physicians: 16.1 per 10,000 population; Dentists: 3.8 per 10,000 population; Hospital beds: 86.8 per 10,000 population; Hospital admissions: 1,631.8 per 10,000 population
Air Quality Index (AQI): Percent of Days: 92.5% good, 7.5% moderate, 0.0% unhealthy for sensitive individuals, 0.0% unhealthy, 0.0% very unhealthy; Annual median: 31; Annual maximum: 64
Transportation: Commute: 90.7% car, 0.7% public transportation, 4.0% walk, 3.1% work from home; Mean travel time to work: 21.6 minutes
2016 Presidential Election: 64.5% Trump, 30.1% Clinton, 4.0% Johnson, 1.4% Stein
National and State Parks: Stony Brook State Park
Additional Information Contacts
Steuben Government . . . . (607) 776-9631
  http://www.steubencony.org

Steuben County Communities

ADDISON (town). Covers a land area of 25.545 square miles and a water area of 0.142 square miles. Located at 42.13° N. Lat; 77.23° W. Long. Elevation is 997 feet.
History: Incorporated 1873.
Population: 2,573; Growth (since 2000): -2.5%; Density: 100.7 persons per square mile; Race: 97.4% White, 0.4% Black/African American, 0.6% Asian, 0.4% American Indian/Alaska Native, 0.0% Native Hawaiian/Other Pacific Islander, 0.3% Two or more races, 1.0% Hispanic of any race; Average household size: 2.52; Median age: 38.4; Age under 18: 26.4%; Age 65 and over: 15.2%; Males per 100 females: 93.7; Marriage status: 26.0% never married, 56.6% now married, 4.5% separated, 5.7% widowed, 11.8% divorced; Foreign born: 2.4%; Speak English only: 97.1%; With disability: 17.4%; Veterans: 9.6%; Ancestry: 19.1% German, 16.2% American, 15.6% English, 13.9% Irish, 7.6% Italian
Employment: 10.2% management, business, and financial, 2.4% computer, engineering, and science, 10.3% education, legal, community service, arts, and media, 4.6% healthcare practitioners, 14.5% service, 29.6% sales and office, 12.6% natural resources, construction, and maintenance, 15.9% production, transportation, and material moving
Income: Per capita: $23,444; Median household: $45,278; Average household: $58,736; Households with income of $100,000 or more: 18.6%; Poverty rate: 13.5%
Educational Attainment: High school diploma or higher: 92.1%; Bachelor's degree or higher: 17.3%; Graduate/professional degree or higher: 9.4%

Addison Central SD (PK-12)
  2014-15 Enrollment: 1,140 . . . . (607) 359-2244
Housing: Homeownership rate: 71.3%; Median home value: $84,200; Median year structure built: 1951; Homeowner vacancy rate: 2.5%; Median selected monthly owner costs: $1,118 with a mortgage, $475 without a mortgage; Median gross rent: $593 per month; Rental vacancy rate: 5.2%
Health Insurance: 88.4% have insurance; 62.8% have private insurance; 39.6% have public insurance; 11.6% do not have insurance; 8.0% of children under 18 do not have insurance
Safety: Violent crime rate: 3.9 per 10,000 population; Property crime rate: 113.6 per 10,000 population
Newspapers: Addison Post (weekly circulation 6,400)
Transportation: Commute: 94.5% car, 0.0% public transportation, 2.8% walk, 2.1% work from home; Mean travel time to work: 23.3 minutes

ADDISON (village). Covers a land area of 1.893 square miles and a water area of 0 square miles. Located at 42.11° N. Lat; 77.23° W. Long. Elevation is 997 feet.
Population: 1,788; Growth (since 2000): -0.5%; Density: 944.6 persons per square mile; Race: 96.8% White, 0.6% Black/African American, 0.4% Asian, 0.6% American Indian/Alaska Native, 0.0% Native Hawaiian/Other Pacific Islander, 0.4% Two or more races, 1.5% Hispanic of any race; Average household size: 2.54; Median age: 36.1; Age under 18: 27.8%; Age 65 and over: 13.0%; Males per 100 females: 91.4; Marriage status: 30.1% never married, 55.8% now married, 4.5% separated, 5.0% widowed, 9.1% divorced; Foreign born: 2.9%; Speak English only: 96.4%; With disability: 15.2%; Veterans: 11.5%; Ancestry: 18.0% German, 16.6% English, 14.4% Irish, 13.8% American, 10.1% Italian
Employment: 8.2% management, business, and financial, 2.9% computer, engineering, and science, 12.5% education, legal, community service, arts, and media, 5.4% healthcare practitioners, 16.1% service, 28.7% sales and office, 11.1% natural resources, construction, and maintenance, 15.0% production, transportation, and material moving
Income: Per capita: $23,119; Median household: $49,821; Average household: $58,217; Households with income of $100,000 or more: 15.9%; Poverty rate: 13.5%
Educational Attainment: High school diploma or higher: 92.6%; Bachelor's degree or higher: 16.0%; Graduate/professional degree or higher: 10.7%

Addison Central SD (PK-12)
  2014-15 Enrollment: 1,140 . . . . (607) 359-2244
Housing: Homeownership rate: 69.6%; Median home value: $80,100; Median year structure built: Before 1940; Homeowner vacancy rate: 3.7%; Median selected monthly owner costs: $1,091 with a mortgage, $456 without a mortgage; Median gross rent: $561 per month; Rental vacancy rate: 7.0%
Health Insurance: 88.6% have insurance; 65.4% have private insurance; 35.2% have public insurance; 11.4% do not have insurance; 10.9% of children under 18 do not have insurance
Newspapers: Addison Post (weekly circulation 6,400)
Transportation: Commute: 93.6% car, 0.0% public transportation, 2.5% walk, 2.9% work from home; Mean travel time to work: 23.6 minutes

ARKPORT (village). Covers a land area of 0.694 square miles and a water area of 0 square miles. Located at 42.39° N. Lat; 77.70° W. Long. Elevation is 1,184 feet.
Population: 760; Growth (since 2000): -8.7%; Density: 1,094.7 persons per square mile; Race: 99.2% White, 0.0% Black/African American, 0.0% Asian, 0.0% American Indian/Alaska Native, 0.0% Native Hawaiian/Other Pacific Islander, 0.0% Two or more races, 0.0% Hispanic of any race; Average household size: 2.20; Median age: 44.2; Age under 18: 22.1%; Age 65 and over: 22.2%; Males per 100 females: 83.1; Marriage status: 24.0% never married, 53.7% now married, 7.1% separated, 10.2% widowed, 12.1% divorced; Foreign born: 1.1%; Speak English only: 96.9%; With disability: 17.5%; Veterans: 14.2%; Ancestry: 26.1% Irish, 22.1% German, 20.3% English, 12.2% Italian, 8.7% American
Employment: 10.9% management, business, and financial, 1.4% computer, engineering, and science, 10.6% education, legal, community service, arts, and media, 2.7% healthcare practitioners, 14.4% service, 27.2% sales and office, 13.6% natural resources, construction, and maintenance, 19.1% production, transportation, and material moving

Income: Per capita: $24,858; Median household: $48,438; Average household: $54,814; Households with income of $100,000 or more: 14.5%; Poverty rate: 4.6%

Educational Attainment: High school diploma or higher: 93.0%; Bachelor's degree or higher: 15.0%; Graduate/professional degree or higher: 5.7%

School District(s)

Arkport Central SD (KG-12)

   2014-15 Enrollment: 460 . . . . (607) 295-7471

Housing: Homeownership rate: 72.2%; Median home value: $88,900; Median year structure built: 1955; Homeowner vacancy rate: 5.0%; Median selected monthly owner costs: $867 with a mortgage, $450 without a mortgage; Median gross rent: $611 per month; Rental vacancy rate: 5.9%

Health Insurance: 93.9% have insurance; 77.8% have private insurance; 35.7% have public insurance; 6.1% do not have insurance; 7.7% of children under 18 do not have insurance

Transportation: Commute: 92.5% car, 0.0% public transportation, 4.1% walk, 1.4% work from home; Mean travel time to work: 17.1 minutes

ATLANTA (unincorporated postal area)

ZCTA: 14808

Covers a land area of 3.369 square miles and a water area of 0 square miles. Located at 42.56° N. Lat; 77.47° W. Long. Elevation is 1,309 feet.

Population: 539; Growth (since 2000): -9.4%; Density: 160.0 persons per square mile; Race: 100.0% White, 0.0% Black/African American, 0.0% Asian, 0.0% American Indian/Alaska Native, 0.0% Native Hawaiian/Other Pacific Islander, 0.0% Two or more races, 0.0% Hispanic of any race; Average household size: 2.40; Median age: 51.3; Age under 18: 20.8%; Age 65 and over: 24.7%; Males per 100 females: 119.7; Marriage status: 30.2% never married, 47.3% now married, 1.8% separated, 7.1% widowed, 15.3% divorced; Foreign born: 1.1%; Speak English only: 99.4%; With disability: 24.9%; Veterans: 9.6%; Ancestry: 16.3% American, 15.6% English, 15.4% German, 13.2% Irish, 8.0% Italian

Employment: 5.1% management, business, and financial, 0.0% computer, engineering, and science, 6.5% education, legal, community service, arts, and media, 0.0% healthcare practitioners, 12.6% service, 29.9% sales and office, 6.5% natural resources, construction, and maintenance, 39.3% production, transportation, and material moving

Income: Per capita: $23,222; Median household: $44,120; Average household: $55,474; Households with income of $100,000 or more: 6.4%; Poverty rate: 7.2%

Educational Attainment: High school diploma or higher: 82.5%; Bachelor's degree or higher: 8.5%; Graduate/professional degree or higher: 4.6%

Housing: Homeownership rate: 81.7%; Median home value: $68,000; Median year structure built: Before 1940; Homeowner vacancy rate: 7.7%; Median selected monthly owner costs: $867 with a mortgage, $493 without a mortgage; Median gross rent: $723 per month; Rental vacancy rate: 0.0%

Health Insurance: 95.9% have insurance; 63.3% have private insurance; 51.6% have public insurance; 4.1% do not have insurance; 0.0% of children under 18 do not have insurance

Transportation: Commute: 84.1% car, 0.0% public transportation, 7.9% walk, 0.0% work from home; Mean travel time to work: 23.4 minutes

AVOCA (town). Covers a land area of 36.249 square miles and a water area of 0.041 square miles. Located at 42.42° N. Lat; 77.45° W. Long. Elevation is 1,194 feet.

History: Settled 1843, incorporated 1883.

Population: 2,240; Growth (since 2000): -3.2%; Density: 61.8 persons per square mile; Race: 97.2% White, 0.4% Black/African American, 0.0% Asian, 0.0% American Indian/Alaska Native, 0.3% Native Hawaiian/Other Pacific Islander, 1.2% Two or more races, 1.8% Hispanic of any race; Average household size: 2.24; Median age: 45.1; Age under 18: 18.3%; Age 65 and over: 19.6%; Males per 100 females: 104.7; Marriage status: 31.9% never married, 47.1% now married, 0.8% separated, 4.7% widowed, 16.3% divorced; Foreign born: 1.7%; Speak English only: 96.9%; With disability: 20.4%; Veterans: 15.9%; Ancestry: 21.2% German, 16.7% English, 15.1% Irish, 15.0% American, 8.6% Italian

Employment: 11.5% management, business, and financial, 3.0% computer, engineering, and science, 10.4% education, legal, community service, arts, and media, 5.3% healthcare practitioners, 17.0% service, 22.3% sales and office, 13.4% natural resources, construction, and maintenance, 17.1% production, transportation, and material moving

Income: Per capita: $22,803; Median household: $40,969; Average household: $52,659; Households with income of $100,000 or more: 12.0%; Poverty rate: 19.9%

Educational Attainment: High school diploma or higher: 89.5%; Bachelor's degree or higher: 16.1%; Graduate/professional degree or higher: 8.0%

School District(s)

Avoca Central SD (PK-12)

   2014-15 Enrollment: 447 . . . . (607) 566-2221

Housing: Homeownership rate: 73.7%; Median home value: $77,200; Median year structure built: 1959; Homeowner vacancy rate: 1.0%; Median selected monthly owner costs: $986 with a mortgage, $358 without a mortgage; Median gross rent: $641 per month; Rental vacancy rate: 0.0%

Health Insurance: 92.1% have insurance; 58.6% have private insurance; 48.2% have public insurance; 7.9% do not have insurance; 0.0% of children under 18 do not have insurance

Transportation: Commute: 93.9% car, 1.0% public transportation, 1.4% walk, 2.8% work from home; Mean travel time to work: 23.3 minutes

AVOCA (village). Covers a land area of 1.326 square miles and a water area of 0.002 square miles. Located at 42.41° N. Lat; 77.42° W. Long. Elevation is 1,194 feet.

Population: 1,033; Growth (since 2000): 2.5%; Density: 779.0 persons per square mile; Race: 98.0% White, 0.4% Black/African American, 0.0% Asian, 0.0% American Indian/Alaska Native, 0.2% Native Hawaiian/Other Pacific Islander, 0.7% Two or more races, 2.8% Hispanic of any race; Average household size: 2.47; Median age: 39.8; Age under 18: 22.4%; Age 65 and over: 12.9%; Males per 100 females: 100.4; Marriage status: 30.8% never married, 50.5% now married, 1.3% separated, 3.4% widowed, 15.3% divorced; Foreign born: 0.3%; Speak English only: 98.1%; With disability: 16.8%; Veterans: 14.2%; Ancestry: 24.8% German, 17.4% Irish, 17.2% English, 10.3% Italian, 6.2% American

Employment: 12.6% management, business, and financial, 3.1% computer, engineering, and science, 9.1% education, legal, community service, arts, and media, 7.1% healthcare practitioners, 15.5% service, 30.5% sales and office, 10.2% natural resources, construction, and maintenance, 12.1% production, transportation, and material moving

Income: Per capita: $21,518; Median household: $47,788; Average household: $55,314; Households with income of $100,000 or more: 9.6%; Poverty rate: 16.9%

Educational Attainment: High school diploma or higher: 94.4%; Bachelor's degree or higher: 15.0%; Graduate/professional degree or higher: 5.3%

School District(s)

Avoca Central SD (PK-12)

   2014-15 Enrollment: 447 . . . . (607) 566-2221

Housing: Homeownership rate: 73.5%; Median home value: $70,600; Median year structure built: Before 1940; Homeowner vacancy rate: 2.3%; Median selected monthly owner costs: $1,026 with a mortgage, $373 without a mortgage; Median gross rent: $619 per month; Rental vacancy rate: 0.0%

Health Insurance: 93.4% have insurance; 62.5% have private insurance; 43.6% have public insurance; 6.6% do not have insurance; 0.0% of children under 18 do not have insurance

Transportation: Commute: 95.1% car, 0.5% public transportation, 2.8% walk, 0.0% work from home; Mean travel time to work: 20.0 minutes

BATH (town). Covers a land area of 95.319 square miles and a water area of 0.559 square miles. Located at 42.32° N. Lat; 77.32° W. Long. Elevation is 1,109 feet.

History: Bath is the site of the first clearing in Steuben County, made in 1793 by Colonel Charles Williamson (1757-1808), agent for the Pulteney Estate. Williamson chose the site of Bath on the Cohocton River as the location of a future metropolis that was to be the trading, industrial, and distribution center for the entire region. He was too energetic to wait for the normal processes of settlement. His plan was to build the city first, which would then attract settlers. Williamson's overhasty promotions cost his principals more than a million dollars, and he was dismissed from his position in 1801. Incorporated in 1816.

Population: 12,277; Growth (since 2000): 1.5%; Density: 128.8 persons per square mile; Race: 95.0% White, 2.8% Black/African American, 0.6% Asian, 0.1% American Indian/Alaska Native, 0.0% Native Hawaiian/Other Pacific Islander, 0.8% Two or more races, 2.6% Hispanic of any race; Average household size: 2.22; Median age: 44.4; Age under 18: 20.4%; Age 65 and over: 19.2%; Males per 100 females: 103.4; Marriage status:

26.4% never married, 47.9% now married, 4.3% separated, 9.6% widowed, 16.0% divorced; Foreign born: 1.9%; Speak English only: 96.6%; With disability: 19.2%; Veterans: 14.1%; Ancestry: 21.4% German, 19.7% American, 14.1% Irish, 10.8% English, 6.9% Italian

Employment: 9.5% management, business, and financial, 3.3% computer, engineering, and science, 11.8% education, legal, community service, arts, and media, 5.9% healthcare practitioners, 21.8% service, 22.6% sales and office, 8.8% natural resources, construction, and maintenance, 16.3% production, transportation, and material moving

Income: Per capita: $22,128; Median household: $40,931; Average household: $50,595; Households with income of $100,000 or more: 10.3%; Poverty rate: 21.2%

Educational Attainment: High school diploma or higher: 86.7%; Bachelor's degree or higher: 16.0%; Graduate/professional degree or higher: 7.4%

School District(s)

Bath Central SD (PK-12)

    2014-15 Enrollment: 1,629 . . . . (607) 776-3301

Housing: Homeownership rate: 63.1%; Median home value: $78,400; Median year structure built: 1962; Homeowner vacancy rate: 1.2%; Median selected monthly owner costs: $1,032 with a mortgage, $445 without a mortgage; Median gross rent: $580 per month; Rental vacancy rate: 4.5%

Health Insurance: 92.5% have insurance; 62.8% have private insurance; 48.4% have public insurance; 7.5% do not have insurance; 2.6% of children under 18 do not have insurance

Hospitals: Bath VA Medical Center (440 beds); Ira Davenport Memorial Hospital (66 beds)

Newspapers: Courier-Advocate (weekly circulation 11,000)

Transportation: Commute: 87.3% car, 1.2% public transportation, 6.1% walk, 2.4% work from home; Mean travel time to work: 18.6 minutes

Additional Information Contacts

Town of Bath . . . . (607) 776-7013
    http://www.townofbathny.org

BATH (village). County seat. Covers a land area of 3.175 square miles and a water area of <.001 square miles. Located at 42.34° N. Lat; 77.32° W. Long. Elevation is 1,109 feet.

Population: 5,720; Growth (since 2000): 1.4%; Density: 1,801.8 persons per square mile; Race: 96.4% White, 1.7% Black/African American, 0.5% Asian, 0.0% American Indian/Alaska Native, 0.0% Native Hawaiian/Other Pacific Islander, 0.8% Two or more races, 1.4% Hispanic of any race; Average household size: 2.08; Median age: 42.3; Age under 18: 19.9%; Age 65 and over: 20.7%; Males per 100 females: 93.1; Marriage status: 28.5% never married, 45.5% now married, 4.1% separated, 12.3% widowed, 13.7% divorced; Foreign born: 2.2%; Speak English only: 95.8%; With disability: 18.2%; Veterans: 12.9%; Ancestry: 24.4% German, 21.0% American, 12.5% Irish, 12.2% English, 8.6% Polish

Employment: 8.7% management, business, and financial, 4.7% computer, engineering, and science, 10.0% education, legal, community service, arts, and media, 7.1% healthcare practitioners, 22.6% service, 28.0% sales and office, 2.8% natural resources, construction, and maintenance, 16.1% production, transportation, and material moving

Income: Per capita: $23,947; Median household: $38,266; Average household: $50,180; Households with income of $100,000 or more: 8.0%; Poverty rate: 18.7%

Educational Attainment: High school diploma or higher: 89.5%; Bachelor's degree or higher: 16.2%; Graduate/professional degree or higher: 7.3%

School District(s)

Bath Central SD (PK-12)

    2014-15 Enrollment: 1,629 . . . . (607) 776-3301

Housing: Homeownership rate: 51.5%; Median home value: $78,800; Median year structure built: 1947; Homeowner vacancy rate: 2.7%; Median selected monthly owner costs: $1,008 with a mortgage, $441 without a mortgage; Median gross rent: $560 per month; Rental vacancy rate: 5.0%

Health Insurance: 91.6% have insurance; 61.1% have private insurance; 49.3% have public insurance; 8.4% do not have insurance; 4.8% of children under 18 do not have insurance

Hospitals: Bath VA Medical Center (440 beds); Ira Davenport Memorial Hospital (66 beds)

Safety: Violent crime rate: 14.1 per 10,000 population; Property crime rate: 252.5 per 10,000 population

Newspapers: Courier-Advocate (weekly circulation 11,000)

Transportation: Commute: 85.1% car, 1.6% public transportation, 8.2% walk, 1.0% work from home; Mean travel time to work: 16.6 minutes

Additional Information Contacts

Village of Bath . . . . (607) 776-3811
    http://www.villageofbath.org

BRADFORD (town). Covers a land area of 25.122 square miles and a water area of 0.114 square miles. Located at 42.33° N. Lat; 77.13° W. Long. Elevation is 1,119 feet.

Population: 826; Growth (since 2000): 8.3%; Density: 32.9 persons per square mile; Race: 99.6% White, 0.0% Black/African American, 0.0% Asian, 0.4% American Indian/Alaska Native, 0.0% Native Hawaiian/Other Pacific Islander, 0.0% Two or more races, 0.4% Hispanic of any race; Average household size: 2.64; Median age: 40.8; Age under 18: 20.6%; Age 65 and over: 13.2%; Males per 100 females: 104.1; Marriage status: 25.6% never married, 57.9% now married, 2.2% separated, 7.4% widowed, 9.0% divorced; Foreign born: 0.5%; Speak English only: 98.5%; With disability: 18.2%; Veterans: 15.9%; Ancestry: 23.6% American, 19.1% German, 15.7% Polish, 12.3% English, 12.2% Irish

Employment: 9.1% management, business, and financial, 5.7% computer, engineering, and science, 7.4% education, legal, community service, arts, and media, 7.4% healthcare practitioners, 17.3% service, 21.2% sales and office, 12.5% natural resources, construction, and maintenance, 19.5% production, transportation, and material moving

Income: Per capita: $20,614; Median household: $49,219; Average household: $53,875; Households with income of $100,000 or more: 7.9%; Poverty rate: 19.1%

Educational Attainment: High school diploma or higher: 81.2%; Bachelor's degree or higher: 12.6%; Graduate/professional degree or higher: 4.3%

School District(s)

Bradford Central SD (PK-12)

    2014-15 Enrollment: 275. . . . . (607) 583-4616

Housing: Homeownership rate: 87.2%; Median home value: $84,800; Median year structure built: 1981; Homeowner vacancy rate: 0.0%; Median selected monthly owner costs: $1,096 with a mortgage, $465 without a mortgage; Median gross rent: $598 per month; Rental vacancy rate: 0.0%

Health Insurance: 91.5% have insurance; 67.7% have private insurance; 37.2% have public insurance; 8.5% do not have insurance; 2.4% of children under 18 do not have insurance

Transportation: Commute: 92.9% car, 0.0% public transportation, 0.6% walk, 6.5% work from home; Mean travel time to work: 24.2 minutes

CAMERON (town). Covers a land area of 46.704 square miles and a water area of 0.058 square miles. Located at 42.23° N. Lat; 77.42° W. Long. Elevation is 1,070 feet.

Population: 911; Growth (since 2000): -11.9%; Density: 19.5 persons per square mile; Race: 98.7% White, 0.0% Black/African American, 0.0% Asian, 0.3% American Indian/Alaska Native, 0.2% Native Hawaiian/Other Pacific Islander, 0.5% Two or more races, 0.2% Hispanic of any race; Average household size: 2.57; Median age: 40.3; Age under 18: 25.8%; Age 65 and over: 14.3%; Males per 100 females: 106.8; Marriage status: 22.2% never married, 52.8% now married, 5.0% separated, 8.0% widowed, 17.0% divorced; Foreign born: 1.5%; Speak English only: 97.3%; With disability: 17.2%; Veterans: 13.0%; Ancestry: 20.4% German, 14.2% Irish, 13.4% American, 11.9% English, 5.7% French

Employment: 8.8% management, business, and financial, 4.0% computer, engineering, and science, 1.4% education, legal, community service, arts, and media, 5.7% healthcare practitioners, 12.3% service, 22.2% sales and office, 19.7% natural resources, construction, and maintenance, 25.9% production, transportation, and material moving

Income: Per capita: $22,275; Median household: $42,632; Average household: $56,608; Households with income of $100,000 or more: 8.2%; Poverty rate: 23.7%

Educational Attainment: High school diploma or higher: 84.6%; Bachelor's degree or higher: 5.8%; Graduate/professional degree or higher: 2.7%

Housing: Homeownership rate: 76.0%; Median home value: $70,200; Median year structure built: 1973; Homeowner vacancy rate: 4.6%; Median selected monthly owner costs: $1,005 with a mortgage, $371 without a mortgage; Median gross rent: $791 per month; Rental vacancy rate: 9.6%

Health Insurance: 86.4% have insurance; 50.5% have private insurance; 48.7% have public insurance; 13.6% do not have insurance; 3.4% of children under 18 do not have insurance

Transportation: Commute: 92.2% car, 0.9% public transportation, 4.3% walk, 1.7% work from home; Mean travel time to work: 29.6 minutes

CAMERON MILLS (unincorporated postal area)

ZCTA: 14820

Covers a land area of 30.740 square miles and a water area of 0.026 square miles. Located at 42.19° N. Lat; 77.36° W. Long. Elevation is 1,033 feet.

Population: 717; Growth (since 2000): -10.8%; Density: 23.3 persons per square mile; Race: 99.2% White, 0.3% Black/African American, 0.0% Asian, 0.0% American Indian/Alaska Native, 0.0% Native Hawaiian/Other Pacific Islander, 0.3% Two or more races, 0.3% Hispanic of any race; Average household size: 2.34; Median age: 50.2; Age under 18: 18.3%; Age 65 and over: 16.9%; Males per 100 females: 100.0; Marriage status: 16.8% never married, 65.4% now married, 3.0% separated, 7.4% widowed, 10.4% divorced; Foreign born: 0.0%; Speak English only: 97.9%; With disability: 15.6%; Veterans: 15.9%; Ancestry: 22.9% American, 15.9% English, 12.3% German, 11.6% Irish, 7.8% Polish

Employment: 9.6% management, business, and financial, 3.9% computer, engineering, and science, 7.1% education, legal, community service, arts, and media, 6.4% healthcare practitioners, 10.7% service, 27.4% sales and office, 19.9% natural resources, construction, and maintenance, 14.9% production, transportation, and material moving

Income: Per capita: $20,792; Median household: $42,045; Average household: $48,408; Households with income of $100,000 or more: 7.2%; Poverty rate: 20.6%

Educational Attainment: High school diploma or higher: 81.3%; Bachelor's degree or higher: 3.6%; Graduate/professional degree or higher: 0.9%

School District(s)

Addison Central SD (PK-12)

   2014-15 Enrollment: 1,140 . . . . (607) 359-2244

Housing: Homeownership rate: 82.7%; Median home value: $81,000; Median year structure built: 1979; Homeowner vacancy rate: 2.3%; Median selected monthly owner costs: $1,113 with a mortgage, $394 without a mortgage; Median gross rent: $607 per month; Rental vacancy rate: 0.0%

Health Insurance: 86.9% have insurance; 54.1% have private insurance; 48.7% have public insurance; 13.1% do not have insurance; 4.6% of children under 18 do not have insurance

Transportation: Commute: 94.7% car, 1.1% public transportation, 0.0% walk, 4.3% work from home; Mean travel time to work: 29.2 minutes

CAMPBELL (CDP).

Covers a land area of 1.761 square miles and a water area of 0 square miles. Located at 42.24° N. Lat; 77.19° W. Long. Elevation is 1,014 feet.

Population: 630; Growth (since 2000): n/a; Density: 357.7 persons per square mile; Race: 97.8% White, 2.2% Black/African American, 0.0% Asian, 0.0% American Indian/Alaska Native, 0.0% Native Hawaiian/Other Pacific Islander, 0.0% Two or more races, 2.4% Hispanic of any race; Average household size: 2.32; Median age: 47.3; Age under 18: 17.0%; Age 65 and over: 8.4%; Males per 100 females: 90.6; Marriage status: 23.4% never married, 58.9% now married, 2.0% separated, 1.4% widowed, 16.3% divorced; Foreign born: 1.7%; Speak English only: 96.8%; With disability: 9.0%; Veterans: 17.2%; Ancestry: 35.4% American, 10.2% English, 7.9% Italian, 7.5% German, 3.8% Polish

Employment: 2.2% management, business, and financial, 0.0% computer, engineering, and science, 6.3% education, legal, community service, arts, and media, 9.3% healthcare practitioners, 22.4% service, 29.2% sales and office, 12.8% natural resources, construction, and maintenance, 17.8% production, transportation, and material moving

Income: Per capita: $23,393; Median household: $40,313; Average household: $54,597; Households with income of $100,000 or more: 16.6%; Poverty rate: 11.1%

Educational Attainment: High school diploma or higher: 92.1%; Bachelor's degree or higher: 8.1%; Graduate/professional degree or higher: 4.6%

School District(s)

Campbell-Savona Central SD (PK-12)

   2014-15 Enrollment: 863 . . . . (607) 527-9800

Housing: Homeownership rate: 79.6%; Median home value: $86,300; Median year structure built: 1961; Homeowner vacancy rate: 0.0%; Median selected monthly owner costs: $1,147 with a mortgage, $435 without a mortgage; Median gross rent: $657 per month; Rental vacancy rate: 0.0%

Health Insurance: 87.8% have insurance; 80.2% have private insurance; 24.4% have public insurance; 12.2% do not have insurance; 0.0% of children under 18 do not have insurance

Transportation: Commute: 97.1% car, 0.0% public transportation, 0.0% walk, 2.9% work from home; Mean travel time to work: 25.1 minutes

CAMPBELL (town).

Covers a land area of 40.685 square miles and a water area of 0.094 square miles. Located at 42.23° N. Lat; 77.17° W. Long. Elevation is 1,014 feet.

Population: 3,372; Growth (since 2000): -8.6%; Density: 82.9 persons per square mile; Race: 99.1% White, 0.4% Black/African American, 0.0% Asian, 0.0% American Indian/Alaska Native, 0.0% Native Hawaiian/Other Pacific Islander, 0.4% Two or more races, 2.1% Hispanic of any race; Average household size: 2.27; Median age: 44.8; Age under 18: 19.8%; Age 65 and over: 19.7%; Males per 100 females: 96.5; Marriage status: 20.0% never married, 60.4% now married, 3.3% separated, 7.5% widowed, 12.1% divorced; Foreign born: 0.9%; Speak English only: 96.2%; With disability: 13.1%; Veterans: 12.1%; Ancestry: 17.8% German, 16.2% English, 16.2% American, 10.6% Irish, 6.9% Italian

Employment: 11.9% management, business, and financial, 3.9% computer, engineering, and science, 6.1% education, legal, community service, arts, and media, 6.9% healthcare practitioners, 16.7% service, 23.6% sales and office, 15.5% natural resources, construction, and maintenance, 15.5% production, transportation, and material moving

Income: Per capita: $25,858; Median household: $46,250; Average household: $58,780; Households with income of $100,000 or more: 16.2%; Poverty rate: 7.0%

Educational Attainment: High school diploma or higher: 91.6%; Bachelor's degree or higher: 14.3%; Graduate/professional degree or higher: 3.6%

School District(s)

Campbell-Savona Central SD (PK-12)

   2014-15 Enrollment: 863 . . . . (607) 527-9800

Housing: Homeownership rate: 82.5%; Median home value: $86,100; Median year structure built: 1976; Homeowner vacancy rate: 0.0%; Median selected monthly owner costs: $1,164 with a mortgage, $403 without a mortgage; Median gross rent: $777 per month; Rental vacancy rate: 0.0%

Health Insurance: 91.9% have insurance; 78.9% have private insurance; 32.0% have public insurance; 8.1% do not have insurance; 9.3% of children under 18 do not have insurance

Transportation: Commute: 93.6% car, 1.8% public transportation, 2.8% walk, 1.8% work from home; Mean travel time to work: 21.7 minutes

CANISTEO (town).

Covers a land area of 54.351 square miles and a water area of 0.009 square miles. Located at 42.24° N. Lat; 77.54° W. Long. Elevation is 1,135 feet.

History: Settled before 1790, incorporated 1873.

Population: 3,339; Growth (since 2000): -6.8%; Density: 61.4 persons per square mile; Race: 98.1% White, 0.9% Black/African American, 0.2% Asian, 0.0% American Indian/Alaska Native, 0.0% Native Hawaiian/Other Pacific Islander, 0.0% Two or more races, 1.1% Hispanic of any race; Average household size: 2.50; Median age: 42.0; Age under 18: 24.0%; Age 65 and over: 17.3%; Males per 100 females: 95.8; Marriage status: 26.6% never married, 53.6% now married, 4.1% separated, 7.3% widowed, 12.5% divorced; Foreign born: 0.7%; Speak English only: 98.7%; With disability: 17.8%; Veterans: 12.9%; Ancestry: 23.7% German, 21.1% Irish, 19.4% English, 10.6% American, 6.2% Italian

Employment: 7.4% management, business, and financial, 1.2% computer, engineering, and science, 9.1% education, legal, community service, arts, and media, 7.9% healthcare practitioners, 21.6% service, 22.9% sales and office, 15.3% natural resources, construction, and maintenance, 14.6% production, transportation, and material moving

Income: Per capita: $20,881; Median household: $49,289; Average household: $52,203; Households with income of $100,000 or more: 9.8%; Poverty rate: 16.5%

Educational Attainment: High school diploma or higher: 89.7%; Bachelor's degree or higher: 15.1%; Graduate/professional degree or higher: 6.5%

School District(s)

Canisteo-Greenwood CSD (PK-12)

   2014-15 Enrollment: 961 . . . . (607) 698-4225

Housing: Homeownership rate: 74.5%; Median home value: $82,900; Median year structure built: 1945; Homeowner vacancy rate: 1.5%; Median selected monthly owner costs: $993 with a mortgage, $368 without a mortgage; Median gross rent: $655 per month; Rental vacancy rate: 0.0%

Health Insurance: 92.0% have insurance; 69.4% have private insurance; 41.0% have public insurance; 8.0% do not have insurance; 8.8% of children under 18 do not have insurance

Transportation: Commute: 91.0% car, 1.7% public transportation, 3.7% walk, 2.0% work from home; Mean travel time to work: 29.9 minutes

CANISTEO (village).

Covers a land area of 0.934 square miles and a water area of 0 square miles. Located at 42.27° N. Lat; 77.61° W. Long. Elevation is 1,135 feet.

Population: 2,298; Growth (since 2000): -1.6%; Density: 2,461.3 persons per square mile; Race: 97.6% White, 1.3% Black/African American, 0.3% Asian, 0.0% American Indian/Alaska Native, 0.0% Native Hawaiian/Other Pacific Islander, 0.0% Two or more races, 1.3% Hispanic of any race; Average household size: 2.58; Median age: 37.8; Age under 18: 28.5%; Age 65 and over: 16.0%; Males per 100 females: 90.8; Marriage status: 27.1% never married, 53.1% now married, 2.8% separated, 7.0% widowed, 12.8% divorced; Foreign born: 0.7%; Speak English only: 98.3%; With disability: 18.3%; Veterans: 10.8%; Ancestry: 22.6% English, 22.6% German, 21.6% Irish, 9.1% American, 7.6% Italian

Employment: 8.0% management, business, and financial, 1.0% computer, engineering, and science, 11.1% education, legal, community service, arts, and media, 8.9% healthcare practitioners, 22.7% service, 21.8% sales and office, 11.3% natural resources, construction, and maintenance, 15.1% production, transportation, and material moving

Income: Per capita: $19,333; Median household: $42,422; Average household: $50,147; Households with income of $100,000 or more: 9.7%; Poverty rate: 16.4%

Educational Attainment: High school diploma or higher: 91.3%; Bachelor's degree or higher: 20.0%; Graduate/professional degree or higher: 8.7%

School District(s)

Canisteo-Greenwood CSD (PK-12)

    2014-15 Enrollment: 961 . . . . (607) 698-4225

Housing: Homeownership rate: 66.9%; Median home value: $76,400; Median year structure built: Before 1940; Homeowner vacancy rate: 2.6%; Median selected monthly owner costs: $907 with a mortgage, $377 without a mortgage; Median gross rent: $677 per month; Rental vacancy rate: 0.0%

Health Insurance: 90.8% have insurance; 68.0% have private insurance; 38.9% have public insurance; 9.2% do not have insurance; 9.9% of children under 18 do not have insurance

Safety: Violent crime rate: 9.0 per 10,000 population; Property crime rate: 58.7 per 10,000 population

Transportation: Commute: 90.6% car, 2.5% public transportation, 3.9% walk, 1.5% work from home; Mean travel time to work: 26.3 minutes

CATON (town).

Covers a land area of 37.565 square miles and a water area of 0.434 square miles. Located at 42.04° N. Lat; 77.02° W. Long. Elevation is 1,424 feet.

Population: 1,912; Growth (since 2000): -8.8%; Density: 50.9 persons per square mile; Race: 98.2% White, 0.4% Black/African American, 0.0% Asian, 0.0% American Indian/Alaska Native, 0.0% Native Hawaiian/Other Pacific Islander, 1.4% Two or more races, 1.4% Hispanic of any race; Average household size: 2.50; Median age: 46.1; Age under 18: 20.9%; Age 65 and over: 17.2%; Males per 100 females: 101.0; Marriage status: 20.3% never married, 67.9% now married, 2.2% separated, 4.1% widowed, 7.7% divorced; Foreign born: 0.3%; Speak English only: 98.3%; With disability: 13.2%; Veterans: 10.0%; Ancestry: 18.6% Irish, 15.4% American, 14.7% German, 9.9% English, 9.9% Italian

Employment: 14.0% management, business, and financial, 6.7% computer, engineering, and science, 8.3% education, legal, community service, arts, and media, 4.3% healthcare practitioners, 16.0% service, 17.9% sales and office, 11.1% natural resources, construction, and maintenance, 21.6% production, transportation, and material moving

Income: Per capita: $26,540; Median household: $62,955; Average household: $66,239; Households with income of $100,000 or more: 18.6%; Poverty rate: 6.9%

Educational Attainment: High school diploma or higher: 88.8%; Bachelor's degree or higher: 15.8%; Graduate/professional degree or higher: 7.0%

Housing: Homeownership rate: 90.7%; Median home value: $100,100; Median year structure built: 1975; Homeowner vacancy rate: 0.0%; Median selected monthly owner costs: $1,125 with a mortgage, $512 without a mortgage; Median gross rent: $884 per month; Rental vacancy rate: 0.0%

Health Insurance: 96.7% have insurance; 78.7% have private insurance; 35.9% have public insurance; 3.3% do not have insurance; 1.0% of children under 18 do not have insurance

Transportation: Commute: 99.5% car, 0.0% public transportation, 0.0% walk, 0.3% work from home; Mean travel time to work: 28.9 minutes

COHOCTON (town).

Covers a land area of 56.083 square miles and a water area of 0.007 square miles. Located at 42.52° N. Lat; 77.48° W. Long. Elevation is 1,319 feet.

Population: 2,554; Growth (since 2000): -2.7%; Density: 45.5 persons per square mile; Race: 97.0% White, 0.1% Black/African American, 0.0% Asian, 0.2% American Indian/Alaska Native, 0.0% Native Hawaiian/Other Pacific Islander, 1.8% Two or more races, 1.6% Hispanic of any race; Average household size: 2.63; Median age: 41.3; Age under 18: 25.5%; Age 65 and over: 16.4%; Males per 100 females: 105.0; Marriage status: 25.4% never married, 57.5% now married, 3.1% separated, 5.6% widowed, 11.6% divorced; Foreign born: 0.4%; Speak English only: 97.9%; With disability: 18.4%; Veterans: 11.1%; Ancestry: 28.2% German, 19.5% English, 13.2% Irish, 10.3% American, 6.4% Italian

Employment: 9.1% management, business, and financial, 1.5% computer, engineering, and science, 7.2% education, legal, community service, arts, and media, 3.7% healthcare practitioners, 19.1% service, 21.3% sales and office, 9.2% natural resources, construction, and maintenance, 28.9% production, transportation, and material moving

Income: Per capita: $22,242; Median household: $44,202; Average household: $58,500; Households with income of $100,000 or more: 14.5%; Poverty rate: 17.1%

Educational Attainment: High school diploma or higher: 85.3%; Bachelor's degree or higher: 10.7%; Graduate/professional degree or higher: 4.1%

School District(s)

Wayland-Cohocton Central SD (PK-12)

    2014-15 Enrollment: 1,412 . . . . (585) 728-2211

Housing: Homeownership rate: 81.3%; Median home value: $78,500; Median year structure built: 1952; Homeowner vacancy rate: 3.5%; Median selected monthly owner costs: $984 with a mortgage, $417 without a mortgage; Median gross rent: $655 per month; Rental vacancy rate: 3.2%

Health Insurance: 94.2% have insurance; 64.0% have private insurance; 45.0% have public insurance; 5.8% do not have insurance; 1.4% of children under 18 do not have insurance

Transportation: Commute: 89.2% car, 0.0% public transportation, 4.0% walk, 2.2% work from home; Mean travel time to work: 27.1 minutes

COHOCTON (village).

Covers a land area of 1.501 square miles and a water area of 0 square miles. Located at 42.50° N. Lat; 77.50° W. Long. Elevation is 1,319 feet.

Population: 1,016; Growth (since 2000): 19.0%; Density: 676.7 persons per square mile; Race: 96.1% White, 0.0% Black/African American, 0.0% Asian, 0.6% American Indian/Alaska Native, 0.0% Native Hawaiian/Other Pacific Islander, 3.3% Two or more races, 0.0% Hispanic of any race; Average household size: 2.99; Median age: 35.9; Age under 18: 30.0%; Age 65 and over: 12.7%; Males per 100 females: 93.5; Marriage status: 29.8% never married, 55.6% now married, 5.3% separated, 5.7% widowed, 9.0% divorced; Foreign born: 0.0%; Speak English only: 99.0%; With disability: 21.4%; Veterans: 10.7%; Ancestry: 23.5% German, 18.0% English, 13.8% Irish, 13.7% American, 5.2% Italian

Employment: 7.5% management, business, and financial, 1.3% computer, engineering, and science, 9.1% education, legal, community service, arts, and media, 1.6% healthcare practitioners, 25.6% service, 15.7% sales and office, 12.5% natural resources, construction, and maintenance, 26.7% production, transportation, and material moving

Income: Per capita: $16,715; Median household: $39,531; Average household: $50,360; Households with income of $100,000 or more: 11.1%; Poverty rate: 26.2%

Educational Attainment: High school diploma or higher: 85.2%; Bachelor's degree or higher: 8.5%; Graduate/professional degree or higher: 2.7%

School District(s)

Wayland-Cohocton Central SD (PK-12)

    2014-15 Enrollment: 1,412 . . . . (585) 728-2211

Housing: Homeownership rate: 73.7%; Median home value: $76,400; Median year structure built: Before 1940; Homeowner vacancy rate: 0.0%; Median selected monthly owner costs: $863 with a mortgage, $417 without a mortgage; Median gross rent: $662 per month; Rental vacancy rate: 6.4%

Health Insurance: 89.6% have insurance; 51.8% have private insurance; 47.9% have public insurance; 10.4% do not have insurance; 3.0% of children under 18 do not have insurance

Transportation: Commute: 89.6% car, 0.0% public transportation, 3.0% walk, 4.6% work from home; Mean travel time to work: 26.9 minutes

COOPERS PLAINS (CDP). Covers a land area of 0.824 square miles and a water area of 0 square miles. Located at 42.18° N. Lat; 77.14° W. Long. Elevation is 984 feet.

Population: 407; Growth (since 2000): n/a; Density: 493.7 persons per square mile; Race: 100.0% White, 0.0% Black/African American, 0.0% Asian, 0.0% American Indian/Alaska Native, 0.0% Native Hawaiian/Other Pacific Islander, 0.0% Two or more races, 0.0% Hispanic of any race; Average household size: 1.92; Median age: 46.6; Age under 18: 10.6%; Age 65 and over: 33.4%; Males per 100 females: 101.3; Marriage status: 35.8% never married, 40.9% now married, 0.0% separated, 15.4% widowed, 7.9% divorced; Foreign born: 0.0%; Speak English only: 100.0%; With disability: 20.1%; Veterans: 15.7%; Ancestry: 24.1% German, 15.0% Scottish, 12.0% American, 9.6% English, 6.9% Swedish

Employment: 0.0% management, business, and financial, 0.0% computer, engineering, and science, 7.6% education, legal, community service, arts, and media, 0.0% healthcare practitioners, 3.3% service, 24.5% sales and office, 51.1% natural resources, construction, and maintenance, 13.6% production, transportation, and material moving

Income: Per capita: $33,994; Median household: $53,696; Average household: $65,101; Households with income of $100,000 or more: 22.2%; Poverty rate: 12.0%

Educational Attainment: High school diploma or higher: 100.0%; Bachelor's degree or higher: 18.3%; Graduate/professional degree or higher: n/a

Housing: Homeownership rate: 77.8%; Median home value: $86,300; Median year structure built: Before 1940; Homeowner vacancy rate: 0.0%; Median selected monthly owner costs: $896 with a mortgage, $281 without a mortgage; Median gross rent: n/a per month; Rental vacancy rate: 0.0%

Health Insurance: 96.6% have insurance; 80.8% have private insurance; 45.5% have public insurance; 3.4% do not have insurance; 0.0% of children under 18 do not have insurance

Transportation: Commute: 100.0% car, 0.0% public transportation, 0.0% walk, 0.0% work from home; Mean travel time to work: 16.7 minutes

CORNING (city). Covers a land area of 3.084 square miles and a water area of 0.177 square miles. Located at 42.15° N. Lat; 77.06° W. Long. Elevation is 932 feet.

History: The glass industry, for which the city is famous, began in 1868. Corning glass Museum and the Rockwell Museum, with the largest collection of Western art in the Eastern U.S. and the world's largest collection of Steuben glass, are located in the city. In 1972 the city was heavily damaged by flooding In the wake of Hurricane Agnes. Settled 1788; Incorporated as a city 1890.

Population: 11,059; Growth (since 2000): 2.0%; Density: 3,586.2 persons per square mile; Race: 90.5% White, 3.6% Black/African American, 2.2% Asian, 0.4% American Indian/Alaska Native, 0.0% Native Hawaiian/Other Pacific Islander, 3.2% Two or more races, 1.7% Hispanic of any race; Average household size: 2.14; Median age: 38.4; Age under 18: 21.6%; Age 65 and over: 14.7%; Males per 100 females: 93.1; Marriage status: 32.4% never married, 46.1% now married, 3.6% separated, 6.8% widowed, 14.7% divorced; Foreign born: 3.8%; Speak English only: 94.4%; With disability: 14.1%; Veterans: 10.4%; Ancestry: 19.9% Irish, 19.0% German, 13.6% English, 12.0% Italian, 11.5% American

Employment: 14.0% management, business, and financial, 9.7% computer, engineering, and science, 11.9% education, legal, community service, arts, and media, 5.4% healthcare practitioners, 20.4% service, 20.4% sales and office, 6.3% natural resources, construction, and maintenance, 11.9% production, transportation, and material moving

Income: Per capita: $30,799; Median household: $51,022; Average household: $66,017; Households with income of $100,000 or more: 19.7%; Poverty rate: 17.9%

Educational Attainment: High school diploma or higher: 93.2%; Bachelor's degree or higher: 34.2%; Graduate/professional degree or higher: 16.2%

School District(s)

Corning City SD (PK-12)
   2014-15 Enrollment: 4,867 . . . . (607) 936-3704

Two-year College(s)

Corning Community College (Public)
   Fall 2014 Enrollment: 4,520 . . . . (607) 962-9011
   2015-16 Tuition: In-state $4,774; Out-of-state $9,004

Housing: Homeownership rate: 49.7%; Median home value: $101,700; Median year structure built: Before 1940; Homeowner vacancy rate: 1.1%; Median selected monthly owner costs: $1,163 with a mortgage, $522 without a mortgage; Median gross rent: $677 per month; Rental vacancy rate: 6.3%

Health Insurance: 90.5% have insurance; 68.6% have private insurance; 35.2% have public insurance; 9.5% do not have insurance; 4.5% of children under 18 do not have insurance

Hospitals: Corning Hospital (99 beds)

Safety: Violent crime rate: 59.4 per 10,000 population; Property crime rate: 327.0 per 10,000 population

Newspapers: The Leader (daily circulation 12,800)

Transportation: Commute: 89.1% car, 0.1% public transportation, 8.1% walk, 1.7% work from home; Mean travel time to work: 15.3 minutes

Additional Information Contacts

City of Corning. . . . . (607) 962-0340
  http://www.cityofcorning.com

CORNING (town). Covers a land area of 36.850 square miles and a water area of 0.503 square miles. Located at 42.15° N. Lat; 77.01° W. Long. Elevation is 932 feet.

Population: 6,294; Growth (since 2000): -2.1%; Density: 170.8 persons per square mile; Race: 95.2% White, 1.7% Black/African American, 2.0% Asian, 0.1% American Indian/Alaska Native, 0.0% Native Hawaiian/Other Pacific Islander, 1.0% Two or more races, 0.7% Hispanic of any race; Average household size: 2.47; Median age: 43.3; Age under 18: 22.8%; Age 65 and over: 17.2%; Males per 100 females: 99.4; Marriage status: 24.4% never married, 62.1% now married, 2.1% separated, 6.4% widowed, 7.0% divorced; Foreign born: 2.0%; Speak English only: 95.9%; With disability: 15.6%; Veterans: 11.0%; Ancestry: 21.5% German, 15.6% Irish, 12.7% English, 11.4% American, 9.7% Italian

Employment: 16.3% management, business, and financial, 8.0% computer, engineering, and science, 11.4% education, legal, community service, arts, and media, 5.7% healthcare practitioners, 17.7% service, 17.4% sales and office, 8.5% natural resources, construction, and maintenance, 15.0% production, transportation, and material moving

Income: Per capita: $32,651; Median household: $55,927; Average household: $80,540; Households with income of $100,000 or more: 22.4%; Poverty rate: 8.5%

Educational Attainment: High school diploma or higher: 88.6%; Bachelor's degree or higher: 27.8%; Graduate/professional degree or higher: 14.9%

School District(s)

Corning City SD (PK-12)
   2014-15 Enrollment: 4,867 . . . . (607) 936-3704

Two-year College(s)

Corning Community College (Public)
   Fall 2014 Enrollment: 4,520 . . . . (607) 962-9011
   2015-16 Tuition: In-state $4,774; Out-of-state $9,004

Housing: Homeownership rate: 80.0%; Median home value: $111,600; Median year structure built: 1960; Homeowner vacancy rate: 0.0%; Median selected monthly owner costs: $1,191 with a mortgage, $462 without a mortgage; Median gross rent: $741 per month; Rental vacancy rate: 3.6%

Health Insurance: 88.9% have insurance; 72.5% have private insurance; 32.3% have public insurance; 11.1% do not have insurance; 8.6% of children under 18 do not have insurance

Hospitals: Corning Hospital (99 beds)

Newspapers: The Leader (daily circulation 12,800)

Transportation: Commute: 96.0% car, 0.2% public transportation, 1.5% walk, 1.6% work from home; Mean travel time to work: 18.5 minutes

Additional Information Contacts

Town of Corning . . . . (607) 936-6114
  http://www.townofcorningny.org

DANSVILLE (town). Covers a land area of 48.368 square miles and a water area of 0.068 square miles. Located at 42.46° N. Lat; 77.66° W. Long.

Population: 1,695; Growth (since 2000): -14.3%; Density: 35.0 persons per square mile; Race: 99.0% White, 0.4% Black/African American, 0.2% Asian, 0.0% American Indian/Alaska Native, 0.0% Native Hawaiian/Other Pacific Islander, 0.0% Two or more races, 0.7% Hispanic of any race; Average household size: 2.48; Median age: 47.7; Age under 18: 20.1%; Age 65 and over: 14.5%; Males per 100 females: 104.0; Marriage status: 24.8% never married, 54.6% now married, 1.5% separated, 5.1% widowed, 15.5% divorced; Foreign born: 0.9%; Speak English only: 98.7%;

With disability: 12.8%; Veterans: 8.9%; Ancestry: 36.0% German, 19.2% Irish, 12.5% English, 8.5% Italian, 6.6% Polish

Employment: 12.2% management, business, and financial, 3.9% computer, engineering, and science, 7.5% education, legal, community service, arts, and media, 6.9% healthcare practitioners, 16.6% service, 19.8% sales and office, 15.1% natural resources, construction, and maintenance, 18.0% production, transportation, and material moving

Income: Per capita: $23,122; Median household: $44,417; Average household: $56,976; Households with income of $100,000 or more: 14.8%; Poverty rate: 15.8%

Educational Attainment: High school diploma or higher: 89.6%; Bachelor's degree or higher: 16.5%; Graduate/professional degree or higher: 7.7%

Housing: Homeownership rate: 82.1%; Median home value: $99,300; Median year structure built: 1979; Homeowner vacancy rate: 0.5%; Median selected monthly owner costs: $1,210 with a mortgage, $489 without a mortgage; Median gross rent: $788 per month; Rental vacancy rate: 6.9%

Health Insurance: 85.5% have insurance; 64.2% have private insurance; 35.9% have public insurance; 14.5% do not have insurance; 11.7% of children under 18 do not have insurance

Transportation: Commute: 92.0% car, 0.0% public transportation, 1.8% walk, 5.9% work from home; Mean travel time to work: 27.5 minutes

---

ERWIN (town). Covers a land area of 38.656 square miles and a water area of 0.501 square miles. Located at 42.13° N. Lat; 77.15° W. Long.

Population: 8,423; Growth (since 2000): 16.5%; Density: 217.9 persons per square mile; Race: 84.6% White, 3.9% Black/African American, 10.6% Asian, 0.0% American Indian/Alaska Native, 0.0% Native Hawaiian/Other Pacific Islander, 0.7% Two or more races, 2.8% Hispanic of any race; Average household size: 2.33; Median age: 39.8; Age under 18: 22.8%; Age 65 and over: 16.7%; Males per 100 females: 95.0; Marriage status: 28.0% never married, 52.3% now married, 2.0% separated, 7.2% widowed, 12.6% divorced; Foreign born: 10.3%; Speak English only: 87.0%; With disability: 9.8%; Veterans: 9.0%; Ancestry: 15.8% Irish, 14.8% German, 12.3% English, 10.3% Italian, 9.7% Polish

Employment: 17.3% management, business, and financial, 15.3% computer, engineering, and science, 13.4% education, legal, community service, arts, and media, 2.6% healthcare practitioners, 15.2% service, 18.7% sales and office, 6.6% natural resources, construction, and maintenance, 10.9% production, transportation, and material moving

Income: Per capita: $39,489; Median household: $66,280; Average household: $94,287; Households with income of $100,000 or more: 29.6%; Poverty rate: 7.8%

Educational Attainment: High school diploma or higher: 93.5%; Bachelor's degree or higher: 42.7%; Graduate/professional degree or higher: 22.6%

Housing: Homeownership rate: 60.7%; Median home value: $122,500; Median year structure built: 1973; Homeowner vacancy rate: 3.2%; Median selected monthly owner costs: $1,320 with a mortgage, $514 without a mortgage; Median gross rent: $851 per month; Rental vacancy rate: 2.5%

Health Insurance: 97.0% have insurance; 82.5% have private insurance; 29.2% have public insurance; 3.0% do not have insurance; 2.0% of children under 18 do not have insurance

Transportation: Commute: 92.7% car, 0.3% public transportation, 1.3% walk, 5.0% work from home; Mean travel time to work: 15.1 minutes

Additional Information Contacts

Town of Erwin . . . . (607) 936-3652
    http://www.erwinny.org

FREMONT (town). Covers a land area of 32.036 square miles and a water area of 0.154 square miles. Located at 42.39° N. Lat; 77.61° W. Long. Elevation is 1,529 feet.

Population: 957; Growth (since 2000): -0.7%; Density: 29.9 persons per square mile; Race: 99.2% White, 0.0% Black/African American, 0.0% Asian, 0.0% American Indian/Alaska Native, 0.0% Native Hawaiian/Other Pacific Islander, 0.8% Two or more races, 2.3% Hispanic of any race; Average household size: 2.24; Median age: 43.3; Age under 18: 19.6%; Age 65 and over: 19.3%; Males per 100 females: 104.0; Marriage status: 24.5% never married, 55.8% now married, 2.5% separated, 7.7% widowed, 11.9% divorced; Foreign born: 2.9%; Speak English only: 97.2%; With disability: 14.0%; Veterans: 10.7%; Ancestry: 24.8% Irish, 23.0% German, 12.9% English, 7.2% Italian, 6.8% American

Employment: 8.4% management, business, and financial, 2.1% computer, engineering, and science, 6.7% education, legal, community service, arts, and media, 11.2% healthcare practitioners, 9.9% service, 19.5% sales and

office, 29.0% natural resources, construction, and maintenance, 13.3% production, transportation, and material moving

Income: Per capita: $26,054; Median household: $55,714; Average household: $59,177; Households with income of $100,000 or more: 13.5%; Poverty rate: 9.5%

Educational Attainment: High school diploma or higher: 94.4%; Bachelor's degree or higher: 16.5%; Graduate/professional degree or higher: 5.5%

Housing: Homeownership rate: 82.9%; Median home value: $86,000; Median year structure built: 1960; Homeowner vacancy rate: 0.0%; Median selected monthly owner costs: $1,133 with a mortgage, $436 without a mortgage; Median gross rent: $630 per month; Rental vacancy rate: 0.0%

Health Insurance: 89.0% have insurance; 73.4% have private insurance; 35.1% have public insurance; 11.0% do not have insurance; 16.0% of children under 18 do not have insurance

Transportation: Commute: 82.1% car, 0.0% public transportation, 5.0% walk, 10.2% work from home; Mean travel time to work: 21.3 minutes

---

GANG MILLS (CDP). Covers a land area of 4.378 square miles and a water area of 0.023 square miles. Located at 42.16° N. Lat; 77.13° W. Long. Elevation is 935 feet.

Population: 4,401; Growth (since 2000): 33.2%; Density: 1,005.3 persons per square mile; Race: 73.5% White, 6.3% Black/African American, 19.1% Asian, 0.0% American Indian/Alaska Native, 0.0% Native Hawaiian/Other Pacific Islander, 0.8% Two or more races, 4.1% Hispanic of any race; Average household size: 2.34; Median age: 39.5; Age under 18: 22.1%; Age 65 and over: 15.4%; Males per 100 females: 95.1; Marriage status: 30.7% never married, 51.6% now married, 1.1% separated, 7.3% widowed, 10.4% divorced; Foreign born: 17.2%; Speak English only: 77.3%; With disability: 10.5%; Veterans: 8.5%; Ancestry: 12.6% Italian, 11.8% German, 11.4% Irish, 10.0% English, 6.9% Polish

Employment: 17.9% management, business, and financial, 19.3% computer, engineering, and science, 11.9% education, legal, community service, arts, and media, 4.3% healthcare practitioners, 14.4% service, 17.7% sales and office, 4.1% natural resources, construction, and maintenance, 10.5% production, transportation, and material moving

Income: Per capita: $42,411; Median household: $84,920; Average household: $104,005; Households with income of $100,000 or more: 36.6%; Poverty rate: 7.9%

Educational Attainment: High school diploma or higher: 92.3%; Bachelor's degree or higher: 51.0%; Graduate/professional degree or higher: 30.0%

Housing: Homeownership rate: 52.7%; Median home value: $175,000; Median year structure built: 1982; Homeowner vacancy rate: 0.0%; Median selected monthly owner costs: $1,595 with a mortgage, $555 without a mortgage; Median gross rent: $1,020 per month; Rental vacancy rate: 3.9%

Health Insurance: 97.6% have insurance; 83.0% have private insurance; 27.9% have public insurance; 2.4% do not have insurance; 1.5% of children under 18 do not have insurance

Transportation: Commute: 96.0% car, 0.0% public transportation, 0.5% walk, 3.4% work from home; Mean travel time to work: 14.5 minutes

---

GREENWOOD (town). Covers a land area of 41.339 square miles and a water area of 0.007 square miles. Located at 42.15° N. Lat; 77.66° W. Long. Elevation is 1,562 feet.

Population: 764; Growth (since 2000): -10.0%; Density: 18.5 persons per square mile; Race: 98.3% White, 0.0% Black/African American, 0.5% Asian, 0.0% American Indian/Alaska Native, 0.0% Native Hawaiian/Other Pacific Islander, 1.2% Two or more races, 0.0% Hispanic of any race; Average household size: 2.42; Median age: 44.7; Age under 18: 22.3%; Age 65 and over: 18.1%; Males per 100 females: 103.8; Marriage status: 23.9% never married, 65.8% now married, 2.5% separated, 5.3% widowed, 5.0% divorced; Foreign born: 1.8%; Speak English only: 99.0%; With disability: 19.0%; Veterans: 10.4%; Ancestry: 24.2% German, 22.1% Irish, 14.0% English, 8.4% Italian, 6.9% Dutch

Employment: 13.0% management, business, and financial, 1.6% computer, engineering, and science, 13.8% education, legal, community service, arts, and media, 3.3% healthcare practitioners, 10.8% service, 16.8% sales and office, 22.2% natural resources, construction, and maintenance, 18.4% production, transportation, and material moving

Income: Per capita: $25,490; Median household: $54,583; Average household: $62,839; Households with income of $100,000 or more: 20.5%; Poverty rate: 10.3%

Educational Attainment: High school diploma or higher: 92.7%; Bachelor's degree or higher: 16.6%; Graduate/professional degree or higher: 9.5%

School District(s)
Canisteo-Greenwood CSD (PK-12)
    2014-15 Enrollment: 961 . . . . (607) 698-4225
Housing: Homeownership rate: 85.4%; Median home value: $91,000; Median year structure built: Before 1940; Homeowner vacancy rate: 0.7%; Median selected monthly owner costs: $911 with a mortgage, $443 without a mortgage; Median gross rent: $626 per month; Rental vacancy rate: 0.0%
Health Insurance: 88.6% have insurance; 73.8% have private insurance; 33.9% have public insurance; 11.4% do not have insurance; 8.8% of children under 18 do not have insurance
Transportation: Commute: 88.6% car, 0.0% public transportation, 3.1% walk, 8.3% work from home; Mean travel time to work: 31.6 minutes

HAMMONDSPORT (village). Covers a land area of 0.345 square miles and a water area of 0.020 square miles. Located at 42.41° N. Lat; 77.22° W. Long. Elevation is 755 feet.
History: Birthplace of Glenn Curtiss, who made aviation experiments in the village. Museum. Incorporated 1871.
Population: 592; Growth (since 2000): -19.0%; Density: 1,715.4 persons per square mile; Race: 97.1% White, 2.4% Black/African American, 0.0% Asian, 0.0% American Indian/Alaska Native, 0.0% Native Hawaiian/Other Pacific Islander, 0.5% Two or more races, 0.2% Hispanic of any race; Average household size: 1.90; Median age: 55.0; Age under 18: 14.0%; Age 65 and over: 27.5%; Males per 100 females: 95.0; Marriage status: 17.4% never married, 55.3% now married, 2.1% separated, 10.5% widowed, 16.7% divorced; Foreign born: 0.7%; Speak English only: 99.2%; With disability: 16.2%; Veterans: 14.2%; Ancestry: 23.5% English, 22.8% German, 20.9% Irish, 15.7% American, 11.1% Italian
Employment: 20.2% management, business, and financial, 1.8% computer, engineering, and science, 20.2% education, legal, community service, arts, and media, 10.3% healthcare practitioners, 17.7% service, 17.7% sales and office, 5.3% natural resources, construction, and maintenance, 6.7% production, transportation, and material moving
Income: Per capita: $36,554; Median household: $56,310; Average household: $69,205; Households with income of $100,000 or more: 21.7%; Poverty rate: 9.0%
Educational Attainment: High school diploma or higher: 95.7%; Bachelor's degree or higher: 45.0%; Graduate/professional degree or higher: 17.9%

School District(s)
Hammondsport Central SD (PK-12)
    2014-15 Enrollment: 483 . . . . (607) 569-5200
Housing: Homeownership rate: 61.2%; Median home value: $129,700; Median year structure built: Before 1940; Homeowner vacancy rate: 0.0%; Median selected monthly owner costs: $1,297 with a mortgage, $560 without a mortgage; Median gross rent: $575 per month; Rental vacancy rate: 0.0%
Health Insurance: 94.1% have insurance; 77.7% have private insurance; 39.6% have public insurance; 5.9% do not have insurance; 6.0% of children under 18 do not have insurance
Safety: Violent crime rate: 0.0 per 10,000 population; Property crime rate: 92.7 per 10,000 population
Transportation: Commute: 79.2% car, 0.0% public transportation, 13.2% walk, 4.2% work from home; Mean travel time to work: 19.3 minutes

HARTSVILLE (town). Covers a land area of 36.143 square miles and a water area of 0.056 square miles. Located at 42.22° N. Lat; 77.66° W. Long. Elevation is 1,480 feet.
Population: 573; Growth (since 2000): -2.1%; Density: 15.9 persons per square mile; Race: 98.8% White, 0.3% Black/African American, 0.0% Asian, 0.0% American Indian/Alaska Native, 0.0% Native Hawaiian/Other Pacific Islander, 0.9% Two or more races, 0.2% Hispanic of any race; Average household size: 2.30; Median age: 46.1; Age under 18: 21.5%; Age 65 and over: 22.5%; Males per 100 females: 116.7; Marriage status: 17.2% never married, 70.3% now married, 1.9% separated, 2.5% widowed, 10.0% divorced; Foreign born: 1.9%; Speak English only: 98.4%; With disability: 12.2%; Veterans: 9.8%; Ancestry: 16.8% German, 16.8% Irish, 10.5% Italian, 9.6% English, 9.1% European
Employment: 11.3% management, business, and financial, 2.3% computer, engineering, and science, 8.6% education, legal, community service, arts, and media, 3.1% healthcare practitioners, 27.2% service,

17.9% sales and office, 18.7% natural resources, construction, and maintenance, 10.9% production, transportation, and material moving
Income: Per capita: $27,090; Median household: $53,984; Average household: $62,422; Households with income of $100,000 or more: 12.4%; Poverty rate: 5.6%
Educational Attainment: High school diploma or higher: 96.7%; Bachelor's degree or higher: 16.5%; Graduate/professional degree or higher: 7.3%
Housing: Homeownership rate: 90.8%; Median home value: $102,000; Median year structure built: 1976; Homeowner vacancy rate: 0.0%; Median selected monthly owner costs: $1,172 with a mortgage, $413 without a mortgage; Median gross rent: $975 per month; Rental vacancy rate: 11.5%
Health Insurance: 92.5% have insurance; 81.0% have private insurance; 34.0% have public insurance; 7.5% do not have insurance; 4.9% of children under 18 do not have insurance
Transportation: Commute: 97.2% car, 0.0% public transportation, 1.2% walk, 1.6% work from home; Mean travel time to work: 24.2 minutes

HORNBY (town). Covers a land area of 40.850 square miles and a water area of 0.038 square miles. Located at 42.24° N. Lat; 77.03° W. Long. Elevation is 1,522 feet.
Population: 1,742; Growth (since 2000): 0.0%; Density: 42.6 persons per square mile; Race: 97.1% White, 1.5% Black/African American, 0.5% Asian, 0.0% American Indian/Alaska Native, 0.2% Native Hawaiian/Other Pacific Islander, 0.7% Two or more races, 0.5% Hispanic of any race; Average household size: 2.60; Median age: 41.4; Age under 18: 24.1%; Age 65 and over: 13.1%; Males per 100 females: 99.5; Marriage status: 25.0% never married, 60.0% now married, 2.3% separated, 3.5% widowed, 11.5% divorced; Foreign born: 0.7%; Speak English only: 98.9%; With disability: 13.7%; Veterans: 9.7%; Ancestry: 19.0% Irish, 16.1% German, 15.8% American, 15.6% English, 13.4% Italian
Employment: 13.6% management, business, and financial, 9.2% computer, engineering, and science, 6.4% education, legal, community service, arts, and media, 3.8% healthcare practitioners, 14.1% service, 21.5% sales and office, 21.4% natural resources, construction, and maintenance, 10.2% production, transportation, and material moving
Income: Per capita: $26,145; Median household: $55,521; Average household: $67,908; Households with income of $100,000 or more: 20.8%; Poverty rate: 8.8%
Educational Attainment: High school diploma or higher: 85.2%; Bachelor's degree or higher: 20.8%; Graduate/professional degree or higher: 9.2%
Housing: Homeownership rate: 90.5%; Median home value: $99,700; Median year structure built: 1973; Homeowner vacancy rate: 1.3%; Median selected monthly owner costs: $1,190 with a mortgage, $517 without a mortgage; Median gross rent: $725 per month; Rental vacancy rate: 12.3%
Health Insurance: 93.6% have insurance; 71.4% have private insurance; 37.4% have public insurance; 6.4% do not have insurance; 2.1% of children under 18 do not have insurance
Transportation: Commute: 96.1% car, 0.0% public transportation, 1.3% walk, 1.9% work from home; Mean travel time to work: 22.1 minutes

HORNELL (city). Covers a land area of 2.837 square miles and a water area of 0 square miles. Located at 42.33° N. Lat; 77.66° W. Long. Elevation is 1,161 feet.
History: Settled 1790, incorporated 1906.
Population: 8,471; Growth (since 2000): -6.1%; Density: 2,985.7 persons per square mile; Race: 94.1% White, 1.2% Black/African American, 0.6% Asian, 0.0% American Indian/Alaska Native, 0.0% Native Hawaiian/Other Pacific Islander, 3.5% Two or more races, 1.8% Hispanic of any race; Average household size: 2.38; Median age: 35.9; Age under 18: 24.9%; Age 65 and over: 13.6%; Males per 100 females: 93.6; Marriage status: 33.8% never married, 45.9% now married, 2.1% separated, 7.3% widowed, 13.0% divorced; Foreign born: 1.2%; Speak English only: 97.1%; With disability: 19.6%; Veterans: 12.2%; Ancestry: 24.8% Irish, 19.4% German, 18.2% Italian, 13.5% English, 8.4% American
Employment: 6.7% management, business, and financial, 3.3% computer, engineering, and science, 10.6% education, legal, community service, arts, and media, 4.9% healthcare practitioners, 23.7% service, 23.8% sales and office, 11.5% natural resources, construction, and maintenance, 15.4% production, transportation, and material moving
Income: Per capita: $19,034; Median household: $38,598; Average household: $45,797; Households with income of $100,000 or more: 7.4%; Poverty rate: 25.9%

Educational Attainment: High school diploma or higher: 88.8%; Bachelor's degree or higher: 16.9%; Graduate/professional degree or higher: 7.6%

School District(s)
Hornell City SD (KG-12)
    2014-15 Enrollment: 1,763 . . . . (607) 324-1302

Two-year College(s)
St James Mercy Hospital School of Radiologic Science (Private, Not-for-profit)
    Fall 2014 Enrollment: 10 . . . . (607) 324-8265

Housing: Homeownership rate: 52.9%; Median home value: $64,900; Median year structure built: Before 1940; Homeowner vacancy rate: 1.2%; Median selected monthly owner costs: $879 with a mortgage, $399 without a mortgage; Median gross rent: $618 per month; Rental vacancy rate: 6.4%

Health Insurance: 92.7% have insurance; 53.3% have private insurance; 54.1% have public insurance; 7.3% do not have insurance; 1.5% of children under 18 do not have insurance

Hospitals: Saint James Mercy Hospital (297 beds)

Safety: Violent crime rate: 2.4 per 10,000 population; Property crime rate: 138.6 per 10,000 population

Newspapers: Evening Tribune (daily circulation 4,200); Hornell Spectator (weekly circulation 14,500)

Transportation: Commute: 88.4% car, 1.2% public transportation, 6.9% walk, 0.7% work from home; Mean travel time to work: 19.6 minutes

Airports: Hornell Municipal (general aviation)

Additional Information Contacts
City of Hornell . . . . (607) 324-7421
    http://www.cityofhornell.com

HORNELLSVILLE (town).
Covers a land area of 43.325 square miles and a water area of 0.216 square miles. Located at 42.33° N. Lat; 77.68° W. Long.

Population: 4,110; Growth (since 2000): 1.7%; Density: 94.9 persons per square mile; Race: 96.4% White, 0.0% Black/African American, 1.1% Asian, 0.3% American Indian/Alaska Native, 0.0% Native Hawaiian/Other Pacific Islander, 1.9% Two or more races, 1.5% Hispanic of any race; Average household size: 2.12; Median age: 48.5; Age under 18: 18.0%; Age 65 and over: 24.4%; Males per 100 females: 89.7; Marriage status: 25.5% never married, 48.9% now married, 3.4% separated, 14.7% widowed, 10.9% divorced; Foreign born: 2.3%; Speak English only: 95.9%; With disability: 19.1%; Veterans: 14.6%; Ancestry: 24.8% Irish, 22.4% German, 22.4% English, 11.7% Italian, 6.6% American

Employment: 13.6% management, business, and financial, 2.1% computer, engineering, and science, 13.2% education, legal, community service, arts, and media, 8.7% healthcare practitioners, 17.8% service, 23.1% sales and office, 12.1% natural resources, construction, and maintenance, 9.5% production, transportation, and material moving

Income: Per capita: $25,844; Median household: $41,830; Average household: $56,114; Households with income of $100,000 or more: 12.8%; Poverty rate: 15.3%

Educational Attainment: High school diploma or higher: 92.4%; Bachelor's degree or higher: 22.4%; Graduate/professional degree or higher: 13.3%

Housing: Homeownership rate: 73.6%; Median home value: $93,200; Median year structure built: 1967; Homeowner vacancy rate: 1.1%; Median selected monthly owner costs: $1,065 with a mortgage, $496 without a mortgage; Median gross rent: $612 per month; Rental vacancy rate: 1.2%

Health Insurance: 93.6% have insurance; 71.7% have private insurance; 41.9% have public insurance; 6.4% do not have insurance; 1.8% of children under 18 do not have insurance

Transportation: Commute: 91.1% car, 0.4% public transportation, 2.9% walk, 4.5% work from home; Mean travel time to work: 18.0 minutes

Additional Information Contacts
Town of Hornellsville . . . . (607) 295-9660
    http://www.townofhornellsville.com

HOWARD (town).
Covers a land area of 60.546 square miles and a water area of 0.220 square miles. Located at 42.34° N. Lat; 77.51° W. Long. Elevation is 1,650 feet.

Population: 1,438; Growth (since 2000): 0.6%; Density: 23.8 persons per square mile; Race: 99.0% White, 0.8% Black/African American, 0.0% Asian, 0.0% American Indian/Alaska Native, 0.0% Native Hawaiian/Other Pacific Islander, 0.2% Two or more races, 0.0% Hispanic of any race; Average household size: 2.48; Median age: 43.9; Age under 18: 24.3%;

Age 65 and over: 15.4%; Males per 100 females: 106.6; Marriage status: 25.8% never married, 61.7% now married, 4.0% separated, 7.3% widowed, 5.2% divorced; Foreign born: 0.6%; Speak English only: 99.0%; With disability: 11.5%; Veterans: 10.3%; Ancestry: 33.8% German, 20.8% Irish, 19.0% English, 9.8% American, 8.2% Dutch

Employment: 6.1% management, business, and financial, 5.6% computer, engineering, and science, 16.5% education, legal, community service, arts, and media, 2.1% healthcare practitioners, 20.0% service, 21.0% sales and office, 12.6% natural resources, construction, and maintenance, 16.1% production, transportation, and material moving

Income: Per capita: $23,176; Median household: $43,438; Average household: $57,974; Households with income of $100,000 or more: 14.4%; Poverty rate: 15.3%

Educational Attainment: High school diploma or higher: 92.1%; Bachelor's degree or higher: 17.6%; Graduate/professional degree or higher: 6.6%

Housing: Homeownership rate: 80.5%; Median home value: $89,700; Median year structure built: 1971; Homeowner vacancy rate: 0.0%; Median selected monthly owner costs: $1,113 with a mortgage, $424 without a mortgage; Median gross rent: $868 per month; Rental vacancy rate: 0.0%

Health Insurance: 93.4% have insurance; 63.0% have private insurance; 45.2% have public insurance; 6.6% do not have insurance; 2.3% of children under 18 do not have insurance

Transportation: Commute: 86.7% car, 1.5% public transportation, 3.5% walk, 7.6% work from home; Mean travel time to work: 24.6 minutes

JASPER (town).
Covers a land area of 52.644 square miles and a water area of 0.023 square miles. Located at 42.14° N. Lat; 77.53° W. Long. Elevation is 1,572 feet.

Population: 1,282; Growth (since 2000): 0.9%; Density: 24.4 persons per square mile; Race: 98.9% White, 0.2% Black/African American, 0.0% Asian, 0.9% American Indian/Alaska Native, 0.0% Native Hawaiian/Other Pacific Islander, 0.0% Two or more races, 0.0% Hispanic of any race; Average household size: 3.18; Median age: 31.3; Age under 18: 34.9%; Age 65 and over: 10.5%; Males per 100 females: 100.3; Marriage status: 24.9% never married, 60.5% now married, 2.5% separated, 6.7% widowed, 7.9% divorced; Foreign born: 1.7%; Speak English only: 74.1%; With disability: 14.2%; Veterans: 12.2%; Ancestry: 25.6% German, 13.7% Pennsylvania German, 11.2% Irish, 10.9% American, 9.8% English

Employment: 13.8% management, business, and financial, 0.9% computer, engineering, and science, 6.3% education, legal, community service, arts, and media, 1.6% healthcare practitioners, 12.4% service, 20.5% sales and office, 21.4% natural resources, construction, and maintenance, 23.1% production, transportation, and material moving

Income: Per capita: $16,284; Median household: $41,176; Average household: $52,535; Households with income of $100,000 or more: 12.7%; Poverty rate: 15.6%

Educational Attainment: High school diploma or higher: 85.4%; Bachelor's degree or higher: 8.1%; Graduate/professional degree or higher: 5.0%

School District(s)
Jasper-Troupsburg Central SD (KG-12)
    2014-15 Enrollment: 538 . . . . (607) 792-3675

Housing: Homeownership rate: 73.9%; Median home value: $92,400; Median year structure built: 1975; Homeowner vacancy rate: 0.0%; Median selected monthly owner costs: $1,104 with a mortgage, $352 without a mortgage; Median gross rent: $525 per month; Rental vacancy rate: 0.0%

Health Insurance: 58.3% have insurance; 41.6% have private insurance; 24.1% have public insurance; 41.7% do not have insurance; 60.7% of children under 18 do not have insurance

Transportation: Commute: 73.0% car, 3.5% public transportation, 10.0% walk, 9.0% work from home; Mean travel time to work: 28.0 minutes

KANONA (unincorporated postal area)
ZCTA: 14856
    Covers a land area of 0.377 square miles and a water area of 0 square miles. Located at 42.38° N. Lat; 77.37° W. Long. Elevation is 1,145 feet.

Population: 118; Growth (since 2000): n/a; Density: 312.9 persons per square mile; Race: 100.0% White, 0.0% Black/African American, 0.0% Asian, 0.0% American Indian/Alaska Native, 0.0% Native Hawaiian/Other Pacific Islander, 0.0% Two or more races, 0.0% Hispanic of any race; Average household size: 1.39; Median age: 68.3; Age under 18: 0.0%; Age 65 and over: 55.1%; Males per 100 females: 117.2; Marriage status: 0.0% never married, 55.1% now married, 0.0% separated, 0.0% widowed, 44.9% divorced; Foreign born: 0.0%; Speak

English only: 100.0%; With disability: 6.8%; Veterans: 28.8%; Ancestry: 48.3% American, 44.9% German, 22.9% Irish, 6.8% English
Employment: 0.0% management, business, and financial, 0.0% computer, engineering, and science, 50.9% education, legal, community service, arts, and media, 0.0% healthcare practitioners, 49.1% service, 0.0% sales and office, 0.0% natural resources, construction, and maintenance, 0.0% production, transportation, and material moving
Income: Per capita: $22,348; Median household: n/a; Average household: $30,780; Households with income of $100,000 or more: n/a; Poverty rate: n/a
Educational Attainment: High school diploma or higher: 79.7%; Bachelor's degree or higher: n/a; Graduate/professional degree or higher: n/a
Housing: Homeownership rate: 69.4%; Median home value: $50,800; Median year structure built: 1981; Homeowner vacancy rate: 0.0%; Median selected monthly owner costs: $0 with a mortgage, $310 without a mortgage; Median gross rent: n/a per month; Rental vacancy rate: 0.0%
Health Insurance: 100.0% have insurance; 100.0% have private insurance; 55.1% have public insurance; 0.0% do not have insurance; 0.0% of children under 18 do not have insurance
Transportation: Commute: 50.9% car, 0.0% public transportation, 49.1% walk, 0.0% work from home; Mean travel time to work: 0.0 minutes

LINDLEY (town). Covers a land area of 37.597 square miles and a water area of 0.271 square miles. Located at 42.04° N. Lat; 77.15° W. Long. Elevation is 1,010 feet.
Population: 2,104; Growth (since 2000): 10.0%; Density: 56.0 persons per square mile; Race: 96.9% White, 0.0% Black/African American, 0.0% Asian, 0.0% American Indian/Alaska Native, 0.0% Native Hawaiian/Other Pacific Islander, 3.1% Two or more races, 1.6% Hispanic of any race; Average household size: 2.56; Median age: 41.7; Age under 18: 26.0%; Age 65 and over: 14.3%; Males per 100 females: 102.6; Marriage status: 29.0% never married, 54.4% now married, 2.9% separated, 2.3% widowed, 14.3% divorced; Foreign born: 1.7%; Speak English only: 97.5%; With disability: 10.3%; Veterans: 11.3%; Ancestry: 22.7% American, 22.0% German, 15.6% Irish, 11.1% English, 4.0% French
Employment: 8.3% management, business, and financial, 3.6% computer, engineering, and science, 5.6% education, legal, community service, arts, and media, 7.1% healthcare practitioners, 15.3% service, 24.7% sales and office, 13.8% natural resources, construction, and maintenance, 21.5% production, transportation, and material moving
Income: Per capita: $24,308; Median household: $47,500; Average household: $63,326; Households with income of $100,000 or more: 18.5%; Poverty rate: 16.3%
Educational Attainment: High school diploma or higher: 91.7%; Bachelor's degree or higher: 15.3%; Graduate/professional degree or higher: 4.2%
Housing: Homeownership rate: 80.4%; Median home value: $98,900; Median year structure built: 1979; Homeowner vacancy rate: 0.0%; Median selected monthly owner costs: $1,170 with a mortgage, $431 without a mortgage; Median gross rent: $749 per month; Rental vacancy rate: 0.0%
Health Insurance: 92.3% have insurance; 62.6% have private insurance; 40.7% have public insurance; 7.7% do not have insurance; 4.6% of children under 18 do not have insurance
Transportation: Commute: 97.1% car, 0.0% public transportation, 1.3% walk, 1.3% work from home; Mean travel time to work: 26.8 minutes

NORTH HORNELL (village). Covers a land area of 0.498 square miles and a water area of 0 square miles. Located at 42.35° N. Lat; 77.66° W. Long. Elevation is 1,165 feet.
Population: 867; Growth (since 2000): 1.9%; Density: 1,741.9 persons per square mile; Race: 94.2% White, 0.2% Black/African American, 5.1% Asian, 0.0% American Indian/Alaska Native, 0.0% Native Hawaiian/Other Pacific Islander, 0.5% Two or more races, 0.5% Hispanic of any race; Average household size: 2.09; Median age: 58.0; Age under 18: 14.1%; Age 65 and over: 34.8%; Males per 100 females: 76.4; Marriage status: 16.8% never married, 55.7% now married, 2.5% separated, 19.8% widowed, 7.6% divorced; Foreign born: 6.7%; Speak English only: 93.6%; With disability: 16.9%; Veterans: 14.5%; Ancestry: 29.6% Irish, 26.5% German, 21.6% English, 11.4% Italian, 4.6% Polish
Employment: 15.6% management, business, and financial, 2.3% computer, engineering, and science, 23.0% education, legal, community service, arts, and media, 9.4% healthcare practitioners, 9.7% service,

30.4% sales and office, 7.1% natural resources, construction, and maintenance, 2.6% production, transportation, and material moving
Income: Per capita: $32,507; Median household: $57,105; Average household: $75,834; Households with income of $100,000 or more: 24.6%; Poverty rate: 6.1%
Educational Attainment: High school diploma or higher: 96.6%; Bachelor's degree or higher: 37.2%; Graduate/professional degree or higher: 21.1%
Housing: Homeownership rate: 87.2%; Median home value: $122,900; Median year structure built: 1949; Homeowner vacancy rate: 0.6%; Median selected monthly owner costs: $1,152 with a mortgage, $460 without a mortgage; Median gross rent: $595 per month; Rental vacancy rate: 0.0%
Health Insurance: 94.7% have insurance; 80.9% have private insurance; 39.1% have public insurance; 5.3% do not have insurance; 0.0% of children under 18 do not have insurance
Transportation: Commute: 91.3% car, 2.0% public transportation, 2.6% walk, 3.5% work from home; Mean travel time to work: 15.8 minutes

PAINTED POST (village). Covers a land area of 1.272 square miles and a water area of 0.060 square miles. Located at 42.16° N. Lat; 77.09° W. Long. Elevation is 942 feet.
History: Settled before 1790; incorporated 1893.
Population: 1,689; Growth (since 2000): -8.3%; Density: 1,327.6 persons per square mile; Race: 94.4% White, 1.1% Black/African American, 2.9% Asian, 0.0% American Indian/Alaska Native, 0.0% Native Hawaiian/Other Pacific Islander, 1.4% Two or more races, 0.9% Hispanic of any race; Average household size: 2.18; Median age: 41.7; Age under 18: 21.9%; Age 65 and over: 24.0%; Males per 100 females: 93.3; Marriage status: 24.4% never married, 54.5% now married, 1.9% separated, 10.3% widowed, 10.9% divorced; Foreign born: 4.1%; Speak English only: 97.7%; With disability: 11.2%; Veterans: 11.0%; Ancestry: 20.5% German, 18.7% English, 18.1% Irish, 9.8% American, 8.2% Italian
Employment: 11.7% management, business, and financial, 9.0% computer, engineering, and science, 23.3% education, legal, community service, arts, and media, 1.3% healthcare practitioners, 20.6% service, 17.4% sales and office, 7.6% natural resources, construction, and maintenance, 9.1% production, transportation, and material moving
Income: Per capita: $27,747; Median household: $51,458; Average household: $60,231; Households with income of $100,000 or more: 16.8%; Poverty rate: 7.2%
Educational Attainment: High school diploma or higher: 91.4%; Bachelor's degree or higher: 36.5%; Graduate/professional degree or higher: 16.8%

School District(s)
Corning City SD (PK-12)
    2014-15 Enrollment: 4,867 . . . . (607) 936-3704
Schuyler-Steuben-Chemung-Tioga-Allegany Boces
    2014-15 Enrollment: n/a . . . . (607) 739-3581
Housing: Homeownership rate: 58.6%; Median home value: $99,100; Median year structure built: 1952; Homeowner vacancy rate: 5.2%; Median selected monthly owner costs: $1,206 with a mortgage, $545 without a mortgage; Median gross rent: $583 per month; Rental vacancy rate: 0.0%
Health Insurance: 93.4% have insurance; 75.7% have private insurance; 37.2% have public insurance; 6.6% do not have insurance; 6.2% of children under 18 do not have insurance
Transportation: Commute: 87.2% car, 1.4% public transportation, 4.0% walk, 5.5% work from home; Mean travel time to work: 14.1 minutes

PERKINSVILLE (unincorporated postal area)
ZCTA: 14529
    Covers a land area of 0.390 square miles and a water area of 0 square miles. Located at 42.54° N. Lat; 77.64° W. Long. Elevation is 1,365 feet.
Population: 183; Growth (since 2000): n/a; Density: 469.2 persons per square mile; Race: 100.0% White, 0.0% Black/African American, 0.0% Asian, 0.0% American Indian/Alaska Native, 0.0% Native Hawaiian/Other Pacific Islander, 0.0% Two or more races, 0.0% Hispanic of any race; Average household size: 2.77; Median age: 61.0; Age under 18: 12.6%; Age 65 and over: 11.5%; Males per 100 females: 97.1; Marriage status: 25.7% never married, 74.3% now married, 0.0% separated, 0.0% widowed, 0.0% divorced; Foreign born: 0.0%; Speak English only: 100.0%; With disability: 5.5%; Veterans: 14.4%; Ancestry: 80.3% German, 18.6% Irish, 6.6% English
Employment: 0.0% management, business, and financial, 0.0% computer, engineering, and science, 17.3% education, legal, community service, arts, and media, 0.0% healthcare practitioners, 17.3% service,

28.3% sales and office, 18.1% natural resources, construction, and maintenance, 18.9% production, transportation, and material moving
Income: Per capita: $30,036; Median household: n/a; Average household: $81,523; Households with income of $100,000 or more: 50.0%; Poverty rate: n/a
Educational Attainment: High school diploma or higher: 100.0%; Bachelor's degree or higher: 8.1%; Graduate/professional degree or higher: 8.1%
Housing: Homeownership rate: 65.2%; Median home value: $125,600; Median year structure built: Before 1940; Homeowner vacancy rate: 0.0%; Median selected monthly owner costs: $0 with a mortgage, $0 without a mortgage; Median gross rent: n/a per month; Rental vacancy rate: 0.0%
Health Insurance: 100.0% have insurance; 100.0% have private insurance; 11.5% have public insurance; 0.0% do not have insurance; 0.0% of children under 18 do not have insurance
Transportation: Commute: 100.0% car, 0.0% public transportation, 0.0% walk, 0.0% work from home; Mean travel time to work: 31.5 minutes

PRATTSBURGH (CDP). Covers a land area of 1.640 square miles and a water area of 0 square miles. Located at 42.52° N. Lat; 77.29° W. Long. Elevation is 1,463 feet.
Population: 753; Growth (since 2000): n/a; Density: 459.0 persons per square mile; Race: 98.9% White, 1.1% Black/African American, 0.0% Asian, 0.0% American Indian/Alaska Native, 0.0% Native Hawaiian/Other Pacific Islander, 0.0% Two or more races, 7.0% Hispanic of any race; Average household size: 2.50; Median age: 41.9; Age under 18: 23.2%; Age 65 and over: 16.9%; Males per 100 females: 85.3; Marriage status: 28.6% never married, 55.9% now married, 3.3% separated, 4.5% widowed, 11.0% divorced; Foreign born: 0.0%; Speak English only: 97.4%; With disability: 20.1%; Veterans: 9.0%; Ancestry: 25.0% German, 17.0% American, 15.5% Irish, 14.5% English, 12.0% Polish
Employment: 6.6% management, business, and financial, 1.4% computer, engineering, and science, 6.3% education, legal, community service, arts, and media, 8.0% healthcare practitioners, 30.6% service, 6.6% sales and office, 25.4% natural resources, construction, and maintenance, 15.1% production, transportation, and material moving
Income: Per capita: $18,081; Median household: $38,988; Average household: $45,533; Households with income of $100,000 or more: 3.4%; Poverty rate: 13.9%
Educational Attainment: High school diploma or higher: 79.6%; Bachelor's degree or higher: 12.9%; Graduate/professional degree or higher: 5.0%

School District(s)
Prattsburgh Central SD (PK-12)
   2014-15 Enrollment: 416. . . . . (607) 522-3795
Housing: Homeownership rate: 60.5%; Median home value: $80,000; Median year structure built: Before 1940; Homeowner vacancy rate: 0.0%; Median selected monthly owner costs: $733 with a mortgage, $421 without a mortgage; Median gross rent: $581 per month; Rental vacancy rate: 11.9%
Health Insurance: 87.4% have insurance; 46.7% have private insurance; 57.9% have public insurance; 12.6% do not have insurance; 6.9% of children under 18 do not have insurance
Transportation: Commute: 89.1% car, 4.9% public transportation, 4.0% walk, 0.0% work from home; Mean travel time to work: 27.5 minutes

PRATTSBURGH (town). Covers a land area of 51.666 square miles and a water area of 0.050 square miles. Located at 42.54° N. Lat; 77.33° W. Long. Elevation is 1,463 feet.
Population: 2,378; Growth (since 2000): 15.2%; Density: 46.0 persons per square mile; Race: 97.9% White, 0.3% Black/African American, 0.2% Asian, 0.0% American Indian/Alaska Native, 0.0% Native Hawaiian/Other Pacific Islander, 0.8% Two or more races, 4.4% Hispanic of any race; Average household size: 2.47; Median age: 45.4; Age under 18: 20.9%; Age 65 and over: 16.3%; Males per 100 females: 100.3; Marriage status: 28.9% never married, 54.9% now married, 2.0% separated, 3.8% widowed, 12.4% divorced; Foreign born: 0.9%; Speak English only: 95.2%; With disability: 11.9%; Veterans: 10.0%; Ancestry: 27.2% German, 15.5% English, 15.3% Irish, 14.2% American, 8.2% Polish
Employment: 10.3% management, business, and financial, 2.9% computer, engineering, and science, 7.0% education, legal, community service, arts, and media, 8.1% healthcare practitioners, 25.5% service,

15.1% sales and office, 15.4% natural resources, construction, and maintenance, 15.8% production, transportation, and material moving
Income: Per capita: $22,513; Median household: $46,486; Average household: $56,258; Households with income of $100,000 or more: 12.1%; Poverty rate: 12.5%
Educational Attainment: High school diploma or higher: 85.7%; Bachelor's degree or higher: 15.1%; Graduate/professional degree or higher: 5.6%

School District(s)
Prattsburgh Central SD (PK-12)
   2014-15 Enrollment: 416. . . . . (607) 522-3795
Housing: Homeownership rate: 82.9%; Median home value: $85,000; Median year structure built: 1978; Homeowner vacancy rate: 0.0%; Median selected monthly owner costs: $1,023 with a mortgage, $394 without a mortgage; Median gross rent: $578 per month; Rental vacancy rate: 8.9%
Health Insurance: 85.9% have insurance; 58.8% have private insurance; 41.2% have public insurance; 14.1% do not have insurance; 15.1% of children under 18 do not have insurance
Transportation: Commute: 91.0% car, 1.7% public transportation, 1.9% walk, 4.8% work from home; Mean travel time to work: 27.9 minutes

PULTENEY (town). Covers a land area of 33.137 square miles and a water area of 3.317 square miles. Located at 42.53° N. Lat; 77.20° W. Long. Elevation is 1,053 feet.
Population: 1,360; Growth (since 2000): -3.2%; Density: 41.0 persons per square mile; Race: 97.8% White, 0.1% Black/African American, 0.2% Asian, 1.0% American Indian/Alaska Native, 0.0% Native Hawaiian/Other Pacific Islander, 0.8% Two or more races, 0.0% Hispanic of any race; Average household size: 2.32; Median age: 45.5; Age under 18: 23.5%; Age 65 and over: 21.8%; Males per 100 females: 96.8; Marriage status: 18.8% never married, 63.0% now married, 4.0% separated, 9.1% widowed, 9.0% divorced; Foreign born: 1.3%; Speak English only: 93.9%; With disability: 16.1%; Veterans: 13.2%; Ancestry: 21.5% German, 14.9% English, 12.3% Irish, 9.5% French, 8.4% American
Employment: 19.1% management, business, and financial, 4.7% computer, engineering, and science, 10.7% education, legal, community service, arts, and media, 6.0% healthcare practitioners, 13.9% service, 11.8% sales and office, 21.0% natural resources, construction, and maintenance, 12.9% production, transportation, and material moving
Income: Per capita: $25,868; Median household: $48,516; Average household: $59,450; Households with income of $100,000 or more: 20.1%; Poverty rate: 17.7%
Educational Attainment: High school diploma or higher: 93.2%; Bachelor's degree or higher: 28.8%; Graduate/professional degree or higher: 17.3%
Housing: Homeownership rate: 90.1%; Median home value: $108,200; Median year structure built: 1964; Homeowner vacancy rate: 2.0%; Median selected monthly owner costs: $1,052 with a mortgage, $490 without a mortgage; Median gross rent: $644 per month; Rental vacancy rate: 13.4%
Health Insurance: 86.1% have insurance; 62.0% have private insurance; 43.4% have public insurance; 13.9% do not have insurance; 16.6% of children under 18 do not have insurance
Transportation: Commute: 86.8% car, 0.0% public transportation, 1.7% walk, 9.7% work from home; Mean travel time to work: 29.8 minutes

RATHBONE (town). Covers a land area of 36.017 square miles and a water area of 0.102 square miles. Located at 42.13° N. Lat; 77.34° W. Long. Elevation is 1,001 feet.
Population: 1,233; Growth (since 2000): 14.2%; Density: 34.2 persons per square mile; Race: 99.0% White, 0.6% Black/African American, 0.0% Asian, 0.0% American Indian/Alaska Native, 0.0% Native Hawaiian/Other Pacific Islander, 0.3% Two or more races, 0.3% Hispanic of any race; Average household size: 2.99; Median age: 35.0; Age under 18: 28.5%; Age 65 and over: 12.7%; Males per 100 females: 110.5; Marriage status: 25.5% never married, 61.8% now married, 2.9% separated, 5.0% widowed, 7.7% divorced; Foreign born: 1.1%; Speak English only: 84.0%; With disability: 13.9%; Veterans: 11.9%; Ancestry: 20.6% German, 19.1% American, 14.2% English, 14.0% Irish, 5.8% Polish
Employment: 8.7% management, business, and financial, 2.8% computer, engineering, and science, 7.6% education, legal, community service, arts, and media, 8.0% healthcare practitioners, 9.7% service, 22.9% sales and office, 19.0% natural resources, construction, and maintenance, 21.2% production, transportation, and material moving

Income: Per capita: $16,009; Median household: $36,125; Average household: $47,957; Households with income of $100,000 or more: 9.9%; Poverty rate: 33.3%
Educational Attainment: High school diploma or higher: 77.4%; Bachelor's degree or higher: 5.4%; Graduate/professional degree or higher: 2.6%
Housing: Homeownership rate: 85.0%; Median home value: $84,300; Median year structure built: 1982; Homeowner vacancy rate: 0.0%; Median selected monthly owner costs: $913 with a mortgage, $361 without a mortgage; Median gross rent: $547 per month; Rental vacancy rate: 0.0%
Health Insurance: 70.5% have insurance; 49.0% have private insurance; 32.6% have public insurance; 29.5% do not have insurance; 38.4% of children under 18 do not have insurance
Transportation: Commute: 91.6% car, 1.7% public transportation, 0.0% walk, 4.3% work from home; Mean travel time to work: 31.3 minutes

REXVILLE (unincorporated postal area)
ZCTA: 14877

Covers a land area of 42.288 square miles and a water area of 0.146 square miles. Located at 42.06° N. Lat; 77.68° W. Long. Elevation is 1,841 feet.
Population: 456; Growth (since 2000): -30.0%; Density: 10.8 persons per square mile; Race: 97.8% White, 0.0% Black/African American, 0.7% Asian, 0.0% American Indian/Alaska Native, 0.0% Native Hawaiian/Other Pacific Islander, 1.5% Two or more races, 0.0% Hispanic of any race; Average household size: 2.39; Median age: 47.2; Age under 18: 21.3%; Age 65 and over: 19.5%; Males per 100 females: 114.4; Marriage status: 23.5% never married, 64.2% now married, 4.0% separated, 4.0% widowed, 8.4% divorced; Foreign born: 4.6%; Speak English only: 94.2%; With disability: 16.0%; Veterans: 10.9%; Ancestry: 28.5% Irish, 25.7% German, 14.0% English, 9.2% American, 7.2% Italian
Employment: 18.5% management, business, and financial, 4.4% computer, engineering, and science, 8.8% education, legal, community service, arts, and media, 7.0% healthcare practitioners, 19.4% service, 13.2% sales and office, 17.6% natural resources, construction, and maintenance, 11.0% production, transportation, and material moving
Income: Per capita: $25,613; Median household: $51,094; Average household: $62,732; Households with income of $100,000 or more: 20.4%; Poverty rate: 15.8%
Educational Attainment: High school diploma or higher: 88.4%; Bachelor's degree or higher: 19.7%; Graduate/professional degree or higher: 10.7%
Housing: Homeownership rate: 79.1%; Median home value: $94,400; Median year structure built: 1964; Homeowner vacancy rate: 0.0%; Median selected monthly owner costs: $1,014 with a mortgage, $470 without a mortgage; Median gross rent: $595 per month; Rental vacancy rate: 0.0%
Health Insurance: 89.0% have insurance; 61.6% have private insurance; 42.5% have public insurance; 11.0% do not have insurance; 11.3% of children under 18 do not have insurance
Transportation: Commute: 79.3% car, 0.0% public transportation, 7.8% walk, 12.0% work from home; Mean travel time to work: 26.4 minutes

RIVERSIDE (village). Covers a land area of 0.301 square miles and a water area of 0.006 square miles. Located at 42.16° N. Lat; 77.08° W. Long. Elevation is 938 feet.
Population: 589; Growth (since 2000): -0.8%; Density: 1,953.7 persons per square mile; Race: 92.7% White, 2.0% Black/African American, 4.2% Asian, 0.0% American Indian/Alaska Native, 0.0% Native Hawaiian/Other Pacific Islander, 1.0% Two or more races, 0.2% Hispanic of any race; Average household size: 2.54; Median age: 37.2; Age under 18: 28.7%; Age 65 and over: 16.3%; Males per 100 females: 96.4; Marriage status: 28.8% never married, 45.5% now married, 3.6% separated, 8.7% widowed, 17.0% divorced; Foreign born: 1.7%; Speak English only: 93.1%; With disability: 13.1%; Veterans: 11.7%; Ancestry: 31.2% German, 14.8% Irish, 13.2% American, 11.4% English, 10.5% Welsh
Employment: 4.5% management, business, and financial, 10.5% computer, engineering, and science, 18.2% education, legal, community service, arts, and media, 1.6% healthcare practitioners, 23.5% service, 17.8% sales and office, 4.5% natural resources, construction, and maintenance, 19.4% production, transportation, and material moving
Income: Per capita: $20,317; Median household: $42,500; Average household: $51,035; Households with income of $100,000 or more: 9.1%; Poverty rate: 16.3%

Educational Attainment: High school diploma or higher: 87.6%; Bachelor's degree or higher: 15.4%; Graduate/professional degree or higher: 4.9%
Housing: Homeownership rate: 81.5%; Median home value: $73,900; Median year structure built: 1945; Homeowner vacancy rate: 0.0%; Median selected monthly owner costs: $871 with a mortgage, $334 without a mortgage; Median gross rent: $863 per month; Rental vacancy rate: 0.0%
Health Insurance: 89.0% have insurance; 66.4% have private insurance; 39.6% have public insurance; 11.0% do not have insurance; 11.8% of children under 18 do not have insurance
Transportation: Commute: 91.8% car, 2.0% public transportation, 3.7% walk, 1.2% work from home; Mean travel time to work: 18.7 minutes

SAVONA (village). Covers a land area of 1.040 square miles and a water area of 0 square miles. Located at 42.28° N. Lat; 77.22° W. Long. Elevation is 1,053 feet.
Population: 809; Growth (since 2000): -1.6%; Density: 778.2 persons per square mile; Race: 91.5% White, 1.4% Black/African American, 2.3% Asian, 0.6% American Indian/Alaska Native, 0.0% Native Hawaiian/Other Pacific Islander, 2.5% Two or more races, 3.5% Hispanic of any race; Average household size: 2.43; Median age: 38.3; Age under 18: 23.6%; Age 65 and over: 12.5%; Males per 100 females: 93.2; Marriage status: 31.0% never married, 41.5% now married, 3.2% separated, 9.3% widowed, 18.2% divorced; Foreign born: 1.9%; Speak English only: 96.6%; With disability: 14.2%; Veterans: 15.2%; Ancestry: 29.3% German, 15.9% Irish, 10.5% English, 8.7% American, 6.8% Dutch
Employment: 4.0% management, business, and financial, 2.6% computer, engineering, and science, 6.8% education, legal, community service, arts, and media, 2.3% healthcare practitioners, 23.9% service, 22.5% sales and office, 24.2% natural resources, construction, and maintenance, 13.7% production, transportation, and material moving
Income: Per capita: $20,115; Median household: $49,500; Average household: $50,143; Households with income of $100,000 or more: 10.2%; Poverty rate: 23.4%
Educational Attainment: High school diploma or higher: 90.3%; Bachelor's degree or higher: 8.6%; Graduate/professional degree or higher: 2.5%

School District(s)
Campbell-Savona Central SD (PK-12)
   2014-15 Enrollment: 863 . . . . (607) 527-9800
Housing: Homeownership rate: 71.7%; Median home value: $82,300; Median year structure built: Before 1940; Homeowner vacancy rate: 0.0%; Median selected monthly owner costs: $1,119 with a mortgage, $371 without a mortgage; Median gross rent: $618 per month; Rental vacancy rate: 0.0%
Health Insurance: 88.5% have insurance; 58.3% have private insurance; 45.4% have public insurance; 11.5% do not have insurance; 5.2% of children under 18 do not have insurance
Transportation: Commute: 93.9% car, 1.5% public transportation, 4.1% walk, 0.6% work from home; Mean travel time to work: 21.8 minutes

SOUTH CORNING (village). Covers a land area of 0.617 square miles and a water area of 0 square miles. Located at 42.13° N. Lat; 77.04° W. Long. Elevation is 951 feet.
Population: 1,060; Growth (since 2000): -7.6%; Density: 1,718.9 persons per square mile; Race: 88.6% White, 5.4% Black/African American, 4.0% Asian, 0.0% American Indian/Alaska Native, 0.0% Native Hawaiian/Other Pacific Islander, 2.1% Two or more races, 0.4% Hispanic of any race; Average household size: 2.24; Median age: 44.2; Age under 18: 16.5%; Age 65 and over: 21.4%; Males per 100 females: 95.7; Marriage status: 26.1% never married, 52.3% now married, 3.1% separated, 10.9% widowed, 10.7% divorced; Foreign born: 4.7%; Speak English only: 94.0%; With disability: 15.2%; Veterans: 8.6%; Ancestry: 21.4% Irish, 21.3% German, 15.7% English, 9.2% Italian, 8.0% American
Employment: 11.9% management, business, and financial, 4.0% computer, engineering, and science, 9.6% education, legal, community service, arts, and media, 5.7% healthcare practitioners, 13.2% service, 23.9% sales and office, 9.6% natural resources, construction, and maintenance, 22.1% production, transportation, and material moving
Income: Per capita: $26,377; Median household: $54,875; Average household: $59,836; Households with income of $100,000 or more: 13.8%; Poverty rate: 7.8%
Educational Attainment: High school diploma or higher: 92.8%; Bachelor's degree or higher: 26.2%; Graduate/professional degree or higher: 10.6%

Housing: Homeownership rate: 71.2%; Median home value: $89,100; Median year structure built: 1954; Homeowner vacancy rate: 0.0%; Median selected monthly owner costs: $1,043 with a mortgage, $490 without a mortgage; Median gross rent: $956 per month; Rental vacancy rate: 8.7%
Health Insurance: 87.8% have insurance; 75.7% have private insurance; 33.0% have public insurance; 12.2% do not have insurance; 7.4% of children under 18 do not have insurance
Transportation: Commute: 96.3% car, 0.0% public transportation, 1.1% walk, 2.0% work from home; Mean travel time to work: 16.7 minutes

THURSTON (town). Covers a land area of 36.353 square miles and a water area of 0.165 square miles. Located at 42.23° N. Lat; 77.28° W. Long. Elevation is 1,263 feet.
Population: 1,213; Growth (since 2000): -7.3%; Density: 33.4 persons per square mile; Race: 99.8% White, 0.0% Black/African American, 0.0% Asian, 0.2% American Indian/Alaska Native, 0.0% Native Hawaiian/Other Pacific Islander, 0.0% Two or more races, 0.5% Hispanic of any race; Average household size: 2.50; Median age: 46.9; Age under 18: 19.8%; Age 65 and over: 15.3%; Males per 100 females: 102.4; Marriage status: 22.7% never married, 58.5% now married, 2.2% separated, 6.4% widowed, 12.4% divorced; Foreign born: 0.5%; Speak English only: 99.4%; With disability: 15.6%; Veterans: 13.4%; Ancestry: 23.1% German, 19.6% American, 17.4% English, 16.2% Irish, 5.9% Dutch
Employment: 11.3% management, business, and financial, 5.9% computer, engineering, and science, 3.0% education, legal, community service, arts, and media, 2.8% healthcare practitioners, 22.9% service, 24.7% sales and office, 11.3% natural resources, construction, and maintenance, 18.0% production, transportation, and material moving
Income: Per capita: $23,008; Median household: $50,385; Average household: $57,448; Households with income of $100,000 or more: 16.0%; Poverty rate: 14.2%
Educational Attainment: High school diploma or higher: 86.6%; Bachelor's degree or higher: 12.5%; Graduate/professional degree or higher: 4.4%
Housing: Homeownership rate: 81.5%; Median home value: $92,300; Median year structure built: 1975; Homeowner vacancy rate: 2.2%; Median selected monthly owner costs: $1,284 with a mortgage, $523 without a mortgage; Median gross rent: $636 per month; Rental vacancy rate: 8.2%
Health Insurance: 92.6% have insurance; 72.0% have private insurance; 36.5% have public insurance; 7.4% do not have insurance; 1.3% of children under 18 do not have insurance
Transportation: Commute: 97.7% car, 0.0% public transportation, 0.6% walk, 1.7% work from home; Mean travel time to work: 22.9 minutes

TROUPSBURG (town). Covers a land area of 61.238 square miles and a water area of 0.028 square miles. Located at 42.07° N. Lat; 77.53° W. Long. Elevation is 1,663 feet.
Population: 1,223; Growth (since 2000): 8.6%; Density: 20.0 persons per square mile; Race: 97.6% White, 0.7% Black/African American, 0.3% Asian, 0.0% American Indian/Alaska Native, 0.0% Native Hawaiian/Other Pacific Islander, 1.4% Two or more races, 0.0% Hispanic of any race; Average household size: 2.98; Median age: 37.5; Age under 18: 31.6%; Age 65 and over: 17.4%; Males per 100 females: 103.6; Marriage status: 24.3% never married, 58.6% now married, 0.9% separated, 8.2% widowed, 8.8% divorced; Foreign born: 1.4%; Speak English only: 86.8%; With disability: 11.1%; Veterans: 7.5%; Ancestry: 18.2% English, 18.2% German, 11.5% American, 10.5% Irish, 7.7% Pennsylvania German
Employment: 16.6% management, business, and financial, 2.7% computer, engineering, and science, 10.8% education, legal, community service, arts, and media, 2.5% healthcare practitioners, 6.0% service, 27.0% sales and office, 17.4% natural resources, construction, and maintenance, 17.0% production, transportation, and material moving
Income: Per capita: $17,891; Median household: $47,375; Average household: $53,284; Households with income of $100,000 or more: 9.5%; Poverty rate: 24.8%
Educational Attainment: High school diploma or higher: 83.7%; Bachelor's degree or higher: 11.2%; Graduate/professional degree or higher: 4.7%

School District(s)
Jasper-Troupsburg Central SD (KG-12)
   2014-15 Enrollment: 538 . . . . (607) 792-3675
Housing: Homeownership rate: 85.2%; Median home value: $87,900; Median year structure built: 1976; Homeowner vacancy rate: 4.8%; Median selected monthly owner costs: $1,091 with a mortgage, $557 without a mortgage; Median gross rent: $644 per month; Rental vacancy rate: 0.0%

Health Insurance: 80.4% have insurance; 58.1% have private insurance; 38.0% have public insurance; 19.6% do not have insurance; 33.2% of children under 18 do not have insurance
Transportation: Commute: 80.5% car, 0.0% public transportation, 12.1% walk, 7.4% work from home; Mean travel time to work: 30.6 minutes

TUSCARORA (town). Covers a land area of 37.627 square miles and a water area of 0.085 square miles. Located at 42.05° N. Lat; 77.26° W. Long.
Population: 1,437; Growth (since 2000): 2.6%; Density: 38.2 persons per square mile; Race: 92.8% White, 0.3% Black/African American, 0.6% Asian, 0.0% American Indian/Alaska Native, 0.0% Native Hawaiian/Other Pacific Islander, 5.8% Two or more races, 0.3% Hispanic of any race; Average household size: 2.39; Median age: 40.1; Age under 18: 24.4%; Age 65 and over: 14.3%; Males per 100 females: 101.8; Marriage status: 26.2% never married, 57.2% now married, 7.6% separated, 5.7% widowed, 11.0% divorced; Foreign born: 2.2%; Speak English only: 93.5%; With disability: 16.4%; Veterans: 9.5%; Ancestry: 24.6% American, 14.1% Irish, 13.8% German, 7.1% English, 5.8% Italian
Employment: 13.0% management, business, and financial, 5.7% computer, engineering, and science, 6.7% education, legal, community service, arts, and media, 9.1% healthcare practitioners, 7.9% service, 16.4% sales and office, 15.7% natural resources, construction, and maintenance, 25.5% production, transportation, and material moving
Income: Per capita: $23,232; Median household: $40,458; Average household: $56,006; Households with income of $100,000 or more: 10.0%; Poverty rate: 27.4%
Educational Attainment: High school diploma or higher: 83.5%; Bachelor's degree or higher: 13.8%; Graduate/professional degree or higher: 5.1%
Housing: Homeownership rate: 79.4%; Median home value: $87,900; Median year structure built: 1975; Homeowner vacancy rate: 0.0%; Median selected monthly owner costs: $1,043 with a mortgage, $535 without a mortgage; Median gross rent: $867 per month; Rental vacancy rate: 0.0%
Health Insurance: 89.3% have insurance; 59.7% have private insurance; 42.2% have public insurance; 10.7% do not have insurance; 8.3% of children under 18 do not have insurance
Transportation: Commute: 94.4% car, 0.0% public transportation, 1.0% walk, 3.3% work from home; Mean travel time to work: 30.9 minutes

URBANA (town). Covers a land area of 40.946 square miles and a water area of 3.231 square miles. Located at 42.41° N. Lat; 77.23° W. Long. Elevation is 728 feet.
Population: 2,263; Growth (since 2000): -11.1%; Density: 55.3 persons per square mile; Race: 97.0% White, 1.8% Black/African American, 0.0% Asian, 0.0% American Indian/Alaska Native, 0.0% Native Hawaiian/Other Pacific Islander, 0.6% Two or more races, 1.2% Hispanic of any race; Average household size: 2.16; Median age: 53.8; Age under 18: 16.2%; Age 65 and over: 25.8%; Males per 100 females: 100.1; Marriage status: 19.0% never married, 57.1% now married, 2.4% separated, 9.2% widowed, 14.6% divorced; Foreign born: 1.8%; Speak English only: 98.7%; With disability: 13.9%; Veterans: 15.7%; Ancestry: 21.2% English, 19.1% German, 16.5% Irish, 11.3% American, 9.5% Italian
Employment: 12.8% management, business, and financial, 4.4% computer, engineering, and science, 16.2% education, legal, community service, arts, and media, 5.6% healthcare practitioners, 17.5% service, 18.7% sales and office, 7.8% natural resources, construction, and maintenance, 17.0% production, transportation, and material moving
Income: Per capita: $32,472; Median household: $56,076; Average household: $73,038; Households with income of $100,000 or more: 18.1%; Poverty rate: 9.8%
Educational Attainment: High school diploma or higher: 90.8%; Bachelor's degree or higher: 30.3%; Graduate/professional degree or higher: 14.2%
Housing: Homeownership rate: 74.1%; Median home value: $144,200; Median year structure built: 1948; Homeowner vacancy rate: 0.0%; Median selected monthly owner costs: $1,375 with a mortgage, $533 without a mortgage; Median gross rent: $611 per month; Rental vacancy rate: 0.0%
Health Insurance: 94.3% have insurance; 76.1% have private insurance; 37.4% have public insurance; 5.7% do not have insurance; 2.5% of children under 18 do not have insurance
Transportation: Commute: 88.6% car, 0.5% public transportation, 5.7% walk, 3.0% work from home; Mean travel time to work: 21.2 minutes

WAYLAND (town). Covers a land area of 38.738 square miles and a water area of 0.600 square miles. Located at 42.52° N. Lat; 77.60° W. Long. Elevation is 1,375 feet.

History: Incorporated 1877.

Population: 4,052; Growth (since 2000): -6.1%; Density: 104.6 persons per square mile; Race: 97.0% White, 1.0% Black/African American, 0.0% Asian, 0.6% American Indian/Alaska Native, 0.0% Native Hawaiian/Other Pacific Islander, 1.4% Two or more races, 0.4% Hispanic of any race; Average household size: 2.26; Median age: 46.1; Age under 18: 20.8%; Age 65 and over: 15.4%; Males per 100 females: 95.0; Marriage status: 25.4% never married, 55.1% now married, 4.8% separated, 6.8% widowed, 12.7% divorced; Foreign born: 0.5%; Speak English only: 98.7%; With disability: 19.7%; Veterans: 11.9%; Ancestry: 38.6% German, 26.4% Irish, 16.1% English, 7.8% American, 5.8% Italian

Employment: 5.6% management, business, and financial, 3.2% computer, engineering, and science, 10.2% education, legal, community service, arts, and media, 5.6% healthcare practitioners, 19.8% service, 20.5% sales and office, 14.6% natural resources, construction, and maintenance, 20.4% production, transportation, and material moving

Income: Per capita: $23,462; Median household: $42,672; Average household: $52,879; Households with income of $100,000 or more: 13.6%; Poverty rate: 17.2%

Educational Attainment: High school diploma or higher: 87.0%; Bachelor's degree or higher: 10.7%; Graduate/professional degree or higher: 5.7%

School District(s)
Wayland-Cohocton Central SD (PK-12)
    2014-15 Enrollment: 1,412 . . . . (585) 728-2211

Housing: Homeownership rate: 72.5%; Median home value: $89,400; Median year structure built: 1956; Homeowner vacancy rate: 1.7%; Median selected monthly owner costs: $1,027 with a mortgage, $421 without a mortgage; Median gross rent: $687 per month; Rental vacancy rate: 6.3%

Health Insurance: 93.5% have insurance; 65.2% have private insurance; 41.7% have public insurance; 6.5% do not have insurance; 5.7% of children under 18 do not have insurance

Transportation: Commute: 89.2% car, 2.0% public transportation, 3.6% walk, 2.9% work from home; Mean travel time to work: 28.5 minutes

Additional Information Contacts
Town of Wayland . . . . (585) 728-5660
    http://townofwayland.org/content

WAYLAND (village). Covers a land area of 1.130 square miles and a water area of 0.058 square miles. Located at 42.56° N. Lat; 77.60° W. Long. Elevation is 1,375 feet.

Population: 1,750; Growth (since 2000): -7.6%; Density: 1,549.2 persons per square mile; Race: 98.2% White, 0.5% Black/African American, 0.0% Asian, 0.2% American Indian/Alaska Native, 0.0% Native Hawaiian/Other Pacific Islander, 1.1% Two or more races, 0.3% Hispanic of any race; Average household size: 2.16; Median age: 43.4; Age under 18: 23.5%; Age 65 and over: 16.8%; Males per 100 females: 94.3; Marriage status: 26.9% never married, 49.4% now married, 2.9% separated, 8.8% widowed, 15.0% divorced; Foreign born: 0.7%; Speak English only: 98.2%; With disability: 19.9%; Veterans: 9.2%; Ancestry: 37.8% German, 18.0% Irish, 14.4% English, 9.7% American, 6.8% Dutch

Employment: 6.5% management, business, and financial, 4.5% computer, engineering, and science, 9.9% education, legal, community service, arts, and media, 8.2% healthcare practitioners, 19.3% service, 22.6% sales and office, 10.6% natural resources, construction, and maintenance, 18.4% production, transportation, and material moving

Income: Per capita: $23,563; Median household: $35,938; Average household: $50,882; Households with income of $100,000 or more: 11.2%; Poverty rate: 15.0%

Educational Attainment: High school diploma or higher: 88.5%; Bachelor's degree or higher: 14.7%; Graduate/professional degree or higher: 7.4%

School District(s)
Wayland-Cohocton Central SD (PK-12)
    2014-15 Enrollment: 1,412 . . . . (585) 728-2211

Housing: Homeownership rate: 60.1%; Median home value: $88,500; Median year structure built: 1941; Homeowner vacancy rate: 2.0%; Median selected monthly owner costs: $1,037 with a mortgage, $484 without a mortgage; Median gross rent: $632 per month; Rental vacancy rate: 9.4%

Health Insurance: 92.5% have insurance; 62.5% have private insurance; 45.9% have public insurance; 7.5% do not have insurance; 6.8% of children under 18 do not have insurance

Safety: Violent crime rate: 0.0 per 10,000 population; Property crime rate: 54.7 per 10,000 population

Transportation: Commute: 87.8% car, 0.8% public transportation, 5.9% walk, 2.9% work from home; Mean travel time to work: 24.4 minutes

WAYNE (town). Covers a land area of 20.582 square miles and a water area of 2.014 square miles. Located at 42.43° N. Lat; 77.14° W. Long. Elevation is 1,168 feet.

Population: 1,019; Growth (since 2000): -12.5%; Density: 49.5 persons per square mile; Race: 96.7% White, 0.6% Black/African American, 2.4% Asian, 0.4% American Indian/Alaska Native, 0.0% Native Hawaiian/Other Pacific Islander, 0.0% Two or more races, 1.0% Hispanic of any race; Average household size: 2.14; Median age: 55.3; Age under 18: 13.5%; Age 65 and over: 29.0%; Males per 100 females: 97.2; Marriage status: 18.3% never married, 65.5% now married, 2.4% separated, 6.7% widowed, 9.4% divorced; Foreign born: 3.4%; Speak English only: 93.5%; With disability: 18.9%; Veterans: 12.4%; Ancestry: 25.2% Irish, 22.2% English, 18.5% German, 9.5% American, 8.8% Italian

Employment: 18.1% management, business, and financial, 2.8% computer, engineering, and science, 11.9% education, legal, community service, arts, and media, 9.4% healthcare practitioners, 15.7% service, 25.5% sales and office, 8.3% natural resources, construction, and maintenance, 8.3% production, transportation, and material moving

Income: Per capita: $38,058; Median household: $60,729; Average household: $79,256; Households with income of $100,000 or more: 28.1%; Poverty rate: 6.4%

Educational Attainment: High school diploma or higher: 93.7%; Bachelor's degree or higher: 37.3%; Graduate/professional degree or higher: 19.0%

Housing: Homeownership rate: 88.9%; Median home value: $179,700; Median year structure built: 1964; Homeowner vacancy rate: 0.0%; Median selected monthly owner costs: $1,405 with a mortgage, $598 without a mortgage; Median gross rent: $950 per month; Rental vacancy rate: 25.4%

Health Insurance: 90.4% have insurance; 75.1% have private insurance; 40.2% have public insurance; 9.6% do not have insurance; 19.6% of children under 18 do not have insurance

Transportation: Commute: 93.8% car, 0.0% public transportation, 2.1% walk, 4.0% work from home; Mean travel time to work: 26.7 minutes

WEST UNION (town). Covers a land area of 40.903 square miles and a water area of 0.146 square miles. Located at 42.04° N. Lat; 77.69° W. Long. Elevation is 2,257 feet.

Population: 366; Growth (since 2000): -8.3%; Density: 8.9 persons per square mile; Race: 97.8% White, 0.0% Black/African American, 0.3% Asian, 0.0% American Indian/Alaska Native, 0.0% Native Hawaiian/Other Pacific Islander, 1.9% Two or more races, 0.0% Hispanic of any race; Average household size: 2.46; Median age: 47.2; Age under 18: 22.4%; Age 65 and over: 19.9%; Males per 100 females: 113.7; Marriage status: 26.0% never married, 63.0% now married, 5.0% separated, 3.3% widowed, 7.7% divorced; Foreign born: 3.8%; Speak English only: 94.3%; With disability: 13.7%; Veterans: 12.3%; Ancestry: 24.3% German, 23.2% Irish, 15.8% English, 11.2% American, 7.1% Italian

Employment: 25.0% management, business, and financial, 4.8% computer, engineering, and science, 1.8% education, legal, community service, arts, and media, 4.8% healthcare practitioners, 19.6% service, 13.1% sales and office, 18.5% natural resources, construction, and maintenance, 12.5% production, transportation, and material moving

Income: Per capita: $22,510; Median household: $41,771; Average household: $56,505; Households with income of $100,000 or more: 13.5%; Poverty rate: 13.4%

Educational Attainment: High school diploma or higher: 85.3%; Bachelor's degree or higher: 11.0%; Graduate/professional degree or higher: 5.9%

Housing: Homeownership rate: 76.5%; Median home value: $96,400; Median year structure built: 1968; Homeowner vacancy rate: 0.0%; Median selected monthly owner costs: $1,089 with a mortgage, $544 without a mortgage; Median gross rent: $595 per month; Rental vacancy rate: 0.0%

Health Insurance: 80.3% have insurance; 53.0% have private insurance; 44.0% have public insurance; 19.7% do not have insurance; 22.0% of children under 18 do not have insurance

Transportation: Commute: 77.2% car, 0.0% public transportation, 10.5% walk, 11.1% work from home; Mean travel time to work: 24.5 minutes

WHEELER (town). Covers a land area of 46.066 square miles and a water area of 0.061 square miles. Located at 42.44° N. Lat; 77.34° W. Long. Elevation is 1,257 feet.

Population: 1,144; Growth (since 2000): -9.4%; Density: 24.8 persons per square mile; Race: 96.4% White, 2.6% Black/African American, 0.2% Asian, 0.0% American Indian/Alaska Native, 0.0% Native Hawaiian/Other Pacific Islander, 0.8% Two or more races, 1.8% Hispanic of any race; Average household size: 2.51; Median age: 40.2; Age under 18: 24.0%; Age 65 and over: 17.3%; Males per 100 females: 106.9; Marriage status: 24.7% never married, 58.6% now married, 2.8% separated, 5.2% widowed, 11.5% divorced; Foreign born: 0.5%; Speak English only: 87.9%; With disability: 15.1%; Veterans: 11.3%; Ancestry: 29.2% German, 24.7% Irish, 9.8% English, 9.2% American, 4.6% Dutch

Employment: 16.0% management, business, and financial, 5.3% computer, engineering, and science, 9.0% education, legal, community service, arts, and media, 2.4% healthcare practitioners, 22.6% service, 15.6% sales and office, 16.2% natural resources, construction, and maintenance, 12.9% production, transportation, and material moving

Income: Per capita: $20,343; Median household: $47,700; Average household: $51,479; Households with income of $100,000 or more: 6.2%; Poverty rate: 13.9%

Educational Attainment: High school diploma or higher: 81.7%; Bachelor's degree or higher: 14.6%; Graduate/professional degree or higher: 6.5%

Housing: Homeownership rate: 82.2%; Median home value: $93,400; Median year structure built: 1977; Homeowner vacancy rate: 1.0%; Median selected monthly owner costs: $1,019 with a mortgage, $479 without a mortgage; Median gross rent: $794 per month; Rental vacancy rate: 0.0%

Health Insurance: 82.1% have insurance; 56.3% have private insurance; 38.6% have public insurance; 17.9% do not have insurance; 22.5% of children under 18 do not have insurance

Transportation: Commute: 84.2% car, 0.7% public transportation, 0.0% walk, 10.8% work from home; Mean travel time to work: 29.8 minutes

WOODHULL (town). Covers a land area of 55.390 square miles and a water area of 0.033 square miles. Located at 42.05° N. Lat; 77.39° W. Long. Elevation is 1,322 feet.

Population: 2,061; Growth (since 2000): 35.2%; Density: 37.2 persons per square mile; Race: 99.6% White, 0.0% Black/African American, 0.0% Asian, 0.3% American Indian/Alaska Native, 0.0% Native Hawaiian/Other Pacific Islander, 0.1% Two or more races, 0.0% Hispanic of any race; Average household size: 2.99; Median age: 36.3; Age under 18: 33.9%; Age 65 and over: 14.8%; Males per 100 females: 101.3; Marriage status: 27.7% never married, 54.6% now married, 2.5% separated, 6.8% widowed, 11.0% divorced; Foreign born: 0.2%; Speak English only: 86.1%; With disability: 12.0%; Veterans: 10.6%; Ancestry: 17.0% American, 15.4% English, 12.8% Irish, 11.2% German, 8.5% Pennsylvania German

Employment: 8.9% management, business, and financial, 0.4% computer, engineering, and science, 11.9% education, legal, community service, arts, and media, 4.9% healthcare practitioners, 22.3% service, 16.5% sales and office, 16.1% natural resources, construction, and maintenance, 19.0% production, transportation, and material moving

Income: Per capita: $16,520; Median household: $42,361; Average household: $48,833; Households with income of $100,000 or more: 7.1%; Poverty rate: 30.6%

Educational Attainment: High school diploma or higher: 81.5%; Bachelor's degree or higher: 10.2%; Graduate/professional degree or higher: 3.5%

Housing: Homeownership rate: 87.2%; Median home value: $83,900; Median year structure built: 1975; Homeowner vacancy rate: 1.6%; Median selected monthly owner costs: $984 with a mortgage, $339 without a mortgage; Median gross rent: $700 per month; Rental vacancy rate: 10.2%

Health Insurance: 78.8% have insurance; 52.8% have private insurance; 38.8% have public insurance; 21.2% do not have insurance; 32.2% of children under 18 do not have insurance

Transportation: Commute: 90.8% car, 1.0% public transportation, 4.1% walk, 4.0% work from home; Mean travel time to work: 29.8 minutes

Suffolk County

Located in southeastern New York; on Long Island, bounded on the south by the Atlantic Ocean, on the east by Block Island Sound, and on the north by Long Island Sound; includes many bays and inlets. Covers a land area of 912.051 square miles, a water area of 1,461.082 square miles, and is located in the Eastern Time Zone at 40.94° N. Lat., 72.69° W. Long. The county was founded in 1683. County seat is Riverhead.

Suffolk County is part of the New York-Newark-Jersey City, NY-NJ-PA Metropolitan Statistical Area. The entire metro area includes: Dutchess County-Putnam County, NY Metropolitan Division (Dutchess County, NY; Putnam County, NY); Nassau County-Suffolk County, NY Metropolitan Division (Nassau County, NY; Suffolk County, NY); Newark, NJ-PA Metropolitan Division (Essex County, NJ; Hunterdon County, NJ; Morris County, NJ; Somerset County, NJ; Sussex County, NJ; Union County, NJ; Pike County, PA); New York-Jersey City-White Plains, NY-NJ Metropolitan Division (Bergen County, NJ; Hudson County, NJ; Middlesex County, NJ; Monmouth County, NJ; Ocean County, NJ; Passaic County, NJ; Bronx County, NY; Kings County, NY; New York County, NY; Orange County, NY; Queens County, NY; Richmond County, NY; Rockland County, NY; Westchester County, NY)

Weather Station: Bridgehampton										Elevation: 60 feet		
	Jan	Feb	Mar	Apr	May	Jun	Jul	Aug	Sep	Oct	Nov	Dec
High	39	40	47	56	66	75	81	80	74	63	54	44
Low	23	25	30	39	48	57	63	63	55	44	37	28
Precip	4.0	3.5	4.9	4.7	3.7	4.2	3.4	4.0	4.4	4.2	4.4	4.3
Snow	7.7	7.9	5.3	0.9	0.0	0.0	0.0	0.0	0.0	tr	0.7	4.0

High and Low temperatures in degrees Fahrenheit; Precipitation and Snow in inches

Weather Station: Islip-Macarthur Arpt										Elevation: 83 feet		
	Jan	Feb	Mar	Apr	May	Jun	Jul	Aug	Sep	Oct	Nov	Dec
High	39	41	48	58	68	77	82	81	74	64	54	44
Low	24	25	31	41	50	60	66	65	58	46	37	28
Precip	3.8	3.0	4.4	4.3	3.8	4.1	3.3	4.3	3.8	4.0	3.6	4.2
Snow	na	na	na	na	na	na	na	na	na	na	na	na

High and Low temperatures in degrees Fahrenheit; Precipitation and Snow in inches

Weather Station: Riverhead Research Farm										Elevation: 100 feet		
	Jan	Feb	Mar	Apr	May	Jun	Jul	Aug	Sep	Oct	Nov	Dec
High	40	42	49	60	71	79	84	83	76	65	55	45
Low	25	26	32	41	50	60	65	65	58	48	40	30
Precip	3.7	3.1	4.5	4.5	3.9	4.1	3.2	3.9	3.8	4.2	4.3	4.0
Snow	8.5	7.6	5.1	0.7	0.0	0.0	0.0	0.0	0.0	0.0	0.5	4.7

High and Low temperatures in degrees Fahrenheit; Precipitation and Snow in inches

Weather Station: Setauket Strong										Elevation: 40 feet		
	Jan	Feb	Mar	Apr	May	Jun	Jul	Aug	Sep	Oct	Nov	Dec
High	40	42	50	61	71	79	83	82	76	65	55	45
Low	25	26	31	41	49	59	65	64	58	47	38	30
Precip	3.4	2.7	4.0	4.4	3.7	3.9	na	3.6	3.8	3.6	3.6	3.5
Snow	2.5	3.3	1.3	0.2	0.0	0.0	0.0	0.0	0.0	0.0	tr	na

High and Low temperatures in degrees Fahrenheit; Precipitation and Snow in inches

Population: 1,501,373; Growth (since 2000): 5.8%; Density: 1,646.2 persons per square mile; Race: 80.9% White, 7.7% Black/African American, 3.8% Asian, 0.2% American Indian/Alaska Native, 0.0% Native Hawaiian/Other Pacific Islander, 2.4% two or more races, 17.8% Hispanic of any race; Average household size: 2.98; Median age: 40.6; Age under 18: 22.7%; Age 65 and over: 14.8%; Males per 100 females: 96.8; Marriage status: 32.4% never married, 53.2% now married, 1.8% separated, 6.3% widowed, 8.1% divorced; Foreign born: 15.1%; Speak English only: 78.0%; With disability: 9.3%; Veterans: 6.4%; Ancestry: 26.1% Italian, 20.4% Irish, 15.2% German, 5.2% Polish, 4.7% English

Religion: Six largest groups: 58.9% Catholicism, 2.2% Lutheran, 1.7% Methodist/Pietist, 1.6% Non-denominational Protestant, 1.4% Judaism, 1.3% Muslim Estimate

Economy: Unemployment rate: 4.2%; Leading industries: 14.3 % construction; 13.5 % retail trade; 11.9 % professional, scientific, and technical services; Farms: 604 totaling 35,975 acres; Company size: 21 employs 1,000 or more persons, 51 employs 500 to 999 persons, 749 employ 100 to 499 persons, 48,010 employ less than 100 persons; Business ownership: 48,272 women-owned, 7,112 Black-owned, 15,418 Hispanic-owned, 7,686 Asian-owned, 715 American Indian/Alaska Native-owned

Employment: 14.4% management, business, and financial, 4.3% computer, engineering, and science, 12.9% education, legal, community service, arts, and media, 6.2% healthcare practitioners, 17.5% service, 25.7% sales and office, 9.4% natural resources, construction, and maintenance, 9.5% production, transportation, and material moving

Income: Per capita: $37,634; Median household: $88,663; Average household: $110,577; Households with income of $100,000 or more: 44.1%; Poverty rate: 7.0%

Educational Attainment: High school diploma or higher: 89.9%; Bachelor's degree or higher: 34.0%; Graduate/professional degree or higher: 15.3%

Housing: Homeownership rate: 79.5%; Median home value: $375,100; Median year structure built: 1968; Homeowner vacancy rate: 1.4%; Median selected monthly owner costs: $2,734 with a mortgage, $1,139 without a mortgage; Median gross rent: $1,544 per month; Rental vacancy rate: 4.6%

Vital Statistics: Birth rate: 103.7 per 10,000 population; Death rate: 81.7 per 10,000 population; Age-adjusted cancer mortality rate: 148.4 deaths per 100,000 population

Health Insurance: 91.6% have insurance; 77.9% have private insurance; 26.2% have public insurance; 8.4% do not have insurance; 3.5% of children under 18 do not have insurance

Health Care: Physicians: 33.0 per 10,000 population; Dentists: 7.9 per 10,000 population; Hospital beds: 31.6 per 10,000 population; Hospital admissions: 1,124.6 per 10,000 population

Air Quality Index (AQI): Percent of Days: 80.0% good, 18.1% moderate, 1.9% unhealthy for sensitive individuals, 0.0% unhealthy, 0.0% very unhealthy; Annual median: 38; Annual maximum: 124

Transportation: Commute: 87.2% car, 6.5% public transportation, 1.6% walk, 3.5% work from home; Mean travel time to work: 31.4 minutes

2016 Presidential Election: 51.8% Trump, 44.9% Clinton, 2.1% Johnson, 1.2% Stein

National and State Parks: Amagansett National Wildlife Refuge; Babylon Marsh State Tidal Wetlands; Belmont Lake State Park; Brookhaven State Park; Caleb Smith State Park; Camp Hero State Park; Captree State Park; Caumsett State Park; Connetquot River State Park; Conscience Point National Wildlife Refuge; Elizabeth Alexandra Morton National Wildlife Refuge; Fire Island National Seashore; Gilgo State Park; Heckscher State Park; Hither Hills State Park; Montauk Downs State Park; Montauk Point State Park; Orient Beach State Park; Petteanger Island State Tidal Wetlands; Robert Moses State Park; Seatuck National Wildlife Refuge; Sunken Meadow State Park; Target Rock National Wildlife Refuge; Wertheim National Wildlife Refuge; Wildwood State Park

Additional Information Contacts
Suffolk Government. . . . . (631) 852-2000
  http://www.suffolkcountyny.gov

Suffolk County Communities

AMAGANSETT (CDP). Covers a land area of 6.527 square miles and a water area of 0.024 square miles. Located at 40.99° N. Lat; 72.13° W. Long. Elevation is 30 feet.

Population: 1,211; Growth (since 2000): 13.5%; Density: 185.5 persons per square mile; Race: 98.0% White, 1.1% Black/African American, 0.6% Asian, 0.0% American Indian/Alaska Native, 0.0% Native Hawaiian/Other Pacific Islander, 0.3% Two or more races, 3.9% Hispanic of any race; Average household size: 2.72; Median age: 50.9; Age under 18: 18.4%; Age 65 and over: 36.7%; Males per 100 females: 107.3; Marriage status: 23.5% never married, 63.5% now married, 0.7% separated, 7.8% widowed, 5.1% divorced; Foreign born: 7.8%; Speak English only: 92.5%; With disability: 13.0%; Veterans: 8.4%; Ancestry: 26.1% Irish, 21.6% German, 19.3% Italian, 12.6% English, 6.9% Russian

Employment: 13.4% management, business, and financial, 3.4% computer, engineering, and science, 11.6% education, legal, community service, arts, and media, 3.3% healthcare practitioners, 20.5% service, 37.0% sales and office, 9.8% natural resources, construction, and maintenance, 1.1% production, transportation, and material moving

Income: Per capita: $55,992; Median household: $93,750; Average household: $146,619; Households with income of $100,000 or more: 49.6%; Poverty rate: 2.6%

Educational Attainment: High school diploma or higher: 96.6%; Bachelor's degree or higher: 49.4%; Graduate/professional degree or higher: 18.0%

School District(s)
Amagansett Union Free SD (PK-06)
  2014-15 Enrollment: 111. . . . . (631) 267-3572

Housing: Homeownership rate: 82.3%; Median home value: $1,650,600; Median year structure built: 1967; Homeowner vacancy rate: 0.0%; Median selected monthly owner costs: $2,486 with a mortgage, $829 without a

mortgage; Median gross rent: $2,545 per month; Rental vacancy rate: 0.0%

Health Insurance: 95.3% have insurance; 88.2% have private insurance; 35.2% have public insurance; 4.7% do not have insurance; 0.0% of children under 18 do not have insurance

Transportation: Commute: 75.3% car, 3.4% public transportation, 7.9% walk, 13.5% work from home; Mean travel time to work: 23.6 minutes

AMITYVILLE (village). Covers a land area of 2.113 square miles and a water area of 0.363 square miles. Located at 40.67° N. Lat; 73.42° W. Long. Elevation is 20 feet.

History: Settled 1780, incorporated 1894.

Population: 9,515; Growth (since 2000): 0.8%; Density: 4,503.2 persons per square mile; Race: 73.2% White, 7.8% Black/African American, 1.5% Asian, 0.0% American Indian/Alaska Native, 0.0% Native Hawaiian/Other Pacific Islander, 3.9% Two or more races, 19.5% Hispanic of any race; Average household size: 2.64; Median age: 46.4; Age under 18: 19.0%; Age 65 and over: 19.2%; Males per 100 females: 91.5; Marriage status: 30.3% never married, 51.5% now married, 1.6% separated, 7.7% widowed, 10.4% divorced; Foreign born: 15.6%; Speak English only: 79.2%; With disability: 11.1%; Veterans: 6.9%; Ancestry: 26.4% Irish, 18.4% Italian, 13.4% German, 5.9% Polish, 5.9% English

Employment: 12.7% management, business, and financial, 8.4% computer, engineering, and science, 9.7% education, legal, community service, arts, and media, 7.8% healthcare practitioners, 18.3% service, 23.1% sales and office, 8.3% natural resources, construction, and maintenance, 11.7% production, transportation, and material moving

Income: Per capita: $36,822; Median household: $83,125; Average household: $98,417; Households with income of $100,000 or more: 42.6%; Poverty rate: 10.9%

Educational Attainment: High school diploma or higher: 92.2%; Bachelor's degree or higher: 38.1%; Graduate/professional degree or higher: 15.0%

School District(s)
Amityville Union Free SD (PK-12)
  2014-15 Enrollment: 3,249 . . . . (631) 565-6019

Two-year College(s)
Island Drafting and Technical Institute (Private, For-profit)
  Fall 2014 Enrollment: 110 . . . . (631) 691-8733
  2015-16 Tuition: In-state $16,200; Out-of-state $16,200

Vocational/Technical School(s)
Branford Hall Career Institute-Amityville (Private, For-profit)
  Fall 2014 Enrollment: 328 . . . . (631) 608-9113
  2015-16 Tuition: $11,250

Housing: Homeownership rate: 63.4%; Median home value: $367,900; Median year structure built: 1955; Homeowner vacancy rate: 6.3%; Median selected monthly owner costs: $2,688 with a mortgage, $1,320 without a mortgage; Median gross rent: $1,431 per month; Rental vacancy rate: 3.1%

Health Insurance: 88.9% have insurance; 73.5% have private insurance; 30.5% have public insurance; 11.1% do not have insurance; 0.5% of children under 18 do not have insurance

Safety: Violent crime rate: 5.3 per 10,000 population; Property crime rate: 137.6 per 10,000 population

Newspapers: Amityville Record (weekly circulation 2,900)

Transportation: Commute: 76.2% car, 14.8% public transportation, 2.7% walk, 4.3% work from home; Mean travel time to work: 33.5 minutes

Additional Information Contacts
Village of Amityville . . . . (631) 264-6000
  http://www.amityville.com

AQUEBOGUE (CDP). Covers a land area of 3.812 square miles and a water area of 0.099 square miles. Located at 40.94° N. Lat; 72.62° W. Long. Elevation is 36 feet.

Population: 1,958; Growth (since 2000): -13.1%; Density: 513.7 persons per square mile; Race: 99.9% White, 0.1% Black/African American, 0.0% Asian, 0.0% American Indian/Alaska Native, 0.0% Native Hawaiian/Other Pacific Islander, 0.0% Two or more races, 12.1% Hispanic of any race; Average household size: 2.51; Median age: 43.6; Age under 18: 15.3%; Age 65 and over: 13.3%; Males per 100 females: 92.4; Marriage status: 40.2% never married, 45.3% now married, 0.0% separated, 5.1% widowed, 9.3% divorced; Foreign born: 9.3%; Speak English only: 87.5%; With disability: 11.3%; Veterans: 12.6%; Ancestry: 30.3% Irish, 22.8% Italian, 17.6% Polish, 17.2% German, 11.4% English

Employment: 13.5% management, business, and financial, 8.1% computer, engineering, and science, 15.1% education, legal, community service, arts, and media, 8.9% healthcare practitioners, 18.4% service, 16.8% sales and office, 12.8% natural resources, construction, and maintenance, 6.3% production, transportation, and material moving
Income: Per capita: $44,817; Median household: $90,847; Average household: $112,400; Households with income of $100,000 or more: 43.2%; Poverty rate: 0.3%
Educational Attainment: High school diploma or higher: 96.6%; Bachelor's degree or higher: 36.9%; Graduate/professional degree or higher: 22.8%

School District(s)
Riverhead Central SD (KG-12)
   2014-15 Enrollment: 5,216 . . . . (631) 369-6717
Housing: Homeownership rate: 83.4%; Median home value: $433,800; Median year structure built: 1980; Homeowner vacancy rate: 0.0%; Median selected monthly owner costs: $2,588 with a mortgage, $1,080 without a mortgage; Median gross rent: n/a per month; Rental vacancy rate: 0.0%
Health Insurance: 84.5% have insurance; 70.2% have private insurance; 21.5% have public insurance; 15.5% do not have insurance; 0.0% of children under 18 do not have insurance
Transportation: Commute: 91.2% car, 1.2% public transportation, 0.0% walk, 4.6% work from home; Mean travel time to work: 24.4 minutes

ASHAROKEN (village). Covers a land area of 1.471 square miles and a water area of 5.015 square miles. Located at 40.94° N. Lat; 73.39° W. Long. Elevation is 13 feet.
Population: 532; Growth (since 2000): -14.9%; Density: 361.7 persons per square mile; Race: 97.6% White, 0.0% Black/African American, 1.3% Asian, 0.6% American Indian/Alaska Native, 0.0% Native Hawaiian/Other Pacific Islander, 0.6% Two or more races, 1.3% Hispanic of any race; Average household size: 2.49; Median age: 57.1; Age under 18: 14.3%; Age 65 and over: 28.9%; Males per 100 females: 107.6; Marriage status: 22.2% never married, 69.6% now married, 1.2% separated, 5.0% widowed, 3.1% divorced; Foreign born: 5.1%; Speak English only: 94.2%; With disability: 10.0%; Veterans: 13.8%; Ancestry: 33.8% Irish, 29.3% Italian, 27.4% German, 8.3% English, 7.3% Norwegian
Employment: 24.9% management, business, and financial, 9.6% computer, engineering, and science, 16.2% education, legal, community service, arts, and media, 8.3% healthcare practitioners, 7.4% service, 27.5% sales and office, 4.8% natural resources, construction, and maintenance, 1.3% production, transportation, and material moving
Income: Per capita: $100,686; Median household: $153,750; Average household: $257,123; Households with income of $100,000 or more: 65.5%; Poverty rate: 3.9%
Educational Attainment: High school diploma or higher: 100.0%; Bachelor's degree or higher: 58.5%; Graduate/professional degree or higher: 26.3%
Housing: Homeownership rate: 87.9%; Median home value: $1,118,200; Median year structure built: 1958; Homeowner vacancy rate: 0.0%; Median selected monthly owner costs: $4,000+ with a mortgage, $1,500+ without a mortgage; Median gross rent: $3,500+ per month; Rental vacancy rate: 0.0%
Health Insurance: 99.1% have insurance; 91.5% have private insurance; 33.3% have public insurance; 0.9% do not have insurance; 0.0% of children under 18 do not have insurance
Safety: Violent crime rate: 0.0 per 10,000 population; Property crime rate: 15.3 per 10,000 population
Transportation: Commute: 83.8% car, 4.8% public transportation, 4.8% walk, 5.7% work from home; Mean travel time to work: 40.6 minutes

BABYLON (town). Covers a land area of 52.319 square miles and a water area of 61.861 square miles. Located at 40.68° N. Lat; 73.32° W. Long. Elevation is 7 feet.
History: The 1st U.S. wireless station was built here by Marconi. Settled 1689, incorporated as a village 1893.
Population: 214,132; Growth (since 2000): 1.1%; Density: 4,092.8 persons per square mile; Race: 69.0% White, 16.5% Black/African American, 3.2% Asian, 0.1% American Indian/Alaska Native, 0.0% Native Hawaiian/Other Pacific Islander, 2.9% Two or more races, 20.5% Hispanic of any race; Average household size: 3.08; Median age: 39.4; Age under 18: 21.7%; Age 65 and over: 13.4%; Males per 100 females: 93.7; Marriage status: 34.8% never married, 50.0% now married, 2.3% separated, 7.0% widowed, 8.2% divorced; Foreign born: 19.6%; Speak

English only: 74.4%; With disability: 10.4%; Veterans: 5.9%; Ancestry: 25.6% Italian, 17.3% Irish, 11.9% German, 5.5% Polish, 3.0% English
Employment: 11.7% management, business, and financial, 3.8% computer, engineering, and science, 10.6% education, legal, community service, arts, and media, 5.5% healthcare practitioners, 19.7% service, 27.3% sales and office, 9.8% natural resources, construction, and maintenance, 11.6% production, transportation, and material moving
Income: Per capita: $31,794; Median household: $80,327; Average household: $94,732; Households with income of $100,000 or more: 38.3%; Poverty rate: 7.1%
Educational Attainment: High school diploma or higher: 87.3%; Bachelor's degree or higher: 25.2%; Graduate/professional degree or higher: 9.4%

School District(s)
Babylon Union Free SD (KG-12)
   2014-15 Enrollment: 1,680 . . . . (631) 893-7925
Housing: Homeownership rate: 73.8%; Median home value: $340,600; Median year structure built: 1960; Homeowner vacancy rate: 1.7%; Median selected monthly owner costs: $2,680 with a mortgage, $1,147 without a mortgage; Median gross rent: $1,487 per month; Rental vacancy rate: 3.7%
Health Insurance: 89.9% have insurance; 74.1% have private insurance; 27.2% have public insurance; 10.1% do not have insurance; 4.1% of children under 18 do not have insurance
Newspapers: Babylon Beacon (weekly circulation 3,400)
Transportation: Commute: 85.4% car, 8.6% public transportation, 2.0% walk, 2.5% work from home; Mean travel time to work: 30.5 minutes
Additional Information Contacts
Town of Babylon . . . . (631) 957-3000
  http://www.townofbabylon.com

BABYLON (village). Covers a land area of 2.445 square miles and a water area of 0.343 square miles. Located at 40.69° N. Lat; 73.33° W. Long. Elevation is 7 feet.
Population: 12,186; Growth (since 2000): -3.4%; Density: 4,984.2 persons per square mile; Race: 89.0% White, 1.4% Black/African American, 4.1% Asian, 0.0% American Indian/Alaska Native, 0.0% Native Hawaiian/Other Pacific Islander, 3.6% Two or more races, 9.1% Hispanic of any race; Average household size: 2.74; Median age: 42.3; Age under 18: 20.8%; Age 65 and over: 14.4%; Males per 100 females: 94.5; Marriage status: 32.2% never married, 54.2% now married, 1.7% separated, 7.2% widowed, 6.3% divorced; Foreign born: 10.6%; Speak English only: 89.1%; With disability: 10.0%; Veterans: 6.2%; Ancestry: 32.9% Italian, 32.0% Irish, 17.9% German, 7.3% English, 5.3% Polish
Employment: 21.1% management, business, and financial, 3.7% computer, engineering, and science, 20.2% education, legal, community service, arts, and media, 4.1% healthcare practitioners, 13.6% service, 22.7% sales and office, 7.9% natural resources, construction, and maintenance, 6.6% production, transportation, and material moving
Income: Per capita: $45,614; Median household: $100,025; Average household: $122,316; Households with income of $100,000 or more: 49.9%; Poverty rate: 4.6%
Educational Attainment: High school diploma or higher: 95.8%; Bachelor's degree or higher: 42.6%; Graduate/professional degree or higher: 20.0%

School District(s)
Babylon Union Free SD (KG-12)
   2014-15 Enrollment: 1,680 . . . . (631) 893-7925
Housing: Homeownership rate: 75.2%; Median home value: $432,100; Median year structure built: 1954; Homeowner vacancy rate: 1.9%; Median selected monthly owner costs: $3,154 with a mortgage, $1,323 without a mortgage; Median gross rent: $1,668 per month; Rental vacancy rate: 0.0%
Health Insurance: 95.5% have insurance; 87.9% have private insurance; 19.4% have public insurance; 4.5% do not have insurance; 1.6% of children under 18 do not have insurance
Newspapers: Babylon Beacon (weekly circulation 3,400)
Transportation: Commute: 78.8% car, 13.4% public transportation, 1.9% walk, 5.5% work from home; Mean travel time to work: 32.9 minutes
Additional Information Contacts
Village of Babylon . . . . (631) 669-1212
  http://www.villageofbabylonny.gov

BAITING HOLLOW (CDP).

Covers a land area of 3.213 square miles and a water area of 0 square miles. Located at 40.96° N. Lat; 72.74° W. Long. Elevation is 105 feet.

Population: 1,542; Growth (since 2000): 6.4%; Density: 480.0 persons per square mile; Race: 96.4% White, 0.9% Black/African American, 2.4% Asian, 0.0% American Indian/Alaska Native, 0.0% Native Hawaiian/Other Pacific Islander, 0.0% Two or more races, 6.9% Hispanic of any race; Average household size: 2.58; Median age: 51.4; Age under 18: 16.9%; Age 65 and over: 25.0%; Males per 100 females: 97.1; Marriage status: 22.2% never married, 68.5% now married, 1.0% separated, 6.4% widowed, 3.0% divorced; Foreign born: 10.6%; Speak English only: 84.1%; With disability: 8.5%; Veterans: 8.5%; Ancestry: 22.8% Irish, 19.6% Italian, 18.1% German, 10.4% Polish, 5.1% English

Employment: 10.6% management, business, and financial, 2.8% computer, engineering, and science, 16.7% education, legal, community service, arts, and media, 2.2% healthcare practitioners, 14.4% service, 35.4% sales and office, 11.6% natural resources, construction, and maintenance, 6.2% production, transportation, and material moving

Income: Per capita: $41,273; Median household: $83,380; Average household: $105,162; Households with income of $100,000 or more: 33.8%; Poverty rate: 3.0%

Educational Attainment: High school diploma or higher: 94.3%; Bachelor's degree or higher: 25.3%; Graduate/professional degree or higher: 11.8%

Housing: Homeownership rate: 88.8%; Median home value: $409,800; Median year structure built: 1986; Homeowner vacancy rate: 2.6%; Median selected monthly owner costs: $3,270 with a mortgage, $1,114 without a mortgage; Median gross rent: $1,806 per month; Rental vacancy rate: 0.0%

Health Insurance: 97.5% have insurance; 89.3% have private insurance; 29.2% have public insurance; 2.5% do not have insurance; 0.0% of children under 18 do not have insurance

Transportation: Commute: 88.2% car, 3.9% public transportation, 0.0% walk, 5.1% work from home; Mean travel time to work: 29.8 minutes

BAY SHORE (CDP).

Covers a land area of 5.368 square miles and a water area of 0.159 square miles. Located at 40.73° N. Lat; 73.25° W. Long. Elevation is 16 feet.

History: Named for its location on Great South Bay. Founded 1708.

Population: 29,670; Growth (since 2000): 24.4%; Density: 5,527.6 persons per square mile; Race: 52.5% White, 22.0% Black/African American, 4.5% Asian, 0.1% American Indian/Alaska Native, 0.0% Native Hawaiian/Other Pacific Islander, 5.1% Two or more races, 36.2% Hispanic of any race; Average household size: 3.12; Median age: 34.1; Age under 18: 24.4%; Age 65 and over: 11.7%; Males per 100 females: 94.1; Marriage status: 39.6% never married, 44.5% now married, 3.1% separated, 5.5% widowed, 10.3% divorced; Foreign born: 23.7%; Speak English only: 65.2%; With disability: 10.5%; Veterans: 5.3%; Ancestry: 13.6% Italian, 12.6% Irish, 8.4% German, 3.2% English, 3.2% Haitian

Employment: 13.4% management, business, and financial, 1.8% computer, engineering, and science, 10.0% education, legal, community service, arts, and media, 3.5% healthcare practitioners, 22.9% service, 24.8% sales and office, 8.2% natural resources, construction, and maintenance, 15.3% production, transportation, and material moving

Income: Per capita: $27,969; Median household: $70,229; Average household: $84,581; Households with income of $100,000 or more: 31.7%; Poverty rate: 9.5%

Educational Attainment: High school diploma or higher: 83.1%; Bachelor's degree or higher: 27.3%; Graduate/professional degree or higher: 10.4%

School District(s)

Bay Shore Union Free SD (KG-12)
    2014-15 Enrollment: 6,033 . . . . (631) 968-1117
Brentwood Union Free SD (PK-12)
    2014-15 Enrollment: 18,648 . . . . (631) 434-2325
Fire Island Union Free SD (PK-06)
    2014-15 Enrollment: 36 . . . . (631) 583-5626

Housing: Homeownership rate: 59.8%; Median home value: $318,000; Median year structure built: 1961; Homeowner vacancy rate: 1.4%; Median selected monthly owner costs: $2,627 with a mortgage, $1,104 without a mortgage; Median gross rent: $1,332 per month; Rental vacancy rate: 2.1%

Health Insurance: 87.2% have insurance; 67.8% have private insurance; 28.4% have public insurance; 12.8% do not have insurance; 7.4% of children under 18 do not have insurance

Hospitals: Southside Hospital (377 beds)

Transportation: Commute: 81.0% car, 10.1% public transportation, 2.7% walk, 2.9% work from home; Mean travel time to work: 31.4 minutes

BAYPORT (CDP).

Covers a land area of 3.720 square miles and a water area of 0.076 square miles. Located at 40.75° N. Lat; 73.06° W. Long. Elevation is 16 feet.

History: Bayport is a hamlet and a census-designated place (CDP) in Suffolk County, Long Island, New York.

Population: 8,305; Growth (since 2000): -4.1%; Density: 2,232.7 persons per square mile; Race: 94.7% White, 0.7% Black/African American, 1.7% Asian, 0.1% American Indian/Alaska Native, 0.0% Native Hawaiian/Other Pacific Islander, 2.3% Two or more races, 3.9% Hispanic of any race; Average household size: 2.64; Median age: 44.8; Age under 18: 22.8%; Age 65 and over: 17.3%; Males per 100 females: 92.2; Marriage status: 25.2% never married, 55.3% now married, 1.7% separated, 8.9% widowed, 10.7% divorced; Foreign born: 4.4%; Speak English only: 93.0%; With disability: 10.3%; Veterans: 7.9%; Ancestry: 34.8% Italian, 26.9% Irish, 26.5% German, 9.5% English, 7.0% Polish

Employment: 17.4% management, business, and financial, 4.3% computer, engineering, and science, 17.3% education, legal, community service, arts, and media, 5.2% healthcare practitioners, 12.1% service, 26.1% sales and office, 9.8% natural resources, construction, and maintenance, 7.8% production, transportation, and material moving

Income: Per capita: $43,567; Median household: $81,955; Average household: $113,430; Households with income of $100,000 or more: 43.9%; Poverty rate: 6.4%

Educational Attainment: High school diploma or higher: 95.0%; Bachelor's degree or higher: 43.2%; Graduate/professional degree or higher: 18.8%

School District(s)

Bayport-Blue Point Union Free SD (KG-12)
    2014-15 Enrollment: 2,388 . . . . (631) 472-7860

Housing: Homeownership rate: 67.9%; Median home value: $438,000; Median year structure built: 1969; Homeowner vacancy rate: 0.0%; Median selected monthly owner costs: $3,473 with a mortgage, $1,404 without a mortgage; Median gross rent: $1,593 per month; Rental vacancy rate: 4.0%

Health Insurance: 96.9% have insurance; 87.2% have private insurance; 27.2% have public insurance; 3.1% do not have insurance; 3.9% of children under 18 do not have insurance

Transportation: Commute: 88.5% car, 6.0% public transportation, 0.2% walk, 4.5% work from home; Mean travel time to work: 32.2 minutes

BAYWOOD (CDP).

Covers a land area of 2.260 square miles and a water area of 0 square miles. Located at 40.75° N. Lat; 73.29° W. Long. Elevation is 59 feet.

Population: 7,249; Growth (since 2000): -4.3%; Density: 3,207.0 persons per square mile; Race: 60.9% White, 18.5% Black/African American, 1.9% Asian, 0.2% American Indian/Alaska Native, 0.0% Native Hawaiian/Other Pacific Islander, 3.7% Two or more races, 31.9% Hispanic of any race; Average household size: 3.23; Median age: 39.0; Age under 18: 24.7%; Age 65 and over: 11.1%; Males per 100 females: 100.5; Marriage status: 35.4% never married, 44.8% now married, 2.1% separated, 8.7% widowed, 11.2% divorced; Foreign born: 15.5%; Speak English only: 72.3%; With disability: 14.5%; Veterans: 7.2%; Ancestry: 21.5% Italian, 12.6% Irish, 7.7% German, 3.4% Jamaican, 3.0% American

Employment: 10.2% management, business, and financial, 2.1% computer, engineering, and science, 8.8% education, legal, community service, arts, and media, 6.6% healthcare practitioners, 22.3% service, 26.3% sales and office, 10.6% natural resources, construction, and maintenance, 13.0% production, transportation, and material moving

Income: Per capita: $27,157; Median household: $74,609; Average household: $83,369; Households with income of $100,000 or more: 33.7%; Poverty rate: 7.3%

Educational Attainment: High school diploma or higher: 86.7%; Bachelor's degree or higher: 18.9%; Graduate/professional degree or higher: 3.9%

Housing: Homeownership rate: 84.0%; Median home value: $285,600; Median year structure built: 1958; Homeowner vacancy rate: 0.4%; Median selected monthly owner costs: $2,268 with a mortgage, $874 without a mortgage; Median gross rent: $1,467 per month; Rental vacancy rate: 0.0%

Health Insurance: 89.5% have insurance; 70.5% have private insurance; 27.6% have public insurance; 10.5% do not have insurance; 3.6% of children under 18 do not have insurance

Transportation: Commute: 85.5% car, 9.8% public transportation, 0.5% walk, 2.0% work from home; Mean travel time to work: 29.2 minutes

BELLE TERRE (village).
Covers a land area of 0.885 square miles and a water area of 0 square miles. Located at 40.96° N. Lat; 73.07° W. Long. Elevation is 161 feet.

Population: 783; Growth (since 2000): -5.9%; Density: 884.9 persons per square mile; Race: 96.6% White, 0.0% Black/African American, 2.0% Asian, 0.0% American Indian/Alaska Native, 0.0% Native Hawaiian/Other Pacific Islander, 1.4% Two or more races, 4.6% Hispanic of any race; Average household size: 2.87; Median age: 44.7; Age under 18: 29.1%; Age 65 and over: 19.0%; Males per 100 females: 101.0; Marriage status: 16.3% never married, 75.9% now married, 0.3% separated, 5.9% widowed, 1.9% divorced; Foreign born: 11.2%; Speak English only: 90.0%; With disability: 5.5%; Veterans: 9.5%; Ancestry: 24.0% Italian, 16.3% Irish, 14.3% German, 7.8% Greek, 5.9% Russian

Employment: 23.4% management, business, and financial, 9.2% computer, engineering, and science, 13.3% education, legal, community service, arts, and media, 19.9% healthcare practitioners, 11.3% service, 17.1% sales and office, 3.8% natural resources, construction, and maintenance, 2.0% production, transportation, and material moving

Income: Per capita: $90,592; Median household: $204,750; Average household: $264,407; Households with income of $100,000 or more: 79.5%; Poverty rate: 5.2%

Educational Attainment: High school diploma or higher: 99.2%; Bachelor's degree or higher: 68.9%; Graduate/professional degree or higher: 44.8%

Housing: Homeownership rate: 98.2%; Median home value: $875,000; Median year structure built: 1973; Homeowner vacancy rate: 3.2%; Median selected monthly owner costs: $4,000+ with a mortgage, $1,500+ without a mortgage; Median gross rent: n/a per month; Rental vacancy rate: 0.0%

Health Insurance: 95.8% have insurance; 87.0% have private insurance; 21.7% have public insurance; 4.2% do not have insurance; 5.7% of children under 18 do not have insurance

Transportation: Commute: 88.0% car, 3.6% public transportation, 0.0% walk, 7.8% work from home; Mean travel time to work: 34.5 minutes

BELLPORT (village).
Covers a land area of 1.445 square miles and a water area of 0.091 square miles. Located at 40.75° N. Lat; 72.94° W. Long. Elevation is 26 feet.

Population: 2,059; Growth (since 2000): -12.9%; Density: 1,424.9 persons per square mile; Race: 95.2% White, 1.0% Black/African American, 1.7% Asian, 0.8% American Indian/Alaska Native, 0.0% Native Hawaiian/Other Pacific Islander, 1.0% Two or more races, 3.0% Hispanic of any race; Average household size: 2.17; Median age: 55.7; Age under 18: 15.4%; Age 65 and over: 29.7%; Males per 100 females: 93.5; Marriage status: 20.5% never married, 62.5% now married, 1.7% separated, 9.3% widowed, 7.7% divorced; Foreign born: 9.4%; Speak English only: 87.3%; With disability: 9.1%; Veterans: 9.0%; Ancestry: 26.6% German, 26.2% Irish, 23.4% Italian, 11.8% English, 7.7% Polish

Employment: 11.9% management, business, and financial, 5.7% computer, engineering, and science, 27.3% education, legal, community service, arts, and media, 5.9% healthcare practitioners, 14.0% service, 24.5% sales and office, 6.5% natural resources, construction, and maintenance, 4.1% production, transportation, and material moving

Income: Per capita: $57,141; Median household: $82,500; Average household: $123,413; Households with income of $100,000 or more: 43.3%; Poverty rate: 4.4%

Educational Attainment: High school diploma or higher: 97.4%; Bachelor's degree or higher: 55.3%; Graduate/professional degree or higher: 35.8%

School District(s)
South Country Central SD (PK-12)
    2014-15 Enrollment: 4,632 . . . . (631) 730-1510

Housing: Homeownership rate: 85.3%; Median home value: $434,200; Median year structure built: 1957; Homeowner vacancy rate: 3.8%; Median selected monthly owner costs: $2,721 with a mortgage, $1,264 without a mortgage; Median gross rent: $1,871 per month; Rental vacancy rate: 3.5%

Health Insurance: 96.2% have insurance; 86.4% have private insurance; 36.6% have public insurance; 3.8% do not have insurance; 2.8% of children under 18 do not have insurance

Transportation: Commute: 78.5% car, 6.1% public transportation, 5.1% walk, 7.8% work from home; Mean travel time to work: 27.5 minutes

Additional Information Contacts
Village of Bellport . . . . (631) 286-0327
  http://www.bellportvillage.com

BLUE POINT (CDP).
Covers a land area of 1.794 square miles and a water area of 0.006 square miles. Located at 40.75° N. Lat; 73.04° W. Long. Elevation is 10 feet.

History: Bluepoint oysters take their name from here.

Population: 4,725; Growth (since 2000): 7.2%; Density: 2,634.4 persons per square mile; Race: 98.8% White, 0.1% Black/African American, 0.7% Asian, 0.0% American Indian/Alaska Native, 0.0% Native Hawaiian/Other Pacific Islander, 0.4% Two or more races, 9.6% Hispanic of any race; Average household size: 2.84; Median age: 42.8; Age under 18: 24.7%; Age 65 and over: 15.7%; Males per 100 females: 96.7; Marriage status: 28.3% never married, 58.0% now married, 1.1% separated, 5.7% widowed, 8.0% divorced; Foreign born: 6.1%; Speak English only: 90.6%; With disability: 6.8%; Veterans: 6.6%; Ancestry: 38.2% Irish, 29.7% German, 28.0% Italian, 6.0% English, 3.0% French

Employment: 14.8% management, business, and financial, 5.0% computer, engineering, and science, 23.3% education, legal, community service, arts, and media, 7.5% healthcare practitioners, 12.7% service, 20.3% sales and office, 9.3% natural resources, construction, and maintenance, 7.1% production, transportation, and material moving

Income: Per capita: $41,212; Median household: $108,704; Average household: $115,341; Households with income of $100,000 or more: 52.1%; Poverty rate: 4.5%

Educational Attainment: High school diploma or higher: 97.5%; Bachelor's degree or higher: 42.4%; Graduate/professional degree or higher: 22.0%

School District(s)
Bayport-Blue Point Union Free SD (KG-12)
    2014-15 Enrollment: 2,388 . . . . (631) 472-7860

Housing: Homeownership rate: 85.2%; Median home value: $384,500; Median year structure built: 1961; Homeowner vacancy rate: 0.8%; Median selected monthly owner costs: $2,801 with a mortgage, $1,280 without a mortgage; Median gross rent: $1,682 per month; Rental vacancy rate: 0.0%

Health Insurance: 94.4% have insurance; 88.1% have private insurance; 19.8% have public insurance; 5.6% do not have insurance; 3.3% of children under 18 do not have insurance

Transportation: Commute: 91.9% car, 3.8% public transportation, 0.4% walk, 3.0% work from home; Mean travel time to work: 30.1 minutes

BOHEMIA (CDP).
Covers a land area of 8.620 square miles and a water area of 0.037 square miles. Located at 40.78° N. Lat; 73.13° W. Long. Elevation is 66 feet.

History: Bohemia was founded in 1855 by Slavic immigrants who were the first Europeans to settle there in large numbers. They came from a mountainous village in the Central European Kingdom of Bohemia, for which the town was named.

Population: 9,977; Growth (since 2000): 1.1%; Density: 1,157.5 persons per square mile; Race: 95.4% White, 0.9% Black/African American, 1.6% Asian, 0.0% American Indian/Alaska Native, 0.0% Native Hawaiian/Other Pacific Islander, 0.6% Two or more races, 8.1% Hispanic of any race; Average household size: 2.85; Median age: 40.6; Age under 18: 24.6%; Age 65 and over: 15.2%; Males per 100 females: 97.0; Marriage status: 31.1% never married, 48.5% now married, 2.0% separated, 7.8% widowed, 12.6% divorced; Foreign born: 5.1%; Speak English only: 89.9%; With disability: 11.5%; Veterans: 5.4%; Ancestry: 36.8% Italian, 28.3% Irish, 19.8% German, 4.6% Polish, 4.0% Russian

Employment: 17.5% management, business, and financial, 3.3% computer, engineering, and science, 14.8% education, legal, community service, arts, and media, 5.3% healthcare practitioners, 16.6% service, 26.2% sales and office, 8.3% natural resources, construction, and maintenance, 8.1% production, transportation, and material moving

Income: Per capita: $33,662; Median household: $82,011; Average household: $94,486; Households with income of $100,000 or more: 42.8%; Poverty rate: 5.9%

Educational Attainment: High school diploma or higher: 92.0%; Bachelor's degree or higher: 28.1%; Graduate/professional degree or higher: 14.1%

School District(s)
Connetquot Central SD (PK-12)
2014-15 Enrollment: 6,244 . . . . (631) 244-2215
Vocational/Technical School(s)
Branford Hall Career Institute-Bohemia Campus (Private, For-profit)
Fall 2014 Enrollment: 682 . . . . (631) 589-1222
2015-16 Tuition: $11,390
Housing: Homeownership rate: 76.0%; Median home value: $389,600; Median year structure built: 1972; Homeowner vacancy rate: 0.0%; Median selected monthly owner costs: $2,861 with a mortgage, $1,159 without a mortgage; Median gross rent: $1,615 per month; Rental vacancy rate: 2.8%
Health Insurance: 96.9% have insurance; 85.8% have private insurance; 23.2% have public insurance; 3.1% do not have insurance; 0.8% of children under 18 do not have insurance
Transportation: Commute: 90.8% car, 6.6% public transportation, 1.3% walk, 0.9% work from home; Mean travel time to work: 31.1 minutes

BRENTWOOD (CDP). Covers a land area of 10.981 square miles and a water area of 0 square miles. Located at 40.78° N. Lat; 73.25° W. Long. Elevation is 79 feet.
History: Josiah Warren led (1851) an experiment in communal living in Brentwood.
Population: 61,374; Growth (since 2000): 13.8%; Density: 5,589.3 persons per square mile; Race: 50.6% White, 15.3% Black/African American, 2.4% Asian, 0.4% American Indian/Alaska Native, 0.0% Native Hawaiian/Other Pacific Islander, 6.4% Two or more races, 66.3% Hispanic of any race; Average household size: 4.36; Median age: 32.5; Age under 18: 26.5%; Age 65 and over: 8.4%; Males per 100 females: 103.6; Marriage status: 45.5% never married, 41.9% now married, 2.6% separated, 4.4% widowed, 8.1% divorced; Foreign born: 42.1%; Speak English only: 30.7%; With disability: 8.1%; Veterans: 3.5%; Ancestry: 4.6% Italian, 3.7% Irish, 3.6% Haitian, 2.2% German, 1.4% American
Employment: 6.2% management, business, and financial, 1.9% computer, engineering, and science, 4.1% education, legal, community service, arts, and media, 3.3% healthcare practitioners, 25.8% service, 22.6% sales and office, 11.8% natural resources, construction, and maintenance, 24.3% production, transportation, and material moving
Income: Per capita: $20,463; Median household: $70,139; Average household: $82,569; Households with income of $100,000 or more: 31.9%; Poverty rate: 11.6%
Educational Attainment: High school diploma or higher: 70.8%; Bachelor's degree or higher: 12.9%; Graduate/professional degree or higher: 4.0%
School District(s)
Brentwood Union Free SD (PK-12)
2014-15 Enrollment: 18,648 . . . . (631) 434-2325
Four-year College(s)
LIU Brentwood (Private, Not-for-profit)
Fall 2014 Enrollment: 216 . . . . (631) 287-8500
Housing: Homeownership rate: 70.3%; Median home value: $278,200; Median year structure built: 1963; Homeowner vacancy rate: 1.0%; Median selected monthly owner costs: $2,351 with a mortgage, $921 without a mortgage; Median gross rent: $1,243 per month; Rental vacancy rate: 5.0%
Health Insurance: 79.0% have insurance; 56.3% have private insurance; 29.2% have public insurance; 21.0% do not have insurance; 7.2% of children under 18 do not have insurance
Transportation: Commute: 89.6% car, 4.3% public transportation, 1.4% walk, 1.1% work from home; Mean travel time to work: 26.2 minutes

BRIDGEHAMPTON (CDP). Covers a land area of 13.010 square miles and a water area of 0.623 square miles. Located at 40.95° N. Lat; 72.31° W. Long. Elevation is 43 feet.
Population: 1,274; Growth (since 2000): -7.7%; Density: 97.9 persons per square mile; Race: 93.7% White, 5.5% Black/African American, 0.8% Asian, 0.0% American Indian/Alaska Native, 0.0% Native Hawaiian/Other Pacific Islander, 0.0% Two or more races, 19.2% Hispanic of any race; Average household size: 2.22; Median age: 49.8; Age under 18: 16.5%; Age 65 and over: 26.5%; Males per 100 females: 101.1; Marriage status: 23.0% never married, 66.5% now married, 2.0% separated, 5.8% widowed, 4.7% divorced; Foreign born: 15.3%; Speak English only: 78.9%; With disability: 8.0%; Veterans: 10.2%; Ancestry: 17.2% English, 16.8% Polish, 16.4% Irish, 14.5% Italian, 12.1% German

Employment: 15.6% management, business, and financial, 0.0% computer, engineering, and science, 9.9% education, legal, community service, arts, and media, 3.1% healthcare practitioners, 21.7% service, 30.2% sales and office, 15.7% natural resources, construction, and maintenance, 3.6% production, transportation, and material moving
Income: Per capita: $62,096; Median household: $77,174; Average household: $135,330; Households with income of $100,000 or more: 43.3%; Poverty rate: 2.8%
Educational Attainment: High school diploma or higher: 93.8%; Bachelor's degree or higher: 39.6%; Graduate/professional degree or higher: 17.0%
School District(s)
Bridgehampton Union Free SD (PK-12)
2014-15 Enrollment: 169 . . . . (631) 537-0271
Housing: Homeownership rate: 87.1%; Median home value: $1,504,200; Median year structure built: 1983; Homeowner vacancy rate: 0.8%; Median selected monthly owner costs: $3,121 with a mortgage, $1,174 without a mortgage; Median gross rent: $1,244 per month; Rental vacancy rate: 0.0%
Health Insurance: 90.8% have insurance; 82.4% have private insurance; 34.1% have public insurance; 9.2% do not have insurance; 0.0% of children under 18 do not have insurance
Newspapers: Dan's Papers (weekly circulation 69,000)
Transportation: Commute: 80.2% car, 4.6% public transportation, 5.5% walk, 8.8% work from home; Mean travel time to work: 18.0 minutes

BRIGHTWATERS (village). Covers a land area of 0.976 square miles and a water area of 0.023 square miles. Located at 40.72° N. Lat; 73.26° W. Long. Elevation is 23 feet.
History: Laid out 1907, incorporated 1916.
Population: 3,102; Growth (since 2000): -4.5%; Density: 3,177.3 persons per square mile; Race: 93.1% White, 1.1% Black/African American, 1.7% Asian, 0.0% American Indian/Alaska Native, 0.0% Native Hawaiian/Other Pacific Islander, 1.7% Two or more races, 6.7% Hispanic of any race; Average household size: 2.85; Median age: 44.0; Age under 18: 23.1%; Age 65 and over: 13.7%; Males per 100 females: 97.6; Marriage status: 28.1% never married, 61.2% now married, 0.9% separated, 6.3% widowed, 4.5% divorced; Foreign born: 5.1%; Speak English only: 91.9%; With disability: 7.2%; Veterans: 9.6%; Ancestry: 34.8% Italian, 33.4% Irish, 16.9% German, 8.0% English, 4.7% Polish
Employment: 19.6% management, business, and financial, 5.0% computer, engineering, and science, 18.3% education, legal, community service, arts, and media, 10.9% healthcare practitioners, 8.8% service, 25.9% sales and office, 6.6% natural resources, construction, and maintenance, 4.9% production, transportation, and material moving
Income: Per capita: $56,379; Median household: $122,692; Average household: $159,211; Households with income of $100,000 or more: 61.9%; Poverty rate: 1.7%
Educational Attainment: High school diploma or higher: 98.6%; Bachelor's degree or higher: 57.3%; Graduate/professional degree or higher: 26.4%
Housing: Homeownership rate: 91.0%; Median home value: $498,200; Median year structure built: 1947; Homeowner vacancy rate: 0.0%; Median selected monthly owner costs: $3,490 with a mortgage, $1,500+ without a mortgage; Median gross rent: $1,265 per month; Rental vacancy rate: 0.0%
Health Insurance: 95.6% have insurance; 91.6% have private insurance; 16.9% have public insurance; 4.4% do not have insurance; 0.0% of children under 18 do not have insurance
Transportation: Commute: 87.5% car, 7.8% public transportation, 1.8% walk, 2.7% work from home; Mean travel time to work: 30.7 minutes

BROOKHAVEN (CDP). Covers a land area of 5.761 square miles and a water area of 0.146 square miles. Located at 40.78° N. Lat; 72.91° W. Long. Elevation is 10 feet.
Population: 3,138; Growth (since 2000): -12.1%; Density: 544.7 persons per square mile; Race: 86.5% White, 7.9% Black/African American, 0.3% Asian, 0.0% American Indian/Alaska Native, 0.0% Native Hawaiian/Other Pacific Islander, 4.1% Two or more races, 7.4% Hispanic of any race; Average household size: 2.48; Median age: 50.5; Age under 18: 21.7%; Age 65 and over: 21.0%; Males per 100 females: 93.2; Marriage status: 27.8% never married, 50.0% now married, 2.9% separated, 9.8% widowed, 12.4% divorced; Foreign born: 8.9%; Speak English only: 85.4%; With disability: 13.0%; Veterans: 10.0%; Ancestry: 24.6% Italian, 23.6% Irish, 14.4% German, 7.9% Polish, 4.9% English

Employment: 16.3% management, business, and financial, 6.1% computer, engineering, and science, 17.6% education, legal, community service, arts, and media, 7.8% healthcare practitioners, 13.6% service, 23.0% sales and office, 6.2% natural resources, construction, and maintenance, 9.4% production, transportation, and material moving
Income: Per capita: $44,939; Median household: $90,833; Average household: $128,449; Households with income of $100,000 or more: 44.1%; Poverty rate: 8.7%
Educational Attainment: High school diploma or higher: 88.4%; Bachelor's degree or higher: 39.2%; Graduate/professional degree or higher: 19.7%

School District(s)
South Country Central SD (PK-12)
   2014-15 Enrollment: 4,632 . . . . (631) 730-1510
Housing: Homeownership rate: 80.8%; Median home value: $400,700; Median year structure built: 1971; Homeowner vacancy rate: 0.7%; Median selected monthly owner costs: $3,021 with a mortgage, $1,261 without a mortgage; Median gross rent: $1,317 per month; Rental vacancy rate: 0.0%
Health Insurance: 95.6% have insurance; 77.1% have private insurance; 35.9% have public insurance; 4.4% do not have insurance; 4.4% of children under 18 do not have insurance
Transportation: Commute: 84.8% car, 7.1% public transportation, 0.6% walk, 6.7% work from home; Mean travel time to work: 33.2 minutes

BROOKHAVEN (town).
Covers a land area of 259.439 square miles and a water area of 272.097 square miles. Located at 40.86° N. Lat; 72.96° W. Long. Elevation is 10 feet.
History: Brookhaven was the home of William Floyd (1743-1821), Revolutionary War soldier, statesman, and signer of the Declaration of Independence.
Population: 488,930; Growth (since 2000): 9.1%; Density: 1,884.6 persons per square mile; Race: 86.1% White, 5.4% Black/African American, 4.6% Asian, 0.2% American Indian/Alaska Native, 0.0% Native Hawaiian/Other Pacific Islander, 2.0% Two or more races, 15.0% Hispanic of any race; Average household size: 2.94; Median age: 39.1; Age under 18: 22.9%; Age 65 and over: 13.3%; Males per 100 females: 97.2; Marriage status: 33.1% never married, 52.6% now married, 1.7% separated, 5.9% widowed, 8.4% divorced; Foreign born: 12.2%; Speak English only: 81.0%; With disability: 9.3%; Veterans: 6.4%; Ancestry: 29.5% Italian, 22.5% Irish, 17.2% German, 4.8% Polish, 4.6% American
Employment: 13.7% management, business, and financial, 5.1% computer, engineering, and science, 12.8% education, legal, community service, arts, and media, 6.6% healthcare practitioners, 17.3% service, 26.0% sales and office, 9.7% natural resources, construction, and maintenance, 8.7% production, transportation, and material moving
Income: Per capita: $35,067; Median household: $87,040; Average household: $102,812; Households with income of $100,000 or more: 42.4%; Poverty rate: 7.7%
Educational Attainment: High school diploma or higher: 91.5%; Bachelor's degree or higher: 31.6%; Graduate/professional degree or higher: 14.9%

School District(s)
South Country Central SD (PK-12)
   2014-15 Enrollment: 4,632 . . . . (631) 730-1510
Housing: Homeownership rate: 79.3%; Median home value: $327,300; Median year structure built: 1973; Homeowner vacancy rate: 1.6%; Median selected monthly owner costs: $2,607 with a mortgage, $1,084 without a mortgage; Median gross rent: $1,601 per month; Rental vacancy rate: 4.8%
Health Insurance: 92.7% have insurance; 79.0% have private insurance; 26.1% have public insurance; 7.3% do not have insurance; 2.8% of children under 18 do not have insurance
Transportation: Commute: 90.4% car, 4.2% public transportation, 1.6% walk, 3.2% work from home; Mean travel time to work: 32.8 minutes
Additional Information Contacts
Town of Brookhaven . . . . (631) 451-6300
   http://www.brookhaven.org

CALVERTON (CDP).
Covers a land area of 28.027 square miles and a water area of 0.501 square miles. Located at 40.92° N. Lat; 72.77° W. Long. Elevation is 30 feet.
History: Calverton was first called "Baiting Hollow Station" when the Long Island Railroad arrived in 1844. The station closed in 1958, but the sheltered shed for the station remained standing as of 2007. The area's

native American name was Conungum or Kanungum, meaning "fixed line" or "boundary."
Population: 6,380; Growth (since 2000): 11.9%; Density: 227.6 persons per square mile; Race: 83.5% White, 10.0% Black/African American, 1.6% Asian, 0.0% American Indian/Alaska Native, 0.0% Native Hawaiian/Other Pacific Islander, 4.8% Two or more races, 8.3% Hispanic of any race; Average household size: 2.13; Median age: 54.3; Age under 18: 12.4%; Age 65 and over: 35.7%; Males per 100 females: 91.5; Marriage status: 24.1% never married, 50.4% now married, 2.9% separated, 15.5% widowed, 9.9% divorced; Foreign born: 9.4%; Speak English only: 91.2%; With disability: 17.8%; Veterans: 14.5%; Ancestry: 23.1% Irish, 20.5% Italian, 16.1% German, 8.8% Polish, 7.6% English
Employment: 8.0% management, business, and financial, 3.0% computer, engineering, and science, 14.6% education, legal, community service, arts, and media, 6.1% healthcare practitioners, 17.9% service, 29.8% sales and office, 14.5% natural resources, construction, and maintenance, 6.2% production, transportation, and material moving
Income: Per capita: $32,739; Median household: $46,176; Average household: $69,639; Households with income of $100,000 or more: 23.2%; Poverty rate: 6.3%
Educational Attainment: High school diploma or higher: 89.9%; Bachelor's degree or higher: 25.3%; Graduate/professional degree or higher: 10.6%

School District(s)
Riverhead Central SD (KG-12)
   2014-15 Enrollment: 5,216 . . . . (631) 369-6717
Riverhead Charter School (KG-06)
   2014-15 Enrollment: 366. . . . . (631) 369-5800
Housing: Homeownership rate: 84.3%; Median home value: $211,000; Median year structure built: 1985; Homeowner vacancy rate: 2.2%; Median selected monthly owner costs: $2,166 with a mortgage, $854 without a mortgage; Median gross rent: $1,400 per month; Rental vacancy rate: 8.2%
Health Insurance: 94.6% have insurance; 76.9% have private insurance; 45.8% have public insurance; 5.4% do not have insurance; 0.0% of children under 18 do not have insurance
Transportation: Commute: 91.8% car, 0.5% public transportation, 2.9% walk, 3.0% work from home; Mean travel time to work: 26.6 minutes

CENTER MORICHES (CDP).
Covers a land area of 5.217 square miles and a water area of 0.415 square miles. Located at 40.80° N. Lat; 72.80° W. Long. Elevation is 26 feet.
History: Center Moriches is a hamlet in Suffolk County, New York. It is the location of the historic Masury Estate Ballroom and Terry-Ketcham Inn, both listed on the National Register of Historic Places.
Population: 8,418; Growth (since 2000): 26.5%; Density: 1,613.6 persons per square mile; Race: 97.0% White, 0.9% Black/African American, 0.7% Asian, 0.0% American Indian/Alaska Native, 0.0% Native Hawaiian/Other Pacific Islander, 0.4% Two or more races, 9.2% Hispanic of any race; Average household size: 3.13; Median age: 39.8; Age under 18: 23.8%; Age 65 and over: 11.0%; Males per 100 females: 102.0; Marriage status: 28.5% never married, 60.3% now married, 0.2% separated, 5.0% widowed, 6.2% divorced; Foreign born: 5.3%; Speak English only: 89.3%; With disability: 7.7%; Veterans: 6.7%; Ancestry: 32.6% Irish, 31.7% Italian, 23.9% German, 8.4% Polish, 7.4% English
Employment: 10.7% management, business, and financial, 1.6% computer, engineering, and science, 13.8% education, legal, community service, arts, and media, 7.0% healthcare practitioners, 22.7% service, 23.8% sales and office, 13.3% natural resources, construction, and maintenance, 7.0% production, transportation, and material moving
Income: Per capita: $35,445; Median household: $89,037; Average household: $109,181; Households with income of $100,000 or more: 41.9%; Poverty rate: 2.5%
Educational Attainment: High school diploma or higher: 91.1%; Bachelor's degree or higher: 24.4%; Graduate/professional degree or higher: 13.3%

School District(s)
Center Moriches Union Free SD (PK-12)
   2014-15 Enrollment: 1,645 . . . . (631) 878-0052
Housing: Homeownership rate: 82.0%; Median home value: $398,500; Median year structure built: 1971; Homeowner vacancy rate: 6.1%; Median selected monthly owner costs: $2,843 with a mortgage, $1,097 without a mortgage; Median gross rent: $1,467 per month; Rental vacancy rate: 0.0%

Health Insurance: 94.5% have insurance; 83.3% have private insurance; 22.6% have public insurance; 5.5% do not have insurance; 1.4% of children under 18 do not have insurance
Newspapers: The Press (weekly circulation 3,000)
Transportation: Commute: 93.9% car, 0.7% public transportation, 1.8% walk, 3.2% work from home; Mean travel time to work: 29.3 minutes

CENTEREACH (CDP). Covers a land area of 8.714 square miles and a water area of 0 square miles. Located at 40.87° N. Lat; 73.08° W. Long. Elevation is 98 feet.
History: Centereach was first called West Middle Island, as was known as New Village until the early 20th century. In 1916, it was discovered that another town in Updstate New York had the same name, and it was changed to Centereach, due to its central location on Long Island.
Population: 32,649; Growth (since 2000): 19.7%; Density: 3,746.5 persons per square mile; Race: 87.4% White, 3.0% Black/African American, 5.5% Asian, 0.5% American Indian/Alaska Native, 0.1% Native Hawaiian/Other Pacific Islander, 1.5% Two or more races, 13.6% Hispanic of any race; Average household size: 3.29; Median age: 39.1; Age under 18: 22.7%; Age 65 and over: 12.3%; Males per 100 females: 99.7; Marriage status: 33.4% never married, 52.6% now married, 1.0% separated, 6.3% widowed, 7.7% divorced; Foreign born: 10.9%; Speak English only: 84.6%; With disability: 9.5%; Veterans: 6.6%; Ancestry: 31.7% Italian, 22.9% Irish, 19.9% German, 5.9% American, 5.0% Polish
Employment: 15.5% management, business, and financial, 4.6% computer, engineering, and science, 11.3% education, legal, community service, arts, and media, 6.1% healthcare practitioners, 15.9% service, 29.2% sales and office, 8.4% natural resources, construction, and maintenance, 9.0% production, transportation, and material moving
Income: Per capita: $33,605; Median household: $94,432; Average household: $106,686; Households with income of $100,000 or more: 47.8%; Poverty rate: 5.3%
Educational Attainment: High school diploma or higher: 93.0%; Bachelor's degree or higher: 29.1%; Graduate/professional degree or higher: 12.4%
School District(s)
Middle Country Central SD (PK-12)
    2014-15 Enrollment: 10,254 . . . . (631) 285-8005
Housing: Homeownership rate: 85.4%; Median home value: $329,900; Median year structure built: 1968; Homeowner vacancy rate: 0.4%; Median selected monthly owner costs: $2,654 with a mortgage, $1,075 without a mortgage; Median gross rent: $2,134 per month; Rental vacancy rate: 10.0%
Health Insurance: 93.4% have insurance; 81.5% have private insurance; 22.5% have public insurance; 6.6% do not have insurance; 2.5% of children under 18 do not have insurance
Transportation: Commute: 94.1% car, 3.5% public transportation, 0.2% walk, 1.6% work from home; Mean travel time to work: 28.1 minutes

CENTERPORT (CDP). Covers a land area of 2.104 square miles and a water area of 0.190 square miles. Located at 40.90° N. Lat; 73.37° W. Long. Elevation is 49 feet.
History: Formerly known as Little Cow Harbor about 1700, Centreport in 1836, and then the present Centerport after 1895. The name refers to its geographic position midway between the east and west boundaries of the township of Huntington.
Population: 5,447; Growth (since 2000): 0.0%; Density: 2,588.5 persons per square mile; Race: 96.7% White, 0.7% Black/African American, 2.1% Asian, 0.0% American Indian/Alaska Native, 0.0% Native Hawaiian/Other Pacific Islander, 0.5% Two or more races, 0.9% Hispanic of any race; Average household size: 2.75; Median age: 45.1; Age under 18: 24.4%; Age 65 and over: 15.9%; Males per 100 females: 91.1; Marriage status: 24.7% never married, 59.6% now married, 1.1% separated, 7.1% widowed, 8.6% divorced; Foreign born: 4.8%; Speak English only: 94.9%; With disability: 9.0%; Veterans: 5.6%; Ancestry: 31.9% Italian, 31.7% Irish, 29.1% German, 12.9% English, 5.0% Russian
Employment: 24.7% management, business, and financial, 7.5% computer, engineering, and science, 20.3% education, legal, community service, arts, and media, 8.9% healthcare practitioners, 6.0% service, 26.3% sales and office, 2.9% natural resources, construction, and maintenance, 3.4% production, transportation, and material moving
Income: Per capita: $55,085; Median household: $103,945; Average household: $149,192; Households with income of $100,000 or more: 54.1%; Poverty rate: 3.2%

Educational Attainment: High school diploma or higher: 97.6%; Bachelor's degree or higher: 60.5%; Graduate/professional degree or higher: 27.7%
School District(s)
Harborfields Central SD (KG-12)
    2014-15 Enrollment: 3,364 . . . . (631) 754-5320
Housing: Homeownership rate: 91.1%; Median home value: $603,100; Median year structure built: 1955; Homeowner vacancy rate: 0.0%; Median selected monthly owner costs: $3,331 with a mortgage, $1,374 without a mortgage; Median gross rent: $1,640 per month; Rental vacancy rate: 0.0%
Health Insurance: 97.3% have insurance; 90.0% have private insurance; 21.2% have public insurance; 2.7% do not have insurance; 0.0% of children under 18 do not have insurance
Transportation: Commute: 70.2% car, 17.0% public transportation, 0.6% walk, 11.1% work from home; Mean travel time to work: 37.9 minutes

CENTRAL ISLIP (CDP). Covers a land area of 7.111 square miles and a water area of 0 square miles. Located at 40.78° N. Lat; 73.19° W. Long. Elevation is 89 feet.
History: Central Islip was home to the Secatogue tribe of Algonquin native-American people before the arrival of European settlers.
Population: 34,960; Growth (since 2000): 9.4%; Density: 4,916.2 persons per square mile; Race: 50.8% White, 24.6% Black/African American, 3.7% Asian, 0.1% American Indian/Alaska Native, 0.1% Native Hawaiian/Other Pacific Islander, 6.9% Two or more races, 49.3% Hispanic of any race; Average household size: 3.63; Median age: 33.6; Age under 18: 25.7%; Age 65 and over: 9.9%; Males per 100 females: 98.5; Marriage status: 44.2% never married, 40.3% now married, 2.6% separated, 6.1% widowed, 9.4% divorced; Foreign born: 33.9%; Speak English only: 46.1%; With disability: 10.3%; Veterans: 4.4%; Ancestry: 6.5% Italian, 5.7% Irish, 4.6% German, 3.2% Haitian, 2.3% Jamaican
Employment: 6.3% management, business, and financial, 2.6% computer, engineering, and science, 6.3% education, legal, community service, arts, and media, 5.5% healthcare practitioners, 24.5% service, 21.8% sales and office, 9.6% natural resources, construction, and maintenance, 23.4% production, transportation, and material moving
Income: Per capita: $22,515; Median household: $66,430; Average household: $76,562; Households with income of $100,000 or more: 27.7%; Poverty rate: 13.1%
Educational Attainment: High school diploma or higher: 71.0%; Bachelor's degree or higher: 15.3%; Graduate/professional degree or higher: 6.3%
School District(s)
Central Islip Union Free SD (PK-12)
    2014-15 Enrollment: 7,302 . . . . (631) 348-4421
Housing: Homeownership rate: 64.4%; Median home value: $252,100; Median year structure built: 1971; Homeowner vacancy rate: 0.0%; Median selected monthly owner costs: $2,327 with a mortgage, $1,026 without a mortgage; Median gross rent: $1,467 per month; Rental vacancy rate: 2.0%
Health Insurance: 80.4% have insurance; 56.9% have private insurance; 32.0% have public insurance; 19.6% do not have insurance; 5.3% of children under 18 do not have insurance
Transportation: Commute: 89.3% car, 6.2% public transportation, 1.8% walk, 0.9% work from home; Mean travel time to work: 27.9 minutes

COLD SPRING HARBOR (CDP). Covers a land area of 3.665 square miles and a water area of 0.169 square miles. Located at 40.86° N. Lat; 73.45° W. Long. Elevation is 33 feet.
History: Was 19th-century whaling port.
Population: 5,076; Growth (since 2000): 2.0%; Density: 1,384.9 persons per square mile; Race: 91.6% White, 0.2% Black/African American, 4.3% Asian, 0.0% American Indian/Alaska Native, 0.0% Native Hawaiian/Other Pacific Islander, 0.8% Two or more races, 5.4% Hispanic of any race; Average household size: 2.85; Median age: 45.4; Age under 18: 25.1%; Age 65 and over: 15.6%; Males per 100 females: 96.3; Marriage status: 24.9% never married, 64.7% now married, 1.3% separated, 4.3% widowed, 6.1% divorced; Foreign born: 10.5%; Speak English only: 86.5%; With disability: 6.9%; Veterans: 6.1%; Ancestry: 29.1% Italian, 24.8% Irish, 16.5% German, 12.6% English, 5.9% American
Employment: 32.1% management, business, and financial, 6.2% computer, engineering, and science, 20.9% education, legal, community service, arts, and media, 5.9% healthcare practitioners, 4.8% service,

25.4% sales and office, 2.5% natural resources, construction, and maintenance, 2.0% production, transportation, and material moving
Income: Per capita: $76,032; Median household: $157,143; Average household: $218,923; Households with income of $100,000 or more: 73.4%; Poverty rate: 1.6%
Educational Attainment: High school diploma or higher: 98.0%; Bachelor's degree or higher: 71.0%; Graduate/professional degree or higher: 36.6%

School District(s)
Cold Spring Harbor Central SD (KG-12)
    2014-15 Enrollment: 1,814 . . . . (631) 367-5931
Housing: Homeownership rate: 88.6%; Median home value: $774,100; Median year structure built: 1958; Homeowner vacancy rate: 0.0%; Median selected monthly owner costs: $3,935 with a mortgage, $1,500+ without a mortgage; Median gross rent: $3,045 per month; Rental vacancy rate: 0.0%
Health Insurance: 97.3% have insurance; 89.4% have private insurance; 17.5% have public insurance; 2.7% do not have insurance; 3.4% of children under 18 do not have insurance
Transportation: Commute: 71.5% car, 18.7% public transportation, 0.5% walk, 7.5% work from home; Mean travel time to work: 36.5 minutes

COMMACK (CDP). Covers a land area of 11.969 square miles and a water area of 0 square miles. Located at 40.84° N. Lat; 73.28° W. Long. Elevation is 131 feet.
History: Commack is home to the oldest Methodist Church building in New York state, built in 1789 as the Comac Church. It is listed on the National Register of Historic Places and is one of the oldest buildings in Commack.
Population: 35,914; Growth (since 2000): -1.2%; Density: 3,000.7 persons per square mile; Race: 90.1% White, 1.7% Black/African American, 5.1% Asian, 0.0% American Indian/Alaska Native, 0.0% Native Hawaiian/Other Pacific Islander, 2.1% Two or more races, 5.5% Hispanic of any race; Average household size: 3.01; Median age: 44.4; Age under 18: 23.5%; Age 65 and over: 17.5%; Males per 100 females: 94.1; Marriage status: 25.9% never married, 61.6% now married, 1.0% separated, 6.8% widowed, 5.7% divorced; Foreign born: 9.9%; Speak English only: 86.2%; With disability: 8.3%; Veterans: 7.5%; Ancestry: 34.1% Italian, 19.1% Irish, 14.0% German, 7.5% Polish, 6.4% Russian
Employment: 20.2% management, business, and financial, 4.7% computer, engineering, and science, 18.7% education, legal, community service, arts, and media, 8.3% healthcare practitioners, 12.8% service, 24.6% sales and office, 5.4% natural resources, construction, and maintenance, 5.2% production, transportation, and material moving
Income: Per capita: $44,040; Median household: $114,463; Average household: $130,758; Households with income of $100,000 or more: 56.8%; Poverty rate: 3.5%
Educational Attainment: High school diploma or higher: 95.7%; Bachelor's degree or higher: 48.8%; Graduate/professional degree or higher: 23.2%

School District(s)
Commack Union Free SD (KG-12)
    2014-15 Enrollment: 6,842 . . . . (631) 912-2010
Housing: Homeownership rate: 91.1%; Median home value: $466,200; Median year structure built: 1964; Homeowner vacancy rate: 0.7%; Median selected monthly owner costs: $3,119 with a mortgage, $1,301 without a mortgage; Median gross rent: $1,609 per month; Rental vacancy rate: 7.2%
Health Insurance: 96.7% have insurance; 88.3% have private insurance; 22.3% have public insurance; 3.3% do not have insurance; 1.6% of children under 18 do not have insurance
Transportation: Commute: 87.5% car, 7.3% public transportation, 0.9% walk, 3.8% work from home; Mean travel time to work: 32.6 minutes

COPIAGUE (CDP). Covers a land area of 3.218 square miles and a water area of 0.028 square miles. Located at 40.67° N. Lat; 73.39° W. Long. Elevation is 23 feet.
History: Copiague is an unincorporated place within the Town of Babylon.
Population: 22,772; Growth (since 2000): 3.9%; Density: 7,075.6 persons per square mile; Race: 73.5% White, 7.6% Black/African American, 1.4% Asian, 0.1% American Indian/Alaska Native, 0.0% Native Hawaiian/Other Pacific Islander, 3.6% Two or more races, 35.7% Hispanic of any race; Average household size: 3.02; Median age: 40.9; Age under 18: 19.5%; Age 65 and over: 12.7%; Males per 100 females: 99.2; Marriage status: 36.3% never married, 47.0% now married, 2.1% separated, 6.9% widowed, 9.7% divorced; Foreign born: 31.4%; Speak English only: 60.4%;

With disability: 9.7%; Veterans: 5.1%; Ancestry: 24.0% Italian, 15.1% Irish, 10.2% German, 6.9% Polish, 2.6% English
Employment: 9.7% management, business, and financial, 2.9% computer, engineering, and science, 6.8% education, legal, community service, arts, and media, 3.8% healthcare practitioners, 22.9% service, 25.3% sales and office, 11.2% natural resources, construction, and maintenance, 17.3% production, transportation, and material moving
Income: Per capita: $28,088; Median household: $66,161; Average household: $81,201; Households with income of $100,000 or more: 30.0%; Poverty rate: 7.5%
Educational Attainment: High school diploma or higher: 79.8%; Bachelor's degree or higher: 18.3%; Graduate/professional degree or higher: 7.0%

School District(s)
Copiague Union Free SD (KG-12)
    2014-15 Enrollment: 5,212 . . . . (631) 842-4015
Vocational/Technical School(s)
Electrical Training Center (Private, For-profit)
    Fall 2014 Enrollment: 141 . . . . (631) 226-8021
    2015-16 Tuition: $9,200
Housing: Homeownership rate: 72.3%; Median home value: $310,500; Median year structure built: 1960; Homeowner vacancy rate: 1.6%; Median selected monthly owner costs: $2,517 with a mortgage, $1,076 without a mortgage; Median gross rent: $1,511 per month; Rental vacancy rate: 2.2%
Health Insurance: 86.2% have insurance; 66.0% have private insurance; 30.2% have public insurance; 13.8% do not have insurance; 7.7% of children under 18 do not have insurance
Transportation: Commute: 82.3% car, 7.5% public transportation, 2.9% walk, 2.1% work from home; Mean travel time to work: 26.8 minutes

CORAM (CDP). Covers a land area of 13.824 square miles and a water area of 0 square miles. Located at 40.88° N. Lat; 73.01° W. Long. Elevation is 95 feet.
History: Coram is the oldest settlement in the central part of the town of Brookhaven. Its early name was "Wincoram." Its first white settler was likely William Satterly, who opened a tavern in 1677.
Population: 40,685; Growth (since 2000): 16.5%; Density: 2,943.0 persons per square mile; Race: 78.6% White, 10.1% Black/African American, 6.2% Asian, 0.2% American Indian/Alaska Native, 0.0% Native Hawaiian/Other Pacific Islander, 2.4% Two or more races, 15.9% Hispanic of any race; Average household size: 2.72; Median age: 40.1; Age under 18: 22.3%; Age 65 and over: 12.7%; Males per 100 females: 93.2; Marriage status: 31.9% never married, 51.2% now married, 2.0% separated, 6.1% widowed, 10.7% divorced; Foreign born: 18.0%; Speak English only: 77.0%; With disability: 8.7%; Veterans: 4.7%; Ancestry: 26.4% Italian, 16.4% Irish, 13.9% German, 5.2% American, 4.4% Polish
Employment: 14.2% management, business, and financial, 4.4% computer, engineering, and science, 12.6% education, legal, community service, arts, and media, 5.8% healthcare practitioners, 19.8% service, 27.6% sales and office, 8.3% natural resources, construction, and maintenance, 7.4% production, transportation, and material moving
Income: Per capita: $35,358; Median household: $80,899; Average household: $94,135; Households with income of $100,000 or more: 37.5%; Poverty rate: 6.1%
Educational Attainment: High school diploma or higher: 92.7%; Bachelor's degree or higher: 35.4%; Graduate/professional degree or higher: 14.9%

School District(s)
Longwood Central SD (KG-12)
    2014-15 Enrollment: 9,211 . . . . (631) 345-2172
Housing: Homeownership rate: 67.3%; Median home value: $309,300; Median year structure built: 1979; Homeowner vacancy rate: 0.4%; Median selected monthly owner costs: $2,678 with a mortgage, $1,018 without a mortgage; Median gross rent: $1,700 per month; Rental vacancy rate: 3.0%
Health Insurance: 93.5% have insurance; 76.9% have private insurance; 26.5% have public insurance; 6.5% do not have insurance; 2.8% of children under 18 do not have insurance
Transportation: Commute: 90.9% car, 5.1% public transportation, 0.4% walk, 3.0% work from home; Mean travel time to work: 37.0 minutes

CUTCHOGUE (CDP).
Covers a land area of 9.723 square miles and a water area of 0.427 square miles. Located at 41.02° N. Lat; 72.49° W. Long. Elevation is 30 feet.

Population: 3,192; Growth (since 2000): 12.0%; Density: 328.3 persons per square mile; Race: 95.7% White, 1.0% Black/African American, 2.4% Asian, 0.0% American Indian/Alaska Native, 0.4% Native Hawaiian/Other Pacific Islander, 0.0% Two or more races, 2.3% Hispanic of any race; Average household size: 2.43; Median age: 51.6; Age under 18: 17.0%; Age 65 and over: 27.3%; Males per 100 females: 102.0; Marriage status: 25.5% never married, 61.1% now married, 2.2% separated, 5.7% widowed, 7.6% divorced; Foreign born: 9.9%; Speak English only: 88.6%; With disability: 10.6%; Veterans: 10.4%; Ancestry: 24.3% Irish, 19.5% Italian, 15.1% English, 14.8% German, 10.2% Polish

Employment: 16.1% management, business, and financial, 4.6% computer, engineering, and science, 15.3% education, legal, community service, arts, and media, 8.4% healthcare practitioners, 12.8% service, 20.0% sales and office, 14.4% natural resources, construction, and maintenance, 8.5% production, transportation, and material moving

Income: Per capita: $45,109; Median household: $86,344; Average household: $109,174; Households with income of $100,000 or more: 40.6%; Poverty rate: 3.3%

Educational Attainment: High school diploma or higher: 94.7%; Bachelor's degree or higher: 45.3%; Graduate/professional degree or higher: 18.6%

School District(s)
Mattituck-Cutchogue Union Free SD (KG-12)
  2014-15 Enrollment: 1,310 . . . . (631) 298-4242

Housing: Homeownership rate: 91.5%; Median home value: $490,000; Median year structure built: 1968; Homeowner vacancy rate: 0.0%; Median selected monthly owner costs: $2,555 with a mortgage, $978 without a mortgage; Median gross rent: $1,785 per month; Rental vacancy rate: 0.0%

Health Insurance: 94.7% have insurance; 84.8% have private insurance; 37.9% have public insurance; 5.3% do not have insurance; 0.0% of children under 18 do not have insurance

Transportation: Commute: 82.3% car, 5.6% public transportation, 2.8% walk, 9.3% work from home; Mean travel time to work: 32.2 minutes

DEER PARK (CDP).
Covers a land area of 6.168 square miles and a water area of 0.004 square miles. Located at 40.76° N. Lat; 73.32° W. Long. Elevation is 85 feet.

History: Deer Park is a residential hamlet located in the pine barrens in the northeast corner of the town of Babylon. It grew out of Jacob Conklin's 1610 settlement of the Half Way Hollow Hills, later Wheatley Heights. Charles Wilson founded Deer Park in 1853 about eleven years after the Long Island Rail Road arrived in 1842.

Population: 27,346; Growth (since 2000): -3.4%; Density: 4,433.8 persons per square mile; Race: 73.0% White, 12.6% Black/African American, 7.4% Asian, 0.0% American Indian/Alaska Native, 0.0% Native Hawaiian/Other Pacific Islander, 2.1% Two or more races, 14.3% Hispanic of any race; Average household size: 3.00; Median age: 40.4; Age under 18: 23.0%; Age 65 and over: 14.7%; Males per 100 females: 93.8; Marriage status: 32.5% never married, 52.3% now married, 2.7% separated, 7.5% widowed, 7.7% divorced; Foreign born: 15.9%; Speak English only: 75.4%; With disability: 10.9%; Veterans: 7.4%; Ancestry: 32.4% Italian, 16.4% Irish, 10.4% German, 4.2% American, 3.2% Polish

Employment: 11.2% management, business, and financial, 4.1% computer, engineering, and science, 13.4% education, legal, community service, arts, and media, 6.1% healthcare practitioners, 20.4% service, 25.1% sales and office, 8.9% natural resources, construction, and maintenance, 10.8% production, transportation, and material moving

Income: Per capita: $34,161; Median household: $83,287; Average household: $98,950; Households with income of $100,000 or more: 42.3%; Poverty rate: 5.6%

Educational Attainment: High school diploma or higher: 90.7%; Bachelor's degree or higher: 27.1%; Graduate/professional degree or higher: 10.5%

School District(s)
Deer Park Union Free SD (PK-12)
  2014-15 Enrollment: 4,280 . . . . (631) 274-4010

Housing: Homeownership rate: 82.9%; Median home value: $351,000; Median year structure built: 1963; Homeowner vacancy rate: 1.2%; Median selected monthly owner costs: $2,718 with a mortgage, $1,057 without a mortgage; Median gross rent: $1,527 per month; Rental vacancy rate: 2.1%

Health Insurance: 92.6% have insurance; 79.3% have private insurance; 26.3% have public insurance; 7.4% do not have insurance; 4.8% of children under 18 do not have insurance

Transportation: Commute: 88.0% car, 6.4% public transportation, 2.3% walk, 2.8% work from home; Mean travel time to work: 29.9 minutes

DERING HARBOR (village).
Covers a land area of 0.246 square miles and a water area of 0.013 square miles. Located at 41.09° N. Lat; 72.34° W. Long. Elevation is 7 feet.

Population: 6; Growth (since 2000): -53.8%; Density: 24.4 persons per square mile; Race: 100.0% White, 0.0% Black/African American, 0.0% Asian, 0.0% American Indian/Alaska Native, 0.0% Native Hawaiian/Other Pacific Islander, 0.0% Two or more races, 0.0% Hispanic of any race; Average household size: 2.00; Median age: 45.0; Age under 18: 0.0%; Age 65 and over: 50.0%; Males per 100 females: 120.0; Marriage status: 50.0% never married, 0.0% now married, 0.0% separated, 16.7% widowed, 33.3% divorced; Foreign born: 0.0%; Speak English only: 100.0%; With disability: 16.7%; Veterans: 0.0%; Ancestry: 100.0% English

Employment: n/a management, business, and financial, n/a computer, engineering, and science, n/a education, legal, community service, arts, and media, n/a healthcare practitioners, n/a service, n/a sales and office, n/a natural resources, construction, and maintenance, n/a production, transportation, and material moving

Income: Per capita: $57,367; Median household: n/a; Average household: n/a; Households with income of $100,000 or more: 66.7%; Poverty rate: n/a

Educational Attainment: High school diploma or higher: 100.0%; Bachelor's degree or higher: 100.0%; Graduate/professional degree or higher: 66.7%

Housing: Homeownership rate: 66.7%; Median home value: n/a; Median year structure built: Before 1940; Homeowner vacancy rate: 0.0%; Median selected monthly owner costs: n/a with a mortgage, n/a without a mortgage; Median gross rent: n/a per month; Rental vacancy rate: 0.0%

Health Insurance: 100.0% have insurance; 100.0% have private insurance; 50.0% have public insurance; 0.0% do not have insurance; 0.0% of children under 18 do not have insurance

Transportation: Commute: n/a car, n/a public transportation, n/a walk, n/a work from home; Mean travel time to work: 0.0 minutes

DIX HILLS (CDP).
Covers a land area of 15.946 square miles and a water area of 0 square miles. Located at 40.80° N. Lat; 73.34° W. Long. Elevation is 203 feet.

History: Settlers traded goods with the Secatogue tribe for land that became Dix Hills in 1699, originally called Dick's Hills. Lore has it that it was named for local native Dick Pechegan. Scholar William Wallace Tooker notes that the addition of the English name "Dick" to the indigenous name "Pechegan" was a common practice. The area was mostly used for farming until after World War II.

Population: 27,374; Growth (since 2000): 5.2%; Density: 1,716.6 persons per square mile; Race: 80.0% White, 4.8% Black/African American, 12.6% Asian, 0.1% American Indian/Alaska Native, 0.2% Native Hawaiian/Other Pacific Islander, 0.9% Two or more races, 5.8% Hispanic of any race; Average household size: 3.25; Median age: 43.6; Age under 18: 23.2%; Age 65 and over: 14.4%; Males per 100 females: 98.9; Marriage status: 29.3% never married, 62.5% now married, 0.7% separated, 4.4% widowed, 3.7% divorced; Foreign born: 17.1%; Speak English only: 78.2%; With disability: 6.2%; Veterans: 3.4%; Ancestry: 24.2% Italian, 13.8% Irish, 11.0% German, 7.4% Polish, 6.2% American

Employment: 20.9% management, business, and financial, 4.7% computer, engineering, and science, 14.4% education, legal, community service, arts, and media, 13.6% healthcare practitioners, 10.4% service, 27.3% sales and office, 3.0% natural resources, construction, and maintenance, 5.7% production, transportation, and material moving

Income: Per capita: $57,158; Median household: $141,250; Average household: $184,220; Households with income of $100,000 or more: 65.7%; Poverty rate: 2.6%

Educational Attainment: High school diploma or higher: 95.1%; Bachelor's degree or higher: 58.6%; Graduate/professional degree or higher: 28.8%

School District(s)
Commack Union Free SD (KG-12)
  2014-15 Enrollment: 6,842 . . . . (631) 912-2010
Half Hollow Hills Central SD (KG-12)
  2014-15 Enrollment: 8,927 . . . . (631) 592-3008

Western Suffolk Boces
  2014-15 Enrollment: n/a . . . . (631) 549-4900
Four-year College(s)
Five Towns College (Private, For-profit)
  Fall 2014 Enrollment: 687 . . . . (631) 424-7000
  2015-16 Tuition: In-state $21,500; Out-of-state $21,500
Housing: Homeownership rate: 93.4%; Median home value: $682,400; Median year structure built: 1968; Homeowner vacancy rate: 0.9%; Median selected monthly owner costs: $3,919 with a mortgage, $1,500+ without a mortgage; Median gross rent: $1,844 per month; Rental vacancy rate: 11.2%
Health Insurance: 95.9% have insurance; 87.6% have private insurance; 19.2% have public insurance; 4.1% do not have insurance; 1.9% of children under 18 do not have insurance
Transportation: Commute: 83.7% car, 9.8% public transportation, 0.7% walk, 5.4% work from home; Mean travel time to work: 35.9 minutes

EAST FARMINGDALE (CDP).
Covers a land area of 5.715 square miles and a water area of 0.020 square miles. Located at 40.73° N. Lat; 73.42° W. Long. Elevation is 69 feet.
History: East Farmingdale's first European settler was Thomas Powell, who arrived in 1687. On October 18, 1695, he purchased a 15-square-mile tract of land from three Native American tribes, known as the Bethpage Purchase.
Population: 6,414; Growth (since 2000): 18.8%; Density: 1,122.3 persons per square mile; Race: 62.8% White, 13.2% Black/African American, 6.4% Asian, 0.0% American Indian/Alaska Native, 0.0% Native Hawaiian/Other Pacific Islander, 6.1% Two or more races, 24.2% Hispanic of any race; Average household size: 3.11; Median age: 34.0; Age under 18: 21.6%; Age 65 and over: 12.1%; Males per 100 females: 100.9; Marriage status: 38.0% never married, 49.5% now married, 1.7% separated, 6.2% widowed, 6.3% divorced; Foreign born: 24.7%; Speak English only: 71.1%; With disability: 6.5%; Veterans: 3.8%; Ancestry: 26.0% Italian, 11.0% Irish, 10.2% German, 5.2% Polish, 2.7% Guyanese
Employment: 13.2% management, business, and financial, 5.3% computer, engineering, and science, 8.2% education, legal, community service, arts, and media, 4.9% healthcare practitioners, 14.5% service, 35.1% sales and office, 11.3% natural resources, construction, and maintenance, 7.6% production, transportation, and material moving
Income: Per capita: $32,320; Median household: $80,317; Average household: $104,160; Households with income of $100,000 or more: 40.8%; Poverty rate: 7.0%
Educational Attainment: High school diploma or higher: 87.9%; Bachelor's degree or higher: 32.4%; Graduate/professional degree or higher: 9.9%
Housing: Homeownership rate: 66.7%; Median home value: $392,500; Median year structure built: 1968; Homeowner vacancy rate: 0.8%; Median selected monthly owner costs: $2,923 with a mortgage, $1,085 without a mortgage; Median gross rent: $1,482 per month; Rental vacancy rate: 8.7%
Health Insurance: 88.7% have insurance; 73.3% have private insurance; 24.6% have public insurance; 11.3% do not have insurance; 2.6% of children under 18 do not have insurance
Transportation: Commute: 77.8% car, 9.4% public transportation, 4.6% walk, 4.7% work from home; Mean travel time to work: 29.8 minutes

EAST HAMPTON (town).
Covers a land area of 74.328 square miles and a water area of 312.224 square miles. Located at 41.09° N. Lat; 72.11° W. Long. Elevation is 33 feet.
History: Birthplace of John Howard Payne, whose home is now a museum. The village has 3 historic districts containing other significant buildings. Settled 1648, incorporated 1920.
Population: 21,844; Growth (since 2000): 10.8%; Density: 293.9 persons per square mile; Race: 90.3% White, 3.7% Black/African American, 2.8% Asian, 1.1% American Indian/Alaska Native, 0.0% Native Hawaiian/Other Pacific Islander, 0.8% Two or more races, 15.7% Hispanic of any race; Average household size: 2.30; Median age: 50.5; Age under 18: 17.1%; Age 65 and over: 23.8%; Males per 100 females: 101.5; Marriage status: 28.1% never married, 56.8% now married, 0.9% separated, 7.4% widowed, 7.8% divorced; Foreign born: 18.5%; Speak English only: 76.6%; With disability: 9.0%; Veterans: 7.4%; Ancestry: 16.4% Irish, 13.8% German, 13.3% Italian, 10.1% English, 5.4% American
Employment: 16.0% management, business, and financial, 3.3% computer, engineering, and science, 15.7% education, legal, community service, arts, and media, 3.8% healthcare practitioners, 19.2% service,

24.3% sales and office, 14.0% natural resources, construction, and maintenance, 3.7% production, transportation, and material moving
Income: Per capita: $56,135; Median household: $81,715; Average household: $128,130; Households with income of $100,000 or more: 40.9%; Poverty rate: 8.6%
Educational Attainment: High school diploma or higher: 93.1%; Bachelor's degree or higher: 47.3%; Graduate/professional degree or higher: 20.9%
School District(s)
East Hampton Union Free SD (KG-12)
  2014-15 Enrollment: 1,835 . . . . (631) 329-4104
Springs Union Free SD (PK-08)
  2014-15 Enrollment: 741 . . . . (631) 324-0144
Housing: Homeownership rate: 80.6%; Median home value: $812,700; Median year structure built: 1978; Homeowner vacancy rate: 2.0%; Median selected monthly owner costs: $2,924 with a mortgage, $1,006 without a mortgage; Median gross rent: $1,598 per month; Rental vacancy rate: 10.4%
Health Insurance: 89.2% have insurance; 77.9% have private insurance; 30.2% have public insurance; 10.8% do not have insurance; 7.1% of children under 18 do not have insurance
Safety: Violent crime rate: 4.5 per 10,000 population; Property crime rate: 147.4 per 10,000 population
Newspapers: East Hampton Star (weekly circulation 15,000); The Independent (weekly circulation 25,000)
Transportation: Commute: 78.8% car, 7.8% public transportation, 3.8% walk, 8.4% work from home; Mean travel time to work: 25.5 minutes
Airports: East Hampton (general aviation)
Additional Information Contacts
Town of East Hampton . . . . (631) 324-4141
  http://www.town.east-hampton.ny.us

EAST HAMPTON (village).
Covers a land area of 4.764 square miles and a water area of 0.138 square miles. Located at 40.95° N. Lat; 72.20° W. Long. Elevation is 33 feet.
Population: 1,148; Growth (since 2000): -13.9%; Density: 241.0 persons per square mile; Race: 97.1% White, 0.3% Black/African American, 1.1% Asian, 0.0% American Indian/Alaska Native, 0.0% Native Hawaiian/Other Pacific Islander, 1.4% Two or more races, 5.1% Hispanic of any race; Average household size: 1.94; Median age: 62.2; Age under 18: 10.5%; Age 65 and over: 43.4%; Males per 100 females: 90.7; Marriage status: 21.8% never married, 53.1% now married, 0.0% separated, 10.3% widowed, 14.9% divorced; Foreign born: 15.2%; Speak English only: 84.6%; With disability: 12.0%; Veterans: 8.9%; Ancestry: 19.6% English, 17.1% German, 14.0% Italian, 12.0% Irish, 7.3% Scottish
Employment: 25.0% management, business, and financial, 2.4% computer, engineering, and science, 20.0% education, legal, community service, arts, and media, 2.4% healthcare practitioners, 13.4% service, 28.2% sales and office, 7.5% natural resources, construction, and maintenance, 1.0% production, transportation, and material moving
Income: Per capita: $111,439; Median household: $104,531; Average household: $214,897; Households with income of $100,000 or more: 53.1%; Poverty rate: 4.7%
Educational Attainment: High school diploma or higher: 96.5%; Bachelor's degree or higher: 63.4%; Graduate/professional degree or higher: 30.7%
School District(s)
East Hampton Union Free SD (KG-12)
  2014-15 Enrollment: 1,835 . . . . (631) 329-4104
Springs Union Free SD (PK-08)
  2014-15 Enrollment: 741 . . . . (631) 324-0144
Housing: Homeownership rate: 74.5%; Median home value: $1,567,700; Median year structure built: 1954; Homeowner vacancy rate: 5.6%; Median selected monthly owner costs: $4,000+ with a mortgage, $1,269 without a mortgage; Median gross rent: $1,985 per month; Rental vacancy rate: 15.5%
Health Insurance: 92.1% have insurance; 82.1% have private insurance; 43.6% have public insurance; 7.9% do not have insurance; 0.0% of children under 18 do not have insurance
Safety: Violent crime rate: 0.0 per 10,000 population; Property crime rate: 464.3 per 10,000 population
Newspapers: East Hampton Star (weekly circulation 15,000); The Independent (weekly circulation 25,000)
Transportation: Commute: 61.0% car, 10.9% public transportation, 15.3% walk, 8.5% work from home; Mean travel time to work: 20.6 minutes

Airports: East Hampton (general aviation)

EAST HAMPTON NORTH (CDP). Covers a land area of 5.639 square miles and a water area of 0 square miles. Located at 40.97° N. Lat; 72.19° W. Long.

Population: 3,979; Growth (since 2000): 10.9%; Density: 705.6 persons per square mile; Race: 92.6% White, 6.2% Black/African American, 0.0% Asian, 0.0% American Indian/Alaska Native, 0.0% Native Hawaiian/Other Pacific Islander, 0.4% Two or more races, 26.2% Hispanic of any race; Average household size: 2.39; Median age: 43.5; Age under 18: 22.3%; Age 65 and over: 16.5%; Males per 100 females: 99.3; Marriage status: 37.1% never married, 51.2% now married, 1.9% separated, 4.4% widowed, 7.3% divorced; Foreign born: 24.4%; Speak English only: 68.4%; With disability: 9.6%; Veterans: 3.8%; Ancestry: 17.4% Irish, 11.6% Italian, 10.4% German, 8.8% English, 6.9% French

Employment: 12.3% management, business, and financial, 3.6% computer, engineering, and science, 18.6% education, legal, community service, arts, and media, 3.0% healthcare practitioners, 15.2% service, 13.8% sales and office, 27.7% natural resources, construction, and maintenance, 5.8% production, transportation, and material moving

Income: Per capita: $48,075; Median household: $61,523; Average household: $114,445; Households with income of $100,000 or more: 42.5%; Poverty rate: 9.2%

Educational Attainment: High school diploma or higher: 86.2%; Bachelor's degree or higher: 36.5%; Graduate/professional degree or higher: 16.1%

Housing: Homeownership rate: 66.4%; Median home value: $742,300; Median year structure built: 1982; Homeowner vacancy rate: 0.0%; Median selected monthly owner costs: $2,892 with a mortgage, $1,172 without a mortgage; Median gross rent: $1,228 per month; Rental vacancy rate: 0.0%

Health Insurance: 82.8% have insurance; 72.4% have private insurance; 22.3% have public insurance; 17.2% do not have insurance; 1.8% of children under 18 do not have insurance

Transportation: Commute: 90.6% car, 1.4% public transportation, 1.6% walk, 6.3% work from home; Mean travel time to work: 18.1 minutes

EAST ISLIP (CDP). Covers a land area of 3.950 square miles and a water area of 0.109 square miles. Located at 40.73° N. Lat; 73.19° W. Long. Elevation is 16 feet.

History: Originally referred to as "East of Islip", the town was named in 1890 by William Nicoll, an English aristocrat who purchased the surrounding land in 1683 to build a family residence.

Population: 13,802; Growth (since 2000): -2.0%; Density: 3,494.3 persons per square mile; Race: 97.4% White, 1.6% Black/African American, 0.2% Asian, 0.0% American Indian/Alaska Native, 0.0% Native Hawaiian/Other Pacific Islander, 0.6% Two or more races, 4.6% Hispanic of any race; Average household size: 3.11; Median age: 41.7; Age under 18: 24.0%; Age 65 and over: 13.4%; Males per 100 females: 96.2; Marriage status: 30.0% never married, 55.1% now married, 1.9% separated, 8.0% widowed, 6.8% divorced; Foreign born: 2.2%; Speak English only: 94.4%; With disability: 8.2%; Veterans: 6.6%; Ancestry: 39.7% Italian, 34.0% Irish, 21.6% German, 5.5% Polish, 4.9% English

Employment: 19.8% management, business, and financial, 4.0% computer, engineering, and science, 18.8% education, legal, community service, arts, and media, 5.7% healthcare practitioners, 12.0% service, 21.5% sales and office, 11.6% natural resources, construction, and maintenance, 6.6% production, transportation, and material moving

Income: Per capita: $42,514; Median household: $115,432; Average household: $130,139; Households with income of $100,000 or more: 57.2%; Poverty rate: 5.3%

Educational Attainment: High school diploma or higher: 94.2%; Bachelor's degree or higher: 39.4%; Graduate/professional degree or higher: 19.8%

School District(s)

East Islip Union Free SD (PK-12)

   2014-15 Enrollment: 3,985 . . . . (631) 224-2000

Housing: Homeownership rate: 90.1%; Median home value: $400,400; Median year structure built: 1958; Homeowner vacancy rate: 0.7%; Median selected monthly owner costs: $2,868 with a mortgage, $1,263 without a mortgage; Median gross rent: $1,550 per month; Rental vacancy rate: 12.4%

Health Insurance: 96.6% have insurance; 90.6% have private insurance; 15.8% have public insurance; 3.4% do not have insurance; 3.1% of children under 18 do not have insurance

Transportation: Commute: 88.1% car, 7.2% public transportation, 1.1% walk, 2.5% work from home; Mean travel time to work: 34.4 minutes

EAST MARION (CDP). Covers a land area of 2.238 square miles and a water area of 0.128 square miles. Located at 41.13° N. Lat; 72.35° W. Long. Elevation is 33 feet.

Population: 915; Growth (since 2000): 21.0%; Density: 408.8 persons per square mile; Race: 96.8% White, 0.0% Black/African American, 0.4% Asian, 0.0% American Indian/Alaska Native, 0.0% Native Hawaiian/Other Pacific Islander, 2.7% Two or more races, 3.6% Hispanic of any race; Average household size: 1.98; Median age: 62.4; Age under 18: 5.8%; Age 65 and over: 43.2%; Males per 100 females: 102.2; Marriage status: 18.5% never married, 56.3% now married, 0.0% separated, 16.0% widowed, 9.2% divorced; Foreign born: 13.1%; Speak English only: 85.5%; With disability: 18.6%; Veterans: 16.7%; Ancestry: 18.1% German, 15.8% Irish, 15.0% Italian, 14.2% English, 10.3% Greek

Employment: 8.0% management, business, and financial, 4.3% computer, engineering, and science, 13.8% education, legal, community service, arts, and media, 6.9% healthcare practitioners, 28.2% service, 16.2% sales and office, 20.2% natural resources, construction, and maintenance, 2.4% production, transportation, and material moving

Income: Per capita: $46,622; Median household: $72,500; Average household: $90,271; Households with income of $100,000 or more: 37.7%; Poverty rate: 1.6%

Educational Attainment: High school diploma or higher: 93.1%; Bachelor's degree or higher: 35.1%; Graduate/professional degree or higher: 18.4%

Housing: Homeownership rate: 89.8%; Median home value: $490,000; Median year structure built: 1974; Homeowner vacancy rate: 5.4%; Median selected monthly owner costs: $2,511 with a mortgage, $778 without a mortgage; Median gross rent: $1,717 per month; Rental vacancy rate: 43.4%

Health Insurance: 85.8% have insurance; 68.7% have private insurance; 46.8% have public insurance; 14.2% do not have insurance; 0.0% of children under 18 do not have insurance

Transportation: Commute: 74.2% car, 3.5% public transportation, 2.4% walk, 19.9% work from home; Mean travel time to work: 31.9 minutes

EAST MORICHES (CDP). Covers a land area of 5.477 square miles and a water area of 0.149 square miles. Located at 40.81° N. Lat; 72.76° W. Long. Elevation is 30 feet.

History: East Moriches is a hamlet (and census-designated place) in Suffolk County, New York. The name Moriches comes from Meritces, a Native American who owned land on Moriches Neck.

Population: 5,428; Growth (since 2000): 19.3%; Density: 991.1 persons per square mile; Race: 96.5% White, 2.5% Black/African American, 0.3% Asian, 0.1% American Indian/Alaska Native, 0.0% Native Hawaiian/Other Pacific Islander, 0.3% Two or more races, 5.1% Hispanic of any race; Average household size: 2.75; Median age: 43.2; Age under 18: 19.8%; Age 65 and over: 14.0%; Males per 100 females: 96.4; Marriage status: 31.1% never married, 54.3% now married, 1.2% separated, 5.9% widowed, 8.7% divorced; Foreign born: 2.0%; Speak English only: 94.2%; With disability: 8.2%; Veterans: 5.1%; Ancestry: 31.2% Italian, 27.6% Irish, 17.3% German, 11.1% English, 5.4% Polish

Employment: 16.2% management, business, and financial, 4.0% computer, engineering, and science, 11.0% education, legal, community service, arts, and media, 7.2% healthcare practitioners, 17.5% service, 24.2% sales and office, 14.0% natural resources, construction, and maintenance, 5.9% production, transportation, and material moving

Income: Per capita: $42,169; Median household: $96,685; Average household: $116,099; Households with income of $100,000 or more: 47.7%; Poverty rate: 5.8%

Educational Attainment: High school diploma or higher: 95.6%; Bachelor's degree or higher: 33.6%; Graduate/professional degree or higher: 17.2%

School District(s)

East Moriches Union Free SD (KG-08)

   2014-15 Enrollment: 755 . . . . (631) 878-0162

Housing: Homeownership rate: 76.1%; Median home value: $392,000; Median year structure built: 1983; Homeowner vacancy rate: 0.0%; Median selected monthly owner costs: $2,884 with a mortgage, $1,260 without a mortgage; Median gross rent: $1,762 per month; Rental vacancy rate: 1.5%

Health Insurance: 94.7% have insurance; 86.8% have private insurance; 18.2% have public insurance; 5.3% do not have insurance; 0.0% of children under 18 do not have insurance
Transportation: Commute: 90.7% car, 2.8% public transportation, 1.2% walk, 5.3% work from home; Mean travel time to work: 34.1 minutes

EAST NORTHPORT (CDP). Covers a land area of 5.161 square miles and a water area of 0 square miles. Located at 40.88° N. Lat; 73.32° W. Long. Elevation is 223 feet.

History: On July 30, 1656, land was purchased from Chief Asharoken, head of the Matinecocks Native American tribe, part of which is known today as East Northport.
Population: 19,682; Growth (since 2000): -5.6%; Density: 3,813.6 persons per square mile; Race: 94.7% White, 1.3% Black/African American, 1.8% Asian, 0.1% American Indian/Alaska Native, 0.1% Native Hawaiian/Other Pacific Islander, 1.0% Two or more races, 7.5% Hispanic of any race; Average household size: 2.79; Median age: 43.9; Age under 18: 22.4%; Age 65 and over: 14.1%; Males per 100 females: 97.8; Marriage status: 29.7% never married, 57.4% now married, 1.7% separated, 5.8% widowed, 7.1% divorced; Foreign born: 7.8%; Speak English only: 89.5%; With disability: 8.1%; Veterans: 7.2%; Ancestry: 31.3% Italian, 27.2% Irish, 20.4% German, 6.1% Polish, 6.0% English
Employment: 17.0% management, business, and financial, 4.5% computer, engineering, and science, 15.4% education, legal, community service, arts, and media, 5.5% healthcare practitioners, 16.5% service, 27.0% sales and office, 8.2% natural resources, construction, and maintenance, 6.0% production, transportation, and material moving
Income: Per capita: $38,606; Median household: $92,899; Average household: $105,250; Households with income of $100,000 or more: 45.9%; Poverty rate: 4.8%
Educational Attainment: High school diploma or higher: 95.1%; Bachelor's degree or higher: 44.4%; Graduate/professional degree or higher: 19.0%

School District(s)
Northport-East Northport Union Free SD (KG-12)
    2014-15 Enrollment: 5,746 . . . . (631) 262-6604
Housing: Homeownership rate: 83.0%; Median home value: $438,100; Median year structure built: 1958; Homeowner vacancy rate: 0.1%; Median selected monthly owner costs: $2,717 with a mortgage, $1,087 without a mortgage; Median gross rent: $1,714 per month; Rental vacancy rate: 0.0%
Health Insurance: 95.4% have insurance; 83.7% have private insurance; 26.9% have public insurance; 4.6% do not have insurance; 0.0% of children under 18 do not have insurance
Transportation: Commute: 85.2% car, 7.7% public transportation, 0.5% walk, 5.5% work from home; Mean travel time to work: 32.2 minutes

EAST PATCHOGUE (CDP). Covers a land area of 8.346 square miles and a water area of 0.131 square miles. Located at 40.77° N. Lat; 72.98° W. Long. Elevation is 23 feet.

History: Patchogue is a village on the south shore of Long Island in Suffolk County, New York.
Population: 22,452; Growth (since 2000): 7.8%; Density: 2,690.2 persons per square mile; Race: 91.9% White, 3.2% Black/African American, 2.1% Asian, 0.0% American Indian/Alaska Native, 0.1% Native Hawaiian/Other Pacific Islander, 1.7% Two or more races, 21.4% Hispanic of any race; Average household size: 2.63; Median age: 42.2; Age under 18: 20.6%; Age 65 and over: 17.2%; Males per 100 females: 95.3; Marriage status: 31.1% never married, 49.7% now married, 3.1% separated, 8.0% widowed, 11.2% divorced; Foreign born: 12.5%; Speak English only: 77.0%; With disability: 12.0%; Veterans: 7.4%; Ancestry: 29.2% Italian, 23.6% Irish, 16.2% German, 4.8% English, 3.6% Polish
Employment: 11.1% management, business, and financial, 5.1% computer, engineering, and science, 12.4% education, legal, community service, arts, and media, 6.9% healthcare practitioners, 15.4% service, 25.6% sales and office, 13.0% natural resources, construction, and maintenance, 10.5% production, transportation, and material moving
Income: Per capita: $32,844; Median household: $68,366; Average household: $84,292; Households with income of $100,000 or more: 33.3%; Poverty rate: 9.8%
Educational Attainment: High school diploma or higher: 86.5%; Bachelor's degree or higher: 24.1%; Graduate/professional degree or higher: 10.6%

School District(s)
South Country Central SD (PK-12)
    2014-15 Enrollment: 4,632 . . . . (631) 730-1510
Housing: Homeownership rate: 60.3%; Median home value: $312,400; Median year structure built: 1971; Homeowner vacancy rate: 1.2%; Median selected monthly owner costs: $2,560 with a mortgage, $1,042 without a mortgage; Median gross rent: $1,376 per month; Rental vacancy rate: 2.2%
Health Insurance: 87.3% have insurance; 73.9% have private insurance; 29.3% have public insurance; 12.7% do not have insurance; 5.4% of children under 18 do not have insurance
Transportation: Commute: 90.7% car, 3.4% public transportation, 1.2% walk, 3.9% work from home; Mean travel time to work: 29.2 minutes

EAST QUOGUE (CDP). Covers a land area of 8.874 square miles and a water area of 2.685 square miles. Located at 40.85° N. Lat; 72.58° W. Long. Elevation is 13 feet.

History: East Quogue, originally settled in 1673 as Fourth Neck, is a hamlet and census-designated place (CDP) in Suffolk County, New York.
Population: 4,589; Growth (since 2000): 7.6%; Density: 517.1 persons per square mile; Race: 94.2% White, 0.3% Black/African American, 0.8% Asian, 0.6% American Indian/Alaska Native, 0.0% Native Hawaiian/Other Pacific Islander, 2.7% Two or more races, 4.1% Hispanic of any race; Average household size: 2.67; Median age: 46.1; Age under 18: 25.6%; Age 65 and over: 17.3%; Males per 100 females: 96.4; Marriage status: 23.0% never married, 64.5% now married, 0.8% separated, 4.7% widowed, 7.7% divorced; Foreign born: 5.6%; Speak English only: 93.2%; With disability: 7.8%; Veterans: 8.9%; Ancestry: 31.9% Irish, 27.2% Italian, 15.8% German, 10.8% Polish, 5.8% English
Employment: 17.8% management, business, and financial, 2.5% computer, engineering, and science, 16.8% education, legal, community service, arts, and media, 6.3% healthcare practitioners, 15.2% service, 25.1% sales and office, 11.3% natural resources, construction, and maintenance, 5.0% production, transportation, and material moving
Income: Per capita: $44,013; Median household: $88,953; Average household: $115,332; Households with income of $100,000 or more: 46.0%; Poverty rate: 3.1%
Educational Attainment: High school diploma or higher: 96.6%; Bachelor's degree or higher: 39.8%; Graduate/professional degree or higher: 22.3%

School District(s)
East Quogue Union Free SD (KG-06)
    2014-15 Enrollment: 432 . . . . (631) 653-5210
Housing: Homeownership rate: 87.4%; Median home value: $473,600; Median year structure built: 1975; Homeowner vacancy rate: 3.8%; Median selected monthly owner costs: $2,662 with a mortgage, $861 without a mortgage; Median gross rent: $1,793 per month; Rental vacancy rate: 10.7%
Health Insurance: 96.0% have insurance; 83.9% have private insurance; 27.3% have public insurance; 4.0% do not have insurance; 0.9% of children under 18 do not have insurance
Transportation: Commute: 90.7% car, 4.0% public transportation, 1.5% walk, 3.3% work from home; Mean travel time to work: 29.9 minutes

EAST SHOREHAM (CDP). Covers a land area of 5.367 square miles and a water area of 0 square miles. Located at 40.95° N. Lat; 72.88° W. Long. Elevation is 121 feet.

Population: 6,455; Growth (since 2000): 11.1%; Density: 1,202.7 persons per square mile; Race: 96.1% White, 0.5% Black/African American, 2.2% Asian, 0.0% American Indian/Alaska Native, 0.0% Native Hawaiian/Other Pacific Islander, 1.0% Two or more races, 9.4% Hispanic of any race; Average household size: 3.18; Median age: 41.4; Age under 18: 26.4%; Age 65 and over: 12.1%; Males per 100 females: 101.8; Marriage status: 25.6% never married, 65.2% now married, 0.7% separated, 3.1% widowed, 6.0% divorced; Foreign born: 8.4%; Speak English only: 91.4%; With disability: 6.6%; Veterans: 6.5%; Ancestry: 30.4% Irish, 27.5% Italian, 22.0% German, 9.8% American, 7.3% Polish
Employment: 11.1% management, business, and financial, 6.2% computer, engineering, and science, 18.5% education, legal, community service, arts, and media, 11.0% healthcare practitioners, 15.5% service, 24.1% sales and office, 4.8% natural resources, construction, and maintenance, 8.8% production, transportation, and material moving
Income: Per capita: $40,072; Median household: $119,628; Average household: $125,780; Households with income of $100,000 or more: 65.4%; Poverty rate: 3.1%

Educational Attainment: High school diploma or higher: 95.4%; Bachelor's degree or higher: 44.9%; Graduate/professional degree or higher: 26.7%

Housing: Homeownership rate: 93.8%; Median home value: $410,200; Median year structure built: 1974; Homeowner vacancy rate: 0.0%; Median selected monthly owner costs: $2,910 with a mortgage, $1,424 without a mortgage; Median gross rent: $2,019 per month; Rental vacancy rate: 20.0%

Health Insurance: 97.4% have insurance; 92.2% have private insurance; 17.3% have public insurance; 2.6% do not have insurance; 0.6% of children under 18 do not have insurance

Transportation: Commute: 94.9% car, 2.4% public transportation, 0.5% walk, 2.1% work from home; Mean travel time to work: 36.5 minutes

---

EASTPORT (CDP). Covers a land area of 5.258 square miles and a water area of 0.130 square miles. Located at 40.84° N. Lat; 72.73° W. Long. Elevation is 30 feet.

Population: 1,869; Growth (since 2000): 28.5%; Density: 355.4 persons per square mile; Race: 96.7% White, 0.0% Black/African American, 2.2% Asian, 0.0% American Indian/Alaska Native, 0.0% Native Hawaiian/Other Pacific Islander, 0.7% Two or more races, 10.5% Hispanic of any race; Average household size: 2.46; Median age: 49.2; Age under 18: 12.9%; Age 65 and over: 24.9%; Males per 100 females: 99.2; Marriage status: 25.0% never married, 65.7% now married, 0.6% separated, 3.0% widowed, 6.3% divorced; Foreign born: 10.4%; Speak English only: 87.7%; With disability: 15.2%; Veterans: 11.7%; Ancestry: 24.9% German, 23.1% Irish, 17.5% Italian, 12.3% English, 7.0% American

Employment: 13.0% management, business, and financial, 1.5% computer, engineering, and science, 6.8% education, legal, community service, arts, and media, 9.7% healthcare practitioners, 29.8% service, 17.4% sales and office, 16.5% natural resources, construction, and maintenance, 5.3% production, transportation, and material moving

Income: Per capita: $41,560; Median household: $100,521; Average household: $105,883; Households with income of $100,000 or more: 50.7%; Poverty rate: 6.8%

Educational Attainment: High school diploma or higher: 94.2%; Bachelor's degree or higher: 39.0%; Graduate/professional degree or higher: 11.5%

School District(s)

Eastport-South Manor CSD (KG-12)
   2014-15 Enrollment: 3,623 . . . . (631) 801-3011

Housing: Homeownership rate: 72.8%; Median home value: $522,600; Median year structure built: 1983; Homeowner vacancy rate: 0.0%; Median selected monthly owner costs: $2,947 with a mortgage, $1,189 without a mortgage; Median gross rent: $1,438 per month; Rental vacancy rate: 0.0%

Health Insurance: 89.5% have insurance; 75.6% have private insurance; 33.4% have public insurance; 10.5% do not have insurance; 0.0% of children under 18 do not have insurance

Transportation: Commute: 79.1% car, 2.4% public transportation, 8.3% walk, 10.2% work from home; Mean travel time to work: 31.7 minutes

---

EATONS NECK (CDP). Covers a land area of 1.005 square miles and a water area of 0 square miles. Located at 40.93° N. Lat; 73.39° W. Long. Elevation is 16 feet.

Population: 1,469; Growth (since 2000): 5.8%; Density: 1,462.3 persons per square mile; Race: 94.3% White, 0.4% Black/African American, 2.9% Asian, 0.0% American Indian/Alaska Native, 0.0% Native Hawaiian/Other Pacific Islander, 2.5% Two or more races, 4.4% Hispanic of any race; Average household size: 2.80; Median age: 47.4; Age under 18: 20.1%; Age 65 and over: 21.0%; Males per 100 females: 96.1; Marriage status: 26.5% never married, 63.3% now married, 0.3% separated, 3.8% widowed, 6.4% divorced; Foreign born: 6.4%; Speak English only: 88.2%; With disability: 9.7%; Veterans: 8.6%; Ancestry: 26.2% Irish, 23.8% German, 23.2% Italian, 8.4% American, 6.9% English

Employment: 18.4% management, business, and financial, 5.1% computer, engineering, and science, 21.7% education, legal, community service, arts, and media, 8.9% healthcare practitioners, 5.7% service, 30.1% sales and office, 5.6% natural resources, construction, and maintenance, 4.5% production, transportation, and material moving

Income: Per capita: $56,510; Median household: $123,971; Average household: $156,427; Households with income of $100,000 or more: 55.0%; Poverty rate: 3.6%

Educational Attainment: High school diploma or higher: 99.3%; Bachelor's degree or higher: 62.3%; Graduate/professional degree or higher: 31.9%

Housing: Homeownership rate: 100.0%; Median home value: $672,500; Median year structure built: 1964; Homeowner vacancy rate: 0.0%; Median selected monthly owner costs: $3,492 with a mortgage, $1,355 without a mortgage; Median gross rent: n/a per month; Rental vacancy rate: 0.0%

Health Insurance: 99.2% have insurance; 93.3% have private insurance; 22.9% have public insurance; 0.8% do not have insurance; 0.0% of children under 18 do not have insurance

Transportation: Commute: 82.6% car, 7.7% public transportation, 2.2% walk, 6.3% work from home; Mean travel time to work: 45.7 minutes

---

ELWOOD (CDP). Covers a land area of 4.782 square miles and a water area of 0 square miles. Located at 40.85° N. Lat; 73.34° W. Long. Elevation is 184 feet.

Population: 10,941; Growth (since 2000): 0.2%; Density: 2,288.1 persons per square mile; Race: 77.3% White, 6.8% Black/African American, 11.3% Asian, 0.0% American Indian/Alaska Native, 0.0% Native Hawaiian/Other Pacific Islander, 1.2% Two or more races, 8.0% Hispanic of any race; Average household size: 3.03; Median age: 43.1; Age under 18: 25.5%; Age 65 and over: 16.8%; Males per 100 females: 94.0; Marriage status: 26.8% never married, 62.7% now married, 0.8% separated, 3.9% widowed, 6.6% divorced; Foreign born: 14.7%; Speak English only: 83.6%; With disability: 9.5%; Veterans: 6.5%; Ancestry: 29.8% Italian, 21.7% Irish, 14.2% German, 6.1% English, 5.5% Polish

Employment: 20.7% management, business, and financial, 7.3% computer, engineering, and science, 14.7% education, legal, community service, arts, and media, 7.4% healthcare practitioners, 13.2% service, 25.3% sales and office, 4.3% natural resources, construction, and maintenance, 7.0% production, transportation, and material moving

Income: Per capita: $45,095; Median household: $104,476; Average household: $134,958; Households with income of $100,000 or more: 52.7%; Poverty rate: 4.3%

Educational Attainment: High school diploma or higher: 92.2%; Bachelor's degree or higher: 46.5%; Graduate/professional degree or higher: 18.6%

School District(s)

Elwood Union Free SD (KG-12)
   2014-15 Enrollment: 2,354 . . . . (631) 266-5400

Housing: Homeownership rate: 92.0%; Median home value: $487,100; Median year structure built: 1964; Homeowner vacancy rate: 0.6%; Median selected monthly owner costs: $3,375 with a mortgage, $1,369 without a mortgage; Median gross rent: $2,059 per month; Rental vacancy rate: 0.0%

Health Insurance: 95.6% have insurance; 82.3% have private insurance; 26.4% have public insurance; 4.4% do not have insurance; 3.3% of children under 18 do not have insurance

Transportation: Commute: 82.7% car, 8.7% public transportation, 0.0% walk, 5.8% work from home; Mean travel time to work: 31.5 minutes

---

FARMINGVILLE (CDP). Covers a land area of 4.124 square miles and a water area of 0 square miles. Located at 40.84° N. Lat; 73.04° W. Long. Elevation is 105 feet.

Population: 15,690; Growth (since 2000): -4.7%; Density: 3,804.6 persons per square mile; Race: 89.9% White, 1.1% Black/African American, 4.4% Asian, 0.0% American Indian/Alaska Native, 0.0% Native Hawaiian/Other Pacific Islander, 1.9% Two or more races, 14.6% Hispanic of any race; Average household size: 3.29; Median age: 38.6; Age under 18: 22.9%; Age 65 and over: 11.3%; Males per 100 females: 99.7; Marriage status: 31.0% never married, 57.8% now married, 1.6% separated, 5.3% widowed, 5.9% divorced; Foreign born: 10.9%; Speak English only: 78.8%; With disability: 8.2%; Veterans: 6.4%; Ancestry: 29.5% Italian, 22.5% Irish, 16.6% German, 5.6% English, 3.9% Polish

Employment: 14.9% management, business, and financial, 5.5% computer, engineering, and science, 7.9% education, legal, community service, arts, and media, 5.0% healthcare practitioners, 17.7% service, 27.7% sales and office, 10.6% natural resources, construction, and maintenance, 10.6% production, transportation, and material moving

Income: Per capita: $33,917; Median household: $95,953; Average household: $107,790; Households with income of $100,000 or more: 46.5%; Poverty rate: 5.6%

Educational Attainment: High school diploma or higher: 92.1%; Bachelor's degree or higher: 23.6%; Graduate/professional degree or higher: 8.5%

Sachem Central SD (KG-12)

    2014-15 Enrollment: 13,882 . . . . (631) 471-1336

Housing: Homeownership rate: 88.1%; Median home value: $332,500; Median year structure built: 1971; Homeowner vacancy rate: 2.3%; Median selected monthly owner costs: $2,544 with a mortgage, $1,088 without a mortgage; Median gross rent: $1,940 per month; Rental vacancy rate: 9.9%

Health Insurance: 89.9% have insurance; 77.6% have private insurance; 22.4% have public insurance; 10.1% do not have insurance; 6.6% of children under 18 do not have insurance

Transportation: Commute: 93.3% car, 3.1% public transportation, 0.1% walk, 2.4% work from home; Mean travel time to work: 31.9 minutes

FIRE ISLAND (CDP). Covers a land area of 9.226 square miles and a water area of 29.044 square miles. Located at 40.64° N. Lat; 73.20° W. Long. Elevation is 3 feet.

Population: 298; Growth (since 2000): -3.9%; Density: 32.3 persons per square mile; Race: 88.9% White, 3.0% Black/African American, 3.7% Asian, 0.0% American Indian/Alaska Native, 0.0% Native Hawaiian/Other Pacific Islander, 1.7% Two or more races, 20.1% Hispanic of any race; Average household size: 2.87; Median age: 36.8; Age under 18: 26.5%; Age 65 and over: 13.1%; Males per 100 females: 121.2; Marriage status: 32.3% never married, 58.8% now married, 0.4% separated, 4.0% widowed, 4.9% divorced; Foreign born: 18.8%; Speak English only: 72.0%; With disability: 12.8%; Veterans: 10.0%; Ancestry: 12.1% English, 11.4% American, 10.7% Irish, 8.7% Italian, 6.4% German

Employment: 16.3% management, business, and financial, 5.9% computer, engineering, and science, 15.6% education, legal, community service, arts, and media, 7.4% healthcare practitioners, 17.0% service, 15.6% sales and office, 5.9% natural resources, construction, and maintenance, 16.3% production, transportation, and material moving

Income: Per capita: $37,717; Median household: $111,250; Average household: $108,235; Households with income of $100,000 or more: 51.0%; Poverty rate: 4.6%

Educational Attainment: High school diploma or higher: 89.6%; Bachelor's degree or higher: 41.5%; Graduate/professional degree or higher: 16.1%

Housing: Homeownership rate: 80.4%; Median home value: $576,100; Median year structure built: 1965; Homeowner vacancy rate: 25.9%; Median selected monthly owner costs: $2,850 with a mortgage, $825 without a mortgage; Median gross rent: $1,300 per month; Rental vacancy rate: 0.0%

Health Insurance: 86.5% have insurance; 75.3% have private insurance; 24.7% have public insurance; 13.5% do not have insurance; 5.1% of children under 18 do not have insurance

Transportation: Commute: 65.7% car, 3.5% public transportation, 4.2% walk, 13.3% work from home; Mean travel time to work: 26.6 minutes

FISHERS ISLAND (CDP). Covers a land area of 4.076 square miles and a water area of 0.147 square miles. Located at 41.27° N. Lat; 71.97° W. Long. Elevation is 16 feet.

Population: 339; Growth (since 2000): 17.3%; Density: 83.2 persons per square mile; Race: 97.6% White, 0.0% Black/African American, 0.0% Asian, 0.0% American Indian/Alaska Native, 0.0% Native Hawaiian/Other Pacific Islander, 2.4% Two or more races, 0.0% Hispanic of any race; Average household size: 2.47; Median age: 52.5; Age under 18: 13.9%; Age 65 and over: 20.4%; Males per 100 females: 100.0; Marriage status: 26.6% never married, 61.6% now married, 0.7% separated, 11.1% widowed, 0.7% divorced; Foreign born: 3.2%; Speak English only: 90.9%; With disability: 2.7%; Veterans: 15.1%; Ancestry: 18.3% Irish, 13.9% German, 12.7% English, 9.4% British, 7.4% Polish

Employment: 17.1% management, business, and financial, 1.6% computer, engineering, and science, 7.8% education, legal, community service, arts, and media, 8.8% healthcare practitioners, 13.0% service, 34.2% sales and office, 8.3% natural resources, construction, and maintenance, 9.3% production, transportation, and material moving

Income: Per capita: $67,122; Median household: $151,083; Average household: $168,193; Households with income of $100,000 or more: 81.3%; Poverty rate: 0.9%

Educational Attainment: High school diploma or higher: 95.4%; Bachelor's degree or higher: 49.5%; Graduate/professional degree or higher: 33.8%

Housing: Homeownership rate: 69.4%; Median home value: $1,058,300; Median year structure built: 1950; Homeowner vacancy rate: 0.0%; Median

selected monthly owner costs: $3,031 with a mortgage, $1,500+ without a mortgage; Median gross rent: $1,381 per month; Rental vacancy rate: 24.6%

Health Insurance: 89.7% have insurance; 88.5% have private insurance; 19.5% have public insurance; 10.3% do not have insurance; 0.0% of children under 18 do not have insurance

Transportation: Commute: 61.1% car, 11.4% public transportation, 24.4% walk, 3.1% work from home; Mean travel time to work: 9.4 minutes

Airports: Elizabeth Field (general aviation)

FLANDERS (CDP). Covers a land area of 11.461 square miles and a water area of 0.174 square miles. Located at 40.89° N. Lat; 72.61° W. Long. Elevation is 7 feet.

Population: 4,906; Growth (since 2000): 34.6%; Density: 428.1 persons per square mile; Race: 78.9% White, 7.7% Black/African American, 2.1% Asian, 0.0% American Indian/Alaska Native, 0.0% Native Hawaiian/Other Pacific Islander, 8.6% Two or more races, 51.0% Hispanic of any race; Average household size: 3.37; Median age: 34.8; Age under 18: 28.0%; Age 65 and over: 10.7%; Males per 100 females: 114.6; Marriage status: 42.4% never married, 44.6% now married, 1.8% separated, 3.0% widowed, 10.0% divorced; Foreign born: 39.3%; Speak English only: 41.1%; With disability: 1.2%; Veterans: 0.4%; Ancestry: 10.8% Polish, 5.8% Norwegian, 5.5% Scottish, 5.3% Italian, 5.3% Irish

Employment: 4.8% management, business, and financial, 1.5% computer, engineering, and science, 11.8% education, legal, community service, arts, and media, 2.3% healthcare practitioners, 31.7% service, 14.2% sales and office, 30.9% natural resources, construction, and maintenance, 2.9% production, transportation, and material moving

Income: Per capita: $26,663; Median household: $63,482; Average household: $86,792; Households with income of $100,000 or more: 32.9%; Poverty rate: 12.8%

Educational Attainment: High school diploma or higher: 61.9%; Bachelor's degree or higher: 21.3%; Graduate/professional degree or higher: 9.5%

Housing: Homeownership rate: 83.8%; Median home value: $297,000; Median year structure built: 1966; Homeowner vacancy rate: 0.0%; Median selected monthly owner costs: $2,278 with a mortgage, $788 without a mortgage; Median gross rent: $1,747 per month; Rental vacancy rate: 0.0%

Health Insurance: 71.6% have insurance; 53.7% have private insurance; 23.3% have public insurance; 28.4% do not have insurance; 8.8% of children under 18 do not have insurance

Transportation: Commute: 93.2% car, 4.3% public transportation, 2.4% walk, 0.0% work from home; Mean travel time to work: 22.2 minutes

FORT SALONGA (CDP). Covers a land area of 9.829 square miles and a water area of 0.111 square miles. Located at 40.90° N. Lat; 73.30° W. Long. Elevation is 33 feet.

History: The name evolved from the Revolutionary War British Fort Salonga, or Fort Slongo, (named after one of the fort's architects) once located near the border of Huntington Township and The Town of Smithtown, overlooking the Long Island Sound.

Population: 9,821; Growth (since 2000): 1.9%; Density: 999.1 persons per square mile; Race: 94.8% White, 1.0% Black/African American, 2.3% Asian, 0.4% American Indian/Alaska Native, 0.0% Native Hawaiian/Other Pacific Islander, 0.6% Two or more races, 4.9% Hispanic of any race; Average household size: 2.89; Median age: 47.1; Age under 18: 25.4%; Age 65 and over: 18.5%; Males per 100 females: 100.5; Marriage status: 25.9% never married, 63.6% now married, 0.3% separated, 5.2% widowed, 5.3% divorced; Foreign born: 5.3%; Speak English only: 94.0%; With disability: 8.9%; Veterans: 8.9%; Ancestry: 35.2% Italian, 27.2% Irish, 20.3% German, 6.8% Polish, 6.8% English

Employment: 22.6% management, business, and financial, 4.0% computer, engineering, and science, 16.1% education, legal, community service, arts, and media, 10.5% healthcare practitioners, 13.2% service, 22.8% sales and office, 7.9% natural resources, construction, and maintenance, 2.9% production, transportation, and material moving

Income: Per capita: $56,464; Median household: $122,554; Average household: $163,819; Households with income of $100,000 or more: 60.0%; Poverty rate: 5.8%

Educational Attainment: High school diploma or higher: 98.0%; Bachelor's degree or higher: 49.3%; Graduate/professional degree or higher: 23.5%

Housing: Homeownership rate: 89.7%; Median home value: $686,700; Median year structure built: 1965; Homeowner vacancy rate: 2.7%; Median

selected monthly owner costs: $3,847 with a mortgage, $1,500+ without a mortgage; Median gross rent: $1,755 per month; Rental vacancy rate: 0.0%

Health Insurance: 97.0% have insurance; 86.8% have private insurance; 24.1% have public insurance; 3.0% do not have insurance; 1.4% of children under 18 do not have insurance

Transportation: Commute: 86.7% car, 7.3% public transportation, 0.0% walk, 4.4% work from home; Mean travel time to work: 34.4 minutes

GILGO (CDP). Covers a land area of 4.996 square miles and a water area of 6.707 square miles. Located at 40.64° N. Lat; 73.38° W. Long.

Population: 208; Growth (since 2000): n/a; Density: 41.6 persons per square mile; Race: 100.0% White, 0.0% Black/African American, 0.0% Asian, 0.0% American Indian/Alaska Native, 0.0% Native Hawaiian/Other Pacific Islander, 0.0% Two or more races, 0.0% Hispanic of any race; Average household size: 2.89; Median age: 54.2; Age under 18: 16.3%; Age 65 and over: 19.2%; Males per 100 females: 118.3; Marriage status: 38.0% never married, 51.0% now married, 0.0% separated, 11.0% widowed, 0.0% divorced; Foreign born: 0.0%; Speak English only: 100.0%; With disability: 0.0%; Veterans: 0.0%; Ancestry: 64.9% Italian, 38.0% Irish, 26.9% German, 12.0% French, 10.6% Canadian

Employment: 20.4% management, business, and financial, 0.0% computer, engineering, and science, 70.4% education, legal, community service, arts, and media, 9.2% healthcare practitioners, 0.0% service, 0.0% sales and office, 0.0% natural resources, construction, and maintenance, 0.0% production, transportation, and material moving

Income: Per capita: $62,076; Median household: $159,479; Average household: $174,238; Households with income of $100,000 or more: 87.5%; Poverty rate: n/a

Educational Attainment: High school diploma or higher: 100.0%; Bachelor's degree or higher: 71.9%; Graduate/professional degree or higher: 29.5%

Housing: Homeownership rate: 100.0%; Median home value: $484,800; Median year structure built: 1958; Homeowner vacancy rate: 0.0%; Median selected monthly owner costs: n/a with a mortgage, $1,034 without a mortgage; Median gross rent: n/a per month; Rental vacancy rate: 0.0%

Health Insurance: 100.0% have insurance; 89.4% have private insurance; 19.2% have public insurance; 0.0% do not have insurance; 0.0% of children under 18 do not have insurance

Transportation: Commute: 90.8% car, 9.2% public transportation, 0.0% walk, 0.0% work from home; Mean travel time to work: 35.2 minutes

GORDON HEIGHTS (CDP). Covers a land area of 1.705 square miles and a water area of 0.014 square miles. Located at 40.86° N. Lat; 72.96° W. Long. Elevation is 154 feet.

Population: 3,866; Growth (since 2000): 25.0%; Density: 2,267.7 persons per square mile; Race: 44.8% White, 48.6% Black/African American, 0.9% Asian, 0.0% American Indian/Alaska Native, 0.0% Native Hawaiian/Other Pacific Islander, 4.0% Two or more races, 28.1% Hispanic of any race; Average household size: 3.45; Median age: 32.7; Age under 18: 32.0%; Age 65 and over: 8.0%; Males per 100 females: 100.2; Marriage status: 42.2% never married, 39.5% now married, 4.8% separated, 3.7% widowed, 14.7% divorced; Foreign born: 16.6%; Speak English only: 73.2%; With disability: 13.4%; Veterans: 5.7%; Ancestry: 12.6% Italian, 4.4% German, 3.5% French, 3.4% Irish, 3.3% American

Employment: 11.2% management, business, and financial, 6.0% computer, engineering, and science, 10.0% education, legal, community service, arts, and media, 6.4% healthcare practitioners, 23.4% service, 20.2% sales and office, 6.4% natural resources, construction, and maintenance, 16.4% production, transportation, and material moving

Income: Per capita: $23,063; Median household: $71,447; Average household: $76,585; Households with income of $100,000 or more: 29.5%; Poverty rate: 16.0%

Educational Attainment: High school diploma or higher: 82.0%; Bachelor's degree or higher: 17.7%; Graduate/professional degree or higher: 7.0%

Housing: Homeownership rate: 69.4%; Median home value: $258,800; Median year structure built: 1986; Homeowner vacancy rate: 2.6%; Median selected monthly owner costs: $2,386 with a mortgage, $1,065 without a mortgage; Median gross rent: $1,687 per month; Rental vacancy rate: 11.5%

Health Insurance: 90.8% have insurance; 60.5% have private insurance; 46.3% have public insurance; 9.2% do not have insurance; 0.0% of children under 18 do not have insurance

Transportation: Commute: 87.8% car, 3.8% public transportation, 1.9% walk, 5.8% work from home; Mean travel time to work: 33.6 minutes

GREAT RIVER (CDP). Covers a land area of 4.597 square miles and a water area of 0.595 square miles. Located at 40.72° N. Lat; 73.16° W. Long. Elevation is 13 feet.

Population: 1,561; Growth (since 2000): 1.0%; Density: 339.6 persons per square mile; Race: 95.7% White, 0.0% Black/African American, 3.6% Asian, 0.0% American Indian/Alaska Native, 0.0% Native Hawaiian/Other Pacific Islander, 0.7% Two or more races, 3.7% Hispanic of any race; Average household size: 2.96; Median age: 46.2; Age under 18: 24.6%; Age 65 and over: 15.4%; Males per 100 females: 105.4; Marriage status: 24.4% never married, 64.2% now married, 0.6% separated, 6.3% widowed, 5.1% divorced; Foreign born: 6.4%; Speak English only: 95.6%; With disability: 8.0%; Veterans: 7.1%; Ancestry: 39.3% Italian, 33.6% Irish, 28.6% German, 8.5% English, 7.4% Polish

Employment: 28.0% management, business, and financial, 2.4% computer, engineering, and science, 24.7% education, legal, community service, arts, and media, 12.1% healthcare practitioners, 5.9% service, 21.4% sales and office, 2.0% natural resources, construction, and maintenance, 3.6% production, transportation, and material moving

Income: Per capita: $53,946; Median household: $128,214; Average household: $157,302; Households with income of $100,000 or more: 68.1%; Poverty rate: 3.1%

Educational Attainment: High school diploma or higher: 97.8%; Bachelor's degree or higher: 52.8%; Graduate/professional degree or higher: 35.2%

Housing: Homeownership rate: 91.7%; Median home value: $663,400; Median year structure built: 1964; Homeowner vacancy rate: 3.2%; Median selected monthly owner costs: $4,000+ with a mortgage, $1,500+ without a mortgage; Median gross rent: $1,782 per month; Rental vacancy rate: 0.0%

Health Insurance: 97.2% have insurance; 92.2% have private insurance; 18.2% have public insurance; 2.8% do not have insurance; 0.0% of children under 18 do not have insurance

Transportation: Commute: 91.5% car, 6.7% public transportation, 0.0% walk, 1.7% work from home; Mean travel time to work: 28.7 minutes

GREENLAWN (CDP). Covers a land area of 3.722 square miles and a water area of 0.003 square miles. Located at 40.86° N. Lat; 73.36° W. Long. Elevation is 226 feet.

Population: 14,481; Growth (since 2000): 9.0%; Density: 3,891.0 persons per square mile; Race: 71.2% White, 16.8% Black/African American, 2.8% Asian, 0.2% American Indian/Alaska Native, 0.0% Native Hawaiian/Other Pacific Islander, 2.6% Two or more races, 14.7% Hispanic of any race; Average household size: 3.09; Median age: 42.1; Age under 18: 26.1%; Age 65 and over: 17.7%; Males per 100 females: 92.4; Marriage status: 31.4% never married, 51.3% now married, 1.9% separated, 8.7% widowed, 8.6% divorced; Foreign born: 17.0%; Speak English only: 78.5%; With disability: 8.2%; Veterans: 6.0%; Ancestry: 21.9% Italian, 15.4% Irish, 13.9% German, 6.2% Polish, 4.9% English

Employment: 19.9% management, business, and financial, 3.5% computer, engineering, and science, 12.2% education, legal, community service, arts, and media, 8.2% healthcare practitioners, 17.7% service, 24.5% sales and office, 5.7% natural resources, construction, and maintenance, 8.4% production, transportation, and material moving

Income: Per capita: $37,974; Median household: $86,563; Average household: $116,048; Households with income of $100,000 or more: 41.2%; Poverty rate: 6.7%

Educational Attainment: High school diploma or higher: 92.4%; Bachelor's degree or higher: 38.3%; Graduate/professional degree or higher: 16.9%

School District(s)

Harborfields Central SD (KG-12)

 2014-15 Enrollment: 3,364 . . . . (631) 754-5320

Housing: Homeownership rate: 79.6%; Median home value: $436,500; Median year structure built: 1961; Homeowner vacancy rate: 0.7%; Median selected monthly owner costs: $2,891 with a mortgage, $1,185 without a mortgage; Median gross rent: $833 per month; Rental vacancy rate: 3.8%

Health Insurance: 92.7% have insurance; 78.7% have private insurance; 27.4% have public insurance; 7.3% do not have insurance; 4.7% of children under 18 do not have insurance

Transportation: Commute: 84.8% car, 10.2% public transportation, 0.5% walk, 3.9% work from home; Mean travel time to work: 31.1 minutes

GREENPORT (village).
Covers a land area of 0.956 square miles and a water area of 0.249 square miles. Located at 41.10° N. Lat; 72.37° W. Long. Elevation is 10 feet.

History: By 1840 pursuit of offshore whaling, practiced by both Native Americans and European residents, had turned into a way of industry with ships leaving Cold Springs Harbor, Sag Harbor, and Greenport on 3-year whaling voyages. Greenport Village Historic District. Incorporated 1838.

Population: 2,234; Growth (since 2000): 9.1%; Density: 2,337.1 persons per square mile; Race: 81.6% White, 13.9% Black/African American, 0.3% Asian, 0.0% American Indian/Alaska Native, 0.0% Native Hawaiian/Other Pacific Islander, 2.6% Two or more races, 23.1% Hispanic of any race; Average household size: 2.44; Median age: 42.0; Age under 18: 20.2%; Age 65 and over: 17.1%; Males per 100 females: 100.8; Marriage status: 37.1% never married, 44.9% now married, 0.9% separated, 7.8% widowed, 10.2% divorced; Foreign born: 18.0%; Speak English only: 77.2%; With disability: 10.7%; Veterans: 7.7%; Ancestry: 19.8% Irish, 11.9% German, 10.1% English, 7.4% Polish, 7.3% Italian

Employment: 8.1% management, business, and financial, 4.9% computer, engineering, and science, 12.5% education, legal, community service, arts, and media, 5.4% healthcare practitioners, 21.2% service, 24.7% sales and office, 15.9% natural resources, construction, and maintenance, 7.3% production, transportation, and material moving

Income: Per capita: $32,438; Median household: $56,212; Average household: $80,122; Households with income of $100,000 or more: 23.6%; Poverty rate: 17.7%

Educational Attainment: High school diploma or higher: 81.0%; Bachelor's degree or higher: 34.9%; Graduate/professional degree or higher: 14.7%

School District(s)
Greenport Union Free SD (KG-12)
   2014-15 Enrollment: 691 . . . . (631) 477-1950

Housing: Homeownership rate: 50.7%; Median home value: $476,300; Median year structure built: Before 1940; Homeowner vacancy rate: 3.8%; Median selected monthly owner costs: $2,117 with a mortgage, $685 without a mortgage; Median gross rent: $1,379 per month; Rental vacancy rate: 13.4%

Health Insurance: 78.0% have insurance; 58.0% have private insurance; 30.3% have public insurance; 22.0% do not have insurance; 4.2% of children under 18 do not have insurance

Hospitals: Eastern Long Island Hospital (90 beds)

Transportation: Commute: 67.2% car, 5.7% public transportation, 18.8% walk, 4.4% work from home; Mean travel time to work: 24.8 minutes

GREENPORT WEST (CDP).
Covers a land area of 3.209 square miles and a water area of 0.125 square miles. Located at 41.09° N. Lat; 72.39° W. Long. Elevation is 7 feet.

Population: 2,002; Growth (since 2000): 19.2%; Density: 623.8 persons per square mile; Race: 98.6% White, 1.4% Black/African American, 0.0% Asian, 0.0% American Indian/Alaska Native, 0.0% Native Hawaiian/Other Pacific Islander, 0.0% Two or more races, 9.4% Hispanic of any race; Average household size: 2.01; Median age: 59.9; Age under 18: 14.2%; Age 65 and over: 43.1%; Males per 100 females: 82.8; Marriage status: 22.7% never married, 53.8% now married, 2.0% separated, 16.9% widowed, 6.6% divorced; Foreign born: 11.0%; Speak English only: 85.8%; With disability: 15.6%; Veterans: 11.6%; Ancestry: 20.5% German, 20.4% Irish, 18.5% Italian, 17.8% Polish, 17.2% English

Employment: 23.7% management, business, and financial, 5.3% computer, engineering, and science, 8.5% education, legal, community service, arts, and media, 1.4% healthcare practitioners, 16.4% service, 15.5% sales and office, 12.8% natural resources, construction, and maintenance, 16.4% production, transportation, and material moving

Income: Per capita: $41,269; Median household: $56,806; Average household: $85,869; Households with income of $100,000 or more: 24.6%; Poverty rate: 15.1%

Educational Attainment: High school diploma or higher: 95.3%; Bachelor's degree or higher: 37.3%; Graduate/professional degree or higher: 18.3%

Housing: Homeownership rate: 77.3%; Median home value: $437,900; Median year structure built: 1987; Homeowner vacancy rate: 3.9%; Median selected monthly owner costs: $2,304 with a mortgage, $646 without a mortgage; Median gross rent: $1,132 per month; Rental vacancy rate: 8.6%

Health Insurance: 94.5% have insurance; 80.0% have private insurance; 60.0% have public insurance; 5.5% do not have insurance; 0.0% of children under 18 do not have insurance

Transportation: Commute: 77.5% car, 3.4% public transportation, 4.3% walk, 9.2% work from home; Mean travel time to work: 21.3 minutes

HALESITE (CDP).
Covers a land area of 0.889 square miles and a water area of 0.092 square miles. Located at 40.89° N. Lat; 73.41° W. Long. Elevation is 26 feet.

Population: 2,810; Growth (since 2000): 8.8%; Density: 3,161.3 persons per square mile; Race: 96.5% White, 2.1% Black/African American, 1.1% Asian, 0.0% American Indian/Alaska Native, 0.0% Native Hawaiian/Other Pacific Islander, 0.4% Two or more races, 4.1% Hispanic of any race; Average household size: 2.64; Median age: 49.5; Age under 18: 19.0%; Age 65 and over: 16.2%; Males per 100 females: 101.0; Marriage status: 16.6% never married, 68.1% now married, 0.9% separated, 7.1% widowed, 8.2% divorced; Foreign born: 8.3%; Speak English only: 94.7%; With disability: 4.6%; Veterans: 7.1%; Ancestry: 40.7% Italian, 25.7% Irish, 13.2% German, 10.6% English, 7.0% American

Employment: 20.8% management, business, and financial, 4.7% computer, engineering, and science, 27.5% education, legal, community service, arts, and media, 6.4% healthcare practitioners, 7.3% service, 25.0% sales and office, 3.0% natural resources, construction, and maintenance, 5.4% production, transportation, and material moving

Income: Per capita: $50,942; Median household: $120,318; Average household: $132,268; Households with income of $100,000 or more: 62.3%; Poverty rate: 1.7%

Educational Attainment: High school diploma or higher: 99.4%; Bachelor's degree or higher: 53.7%; Graduate/professional degree or higher: 30.3%

Housing: Homeownership rate: 90.1%; Median home value: $524,200; Median year structure built: 1953; Homeowner vacancy rate: 0.0%; Median selected monthly owner costs: $3,288 with a mortgage, $1,297 without a mortgage; Median gross rent: n/a per month; Rental vacancy rate: 0.0%

Health Insurance: 96.8% have insurance; 90.7% have private insurance; 18.8% have public insurance; 3.2% do not have insurance; 7.3% of children under 18 do not have insurance

Transportation: Commute: 79.1% car, 11.0% public transportation, 2.6% walk, 7.3% work from home; Mean travel time to work: 32.4 minutes

HAMPTON BAYS (CDP).
Covers a land area of 12.954 square miles and a water area of 5.174 square miles. Located at 40.87° N. Lat; 72.52° W. Long. Elevation is 33 feet.

History: Until 1922 called Good Ground.

Population: 12,866; Growth (since 2000): 5.1%; Density: 993.2 persons per square mile; Race: 94.0% White, 1.3% Black/African American, 1.1% Asian, 0.0% American Indian/Alaska Native, 0.0% Native Hawaiian/Other Pacific Islander, 1.9% Two or more races, 29.7% Hispanic of any race; Average household size: 2.59; Median age: 42.3; Age under 18: 19.4%; Age 65 and over: 17.4%; Males per 100 females: 106.0; Marriage status: 26.7% never married, 56.7% now married, 1.9% separated, 6.9% widowed, 9.8% divorced; Foreign born: 27.5%; Speak English only: 65.3%; With disability: 9.7%; Veterans: 7.4%; Ancestry: 20.8% Irish, 16.4% Italian, 15.7% German, 6.0% English, 5.3% Polish

Employment: 12.6% management, business, and financial, 3.0% computer, engineering, and science, 6.3% education, legal, community service, arts, and media, 5.9% healthcare practitioners, 26.9% service, 21.5% sales and office, 16.1% natural resources, construction, and maintenance, 7.8% production, transportation, and material moving

Income: Per capita: $36,920; Median household: $75,606; Average household: $92,577; Households with income of $100,000 or more: 29.0%; Poverty rate: 6.6%

Educational Attainment: High school diploma or higher: 89.7%; Bachelor's degree or higher: 32.5%; Graduate/professional degree or higher: 12.2%

School District(s)
Hampton Bays Union Free SD (KG-12)
   2014-15 Enrollment: 2,174 . . . . (631) 723-2100

Housing: Homeownership rate: 71.8%; Median home value: $436,700; Median year structure built: 1974; Homeowner vacancy rate: 3.1%; Median selected monthly owner costs: $2,539 with a mortgage, $965 without a mortgage; Median gross rent: $1,676 per month; Rental vacancy rate: 1.8%

Health Insurance: 80.5% have insurance; 62.8% have private insurance; 31.4% have public insurance; 19.5% do not have insurance; 7.0% of children under 18 do not have insurance

Transportation: Commute: 90.1% car, 3.6% public transportation, 1.2% walk, 4.4% work from home; Mean travel time to work: 29.8 minutes

HAUPPAUGE (CDP).

Covers a land area of 10.713 square miles and a water area of 0.148 square miles. Located at 40.82° N. Lat; 73.21° W. Long. Elevation is 62 feet.

History: Happague's name derives from the Native American Algonquian term for "overflowed land."

Population: 20,616; Growth (since 2000): 2.6%; Density: 1,924.4 persons per square mile; Race: 89.7% White, 3.6% Black/African American, 3.7% Asian, 0.1% American Indian/Alaska Native, 0.0% Native Hawaiian/Other Pacific Islander, 0.8% Two or more races, 7.2% Hispanic of any race; Average household size: 2.89; Median age: 44.4; Age under 18: 22.7%; Age 65 and over: 17.0%; Males per 100 females: 96.4; Marriage status: 26.8% never married, 59.3% now married, 1.4% separated, 6.7% widowed, 7.2% divorced; Foreign born: 9.6%; Speak English only: 85.1%; With disability: 8.8%; Veterans: 7.6%; Ancestry: 35.5% Italian, 21.2% Irish, 15.6% German, 5.3% Polish, 4.4% English

Employment: 18.8% management, business, and financial, 6.5% computer, engineering, and science, 13.2% education, legal, community service, arts, and media, 5.4% healthcare practitioners, 16.1% service, 25.6% sales and office, 7.3% natural resources, construction, and maintenance, 7.0% production, transportation, and material moving

Income: Per capita: $41,499; Median household: $105,305; Average household: $117,512; Households with income of $100,000 or more: 51.7%; Poverty rate: 3.5%

Educational Attainment: High school diploma or higher: 96.1%; Bachelor's degree or higher: 44.0%; Graduate/professional degree or higher: 18.8%

School District(s)

Hauppauge Union Free SD (KG-12)
    2014-15 Enrollment: 3,782 . . . . (631) 761-8208

Vocational/Technical School(s)

Long Island Beauty School-Hauppauge (Private, For-profit)
    Fall 2014 Enrollment: 249 . . . . (631) 724-0440
    2015-16 Tuition: $13,200

Housing: Homeownership rate: 84.3%; Median home value: $459,600; Median year structure built: 1968; Homeowner vacancy rate: 1.1%; Median selected monthly owner costs: $2,858 with a mortgage, $1,179 without a mortgage; Median gross rent: $1,865 per month; Rental vacancy rate: 6.4%

Health Insurance: 96.7% have insurance; 88.1% have private insurance; 22.0% have public insurance; 3.3% do not have insurance; 1.5% of children under 18 do not have insurance

Transportation: Commute: 88.2% car, 6.1% public transportation, 0.5% walk, 3.6% work from home; Mean travel time to work: 32.0 minutes

HEAD OF THE HARBOR (village).

Covers a land area of 2.807 square miles and a water area of 0.228 square miles. Located at 40.90° N. Lat; 73.16° W. Long. Elevation is 121 feet.

Population: 1,330; Growth (since 2000): -8.1%; Density: 473.8 persons per square mile; Race: 94.4% White, 0.0% Black/African American, 3.6% Asian, 0.0% American Indian/Alaska Native, 0.0% Native Hawaiian/Other Pacific Islander, 0.5% Two or more races, 4.3% Hispanic of any race; Average household size: 2.70; Median age: 48.3; Age under 18: 20.4%; Age 65 and over: 17.2%; Males per 100 females: 102.2; Marriage status: 28.5% never married, 62.8% now married, 1.1% separated, 6.0% widowed, 2.7% divorced; Foreign born: 6.6%; Speak English only: 91.2%; With disability: 9.1%; Veterans: 7.5%; Ancestry: 32.9% Italian, 22.5% German, 22.5% Irish, 7.4% Russian, 6.4% English

Employment: 19.3% management, business, and financial, 8.8% computer, engineering, and science, 17.2% education, legal, community service, arts, and media, 12.4% healthcare practitioners, 11.8% service, 26.5% sales and office, 1.5% natural resources, construction, and maintenance, 2.5% production, transportation, and material moving

Income: Per capita: $85,636; Median household: $140,673; Average household: $225,897; Households with income of $100,000 or more: 67.9%; Poverty rate: 5.0%

Educational Attainment: High school diploma or higher: 97.4%; Bachelor's degree or higher: 64.1%; Graduate/professional degree or higher: 34.5%

Housing: Homeownership rate: 90.1%; Median home value: $915,300; Median year structure built: 1967; Homeowner vacancy rate: 0.0%; Median selected monthly owner costs: $4,000+ with a mortgage, $1,500+ without a mortgage; Median gross rent: $2,395 per month; Rental vacancy rate: 0.0%

Health Insurance: 95.3% have insurance; 90.1% have private insurance; 20.4% have public insurance; 4.7% do not have insurance; 1.1% of children under 18 do not have insurance

Transportation: Commute: 91.9% car, 3.2% public transportation, 0.0% walk, 4.3% work from home; Mean travel time to work: 25.7 minutes

HOLBROOK (CDP).

Covers a land area of 7.183 square miles and a water area of 0 square miles. Located at 40.79° N. Lat; 73.07° W. Long. Elevation is 118 feet.

History: Holbrook is located in the towns of Islip and Brookhaven, divided by the Main Line of the Long Island Rail Road.

Population: 27,533; Growth (since 2000): 0.1%; Density: 3,833.3 persons per square mile; Race: 92.0% White, 0.8% Black/African American, 2.8% Asian, 0.2% American Indian/Alaska Native, 0.2% Native Hawaiian/Other Pacific Islander, 2.5% Two or more races, 10.7% Hispanic of any race; Average household size: 3.03; Median age: 41.1; Age under 18: 22.9%; Age 65 and over: 14.0%; Males per 100 females: 93.2; Marriage status: 30.3% never married, 53.8% now married, 1.3% separated, 5.7% widowed, 10.2% divorced; Foreign born: 5.8%; Speak English only: 89.6%; With disability: 8.8%; Veterans: 6.0%; Ancestry: 35.9% Italian, 29.2% Irish, 19.3% German, 6.2% Polish, 5.6% English

Employment: 12.3% management, business, and financial, 4.6% computer, engineering, and science, 13.1% education, legal, community service, arts, and media, 6.0% healthcare practitioners, 16.5% service, 29.9% sales and office, 9.3% natural resources, construction, and maintenance, 8.2% production, transportation, and material moving

Income: Per capita: $38,919; Median household: $98,878; Average household: $114,647; Households with income of $100,000 or more: 49.4%; Poverty rate: 2.7%

Educational Attainment: High school diploma or higher: 93.2%; Bachelor's degree or higher: 32.2%; Graduate/professional degree or higher: 14.4%

School District(s)

Sachem Central SD (KG-12)
    2014-15 Enrollment: 13,882 . . . . (631) 471-1336

Housing: Homeownership rate: 79.4%; Median home value: $356,900; Median year structure built: 1975; Homeowner vacancy rate: 0.6%; Median selected monthly owner costs: $2,534 with a mortgage, $1,083 without a mortgage; Median gross rent: $1,751 per month; Rental vacancy rate: 5.4%

Health Insurance: 93.2% have insurance; 85.3% have private insurance; 20.7% have public insurance; 6.8% do not have insurance; 5.6% of children under 18 do not have insurance

Transportation: Commute: 91.1% car, 6.3% public transportation, 0.4% walk, 1.6% work from home; Mean travel time to work: 32.7 minutes

HOLTSVILLE (CDP).

Covers a land area of 7.113 square miles and a water area of 0 square miles. Located at 40.81° N. Lat; 73.04° W. Long. Elevation is 105 feet.

History: Holtsville included only a few farmhouses until 1843, when the Long Island Rail Road opened its Waverly Station. As another post office named Waverly already existed in Upstate New York, the name of the hamlet was changed to Holtsville in 1860, in honor of U.S. Postmaster General Joseph Holt.

Population: 20,081; Growth (since 2000): 18.1%; Density: 2,823.1 persons per square mile; Race: 89.5% White, 5.1% Black/African American, 2.7% Asian, 0.4% American Indian/Alaska Native, 0.0% Native Hawaiian/Other Pacific Islander, 2.0% Two or more races, 13.4% Hispanic of any race; Average household size: 2.98; Median age: 40.3; Age under 18: 22.7%; Age 65 and over: 13.0%; Males per 100 females: 93.5; Marriage status: 31.5% never married, 56.6% now married, 1.3% separated, 4.8% widowed, 7.1% divorced; Foreign born: 9.5%; Speak English only: 84.1%; With disability: 10.5%; Veterans: 7.2%; Ancestry: 34.1% Italian, 23.1% Irish, 17.7% German, 5.2% Polish, 4.6% American

Employment: 16.0% management, business, and financial, 4.9% computer, engineering, and science, 12.2% education, legal, community service, arts, and media, 7.4% healthcare practitioners, 13.4% service, 25.7% sales and office, 11.0% natural resources, construction, and maintenance, 9.4% production, transportation, and material moving

Income: Per capita: $37,089; Median household: $92,194; Average household: $107,167; Households with income of $100,000 or more: 45.0%; Poverty rate: 4.8%

Educational Attainment: High school diploma or higher: 92.5%; Bachelor's degree or higher: 30.6%; Graduate/professional degree or higher: 11.2%

School District(s)
Sachem Central SD (KG-12)
   2014-15 Enrollment: 13,882 . . . . (631) 471-1336
Housing: Homeownership rate: 80.0%; Median home value: $346,500; Median year structure built: 1977; Homeowner vacancy rate: 1.2%; Median selected monthly owner costs: $2,546 with a mortgage, $1,007 without a mortgage; Median gross rent: $1,642 per month; Rental vacancy rate: 2.3%
Health Insurance: 93.9% have insurance; 83.9% have private insurance; 22.8% have public insurance; 6.1% do not have insurance; 2.1% of children under 18 do not have insurance
Transportation: Commute: 90.9% car, 5.6% public transportation, 0.5% walk, 3.1% work from home; Mean travel time to work: 33.6 minutes

---

HUNTINGTON (CDP). Covers a land area of 7.594 square miles and a water area of 0.140 square miles. Located at 40.88° N. Lat; 73.41° W. Long. Elevation is 75 feet.
History: The central business district, called Huntington Village locally, is old and well developed, but it is not incorporated and does not have a village form of government. Huntington is the birthplace of singer Mariah Carey and actor Ralph Macchio. It is also where world-renowned jazz musicians John Coltrane and his wife Alice Coltrane (harpist and pianist) lived in the later years of their life together; he died in Huntington in 1967.
Population: 17,917; Growth (since 2000): -2.6%; Density: 2,359.5 persons per square mile; Race: 93.5% White, 1.5% Black/African American, 1.9% Asian, 0.0% American Indian/Alaska Native, 0.0% Native Hawaiian/Other Pacific Islander, 1.4% Two or more races, 7.5% Hispanic of any race; Average household size: 2.52; Median age: 46.3; Age under 18: 20.2%; Age 65 and over: 17.7%; Males per 100 females: 96.5; Marriage status: 28.0% never married, 57.4% now married, 2.3% separated, 6.3% widowed, 8.3% divorced; Foreign born: 8.7%; Speak English only: 90.4%; With disability: 6.8%; Veterans: 5.2%; Ancestry: 25.7% Italian, 24.5% Irish, 17.8% German, 9.0% English, 7.9% American
Employment: 22.9% management, business, and financial, 5.6% computer, engineering, and science, 23.1% education, legal, community service, arts, and media, 7.4% healthcare practitioners, 9.0% service, 22.8% sales and office, 4.6% natural resources, construction, and maintenance, 4.7% production, transportation, and material moving
Income: Per capita: $60,458; Median household: $110,901; Average household: $151,381; Households with income of $100,000 or more: 54.8%; Poverty rate: 5.3%
Educational Attainment: High school diploma or higher: 96.6%; Bachelor's degree or higher: 63.1%; Graduate/professional degree or higher: 30.6%

School District(s)
Cold Spring Harbor Central SD (KG-12)
   2014-15 Enrollment: 1,814 . . . . (631) 367-5931
Elwood Union Free SD (KG-12)
   2014-15 Enrollment: 2,354 . . . . (631) 266-5400
Huntington Union Free SD (KG-12)
   2014-15 Enrollment: 4,563 . . . . (631) 673-2038
South Huntington Union Free SD (PK-12)
   2014-15 Enrollment: 6,072 . . . . (631) 812-3070
Housing: Homeownership rate: 81.9%; Median home value: $559,000; Median year structure built: 1956; Homeowner vacancy rate: 0.6%; Median selected monthly owner costs: $3,465 with a mortgage, $1,500+ without a mortgage; Median gross rent: $1,781 per month; Rental vacancy rate: 4.9%
Health Insurance: 96.9% have insurance; 89.4% have private insurance; 20.2% have public insurance; 3.1% do not have insurance; 0.2% of children under 18 do not have insurance
Hospitals: Huntington Hospital (408 beds)
Newspapers: Long Islander Newspapers (weekly circulation 33,500)
Transportation: Commute: 77.2% car, 12.4% public transportation, 1.8% walk, 8.0% work from home; Mean travel time to work: 35.4 minutes

---

HUNTINGTON (town). Covers a land area of 94.123 square miles and a water area of 42.988 square miles. Located at 40.88° N. Lat; 73.38° W. Long. Elevation is 75 feet.
History: Named for Huntingdon, England, or to mean "hunting town" for its abundance of game. Seat of Immaculate Conception College, World Friends College. Settled 1653.
Population: 204,240; Growth (since 2000): 4.6%; Density: 2,169.9 persons per square mile; Race: 83.3% White, 4.8% Black/African American, 5.2% Asian, 0.1% American Indian/Alaska Native, 0.0% Native Hawaiian/Other Pacific Islander, 1.3% Two or more races, 12.0% Hispanic of any race; Average household size: 2.92; Median age: 43.7; Age under 18: 23.5%; Age 65 and over: 16.8%; Males per 100 females: 96.9; Marriage status: 28.3% never married, 58.4% now married, 1.4% separated, 6.4% widowed, 7.0% divorced; Foreign born: 14.0%; Speak English only: 81.5%; With disability: 7.7%; Veterans: 5.9%; Ancestry: 25.9% Italian, 19.1% Irish, 15.0% German, 6.0% Polish, 5.6% English
Employment: 19.5% management, business, and financial, 4.8% computer, engineering, and science, 16.6% education, legal, community service, arts, and media, 7.7% healthcare practitioners, 13.7% service, 25.7% sales and office, 5.9% natural resources, construction, and maintenance, 6.0% production, transportation, and material moving
Income: Per capita: $49,067; Median household: $105,451; Average household: $142,000; Households with income of $100,000 or more: 52.6%; Poverty rate: 6.1%
Educational Attainment: High school diploma or higher: 92.7%; Bachelor's degree or higher: 49.9%; Graduate/professional degree or higher: 23.4%

School District(s)
Cold Spring Harbor Central SD (KG-12)
   2014-15 Enrollment: 1,814 . . . . (631) 367-5931
Elwood Union Free SD (KG-12)
   2014-15 Enrollment: 2,354 . . . . (631) 266-5400
Huntington Union Free SD (KG-12)
   2014-15 Enrollment: 4,563 . . . . (631) 673-2038
South Huntington Union Free SD (PK-12)
   2014-15 Enrollment: 6,072 . . . . (631) 812-3070
Housing: Homeownership rate: 84.4%; Median home value: $497,500; Median year structure built: 1962; Homeowner vacancy rate: 0.9%; Median selected monthly owner costs: $3,203 with a mortgage, $1,330 without a mortgage; Median gross rent: $1,676 per month; Rental vacancy rate: 5.9%
Health Insurance: 93.9% have insurance; 82.4% have private insurance; 24.7% have public insurance; 6.1% do not have insurance; 3.0% of children under 18 do not have insurance
Hospitals: Huntington Hospital (408 beds)
Newspapers: Long Islander Newspapers (weekly circulation 33,500)
Transportation: Commute: 81.6% car, 10.5% public transportation, 1.2% walk, 5.5% work from home; Mean travel time to work: 33.3 minutes
Additional Information Contacts
Town of Huntington . . . . (631) 351-3206
   http://www.huntingtonny.gov

HUNTINGTON BAY (village). Covers a land area of 0.998 square miles and a water area of 0.897 square miles. Located at 40.90° N. Lat; 73.41° W. Long. Elevation is 16 feet.
History: Site of capture of Nathan Hale by British forces during American Revolution.
Population: 1,509; Growth (since 2000): 0.9%; Density: 1,511.7 persons per square mile; Race: 96.1% White, 0.0% Black/African American, 2.7% Asian, 0.0% American Indian/Alaska Native, 0.0% Native Hawaiian/Other Pacific Islander, 1.2% Two or more races, 0.9% Hispanic of any race; Average household size: 2.65; Median age: 51.0; Age under 18: 19.0%; Age 65 and over: 22.4%; Males per 100 females: 97.9; Marriage status: 21.5% never married, 68.9% now married, 1.9% separated, 5.8% widowed, 3.8% divorced; Foreign born: 8.7%; Speak English only: 87.8%; With disability: 4.0%; Veterans: 6.8%; Ancestry: 29.7% Irish, 28.6% Italian, 14.6% German, 10.4% English, 5.2% American
Employment: 31.1% management, business, and financial, 2.4% computer, engineering, and science, 16.4% education, legal, community service, arts, and media, 8.3% healthcare practitioners, 5.8% service, 30.1% sales and office, 2.1% natural resources, construction, and maintenance, 3.9% production, transportation, and material moving
Income: Per capita: $96,415; Median household: $177,083; Average household: $252,100; Households with income of $100,000 or more: 70.1%; Poverty rate: 6.5%
Educational Attainment: High school diploma or higher: 99.3%; Bachelor's degree or higher: 74.9%; Graduate/professional degree or higher: 32.6%
Housing: Homeownership rate: 95.3%; Median home value: $1,078,700; Median year structure built: 1950; Homeowner vacancy rate: 0.0%; Median selected monthly owner costs: $4,000+ with a mortgage, $1,500+ without a mortgage; Median gross rent: $2,250 per month; Rental vacancy rate: 0.0%

Health Insurance: 98.7% have insurance; 92.0% have private insurance; 23.7% have public insurance; 1.3% do not have insurance; 0.0% of children under 18 do not have insurance
Safety: Violent crime rate: 0.0 per 10,000 population; Property crime rate: 41.8 per 10,000 population
Transportation: Commute: 74.0% car, 13.8% public transportation, 0.0% walk, 11.8% work from home; Mean travel time to work: 39.2 minutes

HUNTINGTON STATION (CDP).
Covers a land area of 5.474 square miles and a water area of 0.004 square miles. Located at 40.84° N. Lat; 73.40° W. Long. Elevation is 217 feet.
History: Named for Huntingdon, England, or to mean "hunting town". Walt Whitman born here.
Population: 34,088; Growth (since 2000): 14.0%; Density: 6,227.1 persons per square mile; Race: 64.5% White, 9.5% Black/African American, 2.9% Asian, 0.1% American Indian/Alaska Native, 0.0% Native Hawaiian/Other Pacific Islander, 2.0% Two or more races, 37.7% Hispanic of any race; Average household size: 3.31; Median age: 36.5; Age under 18: 27.0%; Age 65 and over: 11.3%; Males per 100 females: 104.4; Marriage status: 36.4% never married, 49.8% now married, 2.2% separated, 5.0% widowed, 8.8% divorced; Foreign born: 25.7%; Speak English only: 59.7%; With disability: 7.8%; Veterans: 5.0%; Ancestry: 18.5% Italian, 13.5% Irish, 10.7% German, 3.7% Polish, 3.3% American
Employment: 10.8% management, business, and financial, 3.8% computer, engineering, and science, 11.4% education, legal, community service, arts, and media, 4.8% healthcare practitioners, 25.1% service, 23.1% sales and office, 9.9% natural resources, construction, and maintenance, 11.0% production, transportation, and material moving
Income: Per capita: $29,269; Median household: $73,591; Average household: $93,294; Households with income of $100,000 or more: 38.3%; Poverty rate: 15.2%
Educational Attainment: High school diploma or higher: 77.6%; Bachelor's degree or higher: 30.9%; Graduate/professional degree or higher: 12.9%

School District(s)
Huntington Union Free SD (KG-12)
    2014-15 Enrollment: 4,563 . . . . (631) 673-2038
South Huntington Union Free SD (PK-12)
    2014-15 Enrollment: 6,072 . . . . (631) 812-3070
Housing: Homeownership rate: 71.8%; Median home value: $352,500; Median year structure built: 1957; Homeowner vacancy rate: 1.3%; Median selected monthly owner costs: $2,578 with a mortgage, $1,150 without a mortgage; Median gross rent: $1,587 per month; Rental vacancy rate: 7.9%
Health Insurance: 82.8% have insurance; 63.5% have private insurance; 28.4% have public insurance; 17.2% do not have insurance; 7.4% of children under 18 do not have insurance
Transportation: Commute: 80.9% car, 10.4% public transportation, 2.4% walk, 4.1% work from home; Mean travel time to work: 27.7 minutes

ISLANDIA (village).
Covers a land area of 2.220 square miles and a water area of 0 square miles. Located at 40.81° N. Lat; 73.17° W. Long. Elevation is 66 feet.
Population: 3,370; Growth (since 2000): 10.2%; Density: 1,518.1 persons per square mile; Race: 69.1% White, 12.5% Black/African American, 9.8% Asian, 0.0% American Indian/Alaska Native, 0.0% Native Hawaiian/Other Pacific Islander, 0.7% Two or more races, 29.1% Hispanic of any race; Average household size: 3.37; Median age: 44.1; Age under 18: 20.6%; Age 65 and over: 14.0%; Males per 100 females: 88.1; Marriage status: 34.8% never married, 48.8% now married, 2.1% separated, 6.0% widowed, 10.4% divorced; Foreign born: 25.4%; Speak English only: 61.7%; With disability: 7.6%; Veterans: 8.1%; Ancestry: 17.1% Italian, 9.5% Irish, 6.8% German, 4.7% Trinidadian and Tobagonian, 2.8% Polish
Employment: 12.2% management, business, and financial, 4.5% computer, engineering, and science, 9.4% education, legal, community service, arts, and media, 4.4% healthcare practitioners, 21.0% service, 25.9% sales and office, 11.2% natural resources, construction, and maintenance, 11.4% production, transportation, and material moving
Income: Per capita: $30,941; Median household: $87,976; Average household: $101,948; Households with income of $100,000 or more: 43.3%; Poverty rate: 3.6%
Educational Attainment: High school diploma or higher: 87.5%; Bachelor's degree or higher: 25.3%; Graduate/professional degree or higher: 9.6%

School District(s)
Central Islip Union Free SD (PK-12)
    2014-15 Enrollment: 7,302 . . . . (631) 348-4421
Vocational/Technical School(s)
New York Institute of Beauty (Private, For-profit)
    Fall 2014 Enrollment: 112 . . . . (631) 582-4737
    2015-16 Tuition: $8,595
Housing: Homeownership rate: 87.9%; Median home value: $313,200; Median year structure built: 1969; Homeowner vacancy rate: 2.9%; Median selected monthly owner costs: $2,591 with a mortgage, $1,083 without a mortgage; Median gross rent: $1,815 per month; Rental vacancy rate: 8.5%
Health Insurance: 91.2% have insurance; 71.1% have private insurance; 27.9% have public insurance; 8.8% do not have insurance; 0.0% of children under 18 do not have insurance
Transportation: Commute: 88.8% car, 5.3% public transportation, 0.0% walk, 3.5% work from home; Mean travel time to work: 29.2 minutes

ISLIP (CDP).
Covers a land area of 4.800 square miles and a water area of 0.119 square miles. Located at 40.74° N. Lat; 73.22° W. Long. Elevation is 13 feet.
History: Islip is one of ten towns in Suffolk County located on the south shore of Long Island. Within the Town of Islip is a smaller, unincorporated hamlet and census-designated place also named Islip.
Population: 18,433; Growth (since 2000): -10.4%; Density: 3,840.2 persons per square mile; Race: 86.2% White, 4.7% Black/African American, 1.9% Asian, 0.0% American Indian/Alaska Native, 0.0% Native Hawaiian/Other Pacific Islander, 0.9% Two or more races, 17.0% Hispanic of any race; Average household size: 2.99; Median age: 41.5; Age under 18: 22.0%; Age 65 and over: 14.2%; Males per 100 females: 95.6; Marriage status: 34.9% never married, 52.5% now married, 1.6% separated, 6.2% widowed, 6.4% divorced; Foreign born: 10.9%; Speak English only: 84.9%; With disability: 9.7%; Veterans: 8.0%; Ancestry: 27.5% Italian, 26.4% Irish, 21.8% German, 4.2% English, 3.6% Polish
Employment: 15.2% management, business, and financial, 4.5% computer, engineering, and science, 13.0% education, legal, community service, arts, and media, 6.0% healthcare practitioners, 16.9% service, 27.2% sales and office, 9.5% natural resources, construction, and maintenance, 7.8% production, transportation, and material moving
Income: Per capita: $40,483; Median household: $97,500; Average household: $117,987; Households with income of $100,000 or more: 47.7%; Poverty rate: 5.6%
Educational Attainment: High school diploma or higher: 92.4%; Bachelor's degree or higher: 32.7%; Graduate/professional degree or higher: 13.1%

School District(s)
Islip Union Free SD (KG-12)
    2014-15 Enrollment: 2,961 . . . . (631) 650-8210
Housing: Homeownership rate: 83.4%; Median home value: $364,700; Median year structure built: 1963; Homeowner vacancy rate: 1.5%; Median selected monthly owner costs: $2,783 with a mortgage, $1,214 without a mortgage; Median gross rent: $1,540 per month; Rental vacancy rate: 6.8%
Health Insurance: 94.3% have insurance; 81.0% have private insurance; 25.3% have public insurance; 5.7% do not have insurance; 2.7% of children under 18 do not have insurance
Transportation: Commute: 89.2% car, 7.4% public transportation, 0.5% walk, 2.5% work from home; Mean travel time to work: 32.4 minutes
Airports: Long Island MacArthur (primary service/small hub)

ISLIP (town).
Covers a land area of 104.114 square miles and a water area of 58.891 square miles. Located at 40.71° N. Lat; 73.20° W. Long. Elevation is 13 feet.
History: Islip is one of ten towns in Suffolk County located on the south shore of Long Island.
Population: 336,747; Growth (since 2000): 4.4%; Density: 3,234.4 persons per square mile; Race: 72.9% White, 10.1% Black/African American, 2.9% Asian, 0.2% American Indian/Alaska Native, 0.0% Native Hawaiian/Other Pacific Islander, 3.9% Two or more races, 29.5% Hispanic of any race; Average household size: 3.28; Median age: 37.7; Age under 18: 24.1%; Age 65 and over: 12.5%; Males per 100 females: 97.2; Marriage status: 35.6% never married, 49.8% now married, 2.1% separated, 6.1% widowed, 8.5% divorced; Foreign born: 19.5%; Speak English only: 69.1%; With disability: 9.6%; Veterans: 5.7%; Ancestry: 22.4% Italian, 18.4% Irish, 13.1% German, 3.4% English, 3.3% Polish

Employment: 12.4% management, business, and financial, 3.4% computer, engineering, and science, 10.9% education, legal, community service, arts, and media, 5.1% healthcare practitioners, 19.3% service, 25.6% sales and office, 9.7% natural resources, construction, and maintenance, 13.8% production, transportation, and material moving
Income: Per capita: $32,425; Median household: $86,864; Average household: $103,042; Households with income of $100,000 or more: 42.6%; Poverty rate: 7.3%
Educational Attainment: High school diploma or higher: 85.3%; Bachelor's degree or higher: 27.5%; Graduate/professional degree or higher: 11.7%

School District(s)
Islip Union Free SD (KG-12)
    2014-15 Enrollment: 2,961 . . . . (631) 650-8210
Housing: Homeownership rate: 76.8%; Median home value: $350,700; Median year structure built: 1965; Homeowner vacancy rate: 1.0%; Median selected monthly owner costs: $2,646 with a mortgage, $1,154 without a mortgage; Median gross rent: $1,510 per month; Rental vacancy rate: 4.0%
Health Insurance: 89.4% have insurance; 73.9% have private insurance; 25.9% have public insurance; 10.6% do not have insurance; 4.3% of children under 18 do not have insurance
Transportation: Commute: 88.2% car, 6.7% public transportation, 1.2% walk, 2.3% work from home; Mean travel time to work: 30.3 minutes
Airports: Long Island MacArthur (primary service/small hub)
Additional Information Contacts
Town of Islip . . . . (631) 224-5490
    http://www.townofislip-ny.gov

ISLIP TERRACE (CDP). Covers a land area of 1.347 square miles and a water area of 0 square miles. Located at 40.75° N. Lat; 73.19° W. Long. Elevation is 23 feet.
Population: 5,327; Growth (since 2000): -5.6%; Density: 3,954.1 persons per square mile; Race: 91.4% White, 2.0% Black/African American, 2.4% Asian, 0.3% American Indian/Alaska Native, 0.0% Native Hawaiian/Other Pacific Islander, 3.3% Two or more races, 14.6% Hispanic of any race; Average household size: 3.10; Median age: 40.6; Age under 18: 24.1%; Age 65 and over: 12.9%; Males per 100 females: 99.7; Marriage status: 30.0% never married, 57.6% now married, 3.6% separated, 5.3% widowed, 7.2% divorced; Foreign born: 5.9%; Speak English only: 88.8%; With disability: 7.1%; Veterans: 6.9%; Ancestry: 37.6% Italian, 33.8% Irish, 21.8% German, 4.2% Polish, 3.6% English
Employment: 13.0% management, business, and financial, 5.8% computer, engineering, and science, 12.6% education, legal, community service, arts, and media, 3.4% healthcare practitioners, 14.8% service, 33.0% sales and office, 10.3% natural resources, construction, and maintenance, 7.0% production, transportation, and material moving
Income: Per capita: $34,906; Median household: $96,856; Average household: $105,788; Households with income of $100,000 or more: 48.9%; Poverty rate: 4.6%
Educational Attainment: High school diploma or higher: 94.2%; Bachelor's degree or higher: 26.6%; Graduate/professional degree or higher: 9.6%

School District(s)
East Islip Union Free SD (PK-12)
    2014-15 Enrollment: 3,985 . . . . (631) 224-2000
Housing: Homeownership rate: 89.6%; Median home value: $344,900; Median year structure built: 1961; Homeowner vacancy rate: 1.5%; Median selected monthly owner costs: $2,832 with a mortgage, $1,202 without a mortgage; Median gross rent: $1,368 per month; Rental vacancy rate: 0.0%
Health Insurance: 93.8% have insurance; 85.4% have private insurance; 20.8% have public insurance; 6.2% do not have insurance; 1.9% of children under 18 do not have insurance
Transportation: Commute: 90.8% car, 6.2% public transportation, 0.3% walk, 2.2% work from home; Mean travel time to work: 32.3 minutes

---

JAMESPORT (CDP). Covers a land area of 4.496 square miles and a water area of 0.027 square miles. Located at 40.96° N. Lat; 72.58° W. Long. Elevation is 16 feet.
Population: 1,355; Growth (since 2000): -11.2%; Density: 301.4 persons per square mile; Race: 98.5% White, 1.5% Black/African American, 0.0% Asian, 0.0% American Indian/Alaska Native, 0.0% Native Hawaiian/Other Pacific Islander, 0.0% Two or more races, 17.3% Hispanic of any race; Average household size: 3.07; Median age: 32.9; Age under 18: 12.5%;

Age 65 and over: 14.5%; Males per 100 females: 97.2; Marriage status: 41.7% never married, 51.0% now married, 0.0% separated, 4.1% widowed, 3.2% divorced; Foreign born: 4.8%; Speak English only: 78.9%; With disability: 3.4%; Veterans: 5.7%; Ancestry: 44.5% German, 20.1% Albanian, 18.7% Norwegian, 8.4% Italian, 8.2% German
Employment: 36.4% management, business, and financial, 3.7% computer, engineering, and science, 21.4% education, legal, community service, arts, and media, 11.0% healthcare practitioners, 0.0% service, 16.3% sales and office, 2.9% natural resources, construction, and maintenance, 8.4% production, transportation, and material moving
Income: Per capita: $36,590; Median household: $80,711; Average household: $108,583; Households with income of $100,000 or more: 41.6%; Poverty rate: 20.7%
Educational Attainment: High school diploma or higher: 100.0%; Bachelor's degree or higher: 48.7%; Graduate/professional degree or higher: 38.9%
Housing: Homeownership rate: 95.2%; Median home value: $378,100; Median year structure built: 1964; Homeowner vacancy rate: 8.4%; Median selected monthly owner costs: $2,694 with a mortgage, $1,050 without a mortgage; Median gross rent: n/a per month; Rental vacancy rate: 0.0%
Health Insurance: 83.9% have insurance; 57.8% have private insurance; 37.0% have public insurance; 16.1% do not have insurance; 0.0% of children under 18 do not have insurance
Transportation: Commute: 82.6% car, 0.0% public transportation, 0.0% walk, 17.4% work from home; Mean travel time to work: 30.4 minutes

---

KINGS PARK (CDP). Covers a land area of 6.199 square miles and a water area of 0.391 square miles. Located at 40.89° N. Lat; 73.25° W. Long. Elevation is 174 feet.
History: Developed as utopian community in 1872; became farm for insane in 1885. State psychiatric center opened 1892.
Population: 17,823; Growth (since 2000): 10.4%; Density: 2,875.0 persons per square mile; Race: 93.0% White, 0.8% Black/African American, 3.0% Asian, 0.0% American Indian/Alaska Native, 0.0% Native Hawaiian/Other Pacific Islander, 0.6% Two or more races, 6.1% Hispanic of any race; Average household size: 2.85; Median age: 43.6; Age under 18: 21.3%; Age 65 and over: 20.5%; Males per 100 females: 93.7; Marriage status: 26.9% never married, 59.0% now married, 1.4% separated, 7.5% widowed, 6.6% divorced; Foreign born: 7.0%; Speak English only: 90.0%; With disability: 10.0%; Veterans: 7.9%; Ancestry: 33.9% Italian, 28.0% Irish, 22.3% German, 7.5% English, 5.7% Polish
Employment: 18.7% management, business, and financial, 4.0% computer, engineering, and science, 14.7% education, legal, community service, arts, and media, 7.3% healthcare practitioners, 14.4% service, 26.8% sales and office, 9.0% natural resources, construction, and maintenance, 5.1% production, transportation, and material moving
Income: Per capita: $42,151; Median household: $98,384; Average household: $119,759; Households with income of $100,000 or more: 49.4%; Poverty rate: 5.3%
Educational Attainment: High school diploma or higher: 93.5%; Bachelor's degree or higher: 40.6%; Graduate/professional degree or higher: 17.4%

School District(s)
Kings Park Central SD (KG-12)
    2014-15 Enrollment: 3,555 . . . . (631) 269-3310
Housing: Homeownership rate: 81.4%; Median home value: $423,600; Median year structure built: 1966; Homeowner vacancy rate: 0.3%; Median selected monthly owner costs: $2,966 with a mortgage, $1,158 without a mortgage; Median gross rent: $1,341 per month; Rental vacancy rate: 4.7%
Health Insurance: 95.5% have insurance; 83.4% have private insurance; 27.6% have public insurance; 4.5% do not have insurance; 0.6% of children under 18 do not have insurance
Transportation: Commute: 86.5% car, 9.0% public transportation, 1.1% walk, 3.2% work from home; Mean travel time to work: 34.4 minutes

---

LAKE GROVE (village). Covers a land area of 2.947 square miles and a water area of 0.001 square miles. Located at 40.86° N. Lat; 73.12° W. Long. Elevation is 118 feet.
Population: 11,262; Growth (since 2000): 9.9%; Density: 3,821.8 persons per square mile; Race: 89.3% White, 1.3% Black/African American, 3.5% Asian, 0.0% American Indian/Alaska Native, 0.0% Native Hawaiian/Other Pacific Islander, 2.6% Two or more races, 10.3% Hispanic of any race; Average household size: 3.02; Median age: 39.4; Age under 18: 22.5%; Age 65 and over: 13.6%; Males per 100 females: 98.6; Marriage status:

31.5% never married, 56.1% now married, 2.0% separated, 5.9% widowed, 6.5% divorced; Foreign born: 14.3%; Speak English only: 83.2%; With disability: 7.9%; Veterans: 5.9%; Ancestry: 39.8% Italian, 24.4% Irish, 18.4% German, 4.9% Polish, 4.2% English

Employment: 16.4% management, business, and financial, 6.9% computer, engineering, and science, 12.2% education, legal, community service, arts, and media, 6.5% healthcare practitioners, 17.6% service, 27.8% sales and office, 6.4% natural resources, construction, and maintenance, 6.1% production, transportation, and material moving

Income: Per capita: $38,573; Median household: $94,960; Average household: $112,664; Households with income of $100,000 or more: 47.0%; Poverty rate: 9.2%

Educational Attainment: High school diploma or higher: 93.4%; Bachelor's degree or higher: 37.3%; Graduate/professional degree or higher: 15.4%

School District(s)

Middle Country Central SD (PK-12)

    2014-15 Enrollment: 10,254 . . . . (631) 285-8005

Sachem Central SD (KG-12)

    2014-15 Enrollment: 13,882 . . . . (631) 471-1336

Housing: Homeownership rate: 81.1%; Median home value: $378,600; Median year structure built: 1969; Homeowner vacancy rate: 1.2%; Median selected monthly owner costs: $2,751 with a mortgage, $1,124 without a mortgage; Median gross rent: $1,786 per month; Rental vacancy rate: 0.0%

Health Insurance: 92.6% have insurance; 83.3% have private insurance; 20.8% have public insurance; 7.4% do not have insurance; 0.9% of children under 18 do not have insurance

Transportation: Commute: 86.7% car, 8.9% public transportation, 1.2% walk, 2.2% work from home; Mean travel time to work: 34.8 minutes

Additional Information Contacts

Village of Lake Grove . . . . (631) 585-2000

    http://www.lakegroveny.gov

LAKE RONKONKOMA (CDP).

Covers a land area of 4.940 square miles and a water area of 0.003 square miles. Located at 40.83° N. Lat; 73.11° W. Long. Elevation is 72 feet.

History: The actual Lake Ronkonkoma, adjacent to the hamlet, is the largest lake on Long Island. It is a "groundwater lake," not fed by streams, with no surface outlet.

Population: 19,943; Growth (since 2000): 1.2%; Density: 4,036.8 persons per square mile; Race: 90.4% White, 2.3% Black/African American, 4.0% Asian, 0.1% American Indian/Alaska Native, 0.0% Native Hawaiian/Other Pacific Islander, 1.7% Two or more races, 11.4% Hispanic of any race; Average household size: 2.89; Median age: 39.5; Age under 18: 23.2%; Age 65 and over: 13.3%; Males per 100 females: 94.6; Marriage status: 31.3% never married, 54.1% now married, 1.6% separated, 6.5% widowed, 8.1% divorced; Foreign born: 11.7%; Speak English only: 81.9%; With disability: 10.2%; Veterans: 7.1%; Ancestry: 32.4% Italian, 27.7% Irish, 16.3% German, 5.6% Polish, 4.4% English

Employment: 13.9% management, business, and financial, 5.4% computer, engineering, and science, 13.8% education, legal, community service, arts, and media, 3.8% healthcare practitioners, 17.0% service, 26.9% sales and office, 10.0% natural resources, construction, and maintenance, 9.1% production, transportation, and material moving

Income: Per capita: $34,517; Median household: $87,296; Average household: $98,473; Households with income of $100,000 or more: 43.9%; Poverty rate: 6.2%

Educational Attainment: High school diploma or higher: 91.8%; Bachelor's degree or higher: 29.0%; Graduate/professional degree or higher: 13.4%

School District(s)

Sachem Central SD (KG-12)

    2014-15 Enrollment: 13,882 . . . . (631) 471-1336

Housing: Homeownership rate: 75.4%; Median home value: $336,800; Median year structure built: 1967; Homeowner vacancy rate: 0.5%; Median selected monthly owner costs: $2,625 with a mortgage, $975 without a mortgage; Median gross rent: $1,370 per month; Rental vacancy rate: 0.0%

Health Insurance: 94.2% have insurance; 81.9% have private insurance; 23.5% have public insurance; 5.8% do not have insurance; 2.3% of children under 18 do not have insurance

Transportation: Commute: 90.6% car, 4.6% public transportation, 1.1% walk, 2.1% work from home; Mean travel time to work: 31.3 minutes

LAUREL (CDP).

Covers a land area of 3.000 square miles and a water area of 0.074 square miles. Located at 40.97° N. Lat; 72.56° W. Long. Elevation is 20 feet.

Population: 1,250; Growth (since 2000): 5.2%; Density: 416.7 persons per square mile; Race: 98.3% White, 0.6% Black/African American, 0.0% Asian, 0.0% American Indian/Alaska Native, 0.0% Native Hawaiian/Other Pacific Islander, 0.6% Two or more races, 0.6% Hispanic of any race; Average household size: 2.33; Median age: 50.8; Age under 18: 11.0%; Age 65 and over: 33.0%; Males per 100 females: 102.9; Marriage status: 29.5% never married, 48.0% now married, 1.4% separated, 14.1% widowed, 8.3% divorced; Foreign born: 4.4%; Speak English only: 97.4%; With disability: 15.5%; Veterans: 11.3%; Ancestry: 35.3% Irish, 24.2% Polish, 20.9% Italian, 17.4% English, 14.7% German

Employment: 8.8% management, business, and financial, 0.0% computer, engineering, and science, 19.8% education, legal, community service, arts, and media, 6.1% healthcare practitioners, 26.4% service, 19.8% sales and office, 19.1% natural resources, construction, and maintenance, 0.0% production, transportation, and material moving

Income: Per capita: $55,106; Median household: $103,723; Average household: $127,213; Households with income of $100,000 or more: 55.9%; Poverty rate: 2.7%

Educational Attainment: High school diploma or higher: 95.2%; Bachelor's degree or higher: 45.6%; Graduate/professional degree or higher: 27.1%

Housing: Homeownership rate: 89.5%; Median home value: $584,200; Median year structure built: 1973; Homeowner vacancy rate: 0.0%; Median selected monthly owner costs: $3,117 with a mortgage, $1,144 without a mortgage; Median gross rent: n/a per month; Rental vacancy rate: 0.0%

Health Insurance: 94.7% have insurance; 72.1% have private insurance; 41.9% have public insurance; 5.3% do not have insurance; 0.0% of children under 18 do not have insurance

Transportation: Commute: 88.1% car, 9.5% public transportation, 1.1% walk, 1.3% work from home; Mean travel time to work: 19.8 minutes

LINDENHURST (village).

Covers a land area of 3.760 square miles and a water area of 0.057 square miles. Located at 40.69° N. Lat; 73.37° W. Long. Elevation is 30 feet.

History: Named for Linden, Germany. Incorporated 1923.

Population: 27,310; Growth (since 2000): -1.8%; Density: 7,262.9 persons per square mile; Race: 91.8% White, 2.0% Black/African American, 1.8% Asian, 0.0% American Indian/Alaska Native, 0.0% Native Hawaiian/Other Pacific Islander, 1.3% Two or more races, 15.4% Hispanic of any race; Average household size: 3.00; Median age: 41.3; Age under 18: 18.9%; Age 65 and over: 12.3%; Males per 100 females: 94.6; Marriage status: 32.3% never married, 53.6% now married, 1.9% separated, 5.8% widowed, 8.3% divorced; Foreign born: 17.1%; Speak English only: 76.1%; With disability: 9.7%; Veterans: 6.3%; Ancestry: 32.5% Italian, 22.7% Irish, 18.5% German, 10.8% Polish, 3.8% English

Employment: 11.4% management, business, and financial, 3.1% computer, engineering, and science, 10.3% education, legal, community service, arts, and media, 4.6% healthcare practitioners, 18.3% service, 29.4% sales and office, 11.9% natural resources, construction, and maintenance, 10.9% production, transportation, and material moving

Income: Per capita: $33,359; Median household: $83,532; Average household: $95,886; Households with income of $100,000 or more: 38.7%; Poverty rate: 5.8%

Educational Attainment: High school diploma or higher: 89.4%; Bachelor's degree or higher: 24.8%; Graduate/professional degree or higher: 8.2%

School District(s)

Lindenhurst Union Free SD (KG-12)

    2014-15 Enrollment: 6,249 . . . . (631) 867-3001

Housing: Homeownership rate: 76.4%; Median home value: $342,200; Median year structure built: 1957; Homeowner vacancy rate: 2.3%; Median selected monthly owner costs: $2,646 with a mortgage, $1,208 without a mortgage; Median gross rent: $1,395 per month; Rental vacancy rate: 8.4%

Health Insurance: 91.3% have insurance; 78.7% have private insurance; 24.1% have public insurance; 8.7% do not have insurance; 4.8% of children under 18 do not have insurance

Transportation: Commute: 85.4% car, 10.0% public transportation, 2.5% walk, 1.1% work from home; Mean travel time to work: 34.3 minutes

Additional Information Contacts

Village of Lindenhurst . . . . (631) 957-7500

    http://www.villageoflindenhurst.com

LLOYD HARBOR (village). Covers a land area of 9.363 square miles and a water area of 1.296 square miles. Located at 40.92° N. Lat; 73.44° W. Long. Elevation is 138 feet.

History: In 1654, the Matinecock Native Americans sold 3,000 acres (12 km_) of what is now called Lloyd Neck to English settlers from Oyster Bay. The Matinecock referred to the region as Caumsett (place by sharp rock). In 1676, James Lloyd acquired the neck, which was then taken over by his son Henry.

Population: 3,684; Growth (since 2000): 0.2%; Density: 393.5 persons per square mile; Race: 94.3% White, 0.3% Black/African American, 4.1% Asian, 0.0% American Indian/Alaska Native, 0.0% Native Hawaiian/Other Pacific Islander, 1.2% Two or more races, 3.1% Hispanic of any race; Average household size: 3.38; Median age: 44.2; Age under 18: 32.8%; Age 65 and over: 14.0%; Males per 100 females: 99.7; Marriage status: 27.5% never married, 67.4% now married, 0.3% separated, 2.9% widowed, 2.2% divorced; Foreign born: 7.4%; Speak English only: 93.8%; With disability: 5.9%; Veterans: 5.9%; Ancestry: 29.0% Irish, 26.9% Italian, 18.1% German, 9.0% American, 8.4% English

Employment: 28.0% management, business, and financial, 3.9% computer, engineering, and science, 21.9% education, legal, community service, arts, and media, 10.0% healthcare practitioners, 8.5% service, 22.9% sales and office, 3.8% natural resources, construction, and maintenance, 1.0% production, transportation, and material moving

Income: Per capita: $98,260; Median household: $202,292; Average household: $332,442; Households with income of $100,000 or more: 78.4%; Poverty rate: 3.3%

Educational Attainment: High school diploma or higher: 98.3%; Bachelor's degree or higher: 76.0%; Graduate/professional degree or higher: 42.7%

Housing: Homeownership rate: 94.4%; Median home value: $1,447,400; Median year structure built: 1966; Homeowner vacancy rate: 1.6%; Median selected monthly owner costs: $4,000+ with a mortgage, $1,500+ without a mortgage; Median gross rent: n/a per month; Rental vacancy rate: 23.1%

Health Insurance: 95.5% have insurance; 88.8% have private insurance; 15.8% have public insurance; 4.5% do not have insurance; 5.0% of children under 18 do not have insurance

Safety: Violent crime rate: 0.0 per 10,000 population; Property crime rate: 37.9 per 10,000 population

Transportation: Commute: 71.7% car, 17.0% public transportation, 1.5% walk, 7.2% work from home; Mean travel time to work: 48.3 minutes

MANORVILLE (CDP). Covers a land area of 25.469 square miles and a water area of 0.042 square miles. Located at 40.86° N. Lat; 72.79° W. Long. Elevation is 52 feet.

Population: 14,501; Growth (since 2000): 30.3%; Density: 569.4 persons per square mile; Race: 95.2% White, 1.6% Black/African American, 0.7% Asian, 0.0% American Indian/Alaska Native, 0.0% Native Hawaiian/Other Pacific Islander, 1.8% Two or more races, 5.7% Hispanic of any race; Average household size: 3.00; Median age: 39.0; Age under 18: 26.3%; Age 65 and over: 11.6%; Males per 100 females: 98.0; Marriage status: 29.1% never married, 56.3% now married, 0.4% separated, 7.4% widowed, 7.1% divorced; Foreign born: 4.1%; Speak English only: 93.7%; With disability: 7.0%; Veterans: 6.4%; Ancestry: 40.1% Italian, 26.7% Irish, 18.9% German, 6.5% Polish, 4.0% English

Employment: 20.4% management, business, and financial, 4.9% computer, engineering, and science, 14.9% education, legal, community service, arts, and media, 7.1% healthcare practitioners, 14.8% service, 20.6% sales and office, 7.6% natural resources, construction, and maintenance, 9.7% production, transportation, and material moving

Income: Per capita: $37,749; Median household: $104,519; Average household: $112,013; Households with income of $100,000 or more: 50.9%; Poverty rate: 4.6%

Educational Attainment: High school diploma or higher: 96.0%; Bachelor's degree or higher: 36.7%; Graduate/professional degree or higher: 16.0%

School District(s)

Eastport-South Manor CSD (KG-12)

   2014-15 Enrollment: 3,623 . . . . (631) 801-3011

Housing: Homeownership rate: 87.0%; Median home value: $407,500; Median year structure built: 1992; Homeowner vacancy rate: 2.1%; Median selected monthly owner costs: $3,228 with a mortgage, $933 without a mortgage; Median gross rent: $1,511 per month; Rental vacancy rate: 0.0%

Health Insurance: 94.8% have insurance; 86.4% have private insurance; 18.6% have public insurance; 5.2% do not have insurance; 3.2% of children under 18 do not have insurance

Transportation: Commute: 96.4% car, 0.7% public transportation, 0.4% walk, 2.5% work from home; Mean travel time to work: 31.6 minutes

MASTIC (CDP). Covers a land area of 3.897 square miles and a water area of 0.085 square miles. Located at 40.81° N. Lat; 72.85° W. Long. Elevation is 30 feet.

History: The hamlet was originally called Forge, and was chaned to Mastic in 1893. The Poospatuck Indian Reservation lies in the town's southern end.

Population: 16,084; Growth (since 2000): 4.2%; Density: 4,127.3 persons per square mile; Race: 83.0% White, 7.7% Black/African American, 4.1% Asian, 0.4% American Indian/Alaska Native, 0.0% Native Hawaiian/Other Pacific Islander, 2.2% Two or more races, 21.5% Hispanic of any race; Average household size: 3.38; Median age: 35.6; Age under 18: 26.5%; Age 65 and over: 7.9%; Males per 100 females: 100.1; Marriage status: 32.3% never married, 54.9% now married, 1.8% separated, 4.0% widowed, 8.9% divorced; Foreign born: 12.6%; Speak English only: 77.0%; With disability: 9.4%; Veterans: 5.8%; Ancestry: 27.7% Italian, 23.0% Irish, 21.3% German, 3.2% English, 3.1% Polish

Employment: 8.4% management, business, and financial, 3.6% computer, engineering, and science, 6.8% education, legal, community service, arts, and media, 6.3% healthcare practitioners, 25.2% service, 23.7% sales and office, 12.8% natural resources, construction, and maintenance, 13.2% production, transportation, and material moving

Income: Per capita: $24,630; Median household: $71,789; Average household: $80,048; Households with income of $100,000 or more: 31.0%; Poverty rate: 12.9%

Educational Attainment: High school diploma or higher: 86.3%; Bachelor's degree or higher: 13.8%; Graduate/professional degree or higher: 4.6%

Housing: Homeownership rate: 78.8%; Median home value: $235,100; Median year structure built: 1975; Homeowner vacancy rate: 3.8%; Median selected monthly owner costs: $2,264 with a mortgage, $1,002 without a mortgage; Median gross rent: $1,617 per month; Rental vacancy rate: 4.5%

Health Insurance: 87.3% have insurance; 66.8% have private insurance; 32.7% have public insurance; 12.7% do not have insurance; 5.4% of children under 18 do not have insurance

Transportation: Commute: 92.2% car, 2.4% public transportation, 2.7% walk, 2.0% work from home; Mean travel time to work: 31.4 minutes

MASTIC BEACH (village). Covers a land area of 4.715 square miles and a water area of 0.265 square miles. Located at 40.77° N. Lat; 72.84° W. Long. Elevation is 7 feet.

History: Mastic Beach is on a peninsula extending into Moriches Bay. Created in 1928, there are marinas, private docks, and several historic sites. There is sailing, swimming, fishing, birding, hiking, camping and shopping.

Population: 14,883; Growth (since 2000): 28.9%; Density: 3,156.6 persons per square mile; Race: 81.7% White, 11.3% Black/African American, 1.7% Asian, 0.2% American Indian/Alaska Native, 0.0% Native Hawaiian/Other Pacific Islander, 4.3% Two or more races, 17.5% Hispanic of any race; Average household size: 3.05; Median age: 35.9; Age under 18: 27.2%; Age 65 and over: 8.0%; Males per 100 females: 98.6; Marriage status: 39.9% never married, 45.4% now married, 2.3% separated, 5.4% widowed, 9.3% divorced; Foreign born: 6.6%; Speak English only: 84.5%; With disability: 10.3%; Veterans: 7.4%; Ancestry: 30.2% Italian, 23.4% Irish, 15.7% German, 3.4% Polish, 3.0% English

Employment: 8.8% management, business, and financial, 4.1% computer, engineering, and science, 9.1% education, legal, community service, arts, and media, 5.1% healthcare practitioners, 16.7% service, 29.2% sales and office, 16.2% natural resources, construction, and maintenance, 10.9% production, transportation, and material moving

Income: Per capita: $25,119; Median household: $62,602; Average household: $74,023; Households with income of $100,000 or more: 29.4%; Poverty rate: 14.6%

Educational Attainment: High school diploma or higher: 86.0%; Bachelor's degree or higher: 13.9%; Graduate/professional degree or higher: 5.5%

School District(s)

William Floyd Union Free SD (KG-12)

   2014-15 Enrollment: 8,832 . . . . (631) 874-1201

Housing: Homeownership rate: 73.3%; Median home value: $188,500; Median year structure built: 1965; Homeowner vacancy rate: 4.2%; Median selected monthly owner costs: $2,093 with a mortgage, $919 without a mortgage; Median gross rent: $1,622 per month; Rental vacancy rate: 0.9%

Health Insurance: 89.3% have insurance; 69.9% have private insurance; 31.0% have public insurance; 10.7% do not have insurance; 5.4% of children under 18 do not have insurance

Transportation: Commute: 94.5% car, 2.4% public transportation, 0.4% walk, 1.9% work from home; Mean travel time to work: 38.8 minutes

MATTITUCK (CDP).
Covers a land area of 8.996 square miles and a water area of 0.364 square miles. Located at 41.00° N. Lat; 72.54° W. Long. Elevation is 16 feet.

History: Mattituck is believed to havebeen named for the Native American "Great Creek." Mattituck Creek has been dredged and is used extensively by pleasure craft on Long Island Sound.

Population: 4,435; Growth (since 2000): 5.6%; Density: 493.0 persons per square mile; Race: 94.2% White, 1.5% Black/African American, 0.5% Asian, 2.7% American Indian/Alaska Native, 0.0% Native Hawaiian/Other Pacific Islander, 1.1% Two or more races, 3.3% Hispanic of any race; Average household size: 2.41; Median age: 49.5; Age under 18: 23.0%; Age 65 and over: 18.4%; Males per 100 females: 98.2; Marriage status: 26.2% never married, 64.1% now married, 0.6% separated, 2.3% widowed, 7.4% divorced; Foreign born: 7.2%; Speak English only: 85.7%; With disability: 13.6%; Veterans: 8.8%; Ancestry: 24.1% Irish, 20.4% German, 17.8% Italian, 12.4% Polish, 11.2% English

Employment: 16.3% management, business, and financial, 2.9% computer, engineering, and science, 17.2% education, legal, community service, arts, and media, 4.5% healthcare practitioners, 16.3% service, 17.3% sales and office, 18.9% natural resources, construction, and maintenance, 6.7% production, transportation, and material moving

Income: Per capita: $43,016; Median household: $75,391; Average household: $103,201; Households with income of $100,000 or more: 36.3%; Poverty rate: 3.3%

Educational Attainment: High school diploma or higher: 94.9%; Bachelor's degree or higher: 40.2%; Graduate/professional degree or higher: 20.5%

School District(s)
Mattituck-Cutchogue Union Free SD (KG-12)
    2014-15 Enrollment: 1,310 . . . . (631) 298-4242
Housing: Homeownership rate: 79.7%; Median home value: $497,900; Median year structure built: 1961; Homeowner vacancy rate: 0.0%; Median selected monthly owner costs: $2,562 with a mortgage, $1,054 without a mortgage; Median gross rent: $1,402 per month; Rental vacancy rate: 0.0%
Health Insurance: 93.6% have insurance; 81.0% have private insurance; 30.9% have public insurance; 6.4% do not have insurance; 7.1% of children under 18 do not have insurance
Newspapers: Suffolk Times (weekly circulation 12,000); The News-Review (weekly circulation 5,000)
Transportation: Commute: 87.5% car, 2.4% public transportation, 1.4% walk, 6.4% work from home; Mean travel time to work: 26.5 minutes
Airports: Mattituck (general aviation)

MEDFORD (CDP).
Covers a land area of 10.797 square miles and a water area of 0 square miles. Located at 40.82° N. Lat; 72.99° W. Long. Elevation is 89 feet.
Population: 24,793; Growth (since 2000): 12.8%; Density: 2,296.3 persons per square mile; Race: 85.9% White, 7.3% Black/African American, 3.1% Asian, 0.2% American Indian/Alaska Native, 0.0% Native Hawaiian/Other Pacific Islander, 1.8% Two or more races, 23.1% Hispanic of any race; Average household size: 3.13; Median age: 38.6; Age under 18: 21.8%; Age 65 and over: 13.3%; Males per 100 females: 96.5; Marriage status: 37.6% never married, 45.6% now married, 2.7% separated, 7.5% widowed, 9.3% divorced; Foreign born: 12.8%; Speak English only: 76.5%; With disability: 8.3%; Veterans: 6.9%; Ancestry: 27.4% Italian, 25.1% Irish, 17.4% German, 3.9% Polish, 3.5% American
Employment: 13.3% management, business, and financial, 4.9% computer, engineering, and science, 9.8% education, legal, community service, arts, and media, 6.4% healthcare practitioners, 19.5% service, 26.4% sales and office, 10.9% natural resources, construction, and maintenance, 8.8% production, transportation, and material moving

Income: Per capita: $32,985; Median household: $91,035; Average household: $100,227; Households with income of $100,000 or more: 43.4%; Poverty rate: 6.6%
Educational Attainment: High school diploma or higher: 89.3%; Bachelor's degree or higher: 24.0%; Graduate/professional degree or higher: 9.3%

School District(s)
Patchogue-Medford Union Free SD (PK-12)
    2014-15 Enrollment: 7,818 . . . . (631) 687-6380
Housing: Homeownership rate: 84.8%; Median home value: $289,900; Median year structure built: 1974; Homeowner vacancy rate: 1.2%; Median selected monthly owner costs: $2,517 with a mortgage, $998 without a mortgage; Median gross rent: $1,732 per month; Rental vacancy rate: 7.9%
Health Insurance: 91.8% have insurance; 79.0% have private insurance; 27.4% have public insurance; 8.2% do not have insurance; 2.4% of children under 18 do not have insurance
Transportation: Commute: 92.1% car, 4.0% public transportation, 0.2% walk, 3.2% work from home; Mean travel time to work: 32.2 minutes

MELVILLE (CDP).
Covers a land area of 12.086 square miles and a water area of <.001 square miles. Located at 40.78° N. Lat; 73.41° W. Long. Elevation is 135 feet.
History: Poet Walt Whitman was born in a shingle-sided farmhouse that still sits, though rather improbably, on a heavily commercial stretch of Route 110 in Melville, squeezed between a film developer and a furniture store.
Population: 18,682; Growth (since 2000): 28.5%; Density: 1,545.8 persons per square mile; Race: 85.2% White, 4.4% Black/African American, 7.5% Asian, 0.0% American Indian/Alaska Native, 0.0% Native Hawaiian/Other Pacific Islander, 1.0% Two or more races, 5.1% Hispanic of any race; Average household size: 2.68; Median age: 49.1; Age under 18: 21.1%; Age 65 and over: 27.2%; Males per 100 females: 89.9; Marriage status: 21.4% never married, 61.5% now married, 1.6% separated, 10.2% widowed, 7.0% divorced; Foreign born: 12.5%; Speak English only: 85.9%; With disability: 8.2%; Veterans: 7.6%; Ancestry: 22.5% Italian, 10.5% Russian, 8.9% Polish, 8.7% Irish, 8.0% German
Employment: 21.4% management, business, and financial, 4.6% computer, engineering, and science, 15.9% education, legal, community service, arts, and media, 8.7% healthcare practitioners, 7.5% service, 36.1% sales and office, 1.4% natural resources, construction, and maintenance, 4.4% production, transportation, and material moving
Income: Per capita: $64,491; Median household: $121,376; Average household: $172,801; Households with income of $100,000 or more: 57.6%; Poverty rate: 4.4%
Educational Attainment: High school diploma or higher: 96.0%; Bachelor's degree or higher: 54.8%; Graduate/professional degree or higher: 27.6%

School District(s)
Half Hollow Hills Central SD (KG-12)
    2014-15 Enrollment: 8,927 . . . . (631) 592-3008
South Huntington Union Free SD (PK-12)
    2014-15 Enrollment: 6,072 . . . . (631) 812-3070
Two-year College(s)
SBI Campus-An Affiliate of Sanford-Brown (Private, For-profit)
    Fall 2014 Enrollment: 240 . . . . (631) 370-3300
Housing: Homeownership rate: 87.2%; Median home value: $623,700; Median year structure built: 1981; Homeowner vacancy rate: 1.3%; Median selected monthly owner costs: $3,521 with a mortgage, $1,241 without a mortgage; Median gross rent: $2,428 per month; Rental vacancy rate: 8.8%
Health Insurance: 98.4% have insurance; 87.0% have private insurance; 30.6% have public insurance; 1.6% do not have insurance; 0.0% of children under 18 do not have insurance
Newspapers: Newsday (daily circulation 368,000)
Transportation: Commute: 84.1% car, 9.6% public transportation, 0.6% walk, 5.7% work from home; Mean travel time to work: 32.1 minutes

MIDDLE ISLAND (CDP).
Covers a land area of 8.239 square miles and a water area of 0.059 square miles. Located at 40.89° N. Lat; 72.95° W. Long. Elevation is 82 feet.
Population: 9,949; Growth (since 2000): 2.5%; Density: 1,207.5 persons per square mile; Race: 81.2% White, 12.3% Black/African American, 3.8% Asian, 0.0% American Indian/Alaska Native, 0.0% Native Hawaiian/Other Pacific Islander, 1.4% Two or more races, 8.6% Hispanic of any race;

Average household size: 2.36; Median age: 43.6; Age under 18: 19.9%; Age 65 and over: 20.2%; Males per 100 females: 92.7; Marriage status: 27.6% never married, 51.2% now married, 1.6% separated, 9.3% widowed, 11.9% divorced; Foreign born: 9.1%; Speak English only: 90.5%; With disability: 12.9%; Veterans: 9.8%; Ancestry: 30.8% Italian, 21.3% Irish, 14.5% German, 7.1% American, 6.8% Polish

Employment: 14.0% management, business, and financial, 4.7% computer, engineering, and science, 12.1% education, legal, community service, arts, and media, 6.1% healthcare practitioners, 16.3% service, 26.4% sales and office, 12.1% natural resources, construction, and maintenance, 8.3% production, transportation, and material moving

Income: Per capita: $33,745; Median household: $68,847; Average household: $80,009; Households with income of $100,000 or more: 31.9%; Poverty rate: 10.7%

Educational Attainment: High school diploma or higher: 93.8%; Bachelor's degree or higher: 28.9%; Graduate/professional degree or higher: 12.4%

School District(s)
Longwood Central SD (KG-12)
  2014-15 Enrollment: 9,211 . . . . (631) 345-2172

Housing: Homeownership rate: 77.5%; Median home value: $270,900; Median year structure built: 1979; Homeowner vacancy rate: 1.5%; Median selected monthly owner costs: $2,255 with a mortgage, $1,092 without a mortgage; Median gross rent: $1,507 per month; Rental vacancy rate: 8.0%

Health Insurance: 93.7% have insurance; 72.1% have private insurance; 38.0% have public insurance; 6.3% do not have insurance; 3.3% of children under 18 do not have insurance

Transportation: Commute: 93.8% car, 3.3% public transportation, 0.8% walk, 2.1% work from home; Mean travel time to work: 36.6 minutes

MILLER PLACE (CDP).
Covers a land area of 6.552 square miles and a water area of 0 square miles. Located at 40.94° N. Lat; 72.99° W. Long. Elevation is 131 feet.

History: Miller Place is named for the Miller family, settlers of the area in the 17th century. For most of its history, the community functioned as an agriculture-based society.

Population: 11,312; Growth (since 2000): 6.9%; Density: 1,726.6 persons per square mile; Race: 91.1% White, 1.4% Black/African American, 5.6% Asian, 0.2% American Indian/Alaska Native, 0.0% Native Hawaiian/Other Pacific Islander, 1.8% Two or more races, 5.3% Hispanic of any race; Average household size: 2.97; Median age: 38.9; Age under 18: 28.8%; Age 65 and over: 13.6%; Males per 100 females: 98.4; Marriage status: 26.6% never married, 60.5% now married, 1.4% separated, 4.5% widowed, 8.4% divorced; Foreign born: 7.2%; Speak English only: 88.6%; With disability: 6.9%; Veterans: 6.2%; Ancestry: 34.8% Italian, 25.3% Irish, 18.1% German, 7.1% American, 4.1% English

Employment: 16.5% management, business, and financial, 5.6% computer, engineering, and science, 17.6% education, legal, community service, arts, and media, 9.0% healthcare practitioners, 15.0% service, 20.0% sales and office, 12.2% natural resources, construction, and maintenance, 4.1% production, transportation, and material moving

Income: Per capita: $42,947; Median household: $106,654; Average household: $126,262; Households with income of $100,000 or more: 52.4%; Poverty rate: 5.4%

Educational Attainment: High school diploma or higher: 97.4%; Bachelor's degree or higher: 46.9%; Graduate/professional degree or higher: 21.6%

School District(s)
Miller Place Union Free SD (KG-12)
  2014-15 Enrollment: 2,820 . . . . (631) 474-2700

Housing: Homeownership rate: 94.4%; Median home value: $426,700; Median year structure built: 1976; Homeowner vacancy rate: 1.2%; Median selected monthly owner costs: $3,014 with a mortgage, $1,327 without a mortgage; Median gross rent: $1,263 per month; Rental vacancy rate: 0.0%

Health Insurance: 98.5% have insurance; 88.6% have private insurance; 21.4% have public insurance; 1.5% do not have insurance; 0.8% of children under 18 do not have insurance

Transportation: Commute: 94.2% car, 4.1% public transportation, 0.4% walk, 1.3% work from home; Mean travel time to work: 36.9 minutes

MONTAUK (CDP).
Covers a land area of 17.479 square miles and a water area of 2.252 square miles. Located at 41.05° N. Lat; 71.95° W. Long. Elevation is 33 feet.

History: Name derived from Montauk word for hilly land. Founded on land bought from Montauks in 1686 by settlers from nearby East Hampton to raise cattle. Site of oldest cattle ranch in U.S.

Population: 3,495; Growth (since 2000): -9.2%; Density: 200.0 persons per square mile; Race: 92.6% White, 3.0% Black/African American, 2.9% Asian, 0.3% American Indian/Alaska Native, 0.0% Native Hawaiian/Other Pacific Islander, 0.8% Two or more races, 9.9% Hispanic of any race; Average household size: 1.96; Median age: 54.4; Age under 18: 9.3%; Age 65 and over: 27.8%; Males per 100 females: 99.8; Marriage status: 27.3% never married, 53.6% now married, 0.0% separated, 13.5% widowed, 5.6% divorced; Foreign born: 13.9%; Speak English only: 83.7%; With disability: 10.9%; Veterans: 10.0%; Ancestry: 18.7% Italian, 17.9% German, 16.8% Irish, 8.4% English, 4.9% American

Employment: 14.1% management, business, and financial, 2.8% computer, engineering, and science, 10.3% education, legal, community service, arts, and media, 5.0% healthcare practitioners, 28.7% service, 24.6% sales and office, 10.2% natural resources, construction, and maintenance, 4.3% production, transportation, and material moving

Income: Per capita: $47,685; Median household: $72,903; Average household: $93,491; Households with income of $100,000 or more: 32.5%; Poverty rate: 12.6%

Educational Attainment: High school diploma or higher: 95.2%; Bachelor's degree or higher: 39.3%; Graduate/professional degree or higher: 13.2%

School District(s)
Montauk Union Free SD (PK-08)
  2014-15 Enrollment: 355 . . . . (631) 668-2474

Housing: Homeownership rate: 78.5%; Median home value: $792,400; Median year structure built: 1977; Homeowner vacancy rate: 0.7%; Median selected monthly owner costs: $2,764 with a mortgage, $950 without a mortgage; Median gross rent: $1,342 per month; Rental vacancy rate: 33.9%

Health Insurance: 89.1% have insurance; 78.4% have private insurance; 32.4% have public insurance; 10.9% do not have insurance; 3.4% of children under 18 do not have insurance

Transportation: Commute: 77.9% car, 5.7% public transportation, 3.2% walk, 10.6% work from home; Mean travel time to work: 26.7 minutes

Airports: Montauk (general aviation)

MORICHES (CDP).
Covers a land area of 2.050 square miles and a water area of 0.227 square miles. Located at 40.81° N. Lat; 72.83° W. Long. Elevation is 23 feet.

Population: 2,703; Growth (since 2000): 16.6%; Density: 1,318.8 persons per square mile; Race: 79.9% White, 8.7% Black/African American, 4.1% Asian, 1.3% American Indian/Alaska Native, 0.0% Native Hawaiian/Other Pacific Islander, 4.3% Two or more races, 3.0% Hispanic of any race; Average household size: 2.12; Median age: 45.8; Age under 18: 21.8%; Age 65 and over: 22.1%; Males per 100 females: 93.6; Marriage status: 28.6% never married, 55.8% now married, 7.2% separated, 8.8% widowed, 6.9% divorced; Foreign born: 8.5%; Speak English only: 86.4%; With disability: 10.3%; Veterans: 6.4%; Ancestry: 40.1% Italian, 26.8% Irish, 11.5% German, 4.6% Polish, 2.9% French

Employment: 17.7% management, business, and financial, 1.0% computer, engineering, and science, 7.3% education, legal, community service, arts, and media, 4.6% healthcare practitioners, 11.5% service, 40.2% sales and office, 9.9% natural resources, construction, and maintenance, 7.9% production, transportation, and material moving

Income: Per capita: $38,996; Median household: $57,656; Average household: $81,798; Households with income of $100,000 or more: 26.9%; Poverty rate: 6.0%

Educational Attainment: High school diploma or higher: 89.6%; Bachelor's degree or higher: 32.4%; Graduate/professional degree or higher: 20.3%

School District(s)
William Floyd Union Free SD (KG-12)
  2014-15 Enrollment: 8,832 . . . . (631) 874-1201

Housing: Homeownership rate: 51.8%; Median home value: $326,900; Median year structure built: 1986; Homeowner vacancy rate: 0.0%; Median selected monthly owner costs: $2,690 with a mortgage, $1,076 without a mortgage; Median gross rent: $1,672 per month; Rental vacancy rate: 0.0%

Health Insurance: 90.5% have insurance; 81.1% have private insurance; 30.3% have public insurance; 9.5% do not have insurance; 16.3% of children under 18 do not have insurance
Transportation: Commute: 91.7% car, 1.6% public transportation, 0.0% walk, 6.7% work from home; Mean travel time to work: 31.5 minutes

MOUNT SINAI (CDP). Covers a land area of 5.999 square miles and a water area of 0.419 square miles. Located at 40.94° N. Lat; 73.02° W. Long. Elevation is 33 feet.
Population: 12,451; Growth (since 2000): 42.6%; Density: 2,075.5 persons per square mile; Race: 92.3% White, 0.3% Black/African American, 3.7% Asian, 0.1% American Indian/Alaska Native, 0.0% Native Hawaiian/Other Pacific Islander, 2.7% Two or more races, 12.4% Hispanic of any race; Average household size: 2.96; Median age: 40.9; Age under 18: 26.2%; Age 65 and over: 17.3%; Males per 100 females: 95.3; Marriage status: 24.0% never married, 65.6% now married, 0.7% separated, 5.7% widowed, 4.8% divorced; Foreign born: 8.7%; Speak English only: 85.3%; With disability: 8.5%; Veterans: 7.3%; Ancestry: 32.2% Italian, 21.3% Irish, 16.3% German, 8.6% American, 7.0% Polish
Employment: 20.4% management, business, and financial, 4.9% computer, engineering, and science, 12.1% education, legal, community service, arts, and media, 7.8% healthcare practitioners, 16.1% service, 27.5% sales and office, 6.4% natural resources, construction, and maintenance, 4.8% production, transportation, and material moving
Income: Per capita: $43,881; Median household: $108,642; Average household: $128,087; Households with income of $100,000 or more: 54.8%; Poverty rate: 6.3%
Educational Attainment: High school diploma or higher: 93.4%; Bachelor's degree or higher: 42.1%; Graduate/professional degree or higher: 18.4%

School District(s)
Mount Sinai Union Free SD (KG-12)
   2014-15 Enrollment: 2,410 . . . . (631) 870-2550
Housing: Homeownership rate: 93.1%; Median home value: $449,500; Median year structure built: 1979; Homeowner vacancy rate: 0.0%; Median selected monthly owner costs: $3,285 with a mortgage, $1,257 without a mortgage; Median gross rent: $1,699 per month; Rental vacancy rate: 6.2%
Health Insurance: 97.1% have insurance; 87.3% have private insurance; 26.3% have public insurance; 2.9% do not have insurance; 0.2% of children under 18 do not have insurance
Transportation: Commute: 89.2% car, 4.6% public transportation, 0.7% walk, 5.5% work from home; Mean travel time to work: 36.4 minutes

NAPEAGUE (CDP). Covers a land area of 3.678 square miles and a water area of 0.080 square miles. Located at 40.99° N. Lat; 72.07° W. Long. Elevation is 7 feet.
Population: 211; Growth (since 2000): -5.4%; Density: 57.4 persons per square mile; Race: 100.0% White, 0.0% Black/African American, 0.0% Asian, 0.0% American Indian/Alaska Native, 0.0% Native Hawaiian/Other Pacific Islander, 0.0% Two or more races, 0.0% Hispanic of any race; Average household size: 1.77; Median age: 60.5; Age under 18: 9.5%; Age 65 and over: 26.5%; Males per 100 females: 92.3; Marriage status: 22.0% never married, 58.6% now married, 0.0% separated, 19.4% widowed, 0.0% divorced; Foreign born: 37.9%; Speak English only: 55.2%; With disability: 17.5%; Veterans: 0.0%; Ancestry: 31.8% Polish, 25.1% Russian, 18.5% German, 15.2% Finnish, 10.4% Norwegian
Employment: 8.3% management, business, and financial, 7.6% computer, engineering, and science, 13.6% education, legal, community service, arts, and media, 7.6% healthcare practitioners, 43.9% service, 16.7% sales and office, 2.3% natural resources, construction, and maintenance, 0.0% production, transportation, and material moving
Income: Per capita: $49,097; Median household: $59,458; Average household: $85,995; Households with income of $100,000 or more: 23.5%; Poverty rate: 17.1%
Educational Attainment: High school diploma or higher: 82.7%; Bachelor's degree or higher: 48.7%; Graduate/professional degree or higher: 20.9%
Housing: Homeownership rate: 68.1%; Median home value: n/a; Median year structure built: 1982; Homeowner vacancy rate: 13.8%; Median selected monthly owner costs: n/a with a mortgage, n/a without a mortgage; Median gross rent: n/a per month; Rental vacancy rate: 0.0%
Health Insurance: 87.2% have insurance; 76.3% have private insurance; 26.5% have public insurance; 12.8% do not have insurance; 0.0% of children under 18 do not have insurance

Transportation: Commute: 21.2% car, 3.0% public transportation, 0.0% walk, 75.8% work from home; Mean travel time to work: 0.0 minutes

NESCONSET (CDP). Covers a land area of 3.821 square miles and a water area of 0.003 square miles. Located at 40.85° N. Lat; 73.15° W. Long. Elevation is 118 feet.
History: Nesconset is a hamlet and census-designated place (CDP) in Suffolk County, Long Island, New York.
Population: 13,876; Growth (since 2000): 15.7%; Density: 3,631.4 persons per square mile; Race: 90.1% White, 1.5% Black/African American, 6.1% Asian, 0.0% American Indian/Alaska Native, 0.0% Native Hawaiian/Other Pacific Islander, 0.8% Two or more races, 4.4% Hispanic of any race; Average household size: 3.03; Median age: 41.6; Age under 18: 24.0%; Age 65 and over: 15.4%; Males per 100 females: 94.6; Marriage status: 27.4% never married, 58.7% now married, 1.3% separated, 5.9% widowed, 8.0% divorced; Foreign born: 10.0%; Speak English only: 89.6%; With disability: 6.2%; Veterans: 5.1%; Ancestry: 40.7% Italian, 29.1% Irish, 17.3% German, 6.2% English, 5.4% Polish
Employment: 18.9% management, business, and financial, 5.5% computer, engineering, and science, 15.9% education, legal, community service, arts, and media, 8.3% healthcare practitioners, 14.5% service, 22.9% sales and office, 9.0% natural resources, construction, and maintenance, 5.0% production, transportation, and material moving
Income: Per capita: $44,487; Median household: $117,946; Average household: $132,790; Households with income of $100,000 or more: 61.3%; Poverty rate: 3.0%
Educational Attainment: High school diploma or higher: 93.6%; Bachelor's degree or higher: 43.2%; Graduate/professional degree or higher: 18.7%

School District(s)
Smithtown Central SD (KG-12)
   2014-15 Enrollment: 9,810 . . . . (631) 382-2006
Housing: Homeownership rate: 86.3%; Median home value: $464,400; Median year structure built: 1974; Homeowner vacancy rate: 0.3%; Median selected monthly owner costs: $2,984 with a mortgage, $1,435 without a mortgage; Median gross rent: $1,456 per month; Rental vacancy rate: 11.5%
Health Insurance: 96.9% have insurance; 89.5% have private insurance; 18.6% have public insurance; 3.1% do not have insurance; 1.7% of children under 18 do not have insurance
Transportation: Commute: 89.2% car, 5.8% public transportation, 0.6% walk, 3.1% work from home; Mean travel time to work: 35.6 minutes

NEW SUFFOLK (CDP). Covers a land area of 0.556 square miles and a water area of 0.054 square miles. Located at 41.00° N. Lat; 72.48° W. Long. Elevation is 26 feet.
Population: 310; Growth (since 2000): -8.0%; Density: 557.1 persons per square mile; Race: 98.1% White, 1.9% Black/African American, 0.0% Asian, 0.0% American Indian/Alaska Native, 0.0% Native Hawaiian/Other Pacific Islander, 0.0% Two or more races, 8.4% Hispanic of any race; Average household size: 1.86; Median age: 59.2; Age under 18: 1.9%; Age 65 and over: 32.9%; Males per 100 females: 84.7; Marriage status: 28.9% never married, 45.7% now married, 0.0% separated, 6.6% widowed, 18.8% divorced; Foreign born: 18.1%; Speak English only: 87.4%; With disability: 13.2%; Veterans: 8.9%; Ancestry: 19.4% Italian, 18.4% German, 17.4% Polish, 14.5% Irish, 13.2% English
Employment: 2.7% management, business, and financial, 0.5% computer, engineering, and science, 16.8% education, legal, community service, arts, and media, 3.2% healthcare practitioners, 21.6% service, 29.7% sales and office, 15.1% natural resources, construction, and maintenance, 10.3% production, transportation, and material moving
Income: Per capita: $50,335; Median household: n/a; Average household: $89,750; Households with income of $100,000 or more: 45.6%; Poverty rate: 13.2%
Educational Attainment: High school diploma or higher: 84.5%; Bachelor's degree or higher: 49.1%; Graduate/professional degree or higher: 26.0%

School District(s)
New Suffolk Common SD (PK-06)
   2014-15 Enrollment: 17. . . . . (631) 734-6940
Housing: Homeownership rate: 71.9%; Median home value: $589,300; Median year structure built: Before 1940; Homeowner vacancy rate: 3.2%; Median selected monthly owner costs: $2,375 with a mortgage, $950 without a mortgage; Median gross rent: $1,604 per month; Rental vacancy rate: 0.0%

Health Insurance: 84.5% have insurance; 71.9% have private insurance; 37.7% have public insurance; 15.5% do not have insurance; 0.0% of children under 18 do not have insurance
Transportation: Commute: 78.6% car, 1.1% public transportation, 5.5% walk, 14.8% work from home; Mean travel time to work: 22.7 minutes

NISSEQUOGUE (village).
Covers a land area of 3.782 square miles and a water area of 0.194 square miles. Located at 40.91° N. Lat; 73.19° W. Long. Elevation is 85 feet.
Population: 1,692; Growth (since 2000): 9.7%; Density: 447.3 persons per square mile; Race: 96.0% White, 2.3% Black/African American, 0.7% Asian, 1.0% American Indian/Alaska Native, 0.0% Native Hawaiian/Other Pacific Islander, 0.0% Two or more races, 1.2% Hispanic of any race; Average household size: 3.05; Median age: 47.0; Age under 18: 25.3%; Age 65 and over: 18.9%; Males per 100 females: 107.5; Marriage status: 23.9% never married, 67.5% now married, 1.0% separated, 4.3% widowed, 4.2% divorced; Foreign born: 7.4%; Speak English only: 94.0%; With disability: 7.1%; Veterans: 4.9%; Ancestry: 35.3% Italian, 23.4% Irish, 21.7% German, 6.0% Polish, 5.2% Czech
Employment: 22.0% management, business, and financial, 6.4% computer, engineering, and science, 17.7% education, legal, community service, arts, and media, 15.1% healthcare practitioners, 7.6% service, 22.0% sales and office, 5.9% natural resources, construction, and maintenance, 3.5% production, transportation, and material moving
Income: Per capita: $83,541; Median household: $170,250; Average household: $256,400; Households with income of $100,000 or more: 76.5%; Poverty rate: 3.5%
Educational Attainment: High school diploma or higher: 96.6%; Bachelor's degree or higher: 59.4%; Graduate/professional degree or higher: 40.0%
Housing: Homeownership rate: 94.0%; Median home value: $931,500; Median year structure built: 1973; Homeowner vacancy rate: 2.3%; Median selected monthly owner costs: $4,000+ with a mortgage, $1,500+ without a mortgage; Median gross rent: $1,950 per month; Rental vacancy rate: 25.6%
Health Insurance: 97.0% have insurance; 91.8% have private insurance; 20.4% have public insurance; 3.0% do not have insurance; 2.6% of children under 18 do not have insurance
Safety: Violent crime rate: 0.0 per 10,000 population; Property crime rate: 56.7 per 10,000 population
Transportation: Commute: 85.9% car, 3.3% public transportation, 1.0% walk, 9.8% work from home; Mean travel time to work: 29.3 minutes

NORTH AMITYVILLE (CDP).
Covers a land area of 2.354 square miles and a water area of 0 square miles. Located at 40.70° N. Lat; 73.41° W. Long. Elevation is 33 feet.
History: North Amityville is a hamlet in Suffolk County, New York.
Population: 19,895; Growth (since 2000): 20.1%; Density: 8,451.0 persons per square mile; Race: 19.2% White, 54.0% Black/African American, 2.5% Asian, 0.4% American Indian/Alaska Native, 0.0% Native Hawaiian/Other Pacific Islander, 3.6% Two or more races, 36.6% Hispanic of any race; Average household size: 3.65; Median age: 32.7; Age under 18: 25.9%; Age 65 and over: 11.5%; Males per 100 females: 85.7; Marriage status: 47.3% never married, 35.8% now married, 3.4% separated, 7.0% widowed, 9.8% divorced; Foreign born: 31.1%; Speak English only: 61.7%; With disability: 10.1%; Veterans: 4.7%; Ancestry: 6.2% Haitian, 4.5% Jamaican, 2.8% Italian, 2.7% American, 1.8% German
Employment: 7.4% management, business, and financial, 2.9% computer, engineering, and science, 7.3% education, legal, community service, arts, and media, 7.1% healthcare practitioners, 29.2% service, 26.9% sales and office, 6.3% natural resources, construction, and maintenance, 12.9% production, transportation, and material moving
Income: Per capita: $21,911; Median household: $70,660; Average household: $75,171; Households with income of $100,000 or more: 27.0%; Poverty rate: 8.0%
Educational Attainment: High school diploma or higher: 76.1%; Bachelor's degree or higher: 18.3%; Graduate/professional degree or higher: 6.8%
Housing: Homeownership rate: 59.8%; Median home value: $270,800; Median year structure built: 1970; Homeowner vacancy rate: 0.7%; Median selected monthly owner costs: $2,585 with a mortgage, $1,078 without a mortgage; Median gross rent: $1,303 per month; Rental vacancy rate: 3.2%

Health Insurance: 82.5% have insurance; 60.2% have private insurance; 32.7% have public insurance; 17.5% do not have insurance; 6.3% of children under 18 do not have insurance
Transportation: Commute: 84.8% car, 8.0% public transportation, 2.4% walk, 1.1% work from home; Mean travel time to work: 27.6 minutes

NORTH BABYLON (CDP).
Covers a land area of 3.370 square miles and a water area of 0.053 square miles. Located at 40.73° N. Lat; 73.33° W. Long. Elevation is 23 feet.
History: North Babylon is a hamlet and census-designated place (CDP) in Suffolk County, New York.
Population: 17,228; Growth (since 2000): -3.6%; Density: 5,112.5 persons per square mile; Race: 81.6% White, 8.2% Black/African American, 2.8% Asian, 0.0% American Indian/Alaska Native, 0.0% Native Hawaiian/Other Pacific Islander, 2.0% Two or more races, 14.7% Hispanic of any race; Average household size: 2.93; Median age: 41.3; Age under 18: 21.7%; Age 65 and over: 14.4%; Males per 100 females: 93.8; Marriage status: 31.0% never married, 54.6% now married, 1.4% separated, 6.7% widowed, 7.7% divorced; Foreign born: 13.0%; Speak English only: 82.4%; With disability: 10.7%; Veterans: 7.1%; Ancestry: 34.8% Italian, 24.6% Irish, 15.2% German, 4.7% Polish, 3.1% English
Employment: 16.1% management, business, and financial, 5.0% computer, engineering, and science, 10.8% education, legal, community service, arts, and media, 6.0% healthcare practitioners, 15.7% service, 27.0% sales and office, 9.3% natural resources, construction, and maintenance, 10.1% production, transportation, and material moving
Income: Per capita: $34,050; Median household: $88,139; Average household: $96,771; Households with income of $100,000 or more: 40.4%; Poverty rate: 5.0%
Educational Attainment: High school diploma or higher: 93.4%; Bachelor's degree or higher: 26.7%; Graduate/professional degree or higher: 10.5%
School District(s)
North Babylon Union Free SD (KG-12)
    2014-15 Enrollment: 4,820 . . . . (631) 620-7011
Housing: Homeownership rate: 81.0%; Median home value: $336,500; Median year structure built: 1958; Homeowner vacancy rate: 2.8%; Median selected monthly owner costs: $2,675 with a mortgage, $1,069 without a mortgage; Median gross rent: $1,745 per month; Rental vacancy rate: 2.3%
Health Insurance: 92.7% have insurance; 80.1% have private insurance; 25.5% have public insurance; 7.3% do not have insurance; 1.4% of children under 18 do not have insurance
Transportation: Commute: 89.4% car, 6.9% public transportation, 1.0% walk, 2.3% work from home; Mean travel time to work: 30.4 minutes
Airports: Republic (commercial service–non-primary)

NORTH BAY SHORE (CDP).
Covers a land area of 3.252 square miles and a water area of 0 square miles. Located at 40.76° N. Lat; 73.26° W. Long. Elevation is 36 feet.
History: North Bay Shore is an unincorporated neighborhood on Long Island in the Town of Islip in Suffolk County. The area is a suburb of New York City.
Population: 20,127; Growth (since 2000): 34.3%; Density: 6,189.2 persons per square mile; Race: 38.4% White, 22.6% Black/African American, 2.4% Asian, 0.9% American Indian/Alaska Native, 0.0% Native Hawaiian/Other Pacific Islander, 11.1% Two or more races, 57.4% Hispanic of any race; Average household size: 4.30; Median age: 31.7; Age under 18: 28.7%; Age 65 and over: 6.8%; Males per 100 females: 103.7; Marriage status: 41.1% never married, 47.6% now married, 3.5% separated, 3.7% widowed, 7.6% divorced; Foreign born: 35.5%; Speak English only: 42.0%; With disability: 11.4%; Veterans: 2.8%; Ancestry: 5.5% Italian, 4.0% American, 4.0% Irish, 3.6% German, 2.6% Jamaican
Employment: 8.3% management, business, and financial, 2.3% computer, engineering, and science, 4.5% education, legal, community service, arts, and media, 2.7% healthcare practitioners, 22.5% service, 24.3% sales and office, 12.9% natural resources, construction, and maintenance, 22.5% production, transportation, and material moving
Income: Per capita: $22,832; Median household: $81,526; Average household: $92,192; Households with income of $100,000 or more: 40.4%; Poverty rate: 10.5%
Educational Attainment: High school diploma or higher: 72.2%; Bachelor's degree or higher: 11.4%; Graduate/professional degree or higher: 3.4%

Housing: Homeownership rate: 74.3%; Median home value: $284,400; Median year structure built: 1964; Homeowner vacancy rate: 1.1%; Median selected monthly owner costs: $2,346 with a mortgage, $1,030 without a mortgage; Median gross rent: $1,389 per month; Rental vacancy rate: 3.0%

Health Insurance: 86.8% have insurance; 59.2% have private insurance; 34.0% have public insurance; 13.2% do not have insurance; 5.1% of children under 18 do not have insurance

Transportation: Commute: 87.8% car, 7.4% public transportation, 0.9% walk, 2.1% work from home; Mean travel time to work: 31.6 minutes

NORTH BELLPORT (CDP). Covers a land area of 4.936 square miles and a water area of 0 square miles. Located at 40.79° N. Lat; 72.95° W. Long. Elevation is 46 feet.

History: North Bellport is a hamlet and census-designated place (CDP) in Suffolk County, New York.

Population: 11,623; Growth (since 2000): 29.0%; Density: 2,354.5 persons per square mile; Race: 68.8% White, 21.2% Black/African American, 3.9% Asian, 0.0% American Indian/Alaska Native, 0.1% Native Hawaiian/Other Pacific Islander, 3.7% Two or more races, 36.8% Hispanic of any race; Average household size: 3.25; Median age: 30.8; Age under 18: 29.9%; Age 65 and over: 6.7%; Males per 100 females: 98.5; Marriage status: 41.3% never married, 43.5% now married, 2.8% separated, 4.9% widowed, 10.3% divorced; Foreign born: 20.7%; Speak English only: 60.3%; With disability: 8.0%; Veterans: 4.0%; Ancestry: 16.0% Italian, 11.3% Irish, 9.1% German, 3.6% English, 2.6% Polish

Employment: 13.0% management, business, and financial, 5.8% computer, engineering, and science, 7.8% education, legal, community service, arts, and media, 4.3% healthcare practitioners, 21.9% service, 20.0% sales and office, 14.8% natural resources, construction, and maintenance, 12.4% production, transportation, and material moving

Income: Per capita: $22,598; Median household: $66,023; Average household: $71,175; Households with income of $100,000 or more: 25.3%; Poverty rate: 20.4%

Educational Attainment: High school diploma or higher: 79.4%; Bachelor's degree or higher: 21.9%; Graduate/professional degree or higher: 10.8%

Housing: Homeownership rate: 62.5%; Median home value: $256,200; Median year structure built: 1979; Homeowner vacancy rate: 0.9%; Median selected monthly owner costs: $2,441 with a mortgage, $886 without a mortgage; Median gross rent: $2,075 per month; Rental vacancy rate: 2.9%

Health Insurance: 86.6% have insurance; 68.2% have private insurance; 32.8% have public insurance; 13.4% do not have insurance; 4.3% of children under 18 do not have insurance

Transportation: Commute: 91.2% car, 5.7% public transportation, 0.5% walk, 2.0% work from home; Mean travel time to work: 32.1 minutes

NORTH GREAT RIVER (CDP). Covers a land area of 2.325 square miles and a water area of 0.023 square miles. Located at 40.76° N. Lat; 73.16° W. Long. Elevation is 30 feet.

Population: 4,091; Growth (since 2000): 4.1%; Density: 1,759.5 persons per square mile; Race: 89.1% White, 0.9% Black/African American, 9.5% Asian, 0.0% American Indian/Alaska Native, 0.0% Native Hawaiian/Other Pacific Islander, 0.3% Two or more races, 8.6% Hispanic of any race; Average household size: 3.30; Median age: 45.3; Age under 18: 18.8%; Age 65 and over: 17.0%; Males per 100 females: 97.9; Marriage status: 36.5% never married, 50.6% now married, 0.6% separated, 6.9% widowed, 6.1% divorced; Foreign born: 12.6%; Speak English only: 81.7%; With disability: 7.7%; Veterans: 5.3%; Ancestry: 33.3% Italian, 29.6% Irish, 25.3% German, 3.8% Welsh, 3.3% English

Employment: 14.9% management, business, and financial, 3.7% computer, engineering, and science, 10.6% education, legal, community service, arts, and media, 3.3% healthcare practitioners, 18.1% service, 27.0% sales and office, 7.8% natural resources, construction, and maintenance, 14.6% production, transportation, and material moving

Income: Per capita: $35,580; Median household: $105,391; Average household: $111,953; Households with income of $100,000 or more: 52.4%; Poverty rate: 4.2%

Educational Attainment: High school diploma or higher: 95.3%; Bachelor's degree or higher: 26.0%; Graduate/professional degree or higher: 6.8%

Housing: Homeownership rate: 84.4%; Median home value: $354,400; Median year structure built: 1966; Homeowner vacancy rate: 2.2%; Median selected monthly owner costs: $2,662 with a mortgage, $1,163 without a

mortgage; Median gross rent: $1,725 per month; Rental vacancy rate: 17.9%

Health Insurance: 97.7% have insurance; 91.9% have private insurance; 22.0% have public insurance; 2.3% do not have insurance; 0.0% of children under 18 do not have insurance

Transportation: Commute: 89.8% car, 5.1% public transportation, 0.9% walk, 3.6% work from home; Mean travel time to work: 27.3 minutes

NORTH HAVEN (village). Covers a land area of 2.713 square miles and a water area of 0 square miles. Located at 41.02° N. Lat; 72.31° W. Long. Elevation is 20 feet.

Population: 846; Growth (since 2000): 13.9%; Density: 311.9 persons per square mile; Race: 99.3% White, 0.0% Black/African American, 0.4% Asian, 0.0% American Indian/Alaska Native, 0.0% Native Hawaiian/Other Pacific Islander, 0.4% Two or more races, 0.8% Hispanic of any race; Average household size: 2.33; Median age: 51.7; Age under 18: 17.6%; Age 65 and over: 25.3%; Males per 100 females: 91.5; Marriage status: 22.2% never married, 64.9% now married, 0.4% separated, 4.9% widowed, 8.0% divorced; Foreign born: 8.5%; Speak English only: 95.4%; With disability: 7.9%; Veterans: 6.9%; Ancestry: 28.1% Irish, 20.4% Italian, 15.0% English, 11.6% German, 6.4% Polish

Employment: 23.7% management, business, and financial, 7.5% computer, engineering, and science, 16.2% education, legal, community service, arts, and media, 3.9% healthcare practitioners, 10.9% service, 20.6% sales and office, 14.5% natural resources, construction, and maintenance, 2.7% production, transportation, and material moving

Income: Per capita: $103,876; Median household: $118,750; Average household: $245,800; Households with income of $100,000 or more: 60.6%; Poverty rate: 3.1%

Educational Attainment: High school diploma or higher: 97.9%; Bachelor's degree or higher: 65.8%; Graduate/professional degree or higher: 31.9%

Housing: Homeownership rate: 91.5%; Median home value: $1,210,500; Median year structure built: 1976; Homeowner vacancy rate: 4.3%; Median selected monthly owner costs: $3,728 with a mortgage, $1,096 without a mortgage; Median gross rent: $3,208 per month; Rental vacancy rate: 4.8%

Health Insurance: 95.9% have insurance; 89.7% have private insurance; 27.4% have public insurance; 4.1% do not have insurance; 2.0% of children under 18 do not have insurance

Transportation: Commute: 73.8% car, 5.6% public transportation, 2.7% walk, 16.2% work from home; Mean travel time to work: 30.0 minutes

NORTH LINDENHURST (CDP). Covers a land area of 1.920 square miles and a water area of 0 square miles. Located at 40.71° N. Lat; 73.39° W. Long. Elevation is 43 feet.

History: North Lindenhurst is a hamlet (and census-designated place) in Suffolk County, New York.

Population: 11,679; Growth (since 2000): -0.7%; Density: 6,084.1 persons per square mile; Race: 82.5% White, 4.1% Black/African American, 3.7% Asian, 0.5% American Indian/Alaska Native, 0.0% Native Hawaiian/Other Pacific Islander, 2.8% Two or more races, 19.5% Hispanic of any race; Average household size: 3.15; Median age: 37.1; Age under 18: 25.7%; Age 65 and over: 11.7%; Males per 100 females: 96.3; Marriage status: 31.0% never married, 54.7% now married, 3.0% separated, 7.4% widowed, 6.9% divorced; Foreign born: 24.6%; Speak English only: 66.7%; With disability: 8.8%; Veterans: 5.2%; Ancestry: 23.9% Italian, 17.8% Irish, 11.4% Polish, 11.3% German, 3.1% Norwegian

Employment: 7.7% management, business, and financial, 3.3% computer, engineering, and science, 8.3% education, legal, community service, arts, and media, 6.8% healthcare practitioners, 18.6% service, 33.9% sales and office, 11.8% natural resources, construction, and maintenance, 9.6% production, transportation, and material moving

Income: Per capita: $28,248; Median household: $70,799; Average household: $85,960; Households with income of $100,000 or more: 34.1%; Poverty rate: 9.0%

Educational Attainment: High school diploma or higher: 85.3%; Bachelor's degree or higher: 21.4%; Graduate/professional degree or higher: 7.3%

Housing: Homeownership rate: 68.3%; Median home value: $339,100; Median year structure built: 1958; Homeowner vacancy rate: 1.1%; Median selected monthly owner costs: $2,734 with a mortgage, $1,159 without a mortgage; Median gross rent: $1,426 per month; Rental vacancy rate: 3.3%

Health Insurance: 89.7% have insurance; 68.6% have private insurance; 30.3% have public insurance; 10.3% do not have insurance; 0.7% of children under 18 do not have insurance

Transportation: Commute: 89.5% car, 6.5% public transportation, 2.4% walk, 1.3% work from home; Mean travel time to work: 29.7 minutes

NORTH PATCHOGUE (CDP). Covers a land area of 1.978 square miles and a water area of 0.052 square miles. Located at 40.78° N. Lat; 73.02° W. Long. Elevation is 49 feet.

History: North Patchogue is a hamlet and census-designated place (CDP) in Suffolk County, New York.

Population: 6,680; Growth (since 2000): -14.6%; Density: 3,377.9 persons per square mile; Race: 92.9% White, 3.9% Black/African American, 0.7% Asian, 0.0% American Indian/Alaska Native, 0.0% Native Hawaiian/Other Pacific Islander, 0.6% Two or more races, 23.5% Hispanic of any race; Average household size: 2.87; Median age: 40.2; Age under 18: 23.3%; Age 65 and over: 13.4%; Males per 100 females: 98.2; Marriage status: 34.0% never married, 53.8% now married, 0.8% separated, 4.9% widowed, 7.3% divorced; Foreign born: 9.3%; Speak English only: 82.5%; With disability: 9.4%; Veterans: 9.2%; Ancestry: 31.9% Italian, 27.9% Irish, 19.9% German, 9.0% English, 2.6% Polish

Employment: 11.4% management, business, and financial, 2.4% computer, engineering, and science, 11.8% education, legal, community service, arts, and media, 10.7% healthcare practitioners, 14.1% service, 32.5% sales and office, 8.6% natural resources, construction, and maintenance, 8.5% production, transportation, and material moving

Income: Per capita: $32,494; Median household: $86,038; Average household: $91,066; Households with income of $100,000 or more: 42.8%; Poverty rate: 6.0%

Educational Attainment: High school diploma or higher: 94.6%; Bachelor's degree or higher: 22.4%; Graduate/professional degree or higher: 10.0%

Housing: Homeownership rate: 89.9%; Median home value: $278,500; Median year structure built: 1959; Homeowner vacancy rate: 2.0%; Median selected monthly owner costs: $2,388 with a mortgage, $1,049 without a mortgage; Median gross rent: $1,558 per month; Rental vacancy rate: 0.0%

Health Insurance: 96.3% have insurance; 86.3% have private insurance; 21.9% have public insurance; 3.7% do not have insurance; 0.0% of children under 18 do not have insurance

Transportation: Commute: 90.6% car, 2.8% public transportation, 2.2% walk, 3.1% work from home; Mean travel time to work: 30.4 minutes

NORTH SEA (CDP). Covers a land area of 11.052 square miles and a water area of 1.041 square miles. Located at 40.93° N. Lat; 72.41° W. Long. Elevation is 16 feet.

Population: 4,441; Growth (since 2000): -1.2%; Density: 401.8 persons per square mile; Race: 94.9% White, 0.5% Black/African American, 1.4% Asian, 0.0% American Indian/Alaska Native, 0.0% Native Hawaiian/Other Pacific Islander, 0.0% Two or more races, 9.7% Hispanic of any race; Average household size: 2.39; Median age: 50.3; Age under 18: 17.3%; Age 65 and over: 25.6%; Males per 100 females: 103.7; Marriage status: 23.8% never married, 61.3% now married, 1.2% separated, 6.4% widowed, 8.5% divorced; Foreign born: 18.0%; Speak English only: 80.7%; With disability: 10.7%; Veterans: 8.1%; Ancestry: 21.5% Irish, 15.0% Italian, 14.1% Polish, 13.7% German, 10.7% English

Employment: 14.0% management, business, and financial, 3.1% computer, engineering, and science, 14.0% education, legal, community service, arts, and media, 4.4% healthcare practitioners, 19.0% service, 27.7% sales and office, 13.6% natural resources, construction, and maintenance, 4.2% production, transportation, and material moving

Income: Per capita: $55,500; Median household: $72,554; Average household: $128,074; Households with income of $100,000 or more: 34.9%; Poverty rate: 5.2%

Educational Attainment: High school diploma or higher: 94.5%; Bachelor's degree or higher: 41.9%; Graduate/professional degree or higher: 15.6%

Housing: Homeownership rate: 74.0%; Median home value: $760,100; Median year structure built: 1977; Homeowner vacancy rate: 2.8%; Median selected monthly owner costs: $2,420 with a mortgage, $825 without a mortgage; Median gross rent: $2,041 per month; Rental vacancy rate: 0.0%

Health Insurance: 90.4% have insurance; 75.9% have private insurance; 33.2% have public insurance; 9.6% do not have insurance; 7.8% of children under 18 do not have insurance

Transportation: Commute: 84.3% car, 6.3% public transportation, 2.8% walk, 6.1% work from home; Mean travel time to work: 28.0 minutes

NORTHAMPTON (CDP). Covers a land area of 11.551 square miles and a water area of 0.100 square miles. Located at 40.88° N. Lat; 72.68° W. Long. Elevation is 151 feet.

Population: 578; Growth (since 2000): 23.5%; Density: 50.0 persons per square mile; Race: 53.3% White, 36.3% Black/African American, 2.9% Asian, 0.0% American Indian/Alaska Native, 0.0% Native Hawaiian/Other Pacific Islander, 7.4% Two or more races, 36.9% Hispanic of any race; Average household size: 2.51; Median age: 36.1; Age under 18: 5.2%; Age 65 and over: 18.9%; Males per 100 females: 108.8; Marriage status: 37.6% never married, 55.7% now married, 3.8% separated, 3.8% widowed, 2.9% divorced; Foreign born: 27.9%; Speak English only: 72.1%; With disability: 20.9%; Veterans: 6.0%; Ancestry: 11.8% English, 10.2% Finnish, 8.7% Italian, 7.1% Polish, 5.2% Irish

Employment: 0.0% management, business, and financial, 0.0% computer, engineering, and science, 10.5% education, legal, community service, arts, and media, 0.0% healthcare practitioners, 26.9% service, 32.0% sales and office, 28.6% natural resources, construction, and maintenance, 2.0% production, transportation, and material moving

Income: Per capita: $26,432; Median household: $51,333; Average household: $61,070; Households with income of $100,000 or more: 29.8%; Poverty rate: 9.0%

Educational Attainment: High school diploma or higher: 73.6%; Bachelor's degree or higher: 4.3%; Graduate/professional degree or higher: 4.3%

Housing: Homeownership rate: 47.8%; Median home value: $278,000; Median year structure built: 1962; Homeowner vacancy rate: 0.0%; Median selected monthly owner costs: $1,417 with a mortgage, $853 without a mortgage; Median gross rent: $1,331 per month; Rental vacancy rate: 0.0%

Health Insurance: 80.1% have insurance; 55.5% have private insurance; 40.1% have public insurance; 19.9% do not have insurance; 0.0% of children under 18 do not have insurance

Transportation: Commute: 85.3% car, 0.0% public transportation, 14.7% walk, 0.0% work from home; Mean travel time to work: 28.7 minutes

NORTHPORT (village). Covers a land area of 2.308 square miles and a water area of 0.222 square miles. Located at 40.90° N. Lat; 73.34° W. Long. Elevation is 59 feet.

History: Although it was known by the name of Northport since at least 1837, the village of Northport was formally incorporated in 1894, the first village to do so in Huntington Township. Over the years Northport has expanded from its original borders, annexing other established communities.

Population: 7,412; Growth (since 2000): -2.6%; Density: 3,211.0 persons per square mile; Race: 93.9% White, 1.1% Black/African American, 3.8% Asian, 0.0% American Indian/Alaska Native, 0.0% Native Hawaiian/Other Pacific Islander, 1.2% Two or more races, 1.8% Hispanic of any race; Average household size: 2.50; Median age: 45.5; Age under 18: 21.7%; Age 65 and over: 17.9%; Males per 100 females: 95.5; Marriage status: 22.0% never married, 63.3% now married, 1.7% separated, 5.3% widowed, 9.3% divorced; Foreign born: 9.5%; Speak English only: 90.8%; With disability: 6.2%; Veterans: 7.2%; Ancestry: 27.1% Italian, 20.0% Irish, 19.6% German, 11.9% English, 7.0% Russian

Employment: 26.3% management, business, and financial, 5.2% computer, engineering, and science, 20.7% education, legal, community service, arts, and media, 7.4% healthcare practitioners, 10.1% service, 21.7% sales and office, 4.4% natural resources, construction, and maintenance, 4.2% production, transportation, and material moving

Income: Per capita: $54,858; Median household: $112,390; Average household: $137,622; Households with income of $100,000 or more: 56.9%; Poverty rate: 2.7%

Educational Attainment: High school diploma or higher: 97.1%; Bachelor's degree or higher: 66.0%; Graduate/professional degree or higher: 31.5%

School District(s)

Kings Park Central SD (KG-12)

    2014-15 Enrollment: 3,555 . . . . (631) 269-3310

Northport-East Northport Union Free SD (KG-12)

    2014-15 Enrollment: 5,746 . . . . (631) 262-6604

Two-year College(s)

Western Suffolk BOCES (Public)

    Fall 2014 Enrollment: 336 . . . . (631) 261-3600

Housing: Homeownership rate: 73.8%; Median home value: $540,500; Median year structure built: 1956; Homeowner vacancy rate: 2.4%; Median selected monthly owner costs: $2,871 with a mortgage, $1,257 without a mortgage; Median gross rent: $1,462 per month; Rental vacancy rate: 11.1%

Health Insurance: 97.4% have insurance; 89.8% have private insurance; 23.0% have public insurance; 2.6% do not have insurance; 3.0% of children under 18 do not have insurance

Hospitals: Northport VA Medical Center (524 beds)

Safety: Violent crime rate: 5.4 per 10,000 population; Property crime rate: 75.5 per 10,000 population

Transportation: Commute: 75.9% car, 14.3% public transportation, 2.9% walk, 3.1% work from home; Mean travel time to work: 37.1 minutes

Additional Information Contacts

Village of Northport . . . . (631) 261-7502
    http://www.northportny.gov

NORTHVILLE (CDP). Covers a land area of 7.404 square miles and a water area of 0.021 square miles. Located at 40.98° N. Lat; 72.63° W. Long. Elevation is 59 feet.

Population: 1,685; Growth (since 2000): 110.4%; Density: 227.6 persons per square mile; Race: 99.0% White, 0.5% Black/African American, 0.0% Asian, 0.0% American Indian/Alaska Native, 0.0% Native Hawaiian/Other Pacific Islander, 0.0% Two or more races, 5.7% Hispanic of any race; Average household size: 2.36; Median age: 49.8; Age under 18: 18.0%; Age 65 and over: 31.2%; Males per 100 females: 99.4; Marriage status: 13.2% never married, 73.4% now married, 5.4% separated, 10.4% widowed, 2.9% divorced; Foreign born: 3.2%; Speak English only: 96.6%; With disability: 15.9%; Veterans: 7.4%; Ancestry: 39.7% Irish, 36.1% German, 11.1% American, 9.5% Italian, 7.8% Polish

Employment: 54.9% management, business, and financial, 0.0% computer, engineering, and science, 0.0% education, legal, community service, arts, and media, 0.0% healthcare practitioners, 5.0% service, 33.4% sales and office, 2.6% natural resources, construction, and maintenance, 4.0% production, transportation, and material moving

Income: Per capita: $34,672; Median household: $68,507; Average household: $81,687; Households with income of $100,000 or more: 30.8%; Poverty rate: 5.1%

Educational Attainment: High school diploma or higher: 98.8%; Bachelor's degree or higher: 39.5%; Graduate/professional degree or higher: 14.7%

Housing: Homeownership rate: 88.3%; Median home value: $412,000; Median year structure built: 1996; Homeowner vacancy rate: 5.7%; Median selected monthly owner costs: $2,893 with a mortgage, $1,077 without a mortgage; Median gross rent: $2,129 per month; Rental vacancy rate: 0.0%

Health Insurance: 99.2% have insurance; 93.2% have private insurance; 33.3% have public insurance; 0.8% do not have insurance; 0.0% of children under 18 do not have insurance

Transportation: Commute: 90.8% car, 2.5% public transportation, 6.7% walk, 0.0% work from home; Mean travel time to work: 27.1 minutes

---

NORTHWEST HARBOR (CDP). Covers a land area of 14.473 square miles and a water area of 1.580 square miles. Located at 41.00° N. Lat; 72.22° W. Long. Elevation is 79 feet.

History: Northwest Harbor is named for the bay on the South Fork of Long Island connecting Sag Harbor, Shelter Island and East Hampton town to Gardiners Bay and the open waters of the Atlantic Ocean. The bay derives its name from being northwest of East Hampton village.

Population: 4,004; Growth (since 2000): 30.9%; Density: 276.6 persons per square mile; Race: 80.4% White, 1.5% Black/African American, 12.2% Asian, 0.0% American Indian/Alaska Native, 0.0% Native Hawaiian/Other Pacific Islander, 1.7% Two or more races, 9.9% Hispanic of any race; Average household size: 2.30; Median age: 49.7; Age under 18: 19.2%; Age 65 and over: 19.0%; Males per 100 females: 96.6; Marriage status: 19.0% never married, 62.9% now married, 1.0% separated, 6.2% widowed, 11.9% divorced; Foreign born: 16.2%; Speak English only: 73.8%; With disability: 5.9%; Veterans: 8.6%; Ancestry: 15.1% Irish, 12.7% Italian, 9.8% Russian, 9.1% German, 8.8% English

Employment: 22.1% management, business, and financial, 4.2% computer, engineering, and science, 16.0% education, legal, community service, arts, and media, 18.0% healthcare practitioners, 18.0% service, 25.6% sales and office, 7.6% natural resources, construction, and maintenance, 4.7% production, transportation, and material moving

Income: Per capita: $64,622; Median household: $93,750; Average household: $148,370; Households with income of $100,000 or more: 42.9%; Poverty rate: 6.5%

Educational Attainment: High school diploma or higher: 98.0%; Bachelor's degree or higher: 56.3%; Graduate/professional degree or higher: 24.2%

Housing: Homeownership rate: 87.7%; Median home value: $937,900; Median year structure built: 1985; Homeowner vacancy rate: 4.1%; Median selected monthly owner costs: $3,030 with a mortgage, $933 without a mortgage; Median gross rent: $3,133 per month; Rental vacancy rate: 0.0%

Health Insurance: 87.2% have insurance; 81.1% have private insurance; 24.1% have public insurance; 12.8% do not have insurance; 30.4% of children under 18 do not have insurance

Transportation: Commute: 78.8% car, 8.2% public transportation, 3.8% walk, 7.2% work from home; Mean travel time to work: 22.7 minutes

---

NOYACK (CDP). Covers a land area of 8.404 square miles and a water area of 0.322 square miles. Located at 40.98° N. Lat; 72.35° W. Long. Elevation is 26 feet.

Population: 3,970; Growth (since 2000): 47.3%; Density: 472.4 persons per square mile; Race: 91.7% White, 2.5% Black/African American, 2.7% Asian, 0.0% American Indian/Alaska Native, 0.0% Native Hawaiian/Other Pacific Islander, 0.5% Two or more races, 23.1% Hispanic of any race; Average household size: 2.51; Median age: 45.8; Age under 18: 19.7%; Age 65 and over: 17.3%; Males per 100 females: 93.1; Marriage status: 32.6% never married, 52.7% now married, 1.2% separated, 6.5% widowed, 8.2% divorced; Foreign born: 27.3%; Speak English only: 70.7%; With disability: 7.9%; Veterans: 5.2%; Ancestry: 20.8% Irish, 16.6% Italian, 13.9% German, 7.8% English, 4.5% American

Employment: 20.9% management, business, and financial, 3.8% computer, engineering, and science, 15.7% education, legal, community service, arts, and media, 3.5% healthcare practitioners, 15.9% service, 19.6% sales and office, 17.6% natural resources, construction, and maintenance, 3.1% production, transportation, and material moving

Income: Per capita: $47,041; Median household: $77,988; Average household: $116,201; Households with income of $100,000 or more: 39.9%; Poverty rate: 11.6%

Educational Attainment: High school diploma or higher: 91.0%; Bachelor's degree or higher: 52.2%; Graduate/professional degree or higher: 19.1%

Housing: Homeownership rate: 82.6%; Median home value: $716,700; Median year structure built: 1972; Homeowner vacancy rate: 2.4%; Median selected monthly owner costs: $2,907 with a mortgage, $881 without a mortgage; Median gross rent: $1,870 per month; Rental vacancy rate: 0.0%

Health Insurance: 78.0% have insurance; 62.6% have private insurance; 27.5% have public insurance; 22.0% do not have insurance; 3.6% of children under 18 do not have insurance

Transportation: Commute: 80.7% car, 5.4% public transportation, 0.4% walk, 13.5% work from home; Mean travel time to work: 22.1 minutes

---

OAK BEACH-CAPTREE (CDP). Covers a land area of 2.756 square miles and a water area of 0.920 square miles. Located at 40.65° N. Lat; 73.27° W. Long.

Population: 134; Growth (since 2000): n/a; Density: 48.6 persons per square mile; Race: 100.0% White, 0.0% Black/African American, 0.0% Asian, 0.0% American Indian/Alaska Native, 0.0% Native Hawaiian/Other Pacific Islander, 0.0% Two or more races, 0.0% Hispanic of any race; Average household size: 1.51; Median age: 62.8; Age under 18: 0.0%; Age 65 and over: 46.3%; Males per 100 females: 100.0; Marriage status: 0.0% never married, 67.9% now married, 0.0% separated, 0.0% widowed, 32.1% divorced; Foreign born: 29.1%; Speak English only: 100.0%; With disability: 0.0%; Veterans: 39.6%; Ancestry: 35.1% English, 29.1% Dutch, 28.4% Polish, 23.9% German, 12.7% Irish

Employment: 0.0% management, business, and financial, 20.8% computer, engineering, and science, 0.0% education, legal, community service, arts, and media, 0.0% healthcare practitioners, 0.0% service, 0.0% sales and office, 79.2% natural resources, construction, and maintenance, 0.0% production, transportation, and material moving

Income: Per capita: $102,182; Median household: n/a; Average household: $156,290; Households with income of $100,000 or more: 63.0%; Poverty rate: n/a

Educational Attainment: High school diploma or higher: 71.6%; Bachelor's degree or higher: 31.3%; Graduate/professional degree or higher: 31.3%

Housing: Homeownership rate: 100.0%; Median home value: $849,500; Median year structure built: 1967; Homeowner vacancy rate: 0.0%; Median selected monthly owner costs: n/a with a mortgage, $1,500+ without a mortgage; Median gross rent: n/a per month; Rental vacancy rate: 0.0%

Health Insurance: 100.0% have insurance; 89.6% have private insurance; 23.9% have public insurance; 0.0% do not have insurance; 0.0% of children under 18 do not have insurance

Transportation: Commute: 100.0% car, 0.0% public transportation, 0.0% walk, 0.0% work from home; Mean travel time to work: 0.0 minutes

---

OAKDALE (CDP).

Covers a land area of 3.417 square miles and a water area of 0.394 square miles. Located at 40.74° N. Lat; 73.13° W. Long. Elevation is 10 feet.

History: Seat of Dowling College.

Population: 7,336; Growth (since 2000): -9.2%; Density: 2,146.7 persons per square mile; Race: 95.7% White, 1.8% Black/African American, 1.3% Asian, 0.0% American Indian/Alaska Native, 0.0% Native Hawaiian/Other Pacific Islander, 0.8% Two or more races, 6.5% Hispanic of any race; Average household size: 2.56; Median age: 45.6; Age under 18: 18.7%; Age 65 and over: 18.3%; Males per 100 females: 91.1; Marriage status: 27.5% never married, 56.7% now married, 1.4% separated, 6.8% widowed, 9.0% divorced; Foreign born: 6.5%; Speak English only: 90.7%; With disability: 13.0%; Veterans: 8.0%; Ancestry: 35.2% Italian, 23.9% Irish, 23.7% German, 6.9% English, 5.6% Polish

Employment: 16.8% management, business, and financial, 4.1% computer, engineering, and science, 18.3% education, legal, community service, arts, and media, 5.4% healthcare practitioners, 20.2% service, 21.1% sales and office, 8.5% natural resources, construction, and maintenance, 5.6% production, transportation, and material moving

Income: Per capita: $40,895; Median household: $84,655; Average household: $104,968; Households with income of $100,000 or more: 43.9%; Poverty rate: 3.3%

Educational Attainment: High school diploma or higher: 94.5%; Bachelor's degree or higher: 33.6%; Graduate/professional degree or higher: 18.3%

School District(s)
Connetquot Central SD (PK-12)
    2014-15 Enrollment: 6,244 . . . . (631) 244-2215

Four-year College(s)
Dowling College (Private, Not-for-profit)
    Fall 2014 Enrollment: 2,453 . . . . (631) 244-3000
    2015-16 Tuition: In-state $29,100; Out-of-state $29,100

Vocational/Technical School(s)
Eastern Suffolk BOCES (Public)
    Fall 2014 Enrollment: n/a . . . . (631) 233-4450
    2015-16 Tuition: $9,940

Housing: Homeownership rate: 84.7%; Median home value: $428,000; Median year structure built: 1969; Homeowner vacancy rate: 2.7%; Median selected monthly owner costs: $2,759 with a mortgage, $1,319 without a mortgage; Median gross rent: $1,585 per month; Rental vacancy rate: 12.9%

Health Insurance: 95.3% have insurance; 82.9% have private insurance; 26.5% have public insurance; 4.7% do not have insurance; 0.9% of children under 18 do not have insurance

Transportation: Commute: 87.5% car, 7.2% public transportation, 1.3% walk, 3.9% work from home; Mean travel time to work: 33.9 minutes

---

OCEAN BEACH (village).

Covers a land area of 0.141 square miles and a water area of 0 square miles. Located at 40.65° N. Lat; 73.16° W. Long. Elevation is 3 feet.

Population: 32; Growth (since 2000): -76.8%; Density: 226.4 persons per square mile; Race: 100.0% White, 0.0% Black/African American, 0.0% Asian, 0.0% American Indian/Alaska Native, 0.0% Native Hawaiian/Other Pacific Islander, 0.0% Two or more races, 0.0% Hispanic of any race; Average household size: 1.78; Median age: 66.0; Age under 18: 0.0%; Age 65 and over: 56.3%; Males per 100 females: 146.9; Marriage status: 21.9% never married, 37.5% now married, 0.0% separated, 12.5% widowed, 28.1% divorced; Foreign born: 9.4%; Speak English only: 100.0%; With disability: 3.1%; Veterans: 18.8%; Ancestry: 28.1% Irish, 21.9% Italian, 15.6% Czech, 15.6% German, 9.4% French

Employment: 46.7% management, business, and financial, 6.7% computer, engineering, and science, 6.7% education, legal, community

service, arts, and media, 6.7% healthcare practitioners, 0.0% service, 20.0% sales and office, 13.3% natural resources, construction, and maintenance, 0.0% production, transportation, and material moving

Income: Per capita: $57,831; Median household: $58,750; Average household: $97,133; Households with income of $100,000 or more: 33.3%; Poverty rate: 3.1%

Educational Attainment: High school diploma or higher: 96.9%; Bachelor's degree or higher: 46.9%; Graduate/professional degree or higher: 28.1%

Housing: Homeownership rate: 100.0%; Median home value: $1,000,000; Median year structure built: 1942; Homeowner vacancy rate: 5.3%; Median selected monthly owner costs: $2,500 with a mortgage, $1,500+ without a mortgage; Median gross rent: n/a per month; Rental vacancy rate: 0.0%

Health Insurance: 84.4% have insurance; 68.8% have private insurance; 56.3% have public insurance; 15.6% do not have insurance; 0.0% of children under 18 do not have insurance

Safety: Violent crime rate: 0.0 per 10,000 population; Property crime rate: 1,875.0 per 10,000 population

Transportation: Commute: 33.3% car, 0.0% public transportation, 20.0% walk, 20.0% work from home; Mean travel time to work: 5.4 minutes

Additional Information Contacts
Village of Ocean Beach . . . . (631) 583-5940
  http://www.villageofoceanbeach.org

OLD FIELD (village).

Covers a land area of 2.070 square miles and a water area of 0.121 square miles. Located at 40.96° N. Lat; 73.15° W. Long. Elevation is 7 feet.

Population: 858; Growth (since 2000): -9.4%; Density: 414.6 persons per square mile; Race: 86.4% White, 0.0% Black/African American, 12.8% Asian, 0.0% American Indian/Alaska Native, 0.0% Native Hawaiian/Other Pacific Islander, 0.5% Two or more races, 3.1% Hispanic of any race; Average household size: 2.71; Median age: 50.6; Age under 18: 20.2%; Age 65 and over: 18.8%; Males per 100 females: 104.5; Marriage status: 19.9% never married, 68.8% now married, 1.5% separated, 7.0% widowed, 4.3% divorced; Foreign born: 17.0%; Speak English only: 84.3%; With disability: 5.7%; Veterans: 6.3%; Ancestry: 16.8% Italian, 13.3% Irish, 11.1% German, 6.9% American, 6.4% Eastern European

Employment: 22.1% management, business, and financial, 6.5% computer, engineering, and science, 17.4% education, legal, community service, arts, and media, 27.3% healthcare practitioners, 2.2% service, 18.6% sales and office, 4.0% natural resources, construction, and maintenance, 2.0% production, transportation, and material moving

Income: Per capita: $120,199; Median household: $208,750; Average household: $326,181; Households with income of $100,000 or more: 77.9%; Poverty rate: 5.0%

Educational Attainment: High school diploma or higher: 99.0%; Bachelor's degree or higher: 78.2%; Graduate/professional degree or higher: 59.7%

Housing: Homeownership rate: 93.3%; Median home value: $1,109,400; Median year structure built: 1967; Homeowner vacancy rate: 3.2%; Median selected monthly owner costs: $4,000+ with a mortgage, $1,500+ without a mortgage; Median gross rent: n/a per month; Rental vacancy rate: 0.0%

Health Insurance: 98.5% have insurance; 90.3% have private insurance; 22.4% have public insurance; 1.5% do not have insurance; 1.7% of children under 18 do not have insurance

Transportation: Commute: 85.4% car, 6.5% public transportation, 1.5% walk, 5.5% work from home; Mean travel time to work: 32.0 minutes

Additional Information Contacts
Village of Old Field . . . . (631) 941-9412
  http://www.oldfieldny.org

ORIENT (CDP).

Covers a land area of 5.122 square miles and a water area of 1.032 square miles. Located at 41.14° N. Lat; 72.26° W. Long. Elevation is 13 feet.

Population: 706; Growth (since 2000): -0.4%; Density: 137.8 persons per square mile; Race: 98.7% White, 0.3% Black/African American, 0.0% Asian, 1.0% American Indian/Alaska Native, 0.0% Native Hawaiian/Other Pacific Islander, 0.0% Two or more races, 1.8% Hispanic of any race; Average household size: 1.95; Median age: 66.3; Age under 18: 6.7%; Age 65 and over: 54.1%; Males per 100 females: 89.5; Marriage status: 20.7% never married, 57.4% now married, 0.6% separated, 10.8% widowed, 11.1% divorced; Foreign born: 1.6%; Speak English only: 94.2%; With disability: 16.1%; Veterans: 21.5%; Ancestry: 31.2% English, 27.3% Irish, 22.4% German, 12.3% Polish, 10.3% Italian

Employment: 28.0% management, business, and financial, 0.0% computer, engineering, and science, 11.8% education, legal, community service, arts, and media, 6.6% healthcare practitioners, 17.7% service, 21.4% sales and office, 7.0% natural resources, construction, and maintenance, 7.4% production, transportation, and material moving
Income: Per capita: $48,563; Median household: $75,375; Average household: $95,914; Households with income of $100,000 or more: 31.4%; Poverty rate: 1.8%
Educational Attainment: High school diploma or higher: 97.1%; Bachelor's degree or higher: 42.0%; Graduate/professional degree or higher: 15.7%

School District(s)

Oysterponds Union Free SD (KG-06)
    2014-15 Enrollment: 73. . . . . (631) 323-2410
Housing: Homeownership rate: 91.8%; Median home value: $645,200; Median year structure built: 1970; Homeowner vacancy rate: 1.8%; Median selected monthly owner costs: $2,000 with a mortgage, $1,005 without a mortgage; Median gross rent: $1,575 per month; Rental vacancy rate: 17.1%
Health Insurance: 98.0% have insurance; 87.7% have private insurance; 55.4% have public insurance; 2.0% do not have insurance; 0.0% of children under 18 do not have insurance
Transportation: Commute: 73.1% car, 7.6% public transportation, 4.4% walk, 12.0% work from home; Mean travel time to work: 28.1 minutes

PATCHOGUE (village). Covers a land area of 2.255 square miles and a water area of 0.262 square miles. Located at 40.76° N. Lat; 73.02° W. Long. Elevation is 20 feet.

History: Patchogue is a village on the south shore of Long Island in Suffolk County, New York.
Population: 12,173; Growth (since 2000): 2.1%; Density: 5,397.2 persons per square mile; Race: 84.3% White, 8.2% Black/African American, 0.1% Asian, 0.6% American Indian/Alaska Native, 0.0% Native Hawaiian/Other Pacific Islander, 1.3% Two or more races, 32.8% Hispanic of any race; Average household size: 2.56; Median age: 35.1; Age under 18: 22.5%; Age 65 and over: 10.1%; Males per 100 females: 100.2; Marriage status: 38.6% never married, 42.1% now married, 2.8% separated, 5.3% widowed, 14.0% divorced; Foreign born: 17.2%; Speak English only: 70.5%; With disability: 10.0%; Veterans: 4.8%; Ancestry: 25.0% Italian, 18.3% Irish, 15.4% German, 6.8% English, 2.3% American
Employment: 11.6% management, business, and financial, 2.3% computer, engineering, and science, 11.8% education, legal, community service, arts, and media, 3.2% healthcare practitioners, 20.0% service, 23.3% sales and office, 11.0% natural resources, construction, and maintenance, 17.0% production, transportation, and material moving
Income: Per capita: $32,621; Median household: $68,117; Average household: $81,060; Households with income of $100,000 or more: 27.7%; Poverty rate: 15.1%
Educational Attainment: High school diploma or higher: 85.9%; Bachelor's degree or higher: 25.8%; Graduate/professional degree or higher: 10.5%

School District(s)

Eastern Suffolk Boces
    2014-15 Enrollment: n/a . . . . (631) 687-3006
Patchogue-Medford Union Free SD (PK-12)
    2014-15 Enrollment: 7,818 . . . . (631) 687-6380

Vocational/Technical School(s)

Eastern Suffolk BOCES (Public)
    Fall 2014 Enrollment: 346 . . . . (631) 233-4450
    2015-16 Tuition: $14,200
Housing: Homeownership rate: 53.7%; Median home value: $289,400; Median year structure built: 1961; Homeowner vacancy rate: 0.0%; Median selected monthly owner costs: $2,218 with a mortgage, $1,052 without a mortgage; Median gross rent: $1,398 per month; Rental vacancy rate: 6.6%
Health Insurance: 83.0% have insurance; 68.7% have private insurance; 27.7% have public insurance; 17.0% do not have insurance; 6.6% of children under 18 do not have insurance
Hospitals: Brookhaven Memorial Hospital Medical Center (321 beds)
Newspapers: Long Island Advance (weekly circulation 11,000)
Transportation: Commute: 83.9% car, 6.8% public transportation, 5.0% walk, 3.6% work from home; Mean travel time to work: 29.8 minutes
Additional Information Contacts
Village of Patchogue . . . . (631) 475-4300
    http://www.patchoguevillage.org

PECONIC (CDP). Covers a land area of 3.380 square miles and a water area of 0.126 square miles. Located at 41.04° N. Lat; 72.46° W. Long. Elevation is 30 feet.

Population: 526; Growth (since 2000): -51.3%; Density: 155.6 persons per square mile; Race: 100.0% White, 0.0% Black/African American, 0.0% Asian, 0.0% American Indian/Alaska Native, 0.0% Native Hawaiian/Other Pacific Islander, 0.0% Two or more races, 0.0% Hispanic of any race; Average household size: 1.86; Median age: 62.4; Age under 18: 4.8%; Age 65 and over: 45.4%; Males per 100 females: 109.5; Marriage status: 20.2% never married, 59.3% now married, 0.0% separated, 10.0% widowed, 10.6% divorced; Foreign born: 9.7%; Speak English only: 94.2%; With disability: 19.4%; Veterans: 12.0%; Ancestry: 23.8% German, 18.6% Irish, 13.7% Polish, 12.4% Italian, 4.9% English
Employment: 9.7% management, business, and financial, 4.9% computer, engineering, and science, 31.1% education, legal, community service, arts, and media, 0.0% healthcare practitioners, 12.4% service, 28.5% sales and office, 0.0% natural resources, construction, and maintenance, 13.5% production, transportation, and material moving
Income: Per capita: $74,231; Median household: $66,442; Average household: $136,901; Households with income of $100,000 or more: 25.1%; Poverty rate: n/a
Educational Attainment: High school diploma or higher: 85.0%; Bachelor's degree or higher: 46.6%; Graduate/professional degree or higher: 30.7%
Housing: Homeownership rate: 95.4%; Median home value: $539,900; Median year structure built: 1971; Homeowner vacancy rate: 0.0%; Median selected monthly owner costs: $1,875 with a mortgage, $841 without a mortgage; Median gross rent: n/a per month; Rental vacancy rate: 0.0%
Health Insurance: 97.5% have insurance; 77.4% have private insurance; 58.7% have public insurance; 2.5% do not have insurance; 0.0% of children under 18 do not have insurance
Transportation: Commute: 73.9% car, 4.5% public transportation, 0.0% walk, 21.6% work from home; Mean travel time to work: 15.9 minutes

POOSPATUCK RESERVATION (reservation). Covers a land area of 0.113 square miles and a water area of 0.057 square miles. Located at 40.79° N. Lat; 72.83° W. Long.

Population: 429; Growth (since 2000): 58.3%; Density: 3,807.4 persons per square mile; Race: 25.6% White, 13.1% Black/African American, 0.0% Asian, 52.4% American Indian/Alaska Native, 0.0% Native Hawaiian/Other Pacific Islander, 8.9% Two or more races, 5.8% Hispanic of any race; Average household size: 3.02; Median age: 33.9; Age under 18: 22.4%; Age 65 and over: 14.7%; Males per 100 females: 88.4; Marriage status: 44.3% never married, 44.9% now married, 3.7% separated, 2.9% widowed, 8.0% divorced; Foreign born: 6.8%; Speak English only: 90.6%; With disability: 10.5%; Veterans: 6.0%; Ancestry: 11.7% Italian, 6.1% German, 4.0% Irish, 4.0% Belizean, 3.3% French
Employment: 15.4% management, business, and financial, 0.0% computer, engineering, and science, 6.8% education, legal, community service, arts, and media, 6.8% healthcare practitioners, 23.5% service, 30.2% sales and office, 9.3% natural resources, construction, and maintenance, 8.0% production, transportation, and material moving
Income: Per capita: $17,612; Median household: $33,438; Average household: $50,420; Households with income of $100,000 or more: 10.5%; Poverty rate: 25.6%
Educational Attainment: High school diploma or higher: 77.3%; Bachelor's degree or higher: 5.0%; Graduate/professional degree or higher: 1.3%
Housing: Homeownership rate: 78.9%; Median home value: $163,500; Median year structure built: 1979; Homeowner vacancy rate: 1.8%; Median selected monthly owner costs: $1,625 with a mortgage, $522 without a mortgage; Median gross rent: $1,219 per month; Rental vacancy rate: 0.0%
Health Insurance: 73.0% have insurance; 44.5% have private insurance; 39.2% have public insurance; 27.0% do not have insurance; 25.0% of children under 18 do not have insurance
Transportation: Commute: 74.1% car, 0.6% public transportation, 19.1% walk, 3.1% work from home; Mean travel time to work: 22.8 minutes

POQUOTT (village). Covers a land area of 0.439 square miles and a water area of 0.147 square miles. Located at 40.95° N. Lat; 73.09° W. Long. Elevation is 66 feet.

Population: 856; Growth (since 2000): -12.2%; Density: 1,948.7 persons per square mile; Race: 87.5% White, 1.9% Black/African American, 6.7% Asian, 0.0% American Indian/Alaska Native, 0.0% Native Hawaiian/Other

Pacific Islander, 2.1% Two or more races, 4.3% Hispanic of any race; Average household size: 2.65; Median age: 49.4; Age under 18: 19.9%; Age 65 and over: 18.9%; Males per 100 females: 97.3; Marriage status: 30.8% never married, 56.6% now married, 1.2% separated, 4.8% widowed, 7.8% divorced; Foreign born: 17.5%; Speak English only: 86.3%; With disability: 7.4%; Veterans: 5.2%; Ancestry: 22.9% Italian, 20.1% German, 19.2% Irish, 7.9% American, 5.8% Russian

Employment: 16.7% management, business, and financial, 9.5% computer, engineering, and science, 24.4% education, legal, community service, arts, and media, 10.0% healthcare practitioners, 16.2% service, 14.6% sales and office, 3.5% natural resources, construction, and maintenance, 5.1% production, transportation, and material moving

Income: Per capita: $69,242; Median household: $120,417; Average household: $184,120; Households with income of $100,000 or more: 61.6%; Poverty rate: 3.6%

Educational Attainment: High school diploma or higher: 96.6%; Bachelor's degree or higher: 63.0%; Graduate/professional degree or higher: 40.9%

Housing: Homeownership rate: 88.2%; Median home value: $566,500; Median year structure built: 1954; Homeowner vacancy rate: 0.0%; Median selected monthly owner costs: $3,338 with a mortgage, $1,356 without a mortgage; Median gross rent: $1,971 per month; Rental vacancy rate: 19.1%

Health Insurance: 94.4% have insurance; 84.1% have private insurance; 23.0% have public insurance; 5.6% do not have insurance; 0.0% of children under 18 do not have insurance

Transportation: Commute: 89.2% car, 3.1% public transportation, 1.0% walk, 6.7% work from home; Mean travel time to work: 26.7 minutes

PORT JEFFERSON (village).

Covers a land area of 3.057 square miles and a water area of 0.027 square miles. Located at 40.94° N. Lat; 73.05° W. Long. Elevation is 3 feet.

History: Port Jefferson at one time was a small ship building community, with the name Drowned Meadow. The community leaders, realizing this was a poor name for the ship building business, eventually changed its name to Port Jefferson in 1836 after President Thomas Jefferson. The town was once a major whaling port, especially in the 1880s. The Village of Port Jefferson was incorporated in 1964.

Population: 7,802; Growth (since 2000): -0.4%; Density: 2,552.3 persons per square mile; Race: 87.9% White, 2.3% Black/African American, 5.7% Asian, 0.0% American Indian/Alaska Native, 0.0% Native Hawaiian/Other Pacific Islander, 2.6% Two or more races, 7.2% Hispanic of any race; Average household size: 2.38; Median age: 47.4; Age under 18: 18.4%; Age 65 and over: 21.7%; Males per 100 females: 97.5; Marriage status: 27.8% never married, 58.5% now married, 0.9% separated, 4.7% widowed, 9.0% divorced; Foreign born: 14.3%; Speak English only: 83.8%; With disability: 7.8%; Veterans: 5.6%; Ancestry: 22.4% Irish, 19.6% Italian, 14.2% German, 7.9% American, 7.9% English

Employment: 17.9% management, business, and financial, 8.5% computer, engineering, and science, 20.4% education, legal, community service, arts, and media, 13.4% healthcare practitioners, 12.5% service, 20.6% sales and office, 3.1% natural resources, construction, and maintenance, 3.5% production, transportation, and material moving

Income: Per capita: $55,294; Median household: $110,681; Average household: $133,239; Households with income of $100,000 or more: 53.7%; Poverty rate: 5.4%

Educational Attainment: High school diploma or higher: 98.3%; Bachelor's degree or higher: 61.3%; Graduate/professional degree or higher: 42.3%

School District(s)

Port Jefferson Union Free SD (PK-12)

    2014-15 Enrollment: 1,175 . . . . (631) 791-4221

Housing: Homeownership rate: 72.6%; Median home value: $495,100; Median year structure built: 1971; Homeowner vacancy rate: 0.6%; Median selected monthly owner costs: $2,860 with a mortgage, $1,192 without a mortgage; Median gross rent: $1,609 per month; Rental vacancy rate: 1.8%

Health Insurance: 96.0% have insurance; 87.6% have private insurance; 27.3% have public insurance; 4.0% do not have insurance; 2.3% of children under 18 do not have insurance

Hospitals: John T Mather Memorial Hospital of Port Jefferson (248 beds); Saint Charles Hospital (231 beds)

Transportation: Commute: 88.7% car, 5.8% public transportation, 1.2% walk, 4.2% work from home; Mean travel time to work: 31.6 minutes

Additional Information Contacts

Village of Port Jefferson . . . . (631) 473-4724
  http://www.portjeff.com

PORT JEFFERSON STATION (CDP).

Covers a land area of 2.666 square miles and a water area of 0 square miles. Located at 40.93° N. Lat; 73.07° W. Long. Elevation is 177 feet.

History: Port Jefferson Station was first called by the Native American name *Comsewogue*.

Population: 8,582; Growth (since 2000): 14.0%; Density: 3,219.1 persons per square mile; Race: 88.7% White, 1.0% Black/African American, 9.0% Asian, 0.2% American Indian/Alaska Native, 0.0% Native Hawaiian/Other Pacific Islander, 1.0% Two or more races, 21.1% Hispanic of any race; Average household size: 3.11; Median age: 36.3; Age under 18: 21.3%; Age 65 and over: 12.2%; Males per 100 females: 95.8; Marriage status: 35.5% never married, 52.2% now married, 1.9% separated, 5.5% widowed, 6.8% divorced; Foreign born: 20.3%; Speak English only: 71.9%; With disability: 8.9%; Veterans: 8.7%; Ancestry: 35.4% Italian, 21.8% Irish, 16.0% German, 10.0% American, 3.2% Polish

Employment: 10.9% management, business, and financial, 9.1% computer, engineering, and science, 18.0% education, legal, community service, arts, and media, 6.8% healthcare practitioners, 17.9% service, 23.4% sales and office, 10.8% natural resources, construction, and maintenance, 3.2% production, transportation, and material moving

Income: Per capita: $32,836; Median household: $86,360; Average household: $99,486; Households with income of $100,000 or more: 39.5%; Poverty rate: 14.2%

Educational Attainment: High school diploma or higher: 92.8%; Bachelor's degree or higher: 37.0%; Graduate/professional degree or higher: 17.4%

School District(s)

Brookhaven-Comsewogue Union Free SD (KG-12)

    2014-15 Enrollment: 3,791 . . . . (631) 474-8105

Housing: Homeownership rate: 74.5%; Median home value: $339,900; Median year structure built: 1968; Homeowner vacancy rate: 1.1%; Median selected monthly owner costs: $2,595 with a mortgage, $1,181 without a mortgage; Median gross rent: $1,585 per month; Rental vacancy rate: 2.2%

Health Insurance: 89.8% have insurance; 76.4% have private insurance; 23.5% have public insurance; 10.2% do not have insurance; 6.8% of children under 18 do not have insurance

Transportation: Commute: 92.0% car, 4.1% public transportation, 3.8% walk, 0.0% work from home; Mean travel time to work: 32.3 minutes

QUIOGUE (CDP).

Note: Statistics that would complete this profile are not available because the CDP was created after the 2010 Census was released.

QUOGUE (village).

Covers a land area of 4.191 square miles and a water area of 0.773 square miles. Located at 40.82° N. Lat; 72.60° W. Long. Elevation is 16 feet.

History: Region originally occupied by Native American tribe of Shinnecocks because of rich hunting and fishing. Nearby Hampton Bays was called Good Ground until 1922. Settled in 1686, when known as Fourth Neck, then Atlanticville, until adoption of present name in 1891.

Population: 854; Growth (since 2000): -16.1%; Density: 203.8 persons per square mile; Race: 95.0% White, 2.7% Black/African American, 1.3% Asian, 0.0% American Indian/Alaska Native, 0.0% Native Hawaiian/Other Pacific Islander, 1.1% Two or more races, 3.7% Hispanic of any race; Average household size: 2.21; Median age: 56.6; Age under 18: 15.2%; Age 65 and over: 27.6%; Males per 100 females: 91.9; Marriage status: 18.2% never married, 62.9% now married, 2.0% separated, 7.0% widowed, 11.9% divorced; Foreign born: 4.3%; Speak English only: 93.9%; With disability: 6.8%; Veterans: 8.4%; Ancestry: 17.7% Italian, 17.4% Irish, 11.6% German, 9.1% European, 7.3% English

Employment: 29.6% management, business, and financial, 0.0% computer, engineering, and science, 12.7% education, legal, community service, arts, and media, 8.5% healthcare practitioners, 5.4% service, 31.5% sales and office, 8.2% natural resources, construction, and maintenance, 4.2% production, transportation, and material moving

Income: Per capita: $57,860; Median household: $85,000; Average household: $127,905; Households with income of $100,000 or more: 42.9%; Poverty rate: 6.2%

Educational Attainment: High school diploma or higher: 98.0%; Bachelor's degree or higher: 58.2%; Graduate/professional degree or higher: 26.8%

Quogue Union Free SD (PK-06)

2014-15 Enrollment: 113 . . . . (631) 653-4285

Housing: Homeownership rate: 81.9%; Median home value: $947,400; Median year structure built: 1982; Homeowner vacancy rate: 0.0%; Median selected monthly owner costs: $3,263 with a mortgage, $1,065 without a mortgage; Median gross rent: $1,667 per month; Rental vacancy rate: 0.0%

Health Insurance: 93.7% have insurance; 81.0% have private insurance; 30.1% have public insurance; 6.3% do not have insurance; 8.5% of children under 18 do not have insurance

Safety: Violent crime rate: 0.0 per 10,000 population; Property crime rate: 303.0 per 10,000 population

Transportation: Commute: 82.4% car, 9.2% public transportation, 0.0% walk, 6.9% work from home; Mean travel time to work: 37.4 minutes

REMSENBURG-SPEONK (CDP). Covers a land area of 3.602 square miles and a water area of 0.081 square miles. Located at 40.82° N. Lat; 72.71° W. Long. Elevation is 30 feet.

Population: 1,867; Growth (since 2000): -30.2%; Density: 518.3 persons per square mile; Race: 92.4% White, 1.1% Black/African American, 4.8% Asian, 0.0% American Indian/Alaska Native, 0.0% Native Hawaiian/Other Pacific Islander, 1.7% Two or more races, 12.3% Hispanic of any race; Average household size: 2.37; Median age: 47.3; Age under 18: 20.9%; Age 65 and over: 20.2%; Males per 100 females: 94.4; Marriage status: 23.1% never married, 63.3% now married, 0.5% separated, 6.1% widowed, 7.5% divorced; Foreign born: 8.8%; Speak English only: 84.1%; With disability: 2.8%; Veterans: 7.0%; Ancestry: 24.0% Italian, 23.9% Irish, 17.7% German, 9.9% English, 5.3% Polish

Employment: 22.3% management, business, and financial, 8.1% computer, engineering, and science, 12.8% education, legal, community service, arts, and media, 3.6% healthcare practitioners, 10.0% service, 16.9% sales and office, 13.0% natural resources, construction, and maintenance, 13.2% production, transportation, and material moving

Income: Per capita: $48,638; Median household: $103,575; Average household: $114,814; Households with income of $100,000 or more: 53.1%; Poverty rate: 10.6%

Educational Attainment: High school diploma or higher: 98.9%; Bachelor's degree or higher: 43.0%; Graduate/professional degree or higher: 17.6%

Remsenburg-Speonk Union Free SD (KG-06)

2014-15 Enrollment: 159 . . . . (631) 325-0203

Housing: Homeownership rate: 84.3%; Median home value: $578,800; Median year structure built: 1978; Homeowner vacancy rate: 5.4%; Median selected monthly owner costs: $2,519 with a mortgage, $914 without a mortgage; Median gross rent: $1,294 per month; Rental vacancy rate: 6.1%

Health Insurance: 88.1% have insurance; 79.1% have private insurance; 27.2% have public insurance; 11.9% do not have insurance; 12.3% of children under 18 do not have insurance

Transportation: Commute: 90.8% car, 1.5% public transportation, 3.4% walk, 2.6% work from home; Mean travel time to work: 25.1 minutes

RIDGE (CDP). Covers a land area of 13.211 square miles and a water area of 0.093 square miles. Located at 40.90° N. Lat; 72.89° W. Long. Elevation is 92 feet.

Population: 12,835; Growth (since 2000): -4.1%; Density: 971.6 persons per square mile; Race: 90.4% White, 4.6% Black/African American, 3.4% Asian, 0.4% American Indian/Alaska Native, 0.0% Native Hawaiian/Other Pacific Islander, 1.1% Two or more races, 4.9% Hispanic of any race; Average household size: 2.38; Median age: 49.4; Age under 18: 19.1%; Age 65 and over: 28.3%; Males per 100 females: 85.0; Marriage status: 23.8% never married, 53.2% now married, 1.0% separated, 11.9% widowed, 11.1% divorced; Foreign born: 5.8%; Speak English only: 93.0%; With disability: 16.7%; Veterans: 10.7%; Ancestry: 31.1% Italian, 26.9% Irish, 24.6% German, 7.6% Polish, 6.6% American

Employment: 13.8% management, business, and financial, 5.8% computer, engineering, and science, 11.6% education, legal, community service, arts, and media, 3.8% healthcare practitioners, 15.2% service, 26.6% sales and office, 10.2% natural resources, construction, and maintenance, 13.0% production, transportation, and material moving

Income: Per capita: $34,717; Median household: $58,885; Average household: $81,513; Households with income of $100,000 or more: 29.1%; Poverty rate: 6.4%

Educational Attainment: High school diploma or higher: 92.1%; Bachelor's degree or higher: 23.1%; Graduate/professional degree or higher: 13.0%

Longwood Central SD (KG-12)

2014-15 Enrollment: 9,211 . . . . (631) 345-2172

Housing: Homeownership rate: 85.7%; Median home value: $255,500; Median year structure built: 1978; Homeowner vacancy rate: 3.8%; Median selected monthly owner costs: $2,259 with a mortgage, $849 without a mortgage; Median gross rent: $1,422 per month; Rental vacancy rate: 18.0%

Health Insurance: 97.5% have insurance; 82.5% have private insurance; 36.9% have public insurance; 2.5% do not have insurance; 0.7% of children under 18 do not have insurance

Transportation: Commute: 94.4% car, 2.3% public transportation, 0.3% walk, 2.5% work from home; Mean travel time to work: 29.4 minutes

RIVERHEAD (CDP). Covers a land area of 15.082 square miles and a water area of 0.305 square miles. Located at 40.95° N. Lat; 72.68° W. Long. Elevation is 13 feet.

Population: 14,258; Growth (since 2000): 35.6%; Density: 945.3 persons per square mile; Race: 68.3% White, 20.6% Black/African American, 1.8% Asian, 1.2% American Indian/Alaska Native, 0.7% Native Hawaiian/Other Pacific Islander, 2.9% Two or more races, 20.2% Hispanic of any race; Average household size: 2.75; Median age: 39.9; Age under 18: 20.3%; Age 65 and over: 19.6%; Males per 100 females: 103.5; Marriage status: 39.6% never married, 43.1% now married, 1.5% separated, 7.5% widowed, 9.7% divorced; Foreign born: 21.6%; Speak English only: 74.2%; With disability: 15.5%; Veterans: 7.6%; Ancestry: 20.3% Irish, 13.6% German, 12.7% Polish, 11.1% Italian, 4.2% African

Employment: 4.6% management, business, and financial, 2.3% computer, engineering, and science, 9.1% education, legal, community service, arts, and media, 1.9% healthcare practitioners, 25.5% service, 29.7% sales and office, 11.8% natural resources, construction, and maintenance, 15.2% production, transportation, and material moving

Income: Per capita: $26,590; Median household: $52,876; Average household: $71,962; Households with income of $100,000 or more: 23.6%; Poverty rate: 15.4%

Educational Attainment: High school diploma or higher: 84.5%; Bachelor's degree or higher: 20.2%; Graduate/professional degree or higher: 7.7%

Riverhead Central SD (KG-12)

2014-15 Enrollment: 5,216 . . . . (631) 369-6717

LIU Riverhead (Private, Not-for-profit)

Fall 2014 Enrollment: 168 . . . . (631) 287-8010

Eastern Suffolk BOCES (Public)

Fall 2014 Enrollment: n/a . . . . (631) 233-4450

2015-16 Tuition: $9,940

Housing: Homeownership rate: 59.2%; Median home value: $312,800; Median year structure built: 1977; Homeowner vacancy rate: 0.7%; Median selected monthly owner costs: $2,203 with a mortgage, $810 without a mortgage; Median gross rent: $1,301 per month; Rental vacancy rate: 1.2%

Health Insurance: 76.6% have insurance; 50.7% have private insurance; 38.6% have public insurance; 23.4% do not have insurance; 10.7% of children under 18 do not have insurance

Hospitals: Peconic Bay Medical Center (214 beds)

Newspapers: Suffolk Life Papers (weekly circulation 570,000)

Transportation: Commute: 82.0% car, 4.6% public transportation, 4.8% walk, 3.4% work from home; Mean travel time to work: 24.1 minutes

RIVERHEAD (town). County seat. Covers a land area of 67.426 square miles and a water area of 133.841 square miles. Located at 40.98° N. Lat; 72.71° W. Long. Elevation is 13 feet.

History: Named for its location at the head of the Peconic River. Museum of Suffolk County Historical Society is here.

Population: 33,769; Growth (since 2000): 22.0%; Density: 500.8 persons per square mile; Race: 84.1% White, 9.5% Black/African American, 1.3% Asian, 0.5% American Indian/Alaska Native, 0.3% Native Hawaiian/Other

Pacific Islander, 2.0% Two or more races, 13.7% Hispanic of any race; Average household size: 2.58; Median age: 45.7; Age under 18: 18.5%; Age 65 and over: 21.7%; Males per 100 females: 99.0; Marriage status: 30.7% never married, 53.3% now married, 1.5% separated, 7.8% widowed, 8.2% divorced; Foreign born: 13.3%; Speak English only: 82.9%; With disability: 13.6%; Veterans: 9.7%; Ancestry: 22.1% Irish, 18.3% German, 17.0% Italian, 10.9% Polish, 5.9% American

Employment: 12.8% management, business, and financial, 3.3% computer, engineering, and science, 12.6% education, legal, community service, arts, and media, 5.4% healthcare practitioners, 20.0% service, 26.6% sales and office, 9.2% natural resources, construction, and maintenance, 10.0% production, transportation, and material moving

Income: Per capita: $34,885; Median household: $64,775; Average household: $89,019; Households with income of $100,000 or more: 34.1%; Poverty rate: 9.3%

Educational Attainment: High school diploma or higher: 90.2%; Bachelor's degree or higher: 28.5%; Graduate/professional degree or higher: 13.4%

School District(s)

Riverhead Central SD (KG-12)
    2014-15 Enrollment: 5,216 . . . . (631) 369-6717

Four-year College(s)

LIU Riverhead (Private, Not-for-profit)
    Fall 2014 Enrollment: 168 . . . . (631) 287-8010

Vocational/Technical School(s)

Eastern Suffolk BOCES (Public)
    Fall 2014 Enrollment: n/a . . . . (631) 233-4450
    2015-16 Tuition: $9,940

Housing: Homeownership rate: 77.7%; Median home value: $355,400; Median year structure built: 1981; Homeowner vacancy rate: 2.0%; Median selected monthly owner costs: $2,523 with a mortgage, $935 without a mortgage; Median gross rent: $1,303 per month; Rental vacancy rate: 2.3%

Health Insurance: 87.0% have insurance; 69.4% have private insurance; 33.7% have public insurance; 13.0% do not have insurance; 5.9% of children under 18 do not have insurance

Hospitals: Peconic Bay Medical Center (214 beds)

Newspapers: Suffolk Life Papers (weekly circulation 570,000)

Transportation: Commute: 87.9% car, 2.7% public transportation, 2.8% walk, 4.0% work from home; Mean travel time to work: 26.8 minutes

Additional Information Contacts

Town of Riverhead . . . . (631) 727-3200
    http://www.townofriverheadny.gov

RIVERSIDE (CDP). Covers a land area of 2.717 square miles and a water area of 0.113 square miles. Located at 40.91° N. Lat; 72.67° W. Long. Elevation is 180 feet.

Population: 4,912; Growth (since 2000): 70.9%; Density: 1,807.8 persons per square mile; Race: 53.9% White, 33.9% Black/African American, 0.3% Asian, 0.0% American Indian/Alaska Native, 0.0% Native Hawaiian/Other Pacific Islander, 8.6% Two or more races, 16.7% Hispanic of any race; Average household size: 2.11; Median age: 36.4; Age under 18: 4.2%; Age 65 and over: 8.4%; Males per 100 females: 178.0; Marriage status: 67.1% never married, 20.2% now married, 1.5% separated, 4.4% widowed, 8.3% divorced; Foreign born: 11.1%; Speak English only: 89.2%; With disability: 12.8%; Veterans: 6.8%; Ancestry: 5.8% English, 2.4% German, 2.3% Irish, 1.9% Italian, 1.0% American

Employment: 6.8% management, business, and financial, 11.1% computer, engineering, and science, 4.7% education, legal, community service, arts, and media, 0.0% healthcare practitioners, 8.4% service, 18.3% sales and office, 42.0% natural resources, construction, and maintenance, 8.7% production, transportation, and material moving

Income: Per capita: $13,403; Median household: $39,571; Average household: $48,282; Households with income of $100,000 or more: 11.8%; Poverty rate: 11.4%

Educational Attainment: High school diploma or higher: 70.9%; Bachelor's degree or higher: 4.9%; Graduate/professional degree or higher: 0.4%

Housing: Homeownership rate: 80.4%; Median home value: $70,400; Median year structure built: 1969; Homeowner vacancy rate: 9.5%; Median selected monthly owner costs: $1,226 with a mortgage, $997 without a mortgage; Median gross rent: $1,622 per month; Rental vacancy rate: 0.0%

Health Insurance: 61.5% have insurance; 49.7% have private insurance; 36.4% have public insurance; 38.5% do not have insurance; 15.8% of children under 18 do not have insurance

Transportation: Commute: 82.6% car, 0.0% public transportation, 14.7% walk, 0.0% work from home; Mean travel time to work: 20.6 minutes

---

ROCKY POINT (CDP). Covers a land area of 11.298 square miles and a water area of 0 square miles. Located at 40.94° N. Lat; 72.94° W. Long. Elevation is 194 feet.

Population: 13,593; Growth (since 2000): 33.5%; Density: 1,203.1 persons per square mile; Race: 95.9% White, 0.5% Black/African American, 0.3% Asian, 0.1% American Indian/Alaska Native, 0.0% Native Hawaiian/Other Pacific Islander, 1.2% Two or more races, 9.4% Hispanic of any race; Average household size: 2.92; Median age: 38.0; Age under 18: 26.1%; Age 65 and over: 10.4%; Males per 100 females: 98.7; Marriage status: 31.2% never married, 54.7% now married, 1.7% separated, 5.1% widowed, 9.0% divorced; Foreign born: 5.1%; Speak English only: 89.4%; With disability: 11.0%; Veterans: 6.9%; Ancestry: 30.9% Italian, 29.8% Irish, 18.6% German, 8.5% American, 5.5% English

Employment: 11.2% management, business, and financial, 4.3% computer, engineering, and science, 17.8% education, legal, community service, arts, and media, 7.0% healthcare practitioners, 15.9% service, 22.8% sales and office, 12.8% natural resources, construction, and maintenance, 8.1% production, transportation, and material moving

Income: Per capita: $35,831; Median household: $91,661; Average household: $102,715; Households with income of $100,000 or more: 44.3%; Poverty rate: 5.3%

Educational Attainment: High school diploma or higher: 94.7%; Bachelor's degree or higher: 35.2%; Graduate/professional degree or higher: 17.6%

School District(s)

Rocky Point Union Free SD (KG-12)
    2014-15 Enrollment: 3,340 . . . . (631) 849-7561

Housing: Homeownership rate: 86.0%; Median home value: $286,900; Median year structure built: 1966; Homeowner vacancy rate: 3.4%; Median selected monthly owner costs: $2,457 with a mortgage, $1,080 without a mortgage; Median gross rent: $1,413 per month; Rental vacancy rate: 21.3%

Health Insurance: 93.3% have insurance; 79.7% have private insurance; 23.8% have public insurance; 6.7% do not have insurance; 1.1% of children under 18 do not have insurance

Newspapers: The North Shore Sun (weekly circulation 5,000)

Transportation: Commute: 92.2% car, 4.1% public transportation, 0.5% walk, 2.9% work from home; Mean travel time to work: 39.1 minutes

---

RONKONKOMA (CDP). Covers a land area of 7.833 square miles and a water area of 0.332 square miles. Located at 40.80° N. Lat; 73.13° W. Long. Elevation is 112 feet.

History: Since 1988, Ronkonkoma has been the end of electrification along the Long Island Rail Road's Main Line. The track between Hicksville and Ronkonkoma is referred to as the Ronkonkoma Branch.

Population: 18,634; Growth (since 2000): -7.0%; Density: 2,378.9 persons per square mile; Race: 91.2% White, 2.0% Black/African American, 4.7% Asian, 0.2% American Indian/Alaska Native, 0.0% Native Hawaiian/Other Pacific Islander, 1.1% Two or more races, 8.6% Hispanic of any race; Average household size: 2.96; Median age: 40.9; Age under 18: 21.7%; Age 65 and over: 13.1%; Males per 100 females: 98.3; Marriage status: 32.1% never married, 55.0% now married, 2.1% separated, 4.7% widowed, 8.2% divorced; Foreign born: 9.6%; Speak English only: 85.7%; With disability: 10.6%; Veterans: 6.4%; Ancestry: 35.7% Italian, 26.5% Irish, 19.6% German, 6.7% Polish, 3.2% English

Employment: 12.0% management, business, and financial, 5.3% computer, engineering, and science, 11.4% education, legal, community service, arts, and media, 6.7% healthcare practitioners, 16.9% service, 30.1% sales and office, 8.4% natural resources, construction, and maintenance, 9.3% production, transportation, and material moving

Income: Per capita: $34,192; Median household: $85,788; Average household: $98,084; Households with income of $100,000 or more: 39.9%; Poverty rate: 4.9%

Educational Attainment: High school diploma or higher: 92.3%; Bachelor's degree or higher: 28.4%; Graduate/professional degree or higher: 12.1%

School District(s)

Connetquot Central SD (PK-12)
    2014-15 Enrollment: 6,244 . . . . (631) 244-2215

Housing: Homeownership rate: 78.0%; Median home value: $338,000; Median year structure built: 1970; Homeowner vacancy rate: 0.8%; Median selected monthly owner costs: $2,489 with a mortgage, $1,114 without a mortgage; Median gross rent: $1,492 per month; Rental vacancy rate: 1.6%

Health Insurance: 91.6% have insurance; 78.9% have private insurance; 25.4% have public insurance; 8.4% do not have insurance; 3.6% of children under 18 do not have insurance

Transportation: Commute: 91.7% car, 5.0% public transportation, 1.1% walk, 1.4% work from home; Mean travel time to work: 28.7 minutes

SAG HARBOR (village).
Covers a land area of 1.804 square miles and a water area of 0.522 square miles. Located at 41.00° N. Lat; 72.29° W. Long. Elevation is 26 feet.

History: An important 19th-century whaling port. National Historic District. The *Long Island Herald* (1791) was L.I.'s first local paper. The Whalers' Church and Whalers' Museum, noted for their architecture, are among its historic buildings. Had first customhouse in N.Y., and first post office on L.I., established 1794. Settled 1720—1730, Incorporated 1846.

Population: 2,075; Growth (since 2000): -10.3%; Density: 1,150.2 persons per square mile; Race: 85.3% White, 12.7% Black/African American, 1.3% Asian, 0.0% American Indian/Alaska Native, 0.0% Native Hawaiian/Other Pacific Islander, 0.8% Two or more races, 18.3% Hispanic of any race; Average household size: 2.36; Median age: 49.1; Age under 18: 16.7%; Age 65 and over: 26.3%; Males per 100 females: 88.4; Marriage status: 23.2% never married, 59.4% now married, 2.2% separated, 8.6% widowed, 8.8% divorced; Foreign born: 22.7%; Speak English only: 77.9%; With disability: 6.5%; Veterans: 6.4%; Ancestry: 16.1% Irish, 15.1% German, 12.2% Italian, 9.9% English, 4.0% Polish

Employment: 13.8% management, business, and financial, 5.6% computer, engineering, and science, 21.0% education, legal, community service, arts, and media, 1.0% healthcare practitioners, 15.5% service, 24.6% sales and office, 14.3% natural resources, construction, and maintenance, 4.1% production, transportation, and material moving

Income: Per capita: $63,995; Median household: $100,900; Average household: $148,922; Households with income of $100,000 or more: 51.1%; Poverty rate: 5.9%

Educational Attainment: High school diploma or higher: 91.9%; Bachelor's degree or higher: 48.7%; Graduate/professional degree or higher: 24.9%

School District(s)
Sag Harbor Union Free SD (PK-12)
   2014-15 Enrollment: 1,014 . . . . (631) 725-5300

Housing: Homeownership rate: 76.8%; Median home value: $918,500; Median year structure built: 1964; Homeowner vacancy rate: 0.7%; Median selected monthly owner costs: $3,106 with a mortgage, $998 without a mortgage; Median gross rent: $1,746 per month; Rental vacancy rate: 5.2%

Health Insurance: 92.7% have insurance; 72.9% have private insurance; 36.6% have public insurance; 7.3% do not have insurance; 2.9% of children under 18 do not have insurance

Safety: Violent crime rate: 4.4 per 10,000 population; Property crime rate: 222.4 per 10,000 population

Newspapers: Sag Harbor Express (weekly circulation 2,500)

Transportation: Commute: 67.1% car, 12.8% public transportation, 8.4% walk, 9.5% work from home; Mean travel time to work: 30.2 minutes

SAGAPONACK (village).
Covers a land area of 4.414 square miles and a water area of 0.240 square miles. Located at 40.93° N. Lat; 72.27° W. Long. Elevation is 23 feet.

Population: 208; Growth (since 2000): -64.3%; Density: 47.1 persons per square mile; Race: 95.2% White, 4.8% Black/African American, 0.0% Asian, 0.0% American Indian/Alaska Native, 0.0% Native Hawaiian/Other Pacific Islander, 0.0% Two or more races, 0.5% Hispanic of any race; Average household size: 2.04; Median age: 50.2; Age under 18: 23.1%; Age 65 and over: 29.8%; Males per 100 females: 93.2; Marriage status: 16.0% never married, 68.6% now married, 0.0% separated, 8.0% widowed, 7.4% divorced; Foreign born: 5.8%; Speak English only: 96.2%; With disability: 4.3%; Veterans: 6.3%; Ancestry: 25.0% German, 14.4% English, 12.5% Irish, 9.1% Italian, 9.1% Russian

Employment: 23.0% management, business, and financial, 0.0% computer, engineering, and science, 32.2% education, legal, community service, arts, and media, 5.7% healthcare practitioners, 3.4% service, 27.6% sales and office, 4.6% natural resources, construction, and maintenance, 3.4% production, transportation, and material moving

Income: Per capita: $137,340; Median household: $196,250; Average household: $280,211; Households with income of $100,000 or more: 81.4%; Poverty rate: 1.0%

Educational Attainment: High school diploma or higher: 100.0%; Bachelor's degree or higher: 68.1%; Graduate/professional degree or higher: 30.0%

School District(s)
Sagaponack Common SD (01-04)
   2014-15 Enrollment: 12 . . . . (631) 537-0651

Housing: Homeownership rate: 95.1%; Median home value: 2 million+; Median year structure built: 1983; Homeowner vacancy rate: 4.0%; Median selected monthly owner costs: $3,222 with a mortgage, $1,330 without a mortgage; Median gross rent: n/a per month; Rental vacancy rate: 0.0%

Health Insurance: 85.6% have insurance; 76.4% have private insurance; 34.6% have public insurance; 14.4% do not have insurance; 20.8% of children under 18 do not have insurance

Transportation: Commute: 43.0% car, 4.7% public transportation, 5.8% walk, 44.2% work from home; Mean travel time to work: 15.5 minutes

SAINT JAMES (CDP).
Covers a land area of 4.559 square miles and a water area of <.001 square miles. Located at 40.88° N. Lat; 73.15° W. Long. Elevation is 151 feet.

History: In the early 20th century, St. James was a popular vacation spot for celebrities of stage and screen, including Lionel, Ethel, and John Barrymore, Buster Keaton, Myrna Loy, and Irving Berlin.

Population: 13,536; Growth (since 2000): 2.0%; Density: 2,968.8 persons per square mile; Race: 94.1% White, 1.1% Black/African American, 2.9% Asian, 0.1% American Indian/Alaska Native, 0.0% Native Hawaiian/Other Pacific Islander, 1.4% Two or more races, 3.9% Hispanic of any race; Average household size: 2.86; Median age: 44.6; Age under 18: 22.3%; Age 65 and over: 19.1%; Males per 100 females: 90.8; Marriage status: 28.4% never married, 56.0% now married, 1.0% separated, 9.0% widowed, 6.5% divorced; Foreign born: 5.4%; Speak English only: 90.2%; With disability: 10.6%; Veterans: 9.3%; Ancestry: 38.1% Italian, 27.2% Irish, 20.5% German, 6.1% English, 4.2% Polish

Employment: 16.2% management, business, and financial, 5.7% computer, engineering, and science, 19.3% education, legal, community service, arts, and media, 6.3% healthcare practitioners, 13.8% service, 23.3% sales and office, 9.1% natural resources, construction, and maintenance, 6.3% production, transportation, and material moving

Income: Per capita: $40,825; Median household: $93,034; Average household: $117,673; Households with income of $100,000 or more: 46.1%; Poverty rate: 4.6%

Educational Attainment: High school diploma or higher: 94.1%; Bachelor's degree or higher: 42.5%; Graduate/professional degree or higher: 20.7%

School District(s)
Smithtown Central SD (KG-12)
   2014-15 Enrollment: 9,810 . . . . (631) 382-2006

Housing: Homeownership rate: 89.5%; Median home value: $427,700; Median year structure built: 1968; Homeowner vacancy rate: 1.8%; Median selected monthly owner costs: $3,010 with a mortgage, $1,124 without a mortgage; Median gross rent: $1,503 per month; Rental vacancy rate: 6.8%

Health Insurance: 96.1% have insurance; 89.5% have private insurance; 23.3% have public insurance; 3.9% do not have insurance; 1.9% of children under 18 do not have insurance

Transportation: Commute: 88.3% car, 6.0% public transportation, 0.9% walk, 4.1% work from home; Mean travel time to work: 32.0 minutes

SALTAIRE (village).
Covers a land area of 0.233 square miles and a water area of 0.051 square miles. Located at 40.64° N. Lat; 73.19° W. Long. Elevation is 3 feet.

Population: 46; Growth (since 2000): 7.0%; Density: 197.6 persons per square mile; Race: 91.3% White, 6.5% Black/African American, 2.2% Asian, 0.0% American Indian/Alaska Native, 0.0% Native Hawaiian/Other Pacific Islander, 0.0% Two or more races, 0.0% Hispanic of any race; Average household size: 2.09; Median age: 44.0; Age under 18: 28.3%; Age 65 and over: 30.4%; Males per 100 females: 105.6; Marriage status: 8.6% never married, 77.1% now married, 0.0% separated, 8.6% widowed, 5.7% divorced; Foreign born: 10.9%; Speak English only: 90.9%; With disability: 15.2%; Veterans: 18.2%; Ancestry: 26.1% German, 26.1% Italian, 17.4% Eastern European, 8.7% Irish, 6.5% English

Employment: 18.2% management, business, and financial, 0.0% computer, engineering, and science, 27.3% education, legal, community

service, arts, and media, 18.2% healthcare practitioners, 18.2% service, 18.2% sales and office, 0.0% natural resources, construction, and maintenance, 0.0% production, transportation, and material moving
Income: Per capita: $82,859; Median household: $161,250; Average household: $180,245; Households with income of $100,000 or more: 63.7%; Poverty rate: n/a
Educational Attainment: High school diploma or higher: 100.0%; Bachelor's degree or higher: 78.8%; Graduate/professional degree or higher: 48.5%
Housing: Homeownership rate: 81.8%; Median home value: $937,500; Median year structure built: 1962; Homeowner vacancy rate: 0.0%; Median selected monthly owner costs: $4,000+ with a mortgage, $850 without a mortgage; Median gross rent: n/a per month; Rental vacancy rate: 33.3%
Health Insurance: 97.8% have insurance; 82.6% have private insurance; 41.3% have public insurance; 2.2% do not have insurance; 0.0% of children under 18 do not have insurance
Transportation: Commute: 13.6% car, 36.4% public transportation, 27.3% walk, 22.7% work from home; Mean travel time to work: 36.2 minutes
Additional Information Contacts
Village of Saltaire . . . . (631) 583-5566
   http://www.saltaire.org

SAYVILLE (CDP).
Covers a land area of 5.289 square miles and a water area of 0.065 square miles. Located at 40.75° N. Lat; 73.09° W. Long. Elevation is 20 feet.
History: The earliest known inhabitants of Sayville were the Secatogue tribe of the Algonquian tribe. It was founded by John Edwards, who built the first house in Sayville in 1761.
Population: 16,621; Growth (since 2000): -0.7%; Density: 3,142.5 persons per square mile; Race: 95.5% White, 0.4% Black/African American, 2.2% Asian, 0.0% American Indian/Alaska Native, 0.2% Native Hawaiian/Other Pacific Islander, 1.3% Two or more races, 4.8% Hispanic of any race; Average household size: 2.79; Median age: 44.3; Age under 18: 22.9%; Age 65 and over: 17.2%; Males per 100 females: 89.5; Marriage status: 26.7% never married, 56.2% now married, 1.3% separated, 9.6% widowed, 7.5% divorced; Foreign born: 4.0%; Speak English only: 94.4%; With disability: 8.3%; Veterans: 8.0%; Ancestry: 35.5% Irish, 31.2% Italian, 22.1% German, 6.2% English, 4.6% Polish
Employment: 17.0% management, business, and financial, 4.0% computer, engineering, and science, 22.6% education, legal, community service, arts, and media, 4.5% healthcare practitioners, 13.1% service, 24.9% sales and office, 7.6% natural resources, construction, and maintenance, 6.5% production, transportation, and material moving
Income: Per capita: $45,099; Median household: $105,712; Average household: $125,576; Households with income of $100,000 or more: 53.3%; Poverty rate: 2.4%
Educational Attainment: High school diploma or higher: 94.7%; Bachelor's degree or higher: 44.7%; Graduate/professional degree or higher: 23.1%

School District(s)
Sayville Union Free SD (KG-12)
   2014-15 Enrollment: 3,048 . . . . (631) 244-6510
Housing: Homeownership rate: 80.4%; Median home value: $423,800; Median year structure built: 1963; Homeowner vacancy rate: 1.6%; Median selected monthly owner costs: $3,071 with a mortgage, $1,245 without a mortgage; Median gross rent: $1,736 per month; Rental vacancy rate: 2.3%
Health Insurance: 96.7% have insurance; 90.0% have private insurance; 20.9% have public insurance; 3.3% do not have insurance; 0.8% of children under 18 do not have insurance
Newspapers: Islip Bulletin (weekly circulation 3,000); Suffolk Co. News (weekly circulation 15,000)
Transportation: Commute: 86.7% car, 8.2% public transportation, 1.0% walk, 3.5% work from home; Mean travel time to work: 34.0 minutes

SELDEN (CDP).
Covers a land area of 4.321 square miles and a water area of 0 square miles. Located at 40.87° N. Lat; 73.05° W. Long. Elevation is 89 feet.
History: The town's early resident was Captain Daniel Roe (1740-1820), who fought in the French and Indian War and served as a captain in the Revolutionary War, and for whom Captain Daniel Roe Highway is named.
Population: 20,123; Growth (since 2000): -8.0%; Density: 4,656.7 persons per square mile; Race: 89.0% White, 3.6% Black/African American, 4.3% Asian, 0.2% American Indian/Alaska Native, 0.0% Native Hawaiian/Other Pacific Islander, 1.2% Two or more races, 20.4% Hispanic of any race;

Average household size: 3.23; Median age: 38.1; Age under 18: 22.2%; Age 65 and over: 12.1%; Males per 100 females: 98.4; Marriage status: 35.1% never married, 51.5% now married, 1.6% separated, 5.3% widowed, 8.1% divorced; Foreign born: 14.7%; Speak English only: 77.7%; With disability: 10.3%; Veterans: 4.9%; Ancestry: 32.0% Italian, 20.6% Irish, 17.2% German, 4.4% American, 3.5% Polish
Employment: 10.2% management, business, and financial, 3.4% computer, engineering, and science, 8.5% education, legal, community service, arts, and media, 5.9% healthcare practitioners, 18.9% service, 33.3% sales and office, 10.7% natural resources, construction, and maintenance, 9.2% production, transportation, and material moving
Income: Per capita: $29,304; Median household: $88,187; Average household: $91,314; Households with income of $100,000 or more: 38.4%; Poverty rate: 7.8%
Educational Attainment: High school diploma or higher: 89.4%; Bachelor's degree or higher: 24.1%; Graduate/professional degree or higher: 10.4%

School District(s)
Middle Country Central SD (PK-12)
   2014-15 Enrollment: 10,254 . . . . (631) 285-8005
Two-year College(s)
Suffolk County Community College (Public)
   Fall 2014 Enrollment: 26,600 . . . . (631) 451-4110
   2015-16 Tuition: In-state $5,100; Out-of-state $9,490
Housing: Homeownership rate: 77.8%; Median home value: $298,400; Median year structure built: 1968; Homeowner vacancy rate: 1.5%; Median selected monthly owner costs: $2,413 with a mortgage, $1,039 without a mortgage; Median gross rent: $1,533 per month; Rental vacancy rate: 0.9%
Health Insurance: 92.2% have insurance; 73.4% have private insurance; 28.5% have public insurance; 7.8% do not have insurance; 1.5% of children under 18 do not have insurance
Transportation: Commute: 91.6% car, 4.1% public transportation, 0.9% walk, 3.0% work from home; Mean travel time to work: 33.8 minutes

SETAUKET-EAST SETAUKET (CDP).
Covers a land area of 8.520 square miles and a water area of 0.805 square miles. Located at 40.93° N. Lat; 73.10° W. Long.
History: The region was first settled in the 1650s. During the American Revolutionary War, the Culper Spy Ring headed by Benjamin Tallmadge passed information about British troop movements gathered in New York City to George Washington. The 1777 Battle of Setauket was fought here.
Population: 14,346; Growth (since 2000): -9.9%; Density: 1,683.8 persons per square mile; Race: 86.2% White, 2.0% Black/African American, 8.7% Asian, 0.1% American Indian/Alaska Native, 0.0% Native Hawaiian/Other Pacific Islander, 2.4% Two or more races, 4.4% Hispanic of any race; Average household size: 2.82; Median age: 44.9; Age under 18: 24.2%; Age 65 and over: 16.6%; Males per 100 females: 94.7; Marriage status: 23.6% never married, 63.9% now married, 2.1% separated, 6.1% widowed, 6.4% divorced; Foreign born: 13.4%; Speak English only: 84.0%; With disability: 6.0%; Veterans: 5.2%; Ancestry: 25.9% Italian, 20.8% Irish, 19.5% German, 6.3% Polish, 5.9% English
Employment: 15.0% management, business, and financial, 9.1% computer, engineering, and science, 21.9% education, legal, community service, arts, and media, 11.1% healthcare practitioners, 10.6% service, 24.8% sales and office, 4.4% natural resources, construction, and maintenance, 3.1% production, transportation, and material moving
Income: Per capita: $54,185; Median household: $125,370; Average household: $151,435; Households with income of $100,000 or more: 62.3%; Poverty rate: 2.5%
Educational Attainment: High school diploma or higher: 97.0%; Bachelor's degree or higher: 59.3%; Graduate/professional degree or higher: 35.3%

School District(s)
Three Village Central SD (KG-12)
   2014-15 Enrollment: 6,784 . . . . (631) 730-4010
Housing: Homeownership rate: 93.9%; Median home value: $462,300; Median year structure built: 1968; Homeowner vacancy rate: 1.8%; Median selected monthly owner costs: $3,077 with a mortgage, $1,402 without a mortgage; Median gross rent: $1,682 per month; Rental vacancy rate: 17.7%
Health Insurance: 97.8% have insurance; 90.7% have private insurance; 20.4% have public insurance; 2.2% do not have insurance; 0.6% of children under 18 do not have insurance

Newspapers: Times-Beacon Record Newspapers (weekly circulation 50,000)
Transportation: Commute: 87.0% car, 4.9% public transportation, 0.8% walk, 6.8% work from home; Mean travel time to work: 31.5 minutes

SHELTER ISLAND (CDP).
Covers a land area of 6.549 square miles and a water area of 0.142 square miles. Located at 41.06° N. Lat; 72.32° W. Long. Elevation is 52 feet.
Population: 1,313; Growth (since 2000): 6.4%; Density: 200.5 persons per square mile; Race: 93.5% White, 0.0% Black/African American, 0.0% Asian, 0.0% American Indian/Alaska Native, 0.0% Native Hawaiian/Other Pacific Islander, 3.0% Two or more races, 6.5% Hispanic of any race; Average household size: 2.41; Median age: 48.6; Age under 18: 25.1%; Age 65 and over: 23.3%; Males per 100 females: 103.5; Marriage status: 17.9% never married, 68.1% now married, 0.0% separated, 6.9% widowed, 7.2% divorced; Foreign born: 7.9%; Speak English only: 90.7%; With disability: 8.5%; Veterans: 18.0%; Ancestry: 39.8% Irish, 29.6% German, 22.0% English, 6.5% Czech, 6.3% Italian
Employment: 18.4% management, business, and financial, 2.8% computer, engineering, and science, 6.6% education, legal, community service, arts, and media, 8.0% healthcare practitioners, 29.1% service, 14.6% sales and office, 12.1% natural resources, construction, and maintenance, 8.4% production, transportation, and material moving
Income: Per capita: $48,568; Median household: $74,855; Average household: $119,519; Households with income of $100,000 or more: 39.3%; Poverty rate: 2.3%
Educational Attainment: High school diploma or higher: 98.0%; Bachelor's degree or higher: 49.0%; Graduate/professional degree or higher: 25.0%

School District(s)
Shelter Island Union Free SD (KG-12)
    2014-15 Enrollment: 224 . . . . (631) 749-0302
Housing: Homeownership rate: 82.4%; Median home value: $660,100; Median year structure built: 1968; Homeowner vacancy rate: 4.9%; Median selected monthly owner costs: $2,611 with a mortgage, $649 without a mortgage; Median gross rent: $1,245 per month; Rental vacancy rate: 0.0%
Health Insurance: 92.2% have insurance; 83.3% have private insurance; 28.7% have public insurance; 7.8% do not have insurance; 4.6% of children under 18 do not have insurance
Newspapers: Shelter Island Reporter (weekly circulation 3,200)
Transportation: Commute: 90.5% car, 5.5% public transportation, 0.0% walk, 4.0% work from home; Mean travel time to work: 27.8 minutes

SHELTER ISLAND (town).
Covers a land area of 12.165 square miles and a water area of 16.944 square miles. Located at 41.06° N. Lat; 72.32° W. Long. Elevation is 52 feet.
Population: 2,812; Growth (since 2000): 26.2%; Density: 231.2 persons per square mile; Race: 96.6% White, 0.1% Black/African American, 0.3% Asian, 0.0% American Indian/Alaska Native, 0.0% Native Hawaiian/Other Pacific Islander, 1.4% Two or more races, 3.0% Hispanic of any race; Average household size: 2.46; Median age: 48.3; Age under 18: 22.7%; Age 65 and over: 28.9%; Males per 100 females: 97.2; Marriage status: 23.4% never married, 61.9% now married, 0.9% separated, 7.8% widowed, 6.8% divorced; Foreign born: 5.7%; Speak English only: 90.8%; With disability: 7.2%; Veterans: 16.0%; Ancestry: 35.1% Irish, 21.9% German, 15.9% English, 10.5% Italian, 10.1% Polish
Employment: 19.6% management, business, and financial, 3.8% computer, engineering, and science, 17.0% education, legal, community service, arts, and media, 4.1% healthcare practitioners, 22.0% service, 15.8% sales and office, 10.7% natural resources, construction, and maintenance, 7.1% production, transportation, and material moving
Income: Per capita: $53,451; Median household: $94,492; Average household: $133,694; Households with income of $100,000 or more: 47.1%; Poverty rate: 1.1%
Educational Attainment: High school diploma or higher: 99.0%; Bachelor's degree or higher: 56.4%; Graduate/professional degree or higher: 28.6%

School District(s)
Shelter Island Union Free SD (KG-12)
    2014-15 Enrollment: 224 . . . . (631) 749-0302
Housing: Homeownership rate: 87.7%; Median home value: $728,400; Median year structure built: 1976; Homeowner vacancy rate: 2.3%; Median selected monthly owner costs: $2,690 with a mortgage, $706 without a

mortgage; Median gross rent: $1,875 per month; Rental vacancy rate: 0.0%
Health Insurance: 94.8% have insurance; 86.7% have private insurance; 31.5% have public insurance; 5.2% do not have insurance; 6.9% of children under 18 do not have insurance
Safety: Violent crime rate: 4.1 per 10,000 population; Property crime rate: 111.6 per 10,000 population
Newspapers: Shelter Island Reporter (weekly circulation 3,200)
Transportation: Commute: 83.2% car, 8.1% public transportation, 0.3% walk, 8.4% work from home; Mean travel time to work: 27.6 minutes

SHELTER ISLAND HEIGHTS (CDP).
Covers a land area of 5.370 square miles and a water area of 0.279 square miles. Located at 41.07° N. Lat; 72.37° W. Long. Elevation is 56 feet.
Population: 1,493; Growth (since 2000): 52.2%; Density: 278.0 persons per square mile; Race: 99.3% White, 0.1% Black/African American, 0.5% Asian, 0.0% American Indian/Alaska Native, 0.0% Native Hawaiian/Other Pacific Islander, 0.0% Two or more races, 0.0% Hispanic of any race; Average household size: 2.51; Median age: 47.8; Age under 18: 20.7%; Age 65 and over: 33.8%; Males per 100 females: 89.5; Marriage status: 27.9% never married, 57.2% now married, 1.7% separated, 8.6% widowed, 6.3% divorced; Foreign born: 3.8%; Speak English only: 90.8%; With disability: 6.1%; Veterans: 14.4%; Ancestry: 31.0% Irish, 16.6% Polish, 15.2% German, 14.3% Italian, 10.1% English
Employment: 20.9% management, business, and financial, 4.8% computer, engineering, and science, 27.9% education, legal, community service, arts, and media, 0.0% healthcare practitioners, 14.4% service, 17.0% sales and office, 9.3% natural resources, construction, and maintenance, 5.6% production, transportation, and material moving
Income: Per capita: $57,730; Median household: $116,579; Average household: $147,045; Households with income of $100,000 or more: 54.1%; Poverty rate: n/a
Educational Attainment: High school diploma or higher: 100.0%; Bachelor's degree or higher: 62.7%; Graduate/professional degree or higher: 31.7%
Housing: Homeownership rate: 92.8%; Median home value: $819,300; Median year structure built: 1979; Homeowner vacancy rate: 0.0%; Median selected monthly owner costs: $2,786 with a mortgage, $1,087 without a mortgage; Median gross rent: n/a per month; Rental vacancy rate: 0.0%
Health Insurance: 97.1% have insurance; 89.6% have private insurance; 33.9% have public insurance; 2.9% do not have insurance; 9.4% of children under 18 do not have insurance
Transportation: Commute: 75.6% car, 10.8% public transportation, 0.6% walk, 13.0% work from home; Mean travel time to work: 27.4 minutes

SHINNECOCK HILLS (CDP).
Covers a land area of 2.839 square miles and a water area of 0.201 square miles. Located at 40.89° N. Lat; 72.46° W. Long. Elevation is 79 feet.
Population: 2,152; Growth (since 2000): 23.0%; Density: 758.0 persons per square mile; Race: 81.2% White, 0.9% Black/African American, 15.2% Asian, 0.0% American Indian/Alaska Native, 0.0% Native Hawaiian/Other Pacific Islander, 1.3% Two or more races, 17.5% Hispanic of any race; Average household size: 2.43; Median age: 35.8; Age under 18: 17.0%; Age 65 and over: 19.7%; Males per 100 females: 104.9; Marriage status: 37.2% never married, 43.9% now married, 0.0% separated, 6.0% widowed, 12.9% divorced; Foreign born: 33.1%; Speak English only: 57.6%; With disability: 4.6%; Veterans: 6.1%; Ancestry: 14.8% German, 11.3% Polish, 10.9% Italian, 10.0% Irish, 6.0% English
Employment: 15.6% management, business, and financial, 1.6% computer, engineering, and science, 10.7% education, legal, community service, arts, and media, 15.2% healthcare practitioners, 12.3% service, 18.2% sales and office, 15.5% natural resources, construction, and maintenance, 10.8% production, transportation, and material moving
Income: Per capita: $46,476; Median household: $71,875; Average household: $121,084; Households with income of $100,000 or more: 41.5%; Poverty rate: 8.2%
Educational Attainment: High school diploma or higher: 97.9%; Bachelor's degree or higher: 50.2%; Graduate/professional degree or higher: 25.4%
Housing: Homeownership rate: 65.8%; Median home value: $701,000; Median year structure built: 1975; Homeowner vacancy rate: 2.9%; Median selected monthly owner costs: $2,459 with a mortgage, $1,210 without a mortgage; Median gross rent: $1,500 per month; Rental vacancy rate: 3.5%

Health Insurance: 78.4% have insurance; 63.0% have private insurance; 30.0% have public insurance; 21.6% do not have insurance; 12.3% of children under 18 do not have insurance
Transportation: Commute: 74.7% car, 14.6% public transportation, 3.9% walk, 6.8% work from home; Mean travel time to work: 26.4 minutes

SHINNECOCK RESERVATION (reservation). Covers a land area of 1.349 square miles and a water area of 0 square miles. Located at 40.87° N. Lat; 72.43° W. Long.
Population: 163; Growth (since 2000): -67.7%; Density: 120.8 persons per square mile; Race: 4.9% White, 0.0% Black/African American, 3.7% Asian, 81.6% American Indian/Alaska Native, 0.0% Native Hawaiian/Other Pacific Islander, 9.8% Two or more races, 0.0% Hispanic of any race; Average household size: 3.98; Median age: 24.5; Age under 18: 28.2%; Age 65 and over: 5.5%; Males per 100 females: 88.1; Marriage status: 44.3% never married, 34.4% now married, 0.0% separated, 14.8% widowed, 6.6% divorced; Foreign born: 2.5%; Speak English only: 91.2%; With disability: 9.8%; Veterans: 7.7%; Ancestry: 5.5% German
Employment: 0.0% management, business, and financial, 0.0% computer, engineering, and science, 17.0% education, legal, community service, arts, and media, 3.8% healthcare practitioners, 30.2% service, 28.3% sales and office, 7.5% natural resources, construction, and maintenance, 13.2% production, transportation, and material moving
Income: Per capita: $18,288; Median household: n/a; Average household: $67,880; Households with income of $100,000 or more: 26.9%; Poverty rate: 20.2%
Educational Attainment: High school diploma or higher: 90.0%; Bachelor's degree or higher: 8.8%; Graduate/professional degree or higher: 3.8%
Housing: Homeownership rate: 87.8%; Median home value: n/a; Median year structure built: 1983; Homeowner vacancy rate: 19.1%; Median selected monthly owner costs: n/a with a mortgage, $550 without a mortgage; Median gross rent: n/a per month; Rental vacancy rate: 0.0%
Health Insurance: 47.2% have insurance; 33.7% have private insurance; 14.7% have public insurance; 52.8% do not have insurance; 76.1% of children under 18 do not have insurance
Transportation: Commute: 100.0% car, 0.0% public transportation, 0.0% walk, 0.0% work from home; Mean travel time to work: 12.7 minutes

SHIRLEY (CDP). Covers a land area of 11.455 square miles and a water area of 0.432 square miles. Located at 40.80° N. Lat; 72.87° W. Long. Elevation is 52 feet.
History: Shirley is notable as the western terminus of Atlantic Crossing 1, a major submarine telecommunications cable linking the United States with the UK, Germany, and the Netherlands. The town is named for Walter T. Shirley, who developed the area on Mastic Bay into an affordable enclave.
Population: 25,691; Growth (since 2000): 1.2%; Density: 2,242.7 persons per square mile; Race: 82.1% White, 7.4% Black/African American, 4.6% Asian, 0.3% American Indian/Alaska Native, 0.0% Native Hawaiian/Other Pacific Islander, 3.1% Two or more races, 18.8% Hispanic of any race; Average household size: 3.36; Median age: 36.7; Age under 18: 22.7%; Age 65 and over: 8.7%; Males per 100 females: 99.4; Marriage status: 33.7% never married, 54.1% now married, 2.3% separated, 3.5% widowed, 8.7% divorced; Foreign born: 15.5%; Speak English only: 75.0%; With disability: 9.6%; Veterans: 4.9%; Ancestry: 34.5% Italian, 20.0% Irish, 16.2% German, 5.9% Polish, 3.2% English
Employment: 11.8% management, business, and financial, 3.2% computer, engineering, and science, 7.9% education, legal, community service, arts, and media, 5.7% healthcare practitioners, 19.2% service, 25.6% sales and office, 13.1% natural resources, construction, and maintenance, 13.4% production, transportation, and material moving
Income: Per capita: $27,702; Median household: $83,569; Average household: $89,675; Households with income of $100,000 or more: 36.7%; Poverty rate: 9.8%
Educational Attainment: High school diploma or higher: 87.7%; Bachelor's degree or higher: 16.3%; Graduate/professional degree or higher: 7.5%
School District(s)
William Floyd Union Free SD (KG-12)
   2014-15 Enrollment: 8,832 . . . . (631) 874-1201
Housing: Homeownership rate: 81.4%; Median home value: $253,700; Median year structure built: 1977; Homeowner vacancy rate: 4.3%; Median selected monthly owner costs: $2,370 with a mortgage, $993 without a

mortgage; Median gross rent: $1,950 per month; Rental vacancy rate: 3.3%
Health Insurance: 89.3% have insurance; 69.6% have private insurance; 29.2% have public insurance; 10.7% do not have insurance; 2.4% of children under 18 do not have insurance
Newspapers: South Shore Press (weekly circulation 45,000)
Transportation: Commute: 91.9% car, 3.9% public transportation, 0.7% walk, 2.5% work from home; Mean travel time to work: 32.3 minutes

SHOREHAM (village). Covers a land area of 0.448 square miles and a water area of 0 square miles. Located at 40.96° N. Lat; 72.91° W. Long. Elevation is 66 feet.
Population: 432; Growth (since 2000): 3.6%; Density: 963.4 persons per square mile; Race: 99.1% White, 0.0% Black/African American, 0.5% Asian, 0.0% American Indian/Alaska Native, 0.0% Native Hawaiian/Other Pacific Islander, 0.5% Two or more races, 2.1% Hispanic of any race; Average household size: 2.57; Median age: 59.0; Age under 18: 13.7%; Age 65 and over: 39.6%; Males per 100 females: 101.1; Marriage status: 18.9% never married, 74.6% now married, 0.8% separated, 4.7% widowed, 1.8% divorced; Foreign born: 7.2%; Speak English only: 93.2%; With disability: 8.3%; Veterans: 5.9%; Ancestry: 29.6% Italian, 23.8% German, 14.4% Irish, 14.1% American, 10.9% English
Employment: 23.8% management, business, and financial, 8.3% computer, engineering, and science, 26.7% education, legal, community service, arts, and media, 8.3% healthcare practitioners, 5.3% service, 23.8% sales and office, 1.5% natural resources, construction, and maintenance, 2.4% production, transportation, and material moving
Income: Per capita: $76,696; Median household: $143,929; Average household: $184,483; Households with income of $100,000 or more: 71.4%; Poverty rate: 1.2%
Educational Attainment: High school diploma or higher: 99.2%; Bachelor's degree or higher: 68.8%; Graduate/professional degree or higher: 50.7%
School District(s)
Shoreham-Wading River Central SD (KG-12)
   2014-15 Enrollment: 2,424 . . . . (631) 821-8105
Housing: Homeownership rate: 97.6%; Median home value: $544,400; Median year structure built: 1960; Homeowner vacancy rate: 0.0%; Median selected monthly owner costs: $3,578 with a mortgage, $1,500+ without a mortgage; Median gross rent: n/a per month; Rental vacancy rate: 42.9%
Health Insurance: 95.8% have insurance; 79.2% have private insurance; 43.3% have public insurance; 4.2% do not have insurance; 0.0% of children under 18 do not have insurance
Transportation: Commute: 76.3% car, 14.1% public transportation, 0.5% walk, 8.1% work from home; Mean travel time to work: 46.0 minutes

SMITHTOWN (CDP). Covers a land area of 11.629 square miles and a water area of 0.485 square miles. Located at 40.86° N. Lat; 73.22° W. Long. Elevation is 59 feet.
History: Smithtown, originally known as "Smithfield," was first settled around 1665. Local legend has it that after rescuing a Native American Chief's kidnapped daughter, Richard Smith was told that the Chief would grant title to all of the land Smith could encircle in one day, on a bull. Smith chose to ride the bull on the longest day of the year (summer solstice)—to enable him to ride longer "in one day." The land he acquired in this way is said to approximate the current town's location. There is a large anatomically correct statue of Smith's bull, known as Whisper, at the fork of Jericho Turnpike and St. Johnland Road.
Population: 25,974; Growth (since 2000): -3.4%; Density: 2,233.6 persons per square mile; Race: 92.1% White, 1.0% Black/African American, 4.5% Asian, 0.0% American Indian/Alaska Native, 0.0% Native Hawaiian/Other Pacific Islander, 1.1% Two or more races, 5.2% Hispanic of any race; Average household size: 2.92; Median age: 44.7; Age under 18: 23.1%; Age 65 and over: 17.5%; Males per 100 females: 94.5; Marriage status: 27.4% never married, 58.1% now married, 1.3% separated, 7.4% widowed, 7.1% divorced; Foreign born: 6.5%; Speak English only: 87.6%; With disability: 8.9%; Veterans: 7.3%; Ancestry: 36.2% Italian, 23.6% Irish, 20.1% German, 6.3% Polish, 5.5% English
Employment: 18.9% management, business, and financial, 4.7% computer, engineering, and science, 15.2% education, legal, community service, arts, and media, 9.2% healthcare practitioners, 12.4% service, 27.1% sales and office, 7.2% natural resources, construction, and maintenance, 5.3% production, transportation, and material moving

Income: Per capita: $45,869; Median household: $113,372; Average household: $134,615; Households with income of $100,000 or more: 58.9%; Poverty rate: 3.6%

Educational Attainment: High school diploma or higher: 94.5%; Bachelor's degree or higher: 45.6%; Graduate/professional degree or higher: 20.4%

School District(s)

Hauppauge Union Free SD (KG-12)
   2014-15 Enrollment: 3,782 . . . . (631) 761-8208
Smithtown Central SD (KG-12)
   2014-15 Enrollment: 9,810 . . . . (631) 382-2006

Housing: Homeownership rate: 85.7%; Median home value: $472,200; Median year structure built: 1967; Homeowner vacancy rate: 1.1%; Median selected monthly owner costs: $3,102 with a mortgage, $1,284 without a mortgage; Median gross rent: $1,281 per month; Rental vacancy rate: 0.7%

Health Insurance: 96.6% have insurance; 89.2% have private insurance; 20.8% have public insurance; 3.4% do not have insurance; 0.9% of children under 18 do not have insurance

Hospitals: Saint Catherine of Siena Hospital (311 beds)

Newspapers: ESP Publications (weekly circulation 31,000); Mid Island News (weekly circulation 2,200); Smithtown News Inc. (weekly circulation 37,000)

Transportation: Commute: 87.0% car, 5.7% public transportation, 0.9% walk, 5.7% work from home; Mean travel time to work: 30.9 minutes

---

SMITHTOWN (town). Covers a land area of 53.698 square miles and a water area of 57.752 square miles. Located at 40.92° N. Lat; 73.18° W. Long. Elevation is 59 feet.

History: Smithtown, originally known as "Smithfield," was first settled around 1665. Legend has it that Richard Smith rescued a Native American Chief's kidnapped daughter, and was granted title to all of the land Smith could encircle in one day, on a bull. In this way, he acquired the current town. A large statue of Smith's bull, known as Whisper, is at the fork of Jericho Turnpike and St. Johnland Road.

Population: 118,373; Growth (since 2000): 2.3%; Density: 2,204.4 persons per square mile; Race: 92.0% White, 1.3% Black/African American, 4.1% Asian, 0.0% American Indian/Alaska Native, 0.0% Native Hawaiian/Other Pacific Islander, 1.2% Two or more races, 4.9% Hispanic of any race; Average household size: 2.94; Median age: 43.9; Age under 18: 23.3%; Age 65 and over: 17.3%; Males per 100 females: 94.8; Marriage status: 26.8% never married, 60.4% now married, 1.2% separated, 6.5% widowed, 6.4% divorced; Foreign born: 7.8%; Speak English only: 88.8%; With disability: 8.5%; Veterans: 7.5%; Ancestry: 36.3% Italian, 25.4% Irish, 18.5% German, 6.2% Polish, 5.6% English

Employment: 19.4% management, business, and financial, 5.2% computer, engineering, and science, 16.2% education, legal, community service, arts, and media, 8.1% healthcare practitioners, 13.4% service, 24.9% sales and office, 7.2% natural resources, construction, and maintenance, 5.6% production, transportation, and material moving

Income: Per capita: $45,518; Median household: $112,693; Average household: $133,009; Households with income of $100,000 or more: 56.5%; Poverty rate: 3.8%

Educational Attainment: High school diploma or higher: 95.1%; Bachelor's degree or higher: 45.7%; Graduate/professional degree or higher: 21.2%

School District(s)

Hauppauge Union Free SD (KG-12)
   2014-15 Enrollment: 3,782 . . . . (631) 761-8208
Smithtown Central SD (KG-12)
   2014-15 Enrollment: 9,810 . . . . (631) 382-2006

Housing: Homeownership rate: 88.1%; Median home value: $460,800; Median year structure built: 1967; Homeowner vacancy rate: 0.9%; Median selected monthly owner costs: $3,070 with a mortgage, $1,273 without a mortgage; Median gross rent: $1,423 per month; Rental vacancy rate: 5.6%

Health Insurance: 96.7% have insurance; 88.6% have private insurance; 21.8% have public insurance; 3.3% do not have insurance; 1.1% of children under 18 do not have insurance

Hospitals: Saint Catherine of Siena Hospital (311 beds)

Newspapers: ESP Publications (weekly circulation 31,000); Mid Island News (weekly circulation 2,200); Smithtown News Inc. (weekly circulation 37,000)

Transportation: Commute: 88.0% car, 6.3% public transportation, 0.7% walk, 4.1% work from home; Mean travel time to work: 32.3 minutes

Additional Information Contacts

Town of Smithtown . . . . (631) 360-7620
   http://www.smithtowninfo.com

SOUND BEACH (CDP). Covers a land area of 1.637 square miles and a water area of 0 square miles. Located at 40.96° N. Lat; 72.97° W. Long. Elevation is 177 feet.

Population: 8,071; Growth (since 2000): -17.7%; Density: 4,931.4 persons per square mile; Race: 96.8% White, 0.1% Black/African American, 1.4% Asian, 0.0% American Indian/Alaska Native, 0.0% Native Hawaiian/Other Pacific Islander, 0.5% Two or more races, 12.0% Hispanic of any race; Average household size: 3.01; Median age: 38.0; Age under 18: 25.8%; Age 65 and over: 8.6%; Males per 100 females: 97.0; Marriage status: 27.8% never married, 57.6% now married, 1.1% separated, 4.0% widowed, 10.5% divorced; Foreign born: 8.0%; Speak English only: 89.3%; With disability: 7.2%; Veterans: 5.1%; Ancestry: 30.5% Italian, 27.5% Irish, 20.6% German, 9.5% American, 4.5% English

Employment: 12.2% management, business, and financial, 5.1% computer, engineering, and science, 9.4% education, legal, community service, arts, and media, 6.7% healthcare practitioners, 23.7% service, 27.8% sales and office, 9.6% natural resources, construction, and maintenance, 5.5% production, transportation, and material moving

Income: Per capita: $35,010; Median household: $90,000; Average household: $102,400; Households with income of $100,000 or more: 43.3%; Poverty rate: 5.6%

Educational Attainment: High school diploma or higher: 94.2%; Bachelor's degree or higher: 36.1%; Graduate/professional degree or higher: 12.6%

Housing: Homeownership rate: 88.6%; Median home value: $285,400; Median year structure built: 1960; Homeowner vacancy rate: 2.8%; Median selected monthly owner costs: $2,616 with a mortgage, $1,102 without a mortgage; Median gross rent: $1,407 per month; Rental vacancy rate: 8.4%

Health Insurance: 94.3% have insurance; 76.1% have private insurance; 26.2% have public insurance; 5.7% do not have insurance; 0.0% of children under 18 do not have insurance

Transportation: Commute: 89.3% car, 4.4% public transportation, 1.3% walk, 3.3% work from home; Mean travel time to work: 39.1 minutes

---

SOUTH HUNTINGTON (CDP). Covers a land area of 3.409 square miles and a water area of 0 square miles. Located at 40.82° N. Lat; 73.39° W. Long. Elevation is 207 feet.

History: South Huntington is the birthplace of Walt Whitman, and a shopping mall named after him is nearby.

Population: 9,724; Growth (since 2000): 2.7%; Density: 2,852.8 persons per square mile; Race: 85.3% White, 2.1% Black/African American, 7.3% Asian, 0.2% American Indian/Alaska Native, 0.0% Native Hawaiian/Other Pacific Islander, 1.0% Two or more races, 12.0% Hispanic of any race; Average household size: 2.80; Median age: 44.8; Age under 18: 18.7%; Age 65 and over: 18.3%; Males per 100 females: 96.7; Marriage status: 28.2% never married, 55.6% now married, 0.9% separated, 7.7% widowed, 8.5% divorced; Foreign born: 13.1%; Speak English only: 79.8%; With disability: 9.5%; Veterans: 5.7%; Ancestry: 29.1% Italian, 25.2% Irish, 18.1% German, 4.5% Russian, 4.3% Polish

Employment: 17.0% management, business, and financial, 5.7% computer, engineering, and science, 16.9% education, legal, community service, arts, and media, 5.0% healthcare practitioners, 14.1% service, 24.5% sales and office, 12.3% natural resources, construction, and maintenance, 4.4% production, transportation, and material moving

Income: Per capita: $38,970; Median household: $87,353; Average household: $109,349; Households with income of $100,000 or more: 43.9%; Poverty rate: 6.5%

Educational Attainment: High school diploma or higher: 94.7%; Bachelor's degree or higher: 41.7%; Graduate/professional degree or higher: 18.4%

Housing: Homeownership rate: 84.0%; Median home value: $419,200; Median year structure built: 1959; Homeowner vacancy rate: 0.7%; Median selected monthly owner costs: $2,822 with a mortgage, $1,212 without a mortgage; Median gross rent: $1,559 per month; Rental vacancy rate: 4.7%

Health Insurance: 95.9% have insurance; 84.7% have private insurance; 27.6% have public insurance; 4.1% do not have insurance; 3.4% of children under 18 do not have insurance

Transportation: Commute: 83.8% car, 9.9% public transportation, 0.4% walk, 4.8% work from home; Mean travel time to work: 34.0 minutes

SOUTH JAMESPORT (unincorporated postal area)
ZCTA: 11970

Covers a land area of 0.562 square miles and a water area of 0.027 square miles. Located at 40.94° N. Lat; 72.58° W. Long. Elevation is 3 feet.

Population: 284; Growth (since 2000): -11.0%; Density: 505.7 persons per square mile; Race: 100.0% White, 0.0% Black/African American, 0.0% Asian, 0.0% American Indian/Alaska Native, 0.0% Native Hawaiian/Other Pacific Islander, 0.0% Two or more races, 0.0% Hispanic of any race; Average household size: 1.89; Median age: 54.8; Age under 18: 0.0%; Age 65 and over: 10.6%; Males per 100 females: 83.2; Marriage status: 38.7% never married, 53.9% now married, 0.0% separated, 0.0% widowed, 7.4% divorced; Foreign born: 0.0%; Speak English only: 100.0%; With disability: 0.0%; Veterans: 5.3%; Ancestry: 47.5% German, 31.3% Irish, 10.6% Italian, 5.3% English, 5.3% Polish

Employment: 25.4% management, business, and financial, 0.0% computer, engineering, and science, 57.5% education, legal, community service, arts, and media, 0.0% healthcare practitioners, 0.0% service, 17.1% sales and office, 0.0% natural resources, construction, and maintenance, 0.0% production, transportation, and material moving

Income: Per capita: $68,007; Median household: n/a; Average household: $122,136; Households with income of $100,000 or more: 65.4%; Poverty rate: n/a

Educational Attainment: High school diploma or higher: 100.0%; Bachelor's degree or higher: 49.6%; Graduate/professional degree or higher: 49.6%

Housing: Homeownership rate: 86.0%; Median home value: $365,800; Median year structure built: 1965; Homeowner vacancy rate: 0.0%; Median selected monthly owner costs: $2,791 with a mortgage, $0 without a mortgage; Median gross rent: n/a per month; Rental vacancy rate: 0.0%

Health Insurance: 81.7% have insurance; 81.7% have private insurance; 10.6% have public insurance; 18.3% do not have insurance; 0.0% of children under 18 do not have insurance

Transportation: Commute: 100.0% car, 0.0% public transportation, 0.0% walk, 0.0% work from home; Mean travel time to work: 0.0 minutes

SOUTHAMPTON (town). Covers a land area of 139.195 square miles and a water area of 154.510 square miles. Located at 40.88° N. Lat; 72.46° W. Long. Elevation is 26 feet.

History: Known for its many fine estates and celebrity residents. Parrish Memorial Art Museum is here, as is Southampton College of Long Island University. Settled 1640 as first English settlement in state, incorporated 1894.

Population: 57,730; Growth (since 2000): 5.5%; Density: 414.7 persons per square mile; Race: 86.8% White, 6.3% Black/African American, 2.2% Asian, 0.1% American Indian/Alaska Native, 0.0% Native Hawaiian/Other Pacific Islander, 2.7% Two or more races, 19.6% Hispanic of any race; Average household size: 2.52; Median age: 44.9; Age under 18: 18.1%; Age 65 and over: 19.5%; Males per 100 females: 104.6; Marriage status: 31.1% never married, 52.8% now married, 1.5% separated, 6.4% widowed, 9.8% divorced; Foreign born: 20.3%; Speak English only: 75.2%; With disability: 8.1%; Veterans: 6.6%; Ancestry: 18.4% Irish, 14.3% Italian, 13.2% German, 8.7% English, 7.3% Polish

Employment: 14.5% management, business, and financial, 3.2% computer, engineering, and science, 12.8% education, legal, community service, arts, and media, 4.8% healthcare practitioners, 20.2% service, 22.3% sales and office, 16.5% natural resources, construction, and maintenance, 5.8% production, transportation, and material moving

Income: Per capita: $45,188; Median household: $79,799; Average household: $119,046; Households with income of $100,000 or more: 39.7%; Poverty rate: 8.1%

Educational Attainment: High school diploma or higher: 88.8%; Bachelor's degree or higher: 37.5%; Graduate/professional degree or higher: 16.4%

School District(s)
Southampton Union Free SD (PK-12)
    2014-15 Enrollment: 1,632 . . . . (631) 591-4510
Tuckahoe Common SD (PK-08)
    2014-15 Enrollment: 349 . . . . (631) 283-3550

Housing: Homeownership rate: 77.9%; Median home value: $598,100; Median year structure built: 1974; Homeowner vacancy rate: 3.2%; Median selected monthly owner costs: $2,663 with a mortgage, $994 without a mortgage; Median gross rent: $1,677 per month; Rental vacancy rate: 3.3%

Health Insurance: 84.5% have insurance; 70.1% have private insurance; 29.7% have public insurance; 15.5% do not have insurance; 6.3% of children under 18 do not have insurance

Hospitals: Southampton Hospital (168 beds)

Transportation: Commute: 83.9% car, 5.5% public transportation, 2.8% walk, 6.7% work from home; Mean travel time to work: 26.4 minutes

Airports: Southampton (general aviation)

Additional Information Contacts
Town of Southampton . . . . (631) 287-5740
    http://www.southamptontownny.gov

SOUTHAMPTON (village). Covers a land area of 6.422 square miles and a water area of 0.797 square miles. Located at 40.88° N. Lat; 72.40° W. Long. Elevation is 26 feet.

Population: 3,193; Growth (since 2000): -19.5%; Density: 497.2 persons per square mile; Race: 74.5% White, 16.7% Black/African American, 3.6% Asian, 0.4% American Indian/Alaska Native, 0.0% Native Hawaiian/Other Pacific Islander, 0.3% Two or more races, 4.3% Hispanic of any race; Average household size: 2.21; Median age: 55.2; Age under 18: 14.1%; Age 65 and over: 32.3%; Males per 100 females: 96.2; Marriage status: 27.2% never married, 44.4% now married, 1.9% separated, 11.9% widowed, 16.5% divorced; Foreign born: 15.4%; Speak English only: 84.3%; With disability: 7.5%; Veterans: 5.4%; Ancestry: 18.3% Irish, 15.8% English, 11.4% German, 9.4% American, 9.3% Italian

Employment: 22.5% management, business, and financial, 1.1% computer, engineering, and science, 17.0% education, legal, community service, arts, and media, 1.1% healthcare practitioners, 20.4% service, 24.7% sales and office, 7.4% natural resources, construction, and maintenance, 5.7% production, transportation, and material moving

Income: Per capita: $69,450; Median household: $96,250; Average household: $162,663; Households with income of $100,000 or more: 49.2%; Poverty rate: 14.9%

Educational Attainment: High school diploma or higher: 92.1%; Bachelor's degree or higher: 50.2%; Graduate/professional degree or higher: 24.0%

School District(s)
Southampton Union Free SD (PK-12)
    2014-15 Enrollment: 1,632 . . . . (631) 591-4510
Tuckahoe Common SD (PK-08)
    2014-15 Enrollment: 349 . . . . (631) 283-3550

Housing: Homeownership rate: 72.8%; Median home value: $1,266,800; Median year structure built: 1959; Homeowner vacancy rate: 3.6%; Median selected monthly owner costs: $3,779 with a mortgage, $1,022 without a mortgage; Median gross rent: $1,574 per month; Rental vacancy rate: 0.0%

Health Insurance: 90.5% have insurance; 82.7% have private insurance; 29.0% have public insurance; 9.5% do not have insurance; 5.8% of children under 18 do not have insurance

Hospitals: Southampton Hospital (168 beds)

Safety: Violent crime rate: 9.3 per 10,000 population; Property crime rate: 294.3 per 10,000 population

Transportation: Commute: 67.6% car, 10.7% public transportation, 2.0% walk, 17.4% work from home; Mean travel time to work: 25.3 minutes

Airports: Southampton (general aviation)

SOUTHOLD (CDP). Covers a land area of 10.465 square miles and a water area of 0.855 square miles. Located at 41.06° N. Lat; 72.43° W. Long. Elevation is 23 feet.

Population: 6,295; Growth (since 2000): 15.2%; Density: 601.6 persons per square mile; Race: 97.8% White, 0.0% Black/African American, 1.1% Asian, 0.0% American Indian/Alaska Native, 0.0% Native Hawaiian/Other Pacific Islander, 0.3% Two or more races, 2.3% Hispanic of any race; Average household size: 2.38; Median age: 54.6; Age under 18: 14.9%; Age 65 and over: 30.1%; Males per 100 females: 95.1; Marriage status: 20.7% never married, 63.2% now married, 1.6% separated, 6.2% widowed, 9.9% divorced; Foreign born: 6.0%; Speak English only: 96.1%; With disability: 9.9%; Veterans: 9.3%; Ancestry: 30.2% Irish, 28.3% German, 24.0% Italian, 14.3% Polish, 12.7% English

Employment: 22.1% management, business, and financial, 2.9% computer, engineering, and science, 13.3% education, legal, community service, arts, and media, 7.9% healthcare practitioners, 14.5% service, 19.7% sales and office, 11.0% natural resources, construction, and maintenance, 8.7% production, transportation, and material moving

Income: Per capita: $52,946; Median household: $89,769; Average household: $121,277; Households with income of $100,000 or more: 46.1%; Poverty rate: 4.8%

Educational Attainment: High school diploma or higher: 97.0%; Bachelor's degree or higher: 35.0%; Graduate/professional degree or higher: 18.2%

School District(s)

Southold Union Free SD (KG-12)

    2014-15 Enrollment: 832 . . . . (631) 765-5400

Housing: Homeownership rate: 87.1%; Median home value: $514,700; Median year structure built: 1974; Homeowner vacancy rate: 4.2%; Median selected monthly owner costs: $2,215 with a mortgage, $1,043 without a mortgage; Median gross rent: $1,372 per month; Rental vacancy rate: 17.7%

Health Insurance: 96.9% have insurance; 90.3% have private insurance; 34.6% have public insurance; 3.1% do not have insurance; 0.0% of children under 18 do not have insurance

Transportation: Commute: 85.4% car, 5.5% public transportation, 4.0% walk, 5.1% work from home; Mean travel time to work: 35.9 minutes

SOUTHOLD (town).
Covers a land area of 53.783 square miles and a water area of 349.917 square miles. Located at 41.14° N. Lat; 72.32° W. Long. Elevation is 23 feet.

History: The Algonquian-speaking Shinnecock tribes lived in eastern Long Island before European colonization. Southold was settled by English colonists in 1640, and in most histories is reported as the first English settlement on Long Island in the future New York State.

Population: 22,204; Growth (since 2000): 7.8%; Density: 412.8 persons per square mile; Race: 95.3% White, 2.1% Black/African American, 0.8% Asian, 0.6% American Indian/Alaska Native, 0.1% Native Hawaiian/Other Pacific Islander, 0.8% Two or more races, 5.2% Hispanic of any race; Average household size: 2.30; Median age: 53.2; Age under 18: 16.0%; Age 65 and over: 28.9%; Males per 100 females: 96.9; Marriage status: 24.8% never married, 58.6% now married, 1.3% separated, 7.8% widowed, 8.8% divorced; Foreign born: 8.7%; Speak English only: 89.6%; With disability: 12.4%; Veterans: 10.5%; Ancestry: 25.1% Irish, 20.6% German, 18.3% Italian, 13.6% English, 13.1% Polish

Employment: 16.7% management, business, and financial, 3.3% computer, engineering, and science, 14.8% education, legal, community service, arts, and media, 6.2% healthcare practitioners, 16.8% service, 20.2% sales and office, 14.2% natural resources, construction, and maintenance, 7.9% production, transportation, and material moving

Income: Per capita: $47,126; Median household: $78,374; Average household: $107,344; Households with income of $100,000 or more: 38.8%; Poverty rate: 6.0%

Educational Attainment: High school diploma or higher: 93.7%; Bachelor's degree or higher: 39.2%; Graduate/professional degree or higher: 19.5%

School District(s)

Southold Union Free SD (KG-12)

    2014-15 Enrollment: 832 . . . . (631) 765-5400

Housing: Homeownership rate: 82.2%; Median home value: $513,100; Median year structure built: 1969; Homeowner vacancy rate: 2.3%; Median selected monthly owner costs: $2,390 with a mortgage, $976 without a mortgage; Median gross rent: $1,417 per month; Rental vacancy rate: 11.4%

Health Insurance: 93.1% have insurance; 81.0% have private insurance; 38.1% have public insurance; 6.9% do not have insurance; 2.6% of children under 18 do not have insurance

Safety: Violent crime rate: 10.0 per 10,000 population; Property crime rate: 158.2 per 10,000 population

Transportation: Commute: 81.5% car, 5.0% public transportation, 5.0% walk, 7.2% work from home; Mean travel time to work: 28.8 minutes

Additional Information Contacts

Town of Southold . . . . (631) 765-1800
  http://southoldtown.northfork.net

SPRINGS (CDP).
Covers a land area of 8.479 square miles and a water area of 0.757 square miles. Located at 41.02° N. Lat; 72.17° W. Long. Elevation is 10 feet.

Population: 6,065; Growth (since 2000): 22.5%; Density: 715.3 persons per square mile; Race: 92.9% White, 1.9% Black/African American, 0.0% Asian, 3.8% American Indian/Alaska Native, 0.0% Native Hawaiian/Other Pacific Islander, 0.5% Two or more races, 20.9% Hispanic of any race; Average household size: 2.52; Median age: 50.8; Age under 18: 18.9%;

Age 65 and over: 22.8%; Males per 100 females: 108.5; Marriage status: 29.2% never married, 58.8% now married, 1.0% separated, 5.2% widowed, 6.9% divorced; Foreign born: 19.6%; Speak English only: 75.2%; With disability: 8.5%; Veterans: 7.2%; Ancestry: 15.6% Irish, 14.1% German, 11.0% Italian, 10.8% English, 8.6% American

Employment: 13.9% management, business, and financial, 1.7% computer, engineering, and science, 17.1% education, legal, community service, arts, and media, 5.5% healthcare practitioners, 18.0% service, 28.8% sales and office, 13.8% natural resources, construction, and maintenance, 1.2% production, transportation, and material moving

Income: Per capita: $51,881; Median household: $83,949; Average household: $128,083; Households with income of $100,000 or more: 40.2%; Poverty rate: 8.1%

Educational Attainment: High school diploma or higher: 93.7%; Bachelor's degree or higher: 48.6%; Graduate/professional degree or higher: 23.3%

Housing: Homeownership rate: 89.8%; Median home value: $660,700; Median year structure built: 1979; Homeowner vacancy rate: 1.5%; Median selected monthly owner costs: $2,631 with a mortgage, $1,026 without a mortgage; Median gross rent: $1,809 per month; Rental vacancy rate: 0.0%

Health Insurance: 92.6% have insurance; 76.4% have private insurance; 34.2% have public insurance; 7.4% do not have insurance; 0.0% of children under 18 do not have insurance

Transportation: Commute: 80.2% car, 12.9% public transportation, 1.3% walk, 5.6% work from home; Mean travel time to work: 32.4 minutes

STONY BROOK (CDP).
Covers a land area of 5.815 square miles and a water area of 0.139 square miles. Located at 40.91° N. Lat; 73.13° W. Long. Elevation is 89 feet.

History: Named for its location, and to promote the town. Restored 1941 to resemble 18th-century village. State University of New York at Stony Brook, one of the university's four graduate centers, and the State University of New York Health Science Center are here.

Population: 13,889; Growth (since 2000): 1.2%; Density: 2,388.6 persons per square mile; Race: 87.0% White, 1.1% Black/African American, 10.9% Asian, 0.0% American Indian/Alaska Native, 0.0% Native Hawaiian/Other Pacific Islander, 0.7% Two or more races, 4.2% Hispanic of any race; Average household size: 2.89; Median age: 45.2; Age under 18: 23.8%; Age 65 and over: 18.7%; Males per 100 females: 95.9; Marriage status: 25.2% never married, 63.7% now married, 1.2% separated, 6.1% widowed, 5.0% divorced; Foreign born: 10.2%; Speak English only: 87.5%; With disability: 7.3%; Veterans: 7.8%; Ancestry: 26.2% Italian, 25.4% Irish, 20.1% German, 6.0% English, 5.3% Russian

Employment: 17.3% management, business, and financial, 11.4% computer, engineering, and science, 20.3% education, legal, community service, arts, and media, 13.3% healthcare practitioners, 10.8% service, 20.0% sales and office, 2.2% natural resources, construction, and maintenance, 4.8% production, transportation, and material moving

Income: Per capita: $53,926; Median household: $132,839; Average household: $154,685; Households with income of $100,000 or more: 65.3%; Poverty rate: 6.7%

Educational Attainment: High school diploma or higher: 97.6%; Bachelor's degree or higher: 64.6%; Graduate/professional degree or higher: 38.1%

School District(s)

Three Village Central SD (KG-12)

    2014-15 Enrollment: 6,784 . . . . (631) 730-4010

Four-year College(s)

Stony Brook University (Public)

    Fall 2014 Enrollment: 24,607 . . . . (631) 632-6000

    2015-16 Tuition: In-state $8,855; Out-of-state $23,935

Housing: Homeownership rate: 89.8%; Median home value: $455,500; Median year structure built: 1966; Homeowner vacancy rate: 0.1%; Median selected monthly owner costs: $3,290 with a mortgage, $1,350 without a mortgage; Median gross rent: $2,301 per month; Rental vacancy rate: 0.0%

Health Insurance: 96.7% have insurance; 91.2% have private insurance; 21.3% have public insurance; 3.3% do not have insurance; 0.6% of children under 18 do not have insurance

Hospitals: University Hospital - Stony Brook (540 beds)

Transportation: Commute: 80.5% car, 6.8% public transportation, 2.1% walk, 9.4% work from home; Mean travel time to work: 31.6 minutes

Airports: Health Sciences Center Unv Hospital (general aviation)

STONY BROOK UNIVERSITY (CDP). Covers a land area of 1.697 square miles and a water area of 0 square miles. Located at 40.91° N. Lat; 73.12° W. Long.

History: Stony Brook is a hamlet and census-designated place (CDP) in the Town of Brookhaven in Suffolk County, New York, on the North Shore of Long Island. It is the home of Stony Brook University.

Population: 9,101; Growth (since 2000): n/a; Density: 5,361.7 persons per square mile; Race: 38.0% White, 9.4% Black/African American, 43.5% Asian, 0.1% American Indian/Alaska Native, 0.0% Native Hawaiian/Other Pacific Islander, 4.4% Two or more races, 10.2% Hispanic of any race; Average household size: 3.06; Median age: 20.6; Age under 18: 2.8%; Age 65 and over: 4.2%; Males per 100 females: 110.0; Marriage status: 94.2% never married, 3.5% now married, 0.0% separated, 2.2% widowed, 0.2% divorced; Foreign born: 31.4%; Speak English only: 43.4%; With disability: 4.8%; Veterans: 3.5%; Ancestry: 10.1% Italian, 9.6% Irish, 6.1% German, 3.8% Polish, 2.9% Russian

Employment: 8.2% management, business, and financial, 10.1% computer, engineering, and science, 21.7% education, legal, community service, arts, and media, 0.8% healthcare practitioners, 15.7% service, 39.4% sales and office, 2.3% natural resources, construction, and maintenance, 1.9% production, transportation, and material moving

Income: Per capita: $5,426; Median household: $142,692; Average household: $110,438; Households with income of $100,000 or more: 65.6%; Poverty rate: n/a

Educational Attainment: High school diploma or higher: 87.5%; Bachelor's degree or higher: 55.6%; Graduate/professional degree or higher: 21.8%

Housing: Homeownership rate: 90.6%; Median home value: $380,800; Median year structure built: 1958; Homeowner vacancy rate: 0.0%; Median selected monthly owner costs: $2,673 with a mortgage, n/a without a mortgage; Median gross rent: n/a per month; Rental vacancy rate: 0.0%

Health Insurance: 97.5% have insurance; 83.1% have private insurance; 15.9% have public insurance; 2.5% do not have insurance; 5.6% of children under 18 do not have insurance

Transportation: Commute: 23.7% car, 13.9% public transportation, 55.3% walk, 5.6% work from home; Mean travel time to work: 19.2 minutes

TERRYVILLE (CDP). Covers a land area of 3.213 square miles and a water area of 0 square miles. Located at 40.91° N. Lat; 73.05° W. Long. Elevation is 151 feet.

Population: 12,296; Growth (since 2000): 16.1%; Density: 3,827.0 persons per square mile; Race: 89.0% White, 3.0% Black/African American, 1.0% Asian, 0.0% American Indian/Alaska Native, 0.0% Native Hawaiian/Other Pacific Islander, 3.4% Two or more races, 22.4% Hispanic of any race; Average household size: 3.29; Median age: 40.9; Age under 18: 25.4%; Age 65 and over: 16.1%; Males per 100 females: 93.5; Marriage status: 29.2% never married, 57.5% now married, 1.4% separated, 6.2% widowed, 7.0% divorced; Foreign born: 15.6%; Speak English only: 78.7%; With disability: 8.8%; Veterans: 6.2%; Ancestry: 27.1% Italian, 17.8% Irish, 11.8% German, 10.7% American, 7.8% Polish

Employment: 11.8% management, business, and financial, 6.3% computer, engineering, and science, 15.5% education, legal, community service, arts, and media, 3.5% healthcare practitioners, 22.5% service, 25.5% sales and office, 7.1% natural resources, construction, and maintenance, 7.9% production, transportation, and material moving

Income: Per capita: $32,333; Median household: $92,567; Average household: $103,795; Households with income of $100,000 or more: 47.5%; Poverty rate: 9.0%

Educational Attainment: High school diploma or higher: 89.9%; Bachelor's degree or higher: 33.0%; Graduate/professional degree or higher: 12.9%

Housing: Homeownership rate: 81.4%; Median home value: $343,300; Median year structure built: 1973; Homeowner vacancy rate: 0.0%; Median selected monthly owner costs: $2,752 with a mortgage, $1,165 without a mortgage; Median gross rent: $1,941 per month; Rental vacancy rate: 4.1%

Health Insurance: 95.1% have insurance; 80.5% have private insurance; 27.6% have public insurance; 4.9% do not have insurance; 1.9% of children under 18 do not have insurance

Transportation: Commute: 94.2% car, 2.3% public transportation, 0.4% walk, 2.4% work from home; Mean travel time to work: 32.2 minutes

TUCKAHOE (CDP). Covers a land area of 4.140 square miles and a water area of 0.458 square miles. Located at 40.90° N. Lat; 72.44° W. Long. Elevation is 49 feet.

Population: 1,169; Growth (since 2000): -32.9%; Density: 282.3 persons per square mile; Race: 70.5% White, 23.7% Black/African American, 1.8% Asian, 0.0% American Indian/Alaska Native, 0.0% Native Hawaiian/Other Pacific Islander, 0.4% Two or more races, 14.8% Hispanic of any race; Average household size: 2.45; Median age: 49.6; Age under 18: 14.6%; Age 65 and over: 24.2%; Males per 100 females: 101.0; Marriage status: 22.8% never married, 64.2% now married, 0.0% separated, 0.5% widowed, 12.4% divorced; Foreign born: 15.6%; Speak English only: 79.6%; With disability: 6.2%; Veterans: 7.8%; Ancestry: 22.6% Irish, 12.8% German, 11.9% English, 7.8% Italian, 5.4% Russian

Employment: 10.7% management, business, and financial, 1.0% computer, engineering, and science, 29.4% education, legal, community service, arts, and media, 10.5% healthcare practitioners, 19.4% service, 15.6% sales and office, 9.5% natural resources, construction, and maintenance, 4.0% production, transportation, and material moving

Income: Per capita: $49,382; Median household: $101,484; Average household: $125,992; Households with income of $100,000 or more: 54.3%; Poverty rate: 4.7%

Educational Attainment: High school diploma or higher: 83.9%; Bachelor's degree or higher: 36.5%; Graduate/professional degree or higher: 17.5%

Housing: Homeownership rate: 78.2%; Median home value: $915,800; Median year structure built: 1982; Homeowner vacancy rate: 0.0%; Median selected monthly owner costs: $2,890 with a mortgage, $1,230 without a mortgage; Median gross rent: $1,710 per month; Rental vacancy rate: 27.1%

Health Insurance: 85.0% have insurance; 76.5% have private insurance; 31.5% have public insurance; 15.0% do not have insurance; 3.5% of children under 18 do not have insurance

Transportation: Commute: 77.7% car, 9.3% public transportation, 5.1% walk, 6.9% work from home; Mean travel time to work: 23.2 minutes

UPTON (unincorporated postal area)
ZCTA: 11973

Covers a land area of 4.408 square miles and a water area of 0.004 square miles. Located at 40.87° N. Lat; 72.88° W. Long. Elevation is 89 feet.

Population: 46; Growth (since 2000): n/a; Density: 10.4 persons per square mile; Race: 13.0% White, 8.7% Black/African American, 78.3% Asian, 0.0% American Indian/Alaska Native, 0.0% Native Hawaiian/Other Pacific Islander, 0.0% Two or more races, 6.5% Hispanic of any race; Average household size: 0.00; Median age: 20.9; Age under 18: 6.5%; Age 65 and over: 0.0%; Males per 100 females: All males; Marriage status: 91.3% never married, 8.7% now married, 0.0% separated, 0.0% widowed, 0.0% divorced; Foreign born: 39.1%; Speak English only: 15.2%; With disability: 0.0%; Veterans: 0.0%; Ancestry: 6.5% Austrian, 6.5% Russian

Employment: 0.0% management, business, and financial, 36.4% computer, engineering, and science, 27.3% education, legal, community service, arts, and media, 0.0% healthcare practitioners, 0.0% service, 36.4% sales and office, 0.0% natural resources, construction, and maintenance, 0.0% production, transportation, and material moving

Income: Per capita: $3,320; Median household: n/a; Average household: n/a; Households with income of $100,000 or more: n/a; Poverty rate: n/a

Educational Attainment: High school diploma or higher: 100.0%; Bachelor's degree or higher: 100.0%; Graduate/professional degree or higher: 100.0%

Housing: Homeownership rate: n/a; Median home value: n/a; Median year structure built: 1965; Homeowner vacancy rate: 0.0%; Median selected monthly owner costs: $0 with a mortgage, $0 without a mortgage; Median gross rent: n/a per month; Rental vacancy rate: 100.0%

Health Insurance: 100.0% have insurance; 100.0% have private insurance; 0.0% have public insurance; 0.0% do not have insurance; 0.0% of children under 18 do not have insurance

Transportation: Commute: 0.0% car, 0.0% public transportation, 100.0% walk, 0.0% work from home; Mean travel time to work: 12.7 minutes

VILLAGE OF THE BRANCH (village).

Covers a land area of 0.948 square miles and a water area of 0.030 square miles. Located at 40.85° N. Lat; 73.18° W. Long. Elevation is 62 feet.

Population: 1,986; Growth (since 2000): 4.8%; Density: 2,095.2 persons per square mile; Race: 96.1% White, 0.0% Black/African American, 2.4% Asian, 0.0% American Indian/Alaska Native, 0.0% Native Hawaiian/Other Pacific Islander, 1.0% Two or more races, 4.4% Hispanic of any race; Average household size: 3.23; Median age: 39.8; Age under 18: 31.6%; Age 65 and over: 13.6%; Males per 100 females: 89.4; Marriage status: 24.2% never married, 65.8% now married, 0.3% separated, 5.3% widowed, 4.7% divorced; Foreign born: 6.0%; Speak English only: 92.8%; With disability: 7.8%; Veterans: 5.2%; Ancestry: 30.9% Italian, 28.0% Irish, 22.2% German, 12.0% Polish, 3.8% English

Employment: 24.2% management, business, and financial, 3.3% computer, engineering, and science, 20.6% education, legal, community service, arts, and media, 10.5% healthcare practitioners, 9.1% service, 22.0% sales and office, 6.6% natural resources, construction, and maintenance, 3.8% production, transportation, and material moving

Income: Per capita: $47,986; Median household: $132,222; Average household: $155,876; Households with income of $100,000 or more: 64.6%; Poverty rate: 3.6%

Educational Attainment: High school diploma or higher: 98.0%; Bachelor's degree or higher: 63.0%; Graduate/professional degree or higher: 35.5%

Housing: Homeownership rate: 90.7%; Median home value: $488,900; Median year structure built: 1968; Homeowner vacancy rate: 0.0%; Median selected monthly owner costs: $3,196 with a mortgage, $1,415 without a mortgage; Median gross rent: $1,879 per month; Rental vacancy rate: 37.8%

Health Insurance: 96.1% have insurance; 91.0% have private insurance; 15.0% have public insurance; 3.9% do not have insurance; 3.0% of children under 18 do not have insurance

Transportation: Commute: 83.2% car, 10.6% public transportation, 0.9% walk, 5.0% work from home; Mean travel time to work: 35.2 minutes

WADING RIVER (CDP).

Covers a land area of 9.803 square miles and a water area of 0.039 square miles. Located at 40.95° N. Lat; 72.82° W. Long. Elevation is 92 feet.

History: Wading River lies in both the Towns of Riverhead and Brookhaven. Its name comes from the original Algonquian name, Pauquaconsuk, meaning "the place where we wade for thick, round-shelled clams." "Wading River" was adopted by the first English colonists.

Population: 7,762; Growth (since 2000): 16.4%; Density: 791.8 persons per square mile; Race: 96.6% White, 0.8% Black/African American, 0.6% Asian, 0.1% American Indian/Alaska Native, 0.0% Native Hawaiian/Other Pacific Islander, 1.0% Two or more races, 8.5% Hispanic of any race; Average household size: 2.76; Median age: 41.8; Age under 18: 23.7%; Age 65 and over: 12.9%; Males per 100 females: 100.1; Marriage status: 22.7% never married, 67.5% now married, 0.6% separated, 3.2% widowed, 6.6% divorced; Foreign born: 6.5%; Speak English only: 90.3%; With disability: 8.7%; Veterans: 9.6%; Ancestry: 23.4% Italian, 20.9% Irish, 20.2% German, 11.3% American, 9.6% Polish

Employment: 17.4% management, business, and financial, 4.5% computer, engineering, and science, 16.4% education, legal, community service, arts, and media, 10.1% healthcare practitioners, 19.7% service, 20.0% sales and office, 4.3% natural resources, construction, and maintenance, 7.5% production, transportation, and material moving

Income: Per capita: $46,227; Median household: $110,417; Average household: $126,205; Households with income of $100,000 or more: 59.7%; Poverty rate: 3.8%

Educational Attainment: High school diploma or higher: 95.0%; Bachelor's degree or higher: 38.3%; Graduate/professional degree or higher: 20.1%

School District(s)

Little Flower Union Free SD (04-12)

 2014-15 Enrollment: 34 . . . . (631) 929-4300

Shoreham-Wading River Central SD (KG-12)

 2014-15 Enrollment: 2,424 . . . . (631) 821-8105

Housing: Homeownership rate: 93.4%; Median home value: $409,400; Median year structure built: 1976; Homeowner vacancy rate: 1.5%; Median selected monthly owner costs: $2,868 with a mortgage, $1,284 without a mortgage; Median gross rent: $1,076 per month; Rental vacancy rate: 0.0%

Health Insurance: 96.6% have insurance; 90.1% have private insurance; 17.6% have public insurance; 3.4% do not have insurance; 3.3% of children under 18 do not have insurance

Newspapers: The Community Journal (weekly circulation 7,000)

Transportation: Commute: 94.0% car, 1.5% public transportation, 0.0% walk, 3.6% work from home; Mean travel time to work: 30.4 minutes

WAINSCOTT (CDP).

Covers a land area of 6.728 square miles and a water area of 0.496 square miles. Located at 40.96° N. Lat; 72.25° W. Long. Elevation is 23 feet.

Population: 753; Growth (since 2000): 19.9%; Density: 111.9 persons per square mile; Race: 95.0% White, 1.9% Black/African American, 0.4% Asian, 0.5% American Indian/Alaska Native, 0.0% Native Hawaiian/Other Pacific Islander, 0.3% Two or more races, 16.9% Hispanic of any race; Average household size: 2.15; Median age: 45.1; Age under 18: 12.1%; Age 65 and over: 24.3%; Males per 100 females: 115.9; Marriage status: 39.4% never married, 49.2% now married, 1.9% separated, 4.5% widowed, 7.0% divorced; Foreign born: 21.1%; Speak English only: 82.1%; With disability: 10.9%; Veterans: 8.0%; Ancestry: 21.5% Italian, 15.3% Irish, 14.7% English, 12.5% German, 5.7% Scottish

Employment: 15.8% management, business, and financial, 11.5% computer, engineering, and science, 15.2% education, legal, community service, arts, and media, 6.0% healthcare practitioners, 12.9% service, 19.2% sales and office, 11.2% natural resources, construction, and maintenance, 8.3% production, transportation, and material moving

Income: Per capita: $40,435; Median household: $61,563; Average household: $90,434; Households with income of $100,000 or more: 37.4%; Poverty rate: 23.1%

Educational Attainment: High school diploma or higher: 88.1%; Bachelor's degree or higher: 42.9%; Graduate/professional degree or higher: 24.7%

School District(s)

Child Development Center of the Hamptons Charter S (KG-05)

 2014-15 Enrollment: 67 . . . . (631) 324-0207

Wainscott Common SD (KG-03)

 2014-15 Enrollment: 21 . . . . (631) 537-1080

Housing: Homeownership rate: 71.9%; Median home value: $1,178,200; Median year structure built: 1985; Homeowner vacancy rate: 0.0%; Median selected monthly owner costs: $3,829 with a mortgage, $1,075 without a mortgage; Median gross rent: $1,338 per month; Rental vacancy rate: 0.0%

Health Insurance: 85.6% have insurance; 73.9% have private insurance; 34.3% have public insurance; 14.4% do not have insurance; 3.5% of children under 18 do not have insurance

Transportation: Commute: 78.3% car, 3.0% public transportation, 7.7% walk, 5.4% work from home; Mean travel time to work: 17.5 minutes

WATER MILL (CDP).

Covers a land area of 10.541 square miles and a water area of 1.483 square miles. Located at 40.92° N. Lat; 72.35° W. Long. Elevation is 33 feet.

Population: 2,273; Growth (since 2000): 31.8%; Density: 215.6 persons per square mile; Race: 94.0% White, 0.0% Black/African American, 4.8% Asian, 0.0% American Indian/Alaska Native, 0.0% Native Hawaiian/Other Pacific Islander, 1.3% Two or more races, 11.8% Hispanic of any race; Average household size: 2.31; Median age: 55.4; Age under 18: 11.0%; Age 65 and over: 24.0%; Males per 100 females: 102.2; Marriage status: 21.9% never married, 61.7% now married, 3.0% separated, 6.7% widowed, 9.8% divorced; Foreign born: 21.7%; Speak English only: 79.4%; With disability: 8.8%; Veterans: 5.0%; Ancestry: 22.0% German, 19.5% English, 12.8% Irish, 9.9% Italian, 6.0% Polish

Employment: 17.0% management, business, and financial, 4.7% computer, engineering, and science, 16.7% education, legal, community service, arts, and media, 5.2% healthcare practitioners, 11.6% service, 24.6% sales and office, 12.2% natural resources, construction, and maintenance, 7.9% production, transportation, and material moving

Income: Per capita: $81,303; Median household: $104,569; Average household: $187,315; Households with income of $100,000 or more: 52.5%; Poverty rate: 7.5%

Educational Attainment: High school diploma or higher: 95.6%; Bachelor's degree or higher: 56.6%; Graduate/professional degree or higher: 31.7%

Housing: Homeownership rate: 91.4%; Median home value: $1,538,100; Median year structure built: 1983; Homeowner vacancy rate: 2.3%; Median selected monthly owner costs: $3,815 with a mortgage, $1,132 without a

mortgage; Median gross rent: $2,635 per month; Rental vacancy rate: 0.0%

Health Insurance: 87.7% have insurance; 78.9% have private insurance; 24.0% have public insurance; 12.3% do not have insurance; 6.4% of children under 18 do not have insurance

Transportation: Commute: 69.3% car, 11.3% public transportation, 2.9% walk, 10.5% work from home; Mean travel time to work: 24.8 minutes

WEST BABYLON (CDP). Covers a land area of 7.767 square miles and a water area of 0.309 square miles. Located at 40.71° N. Lat; 73.36° W. Long. Elevation is 39 feet.

History: West Babylon's first one-room schoolhouse was erected in the early 1800s, on South Country Road (Montauk Highway), just east of Great East Neck Road. During the winter of 1836, poet Walt Whitman taught school in West Babylon.

Population: 42,664; Growth (since 2000): -1.8%; Density: 5,493.1 persons per square mile; Race: 77.0% White, 10.4% Black/African American, 2.6% Asian, 0.1% American Indian/Alaska Native, 0.0% Native Hawaiian/Other Pacific Islander, 2.9% Two or more races, 16.4% Hispanic of any race; Average household size: 3.04; Median age: 41.1; Age under 18: 20.1%; Age 65 and over: 15.0%; Males per 100 females: 91.8; Marriage status: 30.4% never married, 52.9% now married, 1.9% separated, 8.0% widowed, 8.6% divorced; Foreign born: 14.4%; Speak English only: 81.0%; With disability: 11.6%; Veterans: 6.2%; Ancestry: 33.0% Italian, 20.2% Irish, 14.9% German, 5.9% Polish, 3.6% English

Employment: 12.7% management, business, and financial, 3.8% computer, engineering, and science, 10.5% education, legal, community service, arts, and media, 4.9% healthcare practitioners, 16.8% service, 30.5% sales and office, 10.5% natural resources, construction, and maintenance, 10.3% production, transportation, and material moving

Income: Per capita: $33,288; Median household: $82,952; Average household: $98,060; Households with income of $100,000 or more: 40.4%; Poverty rate: 5.7%

Educational Attainment: High school diploma or higher: 88.4%; Bachelor's degree or higher: 22.9%; Graduate/professional degree or higher: 7.6%

School District(s)
West Babylon Union Free SD (KG-12)
    2014-15 Enrollment: 4,074 . . . . (631) 376-7001

Housing: Homeownership rate: 75.5%; Median home value: $337,200; Median year structure built: 1961; Homeowner vacancy rate: 0.6%; Median selected monthly owner costs: $2,672 with a mortgage, $1,230 without a mortgage; Median gross rent: $1,533 per month; Rental vacancy rate: 3.9%

Health Insurance: 92.7% have insurance; 79.3% have private insurance; 25.7% have public insurance; 7.3% do not have insurance; 1.9% of children under 18 do not have insurance

Transportation: Commute: 88.3% car, 7.8% public transportation, 0.8% walk, 2.6% work from home; Mean travel time to work: 31.0 minutes

WEST BAY SHORE (CDP). Covers a land area of 2.193 square miles and a water area of 0.094 square miles. Located at 40.71° N. Lat; 73.27° W. Long. Elevation is 13 feet.

Population: 4,684; Growth (since 2000): -1.9%; Density: 2,136.3 persons per square mile; Race: 88.7% White, 1.7% Black/African American, 3.0% Asian, 0.0% American Indian/Alaska Native, 0.0% Native Hawaiian/Other Pacific Islander, 4.6% Two or more races, 18.8% Hispanic of any race; Average household size: 2.81; Median age: 46.2; Age under 18: 22.5%; Age 65 and over: 21.5%; Males per 100 females: 96.7; Marriage status: 19.9% never married, 62.8% now married, 0.9% separated, 8.6% widowed, 8.7% divorced; Foreign born: 8.3%; Speak English only: 86.8%; With disability: 9.5%; Veterans: 8.4%; Ancestry: 31.9% Italian, 26.4% Irish, 19.0% German, 3.9% English, 3.5% American

Employment: 21.5% management, business, and financial, 4.1% computer, engineering, and science, 16.5% education, legal, community service, arts, and media, 4.7% healthcare practitioners, 9.2% service, 27.0% sales and office, 8.9% natural resources, construction, and maintenance, 7.9% production, transportation, and material moving

Income: Per capita: $48,794; Median household: $103,828; Average household: $133,477; Households with income of $100,000 or more: 53.3%; Poverty rate: 2.4%

Educational Attainment: High school diploma or higher: 96.5%; Bachelor's degree or higher: 42.2%; Graduate/professional degree or higher: 21.4%

Housing: Homeownership rate: 98.0%; Median home value: $419,500; Median year structure built: 1962; Homeowner vacancy rate: 1.5%; Median selected monthly owner costs: $2,992 with a mortgage, $1,422 without a mortgage; Median gross rent: n/a per month; Rental vacancy rate: 0.0%

Health Insurance: 96.7% have insurance; 86.2% have private insurance; 28.7% have public insurance; 3.3% do not have insurance; 2.7% of children under 18 do not have insurance

Transportation: Commute: 83.8% car, 12.3% public transportation, 0.5% walk, 2.3% work from home; Mean travel time to work: 35.1 minutes

WEST HAMPTON DUNES (village). Covers a land area of 0.329 square miles and a water area of 0.085 square miles. Located at 40.78° N. Lat; 72.71° W. Long. Elevation is 7 feet.

Population: 53; Growth (since 2000): 381.8%; Density: 160.9 persons per square mile; Race: 92.5% White, 0.0% Black/African American, 0.0% Asian, 7.5% American Indian/Alaska Native, 0.0% Native Hawaiian/Other Pacific Islander, 0.0% Two or more races, 7.5% Hispanic of any race; Average household size: 1.96; Median age: 67.2; Age under 18: 7.5%; Age 65 and over: 56.6%; Males per 100 females: 139.1; Marriage status: 0.0% never married, 91.8% now married, 0.0% separated, 8.2% widowed, 0.0% divorced; Foreign born: 9.4%; Speak English only: 84.9%; With disability: 7.5%; Veterans: 26.5%; Ancestry: 30.2% Irish, 24.5% Italian, 13.2% German, 13.2% Russian, 9.4% Austrian

Employment: 32.0% management, business, and financial, 0.0% computer, engineering, and science, 28.0% education, legal, community service, arts, and media, 12.0% healthcare practitioners, 0.0% service, 20.0% sales and office, 0.0% natural resources, construction, and maintenance, 8.0% production, transportation, and material moving

Income: Per capita: $89,889; Median household: $129,375; Average household: $178,337; Households with income of $100,000 or more: 77.7%; Poverty rate: n/a

Educational Attainment: High school diploma or higher: 100.0%; Bachelor's degree or higher: 87.8%; Graduate/professional degree or higher: 53.1%

Housing: Homeownership rate: 85.2%; Median home value: 2 million+; Median year structure built: 1988; Homeowner vacancy rate: 0.0%; Median selected monthly owner costs: $4,000+ with a mortgage, $1,500+ without a mortgage; Median gross rent: n/a per month; Rental vacancy rate: 0.0%

Health Insurance: 100.0% have insurance; 77.4% have private insurance; 62.3% have public insurance; 0.0% do not have insurance; 0.0% of children under 18 do not have insurance

Transportation: Commute: 52.0% car, 0.0% public transportation, 24.0% walk, 24.0% work from home; Mean travel time to work: 36.6 minutes

WEST HILLS (CDP). Covers a land area of 4.926 square miles and a water area of 0 square miles. Located at 40.82° N. Lat; 73.43° W. Long. Elevation is 348 feet.

History: The community of West Hills is home to West Hills County Park, the location of Jayne's Hill which is the natural highest point on Long Island (400 feet). This area includes picturesque, well-groomed nature trails, including the historic Walt Whitman Trail.

Population: 5,098; Growth (since 2000): -9.1%; Density: 1,035.0 persons per square mile; Race: 90.9% White, 0.5% Black/African American, 5.3% Asian, 0.6% American Indian/Alaska Native, 0.0% Native Hawaiian/Other Pacific Islander, 0.9% Two or more races, 5.4% Hispanic of any race; Average household size: 2.68; Median age: 47.8; Age under 18: 20.6%; Age 65 and over: 18.1%; Males per 100 females: 97.4; Marriage status: 22.3% never married, 67.1% now married, 1.0% separated, 5.4% widowed, 5.2% divorced; Foreign born: 8.2%; Speak English only: 90.3%; With disability: 7.7%; Veterans: 5.9%; Ancestry: 27.8% Italian, 21.8% Irish, 17.9% German, 6.9% Polish, 5.9% American

Employment: 27.7% management, business, and financial, 3.8% computer, engineering, and science, 25.3% education, legal, community service, arts, and media, 5.4% healthcare practitioners, 6.7% service, 23.8% sales and office, 5.6% natural resources, construction, and maintenance, 1.7% production, transportation, and material moving

Income: Per capita: $57,476; Median household: $114,141; Average household: $152,363; Households with income of $100,000 or more: 57.1%; Poverty rate: 1.6%

Educational Attainment: High school diploma or higher: 96.2%; Bachelor's degree or higher: 56.9%; Graduate/professional degree or higher: 28.8%

Housing: Homeownership rate: 90.9%; Median home value: $547,900; Median year structure built: 1959; Homeowner vacancy rate: 0.4%; Median selected monthly owner costs: $3,207 with a mortgage, $1,460 without a

mortgage; Median gross rent: $2,082 per month; Rental vacancy rate: 0.0%

Health Insurance: 97.0% have insurance; 88.7% have private insurance; 20.3% have public insurance; 3.0% do not have insurance; 2.4% of children under 18 do not have insurance

Transportation: Commute: 80.4% car, 11.8% public transportation, 1.6% walk, 6.2% work from home; Mean travel time to work: 33.9 minutes

---

WEST ISLIP (CDP). Covers a land area of 6.329 square miles and a water area of 0.437 square miles. Located at 40.71° N. Lat; 73.29° W. Long. Elevation is 20 feet.

History: The first people to settle in this area more than one thousand years ago were the Secatogue Indians. An Indian burial ground was discovered north of West Islip beach enabling historians to reconstruct a village of these Indians who lived along the edges of the Great South Bay, Sampawams Creek, Trues Creek and Willetts Creek.

Population: 27,224; Growth (since 2000): -5.8%; Density: 4,301.6 persons per square mile; Race: 94.6% White, 0.6% Black/African American, 1.8% Asian, 0.0% American Indian/Alaska Native, 0.0% Native Hawaiian/Other Pacific Islander, 1.9% Two or more races, 6.7% Hispanic of any race; Average household size: 3.08; Median age: 42.6; Age under 18: 22.5%; Age 65 and over: 14.8%; Males per 100 females: 96.2; Marriage status: 28.3% never married, 57.2% now married, 1.0% separated, 7.4% widowed, 7.1% divorced; Foreign born: 5.6%; Speak English only: 90.7%; With disability: 9.3%; Veterans: 6.6%; Ancestry: 40.0% Italian, 30.9% Irish, 19.5% German, 5.4% English, 5.0% Polish

Employment: 16.6% management, business, and financial, 3.3% computer, engineering, and science, 13.1% education, legal, community service, arts, and media, 7.8% healthcare practitioners, 15.5% service, 28.8% sales and office, 9.0% natural resources, construction, and maintenance, 5.9% production, transportation, and material moving

Income: Per capita: $40,931; Median household: $110,340; Average household: $123,907; Households with income of $100,000 or more: 55.8%; Poverty rate: 4.0%

Educational Attainment: High school diploma or higher: 94.1%; Bachelor's degree or higher: 36.4%; Graduate/professional degree or higher: 16.9%

School District(s)

West Islip Union Free SD (KG-12)

   2014-15 Enrollment: 4,684 . . . . (631) 930-1560

Housing: Homeownership rate: 94.5%; Median home value: $411,500; Median year structure built: 1959; Homeowner vacancy rate: 0.2%; Median selected monthly owner costs: $2,998 with a mortgage, $1,312 without a mortgage; Median gross rent: $1,225 per month; Rental vacancy rate: 5.0%

Health Insurance: 96.1% have insurance; 87.8% have private insurance; 19.3% have public insurance; 3.9% do not have insurance; 1.4% of children under 18 do not have insurance

Hospitals: Good Samaritan Hospital Medical Center (437 beds)

Transportation: Commute: 87.5% car, 7.3% public transportation, 0.9% walk, 3.9% work from home; Mean travel time to work: 30.7 minutes

---

WEST SAYVILLE (CDP). Covers a land area of 2.100 square miles and a water area of 0.007 square miles. Located at 40.73° N. Lat; 73.11° W. Long. Elevation is 13 feet.

History: West Sayville is a hamlet in Suffolk County, New York. It was inhabited by the Secatogue Tribe of the Algonquin Nation. The name Secatogue means "black meadow lands."

Population: 4,712; Growth (since 2000): -5.8%; Density: 2,244.3 persons per square mile; Race: 95.5% White, 0.2% Black/African American, 1.9% Asian, 0.0% American Indian/Alaska Native, 0.0% Native Hawaiian/Other Pacific Islander, 2.1% Two or more races, 3.1% Hispanic of any race; Average household size: 2.90; Median age: 45.1; Age under 18: 20.1%; Age 65 and over: 16.5%; Males per 100 females: 92.4; Marriage status: 30.1% never married, 57.1% now married, 1.3% separated, 7.3% widowed, 5.6% divorced; Foreign born: 3.2%; Speak English only: 95.5%; With disability: 10.5%; Veterans: 7.4%; Ancestry: 33.6% Irish, 26.8% German, 26.4% Italian, 6.9% English, 3.9% American

Employment: 14.1% management, business, and financial, 7.2% computer, engineering, and science, 15.6% education, legal, community service, arts, and media, 4.6% healthcare practitioners, 12.7% service, 27.6% sales and office, 7.1% natural resources, construction, and maintenance, 10.9% production, transportation, and material moving

Income: Per capita: $41,524; Median household: $104,330; Average household: $118,757; Households with income of $100,000 or more: 52.3%; Poverty rate: 2.7%

Educational Attainment: High school diploma or higher: 92.8%; Bachelor's degree or higher: 36.0%; Graduate/professional degree or higher: 15.6%

School District(s)

Sayville Union Free SD (KG-12)

   2014-15 Enrollment: 3,048 . . . . (631) 244-6510

Housing: Homeownership rate: 88.9%; Median home value: $374,100; Median year structure built: 1956; Homeowner vacancy rate: 3.0%; Median selected monthly owner costs: $2,828 with a mortgage, $1,087 without a mortgage; Median gross rent: $1,434 per month; Rental vacancy rate: 0.0%

Health Insurance: 94.9% have insurance; 85.9% have private insurance; 22.8% have public insurance; 5.1% do not have insurance; 1.6% of children under 18 do not have insurance

Transportation: Commute: 87.8% car, 7.9% public transportation, 0.3% walk, 4.0% work from home; Mean travel time to work: 36.9 minutes

---

WESTHAMPTON (CDP). Covers a land area of 12.674 square miles and a water area of 2.191 square miles. Located at 40.85° N. Lat; 72.66° W. Long. Elevation is 36 feet.

History: Like most of Southern Long Island shore zone, suffering from significant beach erosion due to a succession of mid-1990s Atlantic hurricanes. Part of the original Quogue Purchase of 1666. Westhampton's first summerhouse built by Gen. John A. Dix in 1879; then a three-day journey by stage from Brooklyn until L.I. Railroad extended to Sag Harbor in 1870. By 1920s Westhampton and The Hamptons were the summering place for the rich and famous. Incorporated 1928.

Population: 2,935; Growth (since 2000): 2.3%; Density: 231.6 persons per square mile; Race: 94.3% White, 3.6% Black/African American, 0.4% Asian, 0.0% American Indian/Alaska Native, 0.0% Native Hawaiian/Other Pacific Islander, 0.9% Two or more races, 9.4% Hispanic of any race; Average household size: 2.55; Median age: 48.6; Age under 18: 20.3%; Age 65 and over: 26.4%; Males per 100 females: 97.2; Marriage status: 21.5% never married, 54.9% now married, 1.7% separated, 10.7% widowed, 13.0% divorced; Foreign born: 11.3%; Speak English only: 85.1%; With disability: 10.1%; Veterans: 8.1%; Ancestry: 27.7% Irish, 20.6% Italian, 13.8% German, 8.9% American, 8.8% Polish

Employment: 19.0% management, business, and financial, 2.6% computer, engineering, and science, 14.0% education, legal, community service, arts, and media, 3.8% healthcare practitioners, 13.5% service, 31.6% sales and office, 10.3% natural resources, construction, and maintenance, 5.2% production, transportation, and material moving

Income: Per capita: $45,726; Median household: $94,408; Average household: $121,789; Households with income of $100,000 or more: 44.9%; Poverty rate: 9.0%

Educational Attainment: High school diploma or higher: 95.5%; Bachelor's degree or higher: 43.9%; Graduate/professional degree or higher: 20.4%

Housing: Homeownership rate: 78.6%; Median home value: $669,000; Median year structure built: 1977; Homeowner vacancy rate: 7.1%; Median selected monthly owner costs: $2,970 with a mortgage, $1,055 without a mortgage; Median gross rent: $1,771 per month; Rental vacancy rate: 5.4%

Health Insurance: 90.9% have insurance; 76.0% have private insurance; 31.0% have public insurance; 9.1% do not have insurance; 5.5% of children under 18 do not have insurance

Transportation: Commute: 82.7% car, 4.1% public transportation, 2.4% walk, 8.9% work from home; Mean travel time to work: 21.6 minutes

---

WESTHAMPTON BEACH (village). Covers a land area of 2.931 square miles and a water area of 0.072 square miles. Located at 40.81° N. Lat; 72.65° W. Long. Elevation is 7 feet.

Population: 1,918; Growth (since 2000): 0.8%; Density: 654.4 persons per square mile; Race: 92.1% White, 0.9% Black/African American, 1.0% Asian, 1.1% American Indian/Alaska Native, 0.0% Native Hawaiian/Other Pacific Islander, 2.9% Two or more races, 11.6% Hispanic of any race; Average household size: 2.26; Median age: 51.2; Age under 18: 18.4%; Age 65 and over: 30.3%; Males per 100 females: 109.6; Marriage status: 22.2% never married, 58.8% now married, 1.5% separated, 9.4% widowed, 9.6% divorced; Foreign born: 14.5%; Speak English only: 83.7%; With disability: 13.8%; Veterans: 7.5%; Ancestry: 22.4% Irish, 18.5% Italian, 14.0% German, 11.3% English, 8.1% Polish

Employment: 13.0% management, business, and financial, 6.4% computer, engineering, and science, 19.3% education, legal, community service, arts, and media, 6.3% healthcare practitioners, 14.0% service, 24.0% sales and office, 11.9% natural resources, construction, and maintenance, 5.0% production, transportation, and material moving
Income: Per capita: $62,231; Median household: $82,321; Average household: $140,478; Households with income of $100,000 or more: 38.8%; Poverty rate: 11.0%
Educational Attainment: High school diploma or higher: 95.9%; Bachelor's degree or higher: 50.5%; Graduate/professional degree or higher: 24.4%

School District(s)
Westhampton Beach Union Free SD (KG-12)
    2014-15 Enrollment: 1,867 . . . . (631) 288-3800
Housing: Homeownership rate: 75.8%; Median home value: $698,600; Median year structure built: 1966; Homeowner vacancy rate: 7.4%; Median selected monthly owner costs: $2,713 with a mortgage, $1,105 without a mortgage; Median gross rent: $1,775 per month; Rental vacancy rate: 4.3%
Health Insurance: 90.8% have insurance; 73.7% have private insurance; 39.8% have public insurance; 9.2% do not have insurance; 6.3% of children under 18 do not have insurance
Safety: Violent crime rate: 5.6 per 10,000 population; Property crime rate: 203.0 per 10,000 population
Transportation: Commute: 78.0% car, 8.3% public transportation, 4.3% walk, 6.9% work from home; Mean travel time to work: 29.6 minutes
Airports: Francis S Gabreski (general aviation)
Additional Information Contacts
Village of Westhampton Beach . . . . (631) 288-1654
    http://www.whbvillage.com

WHEATLEY HEIGHTS (CDP). Covers a land area of 1.302 square miles and a water area of 0 square miles. Located at 40.76° N. Lat; 73.37° W. Long. Elevation is 102 feet.
Population: 5,220; Growth (since 2000): 4.1%; Density: 4,010.0 persons per square mile; Race: 25.1% White, 62.2% Black/African American, 6.7% Asian, 0.0% American Indian/Alaska Native, 0.0% Native Hawaiian/Other Pacific Islander, 0.8% Two or more races, 10.3% Hispanic of any race; Average household size: 3.68; Median age: 37.9; Age under 18: 25.0%; Age 65 and over: 10.1%; Males per 100 females: 91.6; Marriage status: 39.0% never married, 51.1% now married, 2.2% separated, 4.2% widowed, 5.7% divorced; Foreign born: 20.8%; Speak English only: 79.4%; With disability: 11.2%; Veterans: 3.4%; Ancestry: 9.6% Haitian, 8.1% Italian, 5.4% Irish, 3.7% Jamaican, 3.3% American
Employment: 13.3% management, business, and financial, 4.1% computer, engineering, and science, 16.3% education, legal, community service, arts, and media, 9.7% healthcare practitioners, 14.1% service, 29.8% sales and office, 2.9% natural resources, construction, and maintenance, 9.8% production, transportation, and material moving
Income: Per capita: $32,686; Median household: $97,014; Average household: $116,192; Households with income of $100,000 or more: 48.8%; Poverty rate: 5.9%
Educational Attainment: High school diploma or higher: 92.6%; Bachelor's degree or higher: 40.1%; Graduate/professional degree or higher: 16.3%
Housing: Homeownership rate: 80.0%; Median home value: $388,900; Median year structure built: 1966; Homeowner vacancy rate: 3.4%; Median selected monthly owner costs: $3,037 with a mortgage, $1,223 without a mortgage; Median gross rent: $1,660 per month; Rental vacancy rate: 5.7%
Health Insurance: 91.8% have insurance; 78.4% have private insurance; 21.6% have public insurance; 8.2% do not have insurance; 3.7% of children under 18 do not have insurance
Transportation: Commute: 83.0% car, 13.4% public transportation, 0.0% walk, 2.5% work from home; Mean travel time to work: 33.7 minutes

---

WYANDANCH (CDP). Covers a land area of 4.473 square miles and a water area of 0.003 square miles. Located at 40.75° N. Lat; 73.38° W. Long. Elevation is 56 feet.
History: Wyandanch is named after Chief Wyandanch, a leader of the Montaukett Native American tribe during the 17th century.
Population: 11,558; Growth (since 2000): 9.6%; Density: 2,583.7 persons per square mile; Race: 18.6% White, 64.5% Black/African American, 0.4% Asian, 0.7% American Indian/Alaska Native, 0.0% Native Hawaiian/Other Pacific Islander, 5.9% Two or more races, 30.2% Hispanic of any race;

Average household size: 3.83; Median age: 32.0; Age under 18: 26.7%; Age 65 and over: 8.5%; Males per 100 females: 96.4; Marriage status: 53.2% never married, 35.5% now married, 4.4% separated, 5.4% widowed, 5.9% divorced; Foreign born: 25.1%; Speak English only: 67.1%; With disability: 12.4%; Veterans: 3.9%; Ancestry: 9.5% Haitian, 4.0% Jamaican, 2.5% American, 2.1% British West Indian, 1.6% Italian
Employment: 5.2% management, business, and financial, 1.9% computer, engineering, and science, 6.5% education, legal, community service, arts, and media, 5.4% healthcare practitioners, 32.2% service, 17.2% sales and office, 10.0% natural resources, construction, and maintenance, 21.6% production, transportation, and material moving
Income: Per capita: $20,749; Median household: $57,500; Average household: $74,394; Households with income of $100,000 or more: 26.3%; Poverty rate: 17.2%
Educational Attainment: High school diploma or higher: 77.2%; Bachelor's degree or higher: 14.5%; Graduate/professional degree or higher: 4.2%

School District(s)
Wyandanch Union Free SD (PK-12)
    2014-15 Enrollment: 2,469 . . . . (631) 870-0401
Housing: Homeownership rate: 63.6%; Median home value: $239,300; Median year structure built: 1967; Homeowner vacancy rate: 2.2%; Median selected monthly owner costs: $2,353 with a mortgage, $936 without a mortgage; Median gross rent: $1,743 per month; Rental vacancy rate: 1.1%
Health Insurance: 81.0% have insurance; 53.2% have private insurance; 36.8% have public insurance; 19.0% do not have insurance; 9.7% of children under 18 do not have insurance
Transportation: Commute: 85.7% car, 8.5% public transportation, 2.5% walk, 2.8% work from home; Mean travel time to work: 27.9 minutes

---

YAPHANK (CDP). Covers a land area of 13.649 square miles and a water area of 0.123 square miles. Located at 40.83° N. Lat; 72.92° W. Long. Elevation is 39 feet.
History: US Camp Upton here was a US Army induction center in World Wars I and II.
Population: 5,958; Growth (since 2000): 18.6%; Density: 436.5 persons per square mile; Race: 82.4% White, 8.0% Black/African American, 1.9% Asian, 0.6% American Indian/Alaska Native, 0.0% Native Hawaiian/Other Pacific Islander, 3.5% Two or more races, 9.7% Hispanic of any race; Average household size: 2.82; Median age: 41.4; Age under 18: 18.5%; Age 65 and over: 12.1%; Males per 100 females: 119.4; Marriage status: 36.0% never married, 50.9% now married, 1.2% separated, 4.0% widowed, 9.1% divorced; Foreign born: 7.1%; Speak English only: 89.0%; With disability: 8.9%; Veterans: 6.9%; Ancestry: 31.7% Italian, 23.8% Irish, 22.8% German, 7.6% English, 4.5% Polish
Employment: 18.2% management, business, and financial, 4.0% computer, engineering, and science, 16.7% education, legal, community service, arts, and media, 5.5% healthcare practitioners, 15.2% service, 24.7% sales and office, 8.0% natural resources, construction, and maintenance, 7.5% production, transportation, and material moving
Income: Per capita: $35,649; Median household: $94,896; Average household: $106,370; Households with income of $100,000 or more: 48.7%; Poverty rate: 4.5%
Educational Attainment: High school diploma or higher: 90.6%; Bachelor's degree or higher: 29.5%; Graduate/professional degree or higher: 13.2%

School District(s)
Longwood Central SD (KG-12)
    2014-15 Enrollment: 9,211 . . . . (631) 345-2172
Housing: Homeownership rate: 91.0%; Median home value: $307,600; Median year structure built: 1981; Homeowner vacancy rate: 1.8%; Median selected monthly owner costs: $2,359 with a mortgage, $1,027 without a mortgage; Median gross rent: $1,768 per month; Rental vacancy rate: 0.0%
Health Insurance: 94.8% have insurance; 83.6% have private insurance; 22.5% have public insurance; 5.2% do not have insurance; 0.0% of children under 18 do not have insurance
Transportation: Commute: 93.3% car, 2.3% public transportation, 0.3% walk, 3.9% work from home; Mean travel time to work: 34.1 minutes

Sullivan County

Located in southeastern New York; bounded on the west and southwest by the Delaware River and the Pennsylvania border; drained by the Neversink

River; includes parts of the Catskills and the Shawangunk Range, and many lakes. Covers a land area of 968.132 square miles, a water area of 28.591 square miles, and is located in the Eastern Time Zone at 41.72° N. Lat., 74.76° W. Long. The county was founded in 1809. County seat is Monticello.

Weather Station: Liberty 1 NE   Elevation: 1,548 feet

	Jan	Feb	Mar	Apr	May	Jun	Jul	Aug	Sep	Oct	Nov	Dec
High	30	34	42	55	66	74	79	78	70	59	47	34
Low	12	14	22	33	43	51	56	55	47	36	28	18
Precip	3.7	2.8	3.8	4.6	4.8	5.0	4.9	4.5	4.9	4.5	3.9	4.2
Snow	18.6	12.7	12.7	3.3	tr	0.0	0.0	0.0	0.0	0.3	4.0	15.1

High and Low temperatures in degrees Fahrenheit; Precipitation and Snow in inches

Population: 76,330; Growth (since 2000): 3.2%; Density: 78.8 persons per square mile; Race: 81.2% White, 8.6% Black/African American, 1.6% Asian, 0.2% American Indian/Alaska Native, 0.0% Native Hawaiian/Other Pacific Islander, 3.8% two or more races, 14.6% Hispanic of any race; Average household size: 2.54; Median age: 42.2; Age under 18: 21.7%; Age 65 and over: 16.2%; Males per 100 females: 104.4; Marriage status: 33.4% never married, 49.0% now married, 3.5% separated, 7.4% widowed, 10.2% divorced; Foreign born: 9.9%; Speak English only: 84.8%; With disability: 15.5%; Veterans: 9.0%; Ancestry: 19.3% German, 17.4% Irish, 12.7% Italian, 6.2% English, 5.9% Polish

Religion: Six largest groups: 19.8% Catholicism, 5.6% Judaism, 4.0% Methodist/Pietist, 3.9% Muslim Estimate, 1.7% Hindu, 1.5% Presbyterian-Reformed

Economy: Unemployment rate: 4.7%; Leading Industries: 14.4 % retail trade; 12.6 % accommodation and food services; 11.9 % health care and social assistance; Farms: 321 totaling 53,859 acres; Company size: 0 employ 1,000 or more persons, 4 employ 500 to 999 persons, 24 employ 100 to 499 persons, 1,894 employ less than 100 persons; Business ownership: 2,105 women-owned, 377 Black-owned, 447 Hispanic-owned, 219 Asian-owned, 26 American Indian/Alaska Native-owned

Employment: 9.5% management, business, and financial, 2.2% computer, engineering, and science, 13.0% education, legal, community service, arts, and media, 5.5% healthcare practitioners, 23.1% service, 22.6% sales and office, 12.7% natural resources, construction, and maintenance, 11.3% production, transportation, and material moving

Income: Per capita: $25,742; Median household: $50,710; Average household: $65,585; Households with income of $100,000 or more: 18.2%; Poverty rate: 17.5%

Educational Attainment: High school diploma or higher: 86.0%; Bachelor's degree or higher: 22.2%; Graduate/professional degree or higher: 9.9%

Housing: Homeownership rate: 65.5%; Median home value: $165,900; Median year structure built: 1971; Homeowner vacancy rate: 4.7%; Median selected monthly owner costs: $1,570 with a mortgage, $652 without a mortgage; Median gross rent: $841 per month; Rental vacancy rate: 9.6%

Vital Statistics: Birth rate: 110.0 per 10,000 population; Death rate: 98.7 per 10,000 population; Age-adjusted cancer mortality rate: 161.0 deaths per 10,000 population

Health Insurance: 89.4% have insurance; 62.2% have private insurance; 41.4% have public insurance; 10.6% do not have insurance; 3.2% of children under 18 do not have insurance

Health Care: Physicians: 11.6 per 10,000 population; Dentists: 4.0 per 10,000 population; Hospital beds: 28.7 per 10,000 population; Hospital admissions: 745.8 per 10,000 population

Transportation: Commute: 87.4% car, 2.0% public transportation, 4.0% walk, 5.1% work from home; Mean travel time to work: 29.2 minutes

2016 Presidential Election: 53.6% Trump, 42.3% Clinton, 2.5% Johnson, 1.7% Stein

Additional Information Contacts
Sullivan Government . . . . (845) 794-3000
http://co.sullivan.ny.us

Sullivan County Communities

BARRYVILLE (unincorporated postal area)
ZCTA: 12719
   Covers a land area of 17.233 square miles and a water area of 0.443 square miles. Located at 41.50° N. Lat; 74.90° W. Long. Elevation is 594 feet.
Population: 1,257; Growth (since 2000): 24.2%; Density: 72.9 persons per square mile; Race: 97.1% White, 2.1% Black/African American, 0.0% Asian, 0.3% American Indian/Alaska Native, 0.0% Native

Hawaiian/Other Pacific Islander, 0.0% Two or more races, 3.6% Hispanic of any race; Average household size: 2.31; Median age: 51.6; Age under 18: 13.8%; Age 65 and over: 20.8%; Males per 100 females: 109.5; Marriage status: 33.2% never married, 47.5% now married, 5.5% separated, 7.1% widowed, 12.2% divorced; Foreign born: 14.7%; Speak English only: 88.5%; With disability: 17.8%; Veterans: 9.0%; Ancestry: 35.5% German, 20.6% Irish, 13.7% Italian, 8.2% English, 6.7% Polish

Employment: 14.9% management, business, and financial, 6.2% computer, engineering, and science, 11.6% education, legal, community service, arts, and media, 13.1% healthcare practitioners, 16.9% service, 15.3% sales and office, 10.6% natural resources, construction, and maintenance, 11.4% production, transportation, and material moving

Income: Per capita: $33,989; Median household: $51,607; Average household: $82,949; Households with income of $100,000 or more: 20.0%; Poverty rate: 22.0%

Educational Attainment: High school diploma or higher: 85.1%; Bachelor's degree or higher: 30.2%; Graduate/professional degree or higher: 9.4%

Housing: Homeownership rate: 81.0%; Median home value: $185,500; Median year structure built: 1965; Homeowner vacancy rate: 4.0%; Median selected monthly owner costs: $1,577 with a mortgage, $686 without a mortgage; Median gross rent: $695 per month; Rental vacancy rate: 0.0%

Health Insurance: 89.9% have insurance; 64.4% have private insurance; 43.8% have public insurance; 10.1% do not have insurance; 10.3% of children under 18 do not have insurance

Transportation: Commute: 89.0% car, 0.0% public transportation, 2.0% walk, 6.1% work from home; Mean travel time to work: 42.0 minutes

BETHEL (town).
Covers a land area of 85.265 square miles and a water area of 4.693 square miles. Located at 41.69° N. Lat; 74.85° W. Long. Elevation is 1,325 feet.
History: Site of the 3-day Woodstock rock festival, July 1969.
Population: 4,191; Growth (since 2000): -3.9%; Density: 49.2 persons per square mile; Race: 85.1% White, 4.2% Black/African American, 4.2% Asian, 0.3% American Indian/Alaska Native, 0.0% Native Hawaiian/Other Pacific Islander, 4.1% Two or more races, 9.3% Hispanic of any race; Average household size: 2.33; Median age: 47.3; Age under 18: 14.6%; Age 65 and over: 21.5%; Males per 100 females: 110.6; Marriage status: 36.7% never married, 42.9% now married, 2.3% separated, 8.4% widowed, 12.0% divorced; Foreign born: 9.9%; Speak English only: 89.2%; With disability: 14.2%; Veterans: 9.1%; Ancestry: 21.3% Irish, 18.1% Italian, 16.0% German, 7.0% American, 5.2% Polish

Employment: 11.5% management, business, and financial, 4.3% computer, engineering, and science, 13.4% education, legal, community service, arts, and media, 11.1% healthcare practitioners, 22.8% service, 16.3% sales and office, 14.9% natural resources, construction, and maintenance, 5.7% production, transportation, and material moving

Income: Per capita: $30,084; Median household: $57,689; Average household: $72,875; Households with income of $100,000 or more: 18.1%; Poverty rate: 14.8%

Educational Attainment: High school diploma or higher: 83.9%; Bachelor's degree or higher: 27.5%; Graduate/professional degree or higher: 9.5%

Housing: Homeownership rate: 72.5%; Median home value: $179,600; Median year structure built: 1960; Homeowner vacancy rate: 9.2%; Median selected monthly owner costs: $1,814 with a mortgage, $609 without a mortgage; Median gross rent: $877 per month; Rental vacancy rate: 2.4%

Health Insurance: 88.1% have insurance; 64.1% have private insurance; 41.1% have public insurance; 11.9% do not have insurance; 0.0% of children under 18 do not have insurance

Transportation: Commute: 93.2% car, 0.0% public transportation, 0.0% walk, 5.2% work from home; Mean travel time to work: 28.3 minutes

Additional Information Contacts
Town of Bethel . . . . (845) 583-4350
http://www.town.bethel.ny.us

BLOOMINGBURG (village).
Covers a land area of 0.309 square miles and a water area of 0 square miles. Located at 41.56° N. Lat; 74.44° W. Long. Elevation is 515 feet.
History: Also spelled Bloomingburgh.
Population: 471; Growth (since 2000): 33.4%; Density: 1,525.5 persons per square mile; Race: 81.5% White, 11.0% Black/African American, 0.0% Asian, 0.0% American Indian/Alaska Native, 0.0% Native Hawaiian/Other Pacific Islander, 6.6% Two or more races, 4.9% Hispanic of any race;

Average household size: 2.89; Median age: 31.3; Age under 18: 27.0%; Age 65 and over: 15.9%; Males per 100 females: 92.7; Marriage status: 38.6% never married, 42.3% now married, 4.8% separated, 10.3% widowed, 8.7% divorced; Foreign born: 8.1%; Speak English only: 87.4%; With disability: 12.5%; Veterans: 6.4%; Ancestry: 21.0% Irish, 17.0% Italian, 14.0% German, 10.2% American, 7.9% Polish
Employment: 10.8% management, business, and financial, 0.0% computer, engineering, and science, 5.1% education, legal, community service, arts, and media, 8.2% healthcare practitioners, 31.0% service, 24.7% sales and office, 10.8% natural resources, construction, and maintenance, 9.5% production, transportation, and material moving
Income: Per capita: $16,786; Median household: $45,417; Average household: $48,494; Households with income of $100,000 or more: 11.0%; Poverty rate: 16.8%
Educational Attainment: High school diploma or higher: 88.0%; Bachelor's degree or higher: 9.1%; Graduate/professional degree or higher: 0.7%
Housing: Homeownership rate: 34.4%; Median home value: $203,800; Median year structure built: 1955; Homeowner vacancy rate: 15.2%; Median selected monthly owner costs: $2,050 with a mortgage, $819 without a mortgage; Median gross rent: $877 per month; Rental vacancy rate: 16.7%
Health Insurance: 89.4% have insurance; 59.7% have private insurance; 42.7% have public insurance; 10.6% do not have insurance; 4.7% of children under 18 do not have insurance
Transportation: Commute: 91.1% car, 5.1% public transportation, 1.9% walk, 1.9% work from home; Mean travel time to work: 25.2 minutes

BURLINGHAM (unincorporated postal area)
ZCTA: 12722
Covers a land area of 0.278 square miles and a water area of 0 square miles. Located at 41.59° N. Lat; 74.37° W. Long. Elevation is 400 feet.
Population: 238; Growth (since 2000): n/a; Density: 855.1 persons per square mile; Race: 100.0% White, 0.0% Black/African American, 0.0% Asian, 0.0% American Indian/Alaska Native, 0.0% Native Hawaiian/Other Pacific Islander, 0.0% Two or more races, 0.0% Hispanic of any race; Average household size: 2.83; Median age: 54.8; Age under 18: 17.2%; Age 65 and over: 47.9%; Males per 100 females: 100.0; Marriage status: 29.0% never married, 71.0% now married, 31.9% separated, 0.0% widowed, 0.0% divorced; Foreign born: 0.0%; Speak English only: 100.0%; With disability: 23.9%; Veterans: 28.4%; Ancestry: 35.7% Irish, 31.9% Italian, 12.2% French, 12.2% Yugoslavian
Employment: 0.0% management, business, and financial, 0.0% computer, engineering, and science, 0.0% education, legal, community service, arts, and media, 0.0% healthcare practitioners, 26.3% service, 0.0% sales and office, 0.0% natural resources, construction, and maintenance, 73.7% production, transportation, and material moving
Income: Per capita: $23,646; Median household: n/a; Average household: $62,751; Households with income of $100,000 or more: 23.8%; Poverty rate: n/a
Educational Attainment: High school diploma or higher: 82.8%; Bachelor's degree or higher: n/a; Graduate/professional degree or higher: n/a
Housing: Homeownership rate: 100.0%; Median home value: n/a; Median year structure built: 1989; Homeowner vacancy rate: 0.0%; Median selected monthly owner costs: $0 with a mortgage, $0 without a mortgage; Median gross rent: n/a per month; Rental vacancy rate: 0.0%
Health Insurance: 76.5% have insurance; 44.5% have private insurance; 56.3% have public insurance; 23.5% do not have insurance; 0.0% of children under 18 do not have insurance
Transportation: Commute: 100.0% car, 0.0% public transportation, 0.0% walk, 0.0% work from home; Mean travel time to work: 0.0 minutes

CALLICOON (CDP). Covers a land area of 0.359 square miles and a water area of 0.086 square miles. Located at 41.77° N. Lat; 75.06° W. Long. Elevation is 840 feet.
Population: 172; Growth (since 2000): -20.4%; Density: 479.6 persons per square mile; Race: 83.1% White, 2.9% Black/African American, 0.0% Asian, 0.0% American Indian/Alaska Native, 0.0% Native Hawaiian/Other Pacific Islander, 4.7% Two or more races, 9.3% Hispanic of any race; Average household size: 1.56; Median age: 44.3; Age under 18: 16.9%; Age 65 and over: 7.0%; Males per 100 females: 85.6; Marriage status: 42.3% never married, 34.2% now married, 0.0% separated, 4.0% widowed, 19.5% divorced; Foreign born: 2.9%; Speak English only:

100.0%; With disability: 3.5%; Veterans: 26.6%; Ancestry: 29.7% German, 16.9% Irish, 15.7% Scottish, 14.5% Italian, 9.3% Ukrainian
Employment: 25.4% management, business, and financial, 0.0% computer, engineering, and science, 14.9% education, legal, community service, arts, and media, 0.0% healthcare practitioners, 4.4% service, 25.4% sales and office, 29.8% natural resources, construction, and maintenance, 0.0% production, transportation, and material moving
Income: Per capita: $28,182; Median household: $39,063; Average household: $43,258; Households with income of $100,000 or more: n/a; Poverty rate: n/a
Educational Attainment: High school diploma or higher: 98.5%; Bachelor's degree or higher: 22.2%; Graduate/professional degree or higher: n/a
Housing: Homeownership rate: 52.7%; Median home value: $161,300; Median year structure built: Before 1940; Homeowner vacancy rate: 0.0%; Median selected monthly owner costs: $1,448 with a mortgage, $823 without a mortgage; Median gross rent: n/a per month; Rental vacancy rate: 0.0%
Health Insurance: 83.1% have insurance; 75.6% have private insurance; 34.3% have public insurance; 16.9% do not have insurance; 0.0% of children under 18 do not have insurance
Hospitals: Catskill Regional Medical Center - G Hermann Site
Newspapers: Sullivan County Democrat (weekly circulation 8,300)
Transportation: Commute: 46.5% car, 0.0% public transportation, 41.2% walk, 12.3% work from home; Mean travel time to work: 21.0 minutes

CALLICOON (town). Covers a land area of 48.591 square miles and a water area of 0.355 square miles. Located at 41.84° N. Lat; 74.92° W. Long. Elevation is 840 feet.
History: Seat of St. Joseph Seraphic Seminary.
Population: 2,998; Growth (since 2000): -1.8%; Density: 61.7 persons per square mile; Race: 96.8% White, 0.6% Black/African American, 1.5% Asian, 0.0% American Indian/Alaska Native, 0.0% Native Hawaiian/Other Pacific Islander, 0.6% Two or more races, 4.0% Hispanic of any race; Average household size: 2.24; Median age: 50.1; Age under 18: 18.8%; Age 65 and over: 23.9%; Males per 100 females: 99.3; Marriage status: 16.7% never married, 65.1% now married, 1.2% separated, 5.1% widowed, 13.0% divorced; Foreign born: 6.2%; Speak English only: 94.9%; With disability: 11.5%; Veterans: 8.5%; Ancestry: 31.6% German, 23.5% Irish, 12.3% American, 9.7% Italian, 9.6% English
Employment: 11.2% management, business, and financial, 1.4% computer, engineering, and science, 31.7% education, legal, community service, arts, and media, 3.6% healthcare practitioners, 16.1% service, 12.9% sales and office, 18.1% natural resources, construction, and maintenance, 4.9% production, transportation, and material moving
Income: Per capita: $30,648; Median household: $62,783; Average household: $67,619; Households with income of $100,000 or more: 27.7%; Poverty rate: 9.1%
Educational Attainment: High school diploma or higher: 94.5%; Bachelor's degree or higher: 33.7%; Graduate/professional degree or higher: 20.0%
Housing: Homeownership rate: 77.1%; Median home value: $206,400; Median year structure built: 1973; Homeowner vacancy rate: 4.6%; Median selected monthly owner costs: $1,648 with a mortgage, $641 without a mortgage; Median gross rent: $840 per month; Rental vacancy rate: 2.0%
Health Insurance: 89.6% have insurance; 80.1% have private insurance; 32.4% have public insurance; 10.4% do not have insurance; 3.3% of children under 18 do not have insurance
Hospitals: Catskill Regional Medical Center - G Hermann Site
Newspapers: Sullivan County Democrat (weekly circulation 8,300)
Transportation: Commute: 85.8% car, 1.9% public transportation, 1.7% walk, 10.5% work from home; Mean travel time to work: 31.8 minutes

CALLICOON CENTER (unincorporated postal area)
ZCTA: 12724
Covers a land area of 7.556 square miles and a water area of <.001 square miles. Located at 41.84° N. Lat; 74.96° W. Long. Elevation is 1,253 feet.
Population: 323; Growth (since 2000): 9.1%; Density: 42.7 persons per square mile; Race: 100.0% White, 0.0% Black/African American, 0.0% Asian, 0.0% American Indian/Alaska Native, 0.0% Native Hawaiian/Other Pacific Islander, 0.0% Two or more races, 0.0% Hispanic of any race; Average household size: 2.17; Median age: 43.8; Age under 18: 20.4%; Age 65 and over: 31.9%; Males per 100 females: 100.8; Marriage status: 21.4% never married, 65.0% now married, 0.0%

separated, 9.3% widowed, 4.3% divorced; Foreign born: 0.0%; Speak English only: 100.0%; With disability: 13.9%; Veterans: 16.0%; Ancestry: 52.9% Irish, 32.8% German, 6.2% Danish, 6.2% English, 2.5% American
Employment: 37.1% management, business, and financial, 0.0% computer, engineering, and science, 25.9% education, legal, community service, arts, and media, 0.0% healthcare practitioners, 0.0% service, 17.2% sales and office, 19.8% natural resources, construction, and maintenance, 0.0% production, transportation, and material moving
Income: Per capita: $27,599; Median household: $60,848; Average household: $59,315; Households with income of $100,000 or more: 12.1%; Poverty rate: n/a
Educational Attainment: High school diploma or higher: 91.4%; Bachelor's degree or higher: 6.9%; Graduate/professional degree or higher: n/a
Housing: Homeownership rate: 77.2%; Median home value: n/a; Median year structure built: Before 1940; Homeowner vacancy rate: 0.0%; Median selected monthly owner costs: n/a with a mortgage, n/a without a mortgage; Median gross rent: n/a per month; Rental vacancy rate: 0.0%
Health Insurance: 92.9% have insurance; 92.9% have private insurance; 31.9% have public insurance; 7.1% do not have insurance; 0.0% of children under 18 do not have insurance
Transportation: Commute: 84.5% car, 0.0% public transportation, 0.0% walk, 15.5% work from home; Mean travel time to work: 47.2 minutes

CLARYVILLE (unincorporated postal area)
ZCTA: 12725
Covers a land area of 67.785 square miles and a water area of 0.104 square miles. Located at 41.98° N. Lat; 74.57° W. Long. Elevation is 1,617 feet.
Population: 208; Growth (since 2000): -20.0%; Density: 3.1 persons per square mile; Race: 98.1% White, 0.0% Black/African American, 1.9% Asian, 0.0% American Indian/Alaska Native, 0.0% Native Hawaiian/Other Pacific Islander, 0.0% Two or more races, 2.4% Hispanic of any race; Average household size: 1.98; Median age: 42.5; Age under 18: 28.4%; Age 65 and over: 29.8%; Males per 100 females: 102.2; Marriage status: 25.0% never married, 61.3% now married, 1.3% separated, 9.4% widowed, 4.4% divorced; Foreign born: 2.9%; Speak English only: 96.5%; With disability: 14.9%; Veterans: 12.8%; Ancestry: 33.2% Irish, 22.1% German, 18.3% Russian, 17.3% American, 16.8% Polish
Employment: 12.8% management, business, and financial, 2.6% computer, engineering, and science, 12.8% education, legal, community service, arts, and media, 10.3% healthcare practitioners, 19.2% service, 20.5% sales and office, 15.4% natural resources, construction, and maintenance, 6.4% production, transportation, and material moving
Income: Per capita: $29,900; Median household: $43,750; Average household: $69,646; Households with income of $100,000 or more: 21.1%; Poverty rate: 8.4%
Educational Attainment: High school diploma or higher: 96.4%; Bachelor's degree or higher: 47.5%; Graduate/professional degree or higher: 18.0%
Housing: Homeownership rate: 81.1%; Median home value: $243,800; Median year structure built: 1969; Homeowner vacancy rate: 6.4%; Median selected monthly owner costs: $1,188 with a mortgage, $550 without a mortgage; Median gross rent: n/a per month; Rental vacancy rate: 0.0%
Health Insurance: 95.7% have insurance; 67.8% have private insurance; 55.8% have public insurance; 4.3% do not have insurance; 0.0% of children under 18 do not have insurance
Transportation: Commute: 80.8% car, 2.6% public transportation, 0.0% walk, 12.8% work from home; Mean travel time to work: 37.0 minutes

COCHECTON (town). Covers a land area of 36.241 square miles and a water area of 0.790 square miles. Located at 41.68° N. Lat; 74.99° W. Long. Elevation is 732 feet.
Population: 1,437; Growth (since 2000): 8.2%; Density: 39.7 persons per square mile; Race: 92.6% White, 0.8% Black/African American, 0.6% Asian, 0.5% American Indian/Alaska Native, 0.0% Native Hawaiian/Other Pacific Islander, 1.6% Two or more races, 5.8% Hispanic of any race; Average household size: 2.32; Median age: 47.3; Age under 18: 16.3%; Age 65 and over: 23.2%; Males per 100 females: 100.6; Marriage status: 32.5% never married, 50.8% now married, 1.9% separated, 9.2% widowed, 7.5% divorced; Foreign born: 4.8%; Speak English only: 94.8%;

With disability: 15.9%; Veterans: 11.1%; Ancestry: 29.9% German, 16.7% Irish, 11.8% Italian, 7.9% American, 7.9% English
Employment: 15.2% management, business, and financial, 2.2% computer, engineering, and science, 18.1% education, legal, community service, arts, and media, 3.2% healthcare practitioners, 18.0% service, 18.1% sales and office, 14.6% natural resources, construction, and maintenance, 10.6% production, transportation, and material moving
Income: Per capita: $27,975; Median household: $56,667; Average household: $64,194; Households with income of $100,000 or more: 19.9%; Poverty rate: 12.2%
Educational Attainment: High school diploma or higher: 94.5%; Bachelor's degree or higher: 27.5%; Graduate/professional degree or higher: 12.2%
Housing: Homeownership rate: 80.3%; Median home value: $171,800; Median year structure built: 1965; Homeowner vacancy rate: 4.5%; Median selected monthly owner costs: $1,419 with a mortgage, $623 without a mortgage; Median gross rent: $868 per month; Rental vacancy rate: 11.6%
Health Insurance: 89.7% have insurance; 76.8% have private insurance; 32.7% have public insurance; 10.3% do not have insurance; 6.0% of children under 18 do not have insurance
Transportation: Commute: 88.4% car, 0.8% public transportation, 2.3% walk, 7.7% work from home; Mean travel time to work: 37.8 minutes

DELAWARE (town). Covers a land area of 34.941 square miles and a water area of 0.703 square miles. Located at 41.75° N. Lat; 75.00° W. Long.
Population: 2,620; Growth (since 2000): -3.6%; Density: 75.0 persons per square mile; Race: 86.8% White, 3.0% Black/African American, 2.2% Asian, 0.3% American Indian/Alaska Native, 0.0% Native Hawaiian/Other Pacific Islander, 3.9% Two or more races, 7.1% Hispanic of any race; Average household size: 2.35; Median age: 44.4; Age under 18: 18.1%; Age 65 and over: 16.4%; Males per 100 females: 96.3; Marriage status: 32.4% never married, 52.5% now married, 2.7% separated, 7.0% widowed, 8.0% divorced; Foreign born: 9.2%; Speak English only: 88.2%; With disability: 10.8%; Veterans: 12.5%; Ancestry: 37.1% German, 24.0% Irish, 7.1% Italian, 6.9% English, 6.6% American
Employment: 8.0% management, business, and financial, 1.6% computer, engineering, and science, 11.9% education, legal, community service, arts, and media, 4.1% healthcare practitioners, 24.3% service, 17.2% sales and office, 25.0% natural resources, construction, and maintenance, 8.0% production, transportation, and material moving
Income: Per capita: $29,998; Median household: $61,705; Average household: $73,869; Households with income of $100,000 or more: 23.0%; Poverty rate: 12.0%
Educational Attainment: High school diploma or higher: 95.6%; Bachelor's degree or higher: 27.3%; Graduate/professional degree or higher: 11.2%
Housing: Homeownership rate: 74.2%; Median home value: $214,800; Median year structure built: 1951; Homeowner vacancy rate: 3.4%; Median selected monthly owner costs: $1,585 with a mortgage, $724 without a mortgage; Median gross rent: $873 per month; Rental vacancy rate: 1.9%
Health Insurance: 93.4% have insurance; 76.2% have private insurance; 33.3% have public insurance; 6.6% do not have insurance; 0.0% of children under 18 do not have insurance
Transportation: Commute: 78.9% car, 2.3% public transportation, 8.4% walk, 7.3% work from home; Mean travel time to work: 28.8 minutes

ELDRED (unincorporated postal area)
ZCTA: 12732
Covers a land area of 25.067 square miles and a water area of 0.760 square miles. Located at 41.55° N. Lat; 74.87° W. Long. Elevation is 971 feet.
Population: 788; Growth (since 2000): -12.4%; Density: 31.4 persons per square mile; Race: 93.1% White, 3.0% Black/African American, 2.5% Asian, 0.0% American Indian/Alaska Native, 0.0% Native Hawaiian/Other Pacific Islander, 0.0% Two or more races, 2.9% Hispanic of any race; Average household size: 2.07; Median age: 47.6; Age under 18: 22.1%; Age 65 and over: 20.4%; Males per 100 females: 91.2; Marriage status: 23.7% never married, 59.1% now married, 1.8% separated, 9.1% widowed, 8.1% divorced; Foreign born: 6.6%; Speak English only: 93.5%; With disability: 14.2%; Veterans: 9.3%; Ancestry: 38.5% German, 29.3% Irish, 14.2% American, 9.9% English, 8.0% French
Employment: 13.8% management, business, and financial, 1.4% computer, engineering, and science, 2.3% education, legal, community

service, arts, and media, 3.7% healthcare practitioners, 10.9% service, 27.5% sales and office, 17.5% natural resources, construction, and maintenance, 22.9% production, transportation, and material moving
Income: Per capita: $30,311; Median household: $40,568; Average household: $63,134; Households with income of $100,000 or more: 13.4%; Poverty rate: 12.8%
Educational Attainment: High school diploma or higher: 94.3%; Bachelor's degree or higher: 17.9%; Graduate/professional degree or higher: 4.1%

School District(s)
Eldred Central SD (PK-12)
    2014-15 Enrollment: 629 . . . . (845) 456-1100
Housing: Homeownership rate: 70.3%; Median home value: $171,700; Median year structure built: 1967; Homeowner vacancy rate: 2.2%; Median selected monthly owner costs: $1,205 with a mortgage, $568 without a mortgage; Median gross rent: $926 per month; Rental vacancy rate: 11.7%
Health Insurance: 74.7% have insurance; 58.9% have private insurance; 33.5% have public insurance; 25.3% do not have insurance; 28.2% of children under 18 do not have insurance
Transportation: Commute: 95.1% car, 1.5% public transportation, 1.7% walk, 0.0% work from home; Mean travel time to work: 52.6 minutes

---

FALLSBURG (town). Covers a land area of 77.622 square miles and a water area of 1.488 square miles. Located at 41.74° N. Lat; 74.60° W. Long. Elevation is 1,207 feet.
History: Fallsburg takes its name from a waterfall on the Neversink River and was established in 1826. The town is in the heart of a once popular predominately Jewish summer resort area known as the Catskills Borscht Belt.
Population: 12,879; Growth (since 2000): 5.3%; Density: 165.9 persons per square mile; Race: 67.9% White, 13.7% Black/African American, 2.1% Asian, 0.5% American Indian/Alaska Native, 0.0% Native Hawaiian/Other Pacific Islander, 5.1% Two or more races, 23.9% Hispanic of any race; Average household size: 2.80; Median age: 36.7; Age under 18: 25.9%; Age 65 and over: 12.2%; Males per 100 females: 124.0; Marriage status: 39.9% never married, 44.2% now married, 3.6% separated, 6.1% widowed, 9.9% divorced; Foreign born: 15.3%; Speak English only: 71.8%; With disability: 16.6%; Veterans: 8.3%; Ancestry: 13.7% German, 13.2% Irish, 8.2% Italian, 7.3% Polish, 4.6% English
Employment: 11.0% management, business, and financial, 2.4% computer, engineering, and science, 16.0% education, legal, community service, arts, and media, 2.7% healthcare practitioners, 23.8% service, 23.3% sales and office, 9.2% natural resources, construction, and maintenance, 11.5% production, transportation, and material moving
Income: Per capita: $18,509; Median household: $43,340; Average household: $56,605; Households with income of $100,000 or more: 14.0%; Poverty rate: 28.9%
Educational Attainment: High school diploma or higher: 79.8%; Bachelor's degree or higher: 19.7%; Graduate/professional degree or higher: 11.0%

School District(s)
Fallsburg Central SD (PK-12)
    2014-15 Enrollment: 1,430 . . . . (845) 434-5884
Housing: Homeownership rate: 54.3%; Median home value: $155,800; Median year structure built: 1982; Homeowner vacancy rate: 4.2%; Median selected monthly owner costs: $1,501 with a mortgage, $687 without a mortgage; Median gross rent: $814 per month; Rental vacancy rate: 11.9%
Health Insurance: 88.5% have insurance; 49.9% have private insurance; 50.9% have public insurance; 11.5% do not have insurance; 3.2% of children under 18 do not have insurance
Safety: Violent crime rate: 14.1 per 10,000 population; Property crime rate: 92.1 per 10,000 population
Transportation: Commute: 81.4% car, 1.2% public transportation, 8.8% walk, 6.7% work from home; Mean travel time to work: 18.4 minutes
Additional Information Contacts
Town of Fallsburg . . . . (845) 434-8810
  http://www.townoffallsburg.com

FERNDALE (unincorporated postal area)
ZCTA: 12734
  Covers a land area of 13.772 square miles and a water area of 0.036 square miles. Located at 41.73° N. Lat; 74.75° W. Long. Elevation is 1,345 feet.

Population: 976; Growth (since 2000): 16.6%; Density: 70.9 persons per square mile; Race: 95.9% White, 0.0% Black/African American, 1.5% Asian, 0.0% American Indian/Alaska Native, 0.0% Native Hawaiian/Other Pacific Islander, 0.0% Two or more races, 21.9% Hispanic of any race; Average household size: 2.42; Median age: 48.4; Age under 18: 27.8%; Age 65 and over: 27.0%; Males per 100 females: 114.1; Marriage status: 18.9% never married, 61.6% now married, 5.4% separated, 8.9% widowed, 10.6% divorced; Foreign born: 8.8%; Speak English only: 87.7%; With disability: 12.4%; Veterans: 9.4%; Ancestry: 24.1% German, 19.9% Irish, 10.0% English, 9.7% Italian, 5.0% French
Employment: 13.9% management, business, and financial, 0.0% computer, engineering, and science, 23.7% education, legal, community service, arts, and media, 11.3% healthcare practitioners, 19.1% service, 13.4% sales and office, 13.1% natural resources, construction, and maintenance, 5.5% production, transportation, and material moving
Income: Per capita: $32,054; Median household: $62,632; Average household: $67,893; Households with income of $100,000 or more: 13.7%; Poverty rate: 5.2%
Educational Attainment: High school diploma or higher: 79.8%; Bachelor's degree or higher: 31.0%; Graduate/professional degree or higher: 10.8%
Housing: Homeownership rate: 77.3%; Median home value: $170,300; Median year structure built: 1970; Homeowner vacancy rate: 4.5%; Median selected monthly owner costs: $1,819 with a mortgage, $573 without a mortgage; Median gross rent: $773 per month; Rental vacancy rate: 0.0%
Health Insurance: 94.8% have insurance; 84.9% have private insurance; 28.0% have public insurance; 5.2% do not have insurance; 0.0% of children under 18 do not have insurance
Transportation: Commute: 90.7% car, 0.0% public transportation, 0.0% walk, 9.3% work from home; Mean travel time to work: 22.2 minutes

---

FORESTBURGH (town). Covers a land area of 54.781 square miles and a water area of 1.532 square miles. Located at 41.56° N. Lat; 74.71° W. Long.
Population: 978; Growth (since 2000): 17.4%; Density: 17.9 persons per square mile; Race: 97.3% White, 1.1% Black/African American, 1.1% Asian, 0.0% American Indian/Alaska Native, 0.0% Native Hawaiian/Other Pacific Islander, 0.4% Two or more races, 2.5% Hispanic of any race; Average household size: 2.55; Median age: 49.6; Age under 18: 18.3%; Age 65 and over: 17.6%; Males per 100 females: 99.3; Marriage status: 21.9% never married, 59.6% now married, 2.5% separated, 7.2% widowed, 11.3% divorced; Foreign born: 8.5%; Speak English only: 90.7%; With disability: 14.1%; Veterans: 11.1%; Ancestry: 28.7% German, 24.2% Irish, 17.6% Italian, 9.5% English, 5.1% Russian
Employment: 22.7% management, business, and financial, 3.9% computer, engineering, and science, 15.5% education, legal, community service, arts, and media, 3.9% healthcare practitioners, 15.9% service, 18.4% sales and office, 12.2% natural resources, construction, and maintenance, 7.6% production, transportation, and material moving
Income: Per capita: $46,786; Median household: $72,500; Average household: $114,052; Households with income of $100,000 or more: 34.0%; Poverty rate: 2.5%
Educational Attainment: High school diploma or higher: 90.1%; Bachelor's degree or higher: 34.1%; Graduate/professional degree or higher: 16.7%
Housing: Homeownership rate: 85.2%; Median home value: $210,800; Median year structure built: 1967; Homeowner vacancy rate: 1.8%; Median selected monthly owner costs: $1,913 with a mortgage, $715 without a mortgage; Median gross rent: $913 per month; Rental vacancy rate: 16.4%
Health Insurance: 94.6% have insurance; 78.6% have private insurance; 30.7% have public insurance; 5.4% do not have insurance; 0.0% of children under 18 do not have insurance
Transportation: Commute: 85.0% car, 3.1% public transportation, 1.7% walk, 5.6% work from home; Mean travel time to work: 34.5 minutes

---

FREMONT (town). Covers a land area of 50.186 square miles and a water area of 1.046 square miles. Located at 41.87° N. Lat; 75.03° W. Long.
Population: 1,314; Growth (since 2000): -5.5%; Density: 26.2 persons per square mile; Race: 97.3% White, 1.8% Black/African American, 0.7% Asian, 0.0% American Indian/Alaska Native, 0.0% Native Hawaiian/Other Pacific Islander, 0.0% Two or more races, 3.0% Hispanic of any race; Average household size: 2.41; Median age: 47.0; Age under 18: 16.3%; Age 65 and over: 21.6%; Males per 100 females: 106.4; Marriage status:

27.6% never married, 55.2% now married, 4.0% separated, 7.6% widowed, 9.6% divorced; Foreign born: 4.3%; Speak English only: 95.4%; With disability: 14.4%; Veterans: 7.2%; Ancestry: 30.8% German, 26.0% Irish, 14.5% Italian, 12.2% English, 9.4% American

Employment: 12.4% management, business, and financial, 5.1% computer, engineering, and science, 21.4% education, legal, community service, arts, and media, 1.3% healthcare practitioners, 20.9% service, 23.1% sales and office, 12.3% natural resources, construction, and maintenance, 3.5% production, transportation, and material moving

Income: Per capita: $25,981; Median household: $46,563; Average household: $59,107; Households with income of $100,000 or more: 15.5%; Poverty rate: 7.6%

Educational Attainment: High school diploma or higher: 84.8%; Bachelor's degree or higher: 30.7%; Graduate/professional degree or higher: 13.3%

Housing: Homeownership rate: 83.8%; Median home value: $174,600; Median year structure built: 1960; Homeowner vacancy rate: 2.6%; Median selected monthly owner costs: $1,276 with a mortgage, $544 without a mortgage; Median gross rent: $900 per month; Rental vacancy rate: 0.0%

Health Insurance: 90.4% have insurance; 80.4% have private insurance; 31.4% have public insurance; 9.6% do not have insurance; 4.7% of children under 18 do not have insurance

Transportation: Commute: 82.5% car, 0.5% public transportation, 3.7% walk, 13.3% work from home; Mean travel time to work: 23.5 minutes

FREMONT CENTER (unincorporated postal area)
ZCTA: 12736

Covers a land area of 6.086 square miles and a water area of <.001 square miles. Located at 41.85° N. Lat; 75.02° W. Long. Elevation is 1,240 feet.

Population: 157; Growth (since 2000): 3.3%; Density: 25.8 persons per square mile; Race: 100.0% White, 0.0% Black/African American, 0.0% Asian, 0.0% American Indian/Alaska Native, 0.0% Native Hawaiian/Other Pacific Islander, 0.0% Two or more races, 7.6% Hispanic of any race; Average household size: 2.34; Median age: 48.6; Age under 18: 11.5%; Age 65 and over: 17.8%; Males per 100 females: 114.5; Marriage status: 16.7% never married, 78.0% now married, 8.0% separated, 2.0% widowed, 3.3% divorced; Foreign born: 5.1%; Speak English only: 87.9%; With disability: 25.5%; Veterans: 5.8%; Ancestry: 73.9% German, 51.0% Irish, 7.0% Polish, 6.4% Italian, 3.8% English

Employment: 0.0% management, business, and financial, 0.0% computer, engineering, and science, 14.4% education, legal, community service, arts, and media, 0.0% healthcare practitioners, 15.6% service, 45.6% sales and office, 16.7% natural resources, construction, and maintenance, 7.8% production, transportation, and material moving

Income: Per capita: $20,650; Median household: $35,938; Average household: $47,197; Households with income of $100,000 or more: 4.5%; Poverty rate: 10.8%

Educational Attainment: High school diploma or higher: 92.8%; Bachelor's degree or higher: 12.8%; Graduate/professional degree or higher: 10.4%

Housing: Homeownership rate: 100.0%; Median home value: n/a; Median year structure built: 1973; Homeowner vacancy rate: 0.0%; Median selected monthly owner costs: $735 with a mortgage, $565 without a mortgage; Median gross rent: n/a per month; Rental vacancy rate: 0.0%

Health Insurance: 81.5% have insurance; 67.5% have private insurance; 25.5% have public insurance; 18.5% do not have insurance; 0.0% of children under 18 do not have insurance

Transportation: Commute: 100.0% car, 0.0% public transportation, 0.0% walk, 0.0% work from home; Mean travel time to work: 19.0 minutes

GLEN SPEY (unincorporated postal area)
ZCTA: 12737

Covers a land area of 35.801 square miles and a water area of 2.321 square miles. Located at 41.50° N. Lat; 74.80° W. Long. Elevation is 1,283 feet.

Population: 1,969; Growth (since 2000): 31.3%; Density: 55.0 persons per square mile; Race: 91.2% White, 0.7% Black/African American, 5.6% Asian, 0.4% American Indian/Alaska Native, 0.0% Native Hawaiian/Other Pacific Islander, 0.0% Two or more races, 9.4% Hispanic of any race; Average household size: 2.63; Median age: 41.9; Age under 18: 27.5%; Age 65 and over: 18.4%; Males per 100 females: 101.7; Marriage status: 19.7% never married, 60.7% now married, 0.8%

separated, 5.9% widowed, 13.7% divorced; Foreign born: 14.6%; Speak English only: 82.0%; With disability: 17.7%; Veterans: 5.8%; Ancestry: 24.3% Irish, 17.3% German, 10.6% Italian, 8.4% Polish, 8.3% Ukrainian

Employment: 12.7% management, business, and financial, 5.7% computer, engineering, and science, 13.9% education, legal, community service, arts, and media, 5.1% healthcare practitioners, 16.7% service, 22.9% sales and office, 14.3% natural resources, construction, and maintenance, 8.7% production, transportation, and material moving

Income: Per capita: $27,819; Median household: $65,500; Average household: $72,323; Households with income of $100,000 or more: 21.8%; Poverty rate: 9.1%

Educational Attainment: High school diploma or higher: 91.9%; Bachelor's degree or higher: 30.5%; Graduate/professional degree or higher: 13.8%

School District(s)
Eldred Central SD (PK-12)
   2014-15 Enrollment: 629 . . . . (845) 456-1100

Housing: Homeownership rate: 82.2%; Median home value: $182,900; Median year structure built: 1976; Homeowner vacancy rate: 4.3%; Median selected monthly owner costs: $1,983 with a mortgage, $719 without a mortgage; Median gross rent: $881 per month; Rental vacancy rate: 9.3%

Health Insurance: 91.4% have insurance; 70.2% have private insurance; 36.2% have public insurance; 8.6% do not have insurance; 3.5% of children under 18 do not have insurance

Transportation: Commute: 85.6% car, 3.5% public transportation, 1.9% walk, 7.8% work from home; Mean travel time to work: 40.3 minutes

GLEN WILD (unincorporated postal area)
ZCTA: 12738

Covers a land area of 6.559 square miles and a water area of 0.047 square miles. Located at 41.68° N. Lat; 74.59° W. Long. Elevation is 1,322 feet.

Population: 549; Growth (since 2000): 71.6%; Density: 83.7 persons per square mile; Race: 97.8% White, 0.0% Black/African American, 0.0% Asian, 0.0% American Indian/Alaska Native, 0.0% Native Hawaiian/Other Pacific Islander, 2.2% Two or more races, 23.5% Hispanic of any race; Average household size: 3.05; Median age: 39.5; Age under 18: 33.5%; Age 65 and over: 16.9%; Males per 100 females: 93.9; Marriage status: 19.2% never married, 68.8% now married, 2.5% separated, 9.3% widowed, 2.7% divorced; Foreign born: 0.9%; Speak English only: 95.2%; With disability: 10.7%; Veterans: 17.8%; Ancestry: 30.6% European, 15.7% Irish, 14.8% Scottish, 11.7% Italian, 9.7% American

Employment: 16.6% management, business, and financial, 0.0% computer, engineering, and science, 8.7% education, legal, community service, arts, and media, 9.1% healthcare practitioners, 7.1% service, 43.9% sales and office, 11.5% natural resources, construction, and maintenance, 3.2% production, transportation, and material moving

Income: Per capita: $39,745; Median household: $75,600; Average household: $125,103; Households with income of $100,000 or more: 34.4%; Poverty rate: 2.6%

Educational Attainment: High school diploma or higher: 93.2%; Bachelor's degree or higher: 53.4%; Graduate/professional degree or higher: 8.5%

Housing: Homeownership rate: 76.1%; Median home value: $180,100; Median year structure built: 1974; Homeowner vacancy rate: 13.8%; Median selected monthly owner costs: $1,230 with a mortgage, $857 without a mortgage; Median gross rent: $886 per month; Rental vacancy rate: 0.0%

Health Insurance: 100.0% have insurance; 92.2% have private insurance; 20.4% have public insurance; 0.0% do not have insurance; 0.0% of children under 18 do not have insurance

Transportation: Commute: 96.4% car, 0.0% public transportation, 0.0% walk, 3.6% work from home; Mean travel time to work: 19.7 minutes

GRAHAMSVILLE (unincorporated postal area)
ZCTA: 12740

Covers a land area of 74.355 square miles and a water area of 1.051 square miles. Located at 41.94° N. Lat; 74.43° W. Long. Elevation is 968 feet.

Population: 1,628; Growth (since 2000): -22.0%; Density: 21.9 persons per square mile; Race: 96.6% White, 1.2% Black/African American, 0.0% Asian, 0.0% American Indian/Alaska Native, 0.0% Native Hawaiian/Other Pacific Islander, 1.8% Two or more races, 8.7%

Hispanic of any race; Average household size: 2.50; Median age: 46.5; Age under 18: 16.0%; Age 65 and over: 21.7%; Males per 100 females: 98.5; Marriage status: 30.5% never married, 50.7% now married, 2.2% separated, 8.8% widowed, 10.1% divorced; Foreign born: 3.6%; Speak English only: 95.3%; With disability: 17.6%; Veterans: 11.3%; Ancestry: 24.2% German, 19.0% Irish, 16.2% Italian, 14.8% Dutch, 12.1% English
Employment: 13.8% management, business, and financial, 5.6% computer, engineering, and science, 10.3% education, legal, community service, arts, and media, 4.2% healthcare practitioners, 28.1% service, 21.5% sales and office, 10.1% natural resources, construction, and maintenance, 6.4% production, transportation, and material moving
Income: Per capita: $29,261; Median household: $59,198; Average household: $71,257; Households with income of $100,000 or more: 21.2%; Poverty rate: 11.1%
Educational Attainment: High school diploma or higher: 90.7%; Bachelor's degree or higher: 17.8%; Graduate/professional degree or higher: 10.1%

School District(s)
Tri-Valley Central SD (PK-12)
   2014-15 Enrollment: 1,120 . . . . (845) 985-2296
Housing: Homeownership rate: 79.9%; Median home value: $217,800; Median year structure built: 1976; Homeowner vacancy rate: 5.1%; Median selected monthly owner costs: $1,551 with a mortgage, $503 without a mortgage; Median gross rent: $1,071 per month; Rental vacancy rate: 0.0%
Health Insurance: 94.8% have insurance; 80.6% have private insurance; 37.0% have public insurance; 5.2% do not have insurance; 0.0% of children under 18 do not have insurance
Transportation: Commute: 91.7% car, 0.0% public transportation, 4.2% walk, 1.8% work from home; Mean travel time to work: 32.0 minutes

HANKINS (unincorporated postal area)
ZCTA: 12741
Covers a land area of 8.248 square miles and a water area of 0.122 square miles. Located at 41.84° N. Lat; 75.08° W. Long. Elevation is 807 feet.
Population: 247; Growth (since 2000): -2.0%; Density: 29.9 persons per square mile; Race: 97.2% White, 2.8% Black/African American, 0.0% Asian, 0.0% American Indian/Alaska Native, 0.0% Native Hawaiian/Other Pacific Islander, 0.0% Two or more races, 0.0% Hispanic of any race; Average household size: 1.82; Median age: 54.4; Age under 18: 14.2%; Age 65 and over: 28.7%; Males per 100 females: 104.1; Marriage status: 31.3% never married, 34.3% now married, 1.7% separated, 11.2% widowed, 23.2% divorced; Foreign born: 4.0%; Speak English only: 100.0%; With disability: 25.9%; Veterans: 4.2%; Ancestry: 35.2% German, 21.1% Irish, 15.4% Italian, 12.1% American, 11.7% English
Employment: 14.0% management, business, and financial, 2.3% computer, engineering, and science, 30.2% education, legal, community service, arts, and media, 0.0% healthcare practitioners, 17.4% service, 25.6% sales and office, 7.0% natural resources, construction, and maintenance, 3.5% production, transportation, and material moving
Income: Per capita: $27,442; Median household: $30,000; Average household: $47,182; Households with income of $100,000 or more: 8.8%; Poverty rate: 9.7%
Educational Attainment: High school diploma or higher: 86.1%; Bachelor's degree or higher: 44.9%; Graduate/professional degree or higher: 23.0%
Housing: Homeownership rate: 70.6%; Median home value: $150,000; Median year structure built: 1943; Homeowner vacancy rate: 0.0%; Median selected monthly owner costs: $833 with a mortgage, $575 without a mortgage; Median gross rent: $669 per month; Rental vacancy rate: 0.0%
Health Insurance: 91.9% have insurance; 75.3% have private insurance; 36.0% have public insurance; 8.1% do not have insurance; 0.0% of children under 18 do not have insurance
Transportation: Commute: 89.6% car, 0.0% public transportation, 0.0% walk, 10.4% work from home; Mean travel time to work: 23.2 minutes

HARRIS (unincorporated postal area)
ZCTA: 12742
Covers a land area of 2.150 square miles and a water area of 0.008 square miles. Located at 41.72° N. Lat; 74.72° W. Long. Elevation is 1,181 feet.

Population: 124; Growth (since 2000): -6.1%; Density: 57.7 persons per square mile; Race: 95.2% White, 0.0% Black/African American, 4.8% Asian, 0.0% American Indian/Alaska Native, 0.0% Native Hawaiian/Other Pacific Islander, 0.0% Two or more races, 23.4% Hispanic of any race; Average household size: 2.43; Median age: 32.8; Age under 18: 21.8%; Age 65 and over: 14.5%; Males per 100 females: 101.1; Marriage status: 27.8% never married, 47.4% now married, 0.0% separated, 6.2% widowed, 18.6% divorced; Foreign born: 12.1%; Speak English only: 100.0%; With disability: 16.9%; Veterans: 5.2%; Ancestry: 17.7% Irish, 16.1% Italian, 10.5% German, 7.3% Brazilian, 6.5% American
Employment: 18.6% management, business, and financial, 0.0% computer, engineering, and science, 13.6% education, legal, community service, arts, and media, 0.0% healthcare practitioners, 15.3% service, 37.3% sales and office, 5.1% natural resources, construction, and maintenance, 10.2% production, transportation, and material moving
Income: Per capita: $23,775; Median household: $40,781; Average household: $62,741; Households with income of $100,000 or more: 21.6%; Poverty rate: 6.5%
Educational Attainment: High school diploma or higher: 100.0%; Bachelor's degree or higher: 16.5%; Graduate/professional degree or higher: 12.1%
Housing: Homeownership rate: 47.1%; Median home value: $250,000; Median year structure built: 1957; Homeowner vacancy rate: 0.0%; Median selected monthly owner costs: $1,781 with a mortgage, $0 without a mortgage; Median gross rent: $597 per month; Rental vacancy rate: 0.0%
Health Insurance: 92.7% have insurance; 75.8% have private insurance; 38.7% have public insurance; 7.3% do not have insurance; 0.0% of children under 18 do not have insurance
Hospitals: Catskill Regional Medical Center (263 beds)
Transportation: Commute: 100.0% car, 0.0% public transportation, 0.0% walk, 0.0% work from home; Mean travel time to work: 26.1 minutes

HIGHLAND (town). Covers a land area of 50.056 square miles and a water area of 1.867 square miles. Located at 41.57° N. Lat; 74.89° W. Long.
Population: 2,414; Growth (since 2000): 0.4%; Density: 48.2 persons per square mile; Race: 95.4% White, 2.1% Black/African American, 1.3% Asian, 0.2% American Indian/Alaska Native, 0.0% Native Hawaiian/Other Pacific Islander, 0.4% Two or more races, 3.9% Hispanic of any race; Average household size: 2.21; Median age: 49.1; Age under 18: 19.8%; Age 65 and over: 18.2%; Males per 100 females: 102.4; Marriage status: 27.2% never married, 52.8% now married, 4.8% separated, 9.5% widowed, 10.6% divorced; Foreign born: 12.1%; Speak English only: 90.1%; With disability: 17.1%; Veterans: 7.4%; Ancestry: 35.0% German, 25.8% Irish, 8.4% Italian, 8.3% English, 8.1% Polish
Employment: 15.6% management, business, and financial, 3.1% computer, engineering, and science, 10.5% education, legal, community service, arts, and media, 8.0% healthcare practitioners, 14.0% service, 22.8% sales and office, 13.1% natural resources, construction, and maintenance, 12.9% production, transportation, and material moving
Income: Per capita: $30,767; Median household: $47,105; Average household: $70,064; Households with income of $100,000 or more: 15.5%; Poverty rate: 16.2%
Educational Attainment: High school diploma or higher: 90.8%; Bachelor's degree or higher: 24.5%; Graduate/professional degree or higher: 7.7%
Housing: Homeownership rate: 74.7%; Median home value: $183,100; Median year structure built: 1966; Homeowner vacancy rate: 4.6%; Median selected monthly owner costs: $1,452 with a mortgage, $605 without a mortgage; Median gross rent: $921 per month; Rental vacancy rate: 7.3%
Health Insurance: 83.9% have insurance; 63.2% have private insurance; 36.6% have public insurance; 16.1% do not have insurance; 15.9% of children under 18 do not have insurance
Transportation: Commute: 89.7% car, 1.0% public transportation, 2.2% walk, 5.0% work from home; Mean travel time to work: 44.2 minutes

HIGHLAND LAKE (unincorporated postal area)
ZCTA: 12743
Covers a land area of 8.192 square miles and a water area of 0.623 square miles. Located at 41.55° N. Lat; 74.83° W. Long. Elevation is 1,332 feet.

Population: 246; Growth (since 2000): -18.8%; Density: 30.0 persons per square mile; Race: 97.6% White, 0.0% Black/African American, 2.4% Asian, 0.0% American Indian/Alaska Native, 0.0% Native Hawaiian/Other Pacific Islander, 0.0% Two or more races, 3.7% Hispanic of any race; Average household size: 1.81; Median age: 55.4; Age under 18: 9.8%; Age 65 and over: 30.5%; Males per 100 females: 103.7; Marriage status: 16.4% never married, 36.2% now married, 2.2% separated, 17.2% widowed, 30.2% divorced; Foreign born: 15.0%; Speak English only: 88.0%; With disability: 27.2%; Veterans: 5.4%; Ancestry: 31.3% German, 14.6% English, 13.8% Irish, 8.9% Italian, 5.7% French

Employment: 5.7% management, business, and financial, 0.0% computer, engineering, and science, 39.8% education, legal, community service, arts, and media, 6.8% healthcare practitioners, 10.2% service, 9.1% sales and office, 22.7% natural resources, construction, and maintenance, 5.7% production, transportation, and material moving

Income: Per capita: $37,086; Median household: $51,354; Average household: $68,390; Households with income of $100,000 or more: 22.1%; Poverty rate: 8.5%

Educational Attainment: High school diploma or higher: 94.4%; Bachelor's degree or higher: 23.6%; Graduate/professional degree or higher: 13.0%

Housing: Homeownership rate: 74.3%; Median home value: $192,700; Median year structure built: 1965; Homeowner vacancy rate: 0.0%; Median selected monthly owner costs: $1,708 with a mortgage, $445 without a mortgage; Median gross rent: $1,571 per month; Rental vacancy rate: 0.0%

Health Insurance: 86.2% have insurance; 72.0% have private insurance; 44.7% have public insurance; 13.8% do not have insurance; 16.7% of children under 18 do not have insurance

Transportation: Commute: 78.4% car, 5.7% public transportation, 5.7% walk, 10.2% work from home; Mean travel time to work: 41.9 minutes

HORTONVILLE (CDP). Covers a land area of 0.756 square miles and a water area of 0 square miles. Located at 41.77° N. Lat; 75.02° W. Long. Elevation is 804 feet.

Population: 235; Growth (since 2000): n/a; Density: 310.9 persons per square mile; Race: 98.3% White, 0.0% Black/African American, 0.0% Asian, 0.0% American Indian/Alaska Native, 0.0% Native Hawaiian/Other Pacific Islander, 1.7% Two or more races, 0.0% Hispanic of any race; Average household size: 2.50; Median age: 33.8; Age under 18: 10.2%; Age 65 and over: 21.3%; Males per 100 females: 96.4; Marriage status: 44.5% never married, 49.8% now married, 5.2% separated, 2.4% widowed, 3.3% divorced; Foreign born: 2.6%; Speak English only: 97.3%; With disability: 19.6%; Veterans: 19.4%; Ancestry: 37.0% German, 24.7% Irish, 17.4% American, 9.8% Norwegian, 9.8% Scandinavian

Employment: 6.8% management, business, and financial, 0.0% computer, engineering, and science, 0.0% education, legal, community service, arts, and media, 0.0% healthcare practitioners, 46.6% service, 26.1% sales and office, 11.4% natural resources, construction, and maintenance, 9.1% production, transportation, and material moving

Income: Per capita: $26,524; Median household: $64,773; Average household: $66,595; Households with income of $100,000 or more: 10.6%; Poverty rate: n/a

Educational Attainment: High school diploma or higher: 94.5%; Bachelor's degree or higher: 15.8%; Graduate/professional degree or higher: n/a

Housing: Homeownership rate: 46.8%; Median home value: $134,400; Median year structure built: 1950; Homeowner vacancy rate: 4.3%; Median selected monthly owner costs: n/a with a mortgage, n/a without a mortgage; Median gross rent: $689 per month; Rental vacancy rate: 0.0%

Health Insurance: 100.0% have insurance; 70.6% have private insurance; 51.5% have public insurance; 0.0% do not have insurance; 0.0% of children under 18 do not have insurance

Transportation: Commute: 88.1% car, 0.0% public transportation, 11.9% walk, 0.0% work from home; Mean travel time to work: 27.3 minutes

HURLEYVILLE (unincorporated postal area)
ZCTA: 12747

Covers a land area of 13.954 square miles and a water area of 0.452 square miles. Located at 41.75° N. Lat; 74.69° W. Long. Elevation is 1,319 feet.

Population: 1,399; Growth (since 2000): -27.8%; Density: 100.3 persons per square mile; Race: 68.6% White, 17.8% Black/African American, 2.6% Asian, 0.4% American Indian/Alaska Native, 0.0%

Native Hawaiian/Other Pacific Islander, 1.6% Two or more races, 11.8% Hispanic of any race; Average household size: 2.46; Median age: 46.1; Age under 18: 21.3%; Age 65 and over: 21.6%; Males per 100 females: 95.7; Marriage status: 26.4% never married, 59.7% now married, 5.3% separated, 9.2% widowed, 4.7% divorced; Foreign born: 12.3%; Speak English only: 88.9%; With disability: 12.9%; Veterans: 6.9%; Ancestry: 14.2% Irish, 12.3% German, 8.7% English, 4.6% Italian, 4.1% Polish

Employment: 19.3% management, business, and financial, 1.2% computer, engineering, and science, 18.1% education, legal, community service, arts, and media, 4.3% healthcare practitioners, 14.5% service, 22.4% sales and office, 15.5% natural resources, construction, and maintenance, 4.6% production, transportation, and material moving

Income: Per capita: $28,478; Median household: $62,576; Average household: $69,534; Households with income of $100,000 or more: 17.4%; Poverty rate: 24.4%

Educational Attainment: High school diploma or higher: 88.8%; Bachelor's degree or higher: 37.6%; Graduate/professional degree or higher: 22.9%

Housing: Homeownership rate: 68.1%; Median home value: $172,400; Median year structure built: 1965; Homeowner vacancy rate: 0.0%; Median selected monthly owner costs: $1,552 with a mortgage, $479 without a mortgage; Median gross rent: $858 per month; Rental vacancy rate: 0.0%

Health Insurance: 78.8% have insurance; 62.3% have private insurance; 34.2% have public insurance; 21.2% do not have insurance; 27.2% of children under 18 do not have insurance

Transportation: Commute: 71.6% car, 1.1% public transportation, 7.7% walk, 19.6% work from home; Mean travel time to work: 21.9 minutes

JEFFERSONVILLE (village). Covers a land area of 0.405 square miles and a water area of 0.033 square miles. Located at 41.78° N. Lat; 74.93° W. Long. Elevation is 1,050 feet.

Population: 387; Growth (since 2000): -7.9%; Density: 954.4 persons per square mile; Race: 85.8% White, 3.4% Black/African American, 6.5% Asian, 0.0% American Indian/Alaska Native, 0.0% Native Hawaiian/Other Pacific Islander, 1.8% Two or more races, 7.2% Hispanic of any race; Average household size: 2.33; Median age: 47.6; Age under 18: 15.2%; Age 65 and over: 19.9%; Males per 100 females: 106.3; Marriage status: 34.8% never married, 50.0% now married, 9.1% separated, 8.2% widowed, 7.0% divorced; Foreign born: 18.1%; Speak English only: 81.6%; With disability: 13.7%; Veterans: 5.2%; Ancestry: 22.7% German, 17.6% Irish, 10.6% American, 7.2% European, 7.0% Italian

Employment: 10.9% management, business, and financial, 4.1% computer, engineering, and science, 12.7% education, legal, community service, arts, and media, 5.5% healthcare practitioners, 40.0% service, 10.0% sales and office, 13.2% natural resources, construction, and maintenance, 3.6% production, transportation, and material moving

Income: Per capita: $22,510; Median household: $41,250; Average household: $51,304; Households with income of $100,000 or more: 6.0%; Poverty rate: 25.0%

Educational Attainment: High school diploma or higher: 86.2%; Bachelor's degree or higher: 36.2%; Graduate/professional degree or higher: 14.5%

School District(s)
Sullivan West Central SD (PK-12)
    2014-15 Enrollment: 1,137 . . . . (845) 482-4610

Housing: Homeownership rate: 58.4%; Median home value: $139,200; Median year structure built: Before 1940; Homeowner vacancy rate: 2.2%; Median selected monthly owner costs: $1,396 with a mortgage, $663 without a mortgage; Median gross rent: $783 per month; Rental vacancy rate: 8.8%

Health Insurance: 71.6% have insurance; 56.3% have private insurance; 30.7% have public insurance; 28.4% do not have insurance; 30.5% of children under 18 do not have insurance

Transportation: Commute: 69.0% car, 1.4% public transportation, 11.0% walk, 18.6% work from home; Mean travel time to work: 32.2 minutes

KAUNEONGA LAKE (unincorporated postal area)
ZCTA: 12749

Covers a land area of 2.942 square miles and a water area of 0.026 square miles. Located at 41.70° N. Lat; 74.84° W. Long. Elevation is 1,348 feet.

Population: 321; Growth (since 2000): 27.9%; Density: 109.1 persons per square mile; Race: 100.0% White, 0.0% Black/African American, 0.0% Asian, 0.0% American Indian/Alaska Native, 0.0% Native

Hawaiian/Other Pacific Islander, 0.0% Two or more races, 2.5% Hispanic of any race; Average household size: 1.74; Median age: 59.9; Age under 18: 0.0%; Age 65 and over: 36.1%; Males per 100 females: 106.9; Marriage status: 36.4% never married, 35.5% now married, 0.0% separated, 9.3% widowed, 18.7% divorced; Foreign born: 6.2%; Speak English only: 97.5%; With disability: 4.4%; Veterans: 13.1%; Ancestry: 26.2% Polish, 25.5% Irish, 22.4% German, 18.1% Italian, 5.3% English

Employment: 35.9% management, business, and financial, 0.0% computer, engineering, and science, 3.5% education, legal, community service, arts, and media, 11.8% healthcare practitioners, 14.1% service, 24.7% sales and office, 10.0% natural resources, construction, and maintenance, 0.0% production, transportation, and material moving

Income: Per capita: $35,203; Median household: $46,313; Average household: $63,049; Households with income of $100,000 or more: 26.5%; Poverty rate: 18.7%

Educational Attainment: High school diploma or higher: 93.7%; Bachelor's degree or higher: 25.1%; Graduate/professional degree or higher: 2.4%

Housing: Homeownership rate: 36.2%; Median home value: n/a; Median year structure built: 1965; Homeowner vacancy rate: 9.5%; Median selected monthly owner costs: n/a with a mortgage, n/a without a mortgage; Median gross rent: $643 per month; Rental vacancy rate: 0.0%

Health Insurance: 95.6% have insurance; 85.4% have private insurance; 38.0% have public insurance; 4.4% do not have insurance; 0.0% of children under 18 do not have insurance

Transportation: Commute: 97.1% car, 0.0% public transportation, 0.0% walk, 2.9% work from home; Mean travel time to work: 23.9 minutes

---

KENOZA LAKE (unincorporated postal area)
ZCTA: 12750

Covers a land area of 4.255 square miles and a water area of 0.221 square miles. Located at 41.73° N. Lat; 74.97° W. Long. Elevation is 1,060 feet.

Population: 320; Growth (since 2000): n/a; Density: 75.2 persons per square mile; Race: 87.8% White, 9.4% Black/African American, 0.0% Asian, 2.8% American Indian/Alaska Native, 0.0% Native Hawaiian/Other Pacific Islander, 0.0% Two or more races, 0.0% Hispanic of any race; Average household size: 3.37; Median age: 42.3; Age under 18: 15.9%; Age 65 and over: 6.6%; Males per 100 females: 88.9; Marriage status: 43.2% never married, 50.4% now married, 5.0% separated, 4.3% widowed, 2.1% divorced; Foreign born: 4.7%; Speak English only: 95.3%; With disability: 11.9%; Veterans: 4.1%; Ancestry: 24.4% German, 13.4% French, 12.5% Scotch-Irish, 11.9% American, 7.2% Italian

Employment: 0.0% management, business, and financial, 7.1% computer, engineering, and science, 4.3% education, legal, community service, arts, and media, 3.8% healthcare practitioners, 46.2% service, 11.0% sales and office, 11.9% natural resources, construction, and maintenance, 15.7% production, transportation, and material moving

Income: Per capita: $32,007; Median household: $74,792; Average household: $102,427; Households with income of $100,000 or more: 42.1%; Poverty rate: 12.8%

Educational Attainment: High school diploma or higher: 96.9%; Bachelor's degree or higher: 17.9%; Graduate/professional degree or higher: 10.7%

Housing: Homeownership rate: 73.7%; Median home value: n/a; Median year structure built: 1963; Homeowner vacancy rate: 0.0%; Median selected monthly owner costs: $1,542 with a mortgage, $836 without a mortgage; Median gross rent: $1,223 per month; Rental vacancy rate: 0.0%

Health Insurance: 96.6% have insurance; 67.8% have private insurance; 33.1% have public insurance; 3.4% do not have insurance; 0.0% of children under 18 do not have insurance

Transportation: Commute: 92.9% car, 0.0% public transportation, 0.0% walk, 7.1% work from home; Mean travel time to work: 38.5 minutes

---

KIAMESHA LAKE (unincorporated postal area)
ZCTA: 12751

Covers a land area of 3.417 square miles and a water area of 0.465 square miles. Located at 41.70° N. Lat; 74.66° W. Long. Elevation is 1,417 feet.

Population: 1,286; Growth (since 2000): 232.3%; Density: 376.3 persons per square mile; Race: 71.7% White, 23.0% Black/African American, 1.2% Asian, 0.0% American Indian/Alaska Native, 0.0%

Native Hawaiian/Other Pacific Islander, 0.0% Two or more races, 6.6% Hispanic of any race; Average household size: 3.66; Median age: 20.5; Age under 18: 48.6%; Age 65 and over: 6.6%; Males per 100 females: 98.5; Marriage status: 39.6% never married, 49.7% now married, 0.0% separated, 4.8% widowed, 5.9% divorced; Foreign born: 9.0%; Speak English only: 68.5%; With disability: 9.8%; Veterans: 2.6%; Ancestry: 11.5% German, 9.9% Italian, 6.5% African, 6.1% Hungarian, 5.5% American

Employment: 4.0% management, business, and financial, 3.3% computer, engineering, and science, 9.9% education, legal, community service, arts, and media, 10.9% healthcare practitioners, 35.0% service, 20.8% sales and office, 5.9% natural resources, construction, and maintenance, 10.2% production, transportation, and material moving

Income: Per capita: $15,024; Median household: $49,531; Average household: $53,435; Households with income of $100,000 or more: 13.7%; Poverty rate: 24.6%

Educational Attainment: High school diploma or higher: 84.3%; Bachelor's degree or higher: 11.9%; Graduate/professional degree or higher: 5.4%

Housing: Homeownership rate: 45.8%; Median home value: $152,500; Median year structure built: 1977; Homeowner vacancy rate: 0.0%; Median selected monthly owner costs: $1,174 with a mortgage, $659 without a mortgage; Median gross rent: $961 per month; Rental vacancy rate: 0.0%

Health Insurance: 96.9% have insurance; 39.0% have private insurance; 68.6% have public insurance; 3.1% do not have insurance; 0.0% of children under 18 do not have insurance

Transportation: Commute: 74.0% car, 0.0% public transportation, 17.9% walk, 4.9% work from home; Mean travel time to work: 19.2 minutes

---

LAKE HUNTINGTON (unincorporated postal area)
ZCTA: 12752

Covers a land area of 1.733 square miles and a water area of 0.141 square miles. Located at 41.68° N. Lat; 74.99° W. Long. Elevation is 1,217 feet.

Population: 221; Growth (since 2000): 52.4%; Density: 127.5 persons per square mile; Race: 96.4% White, 3.6% Black/African American, 0.0% Asian, 0.0% American Indian/Alaska Native, 0.0% Native Hawaiian/Other Pacific Islander, 0.0% Two or more races, 5.0% Hispanic of any race; Average household size: 1.89; Median age: 49.3; Age under 18: 9.0%; Age 65 and over: 14.9%; Males per 100 females: 112.3; Marriage status: 44.2% never married, 31.6% now married, 0.0% separated, 12.6% widowed, 11.6% divorced; Foreign born: 0.9%; Speak English only: 98.1%; With disability: 17.2%; Veterans: 8.5%; Ancestry: 33.0% Irish, 32.1% German, 16.3% Italian, 12.7% Polish, 6.8% American

Employment: 20.3% management, business, and financial, 3.4% computer, engineering, and science, 2.5% education, legal, community service, arts, and media, 5.1% healthcare practitioners, 17.8% service, 22.9% sales and office, 11.0% natural resources, construction, and maintenance, 16.9% production, transportation, and material moving

Income: Per capita: $32,058; Median household: $50,781; Average household: $60,429; Households with income of $100,000 or more: 17.9%; Poverty rate: 0.9%

Educational Attainment: High school diploma or higher: 97.1%; Bachelor's degree or higher: 18.9%; Graduate/professional degree or higher: 5.1%

School District(s)
Sullivan West Central SD (PK-12)
   2014-15 Enrollment: 1,137 . . . . (845) 482-4610

Housing: Homeownership rate: 72.6%; Median home value: $178,900; Median year structure built: 1947; Homeowner vacancy rate: 15.8%; Median selected monthly owner costs: $1,306 with a mortgage, $721 without a mortgage; Median gross rent: $631 per month; Rental vacancy rate: 18.4%

Health Insurance: 78.7% have insurance; 73.8% have private insurance; 24.0% have public insurance; 21.3% do not have insurance; 0.0% of children under 18 do not have insurance

Transportation: Commute: 90.2% car, 1.8% public transportation, 2.7% walk, 5.4% work from home; Mean travel time to work: 32.0 minutes

LIBERTY (town). Covers a land area of 79.579 square miles and a water area of 1.158 square miles. Located at 41.81° N. Lat; 74.78° W. Long. Elevation is 1,506 feet.

History: Settled 1793, incorporated 1870.

Population: 9,615; Growth (since 2000): -0.2%; Density: 120.8 persons per square mile; Race: 83.2% White, 6.0% Black/African American, 2.3% Asian, 0.3% American Indian/Alaska Native, 0.0% Native Hawaiian/Other Pacific Islander, 2.8% Two or more races, 22.0% Hispanic of any race; Average household size: 2.63; Median age: 42.2; Age under 18: 22.3%; Age 65 and over: 16.7%; Males per 100 females: 99.0; Marriage status: 32.3% never married, 49.0% now married, 4.3% separated, 9.3% widowed, 9.4% divorced; Foreign born: 12.1%; Speak English only: 81.3%; With disability: 18.7%; Veterans: 7.7%; Ancestry: 17.7% German, 16.5% Irish, 12.3% Italian, 6.9% Polish, 5.4% English

Employment: 6.7% management, business, and financial, 0.8% computer, engineering, and science, 12.7% education, legal, community service, arts, and media, 4.0% healthcare practitioners, 24.1% service, 22.1% sales and office, 11.8% natural resources, construction, and maintenance, 17.7% production, transportation, and material moving

Income: Per capita: $24,907; Median household: $42,878; Average household: $63,010; Households with income of $100,000 or more: 17.3%; Poverty rate: 17.8%

Educational Attainment: High school diploma or higher: 82.0%; Bachelor's degree or higher: 17.1%; Graduate/professional degree or higher: 8.2%

School District(s)
Liberty Central SD (PK-12)
    2014-15 Enrollment: 1,647 . . . . (845) 292-6990
Sullivan Boces
    2014-15 Enrollment: n/a . . . . (845) 295-4016

Vocational/Technical School(s)
Sullivan County BOCES-Practical Nursing Program (Public)
    Fall 2014 Enrollment: 9 . . . . (845) 295-4136

Housing: Homeownership rate: 56.1%; Median home value: $128,600; Median year structure built: 1966; Homeowner vacancy rate: 3.2%; Median selected monthly owner costs: $1,435 with a mortgage, $655 without a mortgage; Median gross rent: $772 per month; Rental vacancy rate: 4.9%

Health Insurance: 89.9% have insurance; 56.2% have private insurance; 44.3% have public insurance; 10.1% do not have insurance; 4.2% of children under 18 do not have insurance

Transportation: Commute: 88.3% car, 1.4% public transportation, 3.8% walk, 3.5% work from home; Mean travel time to work: 23.7 minutes

Additional Information Contacts
Town of Liberty . . . . (845) 292-5110
    http://www.townofliberty.org

LIBERTY (village). Covers a land area of 2.602 square miles and a water area of 0.004 square miles. Located at 41.80° N. Lat; 74.74° W. Long. Elevation is 1,506 feet.

Population: 4,241; Growth (since 2000): 6.7%; Density: 1,629.7 persons per square mile; Race: 75.7% White, 9.1% Black/African American, 1.0% Asian, 0.3% American Indian/Alaska Native, 0.0% Native Hawaiian/Other Pacific Islander, 3.8% Two or more races, 32.1% Hispanic of any race; Average household size: 2.49; Median age: 38.3; Age under 18: 23.0%; Age 65 and over: 17.3%; Males per 100 females: 93.4; Marriage status: 36.7% never married, 43.7% now married, 5.0% separated, 10.1% widowed, 9.5% divorced; Foreign born: 13.9%; Speak English only: 78.3%; With disability: 23.2%; Veterans: 7.7%; Ancestry: 20.0% German, 14.1% Irish, 10.0% Italian, 8.3% Polish, 6.6% Dutch

Employment: 6.3% management, business, and financial, 1.8% computer, engineering, and science, 6.6% education, legal, community service, arts, and media, 2.5% healthcare practitioners, 16.7% service, 23.7% sales and office, 8.7% natural resources, construction, and maintenance, 33.7% production, transportation, and material moving

Income: Per capita: $23,454; Median household: $34,088; Average household: $55,376; Households with income of $100,000 or more: 10.6%; Poverty rate: 23.4%

Educational Attainment: High school diploma or higher: 79.9%; Bachelor's degree or higher: 11.5%; Graduate/professional degree or higher: 3.6%

School District(s)
Liberty Central SD (PK-12)
    2014-15 Enrollment: 1,647 . . . . (845) 292-6990
Sullivan Boces
    2014-15 Enrollment: n/a . . . . (845) 295-4016

Vocational/Technical School(s)
Sullivan County BOCES-Practical Nursing Program (Public)
    Fall 2014 Enrollment: 9 . . . . (845) 295-4136

Housing: Homeownership rate: 35.5%; Median home value: $107,000; Median year structure built: 1960; Homeowner vacancy rate: 4.5%; Median selected monthly owner costs: $1,351 with a mortgage, $671 without a mortgage; Median gross rent: $722 per month; Rental vacancy rate: 4.3%

Health Insurance: 84.7% have insurance; 39.0% have private insurance; 57.4% have public insurance; 15.3% do not have insurance; 9.1% of children under 18 do not have insurance

Safety: Violent crime rate: 57.7 per 10,000 population; Property crime rate: 384.6 per 10,000 population

Transportation: Commute: 86.4% car, 1.0% public transportation, 4.6% walk, 1.4% work from home; Mean travel time to work: 22.9 minutes

Additional Information Contacts
Village of Liberty . . . . (845) 292-2250
    http://www.libertyvillageny.org

LIVINGSTON MANOR (CDP). Covers a land area of 3.081 square miles and a water area of 0.012 square miles. Located at 41.89° N. Lat; 74.82° W. Long. Elevation is 1,401 feet.

Population: 1,104; Growth (since 2000): -18.5%; Density: 358.3 persons per square mile; Race: 86.8% White, 0.0% Black/African American, 0.5% Asian, 0.0% American Indian/Alaska Native, 0.0% Native Hawaiian/Other Pacific Islander, 7.0% Two or more races, 23.0% Hispanic of any race; Average household size: 2.42; Median age: 46.5; Age under 18: 14.7%; Age 65 and over: 14.5%; Males per 100 females: 96.6; Marriage status: 25.5% never married, 59.8% now married, 17.8% separated, 7.5% widowed, 7.2% divorced; Foreign born: 7.4%; Speak English only: 91.4%; With disability: 20.7%; Veterans: 10.2%; Ancestry: 30.7% German, 10.9% Italian, 10.0% Irish, 9.3% Polish, 7.1% English

Employment: 2.7% management, business, and financial, 1.5% computer, engineering, and science, 11.2% education, legal, community service, arts, and media, 0.0% healthcare practitioners, 33.4% service, 25.2% sales and office, 6.5% natural resources, construction, and maintenance, 19.5% production, transportation, and material moving

Income: Per capita: $22,835; Median household: $47,254; Average household: $53,432; Households with income of $100,000 or more: 11.6%; Poverty rate: 19.5%

Educational Attainment: High school diploma or higher: 76.9%; Bachelor's degree or higher: 18.4%; Graduate/professional degree or higher: 6.4%

School District(s)
Livingston Manor Central SD (PK-12)
    2014-15 Enrollment: 501 . . . . (845) 439-4400

Housing: Homeownership rate: 59.9%; Median home value: $87,700; Median year structure built: 1957; Homeowner vacancy rate: 8.1%; Median selected monthly owner costs: $1,527 with a mortgage, $545 without a mortgage; Median gross rent: $921 per month; Rental vacancy rate: 11.6%

Health Insurance: 84.9% have insurance; 56.7% have private insurance; 44.9% have public insurance; 15.1% do not have insurance; 0.0% of children under 18 do not have insurance

Transportation: Commute: 95.1% car, 0.0% public transportation, 1.4% walk, 3.4% work from home; Mean travel time to work: 37.3 minutes

LOCH SHELDRAKE (CDP).

Note: Statistics that would complete this profile are not available because the CDP was created after the 2010 Census was released.

LUMBERLAND (town). Covers a land area of 46.539 square miles and a water area of 2.807 square miles. Located at 41.49° N. Lat; 74.81° W. Long.

Population: 2,437; Growth (since 2000): 25.7%; Density: 52.4 persons per square mile; Race: 92.7% White, 0.5% Black/African American, 4.7% Asian, 0.3% American Indian/Alaska Native, 0.0% Native Hawaiian/Other Pacific Islander, 0.0% Two or more races, 7.8% Hispanic of any race; Average household size: 2.56; Median age: 45.5; Age under 18: 24.6%; Age 65 and over: 20.7%; Males per 100 females: 100.5; Marriage status: 20.9% never married, 58.8% now married, 0.7% separated, 6.1% widowed, 14.1% divorced; Foreign born: 14.9%; Speak English only: 82.6%; With disability: 16.5%; Veterans: 7.8%; Ancestry: 21.6% German, 21.2% Irish, 12.8% Italian, 7.7% Polish, 7.0% English

Employment: 10.6% management, business, and financial, 5.4% computer, engineering, and science, 14.9% education, legal, community service, arts, and media, 5.2% healthcare practitioners, 16.6% service,

22.1% sales and office, 13.8% natural resources, construction, and maintenance, 11.4% production, transportation, and material moving
Income: Per capita: $28,161; Median household: $58,846; Average household: $70,942; Households with income of $100,000 or more: 21.3%; Poverty rate: 12.4%
Educational Attainment: High school diploma or higher: 91.2%; Bachelor's degree or higher: 29.9%; Graduate/professional degree or higher: 12.7%
Housing: Homeownership rate: 84.9%; Median home value: $172,700; Median year structure built: 1974; Homeowner vacancy rate: 3.3%; Median selected monthly owner costs: $1,853 with a mortgage, $766 without a mortgage; Median gross rent: $883 per month; Rental vacancy rate: 8.7%
Health Insurance: 91.8% have insurance; 71.0% have private insurance; 39.0% have public insurance; 8.2% do not have insurance; 3.2% of children under 18 do not have insurance
Transportation: Commute: 86.6% car, 2.9% public transportation, 1.6% walk, 7.9% work from home; Mean travel time to work: 41.5 minutes

MAMAKATING (town). Covers a land area of 96.108 square miles and a water area of 2.561 square miles. Located at 41.59° N. Lat; 74.50° W. Long. Elevation is 577 feet.

Population: 11,795; Growth (since 2000): 7.2%; Density: 122.7 persons per square mile; Race: 89.9% White, 4.1% Black/African American, 0.5% Asian, 0.2% American Indian/Alaska Native, 0.0% Native Hawaiian/Other Pacific Islander, 3.8% Two or more races, 9.3% Hispanic of any race; Average household size: 2.76; Median age: 42.2; Age under 18: 22.1%; Age 65 and over: 13.4%; Males per 100 females: 102.2; Marriage status: 32.1% never married, 50.1% now married, 4.2% separated, 6.7% widowed, 11.2% divorced; Foreign born: 5.7%; Speak English only: 92.3%; With disability: 12.4%; Veterans: 9.1%; Ancestry: 21.1% Italian, 21.0% Irish, 20.7% German, 8.1% English, 7.4% American
Employment: 9.3% management, business, and financial, 2.3% computer, engineering, and science, 7.7% education, legal, community service, arts, and media, 6.5% healthcare practitioners, 21.3% service, 25.7% sales and office, 14.3% natural resources, construction, and maintenance, 12.9% production, transportation, and material moving
Income: Per capita: $26,021; Median household: $53,750; Average household: $68,398; Households with income of $100,000 or more: 21.1%; Poverty rate: 10.6%
Educational Attainment: High school diploma or higher: 89.2%; Bachelor's degree or higher: 18.4%; Graduate/professional degree or higher: 7.2%
Housing: Homeownership rate: 77.2%; Median home value: $176,600; Median year structure built: 1971; Homeowner vacancy rate: 3.5%; Median selected monthly owner costs: $1,825 with a mortgage, $802 without a mortgage; Median gross rent: $998 per month; Rental vacancy rate: 11.5%
Health Insurance: 88.7% have insurance; 70.8% have private insurance; 31.1% have public insurance; 11.3% do not have insurance; 4.8% of children under 18 do not have insurance
Transportation: Commute: 91.9% car, 3.4% public transportation, 0.7% walk, 4.0% work from home; Mean travel time to work: 37.3 minutes
Additional Information Contacts
Town of Mamakating . . . . (845) 888-3002
  http://www.mamakating.org

MONGAUP VALLEY (unincorporated postal area)
ZCTA: 12762
  Covers a land area of 6.342 square miles and a water area of 0.490 square miles. Located at 41.66° N. Lat; 74.79° W. Long. Elevation is 1,112 feet.
Population: 298; Growth (since 2000): -12.9%; Density: 47.0 persons per square mile; Race: 100.0% White, 0.0% Black/African American, 0.0% Asian, 0.0% American Indian/Alaska Native, 0.0% Native Hawaiian/Other Pacific Islander, 0.0% Two or more races, 0.0% Hispanic of any race; Average household size: 1.80; Median age: 44.4; Age under 18: 20.1%; Age 65 and over: 24.2%; Males per 100 females: 101.6; Marriage status: 48.7% never married, 13.2% now married, 2.6% separated, 5.3% widowed, 32.8% divorced; Foreign born: 3.0%; Speak English only: 97.0%; With disability: 10.1%; Veterans: 4.2%; Ancestry: 28.9% American, 19.5% Italian, 15.8% German, 15.4% Irish, 11.4% Russian
Employment: 0.0% management, business, and financial, 0.0% computer, engineering, and science, 7.0% education, legal, community service, arts, and media, 19.0% healthcare practitioners, 16.2% service,

50.7% sales and office, 7.0% natural resources, construction, and maintenance, 0.0% production, transportation, and material moving
Income: Per capita: $31,751; Median household: $39,762; Average household: $56,093; Households with income of $100,000 or more: 6.0%; Poverty rate: 13.8%
Educational Attainment: High school diploma or higher: 80.8%; Bachelor's degree or higher: 39.9%; Graduate/professional degree or higher: 17.8%
Housing: Homeownership rate: 56.6%; Median home value: n/a; Median year structure built: 1978; Homeowner vacancy rate: 0.0%; Median selected monthly owner costs: n/a with a mortgage, n/a without a mortgage; Median gross rent: n/a per month; Rental vacancy rate: 14.3%
Health Insurance: 98.3% have insurance; 72.8% have private insurance; 42.3% have public insurance; 1.7% do not have insurance; 0.0% of children under 18 do not have insurance
Transportation: Commute: 100.0% car, 0.0% public transportation, 0.0% walk, 0.0% work from home; Mean travel time to work: 16.3 minutes

MONTICELLO (village). County seat. Covers a land area of 3.985 square miles and a water area of 0.024 square miles. Located at 41.65° N. Lat; 74.69° W. Long. Elevation is 1,512 feet.
History: Incorporated 1830.
Population: 6,685; Growth (since 2000): 2.7%; Density: 1,677.6 persons per square mile; Race: 42.5% White, 35.6% Black/African American, 0.6% Asian, 0.0% American Indian/Alaska Native, 0.0% Native Hawaiian/Other Pacific Islander, 12.6% Two or more races, 32.4% Hispanic of any race; Average household size: 2.20; Median age: 36.2; Age under 18: 23.2%; Age 65 and over: 13.1%; Males per 100 females: 97.1; Marriage status: 44.8% never married, 37.2% now married, 4.7% separated, 8.0% widowed, 10.0% divorced; Foreign born: 12.9%; Speak English only: 76.1%; With disability: 21.8%; Veterans: 6.7%; Ancestry: 8.6% Irish, 5.6% American, 5.5% German, 4.2% Jamaican, 3.2% Italian
Employment: 3.2% management, business, and financial, 0.6% computer, engineering, and science, 7.1% education, legal, community service, arts, and media, 8.0% healthcare practitioners, 35.7% service, 24.2% sales and office, 7.3% natural resources, construction, and maintenance, 13.9% production, transportation, and material moving
Income: Per capita: $17,593; Median household: $26,376; Average household: $38,272; Households with income of $100,000 or more: 4.4%; Poverty rate: 35.1%
Educational Attainment: High school diploma or higher: 80.0%; Bachelor's degree or higher: 15.4%; Graduate/professional degree or higher: 5.8%

School District(s)
Monticello Central SD (KG-12)
  2014-15 Enrollment: 3,035 . . . . (845) 794-7700
Housing: Homeownership rate: 25.5%; Median home value: $86,600; Median year structure built: 1958; Homeowner vacancy rate: 6.4%; Median selected monthly owner costs: $1,436 with a mortgage, $556 without a mortgage; Median gross rent: $791 per month; Rental vacancy rate: 11.8%
Health Insurance: 86.0% have insurance; 35.6% have private insurance; 60.7% have public insurance; 14.0% do not have insurance; 0.0% of children under 18 do not have insurance
Safety: Violent crime rate: 43.9 per 10,000 population; Property crime rate: 307.5 per 10,000 population
Transportation: Commute: 80.5% car, 4.7% public transportation, 9.2% walk, 3.3% work from home; Mean travel time to work: 27.9 minutes
Airports: Sullivan County International (general aviation)
Additional Information Contacts
Village of Monticello . . . . (845) 794-6130
  http://www.villageofmonticello.com

MOUNTAIN DALE (unincorporated postal area)
ZCTA: 12763
  Covers a land area of 14.269 square miles and a water area of 0.177 square miles. Located at 41.68° N. Lat; 74.52° W. Long. Elevation is 1,010 feet.
Population: 671; Growth (since 2000): -12.4%; Density: 47.0 persons per square mile; Race: 90.6% White, 3.6% Black/African American, 0.0% Asian, 0.0% American Indian/Alaska Native, 0.0% Native Hawaiian/Other Pacific Islander, 0.0% Two or more races, 24.6% Hispanic of any race; Average household size: 2.17; Median age: 53.4; Age under 18: 15.5%; Age 65 and over: 28.0%; Males per 100 females:

112.2; Marriage status: 26.3% never married, 53.7% now married, 2.3% separated, 7.6% widowed, 12.3% divorced; Foreign born: 17.9%; Speak English only: 73.3%; With disability: 13.4%; Veterans: 15.0%; Ancestry: 19.4% Italian, 9.1% Irish, 8.3% English, 6.0% German, 5.5% Polish
Employment: 6.1% management, business, and financial, 6.1% computer, engineering, and science, 3.7% education, legal, community service, arts, and media, 1.4% healthcare practitioners, 29.2% service, 36.6% sales and office, 15.6% natural resources, construction, and maintenance, 1.4% production, transportation, and material moving
Income: Per capita: $29,294; Median household: $58,144; Average household: $62,367; Households with income of $100,000 or more: 11.8%; Poverty rate: 6.2%
Educational Attainment: High school diploma or higher: 86.6%; Bachelor's degree or higher: 15.9%; Graduate/professional degree or higher: 8.0%
Housing: Homeownership rate: 77.4%; Median home value: $136,400; Median year structure built: 1972; Homeowner vacancy rate: 12.2%; Median selected monthly owner costs: $1,483 with a mortgage, $580 without a mortgage; Median gross rent: $780 per month; Rental vacancy rate: 0.0%
Health Insurance: 91.5% have insurance; 70.5% have private insurance; 46.3% have public insurance; 8.5% do not have insurance; 0.0% of children under 18 do not have insurance
Transportation: Commute: 94.9% car, 0.0% public transportation, 2.0% walk, 3.1% work from home; Mean travel time to work: 25.7 minutes

NARROWSBURG (CDP). Covers a land area of 1.366 square miles and a water area of 0.134 square miles. Located at 41.60° N. Lat; 75.06° W. Long. Elevation is 676 feet.

Population: 382; Growth (since 2000): -7.7%; Density: 279.6 persons per square mile; Race: 92.9% White, 6.5% Black/African American, 0.0% Asian, 0.0% American Indian/Alaska Native, 0.0% Native Hawaiian/Other Pacific Islander, 0.5% Two or more races, 1.3% Hispanic of any race; Average household size: 2.09; Median age: 49.7; Age under 18: 7.6%; Age 65 and over: 26.7%; Males per 100 females: 109.2; Marriage status: 24.8% never married, 61.4% now married, 3.9% separated, 4.2% widowed, 9.6% divorced; Foreign born: 4.7%; Speak English only: 95.7%; With disability: 22.0%; Veterans: 10.8%; Ancestry: 30.9% German, 28.3% Irish, 18.1% Italian, 6.8% English, 4.2% American
Employment: 12.6% management, business, and financial, 3.3% computer, engineering, and science, 12.6% education, legal, community service, arts, and media, 7.7% healthcare practitioners, 31.9% service, 25.3% sales and office, 3.8% natural resources, construction, and maintenance, 2.7% production, transportation, and material moving
Income: Per capita: $27,622; Median household: $41,932; Average household: $56,683; Households with income of $100,000 or more: 16.9%; Poverty rate: 11.8%
Educational Attainment: High school diploma or higher: 88.6%; Bachelor's degree or higher: 23.6%; Graduate/professional degree or higher: 10.1%
Housing: Homeownership rate: 71.0%; Median home value: $141,200; Median year structure built: Before 1940; Homeowner vacancy rate: 9.7%; Median selected monthly owner costs: $1,500 with a mortgage, $640 without a mortgage; Median gross rent: $900 per month; Rental vacancy rate: 0.0%
Health Insurance: 78.8% have insurance; 64.7% have private insurance; 33.8% have public insurance; 21.2% do not have insurance; 0.0% of children under 18 do not have insurance
Newspapers: The River Reporter (weekly circulation 4,500)
Transportation: Commute: 74.7% car, 7.1% public transportation, 6.6% walk, 11.5% work from home; Mean travel time to work: 23.7 minutes

NEVERSINK (town). Covers a land area of 82.773 square miles and a water area of 3.491 square miles. Located at 41.87° N. Lat; 74.59° W. Long. Elevation is 1,634 feet.

Population: 3,493; Growth (since 2000): -1.7%; Density: 42.2 persons per square mile; Race: 95.7% White, 1.9% Black/African American, 0.0% Asian, 0.0% American Indian/Alaska Native, 0.0% Native Hawaiian/Other Pacific Islander, 2.4% Two or more races, 3.9% Hispanic of any race; Average household size: 2.61; Median age: 41.4; Age under 18: 23.4%; Age 65 and over: 15.0%; Males per 100 females: 96.5; Marriage status: 28.3% never married, 57.5% now married, 1.2% separated, 6.2% widowed, 7.9% divorced; Foreign born: 4.2%; Speak English only: 96.6%; With disability: 12.3%; Veterans: 13.0%; Ancestry: 22.0% Irish, 21.8% German, 11.9% Italian, 9.3% English, 8.3% Dutch

Employment: 13.0% management, business, and financial, 7.0% computer, engineering, and science, 9.9% education, legal, community service, arts, and media, 2.3% healthcare practitioners, 27.8% service, 19.7% sales and office, 13.7% natural resources, construction, and maintenance, 6.6% production, transportation, and material moving
Income: Per capita: $27,412; Median household: $59,194; Average household: $70,308; Households with income of $100,000 or more: 22.8%; Poverty rate: 7.6%
Educational Attainment: High school diploma or higher: 89.0%; Bachelor's degree or higher: 21.0%; Graduate/professional degree or higher: 9.7%
Housing: Homeownership rate: 81.0%; Median home value: $202,800; Median year structure built: 1978; Homeowner vacancy rate: 2.3%; Median selected monthly owner costs: $1,345 with a mortgage, $507 without a mortgage; Median gross rent: $923 per month; Rental vacancy rate: 9.0%
Health Insurance: 95.5% have insurance; 82.7% have private insurance; 28.7% have public insurance; 4.5% do not have insurance; 0.0% of children under 18 do not have insurance
Transportation: Commute: 95.4% car, 0.3% public transportation, 2.1% walk, 1.1% work from home; Mean travel time to work: 28.3 minutes

NORTH BRANCH (unincorporated postal area)
ZCTA: 12766

Covers a land area of 8.037 square miles and a water area of 0.005 square miles. Located at 41.82° N. Lat; 74.98° W. Long. Elevation is 1,037 feet.
Population: 478; Growth (since 2000): 4.8%; Density: 59.5 persons per square mile; Race: 100.0% White, 0.0% Black/African American, 0.0% Asian, 0.0% American Indian/Alaska Native, 0.0% Native Hawaiian/Other Pacific Islander, 0.0% Two or more races, 5.0% Hispanic of any race; Average household size: 2.78; Median age: 51.3; Age under 18: 12.8%; Age 65 and over: 21.8%; Males per 100 females: 98.6; Marriage status: 18.7% never married, 70.6% now married, 0.0% separated, 2.0% widowed, 8.8% divorced; Foreign born: 11.9%; Speak English only: 94.4%; With disability: 11.3%; Veterans: 11.5%; Ancestry: 35.4% German, 19.9% Irish, 13.0% American, 10.7% British, 8.2% English
Employment: 0.0% management, business, and financial, 0.0% computer, engineering, and science, 29.2% education, legal, community service, arts, and media, 5.5% healthcare practitioners, 4.4% service, 18.6% sales and office, 37.2% natural resources, construction, and maintenance, 5.1% production, transportation, and material moving
Income: Per capita: $32,268; Median household: $70,227; Average household: $81,873; Households with income of $100,000 or more: 36.0%; Poverty rate: 2.7%
Educational Attainment: High school diploma or higher: 85.6%; Bachelor's degree or higher: 21.0%; Graduate/professional degree or higher: 19.4%
Housing: Homeownership rate: 88.4%; Median home value: n/a; Median year structure built: 1983; Homeowner vacancy rate: 4.4%; Median selected monthly owner costs: n/a with a mortgage, n/a without a mortgage; Median gross rent: n/a per month; Rental vacancy rate: 0.0%
Health Insurance: 90.6% have insurance; 86.2% have private insurance; 38.5% have public insurance; 9.4% do not have insurance; 0.0% of children under 18 do not have insurance
Transportation: Commute: 100.0% car, 0.0% public transportation, 0.0% walk, 0.0% work from home; Mean travel time to work: 17.6 minutes

OBERNBURG (unincorporated postal area)
ZCTA: 12767

Covers a land area of 2.957 square miles and a water area of 0.016 square miles. Located at 41.84° N. Lat; 74.99° W. Long. Elevation is 1,657 feet.
Population: 42; Growth (since 2000): n/a; Density: 14.2 persons per square mile; Race: 100.0% White, 0.0% Black/African American, 0.0% Asian, 0.0% American Indian/Alaska Native, 0.0% Native Hawaiian/Other Pacific Islander, 0.0% Two or more races, 21.4% Hispanic of any race; Average household size: 4.67; Median age: 20.8; Age under 18: 42.9%; Age 65 and over: 0.0%; Males per 100 females: 103.2; Marriage status: 42.9% never married, 57.1% now married, 0.0% separated, 0.0% widowed, 0.0% divorced; Foreign born: 0.0%; Speak English only: 100.0%; With disability: 0.0%; Veterans: 0.0%; Ancestry: 85.7% German, 54.8% Irish, 4.8% Portuguese

Employment: 0.0% management, business, and financial, 17.4% computer, engineering, and science, 17.4% education, legal, community service, arts, and media, 0.0% healthcare practitioners, 26.1% service, 26.1% sales and office, 13.0% natural resources, construction, and maintenance, 0.0% production, transportation, and material moving
Income: Per capita: $27,500; Median household: $111,875; Average household: $115,756; Households with income of $100,000 or more: 100.0%; Poverty rate: n/a
Educational Attainment: High school diploma or higher: 100.0%; Bachelor's degree or higher: 20.0%; Graduate/professional degree or higher: n/a
Housing: Homeownership rate: 100.0%; Median home value: $170,800; Median year structure built: Before 1940; Homeowner vacancy rate: 25.0%; Median selected monthly owner costs: $1,344 with a mortgage, $0 without a mortgage; Median gross rent: n/a per month; Rental vacancy rate: 0.0%
Health Insurance: 100.0% have insurance; 100.0% have private insurance; 0.0% have public insurance; 0.0% do not have insurance; 0.0% of children under 18 do not have insurance
Transportation: Commute: 100.0% car, 0.0% public transportation, 0.0% walk, 0.0% work from home; Mean travel time to work: 30.2 minutes

PARKSVILLE (unincorporated postal area)
ZCTA: 12768

Covers a land area of 34.840 square miles and a water area of 0.521 square miles. Located at 41.86° N. Lat; 74.73° W. Long. Elevation is 1,670 feet.
Population: 704; Growth (since 2000): -31.7%; Density: 20.2 persons per square mile; Race: 98.3% White, 1.7% Black/African American, 0.0% Asian, 0.0% American Indian/Alaska Native, 0.0% Native Hawaiian/Other Pacific Islander, 0.0% Two or more races, 16.2% Hispanic of any race; Average household size: 2.11; Median age: 54.6; Age under 18: 17.0%; Age 65 and over: 24.6%; Males per 100 females: 134.6; Marriage status: 28.8% never married, 49.6% now married, 1.3% separated, 10.3% widowed, 11.3% divorced; Foreign born: 13.5%; Speak English only: 79.1%; With disability: 25.4%; Veterans: 10.6%; Ancestry: 24.3% German, 23.7% Irish, 19.9% Italian, 12.5% American, 4.1% English
Employment: 12.0% management, business, and financial, 0.0% computer, engineering, and science, 15.5% education, legal, community service, arts, and media, 0.0% healthcare practitioners, 24.3% service, 29.2% sales and office, 19.0% natural resources, construction, and maintenance, 0.0% production, transportation, and material moving
Income: Per capita: $32,215; Median household: $41,983; Average household: $65,381; Households with income of $100,000 or more: 19.5%; Poverty rate: 9.5%
Educational Attainment: High school diploma or higher: 85.4%; Bachelor's degree or higher: 10.1%; Graduate/professional degree or higher: 5.4%
Housing: Homeownership rate: 68.9%; Median home value: $153,900; Median year structure built: 1973; Homeowner vacancy rate: 0.0%; Median selected monthly owner costs: $1,608 with a mortgage, $561 without a mortgage; Median gross rent: $927 per month; Rental vacancy rate: 0.0%
Health Insurance: 97.9% have insurance; 69.3% have private insurance; 43.6% have public insurance; 2.1% do not have insurance; 0.0% of children under 18 do not have insurance
Transportation: Commute: 88.9% car, 0.0% public transportation, 0.0% walk, 8.1% work from home; Mean travel time to work: 29.9 minutes

PHILLIPSPORT (unincorporated postal area)
ZCTA: 12769

Covers a land area of 4.935 square miles and a water area of 0 square miles. Located at 41.66° N. Lat; 74.47° W. Long. Elevation is 499 feet.
Population: 142; Growth (since 2000): n/a; Density: 28.8 persons per square mile; Race: 100.0% White, 0.0% Black/African American, 0.0% Asian, 0.0% American Indian/Alaska Native, 0.0% Native Hawaiian/Other Pacific Islander, 0.0% Two or more races, 4.2% Hispanic of any race; Average household size: 1.67; Median age: 56.2; Age under 18: 21.8%; Age 65 and over: 7.0%; Males per 100 females: 107.4; Marriage status: 0.0% never married, 27.3% now married, 0.0% separated, 10.7% widowed, 62.0% divorced; Foreign born: 0.0%; Speak English only: 89.3%; With disability: 4.2%; Veterans: 0.0%; Ancestry:

38.0% Russian, 31.7% German, 31.0% Polish, 22.5% Italian, 15.5% English
Employment: 0.0% management, business, and financial, 0.0% computer, engineering, and science, 18.9% education, legal, community service, arts, and media, 43.4% healthcare practitioners, 0.0% service, 18.9% sales and office, 0.0% natural resources, construction, and maintenance, 18.9% production, transportation, and material moving
Income: Per capita: $36,049; Median household: n/a; Average household: $61,854; Households with income of $100,000 or more: 11.8%; Poverty rate: 7.0%
Educational Attainment: High school diploma or higher: 100.0%; Bachelor's degree or higher: 46.8%; Graduate/professional degree or higher: 19.8%
Housing: Homeownership rate: 72.9%; Median home value: $148,900; Median year structure built: 1953; Homeowner vacancy rate: 0.0%; Median selected monthly owner costs: $1,181 with a mortgage, $0 without a mortgage; Median gross rent: n/a per month; Rental vacancy rate: 0.0%
Health Insurance: 83.8% have insurance; 76.8% have private insurance; 14.1% have public insurance; 16.2% do not have insurance; 0.0% of children under 18 do not have insurance
Transportation: Commute: 100.0% car, 0.0% public transportation, 0.0% walk, 0.0% work from home; Mean travel time to work: 0.0 minutes

POND EDDY (unincorporated postal area)
ZCTA: 12770

Covers a land area of 4.499 square miles and a water area of 0.274 square miles. Located at 41.45° N. Lat; 74.84° W. Long. Elevation is 554 feet.
Population: 186; Growth (since 2000): -31.6%; Density: 41.3 persons per square mile; Race: 100.0% White, 0.0% Black/African American, 0.0% Asian, 0.0% American Indian/Alaska Native, 0.0% Native Hawaiian/Other Pacific Islander, 0.0% Two or more races, 2.7% Hispanic of any race; Average household size: 2.04; Median age: 61.6; Age under 18: 14.5%; Age 65 and over: 34.4%; Males per 100 females: 88.5; Marriage status: 9.1% never married, 70.3% now married, 0.0% separated, 12.7% widowed, 7.9% divorced; Foreign born: 17.2%; Speak English only: 92.7%; With disability: 0.0%; Veterans: 18.2%; Ancestry: 53.2% German, 18.8% Italian, 14.5% English, 12.9% American, 2.7% French
Employment: 0.0% management, business, and financial, 0.0% computer, engineering, and science, 18.2% education, legal, community service, arts, and media, 0.0% healthcare practitioners, 19.7% service, 40.9% sales and office, 16.7% natural resources, construction, and maintenance, 4.5% production, transportation, and material moving
Income: Per capita: $32,354; Median household: $49,688; Average household: $63,382; Households with income of $100,000 or more: 17.6%; Poverty rate: 3.8%
Educational Attainment: High school diploma or higher: 96.9%; Bachelor's degree or higher: 10.1%; Graduate/professional degree or higher: 3.1%
Housing: Homeownership rate: 87.9%; Median home value: $157,700; Median year structure built: 1964; Homeowner vacancy rate: 0.0%; Median selected monthly owner costs: n/a with a mortgage, n/a without a mortgage; Median gross rent: n/a per month; Rental vacancy rate: 0.0%
Health Insurance: 97.8% have insurance; 93.5% have private insurance; 38.7% have public insurance; 2.2% do not have insurance; 0.0% of children under 18 do not have insurance
Transportation: Commute: 100.0% car, 0.0% public transportation, 0.0% walk, 0.0% work from home; Mean travel time to work: 34.2 minutes

ROCK HILL (CDP). Covers a land area of 3.657 square miles and a water area of 0.946 square miles. Located at 41.61° N. Lat; 74.58° W. Long. Elevation is 1,378 feet.
Population: 1,497; Growth (since 2000): 41.8%; Density: 409.3 persons per square mile; Race: 90.5% White, 2.9% Black/African American, 5.9% Asian, 0.5% American Indian/Alaska Native, 0.0% Native Hawaiian/Other Pacific Islander, 0.2% Two or more races, 4.5% Hispanic of any race; Average household size: 2.67; Median age: 44.0; Age under 18: 18.4%; Age 65 and over: 18.7%; Males per 100 females: 97.7; Marriage status: 24.8% never married, 58.8% now married, 1.2% separated, 11.1% widowed, 5.3% divorced; Foreign born: 17.3%; Speak English only: 85.9%;

With disability: 13.2%; Veterans: 5.9%; Ancestry: 15.6% Italian, 12.0% German, 10.8% Russian, 8.7% Irish, 6.7% Polish

Employment: 5.4% management, business, and financial, 0.4% computer, engineering, and science, 21.1% education, legal, community service, arts, and media, 21.1% healthcare practitioners, 10.6% service, 31.2% sales and office, 3.4% natural resources, construction, and maintenance, 6.7% production, transportation, and material moving

Income: Per capita: $38,606; Median household: $91,786; Average household: $102,446; Households with income of $100,000 or more: 47.7%; Poverty rate: 4.2%

Educational Attainment: High school diploma or higher: 95.4%; Bachelor's degree or higher: 49.5%; Graduate/professional degree or higher: 21.6%

Housing: Homeownership rate: 87.1%; Median home value: $212,200; Median year structure built: 1975; Homeowner vacancy rate: 4.9%; Median selected monthly owner costs: $2,069 with a mortgage, $850 without a mortgage; Median gross rent: n/a per month; Rental vacancy rate: 39.5%

Health Insurance: 95.3% have insurance; 82.0% have private insurance; 29.5% have public insurance; 4.7% do not have insurance; 0.0% of children under 18 do not have insurance

Transportation: Commute: 94.8% car, 4.3% public transportation, 0.0% walk, 0.9% work from home; Mean travel time to work: 32.1 minutes

---

ROCKLAND (town). Covers a land area of 94.156 square miles and a water area of 1.114 square miles. Located at 41.96° N. Lat; 74.79° W. Long. Elevation is 1,293 feet.

Population: 3,692; Growth (since 2000): -5.6%; Density: 39.2 persons per square mile; Race: 91.6% White, 2.8% Black/African American, 0.2% Asian, 0.2% American Indian/Alaska Native, 0.0% Native Hawaiian/Other Pacific Islander, 3.4% Two or more races, 7.3% Hispanic of any race; Average household size: 2.42; Median age: 45.8; Age under 18: 19.1%; Age 65 and over: 16.3%; Males per 100 females: 101.7; Marriage status: 27.1% never married, 55.0% now married, 7.3% separated, 7.5% widowed, 10.4% divorced; Foreign born: 4.2%; Speak English only: 94.6%; With disability: 14.9%; Veterans: 15.4%; Ancestry: 29.2% German, 16.7% Irish, 16.6% Italian, 9.4% English, 7.9% Polish

Employment: 7.8% management, business, and financial, 0.5% computer, engineering, and science, 16.5% education, legal, community service, arts, and media, 1.7% healthcare practitioners, 29.4% service, 20.5% sales and office, 11.3% natural resources, construction, and maintenance, 12.2% production, transportation, and material moving

Income: Per capita: $32,784; Median household: $51,596; Average household: $77,081; Households with income of $100,000 or more: 17.2%; Poverty rate: 18.1%

Educational Attainment: High school diploma or higher: 86.8%; Bachelor's degree or higher: 22.8%; Graduate/professional degree or higher: 8.2%

Housing: Homeownership rate: 70.2%; Median home value: $149,700; Median year structure built: 1968; Homeowner vacancy rate: 6.9%; Median selected monthly owner costs: $1,397 with a mortgage, $567 without a mortgage; Median gross rent: $910 per month; Rental vacancy rate: 10.8%

Health Insurance: 91.0% have insurance; 66.0% have private insurance; 38.2% have public insurance; 9.0% do not have insurance; 1.8% of children under 18 do not have insurance

Transportation: Commute: 91.4% car, 0.6% public transportation, 3.4% walk, 4.6% work from home; Mean travel time to work: 30.7 minutes

---

ROSCOE (CDP). Covers a land area of 0.718 square miles and a water area of 0.002 square miles. Located at 41.93° N. Lat; 74.92° W. Long. Elevation is 1,296 feet.

Population: 564; Growth (since 2000): -5.5%; Density: 785.4 persons per square mile; Race: 100.0% White, 0.0% Black/African American, 0.0% Asian, 0.0% American Indian/Alaska Native, 0.0% Native Hawaiian/Other Pacific Islander, 0.0% Two or more races, 0.0% Hispanic of any race; Average household size: 2.04; Median age: 48.3; Age under 18: 23.0%; Age 65 and over: 20.0%; Males per 100 females: 88.5; Marriage status: 25.7% never married, 47.9% now married, 0.0% separated, 11.7% widowed, 14.7% divorced; Foreign born: 4.3%; Speak English only: 100.0%; With disability: 11.9%; Veterans: 12.4%; Ancestry: 30.7% Irish, 24.6% German, 20.2% Italian, 14.7% English, 8.9% French

Employment: 15.6% management, business, and financial, 0.0% computer, engineering, and science, 14.5% education, legal, community service, arts, and media, 1.9% healthcare practitioners, 30.5% service, 14.1% sales and office, 11.1% natural resources, construction, and maintenance, 12.2% production, transportation, and material moving

Income: Per capita: $35,244; Median household: $48,438; Average household: $70,197; Households with income of $100,000 or more: 10.5%; Poverty rate: 9.8%

Educational Attainment: High school diploma or higher: 86.4%; Bachelor's degree or higher: 31.6%; Graduate/professional degree or higher: 9.0%

School District(s)
Roscoe Central SD (PK-12)
    2014-15 Enrollment: 297 . . . . (607) 498-4126

Housing: Homeownership rate: 69.7%; Median home value: $158,600; Median year structure built: Before 1940; Homeowner vacancy rate: 0.0%; Median selected monthly owner costs: $1,535 with a mortgage, $600 without a mortgage; Median gross rent: $589 per month; Rental vacancy rate: 16.8%

Health Insurance: 93.1% have insurance; 70.9% have private insurance; 36.2% have public insurance; 6.9% do not have insurance; 0.0% of children under 18 do not have insurance

Transportation: Commute: 73.6% car, 0.0% public transportation, 20.0% walk, 6.4% work from home; Mean travel time to work: 15.1 minutes

---

SMALLWOOD (CDP). Covers a land area of 1.505 square miles and a water area of 0.118 square miles. Located at 41.66° N. Lat; 74.82° W. Long. Elevation is 1,201 feet.

Population: 269; Growth (since 2000): -52.5%; Density: 178.8 persons per square mile; Race: 92.6% White, 0.0% Black/African American, 7.4% Asian, 0.0% American Indian/Alaska Native, 0.0% Native Hawaiian/Other Pacific Islander, 0.0% Two or more races, 14.9% Hispanic of any race; Average household size: 1.64; Median age: 57.7; Age under 18: 4.8%; Age 65 and over: 13.8%; Males per 100 females: 99.3; Marriage status: 27.3% never married, 39.5% now married, 0.0% separated, 0.0% widowed, 33.2% divorced; Foreign born: 8.9%; Speak English only: 100.0%; With disability: 10.0%; Veterans: 9.4%; Ancestry: 18.2% Polish, 17.5% Irish, 16.0% Italian, 13.4% German, 8.9% Norwegian

Employment: 19.7% management, business, and financial, 0.0% computer, engineering, and science, 10.2% education, legal, community service, arts, and media, 22.4% healthcare practitioners, 21.8% service, 6.8% sales and office, 8.8% natural resources, construction, and maintenance, 10.2% production, transportation, and material moving

Income: Per capita: $53,199; Median household: $82,895; Average household: $88,645; Households with income of $100,000 or more: 32.9%; Poverty rate: 10.0%

Educational Attainment: High school diploma or higher: 94.0%; Bachelor's degree or higher: 39.5%; Graduate/professional degree or higher: 16.1%

Housing: Homeownership rate: 74.4%; Median home value: $108,300; Median year structure built: 1944; Homeowner vacancy rate: 24.7%; Median selected monthly owner costs: n/a with a mortgage, n/a without a mortgage; Median gross rent: $1,261 per month; Rental vacancy rate: 0.0%

Health Insurance: 84.4% have insurance; 61.7% have private insurance; 42.4% have public insurance; 15.6% do not have insurance; 0.0% of children under 18 do not have insurance

Transportation: Commute: 81.6% car, 0.0% public transportation, 0.0% walk, 9.6% work from home; Mean travel time to work: 24.6 minutes

---

SOUTH FALLSBURG (CDP). Covers a land area of 5.947 square miles and a water area of 0.155 square miles. Located at 41.73° N. Lat; 74.64° W. Long. Elevation is 1,266 feet.

Population: 3,571; Growth (since 2000): 73.3%; Density: 600.5 persons per square mile; Race: 68.7% White, 9.1% Black/African American, 1.7% Asian, 0.3% American Indian/Alaska Native, 0.0% Native Hawaiian/Other Pacific Islander, 5.4% Two or more races, 36.4% Hispanic of any race; Average household size: 3.94; Median age: 24.0; Age under 18: 43.4%; Age 65 and over: 8.2%; Males per 100 females: 99.0; Marriage status: 43.5% never married, 34.7% now married, 3.3% separated, 10.3% widowed, 11.5% divorced; Foreign born: 20.6%; Speak English only: 58.0%; With disability: 14.4%; Veterans: 2.5%; Ancestry: 10.7% German, 10.6% Polish, 8.5% Irish, 4.1% Russian, 2.8% Czech

Employment: 6.2% management, business, and financial, 0.0% computer, engineering, and science, 19.7% education, legal, community service, arts, and media, 0.0% healthcare practitioners, 29.7% service, 16.3% sales and office, 8.0% natural resources, construction, and maintenance, 20.1% production, transportation, and material moving

Income: Per capita: $12,236; Median household: $32,022; Average household: $45,885; Households with income of $100,000 or more: 10.8%; Poverty rate: 45.3%
Educational Attainment: High school diploma or higher: 63.2%; Bachelor's degree or higher: 13.9%; Graduate/professional degree or higher: 9.5%

Four-year College(s)
Yeshivath Zichron Moshe (Private, Not-for-profit)
    Fall 2014 Enrollment: 194 . . . . (914) 434-5240
    2015-16 Tuition: In-state $11,600; Out-of-state $11,600
Housing: Homeownership rate: 28.1%; Median home value: $167,100; Median year structure built: 1981; Homeowner vacancy rate: 5.3%; Median selected monthly owner costs: $2,049 with a mortgage, $797 without a mortgage; Median gross rent: $899 per month; Rental vacancy rate: 18.6%
Health Insurance: 87.3% have insurance; 26.1% have private insurance; 69.2% have public insurance; 12.7% do not have insurance; 0.0% of children under 18 do not have insurance
Transportation: Commute: 69.0% car, 3.3% public transportation, 19.8% walk, 2.1% work from home; Mean travel time to work: 12.4 minutes

SUMMITVILLE (unincorporated postal area)
ZCTA: 12781
Covers a land area of 4.267 square miles and a water area of 0 square miles. Located at 41.62° N. Lat; 74.47° W. Long. Elevation is 548 feet.
Population: 229; Growth (since 2000): n/a; Density: 53.7 persons per square mile; Race: 93.4% White, 6.6% Black/African American, 0.0% Asian, 0.0% American Indian/Alaska Native, 0.0% Native Hawaiian/Other Pacific Islander, 0.0% Two or more races, 21.8% Hispanic of any race; Average household size: 2.41; Median age: 49.5; Age under 18: 21.0%; Age 65 and over: 6.6%; Males per 100 females: 106.0; Marriage status: 25.5% never married, 70.6% now married, 0.0% separated, 0.0% widowed, 3.9% divorced; Foreign born: 0.0%; Speak English only: 86.0%; With disability: 0.0%; Veterans: 4.4%; Ancestry: 21.8% Irish, 6.6% English, 6.6% German, 4.4% Italian, 3.5% Dutch
Employment: 9.6% management, business, and financial, 0.0% computer, engineering, and science, 0.0% education, legal, community service, arts, and media, 8.5% healthcare practitioners, 0.0% service, 52.1% sales and office, 29.8% natural resources, construction, and maintenance, 0.0% production, transportation, and material moving
Income: Per capita: $21,781; Median household: $58,036; Average household: $51,038; Households with income of $100,000 or more: n/a; Poverty rate: 21.8%
Educational Attainment: High school diploma or higher: 87.8%; Bachelor's degree or higher: 3.9%; Graduate/professional degree or higher: n/a
Housing: Homeownership rate: 91.6%; Median home value: n/a; Median year structure built: 1943; Homeowner vacancy rate: 29.3%; Median selected monthly owner costs: $1,300 with a mortgage, $0 without a mortgage; Median gross rent: n/a per month; Rental vacancy rate: 0.0%
Health Insurance: 95.6% have insurance; 78.2% have private insurance; 24.0% have public insurance; 4.4% do not have insurance; 0.0% of children under 18 do not have insurance
Transportation: Commute: 100.0% car, 0.0% public transportation, 0.0% walk, 0.0% work from home; Mean travel time to work: 34.4 minutes

SWAN LAKE (unincorporated postal area)
ZCTA: 12783
Covers a land area of 33.251 square miles and a water area of 1.096 square miles. Located at 41.74° N. Lat; 74.83° W. Long. Elevation is 1,345 feet.
Population: 2,357; Growth (since 2000): 8.7%; Density: 70.9 persons per square mile; Race: 79.1% White, 6.9% Black/African American, 2.9% Asian, 0.0% American Indian/Alaska Native, 0.0% Native Hawaiian/Other Pacific Islander, 7.6% Two or more races, 15.4% Hispanic of any race; Average household size: 3.25; Median age: 42.8; Age under 18: 16.5%; Age 65 and over: 17.3%; Males per 100 females: 137.3; Marriage status: 37.5% never married, 44.7% now married, 4.2% separated, 8.9% widowed, 8.8% divorced; Foreign born: 12.3%; Speak English only: 79.6%; With disability: 19.4%; Veterans: 3.7%; Ancestry: 21.6% Italian, 15.5% Irish, 9.3% German, 6.9% European, 6.1% Russian
Employment: 12.7% management, business, and financial, 3.8% computer, engineering, and science, 16.5% education, legal, community

service, arts, and media, 3.9% healthcare practitioners, 28.7% service, 15.2% sales and office, 11.2% natural resources, construction, and maintenance, 8.2% production, transportation, and material moving
Income: Per capita: $21,136; Median household: $59,394; Average household: $69,608; Households with income of $100,000 or more: 20.1%; Poverty rate: 16.2%
Educational Attainment: High school diploma or higher: 79.5%; Bachelor's degree or higher: 25.2%; Graduate/professional degree or higher: 9.0%
Housing: Homeownership rate: 80.5%; Median home value: $179,500; Median year structure built: 1968; Homeowner vacancy rate: 2.4%; Median selected monthly owner costs: $2,396 with a mortgage, $707 without a mortgage; Median gross rent: $871 per month; Rental vacancy rate: 0.0%
Health Insurance: 87.6% have insurance; 49.0% have private insurance; 51.7% have public insurance; 12.4% do not have insurance; 0.0% of children under 18 do not have insurance
Transportation: Commute: 84.5% car, 0.0% public transportation, 4.5% walk, 9.2% work from home; Mean travel time to work: 22.2 minutes

THOMPSON (town).
Covers a land area of 84.089 square miles and a water area of 3.408 square miles. Located at 41.65° N. Lat; 74.68° W. Long.
Population: 15,098; Growth (since 2000): 6.4%; Density: 179.5 persons per square mile; Race: 65.3% White, 20.5% Black/African American, 1.6% Asian, 0.1% American Indian/Alaska Native, 0.0% Native Hawaiian/Other Pacific Islander, 6.0% Two or more races, 21.7% Hispanic of any race; Average household size: 2.48; Median age: 37.9; Age under 18: 22.6%; Age 65 and over: 15.6%; Males per 100 females: 99.3; Marriage status: 40.1% never married, 42.4% now married, 3.4% separated, 8.4% widowed, 9.0% divorced; Foreign born: 11.3%; Speak English only: 79.5%; With disability: 17.7%; Veterans: 7.2%; Ancestry: 11.0% Irish, 10.1% German, 9.8% Italian, 4.9% American, 3.8% Polish
Employment: 6.2% management, business, and financial, 0.9% computer, engineering, and science, 9.3% education, legal, community service, arts, and media, 9.1% healthcare practitioners, 26.0% service, 26.7% sales and office, 10.1% natural resources, construction, and maintenance, 11.6% production, transportation, and material moving
Income: Per capita: $23,705; Median household: $39,043; Average household: $57,992; Households with income of $100,000 or more: 14.7%; Poverty rate: 24.2%
Educational Attainment: High school diploma or higher: 84.7%; Bachelor's degree or higher: 21.3%; Graduate/professional degree or higher: 9.0%
Housing: Homeownership rate: 48.7%; Median home value: $143,600; Median year structure built: 1970; Homeowner vacancy rate: 6.0%; Median selected monthly owner costs: $1,553 with a mortgage, $652 without a mortgage; Median gross rent: $814 per month; Rental vacancy rate: 12.8%
Health Insurance: 88.0% have insurance; 49.7% have private insurance; 51.0% have public insurance; 12.0% do not have insurance; 1.5% of children under 18 do not have insurance
Transportation: Commute: 85.7% car, 3.0% public transportation, 6.0% walk, 4.0% work from home; Mean travel time to work: 27.7 minutes
Additional Information Contacts
Town of Thompson . . . . (845) 794-2500
    http://www.townofthompson.com

THOMPSONVILLE (unincorporated postal area)
ZCTA: 12784
Covers a land area of 2.261 square miles and a water area of 0.007 square miles. Located at 41.67° N. Lat; 74.64° W. Long. Elevation is 1,168 feet.
Population: 63; Growth (since 2000): 6.8%; Density: 27.9 persons per square mile; Race: 100.0% White, 0.0% Black/African American, 0.0% Asian, 0.0% American Indian/Alaska Native, 0.0% Native Hawaiian/Other Pacific Islander, 0.0% Two or more races, 0.0% Hispanic of any race; Average household size: 1.75; Median age: 50.3; Age under 18: 22.2%; Age 65 and over: 0.0%; Males per 100 females: 100.0; Marriage status: 22.2% never married, 42.9% now married, 0.0% separated, 0.0% widowed, 34.9% divorced; Foreign born: 0.0%; Speak English only: 100.0%; With disability: 57.1%; Veterans: 28.6%; Ancestry: 77.8% Italian, 44.4% Polish, 22.2% Welsh
Employment: 0.0% management, business, and financial, 0.0% computer, engineering, and science, 0.0% education, legal, community service, arts, and media, 0.0% healthcare practitioners, 0.0% service,

0.0% sales and office, 100.0% natural resources, construction, and maintenance, 0.0% production, transportation, and material moving

Income: Per capita: $11,340; Median household: n/a; Average household: n/a; Households with income of $100,000 or more: n/a; Poverty rate: 34.9%

Educational Attainment: High school diploma or higher: 73.5%; Bachelor's degree or higher: n/a; Graduate/professional degree or higher: n/a

Housing: Homeownership rate: 61.1%; Median home value: n/a; Median year structure built: 1955; Homeowner vacancy rate: 0.0%; Median selected monthly owner costs: $0 with a mortgage, $0 without a mortgage; Median gross rent: n/a per month; Rental vacancy rate: 61.1%

Health Insurance: 57.1% have insurance; 0.0% have private insurance; 57.1% have public insurance; 42.9% do not have insurance; 0.0% of children under 18 do not have insurance

Transportation: Commute: 100.0% car, 0.0% public transportation, 0.0% walk, 0.0% work from home; Mean travel time to work: 0.0 minutes

TUSTEN (town). Covers a land area of 47.205 square miles and a water area of 1.580 square miles. Located at 41.57° N. Lat; 75.00° W. Long. Elevation is 709 feet.

Population: 1,369; Growth (since 2000): -3.3%; Density: 29.0 persons per square mile; Race: 87.7% White, 6.2% Black/African American, 0.0% Asian, 0.4% American Indian/Alaska Native, 0.0% Native Hawaiian/Other Pacific Islander, 5.0% Two or more races, 4.5% Hispanic of any race; Average household size: 2.08; Median age: 51.2; Age under 18: 13.7%; Age 65 and over: 26.4%; Males per 100 females: 109.5; Marriage status: 28.6% never married, 52.6% now married, 3.0% separated, 4.9% widowed, 13.9% divorced; Foreign born: 4.7%; Speak English only: 93.7%; With disability: 18.9%; Veterans: 10.9%; Ancestry: 27.1% German, 22.9% Irish, 12.8% American, 10.9% Italian, 7.1% English

Employment: 9.9% management, business, and financial, 3.2% computer, engineering, and science, 14.1% education, legal, community service, arts, and media, 8.5% healthcare practitioners, 21.1% service, 28.1% sales and office, 6.6% natural resources, construction, and maintenance, 8.5% production, transportation, and material moving

Income: Per capita: $33,514; Median household: $48,750; Average household: $73,362; Households with income of $100,000 or more: 20.0%; Poverty rate: 10.5%

Educational Attainment: High school diploma or higher: 84.3%; Bachelor's degree or higher: 26.2%; Graduate/professional degree or higher: 10.9%

Housing: Homeownership rate: 75.8%; Median home value: $176,500; Median year structure built: 1966; Homeowner vacancy rate: 8.5%; Median selected monthly owner costs: $1,510 with a mortgage, $654 without a mortgage; Median gross rent: $751 per month; Rental vacancy rate: 0.0%

Health Insurance: 88.6% have insurance; 66.3% have private insurance; 45.1% have public insurance; 11.4% do not have insurance; 2.7% of children under 18 do not have insurance

Transportation: Commute: 83.8% car, 5.4% public transportation, 3.6% walk, 6.5% work from home; Mean travel time to work: 33.9 minutes

WESTBROOKVILLE (unincorporated postal area)
ZCTA: 12785

Covers a land area of 16.666 square miles and a water area of 0.894 square miles. Located at 41.53° N. Lat; 74.56° W. Long..

Population: 916; Growth (since 2000): 392.5%; Density: 55.0 persons per square mile; Race: 98.6% White, 0.3% Black/African American, 0.0% Asian, 0.0% American Indian/Alaska Native, 0.0% Native Hawaiian/Other Pacific Islander, 1.1% Two or more races, 6.7% Hispanic of any race; Average household size: 2.59; Median age: 44.6; Age under 18: 17.9%; Age 65 and over: 23.1%; Males per 100 females: 101.6; Marriage status: 19.7% never married, 53.8% now married, 1.5% separated, 8.0% widowed, 18.6% divorced; Foreign born: 0.0%; Speak English only: 97.5%; With disability: 27.1%; Veterans: 7.0%; Ancestry: 26.9% German, 19.7% American, 18.7% English, 18.2% Irish, 17.1% Italian

Employment: 7.7% management, business, and financial, 3.5% computer, engineering, and science, 11.9% education, legal, community service, arts, and media, 8.7% healthcare practitioners, 19.0% service, 31.8% sales and office, 6.8% natural resources, construction, and maintenance, 10.6% production, transportation, and material moving

Income: Per capita: $27,575; Median household: $48,147; Average household: $67,128; Households with income of $100,000 or more: 30.2%; Poverty rate: 11.1%

Educational Attainment: High school diploma or higher: 85.7%; Bachelor's degree or higher: 20.3%; Graduate/professional degree or higher: 5.5%

Housing: Homeownership rate: 74.1%; Median home value: $152,500; Median year structure built: 1966; Homeowner vacancy rate: 6.8%; Median selected monthly owner costs: n/a with a mortgage, n/a without a mortgage; Median gross rent: $1,171 per month; Rental vacancy rate: 0.0%

Health Insurance: 87.8% have insurance; 52.2% have private insurance; 48.4% have public insurance; 12.2% do not have insurance; 0.0% of children under 18 do not have insurance

Transportation: Commute: 100.0% car, 0.0% public transportation, 0.0% walk, 0.0% work from home; Mean travel time to work: 33.3 minutes

WHITE LAKE (unincorporated postal area)
ZCTA: 12786

Covers a land area of 14.963 square miles and a water area of 2.790 square miles. Located at 41.64° N. Lat; 74.86° W. Long. Elevation is 1,335 feet.

Population: 365; Growth (since 2000): -45.1%; Density: 24.4 persons per square mile; Race: 83.0% White, 0.0% Black/African American, 0.0% Asian, 3.6% American Indian/Alaska Native, 0.0% Native Hawaiian/Other Pacific Islander, 0.0% Two or more races, 36.7% Hispanic of any race; Average household size: 1.75; Median age: 62.2; Age under 18: 18.1%; Age 65 and over: 43.6%; Males per 100 females: 97.9; Marriage status: 36.5% never married, 57.2% now married, 6.4% separated, 6.4% widowed, 0.0% divorced; Foreign born: 18.6%; Speak English only: 76.4%; With disability: 7.4%; Veterans: 33.1%; Ancestry: 15.6% English, 14.8% American, 11.5% Irish, 9.0% Italian, 8.8% European

Employment: 0.0% management, business, and financial, 0.0% computer, engineering, and science, 0.0% education, legal, community service, arts, and media, 0.0% healthcare practitioners, 15.5% service, 47.6% sales and office, 36.9% natural resources, construction, and maintenance, 0.0% production, transportation, and material moving

Income: Per capita: $22,635; Median household: $44,201; Average household: $39,475; Households with income of $100,000 or more: n/a; Poverty rate: 27.4%

Educational Attainment: High school diploma or higher: 77.3%; Bachelor's degree or higher: 25.4%; Graduate/professional degree or higher: 7.4%

Housing: Homeownership rate: 63.2%; Median home value: $185,700; Median year structure built: 1949; Homeowner vacancy rate: 0.0%; Median selected monthly owner costs: $1,278 with a mortgage, $383 without a mortgage; Median gross rent: $919 per month; Rental vacancy rate: 0.0%

Health Insurance: 82.5% have insurance; 67.4% have private insurance; 48.5% have public insurance; 17.5% do not have insurance; 0.0% of children under 18 do not have insurance

Transportation: Commute: 100.0% car, 0.0% public transportation, 0.0% walk, 0.0% work from home; Mean travel time to work: 32.9 minutes

WHITE SULPHUR SPRINGS (unincorporated postal area)
ZCTA: 12787

Covers a land area of 3.510 square miles and a water area of 0.002 square miles. Located at 41.80° N. Lat; 74.85° W. Long. Elevation is 1,362 feet.

Population: 455; Growth (since 2000): 104.0%; Density: 129.6 persons per square mile; Race: 97.4% White, 0.0% Black/African American, 2.6% Asian, 0.0% American Indian/Alaska Native, 0.0% Native Hawaiian/Other Pacific Islander, 0.0% Two or more races, 5.7% Hispanic of any race; Average household size: 2.97; Median age: 50.7; Age under 18: 25.1%; Age 65 and over: 22.0%; Males per 100 females: 97.4; Marriage status: 13.8% never married, 65.7% now married, 1.8% separated, 13.5% widowed, 7.0% divorced; Foreign born: 2.2%; Speak English only: 96.7%; With disability: 13.2%; Veterans: 19.1%; Ancestry: 41.5% German, 15.4% Polish, 14.7% Italian, 14.3% English, 11.2% Scandinavian

Employment: 5.6% management, business, and financial, 0.0% computer, engineering, and science, 33.7% education, legal, community

service, arts, and media, 2.8% healthcare practitioners, 20.8% service, 25.3% sales and office, 11.8% natural resources, construction, and maintenance, 0.0% production, transportation, and material moving
Income: Per capita: $27,952; Median household: $58,365; Average household: $81,195; Households with income of $100,000 or more: 36.0%; Poverty rate: 13.8%
Educational Attainment: High school diploma or higher: 83.8%; Bachelor's degree or higher: 31.2%; Graduate/professional degree or higher: 28.0%
Housing: Homeownership rate: 86.3%; Median home value: $138,700; Median year structure built: Before 1940; Homeowner vacancy rate: 22.8%; Median selected monthly owner costs: n/a with a mortgage, n/a without a mortgage; Median gross rent: n/a per month; Rental vacancy rate: 0.0%
Health Insurance: 100.0% have insurance; 61.1% have private insurance; 50.5% have public insurance; 0.0% do not have insurance; 0.0% of children under 18 do not have insurance
Transportation: Commute: 85.6% car, 0.0% public transportation, 0.0% walk, 14.4% work from home; Mean travel time to work: 19.1 minutes

WOODBOURNE (unincorporated postal area)
ZCTA: 12788

Covers a land area of 23.499 square miles and a water area of 0.212 square miles. Located at 41.79° N. Lat; 74.59° W. Long. Elevation is 1,188 feet.
Population: 2,937; Growth (since 2000): 0.1%; Density: 125.0 persons per square mile; Race: 59.2% White, 20.1% Black/African American, 3.1% Asian, 0.9% American Indian/Alaska Native, 0.0% Native Hawaiian/Other Pacific Islander, 6.7% Two or more races, 19.1% Hispanic of any race; Average household size: 2.77; Median age: 41.7; Age under 18: 15.6%; Age 65 and over: 10.5%; Males per 100 females: 178.3; Marriage status: 42.9% never married, 46.6% now married, 3.2% separated, 3.8% widowed, 6.8% divorced; Foreign born: 12.9%; Speak English only: 74.7%; With disability: 15.3%; Veterans: 11.5%; Ancestry: 15.5% Irish, 14.4% German, 11.3% Italian, 8.4% Polish, 6.0% English
Employment: 5.2% management, business, and financial, 1.5% computer, engineering, and science, 12.9% education, legal, community service, arts, and media, 2.7% healthcare practitioners, 24.9% service, 26.7% sales and office, 15.6% natural resources, construction, and maintenance, 10.6% production, transportation, and material moving
Income: Per capita: $14,879; Median household: $40,139; Average household: $51,559; Households with income of $100,000 or more: 11.7%; Poverty rate: 16.3%
Educational Attainment: High school diploma or higher: 83.5%; Bachelor's degree or higher: 15.7%; Graduate/professional degree or higher: 4.5%
Housing: Homeownership rate: 71.1%; Median home value: $167,300; Median year structure built: 1973; Homeowner vacancy rate: 2.4%; Median selected monthly owner costs: $1,227 with a mortgage, $450 without a mortgage; Median gross rent: $871 per month; Rental vacancy rate: 6.1%
Health Insurance: 93.6% have insurance; 57.5% have private insurance; 47.5% have public insurance; 6.4% do not have insurance; 1.3% of children under 18 do not have insurance
Transportation: Commute: 91.4% car, 0.0% public transportation, 4.9% walk, 3.7% work from home; Mean travel time to work: 18.0 minutes

WOODRIDGE (village). Covers a land area of 1.603 square miles and a water area of 0.105 square miles. Located at 41.72° N. Lat; 74.58° W. Long. Elevation is 1,161 feet.
Population: 732; Growth (since 2000): -18.8%; Density: 456.6 persons per square mile; Race: 71.4% White, 8.7% Black/African American, 4.9% Asian, 0.0% American Indian/Alaska Native, 0.0% Native Hawaiian/Other Pacific Islander, 5.6% Two or more races, 24.3% Hispanic of any race; Average household size: 2.22; Median age: 42.5; Age under 18: 23.5%; Age 65 and over: 15.6%; Males per 100 females: 105.1; Marriage status: 38.8% never married, 41.4% now married, 0.9% separated, 6.8% widowed, 12.9% divorced; Foreign born: 16.8%; Speak English only: 66.4%; With disability: 18.6%; Veterans: 6.8%; Ancestry: 12.8% German, 10.7% Italian, 9.8% Irish, 9.0% Polish, 6.7% Russian
Employment: 11.1% management, business, and financial, 2.2% computer, engineering, and science, 6.0% education, legal, community service, arts, and media, 0.0% healthcare practitioners, 30.1% service, 29.4% sales and office, 2.5% natural resources, construction, and maintenance, 18.7% production, transportation, and material moving

Income: Per capita: $20,908; Median household: $32,426; Average household: $46,731; Households with income of $100,000 or more: 15.6%; Poverty rate: 23.1%
Educational Attainment: High school diploma or higher: 77.6%; Bachelor's degree or higher: 20.5%; Graduate/professional degree or higher: 8.7%
Housing: Homeownership rate: 34.2%; Median home value: $101,800; Median year structure built: 1977; Homeowner vacancy rate: 11.0%; Median selected monthly owner costs: $1,488 with a mortgage, $700 without a mortgage; Median gross rent: $650 per month; Rental vacancy rate: 7.3%
Health Insurance: 89.2% have insurance; 48.5% have private insurance; 51.7% have public insurance; 10.8% do not have insurance; 0.0% of children under 18 do not have insurance
Transportation: Commute: 80.9% car, 1.0% public transportation, 10.8% walk, 3.2% work from home; Mean travel time to work: 25.5 minutes

WURTSBORO (village). Covers a land area of 1.266 square miles and a water area of 0 square miles. Located at 41.58° N. Lat; 74.49° W. Long. Elevation is 577 feet.
Population: 1,131; Growth (since 2000): -8.3%; Density: 893.2 persons per square mile; Race: 89.5% White, 7.5% Black/African American, 0.0% Asian, 0.3% American Indian/Alaska Native, 0.0% Native Hawaiian/Other Pacific Islander, 2.6% Two or more races, 7.6% Hispanic of any race; Average household size: 2.23; Median age: 41.6; Age under 18: 16.5%; Age 65 and over: 19.5%; Males per 100 females: 89.1; Marriage status: 36.4% never married, 39.5% now married, 2.9% separated, 9.5% widowed, 14.5% divorced; Foreign born: 3.3%; Speak English only: 93.4%; With disability: 17.1%; Veterans: 7.1%; Ancestry: 28.6% Irish, 21.8% Italian, 19.5% German, 8.9% English, 6.5% American
Employment: 10.2% management, business, and financial, 0.0% computer, engineering, and science, 9.2% education, legal, community service, arts, and media, 1.4% healthcare practitioners, 14.2% service, 32.5% sales and office, 11.1% natural resources, construction, and maintenance, 21.4% production, transportation, and material moving
Income: Per capita: $30,532; Median household: $52,574; Average household: $65,174; Households with income of $100,000 or more: 19.3%; Poverty rate: 16.7%
Educational Attainment: High school diploma or higher: 86.6%; Bachelor's degree or higher: 17.6%; Graduate/professional degree or higher: 7.9%

School District(s)
Monticello Central SD (KG-12)
    2014-15 Enrollment: 3,035 . . . . (845) 794-7700
Housing: Homeownership rate: 60.6%; Median home value: $156,600; Median year structure built: 1975; Homeowner vacancy rate: 4.0%; Median selected monthly owner costs: $1,564 with a mortgage, $759 without a mortgage; Median gross rent: $849 per month; Rental vacancy rate: 8.9%
Health Insurance: 92.0% have insurance; 67.6% have private insurance; 41.9% have public insurance; 8.0% do not have insurance; 0.0% of children under 18 do not have insurance
Transportation: Commute: 87.8% car, 4.7% public transportation, 3.8% walk, 2.8% work from home; Mean travel time to work: 30.1 minutes

YOUNGSVILLE (unincorporated postal area)
ZCTA: 12791

Covers a land area of 6.558 square miles and a water area of 0.010 square miles. Located at 41.82° N. Lat; 74.89° W. Long. Elevation is 1,197 feet.
Population: 672; Growth (since 2000): 50.0%; Density: 102.5 persons per square mile; Race: 89.0% White, 0.0% Black/African American, 9.5% Asian, 0.0% American Indian/Alaska Native, 0.0% Native Hawaiian/Other Pacific Islander, 1.5% Two or more races, 3.4% Hispanic of any race; Average household size: 2.07; Median age: 50.5; Age under 18: 23.5%; Age 65 and over: 14.0%; Males per 100 females: 90.4; Marriage status: 8.9% never married, 69.6% now married, 0.0% separated, 5.1% widowed, 16.3% divorced; Foreign born: 9.5%; Speak English only: 96.8%; With disability: 11.3%; Veterans: 4.9%; Ancestry: 40.6% German, 20.1% American, 11.3% Welsh, 11.2% Italian, 6.7% Guyanese
Employment: 8.9% management, business, and financial, 0.0% computer, engineering, and science, 53.9% education, legal, community service, arts, and media, 2.2% healthcare practitioners, 8.1% service, 7.0% sales and office, 17.5% natural resources, construction, and maintenance, 2.4% production, transportation, and material moving

Income: Per capita: $35,029; Median household: $58,380; Average household: $71,834; Households with income of $100,000 or more: 36.6%; Poverty rate: 18.6%

Educational Attainment: High school diploma or higher: 100.0%; Bachelor's degree or higher: 48.0%; Graduate/professional degree or higher: 36.5%

Housing: Homeownership rate: 64.6%; Median home value: $209,700; Median year structure built: 1964; Homeowner vacancy rate: 0.0%; Median selected monthly owner costs: $2,108 with a mortgage, $821 without a mortgage; Median gross rent: $824 per month; Rental vacancy rate: 0.0%

Health Insurance: 92.3% have insurance; 74.9% have private insurance; 30.1% have public insurance; 7.7% do not have insurance; 0.0% of children under 18 do not have insurance

Transportation: Commute: 100.0% car, 0.0% public transportation, 0.0% walk, 0.0% work from home; Mean travel time to work: 40.1 minutes

YULAN (unincorporated postal area)
ZCTA: 12792

Covers a land area of 3.391 square miles and a water area of 0.002 square miles. Located at 41.51° N. Lat; 74.96° W. Long. Elevation is 1,063 feet.

Population: 361; Growth (since 2000): 22.4%; Density: 106.4 persons per square mile; Race: 95.0% White, 0.0% Black/African American, 2.5% Asian, 0.0% American Indian/Alaska Native, 0.0% Native Hawaiian/Other Pacific Islander, 2.5% Two or more races, 5.0% Hispanic of any race; Average household size: 3.01; Median age: 38.5; Age under 18: 33.5%; Age 65 and over: 4.2%; Males per 100 females: 108.1; Marriage status: 22.9% never married, 72.1% now married, 7.5% separated, 5.0% widowed, 0.0% divorced; Foreign born: 17.2%; Speak English only: 82.5%; With disability: 16.1%; Veterans: 4.2%; Ancestry: 33.2% Irish, 30.2% Polish, 26.9% German, 8.3% Italian, 5.0% Eastern European

Employment: 22.3% management, business, and financial, 0.0% computer, engineering, and science, 10.7% education, legal, community service, arts, and media, 2.7% healthcare practitioners, 14.3% service, 33.0% sales and office, 0.0% natural resources, construction, and maintenance, 17.0% production, transportation, and material moving

Income: Per capita: $16,077; Median household: $36,563; Average household: $46,018; Households with income of $100,000 or more: 4.2%; Poverty rate: 21.6%

Educational Attainment: High school diploma or higher: 93.1%; Bachelor's degree or higher: 33.6%; Graduate/professional degree or higher: 9.5%

Housing: Homeownership rate: 86.7%; Median home value: $151,800; Median year structure built: 1973; Homeowner vacancy rate: 12.6%; Median selected monthly owner costs: $1,703 with a mortgage, $380 without a mortgage; Median gross rent: n/a per month; Rental vacancy rate: 30.4%

Health Insurance: 84.5% have insurance; 61.8% have private insurance; 25.8% have public insurance; 15.5% do not have insurance; 4.1% of children under 18 do not have insurance

Transportation: Commute: 80.4% car, 0.0% public transportation, 0.0% walk, 19.6% work from home; Mean travel time to work: 42.6 minutes

Tioga County

Located in southern New York; bounded on the south by Pennsylvania; crossed by the Susquehanna River. Covers a land area of 518.602 square miles, a water area of 4.278 square miles, and is located in the Eastern Time Zone at 42.18° N. Lat., 76.30° W. Long. The county was founded in 1791. County seat is Owego.

Tioga County is part of the Binghamton, NY Metropolitan Statistical Area. The entire metro area includes: Broome County, NY; Tioga County, NY

Population: 50,199; Growth (since 2000): -3.1%; Density: 96.8 persons per square mile; Race: 96.8% White, 0.8% Black/African American, 0.5% Asian, 0.1% American Indian/Alaska Native, 0.0% Native Hawaiian/Other Pacific Islander, 1.5% two or more races, 1.6% Hispanic of any race; Average household size: 2.50; Median age: 43.6; Age under 18: 22.3%; Age 65 and over: 17.4%; Males per 100 females: 98.3; Marriage status: 25.8% never married, 57.4% now married, 2.2% separated, 6.5% widowed, 10.3% divorced; Foreign born: 2.6%; Speak English only: 96.5%;

With disability: 13.4%; Veterans: 10.6%; Ancestry: 18.5% German, 15.0% Irish, 13.5% English, 9.1% Italian, 8.2% American

Religion: Six largest groups: 11.4% Catholicism, 10.3% Methodist/Pietist, 2.2% Baptist, 2.1% Non-denominational Protestant, 1.8% Holiness, 1.5% Presbyterian-Reformed

Economy: Unemployment rate: 4.9%; Leading industries: 17.0 % retail trade; 13.0 % construction; 13.0 % other services (except public administration); Farms: 536 totaling 107,873 acres; Company size: 1 employs 1,000 or more persons, 0 employ 500 to 999 persons, 11 employs 100 to 499 persons, 802 employ less than 100 persons; Business ownership: 1,020 women-owned, n/a Black-owned, 32 Hispanic-owned, 56 Asian-owned, n/a American Indian/Alaska Native-owned

Employment: 12.9% management, business, and financial, 6.5% computer, engineering, and science, 9.8% education, legal, community service, arts, and media, 6.2% healthcare practitioners, 17.7% service, 22.5% sales and office, 9.4% natural resources, construction, and maintenance, 14.8% production, transportation, and material moving

Income: Per capita: $29,427; Median household: $57,514; Average household: $72,680; Households with income of $100,000 or more: 23.7%; Poverty rate: 9.6%

Educational Attainment: High school diploma or higher: 90.9%; Bachelor's degree or higher: 24.4%; Graduate/professional degree or higher: 9.9%

Housing: Homeownership rate: 78.4%; Median home value: $112,600; Median year structure built: 1965; Homeowner vacancy rate: 0.7%; Median selected monthly owner costs: $1,203 with a mortgage, $491 without a mortgage; Median gross rent: $644 per month; Rental vacancy rate: 2.2%

Vital Statistics: Birth rate: 110.4 per 10,000 population; Death rate: 87.8 per 10,000 population; Age-adjusted cancer mortality rate: 149.0 deaths per 100,000 population

Health Insurance: 92.8% have insurance; 74.2% have private insurance; 33.9% have public insurance; 7.2% do not have insurance; 4.4% of children under 18 do not have insurance

Health Care: Physicians: 7.4 per 10,000 population; Dentists: 1.8 per 10,000 population; Hospital beds: 0.0 per 10,000 population; Hospital admissions: 0.0 per 10,000 population

Transportation: Commute: 93.6% car, 0.5% public transportation, 1.4% walk, 3.3% work from home; Mean travel time to work: 23.3 minutes

2016 Presidential Election: 60.1% Trump, 34.1% Clinton, 4.2% Johnson, 1.5% Stein

National and State Parks: Fairfield State Forest; Ketchumville State Forest; Oakley Corners State Forest; Robinson Hollow State Forest

Additional Information Contacts
Tioga Government . . . . (607) 687-8660
http://www.tiogacountyny.com

Tioga County Communities

APALACHIN (CDP). Covers a land area of 1.459 square miles and a water area of 0 square miles. Located at 42.07° N. Lat; 76.16° W. Long. Elevation is 843 feet.

Population: 1,508; Growth (since 2000): 33.9%; Density: 1,033.4 persons per square mile; Race: 97.5% White, 0.5% Black/African American, 0.7% Asian, 0.9% American Indian/Alaska Native, 0.0% Native Hawaiian/Other Pacific Islander, 0.5% Two or more races, 2.5% Hispanic of any race; Average household size: 2.91; Median age: 42.4; Age under 18: 19.6%; Age 65 and over: 22.2%; Males per 100 females: 105.3; Marriage status: 21.2% never married, 55.3% now married, 1.8% separated, 13.0% widowed, 10.5% divorced; Foreign born: 2.7%; Speak English only: 93.4%; With disability: 15.3%; Veterans: 3.4%; Ancestry: 22.6% German, 17.2% Irish, 9.7% Polish, 7.7% Italian, 7.3% English

Employment: 6.3% management, business, and financial, 6.0% computer, engineering, and science, 7.1% education, legal, community service, arts, and media, 1.9% healthcare practitioners, 26.3% service, 28.6% sales and office, 10.0% natural resources, construction, and maintenance, 13.8% production, transportation, and material moving

Income: Per capita: $25,209; Median household: $51,856; Average household: $72,870; Households with income of $100,000 or more: 22.5%; Poverty rate: 1.4%

Educational Attainment: High school diploma or higher: 92.7%; Bachelor's degree or higher: 11.4%; Graduate/professional degree or higher: 2.0%

School District(s)
Owego-Apalachin Central SD (PK-12)
    2014-15 Enrollment: 2,171 . . . . (607) 687-6224

Vestal Central SD (KG-12)
2014-15 Enrollment: 3,477 . . . . (607) 757-2241
Housing: Homeownership rate: 62.9%; Median home value: $113,000; Median year structure built: 1958; Homeowner vacancy rate: 0.0%; Median selected monthly owner costs: $1,317 with a mortgage, $500 without a mortgage; Median gross rent: $644 per month; Rental vacancy rate: 0.0%
Health Insurance: 94.8% have insurance; 78.9% have private insurance; 32.0% have public insurance; 5.2% do not have insurance; 9.5% of children under 18 do not have insurance
Transportation: Commute: 94.8% car, 1.1% public transportation, 0.0% walk, 3.0% work from home; Mean travel time to work: 24.9 minutes

BARTON (town). Covers a land area of 59.275 square miles and a water area of 0.414 square miles. Located at 42.08° N. Lat; 76.50° W. Long. Elevation is 804 feet.
Population: 8,701; Growth (since 2000): -4.0%; Density: 146.8 persons per square mile; Race: 98.1% White, 1.3% Black/African American, 0.2% Asian, 0.0% American Indian/Alaska Native, 0.0% Native Hawaiian/Other Pacific Islander, 0.4% Two or more races, 0.7% Hispanic of any race; Average household size: 2.38; Median age: 41.3; Age under 18: 23.4%; Age 65 and over: 15.6%; Males per 100 females: 92.1; Marriage status: 27.4% never married, 51.6% now married, 4.1% separated, 8.3% widowed, 12.7% divorced; Foreign born: 1.4%; Speak English only: 97.8%; With disability: 17.5%; Veterans: 12.8%; Ancestry: 18.5% Irish, 15.6% German, 14.6% English, 10.5% Italian, 7.8% American
Employment: 11.6% management, business, and financial, 3.4% computer, engineering, and science, 9.3% education, legal, community service, arts, and media, 9.9% healthcare practitioners, 20.6% service, 18.6% sales and office, 5.8% natural resources, construction, and maintenance, 20.8% production, transportation, and material moving
Income: Per capita: $25,721; Median household: $50,872; Average household: $61,387; Households with income of $100,000 or more: 17.3%; Poverty rate: 15.8%
Educational Attainment: High school diploma or higher: 86.8%; Bachelor's degree or higher: 15.8%; Graduate/professional degree or higher: 8.0%
Housing: Homeownership rate: 66.7%; Median home value: $93,300; Median year structure built: 1952; Homeowner vacancy rate: 0.0%; Median selected monthly owner costs: $1,038 with a mortgage, $427 without a mortgage; Median gross rent: $630 per month; Rental vacancy rate: 3.7%
Health Insurance: 91.1% have insurance; 66.8% have private insurance; 38.4% have public insurance; 8.9% do not have insurance; 6.0% of children under 18 do not have insurance
Transportation: Commute: 94.5% car, 0.0% public transportation, 1.8% walk, 3.0% work from home; Mean travel time to work: 21.1 minutes
Additional Information Contacts
Town of Barton . . . . (607) 565-2261
http://www.townofbarton.org

BERKSHIRE (town). Covers a land area of 30.216 square miles and a water area of 0.010 square miles. Located at 42.30° N. Lat; 76.17° W. Long. Elevation is 1,047 feet.
Population: 1,321; Growth (since 2000): -3.3%; Density: 43.7 persons per square mile; Race: 97.1% White, 0.0% Black/African American, 0.5% Asian, 1.4% American Indian/Alaska Native, 0.0% Native Hawaiian/Other Pacific Islander, 1.1% Two or more races, 0.5% Hispanic of any race; Average household size: 2.65; Median age: 40.6; Age under 18: 25.6%; Age 65 and over: 17.6%; Males per 100 females: 100.9; Marriage status: 25.8% never married, 54.4% now married, 1.4% separated, 5.8% widowed, 14.1% divorced; Foreign born: 1.1%; Speak English only: 97.8%; With disability: 15.3%; Veterans: 16.6%; Ancestry: 16.3% English, 16.1% German, 13.0% American, 9.3% Irish, 6.8% Italian
Employment: 8.5% management, business, and financial, 2.0% computer, engineering, and science, 6.6% education, legal, community service, arts, and media, 3.2% healthcare practitioners, 21.9% service, 24.4% sales and office, 11.4% natural resources, construction, and maintenance, 21.9% production, transportation, and material moving
Income: Per capita: $23,353; Median household: $51,607; Average household: $60,077; Households with income of $100,000 or more: 15.3%; Poverty rate: 15.3%
Educational Attainment: High school diploma or higher: 84.8%; Bachelor's degree or higher: 10.5%; Graduate/professional degree or higher: 3.7%
Housing: Homeownership rate: 89.2%; Median home value: $86,900; Median year structure built: 1972; Homeowner vacancy rate: 4.7%; Median

selected monthly owner costs: $1,127 with a mortgage, $502 without a mortgage; Median gross rent: $720 per month; Rental vacancy rate: 0.0%
Health Insurance: 92.1% have insurance; 65.9% have private insurance; 42.4% have public insurance; 7.9% do not have insurance; 0.0% of children under 18 do not have insurance
Transportation: Commute: 86.1% car, 1.2% public transportation, 4.4% walk, 6.5% work from home; Mean travel time to work: 30.0 minutes
Additional Information Contacts
Town of Berkshire . . . . (607) 657-8131
http://berkshireny.com

CANDOR (town). Covers a land area of 94.510 square miles and a water area of 0.110 square miles. Located at 42.23° N. Lat; 76.33° W. Long. Elevation is 902 feet.
Population: 5,196; Growth (since 2000): -2.3%; Density: 55.0 persons per square mile; Race: 96.1% White, 0.7% Black/African American, 0.0% Asian, 0.2% American Indian/Alaska Native, 0.3% Native Hawaiian/Other Pacific Islander, 2.8% Two or more races, 1.6% Hispanic of any race; Average household size: 2.71; Median age: 39.1; Age under 18: 27.4%; Age 65 and over: 17.9%; Males per 100 females: 95.3; Marriage status: 26.0% never married, 59.7% now married, 1.5% separated, 5.5% widowed, 8.9% divorced; Foreign born: 0.8%; Speak English only: 99.1%; With disability: 13.5%; Veterans: 12.4%; Ancestry: 12.1% American, 11.5% German, 9.7% Irish, 7.2% English, 6.6% Italian
Employment: 8.2% management, business, and financial, 2.1% computer, engineering, and science, 9.3% education, legal, community service, arts, and media, 5.8% healthcare practitioners, 23.9% service, 24.8% sales and office, 12.0% natural resources, construction, and maintenance, 14.1% production, transportation, and material moving
Income: Per capita: $24,350; Median household: $51,143; Average household: $63,527; Households with income of $100,000 or more: 19.7%; Poverty rate: 8.7%
Educational Attainment: High school diploma or higher: 89.4%; Bachelor's degree or higher: 17.1%; Graduate/professional degree or higher: 5.5%

School District(s)
Candor Central SD (KG-12)
2014-15 Enrollment: 762 . . . . (607) 659-5010
Housing: Homeownership rate: 83.2%; Median home value: $90,000; Median year structure built: 1974; Homeowner vacancy rate: 0.4%; Median selected monthly owner costs: $1,136 with a mortgage, $461 without a mortgage; Median gross rent: $639 per month; Rental vacancy rate: 2.3%
Health Insurance: 91.6% have insurance; 74.3% have private insurance; 33.9% have public insurance; 8.4% do not have insurance; 6.7% of children under 18 do not have insurance
Transportation: Commute: 92.3% car, 1.6% public transportation, 1.5% walk, 3.7% work from home; Mean travel time to work: 29.2 minutes
Additional Information Contacts
Town of Candor . . . . (607) 659-3175
http://candorny.us

CANDOR (village). Covers a land area of 0.441 square miles and a water area of 0 square miles. Located at 42.23° N. Lat; 76.34° W. Long. Elevation is 902 feet.
Population: 677; Growth (since 2000): -20.8%; Density: 1,536.9 persons per square mile; Race: 96.6% White, 0.0% Black/African American, 0.0% Asian, 0.0% American Indian/Alaska Native, 2.2% Native Hawaiian/Other Pacific Islander, 1.2% Two or more races, 3.7% Hispanic of any race; Average household size: 2.62; Median age: 36.7; Age under 18: 26.1%; Age 65 and over: 12.1%; Males per 100 females: 88.3; Marriage status: 21.5% never married, 59.3% now married, 3.9% separated, 6.5% widowed, 12.7% divorced; Foreign born: 0.3%; Speak English only: 99.0%; With disability: 17.9%; Veterans: 14.6%; Ancestry: 23.5% Irish, 17.3% German, 13.1% English, 12.9% Italian, 4.6% Polish
Employment: 6.8% management, business, and financial, 6.1% computer, engineering, and science, 13.5% education, legal, community service, arts, and media, 4.2% healthcare practitioners, 15.1% service, 25.4% sales and office, 11.9% natural resources, construction, and maintenance, 17.0% production, transportation, and material moving
Income: Per capita: $22,605; Median household: $50,417; Average household: $58,237; Households with income of $100,000 or more: 17.0%; Poverty rate: 15.6%
Educational Attainment: High school diploma or higher: 90.7%; Bachelor's degree or higher: 21.3%; Graduate/professional degree or higher: 9.3%

Candor Central SD (KG-12)
   2014-15 Enrollment: 762 . . . . (607) 659-5010
Housing: Homeownership rate: 77.5%; Median home value: $90,400; Median year structure built: Before 1940; Homeowner vacancy rate: 3.4%; Median selected monthly owner costs: $1,131 with a mortgage, $448 without a mortgage; Median gross rent: $634 per month; Rental vacancy rate: 10.3%
Health Insurance: 93.5% have insurance; 73.6% have private insurance; 34.7% have public insurance; 6.5% do not have insurance; 0.0% of children under 18 do not have insurance
Transportation: Commute: 83.6% car, 3.9% public transportation, 6.6% walk, 3.6% work from home; Mean travel time to work: 25.0 minutes

LOCKWOOD (unincorporated postal area)
ZCTA: 14859
   Covers a land area of 31.161 square miles and a water area of 0.061 square miles. Located at 42.11° N. Lat; 76.54° W. Long. Elevation is 902 feet.
   Population: 831; Growth (since 2000): -26.9%; Density: 26.7 persons per square mile; Race: 98.6% White, 0.0% Black/African American, 0.4% Asian, 0.0% American Indian/Alaska Native, 0.0% Native Hawaiian/Other Pacific Islander, 1.1% Two or more races, 1.6% Hispanic of any race; Average household size: 2.28; Median age: 48.9; Age under 18: 15.6%; Age 65 and over: 23.7%; Males per 100 females: 97.1; Marriage status: 26.4% never married, 58.9% now married, 0.5% separated, 9.6% widowed, 5.1% divorced; Foreign born: 0.6%; Speak English only: 100.0%; With disability: 15.9%; Veterans: 16.5%; Ancestry: 28.2% American, 18.8% German, 16.5% English, 10.8% Irish, 9.3% Italian
   Employment: 13.5% management, business, and financial, 3.7% computer, engineering, and science, 5.4% education, legal, community service, arts, and media, 7.6% healthcare practitioners, 15.2% service, 22.9% sales and office, 7.9% natural resources, construction, and maintenance, 23.8% production, transportation, and material moving
   Income: Per capita: $26,346; Median household: $50,781; Average household: $59,430; Households with income of $100,000 or more: 18.6%; Poverty rate: 12.5%
   Educational Attainment: High school diploma or higher: 92.2%; Bachelor's degree or higher: 10.4%; Graduate/professional degree or higher: 9.5%
   Housing: Homeownership rate: 84.4%; Median home value: $91,100; Median year structure built: 1963; Homeowner vacancy rate: 0.0%; Median selected monthly owner costs: $989 with a mortgage, $379 without a mortgage; Median gross rent: $341 per month; Rental vacancy rate: 0.0%
   Health Insurance: 90.7% have insurance; 77.4% have private insurance; 39.2% have public insurance; 9.3% do not have insurance; 1.5% of children under 18 do not have insurance
   Transportation: Commute: 97.3% car, 1.7% public transportation, 0.0% walk, 1.0% work from home; Mean travel time to work: 28.5 minutes

NEWARK VALLEY (town). Covers a land area of 50.295 square miles and a water area of 0.100 square miles. Located at 42.23° N. Lat; 76.16° W. Long. Elevation is 968 feet.
   Population: 3,872; Growth (since 2000): -5.5%; Density: 77.0 persons per square mile; Race: 97.3% White, 0.2% Black/African American, 0.0% Asian, 0.6% American Indian/Alaska Native, 0.0% Native Hawaiian/Other Pacific Islander, 1.7% Two or more races, 0.5% Hispanic of any race; Average household size: 2.49; Median age: 46.1; Age under 18: 22.0%; Age 65 and over: 14.4%; Males per 100 females: 101.2; Marriage status: 24.2% never married, 61.5% now married, 3.2% separated, 5.1% widowed, 9.2% divorced; Foreign born: 0.4%; Speak English only: 99.7%; With disability: 12.4%; Veterans: 9.8%; Ancestry: 19.2% German, 14.0% English, 12.7% American, 11.5% Irish, 4.5% Italian
   Employment: 12.6% management, business, and financial, 9.7% computer, engineering, and science, 9.8% education, legal, community service, arts, and media, 5.9% healthcare practitioners, 13.9% service, 17.5% sales and office, 11.2% natural resources, construction, and maintenance, 19.5% production, transportation, and material moving
   Income: Per capita: $35,314; Median household: $55,776; Average household: $85,515; Households with income of $100,000 or more: 24.0%; Poverty rate: 7.5%

Educational Attainment: High school diploma or higher: 90.5%; Bachelor's degree or higher: 23.5%; Graduate/professional degree or higher: 11.5%

Newark Valley Central SD (PK-12)
   2014-15 Enrollment: 1,273 . . . . (607) 642-3221
Housing: Homeownership rate: 81.0%; Median home value: $99,000; Median year structure built: 1964; Homeowner vacancy rate: 0.0%; Median selected monthly owner costs: $1,150 with a mortgage, $553 without a mortgage; Median gross rent: $538 per month; Rental vacancy rate: 0.0%
Health Insurance: 93.8% have insurance; 77.2% have private insurance; 30.3% have public insurance; 6.2% do not have insurance; 2.9% of children under 18 do not have insurance
Transportation: Commute: 97.9% car, 0.2% public transportation, 0.4% walk, 0.6% work from home; Mean travel time to work: 30.0 minutes

NEWARK VALLEY (village). Covers a land area of 0.988 square miles and a water area of 0 square miles. Located at 42.22° N. Lat; 76.19° W. Long. Elevation is 968 feet.
   Population: 1,188; Growth (since 2000): 10.9%; Density: 1,202.7 persons per square mile; Race: 92.5% White, 0.6% Black/African American, 0.1% Asian, 1.9% American Indian/Alaska Native, 0.0% Native Hawaiian/Other Pacific Islander, 4.5% Two or more races, 1.8% Hispanic of any race; Average household size: 2.67; Median age: 33.8; Age under 18: 31.1%; Age 65 and over: 11.6%; Males per 100 females: 89.2; Marriage status: 30.8% never married, 54.5% now married, 5.7% separated, 4.4% widowed, 10.3% divorced; Foreign born: 0.3%; Speak English only: 98.9%; With disability: 13.2%; Veterans: 13.3%; Ancestry: 23.1% German, 13.4% Irish, 13.2% English, 9.6% American, 7.2% Polish
   Employment: 14.2% management, business, and financial, 9.5% computer, engineering, and science, 10.1% education, legal, community service, arts, and media, 3.9% healthcare practitioners, 12.8% service, 17.1% sales and office, 6.4% natural resources, construction, and maintenance, 26.0% production, transportation, and material moving
   Income: Per capita: $25,835; Median household: $48,083; Average household: $67,047; Households with income of $100,000 or more: 24.9%; Poverty rate: 10.2%
   Educational Attainment: High school diploma or higher: 95.7%; Bachelor's degree or higher: 23.0%; Graduate/professional degree or higher: 8.9%

Newark Valley Central SD (PK-12)
   2014-15 Enrollment: 1,273 . . . . (607) 642-3221
Housing: Homeownership rate: 72.1%; Median home value: $91,400; Median year structure built: Before 1940; Homeowner vacancy rate: 0.0%; Median selected monthly owner costs: $1,256 with a mortgage, $565 without a mortgage; Median gross rent: $611 per month; Rental vacancy rate: 0.0%
Health Insurance: 94.4% have insurance; 75.6% have private insurance; 35.1% have public insurance; 5.6% do not have insurance; 6.8% of children under 18 do not have insurance
Transportation: Commute: 95.4% car, 0.6% public transportation, 1.6% walk, 2.4% work from home; Mean travel time to work: 27.6 minutes

NICHOLS (town). Covers a land area of 33.727 square miles and a water area of 0.938 square miles. Located at 42.03° N. Lat; 76.35° W. Long. Elevation is 791 feet.
   Population: 2,721; Growth (since 2000): 5.3%; Density: 80.7 persons per square mile; Race: 97.4% White, 0.4% Black/African American, 0.6% Asian, 0.0% American Indian/Alaska Native, 0.0% Native Hawaiian/Other Pacific Islander, 1.5% Two or more races, 1.7% Hispanic of any race; Average household size: 2.64; Median age: 39.0; Age under 18: 22.7%; Age 65 and over: 16.2%; Males per 100 females: 101.5; Marriage status: 31.9% never married, 49.2% now married, 0.8% separated, 6.3% widowed, 12.5% divorced; Foreign born: 1.2%; Speak English only: 98.4%; With disability: 10.9%; Veterans: 9.8%; Ancestry: 17.6% German, 16.3% English, 12.5% Irish, 6.8% French, 6.2% American
   Employment: 14.3% management, business, and financial, 3.1% computer, engineering, and science, 7.4% education, legal, community service, arts, and media, 5.2% healthcare practitioners, 16.0% service, 21.2% sales and office, 15.9% natural resources, construction, and maintenance, 16.9% production, transportation, and material moving
   Income: Per capita: $22,713; Median household: $47,353; Average household: $58,966; Households with income of $100,000 or more: 15.2%; Poverty rate: 11.4%

Educational Attainment: High school diploma or higher: 91.6%; Bachelor's degree or higher: 14.1%; Graduate/professional degree or higher: 4.6%

Housing: Homeownership rate: 79.7%; Median home value: $95,400; Median year structure built: 1959; Homeowner vacancy rate: 2.6%; Median selected monthly owner costs: $1,063 with a mortgage, $443 without a mortgage; Median gross rent: $618 per month; Rental vacancy rate: 7.9%

Health Insurance: 92.7% have insurance; 76.3% have private insurance; 34.4% have public insurance; 7.3% do not have insurance; 2.1% of children under 18 do not have insurance

Transportation: Commute: 92.9% car, 0.4% public transportation, 0.1% walk, 5.1% work from home; Mean travel time to work: 19.9 minutes

NICHOLS (village). Covers a land area of 0.518 square miles and a water area of 0 square miles. Located at 42.02° N. Lat; 76.37° W. Long. Elevation is 791 feet.

Population: 594; Growth (since 2000): 3.5%; Density: 1,145.7 persons per square mile; Race: 98.8% White, 0.0% Black/African American, 0.0% Asian, 0.0% American Indian/Alaska Native, 0.0% Native Hawaiian/Other Pacific Islander, 1.2% Two or more races, 0.8% Hispanic of any race; Average household size: 2.72; Median age: 39.0; Age under 18: 22.9%; Age 65 and over: 9.8%; Males per 100 females: 96.9; Marriage status: 32.0% never married, 53.8% now married, 0.4% separated, 4.0% widowed, 10.2% divorced; Foreign born: 0.8%; Speak English only: 99.3%; With disability: 9.9%; Veterans: 7.4%; Ancestry: 22.7% German, 15.0% English, 15.0% Irish, 9.6% Italian, 5.4% American

Employment: 9.9% management, business, and financial, 2.2% computer, engineering, and science, 17.0% education, legal, community service, arts, and media, 4.2% healthcare practitioners, 18.9% service, 19.2% sales and office, 6.1% natural resources, construction, and maintenance, 22.4% production, transportation, and material moving

Income: Per capita: $24,127; Median household: $58,750; Average household: $65,915; Households with income of $100,000 or more: 17.4%; Poverty rate: 16.7%

Educational Attainment: High school diploma or higher: 94.7%; Bachelor's degree or higher: 14.7%; Graduate/professional degree or higher: 7.0%

Housing: Homeownership rate: 71.6%; Median home value: $83,400; Median year structure built: Before 1940; Homeowner vacancy rate: 0.0%; Median selected monthly owner costs: $1,113 with a mortgage, $496 without a mortgage; Median gross rent: $613 per month; Rental vacancy rate: 22.5%

Health Insurance: 96.1% have insurance; 79.0% have private insurance; 31.5% have public insurance; 3.9% do not have insurance; 2.2% of children under 18 do not have insurance

Transportation: Commute: 93.9% car, 0.0% public transportation, 0.3% walk, 5.8% work from home; Mean travel time to work: 20.3 minutes

OWEGO (town). Covers a land area of 104.221 square miles and a water area of 1.522 square miles. Located at 42.09° N. Lat; 76.20° W. Long. Elevation is 814 feet.

History: Owego came into existence as Ah-wah-ga, "where the valley widens." Thomas C. Platt born here. Settled in 1787 and incorporated in 1827 on site of Native American village destroyed (1779) in Sullivan campaign.

Population: 19,489; Growth (since 2000): -4.3%; Density: 187.0 persons per square mile; Race: 96.2% White, 0.9% Black/African American, 0.8% Asian, 0.1% American Indian/Alaska Native, 0.0% Native Hawaiian/Other Pacific Islander, 1.8% Two or more races, 2.0% Hispanic of any race; Average household size: 2.54; Median age: 44.1; Age under 18: 21.6%; Age 65 and over: 18.3%; Males per 100 females: 100.4; Marriage status: 24.6% never married, 61.6% now married, 1.8% separated, 6.1% widowed, 7.8% divorced; Foreign born: 4.0%; Speak English only: 94.5%; With disability: 11.5%; Veterans: 9.0%; Ancestry: 21.4% German, 17.7% Irish, 12.0% English, 11.7% Italian, 6.3% Polish

Employment: 15.0% management, business, and financial, 9.9% computer, engineering, and science, 11.1% education, legal, community service, arts, and media, 5.9% healthcare practitioners, 15.6% service, 24.1% sales and office, 8.9% natural resources, construction, and maintenance, 9.4% production, transportation, and material moving

Income: Per capita: $33,122; Median household: $69,832; Average household: $84,128; Households with income of $100,000 or more: 31.2%; Poverty rate: 6.3%

Educational Attainment: High school diploma or higher: 93.8%; Bachelor's degree or higher: 35.3%; Graduate/professional degree or higher: 14.5%

School District(s)

Owego-Apalachin Central SD (PK-12)
    2014-15 Enrollment: 2,171 . . . . (607) 687-6224

Housing: Homeownership rate: 81.0%; Median home value: $137,400; Median year structure built: 1963; Homeowner vacancy rate: 0.5%; Median selected monthly owner costs: $1,349 with a mortgage, $560 without a mortgage; Median gross rent: $638 per month; Rental vacancy rate: 0.0%

Health Insurance: 93.4% have insurance; 78.8% have private insurance; 30.0% have public insurance; 6.6% do not have insurance; 3.9% of children under 18 do not have insurance

Newspapers: Tioga Co Courier (weekly circulation 2,400)

Transportation: Commute: 93.0% car, 0.2% public transportation, 1.8% walk, 3.0% work from home; Mean travel time to work: 20.9 minutes

Additional Information Contacts

Town of Owego . . . . (607) 687-0123
    http://www.townofowego.com

OWEGO (village). County seat. Covers a land area of 2.454 square miles and a water area of 0.215 square miles. Located at 42.10° N. Lat; 76.26° W. Long. Elevation is 814 feet.

Population: 3,807; Growth (since 2000): -2.7%; Density: 1,551.4 persons per square mile; Race: 94.1% White, 1.6% Black/African American, 2.3% Asian, 0.0% American Indian/Alaska Native, 0.0% Native Hawaiian/Other Pacific Islander, 2.1% Two or more races, 4.4% Hispanic of any race; Average household size: 2.21; Median age: 37.5; Age under 18: 17.5%; Age 65 and over: 15.9%; Males per 100 females: 95.3; Marriage status: 38.5% never married, 42.6% now married, 2.2% separated, 8.6% widowed, 10.3% divorced; Foreign born: 5.8%; Speak English only: 92.4%; With disability: 15.1%; Veterans: 8.8%; Ancestry: 20.9% Irish, 18.2% German, 13.6% English, 7.5% Italian, 4.9% American

Employment: 12.5% management, business, and financial, 5.2% computer, engineering, and science, 11.1% education, legal, community service, arts, and media, 5.4% healthcare practitioners, 27.6% service, 21.4% sales and office, 5.4% natural resources, construction, and maintenance, 11.4% production, transportation, and material moving

Income: Per capita: $26,996; Median household: $47,760; Average household: $59,684; Households with income of $100,000 or more: 20.4%; Poverty rate: 13.4%

Educational Attainment: High school diploma or higher: 92.5%; Bachelor's degree or higher: 32.9%; Graduate/professional degree or higher: 14.4%

School District(s)

Owego-Apalachin Central SD (PK-12)
    2014-15 Enrollment: 2,171 . . . . (607) 687-6224

Housing: Homeownership rate: 56.8%; Median home value: $103,200; Median year structure built: Before 1940; Homeowner vacancy rate: 0.0%; Median selected monthly owner costs: $1,539 with a mortgage, $504 without a mortgage; Median gross rent: $586 per month; Rental vacancy rate: 0.0%

Health Insurance: 89.0% have insurance; 69.8% have private insurance; 32.0% have public insurance; 11.0% do not have insurance; 6.0% of children under 18 do not have insurance

Safety: Violent crime rate: 32.0 per 10,000 population; Property crime rate: 315.0 per 10,000 population

Newspapers: Tioga Co Courier (weekly circulation 2,400)

Transportation: Commute: 83.6% car, 0.7% public transportation, 6.8% walk, 1.4% work from home; Mean travel time to work: 20.1 minutes

RICHFORD (town). Covers a land area of 38.187 square miles and a water area of 0.019 square miles. Located at 42.37° N. Lat; 76.19° W. Long. Elevation is 1,115 feet.

Population: 1,013; Growth (since 2000): -13.4%; Density: 26.5 persons per square mile; Race: 98.1% White, 0.0% Black/African American, 0.0% Asian, 0.0% American Indian/Alaska Native, 0.0% Native Hawaiian/Other Pacific Islander, 1.9% Two or more races, 0.4% Hispanic of any race; Average household size: 2.27; Median age: 45.9; Age under 18: 17.9%; Age 65 and over: 12.4%; Males per 100 females: 104.5; Marriage status: 29.3% never married, 49.4% now married, 2.0% separated, 5.9% widowed, 15.3% divorced; Foreign born: 0.8%; Speak English only: 99.2%; With disability: 15.4%; Veterans: 12.5%; Ancestry: 15.7% American, 13.7% English, 9.5% German, 5.3% Irish, 5.3% Italian

Employment: 5.7% management, business, and financial, 3.9% computer, engineering, and science, 7.2% education, legal, community service, arts, and media, 2.0% healthcare practitioners, 18.4% service, 26.6% sales and office, 15.0% natural resources, construction, and maintenance, 21.1% production, transportation, and material moving
Income: Per capita: $24,147; Median household: $39,821; Average household: $53,562; Households with income of $100,000 or more: 9.8%; Poverty rate: 15.6%
Educational Attainment: High school diploma or higher: 81.9%; Bachelor's degree or higher: 12.0%; Graduate/professional degree or higher: 4.4%
Housing: Homeownership rate: 85.9%; Median home value: $74,300; Median year structure built: 1974; Homeowner vacancy rate: 0.0%; Median selected monthly owner costs: $1,168 with a mortgage, $395 without a mortgage; Median gross rent: $619 per month; Rental vacancy rate: 0.0%
Health Insurance: 90.6% have insurance; 65.2% have private insurance; 35.4% have public insurance; 9.4% do not have insurance; 0.0% of children under 18 do not have insurance
Transportation: Commute: 93.1% car, 3.3% public transportation, 0.4% walk, 2.3% work from home; Mean travel time to work: 31.5 minutes

SPENCER (town). Covers a land area of 49.550 square miles and a water area of 0.326 square miles. Located at 42.22° N. Lat; 76.47° W. Long. Elevation is 994 feet.
Population: 3,075; Growth (since 2000): 3.2%; Density: 62.1 persons per square mile; Race: 95.4% White, 0.8% Black/African American, 0.4% Asian, 0.3% American Indian/Alaska Native, 0.0% Native Hawaiian/Other Pacific Islander, 0.9% Two or more races, 4.3% Hispanic of any race; Average household size: 2.51; Median age: 39.3; Age under 18: 25.4%; Age 65 and over: 15.8%; Males per 100 females: 101.6; Marriage status: 28.9% never married, 51.6% now married, 3.2% separated, 7.1% widowed, 12.4% divorced; Foreign born: 4.7%; Speak English only: 93.7%; With disability: 12.5%; Veterans: 7.8%; Ancestry: 22.1% German, 20.0% English, 18.8% Irish, 8.1% American, 7.6% Italian
Employment: 8.5% management, business, and financial, 5.1% computer, engineering, and science, 9.8% education, legal, community service, arts, and media, 4.0% healthcare practitioners, 17.0% service, 27.3% sales and office, 14.1% natural resources, construction, and maintenance, 14.2% production, transportation, and material moving
Income: Per capita: $21,120; Median household: $44,550; Average household: $51,824; Households with income of $100,000 or more: 13.1%; Poverty rate: 12.1%
Educational Attainment: High school diploma or higher: 88.3%; Bachelor's degree or higher: 18.9%; Graduate/professional degree or higher: 6.1%

School District(s)
Spencer-Van Etten Central SD (PK-12)
    2014-15 Enrollment: 924 . . . . (607) 589-7100
Housing: Homeownership rate: 71.5%; Median home value: $107,300; Median year structure built: 1975; Homeowner vacancy rate: 2.7%; Median selected monthly owner costs: $1,211 with a mortgage, $478 without a mortgage; Median gross rent: $925 per month; Rental vacancy rate: 7.2%
Health Insurance: 92.1% have insurance; 68.1% have private insurance; 40.1% have public insurance; 7.9% do not have insurance; 7.7% of children under 18 do not have insurance
Transportation: Commute: 93.3% car, 0.9% public transportation, 1.3% walk, 4.4% work from home; Mean travel time to work: 25.6 minutes

SPENCER (village). Covers a land area of 1.015 square miles and a water area of 0.014 square miles. Located at 42.21° N. Lat; 76.50° W. Long. Elevation is 994 feet.
Population: 993; Growth (since 2000): 35.8%; Density: 978.8 persons per square mile; Race: 98.9% White, 0.7% Black/African American, 0.4% Asian, 0.0% American Indian/Alaska Native, 0.0% Native Hawaiian/Other Pacific Islander, 0.0% Two or more races, 0.5% Hispanic of any race; Average household size: 2.63; Median age: 38.3; Age under 18: 28.7%; Age 65 and over: 16.8%; Males per 100 females: 88.8; Marriage status: 18.8% never married, 58.2% now married, 1.0% separated, 9.3% widowed, 13.7% divorced; Foreign born: 2.0%; Speak English only: 96.5%; With disability: 18.7%; Veterans: 7.9%; Ancestry: 22.6% Irish, 19.6% English, 18.6% German, 8.9% Italian, 6.3% American
Employment: 9.9% management, business, and financial, 5.7% computer, engineering, and science, 12.6% education, legal, community service, arts, and media, 5.7% healthcare practitioners, 16.1% service, 25.7% sales and

office, 12.6% natural resources, construction, and maintenance, 11.6% production, transportation, and material moving
Income: Per capita: $21,625; Median household: $44,773; Average household: $55,919; Households with income of $100,000 or more: 20.3%; Poverty rate: 16.5%
Educational Attainment: High school diploma or higher: 91.0%; Bachelor's degree or higher: 19.4%; Graduate/professional degree or higher: 7.3%

School District(s)
Spencer-Van Etten Central SD (PK-12)
    2014-15 Enrollment: 924 . . . . (607) 589-7100
Housing: Homeownership rate: 59.0%; Median home value: $110,900; Median year structure built: Before 1940; Homeowner vacancy rate: 0.0%; Median selected monthly owner costs: $1,281 with a mortgage, $491 without a mortgage; Median gross rent: $721 per month; Rental vacancy rate: 1.9%
Health Insurance: 88.2% have insurance; 61.2% have private insurance; 41.8% have public insurance; 11.8% do not have insurance; 14.4% of children under 18 do not have insurance
Transportation: Commute: 87.7% car, 0.5% public transportation, 4.0% walk, 7.3% work from home; Mean travel time to work: 25.0 minutes

TIOGA (town). Covers a land area of 58.620 square miles and a water area of 0.839 square miles. Located at 42.11° N. Lat; 76.37° W. Long.
History: This area of New York was settled by distinct cultures of indigenous peoples, including the Owasco, who migrated from the south, and the Point Peninsula Complex peoples. A 2011 paper by archaeologist Dr. John P. Hart argues there was no definable Owasco culture.
Population: 4,811; Growth (since 2000): -0.6%; Density: 82.1 persons per square mile; Race: 97.8% White, 0.0% Black/African American, 1.3% Asian, 0.0% American Indian/Alaska Native, 0.0% Native Hawaiian/Other Pacific Islander, 0.9% Two or more races, 1.2% Hispanic of any race; Average household size: 2.29; Median age: 49.8; Age under 18: 15.6%; Age 65 and over: 21.2%; Males per 100 females: 96.7; Marriage status: 23.3% never married, 56.1% now married, 0.9% separated, 7.3% widowed, 13.3% divorced; Foreign born: 2.7%; Speak English only: 96.6%; With disability: 15.3%; Veterans: 11.9%; Ancestry: 19.9% German, 17.6% English, 9.2% Irish, 8.5% American, 7.1% Italian
Employment: 15.7% management, business, and financial, 4.3% computer, engineering, and science, 8.7% education, legal, community service, arts, and media, 5.9% healthcare practitioners, 19.0% service, 21.4% sales and office, 5.7% natural resources, construction, and maintenance, 19.2% production, transportation, and material moving
Income: Per capita: $33,792; Median household: $59,219; Average household: $75,320; Households with income of $100,000 or more: 27.1%; Poverty rate: 9.6%
Educational Attainment: High school diploma or higher: 93.0%; Bachelor's degree or higher: 19.1%; Graduate/professional degree or higher: 6.3%
Housing: Homeownership rate: 82.0%; Median home value: $110,300; Median year structure built: 1976; Homeowner vacancy rate: 0.0%; Median selected monthly owner costs: $1,181 with a mortgage, $449 without a mortgage; Median gross rent: $715 per month; Rental vacancy rate: 0.0%
Health Insurance: 94.3% have insurance; 73.4% have private insurance; 38.2% have public insurance; 5.7% do not have insurance; 2.4% of children under 18 do not have insurance
Transportation: Commute: 94.4% car, 0.9% public transportation, 0.0% walk, 4.1% work from home; Mean travel time to work: 22.7 minutes

TIOGA CENTER (unincorporated postal area)
ZCTA: 13845
    Covers a land area of 0.388 square miles and a water area of 0.003 square miles. Located at 42.05° N. Lat; 76.35° W. Long. Elevation is 797 feet.
Population: 69; Growth (since 2000): n/a; Density: 177.8 persons per square mile; Race: 100.0% White, 0.0% Black/African American, 0.0% Asian, 0.0% American Indian/Alaska Native, 0.0% Native Hawaiian/Other Pacific Islander, 0.0% Two or more races, 0.0% Hispanic of any race; Average household size: 0.00; Median age: n/a; Age under 18: 0.0%; Age 65 and over: 29.0%; Males per 100 females: 97.6; Marriage status: 71.0% never married, 0.0% now married, 0.0% separated, 29.0% widowed, 0.0% divorced; Foreign born: 0.0%; Speak English only: 100.0%; With disability: 0.0%; Veterans: 0.0%; Ancestry: n/a

Employment: n/a management, business, and financial, n/a computer, engineering, and science, n/a education, legal, community service, arts, and media, n/a healthcare practitioners, n/a service, n/a sales and office, n/a natural resources, construction, and maintenance, n/a production, transportation, and material moving
Income: Per capita: n/a; Median household: n/a; Average household: n/a; Households with income of $100,000 or more: n/a; Poverty rate: n/a
Educational Attainment: High school diploma or higher: 100.0%; Bachelor's degree or higher: n/a; Graduate/professional degree or higher: n/a

School District(s)
Tioga Central SD (PK-12)
    2014-15 Enrollment: 1,023 . . . . (607) 687-8000
Housing: Homeownership rate: 29.0%; Median home value: n/a; Median year structure built: n/a; Homeowner vacancy rate: 0.0%; Median selected monthly owner costs: $0 with a mortgage, $0 without a mortgage; Median gross rent: n/a per month; Rental vacancy rate: 0.0%
Health Insurance: 29.0% have insurance; 0.0% have private insurance; 29.0% have public insurance; 71.0% do not have insurance; 0.0% of children under 18 do not have insurance
Transportation: Commute: n/a car, n/a public transportation, n/a walk, n/a work from home; Mean travel time to work: 0.0 minutes

---

WAVERLY (village). Covers a land area of 2.293 square miles and a water area of 0.027 square miles. Located at 42.01° N. Lat; 76.54° W. Long. Elevation is 817 feet.
History: Incorporated 1853.
Population: 4,328; Growth (since 2000): -6.1%; Density: 1,887.3 persons per square mile; Race: 96.1% White, 2.6% Black/African American, 0.4% Asian, 0.0% American Indian/Alaska Native, 0.0% Native Hawaiian/Other Pacific Islander, 0.8% Two or more races, 1.0% Hispanic of any race; Average household size: 2.17; Median age: 39.4; Age under 18: 20.7%; Age 65 and over: 18.3%; Males per 100 females: 86.0; Marriage status: 32.2% never married, 45.8% now married, 6.3% separated, 10.7% widowed, 11.3% divorced; Foreign born: 1.9%; Speak English only: 97.3%; With disability: 19.5%; Veterans: 13.0%; Ancestry: 23.1% Irish, 15.3% German, 13.5% Italian, 13.2% English, 4.9% American
Employment: 12.6% management, business, and financial, 4.2% computer, engineering, and science, 14.5% education, legal, community service, arts, and media, 10.7% healthcare practitioners, 22.9% service, 16.0% sales and office, 3.5% natural resources, construction, and maintenance, 15.7% production, transportation, and material moving
Income: Per capita: $26,073; Median household: $41,146; Average household: $57,349; Households with income of $100,000 or more: 14.5%; Poverty rate: 18.6%
Educational Attainment: High school diploma or higher: 88.0%; Bachelor's degree or higher: 18.3%; Graduate/professional degree or higher: 9.1%

School District(s)
Waverly Central SD (PK-12)
    2014-15 Enrollment: 1,671 . . . . (607) 565-2841
Housing: Homeownership rate: 55.0%; Median home value: $94,000; Median year structure built: Before 1940; Homeowner vacancy rate: 0.0%; Median selected monthly owner costs: $1,034 with a mortgage, $448 without a mortgage; Median gross rent: $637 per month; Rental vacancy rate: 5.0%
Health Insurance: 91.1% have insurance; 67.2% have private insurance; 36.8% have public insurance; 8.9% do not have insurance; 7.5% of children under 18 do not have insurance
Safety: Violent crime rate: 9.4 per 10,000 population; Property crime rate: 21.1 per 10,000 population
Transportation: Commute: 91.5% car, 0.0% public transportation, 3.4% walk, 3.6% work from home; Mean travel time to work: 16.4 minutes
Additional Information Contacts
Village of Waverly . . . . (607) 565-8106
    http://www.waverlybarton.com

WILLSEYVILLE (unincorporated postal area)
ZCTA: 13864
    Covers a land area of 26.650 square miles and a water area of 0.006 square miles. Located at 42.27° N. Lat; 76.39° W. Long. Elevation is 948 feet.
    Population: 1,006; Growth (since 2000): -7.3%; Density: 37.7 persons per square mile; Race: 98.6% White, 1.4% Black/African American, 0.0% Asian, 0.0% American Indian/Alaska Native, 0.0% Native

Hawaiian/Other Pacific Islander, 0.0% Two or more races, 4.8% Hispanic of any race; Average household size: 2.16; Median age: 45.4; Age under 18: 18.4%; Age 65 and over: 24.5%; Males per 100 females: 100.5; Marriage status: 15.5% never married, 65.4% now married, 3.0% separated, 8.9% widowed, 10.2% divorced; Foreign born: 1.1%; Speak English only: 100.0%; With disability: 17.0%; Veterans: 13.4%; Ancestry: 20.3% Irish, 16.0% German, 12.2% English, 7.7% Italian, 7.2% Dutch
Employment: 24.2% management, business, and financial, 2.2% computer, engineering, and science, 5.5% education, legal, community service, arts, and media, 0.0% healthcare practitioners, 28.5% service, 15.7% sales and office, 18.9% natural resources, construction, and maintenance, 5.1% production, transportation, and material moving
Income: Per capita: $26,300; Median household: $39,057; Average household: $55,324; Households with income of $100,000 or more: 14.2%; Poverty rate: 3.8%
Educational Attainment: High school diploma or higher: 76.9%; Bachelor's degree or higher: 17.7%; Graduate/professional degree or higher: 7.9%
Housing: Homeownership rate: 75.8%; Median home value: $84,200; Median year structure built: 1969; Homeowner vacancy rate: 0.0%; Median selected monthly owner costs: $1,278 with a mortgage, $445 without a mortgage; Median gross rent: $929 per month; Rental vacancy rate: 0.0%
Health Insurance: 89.7% have insurance; 65.9% have private insurance; 44.2% have public insurance; 10.3% do not have insurance; 0.0% of children under 18 do not have insurance
Transportation: Commute: 89.4% car, 2.6% public transportation, 0.0% walk, 0.0% work from home; Mean travel time to work: 24.1 minutes

Tompkins County

Located in west central New York; includes part of Cayuga Lake. Covers a land area of 474.649 square miles, a water area of 16.909 square miles, and is located in the Eastern Time Zone at 42.45° N. Lat., 76.47° W. Long. The county was founded in 1817. County seat is Ithaca.

Tompkins County is part of the Ithaca, NY Metropolitan Statistical Area. The entire metro area includes: Tompkins County, NY

Weather Station: Ithaca Cornell Univ									Elevation: 959 feet			
	Jan	Feb	Mar	Apr	May	Jun	Jul	Aug	Sep	Oct	Nov	Dec
High	31	34	41	55	67	76	80	79	71	59	47	36
Low	15	16	23	34	44	53	58	57	49	39	31	21
Precip	2.0	1.8	2.8	3.3	3.2	3.9	3.9	3.5	3.7	3.3	3.2	2.3
Snow	17.4	12.7	12.2	3.6	0.0	0.0	0.0	0.0	0.0	0.4	4.8	12.9

High and Low temperatures in degrees Fahrenheit; Precipitation and Snow in inches

Population: 103,855; Growth (since 2000): 7.6%; Density: 218.8 persons per square mile; Race: 81.3% White, 4.2% Black/African American, 10.0% Asian, 0.4% American Indian/Alaska Native, 0.0% Native Hawaiian/Other Pacific Islander, 3.3% two or more races, 4.6% Hispanic of any race; Average household size: 2.35; Median age: 30.2; Age under 18: 15.5%; Age 65 and over: 11.8%; Males per 100 females: 97.1; Marriage status: 49.5% never married, 38.8% now married, 1.5% separated, 3.6% widowed, 8.1% divorced; Foreign born: 12.7%; Speak English only: 86.2%; With disability: 9.5%; Veterans: 5.0%; Ancestry: 13.7% German, 12.9% Irish, 11.9% English, 10.1% American, 7.4% Italian
Religion: Six largest groups: 7.2% Catholicism, 4.0% Methodist/Pietist, 2.1% Non-denominational Protestant, 2.0% Presbyterian-Reformed, 1.3% Pentecostal, 1.2% Lutheran
Economy: Unemployment rate: 3.6%; Leading industries: 15.4 % retail trade; 13.9 % accommodation and food services; 11.9 % professional, scientific, and technical services; Farms: 558 totaling 90,774 acres; Company size: 3 employ 1,000 or more persons, 2 employ 500 to 999 persons, 39 employ 100 to 499 persons, 2,317 employ less than 100 persons; Business ownership: 2,989 women-owned, 203 Black-owned, 275 Hispanic-owned, 564 Asian-owned, 51 American Indian/Alaska Native-owned
Employment: 14.1% management, business, and financial, 9.9% computer, engineering, and science, 22.8% education, legal, community service, arts, and media, 5.0% healthcare practitioners, 17.7% service, 18.0% sales and office, 6.1% natural resources, construction, and maintenance, 6.5% production, transportation, and material moving

Income: Per capita: $28,460; Median household: $52,624; Average household: $74,288; Households with income of $100,000 or more: 23.5%; Poverty rate: 20.5%

Educational Attainment: High school diploma or higher: 94.2%; Bachelor's degree or higher: 50.8%; Graduate/professional degree or higher: 28.6%

Housing: Homeownership rate: 55.5%; Median home value: $176,500; Median year structure built: 1970; Homeowner vacancy rate: 1.2%; Median selected monthly owner costs: $1,477 with a mortgage, $626 without a mortgage; Median gross rent: $988 per month; Rental vacancy rate: 2.0%

Vital Statistics: Birth rate: 80.2 per 10,000 population; Death rate: 57.6 per 10,000 population; Age-adjusted cancer mortality rate: 154.3 deaths per 100,000 population

Health Insurance: 94.4% have insurance; 79.9% have private insurance; 24.9% have public insurance; 5.6% do not have insurance; 3.1% of children under 18 do not have insurance

Health Care: Physicians: 25.2 per 10,000 population; Dentists: 5.3 per 10,000 population; Hospital beds: 18.5 per 10,000 population; Hospital admissions: 614.9 per 10,000 population

Air Quality Index (AQI): Percent of Days: 96.7% good, 3.3% moderate, 0.0% unhealthy for sensitive individuals, 0.0% unhealthy, 0.0% very unhealthy; Annual median: 32; Annual maximum: 77

Transportation: Commute: 71.5% car, 6.3% public transportation, 14.6% walk, 5.7% work from home; Mean travel time to work: 18.8 minutes

2016 Presidential Election: 24.7% Trump, 68.7% Clinton, 3.3% Johnson, 3.3% Stein

National and State Parks: Alan Treman State Marine Park; Buttermilk Falls State Park; Danby State Forest; Hammond Hill State Forest; Newfield State Forest; Potato Hill State Forest; Robert H Treman State park; Shindagin Hollow State Forest; Taughannock Falls State Park; Yellow Barn State Forest

Additional Information Contacts

Tompkins Government . . . . (607) 274-5431
   http://www.co.tompkins.ny.us

Tompkins County Communities

BROOKTONDALE (unincorporated postal area)

ZCTA: 14817

Covers a land area of 40.294 square miles and a water area of 0.097 square miles. Located at 42.36° N. Lat; 76.33° W. Long. Elevation is 915 feet.

Population: 2,336; Growth (since 2000): 2.4%; Density: 58.0 persons per square mile; Race: 91.1% White, 4.8% Black/African American, 0.8% Asian, 0.0% American Indian/Alaska Native, 0.0% Native Hawaiian/Other Pacific Islander, 3.4% Two or more races, 2.9% Hispanic of any race; Average household size: 2.35; Median age: 46.4; Age under 18: 14.1%; Age 65 and over: 15.6%; Males per 100 females: 101.9; Marriage status: 34.3% never married, 48.6% now married, 2.3% separated, 5.0% widowed, 12.1% divorced; Foreign born: 4.8%; Speak English only: 98.6%; With disability: 20.5%; Veterans: 4.9%; Ancestry: 23.1% English, 14.8% German, 12.2% American, 10.7% Italian, 9.1% Polish

Employment: 7.7% management, business, and financial, 13.3% computer, engineering, and science, 14.7% education, legal, community service, arts, and media, 7.7% healthcare practitioners, 20.1% service, 24.1% sales and office, 8.0% natural resources, construction, and maintenance, 4.3% production, transportation, and material moving

Income: Per capita: $28,601; Median household: $49,931; Average household: $66,872; Households with income of $100,000 or more: 15.5%; Poverty rate: 6.7%

Educational Attainment: High school diploma or higher: 93.0%; Bachelor's degree or higher: 44.4%; Graduate/professional degree or higher: 24.3%

Housing: Homeownership rate: 85.2%; Median home value: $143,400; Median year structure built: 1967; Homeowner vacancy rate: 0.0%; Median selected monthly owner costs: $1,225 with a mortgage, $488 without a mortgage; Median gross rent: $796 per month; Rental vacancy rate: 0.0%

Health Insurance: 97.7% have insurance; 85.7% have private insurance; 24.4% have public insurance; 2.3% do not have insurance; 0.0% of children under 18 do not have insurance

Transportation: Commute: 84.6% car, 8.7% public transportation, 1.3% walk, 5.0% work from home; Mean travel time to work: 22.5 minutes

CAROLINE (town).

Covers a land area of 54.763 square miles and a water area of 0.130 square miles. Located at 42.36° N. Lat; 76.33° W. Long. Elevation is 968 feet.

Population: 3,358; Growth (since 2000): 15.4%; Density: 61.3 persons per square mile; Race: 93.8% White, 3.3% Black/African American, 0.5% Asian, 0.0% American Indian/Alaska Native, 0.0% Native Hawaiian/Other Pacific Islander, 2.4% Two or more races, 2.0% Hispanic of any race; Average household size: 2.39; Median age: 43.9; Age under 18: 16.3%; Age 65 and over: 13.3%; Males per 100 females: 99.9; Marriage status: 28.2% never married, 52.3% now married, 1.5% separated, 4.0% widowed, 15.4% divorced; Foreign born: 3.3%; Speak English only: 99.0%; With disability: 17.3%; Veterans: 4.4%; Ancestry: 25.3% English, 15.9% Irish, 14.8% German, 14.6% American, 7.8% Italian

Employment: 10.3% management, business, and financial, 11.5% computer, engineering, and science, 17.6% education, legal, community service, arts, and media, 5.3% healthcare practitioners, 19.1% service, 24.8% sales and office, 7.8% natural resources, construction, and maintenance, 3.4% production, transportation, and material moving

Income: Per capita: $31,592; Median household: $67,624; Average household: $74,488; Households with income of $100,000 or more: 21.4%; Poverty rate: 7.2%

Educational Attainment: High school diploma or higher: 94.3%; Bachelor's degree or higher: 52.0%; Graduate/professional degree or higher: 28.2%

Housing: Homeownership rate: 79.7%; Median home value: $160,600; Median year structure built: 1971; Homeowner vacancy rate: 0.0%; Median selected monthly owner costs: $1,334 with a mortgage, $545 without a mortgage; Median gross rent: $900 per month; Rental vacancy rate: 0.0%

Health Insurance: 96.5% have insurance; 81.4% have private insurance; 26.7% have public insurance; 3.5% do not have insurance; 0.0% of children under 18 do not have insurance

Transportation: Commute: 86.4% car, 6.2% public transportation, 2.7% walk, 3.5% work from home; Mean travel time to work: 20.9 minutes

CAYUGA HEIGHTS (village).

Covers a land area of 1.767 square miles and a water area of 0.001 square miles. Located at 42.47° N. Lat; 76.49° W. Long. Elevation is 787 feet.

Population: 3,789; Growth (since 2000): 15.8%; Density: 2,144.6 persons per square mile; Race: 70.9% White, 2.0% Black/African American, 20.1% Asian, 1.3% American Indian/Alaska Native, 0.0% Native Hawaiian/Other Pacific Islander, 0.8% Two or more races, 3.0% Hispanic of any race; Average household size: 2.03; Median age: 31.7; Age under 18: 13.8%; Age 65 and over: 18.4%; Males per 100 females: 94.1; Marriage status: 46.3% never married, 45.1% now married, 1.0% separated, 5.0% widowed, 3.6% divorced; Foreign born: 26.4%; Speak English only: 75.6%; With disability: 11.6%; Veterans: 3.5%; Ancestry: 10.2% English, 9.7% Irish, 9.7% German, 7.7% Italian, 3.5% Dutch

Employment: 15.7% management, business, and financial, 16.1% computer, engineering, and science, 45.2% education, legal, community service, arts, and media, 3.7% healthcare practitioners, 10.0% service, 8.2% sales and office, 0.5% natural resources, construction, and maintenance, 0.6% production, transportation, and material moving

Income: Per capita: $43,673; Median household: $78,285; Average household: $107,544; Households with income of $100,000 or more: 42.7%; Poverty rate: 8.3%

Educational Attainment: High school diploma or higher: 97.5%; Bachelor's degree or higher: 87.3%; Graduate/professional degree or higher: 60.8%

Housing: Homeownership rate: 45.6%; Median home value: $319,500; Median year structure built: 1969; Homeowner vacancy rate: 2.7%; Median selected monthly owner costs: $2,721 with a mortgage, $1,063 without a mortgage; Median gross rent: $1,116 per month; Rental vacancy rate: 4.9%

Health Insurance: 94.7% have insurance; 89.8% have private insurance; 20.3% have public insurance; 5.3% do not have insurance; 0.0% of children under 18 do not have insurance

Safety: Violent crime rate: 0.0 per 10,000 population; Property crime rate: 55.2 per 10,000 population

Transportation: Commute: 61.4% car, 13.5% public transportation, 17.9% walk, 3.2% work from home; Mean travel time to work: 13.5 minutes

DANBY (town). Covers a land area of 53.553 square miles and a water area of 0.222 square miles. Located at 42.33° N. Lat; 76.47° W. Long. Elevation is 1,237 feet.

Population: 3,462; Growth (since 2000): 15.1%; Density: 64.6 persons per square mile; Race: 94.7% White, 1.5% Black/African American, 0.4% Asian, 1.0% American Indian/Alaska Native, 0.0% Native Hawaiian/Other Pacific Islander, 0.8% Two or more races, 2.1% Hispanic of any race; Average household size: 2.39; Median age: 47.9; Age under 18: 16.1%; Age 65 and over: 22.2%; Males per 100 females: 97.6; Marriage status: 25.3% never married, 57.3% now married, 0.7% separated, 4.0% widowed, 13.5% divorced; Foreign born: 5.7%; Speak English only: 95.7%; With disability: 14.3%; Veterans: 7.2%; Ancestry: 20.0% English, 17.5% Irish, 13.4% Italian, 13.3% American, 12.3% German

Employment: 19.0% management, business, and financial, 7.3% computer, engineering, and science, 15.1% education, legal, community service, arts, and media, 4.1% healthcare practitioners, 21.6% service, 20.5% sales and office, 8.6% natural resources, construction, and maintenance, 3.8% production, transportation, and material moving

Income: Per capita: $39,067; Median household: $63,750; Average household: $90,887; Households with income of $100,000 or more: 34.0%; Poverty rate: 8.1%

Educational Attainment: High school diploma or higher: 96.2%; Bachelor's degree or higher: 33.5%; Graduate/professional degree or higher: 15.9%

Housing: Homeownership rate: 91.7%; Median home value: $163,900; Median year structure built: 1969; Homeowner vacancy rate: 0.0%; Median selected monthly owner costs: $1,451 with a mortgage, $574 without a mortgage; Median gross rent: $966 per month; Rental vacancy rate: 0.0%

Health Insurance: 95.2% have insurance; 77.4% have private insurance; 37.8% have public insurance; 4.8% do not have insurance; 2.0% of children under 18 do not have insurance

Transportation: Commute: 87.5% car, 3.1% public transportation, 3.5% walk, 3.0% work from home; Mean travel time to work: 19.8 minutes

DRYDEN (town). Covers a land area of 93.640 square miles and a water area of 0.690 square miles. Located at 42.48° N. Lat; 76.36° W. Long. Elevation is 1,089 feet.

Population: 14,840; Growth (since 2000): 9.7%; Density: 158.5 persons per square mile; Race: 92.9% White, 3.3% Black/African American, 1.6% Asian, 0.2% American Indian/Alaska Native, 0.0% Native Hawaiian/Other Pacific Islander, 1.7% Two or more races, 2.2% Hispanic of any race; Average household size: 2.34; Median age: 41.4; Age under 18: 21.5%; Age 65 and over: 12.5%; Males per 100 females: 100.1; Marriage status: 31.7% never married, 51.0% now married, 2.5% separated, 4.8% widowed, 12.5% divorced; Foreign born: 4.7%; Speak English only: 95.3%; With disability: 9.9%; Veterans: 6.3%; Ancestry: 18.6% German, 18.2% Irish, 16.8% English, 15.2% American, 7.7% Italian

Employment: 13.4% management, business, and financial, 7.6% computer, engineering, and science, 18.7% education, legal, community service, arts, and media, 6.8% healthcare practitioners, 16.5% service, 20.6% sales and office, 7.4% natural resources, construction, and maintenance, 9.0% production, transportation, and material moving

Income: Per capita: $34,570; Median household: $60,689; Average household: $80,373; Households with income of $100,000 or more: 26.2%; Poverty rate: 10.3%

Educational Attainment: High school diploma or higher: 94.6%; Bachelor's degree or higher: 44.8%; Graduate/professional degree or higher: 23.7%

School District(s)
Dryden Central SD (KG-12)
    2014-15 Enrollment: 1,656 . . . . (607) 844-5361
Two-year College(s)
Tompkins Cortland Community College (Public)
    Fall 2014 Enrollment: 5,559 . . . . (607) 844-8211
    2015-16 Tuition: In-state $5,666; Out-of-state $10,616

Housing: Homeownership rate: 68.4%; Median home value: $153,700; Median year structure built: 1974; Homeowner vacancy rate: 0.1%; Median selected monthly owner costs: $1,384 with a mortgage, $545 without a mortgage; Median gross rent: $816 per month; Rental vacancy rate: 0.8%

Health Insurance: 93.7% have insurance; 76.2% have private insurance; 29.6% have public insurance; 6.3% do not have insurance; 2.4% of children under 18 do not have insurance

Transportation: Commute: 88.4% car, 2.9% public transportation, 2.9% walk, 4.4% work from home; Mean travel time to work: 20.2 minutes

Additional Information Contacts
Town of Dryden . . . . (607) 844-8888
    http://www.dryden.ny.us

DRYDEN (village). Covers a land area of 1.756 square miles and a water area of 0.014 square miles. Located at 42.49° N. Lat; 76.30° W. Long. Elevation is 1,089 feet.

Population: 2,014; Growth (since 2000): 9.9%; Density: 1,146.8 persons per square mile; Race: 93.0% White, 2.2% Black/African American, 1.4% Asian, 0.2% American Indian/Alaska Native, 0.0% Native Hawaiian/Other Pacific Islander, 3.2% Two or more races, 10.0% Hispanic of any race; Average household size: 2.26; Median age: 42.8; Age under 18: 24.0%; Age 65 and over: 13.1%; Males per 100 females: 96.9; Marriage status: 31.7% never married, 49.1% now married, 1.1% separated, 6.6% widowed, 12.6% divorced; Foreign born: 7.6%; Speak English only: 90.8%; With disability: 13.8%; Veterans: 9.0%; Ancestry: 21.2% German, 20.4% English, 17.2% Irish, 10.2% American, 8.4% Italian

Employment: 13.3% management, business, and financial, 9.7% computer, engineering, and science, 13.3% education, legal, community service, arts, and media, 8.9% healthcare practitioners, 17.8% service, 23.2% sales and office, 3.5% natural resources, construction, and maintenance, 10.5% production, transportation, and material moving

Income: Per capita: $29,044; Median household: $51,071; Average household: $65,783; Households with income of $100,000 or more: 20.7%; Poverty rate: 11.0%

Educational Attainment: High school diploma or higher: 91.9%; Bachelor's degree or higher: 40.6%; Graduate/professional degree or higher: 16.2%

School District(s)
Dryden Central SD (KG-12)
    2014-15 Enrollment: 1,656 . . . . (607) 844-5361
Two-year College(s)
Tompkins Cortland Community College (Public)
    Fall 2014 Enrollment: 5,559 . . . . (607) 844-8211
    2015-16 Tuition: In-state $5,666; Out-of-state $10,616

Housing: Homeownership rate: 62.6%; Median home value: $147,600; Median year structure built: 1962; Homeowner vacancy rate: 0.0%; Median selected monthly owner costs: $1,334 with a mortgage, $605 without a mortgage; Median gross rent: $761 per month; Rental vacancy rate: 4.7%

Health Insurance: 95.0% have insurance; 72.4% have private insurance; 34.7% have public insurance; 5.0% do not have insurance; 2.9% of children under 18 do not have insurance

Safety: Violent crime rate: 18.6 per 10,000 population; Property crime rate: 302.3 per 10,000 population

Transportation: Commute: 94.3% car, 2.1% public transportation, 0.6% walk, 0.9% work from home; Mean travel time to work: 18.6 minutes

Additional Information Contacts
Village of Dryden . . . . (607) 844-8122
    http://www.dryden-ny.org

EAST ITHACA (CDP). Covers a land area of 1.733 square miles and a water area of 0.050 square miles. Located at 42.43° N. Lat; 76.46° W. Long. Elevation is 804 feet.

Population: 2,322; Growth (since 2000): 5.9%; Density: 1,339.8 persons per square mile; Race: 61.5% White, 3.5% Black/African American, 33.8% Asian, 0.0% American Indian/Alaska Native, 0.0% Native Hawaiian/Other Pacific Islander, 0.6% Two or more races, 3.3% Hispanic of any race; Average household size: 1.99; Median age: 33.6; Age under 18: 13.3%; Age 65 and over: 11.1%; Males per 100 females: 98.3; Marriage status: 49.2% never married, 41.7% now married, 0.6% separated, 1.6% widowed, 7.5% divorced; Foreign born: 34.2%; Speak English only: 69.2%; With disability: 1.3%; Veterans: 2.0%; Ancestry: 19.2% Irish, 16.1% German, 14.6% English, 5.3% Italian, 3.4% British

Employment: 16.1% management, business, and financial, 11.8% computer, engineering, and science, 37.6% education, legal, community service, arts, and media, 6.0% healthcare practitioners, 14.4% service, 11.9% sales and office, 1.4% natural resources, construction, and maintenance, 0.8% production, transportation, and material moving

Income: Per capita: $33,055; Median household: $44,647; Average household: $65,932; Households with income of $100,000 or more: 20.8%; Poverty rate: 22.8%

Educational Attainment: High school diploma or higher: 97.7%; Bachelor's degree or higher: 77.5%; Graduate/professional degree or higher: 40.5%

Housing: Homeownership rate: 38.1%; Median home value: $206,900; Median year structure built: 1981; Homeowner vacancy rate: 0.0%; Median selected monthly owner costs: $1,668 with a mortgage, $585 without a mortgage; Median gross rent: $882 per month; Rental vacancy rate: 0.0%
Health Insurance: 95.0% have insurance; 84.1% have private insurance; 19.7% have public insurance; 5.0% do not have insurance; 0.0% of children under 18 do not have insurance
Transportation: Commute: 61.0% car, 6.5% public transportation, 20.4% walk, 6.0% work from home; Mean travel time to work: 15.9 minutes

ENFIELD (town).
Covers a land area of 36.732 square miles and a water area of 0.104 square miles. Located at 42.44° N. Lat; 76.62° W. Long. Elevation is 1,106 feet.
Population: 3,614; Growth (since 2000): 7.3%; Density: 98.4 persons per square mile; Race: 89.2% White, 3.3% Black/African American, 0.0% Asian, 0.0% American Indian/Alaska Native, 0.0% Native Hawaiian/Other Pacific Islander, 7.3% Two or more races, 3.0% Hispanic of any race; Average household size: 2.42; Median age: 45.4; Age under 18: 16.8%; Age 65 and over: 13.1%; Males per 100 females: 95.2; Marriage status: 30.4% never married, 53.5% now married, 1.0% separated, 3.9% widowed, 12.2% divorced; Foreign born: 1.2%; Speak English only: 96.1%; With disability: 17.1%; Veterans: 8.2%; Ancestry: 17.3% English, 17.2% Irish, 11.5% German, 8.7% American, 8.0% Italian
Employment: 10.3% management, business, and financial, 4.2% computer, engineering, and science, 9.9% education, legal, community service, arts, and media, 3.3% healthcare practitioners, 29.7% service, 19.9% sales and office, 9.7% natural resources, construction, and maintenance, 13.1% production, transportation, and material moving
Income: Per capita: $27,899; Median household: $56,000; Average household: $66,467; Households with income of $100,000 or more: 14.2%; Poverty rate: 10.9%
Educational Attainment: High school diploma or higher: 86.5%; Bachelor's degree or higher: 27.4%; Graduate/professional degree or higher: 5.3%
Housing: Homeownership rate: 72.3%; Median home value: $118,800; Median year structure built: 1986; Homeowner vacancy rate: 1.0%; Median selected monthly owner costs: $1,236 with a mortgage, $523 without a mortgage; Median gross rent: $906 per month; Rental vacancy rate: 5.3%
Health Insurance: 94.2% have insurance; 70.7% have private insurance; 34.9% have public insurance; 5.8% do not have insurance; 3.6% of children under 18 do not have insurance
Transportation: Commute: 88.0% car, 1.1% public transportation, 1.2% walk, 9.0% work from home; Mean travel time to work: 22.2 minutes

ETNA (unincorporated postal area)
ZCTA: 13062

Covers a land area of 0.180 square miles and a water area of 0.007 square miles. Located at 42.48° N. Lat; 76.38° W. Long. Elevation is 1,020 feet.
Population: 261; Growth (since 2000): 99.2%; Density: 1,446.9 persons per square mile; Race: 100.0% White, 0.0% Black/African American, 0.0% Asian, 0.0% American Indian/Alaska Native, 0.0% Native Hawaiian/Other Pacific Islander, 0.0% Two or more races, 0.0% Hispanic of any race; Average household size: 3.39; Median age: 18.7; Age under 18: 42.5%; Age 65 and over: 2.7%; Males per 100 females: 94.4; Marriage status: 36.8% never married, 52.9% now married, 14.4% separated, 0.0% widowed, 10.3% divorced; Foreign born: 0.0%; Speak English only: 100.0%; With disability: 2.7%; Veterans: 4.7%; Ancestry: 57.1% English, 11.9% Polish, 9.6% Italian, 8.8% German, 8.4% American
Employment: 0.0% management, business, and financial, 0.0% computer, engineering, and science, 0.0% education, legal, community service, arts, and media, 0.0% healthcare practitioners, 9.0% service, 66.4% sales and office, 0.0% natural resources, construction, and maintenance, 24.6% production, transportation, and material moving
Income: Per capita: $16,243; Median household: n/a; Average household: $55,388; Households with income of $100,000 or more: n/a; Poverty rate: n/a
Educational Attainment: High school diploma or higher: 100.0%; Bachelor's degree or higher: 32.7%; Graduate/professional degree or higher: n/a
Housing: Homeownership rate: 100.0%; Median home value: n/a; Median year structure built: 1951; Homeowner vacancy rate: 0.0%; Median selected monthly owner costs: $0 with a mortgage, $468 without

a mortgage; Median gross rent: n/a per month; Rental vacancy rate: 0.0%
Health Insurance: 82.8% have insurance; 78.9% have private insurance; 6.5% have public insurance; 17.2% do not have insurance; 0.0% of children under 18 do not have insurance
Transportation: Commute: 100.0% car, 0.0% public transportation, 0.0% walk, 0.0% work from home; Mean travel time to work: 31.8 minutes

FOREST HOME (CDP).
Covers a land area of 0.251 square miles and a water area of 0.023 square miles. Located at 42.45° N. Lat; 76.47° W. Long. Elevation is 922 feet.
Population: 555; Growth (since 2000): -41.0%; Density: 2,209.6 persons per square mile; Race: 45.9% White, 3.2% Black/African American, 49.0% Asian, 0.0% American Indian/Alaska Native, 0.0% Native Hawaiian/Other Pacific Islander, 1.8% Two or more races, 13.7% Hispanic of any race; Average household size: 2.07; Median age: 30.1; Age under 18: 15.0%; Age 65 and over: 9.2%; Males per 100 females: 102.8; Marriage status: 44.5% never married, 52.6% now married, 0.6% separated, 0.0% widowed, 2.8% divorced; Foreign born: 64.0%; Speak English only: 44.8%; With disability: 2.2%; Veterans: 3.2%; Ancestry: 10.5% German, 6.3% English, 6.1% Irish, 2.9% Finnish, 2.9% Russian
Employment: 9.0% management, business, and financial, 29.1% computer, engineering, and science, 52.9% education, legal, community service, arts, and media, 0.0% healthcare practitioners, 1.3% service, 4.9% sales and office, 2.7% natural resources, construction, and maintenance, 0.0% production, transportation, and material moving
Income: Per capita: $30,096; Median household: $32,778; Average household: $60,271; Households with income of $100,000 or more: 17.9%; Poverty rate: 22.4%
Educational Attainment: High school diploma or higher: 99.0%; Bachelor's degree or higher: 87.8%; Graduate/professional degree or higher: 60.9%
Housing: Homeownership rate: 21.3%; Median home value: $445,000; Median year structure built: 1968; Homeowner vacancy rate: 0.0%; Median selected monthly owner costs: $3,536 with a mortgage, $950 without a mortgage; Median gross rent: $1,112 per month; Rental vacancy rate: 10.5%
Health Insurance: 96.9% have insurance; 89.5% have private insurance; 15.7% have public insurance; 3.1% do not have insurance; 3.6% of children under 18 do not have insurance
Transportation: Commute: 17.5% car, 34.0% public transportation, 30.6% walk, 9.2% work from home; Mean travel time to work: 15.2 minutes

FREEVILLE (village).
Covers a land area of 1.058 square miles and a water area of 0.037 square miles. Located at 42.51° N. Lat; 76.35° W. Long. Elevation is 1,043 feet.
Population: 524; Growth (since 2000): 3.8%; Density: 495.1 persons per square mile; Race: 93.1% White, 2.3% Black/African American, 0.8% Asian, 0.0% American Indian/Alaska Native, 0.0% Native Hawaiian/Other Pacific Islander, 3.8% Two or more races, 0.0% Hispanic of any race; Average household size: 2.53; Median age: 42.5; Age under 18: 20.0%; Age 65 and over: 10.1%; Males per 100 females: 98.5; Marriage status: 29.7% never married, 58.1% now married, 1.6% separated, 3.2% widowed, 9.0% divorced; Foreign born: 1.0%; Speak English only: 98.6%; With disability: 10.1%; Veterans: 10.0%; Ancestry: 26.5% German, 23.7% English, 18.1% Irish, 10.3% Italian, 9.0% American
Employment: 10.3% management, business, and financial, 11.0% computer, engineering, and science, 18.6% education, legal, community service, arts, and media, 3.8% healthcare practitioners, 25.2% service, 15.5% sales and office, 10.0% natural resources, construction, and maintenance, 5.5% production, transportation, and material moving
Income: Per capita: $30,514; Median household: $64,375; Average household: $76,861; Households with income of $100,000 or more: 28.0%; Poverty rate: 10.9%
Educational Attainment: High school diploma or higher: 99.2%; Bachelor's degree or higher: 49.2%; Graduate/professional degree or higher: 23.0%

School District(s)
Dryden Central SD (KG-12)
    2014-15 Enrollment: 1,656 . . . . (607) 844-5361
George Junior Republic Union Free SD (07-12)
    2014-15 Enrollment: 133 . . . . (607) 844-6343
Housing: Homeownership rate: 70.5%; Median home value: $147,100; Median year structure built: Before 1940; Homeowner vacancy rate: 3.9%;

Median selected monthly owner costs: $1,346 with a mortgage, $536 without a mortgage; Median gross rent: $769 per month; Rental vacancy rate: 0.0%
Health Insurance: 91.6% have insurance; 77.5% have private insurance; 23.3% have public insurance; 8.4% do not have insurance; 0.0% of children under 18 do not have insurance
Transportation: Commute: 81.5% car, 2.8% public transportation, 5.6% walk, 4.5% work from home; Mean travel time to work: 19.3 minutes

GROTON (town).
Covers a land area of 49.406 square miles and a water area of 0.133 square miles. Located at 42.58° N. Lat; 76.36° W. Long. Elevation is 997 feet.
History: Incorporated 1860.
Population: 6,097; Growth (since 2000): 5.2%; Density: 123.4 persons per square mile; Race: 96.4% White, 0.5% Black/African American, 1.5% Asian, 0.3% American Indian/Alaska Native, 0.0% Native Hawaiian/Other Pacific Islander, 1.2% Two or more races, 4.0% Hispanic of any race; Average household size: 2.36; Median age: 42.2; Age under 18: 20.3%; Age 65 and over: 16.0%; Males per 100 females: 96.3; Marriage status: 32.7% never married, 51.3% now married, 1.6% separated, 5.8% widowed, 10.2% divorced; Foreign born: 1.7%; Speak English only: 97.5%; With disability: 14.3%; Veterans: 9.2%; Ancestry: 22.4% German, 17.4% English, 15.7% American, 12.9% Irish, 6.9% Dutch
Employment: 15.6% management, business, and financial, 5.5% computer, engineering, and science, 9.4% education, legal, community service, arts, and media, 5.6% healthcare practitioners, 19.2% service, 18.6% sales and office, 13.0% natural resources, construction, and maintenance, 13.0% production, transportation, and material moving
Income: Per capita: $28,152; Median household: $54,113; Average household: $65,532; Households with income of $100,000 or more: 22.6%; Poverty rate: 10.6%
Educational Attainment: High school diploma or higher: 91.5%; Bachelor's degree or higher: 19.8%; Graduate/professional degree or higher: 7.4%

School District(s)
Groton Central SD (PK-12)
    2014-15 Enrollment: 840. . . . . (607) 898-5301
Housing: Homeownership rate: 72.3%; Median home value: $121,400; Median year structure built: 1950; Homeowner vacancy rate: 3.1%; Median selected monthly owner costs: $1,287 with a mortgage, $490 without a mortgage; Median gross rent: $791 per month; Rental vacancy rate: 0.0%
Health Insurance: 92.8% have insurance; 72.7% have private insurance; 32.3% have public insurance; 7.2% do not have insurance; 1.2% of children under 18 do not have insurance
Transportation: Commute: 89.3% car, 2.1% public transportation, 5.2% walk, 3.1% work from home; Mean travel time to work: 25.9 minutes
Additional Information Contacts
Town of Groton . . . . (607) 898-5035
    http://townofgrotonny.org

GROTON (village).
Covers a land area of 1.738 square miles and a water area of <.001 square miles. Located at 42.58° N. Lat; 76.36° W. Long. Elevation is 997 feet.
Population: 2,536; Growth (since 2000): 2.7%; Density: 1,459.1 persons per square mile; Race: 94.7% White, 0.9% Black/African American, 0.9% Asian, 0.6% American Indian/Alaska Native, 0.0% Native Hawaiian/Other Pacific Islander, 2.4% Two or more races, 2.1% Hispanic of any race; Average household size: 2.35; Median age: 38.4; Age under 18: 21.6%; Age 65 and over: 15.3%; Males per 100 females: 88.4; Marriage status: 35.3% never married, 46.9% now married, 2.4% separated, 8.1% widowed, 9.8% divorced; Foreign born: 3.2%; Speak English only: 95.5%; With disability: 14.6%; Veterans: 7.8%; Ancestry: 17.8% German, 17.6% Irish, 17.0% English, 10.4% American, 8.0% Italian
Employment: 13.4% management, business, and financial, 2.9% computer, engineering, and science, 13.2% education, legal, community service, arts, and media, 6.4% healthcare practitioners, 18.2% service, 22.4% sales and office, 10.1% natural resources, construction, and maintenance, 13.2% production, transportation, and material moving
Income: Per capita: $24,521; Median household: $48,403; Average household: $58,205; Households with income of $100,000 or more: 16.2%; Poverty rate: 13.8%
Educational Attainment: High school diploma or higher: 91.1%; Bachelor's degree or higher: 22.5%; Graduate/professional degree or higher: 9.7%

School District(s)
Groton Central SD (PK-12)
    2014-15 Enrollment: 840. . . . . (607) 898-5301
Housing: Homeownership rate: 63.1%; Median home value: $113,300; Median year structure built: Before 1940; Homeowner vacancy rate: 6.6%; Median selected monthly owner costs: $1,113 with a mortgage, $462 without a mortgage; Median gross rent: $626 per month; Rental vacancy rate: 0.0%
Health Insurance: 91.5% have insurance; 69.2% have private insurance; 37.5% have public insurance; 8.5% do not have insurance; 0.7% of children under 18 do not have insurance
Safety: Violent crime rate: 12.4 per 10,000 population; Property crime rate: 197.9 per 10,000 population
Transportation: Commute: 86.9% car, 2.8% public transportation, 6.5% walk, 2.8% work from home; Mean travel time to work: 25.9 minutes

ITHACA (city).
County seat. Covers a land area of 5.388 square miles and a water area of 0.684 square miles. Located at 42.44° N. Lat; 76.50° W. Long. Elevation is 410 feet.
History: Detachments of General John Sullivan's expedition crossed the site of Ithaca in 1779. The first settlers came in 1788 and 1789, but when the site was included within the Military Tract and title given to Revolutionary War veterans, these pioneers were obliged to move on. The land was later acquired by Simeon De Witt, surveyor-general of New York State, who gave the place its name. Solid growth began after the opening of Cornell University in 1868. In 1888, Ithaca became a city. For several years beginning in 1914, Ithaca was a center of the motion picture industry.
Population: 30,565; Growth (since 2000): 4.4%; Density: 5,672.6 persons per square mile; Race: 69.8% White, 7.4% Black/African American, 17.0% Asian, 0.3% American Indian/Alaska Native, 0.0% Native Hawaiian/Other Pacific Islander, 4.7% Two or more races, 7.1% Hispanic of any race; Average household size: 2.38; Median age: 21.8; Age under 18: 8.9%; Age 65 and over: 5.3%; Males per 100 females: 101.5; Marriage status: 77.1% never married, 17.2% now married, 1.4% separated, 1.4% widowed, 4.3% divorced; Foreign born: 17.2%; Speak English only: 80.1%; With disability: 8.0%; Veterans: 1.6%; Ancestry: 9.7% Irish, 9.1% German, 7.1% American, 6.7% Italian, 6.0% English
Employment: 11.0% management, business, and financial, 14.1% computer, engineering, and science, 29.3% education, legal, community service, arts, and media, 2.4% healthcare practitioners, 17.6% service, 16.3% sales and office, 3.7% natural resources, construction, and maintenance, 5.6% production, transportation, and material moving
Income: Per capita: $17,233; Median household: $30,436; Average household: $50,775; Households with income of $100,000 or more: 13.7%; Poverty rate: 44.8%
Educational Attainment: High school diploma or higher: 94.2%; Bachelor's degree or higher: 62.9%; Graduate/professional degree or higher: 38.0%

School District(s)
Ithaca City SD (PK-12)
    2014-15 Enrollment: 5,384 . . . . (607) 274-2101
New Roots Charter School (09-12)
    2014-15 Enrollment: 155. . . . . (607) 882-9220
Tompkins-Seneca-Tioga Boces
    2014-15 Enrollment: n/a . . . . (607) 257-1551
Four-year College(s)
Cornell University (Private, Not-for-profit)
    Fall 2014 Enrollment: 21,679 . . . . (607) 255-2000
    2015-16 Tuition: In-state $49,116; Out-of-state $49,116
Ithaca College (Private, Not-for-profit)
    Fall 2014 Enrollment: 6,587 . . . . (607) 274-3011
    2015-16 Tuition: In-state $40,658; Out-of-state $40,658
Vocational/Technical School(s)
Finger Lakes School of Massage (Private, For-profit)
    Fall 2014 Enrollment: 51 . . . . (607) 272-9026
    2015-16 Tuition: $15,500
Housing: Homeownership rate: 26.4%; Median home value: $220,400; Median year structure built: Before 1940; Homeowner vacancy rate: 2.7%; Median selected monthly owner costs: $1,649 with a mortgage, $730 without a mortgage; Median gross rent: $1,019 per month; Rental vacancy rate: 1.9%
Health Insurance: 94.4% have insurance; 82.5% have private insurance; 17.3% have public insurance; 5.6% do not have insurance; 9.4% of children under 18 do not have insurance

Hospitals: Cayuga Medical Center at Ithaca (204 beds)
Newspapers: Ithaca Journal (daily circulation 16,400); Ithaca Times (weekly circulation 22,000)
Transportation: Commute: 40.2% car, 10.6% public transportation, 40.2% walk, 6.4% work from home; Mean travel time to work: 15.4 minutes
Airports: Ithaca Tompkins Regional (primary service/non-hub)
Additional Information Contacts
City of Ithaca . . . . (607) 274-6570
    http://www.ci.ithaca.ny.us

ITHACA (town).

Covers a land area of 28.946 square miles and a water area of 1.340 square miles. Located at 42.41° N. Lat; 76.54° W. Long. Elevation is 410 feet.
History: Settled 1789, Incorporated as a city 1888.
Population: 20,254; Growth (since 2000): 11.3%; Density: 699.7 persons per square mile; Race: 73.6% White, 4.3% Black/African American, 16.4% Asian, 0.4% American Indian/Alaska Native, 0.0% Native Hawaiian/Other Pacific Islander, 3.3% Two or more races, 5.1% Hispanic of any race; Average household size: 2.21; Median age: 27.2; Age under 18: 13.4%; Age 65 and over: 12.7%; Males per 100 females: 89.1; Marriage status: 53.2% never married, 37.3% now married, 0.6% separated, 4.4% widowed, 5.0% divorced; Foreign born: 23.7%; Speak English only: 77.6%; With disability: 8.6%; Veterans: 4.0%; Ancestry: 12.0% German, 11.1% Irish, 9.6% English, 6.6% Italian, 5.3% American
Employment: 13.8% management, business, and financial, 11.6% computer, engineering, and science, 32.6% education, legal, community service, arts, and media, 5.1% healthcare practitioners, 16.1% service, 14.8% sales and office, 2.8% natural resources, construction, and maintenance, 3.1% production, transportation, and material moving
Income: Per capita: $28,671; Median household: $55,153; Average household: $81,282; Households with income of $100,000 or more: 27.2%; Poverty rate: 17.2%
Educational Attainment: High school diploma or higher: 96.7%; Bachelor's degree or higher: 70.0%; Graduate/professional degree or higher: 44.2%

School District(s)
Ithaca City SD (PK-12)
    2014-15 Enrollment: 5,384 . . . . (607) 274-2101
New Roots Charter School (09-12)
    2014-15 Enrollment: 155. . . . . (607) 882-9220
Tompkins-Seneca-Tioga Boces
    2014-15 Enrollment: n/a . . . . (607) 257-1551

Four-year College(s)
Cornell University (Private, Not-for-profit)
    Fall 2014 Enrollment: 21,679 . . . . (607) 255-2000
    2015-16 Tuition: In-state $49,116; Out-of-state $49,116
Ithaca College (Private, Not-for-profit)
    Fall 2014 Enrollment: 6,587 . . . . (607) 274-3011
    2015-16 Tuition: In-state $40,658; Out-of-state $40,658

Vocational/Technical School(s)
Finger Lakes School of Massage (Private, For-profit)
    Fall 2014 Enrollment: 51 . . . . (607) 272-9026
    2015-16 Tuition: $15,500
Housing: Homeownership rate: 47.2%; Median home value: $239,700; Median year structure built: 1973; Homeowner vacancy rate: 1.1%; Median selected monthly owner costs: $1,991 with a mortgage, $857 without a mortgage; Median gross rent: $1,071 per month; Rental vacancy rate: 2.7%
Health Insurance: 96.1% have insurance; 86.4% have private insurance; 20.6% have public insurance; 3.9% do not have insurance; 1.3% of children under 18 do not have insurance
Hospitals: Cayuga Medical Center at Ithaca (204 beds)
Newspapers: Ithaca Journal (daily circulation 16,400); Ithaca Times (weekly circulation 22,000)
Transportation: Commute: 62.6% car, 7.4% public transportation, 18.9% walk, 8.2% work from home; Mean travel time to work: 15.4 minutes
Airports: Ithaca Tompkins Regional (primary service/non-hub)
Additional Information Contacts
Town of Ithaca. . . . . (607) 273-1721
    http://www.town.ithaca.ny.us

JACKSONVILLE (unincorporated postal area)
ZCTA: 14854
    Covers a land area of 0.023 square miles and a water area of 0 square miles. Located at 42.51° N. Lat; 76.61° W. Long. Elevation is 1,024 feet.

Population: 15; Growth (since 2000): n/a; Density: 659.0 persons per square mile; Race: 100.0% White, 0.0% Black/African American, 0.0% Asian, 0.0% American Indian/Alaska Native, 0.0% Native Hawaiian/Other Pacific Islander, 0.0% Two or more races, 0.0% Hispanic of any race; Average household size: 2.14; Median age: n/a; Age under 18: 0.0%; Age 65 and over: 0.0%; Males per 100 females: 48.0; Marriage status: 0.0% never married, 100.0% now married, 0.0% separated, 0.0% widowed, 0.0% divorced; Foreign born: 0.0%; Speak English only: 100.0%; With disability: 0.0%; Veterans: 0.0%; Ancestry: n/a
Employment: 0.0% management, business, and financial, 46.7% computer, engineering, and science, 0.0% education, legal, community service, arts, and media, 53.3% healthcare practitioners, 0.0% service, 0.0% sales and office, 0.0% natural resources, construction, and maintenance, 0.0% production, transportation, and material moving
Income: Per capita: n/a; Median household: n/a; Average household: n/a; Households with income of $100,000 or more: 100.0%; Poverty rate: n/a
Educational Attainment: High school diploma or higher: 100.0%; Bachelor's degree or higher: 46.7%; Graduate/professional degree or higher: n/a
Housing: Homeownership rate: 100.0%; Median home value: n/a; Median year structure built: n/a; Homeowner vacancy rate: 0.0%; Median selected monthly owner costs: $0 with a mortgage, $0 without a mortgage; Median gross rent: n/a per month; Rental vacancy rate: 0.0%
Health Insurance: 100.0% have insurance; 100.0% have private insurance; 0.0% have public insurance; 0.0% do not have insurance; 0.0% of children under 18 do not have insurance
Transportation: Commute: 100.0% car, 0.0% public transportation, 0.0% walk, 0.0% work from home; Mean travel time to work: 0.0 minutes

LANSING (town).

Covers a land area of 60.490 square miles and a water area of 9.452 square miles. Located at 42.57° N. Lat; 76.53° W. Long. Elevation is 928 feet.
Population: 11,347; Growth (since 2000): 7.9%; Density: 187.6 persons per square mile; Race: 80.9% White, 1.7% Black/African American, 12.3% Asian, 0.5% American Indian/Alaska Native, 0.0% Native Hawaiian/Other Pacific Islander, 3.9% Two or more races, 4.2% Hispanic of any race; Average household size: 2.34; Median age: 38.5; Age under 18: 22.0%; Age 65 and over: 14.9%; Males per 100 females: 101.0; Marriage status: 28.4% never married, 56.5% now married, 0.7% separated, 4.3% widowed, 10.7% divorced; Foreign born: 15.0%; Speak English only: 82.7%; With disability: 5.2%; Veterans: 8.0%; Ancestry: 15.3% German, 13.3% English, 12.7% Irish, 11.9% American, 8.2% Italian
Employment: 21.6% management, business, and financial, 10.7% computer, engineering, and science, 24.8% education, legal, community service, arts, and media, 4.7% healthcare practitioners, 12.1% service, 16.9% sales and office, 3.9% natural resources, construction, and maintenance, 5.3% production, transportation, and material moving
Income: Per capita: $46,299; Median household: $67,721; Average household: $109,058; Households with income of $100,000 or more: 35.0%; Poverty rate: 9.7%
Educational Attainment: High school diploma or higher: 96.1%; Bachelor's degree or higher: 61.1%; Graduate/professional degree or higher: 35.5%

School District(s)
Lansing Central SD (KG-12)
    2014-15 Enrollment: 1,175 . . . . (607) 533-3020
Housing: Homeownership rate: 60.3%; Median home value: $239,300; Median year structure built: 1978; Homeowner vacancy rate: 1.5%; Median selected monthly owner costs: $1,865 with a mortgage, $711 without a mortgage; Median gross rent: $1,139 per month; Rental vacancy rate: 0.0%
Health Insurance: 95.5% have insurance; 87.4% have private insurance; 20.8% have public insurance; 4.5% do not have insurance; 0.0% of children under 18 do not have insurance
Transportation: Commute: 81.6% car, 8.8% public transportation, 2.5% walk, 6.2% work from home; Mean travel time to work: 18.1 minutes
Additional Information Contacts
Town of Lansing . . . . (607) 533-4142
    http://www.lansingtown.com

LANSING (village). Covers a land area of 4.610 square miles and a water area of 0.019 square miles. Located at 42.49° N. Lat; 76.49° W. Long. Elevation is 928 feet.
Population: 3,629; Growth (since 2000): 6.2%; Density: 787.2 persons per square mile; Race: 66.7% White, 3.2% Black/African American, 26.1% Asian, 0.8% American Indian/Alaska Native, 0.0% Native Hawaiian/Other Pacific Islander, 2.9% Two or more races, 8.3% Hispanic of any race; Average household size: 2.00; Median age: 33.9; Age under 18: 17.8%; Age 65 and over: 12.8%; Males per 100 females: 102.0; Marriage status: 37.5% never married, 45.5% now married, 0.4% separated, 3.4% widowed, 13.6% divorced; Foreign born: 35.9%; Speak English only: 65.2%; With disability: 3.0%; Veterans: 8.0%; Ancestry: 12.3% German, 10.0% Irish, 9.6% American, 8.5% English, 5.8% Italian
Employment: 21.3% management, business, and financial, 15.8% computer, engineering, and science, 26.9% education, legal, community service, arts, and media, 7.4% healthcare practitioners, 8.1% service, 17.2% sales and office, 0.0% natural resources, construction, and maintenance, 3.3% production, transportation, and material moving
Income: Per capita: $46,161; Median household: $61,232; Average household: $94,433; Households with income of $100,000 or more: 27.7%; Poverty rate: 12.6%
Educational Attainment: High school diploma or higher: 98.6%; Bachelor's degree or higher: 70.5%; Graduate/professional degree or higher: 47.1%

School District(s)
Lansing Central SD (KG-12)
    2014-15 Enrollment: 1,175 . . . . (607) 533-3020
Housing: Homeownership rate: 30.8%; Median home value: $315,200; Median year structure built: 1977; Homeowner vacancy rate: 2.8%; Median selected monthly owner costs: $2,692 with a mortgage, $717 without a mortgage; Median gross rent: $1,173 per month; Rental vacancy rate: 0.0%
Health Insurance: 94.1% have insurance; 87.6% have private insurance; 16.7% have public insurance; 5.9% do not have insurance; 0.0% of children under 18 do not have insurance
Transportation: Commute: 68.5% car, 25.0% public transportation, 2.8% walk, 2.1% work from home; Mean travel time to work: 18.8 minutes
Additional Information Contacts
Village of Lansing . . . . (607) 257-0424
    http://www.vlansing.org

MCLEAN (unincorporated postal area)
ZCTA: 13102
    Covers a land area of 0.058 square miles and a water area of 0.001 square miles. Located at 42.55° N. Lat; 76.29° W. Long..
Population: 9; Growth (since 2000): n/a; Density: 154.6 persons per square mile; Race: 100.0% White, 0.0% Black/African American, 0.0% Asian, 0.0% American Indian/Alaska Native, 0.0% Native Hawaiian/Other Pacific Islander, 0.0% Two or more races, 0.0% Hispanic of any race; Average household size: 0.00; Median age: n/a; Age under 18: 0.0%; Age 65 and over: 0.0%; Males per 100 females: 117.9; Marriage status: 100.0% never married, 0.0% now married, 0.0% separated, 0.0% widowed, 0.0% divorced; Foreign born: 0.0%; Speak English only: 100.0%; With disability: 0.0%; Veterans: 0.0%; Ancestry: 100.0% Italian
Employment: n/a management, business, and financial, n/a computer, engineering, and science, n/a education, legal, community service, arts, and media, n/a healthcare practitioners, n/a service, n/a sales and office, n/a natural resources, construction, and maintenance, n/a production, transportation, and material moving
Income: Per capita: n/a; Median household: n/a; Average household: n/a; Households with income of $100,000 or more: n/a; Poverty rate: n/a
Educational Attainment: High school diploma or higher: 100.0%; Bachelor's degree or higher: n/a; Graduate/professional degree or higher: n/a

School District(s)
Dryden Central SD (KG-12)
    2014-15 Enrollment: 1,656 . . . . (607) 844-5361
Housing: Homeownership rate: n/a; Median home value: n/a; Median year structure built: n/a; Homeowner vacancy rate: 0.0%; Median selected monthly owner costs: $0 with a mortgage, $0 without a mortgage; Median gross rent: n/a per month; Rental vacancy rate: 0.0%
Health Insurance: 100.0% have insurance; 0.0% have private insurance; 100.0% have public insurance; 0.0% do not have insurance; 0.0% of children under 18 do not have insurance

Transportation: Commute: n/a car, n/a public transportation, n/a walk, n/a work from home; Mean travel time to work: 0.0 minutes

NEWFIELD (town). Covers a land area of 58.841 square miles and a water area of 0.127 square miles. Located at 42.34° N. Lat; 76.61° W. Long. Elevation is 1,050 feet.
Population: 5,292; Growth (since 2000): 3.6%; Density: 89.9 persons per square mile; Race: 93.0% White, 3.0% Black/African American, 2.2% Asian, 0.3% American Indian/Alaska Native, 0.0% Native Hawaiian/Other Pacific Islander, 0.8% Two or more races, 4.1% Hispanic of any race; Average household size: 2.53; Median age: 40.3; Age under 18: 19.8%; Age 65 and over: 18.3%; Males per 100 females: 94.7; Marriage status: 34.5% never married, 49.3% now married, 2.8% separated, 6.2% widowed, 9.9% divorced; Foreign born: 3.5%; Speak English only: 93.3%; With disability: 11.8%; Veterans: 9.5%; Ancestry: 17.0% German, 14.6% American, 12.1% Irish, 11.0% English, 9.5% Italian
Employment: 11.9% management, business, and financial, 4.0% computer, engineering, and science, 8.5% education, legal, community service, arts, and media, 7.7% healthcare practitioners, 24.5% service, 20.0% sales and office, 15.6% natural resources, construction, and maintenance, 7.9% production, transportation, and material moving
Income: Per capita: $23,684; Median household: $44,352; Average household: $57,685; Households with income of $100,000 or more: 16.1%; Poverty rate: 20.6%
Educational Attainment: High school diploma or higher: 86.0%; Bachelor's degree or higher: 25.7%; Graduate/professional degree or higher: 10.5%

School District(s)
Newfield Central SD (PK-12)
    2014-15 Enrollment: 807 . . . . (607) 564-9955
Housing: Homeownership rate: 70.7%; Median home value: $121,900; Median year structure built: 1987; Homeowner vacancy rate: 0.0%; Median selected monthly owner costs: $1,181 with a mortgage, $480 without a mortgage; Median gross rent: $808 per month; Rental vacancy rate: 0.0%
Health Insurance: 89.4% have insurance; 55.5% have private insurance; 46.1% have public insurance; 10.6% do not have insurance; 6.6% of children under 18 do not have insurance
Transportation: Commute: 91.0% car, 0.6% public transportation, 2.2% walk, 3.5% work from home; Mean travel time to work: 23.1 minutes
Additional Information Contacts
Town of Newfield . . . . (607) 564-9981
    http://newfieldny.org

NEWFIELD HAMLET (CDP). Covers a land area of 1.257 square miles and a water area of <.001 square miles. Located at 42.36° N. Lat; 76.59° W. Long. Elevation is 1,050 feet.
Population: 699; Growth (since 2000): 8.0%; Density: 556.0 persons per square mile; Race: 100.0% White, 0.0% Black/African American, 0.0% Asian, 0.0% American Indian/Alaska Native, 0.0% Native Hawaiian/Other Pacific Islander, 0.0% Two or more races, 3.0% Hispanic of any race; Average household size: 1.98; Median age: 54.4; Age under 18: 7.6%; Age 65 and over: 26.9%; Males per 100 females: 89.8; Marriage status: 21.0% never married, 42.9% now married, 2.2% separated, 12.5% widowed, 23.5% divorced; Foreign born: 2.1%; Speak English only: 97.0%; With disability: 18.0%; Veterans: 2.3%; Ancestry: 25.5% German, 20.5% Dutch, 16.7% Irish, 11.0% American, 9.6% English
Employment: 19.6% management, business, and financial, 3.7% computer, engineering, and science, 12.6% education, legal, community service, arts, and media, 15.6% healthcare practitioners, 19.3% service, 25.5% sales and office, 0.0% natural resources, construction, and maintenance, 3.7% production, transportation, and material moving
Income: Per capita: $28,762; Median household: $47,411; Average household: $54,834; Households with income of $100,000 or more: 17.0%; Poverty rate: 4.4%
Educational Attainment: High school diploma or higher: 75.6%; Bachelor's degree or higher: 31.9%; Graduate/professional degree or higher: 15.5%
Housing: Homeownership rate: 79.0%; Median home value: $105,300; Median year structure built: 1963; Homeowner vacancy rate: 0.0%; Median selected monthly owner costs: $950 with a mortgage, n/a without a mortgage; Median gross rent: n/a per month; Rental vacancy rate: 0.0%
Health Insurance: 95.3% have insurance; 62.4% have private insurance; 41.9% have public insurance; 4.7% do not have insurance; 0.0% of children under 18 do not have insurance

Transportation: Commute: 84.2% car, 4.0% public transportation, 0.0% walk, 0.0% work from home; Mean travel time to work: 28.2 minutes

NORTHEAST ITHACA (CDP). Covers a land area of 1.469 square miles and a water area of 0.004 square miles. Located at 42.47° N. Lat; 76.46° W. Long.

Population: 3,103; Growth (since 2000): 16.9%; Density: 2,111.6 persons per square mile; Race: 58.6% White, 6.2% Black/African American, 32.5% Asian, 0.0% American Indian/Alaska Native, 0.0% Native Hawaiian/Other Pacific Islander, 2.8% Two or more races, 2.7% Hispanic of any race; Average household size: 2.57; Median age: 31.6; Age under 18: 23.1%; Age 65 and over: 9.4%; Males per 100 females: 98.6; Marriage status: 34.2% never married, 58.0% now married, 0.6% separated, 3.3% widowed, 4.4% divorced; Foreign born: 45.2%; Speak English only: 58.7%; With disability: 6.0%; Veterans: 3.6%; Ancestry: 10.9% German, 9.0% English, 8.1% Irish, 4.3% Polish, 4.2% Israeli

Employment: 13.1% management, business, and financial, 16.9% computer, engineering, and science, 32.8% education, legal, community service, arts, and media, 6.1% healthcare practitioners, 12.7% service, 15.5% sales and office, 0.6% natural resources, construction, and maintenance, 2.4% production, transportation, and material moving

Income: Per capita: $29,760; Median household: $54,444; Average household: $76,285; Households with income of $100,000 or more: 24.0%; Poverty rate: 20.3%

Educational Attainment: High school diploma or higher: 97.9%; Bachelor's degree or higher: 79.6%; Graduate/professional degree or higher: 53.9%

Housing: Homeownership rate: 44.6%; Median home value: $239,900; Median year structure built: 1969; Homeowner vacancy rate: 3.4%; Median selected monthly owner costs: $2,058 with a mortgage, $828 without a mortgage; Median gross rent: $1,164 per month; Rental vacancy rate: 0.0%

Health Insurance: 93.3% have insurance; 86.6% have private insurance; 16.1% have public insurance; 6.7% do not have insurance; 2.5% of children under 18 do not have insurance

Transportation: Commute: 76.5% car, 11.4% public transportation, 5.1% walk, 5.6% work from home; Mean travel time to work: 16.7 minutes

NORTHWEST ITHACA (CDP). Covers a land area of 2.908 square miles and a water area of 0.662 square miles. Located at 42.47° N. Lat; 76.54° W. Long. Elevation is 915 feet.

Population: 1,193; Growth (since 2000): 7.0%; Density: 410.3 persons per square mile; Race: 92.5% White, 4.8% Black/African American, 0.8% Asian, 0.0% American Indian/Alaska Native, 0.0% Native Hawaiian/Other Pacific Islander, 0.6% Two or more races, 10.3% Hispanic of any race; Average household size: 1.98; Median age: 53.2; Age under 18: 12.9%; Age 65 and over: 34.5%; Males per 100 females: 82.3; Marriage status: 26.6% never married, 46.0% now married, 2.4% separated, 16.5% widowed, 10.9% divorced; Foreign born: 27.1%; Speak English only: 72.6%; With disability: 16.1%; Veterans: 11.2%; Ancestry: 14.8% German, 11.2% American, 10.0% English, 9.6% Italian, 6.8% Irish

Employment: 16.6% management, business, and financial, 5.5% computer, engineering, and science, 23.1% education, legal, community service, arts, and media, 12.9% healthcare practitioners, 19.9% service, 15.9% sales and office, 4.6% natural resources, construction, and maintenance, 1.4% production, transportation, and material moving

Income: Per capita: $37,237; Median household: $49,948; Average household: $81,413; Households with income of $100,000 or more: 20.4%; Poverty rate: 19.8%

Educational Attainment: High school diploma or higher: 91.8%; Bachelor's degree or higher: 44.8%; Graduate/professional degree or higher: 32.3%

Housing: Homeownership rate: 40.3%; Median home value: $264,500; Median year structure built: 1980; Homeowner vacancy rate: 0.0%; Median selected monthly owner costs: $2,081 with a mortgage, $1,014 without a mortgage; Median gross rent: $927 per month; Rental vacancy rate: 8.7%

Health Insurance: 97.2% have insurance; 71.7% have private insurance; 46.4% have public insurance; 2.8% do not have insurance; 0.0% of children under 18 do not have insurance

Transportation: Commute: 79.4% car, 1.6% public transportation, 5.5% walk, 9.5% work from home; Mean travel time to work: 27.0 minutes

SLATERVILLE SPRINGS (unincorporated postal area)
ZCTA: 14881

Covers a land area of 1.229 square miles and a water area of 0.001 square miles. Located at 42.40° N. Lat; 76.36° W. Long. Elevation is 1,112 feet.

Population: 278; Growth (since 2000): 72.7%; Density: 226.3 persons per square mile; Race: 100.0% White, 0.0% Black/African American, 0.0% Asian, 0.0% American Indian/Alaska Native, 0.0% Native Hawaiian/Other Pacific Islander, 0.0% Two or more races, 0.0% Hispanic of any race; Average household size: 2.14; Median age: 44.3; Age under 18: 0.0%; Age 65 and over: 11.2%; Males per 100 females: 90.1; Marriage status: 5.4% never married, 27.0% now married, 0.0% separated, 5.8% widowed, 61.9% divorced; Foreign born: 0.0%; Speak English only: 100.0%; With disability: 37.4%; Veterans: 0.0%; Ancestry: 56.8% American, 23.7% English, 14.0% French, 12.6% Scotch-Irish, 10.8% Irish

Employment: 0.0% management, business, and financial, 0.0% computer, engineering, and science, 0.0% education, legal, community service, arts, and media, 0.0% healthcare practitioners, 44.0% service, 56.0% sales and office, 0.0% natural resources, construction, and maintenance, 0.0% production, transportation, and material moving

Income: Per capita: $38,466; Median household: n/a; Average household: $74,216; Households with income of $100,000 or more: 53.1%; Poverty rate: 5.4%

Educational Attainment: High school diploma or higher: 89.6%; Bachelor's degree or higher: 52.2%; Graduate/professional degree or higher: 5.8%

School District(s)

Ithaca City SD (PK-12)
    2014-15 Enrollment: 5,384 . . . . (607) 274-2101

Housing: Homeownership rate: 24.6%; Median home value: n/a; Median year structure built: 1977; Homeowner vacancy rate: 0.0%; Median selected monthly owner costs: $0 with a mortgage, $0 without a mortgage; Median gross rent: $929 per month; Rental vacancy rate: 0.0%

Health Insurance: 75.2% have insurance; 27.0% have private insurance; 54.0% have public insurance; 24.8% do not have insurance; 0.0% of children under 18 do not have insurance

Transportation: Commute: 100.0% car, 0.0% public transportation, 0.0% walk, 0.0% work from home; Mean travel time to work: 0.0 minutes

SOUTH HILL (CDP). Covers a land area of 5.896 square miles and a water area of 0.094 square miles. Located at 42.41° N. Lat; 76.49° W. Long. Elevation is 778 feet.

Population: 6,501; Growth (since 2000): 8.3%; Density: 1,102.6 persons per square mile; Race: 85.6% White, 4.8% Black/African American, 2.9% Asian, 0.2% American Indian/Alaska Native, 0.0% Native Hawaiian/Other Pacific Islander, 3.5% Two or more races, 6.1% Hispanic of any race; Average household size: 2.35; Median age: 20.0; Age under 18: 6.8%; Age 65 and over: 5.8%; Males per 100 females: 80.0; Marriage status: 78.3% never married, 17.1% now married, 0.4% separated, 3.1% widowed, 1.5% divorced; Foreign born: 7.7%; Speak English only: 91.3%; With disability: 8.9%; Veterans: 2.7%; Ancestry: 10.5% German, 10.3% Irish, 7.3% English, 6.7% Italian, 5.4% Polish

Employment: 9.4% management, business, and financial, 7.5% computer, engineering, and science, 23.1% education, legal, community service, arts, and media, 3.9% healthcare practitioners, 24.5% service, 21.0% sales and office, 4.9% natural resources, construction, and maintenance, 5.7% production, transportation, and material moving

Income: Per capita: $14,826; Median household: $59,688; Average household: $82,168; Households with income of $100,000 or more: 27.5%; Poverty rate: 16.1%

Educational Attainment: High school diploma or higher: 98.0%; Bachelor's degree or higher: 57.4%; Graduate/professional degree or higher: 37.3%

Housing: Homeownership rate: 63.1%; Median home value: $207,200; Median year structure built: 1969; Homeowner vacancy rate: 0.0%; Median selected monthly owner costs: $2,028 with a mortgage, $787 without a mortgage; Median gross rent: $1,229 per month; Rental vacancy rate: 0.8%

Health Insurance: 98.0% have insurance; 92.2% have private insurance; 12.2% have public insurance; 2.0% do not have insurance; 2.9% of children under 18 do not have insurance

Transportation: Commute: 53.6% car, 0.1% public transportation, 34.4% walk, 10.5% work from home; Mean travel time to work: 12.7 minutes

TRUMANSBURG (village). Covers a land area of 1.387 square miles and a water area of 0.004 square miles. Located at 42.54° N. Lat; 76.66° W. Long. Elevation is 965 feet.

History: Settled 1792; incorporated 1865.

Population: 1,637; Growth (since 2000): 3.5%; Density: 1,180.2 persons per square mile; Race: 99.1% White, 0.2% Black/African American, 0.4% Asian, 0.0% American Indian/Alaska Native, 0.0% Native Hawaiian/Other Pacific Islander, 0.3% Two or more races, 0.8% Hispanic of any race; Average household size: 2.25; Median age: 47.7; Age under 18: 18.3%; Age 65 and over: 23.0%; Males per 100 females: 84.3; Marriage status: 26.1% never married, 54.2% now married, 5.3% separated, 5.3% widowed, 14.3% divorced; Foreign born: 2.9%; Speak English only: 95.6%; With disability: 14.1%; Veterans: 8.8%; Ancestry: 23.1% English, 18.8% German, 18.0% Irish, 13.2% American, 9.9% Italian

Employment: 16.4% management, business, and financial, 5.8% computer, engineering, and science, 17.4% education, legal, community service, arts, and media, 6.6% healthcare practitioners, 17.9% service, 24.7% sales and office, 4.2% natural resources, construction, and maintenance, 7.1% production, transportation, and material moving

Income: Per capita: $31,663; Median household: $47,955; Average household: $69,307; Households with income of $100,000 or more: 22.9%; Poverty rate: 16.8%

Educational Attainment: High school diploma or higher: 96.9%; Bachelor's degree or higher: 41.2%; Graduate/professional degree or higher: 20.1%

School District(s)

Trumansburg Central SD (PK-12)

 2014-15 Enrollment: 1,061 . . . . (607) 387-7551

Housing: Homeownership rate: 64.4%; Median home value: $201,200; Median year structure built: Before 1940; Homeowner vacancy rate: 0.0%; Median selected monthly owner costs: $1,490 with a mortgage, $657 without a mortgage; Median gross rent: $859 per month; Rental vacancy rate: 13.1%

Health Insurance: 91.9% have insurance; 67.0% have private insurance; 41.5% have public insurance; 8.1% do not have insurance; 1.3% of children under 18 do not have insurance

Safety: Violent crime rate: 16.3 per 10,000 population; Property crime rate: 489.4 per 10,000 population

Newspapers: Finger Lakes Community Papers (weekly circulation 7,000)

Transportation: Commute: 83.0% car, 4.9% public transportation, 4.6% walk, 6.5% work from home; Mean travel time to work: 26.0 minutes

Additional Information Contacts

Village of Trumansburg. . . . . (607) 387-6501
 http://www.trumansburg-ny.gov

ULYSSES (town). Covers a land area of 32.889 square miles and a water area of 4.026 square miles. Located at 42.51° N. Lat; 76.62° W. Long.

Population: 5,026; Growth (since 2000): 5.3%; Density: 152.8 persons per square mile; Race: 94.3% White, 0.4% Black/African American, 1.3% Asian, 0.9% American Indian/Alaska Native, 0.0% Native Hawaiian/Other Pacific Islander, 3.1% Two or more races, 2.2% Hispanic of any race; Average household size: 2.40; Median age: 45.4; Age under 18: 20.4%; Age 65 and over: 18.6%; Males per 100 females: 89.8; Marriage status: 28.6% never married, 55.2% now married, 3.1% separated, 4.0% widowed, 12.2% divorced; Foreign born: 3.1%; Speak English only: 96.3%; With disability: 9.3%; Veterans: 7.7%; Ancestry: 18.0% German, 16.9% Irish, 15.6% English, 13.9% American, 9.3% Italian

Employment: 16.0% management, business, and financial, 6.4% computer, engineering, and science, 15.6% education, legal, community service, arts, and media, 9.7% healthcare practitioners, 18.5% service, 20.5% sales and office, 5.6% natural resources, construction, and maintenance, 7.7% production, transportation, and material moving

Income: Per capita: $33,969; Median household: $64,085; Average household: $81,326; Households with income of $100,000 or more: 30.6%; Poverty rate: 12.2%

Educational Attainment: High school diploma or higher: 97.4%; Bachelor's degree or higher: 42.9%; Graduate/professional degree or higher: 23.0%

Housing: Homeownership rate: 77.6%; Median home value: $211,900; Median year structure built: 1951; Homeowner vacancy rate: 1.5%; Median selected monthly owner costs: $1,419 with a mortgage, $804 without a mortgage; Median gross rent: $816 per month; Rental vacancy rate: 13.5%

Health Insurance: 93.3% have insurance; 73.7% have private insurance; 34.3% have public insurance; 6.7% do not have insurance; 1.0% of children under 18 do not have insurance

Transportation: Commute: 88.2% car, 4.4% public transportation, 2.1% walk, 4.3% work from home; Mean travel time to work: 23.2 minutes

Additional Information Contacts

Town of Ulysses . . . . (607) 387-5767
 http://www.ulysses.ny.us

Ulster County

Located in southeastern New York, mainly in the Catskills; bounded on the east by the Hudson River; drained by the Wallkill River; includes part of the Shawangunk Range and several small lakes. Covers a land area of 1,124.235 square miles, a water area of 36.525 square miles, and is located in the Eastern Time Zone at 41.95° N. Lat., 74.27° W. Long. The county was founded in 1683. County seat is Kingston.

Ulster County is part of the Kingston, NY Metropolitan Statistical Area. The entire metro area includes: Ulster County, NY

Weather Station: Mohonk Lake   Elevation: 1,245 feet

	Jan	Feb	Mar	Apr	May	Jun	Jul	Aug	Sep	Oct	Nov	Dec
High	32	36	45	59	69	77	81	79	71	60	48	37
Low	18	20	27	38	49	58	63	62	55	44	34	24
Precip	3.6	3.1	4.4	4.4	4.8	4.6	4.8	4.3	4.7	4.7	4.0	4.2
Snow	16.5	12.7	12.4	2.9	tr	0.0	0.0	0.0	0.0	0.1	3.2	13.4

High and Low temperatures in degrees Fahrenheit; Precipitation and Snow in inches

Weather Station: Slide Mountain   Elevation: 2,649 feet

	Jan	Feb	Mar	Apr	May	Jun	Jul	Aug	Sep	Oct	Nov	Dec
High	27	30	37	49	61	68	72	71	64	54	42	31
Low	11	12	19	31	41	50	54	53	46	36	27	16
Precip	4.4	3.9	5.3	5.5	5.5	5.5	5.5	4.9	5.8	6.0	5.7	4.9
Snow	24.3	18.9	20.0	6.3	0.3	0.0	0.0	0.0	0.0	2.0	7.5	20.1

High and Low temperatures in degrees Fahrenheit; Precipitation and Snow in inches

Population: 181,300; Growth (since 2000): 2.0%; Density: 161.3 persons per square mile; Race: 86.6% White, 5.9% Black/African American, 1.9% Asian, 0.1% American Indian/Alaska Native, 0.0% Native Hawaiian/Other Pacific Islander, 3.7% two or more races, 9.5% Hispanic of any race; Average household size: 2.44; Median age: 43.1; Age under 18: 18.9%; Age 65 and over: 16.7%; Males per 100 females: 99.0; Marriage status: 33.5% never married, 49.3% now married, 2.4% separated, 6.9% widowed, 10.4% divorced; Foreign born: 7.5%; Speak English only: 88.4%; With disability: 13.8%; Veterans: 7.4%; Ancestry: 20.8% Irish, 19.8% Italian, 19.3% German, 8.7% English, 5.5% Polish

Religion: Six largest groups: 27.5% Catholicism, 3.6% Methodist/Pietist, 3.0% Presbyterian-Reformed, 1.4% Lutheran, 0.9% Non-denominational Protestant, 0.8% Muslim Estimate

Economy: Unemployment rate: 4.2%; Leading industries: 15.3 % retail trade; 12.4 % accommodation and food services; 11.7 % construction; Farms: 486 totaling 71,222 acres; Company size: 0 employ 1,000 or more persons, 4 employ 500 to 999 persons, 63 employ 100 to 499 persons, 4,660 employ less than 100 persons; Business ownership: 6,287 women-owned, 658 Black-owned, 815 Hispanic-owned, 311 Asian-owned, 65 American Indian/Alaska Native-owned

Employment: 12.7% management, business, and financial, 4.6% computer, engineering, and science, 15.2% education, legal, community service, arts, and media, 6.4% healthcare practitioners, 18.0% service, 23.7% sales and office, 9.4% natural resources, construction, and maintenance, 10.0% production, transportation, and material moving

Income: Per capita: $30,732; Median household: $58,918; Average household: $77,109; Households with income of $100,000 or more: 25.8%; Poverty rate: 12.8%

Educational Attainment: High school diploma or higher: 89.7%; Bachelor's degree or higher: 30.1%; Graduate/professional degree or higher: 13.6%

Housing: Homeownership rate: 69.0%; Median home value: $222,800; Median year structure built: 1963; Homeowner vacancy rate: 2.6%; Median selected monthly owner costs: $1,889 with a mortgage, $742 without a mortgage; Median gross rent: $1,013 per month; Rental vacancy rate: 6.0%

Vital Statistics: Birth rate: 88.9 per 10,000 population; Death rate: 91.1 per 10,000 population; Age-adjusted cancer mortality rate: 166.6 deaths per 100,000 population

Health Insurance: 90.6% have insurance; 70.0% have private insurance; 34.7% have public insurance; 9.4% do not have insurance; 2.9% of children under 18 do not have insurance

Health Care: Physicians: 19.3 per 10,000 population; Dentists: 6.1 per 10,000 population; Hospital beds: 16.3 per 10,000 population; Hospital admissions: 697.2 per 10,000 population

Transportation: Commute: 85.6% car, 2.4% public transportation, 4.4% walk, 6.2% work from home; Mean travel time to work: 27.6 minutes

2016 Presidential Election: 41.8% Trump, 52.9% Clinton, 2.8% Johnson, 2.5% Stein

National and State Parks: Bristol Beach State Park; Catskill State Park; Senate House State Historic Site; Shawangunk Grasslands National Wildlife Refuge; Turkey Point State Open Space Area

Additional Information Contacts

Ulster Government . . . . (845) 340-3288
    http://www.co.ulster.ny.us

Ulster County Communities

ACCORD (CDP). Covers a land area of 3.400 square miles and a water area of 0.043 square miles. Located at 41.80° N. Lat; 74.23° W. Long. Elevation is 253 feet.

Population: 762; Growth (since 2000): 22.5%; Density: 224.1 persons per square mile; Race: 79.3% White, 2.0% Black/African American, 0.0% Asian, 0.0% American Indian/Alaska Native, 0.0% Native Hawaiian/Other Pacific Islander, 16.4% Two or more races, 2.4% Hispanic of any race; Average household size: 4.06; Median age: 27.1; Age under 18: 37.5%; Age 65 and over: 6.0%; Males per 100 females: 100.0; Marriage status: 35.3% never married, 49.6% now married, 14.7% separated, 6.6% widowed, 8.4% divorced; Foreign born: 2.4%; Speak English only: 91.5%; With disability: 16.4%; Veterans: 8.7%; Ancestry: 24.8% Scandinavian, 22.6% Irish, 21.9% Italian, 20.5% German, 2.6% Scotch-Irish

Employment: 1.8% management, business, and financial, 1.5% computer, engineering, and science, 10.3% education, legal, community service, arts, and media, 17.7% healthcare practitioners, 35.4% service, 23.6% sales and office, 8.6% natural resources, construction, and maintenance, 1.2% production, transportation, and material moving

Income: Per capita: $30,859; Median household: $112,083; Average household: $148,866; Households with income of $100,000 or more: 72.6%; Poverty rate: 6.0%

Educational Attainment: High school diploma or higher: 93.0%; Bachelor's degree or higher: 11.9%; Graduate/professional degree or higher: 3.4%

School District(s)

Rondout Valley Central SD (PK-12)
    2014-15 Enrollment: 1,966 . . . . (845) 687-2400

Housing: Homeownership rate: 71.5%; Median home value: n/a; Median year structure built: 1968; Homeowner vacancy rate: 11.9%; Median selected monthly owner costs: n/a with a mortgage, n/a without a mortgage; Median gross rent: $1,360 per month; Rental vacancy rate: 0.0%

Health Insurance: 95.4% have insurance; 80.7% have private insurance; 49.6% have public insurance; 4.6% do not have insurance; 0.0% of children under 18 do not have insurance

Transportation: Commute: 98.4% car, 0.0% public transportation, 1.6% walk, 0.0% work from home; Mean travel time to work: 25.6 minutes

BEARSVILLE (unincorporated postal area)
ZCTA: 12409

Covers a land area of 14.268 square miles and a water area of 0.223 square miles. Located at 42.04° N. Lat; 74.18° W. Long. Elevation is 699 feet.

Population: 693; Growth (since 2000): 49.4%; Density: 48.6 persons per square mile; Race: 95.8% White, 0.3% Black/African American, 2.3% Asian, 0.0% American Indian/Alaska Native, 0.0% Native Hawaiian/Other Pacific Islander, 1.6% Two or more races, 1.3% Hispanic of any race; Average household size: 2.05; Median age: 57.9; Age under 18: 12.3%; Age 65 and over: 30.9%; Males per 100 females: 84.4; Marriage status: 27.4% never married, 47.1% now married, 0.0% separated, 4.8% widowed, 20.7% divorced; Foreign born: 8.7%; Speak English only: 93.8%; With disability: 11.7%; Veterans: 7.2%; Ancestry: 15.0% German, 12.7% French, 12.0% Russian, 9.8% Irish, 9.4% Italian

Employment: 24.1% management, business, and financial, 3.8% computer, engineering, and science, 22.2% education, legal, community service, arts, and media, 0.0% healthcare practitioners, 17.0% service,

18.6% sales and office, 14.2% natural resources, construction, and maintenance, 0.0% production, transportation, and material moving

Income: Per capita: $48,424; Median household: $65,625; Average household: $99,169; Households with income of $100,000 or more: 38.7%; Poverty rate: 11.0%

Educational Attainment: High school diploma or higher: 96.8%; Bachelor's degree or higher: 56.9%; Graduate/professional degree or higher: 24.3%

Housing: Homeownership rate: 82.6%; Median home value: $399,100; Median year structure built: Before 1940; Homeowner vacancy rate: 7.2%; Median selected monthly owner costs: $2,283 with a mortgage, $1,063 without a mortgage; Median gross rent: $1,125 per month; Rental vacancy rate: 0.0%

Health Insurance: 92.4% have insurance; 71.7% have private insurance; 42.7% have public insurance; 7.6% do not have insurance; 0.0% of children under 18 do not have insurance

Transportation: Commute: 81.1% car, 4.5% public transportation, 2.1% walk, 12.3% work from home; Mean travel time to work: 36.7 minutes

BIG INDIAN (unincorporated postal area)
ZCTA: 12410

Covers a land area of 41.181 square miles and a water area of 0.036 square miles. Located at 42.07° N. Lat; 74.42° W. Long. Elevation is 1,217 feet.

Population: 594; Growth (since 2000): -27.6%; Density: 14.4 persons per square mile; Race: 99.2% White, 0.0% Black/African American, 0.0% Asian, 0.0% American Indian/Alaska Native, 0.0% Native Hawaiian/Other Pacific Islander, 0.8% Two or more races, 1.5% Hispanic of any race; Average household size: 2.11; Median age: 53.8; Age under 18: 19.7%; Age 65 and over: 24.9%; Males per 100 females: 107.9; Marriage status: 24.3% never married, 48.4% now married, 1.2% separated, 9.6% widowed, 17.7% divorced; Foreign born: 3.5%; Speak English only: 91.4%; With disability: 10.9%; Veterans: 7.3%; Ancestry: 24.1% German, 22.9% Irish, 13.1% Italian, 9.9% Dutch, 7.6% Scotch-Irish

Employment: 35.0% management, business, and financial, 0.0% computer, engineering, and science, 20.7% education, legal, community service, arts, and media, 0.0% healthcare practitioners, 14.3% service, 12.4% sales and office, 10.2% natural resources, construction, and maintenance, 7.5% production, transportation, and material moving

Income: Per capita: $32,699; Median household: $60,469; Average household: $68,660; Households with income of $100,000 or more: 23.5%; Poverty rate: 5.9%

Educational Attainment: High school diploma or higher: 95.8%; Bachelor's degree or higher: 28.9%; Graduate/professional degree or higher: 8.1%

Housing: Homeownership rate: 89.0%; Median home value: $214,000; Median year structure built: 1954; Homeowner vacancy rate: 0.0%; Median selected monthly owner costs: $1,900 with a mortgage, $525 without a mortgage; Median gross rent: $828 per month; Rental vacancy rate: 43.6%

Health Insurance: 96.3% have insurance; 87.2% have private insurance; 26.6% have public insurance; 3.7% do not have insurance; 4.3% of children under 18 do not have insurance

Transportation: Commute: 79.7% car, 0.0% public transportation, 0.8% walk, 5.5% work from home; Mean travel time to work: 41.8 minutes

BLOOMINGTON (unincorporated postal area)
ZCTA: 12411

Covers a land area of 0.937 square miles and a water area of 0.019 square miles. Located at 41.88° N. Lat; 74.04° W. Long. Elevation is 184 feet.

Population: 511; Growth (since 2000): 33.8%; Density: 545.2 persons per square mile; Race: 93.2% White, 2.7% Black/African American, 0.0% Asian, 0.0% American Indian/Alaska Native, 0.0% Native Hawaiian/Other Pacific Islander, 4.1% Two or more races, 0.0% Hispanic of any race; Average household size: 3.19; Median age: 41.2; Age under 18: 28.2%; Age 65 and over: 12.1%; Males per 100 females: 97.2; Marriage status: 28.8% never married, 62.8% now married, 0.0% separated, 0.0% widowed, 8.4% divorced; Foreign born: 3.1%; Speak English only: 93.0%; With disability: 6.5%; Veterans: 11.7%; Ancestry: 47.9% Italian, 35.2% German, 13.9% Irish, 8.8% Polish, 7.6% French

Employment: 9.2% management, business, and financial, 0.0% computer, engineering, and science, 18.7% education, legal, community service, arts, and media, 2.5% healthcare practitioners, 7.1% service,

29.3% sales and office, 18.7% natural resources, construction, and maintenance, 14.5% production, transportation, and material moving
Income: Per capita: $21,665; Median household: $81,518; Average household: $68,414; Households with income of $100,000 or more: 5.6%; Poverty rate: 10.5%
Educational Attainment: High school diploma or higher: 89.5%; Bachelor's degree or higher: 19.6%; Graduate/professional degree or higher: 17.0%
Housing: Homeownership rate: 100.0%; Median home value: $218,600; Median year structure built: 1968; Homeowner vacancy rate: 0.0%; Median selected monthly owner costs: $1,958 with a mortgage, $730 without a mortgage; Median gross rent: n/a per month; Rental vacancy rate: 100.0%
Health Insurance: 100.0% have insurance; 83.8% have private insurance; 28.0% have public insurance; 0.0% do not have insurance; 0.0% of children under 18 do not have insurance
Transportation: Commute: 93.6% car, 0.0% public transportation, 0.0% walk, 6.4% work from home; Mean travel time to work: 24.3 minutes

BOICEVILLE (unincorporated postal area)
ZCTA: 12412
Covers a land area of 6.070 square miles and a water area of 0 square miles. Located at 42.01° N. Lat; 74.28° W. Long. Elevation is 630 feet.
Population: 532; Growth (since 2000): -42.6%; Density: 87.6 persons per square mile; Race: 72.2% White, 7.7% Black/African American, 3.2% Asian, 0.0% American Indian/Alaska Native, 0.0% Native Hawaiian/Other Pacific Islander, 5.8% Two or more races, 11.1% Hispanic of any race; Average household size: 1.79; Median age: 49.7; Age under 18: 19.2%; Age 65 and over: 18.0%; Males per 100 females: 103.3; Marriage status: 25.6% never married, 44.2% now married, 18.8% separated, 15.6% widowed, 14.7% divorced; Foreign born: 14.3%; Speak English only: 82.4%; With disability: 1.5%; Veterans: 9.5%; Ancestry: 24.8% German, 23.1% Irish, 16.0% Norwegian, 14.8% Italian, 9.6% English
Employment: 4.2% management, business, and financial, 9.5% computer, engineering, and science, 40.0% education, legal, community service, arts, and media, 8.9% healthcare practitioners, 9.5% service, 14.7% sales and office, 0.0% natural resources, construction, and maintenance, 13.2% production, transportation, and material moving
Income: Per capita: $49,953; Median household: $50,568; Average household: $86,449; Households with income of $100,000 or more: 11.4%; Poverty rate: 26.5%
Educational Attainment: High school diploma or higher: 90.5%; Bachelor's degree or higher: 17.0%; Graduate/professional degree or higher: 8.9%

School District(s)
Onteora Central SD (KG-12)
    2014-15 Enrollment: 1,415 . . . . (845) 657-8851
Housing: Homeownership rate: 58.4%; Median home value: $180,700; Median year structure built: 1969; Homeowner vacancy rate: 0.0%; Median selected monthly owner costs: $1,460 with a mortgage, $0 without a mortgage; Median gross rent: $930 per month; Rental vacancy rate: 0.0%
Health Insurance: 89.8% have insurance; 60.7% have private insurance; 51.1% have public insurance; 10.2% do not have insurance; 0.0% of children under 18 do not have insurance
Transportation: Commute: 82.6% car, 0.0% public transportation, 0.0% walk, 17.4% work from home; Mean travel time to work: 36.1 minutes

CHICHESTER (unincorporated postal area)
ZCTA: 12416
Covers a land area of 5.085 square miles and a water area of <.001 square miles. Located at 42.10° N. Lat; 74.28° W. Long. Elevation is 965 feet.
Population: 127; Growth (since 2000): 46.0%; Density: 25.0 persons per square mile; Race: 100.0% White, 0.0% Black/African American, 0.0% Asian, 0.0% American Indian/Alaska Native, 0.0% Native Hawaiian/Other Pacific Islander, 0.0% Two or more races, 0.0% Hispanic of any race; Average household size: 1.28; Median age: 59.4; Age under 18: 2.4%; Age 65 and over: 30.7%; Males per 100 females: 102.2; Marriage status: 51.6% never married, 28.2% now married, 0.0% separated, 11.3% widowed, 8.9% divorced; Foreign born: 0.0%; Speak English only: 100.0%; With disability: 19.7%; Veterans: 0.0%; Ancestry: 26.8% Russian, 19.7% Polish, 11.8% English, 8.7% Italian, 8.7% Scottish

Employment: 0.0% management, business, and financial, 0.0% computer, engineering, and science, 9.3% education, legal, community service, arts, and media, 0.0% healthcare practitioners, 44.4% service, 20.4% sales and office, 0.0% natural resources, construction, and maintenance, 25.9% production, transportation, and material moving
Income: Per capita: $22,115; Median household: $25,050; Average household: $28,107; Households with income of $100,000 or more: 3.0%; Poverty rate: 17.3%
Educational Attainment: High school diploma or higher: 90.1%; Bachelor's degree or higher: 40.5%; Graduate/professional degree or higher: 32.4%
Housing: Homeownership rate: 97.0%; Median home value: $208,800; Median year structure built: 1960; Homeowner vacancy rate: 5.9%; Median selected monthly owner costs: $1,181 with a mortgage, $634 without a mortgage; Median gross rent: n/a per month; Rental vacancy rate: 0.0%
Health Insurance: 85.8% have insurance; 77.2% have private insurance; 39.4% have public insurance; 14.2% do not have insurance; 100.0% of children under 18 do not have insurance
Transportation: Commute: 100.0% car, 0.0% public transportation, 0.0% walk, 0.0% work from home; Mean travel time to work: 0.0 minutes

CLINTONDALE (CDP). Covers a land area of 5.572 square miles and a water area of 0.039 square miles. Located at 41.69° N. Lat; 74.05° W. Long. Elevation is 545 feet.
Population: 1,391; Growth (since 2000): -2.3%; Density: 249.6 persons per square mile; Race: 84.3% White, 5.9% Black/African American, 2.6% Asian, 0.0% American Indian/Alaska Native, 0.0% Native Hawaiian/Other Pacific Islander, 7.3% Two or more races, 3.5% Hispanic of any race; Average household size: 2.06; Median age: 51.2; Age under 18: 12.4%; Age 65 and over: 22.4%; Males per 100 females: 101.9; Marriage status: 24.3% never married, 44.4% now married, 0.0% separated, 18.4% widowed, 12.9% divorced; Foreign born: 6.9%; Speak English only: 96.4%; With disability: 34.2%; Veterans: 8.9%; Ancestry: 37.0% German, 21.7% Italian, 15.4% English, 12.9% Irish, 6.7% Czech
Employment: 16.6% management, business, and financial, 7.0% computer, engineering, and science, 16.3% education, legal, community service, arts, and media, 3.0% healthcare practitioners, 5.8% service, 29.1% sales and office, 17.3% natural resources, construction, and maintenance, 5.0% production, transportation, and material moving
Income: Per capita: $36,256; Median household: $52,726; Average household: $72,538; Households with income of $100,000 or more: 26.0%; Poverty rate: 11.3%
Educational Attainment: High school diploma or higher: 89.3%; Bachelor's degree or higher: 28.4%; Graduate/professional degree or higher: 6.4%
Housing: Homeownership rate: 44.4%; Median home value: $260,100; Median year structure built: 1960; Homeowner vacancy rate: 0.0%; Median selected monthly owner costs: $2,344 with a mortgage, $776 without a mortgage; Median gross rent: $886 per month; Rental vacancy rate: 0.0%
Health Insurance: 90.5% have insurance; 71.9% have private insurance; 32.8% have public insurance; 9.5% do not have insurance; 1.2% of children under 18 do not have insurance
Transportation: Commute: 77.2% car, 12.8% public transportation, 0.0% walk, 10.1% work from home; Mean travel time to work: 35.6 minutes

CONNELLY (unincorporated postal area)
ZCTA: 12417
Covers a land area of 0.316 square miles and a water area of 0.029 square miles. Located at 41.91° N. Lat; 73.99° W. Long. Elevation is 23 feet.
Population: 757; Growth (since 2000): n/a; Density: 2,399.3 persons per square mile; Race: 70.5% White, 15.2% Black/African American, 0.0% Asian, 0.0% American Indian/Alaska Native, 0.0% Native Hawaiian/Other Pacific Islander, 12.3% Two or more races, 2.0% Hispanic of any race; Average household size: 3.13; Median age: 33.8; Age under 18: 16.4%; Age 65 and over: 20.5%; Males per 100 females: 90.5; Marriage status: 32.9% never married, 44.2% now married, 0.0% separated, 15.2% widowed, 7.7% divorced; Foreign born: 2.8%; Speak English only: 100.0%; With disability: 15.5%; Veterans: 1.7%; Ancestry: 29.6% German, 27.6% Irish, 14.7% Italian, 13.3% English, 12.4% Swedish
Employment: 23.6% management, business, and financial, 0.0% computer, engineering, and science, 0.0% education, legal, community service, arts, and media, 10.6% healthcare practitioners, 32.7% service,

16.6% sales and office, 7.8% natural resources, construction, and maintenance, 8.6% production, transportation, and material moving
Income: Per capita: $19,807; Median household: $50,549; Average household: $57,654; Households with income of $100,000 or more: 16.9%; Poverty rate: 11.8%
Educational Attainment: High school diploma or higher: 83.0%; Bachelor's degree or higher: 4.4%; Graduate/professional degree or higher: n/a
Housing: Homeownership rate: 68.2%; Median home value: $99,800; Median year structure built: 1948; Homeowner vacancy rate: 0.0%; Median selected monthly owner costs: $1,648 with a mortgage, $606 without a mortgage; Median gross rent: $1,042 per month; Rental vacancy rate: 17.2%
Health Insurance: 93.9% have insurance; 55.2% have private insurance; 46.6% have public insurance; 6.1% do not have insurance; 0.0% of children under 18 do not have insurance
Transportation: Commute: 94.8% car, 0.0% public transportation, 0.0% walk, 5.2% work from home; Mean travel time to work: 20.5 minutes

COTTEKILL (unincorporated postal area)
ZCTA: 12419
Covers a land area of 2.395 square miles and a water area of 0.021 square miles. Located at 41.86° N. Lat; 74.10° W. Long. Elevation is 253 feet.
Population: 554; Growth (since 2000): 75.9%; Density: 231.3 persons per square mile; Race: 92.2% White, 4.3% Black/African American, 0.0% Asian, 2.2% American Indian/Alaska Native, 0.0% Native Hawaiian/Other Pacific Islander, 1.3% Two or more races, 4.3% Hispanic of any race; Average household size: 2.60; Median age: 34.8; Age under 18: 14.6%; Age 65 and over: 8.5%; Males per 100 females: 96.2; Marriage status: 47.5% never married, 25.5% now married, 9.0% separated, 5.0% widowed, 22.0% divorced; Foreign born: 0.0%; Speak English only: 96.1%; With disability: 14.3%; Veterans: 9.9%; Ancestry: 36.8% German, 18.8% Irish, 8.5% Italian, 8.5% Polish, 6.5% English
Employment: 4.8% management, business, and financial, 7.7% computer, engineering, and science, 8.1% education, legal, community service, arts, and media, 17.3% healthcare practitioners, 18.5% service, 23.4% sales and office, 0.0% natural resources, construction, and maintenance, 20.2% production, transportation, and material moving
Income: Per capita: $21,771; Median household: $55,893; Average household: $55,726; Households with income of $100,000 or more: 16.9%; Poverty rate: 25.8%
Educational Attainment: High school diploma or higher: 100.0%; Bachelor's degree or higher: 21.8%; Graduate/professional degree or higher: 3.1%

School District(s)
Rondout Valley Central SD (PK-12)
    2014-15 Enrollment: 1,966 . . . . (845) 687-2400
Housing: Homeownership rate: 52.6%; Median home value: $213,000; Median year structure built: 1959; Homeowner vacancy rate: 0.0%; Median selected monthly owner costs: $1,806 with a mortgage, $0 without a mortgage; Median gross rent: $934 per month; Rental vacancy rate: 0.0%
Health Insurance: 91.7% have insurance; 46.9% have private insurance; 47.1% have public insurance; 8.3% do not have insurance; 0.0% of children under 18 do not have insurance
Transportation: Commute: 94.0% car, 0.0% public transportation, 0.0% walk, 0.0% work from home; Mean travel time to work: 27.3 minutes

CRAGSMOOR (CDP). Covers a land area of 4.351 square miles and a water area of 0 square miles. Located at 41.67° N. Lat; 74.39° W. Long. Elevation is 1,863 feet.
Population: 608; Growth (since 2000): 28.3%; Density: 139.7 persons per square mile; Race: 94.7% White, 0.0% Black/African American, 0.0% Asian, 0.0% American Indian/Alaska Native, 0.0% Native Hawaiian/Other Pacific Islander, 0.0% Two or more races, 5.3% Hispanic of any race; Average household size: 2.23; Median age: 55.1; Age under 18: 15.8%; Age 65 and over: 25.3%; Males per 100 females: 102.3; Marriage status: 5.7% never married, 66.4% now married, 0.0% separated, 2.1% widowed, 25.8% divorced; Foreign born: 5.3%; Speak English only: 94.5%; With disability: 15.6%; Veterans: 3.5%; Ancestry: 35.9% German, 19.6% Irish, 9.9% Polish, 8.9% Italian, 6.3% English
Employment: 0.0% management, business, and financial, 22.2% computer, engineering, and science, 42.2% education, legal, community service, arts, and media, 0.0% healthcare practitioners, 4.1% service,

7.4% sales and office, 14.8% natural resources, construction, and maintenance, 9.3% production, transportation, and material moving
Income: Per capita: $38,701; Median household: $86,250; Average household: $86,681; Households with income of $100,000 or more: 35.9%; Poverty rate: 3.5%
Educational Attainment: High school diploma or higher: 93.5%; Bachelor's degree or higher: 42.4%; Graduate/professional degree or higher: 25.7%
Housing: Homeownership rate: 85.0%; Median home value: $205,400; Median year structure built: 1953; Homeowner vacancy rate: 0.0%; Median selected monthly owner costs: $1,632 with a mortgage, $384 without a mortgage; Median gross rent: n/a per month; Rental vacancy rate: 0.0%
Health Insurance: 88.2% have insurance; 83.2% have private insurance; 28.8% have public insurance; 11.8% do not have insurance; 0.0% of children under 18 do not have insurance
Transportation: Commute: 65.6% car, 7.0% public transportation, 0.0% walk, 27.4% work from home; Mean travel time to work: 35.3 minutes

DENNING (town). Covers a land area of 105.666 square miles and a water area of 0.099 square miles. Located at 41.96° N. Lat; 74.48° W. Long. Elevation is 1,959 feet.
Population: 611; Growth (since 2000): 18.4%; Density: 5.8 persons per square mile; Race: 96.4% White, 1.8% Black/African American, 0.7% Asian, 0.0% American Indian/Alaska Native, 0.0% Native Hawaiian/Other Pacific Islander, 0.0% Two or more races, 5.9% Hispanic of any race; Average household size: 2.71; Median age: 40.7; Age under 18: 26.7%; Age 65 and over: 19.1%; Males per 100 females: 106.4; Marriage status: 32.4% never married, 60.0% now married, 1.2% separated, 2.1% widowed, 5.5% divorced; Foreign born: 1.3%; Speak English only: 96.9%; With disability: 15.5%; Veterans: 9.8%; Ancestry: 33.2% Irish, 19.5% German, 16.7% Dutch, 14.2% Italian, 12.4% Polish
Employment: 14.9% management, business, and financial, 4.4% computer, engineering, and science, 10.4% education, legal, community service, arts, and media, 5.2% healthcare practitioners, 27.3% service, 13.7% sales and office, 17.3% natural resources, construction, and maintenance, 6.8% production, transportation, and material moving
Income: Per capita: $26,111; Median household: $64,167; Average household: $74,500; Households with income of $100,000 or more: 24.3%; Poverty rate: 6.0%
Educational Attainment: High school diploma or higher: 88.6%; Bachelor's degree or higher: 30.7%; Graduate/professional degree or higher: 20.8%
Housing: Homeownership rate: 77.1%; Median home value: $210,900; Median year structure built: 1972; Homeowner vacancy rate: 4.1%; Median selected monthly owner costs: $1,520 with a mortgage, $523 without a mortgage; Median gross rent: $1,056 per month; Rental vacancy rate: 0.0%
Health Insurance: 97.4% have insurance; 68.9% have private insurance; 44.2% have public insurance; 2.6% do not have insurance; 0.0% of children under 18 do not have insurance
Transportation: Commute: 90.6% car, 0.8% public transportation, 0.8% walk, 6.6% work from home; Mean travel time to work: 33.0 minutes

EAST KINGSTON (CDP). Covers a land area of 0.674 square miles and a water area of 0.022 square miles. Located at 41.95° N. Lat; 73.97° W. Long. Elevation is 151 feet.
Population: 391; Growth (since 2000): 37.2%; Density: 580.3 persons per square mile; Race: 96.4% White, 0.0% Black/African American, 0.0% Asian, 0.0% American Indian/Alaska Native, 0.0% Native Hawaiian/Other Pacific Islander, 3.6% Two or more races, 10.5% Hispanic of any race; Average household size: 3.26; Median age: 33.6; Age under 18: 33.2%; Age 65 and over: 16.6%; Males per 100 females: 110.7; Marriage status: 20.1% never married, 58.7% now married, 17.0% separated, 9.2% widowed, 12.0% divorced; Foreign born: 0.0%; Speak English only: 100.0%; With disability: 18.2%; Veterans: 10.0%; Ancestry: 52.7% Italian, 24.8% English, 24.8% Irish, 21.2% Dutch, 9.2% Greek
Employment: 21.0% management, business, and financial, 0.0% computer, engineering, and science, 0.0% education, legal, community service, arts, and media, 4.8% healthcare practitioners, 15.0% service, 14.4% sales and office, 44.9% natural resources, construction, and maintenance, 0.0% production, transportation, and material moving
Income: Per capita: $15,316; Median household: $41,750; Average household: $46,376; Households with income of $100,000 or more: n/a; Poverty rate: 30.4%

Educational Attainment: High school diploma or higher: 94.5%; Bachelor's degree or higher: 3.4%; Graduate/professional degree or higher: n/a
Housing: Homeownership rate: 64.2%; Median home value: $184,700; Median year structure built: Before 1940; Homeowner vacancy rate: 0.0%; Median selected monthly owner costs: n/a with a mortgage, n/a without a mortgage; Median gross rent: $983 per month; Rental vacancy rate: 0.0%
Health Insurance: 93.9% have insurance; 56.5% have private insurance; 54.0% have public insurance; 6.1% do not have insurance; 0.0% of children under 18 do not have insurance
Transportation: Commute: 100.0% car, 0.0% public transportation, 0.0% walk, 0.0% work from home; Mean travel time to work: 23.1 minutes

ELLENVILLE (village). Covers a land area of 8.725 square miles and a water area of 0.087 square miles. Located at 41.71° N. Lat; 74.36° W. Long. Elevation is 338 feet.
History: Incorporated 1856.
Population: 4,131; Growth (since 2000): 0.0%; Density: 473.5 persons per square mile; Race: 64.4% White, 11.1% Black/African American, 0.0% Asian, 0.0% American Indian/Alaska Native, 0.0% Native Hawaiian/Other Pacific Islander, 10.8% Two or more races, 32.9% Hispanic of any race; Average household size: 2.80; Median age: 34.5; Age under 18: 31.1%; Age 65 and over: 10.7%; Males per 100 females: 94.1; Marriage status: 31.7% never married, 51.6% now married, 3.6% separated, 4.9% widowed, 11.8% divorced; Foreign born: 9.9%; Speak English only: 82.4%; With disability: 18.0%; Veterans: 8.1%; Ancestry: 21.9% Irish, 10.1% Italian, 7.6% German, 7.4% Dutch, 6.0% American
Employment: 9.6% management, business, and financial, 0.0% computer, engineering, and science, 14.1% education, legal, community service, arts, and media, 0.4% healthcare practitioners, 23.5% service, 27.9% sales and office, 9.7% natural resources, construction, and maintenance, 14.9% production, transportation, and material moving
Income: Per capita: $21,921; Median household: $45,800; Average household: $61,427; Households with income of $100,000 or more: 14.3%; Poverty rate: 17.5%
Educational Attainment: High school diploma or higher: 79.8%; Bachelor's degree or higher: 17.7%; Graduate/professional degree or higher: 9.8%

School District(s)
Ellenville Central SD (PK-12)
   2014-15 Enrollment: 1,786 . . . . (845) 647-0100
Housing: Homeownership rate: 54.5%; Median home value: $152,400; Median year structure built: 1952; Homeowner vacancy rate: 2.1%; Median selected monthly owner costs: $1,702 with a mortgage, $823 without a mortgage; Median gross rent: $948 per month; Rental vacancy rate: 6.6%
Health Insurance: 95.0% have insurance; 59.7% have private insurance; 51.8% have public insurance; 5.0% do not have insurance; 1.7% of children under 18 do not have insurance
Hospitals: Ellenville Regional Hospital (35 beds)
Safety: Violent crime rate: 14.7 per 10,000 population; Property crime rate: 244.7 per 10,000 population
Newspapers: Shawangunk Journal (weekly circulation 3,500)
Transportation: Commute: 81.5% car, 1.8% public transportation, 13.4% walk, 1.6% work from home; Mean travel time to work: 28.5 minutes
Additional Information Contacts
Village of Ellenville . . . . (845) 647-7080
   http://villageofellenville.sharepoint.com/Pages/default.aspx

ESOPUS (town). Covers a land area of 37.312 square miles and a water area of 4.628 square miles. Located at 41.83° N. Lat; 73.99° W. Long. Elevation is 125 feet.
History: Seat of Mt. St. Alphonsus Theological Seminary. John Burroughs lived near here. Town was formed in 1811, and was partly annexed by Kingston in 1818.
Population: 8,957; Growth (since 2000): -4.0%; Density: 240.1 persons per square mile; Race: 94.3% White, 2.6% Black/African American, 1.4% Asian, 0.0% American Indian/Alaska Native, 0.0% Native Hawaiian/Other Pacific Islander, 1.5% Two or more races, 3.9% Hispanic of any race; Average household size: 2.51; Median age: 42.7; Age under 18: 18.0%; Age 65 and over: 16.9%; Males per 100 females: 93.4; Marriage status: 32.2% never married, 49.6% now married, 3.7% separated, 6.7% widowed, 11.5% divorced; Foreign born: 5.6%; Speak English only: 93.5%; With disability: 12.7%; Veterans: 6.7%; Ancestry: 29.3% Irish, 22.6% German, 17.9% Italian, 10.4% American, 7.5% English

Employment: 13.6% management, business, and financial, 4.0% computer, engineering, and science, 15.0% education, legal, community service, arts, and media, 7.7% healthcare practitioners, 19.1% service, 25.6% sales and office, 8.2% natural resources, construction, and maintenance, 6.7% production, transportation, and material moving
Income: Per capita: $30,867; Median household: $67,536; Average household: $79,797; Households with income of $100,000 or more: 25.8%; Poverty rate: 8.6%
Educational Attainment: High school diploma or higher: 91.6%; Bachelor's degree or higher: 27.7%; Graduate/professional degree or higher: 13.3%
Housing: Homeownership rate: 73.7%; Median home value: $207,700; Median year structure built: 1966; Homeowner vacancy rate: 4.0%; Median selected monthly owner costs: $1,645 with a mortgage, $723 without a mortgage; Median gross rent: $1,090 per month; Rental vacancy rate: 5.5%
Health Insurance: 88.0% have insurance; 68.9% have private insurance; 31.3% have public insurance; 12.0% do not have insurance; 8.6% of children under 18 do not have insurance
Transportation: Commute: 84.8% car, 1.8% public transportation, 5.6% walk, 7.5% work from home; Mean travel time to work: 23.8 minutes
Additional Information Contacts
Town of Esopus . . . . (845) 331-3709
   http://www.esopus.com

GARDINER (CDP). Covers a land area of 3.863 square miles and a water area of 0 square miles. Located at 41.68° N. Lat; 74.15° W. Long. Elevation is 315 feet.
Population: 643; Growth (since 2000): -24.9%; Density: 166.5 persons per square mile; Race: 94.7% White, 0.0% Black/African American, 0.0% Asian, 0.0% American Indian/Alaska Native, 0.0% Native Hawaiian/Other Pacific Islander, 3.3% Two or more races, 5.3% Hispanic of any race; Average household size: 2.26; Median age: 50.1; Age under 18: 16.3%; Age 65 and over: 15.6%; Males per 100 females: 95.5; Marriage status: 31.4% never married, 60.9% now married, 0.0% separated, 1.6% widowed, 6.0% divorced; Foreign born: 2.3%; Speak English only: 95.3%; With disability: 10.4%; Veterans: 0.0%; Ancestry: 39.0% Italian, 31.4% German, 26.4% Irish, 7.5% English, 6.4% Dutch
Employment: 11.5% management, business, and financial, 4.7% computer, engineering, and science, 17.2% education, legal, community service, arts, and media, 0.0% healthcare practitioners, 7.7% service, 34.6% sales and office, 20.4% natural resources, construction, and maintenance, 3.8% production, transportation, and material moving
Income: Per capita: $28,429; Median household: $56,917; Average household: $64,350; Households with income of $100,000 or more: 20.7%; Poverty rate: 10.0%
Educational Attainment: High school diploma or higher: 91.8%; Bachelor's degree or higher: 40.7%; Graduate/professional degree or higher: 21.3%
Housing: Homeownership rate: 73.7%; Median home value: $237,800; Median year structure built: 1949; Homeowner vacancy rate: 17.6%; Median selected monthly owner costs: $1,835 with a mortgage, $1,296 without a mortgage; Median gross rent: $1,042 per month; Rental vacancy rate: 0.0%
Health Insurance: 84.6% have insurance; 76.2% have private insurance; 19.3% have public insurance; 15.4% do not have insurance; 0.0% of children under 18 do not have insurance
Transportation: Commute: 95.2% car, 0.0% public transportation, 0.0% walk, 4.8% work from home; Mean travel time to work: 21.4 minutes

GARDINER (town). Covers a land area of 43.435 square miles and a water area of 0.510 square miles. Located at 41.69° N. Lat; 74.19° W. Long. Elevation is 315 feet.
History: A 17th-century gristmill is here.
Population: 5,708; Growth (since 2000): 9.0%; Density: 131.4 persons per square mile; Race: 94.4% White, 3.7% Black/African American, 0.0% Asian, 0.0% American Indian/Alaska Native, 0.0% Native Hawaiian/Other Pacific Islander, 0.8% Two or more races, 8.1% Hispanic of any race; Average household size: 2.67; Median age: 44.9; Age under 18: 21.3%; Age 65 and over: 16.2%; Males per 100 females: 100.7; Marriage status: 29.8% never married, 58.4% now married, 0.9% separated, 3.6% widowed, 8.1% divorced; Foreign born: 7.5%; Speak English only: 92.8%; With disability: 11.6%; Veterans: 5.5%; Ancestry: 22.7% Irish, 19.9% Italian, 19.0% German, 9.1% American, 8.3% English

Employment: 15.5% management, business, and financial, 6.8% computer, engineering, and science, 24.0% education, legal, community service, arts, and media, 6.3% healthcare practitioners, 10.3% service, 13.4% sales and office, 14.3% natural resources, construction, and maintenance, 9.6% production, transportation, and material moving
Income: Per capita: $40,938; Median household: $83,182; Average household: $108,609; Households with income of $100,000 or more: 39.8%; Poverty rate: 11.7%
Educational Attainment: High school diploma or higher: 95.5%; Bachelor's degree or higher: 47.3%; Graduate/professional degree or higher: 24.9%
Housing: Homeownership rate: 79.7%; Median home value: $330,200; Median year structure built: 1978; Homeowner vacancy rate: 2.6%; Median selected monthly owner costs: $2,088 with a mortgage, $978 without a mortgage; Median gross rent: $1,065 per month; Rental vacancy rate: 0.0%
Health Insurance: 90.4% have insurance; 77.8% have private insurance; 23.5% have public insurance; 9.6% do not have insurance; 4.2% of children under 18 do not have insurance
Transportation: Commute: 87.0% car, 2.6% public transportation, 2.3% walk, 7.1% work from home; Mean travel time to work: 31.0 minutes
Additional Information Contacts
Town of Gardiner . . . . (845) 255-9675
  http://www.townofgardiner.org

GLASCO (CDP).
Covers a land area of 1.762 square miles and a water area of 0.683 square miles. Located at 42.05° N. Lat; 73.95° W. Long. Elevation is 151 feet.
Population: 2,464; Growth (since 2000): 45.6%; Density: 1,398.1 persons per square mile; Race: 89.3% White, 7.6% Black/African American, 1.9% Asian, 0.0% American Indian/Alaska Native, 0.0% Native Hawaiian/Other Pacific Islander, 1.1% Two or more races, 5.8% Hispanic of any race; Average household size: 2.72; Median age: 41.5; Age under 18: 25.0%; Age 65 and over: 20.1%; Males per 100 females: 82.0; Marriage status: 35.4% never married, 45.2% now married, 1.5% separated, 10.3% widowed, 9.2% divorced; Foreign born: 12.0%; Speak English only: 85.1%; With disability: 20.5%; Veterans: 8.5%; Ancestry: 29.0% Italian, 18.9% Irish, 14.3% German, 10.8% Dutch, 7.4% Jamaican
Employment: 16.9% management, business, and financial, 1.4% computer, engineering, and science, 8.9% education, legal, community service, arts, and media, 9.2% healthcare practitioners, 24.4% service, 14.4% sales and office, 7.3% natural resources, construction, and maintenance, 17.5% production, transportation, and material moving
Income: Per capita: $23,912; Median household: $54,459; Average household: $63,265; Households with income of $100,000 or more: 20.5%; Poverty rate: 11.8%
Educational Attainment: High school diploma or higher: 80.0%; Bachelor's degree or higher: 18.4%; Graduate/professional degree or higher: 8.4%
School District(s)
Saugerties Central SD (KG-12)
  2014-15 Enrollment: 2,710 . . . . (845) 247-6501
Housing: Homeownership rate: 66.0%; Median home value: $211,300; Median year structure built: 1972; Homeowner vacancy rate: 0.0%; Median selected monthly owner costs: $2,077 with a mortgage, $713 without a mortgage; Median gross rent: $1,114 per month; Rental vacancy rate: 6.4%
Health Insurance: 96.0% have insurance; 73.2% have private insurance; 39.6% have public insurance; 4.0% do not have insurance; 0.0% of children under 18 do not have insurance
Transportation: Commute: 97.1% car, 0.0% public transportation, 0.4% walk, 1.7% work from home; Mean travel time to work: 22.8 minutes

GLENFORD (unincorporated postal area)
ZCTA: 12433
Covers a land area of 3.820 square miles and a water area of 0.086 square miles. Located at 42.00° N. Lat; 74.16° W. Long. Elevation is 659 feet.
Population: 486; Growth (since 2000): 20.3%; Density: 127.2 persons per square mile; Race: 83.7% White, 5.1% Black/African American, 1.4% Asian, 0.0% American Indian/Alaska Native, 0.0% Native Hawaiian/Other Pacific Islander, 5.8% Two or more races, 3.7% Hispanic of any race; Average household size: 2.42; Median age: 46.0; Age under 18: 16.5%; Age 65 and over: 20.4%; Males per 100 females: 98.8; Marriage status: 18.0% never married, 73.9% now married, 2.5%

separated, 4.2% widowed, 3.9% divorced; Foreign born: 6.6%; Speak English only: 93.2%; With disability: 13.2%; Veterans: 18.2%; Ancestry: 30.2% Irish, 18.3% German, 15.6% English, 11.1% Welsh, 8.2% Polish
Employment: 9.6% management, business, and financial, 0.0% computer, engineering, and science, 33.1% education, legal, community service, arts, and media, 7.5% healthcare practitioners, 10.0% service, 33.1% sales and office, 6.7% natural resources, construction, and maintenance, 0.0% production, transportation, and material moving
Income: Per capita: $53,934; Median household: $134,261; Average household: $138,291; Households with income of $100,000 or more: 61.8%; Poverty rate: 2.3%
Educational Attainment: High school diploma or higher: 97.8%; Bachelor's degree or higher: 65.2%; Graduate/professional degree or higher: 38.6%
Housing: Homeownership rate: 85.1%; Median home value: $296,100; Median year structure built: 1974; Homeowner vacancy rate: 0.0%; Median selected monthly owner costs: $2,667 with a mortgage, $555 without a mortgage; Median gross rent: n/a per month; Rental vacancy rate: 14.5%
Health Insurance: 89.7% have insurance; 73.0% have private insurance; 45.5% have public insurance; 10.3% do not have insurance; 0.0% of children under 18 do not have insurance
Transportation: Commute: 90.5% car, 2.9% public transportation, 0.0% walk, 6.7% work from home; Mean travel time to work: 20.7 minutes

GREENFIELD PARK (unincorporated postal area)
ZCTA: 12435
Covers a land area of 9.957 square miles and a water area of 0.077 square miles. Located at 41.73° N. Lat; 74.51° W. Long. Elevation is 873 feet.
Population: 354; Growth (since 2000): 35.6%; Density: 35.6 persons per square mile; Race: 100.0% White, 0.0% Black/African American, 0.0% Asian, 0.0% American Indian/Alaska Native, 0.0% Native Hawaiian/Other Pacific Islander, 0.0% Two or more races, 18.4% Hispanic of any race; Average household size: 2.95; Median age: 44.6; Age under 18: 15.8%; Age 65 and over: 17.5%; Males per 100 females: 109.0; Marriage status: 27.2% never married, 54.0% now married, 0.0% separated, 8.4% widowed, 10.4% divorced; Foreign born: 23.4%; Speak English only: 59.6%; With disability: 8.5%; Veterans: 0.0%; Ancestry: 14.7% Albanian, 9.9% German, 5.6% Dutch, 4.5% Italian, 3.4% French Canadian
Employment: 3.5% management, business, and financial, 4.7% computer, engineering, and science, 16.3% education, legal, community service, arts, and media, 0.0% healthcare practitioners, 24.4% service, 21.5% sales and office, 15.1% natural resources, construction, and maintenance, 14.5% production, transportation, and material moving
Income: Per capita: $18,195; Median household: $34,205; Average household: $48,104; Households with income of $100,000 or more: 6.7%; Poverty rate: 9.6%
Educational Attainment: High school diploma or higher: 95.8%; Bachelor's degree or higher: 23.5%; Graduate/professional degree or higher: n/a
Housing: Homeownership rate: 58.3%; Median home value: $231,000; Median year structure built: 1963; Homeowner vacancy rate: 0.0%; Median selected monthly owner costs: $1,705 with a mortgage, $0 without a mortgage; Median gross rent: $1,000 per month; Rental vacancy rate: 0.0%
Health Insurance: 94.1% have insurance; 66.9% have private insurance; 41.2% have public insurance; 5.9% do not have insurance; 0.0% of children under 18 do not have insurance
Transportation: Commute: 100.0% car, 0.0% public transportation, 0.0% walk, 0.0% work from home; Mean travel time to work: 22.5 minutes

HARDENBURGH (town).
Covers a land area of 80.787 square miles and a water area of 0.235 square miles. Located at 42.05° N. Lat; 74.62° W. Long.
Population: 221; Growth (since 2000): 6.3%; Density: 2.7 persons per square mile; Race: 98.6% White, 0.0% Black/African American, 0.5% Asian, 0.0% American Indian/Alaska Native, 0.0% Native Hawaiian/Other Pacific Islander, 0.9% Two or more races, 0.0% Hispanic of any race; Average household size: 2.17; Median age: 58.3; Age under 18: 16.3%; Age 65 and over: 19.5%; Males per 100 females: 116.4; Marriage status: 18.8% never married, 64.6% now married, 2.1% separated, 7.3% widowed, 9.4% divorced; Foreign born: 0.5%; Speak English only: 95.6%;

With disability: 18.6%; Veterans: 6.5%; Ancestry: 24.9% German, 24.9% Italian, 20.4% Irish, 15.4% English, 11.8% Scottish

Employment: 29.5% management, business, and financial, 1.9% computer, engineering, and science, 13.3% education, legal, community service, arts, and media, 4.8% healthcare practitioners, 21.9% service, 7.6% sales and office, 12.4% natural resources, construction, and maintenance, 8.6% production, transportation, and material moving

Income: Per capita: $26,571; Median household: $44,375; Average household: $56,552; Households with income of $100,000 or more: 10.8%; Poverty rate: 18.6%

Educational Attainment: High school diploma or higher: 90.7%; Bachelor's degree or higher: 37.8%; Graduate/professional degree or higher: 10.5%

Housing: Homeownership rate: 62.7%; Median home value: $187,500; Median year structure built: 1969; Homeowner vacancy rate: 8.0%; Median selected monthly owner costs: $1,275 with a mortgage, $675 without a mortgage; Median gross rent: n/a per month; Rental vacancy rate: 9.5%

Health Insurance: 95.9% have insurance; 72.9% have private insurance; 37.6% have public insurance; 4.1% do not have insurance; 5.6% of children under 18 do not have insurance

Transportation: Commute: 47.6% car, 1.0% public transportation, 39.8% walk, 9.7% work from home; Mean travel time to work: 21.5 minutes

---

HIGH FALLS (CDP). Covers a land area of 1.196 square miles and a water area of 0 square miles. Located at 41.83° N. Lat; 74.12° W. Long. Elevation is 161 feet.

Population: 905; Growth (since 2000): 44.3%; Density: 756.6 persons per square mile; Race: 97.7% White, 0.1% Black/African American, 1.2% Asian, 0.1% American Indian/Alaska Native, 0.0% Native Hawaiian/Other Pacific Islander, 0.9% Two or more races, 2.8% Hispanic of any race; Average household size: 2.60; Median age: 45.8; Age under 18: 13.5%; Age 65 and over: 16.0%; Males per 100 females: 93.5; Marriage status: 36.5% never married, 54.8% now married, 7.0% separated, 2.1% widowed, 6.6% divorced; Foreign born: 0.0%; Speak English only: 99.9%; With disability: 22.2%; Veterans: 2.7%; Ancestry: 39.0% Irish, 32.6% Italian, 17.6% German, 11.2% Polish, 9.1% French

Employment: 13.3% management, business, and financial, 0.0% computer, engineering, and science, 21.9% education, legal, community service, arts, and media, 6.4% healthcare practitioners, 29.0% service, 18.6% sales and office, 2.7% natural resources, construction, and maintenance, 8.1% production, transportation, and material moving

Income: Per capita: $26,409; Median household: n/a; Average household: $63,052; Households with income of $100,000 or more: 21.4%; Poverty rate: 19.4%

Educational Attainment: High school diploma or higher: 94.9%; Bachelor's degree or higher: 24.3%; Graduate/professional degree or higher: 9.8%

Housing: Homeownership rate: 70.4%; Median home value: $196,800; Median year structure built: 1951; Homeowner vacancy rate: 0.0%; Median selected monthly owner costs: n/a with a mortgage, n/a without a mortgage; Median gross rent: n/a per month; Rental vacancy rate: 0.0%

Health Insurance: 78.0% have insurance; 71.6% have private insurance; 15.4% have public insurance; 22.0% do not have insurance; 0.0% of children under 18 do not have insurance

Transportation: Commute: 96.7% car, 0.0% public transportation, 0.0% walk, 3.3% work from home; Mean travel time to work: 25.2 minutes

---

HIGHLAND (CDP). Covers a land area of 4.686 square miles and a water area of 0.390 square miles. Located at 41.72° N. Lat; 73.96° W. Long. Elevation is 174 feet.

Population: 5,189; Growth (since 2000): 2.5%; Density: 1,107.4 persons per square mile; Race: 87.7% White, 4.9% Black/African American, 5.0% Asian, 0.0% American Indian/Alaska Native, 0.0% Native Hawaiian/Other Pacific Islander, 2.0% Two or more races, 11.0% Hispanic of any race; Average household size: 2.25; Median age: 42.1; Age under 18: 22.4%; Age 65 and over: 17.4%; Males per 100 females: 88.7; Marriage status: 30.3% never married, 52.8% now married, 3.0% separated, 9.0% widowed, 7.9% divorced; Foreign born: 8.5%; Speak English only: 89.1%; With disability: 8.7%; Veterans: 8.1%; Ancestry: 25.6% Italian, 15.9% German, 13.4% Irish, 6.3% Polish, 6.3% English

Employment: 17.6% management, business, and financial, 9.0% computer, engineering, and science, 8.1% education, legal, community service, arts, and media, 11.5% healthcare practitioners, 20.2% service, 26.4% sales and office, 4.8% natural resources, construction, and maintenance, 2.4% production, transportation, and material moving

Income: Per capita: $30,500; Median household: $59,406; Average household: $70,011; Households with income of $100,000 or more: 27.2%; Poverty rate: 14.4%

Educational Attainment: High school diploma or higher: 87.1%; Bachelor's degree or higher: 30.0%; Graduate/professional degree or higher: 9.8%

School District(s)

Highland Central SD (KG-12)

    2014-15 Enrollment: 1,824 . . . . (845) 691-1014

Housing: Homeownership rate: 63.9%; Median home value: $223,800; Median year structure built: 1966; Homeowner vacancy rate: 3.0%; Median selected monthly owner costs: $1,939 with a mortgage, $861 without a mortgage; Median gross rent: $1,115 per month; Rental vacancy rate: 16.3%

Health Insurance: 96.4% have insurance; 76.1% have private insurance; 33.9% have public insurance; 3.6% do not have insurance; 0.0% of children under 18 do not have insurance

Transportation: Commute: 93.0% car, 0.6% public transportation, 0.0% walk, 5.8% work from home; Mean travel time to work: 23.4 minutes

---

HIGHMOUNT (unincorporated postal area)

ZCTA: 12441

    Covers a land area of 6.327 square miles and a water area of 0.001 square miles. Located at 42.13° N. Lat; 74.51° W. Long. Elevation is 1,857 feet.

Population: 33; Growth (since 2000): n/a; Density: 5.2 persons per square mile; Race: 100.0% White, 0.0% Black/African American, 0.0% Asian, 0.0% American Indian/Alaska Native, 0.0% Native Hawaiian/Other Pacific Islander, 0.0% Two or more races, 0.0% Hispanic of any race; Average household size: 2.36; Median age: 49.5; Age under 18: 27.3%; Age 65 and over: 30.3%; Males per 100 females: 119.2; Marriage status: 16.7% never married, 83.3% now married, 0.0% separated, 0.0% widowed, 0.0% divorced; Foreign born: 15.2%; Speak English only: 54.5%; With disability: 0.0%; Veterans: 20.8%; Ancestry: 42.4% Italian, 27.3% French, 15.2% English, 15.2% Irish, 12.1% German

Employment: 0.0% management, business, and financial, 0.0% computer, engineering, and science, 64.3% education, legal, community service, arts, and media, 0.0% healthcare practitioners, 0.0% service, 0.0% sales and office, 0.0% natural resources, construction, and maintenance, 35.7% production, transportation, and material moving

Income: Per capita: $46,564; Median household: $116,500; Average household: $109,757; Households with income of $100,000 or more: 71.4%; Poverty rate: n/a

Educational Attainment: High school diploma or higher: 100.0%; Bachelor's degree or higher: 100.0%; Graduate/professional degree or higher: 100.0%

Housing: Homeownership rate: 100.0%; Median home value: $275,000; Median year structure built: 1986; Homeowner vacancy rate: 0.0%; Median selected monthly owner costs: $0 with a mortgage, $0 without a mortgage; Median gross rent: n/a per month; Rental vacancy rate: 0.0%

Health Insurance: 100.0% have insurance; 84.8% have private insurance; 30.3% have public insurance; 0.0% do not have insurance; 0.0% of children under 18 do not have insurance

Transportation: Commute: 100.0% car, 0.0% public transportation, 0.0% walk, 0.0% work from home; Mean travel time to work: 0.0 minutes

---

HILLSIDE (CDP). Covers a land area of 0.825 square miles and a water area of 0.003 square miles. Located at 41.92° N. Lat; 74.03° W. Long. Elevation is 318 feet.

Population: 855; Growth (since 2000): -3.1%; Density: 1,036.1 persons per square mile; Race: 99.2% White, 0.8% Black/African American, 0.0% Asian, 0.0% American Indian/Alaska Native, 0.0% Native Hawaiian/Other Pacific Islander, 0.0% Two or more races, 0.0% Hispanic of any race; Average household size: 2.66; Median age: 51.5; Age under 18: 21.2%; Age 65 and over: 22.1%; Males per 100 females: 98.4; Marriage status: 21.0% never married, 68.2% now married, 0.0% separated, 7.1% widowed, 3.7% divorced; Foreign born: 13.3%; Speak English only: 85.3%; With disability: 10.9%; Veterans: 9.2%; Ancestry: 25.7% Italian, 22.7% Irish, 21.6% German, 12.2% English, 10.6% Russian

Employment: 24.2% management, business, and financial, 5.6% computer, engineering, and science, 21.6% education, legal, community service, arts, and media, 10.0% healthcare practitioners, 8.7% service,

16.0% sales and office, 11.1% natural resources, construction, and maintenance, 2.9% production, transportation, and material moving
Income: Per capita: $50,112; Median household: $96,563; Average household: $131,369; Households with income of $100,000 or more: 47.6%; Poverty rate: 2.3%
Educational Attainment: High school diploma or higher: 89.6%; Bachelor's degree or higher: 52.1%; Graduate/professional degree or higher: 31.3%
Housing: Homeownership rate: 98.4%; Median home value: $285,100; Median year structure built: 1967; Homeowner vacancy rate: 2.2%; Median selected monthly owner costs: $2,311 with a mortgage, $887 without a mortgage; Median gross rent: n/a per month; Rental vacancy rate: 0.0%
Health Insurance: 96.8% have insurance; 84.3% have private insurance; 28.4% have public insurance; 3.2% do not have insurance; 0.0% of children under 18 do not have insurance
Transportation: Commute: 91.9% car, 1.6% public transportation, 2.2% walk, 2.7% work from home; Mean travel time to work: 19.0 minutes

HURLEY (CDP). Covers a land area of 5.486 square miles and a water area of 0.032 square miles. Located at 41.91° N. Lat; 74.06° W. Long. Elevation is 197 feet.
Population: 3,452; Growth (since 2000): -3.1%; Density: 629.3 persons per square mile; Race: 94.6% White, 1.7% Black/African American, 1.6% Asian, 0.2% American Indian/Alaska Native, 0.0% Native Hawaiian/Other Pacific Islander, 1.4% Two or more races, 2.5% Hispanic of any race; Average household size: 2.49; Median age: 49.5; Age under 18: 19.1%; Age 65 and over: 19.8%; Males per 100 females: 95.7; Marriage status: 22.7% never married, 61.7% now married, 2.9% separated, 7.3% widowed, 8.2% divorced; Foreign born: 4.3%; Speak English only: 93.0%; With disability: 10.8%; Veterans: 7.9%; Ancestry: 27.9% Italian, 24.7% German, 19.4% Irish, 11.5% English, 7.3% French
Employment: 14.6% management, business, and financial, 3.5% computer, engineering, and science, 14.3% education, legal, community service, arts, and media, 5.2% healthcare practitioners, 18.0% service, 31.3% sales and office, 5.3% natural resources, construction, and maintenance, 7.8% production, transportation, and material moving
Income: Per capita: $42,013; Median household: $78,906; Average household: $101,895; Households with income of $100,000 or more: 39.3%; Poverty rate: 7.1%
Educational Attainment: High school diploma or higher: 95.4%; Bachelor's degree or higher: 44.7%; Graduate/professional degree or higher: 19.9%

School District(s)
Kingston City SD (PK-12)
   2014-15 Enrollment: 6,471 . . . . (845) 943-3003
Housing: Homeownership rate: 88.0%; Median home value: $235,700; Median year structure built: 1962; Homeowner vacancy rate: 1.0%; Median selected monthly owner costs: $1,980 with a mortgage, $685 without a mortgage; Median gross rent: $1,144 per month; Rental vacancy rate: 0.0%
Health Insurance: 94.8% have insurance; 78.0% have private insurance; 32.7% have public insurance; 5.2% do not have insurance; 2.6% of children under 18 do not have insurance
Transportation: Commute: 92.3% car, 2.5% public transportation, 0.0% walk, 4.5% work from home; Mean travel time to work: 23.3 minutes

HURLEY (town). Covers a land area of 29.911 square miles and a water area of 6.056 square miles. Located at 41.96° N. Lat; 74.12° W. Long. Elevation is 197 feet.
History: In 1662, Peter Stuyvesant, Dutch Governor of Niew Amsterdam, established the village of Niew Dorp on the site of an earlier Native American Settlement. On June 7, 1663, during the Esopus Wars, the village was attacked and destroyed. On September 17, 1669, the abandoned village was resettled and renamed Hurley after Francis Lovelace, Baron Hurley of Ireland.
Population: 6,225; Growth (since 2000): -5.2%; Density: 208.1 persons per square mile; Race: 95.5% White, 1.4% Black/African American, 0.1% Asian, 0.1% American Indian/Alaska Native, 0.0% Native Hawaiian/Other Pacific Islander, 1.2% Two or more races, 2.8% Hispanic of any race; Average household size: 2.31; Median age: 51.5; Age under 18: 17.6%; Age 65 and over: 22.4%; Males per 100 females: 92.9; Marriage status: 19.6% never married, 62.1% now married, 3.5% separated, 7.4% widowed, 10.9% divorced; Foreign born: 4.2%; Speak English only: 95.1%; With disability: 13.1%; Veterans: 10.5%; Ancestry: 25.8% German, 21.5% Irish, 20.3% Italian, 13.0% English, 7.1% French

Employment: 13.6% management, business, and financial, 3.4% computer, engineering, and science, 21.7% education, legal, community service, arts, and media, 5.8% healthcare practitioners, 16.5% service, 26.2% sales and office, 6.5% natural resources, construction, and maintenance, 6.3% production, transportation, and material moving
Income: Per capita: $39,681; Median household: $67,717; Average household: $91,363; Households with income of $100,000 or more: 33.6%; Poverty rate: 7.7%
Educational Attainment: High school diploma or higher: 95.2%; Bachelor's degree or higher: 43.8%; Graduate/professional degree or higher: 24.0%

School District(s)
Kingston City SD (PK-12)
   2014-15 Enrollment: 6,471 . . . . (845) 943-3003
Housing: Homeownership rate: 90.1%; Median home value: $245,800; Median year structure built: 1963; Homeowner vacancy rate: 0.0%; Median selected monthly owner costs: $1,833 with a mortgage, $628 without a mortgage; Median gross rent: $1,188 per month; Rental vacancy rate: 3.3%
Health Insurance: 92.3% have insurance; 75.7% have private insurance; 34.6% have public insurance; 7.7% do not have insurance; 5.7% of children under 18 do not have insurance
Transportation: Commute: 89.2% car, 3.5% public transportation, 0.6% walk, 6.0% work from home; Mean travel time to work: 25.5 minutes
Additional Information Contacts
Town of Hurley . . . . (845) 331-7474
   http://townofhurley.org/content

KERHONKSON (CDP). Covers a land area of 5.277 square miles and a water area of 0.018 square miles. Located at 41.78° N. Lat; 74.30° W. Long. Elevation is 262 feet.
Population: 2,247; Growth (since 2000): 29.7%; Density: 425.8 persons per square mile; Race: 96.5% White, 2.8% Black/African American, 0.0% Asian, 0.0% American Indian/Alaska Native, 0.0% Native Hawaiian/Other Pacific Islander, 0.7% Two or more races, 7.6% Hispanic of any race; Average household size: 3.02; Median age: 33.8; Age under 18: 28.1%; Age 65 and over: 14.1%; Males per 100 females: 97.7; Marriage status: 33.2% never married, 37.7% now married, 2.2% separated, 12.9% widowed, 16.2% divorced; Foreign born: 5.7%; Speak English only: 85.4%; With disability: 16.3%; Veterans: 6.3%; Ancestry: 30.8% German, 19.4% Irish, 17.4% English, 16.8% Norwegian, 10.9% Italian
Employment: 8.8% management, business, and financial, 2.0% computer, engineering, and science, 9.6% education, legal, community service, arts, and media, 4.5% healthcare practitioners, 33.6% service, 23.7% sales and office, 12.2% natural resources, construction, and maintenance, 5.6% production, transportation, and material moving
Income: Per capita: $18,040; Median household: $48,453; Average household: $51,587; Households with income of $100,000 or more: 16.0%; Poverty rate: 13.6%
Educational Attainment: High school diploma or higher: 82.8%; Bachelor's degree or higher: 22.0%; Graduate/professional degree or higher: 5.4%

School District(s)
Rondout Valley Central SD (PK-12)
   2014-15 Enrollment: 1,966 . . . . (845) 687-2400
Housing: Homeownership rate: 75.0%; Median home value: $156,500; Median year structure built: 1964; Homeowner vacancy rate: 11.4%; Median selected monthly owner costs: $1,533 with a mortgage, $559 without a mortgage; Median gross rent: $947 per month; Rental vacancy rate: 6.1%
Health Insurance: 90.0% have insurance; 52.5% have private insurance; 47.1% have public insurance; 10.0% do not have insurance; 2.1% of children under 18 do not have insurance
Transportation: Commute: 91.2% car, 3.5% public transportation, 0.0% walk, 5.3% work from home; Mean travel time to work: 28.8 minutes

KINGSTON (city). County seat. Covers a land area of 7.486 square miles and a water area of 1.287 square miles. Located at 41.93° N. Lat; 74.00° W. Long. Elevation is 197 feet.
History: In 1615, Dutch traders established a trading post at the present site of Kingston and named it Esopus. A group of Dutch colonists from Albany made the first permanent settlement in 1653. In 1658, Director General Peter Stuyvesant erected a stockade and blockhouse and in 1661 granted a charter to the village, which he called Wiltwyck. In 1669, the English Governor Francis Lovelace gave it its present name in honor of

Kingston L'Isle, his family seat in England. Kingston was the site of the New York government during 1777. Boat building and the cement industry both began about 1830.

Population: 23,625; Growth (since 2000): 0.7%; Density: 3,155.7 persons per square mile; Race: 70.8% White, 16.7% Black/African American, 2.7% Asian, 0.2% American Indian/Alaska Native, 0.0% Native Hawaiian/Other Pacific Islander, 8.0% Two or more races, 15.9% Hispanic of any race; Average household size: 2.36; Median age: 39.2; Age under 18: 22.2%; Age 65 and over: 15.6%; Males per 100 females: 92.7; Marriage status: 38.6% never married, 41.5% now married, 4.3% separated, 8.0% widowed, 11.9% divorced; Foreign born: 11.7%; Speak English only: 83.0%; With disability: 18.2%; Veterans: 5.6%; Ancestry: 17.8% Irish, 16.5% Italian, 15.6% German, 5.5% English, 5.3% Polish

Employment: 14.0% management, business, and financial, 2.2% computer, engineering, and science, 12.4% education, legal, community service, arts, and media, 5.7% healthcare practitioners, 23.8% service, 25.1% sales and office, 5.4% natural resources, construction, and maintenance, 11.5% production, transportation, and material moving

Income: Per capita: $23,955; Median household: $40,757; Average household: $55,498; Households with income of $100,000 or more: 15.1%; Poverty rate: 18.6%

Educational Attainment: High school diploma or higher: 84.5%; Bachelor's degree or higher: 22.1%; Graduate/professional degree or higher: 9.1%

School District(s)

Kingston City SD (PK-12)
    2014-15 Enrollment: 6,471 . . . . (845) 943-3003

Housing: Homeownership rate: 44.3%; Median home value: $171,500; Median year structure built: Before 1940; Homeowner vacancy rate: 2.9%; Median selected monthly owner costs: $1,670 with a mortgage, $770 without a mortgage; Median gross rent: $1,005 per month; Rental vacancy rate: 5.1%

Health Insurance: 90.4% have insurance; 52.2% have private insurance; 49.7% have public insurance; 9.6% do not have insurance; 2.7% of children under 18 do not have insurance

Hospitals: Health Alliance Hospital Broadway Campus (150 beds); Health Alliance Hospital Mary's Avenue Campus (222 beds)

Safety: Violent crime rate: 30.2 per 10,000 population; Property crime rate: 281.0 per 10,000 population

Newspapers: Daily Freeman (daily circulation 19,300); Ulster Publishing (weekly circulation 5,500)

Transportation: Commute: 81.4% car, 2.9% public transportation, 7.5% walk, 4.9% work from home; Mean travel time to work: 22.8 minutes

Airports: Kingston-Ulster (general aviation)

Additional Information Contacts

City of Kingston . . . . (845) 331-0080
    http://www.ci.kingston.ny.us

KINGSTON (town).
Covers a land area of 7.702 square miles and a water area of 0.048 square miles. Located at 41.98° N. Lat; 74.04° W. Long. Elevation is 197 feet.

History: First permanent settlement (Wiltwyck) was established in 1652. Served as the first capital of New York State until it was burned by the British in Oct. 1777. Many old Dutch stone houses; the Senate house (1676 meeting place of the first state legislature); the old Dutch church (1659) and cemetery (1661); and the burial place of James Clinton. Incorporated as a village 1805, and as a city through the union (1872) of Kingston and Rondout.

Population: 929; Growth (since 2000): 2.3%; Density: 120.6 persons per square mile; Race: 93.4% White, 0.6% Black/African American, 0.8% Asian, 0.1% American Indian/Alaska Native, 0.0% Native Hawaiian/Other Pacific Islander, 4.6% Two or more races, 3.3% Hispanic of any race; Average household size: 2.19; Median age: 48.6; Age under 18: 17.7%; Age 65 and over: 14.0%; Males per 100 females: 101.6; Marriage status: 27.0% never married, 50.4% now married, 2.4% separated, 6.4% widowed, 16.1% divorced; Foreign born: 2.2%; Speak English only: 96.3%; With disability: 10.3%; Veterans: 9.4%; Ancestry: 30.8% German, 27.6% Irish, 16.5% Italian, 6.7% Dutch, 6.4% English

Employment: 10.6% management, business, and financial, 2.3% computer, engineering, and science, 14.6% education, legal, community service, arts, and media, 10.0% healthcare practitioners, 18.4% service, 24.1% sales and office, 13.1% natural resources, construction, and maintenance, 7.0% production, transportation, and material moving

Income: Per capita: $34,498; Median household: $60,114; Average household: $74,074; Households with income of $100,000 or more: 22.1%; Poverty rate: 7.0%

Educational Attainment: High school diploma or higher: 89.4%; Bachelor's degree or higher: 25.6%; Graduate/professional degree or higher: 13.2%

School District(s)

Kingston City SD (PK-12)
    2014-15 Enrollment: 6,471 . . . . (845) 943-3003

Housing: Homeownership rate: 90.8%; Median home value: $186,200; Median year structure built: 1973; Homeowner vacancy rate: 0.0%; Median selected monthly owner costs: $1,543 with a mortgage, $676 without a mortgage; Median gross rent: $1,109 per month; Rental vacancy rate: 0.0%

Health Insurance: 89.9% have insurance; 76.6% have private insurance; 24.1% have public insurance; 10.1% do not have insurance; 12.8% of children under 18 do not have insurance

Hospitals: Health Alliance Hospital Broadway Campus (150 beds); Health Alliance Hospital Mary's Avenue Campus (222 beds)

Newspapers: Daily Freeman (daily circulation 19,300); Ulster Publishing (weekly circulation 5,500)

Transportation: Commute: 91.4% car, 0.6% public transportation, 0.0% walk, 8.1% work from home; Mean travel time to work: 26.0 minutes

Airports: Kingston-Ulster (general aviation)

Additional Information Contacts

Town of Kingston. . . . . (845) 336-8853
    http://www.townkingstonny.us

LAKE HILL (unincorporated postal area)
ZCTA: 12448

Covers a land area of 11.661 square miles and a water area of 0.243 square miles. Located at 42.09° N. Lat; 74.16° W. Long. Elevation is 1,109 feet.

Population: 429; Growth (since 2000): 96.8%; Density: 36.8 persons per square mile; Race: 100.0% White, 0.0% Black/African American, 0.0% Asian, 0.0% American Indian/Alaska Native, 0.0% Native Hawaiian/Other Pacific Islander, 0.0% Two or more races, 0.0% Hispanic of any race; Average household size: 1.71; Median age: 58.6; Age under 18: 11.4%; Age 65 and over: 30.1%; Males per 100 females: 103.1; Marriage status: 20.8% never married, 65.8% now married, 0.0% separated, 1.5% widowed, 11.8% divorced; Foreign born: 11.9%; Speak English only: 88.7%; With disability: 12.6%; Veterans: 6.1%; Ancestry: 23.8% Italian, 19.3% Russian, 18.9% English, 15.2% Irish, 14.2% Polish

Employment: 31.6% management, business, and financial, 0.0% computer, engineering, and science, 28.8% education, legal, community service, arts, and media, 0.0% healthcare practitioners, 3.6% service, 31.2% sales and office, 4.8% natural resources, construction, and maintenance, 0.0% production, transportation, and material moving

Income: Per capita: $70,017; Median household: $61,648; Average household: $119,271; Households with income of $100,000 or more: 26.7%; Poverty rate: 2.3%

Educational Attainment: High school diploma or higher: 100.0%; Bachelor's degree or higher: 67.1%; Graduate/professional degree or higher: 33.2%

Housing: Homeownership rate: 86.9%; Median home value: $250,000; Median year structure built: Before 1940; Homeowner vacancy rate: 9.5%; Median selected monthly owner costs: $1,586 with a mortgage, $852 without a mortgage; Median gross rent: n/a per month; Rental vacancy rate: 0.0%

Health Insurance: 87.9% have insurance; 80.9% have private insurance; 33.6% have public insurance; 12.1% do not have insurance; 0.0% of children under 18 do not have insurance

Transportation: Commute: 83.2% car, 8.0% public transportation, 0.0% walk, 8.8% work from home; Mean travel time to work: 45.5 minutes

LAKE KATRINE (CDP).
Covers a land area of 2.254 square miles and a water area of 0.040 square miles. Located at 41.99° N. Lat; 73.99° W. Long. Elevation is 184 feet.

Population: 2,322; Growth (since 2000): -3.1%; Density: 1,030.0 persons per square mile; Race: 83.5% White, 4.3% Black/African American, 3.8% Asian, 0.0% American Indian/Alaska Native, 0.0% Native Hawaiian/Other Pacific Islander, 8.4% Two or more races, 2.2% Hispanic of any race; Average household size: 2.08; Median age: 53.3; Age under 18: 12.4%; Age 65 and over: 27.4%; Males per 100 females: 89.6; Marriage status: 33.8% never married, 44.7% now married, 3.1% separated, 14.1%

widowed, 7.4% divorced; Foreign born: 4.5%; Speak English only: 91.8%; With disability: 18.4%; Veterans: 9.7%; Ancestry: 22.0% Irish, 18.2% Italian, 16.9% German, 8.3% Dutch, 6.1% English
Employment: 6.4% management, business, and financial, 7.5% computer, engineering, and science, 8.4% education, legal, community service, arts, and media, 9.2% healthcare practitioners, 20.3% service, 28.1% sales and office, 11.9% natural resources, construction, and maintenance, 8.2% production, transportation, and material moving
Income: Per capita: $26,954; Median household: $31,250; Average household: $53,569; Households with income of $100,000 or more: 16.0%; Poverty rate: 26.0%
Educational Attainment: High school diploma or higher: 86.0%; Bachelor's degree or higher: 20.4%; Graduate/professional degree or higher: 10.1%

School District(s)
Kingston City SD (PK-12)
   2014-15 Enrollment: 6,471 . . . . (845) 943-3003
Housing: Homeownership rate: 50.9%; Median home value: $163,900; Median year structure built: 1973; Homeowner vacancy rate: 0.0%; Median selected monthly owner costs: $1,362 with a mortgage, $687 without a mortgage; Median gross rent: $1,067 per month; Rental vacancy rate: 0.0%
Health Insurance: 94.5% have insurance; 62.5% have private insurance; 49.4% have public insurance; 5.5% do not have insurance; 0.0% of children under 18 do not have insurance
Transportation: Commute: 88.3% car, 0.0% public transportation, 1.6% walk, 7.6% work from home; Mean travel time to work: 19.2 minutes

LINCOLN PARK (CDP).
Covers a land area of 1.434 square miles and a water area of 0.030 square miles. Located at 41.96° N. Lat; 74.00° W. Long. Elevation is 187 feet.
Population: 2,082; Growth (since 2000): -10.9%; Density: 1,452.0 persons per square mile; Race: 89.4% White, 5.9% Black/African American, 3.9% Asian, 0.3% American Indian/Alaska Native, 0.0% Native Hawaiian/Other Pacific Islander, 0.0% Two or more races, 1.4% Hispanic of any race; Average household size: 1.92; Median age: 48.1; Age under 18: 19.6%; Age 65 and over: 26.6%; Males per 100 females: 84.1; Marriage status: 25.4% never married, 46.0% now married, 1.8% separated, 19.1% widowed, 9.5% divorced; Foreign born: 6.7%; Speak English only: 92.3%; With disability: 14.5%; Veterans: 6.9%; Ancestry: 28.2% German, 20.8% Irish, 17.5% Italian, 11.1% Dutch, 11.1% English
Employment: 8.3% management, business, and financial, 7.4% computer, engineering, and science, 9.1% education, legal, community service, arts, and media, 10.4% healthcare practitioners, 19.6% service, 34.6% sales and office, 4.7% natural resources, construction, and maintenance, 5.8% production, transportation, and material moving
Income: Per capita: $23,407; Median household: $27,500; Average household: $44,415; Households with income of $100,000 or more: 11.9%; Poverty rate: 18.6%
Educational Attainment: High school diploma or higher: 85.2%; Bachelor's degree or higher: 16.3%; Graduate/professional degree or higher: 7.1%
Housing: Homeownership rate: 45.4%; Median home value: $178,900; Median year structure built: 1967; Homeowner vacancy rate: 4.3%; Median selected monthly owner costs: $1,537 with a mortgage, $566 without a mortgage; Median gross rent: $861 per month; Rental vacancy rate: 0.0%
Health Insurance: 95.5% have insurance; 69.0% have private insurance; 49.7% have public insurance; 4.5% do not have insurance; 0.0% of children under 18 do not have insurance
Transportation: Commute: 95.0% car, 1.7% public transportation, 2.0% walk, 0.0% work from home; Mean travel time to work: 20.5 minutes

LLOYD (town).
Covers a land area of 31.266 square miles and a water area of 2.019 square miles. Located at 41.71° N. Lat; 74.00° W. Long. Elevation is 381 feet.
Population: 10,681; Growth (since 2000): 7.4%; Density: 341.6 persons per square mile; Race: 89.3% White, 5.7% Black/African American, 2.5% Asian, 0.0% American Indian/Alaska Native, 0.0% Native Hawaiian/Other Pacific Islander, 2.3% Two or more races, 8.3% Hispanic of any race; Average household size: 2.43; Median age: 42.1; Age under 18: 22.3%; Age 65 and over: 16.3%; Males per 100 females: 95.3; Marriage status: 31.0% never married, 51.8% now married, 1.9% separated, 8.0% widowed, 9.2% divorced; Foreign born: 7.2%; Speak English only: 91.1%; With disability: 10.5%; Veterans: 9.0%; Ancestry: 28.7% Italian, 17.0% Irish, 15.7% German, 6.5% American, 6.5% English

Employment: 13.9% management, business, and financial, 8.2% computer, engineering, and science, 11.6% education, legal, community service, arts, and media, 8.1% healthcare practitioners, 18.4% service, 24.7% sales and office, 8.2% natural resources, construction, and maintenance, 6.8% production, transportation, and material moving
Income: Per capita: $32,106; Median household: $63,281; Average household: $78,603; Households with income of $100,000 or more: 31.1%; Poverty rate: 9.0%
Educational Attainment: High school diploma or higher: 89.1%; Bachelor's degree or higher: 30.5%; Graduate/professional degree or higher: 13.5%
Housing: Homeownership rate: 70.2%; Median home value: $238,200; Median year structure built: 1968; Homeowner vacancy rate: 2.2%; Median selected monthly owner costs: $2,110 with a mortgage, $837 without a mortgage; Median gross rent: $1,069 per month; Rental vacancy rate: 12.0%
Health Insurance: 94.7% have insurance; 78.0% have private insurance; 31.3% have public insurance; 5.3% do not have insurance; 0.5% of children under 18 do not have insurance
Safety: Violent crime rate: 8.5 per 10,000 population; Property crime rate: 87.1 per 10,000 population
Transportation: Commute: 92.1% car, 1.1% public transportation, 0.7% walk, 5.6% work from home; Mean travel time to work: 24.4 minutes
Additional Information Contacts
Town of Lloyd . . . . (845) 691-8011
   http://www.townoflloyd.com

MALDEN-ON-HUDSON (CDP).
Covers a land area of 0.501 square miles and a water area of 0 square miles. Located at 42.09° N. Lat; 73.94° W. Long. Elevation is 85 feet.
Population: 202; Growth (since 2000): n/a; Density: 403.2 persons per square mile; Race: 100.0% White, 0.0% Black/African American, 0.0% Asian, 0.0% American Indian/Alaska Native, 0.0% Native Hawaiian/Other Pacific Islander, 0.0% Two or more races, 12.4% Hispanic of any race; Average household size: 1.74; Median age: 49.5; Age under 18: 19.3%; Age 65 and over: 33.2%; Males per 100 females: 88.4; Marriage status: 32.4% never married, 25.7% now married, 0.0% separated, 29.6% widowed, 12.3% divorced; Foreign born: 26.2%; Speak English only: 61.4%; With disability: 38.6%; Veterans: 0.0%; Ancestry: 34.7% German, 26.2% French, 19.8% Irish, 15.3% English, 8.4% Dutch
Employment: 0.0% management, business, and financial, 0.0% computer, engineering, and science, 0.0% education, legal, community service, arts, and media, 0.0% healthcare practitioners, 42.3% service, 0.0% sales and office, 22.7% natural resources, construction, and maintenance, 35.1% production, transportation, and material moving
Income: Per capita: $37,189; Median household: $34,434; Average household: $64,398; Households with income of $100,000 or more: 14.7%; Poverty rate: n/a
Educational Attainment: High school diploma or higher: 76.1%; Bachelor's degree or higher: 19.6%; Graduate/professional degree or higher: 10.4%
Housing: Homeownership rate: 81.0%; Median home value: $343,400; Median year structure built: Before 1940; Homeowner vacancy rate: 0.0%; Median selected monthly owner costs: n/a with a mortgage, n/a without a mortgage; Median gross rent: n/a per month; Rental vacancy rate: 0.0%
Health Insurance: 89.1% have insurance; 69.8% have private insurance; 45.5% have public insurance; 10.9% do not have insurance; 0.0% of children under 18 do not have insurance
Transportation: Commute: 66.0% car, 0.0% public transportation, 16.5% walk, 0.0% work from home; Mean travel time to work: 0.0 minutes

MARBLETOWN (town).
Covers a land area of 54.471 square miles and a water area of 0.709 square miles. Located at 41.87° N. Lat; 74.16° W. Long. Elevation is 223 feet.
Population: 5,585; Growth (since 2000): -4.6%; Density: 102.5 persons per square mile; Race: 92.4% White, 0.9% Black/African American, 1.8% Asian, 0.0% American Indian/Alaska Native, 0.0% Native Hawaiian/Other Pacific Islander, 4.2% Two or more races, 2.3% Hispanic of any race; Average household size: 2.30; Median age: 45.7; Age under 18: 19.1%; Age 65 and over: 17.7%; Males per 100 females: 97.4; Marriage status: 27.8% never married, 55.7% now married, 1.1% separated, 6.9% widowed, 9.6% divorced; Foreign born: 4.7%; Speak English only: 95.5%; With disability: 12.7%; Veterans: 7.6%; Ancestry: 20.9% Irish, 19.9% German, 14.7% English, 14.1% Italian, 6.8% Dutch

Employment: 20.4% management, business, and financial, 3.1% computer, engineering, and science, 23.5% education, legal, community service, arts, and media, 7.4% healthcare practitioners, 9.0% service, 19.8% sales and office, 7.0% natural resources, construction, and maintenance, 9.8% production, transportation, and material moving
Income: Per capita: $37,370; Median household: $62,278; Average household: $86,988; Households with income of $100,000 or more: 28.7%; Poverty rate: 9.4%
Educational Attainment: High school diploma or higher: 94.5%; Bachelor's degree or higher: 46.2%; Graduate/professional degree or higher: 24.6%
Housing: Homeownership rate: 81.8%; Median home value: $264,200; Median year structure built: 1963; Homeowner vacancy rate: 0.0%; Median selected monthly owner costs: $1,912 with a mortgage, $699 without a mortgage; Median gross rent: $1,165 per month; Rental vacancy rate: 5.7%
Health Insurance: 94.1% have insurance; 80.9% have private insurance; 26.6% have public insurance; 5.9% do not have insurance; 3.0% of children under 18 do not have insurance
Transportation: Commute: 85.1% car, 2.6% public transportation, 4.9% walk, 6.4% work from home; Mean travel time to work: 30.3 minutes
Additional Information Contacts
Town of Marbletown . . . . (845) 687-9673
   http://www.marbletown.net

MARLBORO (CDP). Covers a land area of 4.456 square miles and a water area of 0.636 square miles. Located at 41.60° N. Lat; 73.98° W. Long. Elevation is 177 feet.
History: Also spelled Marlborough.
Population: 3,518; Growth (since 2000): 50.4%; Density: 789.6 persons per square mile; Race: 92.1% White, 5.0% Black/African American, 1.9% Asian, 0.0% American Indian/Alaska Native, 0.0% Native Hawaiian/Other Pacific Islander, 0.5% Two or more races, 2.2% Hispanic of any race; Average household size: 2.49; Median age: 37.8; Age under 18: 27.8%; Age 65 and over: 18.0%; Males per 100 females: 94.0; Marriage status: 25.6% never married, 53.8% now married, 1.0% separated, 5.2% widowed, 15.4% divorced; Foreign born: 6.4%; Speak English only: 91.5%; With disability: 11.7%; Veterans: 9.7%; Ancestry: 42.7% Italian, 22.4% Irish, 14.1% German, 8.4% English, 3.6% Hungarian
Employment: 16.6% management, business, and financial, 3.4% computer, engineering, and science, 7.6% education, legal, community service, arts, and media, 10.7% healthcare practitioners, 14.2% service, 25.6% sales and office, 8.7% natural resources, construction, and maintenance, 13.3% production, transportation, and material moving
Income: Per capita: $30,901; Median household: $65,082; Average household: $76,631; Households with income of $100,000 or more: 27.2%; Poverty rate: 4.1%
Educational Attainment: High school diploma or higher: 92.7%; Bachelor's degree or higher: 29.4%; Graduate/professional degree or higher: 11.5%

School District(s)
Marlboro Central SD (KG-12)
   2014-15 Enrollment: 1,972 . . . . (845) 236-5802
Housing: Homeownership rate: 60.5%; Median home value: $242,800; Median year structure built: 1970; Homeowner vacancy rate: 6.3%; Median selected monthly owner costs: $2,601 with a mortgage, $1,001 without a mortgage; Median gross rent: $935 per month; Rental vacancy rate: 12.2%
Health Insurance: 97.6% have insurance; 80.5% have private insurance; 32.1% have public insurance; 2.4% do not have insurance; 2.1% of children under 18 do not have insurance
Transportation: Commute: 88.4% car, 3.1% public transportation, 3.4% walk, 2.6% work from home; Mean travel time to work: 34.1 minutes

MARLBOROUGH (town). Covers a land area of 24.470 square miles and a water area of 2.029 square miles. Located at 41.64° N. Lat; 73.99° W. Long.
Population: 8,773; Growth (since 2000): 6.2%; Density: 358.5 persons per square mile; Race: 90.2% White, 3.2% Black/African American, 1.3% Asian, 0.0% American Indian/Alaska Native, 0.0% Native Hawaiian/Other Pacific Islander, 2.8% Two or more races, 6.1% Hispanic of any race; Average household size: 2.54; Median age: 41.9; Age under 18: 22.3%; Age 65 and over: 16.2%; Males per 100 females: 97.1; Marriage status: 30.5% never married, 49.9% now married, 1.1% separated, 6.1% widowed, 13.5% divorced; Foreign born: 6.8%; Speak English only: 91.0%;

With disability: 13.0%; Veterans: 9.1%; Ancestry: 34.7% Italian, 21.4% Irish, 17.1% German, 9.3% English, 5.1% American
Employment: 13.2% management, business, and financial, 4.5% computer, engineering, and science, 13.0% education, legal, community service, arts, and media, 7.3% healthcare practitioners, 13.0% service, 24.5% sales and office, 12.7% natural resources, construction, and maintenance, 11.8% production, transportation, and material moving
Income: Per capita: $31,491; Median household: $65,957; Average household: $78,435; Households with income of $100,000 or more: 29.1%; Poverty rate: 9.2%
Educational Attainment: High school diploma or higher: 91.4%; Bachelor's degree or higher: 30.1%; Graduate/professional degree or higher: 13.4%
Housing: Homeownership rate: 67.2%; Median home value: $250,600; Median year structure built: 1972; Homeowner vacancy rate: 3.5%; Median selected monthly owner costs: $2,478 with a mortgage, $967 without a mortgage; Median gross rent: $1,003 per month; Rental vacancy rate: 6.5%
Health Insurance: 93.0% have insurance; 78.7% have private insurance; 28.0% have public insurance; 7.0% do not have insurance; 5.1% of children under 18 do not have insurance
Safety: Violent crime rate: 11.5 per 10,000 population; Property crime rate: 90.9 per 10,000 population
Transportation: Commute: 91.0% car, 2.3% public transportation, 1.8% walk, 4.1% work from home; Mean travel time to work: 33.9 minutes
Additional Information Contacts
Town of Marlborough . . . . (845) 795-5100
   http://www.townofmarlboroughny.org

MILTON (CDP). Covers a land area of 2.962 square miles and a water area of 0.049 square miles. Located at 41.66° N. Lat; 73.97° W. Long. Elevation is 148 feet.
Population: 1,521; Growth (since 2000): 21.6%; Density: 513.4 persons per square mile; Race: 95.9% White, 0.1% Black/African American, 2.6% Asian, 0.0% American Indian/Alaska Native, 0.0% Native Hawaiian/Other Pacific Islander, 1.4% Two or more races, 4.7% Hispanic of any race; Average household size: 2.61; Median age: 45.9; Age under 18: 14.4%; Age 65 and over: 15.8%; Males per 100 females: 103.9; Marriage status: 38.4% never married, 44.1% now married, 0.6% separated, 5.3% widowed, 12.2% divorced; Foreign born: 2.7%; Speak English only: 95.3%; With disability: 13.1%; Veterans: 10.2%; Ancestry: 31.9% Italian, 28.8% German, 23.1% Irish, 19.6% English, 6.8% Polish
Employment: 9.1% management, business, and financial, 1.1% computer, engineering, and science, 16.5% education, legal, community service, arts, and media, 7.2% healthcare practitioners, 9.1% service, 23.5% sales and office, 16.5% natural resources, construction, and maintenance, 17.2% production, transportation, and material moving
Income: Per capita: $28,785; Median household: $60,972; Average household: $73,240; Households with income of $100,000 or more: 20.1%; Poverty rate: 11.3%
Educational Attainment: High school diploma or higher: 94.3%; Bachelor's degree or higher: 24.7%; Graduate/professional degree or higher: 8.9%

School District(s)
Marlboro Central SD (KG-12)
   2014-15 Enrollment: 1,972 . . . . (845) 236-5802
Housing: Homeownership rate: 69.9%; Median home value: $217,500; Median year structure built: 1966; Homeowner vacancy rate: 0.0%; Median selected monthly owner costs: $2,311 with a mortgage, $951 without a mortgage; Median gross rent: $1,094 per month; Rental vacancy rate: 0.0%
Health Insurance: 95.0% have insurance; 82.2% have private insurance; 25.8% have public insurance; 5.0% do not have insurance; 0.0% of children under 18 do not have insurance
Transportation: Commute: 93.5% car, 0.1% public transportation, 0.0% walk, 6.3% work from home; Mean travel time to work: 32.2 minutes

MODENA (unincorporated postal area)
ZCTA: 12548
   Covers a land area of 5.871 square miles and a water area of 0.208 square miles. Located at 41.66° N. Lat; 74.10° W. Long. Elevation is 456 feet.
   Population: 1,417; Growth (since 2000): -7.3%; Density: 241.4 persons per square mile; Race: 87.7% White, 8.0% Black/African American, 0.6% Asian, 0.0% American Indian/Alaska Native, 0.0% Native

Hawaiian/Other Pacific Islander, 1.2% Two or more races, 19.0% Hispanic of any race; Average household size: 2.40; Median age: 46.4; Age under 18: 19.5%; Age 65 and over: 13.0%; Males per 100 females: 102.2; Marriage status: 30.7% never married, 57.7% now married, 1.9% separated, 5.3% widowed, 6.3% divorced; Foreign born: 9.0%; Speak English only: 93.3%; With disability: 14.9%; Veterans: 2.7%; Ancestry: 30.5% Irish, 20.0% Italian, 19.3% German, 7.9% Polish, 7.3% Jamaican **Employment:** 3.4% management, business, and financial, 5.7% computer, engineering, and science, 5.9% education, legal, community service, arts, and media, 4.9% healthcare practitioners, 23.1% service, 30.2% sales and office, 9.4% natural resources, construction, and maintenance, 17.2% production, transportation, and material moving **Income:** Per capita: $27,003; Median household: $56,625; Average household: $62,617; Households with income of $100,000 or more: 22.9%; Poverty rate: 20.2% **Educational Attainment:** High school diploma or higher: 90.7%; Bachelor's degree or higher: 11.8%; Graduate/professional degree or higher: 5.2% **Housing:** Homeownership rate: 62.5%; Median home value: $211,900; Median year structure built: 1975; Homeowner vacancy rate: 0.0%; Median selected monthly owner costs: $2,066 with a mortgage, $417 without a mortgage; Median gross rent: $1,071 per month; Rental vacancy rate: 0.0% **Health Insurance:** 87.9% have insurance; 69.0% have private insurance; 30.3% have public insurance; 12.1% do not have insurance; 0.0% of children under 18 do not have insurance **Transportation:** Commute: 94.2% car, 0.0% public transportation, 0.0% walk, 4.3% work from home; Mean travel time to work: 27.0 minutes

MOUNT MARION (unincorporated postal area)
ZCTA: 12456

Covers a land area of 0.540 square miles and a water area of 0.020 square miles. Located at 42.03° N. Lat; 74.00° W. Long. Elevation is 174 feet.
Population: 701; Growth (since 2000): 7.4%; Density: 1,297.6 persons per square mile; Race: 93.6% White, 0.0% Black/African American, 0.0% Asian, 1.1% American Indian/Alaska Native, 0.0% Native Hawaiian/Other Pacific Islander, 5.3% Two or more races, 14.0% Hispanic of any race; Average household size: 3.34; Median age: 39.4; Age under 18: 27.0%; Age 65 and over: 10.4%; Males per 100 females: 99.7; Marriage status: 25.5% never married, 68.3% now married, 0.0% separated, 3.2% widowed, 3.0% divorced; Foreign born: 3.3%; Speak English only: 96.0%; With disability: 17.7%; Veterans: 8.6%; Ancestry: 24.8% Irish, 23.1% Italian, 15.3% Dutch, 11.4% German, 10.6% Scottish
Employment: 7.2% management, business, and financial, 0.0% computer, engineering, and science, 0.0% education, legal, community service, arts, and media, 9.4% healthcare practitioners, 25.9% service, 20.1% sales and office, 26.6% natural resources, construction, and maintenance, 10.8% production, transportation, and material moving **Income:** Per capita: $18,306; Median household: $47,656; Average household: $57,216; Households with income of $100,000 or more: 6.2%; Poverty rate: 1.4% **Educational Attainment:** High school diploma or higher: 83.8%; Bachelor's degree or higher: 10.4%; Graduate/professional degree or higher: 2.2% **Housing:** Homeownership rate: 87.1%; Median home value: $134,000; Median year structure built: 1955; Homeowner vacancy rate: 0.0%; Median selected monthly owner costs: $1,339 with a mortgage, $614 without a mortgage; Median gross rent: $1,313 per month; Rental vacancy rate: 0.0% **Health Insurance:** 90.7% have insurance; 66.9% have private insurance; 35.5% have public insurance; 9.3% do not have insurance; 13.8% of children under 18 do not have insurance **Transportation:** Commute: 89.7% car, 0.0% public transportation, 7.6% walk, 2.7% work from home; Mean travel time to work: 22.7 minutes

MOUNT TREMPER (unincorporated postal area)
ZCTA: 12457

Covers a land area of 13.973 square miles and a water area of 0 square miles. Located at 42.04° N. Lat; 74.25° W. Long. Elevation is 725 feet.
Population: 865; Growth (since 2000): -23.0%; Density: 61.9 persons per square mile; Race: 96.9% White, 0.2% Black/African American, 1.5% Asian, 0.0% American Indian/Alaska Native, 0.0% Native Hawaiian/Other Pacific Islander, 1.4% Two or more races, 3.7%

Hispanic of any race; Average household size: 1.80; Median age: 54.4; Age under 18: 8.9%; Age 65 and over: 22.4%; Males per 100 females: 108.5; Marriage status: 25.1% never married, 53.5% now married, 1.5% separated, 7.6% widowed, 13.8% divorced; Foreign born: 12.8%; Speak English only: 92.9%; With disability: 21.2%; Veterans: 4.9%; Ancestry: 19.8% Italian, 18.8% Dutch, 17.9% French, 16.6% German, 14.8% Irish **Employment:** 25.6% management, business, and financial, 5.2% computer, engineering, and science, 9.8% education, legal, community service, arts, and media, 7.8% healthcare practitioners, 9.3% service, 31.3% sales and office, 5.2% natural resources, construction, and maintenance, 5.9% production, transportation, and material moving **Income:** Per capita: $35,168; Median household: n/a; Average household: $65,222; Households with income of $100,000 or more: 12.4%; Poverty rate: 24.5% **Educational Attainment:** High school diploma or higher: 86.8%; Bachelor's degree or higher: 48.5%; Graduate/professional degree or higher: 25.4% **Housing:** Homeownership rate: 71.0%; Median home value: $263,200; Median year structure built: 1957; Homeowner vacancy rate: 4.2%; Median selected monthly owner costs: $2,176 with a mortgage, $629 without a mortgage; Median gross rent: $755 per month; Rental vacancy rate: 0.0% **Health Insurance:** 89.5% have insurance; 66.1% have private insurance; 35.0% have public insurance; 10.5% do not have insurance; 2.6% of children under 18 do not have insurance **Transportation:** Commute: 67.7% car, 0.8% public transportation, 0.0% walk, 30.0% work from home; Mean travel time to work: 35.1 minutes

NAPANOCH (CDP).
Covers a land area of 1.220 square miles and a water area of 0.025 square miles. Located at 41.75° N. Lat; 74.37° W. Long. Elevation is 312 feet.
Population: 1,096; Growth (since 2000): -6.2%; Density: 898.0 persons per square mile; Race: 91.1% White, 0.6% Black/African American, 1.7% Asian, 0.0% American Indian/Alaska Native, 0.0% Native Hawaiian/Other Pacific Islander, 6.5% Two or more races, 16.1% Hispanic of any race; Average household size: 2.38; Median age: 38.4; Age under 18: 21.3%; Age 65 and over: 11.7%; Males per 100 females: 92.5; Marriage status: 32.1% never married, 53.1% now married, 0.7% separated, 3.8% widowed, 11.0% divorced; Foreign born: 4.1%; Speak English only: 81.5%; With disability: 11.8%; Veterans: 5.7%; Ancestry: 29.5% German, 17.4% Italian, 8.7% Irish, 8.3% English, 4.5% Dutch **Employment:** 10.0% management, business, and financial, 1.7% computer, engineering, and science, 12.1% education, legal, community service, arts, and media, 6.3% healthcare practitioners, 34.3% service, 11.1% sales and office, 12.1% natural resources, construction, and maintenance, 12.5% production, transportation, and material moving **Income:** Per capita: $25,429; Median household: $42,363; Average household: $58,776; Households with income of $100,000 or more: 20.9%; Poverty rate: 18.2% **Educational Attainment:** High school diploma or higher: 94.7%; Bachelor's degree or higher: 17.4%; Graduate/professional degree or higher: 6.9% **Housing:** Homeownership rate: 75.0%; Median home value: $122,100; Median year structure built: 1963; Homeowner vacancy rate: 5.2%; Median selected monthly owner costs: $1,463 with a mortgage, $666 without a mortgage; Median gross rent: $800 per month; Rental vacancy rate: 17.9% **Health Insurance:** 92.0% have insurance; 82.8% have private insurance; 19.3% have public insurance; 8.0% do not have insurance; 0.0% of children under 18 do not have insurance **Transportation:** Commute: 97.1% car, 0.0% public transportation, 0.0% walk, 2.9% work from home; Mean travel time to work: 25.0 minutes

NEW PALTZ (town).
Covers a land area of 33.875 square miles and a water area of 0.432 square miles. Located at 41.76° N. Lat; 74.09° W. Long. Elevation is 239 feet.
History: State University of N.Y. College at New Paltz is here. Settled by Huguenots in 1677; incorporated 1887.
Population: 14,193; Growth (since 2000): 10.6%; Density: 419.0 persons per square mile; Race: 84.4% White, 3.7% Black/African American, 5.2% Asian, 0.5% American Indian/Alaska Native, 0.0% Native Hawaiian/Other Pacific Islander, 3.5% Two or more races, 12.9% Hispanic of any race; Average household size: 2.40; Median age: 26.0; Age under 18: 13.3%; Age 65 and over: 13.6%; Males per 100 females: 83.9; Marriage status: 54.9% never married, 32.9% now married, 2.0% separated, 4.8% widowed, 7.4% divorced; Foreign born: 9.7%; Speak English only: 82.5%;

With disability: 10.8%; Veterans: 4.0%; Ancestry: 22.2% Italian, 18.2% Irish, 14.9% German, 8.1% English, 6.4% Polish
Employment: 8.9% management, business, and financial, 7.7% computer, engineering, and science, 22.2% education, legal, community service, arts, and media, 6.0% healthcare practitioners, 17.6% service, 26.1% sales and office, 5.4% natural resources, construction, and maintenance, 6.0% production, transportation, and material moving
Income: Per capita: $28,334; Median household: $67,642; Average household: $82,433; Households with income of $100,000 or more: 29.8%; Poverty rate: 16.6%
Educational Attainment: High school diploma or higher: 94.2%; Bachelor's degree or higher: 57.3%; Graduate/professional degree or higher: 29.8%

School District(s)
New Paltz Central SD (PK-12)
    2014-15 Enrollment: 2,289 . . . . (845) 256-4020
Ulster Boces
    2014-15 Enrollment: n/a . . . . (845) 255-3040

Four-year College(s)
State University of New York at New Paltz (Public)
    Fall 2014 Enrollment: 7,692 . . . . (877) 696-7411
    2015-16 Tuition: In-state $7,737; Out-of-state $17,587
Housing: Homeownership rate: 55.0%; Median home value: $297,300; Median year structure built: 1972; Homeowner vacancy rate: 2.6%; Median selected monthly owner costs: $2,369 with a mortgage, $949 without a mortgage; Median gross rent: $1,102 per month; Rental vacancy rate: 5.1%
Health Insurance: 93.7% have insurance; 79.4% have private insurance; 25.6% have public insurance; 6.3% do not have insurance; 0.3% of children under 18 do not have insurance
Safety: Violent crime rate: 24.8 per 10,000 population; Property crime rate: 132.4 per 10,000 population
Newspapers: New Paltz Times (weekly circulation 4,600)
Transportation: Commute: 72.0% car, 2.2% public transportation, 17.9% walk, 5.6% work from home; Mean travel time to work: 26.6 minutes
Additional Information Contacts
Town of New Paltz . . . . (845) 255-0604
    http://www.townofnewpaltz.org

NEW PALTZ (village). Covers a land area of 1.715 square miles and a water area of 0.037 square miles. Located at 41.75° N. Lat; 74.08° W. Long. Elevation is 239 feet.
Population: 7,055; Growth (since 2000): 16.9%; Density: 4,113.1 persons per square mile; Race: 78.9% White, 5.1% Black/African American, 7.8% Asian, 0.2% American Indian/Alaska Native, 0.0% Native Hawaiian/Other Pacific Islander, 3.9% Two or more races, 14.4% Hispanic of any race; Average household size: 2.09; Median age: 21.5; Age under 18: 8.1%; Age 65 and over: 9.4%; Males per 100 females: 71.5; Marriage status: 75.2% never married, 15.2% now married, 1.2% separated, 5.0% widowed, 4.6% divorced; Foreign born: 13.1%; Speak English only: 76.2%; With disability: 9.0%; Veterans: 2.0%; Ancestry: 21.1% Italian, 20.0% Irish, 13.4% German, 7.0% Polish, 6.8% English
Employment: 5.6% management, business, and financial, 6.3% computer, engineering, and science, 23.5% education, legal, community service, arts, and media, 3.1% healthcare practitioners, 24.8% service, 28.5% sales and office, 3.5% natural resources, construction, and maintenance, 4.6% production, transportation, and material moving
Income: Per capita: $17,968; Median household: $41,421; Average household: $57,869; Households with income of $100,000 or more: 15.8%; Poverty rate: 31.5%
Educational Attainment: High school diploma or higher: 94.4%; Bachelor's degree or higher: 67.3%; Graduate/professional degree or higher: 36.5%

School District(s)
New Paltz Central SD (PK-12)
    2014-15 Enrollment: 2,289 . . . . (845) 256-4020
Ulster Boces
    2014-15 Enrollment: n/a . . . . (845) 255-3040

Four-year College(s)
State University of New York at New Paltz (Public)
    Fall 2014 Enrollment: 7,692 . . . . (877) 696-7411
    2015-16 Tuition: In-state $7,737; Out-of-state $17,587
Housing: Homeownership rate: 30.0%; Median home value: $283,200; Median year structure built: 1972; Homeowner vacancy rate: 0.0%; Median selected monthly owner costs: $2,514 with a mortgage, $840 without a

mortgage; Median gross rent: $1,108 per month; Rental vacancy rate: 7.4%
Health Insurance: 92.8% have insurance; 79.6% have private insurance; 20.5% have public insurance; 7.2% do not have insurance; 1.1% of children under 18 do not have insurance
Newspapers: New Paltz Times (weekly circulation 4,600)
Transportation: Commute: 55.2% car, 2.3% public transportation, 34.6% walk, 4.7% work from home; Mean travel time to work: 22.1 minutes
Additional Information Contacts
Village of New Paltz . . . . (845) 255-0130
    http://villageofnewpaltz.org

OLIVE (town). Covers a land area of 58.450 square miles and a water area of 6.743 square miles. Located at 41.95° N. Lat; 74.27° W. Long.
Population: 4,376; Growth (since 2000): -4.4%; Density: 74.9 persons per square mile; Race: 92.0% White, 1.7% Black/African American, 1.1% Asian, 0.0% American Indian/Alaska Native, 1.9% Native Hawaiian/Other Pacific Islander, 2.0% Two or more races, 4.4% Hispanic of any race; Average household size: 2.13; Median age: 51.5; Age under 18: 16.5%; Age 65 and over: 20.5%; Males per 100 females: 99.6; Marriage status: 24.4% never married, 56.6% now married, 3.2% separated, 6.1% widowed, 12.9% divorced; Foreign born: 8.2%; Speak English only: 87.6%; With disability: 9.8%; Veterans: 8.8%; Ancestry: 26.6% Irish, 21.3% German, 16.1% Italian, 10.5% English, 8.0% Polish
Employment: 9.1% management, business, and financial, 7.1% computer, engineering, and science, 18.2% education, legal, community service, arts, and media, 7.8% healthcare practitioners, 15.2% service, 24.5% sales and office, 7.2% natural resources, construction, and maintenance, 10.8% production, transportation, and material moving
Income: Per capita: $37,865; Median household: $60,195; Average household: $78,816; Households with income of $100,000 or more: 25.2%; Poverty rate: 11.0%
Educational Attainment: High school diploma or higher: 88.2%; Bachelor's degree or higher: 37.3%; Graduate/professional degree or higher: 17.0%
Housing: Homeownership rate: 76.0%; Median home value: $258,800; Median year structure built: 1970; Homeowner vacancy rate: 0.0%; Median selected monthly owner costs: $1,906 with a mortgage, $676 without a mortgage; Median gross rent: $877 per month; Rental vacancy rate: 0.0%
Health Insurance: 93.9% have insurance; 72.9% have private insurance; 36.8% have public insurance; 6.1% do not have insurance; 0.0% of children under 18 do not have insurance
Safety: Violent crime rate: 0.0 per 10,000 population; Property crime rate: 34.6 per 10,000 population
Transportation: Commute: 86.4% car, 3.6% public transportation, 0.8% walk, 8.9% work from home; Mean travel time to work: 32.2 minutes
Additional Information Contacts
Town of Olive . . . . (845) 657-8118
    http://town.olive.ny.us

OLIVEBRIDGE (unincorporated postal area)
ZCTA: 12461
    Covers a land area of 23.889 square miles and a water area of 0.023 square miles. Located at 41.90° N. Lat; 74.27° W. Long. Elevation is 571 feet.
Population: 1,822; Growth (since 2000): 2.3%; Density: 76.3 persons per square mile; Race: 93.0% White, 0.2% Black/African American, 1.6% Asian, 0.0% American Indian/Alaska Native, 4.7% Native Hawaiian/Other Pacific Islander, 0.5% Two or more races, 1.7% Hispanic of any race; Average household size: 2.19; Median age: 49.1; Age under 18: 20.3%; Age 65 and over: 17.5%; Males per 100 females: 99.8; Marriage status: 22.4% never married, 57.0% now married, 2.2% separated, 2.6% widowed, 18.0% divorced; Foreign born: 6.9%; Speak English only: 89.5%; With disability: 9.2%; Veterans: 14.8%; Ancestry: 27.6% Irish, 19.1% Italian, 16.1% German, 11.6% English, 9.1% American
Employment: 10.2% management, business, and financial, 8.5% computer, engineering, and science, 14.9% education, legal, community service, arts, and media, 9.3% healthcare practitioners, 16.8% service, 27.6% sales and office, 5.3% natural resources, construction, and maintenance, 7.5% production, transportation, and material moving
Income: Per capita: $39,920; Median household: $63,445; Average household: $87,361; Households with income of $100,000 or more: 35.5%; Poverty rate: 9.6%

Educational Attainment: High school diploma or higher: 87.8%; Bachelor's degree or higher: 39.8%; Graduate/professional degree or higher: 18.5%
Housing: Homeownership rate: 72.6%; Median home value: $279,000; Median year structure built: 1972; Homeowner vacancy rate: 0.0%; Median selected monthly owner costs: $2,291 with a mortgage, $705 without a mortgage; Median gross rent: $820 per month; Rental vacancy rate: 0.0%
Health Insurance: 93.7% have insurance; 65.1% have private insurance; 35.1% have public insurance; 6.3% do not have insurance; 0.0% of children under 18 do not have insurance
Transportation: Commute: 84.2% car, 8.5% public transportation, 1.8% walk, 4.7% work from home; Mean travel time to work: 37.6 minutes

PHOENICIA (CDP). Covers a land area of 0.456 square miles and a water area of 0 square miles. Located at 42.08° N. Lat; 74.31° W. Long. Elevation is 827 feet.
Population: 215; Growth (since 2000): -43.6%; Density: 471.9 persons per square mile; Race: 100.0% White, 0.0% Black/African American, 0.0% Asian, 0.0% American Indian/Alaska Native, 0.0% Native Hawaiian/Other Pacific Islander, 0.0% Two or more races, 0.0% Hispanic of any race; Average household size: 1.38; Median age: 64.4; Age under 18: 4.7%; Age 65 and over: 47.9%; Males per 100 females: 87.3; Marriage status: 52.7% never married, 18.0% now married, 5.9% separated, 6.8% widowed, 22.4% divorced; Foreign born: 13.5%; Speak English only: 86.2%; With disability: 33.5%; Veterans: 14.6%; Ancestry: 63.7% German, 45.6% English, 13.5% French, 13.5% Polish, 9.3% Greek
Employment: 0.0% management, business, and financial, 0.0% computer, engineering, and science, 24.0% education, legal, community service, arts, and media, 10.0% healthcare practitioners, 24.0% service, 0.0% sales and office, 42.0% natural resources, construction, and maintenance, 0.0% production, transportation, and material moving
Income: Per capita: $29,365; Median household: $37,586; Average household: $37,864; Households with income of $100,000 or more: 4.5%; Poverty rate: 5.6%
Educational Attainment: High school diploma or higher: 100.0%; Bachelor's degree or higher: 34.1%; Graduate/professional degree or higher: 29.8%
School District(s)
Onteora Central SD (KG-12)
    2014-15 Enrollment: 1,415 . . . . (845) 657-8851
Housing: Homeownership rate: 53.2%; Median home value: $140,100; Median year structure built: Before 1940; Homeowner vacancy rate: 23.9%; Median selected monthly owner costs: n/a with a mortgage, $409 without a mortgage; Median gross rent: $767 per month; Rental vacancy rate: 0.0%
Health Insurance: 90.2% have insurance; 69.8% have private insurance; 81.9% have public insurance; 9.8% do not have insurance; 0.0% of children under 18 do not have insurance
Transportation: Commute: 90.0% car, 0.0% public transportation, 0.0% walk, 10.0% work from home; Mean travel time to work: 0.0 minutes

PINE HILL (CDP). Covers a land area of 2.078 square miles and a water area of 0.010 square miles. Located at 42.13° N. Lat; 74.47° W. Long. Elevation is 1,499 feet.
Population: 172; Growth (since 2000): -44.2%; Density: 82.8 persons per square mile; Race: 100.0% White, 0.0% Black/African American, 0.0% Asian, 0.0% American Indian/Alaska Native, 0.0% Native Hawaiian/Other Pacific Islander, 0.0% Two or more races, 0.0% Hispanic of any race; Average household size: 2.07; Median age: 61.8; Age under 18: 13.4%; Age 65 and over: 30.8%; Males per 100 females: 99.3; Marriage status: 21.5% never married, 45.0% now married, 3.4% separated, 3.4% widowed, 30.2% divorced; Foreign born: 21.5%; Speak English only: 87.7%; With disability: 13.4%; Veterans: 2.7%; Ancestry: 32.6% German, 25.6% Italian, 25.0% American, 15.1% Irish, 5.2% Dutch
Employment: 0.0% management, business, and financial, 0.0% computer, engineering, and science, 18.5% education, legal, community service, arts, and media, 0.0% healthcare practitioners, 37.0% service, 16.0% sales and office, 22.2% natural resources, construction, and maintenance, 6.2% production, transportation, and material moving
Income: Per capita: $27,544; Median household: $52,938; Average household: $55,960; Households with income of $100,000 or more: 20.5%; Poverty rate: 14.4%

Educational Attainment: High school diploma or higher: 91.0%; Bachelor's degree or higher: 30.6%; Graduate/professional degree or higher: 22.5%
Housing: Homeownership rate: 88.0%; Median home value: n/a; Median year structure built: Before 1940; Homeowner vacancy rate: 15.1%; Median selected monthly owner costs: n/a with a mortgage, n/a without a mortgage; Median gross rent: n/a per month; Rental vacancy rate: 41.2%
Health Insurance: 91.3% have insurance; 52.9% have private insurance; 41.3% have public insurance; 8.7% do not have insurance; 0.0% of children under 18 do not have insurance
Transportation: Commute: 100.0% car, 0.0% public transportation, 0.0% walk, 0.0% work from home; Mean travel time to work: 0.0 minutes

PLATTEKILL (CDP). Covers a land area of 2.550 square miles and a water area of 0.073 square miles. Located at 41.62° N. Lat; 74.06° W. Long. Elevation is 568 feet.
Population: 1,240; Growth (since 2000): 18.1%; Density: 486.3 persons per square mile; Race: 70.0% White, 18.5% Black/African American, 0.0% Asian, 0.0% American Indian/Alaska Native, 0.0% Native Hawaiian/Other Pacific Islander, 0.0% Two or more races, 30.9% Hispanic of any race; Average household size: 2.73; Median age: 40.7; Age under 18: 23.1%; Age 65 and over: 14.6%; Males per 100 females: 97.8; Marriage status: 43.2% never married, 42.3% now married, 0.0% separated, 6.0% widowed, 8.5% divorced; Foreign born: 9.5%; Speak English only: 73.7%; With disability: 21.8%; Veterans: 3.2%; Ancestry: 18.4% Irish, 13.8% Italian, 11.5% German, 9.5% American, 9.3% European
Employment: 7.6% management, business, and financial, 4.9% computer, engineering, and science, 10.6% education, legal, community service, arts, and media, 5.8% healthcare practitioners, 27.0% service, 18.7% sales and office, 5.2% natural resources, construction, and maintenance, 20.2% production, transportation, and material moving
Income: Per capita: $18,878; Median household: $33,892; Average household: $49,740; Households with income of $100,000 or more: 10.4%; Poverty rate: 25.9%
Educational Attainment: High school diploma or higher: 79.0%; Bachelor's degree or higher: 25.8%; Graduate/professional degree or higher: 9.3%
School District(s)
Wallkill Central SD (KG-12)
    2014-15 Enrollment: 3,102 . . . . (845) 895-7101
Housing: Homeownership rate: 59.1%; Median home value: $223,200; Median year structure built: 1974; Homeowner vacancy rate: 4.9%; Median selected monthly owner costs: $1,806 with a mortgage, $1,500+ without a mortgage; Median gross rent: $852 per month; Rental vacancy rate: 7.9%
Health Insurance: 85.7% have insurance; 64.6% have private insurance; 32.9% have public insurance; 14.3% do not have insurance; 0.0% of children under 18 do not have insurance
Transportation: Commute: 81.8% car, 8.4% public transportation, 0.0% walk, 9.8% work from home; Mean travel time to work: 36.5 minutes

PLATTEKILL (town). Covers a land area of 35.111 square miles and a water area of 0.628 square miles. Located at 41.65° N. Lat; 74.07° W. Long. Elevation is 568 feet.
History: The town was settled early in the 18th century. The Town of Plattekill was established in 1800 from part of the Town of Marlborough.
Population: 10,388; Growth (since 2000): 5.0%; Density: 295.9 persons per square mile; Race: 87.3% White, 7.0% Black/African American, 1.0% Asian, 0.0% American Indian/Alaska Native, 0.0% Native Hawaiian/Other Pacific Islander, 2.2% Two or more races, 16.7% Hispanic of any race; Average household size: 2.57; Median age: 44.3; Age under 18: 18.9%; Age 65 and over: 15.8%; Males per 100 females: 97.6; Marriage status: 30.1% never married, 52.2% now married, 1.9% separated, 7.9% widowed, 9.8% divorced; Foreign born: 6.5%; Speak English only: 84.8%; With disability: 18.9%; Veterans: 6.8%; Ancestry: 20.6% Italian, 19.2% Irish, 18.7% German, 6.6% English, 5.2% American
Employment: 8.9% management, business, and financial, 5.7% computer, engineering, and science, 12.4% education, legal, community service, arts, and media, 6.4% healthcare practitioners, 15.0% service, 29.4% sales and office, 8.4% natural resources, construction, and maintenance, 13.7% production, transportation, and material moving
Income: Per capita: $29,844; Median household: $58,061; Average household: $73,417; Households with income of $100,000 or more: 26.6%; Poverty rate: 13.3%

Educational Attainment: High school diploma or higher: 87.8%; Bachelor's degree or higher: 21.6%; Graduate/professional degree or higher: 6.5%

School District(s)
Wallkill Central SD (KG-12)
  2014-15 Enrollment: 3,102 . . . . (845) 895-7101
Housing: Homeownership rate: 71.7%; Median home value: $209,100; Median year structure built: 1977; Homeowner vacancy rate: 2.6%; Median selected monthly owner costs: $2,112 with a mortgage, $750 without a mortgage; Median gross rent: $975 per month; Rental vacancy rate: 6.3%
Health Insurance: 89.8% have insurance; 72.3% have private insurance; 30.1% have public insurance; 10.2% do not have insurance; 6.9% of children under 18 do not have insurance
Safety: Violent crime rate: 9.7 per 10,000 population; Property crime rate: 59.2 per 10,000 population
Transportation: Commute: 90.1% car, 3.0% public transportation, 1.5% walk, 4.2% work from home; Mean travel time to work: 29.6 minutes
Additional Information Contacts
Town of Plattekill . . . . (845) 883-7331
  http://town.plattekill.ny.us

PORT EWEN (CDP). Covers a land area of 1.973 square miles and a water area of 0.653 square miles. Located at 41.90° N. Lat; 73.98° W. Long. Elevation is 184 feet.
Population: 3,413; Growth (since 2000): -6.5%; Density: 1,729.8 persons per square mile; Race: 88.7% White, 3.9% Black/African American, 3.5% Asian, 0.0% American Indian/Alaska Native, 0.0% Native Hawaiian/Other Pacific Islander, 3.4% Two or more races, 3.1% Hispanic of any race; Average household size: 2.35; Median age: 46.7; Age under 18: 15.7%; Age 65 and over: 22.7%; Males per 100 females: 86.8; Marriage status: 31.4% never married, 47.8% now married, 3.9% separated, 9.8% widowed, 11.0% divorced; Foreign born: 7.6%; Speak English only: 91.1%; With disability: 15.6%; Veterans: 7.6%; Ancestry: 28.2% German, 27.0% Irish, 19.3% Italian, 7.8% English, 5.0% Polish
Employment: 18.7% management, business, and financial, 4.9% computer, engineering, and science, 9.7% education, legal, community service, arts, and media, 9.4% healthcare practitioners, 21.6% service, 22.6% sales and office, 7.4% natural resources, construction, and maintenance, 5.7% production, transportation, and material moving
Income: Per capita: $31,980; Median household: $56,738; Average household: $72,102; Households with income of $100,000 or more: 22.5%; Poverty rate: 5.1%
Educational Attainment: High school diploma or higher: 89.9%; Bachelor's degree or higher: 23.0%; Graduate/professional degree or higher: 11.5%

School District(s)
Kingston City SD (PK-12)
  2014-15 Enrollment: 6,471 . . . . (845) 943-3003
Vocational/Technical School(s)
Ulster BOCES School of Practical Nursing (Public)
  Fall 2014 Enrollment: 143 . . . . (845) 331-5050
  2015-16 Tuition: $12,219
Housing: Homeownership rate: 73.1%; Median home value: $191,400; Median year structure built: 1965; Homeowner vacancy rate: 2.9%; Median selected monthly owner costs: $1,757 with a mortgage, $694 without a mortgage; Median gross rent: $1,019 per month; Rental vacancy rate: 11.4%
Health Insurance: 91.0% have insurance; 68.4% have private insurance; 40.4% have public insurance; 9.0% do not have insurance; 0.0% of children under 18 do not have insurance
Transportation: Commute: 87.7% car, 4.4% public transportation, 1.8% walk, 6.1% work from home; Mean travel time to work: 22.3 minutes

RIFTON (CDP). Covers a land area of 1.175 square miles and a water area of 0 square miles. Located at 41.83° N. Lat; 74.04° W. Long. Elevation is 180 feet.
Population: 609; Growth (since 2000): 21.6%; Density: 518.1 persons per square mile; Race: 100.0% White, 0.0% Black/African American, 0.0% Asian, 0.0% American Indian/Alaska Native, 0.0% Native Hawaiian/Other Pacific Islander, 0.0% Two or more races, 0.0% Hispanic of any race; Average household size: 3.29; Median age: 30.6; Age under 18: 36.1%; Age 65 and over: 1.3%; Males per 100 females: 95.7; Marriage status: 33.9% never married, 51.4% now married, 0.0% separated, 0.0% widowed, 14.7% divorced; Foreign born: 4.8%; Speak English only:

100.0%; With disability: 7.9%; Veterans: 0.0%; Ancestry: 30.4% American, 20.4% Scottish, 14.6% Polish, 10.3% Irish, 4.8% Italian
Employment: 7.5% management, business, and financial, 3.1% computer, engineering, and science, 43.1% education, legal, community service, arts, and media, 7.1% healthcare practitioners, 16.9% service, 11.4% sales and office, 11.0% natural resources, construction, and maintenance, 0.0% production, transportation, and material moving
Income: Per capita: $18,585; Median household: $52,974; Average household: $59,579; Households with income of $100,000 or more: 9.7%; Poverty rate: 10.8%
Educational Attainment: High school diploma or higher: 100.0%; Bachelor's degree or higher: 48.3%; Graduate/professional degree or higher: 30.8%
Housing: Homeownership rate: 53.0%; Median home value: $255,000; Median year structure built: 1952; Homeowner vacancy rate: 0.0%; Median selected monthly owner costs: $1,970 with a mortgage, n/a without a mortgage; Median gross rent: $1,316 per month; Rental vacancy rate: 0.0%
Health Insurance: 78.3% have insurance; 73.7% have private insurance; 7.6% have public insurance; 21.7% do not have insurance; 0.0% of children under 18 do not have insurance
Transportation: Commute: 89.0% car, 0.0% public transportation, 11.0% walk, 0.0% work from home; Mean travel time to work: 20.5 minutes

ROCHESTER (town). Covers a land area of 89.303 square miles and a water area of 0.416 square miles. Located at 41.81° N. Lat; 74.27° W. Long.
Population: 7,261; Growth (since 2000): 3.5%; Density: 81.3 persons per square mile; Race: 92.4% White, 1.3% Black/African American, 0.2% Asian, 0.0% American Indian/Alaska Native, 0.0% Native Hawaiian/Other Pacific Islander, 5.7% Two or more races, 4.2% Hispanic of any race; Average household size: 2.56; Median age: 44.2; Age under 18: 22.4%; Age 65 and over: 15.8%; Males per 100 females: 101.5; Marriage status: 25.2% never married, 57.0% now married, 3.2% separated, 8.8% widowed, 9.1% divorced; Foreign born: 4.5%; Speak English only: 92.2%; With disability: 14.6%; Veterans: 8.6%; Ancestry: 24.6% German, 20.7% Irish, 20.6% Italian, 10.0% English, 7.0% Norwegian
Employment: 15.1% management, business, and financial, 5.9% computer, engineering, and science, 12.4% education, legal, community service, arts, and media, 4.7% healthcare practitioners, 22.0% service, 28.1% sales and office, 7.8% natural resources, construction, and maintenance, 4.0% production, transportation, and material moving
Income: Per capita: $37,903; Median household: $67,043; Average household: $97,590; Households with income of $100,000 or more: 31.2%; Poverty rate: 6.9%
Educational Attainment: High school diploma or higher: 88.9%; Bachelor's degree or higher: 31.4%; Graduate/professional degree or higher: 11.9%
Housing: Homeownership rate: 81.6%; Median home value: $220,100; Median year structure built: 1977; Homeowner vacancy rate: 5.1%; Median selected monthly owner costs: $1,695 with a mortgage, $639 without a mortgage; Median gross rent: $1,073 per month; Rental vacancy rate: 12.5%
Health Insurance: 90.6% have insurance; 69.5% have private insurance; 36.3% have public insurance; 9.4% do not have insurance; 3.3% of children under 18 do not have insurance
Transportation: Commute: 87.0% car, 5.2% public transportation, 0.3% walk, 6.4% work from home; Mean travel time to work: 33.0 minutes
Additional Information Contacts
Town of Rochester . . . . (845) 626-7384
  http://www.townofrochester.net/Pages/index

ROSENDALE (town). Covers a land area of 19.979 square miles and a water area of 0.767 square miles. Located at 41.85° N. Lat; 74.08° W. Long. Elevation is 66 feet.
History: Incorporated 1890.
Population: 6,017; Growth (since 2000): -5.3%; Density: 301.2 persons per square mile; Race: 95.3% White, 2.7% Black/African American, 0.3% Asian, 0.3% American Indian/Alaska Native, 0.0% Native Hawaiian/Other Pacific Islander, 1.2% Two or more races, 5.5% Hispanic of any race; Average household size: 2.52; Median age: 42.4; Age under 18: 17.9%; Age 65 and over: 16.8%; Males per 100 females: 95.1; Marriage status: 36.0% never married, 49.2% now married, 4.2% separated, 5.3% widowed, 9.5% divorced; Foreign born: 2.2%; Speak English only: 97.7%;

With disability: 12.3%; Veterans: 7.4%; Ancestry: 27.8% Irish, 25.8% Italian, 22.4% German, 7.0% English, 6.4% Polish
Employment: 10.9% management, business, and financial, 3.2% computer, engineering, and science, 18.1% education, legal, community service, arts, and media, 6.2% healthcare practitioners, 21.5% service, 17.0% sales and office, 12.5% natural resources, construction, and maintenance, 10.7% production, transportation, and material moving
Income: Per capita: $31,093; Median household: $63,786; Average household: $76,331; Households with income of $100,000 or more: 22.0%; Poverty rate: 8.7%
Educational Attainment: High school diploma or higher: 91.1%; Bachelor's degree or higher: 32.5%; Graduate/professional degree or higher: 12.4%
Housing: Homeownership rate: 74.2%; Median home value: $196,700; Median year structure built: 1954; Homeowner vacancy rate: 0.0%; Median selected monthly owner costs: $1,740 with a mortgage, $699 without a mortgage; Median gross rent: $1,127 per month; Rental vacancy rate: 7.8%
Health Insurance: 88.3% have insurance; 69.2% have private insurance; 37.2% have public insurance; 11.7% do not have insurance; 1.9% of children under 18 do not have insurance
Safety: Violent crime rate: 1.7 per 10,000 population; Property crime rate: 55.4 per 10,000 population
Transportation: Commute: 91.7% car, 2.6% public transportation, 1.7% walk, 2.9% work from home; Mean travel time to work: 27.8 minutes
Additional Information Contacts
Town of Rosendale . . . . (845) 658-3159
  http://www.townofrosendale.com

ROSENDALE HAMLET (CDP). Covers a land area of 1.904 square miles and a water area of 0.055 square miles. Located at 41.85° N. Lat; 74.07° W. Long.
Population: 1,453; Growth (since 2000): 5.7%; Density: 763.1 persons per square mile; Race: 98.6% White, 0.9% Black/African American, 0.0% Asian, 0.0% American Indian/Alaska Native, 0.0% Native Hawaiian/Other Pacific Islander, 0.3% Two or more races, 11.9% Hispanic of any race; Average household size: 2.41; Median age: 39.1; Age under 18: 24.0%; Age 65 and over: 20.5%; Males per 100 females: 91.6; Marriage status: 36.0% never married, 47.4% now married, 0.0% separated, 4.9% widowed, 11.7% divorced; Foreign born: 0.3%; Speak English only: 96.5%; With disability: 11.3%; Veterans: 4.0%; Ancestry: 30.0% Irish, 26.8% Italian, 12.7% German, 7.0% English, 5.7% Polish
Employment: 17.3% management, business, and financial, 7.5% computer, engineering, and science, 31.1% education, legal, community service, arts, and media, 4.5% healthcare practitioners, 15.6% service, 4.3% sales and office, 12.1% natural resources, construction, and maintenance, 7.6% production, transportation, and material moving
Income: Per capita: $28,090; Median household: $58,618; Average household: $66,546; Households with income of $100,000 or more: 18.3%; Poverty rate: 6.6%
Educational Attainment: High school diploma or higher: 92.3%; Bachelor's degree or higher: 31.2%; Graduate/professional degree or higher: 9.4%
Housing: Homeownership rate: 65.4%; Median home value: $191,300; Median year structure built: 1952; Homeowner vacancy rate: 0.0%; Median selected monthly owner costs: $1,318 with a mortgage, $620 without a mortgage; Median gross rent: $936 per month; Rental vacancy rate: 3.7%
Health Insurance: 88.3% have insurance; 62.2% have private insurance; 50.1% have public insurance; 11.7% do not have insurance; 0.0% of children under 18 do not have insurance
Transportation: Commute: 95.9% car, 1.2% public transportation, 1.6% walk, 1.3% work from home; Mean travel time to work: 19.3 minutes

RUBY (unincorporated postal area)
ZCTA: 12475
  Covers a land area of 1.229 square miles and a water area of 0 square miles. Located at 42.02° N. Lat; 74.02° W. Long. Elevation is 312 feet.
Population: 217; Growth (since 2000): n/a; Density: 176.6 persons per square mile; Race: 100.0% White, 0.0% Black/African American, 0.0% Asian, 0.0% American Indian/Alaska Native, 0.0% Native Hawaiian/Other Pacific Islander, 0.0% Two or more races, 0.0% Hispanic of any race; Average household size: 1.58; Median age: 59.5; Age under 18: 12.4%; Age 65 and over: 7.4%; Males per 100 females: 108.2; Marriage status: 14.2% never married, 64.7% now married, 0.0% separated, 0.0% widowed, 21.1% divorced; Foreign born: 0.0%; Speak

English only: 100.0%; With disability: 18.4%; Veterans: 4.2%; Ancestry: 38.7% Irish, 31.3% Italian, 30.9% German, 18.4% Polish, 12.0% English
Employment: 21.6% management, business, and financial, 0.0% computer, engineering, and science, 29.6% education, legal, community service, arts, and media, 0.0% healthcare practitioners, 19.2% service, 15.2% sales and office, 8.0% natural resources, construction, and maintenance, 6.4% production, transportation, and material moving
Income: Per capita: $34,328; Median household: n/a; Average household: $54,160; Households with income of $100,000 or more: 26.3%; Poverty rate: 18.4%
Educational Attainment: High school diploma or higher: 100.0%; Bachelor's degree or higher: 9.5%; Graduate/professional degree or higher: 9.5%
Housing: Homeownership rate: 92.7%; Median home value: n/a; Median year structure built: Before 1940; Homeowner vacancy rate: 0.0%; Median selected monthly owner costs: n/a with a mortgage, n/a without a mortgage; Median gross rent: n/a per month; Rental vacancy rate: 0.0%
Health Insurance: 77.4% have insurance; 59.0% have private insurance; 22.1% have public insurance; 22.6% do not have insurance; 0.0% of children under 18 do not have insurance
Transportation: Commute: 92.8% car, 0.0% public transportation, 0.0% walk, 7.2% work from home; Mean travel time to work: 17.8 minutes

SAUGERTIES (town). Covers a land area of 64.574 square miles and a water area of 3.386 square miles. Located at 42.09° N. Lat; 73.99° W. Long. Elevation is 154 feet.
History: Former summer resort. Incorporated 1831.
Population: 19,319; Growth (since 2000): -2.8%; Density: 299.2 persons per square mile; Race: 92.6% White, 1.8% Black/African American, 1.4% Asian, 0.1% American Indian/Alaska Native, 0.0% Native Hawaiian/Other Pacific Islander, 3.2% Two or more races, 7.1% Hispanic of any race; Average household size: 2.54; Median age: 43.9; Age under 18: 19.4%; Age 65 and over: 16.3%; Males per 100 females: 95.2; Marriage status: 32.4% never married, 49.7% now married, 1.8% separated, 8.0% widowed, 10.0% divorced; Foreign born: 6.5%; Speak English only: 90.8%; With disability: 14.6%; Veterans: 8.4%; Ancestry: 26.2% Irish, 25.2% German, 20.0% Italian, 9.4% English, 8.0% Dutch
Employment: 12.7% management, business, and financial, 2.8% computer, engineering, and science, 12.3% education, legal, community service, arts, and media, 6.0% healthcare practitioners, 17.8% service, 23.6% sales and office, 13.3% natural resources, construction, and maintenance, 11.6% production, transportation, and material moving
Income: Per capita: $30,883; Median household: $58,272; Average household: $76,815; Households with income of $100,000 or more: 24.3%; Poverty rate: 9.1%
Educational Attainment: High school diploma or higher: 89.6%; Bachelor's degree or higher: 24.4%; Graduate/professional degree or higher: 10.3%

School District(s)
Saugerties Central SD (KG-12)
  2014-15 Enrollment: 2,710 . . . . (845) 247-6501
Housing: Homeownership rate: 71.6%; Median home value: $205,700; Median year structure built: 1962; Homeowner vacancy rate: 1.8%; Median selected monthly owner costs: $1,812 with a mortgage, $743 without a mortgage; Median gross rent: $1,014 per month; Rental vacancy rate: 7.6%
Health Insurance: 91.3% have insurance; 72.1% have private insurance; 34.0% have public insurance; 8.7% do not have insurance; 0.8% of children under 18 do not have insurance
Safety: Violent crime rate: 4.2 per 10,000 population; Property crime rate: 86.1 per 10,000 population
Newspapers: Saugerties Post-Star (weekly circulation 2,500)
Transportation: Commute: 89.9% car, 1.4% public transportation, 3.0% walk, 4.7% work from home; Mean travel time to work: 24.7 minutes
Additional Information Contacts
Town of Saugerties . . . . (845) 246-2800
  http://www.saugerties.ny.us

SAUGERTIES (village). Covers a land area of 1.784 square miles and a water area of 0.477 square miles. Located at 42.08° N. Lat; 73.94° W. Long. Elevation is 154 feet.
Population: 3,940; Growth (since 2000): -20.5%; Density: 2,209.1 persons per square mile; Race: 92.5% White, 1.0% Black/African American, 0.0% Asian, 0.2% American Indian/Alaska Native, 0.0% Native Hawaiian/Other

Pacific Islander, 3.2% Two or more races, 14.1% Hispanic of any race; Average household size: 2.26; Median age: 40.2; Age under 18: 18.6%; Age 65 and over: 16.1%; Males per 100 females: 93.9; Marriage status: 39.1% never married, 40.3% now married, 2.6% separated, 8.1% widowed, 12.4% divorced; Foreign born: 8.7%; Speak English only: 87.4%; With disability: 16.4%; Veterans: 7.6%; Ancestry: 25.2% German, 24.9% Irish, 19.2% Italian, 9.6% English, 7.5% French

Employment: 10.0% management, business, and financial, 2.0% computer, engineering, and science, 15.4% education, legal, community service, arts, and media, 1.2% healthcare practitioners, 19.9% service, 28.9% sales and office, 14.7% natural resources, construction, and maintenance, 7.9% production, transportation, and material moving

Income: Per capita: $26,284; Median household: $44,350; Average household: $59,092; Households with income of $100,000 or more: 18.1%; Poverty rate: 12.8%

Educational Attainment: High school diploma or higher: 85.8%; Bachelor's degree or higher: 24.2%; Graduate/professional degree or higher: 10.3%

School District(s)

Saugerties Central SD (KG-12)

   2014-15 Enrollment: 2,710 . . . . (845) 247-6501

Housing: Homeownership rate: 45.2%; Median home value: $203,500; Median year structure built: 1940; Homeowner vacancy rate: 3.6%; Median selected monthly owner costs: $2,062 with a mortgage, $804 without a mortgage; Median gross rent: $927 per month; Rental vacancy rate: 6.5%

Health Insurance: 87.5% have insurance; 65.5% have private insurance; 35.9% have public insurance; 12.5% do not have insurance; 0.0% of children under 18 do not have insurance

Newspapers: Saugerties Post-Star (weekly circulation 2,500)

Transportation: Commute: 79.0% car, 3.9% public transportation, 7.7% walk, 6.8% work from home; Mean travel time to work: 22.1 minutes

SAUGERTIES SOUTH (CDP). Covers a land area of 0.953 square miles and a water area of 0.210 square miles. Located at 42.06° N. Lat; 73.95° W. Long.

Population: 2,119; Growth (since 2000): -7.3%; Density: 2,224.4 persons per square mile; Race: 90.7% White, 2.1% Black/African American, 4.2% Asian, 0.0% American Indian/Alaska Native, 0.0% Native Hawaiian/Other Pacific Islander, 1.9% Two or more races, 6.4% Hispanic of any race; Average household size: 2.44; Median age: 42.9; Age under 18: 19.2%; Age 65 and over: 17.0%; Males per 100 females: 92.0; Marriage status: 32.4% never married, 48.3% now married, 2.2% separated, 9.0% widowed, 10.4% divorced; Foreign born: 5.0%; Speak English only: 90.6%; With disability: 14.1%; Veterans: 13.1%; Ancestry: 25.0% Irish, 22.3% German, 14.1% English, 12.4% Italian, 5.3% American

Employment: 9.8% management, business, and financial, 4.6% computer, engineering, and science, 13.5% education, legal, community service, arts, and media, 2.5% healthcare practitioners, 18.9% service, 29.2% sales and office, 8.3% natural resources, construction, and maintenance, 13.2% production, transportation, and material moving

Income: Per capita: $32,388; Median household: $62,386; Average household: $76,549; Households with income of $100,000 or more: 26.9%; Poverty rate: 7.7%

Educational Attainment: High school diploma or higher: 92.2%; Bachelor's degree or higher: 18.4%; Graduate/professional degree or higher: 12.4%

Housing: Homeownership rate: 74.0%; Median home value: $190,500; Median year structure built: 1965; Homeowner vacancy rate: 0.0%; Median selected monthly owner costs: $1,687 with a mortgage, $738 without a mortgage; Median gross rent: $998 per month; Rental vacancy rate: 2.2%

Health Insurance: 95.4% have insurance; 87.0% have private insurance; 30.6% have public insurance; 4.6% do not have insurance; 0.0% of children under 18 do not have insurance

Transportation: Commute: 91.1% car, 0.0% public transportation, 5.4% walk, 3.4% work from home; Mean travel time to work: 23.0 minutes

SHANDAKEN (town). Covers a land area of 119.784 square miles and a water area of 0.058 square miles. Located at 42.03° N. Lat; 74.36° W. Long. Elevation is 1,056 feet.

Population: 2,953; Growth (since 2000): -8.7%; Density: 24.7 persons per square mile; Race: 92.4% White, 0.3% Black/African American, 2.6% Asian, 0.1% American Indian/Alaska Native, 0.0% Native Hawaiian/Other Pacific Islander, 0.6% Two or more races, 3.3% Hispanic of any race; Average household size: 1.94; Median age: 58.2; Age under 18: 9.9%; Age 65 and over: 26.8%; Males per 100 females: 101.2; Marriage status:

31.1% never married, 48.6% now married, 1.3% separated, 6.7% widowed, 13.6% divorced; Foreign born: 11.7%; Speak English only: 89.4%; With disability: 16.8%; Veterans: 6.8%; Ancestry: 19.1% German, 14.9% Italian, 13.1% English, 11.4% Dutch, 10.8% Polish

Employment: 16.5% management, business, and financial, 1.9% computer, engineering, and science, 18.0% education, legal, community service, arts, and media, 2.9% healthcare practitioners, 14.9% service, 17.7% sales and office, 14.9% natural resources, construction, and maintenance, 13.3% production, transportation, and material moving

Income: Per capita: $32,834; Median household: $48,365; Average household: $62,057; Households with income of $100,000 or more: 17.5%; Poverty rate: 10.1%

Educational Attainment: High school diploma or higher: 91.0%; Bachelor's degree or higher: 31.5%; Graduate/professional degree or higher: 17.1%

Housing: Homeownership rate: 80.9%; Median home value: $205,600; Median year structure built: 1955; Homeowner vacancy rate: 8.3%; Median selected monthly owner costs: $1,665 with a mortgage, $525 without a mortgage; Median gross rent: $740 per month; Rental vacancy rate: 15.7%

Health Insurance: 85.6% have insurance; 70.4% have private insurance; 36.0% have public insurance; 14.4% do not have insurance; 15.7% of children under 18 do not have insurance

Safety: Violent crime rate: 10.0 per 10,000 population; Property crime rate: 116.7 per 10,000 population

Transportation: Commute: 78.8% car, 5.5% public transportation, 0.0% walk, 10.7% work from home; Mean travel time to work: 41.8 minutes

SHAWANGUNK (town). Covers a land area of 56.056 square miles and a water area of 0.494 square miles. Located at 41.63° N. Lat; 74.27° W. Long. Elevation is 299 feet.

History: The town's name comes from the Dutch translation of the Lenape's "Scha-WAN-gunk" meaning "it is smokey air" referring to the nearby Catskill Mountains, known as the "Hidden Mountains."

Population: 14,190; Growth (since 2000): 18.0%; Density: 253.1 persons per square mile; Race: 86.4% White, 7.5% Black/African American, 1.6% Asian, 0.1% American Indian/Alaska Native, 0.0% Native Hawaiian/Other Pacific Islander, 3.1% Two or more races, 10.1% Hispanic of any race; Average household size: 2.82; Median age: 39.4; Age under 18: 18.0%; Age 65 and over: 10.9%; Males per 100 females: 131.2; Marriage status: 33.0% never married, 54.2% now married, 1.4% separated, 4.9% widowed, 7.8% divorced; Foreign born: 5.4%; Speak English only: 86.8%; With disability: 8.2%; Veterans: 8.3%; Ancestry: 18.9% Irish, 18.9% German, 17.4% Italian, 10.4% English, 6.3% Polish

Employment: 11.1% management, business, and financial, 4.7% computer, engineering, and science, 12.6% education, legal, community service, arts, and media, 6.8% healthcare practitioners, 19.2% service, 21.7% sales and office, 10.8% natural resources, construction, and maintenance, 13.1% production, transportation, and material moving

Income: Per capita: $26,105; Median household: $82,861; Average household: $91,817; Households with income of $100,000 or more: 41.4%; Poverty rate: 22.4%

Educational Attainment: High school diploma or higher: 92.6%; Bachelor's degree or higher: 19.9%; Graduate/professional degree or higher: 7.0%

Housing: Homeownership rate: 79.2%; Median home value: $260,700; Median year structure built: 1974; Homeowner vacancy rate: 2.1%; Median selected monthly owner costs: $2,075 with a mortgage, $775 without a mortgage; Median gross rent: $962 per month; Rental vacancy rate: 0.0%

Health Insurance: 81.9% have insurance; 70.0% have private insurance; 21.7% have public insurance; 18.1% do not have insurance; 3.0% of children under 18 do not have insurance

Safety: Violent crime rate: 4.2 per 10,000 population; Property crime rate: 58.0 per 10,000 population

Transportation: Commute: 85.6% car, 1.2% public transportation, 4.1% walk, 8.1% work from home; Mean travel time to work: 34.0 minutes

Additional Information Contacts

Town of Shawangunk . . . . (845) 895-2611

  http://www.shawangunk.org

SHOKAN (CDP). Covers a land area of 3.891 square miles and a water area of 0 square miles. Located at 41.98° N. Lat; 74.21° W. Long. Elevation is 709 feet.

Population: 1,111; Growth (since 2000): -11.3%; Density: 285.5 persons per square mile; Race: 93.2% White, 2.8% Black/African American, 0.0% Asian, 0.0% American Indian/Alaska Native, 0.0% Native Hawaiian/Other

Pacific Islander, 4.1% Two or more races, 9.3% Hispanic of any race; Average household size: 2.05; Median age: 53.0; Age under 18: 9.2%; Age 65 and over: 27.5%; Males per 100 females: 98.5; Marriage status: 26.7% never married, 60.2% now married, 0.7% separated, 6.5% widowed, 6.6% divorced; Foreign born: 8.7%; Speak English only: 85.4%; With disability: 14.5%; Veterans: 1.6%; Ancestry: 23.2% Italian, 20.8% German, 17.4% Irish, 8.5% Dutch, 7.7% English

Employment: 0.0% management, business, and financial, 4.0% computer, engineering, and science, 17.9% education, legal, community service, arts, and media, 4.3% healthcare practitioners, 14.0% service, 28.4% sales and office, 8.7% natural resources, construction, and maintenance, 22.6% production, transportation, and material moving

Income: Per capita: $32,022; Median household: $54,112; Average household: $62,778; Households with income of $100,000 or more: 15.1%; Poverty rate: 12.4%

Educational Attainment: High school diploma or higher: 83.4%; Bachelor's degree or higher: 29.9%; Graduate/professional degree or higher: 15.4%

Housing: Homeownership rate: 86.0%; Median home value: $233,800; Median year structure built: 1969; Homeowner vacancy rate: 0.0%; Median selected monthly owner costs: $1,643 with a mortgage, $578 without a mortgage; Median gross rent: $1,019 per month; Rental vacancy rate: 0.0%

Health Insurance: 96.8% have insurance; 83.3% have private insurance; 40.5% have public insurance; 3.2% do not have insurance; 0.0% of children under 18 do not have insurance

Transportation: Commute: 94.5% car, 0.0% public transportation, 0.0% walk, 5.5% work from home; Mean travel time to work: 26.5 minutes

SPRING GLEN (unincorporated postal area)
ZCTA: 12483

Covers a land area of 3.324 square miles and a water area of 0.030 square miles. Located at 41.67° N. Lat; 74.42° W. Long. Elevation is 400 feet.

Population: 336; Growth (since 2000): n/a; Density: 101.1 persons per square mile; Race: 71.4% White, 0.0% Black/African American, 1.5% Asian, 0.0% American Indian/Alaska Native, 0.0% Native Hawaiian/Other Pacific Islander, 0.0% Two or more races, 27.1% Hispanic of any race; Average household size: 1.90; Median age: 40.5; Age under 18: 15.5%; Age 65 and over: 20.5%; Males per 100 females: 90.4; Marriage status: 18.7% never married, 50.4% now married, 7.0% separated, 17.3% widowed, 13.7% divorced; Foreign born: 15.5%; Speak English only: 83.8%; With disability: 5.7%; Veterans: 0.0%; Ancestry: 48.2% Irish, 36.3% German, 15.5% Italian, 13.7% French, 9.8% Polish

Employment: 0.0% management, business, and financial, 0.0% computer, engineering, and science, 0.0% education, legal, community service, arts, and media, 0.0% healthcare practitioners, 41.2% service, 33.5% sales and office, 7.7% natural resources, construction, and maintenance, 17.6% production, transportation, and material moving

Income: Per capita: $25,368; Median household: $35,865; Average household: $48,983; Households with income of $100,000 or more: 11.3%; Poverty rate: n/a

Educational Attainment: High school diploma or higher: 85.2%; Bachelor's degree or higher: 7.2%; Graduate/professional degree or higher: 7.2%

Housing: Homeownership rate: 41.8%; Median home value: n/a; Median year structure built: 1956; Homeowner vacancy rate: 0.0%; Median selected monthly owner costs: $0 with a mortgage, $771 without a mortgage; Median gross rent: n/a per month; Rental vacancy rate: 0.0%

Health Insurance: 74.7% have insurance; 40.5% have private insurance; 43.5% have public insurance; 25.3% do not have insurance; 0.0% of children under 18 do not have insurance

Transportation: Commute: 92.3% car, 7.7% public transportation, 0.0% walk, 0.0% work from home; Mean travel time to work: 35.6 minutes

STONE RIDGE (CDP). Covers a land area of 5.190 square miles and a water area of 0.040 square miles. Located at 41.85° N. Lat; 74.15° W. Long. Elevation is 364 feet.

Population: 1,256; Growth (since 2000): 7.1%; Density: 242.0 persons per square mile; Race: 82.9% White, 0.2% Black/African American, 7.0% Asian, 0.0% American Indian/Alaska Native, 0.0% Native Hawaiian/Other Pacific Islander, 9.9% Two or more races, 1.4% Hispanic of any race; Average household size: 2.85; Median age: 34.3; Age under 18: 25.0%;

Age 65 and over: 11.7%; Males per 100 females: 92.9; Marriage status: 41.1% never married, 51.5% now married, 1.7% separated, 4.9% widowed, 2.5% divorced; Foreign born: 6.2%; Speak English only: 94.4%; With disability: 6.2%; Veterans: 7.9%; Ancestry: 22.4% Irish, 17.3% Dutch, 12.6% Italian, 12.2% English, 10.6% German

Employment: 13.3% management, business, and financial, 0.0% computer, engineering, and science, 25.2% education, legal, community service, arts, and media, 1.6% healthcare practitioners, 14.6% service, 23.1% sales and office, 20.1% natural resources, construction, and maintenance, 2.1% production, transportation, and material moving

Income: Per capita: $26,970; Median household: $70,500; Average household: $78,178; Households with income of $100,000 or more: 32.3%; Poverty rate: 2.9%

Educational Attainment: High school diploma or higher: 92.6%; Bachelor's degree or higher: 44.3%; Graduate/professional degree or higher: 25.9%

School District(s)
Rondout Valley Central SD (PK-12)
    2014-15 Enrollment: 1,966 . . . . (845) 687-2400
Two-year College(s)
Ulster County Community College (Public)
    Fall 2014 Enrollment: 3,594 . . . . (845) 687-5000
    2015-16 Tuition: In-state $4,942; Out-of-state $9,172

Housing: Homeownership rate: 68.9%; Median home value: $246,800; Median year structure built: 1960; Homeowner vacancy rate: 0.0%; Median selected monthly owner costs: $2,178 with a mortgage, $713 without a mortgage; Median gross rent: $1,137 per month; Rental vacancy rate: 16.1%

Health Insurance: 90.4% have insurance; 70.8% have private insurance; 29.1% have public insurance; 9.6% do not have insurance; 2.2% of children under 18 do not have insurance

Transportation: Commute: 91.6% car, 5.2% public transportation, 0.0% walk, 3.2% work from home; Mean travel time to work: 29.0 minutes

TILLSON (CDP). Covers a land area of 2.345 square miles and a water area of 0.024 square miles. Located at 41.83° N. Lat; 74.07° W. Long. Elevation is 233 feet.

Population: 1,597; Growth (since 2000): -6.6%; Density: 681.0 persons per square mile; Race: 92.5% White, 5.6% Black/African American, 0.6% Asian, 0.0% American Indian/Alaska Native, 0.0% Native Hawaiian/Other Pacific Islander, 0.8% Two or more races, 4.7% Hispanic of any race; Average household size: 2.54; Median age: 41.8; Age under 18: 16.8%; Age 65 and over: 12.8%; Males per 100 females: 91.5; Marriage status: 42.9% never married, 44.1% now married, 3.7% separated, 7.5% widowed, 5.4% divorced; Foreign born: 4.5%; Speak English only: 98.6%; With disability: 14.7%; Veterans: 5.0%; Ancestry: 28.8% Italian, 21.5% German, 19.4% Irish, 8.8% English, 5.0% Polish

Employment: 10.9% management, business, and financial, 2.1% computer, engineering, and science, 12.2% education, legal, community service, arts, and media, 11.2% healthcare practitioners, 24.5% service, 25.3% sales and office, 6.5% natural resources, construction, and maintenance, 7.1% production, transportation, and material moving

Income: Per capita: $31,058; Median household: $70,068; Average household: $78,459; Households with income of $100,000 or more: 27.2%; Poverty rate: 12.3%

Educational Attainment: High school diploma or higher: 85.3%; Bachelor's degree or higher: 35.5%; Graduate/professional degree or higher: 13.3%

Housing: Homeownership rate: 76.4%; Median home value: $216,400; Median year structure built: 1958; Homeowner vacancy rate: 0.0%; Median selected monthly owner costs: $1,951 with a mortgage, $792 without a mortgage; Median gross rent: $1,422 per month; Rental vacancy rate: 0.0%

Health Insurance: 92.9% have insurance; 77.6% have private insurance; 28.8% have public insurance; 7.1% do not have insurance; 7.1% of children under 18 do not have insurance

Transportation: Commute: 91.0% car, 3.0% public transportation, 1.1% walk, 2.5% work from home; Mean travel time to work: 32.7 minutes

ULSTER (town). Covers a land area of 26.803 square miles and a water area of 2.077 square miles. Located at 41.97° N. Lat; 74.01° W. Long.

Population: 12,251; Growth (since 2000): -2.3%; Density: 457.1 persons per square mile; Race: 89.0% White, 3.9% Black/African American, 3.5% Asian, 0.5% American Indian/Alaska Native, 0.0% Native Hawaiian/Other

Pacific Islander, 2.9% Two or more races, 5.1% Hispanic of any race; Average household size: 2.35; Median age: 47.1; Age under 18: 16.9%; Age 65 and over: 21.3%; Males per 100 females: 93.8; Marriage status: 31.1% never married, 49.7% now married, 1.7% separated, 10.1% widowed, 9.1% divorced; Foreign born: 7.4%; Speak English only: 90.0%; With disability: 13.5%; Veterans: 8.6%; Ancestry: 22.2% Irish, 22.0% Italian, 20.1% German, 10.6% English, 7.6% Dutch

Employment: 10.4% management, business, and financial, 4.6% computer, engineering, and science, 10.3% education, legal, community service, arts, and media, 8.4% healthcare practitioners, 17.0% service, 27.6% sales and office, 11.0% natural resources, construction, and maintenance, 10.6% production, transportation, and material moving

Income: Per capita: $28,325; Median household: $46,734; Average household: $64,986; Households with income of $100,000 or more: 19.3%; Poverty rate: 13.4%

Educational Attainment: High school diploma or higher: 86.7%; Bachelor's degree or higher: 21.5%; Graduate/professional degree or higher: 9.4%

Housing: Homeownership rate: 68.5%; Median home value: $184,900; Median year structure built: 1966; Homeowner vacancy rate: 2.0%; Median selected monthly owner costs: $1,824 with a mortgage, $693 without a mortgage; Median gross rent: $955 per month; Rental vacancy rate: 1.5%

Health Insurance: 91.5% have insurance; 68.0% have private insurance; 40.2% have public insurance; 8.5% do not have insurance; 1.5% of children under 18 do not have insurance

Safety: Violent crime rate: 7.4 per 10,000 population; Property crime rate: 310.4 per 10,000 population

Transportation: Commute: 91.8% car, 1.2% public transportation, 1.7% walk, 4.1% work from home; Mean travel time to work: 21.5 minutes

Additional Information Contacts

Town of Ulster . . . . (845) 382-2455
  http://townofulster.org/content

ULSTER PARK (unincorporated postal area)

ZCTA: 12487

Covers a land area of 15.704 square miles and a water area of 0.284 square miles. Located at 41.87° N. Lat; 74.00° W. Long. Elevation is 157 feet.

Population: 3,326; Growth (since 2000): -13.7%; Density: 211.8 persons per square mile; Race: 96.4% White, 2.1% Black/African American, 1.3% Asian, 0.0% American Indian/Alaska Native, 0.0% Native Hawaiian/Other Pacific Islander, 0.2% Two or more races, 6.3% Hispanic of any race; Average household size: 2.43; Median age: 42.9; Age under 18: 15.4%; Age 65 and over: 16.9%; Males per 100 females: 93.7; Marriage status: 29.1% never married, 47.9% now married, 3.4% separated, 6.9% widowed, 16.2% divorced; Foreign born: 5.4%; Speak English only: 90.2%; With disability: 9.7%; Veterans: 10.4%; Ancestry: 32.6% Irish, 19.2% Italian, 18.4% German, 10.3% American, 7.8% Dutch

Employment: 11.1% management, business, and financial, 5.7% computer, engineering, and science, 14.2% education, legal, community service, arts, and media, 2.1% healthcare practitioners, 17.7% service, 33.4% sales and office, 9.0% natural resources, construction, and maintenance, 6.7% production, transportation, and material moving

Income: Per capita: $33,352; Median household: $71,736; Average household: $85,527; Households with income of $100,000 or more: 30.8%; Poverty rate: 8.7%

Educational Attainment: High school diploma or higher: 94.4%; Bachelor's degree or higher: 27.8%; Graduate/professional degree or higher: 9.5%

School District(s)

Kingston City SD (PK-12)
  2014-15 Enrollment: 6,471 . . . . (845) 943-3003

Housing: Homeownership rate: 71.3%; Median home value: $209,000; Median year structure built: 1973; Homeowner vacancy rate: 5.4%; Median selected monthly owner costs: $1,410 with a mortgage, $724 without a mortgage; Median gross rent: $1,150 per month; Rental vacancy rate: 4.7%

Health Insurance: 87.5% have insurance; 72.0% have private insurance; 26.6% have public insurance; 12.5% do not have insurance; 15.5% of children under 18 do not have insurance

Transportation: Commute: 84.1% car, 0.4% public transportation, 11.2% walk, 4.3% work from home; Mean travel time to work: 22.7 minutes

WALKER VALLEY (CDP). Covers a land area of 2.120 square miles and a water area of 0.010 square miles. Located at 41.64° N. Lat; 74.38° W. Long. Elevation is 663 feet.

Population: 829; Growth (since 2000): 9.4%; Density: 391.0 persons per square mile; Race: 95.4% White, 0.0% Black/African American, 0.0% Asian, 0.0% American Indian/Alaska Native, 0.0% Native Hawaiian/Other Pacific Islander, 4.6% Two or more races, 3.0% Hispanic of any race; Average household size: 2.73; Median age: 38.0; Age under 18: 45.2%; Age 65 and over: 12.2%; Males per 100 females: 106.0; Marriage status: 7.0% never married, 70.0% now married, 2.5% separated, 18.8% widowed, 4.2% divorced; Foreign born: 0.0%; Speak English only: 94.1%; With disability: 11.1%; Veterans: 6.8%; Ancestry: 22.8% Italian, 18.5% German, 14.0% Irish, 10.3% English, 4.3% Swedish

Employment: 14.1% management, business, and financial, 0.0% computer, engineering, and science, 3.5% education, legal, community service, arts, and media, 11.5% healthcare practitioners, 14.4% service, 39.1% sales and office, 6.2% natural resources, construction, and maintenance, 11.2% production, transportation, and material moving

Income: Per capita: $31,622; Median household: $88,994; Average household: $85,345; Households with income of $100,000 or more: 35.2%; Poverty rate: 5.8%

Educational Attainment: High school diploma or higher: 96.0%; Bachelor's degree or higher: 20.0%; Graduate/professional degree or higher: 8.6%

Housing: Homeownership rate: 84.2%; Median home value: $196,600; Median year structure built: 1971; Homeowner vacancy rate: 0.0%; Median selected monthly owner costs: $1,961 with a mortgage, $668 without a mortgage; Median gross rent: n/a per month; Rental vacancy rate: 0.0%

Health Insurance: 100.0% have insurance; 88.7% have private insurance; 15.6% have public insurance; 0.0% do not have insurance; 0.0% of children under 18 do not have insurance

Transportation: Commute: 94.1% car, 2.4% public transportation, 0.0% walk, 3.5% work from home; Mean travel time to work: 46.3 minutes

WALLKILL (CDP). Covers a land area of 3.067 square miles and a water area of 0 square miles. Located at 41.61° N. Lat; 74.16° W. Long. Elevation is 262 feet.

Population: 2,227; Growth (since 2000): 3.9%; Density: 726.1 persons per square mile; Race: 88.2% White, 5.3% Black/African American, 3.2% Asian, 0.0% American Indian/Alaska Native, 0.0% Native Hawaiian/Other Pacific Islander, 0.0% Two or more races, 4.7% Hispanic of any race; Average household size: 2.56; Median age: 41.2; Age under 18: 24.9%; Age 65 and over: 14.5%; Males per 100 females: 97.8; Marriage status: 31.6% never married, 50.3% now married, 1.2% separated, 5.9% widowed, 12.2% divorced; Foreign born: 5.3%; Speak English only: 89.8%; With disability: 7.5%; Veterans: 5.6%; Ancestry: 24.8% German, 22.0% Irish, 19.1% Italian, 13.7% English, 11.6% American

Employment: 10.9% management, business, and financial, 4.3% computer, engineering, and science, 19.1% education, legal, community service, arts, and media, 1.4% healthcare practitioners, 17.9% service, 24.3% sales and office, 13.2% natural resources, construction, and maintenance, 8.8% production, transportation, and material moving

Income: Per capita: $31,419; Median household: $71,701; Average household: $79,589; Households with income of $100,000 or more: 34.0%; Poverty rate: 4.0%

Educational Attainment: High school diploma or higher: 90.9%; Bachelor's degree or higher: 35.6%; Graduate/professional degree or higher: 12.8%

School District(s)

Wallkill Central SD (KG-12)
  2014-15 Enrollment: 3,102 . . . . (845) 895-7101

Housing: Homeownership rate: 55.7%; Median home value: $203,400; Median year structure built: 1967; Homeowner vacancy rate: 6.9%; Median selected monthly owner costs: $2,067 with a mortgage, $960 without a mortgage; Median gross rent: $953 per month; Rental vacancy rate: 0.0%

Health Insurance: 93.1% have insurance; 82.1% have private insurance; 24.9% have public insurance; 6.9% do not have insurance; 1.6% of children under 18 do not have insurance

Transportation: Commute: 91.7% car, 0.0% public transportation, 3.4% walk, 1.2% work from home; Mean travel time to work: 28.8 minutes

WATCHTOWER (CDP).

Covers a land area of 0.777 square miles and a water area of 0 square miles. Located at 41.64° N. Lat; 74.26° W. Long. Elevation is 344 feet.

Population: 2,603; Growth (since 2000): n/a; Density: 3,349.2 persons per square mile; Race: 79.0% White, 10.9% Black/African American, 5.2% Asian, 0.0% American Indian/Alaska Native, 0.0% Native Hawaiian/Other Pacific Islander, 4.1% Two or more races, 21.3% Hispanic of any race; Average household size: 0.00; Median age: 32.8; Age under 18: 3.0%; Age 65 and over: 6.6%; Males per 100 females: 183.5; Marriage status: 46.9% never married, 50.4% now married, 0.3% separated, 0.2% widowed, 2.5% divorced; Foreign born: 10.6%; Speak English only: 73.9%; With disability: 1.7%; Veterans: 0.0%; Ancestry: 10.9% German, 9.0% English, 8.8% Irish, 8.7% American, 4.3% European

Employment: 0.0% management, business, and financial, 0.0% computer, engineering, and science, 19.1% education, legal, community service, arts, and media, 0.0% healthcare practitioners, 31.7% service, 0.0% sales and office, 0.0% natural resources, construction, and maintenance, 49.2% production, transportation, and material moving

Income: Per capita: $4,550; Median household: n/a; Average household: n/a; Households with income of $100,000 or more: n/a; Poverty rate: 88.7%

Educational Attainment: High school diploma or higher: 99.5%; Bachelor's degree or higher: 10.8%; Graduate/professional degree or higher: 2.4%

Housing: Homeownership rate: n/a; Median home value: n/a; Median year structure built: n/a; Homeowner vacancy rate: 0.0%; Median selected monthly owner costs: n/a with a mortgage, n/a without a mortgage; Median gross rent: n/a per month; Rental vacancy rate: 0.0%

Health Insurance: 34.9% have insurance; 20.8% have private insurance; 14.8% have public insurance; 65.1% do not have insurance; 74.7% of children under 18 do not have insurance

Transportation: Commute: 2.9% car, 0.0% public transportation, 25.6% walk, 71.5% work from home; Mean travel time to work: 0.0 minutes

WAWARSING (town).

Covers a land area of 130.505 square miles and a water area of 3.358 square miles. Located at 41.75° N. Lat; 74.42° W. Long. Elevation is 295 feet.

Population: 13,147; Growth (since 2000): 2.0%; Density: 100.7 persons per square mile; Race: 72.8% White, 12.0% Black/African American, 0.9% Asian, 0.2% American Indian/Alaska Native, 0.0% Native Hawaiian/Other Pacific Islander, 6.9% Two or more races, 21.6% Hispanic of any race; Average household size: 2.52; Median age: 40.8; Age under 18: 19.5%; Age 65 and over: 14.1%; Males per 100 females: 128.3; Marriage status: 34.7% never married, 46.5% now married, 2.8% separated, 5.8% widowed, 13.0% divorced; Foreign born: 9.4%; Speak English only: 81.0%; With disability: 18.0%; Veterans: 6.9%; Ancestry: 18.7% Irish, 16.0% German, 11.3% Italian, 6.9% English, 5.5% American

Employment: 8.4% management, business, and financial, 2.8% computer, engineering, and science, 13.8% education, legal, community service, arts, and media, 4.2% healthcare practitioners, 23.7% service, 20.2% sales and office, 12.0% natural resources, construction, and maintenance, 15.1% production, transportation, and material moving

Income: Per capita: $22,255; Median household: $46,603; Average household: $62,225; Households with income of $100,000 or more: 17.5%; Poverty rate: 15.8%

Educational Attainment: High school diploma or higher: 83.8%; Bachelor's degree or higher: 18.3%; Graduate/professional degree or higher: 7.4%

Housing: Homeownership rate: 65.5%; Median home value: $159,800; Median year structure built: 1958; Homeowner vacancy rate: 5.0%; Median selected monthly owner costs: $1,540 with a mortgage, $672 without a mortgage; Median gross rent: $893 per month; Rental vacancy rate: 8.4%

Health Insurance: 90.7% have insurance; 62.8% have private insurance; 44.2% have public insurance; 9.3% do not have insurance; 1.6% of children under 18 do not have insurance

Transportation: Commute: 88.0% car, 2.1% public transportation, 5.5% walk, 4.0% work from home; Mean travel time to work: 31.2 minutes

Additional Information Contacts

Town of Wawarsing . . . . (845) 647-7800
http://www.townofwawarsing.net

WEST HURLEY (CDP).

Covers a land area of 3.787 square miles and a water area of <.001 square miles. Located at 42.01° N. Lat; 74.11° W. Long. Elevation is 597 feet.

Population: 2,034; Growth (since 2000): -3.4%; Density: 537.1 persons per square mile; Race: 95.6% White, 1.1% Black/African American, 0.0% Asian, 0.0% American Indian/Alaska Native, 0.0% Native Hawaiian/Other Pacific Islander, 0.2% Two or more races, 4.5% Hispanic of any race; Average household size: 2.18; Median age: 55.0; Age under 18: 14.4%; Age 65 and over: 27.5%; Males per 100 females: 84.7; Marriage status: 18.1% never married, 58.6% now married, 3.7% separated, 8.5% widowed, 14.8% divorced; Foreign born: 4.1%; Speak English only: 95.5%; With disability: 13.4%; Veterans: 12.7%; Ancestry: 27.6% Irish, 22.4% German, 17.1% English, 13.9% Italian, 6.6% French

Employment: 13.0% management, business, and financial, 3.0% computer, engineering, and science, 27.7% education, legal, community service, arts, and media, 6.3% healthcare practitioners, 17.8% service, 22.1% sales and office, 1.5% natural resources, construction, and maintenance, 8.6% production, transportation, and material moving

Income: Per capita: $36,200; Median household: $54,656; Average household: $78,835; Households with income of $100,000 or more: 27.6%; Poverty rate: 8.1%

Educational Attainment: High school diploma or higher: 92.4%; Bachelor's degree or higher: 40.2%; Graduate/professional degree or higher: 24.9%

Housing: Homeownership rate: 87.4%; Median home value: $255,000; Median year structure built: 1962; Homeowner vacancy rate: 0.0%; Median selected monthly owner costs: $1,718 with a mortgage, $700 without a mortgage; Median gross rent: $1,105 per month; Rental vacancy rate: 0.0%

Health Insurance: 93.8% have insurance; 74.6% have private insurance; 40.3% have public insurance; 6.2% do not have insurance; 0.0% of children under 18 do not have insurance

Transportation: Commute: 83.5% car, 6.4% public transportation, 2.0% walk, 7.2% work from home; Mean travel time to work: 30.1 minutes

WEST PARK (unincorporated postal area)

ZCTA: 12493

Covers a land area of 6.894 square miles and a water area of 0.021 square miles. Located at 41.79° N. Lat; 73.97° W. Long. Elevation is 102 feet.

Population: 321; Growth (since 2000): -41.3%; Density: 46.6 persons per square mile; Race: 92.2% White, 0.9% Black/African American, 0.3% Asian, 0.0% American Indian/Alaska Native, 0.0% Native Hawaiian/Other Pacific Islander, 0.9% Two or more races, 7.5% Hispanic of any race; Average household size: 1.83; Median age: 31.7; Age under 18: 16.5%; Age 65 and over: 5.3%; Males per 100 females: 113.4; Marriage status: 58.5% never married, 26.1% now married, 0.0% separated, 0.0% widowed, 15.5% divorced; Foreign born: 0.0%; Speak English only: 92.7%; With disability: 12.0%; Veterans: 0.0%; Ancestry: 67.0% Irish, 47.4% Italian, 30.5% German, 5.3% Polish, 3.7% American

Employment: 0.0% management, business, and financial, 0.0% computer, engineering, and science, 44.3% education, legal, community service, arts, and media, 41.3% healthcare practitioners, 0.0% service, 14.4% sales and office, 0.0% natural resources, construction, and maintenance, 0.0% production, transportation, and material moving

Income: Per capita: $38,526; Median household: $85,547; Average household: $79,749; Households with income of $100,000 or more: n/a; Poverty rate: 16.0%

Educational Attainment: High school diploma or higher: 100.0%; Bachelor's degree or higher: 57.0%; Graduate/professional degree or higher: 31.2%

School District(s)

West Park Union Free SD

2014-15 Enrollment: n/a . . . . (845) 384-6710

Housing: Homeownership rate: 31.3%; Median home value: $173,400; Median year structure built: Before 1940; Homeowner vacancy rate: 0.0%; Median selected monthly owner costs: $0 with a mortgage, $0 without a mortgage; Median gross rent: $964 per month; Rental vacancy rate: 0.0%

Health Insurance: 100.0% have insurance; 88.0% have private insurance; 17.7% have public insurance; 0.0% do not have insurance; 0.0% of children under 18 do not have insurance

Transportation: Commute: 100.0% car, 0.0% public transportation, 0.0% walk, 0.0% work from home; Mean travel time to work: 0.0 minutes

WEST SHOKAN (unincorporated postal area)
ZCTA: 12494

Covers a land area of 18.744 square miles and a water area of 0 square miles. Located at 41.96° N. Lat; 74.29° W. Long. Elevation is 666 feet.
Population: 740; Growth (since 2000): 3.6%; Density: 39.5 persons per square mile; Race: 100.0% White, 0.0% Black/African American, 0.0% Asian, 0.0% American Indian/Alaska Native, 0.0% Native Hawaiian/Other Pacific Islander, 0.0% Two or more races, 0.0% Hispanic of any race; Average household size: 2.33; Median age: 51.8; Age under 18: 17.8%; Age 65 and over: 20.9%; Males per 100 females: 97.4; Marriage status: 23.6% never married, 57.3% now married, 0.0% separated, 7.8% widowed, 11.4% divorced; Foreign born: 6.6%; Speak English only: 88.8%; With disability: 10.8%; Veterans: 7.2%; Ancestry: 36.6% Irish, 32.4% German, 18.2% Ukrainian, 16.5% Polish, 14.1% English
Employment: 18.9% management, business, and financial, 0.0% computer, engineering, and science, 15.6% education, legal, community service, arts, and media, 11.3% healthcare practitioners, 20.2% service, 15.3% sales and office, 15.3% natural resources, construction, and maintenance, 3.3% production, transportation, and material moving
Income: Per capita: $30,837; Median household: $59,844; Average household: $69,368; Households with income of $100,000 or more: 23.3%; Poverty rate: 0.8%
Educational Attainment: High school diploma or higher: 91.9%; Bachelor's degree or higher: 48.4%; Graduate/professional degree or higher: 15.8%
Housing: Homeownership rate: 79.6%; Median home value: $274,700; Median year structure built: 1961; Homeowner vacancy rate: 0.0%; Median selected monthly owner costs: $2,190 with a mortgage, $688 without a mortgage; Median gross rent: n/a per month; Rental vacancy rate: 0.0%
Health Insurance: 96.2% have insurance; 86.5% have private insurance; 28.5% have public insurance; 3.8% do not have insurance; 0.0% of children under 18 do not have insurance
Transportation: Commute: 81.1% car, 0.0% public transportation, 0.0% walk, 18.9% work from home; Mean travel time to work: 25.4 minutes

WILLOW (unincorporated postal area)
ZCTA: 12495

Covers a land area of 9.140 square miles and a water area of 0 square miles. Located at 42.08° N. Lat; 74.24° W. Long. Elevation is 1,093 feet.
Population: 361; Growth (since 2000): 91.0%; Density: 39.5 persons per square mile; Race: 96.4% White, 3.6% Black/African American, 0.0% Asian, 0.0% American Indian/Alaska Native, 0.0% Native Hawaiian/Other Pacific Islander, 0.0% Two or more races, 12.5% Hispanic of any race; Average household size: 2.15; Median age: 47.5; Age under 18: 6.9%; Age 65 and over: 27.1%; Males per 100 females: 100.8; Marriage status: 20.8% never married, 71.4% now married, 0.0% separated, 3.9% widowed, 3.9% divorced; Foreign born: 10.0%; Speak English only: 87.5%; With disability: 6.9%; Veterans: 0.0%; Ancestry: 26.0% German, 23.0% Italian, 21.6% Polish, 20.2% Irish, 10.2% English
Employment: 20.0% management, business, and financial, 19.5% computer, engineering, and science, 29.8% education, legal, community service, arts, and media, 0.0% healthcare practitioners, 11.7% service, 13.2% sales and office, 5.9% natural resources, construction, and maintenance, 0.0% production, transportation, and material moving
Income: Per capita: $44,974; Median household: $82,857; Average household: $96,180; Households with income of $100,000 or more: 38.7%; Poverty rate: 22.4%
Educational Attainment: High school diploma or higher: 82.6%; Bachelor's degree or higher: 46.0%; Graduate/professional degree or higher: 26.2%
Housing: Homeownership rate: 84.5%; Median home value: $483,300; Median year structure built: 1958; Homeowner vacancy rate: 6.0%; Median selected monthly owner costs: $2,132 with a mortgage, $813 without a mortgage; Median gross rent: n/a per month; Rental vacancy rate: 0.0%
Health Insurance: 86.4% have insurance; 77.3% have private insurance; 27.4% have public insurance; 13.6% do not have insurance; 0.0% of children under 18 do not have insurance
Transportation: Commute: 60.5% car, 0.0% public transportation, 5.4% walk, 27.8% work from home; Mean travel time to work: 33.5 minutes

WOODSTOCK (CDP).
Covers a land area of 5.916 square miles and a water area of 0.009 square miles. Located at 42.05° N. Lat; 74.11° W. Long. Elevation is 561 feet.
Population: 1,766; Growth (since 2000): -19.3%; Density: 298.5 persons per square mile; Race: 87.5% White, 2.8% Black/African American, 1.9% Asian, 0.0% American Indian/Alaska Native, 0.0% Native Hawaiian/Other Pacific Islander, 4.4% Two or more races, 7.4% Hispanic of any race; Average household size: 1.74; Median age: 62.5; Age under 18: 5.0%; Age 65 and over: 41.5%; Males per 100 females: 86.1; Marriage status: 29.6% never married, 51.2% now married, 2.3% separated, 6.0% widowed, 13.1% divorced; Foreign born: 10.1%; Speak English only: 86.9%; With disability: 15.2%; Veterans: 10.7%; Ancestry: 13.6% German, 12.3% Russian, 11.9% English, 10.6% Polish, 7.5% Irish
Employment: 22.1% management, business, and financial, 11.7% computer, engineering, and science, 24.4% education, legal, community service, arts, and media, 7.1% healthcare practitioners, 10.7% service, 14.7% sales and office, 4.4% natural resources, construction, and maintenance, 4.9% production, transportation, and material moving
Income: Per capita: $56,465; Median household: $57,485; Average household: $96,229; Households with income of $100,000 or more: 28.4%; Poverty rate: 13.3%
Educational Attainment: High school diploma or higher: 97.2%; Bachelor's degree or higher: 54.9%; Graduate/professional degree or higher: 28.9%

School District(s)
Onteora Central SD (KG-12)
   2014-15 Enrollment: 1,415 . . . . (845) 657-8851
Housing: Homeownership rate: 77.6%; Median home value: $288,000; Median year structure built: 1953; Homeowner vacancy rate: 0.0%; Median selected monthly owner costs: $2,063 with a mortgage, $812 without a mortgage; Median gross rent: $1,038 per month; Rental vacancy rate: 9.3%
Health Insurance: 93.0% have insurance; 61.1% have private insurance; 59.2% have public insurance; 7.0% do not have insurance; 0.0% of children under 18 do not have insurance
Transportation: Commute: 52.7% car, 3.8% public transportation, 3.0% walk, 37.4% work from home; Mean travel time to work: 22.6 minutes

WOODSTOCK (town).
Covers a land area of 67.289 square miles and a water area of 0.544 square miles. Located at 42.06° N. Lat; 74.17° W. Long. Elevation is 561 feet.
History: Best known for its association with the famous 3-day music festival in 1969, Woodstock had a reputation as an artists ' colony and progressive retreat long before the 1960s. A tannery center in the 19th century, it became an art colony in 1902. In 1906 the Manhattan-based Arts Student League opened a summer school here, and the adjacent Maverick colony drew social reformers, artists, and performers. To this day the village remains a magnet for tourists, artists, and drifters.
Population: 5,890; Growth (since 2000): -5.6%; Density: 87.5 persons per square mile; Race: 91.6% White, 2.3% Black/African American, 1.9% Asian, 0.0% American Indian/Alaska Native, 0.0% Native Hawaiian/Other Pacific Islander, 3.2% Two or more races, 4.6% Hispanic of any race; Average household size: 1.99; Median age: 56.5; Age under 18: 13.3%; Age 65 and over: 29.7%; Males per 100 females: 91.3; Marriage status: 24.7% never married, 56.5% now married, 0.9% separated, 5.3% widowed, 13.5% divorced; Foreign born: 8.9%; Speak English only: 90.3%; With disability: 13.0%; Veterans: 8.2%; Ancestry: 16.5% German, 12.9% Italian, 12.1% Irish, 11.8% English, 11.4% Russian
Employment: 21.4% management, business, and financial, 9.7% computer, engineering, and science, 25.0% education, legal, community service, arts, and media, 5.8% healthcare practitioners, 11.1% service, 16.9% sales and office, 6.5% natural resources, construction, and maintenance, 3.6% production, transportation, and material moving
Income: Per capita: $54,844; Median household: $67,029; Average household: $108,938; Households with income of $100,000 or more: 34.9%; Poverty rate: 10.1%
Educational Attainment: High school diploma or higher: 96.3%; Bachelor's degree or higher: 58.1%; Graduate/professional degree or higher: 29.0%

School District(s)
Onteora Central SD (KG-12)
   2014-15 Enrollment: 1,415 . . . . (845) 657-8851
Housing: Homeownership rate: 82.0%; Median home value: $311,700; Median year structure built: 1956; Homeowner vacancy rate: 3.1%; Median selected monthly owner costs: $2,134 with a mortgage, $846 without a

mortgage; Median gross rent: $1,073 per month; Rental vacancy rate: 8.4%

Health Insurance: 92.0% have insurance; 72.6% have private insurance; 41.3% have public insurance; 8.0% do not have insurance; 0.9% of children under 18 do not have insurance

Safety: Violent crime rate: 6.8 per 10,000 population; Property crime rate: 107.2 per 10,000 population

Transportation: Commute: 67.2% car, 4.2% public transportation, 2.7% walk, 22.8% work from home; Mean travel time to work: 30.1 minutes

Additional Information Contacts

Town of Woodstock.................................. (845) 679-2113
   http://www.woodstockny.org

ZENA (CDP). Covers a land area of 2.935 square miles and a water area of 0 square miles. Located at 42.02° N. Lat; 74.09° W. Long. Elevation is 377 feet.

Population: 1,385; Growth (since 2000): 23.8%; Density: 471.9 persons per square mile; Race: 87.1% White, 4.1% Black/African American, 2.7% Asian, 0.0% American Indian/Alaska Native, 0.0% Native Hawaiian/Other Pacific Islander, 6.1% Two or more races, 3.5% Hispanic of any race; Average household size: 2.76; Median age: 45.7; Age under 18: 25.6%; Age 65 and over: 18.1%; Males per 100 females: 92.4; Marriage status: 25.6% never married, 62.6% now married, 0.0% separated, 4.7% widowed, 7.2% divorced; Foreign born: 4.1%; Speak English only: 93.7%; With disability: 12.1%; Veterans: 7.0%; Ancestry: 21.2% German, 20.5% Irish, 18.0% Italian, 11.6% Polish, 11.4% Russian

Employment: 18.2% management, business, and financial, 9.6% computer, engineering, and science, 22.0% education, legal, community service, arts, and media, 10.9% healthcare practitioners, 11.8% service, 19.5% sales and office, 3.4% natural resources, construction, and maintenance, 4.6% production, transportation, and material moving

Income: Per capita: $42,441; Median household: $87,480; Average household: $116,407; Households with income of $100,000 or more: 46.0%; Poverty rate: 2.1%

Educational Attainment: High school diploma or higher: 98.6%; Bachelor's degree or higher: 57.4%; Graduate/professional degree or higher: 27.4%

Housing: Homeownership rate: 89.4%; Median home value: $273,500; Median year structure built: 1964; Homeowner vacancy rate: 5.1%; Median selected monthly owner costs: $2,127 with a mortgage, $1,024 without a mortgage; Median gross rent: n/a per month; Rental vacancy rate: 0.0%

Health Insurance: 96.2% have insurance; 85.5% have private insurance; 28.2% have public insurance; 3.8% do not have insurance; 0.0% of children under 18 do not have insurance

Transportation: Commute: 81.9% car, 0.0% public transportation, 1.1% walk, 12.2% work from home; Mean travel time to work: 24.6 minutes

Warren County

Located in eastern New York, in the Adirondacks; bounded on the east by Lake George; drained by the Hudson and Schroon Rivers. Covers a land area of 866.952 square miles, a water area of 64.652 square miles, and is located in the Eastern Time Zone at 43.56° N. Lat., 73.84° W. Long. The county was founded in 1813. County seat is Lake George.

Warren County is part of the Glens Falls, NY Metropolitan Statistical Area. The entire metro area includes: Warren County, NY; Washington County, NY

Weather Station: Glens Falls Arpt   Elevation: 320 feet

	Jan	Feb	Mar	Apr	May	Jun	Jul	Aug	Sep	Oct	Nov	Dec
High	29	33	42	57	68	77	81	79	71	58	46	34
Low	9	11	21	34	44	53	58	56	48	36	28	17
Precip	2.9	2.0	3.0	3.0	3.6	3.5	4.1	3.6	3.3	3.4	3.3	3.0
Snow	na	13.2	12.8	2.4	tr	0.0	tr	na	na	na	na	na

High and Low temperatures in degrees Fahrenheit; Precipitation and Snow in inches

Weather Station: Glens Falls Farm   Elevation: 503 feet

	Jan	Feb	Mar	Apr	May	Jun	Jul	Aug	Sep	Oct	Nov	Dec
High	31	35	44	59	70	79	82	80	73	60	48	35
Low	11	12	22	34	45	54	59	57	50	38	29	18
Precip	3.3	2.7	3.6	3.7	4.0	4.2	4.6	4.2	3.9	4.0	4.1	3.7
Snow	19.0	12.4	11.3	2.0	0.0	0.0	0.0	0.0	0.0	tr	2.5	12.4

High and Low temperatures in degrees Fahrenheit; Precipitation and Snow in inches

Population: 65,180; Growth (since 2000): 3.0%; Density: 75.2 persons per square mile; Race: 96.2% White, 1.2% Black/African American, 0.9% Asian, 0.3% American Indian/Alaska Native, 0.0% Native Hawaiian/Other Pacific Islander, 1.1% two or more races, 2.1% Hispanic of any race; Average household size: 2.40; Median age: 45.2; Age under 18: 19.4%; Age 65 and over: 19.1%; Males per 100 females: 95.4; Marriage status: 29.5% never married, 51.0% now married, 2.6% separated, 7.4% widowed, 12.1% divorced; Foreign born: 3.4%; Speak English only: 95.1%; With disability: 14.1%; Veterans: 9.7%; Ancestry: 20.2% Irish, 15.4% German, 14.0% English, 11.5% Italian, 10.6% French

Religion: Six largest groups: 22.1% Catholicism, 3.2% Methodist/Pietist, 2.1% Presbyterian-Reformed, 1.7% Episcopalianism/Anglicanism, 1.4% Holiness, 1.3% Baptist

Economy: Unemployment rate: 4.6%; Leading industries: 18.6 % retail trade; 18.5 % accommodation and food services; 11.6 % health care and social assistance; Farms: 117 totaling 9,528 acres; Company size: 1 employs 1,000 or more persons, 4 employ 500 to 999 persons, 39 employ 100 to 499 persons, 2,262 employ less than 100 persons; Business ownership: 1,902 women-owned, n/a Black-owned, 62 Hispanic-owned, 95 Asian-owned, 36 American Indian/Alaska Native-owned

Employment: 12.9% management, business, and financial, 3.9% computer, engineering, and science, 12.0% education, legal, community service, arts, and media, 6.7% healthcare practitioners, 19.5% service, 24.4% sales and office, 8.3% natural resources, construction, and maintenance, 12.2% production, transportation, and material moving

Income: Per capita: $30,611; Median household: $56,798; Average household: $71,951; Households with income of $100,000 or more: 21.4%; Poverty rate: 12.0%

Educational Attainment: High school diploma or higher: 90.9%; Bachelor's degree or higher: 28.2%; Graduate/professional degree or higher: 13.2%

Housing: Homeownership rate: 70.5%; Median home value: $189,700; Median year structure built: 1971; Homeowner vacancy rate: 1.2%; Median selected monthly owner costs: $1,409 with a mortgage, $551 without a mortgage; Median gross rent: $862 per month; Rental vacancy rate: 7.4%

Vital Statistics: Birth rate: 96.3 per 10,000 population; Death rate: 98.9 per 10,000 population; Age-adjusted cancer mortality rate: 206.0 deaths per 100,000 population

Health Insurance: 91.8% have insurance; 72.6% have private insurance; 36.5% have public insurance; 8.2% do not have insurance; 4.9% of children under 18 do not have insurance

Health Care: Physicians: 34.9 per 10,000 population; Dentists: 9.3 per 10,000 population; Hospital beds: 55.7 per 10,000 population; Hospital admissions: 2,289.2 per 10,000 population

Transportation: Commute: 89.9% car, 1.0% public transportation, 3.7% walk, 3.8% work from home; Mean travel time to work: 22.9 minutes

2016 Presidential Election: 50.9% Trump, 42.3% Clinton, 4.1% Johnson, 2.8% Stein

National and State Parks: Lake George Beach State Park

Additional Information Contacts

Warren Government .... (518) 761-6539
   http://www.co.warren.ny.us

Warren County Communities

ADIRONDACK (unincorporated postal area)

ZCTA: 12808

   Covers a land area of 22.184 square miles and a water area of 2.850 square miles. Located at 43.76° N. Lat; 73.72° W. Long. Elevation is 814 feet.

   Population: 412; Growth (since 2000): 44.6%; Density: 18.6 persons per square mile; Race: 100.0% White, 0.0% Black/African American, 0.0% Asian, 0.0% American Indian/Alaska Native, 0.0% Native Hawaiian/Other Pacific Islander, 0.0% Two or more races, 0.0% Hispanic of any race; Average household size: 1.99; Median age: 65.2; Age under 18: 4.1%; Age 65 and over: 51.0%; Males per 100 females: 104.0; Marriage status: 14.3% never married, 67.7% now married, 1.3% separated, 7.8% widowed, 10.3% divorced; Foreign born: 3.4%; Speak English only: 98.8%; With disability: 20.6%; Veterans: 17.7%; Ancestry: 29.1% American, 16.3% German, 13.1% English, 12.4% Italian, 7.8% Swedish

   Employment: 5.1% management, business, and financial, 3.4% computer, engineering, and science, 8.5% education, legal, community service, arts, and media, 5.1% healthcare practitioners, 36.2% service,

24.9% sales and office, 7.9% natural resources, construction, and maintenance, 9.0% production, transportation, and material moving
Income: Per capita: $45,242; Median household: $76,458; Average household: $88,035; Households with income of $100,000 or more: 32.8%; Poverty rate: 1.0%
Educational Attainment: High school diploma or higher: 89.5%; Bachelor's degree or higher: 34.5%; Graduate/professional degree or higher: 23.3%
Housing: Homeownership rate: 100.0%; Median home value: $317,200; Median year structure built: 1980; Homeowner vacancy rate: 9.2%; Median selected monthly owner costs: $1,760 with a mortgage, $456 without a mortgage; Median gross rent: n/a per month; Rental vacancy rate: 100.0%
Health Insurance: 97.1% have insurance; 86.4% have private insurance; 57.3% have public insurance; 2.9% do not have insurance; 0.0% of children under 18 do not have insurance
Transportation: Commute: 85.3% car, 0.0% public transportation, 0.0% walk, 13.0% work from home; Mean travel time to work: 32.8 minutes

ATHOL (unincorporated postal area)
ZCTA: 12810
Covers a land area of 66.404 square miles and a water area of 1.140 square miles. Located at 43.49° N. Lat; 73.99° W. Long. Elevation is 787 feet.
Population: 724; Growth (since 2000): 12.6%; Density: 10.9 persons per square mile; Race: 99.0% White, 0.0% Black/African American, 0.3% Asian, 0.0% American Indian/Alaska Native, 0.0% Native Hawaiian/Other Pacific Islander, 0.7% Two or more races, 1.9% Hispanic of any race; Average household size: 2.50; Median age: 46.5; Age under 18: 20.4%; Age 65 and over: 11.0%; Males per 100 females: 112.5; Marriage status: 25.9% never married, 47.4% now married, 2.4% separated, 9.4% widowed, 17.3% divorced; Foreign born: 1.2%; Speak English only: 97.0%; With disability: 13.0%; Veterans: 8.5%; Ancestry: 24.2% English, 20.2% German, 17.4% Irish, 7.0% Italian, 6.9% French
Employment: 10.0% management, business, and financial, 4.7% computer, engineering, and science, 2.9% education, legal, community service, arts, and media, 3.2% healthcare practitioners, 16.6% service, 23.7% sales and office, 16.6% natural resources, construction, and maintenance, 22.2% production, transportation, and material moving
Income: Per capita: $25,551; Median household: $57,500; Average household: $60,551; Households with income of $100,000 or more: 8.6%; Poverty rate: 10.8%
Educational Attainment: High school diploma or higher: 81.9%; Bachelor's degree or higher: 8.9%; Graduate/professional degree or higher: 3.6%
Housing: Homeownership rate: 89.7%; Median home value: $116,200; Median year structure built: 1975; Homeowner vacancy rate: 3.7%; Median selected monthly owner costs: $1,054 with a mortgage, $471 without a mortgage; Median gross rent: $675 per month; Rental vacancy rate: 0.0%
Health Insurance: 89.5% have insurance; 66.2% have private insurance; 33.7% have public insurance; 10.5% do not have insurance; 0.0% of children under 18 do not have insurance
Transportation: Commute: 93.4% car, 0.0% public transportation, 6.1% walk, 0.5% work from home; Mean travel time to work: 30.4 minutes

BAKERS MILLS (unincorporated postal area)
ZCTA: 12811
Covers a land area of 1.722 square miles and a water area of 0 square miles. Located at 43.61° N. Lat; 74.03° W. Long. Elevation is 1,594 feet.
Population: 67; Growth (since 2000): n/a; Density: 38.9 persons per square mile; Race: 100.0% White, 0.0% Black/African American, 0.0% Asian, 0.0% American Indian/Alaska Native, 0.0% Native Hawaiian/Other Pacific Islander, 0.0% Two or more races, 0.0% Hispanic of any race; Average household size: 2.09; Median age: 45.9; Age under 18: 0.0%; Age 65 and over: 25.4%; Males per 100 females: 95.4; Marriage status: 29.9% never married, 44.8% now married, 0.0% separated, 0.0% widowed, 25.4% divorced; Foreign born: 0.0%; Speak English only: 100.0%; With disability: 44.8%; Veterans: 25.4%; Ancestry: 77.6% Irish, 52.2% French
Employment: 0.0% management, business, and financial, 0.0% computer, engineering, and science, 0.0% education, legal, community service, arts, and media, 0.0% healthcare practitioners, 0.0% service, 50.0% sales and office, 0.0% natural resources, construction, and maintenance, 50.0% production, transportation, and material moving

Income: Per capita: $11,590; Median household: n/a; Average household: n/a; Households with income of $100,000 or more: n/a; Poverty rate: n/a
Educational Attainment: High school diploma or higher: 100.0%; Bachelor's degree or higher: n/a; Graduate/professional degree or higher: n/a
Housing: Homeownership rate: 100.0%; Median home value: n/a; Median year structure built: 1976; Homeowner vacancy rate: 0.0%; Median selected monthly owner costs: $0 with a mortgage, $0 without a mortgage; Median gross rent: n/a per month; Rental vacancy rate: 0.0%
Health Insurance: 100.0% have insurance; 74.6% have private insurance; 25.4% have public insurance; 0.0% do not have insurance; 0.0% of children under 18 do not have insurance
Transportation: Commute: 100.0% car, 0.0% public transportation, 0.0% walk, 0.0% work from home; Mean travel time to work: 0.0 minutes

BOLTON (town). Covers a land area of 63.270 square miles and a water area of 26.771 square miles. Located at 43.58° N. Lat; 73.66° W. Long. Elevation is 374 feet.
Population: 2,279; Growth (since 2000): 7.7%; Density: 36.0 persons per square mile; Race: 94.0% White, 1.9% Black/African American, 0.6% Asian, 0.0% American Indian/Alaska Native, 0.0% Native Hawaiian/Other Pacific Islander, 0.0% Two or more races, 1.4% Hispanic of any race; Average household size: 2.27; Median age: 49.9; Age under 18: 13.6%; Age 65 and over: 24.1%; Males per 100 females: 104.8; Marriage status: 22.4% never married, 61.4% now married, 1.3% separated, 7.1% widowed, 9.1% divorced; Foreign born: 5.8%; Speak English only: 91.6%; With disability: 15.9%; Veterans: 9.0%; Ancestry: 22.4% English, 19.1% Irish, 17.6% German, 11.1% French, 6.6% Italian
Employment: 29.0% management, business, and financial, 2.2% computer, engineering, and science, 6.0% education, legal, community service, arts, and media, 8.3% healthcare practitioners, 12.6% service, 21.1% sales and office, 12.9% natural resources, construction, and maintenance, 7.9% production, transportation, and material moving
Income: Per capita: $37,050; Median household: $59,320; Average household: $82,431; Households with income of $100,000 or more: 23.7%; Poverty rate: 3.4%
Educational Attainment: High school diploma or higher: 96.1%; Bachelor's degree or higher: 40.9%; Graduate/professional degree or higher: 14.0%
Housing: Homeownership rate: 77.7%; Median home value: $306,400; Median year structure built: 1976; Homeowner vacancy rate: 0.9%; Median selected monthly owner costs: $1,580 with a mortgage, $541 without a mortgage; Median gross rent: $1,000 per month; Rental vacancy rate: 9.3%
Health Insurance: 93.2% have insurance; 76.6% have private insurance; 35.9% have public insurance; 6.8% do not have insurance; 0.0% of children under 18 do not have insurance
Safety: Violent crime rate: 4.3 per 10,000 population; Property crime rate: 69.5 per 10,000 population
Transportation: Commute: 90.9% car, 0.9% public transportation, 1.8% walk, 6.5% work from home; Mean travel time to work: 25.9 minutes

BOLTON LANDING (CDP). Covers a land area of 1.062 square miles and a water area of 0.176 square miles. Located at 43.56° N. Lat; 73.66° W. Long. Elevation is 361 feet.
Population: 416; Growth (since 2000): n/a; Density: 391.5 persons per square mile; Race: 89.2% White, 8.7% Black/African American, 0.0% Asian, 0.0% American Indian/Alaska Native, 0.0% Native Hawaiian/Other Pacific Islander, 0.0% Two or more races, 2.2% Hispanic of any race; Average household size: 2.48; Median age: 44.1; Age under 18: 24.0%; Age 65 and over: 15.6%; Males per 100 females: 101.2; Marriage status: 12.7% never married, 79.8% now married, 0.0% separated, 1.9% widowed, 5.6% divorced; Foreign born: 6.3%; Speak English only: 92.3%; With disability: 12.3%; Veterans: 10.4%; Ancestry: 32.7% Irish, 25.0% English, 23.3% German, 16.1% American, 11.8% Scottish
Employment: 53.5% management, business, and financial, 0.0% computer, engineering, and science, 10.4% education, legal, community service, arts, and media, 7.9% healthcare practitioners, 12.9% service, 9.4% sales and office, 3.0% natural resources, construction, and maintenance, 3.0% production, transportation, and material moving
Income: Per capita: $46,624; Median household: $90,000; Average household: $114,662; Households with income of $100,000 or more: 31.6%; Poverty rate: 1.4%

Educational Attainment: High school diploma or higher: 100.0%; Bachelor's degree or higher: 57.0%; Graduate/professional degree or higher: 6.6%

School District(s)
Bolton Central SD (PK-12)
   2014-15 Enrollment: 196. . . . . (518) 644-2400
Housing: Homeownership rate: 70.8%; Median home value: $392,900; Median year structure built: 1969; Homeowner vacancy rate: 0.0%; Median selected monthly owner costs: $2,838 with a mortgage, $331 without a mortgage; Median gross rent: $948 per month; Rental vacancy rate: 21.0%
Health Insurance: 97.1% have insurance; 89.9% have private insurance; 17.8% have public insurance; 2.9% do not have insurance; 0.0% of children under 18 do not have insurance
Transportation: Commute: 92.1% car, 5.0% public transportation, 0.0% walk, 3.0% work from home; Mean travel time to work: 27.2 minutes

BRANT LAKE (unincorporated postal area)
ZCTA: 12815

Covers a land area of 36.592 square miles and a water area of 2.976 square miles. Located at 43.70° N. Lat; 73.67° W. Long. Elevation is 794 feet.
Population: 1,103; Growth (since 2000): 15.5%; Density: 30.1 persons per square mile; Race: 91.3% White, 1.4% Black/African American, 0.0% Asian, 0.4% American Indian/Alaska Native, 0.0% Native Hawaiian/Other Pacific Islander, 7.0% Two or more races, 0.5% Hispanic of any race; Average household size: 2.48; Median age: 54.2; Age under 18: 17.0%; Age 65 and over: 28.4%; Males per 100 females: 98.9; Marriage status: 20.8% never married, 66.1% now married, 2.8% separated, 7.9% widowed, 5.2% divorced; Foreign born: 2.9%; Speak English only: 93.6%; With disability: 13.8%; Veterans: 15.9%; Ancestry: 19.8% German, 18.9% English, 15.1% Irish, 11.7% Italian, 10.2% American
Employment: 4.9% management, business, and financial, 2.7% computer, engineering, and science, 10.5% education, legal, community service, arts, and media, 1.2% healthcare practitioners, 22.6% service, 33.5% sales and office, 10.3% natural resources, construction, and maintenance, 14.2% production, transportation, and material moving
Income: Per capita: $30,685; Median household: $60,458; Average household: $72,851; Households with income of $100,000 or more: 24.4%; Poverty rate: 14.4%
Educational Attainment: High school diploma or higher: 85.4%; Bachelor's degree or higher: 26.7%; Graduate/professional degree or higher: 13.2%
Housing: Homeownership rate: 90.5%; Median home value: $227,300; Median year structure built: 1976; Homeowner vacancy rate: 2.7%; Median selected monthly owner costs: $1,149 with a mortgage, $523 without a mortgage; Median gross rent: $698 per month; Rental vacancy rate: 16.0%
Health Insurance: 96.4% have insurance; 68.1% have private insurance; 51.7% have public insurance; 3.6% do not have insurance; 0.0% of children under 18 do not have insurance
Transportation: Commute: 95.6% car, 0.0% public transportation, 0.2% walk, 4.2% work from home; Mean travel time to work: 29.3 minutes

CHESTER (town). Covers a land area of 84.190 square miles and a water area of 2.860 square miles. Located at 43.69° N. Lat; 73.87° W. Long.
Population: 3,330; Growth (since 2000): -7.9%; Density: 39.6 persons per square mile; Race: 99.7% White, 0.2% Black/African American, 0.0% Asian, 0.0% American Indian/Alaska Native, 0.0% Native Hawaiian/Other Pacific Islander, 0.1% Two or more races, 0.1% Hispanic of any race; Average household size: 2.69; Median age: 43.2; Age under 18: 25.1%; Age 65 and over: 17.5%; Males per 100 females: 99.5; Marriage status: 26.2% never married, 60.6% now married, 1.3% separated, 6.7% widowed, 6.4% divorced; Foreign born: 1.9%; Speak English only: 94.7%; With disability: 9.9%; Veterans: 8.4%; Ancestry: 22.7% Irish, 17.6% English, 16.8% German, 6.4% American, 5.1% Italian
Employment: 10.1% management, business, and financial, 2.9% computer, engineering, and science, 14.8% education, legal, community service, arts, and media, 2.5% healthcare practitioners, 23.5% service, 19.0% sales and office, 12.8% natural resources, construction, and maintenance, 14.2% production, transportation, and material moving
Income: Per capita: $22,263; Median household: $46,860; Average household: $58,357; Households with income of $100,000 or more: 20.0%; Poverty rate: 22.8%

Educational Attainment: High school diploma or higher: 91.2%; Bachelor's degree or higher: 26.8%; Graduate/professional degree or higher: 12.9%
Housing: Homeownership rate: 82.1%; Median home value: $187,400; Median year structure built: 1971; Homeowner vacancy rate: 0.0%; Median selected monthly owner costs: $1,196 with a mortgage, $560 without a mortgage; Median gross rent: $769 per month; Rental vacancy rate: 21.1%
Health Insurance: 90.5% have insurance; 68.5% have private insurance; 36.3% have public insurance; 9.5% do not have insurance; 11.0% of children under 18 do not have insurance
Transportation: Commute: 80.8% car, 0.4% public transportation, 8.3% walk, 10.4% work from home; Mean travel time to work: 23.6 minutes

CHESTERTOWN (CDP). Covers a land area of 3.843 square miles and a water area of 0.013 square miles. Located at 43.64° N. Lat; 73.78° W. Long. Elevation is 843 feet.
Population: 764; Growth (since 2000): n/a; Density: 198.8 persons per square mile; Race: 99.7% White, 0.0% Black/African American, 0.0% Asian, 0.0% American Indian/Alaska Native, 0.0% Native Hawaiian/Other Pacific Islander, 0.3% Two or more races, 0.5% Hispanic of any race; Average household size: 2.82; Median age: 42.4; Age under 18: 34.7%; Age 65 and over: 11.0%; Males per 100 females: 94.5; Marriage status: 21.8% never married, 61.7% now married, 1.5% separated, 10.4% widowed, 6.0% divorced; Foreign born: 0.0%; Speak English only: 99.7%; With disability: 11.8%; Veterans: 7.2%; Ancestry: 30.0% English, 21.5% German, 13.2% Irish, 5.2% American, 4.6% Italian
Employment: 4.0% management, business, and financial, 10.8% computer, engineering, and science, 12.4% education, legal, community service, arts, and media, 0.0% healthcare practitioners, 16.4% service, 27.9% sales and office, 17.0% natural resources, construction, and maintenance, 11.5% production, transportation, and material moving
Income: Per capita: $17,708; Median household: $46,761; Average household: $48,728; Households with income of $100,000 or more: n/a; Poverty rate: 13.2%
Educational Attainment: High school diploma or higher: 92.9%; Bachelor's degree or higher: 22.6%; Graduate/professional degree or higher: 9.3%

School District(s)
North Warren Central SD (PK-12)
   2014-15 Enrollment: 557. . . . . (518) 494-3015
Housing: Homeownership rate: 72.9%; Median home value: $187,700; Median year structure built: 1961; Homeowner vacancy rate: 0.0%; Median selected monthly owner costs: $1,386 with a mortgage, $550 without a mortgage; Median gross rent: $728 per month; Rental vacancy rate: 0.0%
Health Insurance: 91.9% have insurance; 79.7% have private insurance; 23.0% have public insurance; 8.1% do not have insurance; 0.0% of children under 18 do not have insurance
Transportation: Commute: 88.5% car, 0.0% public transportation, 0.0% walk, 11.5% work from home; Mean travel time to work: 25.8 minutes

DIAMOND POINT (unincorporated postal area)
ZCTA: 12824

Covers a land area of 15.164 square miles and a water area of 0.487 square miles. Located at 43.52° N. Lat; 73.73° W. Long. Elevation is 331 feet.
Population: 1,114; Growth (since 2000): 51.6%; Density: 73.5 persons per square mile; Race: 99.4% White, 0.6% Black/African American, 0.0% Asian, 0.0% American Indian/Alaska Native, 0.0% Native Hawaiian/Other Pacific Islander, 0.0% Two or more races, 0.0% Hispanic of any race; Average household size: 2.43; Median age: 55.7; Age under 18: 12.2%; Age 65 and over: 21.6%; Males per 100 females: 101.4; Marriage status: 20.3% never married, 61.4% now married, 0.9% separated, 4.3% widowed, 13.9% divorced; Foreign born: 5.7%; Speak English only: 93.9%; With disability: 14.9%; Veterans: 8.6%; Ancestry: 23.4% English, 20.2% German, 15.1% French, 14.0% Irish, 9.9% Italian
Employment: 18.1% management, business, and financial, 4.2% computer, engineering, and science, 7.5% education, legal, community service, arts, and media, 12.0% healthcare practitioners, 10.6% service, 30.1% sales and office, 7.1% natural resources, construction, and maintenance, 10.3% production, transportation, and material moving
Income: Per capita: $38,444; Median household: $61,650; Average household: $90,349; Households with income of $100,000 or more: 33.8%; Poverty rate: 2.4%

Educational Attainment: High school diploma or higher: 96.7%; Bachelor's degree or higher: 41.3%; Graduate/professional degree or higher: 18.7%

Housing: Homeownership rate: 85.4%; Median home value: $283,000; Median year structure built: 1972; Homeowner vacancy rate: 0.0%; Median selected monthly owner costs: $1,543 with a mortgage, $596 without a mortgage; Median gross rent: $1,235 per month; Rental vacancy rate: 6.9%

Health Insurance: 91.6% have insurance; 80.9% have private insurance; 29.0% have public insurance; 8.4% do not have insurance; 0.0% of children under 18 do not have insurance

Transportation: Commute: 88.9% car, 0.0% public transportation, 4.2% walk, 6.9% work from home; Mean travel time to work: 32.0 minutes

GLENS FALLS (city). Covers a land area of 3.851 square miles and a water area of 0.138 square miles. Located at 43.31° N. Lat; 73.65° W. Long. Elevation is 344 feet.

History: The site of Glens Falls was part of the Queensbury Patent, 23,000 acres of land granted in 1759 to 23 men. The water power provided by the 60-foot falls in the Hudson River determined the location of the settlement. During the Revolution the village was destroyed by the British. In 1788, Colonel John Glen of Schenectady acquired land and built mills here. There followed a succession of industrial activities, beginning with lumbering and followed by the manufacture of lime, cement, paper and cellulose.

Population: 14,496; Growth (since 2000): 1.0%; Density: 3,764.2 persons per square mile; Race: 94.0% White, 1.4% Black/African American, 1.6% Asian, 0.3% American Indian/Alaska Native, 0.1% Native Hawaiian/Other Pacific Islander, 2.3% Two or more races, 4.2% Hispanic of any race; Average household size: 2.22; Median age: 38.8; Age under 18: 18.4%; Age 65 and over: 13.4%; Males per 100 females: 94.3; Marriage status: 42.1% never married, 37.6% now married, 2.6% separated, 5.7% widowed, 14.6% divorced; Foreign born: 3.3%; Speak English only: 95.1%; With disability: 15.4%; Veterans: 9.7%; Ancestry: 18.7% Irish, 13.0% American, 12.7% English, 11.7% French, 11.5% German

Employment: 12.4% management, business, and financial, 4.4% computer, engineering, and science, 11.8% education, legal, community service, arts, and media, 6.6% healthcare practitioners, 21.8% service, 25.4% sales and office, 5.5% natural resources, construction, and maintenance, 12.2% production, transportation, and material moving

Income: Per capita: $26,796; Median household: $45,395; Average household: $57,826; Households with income of $100,000 or more: 15.4%; Poverty rate: 16.1%

Educational Attainment: High school diploma or higher: 89.3%; Bachelor's degree or higher: 25.7%; Graduate/professional degree or higher: 10.9%

School District(s)

Glens Falls City SD (PK-12)
    2014-15 Enrollment: 2,038 . . . . (518) 792-1212
Glens Falls Common SD (KG-06)
    2014-15 Enrollment: 182 . . . . (518) 792-3231

Vocational/Technical School(s)

Adirondack Beauty School (Private, For-profit)
    Fall 2014 Enrollment: 34 . . . . (518) 745-1646
    2015-16 Tuition: $10,100

Housing: Homeownership rate: 50.3%; Median home value: $146,900; Median year structure built: Before 1940; Homeowner vacancy rate: 0.6%; Median selected monthly owner costs: $1,346 with a mortgage, $497 without a mortgage; Median gross rent: $806 per month; Rental vacancy rate: 6.1%

Health Insurance: 90.8% have insurance; 66.2% have private insurance; 37.2% have public insurance; 9.2% do not have insurance; 2.5% of children under 18 do not have insurance

Hospitals: Glens Falls Hospital (410 beds)

Safety: Violent crime rate: 25.1 per 10,000 population; Property crime rate: 163.6 per 10,000 population

Newspapers: Post-Star (daily circulation 33,300); The Chronicle (weekly circulation 30,000)

Transportation: Commute: 83.9% car, 2.6% public transportation, 7.9% walk, 3.3% work from home; Mean travel time to work: 17.6 minutes; Amtrak: Train service available.

Airports: Floyd Bennett Memorial (general aviation)

Additional Information Contacts

City of Glens Falls . . . . (518) 761-3803
    http://www.cityofglensfalls.com

GLENS FALLS NORTH (CDP). Covers a land area of 8.232 square miles and a water area of 0.088 square miles. Located at 43.33° N. Lat; 73.68° W. Long.

History: Glens Falls North is a census-designated place (CDP) in Warren County, New York. Its residents call it not Glens Falls North, but the Town of Queensbury.

Population: 8,494; Growth (since 2000): 5.4%; Density: 1,031.8 persons per square mile; Race: 95.4% White, 1.0% Black/African American, 1.8% Asian, 0.0% American Indian/Alaska Native, 0.0% Native Hawaiian/Other Pacific Islander, 1.2% Two or more races, 2.3% Hispanic of any race; Average household size: 2.34; Median age: 43.8; Age under 18: 21.2%; Age 65 and over: 21.2%; Males per 100 females: 87.8; Marriage status: 26.2% never married, 52.6% now married, 2.2% separated, 10.1% widowed, 11.1% divorced; Foreign born: 6.3%; Speak English only: 90.8%; With disability: 14.3%; Veterans: 10.5%; Ancestry: 23.3% Irish, 17.2% Italian, 15.5% German, 11.5% English, 11.4% American

Employment: 12.0% management, business, and financial, 3.1% computer, engineering, and science, 17.0% education, legal, community service, arts, and media, 9.1% healthcare practitioners, 17.6% service, 23.4% sales and office, 6.8% natural resources, construction, and maintenance, 11.1% production, transportation, and material moving

Income: Per capita: $33,241; Median household: $59,938; Average household: $77,482; Households with income of $100,000 or more: 22.2%; Poverty rate: 10.0%

Educational Attainment: High school diploma or higher: 95.2%; Bachelor's degree or higher: 33.9%; Graduate/professional degree or higher: 16.9%

Housing: Homeownership rate: 62.5%; Median home value: $209,100; Median year structure built: 1975; Homeowner vacancy rate: 2.2%; Median selected monthly owner costs: $1,554 with a mortgage, $526 without a mortgage; Median gross rent: $865 per month; Rental vacancy rate: 9.1%

Health Insurance: 94.6% have insurance; 82.7% have private insurance; 31.2% have public insurance; 5.4% do not have insurance; 11.0% of children under 18 do not have insurance

Transportation: Commute: 90.7% car, 1.7% public transportation, 2.7% walk, 4.3% work from home; Mean travel time to work: 21.0 minutes

HAGUE (town). Covers a land area of 63.760 square miles and a water area of 15.859 square miles. Located at 43.69° N. Lat; 73.55° W. Long. Elevation is 331 feet.

Population: 824; Growth (since 2000): -3.5%; Density: 12.9 persons per square mile; Race: 97.2% White, 0.0% Black/African American, 1.0% Asian, 0.0% American Indian/Alaska Native, 0.0% Native Hawaiian/Other Pacific Islander, 1.8% Two or more races, 0.5% Hispanic of any race; Average household size: 2.19; Median age: 59.0; Age under 18: 15.0%; Age 65 and over: 34.0%; Males per 100 females: 97.5; Marriage status: 14.1% never married, 74.5% now married, 1.6% separated, 5.6% widowed, 5.8% divorced; Foreign born: 3.6%; Speak English only: 93.1%; With disability: 12.9%; Veterans: 12.3%; Ancestry: 17.7% German, 15.8% English, 15.3% Irish, 10.1% Italian, 10.0% Scottish

Employment: 12.5% management, business, and financial, 3.5% computer, engineering, and science, 10.3% education, legal, community service, arts, and media, 5.2% healthcare practitioners, 15.5% service, 16.8% sales and office, 17.9% natural resources, construction, and maintenance, 18.2% production, transportation, and material moving

Income: Per capita: $34,612; Median household: $65,000; Average household: $75,193; Households with income of $100,000 or more: 25.9%; Poverty rate: 7.9%

Educational Attainment: High school diploma or higher: 91.9%; Bachelor's degree or higher: 35.0%; Graduate/professional degree or higher: 21.8%

Housing: Homeownership rate: 91.5%; Median home value: $258,900; Median year structure built: 1962; Homeowner vacancy rate: 4.1%; Median selected monthly owner costs: $1,295 with a mortgage, $650 without a mortgage; Median gross rent: $813 per month; Rental vacancy rate: 0.0%

Health Insurance: 87.0% have insurance; 69.9% have private insurance; 48.2% have public insurance; 13.0% do not have insurance; 33.1% of children under 18 do not have insurance

Transportation: Commute: 93.6% car, 1.1% public transportation, 0.6% walk, 4.7% work from home; Mean travel time to work: 29.3 minutes

HORICON (town). Covers a land area of 65.767 square miles and a water area of 6.100 square miles. Located at 43.72° N. Lat; 73.71° W. Long.

Population: 1,722; Growth (since 2000): 16.4%; Density: 26.2 persons per square mile; Race: 94.4% White, 0.9% Black/African American, 0.0% Asian, 0.2% American Indian/Alaska Native, 0.0% Native Hawaiian/Other Pacific Islander, 4.5% Two or more races, 0.3% Hispanic of any race; Average household size: 2.34; Median age: 56.2; Age under 18: 13.0%; Age 65 and over: 34.1%; Males per 100 females: 100.4; Marriage status: 18.4% never married, 66.9% now married, 2.1% separated, 8.0% widowed, 6.7% divorced; Foreign born: 2.7%; Speak English only: 95.7%; With disability: 15.3%; Veterans: 16.1%; Ancestry: 18.2% German, 17.8% English, 15.4% Irish, 14.9% American, 10.9% Italian

Employment: 5.8% management, business, and financial, 3.0% computer, engineering, and science, 9.3% education, legal, community service, arts, and media, 1.9% healthcare practitioners, 23.0% service, 32.1% sales and office, 11.8% natural resources, construction, and maintenance, 13.1% production, transportation, and material moving

Income: Per capita: $35,597; Median household: $65,804; Average household: $80,060; Households with income of $100,000 or more: 27.3%; Poverty rate: 9.5%

Educational Attainment: High school diploma or higher: 87.9%; Bachelor's degree or higher: 28.6%; Graduate/professional degree or higher: 15.8%

Housing: Homeownership rate: 93.7%; Median home value: $253,100; Median year structure built: 1977; Homeowner vacancy rate: 4.5%; Median selected monthly owner costs: $1,219 with a mortgage, $489 without a mortgage; Median gross rent: $698 per month; Rental vacancy rate: 31.3%

Health Insurance: 97.0% have insurance; 75.2% have private insurance; 50.8% have public insurance; 3.0% do not have insurance; 0.0% of children under 18 do not have insurance

Transportation: Commute: 92.8% car, 0.0% public transportation, 0.1% walk, 6.7% work from home; Mean travel time to work: 28.9 minutes

JOHNSBURG (town). Covers a land area of 203.976 square miles and a water area of 2.768 square miles. Located at 43.66° N. Lat; 74.07° W. Long. Elevation is 1,283 feet.

Population: 1,822; Growth (since 2000): -25.6%; Density: 8.9 persons per square mile; Race: 96.7% White, 0.0% Black/African American, 0.3% Asian, 0.0% American Indian/Alaska Native, 0.0% Native Hawaiian/Other Pacific Islander, 3.0% Two or more races, 0.0% Hispanic of any race; Average household size: 2.38; Median age: 50.8; Age under 18: 17.6%; Age 65 and over: 24.3%; Males per 100 females: 96.2; Marriage status: 17.3% never married, 64.8% now married, 3.2% separated, 8.1% widowed, 9.8% divorced; Foreign born: 1.4%; Speak English only: 96.3%; With disability: 18.7%; Veterans: 10.1%; Ancestry: 21.9% Irish, 15.9% German, 15.8% English, 13.8% French, 8.9% Italian

Employment: 13.1% management, business, and financial, 3.3% computer, engineering, and science, 10.2% education, legal, community service, arts, and media, 4.5% healthcare practitioners, 18.0% service, 20.5% sales and office, 15.0% natural resources, construction, and maintenance, 15.4% production, transportation, and material moving

Income: Per capita: $22,622; Median household: $46,786; Average household: $52,607; Households with income of $100,000 or more: 12.3%; Poverty rate: 15.5%

Educational Attainment: High school diploma or higher: 89.3%; Bachelor's degree or higher: 24.2%; Graduate/professional degree or higher: 9.9%

Housing: Homeownership rate: 83.8%; Median home value: $153,800; Median year structure built: 1968; Homeowner vacancy rate: 1.0%; Median selected monthly owner costs: $1,173 with a mortgage, $457 without a mortgage; Median gross rent: $754 per month; Rental vacancy rate: 0.0%

Health Insurance: 86.4% have insurance; 64.2% have private insurance; 42.4% have public insurance; 13.6% do not have insurance; 15.0% of children under 18 do not have insurance

Transportation: Commute: 97.5% car, 0.0% public transportation, 0.0% walk, 2.5% work from home; Mean travel time to work: 23.3 minutes

KATTSKILL BAY (unincorporated postal area)
ZCTA: 12844

Covers a land area of 2.737 square miles and a water area of 0 square miles. Located at 43.49° N. Lat; 73.62° W. Long..

Population: 263; Growth (since 2000): -2.2%; Density: 96.1 persons per square mile; Race: 92.8% White, 2.7% Black/African American, 0.8% Asian, 0.4% American Indian/Alaska Native, 0.0% Native

Hawaiian/Other Pacific Islander, 1.5% Two or more races, 2.3% Hispanic of any race; Average household size: 1.90; Median age: 53.0; Age under 18: 16.3%; Age 65 and over: 37.3%; Males per 100 females: 103.1; Marriage status: 23.3% never married, 55.9% now married, 0.9% separated, 4.4% widowed, 16.3% divorced; Foreign born: 4.6%; Speak English only: 97.0%; With disability: 13.7%; Veterans: 15.9%; Ancestry: 43.7% Irish, 22.4% French, 22.4% German, 18.3% English, 11.0% Slovak

Employment: 12.1% management, business, and financial, 0.0% computer, engineering, and science, 18.2% education, legal, community service, arts, and media, 18.9% healthcare practitioners, 6.1% service, 7.6% sales and office, 25.8% natural resources, construction, and maintenance, 11.4% production, transportation, and material moving

Income: Per capita: $34,329; Median household: $60,000; Average household: $72,499; Households with income of $100,000 or more: 13.2%; Poverty rate: 15.4%

Educational Attainment: High school diploma or higher: 97.9%; Bachelor's degree or higher: 53.9%; Graduate/professional degree or higher: 22.5%

Housing: Homeownership rate: 88.5%; Median home value: n/a; Median year structure built: 1966; Homeowner vacancy rate: 17.6%; Median selected monthly owner costs: $1,448 with a mortgage, $1,500 without a mortgage; Median gross rent: n/a per month; Rental vacancy rate: 0.0%

Health Insurance: 96.6% have insurance; 91.6% have private insurance; 38.0% have public insurance; 3.4% do not have insurance; 0.0% of children under 18 do not have insurance

Transportation: Commute: 85.6% car, 0.0% public transportation, 8.0% walk, 6.4% work from home; Mean travel time to work: 23.4 minutes

LAKE GEORGE (town). Covers a land area of 30.069 square miles and a water area of 2.549 square miles. Located at 43.44° N. Lat; 73.72° W. Long. Elevation is 344 feet.

History: Vestiges of Fort William Henry, built by Sir William Johnson, and Fort George are in the village. Incorporated 1903.

Population: 3,494; Growth (since 2000): -2.3%; Density: 116.2 persons per square mile; Race: 99.1% White, 0.1% Black/African American, 0.1% Asian, 0.0% American Indian/Alaska Native, 0.0% Native Hawaiian/Other Pacific Islander, 0.7% Two or more races, 0.7% Hispanic of any race; Average household size: 2.33; Median age: 50.4; Age under 18: 15.0%; Age 65 and over: 22.1%; Males per 100 females: 101.9; Marriage status: 26.8% never married, 55.2% now married, 2.8% separated, 7.0% widowed, 11.0% divorced; Foreign born: 5.1%; Speak English only: 93.8%; With disability: 10.4%; Veterans: 9.5%; Ancestry: 25.7% Irish, 17.9% German, 16.8% Italian, 10.8% English, 7.2% French

Employment: 15.2% management, business, and financial, 3.9% computer, engineering, and science, 14.8% education, legal, community service, arts, and media, 6.8% healthcare practitioners, 23.1% service, 22.5% sales and office, 4.8% natural resources, construction, and maintenance, 9.0% production, transportation, and material moving

Income: Per capita: $35,613; Median household: $63,846; Average household: $81,376; Households with income of $100,000 or more: 24.9%; Poverty rate: 11.1%

Educational Attainment: High school diploma or higher: 92.1%; Bachelor's degree or higher: 32.0%; Graduate/professional degree or higher: 15.4%

School District(s)

Lake George Central SD (KG-12)

    2014-15 Enrollment: 867 . . . . (518) 668-5456

Housing: Homeownership rate: 74.4%; Median home value: $252,200; Median year structure built: 1973; Homeowner vacancy rate: 0.0%; Median selected monthly owner costs: $1,516 with a mortgage, $573 without a mortgage; Median gross rent: $968 per month; Rental vacancy rate: 9.7%

Health Insurance: 89.0% have insurance; 68.9% have private insurance; 38.1% have public insurance; 11.0% do not have insurance; 0.0% of children under 18 do not have insurance

Transportation: Commute: 86.9% car, 0.7% public transportation, 6.0% walk, 4.4% work from home; Mean travel time to work: 22.7 minutes

LAKE GEORGE (village). County seat. Covers a land area of 0.586 square miles and a water area of 0 square miles. Located at 43.43° N. Lat; 73.72° W. Long. Elevation is 344 feet.

Population: 851; Growth (since 2000): -13.6%; Density: 1,452.1 persons per square mile; Race: 97.3% White, 0.4% Black/African American, 0.0% Asian, 0.0% American Indian/Alaska Native, 0.0% Native Hawaiian/Other

Pacific Islander, 2.4% Two or more races, 0.8% Hispanic of any race; Average household size: 2.21; Median age: 48.1; Age under 18: 11.9%; Age 65 and over: 19.2%; Males per 100 females: 95.7; Marriage status: 35.2% never married, 45.1% now married, 0.9% separated, 5.1% widowed, 14.6% divorced; Foreign born: 6.0%; Speak English only: 92.7%; With disability: 12.7%; Veterans: 6.6%; Ancestry: 23.5% Irish, 22.4% German, 15.5% Italian, 12.0% English, 11.3% Polish

Employment: 15.6% management, business, and financial, 5.0% computer, engineering, and science, 7.9% education, legal, community service, arts, and media, 11.2% healthcare practitioners, 34.8% service, 18.3% sales and office, 3.1% natural resources, construction, and maintenance, 4.2% production, transportation, and material moving

Income: Per capita: $42,874; Median household: $63,026; Average household: $92,088; Households with income of $100,000 or more: 29.6%; Poverty rate: 7.8%

Educational Attainment: High school diploma or higher: 88.2%; Bachelor's degree or higher: 27.9%; Graduate/professional degree or higher: 10.0%

School District(s)

Lake George Central SD (KG-12)

   2014-15 Enrollment: 867 . . . . (518) 668-5456

Housing: Homeownership rate: 50.5%; Median home value: $250,500; Median year structure built: 1955; Homeowner vacancy rate: 0.0%; Median selected monthly owner costs: $1,292 with a mortgage, $629 without a mortgage; Median gross rent: $850 per month; Rental vacancy rate: 17.4%

Health Insurance: 89.6% have insurance; 68.8% have private insurance; 32.6% have public insurance; 10.4% do not have insurance; 0.0% of children under 18 do not have insurance

Transportation: Commute: 83.5% car, 0.0% public transportation, 8.7% walk, 7.8% work from home; Mean travel time to work: 19.9 minutes

LAKE LUZERNE (town). Covers a land area of 52.519 square miles and a water area of 1.540 square miles. Located at 43.35° N. Lat; 73.79° W. Long. Elevation is 564 feet.

History: Also called Luzerne.

Population: 3,321; Growth (since 2000): 3.2%; Density: 63.2 persons per square mile; Race: 99.3% White, 0.4% Black/African American, 0.3% Asian, 0.0% American Indian/Alaska Native, 0.0% Native Hawaiian/Other Pacific Islander, 0.0% Two or more races, 2.1% Hispanic of any race; Average household size: 2.64; Median age: 43.9; Age under 18: 16.5%; Age 65 and over: 19.2%; Males per 100 females: 99.1; Marriage status: 30.3% never married, 48.1% now married, 5.1% separated, 11.6% widowed, 10.0% divorced; Foreign born: 0.8%; Speak English only: 98.6%; With disability: 21.3%; Veterans: 6.5%; Ancestry: 22.5% Irish, 19.4% German, 16.6% French, 11.0% English, 8.3% Italian

Employment: 8.2% management, business, and financial, 1.8% computer, engineering, and science, 7.6% education, legal, community service, arts, and media, 6.0% healthcare practitioners, 17.9% service, 23.9% sales and office, 19.7% natural resources, construction, and maintenance, 15.0% production, transportation, and material moving

Income: Per capita: $24,807; Median household: $53,265; Average household: $62,552; Households with income of $100,000 or more: 15.5%; Poverty rate: 9.4%

Educational Attainment: High school diploma or higher: 85.5%; Bachelor's degree or higher: 16.3%; Graduate/professional degree or higher: 6.7%

School District(s)

Hadley-Luzerne Central SD (PK-12)

   2014-15 Enrollment: 777 . . . . (518) 696-2378

Housing: Homeownership rate: 81.8%; Median home value: $169,000; Median year structure built: 1977; Homeowner vacancy rate: 2.0%; Median selected monthly owner costs: $1,305 with a mortgage, $554 without a mortgage; Median gross rent: $957 per month; Rental vacancy rate: 0.0%

Health Insurance: 87.4% have insurance; 70.6% have private insurance; 35.5% have public insurance; 12.6% do not have insurance; 9.1% of children under 18 do not have insurance

Transportation: Commute: 91.9% car, 0.0% public transportation, 1.3% walk, 3.2% work from home; Mean travel time to work: 34.5 minutes

NORTH CREEK (CDP). Covers a land area of 1.595 square miles and a water area of 0.051 square miles. Located at 43.69° N. Lat; 73.99° W. Long. Elevation is 1,030 feet.

Population: 446; Growth (since 2000): n/a; Density: 279.7 persons per square mile; Race: 100.0% White, 0.0% Black/African American, 0.0% Asian, 0.0% American Indian/Alaska Native, 0.0% Native Hawaiian/Other

Pacific Islander, 0.0% Two or more races, 0.0% Hispanic of any race; Average household size: 2.23; Median age: 63.7; Age under 18: 6.3%; Age 65 and over: 46.4%; Males per 100 females: 96.8; Marriage status: 20.4% never married, 43.3% now married, 1.2% separated, 23.1% widowed, 13.2% divorced; Foreign born: 2.2%; Speak English only: 91.6%; With disability: 19.0%; Veterans: 14.1%; Ancestry: 26.5% American, 18.8% English, 12.3% Italian, 12.1% Irish, 9.4% French

Employment: 16.7% management, business, and financial, 0.0% computer, engineering, and science, 6.7% education, legal, community service, arts, and media, 8.7% healthcare practitioners, 42.0% service, 6.0% sales and office, 0.0% natural resources, construction, and maintenance, 20.0% production, transportation, and material moving

Income: Per capita: $22,447; Median household: $37,969; Average household: $49,109; Households with income of $100,000 or more: 14.1%; Poverty rate: 9.9%

Educational Attainment: High school diploma or higher: 80.4%; Bachelor's degree or higher: 19.4%; Graduate/professional degree or higher: 12.9%

School District(s)

Johnsburg Central SD (PK-12)

   2014-15 Enrollment: 354 . . . . (518) 251-2814

Housing: Homeownership rate: 68.1%; Median home value: $149,300; Median year structure built: 1972; Homeowner vacancy rate: 0.0%; Median selected monthly owner costs: $1,438 with a mortgage, $592 without a mortgage; Median gross rent: $625 per month; Rental vacancy rate: 0.0%

Health Insurance: 90.6% have insurance; 58.7% have private insurance; 60.9% have public insurance; 9.4% do not have insurance; 0.0% of children under 18 do not have insurance

Transportation: Commute: 100.0% car, 0.0% public transportation, 0.0% walk, 0.0% work from home; Mean travel time to work: 23.9 minutes

NORTH RIVER (unincorporated postal area)
ZCTA: 12856

   Covers a land area of 63.591 square miles and a water area of 1.073 square miles. Located at 43.67° N. Lat; 74.14° W. Long. Elevation is 1,073 feet.

Population: 70; Growth (since 2000): -68.8%; Density: 1.1 persons per square mile; Race: 100.0% White, 0.0% Black/African American, 0.0% Asian, 0.0% American Indian/Alaska Native, 0.0% Native Hawaiian/Other Pacific Islander, 0.0% Two or more races, 0.0% Hispanic of any race; Average household size: 2.69; Median age: 53.0; Age under 18: 12.9%; Age 65 and over: 15.7%; Males per 100 females: 94.8; Marriage status: 38.6% never married, 54.3% now married, 8.6% separated, 7.1% widowed, 0.0% divorced; Foreign born: 8.6%; Speak English only: 100.0%; With disability: 0.0%; Veterans: 0.0%; Ancestry: 80.0% English, 35.7% German, 22.9% Scottish, 11.4% Irish

Employment: 0.0% management, business, and financial, 0.0% computer, engineering, and science, 35.7% education, legal, community service, arts, and media, 0.0% healthcare practitioners, 23.8% service, 0.0% sales and office, 40.5% natural resources, construction, and maintenance, 0.0% production, transportation, and material moving

Income: Per capita: $29,410; Median household: n/a; Average household: $73,923; Households with income of $100,000 or more: 30.8%; Poverty rate: 8.6%

Educational Attainment: High school diploma or higher: 100.0%; Bachelor's degree or higher: 60.4%; Graduate/professional degree or higher: 15.1%

Housing: Homeownership rate: 100.0%; Median home value: $256,300; Median year structure built: 1983; Homeowner vacancy rate: 18.8%; Median selected monthly owner costs: $0 with a mortgage, $525 without a mortgage; Median gross rent: n/a per month; Rental vacancy rate: 0.0%

Health Insurance: 100.0% have insurance; 100.0% have private insurance; 15.7% have public insurance; 0.0% do not have insurance; 0.0% of children under 18 do not have insurance

Transportation: Commute: 76.2% car, 0.0% public transportation, 0.0% walk, 23.8% work from home; Mean travel time to work: 0.0 minutes

POTTERSVILLE (CDP). Covers a land area of 2.279 square miles and a water area of 0.047 square miles. Located at 43.74° N. Lat; 73.82° W. Long. Elevation is 846 feet.

Population: 489; Growth (since 2000): n/a; Density: 214.6 persons per square mile; Race: 98.6% White, 1.4% Black/African American, 0.0% Asian, 0.0% American Indian/Alaska Native, 0.0% Native Hawaiian/Other Pacific Islander, 0.0% Two or more races, 0.0% Hispanic of any race;

Average household size: 4.15; Median age: 25.4; Age under 18: 34.4%; Age 65 and over: 9.0%; Males per 100 females: 91.9; Marriage status: 49.2% never married, 47.1% now married, 0.0% separated, 0.0% widowed, 3.7% divorced; Foreign born: 4.3%; Speak English only: 96.2%; With disability: 11.2%; Veterans: 0.0%; Ancestry: 19.8% Irish, 18.6% German, 5.5% American, 3.5% Polish, 2.0% Hungarian

Employment: 0.0% management, business, and financial, 0.0% computer, engineering, and science, 0.0% education, legal, community service, arts, and media, 0.0% healthcare practitioners, 80.5% service, 2.9% sales and office, 8.0% natural resources, construction, and maintenance, 8.6% production, transportation, and material moving

Income: Per capita: $7,215; Median household: n/a; Average household: $26,094; Households with income of $100,000 or more: n/a; Poverty rate: 72.7%

Educational Attainment: High school diploma or higher: 79.9%; Bachelor's degree or higher: 2.5%; Graduate/professional degree or higher: n/a

Two-year College(s)
Word of Life Bible Institute (Private, Not-for-profit, Interdenominational)
    Fall 2014 Enrollment: 569 . . . . (518) 494-4723
    2015-16 Tuition: In-state $9,290; Out-of-state $9,290

Housing: Homeownership rate: 41.6%; Median home value: $93,900; Median year structure built: 1962; Homeowner vacancy rate: 0.0%; Median selected monthly owner costs: n/a with a mortgage, n/a without a mortgage; Median gross rent: n/a per month; Rental vacancy rate: 0.0%

Health Insurance: 64.8% have insurance; 44.2% have private insurance; 29.7% have public insurance; 35.2% do not have insurance; 54.8% of children under 18 do not have insurance

Transportation: Commute: 41.4% car, 0.0% public transportation, 58.6% walk, 0.0% work from home; Mean travel time to work: 13.1 minutes

QUEENSBURY (town).
Covers a land area of 62.830 square miles and a water area of 2.009 square miles. Located at 43.37° N. Lat; 73.67° W. Long. Elevation is 315 feet.

Population: 27,753; Growth (since 2000): 9.1%; Density: 441.7 persons per square mile; Race: 95.8% White, 1.7% Black/African American, 1.1% Asian, 0.4% American Indian/Alaska Native, 0.0% Native Hawaiian/Other Pacific Islander, 0.7% Two or more races, 1.8% Hispanic of any race; Average household size: 2.47; Median age: 45.8; Age under 18: 21.0%; Age 65 and over: 20.1%; Males per 100 females: 92.6; Marriage status: 27.4% never married, 52.3% now married, 2.5% separated, 7.8% widowed, 12.5% divorced; Foreign born: 3.8%; Speak English only: 95.0%; With disability: 12.8%; Veterans: 9.3%; Ancestry: 21.3% Irish, 15.2% German, 13.4% English, 13.4% Italian, 11.6% French

Employment: 13.4% management, business, and financial, 3.9% computer, engineering, and science, 13.0% education, legal, community service, arts, and media, 7.5% healthcare practitioners, 18.0% service, 25.6% sales and office, 7.2% natural resources, construction, and maintenance, 11.3% production, transportation, and material moving

Income: Per capita: $34,263; Median household: $64,060; Average household: $83,267; Households with income of $100,000 or more: 26.8%; Poverty rate: 8.8%

Educational Attainment: High school diploma or higher: 93.2%; Bachelor's degree or higher: 31.4%; Graduate/professional degree or higher: 15.3%

School District(s)
Queensbury Union Free SD (KG-12)
    2014-15 Enrollment: 3,426 . . . . (518) 824-5602

Two-year College(s)
Adirondack Community College (Public)
    Fall 2014 Enrollment: 4,247 . . . . (518) 743-2200
    2015-16 Tuition: In-state $4,423; Out-of-state $8,407

Housing: Homeownership rate: 73.4%; Median home value: $216,100; Median year structure built: 1981; Homeowner vacancy rate: 0.7%; Median selected monthly owner costs: $1,544 with a mortgage, $608 without a mortgage; Median gross rent: $978 per month; Rental vacancy rate: 6.6%

Health Insurance: 93.9% have insurance; 79.4% have private insurance; 32.7% have public insurance; 6.1% do not have insurance; 5.3% of children under 18 do not have insurance

Transportation: Commute: 93.1% car, 0.6% public transportation, 1.2% walk, 3.4% work from home; Mean travel time to work: 23.3 minutes

Additional Information Contacts
Town of Queensbury . . . . (518) 761-8234
    http://www.queensbury.net

SILVER BAY (unincorporated postal area)
ZCTA: 12874

Covers a land area of 21.418 square miles and a water area of 0.307 square miles. Located at 43.69° N. Lat; 73.55° W. Long. Elevation is 348 feet.

Population: 142; Growth (since 2000): -19.3%; Density: 6.6 persons per square mile; Race: 95.1% White, 0.0% Black/African American, 0.0% Asian, 0.0% American Indian/Alaska Native, 0.0% Native Hawaiian/Other Pacific Islander, 4.9% Two or more races, 1.4% Hispanic of any race; Average household size: 1.69; Median age: 68.8; Age under 18: 2.1%; Age 65 and over: 61.3%; Males per 100 females: 105.8; Marriage status: 1.4% never married, 84.9% now married, 0.0% separated, 7.2% widowed, 6.5% divorced; Foreign born: 1.4%; Speak English only: 93.7%; With disability: 19.7%; Veterans: 18.7%; Ancestry: 31.0% German, 21.8% English, 12.7% Irish, 9.9% French, 6.3% American

Employment: 18.5% management, business, and financial, 11.1% computer, engineering, and science, 27.8% education, legal, community service, arts, and media, 7.4% healthcare practitioners, 0.0% service, 29.6% sales and office, 5.6% natural resources, construction, and maintenance, 0.0% production, transportation, and material moving

Income: Per capita: $53,814; Median household: $69,583; Average household: $91,449; Households with income of $100,000 or more: 44.1%; Poverty rate: 2.8%

Educational Attainment: High school diploma or higher: 100.0%; Bachelor's degree or higher: 62.6%; Graduate/professional degree or higher: 37.4%

Housing: Homeownership rate: 94.0%; Median home value: $589,800; Median year structure built: 1956; Homeowner vacancy rate: 8.1%; Median selected monthly owner costs: $1,594 with a mortgage, $725 without a mortgage; Median gross rent: n/a per month; Rental vacancy rate: 0.0%

Health Insurance: 98.6% have insurance; 93.0% have private insurance; 64.1% have public insurance; 1.4% do not have insurance; 0.0% of children under 18 do not have insurance

Transportation: Commute: 90.4% car, 0.0% public transportation, 0.0% walk, 9.6% work from home; Mean travel time to work: 36.5 minutes

STONY CREEK (town).
Covers a land area of 82.162 square miles and a water area of 1.042 square miles. Located at 43.42° N. Lat; 74.03° W. Long. Elevation is 827 feet.

Population: 786; Growth (since 2000): 5.8%; Density: 9.6 persons per square mile; Race: 95.9% White, 0.0% Black/African American, 1.3% Asian, 0.0% American Indian/Alaska Native, 0.0% Native Hawaiian/Other Pacific Islander, 2.8% Two or more races, 1.7% Hispanic of any race; Average household size: 2.41; Median age: 52.0; Age under 18: 16.9%; Age 65 and over: 26.7%; Males per 100 females: 102.9; Marriage status: 21.2% never married, 50.5% now married, 3.3% separated, 10.2% widowed, 18.1% divorced; Foreign born: 0.8%; Speak English only: 98.1%; With disability: 18.4%; Veterans: 17.8%; Ancestry: 24.9% English, 18.3% German, 17.9% Irish, 12.2% American, 7.6% Italian

Employment: 6.1% management, business, and financial, 1.3% computer, engineering, and science, 12.1% education, legal, community service, arts, and media, 6.7% healthcare practitioners, 27.4% service, 23.6% sales and office, 12.1% natural resources, construction, and maintenance, 10.8% production, transportation, and material moving

Income: Per capita: $24,142; Median household: $50,500; Average household: $55,646; Households with income of $100,000 or more: 11.7%; Poverty rate: 15.1%

Educational Attainment: High school diploma or higher: 87.4%; Bachelor's degree or higher: 11.2%; Graduate/professional degree or higher: 6.6%

Housing: Homeownership rate: 87.4%; Median home value: $139,400; Median year structure built: 1969; Homeowner vacancy rate: 7.5%; Median selected monthly owner costs: $1,078 with a mortgage, $439 without a mortgage; Median gross rent: $790 per month; Rental vacancy rate: 16.0%

Health Insurance: 84.5% have insurance; 64.9% have private insurance; 40.7% have public insurance; 15.5% do not have insurance; 0.0% of children under 18 do not have insurance

Transportation: Commute: 92.7% car, 1.0% public transportation, 0.6% walk, 2.9% work from home; Mean travel time to work: 38.2 minutes

THURMAN (town). Covers a land area of 91.098 square miles and a water area of 1.678 square miles. Located at 43.49° N. Lat; 73.99° W. Long. Elevation is 1,316 feet.
Population: 1,304; Growth (since 2000): 8.8%; Density: 14.3 persons per square mile; Race: 98.2% White, 1.0% Black/African American, 0.2% Asian, 0.0% American Indian/Alaska Native, 0.0% Native Hawaiian/Other Pacific Islander, 0.6% Two or more races, 1.2% Hispanic of any race; Average household size: 2.63; Median age: 45.5; Age under 18: 22.0%; Age 65 and over: 16.6%; Males per 100 females: 104.9; Marriage status: 23.4% never married, 53.0% now married, 1.8% separated, 8.2% widowed, 15.4% divorced; Foreign born: 1.0%; Speak English only: 98.0%; With disability: 16.2%; Veterans: 10.9%; Ancestry: 21.3% German, 18.9% English, 18.0% Irish, 6.2% Italian, 6.1% American
Employment: 9.4% management, business, and financial, 3.8% computer, engineering, and science, 6.3% education, legal, community service, arts, and media, 4.2% healthcare practitioners, 18.7% service, 20.9% sales and office, 15.4% natural resources, construction, and maintenance, 21.4% production, transportation, and material moving
Income: Per capita: $23,766; Median household: $50,234; Average household: $59,388; Households with income of $100,000 or more: 11.1%; Poverty rate: 15.7%
Educational Attainment: High school diploma or higher: 84.4%; Bachelor's degree or higher: 12.6%; Graduate/professional degree or higher: 5.3%
Housing: Homeownership rate: 89.5%; Median home value: $131,700; Median year structure built: 1977; Homeowner vacancy rate: 2.2%; Median selected monthly owner costs: $1,068 with a mortgage, $496 without a mortgage; Median gross rent: $817 per month; Rental vacancy rate: 0.0%
Health Insurance: 89.3% have insurance; 60.7% have private insurance; 43.1% have public insurance; 10.7% do not have insurance; 0.0% of children under 18 do not have insurance
Transportation: Commute: 89.8% car, 0.0% public transportation, 7.3% walk, 2.9% work from home; Mean travel time to work: 31.0 minutes

WARRENSBURG (CDP). Covers a land area of 11.028 square miles and a water area of 0.319 square miles. Located at 43.52° N. Lat; 73.77° W. Long. Elevation is 745 feet.
Population: 3,170; Growth (since 2000): -1.2%; Density: 287.4 persons per square mile; Race: 99.1% White, 0.6% Black/African American, 0.0% Asian, 0.0% American Indian/Alaska Native, 0.0% Native Hawaiian/Other Pacific Islander, 0.3% Two or more races, 2.8% Hispanic of any race; Average household size: 2.52; Median age: 40.3; Age under 18: 23.3%; Age 65 and over: 15.3%; Males per 100 females: 92.1; Marriage status: 23.0% never married, 56.8% now married, 3.1% separated, 7.5% widowed, 12.7% divorced; Foreign born: 4.7%; Speak English only: 95.6%; With disability: 14.0%; Veterans: 10.0%; Ancestry: 17.2% German, 16.5% English, 11.7% Irish, 8.8% American, 8.7% Italian
Employment: 8.7% management, business, and financial, 7.1% computer, engineering, and science, 11.8% education, legal, community service, arts, and media, 5.6% healthcare practitioners, 21.0% service, 22.3% sales and office, 8.9% natural resources, construction, and maintenance, 14.7% production, transportation, and material moving
Income: Per capita: $24,453; Median household: $48,304; Average household: $59,708; Households with income of $100,000 or more: 12.3%; Poverty rate: 16.7%
Educational Attainment: High school diploma or higher: 83.1%; Bachelor's degree or higher: 22.5%; Graduate/professional degree or higher: 10.7%

School District(s)
Warrensburg Central SD (PK-12)
    2014-15 Enrollment: 782 . . . . (518) 623-2861
Housing: Homeownership rate: 73.2%; Median home value: $121,200; Median year structure built: 1957; Homeowner vacancy rate: 4.9%; Median selected monthly owner costs: $1,270 with a mortgage, $477 without a mortgage; Median gross rent: $700 per month; Rental vacancy rate: 12.3%
Health Insurance: 89.7% have insurance; 59.5% have private insurance; 48.3% have public insurance; 10.3% do not have insurance; 1.2% of children under 18 do not have insurance
Transportation: Commute: 94.0% car, 0.0% public transportation, 3.9% walk, 1.3% work from home; Mean travel time to work: 21.3 minutes

WARRENSBURG (town). Covers a land area of 63.461 square miles and a water area of 1.338 square miles. Located at 43.52° N. Lat; 73.81° W. Long. Elevation is 745 feet.
Population: 4,049; Growth (since 2000): -4.8%; Density: 63.8 persons per square mile; Race: 99.3% White, 0.4% Black/African American, 0.0% Asian, 0.0% American Indian/Alaska Native, 0.0% Native Hawaiian/Other Pacific Islander, 0.3% Two or more races, 2.3% Hispanic of any race; Average household size: 2.46; Median age: 44.7; Age under 18: 20.9%; Age 65 and over: 16.3%; Males per 100 females: 95.9; Marriage status: 24.0% never married, 56.2% now married, 2.4% separated, 7.3% widowed, 12.5% divorced; Foreign born: 4.2%; Speak English only: 95.1%; With disability: 14.3%; Veterans: 10.8%; Ancestry: 18.3% German, 14.3% English, 13.8% Irish, 10.7% American, 10.3% Italian
Employment: 10.9% management, business, and financial, 6.5% computer, engineering, and science, 11.9% education, legal, community service, arts, and media, 8.2% healthcare practitioners, 18.8% service, 21.5% sales and office, 7.5% natural resources, construction, and maintenance, 14.7% production, transportation, and material moving
Income: Per capita: $27,040; Median household: $55,625; Average household: $64,671; Households with income of $100,000 or more: 15.6%; Poverty rate: 15.8%
Educational Attainment: High school diploma or higher: 85.4%; Bachelor's degree or higher: 24.2%; Graduate/professional degree or higher: 12.1%

School District(s)
Warrensburg Central SD (PK-12)
    2014-15 Enrollment: 782 . . . . (518) 623-2861
Housing: Homeownership rate: 75.3%; Median home value: $143,100; Median year structure built: 1970; Homeowner vacancy rate: 3.7%; Median selected monthly owner costs: $1,244 with a mortgage, $511 without a mortgage; Median gross rent: $729 per month; Rental vacancy rate: 14.4%
Health Insurance: 91.0% have insurance; 63.4% have private insurance; 46.3% have public insurance; 9.0% do not have insurance; 1.1% of children under 18 do not have insurance
Transportation: Commute: 94.5% car, 0.0% public transportation, 3.5% walk, 1.3% work from home; Mean travel time to work: 20.9 minutes
Additional Information Contacts
Town of Warrensburg . . . . (518) 623-4561
   http://townofwarrensburg.org

WEST GLENS FALLS (CDP). Covers a land area of 4.682 square miles and a water area of 0.131 square miles. Located at 43.30° N. Lat; 73.69° W. Long. Elevation is 381 feet.
History: West Glens Falls is a census-designated place (CDP) and hamlet in Warren County, New York.
Population: 7,670; Growth (since 2000): 14.1%; Density: 1,638.2 persons per square mile; Race: 93.2% White, 3.3% Black/African American, 2.0% Asian, 1.4% American Indian/Alaska Native, 0.0% Native Hawaiian/Other Pacific Islander, 0.0% Two or more races, 0.9% Hispanic of any race; Average household size: 2.68; Median age: 41.8; Age under 18: 25.7%; Age 65 and over: 14.1%; Males per 100 females: 93.5; Marriage status: 32.9% never married, 43.0% now married, 3.5% separated, 9.3% widowed, 14.8% divorced; Foreign born: 3.0%; Speak English only: 96.0%; With disability: 15.4%; Veterans: 8.9%; Ancestry: 17.1% Irish, 16.5% French, 15.3% German, 11.8% English, 10.6% Italian
Employment: 10.5% management, business, and financial, 4.6% computer, engineering, and science, 10.1% education, legal, community service, arts, and media, 6.4% healthcare practitioners, 19.6% service, 29.0% sales and office, 5.3% natural resources, construction, and maintenance, 14.5% production, transportation, and material moving
Income: Per capita: $26,273; Median household: $52,701; Average household: $69,303; Households with income of $100,000 or more: 18.6%; Poverty rate: 12.4%
Educational Attainment: High school diploma or higher: 90.8%; Bachelor's degree or higher: 17.4%; Graduate/professional degree or higher: 8.7%
Housing: Homeownership rate: 76.9%; Median home value: $148,600; Median year structure built: 1981; Homeowner vacancy rate: 0.0%; Median selected monthly owner costs: $1,309 with a mortgage, $562 without a mortgage; Median gross rent: $1,059 per month; Rental vacancy rate: 0.0%
Health Insurance: 92.0% have insurance; 65.8% have private insurance; 38.0% have public insurance; 8.0% do not have insurance; 1.4% of children under 18 do not have insurance

Transportation: Commute: 91.6% car, 0.0% public transportation, 1.2% walk, 2.5% work from home; Mean travel time to work: 24.8 minutes

WEVERTOWN (unincorporated postal area)

ZCTA: 12886

Covers a land area of 14.478 square miles and a water area of 0.053 square miles. Located at 43.68° N. Lat; 73.93° W. Long. Elevation is 1,066 feet.

Population: 201; Growth (since 2000): 139.3%; Density: 13.9 persons per square mile; Race: 97.0% White, 0.0% Black/African American, 0.0% Asian, 0.0% American Indian/Alaska Native, 0.0% Native Hawaiian/Other Pacific Islander, 3.0% Two or more races, 0.0% Hispanic of any race; Average household size: 2.43; Median age: 45.6; Age under 18: 15.9%; Age 65 and over: 6.0%; Males per 100 females: 99.3; Marriage status: 21.0% never married, 72.2% now married, 0.0% separated, 6.8% widowed, 0.0% divorced; Foreign born: 0.0%; Speak English only: 96.6%; With disability: 21.4%; Veterans: 0.0%; Ancestry: 25.4% German, 18.9% Dutch, 16.4% Irish, 13.4% French, 8.0% European

Employment: 37.3% management, business, and financial, 11.1% computer, engineering, and science, 4.0% education, legal, community service, arts, and media, 4.8% healthcare practitioners, 15.1% service, 14.3% sales and office, 4.0% natural resources, construction, and maintenance, 9.5% production, transportation, and material moving

Income: Per capita: $31,644; Median household: n/a; Average household: $74,375; Households with income of $100,000 or more: 48.8%; Poverty rate: 12.9%

Educational Attainment: High school diploma or higher: 87.3%; Bachelor's degree or higher: 42.0%; Graduate/professional degree or higher: 17.3%

Housing: Homeownership rate: 83.8%; Median home value: $103,900; Median year structure built: 1962; Homeowner vacancy rate: 0.0%; Median selected monthly owner costs: $1,125 with a mortgage, $338 without a mortgage; Median gross rent: n/a per month; Rental vacancy rate: 0.0%

Health Insurance: 100.0% have insurance; 85.1% have private insurance; 18.4% have public insurance; 0.0% do not have insurance; 0.0% of children under 18 do not have insurance

Transportation: Commute: 100.0% car, 0.0% public transportation, 0.0% walk, 0.0% work from home; Mean travel time to work: 16.8 minutes

Washington County

Located in eastern New York; bounded on the northwest by Lake George, on the east by Vermont, and on the west by the Hudson River; drained by the Poultney, Mettawee, and Hoosic Rivers; includes part of Lake Champlain. Covers a land area of 831.184 square miles, a water area of 14.704 square miles, and is located in the Eastern Time Zone at 43.31° N. Lat., 73.44° W. Long. The county was founded in 1772. County seat is Hudson Falls.

Washington County is part of the Glens Falls, NY Metropolitan Statistical Area. The entire metro area includes: Warren County, NY; Washington County, NY

Weather Station: Whitehall   Elevation: 119 feet

	Jan	Feb	Mar	Apr	May	Jun	Jul	Aug	Sep	Oct	Nov	Dec
High	30	34	44	59	71	80	84	82	73	61	47	35
Low	12	14	24	36	47	57	61	60	52	41	32	20
Precip	3.0	2.5	3.0	3.2	3.7	3.9	4.5	4.2	3.7	3.7	3.6	3.2
Snow	16.6	12.0	12.5	2.2	0.0	0.0	0.0	0.0	0.0	tr	2.7	13.6

High and Low temperatures in degrees Fahrenheit; Precipitation and Snow in inches

Population: 62,700; Growth (since 2000): 2.7%; Density: 75.4 persons per square mile; Race: 94.0% White, 3.2% Black/African American, 0.5% Asian, 0.2% American Indian/Alaska Native, 0.0% Native Hawaiian/Other Pacific Islander, 1.4% two or more races, 2.5% Hispanic of any race; Average household size: 2.45; Median age: 42.9; Age under 18: 20.0%; Age 65 and over: 16.6%; Males per 100 females: 107.6; Marriage status: 30.2% never married, 51.5% now married, 2.4% separated, 6.4% widowed, 11.9% divorced; Foreign born: 2.4%; Speak English only: 96.7%; With disability: 14.3%; Veterans: 10.4%; Ancestry: 20.4% Irish, 17.4% American, 12.4% English, 11.4% French, 10.8% German

Religion: Six largest groups: 21.5% Catholicism, 5.2% Methodist/Pietist, 2.5% Baptist, 2.0% Presbyterian-Reformed, 1.2% Non-denominational Protestant, 0.8% Episcopalianism/Anglicanism

Economy: Unemployment rate: 4.1%; Leading industries: 17.4 % retail trade; 13.7 % construction; 11.2 % other services (except public administration); Farms: 851 totaling 189,391 acres; Company size: 0 employ 1,000 or more persons, 0 employ 500 to 999 persons, 19 employ 100 to 499 persons, 1,030 employ less than 100 persons; Business ownership: 1,484 women-owned, n/a Black-owned, 54 Hispanic-owned, 36 Asian-owned, 34 American Indian/Alaska Native-owned

Employment: 10.4% management, business, and financial, 2.9% computer, engineering, and science, 9.1% education, legal, community service, arts, and media, 5.0% healthcare practitioners, 19.7% service, 22.2% sales and office, 12.9% natural resources, construction, and maintenance, 17.9% production, transportation, and material moving

Income: Per capita: $24,345; Median household: $51,143; Average household: $61,813; Households with income of $100,000 or more: 15.8%; Poverty rate: 13.5%

Educational Attainment: High school diploma or higher: 88.5%; Bachelor's degree or higher: 19.4%; Graduate/professional degree or higher: 7.7%

Housing: Homeownership rate: 72.3%; Median home value: $142,700; Median year structure built: 1960; Homeowner vacancy rate: 2.3%; Median selected monthly owner costs: $1,317 with a mortgage, $540 without a mortgage; Median gross rent: $803 per month; Rental vacancy rate: 2.4%

Vital Statistics: Birth rate: 95.0 per 10,000 population; Death rate: 100.9 per 10,000 population; Age-adjusted cancer mortality rate: 166.3 deaths per 100,000 population

Health Insurance: 91.1% have insurance; 68.5% have private insurance; 39.3% have public insurance; 8.9% do not have insurance; 5.5% of children under 18 do not have insurance

Health Care: Physicians: 5.4 per 10,000 population; Dentists: 2.2 per 10,000 population; Hospital beds: 0.0 per 10,000 population; Hospital admissions: 0.0 per 10,000 population

Transportation: Commute: 89.7% car, 0.9% public transportation, 3.1% walk, 5.3% work from home; Mean travel time to work: 25.5 minutes

2016 Presidential Election: 56.2% Trump, 37.6% Clinton, 3.8% Johnson, 2.4% Stein

National and State Parks: Carters Pond State Wildlife Management Area

Additional Information Contacts

Washington Government . . . . (518) 746-2210
  http://www.co.washington.ny.us

Washington County Communities

ARGYLE (town). Covers a land area of 56.536 square miles and a water area of 1.260 square miles. Located at 43.23° N. Lat; 73.48° W. Long. Elevation is 285 feet.

Population: 3,756; Growth (since 2000): 1.8%; Density: 66.4 persons per square mile; Race: 98.8% White, 0.6% Black/African American, 0.0% Asian, 0.0% American Indian/Alaska Native, 0.0% Native Hawaiian/Other Pacific Islander, 0.6% Two or more races, 0.0% Hispanic of any race; Average household size: 2.41; Median age: 47.0; Age under 18: 16.3%; Age 65 and over: 20.2%; Males per 100 females: 100.6; Marriage status: 25.1% never married, 62.7% now married, 0.2% separated, 7.6% widowed, 4.6% divorced; Foreign born: 1.5%; Speak English only: 98.9%; With disability: 11.3%; Veterans: 8.5%; Ancestry: 22.8% Irish, 13.7% German, 13.3% English, 13.3% American, 13.2% French

Employment: 11.7% management, business, and financial, 4.2% computer, engineering, and science, 9.6% education, legal, community service, arts, and media, 4.0% healthcare practitioners, 13.5% service, 21.5% sales and office, 15.9% natural resources, construction, and maintenance, 19.6% production, transportation, and material moving

Income: Per capita: $28,659; Median household: $60,823; Average household: $69,340; Households with income of $100,000 or more: 18.7%; Poverty rate: 11.0%

Educational Attainment: High school diploma or higher: 94.4%; Bachelor's degree or higher: 21.4%; Graduate/professional degree or higher: 8.9%

School District(s)

Argyle Central SD (KG-12)
  2014-15 Enrollment: 549 . . . . (518) 638-8243

Housing: Homeownership rate: 86.0%; Median home value: $154,900; Median year structure built: 1977; Homeowner vacancy rate: 1.8%; Median

selected monthly owner costs: $1,274 with a mortgage, $505 without a mortgage; Median gross rent: $800 per month; Rental vacancy rate: 0.0%
Health Insurance: 92.2% have insurance; 78.9% have private insurance; 30.4% have public insurance; 7.8% do not have insurance; 1.2% of children under 18 do not have insurance
Transportation: Commute: 88.2% car, 0.0% public transportation, 3.3% walk, 7.9% work from home; Mean travel time to work: 30.0 minutes

ARGYLE (village). Covers a land area of 0.350 square miles and a water area of 0 square miles. Located at 43.24° N. Lat; 73.49° W. Long. Elevation is 285 feet.
Population: 379; Growth (since 2000): 31.1%; Density: 1,083.1 persons per square mile; Race: 97.9% White, 0.8% Black/African American, 0.0% Asian, 0.0% American Indian/Alaska Native, 0.0% Native Hawaiian/Other Pacific Islander, 1.3% Two or more races, 0.0% Hispanic of any race; Average household size: 2.63; Median age: 35.0; Age under 18: 25.6%; Age 65 and over: 15.0%; Males per 100 females: 98.7; Marriage status: 30.4% never married, 56.2% now married, 0.3% separated, 6.0% widowed, 7.4% divorced; Foreign born: 1.1%; Speak English only: 99.2%; With disability: 8.4%; Veterans: 7.8%; Ancestry: 20.3% Irish, 19.3% German, 15.6% American, 13.5% English, 11.9% French
Employment: 7.6% management, business, and financial, 0.5% computer, engineering, and science, 13.0% education, legal, community service, arts, and media, 4.9% healthcare practitioners, 17.8% service, 16.8% sales and office, 17.8% natural resources, construction, and maintenance, 21.6% production, transportation, and material moving
Income: Per capita: $24,276; Median household: $53,500; Average household: $65,067; Households with income of $100,000 or more: 26.4%; Poverty rate: 6.1%
Educational Attainment: High school diploma or higher: 92.4%; Bachelor's degree or higher: 28.8%; Graduate/professional degree or higher: 14.8%
School District(s)
Argyle Central SD (KG-12)
 2014-15 Enrollment: 549. . . . . (518) 638-8243
Housing: Homeownership rate: 68.8%; Median home value: $114,800; Median year structure built: Before 1940; Homeowner vacancy rate: 1.0%; Median selected monthly owner costs: $1,184 with a mortgage, $559 without a mortgage; Median gross rent: $682 per month; Rental vacancy rate: 0.0%
Health Insurance: 85.2% have insurance; 61.7% have private insurance; 34.6% have public insurance; 14.8% do not have insurance; 7.2% of children under 18 do not have insurance
Transportation: Commute: 90.2% car, 0.0% public transportation, 4.4% walk, 3.8% work from home; Mean travel time to work: 22.7 minutes

CAMBRIDGE (town). Covers a land area of 36.357 square miles and a water area of 0.127 square miles. Located at 43.01° N. Lat; 73.45° W. Long. Elevation is 489 feet.
History: Cambridge Historical District within the village. Its weekly, *Washington County Post,* was founded in 1787. Settled c.1761, incorporated 1866.
Population: 1,959; Growth (since 2000): -9.0%; Density: 53.9 persons per square mile; Race: 98.0% White, 0.1% Black/African American, 0.7% Asian, 0.0% American Indian/Alaska Native, 0.0% Native Hawaiian/Other Pacific Islander, 1.2% Two or more races, 0.4% Hispanic of any race; Average household size: 2.45; Median age: 46.2; Age under 18: 23.7%; Age 65 and over: 19.6%; Males per 100 females: 108.4; Marriage status: 19.2% never married, 64.8% now married, 2.5% separated, 5.1% widowed, 10.8% divorced; Foreign born: 1.5%; Speak English only: 99.1%; With disability: 7.9%; Veterans: 8.2%; Ancestry: 18.4% German, 17.5% American, 17.4% English, 14.6% Irish, 8.0% French
Employment: 19.6% management, business, and financial, 3.5% computer, engineering, and science, 12.0% education, legal, community service, arts, and media, 4.6% healthcare practitioners, 14.2% service, 19.0% sales and office, 14.2% natural resources, construction, and maintenance, 12.9% production, transportation, and material moving
Income: Per capita: $32,114; Median household: $63,902; Average household: $77,037; Households with income of $100,000 or more: 27.1%; Poverty rate: 11.7%
Educational Attainment: High school diploma or higher: 96.7%; Bachelor's degree or higher: 38.8%; Graduate/professional degree or higher: 21.1%

School District(s)
Cambridge Central SD (PK-12)
 2014-15 Enrollment: 890. . . . . (518) 677-2653
Housing: Homeownership rate: 83.0%; Median home value: $216,700; Median year structure built: 1949; Homeowner vacancy rate: 1.8%; Median selected monthly owner costs: $1,743 with a mortgage, $691 without a mortgage; Median gross rent: $763 per month; Rental vacancy rate: 12.8%
Health Insurance: 95.9% have insurance; 81.1% have private insurance; 31.3% have public insurance; 4.1% do not have insurance; 0.0% of children under 18 do not have insurance
Newspapers: Cambridge Eagle (weekly circulation 4,400)
Transportation: Commute: 86.3% car, 0.0% public transportation, 3.7% walk, 9.0% work from home; Mean travel time to work: 30.2 minutes

CAMBRIDGE (village). Covers a land area of 1.678 square miles and a water area of 0 square miles. Located at 43.03° N. Lat; 73.38° W. Long. Elevation is 489 feet.
Population: 1,715; Growth (since 2000): -10.9%; Density: 1,022.3 persons per square mile; Race: 97.8% White, 0.1% Black/African American, 0.0% Asian, 0.0% American Indian/Alaska Native, 0.0% Native Hawaiian/Other Pacific Islander, 2.1% Two or more races, 0.9% Hispanic of any race; Average household size: 2.14; Median age: 42.7; Age under 18: 22.9%; Age 65 and over: 19.0%; Males per 100 females: 89.5; Marriage status: 22.7% never married, 50.3% now married, 1.2% separated, 11.9% widowed, 15.1% divorced; Foreign born: 0.9%; Speak English only: 99.6%; With disability: 13.0%; Veterans: 7.9%; Ancestry: 29.9% Irish, 19.1% German, 15.6% American, 14.0% Italian, 8.8% English
Employment: 11.4% management, business, and financial, 3.1% computer, engineering, and science, 12.0% education, legal, community service, arts, and media, 6.8% healthcare practitioners, 13.1% service, 16.6% sales and office, 10.7% natural resources, construction, and maintenance, 26.3% production, transportation, and material moving
Income: Per capita: $24,303; Median household: $43,750; Average household: $51,647; Households with income of $100,000 or more: 13.0%; Poverty rate: 16.1%
Educational Attainment: High school diploma or higher: 86.3%; Bachelor's degree or higher: 26.7%; Graduate/professional degree or higher: 12.6%
School District(s)
Cambridge Central SD (PK-12)
 2014-15 Enrollment: 890. . . . . (518) 677-2653
Housing: Homeownership rate: 60.8%; Median home value: $147,400; Median year structure built: 1943; Homeowner vacancy rate: 0.0%; Median selected monthly owner costs: $1,254 with a mortgage, $580 without a mortgage; Median gross rent: $806 per month; Rental vacancy rate: 6.0%
Health Insurance: 90.0% have insurance; 62.6% have private insurance; 45.0% have public insurance; 10.0% do not have insurance; 2.0% of children under 18 do not have insurance
Safety: Violent crime rate: 21.9 per 10,000 population; Property crime rate: 104.1 per 10,000 population
Newspapers: Cambridge Eagle (weekly circulation 4,400)
Transportation: Commute: 89.6% car, 0.0% public transportation, 5.5% walk, 2.9% work from home; Mean travel time to work: 28.6 minutes

CLEMONS (unincorporated postal area)
ZCTA: 12819
 Covers a land area of 28.976 square miles and a water area of 0.464 square miles. Located at 43.59° N. Lat; 73.47° W. Long. Elevation is 377 feet.
 Population: 309; Growth (since 2000): -15.1%; Density: 10.7 persons per square mile; Race: 97.4% White, 0.0% Black/African American, 1.3% Asian, 0.0% American Indian/Alaska Native, 0.0% Native Hawaiian/Other Pacific Islander, 1.3% Two or more races, 6.1% Hispanic of any race; Average household size: 2.16; Median age: 55.6; Age under 18: 15.9%; Age 65 and over: 27.2%; Males per 100 females: 97.5; Marriage status: 20.1% never married, 56.4% now married, 4.4% separated, 6.2% widowed, 17.2% divorced; Foreign born: 3.2%; Speak English only: 93.9%; With disability: 20.1%; Veterans: 13.5%; Ancestry: 15.2% American, 13.6% French, 10.7% English, 10.7% Irish, 6.8% German
 Employment: 4.1% management, business, and financial, 2.5% computer, engineering, and science, 3.3% education, legal, community service, arts, and media, 3.3% healthcare practitioners, 28.1% service, 23.1% sales and office, 15.7% natural resources, construction, and maintenance, 19.8% production, transportation, and material moving

Income: Per capita: $23,297; Median household: $43,839; Average household: $51,523; Households with income of $100,000 or more: 6.3%; Poverty rate: 13.7%

Educational Attainment: High school diploma or higher: 82.7%; Bachelor's degree or higher: 10.5%; Graduate/professional degree or higher: 4.8%

Housing: Homeownership rate: 81.8%; Median home value: $104,700; Median year structure built: 1971; Homeowner vacancy rate: 0.0%; Median selected monthly owner costs: $1,260 with a mortgage, $444 without a mortgage; Median gross rent: n/a per month; Rental vacancy rate: 0.0%

Health Insurance: 89.3% have insurance; 69.6% have private insurance; 43.7% have public insurance; 10.7% do not have insurance; 12.2% of children under 18 do not have insurance

Transportation: Commute: 87.8% car, 0.0% public transportation, 4.3% walk, 7.8% work from home; Mean travel time to work: 36.9 minutes

COMSTOCK (unincorporated postal area)
ZCTA: 12821

Covers a land area of 5.548 square miles and a water area of 0.061 square miles. Located at 43.45° N. Lat; 73.42° W. Long. Elevation is 128 feet.

Population: 2,816; Growth (since 2000): -12.5%; Density: 507.5 persons per square mile; Race: 37.8% White, 47.9% Black/African American, 1.2% Asian, 0.2% American Indian/Alaska Native, 0.0% Native Hawaiian/Other Pacific Islander, 6.6% Two or more races, 19.3% Hispanic of any race; Average household size: 2.28; Median age: 35.6; Age under 18: 3.5%; Age 65 and over: 4.4%; Males per 100 females: ***.*; Marriage status: 63.0% never married, 21.3% now married, 2.6% separated, 3.5% widowed, 12.3% divorced; Foreign born: 9.0%; Speak English only: 77.1%; With disability: 23.9%; Veterans: 3.5%; Ancestry: 15.6% American, 8.1% Italian, 7.1% Irish, 5.0% English, 2.7% German

Employment: 39.5% management, business, and financial, 0.0% computer, engineering, and science, 4.2% education, legal, community service, arts, and media, 0.0% healthcare practitioners, 15.1% service, 23.5% sales and office, 7.6% natural resources, construction, and maintenance, 10.1% production, transportation, and material moving

Income: Per capita: $3,450; Median household: $34,000; Average household: $43,622; Households with income of $100,000 or more: 9.6%; Poverty rate: n/a

Educational Attainment: High school diploma or higher: 72.0%; Bachelor's degree or higher: 5.6%; Graduate/professional degree or higher: 0.3%

Housing: Homeownership rate: 65.2%; Median home value: $126,700; Median year structure built: 1978; Homeowner vacancy rate: 0.0%; Median selected monthly owner costs: $0 with a mortgage, $375 without a mortgage; Median gross rent: $986 per month; Rental vacancy rate: 0.0%

Health Insurance: 87.4% have insurance; 55.7% have private insurance; 51.2% have public insurance; 12.6% do not have insurance; 0.0% of children under 18 do not have insurance

Transportation: Commute: 51.3% car, 0.0% public transportation, 21.0% walk, 18.5% work from home; Mean travel time to work: 15.6 minutes

COSSAYUNA (unincorporated postal area)
ZCTA: 12823

Covers a land area of 4.261 square miles and a water area of 0.081 square miles. Located at 43.18° N. Lat; 73.41° W. Long. Elevation is 479 feet.

Population: 369; Growth (since 2000): 94.2%; Density: 86.6 persons per square mile; Race: 100.0% White, 0.0% Black/African American, 0.0% Asian, 0.0% American Indian/Alaska Native, 0.0% Native Hawaiian/Other Pacific Islander, 0.0% Two or more races, 0.0% Hispanic of any race; Average household size: 2.44; Median age: 54.7; Age under 18: 13.6%; Age 65 and over: 17.1%; Males per 100 females: 100.0; Marriage status: 19.1% never married, 37.3% now married, 0.0% separated, 6.3% widowed, 37.3% divorced; Foreign born: 0.0%; Speak English only: 100.0%; With disability: 7.6%; Veterans: 17.6%; Ancestry: 60.7% American, 12.2% Irish, 9.2% Dutch, 7.9% French, 5.7% German

Employment: 12.8% management, business, and financial, 0.0% computer, engineering, and science, 0.0% education, legal, community service, arts, and media, 0.0% healthcare practitioners, 43.2% service, 0.0% sales and office, 32.4% natural resources, construction, and maintenance, 11.5% production, transportation, and material moving

Income: Per capita: $26,705; Median household: $82,639; Average household: $63,198; Households with income of $100,000 or more: 28.5%; Poverty rate: 22.2%

Educational Attainment: High school diploma or higher: 74.3%; Bachelor's degree or higher: 7.5%; Graduate/professional degree or higher: n/a

Housing: Homeownership rate: 89.4%; Median home value: n/a; Median year structure built: 1992; Homeowner vacancy rate: 0.0%; Median selected monthly owner costs: $1,627 with a mortgage, $0 without a mortgage; Median gross rent: n/a per month; Rental vacancy rate: 0.0%

Health Insurance: 90.8% have insurance; 77.8% have private insurance; 41.7% have public insurance; 9.2% do not have insurance; 0.0% of children under 18 do not have insurance

Transportation: Commute: 100.0% car, 0.0% public transportation, 0.0% walk, 0.0% work from home; Mean travel time to work: 0.0 minutes

DRESDEN (town). Covers a land area of 52.254 square miles and a water area of 2.745 square miles. Located at 43.59° N. Lat; 73.47° W. Long. Elevation is 138 feet.

Population: 548; Growth (since 2000): -19.1%; Density: 10.5 persons per square mile; Race: 95.6% White, 0.0% Black/African American, 0.7% Asian, 0.0% American Indian/Alaska Native, 0.0% Native Hawaiian/Other Pacific Islander, 3.6% Two or more races, 5.1% Hispanic of any race; Average household size: 2.19; Median age: 56.4; Age under 18: 16.2%; Age 65 and over: 26.3%; Males per 100 females: 95.2; Marriage status: 14.4% never married, 60.3% now married, 3.4% separated, 7.8% widowed, 17.5% divorced; Foreign born: 3.5%; Speak English only: 95.4%; With disability: 17.0%; Veterans: 14.8%; Ancestry: 15.5% French, 14.2% English, 13.9% Irish, 10.8% German, 9.7% Italian

Employment: 6.4% management, business, and financial, 1.5% computer, engineering, and science, 5.9% education, legal, community service, arts, and media, 5.4% healthcare practitioners, 23.5% service, 21.6% sales and office, 14.2% natural resources, construction, and maintenance, 21.6% production, transportation, and material moving

Income: Per capita: $26,233; Median household: $43,625; Average household: $61,143; Households with income of $100,000 or more: 8.0%; Poverty rate: 11.4%

Educational Attainment: High school diploma or higher: 87.7%; Bachelor's degree or higher: 20.6%; Graduate/professional degree or higher: 11.1%

Housing: Homeownership rate: 79.6%; Median home value: $163,000; Median year structure built: 1968; Homeowner vacancy rate: 0.0%; Median selected monthly owner costs: $1,232 with a mortgage, $631 without a mortgage; Median gross rent: n/a per month; Rental vacancy rate: 10.5%

Health Insurance: 91.6% have insurance; 67.0% have private insurance; 47.1% have public insurance; 8.4% do not have insurance; 6.7% of children under 18 do not have insurance

Transportation: Commute: 88.4% car, 0.0% public transportation, 2.5% walk, 6.1% work from home; Mean travel time to work: 30.6 minutes

EASTON (town). Covers a land area of 62.304 square miles and a water area of 0.934 square miles. Located at 43.03° N. Lat; 73.54° W. Long. Elevation is 436 feet.

Population: 2,329; Growth (since 2000): 3.1%; Density: 37.4 persons per square mile; Race: 98.9% White, 0.0% Black/African American, 0.3% Asian, 0.0% American Indian/Alaska Native, 0.0% Native Hawaiian/Other Pacific Islander, 0.8% Two or more races, 1.0% Hispanic of any race; Average household size: 2.43; Median age: 47.5; Age under 18: 22.5%; Age 65 and over: 19.7%; Males per 100 females: 103.1; Marriage status: 19.5% never married, 66.6% now married, 2.5% separated, 6.8% widowed, 7.1% divorced; Foreign born: 1.3%; Speak English only: 97.9%; With disability: 13.4%; Veterans: 9.0%; Ancestry: 23.1% Irish, 20.6% English, 12.2% American, 11.8% German, 9.4% Italian

Employment: 20.7% management, business, and financial, 5.1% computer, engineering, and science, 14.1% education, legal, community service, arts, and media, 4.2% healthcare practitioners, 14.4% service, 18.8% sales and office, 13.5% natural resources, construction, and maintenance, 9.2% production, transportation, and material moving

Income: Per capita: $34,623; Median household: $69,883; Average household: $84,737; Households with income of $100,000 or more: 30.4%; Poverty rate: 3.0%

Educational Attainment: High school diploma or higher: 92.4%; Bachelor's degree or higher: 36.9%; Graduate/professional degree or higher: 15.6%

Housing: Homeownership rate: 85.2%; Median home value: $214,400; Median year structure built: 1956; Homeowner vacancy rate: 0.0%; Median selected monthly owner costs: $1,599 with a mortgage, $618 without a mortgage; Median gross rent: $900 per month; Rental vacancy rate: 0.0%
Health Insurance: 95.8% have insurance; 86.6% have private insurance; 26.8% have public insurance; 4.2% do not have insurance; 0.6% of children under 18 do not have insurance
Transportation: Commute: 88.0% car, 0.0% public transportation, 3.9% walk, 7.6% work from home; Mean travel time to work: 27.2 minutes

FORT ANN (town).
Covers a land area of 108.999 square miles and a water area of 1.780 square miles. Located at 43.46° N. Lat; 73.53° W. Long. Elevation is 157 feet.
Population: 6,172; Growth (since 2000): -3.8%; Density: 56.6 persons per square mile; Race: 69.7% White, 22.9% Black/African American, 0.7% Asian, 0.1% American Indian/Alaska Native, 0.0% Native Hawaiian/Other Pacific Islander, 3.7% Two or more races, 9.4% Hispanic of any race; Average household size: 2.51; Median age: 40.3; Age under 18: 12.1%; Age 65 and over: 11.9%; Males per 100 females: 237.1; Marriage status: 42.9% never married, 40.0% now married, 1.9% separated, 5.2% widowed, 11.8% divorced; Foreign born: 5.2%; Speak English only: 86.9%; With disability: 15.9%; Veterans: 6.3%; Ancestry: 16.4% American, 11.4% English, 11.3% Irish, 8.9% Italian, 8.2% French
Employment: 11.9% management, business, and financial, 1.0% computer, engineering, and science, 12.8% education, legal, community service, arts, and media, 4.0% healthcare practitioners, 19.7% service, 19.6% sales and office, 15.4% natural resources, construction, and maintenance, 15.6% production, transportation, and material moving
Income: Per capita: $16,715; Median household: $58,033; Average household: $67,592; Households with income of $100,000 or more: 16.3%; Poverty rate: 6.3%
Educational Attainment: High school diploma or higher: 81.2%; Bachelor's degree or higher: 12.0%; Graduate/professional degree or higher: 4.7%

School District(s)
Fort Ann Central SD (PK-12)
  2014-15 Enrollment: 484 . . . . (518) 639-5594
Housing: Homeownership rate: 82.7%; Median home value: $151,000; Median year structure built: 1974; Homeowner vacancy rate: 4.6%; Median selected monthly owner costs: $1,329 with a mortgage, $544 without a mortgage; Median gross rent: $949 per month; Rental vacancy rate: 2.3%
Health Insurance: 93.2% have insurance; 73.8% have private insurance; 36.7% have public insurance; 6.8% do not have insurance; 5.8% of children under 18 do not have insurance
Transportation: Commute: 92.7% car, 0.0% public transportation, 3.3% walk, 2.3% work from home; Mean travel time to work: 24.1 minutes
Additional Information Contacts
Town of Fort Ann. . . . . (518) 639-8929
  http://www.fortann.us

FORT ANN (village).
Covers a land area of 0.293 square miles and a water area of 0.015 square miles. Located at 43.42° N. Lat; 73.49° W. Long. Elevation is 157 feet.
Population: 545; Growth (since 2000): 15.7%; Density: 1,862.7 persons per square mile; Race: 93.4% White, 0.6% Black/African American, 0.4% Asian, 0.0% American Indian/Alaska Native, 0.0% Native Hawaiian/Other Pacific Islander, 5.7% Two or more races, 5.1% Hispanic of any race; Average household size: 2.58; Median age: 35.7; Age under 18: 27.0%; Age 65 and over: 11.4%; Males per 100 females: 96.0; Marriage status: 28.7% never married, 57.1% now married, 2.8% separated, 5.6% widowed, 8.6% divorced; Foreign born: 0.9%; Speak English only: 95.5%; With disability: 10.6%; Veterans: 9.5%; Ancestry: 29.5% Irish, 18.7% American, 15.8% French, 10.5% German, 8.6% English
Employment: 6.0% management, business, and financial, 0.7% computer, engineering, and science, 12.5% education, legal, community service, arts, and media, 6.4% healthcare practitioners, 18.9% service, 14.6% sales and office, 14.9% natural resources, construction, and maintenance, 26.0% production, transportation, and material moving
Income: Per capita: $25,108; Median household: $68,482; Average household: $67,245; Households with income of $100,000 or more: 18.5%; Poverty rate: 8.1%
Educational Attainment: High school diploma or higher: 93.6%; Bachelor's degree or higher: 12.8%; Graduate/professional degree or higher: 7.2%

School District(s)
Fort Ann Central SD (PK-12)
  2014-15 Enrollment: 484 . . . . (518) 639-5594
Housing: Homeownership rate: 66.8%; Median home value: $119,300; Median year structure built: Before 1940; Homeowner vacancy rate: 4.1%; Median selected monthly owner costs: $1,400 with a mortgage, $537 without a mortgage; Median gross rent: $791 per month; Rental vacancy rate: 7.9%
Health Insurance: 85.9% have insurance; 70.1% have private insurance; 26.1% have public insurance; 14.1% do not have insurance; 23.8% of children under 18 do not have insurance
Transportation: Commute: 92.0% car, 0.0% public transportation, 6.5% walk, 0.8% work from home; Mean travel time to work: 24.5 minutes

FORT EDWARD (town).
Covers a land area of 26.630 square miles and a water area of 0.796 square miles. Located at 43.23° N. Lat; 73.56° W. Long. Elevation is 138 feet.
History: Fort built here in 1755 to protect portage between the Hudson River and Lake Champlain; it was occupied by Burgoyne in 1777. Incorporated 1849.
Population: 6,241; Growth (since 2000): 5.9%; Density: 234.4 persons per square mile; Race: 95.9% White, 3.2% Black/African American, 0.0% Asian, 0.0% American Indian/Alaska Native, 0.0% Native Hawaiian/Other Pacific Islander, 0.8% Two or more races, 1.8% Hispanic of any race; Average household size: 2.56; Median age: 41.8; Age under 18: 20.0%; Age 65 and over: 16.9%; Males per 100 females: 98.9; Marriage status: 37.3% never married, 44.0% now married, 4.2% separated, 5.4% widowed, 13.3% divorced; Foreign born: 0.8%; Speak English only: 98.4%; With disability: 21.9%; Veterans: 11.1%; Ancestry: 25.5% Irish, 16.6% English, 16.1% French, 13.9% Italian, 13.7% German
Employment: 4.0% management, business, and financial, 2.7% computer, engineering, and science, 8.8% education, legal, community service, arts, and media, 8.8% healthcare practitioners, 16.1% service, 28.1% sales and office, 14.1% natural resources, construction, and maintenance, 17.4% production, transportation, and material moving
Income: Per capita: $23,421; Median household: $49,164; Average household: $60,568; Households with income of $100,000 or more: 8.5%; Poverty rate: 12.2%
Educational Attainment: High school diploma or higher: 88.4%; Bachelor's degree or higher: 15.0%; Graduate/professional degree or higher: 2.8%

School District(s)
Fort Edward Union Free SD (PK-12)
  2014-15 Enrollment: 571 . . . . (518) 747-4594
Washington-Saratoga-Warren-Hamilton-Essex Boces
  2014-15 Enrollment: n/a . . . . (518) 746-3310
Housing: Homeownership rate: 64.0%; Median home value: $102,600; Median year structure built: 1944; Homeowner vacancy rate: 0.0%; Median selected monthly owner costs: $1,236 with a mortgage, $503 without a mortgage; Median gross rent: $833 per month; Rental vacancy rate: 5.7%
Health Insurance: 95.8% have insurance; 63.0% have private insurance; 49.7% have public insurance; 4.2% do not have insurance; 1.8% of children under 18 do not have insurance
Transportation: Commute: 90.2% car, 0.7% public transportation, 2.1% walk, 5.2% work from home; Mean travel time to work: 21.5 minutes; Amtrak: Train service available.
Additional Information Contacts
Town of Fort Edward . . . . (518) 747-4023
  http://www.fortedward.net

FORT EDWARD (village).
Covers a land area of 1.756 square miles and a water area of 0.180 square miles. Located at 43.27° N. Lat; 73.58° W. Long. Elevation is 138 feet.
Population: 3,318; Growth (since 2000): 5.6%; Density: 1,889.2 persons per square mile; Race: 99.3% White, 0.0% Black/African American, 0.0% Asian, 0.0% American Indian/Alaska Native, 0.0% Native Hawaiian/Other Pacific Islander, 0.7% Two or more races, 2.0% Hispanic of any race; Average household size: 2.39; Median age: 40.2; Age under 18: 21.6%; Age 65 and over: 13.4%; Males per 100 females: 95.3; Marriage status: 38.1% never married, 46.5% now married, 3.9% separated, 3.0% widowed, 12.4% divorced; Foreign born: 0.4%; Speak English only: 98.9%; With disability: 20.0%; Veterans: 13.5%; Ancestry: 20.3% French, 19.2% Irish, 18.4% Italian, 18.1% English, 17.1% German
Employment: 2.9% management, business, and financial, 2.0% computer, engineering, and science, 8.9% education, legal, community service, arts,

and media, 7.4% healthcare practitioners, 21.2% service, 21.6% sales and office, 15.1% natural resources, construction, and maintenance, 21.0% production, transportation, and material moving
Income: Per capita: $22,633; Median household: $48,827; Average household: $53,777; Households with income of $100,000 or more: 4.8%; Poverty rate: 15.0%
Educational Attainment: High school diploma or higher: 89.1%; Bachelor's degree or higher: 14.6%; Graduate/professional degree or higher: 2.1%

School District(s)
Fort Edward Union Free SD (PK-12)
   2014-15 Enrollment: 571 . . . . (518) 747-4594
Washington-Saratoga-Warren-Hamilton-Essex Boces
   2014-15 Enrollment: n/a . . . . (518) 746-3310
Housing: Homeownership rate: 64.7%; Median home value: $95,700; Median year structure built: Before 1940; Homeowner vacancy rate: 0.0%; Median selected monthly owner costs: $1,220 with a mortgage, $507 without a mortgage; Median gross rent: $763 per month; Rental vacancy rate: 9.3%
Health Insurance: 95.4% have insurance; 70.0% have private insurance; 44.2% have public insurance; 4.6% do not have insurance; 3.2% of children under 18 do not have insurance
Safety: Violent crime rate: 30.7 per 10,000 population; Property crime rate: 15.3 per 10,000 population
Transportation: Commute: 93.5% car, 1.2% public transportation, 2.4% walk, 0.7% work from home; Mean travel time to work: 22.3 minutes; Amtrak: Train service available.

GRANVILLE (town). Covers a land area of 55.618 square miles and a water area of 0.500 square miles. Located at 43.42° N. Lat; 73.31° W. Long. Elevation is 410 feet.
History: Granville, on the eastern border of Washington County, New York, contains a village of the same name. Granville is named for John Carteret, 2nd Earl Granvilleand has been called the "Colored Slate Capital of the World" for the various colored slate mined in its quaries, including green, gray, gray black, purple, mottled green and purple, and red.
Population: 6,556; Growth (since 2000): 1.5%; Density: 117.9 persons per square mile; Race: 96.9% White, 0.9% Black/African American, 0.7% Asian, 0.3% American Indian/Alaska Native, 0.0% Native Hawaiian/Other Pacific Islander, 0.7% Two or more races, 1.5% Hispanic of any race; Average household size: 2.52; Median age: 45.3; Age under 18: 20.8%; Age 65 and over: 18.6%; Males per 100 females: 97.6; Marriage status: 29.9% never married, 46.1% now married, 3.2% separated, 6.6% widowed, 17.4% divorced; Foreign born: 3.4%; Speak English only: 97.4%; With disability: 13.2%; Veterans: 14.6%; Ancestry: 25.2% American, 14.8% Irish, 12.1% German, 10.3% English, 9.5% French
Employment: 9.9% management, business, and financial, 3.2% computer, engineering, and science, 5.2% education, legal, community service, arts, and media, 4.7% healthcare practitioners, 21.3% service, 24.6% sales and office, 10.9% natural resources, construction, and maintenance, 20.2% production, transportation, and material moving
Income: Per capita: $22,034; Median household: $44,200; Average household: $55,027; Households with income of $100,000 or more: 13.7%; Poverty rate: 16.1%
Educational Attainment: High school diploma or higher: 86.1%; Bachelor's degree or higher: 14.0%; Graduate/professional degree or higher: 5.7%

School District(s)
Granville Central SD (PK-12)
   2014-15 Enrollment: 1,144 . . . . (518) 642-1051
Housing: Homeownership rate: 66.5%; Median home value: $117,600; Median year structure built: 1955; Homeowner vacancy rate: 1.6%; Median selected monthly owner costs: $1,370 with a mortgage, $562 without a mortgage; Median gross rent: $682 per month; Rental vacancy rate: 3.3%
Health Insurance: 88.7% have insurance; 64.9% have private insurance; 40.2% have public insurance; 11.3% do not have insurance; 7.2% of children under 18 do not have insurance
Newspapers: Manchester Newspapers (weekly circulation 51,000); Northshire Free Press (weekly circulation 8,000)
Transportation: Commute: 90.1% car, 0.2% public transportation, 4.8% walk, 5.0% work from home; Mean travel time to work: 26.8 minutes
Additional Information Contacts
Town of Granville . . . . (518) 642-2640
   http://granvillevillage.com

GRANVILLE (village). Covers a land area of 1.570 square miles and a water area of <.001 square miles. Located at 43.41° N. Lat; 73.27° W. Long. Elevation is 410 feet.
Population: 2,321; Growth (since 2000): -12.2%; Density: 1,477.9 persons per square mile; Race: 95.9% White, 0.1% Black/African American, 1.3% Asian, 0.8% American Indian/Alaska Native, 0.0% Native Hawaiian/Other Pacific Islander, 1.6% Two or more races, 2.5% Hispanic of any race; Average household size: 2.20; Median age: 46.3; Age under 18: 21.8%; Age 65 and over: 22.0%; Males per 100 females: 85.9; Marriage status: 24.3% never married, 49.0% now married, 7.2% separated, 9.5% widowed, 17.1% divorced; Foreign born: 3.7%; Speak English only: 97.4%; With disability: 13.3%; Veterans: 11.7%; Ancestry: 20.8% Irish, 14.8% American, 12.0% German, 11.2% French, 10.3% Italian
Employment: 7.7% management, business, and financial, 6.6% computer, engineering, and science, 14.4% education, legal, community service, arts, and media, 7.4% healthcare practitioners, 20.9% service, 21.3% sales and office, 7.9% natural resources, construction, and maintenance, 13.6% production, transportation, and material moving
Income: Per capita: $21,901; Median household: $38,194; Average household: $47,517; Households with income of $100,000 or more: 11.6%; Poverty rate: 18.8%
Educational Attainment: High school diploma or higher: 85.3%; Bachelor's degree or higher: 17.9%; Graduate/professional degree or higher: 8.0%

School District(s)
Granville Central SD (PK-12)
   2014-15 Enrollment: 1,144 . . . . (518) 642-1051
Housing: Homeownership rate: 55.6%; Median home value: $110,800; Median year structure built: Before 1940; Homeowner vacancy rate: 4.6%; Median selected monthly owner costs: $1,334 with a mortgage, $569 without a mortgage; Median gross rent: $589 per month; Rental vacancy rate: 5.8%
Health Insurance: 93.2% have insurance; 66.4% have private insurance; 41.6% have public insurance; 6.8% do not have insurance; 1.6% of children under 18 do not have insurance
Safety: Violent crime rate: 24.5 per 10,000 population; Property crime rate: 106.0 per 10,000 population
Newspapers: Manchester Newspapers (weekly circulation 51,000); Northshire Free Press (weekly circulation 8,000)
Transportation: Commute: 81.3% car, 0.5% public transportation, 13.0% walk, 5.2% work from home; Mean travel time to work: 27.5 minutes

GREENWICH (town). Covers a land area of 43.663 square miles and a water area of 0.598 square miles. Located at 43.15° N. Lat; 73.48° W. Long. Elevation is 374 feet.
History: Incorporated 1809.
Population: 4,911; Growth (since 2000): 0.3%; Density: 112.5 persons per square mile; Race: 96.8% White, 0.1% Black/African American, 1.9% Asian, 1.1% American Indian/Alaska Native, 0.0% Native Hawaiian/Other Pacific Islander, 0.1% Two or more races, 1.1% Hispanic of any race; Average household size: 2.52; Median age: 43.8; Age under 18: 20.4%; Age 65 and over: 15.1%; Males per 100 females: 97.3; Marriage status: 25.1% never married, 56.2% now married, 1.6% separated, 6.5% widowed, 12.2% divorced; Foreign born: 3.2%; Speak English only: 96.9%; With disability: 9.3%; Veterans: 12.7%; Ancestry: 23.9% Irish, 14.7% French, 12.7% American, 12.6% Italian, 12.5% English
Employment: 8.6% management, business, and financial, 5.8% computer, engineering, and science, 11.3% education, legal, community service, arts, and media, 5.8% healthcare practitioners, 18.1% service, 18.5% sales and office, 12.3% natural resources, construction, and maintenance, 19.6% production, transportation, and material moving
Income: Per capita: $27,787; Median household: $54,694; Average household: $69,400; Households with income of $100,000 or more: 27.7%; Poverty rate: 7.6%
Educational Attainment: High school diploma or higher: 90.6%; Bachelor's degree or higher: 25.7%; Graduate/professional degree or higher: 12.6%

School District(s)
Greenwich Central SD (KG-12)
   2014-15 Enrollment: 1,038 . . . . (518) 692-9542
Housing: Homeownership rate: 73.9%; Median home value: $158,000; Median year structure built: 1955; Homeowner vacancy rate: 3.1%; Median selected monthly owner costs: $1,610 with a mortgage, $599 without a mortgage; Median gross rent: $731 per month; Rental vacancy rate: 0.0%

Health Insurance: 89.4% have insurance; 71.8% have private insurance; 33.4% have public insurance; 10.6% do not have insurance; 5.9% of children under 18 do not have insurance
Newspapers: Greenwich Journal & Salem Press (weekly circulation 1,800)
Transportation: Commute: 90.6% car, 0.7% public transportation, 2.8% walk, 4.9% work from home; Mean travel time to work: 28.3 minutes
Additional Information Contacts
Town of Greenwich . . . . (518) 692-7611
    http://www.greenwichny.org

GREENWICH (village). Covers a land area of 1.477 square miles and a water area of 0 square miles. Located at 43.09° N. Lat; 73.50° W. Long. Elevation is 374 feet.
Population: 1,885; Growth (since 2000): -0.9%; Density: 1,276.3 persons per square mile; Race: 97.6% White, 0.1% Black/African American, 0.5% Asian, 0.6% American Indian/Alaska Native, 0.0% Native Hawaiian/Other Pacific Islander, 1.2% Two or more races, 2.8% Hispanic of any race; Average household size: 2.44; Median age: 40.9; Age under 18: 24.0%; Age 65 and over: 13.7%; Males per 100 females: 93.6; Marriage status: 27.3% never married, 57.0% now married, 3.6% separated, 6.3% widowed, 9.3% divorced; Foreign born: 3.0%; Speak English only: 94.7%; With disability: 10.1%; Veterans: 11.4%; Ancestry: 33.3% Irish, 15.6% German, 14.7% English, 8.4% American, 7.9% Italian
Employment: 8.6% management, business, and financial, 3.6% computer, engineering, and science, 14.4% education, legal, community service, arts, and media, 5.0% healthcare practitioners, 18.1% service, 23.8% sales and office, 10.6% natural resources, construction, and maintenance, 16.0% production, transportation, and material moving
Income: Per capita: $27,865; Median household: $46,146; Average household: $67,475; Households with income of $100,000 or more: 22.8%; Poverty rate: 11.5%
Educational Attainment: High school diploma or higher: 93.6%; Bachelor's degree or higher: 29.6%; Graduate/professional degree or higher: 14.3%
School District(s)
Greenwich Central SD (KG-12)
    2014-15 Enrollment: 1,038 . . . . (518) 692-9542
Housing: Homeownership rate: 54.4%; Median home value: $151,100; Median year structure built: Before 1940; Homeowner vacancy rate: 0.0%; Median selected monthly owner costs: $1,613 with a mortgage, $736 without a mortgage; Median gross rent: $719 per month; Rental vacancy rate: 0.0%
Health Insurance: 90.0% have insurance; 73.4% have private insurance; 27.8% have public insurance; 10.0% do not have insurance; 3.5% of children under 18 do not have insurance
Safety: Violent crime rate: 0.0 per 10,000 population; Property crime rate: 74.7 per 10,000 population
Newspapers: Greenwich Journal & Salem Press (weekly circulation 1,800)
Transportation: Commute: 83.4% car, 0.0% public transportation, 7.3% walk, 6.4% work from home; Mean travel time to work: 26.6 minutes

HAMPTON (town). Covers a land area of 22.242 square miles and a water area of 0.348 square miles. Located at 43.55° N. Lat; 73.29° W. Long. Elevation is 427 feet.
Population: 863; Growth (since 2000): -0.9%; Density: 38.8 persons per square mile; Race: 98.0% White, 1.6% Black/African American, 0.0% Asian, 0.0% American Indian/Alaska Native, 0.0% Native Hawaiian/Other Pacific Islander, 0.1% Two or more races, 1.6% Hispanic of any race; Average household size: 2.42; Median age: 44.3; Age under 18: 21.3%; Age 65 and over: 16.3%; Males per 100 females: 103.0; Marriage status: 23.4% never married, 57.5% now married, 2.5% separated, 6.0% widowed, 13.0% divorced; Foreign born: 2.1%; Speak English only: 96.2%; With disability: 13.0%; Veterans: 10.9%; Ancestry: 22.7% American, 19.8% Irish, 18.4% French, 11.2% English, 8.8% Italian
Employment: 11.3% management, business, and financial, 2.4% computer, engineering, and science, 8.2% education, legal, community service, arts, and media, 2.4% healthcare practitioners, 15.4% service, 24.5% sales and office, 12.3% natural resources, construction, and maintenance, 23.6% production, transportation, and material moving
Income: Per capita: $25,532; Median household: $48,750; Average household: $61,490; Households with income of $100,000 or more: 19.3%; Poverty rate: 8.6%

Educational Attainment: High school diploma or higher: 86.0%; Bachelor's degree or higher: 14.7%; Graduate/professional degree or higher: 4.9%
Housing: Homeownership rate: 81.3%; Median home value: $135,500; Median year structure built: 1981; Homeowner vacancy rate: 2.7%; Median selected monthly owner costs: $1,304 with a mortgage, $463 without a mortgage; Median gross rent: $832 per month; Rental vacancy rate: 0.0%
Health Insurance: 94.6% have insurance; 75.9% have private insurance; 33.1% have public insurance; 5.4% do not have insurance; 2.7% of children under 18 do not have insurance
Transportation: Commute: 93.5% car, 0.2% public transportation, 0.0% walk, 5.6% work from home; Mean travel time to work: 28.8 minutes

HARTFORD (town). Covers a land area of 43.384 square miles and a water area of 0.105 square miles. Located at 43.36° N. Lat; 73.41° W. Long. Elevation is 390 feet.
Population: 2,341; Growth (since 2000): 2.7%; Density: 54.0 persons per square mile; Race: 98.0% White, 0.1% Black/African American, 0.3% Asian, 0.2% American Indian/Alaska Native, 0.0% Native Hawaiian/Other Pacific Islander, 1.4% Two or more races, 3.8% Hispanic of any race; Average household size: 2.56; Median age: 44.1; Age under 18: 19.3%; Age 65 and over: 12.9%; Males per 100 females: 101.9; Marriage status: 26.3% never married, 62.3% now married, 1.0% separated, 4.4% widowed, 7.0% divorced; Foreign born: 1.9%; Speak English only: 97.6%; With disability: 11.1%; Veterans: 7.7%; Ancestry: 29.5% American, 15.3% Irish, 12.5% French, 9.1% English, 7.0% Italian
Employment: 9.7% management, business, and financial, 3.8% computer, engineering, and science, 10.9% education, legal, community service, arts, and media, 3.4% healthcare practitioners, 19.7% service, 17.6% sales and office, 16.8% natural resources, construction, and maintenance, 18.1% production, transportation, and material moving
Income: Per capita: $26,717; Median household: $58,641; Average household: $67,310; Households with income of $100,000 or more: 20.7%; Poverty rate: 6.7%
Educational Attainment: High school diploma or higher: 87.2%; Bachelor's degree or higher: 18.6%; Graduate/professional degree or higher: 6.6%
School District(s)
Hartford Central SD (PK-12)
    2014-15 Enrollment: 487 . . . . (518) 632-5931
Housing: Homeownership rate: 85.9%; Median home value: $143,500; Median year structure built: 1981; Homeowner vacancy rate: 0.0%; Median selected monthly owner costs: $1,389 with a mortgage, $539 without a mortgage; Median gross rent: $815 per month; Rental vacancy rate: 0.0%
Health Insurance: 89.4% have insurance; 73.7% have private insurance; 28.4% have public insurance; 10.6% do not have insurance; 15.3% of children under 18 do not have insurance
Transportation: Commute: 95.2% car, 0.3% public transportation, 0.4% walk, 3.4% work from home; Mean travel time to work: 24.3 minutes

HEBRON (town). Covers a land area of 56.108 square miles and a water area of 0.310 square miles. Located at 43.26° N. Lat; 73.35° W. Long.
Population: 1,769; Growth (since 2000): -0.2%; Density: 31.5 persons per square mile; Race: 94.2% White, 2.1% Black/African American, 0.5% Asian, 0.5% American Indian/Alaska Native, 0.0% Native Hawaiian/Other Pacific Islander, 2.3% Two or more races, 2.1% Hispanic of any race; Average household size: 2.28; Median age: 47.0; Age under 18: 17.1%; Age 65 and over: 13.1%; Males per 100 females: 104.1; Marriage status: 30.0% never married, 52.9% now married, 0.9% separated, 5.0% widowed, 12.1% divorced; Foreign born: 1.1%; Speak English only: 96.4%; With disability: 12.2%; Veterans: 10.0%; Ancestry: 17.5% American, 12.7% Irish, 10.2% French, 9.5% English, 8.5% German
Employment: 13.3% management, business, and financial, 1.7% computer, engineering, and science, 9.2% education, legal, community service, arts, and media, 5.7% healthcare practitioners, 14.3% service, 20.8% sales and office, 20.5% natural resources, construction, and maintenance, 14.5% production, transportation, and material moving
Income: Per capita: $25,046; Median household: $50,524; Average household: $57,157; Households with income of $100,000 or more: 12.3%; Poverty rate: 21.2%
Educational Attainment: High school diploma or higher: 85.9%; Bachelor's degree or higher: 22.3%; Graduate/professional degree or higher: 9.9%

Housing: Homeownership rate: 85.0%; Median home value: $137,700; Median year structure built: 1983; Homeowner vacancy rate: 5.8%; Median selected monthly owner costs: $1,288 with a mortgage, $487 without a mortgage; Median gross rent: $695 per month; Rental vacancy rate: 6.5%
Health Insurance: 87.8% have insurance; 54.8% have private insurance; 43.2% have public insurance; 12.2% do not have insurance; 2.3% of children under 18 do not have insurance
Transportation: Commute: 87.8% car, 0.4% public transportation, 6.0% walk, 3.8% work from home; Mean travel time to work: 32.0 minutes

HUDSON FALLS (village). County seat. Covers a land area of 1.832 square miles and a water area of 0.058 square miles. Located at 43.30° N. Lat; 73.58° W. Long. Elevation is 295 feet.
History: Settlers arrived in Hudson Falls in the 1760's and built gristmills and sawmills on the river near the 70-foot falls. The Burgoyne campaign delayed development and then the settlement was burned in 1780 by Sir Guy Carleton. In the 19th century, pulpwood, floated down the Hudson River from the Adirondack forests, helped to establish paper manufacturing as the dominant industry.
Population: 7,239; Growth (since 2000): 4.5%; Density: 3,951.6 persons per square mile; Race: 96.4% White, 1.1% Black/African American, 0.0% Asian, 0.0% American Indian/Alaska Native, 0.0% Native Hawaiian/Other Pacific Islander, 2.1% Two or more races, 1.4% Hispanic of any race; Average household size: 2.54; Median age: 36.0; Age under 18: 23.9%; Age 65 and over: 14.2%; Males per 100 females: 92.3; Marriage status: 36.2% never married, 42.9% now married, 2.6% separated, 6.5% widowed, 14.3% divorced; Foreign born: 1.2%; Speak English only: 99.1%; With disability: 16.5%; Veterans: 10.8%; Ancestry: 24.3% Irish, 18.1% American, 16.2% Italian, 13.3% French, 12.7% English
Employment: 6.8% management, business, and financial, 1.0% computer, engineering, and science, 7.2% education, legal, community service, arts, and media, 4.7% healthcare practitioners, 31.7% service, 23.3% sales and office, 8.5% natural resources, construction, and maintenance, 16.8% production, transportation, and material moving
Income: Per capita: $19,618; Median household: $42,392; Average household: $49,697; Households with income of $100,000 or more: 9.1%; Poverty rate: 24.9%
Educational Attainment: High school diploma or higher: 85.7%; Bachelor's degree or higher: 12.6%; Graduate/professional degree or higher: 4.6%

School District(s)
Hudson Falls Central SD (PK-12)
    2014-15 Enrollment: 2,403 . . . . (518) 747-2121
Vocational/Technical School(s)
Washington Saratoga Warren Hamilton Essex BOCES-Practical Nursing Program (Public)
    Fall 2014 Enrollment: 30 . . . . (518) 746-3508
    2015-16 Tuition: $11,484
Housing: Homeownership rate: 54.1%; Median home value: $128,800; Median year structure built: Before 1940; Homeowner vacancy rate: 6.7%; Median selected monthly owner costs: $1,164 with a mortgage, $463 without a mortgage; Median gross rent: $742 per month; Rental vacancy rate: 0.0%
Health Insurance: 87.8% have insurance; 57.7% have private insurance; 44.5% have public insurance; 12.2% do not have insurance; 6.9% of children under 18 do not have insurance
Safety: Violent crime rate: 29.1 per 10,000 population; Property crime rate: 124.9 per 10,000 population
Transportation: Commute: 86.8% car, 4.5% public transportation, 0.7% walk, 5.0% work from home; Mean travel time to work: 23.3 minutes
Additional Information Contacts
Village of Hudson Falls . . . . (518) 747-5426
    http://www.villageofhudsonfalls.com

HULETTS LANDING (unincorporated postal area)
ZCTA: 12841
    Covers a land area of 16.967 square miles and a water area of 0.041 square miles. Located at 43.61° N. Lat; 73.53° W. Long. Elevation is 371 feet.
    Population: 100; Growth (since 2000): 14.9%; Density: 5.9 persons per square mile; Race: 100.0% White, 0.0% Black/African American, 0.0% Asian, 0.0% American Indian/Alaska Native, 0.0% Native Hawaiian/Other Pacific Islander, 0.0% Two or more races, 0.0% Hispanic of any race; Average household size: 1.61; Median age: 68.2; Age under 18: 0.0%; Age 65 and over: 51.0%; Males per 100 females:

87.8; Marriage status: 0.0% never married, 63.0% now married, 0.0% separated, 17.0% widowed, 20.0% divorced; Foreign born: 9.0%; Speak English only: 94.0%; With disability: 14.0%; Veterans: 16.0%; Ancestry: 36.0% English, 27.0% French, 19.0% German, 11.0% Scottish, 11.0% Swedish
    Employment: 10.7% management, business, and financial, 0.0% computer, engineering, and science, 28.6% education, legal, community service, arts, and media, 0.0% healthcare practitioners, 0.0% service, 46.4% sales and office, 14.3% natural resources, construction, and maintenance, 0.0% production, transportation, and material moving
    Income: Per capita: $42,708; Median household: $27,500; Average household: $81,187; Households with income of $100,000 or more: 9.7%; Poverty rate: n/a
    Educational Attainment: High school diploma or higher: 100.0%; Bachelor's degree or higher: 57.0%; Graduate/professional degree or higher: 32.0%
    Housing: Homeownership rate: 85.5%; Median home value: $334,600; Median year structure built: 1959; Homeowner vacancy rate: 0.0%; Median selected monthly owner costs: $1,563 with a mortgage, $975 without a mortgage; Median gross rent: n/a per month; Rental vacancy rate: 0.0%
    Health Insurance: 94.0% have insurance; 61.0% have private insurance; 58.0% have public insurance; 6.0% do not have insurance; 0.0% of children under 18 do not have insurance
    Transportation: Commute: 78.6% car, 0.0% public transportation, 0.0% walk, 0.0% work from home; Mean travel time to work: 13.8 minutes

JACKSON (town). Covers a land area of 37.160 square miles and a water area of 0.406 square miles. Located at 43.08° N. Lat; 73.38° W. Long.
Population: 1,822; Growth (since 2000): 6.1%; Density: 49.0 persons per square mile; Race: 98.1% White, 0.5% Black/African American, 0.3% Asian, 0.0% American Indian/Alaska Native, 0.0% Native Hawaiian/Other Pacific Islander, 0.7% Two or more races, 1.8% Hispanic of any race; Average household size: 2.17; Median age: 50.1; Age under 18: 17.3%; Age 65 and over: 25.8%; Males per 100 females: 104.8; Marriage status: 22.3% never married, 53.9% now married, 4.3% separated, 6.8% widowed, 17.0% divorced; Foreign born: 1.4%; Speak English only: 97.6%; With disability: 16.0%; Veterans: 14.7%; Ancestry: 20.0% Irish, 18.4% German, 12.3% Polish, 12.2% American, 10.8% English
Employment: 14.7% management, business, and financial, 3.7% computer, engineering, and science, 12.0% education, legal, community service, arts, and media, 5.6% healthcare practitioners, 12.4% service, 20.3% sales and office, 13.1% natural resources, construction, and maintenance, 18.1% production, transportation, and material moving
Income: Per capita: $27,918; Median household: $50,449; Average household: $60,620; Households with income of $100,000 or more: 15.9%; Poverty rate: 9.3%
Educational Attainment: High school diploma or higher: 89.7%; Bachelor's degree or higher: 26.5%; Graduate/professional degree or higher: 8.9%
Housing: Homeownership rate: 76.6%; Median home value: $169,200; Median year structure built: 1967; Homeowner vacancy rate: 0.0%; Median selected monthly owner costs: $1,545 with a mortgage, $604 without a mortgage; Median gross rent: $818 per month; Rental vacancy rate: 0.0%
Health Insurance: 93.4% have insurance; 74.3% have private insurance; 43.4% have public insurance; 6.6% do not have insurance; 2.9% of children under 18 do not have insurance
Transportation: Commute: 91.0% car, 0.0% public transportation, 2.3% walk, 4.5% work from home; Mean travel time to work: 32.3 minutes

KINGSBURY (town). Covers a land area of 39.678 square miles and a water area of 0.327 square miles. Located at 43.34° N. Lat; 73.55° W. Long. Elevation is 305 feet.
Population: 12,667; Growth (since 2000): 13.4%; Density: 319.2 persons per square mile; Race: 95.0% White, 1.7% Black/African American, 0.0% Asian, 0.0% American Indian/Alaska Native, 0.0% Native Hawaiian/Other Pacific Islander, 2.3% Two or more races, 2.7% Hispanic of any race; Average household size: 2.55; Median age: 37.7; Age under 18: 22.7%; Age 65 and over: 14.1%; Males per 100 females: 96.4; Marriage status: 33.0% never married, 48.2% now married, 2.5% separated, 7.2% widowed, 11.5% divorced; Foreign born: 2.0%; Speak English only: 97.8%; With disability: 14.6%; Veterans: 11.3%; Ancestry: 26.2% Irish, 16.7% American, 14.7% Italian, 12.0% English, 10.9% French

Employment: 8.9% management, business, and financial, 2.0% computer, engineering, and science, 6.9% education, legal, community service, arts, and media, 3.8% healthcare practitioners, 25.7% service, 26.4% sales and office, 9.8% natural resources, construction, and maintenance, 16.4% production, transportation, and material moving
Income: Per capita: $22,361; Median household: $44,834; Average household: $56,363; Households with income of $100,000 or more: 12.6%; Poverty rate: 18.5%
Educational Attainment: High school diploma or higher: 88.0%; Bachelor's degree or higher: 16.1%; Graduate/professional degree or higher: 6.1%
Housing: Homeownership rate: 58.5%; Median home value: $139,100; Median year structure built: 1956; Homeowner vacancy rate: 3.7%; Median selected monthly owner costs: $1,252 with a mortgage, $463 without a mortgage; Median gross rent: $836 per month; Rental vacancy rate: 2.1%
Health Insurance: 88.9% have insurance; 63.8% have private insurance; 40.5% have public insurance; 11.1% do not have insurance; 7.5% of children under 18 do not have insurance
Transportation: Commute: 90.2% car, 2.7% public transportation, 0.6% walk, 5.0% work from home; Mean travel time to work: 22.1 minutes

MIDDLE GRANVILLE (unincorporated postal area)
ZCTA: 12849

Covers a land area of 2.719 square miles and a water area of 0.011 square miles. Located at 43.45° N. Lat; 73.30° W. Long. Elevation is 371 feet.

Population: 623; Growth (since 2000): 40.0%; Density: 229.1 persons per square mile; Race: 100.0% White, 0.0% Black/African American, 0.0% Asian, 0.0% American Indian/Alaska Native, 0.0% Native Hawaiian/Other Pacific Islander, 0.0% Two or more races, 0.0% Hispanic of any race; Average household size: 3.35; Median age: 37.8; Age under 18: 17.5%; Age 65 and over: 4.8%; Males per 100 females: 94.4; Marriage status: 35.3% never married, 52.5% now married, 0.0% separated, 0.0% widowed, 12.2% divorced; Foreign born: 0.0%; Speak English only: 100.0%; With disability: 2.9%; Veterans: 20.0%; Ancestry: 54.9% American, 19.1% French, 16.7% Welsh, 10.0% Irish, 9.0% German
Employment: 28.0% management, business, and financial, 0.0% computer, engineering, and science, 0.0% education, legal, community service, arts, and media, 0.0% healthcare practitioners, 22.6% service, 10.7% sales and office, 6.6% natural resources, construction, and maintenance, 32.1% production, transportation, and material moving
Income: Per capita: $23,449; Median household: $70,263; Average household: $79,731; Households with income of $100,000 or more: 22.5%; Poverty rate: 9.1%
Educational Attainment: High school diploma or higher: 92.2%; Bachelor's degree or higher: 4.6%; Graduate/professional degree or higher: n/a

School District(s)
Granville Central SD (PK-12)
   2014-15 Enrollment: 1,144 . . . . (518) 642-1051
Housing: Homeownership rate: 100.0%; Median home value: $120,200; Median year structure built: 1978; Homeowner vacancy rate: 0.0%; Median selected monthly owner costs: $1,546 with a mortgage, $0 without a mortgage; Median gross rent: n/a per month; Rental vacancy rate: 0.0%
Health Insurance: 95.3% have insurance; 78.5% have private insurance; 19.6% have public insurance; 4.7% do not have insurance; 0.0% of children under 18 do not have insurance
Transportation: Commute: 92.9% car, 0.0% public transportation, 0.0% walk, 7.1% work from home; Mean travel time to work: 26.1 minutes

PUTNAM (town). Covers a land area of 32.791 square miles and a water area of 2.627 square miles. Located at 43.75° N. Lat; 73.42° W. Long. Elevation is 335 feet.
Population: 742; Growth (since 2000): 15.0%; Density: 22.6 persons per square mile; Race: 100.0% White, 0.0% Black/African American, 0.0% Asian, 0.0% American Indian/Alaska Native, 0.0% Native Hawaiian/Other Pacific Islander, 0.0% Two or more races, 0.5% Hispanic of any race; Average household size: 2.31; Median age: 51.0; Age under 18: 22.5%; Age 65 and over: 23.5%; Males per 100 females: 100.3; Marriage status: 19.5% never married, 65.2% now married, 2.4% separated, 5.2% widowed, 10.1% divorced; Foreign born: 3.1%; Speak English only: 99.3%; With disability: 14.6%; Veterans: 9.1%; Ancestry: 20.1% French, 18.9% Irish, 18.5% American, 11.9% German, 11.7% English

Employment: 19.1% management, business, and financial, 1.0% computer, engineering, and science, 15.0% education, legal, community service, arts, and media, 0.7% healthcare practitioners, 18.1% service, 15.4% sales and office, 19.5% natural resources, construction, and maintenance, 11.3% production, transportation, and material moving
Income: Per capita: $38,021; Median household: $63,125; Average household: $84,011; Households with income of $100,000 or more: 25.9%; Poverty rate: 8.4%
Educational Attainment: High school diploma or higher: 90.7%; Bachelor's degree or higher: 26.8%; Graduate/professional degree or higher: 12.0%
Housing: Homeownership rate: 86.0%; Median home value: $160,800; Median year structure built: 1964; Homeowner vacancy rate: 12.1%; Median selected monthly owner costs: $1,080 with a mortgage, $533 without a mortgage; Median gross rent: $907 per month; Rental vacancy rate: 0.0%
Health Insurance: 91.6% have insurance; 73.0% have private insurance; 36.3% have public insurance; 8.4% do not have insurance; 5.4% of children under 18 do not have insurance
Transportation: Commute: 92.5% car, 0.0% public transportation, 0.0% walk, 6.8% work from home; Mean travel time to work: 29.8 minutes

PUTNAM STATION (unincorporated postal area)
ZCTA: 12861

Covers a land area of 32.791 square miles and a water area of 0.566 square miles. Located at 43.75° N. Lat; 73.42° W. Long. Elevation is 118 feet.

Population: 742; Growth (since 2000): 15.0%; Density: 22.6 persons per square mile; Race: 100.0% White, 0.0% Black/African American, 0.0% Asian, 0.0% American Indian/Alaska Native, 0.0% Native Hawaiian/Other Pacific Islander, 0.0% Two or more races, 0.5% Hispanic of any race; Average household size: 2.31; Median age: 51.0; Age under 18: 22.5%; Age 65 and over: 23.5%; Males per 100 females: 100.3; Marriage status: 19.5% never married, 65.2% now married, 2.4% separated, 5.2% widowed, 10.1% divorced; Foreign born: 3.1%; Speak English only: 99.3%; With disability: 14.6%; Veterans: 9.1%; Ancestry: 20.1% French, 18.9% Irish, 18.5% American, 11.9% German, 11.7% English
Employment: 19.1% management, business, and financial, 1.0% computer, engineering, and science, 15.0% education, legal, community service, arts, and media, 0.7% healthcare practitioners, 18.1% service, 15.4% sales and office, 19.5% natural resources, construction, and maintenance, 11.3% production, transportation, and material moving
Income: Per capita: $38,021; Median household: $63,125; Average household: $84,011; Households with income of $100,000 or more: 25.9%; Poverty rate: 8.4%
Educational Attainment: High school diploma or higher: 90.7%; Bachelor's degree or higher: 26.8%; Graduate/professional degree or higher: 12.0%

School District(s)
Putnam Central SD (PK-06)
   2014-15 Enrollment: 30 . . . . (518) 547-8266
Housing: Homeownership rate: 86.0%; Median home value: $160,800; Median year structure built: 1964; Homeowner vacancy rate: 12.1%; Median selected monthly owner costs: $1,080 with a mortgage, $533 without a mortgage; Median gross rent: $907 per month; Rental vacancy rate: 0.0%
Health Insurance: 91.6% have insurance; 73.0% have private insurance; 36.3% have public insurance; 8.4% do not have insurance; 5.4% of children under 18 do not have insurance
Transportation: Commute: 92.5% car, 0.0% public transportation, 0.0% walk, 6.8% work from home; Mean travel time to work: 29.8 minutes

SALEM (town). Covers a land area of 52.362 square miles and a water area of 0.058 square miles. Located at 43.16° N. Lat; 73.32° W. Long. Elevation is 482 feet.
History: Settled 1764, incorporated 1803.
Population: 2,694; Growth (since 2000): -0.3%; Density: 51.4 persons per square mile; Race: 98.4% White, 0.4% Black/African American, 0.4% Asian, 0.0% American Indian/Alaska Native, 0.0% Native Hawaiian/Other Pacific Islander, 0.7% Two or more races, 3.7% Hispanic of any race; Average household size: 2.35; Median age: 46.2; Age under 18: 21.7%; Age 65 and over: 18.4%; Males per 100 females: 100.4; Marriage status: 27.4% never married, 55.5% now married, 0.8% separated, 6.9% widowed, 10.3% divorced; Foreign born: 5.2%; Speak English only: 96.1%;

With disability: 11.7%; Veterans: 9.1%; Ancestry: 17.7% German, 17.7% Irish, 17.3% American, 12.7% English, 8.4% Italian
Employment: 11.5% management, business, and financial, 1.3% computer, engineering, and science, 12.0% education, legal, community service, arts, and media, 7.5% healthcare practitioners, 14.4% service, 21.6% sales and office, 15.4% natural resources, construction, and maintenance, 16.2% production, transportation, and material moving
Income: Per capita: $26,023; Median household: $54,286; Average household: $61,312; Households with income of $100,000 or more: 12.4%; Poverty rate: 13.1%
Educational Attainment: High school diploma or higher: 94.2%; Bachelor's degree or higher: 32.5%; Graduate/professional degree or higher: 12.4%

School District(s)
Salem Central SD (KG-12)
  2014-15 Enrollment: 509. . . . . (518) 854-7855
Housing: Homeownership rate: 84.0%; Median home value: $150,500; Median year structure built: 1951; Homeowner vacancy rate: 2.6%; Median selected monthly owner costs: $1,167 with a mortgage, $552 without a mortgage; Median gross rent: $802 per month; Rental vacancy rate: 0.0%
Health Insurance: 90.3% have insurance; 70.9% have private insurance; 36.6% have public insurance; 9.7% do not have insurance; 9.7% of children under 18 do not have insurance
Transportation: Commute: 84.7% car, 0.6% public transportation, 4.1% walk, 9.9% work from home; Mean travel time to work: 26.5 minutes

SALEM (village).
Covers a land area of 2.928 square miles and a water area of 0 square miles. Located at 43.17° N. Lat; 73.33° W. Long. Elevation is 482 feet.
Population: 698; Growth (since 2000): -27.6%; Density: 238.3 persons per square mile; Race: 98.9% White, 0.4% Black/African American, 0.0% Asian, 0.0% American Indian/Alaska Native, 0.0% Native Hawaiian/Other Pacific Islander, 0.7% Two or more races, 4.4% Hispanic of any race; Average household size: 2.12; Median age: 48.4; Age under 18: 20.6%; Age 65 and over: 23.5%; Males per 100 females: 93.1; Marriage status: 30.6% never married, 48.3% now married, 1.0% separated, 9.3% widowed, 11.9% divorced; Foreign born: 3.7%; Speak English only: 95.1%; With disability: 14.5%; Veterans: 9.6%; Ancestry: 23.5% Irish, 21.5% German, 11.9% American, 11.6% English, 11.2% Italian
Employment: 8.7% management, business, and financial, 2.4% computer, engineering, and science, 14.9% education, legal, community service, arts, and media, 7.8% healthcare practitioners, 18.5% service, 26.9% sales and office, 6.6% natural resources, construction, and maintenance, 14.3% production, transportation, and material moving
Income: Per capita: $26,803; Median household: $47,083; Average household: $57,283; Households with income of $100,000 or more: 8.8%; Poverty rate: 8.2%
Educational Attainment: High school diploma or higher: 91.3%; Bachelor's degree or higher: 28.7%; Graduate/professional degree or higher: 15.0%

School District(s)
Salem Central SD (KG-12)
  2014-15 Enrollment: 509. . . . . (518) 854-7855
Housing: Homeownership rate: 74.8%; Median home value: $116,700; Median year structure built: Before 1940; Homeowner vacancy rate: 5.0%; Median selected monthly owner costs: $1,239 with a mortgage, $643 without a mortgage; Median gross rent: $661 per month; Rental vacancy rate: 0.0%
Health Insurance: 89.5% have insurance; 70.8% have private insurance; 44.4% have public insurance; 10.5% do not have insurance; 9.7% of children under 18 do not have insurance
Transportation: Commute: 89.3% car, 0.0% public transportation, 6.4% walk, 4.3% work from home; Mean travel time to work: 28.7 minutes

SHUSHAN (unincorporated postal area)
ZCTA: 12873
  Covers a land area of 21.118 square miles and a water area of <.001 square miles. Located at 43.12° N. Lat; 73.31° W. Long. Elevation is 469 feet.
Population: 695; Growth (since 2000): -14.0%; Density: 32.9 persons per square mile; Race: 100.0% White, 0.0% Black/African American, 0.0% Asian, 0.0% American Indian/Alaska Native, 0.0% Native Hawaiian/Other Pacific Islander, 0.0% Two or more races, 0.0% Hispanic of any race; Average household size: 2.18; Median age: 50.6; Age under 18: 15.4%; Age 65 and over: 21.2%; Males per 100 females:

100.5; Marriage status: 30.0% never married, 53.2% now married, 0.6% separated, 4.2% widowed, 12.6% divorced; Foreign born: 1.6%; Speak English only: 97.5%; With disability: 11.8%; Veterans: 10.0%; Ancestry: 18.0% English, 17.1% Italian, 16.1% Irish, 13.5% American, 10.1% German
Employment: 14.1% management, business, and financial, 3.0% computer, engineering, and science, 9.4% education, legal, community service, arts, and media, 7.5% healthcare practitioners, 10.5% service, 19.9% sales and office, 21.5% natural resources, construction, and maintenance, 14.1% production, transportation, and material moving
Income: Per capita: $28,567; Median household: $48,750; Average household: $61,433; Households with income of $100,000 or more: 12.5%; Poverty rate: 9.8%
Educational Attainment: High school diploma or higher: 95.4%; Bachelor's degree or higher: 43.2%; Graduate/professional degree or higher: 17.0%
Housing: Homeownership rate: 96.5%; Median home value: $163,100; Median year structure built: 1951; Homeowner vacancy rate: 0.0%; Median selected monthly owner costs: $1,167 with a mortgage, $472 without a mortgage; Median gross rent: n/a per month; Rental vacancy rate: 0.0%
Health Insurance: 88.5% have insurance; 73.1% have private insurance; 36.0% have public insurance; 11.5% do not have insurance; 25.2% of children under 18 do not have insurance
Transportation: Commute: 79.7% car, 1.8% public transportation, 0.0% walk, 17.3% work from home; Mean travel time to work: 29.2 minutes

WHITE CREEK (town).
Covers a land area of 47.923 square miles and a water area of 0.053 square miles. Located at 42.99° N. Lat; 73.32° W. Long. Elevation is 656 feet.
Population: 3,319; Growth (since 2000): -2.7%; Density: 69.3 persons per square mile; Race: 96.6% White, 0.0% Black/African American, 1.7% Asian, 0.0% American Indian/Alaska Native, 0.0% Native Hawaiian/Other Pacific Islander, 1.7% Two or more races, 0.5% Hispanic of any race; Average household size: 2.19; Median age: 44.4; Age under 18: 20.6%; Age 65 and over: 21.6%; Males per 100 females: 93.5; Marriage status: 22.7% never married, 55.7% now married, 3.4% separated, 7.2% widowed, 14.4% divorced; Foreign born: 1.6%; Speak English only: 99.0%; With disability: 16.8%; Veterans: 10.0%; Ancestry: 25.7% Irish, 20.4% American, 12.8% German, 10.9% English, 10.0% Italian
Employment: 12.5% management, business, and financial, 2.5% computer, engineering, and science, 10.2% education, legal, community service, arts, and media, 7.3% healthcare practitioners, 14.6% service, 14.1% sales and office, 11.7% natural resources, construction, and maintenance, 27.1% production, transportation, and material moving
Income: Per capita: $24,337; Median household: $43,918; Average household: $53,802; Households with income of $100,000 or more: 12.2%; Poverty rate: 11.4%
Educational Attainment: High school diploma or higher: 88.1%; Bachelor's degree or higher: 21.4%; Graduate/professional degree or higher: 10.4%
Housing: Homeownership rate: 78.5%; Median home value: $149,400; Median year structure built: 1969; Homeowner vacancy rate: 0.0%; Median selected monthly owner costs: $1,185 with a mortgage, $607 without a mortgage; Median gross rent: $812 per month; Rental vacancy rate: 0.0%
Health Insurance: 93.3% have insurance; 70.6% have private insurance; 43.8% have public insurance; 6.7% do not have insurance; 2.0% of children under 18 do not have insurance
Transportation: Commute: 86.4% car, 0.0% public transportation, 8.2% walk, 5.0% work from home; Mean travel time to work: 26.1 minutes

WHITEHALL (town).
Covers a land area of 57.176 square miles and a water area of 1.729 square miles. Located at 43.54° N. Lat; 73.39° W. Long. Elevation is 157 feet.
History: Settled 1759, incorporated 1806.
Population: 4,011; Growth (since 2000): -0.6%; Density: 70.2 persons per square mile; Race: 96.6% White, 1.1% Black/African American, 0.0% Asian, 1.4% American Indian/Alaska Native, 0.0% Native Hawaiian/Other Pacific Islander, 0.3% Two or more races, 0.7% Hispanic of any race; Average household size: 2.41; Median age: 37.4; Age under 18: 23.4%; Age 65 and over: 15.1%; Males per 100 females: 103.9; Marriage status: 31.3% never married, 51.4% now married, 2.7% separated, 7.1% widowed, 10.2% divorced; Foreign born: 0.5%; Speak English only: 98.1%; With disability: 16.9%; Veterans: 8.6%; Ancestry: 24.4% American, 17.8% Irish, 15.2% French, 9.6% Italian, 8.3% English

Employment: 6.9% management, business, and financial, 1.7% computer, engineering, and science, 6.0% education, legal, community service, arts, and media, 4.1% healthcare practitioners, 30.9% service, 18.9% sales and office, 10.5% natural resources, construction, and maintenance, 21.0% production, transportation, and material moving

Income: Per capita: $22,073; Median household: $41,454; Average household: $52,169; Households with income of $100,000 or more: 10.3%; Poverty rate: 24.9%

Educational Attainment: High school diploma or higher: 88.5%; Bachelor's degree or higher: 11.5%; Graduate/professional degree or higher: 2.3%

School District(s)
Whitehall Central SD (PK-12)
    2014-15 Enrollment: 799 . . . . (518) 499-1772

Housing: Homeownership rate: 63.3%; Median home value: $90,700; Median year structure built: Before 1940; Homeowner vacancy rate: 2.6%; Median selected monthly owner costs: $1,177 with a mortgage, $526 without a mortgage; Median gross rent: $799 per month; Rental vacancy rate: 0.0%

Health Insurance: 89.0% have insurance; 56.6% have private insurance; 49.3% have public insurance; 11.0% do not have insurance; 7.0% of children under 18 do not have insurance

Transportation: Commute: 88.8% car, 0.9% public transportation, 7.3% walk, 2.7% work from home; Mean travel time to work: 23.1 minutes; Amtrak: Train service available.

Additional Information Contacts
Town of Whitehall . . . . (518) 499-1535
    http://www.whitehallny.info/Town.html

WHITEHALL (village). Covers a land area of 4.703 square miles and a water area of 0.212 square miles. Located at 43.56° N. Lat; 73.42° W. Long. Elevation is 157 feet.

Population: 2,769; Growth (since 2000): 3.8%; Density: 588.8 persons per square mile; Race: 96.7% White, 1.6% Black/African American, 0.0% Asian, 0.5% American Indian/Alaska Native, 0.0% Native Hawaiian/Other Pacific Islander, 0.4% Two or more races, 1.1% Hispanic of any race; Average household size: 2.41; Median age: 34.4; Age under 18: 26.0%; Age 65 and over: 12.7%; Males per 100 females: 104.1; Marriage status: 34.7% never married, 44.1% now married, 4.0% separated, 7.9% widowed, 13.2% divorced; Foreign born: 0.8%; Speak English only: 98.9%; With disability: 16.6%; Veterans: 8.8%; Ancestry: 27.9% American, 18.2% Irish, 16.2% French, 10.6% Italian, 7.0% English

Employment: 7.9% management, business, and financial, 2.7% computer, engineering, and science, 9.3% education, legal, community service, arts, and media, 4.9% healthcare practitioners, 30.8% service, 16.4% sales and office, 7.8% natural resources, construction, and maintenance, 20.2% production, transportation, and material moving

Income: Per capita: $19,738; Median household: $37,931; Average household: $47,502; Households with income of $100,000 or more: 7.6%; Poverty rate: 30.1%

Educational Attainment: High school diploma or higher: 85.5%; Bachelor's degree or higher: 12.9%; Graduate/professional degree or higher: 2.6%

School District(s)
Whitehall Central SD (PK-12)
    2014-15 Enrollment: 799 . . . . (518) 499-1772

Housing: Homeownership rate: 51.0%; Median home value: $81,400; Median year structure built: Before 1940; Homeowner vacancy rate: 4.6%; Median selected monthly owner costs: $1,130 with a mortgage, $550 without a mortgage; Median gross rent: $829 per month; Rental vacancy rate: 0.0%

Health Insurance: 87.4% have insurance; 47.7% have private insurance; 53.9% have public insurance; 12.6% do not have insurance; 5.0% of children under 18 do not have insurance

Safety: Violent crime rate: 38.8 per 10,000 population; Property crime rate: 69.9 per 10,000 population

Transportation: Commute: 92.6% car, 1.3% public transportation, 2.5% walk, 3.0% work from home; Mean travel time to work: 24.3 minutes; Amtrak: Train service available.

Wayne County

Located in western New York; bounded on the north by Lake Ontario; drained by the Clyde River. Covers a land area of 603.826 square miles, a water area of 779.225 square miles, and is located in the Eastern Time

Zone at 43.46° N. Lat., 77.06° W. Long. The county was founded in 1823. County seat is Lyons.

Wayne County is part of the Rochester, NY Metropolitan Statistical Area. The entire metro area includes: Livingston County, NY; Monroe County, NY; Ontario County, NY; Orleans County, NY; Wayne County, NY; Yates County, NY

Weather Station: Sodus Center									Elevation: 419 feet			
	Jan	Feb	Mar	Apr	May	Jun	Jul	Aug	Sep	Oct	Nov	Dec
High	33	35	44	57	69	78	81	80	73	60	49	37
Low	18	19	26	37	46	55	61	60	53	42	34	24
Precip	2.7	2.1	2.7	3.1	3.2	3.5	3.3	3.3	3.7	4.0	4.0	3.2
Snow	29.7	16.3	12.9	2.8	0.1	0.0	0.0	0.0	0.0	0.1	7.1	23.7

High and Low temperatures in degrees Fahrenheit; Precipitation and Snow in inches

Population: 92,416; Growth (since 2000): -1.4%; Density: 153.1 persons per square mile; Race: 93.1% White, 3.4% Black/African American, 0.6% Asian, 0.2% American Indian/Alaska Native, 0.1% Native Hawaiian/Other Pacific Islander, 1.6% two or more races, 4.0% Hispanic of any race; Average household size: 2.48; Median age: 43.1; Age under 18: 22.5%; Age 65 and over: 16.0%; Males per 100 females: 98.5; Marriage status: 27.8% never married, 55.1% now married, 2.4% separated, 6.5% widowed, 10.6% divorced; Foreign born: 2.8%; Speak English only: 95.7%; With disability: 14.0%; Veterans: 9.1%; Ancestry: 22.4% German, 16.2% Irish, 14.8% English, 14.0% Italian, 12.5% Dutch

Religion: Six largest groups: 16.4% Catholicism, 5.2% Methodist/Pietist, 3.1% Presbyterian-Reformed, 2.4% Baptist, 2.1% Non-denominational Protestant, 1.3% Holiness

Economy: Unemployment rate: 4.6%; Leading industries: 15.2 % construction; 15.2 % retail trade; 11.5 % other services (except public administration); Farms: 873 totaling 179,109 acres; Company size: 0 employ 1,000 or more persons, 4 employ 500 to 999 persons, 30 employ 100 to 499 persons, 1,686 employ less than 100 persons; Business ownership: 1,837 women-owned, 50 Black-owned, 170 Hispanic-owned, 132 Asian-owned, 37 American Indian/Alaska Native-owned

Employment: 11.9% management, business, and financial, 4.9% computer, engineering, and science, 10.2% education, legal, community service, arts, and media, 6.0% healthcare practitioners, 16.8% service, 21.7% sales and office, 11.5% natural resources, construction, and maintenance, 17.0% production, transportation, and material moving

Income: Per capita: $25,609; Median household: $50,798; Average household: $63,372; Households with income of $100,000 or more: 17.5%; Poverty rate: 12.7%

Educational Attainment: High school diploma or higher: 89.6%; Bachelor's degree or higher: 20.6%; Graduate/professional degree or higher: 8.3%

Housing: Homeownership rate: 77.6%; Median home value: $112,900; Median year structure built: 1964; Homeowner vacancy rate: 1.7%; Median selected monthly owner costs: $1,234 with a mortgage, $518 without a mortgage; Median gross rent: $694 per month; Rental vacancy rate: 5.8%

Vital Statistics: Birth rate: 108.7 per 10,000 population; Death rate: 88.4 per 10,000 population; Age-adjusted cancer mortality rate: 191.4 deaths per 100,000 population

Health Insurance: 91.7% have insurance; 71.0% have private insurance; 34.7% have public insurance; 8.3% do not have insurance; 6.2% of children under 18 do not have insurance

Health Care: Physicians: 7.0 per 10,000 population; Dentists: 4.5 per 10,000 population; Hospital beds: 30.3 per 10,000 population; Hospital admissions: 561.3 per 10,000 population

Air Quality Index (AQI): Percent of Days: 98.4% good, 1.6% moderate, 0.0% unhealthy for sensitive individuals, 0.0% unhealthy, 0.0% very unhealthy; Annual median: 31; Annual maximum: 77

Transportation: Commute: 92.4% car, 0.7% public transportation, 2.2% walk, 3.4% work from home; Mean travel time to work: 24.5 minutes

2016 Presidential Election: 59.4% Trump, 34.3% Clinton, 4.9% Johnson, 1.4% Stein

Additional Information Contacts
Wayne Government . . . . (315) 946-5400
    http://www.co.wayne.ny.us

Wayne County Communities

ARCADIA (town). Covers a land area of 52.033 square miles and a water area of 0.111 square miles. Located at 43.10° N. Lat; 77.08° W. Long.

Population: 13,978; Growth (since 2000): -6.1%; Density: 268.6 persons per square mile; Race: 88.3% White, 6.6% Black/African American, 0.7% Asian, 0.2% American Indian/Alaska Native, 0.1% Native Hawaiian/Other Pacific Islander, 2.4% Two or more races, 6.0% Hispanic of any race; Average household size: 2.30; Median age: 45.1; Age under 18: 20.0%; Age 65 and over: 17.4%; Males per 100 females: 93.6; Marriage status: 32.7% never married, 46.8% now married, 2.7% separated, 7.6% widowed, 12.8% divorced; Foreign born: 2.8%; Speak English only: 95.3%; With disability: 19.9%; Veterans: 9.5%; Ancestry: 17.9% German, 15.9% Dutch, 15.0% Irish, 14.7% English, 13.1% Italian

Employment: 10.8% management, business, and financial, 2.3% computer, engineering, and science, 8.1% education, legal, community service, arts, and media, 7.7% healthcare practitioners, 20.1% service, 21.9% sales and office, 9.5% natural resources, construction, and maintenance, 19.7% production, transportation, and material moving

Income: Per capita: $22,158; Median household: $38,168; Average household: $50,097; Households with income of $100,000 or more: 10.9%; Poverty rate: 19.1%

Educational Attainment: High school diploma or higher: 88.2%; Bachelor's degree or higher: 15.5%; Graduate/professional degree or higher: 6.7%

Housing: Homeownership rate: 65.9%; Median home value: $92,500; Median year structure built: 1954; Homeowner vacancy rate: 1.4%; Median selected monthly owner costs: $1,136 with a mortgage, $498 without a mortgage; Median gross rent: $657 per month; Rental vacancy rate: 3.9%

Health Insurance: 93.1% have insurance; 63.0% have private insurance; 45.4% have public insurance; 6.9% do not have insurance; 2.3% of children under 18 do not have insurance

Transportation: Commute: 90.0% car, 1.8% public transportation, 4.7% walk, 3.1% work from home; Mean travel time to work: 19.5 minutes

Additional Information Contacts

Town of Arcadia . . . . (315) 331-1222

BUTLER (town). Covers a land area of 37.090 square miles and a water area of 0.079 square miles. Located at 43.18° N. Lat; 76.77° W. Long.

Population: 1,839; Growth (since 2000): -19.2%; Density: 49.6 persons per square mile; Race: 97.5% White, 1.1% Black/African American, 0.0% Asian, 0.0% American Indian/Alaska Native, 0.0% Native Hawaiian/Other Pacific Islander, 1.4% Two or more races, 3.7% Hispanic of any race; Average household size: 2.44; Median age: 44.3; Age under 18: 21.5%; Age 65 and over: 18.0%; Males per 100 females: 108.9; Marriage status: 27.0% never married, 56.9% now married, 3.3% separated, 6.1% widowed, 10.0% divorced; Foreign born: 2.0%; Speak English only: 97.2%; With disability: 17.4%; Veterans: 9.3%; Ancestry: 23.2% German, 16.2% English, 14.4% Irish, 10.0% American, 8.9% Dutch

Employment: 9.4% management, business, and financial, 2.7% computer, engineering, and science, 5.7% education, legal, community service, arts, and media, 3.9% healthcare practitioners, 10.8% service, 19.2% sales and office, 19.6% natural resources, construction, and maintenance, 28.7% production, transportation, and material moving

Income: Per capita: $20,015; Median household: $40,238; Average household: $49,421; Households with income of $100,000 or more: 10.3%; Poverty rate: 15.2%

Educational Attainment: High school diploma or higher: 82.3%; Bachelor's degree or higher: 6.8%; Graduate/professional degree or higher: 3.4%

Housing: Homeownership rate: 80.9%; Median home value: $88,700; Median year structure built: 1972; Homeowner vacancy rate: 0.0%; Median selected monthly owner costs: $1,034 with a mortgage, $426 without a mortgage; Median gross rent: $498 per month; Rental vacancy rate: 0.0%

Health Insurance: 84.8% have insurance; 57.9% have private insurance; 41.6% have public insurance; 15.2% do not have insurance; 14.2% of children under 18 do not have insurance

Transportation: Commute: 87.6% car, 0.0% public transportation, 7.4% walk, 2.6% work from home; Mean travel time to work: 30.0 minutes

CLYDE (village). Covers a land area of 2.198 square miles and a water area of 0.059 square miles. Located at 43.08° N. Lat; 76.87° W. Long. Elevation is 400 feet.

History: Incorporated 1835.

Population: 2,012; Growth (since 2000): -11.3%; Density: 915.3 persons per square mile; Race: 93.1% White, 4.0% Black/African American, 0.7% Asian, 0.7% American Indian/Alaska Native, 0.0% Native Hawaiian/Other Pacific Islander, 1.4% Two or more races, 6.9% Hispanic of any race; Average household size: 2.97; Median age: 33.3; Age under 18: 33.3%; Age 65 and over: 13.8%; Males per 100 females: 94.7; Marriage status: 31.9% never married, 50.5% now married, 4.4% separated, 6.1% widowed, 11.5% divorced; Foreign born: 2.2%; Speak English only: 94.4%; With disability: 16.5%; Veterans: 9.1%; Ancestry: 23.2% Italian, 20.2% German, 13.8% Irish, 12.5% English, 7.6% Dutch

Employment: 7.0% management, business, and financial, 5.1% computer, engineering, and science, 12.8% education, legal, community service, arts, and media, 6.1% healthcare practitioners, 18.2% service, 21.5% sales and office, 9.8% natural resources, construction, and maintenance, 19.6% production, transportation, and material moving

Income: Per capita: $19,001; Median household: $43,400; Average household: $55,268; Households with income of $100,000 or more: 14.2%; Poverty rate: 19.1%

Educational Attainment: High school diploma or higher: 85.3%; Bachelor's degree or higher: 12.3%; Graduate/professional degree or higher: 5.6%

School District(s)

Clyde-Savannah Central SD (PK-12)

   2014-15 Enrollment: 847 . . . . (315) 902-3000

Housing: Homeownership rate: 71.5%; Median home value: $73,000; Median year structure built: Before 1940; Homeowner vacancy rate: 6.2%; Median selected monthly owner costs: $967 with a mortgage, $483 without a mortgage; Median gross rent: $731 per month; Rental vacancy rate: 34.0%

Health Insurance: 93.7% have insurance; 68.1% have private insurance; 38.6% have public insurance; 6.3% do not have insurance; 0.9% of children under 18 do not have insurance

Safety: Violent crime rate: 5.0 per 10,000 population; Property crime rate: 154.9 per 10,000 population

Transportation: Commute: 87.7% car, 0.0% public transportation, 7.5% walk, 3.5% work from home; Mean travel time to work: 26.1 minutes

GALEN (town). Covers a land area of 59.477 square miles and a water area of 0.581 square miles. Located at 43.07° N. Lat; 76.88° W. Long.

Population: 4,219; Growth (since 2000): -5.0%; Density: 70.9 persons per square mile; Race: 92.9% White, 2.1% Black/African American, 1.4% Asian, 1.7% American Indian/Alaska Native, 0.0% Native Hawaiian/Other Pacific Islander, 1.3% Two or more races, 5.4% Hispanic of any race; Average household size: 2.96; Median age: 34.6; Age under 18: 30.2%; Age 65 and over: 15.4%; Males per 100 females: 99.8; Marriage status: 28.4% never married, 56.1% now married, 3.4% separated, 7.1% widowed, 8.4% divorced; Foreign born: 1.9%; Speak English only: 92.2%; With disability: 14.1%; Veterans: 6.9%; Ancestry: 23.2% German, 17.8% Italian, 14.2% English, 10.8% Irish, 9.8% Dutch

Employment: 8.5% management, business, and financial, 3.5% computer, engineering, and science, 10.1% education, legal, community service, arts, and media, 4.9% healthcare practitioners, 15.2% service, 18.0% sales and office, 17.3% natural resources, construction, and maintenance, 22.5% production, transportation, and material moving

Income: Per capita: $20,337; Median household: $53,406; Average household: $58,923; Households with income of $100,000 or more: 11.1%; Poverty rate: 11.8%

Educational Attainment: High school diploma or higher: 82.1%; Bachelor's degree or higher: 11.0%; Graduate/professional degree or higher: 5.3%

Housing: Homeownership rate: 83.2%; Median home value: $83,700; Median year structure built: 1944; Homeowner vacancy rate: 4.1%; Median selected monthly owner costs: $976 with a mortgage, $473 without a mortgage; Median gross rent: $737 per month; Rental vacancy rate: 29.3%

Health Insurance: 77.9% have insurance; 57.6% have private insurance; 32.2% have public insurance; 22.1% do not have insurance; 26.5% of children under 18 do not have insurance

Transportation: Commute: 89.7% car, 0.0% public transportation, 3.6% walk, 5.2% work from home; Mean travel time to work: 25.4 minutes

HURON (town). Covers a land area of 39.392 square miles and a water area of 3.710 square miles. Located at 43.25° N. Lat; 76.90° W. Long. Elevation is 390 feet.

Population: 2,248; Growth (since 2000): 6.2%; Density: 57.1 persons per square mile; Race: 87.7% White, 4.9% Black/African American, 2.1% Asian, 0.0% American Indian/Alaska Native, 0.0% Native Hawaiian/Other Pacific Islander, 1.6% Two or more races, 9.0% Hispanic of any race; Average household size: 2.54; Median age: 45.9; Age under 18: 19.4%; Age 65 and over: 19.2%; Males per 100 females: 107.6; Marriage status: 25.5% never married, 61.8% now married, 2.0% separated, 4.1% widowed, 8.6% divorced; Foreign born: 4.8%; Speak English only: 91.3%; With disability: 12.1%; Veterans: 12.5%; Ancestry: 23.0% German, 14.9% Irish, 14.5% English, 10.8% Dutch, 5.6% French

Employment: 19.1% management, business, and financial, 5.0% computer, engineering, and science, 7.7% education, legal, community service, arts, and media, 4.3% healthcare practitioners, 18.0% service, 17.6% sales and office, 12.5% natural resources, construction, and maintenance, 15.9% production, transportation, and material moving

Income: Per capita: $31,404; Median household: $68,800; Average household: $83,384; Households with income of $100,000 or more: 30.5%; Poverty rate: 15.6%

Educational Attainment: High school diploma or higher: 92.5%; Bachelor's degree or higher: 26.5%; Graduate/professional degree or higher: 10.8%

Housing: Homeownership rate: 83.3%; Median home value: $163,900; Median year structure built: 1963; Homeowner vacancy rate: 2.0%; Median selected monthly owner costs: $1,331 with a mortgage, $627 without a mortgage; Median gross rent: $638 per month; Rental vacancy rate: 4.2%

Health Insurance: 92.0% have insurance; 70.9% have private insurance; 39.8% have public insurance; 8.0% do not have insurance; 2.3% of children under 18 do not have insurance

Transportation: Commute: 89.6% car, 0.0% public transportation, 1.1% walk, 9.3% work from home; Mean travel time to work: 31.2 minutes

LYONS (town). Covers a land area of 37.485 square miles and a water area of 0.111 square miles. Located at 43.09° N. Lat; 77.00° W. Long. Elevation is 410 feet.

History: Settled 1800; incorporated 1831.

Population: 5,583; Growth (since 2000): -4.3%; Density: 148.9 persons per square mile; Race: 91.0% White, 5.9% Black/African American, 0.3% Asian, 0.3% American Indian/Alaska Native, 0.0% Native Hawaiian/Other Pacific Islander, 1.3% Two or more races, 4.0% Hispanic of any race; Average household size: 2.37; Median age: 43.3; Age under 18: 18.5%; Age 65 and over: 20.6%; Males per 100 females: 96.0; Marriage status: 33.9% never married, 47.2% now married, 3.1% separated, 6.3% widowed, 12.6% divorced; Foreign born: 2.8%; Speak English only: 97.9%; With disability: 17.4%; Veterans: 7.3%; Ancestry: 25.2% German, 17.0% Irish, 14.6% Italian, 12.1% Dutch, 11.7% English

Employment: 7.6% management, business, and financial, 3.0% computer, engineering, and science, 15.8% education, legal, community service, arts, and media, 5.9% healthcare practitioners, 18.6% service, 19.8% sales and office, 13.5% natural resources, construction, and maintenance, 15.8% production, transportation, and material moving

Income: Per capita: $21,549; Median household: $44,597; Average household: $51,947; Households with income of $100,000 or more: 11.0%; Poverty rate: 21.5%

Educational Attainment: High school diploma or higher: 85.7%; Bachelor's degree or higher: 15.3%; Graduate/professional degree or higher: 7.1%

School District(s)
Lyons Central SD (PK-12)
    2014-15 Enrollment: 943. . . . . (315) 946-2200

Housing: Homeownership rate: 68.8%; Median home value: $69,100; Median year structure built: Before 1940; Homeowner vacancy rate: 3.0%; Median selected monthly owner costs: $1,021 with a mortgage, $521 without a mortgage; Median gross rent: $633 per month; Rental vacancy rate: 4.2%

Health Insurance: 92.8% have insurance; 67.2% have private insurance; 42.5% have public insurance; 7.2% do not have insurance; 3.6% of children under 18 do not have insurance

Transportation: Commute: 93.6% car, 1.3% public transportation, 3.8% walk, 0.9% work from home; Mean travel time to work: 24.2 minutes

Additional Information Contacts
Town of Lyons. . . . . (315) 946-6252
    http://www.lyonsny.com/thetown

LYONS (village). County seat. Covers a land area of 4.074 square miles and a water area of 0.077 square miles. Located at 43.06° N. Lat; 76.99° W. Long. Elevation is 410 feet.

Population: 3,241; Growth (since 2000): -12.3%; Density: 795.6 persons per square mile; Race: 87.9% White, 7.7% Black/African American, 0.6% Asian, 0.0% American Indian/Alaska Native, 0.0% Native Hawaiian/Other Pacific Islander, 2.2% Two or more races, 2.9% Hispanic of any race; Average household size: 2.24; Median age: 41.1; Age under 18: 21.8%; Age 65 and over: 17.7%; Males per 100 females: 92.4; Marriage status: 35.3% never married, 41.5% now married, 4.9% separated, 6.3% widowed, 16.9% divorced; Foreign born: 0.9%; Speak English only: 99.3%; With disability: 19.4%; Veterans: 6.3%; Ancestry: 22.2% German, 20.8% Italian, 19.4% Irish, 13.1% Dutch, 10.0% French

Employment: 4.6% management, business, and financial, 4.2% computer, engineering, and science, 10.8% education, legal, community service, arts, and media, 5.4% healthcare practitioners, 17.4% service, 27.4% sales and office, 11.4% natural resources, construction, and maintenance, 18.7% production, transportation, and material moving

Income: Per capita: $20,702; Median household: $35,318; Average household: $45,418; Households with income of $100,000 or more: 11.3%; Poverty rate: 23.2%

Educational Attainment: High school diploma or higher: 84.6%; Bachelor's degree or higher: 11.2%; Graduate/professional degree or higher: 5.9%

School District(s)
Lyons Central SD (PK-12)
    2014-15 Enrollment: 943. . . . . (315) 946-2200

Housing: Homeownership rate: 60.9%; Median home value: $62,400; Median year structure built: Before 1940; Homeowner vacancy rate: 2.6%; Median selected monthly owner costs: $947 with a mortgage, $502 without a mortgage; Median gross rent: $614 per month; Rental vacancy rate: 5.1%

Health Insurance: 93.1% have insurance; 63.2% have private insurance; 45.4% have public insurance; 6.9% do not have insurance; 3.7% of children under 18 do not have insurance

Transportation: Commute: 92.5% car, 2.0% public transportation, 5.5% walk, 0.0% work from home; Mean travel time to work: 21.4 minutes

MACEDON (town). Covers a land area of 38.681 square miles and a water area of 0.177 square miles. Located at 43.08° N. Lat; 77.31° W. Long. Elevation is 472 feet.

Population: 9,053; Growth (since 2000): 4.2%; Density: 234.0 persons per square mile; Race: 97.0% White, 0.4% Black/African American, 0.1% Asian, 0.0% American Indian/Alaska Native, 0.0% Native Hawaiian/Other Pacific Islander, 1.6% Two or more races, 3.8% Hispanic of any race; Average household size: 2.61; Median age: 40.7; Age under 18: 23.8%; Age 65 and over: 12.4%; Males per 100 females: 99.5; Marriage status: 29.0% never married, 57.5% now married, 1.0% separated, 4.2% widowed, 9.4% divorced; Foreign born: 2.4%; Speak English only: 97.4%; With disability: 11.6%; Veterans: 8.3%; Ancestry: 24.8% German, 19.5% Irish, 16.5% Italian, 13.6% English, 6.6% American

Employment: 11.3% management, business, and financial, 7.5% computer, engineering, and science, 12.3% education, legal, community service, arts, and media, 6.1% healthcare practitioners, 20.4% service, 19.2% sales and office, 9.9% natural resources, construction, and maintenance, 13.3% production, transportation, and material moving

Income: Per capita: $27,426; Median household: $55,893; Average household: $71,057; Households with income of $100,000 or more: 21.9%; Poverty rate: 6.2%

Educational Attainment: High school diploma or higher: 94.0%; Bachelor's degree or higher: 26.0%; Graduate/professional degree or higher: 9.5%

School District(s)
Palmyra-Macedon Central SD (KG-12)
    2014-15 Enrollment: 1,934 . . . . (315) 597-3401

Housing: Homeownership rate: 78.0%; Median home value: $136,400; Median year structure built: 1980; Homeowner vacancy rate: 2.8%; Median selected monthly owner costs: $1,420 with a mortgage, $554 without a mortgage; Median gross rent: $761 per month; Rental vacancy rate: 3.3%

Health Insurance: 91.4% have insurance; 78.1% have private insurance; 24.8% have public insurance; 8.6% do not have insurance; 4.4% of children under 18 do not have insurance

Safety: Violent crime rate: 2.2 per 10,000 population; Property crime rate: 82.6 per 10,000 population

Newspapers: Times of Wayne County (weekly circulation 12,500)

Transportation: Commute: 93.6% car, 0.0% public transportation, 0.3% walk, 4.7% work from home; Mean travel time to work: 24.3 minutes

Additional Information Contacts

Town of Macedon . . . . (315) 986-5932
  http://www.macedontown.net/s2

MACEDON (village). Covers a land area of 1.225 square miles and a water area of 0.007 square miles. Located at 43.07° N. Lat; 77.30° W. Long. Elevation is 472 feet.

Population: 1,591; Growth (since 2000): 6.4%; Density: 1,298.6 persons per square mile; Race: 97.7% White, 1.7% Black/African American, 0.0% Asian, 0.0% American Indian/Alaska Native, 0.3% Native Hawaiian/Other Pacific Islander, 0.4% Two or more races, 5.4% Hispanic of any race; Average household size: 2.72; Median age: 40.0; Age under 18: 25.5%; Age 65 and over: 8.7%; Males per 100 females: 101.2; Marriage status: 22.8% never married, 62.6% now married, 1.9% separated, 5.8% widowed, 8.9% divorced; Foreign born: 1.7%; Speak English only: 98.0%; With disability: 9.9%; Veterans: 5.3%; Ancestry: 24.1% German, 23.9% Italian, 15.1% Irish, 13.5% English, 6.8% American

Employment: 15.7% management, business, and financial, 7.7% computer, engineering, and science, 17.4% education, legal, community service, arts, and media, 7.0% healthcare practitioners, 19.0% service, 18.7% sales and office, 6.1% natural resources, construction, and maintenance, 8.3% production, transportation, and material moving

Income: Per capita: $27,328; Median household: $67,969; Average household: $74,094; Households with income of $100,000 or more: 24.9%; Poverty rate: 7.4%

Educational Attainment: High school diploma or higher: 95.2%; Bachelor's degree or higher: 38.1%; Graduate/professional degree or higher: 14.4%

School District(s)

Palmyra-Macedon Central SD (KG-12)
  2014-15 Enrollment: 1,934 . . . . (315) 597-3401

Housing: Homeownership rate: 82.2%; Median home value: $123,200; Median year structure built: 1968; Homeowner vacancy rate: 0.6%; Median selected monthly owner costs: $1,439 with a mortgage, $595 without a mortgage; Median gross rent: $745 per month; Rental vacancy rate: 14.0%

Health Insurance: 96.6% have insurance; 81.5% have private insurance; 23.1% have public insurance; 3.4% do not have insurance; 0.0% of children under 18 do not have insurance

Newspapers: Times of Wayne County (weekly circulation 12,500)

Transportation: Commute: 93.3% car, 0.0% public transportation, 1.5% walk, 3.3% work from home; Mean travel time to work: 25.7 minutes

MARION (CDP). Covers a land area of 3.053 square miles and a water area of 0.006 square miles. Located at 43.14° N. Lat; 77.19° W. Long. Elevation is 459 feet.

Population: 1,403; Growth (since 2000): n/a; Density: 459.6 persons per square mile; Race: 97.6% White, 2.4% Black/African American, 0.0% Asian, 0.0% American Indian/Alaska Native, 0.0% Native Hawaiian/Other Pacific Islander, 0.0% Two or more races, 0.0% Hispanic of any race; Average household size: 2.37; Median age: 38.6; Age under 18: 29.9%; Age 65 and over: 17.4%; Males per 100 females: 92.2; Marriage status: 23.9% never married, 57.4% now married, 0.8% separated, 11.5% widowed, 7.1% divorced; Foreign born: 0.0%; Speak English only: 100.0%; With disability: 13.0%; Veterans: 3.5%; Ancestry: 26.6% Irish, 21.8% Dutch, 19.8% English, 18.7% German, 16.9% Italian

Employment: 5.0% management, business, and financial, 8.7% computer, engineering, and science, 20.0% education, legal, community service, arts, and media, 3.5% healthcare practitioners, 11.4% service, 26.3% sales and office, 5.4% natural resources, construction, and maintenance, 19.7% production, transportation, and material moving

Income: Per capita: $23,123; Median household: $40,993; Average household: $54,989; Households with income of $100,000 or more: 10.5%; Poverty rate: 6.3%

Educational Attainment: High school diploma or higher: 87.1%; Bachelor's degree or higher: 24.5%; Graduate/professional degree or higher: 9.4%

School District(s)

Marion Central SD (PK-12)
  2014-15 Enrollment: 794 . . . . (315) 926-2300

Housing: Homeownership rate: 63.4%; Median home value: $109,700; Median year structure built: 1958; Homeowner vacancy rate: 0.0%; Median selected monthly owner costs: $1,127 with a mortgage, $464 without a mortgage; Median gross rent: $705 per month; Rental vacancy rate: 0.0%

Health Insurance: 97.3% have insurance; 75.0% have private insurance; 39.7% have public insurance; 2.7% do not have insurance; 1.7% of children under 18 do not have insurance

Transportation: Commute: 93.3% car, 1.5% public transportation, 3.8% walk, 1.5% work from home; Mean travel time to work: 25.8 minutes

MARION (town). Covers a land area of 29.147 square miles and a water area of 0.103 square miles. Located at 43.17° N. Lat; 77.19° W. Long. Elevation is 459 feet.

Population: 4,679; Growth (since 2000): -5.9%; Density: 160.5 persons per square mile; Race: 96.5% White, 1.5% Black/African American, 1.4% Asian, 0.0% American Indian/Alaska Native, 0.0% Native Hawaiian/Other Pacific Islander, 0.5% Two or more races, 0.8% Hispanic of any race; Average household size: 2.41; Median age: 45.4; Age under 18: 23.0%; Age 65 and over: 15.1%; Males per 100 females: 95.1; Marriage status: 22.3% never married, 62.6% now married, 2.8% separated, 6.3% widowed, 8.9% divorced; Foreign born: 3.5%; Speak English only: 97.2%; With disability: 9.8%; Veterans: 8.9%; Ancestry: 25.0% German, 24.6% Dutch, 15.3% Irish, 15.2% English, 10.0% Italian

Employment: 14.1% management, business, and financial, 4.6% computer, engineering, and science, 9.7% education, legal, community service, arts, and media, 5.8% healthcare practitioners, 11.8% service, 27.0% sales and office, 8.4% natural resources, construction, and maintenance, 18.5% production, transportation, and material moving

Income: Per capita: $28,336; Median household: $58,382; Average household: $67,668; Households with income of $100,000 or more: 18.0%; Poverty rate: 7.5%

Educational Attainment: High school diploma or higher: 92.5%; Bachelor's degree or higher: 20.7%; Graduate/professional degree or higher: 7.4%

School District(s)

Marion Central SD (PK-12)
  2014-15 Enrollment: 794 . . . . (315) 926-2300

Housing: Homeownership rate: 86.3%; Median home value: $118,500; Median year structure built: 1972; Homeowner vacancy rate: 0.0%; Median selected monthly owner costs: $1,166 with a mortgage, $515 without a mortgage; Median gross rent: $699 per month; Rental vacancy rate: 8.0%

Health Insurance: 93.2% have insurance; 79.3% have private insurance; 28.1% have public insurance; 6.8% do not have insurance; 4.6% of children under 18 do not have insurance

Transportation: Commute: 92.6% car, 0.4% public transportation, 3.0% walk, 3.3% work from home; Mean travel time to work: 25.2 minutes

Additional Information Contacts

Town of Marion . . . . (315) 926-4271
  http://www.townofmarionny.com

NEWARK (village). Covers a land area of 5.406 square miles and a water area of 0.005 square miles. Located at 43.04° N. Lat; 77.09° W. Long. Elevation is 443 feet.

History: Incorporated 1839.

Population: 8,965; Growth (since 2000): -7.4%; Density: 1,658.3 persons per square mile; Race: 85.2% White, 9.8% Black/African American, 0.4% Asian, 0.0% American Indian/Alaska Native, 0.2% Native Hawaiian/Other Pacific Islander, 2.0% Two or more races, 8.3% Hispanic of any race; Average household size: 2.28; Median age: 42.3; Age under 18: 20.3%; Age 65 and over: 16.5%; Males per 100 females: 90.5; Marriage status: 37.1% never married, 45.1% now married, 3.6% separated, 7.4% widowed, 10.4% divorced; Foreign born: 3.0%; Speak English only: 94.5%; With disability: 24.9%; Veterans: 8.3%; Ancestry: 17.3% German, 15.5% English, 15.1% Irish, 13.8% Italian, 12.3% Dutch

Employment: 8.8% management, business, and financial, 2.5% computer, engineering, and science, 9.5% education, legal, community service, arts, and media, 5.8% healthcare practitioners, 23.7% service, 20.0% sales and office, 7.7% natural resources, construction, and maintenance, 22.0% production, transportation, and material moving

Income: Per capita: $19,236; Median household: $31,121; Average household: $42,676; Households with income of $100,000 or more: 6.2%; Poverty rate: 21.8%

Educational Attainment: High school diploma or higher: 84.6%; Bachelor's degree or higher: 15.4%; Graduate/professional degree or higher: 6.4%

School District(s)

Newark Central SD (PK-12)
  2014-15 Enrollment: 2,193 . . . . (315) 332-3217

Wayne-Finger Lakes Boces
  2014-15 Enrollment: n/a . . . . (315) 332-7284
                Vocational/Technical School(s)
Wayne Finger Lakes BOCES-Practical Nursing Program (Public)
  Fall 2014 Enrollment: 302 . . . . (315) 332-7375
  2015-16 Tuition: $17,350
Housing: Homeownership rate: 50.5%; Median home value: $84,100;
Median year structure built: 1951; Homeowner vacancy rate: 1.6%; Median
selected monthly owner costs: $1,069 with a mortgage, $489 without a
mortgage; Median gross rent: $649 per month; Rental vacancy rate: 4.2%
Health Insurance: 93.7% have insurance; 57.3% have private insurance;
49.1% have public insurance; 6.3% do not have insurance; 0.5% of
children under 18 do not have insurance
Hospitals: Newark - Wayne Community Hospital
Safety: Violent crime rate: 37.3 per 10,000 population; Property crime rate:
300.7 per 10,000 population
Newspapers: Newark Courier-Gazette (weekly circulation 3,600)
Transportation: Commute: 88.5% car, 3.0% public transportation, 7.8%
walk, 0.5% work from home; Mean travel time to work: 18.0 minutes
Additional Information Contacts
Village of Newark . . . . (315) 331-4770
  http://www.villageofnewark.com

NORTH ROSE (CDP). Covers a land area of 1.690 square miles and
a water area of 0 square miles. Located at 43.19° N. Lat; 76.89° W. Long.
Elevation is 387 feet.
Population: 544; Growth (since 2000): n/a; Density: 321.8 persons per
square mile; Race: 84.4% White, 15.6% Black/African American, 0.0%
Asian, 0.0% American Indian/Alaska Native, 0.0% Native Hawaiian/Other
Pacific Islander, 0.0% Two or more races, 14.3% Hispanic of any race;
Average household size: 2.24; Median age: 52.2; Age under 18: 18.4%;
Age 65 and over: 16.4%; Males per 100 females: 88.7; Marriage status:
29.9% never married, 51.8% now married, 0.0% separated, 11.8%
widowed, 6.5% divorced; Foreign born: 5.1%; Speak English only: 85.1%;
With disability: 9.2%; Veterans: 7.4%; Ancestry: 26.3% German, 18.0%
English, 14.9% Irish, 14.5% Italian, 7.5% Dutch
Employment: 11.0% management, business, and financial, 4.6%
computer, engineering, and science, 21.1% education, legal, community
service, arts, and media, 0.0% healthcare practitioners, 6.3% service,
20.3% sales and office, 22.4% natural resources, construction, and
maintenance, 14.3% production, transportation, and material moving
Income: Per capita: $22,810; Median household: $42,250; Average
household: $50,698; Households with income of $100,000 or more: 5.3%;
Poverty rate: 2.0%
Educational Attainment: High school diploma or higher: 83.7%;
Bachelor's degree or higher: 11.5%; Graduate/professional degree or
higher: 7.6%
                School District(s)
North Rose-Wolcott Central SD (KG-12)
  2014-15 Enrollment: 1,315 . . . . (315) 594-3141
Housing: Homeownership rate: 81.9%; Median home value: $91,300;
Median year structure built: Before 1940; Homeowner vacancy rate: 7.0%;
Median selected monthly owner costs: $788 with a mortgage, $386 without
a mortgage; Median gross rent: n/a per month; Rental vacancy rate: 0.0%
Health Insurance: 89.3% have insurance; 65.1% have private insurance;
31.8% have public insurance; 10.7% do not have insurance; 0.0% of
children under 18 do not have insurance
Transportation: Commute: 97.9% car, 0.0% public transportation, 0.0%
walk, 2.1% work from home; Mean travel time to work: 19.4 minutes

ONTARIO (CDP). Covers a land area of 3.796 square miles and a
water area of 0 square miles. Located at 43.22° N. Lat; 77.28° W. Long.
Elevation is 440 feet.
Population: 2,190; Growth (since 2000): n/a; Density: 576.9 persons per
square mile; Race: 100.0% White, 0.0% Black/African American, 0.0%
Asian, 0.0% American Indian/Alaska Native, 0.0% Native Hawaiian/Other
Pacific Islander, 0.0% Two or more races, 7.0% Hispanic of any race;
Average household size: 2.10; Median age: 46.1; Age under 18: 17.2%;
Age 65 and over: 16.9%; Males per 100 females: 92.9; Marriage status:
26.2% never married, 48.4% now married, 6.2% separated, 12.7%
widowed, 12.7% divorced; Foreign born: 5.0%; Speak English only: 94.8%;
With disability: 14.8%; Veterans: 8.4%; Ancestry: 20.3% German, 19.9%
Italian, 17.3% English, 7.8% Irish, 6.1% American
Employment: 5.4% management, business, and financial, 8.7% computer,
engineering, and science, 5.8% education, legal, community service, arts,

and media, 3.4% healthcare practitioners, 15.4% service, 30.1% sales and
office, 6.6% natural resources, construction, and maintenance, 24.5%
production, transportation, and material moving
Income: Per capita: $23,100; Median household: $29,025; Average
household: $48,091; Households with income of $100,000 or more: 14.3%;
Poverty rate: 20.4%
Educational Attainment: High school diploma or higher: 88.3%;
Bachelor's degree or higher: 18.6%; Graduate/professional degree or
higher: 6.9%
Housing: Homeownership rate: 71.9%; Median home value: $87,100;
Median year structure built: 1981; Homeowner vacancy rate: 0.0%; Median
selected monthly owner costs: $1,212 with a mortgage, $428 without a
mortgage; Median gross rent: $349 per month; Rental vacancy rate: 0.0%
Health Insurance: 82.9% have insurance; 63.7% have private insurance;
33.1% have public insurance; 17.1% do not have insurance; 8.2% of
children under 18 do not have insurance
Transportation: Commute: 96.3% car, 0.0% public transportation, 3.7%
walk, 0.0% work from home; Mean travel time to work: 20.7 minutes

ONTARIO (town). Covers a land area of 32.412 square miles and a
water area of 0.086 square miles. Located at 43.25° N. Lat; 77.32° W.
Long. Elevation is 440 feet.
Population: 10,126; Growth (since 2000): 3.6%; Density: 312.4 persons
per square mile; Race: 94.5% White, 3.0% Black/African American, 1.5%
Asian, 0.0% American Indian/Alaska Native, 0.0% Native Hawaiian/Other
Pacific Islander, 0.8% Two or more races, 2.9% Hispanic of any race;
Average household size: 2.38; Median age: 44.7; Age under 18: 21.7%;
Age 65 and over: 16.2%; Males per 100 females: 98.1; Marriage status:
23.8% never married, 59.5% now married, 2.2% separated, 7.1%
widowed, 9.5% divorced; Foreign born: 3.4%; Speak English only: 96.9%;
With disability: 12.4%; Veterans: 9.8%; Ancestry: 28.6% German, 19.8%
Italian, 16.9% English, 13.4% Irish, 10.4% Dutch
Employment: 10.3% management, business, and financial, 5.8%
computer, engineering, and science, 11.7% education, legal, community
service, arts, and media, 7.4% healthcare practitioners, 12.9% service,
23.8% sales and office, 9.6% natural resources, construction, and
maintenance, 18.5% production, transportation, and material moving
Income: Per capita: $30,040; Median household: $59,543; Average
household: $70,849; Households with income of $100,000 or more: 23.6%;
Poverty rate: 7.4%
Educational Attainment: High school diploma or higher: 93.1%;
Bachelor's degree or higher: 25.0%; Graduate/professional degree or
higher: 10.8%
Housing: Homeownership rate: 82.7%; Median home value: $152,600;
Median year structure built: 1977; Homeowner vacancy rate: 0.8%; Median
selected monthly owner costs: $1,427 with a mortgage, $568 without a
mortgage; Median gross rent: $752 per month; Rental vacancy rate: 0.0%
Health Insurance: 93.8% have insurance; 81.2% have private insurance;
27.1% have public insurance; 6.2% do not have insurance; 3.7% of
children under 18 do not have insurance
Transportation: Commute: 97.0% car, 0.3% public transportation, 1.2%
walk, 1.0% work from home; Mean travel time to work: 23.3 minutes
Additional Information Contacts
Town of Ontario. . . . . (315) 524-7105
  http://www.ontariotown.org

PALMYRA (town). Covers a land area of 33.435 square miles and a
water area of 0.234 square miles. Located at 43.08° N. Lat; 77.19° W.
Long. Elevation is 486 feet.
History: Joseph Smith, founder and first president of the Mormon Church,
lived and published *The Book of Mormon* here. Hill Cumorah Center
pageant held each August atop the glacial drumlin where Smith buried his
tablets four miles south of villlage.
Population: 7,802; Growth (since 2000): 1.7%; Density: 233.3 persons per
square mile; Race: 96.5% White, 0.3% Black/African American, 0.7%
Asian, 0.0% American Indian/Alaska Native, 0.0% Native Hawaiian/Other
Pacific Islander, 2.5% Two or more races, 3.6% Hispanic of any race;
Average household size: 2.32; Median age: 43.8; Age under 18: 20.3%;
Age 65 and over: 15.4%; Males per 100 females: 98.2; Marriage status:
28.7% never married, 49.7% now married, 2.6% separated, 8.0%
widowed, 13.6% divorced; Foreign born: 1.5%; Speak English only: 96.7%;
With disability: 11.8%; Veterans: 9.5%; Ancestry: 21.0% Irish, 20.9%
German, 13.1% English, 12.8% Dutch, 12.3% Italian
Employment: 12.2% management, business, and financial, 4.5%
computer, engineering, and science, 8.0% education, legal, community

service, arts, and media, 3.8% healthcare practitioners, 17.1% service, 25.0% sales and office, 10.4% natural resources, construction, and maintenance, 19.0% production, transportation, and material moving
Income: Per capita: $24,765; Median household: $42,304; Average household: $56,643; Households with income of $100,000 or more: 14.6%; Poverty rate: 16.6%
Educational Attainment: High school diploma or higher: 89.0%; Bachelor's degree or higher: 16.8%; Graduate/professional degree or higher: 5.5%

School District(s)
Palmyra-Macedon Central SD (KG-12)
 2014-15 Enrollment: 1,934 . . . . (315) 597-3401
Housing: Homeownership rate: 65.5%; Median home value: $101,800; Median year structure built: 1958; Homeowner vacancy rate: 5.0%; Median selected monthly owner costs: $1,204 with a mortgage, $479 without a mortgage; Median gross rent: $712 per month; Rental vacancy rate: 1.3%
Health Insurance: 87.9% have insurance; 62.4% have private insurance; 37.2% have public insurance; 12.1% do not have insurance; 4.6% of children under 18 do not have insurance
Newspapers: Palmyra Courier-Journal (weekly circulation 2,700)
Transportation: Commute: 93.6% car, 0.6% public transportation, 1.7% walk, 3.7% work from home; Mean travel time to work: 25.4 minutes
Additional Information Contacts
Town of Palmyra . . . . (315) 597-5521
 http://www.palmyrany.com

PALMYRA (village).
Covers a land area of 1.347 square miles and a water area of 0 square miles. Located at 43.06° N. Lat; 77.23° W. Long. Elevation is 486 feet.
Population: 3,446; Growth (since 2000): -1.3%; Density: 2,558.5 persons per square mile; Race: 96.1% White, 0.2% Black/African American, 0.0% Asian, 0.0% American Indian/Alaska Native, 0.0% Native Hawaiian/Other Pacific Islander, 3.7% Two or more races, 4.4% Hispanic of any race; Average household size: 2.29; Median age: 42.0; Age under 18: 19.4%; Age 65 and over: 13.3%; Males per 100 females: 95.9; Marriage status: 34.2% never married, 41.1% now married, 2.3% separated, 9.3% widowed, 15.3% divorced; Foreign born: 0.2%; Speak English only: 98.3%; With disability: 12.2%; Veterans: 8.6%; Ancestry: 22.7% Irish, 17.4% German, 12.9% Dutch, 11.8% Italian, 10.9% English
Employment: 13.1% management, business, and financial, 4.6% computer, engineering, and science, 6.6% education, legal, community service, arts, and media, 3.9% healthcare practitioners, 22.8% service, 26.1% sales and office, 6.1% natural resources, construction, and maintenance, 16.9% production, transportation, and material moving
Income: Per capita: $22,754; Median household: $38,577; Average household: $51,019; Households with income of $100,000 or more: 9.9%; Poverty rate: 22.1%
Educational Attainment: High school diploma or higher: 90.3%; Bachelor's degree or higher: 16.4%; Graduate/professional degree or higher: 5.3%

School District(s)
Palmyra-Macedon Central SD (KG-12)
 2014-15 Enrollment: 1,934 . . . . (315) 597-3401
Housing: Homeownership rate: 50.2%; Median home value: $91,000; Median year structure built: 1943; Homeowner vacancy rate: 5.2%; Median selected monthly owner costs: $1,162 with a mortgage, $522 without a mortgage; Median gross rent: $707 per month; Rental vacancy rate: 2.0%
Health Insurance: 84.4% have insurance; 58.4% have private insurance; 36.8% have public insurance; 15.6% do not have insurance; 7.0% of children under 18 do not have insurance
Safety: Violent crime rate: 8.8 per 10,000 population; Property crime rate: 70.3 per 10,000 population
Newspapers: Palmyra Courier-Journal (weekly circulation 2,700)
Transportation: Commute: 93.6% car, 0.6% public transportation, 2.4% walk, 2.8% work from home; Mean travel time to work: 25.9 minutes
Additional Information Contacts
Village of Palmyra . . . . (315) 597-4849
 http://www.palmyrany.com

PULTNEYVILLE (CDP).
Covers a land area of 2.242 square miles and a water area of <.001 square miles. Located at 43.27° N. Lat; 77.17° W. Long. Elevation is 272 feet.
Population: 458; Growth (since 2000): n/a; Density: 204.3 persons per square mile; Race: 100.0% White, 0.0% Black/African American, 0.0% Asian, 0.0% American Indian/Alaska Native, 0.0% Native Hawaiian/Other

Pacific Islander, 0.0% Two or more races, 0.0% Hispanic of any race; Average household size: 2.31; Median age: 44.3; Age under 18: 24.7%; Age 65 and over: 20.7%; Males per 100 females: 94.4; Marriage status: 18.1% never married, 70.5% now married, 2.5% separated, 11.4% widowed, 0.0% divorced; Foreign born: 1.7%; Speak English only: 98.2%; With disability: 9.4%; Veterans: 2.0%; Ancestry: 57.0% Dutch, 36.9% German, 23.4% Irish, 19.7% English, 6.1% Italian
Employment: 11.4% management, business, and financial, 7.6% computer, engineering, and science, 17.5% education, legal, community service, arts, and media, 10.4% healthcare practitioners, 3.8% service, 22.3% sales and office, 14.7% natural resources, construction, and maintenance, 12.3% production, transportation, and material moving
Income: Per capita: $39,518; Median household: $74,444; Average household: $89,492; Households with income of $100,000 or more: 26.3%; Poverty rate: n/a
Educational Attainment: High school diploma or higher: 97.9%; Bachelor's degree or higher: 40.2%; Graduate/professional degree or higher: 25.1%
Housing: Homeownership rate: 96.5%; Median home value: $140,600; Median year structure built: 1942; Homeowner vacancy rate: 0.0%; Median selected monthly owner costs: $1,578 with a mortgage, $550 without a mortgage; Median gross rent: n/a per month; Rental vacancy rate: 0.0%
Health Insurance: 100.0% have insurance; 96.3% have private insurance; 20.7% have public insurance; 0.0% do not have insurance; 0.0% of children under 18 do not have insurance
Transportation: Commute: 89.1% car, 0.0% public transportation, 0.0% walk, 10.9% work from home; Mean travel time to work: 36.8 minutes

RED CREEK (village).
Covers a land area of 0.909 square miles and a water area of 0.027 square miles. Located at 43.25° N. Lat; 76.72° W. Long. Elevation is 341 feet.
Population: 646; Growth (since 2000): 24.0%; Density: 710.9 persons per square mile; Race: 95.7% White, 4.3% Black/African American, 0.0% Asian, 0.0% American Indian/Alaska Native, 0.0% Native Hawaiian/Other Pacific Islander, 0.0% Two or more races, 2.2% Hispanic of any race; Average household size: 2.94; Median age: 27.8; Age under 18: 40.1%; Age 65 and over: 10.2%; Males per 100 females: 102.3; Marriage status: 36.9% never married, 49.2% now married, 3.8% separated, 7.6% widowed, 6.3% divorced; Foreign born: 0.0%; Speak English only: 97.8%; With disability: 20.3%; Veterans: 12.9%; Ancestry: 20.0% Irish, 13.6% German, 9.8% Dutch, 8.7% English, 5.4% Italian
Employment: 4.9% management, business, and financial, 2.4% computer, engineering, and science, 17.5% education, legal, community service, arts, and media, 4.9% healthcare practitioners, 14.1% service, 25.2% sales and office, 14.6% natural resources, construction, and maintenance, 16.5% production, transportation, and material moving
Income: Per capita: $16,858; Median household: $34,028; Average household: $49,582; Households with income of $100,000 or more: 10.5%; Poverty rate: 24.1%
Educational Attainment: High school diploma or higher: 84.9%; Bachelor's degree or higher: 11.4%; Graduate/professional degree or higher: 7.4%

School District(s)
Red Creek Central SD (PK-12)
 2014-15 Enrollment: 979 . . . . (315) 754-2010
Housing: Homeownership rate: 65.9%; Median home value: $76,800; Median year structure built: Before 1940; Homeowner vacancy rate: 0.0%; Median selected monthly owner costs: $1,007 with a mortgage, $433 without a mortgage; Median gross rent: $595 per month; Rental vacancy rate: 7.4%
Health Insurance: 81.9% have insurance; 33.9% have private insurance; 53.9% have public insurance; 18.1% do not have insurance; 22.0% of children under 18 do not have insurance
Newspapers: The Lakeshore News (weekly circulation 3,500)
Transportation: Commute: 85.2% car, 0.0% public transportation, 13.8% walk, 0.0% work from home; Mean travel time to work: 32.1 minutes

ROSE (town).
Covers a land area of 33.896 square miles and a water area of 0.006 square miles. Located at 43.16° N. Lat; 76.90° W. Long. Elevation is 420 feet.
Population: 2,558; Growth (since 2000): 4.8%; Density: 75.5 persons per square mile; Race: 95.3% White, 3.6% Black/African American, 0.0% Asian, 0.2% American Indian/Alaska Native, 0.0% Native Hawaiian/Other Pacific Islander, 0.8% Two or more races, 4.3% Hispanic of any race; Average household size: 2.84; Median age: 39.6; Age under 18: 24.3%;

Age 65 and over: 14.9%; Males per 100 females: 93.2; Marriage status: 30.8% never married, 52.4% now married, 1.0% separated, 7.1% widowed, 9.7% divorced; Foreign born: 1.4%; Speak English only: 93.5%; With disability: 17.2%; Veterans: 8.5%; Ancestry: 25.4% German, 15.2% Irish, 12.4% Italian, 11.0% English, 10.4% Dutch
Employment: 7.0% management, business, and financial, 4.0% computer, engineering, and science, 10.2% education, legal, community service, arts, and media, 4.0% healthcare practitioners, 11.3% service, 22.2% sales and office, 14.7% natural resources, construction, and maintenance, 26.6% production, transportation, and material moving
Income: Per capita: $21,740; Median household: $46,750; Average household: $61,866; Households with income of $100,000 or more: 10.7%; Poverty rate: 12.8%
Educational Attainment: High school diploma or higher: 84.5%; Bachelor's degree or higher: 15.5%; Graduate/professional degree or higher: 7.6%
Housing: Homeownership rate: 87.0%; Median home value: $83,500; Median year structure built: 1944; Homeowner vacancy rate: 1.9%; Median selected monthly owner costs: $1,112 with a mortgage, $438 without a mortgage; Median gross rent: $831 per month; Rental vacancy rate: 0.0%
Health Insurance: 85.5% have insurance; 62.0% have private insurance; 34.7% have public insurance; 14.5% do not have insurance; 21.9% of children under 18 do not have insurance
Transportation: Commute: 94.4% car, 0.0% public transportation, 2.7% walk, 1.9% work from home; Mean travel time to work: 24.6 minutes

SAVANNAH (CDP). Covers a land area of 1.180 square miles and a water area of 0 square miles. Located at 43.07° N. Lat; 76.76° W. Long. Elevation is 420 feet.
Population: 405; Growth (since 2000): n/a; Density: 343.3 persons per square mile; Race: 97.0% White, 0.7% Black/African American, 0.0% Asian, 1.7% American Indian/Alaska Native, 0.0% Native Hawaiian/Other Pacific Islander, 0.5% Two or more races, 0.2% Hispanic of any race; Average household size: 2.04; Median age: 48.5; Age under 18: 20.0%; Age 65 and over: 22.0%; Males per 100 females: 88.5; Marriage status: 24.1% never married, 53.2% now married, 10.0% separated, 5.9% widowed, 16.8% divorced; Foreign born: 0.0%; Speak English only: 99.7%; With disability: 18.8%; Veterans: 10.8%; Ancestry: 31.6% Irish, 14.8% Italian, 14.3% English, 13.3% German, 13.1% Dutch
Employment: 5.1% management, business, and financial, 1.7% computer, engineering, and science, 11.9% education, legal, community service, arts, and media, 2.8% healthcare practitioners, 9.7% service, 26.1% sales and office, 7.4% natural resources, construction, and maintenance, 35.2% production, transportation, and material moving
Income: Per capita: $24,110; Median household: $38,929; Average household: $49,062; Households with income of $100,000 or more: 9.8%; Poverty rate: 8.9%
Educational Attainment: High school diploma or higher: 79.2%; Bachelor's degree or higher: 11.1%; Graduate/professional degree or higher: 1.0%
Housing: Homeownership rate: 77.8%; Median home value: $70,100; Median year structure built: 1957; Homeowner vacancy rate: 0.0%; Median selected monthly owner costs: $829 with a mortgage, $497 without a mortgage; Median gross rent: $488 per month; Rental vacancy rate: 14.0%
Health Insurance: 84.4% have insurance; 66.9% have private insurance; 29.4% have public insurance; 15.6% do not have insurance; 21.0% of children under 18 do not have insurance
Transportation: Commute: 90.9% car, 2.3% public transportation, 4.5% walk, 2.3% work from home; Mean travel time to work: 24.5 minutes

SAVANNAH (town). Covers a land area of 35.968 square miles and a water area of 0.211 square miles. Located at 43.08° N. Lat; 76.75° W. Long. Elevation is 420 feet.
Population: 1,439; Growth (since 2000): -21.7%; Density: 40.0 persons per square mile; Race: 98.0% White, 0.4% Black/African American, 0.0% Asian, 0.8% American Indian/Alaska Native, 0.0% Native Hawaiian/Other Pacific Islander, 0.8% Two or more races, 5.0% Hispanic of any race; Average household size: 2.33; Median age: 46.4; Age under 18: 22.2%; Age 65 and over: 20.2%; Males per 100 females: 99.1; Marriage status: 23.3% never married, 56.5% now married, 3.8% separated, 6.5% widowed, 13.7% divorced; Foreign born: 0.3%; Speak English only: 98.4%; With disability: 20.2%; Veterans: 11.3%; Ancestry: 22.5% German, 16.4% Irish, 15.7% English, 11.5% Italian, 9.7% Dutch
Employment: 7.6% management, business, and financial, 3.3% computer, engineering, and science, 9.7% education, legal, community service, arts,

and media, 6.9% healthcare practitioners, 9.4% service, 20.8% sales and office, 13.5% natural resources, construction, and maintenance, 28.7% production, transportation, and material moving
Income: Per capita: $22,840; Median household: $44,792; Average household: $52,564; Households with income of $100,000 or more: 10.1%; Poverty rate: 11.9%
Educational Attainment: High school diploma or higher: 81.1%; Bachelor's degree or higher: 9.9%; Graduate/professional degree or higher: 4.1%
Housing: Homeownership rate: 80.9%; Median home value: $79,200; Median year structure built: 1971; Homeowner vacancy rate: 1.4%; Median selected monthly owner costs: $962 with a mortgage, $465 without a mortgage; Median gross rent: $892 per month; Rental vacancy rate: 5.6%
Health Insurance: 89.7% have insurance; 65.7% have private insurance; 39.4% have public insurance; 10.3% do not have insurance; 6.6% of children under 18 do not have insurance
Transportation: Commute: 92.1% car, 2.5% public transportation, 1.3% walk, 2.7% work from home; Mean travel time to work: 30.2 minutes

SODUS (town). Covers a land area of 67.268 square miles and a water area of 1.979 square miles. Located at 43.22° N. Lat; 77.05° W. Long. Elevation is 436 feet.
History: The raising of silkworms was attempted in Sodus in the 1830s. The attempt failed because mulberry trees could not withstand the severe winters. The lotuses of nearby Sodus Bay are famous. Incorporated in 1918.
Population: 8,264; Growth (since 2000): -7.7%; Density: 122.9 persons per square mile; Race: 88.6% White, 5.5% Black/African American, 0.5% Asian, 0.4% American Indian/Alaska Native, 0.0% Native Hawaiian/Other Pacific Islander, 2.8% Two or more races, 5.3% Hispanic of any race; Average household size: 2.50; Median age: 42.4; Age under 18: 21.7%; Age 65 and over: 18.4%; Males per 100 females: 98.3; Marriage status: 27.2% never married, 53.4% now married, 3.3% separated, 7.4% widowed, 12.1% divorced; Foreign born: 3.1%; Speak English only: 94.4%; With disability: 15.2%; Veterans: 9.3%; Ancestry: 20.0% German, 16.0% English, 15.7% Dutch, 15.5% Irish, 9.1% Italian
Employment: 9.2% management, business, and financial, 2.1% computer, engineering, and science, 8.0% education, legal, community service, arts, and media, 6.2% healthcare practitioners, 23.5% service, 17.6% sales and office, 15.0% natural resources, construction, and maintenance, 18.4% production, transportation, and material moving
Income: Per capita: $22,497; Median household: $46,189; Average household: $56,020; Households with income of $100,000 or more: 14.2%; Poverty rate: 19.2%
Educational Attainment: High school diploma or higher: 86.4%; Bachelor's degree or higher: 16.4%; Graduate/professional degree or higher: 6.4%

School District(s)
Sodus Central SD (PK-12)
　　2014-15 Enrollment: 1,134 . . . . (315) 483-5201
Housing: Homeownership rate: 77.7%; Median home value: $90,000; Median year structure built: 1955; Homeowner vacancy rate: 1.6%; Median selected monthly owner costs: $1,118 with a mortgage, $518 without a mortgage; Median gross rent: $724 per month; Rental vacancy rate: 10.9%
Health Insurance: 91.9% have insurance; 64.2% have private insurance; 43.4% have public insurance; 8.1% do not have insurance; 5.1% of children under 18 do not have insurance
Transportation: Commute: 89.3% car, 1.4% public transportation, 1.4% walk, 3.0% work from home; Mean travel time to work: 25.2 minutes
Additional Information Contacts
Town of Sodus . . . . (315) 576-3818
　　http://sodusny.org

SODUS (village). Covers a land area of 0.941 square miles and a water area of 0 square miles. Located at 43.24° N. Lat; 77.06° W. Long. Elevation is 436 feet.
Population: 2,374; Growth (since 2000): 36.8%; Density: 2,523.0 persons per square mile; Race: 80.0% White, 13.6% Black/African American, 0.5% Asian, 0.9% American Indian/Alaska Native, 0.0% Native Hawaiian/Other Pacific Islander, 3.1% Two or more races, 11.8% Hispanic of any race; Average household size: 2.64; Median age: 31.7; Age under 18: 30.9%; Age 65 and over: 10.3%; Males per 100 females: 89.5; Marriage status: 38.3% never married, 48.4% now married, 3.5% separated, 5.7% widowed, 7.6% divorced; Foreign born: 3.8%; Speak English only: 93.2%;

With disability: 15.8%; Veterans: 9.4%; Ancestry: 16.8% German, 15.8% Dutch, 13.5% English, 11.9% Irish, 6.9% American

Employment: 3.9% management, business, and financial, 2.7% computer, engineering, and science, 7.1% education, legal, community service, arts, and media, 4.5% healthcare practitioners, 30.2% service, 15.3% sales and office, 10.2% natural resources, construction, and maintenance, 26.2% production, transportation, and material moving

Income: Per capita: $18,776; Median household: $35,250; Average household: $49,611; Households with income of $100,000 or more: 8.8%; Poverty rate: 19.6%

Educational Attainment: High school diploma or higher: 85.4%; Bachelor's degree or higher: 14.2%; Graduate/professional degree or higher: 4.6%

School District(s)

Sodus Central SD (PK-12)

    2014-15 Enrollment: 1,134 . . . . (315) 483-5201

Housing: Homeownership rate: 57.2%; Median home value: $75,900; Median year structure built: Before 1940; Homeowner vacancy rate: 0.0%; Median selected monthly owner costs: $1,036 with a mortgage, $467 without a mortgage; Median gross rent: $667 per month; Rental vacancy rate: 6.9%

Health Insurance: 93.6% have insurance; 59.7% have private insurance; 46.3% have public insurance; 6.4% do not have insurance; 2.5% of children under 18 do not have insurance

Safety: Violent crime rate: 0.0 per 10,000 population; Property crime rate: 102.6 per 10,000 population

Transportation: Commute: 85.4% car, 3.6% public transportation, 4.7% walk, 2.2% work from home; Mean travel time to work: 25.9 minutes

SODUS POINT (village).

Covers a land area of 1.468 square miles and a water area of 0.006 square miles. Located at 43.26° N. Lat; 77.00° W. Long. Elevation is 276 feet.

History: Fired upon by British in War of 1812.

Population: 981; Growth (since 2000): -15.4%; Density: 668.3 persons per square mile; Race: 92.5% White, 3.5% Black/African American, 0.2% Asian, 0.1% American Indian/Alaska Native, 0.0% Native Hawaiian/Other Pacific Islander, 3.8% Two or more races, 1.0% Hispanic of any race; Average household size: 2.28; Median age: 48.6; Age under 18: 21.4%; Age 65 and over: 27.1%; Males per 100 females: 105.0; Marriage status: 22.8% never married, 57.2% now married, 3.6% separated, 9.0% widowed, 11.0% divorced; Foreign born: 2.1%; Speak English only: 97.8%; With disability: 12.5%; Veterans: 10.9%; Ancestry: 27.2% Irish, 22.1% German, 17.3% English, 12.3% Dutch, 10.4% Italian

Employment: 9.4% management, business, and financial, 3.1% computer, engineering, and science, 11.0% education, legal, community service, arts, and media, 10.1% healthcare practitioners, 19.2% service, 21.6% sales and office, 13.1% natural resources, construction, and maintenance, 12.4% production, transportation, and material moving

Income: Per capita: $30,209; Median household: $51,000; Average household: $67,437; Households with income of $100,000 or more: 19.8%; Poverty rate: 17.0%

Educational Attainment: High school diploma or higher: 96.2%; Bachelor's degree or higher: 24.8%; Graduate/professional degree or higher: 8.9%

Housing: Homeownership rate: 85.1%; Median home value: $127,500; Median year structure built: 1949; Homeowner vacancy rate: 2.3%; Median selected monthly owner costs: $1,272 with a mortgage, $590 without a mortgage; Median gross rent: $912 per month; Rental vacancy rate: 22.9%

Health Insurance: 97.5% have insurance; 74.5% have private insurance; 42.5% have public insurance; 2.5% do not have insurance; 0.0% of children under 18 do not have insurance

Safety: Violent crime rate: 11.4 per 10,000 population; Property crime rate: 22.9 per 10,000 population

Transportation: Commute: 91.8% car, 0.0% public transportation, 1.7% walk, 4.6% work from home; Mean travel time to work: 28.7 minutes

Additional Information Contacts

Village of Sodus Point . . . . (315) 483-9881

    http://www.soduspoint.info

WALWORTH (town).

Covers a land area of 33.853 square miles and a water area of 0.043 square miles. Located at 43.16° N. Lat; 77.31° W. Long. Elevation is 541 feet.

Population: 9,397; Growth (since 2000): 11.8%; Density: 277.6 persons per square mile; Race: 97.1% White, 1.1% Black/African American, 0.2% Asian, 0.2% American Indian/Alaska Native, 0.0% Native Hawaiian/Other

Pacific Islander, 1.1% Two or more races, 1.7% Hispanic of any race; Average household size: 2.77; Median age: 40.5; Age under 18: 27.1%; Age 65 and over: 11.8%; Males per 100 females: 99.3; Marriage status: 23.1% never married, 66.4% now married, 1.3% separated, 4.9% widowed, 5.6% divorced; Foreign born: 3.3%; Speak English only: 96.6%; With disability: 7.7%; Veterans: 8.8%; Ancestry: 24.4% Italian, 23.7% German, 20.3% Irish, 18.8% English, 6.6% Dutch

Employment: 17.9% management, business, and financial, 10.2% computer, engineering, and science, 11.2% education, legal, community service, arts, and media, 6.9% healthcare practitioners, 13.0% service, 24.2% sales and office, 8.2% natural resources, construction, and maintenance, 8.5% production, transportation, and material moving

Income: Per capita: $31,654; Median household: $74,719; Average household: $87,124; Households with income of $100,000 or more: 34.5%; Poverty rate: 2.6%

Educational Attainment: High school diploma or higher: 96.8%; Bachelor's degree or higher: 40.3%; Graduate/professional degree or higher: 15.2%

School District(s)

Gananda Central SD (KG-12)

    2014-15 Enrollment: 1,035 . . . . (315) 986-3521

Housing: Homeownership rate: 93.2%; Median home value: $154,100; Median year structure built: 1982; Homeowner vacancy rate: 0.8%; Median selected monthly owner costs: $1,575 with a mortgage, $582 without a mortgage; Median gross rent: $700 per month; Rental vacancy rate: 16.7%

Health Insurance: 98.6% have insurance; 88.4% have private insurance; 21.7% have public insurance; 1.4% do not have insurance; 0.0% of children under 18 do not have insurance

Transportation: Commute: 95.0% car, 0.7% public transportation, 0.0% walk, 3.7% work from home; Mean travel time to work: 26.1 minutes

Additional Information Contacts

Town of Walworth . . . . (315) 986-1400

    http://www.townwalworthny.com

WILLIAMSON (CDP).

Covers a land area of 3.840 square miles and a water area of 0.004 square miles. Located at 43.22° N. Lat; 77.18° W. Long. Elevation is 443 feet.

Population: 2,324; Growth (since 2000): n/a; Density: 605.2 persons per square mile; Race: 97.8% White, 1.3% Black/African American, 0.2% Asian, 0.0% American Indian/Alaska Native, 0.0% Native Hawaiian/Other Pacific Islander, 0.2% Two or more races, 1.1% Hispanic of any race; Average household size: 2.26; Median age: 45.9; Age under 18: 15.4%; Age 65 and over: 15.1%; Males per 100 females: 93.3; Marriage status: 26.2% never married, 50.4% now married, 5.2% separated, 6.7% widowed, 16.6% divorced; Foreign born: 2.7%; Speak English only: 95.4%; With disability: 13.9%; Veterans: 7.8%; Ancestry: 23.8% Dutch, 20.1% German, 15.7% English, 13.0% Irish, 8.6% Italian

Employment: 15.5% management, business, and financial, 3.1% computer, engineering, and science, 9.4% education, legal, community service, arts, and media, 5.2% healthcare practitioners, 14.7% service, 26.4% sales and office, 12.9% natural resources, construction, and maintenance, 12.9% production, transportation, and material moving

Income: Per capita: $24,873; Median household: $47,269; Average household: $55,892; Households with income of $100,000 or more: 10.9%; Poverty rate: 10.0%

Educational Attainment: High school diploma or higher: 92.7%; Bachelor's degree or higher: 17.6%; Graduate/professional degree or higher: 7.9%

School District(s)

Williamson Central SD (PK-12)

    2014-15 Enrollment: 1,128 . . . . (315) 589-9661

Housing: Homeownership rate: 69.5%; Median home value: $99,800; Median year structure built: 1947; Homeowner vacancy rate: 0.0%; Median selected monthly owner costs: $1,160 with a mortgage, $589 without a mortgage; Median gross rent: $589 per month; Rental vacancy rate: 2.8%

Health Insurance: 95.6% have insurance; 79.9% have private insurance; 30.7% have public insurance; 4.4% do not have insurance; 0.0% of children under 18 do not have insurance

Newspapers: Sun & Record (weekly circulation 3,500)

Transportation: Commute: 97.7% car, 0.0% public transportation, 0.0% walk, 2.0% work from home; Mean travel time to work: 26.3 minutes

WILLIAMSON (town). Covers a land area of 34.640 square miles and a water area of 0.015 square miles. Located at 43.25° N. Lat; 77.19° W. Long. Elevation is 443 feet.
Population: 6,884; Growth (since 2000): 1.6%; Density: 198.7 persons per square mile; Race: 90.4% White, 5.6% Black/African American, 0.3% Asian, 0.6% American Indian/Alaska Native, 0.8% Native Hawaiian/Other Pacific Islander, 1.8% Two or more races, 4.8% Hispanic of any race; Average household size: 2.56; Median age: 44.4; Age under 18: 21.3%; Age 65 and over: 16.9%; Males per 100 females: 100.0; Marriage status: 27.1% never married, 55.6% now married, 2.5% separated, 6.6% widowed, 10.7% divorced; Foreign born: 4.1%; Speak English only: 92.2%; With disability: 13.8%; Veterans: 8.8%; Ancestry: 21.3% Dutch, 19.1% German, 13.6% Irish, 12.7% English, 8.7% American
Employment: 13.4% management, business, and financial, 5.8% computer, engineering, and science, 11.3% education, legal, community service, arts, and media, 5.3% healthcare practitioners, 15.2% service, 22.5% sales and office, 14.1% natural resources, construction, and maintenance, 12.4% production, transportation, and material moving
Income: Per capita: $29,492; Median household: $55,203; Average household: $75,363; Households with income of $100,000 or more: 19.6%; Poverty rate: 11.9%
Educational Attainment: High school diploma or higher: 89.2%; Bachelor's degree or higher: 24.1%; Graduate/professional degree or higher: 10.5%

School District(s)
Williamson Central SD (PK-12)
    2014-15 Enrollment: 1,128 . . . . (315) 589-9661
Housing: Homeownership rate: 82.5%; Median home value: $123,800; Median year structure built: 1954; Homeowner vacancy rate: 0.4%; Median selected monthly owner costs: $1,360 with a mortgage, $575 without a mortgage; Median gross rent: $646 per month; Rental vacancy rate: 11.7%
Health Insurance: 93.4% have insurance; 77.2% have private insurance; 32.8% have public insurance; 6.6% do not have insurance; 10.5% of children under 18 do not have insurance
Newspapers: Sun & Record (weekly circulation 3,500)
Transportation: Commute: 90.9% car, 0.0% public transportation, 1.5% walk, 6.3% work from home; Mean travel time to work: 25.2 minutes
Additional Information Contacts
Town of Williamson . . . . (315) 589-8100
    http://town.williamson.ny.us

WOLCOTT (town). Covers a land area of 39.050 square miles and a water area of 0.901 square miles. Located at 43.27° N. Lat; 76.77° W. Long. Elevation is 371 feet.
History: Incorporated 1873.
Population: 4,347; Growth (since 2000): -7.4%; Density: 111.3 persons per square mile; Race: 93.3% White, 4.9% Black/African American, 0.0% Asian, 0.0% American Indian/Alaska Native, 0.0% Native Hawaiian/Other Pacific Islander, 1.3% Two or more races, 2.3% Hispanic of any race; Average household size: 2.42; Median age: 40.1; Age under 18: 24.7%; Age 65 and over: 14.4%; Males per 100 females: 109.4; Marriage status: 28.1% never married, 55.0% now married, 2.5% separated, 5.2% widowed, 11.7% divorced; Foreign born: 1.2%; Speak English only: 96.6%; With disability: 16.9%; Veterans: 11.0%; Ancestry: 18.3% German, 15.4% Irish, 14.1% English, 10.4% American, 6.6% Italian
Employment: 14.9% management, business, and financial, 2.1% computer, engineering, and science, 8.4% education, legal, community service, arts, and media, 3.6% healthcare practitioners, 20.5% service, 16.7% sales and office, 16.6% natural resources, construction, and maintenance, 17.3% production, transportation, and material moving
Income: Per capita: $20,768; Median household: $43,199; Average household: $50,894; Households with income of $100,000 or more: 6.8%; Poverty rate: 15.3%
Educational Attainment: High school diploma or higher: 85.0%; Bachelor's degree or higher: 9.6%; Graduate/professional degree or higher: 4.7%

School District(s)
North Rose-Wolcott Central SD (KG-12)
    2014-15 Enrollment: 1,315 . . . . (315) 594-3141
Housing: Homeownership rate: 75.0%; Median home value: $81,700; Median year structure built: 1958; Homeowner vacancy rate: 0.7%; Median selected monthly owner costs: $1,008 with a mortgage, $470 without a mortgage; Median gross rent: $577 per month; Rental vacancy rate: 5.5%

Health Insurance: 89.5% have insurance; 59.4% have private insurance; 42.5% have public insurance; 10.5% do not have insurance; 7.9% of children under 18 do not have insurance
Transportation: Commute: 87.7% car, 0.0% public transportation, 6.3% walk, 2.3% work from home; Mean travel time to work: 26.7 minutes
Additional Information Contacts
Town of Wolcott . . . . (315) 594-9431
    http://www.wolcottny.org/townindex.php

WOLCOTT (village). Covers a land area of 1.948 square miles and a water area of 0.019 square miles. Located at 43.22° N. Lat; 76.81° W. Long. Elevation is 371 feet.
Population: 1,723; Growth (since 2000): 0.6%; Density: 884.7 persons per square mile; Race: 94.5% White, 2.9% Black/African American, 0.0% Asian, 0.0% American Indian/Alaska Native, 0.0% Native Hawaiian/Other Pacific Islander, 2.2% Two or more races, 3.4% Hispanic of any race; Average household size: 2.30; Median age: 37.6; Age under 18: 25.0%; Age 65 and over: 14.2%; Males per 100 females: 97.8; Marriage status: 36.8% never married, 37.7% now married, 4.0% separated, 7.7% widowed, 17.8% divorced; Foreign born: 3.0%; Speak English only: 97.9%; With disability: 23.7%; Veterans: 8.5%; Ancestry: 14.2% German, 13.1% American, 12.1% English, 11.7% Irish, 9.7% Dutch
Employment: 10.4% management, business, and financial, 2.2% computer, engineering, and science, 7.7% education, legal, community service, arts, and media, 4.6% healthcare practitioners, 29.1% service, 17.3% sales and office, 12.4% natural resources, construction, and maintenance, 16.4% production, transportation, and material moving
Income: Per capita: $19,862; Median household: $33,021; Average household: $44,689; Households with income of $100,000 or more: 9.1%; Poverty rate: 25.0%
Educational Attainment: High school diploma or higher: 84.1%; Bachelor's degree or higher: 11.7%; Graduate/professional degree or higher: 5.4%

School District(s)
North Rose-Wolcott Central SD (KG-12)
    2014-15 Enrollment: 1,315 . . . . (315) 594-3141
Housing: Homeownership rate: 57.6%; Median home value: $77,600; Median year structure built: 1946; Homeowner vacancy rate: 0.0%; Median selected monthly owner costs: $916 with a mortgage, $467 without a mortgage; Median gross rent: $464 per month; Rental vacancy rate: 5.7%
Health Insurance: 91.6% have insurance; 55.9% have private insurance; 48.8% have public insurance; 8.4% do not have insurance; 3.3% of children under 18 do not have insurance
Safety: Violent crime rate: 0.0 per 10,000 population; Property crime rate: 24.4 per 10,000 population
Transportation: Commute: 86.7% car, 0.0% public transportation, 10.4% walk, 1.6% work from home; Mean travel time to work: 24.7 minutes

Westchester County

Located in southeastern New York; bounded on the west by the Hudson River, on the southeast by Long Island Sound, and on the east by Connecticut; drained by the Byram, Mianus, and Rippowam Rivers. Covers a land area of 430.497 square miles, a water area of 69.498 square miles, and is located in the Eastern Time Zone at 41.15° N. Lat., 73.75° W. Long. The county was founded in 1683. County seat is White Plains.

Westchester County is part of the New York-Newark-Jersey City, NY-NJ-PA Metropolitan Statistical Area. The entire metro area includes: Dutchess County-Putnam County, NY Metropolitan Division (Dutchess County, NY; Putnam County, NY); Nassau County-Suffolk County, NY Metropolitan Division (Nassau County, NY; Suffolk County, NY); Newark, NJ-PA Metropolitan Division (Essex County, NJ; Hunterdon County, NJ; Morris County, NJ; Somerset County, NJ; Sussex County, NJ; Union County, NJ; Pike County, PA); New York-Jersey City-White Plains, NY-NJ Metropolitan Division (Bergen County, NJ; Hudson County, NJ; Middlesex County, NJ; Monmouth County, NJ; Ocean County, NJ; Passaic County, NJ; Bronx County, NY; Kings County, NY; New York County, NY; Orange County, NY; Queens County, NY; Richmond County, NY; Rockland County, NY; Westchester County, NY)

Weather Station: Dobbs Ferry Ardsley   Elevation: 200 feet

	Jan	Feb	Mar	Apr	May	Jun	Jul	Aug	Sep	Oct	Nov	Dec
High	39	42	50	62	72	81	85	84	76	65	54	43
Low	23	25	31	40	50	59	64	64	56	45	36	28
Precip	3.8	3.0	4.5	4.7	4.5	4.4	4.6	4.2	4.6	4.5	4.4	4.3
Snow	9.0	8.4	5.7	0.9	tr	0.0	0.0	0.0	0.0	0.1	0.7	5.8

High and Low temperatures in degrees Fahrenheit; Precipitation and Snow in inches

Weather Station: Yorktown Heights 1 W   Elevation: 669 feet

	Jan	Feb	Mar	Apr	May	Jun	Jul	Aug	Sep	Oct	Nov	Dec
High	34	38	47	59	69	78	82	81	73	62	51	40
Low	19	21	28	39	49	58	63	62	54	43	35	25
Precip	3.6	3.0	4.0	4.6	4.4	4.8	4.8	4.4	4.5	4.5	4.4	3.9
Snow	11.0	10.3	7.7	2.1	0.0	0.0	0.0	0.0	0.0	tr	1.3	7.6

High and Low temperatures in degrees Fahrenheit; Precipitation and Snow in inches

Population: 967,315; Growth (since 2000): 4.7%; Density: 2,247.0 persons per square mile; Race: 66.6% White, 14.4% Black/African American, 5.7% Asian, 0.4% American Indian/Alaska Native, 0.0% Native Hawaiian/Other Pacific Islander, 3.0% two or more races, 23.3% Hispanic of any race; Average household size: 2.75; Median age: 40.3; Age under 18: 23.2%; Age 65 and over: 15.3%; Males per 100 females: 92.7; Marriage status: 34.0% never married, 52.4% now married, 2.2% separated, 5.8% widowed, 7.8% divorced; Foreign born: 25.3%; Speak English only: 66.9%; With disability: 9.0%; Veterans: 4.6%; Ancestry: 18.0% Italian, 12.1% Irish, 6.7% German, 5.2% American, 3.5% Polish

Religion: Six largest groups: 45.9% Catholicism, 5.2% Judaism, 1.7% Methodist/Pietist, 1.6% Baptist, 1.5% Episcopalianism/Anglicanism, 1.4% Presbyterian-Reformed

Economy: Unemployment rate: 4.3%; Leading industries: 13.2 % professional, scientific, and technical services; 12.1 % retail trade; 11.2 % health care and social assistance; Farms: 131 totaling 7,752 acres; Company size: 23 employ 1,000 or more persons, 42 employ 500 to 999 persons, 511 employs 100 to 499 persons, 31,116 employ less than 100 persons; Business ownership: 39,870 women-owned, 9,982 Black-owned, 16,965 Hispanic-owned, 7,206 Asian-owned, 698 American Indian/Alaska Native-owned

Employment: 19.0% management, business, and financial, 4.4% computer, engineering, and science, 16.3% education, legal, community service, arts, and media, 6.7% healthcare practitioners, 18.8% service, 22.1% sales and office, 6.5% natural resources, construction, and maintenance, 6.2% production, transportation, and material moving

Income: Per capita: $48,885; Median household: $83,958; Average household: $134,714; Households with income of $100,000 or more: 43.7%; Poverty rate: 9.6%

Educational Attainment: High school diploma or higher: 87.5%; Bachelor's degree or higher: 46.7%; Graduate/professional degree or higher: 23.1%

Housing: Homeownership rate: 61.5%; Median home value: $506,900; Median year structure built: 1956; Homeowner vacancy rate: 1.9%; Median selected monthly owner costs: $3,289 with a mortgage, $1,362 without a mortgage; Median gross rent: $1,364 per month; Rental vacancy rate: 6.5%

Vital Statistics: Birth rate: 109.6 per 10,000 population; Death rate: 73.5 per 10,000 population; Age-adjusted cancer mortality rate: 134.4 deaths per 100,000 population

Health Insurance: 90.4% have insurance; 73.6% have private insurance; 28.0% have public insurance; 9.6% do not have insurance; 2.8% of children under 18 do not have insurance

Health Care: Physicians: 66.2 per 10,000 population; Dentists: 10.6 per 10,000 population; Hospital beds: 38.3 per 10,000 population; Hospital admissions: 1,254.5 per 10,000 population

Air Quality Index (AQI): Percent of Days: 81.9% good, 17.5% moderate, 0.5% unhealthy for sensitive individuals, 0.0% unhealthy, 0.0% very unhealthy; Annual median: 36; Annual maximum: 116

Transportation: Commute: 66.4% car, 21.8% public transportation, 5.2% walk, 5.0% work from home; Mean travel time to work: 32.9 minutes

2016 Presidential Election: 31.5% Trump, 65.5% Clinton, 1.9% Johnson, 1.0% Stein

National and State Parks: Brinton Brook National Audubon Society Sanctuary; Echo Lake State Park; John Jay Homestead State Historic Site; Mohansic State Park; Saint Pauls Church National Historic Site; Titus Mill Pond State Tidal Wetlands

Additional Information Contacts
Westchester Government . . . . (914) 995-2900
  http://www3.westchestergov.com

Westchester County Communities

AMAWALK (unincorporated postal area)
ZCTA: 10501
  Covers a land area of 1.399 square miles and a water area of 0.001 square miles. Located at 41.30° N. Lat; 73.76° W. Long. Elevation is 413 feet.
Population: 1,226; Growth (since 2000): 45.4%; Density: 876.1 persons per square mile; Race: 91.6% White, 0.0% Black/African American, 1.1% Asian, 0.0% American Indian/Alaska Native, 0.0% Native Hawaiian/Other Pacific Islander, 3.9% Two or more races, 6.6% Hispanic of any race; Average household size: 3.07; Median age: 47.6; Age under 18: 21.8%; Age 65 and over: 16.1%; Males per 100 females: 103.8; Marriage status: 22.5% never married, 66.2% now married, 0.0% separated, 4.6% widowed, 6.7% divorced; Foreign born: 10.3%; Speak English only: 84.3%; With disability: 14.5%; Veterans: 4.2%; Ancestry: 40.2% Italian, 26.5% Irish, 14.4% German, 11.7% American, 5.1% Polish

Employment: 29.5% management, business, and financial, 4.0% computer, engineering, and science, 17.9% education, legal, community service, arts, and media, 5.4% healthcare practitioners, 4.9% service, 28.7% sales and office, 6.2% natural resources, construction, and maintenance, 3.5% production, transportation, and material moving

Income: Per capita: $56,962; Median household: $141,563; Average household: $168,224; Households with income of $100,000 or more: 67.6%; Poverty rate: 0.4%

Educational Attainment: High school diploma or higher: 95.6%; Bachelor's degree or higher: 48.8%; Graduate/professional degree or higher: 17.2%

Housing: Homeownership rate: 97.7%; Median home value: $606,000; Median year structure built: 1971; Homeowner vacancy rate: 0.0%; Median selected monthly owner costs: $3,573 with a mortgage, $1,289 without a mortgage; Median gross rent: n/a per month; Rental vacancy rate: 0.0%

Health Insurance: 97.6% have insurance; 87.2% have private insurance; 22.5% have public insurance; 2.4% do not have insurance; 0.0% of children under 18 do not have insurance

Transportation: Commute: 91.3% car, 5.8% public transportation, 0.0% walk, 2.8% work from home; Mean travel time to work: 38.4 minutes

ARDSLEY (village).
Covers a land area of 1.323 square miles and a water area of 0 square miles. Located at 41.01° N. Lat; 73.84° W. Long. Elevation is 210 feet.

History: The town took the name "Ardsley" after the name of a local baron's estate, and the first village postmaster was appointed in 1883. Incorporated in 1896, Ardsley would continue to grow at a steady pace, until a fire destroyed the village center in 1914.

Population: 4,542; Growth (since 2000): 6.4%; Density: 3,434.2 persons per square mile; Race: 69.0% White, 4.8% Black/African American, 19.3% Asian, 0.0% American Indian/Alaska Native, 0.0% Native Hawaiian/Other Pacific Islander, 3.2% Two or more races, 12.1% Hispanic of any race; Average household size: 2.93; Median age: 45.5; Age under 18: 23.0%; Age 65 and over: 18.8%; Males per 100 females: 88.4; Marriage status: 29.2% never married, 60.0% now married, 0.2% separated, 5.2% widowed, 5.7% divorced; Foreign born: 29.5%; Speak English only: 65.6%; With disability: 9.4%; Veterans: 3.7%; Ancestry: 16.8% Irish, 14.4% Italian, 6.1% Polish, 5.9% Russian, 4.9% German

Employment: 23.2% management, business, and financial, 8.3% computer, engineering, and science, 24.5% education, legal, community service, arts, and media, 8.4% healthcare practitioners, 12.8% service, 17.8% sales and office, 1.2% natural resources, construction, and maintenance, 3.8% production, transportation, and material moving

Income: Per capita: $65,176; Median household: $141,447; Average household: $187,037; Households with income of $100,000 or more: 62.4%; Poverty rate: 1.6%

Educational Attainment: High school diploma or higher: 94.0%; Bachelor's degree or higher: 68.2%; Graduate/professional degree or higher: 36.6%

School District(s)
Ardsley Union Free SD (KG-12)
  2014-15 Enrollment: 2,089 . . . . (914) 693-6300

Housing: Homeownership rate: 82.8%; Median home value: $616,600; Median year structure built: 1956; Homeowner vacancy rate: 0.0%; Median selected monthly owner costs: $3,732 with a mortgage, $1,500+ without a

mortgage; Median gross rent: $1,238 per month; Rental vacancy rate: 7.7%

Health Insurance: 93.3% have insurance; 85.6% have private insurance; 23.8% have public insurance; 6.7% do not have insurance; 3.9% of children under 18 do not have insurance

Safety: Violent crime rate: 0.0 per 10,000 population; Property crime rate: 67.7 per 10,000 population

Transportation: Commute: 72.4% car, 19.0% public transportation, 4.3% walk, 2.6% work from home; Mean travel time to work: 32.1 minutes

Additional Information Contacts
Village of Ardsley.................................. (914) 693-1550
   http://www.ardsleyvillage.com

ARDSLEY ON HUDSON (unincorporated postal area)
ZCTA: 10503

Covers a land area of 0.015 square miles and a water area of 0 square miles. Located at 41.03° N. Lat; 73.88° W. Long..

Population: 168; Growth (since 2000): 46.1%; Density: 11,302.5 persons per square mile; Race: 81.0% White, 0.0% Black/African American, 9.5% Asian, 0.0% American Indian/Alaska Native, 0.0% Native Hawaiian/Other Pacific Islander, 0.0% Two or more races, 9.5% Hispanic of any race; Average household size: 1.58; Median age: 60.4; Age under 18: 0.0%; Age 65 and over: 26.8%; Males per 100 females: 63.6; Marriage status: 0.0% never married, 81.5% now married, 8.3% separated, 9.5% widowed, 8.9% divorced; Foreign born: 9.5%; Speak English only: 72.6%; With disability: 8.3%; Veterans: 0.0%; Ancestry: 26.8% German, 10.1% English, 9.5% Polish, 8.9% French, 8.9% Hungarian

Employment: 42.1% management, business, and financial, 0.0% computer, engineering, and science, 38.2% education, legal, community service, arts, and media, 0.0% healthcare practitioners, 0.0% service, 19.7% sales and office, 0.0% natural resources, construction, and maintenance, 0.0% production, transportation, and material moving

Income: Per capita: $89,493; Median household: n/a; Average household: $141,105; Households with income of $100,000 or more: 57.6%; Poverty rate: 8.3%

Educational Attainment: High school diploma or higher: 100.0%; Bachelor's degree or higher: 82.7%; Graduate/professional degree or higher: 73.2%

Housing: Homeownership rate: 100.0%; Median home value: $575,700; Median year structure built: Before 1940; Homeowner vacancy rate: 0.0%; Median selected monthly owner costs: n/a with a mortgage, n/a without a mortgage; Median gross rent: n/a per month; Rental vacancy rate: 0.0%

Health Insurance: 100.0% have insurance; 91.7% have private insurance; 26.8% have public insurance; 0.0% do not have insurance; 0.0% of children under 18 do not have insurance

Transportation: Commute: 59.2% car, 18.4% public transportation, 0.0% walk, 22.4% work from home; Mean travel time to work: 0.0 minutes

ARMONK (CDP). Covers a land area of 5.966 square miles and a water area of 0.093 square miles. Located at 41.13° N. Lat; 73.72° W. Long. Elevation is 387 feet.

History: The Indians of North Castle were the Siwanoys, who belonged to the Wappinger Confederacy, and were part of the Algonkian-speaking group. They gave the name of Armonck (the name the Indians called Byram River) undoubtedly gave us thw hamlet name of Armonk.

Population: 4,541; Growth (since 2000): 31.2%; Density: 761.1 persons per square mile; Race: 94.8% White, 0.7% Black/African American, 2.6% Asian, 0.0% American Indian/Alaska Native, 0.0% Native Hawaiian/Other Pacific Islander, 0.7% Two or more races, 10.5% Hispanic of any race; Average household size: 3.29; Median age: 39.8; Age under 18: 32.7%; Age 65 and over: 14.2%; Males per 100 females: 97.0; Marriage status: 26.9% never married, 66.0% now married, 1.7% separated, 3.5% widowed, 3.5% divorced; Foreign born: 9.3%; Speak English only: 82.6%; With disability: 6.7%; Veterans: 5.4%; Ancestry: 23.0% Italian, 12.0% Irish, 9.2% German, 7.8% Russian, 7.5% Eastern European

Employment: 33.4% management, business, and financial, 7.2% computer, engineering, and science, 16.0% education, legal, community service, arts, and media, 10.1% healthcare practitioners, 6.8% service, 23.5% sales and office, 2.1% natural resources, construction, and maintenance, 0.9% production, transportation, and material moving

Income: Per capita: $94,278; Median household: $183,036; Average household: $303,240; Households with income of $100,000 or more: 72.7%; Poverty rate: 1.9%

Educational Attainment: High school diploma or higher: 97.5%; Bachelor's degree or higher: 75.0%; Graduate/professional degree or higher: 36.5%

School District(s)
Byram Hills Central SD (KG-12)
   2014-15 Enrollment: 2,549 .... (914) 273-4082

Housing: Homeownership rate: 90.6%; Median home value: $907,400; Median year structure built: 1968; Homeowner vacancy rate: 4.5%; Median selected monthly owner costs: $4,000+ with a mortgage, $1,500+ without a mortgage; Median gross rent: $3,500+ per month; Rental vacancy rate: 6.5%

Health Insurance: 96.0% have insurance; 92.8% have private insurance; 13.4% have public insurance; 4.0% do not have insurance; 2.8% of children under 18 do not have insurance

Transportation: Commute: 79.1% car, 15.7% public transportation, 1.0% walk, 4.2% work from home; Mean travel time to work: 31.9 minutes

BALDWIN PLACE (unincorporated postal area)
ZCTA: 10505

Covers a land area of 0.652 square miles and a water area of 0 square miles. Located at 41.34° N. Lat; 73.75° W. Long..

Population: 868; Growth (since 2000): n/a; Density: 1,330.5 persons per square mile; Race: 85.9% White, 1.5% Black/African American, 12.6% Asian, 0.0% American Indian/Alaska Native, 0.0% Native Hawaiian/Other Pacific Islander, 0.0% Two or more races, 7.4% Hispanic of any race; Average household size: 3.25; Median age: 36.9; Age under 18: 39.5%; Age 65 and over: 13.2%; Males per 100 females: 98.4; Marriage status: 31.5% never married, 66.7% now married, 0.0% separated, 0.0% widowed, 1.9% divorced; Foreign born: 7.5%; Speak English only: 80.4%; With disability: 13.7%; Veterans: 8.2%; Ancestry: 30.9% Italian, 18.4% Irish, 15.7% American, 6.5% German, 4.5% Russian

Employment: 29.2% management, business, and financial, 0.0% computer, engineering, and science, 13.2% education, legal, community service, arts, and media, 12.6% healthcare practitioners, 18.8% service, 21.6% sales and office, 1.7% natural resources, construction, and maintenance, 2.8% production, transportation, and material moving

Income: Per capita: $50,365; Median household: $143,750; Average household: $162,688; Households with income of $100,000 or more: 59.2%; Poverty rate: n/a

Educational Attainment: High school diploma or higher: 100.0%; Bachelor's degree or higher: 56.3%; Graduate/professional degree or higher: 38.8%

Housing: Homeownership rate: 64.8%; Median home value: $757,500; Median year structure built: 2002; Homeowner vacancy rate: 0.0%; Median selected monthly owner costs: $4,000 with a mortgage, $1,380 without a mortgage; Median gross rent: $1,316 per month; Rental vacancy rate: 0.0%

Health Insurance: 94.7% have insurance; 80.9% have private insurance; 26.3% have public insurance; 5.3% do not have insurance; 4.4% of children under 18 do not have insurance

Transportation: Commute: 81.7% car, 11.5% public transportation, 0.0% walk, 6.7% work from home; Mean travel time to work: 42.9 minutes

BEDFORD (CDP). Covers a land area of 3.507 square miles and a water area of 0.048 square miles. Located at 41.20° N. Lat; 73.65° W. Long. Elevation is 377 feet.

Population: 2,044; Growth (since 2000): 18.6%; Density: 582.8 persons per square mile; Race: 92.5% White, 1.9% Black/African American, 3.7% Asian, 0.0% American Indian/Alaska Native, 0.0% Native Hawaiian/Other Pacific Islander, 1.5% Two or more races, 3.2% Hispanic of any race; Average household size: 3.03; Median age: 44.4; Age under 18: 28.0%; Age 65 and over: 17.2%; Males per 100 females: 99.1; Marriage status: 22.2% never married, 66.6% now married, 0.0% separated, 6.9% widowed, 4.3% divorced; Foreign born: 9.5%; Speak English only: 93.7%; With disability: 6.7%; Veterans: 3.8%; Ancestry: 26.1% Irish, 21.4% Italian, 16.0% German, 15.5% English, 6.0% American

Employment: 33.0% management, business, and financial, 4.4% computer, engineering, and science, 19.7% education, legal, community service, arts, and media, 5.8% healthcare practitioners, 13.9% service,

21.0% sales and office, 2.3% natural resources, construction, and maintenance, 0.0% production, transportation, and material moving
Income: Per capita: $82,141; Median household: $188,705; Average household: $246,422; Households with income of $100,000 or more: 74.9%; Poverty rate: 3.0%
Educational Attainment: High school diploma or higher: 96.6%; Bachelor's degree or higher: 69.8%; Graduate/professional degree or higher: 30.2%

School District(s)
Bedford Central SD (PK-12)
   2014-15 Enrollment: 4,390 . . . . (914) 241-6010
Housing: Homeownership rate: 95.1%; Median home value: $848,300; Median year structure built: 1961; Homeowner vacancy rate: 0.0%; Median selected monthly owner costs: $3,917 with a mortgage, $1,500+ without a mortgage; Median gross rent: n/a per month; Rental vacancy rate: 41.1%
Health Insurance: 99.6% have insurance; 94.4% have private insurance; 16.1% have public insurance; 0.4% do not have insurance; 0.0% of children under 18 do not have insurance
Transportation: Commute: 63.2% car, 23.4% public transportation, 0.8% walk, 12.6% work from home; Mean travel time to work: 45.8 minutes

BEDFORD (town).
Covers a land area of 37.173 square miles and a water area of 2.247 square miles. Located at 41.23° N. Lat; 73.66° W. Long. Elevation is 377 feet.
History: Caramoor Art and Music Center. Maximum-security Tacoma Correctional Facility for Women is at nearby Bedford Hills village. Also known as Bedford Village.
Population: 17,739; Growth (since 2000): -2.2%; Density: 477.2 persons per square mile; Race: 79.2% White, 6.1% Black/African American, 3.5% Asian, 0.3% American Indian/Alaska Native, 0.0% Native Hawaiian/Other Pacific Islander, 2.7% Two or more races, 14.2% Hispanic of any race; Average household size: 2.94; Median age: 41.1; Age under 18: 26.5%; Age 65 and over: 12.8%; Males per 100 females: 84.3; Marriage status: 31.0% never married, 58.0% now married, 1.4% separated, 4.1% widowed, 6.9% divorced; Foreign born: 15.5%; Speak English only: 80.3%; With disability: 5.2%; Veterans: 4.9%; Ancestry: 20.4% Italian, 15.4% Irish, 11.9% German, 8.0% English, 5.9% Russian
Employment: 27.7% management, business, and financial, 3.8% computer, engineering, and science, 20.2% education, legal, community service, arts, and media, 7.2% healthcare practitioners, 17.1% service, 18.8% sales and office, 3.7% natural resources, construction, and maintenance, 1.4% production, transportation, and material moving
Income: Per capita: $71,544; Median household: $127,644; Average household: $226,076; Households with income of $100,000 or more: 59.4%; Poverty rate: 6.2%
Educational Attainment: High school diploma or higher: 88.4%; Bachelor's degree or higher: 57.9%; Graduate/professional degree or higher: 27.8%

School District(s)
Bedford Central SD (PK-12)
   2014-15 Enrollment: 4,390 . . . . (914) 241-6010
Housing: Homeownership rate: 74.8%; Median home value: $771,000; Median year structure built: 1961; Homeowner vacancy rate: 3.9%; Median selected monthly owner costs: $4,000+ with a mortgage, $1,500+ without a mortgage; Median gross rent: $1,421 per month; Rental vacancy rate: 7.5%
Health Insurance: 91.1% have insurance; 78.7% have private insurance; 22.7% have public insurance; 8.9% do not have insurance; 3.1% of children under 18 do not have insurance
Safety: Violent crime rate: 2.2 per 10,000 population; Property crime rate: 44.9 per 10,000 population
Transportation: Commute: 64.4% car, 22.0% public transportation, 2.5% walk, 10.3% work from home; Mean travel time to work: 39.2 minutes
Additional Information Contacts
Town of Bedford . . . . (914) 666-4534
   http://www.bedfordny.info

BEDFORD HILLS (CDP).
Covers a land area of 1.006 square miles and a water area of 0 square miles. Located at 41.24° N. Lat; 73.69° W. Long. Elevation is 341 feet.
Population: 3,271; Growth (since 2000): n/a; Density: 3,251.2 persons per square mile; Race: 59.4% White, 5.9% Black/African American, 1.4% Asian, 0.0% American Indian/Alaska Native, 0.0% Native Hawaiian/Other Pacific Islander, 0.0% Two or more races, 46.8% Hispanic of any race; Average household size: 2.63; Median age: 34.8; Age under 18: 29.9%;

Age 65 and over: 11.5%; Males per 100 females: 97.8; Marriage status: 37.9% never married, 55.3% now married, 1.5% separated, 3.2% widowed, 3.6% divorced; Foreign born: 35.3%; Speak English only: 52.2%; With disability: 4.5%; Veterans: 4.7%; Ancestry: 17.0% Italian, 8.7% German, 8.1% Irish, 4.2% Norwegian, 4.0% Russian
Employment: 10.3% management, business, and financial, 3.8% computer, engineering, and science, 15.6% education, legal, community service, arts, and media, 7.4% healthcare practitioners, 36.6% service, 14.7% sales and office, 10.4% natural resources, construction, and maintenance, 1.3% production, transportation, and material moving
Income: Per capita: $28,485; Median household: $42,155; Average household: $74,454; Households with income of $100,000 or more: 28.7%; Poverty rate: 11.3%
Educational Attainment: High school diploma or higher: 73.1%; Bachelor's degree or higher: 34.1%; Graduate/professional degree or higher: 18.8%

School District(s)
Bedford Central SD (PK-12)
   2014-15 Enrollment: 4,390 . . . . (914) 241-6010
Housing: Homeownership rate: 41.9%; Median home value: $470,700; Median year structure built: 1963; Homeowner vacancy rate: 0.0%; Median selected monthly owner costs: $2,687 with a mortgage, $966 without a mortgage; Median gross rent: $1,358 per month; Rental vacancy rate: 0.0%
Health Insurance: 69.3% have insurance; 42.9% have private insurance; 31.9% have public insurance; 30.7% do not have insurance; 14.9% of children under 18 do not have insurance
Newspapers: Record-Review (weekly circulation 4,000)
Transportation: Commute: 83.7% car, 12.0% public transportation, 1.4% walk, 2.8% work from home; Mean travel time to work: 33.9 minutes

BRIARCLIFF MANOR (village).
Covers a land area of 5.962 square miles and a water area of 0.850 square miles. Located at 41.14° N. Lat; 73.85° W. Long. Elevation is 249 feet.
History: Settled 1896, incorporated 1902.
Population: 7,739; Growth (since 2000): 0.6%; Density: 1,298.1 persons per square mile; Race: 79.2% White, 3.0% Black/African American, 11.0% Asian, 0.0% American Indian/Alaska Native, 0.2% Native Hawaiian/Other Pacific Islander, 4.6% Two or more races, 6.3% Hispanic of any race; Average household size: 2.68; Median age: 46.1; Age under 18: 21.8%; Age 65 and over: 17.9%; Males per 100 females: 92.3; Marriage status: 27.6% never married, 60.5% now married, 0.9% separated, 7.0% widowed, 4.9% divorced; Foreign born: 12.6%; Speak English only: 84.8%; With disability: 9.7%; Veterans: 5.8%; Ancestry: 18.1% Italian, 12.9% Irish, 8.8% American, 8.5% Russian, 8.4% German
Employment: 27.2% management, business, and financial, 6.1% computer, engineering, and science, 21.1% education, legal, community service, arts, and media, 11.4% healthcare practitioners, 7.2% service, 23.1% sales and office, 1.8% natural resources, construction, and maintenance, 2.1% production, transportation, and material moving
Income: Per capita: $76,256; Median household: $141,170; Average household: $220,241; Households with income of $100,000 or more: 67.5%; Poverty rate: 2.2%
Educational Attainment: High school diploma or higher: 95.5%; Bachelor's degree or higher: 70.4%; Graduate/professional degree or higher: 39.1%

School District(s)
Briarcliff Manor Union Free SD (KG-12)
   2014-15 Enrollment: 1,527 . . . . (914) 432-8115
Housing: Homeownership rate: 83.0%; Median home value: $666,700; Median year structure built: 1965; Homeowner vacancy rate: 0.4%; Median selected monthly owner costs: $4,000+ with a mortgage, $1,500+ without a mortgage; Median gross rent: $1,384 per month; Rental vacancy rate: 0.0%
Health Insurance: 98.5% have insurance; 92.3% have private insurance; 20.1% have public insurance; 1.5% do not have insurance; 0.4% of children under 18 do not have insurance
Safety: Violent crime rate: 0.0 per 10,000 population; Property crime rate: 39.9 per 10,000 population
Transportation: Commute: 54.9% car, 27.7% public transportation, 4.0% walk, 13.1% work from home; Mean travel time to work: 39.3 minutes
Additional Information Contacts
Village of Briarcliff Manor . . . . (914) 941-4800
   http://www.briarcliffmanor.org/pages/index

BRONXVILLE (village). Covers a land area of 0.962 square miles and a water area of 0 square miles. Located at 40.94° N. Lat; 73.83° W. Long. Elevation is 92 feet.

History: Seat of Sarah Lawrence College. Settled 1664, incorporated 1898.

Population: 6,409; Growth (since 2000): -2.0%; Density: 6,662.3 persons per square mile; Race: 89.9% White, 0.7% Black/African American, 5.8% Asian, 0.0% American Indian/Alaska Native, 0.0% Native Hawaiian/Other Pacific Islander, 2.8% Two or more races, 4.7% Hispanic of any race; Average household size: 2.85; Median age: 40.9; Age under 18: 29.5%; Age 65 and over: 13.4%; Males per 100 females: 88.7; Marriage status: 26.4% never married, 61.7% now married, 1.0% separated, 5.5% widowed, 6.3% divorced; Foreign born: 13.5%; Speak English only: 84.6%; With disability: 4.6%; Veterans: 3.4%; Ancestry: 26.2% Irish, 16.1% German, 13.9% English, 13.6% Italian, 5.1% American

Employment: 36.3% management, business, and financial, 2.9% computer, engineering, and science, 24.0% education, legal, community service, arts, and media, 9.2% healthcare practitioners, 5.7% service, 19.4% sales and office, 1.9% natural resources, construction, and maintenance, 0.6% production, transportation, and material moving

Income: Per capita: $108,627; Median household: $198,839; Average household: $317,063; Households with income of $100,000 or more: 72.7%; Poverty rate: 3.0%

Educational Attainment: High school diploma or higher: 98.7%; Bachelor's degree or higher: 81.3%; Graduate/professional degree or higher: 47.8%

School District(s)
Bronxville Union Free SD (KG-12)
    2014-15 Enrollment: 1,716 . . . . (914) 395-0500

Four-year College(s)
Concordia College-New York (Private, Not-for-profit, Lutheran Church - Missouri Synod)
    Fall 2014 Enrollment: 1,037 . . . . (914) 337-9300
    2015-16 Tuition: In-state $29,700; Out-of-state $29,700
Sarah Lawrence College (Private, Not-for-profit)
    Fall 2014 Enrollment: 1,761 . . . . (914) 337-0700
    2015-16 Tuition: In-state $51,038; Out-of-state $51,038

Housing: Homeownership rate: 79.7%; Median home value: $916,700; Median year structure built: Before 1940; Homeowner vacancy rate: 3.2%; Median selected monthly owner costs: $4,000+ with a mortgage, $1,500+ without a mortgage; Median gross rent: $2,512 per month; Rental vacancy rate: 0.0%

Health Insurance: 98.5% have insurance; 92.5% have private insurance; 16.7% have public insurance; 1.5% do not have insurance; 0.0% of children under 18 do not have insurance

Hospitals: Lawrence Hospital Center (281 beds)

Transportation: Commute: 41.4% car, 45.2% public transportation, 5.7% walk, 6.7% work from home; Mean travel time to work: 39.1 minutes

Additional Information Contacts
Village of Bronxville . . . . (914) 337-6500
    http://villageofbronxville.com

BUCHANAN (village). Covers a land area of 1.382 square miles and a water area of 0.339 square miles. Located at 41.26° N. Lat; 73.95° W. Long. Elevation is 39 feet.

History: Incorporated 1928.

Population: 2,218; Growth (since 2000): 1.3%; Density: 1,605.4 persons per square mile; Race: 77.0% White, 2.3% Black/African American, 2.3% Asian, 0.0% American Indian/Alaska Native, 0.0% Native Hawaiian/Other Pacific Islander, 4.8% Two or more races, 17.4% Hispanic of any race; Average household size: 2.72; Median age: 44.4; Age under 18: 22.2%; Age 65 and over: 14.0%; Males per 100 females: 101.1; Marriage status: 23.5% never married, 64.5% now married, 2.6% separated, 6.3% widowed, 5.7% divorced; Foreign born: 15.6%; Speak English only: 77.9%; With disability: 13.4%; Veterans: 7.6%; Ancestry: 27.1% Irish, 24.3% Italian, 17.7% German, 7.5% Polish, 7.4% English

Employment: 15.0% management, business, and financial, 4.5% computer, engineering, and science, 11.3% education, legal, community service, arts, and media, 7.8% healthcare practitioners, 17.5% service, 25.7% sales and office, 8.4% natural resources, construction, and maintenance, 9.9% production, transportation, and material moving

Income: Per capita: $42,166; Median household: $97,935; Average household: $111,920; Households with income of $100,000 or more: 47.7%; Poverty rate: 5.5%

Educational Attainment: High school diploma or higher: 92.5%; Bachelor's degree or higher: 33.8%; Graduate/professional degree or higher: 14.3%

School District(s)
Hendrick Hudson Central SD (KG-12)
    2014-15 Enrollment: 2,366 . . . . (914) 257-5100

Housing: Homeownership rate: 75.9%; Median home value: $376,200; Median year structure built: 1952; Homeowner vacancy rate: 4.1%; Median selected monthly owner costs: $2,584 with a mortgage, $1,089 without a mortgage; Median gross rent: $1,494 per month; Rental vacancy rate: 7.5%

Health Insurance: 94.5% have insurance; 82.6% have private insurance; 24.2% have public insurance; 5.5% do not have insurance; 2.2% of children under 18 do not have insurance

Transportation: Commute: 89.6% car, 7.7% public transportation, 0.0% walk, 2.4% work from home; Mean travel time to work: 32.5 minutes

Additional Information Contacts
Village of Buchanan . . . . (914) 737-1033
    http://villageofbuchanan.com

CHAPPAQUA (CDP). Covers a land area of 0.450 square miles and a water area of 0 square miles. Located at 41.16° N. Lat; 73.77° W. Long. Elevation is 492 feet.

History: Originally a Quaker community; later estate area. Horace Greeley lived here.

Population: 1,287; Growth (since 2000): -86.4%; Density: 2,859.9 persons per square mile; Race: 85.2% White, 7.2% Black/African American, 5.2% Asian, 0.0% American Indian/Alaska Native, 0.0% Native Hawaiian/Other Pacific Islander, 2.3% Two or more races, 3.8% Hispanic of any race; Average household size: 2.62; Median age: 40.2; Age under 18: 19.9%; Age 65 and over: 20.7%; Males per 100 females: 88.2; Marriage status: 32.1% never married, 55.6% now married, 0.0% separated, 4.4% widowed, 7.9% divorced; Foreign born: 12.7%; Speak English only: 81.0%; With disability: 9.2%; Veterans: 10.2%; Ancestry: 17.9% Italian, 14.5% Irish, 10.6% German, 10.3% French, 8.5% Russian

Employment: 16.1% management, business, and financial, 9.0% computer, engineering, and science, 20.9% education, legal, community service, arts, and media, 10.1% healthcare practitioners, 18.8% service, 22.2% sales and office, 0.0% natural resources, construction, and maintenance, 2.8% production, transportation, and material moving

Income: Per capita: $58,165; Median household: $113,300; Average household: $148,443; Households with income of $100,000 or more: 60.6%; Poverty rate: 3.3%

Educational Attainment: High school diploma or higher: 96.1%; Bachelor's degree or higher: 83.3%; Graduate/professional degree or higher: 45.1%

School District(s)
Chappaqua Central SD (KG-12)
    2014-15 Enrollment: 3,943 . . . . (914) 238-7200

Housing: Homeownership rate: 77.4%; Median home value: $577,600; Median year structure built: 1951; Homeowner vacancy rate: 0.0%; Median selected monthly owner costs: $3,327 with a mortgage, $1,230 without a mortgage; Median gross rent: $1,427 per month; Rental vacancy rate: 0.0%

Health Insurance: 92.8% have insurance; 82.0% have private insurance; 23.0% have public insurance; 7.2% do not have insurance; 0.0% of children under 18 do not have insurance

Transportation: Commute: 53.0% car, 30.6% public transportation, 8.5% walk, 7.9% work from home; Mean travel time to work: 39.8 minutes

CORTLANDT (town). Covers a land area of 39.255 square miles and a water area of 10.761 square miles. Located at 41.26° N. Lat; 73.90° W. Long.

History: The Bear Mountain Bridge Road and Toll House, and the site of Old Croton Dam, both in Cortlandt, are listed on the National Register of Historic Places.

Population: 42,442; Growth (since 2000): 10.3%; Density: 1,081.2 persons per square mile; Race: 79.3% White, 7.5% Black/African American, 3.6% Asian, 0.2% American Indian/Alaska Native, 0.0% Native Hawaiian/Other Pacific Islander, 3.2% Two or more races, 16.2% Hispanic of any race; Average household size: 2.73; Median age: 43.9; Age under 18: 23.7%; Age 65 and over: 16.3%; Males per 100 females: 96.4; Marriage status: 26.1% never married, 58.7% now married, 1.6% separated, 6.3% widowed, 8.9% divorced; Foreign born: 15.8%; Speak

English only: 80.0%; With disability: 10.1%; Veterans: 6.8%; Ancestry: 23.6% Italian, 17.7% Irish, 11.6% German, 5.3% English, 5.3% Polish
Employment: 19.6% management, business, and financial, 5.1% computer, engineering, and science, 20.5% education, legal, community service, arts, and media, 6.3% healthcare practitioners, 16.9% service, 19.5% sales and office, 6.2% natural resources, construction, and maintenance, 5.8% production, transportation, and material moving
Income: Per capita: $47,882; Median household: $100,593; Average household: $131,247; Households with income of $100,000 or more: 50.4%; Poverty rate: 5.1%
Educational Attainment: High school diploma or higher: 92.4%; Bachelor's degree or higher: 48.1%; Graduate/professional degree or higher: 24.6%
Housing: Homeownership rate: 75.6%; Median home value: $414,900; Median year structure built: 1961; Homeowner vacancy rate: 1.0%; Median selected monthly owner costs: $3,011 with a mortgage, $1,262 without a mortgage; Median gross rent: $1,379 per month; Rental vacancy rate: 4.8%
Health Insurance: 93.5% have insurance; 82.0% have private insurance; 24.3% have public insurance; 6.5% do not have insurance; 2.8% of children under 18 do not have insurance
Transportation: Commute: 78.0% car, 14.4% public transportation, 1.8% walk, 4.7% work from home; Mean travel time to work: 38.8 minutes
Additional Information Contacts
Town of Cortlandt . . . . (914) 734-1020
    http://www.townofcortlandt.com

CORTLANDT MANOR (unincorporated postal area)
ZCTA: 10567
Covers a land area of 22.137 square miles and a water area of 0.453 square miles. Located at 41.29° N. Lat; 73.90° W. Long..
Population: 20,741; Growth (since 2000): 16.5%; Density: 936.9 persons per square mile; Race: 79.2% White, 8.1% Black/African American, 3.1% Asian, 0.2% American Indian/Alaska Native, 0.0% Native Hawaiian/Other Pacific Islander, 2.9% Two or more races, 18.0% Hispanic of any race; Average household size: 2.93; Median age: 43.8; Age under 18: 25.5%; Age 65 and over: 16.1%; Males per 100 females: 97.6; Marriage status: 24.9% never married, 61.4% now married, 0.8% separated, 6.7% widowed, 7.0% divorced; Foreign born: 15.0%; Speak English only: 80.4%; With disability: 9.2%; Veterans: 6.6%; Ancestry: 24.3% Italian, 15.0% Irish, 11.4% German, 5.3% Polish, 5.0% English
Employment: 20.9% management, business, and financial, 3.9% computer, engineering, and science, 24.6% education, legal, community service, arts, and media, 7.8% healthcare practitioners, 13.9% service, 18.6% sales and office, 4.3% natural resources, construction, and maintenance, 5.9% production, transportation, and material moving
Income: Per capita: $48,302; Median household: $119,521; Average household: $142,084; Households with income of $100,000 or more: 56.4%; Poverty rate: 4.5%
Educational Attainment: High school diploma or higher: 93.5%; Bachelor's degree or higher: 49.8%; Graduate/professional degree or higher: 27.3%

School District(s)
Hendrick Hudson Central SD (KG-12)
    2014-15 Enrollment: 2,366 . . . . (914) 257-5100
Lakeland Central SD (PK-12)
    2014-15 Enrollment: 5,900 . . . . (914) 245-1700
Housing: Homeownership rate: 90.2%; Median home value: $398,700; Median year structure built: 1966; Homeowner vacancy rate: 1.4%; Median selected monthly owner costs: $2,965 with a mortgage, $1,335 without a mortgage; Median gross rent: $1,664 per month; Rental vacancy rate: 3.5%
Health Insurance: 95.7% have insurance; 86.7% have private insurance; 21.7% have public insurance; 4.3% do not have insurance; 1.4% of children under 18 do not have insurance
Hospitals: Hudson Valley Hospital Center (120 beds)
Transportation: Commute: 79.9% car, 13.1% public transportation, 1.1% walk, 4.5% work from home; Mean travel time to work: 41.4 minutes

CROMPOND (CDP). Covers a land area of 2.420 square miles and a water area of 0.020 square miles. Located at 41.30° N. Lat; 73.84° W. Long. Elevation is 420 feet.
Population: 2,466; Growth (since 2000): 20.3%; Density: 1,019.2 persons per square mile; Race: 84.5% White, 3.7% Black/African American, 2.1%

Asian, 0.0% American Indian/Alaska Native, 0.0% Native Hawaiian/Other Pacific Islander, 3.3% Two or more races, 9.9% Hispanic of any race; Average household size: 2.69; Median age: 47.7; Age under 18: 22.6%; Age 65 and over: 20.0%; Males per 100 females: 85.1; Marriage status: 19.8% never married, 63.1% now married, 0.5% separated, 9.2% widowed, 7.9% divorced; Foreign born: 6.2%; Speak English only: 91.7%; With disability: 6.8%; Veterans: 7.0%; Ancestry: 37.8% Italian, 16.2% Irish, 8.5% American, 6.9% German, 6.4% English
Employment: 24.0% management, business, and financial, 4.0% computer, engineering, and science, 14.7% education, legal, community service, arts, and media, 9.0% healthcare practitioners, 11.2% service, 18.3% sales and office, 12.1% natural resources, construction, and maintenance, 6.8% production, transportation, and material moving
Income: Per capita: $57,328; Median household: $138,281; Average household: $162,900; Households with income of $100,000 or more: 62.6%; Poverty rate: 1.3%
Educational Attainment: High school diploma or higher: 91.9%; Bachelor's degree or higher: 46.4%; Graduate/professional degree or higher: 21.4%

School District(s)
Lakeland Central SD (PK-12)
    2014-15 Enrollment: 5,900 . . . . (914) 245-1700
Housing: Homeownership rate: 92.8%; Median home value: $524,600; Median year structure built: 1975; Homeowner vacancy rate: 0.0%; Median selected monthly owner costs: $3,360 with a mortgage, $1,500+ without a mortgage; Median gross rent: $1,212 per month; Rental vacancy rate: 0.0%
Health Insurance: 94.8% have insurance; 86.1% have private insurance; 16.6% have public insurance; 5.2% do not have insurance; 5.7% of children under 18 do not have insurance
Transportation: Commute: 86.7% car, 7.8% public transportation, 0.9% walk, 3.8% work from home; Mean travel time to work: 32.9 minutes

CROSS RIVER (unincorporated postal area)
ZCTA: 10518
Covers a land area of 3.448 square miles and a water area of 0.054 square miles. Located at 41.27° N. Lat; 73.59° W. Long. Elevation is 338 feet.
Population: 1,502; Growth (since 2000): -3.2%; Density: 435.6 persons per square mile; Race: 94.7% White, 0.0% Black/African American, 3.1% Asian, 0.0% American Indian/Alaska Native, 0.0% Native Hawaiian/Other Pacific Islander, 0.0% Two or more races, 0.0% Hispanic of any race; Average household size: 2.93; Median age: 49.8; Age under 18: 25.0%; Age 65 and over: 17.3%; Males per 100 females: 90.4; Marriage status: 21.5% never married, 65.1% now married, 0.0% separated, 8.0% widowed, 5.5% divorced; Foreign born: 5.7%; Speak English only: 95.7%; With disability: 8.9%; Veterans: 7.0%; Ancestry: 24.2% Irish, 20.9% Italian, 18.2% American, 17.4% English, 7.8% Polish
Employment: 25.0% management, business, and financial, 10.6% computer, engineering, and science, 30.0% education, legal, community service, arts, and media, 8.8% healthcare practitioners, 6.0% service, 19.7% sales and office, 0.0% natural resources, construction, and maintenance, 0.0% production, transportation, and material moving
Income: Per capita: $66,953; Median household: $187,898; Average household: $193,774; Households with income of $100,000 or more: 69.0%; Poverty rate: 6.4%
Educational Attainment: High school diploma or higher: 97.3%; Bachelor's degree or higher: 77.7%; Graduate/professional degree or higher: 35.0%

School District(s)
Katonah-Lewisboro Union Free SD (KG-12)
    2014-15 Enrollment: 3,233 . . . . (914) 763-7003
Housing: Homeownership rate: 92.2%; Median home value: $780,400; Median year structure built: 1986; Homeowner vacancy rate: 0.0%; Median selected monthly owner costs: $4,000 with a mortgage, $1,500 without a mortgage; Median gross rent: n/a per month; Rental vacancy rate: 0.0%
Health Insurance: 94.7% have insurance; 90.4% have private insurance; 19.9% have public insurance; 5.3% do not have insurance; 3.7% of children under 18 do not have insurance
Newspapers: Lewisboro Ledger (weekly circulation 2,100)
Transportation: Commute: 67.3% car, 21.8% public transportation, 0.0% walk, 8.1% work from home; Mean travel time to work: 40.1 minutes

CROTON FALLS (unincorporated postal area)

ZCTA: 10519

Covers a land area of 0.744 square miles and a water area of 0.025 square miles. Located at 41.35° N. Lat; 73.65° W. Long. Elevation is 269 feet.

Population: 207; Growth (since 2000): 32.7%; Density: 278.2 persons per square mile; Race: 100.0% White, 0.0% Black/African American, 0.0% Asian, 0.0% American Indian/Alaska Native, 0.0% Native Hawaiian/Other Pacific Islander, 0.0% Two or more races, 0.0% Hispanic of any race; Average household size: 2.17; Median age: 49.2; Age under 18: 0.0%; Age 65 and over: 18.8%; Males per 100 females: 91.5; Marriage status: 21.3% never married, 65.2% now married, 0.0% separated, 13.5% widowed, 0.0% divorced; Foreign born: 27.5%; Speak English only: 86.5%; With disability: 13.5%; Veterans: 4.8%; Ancestry: 34.8% European, 26.6% German, 19.8% Jamaican, 14.0% American, 13.0% Dutch

Employment: 0.0% management, business, and financial, 26.5% computer, engineering, and science, 1.7% education, legal, community service, arts, and media, 47.0% healthcare practitioners, 0.0% service, 24.8% sales and office, 0.0% natural resources, construction, and maintenance, 0.0% production, transportation, and material moving

Income: Per capita: $89,248; Median household: n/a; Average household: $191,300; Households with income of $100,000 or more: 59.6%; Poverty rate: 0.5%

Educational Attainment: High school diploma or higher: 100.0%; Bachelor's degree or higher: 53.6%; Graduate/professional degree or higher: 34.9%

Housing: Homeownership rate: 100.0%; Median home value: n/a; Median year structure built: Before 1940; Homeowner vacancy rate: 0.0%; Median selected monthly owner costs: $4,000 with a mortgage, $0 without a mortgage; Median gross rent: n/a per month; Rental vacancy rate: 0.0%

Health Insurance: 100.0% have insurance; 99.5% have private insurance; 18.8% have public insurance; 0.0% do not have insurance; 0.0% of children under 18 do not have insurance

Transportation: Commute: 71.8% car, 26.5% public transportation, 1.7% walk, 0.0% work from home; Mean travel time to work: 0.0 minutes

CROTON-ON-HUDSON (village).

Covers a land area of 4.642 square miles and a water area of 6.038 square miles. Located at 41.21° N. Lat; 73.90° W. Long. Elevation is 161 feet.

History: During 1920s, fashionable haven for intellectuals such as Edna St. Vincent Millay, Doris Stevens, Stuart Chase and John Reed. Van Cortlandt Manor, a restored 18th-century Dutch-English manorhouse on 20 acres of what was once 86,000-acre estate is located here. Settled 1609, Incorporated 1898.

Population: 8,202; Growth (since 2000): 7.8%; Density: 1,766.7 persons per square mile; Race: 80.5% White, 8.4% Black/African American, 4.1% Asian, 0.4% American Indian/Alaska Native, 0.0% Native Hawaiian/Other Pacific Islander, 4.2% Two or more races, 14.5% Hispanic of any race; Average household size: 2.76; Median age: 42.1; Age under 18: 26.9%; Age 65 and over: 13.3%; Males per 100 females: 92.3; Marriage status: 23.2% never married, 62.2% now married, 2.5% separated, 5.9% widowed, 8.7% divorced; Foreign born: 17.5%; Speak English only: 78.5%; With disability: 6.0%; Veterans: 5.1%; Ancestry: 21.6% Italian, 18.1% Irish, 10.7% German, 6.0% Polish, 4.8% English

Employment: 23.1% management, business, and financial, 6.6% computer, engineering, and science, 21.6% education, legal, community service, arts, and media, 5.6% healthcare practitioners, 17.9% service, 17.0% sales and office, 4.2% natural resources, construction, and maintenance, 3.8% production, transportation, and material moving

Income: Per capita: $57,165; Median household: $131,475; Average household: $159,812; Households with income of $100,000 or more: 58.3%; Poverty rate: 3.1%

Educational Attainment: High school diploma or higher: 93.1%; Bachelor's degree or higher: 60.9%; Graduate/professional degree or higher: 32.5%

School District(s)

Croton-Harmon Union Free SD (KG-12)

    2014-15 Enrollment: 1,666 . . . . (914) 271-4793

Housing: Homeownership rate: 72.3%; Median home value: $503,600; Median year structure built: 1953; Homeowner vacancy rate: 0.0%; Median selected monthly owner costs: $3,261 with a mortgage, $1,315 without a mortgage; Median gross rent: $1,485 per month; Rental vacancy rate: 0.0%

Health Insurance: 88.4% have insurance; 77.7% have private insurance; 20.4% have public insurance; 11.6% do not have insurance; 6.2% of children under 18 do not have insurance

Safety: Violent crime rate: 4.8 per 10,000 population; Property crime rate: 32.6 per 10,000 population

Newspapers: The Gazette (weekly circulation 3,000)

Transportation: Commute: 64.8% car, 25.0% public transportation, 3.3% walk, 6.2% work from home; Mean travel time to work: 39.9 minutes; Amtrak: Train service available.

CRUGERS (CDP).

Covers a land area of 0.661 square miles and a water area of 0.574 square miles. Located at 41.23° N. Lat; 73.93° W. Long. Elevation is 98 feet.

Population: 1,720; Growth (since 2000): -1.8%; Density: 2,603.6 persons per square mile; Race: 78.6% White, 4.4% Black/African American, 2.3% Asian, 0.0% American Indian/Alaska Native, 0.0% Native Hawaiian/Other Pacific Islander, 0.5% Two or more races, 17.2% Hispanic of any race; Average household size: 1.84; Median age: 62.9; Age under 18: 10.5%; Age 65 and over: 44.8%; Males per 100 females: 81.3; Marriage status: 28.8% never married, 42.2% now married, 3.8% separated, 13.6% widowed, 15.5% divorced; Foreign born: 21.8%; Speak English only: 80.2%; With disability: 21.1%; Veterans: 12.6%; Ancestry: 23.0% Irish, 16.7% Italian, 7.9% Norwegian, 6.9% Danish, 6.0% German

Employment: 10.4% management, business, and financial, 5.3% computer, engineering, and science, 4.6% education, legal, community service, arts, and media, 2.9% healthcare practitioners, 32.4% service, 26.1% sales and office, 14.1% natural resources, construction, and maintenance, 4.2% production, transportation, and material moving

Income: Per capita: $27,833; Median household: $38,301; Average household: $52,904; Households with income of $100,000 or more: 12.9%; Poverty rate: 8.5%

Educational Attainment: High school diploma or higher: 74.2%; Bachelor's degree or higher: 29.8%; Graduate/professional degree or higher: 8.1%

Housing: Homeownership rate: 19.1%; Median home value: $420,800; Median year structure built: 1959; Homeowner vacancy rate: 0.0%; Median selected monthly owner costs: $3,658 with a mortgage, $1,412 without a mortgage; Median gross rent: $1,089 per month; Rental vacancy rate: 3.0%

Health Insurance: 86.4% have insurance; 66.3% have private insurance; 49.2% have public insurance; 13.6% do not have insurance; 0.0% of children under 18 do not have insurance

Transportation: Commute: 80.2% car, 13.9% public transportation, 3.5% walk, 1.3% work from home; Mean travel time to work: 34.2 minutes

DOBBS FERRY (village).

Covers a land area of 2.429 square miles and a water area of 0.752 square miles. Located at 41.01° N. Lat; 73.87° W. Long. Elevation is 210 feet.

History: Named for Jeremiah Dobbs, who operated a ferry across the Hudson River. Site of Livingston Manor, where George Washington and Marshal Rochambeau of France are said to have planned the Yorktown Campaign. Seat of Mercy College. Incorporated 1873.

Population: 11,055; Growth (since 2000): 4.1%; Density: 4,550.8 persons per square mile; Race: 79.1% White, 7.1% Black/African American, 7.8% Asian, 0.3% American Indian/Alaska Native, 0.0% Native Hawaiian/Other Pacific Islander, 1.9% Two or more races, 10.3% Hispanic of any race; Average household size: 2.70; Median age: 41.8; Age under 18: 20.4%; Age 65 and over: 15.7%; Males per 100 females: 91.4; Marriage status: 34.2% never married, 52.2% now married, 1.5% separated, 6.2% widowed, 7.3% divorced; Foreign born: 18.4%; Speak English only: 78.2%; With disability: 7.3%; Veterans: 6.3%; Ancestry: 19.8% Italian, 19.4% Irish, 12.1% German, 6.7% Polish, 5.4% Russian

Employment: 22.6% management, business, and financial, 6.4% computer, engineering, and science, 21.5% education, legal, community service, arts, and media, 9.1% healthcare practitioners, 15.5% service, 17.5% sales and office, 2.7% natural resources, construction, and maintenance, 4.5% production, transportation, and material moving

Income: Per capita: $53,820; Median household: $116,671; Average household: $156,335; Households with income of $100,000 or more: 58.6%; Poverty rate: 4.4%

Educational Attainment: High school diploma or higher: 94.9%; Bachelor's degree or higher: 56.9%; Graduate/professional degree or higher: 30.7%

School District(s)

Dobbs Ferry Union Free SD (KG-12)
  2014-15 Enrollment: 1,472 . . . . (914) 693-1506
Greenburgh Eleven Union Free SD (KG-12)
  2014-15 Enrollment: 117 . . . . (914) 693-8500
Greenburgh-North Castle Union Free SD (07-12)
  2014-15 Enrollment: 21 . . . . (914) 693-4309

Four-year College(s)

Mercy College (Private, Not-for-profit)
  Fall 2014 Enrollment: 11,272 . . . . (800) 637-2969
  2015-16 Tuition: In-state $18,076; Out-of-state $18,076

Housing: Homeownership rate: 60.6%; Median home value: $582,900; Median year structure built: 1955; Homeowner vacancy rate: 0.0%; Median selected monthly owner costs: $3,359 with a mortgage, $1,500+ without a mortgage; Median gross rent: $1,631 per month; Rental vacancy rate: 3.3%

Health Insurance: 93.1% have insurance; 81.7% have private insurance; 20.7% have public insurance; 6.9% do not have insurance; 1.6% of children under 18 do not have insurance

Safety: Violent crime rate: 8.1 per 10,000 population; Property crime rate: 80.7 per 10,000 population

Newspapers: Rivertowns Enterprise (weekly circulation 6,200)

Transportation: Commute: 66.6% car, 22.5% public transportation, 4.6% walk, 5.4% work from home; Mean travel time to work: 31.3 minutes

Additional Information Contacts

Village of Dobbs Ferry . . . . (914) 231-8504
  http://www.dobbsferry.com

EASTCHESTER (CDP). Covers a land area of 3.294 square miles and a water area of 0.088 square miles. Located at 40.96° N. Lat; 73.81° W. Long. Elevation is 23 feet.

History: Laws for the region (of which Eastchester CDP is a part) were established in 1665, under an agreement called the "Eastchester Covenant." The covenant was a rare document for this period. It contained 26 provisions, such items as: education of children, disposition and upkeep of property, and support of a minister.

Population: 19,885; Growth (since 2000): 7.1%; Density: 6,037.6 persons per square mile; Race: 85.4% White, 3.0% Black/African American, 8.1% Asian, 0.1% American Indian/Alaska Native, 0.0% Native Hawaiian/Other Pacific Islander, 2.2% Two or more races, 5.8% Hispanic of any race; Average household size: 2.54; Median age: 43.5; Age under 18: 21.9%; Age 65 and over: 19.4%; Males per 100 females: 89.4; Marriage status: 28.9% never married, 56.9% now married, 1.1% separated, 7.6% widowed, 6.7% divorced; Foreign born: 17.6%; Speak English only: 79.2%; With disability: 8.0%; Veterans: 5.5%; Ancestry: 43.2% Italian, 17.1% Irish, 7.7% American, 7.1% German, 3.2% Russian

Employment: 22.8% management, business, and financial, 5.1% computer, engineering, and science, 19.4% education, legal, community service, arts, and media, 6.5% healthcare practitioners, 11.0% service, 26.8% sales and office, 5.1% natural resources, construction, and maintenance, 3.4% production, transportation, and material moving

Income: Per capita: $57,762; Median household: $104,293; Average household: $144,059; Households with income of $100,000 or more: 51.4%; Poverty rate: 2.8%

Educational Attainment: High school diploma or higher: 93.7%; Bachelor's degree or higher: 55.4%; Graduate/professional degree or higher: 26.2%

School District(s)

Eastchester Union Free SD (KG-12)
  2014-15 Enrollment: 3,200 . . . . (914) 793-6130
Tuckahoe Union Free SD (KG-12)
  2014-15 Enrollment: 1,070 . . . . (914) 337-6600

Housing: Homeownership rate: 82.9%; Median home value: $555,900; Median year structure built: 1950; Homeowner vacancy rate: 0.8%; Median selected monthly owner costs: $3,255 with a mortgage, $1,420 without a mortgage; Median gross rent: $1,646 per month; Rental vacancy rate: 8.1%

Health Insurance: 96.8% have insurance; 88.6% have private insurance; 21.9% have public insurance; 3.2% do not have insurance; 0.6% of children under 18 do not have insurance

Transportation: Commute: 72.2% car, 20.7% public transportation, 3.2% walk, 3.7% work from home; Mean travel time to work: 30.9 minutes

---

EASTCHESTER (town). Covers a land area of 4.853 square miles and a water area of 0.088 square miles. Located at 40.95° N. Lat; 73.81° W. Long. Elevation is 23 feet.

History: Named for the town of Chester in England. Once a township (formed 1788) extending from the present Bronx North to Scarsdale; Mt. Vernon city was separated from it in 1892; the section South of Mt. Vernon was annexed by N.Y. city in 1895.

Population: 32,880; Growth (since 2000): 5.0%; Density: 6,775.1 persons per square mile; Race: 83.7% White, 4.8% Black/African American, 7.6% Asian, 0.0% American Indian/Alaska Native, 0.0% Native Hawaiian/Other Pacific Islander, 2.5% Two or more races, 5.9% Hispanic of any race; Average household size: 2.54; Median age: 42.0; Age under 18: 22.7%; Age 65 and over: 17.5%; Males per 100 females: 88.7; Marriage status: 30.0% never married, 55.0% now married, 1.3% separated, 6.8% widowed, 8.3% divorced; Foreign born: 17.9%; Speak English only: 78.4%; With disability: 7.7%; Veterans: 4.9%; Ancestry: 34.7% Italian, 18.3% Irish, 8.6% German, 6.4% American, 5.0% English

Employment: 24.1% management, business, and financial, 4.6% computer, engineering, and science, 21.8% education, legal, community service, arts, and media, 6.9% healthcare practitioners, 10.7% service, 24.1% sales and office, 4.9% natural resources, construction, and maintenance, 3.0% production, transportation, and material moving

Income: Per capita: $66,592; Median household: $105,318; Average household: $167,976; Households with income of $100,000 or more: 51.9%; Poverty rate: 3.2%

Educational Attainment: High school diploma or higher: 94.5%; Bachelor's degree or higher: 59.1%; Graduate/professional degree or higher: 30.2%

School District(s)

Eastchester Union Free SD (KG-12)
  2014-15 Enrollment: 3,200 . . . . (914) 793-6130
Tuckahoe Union Free SD (KG-12)
  2014-15 Enrollment: 1,070 . . . . (914) 337-6600

Housing: Homeownership rate: 75.1%; Median home value: $579,200; Median year structure built: 1948; Homeowner vacancy rate: 1.1%; Median selected monthly owner costs: $3,353 with a mortgage, $1,452 without a mortgage; Median gross rent: $1,750 per month; Rental vacancy rate: 3.6%

Health Insurance: 96.5% have insurance; 88.1% have private insurance; 21.3% have public insurance; 3.5% do not have insurance; 0.3% of children under 18 do not have insurance

Safety: Violent crime rate: 3.0 per 10,000 population; Property crime rate: 85.1 per 10,000 population

Transportation: Commute: 61.6% car, 28.6% public transportation, 4.6% walk, 4.7% work from home; Mean travel time to work: 33.0 minutes

Additional Information Contacts

Town of Eastchester . . . . (914) 771-3351
  http://www.eastchester.org

ELMSFORD (village). Covers a land area of 1.027 square miles and a water area of 0 square miles. Located at 41.05° N. Lat; 73.81° W. Long. Elevation is 177 feet.

History: Incorporated 1910.

Population: 4,765; Growth (since 2000): 1.9%; Density: 4,641.0 persons per square mile; Race: 43.2% White, 24.0% Black/African American, 9.3% Asian, 0.0% American Indian/Alaska Native, 0.0% Native Hawaiian/Other Pacific Islander, 2.2% Two or more races, 36.2% Hispanic of any race; Average household size: 3.09; Median age: 36.0; Age under 18: 21.4%; Age 65 and over: 9.7%; Males per 100 females: 103.8; Marriage status: 38.6% never married, 50.3% now married, 3.1% separated, 4.4% widowed, 6.7% divorced; Foreign born: 41.1%; Speak English only: 53.7%; With disability: 6.9%; Veterans: 3.3%; Ancestry: 9.4% Irish, 8.4% Jamaican, 8.2% Italian, 7.0% American, 3.9% German

Employment: 13.5% management, business, and financial, 7.2% computer, engineering, and science, 9.1% education, legal, community service, arts, and media, 2.5% healthcare practitioners, 34.3% service, 20.3% sales and office, 6.4% natural resources, construction, and maintenance, 6.6% production, transportation, and material moving

Income: Per capita: $34,036; Median household: $83,995; Average household: $101,002; Households with income of $100,000 or more: 37.5%; Poverty rate: 14.0%

Educational Attainment: High school diploma or higher: 83.3%; Bachelor's degree or higher: 35.3%; Graduate/professional degree or higher: 17.2%

School District(s)
Elmsford Union Free SD (PK-12)
   2014-15 Enrollment: 1,015 . . . . (914) 592-6632
Housing: Homeownership rate: 49.7%; Median home value: $388,700; Median year structure built: 1955; Homeowner vacancy rate: 1.6%; Median selected monthly owner costs: $3,026 with a mortgage, $1,162 without a mortgage; Median gross rent: $1,648 per month; Rental vacancy rate: 3.5%
Health Insurance: 83.3% have insurance; 68.7% have private insurance; 23.4% have public insurance; 16.7% do not have insurance; 2.3% of children under 18 do not have insurance
Safety: Violent crime rate: 10.4 per 10,000 population; Property crime rate: 58.3 per 10,000 population
Transportation: Commute: 76.4% car, 13.4% public transportation, 6.2% walk, 3.4% work from home; Mean travel time to work: 23.6 minutes
Additional Information Contacts
Village of Elmsford . . . . (914) 592-6555
   http://www.elmsfordny.org

FAIRVIEW (CDP). Covers a land area of 0.428 square miles and a water area of 0.003 square miles. Located at 41.04° N. Lat; 73.80° W. Long. Elevation is 217 feet.
Population: 2,874; Growth (since 2000): -0.5%; Density: 6,712.8 persons per square mile; Race: 13.4% White, 59.8% Black/African American, 3.7% Asian, 2.3% American Indian/Alaska Native, 2.3% Native Hawaiian/Other Pacific Islander, 7.0% Two or more races, 22.2% Hispanic of any race; Average household size: 2.92; Median age: 35.5; Age under 18: 22.9%; Age 65 and over: 12.2%; Males per 100 females: 88.0; Marriage status: 55.3% never married, 30.0% now married, 0.5% separated, 6.5% widowed, 8.2% divorced; Foreign born: 33.2%; Speak English only: 66.3%; With disability: 7.6%; Veterans: 3.7%; Ancestry: 9.1% Jamaican, 6.7% African, 5.4% Haitian, 2.0% Irish, 1.8% Guyanese
Employment: 8.2% management, business, and financial, 0.0% computer, engineering, and science, 9.8% education, legal, community service, arts, and media, 7.0% healthcare practitioners, 36.8% service, 25.2% sales and office, 5.2% natural resources, construction, and maintenance, 7.8% production, transportation, and material moving
Income: Per capita: $23,554; Median household: $43,512; Average household: $65,223; Households with income of $100,000 or more: 23.3%; Poverty rate: 16.8%
Educational Attainment: High school diploma or higher: 82.8%; Bachelor's degree or higher: 19.7%; Graduate/professional degree or higher: 4.7%
Housing: Homeownership rate: 36.2%; Median home value: $343,800; Median year structure built: 1966; Homeowner vacancy rate: 0.0%; Median selected monthly owner costs: $3,032 with a mortgage, $983 without a mortgage; Median gross rent: $1,296 per month; Rental vacancy rate: 3.3%
Health Insurance: 85.5% have insurance; 47.8% have private insurance; 43.1% have public insurance; 14.5% do not have insurance; 0.0% of children under 18 do not have insurance
Transportation: Commute: 69.3% car, 14.7% public transportation, 9.7% walk, 5.9% work from home; Mean travel time to work: 20.7 minutes

GOLDEN'S BRIDGE (CDP). Covers a land area of 2.430 square miles and a water area of 0.133 square miles. Located at 41.28° N. Lat; 73.67° W. Long. Elevation is 217 feet.
Population: 1,694; Growth (since 2000): 7.4%; Density: 697.2 persons per square mile; Race: 89.6% White, 2.4% Black/African American, 5.8% Asian, 0.0% American Indian/Alaska Native, 0.0% Native Hawaiian/Other Pacific Islander, 1.7% Two or more races, 1.7% Hispanic of any race; Average household size: 2.62; Median age: 43.7; Age under 18: 32.2%; Age 65 and over: 11.5%; Males per 100 females: 92.4; Marriage status: 22.3% never married, 61.7% now married, 0.7% separated, 5.5% widowed, 10.6% divorced; Foreign born: 12.0%; Speak English only: 89.6%; With disability: 3.5%; Veterans: 4.3%; Ancestry: 19.4% Italian, 11.4% Irish, 8.4% Eastern European, 8.4% English, 7.4% German
Employment: 32.2% management, business, and financial, 7.3% computer, engineering, and science, 22.9% education, legal, community service, arts, and media, 14.2% healthcare practitioners, 8.3% service, 11.2% sales and office, 1.1% natural resources, construction, and maintenance, 2.7% production, transportation, and material moving
Income: Per capita: $63,183; Median household: $122,406; Average household: $164,776; Households with income of $100,000 or more: 67.1%; Poverty rate: 2.2%

Educational Attainment: High school diploma or higher: 99.2%; Bachelor's degree or higher: 81.5%; Graduate/professional degree or higher: 43.7%
School District(s)
Katonah-Lewisboro Union Free SD (KG-12)
   2014-15 Enrollment: 3,233 . . . . (914) 763-7003
Housing: Homeownership rate: 90.9%; Median home value: $549,300; Median year structure built: 1975; Homeowner vacancy rate: 3.1%; Median selected monthly owner costs: $3,132 with a mortgage, $1,376 without a mortgage; Median gross rent: n/a per month; Rental vacancy rate: 0.0%
Health Insurance: 99.5% have insurance; 91.3% have private insurance; 16.7% have public insurance; 0.5% do not have insurance; 0.0% of children under 18 do not have insurance
Transportation: Commute: 75.4% car, 19.8% public transportation, 0.0% walk, 4.8% work from home; Mean travel time to work: 39.7 minutes

GRANITE SPRINGS (unincorporated postal area)
ZCTA: 10527
   Covers a land area of 2.444 square miles and a water area of 0.008 square miles. Located at 41.32° N. Lat; 73.77° W. Long. Elevation is 515 feet.
Population: 877; Growth (since 2000): -20.1%; Density: 358.8 persons per square mile; Race: 96.7% White, 0.2% Black/African American, 2.5% Asian, 0.0% American Indian/Alaska Native, 0.0% Native Hawaiian/Other Pacific Islander, 0.0% Two or more races, 1.5% Hispanic of any race; Average household size: 3.05; Median age: 44.6; Age under 18: 30.6%; Age 65 and over: 15.4%; Males per 100 females: 102.2; Marriage status: 21.1% never married, 73.0% now married, 4.7% separated, 0.0% widowed, 5.9% divorced; Foreign born: 3.8%; Speak English only: 93.8%; With disability: 8.3%; Veterans: 6.2%; Ancestry: 24.4% Italian, 23.5% Irish, 9.1% German, 7.4% Scottish, 6.0% English
Employment: 20.4% management, business, and financial, 2.7% computer, engineering, and science, 18.6% education, legal, community service, arts, and media, 11.9% healthcare practitioners, 11.1% service, 29.2% sales and office, 4.2% natural resources, construction, and maintenance, 1.9% production, transportation, and material moving
Income: Per capita: $53,237; Median household: $152,212; Average household: $164,764; Households with income of $100,000 or more: 73.5%; Poverty rate: 3.4%
Educational Attainment: High school diploma or higher: 99.0%; Bachelor's degree or higher: 65.1%; Graduate/professional degree or higher: 39.1%
Housing: Homeownership rate: 100.0%; Median home value: $627,500; Median year structure built: 1977; Homeowner vacancy rate: 0.0%; Median selected monthly owner costs: $3,807 with a mortgage, $1,500 without a mortgage; Median gross rent: n/a per month; Rental vacancy rate: 0.0%
Health Insurance: 98.4% have insurance; 91.8% have private insurance; 18.9% have public insurance; 1.6% do not have insurance; 0.0% of children under 18 do not have insurance
Transportation: Commute: 82.0% car, 14.9% public transportation, 0.0% walk, 3.2% work from home; Mean travel time to work: 38.5 minutes

GREENBURGH (town). Covers a land area of 30.309 square miles and a water area of 5.805 square miles. Located at 41.03° N. Lat; 73.84° W. Long. Elevation is 348 feet.
History: The Romer-Van Tassel House served as the first town hall from 1793 to the early 19th century. It was added to the National Register of Historic Places in 1994.
Population: 90,809; Growth (since 2000): 4.7%; Density: 2,996.1 persons per square mile; Race: 68.2% White, 13.4% Black/African American, 9.7% Asian, 0.4% American Indian/Alaska Native, 0.1% Native Hawaiian/Other Pacific Islander, 3.4% Two or more races, 14.3% Hispanic of any race; Average household size: 2.69; Median age: 43.0; Age under 18: 22.4%; Age 65 and over: 16.8%; Males per 100 females: 89.5; Marriage status: 31.4% never married, 56.2% now married, 1.5% separated, 5.1% widowed, 7.3% divorced; Foreign born: 22.9%; Speak English only: 72.1%; With disability: 7.6%; Veterans: 4.7%; Ancestry: 14.4% Italian, 13.4% Irish, 8.8% German, 5.2% Russian, 4.8% American
Employment: 22.2% management, business, and financial, 6.9% computer, engineering, and science, 20.8% education, legal, community service, arts, and media, 8.1% healthcare practitioners, 15.1% service, 19.4% sales and office, 3.7% natural resources, construction, and maintenance, 3.8% production, transportation, and material moving

Income: Per capita: $60,248; Median household: $115,754; Average household: $163,030; Households with income of $100,000 or more: 56.9%; Poverty rate: 4.6%

Educational Attainment: High school diploma or higher: 93.1%; Bachelor's degree or higher: 61.2%; Graduate/professional degree or higher: 34.2%

Housing: Homeownership rate: 73.5%; Median home value: $538,700; Median year structure built: 1958; Homeowner vacancy rate: 1.0%; Median selected monthly owner costs: $3,397 with a mortgage, $1,500+ without a mortgage; Median gross rent: $1,657 per month; Rental vacancy rate: 4.0%

Health Insurance: 93.9% have insurance; 83.7% have private insurance; 22.1% have public insurance; 6.1% do not have insurance; 2.3% of children under 18 do not have insurance

Safety: Violent crime rate: 10.6 per 10,000 population; Property crime rate: 138.4 per 10,000 population

Transportation: Commute: 68.3% car, 21.5% public transportation, 3.6% walk, 5.8% work from home; Mean travel time to work: 32.6 minutes

Additional Information Contacts

Town of Greenburgh . . . . (914) 993-1500
   http://www.greenburghny.com

GREENVILLE (CDP). Covers a land area of 2.562 square miles and a water area of 0.035 square miles. Located at 41.00° N. Lat; 73.82° W. Long. Elevation is 249 feet.

History: Residents popularly refer to the Greenville area as "Edgemont". Edgemont was originally a development designed by different architects for summer homes for Manhattanites.

Population: 7,543; Growth (since 2000): -12.8%; Density: 2,943.9 persons per square mile; Race: 73.3% White, 2.7% Black/African American, 19.8% Asian, 0.0% American Indian/Alaska Native, 0.0% Native Hawaiian/Other Pacific Islander, 3.9% Two or more races, 2.9% Hispanic of any race; Average household size: 3.11; Median age: 43.6; Age under 18: 29.4%; Age 65 and over: 13.1%; Males per 100 females: 94.4; Marriage status: 26.1% never married, 63.9% now married, 0.9% separated, 3.2% widowed, 6.8% divorced; Foreign born: 22.5%; Speak English only: 71.3%; With disability: 5.3%; Veterans: 3.6%; Ancestry: 9.5% German, 9.5% Russian, 8.3% Italian, 5.9% Irish, 5.8% Polish

Employment: 25.5% management, business, and financial, 12.5% computer, engineering, and science, 26.8% education, legal, community service, arts, and media, 10.1% healthcare practitioners, 4.8% service, 14.7% sales and office, 2.9% natural resources, construction, and maintenance, 2.8% production, transportation, and material moving

Income: Per capita: $89,556; Median household: $200,952; Average household: $278,501; Households with income of $100,000 or more: 77.0%; Poverty rate: 4.6%

Educational Attainment: High school diploma or higher: 96.3%; Bachelor's degree or higher: 80.9%; Graduate/professional degree or higher: 54.1%

Housing: Homeownership rate: 92.4%; Median home value: $848,300; Median year structure built: 1956; Homeowner vacancy rate: 0.0%; Median selected monthly owner costs: $4,000+ with a mortgage, $1,500+ without a mortgage; Median gross rent: $2,375 per month; Rental vacancy rate: 0.0%

Health Insurance: 97.1% have insurance; 92.5% have private insurance; 14.9% have public insurance; 2.9% do not have insurance; 0.0% of children under 18 do not have insurance

Transportation: Commute: 51.5% car, 38.1% public transportation, 0.7% walk, 8.8% work from home; Mean travel time to work: 41.1 minutes

---

HARRISON (town/village). Covers a land area of 16.766 square miles and a water area of 0.603 square miles. Located at 41.03° N. Lat; 73.72° W. Long. Elevation is 69 feet.

History: Harrison was established in 1696 by John Harrison, who was given 24 hours to ride his horse around an area which would become his as payment to a debt owed him by the King. The town is named for Harrison, and was incorporated as a town on March 7, 1788.

Population: 27,998; Growth (since 2000): 15.9%; Density: 1,670.0 persons per square mile; Race: 81.3% White, 4.2% Black/African American, 7.0% Asian, 0.5% American Indian/Alaska Native, 0.0% Native Hawaiian/Other Pacific Islander, 2.6% Two or more races, 17.3% Hispanic of any race; Average household size: 2.93; Median age: 36.1; Age under 18: 21.3%; Age 65 and over: 14.4%; Males per 100 females: 88.5; Marriage status: 40.8% never married, 47.7% now married, 1.1% separated, 4.7% widowed, 6.7% divorced; Foreign born: 25.0%; Speak

English only: 64.1%; With disability: 8.4%; Veterans: 3.5%; Ancestry: 26.1% Italian, 11.0% Irish, 10.2% American, 7.9% German, 4.3% Russian

Employment: 24.6% management, business, and financial, 3.5% computer, engineering, and science, 14.9% education, legal, community service, arts, and media, 5.0% healthcare practitioners, 17.3% service, 26.7% sales and office, 5.3% natural resources, construction, and maintenance, 2.6% production, transportation, and material moving

Income: Per capita: $60,166; Median household: $104,469; Average household: $198,972; Households with income of $100,000 or more: 54.2%; Poverty rate: 7.9%

Educational Attainment: High school diploma or higher: 90.8%; Bachelor's degree or higher: 49.9%; Graduate/professional degree or higher: 21.0%

School District(s)

Harrison Central SD (KG-12)
   2014-15 Enrollment: 3,558 . . . . (914) 630-3021

Vocational/Technical School(s)

Southern Westchester BOCES-Practical Nursing Program (Public)
   Fall 2014 Enrollment: 165 . . . . (914) 592-0849
   2015-16 Tuition: $12,775

Housing: Homeownership rate: 64.3%; Median home value: $761,200; Median year structure built: 1958; Homeowner vacancy rate: 0.2%; Median selected monthly owner costs: $3,771 with a mortgage, $1,500+ without a mortgage; Median gross rent: $1,860 per month; Rental vacancy rate: 1.3%

Health Insurance: 92.4% have insurance; 80.4% have private insurance; 21.6% have public insurance; 7.6% do not have insurance; 6.1% of children under 18 do not have insurance

Safety: Violent crime rate: 1.4 per 10,000 population; Property crime rate: 39.2 per 10,000 population

Transportation: Commute: 63.9% car, 18.8% public transportation, 9.7% walk, 5.6% work from home; Mean travel time to work: 28.2 minutes

Additional Information Contacts

Village and Town of Harrison . . . . (914) 670-3000
   http://www.harrison-ny.gov

HARTSDALE (CDP). Covers a land area of 0.895 square miles and a water area of 0 square miles. Located at 41.02° N. Lat; 73.80° W. Long. Elevation is 184 feet.

History: The intersection of Central Park Avenue and Hartsdale Avenue was named "Hart's Corners" after Robert Hart, one of these farmers who successfully bid for the land, and in the mid 1800s the entire area became known as "Hartsdale".

Population: 5,146; Growth (since 2000): -47.7%; Density: 5,749.4 persons per square mile; Race: 67.2% White, 3.7% Black/African American, 18.9% Asian, 0.0% American Indian/Alaska Native, 0.0% Native Hawaiian/Other Pacific Islander, 3.7% Two or more races, 13.6% Hispanic of any race; Average household size: 2.05; Median age: 47.9; Age under 18: 16.8%; Age 65 and over: 24.3%; Males per 100 females: 80.9; Marriage status: 29.6% never married, 53.4% now married, 2.6% separated, 3.4% widowed, 13.6% divorced; Foreign born: 33.1%; Speak English only: 64.2%; With disability: 6.6%; Veterans: 2.1%; Ancestry: 15.1% Italian, 14.1% Irish, 8.1% German, 6.0% Polish, 5.7% Russian

Employment: 26.4% management, business, and financial, 7.9% computer, engineering, and science, 22.5% education, legal, community service, arts, and media, 6.1% healthcare practitioners, 9.2% service, 22.8% sales and office, 2.9% natural resources, construction, and maintenance, 2.2% production, transportation, and material moving

Income: Per capita: $61,619; Median household: $84,601; Average household: $126,764; Households with income of $100,000 or more: 44.3%; Poverty rate: 5.9%

Educational Attainment: High school diploma or higher: 94.3%; Bachelor's degree or higher: 62.0%; Graduate/professional degree or higher: 33.2%

School District(s)

Greenburgh Central SD (PK-12)
   2014-15 Enrollment: 1,893 . . . . (914) 761-6000

Housing: Homeownership rate: 72.9%; Median home value: $291,800; Median year structure built: 1960; Homeowner vacancy rate: 3.5%; Median selected monthly owner costs: $2,072 with a mortgage, $763 without a mortgage; Median gross rent: $1,622 per month; Rental vacancy rate: 7.8%

Health Insurance: 95.4% have insurance; 81.6% have private insurance; 29.8% have public insurance; 4.6% do not have insurance; 0.0% of children under 18 do not have insurance

Transportation: Commute: 54.8% car, 28.3% public transportation, 5.6% walk, 8.6% work from home; Mean travel time to work: 37.2 minutes

HASTINGS-ON-HUDSON (village). Covers a land area of 1.952 square miles and a water area of 0.961 square miles. Located at 40.99° N. Lat; 73.88° W. Long. Elevation is 125 feet.

History: Incorporated 1879.

Population: 7,951; Growth (since 2000): 4.0%; Density: 4,072.5 persons per square mile; Race: 89.4% White, 4.2% Black/African American, 3.2% Asian, 0.0% American Indian/Alaska Native, 0.0% Native Hawaiian/Other Pacific Islander, 2.1% Two or more races, 6.2% Hispanic of any race; Average household size: 2.57; Median age: 45.1; Age under 18: 25.8%; Age 65 and over: 19.0%; Males per 100 females: 89.4; Marriage status: 26.5% never married, 60.1% now married, 1.3% separated, 5.4% widowed, 7.9% divorced; Foreign born: 13.4%; Speak English only: 86.2%; With disability: 7.6%; Veterans: 5.5%; Ancestry: 19.4% Irish, 11.3% German, 10.1% Italian, 9.7% Russian, 8.0% Polish

Employment: 25.0% management, business, and financial, 10.1% computer, engineering, and science, 28.4% education, legal, community service, arts, and media, 10.0% healthcare practitioners, 8.9% service, 12.7% sales and office, 3.0% natural resources, construction, and maintenance, 2.0% production, transportation, and material moving

Income: Per capita: $63,877; Median household: $124,276; Average household: $170,681; Households with income of $100,000 or more: 59.8%; Poverty rate: 4.0%

Educational Attainment: High school diploma or higher: 97.1%; Bachelor's degree or higher: 74.3%; Graduate/professional degree or higher: 45.0%

School District(s)
Greenburgh-Graham Union Free SD (KG-12)
   2014-15 Enrollment: 79 . . . . (914) 478-1106
Hastings-On-Hudson Union Free SD (KG-12)
   2014-15 Enrollment: 1,551 . . . . (914) 478-6205

Housing: Homeownership rate: 69.2%; Median home value: $648,400; Median year structure built: Before 1940; Homeowner vacancy rate: 1.2%; Median selected monthly owner costs: $3,780 with a mortgage, $1,500+ without a mortgage; Median gross rent: $1,653 per month; Rental vacancy rate: 0.0%

Health Insurance: 96.4% have insurance; 82.9% have private insurance; 24.6% have public insurance; 3.6% do not have insurance; 3.2% of children under 18 do not have insurance

Safety: Violent crime rate: 6.2 per 10,000 population; Property crime rate: 68.7 per 10,000 population

Transportation: Commute: 57.5% car, 28.7% public transportation, 4.1% walk, 8.5% work from home; Mean travel time to work: 38.0 minutes

Additional Information Contacts
Village of Hastings-on-Hudson . . . . (914) 478-3400
   http://www.hastingsgov.org

HAWTHORNE (CDP). Covers a land area of 1.093 square miles and a water area of 0 square miles. Located at 41.10° N. Lat; 73.80° W. Long. Elevation is 282 feet.

Population: 4,583; Growth (since 2000): -9.8%; Density: 4,193.2 persons per square mile; Race: 90.6% White, 1.1% Black/African American, 4.3% Asian, 0.0% American Indian/Alaska Native, 0.0% Native Hawaiian/Other Pacific Islander, 0.3% Two or more races, 8.4% Hispanic of any race; Average household size: 2.88; Median age: 45.1; Age under 18: 21.9%; Age 65 and over: 17.7%; Males per 100 females: 95.8; Marriage status: 27.7% never married, 60.8% now married, 2.0% separated, 3.8% widowed, 7.7% divorced; Foreign born: 15.4%; Speak English only: 81.1%; With disability: 8.9%; Veterans: 6.8%; Ancestry: 48.8% Italian, 21.9% Irish, 9.8% German, 4.5% Polish, 4.2% English

Employment: 20.2% management, business, and financial, 6.0% computer, engineering, and science, 14.6% education, legal, community service, arts, and media, 5.0% healthcare practitioners, 14.7% service, 24.0% sales and office, 9.3% natural resources, construction, and maintenance, 6.2% production, transportation, and material moving

Income: Per capita: $42,391; Median household: $105,227; Average household: $120,771; Households with income of $100,000 or more: 51.4%; Poverty rate: 3.0%

Educational Attainment: High school diploma or higher: 90.3%; Bachelor's degree or higher: 41.4%; Graduate/professional degree or higher: 17.0%

School District(s)
Hawthorne-Cedar Knolls Union Free SD (KG-12)
   2014-15 Enrollment: 261 . . . . (914) 749-2903
Mount Pleasant Central SD (KG-12)
   2014-15 Enrollment: 1,923 . . . . (914) 769-5500

Housing: Homeownership rate: 86.1%; Median home value: $494,500; Median year structure built: 1957; Homeowner vacancy rate: 0.0%; Median selected monthly owner costs: $3,228 with a mortgage, $1,302 without a mortgage; Median gross rent: $1,204 per month; Rental vacancy rate: 0.0%

Health Insurance: 97.3% have insurance; 87.1% have private insurance; 24.2% have public insurance; 2.7% do not have insurance; 0.0% of children under 18 do not have insurance

Transportation: Commute: 83.5% car, 12.1% public transportation, 0.0% walk, 4.4% work from home; Mean travel time to work: 30.8 minutes

HERITAGE HILLS (CDP). Covers a land area of 1.864 square miles and a water area of 0.039 square miles. Located at 41.34° N. Lat; 73.70° W. Long. Elevation is 587 feet.

History: This community in Northern Westchester is located in the town of Somers, N.Y. and was designed to enhance the quality of living for its residents. It is a self contained complex of over 2,500 units on 1,100 acres of beautiful countryside, 40% of which will remain as open space.

Population: 4,024; Growth (since 2000): 9.3%; Density: 2,159.3 persons per square mile; Race: 97.0% White, 0.4% Black/African American, 0.8% Asian, 1.0% American Indian/Alaska Native, 0.0% Native Hawaiian/Other Pacific Islander, 0.0% Two or more races, 4.6% Hispanic of any race; Average household size: 1.76; Median age: 70.5; Age under 18: 5.9%; Age 65 and over: 66.7%; Males per 100 females: 65.0; Marriage status: 11.1% never married, 63.8% now married, 1.4% separated, 15.5% widowed, 9.6% divorced; Foreign born: 8.7%; Speak English only: 88.4%; With disability: 19.1%; Veterans: 18.3%; Ancestry: 31.9% Italian, 16.2% Irish, 10.6% German, 7.6% English, 6.3% Polish

Employment: 15.9% management, business, and financial, 6.3% computer, engineering, and science, 19.1% education, legal, community service, arts, and media, 6.4% healthcare practitioners, 4.8% service, 33.5% sales and office, 10.6% natural resources, construction, and maintenance, 3.4% production, transportation, and material moving

Income: Per capita: $53,997; Median household: $74,886; Average household: $94,965; Households with income of $100,000 or more: 35.0%; Poverty rate: 4.8%

Educational Attainment: High school diploma or higher: 95.5%; Bachelor's degree or higher: 50.5%; Graduate/professional degree or higher: 20.6%

Housing: Homeownership rate: 85.0%; Median home value: $387,600; Median year structure built: 1985; Homeowner vacancy rate: 0.0%; Median selected monthly owner costs: $2,100 with a mortgage, $1,045 without a mortgage; Median gross rent: $2,500 per month; Rental vacancy rate: 10.0%

Health Insurance: 97.8% have insurance; 81.7% have private insurance; 71.9% have public insurance; 2.2% do not have insurance; 0.0% of children under 18 do not have insurance

Transportation: Commute: 87.1% car, 6.4% public transportation, 0.0% walk, 6.5% work from home; Mean travel time to work: 34.9 minutes

IRVINGTON (village). Covers a land area of 2.773 square miles and a water area of 1.290 square miles. Located at 41.03° N. Lat; 73.87° W. Long. Elevation is 125 feet.

History: Here at Nevis, once the estate of Alexander Hamilton's son, are a Columbia University arboretum and a children's Museum. Originally called Dearman; renamed (1857) for Washington Irving, who bought the estate Sunnyside (extant) here in 1835. Settled c.1655, Incorporated 1872.

Population: 6,540; Growth (since 2000): -1.4%; Density: 2,358.2 persons per square mile; Race: 86.5% White, 0.8% Black/African American, 9.8% Asian, 0.1% American Indian/Alaska Native, 0.0% Native Hawaiian/Other Pacific Islander, 1.3% Two or more races, 7.5% Hispanic of any race; Average household size: 2.73; Median age: 45.4; Age under 18: 26.7%; Age 65 and over: 14.7%; Males per 100 females: 90.6; Marriage status: 20.6% never married, 69.2% now married, 2.4% separated, 5.2% widowed, 5.0% divorced; Foreign born: 14.0%; Speak English only: 80.7%; With disability: 7.0%; Veterans: 4.5%; Ancestry: 21.1% Irish, 17.0% Italian, 10.5% German, 8.6% American, 5.4% English

Employment: 26.4% management, business, and financial, 7.7% computer, engineering, and science, 27.2% education, legal, community service, arts, and media, 9.7% healthcare practitioners, 8.4% service,

15.4% sales and office, 4.8% natural resources, construction, and maintenance, 0.4% production, transportation, and material moving

Income: Per capita: $85,540; Median household: $138,051; Average household: $232,353; Households with income of $100,000 or more: 67.4%; Poverty rate: 2.7%

Educational Attainment: High school diploma or higher: 95.7%; Bachelor's degree or higher: 71.3%; Graduate/professional degree or higher: 41.0%

School District(s)

Abbott Union Free SD

    2014-15 Enrollment: n/a . . . . (914) 428-3043

Irvington Union Free SD (KG-12)

    2014-15 Enrollment: 1,769 . . . . (914) 591-8501

Housing: Homeownership rate: 79.4%; Median home value: $633,900; Median year structure built: 1956; Homeowner vacancy rate: 2.3%; Median selected monthly owner costs: $4,000+ with a mortgage, $1,500+ without a mortgage; Median gross rent: $1,786 per month; Rental vacancy rate: 7.7%

Health Insurance: 96.6% have insurance; 90.5% have private insurance; 17.4% have public insurance; 3.4% do not have insurance; 0.0% of children under 18 do not have insurance

Safety: Violent crime rate: 1.5 per 10,000 population; Property crime rate: 36.3 per 10,000 population

Transportation: Commute: 68.1% car, 22.5% public transportation, 2.6% walk, 6.8% work from home; Mean travel time to work: 33.5 minutes

Additional Information Contacts

Village of Irvington. . . . . (914) 591-7070

    http://www.irvingtonny.gov

JEFFERSON VALLEY-YORKTOWN (CDP).

Covers a land area of 6.926 square miles and a water area of 0.096 square miles. Located at 41.32° N. Lat; 73.80° W. Long.

Population: 14,923; Growth (since 2000): 0.2%; Density: 2,154.7 persons per square mile; Race: 90.3% White, 2.4% Black/African American, 3.4% Asian, 0.5% American Indian/Alaska Native, 0.0% Native Hawaiian/Other Pacific Islander, 1.9% Two or more races, 9.4% Hispanic of any race; Average household size: 2.83; Median age: 45.5; Age under 18: 25.0%; Age 65 and over: 20.0%; Males per 100 females: 91.3; Marriage status: 25.0% never married, 60.2% now married, 1.0% separated, 7.5% widowed, 7.2% divorced; Foreign born: 9.9%; Speak English only: 85.5%; With disability: 10.2%; Veterans: 5.0%; Ancestry: 40.2% Italian, 21.4% Irish, 9.9% German, 6.5% Polish, 4.7% Russian

Employment: 17.5% management, business, and financial, 4.9% computer, engineering, and science, 21.2% education, legal, community service, arts, and media, 7.3% healthcare practitioners, 11.5% service, 26.6% sales and office, 5.6% natural resources, construction, and maintenance, 5.4% production, transportation, and material moving

Income: Per capita: $42,889; Median household: $110,655; Average household: $119,100; Households with income of $100,000 or more: 55.0%; Poverty rate: 1.1%

Educational Attainment: High school diploma or higher: 95.2%; Bachelor's degree or higher: 45.9%; Graduate/professional degree or higher: 21.7%

Housing: Homeownership rate: 89.8%; Median home value: $405,200; Median year structure built: 1968; Homeowner vacancy rate: 0.6%; Median selected monthly owner costs: $3,129 with a mortgage, $1,049 without a mortgage; Median gross rent: $1,371 per month; Rental vacancy rate: 0.0%

Health Insurance: 97.7% have insurance; 89.4% have private insurance; 23.4% have public insurance; 2.3% do not have insurance; 1.6% of children under 18 do not have insurance

Transportation: Commute: 89.1% car, 6.4% public transportation, 0.6% walk, 3.3% work from home; Mean travel time to work: 38.9 minutes

KATONAH (CDP).

Covers a land area of 0.725 square miles and a water area of 0.079 square miles. Located at 41.26° N. Lat; 73.69° W. Long. Elevation is 236 feet.

Population: 2,196; Growth (since 2000): n/a; Density: 3,027.0 persons per square mile; Race: 71.9% White, 7.1% Black/African American, 6.5% Asian, 0.0% American Indian/Alaska Native, 0.0% Native Hawaiian/Other Pacific Islander, 7.8% Two or more races, 8.4% Hispanic of any race; Average household size: 3.37; Median age: 39.8; Age under 18: 29.9%; Age 65 and over: 8.8%; Males per 100 females: 88.0; Marriage status: 32.6% never married, 57.9% now married, 3.3% separated, 2.4% widowed, 7.0% divorced; Foreign born: 13.2%; Speak English only: 86.4%;

With disability: 3.5%; Veterans: 4.5%; Ancestry: 18.5% German, 17.0% Irish, 13.1% Russian, 11.8% Italian, 11.4% English

Employment: 25.4% management, business, and financial, 5.1% computer, engineering, and science, 19.2% education, legal, community service, arts, and media, 6.7% healthcare practitioners, 20.6% service, 15.5% sales and office, 2.2% natural resources, construction, and maintenance, 5.3% production, transportation, and material moving

Income: Per capita: $46,017; Median household: $109,952; Average household: $147,212; Households with income of $100,000 or more: 53.9%; Poverty rate: 6.6%

Educational Attainment: High school diploma or higher: 94.7%; Bachelor's degree or higher: 72.3%; Graduate/professional degree or higher: 33.5%

School District(s)

Katonah-Lewisboro Union Free SD (KG-12)

    2014-15 Enrollment: 3,233 . . . . (914) 763-7003

Housing: Homeownership rate: 74.9%; Median home value: $706,900; Median year structure built: Before 1940; Homeowner vacancy rate: 0.0%; Median selected monthly owner costs: $4,000+ with a mortgage, $1,500+ without a mortgage; Median gross rent: $1,977 per month; Rental vacancy rate: 0.0%

Health Insurance: 95.3% have insurance; 86.7% have private insurance; 19.2% have public insurance; 4.7% do not have insurance; 0.0% of children under 18 do not have insurance

Transportation: Commute: 66.5% car, 18.6% public transportation, 0.0% walk, 15.0% work from home; Mean travel time to work: 30.8 minutes

LAKE MOHEGAN (CDP).

Covers a land area of 2.876 square miles and a water area of 0.199 square miles. Located at 41.31° N. Lat; 73.85° W. Long. Elevation is 522 feet.

History: Lake Mohegan is a census-designated place (CDP) located in the town of Yorktown in Westchester County, New York.

Population: 5,663; Growth (since 2000): -5.3%; Density: 1,969.2 persons per square mile; Race: 83.7% White, 4.8% Black/African American, 4.1% Asian, 0.0% American Indian/Alaska Native, 0.0% Native Hawaiian/Other Pacific Islander, 0.7% Two or more races, 24.3% Hispanic of any race; Average household size: 2.64; Median age: 42.3; Age under 18: 24.1%; Age 65 and over: 12.9%; Males per 100 females: 95.2; Marriage status: 34.2% never married, 46.0% now married, 0.9% separated, 7.2% widowed, 12.6% divorced; Foreign born: 15.5%; Speak English only: 79.9%; With disability: 7.8%; Veterans: 4.8%; Ancestry: 28.2% Italian, 19.9% Irish, 11.2% German, 4.5% English, 4.4% American

Employment: 17.1% management, business, and financial, 3.4% computer, engineering, and science, 15.3% education, legal, community service, arts, and media, 5.6% healthcare practitioners, 16.5% service, 25.1% sales and office, 6.6% natural resources, construction, and maintenance, 10.5% production, transportation, and material moving

Income: Per capita: $40,182; Median household: $104,531; Average household: $108,947; Households with income of $100,000 or more: 52.9%; Poverty rate: 4.7%

Educational Attainment: High school diploma or higher: 94.4%; Bachelor's degree or higher: 44.7%; Graduate/professional degree or higher: 17.0%

Housing: Homeownership rate: 80.0%; Median home value: $339,400; Median year structure built: 1965; Homeowner vacancy rate: 1.0%; Median selected monthly owner costs: $2,710 with a mortgage, $965 without a mortgage; Median gross rent: $1,584 per month; Rental vacancy rate: 0.0%

Health Insurance: 94.9% have insurance; 83.0% have private insurance; 21.5% have public insurance; 5.1% do not have insurance; 4.6% of children under 18 do not have insurance

Transportation: Commute: 83.3% car, 10.0% public transportation, 0.4% walk, 4.4% work from home; Mean travel time to work: 39.1 minutes

LARCHMONT (village).

Covers a land area of 1.077 square miles and a water area of 0.002 square miles. Located at 40.93° N. Lat; 73.75° W. Long. Elevation is 52 feet.

History: Joyce Kilmer lived here. Developed c.1845, incorporated 1891.

Population: 6,005; Growth (since 2000): -7.4%; Density: 5,573.8 persons per square mile; Race: 89.3% White, 1.8% Black/African American, 2.2% Asian, 0.3% American Indian/Alaska Native, 0.0% Native Hawaiian/Other Pacific Islander, 4.5% Two or more races, 8.0% Hispanic of any race; Average household size: 2.89; Median age: 37.5; Age under 18: 32.3%; Age 65 and over: 11.9%; Males per 100 females: 95.5; Marriage status: 17.8% never married, 72.2% now married, 2.4% separated, 3.2%

widowed, 6.7% divorced; Foreign born: 18.1%; Speak English only: 78.1%; With disability: 3.0%; Veterans: 4.1%; Ancestry: 21.1% American, 17.2% Italian, 10.9% Irish, 9.5% English, 7.6% German

Employment: 34.8% management, business, and financial, 7.3% computer, engineering, and science, 22.5% education, legal, community service, arts, and media, 6.3% healthcare practitioners, 7.0% service, 16.9% sales and office, 2.5% natural resources, construction, and maintenance, 2.6% production, transportation, and material moving

Income: Per capita: $89,101; Median household: $152,284; Average household: $257,534; Households with income of $100,000 or more: 70.0%; Poverty rate: 4.6%

Educational Attainment: High school diploma or higher: 98.2%; Bachelor's degree or higher: 83.9%; Graduate/professional degree or higher: 44.2%

School District(s)

Mamaroneck Union Free SD (PK-12)

    2014-15 Enrollment: 5,218 . . . . (914) 220-3005

Housing: Homeownership rate: 70.6%; Median home value: $1,044,800; Median year structure built: Before 1940; Homeowner vacancy rate: 0.0%; Median selected monthly owner costs: $4,000+ with a mortgage, $1,500+ without a mortgage; Median gross rent: $1,722 per month; Rental vacancy rate: 0.0%

Health Insurance: 98.4% have insurance; 92.4% have private insurance; 16.0% have public insurance; 1.6% do not have insurance; 0.0% of children under 18 do not have insurance

Safety: Violent crime rate: 6.5 per 10,000 population; Property crime rate: 94.0 per 10,000 population

Transportation: Commute: 37.4% car, 52.5% public transportation, 1.2% walk, 7.6% work from home; Mean travel time to work: 47.5 minutes

Additional Information Contacts

Village of Larchmont . . . . (914) 834-6230
    http://www.villageoflarchmont.org

LEWISBORO (town). Covers a land area of 27.746 square miles and a water area of 1.416 square miles. Located at 41.27° N. Lat; 73.59° W. Long. Elevation is 728 feet.

History: The town was formed in 1747 as the "Town of Salem." John Lewis, a financier, requested that the town be given his name and established a fund for the town, though he did not follow through on his promise of a railroad link.

Population: 12,642; Growth (since 2000): 2.6%; Density: 455.6 persons per square mile; Race: 91.9% White, 3.1% Black/African American, 2.7% Asian, 0.2% American Indian/Alaska Native, 0.0% Native Hawaiian/Other Pacific Islander, 1.5% Two or more races, 4.4% Hispanic of any race; Average household size: 2.77; Median age: 45.6; Age under 18: 24.6%; Age 65 and over: 14.2%; Males per 100 females: 96.7; Marriage status: 26.2% never married, 62.6% now married, 0.7% separated, 4.4% widowed, 6.9% divorced; Foreign born: 9.6%; Speak English only: 90.6%; With disability: 5.3%; Veterans: 4.8%; Ancestry: 23.6% Italian, 18.4% Irish, 11.6% German, 8.4% American, 7.8% English

Employment: 26.8% management, business, and financial, 5.7% computer, engineering, and science, 22.0% education, legal, community service, arts, and media, 7.3% healthcare practitioners, 9.8% service, 20.8% sales and office, 4.5% natural resources, construction, and maintenance, 3.1% production, transportation, and material moving

Income: Per capita: $70,387; Median household: $135,478; Average household: $191,959; Households with income of $100,000 or more: 65.1%; Poverty rate: 2.3%

Educational Attainment: High school diploma or higher: 98.1%; Bachelor's degree or higher: 74.4%; Graduate/professional degree or higher: 37.8%

Housing: Homeownership rate: 91.3%; Median home value: $649,000; Median year structure built: 1975; Homeowner vacancy rate: 1.2%; Median selected monthly owner costs: $3,809 with a mortgage, $1,500+ without a mortgage; Median gross rent: $2,032 per month; Rental vacancy rate: 5.5%

Health Insurance: 94.8% have insurance; 86.2% have private insurance; 18.8% have public insurance; 5.2% do not have insurance; 3.8% of children under 18 do not have insurance

Safety: Violent crime rate: 0.0 per 10,000 population; Property crime rate: 0.8 per 10,000 population

Transportation: Commute: 76.3% car, 12.6% public transportation, 1.9% walk, 8.5% work from home; Mean travel time to work: 39.9 minutes

Additional Information Contacts

Town of Lewisboro . . . . (914) 763-3511
    http://www.lewisborogov.com

LINCOLNDALE (CDP). Covers a land area of 0.958 square miles and a water area of 0.041 square miles. Located at 41.33° N. Lat; 73.72° W. Long. Elevation is 338 feet.

Population: 1,537; Growth (since 2000): -23.8%; Density: 1,605.2 persons per square mile; Race: 95.3% White, 0.0% Black/African American, 0.9% Asian, 0.0% American Indian/Alaska Native, 0.8% Native Hawaiian/Other Pacific Islander, 0.0% Two or more races, 8.5% Hispanic of any race; Average household size: 3.02; Median age: 36.2; Age under 18: 25.6%; Age 65 and over: 9.5%; Males per 100 females: 95.5; Marriage status: 28.0% never married, 57.7% now married, 4.8% separated, 3.9% widowed, 10.4% divorced; Foreign born: 7.4%; Speak English only: 90.3%; With disability: 3.1%; Veterans: 5.2%; Ancestry: 34.9% Irish, 34.9% Italian, 18.2% German, 8.8% American, 6.0% English

Employment: 18.8% management, business, and financial, 0.0% computer, engineering, and science, 27.8% education, legal, community service, arts, and media, 0.8% healthcare practitioners, 11.6% service, 33.1% sales and office, 3.7% natural resources, construction, and maintenance, 4.1% production, transportation, and material moving

Income: Per capita: $39,515; Median household: $108,299; Average household: $117,091; Households with income of $100,000 or more: 61.7%; Poverty rate: 3.4%

Educational Attainment: High school diploma or higher: 98.0%; Bachelor's degree or higher: 49.5%; Graduate/professional degree or higher: 21.6%

School District(s)

Somers Central SD (KG-12)

    2014-15 Enrollment: 3,285 . . . . (914) 277-2400

Housing: Homeownership rate: 81.7%; Median home value: $368,100; Median year structure built: 1956; Homeowner vacancy rate: 0.0%; Median selected monthly owner costs: $2,566 with a mortgage, $1,150 without a mortgage; Median gross rent: $2,578 per month; Rental vacancy rate: 0.0%

Health Insurance: 94.1% have insurance; 85.6% have private insurance; 18.5% have public insurance; 5.9% do not have insurance; 0.0% of children under 18 do not have insurance

Transportation: Commute: 85.0% car, 11.6% public transportation, 1.5% walk, 1.9% work from home; Mean travel time to work: 34.2 minutes

MAMARONECK (town). Covers a land area of 6.654 square miles and a water area of 7.410 square miles. Located at 40.92° N. Lat; 73.74° W. Long. Elevation is 47 feet.

History: Initially a farming community. Settled 1661, incorporated 1895.

Population: 29,657; Growth (since 2000): 2.4%; Density: 4,457.0 persons per square mile; Race: 82.4% White, 3.3% Black/African American, 4.4% Asian, 0.1% American Indian/Alaska Native, 0.0% Native Hawaiian/Other Pacific Islander, 3.0% Two or more races, 14.7% Hispanic of any race; Average household size: 2.71; Median age: 40.7; Age under 18: 26.8%; Age 65 and over: 15.9%; Males per 100 females: 93.9; Marriage status: 26.2% never married, 61.4% now married, 1.5% separated, 5.3% widowed, 7.1% divorced; Foreign born: 21.0%; Speak English only: 71.4%; With disability: 7.7%; Veterans: 4.5%; Ancestry: 15.8% Italian, 13.7% Irish, 10.8% American, 7.4% German, 5.6% Russian

Employment: 29.7% management, business, and financial, 5.4% computer, engineering, and science, 21.1% education, legal, community service, arts, and media, 4.2% healthcare practitioners, 12.2% service, 19.2% sales and office, 4.4% natural resources, construction, and maintenance, 3.7% production, transportation, and material moving

Income: Per capita: $73,499; Median household: $114,273; Average household: $200,593; Households with income of $100,000 or more: 55.0%; Poverty rate: 6.8%

Educational Attainment: High school diploma or higher: 92.4%; Bachelor's degree or higher: 66.5%; Graduate/professional degree or higher: 34.5%

School District(s)

Mamaroneck Union Free SD (PK-12)

    2014-15 Enrollment: 5,218 . . . . (914) 220-3005

Rye Neck Union Free SD (KG-12)

    2014-15 Enrollment: 1,552 . . . . (914) 777-5200

Housing: Homeownership rate: 69.4%; Median home value: $816,300; Median year structure built: 1942; Homeowner vacancy rate: 2.4%; Median selected monthly owner costs: $4,000+ with a mortgage, $1,500+ without a

mortgage; Median gross rent: $1,569 per month; Rental vacancy rate: 2.8%

Health Insurance: 95.2% have insurance; 83.8% have private insurance; 22.5% have public insurance; 4.8% do not have insurance; 2.4% of children under 18 do not have insurance

Safety: Violent crime rate: 6.5 per 10,000 population; Property crime rate: 79.1 per 10,000 population

Transportation: Commute: 47.9% car, 36.4% public transportation, 4.6% walk, 8.4% work from home; Mean travel time to work: 37.4 minutes

Additional Information Contacts

Town of Mamaroneck . . . . (914) 381-7870
http://www.townofmamaroneck.org

MAMARONECK (village). Covers a land area of 3.170 square miles and a water area of 3.407 square miles. Located at 40.93° N. Lat; 73.73° W. Long. Elevation is 47 feet.

Population: 19,219; Growth (since 2000): 2.5%; Density: 6,063.3 persons per square mile; Race: 75.7% White, 6.5% Black/African American, 5.1% Asian, 0.2% American Indian/Alaska Native, 0.0% Native Hawaiian/Other Pacific Islander, 2.8% Two or more races, 20.6% Hispanic of any race; Average household size: 2.63; Median age: 41.5; Age under 18: 24.4%; Age 65 and over: 15.5%; Males per 100 females: 95.1; Marriage status: 31.4% never married, 53.7% now married, 1.8% separated, 6.3% widowed, 8.7% divorced; Foreign born: 26.1%; Speak English only: 64.7%; With disability: 9.0%; Veterans: 4.5%; Ancestry: 24.1% Italian, 12.3% Irish, 8.4% American, 6.9% German, 4.0% French

Employment: 23.3% management, business, and financial, 4.7% computer, engineering, and science, 15.3% education, legal, community service, arts, and media, 4.8% healthcare practitioners, 17.1% service, 19.7% sales and office, 7.8% natural resources, construction, and maintenance, 7.3% production, transportation, and material moving

Income: Per capita: $55,008; Median household: $82,035; Average household: $146,535; Households with income of $100,000 or more: 42.9%; Poverty rate: 8.5%

Educational Attainment: High school diploma or higher: 87.7%; Bachelor's degree or higher: 49.3%; Graduate/professional degree or higher: 25.1%

School District(s)

Mamaroneck Union Free SD (PK-12)
    2014-15 Enrollment: 5,218 . . . . (914) 220-3005
Rye Neck Union Free SD (KG-12)
    2014-15 Enrollment: 1,552 . . . . (914) 777-5200

Housing: Homeownership rate: 56.8%; Median home value: $591,600; Median year structure built: 1951; Homeowner vacancy rate: 2.7%; Median selected monthly owner costs: $3,580 with a mortgage, $1,451 without a mortgage; Median gross rent: $1,646 per month; Rental vacancy rate: 3.0%

Health Insurance: 91.6% have insurance; 75.1% have private insurance; 27.5% have public insurance; 8.4% do not have insurance; 4.3% of children under 18 do not have insurance

Safety: Violent crime rate: 3.1 per 10,000 population; Property crime rate: 70.7 per 10,000 population

Transportation: Commute: 61.7% car, 24.2% public transportation, 5.1% walk, 5.0% work from home; Mean travel time to work: 31.3 minutes

Additional Information Contacts

Village of Mamaroneck . . . . (914) 777-7722
http://www.village.mamaroneck.ny.us

MARYKNOLL (unincorporated postal area)
ZCTA: 10545

Covers a land area of 0.126 square miles and a water area of 0 square miles. Located at 41.18° N. Lat; 73.84° W. Long..

Population: 129; Growth (since 2000): n/a; Density: 1,024.3 persons per square mile; Race: 86.8% White, 7.0% Black/African American, 0.0% Asian, 0.0% American Indian/Alaska Native, 0.0% Native Hawaiian/Other Pacific Islander, 0.0% Two or more races, 18.6% Hispanic of any race; Average household size: 0.00; Median age: 35.2; Age under 18: 0.0%; Age 65 and over: 30.2%; Males per 100 females: ***.*; Marriage status: 86.0% never married, 14.0% now married, 0.0% separated, 0.0% widowed, 0.0% divorced; Foreign born: 21.7%; Speak English only: 58.9%; With disability: 7.0%; Veterans: 0.0%; Ancestry: 38.8% Irish, 23.3% Italian, 20.2% American, 8.5% German, 7.8% Armenian

Employment: 0.0% management, business, and financial, 0.0% computer, engineering, and science, 37.0% education, legal, community

service, arts, and media, 0.0% healthcare practitioners, 29.6% service, 0.0% sales and office, 0.0% natural resources, construction, and maintenance, 33.3% production, transportation, and material moving

Income: Per capita: $9,875; Median household: n/a; Average household: n/a; Households with income of $100,000 or more: n/a; Poverty rate: 79.1%

Educational Attainment: High school diploma or higher: 100.0%; Bachelor's degree or higher: 71.7%; Graduate/professional degree or higher: 32.5%

Housing: Homeownership rate: n/a; Median home value: n/a; Median year structure built: n/a; Homeowner vacancy rate: 0.0%; Median selected monthly owner costs: $0 with a mortgage, $0 without a mortgage; Median gross rent: n/a per month; Rental vacancy rate: 0.0%

Health Insurance: 72.1% have insurance; 42.6% have private insurance; 37.2% have public insurance; 27.9% do not have insurance; 0.0% of children under 18 do not have insurance

Transportation: Commute: 0.0% car, 0.0% public transportation, 66.7% walk, 33.3% work from home; Mean travel time to work: 0.0 minutes

MILLWOOD (unincorporated postal area)
ZCTA: 10546

Covers a land area of 1.123 square miles and a water area of 0.005 square miles. Located at 41.20° N. Lat; 73.80° W. Long. Elevation is 361 feet.

Population: 1,265; Growth (since 2000): 3.3%; Density: 1,126.4 persons per square mile; Race: 70.8% White, 0.3% Black/African American, 14.0% Asian, 0.0% American Indian/Alaska Native, 0.0% Native Hawaiian/Other Pacific Islander, 4.1% Two or more races, 12.6% Hispanic of any race; Average household size: 2.91; Median age: 45.1; Age under 18: 22.4%; Age 65 and over: 16.1%; Males per 100 females: 97.1; Marriage status: 19.3% never married, 70.2% now married, 0.7% separated, 3.3% widowed, 7.1% divorced; Foreign born: 23.9%; Speak English only: 84.7%; With disability: 5.2%; Veterans: 0.5%; Ancestry: 14.2% Polish, 10.9% German, 9.5% Hungarian, 7.9% Trinidadian and Tobagonian, 7.3% American

Employment: 32.1% management, business, and financial, 7.6% computer, engineering, and science, 14.2% education, legal, community service, arts, and media, 12.1% healthcare practitioners, 5.5% service, 21.5% sales and office, 0.0% natural resources, construction, and maintenance, 7.1% production, transportation, and material moving

Income: Per capita: $57,776; Median household: $115,278; Average household: $166,804; Households with income of $100,000 or more: 55.5%; Poverty rate: 0.6%

Educational Attainment: High school diploma or higher: 92.2%; Bachelor's degree or higher: 66.1%; Graduate/professional degree or higher: 41.8%

Housing: Homeownership rate: 89.4%; Median home value: $648,400; Median year structure built: 1980; Homeowner vacancy rate: 5.4%; Median selected monthly owner costs: $4,000 with a mortgage, $1,428 without a mortgage; Median gross rent: $3,189 per month; Rental vacancy rate: 0.0%

Health Insurance: 100.0% have insurance; 90.8% have private insurance; 19.6% have public insurance; 0.0% do not have insurance; 0.0% of children under 18 do not have insurance

Transportation: Commute: 78.8% car, 15.4% public transportation, 0.0% walk, 5.8% work from home; Mean travel time to work: 36.2 minutes

MOHEGAN LAKE (unincorporated postal area)
ZCTA: 10547

Covers a land area of 5.066 square miles and a water area of 0.199 square miles. Located at 41.31° N. Lat; 73.85° W. Long. Elevation is 472 feet.

Population: 7,045; Growth (since 2000): -17.5%; Density: 1,390.7 persons per square mile; Race: 80.1% White, 9.6% Black/African American, 4.0% Asian, 0.0% American Indian/Alaska Native, 0.0% Native Hawaiian/Other Pacific Islander, 1.2% Two or more races, 17.6% Hispanic of any race; Average household size: 2.59; Median age: 41.7; Age under 18: 21.2%; Age 65 and over: 11.5%; Males per 100 females: 96.6; Marriage status: 37.6% never married, 45.5% now married, 1.8% separated, 4.5% widowed, 12.3% divorced; Foreign born: 14.1%; Speak English only: 82.0%; With disability: 10.1%; Veterans: 5.0%; Ancestry: 28.6% Italian, 20.5% Irish, 11.3% German, 5.2% American, 4.9% English

Employment: 17.5% management, business, and financial, 2.8% computer, engineering, and science, 12.0% education, legal, community service, arts, and media, 5.7% healthcare practitioners, 19.3% service, 24.3% sales and office, 7.1% natural resources, construction, and maintenance, 11.3% production, transportation, and material moving
Income: Per capita: $39,767; Median household: $94,982; Average household: $106,680; Households with income of $100,000 or more: 49.5%; Poverty rate: 8.5%
Educational Attainment: High school diploma or higher: 91.8%; Bachelor's degree or higher: 41.0%; Graduate/professional degree or higher: 16.1%

School District(s)
Lakeland Central SD (PK-12)
   2014-15 Enrollment: 5,900 . . . . (914) 245-1700
Housing: Homeownership rate: 73.5%; Median home value: $341,300; Median year structure built: 1964; Homeowner vacancy rate: 0.9%; Median selected monthly owner costs: $2,828 with a mortgage, $981 without a mortgage; Median gross rent: $1,381 per month; Rental vacancy rate: 3.3%
Health Insurance: 93.6% have insurance; 78.3% have private insurance; 24.9% have public insurance; 6.4% do not have insurance; 6.3% of children under 18 do not have insurance
Transportation: Commute: 84.9% car, 9.6% public transportation, 2.0% walk, 1.3% work from home; Mean travel time to work: 37.2 minutes

MONTROSE (CDP).
Covers a land area of 1.614 square miles and a water area of 0.052 square miles. Located at 41.24° N. Lat; 73.94° W. Long. Elevation is 115 feet.
Population: 2,659; Growth (since 2000): n/a; Density: 1,647.3 persons per square mile; Race: 87.4% White, 2.2% Black/African American, 1.3% Asian, 0.3% American Indian/Alaska Native, 0.0% Native Hawaiian/Other Pacific Islander, 2.0% Two or more races, 16.0% Hispanic of any race; Average household size: 2.45; Median age: 47.6; Age under 18: 20.0%; Age 65 and over: 17.6%; Males per 100 females: 97.0; Marriage status: 22.0% never married, 55.2% now married, 0.1% separated, 9.9% widowed, 13.0% divorced; Foreign born: 10.8%; Speak English only: 85.7%; With disability: 12.6%; Veterans: 8.6%; Ancestry: 33.6% Italian, 28.8% Irish, 13.0% German, 6.0% English, 4.9% American
Employment: 13.4% management, business, and financial, 8.5% computer, engineering, and science, 16.1% education, legal, community service, arts, and media, 5.7% healthcare practitioners, 19.5% service, 23.8% sales and office, 8.3% natural resources, construction, and maintenance, 4.7% production, transportation, and material moving
Income: Per capita: $43,678; Median household: $78,125; Average household: $105,407; Households with income of $100,000 or more: 38.7%; Poverty rate: 7.4%
Educational Attainment: High school diploma or higher: 96.7%; Bachelor's degree or higher: 37.5%; Graduate/professional degree or higher: 12.9%

School District(s)
Hendrick Hudson Central SD (KG-12)
   2014-15 Enrollment: 2,366 . . . . (914) 257-5100
Housing: Homeownership rate: 80.4%; Median home value: $345,300; Median year structure built: 1960; Homeowner vacancy rate: 0.0%; Median selected monthly owner costs: $2,721 with a mortgage, $883 without a mortgage; Median gross rent: $1,438 per month; Rental vacancy rate: 20.9%
Health Insurance: 95.1% have insurance; 84.8% have private insurance; 30.4% have public insurance; 4.9% do not have insurance; 1.1% of children under 18 do not have insurance
Hospitals: VA Hudson Valley Healthcare System
Transportation: Commute: 82.7% car, 13.0% public transportation, 0.0% walk, 4.3% work from home; Mean travel time to work: 31.9 minutes

MOUNT KISCO (town/village).
Covers a land area of 3.035 square miles and a water area of 0.030 square miles. Located at 41.20° N. Lat; 73.73° W. Long. Elevation is 305 feet.
Population: 11,060; Growth (since 2000): 10.8%; Density: 3,643.9 persons per square mile; Race: 59.2% White, 6.2% Black/African American, 3.3% Asian, 0.0% American Indian/Alaska Native, 0.0% Native Hawaiian/Other Pacific Islander, 2.5% Two or more races, 44.9% Hispanic of any race; Average household size: 2.75; Median age: 36.6; Age under 18: 22.5%; Age 65 and over: 12.6%; Males per 100 females: 107.4; Marriage status: 38.4% never married, 50.6% now married, 1.5% separated, 3.7% widowed, 7.3% divorced; Foreign born: 38.3%; Speak

English only: 51.0%; With disability: 8.3%; Veterans: 4.0%; Ancestry: 15.7% Italian, 13.5% Irish, 7.1% German, 3.6% American, 3.1% Polish
Employment: 13.0% management, business, and financial, 3.4% computer, engineering, and science, 12.3% education, legal, community service, arts, and media, 4.5% healthcare practitioners, 36.6% service, 15.9% sales and office, 9.0% natural resources, construction, and maintenance, 5.2% production, transportation, and material moving
Income: Per capita: $35,041; Median household: $68,556; Average household: $94,183; Households with income of $100,000 or more: 33.2%; Poverty rate: 14.0%
Educational Attainment: High school diploma or higher: 82.2%; Bachelor's degree or higher: 39.7%; Graduate/professional degree or higher: 18.1%

School District(s)
Bedford Central SD (PK-12)
   2014-15 Enrollment: 4,390 . . . . (914) 241-6010
Four-year College(s)
Yeshiva of Nitra Rabbinical College (Private, Not-for-profit)
   Fall 2014 Enrollment: 267 . . . . (718) 384-5460
   2015-16 Tuition: In-state $8,200; Out-of-state $8,200
Vocational/Technical School(s)
Finger Lakes School of Massage (Private, For-profit)
   Fall 2014 Enrollment: 61 . . . . (914) 241-7363
   2015-16 Tuition: $17,000
Housing: Homeownership rate: 53.1%; Median home value: $402,200; Median year structure built: 1966; Homeowner vacancy rate: 0.9%; Median selected monthly owner costs: $2,535 with a mortgage, $1,029 without a mortgage; Median gross rent: $1,363 per month; Rental vacancy rate: 2.8%
Health Insurance: 79.4% have insurance; 58.5% have private insurance; 30.0% have public insurance; 20.6% do not have insurance; 2.0% of children under 18 do not have insurance
Hospitals: Northern Westchester Hospital (233 beds)
Transportation: Commute: 72.1% car, 9.9% public transportation, 8.3% walk, 3.9% work from home; Mean travel time to work: 26.9 minutes
Additional Information Contacts
Village and Town of Mount Kisco . . . . (914) 241-0500
   http://www.mountkisco.org

MOUNT PLEASANT (town).
Covers a land area of 27.423 square miles and a water area of 5.335 square miles. Located at 41.10° N. Lat; 73.82° W. Long. Elevation is 259 feet.
History: Mount Pleasant is home to the John D. Rockefeller Estate which was added to the National Register of Historic Places in 1976 as a National Historic Landmark.
Population: 44,528; Growth (since 2000): 3.0%; Density: 1,623.8 persons per square mile; Race: 79.1% White, 4.2% Black/African American, 5.3% Asian, 0.3% American Indian/Alaska Native, 0.0% Native Hawaiian/Other Pacific Islander, 3.2% Two or more races, 18.9% Hispanic of any race; Average household size: 2.90; Median age: 40.3; Age under 18: 23.3%; Age 65 and over: 14.6%; Males per 100 females: 101.8; Marriage status: 33.2% never married, 55.3% now married, 1.7% separated, 5.2% widowed, 6.3% divorced; Foreign born: 20.3%; Speak English only: 71.8%; With disability: 7.7%; Veterans: 4.5%; Ancestry: 29.0% Italian, 16.0% Irish, 8.9% German, 5.1% American, 4.4% English
Employment: 21.2% management, business, and financial, 5.0% computer, engineering, and science, 17.2% education, legal, community service, arts, and media, 6.9% healthcare practitioners, 16.8% service, 20.3% sales and office, 6.5% natural resources, construction, and maintenance, 6.2% production, transportation, and material moving
Income: Per capita: $47,484; Median household: $102,142; Average household: $143,688; Households with income of $100,000 or more: 51.2%; Poverty rate: 7.7%
Educational Attainment: High school diploma or higher: 88.9%; Bachelor's degree or higher: 50.7%; Graduate/professional degree or higher: 25.0%
Housing: Homeownership rate: 70.2%; Median home value: $610,900; Median year structure built: 1956; Homeowner vacancy rate: 1.5%; Median selected monthly owner costs: $3,692 with a mortgage, $1,500+ without a mortgage; Median gross rent: $1,373 per month; Rental vacancy rate: 2.0%
Health Insurance: 93.9% have insurance; 82.1% have private insurance; 23.1% have public insurance; 6.1% do not have insurance; 1.7% of children under 18 do not have insurance

Safety: Violent crime rate: 6.4 per 10,000 population; Property crime rate: 72.7 per 10,000 population

Transportation: Commute: 71.3% car, 16.3% public transportation, 6.6% walk, 4.9% work from home; Mean travel time to work: 30.0 minutes

Additional Information Contacts

Town of Mount Pleasant . . . . (914) 742-2300
  http://www.mtpleasantny.com

MOUNT VERNON (city). Covers a land area of 4.386 square miles and a water area of 0.017 square miles. Located at 40.91° N. Lat; 73.83° W. Long. Elevation is 112 feet.

History: Named for George Washington's estate on the Potomac River, which was named for Edward Vernon, British admiral. John Peter Zenger was arrested here for libel in 1733. The city itself was not founded until 1851, when a cooperative group, the Industrial Home Association, bought the land and built a planned community. St. Paul's Church (c.1761), a national historic site, is here. The city, which has a large French-American population, has been the scene of a great deal of controversy over school and housing integration in the 1970s, 1980s, and 1990s.

Population: 68,221; Growth (since 2000): -0.2%; Density: 15,555.4 persons per square mile; Race: 22.5% White, 65.3% Black/African American, 2.2% Asian, 0.4% American Indian/Alaska Native, 0.0% Native Hawaiian/Other Pacific Islander, 3.1% Two or more races, 15.2% Hispanic of any race; Average household size: 2.70; Median age: 37.4; Age under 18: 22.8%; Age 65 and over: 13.5%; Males per 100 females: 83.3; Marriage status: 44.7% never married, 38.1% now married, 3.6% separated, 6.5% widowed, 10.7% divorced; Foreign born: 33.9%; Speak English only: 76.8%; With disability: 11.0%; Veterans: 3.8%; Ancestry: 20.5% Jamaican, 6.4% Italian, 3.6% Irish, 3.2% American, 2.6% Haitian

Employment: 12.4% management, business, and financial, 2.4% computer, engineering, and science, 12.3% education, legal, community service, arts, and media, 7.7% healthcare practitioners, 26.9% service, 22.6% sales and office, 7.6% natural resources, construction, and maintenance, 8.2% production, transportation, and material moving

Income: Per capita: $27,378; Median household: $50,952; Average household: $70,868; Households with income of $100,000 or more: 22.2%; Poverty rate: 15.3%

Educational Attainment: High school diploma or higher: 84.6%; Bachelor's degree or higher: 27.8%; Graduate/professional degree or higher: 11.1%

School District(s)

Amani Public Charter School (05-05)
  2014-15 Enrollment: 336 . . . . (914) 668-6450
Mount Vernon SD (PK-12)
  2014-15 Enrollment: 8,684 . . . . (914) 665-5000

Two-year College(s)

Montefiore School of Nursing (Private, Not-for-profit)
  Fall 2014 Enrollment: n/a . . . . (914) 361-6221

Vocational/Technical School(s)

Westchester School of Beauty Culture (Private, For-profit)
  Fall 2014 Enrollment: 87 . . . . (914) 699-2344
  2015-16 Tuition: $10,346

Housing: Homeownership rate: 39.1%; Median home value: $361,700; Median year structure built: 1944; Homeowner vacancy rate: 4.2%; Median selected monthly owner costs: $2,870 with a mortgage, $1,199 without a mortgage; Median gross rent: $1,216 per month; Rental vacancy rate: 7.5%

Health Insurance: 87.4% have insurance; 60.3% have private insurance; 38.5% have public insurance; 12.6% do not have insurance; 3.9% of children under 18 do not have insurance

Hospitals: Montefiore Mount Vernon Hospital (228 beds)

Safety: Violent crime rate: 69.3 per 10,000 population; Property crime rate: 164.1 per 10,000 population

Transportation: Commute: 62.2% car, 26.5% public transportation, 6.5% walk, 3.3% work from home; Mean travel time to work: 33.7 minutes

Additional Information Contacts

City of Mount Vernon . . . . (914) 665-2300
  http://www.cmvny.com

NEW CASTLE (town). Covers a land area of 23.236 square miles and a water area of 0.383 square miles. Located at 41.18° N. Lat; 73.77° W. Long.

History: In 1696 Caleb Heathcote purchases a large tract of land including what is now New Castle from Wampus and other Native American

sachems. In 1730 Quakers begin settling in the northern and western parts of North Castle, which will become New Castle.

Population: 17,897; Growth (since 2000): 2.3%; Density: 770.2 persons per square mile; Race: 87.5% White, 1.5% Black/African American, 7.0% Asian, 0.4% American Indian/Alaska Native, 0.0% Native Hawaiian/Other Pacific Islander, 2.0% Two or more races, 5.1% Hispanic of any race; Average household size: 3.07; Median age: 41.9; Age under 18: 29.1%; Age 65 and over: 11.9%; Males per 100 females: 99.2; Marriage status: 23.3% never married, 70.5% now married, 0.5% separated, 3.0% widowed, 3.2% divorced; Foreign born: 12.4%; Speak English only: 86.5%; With disability: 5.0%; Veterans: 3.2%; Ancestry: 15.1% Italian, 13.2% Irish, 11.6% German, 7.5% American, 7.2% Polish

Employment: 32.7% management, business, and financial, 5.5% computer, engineering, and science, 24.1% education, legal, community service, arts, and media, 8.6% healthcare practitioners, 5.8% service, 19.8% sales and office, 1.1% natural resources, construction, and maintenance, 2.3% production, transportation, and material moving

Income: Per capita: $90,345; Median household: $199,426; Average household: $277,541; Households with income of $100,000 or more: 78.4%; Poverty rate: 2.5%

Educational Attainment: High school diploma or higher: 97.8%; Bachelor's degree or higher: 84.0%; Graduate/professional degree or higher: 48.0%

Housing: Homeownership rate: 93.0%; Median home value: $872,100; Median year structure built: 1964; Homeowner vacancy rate: 1.5%; Median selected monthly owner costs: $4,000+ with a mortgage, $1,500+ without a mortgage; Median gross rent: $1,557 per month; Rental vacancy rate: 0.0%

Health Insurance: 97.3% have insurance; 92.9% have private insurance; 13.1% have public insurance; 2.7% do not have insurance; 0.6% of children under 18 do not have insurance

Safety: Violent crime rate: 1.1 per 10,000 population; Property crime rate: 31.6 per 10,000 population

Transportation: Commute: 57.5% car, 29.6% public transportation, 2.4% walk, 10.4% work from home; Mean travel time to work: 41.7 minutes

Additional Information Contacts

Town of New Castle . . . . (914) 238-7269
  http://www.mynewcastle.org

NEW ROCHELLE (city). Covers a land area of 10.350 square miles and a water area of 2.885 square miles. Located at 40.92° N. Lat; 73.78° W. Long. Elevation is 85 feet.

History: New Rochelle occupies the site of the villages of the Siwanoy, principal nation of the Wappinger confederacy. In 1689, a group of Huguenot refugees purchased a tract of 6,000 acres and named the settlement for their old home in France, La Rochelle. New Rochelle was incorporated as a village in 1857 and as a city in 1899.

Population: 79,027; Growth (since 2000): 9.5%; Density: 7,635.3 persons per square mile; Race: 63.8% White, 18.6% Black/African American, 4.2% Asian, 0.1% American Indian/Alaska Native, 0.0% Native Hawaiian/Other Pacific Islander, 3.5% Two or more races, 28.3% Hispanic of any race; Average household size: 2.68; Median age: 39.3; Age under 18: 21.7%; Age 65 and over: 15.1%; Males per 100 females: 92.3; Marriage status: 35.4% never married, 49.7% now married, 2.3% separated, 6.8% widowed, 8.1% divorced; Foreign born: 29.1%; Speak English only: 60.3%; With disability: 9.9%; Veterans: 4.5%; Ancestry: 17.9% Italian, 8.3% Irish, 4.6% American, 4.1% German, 3.5% Polish

Employment: 16.2% management, business, and financial, 3.5% computer, engineering, and science, 15.0% education, legal, community service, arts, and media, 7.6% healthcare practitioners, 20.0% service, 22.4% sales and office, 8.4% natural resources, construction, and maintenance, 6.9% production, transportation, and material moving

Income: Per capita: $41,485; Median household: $70,036; Average household: $112,366; Households with income of $100,000 or more: 37.3%; Poverty rate: 11.1%

Educational Attainment: High school diploma or higher: 82.9%; Bachelor's degree or higher: 42.2%; Graduate/professional degree or higher: 21.6%

School District(s)

New Rochelle City SD (PK-12)
  2014-15 Enrollment: 10,992 . . . . (914) 576-4200

Four-year College(s)

Iona College (Private, Not-for-profit, Roman Catholic)
  Fall 2014 Enrollment: 3,909 . . . . (914) 633-2000
  2015-16 Tuition: In-state $35,324; Out-of-state $35,324

The College of New Rochelle (Private, Not-for-profit)
    Fall 2014 Enrollment: 3,740 . . . . (914) 654-5000
    2015-16 Tuition: In-state $33,600; Out-of-state $33,600
Housing: Homeownership rate: 49.6%; Median home value: $552,600;
Median year structure built: 1951; Homeowner vacancy rate: 1.8%; Median
selected monthly owner costs: $3,452 with a mortgage, $1,500+ without a
mortgage; Median gross rent: $1,359 per month; Rental vacancy rate:
4.2%
Health Insurance: 88.6% have insurance; 68.0% have private insurance;
30.9% have public insurance; 11.4% do not have insurance; 2.2% of
children under 18 do not have insurance
Hospitals: Montefiore New Rochelle Hospital (476 beds)
Safety: Violent crime rate: 21.3 per 10,000 population; Property crime rate:
159.8 per 10,000 population
Newspapers: Westchester Guardian (weekly circulation 15,000)
Transportation: Commute: 63.6% car, 21.8% public transportation, 7.5%
walk, 5.3% work from home; Mean travel time to work: 30.7 minutes;
Amtrak: Train service available.
Additional Information Contacts
City of New Rochelle . . . . (914) 654-2000
    http://www.newrochelleny.com

NORTH CASTLE (town). Covers a land area of 23.757 square miles
and a water area of 2.604 square miles. Located at 41.14° N. Lat; 73.69°
W. Long. Elevation is 597 feet.
History: Town got its name from a barrier built by the Mohicans to protect
themselves from attack.
Population: 12,141; Growth (since 2000): 11.9%; Density: 511.0 persons
per square mile; Race: 90.7% White, 1.4% Black/African American, 3.3%
Asian, 0.4% American Indian/Alaska Native, 0.0% Native Hawaiian/Other
Pacific Islander, 1.8% Two or more races, 9.0% Hispanic of any race;
Average household size: 3.12; Median age: 41.5; Age under 18: 29.4%;
Age 65 and over: 13.7%; Males per 100 females: 98.2; Marriage status:
24.1% never married, 66.6% now married, 0.9% separated, 3.1%
widowed, 6.2% divorced; Foreign born: 11.5%; Speak English only: 81.1%;
With disability: 6.2%; Veterans: 4.7%; Ancestry: 23.5% Italian, 11.3% Irish,
10.3% German, 7.7% Russian, 7.1% American
Employment: 28.7% management, business, and financial, 5.4%
computer, engineering, and science, 17.2% education, legal, community
service, arts, and media, 8.5% healthcare practitioners, 11.4% service,
23.1% sales and office, 3.5% natural resources, construction, and
maintenance, 2.2% production, transportation, and material moving
Income: Per capita: $94,458; Median household: $172,167; Average
household: $289,857; Households with income of $100,000 or more:
71.7%; Poverty rate: 2.0%
Educational Attainment: High school diploma or higher: 96.5%;
Bachelor's degree or higher: 69.3%; Graduate/professional degree or
higher: 36.0%
Housing: Homeownership rate: 87.6%; Median home value: $907,600;
Median year structure built: 1966; Homeowner vacancy rate: 2.9%; Median
selected monthly owner costs: $4,000+ with a mortgage, $1,500+ without a
mortgage; Median gross rent: $2,101 per month; Rental vacancy rate:
6.4%
Health Insurance: 95.9% have insurance; 90.7% have private insurance;
15.3% have public insurance; 4.1% do not have insurance; 2.2% of
children under 18 do not have insurance
Safety: Violent crime rate: 3.2 per 10,000 population; Property crime rate:
47.9 per 10,000 population
Transportation: Commute: 74.0% car, 16.0% public transportation, 1.1%
walk, 7.8% work from home; Mean travel time to work: 33.8 minutes
Additional Information Contacts
Town of North Castle . . . . (914) 273-3321
    http://www.northcastleny.com

NORTH SALEM (town). Covers a land area of 21.326 square miles
and a water area of 1.519 square miles. Located at 41.34° N. Lat; 73.60°
W. Long. Elevation is 505 feet.
History: DeLancey Town Hall, a restored 18th-century Georgian manor, is
on the National Register of Historic Places; Museum, Japanese Stroll
Garden also here.
Population: 5,182; Growth (since 2000): 0.2%; Density: 243.0 persons per
square mile; Race: 90.7% White, 1.9% Black/African American, 1.1%
Asian, 0.2% American Indian/Alaska Native, 0.0% Native Hawaiian/Other
Pacific Islander, 1.6% Two or more races, 9.3% Hispanic of any race;
Average household size: 2.62; Median age: 50.2; Age under 18: 20.0%;

Age 65 and over: 22.1%; Males per 100 females: 94.1; Marriage status:
23.1% never married, 63.7% now married, 1.3% separated, 5.3%
widowed, 7.9% divorced; Foreign born: 14.0%; Speak English only: 86.4%;
With disability: 8.5%; Veterans: 7.5%; Ancestry: 24.0% Italian, 17.5% Irish,
13.4% German, 7.2% English, 4.7% American
Employment: 27.8% management, business, and financial, 4.5%
computer, engineering, and science, 15.2% education, legal, community
service, arts, and media, 7.4% healthcare practitioners, 9.9% service,
27.5% sales and office, 2.4% natural resources, construction, and
maintenance, 5.3% production, transportation, and material moving
Income: Per capita: $68,466; Median household: $124,868; Average
household: $186,684; Households with income of $100,000 or more:
62.9%; Poverty rate: 4.2%
Educational Attainment: High school diploma or higher: 94.3%;
Bachelor's degree or higher: 58.7%; Graduate/professional degree or
higher: 19.9%
School District(s)
North Salem Central SD (KG-12)
    2014-15 Enrollment: 1,169 . . . . (914) 669-5414
Housing: Homeownership rate: 82.8%; Median home value: $578,200;
Median year structure built: 1961; Homeowner vacancy rate: 6.3%; Median
selected monthly owner costs: $3,535 with a mortgage, $1,395 without a
mortgage; Median gross rent: $1,777 per month; Rental vacancy rate:
0.0%
Health Insurance: 97.9% have insurance; 87.0% have private insurance;
26.3% have public insurance; 2.1% do not have insurance; 0.0% of
children under 18 do not have insurance
Transportation: Commute: 75.0% car, 10.7% public transportation, 1.2%
walk, 11.9% work from home; Mean travel time to work: 37.8 minutes
Additional Information Contacts
Town of North Salem . . . . (914) 669-5577
    http://www.northsalemny.org

OSSINING (town). Covers a land area of 11.556 square miles and a
water area of 4.168 square miles. Located at 41.16° N. Lat; 73.86° W.
Long. Elevation is 161 feet.
History: Ossining is the site of Sing Sing state prison (built 1825—1828).
This prison was long known for its extreme discipline, but under Thomas
Mott Osborne and Lewis Edward Lawes, notable reforms were introduced.
By end of 19th century, second-largest industrial center in Westchester.
Brickyards produced bricks for Old Croton Aqueduct. Maryknoll, the
headquarters of the Catholic Foreign Mission Society, is nearby. Settled
c.1750, Incorporated 1813 as Sing Sing, renamed 1901.
Population: 38,136; Growth (since 2000): 4.4%; Density: 3,300.1 persons
per square mile; Race: 56.8% White, 12.6% Black/African American, 6.0%
Asian, 1.7% American Indian/Alaska Native, 0.0% Native Hawaiian/Other
Pacific Islander, 3.4% Two or more races, 34.3% Hispanic of any race;
Average household size: 2.86; Median age: 39.9; Age under 18: 21.9%;
Age 65 and over: 13.3%; Males per 100 females: 104.3; Marriage status:
34.5% never married, 51.8% now married, 2.4% separated, 5.3%
widowed, 8.4% divorced; Foreign born: 30.6%; Speak English only: 57.8%;
With disability: 8.0%; Veterans: 4.5%; Ancestry: 12.9% Italian, 10.9% Irish,
5.8% German, 3.8% English, 3.5% American
Employment: 15.5% management, business, and financial, 4.3%
computer, engineering, and science, 14.2% education, legal, community
service, arts, and media, 6.1% healthcare practitioners, 21.1% service,
22.8% sales and office, 10.4% natural resources, construction, and
maintenance, 5.6% production, transportation, and material moving
Income: Per capita: $40,732; Median household: $79,688; Average
household: $122,859; Households with income of $100,000 or more:
42.9%; Poverty rate: 11.0%
Educational Attainment: High school diploma or higher: 80.0%;
Bachelor's degree or higher: 43.5%; Graduate/professional degree or
higher: 22.5%
School District(s)
Ossining Union Free SD (PK-12)
    2014-15 Enrollment: 4,912 . . . . (914) 941-7700
Four-year College(s)
Kehilath Yakov Rabbinical Seminary (Private, Not-for-profit, Jewish)
    Fall 2014 Enrollment: 125 . . . . (718) 963-1212
    2015-16 Tuition: In-state $9,400; Out-of-state $9,400
Housing: Homeownership rate: 60.1%; Median home value: $447,200;
Median year structure built: 1961; Homeowner vacancy rate: 1.4%; Median
selected monthly owner costs: $3,287 with a mortgage, $1,447 without a

mortgage; Median gross rent: $1,422 per month; Rental vacancy rate: 4.4%

Health Insurance: 85.3% have insurance; 68.5% have private insurance; 26.5% have public insurance; 14.7% do not have insurance; 2.1% of children under 18 do not have insurance

Transportation: Commute: 68.5% car, 15.9% public transportation, 7.8% walk, 6.0% work from home; Mean travel time to work: 31.1 minutes

Additional Information Contacts

Town of Ossining . . . . (914) 762-6000
  http://www.townofossining.com

OSSINING (village). Covers a land area of 3.149 square miles and a water area of 3.283 square miles. Located at 41.16° N. Lat; 73.87° W. Long. Elevation is 161 feet.

Population: 25,311; Growth (since 2000): 5.4%; Density: 8,037.1 persons per square mile; Race: 44.8% White, 17.0% Black/African American, 4.7% Asian, 2.6% American Indian/Alaska Native, 0.0% Native Hawaiian/Other Pacific Islander, 3.4% Two or more races, 47.5% Hispanic of any race; Average household size: 2.99; Median age: 37.1; Age under 18: 23.1%; Age 65 and over: 10.1%; Males per 100 females: 113.0; Marriage status: 37.1% never married, 48.4% now married, 3.3% separated, 4.9% widowed, 9.5% divorced; Foreign born: 39.5%; Speak English only: 45.7%; With disability: 7.0%; Veterans: 3.7%; Ancestry: 9.6% Italian, 8.6% Irish, 4.3% Jamaican, 2.9% German, 2.8% English

Employment: 11.4% management, business, and financial, 2.8% computer, engineering, and science, 11.3% education, legal, community service, arts, and media, 4.5% healthcare practitioners, 27.2% service, 21.8% sales and office, 13.7% natural resources, construction, and maintenance, 7.3% production, transportation, and material moving

Income: Per capita: $28,075; Median household: $61,746; Average household: $87,267; Households with income of $100,000 or more: 31.8%; Poverty rate: 13.8%

Educational Attainment: High school diploma or higher: 72.1%; Bachelor's degree or higher: 31.2%; Graduate/professional degree or higher: 14.9%

School District(s)
Ossining Union Free SD (PK-12)
  2014-15 Enrollment: 4,912 . . . . (914) 941-7700

Four-year College(s)
Kehilath Yakov Rabbinical Seminary (Private, Not-for-profit, Jewish)
  Fall 2014 Enrollment: 125 . . . . (718) 963-1212
  2015-16 Tuition: In-state $9,400; Out-of-state $9,400

Housing: Homeownership rate: 46.3%; Median home value: $377,800; Median year structure built: 1958; Homeowner vacancy rate: 2.1%; Median selected monthly owner costs: $3,025 with a mortgage, $1,214 without a mortgage; Median gross rent: $1,418 per month; Rental vacancy rate: 5.1%

Health Insurance: 79.0% have insurance; 58.3% have private insurance; 28.3% have public insurance; 21.0% do not have insurance; 2.9% of children under 18 do not have insurance

Safety: Violent crime rate: 14.6 per 10,000 population; Property crime rate: 79.8 per 10,000 population

Transportation: Commute: 70.7% car, 13.2% public transportation, 10.0% walk, 3.6% work from home; Mean travel time to work: 28.6 minutes

Additional Information Contacts

Village of Ossining . . . . (914) 762-8428
  http://www.villageofossining.org

PEEKSKILL (city). Covers a land area of 4.368 square miles and a water area of 1.230 square miles. Located at 41.29° N. Lat; 73.92° W. Long. Elevation is 128 feet.

History: Named for Jan Peeck, a Dutch trader from New Amsterdam. In the American Revolution, Peekskill was attacked and burned (1777) by the British; after the war the city became a prominent trade center. In 19th century had foundries based on Putnam County iron deposits. Peter Cooper and Henry Ward Beecher born here. St. Peter's Church, dedicated in 1767, has been restored. Settled 1665. Incorporated as a village 1816, as a city 1940.

Population: 23,928; Growth (since 2000): 6.6%; Density: 5,478.6 persons per square mile; Race: 45.3% White, 21.0% Black/African American, 2.8% Asian, 0.4% American Indian/Alaska Native, 0.0% Native Hawaiian/Other Pacific Islander, 5.5% Two or more races, 36.9% Hispanic of any race; Average household size: 2.62; Median age: 39.3; Age under 18: 21.5%; Age 65 and over: 14.6%; Males per 100 females: 95.6; Marriage status: 34.6% never married, 48.5% now married, 3.4% separated, 5.6%

widowed, 11.2% divorced; Foreign born: 28.5%; Speak English only: 63.9%; With disability: 11.9%; Veterans: 6.4%; Ancestry: 12.3% Italian, 11.6% Irish, 6.8% German, 4.7% Jamaican, 3.6% English

Employment: 11.4% management, business, and financial, 3.8% computer, engineering, and science, 11.2% education, legal, community service, arts, and media, 5.1% healthcare practitioners, 28.1% service, 20.2% sales and office, 8.1% natural resources, construction, and maintenance, 12.1% production, transportation, and material moving

Income: Per capita: $30,200; Median household: $52,125; Average household: $76,305; Households with income of $100,000 or more: 26.7%; Poverty rate: 11.8%

Educational Attainment: High school diploma or higher: 80.8%; Bachelor's degree or higher: 26.8%; Graduate/professional degree or higher: 10.6%

School District(s)
Peekskill City SD (PK-12)
  2014-15 Enrollment: 3,363 . . . . (914) 737-3300

Four-year College(s)
Ohr Hameir Theological Seminary (Private, Not-for-profit)
  Fall 2014 Enrollment: 96 . . . . (914) 736-1500
  2015-16 Tuition: In-state $10,000; Out-of-state $10,000

Vocational/Technical School(s)
Empire Beauty School-Peekskill (Private, For-profit)
  Fall 2014 Enrollment: 31 . . . . (800) 920-4593
  2015-16 Tuition: $11,750

Housing: Homeownership rate: 49.6%; Median home value: $298,700; Median year structure built: 1962; Homeowner vacancy rate: 3.3%; Median selected monthly owner costs: $2,435 with a mortgage, $946 without a mortgage; Median gross rent: $1,252 per month; Rental vacancy rate: 3.3%

Health Insurance: 86.4% have insurance; 60.5% have private insurance; 37.1% have public insurance; 13.6% do not have insurance; 2.9% of children under 18 do not have insurance

Safety: Violent crime rate: 16.1 per 10,000 population; Property crime rate: 117.1 per 10,000 population

Transportation: Commute: 72.3% car, 18.0% public transportation, 5.1% walk, 3.4% work from home; Mean travel time to work: 34.3 minutes

Additional Information Contacts

City of Peekskill . . . . (914) 737-3400
  http://www.cityofpeekskill.com

PELHAM (town). Covers a land area of 2.172 square miles and a water area of 0.046 square miles. Located at 40.90° N. Lat; 73.81° W. Long. Elevation is 72 feet.

History: Settled in 17th century; incorporated 1896.

Population: 12,560; Growth (since 2000): 5.8%; Density: 5,782.8 persons per square mile; Race: 76.3% White, 9.4% Black/African American, 7.3% Asian, 0.0% American Indian/Alaska Native, 0.0% Native Hawaiian/Other Pacific Islander, 3.9% Two or more races, 11.2% Hispanic of any race; Average household size: 3.21; Median age: 39.8; Age under 18: 27.7%; Age 65 and over: 13.5%; Males per 100 females: 96.4; Marriage status: 29.5% never married, 59.0% now married, 1.5% separated, 5.4% widowed, 6.1% divorced; Foreign born: 17.5%; Speak English only: 78.3%; With disability: 4.0%; Veterans: 5.1%; Ancestry: 22.6% Italian, 18.4% Irish, 9.6% English, 9.4% German, 4.5% American

Employment: 31.2% management, business, and financial, 4.4% computer, engineering, and science, 22.2% education, legal, community service, arts, and media, 5.7% healthcare practitioners, 11.7% service, 16.6% sales and office, 4.5% natural resources, construction, and maintenance, 3.8% production, transportation, and material moving

Income: Per capita: $76,495; Median household: $151,607; Average household: $240,089; Households with income of $100,000 or more: 67.1%; Poverty rate: 2.8%

Educational Attainment: High school diploma or higher: 94.8%; Bachelor's degree or higher: 62.8%; Graduate/professional degree or higher: 33.1%

School District(s)
Pelham Union Free SD (KG-12)
  2014-15 Enrollment: 2,810 . . . . (914) 738-3434

Housing: Homeownership rate: 79.4%; Median home value: $734,500; Median year structure built: Before 1940; Homeowner vacancy rate: 1.7%; Median selected monthly owner costs: $4,000+ with a mortgage, $1,500+ without a mortgage; Median gross rent: $1,728 per month; Rental vacancy rate: 9.5%

Health Insurance: 95.4% have insurance; 87.9% have private insurance; 16.9% have public insurance; 4.6% do not have insurance; 1.3% of children under 18 do not have insurance
Newspapers: Norway Times (weekly circulation 7,000); Pelham Weekly (weekly circulation 2,100)
Transportation: Commute: 64.3% car, 26.6% public transportation, 2.9% walk, 4.3% work from home; Mean travel time to work: 34.6 minutes
Additional Information Contacts
Town of Pelham . . . . (914) 738-0777
  http://townofpelham.com

PELHAM (village). Covers a land area of 0.829 square miles and a water area of 0.005 square miles. Located at 40.91° N. Lat; 73.81° W. Long. Elevation is 72 feet.
History: On June 27, 1654, Thomas Pell purchased 9,166 acres (37.09 sq. km.) from the Native American tribe of the Siwanoys. Among the land that he purchased, of course, was all the land that constitutes today's Village of Pelham. Upon his death in 1669, Thomas Pell left the land to his nephew and sole heir, John Pell.
Population: 6,993; Growth (since 2000): 9.3%; Density: 8,432.9 persons per square mile; Race: 68.1% White, 12.5% Black/African American, 8.9% Asian, 0.0% American Indian/Alaska Native, 0.0% Native Hawaiian/Other Pacific Islander, 4.8% Two or more races, 15.6% Hispanic of any race; Average household size: 3.20; Median age: 39.7; Age under 18: 26.7%; Age 65 and over: 12.5%; Males per 100 females: 95.8; Marriage status: 30.8% never married, 57.8% now married, 2.6% separated, 3.9% widowed, 7.5% divorced; Foreign born: 19.5%; Speak English only: 73.9%; With disability: 5.4%; Veterans: 4.7%; Ancestry: 19.4% Irish, 17.3% Italian, 10.2% German, 8.6% English, 3.1% American
Employment: 27.5% management, business, and financial, 4.2% computer, engineering, and science, 20.0% education, legal, community service, arts, and media, 4.7% healthcare practitioners, 14.2% service, 16.9% sales and office, 6.1% natural resources, construction, and maintenance, 6.4% production, transportation, and material moving
Income: Per capita: $66,778; Median household: $123,672; Average household: $208,521; Households with income of $100,000 or more: 62.1%; Poverty rate: 2.9%
Educational Attainment: High school diploma or higher: 92.7%; Bachelor's degree or higher: 55.4%; Graduate/professional degree or higher: 30.1%

School District(s)
Pelham Union Free SD (KG-12)
  2014-15 Enrollment: 2,810 . . . . (914) 738-3434
Housing: Homeownership rate: 68.4%; Median home value: $639,300; Median year structure built: Before 1940; Homeowner vacancy rate: 2.0%; Median selected monthly owner costs: $4,000+ with a mortgage, $1,500+ without a mortgage; Median gross rent: $1,720 per month; Rental vacancy rate: 8.6%
Health Insurance: 94.4% have insurance; 86.8% have private insurance; 17.7% have public insurance; 5.6% do not have insurance; 1.4% of children under 18 do not have insurance
Safety: Violent crime rate: 5.7 per 10,000 population; Property crime rate: 104.9 per 10,000 population
Newspapers: Norway Times (weekly circulation 7,000); Pelham Weekly (weekly circulation 2,100)
Transportation: Commute: 59.7% car, 28.6% public transportation, 4.4% walk, 4.2% work from home; Mean travel time to work: 35.0 minutes
Additional Information Contacts
Village of Pelham . . . . (914) 738-2015
  http://www.pelhamgov.com

PELHAM MANOR (village). Covers a land area of 1.343 square miles and a water area of 0.041 square miles. Located at 40.89° N. Lat; 73.81° W. Long. Elevation is 62 feet.
History: Settled in mid-17th century; incorporated 1891.
Population: 5,567; Growth (since 2000): 1.8%; Density: 4,146.2 persons per square mile; Race: 86.5% White, 5.5% Black/African American, 5.2% Asian, 0.0% American Indian/Alaska Native, 0.0% Native Hawaiian/Other Pacific Islander, 2.7% Two or more races, 5.6% Hispanic of any race; Average household size: 3.22; Median age: 39.9; Age under 18: 28.9%; Age 65 and over: 14.7%; Males per 100 females: 97.1; Marriage status: 27.9% never married, 60.5% now married, 0.1% separated, 7.3% widowed, 4.3% divorced; Foreign born: 15.0%; Speak English only: 83.9%; With disability: 2.3%; Veterans: 5.6%; Ancestry: 29.3% Italian, 17.0% Irish, 10.8% English, 8.4% German, 6.1% American

Employment: 35.9% management, business, and financial, 4.6% computer, engineering, and science, 25.0% education, legal, community service, arts, and media, 7.0% healthcare practitioners, 8.4% service, 16.1% sales and office, 2.3% natural resources, construction, and maintenance, 0.6% production, transportation, and material moving
Income: Per capita: $88,701; Median household: $188,659; Average household: $280,081; Households with income of $100,000 or more: 73.5%; Poverty rate: 2.8%
Educational Attainment: High school diploma or higher: 97.6%; Bachelor's degree or higher: 72.3%; Graduate/professional degree or higher: 37.1%
Housing: Homeownership rate: 93.4%; Median home value: $821,400; Median year structure built: Before 1940; Homeowner vacancy rate: 1.4%; Median selected monthly owner costs: $4,000+ with a mortgage, $1,500+ without a mortgage; Median gross rent: $1,758 per month; Rental vacancy rate: 14.3%
Health Insurance: 96.6% have insurance; 89.2% have private insurance; 15.9% have public insurance; 3.4% do not have insurance; 1.2% of children under 18 do not have insurance
Safety: Violent crime rate: 12.5 per 10,000 population; Property crime rate: 158.8 per 10,000 population
Transportation: Commute: 70.2% car, 23.9% public transportation, 0.9% walk, 4.5% work from home; Mean travel time to work: 34.2 minutes
Additional Information Contacts
Village of Pelham Manor . . . . (914) 738-8820
  http://www.pelhammanor.org

PLEASANTVILLE (village). Covers a land area of 1.824 square miles and a water area of 0.002 square miles. Located at 41.13° N. Lat; 73.78° W. Long. Elevation is 292 feet.
History: French Huguenot Isaac See (sometimes spelled Sie) settled here as an agent for Dutch landowner Frederick Philipse in 1695, thus beginning the modern history of Pleasantville.
Population: 7,125; Growth (since 2000): -0.7%; Density: 3,905.2 persons per square mile; Race: 87.1% White, 3.6% Black/African American, 3.2% Asian, 0.0% American Indian/Alaska Native, 0.0% Native Hawaiian/Other Pacific Islander, 1.1% Two or more races, 10.9% Hispanic of any race; Average household size: 2.56; Median age: 42.3; Age under 18: 23.5%; Age 65 and over: 15.7%; Males per 100 females: 95.4; Marriage status: 28.6% never married, 57.2% now married, 1.5% separated, 5.6% widowed, 8.6% divorced; Foreign born: 13.8%; Speak English only: 83.9%; With disability: 7.0%; Veterans: 5.3%; Ancestry: 28.8% Italian, 24.8% Irish, 14.0% German, 8.6% English, 5.8% American
Employment: 31.5% management, business, and financial, 5.1% computer, engineering, and science, 23.0% education, legal, community service, arts, and media, 6.0% healthcare practitioners, 9.8% service, 17.9% sales and office, 2.8% natural resources, construction, and maintenance, 4.0% production, transportation, and material moving
Income: Per capita: $53,278; Median household: $105,625; Average household: $141,320; Households with income of $100,000 or more: 54.3%; Poverty rate: 2.1%
Educational Attainment: High school diploma or higher: 95.0%; Bachelor's degree or higher: 57.7%; Graduate/professional degree or higher: 26.5%

School District(s)
Mount Pleasant-Cottage Union Free SD (KG-12)
  2014-15 Enrollment: 221 . . . . (914) 769-0456
Pleasantville Union Free SD (KG-12)
  2014-15 Enrollment: 1,772 . . . . (914) 741-1400
Housing: Homeownership rate: 72.8%; Median home value: $578,800; Median year structure built: 1953; Homeowner vacancy rate: 4.5%; Median selected monthly owner costs: $3,453 with a mortgage, $1,426 without a mortgage; Median gross rent: $1,316 per month; Rental vacancy rate: 1.9%
Health Insurance: 96.4% have insurance; 89.0% have private insurance; 20.9% have public insurance; 3.6% do not have insurance; 3.1% of children under 18 do not have insurance
Safety: Violent crime rate: 5.6 per 10,000 population; Property crime rate: 104.3 per 10,000 population
Transportation: Commute: 74.6% car, 17.6% public transportation, 5.0% walk, 1.7% work from home; Mean travel time to work: 29.8 minutes
Additional Information Contacts
Village of Pleasantville . . . . (914) 769-1900
  http://www.pleasantville-ny.gov

PORT CHESTER (village).
Covers a land area of 2.331 square miles and a water area of 0.071 square miles. Located at 41.00° N. Lat; 73.67° W. Long. Elevation is 43 feet.

History: Named for Chester, England, and for its location as a port on Long Island Sound. Gen. Israel Putnam had his headquarters here 1777—1778. Several Colonial homes remain. Previously called Saw Pits, village was renamed in 1837. Settled after 1660. Incorporated 1868.

Population: 29,406; Growth (since 2000): 5.5%; Density: 12,617.2 persons per square mile; Race: 48.5% White, 5.8% Black/African American, 1.4% Asian, 1.0% American Indian/Alaska Native, 0.1% Native Hawaiian/Other Pacific Islander, 1.8% Two or more races, 63.8% Hispanic of any race; Average household size: 3.21; Median age: 35.9; Age under 18: 22.3%; Age 65 and over: 10.6%; Males per 100 females: 110.3; Marriage status: 41.4% never married, 48.2% now married, 4.3% separated, 4.1% widowed, 6.3% divorced; Foreign born: 45.6%; Speak English only: 34.7%; With disability: 10.2%; Veterans: 3.0%; Ancestry: 12.0% Italian, 7.0% American, 5.5% Irish, 1.4% German, 1.3% English

Employment: 8.2% management, business, and financial, 1.6% computer, engineering, and science, 6.7% education, legal, community service, arts, and media, 2.7% healthcare practitioners, 38.2% service, 20.3% sales and office, 10.8% natural resources, construction, and maintenance, 11.5% production, transportation, and material moving

Income: Per capita: $25,952; Median household: $55,437; Average household: $79,418; Households with income of $100,000 or more: 25.5%; Poverty rate: 13.3%

Educational Attainment: High school diploma or higher: 68.3%; Bachelor's degree or higher: 20.7%; Graduate/professional degree or higher: 7.2%

School District(s)
Port Chester-Rye Union Free SD (KG-12)
   2014-15 Enrollment: 4,561 . . . . (914) 934-7901

Housing: Homeownership rate: 42.7%; Median home value: $436,700; Median year structure built: 1946; Homeowner vacancy rate: 2.1%; Median selected monthly owner costs: $3,085 with a mortgage, $1,359 without a mortgage; Median gross rent: $1,419 per month; Rental vacancy rate: 2.3%

Health Insurance: 72.0% have insurance; 49.3% have private insurance; 29.3% have public insurance; 28.0% do not have insurance; 6.5% of children under 18 do not have insurance

Safety: Violent crime rate: 25.3 per 10,000 population; Property crime rate: 175.7 per 10,000 population

Newspapers: Hometown Media (weekly circulation 38,000); Westmore News (weekly circulation 3,500)

Transportation: Commute: 60.7% car, 14.4% public transportation, 12.9% walk, 2.1% work from home; Mean travel time to work: 23.5 minutes

Additional Information Contacts
Village of Port Chester . . . . (914) 939-5202
  http://www.portchesterny.com

POUND RIDGE (town).
Covers a land area of 22.638 square miles and a water area of 0.803 square miles. Located at 41.21° N. Lat; 73.58° W. Long. Elevation is 620 feet.

History: Originally home to the Siwanoy and Kitchawong Indians (Mohican tribes, a subgroup of the Algonquians), the town takes its name from a tribal "pound" or enclosure for game that was on one of the area's many "ridges". The Indians led a relatively peaceful life of planting, hunting, and fishing.

Population: 5,209; Growth (since 2000): 10.2%; Density: 230.1 persons per square mile; Race: 93.9% White, 0.5% Black/African American, 5.5% Asian, 0.0% American Indian/Alaska Native, 0.0% Native Hawaiian/Other Pacific Islander, 0.1% Two or more races, 2.4% Hispanic of any race; Average household size: 2.73; Median age: 47.9; Age under 18: 24.2%; Age 65 and over: 18.6%; Males per 100 females: 96.7; Marriage status: 22.5% never married, 66.0% now married, 1.5% separated, 4.4% widowed, 7.2% divorced; Foreign born: 9.1%; Speak English only: 91.0%; With disability: 5.8%; Veterans: 7.1%; Ancestry: 26.6% Italian, 12.4% German, 11.8% Irish, 7.9% American, 7.8% Polish

Employment: 35.9% management, business, and financial, 5.8% computer, engineering, and science, 22.7% education, legal, community service, arts, and media, 6.7% healthcare practitioners, 9.8% service, 12.2% sales and office, 2.9% natural resources, construction, and maintenance, 4.2% production, transportation, and material moving

Income: Per capita: $107,333; Median household: $176,591; Average household: $291,216; Households with income of $100,000 or more: 74.0%; Poverty rate: 3.4%

Educational Attainment: High school diploma or higher: 98.3%; Bachelor's degree or higher: 73.3%; Graduate/professional degree or higher: 39.4%

School District(s)
Bedford Central SD (PK-12)
   2014-15 Enrollment: 4,390 . . . . (914) 241-6010

Housing: Homeownership rate: 86.9%; Median home value: $927,300; Median year structure built: 1969; Homeowner vacancy rate: 1.4%; Median selected monthly owner costs: $4,000+ with a mortgage, $1,500+ without a mortgage; Median gross rent: $1,726 per month; Rental vacancy rate: 0.0%

Health Insurance: 94.6% have insurance; 89.2% have private insurance; 19.1% have public insurance; 5.4% do not have insurance; 2.4% of children under 18 do not have insurance

Safety: Violent crime rate: 3.8 per 10,000 population; Property crime rate: 41.8 per 10,000 population

Transportation: Commute: 65.1% car, 14.1% public transportation, 3.8% walk, 15.7% work from home; Mean travel time to work: 41.6 minutes

Additional Information Contacts
Town of Pound Ridge . . . . (914) 764-5511
  http://www.townofpoundridge.com

PURCHASE (unincorporated postal area)
ZCTA: 10577

Covers a land area of 6.717 square miles and a water area of 0.033 square miles. Located at 41.04° N. Lat; 73.71° W. Long. Elevation is 351 feet.

Population: 6,486; Growth (since 2000): 87.8%; Density: 965.6 persons per square mile; Race: 72.8% White, 13.4% Black/African American, 6.7% Asian, 0.1% American Indian/Alaska Native, 0.0% Native Hawaiian/Other Pacific Islander, 4.2% Two or more races, 12.9% Hispanic of any race; Average household size: 3.06; Median age: 20.4; Age under 18: 10.4%; Age 65 and over: 7.4%; Males per 100 females: 78.3; Marriage status: 72.7% never married, 25.5% now married, 0.1% separated, 0.9% widowed, 0.8% divorced; Foreign born: 14.9%; Speak English only: 76.7%; With disability: 6.5%; Veterans: 2.2%; Ancestry: 19.1% Italian, 13.0% Irish, 12.6% German, 8.9% American, 6.7% Polish

Employment: 20.9% management, business, and financial, 2.7% computer, engineering, and science, 15.4% education, legal, community service, arts, and media, 4.4% healthcare practitioners, 21.4% service, 33.3% sales and office, 1.3% natural resources, construction, and maintenance, 0.5% production, transportation, and material moving

Income: Per capita: $54,634; Median household: $216,250; Average household: $402,826; Households with income of $100,000 or more: 79.4%; Poverty rate: 9.1%

Educational Attainment: High school diploma or higher: 95.0%; Bachelor's degree or higher: 71.8%; Graduate/professional degree or higher: 37.4%

School District(s)
Harrison Central SD (KG-12)
   2014-15 Enrollment: 3,558 . . . . (914) 630-3021

Four-year College(s)
LIU Hudson at Westchester (Private, Not-for-profit)
   Fall 2014 Enrollment: 158 . . . . (914) 831-2700
Manhattanville College (Private, Not-for-profit)
   Fall 2014 Enrollment: 2,865 . . . . (914) 694-2200
   2013-14 Tuition: In-state $36,220; Out-of-state $36,220
SUNY at Purchase College (Public)
   Fall 2014 Enrollment: 4,225 . . . . (914) 251-6000
   2013-14 Tuition: In-state $8,267; Out-of-state $18,117

Two-year College(s)
LIU Hudson at Westchester (Private, Not-for-profit)
   Fall 2014 Enrollment: 158 . . . . (914) 831-2700
Manhattanville College (Private, Not-for-profit)
   Fall 2014 Enrollment: 2,865 . . . . (914) 694-2200
   2013-14 Tuition: In-state $36,220; Out-of-state $36,220
SUNY at Purchase College (Public)
   Fall 2014 Enrollment: 4,225 . . . . (914) 251-6000
   2013-14 Tuition: In-state $8,267; Out-of-state $18,117

Vocational/Technical School(s)
LIU Hudson at Westchester (Private, Not-for-profit)
   Fall 2014 Enrollment: 158 . . . . (914) 831-2700
Manhattanville College (Private, Not-for-profit)
   Fall 2014 Enrollment: 2,865 . . . . (914) 694-2200
   2015-16 Tuition: In-state $36,220; Out-of-state $36,220

SUNY at Purchase College (Public)
  Fall 2014 Enrollment: 4,225 . . . . (914) 251-6000
  2015-16 Tuition: In-state $8,267; Out-of-state $18,117
  Housing: Homeownership rate: 88.2%; Median home value:
  $1,159,900; Median year structure built: 1970; Homeowner vacancy
  rate: 1.8%; Median selected monthly owner costs: $4,000 with a
  mortgage, $1,500 without a mortgage; Median gross rent: $3,132 per
  month; Rental vacancy rate: 0.0%
  Health Insurance: 95.2% have insurance; 85.9% have private
  insurance; 16.3% have public insurance; 4.8% do not have insurance;
  3.6% of children under 18 do not have insurance
  Transportation: Commute: 42.8% car, 14.1% public transportation,
  30.5% walk, 10.3% work from home; Mean travel time to work: 20.9
  minutes

PURDYS (unincorporated postal area)
ZCTA: 10578
  Covers a land area of 1.584 square miles and a water area of 0.168
  square miles. Located at 41.32° N. Lat; 73.68° W. Long. Elevation is
  253 feet.
  Population: 714; Growth (since 2000): 8.0%; Density: 450.8 persons
  per square mile; Race: 83.9% White, 0.0% Black/African American,
  1.4% Asian, 0.0% American Indian/Alaska Native, 0.0% Native
  Hawaiian/Other Pacific Islander, 0.0% Two or more races, 20.0%
  Hispanic of any race; Average household size: 2.66; Median age: 45.5;
  Age under 18: 22.7%; Age 65 and over: 6.4%; Males per 100 females:
  92.9; Marriage status: 31.1% never married, 57.8% now married, 0.0%
  separated, 5.2% widowed, 6.0% divorced; Foreign born: 22.3%; Speak
  English only: 72.8%; With disability: 4.8%; Veterans: 1.8%; Ancestry:
  18.5% Italian, 12.7% German, 12.6% Russian, 10.4% Irish, 9.4%
  English
  Employment: 9.6% management, business, and financial, 14.0%
  computer, engineering, and science, 30.0% education, legal, community
  service, arts, and media, 2.5% healthcare practitioners, 0.0% service,
  21.1% sales and office, 17.4% natural resources, construction, and
  maintenance, 5.4% production, transportation, and material moving
  Income: Per capita: $43,199; Median household: $115,714; Average
  household: $112,044; Households with income of $100,000 or more:
  58.2%; Poverty rate: 1.7%
  Educational Attainment: High school diploma or higher: 94.6%;
  Bachelor's degree or higher: 54.9%; Graduate/professional degree or
  higher: 24.2%
  Housing: Homeownership rate: 81.7%; Median home value: $464,500;
  Median year structure built: 1955; Homeowner vacancy rate: 0.0%;
  Median selected monthly owner costs: n/a with a mortgage, n/a without
  a mortgage; Median gross rent: $1,799 per month; Rental vacancy rate:
  0.0%
  Health Insurance: 87.7% have insurance; 86.0% have private
  insurance; 8.1% have public insurance; 12.3% do not have insurance;
  0.0% of children under 18 do not have insurance
  Transportation: Commute: 93.5% car, 4.8% public transportation, 0.0%
  walk, 1.8% work from home; Mean travel time to work: 36.6 minutes

RYE (city). Covers a land area of 5.848 square miles and a water area of
14.173 square miles. Located at 40.94° N. Lat; 73.69° W. Long. Elevation
is 26 feet.
  History: Named for Rye in Sussex, England. In colonial times, Rye was
  the first stop on the Boston Post Road after N.Y. city. The old Square
  House, an inn where many Revolutionary notables stayed, is now a
  museum. Playland, a large county-owned amusement park, is on the
  beach here. Chief Justice John Jay is buried in Rye. Settled 1660.
  Incorporated as a city 1942.
  Population: 15,944; Growth (since 2000): 6.6%; Density: 2,726.3 persons
  per square mile; Race: 90.0% White, 0.7% Black/African American, 5.3%
  Asian, 0.3% American Indian/Alaska Native, 0.0% Native Hawaiian/Other
  Pacific Islander, 2.0% Two or more races, 6.5% Hispanic of any race;
  Average household size: 2.89; Median age: 41.9; Age under 18: 30.8%;
  Age 65 and over: 15.5%; Males per 100 females: 92.7; Marriage status:
  20.8% never married, 67.5% now married, 1.9% separated, 6.1%
  widowed, 5.6% divorced; Foreign born: 14.4%; Speak English only: 81.2%;
  With disability: 7.9%; Veterans: 5.9%; Ancestry: 20.4% Irish, 16.5% Italian,
  13.0% American, 12.5% German, 8.8% English
  Employment: 29.7% management, business, and financial, 3.8%
  computer, engineering, and science, 18.2% education, legal, community
  service, arts, and media, 6.0% healthcare practitioners, 9.7% service,

26.0% sales and office, 3.1% natural resources, construction, and
maintenance, 3.4% production, transportation, and material moving
  Income: Per capita: $90,548; Median household: $155,273; Average
  household: $257,949; Households with income of $100,000 or more:
  66.5%; Poverty rate: 3.6%
  Educational Attainment: High school diploma or higher: 97.0%;
  Bachelor's degree or higher: 74.0%; Graduate/professional degree or
  higher: 37.6%
School District(s)
Rye City SD (KG-12)
  2014-15 Enrollment: 3,360 . . . . (914) 967-6108
  Housing: Homeownership rate: 73.8%; Median home value: $1,055,100;
  Median year structure built: 1953; Homeowner vacancy rate: 1.8%; Median
  selected monthly owner costs: $4,000+ with a mortgage, $1,500+ without a
  mortgage; Median gross rent: $1,878 per month; Rental vacancy rate:
  0.0%
  Health Insurance: 96.9% have insurance; 88.1% have private insurance;
  20.0% have public insurance; 3.1% do not have insurance; 0.9% of
  children under 18 do not have insurance
  Safety: Violent crime rate: 0.6 per 10,000 population; Property crime rate:
  29.9 per 10,000 population
  Transportation: Commute: 55.4% car, 33.4% public transportation, 3.0%
  walk, 6.8% work from home; Mean travel time to work: 36.1 minutes
  Additional Information Contacts
  City of Rye. . . . . (914) 967-5400
    http://www.ryeny.gov

RYE (town). Covers a land area of 6.919 square miles and a water area
of 0.435 square miles. Located at 41.01° N. Lat; 73.69° W. Long. Elevation
is 26 feet.
  Population: 46,650; Growth (since 2000): 6.3%; Density: 6,742.5 persons
  per square mile; Race: 61.7% White, 5.2% Black/African American, 2.8%
  Asian, 0.7% American Indian/Alaska Native, 0.0% Native Hawaiian/Other
  Pacific Islander, 1.8% Two or more races, 44.4% Hispanic of any race;
  Average household size: 3.02; Median age: 38.4; Age under 18: 23.3%;
  Age 65 and over: 13.0%; Males per 100 females: 102.9; Marriage status:
  36.3% never married, 52.4% now married, 3.1% separated, 4.9%
  widowed, 6.4% divorced; Foreign born: 35.7%; Speak English only: 49.6%;
  With disability: 9.2%; Veterans: 3.9%; Ancestry: 17.1% Italian, 9.4%
  American, 7.2% Irish, 3.8% German, 3.2% Polish
  Employment: 14.2% management, business, and financial, 1.8%
  computer, engineering, and science, 10.4% education, legal, community
  service, arts, and media, 3.8% healthcare practitioners, 29.5% service,
  21.9% sales and office, 9.0% natural resources, construction, and
  maintenance, 9.4% production, transportation, and material moving
  Income: Per capita: $39,514; Median household: $73,276; Average
  household: $116,639; Households with income of $100,000 or more:
  36.9%; Poverty rate: 10.0%
  Educational Attainment: High school diploma or higher: 76.7%;
  Bachelor's degree or higher: 35.1%; Graduate/professional degree or
  higher: 15.3%
School District(s)
Rye City SD (KG-12)
  2014-15 Enrollment: 3,360 . . . . (914) 967-6108
  Housing: Homeownership rate: 54.4%; Median home value: $536,700;
  Median year structure built: 1952; Homeowner vacancy rate: 3.1%; Median
  selected monthly owner costs: $3,519 with a mortgage, $1,430 without a
  mortgage; Median gross rent: $1,489 per month; Rental vacancy rate:
  3.1%
  Health Insurance: 79.9% have insurance; 61.4% have private insurance;
  26.8% have public insurance; 20.1% do not have insurance; 4.5% of
  children under 18 do not have insurance
  Transportation: Commute: 63.3% car, 17.1% public transportation, 9.2%
  walk, 3.5% work from home; Mean travel time to work: 26.1 minutes
  Additional Information Contacts
  Town of Rye . . . . (914) 939-3570
    http://www.townofryeny.com

RYE BROOK (village). Covers a land area of 3.433 square miles and
a water area of 0.031 square miles. Located at 41.03° N. Lat; 73.69° W.
Long. Elevation is 249 feet.
  History: Prior to the village's establishment on July 7, 1982, the area was
  an unincorporated section of the Town of Rye. The population was 8,602
  according to the 2000 census. Rye Brook has been designated as a Tree
  City USA for 14 years.

Population: 9,510; Growth (since 2000): 10.6%; Density: 2,770.4 persons per square mile; Race: 84.1% White, 2.6% Black/African American, 6.2% Asian, 0.0% American Indian/Alaska Native, 0.0% Native Hawaiian/Other Pacific Islander, 1.0% Two or more races, 11.4% Hispanic of any race; Average household size: 2.72; Median age: 45.7; Age under 18: 25.1%; Age 65 and over: 21.0%; Males per 100 females: 88.4; Marriage status: 24.4% never married, 63.0% now married, 0.2% separated, 6.9% widowed, 5.8% divorced; Foreign born: 16.9%; Speak English only: 77.1%; With disability: 8.0%; Veterans: 6.7%; Ancestry: 19.3% Italian, 14.3% American, 9.9% Russian, 8.5% Irish, 8.3% Polish

Employment: 27.1% management, business, and financial, 1.4% computer, engineering, and science, 21.0% education, legal, community service, arts, and media, 7.0% healthcare practitioners, 9.8% service, 26.8% sales and office, 4.0% natural resources, construction, and maintenance, 2.9% production, transportation, and material moving

Income: Per capita: $72,602; Median household: $131,488; Average household: $196,905; Households with income of $100,000 or more: 58.4%; Poverty rate: 5.0%

Educational Attainment: High school diploma or higher: 91.8%; Bachelor's degree or higher: 67.2%; Graduate/professional degree or higher: 32.3%

School District(s)

Blind Brook-Rye Union Free SD (KG-12)
  2014-15 Enrollment: 1,499 . . . . (914) 937-3600
Westchester Boces
  2014-15 Enrollment: n/a . . . . (914) 937-3820

Housing: Homeownership rate: 79.2%; Median home value: $730,100; Median year structure built: 1962; Homeowner vacancy rate: 3.3%; Median selected monthly owner costs: $4,000+ with a mortgage, $1,500+ without a mortgage; Median gross rent: $1,694 per month; Rental vacancy rate: 7.8%

Health Insurance: 92.6% have insurance; 81.1% have private insurance; 25.0% have public insurance; 7.4% do not have insurance; 1.5% of children under 18 do not have insurance

Safety: Violent crime rate: 2.1 per 10,000 population; Property crime rate: 60.4 per 10,000 population

Transportation: Commute: 64.0% car, 26.5% public transportation, 1.2% walk, 8.3% work from home; Mean travel time to work: 33.8 minutes

Additional Information Contacts
Village of Rye Brook . . . . (914) 939-1121
  http://www.ryebrook.org

SCARSDALE (town/village). Covers a land area of 6.660 square miles and a water area of 0.008 square miles. Located at 40.99° N. Lat; 73.78° W. Long. Elevation is 217 feet.

Population: 17,621; Growth (since 2000): -1.1%; Density: 2,645.7 persons per square mile; Race: 83.0% White, 0.8% Black/African American, 13.6% Asian, 0.0% American Indian/Alaska Native, 0.0% Native Hawaiian/Other Pacific Islander, 2.3% Two or more races, 4.4% Hispanic of any race; Average household size: 3.21; Median age: 42.5; Age under 18: 32.1%; Age 65 and over: 14.1%; Males per 100 females: 95.1; Marriage status: 20.2% never married, 74.1% now married, 0.9% separated, 2.8% widowed, 2.9% divorced; Foreign born: 22.2%; Speak English only: 76.1%; With disability: 5.4%; Veterans: 4.2%; Ancestry: 11.0% Russian, 8.5% Italian, 7.8% German, 7.3% Polish, 6.6% American

Employment: 33.5% management, business, and financial, 5.5% computer, engineering, and science, 25.9% education, legal, community service, arts, and media, 9.5% healthcare practitioners, 3.9% service, 20.2% sales and office, 0.7% natural resources, construction, and maintenance, 0.8% production, transportation, and material moving

Income: Per capita: $116,456; Median household: $242,782; Average household: $371,194; Households with income of $100,000 or more: 83.0%; Poverty rate: 2.3%

Educational Attainment: High school diploma or higher: 98.8%; Bachelor's degree or higher: 87.0%; Graduate/professional degree or higher: 56.5%

School District(s)

Eastchester Union Free SD (KG-12)
  2014-15 Enrollment: 3,200 . . . . (914) 793-6130
Edgemont Union Free SD (KG-12)
  2014-15 Enrollment: 1,925 . . . . (914) 472-7768
Scarsdale Union Free SD (KG-12)
  2014-15 Enrollment: 4,851 . . . . (914) 721-2410

Housing: Homeownership rate: 90.7%; Median home value: $1,230,600; Median year structure built: 1941; Homeowner vacancy rate: 0.6%; Median

selected monthly owner costs: $4,000+ with a mortgage, $1,500+ without a mortgage; Median gross rent: $3,500+ per month; Rental vacancy rate: 4.5%

Health Insurance: 98.3% have insurance; 92.1% have private insurance; 15.5% have public insurance; 1.7% do not have insurance; 0.2% of children under 18 do not have insurance

Safety: Violent crime rate: 1.7 per 10,000 population; Property crime rate: 81.7 per 10,000 population

Newspapers: Scarsdale Inquirer (weekly circulation 6,500)

Transportation: Commute: 42.0% car, 44.8% public transportation, 0.8% walk, 11.4% work from home; Mean travel time to work: 44.0 minutes

Additional Information Contacts
Village and Town of Scarsdale . . . . (914) 722-1175
  http://www.scarsdale.com

SCOTTS CORNERS (CDP). Covers a land area of 1.773 square miles and a water area of 0 square miles. Located at 41.19° N. Lat; 73.56° W. Long. Elevation is 397 feet.

Population: 563; Growth (since 2000): -9.8%; Density: 317.5 persons per square mile; Race: 100.0% White, 0.0% Black/African American, 0.0% Asian, 0.0% American Indian/Alaska Native, 0.0% Native Hawaiian/Other Pacific Islander, 0.0% Two or more races, 4.4% Hispanic of any race; Average household size: 2.20; Median age: 57.4; Age under 18: 12.3%; Age 65 and over: 36.9%; Males per 100 females: 95.9; Marriage status: 18.2% never married, 54.7% now married, 6.5% separated, 3.1% widowed, 24.0% divorced; Foreign born: 17.9%; Speak English only: 89.2%; With disability: 14.0%; Veterans: 15.6%; Ancestry: 30.2% Italian, 14.7% Polish, 12.4% European, 11.0% Irish, 8.9% German

Employment: 30.6% management, business, and financial, 0.0% computer, engineering, and science, 24.6% education, legal, community service, arts, and media, 19.8% healthcare practitioners, 2.8% service, 3.6% sales and office, 18.7% natural resources, construction, and maintenance, 0.0% production, transportation, and material moving

Income: Per capita: $84,152; Median household: $78,594; Average household: $188,186; Households with income of $100,000 or more: 45.0%; Poverty rate: 10.7%

Educational Attainment: High school diploma or higher: 96.1%; Bachelor's degree or higher: 47.9%; Graduate/professional degree or higher: 37.9%

Housing: Homeownership rate: 76.1%; Median home value: $895,500; Median year structure built: 1965; Homeowner vacancy rate: 0.0%; Median selected monthly owner costs: $4,000+ with a mortgage, $1,500+ without a mortgage; Median gross rent: $1,469 per month; Rental vacancy rate: 0.0%

Health Insurance: 89.9% have insurance; 76.0% have private insurance; 39.6% have public insurance; 10.1% do not have insurance; 0.0% of children under 18 do not have insurance

Transportation: Commute: 57.5% car, 6.3% public transportation, 4.8% walk, 27.8% work from home; Mean travel time to work: 40.0 minutes

SHENOROCK (CDP). Covers a land area of 0.700 square miles and a water area of 0.029 square miles. Located at 41.33° N. Lat; 73.74° W. Long. Elevation is 509 feet.

Population: 1,874; Growth (since 2000): -0.7%; Density: 2,677.6 persons per square mile; Race: 86.0% White, 2.7% Black/African American, 8.1% Asian, 0.6% American Indian/Alaska Native, 0.0% Native Hawaiian/Other Pacific Islander, 0.0% Two or more races, 14.2% Hispanic of any race; Average household size: 2.96; Median age: 40.9; Age under 18: 27.2%; Age 65 and over: 11.3%; Males per 100 females: 94.9; Marriage status: 26.3% never married, 68.1% now married, 3.2% separated, 4.1% widowed, 1.4% divorced; Foreign born: 15.6%; Speak English only: 83.2%; With disability: 7.8%; Veterans: 8.1%; Ancestry: 31.1% Italian, 16.6% Irish, 10.3% German, 8.1% Polish, 4.5% English

Employment: 18.9% management, business, and financial, 5.5% computer, engineering, and science, 14.9% education, legal, community service, arts, and media, 7.4% healthcare practitioners, 9.4% service, 29.0% sales and office, 10.7% natural resources, construction, and maintenance, 4.2% production, transportation, and material moving

Income: Per capita: $40,702; Median household: $120,357; Average household: $116,726; Households with income of $100,000 or more: 60.5%; Poverty rate: 0.4%

Educational Attainment: High school diploma or higher: 93.8%; Bachelor's degree or higher: 36.8%; Graduate/professional degree or higher: 14.9%

Housing: Homeownership rate: 91.2%; Median home value: $365,600; Median year structure built: 1947; Homeowner vacancy rate: 8.8%; Median selected monthly owner costs: $2,752 with a mortgage, $803 without a mortgage; Median gross rent: $1,944 per month; Rental vacancy rate: 0.0%
Health Insurance: 97.1% have insurance; 92.9% have private insurance; 13.7% have public insurance; 2.9% do not have insurance; 2.2% of children under 18 do not have insurance
Transportation: Commute: 84.4% car, 8.6% public transportation, 1.2% walk, 5.8% work from home; Mean travel time to work: 31.2 minutes

SHRUB OAK (CDP).
Covers a land area of 1.580 square miles and a water area of 0.027 square miles. Located at 41.33° N. Lat; 73.83° W. Long. Elevation is 440 feet.
Population: 1,997; Growth (since 2000): 10.2%; Density: 1,263.6 persons per square mile; Race: 89.1% White, 1.0% Black/African American, 0.4% Asian, 1.1% American Indian/Alaska Native, 0.0% Native Hawaiian/Other Pacific Islander, 0.0% Two or more races, 20.4% Hispanic of any race; Average household size: 2.40; Median age: 52.8; Age under 18: 11.7%; Age 65 and over: 25.4%; Males per 100 females: 89.2; Marriage status: 31.2% never married, 56.9% now married, 1.6% separated, 7.0% widowed, 4.8% divorced; Foreign born: 16.9%; Speak English only: 85.4%; With disability: 15.4%; Veterans: 10.3%; Ancestry: 41.4% Italian, 27.8% Irish, 13.3% German, 5.6% English, 5.5% Russian
Employment: 12.8% management, business, and financial, 2.3% computer, engineering, and science, 16.6% education, legal, community service, arts, and media, 14.3% healthcare practitioners, 13.8% service, 24.5% sales and office, 7.7% natural resources, construction, and maintenance, 8.0% production, transportation, and material moving
Income: Per capita: $37,623; Median household: $73,054; Average household: $87,289; Households with income of $100,000 or more: 31.1%; Poverty rate: 0.4%
Educational Attainment: High school diploma or higher: 89.7%; Bachelor's degree or higher: 39.8%; Graduate/professional degree or higher: 15.7%

School District(s)
Lakeland Central SD (PK-12)
    2014-15 Enrollment: 5,900 . . . . (914) 245-1700
Housing: Homeownership rate: 80.1%; Median home value: $320,600; Median year structure built: 1960; Homeowner vacancy rate: 0.0%; Median selected monthly owner costs: $2,626 with a mortgage, $1,409 without a mortgage; Median gross rent: $1,144 per month; Rental vacancy rate: 0.0%
Health Insurance: 94.0% have insurance; 82.9% have private insurance; 37.8% have public insurance; 6.0% do not have insurance; 0.0% of children under 18 do not have insurance
Transportation: Commute: 92.1% car, 4.5% public transportation, 0.0% walk, 3.4% work from home; Mean travel time to work: 29.5 minutes

SLEEPY HOLLOW (village).
Covers a land area of 2.161 square miles and a water area of 2.919 square miles. Located at 41.10° N. Lat; 73.87° W. Long. Elevation is 89 feet.
History: Sleepy Hollow is a village in the town of Mount Pleasant in Westchester County, New York. It is known as the setting of "The Legend of Sleepy Hollow," a short story by Washington Irving, who lived in neighboring Tarrytown and is buried in Sleepy Hollow Cemetery.
Population: 10,074; Growth (since 2000): 9.4%; Density: 4,662.5 persons per square mile; Race: 62.2% White, 5.3% Black/African American, 2.1% Asian, 1.1% American Indian/Alaska Native, 0.0% Native Hawaiian/Other Pacific Islander, 5.7% Two or more races, 48.1% Hispanic of any race; Average household size: 2.69; Median age: 40.5; Age under 18: 23.8%; Age 65 and over: 16.2%; Males per 100 females: 94.2; Marriage status: 32.1% never married, 54.2% now married, 3.0% separated, 5.6% widowed, 8.1% divorced; Foreign born: 39.8%; Speak English only: 43.8%; With disability: 10.8%; Veterans: 4.4%; Ancestry: 10.7% Italian, 10.2% Irish, 4.4% German, 4.3% Portuguese, 4.3% English
Employment: 13.3% management, business, and financial, 3.9% computer, engineering, and science, 12.1% education, legal, community service, arts, and media, 4.4% healthcare practitioners, 25.6% service, 18.7% sales and office, 11.0% natural resources, construction, and maintenance, 11.1% production, transportation, and material moving
Income: Per capita: $37,170; Median household: $52,740; Average household: $98,834; Households with income of $100,000 or more: 27.6%; Poverty rate: 18.6%

Educational Attainment: High school diploma or higher: 75.8%; Bachelor's degree or higher: 38.3%; Graduate/professional degree or higher: 17.7%

School District(s)
Pocantico Hills Central SD (PK-08)
    2014-15 Enrollment: 281 . . . . (914) 631-2440
Union Free SD of the Tarrytowns (PK-12)
    2014-15 Enrollment: 2,736 . . . . (914) 631-9404
Housing: Homeownership rate: 38.5%; Median home value: $575,100; Median year structure built: 1944; Homeowner vacancy rate: 0.0%; Median selected monthly owner costs: $3,965 with a mortgage, $1,500+ without a mortgage; Median gross rent: $1,314 per month; Rental vacancy rate: 0.0%
Health Insurance: 86.5% have insurance; 59.1% have private insurance; 38.4% have public insurance; 13.5% do not have insurance; 1.7% of children under 18 do not have insurance
Hospitals: Phelps Memorial Hospital Assn (235 beds)
Safety: Violent crime rate: 7.8 per 10,000 population; Property crime rate: 33.0 per 10,000 population
Transportation: Commute: 56.1% car, 21.5% public transportation, 15.7% walk, 4.4% work from home; Mean travel time to work: 27.6 minutes
Additional Information Contacts
Village of Sleepy Hollow . . . . (914) 366-5106
    http://www.sleepyhollowny.gov

SOMERS (town).
Covers a land area of 29.642 square miles and a water area of 2.518 square miles. Located at 41.30° N. Lat; 73.72° W. Long. Elevation is 279 feet.
History: Formerly a rural, summer lake community. Early Dutch settlement, it was incorporated 1778 as Stephentown. Renamed Somerstown for US naval hero Captain Richard Somers.
Population: 21,073; Growth (since 2000): 14.9%; Density: 710.9 persons per square mile; Race: 91.5% White, 0.9% Black/African American, 4.3% Asian, 0.2% American Indian/Alaska Native, 0.1% Native Hawaiian/Other Pacific Islander, 1.0% Two or more races, 7.0% Hispanic of any race; Average household size: 2.69; Median age: 47.3; Age under 18: 24.2%; Age 65 and over: 23.9%; Males per 100 females: 91.0; Marriage status: 21.3% never married, 63.8% now married, 1.8% separated, 7.9% widowed, 7.0% divorced; Foreign born: 10.9%; Speak English only: 86.2%; With disability: 9.3%; Veterans: 8.0%; Ancestry: 32.0% Italian, 21.3% Irish, 12.7% German, 6.5% English, 5.3% American
Employment: 26.2% management, business, and financial, 6.6% computer, engineering, and science, 17.0% education, legal, community service, arts, and media, 6.9% healthcare practitioners, 7.6% service, 25.7% sales and office, 6.4% natural resources, construction, and maintenance, 3.6% production, transportation, and material moving
Income: Per capita: $56,542; Median household: $115,696; Average household: $152,986; Households with income of $100,000 or more: 58.6%; Poverty rate: 2.3%
Educational Attainment: High school diploma or higher: 95.7%; Bachelor's degree or higher: 55.8%; Graduate/professional degree or higher: 25.9%

School District(s)
Somers Central SD (KG-12)
    2014-15 Enrollment: 3,285 . . . . (914) 277-2400
Housing: Homeownership rate: 89.7%; Median home value: $493,800; Median year structure built: 1977; Homeowner vacancy rate: 0.8%; Median selected monthly owner costs: $3,036 with a mortgage, $1,142 without a mortgage; Median gross rent: $2,136 per month; Rental vacancy rate: 4.7%
Health Insurance: 96.1% have insurance; 87.8% have private insurance; 27.6% have public insurance; 3.9% do not have insurance; 1.5% of children under 18 do not have insurance
Transportation: Commute: 82.1% car, 9.5% public transportation, 0.8% walk, 7.2% work from home; Mean travel time to work: 36.2 minutes
Additional Information Contacts
Town of Somers . . . . (914) 277-3323
    http://www.somersny.com

SOUTH SALEM (unincorporated postal area)
ZCTA: 10590
    Covers a land area of 13.497 square miles and a water area of 0.520 square miles. Located at 41.26° N. Lat; 73.54° W. Long. Elevation is 541 feet.

Population: 7,111; Growth (since 2000): -1.4%; Density: 526.9 persons per square mile; Race: 90.3% White, 4.0% Black/African American, 2.7% Asian, 0.4% American Indian/Alaska Native, 0.0% Native Hawaiian/Other Pacific Islander, 2.3% Two or more races, 5.8% Hispanic of any race; Average household size: 2.78; Median age: 44.6; Age under 18: 25.1%; Age 65 and over: 12.6%; Males per 100 females: 98.2; Marriage status: 27.5% never married, 62.2% now married, 0.8% separated, 3.9% widowed, 6.3% divorced; Foreign born: 9.1%; Speak English only: 90.9%; With disability: 5.6%; Veterans: 4.5%; Ancestry: 19.8% Italian, 17.5% Irish, 12.0% German, 9.2% American, 9.1% Polish

Employment: 30.3% management, business, and financial, 6.4% computer, engineering, and science, 18.1% education, legal, community service, arts, and media, 5.2% healthcare practitioners, 8.2% service, 20.8% sales and office, 6.4% natural resources, construction, and maintenance, 4.6% production, transportation, and material moving

Income: Per capita: $64,799; Median household: $131,607; Average household: $177,402; Households with income of $100,000 or more: 60.9%; Poverty rate: 1.7%

Educational Attainment: High school diploma or higher: 98.7%; Bachelor's degree or higher: 69.8%; Graduate/professional degree or higher: 30.9%

School District(s)
Katonah-Lewisboro Union Free SD (KG-12)
    2014-15 Enrollment: 3,233 . . . . (914) 763-7003

Housing: Homeownership rate: 91.8%; Median home value: $590,100; Median year structure built: 1971; Homeowner vacancy rate: 1.3%; Median selected monthly owner costs: $3,524 with a mortgage, $1,238 without a mortgage; Median gross rent: $1,890 per month; Rental vacancy rate: 0.0%

Health Insurance: 92.8% have insurance; 82.8% have private insurance; 18.6% have public insurance; 7.2% do not have insurance; 5.8% of children under 18 do not have insurance

Transportation: Commute: 78.4% car, 9.2% public transportation, 3.0% walk, 8.7% work from home; Mean travel time to work: 39.3 minutes

---

TARRYTOWN (village). Covers a land area of 2.926 square miles and a water area of 2.753 square miles. Located at 41.07° N. Lat; 73.87° W. Long. Elevation is 121 feet.

History: Named for a variation of the Dutch translation of "wheat". Of interest are Sunnyside, the home of Washington Irving; Sleepy Hollow cemetery, where Irving is buried; Philipsburg Manor, an estate; and Lyndhurst (1838), a Gothic Revival mansion. Philipsburg Manor, an early trading center complex northwest of village center, includes a Dutch farmhouse (c.1683) and a restored operating gristmill. Settled in the 17th century by Dutch. Incorporated 1870.

Population: 11,452; Growth (since 2000): 3.3%; Density: 3,913.4 persons per square mile; Race: 75.4% White, 8.3% Black/African American, 6.1% Asian, 0.1% American Indian/Alaska Native, 0.0% Native Hawaiian/Other Pacific Islander, 2.7% Two or more races, 22.5% Hispanic of any race; Average household size: 2.61; Median age: 40.1; Age under 18: 21.1%; Age 65 and over: 15.1%; Males per 100 females: 87.7; Marriage status: 37.1% never married, 51.8% now married, 1.2% separated, 4.6% widowed, 6.5% divorced; Foreign born: 20.5%; Speak English only: 71.7%; With disability: 7.4%; Veterans: 4.3%; Ancestry: 16.8% Irish, 16.0% Italian, 11.0% German, 7.1% American, 5.7% Russian

Employment: 23.9% management, business, and financial, 5.5% computer, engineering, and science, 20.2% education, legal, community service, arts, and media, 5.4% healthcare practitioners, 14.1% service, 22.3% sales and office, 5.8% natural resources, construction, and maintenance, 2.9% production, transportation, and material moving

Income: Per capita: $51,107; Median household: $102,750; Average household: $134,936; Households with income of $100,000 or more: 51.4%; Poverty rate: 4.0%

Educational Attainment: High school diploma or higher: 92.0%; Bachelor's degree or higher: 55.7%; Graduate/professional degree or higher: 31.2%

School District(s)
Union Free SD of the Tarrytowns (PK-12)
    2014-15 Enrollment: 2,736 . . . . (914) 631-9404
Vocational/Technical School(s)
New York School of Esthetics & Day Spa (Private, For-profit)
    Fall 2014 Enrollment: 77 . . . . (914) 631-4432
    2015-16 Tuition: $7,375

Housing: Homeownership rate: 63.8%; Median home value: $538,400; Median year structure built: 1954; Homeowner vacancy rate: 1.6%; Median

selected monthly owner costs: $3,215 with a mortgage, $1,500+ without a mortgage; Median gross rent: $1,580 per month; Rental vacancy rate: 0.0%

Health Insurance: 93.4% have insurance; 86.7% have private insurance; 20.1% have public insurance; 6.6% do not have insurance; 2.9% of children under 18 do not have insurance

Safety: Violent crime rate: 7.8 per 10,000 population; Property crime rate: 47.4 per 10,000 population

Newspapers: The Hudson Independent (weekly circulation 13,700)

Transportation: Commute: 65.7% car, 23.5% public transportation, 6.4% walk, 4.1% work from home; Mean travel time to work: 32.8 minutes

Additional Information Contacts
Village of Tarrytown. . . . . (914) 631-1652
    http://www.tarrytowngov.com/pages/index

THORNWOOD (CDP). Covers a land area of 1.107 square miles and a water area of 0 square miles. Located at 41.12° N. Lat; 73.78° W. Long. Elevation is 269 feet.

History: Thornwood once had a large and thriving marble quarry near its heart, the intersection of Route 141 and Kensico Road (known as Four Corners). The quarry pit was filled in in the mid 1980s and the Town Center shopping center constructed over it.

Population: 4,054; Growth (since 2000): -32.2%; Density: 3,661.6 persons per square mile; Race: 91.8% White, 0.0% Black/African American, 2.5% Asian, 0.2% American Indian/Alaska Native, 0.0% Native Hawaiian/Other Pacific Islander, 1.5% Two or more races, 8.6% Hispanic of any race; Average household size: 3.14; Median age: 39.1; Age under 18: 20.9%; Age 65 and over: 14.6%; Males per 100 females: 98.7; Marriage status: 32.2% never married, 55.1% now married, 2.4% separated, 6.0% widowed, 6.7% divorced; Foreign born: 13.2%; Speak English only: 79.7%; With disability: 5.3%; Veterans: 4.5%; Ancestry: 54.8% Italian, 17.9% Irish, 11.0% German, 5.6% Albanian, 4.7% American

Employment: 14.3% management, business, and financial, 5.0% computer, engineering, and science, 16.7% education, legal, community service, arts, and media, 5.3% healthcare practitioners, 19.9% service, 20.5% sales and office, 10.6% natural resources, construction, and maintenance, 7.7% production, transportation, and material moving

Income: Per capita: $41,066; Median household: $119,327; Average household: $126,705; Households with income of $100,000 or more: 56.5%; Poverty rate: 3.1%

Educational Attainment: High school diploma or higher: 92.1%; Bachelor's degree or higher: 44.8%; Graduate/professional degree or higher: 19.3%

School District(s)
Mount Pleasant Central SD (KG-12)
    2014-15 Enrollment: 1,923 . . . . (914) 769-5500

Housing: Homeownership rate: 75.6%; Median home value: $575,900; Median year structure built: 1956; Homeowner vacancy rate: 0.0%; Median selected monthly owner costs: $3,185 with a mortgage, $1,321 without a mortgage; Median gross rent: $1,521 per month; Rental vacancy rate: 18.8%

Health Insurance: 94.3% have insurance; 90.4% have private insurance; 15.8% have public insurance; 5.7% do not have insurance; 3.8% of children under 18 do not have insurance

Transportation: Commute: 79.8% car, 10.6% public transportation, 1.1% walk, 7.5% work from home; Mean travel time to work: 27.3 minutes

---

TUCKAHOE (village). Covers a land area of 0.598 square miles and a water area of 0 square miles. Located at 40.95° N. Lat; 73.82° W. Long. Elevation is 112 feet.

History: Settled 1684; incorporated 1903.

Population: 6,586; Growth (since 2000): 6.0%; Density: 11,021.7 persons per square mile; Race: 72.6% White, 14.1% Black/African American, 7.8% Asian, 0.0% American Indian/Alaska Native, 0.0% Native Hawaiian/Other Pacific Islander, 3.2% Two or more races, 7.4% Hispanic of any race; Average household size: 2.32; Median age: 38.9; Age under 18: 18.6%; Age 65 and over: 15.6%; Males per 100 females: 86.6; Marriage status: 36.4% never married, 43.4% now married, 2.3% separated, 5.7% widowed, 14.6% divorced; Foreign born: 22.7%; Speak English only: 70.2%; With disability: 9.8%; Veterans: 4.3%; Ancestry: 29.6% Italian, 13.9% Irish, 6.0% German, 4.3% African, 3.4% American

Employment: 18.1% management, business, and financial, 4.6% computer, engineering, and science, 27.2% education, legal, community service, arts, and media, 6.2% healthcare practitioners, 13.6% service,

19.8% sales and office, 6.8% natural resources, construction, and maintenance, 3.6% production, transportation, and material moving
Income: Per capita: $52,348; Median household: $69,906; Average household: $119,698; Households with income of $100,000 or more: 37.1%; Poverty rate: 4.7%
Educational Attainment: High school diploma or higher: 93.5%; Bachelor's degree or higher: 52.3%; Graduate/professional degree or higher: 27.6%
Housing: Homeownership rate: 49.8%; Median home value: $486,200; Median year structure built: 1957; Homeowner vacancy rate: 0.0%; Median selected monthly owner costs: $3,021 with a mortgage, $1,460 without a mortgage; Median gross rent: $1,723 per month; Rental vacancy rate: 0.0%
Health Insurance: 93.8% have insurance; 82.3% have private insurance; 23.7% have public insurance; 6.2% do not have insurance; 0.0% of children under 18 do not have insurance
Safety: Violent crime rate: 1.5 per 10,000 population; Property crime rate: 66.1 per 10,000 population
Transportation: Commute: 47.1% car, 37.9% public transportation, 7.5% walk, 5.9% work from home; Mean travel time to work: 34.6 minutes
Additional Information Contacts
Village of Tuckahoe . . . . (914) 961-3100
   http://www.tuckahoe.com

VALHALLA (CDP). Covers a land area of 0.830 square miles and a water area of 0 square miles. Located at 41.08° N. Lat; 73.78° W. Long. Elevation is 256 feet.
Population: 3,352; Growth (since 2000): -37.7%; Density: 4,038.6 persons per square mile; Race: 82.7% White, 0.8% Black/African American, 8.9% Asian, 0.0% American Indian/Alaska Native, 0.0% Native Hawaiian/Other Pacific Islander, 6.3% Two or more races, 18.9% Hispanic of any race; Average household size: 3.01; Median age: 43.4; Age under 18: 19.6%; Age 65 and over: 16.5%; Males per 100 females: 94.1; Marriage status: 33.0% never married, 52.4% now married, 0.5% separated, 10.4% widowed, 4.2% divorced; Foreign born: 23.7%; Speak English only: 63.5%; With disability: 9.9%; Veterans: 2.9%; Ancestry: 27.1% Italian, 17.5% Irish, 11.6% German, 5.1% Croatian, 4.7% Polish
Employment: 17.3% management, business, and financial, 4.4% computer, engineering, and science, 18.3% education, legal, community service, arts, and media, 8.9% healthcare practitioners, 22.0% service, 19.5% sales and office, 3.3% natural resources, construction, and maintenance, 6.4% production, transportation, and material moving
Income: Per capita: $46,506; Median household: $106,413; Average household: $135,915; Households with income of $100,000 or more: 56.1%; Poverty rate: 1.6%
Educational Attainment: High school diploma or higher: 87.6%; Bachelor's degree or higher: 50.7%; Graduate/professional degree or higher: 25.2%
School District(s)
Greenburgh-North Castle Union Free SD (07-12)
   2014-15 Enrollment: 21 . . . . (914) 693-4309
Mount Pleasant-Blythedale Union Free SD (PK-12)
   2014-15 Enrollment: 105 . . . . (914) 347-1800
Valhalla Union Free SD (KG-12)
   2014-15 Enrollment: 1,517 . . . . (914) 683-5040
Four-year College(s)
New York Medical College (Private, Not-for-profit, Jewish)
   Fall 2014 Enrollment: 1,482 . . . . (914) 594-4000
Two-year College(s)
SUNY Westchester Community College (Public)
   Fall 2014 Enrollment: 13,916 . . . . (914) 606-6600
   2015-16 Tuition: In-state $4,723; Out-of-state $12,213
Housing: Homeownership rate: 75.0%; Median home value: $562,400; Median year structure built: 1956; Homeowner vacancy rate: 0.0%; Median selected monthly owner costs: $3,462 with a mortgage, $1,418 without a mortgage; Median gross rent: $1,989 per month; Rental vacancy rate: 0.0%
Health Insurance: 94.8% have insurance; 86.6% have private insurance; 23.6% have public insurance; 5.2% do not have insurance; 2.1% of children under 18 do not have insurance
Hospitals: Westchester Medical Center (635 beds)
Transportation: Commute: 73.6% car, 19.9% public transportation, 2.5% walk, 4.0% work from home; Mean travel time to work: 31.2 minutes

VERPLANCK (CDP). Covers a land area of 0.622 square miles and a water area of 0.104 square miles. Located at 41.26° N. Lat; 73.96° W. Long. Elevation is 59 feet.
Population: 1,662; Growth (since 2000): 113.9%; Density: 2,670.8 persons per square mile; Race: 77.4% White, 1.9% Black/African American, 4.7% Asian, 0.0% American Indian/Alaska Native, 0.0% Native Hawaiian/Other Pacific Islander, 5.4% Two or more races, 18.8% Hispanic of any race; Average household size: 2.65; Median age: 36.9; Age under 18: 25.5%; Age 65 and over: 11.0%; Males per 100 females: 92.1; Marriage status: 32.2% never married, 49.4% now married, 1.7% separated, 6.8% widowed, 11.5% divorced; Foreign born: 17.3%; Speak English only: 77.7%; With disability: 15.6%; Veterans: 4.2%; Ancestry: 30.2% Italian, 28.8% Irish, 7.8% English, 6.5% Greek, 5.3% German
Employment: 10.2% management, business, and financial, 0.0% computer, engineering, and science, 10.4% education, legal, community service, arts, and media, 0.0% healthcare practitioners, 31.3% service, 19.9% sales and office, 21.1% natural resources, construction, and maintenance, 7.1% production, transportation, and material moving
Income: Per capita: $26,693; Median household: $54,716; Average household: $68,668; Households with income of $100,000 or more: 20.7%; Poverty rate: 8.0%
Educational Attainment: High school diploma or higher: 78.6%; Bachelor's degree or higher: 9.9%; Graduate/professional degree or higher: 7.2%
Housing: Homeownership rate: 49.6%; Median home value: $296,300; Median year structure built: 1947; Homeowner vacancy rate: 0.0%; Median selected monthly owner costs: $3,082 with a mortgage, $795 without a mortgage; Median gross rent: $1,361 per month; Rental vacancy rate: 11.0%
Health Insurance: 89.5% have insurance; 63.7% have private insurance; 32.3% have public insurance; 10.5% do not have insurance; 0.0% of children under 18 do not have insurance
Transportation: Commute: 84.4% car, 4.0% public transportation, 7.2% walk, 2.9% work from home; Mean travel time to work: 28.5 minutes

WACCABUC (unincorporated postal area)
ZCTA: 10597
   Covers a land area of 3.339 square miles and a water area of 0.249 square miles. Located at 41.29° N. Lat; 73.60° W. Long. Elevation is 554 feet.
Population: 1,058; Growth (since 2000): 137.8%; Density: 316.9 persons per square mile; Race: 99.1% White, 0.0% Black/African American, 0.9% Asian, 0.0% American Indian/Alaska Native, 0.0% Native Hawaiian/Other Pacific Islander, 0.0% Two or more races, 9.9% Hispanic of any race; Average household size: 3.25; Median age: 46.9; Age under 18: 19.1%; Age 65 and over: 26.1%; Males per 100 females: 100.4; Marriage status: 33.7% never married, 57.3% now married, 0.0% separated, 3.9% widowed, 5.2% divorced; Foreign born: 10.7%; Speak English only: 87.1%; With disability: 0.0%; Veterans: 5.5%; Ancestry: 41.1% Italian, 27.7% Russian, 27.6% Irish, 20.5% German, 8.2% Estonian
Employment: 21.0% management, business, and financial, 0.0% computer, engineering, and science, 25.9% education, legal, community service, arts, and media, 5.3% healthcare practitioners, 20.5% service, 23.5% sales and office, 1.9% natural resources, construction, and maintenance, 1.9% production, transportation, and material moving
Income: Per capita: $82,436; Median household: $207,895; Average household: $263,442; Households with income of $100,000 or more: 83.4%; Poverty rate: 0.9%
Educational Attainment: High school diploma or higher: 98.5%; Bachelor's degree or higher: 85.9%; Graduate/professional degree or higher: 47.2%
Housing: Homeownership rate: 100.0%; Median home value: $976,500; Median year structure built: 1982; Homeowner vacancy rate: 0.0%; Median selected monthly owner costs: $4,000 with a mortgage, $1,500 without a mortgage; Median gross rent: n/a per month; Rental vacancy rate: 0.0%
Health Insurance: 99.1% have insurance; 90.5% have private insurance; 23.8% have public insurance; 0.9% do not have insurance; 0.0% of children under 18 do not have insurance
Transportation: Commute: 88.8% car, 11.2% public transportation, 0.0% walk, 0.0% work from home; Mean travel time to work: 34.5 minutes

WEST HARRISON (unincorporated postal area)
ZCTA: 10604

Covers a land area of 6.813 square miles and a water area of 1.252 square miles. Located at 41.06° N. Lat; 73.74° W. Long..

Population: 11,808; Growth (since 2000): 13.2%; Density: 1,733.1 persons per square mile; Race: 79.8% White, 3.8% Black/African American, 5.7% Asian, 0.0% American Indian/Alaska Native, 0.0% Native Hawaiian/Other Pacific Islander, 1.9% Two or more races, 30.3% Hispanic of any race; Average household size: 3.05; Median age: 41.1; Age under 18: 20.8%; Age 65 and over: 17.1%; Males per 100 females: 92.0; Marriage status: 33.3% never married, 48.9% now married, 0.9% separated, 5.7% widowed, 12.1% divorced; Foreign born: 35.7%; Speak English only: 50.0%; With disability: 9.5%; Veterans: 3.8%; Ancestry: 24.5% Italian, 9.7% American, 6.0% Irish, 5.0% German, 2.5% English

Employment: 18.9% management, business, and financial, 5.4% computer, engineering, and science, 9.0% education, legal, community service, arts, and media, 6.2% healthcare practitioners, 25.4% service, 21.4% sales and office, 7.4% natural resources, construction, and maintenance, 6.2% production, transportation, and material moving

Income: Per capita: $48,645; Median household: $87,396; Average household: $144,359; Households with income of $100,000 or more: 43.2%; Poverty rate: 11.3%

Educational Attainment: High school diploma or higher: 86.6%; Bachelor's degree or higher: 36.5%; Graduate/professional degree or higher: 15.9%

School District(s)
Harrison Central SD (KG-12)

2014-15 Enrollment: 3,558 . . . . (914) 630-3021

Housing: Homeownership rate: 56.8%; Median home value: $654,000; Median year structure built: 1960; Homeowner vacancy rate: 1.1%; Median selected monthly owner costs: $3,448 with a mortgage, $1,493 without a mortgage; Median gross rent: $1,683 per month; Rental vacancy rate: 2.5%

Health Insurance: 86.1% have insurance; 66.9% have private insurance; 27.3% have public insurance; 13.9% do not have insurance; 9.1% of children under 18 do not have insurance

Transportation: Commute: 77.0% car, 10.9% public transportation, 5.0% walk, 4.0% work from home; Mean travel time to work: 25.2 minutes

WHITE PLAINS (city). County seat. Covers a land area of 9.768 square miles and a water area of 0.117 square miles. Located at 41.03° N. Lat; 73.75° W. Long. Elevation is 213 feet.

History: Named for the Weckquaeskeck word "quaropas," meaning "white marshes or plains". Settled by Puritans in 1683. The state convention that ratified the Declaration of Independence met (1776) here. The battle of White Plains (1776), a principal engagement of the American Revolution occurred here. Gen. George Washington briefly made his headquarters here at Elijah Miller House, which still stands. Other buildings from the revolutionary period are also preserved. Incorporated as a village 1866 (originally named Quarrapas by Siwanoy people), as a city 1916.

Population: 57,790; Growth (since 2000): 8.9%; Density: 5,916.4 persons per square mile; Race: 62.0% White, 12.3% Black/African American, 7.2% Asian, 1.0% American Indian/Alaska Native, 0.0% Native Hawaiian/Other Pacific Islander, 4.6% Two or more races, 34.4% Hispanic of any race; Average household size: 2.57; Median age: 38.3; Age under 18: 20.6%; Age 65 and over: 15.6%; Males per 100 females: 92.7; Marriage status: 35.4% never married, 49.7% now married, 2.6% separated, 6.1% widowed, 8.7% divorced; Foreign born: 32.6%; Speak English only: 54.9%; With disability: 8.2%; Veterans: 3.5%; Ancestry: 13.2% Italian, 8.0% Irish, 5.2% American, 5.1% German, 3.3% Russian

Employment: 19.0% management, business, and financial, 5.0% computer, engineering, and science, 16.1% education, legal, community service, arts, and media, 5.8% healthcare practitioners, 22.9% service, 20.6% sales and office, 5.2% natural resources, construction, and maintenance, 5.4% production, transportation, and material moving

Income: Per capita: $45,909; Median household: $80,442; Average household: $117,392; Households with income of $100,000 or more: 41.3%; Poverty rate: 12.2%

Educational Attainment: High school diploma or higher: 85.8%; Bachelor's degree or higher: 49.0%; Graduate/professional degree or higher: 24.8%

School District(s)
Greenburgh Central SD (PK-12)

2014-15 Enrollment: 1,893 . . . . (914) 761-6000

Valhalla Union Free SD (KG-12)

2014-15 Enrollment: 1,517 . . . . (914) 683-5040

White Plains City SD (PK-12)

2014-15 Enrollment: 7,106 . . . . (914) 422-2019

Four-year College(s)
The College of Westchester (Private, For-profit)

Fall 2014 Enrollment: 1,125 . . . . (914) 948-4442

2015-16 Tuition: In-state $21,015; Out-of-state $21,015

Two-year College(s)
Center for Ultrasound Research & Education (Private, For-profit)

Fall 2014 Enrollment: n/a . . . . (855) 843-2873

Vocational/Technical School(s)
Westchester School for Dental Assistant (Private, For-profit)

Fall 2014 Enrollment: n/a . . . . (914) 682-9001

2015-16 Tuition: $9,500

Housing: Homeownership rate: 50.9%; Median home value: $511,600; Median year structure built: 1956; Homeowner vacancy rate: 1.9%; Median selected monthly owner costs: $3,094 with a mortgage, $1,306 without a mortgage; Median gross rent: $1,554 per month; Rental vacancy rate: 2.2%

Health Insurance: 85.6% have insurance; 67.7% have private insurance; 28.2% have public insurance; 14.4% do not have insurance; 3.1% of children under 18 do not have insurance

Hospitals: White Plains Hospital Center (307 beds); Winifred Masterson Burke Rehabilitation Hospital (150 beds)

Safety: Violent crime rate: 17.5 per 10,000 population; Property crime rate: 174.4 per 10,000 population

Newspapers: Journal News (daily circulation 122,000); Review Press (weekly circulation 5,500); White Plains Times (weekly circulation 25,000)

Transportation: Commute: 65.5% car, 19.5% public transportation, 8.2% walk, 4.5% work from home; Mean travel time to work: 26.8 minutes

Airports: Westchester County (primary service/small hub)

Additional Information Contacts

City of White Plains . . . . (914) 422-1200

http://www.ci.white-plains.ny.us

YONKERS (city). Covers a land area of 18.012 square miles and a water area of 2.285 square miles. Located at 40.95° N. Lat; 73.87° W. Long. Elevation is 82 feet.

History: Named for Adriaen Van der Donck, whose title was "jonkheer," purchaser of the land. The village of Nappeckamack stood on the site of Yonkers before the Kekeskick Purchase (1639) made by the Dutch West India Company. The city site was included in a grant of land made in 1646 by the company to Adriaen Cornelissen Van der Donck, the first lawyer and first historian of New Netherland. By reason of his wealth and social position, Van der Donck enjoyed the courtesy title of "jonker," the Dutch equivalent of "his young lordship," from which was derived the name of the city.

Population: 199,435; Growth (since 2000): 1.7%; Density: 11,072.3 persons per square mile; Race: 58.6% White, 17.2% Black/African American, 6.8% Asian, 0.3% American Indian/Alaska Native, 0.0% Native Hawaiian/Other Pacific Islander, 3.2% Two or more races, 35.5% Hispanic of any race; Average household size: 2.69; Median age: 37.9; Age under 18: 22.1%; Age 65 and over: 15.4%; Males per 100 females: 90.0; Marriage status: 39.7% never married, 45.7% now married, 3.3% separated, 6.4% widowed, 8.2% divorced; Foreign born: 30.6%; Speak English only: 53.4%; With disability: 10.9%; Veterans: 4.1%; Ancestry: 15.0% Italian, 11.4% Irish, 3.5% German, 3.2% American, 2.4% Polish

Employment: 12.6% management, business, and financial, 3.8% computer, engineering, and science, 12.3% education, legal, community service, arts, and media, 6.9% healthcare practitioners, 21.4% service, 25.2% sales and office, 8.7% natural resources, construction, and maintenance, 9.0% production, transportation, and material moving

Income: Per capita: $30,263; Median household: $59,049; Average household: $79,292; Households with income of $100,000 or more: 28.1%; Poverty rate: 16.7%

Educational Attainment: High school diploma or higher: 83.0%; Bachelor's degree or higher: 31.1%; Graduate/professional degree or higher: 13.2%

School District(s)
Charter School of Educational Excellence (KG-08)

2014-15 Enrollment: 660 . . . . (914) 476-5070

Greenburgh-North Castle Union Free SD (07-12)

2014-15 Enrollment: 21 . . . . (914) 693-4309

Yonkers City SD (PK-12)
  2014-15 Enrollment: 26,828 . . . . (914) 376-8100
Four-year College(s)
Saint Vladimirs Orthodox Theological Seminary (Private, Not-for-profit, Russian Orthodox)
  Fall 2014 Enrollment: 88 . . . . (914) 961-8313
Two-year College(s)
Cochran School of Nursing (Private, Not-for-profit)
  Fall 2014 Enrollment: 93 . . . . (914) 964-4296

Housing: Homeownership rate: 47.5%; Median home value: $382,300; Median year structure built: 1954; Homeowner vacancy rate: 2.5%; Median selected monthly owner costs: $2,497 with a mortgage, $1,038 without a mortgage; Median gross rent: $1,227 per month; Rental vacancy rate: 11.8%

Health Insurance: 88.2% have insurance; 62.6% have private insurance; 36.8% have public insurance; 11.8% do not have insurance; 4.0% of children under 18 do not have insurance

Hospitals: Saint John's Riverside Hospital (407 beds); Saint Joseph's Medical Center (194 beds)

Safety: Violent crime rate: 47.1 per 10,000 population; Property crime rate: 99.5 per 10,000 population

Newspapers: Martinelli Publications (weekly circulation 52,000)

Transportation: Commute: 65.1% car, 26.4% public transportation, 5.1% walk, 2.4% work from home; Mean travel time to work: 33.2 minutes; Amtrak: Train service available.

Additional Information Contacts
City of Yonkers . . . . (914) 377-6020
  http://www.cityofyonkers.com

YORKTOWN (town). Covers a land area of 36.645 square miles and a water area of 2.612 square miles. Located at 41.27° N. Lat; 73.82° W. Long. Elevation is 505 feet.

History: Nearby, at Crompound (2.5 miles east of Peekskill), is the former anarchist Mohegan colony designed by Lewis Mumford in 1923 and led by American Harry Kelly and Englishmen Joseph Cohen and Leonard Abbott. Also known as the twelve Mohegan Colony and the Modern School Movement, the colony flourished both here and in the Stetton colony in N.J.

Population: 36,746; Growth (since 2000): 1.2%; Density: 1,002.8 persons per square mile; Race: 88.2% White, 3.4% Black/African American, 4.2% Asian, 0.3% American Indian/Alaska Native, 0.0% Native Hawaiian/Other Pacific Islander, 1.4% Two or more races, 12.4% Hispanic of any race; Average household size: 2.78; Median age: 44.9; Age under 18: 22.9%; Age 65 and over: 17.9%; Males per 100 females: 93.0; Marriage status: 27.7% never married, 57.1% now married, 1.1% separated, 6.8% widowed, 8.4% divorced; Foreign born: 11.9%; Speak English only: 84.0%; With disability: 9.4%; Veterans: 5.5%; Ancestry: 34.7% Italian, 20.0% Irish, 11.1% German, 5.3% American, 5.0% Polish

Employment: 19.9% management, business, and financial, 5.0% computer, engineering, and science, 20.6% education, legal, community service, arts, and media, 6.6% healthcare practitioners, 12.7% service, 23.0% sales and office, 5.5% natural resources, construction, and maintenance, 6.7% production, transportation, and material moving

Income: Per capita: $48,697; Median household: $107,906; Average household: $134,591; Households with income of $100,000 or more: 53.8%; Poverty rate: 2.2%

Educational Attainment: High school diploma or higher: 94.2%; Bachelor's degree or higher: 50.5%; Graduate/professional degree or higher: 23.1%

Housing: Homeownership rate: 85.4%; Median home value: $408,700; Median year structure built: 1968; Homeowner vacancy rate: 1.0%; Median selected monthly owner costs: $3,087 with a mortgage, $1,209 without a mortgage; Median gross rent: $1,346 per month; Rental vacancy rate: 0.0%

Health Insurance: 96.4% have insurance; 87.2% have private insurance; 22.7% have public insurance; 3.6% do not have insurance; 2.4% of children under 18 do not have insurance

Safety: Violent crime rate: 3.8 per 10,000 population; Property crime rate: 79.3 per 10,000 population

Transportation: Commute: 85.8% car, 7.2% public transportation, 1.3% walk, 4.9% work from home; Mean travel time to work: 36.2 minutes

Additional Information Contacts
Town of Yorktown . . . . (914) 962-5722
  http://www.yorktownny.org

YORKTOWN HEIGHTS (CDP). Covers a land area of 0.914 square miles and a water area of 0.003 square miles. Located at 41.27° N. Lat; 73.77° W. Long. Elevation is 492 feet.

Population: 1,964; Growth (since 2000): -75.4%; Density: 2,148.3 persons per square mile; Race: 79.1% White, 13.0% Black/African American, 6.7% Asian, 0.0% American Indian/Alaska Native, 0.0% Native Hawaiian/Other Pacific Islander, 0.0% Two or more races, 1.0% Hispanic of any race; Average household size: 3.10; Median age: 42.7; Age under 18: 23.8%; Age 65 and over: 12.7%; Males per 100 females: 94.9; Marriage status: 31.7% never married, 50.5% now married, 0.8% separated, 3.0% widowed, 14.8% divorced; Foreign born: 11.0%; Speak English only: 88.9%; With disability: 10.5%; Veterans: 6.6%; Ancestry: 46.2% Italian, 14.1% German, 12.5% English, 9.5% Irish, 4.2% Danish

Employment: 14.3% management, business, and financial, 5.4% computer, engineering, and science, 21.1% education, legal, community service, arts, and media, 7.2% healthcare practitioners, 10.1% service, 27.0% sales and office, 1.3% natural resources, construction, and maintenance, 13.6% production, transportation, and material moving

Income: Per capita: $69,827; Median household: $95,988; Average household: $211,618; Households with income of $100,000 or more: 46.0%; Poverty rate: 1.1%

Educational Attainment: High school diploma or higher: 97.1%; Bachelor's degree or higher: 56.8%; Graduate/professional degree or higher: 20.8%

School District(s)
Lakeland Central SD (PK-12)
  2014-15 Enrollment: 5,900 . . . . (914) 245-1700
Putnam-Northern Westchester Boces
  2014-15 Enrollment: n/a . . . . (845) 248-2301
Yorktown Central SD (KG-12)
  2014-15 Enrollment: 3,470 . . . . (914) 243-8000
Vocational/Technical School(s)
Putnam Westchester BOCES-Practical Nursing Program (Public)
  Fall 2014 Enrollment: 42 . . . . (914) 245-2700
  2015-16 Tuition: $13,000

Housing: Homeownership rate: 75.2%; Median home value: $417,000; Median year structure built: 1963; Homeowner vacancy rate: 0.0%; Median selected monthly owner costs: $3,325 with a mortgage, $1,088 without a mortgage; Median gross rent: $1,237 per month; Rental vacancy rate: 0.0%

Health Insurance: 98.8% have insurance; 85.5% have private insurance; 23.4% have public insurance; 1.2% do not have insurance; 0.0% of children under 18 do not have insurance

Newspapers: North County News (weekly circulation 10,000)

Transportation: Commute: 97.7% car, 0.0% public transportation, 0.0% walk, 2.3% work from home; Mean travel time to work: 30.1 minutes

Wyoming County

Located in western New York; drained by the Genesee River. Covers a land area of 592.746 square miles, a water area of 3.541 square miles, and is located in the Eastern Time Zone at 42.70° N. Lat., 78.23° W. Long. The county was founded in 1841. County seat is Warsaw.

Weather Station: Warsaw 6 SW   Elevation: 1,819 feet

	Jan	Feb	Mar	Apr	May	Jun	Jul	Aug	Sep	Oct	Nov	Dec
High	28	30	38	52	64	72	76	75	68	56	44	32
Low	13	14	20	33	43	53	57	56	49	38	29	19
Precip	3.2	2.5	3.2	3.4	4.0	4.6	4.5	3.7	4.6	4.0	3.9	3.7
Snow	35.3	25.5	20.7	6.1	0.2	0.0	0.0	0.0	0.0	0.6	12.4	29.7

High and Low temperatures in degrees Fahrenheit; Precipitation and Snow in inches

Population: 41,446; Growth (since 2000): -4.6%; Density: 69.9 persons per square mile; Race: 91.8% White, 5.7% Black/African American, 0.4% Asian, 0.3% American Indian/Alaska Native, 0.0% Native Hawaiian/Other Pacific Islander, 1.3% two or more races, 3.2% Hispanic of any race; Average household size: 2.38; Median age: 41.1; Age under 18: 19.9%; Age 65 and over: 15.0%; Males per 100 females: 119.5; Marriage status: 30.7% never married, 53.1% now married, 2.1% separated, 5.7% widowed, 10.5% divorced; Foreign born: 1.7%; Speak English only: 95.7%; With disability: 13.1%; Veterans: 9.3%; Ancestry: 33.1% German, 15.8% Irish, 12.9% English, 10.7% Polish, 9.1% Italian

Religion: Six largest groups: 18.9% Catholicism, 4.7% Methodist/Pietist, 4.3% Presbyterian-Reformed, 1.6% Baptist, 1.2% Non-denominational Protestant, 1.0% Episcopalianism/Anglicanism

Economy: Unemployment rate: 4.6%; Leading industries: 16.8 % retail trade; 13.0 % other services (except public administration); 12.9 % construction; Farms: 713 totaling 225,864 acres; Company size: 0 employ 1,000 or more persons, 3 employ 500 to 999 persons, 10 employ 100 to 499 persons, 772 employ less than 100 persons; Business ownership: 799 women-owned, n/a Black-owned, n/a Hispanic-owned, n/a Asian-owned, n/a American Indian/Alaska Native-owned

Employment: 11.2% management, business, and financial, 2.9% computer, engineering, and science, 7.7% education, legal, community service, arts, and media, 5.6% healthcare practitioners, 17.7% service, 23.3% sales and office, 14.9% natural resources, construction, and maintenance, 16.6% production, transportation, and material moving

Income: Per capita: $23,960; Median household: $52,564; Average household: $62,150; Households with income of $100,000 or more: 15.7%; Poverty rate: 11.8%

Educational Attainment: High school diploma or higher: 87.2%; Bachelor's degree or higher: 15.2%; Graduate/professional degree or higher: 5.4%

Housing: Homeownership rate: 75.2%; Median home value: $102,000; Median year structure built: 1951; Homeowner vacancy rate: 1.0%; Median selected monthly owner costs: $1,121 with a mortgage, $453 without a mortgage; Median gross rent: $589 per month; Rental vacancy rate: 2.6%

Vital Statistics: Birth rate: 93.6 per 10,000 population; Death rate: 79.5 per 10,000 population; Age-adjusted cancer mortality rate: 183.3 deaths per 100,000 population

Health Insurance: 92.7% have insurance; 74.0% have private insurance; 34.2% have public insurance; 7.3% do not have insurance; 5.8% of children under 18 do not have insurance

Health Care: Physicians: 8.0 per 10,000 population; Dentists: 4.1 per 10,000 population; Hospital beds: 18.1 per 10,000 population; Hospital admissions: 604.8 per 10,000 population

Transportation: Commute: 91.9% car, 0.4% public transportation, 3.7% walk, 2.5% work from home; Mean travel time to work: 25.4 minutes

2016 Presidential Election: 72.3% Trump, 22.7% Clinton, 3.9% Johnson, 1.0% Stein

National and State Parks: Letchworth State Park; Silver Lake State Park

Additional Information Contacts

Wyoming Government . . . . (716) 786-8810
  http://www.wyomingco.net

Wyoming County Communities

ARCADE (town). Covers a land area of 47.004 square miles and a water area of 0.106 square miles. Located at 42.57° N. Lat; 78.37° W. Long. Elevation is 1,476 feet.

Population: 4,158; Growth (since 2000): -0.6%; Density: 88.5 persons per square mile; Race: 95.8% White, 1.8% Black/African American, 1.4% Asian, 0.1% American Indian/Alaska Native, 0.0% Native Hawaiian/Other Pacific Islander, 0.7% Two or more races, 2.3% Hispanic of any race; Average household size: 2.32; Median age: 39.1; Age under 18: 23.4%; Age 65 and over: 15.6%; Males per 100 females: 95.3; Marriage status: 31.5% never married, 48.1% now married, 2.7% separated, 9.7% widowed, 10.7% divorced; Foreign born: 1.3%; Speak English only: 97.2%; With disability: 14.9%; Veterans: 8.3%; Ancestry: 39.4% German, 16.9% English, 14.5% Irish, 11.2% Italian, 9.8% Polish

Employment: 8.2% management, business, and financial, 1.7% computer, engineering, and science, 8.5% education, legal, community service, arts, and media, 5.3% healthcare practitioners, 20.5% service, 25.9% sales and office, 8.2% natural resources, construction, and maintenance, 21.8% production, transportation, and material moving

Income: Per capita: $22,614; Median household: $41,384; Average household: $52,658; Households with income of $100,000 or more: 11.3%; Poverty rate: 19.0%

Educational Attainment: High school diploma or higher: 87.6%; Bachelor's degree or higher: 17.8%; Graduate/professional degree or higher: 6.8%

School District(s)

Yorkshire-Pioneer Central SD (PK-12)
  2014-15 Enrollment: 2,585 . . . . (716) 492-9304

Housing: Homeownership rate: 74.2%; Median home value: $104,300; Median year structure built: 1969; Homeowner vacancy rate: 1.6%; Median selected monthly owner costs: $1,108 with a mortgage, $347 without a mortgage; Median gross rent: $599 per month; Rental vacancy rate: 4.7%

Health Insurance: 94.6% have insurance; 68.8% have private insurance; 40.0% have public insurance; 5.4% do not have insurance; 3.2% of children under 18 do not have insurance

Newspapers: Arcade Herald (weekly circulation 5,000)

Transportation: Commute: 92.7% car, 0.0% public transportation, 3.9% walk, 1.5% work from home; Mean travel time to work: 22.9 minutes

ARCADE (village). Covers a land area of 2.649 square miles and a water area of 0.003 square miles. Located at 42.53° N. Lat; 78.44° W. Long. Elevation is 1,476 feet.

Population: 2,214; Growth (since 2000): 9.3%; Density: 835.7 persons per square mile; Race: 96.4% White, 0.0% Black/African American, 2.1% Asian, 0.2% American Indian/Alaska Native, 0.0% Native Hawaiian/Other Pacific Islander, 0.9% Two or more races, 2.1% Hispanic of any race; Average household size: 2.34; Median age: 33.0; Age under 18: 29.3%; Age 65 and over: 10.9%; Males per 100 females: 90.5; Marriage status: 33.1% never married, 43.7% now married, 3.3% separated, 8.2% widowed, 15.0% divorced; Foreign born: 1.9%; Speak English only: 95.8%; With disability: 13.2%; Veterans: 8.5%; Ancestry: 42.1% German, 16.0% English, 12.4% Irish, 12.1% Italian, 9.9% Polish

Employment: 9.5% management, business, and financial, 3.0% computer, engineering, and science, 7.0% education, legal, community service, arts, and media, 4.9% healthcare practitioners, 21.3% service, 31.3% sales and office, 5.5% natural resources, construction, and maintenance, 17.3% production, transportation, and material moving

Income: Per capita: $22,487; Median household: $39,205; Average household: $53,271; Households with income of $100,000 or more: 11.8%; Poverty rate: 21.0%

Educational Attainment: High school diploma or higher: 87.9%; Bachelor's degree or higher: 19.6%; Graduate/professional degree or higher: 6.8%

School District(s)

Yorkshire-Pioneer Central SD (PK-12)
  2014-15 Enrollment: 2,585 . . . . (716) 492-9304

Housing: Homeownership rate: 60.8%; Median home value: $102,800; Median year structure built: 1943; Homeowner vacancy rate: 0.0%; Median selected monthly owner costs: $1,038 with a mortgage, $428 without a mortgage; Median gross rent: $582 per month; Rental vacancy rate: 3.6%

Health Insurance: 92.3% have insurance; 66.9% have private insurance; 37.7% have public insurance; 7.7% do not have insurance; 4.8% of children under 18 do not have insurance

Safety: Violent crime rate: 0.0 per 10,000 population; Property crime rate: 125.7 per 10,000 population

Newspapers: Arcade Herald (weekly circulation 5,000)

Transportation: Commute: 90.3% car, 0.0% public transportation, 6.0% walk, 1.9% work from home; Mean travel time to work: 22.6 minutes

Additional Information Contacts

Village of Arcade . . . . (585) 492-1111
  http://www.villageofarcade.org

ATTICA (town). Covers a land area of 35.712 square miles and a water area of 0.315 square miles. Located at 42.82° N. Lat; 78.25° W. Long. Elevation is 981 feet.

Population: 7,520; Growth (since 2000): 24.8%; Density: 210.6 persons per square mile; Race: 66.2% White, 28.0% Black/African American, 0.6% Asian, 1.1% American Indian/Alaska Native, 0.0% Native Hawaiian/Other Pacific Islander, 2.4% Two or more races, 9.5% Hispanic of any race; Average household size: 2.49; Median age: 36.1; Age under 18: 12.6%; Age 65 and over: 7.6%; Males per 100 females: 283.4; Marriage status: 48.0% never married, 39.3% now married, 3.2% separated, 3.2% widowed, 9.5% divorced; Foreign born: 3.6%; Speak English only: 88.3%; With disability: 7.8%; Veterans: 6.5%; Ancestry: 19.6% German, 9.8% Irish, 7.3% Italian, 7.0% English, 6.6% Polish

Employment: 8.7% management, business, and financial, 4.0% computer, engineering, and science, 6.2% education, legal, community service, arts, and media, 6.4% healthcare practitioners, 22.8% service, 24.9% sales and office, 10.3% natural resources, construction, and maintenance, 16.7% production, transportation, and material moving

Income: Per capita: $13,620; Median household: $59,533; Average household: $63,660; Households with income of $100,000 or more: 16.6%; Poverty rate: 6.4%

Educational Attainment: High school diploma or higher: 79.6%; Bachelor's degree or higher: 9.3%; Graduate/professional degree or higher: 3.9%

School District(s)

Attica Central SD (KG-12)
2014-15 Enrollment: 1,374 . . . . (585) 591-2173
Housing: Homeownership rate: 65.8%; Median home value: $108,600;
Median year structure built: Before 1940; Homeowner vacancy rate: 1.5%;
Median selected monthly owner costs: $1,069 with a mortgage, $486
without a mortgage; Median gross rent: $597 per month; Rental vacancy
rate: 6.1%
Health Insurance: 94.7% have insurance; 81.8% have private insurance;
27.0% have public insurance; 5.3% do not have insurance; 1.1% of
children under 18 do not have insurance
Transportation: Commute: 92.6% car, 0.5% public transportation, 2.7%
walk, 3.7% work from home; Mean travel time to work: 23.2 minutes
Additional Information Contacts
Town of Attica . . . . (585) 591-2920
http://www.townofattica.net

ATTICA (village). Covers a land area of 1.691 square miles and a water
area of 0 square miles. Located at 42.86° N. Lat; 78.28° W. Long.
Elevation is 981 feet.
Population: 2,643; Growth (since 2000): 1.8%; Density: 1,562.5 persons
per square mile; Race: 95.6% White, 0.0% Black/African American, 0.6%
Asian, 0.4% American Indian/Alaska Native, 0.0% Native Hawaiian/Other
Pacific Islander, 3.3% Two or more races, 0.7% Hispanic of any race;
Average household size: 2.55; Median age: 31.5; Age under 18: 29.4%;
Age 65 and over: 10.5%; Males per 100 females: 93.7; Marriage status:
32.3% never married, 52.4% now married, 3.1% separated, 5.2%
widowed, 10.2% divorced; Foreign born: 0.8%; Speak English only: 97.4%;
With disability: 6.7%; Veterans: 8.8%; Ancestry: 30.6% German, 12.5%
Irish, 11.9% English, 10.3% Polish, 8.9% Italian
Employment: 4.5% management, business, and financial, 3.4% computer,
engineering, and science, 6.4% education, legal, community service, arts,
and media, 6.7% healthcare practitioners, 24.8% service, 28.4% sales and
office, 10.2% natural resources, construction, and maintenance, 15.7%
production, transportation, and material moving
Income: Per capita: $21,797; Median household: $54,265; Average
household: $55,830; Households with income of $100,000 or more: 9.7%;
Poverty rate: 10.4%
Educational Attainment: High school diploma or higher: 90.7%;
Bachelor's degree or higher: 19.3%; Graduate/professional degree or
higher: 7.4%

School District(s)
Attica Central SD (KG-12)
2014-15 Enrollment: 1,374 . . . . (585) 591-2173
Housing: Homeownership rate: 55.3%; Median home value: $89,800;
Median year structure built: Before 1940; Homeowner vacancy rate: 2.7%;
Median selected monthly owner costs: $1,000 with a mortgage, $488
without a mortgage; Median gross rent: $600 per month; Rental vacancy
rate: 7.0%
Health Insurance: 93.6% have insurance; 77.4% have private insurance;
31.5% have public insurance; 6.4% do not have insurance; 1.3% of
children under 18 do not have insurance
Transportation: Commute: 94.0% car, 0.8% public transportation, 3.6%
walk, 0.9% work from home; Mean travel time to work: 23.2 minutes
Additional Information Contacts
Village of Attica . . . . (585) 591-0898
http://attica.org

BENNINGTON (town). Covers a land area of 55.049 square miles
and a water area of 0.215 square miles. Located at 42.82° N. Lat; 78.39°
W. Long. Elevation is 1,207 feet.
Population: 3,316; Growth (since 2000): -1.0%; Density: 60.2 persons per
square mile; Race: 97.8% White, 0.0% Black/African American, 0.3%
Asian, 0.0% American Indian/Alaska Native, 0.0% Native Hawaiian/Other
Pacific Islander, 1.6% Two or more races, 2.5% Hispanic of any race;
Average household size: 2.39; Median age: 48.2; Age under 18: 18.2%;
Age 65 and over: 18.6%; Males per 100 females: 107.0; Marriage status:
22.3% never married, 64.7% now married, 1.2% separated, 4.9%
widowed, 8.1% divorced; Foreign born: 1.4%; Speak English only: 97.6%;
With disability: 10.1%; Veterans: 11.7%; Ancestry: 37.0% German, 24.8%
Polish, 13.8% Irish, 8.0% English, 7.9% American
Employment: 10.1% management, business, and financial, 3.7%
computer, engineering, and science, 10.1% education, legal, community
service, arts, and media, 5.2% healthcare practitioners, 18.8% service,

22.1% sales and office, 14.9% natural resources, construction, and
maintenance, 15.1% production, transportation, and material moving
Income: Per capita: $30,404; Median household: $64,363; Average
household: $71,559; Households with income of $100,000 or more: 20.8%;
Poverty rate: 4.0%
Educational Attainment: High school diploma or higher: 91.5%;
Bachelor's degree or higher: 20.3%; Graduate/professional degree or
higher: 5.8%
Housing: Homeownership rate: 85.0%; Median home value: $149,900;
Median year structure built: 1972; Homeowner vacancy rate: 0.0%; Median
selected monthly owner costs: $1,413 with a mortgage, $535 without a
mortgage; Median gross rent: $576 per month; Rental vacancy rate: 0.0%
Health Insurance: 94.4% have insurance; 81.1% have private insurance;
33.2% have public insurance; 5.6% do not have insurance; 1.8% of
children under 18 do not have insurance
Transportation: Commute: 92.1% car, 0.5% public transportation, 3.6%
walk, 1.6% work from home; Mean travel time to work: 27.9 minutes

BLISS (CDP). Covers a land area of 9.792 square miles and a water
area of 0 square miles. Located at 42.58° N. Lat; 78.25° W. Long.
Elevation is 1,745 feet.
Population: 613; Growth (since 2000): n/a; Density: 62.6 persons per
square mile; Race: 99.0% White, 1.0% Black/African American, 0.0%
Asian, 0.0% American Indian/Alaska Native, 0.0% Native Hawaiian/Other
Pacific Islander, 0.0% Two or more races, 0.0% Hispanic of any race;
Average household size: 2.80; Median age: 35.4; Age under 18: 25.3%;
Age 65 and over: 11.1%; Males per 100 females: 92.3; Marriage status:
31.6% never married, 46.3% now married, 2.7% separated, 9.1%
widowed, 13.0% divorced; Foreign born: 0.0%; Speak English only: 99.5%;
With disability: 14.8%; Veterans: 6.1%; Ancestry: 29.5% German, 29.0%
Irish, 11.9% European, 10.4% Italian, 10.3% Polish
Employment: 15.9% management, business, and financial, 2.4%
computer, engineering, and science, 1.0% education, legal, community
service, arts, and media, 4.1% healthcare practitioners, 14.5% service,
29.1% sales and office, 15.5% natural resources, construction, and
maintenance, 17.6% production, transportation, and material moving
Income: Per capita: $22,678; Median household: $60,469; Average
household: $62,087; Households with income of $100,000 or more: 20.5%;
Poverty rate: 15.0%
Educational Attainment: High school diploma or higher: 92.2%;
Bachelor's degree or higher: 14.3%; Graduate/professional degree or
higher: 5.9%
Housing: Homeownership rate: 90.4%; Median home value: $82,300;
Median year structure built: 1961; Homeowner vacancy rate: 0.0%; Median
selected monthly owner costs: $979 with a mortgage, $412 without a
mortgage; Median gross rent: n/a per month; Rental vacancy rate: 0.0%
Health Insurance: 93.8% have insurance; 77.0% have private insurance;
29.4% have public insurance; 6.2% do not have insurance; 10.3% of
children under 18 do not have insurance
Transportation: Commute: 96.2% car, 0.0% public transportation, 0.0%
walk, 0.0% work from home; Mean travel time to work: 34.3 minutes

CASTILE (town). Covers a land area of 36.980 square miles and a
water area of 1.415 square miles. Located at 42.66° N. Lat; 78.02° W.
Long. Elevation is 1,355 feet.
Population: 2,862; Growth (since 2000): -0.4%; Density: 77.4 persons per
square mile; Race: 97.8% White, 0.9% Black/African American, 0.2%
Asian, 0.2% American Indian/Alaska Native, 0.0% Native Hawaiian/Other
Pacific Islander, 0.9% Two or more races, 4.3% Hispanic of any race;
Average household size: 2.34; Median age: 46.8; Age under 18: 19.8%;
Age 65 and over: 21.4%; Males per 100 females: 99.0; Marriage status:
20.0% never married, 63.6% now married, 4.4% separated, 5.8%
widowed, 10.6% divorced; Foreign born: 2.8%; Speak English only: 96.0%;
With disability: 19.0%; Veterans: 11.9%; Ancestry: 29.6% German, 18.5%
English, 17.0% Irish, 9.4% Italian, 7.0% Polish
Employment: 16.3% management, business, and financial, 1.1%
computer, engineering, and science, 11.1% education, legal, community
service, arts, and media, 2.8% healthcare practitioners, 14.1% service,
24.8% sales and office, 17.4% natural resources, construction, and
maintenance, 12.4% production, transportation, and material moving
Income: Per capita: $28,194; Median household: $53,409; Average
household: $62,355; Households with income of $100,000 or more: 15.7%;
Poverty rate: 11.0%

Educational Attainment: High school diploma or higher: 91.5%; Bachelor's degree or higher: 21.8%; Graduate/professional degree or higher: 9.5%

Housing: Homeownership rate: 82.9%; Median home value: $88,000; Median year structure built: 1943; Homeowner vacancy rate: 0.0%; Median selected monthly owner costs: $1,017 with a mortgage, $404 without a mortgage; Median gross rent: $642 per month; Rental vacancy rate: 6.8%

Health Insurance: 96.7% have insurance; 77.6% have private insurance; 36.1% have public insurance; 3.3% do not have insurance; 3.4% of children under 18 do not have insurance

Transportation: Commute: 90.6% car, 0.4% public transportation, 4.2% walk, 4.3% work from home; Mean travel time to work: 21.9 minutes

CASTILE (village).
Covers a land area of 1.352 square miles and a water area of 0 square miles. Located at 42.63° N. Lat; 78.05° W. Long. Elevation is 1,355 feet.

Population: 922; Growth (since 2000): -12.3%; Density: 682.0 persons per square mile; Race: 100.0% White, 0.0% Black/African American, 0.0% Asian, 0.0% American Indian/Alaska Native, 0.0% Native Hawaiian/Other Pacific Islander, 0.0% Two or more races, 0.8% Hispanic of any race; Average household size: 2.36; Median age: 41.8; Age under 18: 19.3%; Age 65 and over: 14.6%; Males per 100 females: 93.0; Marriage status: 27.8% never married, 59.3% now married, 7.8% separated, 3.7% widowed, 9.2% divorced; Foreign born: 1.0%; Speak English only: 96.9%; With disability: 19.1%; Veterans: 8.3%; Ancestry: 28.0% German, 24.5% English, 18.8% Irish, 11.6% Italian, 6.7% Polish

Employment: 13.3% management, business, and financial, 2.2% computer, engineering, and science, 10.5% education, legal, community service, arts, and media, 3.5% healthcare practitioners, 22.1% service, 25.4% sales and office, 12.3% natural resources, construction, and maintenance, 10.7% production, transportation, and material moving

Income: Per capita: $24,081; Median household: $47,045; Average household: $56,715; Households with income of $100,000 or more: 15.2%; Poverty rate: 18.8%

Educational Attainment: High school diploma or higher: 91.0%; Bachelor's degree or higher: 18.7%; Graduate/professional degree or higher: 6.7%

Housing: Homeownership rate: 67.2%; Median home value: $82,300; Median year structure built: Before 1940; Homeowner vacancy rate: 0.0%; Median selected monthly owner costs: $1,003 with a mortgage, $362 without a mortgage; Median gross rent: $621 per month; Rental vacancy rate: 0.0%

Health Insurance: 95.9% have insurance; 72.2% have private insurance; 38.9% have public insurance; 4.1% do not have insurance; 3.9% of children under 18 do not have insurance

Transportation: Commute: 96.7% car, 0.0% public transportation, 1.6% walk, 0.2% work from home; Mean travel time to work: 22.9 minutes

COVINGTON (town).
Covers a land area of 26.138 square miles and a water area of 0 square miles. Located at 42.83° N. Lat; 78.01° W. Long. Elevation is 1,102 feet.

Population: 1,002; Growth (since 2000): -26.2%; Density: 38.3 persons per square mile; Race: 96.5% White, 0.5% Black/African American, 0.0% Asian, 0.8% American Indian/Alaska Native, 0.0% Native Hawaiian/Other Pacific Islander, 2.2% Two or more races, 0.8% Hispanic of any race; Average household size: 2.34; Median age: 47.2; Age under 18: 17.9%; Age 65 and over: 14.7%; Males per 100 females: 105.0; Marriage status: 25.8% never married, 58.4% now married, 2.2% separated, 7.8% widowed, 8.0% divorced; Foreign born: 1.2%; Speak English only: 98.2%; With disability: 12.6%; Veterans: 7.8%; Ancestry: 35.8% German, 22.7% Irish, 19.4% English, 14.8% American, 10.0% Italian

Employment: 11.4% management, business, and financial, 1.1% computer, engineering, and science, 8.2% education, legal, community service, arts, and media, 8.9% healthcare practitioners, 10.2% service, 24.7% sales and office, 21.2% natural resources, construction, and maintenance, 14.3% production, transportation, and material moving

Income: Per capita: $28,443; Median household: $61,000; Average household: $66,452; Households with income of $100,000 or more: 19.4%; Poverty rate: 9.2%

Educational Attainment: High school diploma or higher: 89.2%; Bachelor's degree or higher: 16.8%; Graduate/professional degree or higher: 8.2%

Housing: Homeownership rate: 86.2%; Median home value: $106,400; Median year structure built: 1971; Homeowner vacancy rate: 1.8%; Median

selected monthly owner costs: $1,140 with a mortgage, $470 without a mortgage; Median gross rent: $619 per month; Rental vacancy rate: 0.0%

Health Insurance: 94.8% have insurance; 80.9% have private insurance; 34.1% have public insurance; 5.2% do not have insurance; 1.7% of children under 18 do not have insurance

Transportation: Commute: 95.9% car, 0.6% public transportation, 0.6% walk, 2.6% work from home; Mean travel time to work: 25.5 minutes

COWLESVILLE (unincorporated postal area)
ZCTA: 14037

Covers a land area of 17.307 square miles and a water area of 0.008 square miles. Located at 42.80° N. Lat; 78.45° W. Long. Elevation is 945 feet.

Population: 914; Growth (since 2000): -14.3%; Density: 52.8 persons per square mile; Race: 99.0% White, 0.0% Black/African American, 0.0% Asian, 0.0% American Indian/Alaska Native, 0.0% Native Hawaiian/Other Pacific Islander, 0.0% Two or more races, 1.8% Hispanic of any race; Average household size: 2.31; Median age: 50.4; Age under 18: 18.2%; Age 65 and over: 22.1%; Males per 100 females: 105.3; Marriage status: 19.6% never married, 65.9% now married, 0.5% separated, 4.1% widowed, 10.4% divorced; Foreign born: 0.4%; Speak English only: 96.6%; With disability: 10.9%; Veterans: 11.8%; Ancestry: 34.5% German, 28.8% Polish, 12.4% American, 7.4% English, 6.7% Irish

Employment: 8.8% management, business, and financial, 6.9% computer, engineering, and science, 10.2% education, legal, community service, arts, and media, 6.7% healthcare practitioners, 24.7% service, 19.8% sales and office, 12.4% natural resources, construction, and maintenance, 10.6% production, transportation, and material moving

Income: Per capita: $28,006; Median household: $68,056; Average household: $64,016; Households with income of $100,000 or more: 24.7%; Poverty rate: 8.8%

Educational Attainment: High school diploma or higher: 93.2%; Bachelor's degree or higher: 26.9%; Graduate/professional degree or higher: 8.1%

Housing: Homeownership rate: 83.8%; Median home value: $161,100; Median year structure built: 1961; Homeowner vacancy rate: 0.0%; Median selected monthly owner costs: $1,425 with a mortgage, $472 without a mortgage; Median gross rent: $524 per month; Rental vacancy rate: 0.0%

Health Insurance: 92.6% have insurance; 79.2% have private insurance; 35.4% have public insurance; 7.4% do not have insurance; 0.0% of children under 18 do not have insurance

Transportation: Commute: 90.4% car, 0.0% public transportation, 2.7% walk, 2.0% work from home; Mean travel time to work: 27.9 minutes

DALE (unincorporated postal area)
ZCTA: 14039

Covers a land area of 1.868 square miles and a water area of 0 square miles. Located at 42.85° N. Lat; 78.17° W. Long. Elevation is 1,201 feet.

Population: 119; Growth (since 2000): 1.7%; Density: 63.7 persons per square mile; Race: 100.0% White, 0.0% Black/African American, 0.0% Asian, 0.0% American Indian/Alaska Native, 0.0% Native Hawaiian/Other Pacific Islander, 0.0% Two or more races, 0.0% Hispanic of any race; Average household size: 2.64; Median age: 32.7; Age under 18: 26.1%; Age 65 and over: 7.6%; Males per 100 females: 102.0; Marriage status: 20.5% never married, 58.0% now married, 0.0% separated, 0.0% widowed, 21.6% divorced; Foreign born: 0.0%; Speak English only: 100.0%; With disability: 9.2%; Veterans: 11.4%; Ancestry: 23.5% Irish, 18.5% German, 13.4% Polish, 7.6% American, 6.7% French

Employment: 5.9% management, business, and financial, 0.0% computer, engineering, and science, 3.9% education, legal, community service, arts, and media, 0.0% healthcare practitioners, 11.8% service, 19.6% sales and office, 23.5% natural resources, construction, and maintenance, 35.3% production, transportation, and material moving

Income: Per capita: $25,452; Median household: $48,750; Average household: $65,533; Households with income of $100,000 or more: 24.4%; Poverty rate: 13.4%

Educational Attainment: High school diploma or higher: 100.0%; Bachelor's degree or higher: 16.5%; Graduate/professional degree or higher: 2.4%

Housing: Homeownership rate: 64.4%; Median home value: $83,000; Median year structure built: Before 1940; Homeowner vacancy rate: 0.0%; Median selected monthly owner costs: $1,092 with a mortgage,

$0 without a mortgage; Median gross rent: $519 per month; Rental vacancy rate: 0.0%
Health Insurance: 89.9% have insurance; 78.2% have private insurance; 19.3% have public insurance; 10.1% do not have insurance; 0.0% of children under 18 do not have insurance
Transportation: Commute: 100.0% car, 0.0% public transportation, 0.0% walk, 0.0% work from home; Mean travel time to work: 44.9 minutes

EAGLE (town). Covers a land area of 36.283 square miles and a water area of 0.187 square miles. Located at 42.56° N. Lat; 78.25° W. Long. Elevation is 1,768 feet.
Population: 1,332; Growth (since 2000): 11.6%; Density: 36.7 persons per square mile; Race: 99.5% White, 0.5% Black/African American, 0.0% Asian, 0.0% American Indian/Alaska Native, 0.0% Native Hawaiian/Other Pacific Islander, 0.0% Two or more races, 1.3% Hispanic of any race; Average household size: 2.84; Median age: 36.9; Age under 18: 27.6%; Age 65 and over: 11.9%; Males per 100 females: 101.4; Marriage status: 27.6% never married, 54.2% now married, 1.3% separated, 6.2% widowed, 12.0% divorced; Foreign born: 0.6%; Speak English only: 93.6%; With disability: 11.9%; Veterans: 7.6%; Ancestry: 29.1% German, 19.1% Irish, 14.3% Polish, 10.9% English, 8.6% Italian
Employment: 14.0% management, business, and financial, 2.0% computer, engineering, and science, 3.4% education, legal, community service, arts, and media, 4.0% healthcare practitioners, 15.5% service, 22.4% sales and office, 18.0% natural resources, construction, and maintenance, 20.6% production, transportation, and material moving
Income: Per capita: $21,160; Median household: $55,104; Average household: $59,729; Households with income of $100,000 or more: 16.8%; Poverty rate: 12.4%
Educational Attainment: High school diploma or higher: 88.5%; Bachelor's degree or higher: 12.3%; Graduate/professional degree or higher: 3.6%
Housing: Homeownership rate: 88.3%; Median home value: $86,300; Median year structure built: 1967; Homeowner vacancy rate: 2.6%; Median selected monthly owner costs: $1,054 with a mortgage, $412 without a mortgage; Median gross rent: $714 per month; Rental vacancy rate: 0.0%
Health Insurance: 88.9% have insurance; 71.3% have private insurance; 30.0% have public insurance; 11.1% do not have insurance; 20.7% of children under 18 do not have insurance
Transportation: Commute: 92.7% car, 0.5% public transportation, 2.2% walk, 1.4% work from home; Mean travel time to work: 33.8 minutes

GAINESVILLE (town). Covers a land area of 35.570 square miles and a water area of 0.138 square miles. Located at 42.65° N. Lat; 78.13° W. Long. Elevation is 1,617 feet.
Population: 2,242; Growth (since 2000): -3.9%; Density: 63.0 persons per square mile; Race: 96.4% White, 0.0% Black/African American, 1.1% Asian, 0.7% American Indian/Alaska Native, 0.0% Native Hawaiian/Other Pacific Islander, 1.4% Two or more races, 1.9% Hispanic of any race; Average household size: 2.58; Median age: 41.5; Age under 18: 23.7%; Age 65 and over: 14.2%; Males per 100 females: 102.8; Marriage status: 33.9% never married, 47.4% now married, 0.7% separated, 7.2% widowed, 11.5% divorced; Foreign born: 1.8%; Speak English only: 98.7%; With disability: 15.8%; Veterans: 8.5%; Ancestry: 29.4% German, 17.2% English, 9.3% Irish, 8.7% Italian, 8.7% American
Employment: 13.9% management, business, and financial, 2.7% computer, engineering, and science, 5.9% education, legal, community service, arts, and media, 2.2% healthcare practitioners, 23.9% service, 20.7% sales and office, 13.3% natural resources, construction, and maintenance, 17.4% production, transportation, and material moving
Income: Per capita: $22,822; Median household: $50,333; Average household: $58,553; Households with income of $100,000 or more: 13.4%; Poverty rate: 11.5%
Educational Attainment: High school diploma or higher: 88.9%; Bachelor's degree or higher: 11.7%; Graduate/professional degree or higher: 3.8%

School District(s)
Letchworth Central SD (PK-12)
    2014-15 Enrollment: 942 . . . . (585) 493-5450
Housing: Homeownership rate: 80.8%; Median home value: $79,500; Median year structure built: Before 1940; Homeowner vacancy rate: 0.0%; Median selected monthly owner costs: $905 with a mortgage, $470 without a mortgage; Median gross rent: $601 per month; Rental vacancy rate: 2.3%

Health Insurance: 90.7% have insurance; 69.6% have private insurance; 36.2% have public insurance; 9.3% do not have insurance; 10.2% of children under 18 do not have insurance
Transportation: Commute: 91.3% car, 0.8% public transportation, 4.5% walk, 1.6% work from home; Mean travel time to work: 21.2 minutes

GAINESVILLE (village). Covers a land area of 0.856 square miles and a water area of 0 square miles. Located at 42.64° N. Lat; 78.13° W. Long. Elevation is 1,617 feet.
Population: 204; Growth (since 2000): -32.9%; Density: 238.3 persons per square mile; Race: 100.0% White, 0.0% Black/African American, 0.0% Asian, 0.0% American Indian/Alaska Native, 0.0% Native Hawaiian/Other Pacific Islander, 0.0% Two or more races, 0.0% Hispanic of any race; Average household size: 2.22; Median age: 50.6; Age under 18: 17.6%; Age 65 and over: 20.1%; Males per 100 females: 110.1; Marriage status: 26.5% never married, 61.1% now married, 4.3% separated, 4.9% widowed, 7.6% divorced; Foreign born: 1.0%; Speak English only: 99.5%; With disability: 17.2%; Veterans: 7.1%; Ancestry: 39.2% German, 27.0% English, 15.7% Irish, 10.3% Italian, 7.4% Polish
Employment: 3.9% management, business, and financial, 3.9% computer, engineering, and science, 2.0% education, legal, community service, arts, and media, 2.0% healthcare practitioners, 30.4% service, 24.5% sales and office, 21.6% natural resources, construction, and maintenance, 11.8% production, transportation, and material moving
Income: Per capita: $22,342; Median household: $41,250; Average household: $48,810; Households with income of $100,000 or more: 8.7%; Poverty rate: 4.4%
Educational Attainment: High school diploma or higher: 91.1%; Bachelor's degree or higher: 11.5%; Graduate/professional degree or higher: 2.5%

School District(s)
Letchworth Central SD (PK-12)
    2014-15 Enrollment: 942 . . . . (585) 493-5450
Housing: Homeownership rate: 83.7%; Median home value: $71,600; Median year structure built: Before 1940; Homeowner vacancy rate: 0.0%; Median selected monthly owner costs: $673 with a mortgage, $431 without a mortgage; Median gross rent: $568 per month; Rental vacancy rate: 21.1%
Health Insurance: 94.6% have insurance; 64.2% have private insurance; 47.5% have public insurance; 5.4% do not have insurance; 0.0% of children under 18 do not have insurance
Transportation: Commute: 92.0% car, 0.0% public transportation, 2.0% walk, 2.0% work from home; Mean travel time to work: 25.5 minutes

GENESEE FALLS (town). Covers a land area of 15.615 square miles and a water area of 0.086 square miles. Located at 42.57° N. Lat; 78.06° W. Long.
Population: 340; Growth (since 2000): -26.1%; Density: 21.8 persons per square mile; Race: 97.1% White, 0.0% Black/African American, 2.9% Asian, 0.0% American Indian/Alaska Native, 0.0% Native Hawaiian/Other Pacific Islander, 0.0% Two or more races, 2.1% Hispanic of any race; Average household size: 1.86; Median age: 47.9; Age under 18: 9.7%; Age 65 and over: 18.8%; Males per 100 females: 96.4; Marriage status: 26.2% never married, 54.2% now married, 2.5% separated, 8.1% widowed, 11.5% divorced; Foreign born: 1.2%; Speak English only: 99.7%; With disability: 18.8%; Veterans: 10.7%; Ancestry: 27.1% German, 20.0% English, 17.9% Irish, 11.8% American, 10.0% Italian
Employment: 10.5% management, business, and financial, 6.1% computer, engineering, and science, 7.2% education, legal, community service, arts, and media, 5.5% healthcare practitioners, 16.6% service, 22.1% sales and office, 8.8% natural resources, construction, and maintenance, 23.2% production, transportation, and material moving
Income: Per capita: $25,535; Median household: $41,625; Average household: $47,080; Households with income of $100,000 or more: 5.5%; Poverty rate: 12.4%
Educational Attainment: High school diploma or higher: 88.1%; Bachelor's degree or higher: 14.3%; Graduate/professional degree or higher: 3.1%
Housing: Homeownership rate: 75.4%; Median home value: $72,500; Median year structure built: 1964; Homeowner vacancy rate: 0.7%; Median selected monthly owner costs: $1,040 with a mortgage, $384 without a mortgage; Median gross rent: $596 per month; Rental vacancy rate: 0.0%
Health Insurance: 86.2% have insurance; 70.3% have private insurance; 31.5% have public insurance; 13.8% do not have insurance; 9.1% of children under 18 do not have insurance

Transportation: Commute: 87.7% car, 0.6% public transportation, 2.8% walk, 8.4% work from home; Mean travel time to work: 25.2 minutes

JAVA (town). Covers a land area of 47.128 square miles and a water area of 0.202 square miles. Located at 42.65° N. Lat; 78.39° W. Long. Elevation is 1,522 feet.
Population: 1,925; Growth (since 2000): -13.4%; Density: 40.8 persons per square mile; Race: 97.3% White, 0.6% Black/African American, 0.0% Asian, 0.0% American Indian/Alaska Native, 0.0% Native Hawaiian/Other Pacific Islander, 2.1% Two or more races, 0.0% Hispanic of any race; Average household size: 2.34; Median age: 42.0; Age under 18: 19.8%; Age 65 and over: 15.3%; Males per 100 females: 106.5; Marriage status: 29.2% never married, 56.8% now married, 0.8% separated, 4.5% widowed, 9.6% divorced; Foreign born: 0.8%; Speak English only: 98.0%; With disability: 9.3%; Veterans: 10.2%; Ancestry: 46.9% German, 24.2% Irish, 16.7% Polish, 13.7% English, 5.2% Italian
Employment: 14.3% management, business, and financial, 2.0% computer, engineering, and science, 7.4% education, legal, community service, arts, and media, 3.5% healthcare practitioners, 15.9% service, 22.6% sales and office, 15.5% natural resources, construction, and maintenance, 18.9% production, transportation, and material moving
Income: Per capita: $25,472; Median household: $50,278; Average household: $59,434; Households with income of $100,000 or more: 13.1%; Poverty rate: 6.0%
Educational Attainment: High school diploma or higher: 90.9%; Bachelor's degree or higher: 16.4%; Graduate/professional degree or higher: 5.1%
Housing: Homeownership rate: 80.0%; Median home value: $129,900; Median year structure built: 1952; Homeowner vacancy rate: 0.0%; Median selected monthly owner costs: $1,264 with a mortgage, $461 without a mortgage; Median gross rent: $666 per month; Rental vacancy rate: 0.0%
Health Insurance: 91.6% have insurance; 78.5% have private insurance; 27.2% have public insurance; 8.4% do not have insurance; 2.6% of children under 18 do not have insurance
Transportation: Commute: 92.0% car, 0.3% public transportation, 3.7% walk, 3.6% work from home; Mean travel time to work: 28.1 minutes

JAVA CENTER (unincorporated postal area)
ZCTA: 14082
Covers a land area of 9.929 square miles and a water area of 0.111 square miles. Located at 42.66° N. Lat; 78.38° W. Long. Elevation is 1,522 feet.
Population: 348; Growth (since 2000): -18.7%; Density: 35.0 persons per square mile; Race: 100.0% White, 0.0% Black/African American, 0.0% Asian, 0.0% American Indian/Alaska Native, 0.0% Native Hawaiian/Other Pacific Islander, 0.0% Two or more races, 0.0% Hispanic of any race; Average household size: 2.00; Median age: 55.7; Age under 18: 10.3%; Age 65 and over: 19.8%; Males per 100 females: 105.8; Marriage status: 23.0% never married, 64.4% now married, 0.0% separated, 3.8% widowed, 8.8% divorced; Foreign born: 0.0%; Speak English only: 100.0%; With disability: 9.8%; Veterans: 8.3%; Ancestry: 63.5% German, 29.0% Irish, 12.9% Italian, 12.4% Polish, 8.6% English
Employment: 14.0% management, business, and financial, 0.0% computer, engineering, and science, 13.5% education, legal, community service, arts, and media, 1.6% healthcare practitioners, 6.7% service, 28.0% sales and office, 11.9% natural resources, construction, and maintenance, 24.4% production, transportation, and material moving
Income: Per capita: $27,462; Median household: $44,063; Average household: $53,608; Households with income of $100,000 or more: 6.9%; Poverty rate: 2.6%
Educational Attainment: High school diploma or higher: 83.4%; Bachelor's degree or higher: 17.9%; Graduate/professional degree or higher: 5.2%
Housing: Homeownership rate: 81.0%; Median home value: $161,300; Median year structure built: 1956; Homeowner vacancy rate: 0.0%; Median selected monthly owner costs: $1,388 with a mortgage, $416 without a mortgage; Median gross rent: $689 per month; Rental vacancy rate: 0.0%
Health Insurance: 100.0% have insurance; 80.2% have private insurance; 33.9% have public insurance; 0.0% do not have insurance; 0.0% of children under 18 do not have insurance
Transportation: Commute: 88.6% car, 1.6% public transportation, 2.1% walk, 7.8% work from home; Mean travel time to work: 25.6 minutes

MIDDLEBURY (town). Covers a land area of 35.643 square miles and a water area of 0.025 square miles. Located at 42.82° N. Lat; 78.13° W. Long.
Population: 1,462; Growth (since 2000): -3.1%; Density: 41.0 persons per square mile; Race: 98.2% White, 1.8% Black/African American, 0.0% Asian, 0.0% American Indian/Alaska Native, 0.0% Native Hawaiian/Other Pacific Islander, 0.0% Two or more races, 1.0% Hispanic of any race; Average household size: 2.43; Median age: 42.7; Age under 18: 21.4%; Age 65 and over: 16.5%; Males per 100 females: 105.6; Marriage status: 26.6% never married, 61.5% now married, 1.6% separated, 2.6% widowed, 9.3% divorced; Foreign born: 1.6%; Speak English only: 98.0%; With disability: 17.4%; Veterans: 9.3%; Ancestry: 28.2% German, 22.5% Irish, 19.3% English, 8.5% Italian, 7.3% American
Employment: 15.3% management, business, and financial, 2.7% computer, engineering, and science, 14.4% education, legal, community service, arts, and media, 3.8% healthcare practitioners, 16.4% service, 21.3% sales and office, 11.3% natural resources, construction, and maintenance, 14.9% production, transportation, and material moving
Income: Per capita: $28,894; Median household: $59,231; Average household: $70,128; Households with income of $100,000 or more: 24.4%; Poverty rate: 8.8%
Educational Attainment: High school diploma or higher: 93.7%; Bachelor's degree or higher: 26.4%; Graduate/professional degree or higher: 8.5%
Housing: Homeownership rate: 82.2%; Median home value: $101,500; Median year structure built: Before 1940; Homeowner vacancy rate: 2.2%; Median selected monthly owner costs: $1,219 with a mortgage, $466 without a mortgage; Median gross rent: $567 per month; Rental vacancy rate: 0.0%
Health Insurance: 93.2% have insurance; 77.9% have private insurance; 33.7% have public insurance; 6.8% do not have insurance; 3.8% of children under 18 do not have insurance
Transportation: Commute: 95.3% car, 0.2% public transportation, 1.1% walk, 2.9% work from home; Mean travel time to work: 29.3 minutes

NORTH JAVA (unincorporated postal area)
ZCTA: 14113
Covers a land area of 17.021 square miles and a water area of <.001 square miles. Located at 42.67° N. Lat; 78.34° W. Long. Elevation is 1,562 feet.
Population: 602; Growth (since 2000): -22.3%; Density: 35.4 persons per square mile; Race: 98.5% White, 0.0% Black/African American, 0.0% Asian, 0.0% American Indian/Alaska Native, 0.0% Native Hawaiian/Other Pacific Islander, 1.5% Two or more races, 1.7% Hispanic of any race; Average household size: 2.29; Median age: 43.2; Age under 18: 10.0%; Age 65 and over: 12.5%; Males per 100 females: 109.2; Marriage status: 30.0% never married, 49.1% now married, 1.3% separated, 7.5% widowed, 13.4% divorced; Foreign born: 3.2%; Speak English only: 95.8%; With disability: 10.1%; Veterans: 13.7%; Ancestry: 49.0% German, 28.7% Irish, 18.3% Polish, 10.5% English, 3.8% Italian
Employment: 11.5% management, business, and financial, 0.0% computer, engineering, and science, 5.4% education, legal, community service, arts, and media, 1.3% healthcare practitioners, 25.2% service, 21.2% sales and office, 20.4% natural resources, construction, and maintenance, 15.0% production, transportation, and material moving
Income: Per capita: $26,348; Median household: $41,359; Average household: $59,602; Households with income of $100,000 or more: 7.3%; Poverty rate: 13.1%
Educational Attainment: High school diploma or higher: 96.0%; Bachelor's degree or higher: 16.4%; Graduate/professional degree or higher: 6.4%
Housing: Homeownership rate: 76.8%; Median home value: $120,200; Median year structure built: 1944; Homeowner vacancy rate: 0.0%; Median selected monthly owner costs: $1,028 with a mortgage, $510 without a mortgage; Median gross rent: $588 per month; Rental vacancy rate: 0.0%
Health Insurance: 82.9% have insurance; 72.9% have private insurance; 21.6% have public insurance; 17.1% do not have insurance; 8.3% of children under 18 do not have insurance
Transportation: Commute: 88.2% car, 0.0% public transportation, 8.6% walk, 3.2% work from home; Mean travel time to work: 29.9 minutes

ORANGEVILLE (town). Covers a land area of 35.560 square miles and a water area of 0.082 square miles. Located at 42.74° N. Lat; 78.25° W. Long.

Population: 1,612; Growth (since 2000): 23.9%; Density: 45.3 persons per square mile; Race: 99.0% White, 0.0% Black/African American, 0.2% Asian, 0.0% American Indian/Alaska Native, 0.0% Native Hawaiian/Other Pacific Islander, 0.3% Two or more races, 1.6% Hispanic of any race; Average household size: 2.52; Median age: 41.5; Age under 18: 19.0%; Age 65 and over: 15.4%; Males per 100 females: 108.5; Marriage status: 26.1% never married, 64.2% now married, 0.7% separated, 3.0% widowed, 6.7% divorced; Foreign born: 1.5%; Speak English only: 97.7%; With disability: 11.0%; Veterans: 9.0%; Ancestry: 49.3% German, 16.0% Polish, 10.2% English, 10.2% Irish, 8.0% Italian

Employment: 13.7% management, business, and financial, 6.7% computer, engineering, and science, 5.9% education, legal, community service, arts, and media, 5.5% healthcare practitioners, 16.2% service, 23.5% sales and office, 18.6% natural resources, construction, and maintenance, 9.9% production, transportation, and material moving

Income: Per capita: $27,548; Median household: $59,922; Average household: $68,543; Households with income of $100,000 or more: 18.8%; Poverty rate: 6.0%

Educational Attainment: High school diploma or higher: 93.4%; Bachelor's degree or higher: 21.4%; Graduate/professional degree or higher: 5.0%

Housing: Homeownership rate: 85.9%; Median home value: $134,500; Median year structure built: 1971; Homeowner vacancy rate: 0.0%; Median selected monthly owner costs: $1,256 with a mortgage, $589 without a mortgage; Median gross rent: $630 per month; Rental vacancy rate: 0.0%

Health Insurance: 96.7% have insurance; 84.9% have private insurance; 28.0% have public insurance; 3.3% do not have insurance; 2.3% of children under 18 do not have insurance

Transportation: Commute: 88.3% car, 0.5% public transportation, 3.4% walk, 7.8% work from home; Mean travel time to work: 27.2 minutes

PERRY (town). Covers a land area of 36.405 square miles and a water area of 0.242 square miles. Located at 42.75° N. Lat; 78.01° W. Long. Elevation is 1,371 feet.

History: In 1833, the Reverend William Arthur became pastor of the First Baptist Church in Perry. His son, Chester Alan Arthur, then four yeas old, was destined to become the 21st President of the United States.

Population: 4,497; Growth (since 2000): -32.4%; Density: 123.5 persons per square mile; Race: 99.8% White, 0.2% Black/African American, 0.0% Asian, 0.0% American Indian/Alaska Native, 0.0% Native Hawaiian/Other Pacific Islander, 0.0% Two or more races, 0.5% Hispanic of any race; Average household size: 2.41; Median age: 38.5; Age under 18: 24.7%; Age 65 and over: 17.1%; Males per 100 females: 94.8; Marriage status: 26.1% never married, 59.0% now married, 1.3% separated, 4.5% widowed, 10.4% divorced; Foreign born: 0.9%; Speak English only: 97.2%; With disability: 13.3%; Veterans: 12.7%; Ancestry: 29.4% German, 20.7% Irish, 13.4% English, 12.9% Italian, 10.7% Polish

Employment: 9.3% management, business, and financial, 4.6% computer, engineering, and science, 11.4% education, legal, community service, arts, and media, 5.5% healthcare practitioners, 15.3% service, 17.1% sales and office, 16.6% natural resources, construction, and maintenance, 20.3% production, transportation, and material moving

Income: Per capita: $25,784; Median household: $50,617; Average household: $62,583; Households with income of $100,000 or more: 10.9%; Poverty rate: 12.9%

Educational Attainment: High school diploma or higher: 88.1%; Bachelor's degree or higher: 16.6%; Graduate/professional degree or higher: 6.0%

School District(s)

Perry Central SD (PK-12)
    2014-15 Enrollment: 864 . . . . (585) 237-0270

Housing: Homeownership rate: 69.5%; Median home value: $82,800; Median year structure built: Before 1940; Homeowner vacancy rate: 0.0%; Median selected monthly owner costs: $1,064 with a mortgage, $428 without a mortgage; Median gross rent: $589 per month; Rental vacancy rate: 4.6%

Health Insurance: 88.4% have insurance; 66.3% have private insurance; 37.2% have public insurance; 11.6% do not have insurance; 9.5% of children under 18 do not have insurance

Newspapers: Perry Herald (weekly circulation 900)

Transportation: Commute: 92.5% car, 0.0% public transportation, 3.2% walk, 0.6% work from home; Mean travel time to work: 25.0 minutes

Additional Information Contacts
Town of Perry . . . . (585) 237-2241
    http://www.townofperryny.com

PERRY (village). Covers a land area of 2.337 square miles and a water area of 0.112 square miles. Located at 42.72° N. Lat; 78.01° W. Long. Elevation is 1,371 feet.

Population: 3,462; Growth (since 2000): -12.2%; Density: 1,481.1 persons per square mile; Race: 99.2% White, 0.3% Black/African American, 0.0% Asian, 0.0% American Indian/Alaska Native, 0.0% Native Hawaiian/Other Pacific Islander, 0.5% Two or more races, 0.7% Hispanic of any race; Average household size: 2.32; Median age: 35.4; Age under 18: 25.4%; Age 65 and over: 17.2%; Males per 100 females: 91.0; Marriage status: 27.8% never married, 55.6% now married, 1.3% separated, 5.4% widowed, 11.2% divorced; Foreign born: 0.9%; Speak English only: 96.9%; With disability: 14.4%; Veterans: 14.4%; Ancestry: 25.2% German, 20.8% Irish, 14.3% English, 13.4% Italian, 11.6% Polish

Employment: 9.1% management, business, and financial, 4.2% computer, engineering, and science, 13.6% education, legal, community service, arts, and media, 7.6% healthcare practitioners, 16.3% service, 16.6% sales and office, 12.3% natural resources, construction, and maintenance, 20.3% production, transportation, and material moving

Income: Per capita: $24,007; Median household: $46,462; Average household: $56,550; Households with income of $100,000 or more: 7.2%; Poverty rate: 14.6%

Educational Attainment: High school diploma or higher: 86.7%; Bachelor's degree or higher: 18.0%; Graduate/professional degree or higher: 5.6%

School District(s)

Perry Central SD (PK-12)
    2014-15 Enrollment: 864 . . . . (585) 237-0270

Housing: Homeownership rate: 63.7%; Median home value: $76,500; Median year structure built: Before 1940; Homeowner vacancy rate: 0.0%; Median selected monthly owner costs: $991 with a mortgage, $420 without a mortgage; Median gross rent: $590 per month; Rental vacancy rate: 4.9%

Health Insurance: 90.8% have insurance; 67.2% have private insurance; 40.1% have public insurance; 9.2% do not have insurance; 1.5% of children under 18 do not have insurance

Safety: Violent crime rate: 19.9 per 10,000 population; Property crime rate: 170.6 per 10,000 population

Newspapers: Perry Herald (weekly circulation 900)

Transportation: Commute: 91.7% car, 0.0% public transportation, 3.4% walk, 0.3% work from home; Mean travel time to work: 21.3 minutes

Additional Information Contacts
Village of Perry . . . . (585) 237-2216
    http://www.villageofperry.com

PIKE (CDP). Covers a land area of 1.494 square miles and a water area of <.001 square miles. Located at 42.55° N. Lat; 78.15° W. Long. Elevation is 1,545 feet.

Population: 233; Growth (since 2000): -39.0%; Density: 156.0 persons per square mile; Race: 91.0% White, 6.9% Black/African American, 0.0% Asian, 0.0% American Indian/Alaska Native, 0.0% Native Hawaiian/Other Pacific Islander, 2.1% Two or more races, 0.0% Hispanic of any race; Average household size: 2.18; Median age: 48.4; Age under 18: 24.5%; Age 65 and over: 15.0%; Males per 100 females: 101.6; Marriage status: 35.3% never married, 46.7% now married, 0.0% separated, 1.6% widowed, 16.3% divorced; Foreign born: 0.0%; Speak English only: 100.0%; With disability: 17.6%; Veterans: 14.2%; Ancestry: 35.2% German, 24.9% English, 11.2% Irish, 10.7% Polish, 8.6% Welsh

Employment: 7.4% management, business, and financial, 0.0% computer, engineering, and science, 3.2% education, legal, community service, arts, and media, 13.8% healthcare practitioners, 23.4% service, 10.6% sales and office, 28.7% natural resources, construction, and maintenance, 12.8% production, transportation, and material moving

Income: Per capita: $20,289; Median household: $34,653; Average household: $45,056; Households with income of $100,000 or more: 9.3%; Poverty rate: 27.5%

Educational Attainment: High school diploma or higher: 90.3%; Bachelor's degree or higher: 4.5%; Graduate/professional degree or higher: 2.6%

Housing: Homeownership rate: 76.6%; Median home value: $53,300; Median year structure built: Before 1940; Homeowner vacancy rate: 0.0%; Median selected monthly owner costs: $856 with a mortgage, $405 without

a mortgage; Median gross rent: $688 per month; Rental vacancy rate: 0.0%

Health Insurance: 92.3% have insurance; 60.1% have private insurance; 50.6% have public insurance; 7.7% do not have insurance; 0.0% of children under 18 do not have insurance

Transportation: Commute: 100.0% car, 0.0% public transportation, 0.0% walk, 0.0% work from home; Mean travel time to work: 33.9 minutes

---

PIKE (town). Covers a land area of 31.084 square miles and a water area of 0.145 square miles. Located at 42.57° N. Lat; 78.14° W. Long. Elevation is 1,545 feet.

Population: 1,013; Growth (since 2000): -6.7%; Density: 32.6 persons per square mile; Race: 95.2% White, 1.6% Black/African American, 1.5% Asian, 0.0% American Indian/Alaska Native, 0.0% Native Hawaiian/Other Pacific Islander, 1.8% Two or more races, 2.5% Hispanic of any race; Average household size: 2.42; Median age: 43.7; Age under 18: 25.5%; Age 65 and over: 12.9%; Males per 100 females: 104.4; Marriage status: 25.7% never married, 57.9% now married, 5.5% separated, 2.1% widowed, 14.3% divorced; Foreign born: 1.0%; Speak English only: 96.5%; With disability: 14.3%; Veterans: 17.2%; Ancestry: 28.6% German, 15.8% English, 15.3% Irish, 13.0% American, 8.2% Polish

Employment: 7.1% management, business, and financial, 3.2% computer, engineering, and science, 6.1% education, legal, community service, arts, and media, 7.4% healthcare practitioners, 16.0% service, 20.3% sales and office, 27.1% natural resources, construction, and maintenance, 12.8% production, transportation, and material moving

Income: Per capita: $24,860; Median household: $49,922; Average household: $60,180; Households with income of $100,000 or more: 15.1%; Poverty rate: 15.4%

Educational Attainment: High school diploma or higher: 91.4%; Bachelor's degree or higher: 11.2%; Graduate/professional degree or higher: 6.4%

Housing: Homeownership rate: 84.2%; Median home value: $75,000; Median year structure built: 1965; Homeowner vacancy rate: 0.0%; Median selected monthly owner costs: $1,129 with a mortgage, $448 without a mortgage; Median gross rent: $667 per month; Rental vacancy rate: 0.0%

Health Insurance: 91.0% have insurance; 74.9% have private insurance; 34.8% have public insurance; 9.0% do not have insurance; 4.7% of children under 18 do not have insurance

Transportation: Commute: 93.5% car, 1.5% public transportation, 1.3% walk, 2.0% work from home; Mean travel time to work: 27.9 minutes

---

PORTAGEVILLE (unincorporated postal area)
ZCTA: 14536

Covers a land area of 18.222 square miles and a water area of 0.164 square miles. Located at 42.54° N. Lat; 78.08° W. Long. Elevation is 1,115 feet.

Population: 525; Growth (since 2000): -20.9%; Density: 28.8 persons per square mile; Race: 97.0% White, 0.0% Black/African American, 1.9% Asian, 0.0% American Indian/Alaska Native, 0.0% Native Hawaiian/Other Pacific Islander, 1.1% Two or more races, 6.9% Hispanic of any race; Average household size: 2.09; Median age: 47.4; Age under 18: 18.7%; Age 65 and over: 19.6%; Males per 100 females: 103.3; Marriage status: 19.8% never married, 62.2% now married, 2.7% separated, 7.3% widowed, 10.7% divorced; Foreign born: 2.1%; Speak English only: 94.4%; With disability: 18.3%; Veterans: 13.3%; Ancestry: 26.5% German, 23.4% American, 13.9% Irish, 10.5% English, 7.8% Dutch

Employment: 12.2% management, business, and financial, 5.0% computer, engineering, and science, 4.5% education, legal, community service, arts, and media, 5.9% healthcare practitioners, 14.0% service, 28.8% sales and office, 14.4% natural resources, construction, and maintenance, 15.3% production, transportation, and material moving

Income: Per capita: $23,355; Median household: $42,438; Average household: $48,690; Households with income of $100,000 or more: 8.4%; Poverty rate: 17.6%

Educational Attainment: High school diploma or higher: 85.8%; Bachelor's degree or higher: 9.0%; Graduate/professional degree or higher: 3.5%

Housing: Homeownership rate: 77.7%; Median home value: $71,500; Median year structure built: 1962; Homeowner vacancy rate: 4.9%; Median selected monthly owner costs: $987 with a mortgage, $405 without a mortgage; Median gross rent: $600 per month; Rental vacancy rate: 0.0%

Health Insurance: 87.6% have insurance; 65.9% have private insurance; 40.0% have public insurance; 12.4% do not have insurance; 3.1% of children under 18 do not have insurance

Transportation: Commute: 94.6% car, 0.5% public transportation, 0.5% walk, 4.1% work from home; Mean travel time to work: 30.2 minutes

---

SHELDON (town). Covers a land area of 47.348 square miles and a water area of 0.025 square miles. Located at 42.75° N. Lat; 78.38° W. Long. Elevation is 1,512 feet.

Population: 2,383; Growth (since 2000): -7.0%; Density: 50.3 persons per square mile; Race: 95.8% White, 3.4% Black/African American, 0.2% Asian, 0.0% American Indian/Alaska Native, 0.0% Native Hawaiian/Other Pacific Islander, 0.6% Two or more races, 1.1% Hispanic of any race; Average household size: 2.44; Median age: 45.7; Age under 18: 20.4%; Age 65 and over: 17.3%; Males per 100 females: 110.9; Marriage status: 27.0% never married, 58.9% now married, 2.1% separated, 4.7% widowed, 9.3% divorced; Foreign born: 1.7%; Speak English only: 97.0%; With disability: 10.3%; Veterans: 9.6%; Ancestry: 50.2% German, 17.4% Irish, 15.6% Polish, 8.7% English, 7.5% American

Employment: 12.0% management, business, and financial, 0.6% computer, engineering, and science, 8.5% education, legal, community service, arts, and media, 3.0% healthcare practitioners, 16.6% service, 23.7% sales and office, 17.6% natural resources, construction, and maintenance, 17.9% production, transportation, and material moving

Income: Per capita: $27,604; Median household: $56,927; Average household: $66,841; Households with income of $100,000 or more: 16.0%; Poverty rate: 8.5%

Educational Attainment: High school diploma or higher: 90.7%; Bachelor's degree or higher: 13.2%; Graduate/professional degree or higher: 5.1%

Housing: Homeownership rate: 77.8%; Median home value: $135,600; Median year structure built: 1962; Homeowner vacancy rate: 0.0%; Median selected monthly owner costs: $1,135 with a mortgage, $469 without a mortgage; Median gross rent: $657 per month; Rental vacancy rate: 0.0%

Health Insurance: 95.2% have insurance; 80.9% have private insurance; 28.4% have public insurance; 4.8% do not have insurance; 0.0% of children under 18 do not have insurance

Transportation: Commute: 88.9% car, 0.6% public transportation, 5.4% walk, 3.9% work from home; Mean travel time to work: 31.9 minutes

---

SILVER LAKE (unincorporated postal area)
ZCTA: 14549

Covers a land area of 0.112 square miles and a water area of 0 square miles. Located at 42.70° N. Lat; 78.02° W. Long. Elevation is 1,375 feet.

Population: 23; Growth (since 2000): n/a; Density: 204.7 persons per square mile; Race: 100.0% White, 0.0% Black/African American, 0.0% Asian, 0.0% American Indian/Alaska Native, 0.0% Native Hawaiian/Other Pacific Islander, 0.0% Two or more races, 0.0% Hispanic of any race; Average household size: 1.64; Median age: 60.7; Age under 18: 17.4%; Age 65 and over: 43.5%; Males per 100 females: 71.7; Marriage status: 17.4% never married, 43.5% now married, 0.0% separated, 0.0% widowed, 39.1% divorced; Foreign born: 0.0%; Speak English only: 100.0%; With disability: 0.0%; Veterans: 0.0%; Ancestry: 65.2% English, 21.7% Irish, 21.7% Italian

Employment: 0.0% management, business, and financial, 0.0% computer, engineering, and science, 35.7% education, legal, community service, arts, and media, 0.0% healthcare practitioners, 0.0% service, 64.3% sales and office, 0.0% natural resources, construction, and maintenance, 0.0% production, transportation, and material moving

Income: Per capita: $29,335; Median household: $31,944; Average household: $48,193; Households with income of $100,000 or more: n/a; Poverty rate: n/a

Educational Attainment: High school diploma or higher: 100.0%; Bachelor's degree or higher: 78.9%; Graduate/professional degree or higher: 52.6%

Housing: Homeownership rate: 71.4%; Median home value: n/a; Median year structure built: 1943; Homeowner vacancy rate: 0.0%; Median selected monthly owner costs: $0 with a mortgage, $0 without a mortgage; Median gross rent: n/a per month; Rental vacancy rate: 0.0%

Health Insurance: 100.0% have insurance; 100.0% have private insurance; 43.5% have public insurance; 0.0% do not have insurance; 0.0% of children under 18 do not have insurance

Transportation: Commute: 64.3% car, 35.7% public transportation, 0.0% walk, 0.0% work from home; Mean travel time to work: 0.0 minutes

SILVER SPRINGS (village). Covers a land area of 0.952 square miles and a water area of 0.027 square miles. Located at 42.66° N. Lat; 78.08° W. Long. Elevation is 1,414 feet.
Population: 951; Growth (since 2000): 12.7%; Density: 998.6 persons per square mile; Race: 93.9% White, 0.0% Black/African American, 1.2% Asian, 1.4% American Indian/Alaska Native, 0.0% Native Hawaiian/Other Pacific Islander, 2.9% Two or more races, 4.1% Hispanic of any race; Average household size: 2.51; Median age: 39.8; Age under 18: 25.4%; Age 65 and over: 13.9%; Males per 100 females: 89.3; Marriage status: 39.8% never married, 33.1% now married, 0.7% separated, 10.8% widowed, 16.3% divorced; Foreign born: 2.3%; Speak English only: 97.9%; With disability: 20.7%; Veterans: 5.4%; Ancestry: 28.2% German, 13.9% English, 11.5% Irish, 9.7% Polish, 9.3% Italian
Employment: 9.0% management, business, and financial, 3.2% computer, engineering, and science, 2.3% education, legal, community service, arts, and media, 3.0% healthcare practitioners, 28.9% service, 24.3% sales and office, 16.9% natural resources, construction, and maintenance, 12.3% production, transportation, and material moving
Income: Per capita: $19,935; Median household: $39,519; Average household: $49,722; Households with income of $100,000 or more: 10.3%; Poverty rate: 21.8%
Educational Attainment: High school diploma or higher: 83.1%; Bachelor's degree or higher: 7.7%; Graduate/professional degree or higher: 1.1%
Housing: Homeownership rate: 66.5%; Median home value: $76,200; Median year structure built: Before 1940; Homeowner vacancy rate: 0.0%; Median selected monthly owner costs: $864 with a mortgage, $457 without a mortgage; Median gross rent: $591 per month; Rental vacancy rate: 0.0%
Health Insurance: 87.3% have insurance; 55.8% have private insurance; 46.2% have public insurance; 12.7% do not have insurance; 12.0% of children under 18 do not have insurance
Transportation: Commute: 83.8% car, 2.1% public transportation, 9.8% walk, 2.1% work from home; Mean travel time to work: 19.4 minutes

STRYKERSVILLE (CDP). Covers a land area of 3.420 square miles and a water area of 0 square miles. Located at 42.71° N. Lat; 78.45° W. Long. Elevation is 1,083 feet.
Population: 719; Growth (since 2000): n/a; Density: 210.2 persons per square mile; Race: 96.9% White, 3.1% Black/African American, 0.0% Asian, 0.0% American Indian/Alaska Native, 0.0% Native Hawaiian/Other Pacific Islander, 0.0% Two or more races, 0.0% Hispanic of any race; Average household size: 2.66; Median age: 38.2; Age under 18: 30.6%; Age 65 and over: 13.4%; Males per 100 females: 93.1; Marriage status: 30.1% never married, 53.8% now married, 0.0% separated, 7.0% widowed, 9.1% divorced; Foreign born: 0.0%; Speak English only: 97.6%; With disability: 5.8%; Veterans: 3.6%; Ancestry: 52.0% German, 20.6% Polish, 16.8% Irish, 7.8% English, 7.8% French
Employment: 19.5% management, business, and financial, 0.0% computer, engineering, and science, 4.4% education, legal, community service, arts, and media, 2.6% healthcare practitioners, 14.2% service, 29.7% sales and office, 11.9% natural resources, construction, and maintenance, 17.7% production, transportation, and material moving
Income: Per capita: $25,905; Median household: $55,682; Average household: $68,402; Households with income of $100,000 or more: 20.7%; Poverty rate: 2.6%
Educational Attainment: High school diploma or higher: 94.9%; Bachelor's degree or higher: 20.5%; Graduate/professional degree or higher: 4.8%
Housing: Homeownership rate: 77.0%; Median home value: $140,900; Median year structure built: 1958; Homeowner vacancy rate: 0.0%; Median selected monthly owner costs: $1,303 with a mortgage, $461 without a mortgage; Median gross rent: $538 per month; Rental vacancy rate: 0.0%
Health Insurance: 98.5% have insurance; 88.5% have private insurance; 22.9% have public insurance; 1.5% do not have insurance; 0.0% of children under 18 do not have insurance
Transportation: Commute: 87.9% car, 0.0% public transportation, 9.4% walk, 1.2% work from home; Mean travel time to work: 34.6 minutes

VARYSBURG (unincorporated postal area)
ZCTA: 14167
   Covers a land area of 37.669 square miles and a water area of 0.004 square miles. Located at 42.75° N. Lat; 78.32° W. Long. Elevation is 1,158 feet.

Population: 1,812; Growth (since 2000): 10.1%; Density: 48.1 persons per square mile; Race: 95.1% White, 3.2% Black/African American, 0.4% Asian, 0.0% American Indian/Alaska Native, 0.0% Native Hawaiian/Other Pacific Islander, 0.8% Two or more races, 2.3% Hispanic of any race; Average household size: 2.47; Median age: 42.6; Age under 18: 19.7%; Age 65 and over: 15.1%; Males per 100 females: 117.1; Marriage status: 28.9% never married, 59.0% now married, 2.5% separated, 2.2% widowed, 9.9% divorced; Foreign born: 2.0%; Speak English only: 96.9%; With disability: 9.5%; Veterans: 10.8%; Ancestry: 49.2% German, 19.3% Polish, 10.5% Irish, 9.5% English, 9.1% Italian
Employment: 10.4% management, business, and financial, 2.7% computer, engineering, and science, 7.5% education, legal, community service, arts, and media, 3.7% healthcare practitioners, 12.4% service, 26.0% sales and office, 22.9% natural resources, construction, and maintenance, 14.3% production, transportation, and material moving
Income: Per capita: $26,602; Median household: $59,306; Average household: $65,507; Households with income of $100,000 or more: 16.9%; Poverty rate: 10.4%
Educational Attainment: High school diploma or higher: 92.9%; Bachelor's degree or higher: 14.4%; Graduate/professional degree or higher: 4.4%

School District(s)
Attica Central SD (KG-12)
   2014-15 Enrollment: 1,374 . . . . (585) 591-2173
Housing: Homeownership rate: 77.5%; Median home value: $138,000; Median year structure built: 1967; Homeowner vacancy rate: 0.0%; Median selected monthly owner costs: $1,175 with a mortgage, $546 without a mortgage; Median gross rent: $656 per month; Rental vacancy rate: 0.0%
Health Insurance: 93.6% have insurance; 78.6% have private insurance; 30.3% have public insurance; 6.4% do not have insurance; 2.0% of children under 18 do not have insurance
Transportation: Commute: 83.6% car, 0.4% public transportation, 6.7% walk, 8.1% work from home; Mean travel time to work: 30.4 minutes

WARSAW (town). Covers a land area of 35.416 square miles and a water area of 0.050 square miles. Located at 42.74° N. Lat; 78.13° W. Long. Elevation is 1,014 feet.
Population: 4,989; Growth (since 2000): -8.0%; Density: 140.9 persons per square mile; Race: 96.6% White, 0.3% Black/African American, 0.0% Asian, 0.0% American Indian/Alaska Native, 0.0% Native Hawaiian/Other Pacific Islander, 2.3% Two or more races, 1.9% Hispanic of any race; Average household size: 2.15; Median age: 44.9; Age under 18: 19.6%; Age 65 and over: 18.2%; Males per 100 females: 91.4; Marriage status: 25.6% never married, 48.7% now married, 1.7% separated, 9.7% widowed, 16.0% divorced; Foreign born: 0.9%; Speak English only: 98.3%; With disability: 15.4%; Veterans: 7.8%; Ancestry: 37.5% German, 17.3% Irish, 15.9% English, 11.0% Italian, 8.5% Polish
Employment: 9.7% management, business, and financial, 3.0% computer, engineering, and science, 2.4% education, legal, community service, arts, and media, 11.4% healthcare practitioners, 16.6% service, 28.4% sales and office, 14.4% natural resources, construction, and maintenance, 14.2% production, transportation, and material moving
Income: Per capita: $27,305; Median household: $45,035; Average household: $59,678; Households with income of $100,000 or more: 16.6%; Poverty rate: 20.7%
Educational Attainment: High school diploma or higher: 83.3%; Bachelor's degree or higher: 11.6%; Graduate/professional degree or higher: 3.9%

School District(s)
Warsaw Central SD (KG-12)
   2014-15 Enrollment: 899 . . . . (585) 786-8000
Housing: Homeownership rate: 60.2%; Median home value: $96,300; Median year structure built: Before 1940; Homeowner vacancy rate: 2.7%; Median selected monthly owner costs: $1,023 with a mortgage, $499 without a mortgage; Median gross rent: $559 per month; Rental vacancy rate: 0.0%
Health Insurance: 90.2% have insurance; 64.5% have private insurance; 40.6% have public insurance; 9.8% do not have insurance; 11.8% of children under 18 do not have insurance
Hospitals: Wyoming County Community Hospital (264 beds)
Newspapers: Warsaw's Country Courier (weekly circulation 2,000)
Transportation: Commute: 92.0% car, 0.3% public transportation, 5.3% walk, 0.5% work from home; Mean travel time to work: 21.6 minutes

WARSAW (village). County seat. Covers a land area of 4.106 square miles and a water area of 0 square miles. Located at 42.74° N. Lat; 78.14° W. Long. Elevation is 1,014 feet.

Population: 3,519; Growth (since 2000): -7.7%; Density: 857.1 persons per square mile; Race: 95.2% White, 0.4% Black/African American, 0.0% Asian, 0.0% American Indian/Alaska Native, 0.0% Native Hawaiian/Other Pacific Islander, 3.2% Two or more races, 2.7% Hispanic of any race; Average household size: 2.10; Median age: 43.9; Age under 18: 19.0%; Age 65 and over: 18.8%; Males per 100 females: 90.5; Marriage status: 27.3% never married, 42.0% now married, 2.4% separated, 10.9% widowed, 19.7% divorced; Foreign born: 1.3%; Speak English only: 97.6%; With disability: 17.3%; Veterans: 7.3%; Ancestry: 34.6% German, 17.6% English, 14.8% Irish, 11.7% Italian, 10.7% American
Employment: 12.4% management, business, and financial, 3.7% computer, engineering, and science, 3.5% education, legal, community service, arts, and media, 11.4% healthcare practitioners, 19.0% service, 22.6% sales and office, 13.4% natural resources, construction, and maintenance, 14.0% production, transportation, and material moving
Income: Per capita: $23,000; Median household: $39,567; Average household: $48,887; Households with income of $100,000 or more: 15.1%; Poverty rate: 24.1%
Educational Attainment: High school diploma or higher: 79.3%; Bachelor's degree or higher: 11.3%; Graduate/professional degree or higher: 3.9%

School District(s)
Warsaw Central SD (KG-12)
   2014-15 Enrollment: 899. . . . . (585) 786-8000
Housing: Homeownership rate: 55.1%; Median home value: $87,800; Median year structure built: Before 1940; Homeowner vacancy rate: 0.0%; Median selected monthly owner costs: $1,009 with a mortgage, $467 without a mortgage; Median gross rent: $562 per month; Rental vacancy rate: 0.0%
Health Insurance: 92.7% have insurance; 63.0% have private insurance; 45.8% have public insurance; 7.3% do not have insurance; 5.2% of children under 18 do not have insurance
Hospitals: Wyoming County Community Hospital (264 beds)
Safety: Violent crime rate: 17.8 per 10,000 population; Property crime rate: 231.9 per 10,000 population
Newspapers: Warsaw's Country Courier (weekly circulation 2,000)
Transportation: Commute: 89.8% car, 0.4% public transportation, 6.1% walk, 0.8% work from home; Mean travel time to work: 19.1 minutes

WETHERSFIELD (town). Covers a land area of 35.810 square miles and a water area of 0.307 square miles. Located at 42.65° N. Lat; 78.24° W. Long.

Population: 793; Growth (since 2000): -11.0%; Density: 22.1 persons per square mile; Race: 99.5% White, 0.0% Black/African American, 0.0% Asian, 0.5% American Indian/Alaska Native, 0.0% Native Hawaiian/Other Pacific Islander, 0.0% Two or more races, 2.0% Hispanic of any race; Average household size: 2.57; Median age: 38.8; Age under 18: 25.3%; Age 65 and over: 9.3%; Males per 100 females: 112.8; Marriage status: 23.6% never married, 62.9% now married, 0.6% separated, 7.1% widowed, 6.4% divorced; Foreign born: 1.6%; Speak English only: 96.1%; With disability: 10.7%; Veterans: 8.4%; Ancestry: 32.3% German, 22.8% Irish, 10.7% Polish, 9.7% Italian, 9.6% English
Employment: 12.8% management, business, and financial, 1.9% computer, engineering, and science, 6.5% education, legal, community service, arts, and media, 5.6% healthcare practitioners, 18.9% service, 21.5% sales and office, 20.1% natural resources, construction, and maintenance, 12.6% production, transportation, and material moving
Income: Per capita: $24,878; Median household: $54,886; Average household: $64,737; Households with income of $100,000 or more: 22.1%; Poverty rate: 15.5%
Educational Attainment: High school diploma or higher: 91.4%; Bachelor's degree or higher: 13.5%; Graduate/professional degree or higher: 6.0%
Housing: Homeownership rate: 76.4%; Median home value: $94,200; Median year structure built: 1972; Homeowner vacancy rate: 4.1%; Median selected monthly owner costs: $1,130 with a mortgage, $443 without a mortgage; Median gross rent: $781 per month; Rental vacancy rate: 0.0%
Health Insurance: 91.4% have insurance; 68.9% have private insurance; 31.3% have public insurance; 8.6% do not have insurance; 4.0% of children under 18 do not have insurance
Transportation: Commute: 90.0% car, 0.0% public transportation, 4.6% walk, 4.4% work from home; Mean travel time to work: 30.7 minutes

WYOMING (village). Covers a land area of 0.669 square miles and a water area of 0 square miles. Located at 42.82° N. Lat; 78.08° W. Long. Elevation is 988 feet.

Population: 381; Growth (since 2000): -25.7%; Density: 569.6 persons per square mile; Race: 100.0% White, 0.0% Black/African American, 0.0% Asian, 0.0% American Indian/Alaska Native, 0.0% Native Hawaiian/Other Pacific Islander, 0.0% Two or more races, 0.0% Hispanic of any race; Average household size: 2.54; Median age: 40.8; Age under 18: 26.5%; Age 65 and over: 17.3%; Males per 100 females: 100.9; Marriage status: 32.2% never married, 51.6% now married, 0.6% separated, 3.8% widowed, 12.4% divorced; Foreign born: 0.8%; Speak English only: 96.5%; With disability: 18.4%; Veterans: 11.4%; Ancestry: 21.0% German, 19.4% English, 13.6% Irish, 10.5% American, 7.9% Italian
Employment: 15.2% management, business, and financial, 1.3% computer, engineering, and science, 16.5% education, legal, community service, arts, and media, 6.3% healthcare practitioners, 13.9% service, 19.6% sales and office, 12.0% natural resources, construction, and maintenance, 15.2% production, transportation, and material moving
Income: Per capita: $22,308; Median household: $47,917; Average household: $57,037; Households with income of $100,000 or more: 12.6%; Poverty rate: 11.0%
Educational Attainment: High school diploma or higher: 94.1%; Bachelor's degree or higher: 19.2%; Graduate/professional degree or higher: 4.3%

School District(s)
Wyoming Central SD (KG-08)
   2014-15 Enrollment: 123. . . . . (585) 495-6222
Housing: Homeownership rate: 78.0%; Median home value: $93,200; Median year structure built: Before 1940; Homeowner vacancy rate: 0.0%; Median selected monthly owner costs: $1,071 with a mortgage, $404 without a mortgage; Median gross rent: $579 per month; Rental vacancy rate: 0.0%
Health Insurance: 95.8% have insurance; 79.8% have private insurance; 33.1% have public insurance; 4.2% do not have insurance; 4.0% of children under 18 do not have insurance
Transportation: Commute: 96.1% car, 0.7% public transportation, 0.0% walk, 0.7% work from home; Mean travel time to work: 27.7 minutes

Yates County

Located in west central New York; bounded on the east by Seneca Lake; includes parts of Keuka and Canandaigua Lakes. Covers a land area of 338.143 square miles, a water area of 37.647 square miles, and is located in the Eastern Time Zone at 42.64° N. Lat., 77.10° W. Long. The county was founded in 1823. County seat is Penn Yan.

Yates County is part of the Rochester, NY Metropolitan Statistical Area. The entire metro area includes: Livingston County, NY; Monroe County, NY; Ontario County, NY; Orleans County, NY; Wayne County, NY; Yates County, NY

Population: 25,187; Growth (since 2000): 2.3%; Density: 74.5 persons per square mile; Race: 97.2% White, 1.0% Black/African American, 0.5% Asian, 0.1% American Indian/Alaska Native, 0.0% Native Hawaiian/Other Pacific Islander, 0.9% two or more races, 2.0% Hispanic of any race; Average household size: 2.46; Median age: 41.5; Age under 18: 23.2%; Age 65 and over: 17.8%; Males per 100 females: 93.9; Marriage status: 29.4% never married, 55.2% now married, 2.3% separated, 5.2% widowed, 10.3% divorced; Foreign born: 1.8%; Speak English only: 86.7%; With disability: 13.2%; Veterans: 9.4%; Ancestry: 23.4% German, 16.4% English, 15.9% Irish, 11.0% American, 5.8% Italian
Religion: Six largest groups: 11.3% Catholicism, 8.3% Methodist/Pietist, 4.0% Baptist, 2.0% Presbyterian-Reformed, 1.9% Lutheran, 0.8% Non-denominational Protestant
Economy: Unemployment rate: 4.0%; Leading industries: 16.5 % retail trade; 15.9 % construction; 12.0 % other services (except public administration); Farms: 919 totaling 126,946 acres; Company size: 0 employ 1,000 or more persons, 1 employs 500 to 999 persons, 4 employ 100 to 499 persons, 535 employ less than 100 persons; Business ownership: 557 women-owned, n/a Black-owned, n/a Hispanic-owned, n/a Asian-owned, n/a American Indian/Alaska Native-owned
Employment: 13.9% management, business, and financial, 2.0% computer, engineering, and science, 11.1% education, legal, community service, arts, and media, 4.3% healthcare practitioners, 20.5% service,

21.8% sales and office, 12.7% natural resources, construction, and maintenance, 13.7% production, transportation, and material moving
Income: Per capita: $25,224; Median household: $49,510; Average household: $65,445; Households with income of $100,000 or more: 18.0%; Poverty rate: 14.4%
Educational Attainment: High school diploma or higher: 85.8%; Bachelor's degree or higher: 23.7%; Graduate/professional degree or higher: 11.5%
Housing: Homeownership rate: 76.6%; Median home value: $124,200; Median year structure built: 1961; Homeowner vacancy rate: 1.1%; Median selected monthly owner costs: $1,108 with a mortgage, $520 without a mortgage; Median gross rent: $688 per month; Rental vacancy rate: 3.4%
Vital Statistics: Birth rate: 121.8 per 10,000 population; Death rate: 100.6 per 10,000 population; Age-adjusted cancer mortality rate: 177.7 deaths per 100,000 population
Health Insurance: 79.8% have insurance; 59.6% have private insurance; 35.1% have public insurance; 20.2% do not have insurance; 34.1% of children under 18 do not have insurance
Health Care: Physicians: 8.4 per 10,000 population; Dentists: 4.8 per 10,000 population; Hospital beds: 74.0 per 10,000 population; Hospital admissions: 367.6 per 10,000 population
Transportation: Commute: 80.4% car, 0.3% public transportation, 8.2% walk, 7.8% work from home; Mean travel time to work: 22.8 minutes
2016 Presidential Election: 56.8% Trump, 36.7% Clinton, 5.0% Johnson, 1.5% Stein
National and State Parks: Keuka Lake State Park
Additional Information Contacts
Yates Government . . . . (315) 536-5120
http://www.yatescounty.org

Yates County Communities

BARRINGTON (town). Covers a land area of 35.753 square miles and a water area of 1.378 square miles. Located at 42.52° N. Lat; 77.05° W. Long. Elevation is 1,565 feet.
Population: 1,480; Growth (since 2000): 6.0%; Density: 41.4 persons per square mile; Race: 98.4% White, 0.9% Black/African American, 0.1% Asian, 0.0% American Indian/Alaska Native, 0.0% Native Hawaiian/Other Pacific Islander, 0.3% Two or more races, 0.9% Hispanic of any race; Average household size: 2.51; Median age: 44.0; Age under 18: 23.6%; Age 65 and over: 19.5%; Males per 100 females: 93.4; Marriage status: 22.3% never married, 66.4% now married, 1.6% separated, 3.8% widowed, 7.5% divorced; Foreign born: 0.7%; Speak English only: 76.5%; With disability: 11.1%; Veterans: 9.9%; Ancestry: 27.1% German, 19.1% American, 11.4% Irish, 11.0% Swiss, 10.7% English
Employment: 19.6% management, business, and financial, 0.5% computer, engineering, and science, 7.2% education, legal, community service, arts, and media, 6.1% healthcare practitioners, 19.5% service, 16.7% sales and office, 15.6% natural resources, construction, and maintenance, 14.8% production, transportation, and material moving
Income: Per capita: $28,409; Median household: $49,097; Average household: $72,624; Households with income of $100,000 or more: 19.6%; Poverty rate: 11.0%
Educational Attainment: High school diploma or higher: 80.5%; Bachelor's degree or higher: 22.7%; Graduate/professional degree or higher: 13.0%
Housing: Homeownership rate: 90.8%; Median home value: $129,200; Median year structure built: 1980; Homeowner vacancy rate: 0.5%; Median selected monthly owner costs: $1,092 with a mortgage, $436 without a mortgage; Median gross rent: $881 per month; Rental vacancy rate: 0.0%
Health Insurance: 69.9% have insurance; 55.9% have private insurance; 28.7% have public insurance; 30.1% do not have insurance; 49.0% of children under 18 do not have insurance
Transportation: Commute: 72.4% car, 0.0% public transportation, 6.5% walk, 13.9% work from home; Mean travel time to work: 23.8 minutes

BELLONA (unincorporated postal area)
ZCTA: 14415
Covers a land area of 1.452 square miles and a water area of 0 square miles. Located at 42.76° N. Lat; 77.02° W. Long. Elevation is 725 feet.
Population: 140; Growth (since 2000): 125.8%; Density: 96.4 persons per square mile; Race: 100.0% White, 0.0% Black/African American, 0.0% Asian, 0.0% American Indian/Alaska Native, 0.0% Native Hawaiian/Other Pacific Islander, 0.0% Two or more races, 0.0% Hispanic of any race; Average household size: 2.19; Median age: 53.5;

Age under 18: 7.1%; Age 65 and over: 9.3%; Males per 100 females: 83.3; Marriage status: 25.9% never married, 53.3% now married, 4.4% separated, 14.1% widowed, 6.7% divorced; Foreign born: 0.0%; Speak English only: 95.7%; With disability: 9.3%; Veterans: 11.5%; Ancestry: 33.6% English, 30.0% American, 17.1% Irish, 5.7% Scottish, 5.0% British
Employment: 11.1% management, business, and financial, 0.0% computer, engineering, and science, 13.1% education, legal, community service, arts, and media, 0.0% healthcare practitioners, 43.4% service, 13.1% sales and office, 12.1% natural resources, construction, and maintenance, 7.1% production, transportation, and material moving
Income: Per capita: $24,797; Median household: $37,708; Average household: $56,661; Households with income of $100,000 or more: 23.4%; Poverty rate: n/a
Educational Attainment: High school diploma or higher: 94.3%; Bachelor's degree or higher: 14.2%; Graduate/professional degree or higher: 6.6%
Housing: Homeownership rate: 81.3%; Median home value: $86,700; Median year structure built: Before 1940; Homeowner vacancy rate: 0.0%; Median selected monthly owner costs: n/a with a mortgage, n/a without a mortgage; Median gross rent: n/a per month; Rental vacancy rate: 0.0%
Health Insurance: 82.1% have insurance; 52.9% have private insurance; 38.6% have public insurance; 17.9% do not have insurance; 0.0% of children under 18 do not have insurance
Transportation: Commute: 100.0% car, 0.0% public transportation, 0.0% walk, 0.0% work from home; Mean travel time to work: 20.2 minutes

BENTON (town). Covers a land area of 41.473 square miles and a water area of 2.964 square miles. Located at 42.72° N. Lat; 77.05° W. Long. Elevation is 837 feet.
Population: 2,829; Growth (since 2000): 7.2%; Density: 68.2 persons per square mile; Race: 98.1% White, 1.2% Black/African American, 0.0% Asian, 0.0% American Indian/Alaska Native, 0.0% Native Hawaiian/Other Pacific Islander, 0.2% Two or more races, 0.4% Hispanic of any race; Average household size: 2.74; Median age: 45.6; Age under 18: 26.1%; Age 65 and over: 23.9%; Males per 100 females: 94.6; Marriage status: 22.7% never married, 59.2% now married, 0.3% separated, 11.6% widowed, 6.6% divorced; Foreign born: 2.2%; Speak English only: 73.8%; With disability: 11.4%; Veterans: 10.6%; Ancestry: 26.9% German, 19.6% English, 14.5% Irish, 13.4% American, 9.6% Swiss
Employment: 21.0% management, business, and financial, 2.6% computer, engineering, and science, 10.6% education, legal, community service, arts, and media, 1.3% healthcare practitioners, 16.2% service, 22.4% sales and office, 13.9% natural resources, construction, and maintenance, 11.9% production, transportation, and material moving
Income: Per capita: $24,201; Median household: $56,875; Average household: $70,277; Households with income of $100,000 or more: 20.0%; Poverty rate: 8.3%
Educational Attainment: High school diploma or higher: 77.3%; Bachelor's degree or higher: 14.8%; Graduate/professional degree or higher: 5.3%
Housing: Homeownership rate: 83.3%; Median home value: $144,300; Median year structure built: Before 1940; Homeowner vacancy rate: 0.0%; Median selected monthly owner costs: $1,150 with a mortgage, $473 without a mortgage; Median gross rent: $692 per month; Rental vacancy rate: 8.1%
Health Insurance: 68.7% have insurance; 56.8% have private insurance; 29.3% have public insurance; 31.3% do not have insurance; 61.2% of children under 18 do not have insurance
Transportation: Commute: 79.2% car, 0.0% public transportation, 8.7% walk, 9.0% work from home; Mean travel time to work: 19.8 minutes

BRANCHPORT (unincorporated postal area)
ZCTA: 14418
Covers a land area of 37.364 square miles and a water area of 0.040 square miles. Located at 42.60° N. Lat; 77.22° W. Long. Elevation is 741 feet.
Population: 1,404; Growth (since 2000): -5.2%; Density: 37.6 persons per square mile; Race: 99.8% White, 0.0% Black/African American, 0.0% Asian, 0.0% American Indian/Alaska Native, 0.0% Native Hawaiian/Other Pacific Islander, 0.2% Two or more races, 2.0% Hispanic of any race; Average household size: 2.59; Median age: 44.9; Age under 18: 19.0%; Age 65 and over: 17.1%; Males per 100 females:

99.5; Marriage status: 27.2% never married, 64.9% now married, 5.0% separated, 0.8% widowed, 7.0% divorced; Foreign born: 0.9%; Speak English only: 97.8%; With disability: 14.8%; Veterans: 9.2%; Ancestry: 23.6% English, 21.0% German, 16.7% Irish, 8.2% American, 7.9% Dutch

Employment: 9.5% management, business, and financial, 6.3% computer, engineering, and science, 2.6% education, legal, community service, arts, and media, 7.5% healthcare practitioners, 10.5% service, 24.6% sales and office, 15.0% natural resources, construction, and maintenance, 23.9% production, transportation, and material moving

Income: Per capita: $31,221; Median household: $59,236; Average household: $80,698; Households with income of $100,000 or more: 28.8%; Poverty rate: 5.8%

Educational Attainment: High school diploma or higher: 91.0%; Bachelor's degree or higher: 21.3%; Graduate/professional degree or higher: 8.8%

Housing: Homeownership rate: 87.8%; Median home value: $141,200; Median year structure built: 1971; Homeowner vacancy rate: 0.0%; Median selected monthly owner costs: $1,099 with a mortgage, $722 without a mortgage; Median gross rent: $976 per month; Rental vacancy rate: 0.0%

Health Insurance: 87.5% have insurance; 69.7% have private insurance; 28.0% have public insurance; 12.5% do not have insurance; 36.3% of children under 18 do not have insurance

Transportation: Commute: 88.9% car, 0.0% public transportation, 3.4% walk, 7.3% work from home; Mean travel time to work: 26.2 minutes

---

DRESDEN (village). Covers a land area of 0.302 square miles and a water area of 0.006 square miles. Located at 42.68° N. Lat; 76.96° W. Long. Elevation is 509 feet.

Population: 452; Growth (since 2000): 47.2%; Density: 1,497.9 persons per square mile; Race: 92.0% White, 0.0% Black/African American, 0.0% Asian, 0.9% American Indian/Alaska Native, 0.9% Native Hawaiian/Other Pacific Islander, 6.2% Two or more races, 20.1% Hispanic of any race; Average household size: 2.68; Median age: 35.6; Age under 18: 24.6%; Age 65 and over: 9.5%; Males per 100 females: 115.4; Marriage status: 33.8% never married, 52.8% now married, 4.0% separated, 2.6% widowed, 10.8% divorced; Foreign born: 16.4%; Speak English only: 79.7%; With disability: 24.1%; Veterans: 5.6%; Ancestry: 15.5% German, 13.7% Irish, 12.2% Italian, 9.1% English, 8.4% American

Employment: 9.7% management, business, and financial, 0.5% computer, engineering, and science, 14.4% education, legal, community service, arts, and media, 0.5% healthcare practitioners, 17.9% service, 20.5% sales and office, 19.5% natural resources, construction, and maintenance, 16.9% production, transportation, and material moving

Income: Per capita: $19,921; Median household: $50,469; Average household: $61,440; Households with income of $100,000 or more: 13.9%; Poverty rate: 33.2%

Educational Attainment: High school diploma or higher: 64.3%; Bachelor's degree or higher: 17.7%; Graduate/professional degree or higher: 6.7%

Housing: Homeownership rate: 70.9%; Median home value: $87,900; Median year structure built: Before 1940; Homeowner vacancy rate: 0.0%; Median selected monthly owner costs: $880 with a mortgage, $503 without a mortgage; Median gross rent: $923 per month; Rental vacancy rate: 10.2%

Health Insurance: 86.9% have insurance; 50.4% have private insurance; 43.8% have public insurance; 13.1% do not have insurance; 3.6% of children under 18 do not have insurance

Transportation: Commute: 94.3% car, 0.0% public transportation, 0.5% walk, 0.0% work from home; Mean travel time to work: 24.5 minutes

---

DUNDEE (village). Covers a land area of 1.124 square miles and a water area of 0 square miles. Located at 42.52° N. Lat; 76.98° W. Long. Elevation is 984 feet.

History: Incorporated 1847.

Population: 1,448; Growth (since 2000): -14.3%; Density: 1,288.3 persons per square mile; Race: 96.6% White, 1.0% Black/African American, 0.3% Asian, 0.0% American Indian/Alaska Native, 0.0% Native Hawaiian/Other Pacific Islander, 1.5% Two or more races, 2.6% Hispanic of any race; Average household size: 2.11; Median age: 41.1; Age under 18: 21.6%; Age 65 and over: 15.1%; Males per 100 females: 93.2; Marriage status: 28.4% never married, 48.5% now married, 4.2% separated, 7.0% widowed, 16.0% divorced; Foreign born: 1.1%; Speak English only: 97.9%;

With disability: 14.2%; Veterans: 10.0%; Ancestry: 21.0% American, 18.9% German, 15.8% English, 15.3% Irish, 10.3% Dutch

Employment: 9.6% management, business, and financial, 1.1% computer, engineering, and science, 9.7% education, legal, community service, arts, and media, 7.1% healthcare practitioners, 22.1% service, 16.3% sales and office, 6.3% natural resources, construction, and maintenance, 27.9% production, transportation, and material moving

Income: Per capita: $26,898; Median household: $40,214; Average household: $60,264; Households with income of $100,000 or more: 11.7%; Poverty rate: 16.2%

Educational Attainment: High school diploma or higher: 86.0%; Bachelor's degree or higher: 13.2%; Graduate/professional degree or higher: 5.8%

School District(s)

Dundee Central SD (PK-12)

   2014-15 Enrollment: 763 . . . . (607) 243-5533

Housing: Homeownership rate: 53.8%; Median home value: $79,800; Median year structure built: Before 1940; Homeowner vacancy rate: 2.9%; Median selected monthly owner costs: $913 with a mortgage, $429 without a mortgage; Median gross rent: $577 per month; Rental vacancy rate: 0.0%

Health Insurance: 91.2% have insurance; 61.5% have private insurance; 42.4% have public insurance; 8.8% do not have insurance; 3.8% of children under 18 do not have insurance

Newspapers: The Observer (weekly circulation 2,100); Watkins Glen Review/Express (weekly circulation 3,000)

Transportation: Commute: 82.6% car, 0.0% public transportation, 11.1% walk, 5.4% work from home; Mean travel time to work: 19.1 minutes

---

HIMROD (unincorporated postal area)

ZCTA: 14842

   Covers a land area of 16.731 square miles and a water area of 0.007 square miles. Located at 42.60° N. Lat; 76.98° W. Long. Elevation is 797 feet.

Population: 828; Growth (since 2000): -8.9%; Density: 49.5 persons per square mile; Race: 100.0% White, 0.0% Black/African American, 0.0% Asian, 0.0% American Indian/Alaska Native, 0.0% Native Hawaiian/Other Pacific Islander, 0.0% Two or more races, 0.0% Hispanic of any race; Average household size: 1.99; Median age: 53.8; Age under 18: 13.9%; Age 65 and over: 21.0%; Males per 100 females: 100.9; Marriage status: 34.2% never married, 38.0% now married, 2.0% separated, 7.3% widowed, 20.5% divorced; Foreign born: 0.4%; Speak English only: 90.6%; With disability: 4.3%; Veterans: 11.8%; Ancestry: 37.3% Irish, 27.4% German, 10.7% English, 8.8% Swiss, 7.7% Austrian

Employment: 21.6% management, business, and financial, 0.0% computer, engineering, and science, 25.2% education, legal, community service, arts, and media, 2.2% healthcare practitioners, 18.3% service, 7.1% sales and office, 8.8% natural resources, construction, and maintenance, 16.8% production, transportation, and material moving

Income: Per capita: $34,067; Median household: $53,278; Average household: $65,365; Households with income of $100,000 or more: 2.9%; Poverty rate: 11.2%

Educational Attainment: High school diploma or higher: 94.2%; Bachelor's degree or higher: 36.3%; Graduate/professional degree or higher: 26.9%

Housing: Homeownership rate: 97.6%; Median home value: $121,300; Median year structure built: 1982; Homeowner vacancy rate: 0.0%; Median selected monthly owner costs: n/a with a mortgage, n/a without a mortgage; Median gross rent: n/a per month; Rental vacancy rate: 0.0%

Health Insurance: 75.2% have insurance; 69.2% have private insurance; 29.5% have public insurance; 24.8% do not have insurance; 37.4% of children under 18 do not have insurance

Transportation: Commute: 89.8% car, 0.0% public transportation, 4.9% walk, 2.9% work from home; Mean travel time to work: 36.6 minutes

---

ITALY (town). Covers a land area of 40.140 square miles and a water area of 0.122 square miles. Located at 42.62° N. Lat; 77.31° W. Long. Elevation is 1,109 feet.

Population: 1,053; Growth (since 2000): -3.1%; Density: 26.2 persons per square mile; Race: 98.7% White, 0.0% Black/African American, 0.0% Asian, 0.0% American Indian/Alaska Native, 0.0% Native Hawaiian/Other Pacific Islander, 1.3% Two or more races, 0.6% Hispanic of any race; Average household size: 2.31; Median age: 45.9; Age under 18: 22.0%; Age 65 and over: 17.3%; Males per 100 females: 103.0; Marriage status:

17.7% never married, 63.8% now married, 1.8% separated, 2.7% widowed, 15.8% divorced; Foreign born: 0.4%; Speak English only: 97.3%; With disability: 12.6%; Veterans: 8.6%; Ancestry: 18.9% German, 18.6% English, 14.1% Irish, 7.7% Italian, 7.3% American

Employment: 9.6% management, business, and financial, 1.3% computer, engineering, and science, 6.5% education, legal, community service, arts, and media, 8.5% healthcare practitioners, 20.2% service, 17.0% sales and office, 17.9% natural resources, construction, and maintenance, 18.8% production, transportation, and material moving

Income: Per capita: $24,290; Median household: $49,839; Average household: $57,173; Households with income of $100,000 or more: 10.5%; Poverty rate: 19.4%

Educational Attainment: High school diploma or higher: 89.7%; Bachelor's degree or higher: 19.1%; Graduate/professional degree or higher: 7.0%

Housing: Homeownership rate: 87.9%; Median home value: $92,600; Median year structure built: 1973; Homeowner vacancy rate: 3.4%; Median selected monthly owner costs: $1,079 with a mortgage, $450 without a mortgage; Median gross rent: $645 per month; Rental vacancy rate: 12.7%

Health Insurance: 91.8% have insurance; 53.7% have private insurance; 52.1% have public insurance; 8.2% do not have insurance; 6.0% of children under 18 do not have insurance

Transportation: Commute: 92.5% car, 0.9% public transportation, 0.9% walk, 4.9% work from home; Mean travel time to work: 34.7 minutes

JERUSALEM (town).
Covers a land area of 58.639 square miles and a water area of 6.762 square miles. Located at 42.61° N. Lat; 77.16° W. Long.

Population: 4,475; Growth (since 2000): -1.1%; Density: 76.3 persons per square mile; Race: 96.4% White, 1.0% Black/African American, 1.4% Asian, 0.4% American Indian/Alaska Native, 0.0% Native Hawaiian/Other Pacific Islander, 0.8% Two or more races, 0.9% Hispanic of any race; Average household size: 2.36; Median age: 39.7; Age under 18: 15.4%; Age 65 and over: 18.4%; Males per 100 females: 82.1; Marriage status: 34.2% never married, 57.0% now married, 2.0% separated, 1.4% widowed, 7.5% divorced; Foreign born: 2.7%; Speak English only: 94.1%; With disability: 11.3%; Veterans: 8.8%; Ancestry: 22.3% English, 21.8% German, 18.5% Irish, 7.5% Italian, 5.9% Polish

Employment: 9.8% management, business, and financial, 1.6% computer, engineering, and science, 7.8% education, legal, community service, arts, and media, 3.1% healthcare practitioners, 19.2% service, 32.2% sales and office, 10.6% natural resources, construction, and maintenance, 15.7% production, transportation, and material moving

Income: Per capita: $28,297; Median household: $57,778; Average household: $80,036; Households with income of $100,000 or more: 29.6%; Poverty rate: 9.4%

Educational Attainment: High school diploma or higher: 86.1%; Bachelor's degree or higher: 28.7%; Graduate/professional degree or higher: 13.7%

Housing: Homeownership rate: 85.3%; Median home value: $160,800; Median year structure built: 1971; Homeowner vacancy rate: 2.3%; Median selected monthly owner costs: $1,222 with a mortgage, $653 without a mortgage; Median gross rent: $844 per month; Rental vacancy rate: 0.0%

Health Insurance: 89.3% have insurance; 73.9% have private insurance; 28.3% have public insurance; 10.7% do not have insurance; 26.9% of children under 18 do not have insurance

Transportation: Commute: 77.8% car, 0.1% public transportation, 12.5% walk, 7.8% work from home; Mean travel time to work: 18.3 minutes

Additional Information Contacts

Town of Jerusalem . . . . (315) 595-6668
   http://www.jerusalem-ny.org

KEUKA PARK (CDP).
Covers a land area of 0.678 square miles and a water area of 0.559 square miles. Located at 42.61° N. Lat; 77.09° W. Long. Elevation is 774 feet.

Population: 875; Growth (since 2000): n/a; Density: 1,290.9 persons per square mile; Race: 83.1% White, 4.6% Black/African American, 6.1% Asian, 2.1% American Indian/Alaska Native, 0.0% Native Hawaiian/Other Pacific Islander, 4.2% Two or more races, 1.5% Hispanic of any race; Average household size: 1.67; Median age: 20.2; Age under 18: 2.1%; Age 65 and over: 7.8%; Males per 100 females: 50.6; Marriage status: 91.7% never married, 6.0% now married, 0.0% separated, 1.2% widowed, 1.2% divorced; Foreign born: 6.1%; Speak English only: 92.9%; With disability: 9.0%; Veterans: 2.0%; Ancestry: 28.9% Irish, 20.8% Italian, 11.1% German, 10.3% Polish, 9.5% English

Employment: 0.0% management, business, and financial, 0.0% computer, engineering, and science, 6.7% education, legal, community service, arts, and media, 3.0% healthcare practitioners, 38.2% service, 52.1% sales and office, 0.0% natural resources, construction, and maintenance, 0.0% production, transportation, and material moving

Income: Per capita: $4,913; Median household: $30,278; Average household: $32,256; Households with income of $100,000 or more: n/a; Poverty rate: n/a

Educational Attainment: High school diploma or higher: 100.0%; Bachelor's degree or higher: 32.1%; Graduate/professional degree or higher: 7.7%

Four-year College(s)
Keuka College (Private, Not-for-profit, Baptist)
   Fall 2014 Enrollment: 1,997 . . . . (315) 279-5000
   2015-16 Tuition: In-state $28,917; Out-of-state $28,917

Housing: Homeownership rate: 53.8%; Median home value: n/a; Median year structure built: Before 1940; Homeowner vacancy rate: 0.0%; Median selected monthly owner costs: n/a with a mortgage, n/a without a mortgage; Median gross rent: $1,313 per month; Rental vacancy rate: 0.0%

Health Insurance: 93.4% have insurance; 79.9% have private insurance; 18.4% have public insurance; 6.6% do not have insurance; 0.0% of children under 18 do not have insurance

Transportation: Commute: 28.2% car, 0.0% public transportation, 62.2% walk, 9.7% work from home; Mean travel time to work: 7.2 minutes

MIDDLESEX (town).
Covers a land area of 30.875 square miles and a water area of 3.229 square miles. Located at 42.72° N. Lat; 77.29° W. Long. Elevation is 771 feet.

Population: 1,465; Growth (since 2000): 8.9%; Density: 47.4 persons per square mile; Race: 96.0% White, 1.8% Black/African American, 0.2% Asian, 0.0% American Indian/Alaska Native, 0.1% Native Hawaiian/Other Pacific Islander, 1.4% Two or more races, 2.2% Hispanic of any race; Average household size: 2.34; Median age: 46.4; Age under 18: 19.7%; Age 65 and over: 14.9%; Males per 100 females: 99.6; Marriage status: 18.8% never married, 64.0% now married, 1.5% separated, 7.0% widowed, 10.3% divorced; Foreign born: 1.4%; Speak English only: 96.4%; With disability: 13.2%; Veterans: 10.8%; Ancestry: 23.6% German, 16.3% Irish, 14.8% English, 10.2% American, 9.2% Italian

Employment: 12.7% management, business, and financial, 3.7% computer, engineering, and science, 9.2% education, legal, community service, arts, and media, 8.1% healthcare practitioners, 17.6% service, 19.7% sales and office, 15.6% natural resources, construction, and maintenance, 13.3% production, transportation, and material moving

Income: Per capita: $27,778; Median household: $60,893; Average household: $67,429; Households with income of $100,000 or more: 17.4%; Poverty rate: 9.6%

Educational Attainment: High school diploma or higher: 94.1%; Bachelor's degree or higher: 27.1%; Graduate/professional degree or higher: 9.1%

Housing: Homeownership rate: 88.8%; Median home value: $130,000; Median year structure built: 1972; Homeowner vacancy rate: 0.0%; Median selected monthly owner costs: $1,151 with a mortgage, $554 without a mortgage; Median gross rent: $710 per month; Rental vacancy rate: 10.7%

Health Insurance: 92.9% have insurance; 72.9% have private insurance; 31.5% have public insurance; 7.1% do not have insurance; 4.5% of children under 18 do not have insurance

Transportation: Commute: 93.8% car, 0.0% public transportation, 2.2% walk, 3.0% work from home; Mean travel time to work: 32.6 minutes

MILO (town).
Covers a land area of 38.434 square miles and a water area of 5.901 square miles. Located at 42.61° N. Lat; 77.01° W. Long.

Population: 6,900; Growth (since 2000): -1.8%; Density: 179.5 persons per square mile; Race: 96.5% White, 1.4% Black/African American, 0.9% Asian, 0.0% American Indian/Alaska Native, 0.0% Native Hawaiian/Other Pacific Islander, 1.1% Two or more races, 0.9% Hispanic of any race; Average household size: 2.23; Median age: 44.3; Age under 18: 23.0%; Age 65 and over: 18.0%; Males per 100 females: 92.3; Marriage status: 34.4% never married, 44.0% now married, 3.9% separated, 6.4% widowed, 15.3% divorced; Foreign born: 1.0%; Speak English only: 90.5%; With disability: 18.1%; Veterans: 9.5%; Ancestry: 25.3% German, 21.6% Irish, 16.9% English, 9.4% American, 6.0% Dutch

Employment: 14.5% management, business, and financial, 2.5% computer, engineering, and science, 12.7% education, legal, community service, arts, and media, 4.4% healthcare practitioners, 23.9% service,

17.6% sales and office, 12.1% natural resources, construction, and maintenance, 12.3% production, transportation, and material moving
Income: Per capita: $23,707; Median household: $42,583; Average household: $53,902; Households with income of $100,000 or more: 11.2%; Poverty rate: 19.0%
Educational Attainment: High school diploma or higher: 88.8%; Bachelor's degree or higher: 26.2%; Graduate/professional degree or higher: 13.0%
Housing: Homeownership rate: 65.6%; Median home value: $113,500; Median year structure built: 1947; Homeowner vacancy rate: 0.4%; Median selected monthly owner costs: $1,028 with a mortgage, $496 without a mortgage; Median gross rent: $651 per month; Rental vacancy rate: 4.0%
Health Insurance: 79.7% have insurance; 55.6% have private insurance; 41.7% have public insurance; 20.3% do not have insurance; 30.5% of children under 18 do not have insurance
Transportation: Commute: 78.3% car, 0.6% public transportation, 11.5% walk, 6.0% work from home; Mean travel time to work: 21.7 minutes
Additional Information Contacts
Town of Milo . . . . (315) 536-8911
   http://www.townofmilo.com

PENN YAN (village).
County seat. Covers a land area of 2.381 square miles and a water area of 0.056 square miles. Located at 42.66° N. Lat; 77.05° W. Long. Elevation is 728 feet.
History: Controversy between the settlers from Pennsylvania and New England over a name for this place was compromised by combining the first syllables of Pennsylvania and Yankee.
Population: 4,815; Growth (since 2000): -7.7%; Density: 2,021.9 persons per square mile; Race: 94.2% White, 2.6% Black/African American, 1.2% Asian, 0.0% American Indian/Alaska Native, 0.0% Native Hawaiian/Other Pacific Islander, 1.6% Two or more races, 1.5% Hispanic of any race; Average household size: 2.11; Median age: 44.4; Age under 18: 23.0%; Age 65 and over: 20.4%; Males per 100 females: 86.7; Marriage status: 35.1% never married, 38.1% now married, 3.5% separated, 9.8% widowed, 17.0% divorced; Foreign born: 1.9%; Speak English only: 97.1%; With disability: 20.2%; Veterans: 10.0%; Ancestry: 21.7% Irish, 19.0% English, 17.5% German, 9.8% American, 7.5% Dutch
Employment: 11.0% management, business, and financial, 3.5% computer, engineering, and science, 11.9% education, legal, community service, arts, and media, 4.3% healthcare practitioners, 28.9% service, 20.6% sales and office, 10.2% natural resources, construction, and maintenance, 9.6% production, transportation, and material moving
Income: Per capita: $20,865; Median household: $33,586; Average household: $45,964; Households with income of $100,000 or more: 8.7%; Poverty rate: 26.3%
Educational Attainment: High school diploma or higher: 86.1%; Bachelor's degree or higher: 22.2%; Graduate/professional degree or higher: 9.3%

School District(s)
Penn Yan Central SD (PK-12)
   2014-15 Enrollment: 1,512 . . . . (315) 536-3371
Housing: Homeownership rate: 50.3%; Median home value: $104,400; Median year structure built: Before 1940; Homeowner vacancy rate: 0.0%; Median selected monthly owner costs: $1,007 with a mortgage, $479 without a mortgage; Median gross rent: $656 per month; Rental vacancy rate: 3.2%
Health Insurance: 86.9% have insurance; 54.1% have private insurance; 49.2% have public insurance; 13.1% do not have insurance; 14.8% of children under 18 do not have insurance
Hospitals: Soldiers & Sailors Memorial Hospital of Yates (186 beds)
Safety: Violent crime rate: 6.0 per 10,000 population; Property crime rate: 131.0 per 10,000 population
Newspapers: The Chronicle-Express (weekly circulation 3,900)
Transportation: Commute: 77.8% car, 0.9% public transportation, 16.8% walk, 4.5% work from home; Mean travel time to work: 16.1 minutes
Airports: Penn Yan (general aviation)
Additional Information Contacts
Village of Penn Yan. . . . . (315) 536-3015
   http://www.villageofpennyan.com

POTTER (town).
Covers a land area of 37.238 square miles and a water area of 0 square miles. Located at 42.71° N. Lat; 77.18° W. Long. Elevation is 896 feet.
Population: 1,989; Growth (since 2000): 8.7%; Density: 53.4 persons per square mile; Race: 98.6% White, 0.6% Black/African American, 0.1%

Asian, 0.2% American Indian/Alaska Native, 0.0% Native Hawaiian/Other Pacific Islander, 0.6% Two or more races, 4.2% Hispanic of any race; Average household size: 3.00; Median age: 33.8; Age under 18: 30.0%; Age 65 and over: 11.5%; Males per 100 females: 99.5; Marriage status: 32.0% never married, 56.6% now married, 2.7% separated, 4.0% widowed, 7.4% divorced; Foreign born: 1.9%; Speak English only: 79.1%; With disability: 8.2%; Veterans: 5.0%; Ancestry: 22.1% German, 12.1% English, 10.2% Italian, 10.0% American, 9.9% Irish
Employment: 14.7% management, business, and financial, 0.9% computer, engineering, and science, 11.5% education, legal, community service, arts, and media, 3.3% healthcare practitioners, 21.4% service, 19.0% sales and office, 20.2% natural resources, construction, and maintenance, 9.0% production, transportation, and material moving
Income: Per capita: $22,222; Median household: $49,643; Average household: $65,491; Households with income of $100,000 or more: 18.9%; Poverty rate: 17.0%
Educational Attainment: High school diploma or higher: 83.5%; Bachelor's degree or higher: 12.9%; Graduate/professional degree or higher: 4.8%
Housing: Homeownership rate: 84.2%; Median home value: $118,300; Median year structure built: 1968; Homeowner vacancy rate: 2.4%; Median selected monthly owner costs: $1,186 with a mortgage, $526 without a mortgage; Median gross rent: $725 per month; Rental vacancy rate: 0.0%
Health Insurance: 68.8% have insurance; 51.8% have private insurance; 29.3% have public insurance; 31.2% do not have insurance; 39.9% of children under 18 do not have insurance
Transportation: Commute: 81.1% car, 0.0% public transportation, 3.7% walk, 8.4% work from home; Mean travel time to work: 27.4 minutes

RUSHVILLE (village).
Covers a land area of 0.639 square miles and a water area of 0 square miles. Located at 42.76° N. Lat; 77.23° W. Long. Elevation is 876 feet.
Population: 679; Growth (since 2000): 9.3%; Density: 1,062.1 persons per square mile; Race: 96.8% White, 0.7% Black/African American, 0.0% Asian, 0.6% American Indian/Alaska Native, 0.0% Native Hawaiian/Other Pacific Islander, 1.9% Two or more races, 7.1% Hispanic of any race; Average household size: 2.44; Median age: 42.7; Age under 18: 22.7%; Age 65 and over: 14.3%; Males per 100 females: 91.8; Marriage status: 35.8% never married, 48.0% now married, 3.6% separated, 7.8% widowed, 8.4% divorced; Foreign born: 1.0%; Speak English only: 98.1%; With disability: 14.7%; Veterans: 3.4%; Ancestry: 20.5% English, 18.9% American, 18.0% Italian, 13.4% Irish, 13.3% German
Employment: 3.8% management, business, and financial, 0.0% computer, engineering, and science, 7.6% education, legal, community service, arts, and media, 2.1% healthcare practitioners, 39.2% service, 15.6% sales and office, 18.4% natural resources, construction, and maintenance, 13.2% production, transportation, and material moving
Income: Per capita: $24,941; Median household: $37,386; Average household: $57,191; Households with income of $100,000 or more: 11.9%; Poverty rate: 28.1%
Educational Attainment: High school diploma or higher: 89.7%; Bachelor's degree or higher: 7.7%; Graduate/professional degree or higher: 2.8%

School District(s)
Gorham-Middlesex Central SD (Marcus Whitman) (PK-12)
   2014-15 Enrollment: 1,286 . . . . (585) 554-4848
Housing: Homeownership rate: 65.2%; Median home value: $113,100; Median year structure built: Before 1940; Homeowner vacancy rate: 7.4%; Median selected monthly owner costs: $1,329 with a mortgage, $450 without a mortgage; Median gross rent: $507 per month; Rental vacancy rate: 0.0%
Health Insurance: 83.1% have insurance; 50.2% have private insurance; 44.5% have public insurance; 16.9% do not have insurance; 3.2% of children under 18 do not have insurance
Transportation: Commute: 89.5% car, 2.8% public transportation, 2.4% walk, 4.2% work from home; Mean travel time to work: 29.5 minutes

STARKEY (town).
Covers a land area of 32.831 square miles and a water area of 6.375 square miles. Located at 42.52° N. Lat; 76.94° W. Long. Elevation is 804 feet.
Population: 3,531; Growth (since 2000): 1.9%; Density: 107.6 persons per square mile; Race: 97.6% White, 1.0% Black/African American, 0.1% Asian, 0.0% American Indian/Alaska Native, 0.0% Native Hawaiian/Other Pacific Islander, 0.7% Two or more races, 4.6% Hispanic of any race; Average household size: 2.62; Median age: 34.2; Age under 18: 28.8%;

Age 65 and over: 16.5%; Males per 100 females: 101.1; Marriage status: 28.1% never married, 57.7% now married, 1.8% separated, 4.8% widowed, 9.5% divorced; Foreign born: 1.6%; Speak English only: 84.8%; With disability: 10.6%; Veterans: 11.0%; Ancestry: 21.1% German, 18.4% American, 13.1% English, 11.3% Dutch, 9.7% Irish

Employment: 8.7% management, business, and financial, 1.4% computer, engineering, and science, 14.9% education, legal, community service, arts, and media, 5.2% healthcare practitioners, 22.9% service, 22.5% sales and office, 6.4% natural resources, construction, and maintenance, 18.0% production, transportation, and material moving

Income: Per capita: $25,124; Median household: $50,169; Average household: $68,823; Households with income of $100,000 or more: 20.6%; Poverty rate: 15.0%

Educational Attainment: High school diploma or higher: 86.8%; Bachelor's degree or higher: 23.9%; Graduate/professional degree or higher: 15.2%

Housing: Homeownership rate: 64.1%; Median home value: $107,000; Median year structure built: 1961; Homeowner vacancy rate: 1.3%; Median selected monthly owner costs: $947 with a mortgage, $496 without a mortgage; Median gross rent: $695 per month; Rental vacancy rate: 0.0%

Health Insurance: 80.1% have insurance; 55.4% have private insurance; 38.9% have public insurance; 19.9% do not have insurance; 29.9% of children under 18 do not have insurance

Transportation: Commute: 82.2% car, 0.6% public transportation, 5.6% walk, 9.1% work from home; Mean travel time to work: 21.4 minutes

---

TORREY (town). Covers a land area of 22.760 square miles and a water area of 10.915 square miles. Located at 42.67° N. Lat; 76.95° W. Long. Elevation is 509 feet.

Population: 1,465; Growth (since 2000): 12.1%; Density: 64.4 persons per square mile; Race: 96.6% White, 0.0% Black/African American, 0.0% Asian, 0.4% American Indian/Alaska Native, 0.3% Native Hawaiian/Other Pacific Islander, 2.7% Two or more races, 7.0% Hispanic of any race; Average household size: 2.67; Median age: 39.6; Age under 18: 23.9%; Age 65 and over: 16.0%; Males per 100 females: 105.4; Marriage status: 28.4% never married, 61.2% now married, 2.5% separated, 3.6% widowed, 6.8% divorced; Foreign born: 5.5%; Speak English only: 78.3%; With disability: 15.0%; Veterans: 9.6%; Ancestry: 20.0% German, 11.6% Irish, 9.6% English, 9.0% Italian, 8.7% American

Employment: 20.6% management, business, and financial, 2.4% computer, engineering, and science, 13.6% education, legal, community service, arts, and media, 3.9% healthcare practitioners, 14.7% service, 20.6% sales and office, 14.7% natural resources, construction, and maintenance, 9.4% production, transportation, and material moving

Income: Per capita: $24,178; Median household: $55,069; Average household: $68,642; Households with income of $100,000 or more: 17.0%; Poverty rate: 15.7%

Educational Attainment: High school diploma or higher: 80.0%; Bachelor's degree or higher: 28.4%; Graduate/professional degree or higher: 14.2%

Housing: Homeownership rate: 85.1%; Median home value: $159,000; Median year structure built: 1962; Homeowner vacancy rate: 0.7%; Median selected monthly owner costs: $1,295 with a mortgage, $600 without a mortgage; Median gross rent: $725 per month; Rental vacancy rate: 6.0%

Health Insurance: 73.8% have insurance; 54.1% have private insurance; 31.9% have public insurance; 26.2% do not have insurance; 38.3% of children under 18 do not have insurance

Transportation: Commute: 80.6% car, 0.0% public transportation, 2.4% walk, 11.5% work from home; Mean travel time to work: 24.7 minutes;

Place Name Index

Accord (CDP) Ulster County, 679
Acra (unincorporated) Greene County, 249
Adams (town) Jefferson County, 275
Adams (village) Jefferson County, 276
Adams Center (CDP) Jefferson County, 276
Addison (town) Steuben County, 588
Addison (village) Steuben County, 588
Adirondack (unincorporated) Warren County, 699
Afton (town) Chenango County, 127
Afton (village) Chenango County, 127
Airmont (village) Rockland County, 523
Akron (village) Erie County, 195
Alabama (town) Genesee County, 242
Albany (city) Albany County, 45
Albany County, 45
Albertson (CDP) Nassau County, 341
Albion (town) Orleans County, 479
Albion (village) Orleans County, 479
Albion (town) Oswego County, 483
Alcove (unincorporated) Albany County, 46
Alden (town) Erie County, 196
Alden (village) Erie County, 196
Alder Creek (unincorporated) Oneida County, 414
Alexander (town) Genesee County, 242
Alexander (village) Genesee County, 243
Alexandria (town) Jefferson County, 276
Alexandria Bay (village) Jefferson County, 276
Alfred (town) Allegany County, 55
Alfred (village) Allegany County, 56
Alfred Station (unincorporated) Allegany County, 56
Allegany (town) Cattaraugus County, 79
Allegany (village) Cattaraugus County, 79
Allegany County, 55
Allegany Reservation (reservation) Cattaraugus County, 80
Allen (town) Allegany County, 56
Allentown (unincorporated) Allegany County, 56
Alma (town) Allegany County, 57
Almond (town) Allegany County, 57
Almond (village) Allegany County, 57
Alpine (unincorporated) Schuyler County, 579
Alplaus (unincorporated) Schenectady County, 566
Altamont (village) Albany County, 46
Altmar (village) Oswego County, 484
Altona (town) Clinton County, 137
Altona (CDP) Clinton County, 137
Amagansett (CDP) Suffolk County, 603
Amawalk (unincorporated) Westchester County, 725
Amboy (town) Oswego County, 484
Amenia (town) Dutchess County, 178
Amenia (CDP) Dutchess County, 177
Ames (village) Montgomery County, 334
Amherst (town) Erie County, 196
Amity (town) Allegany County, 57
Amityville (village) Suffolk County, 603
Amsterdam (town) Montgomery County, 335
Amsterdam (city) Montgomery County, 335
Ancram (town) Columbia County, 147
Ancramdale (unincorporated) Columbia County, 147
Andes (town) Delaware County, 164
Andes (CDP) Delaware County, 164
Andover (town) Allegany County, 58
Andover (village) Allegany County, 58
Angelica (town) Allegany County, 58
Angelica (village) Allegany County, 58
Angola (village) Erie County, 197
Angola on the Lake (CDP) Erie County, 197

Annandale on Hudson (unincorporated) Dutchess County, 178
Annsville (town) Oneida County, 414
Antwerp (town) Jefferson County, 277
Antwerp (village) Jefferson County, 277
Apalachin (CDP) Tioga County, 665
Appleton (unincorporated) Niagara County, 405
Apulia Station (unincorporated) Onondaga County, 433
Aquebogue (CDP) Suffolk County, 603
Arcade (town) Wyoming County, 751
Arcade (village) Wyoming County, 751
Arcadia (town) Wayne County, 717
Arden (unincorporated) Orange County, 457
Ardsley (village) Westchester County, 725
Ardsley on Hudson (unincorporated) Westchester County, 726
Argyle (town) Washington County, 707
Argyle (village) Washington County, 708
Arietta (town) Hamilton County, 261
Arkport (village) Steuben County, 588
Arkville (unincorporated) Delaware County, 165
Arkwright (town) Chautauqua County, 105
Arlington (CDP) Dutchess County, 178
Armonk (CDP) Westchester County, 726
Arverne (unincorporated) Queens County, 389
Asharoken (village) Suffolk County, 604
Ashford (town) Cattaraugus County, 80
Ashland (town) Chemung County, 120
Ashland (town) Greene County, 249
Ashville (unincorporated) Chautauqua County, 105
Astoria (unincorporated) Queens County, 389
Athens (town) Greene County, 250
Athens (village) Greene County, 250
Athol (unincorporated) Warren County, 700
Atlanta (unincorporated) Steuben County, 589
Atlantic Beach (village) Nassau County, 341
Attica (town) Wyoming County, 751
Attica (village) Wyoming County, 752
Au Sable (town) Clinton County, 137
Au Sable Forks (CDP) Clinton County, 138
Auburn (city) Cayuga County, 94
Augusta (town) Oneida County, 415
Aurelius (town) Cayuga County, 95
Aurora (village) Cayuga County, 95
Aurora (town) Erie County, 197
Austerlitz (town) Columbia County, 147
Ava (town) Oneida County, 415
Averill Park (CDP) Rensselaer County, 513
Avoca (town) Steuben County, 589
Avoca (village) Steuben County, 589
Avon (town) Livingston County, 300
Avon (village) Livingston County, 301
Babylon (town) Suffolk County, 604
Babylon (village) Suffolk County, 604
Bainbridge (town) Chenango County, 128
Bainbridge (village) Chenango County, 128
Baiting Hollow (CDP) Suffolk County, 605
Bakers Mills (unincorporated) Warren County, 700
Baldwin (town) Chemung County, 120
Baldwin (CDP) Nassau County, 342
Baldwin Harbor (CDP) Nassau County, 342
Baldwin Place (unincorporated) Westchester County, 726
Baldwinsville (village) Onondaga County, 433
Ballston (town) Saratoga County, 554
Ballston Lake (unincorporated) Saratoga County, 554
Ballston Spa (village) Saratoga County, 555
Balmville (CDP) Orange County, 458
Bangor (town) Franklin County, 228
Bardonia (CDP) Rockland County, 524

Barker (town) Broome County, 70
Barker (village) Niagara County, 405
Barneveld (village) Oneida County, 415
Barnum Island (CDP) Nassau County, 342
Barre (town) Orleans County, 479
Barrington (town) Yates County, 760
Barrytown (unincorporated) Dutchess County, 178
Barryville (unincorporated) Sullivan County, 649
Barton (town) Tioga County, 666
Basom (unincorporated) Genesee County, 243
Batavia (town) Genesee County, 243
Batavia (city) Genesee County, 243
Bath (town) Steuben County, 589
Bath (village) Steuben County, 590
Baxter Estates (village) Nassau County, 342
Bay Park (CDP) Nassau County, 343
Bay Shore (CDP) Suffolk County, 605
Bayport (CDP) Suffolk County, 605
Bayside (unincorporated) Queens County, 390
Bayville (village) Nassau County, 343
Baywood (CDP) Suffolk County, 605
Beacon (city) Dutchess County, 179
Bearsville (unincorporated) Ulster County, 679
Beaver Dam Lake (CDP) Orange County, 458
Beaver Dams (unincorporated) Schuyler County, 579
Beaver Falls (unincorporated) Lewis County, 292
Bedford (town) Westchester County, 727
Bedford (CDP) Westchester County, 726
Bedford Hills (CDP) Westchester County, 727
Beekman (town) Dutchess County, 179
Beekmantown (town) Clinton County, 138
Belfast (town) Allegany County, 59
Belfast (CDP) Allegany County, 59
Belle Terre (village) Suffolk County, 606
Bellerose (village) Nassau County, 343
Bellerose Terrace (CDP) Nassau County, 343
Belleville (CDP) Jefferson County, 277
Bellmont (town) Franklin County, 228
Bellmore (CDP) Nassau County, 344
Bellona (unincorporated) Yates County, 760
Bellport (village) Suffolk County, 606
Belmont (village) Allegany County, 59
Bemus Point (village) Chautauqua County, 105
Bennington (town) Wyoming County, 752
Benson (town) Hamilton County, 262
Benton (town) Yates County, 760
Bergen (town) Genesee County, 244
Bergen (village) Genesee County, 244
Berkshire (town) Tioga County, 666
Berlin (town) Rensselaer County, 513
Berne (town) Albany County, 47
Bernhards Bay (unincorporated) Oswego County, 484
Bethany (town) Genesee County, 244
Bethel (town) Sullivan County, 649
Bethlehem (town) Albany County, 47
Bethpage (CDP) Nassau County, 344
Big Flats (town) Chemung County, 121
Big Flats (CDP) Chemung County, 120
Big Indian (unincorporated) Ulster County, 679
Billington Heights (CDP) Erie County, 197
Binghamton (town) Broome County, 70
Binghamton (city) Broome County, 70
Binghamton University (CDP) Broome County, 71
Birdsall (town) Allegany County, 59
Black Brook (town) Clinton County, 138
Black Creek (unincorporated) Allegany County, 60
Black River (village) Jefferson County, 277
Blasdell (village) Erie County, 198
Blauvelt (CDP) Rockland County, 524

CDP = Census Designated Place

CDP = Census Designated Place

Chatham (town) Columbia County, 148
Chatham (village) Columbia County, 148
Chaumont (village) Jefferson County, 280
Chautauqua (town) Chautauqua County, 107
Chautauqua (CDP) Chautauqua County, 107
Chautauqua County, 104
Chazy (town) Clinton County, 139
Chazy (CDP) Clinton County, 139
Cheektowaga (town) Erie County, 200
Cheektowaga (CDP) Erie County, 200
Chelsea (unincorporated) Dutchess County, 180
Chemung (town) Chemung County, 121
Chemung County, 119
Chenango (town) Broome County, 71
Chenango Bridge (CDP) Broome County, 71
Chenango County, 127
Chenango Forks (unincorporated) Broome County, 72
Cherry Creek (town) Chautauqua County, 108
Cherry Creek (village) Chautauqua County, 108
Cherry Plain (unincorporated) Rensselaer County, 514
Cherry Valley (town) Otsego County, 495
Cherry Valley (village) Otsego County, 496
Chester (town) Orange County, 459
Chester (village) Orange County, 459
Chester (town) Warren County, 701
Chesterfield (town) Essex County, 218
Chestertown (CDP) Warren County, 701
Chestnut Ridge (village) Rockland County, 524
Chichester (unincorporated) Ulster County, 680
Childwold (unincorporated) Saint Lawrence County, 538
Chili (town) Monroe County, 324
Chippewa Bay (unincorporated) Saint Lawrence County, 538
Chittenango (village) Madison County, 315
Churchville (village) Monroe County, 324
Churubusco (unincorporated) Clinton County, 140
Cicero (town) Onondaga County, 435
Cincinnatus (town) Cortland County, 158
Circleville (unincorporated) Orange County, 459
Clare (town) Saint Lawrence County, 539
Clarence (town) Erie County, 201
Clarence (CDP) Erie County, 201
Clarence Center (CDP) Erie County, 201
Clarendon (town) Orleans County, 480
Clark Mills (CDP) Oneida County, 418
Clarkson (town) Monroe County, 325
Clarkson (CDP) Monroe County, 324
Clarkstown (town) Rockland County, 524
Clarksville (town) Allegany County, 62
Claryville (unincorporated) Sullivan County, 651
Claverack (town) Columbia County, 148
Claverack-Red Mills (CDP) Columbia County, 149
Clay (town) Onondaga County, 435
Clayton (town) Jefferson County, 280
Clayton (village) Jefferson County, 280
Clayville (village) Oneida County, 418
Clemons (unincorporated) Washington County, 708
Clermont (town) Columbia County, 149
Cleveland (village) Oswego County, 485
Clifton (town) Saint Lawrence County, 539
Clifton Park (town) Saratoga County, 556
Clifton Springs (village) Ontario County, 450
Climax (unincorporated) Greene County, 251
Clinton (town) Clinton County, 140
Clinton (town) Dutchess County, 180
Clinton (village) Oneida County, 418
Clinton Corners (unincorporated) Dutchess County, 180

Clinton County, 136
Clintondale (CDP) Ulster County, 680
Clyde (village) Wayne County, 717
Clymer (town) Chautauqua County, 108
Cobleskill (town) Schoharie County, 572
Cobleskill (village) Schoharie County, 572
Cochecton (town) Sullivan County, 651
Coeymans (town) Albany County, 47
Coeymans Hollow (unincorporated) Albany County, 47
Cohocton (town) Steuben County, 592
Cohocton (village) Steuben County, 592
Cohoes (city) Albany County, 48
Colchester (town) Delaware County, 166
Cold Brook (village) Herkimer County, 266
Cold Spring (village) Putnam County, 509
Cold Spring Harbor (CDP) Suffolk County, 609
Colden (town) Erie County, 201
Coldspring (town) Cattaraugus County, 81
Colesville (town) Broome County, 72
College Point (unincorporated) Queens County, 391
Collins (town) Erie County, 202
Collins Center (unincorporated) Erie County, 202
Colonie (town) Albany County, 48
Colonie (village) Albany County, 48
Colton (town) Saint Lawrence County, 539
Colton (CDP) Saint Lawrence County, 539
Columbia (town) Herkimer County, 266
Columbia County, 146
Columbus (town) Chenango County, 128
Commack (CDP) Suffolk County, 610
Comstock (unincorporated) Washington County, 709
Concord (town) Erie County, 202
Conesus (town) Livingston County, 302
Conesus Hamlet (CDP) Livingston County, 302
Conesus Lake (CDP) Livingston County, 302
Conesville (town) Schoharie County, 573
Conewango (town) Cattaraugus County, 81
Conewango Valley (unincorporated) Cattaraugus County, 81
Congers (CDP) Rockland County, 525
Conklin (town) Broome County, 72
Connelly (unincorporated) Ulster County, 680
Conquest (town) Cayuga County, 96
Constable (town) Franklin County, 230
Constableville (village) Lewis County, 293
Constantia (town) Oswego County, 485
Constantia (CDP) Oswego County, 485
Coopers Plains (CDP) Steuben County, 593
Cooperstown (village) Otsego County, 496
Copake (town) Columbia County, 149
Copake Falls (unincorporated) Columbia County, 149
Copake Lake (CDP) Columbia County, 150
Copenhagen (village) Lewis County, 293
Copiague (CDP) Suffolk County, 610
Coram (CDP) Suffolk County, 610
Corfu (village) Genesee County, 245
Corinth (town) Saratoga County, 556
Corinth (village) Saratoga County, 556
Corning (town) Steuben County, 593
Corning (city) Steuben County, 593
Cornwall (town) Orange County, 460
Cornwall-on-Hudson (village) Orange County, 460
Cornwallville (unincorporated) Greene County, 252
Corona (unincorporated) Queens County, 391
Cortland (city) Cortland County, 158
Cortland County, 157
Cortland West (CDP) Cortland County, 159

Cortlandt (town) Westchester County, 728
Cortlandt Manor (unincorporated) Westchester County, 729
Cortlandville (town) Cortland County, 159
Cossayuna (unincorporated) Washington County, 709
Cottekill (unincorporated) Ulster County, 681
Country Knolls (CDP) Saratoga County, 556
Cove Neck (village) Nassau County, 345
Coventry (town) Chenango County, 128
Covert (town) Seneca County, 583
Covington (town) Wyoming County, 753
Cowlesville (unincorporated) Wyoming County, 753
Coxsackie (town) Greene County, 252
Coxsackie (village) Greene County, 252
Cragsmoor (CDP) Ulster County, 681
Cranberry Lake (CDP) Saint Lawrence County, 539
Craryville (unincorporated) Columbia County, 150
Crawford (town) Orange County, 460
Croghan (town) Lewis County, 294
Croghan (village) Lewis County, 294
Crompond (CDP) Westchester County, 729
Cropseyville (unincorporated) Rensselaer County, 515
Cross River (unincorporated) Westchester County, 729
Croton Falls (unincorporated) Westchester County, 730
Croton-on-Hudson (village) Westchester County, 730
Crown Heights (CDP) Dutchess County, 180
Crown Point (town) Essex County, 218
Crugers (CDP) Westchester County, 730
Crystal Beach (CDP) Ontario County, 450
Cuba (town) Allegany County, 62
Cuba (village) Allegany County, 62
Cuddebackville (unincorporated) Orange County, 461
Cumberland Head (CDP) Clinton County, 140
Cumminsville (CDP) Livingston County, 302
Cutchogue (CDP) Suffolk County, 611
Cuyler (town) Cortland County, 159
Cuylerville (CDP) Livingston County, 302
Dale (unincorporated) Wyoming County, 753
Dalton (CDP) Livingston County, 303
Danby (town) Tompkins County, 672
Dannemora (town) Clinton County, 140
Dannemora (village) Clinton County, 141
Dansville (village) Livingston County, 303
Dansville (town) Steuben County, 593
Danube (town) Herkimer County, 266
Darien (town) Genesee County, 245
Darien Center (unincorporated) Genesee County, 245
Davenport (town) Delaware County, 166
Davenport Center (CDP) Delaware County, 166
Day (town) Saratoga County, 557
Dayton (town) Cattaraugus County, 82
De Kalb (town) Saint Lawrence County, 540
De Peyster (town) Saint Lawrence County, 540
De Witt (town) Onondaga County, 435
Deansboro (unincorporated) Oneida County, 418
Decatur (town) Otsego County, 496
Deer Park (CDP) Suffolk County, 611
Deerfield (town) Oneida County, 419
Deerpark (town) Orange County, 461
Deferiet (village) Jefferson County, 280
DeKalb Junction (CDP) Saint Lawrence County, 540
Delancey (unincorporated) Delaware County, 166

CDP = Census Designated Place

CDP = Census Designated Place

Florida (village) Orange County, 461
Flower Hill (village) Nassau County, 349
Floyd (town) Oneida County, 419
Flushing (unincorporated) Queens County, 393
Fly Creek (unincorporated) Otsego County, 498
Fonda (village) Montgomery County, 336
Forest Hills (unincorporated) Queens County, 394
Forest Home (CDP) Tompkins County, 673
Forestburgh (town) Sullivan County, 652
Forestport (town) Oneida County, 420
Forestville (village) Chautauqua County, 111
Fort Ann (town) Washington County, 710
Fort Ann (village) Washington County, 710
Fort Covington (town) Franklin County, 231
Fort Covington Hamlet (CDP) Franklin County, 231
Fort Drum (CDP) Jefferson County, 282
Fort Edward (town) Washington County, 710
Fort Edward (village) Washington County, 710
Fort Hunter (unincorporated) Montgomery County, 337
Fort Johnson (village) Montgomery County, 337
Fort Montgomery (CDP) Orange County, 462
Fort Plain (village) Montgomery County, 337
Fort Salonga (CDP) Suffolk County, 616
Fowler (town) Saint Lawrence County, 541
Fowlerville (CDP) Livingston County, 303
Frankfort (town) Herkimer County, 267
Frankfort (village) Herkimer County, 268
Franklin (town) Delaware County, 169
Franklin (village) Delaware County, 169
Franklin (town) Franklin County, 231
Franklin County, 227
Franklin Springs (unincorporated) Oneida County, 420
Franklin Square (CDP) Nassau County, 349
Franklinville (town) Cattaraugus County, 83
Franklinville (village) Cattaraugus County, 84
Fredonia (village) Chautauqua County, 111
Freedom (town) Cattaraugus County, 84
Freedom Plains (CDP) Dutchess County, 182
Freehold (unincorporated) Greene County, 254
Freeport (village) Nassau County, 349
Freetown (town) Cortland County, 159
Freeville (village) Tompkins County, 673
Fremont (town) Steuben County, 594
Fremont (town) Sullivan County, 652
Fremont Center (unincorporated) Sullivan County, 653
French Creek (town) Chautauqua County, 111
Fresh Meadows (unincorporated) Queens County, 394
Frewsburg (CDP) Chautauqua County, 111
Friendship (town) Allegany County, 63
Friendship (village) Allegany County, 63
Fulton (city) Oswego County, 486
Fulton (town) Schoharie County, 573
Fulton County, 237
Fultonham (unincorporated) Schoharie County, 574
Fultonville (village) Montgomery County, 337
Gabriels (unincorporated) Franklin County, 232
Gaines (town) Orleans County, 480
Gainesville (town) Wyoming County, 754
Gainesville (village) Wyoming County, 754
Galen (town) Wayne County, 717
Galeville (CDP) Onondaga County, 438
Gallatin (town) Columbia County, 151
Galway (town) Saratoga County, 557
Galway (village) Saratoga County, 557
Gang Mills (CDP) Steuben County, 594
Gansevoort (unincorporated) Saratoga County, 558

Garden City (village) Nassau County, 350
Garden City Park (CDP) Nassau County, 350
Garden City South (CDP) Nassau County, 350
Gardiner (town) Ulster County, 682
Gardiner (CDP) Ulster County, 682
Gardnertown (CDP) Orange County, 462
Garnerville (unincorporated) Rockland County, 525
Garrattsville (unincorporated) Otsego County, 498
Garrison (unincorporated) Putnam County, 509
Gasport (CDP) Niagara County, 406
Gates (town) Monroe County, 326
Gates (CDP) Monroe County, 325
Geddes (town) Onondaga County, 438
Genesee (town) Allegany County, 63
Genesee County, 242
Genesee Falls (town) Wyoming County, 754
Geneseo (town) Livingston County, 304
Geneseo (village) Livingston County, 304
Geneva (town) Ontario County, 451
Geneva (city) Ontario County, 451
Genoa (town) Cayuga County, 97
Georgetown (town) Madison County, 316
German (town) Chenango County, 129
German Flatts (town) Herkimer County, 268
Germantown (town) Columbia County, 151
Germantown (CDP) Columbia County, 151
Gerry (town) Chautauqua County, 112
Getzville (unincorporated) Erie County, 206
Ghent (town) Columbia County, 152
Ghent (CDP) Columbia County, 151
Gilbertsville (village) Otsego County, 498
Gilboa (town) Schoharie County, 574
Gilgo (CDP) Suffolk County, 617
Glasco (CDP) Ulster County, 683
Glen (town) Montgomery County, 338
Glen Aubrey (CDP) Broome County, 74
Glen Cove (city) Nassau County, 350
Glen Head (CDP) Nassau County, 351
Glen Oaks (unincorporated) Queens County, 394
Glen Park (village) Jefferson County, 283
Glen Spey (unincorporated) Sullivan County, 653
Glen Wild (unincorporated) Sullivan County, 653
Glenfield (unincorporated) Lewis County, 294
Glenford (unincorporated) Ulster County, 683
Glenham (unincorporated) Dutchess County, 182
Glenmont (unincorporated) Albany County, 49
Glens Falls (city) Warren County, 702
Glens Falls North (CDP) Warren County, 702
Glenville (town) Schenectady County, 567
Glenwood (unincorporated) Erie County, 206
Glenwood Landing (CDP) Nassau County, 351
Gloversville (city) Fulton County, 239
Golden's Bridge (CDP) Westchester County, 732
Gordon Heights (CDP) Suffolk County, 617
Gorham (town) Ontario County, 452
Gorham (CDP) Ontario County, 451
Goshen (town) Orange County, 462
Goshen (village) Orange County, 462
Gouverneur (town) Saint Lawrence County, 541
Gouverneur (village) Saint Lawrence County, 541
Gowanda (village) Cattaraugus County, 84
Grafton (town) Rensselaer County, 516
Grahamsville (unincorporated) Sullivan County, 653
Granby (town) Oswego County, 486
Grand Gorge (unincorporated) Delaware County, 170
Grand Island (town) Erie County, 206

Grand View-on-Hudson (village) Rockland County, 525
Grandyle Village (CDP) Erie County, 207
Granger (town) Allegany County, 64
Granite Springs (unincorporated) Westchester County, 732
Granville (town) Washington County, 711
Granville (village) Washington County, 711
Great Bend (CDP) Jefferson County, 283
Great Neck (village) Nassau County, 351
Great Neck Estates (village) Nassau County, 352
Great Neck Gardens (CDP) Nassau County, 352
Great Neck Plaza (village) Nassau County, 352
Great River (CDP) Suffolk County, 617
Great Valley (town) Cattaraugus County, 84
Greece (town) Monroe County, 326
Greece (CDP) Monroe County, 326
Green Island (town/village) Albany County, 50
Greenburgh (town) Westchester County, 732
Greene (town) Chenango County, 129
Greene (village) Chenango County, 129
Greene County, 249
Greenfield (town) Saratoga County, 558
Greenfield Center (unincorporated) Saratoga County, 558
Greenfield Park (unincorporated) Ulster County, 683
Greenhurst (unincorporated) Chautauqua County, 112
Greenlawn (CDP) Suffolk County, 617
Greenport (town) Columbia County, 152
Greenport (village) Suffolk County, 618
Greenport West (CDP) Suffolk County, 618
Greenvale (CDP) Nassau County, 352
Greenville (town) Greene County, 254
Greenville (CDP) Greene County, 254
Greenville (town) Orange County, 463
Greenville (CDP) Westchester County, 733
Greenwich (town) Washington County, 711
Greenwich (village) Washington County, 712
Greenwood (town) Steuben County, 594
Greenwood Lake (village) Orange County, 463
Greig (town) Lewis County, 295
Greigsville (CDP) Livingston County, 304
Groton (town) Tompkins County, 674
Groton (village) Tompkins County, 674
Grove (town) Allegany County, 64
Groveland (town) Livingston County, 305
Groveland Station (CDP) Livingston County, 305
Guilderland (town) Albany County, 50
Guilderland Center (unincorporated) Albany County, 50
Guilford (town) Chenango County, 130
Guilford (CDP) Chenango County, 129
Hadley (town) Saratoga County, 559
Hadley (CDP) Saratoga County, 558
Hagaman (village) Montgomery County, 338
Hague (town) Warren County, 702
Hailesboro (CDP) Saint Lawrence County, 542
Haines Falls (unincorporated) Greene County, 254
Halcott (town) Greene County, 255
Halcottsville (unincorporated) Delaware County, 170
Halesite (CDP) Suffolk County, 618
Halfmoon (town) Saratoga County, 559
Hall (CDP) Ontario County, 452
Hamburg (town) Erie County, 207
Hamburg (village) Erie County, 207
Hamden (town) Delaware County, 170
Hamilton (town) Madison County, 317
Hamilton (village) Madison County, 317

CDP = Census Designated Place

CDP = Census Designated Place

CDP = Census Designated Place

Maplecrest (unincorporated) Greene County, 257
Marathon (town) Cortland County, 161
Marathon (village) Cortland County, 161
Marbletown (town) Ulster County, 687
Marcellus (town) Onondaga County, 440
Marcellus (village) Onondaga County, 441
Marcy (town) Oneida County, 422
Margaretville (village) Delaware County, 172
Mariaville Lake (CDP) Schenectady County, 568
Marietta (unincorporated) Onondaga County, 441
Marilla (town) Erie County, 210
Marion (town) Wayne County, 719
Marion (CDP) Wayne County, 719
Marlboro (CDP) Ulster County, 688
Marlborough (town) Ulster County, 688
Marshall (town) Oneida County, 422
Martinsburg (town) Lewis County, 297
Martville (unincorporated) Cayuga County, 98
Maryknoll (unincorporated) Westchester County, 737
Maryland (town) Otsego County, 499
Masonville (town) Delaware County, 172
Maspeth (unincorporated) Queens County, 398
Massapequa (CDP) Nassau County, 361
Massapequa Park (village) Nassau County, 362
Massena (town) Saint Lawrence County, 545
Massena (village) Saint Lawrence County, 545
Mastic (CDP) Suffolk County, 624
Mastic Beach (village) Suffolk County, 624
Matinecock (village) Nassau County, 362
Mattituck (CDP) Suffolk County, 625
Mattydale (CDP) Onondaga County, 441
Maybrook (village) Orange County, 466
Mayfield (town) Fulton County, 240
Mayfield (village) Fulton County, 240
Mayville (village) Chautauqua County, 115
McDonough (town) Chenango County, 130
McGraw (village) Cortland County, 161
McLean (unincorporated) Tompkins County, 676
Mechanicstown (CDP) Orange County, 466
Mechanicville (city) Saratoga County, 559
Medford (CDP) Suffolk County, 625
Medina (village) Orleans County, 481
Medusa (unincorporated) Albany County, 51
Melrose (unincorporated) Rensselaer County, 517
Melrose Park (CDP) Cayuga County, 99
Melville (CDP) Suffolk County, 625
Memphis (unincorporated) Onondaga County, 442
Menands (village) Albany County, 51
Mendon (town) Monroe County, 328
Mentz (town) Cayuga County, 99
Meredith (town) Delaware County, 172
Meridale (unincorporated) Delaware County, 173
Meridian (village) Cayuga County, 99
Merrick (CDP) Nassau County, 362
Merritt Park (CDP) Dutchess County, 185
Mexico (town) Oswego County, 488
Mexico (village) Oswego County, 488
Middle Granville (unincorporated) Washington County, 714
Middle Grove (unincorporated) Saratoga County, 560
Middle Island (CDP) Suffolk County, 625
Middle Village (unincorporated) Queens County, 398
Middleburgh (town) Schoharie County, 575
Middleburgh (village) Schoharie County, 575
Middlebury (town) Wyoming County, 755
Middlefield (town) Otsego County, 500
Middleport (village) Niagara County, 408

Middlesex (town) Yates County, 762
Middletown (town) Delaware County, 173
Middletown (city) Orange County, 466
Middleville (village) Herkimer County, 270
Milan (town) Dutchess County, 185
Milford (town) Otsego County, 500
Milford (village) Otsego County, 500
Mill Neck (village) Nassau County, 362
Millbrook (village) Dutchess County, 185
Miller Place (CDP) Suffolk County, 626
Millerton (village) Dutchess County, 186
Millport (village) Chemung County, 124
Millwood (unincorporated) Westchester County, 737
Milo (town) Yates County, 762
Milton (town) Saratoga County, 560
Milton (CDP) Saratoga County, 560
Milton (CDP) Ulster County, 688
Mina (town) Chautauqua County, 115
Minden (town) Montgomery County, 338
Mineola (village) Nassau County, 363
Minerva (town) Essex County, 220
Minetto (town) Oswego County, 488
Minetto (CDP) Oswego County, 488
Mineville (CDP) Essex County, 220
Minisink (town) Orange County, 467
Minoa (village) Onondaga County, 442
Modena (unincorporated) Ulster County, 688
Mohawk (village) Herkimer County, 271
Mohawk (town) Montgomery County, 338
Mohegan Lake (unincorporated) Westchester County, 737
Moira (town) Franklin County, 233
Mongaup Valley (unincorporated) Sullivan County, 658
Monroe (town) Orange County, 467
Monroe (village) Orange County, 467
Monroe County, 323
Monsey (CDP) Rockland County, 527
Montague (town) Lewis County, 297
Montauk (CDP) Suffolk County, 626
Montebello (village) Rockland County, 527
Montezuma (town) Cayuga County, 99
Montgomery (town) Orange County, 468
Montgomery (village) Orange County, 468
Montgomery County, 334
Monticello (village) Sullivan County, 658
Montour (town) Schuyler County, 580
Montour Falls (village) Schuyler County, 581
Montrose (CDP) Westchester County, 738
Mooers (town) Clinton County, 142
Mooers (CDP) Clinton County, 142
Mooers Forks (unincorporated) Clinton County, 143
Moravia (town) Cayuga County, 100
Moravia (village) Cayuga County, 100
Moreau (town) Saratoga County, 560
Morehouse (town) Hamilton County, 264
Moriah (town) Essex County, 221
Moriah Center (unincorporated) Essex County, 221
Moriches (CDP) Suffolk County, 626
Morris (town) Otsego County, 500
Morris (village) Otsego County, 501
Morrisonville (CDP) Clinton County, 143
Morristown (town) Saint Lawrence County, 546
Morristown (village) Saint Lawrence County, 546
Morrisville (village) Madison County, 319
Mount Hope (town) Orange County, 468
Mount Ivy (CDP) Rockland County, 527
Mount Kisco (town/village) Westchester County, 738
Mount Marion (unincorporated) Ulster County, 689

Mount Morris (town) Livingston County, 308
Mount Morris (village) Livingston County, 308
Mount Pleasant (town) Westchester County, 738
Mount Sinai (CDP) Suffolk County, 627
Mount Tremper (unincorporated) Ulster County, 689
Mount Upton (unincorporated) Chenango County, 130
Mount Vernon (city) Westchester County, 739
Mount Vision (unincorporated) Otsego County, 501
Mountain Dale (unincorporated) Sullivan County, 658
Mountain Lodge Park (CDP) Orange County, 468
Mountainville (unincorporated) Orange County, 469
Mumford (unincorporated) Monroe County, 328
Munnsville (village) Madison County, 320
Munsey Park (village) Nassau County, 363
Munsons Corners (CDP) Cortland County, 162
Murray (town) Orleans County, 482
Muttontown (village) Nassau County, 363
Myers Corner (CDP) Dutchess County, 186
Nanticoke (town) Broome County, 76
Nanuet (CDP) Rockland County, 528
Napanoch (CDP) Ulster County, 689
Napeague (CDP) Suffolk County, 627
Naples (town) Ontario County, 453
Naples (village) Ontario County, 454
Napoli (town) Cattaraugus County, 88
Narrowsburg (CDP) Sullivan County, 659
Nassau (town) Rensselaer County, 518
Nassau (village) Rensselaer County, 518
Nassau County, 340
Natural Bridge (CDP) Jefferson County, 286
Nedrow (CDP) Onondaga County, 442
Nelliston (village) Montgomery County, 339
Nelson (town) Madison County, 320
Nelsonville (village) Putnam County, 510
Nesconset (CDP) Suffolk County, 627
Neversink (town) Sullivan County, 659
New Albion (town) Cattaraugus County, 88
New Baltimore (town) Greene County, 257
New Berlin (town) Chenango County, 131
New Berlin (village) Chenango County, 131
New Bremen (town) Lewis County, 297
New Cassel (CDP) Nassau County, 363
New Castle (town) Westchester County, 739
New City (CDP) Rockland County, 528
New Hampton (unincorporated) Orange County, 469
New Hartford (town) Oneida County, 422
New Hartford (village) Oneida County, 422
New Haven (town) Oswego County, 489
New Hempstead (village) Rockland County, 528
New Hudson (town) Allegany County, 65
New Hyde Park (village) Nassau County, 364
New Kingston (unincorporated) Delaware County, 173
New Lebanon (town) Columbia County, 154
New Lisbon (town) Otsego County, 501
New Paltz (town) Ulster County, 689
New Paltz (village) Ulster County, 690
New Rochelle (city) Westchester County, 739
New Russia (unincorporated) Essex County, 221
New Scotland (town) Albany County, 52
New Square (village) Rockland County, 528
New Suffolk (CDP) Suffolk County, 627
New Windsor (town) Orange County, 469
New Windsor (CDP) Orange County, 469
New Woodstock (unincorporated) Madison County, 320
New York (city), 379

CDP = Census Designated Place

New York Mills (village) Oneida County, 423
Newark (village) Wayne County, 719
Newark Valley (town) Tioga County, 667
Newark Valley (village) Tioga County, 667
Newburgh (town) Orange County, 470
Newburgh (city) Orange County, 470
Newcomb (town) Essex County, 221
Newfane (town) Niagara County, 408
Newfane (CDP) Niagara County, 408
Newfield (town) Tompkins County, 676
Newfield Hamlet (CDP) Tompkins County, 676
Newport (town) Herkimer County, 271
Newport (village) Herkimer County, 271
Newstead (town) Erie County, 211
Newton Falls (unincorporated) Saint Lawrence
    County, 546
Niagara (town) Niagara County, 408
Niagara County, 404
Niagara Falls (city) Niagara County, 409
Niagara University (unincorporated) Niagara
    County, 409
Nichols (town) Tioga County, 667
Nichols (village) Tioga County, 668
Nicholville (unincorporated) Saint Lawrence
    County, 546
Niles (town) Cayuga County, 100
Nineveh (unincorporated) Broome County, 76
Niskayuna (town) Schenectady County, 568
Nissequogue (village) Suffolk County, 628
Niverville (CDP) Columbia County, 154
Norfolk (town) Saint Lawrence County, 547
Norfolk (CDP) Saint Lawrence County, 547
North Amityville (CDP) Suffolk County, 628
North Babylon (CDP) Suffolk County, 628
North Ballston Spa (CDP) Saratoga County, 561
North Bangor (unincorporated) Franklin County,
    233
North Bay (unincorporated) Oneida County, 423
North Bay Shore (CDP) Suffolk County, 628
North Bellmore (CDP) Nassau County, 364
North Bellport (CDP) Suffolk County, 629
North Blenheim (unincorporated) Schoharie
    County, 575
North Boston (CDP) Erie County, 211
North Branch (unincorporated) Sullivan County,
    659
North Brookfield (unincorporated) Madison
    County, 320
North Castle (town) Westchester County, 740
North Chatham (unincorporated) Columbia
    County, 155
North Chili (unincorporated) Monroe County,
    328
North Collins (town) Erie County, 211
North Collins (village) Erie County, 211
North Creek (CDP) Warren County, 704
North Dansville (town) Livingston County, 309
North East (town) Dutchess County, 186
North Elba (town) Essex County, 222
North Gates (CDP) Monroe County, 329
North Great River (CDP) Suffolk County, 629
North Greenbush (town) Rensselaer County,
    518
North Harmony (town) Chautauqua County, 115
North Haven (village) Suffolk County, 629
North Hempstead (town) Nassau County, 364
North Hills (village) Nassau County, 365
North Hornell (village) Steuben County, 597
North Hudson (town) Essex County, 222
North Java (unincorporated) Wyoming County,
    755
North Lawrence (unincorporated) Saint
    Lawrence County, 547
North Lindenhurst (CDP) Suffolk County, 629

North Lynbrook (CDP) Nassau County, 365
North Massapequa (CDP) Nassau County, 365
North Merrick (CDP) Nassau County, 365
North New Hyde Park (CDP) Nassau County,
    366
North Norwich (town) Chenango County, 131
North Patchogue (CDP) Suffolk County, 630
North Pitcher (unincorporated) Chenango
    County, 131
North River (unincorporated) Warren County,
    704
North Rose (CDP) Wayne County, 720
North Salem (town) Westchester County, 740
North Sea (CDP) Suffolk County, 630
North Syracuse (village) Onondaga County, 442
North Tonawanda (city) Niagara County, 410
North Valley Stream (CDP) Nassau County, 366
North Wantagh (CDP) Nassau County, 366
Northampton (town) Fulton County, 240
Northampton (CDP) Suffolk County, 630
Northeast Ithaca (CDP) Tompkins County, 677
Northport (village) Suffolk County, 630
Northumberland (town) Saratoga County, 561
Northville (village) Fulton County, 241
Northville (CDP) Suffolk County, 631
Northwest Harbor (CDP) Suffolk County, 631
Northwest Ithaca (CDP) Tompkins County, 677
Norway (town) Herkimer County, 271
Norwich (town) Chenango County, 132
Norwich (city) Chenango County, 132
Norwood (village) Saint Lawrence County, 547
Noyack (CDP) Suffolk County, 631
Nunda (town) Livingston County, 309
Nunda (village) Livingston County, 309
Nyack (village) Rockland County, 529
Oak Beach-Captree (CDP) Suffolk County, 631
Oak Hill (unincorporated) Greene County, 258
Oakdale (CDP) Suffolk County, 632
Oakfield (town) Genesee County, 247
Oakfield (village) Genesee County, 247
Oakland Gardens (unincorporated) Queens
    County, 398
Obernburg (unincorporated) Sullivan County,
    659
Ocean Beach (village) Suffolk County, 632
Oceanside (CDP) Nassau County, 366
Odessa (village) Schuyler County, 581
Ogden (town) Monroe County, 329
Ogdensburg (city) Saint Lawrence County, 548
Ohio (town) Herkimer County, 272
Oil Springs Reservation (reservation) Allegany
    County, 65
Olcott (CDP) Niagara County, 410
Old Bethpage (CDP) Nassau County, 367
Old Brookville (village) Nassau County, 367
Old Chatham (unincorporated) Columbia
    County, 155
Old Field (village) Suffolk County, 632
Old Forge (CDP) Herkimer County, 272
Old Westbury (village) Nassau County, 367
Olean (town) Cattaraugus County, 89
Olean (city) Cattaraugus County, 88
Olive (town) Ulster County, 690
Olivebridge (unincorporated) Ulster County, 690
Olmstedville (unincorporated) Essex County,
    222
Oneida (city) Madison County, 321
Oneida Castle (village) Oneida County, 423
Oneida County, 413
Oneonta (town) Otsego County, 502
Oneonta (city) Otsego County, 501
Onondaga (town) Onondaga County, 443
Onondaga County, 433

Onondaga Nation Reservation (reservation)
    Onondaga County, 443
Ontario (town) Wayne County, 720
Ontario (CDP) Wayne County, 720
Ontario County, 448
Oppenheim (town) Fulton County, 241
Orange (town) Schuyler County, 581
Orange County, 457
Orange Lake (CDP) Orange County, 470
Orangeburg (CDP) Rockland County, 529
Orangetown (town) Rockland County, 529
Orangeville (town) Wyoming County, 756
Orchard Park (town) Erie County, 212
Orchard Park (village) Erie County, 212
Orient (CDP) Suffolk County, 632
Oriskany (village) Oneida County, 423
Oriskany Falls (village) Oneida County, 424
Orleans (town) Jefferson County, 286
Orleans County, 478
Orwell (town) Oswego County, 489
Osceola (town) Lewis County, 298
Ossian (town) Livingston County, 309
Ossining (town) Westchester County, 740
Ossining (village) Westchester County, 741
Oswegatchie (town) Saint Lawrence County,
    548
Oswego (town) Oswego County, 490
Oswego (city) Oswego County, 489
Oswego County, 483
Otego (town) Otsego County, 502
Otego (village) Otsego County, 502
Otisco (town) Onondaga County, 443
Otisville (village) Orange County, 471
Otsego (town) Otsego County, 503
Otsego County, 494
Otselic (town) Chenango County, 132
Otto (town) Cattaraugus County, 89
Ovid (town) Seneca County, 584
Ovid (village) Seneca County, 585
Owasco (town) Cayuga County, 100
Owego (town) Tioga County, 668
Owego (village) Tioga County, 668
Owls Head (unincorporated) Franklin County,
    234
Oxbow (CDP) Jefferson County, 286
Oxford (town) Chenango County, 133
Oxford (village) Chenango County, 133
Oyster Bay (town) Nassau County, 368
Oyster Bay (CDP) Nassau County, 368
Oyster Bay Cove (village) Nassau County, 368
Ozone Park (unincorporated) Queens County,
    399
Painted Post (village) Steuben County, 597
Palatine (town) Montgomery County, 339
Palatine Bridge (village) Montgomery County,
    339
Palenville (CDP) Greene County, 258
Palermo (town) Oswego County, 490
Palisades (unincorporated) Rockland County,
    530
Palmyra (town) Wayne County, 720
Palmyra (village) Wayne County, 721
Pamelia (town) Jefferson County, 286
Pamelia Center (CDP) Jefferson County, 287
Panama (village) Chautauqua County, 115
Paradox (unincorporated) Essex County, 222
Parc (CDP) Clinton County, 143
Paris (town) Oneida County, 424
Parish (town) Oswego County, 490
Parish (village) Oswego County, 490
Parishville (town) Saint Lawrence County, 549
Parishville (CDP) Saint Lawrence County, 548
Parksville (unincorporated) Sullivan County, 660
Parma (town) Monroe County, 329

CDP = Census Designated Place

CDP = Census Designated Place

Ridgewood (unincorporated) Queens County, 401

Rifton (CDP) Ulster County, 692

Riga (town) Monroe County, 330

Ripley (town) Chautauqua County, 117

Ripley (CDP) Chautauqua County, 116

Riverhead (town) Suffolk County, 635

Riverhead (CDP) Suffolk County, 635

Riverside (village) Steuben County, 599

Riverside (CDP) Suffolk County, 636

Rochester (city) Monroe County, 331

Rochester (town) Ulster County, 692

Rock City Falls (unincorporated) Saratoga County, 562

Rock Hill (CDP) Sullivan County, 660

Rock Stream (unincorporated) Schuyler County, 582

Rock Tavern (unincorporated) Orange County, 472

Rockaway Park (unincorporated) Queens County, 401

Rockland (town) Sullivan County, 661

Rockland County, 523

Rockville Centre (village) Nassau County, 370

Rocky Point (CDP) Suffolk County, 636

Rodman (town) Jefferson County, 288

Rodman (CDP) Jefferson County, 288

Rome (city) Oneida County, 425

Romulus (town) Seneca County, 585

Romulus (CDP) Seneca County, 585

Ronkonkoma (CDP) Suffolk County, 636

Roosevelt (CDP) Nassau County, 371

Root (town) Montgomery County, 339

Roscoe (CDP) Sullivan County, 661

Rose (town) Wayne County, 721

Roseboom (town) Otsego County, 504

Rosedale (unincorporated) Queens County, 401

Rosendale (town) Ulster County, 692

Rosendale Hamlet (CDP) Ulster County, 693

Roslyn (village) Nassau County, 371

Roslyn Estates (village) Nassau County, 371

Roslyn Harbor (village) Nassau County, 372

Roslyn Heights (CDP) Nassau County, 372

Rossie (town) Saint Lawrence County, 551

Rotterdam (town) Schenectady County, 569

Rotterdam (CDP) Schenectady County, 569

Rotterdam Junction (unincorporated) Schenectady County, 569

Round Lake (village) Saratoga County, 562

Round Top (unincorporated) Greene County, 259

Rouses Point (village) Clinton County, 145

Roxbury (town) Delaware County, 173

Royalton (town) Niagara County, 411

Ruby (unincorporated) Ulster County, 693

Rush (town) Monroe County, 332

Rushford (town) Allegany County, 66

Rushford (CDP) Allegany County, 66

Rushville (village) Yates County, 763

Russell (town) Saint Lawrence County, 551

Russell Gardens (village) Nassau County, 372

Russia (town) Herkimer County, 272

Rutland (town) Jefferson County, 288

Rye (town) Westchester County, 744

Rye (city) Westchester County, 744

Rye Brook (village) Westchester County, 744

Sabael (unincorporated) Hamilton County, 265

Sackets Harbor (village) Jefferson County, 289

Saddle Rock (village) Nassau County, 372

Saddle Rock Estates (CDP) Nassau County, 373

Sag Harbor (village) Suffolk County, 637

Sagaponack (village) Suffolk County, 637

Saint Albans (unincorporated) Queens County, 402

Saint Armand (town) Essex County, 223

Saint Bonaventure (CDP) Cattaraugus County, 91

Saint James (CDP) Suffolk County, 637

Saint Johnsville (town) Montgomery County, 339

Saint Johnsville (village) Montgomery County, 340

Saint Lawrence County, 536

Saint Regis Falls (CDP) Franklin County, 235

Saint Regis Mohawk Reservation (reservation) Franklin County, 235

Salamanca (town) Cattaraugus County, 91

Salamanca (city) Cattaraugus County, 91

Salem (town) Washington County, 714

Salem (village) Washington County, 715

Salina (town) Onondaga County, 444

Salisbury (town) Herkimer County, 273

Salisbury (CDP) Nassau County, 373

Salisbury Center (unincorporated) Herkimer County, 273

Salisbury Mills (CDP) Orange County, 472

Salt Point (CDP) Dutchess County, 191

Saltaire (village) Suffolk County, 637

Sanborn (CDP) Niagara County, 411

Sand Lake (town) Rensselaer County, 520

Sand Ridge (CDP) Oswego County, 492

Sands Point (village) Nassau County, 373

Sandy Creek (town) Oswego County, 492

Sandy Creek (village) Oswego County, 492

Sanford (town) Broome County, 77

Sangerfield (town) Oneida County, 425

Santa Clara (town) Franklin County, 235

Saranac (town) Clinton County, 145

Saranac Lake (village) Franklin County, 235

Saratoga (town) Saratoga County, 562

Saratoga County, 554

Saratoga Springs (city) Saratoga County, 563

Sardinia (town) Erie County, 212

Saugerties (town) Ulster County, 693

Saugerties (village) Ulster County, 693

Saugerties South (CDP) Ulster County, 694

Sauquoit (unincorporated) Oneida County, 426

Savannah (town) Wayne County, 722

Savannah (CDP) Wayne County, 722

Savona (village) Steuben County, 599

Sayville (CDP) Suffolk County, 638

Scarsdale (town/village) Westchester County, 745

Schaghticoke (town) Rensselaer County, 520

Schaghticoke (village) Rensselaer County, 520

Schenectady (city) Schenectady County, 569

Schenectady County, 566

Schenevus (CDP) Otsego County, 504

Schodack (town) Rensselaer County, 521

Schodack Landing (unincorporated) Rensselaer County, 521

Schoharie (town) Schoharie County, 576

Schoharie (village) Schoharie County, 576

Schoharie County, 570

Schroeppel (town) Oswego County, 493

Schroon (town) Essex County, 224

Schroon Lake (CDP) Essex County, 224

Schuyler (town) Herkimer County, 273

Schuyler County, 578

Schuyler Falls (town) Clinton County, 146

Schuylerville (village) Saratoga County, 563

Scio (town) Allegany County, 66

Scio (CDP) Allegany County, 66

Scipio (town) Cayuga County, 101

Scipio Center (unincorporated) Cayuga County, 101

Scotchtown (CDP) Orange County, 472

Scotia (village) Schenectady County, 570

Scott (town) Cortland County, 162

Scotts Corners (CDP) Westchester County, 745

Scottsburg (CDP) Livingston County, 310

Scottsville (village) Monroe County, 332

Scriba (town) Oswego County, 493

Sea Cliff (village) Nassau County, 373

Seaford (CDP) Nassau County, 374

Searingtown (CDP) Nassau County, 374

Selden (CDP) Suffolk County, 638

Selkirk (unincorporated) Albany County, 53

Sempronius (town) Cayuga County, 101

Seneca (town) Ontario County, 455

Seneca County, 582

Seneca Falls (town) Seneca County, 585

Seneca Falls (CDP) Seneca County, 586

Seneca Knolls (CDP) Onondaga County, 444

Sennett (town) Cayuga County, 102

Setauket-East Setauket (CDP) Suffolk County, 638

Severance (unincorporated) Essex County, 224

Seward (town) Schoharie County, 576

Shandaken (town) Ulster County, 694

Sharon (town) Schoharie County, 577

Sharon Springs (village) Schoharie County, 577

Shawangunk (town) Ulster County, 694

Shelby (town) Orleans County, 482

Sheldon (town) Wyoming County, 757

Shelter Island (town) Suffolk County, 639

Shelter Island (CDP) Suffolk County, 639

Shelter Island Heights (CDP) Suffolk County, 639

Shenorock (CDP) Westchester County, 745

Sherburne (town) Chenango County, 134

Sherburne (village) Chenango County, 134

Sheridan (town) Chautauqua County, 117

Sherman (town) Chautauqua County, 117

Sherman (village) Chautauqua County, 117

Sherrill (city) Oneida County, 426

Shinnecock Hills (CDP) Suffolk County, 639

Shinnecock Reservation (reservation) Suffolk County, 640

Shirley (CDP) Suffolk County, 640

Shokan (CDP) Ulster County, 694

Shoreham (village) Suffolk County, 640

Shortsville (village) Ontario County, 455

Shrub Oak (CDP) Westchester County, 746

Shushan (unincorporated) Washington County, 715

Sidney (town) Delaware County, 174

Sidney (village) Delaware County, 174

Sidney Center (unincorporated) Delaware County, 174

Silver Bay (unincorporated) Warren County, 705

Silver Creek (village) Chautauqua County, 118

Silver Lake (unincorporated) Wyoming County, 757

Silver Springs (village) Wyoming County, 758

Sinclairville (village) Chautauqua County, 118

Skaneateles (town) Onondaga County, 444

Skaneateles (village) Onondaga County, 444

Skaneateles Falls (unincorporated) Onondaga County, 445

Slate Hill (unincorporated) Orange County, 473

Slaterville Springs (unincorporated) Tompkins County, 677

Sleepy Hollow (village) Westchester County, 746

Slingerlands (unincorporated) Albany County, 53

Sloan (village) Erie County, 213

Sloansville (unincorporated) Schoharie County, 577

CDP = Census Designated Place

CDP = Census Designated Place

Tuscarora Nation Reservation (reservation) Niagara County, 412
Tusten (town) Sullivan County, 663
Tuxedo (town) Orange County, 474
Tuxedo Park (village) Orange County, 474
Tyre (town) Seneca County, 586
Tyrone (town) Schuyler County, 582
Ulster (town) Ulster County, 695
Ulster County, 678
Ulster Park (unincorporated) Ulster County, 696
Ulysses (town) Tompkins County, 678
Unadilla (town) Otsego County, 505
Unadilla (village) Otsego County, 505
Union (town) Broome County, 77
Union Springs (village) Cayuga County, 103
Union Vale (town) Dutchess County, 193
Uniondale (CDP) Nassau County, 376
Unionville (village) Orange County, 475
University at Buffalo (CDP) Erie County, 215
University Gardens (CDP) Nassau County, 376
Upper Brookville (village) Nassau County, 377
Upper Jay (unincorporated) Essex County, 225
Upper Nyack (village) Rockland County, 534
Upton (unincorporated) Suffolk County, 644
Urbana (town) Steuben County, 600
Utica (city) Oneida County, 427
Vails Gate (CDP) Orange County, 475
Valatie (village) Columbia County, 157
Valhalla (CDP) Westchester County, 748
Valley Cottage (CDP) Rockland County, 534
Valley Falls (village) Rensselaer County, 522
Valley Stream (village) Nassau County, 377
Van Buren (town) Onondaga County, 447
Van Etten (town) Chemung County, 125
Van Etten (village) Chemung County, 126
Van Hornesville (unincorporated) Herkimer County, 274
Varick (town) Seneca County, 586
Varysburg (unincorporated) Wyoming County, 758
Venice (town) Cayuga County, 103
Verbank (unincorporated) Dutchess County, 193
Vermontville (unincorporated) Franklin County, 236
Vernon (town) Oneida County, 428
Vernon (village) Oneida County, 428
Vernon Center (unincorporated) Oneida County, 428
Verona (town) Oneida County, 429
Verona (CDP) Oneida County, 429
Verona Beach (unincorporated) Oneida County, 429
Verplanck (CDP) Westchester County, 748
Versailles (unincorporated) Cattaraugus County, 92
Vestal (town) Broome County, 77
Veteran (town) Chemung County, 126
Victor (town) Ontario County, 456
Victor (village) Ontario County, 456
Victory (town) Cayuga County, 103
Victory (village) Saratoga County, 564
Victory Mills (unincorporated) Saratoga County, 564
Vienna (town) Oneida County, 430
Village Green (CDP) Onondaga County, 447
Village of the Branch (village) Suffolk County, 645
Villenova (town) Chautauqua County, 119
Viola (CDP) Rockland County, 534
Virgil (town) Cortland County, 163
Volney (town) Oswego County, 493
Voorheesville (village) Albany County, 54
Waccabuc (unincorporated) Westchester County, 748

Waddington (town) Saint Lawrence County, 552
Waddington (village) Saint Lawrence County, 553
Wading River (CDP) Suffolk County, 645
Wadsworth (CDP) Livingston County, 311
Wainscott (CDP) Suffolk County, 645
Walden (village) Orange County, 475
Wales (town) Erie County, 215
Wales Center (unincorporated) Erie County, 215
Walker Valley (CDP) Ulster County, 696
Wallkill (town) Orange County, 475
Wallkill (CDP) Ulster County, 696
Walton (town) Delaware County, 176
Walton (village) Delaware County, 176
Walton Park (CDP) Orange County, 476
Walworth (town) Wayne County, 723
Wampsville (village) Madison County, 322
Wanakah (CDP) Erie County, 216
Wanakena (unincorporated) Saint Lawrence County, 553
Wantagh (CDP) Nassau County, 377
Wappinger (town) Dutchess County, 194
Wappingers Falls (village) Dutchess County, 194
Ward (town) Allegany County, 67
Warners (unincorporated) Onondaga County, 447
Warnerville (unincorporated) Schoharie County, 578
Warren (town) Herkimer County, 274
Warren County, 699
Warrensburg (town) Warren County, 706
Warrensburg (CDP) Warren County, 706
Warsaw (town) Wyoming County, 758
Warsaw (village) Wyoming County, 759
Warwick (town) Orange County, 476
Warwick (village) Orange County, 476
Washington (town) Dutchess County, 194
Washington County, 707
Washington Heights (CDP) Orange County, 477
Washington Mills (CDP) Oneida County, 430
Washingtonville (village) Orange County, 477
Wassaic (unincorporated) Dutchess County, 194
Watchtower (CDP) Ulster County, 697
Water Mill (CDP) Suffolk County, 645
Waterford (town) Saratoga County, 565
Waterford (village) Saratoga County, 565
Waterloo (town) Seneca County, 587
Waterloo (village) Seneca County, 587
Waterport (unincorporated) Orleans County, 482
Watertown (town) Jefferson County, 290
Watertown (city) Jefferson County, 290
Waterville (village) Oneida County, 430
Watervliet (city) Albany County, 54
Watkins Glen (village) Schuyler County, 582
Watson (town) Lewis County, 299
Waverly (town) Franklin County, 236
Waverly (village) Tioga County, 670
Wawarsing (town) Ulster County, 697
Wawayanda (town) Orange County, 477
Wayland (town) Steuben County, 601
Wayland (village) Steuben County, 601
Wayne (town) Steuben County, 601
Wayne County, 716
Webb (town) Herkimer County, 274
Webster (town) Monroe County, 333
Webster (village) Monroe County, 333
Websters Crossing (CDP) Livingston County, 312
Weedsport (village) Cayuga County, 104
Wellesley Island (unincorporated) Jefferson County, 291
Wells (town) Hamilton County, 265

Wells Bridge (unincorporated) Otsego County, 506
Wellsburg (village) Chemung County, 126
Wellsville (town) Allegany County, 67
Wellsville (village) Allegany County, 68
Wesley Hills (village) Rockland County, 535
West Almond (town) Allegany County, 68
West Babylon (CDP) Suffolk County, 646
West Bay Shore (CDP) Suffolk County, 646
West Bloomfield (town) Ontario County, 456
West Carthage (village) Jefferson County, 291
West Chazy (CDP) Clinton County, 146
West Coxsackie (unincorporated) Greene County, 260
West Davenport (unincorporated) Delaware County, 176
West Eaton (unincorporated) Madison County, 322
West Edmeston (unincorporated) Madison County, 322
West Elmira (CDP) Chemung County, 126
West End (CDP) Otsego County, 506
West Falls (unincorporated) Erie County, 216
West Fulton (unincorporated) Schoharie County, 578
West Glens Falls (CDP) Warren County, 706
West Hampton Dunes (village) Suffolk County, 646
West Harrison (unincorporated) Westchester County, 749
West Haverstraw (village) Rockland County, 535
West Hempstead (CDP) Nassau County, 377
West Henrietta (unincorporated) Monroe County, 333
West Hills (CDP) Suffolk County, 646
West Hurley (CDP) Ulster County, 697
West Islip (CDP) Suffolk County, 647
West Kill (unincorporated) Greene County, 260
West Lebanon (unincorporated) Columbia County, 157
West Leyden (unincorporated) Lewis County, 299
West Monroe (town) Oswego County, 494
West Nyack (CDP) Rockland County, 535
West Oneonta (unincorporated) Otsego County, 506
West Park (unincorporated) Ulster County, 697
West Point (CDP) Orange County, 477
West Sand Lake (CDP) Rensselaer County, 522
West Sayville (CDP) Suffolk County, 647
West Seneca (CDP) Erie County, 216
West Shokan (unincorporated) Ulster County, 698
West Sparta (town) Livingston County, 312
West Stockholm (unincorporated) Saint Lawrence County, 553
West Turin (town) Lewis County, 299
West Union (town) Steuben County, 601
West Valley (CDP) Cattaraugus County, 93
West Winfield (village) Herkimer County, 274
Westbrookville (unincorporated) Sullivan County, 663
Westbury (village) Nassau County, 378
Westchester County, 724
Westdale (unincorporated) Oneida County, 430
Westerlo (town) Albany County, 54
Western (town) Oneida County, 431
Westernville (unincorporated) Oneida County, 431
Westfield (town) Chautauqua County, 119
Westfield (village) Chautauqua County, 119
Westford (town) Otsego County, 506
Westhampton (CDP) Suffolk County, 647
Westhampton Beach (village) Suffolk County, 647

CDP = Census Designated Place

CDP = Census Designated Place

Comparative Statistics

This section compares the 100 largest cities by population in the state, by the following data points:

Population

Place	2000 Census	2010 Census	Current Estimate[1]	Population Growth Since 2000 (%)
Albany city *Albany Co.*	95,658	97,856	98,468	2.9
Amherst town *Erie Co.*	116,510	122,366	124,044	6.5
Babylon town *Suffolk Co.*	211,792	213,603	214,132	1.1
Bay Shore cdp *Suffolk Co.*	23,852	26,337	29,670	24.4
Bethlehem town *Albany Co.*	31,304	33,656	34,430	10.0
Binghamton city *Broome Co.*	47,380	47,376	46,495	-1.9
Brentwood cdp *Suffolk Co.*	53,917	60,664	61,374	13.8
Brighton cdp *Monroe Co.*	35,584	36,609	36,929	3.8
Bronx borough *Bronx Co.*	1,332,650	1,385,108	1,428,357	7.2
Brookhaven town *Suffolk Co.*	448,248	486,040	488,930	9.1
Brooklyn borough *Kings Co.*	2,465,326	2,504,700	2,595,259	5.3
Buffalo city *Erie Co.*	292,648	261,310	259,517	-11.3
Carmel town *Putnam Co.*	33,006	34,305	34,376	4.2
Centereach cdp *Suffolk Co.*	27,285	31,578	32,649	19.7
Central Islip cdp *Suffolk Co.*	31,950	34,450	34,960	9.4
Cheektowaga town *Erie Co.*	94,019	88,226	87,858	-6.6
Cicero town *Onondaga Co.*	27,982	31,632	31,648	13.1
Clarence town *Erie Co.*	26,123	30,673	31,376	20.1
Clarkstown town *Rockland Co.*	82,082	84,187	86,334	5.2
Clay town *Onondaga Co.*	58,805	58,206	59,294	0.8
Clifton Park town *Saratoga Co.*	32,995	36,705	37,046	12.3
Colonie town *Albany Co.*	79,258	81,591	82,750	4.4
Commack cdp *Suffolk Co.*	36,367	36,124	35,914	-1.2
Coram cdp *Suffolk Co.*	34,923	39,113	40,685	16.5
Cortlandt town *Westchester Co.*	38,467	41,592	42,442	10.3
East Fishkill town *Dutchess Co.*	25,589	29,029	29,276	14.4
East Meadow cdp *Nassau Co.*	37,461	38,132	37,836	1.0
Eastchester town *Westchester Co.*	31,318	32,363	32,880	5.0
Elmont cdp *Nassau Co.*	32,657	33,198	37,388	14.5
Franklin Square cdp *Nassau Co.*	29,342	29,320	31,544	7.5
Freeport village *Nassau Co.*	43,783	42,860	43,251	-1.2
Glenville town *Schenectady Co.*	28,183	29,480	29,489	4.6
Greece town *Monroe Co.*	94,141	96,095	96,674	2.7
Greenburgh town *Westchester Co.*	86,764	88,400	90,809	4.7
Guilderland town *Albany Co.*	32,688	35,303	35,675	9.1
Hamburg town *Erie Co.*	56,259	56,936	57,712	2.6
Haverstraw town *Rockland Co.*	33,811	36,634	37,261	10.2
Hempstead town *Nassau Co.*	755,924	759,757	767,916	1.6
Hempstead village *Nassau Co.*	56,554	53,891	55,105	-2.6
Henrietta town *Monroe Co.*	39,028	42,581	43,453	11.3
Hicksville cdp *Nassau Co.*	41,260	41,547	42,333	2.6
Huntington town *Suffolk Co.*	195,289	203,264	204,240	4.6
Huntington Station cdp *Suffolk Co.*	29,910	33,029	34,088	14.0
Irondequoit cdp *Monroe Co.*	52,354	51,692	51,337	-1.9
Islip town *Suffolk Co.*	322,612	335,543	336,747	4.4
Ithaca city *Tompkins Co.*	29,287	30,014	30,565	4.4
Jamestown city *Chautauqua Co.*	31,730	31,146	30,546	-3.7
Lancaster town *Erie Co.*	39,019	41,604	42,492	8.9
Levittown cdp *Nassau Co.*	53,067	51,881	51,593	-2.8
Long Beach city *Nassau Co.*	35,462	33,275	33,470	-5.6

Place	2000 Census	2010 Census	Current Estimate[1]	Population Growth Since 2000 (%)
Mamaroneck town *Westchester Co.*	28,967	29,156	29,657	2.4
Manhattan borough *New York Co.*	1,537,195	1,585,873	1,629,507	6.0
Manlius town *Onondaga Co.*	31,872	32,370	32,400	1.7
Monroe town *Orange Co.*	31,407	39,912	41,756	33.0
Mount Pleasant town *Westchester Co.*	43,221	43,724	44,528	3.0
Mount Vernon city *Westchester Co.*	68,381	67,292	68,221	-0.2
New City cdp *Rockland Co.*	34,038	33,559	33,722	-0.9
New Rochelle city *Westchester Co.*	72,182	77,062	79,027	9.5
New York city *New York Co.*	8,008,278	8,175,133	8,426,743	5.2
Newburgh town *Orange Co.*	27,568	29,801	30,664	11.2
Niagara Falls city *Niagara Co.*	55,593	50,193	49,435	-11.1
North Hempstead town *Nassau Co.*	222,611	226,322	229,105	2.9
North Tonawanda city *Niagara Co.*	33,262	31,568	31,077	-6.6
Oceanside cdp *Nassau Co.*	32,733	32,109	30,371	-7.2
Orangetown town *Rockland Co.*	47,711	49,212	50,095	5.0
Orchard Park town *Erie Co.*	27,637	29,054	29,466	6.6
Ossining town *Westchester Co.*	36,534	37,674	38,136	4.4
Oyster Bay town *Nassau Co.*	293,925	293,214	296,876	1.0
Penfield town *Monroe Co.*	34,645	36,242	36,984	6.8
Perinton town *Monroe Co.*	46,090	46,462	46,557	1.0
Pittsford town *Monroe Co.*	27,219	29,405	29,608	8.8
Port Chester village *Westchester Co.*	27,867	28,967	29,406	5.5
Poughkeepsie town *Dutchess Co.*	42,777	43,341	44,786	4.7
Poughkeepsie city *Dutchess Co.*	29,871	32,736	30,635	2.6
Queens borough *Queens Co.*	2,229,379	2,230,722	2,301,139	3.2
Ramapo town *Rockland Co.*	108,905	126,595	131,648	20.9
Riverhead town *Suffolk Co.*	27,680	33,506	33,769	22.0
Rochester city *Monroe Co.*	219,773	210,565	210,745	-4.1
Rome city *Oneida Co.*	34,950	33,725	32,916	-5.8
Rye town *Westchester Co.*	43,880	45,928	46,650	6.3
Salina town *Onondaga Co.*	33,290	33,710	33,598	0.9
Schenectady city *Schenectady Co.*	61,821	66,135	65,735	6.3
Smithtown town *Suffolk Co.*	115,715	117,801	118,373	2.3
Southampton town *Suffolk Co.*	54,712	56,790	57,730	5.5
Spring Valley village *Rockland Co.*	25,464	31,347	32,221	26.5
Staten Island borough *Richmond Co.*	443,728	468,730	472,481	6.5
Syracuse city *Onondaga Co.*	147,306	145,170	144,564	-1.9
Tonawanda town *Erie Co.*	78,155	73,567	73,420	-6.1
Tonawanda cdp *Erie Co.*	61,729	58,144	58,149	-5.8
Troy city *Rensselaer Co.*	49,170	50,129	49,933	1.6
Union town *Broome Co.*	56,298	56,346	55,474	-1.5
Utica city *Oneida Co.*	60,651	62,235	61,628	1.6
Valley Stream village *Nassau Co.*	36,368	37,511	37,838	4.0
Warwick town *Orange Co.*	30,764	32,065	31,446	2.2
Webster town *Monroe Co.*	37,926	42,641	43,750	15.4
West Babylon cdp *Suffolk Co.*	43,452	43,213	42,664	-1.8
West Seneca cdp *Erie Co.*	45,943	44,711	45,089	-1.9
White Plains city *Westchester Co.*	53,077	56,853	57,790	8.9
Yonkers city *Westchester Co.*	196,086	195,976	199,435	1.7
Yorktown town *Westchester Co.*	36,318	36,081	36,746	1.2

NOTE: (1) Current population is based on the American Community Survey's 2011-2015 Five-Year Estimate.
SOURCE: U.S. Census Bureau, Census 2010, Census 2000; U.S. Census Bureau, American Community Survey, 2011-2015 Five-Year Estimates

Physical Characteristics

Place	Density (persons per square mile)	Land Area (square miles)	Water Area (square miles)	Elevation (feet)
Albany city *Albany Co.*	4,603.8	21.40	0.50	148
Amherst town *Erie Co.*	2,331.5	53.20	0.40	597
Babylon town *Suffolk Co.*	4,092.8	52.30	61.90	7
Bay Shore cdp *Suffolk Co.*	5,527.6	5.40	0.20	16
Bethlehem town *Albany Co.*	702.2	49.00	0.80	210
Binghamton city *Broome Co.*	4,432.8	10.50	0.60	866
Brentwood cdp *Suffolk Co.*	5,589.3	11.00	0.00	79
Brighton cdp *Monroe Co.*	2,395.6	15.40	0.20	446
Bronx borough *Bronx Co.*	33,930.7	42.10	15.40	49
Brookhaven town *Suffolk Co.*	1,884.6	259.40	272.10	10
Brooklyn borough *Kings Co.*	36,648.0	70.80	26.10	49
Buffalo city *Erie Co.*	6,426.2	40.40	12.10	600
Carmel town *Putnam Co.*	957.4	35.90	4.80	561
Centereach cdp *Suffolk Co.*	3,746.5	8.70	0.00	98
Central Islip cdp *Suffolk Co.*	4,916.2	7.10	0.00	89
Cheektowaga town *Erie Co.*	2,986.1	29.40	0.10	650
Cicero town *Onondaga Co.*	655.6	48.30	0.20	394
Clarence town *Erie Co.*	586.4	53.50	0.10	738
Clarkstown town *Rockland Co.*	2,243.9	38.50	8.60	n/a
Clay town *Onondaga Co.*	1,236.4	48.00	0.90	394
Clifton Park town *Saratoga Co.*	768.6	48.20	2.00	344
Colonie town *Albany Co.*	1,479.2	55.90	1.90	312
Commack cdp *Suffolk Co.*	3,000.7	12.00	0.00	131
Coram cdp *Suffolk Co.*	2,943.0	13.80	0.00	95
Cortlandt town *Westchester Co.*	1,081.2	39.30	10.80	n/a
East Fishkill town *Dutchess Co.*	518.1	56.50	0.90	276
East Meadow cdp *Nassau Co.*	6,001.9	6.30	0.00	72
Eastchester town *Westchester Co.*	6,775.1	4.90	0.10	23
Elmont cdp *Nassau Co.*	11,098.6	3.40	0.00	39
Franklin Square cdp *Nassau Co.*	10,961.6	2.90	0.00	66
Freeport village *Nassau Co.*	9,345.0	4.60	0.20	20
Glenville town *Schenectady Co.*	599.5	49.20	1.50	705
Greece town *Monroe Co.*	2,034.5	47.50	3.90	430
Greenburgh town *Westchester Co.*	2,996.1	30.30	5.80	348
Guilderland town *Albany Co.*	616.1	57.90	0.90	207
Hamburg town *Erie Co.*	1,396.7	41.30	0.00	820
Haverstraw town *Rockland Co.*	1,681.8	22.20	5.30	33
Hempstead town *Nassau Co.*	6,475.5	118.60	73.00	56
Hempstead village *Nassau Co.*	14,965.9	3.70	0.00	56
Henrietta town *Monroe Co.*	1,229.2	35.40	0.30	600
Hicksville cdp *Nassau Co.*	6,233.7	6.80	0.00	148
Huntington town *Suffolk Co.*	2,169.9	94.10	43.00	75
Huntington Station cdp *Suffolk Co.*	6,227.1	5.50	0.00	217
Irondequoit cdp *Monroe Co.*	3,422.2	15.00	1.80	381
Islip town *Suffolk Co.*	3,234.4	104.10	58.90	13
Ithaca city *Tompkins Co.*	5,672.6	5.40	0.70	410
Jamestown city *Chautauqua Co.*	3,418.9	8.90	0.10	1,378
Lancaster town *Erie Co.*	1,127.0	37.70	0.20	669
Levittown cdp *Nassau Co.*	7,574.9	6.80	0.00	85
Long Beach city *Nassau Co.*	15,112.9	2.20	1.70	7

Place	Density (persons per square mile)	Land Area (square miles)	Water Area (square miles)	Elevation (feet)
Mamaroneck town *Westchester Co.*	4,457.0	6.70	7.40	47
Manhattan borough *New York Co.*	71,379.8	22.80	10.80	115
Manlius town *Onondaga Co.*	658.3	49.20	0.70	591
Monroe town *Orange Co.*	2,090.3	20.00	1.30	643
Mount Pleasant town *Westchester Co.*	1,623.8	27.40	5.30	259
Mount Vernon city *Westchester Co.*	15,555.4	4.40	0.00	112
New City cdp *Rockland Co.*	2,164.1	15.60	0.80	157
New Rochelle city *Westchester Co.*	7,635.3	10.40	2.90	85
New York city *New York Co.*	27,843.8	302.60	165.80	87
Newburgh town *Orange Co.*	718.5	42.70	4.30	131
Niagara Falls city *Niagara Co.*	3,509.5	14.10	2.70	614
North Hempstead town *Nassau Co.*	4,281.4	53.50	15.60	102
North Tonawanda city *Niagara Co.*	3,076.8	10.10	0.80	574
Oceanside cdp *Nassau Co.*	6,143.4	4.90	0.50	13
Orangetown town *Rockland Co.*	2,078.8	24.10	7.30	200
Orchard Park town *Erie Co.*	766.5	38.40	0.10	863
Ossining town *Westchester Co.*	3,300.1	11.60	4.20	161
Oyster Bay town *Nassau Co.*	2,861.5	103.70	65.70	49
Penfield town *Monroe Co.*	993.9	37.20	0.60	423
Perinton town *Monroe Co.*	1,361.9	34.20	0.40	n/a
Pittsford town *Monroe Co.*	1,277.3	23.20	0.20	492
Port Chester village *Westchester Co.*	12,617.2	2.30	0.10	43
Poughkeepsie town *Dutchess Co.*	1,570.7	28.50	2.60	200
Poughkeepsie city *Dutchess Co.*	5,955.6	5.10	0.60	200
Queens borough *Queens Co.*	21,202.4	108.50	69.70	43
Ramapo town *Rockland Co.*	2,151.2	61.20	0.70	331
Riverhead town *Suffolk Co.*	500.8	67.40	133.80	13
Rochester city *Monroe Co.*	5,889.9	35.80	1.40	505
Rome city *Oneida Co.*	440.1	74.80	0.80	456
Rye town *Westchester Co.*	6,742.5	6.90	0.40	26
Salina town *Onondaga Co.*	2,443.5	13.70	1.30	n/a
Schenectady city *Schenectady Co.*	6,098.2	10.80	0.20	243
Smithtown town *Suffolk Co.*	2,204.4	53.70	57.80	59
Southampton town *Suffolk Co.*	414.7	139.20	154.50	26
Spring Valley village *Rockland Co.*	15,984.8	2.00	0.00	446
Staten Island borough *Richmond Co.*	8,094.5	58.40	43.90	161
Syracuse city *Onondaga Co.*	5,772.5	25.00	0.60	397
Tonawanda town *Erie Co.*	3,918.9	18.70	1.50	574
Tonawanda cdp *Erie Co.*	3,361.3	17.30	1.30	574
Troy city *Rensselaer Co.*	4,821.1	10.40	0.70	33
Union town *Broome Co.*	1,564.8	35.50	0.50	846
Utica city *Oneida Co.*	3,677.3	16.80	0.30	456
Valley Stream village *Nassau Co.*	10,866.3	3.50	0.00	16
Warwick town *Orange Co.*	310.3	101.30	3.50	518
Webster town *Monroe Co.*	1,304.8	33.50	1.70	446
West Babylon cdp *Suffolk Co.*	5,493.1	7.80	0.30	39
West Seneca cdp *Erie Co.*	2,111.2	21.40	0.10	597
White Plains city *Westchester Co.*	5,916.4	9.80	0.10	213
Yonkers city *Westchester Co.*	11,072.3	18.00	2.30	82
Yorktown town *Westchester Co.*	1,002.8	36.60	2.60	505

SOURCE: U.S. Census Bureau, Census 2010; U.S. Census Bureau, American Community Survey, 2011-2015 Five-Year Estimates

Population by Race/Hispanic Origin

Place	White[1] (%)	Black[1] (%)	Asian[1] (%)	AIAN[1,2] (%)	NHOPI[1,3] (%)	Two or More Races (%)	Hispanic[4] (%)
Albany city *Albany Co.*	55.5	29.9	7.0	0.3	0.1	5.0	9.6
Amherst town *Erie Co.*	82.3	5.8	8.4	0.3	0.0	2.3	3.1
Babylon town *Suffolk Co.*	69.0	16.5	3.2	0.1	0.0	2.9	20.5
Bay Shore cdp *Suffolk Co.*	52.5	22.0	4.5	0.1	0.0	5.1	36.2
Bethlehem town *Albany Co.*	91.1	2.5	4.0	0.0	0.0	2.0	1.7
Binghamton city *Broome Co.*	75.9	13.9	4.6	0.4	0.1	3.6	7.0
Brentwood cdp *Suffolk Co.*	50.6	15.3	2.4	0.4	0.0	6.4	66.3
Brighton cdp *Monroe Co.*	79.4	6.2	10.8	0.2	0.0	2.8	4.1
Bronx borough *Bronx Co.*	21.0	33.3	3.7	0.6	0.0	3.6	54.6
Brookhaven town *Suffolk Co.*	86.1	5.4	4.6	0.2	0.0	2.0	15.0
Brooklyn borough *Kings Co.*	43.4	33.5	11.5	0.3	0.0	2.4	19.6
Buffalo city *Erie Co.*	48.5	37.3	4.4	0.4	0.0	3.8	10.8
Carmel town *Putnam Co.*	90.7	1.3	2.8	0.8	0.0	1.7	11.3
Centereach cdp *Suffolk Co.*	87.4	3.0	5.5	0.5	0.1	1.5	13.6
Central Islip cdp *Suffolk Co.*	50.8	24.6	3.7	0.1	0.1	6.9	49.3
Cheektowaga town *Erie Co.*	85.5	9.7	1.8	0.2	0.1	1.8	3.1
Cicero town *Onondaga Co.*	95.3	1.4	0.9	0.4	0.0	1.8	1.7
Clarence town *Erie Co.*	92.2	1.3	4.9	0.0	0.2	1.1	1.8
Clarkstown town *Rockland Co.*	71.3	9.6	11.3	0.2	0.0	3.2	13.2
Clay town *Onondaga Co.*	90.0	4.9	1.9	0.4	0.0	2.5	3.4
Clifton Park town *Saratoga Co.*	90.6	2.3	4.6	0.0	0.1	1.6	3.4
Colonie town *Albany Co.*	83.1	5.8	7.2	0.0	0.1	2.6	4.5
Commack cdp *Suffolk Co.*	90.1	1.7	5.1	0.0	0.0	2.1	5.5
Coram cdp *Suffolk Co.*	78.6	10.1	6.2	0.2	0.0	2.4	15.9
Cortlandt town *Westchester Co.*	79.3	7.5	3.6	0.2	0.0	3.2	16.2
East Fishkill town *Dutchess Co.*	88.0	2.7	3.9	0.1	0.0	2.7	7.2
East Meadow cdp *Nassau Co.*	76.3	5.4	11.4	0.6	0.0	2.0	13.3
Eastchester town *Westchester Co.*	83.7	4.8	7.6	0.0	0.0	2.5	5.9
Elmont cdp *Nassau Co.*	20.7	45.8	14.3	0.2	0.0	5.4	21.0
Franklin Square cdp *Nassau Co.*	74.8	3.4	10.3	0.0	0.0	3.1	16.5
Freeport village *Nassau Co.*	39.3	32.8	1.7	2.0	0.0	12.0	42.5
Glenville town *Schenectady Co.*	94.5	1.7	1.1	0.0	0.0	2.1	3.1
Greece town *Monroe Co.*	87.9	6.7	2.0	0.2	0.0	1.3	5.1
Greenburgh town *Westchester Co.*	68.2	13.4	9.7	0.4	0.1	3.4	14.3
Guilderland town *Albany Co.*	86.3	4.0	7.1	0.1	0.1	1.4	2.9
Hamburg town *Erie Co.*	96.0	1.3	0.4	0.2	0.0	1.4	2.4
Haverstraw town *Rockland Co.*	56.9	16.0	4.1	0.2	0.0	3.3	44.8
Hempstead town *Nassau Co.*	65.2	16.9	5.7	0.3	0.0	3.9	18.9
Hempstead village *Nassau Co.*	16.7	48.2	1.7	0.1	0.0	4.1	43.3
Henrietta town *Monroe Co.*	78.4	9.0	7.3	0.5	0.0	3.1	4.8
Hicksville cdp *Nassau Co.*	68.8	3.8	21.5	0.1	0.0	3.3	13.0
Huntington town *Suffolk Co.*	83.3	4.8	5.2	0.1	0.0	1.3	12.0
Huntington Station cdp *Suffolk Co.*	64.5	9.5	2.9	0.1	0.0	2.0	37.7
Irondequoit cdp *Monroe Co.*	85.0	9.3	1.6	0.1	0.0	2.2	7.3
Islip town *Suffolk Co.*	72.9	10.1	2.9	0.2	0.0	3.9	29.5
Ithaca city *Tompkins Co.*	69.8	7.4	17.0	0.3	0.0	4.7	7.1
Jamestown city *Chautauqua Co.*	87.7	4.7	0.7	0.8	0.1	3.1	9.2
Lancaster town *Erie Co.*	96.8	0.8	0.7	0.1	0.0	1.2	2.0
Levittown cdp *Nassau Co.*	86.6	0.8	6.6	0.0	0.0	2.4	12.1
Long Beach city *Nassau Co.*	81.5	6.2	3.8	0.1	0.0	2.4	14.5

Place	White[1] (%)	Black[1] (%)	Asian[1] (%)	AIAN[1,2] (%)	NHOPI[1,3] (%)	Two or More Races (%)	Hispanic[4] (%)
Mamaroneck town *Westchester Co.*	82.4	3.3	4.4	0.1	0.0	3.0	14.7
Manhattan borough *New York Co.*	56.4	15.0	11.7	0.4	0.1	4.1	25.8
Manlius town *Onondaga Co.*	89.7	2.8	3.8	0.3	0.0	2.6	1.8
Monroe town *Orange Co.*	89.4	2.4	2.6	0.4	0.0	1.7	9.6
Mount Pleasant town *Westchester Co.*	79.1	4.2	5.3	0.3	0.0	3.2	18.9
Mount Vernon city *Westchester Co.*	22.5	65.3	2.2	0.4	0.0	3.1	15.2
New City cdp *Rockland Co.*	75.6	8.0	11.3	0.0	0.0	3.8	7.9
New Rochelle city *Westchester Co.*	63.8	18.6	4.2	0.1	0.0	3.5	28.3
New York city *New York Co.*	43.3	24.5	13.5	0.4	0.0	3.2	28.9
Newburgh town *Orange Co.*	76.9	10.1	2.3	0.0	0.0	4.0	18.6
Niagara Falls city *Niagara Co.*	70.0	23.0	1.0	1.3	0.0	4.0	2.7
North Hempstead town *Nassau Co.*	68.9	5.7	16.6	0.2	0.1	2.7	13.7
North Tonawanda city *Niagara Co.*	95.6	1.4	0.9	0.3	0.0	1.5	1.9
Oceanside cdp *Nassau Co.*	92.3	0.7	2.8	0.4	0.0	1.3	9.8
Orangetown town *Rockland Co.*	82.1	5.5	8.5	0.5	0.0	1.7	9.6
Orchard Park town *Erie Co.*	96.8	0.7	1.3	0.1	0.0	0.7	1.6
Ossining town *Westchester Co.*	56.8	12.6	6.0	1.7	0.0	3.4	34.3
Oyster Bay town *Nassau Co.*	83.7	2.5	10.3	0.1	0.0	1.7	8.1
Penfield town *Monroe Co.*	91.9	1.8	2.9	0.1	0.1	2.7	3.6
Perinton town *Monroe Co.*	93.5	1.1	3.2	0.1	0.0	1.8	2.1
Pittsford town *Monroe Co.*	87.7	2.5	7.5	0.0	0.0	1.7	2.5
Port Chester village *Westchester Co.*	48.5	5.8	1.4	1.0	0.1	1.8	63.8
Poughkeepsie town *Dutchess Co.*	74.6	11.3	6.6	0.4	0.1	3.1	11.9
Poughkeepsie city *Dutchess Co.*	43.6	36.4	2.4	0.4	0.0	6.0	21.3
Queens borough *Queens Co.*	41.1	18.5	24.4	0.4	0.0	3.4	27.9
Ramapo town *Rockland Co.*	68.9	16.6	3.1	0.2	0.0	1.8	13.9
Riverhead town *Suffolk Co.*	84.1	9.5	1.3	0.5	0.3	2.0	13.7
Rochester city *Monroe Co.*	45.1	41.1	3.7	0.9	0.0	4.5	17.4
Rome city *Oneida Co.*	88.1	5.3	1.2	0.2	0.0	2.8	6.4
Rye town *Westchester Co.*	61.7	5.2	2.8	0.7	0.0	1.8	44.4
Salina town *Onondaga Co.*	88.7	4.9	2.0	0.2	0.0	3.5	3.2
Schenectady city *Schenectady Co.*	59.9	21.2	6.0	0.5	0.0	5.4	10.9
Smithtown town *Suffolk Co.*	92.0	1.3	4.1	0.0	0.0	1.2	4.9
Southampton town *Suffolk Co.*	86.8	6.3	2.2	0.1	0.0	2.7	19.6
Spring Valley village *Rockland Co.*	30.0	39.9	2.9	0.0	0.0	2.2	29.3
Staten Island borough *Richmond Co.*	75.3	10.5	8.0	0.2	0.0	2.2	17.8
Syracuse city *Onondaga Co.*	55.2	29.3	6.6	1.1	0.0	5.4	8.4
Tonawanda town *Erie Co.*	90.9	3.7	2.5	0.3	0.0	1.9	3.3
Tonawanda cdp *Erie Co.*	90.5	3.7	3.1	0.3	0.0	1.7	3.3
Troy city *Rensselaer Co.*	71.9	16.0	4.0	0.2	0.0	6.7	8.8
Union town *Broome Co.*	87.1	4.3	4.2	0.1	0.1	2.8	3.6
Utica city *Oneida Co.*	65.4	15.6	9.9	0.3	0.1	5.0	11.4
Valley Stream village *Nassau Co.*	46.1	20.6	14.3	0.1	0.0	3.6	29.3
Warwick town *Orange Co.*	85.8	5.7	0.9	0.1	0.0	4.2	11.0
Webster town *Monroe Co.*	93.1	1.4	3.3	0.0	0.0	1.8	2.1
West Babylon cdp *Suffolk Co.*	77.0	10.4	2.6	0.1	0.0	2.9	16.4
West Seneca cdp *Erie Co.*	95.6	2.1	0.3	0.1	0.0	1.3	1.9
White Plains city *Westchester Co.*	62.0	12.3	7.2	1.0	0.0	4.6	34.4
Yonkers city *Westchester Co.*	58.6	17.2	6.8	0.3	0.0	3.2	35.5
Yorktown town *Westchester Co.*	88.2	3.4	4.2	0.3	0.0	1.4	12.4

NOTE: (1) Exclude multiple race combinations; (2) American Indian/Alaska Native; (3) Native Hawaiian/Other Pacific Islander; (4) May be of any race
SOURCE: U.S. Census Bureau, American Community Survey, 2011-2015 Five-Year Estimates

Average Household Size, Age, and Male/Female Ratio

Place	Average Household Size (persons)	Median Age (years)	Age Under 18 (%)	Age 65 and Over (%)	Males per 100 Females
Albany city *Albany Co.*	2.20	31.2	17.1	12.4	89.7
Amherst town *Erie Co.*	2.30	40.6	19.5	18.7	92.1
Babylon town *Suffolk Co.*	3.10	39.4	21.7	13.4	92.0
Bay Shore cdp *Suffolk Co.*	3.10	34.1	24.4	11.7	99.6
Bethlehem town *Albany Co.*	2.60	43.3	23.0	15.8	95.4
Binghamton city *Broome Co.*	2.30	36.2	18.6	16.7	96.2
Brentwood cdp *Suffolk Co.*	4.40	32.5	26.5	8.4	99.3
Brighton cdp *Monroe Co.*	2.20	38.9	18.0	18.6	87.9
Bronx borough *Bronx Co.*	2.90	33.2	25.7	11.1	89.0
Brookhaven town *Suffolk Co.*	2.90	39.1	22.9	13.3	98.8
Brooklyn borough *Kings Co.*	2.70	34.4	23.4	11.9	90.0
Buffalo city *Erie Co.*	2.30	33.1	22.9	11.8	91.3
Carmel town *Putnam Co.*	2.90	42.5	22.7	13.6	98.5
Centereach cdp *Suffolk Co.*	3.30	39.1	22.7	12.3	99.3
Central Islip cdp *Suffolk Co.*	3.60	33.6	25.7	9.9	103.7
Cheektowaga town *Erie Co.*	2.20	43.0	18.1	19.2	91.1
Cicero town *Onondaga Co.*	2.60	40.1	24.1	12.8	95.2
Clarence town *Erie Co.*	2.70	44.4	25.0	15.9	95.3
Clarkstown town *Rockland Co.*	2.90	44.3	21.8	18.2	93.8
Clay town *Onondaga Co.*	2.50	39.3	22.8	13.6	96.2
Clifton Park town *Saratoga Co.*	2.60	42.7	24.0	15.8	95.8
Colonie town *Albany Co.*	2.50	41.4	19.2	16.4	93.4
Commack cdp *Suffolk Co.*	3.00	44.4	23.5	17.5	96.2
Coram cdp *Suffolk Co.*	2.70	40.1	22.3	12.7	91.6
Cortlandt town *Westchester Co.*	2.70	43.9	23.7	16.3	95.0
East Fishkill town *Dutchess Co.*	3.10	42.6	24.5	12.9	100.3
East Meadow cdp *Nassau Co.*	2.90	43.2	18.8	18.2	99.4
Eastchester town *Westchester Co.*	2.50	42.0	22.7	17.5	88.4
Elmont cdp *Nassau Co.*	3.80	37.0	20.8	11.7	94.5
Franklin Square cdp *Nassau Co.*	3.20	40.6	21.5	16.1	95.0
Freeport village *Nassau Co.*	3.20	37.2	23.4	13.7	94.3
Glenville town *Schenectady Co.*	2.60	44.1	21.6	18.7	89.4
Greece town *Monroe Co.*	2.40	43.4	19.7	18.1	90.1
Greenburgh town *Westchester Co.*	2.70	43.0	22.4	16.8	92.8
Guilderland town *Albany Co.*	2.40	39.8	19.7	14.8	95.5
Hamburg town *Erie Co.*	2.40	42.5	20.6	17.0	91.2
Haverstraw town *Rockland Co.*	3.10	36.0	23.9	12.0	94.4
Hempstead town *Nassau Co.*	3.10	40.0	22.7	14.9	94.7
Hempstead village *Nassau Co.*	3.40	34.2	24.9	10.0	98.3
Henrietta town *Monroe Co.*	2.50	33.9	18.4	13.4	112.7
Hicksville cdp *Nassau Co.*	3.20	43.0	18.4	16.2	97.4
Huntington town *Suffolk Co.*	2.90	43.7	23.5	16.8	94.3
Huntington Station cdp *Suffolk Co.*	3.30	36.5	27.0	11.3	103.3
Irondequoit cdp *Monroe Co.*	2.30	43.7	19.8	18.9	86.9
Islip town *Suffolk Co.*	3.30	37.7	24.1	12.5	97.3
Ithaca city *Tompkins Co.*	2.40	21.8	8.9	5.3	101.6
Jamestown city *Chautauqua Co.*	2.30	37.3	24.5	15.4	96.9
Lancaster town *Erie Co.*	2.50	41.6	23.0	15.0	96.0
Levittown cdp *Nassau Co.*	3.10	41.1	21.4	15.1	93.6
Long Beach city *Nassau Co.*	2.20	44.5	15.5	17.8	83.9

Place	Average Household Size (persons)	Median Age (years)	Age Under 18 (%)	Age 65 and Over (%)	Males per 100 Females
Mamaroneck town *Westchester Co.*	2.70	40.7	26.8	15.9	93.2
Manhattan borough *New York Co.*	2.10	36.6	14.6	14.1	89.5
Manlius town *Onondaga Co.*	2.40	45.3	23.5	18.3	88.4
Monroe town *Orange Co.*	4.00	21.7	44.1	5.8	95.7
Mount Pleasant town *Westchester Co.*	2.90	40.3	23.3	14.6	102.9
Mount Vernon city *Westchester Co.*	2.70	37.4	22.8	13.5	83.8
New City cdp *Rockland Co.*	3.00	44.9	21.7	18.5	96.8
New Rochelle city *Westchester Co.*	2.70	39.3	21.7	15.1	97.2
New York city *New York Co.*	2.70	35.8	21.3	12.7	91.0
Newburgh town *Orange Co.*	2.80	41.2	22.5	14.7	95.3
Niagara Falls city *Niagara Co.*	2.30	39.2	22.1	14.9	90.2
North Hempstead town *Nassau Co.*	3.00	42.5	23.3	18.2	93.5
North Tonawanda city *Niagara Co.*	2.30	42.8	18.5	16.9	96.5
Oceanside cdp *Nassau Co.*	2.80	44.3	19.7	16.9	94.0
Orangetown town *Rockland Co.*	2.60	42.8	21.7	18.3	96.1
Orchard Park town *Erie Co.*	2.50	45.6	22.2	18.6	89.7
Ossining town *Westchester Co.*	2.90	39.9	21.9	13.3	101.2
Oyster Bay town *Nassau Co.*	3.00	43.7	21.6	17.1	93.3
Penfield town *Monroe Co.*	2.50	44.8	23.4	18.9	89.5
Perinton town *Monroe Co.*	2.40	45.2	21.5	18.3	92.4
Pittsford town *Monroe Co.*	2.60	43.1	22.5	18.8	87.5
Port Chester village *Westchester Co.*	3.20	35.9	22.3	10.6	107.0
Poughkeepsie town *Dutchess Co.*	2.60	35.6	20.3	14.5	89.1
Poughkeepsie city *Dutchess Co.*	2.40	36.4	23.4	14.0	93.9
Queens borough *Queens Co.*	2.90	37.7	20.5	13.4	94.1
Ramapo town *Rockland Co.*	3.70	28.4	35.8	11.1	99.2
Riverhead town *Suffolk Co.*	2.60	45.7	18.5	21.7	95.3
Rochester city *Monroe Co.*	2.30	31.0	24.1	9.8	94.3
Rome city *Oneida Co.*	2.30	40.1	20.6	17.5	105.4
Rye town *Westchester Co.*	3.00	38.4	23.3	13.0	101.1
Salina town *Onondaga Co.*	2.20	43.5	19.2	19.4	95.5
Schenectady city *Schenectady Co.*	2.60	35.1	22.0	12.5	95.1
Smithtown town *Suffolk Co.*	2.90	43.9	23.3	17.3	96.7
Southampton town *Suffolk Co.*	2.50	44.9	18.1	19.5	110.7
Spring Valley village *Rockland Co.*	3.70	28.8	33.3	7.8	97.1
Staten Island borough *Richmond Co.*	2.80	39.3	22.5	14.1	93.8
Syracuse city *Onondaga Co.*	2.40	29.9	22.6	11.3	89.1
Tonawanda town *Erie Co.*	2.20	43.0	19.0	19.0	91.3
Tonawanda cdp *Erie Co.*	2.20	43.3	19.3	19.4	90.5
Troy city *Rensselaer Co.*	2.30	30.6	19.3	11.3	97.7
Union town *Broome Co.*	2.30	41.1	20.9	18.0	93.0
Utica city *Oneida Co.*	2.50	34.0	25.5	14.8	93.5
Valley Stream village *Nassau Co.*	3.30	38.4	23.6	13.5	96.4
Warwick town *Orange Co.*	2.60	43.7	23.6	15.1	104.5
Webster town *Monroe Co.*	2.50	42.7	23.1	17.5	91.8
West Babylon cdp *Suffolk Co.*	3.00	41.1	20.1	15.0	91.2
West Seneca cdp *Erie Co.*	2.30	45.1	19.2	20.4	91.9
White Plains city *Westchester Co.*	2.60	38.3	20.6	15.6	93.0
Yonkers city *Westchester Co.*	2.70	37.9	22.1	15.4	89.6
Yorktown town *Westchester Co.*	2.80	44.9	22.9	17.9	89.3

SOURCE: U.S. Census Bureau, American Community Survey, 2011-2015 Five-Year Estimates

Foreign Born, Language Spoken, Disabled Persons, and Veterans

Place	Foreign Born (%)	Speak English Only at Home (%)	With a Disability (%)	Veterans (%)
Albany city *Albany Co.*	11.50	84.4	12.1	4.3
Amherst town *Erie Co.*	12.90	84.8	10.3	7.0
Babylon town *Suffolk Co.*	19.60	74.4	10.4	5.9
Bay Shore cdp *Suffolk Co.*	23.70	65.2	10.5	5.3
Bethlehem town *Albany Co.*	6.20	92.3	9.9	7.4
Binghamton city *Broome Co.*	9.10	86.3	18.3	6.9
Brentwood cdp *Suffolk Co.*	42.10	30.7	8.1	3.5
Brighton cdp *Monroe Co.*	18.00	81.0	10.8	6.2
Bronx borough *Bronx Co.*	34.40	41.7	13.6	2.9
Brookhaven town *Suffolk Co.*	12.20	81.0	9.3	6.4
Brooklyn borough *Kings Co.*	37.50	53.4	9.9	2.3
Buffalo city *Erie Co.*	8.80	83.4	16.5	6.8
Carmel town *Putnam Co.*	12.70	81.2	9.8	5.7
Centereach cdp *Suffolk Co.*	10.90	84.6	9.5	6.6
Central Islip cdp *Suffolk Co.*	33.90	46.1	10.3	4.4
Cheektowaga town *Erie Co.*	5.10	92.7	13.5	10.1
Cicero town *Onondaga Co.*	2.90	95.9	9.8	7.8
Clarence town *Erie Co.*	7.30	91.7	8.5	7.1
Clarkstown town *Rockland Co.*	22.10	70.6	9.0	5.1
Clay town *Onondaga Co.*	5.20	92.9	9.6	8.9
Clifton Park town *Saratoga Co.*	7.00	90.2	7.5	9.0
Colonie town *Albany Co.*	10.30	86.0	11.0	7.7
Commack cdp *Suffolk Co.*	9.90	86.2	8.3	7.5
Coram cdp *Suffolk Co.*	18.00	77.0	8.7	4.7
Cortlandt town *Westchester Co.*	15.80	80.0	10.1	6.8
East Fishkill town *Dutchess Co.*	10.10	85.9	10.9	7.1
East Meadow cdp *Nassau Co.*	18.80	73.6	9.0	6.4
Eastchester town *Westchester Co.*	17.90	78.4	7.7	4.9
Elmont cdp *Nassau Co.*	43.40	51.8	7.5	2.3
Franklin Square cdp *Nassau Co.*	22.70	63.7	8.0	5.3
Freeport village *Nassau Co.*	31.30	56.7	8.5	4.2
Glenville town *Schenectady Co.*	3.40	95.1	12.1	9.6
Greece town *Monroe Co.*	6.60	90.6	11.6	7.8
Greenburgh town *Westchester Co.*	22.90	72.1	7.6	4.7
Guilderland town *Albany Co.*	8.50	90.2	7.8	6.5
Hamburg town *Erie Co.*	2.90	96.0	10.8	9.1
Haverstraw town *Rockland Co.*	27.80	54.3	11.5	5.0
Hempstead town *Nassau Co.*	21.80	72.5	8.4	5.1
Hempstead village *Nassau Co.*	39.90	53.0	6.6	3.2
Henrietta town *Monroe Co.*	11.40	86.1	11.7	7.8
Hicksville cdp *Nassau Co.*	27.60	65.8	8.6	6.1
Huntington town *Suffolk Co.*	14.00	81.5	7.7	5.9
Huntington Station cdp *Suffolk Co.*	25.70	59.7	7.8	5.0
Irondequoit cdp *Monroe Co.*	7.50	87.5	12.8	8.2
Islip town *Suffolk Co.*	19.50	69.1	9.6	5.7
Ithaca city *Tompkins Co.*	17.20	80.1	8.0	1.6
Jamestown city *Chautauqua Co.*	1.60	91.3	18.6	9.5
Lancaster town *Erie Co.*	3.30	95.1	9.5	8.3
Levittown cdp *Nassau Co.*	12.70	83.7	10.4	6.3
Long Beach city *Nassau Co.*	16.60	79.1	9.8	5.4

Place	Foreign Born (%)	Speak English Only at Home (%)	With a Disability (%)	Veterans (%)
Mamaroneck town *Westchester Co.*	21.00	71.4	7.7	4.5
Manhattan borough *New York Co.*	28.90	59.7	9.8	2.5
Manlius town *Onondaga Co.*	7.40	91.4	9.7	8.8
Monroe town *Orange Co.*	9.90	42.6	6.4	4.4
Mount Pleasant town *Westchester Co.*	20.30	71.8	7.7	4.5
Mount Vernon city *Westchester Co.*	33.90	76.8	11.0	3.8
New City cdp *Rockland Co.*	19.20	74.5	8.7	5.7
New Rochelle city *Westchester Co.*	29.10	60.3	9.9	4.5
New York city *New York Co.*	37.20	50.9	10.4	2.7
Newburgh town *Orange Co.*	9.30	80.0	11.3	8.4
Niagara Falls city *Niagara Co.*	5.00	95.1	16.8	8.8
North Hempstead town *Nassau Co.*	29.00	61.7	7.9	4.5
North Tonawanda city *Niagara Co.*	3.40	95.5	14.7	10.1
Oceanside cdp *Nassau Co.*	11.90	83.7	8.8	5.5
Orangetown town *Rockland Co.*	15.30	81.1	10.7	5.5
Orchard Park town *Erie Co.*	3.80	96.0	8.8	8.6
Ossining town *Westchester Co.*	30.60	57.8	8.0	4.5
Oyster Bay town *Nassau Co.*	15.40	79.5	8.7	6.2
Penfield town *Monroe Co.*	7.00	91.6	10.1	8.1
Perinton town *Monroe Co.*	6.40	93.8	8.5	7.8
Pittsford town *Monroe Co.*	10.30	88.0	7.5	6.9
Port Chester village *Westchester Co.*	45.60	34.7	10.2	3.0
Poughkeepsie town *Dutchess Co.*	13.80	81.4	12.2	5.8
Poughkeepsie city *Dutchess Co.*	19.60	76.6	15.8	6.1
Queens borough *Queens Co.*	47.80	43.7	9.5	2.7
Ramapo town *Rockland Co.*	22.20	48.8	7.4	3.3
Riverhead town *Suffolk Co.*	13.30	82.9	13.6	9.7
Rochester city *Monroe Co.*	9.00	80.2	17.3	4.7
Rome city *Oneida Co.*	3.30	92.2	17.6	12.2
Rye town *Westchester Co.*	35.70	49.6	9.2	3.9
Salina town *Onondaga Co.*	5.80	92.7	13.3	10.5
Schenectady city *Schenectady Co.*	14.50	86.0	15.0	6.3
Smithtown town *Suffolk Co.*	7.80	88.8	8.5	7.5
Southampton town *Suffolk Co.*	20.30	75.2	8.1	6.6
Spring Valley village *Rockland Co.*	41.90	34.7	6.6	2.2
Staten Island borough *Richmond Co.*	21.60	69.6	9.9	5.0
Syracuse city *Onondaga Co.*	11.90	81.9	15.4	5.5
Tonawanda town *Erie Co.*	5.00	93.1	13.9	8.8
Tonawanda cdp *Erie Co.*	5.60	92.4	14.0	8.7
Troy city *Rensselaer Co.*	7.80	87.5	14.6	5.6
Union town *Broome Co.*	6.80	91.0	14.0	9.2
Utica city *Oneida Co.*	18.90	72.3	19.8	6.8
Valley Stream village *Nassau Co.*	34.20	58.0	9.6	5.1
Warwick town *Orange Co.*	6.80	89.0	12.6	9.6
Webster town *Monroe Co.*	8.90	90.2	9.6	7.0
West Babylon cdp *Suffolk Co.*	14.40	81.0	11.6	6.2
West Seneca cdp *Erie Co.*	2.60	95.0	13.4	9.1
White Plains city *Westchester Co.*	32.60	54.9	8.2	3.5
Yonkers city *Westchester Co.*	30.60	53.4	10.9	4.1
Yorktown town *Westchester Co.*	11.90	84.0	9.4	5.5

SOURCE: U.S. Census Bureau, American Community Survey, 2011-2015 Five-Year Estimates

Five Largest Ancestry Groups

Place	Group 1	Group 2	Group 3	Group 4	Group 5
Albany city *Albany Co.*	Irish (15.0%)	Italian (13.0%)	German (9.8%)	English (5.2%)	Polish (3.9%)
Amherst town *Erie Co.*	German (25.3%)	Italian (19.5%)	Irish (17.0%)	Polish (13.5%)	English (8.7%)
Babylon town *Suffolk Co.*	Italian (25.6%)	Irish (17.3%)	German (11.9%)	Polish (5.5%)	English (3.0%)
Bay Shore cdp *Suffolk Co.*	Italian (13.6%)	Irish (12.6%)	German (8.4%)	English (3.2%)	Haitian (3.2%)
Bethlehem town *Albany Co.*	Irish (28.9%)	German (19.5%)	Italian (15.6%)	English (12.9%)	American (6.1%)
Binghamton city *Broome Co.*	Irish (20.3%)	German (13.6%)	Italian (13.5%)	English (8.6%)	Polish (4.5%)
Brentwood cdp *Suffolk Co.*	Italian (4.6%)	Irish (3.7%)	Haitian (3.6%)	German (2.2%)	American (1.4%)
Brighton cdp *Monroe Co.*	German (18.2%)	Irish (15.4%)	Italian (12.8%)	English (12.6%)	Polish (5.9%)
Bronx borough *Bronx Co.*	Jamaican (4.6%)	Italian (3.3%)	American (2.7%)	African (2.3%)	Irish (2.2%)
Brookhaven town *Suffolk Co.*	Italian (29.5%)	Irish (22.5%)	German (17.2%)	Polish (4.8%)	American (4.6%)
Brooklyn borough *Kings Co.*	American (5.7%)	Italian (5.2%)	Jamaican (3.3%)	Irish (3.2%)	Russian (3.1%)
Buffalo city *Erie Co.*	Irish (12.6%)	German (12.4%)	Italian (10.8%)	Polish (9.5%)	English (3.8%)
Carmel town *Putnam Co.*	Italian (33.3%)	Irish (26.2%)	German (11.8%)	American (5.3%)	Polish (5.2%)
Centereach cdp *Suffolk Co.*	Italian (31.7%)	Irish (22.9%)	German (19.9%)	American (5.9%)	Polish (5.0%)
Central Islip cdp *Suffolk Co.*	Italian (6.5%)	Irish (5.7%)	German (4.6%)	Haitian (3.2%)	Jamaican (2.3%)
Cheektowaga town *Erie Co.*	Polish (32.8%)	German (26.2%)	Italian (15.5%)	Irish (13.7%)	English (4.8%)
Cicero town *Onondaga Co.*	Irish (25.5%)	Italian (23.5%)	German (21.7%)	English (11.1%)	Polish (8.5%)
Clarence town *Erie Co.*	German (31.8%)	Italian (24.6%)	Irish (19.6%)	Polish (14.8%)	English (8.8%)
Clarkstown town *Rockland Co.*	Italian (21.0%)	Irish (17.7%)	German (7.4%)	American (5.6%)	Polish (4.8%)
Clay town *Onondaga Co.*	Irish (24.6%)	Italian (22.2%)	German (20.2%)	English (11.3%)	Polish (6.9%)
Clifton Park town *Saratoga Co.*	Irish (24.4%)	Italian (20.5%)	German (16.8%)	English (10.9%)	Polish (7.2%)
Colonie town *Albany Co.*	Irish (26.6%)	Italian (19.7%)	German (15.9%)	English (8.3%)	Polish (6.7%)
Commack cdp *Suffolk Co.*	Italian (34.1%)	Irish (19.1%)	German (14.0%)	Polish (7.5%)	Russian (6.4%)
Coram cdp *Suffolk Co.*	Italian (26.4%)	Irish (16.4%)	German (13.9%)	American (5.2%)	Polish (4.4%)
Cortlandt town *Westchester Co.*	Italian (23.6%)	Irish (17.7%)	German (11.6%)	English (5.3%)	Polish (5.3%)
East Fishkill town *Dutchess Co.*	Italian (31.6%)	Irish (23.4%)	German (14.0%)	English (7.3%)	Polish (5.7%)
East Meadow cdp *Nassau Co.*	Italian (22.0%)	Irish (13.6%)	German (10.6%)	American (5.9%)	Polish (5.3%)
Eastchester town *Westchester Co.*	Italian (34.7%)	Irish (18.3%)	German (8.6%)	American (6.4%)	English (5.0%)
Elmont cdp *Nassau Co.*	Haitian (15.1%)	Jamaican (9.7%)	Italian (7.6%)	German (3.7%)	Irish (3.2%)
Franklin Square cdp *Nassau Co.*	Italian (38.2%)	Irish (15.5%)	German (7.5%)	Polish (3.9%)	Greek (2.8%)
Freeport village *Nassau Co.*	Irish (6.9%)	Italian (5.9%)	German (4.0%)	American (3.9%)	Jamaican (3.8%)
Glenville town *Schenectady Co.*	Irish (23.5%)	Italian (21.6%)	German (19.8%)	English (12.3%)	Polish (9.0%)
Greece town *Monroe Co.*	Italian (26.2%)	German (24.1%)	Irish (18.0%)	English (10.8%)	Polish (4.9%)
Greenburgh town *Westchester Co.*	Italian (14.4%)	Irish (13.4%)	German (8.8%)	Russian (5.2%)	American (4.8%)
Guilderland town *Albany Co.*	Irish (23.1%)	Italian (19.8%)	German (18.1%)	English (11.9%)	Polish (5.7%)
Hamburg town *Erie Co.*	German (31.4%)	Irish (24.6%)	Polish (23.7%)	Italian (16.4%)	English (7.6%)
Haverstraw town *Rockland Co.*	Italian (13.5%)	Irish (11.9%)	German (6.2%)	Haitian (4.8%)	American (4.0%)
Hempstead town *Nassau Co.*	Italian (19.2%)	Irish (14.8%)	German (8.6%)	American (4.4%)	Polish (4.0%)
Hempstead village *Nassau Co.*	Jamaican (7.0%)	Haitian (3.0%)	American (2.3%)	Italian (2.0%)	Irish (1.8%)
Henrietta town *Monroe Co.*	German (19.4%)	Irish (13.8%)	Italian (13.6%)	English (9.7%)	American (6.0%)
Hicksville cdp *Nassau Co.*	Italian (19.7%)	Irish (18.6%)	German (10.6%)	English (4.2%)	Polish (3.5%)
Huntington town *Suffolk Co.*	Italian (25.9%)	Irish (19.1%)	German (15.0%)	Polish (6.0%)	English (5.6%)
Huntington Station cdp *Suffolk Co.*	Italian (18.5%)	Irish (13.5%)	German (10.7%)	Polish (3.7%)	American (3.3%)
Irondequoit cdp *Monroe Co.*	German (21.7%)	Italian (21.5%)	Irish (14.7%)	English (11.4%)	Polish (6.1%)
Islip town *Suffolk Co.*	Italian (22.4%)	Irish (18.4%)	German (13.1%)	English (3.4%)	Polish (3.3%)
Ithaca city *Tompkins Co.*	Irish (9.7%)	German (9.1%)	American (7.1%)	Italian (6.7%)	English (6.0%)
Jamestown city *Chautauqua Co.*	German (16.3%)	Swedish (15.6%)	Italian (14.7%)	Irish (14.4%)	English (10.8%)
Lancaster town *Erie Co.*	German (32.9%)	Polish (32.2%)	Italian (22.3%)	Irish (16.1%)	English (6.4%)
Levittown cdp *Nassau Co.*	Italian (30.5%)	Irish (22.4%)	German (13.8%)	Polish (5.0%)	English (4.1%)
Long Beach city *Nassau Co.*	Irish (23.1%)	Italian (18.4%)	German (8.9%)	American (5.8%)	Russian (5.5%)

Place	Group 1	Group 2	Group 3	Group 4	Group 5
Mamaroneck town *Westchester Co.*	Italian (15.8%)	Irish (13.7%)	American (10.8%)	German (7.4%)	Russian (5.6%)
Manhattan borough *New York Co.*	Irish (7.1%)	German (6.3%)	Italian (6.2%)	American (5.6%)	Russian (4.4%)
Manlius town *Onondaga Co.*	Irish (25.3%)	German (19.1%)	Italian (16.2%)	English (13.2%)	Polish (5.3%)
Monroe town *Orange Co.*	American (15.2%)	Italian (11.7%)	Irish (10.8%)	Hungarian (9.6%)	German (5.7%)
Mount Pleasant town *Westchester Co.*	Italian (29.0%)	Irish (16.0%)	German (8.9%)	American (5.1%)	English (4.4%)
Mount Vernon city *Westchester Co.*	Jamaican (20.5%)	Italian (6.4%)	Irish (3.6%)	American (3.2%)	Haitian (2.6%)
New City cdp *Rockland Co.*	Italian (19.5%)	Irish (15.0%)	German (7.5%)	Russian (6.9%)	American (6.4%)
New Rochelle city *Westchester Co.*	Italian (17.9%)	Irish (8.3%)	American (4.6%)	German (4.1%)	Polish (3.5%)
New York city *New York Co.*	Italian (6.7%)	American (4.6%)	Irish (4.5%)	German (3.0%)	Jamaican (2.7%)
Newburgh town *Orange Co.*	Italian (25.4%)	Irish (19.4%)	German (11.3%)	American (9.8%)	English (7.2%)
Niagara Falls city *Niagara Co.*	Italian (20.5%)	German (13.5%)	Irish (12.7%)	American (8.8%)	Polish (7.9%)
North Hempstead town *Nassau Co.*	Italian (14.7%)	Irish (10.3%)	German (7.1%)	American (6.7%)	Polish (5.3%)
North Tonawanda city *Niagara Co.*	German (32.9%)	Polish (21.5%)	Irish (19.5%)	Italian (17.9%)	English (10.4%)
Oceanside cdp *Nassau Co.*	Italian (29.1%)	Irish (18.7%)	German (9.5%)	Russian (6.2%)	American (6.1%)
Orangetown town *Rockland Co.*	Irish (30.9%)	Italian (17.8%)	German (11.0%)	English (5.8%)	American (5.6%)
Orchard Park town *Erie Co.*	German (29.9%)	Irish (24.3%)	Polish (21.3%)	Italian (19.5%)	English (8.7%)
Ossining town *Westchester Co.*	Italian (12.9%)	Irish (10.9%)	German (5.8%)	English (3.8%)	American (3.5%)
Oyster Bay town *Nassau Co.*	Italian (28.8%)	Irish (19.6%)	German (12.6%)	Polish (5.9%)	Russian (4.4%)
Penfield town *Monroe Co.*	German (24.5%)	Italian (23.5%)	Irish (17.4%)	English (15.0%)	Polish (6.9%)
Perinton town *Monroe Co.*	German (24.6%)	Irish (22.6%)	Italian (21.8%)	English (14.3%)	Polish (6.9%)
Pittsford town *Monroe Co.*	Irish (19.1%)	German (18.7%)	Italian (16.4%)	English (15.3%)	Polish (6.5%)
Port Chester village *Westchester Co.*	Italian (12.0%)	American (7.0%)	Irish (5.5%)	German (1.4%)	English (1.3%)
Poughkeepsie town *Dutchess Co.*	Italian (21.0%)	Irish (18.8%)	German (13.1%)	English (7.3%)	Polish (4.7%)
Poughkeepsie city *Dutchess Co.*	Italian (11.9%)	Irish (11.4%)	German (7.7%)	Jamaican (7.3%)	American (4.3%)
Queens borough *Queens Co.*	Italian (5.7%)	Irish (4.0%)	American (3.8%)	Guyanese (2.8%)	Jamaican (2.8%)
Ramapo town *Rockland Co.*	European (11.1%)	Hungarian (7.4%)	Haitian (7.3%)	American (6.9%)	Italian (6.8%)
Riverhead town *Suffolk Co.*	Irish (22.1%)	German (18.3%)	Italian (17.0%)	Polish (10.9%)	American (5.9%)
Rochester city *Monroe Co.*	German (9.0%)	Irish (8.8%)	Italian (8.1%)	English (5.1%)	American (2.5%)
Rome city *Oneida Co.*	Italian (22.2%)	Irish (16.9%)	American (16.4%)	German (15.5%)	English (8.5%)
Rye town *Westchester Co.*	Italian (17.1%)	American (9.4%)	Irish (7.2%)	German (3.8%)	Polish (3.2%)
Salina town *Onondaga Co.*	Italian (26.7%)	Irish (22.6%)	German (20.7%)	English (12.1%)	Polish (7.3%)
Schenectady city *Schenectady Co.*	Italian (13.9%)	Irish (11.1%)	German (9.2%)	Polish (5.7%)	English (5.4%)
Smithtown town *Suffolk Co.*	Italian (36.3%)	Irish (25.4%)	German (18.5%)	Polish (6.2%)	English (5.6%)
Southampton town *Suffolk Co.*	Irish (18.4%)	Italian (14.3%)	German (13.2%)	English (8.7%)	Polish (7.3%)
Spring Valley village *Rockland Co.*	Haitian (20.2%)	American (5.5%)	European (5.3%)	Jamaican (3.6%)	Hungarian (2.8%)
Staten Island borough *Richmond Co.*	Italian (31.4%)	Irish (12.5%)	German (4.4%)	American (4.4%)	Polish (3.9%)
Syracuse city *Onondaga Co.*	Irish (14.4%)	Italian (12.6%)	German (11.2%)	English (5.0%)	Polish (4.2%)
Tonawanda town *Erie Co.*	German (29.3%)	Italian (25.2%)	Irish (21.7%)	Polish (14.7%)	English (9.0%)
Tonawanda cdp *Erie Co.*	German (29.3%)	Italian (23.2%)	Irish (21.0%)	Polish (15.5%)	English (9.0%)
Troy city *Rensselaer Co.*	Irish (20.9%)	Italian (15.3%)	German (10.9%)	French (7.9%)	English (6.9%)
Union town *Broome Co.*	Irish (17.4%)	Italian (16.4%)	German (15.8%)	English (10.6%)	Polish (7.7%)
Utica city *Oneida Co.*	Italian (18.5%)	Irish (9.7%)	German (9.0%)	Polish (7.1%)	Yugoslavian (5.8%)
Valley Stream village *Nassau Co.*	Italian (14.9%)	Irish (8.9%)	German (4.9%)	American (4.2%)	Haitian (2.4%)
Warwick town *Orange Co.*	Irish (25.8%)	Italian (18.3%)	German (16.3%)	American (11.9%)	English (8.4%)
Webster town *Monroe Co.*	Italian (27.9%)	German (23.9%)	Irish (19.0%)	English (11.4%)	Polish (6.5%)
West Babylon cdp *Suffolk Co.*	Italian (33.0%)	Irish (20.2%)	German (14.9%)	Polish (5.9%)	English (3.6%)
West Seneca cdp *Erie Co.*	German (31.7%)	Polish (27.1%)	Irish (24.4%)	Italian (19.1%)	English (6.5%)
White Plains city *Westchester Co.*	Italian (13.2%)	Irish (8.0%)	American (5.2%)	German (5.1%)	Russian (3.3%)
Yonkers city *Westchester Co.*	Italian (15.0%)	Irish (11.4%)	German (3.5%)	American (3.2%)	Polish (2.4%)
Yorktown town *Westchester Co.*	Italian (34.7%)	Irish (20.0%)	German (11.1%)	American (5.3%)	Polish (5.0%)

NOTE: "French" excludes Basque; Please refer to the User Guide for more information.
SOURCE: U.S. Census Bureau, American Community Survey, 2011-2015 Five-Year Estimates

Marriage Status

Place	Never Married (%)	Now Married[1] (%)	Separated (%)	Widowed (%)	Divorced (%)
Albany city *Albany Co.*	60.7	25.7	1.8	5.7	7.9
Amherst town *Erie Co.*	34.6	49.6	1.3	7.2	8.6
Babylon town *Suffolk Co.*	34.8	50.0	2.3	7.0	8.2
Bay Shore cdp *Suffolk Co.*	39.6	44.5	3.1	5.5	10.3
Bethlehem town *Albany Co.*	27.3	58.2	0.9	6.7	7.9
Binghamton city *Broome Co.*	47.6	31.9	2.8	8.0	12.5
Brentwood cdp *Suffolk Co.*	45.5	41.9	2.6	4.4	8.1
Brighton cdp *Monroe Co.*	34.7	48.0	1.2	8.1	9.2
Bronx borough *Bronx Co.*	48.8	36.4	5.5	5.5	9.2
Brookhaven town *Suffolk Co.*	33.1	52.6	1.7	5.9	8.4
Brooklyn borough *Kings Co.*	43.9	43.3	3.2	5.6	7.3
Buffalo city *Erie Co.*	51.2	31.5	3.3	6.5	10.8
Carmel town *Putnam Co.*	27.8	59.4	0.8	5.2	7.6
Centereach cdp *Suffolk Co.*	33.4	52.6	1.0	6.3	7.7
Central Islip cdp *Suffolk Co.*	44.2	40.3	2.6	6.1	9.4
Cheektowaga town *Erie Co.*	34.6	45.7	1.3	7.9	11.9
Cicero town *Onondaga Co.*	27.5	57.4	2.0	5.3	9.9
Clarence town *Erie Co.*	24.8	62.0	1.0	6.2	7.0
Clarkstown town *Rockland Co.*	28.7	58.1	1.7	6.3	6.9
Clay town *Onondaga Co.*	30.9	53.1	1.7	5.2	10.8
Clifton Park town *Saratoga Co.*	23.3	63.1	1.2	4.8	8.7
Colonie town *Albany Co.*	34.7	50.0	2.2	5.8	9.4
Commack cdp *Suffolk Co.*	25.9	61.6	1.0	6.8	5.7
Coram cdp *Suffolk Co.*	31.9	51.2	2.0	6.1	10.7
Cortlandt town *Westchester Co.*	26.1	58.7	1.6	6.3	8.9
East Fishkill town *Dutchess Co.*	26.2	62.2	1.7	4.9	6.7
East Meadow cdp *Nassau Co.*	29.2	53.6	1.7	10.3	7.0
Eastchester town *Westchester Co.*	30.0	55.0	1.3	6.8	8.3
Elmont cdp *Nassau Co.*	39.7	47.3	2.5	5.4	7.6
Franklin Square cdp *Nassau Co.*	31.9	55.2	1.0	6.9	5.9
Freeport village *Nassau Co.*	42.4	42.1	3.2	5.9	9.6
Glenville town *Schenectady Co.*	28.4	53.8	1.2	8.1	9.6
Greece town *Monroe Co.*	30.4	50.8	1.5	7.7	11.1
Greenburgh town *Westchester Co.*	31.4	56.2	1.5	5.1	7.3
Guilderland town *Albany Co.*	34.9	50.4	1.6	5.8	8.8
Hamburg town *Erie Co.*	29.2	52.2	1.3	7.1	11.4
Haverstraw town *Rockland Co.*	39.3	48.5	3.7	4.7	7.4
Hempstead town *Nassau Co.*	33.9	53.0	1.9	6.5	6.7
Hempstead village *Nassau Co.*	49.9	36.7	3.5	5.3	8.1
Henrietta town *Monroe Co.*	41.4	45.5	1.7	3.9	9.1
Hicksville cdp *Nassau Co.*	31.5	57.1	1.2	6.3	5.0
Huntington town *Suffolk Co.*	28.3	58.4	1.4	6.4	7.0
Huntington Station cdp *Suffolk Co.*	36.4	49.8	2.2	5.0	8.8
Irondequoit cdp *Monroe Co.*	30.5	49.6	1.8	7.8	12.0
Islip town *Suffolk Co.*	35.6	49.8	2.1	6.1	8.5
Ithaca city *Tompkins Co.*	77.1	17.2	1.4	1.4	4.3
Jamestown city *Chautauqua Co.*	34.1	43.5	3.3	7.6	14.8
Lancaster town *Erie Co.*	27.9	56.8	1.6	6.8	8.5
Levittown cdp *Nassau Co.*	30.2	56.6	1.9	6.6	6.6
Long Beach city *Nassau Co.*	37.9	42.3	2.1	7.1	12.7

Place	Never Married (%)	Now Married[1] (%)	Separated (%)	Widowed (%)	Divorced (%)
Mamaroneck town Westchester Co.	26.2	61.4	1.5	5.3	7.1
Manhattan borough New York Co.	50.7	35.8	2.9	4.8	8.8
Manlius town Onondaga Co.	23.6	59.4	1.4	6.8	10.2
Monroe town Orange Co.	29.4	63.1	1.0	3.0	4.4
Mount Pleasant town Westchester Co.	33.2	55.3	1.7	5.2	6.3
Mount Vernon city Westchester Co.	44.7	38.1	3.6	6.5	10.7
New City cdp Rockland Co.	26.6	63.4	1.1	4.9	5.1
New Rochelle city Westchester Co.	35.4	49.7	2.3	6.8	8.1
New York city New York Co.	44.0	42.5	3.3	5.6	8.0
Newburgh town Orange Co.	30.0	54.4	1.9	5.8	9.8
Niagara Falls city Niagara Co.	40.7	39.1	2.9	7.8	12.4
North Hempstead town Nassau Co.	28.7	58.1	1.4	6.9	6.4
North Tonawanda city Niagara Co.	32.6	47.8	1.8	7.8	11.7
Oceanside cdp Nassau Co.	29.6	58.7	1.1	6.6	5.1
Orangetown town Rockland Co.	33.7	52.2	1.5	6.8	7.3
Orchard Park town Erie Co.	25.3	59.7	1.4	6.6	8.4
Ossining town Westchester Co.	34.5	51.8	2.4	5.3	8.4
Oyster Bay town Nassau Co.	27.9	59.3	1.3	6.9	6.0
Penfield town Monroe Co.	24.9	59.6	1.6	6.7	8.7
Perinton town Monroe Co.	25.2	58.8	1.4	6.0	10.0
Pittsford town Monroe Co.	29.4	59.7	1.0	5.4	5.6
Port Chester village Westchester Co.	41.4	48.2	4.3	4.1	6.3
Poughkeepsie town Dutchess Co.	40.0	46.2	1.8	5.9	7.9
Poughkeepsie city Dutchess Co.	46.4	36.1	3.2	7.1	10.4
Queens borough Queens Co.	38.3	48.1	2.8	5.9	7.7
Ramapo town Rockland Co.	33.4	55.6	1.8	5.2	5.9
Riverhead town Suffolk Co.	30.7	53.3	1.5	7.8	8.2
Rochester city Monroe Co.	55.3	28.6	4.3	5.4	10.7
Rome city Oneida Co.	36.4	40.7	2.9	9.0	13.9
Rye town Westchester Co.	36.3	52.4	3.1	4.9	6.4
Salina town Onondaga Co.	33.2	46.9	2.4	7.9	12.0
Schenectady city Schenectady Co.	45.0	36.7	3.1	7.5	10.9
Smithtown town Suffolk Co.	26.8	60.4	1.2	6.5	6.4
Southampton town Suffolk Co.	31.1	52.8	1.5	6.4	9.8
Spring Valley village Rockland Co.	41.8	46.7	3.9	4.2	7.3
Staten Island borough Richmond Co.	33.5	53.0	1.8	6.7	6.8
Syracuse city Onondaga Co.	54.4	29.7	3.4	5.8	10.0
Tonawanda town Erie Co.	31.6	48.5	1.5	8.6	11.3
Tonawanda cdp Erie Co.	30.7	49.0	1.5	8.9	11.4
Troy city Rensselaer Co.	55.2	30.6	2.6	5.1	9.1
Union town Broome Co.	32.7	47.6	2.5	7.5	12.2
Utica city Oneida Co.	44.2	35.8	2.6	8.1	11.9
Valley Stream village Nassau Co.	33.6	53.3	1.9	6.1	7.1
Warwick town Orange Co.	26.8	56.6	2.2	5.8	10.8
Webster town Monroe Co.	23.7	60.7	1.5	7.0	8.7
West Babylon cdp Suffolk Co.	30.4	52.9	1.9	8.0	8.6
West Seneca cdp Erie Co.	28.8	52.4	1.3	9.4	9.4
White Plains city Westchester Co.	35.4	49.7	2.6	6.1	8.7
Yonkers city Westchester Co.	39.7	45.7	3.3	6.4	8.2
Yorktown town Westchester Co.	27.7	57.1	1.1	6.8	8.4

NOTE: (1) Includes separated.
SOURCE: U.S. Census Bureau, American Community Survey, 2011-2015 Five-Year Estimates

Employment by Occupation

Place	MBF[1] (%)	CES[2] (%)	ELCAM[3] (%)	HPT[4] (%)	S[5] (%)	SO[6] (%)	NRCM[7] (%)	PTMM[8] (%)
Albany city Albany Co.	12.5	7.1	13.9	5.7	24.2	25.9	4.4	6.3
Amherst town Erie Co.	19.1	6.8	17.3	9.0	13.9	24.4	3.9	5.6
Babylon town Suffolk Co.	11.7	3.8	10.6	5.5	19.7	27.3	9.8	11.6
Bay Shore cdp Suffolk Co.	13.4	1.8	10.0	3.5	22.9	24.8	8.2	15.3
Bethlehem town Albany Co.	19.4	9.8	18.9	8.5	11.2	22.0	4.8	5.6
Binghamton city Broome Co.	9.2	5.0	14.1	5.3	22.1	27.9	7.2	9.1
Brentwood cdp Suffolk Co.	6.2	1.9	4.1	3.3	25.8	22.6	11.8	24.3
Brighton cdp Monroe Co.	16.0	12.6	23.1	12.1	11.1	17.4	2.9	4.9
Bronx borough Bronx Co.	8.1	2.0	10.0	4.2	33.3	24.2	7.1	11.0
Brookhaven town Suffolk Co.	13.7	5.1	12.8	6.6	17.3	26.0	9.7	8.7
Brooklyn borough Kings Co.	13.1	4.2	16.5	4.8	24.1	22.3	6.3	8.8
Buffalo city Erie Co.	10.3	3.4	13.3	5.6	25.1	24.2	5.3	12.7
Carmel town Putnam Co.	14.6	3.9	15.1	6.6	16.5	25.0	12.1	6.2
Centereach cdp Suffolk Co.	15.5	4.6	11.3	6.1	15.9	29.2	8.4	9.0
Central Islip cdp Suffolk Co.	6.3	2.6	6.3	5.5	24.5	21.8	9.6	23.4
Cheektowaga town Erie Co.	11.4	3.6	8.6	6.5	18.2	30.6	6.9	14.1
Cicero town Onondaga Co.	14.2	5.3	10.3	7.0	15.8	28.1	7.3	11.9
Clarence town Erie Co.	23.0	4.6	15.4	9.8	14.0	22.3	5.4	5.6
Clarkstown town Rockland Co.	18.1	6.1	15.9	9.9	14.5	23.9	5.8	5.8
Clay town Onondaga Co.	14.5	5.9	10.7	8.0	15.9	28.8	6.4	9.8
Clifton Park town Saratoga Co.	22.0	12.8	14.8	8.3	9.4	22.0	5.2	5.4
Colonie town Albany Co.	17.4	7.8	10.8	7.4	15.8	27.9	5.5	7.4
Commack cdp Suffolk Co.	20.2	4.7	18.7	8.3	12.8	24.6	5.4	5.2
Coram cdp Suffolk Co.	14.2	4.4	12.6	5.8	19.8	27.6	8.3	7.4
Cortlandt town Westchester Co.	19.6	5.1	20.5	6.3	16.9	19.5	6.2	5.8
East Fishkill town Dutchess Co.	20.6	6.1	12.3	6.5	16.3	23.2	8.7	6.3
East Meadow cdp Nassau Co.	15.8	5.4	14.0	8.0	16.3	28.8	5.6	6.2
Eastchester town Westchester Co.	24.1	4.6	21.8	6.9	10.7	24.1	4.9	3.0
Elmont cdp Nassau Co.	10.9	2.2	9.5	9.8	24.7	25.4	8.2	9.3
Franklin Square cdp Nassau Co.	12.9	3.4	11.2	6.6	18.1	29.6	10.1	8.1
Freeport village Nassau Co.	10.5	2.1	11.7	6.0	22.8	25.6	8.7	12.7
Glenville town Schenectady Co.	14.9	6.8	13.1	8.3	14.9	27.1	6.4	8.6
Greece town Monroe Co.	13.7	6.1	10.2	6.7	18.2	27.4	6.2	11.6
Greenburgh town Westchester Co.	22.2	6.9	20.8	8.1	15.1	19.4	3.7	3.8
Guilderland town Albany Co.	16.6	10.3	17.3	7.7	12.7	26.2	4.0	5.3
Hamburg town Erie Co.	13.7	4.4	11.5	7.3	18.9	25.3	7.6	11.4
Haverstraw town Rockland Co.	8.8	3.5	10.0	6.7	27.2	23.2	8.4	12.2
Hempstead town Nassau Co.	15.2	3.6	14.2	7.3	17.9	26.4	7.3	8.1
Hempstead village Nassau Co.	8.2	1.8	6.3	3.8	32.0	23.1	11.3	13.6
Henrietta town Monroe Co.	12.3	10.3	10.8	6.7	17.0	26.7	5.6	10.5
Hicksville cdp Nassau Co.	14.8	4.1	12.3	7.4	15.9	29.0	7.6	8.9
Huntington town Suffolk Co.	19.5	4.8	16.6	7.7	13.7	25.7	5.9	6.0
Huntington Station cdp Suffolk Co.	10.8	3.8	11.4	4.8	25.1	23.1	9.9	11.0
Irondequoit cdp Monroe Co.	16.2	7.0	12.5	7.5	16.2	24.5	5.7	10.3
Islip town Suffolk Co.	12.4	3.4	10.9	5.1	19.3	25.6	9.7	13.8
Ithaca city Tompkins Co.	11.0	14.1	29.3	2.4	17.6	16.3	3.7	5.6
Jamestown city Chautauqua Co.	8.8	2.5	10.1	4.5	20.9	25.5	8.4	19.3
Lancaster town Erie Co.	16.7	5.2	10.2	6.4	15.4	27.7	6.5	12.0
Levittown cdp Nassau Co.	14.2	4.3	13.8	5.3	17.0	29.5	7.6	8.2
Long Beach city Nassau Co.	17.8	3.8	18.5	5.0	17.4	25.8	6.7	4.9

Place	MBF[1] (%)	CES[2] (%)	ELCAM[3] (%)	HPT[4] (%)	S[5] (%)	SO[6] (%)	NRCM[7] (%)	PTMM[8] (%)
Mamaroneck town *Westchester Co.*	29.7	5.4	21.1	4.2	12.2	19.2	4.4	3.7
Manhattan borough *New York Co.*	26.2	6.0	22.0	5.0	13.8	20.7	2.1	4.1
Manlius town *Onondaga Co.*	18.2	5.7	20.9	10.4	11.4	22.6	4.8	5.9
Monroe town *Orange Co.*	14.1	4.5	16.6	6.0	15.8	28.9	5.2	8.9
Mount Pleasant town *Westchester Co.*	21.2	5.0	17.2	6.9	16.8	20.3	6.5	6.2
Mount Vernon city *Westchester Co.*	12.4	2.4	12.3	7.7	26.9	22.6	7.6	8.2
New City cdp *Rockland Co.*	20.4	6.0	17.2	11.7	12.0	22.6	4.8	5.4
New Rochelle city *Westchester Co.*	16.2	3.5	15.0	7.6	20.0	22.4	8.4	6.9
New York city *New York Co.*	15.1	4.2	15.1	5.0	23.1	22.8	6.1	8.6
Newburgh town *Orange Co.*	13.9	4.5	11.7	5.4	20.1	26.0	9.7	8.7
Niagara Falls city *Niagara Co.*	8.6	2.8	9.8	4.4	25.2	29.2	7.2	12.8
North Hempstead town *Nassau Co.*	19.7	5.3	15.1	11.0	12.9	25.4	4.9	5.7
North Tonawanda city *Niagara Co.*	11.8	4.5	9.8	6.3	18.5	27.6	7.1	14.3
Oceanside cdp *Nassau Co.*	17.2	4.2	17.5	4.8	15.2	29.3	4.9	7.0
Orangetown town *Rockland Co.*	19.2	5.9	18.8	7.0	16.7	21.2	7.0	4.3
Orchard Park town *Erie Co.*	20.0	5.7	14.2	8.3	14.9	23.6	4.3	9.0
Ossining town *Westchester Co.*	15.5	4.3	14.2	6.1	21.1	22.8	10.4	5.6
Oyster Bay town *Nassau Co.*	19.7	4.8	15.2	7.5	13.5	26.9	6.4	5.9
Penfield town *Monroe Co.*	20.4	10.0	14.1	7.8	13.0	24.7	3.7	6.3
Perinton town *Monroe Co.*	20.4	9.8	15.7	6.4	14.2	22.9	4.6	6.0
Pittsford town *Monroe Co.*	21.5	7.6	21.1	10.8	11.6	22.7	1.8	3.0
Port Chester village *Westchester Co.*	8.2	1.6	6.7	2.7	38.2	20.3	10.8	11.5
Poughkeepsie town *Dutchess Co.*	13.4	7.2	15.4	5.9	20.1	24.9	5.3	8.0
Poughkeepsie city *Dutchess Co.*	8.9	5.0	11.0	5.1	29.9	23.1	7.6	9.5
Queens borough *Queens Co.*	12.4	3.8	11.0	5.1	24.8	24.0	8.2	10.7
Ramapo town *Rockland Co.*	13.7	3.9	16.7	7.2	20.1	24.4	7.0	7.1
Riverhead town *Suffolk Co.*	12.8	3.3	12.6	5.4	20.0	26.6	9.2	10.0
Rochester city *Monroe Co.*	9.2	5.0	12.3	6.2	25.6	24.2	4.5	13.1
Rome city *Oneida Co.*	13.1	4.8	11.8	6.9	20.0	24.1	6.5	12.8
Rye town *Westchester Co.*	14.2	1.8	10.4	3.8	29.5	21.9	9.0	9.4
Salina town *Onondaga Co.*	14.5	5.5	11.7	6.1	16.2	28.5	6.2	11.3
Schenectady city *Schenectady Co.*	9.8	4.0	11.4	5.2	25.2	25.8	6.5	12.1
Smithtown town *Suffolk Co.*	19.4	5.2	16.2	8.1	13.4	24.9	7.2	5.6
Southampton town *Suffolk Co.*	14.5	3.2	12.8	4.8	20.2	22.3	16.5	5.8
Spring Valley village *Rockland Co.*	7.9	1.7	8.9	4.8	34.6	22.1	9.3	10.7
Staten Island borough *Richmond Co.*	13.5	4.4	14.1	7.3	19.5	24.3	9.0	8.0
Syracuse city *Onondaga Co.*	10.3	4.1	14.7	5.8	24.4	24.8	5.6	10.3
Tonawanda town *Erie Co.*	14.0	4.5	13.1	6.5	16.9	29.4	6.0	9.6
Tonawanda cdp *Erie Co.*	13.6	4.9	12.4	6.7	16.7	28.9	6.4	10.3
Troy city *Rensselaer Co.*	10.3	6.9	14.5	4.2	20.8	27.9	5.7	9.7
Union town *Broome Co.*	10.4	8.0	12.3	7.9	19.5	26.1	5.9	9.9
Utica city *Oneida Co.*	8.4	3.1	12.0	5.8	27.4	23.7	5.1	14.7
Valley Stream village *Nassau Co.*	12.4	3.9	11.0	9.0	19.4	27.2	8.8	8.2
Warwick town *Orange Co.*	15.2	5.0	12.7	5.3	16.5	24.7	11.0	9.6
Webster town *Monroe Co.*	17.8	9.1	11.5	7.0	12.6	25.8	7.2	8.9
West Babylon cdp *Suffolk Co.*	12.7	3.8	10.5	4.9	16.8	30.5	10.5	10.3
West Seneca cdp *Erie Co.*	13.3	4.6	10.1	7.6	16.6	28.5	6.6	12.6
White Plains city *Westchester Co.*	19.0	5.0	16.1	5.8	22.9	20.6	5.2	5.4
Yonkers city *Westchester Co.*	12.6	3.8	12.3	6.9	21.4	25.2	8.7	9.0
Yorktown town *Westchester Co.*	19.9	5.0	20.6	6.6	12.7	23.0	5.5	6.7

NOTES: (1) Management, business, and financial occupations; (2) Computer, engineering, and science occupations; (3) Education, legal, community service, arts, and media occupations; (4) Healthcare practitioners and technical occupations; (5) Service occupations; (6) Sales and office occupations; (7) Natural resources, construction, and maintenance occupations; (8) Production, transportation, and material moving occupations
SOURCE: U.S. Census Bureau, American Community Survey, 2011-2015 Five-Year Estimates

Educational Attainment

Place	Percent of Population 25 Years and Over with:		
	High School Diploma or Higher[1]	Bachelor's Degree or Higher	Graduate/Professional Degree
Albany city *Albany Co.*	89.6	36.4	16.8
Amherst town *Erie Co.*	95.4	53.4	27.8
Babylon town *Suffolk Co.*	87.3	25.2	9.4
Bay Shore cdp *Suffolk Co.*	83.1	27.3	10.4
Bethlehem town *Albany Co.*	96.7	56.3	32.4
Binghamton city *Broome Co.*	84.4	23.4	10.6
Brentwood cdp *Suffolk Co.*	70.8	12.9	4.0
Brighton cdp *Monroe Co.*	94.4	61.9	35.2
Bronx borough *Bronx Co.*	70.6	18.9	6.6
Brookhaven town *Suffolk Co.*	91.5	31.6	14.9
Brooklyn borough *Kings Co.*	79.3	32.8	12.8
Buffalo city *Erie Co.*	82.7	24.6	11.2
Carmel town *Putnam Co.*	93.3	38.5	17.2
Centereach cdp *Suffolk Co.*	93.0	29.1	12.4
Central Islip cdp *Suffolk Co.*	71.0	15.3	6.3
Cheektowaga town *Erie Co.*	90.3	21.4	7.5
Cicero town *Onondaga Co.*	94.3	29.7	12.0
Clarence town *Erie Co.*	96.3	49.5	25.2
Clarkstown town *Rockland Co.*	91.3	49.6	22.5
Clay town *Onondaga Co.*	93.9	32.2	11.8
Clifton Park town *Saratoga Co.*	96.8	56.6	25.7
Colonie town *Albany Co.*	93.9	39.0	16.8
Commack cdp *Suffolk Co.*	95.7	48.8	23.2
Coram cdp *Suffolk Co.*	92.7	35.4	14.9
Cortlandt town *Westchester Co.*	92.4	48.1	24.6
East Fishkill town *Dutchess Co.*	92.6	40.1	17.0
East Meadow cdp *Nassau Co.*	91.1	36.7	15.3
Eastchester town *Westchester Co.*	94.5	59.1	30.2
Elmont cdp *Nassau Co.*	86.2	28.7	10.1
Franklin Square cdp *Nassau Co.*	88.4	28.5	9.9
Freeport village *Nassau Co.*	81.2	26.4	11.6
Glenville town *Schenectady Co.*	95.0	34.8	16.6
Greece town *Monroe Co.*	91.9	28.3	10.3
Greenburgh town *Westchester Co.*	93.1	61.2	34.2
Guilderland town *Albany Co.*	96.8	49.1	25.7
Hamburg town *Erie Co.*	93.6	30.7	12.5
Haverstraw town *Rockland Co.*	82.6	28.1	11.6
Hempstead town *Nassau Co.*	89.6	38.1	16.6
Hempstead village *Nassau Co.*	71.2	17.0	6.6
Henrietta town *Monroe Co.*	92.3	36.8	14.6
Hicksville cdp *Nassau Co.*	90.8	36.0	12.9
Huntington town *Suffolk Co.*	92.7	49.9	23.4
Huntington Station cdp *Suffolk Co.*	77.6	30.9	12.9
Irondequoit cdp *Monroe Co.*	91.9	34.8	13.1
Islip town *Suffolk Co.*	85.3	27.5	11.7
Ithaca city *Tompkins Co.*	94.2	62.9	38.0
Jamestown city *Chautauqua Co.*	85.9	18.3	7.5
Lancaster town *Erie Co.*	95.0	31.5	12.1
Levittown cdp *Nassau Co.*	92.4	31.3	12.3
Long Beach city *Nassau Co.*	93.9	45.9	21.2

Place	Percent of Population 25 Years and Over with:		
	High School Diploma or Higher[1]	Bachelor's Degree or Higher	Graduate/Professional Degree
Mamaroneck town *Westchester Co.*	92.4	66.5	34.5
Manhattan borough *New York Co.*	86.6	59.9	28.4
Manlius town *Onondaga Co.*	96.9	52.7	27.4
Monroe town *Orange Co.*	83.9	33.1	11.6
Mount Pleasant town *Westchester Co.*	88.9	50.7	25.0
Mount Vernon city *Westchester Co.*	84.6	27.8	11.1
New City cdp *Rockland Co.*	93.7	57.7	27.6
New Rochelle city *Westchester Co.*	82.9	42.2	21.6
New York city *New York Co.*	80.3	35.7	14.6
Newburgh town *Orange Co.*	91.1	29.2	12.1
Niagara Falls city *Niagara Co.*	85.6	17.4	7.5
North Hempstead town *Nassau Co.*	90.7	53.1	25.6
North Tonawanda city *Niagara Co.*	92.1	25.1	9.0
Oceanside cdp *Nassau Co.*	94.3	44.2	19.8
Orangetown town *Rockland Co.*	91.0	50.6	23.4
Orchard Park town *Erie Co.*	95.9	44.9	20.7
Ossining town *Westchester Co.*	80.0	43.5	22.5
Oyster Bay town *Nassau Co.*	94.1	47.0	20.9
Penfield town *Monroe Co.*	94.0	51.2	24.6
Perinton town *Monroe Co.*	96.9	54.9	26.0
Pittsford town *Monroe Co.*	98.0	73.1	39.9
Port Chester village *Westchester Co.*	68.3	20.7	7.2
Poughkeepsie town *Dutchess Co.*	90.5	36.8	17.1
Poughkeepsie city *Dutchess Co.*	79.6	23.4	9.7
Queens borough *Queens Co.*	80.4	30.4	11.1
Ramapo town *Rockland Co.*	83.1	32.5	14.6
Riverhead town *Suffolk Co.*	90.2	28.5	13.4
Rochester city *Monroe Co.*	80.5	23.8	9.7
Rome city *Oneida Co.*	87.8	19.3	8.0
Rye town *Westchester Co.*	76.7	35.1	15.3
Salina town *Onondaga Co.*	91.1	26.1	9.9
Schenectady city *Schenectady Co.*	84.3	21.1	8.3
Smithtown town *Suffolk Co.*	95.1	45.7	21.2
Southampton town *Suffolk Co.*	88.8	37.5	16.4
Spring Valley village *Rockland Co.*	69.3	17.1	5.6
Staten Island borough *Richmond Co.*	88.7	30.8	12.4
Syracuse city *Onondaga Co.*	80.2	26.4	12.2
Tonawanda town *Erie Co.*	93.0	32.9	14.7
Tonawanda cdp *Erie Co.*	93.0	32.7	14.2
Troy city *Rensselaer Co.*	84.7	25.2	10.1
Union town *Broome Co.*	91.9	29.6	12.5
Utica city *Oneida Co.*	79.1	16.4	5.7
Valley Stream village *Nassau Co.*	89.8	34.0	10.5
Warwick town *Orange Co.*	94.4	35.6	14.7
Webster town *Monroe Co.*	95.2	43.2	19.4
West Babylon cdp *Suffolk Co.*	88.4	22.9	7.6
West Seneca cdp *Erie Co.*	92.9	27.4	10.9
White Plains city *Westchester Co.*	85.8	49.0	24.8
Yonkers city *Westchester Co.*	83.0	31.1	13.2
Yorktown town *Westchester Co.*	94.2	50.5	23.1

NOTE: (1) Includes General Equivalency Diploma (GED)
SOURCE: U.S. Census Bureau, American Community Survey, 2011-2015 Five-Year Estimates

Health Insurance

Place	Percent of Total Population with:				Percent of Population[1] Under Age 18 without Health Insurance
	Any Insurance	Private Insurance	Public Insurance	No Insurance	
Albany city *Albany Co.*	90.8	65.9	35.9	9.2	2.6
Amherst town *Erie Co.*	96.6	84.4	28.2	3.4	1.5
Babylon town *Suffolk Co.*	89.9	74.1	27.2	10.1	4.1
Bay Shore cdp *Suffolk Co.*	87.2	67.8	28.4	12.8	7.4
Bethlehem town *Albany Co.*	97.3	89.5	22.9	2.7	2.3
Binghamton city *Broome Co.*	91.6	54.4	49.7	8.4	2.6
Brentwood cdp *Suffolk Co.*	79.0	56.3	29.2	21.0	7.2
Brighton cdp *Monroe Co.*	94.5	84.4	24.0	5.5	3.8
Bronx borough *Bronx Co.*	86.3	43.1	52.0	13.7	3.8
Brookhaven town *Suffolk Co.*	92.7	79.0	26.1	7.3	2.8
Brooklyn borough *Kings Co.*	88.0	51.4	43.4	12.0	3.2
Buffalo city *Erie Co.*	91.5	49.8	52.0	8.5	2.7
Carmel town *Putnam Co.*	92.5	83.1	21.0	7.5	3.6
Centereach cdp *Suffolk Co.*	93.4	81.5	22.5	6.6	2.5
Central Islip cdp *Suffolk Co.*	80.4	56.9	32.0	19.6	5.3
Cheektowaga town *Erie Co.*	94.3	76.3	34.9	5.7	2.6
Cicero town *Onondaga Co.*	96.1	81.5	26.4	3.9	1.4
Clarence town *Erie Co.*	96.4	87.0	22.3	3.6	2.5
Clarkstown town *Rockland Co.*	93.8	80.9	27.0	6.2	2.5
Clay town *Onondaga Co.*	94.7	80.8	28.3	5.3	2.5
Clifton Park town *Saratoga Co.*	97.6	90.8	20.6	2.4	1.3
Colonie town *Albany Co.*	96.2	84.8	27.1	3.8	2.1
Commack cdp *Suffolk Co.*	96.7	88.3	22.3	3.3	1.6
Coram cdp *Suffolk Co.*	93.5	76.9	26.5	6.5	2.8
Cortlandt town *Westchester Co.*	93.5	82.0	24.3	6.5	2.8
East Fishkill town *Dutchess Co.*	94.5	83.6	21.6	5.5	4.6
East Meadow cdp *Nassau Co.*	93.4	82.4	25.4	6.6	2.8
Eastchester town *Westchester Co.*	96.5	88.1	21.3	3.5	0.3
Elmont cdp *Nassau Co.*	88.2	68.9	27.4	11.8	4.8
Franklin Square cdp *Nassau Co.*	94.2	79.7	26.1	5.8	1.1
Freeport village *Nassau Co.*	84.4	64.0	31.6	15.6	10.1
Glenville town *Schenectady Co.*	96.0	82.7	29.0	4.0	2.5
Greece town *Monroe Co.*	93.8	77.6	32.4	6.2	2.4
Greenburgh town *Westchester Co.*	93.9	83.7	22.1	6.1	2.3
Guilderland town *Albany Co.*	96.4	87.6	22.8	3.6	0.6
Hamburg town *Erie Co.*	96.1	81.6	28.9	3.9	2.5
Haverstraw town *Rockland Co.*	87.5	62.1	35.4	12.5	4.5
Hempstead town *Nassau Co.*	91.6	77.1	26.0	8.4	3.3
Hempstead village *Nassau Co.*	77.5	45.0	38.3	22.5	5.9
Henrietta town *Monroe Co.*	95.0	81.8	26.4	5.0	2.4
Hicksville cdp *Nassau Co.*	93.4	80.6	25.2	6.6	2.0
Huntington town *Suffolk Co.*	93.9	82.4	24.7	6.1	3.0
Huntington Station cdp *Suffolk Co.*	82.8	63.5	28.4	17.2	7.4
Irondequoit cdp *Monroe Co.*	95.5	78.1	33.7	4.5	3.2
Islip town *Suffolk Co.*	89.4	73.9	25.9	10.6	4.3
Ithaca city *Tompkins Co.*	94.4	82.5	17.3	5.6	9.4
Jamestown city *Chautauqua Co.*	92.3	54.8	51.3	7.7	5.7
Lancaster town *Erie Co.*	95.9	84.0	26.2	4.1	1.9
Levittown cdp *Nassau Co.*	95.6	85.6	22.8	4.4	1.2
Long Beach city *Nassau Co.*	89.8	75.7	27.0	10.2	0.4

Place	Percent of Total Population with:				Percent of Population[1] Under Age 18 without Health Insurance
	Any Insurance	Private Insurance	Public Insurance	No Insurance	
Mamaroneck town *Westchester Co.*	95.2	83.8	22.5	4.8	2.4
Manhattan borough *New York Co.*	91.1	67.3	31.8	8.9	3.2
Manlius town *Onondaga Co.*	96.5	83.1	29.4	3.5	2.0
Monroe town *Orange Co.*	96.3	51.4	52.5	3.7	1.1
Mount Pleasant town *Westchester Co.*	93.9	82.1	23.1	6.1	1.7
Mount Vernon city *Westchester Co.*	87.4	60.3	38.5	12.6	3.9
New City cdp *Rockland Co.*	96.0	85.8	25.2	4.0	1.4
New Rochelle city *Westchester Co.*	88.6	68.0	30.9	11.4	2.2
New York city *New York Co.*	87.6	55.0	40.3	12.4	3.6
Newburgh town *Orange Co.*	92.4	77.8	27.4	7.6	3.6
Niagara Falls city *Niagara Co.*	92.6	58.1	51.3	7.4	2.1
North Hempstead town *Nassau Co.*	92.5	81.1	24.5	7.5	3.9
North Tonawanda city *Niagara Co.*	93.7	76.0	34.3	6.3	1.7
Oceanside cdp *Nassau Co.*	95.7	85.5	22.9	4.3	1.2
Orangetown town *Rockland Co.*	93.8	80.9	26.5	6.2	6.3
Orchard Park town *Erie Co.*	98.0	90.3	23.7	2.0	1.8
Ossining town *Westchester Co.*	85.3	68.5	26.5	14.7	2.1
Oyster Bay town *Nassau Co.*	95.7	86.0	23.3	4.3	1.6
Penfield town *Monroe Co.*	97.1	86.2	26.6	2.9	1.5
Perinton town *Monroe Co.*	96.8	86.6	25.5	3.2	1.7
Pittsford town *Monroe Co.*	98.5	92.7	22.2	1.5	0.6
Port Chester village *Westchester Co.*	72.0	49.3	29.3	28.0	6.5
Poughkeepsie town *Dutchess Co.*	93.9	77.7	28.7	6.1	2.6
Poughkeepsie city *Dutchess Co.*	85.5	51.9	46.6	14.5	3.1
Queens borough *Queens Co.*	84.4	54.5	37.4	15.6	4.4
Ramapo town *Rockland Co.*	89.4	51.1	46.9	10.6	3.8
Riverhead town *Suffolk Co.*	87.0	69.4	33.7	13.0	5.9
Rochester city *Monroe Co.*	90.1	50.0	50.2	9.9	4.4
Rome city *Oneida Co.*	93.2	66.7	44.7	6.8	2.3
Rye town *Westchester Co.*	79.9	61.4	26.8	20.1	4.5
Salina town *Onondaga Co.*	93.1	74.7	35.9	6.9	2.4
Schenectady city *Schenectady Co.*	89.6	55.7	45.6	10.4	4.0
Smithtown town *Suffolk Co.*	96.7	88.6	21.8	3.3	1.1
Southampton town *Suffolk Co.*	84.5	70.1	29.7	15.5	6.3
Spring Valley village *Rockland Co.*	76.9	35.5	46.9	23.1	6.1
Staten Island borough *Richmond Co.*	92.8	70.3	31.6	7.2	2.9
Syracuse city *Onondaga Co.*	90.3	55.4	46.9	9.7	5.0
Tonawanda town *Erie Co.*	96.3	78.3	34.4	3.7	0.8
Tonawanda cdp *Erie Co.*	96.2	78.3	34.8	3.8	0.8
Troy city *Rensselaer Co.*	92.8	63.5	40.0	7.2	1.5
Union town *Broome Co.*	92.8	68.1	40.3	7.2	3.9
Utica city *Oneida Co.*	91.8	45.5	57.7	8.2	3.1
Valley Stream village *Nassau Co.*	90.4	70.3	29.7	9.6	4.0
Warwick town *Orange Co.*	94.0	82.2	24.8	6.0	2.8
Webster town *Monroe Co.*	96.6	84.1	27.5	3.4	2.7
West Babylon cdp *Suffolk Co.*	92.7	79.3	25.7	7.3	1.9
West Seneca cdp *Erie Co.*	94.9	79.9	32.8	5.1	2.7
White Plains city *Westchester Co.*	85.6	67.7	28.2	14.4	3.1
Yonkers city *Westchester Co.*	88.2	62.6	36.8	11.8	4.0
Yorktown town *Westchester Co.*	96.4	87.2	22.7	3.6	2.4

NOTE: (1) Civilian noninstitutionalized population.
SOURCE: U.S. Census Bureau, American Community Survey, 2011-2015 Five-Year Estimates

Income and Poverty

Place	Average Household Income ($)	Median Household Income ($)	Per Capita Income ($)	Households w/$100,000+ Income (%)	Poverty Rate (%)
Albany city *Albany Co.*	57,274	40,949	24,912	15.2	26.8
Amherst town *Erie Co.*	92,050	68,294	37,506	33.2	10.2
Babylon town *Suffolk Co.*	94,732	80,327	31,794	38.3	7.1
Bay Shore cdp *Suffolk Co.*	84,581	70,229	27,969	31.7	9.5
Bethlehem town *Albany Co.*	115,120	93,366	45,215	45.9	4.3
Binghamton city *Broome Co.*	44,614	29,824	19,891	9.6	33.9
Brentwood cdp *Suffolk Co.*	82,569	70,139	20,463	31.9	11.6
Brighton cdp *Monroe Co.*	92,493	66,149	41,519	30.6	9.5
Bronx borough *Bronx Co.*	50,191	34,299	18,456	12.4	30.7
Brookhaven town *Suffolk Co.*	102,812	87,040	35,067	42.4	7.7
Brooklyn borough *Kings Co.*	71,957	48,201	26,774	22.2	23.2
Buffalo city *Erie Co.*	46,918	31,918	20,751	9.8	31.4
Carmel town *Putnam Co.*	120,711	103,438	41,585	51.4	3.2
Centereach cdp *Suffolk Co.*	106,686	94,432	33,605	47.8	5.3
Central Islip cdp *Suffolk Co.*	76,562	66,430	22,515	27.7	13.1
Cheektowaga town *Erie Co.*	56,853	48,662	25,764	13.5	10.9
Cicero town *Onondaga Co.*	81,482	68,409	32,092	28.5	7.8
Clarence town *Erie Co.*	117,313	90,459	43,841	44.4	4.0
Clarkstown town *Rockland Co.*	127,739	104,050	44,842	52.6	5.6
Clay town *Onondaga Co.*	75,117	64,717	30,355	25.0	8.9
Clifton Park town *Saratoga Co.*	109,802	95,100	43,401	48.5	2.5
Colonie town *Albany Co.*	88,857	71,658	35,473	32.7	6.9
Commack cdp *Suffolk Co.*	130,758	114,463	44,040	56.8	3.5
Coram cdp *Suffolk Co.*	94,135	80,899	35,358	37.5	6.1
Cortlandt town *Westchester Co.*	131,247	100,593	47,882	50.4	5.1
East Fishkill town *Dutchess Co.*	118,440	101,377	39,457	51.0	3.2
East Meadow cdp *Nassau Co.*	110,726	94,214	37,369	47.7	4.4
Eastchester town *Westchester Co.*	167,976	105,318	66,592	51.9	3.2
Elmont cdp *Nassau Co.*	103,060	89,523	28,633	43.4	8.0
Franklin Square cdp *Nassau Co.*	103,846	96,568	32,998	47.7	5.4
Freeport village *Nassau Co.*	87,631	72,574	28,357	33.8	13.8
Glenville town *Schenectady Co.*	78,321	67,308	31,712	28.2	4.9
Greece town *Monroe Co.*	68,464	55,061	29,061	20.6	9.3
Greenburgh town *Westchester Co.*	163,030	115,754	60,248	56.9	4.6
Guilderland town *Albany Co.*	101,141	78,131	41,460	37.4	5.8
Hamburg town *Erie Co.*	75,265	62,383	31,766	26.1	7.9
Haverstraw town *Rockland Co.*	91,530	73,117	29,883	34.6	11.7
Hempstead town *Nassau Co.*	117,518	94,999	38,126	47.6	7.0
Hempstead village *Nassau Co.*	70,983	55,417	21,879	25.3	20.7
Henrietta town *Monroe Co.*	72,154	61,762	27,436	24.5	12.2
Hicksville cdp *Nassau Co.*	113,519	95,030	37,215	48.7	4.4
Huntington town *Suffolk Co.*	142,000	105,451	49,067	52.6	6.1
Huntington Station cdp *Suffolk Co.*	93,294	73,591	29,269	38.3	15.2
Irondequoit cdp *Monroe Co.*	66,379	54,275	29,570	19.0	8.5
Islip town *Suffolk Co.*	103,042	86,864	32,425	42.6	7.3
Ithaca city *Tompkins Co.*	50,775	30,436	17,233	13.7	44.8
Jamestown city *Chautauqua Co.*	42,948	30,950	18,796	7.4	29.3
Lancaster town *Erie Co.*	80,639	67,223	32,389	31.0	5.8
Levittown cdp *Nassau Co.*	108,764	98,810	35,783	49.5	3.0
Long Beach city *Nassau Co.*	104,685	84,831	46,925	42.5	7.0

Place	Average Household Income ($)	Median Household Income ($)	Per Capita Income ($)	Households w/$100,000+ Income (%)	Poverty Rate (%)
Mamaroneck town Westchester Co.	200,593	114,273	73,499	55.0	6.8
Manhattan borough New York Co.	135,687	72,871	64,993	39.6	17.9
Manlius town Onondaga Co.	100,151	75,316	41,620	37.2	5.7
Monroe town Orange Co.	87,705	65,523	22,531	35.2	32.7
Mount Pleasant town Westchester Co.	143,688	102,142	47,484	51.2	7.7
Mount Vernon city Westchester Co.	70,868	50,952	27,378	22.2	15.3
New City cdp Rockland Co.	145,336	119,528	48,389	60.7	4.5
New Rochelle city Westchester Co.	112,366	70,036	41,485	37.3	11.1
New York city New York Co.	85,704	53,373	33,078	26.3	20.6
Newburgh town Orange Co.	95,188	79,654	34,628	37.7	6.4
Niagara Falls city Niagara Co.	44,388	31,560	19,964	8.2	26.7
North Hempstead town Nassau Co.	152,374	104,698	51,999	52.5	5.2
North Tonawanda city Niagara Co.	64,256	48,235	29,140	18.2	10.1
Oceanside cdp Nassau Co.	113,279	95,690	41,111	47.9	5.5
Orangetown town Rockland Co.	120,135	92,257	44,117	47.1	8.1
Orchard Park town Erie Co.	112,008	85,660	44,218	41.9	2.4
Ossining town Westchester Co.	122,859	79,688	40,732	42.9	11.0
Oyster Bay town Nassau Co.	146,462	112,162	49,697	55.9	3.7
Penfield town Monroe Co.	98,877	78,469	39,801	36.9	4.3
Perinton town Monroe Co.	99,623	79,105	41,386	37.8	6.1
Pittsford town Monroe Co.	147,754	103,546	52,317	52.3	3.9
Port Chester village Westchester Co.	79,418	55,437	25,952	25.5	13.3
Poughkeepsie town Dutchess Co.	84,455	70,480	29,308	31.9	10.9
Poughkeepsie city Dutchess Co.	56,370	38,919	23,745	14.0	24.1
Queens borough Queens Co.	75,162	57,720	26,876	25.5	15.1
Ramapo town Rockland Co.	91,351	66,911	25,046	33.1	24.9
Riverhead town Suffolk Co.	89,019	64,775	34,885	34.1	9.3
Rochester city Monroe Co.	43,682	30,960	19,158	8.4	33.5
Rome city Oneida Co.	57,459	43,323	24,391	14.7	18.6
Rye town Westchester Co.	116,639	73,276	39,514	36.9	10.0
Salina town Onondaga Co.	62,010	52,259	28,213	15.5	11.1
Schenectady city Schenectady Co.	50,740	40,755	21,257	11.1	22.8
Smithtown town Suffolk Co.	133,009	112,693	45,518	56.5	3.8
Southampton town Suffolk Co.	119,046	79,799	45,188	39.7	8.1
Spring Valley village Rockland Co.	65,658	45,326	19,103	16.5	25.7
Staten Island borough Richmond Co.	90,236	73,197	32,041	35.2	12.5
Syracuse city Onondaga Co.	47,578	31,881	19,558	11.0	34.8
Tonawanda town Erie Co.	64,211	53,760	29,162	17.9	9.8
Tonawanda cdp Erie Co.	64,582	54,345	29,084	17.5	10.1
Troy city Rensselaer Co.	51,553	38,954	21,445	13.5	26.1
Union town Broome Co.	60,123	45,958	26,540	17.7	14.5
Utica city Oneida Co.	44,062	30,504	17,879	8.4	32.2
Valley Stream village Nassau Co.	105,515	90,018	33,303	44.6	7.5
Warwick town Orange Co.	110,976	84,807	42,407	41.2	5.3
Webster town Monroe Co.	83,676	69,987	33,926	30.4	6.9
West Babylon cdp Suffolk Co.	98,060	82,952	33,288	40.4	5.7
West Seneca cdp Erie Co.	67,732	59,265	29,643	21.2	6.7
White Plains city Westchester Co.	117,392	80,442	45,909	41.3	12.2
Yonkers city Westchester Co.	79,292	59,049	30,263	28.1	16.7
Yorktown town Westchester Co.	134,591	107,906	48,697	53.8	2.2

SOURCE: U.S. Census Bureau, American Community Survey, 2011-2015 Five-Year Estimates

Housing

Place	Homeownership Rate (%)	Median Home Value ($)	Median Year Structure Built	Homeowner Vacancy Rate (%)	Median Gross Rent ($/month)	Rental Vacancy Rate (%)
Albany city *Albany Co.*	37.5	$171,400	Before 1940	2.7	$857	6.9
Amherst town *Erie Co.*	70.3	$177,400	1969	0.7	$958	1.7
Babylon town *Suffolk Co.*	73.8	$340,600	1960	1.7	$1,487	3.7
Bay Shore cdp *Suffolk Co.*	59.8	$318,000	1961	1.4	$1,332	2.1
Bethlehem town *Albany Co.*	78.3	$271,900	1974	1.5	$1,094	8.2
Binghamton city *Broome Co.*	45.5	$85,300	1940	4.7	$657	8.3
Brentwood cdp *Suffolk Co.*	70.3	$278,200	1963	1.0	$1,243	5.0
Brighton cdp *Monroe Co.*	56.1	$170,300	1961	0.4	$943	7.1
Bronx borough *Bronx Co.*	19.0	$363,400	1949	2.7	$1,074	2.8
Brookhaven town *Suffolk Co.*	79.3	$327,300	1973	1.6	$1,601	4.8
Brooklyn borough *Kings Co.*	29.3	$570,200	Before 1940	2.3	$1,215	3.7
Buffalo city *Erie Co.*	41.5	$68,800	Before 1940	0.9	$699	5.5
Carmel town *Putnam Co.*	83.5	$379,300	1969	0.4	$1,177	3.2
Centereach cdp *Suffolk Co.*	85.4	$329,900	1968	0.4	$2,134	10.0
Central Islip cdp *Suffolk Co.*	64.4	$252,100	1971	0.0	$1,467	2.0
Cheektowaga town *Erie Co.*	70.9	$99,400	1959	1.4	$765	3.9
Cicero town *Onondaga Co.*	79.4	$147,200	1979	0.9	$825	3.7
Clarence town *Erie Co.*	83.0	$247,800	1981	0.6	$892	2.1
Clarkstown town *Rockland Co.*	79.6	$444,800	1971	0.7	$1,423	4.7
Clay town *Onondaga Co.*	73.6	$139,500	1975	1.0	$862	5.5
Clifton Park town *Saratoga Co.*	80.7	$276,800	1982	0.5	$1,125	5.0
Colonie town *Albany Co.*	70.8	$219,000	1967	0.6	$1,030	2.5
Commack cdp *Suffolk Co.*	91.1	$466,200	1964	0.7	$1,609	7.2
Coram cdp *Suffolk Co.*	67.3	$309,300	1979	0.4	$1,700	3.0
Cortlandt town *Westchester Co.*	75.6	$414,900	1961	1.0	$1,379	4.8
East Fishkill town *Dutchess Co.*	90.8	$348,400	1979	1.1	$1,221	8.5
East Meadow cdp *Nassau Co.*	86.3	$388,000	1956	0.4	$1,901	4.1
Eastchester town *Westchester Co.*	75.1	$579,200	1948	1.1	$1,750	3.6
Elmont cdp *Nassau Co.*	80.6	$368,700	1953	2.3	$1,608	0.8
Franklin Square cdp *Nassau Co.*	82.8	$427,900	1953	1.2	$1,469	2.9
Freeport village *Nassau Co.*	67.5	$312,800	1952	1.3	$1,360	2.6
Glenville town *Schenectady Co.*	76.3	$183,000	1958	1.2	$945	7.9
Greece town *Monroe Co.*	73.3	$128,400	1970	1.3	$850	7.8
Greenburgh town *Westchester Co.*	73.5	$538,700	1958	1.0	$1,657	4.0
Guilderland town *Albany Co.*	68.1	$249,000	1975	1.4	$1,111	4.9
Hamburg town *Erie Co.*	73.2	$145,600	1968	0.4	$775	3.5
Haverstraw town *Rockland Co.*	60.8	$309,300	1971	1.5	$1,357	2.4
Hempstead town *Nassau Co.*	80.5	$407,200	1953	1.2	$1,484	4.3
Hempstead village *Nassau Co.*	43.5	$308,400	1956	2.6	$1,287	6.6
Henrietta town *Monroe Co.*	71.0	$139,400	1974	1.1	$944	4.1
Hicksville cdp *Nassau Co.*	85.7	$398,100	1954	0.8	$1,698	9.2
Huntington town *Suffolk Co.*	84.4	$497,500	1962	0.9	$1,676	5.9
Huntington Station cdp *Suffolk Co.*	71.8	$352,500	1957	1.3	$1,587	7.9
Irondequoit cdp *Monroe Co.*	78.3	$117,500	1955	1.3	$822	6.4
Islip town *Suffolk Co.*	76.8	$350,700	1965	1.0	$1,510	4.0
Ithaca city *Tompkins Co.*	26.4	$220,400	Before 1940	2.7	$1,019	1.9
Jamestown city *Chautauqua Co.*	51.1	$63,600	Before 1940	1.8	$587	10.5
Lancaster town *Erie Co.*	77.1	$167,200	1972	0.7	$707	3.2
Levittown cdp *Nassau Co.*	90.8	$357,400	1952	0.3	$1,852	4.9
Long Beach city *Nassau Co.*	56.8	$459,200	1956	4.0	$1,637	3.7

Place	Homeownership Rate (%)	Median Home Value ($)	Median Year Structure Built	Homeowner Vacancy Rate (%)	Median Gross Rent ($/month)	Rental Vacancy Rate (%)
Mamaroneck town *Westchester Co.*	69.4	$816,300	1942	2.4	$1,569	2.8
Manhattan borough *New York Co.*	22.9	$848,700	1949	2.6	$1,519	4.0
Manlius town *Onondaga Co.*	79.5	$171,700	1969	0.1	$878	4.2
Monroe town *Orange Co.*	61.6	$324,400	1984	2.4	$1,198	0.9
Mount Pleasant town *Westchester Co.*	70.2	$610,900	1956	1.5	$1,373	2.0
Mount Vernon city *Westchester Co.*	39.1	$361,700	1944	4.2	$1,216	7.5
New City cdp *Rockland Co.*	90.1	$473,100	1970	0.6	$1,237	6.9
New Rochelle city *Westchester Co.*	49.6	$552,600	1951	1.8	$1,359	4.2
New York city *New York Co.*	31.8	$494,800	1949	2.1	$1,255	3.5
Newburgh town *Orange Co.*	81.4	$252,500	1969	1.6	$1,296	8.9
Niagara Falls city *Niagara Co.*	56.6	$67,400	1941	10.7	$638	18.2
North Hempstead town *Nassau Co.*	78.3	$623,400	1954	1.1	$1,692	5.1
North Tonawanda city *Niagara Co.*	67.7	$107,500	1954	0.0	$666	4.4
Oceanside cdp *Nassau Co.*	87.7	$441,000	1955	0.9	$1,256	4.3
Orangetown town *Rockland Co.*	72.3	$464,100	1961	2.1	$1,384	6.4
Orchard Park town *Erie Co.*	78.9	$209,400	1972	0.3	$892	14.6
Ossining town *Westchester Co.*	60.1	$447,200	1961	1.4	$1,422	4.4
Oyster Bay town *Nassau Co.*	87.5	$470,800	1957	1.1	$1,722	5.4
Penfield town *Monroe Co.*	81.8	$179,800	1976	1.0	$894	11.8
Perinton town *Monroe Co.*	77.9	$192,600	1975	1.0	$912	3.2
Pittsford town *Monroe Co.*	86.5	$262,200	1971	1.3	$1,059	5.6
Port Chester village *Westchester Co.*	42.7	$436,700	1946	2.1	$1,419	2.3
Poughkeepsie town *Dutchess Co.*	69.2	$240,200	1965	2.5	$1,142	4.7
Poughkeepsie city *Dutchess Co.*	36.2	$196,800	1950	5.2	$1,027	9.0
Queens borough *Queens Co.*	43.6	$450,300	1951	1.7	$1,367	3.0
Ramapo town *Rockland Co.*	58.5	$400,500	1970	1.7	$1,264	4.3
Riverhead town *Suffolk Co.*	77.7	$355,400	1981	2.0	$1,303	2.3
Rochester city *Monroe Co.*	36.9	$76,200	Before 1940	1.5	$770	6.7
Rome city *Oneida Co.*	54.4	$90,500	1951	2.1	$713	4.9
Rye town *Westchester Co.*	54.4	$536,700	1952	3.1	$1,489	3.1
Salina town *Onondaga Co.*	66.6	$108,800	1959	2.6	$848	3.1
Schenectady city *Schenectady Co.*	48.4	$114,400	Before 1940	3.2	$811	6.9
Smithtown town *Suffolk Co.*	88.1	$460,800	1967	0.9	$1,423	5.6
Southampton town *Suffolk Co.*	77.9	$598,100	1974	3.2	$1,677	3.3
Spring Valley village *Rockland Co.*	31.0	$253,400	1970	2.0	$1,204	7.3
Staten Island borough *Richmond Co.*	68.8	$439,500	1972	1.8	$1,169	6.9
Syracuse city *Onondaga Co.*	38.6	$88,800	1945	3.3	$730	6.9
Tonawanda town *Erie Co.*	71.0	$117,000	1953	0.5	$753	4.9
Tonawanda cdp *Erie Co.*	72.2	$118,600	1955	0.6	$773	4.8
Troy city *Rensselaer Co.*	38.2	$143,800	Before 1940	1.5	$842	3.0
Union town *Broome Co.*	59.5	$107,800	1954	2.1	$725	6.8
Utica city *Oneida Co.*	46.4	$89,200	Before 1940	2.4	$666	5.3
Valley Stream village *Nassau Co.*	80.1	$371,000	1950	1.4	$1,581	1.0
Warwick town *Orange Co.*	79.1	$305,900	1970	2.5	$1,144	3.8
Webster town *Monroe Co.*	77.9	$175,200	1980	1.0	$954	1.5
West Babylon cdp *Suffolk Co.*	75.5	$337,200	1961	0.6	$1,533	3.9
West Seneca cdp *Erie Co.*	76.3	$132,900	1964	0.6	$745	1.7
White Plains city *Westchester Co.*	50.9	$511,600	1956	1.9	$1,554	2.2
Yonkers city *Westchester Co.*	47.5	$382,300	1954	2.5	$1,227	11.8
Yorktown town *Westchester Co.*	85.4	$408,700	1968	1.0	$1,346	0.0

SOURCE: U.S. Census Bureau, American Community Survey, 2011-2015 Five-Year Estimates

Commute to Work

Place	Automobile (%)	Public Transportation (%)	Walk (%)	Work from Home (%)	Mean Travel Time to Work (minutes)
Albany city *Albany Co.*	71.1	14.4	10.3	2.4	19.1
Amherst town *Erie Co.*	90.4	1.9	3.2	3.5	19.4
Babylon town *Suffolk Co.*	85.4	8.6	2.0	2.5	30.5
Bay Shore cdp *Suffolk Co.*	81.0	10.1	2.7	2.9	31.4
Bethlehem town *Albany Co.*	90.6	1.4	1.1	5.9	20.9
Binghamton city *Broome Co.*	79.1	8.6	7.1	2.9	18.0
Brentwood cdp *Suffolk Co.*	89.6	4.3	1.4	1.1	26.2
Brighton cdp *Monroe Co.*	88.7	4.1	2.1	4.0	16.0
Bronx borough *Bronx Co.*	27.3	59.7	8.0	3.3	43.0
Brookhaven town *Suffolk Co.*	90.4	4.2	1.6	3.2	32.8
Brooklyn borough *Kings Co.*	23.0	61.7	8.8	3.9	41.7
Buffalo city *Erie Co.*	77.7	11.7	6.1	2.4	20.9
Carmel town *Putnam Co.*	88.4	6.8	0.9	3.5	36.9
Centereach cdp *Suffolk Co.*	94.1	3.5	0.2	1.6	28.1
Central Islip cdp *Suffolk Co.*	89.3	6.2	1.8	0.9	27.9
Cheektowaga town *Erie Co.*	95.1	1.1	1.5	1.2	19.4
Cicero town *Onondaga Co.*	94.3	0.5	1.3	2.7	19.4
Clarence town *Erie Co.*	92.8	0.5	0.9	5.1	20.8
Clarkstown town *Rockland Co.*	86.1	7.1	1.4	4.6	31.9
Clay town *Onondaga Co.*	93.7	0.9	1.7	3.0	20.0
Clifton Park town *Saratoga Co.*	92.3	0.8	0.5	5.8	25.1
Colonie town *Albany Co.*	91.8	2.3	2.2	2.4	19.4
Commack cdp *Suffolk Co.*	87.5	7.3	0.9	3.8	32.6
Coram cdp *Suffolk Co.*	90.9	5.1	0.4	3.0	37.0
Cortlandt town *Westchester Co.*	78.0	14.4	1.8	4.7	38.8
East Fishkill town *Dutchess Co.*	90.4	3.7	0.3	5.1	37.4
East Meadow cdp *Nassau Co.*	85.0	9.0	1.6	3.7	32.1
Eastchester town *Westchester Co.*	61.6	28.6	4.6	4.7	33.0
Elmont cdp *Nassau Co.*	72.6	21.5	2.7	1.9	39.5
Franklin Square cdp *Nassau Co.*	84.3	11.8	1.4	2.2	34.4
Freeport village *Nassau Co.*	76.2	14.2	5.8	2.4	30.7
Glenville town *Schenectady Co.*	92.5	1.0	2.8	2.8	23.0
Greece town *Monroe Co.*	94.7	1.0	0.9	2.6	20.5
Greenburgh town *Westchester Co.*	68.3	21.5	3.6	5.8	32.6
Guilderland town *Albany Co.*	90.7	1.4	2.6	3.7	21.4
Hamburg town *Erie Co.*	94.1	0.8	1.8	2.2	22.4
Haverstraw town *Rockland Co.*	83.2	8.5	2.5	3.7	30.5
Hempstead town *Nassau Co.*	76.3	16.9	2.6	3.2	35.1
Hempstead village *Nassau Co.*	66.4	24.5	4.7	2.1	32.9
Henrietta town *Monroe Co.*	90.3	1.3	4.9	2.7	17.8
Hicksville cdp *Nassau Co.*	79.5	11.9	2.9	2.8	33.4
Huntington town *Suffolk Co.*	81.6	10.5	1.2	5.5	33.3
Huntington Station cdp *Suffolk Co.*	80.9	10.4	2.4	4.1	27.7
Irondequoit cdp *Monroe Co.*	93.8	0.9	0.7	3.2	20.0
Islip town *Suffolk Co.*	88.2	6.7	1.2	2.3	30.3
Ithaca city *Tompkins Co.*	40.2	10.6	40.2	6.4	15.4
Jamestown city *Chautauqua Co.*	89.3	0.4	6.0	2.3	14.7
Lancaster town *Erie Co.*	95.9	0.4	0.5	2.5	21.9
Levittown cdp *Nassau Co.*	83.9	11.5	1.5	1.7	32.2
Long Beach city *Nassau Co.*	70.1	19.0	5.2	3.8	40.3

Place	Automobile (%)	Public Trans-portation (%)	Walk (%)	Work from Home (%)	Mean Travel Time to Work (minutes)
Mamaroneck town *Westchester Co.*	47.9	36.4	4.6	8.4	37.4
Manhattan borough *New York Co.*	8.0	59.2	20.7	6.8	31.1
Manlius town *Onondaga Co.*	92.7	0.5	1.6	4.7	21.6
Monroe town *Orange Co.*	70.3	12.7	9.7	5.0	33.3
Mount Pleasant town *Westchester Co.*	71.3	16.3	6.6	4.9	30.0
Mount Vernon city *Westchester Co.*	62.2	26.5	6.5	3.3	33.7
New City cdp *Rockland Co.*	87.1	6.8	0.6	4.4	33.1
New Rochelle city *Westchester Co.*	63.6	21.8	7.5	5.3	30.7
New York city *New York Co.*	26.7	56.5	10.2	4.0	39.9
Newburgh town *Orange Co.*	90.7	5.0	0.5	3.4	30.7
Niagara Falls city *Niagara Co.*	88.7	4.0	4.0	1.3	17.8
North Hempstead town *Nassau Co.*	71.9	19.2	3.3	4.6	34.8
North Tonawanda city *Niagara Co.*	94.6	0.6	1.5	1.7	20.3
Oceanside cdp *Nassau Co.*	80.0	13.1	1.3	5.1	34.0
Orangetown town *Rockland Co.*	83.1	7.2	3.2	5.8	31.3
Orchard Park town *Erie Co.*	94.5	0.5	1.2	3.2	22.0
Ossining town *Westchester Co.*	68.5	15.9	7.8	6.0	31.1
Oyster Bay town *Nassau Co.*	80.1	12.9	1.9	4.0	34.4
Penfield town *Monroe Co.*	91.3	0.6	1.3	6.0	19.4
Perinton town *Monroe Co.*	91.5	0.8	1.5	5.8	20.1
Pittsford town *Monroe Co.*	83.8	0.2	5.8	8.5	17.9
Port Chester village *Westchester Co.*	60.7	14.4	12.9	2.1	23.5
Poughkeepsie town *Dutchess Co.*	77.0	4.5	11.4	6.1	25.8
Poughkeepsie city *Dutchess Co.*	73.1	9.0	10.9	2.2	23.8
Queens borough *Queens Co.*	38.0	52.3	5.8	2.4	42.6
Ramapo town *Rockland Co.*	75.7	11.1	6.1	4.9	28.7
Riverhead town *Suffolk Co.*	87.9	2.7	2.8	4.0	26.8
Rochester city *Monroe Co.*	80.1	8.8	6.6	2.4	19.6
Rome city *Oneida Co.*	89.3	0.8	5.3	3.0	17.8
Rye town *Westchester Co.*	63.3	17.1	9.2	3.5	26.1
Salina town *Onondaga Co.*	92.2	1.8	2.1	2.9	18.0
Schenectady city *Schenectady Co.*	80.5	9.0	5.5	2.9	22.7
Smithtown town *Suffolk Co.*	88.0	6.3	0.7	4.1	32.3
Southampton town *Suffolk Co.*	83.9	5.5	2.8	6.7	26.4
Spring Valley village *Rockland Co.*	72.1	16.8	5.5	2.3	27.3
Staten Island borough *Richmond Co.*	64.5	29.8	2.5	2.3	42.6
Syracuse city *Onondaga Co.*	73.8	9.4	11.1	3.1	18.3
Tonawanda town *Erie Co.*	92.9	2.0	2.0	1.6	19.6
Tonawanda cdp *Erie Co.*	93.4	2.1	1.9	1.3	19.6
Troy city *Rensselaer Co.*	78.4	5.8	11.9	2.6	20.3
Union town *Broome Co.*	87.1	3.2	4.9	3.6	17.3
Utica city *Oneida Co.*	86.6	3.7	5.9	2.3	17.5
Valley Stream village *Nassau Co.*	74.0	21.2	2.0	1.6	40.3
Warwick town *Orange Co.*	84.6	4.8	3.4	6.8	40.4
Webster town *Monroe Co.*	94.0	0.3	1.1	3.6	20.6
West Babylon cdp *Suffolk Co.*	88.3	7.8	0.8	2.6	31.0
West Seneca cdp *Erie Co.*	94.7	1.1	1.7	2.0	20.8
White Plains city *Westchester Co.*	65.5	19.5	8.2	4.5	26.8
Yonkers city *Westchester Co.*	65.1	26.4	5.1	2.4	33.2
Yorktown town *Westchester Co.*	85.8	7.2	1.3	4.9	36.2

SOURCE: U.S. Census Bureau, American Community Survey, 2011-2015 Five-Year Estimates

Crime

Place	Violent Crime Rate (crimes per 10,000 population)	Property Crime Rate (crimes per 10,000 population)
Albany city *Albany Co.*	80.3	325.1
Amherst town *Erie Co.*	9.7	159.4
Babylon town *Suffolk Co.*	n/a	n/a
Bay Shore cdp *Suffolk Co.*	n/a	n/a
Bethlehem town *Albany Co.*	6.9	131.6
Binghamton city *Broome Co.*	67.3	454.3
Brentwood cdp *Suffolk Co.*	n/a	n/a
Brighton cdp *Monroe Co.*	5.9	209.6
Bronx borough *Bronx Co.*	n/a	n/a
Brookhaven town *Suffolk Co.*	n/a	n/a
Brooklyn borough *Kings Co.*	n/a	n/a
Buffalo city *Erie Co.*	111.9	433.0
Carmel town *Putnam Co.*	2.0	45.6
Centereach cdp *Suffolk Co.*	n/a	n/a
Central Islip cdp *Suffolk Co.*	n/a	n/a
Cheektowaga town *Erie Co.*	24.4	302.9
Cicero town *Onondaga Co.*	5.1	109.9
Clarence town *Erie Co.*	n/a	n/a
Clarkstown town *Rockland Co.*	13.3	172.5
Clay town *Onondaga Co.*	n/a	n/a
Clifton Park town *Saratoga Co.*	n/a	n/a
Colonie town *Albany Co.*	9.3	249.8
Commack cdp *Suffolk Co.*	n/a	n/a
Coram cdp *Suffolk Co.*	n/a	n/a
Cortlandt town *Westchester Co.*	n/a	n/a
East Fishkill town *Dutchess Co.*	3.4	58.5
East Meadow cdp *Nassau Co.*	n/a	n/a
Eastchester town *Westchester Co.*	3.0	85.1
Elmont cdp *Nassau Co.*	n/a	n/a
Franklin Square cdp *Nassau Co.*	n/a	n/a
Freeport village *Nassau Co.*	32.0	161.3
Glenville town *Schenectady Co.*	5.0	200.7
Greece town *Monroe Co.*	17.4	251.0
Greenburgh town *Westchester Co.*	10.6	138.4
Guilderland town *Albany Co.*	2.9	167.7
Hamburg town *Erie Co.*	5.9	197.6
Haverstraw town *Rockland Co.*	13.0	91.2
Hempstead town *Nassau Co.*	n/a	n/a
Hempstead village *Nassau Co.*	72.1	128.2
Henrietta town *Monroe Co.*	n/a	n/a
Hicksville cdp *Nassau Co.*	n/a	n/a
Huntington town *Suffolk Co.*	n/a	n/a
Huntington Station cdp *Suffolk Co.*	n/a	n/a
Irondequoit cdp *Monroe Co.*	19.3	261.8
Islip town *Suffolk Co.*	n/a	n/a
Ithaca city *Tompkins Co.*	n/a	n/a
Jamestown city *Chautauqua Co.*	78.3	334.4
Lancaster town *Erie Co.*	6.7	117.4
Levittown cdp *Nassau Co.*	n/a	n/a
Long Beach city *Nassau Co.*	13.0	93.3

Place	Violent Crime Rate (crimes per 10,000 population)	Property Crime Rate (crimes per 10,000 population)
Mamaroneck town *Westchester Co.*	6.5	79.1
Manhattan borough *New York Co.*	n/a	n/a
Manlius town *Onondaga Co.*	4.5	165.4
Monroe town *Orange Co.*	n/a	n/a
Mount Pleasant town *Westchester Co.*	6.4	72.7
Mount Vernon city *Westchester Co.*	69.3	164.1
New City cdp *Rockland Co.*	n/a	n/a
New Rochelle city *Westchester Co.*	21.3	159.8
New York city *New York Co.*	58.6	151.9
Newburgh town *Orange Co.*	9.7	337.0
Niagara Falls city *Niagara Co.*	113.3	515.6
North Hempstead town *Nassau Co.*	n/a	n/a
North Tonawanda city *Niagara Co.*	13.6	150.8
Oceanside cdp *Nassau Co.*	n/a	n/a
Orangetown town *Rockland Co.*	7.9	78.3
Orchard Park town *Erie Co.*	5.4	87.6
Ossining town *Westchester Co.*	n/a	n/a
Oyster Bay town *Nassau Co.*	n/a	n/a
Penfield town *Monroe Co.*	n/a	n/a
Perinton town *Monroe Co.*	n/a	n/a
Pittsford town *Monroe Co.*	n/a	n/a
Port Chester village *Westchester Co.*	25.3	175.7
Poughkeepsie town *Dutchess Co.*	10.3	297.6
Poughkeepsie city *Dutchess Co.*	79.2	224.2
Queens borough *Queens Co.*	n/a	n/a
Ramapo town *Rockland Co.*	8.6	68.4
Riverhead town *Suffolk Co.*	n/a	n/a
Rochester city *Monroe Co.*	87.6	393.8
Rome city *Oneida Co.*	12.4	190.9
Rye town *Westchester Co.*	n/a	n/a
Salina town *Onondaga Co.*	n/a	n/a
Schenectady city *Schenectady Co.*	n/a	n/a
Smithtown town *Suffolk Co.*	n/a	n/a
Southampton town *Suffolk Co.*	n/a	n/a
Spring Valley village *Rockland Co.*	47.3	112.2
Staten Island borough *Richmond Co.*	n/a	n/a
Syracuse city *Onondaga Co.*	79.3	353.2
Tonawanda town *Erie Co.*	24.3	190.3
Tonawanda cdp *Erie Co.*	n/a	n/a
Troy city *Rensselaer Co.*	85.8	403.6
Union town *Broome Co.*	n/a	n/a
Utica city *Oneida Co.*	57.1	359.4
Valley Stream village *Nassau Co.*	n/a	n/a
Warwick town *Orange Co.*	5.5	80.8
Webster town *Monroe Co.*	5.4	114.0
West Babylon cdp *Suffolk Co.*	n/a	n/a
West Seneca cdp *Erie Co.*	9.9	142.9
White Plains city *Westchester Co.*	17.5	174.4
Yonkers city *Westchester Co.*	47.1	99.5
Yorktown town *Westchester Co.*	3.8	79.3

NOTE: n/a not available.
SOURCE: Federal Bureau of Investigation, Uniform Crime Reports, 2015

Community Rankings

This section ranks incorporated places and CDPs (Census Designated Places) with populations of 2,500 or more. Unincorporated postal areas were not considered. For each topic below, you will find two tables, one in Descending Order—highest to lowest, and one in Ascending Order—lowest to highest. Six topics are exceptions to this rule, and only include Descending Order—Water Area, Ancestry (five tables), American Indian/Alaska Native Population, Native Hawaiian/Other Pacific Islander, Homeowner Vacancy Rate, and Commute to Work: Public Transportation. This is because there are an extraordinarily large number of places that place at the bottom of these topics with zero numbers.

Land Area

Top 150 Places Ranked in *Descending* Order

State Rank	Sq. Miles	Place		State Rank	Sq. Miles	Place
1	302.643	**New York** (city)		76	66.378	**Pompey** (town) Onondaga County
2	259.439	**Brookhaven** (town) Suffolk County		77	65.498	**Oswegatchie** (town) Saint Lawrence County
3	196.866	**Harrietstown** (town) Franklin County		78	64.951	**Phelps** (town) Ontario County
4	179.182	**Croghan** (town) Lewis County		79	64.943	**Theresa** (town) Jefferson County
5	158.822	**Hancock** (town) Delaware County		80	64.574	**Saugerties** (town) Ulster County
6	151.654	**North Elba** (town) Essex County		81	64.491	**Moriah** (town) Essex County
7	139.195	**Southampton** (town) Suffolk County		82	64.198	**Delhi** (town) Delaware County
8	130.505	**Wawarsing** (town) Ulster County		83	64.030	**Berne** (town) Albany County
9	119.784	**Shandaken** (town) Ulster County		84	63.461	**Warrensburg** (town) Warren County
10	118.587	**Hempstead** (town) Nassau County		85	63.032	**Hoosick** (town) Rensselaer County
11	117.348	**Tupper Lake** (town) Franklin County		86	62.830	**Queensbury** (town) Warren County
12	115.286	**Saranac** (town) Clinton County		87	62.107	**Wallkill** (town) Orange County
13	108.999	**Fort Ann** (town) Washington County		88	61.927	**Schodack** (town) Rensselaer County
14	108.532	**Queens** (borough) Queens County		89	61.716	**Guilford** (town) Chenango County
15	108.280	**Lisbon** (town) Saint Lawrence County		90	61.715	**Lysander** (town) Onondaga County
16	104.765	**Canton** (town) Saint Lawrence County		91	61.628	**Pittstown** (town) Rensselaer County
17	104.221	**Owego** (town) Tioga County		92	61.448	**Vienna** (town) Oneida County
18	104.114	**Islip** (town) Suffolk County		93	61.198	**Ramapo** (town) Rockland County
19	103.747	**Oyster Bay** (town) Nassau County		94	60.490	**Lansing** (town) Tompkins County
20	102.369	**Hector** (town) Schuyler County		95	60.439	**Catskill** (town) Greene County
21	101.519	**Malone** (town) Franklin County		96	60.425	**Beekmantown** (town) Clinton County
22	101.403	**Potsdam** (town) Saint Lawrence County		97	60.252	**Pierrepont** (town) Saint Lawrence County
23	101.340	**Warwick** (town) Orange County		98	60.167	**Annsville** (town) Oneida County
24	100.983	**Altona** (town) Clinton County		99	60.063	**Oxford** (town) Chenango County
25	96.837	**Walton** (town) Delaware County		100	59.828	**Cairo** (town) Greene County
26	96.674	**Middletown** (town) Delaware County		101	59.477	**Galen** (town) Wayne County
27	96.108	**Mamakating** (town) Sullivan County		102	59.275	**Barton** (town) Tioga County
28	95.319	**Bath** (town) Steuben County		103	59.132	**Brownville** (town) Jefferson County
29	94.510	**Candor** (town) Tioga County		104	59.080	**Dannemora** (town) Clinton County
30	94.156	**Rockland** (town) Sullivan County		105	58.841	**Newfield** (town) Tompkins County
31	94.123	**Huntington** (town) Suffolk County		106	58.639	**Jerusalem** (town) Yates County
32	93.897	**Stockholm** (town) Saint Lawrence County		107	58.620	**Tioga** (town) Tioga County
33	93.640	**Dryden** (town) Tompkins County		108	58.450	**Olive** (town) Ulster County
34	91.743	**Windsor** (town) Broome County		109	58.385	**Mayfield** (town) Fulton County
35	90.419	**Hunter** (town) Greene County		110	58.370	**Staten Island** (borough) Richmond County
36	90.098	**Sanford** (town) Broome County		111	58.170	**Washington** (town) Dutchess County
37	89.303	**Rochester** (town) Ulster County		112	57.902	**Guilderland** (town) Albany County
38	87.632	**Mooers** (town) Clinton County		113	57.880	**Stephentown** (town) Rensselaer County
39	85.265	**Bethel** (town) Sullivan County		114	57.791	**Westerlo** (town) Albany County
40	85.146	**Ellisburg** (town) Jefferson County		115	57.741	**Onondaga** (town) Onondaga County
41	84.190	**Chester** (town) Warren County		116	57.499	**New Scotland** (town) Albany County
42	84.089	**Thompson** (town) Sullivan County		117	57.248	**Richland** (town) Oswego County
43	82.773	**Neversink** (town) Sullivan County		118	57.176	**Whitehall** (town) Washington County
44	82.360	**Clayton** (town) Jefferson County		119	56.962	**Russia** (town) Herkimer County
45	81.433	**Ticonderoga** (town) Essex County		120	56.796	**Canandaigua** (town) Ontario County
46	79.579	**Liberty** (town) Sullivan County		121	56.765	**Constantia** (town) Oswego County
47	79.036	**Chesterfield** (town) Essex County		122	56.763	**Corinth** (town) Saratoga County
48	78.887	**Peru** (town) Clinton County		123	56.740	**Norfolk** (town) Saint Lawrence County
49	78.623	**Wilna** (town) Jefferson County		124	56.536	**Argyle** (town) Washington County
50	78.347	**Colesville** (town) Broome County		125	56.503	**East Fishkill** (town) Dutchess County
51	77.822	**Brookfield** (town) Madison County		126	56.353	**Cape Vincent** (town) Jefferson County
52	77.622	**Fallsburg** (town) Sullivan County		127	56.083	**Cohocton** (town) Steuben County
53	75.077	**Greene** (town) Chenango County		128	56.056	**Shawangunk** (town) Ulster County
54	74.791	**Rome** (city) Oneida County		129	55.943	**Colonie** (town) Albany County
55	74.328	**East Hampton** (town) Suffolk County		130	55.618	**Granville** (town) Washington County
56	73.643	**Le Ray** (town) Jefferson County		131	55.589	**New Bremen** (town) Lewis County
57	73.163	**Sullivan** (town) Madison County		132	55.190	**Dover** (town) Dutchess County
58	72.657	**Alexandria** (town) Jefferson County		133	55.049	**Bennington** (town) Wyoming County
59	71.878	**Boonville** (town) Oneida County		134	54.819	**Fayette** (town) Seneca County
60	71.423	**Orleans** (town) Jefferson County		135	54.763	**Caroline** (town) Tompkins County
61	71.217	**Gouverneur** (town) Saint Lawrence County		136	54.471	**Marbletown** (town) Ulster County
62	70.923	**Allegany** (town) Cattaraugus County		137	54.351	**Canisteo** (town) Steuben County
63	70.816	**Brooklyn** (borough) Kings County		138	54.153	**Chazy** (town) Clinton County
64	70.782	**Duanesburg** (town) Schenectady County		139	54.013	**Camden** (town) Oneida County
65	70.214	**Johnstown** (town) Fulton County		140	53.890	**Otsego** (town) Otsego County
66	69.966	**Royalton** (town) Niagara County		141	53.783	**Southold** (town) Suffolk County
67	69.934	**Concord** (town) Erie County		142	53.698	**Smithtown** (town) Suffolk County
68	69.230	**Verona** (town) Oneida County		143	53.553	**Danby** (town) Tompkins County
69	67.688	**Jay** (town) Essex County		144	53.512	**North Hempstead** (town) Nassau County
70	67.426	**Riverhead** (town) Suffolk County		145	53.503	**Clarence** (town) Erie County
71	67.388	**Greenfield** (town) Saratoga County		146	53.227	**Chatham** (town) Columbia County
72	67.289	**Woodstock** (town) Ulster County		147	53.203	**Amherst** (town) Erie County
73	67.268	**Sodus** (town) Wayne County		148	52.519	**Lake Luzerne** (town) Warren County
74	67.099	**Chautauqua** (town) Chautauqua County		149	52.378	**Hartland** (town) Niagara County
75	66.502	**Deerpark** (town) Orange County		150	52.362	**Salem** (town) Washington County

Note: This section ranks incorporated places and CDPs (Census Designated Places) with populations of 2,500 or more. Unincorporated postal areas were not considered. Please refer to the User Guide for additional information.

Land Area

Top 150 Places Ranked in *Ascending* Order

State Rank	Sq. Miles	Place	State Rank	Sq. Miles	Place
1	0.172	**Kaser** (village) Rockland County	76	1.154	**Village Green** (CDP) Onondaga County
2	0.312	**Great Neck Plaza** (village) Nassau County	77	1.160	**Silver Creek** (village) Chautauqua County
3	0.324	**SUNY Oswego** (CDP) Oswego County	78	1.180	**New York Mills** (village) Oneida County
4	0.356	**New Square** (village) Rockland County	79	1.190	**Alfred** (village) Allegany County
5	0.404	**Garden City South** (CDP) Nassau County	80	1.204	**Wanakah** (CDP) Erie County
6	0.408	**Thomaston** (village) Nassau County	81	1.205	**Baldwin Harbor** (CDP) Nassau County
7	0.428	**Fairview** (CDP) Westchester County	82	1.233	**Oyster Bay** (CDP) Nassau County
8	0.445	**Island Park** (village) Nassau County	83	1.243	**Lyncourt** (CDP) Onondaga County
9	0.465	**Manorhaven** (village) Nassau County	84	1.260	**Williamsville** (village) Erie County
10	0.478	**Port Washington North** (village) Nassau County	85	1.273	**Minoa** (village) Onondaga County
11	0.518	**Munsey Park** (village) Nassau County	86	1.297	**Hillcrest** (CDP) Rockland County
12	0.533	**University Gardens** (CDP) Nassau County	87	1.302	**Wheatley Heights** (CDP) Suffolk County
13	0.569	**East Williston** (village) Nassau County	88	1.323	**Ardsley** (village) Westchester County
14	0.573	**Herricks** (CDP) Nassau County	89	1.325	**East Rochester** (town/village) Monroe County
15	0.578	**South Hempstead** (CDP) Nassau County	90	1.329	**Great Neck** (village) Nassau County
16	0.591	**Manhasset Hills** (CDP) Nassau County	91	1.337	**Spencerport** (village) Monroe County
17	0.598	**Tuckahoe** (village) Westchester County	92	1.343	**Pelham Manor** (village) Westchester County
18	0.605	**South Nyack** (village) Rockland County	93	1.345	**Watervliet** (city) Albany County
19	0.626	**Williston Park** (village) Nassau County	94	1.346	**Orchard Park** (village) Erie County
20	0.645	**Roslyn** (village) Nassau County	95	1.347	**Palmyra** (village) Wayne County
21	0.668	**Arlington** (CDP) Dutchess County	96	1.347	**Islip Terrace** (CDP) Suffolk County
22	0.671	**Yorkville** (village) Oneida County	97	1.354	**Maybrook** (village) Orange County
23	0.675	**Cedarhurst** (village) Nassau County	98	1.358	**South Glens Falls** (village) Saratoga County
24	0.679	**Piermont** (village) Rockland County	99	1.364	**Westvale** (CDP) Onondaga County
25	0.680	**Albertson** (CDP) Nassau County	100	1.371	**Lake Placid** (village) Essex County
26	0.747	**Green Island** (town/village) Albany County	101	1.373	**Victor** (village) Ontario County
27	0.757	**Great Neck Estates** (village) Nassau County	102	1.373	**University at Buffalo** (CDP) Erie County
28	0.770	**Nyack** (village) Rockland County	103	1.404	**Plainedge** (CDP) Nassau County
29	0.775	**Binghamton University** (CDP) Broome County	104	1.406	**Montgomery** (village) Orange County
30	0.777	**Watchtower** (CDP) Ulster County	105	1.414	**Skaneateles** (village) Onondaga County
31	0.786	**Sloan** (village) Erie County	106	1.417	**Floral Park** (village) Nassau County
32	0.829	**Pelham** (village) Westchester County	107	1.435	**Kenmore** (village) Erie County
33	0.830	**Valhalla** (CDP) Westchester County	108	1.450	**Bayville** (village) Nassau County
34	0.841	**Mechanicville** (city) Saratoga County	109	1.467	**Mount Ivy** (CDP) Rockland County
35	0.844	**Crown Heights** (CDP) Dutchess County	110	1.467	**Ravena** (village) Albany County
36	0.860	**New Hyde Park** (village) Nassau County	111	1.469	**Northeast Ithaca** (CDP) Tompkins County
37	0.873	**South Valley Stream** (CDP) Nassau County	112	1.476	**Roslyn Heights** (CDP) Nassau County
38	0.876	**Mohawk** (village) Herkimer County	113	1.479	**New Cassel** (CDP) Nassau County
39	0.881	**Hewlett** (CDP) Nassau County	114	1.483	**Lakeland** (CDP) Onondaga County
40	0.889	**Halesite** (CDP) Suffolk County	115	1.487	**Milton** (CDP) Saratoga County
41	0.895	**Hartsdale** (CDP) Westchester County	116	1.519	**West Haverstraw** (village) Rockland County
42	0.914	**Locust Valley** (CDP) Nassau County	117	1.523	**Rhinebeck** (village) Dutchess County
43	0.929	**Searingtown** (CDP) Nassau County	118	1.541	**Walton** (village) Delaware County
44	0.935	**Carle Place** (CDP) Nassau County	119	1.581	**Inwood** (CDP) Nassau County
45	0.962	**Bronxville** (village) Westchester County	120	1.589	**Fairport** (village) Monroe County
46	0.972	**Glenwood Landing** (CDP) Nassau County	121	1.593	**Gowanda** (village) Cattaraugus County
47	0.976	**Brightwaters** (village) Suffolk County	122	1.598	**Hoosick Falls** (village) Rensselaer County
48	0.984	**Garden City Park** (CDP) Nassau County	123	1.599	**Ballston Spa** (village) Saratoga County
49	1.000	**Lakeview** (CDP) Nassau County	124	1.614	**Montrose** (CDP) Westchester County
50	1.004	**Harriman** (village) Orange County	125	1.618	**Flower Hill** (village) Nassau County
51	1.006	**Bedford Hills** (CDP) Westchester County	126	1.622	**East Syracuse** (village) Onondaga County
52	1.014	**Frankfort** (village) Herkimer County	127	1.637	**Sound Beach** (CDP) Suffolk County
53	1.017	**East Rockaway** (village) Nassau County	128	1.639	**Glen Head** (CDP) Nassau County
54	1.027	**Elmsford** (village) Westchester County	129	1.654	**Solvay** (village) Onondaga County
55	1.047	**East Norwich** (CDP) Nassau County	130	1.685	**Scotia** (village) Schenectady County
56	1.050	**Whitesboro** (village) Oneida County	131	1.691	**Attica** (village) Wyoming County
57	1.058	**Malverne** (village) Nassau County	132	1.697	**Stony Brook University** (CDP) Suffolk County
58	1.061	**Vails Gate** (CDP) Orange County	133	1.705	**Gordon Heights** (CDP) Suffolk County
59	1.067	**Corinth** (village) Saratoga County	134	1.715	**New Paltz** (village) Ulster County
60	1.077	**Larchmont** (village) Westchester County	135	1.719	**North Merrick** (CDP) Nassau County
61	1.082	**Scottsville** (village) Monroe County	136	1.737	**Salisbury** (CDP) Nassau County
62	1.090	**Highland Falls** (village) Orange County	137	1.738	**Groton** (village) Tompkins County
63	1.093	**Falconer** (village) Chautauqua County	138	1.739	**Lido Beach** (CDP) Nassau County
64	1.093	**Hawthorne** (CDP) Westchester County	139	1.746	**Fayetteville** (village) Onondaga County
65	1.097	**Lewiston** (village) Niagara County	140	1.756	**Fort Edward** (village) Washington County
66	1.107	**Thornwood** (CDP) Westchester County	141	1.767	**Cayuga Heights** (village) Tompkins County
67	1.108	**Wappingers Falls** (village) Dutchess County	142	1.770	**Roosevelt** (CDP) Nassau County
68	1.109	**Kiryas Joel** (village) Orange County	143	1.775	**Spackenkill** (CDP) Dutchess County
69	1.115	**Sea Cliff** (village) Nassau County	144	1.780	**Hilton** (village) Monroe County
70	1.120	**Brinckerhoff** (CDP) Dutchess County	145	1.784	**Saugerties** (village) Ulster County
71	1.121	**Farmingdale** (village) Nassau County	146	1.785	**Manlius** (village) Onondaga County
72	1.123	**Blasdell** (village) Erie County	147	1.794	**Blue Point** (CDP) Suffolk County
73	1.146	**Elmira Heights** (village) Chemung County	148	1.824	**Pleasantville** (village) Westchester County
74	1.148	**Dannemora** (village) Clinton County	149	1.827	**Thiells** (CDP) Rockland County
75	1.152	**Galeville** (CDP) Onondaga County	150	1.832	**Hudson Falls** (village) Washington County

Note: *This section ranks incorporated places and CDPs (Census Designated Places) with populations of 2,500 or more. Unincorporated postal areas were not considered. Please refer to the User Guide for additional information.*

Water Area

Top 150 Places Ranked in *Descending* Order

State Rank	Sq. Miles	Place	State Rank	Sq. Miles	Place
1	349.917	**Southold** (town) Suffolk County	76	4.737	**North Elba** (town) Essex County
2	312.224	**East Hampton** (town) Suffolk County	77	4.693	**Bethel** (town) Sullivan County
3	272.097	**Brookhaven** (town) Suffolk County	78	4.659	**Porter** (town) Niagara County
4	165.841	**New York** (city)	79	4.655	**Fishkill** (town) Dutchess County
5	154.510	**Southampton** (town) Suffolk County	80	4.628	**Esopus** (town) Ulster County
6	133.841	**Riverhead** (town) Suffolk County	81	4.315	**Gorham** (town) Ontario County
7	73.000	**Hempstead** (town) Nassau County	82	4.265	**Newburgh** (town) Orange County
8	71.488	**Hounsfield** (town) Jefferson County	83	4.168	**Ossining** (town) Westchester County
9	69.675	**Queens** (borough) Queens County	84	4.157	**Sandy Creek** (town) Oswego County
10	65.652	**Oyster Bay** (town) Nassau County	85	4.068	**Rhinebeck** (town) Dutchess County
11	61.861	**Babylon** (town) Suffolk County	86	4.026	**Ulysses** (town) Tompkins County
12	58.891	**Islip** (town) Suffolk County	87	4.010	**Lewiston** (town) Niagara County
13	57.752	**Smithtown** (town) Suffolk County	88	3.975	**Stony Point** (town) Rockland County
14	43.921	**Staten Island** (borough) Richmond County	89	3.875	**Greece** (town) Monroe County
15	42.988	**Huntington** (town) Suffolk County	90	3.871	**Red Hook** (town) Dutchess County
16	42.915	**Constantia** (town) Oswego County	91	3.726	**Catskill** (town) Greene County
17	33.628	**Vienna** (town) Oneida County	92	3.614	**Oswego** (city) Oswego County
18	33.499	**Cape Vincent** (town) Jefferson County	93	3.546	**Warwick** (town) Orange County
19	26.336	**Chesterfield** (town) Essex County	94	3.532	**Malta** (town) Saratoga County
20	26.102	**Brooklyn** (borough) Kings County	95	3.491	**Neversink** (town) Sullivan County
21	22.288	**Plattsburgh** (town) Clinton County	96	3.456	**Russia** (town) Herkimer County
22	21.671	**Clayton** (town) Jefferson County	97	3.408	**Thompson** (town) Sullivan County
23	16.944	**Shelter Island** (town) Suffolk County	98	3.407	**Mamaroneck** (village) Westchester County
24	16.814	**Harrietstown** (town) Franklin County	99	3.386	**Saugerties** (town) Ulster County
25	15.598	**North Hempstead** (town) Nassau County	100	3.358	**Wawarsing** (town) Ulster County
26	15.382	**Bronx** (borough) Bronx County	101	3.342	**Scriba** (town) Oswego County
27	15.342	**Louisville** (town) Saint Lawrence County	102	3.283	**Ossining** (village) Westchester County
28	14.173	**Rye** (city) Westchester County	103	3.245	**Southeast** (town) Putnam County
29	13.613	**Northampton** (town) Fulton County	104	3.242	**Seneca Falls** (town) Seneca County
30	13.591	**Romulus** (town) Seneca County	105	3.216	**Pittstown** (town) Rensselaer County
31	13.492	**Peru** (town) Clinton County	106	3.195	**Hyde Park** (town) Dutchess County
32	12.754	**Tupper Lake** (town) Franklin County	107	3.181	**Ogdensburg** (city) Saint Lawrence County
33	12.589	**Glen Cove** (city) Nassau County	108	3.104	**Geddes** (town) Onondaga County
34	12.110	**Buffalo** (city) Erie County	109	3.060	**Highlands** (town) Orange County
35	11.900	**Alexandria** (town) Jefferson County	110	3.057	**Haverstraw** (village) Rockland County
36	11.774	**Massena** (town) Saint Lawrence County	111	3.038	**Coeymans** (town) Albany County
37	11.583	**Fayette** (town) Seneca County	112	2.994	**New Windsor** (town) Orange County
38	10.762	**Manhattan** (borough) New York County	113	2.994	**Hancock** (town) Delaware County
39	10.761	**Cortlandt** (town) Westchester County	114	2.980	**Conesus** (town) Livingston County
40	10.214	**Hector** (town) Schuyler County	115	2.964	**Benton** (town) Yates County
41	9.452	**Lansing** (town) Tompkins County	116	2.919	**Sleepy Hollow** (village) Westchester County
42	9.202	**Beekmantown** (town) Clinton County	117	2.894	**Lysander** (town) Onondaga County
43	8.593	**Clarkstown** (town) Rockland County	118	2.885	**New Rochelle** (city) Westchester County
44	8.059	**Broadalbin** (town) Fulton County	119	2.860	**Chester** (town) Warren County
45	7.585	**Champlain** (town) Clinton County	120	2.849	**Croghan** (town) Lewis County
46	7.410	**Mamaroneck** (town) Westchester County	121	2.822	**Kent** (town) Putnam County
47	7.320	**Brownville** (town) Jefferson County	122	2.812	**Livonia** (town) Livingston County
48	7.268	**Orangetown** (town) Rockland County	123	2.801	**Richland** (town) Oswego County
49	7.163	**Chazy** (town) Clinton County	124	2.785	**Philipstown** (town) Putnam County
50	7.012	**Ticonderoga** (town) Essex County	125	2.753	**Tarrytown** (village) Westchester County
51	6.762	**Jerusalem** (town) Yates County	126	2.742	**Niagara Falls** (city) Niagara County
52	6.759	**Dannemora** (town) Clinton County	127	2.685	**East Quogue** (CDP) Suffolk County
53	6.743	**Olive** (town) Ulster County	128	2.630	**Poughkeepsie** (town) Dutchess County
54	6.620	**Orleans** (town) Jefferson County	129	2.622	**Athens** (town) Greene County
55	6.619	**Moriah** (town) Essex County	130	2.612	**Yorktown** (town) Westchester County
56	6.375	**Starkey** (town) Yates County	131	2.604	**North Castle** (town) Westchester County
57	6.299	**Mayfield** (town) Fulton County	132	2.594	**Owasco** (town) Cayuga County
58	6.220	**Skaneateles** (town) Onondaga County	133	2.561	**Mamakating** (town) Sullivan County
59	6.056	**Hurley** (town) Ulster County	134	2.549	**Lake George** (town) Warren County
60	6.038	**Croton-on-Hudson** (village) Westchester County	135	2.544	**Cato** (town) Cayuga County
61	5.901	**Milo** (town) Yates County	136	2.518	**Somers** (town) Westchester County
62	5.805	**Greenburgh** (town) Westchester County	137	2.487	**Lido Beach** (CDP) Nassau County
63	5.735	**Canandaigua** (town) Ontario County	138	2.480	**Fleming** (town) Cayuga County
64	5.705	**Oswegatchie** (town) Saint Lawrence County	139	2.383	**Stillwater** (town) Saratoga County
65	5.636	**Lisbon** (town) Saint Lawrence County	140	2.339	**Saratoga** (town) Saratoga County
66	5.335	**Mount Pleasant** (town) Westchester County	141	2.315	**New Haven** (town) Oswego County
67	5.260	**Haverstraw** (town) Rockland County	142	2.299	**Tuxedo** (town) Orange County
68	5.174	**Hampton Bays** (CDP) Suffolk County	143	2.285	**Yonkers** (city) Westchester County
69	5.162	**Otsego** (town) Otsego County	144	2.252	**Montauk** (CDP) Suffolk County
70	5.050	**Conesus Lake** (CDP) Livingston County	145	2.247	**Bedford** (town) Westchester County
71	5.020	**Grand Island** (town) Erie County	146	2.191	**Westhampton** (CDP) Suffolk County
72	4.841	**West Monroe** (town) Oswego County	147	2.114	**Schaghticoke** (town) Rensselaer County
73	4.789	**Theresa** (town) Jefferson County	148	2.077	**Ulster** (town) Ulster County
74	4.786	**Carmel** (town) Putnam County	149	2.057	**Wilson** (town) Niagara County
75	4.740	**Au Sable** (town) Clinton County	150	2.055	**Carmel Hamlet** (CDP) Putnam County

Note: This section ranks incorporated places and CDPs (Census Designated Places) with populations of 2,500 or more. Unincorporated postal areas were not considered. Please refer to the User Guide for additional information.

Elevation

Top 150 Places Ranked in *Descending* Order

State Rank	Feet	Place	State Rank	Feet	Place
1	1,965	**North Elba** (town) Essex County	75	1,129	**Russia** (town) Herkimer County
2	1,854	**Harrietstown** (town) Franklin County	77	1,125	**Homer** (town) Cortland County
3	1,818	**Stamford** (town) Delaware County	77	1,125	**Homer** (village) Cortland County
4	1,801	**Lake Placid** (village) Essex County	79	1,122	**Hamilton** (town) Madison County
5	1,765	**Alfred** (town) Allegany County	79	1,122	**Hamilton** (village) Madison County
5	1,765	**Alfred** (village) Allegany County	81	1,112	**Laurens** (town) Otsego County
7	1,673	**Pompey** (town) Onondaga County	81	1,112	**New Berlin** (town) Chenango County
8	1,634	**Neversink** (town) Sullivan County	81	1,112	**Oneonta** (city) Otsego County
9	1,598	**Tupper Lake** (town) Franklin County	81	1,112	**Oneonta** (town) Otsego County
9	1,598	**Tupper Lake** (village) Franklin County	85	1,109	**Bath** (town) Steuben County
11	1,591	**Franklinville** (town) Cattaraugus County	85	1,109	**Bath** (village) Steuben County
12	1,588	**Hunter** (town) Greene County	87	1,106	**Enfield** (town) Tompkins County
13	1,545	**Saranac Lake** (village) Franklin County	87	1,106	**Holland** (town) Erie County
14	1,512	**Monticello** (village) Sullivan County	89	1,096	**Richmondville** (town) Schoharie County
14	1,512	**Wellsville** (town) Allegany County	90	1,089	**Dryden** (town) Tompkins County
14	1,512	**Wellsville** (village) Allegany County	91	1,079	**Colden** (town) Erie County
17	1,506	**Liberty** (town) Sullivan County	92	1,070	**East Bloomfield** (town) Ontario County
17	1,506	**Liberty** (village) Sullivan County	92	1,070	**Otego** (town) Otsego County
19	1,496	**Cuba** (town) Allegany County	92	1,070	**Triangle** (town) Broome County
20	1,489	**Paris** (town) Oneida County	95	1,056	**Shandaken** (town) Ulster County
21	1,486	**Guilford** (town) Chenango County	96	1,050	**Newfield** (town) Tompkins County
22	1,480	**Otisco** (town) Onondaga County	97	1,047	**Sherburne** (town) Chenango County
23	1,476	**Arcade** (town) Wyoming County	98	1,037	**Greenville** (town) Orange County
24	1,447	**Olean** (city) Cattaraugus County	99	1,033	**Livonia** (town) Livingston County
25	1,434	**Yorkshire** (town) Cattaraugus County	100	1,014	**Campbell** (town) Steuben County
26	1,430	**Portville** (town) Cattaraugus County	100	1,014	**Norwich** (city) Chenango County
27	1,421	**Allegany** (town) Cattaraugus County	100	1,014	**Norwich** (town) Chenango County
28	1,414	**Dannemora** (town) Clinton County	100	1,014	**Warsaw** (town) Wyoming County
28	1,414	**Dannemora** (village) Clinton County	100	1,014	**Warsaw** (village) Wyoming County
30	1,404	**Virgil** (town) Cortland County	105	1,010	**Unadilla** (town) Otsego County
31	1,394	**Sardinia** (town) Erie County	106	1,001	**Afton** (town) Chenango County
32	1,381	**Brookfield** (town) Madison County	106	1,001	**Darien** (town) Genesee County
32	1,381	**Salamanca** (city) Cattaraugus County	108	997	**Addison** (town) Steuben County
34	1,378	**Jamestown** (city) Chautauqua County	108	997	**Champion** (town) Jefferson County
35	1,375	**Wayland** (town) Steuben County	108	997	**Groton** (town) Tompkins County
36	1,371	**Delhi** (town) Delaware County	108	997	**Groton** (village) Tompkins County
36	1,371	**Delhi** (village) Delaware County	112	994	**Bainbridge** (town) Chenango County
36	1,371	**Perry** (town) Wyoming County	112	994	**Spencer** (town) Tioga County
36	1,371	**Perry** (village) Wyoming County	114	991	**Sidney** (town) Delaware County
40	1,365	**Busti** (town) Chautauqua County	114	991	**Sidney** (village) Delaware County
41	1,362	**Chautauqua** (town) Chautauqua County	116	981	**Attica** (town) Wyoming County
42	1,355	**Castile** (town) Wyoming County	116	981	**Attica** (village) Wyoming County
42	1,355	**Oswegatchie** (town) Saint Lawrence County	118	974	**Lisle** (town) Broome County
44	1,352	**Concord** (town) Erie County	119	971	**Berne** (town) Albany County
45	1,329	**Springville** (village) Erie County	119	971	**Denmark** (town) Lewis County
46	1,325	**Bethel** (town) Sullivan County	119	971	**Oxford** (town) Chenango County
46	1,325	**Lakewood** (village) Chautauqua County	122	968	**Caroline** (town) Tompkins County
48	1,319	**Cohocton** (town) Steuben County	122	968	**Newark Valley** (town) Tioga County
49	1,306	**Davenport** (town) Delaware County	124	955	**Pavilion** (town) Genesee County
50	1,293	**Rockland** (town) Sullivan County	125	948	**West Bloomfield** (town) Ontario County
51	1,276	**Randolph** (town) Cattaraugus County	125	948	**Windsor** (town) Broome County
52	1,266	**South Fallsburg** (CDP) Sullivan County	127	942	**Boston** (town) Erie County
53	1,263	**Falconer** (village) Chautauqua County	127	942	**Nunda** (town) Livingston County
54	1,253	**Caneadea** (town) Allegany County	129	935	**Gang Mills** (CDP) Steuben County
55	1,250	**Tully** (town) Onondaga County	130	932	**Alexander** (town) Genesee County
56	1,247	**Sangerfield** (town) Oneida County	130	932	**Corning** (city) Steuben County
57	1,237	**Danby** (town) Tompkins County	130	932	**Corning** (town) Steuben County
58	1,234	**Knox** (town) Albany County	133	928	**Lansing** (town) Tompkins County
59	1,224	**Cazenovia** (town) Madison County	133	928	**Lansing** (village) Tompkins County
59	1,224	**Cazenovia** (village) Madison County	135	922	**Cobleskill** (town) Schoharie County
61	1,207	**Bennington** (town) Wyoming County	135	922	**Cobleskill** (village) Schoharie County
61	1,207	**Fallsburg** (town) Sullivan County	135	922	**Hancock** (town) Delaware County
61	1,207	**Milford** (town) Otsego County	138	919	**East Aurora** (village) Erie County
61	1,207	**Walton** (town) Delaware County	138	919	**Greene** (town) Chenango County
61	1,207	**Walton** (village) Delaware County	140	912	**Maine** (town) Broome County
66	1,204	**Eaton** (town) Madison County	141	902	**Big Flats** (CDP) Chemung County
66	1,204	**Madison** (town) Madison County	141	902	**Big Flats** (town) Chemung County
68	1,197	**Conesus** (town) Livingston County	141	902	**Candor** (town) Tioga County
69	1,178	**Sanford** (town) Broome County	141	902	**Fleming** (town) Cayuga County
70	1,165	**Westerlo** (town) Albany County	145	896	**Chenango Bridge** (CDP) Broome County
71	1,161	**Hornell** (city) Steuben County	145	896	**Horseheads** (town) Chemung County
72	1,148	**Boonville** (town) Oneida County	145	896	**Horseheads** (village) Chemung County
73	1,135	**Canisteo** (town) Steuben County	145	896	**Le Roy** (town) Genesee County
74	1,132	**LaFayette** (town) Onondaga County	145	896	**Le Roy** (village) Genesee County
75	1,129	**Cortland** (city) Cortland County	150	892	**Batavia** (city) Genesee County

Note: This section ranks incorporated places and CDPs (Census Designated Places) with populations of 2,500 or more. Unincorporated postal areas were not considered. Please refer to the User Guide for additional information.

Elevation

Top 150 Places Ranked in *Ascending* Order

State Rank	Feet	Place
1	3	**Port Jefferson** (village) Suffolk County
2	7	**Babylon** (town) Suffolk County
2	7	**Babylon** (village) Suffolk County
2	7	**Flanders** (CDP) Suffolk County
2	7	**Inwood** (CDP) Nassau County
2	7	**Island Park** (village) Nassau County
2	7	**Lido Beach** (CDP) Nassau County
2	7	**Long Beach** (city) Nassau County
2	7	**Mastic Beach** (village) Suffolk County
10	10	**Blue Point** (CDP) Suffolk County
10	10	**Brookhaven** (CDP) Suffolk County
10	10	**Brookhaven** (town) Suffolk County
10	10	**East Rockaway** (village) Nassau County
10	10	**Oakdale** (CDP) Suffolk County
10	10	**Seaford** (CDP) Nassau County
10	10	**South Valley Stream** (CDP) Nassau County
10	10	**Springs** (CDP) Suffolk County
18	13	**Baldwin Harbor** (CDP) Nassau County
18	13	**East Quogue** (CDP) Suffolk County
18	13	**Islip** (CDP) Suffolk County
18	13	**Islip** (town) Suffolk County
18	13	**Manorhaven** (village) Nassau County
18	13	**Oceanside** (CDP) Nassau County
18	13	**Riverhead** (CDP) Suffolk County
18	13	**Riverhead** (town) Suffolk County
18	13	**West Bay Shore** (CDP) Suffolk County
18	13	**West Sayville** (CDP) Suffolk County
28	16	**Bay Shore** (CDP) Suffolk County
28	16	**Bayport** (CDP) Suffolk County
28	16	**East Islip** (CDP) Suffolk County
28	16	**East Massapequa** (CDP) Nassau County
28	16	**Mattituck** (CDP) Suffolk County
28	16	**Merrick** (CDP) Nassau County
28	16	**North Sea** (CDP) Suffolk County
28	16	**Rensselaer** (city) Rensselaer County
28	16	**Valley Stream** (village) Nassau County
37	20	**Amityville** (village) Suffolk County
37	20	**Bellmore** (CDP) Nassau County
37	20	**Freeport** (village) Nassau County
37	20	**Lynbrook** (village) Nassau County
37	20	**Patchogue** (village) Suffolk County
37	20	**Sayville** (CDP) Suffolk County
37	20	**West Islip** (CDP) Suffolk County
44	23	**Baldwin** (CDP) Nassau County
44	23	**Brightwaters** (village) Suffolk County
44	23	**Copiague** (CDP) Suffolk County
44	23	**East Patchogue** (CDP) Suffolk County
44	23	**Eastchester** (CDP) Westchester County
44	23	**Eastchester** (town) Westchester County
44	23	**Glen Cove** (city) Nassau County
44	23	**Green Island** (town/village) Albany County
44	23	**Hewlett** (CDP) Nassau County
44	23	**Islip Terrace** (CDP) Suffolk County
44	23	**Lawrence** (village) Nassau County
44	23	**Massapequa** (CDP) Nassau County
44	23	**Massapequa Park** (village) Nassau County
44	23	**Moriches** (CDP) Suffolk County
44	23	**North Babylon** (CDP) Suffolk County
44	23	**Southold** (CDP) Suffolk County
44	23	**Southold** (town) Suffolk County
44	23	**Woodmere** (CDP) Nassau County
62	26	**Athens** (town) Greene County
62	26	**Center Moriches** (CDP) Suffolk County
62	26	**Halesite** (CDP) Suffolk County
62	26	**Kings Point** (village) Nassau County
62	26	**Noyack** (CDP) Suffolk County
62	26	**Rockville Centre** (village) Nassau County
62	26	**Rye** (city) Westchester County
62	26	**Rye** (town) Westchester County
62	26	**Southampton** (town) Suffolk County
62	26	**Southampton** (village) Suffolk County
62	26	**Wantagh** (CDP) Suffolk County
73	30	**Calverton** (CDP) Suffolk County
73	30	**Cedarhurst** (village) Nassau County
73	30	**Cutchogue** (CDP) Suffolk County

State Rank	Feet	Place
73	30	**East Moriches** (CDP) Suffolk County
73	30	**Lindenhurst** (village) Suffolk County
73	30	**Mastic** (CDP) Suffolk County
73	30	**North Great River** (CDP) Suffolk County
73	30	**Port Washington North** (village) Nassau County
73	30	**Watervliet** (city) Albany County
82	33	**Cold Spring Harbor** (CDP) Suffolk County
82	33	**East Hampton** (town) Suffolk County
82	33	**Fort Salonga** (CDP) Suffolk County
82	33	**Hampton Bays** (CDP) Suffolk County
82	33	**Haverstraw** (town) Rockland County
82	33	**Haverstraw** (village) Rockland County
82	33	**Montauk** (CDP) Suffolk County
82	33	**Mount Sinai** (CDP) Suffolk County
82	33	**North Amityville** (CDP) Suffolk County
82	33	**Troy** (city) Rensselaer County
92	36	**Menands** (village) Albany County
92	36	**North Bay Shore** (CDP) Suffolk County
92	36	**North Wantagh** (CDP) Nassau County
92	36	**Westhampton** (CDP) Suffolk County
96	39	**Bayville** (village) Nassau County
96	39	**Elmont** (CDP) Nassau County
96	39	**Lakeview** (CDP) Nassau County
96	39	**Malverne** (village) Nassau County
96	39	**North Valley Stream** (CDP) Nassau County
96	39	**Roosevelt** (CDP) Nassau County
96	39	**Roslyn** (village) Nassau County
96	39	**West Babylon** (CDP) Suffolk County
96	39	**Yaphank** (CDP) Suffolk County
105	43	**Catskill** (town) Greene County
105	43	**Catskill** (village) Greene County
105	43	**North Lindenhurst** (CDP) Suffolk County
105	43	**Port Chester** (village) Westchester County
105	43	**Queens** (borough) Queens County
105	43	**Sands Point** (village) Nassau County
105	43	**South Hempstead** (CDP) Nassau County
105	43	**Tappan** (CDP) Rockland County
113	46	**North Bellmore** (CDP) Nassau County
113	46	**North Bellport** (CDP) Suffolk County
113	46	**North Merrick** (CDP) Nassau County
116	47	**Mamaroneck** (town) Westchester County
116	47	**Mamaroneck** (village) Westchester County
118	49	**Bronx** (borough) Bronx County
118	49	**Brooklyn** (borough) Kings County
118	49	**Centerport** (CDP) Suffolk County
118	49	**North Massapequa** (CDP) Nassau County
118	49	**North Patchogue** (CDP) Suffolk County
118	49	**Oyster Bay** (CDP) Nassau County
118	49	**Oyster Bay** (town) Nassau County
125	52	**Larchmont** (village) Westchester County
125	52	**Manorville** (CDP) Suffolk County
125	52	**Shelter Island** (town) Suffolk County
125	52	**Shirley** (CDP) Suffolk County
125	52	**Uniondale** (CDP) Nassau County
130	56	**Hempstead** (town) Nassau County
130	56	**Hempstead** (village) Nassau County
130	56	**Wyandanch** (CDP) Suffolk County
133	59	**Baywood** (CDP) Suffolk County
133	59	**Coeymans** (town) Albany County
133	59	**Northport** (village) Suffolk County
133	59	**Smithtown** (CDP) Suffolk County
133	59	**Smithtown** (town) Suffolk County
133	59	**South Farmingdale** (CDP) Nassau County
139	62	**Hauppauge** (CDP) Suffolk County
139	62	**Pelham Manor** (village) Westchester County
141	66	**Bohemia** (CDP) Suffolk County
141	66	**Franklin Square** (CDP) Nassau County
141	66	**Islandia** (village) Suffolk County
141	66	**Plainedge** (CDP) Nassau County
141	66	**Rosendale** (town) Ulster County
146	69	**East Farmingdale** (CDP) Suffolk County
146	69	**Harrison** (town/village) Westchester County
146	69	**Waterford** (town) Saratoga County
146	69	**West Hempstead** (CDP) Nassau County
150	72	**East Meadow** (CDP) Nassau County

Note: *This section ranks incorporated places and CDPs (Census Designated Places) with populations of 2,500 or more. Unincorporated postal areas were not considered. Please refer to the User Guide for additional information.*

Population

Top 150 Places Ranked in *Descending* Order

State Rank	Number	Place	State Rank	Number	Place
1	8,426,743	**New York** (city)	76	33,769	**Riverhead** (town) Suffolk County
2	2,595,259	**Brooklyn** (borough) Kings County	77	33,722	**New City** (CDP) Rockland County
3	2,301,139	**Queens** (borough) Queens County	78	33,598	**Salina** (town) Onondaga County
4	1,629,507	**Manhattan** (borough) New York County	79	33,470	**Long Beach** (city) Nassau County
5	1,428,357	**Bronx** (borough) Bronx County	80	32,916	**Rome** (city) Oneida County
6	767,916	**Hempstead** (town) Nassau County	81	32,880	**Eastchester** (town) Westchester County
7	488,930	**Brookhaven** (town) Suffolk County	82	32,649	**Centereach** (CDP) Suffolk County
8	472,481	**Staten Island** (borough) Richmond County	83	32,400	**Manlius** (town) Onondaga County
9	336,747	**Islip** (town) Suffolk County	84	32,221	**Spring Valley** (village) Rockland County
10	296,876	**Oyster Bay** (town) Nassau County	85	31,648	**Cicero** (town) Onondaga County
11	259,517	**Buffalo** (city) Erie County	86	31,544	**Franklin Square** (CDP) Nassau County
12	229,105	**North Hempstead** (town) Nassau County	87	31,446	**Warwick** (town) Orange County
13	214,132	**Babylon** (town) Suffolk County	88	31,376	**Clarence** (town) Erie County
14	210,745	**Rochester** (city) Monroe County	89	31,077	**North Tonawanda** (city) Niagara County
15	204,240	**Huntington** (town) Suffolk County	90	30,664	**Newburgh** (town) Orange County
16	199,435	**Yonkers** (city) Westchester County	91	30,635	**Poughkeepsie** (city) Dutchess County
17	144,564	**Syracuse** (city) Onondaga County	92	30,565	**Ithaca** (city) Tompkins County
18	131,648	**Ramapo** (town) Rockland County	93	30,546	**Jamestown** (city) Chautauqua County
19	124,044	**Amherst** (town) Erie County	94	30,371	**Oceanside** (CDP) Nassau County
20	118,373	**Smithtown** (town) Suffolk County	95	29,670	**Bay Shore** (CDP) Suffolk County
21	98,468	**Albany** (city) Albany County	96	29,657	**Mamaroneck** (town) Westchester County
22	96,674	**Greece** (town) Monroe County	97	29,608	**Pittsford** (town) Monroe County
23	90,809	**Greenburgh** (town) Westchester County	98	29,489	**Glenville** (town) Schenectady County
24	87,858	**Cheektowaga** (town) Erie County	99	29,466	**Orchard Park** (town) Erie County
25	86,334	**Clarkstown** (town) Rockland County	100	29,406	**Port Chester** (village) Westchester County
26	82,750	**Colonie** (town) Albany County	101	29,276	**East Fishkill** (town) Dutchess County
27	79,027	**New Rochelle** (city) Westchester County	102	29,174	**Rotterdam** (town) Schenectady County
28	74,905	**Cheektowaga** (CDP) Erie County	103	28,817	**Elmira** (city) Chemung County
29	73,420	**Tonawanda** (town) Erie County	104	28,738	**Chili** (town) Monroe County
30	68,221	**Mount Vernon** (city) Westchester County	105	28,651	**Gates** (town) Monroe County
31	65,735	**Schenectady** (city) Schenectady County	106	28,495	**Newburgh** (city) Orange County
32	61,628	**Utica** (city) Oneida County	107	28,243	**Vestal** (town) Broome County
33	61,374	**Brentwood** (CDP) Suffolk County	108	28,023	**Wallkill** (town) Orange County
34	59,294	**Clay** (town) Onondaga County	109	27,998	**Harrison** (town/village) Westchester County
35	58,149	**Tonawanda** (CDP) Erie County	110	27,828	**Middletown** (city) Orange County
36	57,790	**White Plains** (city) Westchester County	111	27,753	**Queensbury** (town) Warren County
37	57,730	**Southampton** (town) Suffolk County	112	27,533	**Holbrook** (CDP) Suffolk County
38	57,712	**Hamburg** (town) Erie County	113	27,374	**Dix Hills** (CDP) Suffolk County
39	55,474	**Union** (town) Broome County	114	27,346	**Deer Park** (CDP) Suffolk County
40	55,105	**Hempstead** (village) Nassau County	115	27,310	**Lindenhurst** (village) Suffolk County
41	51,593	**Levittown** (CDP) Nassau County	116	27,264	**Auburn** (city) Cayuga County
42	51,337	**Irondequoit** (CDP) Monroe County	117	27,250	**Watertown** (city) Jefferson County
43	50,095	**Orangetown** (town) Rockland County	118	27,245	**Glen Cove** (city) Nassau County
44	49,933	**Troy** (city) Rensselaer County	119	27,244	**Saratoga Springs** (city) Saratoga County
45	49,435	**Niagara Falls** (city) Niagara County	120	27,224	**West Islip** (CDP) Suffolk County
46	46,650	**Rye** (town) Westchester County	121	27,147	**Wappinger** (town) Dutchess County
47	46,557	**Perinton** (town) Monroe County	122	26,199	**Plainview** (CDP) Nassau County
48	46,495	**Binghamton** (city) Broome County	123	25,974	**Smithtown** (CDP) Suffolk County
49	45,089	**West Seneca** (CDP) Erie County	124	25,959	**New Windsor** (town) Orange County
50	44,786	**Poughkeepsie** (town) Dutchess County	125	25,738	**De Witt** (town) Onondaga County
51	44,528	**Mount Pleasant** (town) Westchester County	126	25,691	**Shirley** (CDP) Suffolk County
52	43,750	**Webster** (town) Monroe County	127	25,311	**Ossining** (village) Westchester County
53	43,453	**Henrietta** (town) Monroe County	128	25,092	**Uniondale** (CDP) Nassau County
54	43,251	**Freeport** (village) Nassau County	129	24,793	**Medford** (CDP) Suffolk County
55	42,664	**West Babylon** (CDP) Suffolk County	130	24,481	**Baldwin** (CDP) Nassau County
56	42,492	**Lancaster** (town) Erie County	131	24,333	**Camillus** (town) Onondaga County
57	42,442	**Cortlandt** (town) Westchester County	132	24,155	**Rockville Centre** (village) Nassau County
58	42,333	**Hicksville** (CDP) Nassau County	133	23,928	**Peekskill** (city) Westchester County
59	41,756	**Monroe** (town) Orange County	134	23,625	**Kingston** (city) Ulster County
60	40,685	**Coram** (CDP) Suffolk County	135	23,505	**Fishkill** (town) Dutchess County
61	38,136	**Ossining** (town) Westchester County	136	23,194	**Montgomery** (town) Orange County
62	37,838	**Valley Stream** (village) Nassau County	137	23,145	**Onondaga** (town) Onondaga County
63	37,836	**East Meadow** (CDP) Nassau County	138	22,847	**Halfmoon** (town) Saratoga County
64	37,388	**Elmont** (CDP) Nassau County	139	22,772	**Copiague** (CDP) Suffolk County
65	37,261	**Haverstraw** (town) Rockland County	140	22,575	**Garden City** (village) Nassau County
66	37,046	**Clifton Park** (town) Saratoga County	141	22,452	**East Patchogue** (CDP) Suffolk County
67	36,984	**Penfield** (town) Monroe County	142	22,385	**Le Ray** (town) Jefferson County
68	36,929	**Brighton** (CDP) Monroe County	143	22,369	**Lysander** (town) Onondaga County
69	36,746	**Yorktown** (town) Westchester County	144	22,204	**Southold** (town) Suffolk County
70	35,914	**Commack** (CDP) Suffolk County	145	22,128	**Massapequa** (CDP) Nassau County
71	35,675	**Guilderland** (town) Albany County	146	22,090	**New Hartford** (town) Oneida County
72	34,960	**Central Islip** (CDP) Suffolk County	147	22,050	**Niskayuna** (town) Schenectady County
73	34,430	**Bethlehem** (town) Albany County	148	21,844	**East Hampton** (town) Suffolk County
74	34,376	**Carmel** (town) Putnam County	149	21,749	**Kiryas Joel** (village) Orange County
75	34,088	**Huntington Station** (CDP) Suffolk County	150	21,382	**Hyde Park** (town) Dutchess County

Note: *This section ranks incorporated places and CDPs (Census Designated Places) with populations of 2,500 or more. Unincorporated postal areas were not considered. Please refer to the User Guide for additional information.*

Population

Top 150 Places Ranked in *Ascending* Order

State Rank	Number	Place	State Rank	Number	Place
1	2,505	**Mount Morris** (village) Livingston County	76	2,742	**Seneca** (town) Ontario County
2	2,507	**Conesus** (town) Livingston County	77	2,747	**Lakeland** (CDP) Onondaga County
3	2,513	**Bangor** (town) Franklin County	77	2,747	**Somerset** (town) Niagara County
4	2,529	**Sangerfield** (town) Oneida County	79	2,749	**North Boston** (CDP) Erie County
5	2,531	**West Bloomfield** (town) Ontario County	80	2,751	**Aurelius** (town) Cayuga County
6	2,532	**Yates** (town) Orleans County	80	2,751	**East Norwich** (CDP) Nassau County
7	2,536	**Groton** (village) Tompkins County	82	2,753	**Coxsackie** (village) Greene County
8	2,539	**Lake Placid** (village) Essex County	83	2,755	**Horseheads North** (CDP) Chemung County
9	2,545	**Corinth** (village) Saratoga County	83	2,755	**Stockport** (town) Columbia County
10	2,550	**Randolph** (town) Cattaraugus County	85	2,768	**Victor** (village) Ontario County
11	2,551	**Chemung** (town) Chemung County	86	2,769	**Knox** (town) Albany County
12	2,553	**Skaneateles** (village) Onondaga County	86	2,769	**Whitehall** (village) Washington County
13	2,554	**Cohocton** (town) Steuben County	88	2,779	**Roslyn** (village) Nassau County
14	2,555	**Pavilion** (town) Genesee County	89	2,794	**Sardinia** (town) Erie County
14	2,555	**Sanford** (town) Broome County	90	2,795	**Chenango Bridge** (CDP) Broome County
16	2,557	**Piermont** (village) Rockland County	91	2,806	**Jay** (town) Essex County
16	2,557	**Pine Plains** (town) Dutchess County	92	2,807	**Afton** (town) Chenango County
18	2,558	**Rose** (town) Wayne County	93	2,809	**Great Neck Estates** (village) Nassau County
19	2,560	**Brookfield** (town) Madison County	94	2,810	**Halesite** (CDP) Suffolk County
19	2,560	**Frankfort** (village) Herkimer County	95	2,812	**Shelter Island** (town) Suffolk County
19	2,560	**Otisco** (town) Onondaga County	96	2,815	**Cazenovia** (village) Madison County
22	2,569	**Stamford** (town) Delaware County	97	2,820	**Voorheesville** (village) Albany County
23	2,571	**Mohawk** (village) Herkimer County	98	2,823	**Berne** (town) Albany County
24	2,573	**Addison** (town) Steuben County	99	2,829	**Benton** (town) Yates County
24	2,573	**Caneadea** (town) Allegany County	100	2,830	**Crown Heights** (CDP) Dutchess County
24	2,573	**Falconer** (village) Chautauqua County	101	2,836	**Wanakah** (CDP) Erie County
24	2,573	**Richmondville** (town) Schoharie County	102	2,845	**West Sand Lake** (CDP) Rensselaer County
28	2,576	**Saint Johnsville** (town) Montgomery County	103	2,860	**Akron** (village) Erie County
29	2,579	**Blasdell** (village) Erie County	104	2,862	**Castile** (town) Wyoming County
30	2,584	**Conesus Lake** (CDP) Livingston County	105	2,865	**Florida** (village) Orange County
31	2,585	**East Williston** (village) Nassau County	106	2,869	**Cape Vincent** (town) Jefferson County
31	2,585	**Pierrepont** (town) Saint Lawrence County	107	2,873	**Guilford** (town) Chenango County
33	2,586	**Russia** (town) Herkimer County	108	2,874	**Fairview** (CDP) Westchester County
34	2,590	**Alden** (village) Erie County	109	2,876	**Orleans** (town) Jefferson County
35	2,597	**Alexander** (town) Genesee County	110	2,885	**Denmark** (town) Lewis County
36	2,598	**Lewiston** (village) Niagara County	111	2,886	**New Haven** (town) Oswego County
36	2,598	**Silver Creek** (village) Chautauqua County	112	2,891	**Stephentown** (town) Rensselaer County
38	2,600	**Lido Beach** (CDP) Nassau County	113	2,893	**Davenport** (town) Delaware County
39	2,602	**Brinckerhoff** (CDP) Dutchess County	114	2,894	**Moira** (town) Franklin County
40	2,603	**Watchtower** (CDP) Ulster County	115	2,905	**Triangle** (town) Broome County
41	2,604	**New Berlin** (town) Chenango County	116	2,907	**Altona** (town) Clinton County
41	2,604	**Virgil** (town) Cortland County	117	2,930	**Franklinville** (town) Cattaraugus County
43	2,610	**Cato** (town) Cayuga County	118	2,935	**Westhampton** (CDP) Suffolk County
44	2,616	**Scottsville** (village) Monroe County	119	2,951	**Lakewood** (village) Chautauqua County
45	2,617	**Fleming** (town) Cayuga County	120	2,953	**Shandaken** (town) Ulster County
46	2,620	**Catlin** (town) Chemung County	121	2,957	**Carlton** (town) Orleans County
46	2,620	**Delaware** (town) Sullivan County	122	2,973	**Theresa** (town) Jefferson County
48	2,622	**Sheridan** (town) Chautauqua County	123	2,979	**Madison** (town) Madison County
49	2,624	**Thomaston** (village) Nassau County	124	2,982	**Milford** (town) Otsego County
50	2,626	**Northampton** (town) Fulton County	125	2,984	**Cornwall-on-Hudson** (village) Orange County
51	2,629	**Green Island** (town/village) Albany County	126	2,994	**Annsville** (town) Oneida County
51	2,629	**Rhinebeck** (village) Dutchess County	127	2,998	**Callicoon** (town) Sullivan County
53	2,639	**Elma Center** (CDP) Erie County	128	3,007	**Nunda** (town) Livingston County
54	2,642	**Yorkville** (village) Oneida County	129	3,011	**North East** (town) Dutchess County
55	2,643	**Attica** (village) Wyoming County	130	3,026	**Walton** (village) Delaware County
56	2,656	**Gowanda** (village) Cattaraugus County	131	3,027	**Lake Success** (village) Nassau County
57	2,659	**Montrose** (CDP) Westchester County	132	3,030	**Wales** (town) Erie County
58	2,678	**Hunter** (town) Greene County	133	3,034	**Sterling** (town) Cayuga County
59	2,693	**Kendall** (town) Orleans County	134	3,036	**Wynantskill** (CDP) Rensselaer County
60	2,694	**Salem** (town) Washington County	135	3,043	**East Syracuse** (village) Onondaga County
61	2,695	**Durham** (town) Greene County	136	3,049	**Otego** (town) Otsego County
62	2,700	**Barker** (town) Broome County	137	3,068	**Bergen** (town) Genesee County
63	2,703	**Moriches** (CDP) Suffolk County	138	3,073	**Sherrill** (city) Oneida County
64	2,704	**Harriman** (village) Orange County	139	3,075	**Spencer** (town) Tioga County
65	2,705	**Florida** (town) Montgomery County	140	3,078	**Delhi** (village) Delaware County
66	2,709	**Lisle** (town) Broome County	141	3,093	**Maybrook** (village) Orange County
67	2,711	**New Bremen** (town) Lewis County	142	3,094	**Schoharie** (town) Schoharie County
68	2,715	**Munsey Park** (village) Nassau County	143	3,102	**Brightwaters** (village) Suffolk County
68	2,715	**Sands Point** (village) Nassau County	144	3,103	**Northeast Ithaca** (CDP) Tompkins County
70	2,720	**Chesterfield** (town) Essex County	145	3,106	**Sloatsburg** (village) Rockland County
70	2,720	**Honeoye Falls** (village) Monroe County	146	3,116	**Darien** (town) Genesee County
72	2,721	**Nichols** (town) Tioga County	147	3,118	**Greenwood Lake** (village) Orange County
73	2,734	**Tully** (town) Onondaga County	148	3,123	**Croghan** (town) Lewis County
74	2,740	**Laurens** (town) Otsego County	148	3,123	**Ticonderoga** (CDP) Essex County
75	2,741	**Balmville** (CDP) Orange County	150	3,136	**Au Sable** (town) Clinton County

Note: This section ranks incorporated places and CDPs (Census Designated Places) with populations of 2,500 or more. Unincorporated postal areas were not considered. Please refer to the User Guide for additional information.

Population Growth Since 2000

Top 150 Places Ranked in *Descending* Order

State Rank	Percent	Place
1	560.9	**East Garden City** (CDP) Nassau County
2	114.1	**Romulus** (town) Seneca County
3	113.7	**Big Flats** (CDP) Chemung County
4	73.3	**South Fallsburg** (CDP) Sullivan County
5	70.9	**Riverside** (CDP) Suffolk County
6	66.8	**Brookville** (village) Nassau County
7	65.5	**Kiryas Joel** (village) Orange County
8	63.1	**New Square** (village) Rockland County
9	50.7	**Kaser** (village) Rockland County
10	50.4	**Marlboro** (CDP) Ulster County
11	47.3	**Noyack** (CDP) Suffolk County
12	45.3	**Victor** (town) Ontario County
13	44.8	**Monsey** (CDP) Rockland County
14	42.6	**Mount Sinai** (CDP) Suffolk County
15	35.8	**Canandaigua** (town) Ontario County
16	35.6	**Riverhead** (CDP) Suffolk County
17	34.6	**Flanders** (CDP) Suffolk County
18	34.3	**North Bay Shore** (CDP) Suffolk County
19	33.5	**Rocky Point** (CDP) Suffolk County
20	33.2	**Gang Mills** (CDP) Steuben County
21	33.0	**Monroe** (town) Orange County
22	32.4	**Wilton** (town) Saratoga County
23	32.2	**Stamford** (town) Delaware County
24	31.4	**Milton** (CDP) Saratoga County
25	31.2	**Armonk** (CDP) Westchester County
26	31.1	**Orangeburg** (CDP) Rockland County
27	30.9	**Northwest Harbor** (CDP) Suffolk County
28	30.3	**Manorville** (CDP) Suffolk County
29	29.7	**Wheatfield** (town) Niagara County
30	29.0	**North Bellport** (CDP) Suffolk County
31	28.9	**Mastic Beach** (village) Suffolk County
32	28.5	**Melville** (CDP) Suffolk County
33	27.8	**Brewerton** (CDP) Onondaga County
34	26.9	**Beekman** (town) Dutchess County
35	26.5	**Center Moriches** (CDP) Suffolk County
35	26.5	**Spring Valley** (village) Rockland County
37	26.2	**Shelter Island** (town) Suffolk County
38	25.9	**Minisink** (town) Orange County
39	25.2	**Montebello** (village) Rockland County
40	25.0	**Gordon Heights** (CDP) Suffolk County
41	24.8	**Attica** (town) Wyoming County
42	24.4	**Bay Shore** (CDP) Suffolk County
43	23.8	**Myers Corner** (CDP) Dutchess County
44	23.7	**Halfmoon** (town) Saratoga County
45	23.2	**Theresa** (town) Jefferson County
46	22.9	**Scottsville** (village) Monroe County
47	22.6	**Calcium** (CDP) Jefferson County
48	22.5	**Springs** (CDP) Suffolk County
49	22.4	**Greenville** (town) Orange County
49	22.4	**Rensselaer** (city) Rensselaer County
51	22.0	**Riverhead** (town) Suffolk County
52	21.7	**Jay** (town) Essex County
53	21.1	**Woodbury** (town) Orange County
54	20.9	**Ramapo** (town) Rockland County
55	20.7	**North Hills** (village) Nassau County
56	20.5	**Newfane** (CDP) Niagara County
56	20.5	**Pomona** (village) Rockland County
58	20.3	**Saint Regis Mohawk Reservation** (reservation) Franklin County
59	20.1	**Clarence** (town) Erie County
59	20.1	**Harriman** (village) Orange County
59	20.1	**North Amityville** (CDP) Suffolk County
62	20.0	**Wesley Hills** (village) Rockland County
62	20.0	**West Nyack** (CDP) Rockland County
64	19.7	**Centereach** (CDP) Suffolk County
65	19.5	**Farmington** (town) Ontario County
65	19.5	**Haverstraw** (village) Rockland County
67	19.3	**East Moriches** (CDP) Suffolk County
68	19.2	**Delhi** (village) Delaware County
69	18.8	**East Farmingdale** (CDP) Suffolk County
70	18.6	**Montgomery** (village) Orange County
70	18.6	**Yaphank** (CDP) Suffolk County
72	18.3	**Hamptonburgh** (town) Orange County
72	18.3	**Pompey** (town) Onondaga County
74	18.1	**Holtsville** (CDP) Suffolk County
74	18.1	**Port Washington North** (village) Nassau County
76	18.0	**Shawangunk** (town) Ulster County
77	17.7	**Crawford** (town) Orange County
78	17.6	**Mechanicstown** (CDP) Orange County
79	17.2	**Lakeview** (CDP) Nassau County
80	17.0	**Bangor** (town) Franklin County
81	16.9	**Ballston** (town) Saratoga County
81	16.9	**New Paltz** (village) Ulster County
81	16.9	**Northeast Ithaca** (CDP) Tompkins County
84	16.8	**South Valley Stream** (CDP) Nassau County
85	16.7	**Orleans** (town) Jefferson County
86	16.6	**Moriches** (CDP) Suffolk County
86	16.6	**West Sand Lake** (CDP) Rensselaer County
88	16.5	**Coram** (CDP) Suffolk County
88	16.5	**Erwin** (town) Steuben County
90	16.4	**Wading River** (CDP) Suffolk County
91	16.3	**East Greenbush** (CDP) Rensselaer County
92	16.1	**Terryville** (CDP) Suffolk County
93	16.0	**Fishkill** (town) Dutchess County
93	16.0	**Lysander** (town) Onondaga County
95	15.9	**Batavia** (town) Genesee County
95	15.9	**Harrison** (town/village) Westchester County
95	15.9	**Wawayanda** (town) Orange County
98	15.8	**Carmel Hamlet** (CDP) Putnam County
98	15.8	**Cayuga Heights** (village) Tompkins County
98	15.8	**Hamilton** (village) Madison County
101	15.7	**Nesconset** (CDP) Suffolk County
102	15.4	**Caroline** (town) Tompkins County
102	15.4	**Fort Drum** (CDP) Jefferson County
102	15.4	**Green Island** (town/village) Albany County
102	15.4	**Webster** (town) Monroe County
106	15.3	**Hamilton** (town) Madison County
107	15.2	**Southold** (CDP) Suffolk County
108	15.1	**Danby** (town) Tompkins County
109	14.9	**Somers** (town) Westchester County
110	14.7	**Malta** (town) Saratoga County
111	14.5	**Elmont** (CDP) Nassau County
112	14.4	**East Fishkill** (town) Dutchess County
113	14.1	**Laurens** (town) Otsego County
113	14.1	**West Glens Falls** (CDP) Warren County
115	14.0	**Chester** (village) Orange County
115	14.0	**Huntington Station** (CDP) Suffolk County
115	14.0	**Port Jefferson Station** (CDP) Suffolk County
118	13.9	**Virgil** (town) Cortland County
119	13.8	**Brentwood** (CDP) Suffolk County
119	13.8	**Victor** (village) Ontario County
121	13.6	**Saranac Lake** (village) Franklin County
121	13.6	**Wallkill** (town) Orange County
123	13.5	**New Windsor** (town) Orange County
124	13.4	**Kingsbury** (town) Washington County
125	13.3	**Canton** (village) Saint Lawrence County
126	13.1	**Cicero** (town) Onondaga County
127	13.0	**North Valley Stream** (CDP) Nassau County
128	12.9	**Airmont** (village) Rockland County
128	12.9	**Chesterfield** (town) Essex County
128	12.9	**Gorham** (town) Ontario County
128	12.9	**Le Ray** (town) Jefferson County
132	12.8	**Medford** (CDP) Suffolk County
133	12.7	**Harris Hill** (CDP) Erie County
134	12.6	**Clarkson** (town) Monroe County
135	12.3	**Avon** (village) Livingston County
135	12.3	**Clifton Park** (town) Saratoga County
135	12.3	**North Greenbush** (town) Rensselaer County
138	12.0	**Cutchogue** (CDP) Suffolk County
139	11.9	**Calverton** (CDP) Suffolk County
139	11.9	**North Castle** (town) Westchester County
139	11.9	**Northumberland** (town) Saratoga County
142	11.8	**Nanuet** (CDP) Rockland County
142	11.8	**Poestenkill** (town) Rensselaer County
142	11.8	**Walworth** (town) Wayne County
145	11.7	**Hopewell** (town) Ontario County
145	11.7	**Pawling** (town) Dutchess County
145	11.7	**Walden** (village) Orange County
148	11.6	**Stillwater** (town) Saratoga County
149	11.4	**Florida** (village) Orange County
150	11.3	**Henrietta** (town) Monroe County

Note: *This section ranks incorporated places and CDPs (Census Designated Places) with populations of 2,500 or more. Unincorporated postal areas were not considered. Please refer to the User Guide for additional information.*

Population Growth Since 2000

Top 150 Places Ranked in *Ascending* Order

State Rank	Percent	Place
1	-68.8	**Arlington** (CDP) Dutchess County
2	-47.7	**Hartsdale** (CDP) Westchester County
3	-37.7	**Valhalla** (CDP) Westchester County
4	-32.4	**Perry** (town) Wyoming County
5	-32.2	**Thornwood** (CDP) Westchester County
6	-25.5	**Red Oaks Mill** (CDP) Dutchess County
7	-24.3	**Albion** (village) Orleans County
8	-23.3	**Mount Morris** (village) Livingston County
9	-22.1	**Murray** (town) Orleans County
10	-21.2	**Collins** (town) Erie County
11	-20.5	**Saugerties** (village) Ulster County
12	-19.5	**Southampton** (village) Suffolk County
13	-18.7	**Bardonia** (CDP) Rockland County
14	-17.9	**Balmville** (CDP) Orange County
15	-17.7	**Sound Beach** (CDP) Suffolk County
16	-14.6	**Hewlett** (CDP) Nassau County
16	-14.6	**North Patchogue** (CDP) Suffolk County
16	-14.6	**Rhinebeck** (village) Dutchess County
19	-14.2	**Cape Vincent** (town) Jefferson County
20	-13.5	**Groveland** (town) Livingston County
21	-13.3	**Spackenkill** (CDP) Dutchess County
22	-12.8	**Greenville** (CDP) Westchester County
23	-12.7	**Hudson** (city) Columbia County
24	-12.3	**Lyons** (town) Wayne County
25	-12.2	**Perry** (village) Wyoming County
26	-12.1	**Brookhaven** (CDP) Suffolk County
27	-12.0	**Moravia** (town) Cayuga County
28	-11.6	**Gaines** (town) Orleans County
28	-11.6	**Portland** (town) Chautauqua County
28	-11.6	**Sterling** (town) Cayuga County
31	-11.3	**Buffalo** (city) Erie County
31	-11.3	**Wellsville** (village) Allegany County
33	-11.1	**Niagara Falls** (city) Niagara County
33	-11.1	**Ogdensburg** (city) Saint Lawrence County
35	-10.6	**Village Green** (CDP) Onondaga County
36	-10.4	**Islip** (CDP) Suffolk County
37	-10.3	**Silver Creek** (village) Chautauqua County
38	-10.1	**Conklin** (town) Broome County
39	-10.0	**Catskill** (village) Greene County
40	-9.9	**Setauket-East Setauket** (CDP) Suffolk County
41	-9.8	**Hawthorne** (CDP) Westchester County
42	-9.6	**Merrick** (CDP) Nassau County
43	-9.4	**Lakewood** (village) Chautauqua County
43	-9.4	**Middletown** (town) Delaware County
43	-9.4	**Tupper Lake** (village) Franklin County
46	-9.2	**Montauk** (CDP) Suffolk County
46	-9.2	**Oakdale** (CDP) Suffolk County
48	-9.1	**West Hills** (CDP) Suffolk County
49	-8.9	**Gouverneur** (village) Saint Lawrence County
49	-8.9	**South Lockport** (CDP) Niagara County
49	-8.9	**Yorkshire** (town) Cattaraugus County
52	-8.7	**Hancock** (town) Delaware County
52	-8.7	**Hanover** (town) Chautauqua County
52	-8.7	**Shandaken** (town) Ulster County
55	-8.6	**Campbell** (town) Steuben County
55	-8.6	**Eden** (CDP) Erie County
55	-8.6	**Greenwood Lake** (village) Orange County
58	-8.5	**Coeymans** (town) Albany County
59	-8.4	**Depew** (village) Erie County
59	-8.4	**Niagara** (town) Niagara County
61	-8.3	**Dannemora** (town) Clinton County
62	-8.1	**Olean** (city) Cattaraugus County
63	-8.0	**Altona** (town) Clinton County
63	-8.0	**Lido Beach** (CDP) Nassau County
63	-8.0	**Scriba** (town) Oswego County
63	-8.0	**Selden** (CDP) Suffolk County
63	-8.0	**Warsaw** (town) Wyoming County
63	-8.0	**Westfield** (town) Chautauqua County
69	-7.9	**Brutus** (town) Cayuga County
69	-7.9	**Caledonia** (town) Livingston County
69	-7.9	**Chester** (town) Warren County
69	-7.9	**Lancaster** (village) Erie County
73	-7.7	**Penn Yan** (village) Yates County
73	-7.7	**Sodus** (town) Wayne County
73	-7.7	**Warsaw** (village) Wyoming County
76	-7.6	**Sheridan** (town) Chautauqua County
76	-7.6	**Sidney** (town) Delaware County
78	-7.5	**Medina** (village) Orleans County
79	-7.4	**Claverack** (town) Columbia County
79	-7.4	**Larchmont** (village) Westchester County
79	-7.4	**Newark** (village) Wayne County
79	-7.4	**Wolcott** (town) Wayne County
83	-7.3	**Akron** (village) Erie County
83	-7.3	**Evans** (town) Erie County
83	-7.3	**Portville** (town) Cattaraugus County
86	-7.2	**Ellicott** (town) Chautauqua County
86	-7.2	**Oceanside** (CDP) Nassau County
86	-7.2	**Wheatland** (town) Monroe County
89	-7.1	**Lima** (town) Livingston County
89	-7.1	**Locust Valley** (CDP) Nassau County
89	-7.1	**New Berlin** (town) Chenango County
92	-7.0	**Dix** (town) Schuyler County
92	-7.0	**Kenmore** (village) Erie County
92	-7.0	**Ronkonkoma** (CDP) Suffolk County
92	-7.0	**Tonawanda** (city) Erie County
96	-6.9	**Elmira** (city) Chemung County
97	-6.8	**Canandaigua** (city) Ontario County
97	-6.8	**Canisteo** (town) Steuben County
99	-6.7	**Salamanca** (city) Cattaraugus County
100	-6.6	**Batavia** (city) Genesee County
100	-6.6	**Cheektowaga** (town) Erie County
100	-6.6	**Fairport** (village) Monroe County
100	-6.6	**Lewiston** (village) Niagara County
100	-6.6	**North Tonawanda** (city) Niagara County
105	-6.5	**Gowanda** (village) Cattaraugus County
105	-6.5	**Haviland** (CDP) Dutchess County
105	-6.5	**Port Ewen** (CDP) Ulster County
108	-6.4	**Cheektowaga** (CDP) Erie County
108	-6.4	**Fairmount** (CDP) Onondaga County
108	-6.4	**Lockport** (city) Niagara County
108	-6.4	**Marilla** (town) Erie County
112	-6.3	**Aurelius** (town) Cayuga County
112	-6.3	**Dunkirk** (city) Chautauqua County
112	-6.3	**East Aurora** (village) Erie County
112	-6.3	**Franklinville** (town) Cattaraugus County
112	-6.3	**Ilion** (village) Herkimer County
117	-6.2	**Schoharie** (town) Schoharie County
118	-6.1	**Arcadia** (town) Wayne County
118	-6.1	**Dansville** (village) Livingston County
118	-6.1	**Hornell** (city) Steuben County
118	-6.1	**Stockport** (town) Columbia County
118	-6.1	**Tonawanda** (town) Erie County
118	-6.1	**Waverly** (village) Tioga County
118	-6.1	**Wayland** (town) Steuben County
125	-6.0	**Lake Erie Beach** (CDP) Erie County
125	-6.0	**Little Falls** (city) Herkimer County
125	-6.0	**Vienna** (town) Oneida County
125	-6.0	**Westmere** (CDP) Albany County
125	-6.0	**Woodbury** (CDP) Nassau County
130	-5.9	**Busti** (town) Chautauqua County
130	-5.9	**Hamburg** (village) Erie County
130	-5.9	**Marion** (town) Wayne County
133	-5.8	**Bayville** (village) Nassau County
133	-5.8	**Firthcliffe** (CDP) Orange County
133	-5.8	**Rome** (city) Oneida County
133	-5.8	**Tonawanda** (CDP) Erie County
133	-5.8	**West Islip** (CDP) Suffolk County
133	-5.8	**West Sayville** (CDP) Suffolk County
139	-5.7	**Afton** (town) Chenango County
139	-5.7	**Chautauqua** (town) Chautauqua County
139	-5.7	**Dannemora** (village) Clinton County
139	-5.7	**Guilford** (town) Chenango County
143	-5.6	**East Northport** (CDP) Suffolk County
143	-5.6	**Holland** (town) Erie County
143	-5.6	**Islip Terrace** (CDP) Suffolk County
143	-5.6	**Lee** (town) Oneida County
143	-5.6	**Long Beach** (city) Nassau County
143	-5.6	**Rockland** (town) Sullivan County
143	-5.6	**Woodstock** (town) Ulster County
150	-5.5	**Cuba** (town) Allegany County

Note: This section ranks incorporated places and CDPs (Census Designated Places) with populations of 2,500 or more. Unincorporated postal areas were not considered. Please refer to the User Guide for additional information.

Population Density

Top 150 Places Ranked in *Descending* Order

State Rank	Pop./ Sq. Mi.	Place	State Rank	Pop./ Sq. Mi.	Place
1	71,379.8	**Manhattan** (borough) New York County	76	6,654.2	**Plainedge** (CDP) Nassau County
2	36,648.0	**Brooklyn** (borough) Kings County	77	6,569.4	**Lakeview** (CDP) Nassau County
3	33,930.7	**Bronx** (borough) Bronx County	78	6,475.5	**Hempstead** (town) Nassau County
4	29,010.4	**Kaser** (village) Rockland County	79	6,438.6	**Thomaston** (village) Nassau County
5	27,843.8	**New York** (city)	80	6,433.7	**Westbury** (village) Nassau County
6	22,036.0	**Great Neck Plaza** (village) Nassau County	81	6,426.2	**Buffalo** (city) Erie County
7	21,202.4	**Queens** (borough) Queens County	82	6,407.6	**Baldwin Harbor** (CDP) Nassau County
8	21,161.6	**New Square** (village) Rockland County	83	6,356.0	**Inwood** (CDP) Nassau County
9	19,618.5	**Kiryas Joel** (village) Orange County	84	6,351.3	**Manhasset Hills** (CDP) Nassau County
10	15,984.8	**Spring Valley** (village) Rockland County	85	6,259.5	**North Massapequa** (CDP) Nassau County
11	15,555.4	**Mount Vernon** (city) Westchester County	86	6,233.7	**Hicksville** (CDP) Nassau County
12	15,112.9	**Long Beach** (city) Nassau County	87	6,227.1	**Huntington Station** (CDP) Suffolk County
13	14,965.9	**Hempstead** (village) Nassau County	88	6,219.7	**Massapequa** (CDP) Nassau County
14	14,379.1	**Manorhaven** (village) Nassau County	89	6,191.7	**Mechanicville** (city) Saratoga County
15	12,617.2	**Port Chester** (village) Westchester County	90	6,189.2	**North Bay Shore** (CDP) Suffolk County
16	11,704.7	**Williston Park** (village) Nassau County	91	6,157.6	**North Wantagh** (CDP) Nassau County
17	11,386.6	**New Hyde Park** (village) Nassau County	92	6,143.4	**Oceanside** (CDP) Nassau County
18	11,354.3	**Floral Park** (village) Nassau County	93	6,107.8	**Haverstraw** (village) Rockland County
19	11,098.6	**Elmont** (CDP) Nassau County	94	6,098.2	**Schenectady** (city) Schenectady County
20	11,072.3	**Yonkers** (city) Westchester County	95	6,084.1	**North Lindenhurst** (CDP) Suffolk County
21	11,021.7	**Tuckahoe** (village) Westchester County	96	6,063.3	**Mamaroneck** (village) Westchester County
22	10,969.5	**SUNY Oswego** (CDP) Oswego County	97	6,037.6	**Eastchester** (CDP) Westchester County
23	10,961.6	**Franklin Square** (CDP) Nassau County	98	6,001.9	**East Meadow** (CDP) Nassau County
24	10,866.3	**Valley Stream** (village) Nassau County	99	5,997.2	**Seaford** (CDP) Nassau County
25	10,639.0	**Kenmore** (village) Erie County	100	5,955.6	**Poughkeepsie** (city) Dutchess County
26	10,550.4	**Garden City South** (CDP) Nassau County	101	5,916.4	**White Plains** (city) Westchester County
27	10,547.9	**Island Park** (village) Nassau County	102	5,889.9	**Rochester** (city) Monroe County
28	10,098.3	**Mineola** (village) Nassau County	103	5,866.1	**South Nyack** (village) Rockland County
29	9,859.9	**Cedarhurst** (village) Nassau County	104	5,823.2	**Arlington** (CDP) Dutchess County
30	9,711.0	**Lynbrook** (village) Nassau County	105	5,782.8	**Pelham** (town) Westchester County
31	9,710.4	**East Rockaway** (village) Nassau County	106	5,772.5	**Syracuse** (city) Onondaga County
32	9,571.4	**North Valley Stream** (CDP) Nassau County	107	5,768.7	**East Massapequa** (CDP) Nassau County
33	9,401.9	**Roosevelt** (CDP) Nassau County	108	5,749.4	**Hartsdale** (CDP) Westchester County
34	9,399.4	**New Cassel** (CDP) Nassau County	109	5,672.6	**Ithaca** (city) Tompkins County
35	9,345.0	**Freeport** (village) Nassau County	110	5,639.7	**Hillcrest** (CDP) Rockland County
36	9,270.8	**Uniondale** (CDP) Nassau County	111	5,589.3	**Brentwood** (CDP) Suffolk County
37	9,240.4	**Monsey** (CDP) Rockland County	112	5,573.8	**Larchmont** (village) Westchester County
38	8,794.6	**Nyack** (village) Rockland County	113	5,527.6	**Bay Shore** (CDP) Suffolk County
39	8,451.0	**North Amityville** (CDP) Suffolk County	114	5,510.6	**Carle Place** (CDP) Nassau County
40	8,432.9	**Pelham** (village) Westchester County	115	5,497.4	**Eggertsville** (CDP) Erie County
41	8,350.9	**Garden City Park** (CDP) Nassau County	116	5,493.1	**West Babylon** (CDP) Suffolk County
42	8,261.8	**Baldwin** (CDP) Nassau County	117	5,482.4	**Middletown** (city) Orange County
43	8,094.5	**Staten Island** (borough) Richmond County	118	5,478.6	**Peekskill** (city) Westchester County
44	8,084.7	**Malverne** (village) Nassau County	119	5,449.9	**South Hempstead** (CDP) Nassau County
45	8,037.1	**Ossining** (village) Westchester County	120	5,397.2	**Patchogue** (village) Suffolk County
46	7,845.4	**Binghamton University** (CDP) Broome County	121	5,361.7	**Stony Brook University** (CDP) Suffolk County
47	7,772.1	**Massapequa Park** (village) Nassau County	122	5,320.1	**Oyster Bay** (CDP) Nassau County
48	7,730.7	**University Gardens** (CDP) Nassau County	123	5,238.3	**Munsey Park** (village) Nassau County
49	7,693.7	**North New Hyde Park** (CDP) Nassau County	124	5,225.4	**Suffern** (village) Rockland County
50	7,691.3	**North Bellmore** (CDP) Nassau County	125	5,131.4	**Searingtown** (CDP) Nassau County
51	7,635.3	**New Rochelle** (city) Westchester County	126	5,118.2	**Merrick** (CDP) Nassau County
52	7,621.2	**Herricks** (CDP) Nassau County	127	5,112.5	**North Babylon** (CDP) Suffolk County
53	7,611.3	**Watervliet** (city) Albany County	128	5,041.3	**East Rochester** (town/village) Monroe County
54	7,596.2	**Great Neck** (village) Nassau County	129	4,984.2	**Babylon** (village) Suffolk County
55	7,574.9	**Levittown** (CDP) Nassau County	130	4,944.5	**Wantagh** (CDP) Nassau County
56	7,572.5	**Albertson** (CDP) Nassau County	131	4,931.4	**Sound Beach** (CDP) Suffolk County
57	7,547.8	**South Valley Stream** (CDP) Nassau County	132	4,916.2	**Central Islip** (CDP) Suffolk County
58	7,494.5	**Farmingdale** (village) Nassau County	133	4,913.7	**Cortland** (city) Cortland County
59	7,490.2	**Newburgh** (city) Orange County	134	4,894.7	**Wappingers Falls** (village) Dutchess County
60	7,438.7	**Rockville Centre** (village) Nassau County	135	4,833.3	**Mount Ivy** (CDP) Rockland County
61	7,262.9	**Lindenhurst** (village) Suffolk County	136	4,821.1	**Troy** (city) Rensselaer County
62	7,177.8	**Salisbury** (CDP) Nassau County	137	4,722.2	**Roslyn Heights** (CDP) Nassau County
63	7,159.4	**West Hempstead** (CDP) Nassau County	138	4,662.5	**Sleepy Hollow** (village) Westchester County
64	7,075.6	**Copiague** (CDP) Suffolk County	139	4,656.7	**Selden** (CDP) Suffolk County
65	7,026.2	**North Merrick** (CDP) Nassau County	140	4,641.0	**Elmsford** (village) Westchester County
66	6,845.7	**Hewlett** (CDP) Nassau County	141	4,637.4	**Bayville** (village) Nassau County
67	6,822.6	**South Farmingdale** (CDP) Nassau County	142	4,610.4	**Sloan** (village) Erie County
68	6,809.7	**West Haverstraw** (village) Rockland County	143	4,603.8	**Albany** (city) Albany County
69	6,775.1	**Eastchester** (town) Westchester County	144	4,594.7	**Scotia** (village) Schenectady County
70	6,750.3	**Woodmere** (CDP) Nassau County	145	4,570.0	**Plainview** (CDP) Nassau County
71	6,742.6	**Rye** (town) Westchester County	146	4,562.5	**Bethpage** (CDP) Nassau County
72	6,729.2	**Bellmore** (CDP) Nassau County	147	4,550.8	**Dobbs Ferry** (village) Westchester County
73	6,712.8	**Fairview** (CDP) Westchester County	148	4,545.6	**East Williston** (village) Nassau County
74	6,679.7	**Port Washington North** (village) Nassau County	149	4,507.4	**Sea Cliff** (village) Nassau County
75	6,662.3	**Bronxville** (village) Westchester County	150	4,503.2	**Amityville** (village) Suffolk County

Note: *This section ranks incorporated places and CDPs (Census Designated Places) with populations of 2,500 or more. Unincorporated postal areas were not considered. Please refer to the User Guide for additional information.*

Population Density

Top 150 Places Ranked in *Ascending* Order

State Rank	Pop./ Sq. Mi.	Place	State Rank	Pop./ Sq. Mi.	Place
1	17.4	**Croghan** (town) Lewis County	76	66.4	**Argyle** (town) Washington County
2	19.8	**Hancock** (town) Delaware County	77	66.7	**Sterling** (town) Cayuga County
3	24.7	**Shandaken** (town) Ulster County	78	66.8	**Otego** (town) Otsego County
4	28.4	**Sanford** (town) Broome County	79	67.5	**Oswegatchie** (town) Saint Lawrence County
5	28.8	**Altona** (town) Clinton County	79	67.5	**Windsor** (town) Broome County
5	28.8	**Harrietstown** (town) Franklin County	81	67.7	**Yates** (town) Orleans County
7	29.6	**Hunter** (town) Greene County	82	67.8	**Carlton** (town) Orleans County
8	32.9	**Brookfield** (town) Madison County	83	68.2	**Benton** (town) Yates County
9	34.4	**Chesterfield** (town) Essex County	84	68.4	**York** (town) Livingston County
10	34.7	**Saranac** (town) Clinton County	85	69.0	**Catlin** (town) Chemung County
11	37.9	**Lisbon** (town) Saint Lawrence County	86	69.3	**White Creek** (town) Washington County
12	38.0	**Middletown** (town) Delaware County	87	69.8	**North East** (town) Dutchess County
13	39.2	**Rockland** (town) Sullivan County	88	70.0	**Rutland** (town) Jefferson County
13	39.2	**Stockholm** (town) Saint Lawrence County	89	70.2	**Whitehall** (town) Washington County
15	39.6	**Chester** (town) Warren County	90	70.4	**Sheridan** (town) Chautauqua County
16	40.3	**Orleans** (town) Jefferson County	91	70.7	**Randolph** (town) Cattaraugus County
17	41.1	**Mooers** (town) Clinton County	92	70.9	**Galen** (town) Wayne County
18	41.5	**Jay** (town) Essex County	93	71.1	**Otsego** (town) Otsego County
19	42.0	**Ellisburg** (town) Jefferson County	94	71.5	**Fayette** (town) Seneca County
20	42.2	**Neversink** (town) Sullivan County	95	71.7	**Pavilion** (town) Genesee County
21	42.9	**Pierrepont** (town) Saint Lawrence County	96	72.2	**Caneadea** (town) Allegany County
22	44.1	**Berne** (town) Albany County	97	72.6	**Greene** (town) Chenango County
23	45.4	**Russia** (town) Herkimer County	98	72.9	**Hounsfield** (town) Jefferson County
24	45.5	**Cohocton** (town) Steuben County	99	73.0	**Madison** (town) Madison County
25	45.8	**Theresa** (town) Jefferson County	100	73.2	**Alexander** (town) Genesee County
26	46.6	**Guilford** (town) Chenango County	101	74.0	**Somerset** (town) Niagara County
27	48.8	**Hector** (town) Schuyler County	102	74.2	**Middleburgh** (town) Schoharie County
27	48.8	**New Bremen** (town) Lewis County	103	74.3	**Moriah** (town) Essex County
29	49.2	**Bethel** (town) Sullivan County	104	74.9	**Olive** (town) Ulster County
30	49.8	**Annsville** (town) Oneida County	105	75.0	**Delaware** (town) Sullivan County
31	49.9	**Stephentown** (town) Rensselaer County	106	75.5	**Rose** (town) Wayne County
32	50.5	**Tupper Lake** (town) Franklin County	107	76.2	**Chatham** (town) Columbia County
33	50.9	**Cape Vincent** (town) Jefferson County	107	76.2	**Conesus** (town) Livingston County
34	51.4	**Salem** (town) Washington County	109	76.3	**Jerusalem** (town) Yates County
35	51.6	**Chemung** (town) Chemung County	110	76.4	**Tuxedo** (town) Orange County
36	53.0	**Stamford** (town) Delaware County	111	76.6	**Stanford** (town) Dutchess County
37	54.0	**Florida** (town) Montgomery County	112	76.7	**Triangle** (town) Broome County
38	54.4	**Seneca** (town) Ontario County	113	77.0	**Newark Valley** (town) Tioga County
39	54.6	**Durham** (town) Greene County	114	77.4	**Castile** (town) Wyoming County
40	55.0	**Candor** (town) Tioga County	115	77.5	**Hartland** (town) Niagara County
40	55.0	**Virgil** (town) Cortland County	116	77.6	**Cato** (town) Cayuga County
42	55.7	**Sardinia** (town) Erie County	117	77.8	**Delhi** (town) Delaware County
43	56.1	**Davenport** (town) Delaware County	118	78.4	**Richmond** (town) Ontario County
43	56.1	**Walton** (town) Delaware County	119	78.5	**Chazy** (town) Clinton County
45	56.4	**New Berlin** (town) Chenango County	120	78.8	**Palatine** (town) Montgomery County
46	56.6	**Fort Ann** (town) Washington County	121	79.6	**New Baltimore** (town) Greene County
46	56.6	**Franklinville** (town) Cattaraugus County	122	79.9	**Dannemora** (town) Clinton County
48	57.0	**Denmark** (town) Lewis County	123	80.2	**Au Sable** (town) Clinton County
49	57.1	**North Elba** (town) Essex County	124	80.7	**Nichols** (town) Tioga County
50	57.5	**Alexandria** (town) Jefferson County	125	80.8	**Galway** (town) Saratoga County
51	57.8	**Lisle** (town) Broome County	126	81.1	**Nunda** (town) Livingston County
52	58.3	**Bangor** (town) Franklin County	127	81.2	**Washington** (town) Dutchess County
53	58.7	**Westerlo** (town) Albany County	128	81.3	**Rochester** (town) Ulster County
54	60.2	**Bennington** (town) Wyoming County	129	81.7	**Norfolk** (town) Saint Lawrence County
55	61.2	**Afton** (town) Chenango County	130	82.0	**Kendall** (town) Orleans County
56	61.3	**Caroline** (town) Tompkins County	130	82.0	**North Collins** (town) Erie County
57	61.4	**Canisteo** (town) Steuben County	132	82.1	**Sangerfield** (town) Oneida County
58	61.5	**Ticonderoga** (town) Essex County	132	82.1	**Tioga** (town) Tioga County
59	61.7	**Callicoon** (town) Sullivan County	134	82.4	**Wilna** (town) Jefferson County
60	62.1	**Spencer** (town) Tioga County	135	82.7	**Minden** (town) Montgomery County
61	63.2	**Lake Luzerne** (town) Warren County	136	82.9	**Campbell** (town) Steuben County
62	63.3	**Boonville** (town) Oneida County	137	83.6	**Pine Plains** (town) Dutchess County
63	63.6	**Clayton** (town) Jefferson County	138	85.1	**Wales** (town) Erie County
64	63.8	**Warrensburg** (town) Warren County	139	85.2	**Groveland** (town) Livingston County
65	64.0	**Moira** (town) Franklin County	140	85.3	**Richmondville** (town) Schoharie County
65	64.0	**Oxford** (town) Chenango County	141	85.7	**Schuyler** (town) Herkimer County
67	64.6	**Danby** (town) Tompkins County	142	85.9	**Canajoharie** (town) Montgomery County
68	64.7	**Milford** (town) Otsego County	143	86.0	**Veteran** (town) Chemung County
69	65.0	**Louisville** (town) Saint Lawrence County	144	86.7	**Otisco** (town) Onondaga County
70	65.2	**Barker** (town) Broome County	145	87.1	**Constantia** (town) Oswego County
70	65.2	**Laurens** (town) Otsego County	146	87.2	**Gorham** (town) Ontario County
72	65.6	**Chautauqua** (town) Chautauqua County	147	87.5	**Woodstock** (town) Ulster County
73	65.8	**Darien** (town) Genesee County	148	87.6	**Mount Morris** (town) Livingston County
74	66.0	**Colesville** (town) Broome County	149	87.7	**Copake** (town) Columbia County
75	66.3	**Knox** (town) Albany County	150	88.5	**Arcade** (town) Wyoming County

Note: *This section ranks incorporated places and CDPs (Census Designated Places) with populations of 2,500 or more. Unincorporated postal areas were not considered. Please refer to the User Guide for additional information.*

White Population

Top 150 Places Ranked in *Descending* Order

State Rank	Percent	Place	State Rank	Percent	Place
1	100.0	**Marilla** (town) Erie County	70	98.3	**West Bloomfield** (town) Ontario County
1	100.0	**Pittstown** (town) Rensselaer County	77	98.2	**Boonville** (town) Oneida County
3	99.8	**Eden** (CDP) Erie County	77	98.2	**Carroll** (town) Chautauqua County
3	99.8	**Eden** (town) Erie County	77	98.2	**Conesus** (town) Livingston County
3	99.8	**Perry** (town) Wyoming County	77	98.2	**Holland** (town) Erie County
6	99.7	**Chester** (town) Warren County	77	98.2	**Knox** (town) Albany County
6	99.7	**Kiryas Joel** (village) Orange County	77	98.2	**Mohawk** (village) Herkimer County
6	99.7	**North Boston** (CDP) Erie County	83	98.1	**Barton** (town) Tioga County
6	99.7	**Pendleton** (town) Niagara County	83	98.1	**Benton** (town) Yates County
10	99.6	**Brookfield** (town) Madison County	83	98.1	**Canisteo** (town) Steuben County
10	99.6	**Middleburgh** (town) Schoharie County	83	98.1	**Skaneateles** (town) Onondaga County
10	99.6	**Schuyler** (town) Herkimer County	83	98.1	**Stockholm** (town) Saint Lawrence County
10	99.6	**Westfield** (village) Chautauqua County	83	98.1	**Verona** (town) Oneida County
14	99.5	**Westfield** (town) Chautauqua County	83	98.1	**Wanakah** (CDP) Erie County
15	99.4	**Kaser** (village) Rockland County	90	98.0	**Alden** (village) Erie County
16	99.3	**Alexander** (town) Genesee County	90	98.0	**Amsterdam** (town) Montgomery County
16	99.3	**Clayton** (town) Jefferson County	90	98.0	**Cuba** (town) Allegany County
16	99.3	**Elma Center** (CDP) Erie County	90	98.0	**Lisbon** (town) Saint Lawrence County
16	99.3	**Fort Edward** (village) Washington County	90	98.0	**Milford** (town) Otsego County
16	99.3	**Lake Luzerne** (town) Warren County	90	98.0	**Sand Lake** (town) Rensselaer County
16	99.3	**Poestenkill** (town) Rensselaer County	90	98.0	**Skaneateles** (village) Onondaga County
16	99.3	**Sardinia** (town) Erie County	90	98.0	**Yorkshire** (town) Cattaraugus County
16	99.3	**Warrensburg** (town) Warren County	98	97.9	**Alexandria** (town) Jefferson County
16	99.3	**Whitesboro** (village) Oneida County	98	97.9	**Barker** (town) Broome County
25	99.2	**Owasco** (town) Cayuga County	98	97.9	**Chazy** (town) Clinton County
25	99.2	**Perry** (village) Wyoming County	98	97.9	**Durham** (town) Greene County
25	99.2	**Sangerfield** (town) Oneida County	98	97.9	**Tupper Lake** (village) Franklin County
28	99.1	**Boston** (town) Erie County	103	97.8	**Bennington** (town) Wyoming County
28	99.1	**Campbell** (town) Steuben County	103	97.8	**Brutus** (town) Cayuga County
28	99.1	**Chittenango** (village) Madison County	103	97.8	**Castile** (town) Wyoming County
28	99.1	**Lake George** (town) Warren County	103	97.8	**Elbridge** (town) Onondaga County
28	99.1	**Lakeland** (CDP) Onondaga County	103	97.8	**Lisle** (town) Broome County
28	99.1	**Warrensburg** (CDP) Warren County	103	97.8	**Newfane** (town) Niagara County
34	99.0	**East Bloomfield** (town) Ontario County	103	97.8	**North Collins** (town) Erie County
34	99.0	**Laurens** (town) Otsego County	103	97.8	**Nunda** (town) Livingston County
34	99.0	**New Square** (village) Rockland County	103	97.8	**Palermo** (town) Oswego County
34	99.0	**Stephentown** (town) Rensselaer County	103	97.8	**Pierrepont** (town) Saint Lawrence County
38	98.9	**Aurelius** (town) Cayuga County	103	97.8	**Southold** (CDP) Suffolk County
38	98.9	**Newfane** (CDP) Niagara County	103	97.8	**Tioga** (town) Tioga County
38	98.9	**Otisco** (town) Onondaga County	115	97.7	**Hector** (town) Schuyler County
38	98.9	**Walton** (village) Delaware County	115	97.7	**Hoosick** (town) Rensselaer County
42	98.8	**Argyle** (town) Washington County	115	97.7	**Orleans** (town) Jefferson County
42	98.8	**Bangor** (town) Franklin County	115	97.7	**Schuyler Falls** (town) Clinton County
42	98.8	**Blue Point** (CDP) Suffolk County	115	97.7	**Ticonderoga** (CDP) Essex County
42	98.8	**Conklin** (town) Broome County	115	97.7	**Ticonderoga** (town) Essex County
42	98.8	**Richland** (town) Oswego County	121	97.6	**Charlton** (town) Saratoga County
47	98.7	**Colesville** (town) Broome County	121	97.6	**Ellery** (town) Chautauqua County
47	98.7	**North Dansville** (town) Livingston County	121	97.6	**Maine** (town) Broome County
47	98.7	**Stillwater** (town) Saratoga County	121	97.6	**Norwich** (town) Chenango County
47	98.7	**Sullivan** (town) Madison County	121	97.6	**Oakfield** (town) Genesee County
51	98.6	**Chenango Bridge** (CDP) Broome County	121	97.6	**Royalton** (town) Niagara County
51	98.6	**Colden** (town) Erie County	121	97.6	**Saint Johnsville** (town) Montgomery County
51	98.6	**Madison** (town) Madison County	121	97.6	**Stamford** (town) Delaware County
51	98.6	**Milton** (CDP) Saratoga County	121	97.6	**Starkey** (town) Yates County
51	98.6	**Pavilion** (town) Genesee County	121	97.6	**Unadilla** (town) Otsego County
51	98.6	**Sterling** (town) Cayuga County	121	97.6	**West Monroe** (town) Oswego County
51	98.6	**Vienna** (town) Oneida County	121	97.6	**Westerlo** (town) Albany County
58	98.5	**Elma** (town) Erie County	133	97.5	**Afton** (town) Chenango County
58	98.5	**Manheim** (town) Herkimer County	133	97.5	**Hoosick Falls** (village) Rensselaer County
58	98.5	**Orchard Park** (village) Erie County	133	97.5	**New Haven** (town) Oswego County
58	98.5	**Sandy Creek** (town) Oswego County	133	97.5	**Sherburne** (town) Chenango County
58	98.5	**Seneca** (town) Ontario County	133	97.5	**Wellsville** (village) Allegany County
58	98.5	**Walton** (town) Delaware County	133	97.5	**Whitestown** (town) Oneida County
64	98.4	**Croghan** (town) Lewis County	133	97.5	**Windsor** (town) Broome County
64	98.4	**Dansville** (village) Livingston County	133	97.5	**Yorkville** (village) Oneida County
64	98.4	**Greenville** (town) Greene County	141	97.4	**Addison** (town) Steuben County
64	98.4	**Lido Beach** (CDP) Nassau County	141	97.4	**Conesus Lake** (CDP) Livingston County
64	98.4	**Northampton** (town) Fulton County	141	97.4	**East Islip** (CDP) Suffolk County
64	98.4	**Salem** (town) Washington County	141	97.4	**Granby** (town) Oswego County
70	98.3	**Chemung** (town) Chemung County	141	97.4	**Horseheads North** (CDP) Chemung County
70	98.3	**Darien** (town) Genesee County	141	97.4	**Nichols** (town) Tioga County
70	98.3	**Lawrence** (village) Nassau County	141	97.4	**Schoharie** (town) Schoharie County
70	98.3	**Mayfield** (town) Fulton County	141	97.4	**Stockport** (town) Columbia County
70	98.3	**Portville** (town) Cattaraugus County	141	97.4	**Trenton** (town) Oneida County
70	98.3	**Volney** (town) Oswego County	141	97.4	**Triangle** (town) Broome County

Note: *This section ranks incorporated places and CDPs (Census Designated Places) with populations of 2,500 or more. Unincorporated postal areas were not considered. Please refer to the User Guide for additional information.*

White Population

Top 150 Places Ranked in *Ascending* Order

State Rank	Percent	Place
1	6.0	**Saint Regis Mohawk Reservation** (reservation) Franklin County
2	13.0	**Lakeview** (CDP) Nassau County
3	13.4	**Fairview** (CDP) Westchester County
4	15.7	**Roosevelt** (CDP) Nassau County
5	16.7	**Hempstead** (village) Nassau County
6	18.6	**Wyandanch** (CDP) Suffolk County
7	19.2	**North Amityville** (CDP) Suffolk County
8	20.7	**Elmont** (CDP) Nassau County
9	21.0	**Bronx** (borough) Bronx County
10	22.0	**New Cassel** (CDP) Nassau County
11	22.2	**Hillcrest** (CDP) Rockland County
12	22.5	**Mount Vernon** (city) Westchester County
13	22.7	**Uniondale** (CDP) Nassau County
14	25.1	**Wheatley Heights** (CDP) Suffolk County
15	25.2	**North Valley Stream** (CDP) Nassau County
16	30.0	**Spring Valley** (village) Rockland County
17	30.6	**Inwood** (CDP) Nassau County
18	37.3	**Newburgh** (city) Orange County
19	38.0	**Stony Brook University** (CDP) Suffolk County
20	38.4	**North Bay Shore** (CDP) Suffolk County
21	39.3	**Freeport** (village) Nassau County
22	41.1	**Queens** (borough) Queens County
23	42.5	**Monticello** (village) Sullivan County
23	42.5	**South Valley Stream** (CDP) Nassau County
25	43.2	**Elmsford** (village) Westchester County
26	43.3	**New York** (city)
27	43.4	**Brooklyn** (borough) Kings County
28	43.6	**Poughkeepsie** (city) Dutchess County
29	44.8	**Gordon Heights** (CDP) Suffolk County
29	44.8	**Ossining** (village) Westchester County
31	45.1	**Rochester** (city) Monroe County
32	45.3	**Peekskill** (city) Westchester County
33	46.1	**Valley Stream** (village) Nassau County
34	46.2	**Middletown** (city) Orange County
35	46.4	**Haverstraw** (village) Rockland County
36	47.4	**Westbury** (village) Nassau County
37	48.3	**Manhasset Hills** (CDP) Nassau County
38	48.5	**Buffalo** (city) Erie County
38	48.5	**Port Chester** (village) Westchester County
40	48.9	**Dannemora** (village) Clinton County
41	49.0	**Baldwin** (CDP) Nassau County
42	50.1	**Garden City Park** (CDP) Nassau County
43	50.6	**Brentwood** (CDP) Suffolk County
44	50.8	**Central Islip** (CDP) Suffolk County
45	51.6	**Searingtown** (CDP) Nassau County
46	52.0	**Wappingers Falls** (village) Dutchess County
47	52.1	**Herricks** (CDP) Nassau County
48	52.5	**Bay Shore** (CDP) Suffolk County
49	52.6	**University Gardens** (CDP) Nassau County
50	53.3	**Harriman** (village) Orange County
51	53.6	**Lake Success** (village) Nassau County
52	53.9	**Riverside** (CDP) Suffolk County
53	54.8	**Mechanicstown** (CDP) Orange County
54	54.9	**Vails Gate** (CDP) Orange County
55	55.0	**Scotchtown** (CDP) Orange County
56	55.1	**Dannemora** (town) Clinton County
57	55.2	**Syracuse** (city) Onondaga County
58	55.5	**Albany** (city) Albany County
59	55.6	**West Haverstraw** (village) Rockland County
60	56.2	**University at Buffalo** (CDP) Erie County
61	56.4	**Manhattan** (borough) New York County
62	56.8	**Ossining** (town) Westchester County
63	56.9	**Haverstraw** (town) Rockland County
64	57.3	**Calcium** (CDP) Jefferson County
64	57.3	**Mount Ivy** (CDP) Rockland County
66	58.4	**Arlington** (CDP) Dutchess County
67	58.6	**Northeast Ithaca** (CDP) Tompkins County
67	58.6	**Yonkers** (city) Westchester County
69	59.2	**Baldwin Harbor** (CDP) Nassau County
69	59.2	**Mount Kisco** (town/village) Westchester County
71	59.4	**Bedford Hills** (CDP) Westchester County
72	59.9	**Hudson** (city) Columbia County
72	59.9	**Schenectady** (city) Schenectady County
74	60.3	**Chestnut Ridge** (village) Rockland County
74	60.3	**New Hyde Park** (village) Nassau County

State Rank	Percent	Place
76	60.6	**North New Hyde Park** (CDP) Nassau County
77	60.9	**Baywood** (CDP) Suffolk County
78	61.7	**Rye** (town) Westchester County
79	62.0	**White Plains** (city) Westchester County
80	62.2	**Sleepy Hollow** (village) Westchester County
81	62.4	**Binghamton University** (CDP) Broome County
81	62.4	**Glen Cove** (city) Nassau County
83	62.5	**Nanuet** (CDP) Rockland County
84	62.8	**East Farmingdale** (CDP) Suffolk County
85	63.6	**Jericho** (CDP) Nassau County
86	63.8	**New Rochelle** (city) Westchester County
87	64.0	**Wallkill** (town) Orange County
88	64.4	**Ellenville** (village) Ulster County
89	64.5	**Huntington Station** (CDP) Suffolk County
90	64.6	**Roslyn Heights** (CDP) Nassau County
91	65.2	**Hempstead** (town) Nassau County
92	65.3	**Thompson** (town) Sullivan County
93	65.4	**Utica** (city) Oneida County
94	65.8	**New Hempstead** (village) Rockland County
95	65.9	**Chester** (village) Orange County
96	66.0	**Old Westbury** (village) Nassau County
97	66.2	**Attica** (town) Wyoming County
98	66.5	**Romulus** (town) Seneca County
99	66.7	**Lansing** (village) Tompkins County
100	67.2	**Hartsdale** (CDP) Westchester County
101	67.7	**Beacon** (city) Dutchess County
101	67.7	**Highland Falls** (village) Orange County
103	67.9	**Balmville** (CDP) Orange County
103	67.9	**Fallsburg** (town) Sullivan County
105	68.0	**Pomona** (village) Rockland County
106	68.1	**Pelham** (village) Westchester County
107	68.2	**Greenburgh** (town) Westchester County
107	68.2	**Menands** (village) Albany County
109	68.3	**Riverhead** (CDP) Suffolk County
110	68.7	**South Fallsburg** (CDP) Sullivan County
111	68.8	**Hicksville** (CDP) Nassau County
111	68.8	**New Windsor** (town) Orange County
111	68.8	**North Bellport** (CDP) Suffolk County
114	68.9	**North Hempstead** (town) Nassau County
114	68.9	**Ramapo** (town) Rockland County
116	69.0	**Ardsley** (village) Westchester County
116	69.0	**Babylon** (town) Suffolk County
118	69.1	**Islandia** (village) Suffolk County
119	69.2	**Manorhaven** (village) Nassau County
120	69.3	**Fort Drum** (CDP) Jefferson County
120	69.3	**Le Ray** (town) Jefferson County
122	69.6	**Salamanca** (city) Cattaraugus County
123	69.7	**Fort Ann** (town) Washington County
123	69.7	**Muttontown** (village) Nassau County
125	69.8	**Ithaca** (city) Tompkins County
126	70.0	**Niagara Falls** (city) Niagara County
127	70.1	**New Windsor** (CDP) Orange County
128	70.2	**Groveland** (town) Livingston County
129	70.8	**Kingston** (city) Ulster County
130	70.9	**Cayuga Heights** (village) Tompkins County
131	71.2	**East Garden City** (CDP) Nassau County
131	71.2	**Greenlawn** (CDP) Suffolk County
131	71.2	**Mount Hope** (town) Orange County
134	71.3	**Clarkstown** (town) Rockland County
135	71.5	**Orange Lake** (CDP) Orange County
136	71.9	**Troy** (city) Rensselaer County
137	72.1	**Syosset** (CDP) Nassau County
138	72.4	**Albion** (town) Orleans County
139	72.6	**Tuckahoe** (village) Westchester County
140	72.7	**South Hempstead** (CDP) Nassau County
141	72.8	**Wawarsing** (town) Ulster County
141	72.8	**West Hempstead** (CDP) Nassau County
143	72.9	**Islip** (town) Suffolk County
144	73.0	**Deer Park** (CDP) Suffolk County
145	73.2	**Amityville** (village) Suffolk County
146	73.3	**Greenville** (CDP) Westchester County
146	73.3	**Nyack** (village) Rockland County
148	73.5	**Copiague** (CDP) Suffolk County
148	73.5	**Gang Mills** (CDP) Steuben County
150	73.6	**Ithaca** (town) Tompkins County

Note: *This section ranks incorporated places and CDPs (Census Designated Places) with populations of 2,500 or more. Unincorporated postal areas were not considered. Please refer to the User Guide for additional information.*

Black/African American Population

Top 150 Places Ranked in *Descending* Order

State Rank	Percent	Place	State Rank	Percent	Place
1	75.4	**Lakeview** (CDP) Nassau County	76	16.7	**Kingston** (city) Ulster County
2	65.3	**Mount Vernon** (city) Westchester County	76	16.7	**Southampton** (village) Suffolk County
3	64.5	**Wyandanch** (CDP) Suffolk County	78	16.6	**Haverstraw** (village) Rockland County
4	62.2	**Wheatley Heights** (CDP) Suffolk County	78	16.6	**Ramapo** (town) Rockland County
5	60.5	**Roosevelt** (CDP) Nassau County	80	16.5	**Babylon** (village) Suffolk County
6	59.8	**Fairview** (CDP) Westchester County	80	16.5	**East Garden City** (CDP) Nassau County
7	56.9	**Hillcrest** (CDP) Rockland County	82	16.2	**Malone** (town) Franklin County
8	54.9	**North Valley Stream** (CDP) Nassau County	83	16.1	**Maybrook** (village) Orange County
9	54.0	**North Amityville** (CDP) Suffolk County	84	16.0	**Haverstraw** (town) Rockland County
10	48.6	**Gordon Heights** (CDP) Suffolk County	84	16.0	**Troy** (city) Rensselaer County
11	48.2	**Hempstead** (village) Nassau County	86	15.8	**Cape Vincent** (town) Jefferson County
12	46.3	**Uniondale** (CDP) Nassau County	87	15.6	**Utica** (city) Oneida County
13	45.8	**Elmont** (CDP) Nassau County	88	15.4	**Pomona** (village) Rockland County
14	41.1	**Rochester** (city) Monroe County	89	15.3	**Brentwood** (CDP) Suffolk County
15	39.9	**Dannemora** (village) Clinton County	89	15.3	**Collins** (town) Erie County
15	39.9	**Spring Valley** (village) Rockland County	91	15.2	**Eggertsville** (CDP) Erie County
17	38.8	**New Cassel** (CDP) Nassau County	92	15.0	**Manhattan** (borough) New York County
18	37.3	**Buffalo** (city) Erie County	93	14.9	**Gardnertown** (CDP) Orange County
19	36.4	**Poughkeepsie** (city) Dutchess County	94	14.5	**Elmira** (city) Chemung County
20	35.6	**Monticello** (village) Sullivan County	95	14.4	**South Hempstead** (CDP) Nassau County
21	34.6	**Dannemora** (town) Clinton County	96	14.2	**New Hempstead** (village) Rockland County
22	33.9	**Riverside** (CDP) Suffolk County	97	14.1	**Tuckahoe** (village) Westchester County
23	33.5	**Brooklyn** (borough) Kings County	98	14.0	**Nanuet** (CDP) Rockland County
24	33.3	**Bronx** (borough) Bronx County	99	13.9	**Binghamton** (city) Broome County
25	33.2	**South Valley Stream** (CDP) Nassau County	99	13.9	**New Windsor** (town) Orange County
26	32.8	**Freeport** (village) Nassau County	101	13.8	**Highland Falls** (village) Orange County
27	31.7	**Baldwin** (CDP) Nassau County	101	13.8	**Montebello** (village) Rockland County
28	30.2	**Romulus** (town) Seneca County	103	13.7	**Fallsburg** (town) Sullivan County
29	29.9	**Albany** (city) Albany County	103	13.7	**Le Ray** (town) Jefferson County
30	29.3	**Syracuse** (city) Onondaga County	105	13.4	**Fort Drum** (CDP) Jefferson County
31	29.2	**Newburgh** (city) Orange County	105	13.4	**Greenburgh** (town) Westchester County
32	28.6	**Baldwin Harbor** (CDP) Nassau County	107	13.2	**East Farmingdale** (CDP) Suffolk County
33	28.0	**Attica** (town) Wyoming County	108	13.0	**Delhi** (village) Delaware County
34	25.9	**Mechanicstown** (CDP) Orange County	108	13.0	**Menands** (village) Albany County
35	25.2	**Scotchtown** (CDP) Orange County	110	12.8	**Albion** (village) Orleans County
36	24.6	**Central Islip** (CDP) Suffolk County	111	12.7	**Marcy** (town) Oneida County
37	24.5	**New York** (city)	112	12.6	**Deer Park** (CDP) Suffolk County
38	24.2	**Groveland** (town) Livingston County	112	12.6	**Ossining** (town) Westchester County
39	24.1	**Calcium** (CDP) Jefferson County	114	12.5	**Islandia** (village) Suffolk County
40	24.0	**Elmsford** (village) Westchester County	114	12.5	**Pelham** (village) Westchester County
41	23.9	**Chestnut Ridge** (village) Rockland County	116	12.3	**Fairview** (CDP) Dutchess County
42	23.4	**Inwood** (CDP) Nassau County	116	12.3	**Middle Island** (CDP) Suffolk County
43	23.0	**Niagara Falls** (city) Niagara County	116	12.3	**White Plains** (city) Westchester County
44	22.9	**Fort Ann** (town) Washington County	119	12.2	**Scottsville** (village) Monroe County
44	22.9	**Westbury** (village) Nassau County	120	12.0	**Wawarsing** (town) Ulster County
46	22.6	**Middletown** (city) Orange County	121	11.9	**South Nyack** (village) Rockland County
46	22.6	**North Bay Shore** (CDP) Suffolk County	122	11.8	**Brinckerhoff** (CDP) Dutchess County
48	22.0	**Bay Shore** (CDP) Suffolk County	123	11.7	**Geneva** (city) Ontario County
49	21.6	**Arlington** (CDP) Dutchess County	123	11.7	**New Windsor** (village) Orange County
50	21.5	**Catskill** (village) Greene County	123	11.7	**Wappingers Falls** (village) Dutchess County
51	21.2	**North Bellport** (CDP) Suffolk County	126	11.6	**Red Oaks Mill** (CDP) Dutchess County
51	21.2	**Schenectady** (city) Schenectady County	127	11.3	**Gates** (CDP) Monroe County
53	21.1	**Vails Gate** (CDP) Orange County	127	11.3	**Mastic Beach** (village) Suffolk County
54	21.0	**Peekskill** (city) Westchester County	127	11.3	**Poughkeepsie** (town) Dutchess County
55	20.6	**Hudson** (city) Columbia County	130	11.2	**North Elba** (town) Essex County
55	20.6	**Riverhead** (CDP) Suffolk County	130	11.2	**Wheatland** (town) Monroe County
55	20.6	**Valley Stream** (village) Nassau County	132	11.1	**Cheektowaga** (CDP) Erie County
58	20.5	**Thompson** (town) Sullivan County	132	11.1	**Ellenville** (village) Ulster County
59	19.7	**Albion** (town) Orleans County	132	11.1	**Port Jervis** (city) Orange County
59	19.7	**Beacon** (city) Dutchess County	135	11.0	**Orange Lake** (CDP) Orange County
61	19.6	**Harriman** (village) Orange County	136	10.9	**Watchtower** (CDP) Ulster County
62	18.7	**Mount Hope** (town) Orange County	137	10.8	**Fishkill** (town) Dutchess County
63	18.6	**New Rochelle** (city) Westchester County	137	10.8	**Lackawanna** (city) Erie County
64	18.5	**Baywood** (CDP) Suffolk County	139	10.7	**Balmville** (CDP) Orange County
64	18.5	**Chester** (village) Orange County	139	10.7	**Catskill** (town) Greene County
64	18.5	**Queens** (borough) Queens County	141	10.6	**SUNY Oswego** (CDP) Oswego County
67	18.1	**Coxsackie** (town) Greene County	142	10.5	**Beekman** (town) Dutchess County
68	17.9	**Wallkill** (town) Orange County	142	10.5	**Gates** (town) Monroe County
69	17.3	**Nyack** (village) Rockland County	142	10.5	**Staten Island** (borough) Richmond County
70	17.2	**Yonkers** (city) Westchester County	145	10.4	**West Babylon** (CDP) Suffolk County
71	17.1	**Mount Ivy** (CDP) Rockland County	146	10.3	**Manhasset** (CDP) Nassau County
71	17.1	**West Haverstraw** (village) Rockland County	147	10.1	**Coram** (CDP) Suffolk County
73	17.0	**Ossining** (village) Westchester County	147	10.1	**East Massapequa** (CDP) Nassau County
74	16.9	**Hempstead** (town) Nassau County	147	10.1	**Galeville** (CDP) Onondaga County
75	16.8	**Greenlawn** (CDP) Suffolk County	147	10.1	**Islip** (town) Suffolk County

Note: *This section ranks incorporated places and CDPs (Census Designated Places) with populations of 2,500 or more. Unincorporated postal areas were not considered. Please refer to the User Guide for additional information.*

Black/African American Population

Top 150 Places Ranked in *Ascending* Order

State Rank	Percent	Place
1	0.0	**Albertson** (CDP) Nassau County
1	0.0	**Attica** (village) Wyoming County
1	0.0	**Bainbridge** (town) Chenango County
1	0.0	**Bangor** (town) Franklin County
1	0.0	**Barker** (town) Broome County
1	0.0	**Bennington** (town) Wyoming County
1	0.0	**Bergen** (town) Genesee County
1	0.0	**Brewerton** (CDP) Onondaga County
1	0.0	**Brookfield** (town) Madison County
1	0.0	**Cedarhurst** (village) Nassau County
1	0.0	**Chittenango** (village) Madison County
1	0.0	**Clarkson** (CDP) Monroe County
1	0.0	**Conesus** (town) Livingston County
1	0.0	**Conesus Lake** (CDP) Livingston County
1	0.0	**Constantia** (town) Oswego County
1	0.0	**Cuba** (town) Allegany County
1	0.0	**East Norwich** (CDP) Nassau County
1	0.0	**Elbridge** (town) Onondaga County
1	0.0	**Elma** (town) Erie County
1	0.0	**Falconer** (village) Chautauqua County
1	0.0	**Firthcliffe** (CDP) Orange County
1	0.0	**Fort Edward** (village) Washington County
1	0.0	**Galway** (town) Saratoga County
1	0.0	**Great Neck Estates** (village) Nassau County
1	0.0	**Hartland** (town) Niagara County
1	0.0	**Hastings** (town) Oswego County
1	0.0	**Hector** (town) Schuyler County
1	0.0	**Holland** (town) Erie County
1	0.0	**Hornellsville** (town) Steuben County
1	0.0	**Kaser** (village) Rockland County
1	0.0	**Kiryas Joel** (village) Orange County
1	0.0	**Lake Erie Beach** (CDP) Erie County
1	0.0	**Lakeland** (CDP) Onondaga County
1	0.0	**Lancaster** (village) Erie County
1	0.0	**Lewiston** (village) Niagara County
1	0.0	**Lisbon** (town) Saint Lawrence County
1	0.0	**Lisle** (town) Broome County
1	0.0	**Louisville** (town) Saint Lawrence County
1	0.0	**Maine** (town) Broome County
1	0.0	**Manhasset Hills** (CDP) Nassau County
1	0.0	**Marilla** (town) Erie County
1	0.0	**Mayfield** (town) Fulton County
1	0.0	**Milton** (CDP) Saratoga County
1	0.0	**Minden** (town) Montgomery County
1	0.0	**Munsey Park** (village) Nassau County
1	0.0	**New Berlin** (town) Chenango County
1	0.0	**North Boston** (CDP) Erie County
1	0.0	**Otisco** (town) Onondaga County
1	0.0	**Owasco** (town) Cayuga County
1	0.0	**Palermo** (town) Oswego County
1	0.0	**Pendleton** (town) Niagara County
1	0.0	**Pittstown** (town) Rensselaer County
1	0.0	**Poestenkill** (town) Rensselaer County
1	0.0	**Richmond** (town) Ontario County
1	0.0	**Sardinia** (town) Erie County
1	0.0	**Schuyler Falls** (town) Clinton County
1	0.0	**Seaford** (CDP) Nassau County
1	0.0	**Sidney** (town) Delaware County
1	0.0	**Sidney** (village) Delaware County
1	0.0	**Skaneateles** (town) Onondaga County
1	0.0	**Southold** (CDP) Suffolk County
1	0.0	**Stephentown** (town) Rensselaer County
1	0.0	**Thornwood** (CDP) Westchester County
1	0.0	**Tioga** (town) Tioga County
1	0.0	**Trenton** (town) Oneida County
1	0.0	**Union Vale** (town) Dutchess County
1	0.0	**Victor** (village) Ontario County
1	0.0	**Vienna** (town) Oneida County
1	0.0	**Village Green** (CDP) Onondaga County
1	0.0	**Wales** (town) Erie County
1	0.0	**Wanakah** (CDP) Erie County
1	0.0	**West Bloomfield** (town) Ontario County
1	0.0	**White Creek** (town) Washington County
1	0.0	**Yorkshire** (town) Cattaraugus County
1	0.0	**Yorkville** (village) Oneida County
76	0.1	**Afton** (town) Chenango County
76	0.1	**Blue Point** (CDP) Suffolk County
76	0.1	**Boonville** (town) Oneida County
76	0.1	**Brutus** (town) Cayuga County
76	0.1	**Cohocton** (town) Steuben County
76	0.1	**Colden** (town) Erie County
76	0.1	**Eden** (CDP) Erie County
76	0.1	**Eden** (town) Erie County
76	0.1	**Elma Center** (CDP) Erie County
76	0.1	**Fairport** (village) Monroe County
76	0.1	**Greenwich** (town) Washington County
76	0.1	**Lake George** (town) Warren County
76	0.1	**Lido Beach** (CDP) Nassau County
76	0.1	**Madison** (town) Madison County
76	0.1	**New Haven** (town) Oswego County
76	0.1	**New Square** (village) Rockland County
76	0.1	**Northampton** (town) Fulton County
76	0.1	**Old Bethpage** (CDP) Nassau County
76	0.1	**Saint Regis Mohawk Reservation** (reservation) Franklin County
76	0.1	**Schuyler** (town) Herkimer County
76	0.1	**Shelter Island** (town) Suffolk County
76	0.1	**Skaneateles** (village) Onondaga County
76	0.1	**Sound Beach** (CDP) Suffolk County
76	0.1	**Ticonderoga** (CDP) Essex County
76	0.1	**Tupper Lake** (village) Franklin County
76	0.1	**Volney** (town) Oswego County
102	0.2	**Chester** (town) Warren County
102	0.2	**Cold Spring Harbor** (CDP) Suffolk County
102	0.2	**Cornwall-on-Hudson** (village) Orange County
102	0.2	**Cortlandville** (town) Cortland County
102	0.2	**Darien** (town) Genesee County
102	0.2	**Duanesburg** (town) Schenectady County
102	0.2	**East Hills** (village) Nassau County
102	0.2	**Fleming** (town) Cayuga County
102	0.2	**Kendall** (town) Orleans County
102	0.2	**Kirkwood** (town) Broome County
102	0.2	**Mahopac** (CDP) Putnam County
102	0.2	**Massena** (town) Saint Lawrence County
102	0.2	**Massena** (village) Saint Lawrence County
102	0.2	**Mohawk** (village) Herkimer County
102	0.2	**New Scotland** (town) Albany County
102	0.2	**Newark Valley** (town) Tioga County
102	0.2	**Newfane** (town) Niagara County
102	0.2	**Palmyra** (village) Wayne County
102	0.2	**Perry** (town) Wyoming County
102	0.2	**Pierrepont** (town) Saint Lawrence County
102	0.2	**Plainedge** (CDP) Nassau County
102	0.2	**Portville** (town) Cattaraugus County
102	0.2	**Randolph** (town) Cattaraugus County
102	0.2	**Sandy Creek** (town) Oswego County
102	0.2	**Seneca** (town) Ontario County
102	0.2	**Somerset** (town) Niagara County
102	0.2	**Theresa** (town) Jefferson County
102	0.2	**Veteran** (town) Chemung County
102	0.2	**Walton** (town) Delaware County
102	0.2	**West Sayville** (CDP) Suffolk County
102	0.2	**Westmoreland** (town) Oneida County
133	0.3	**Bayville** (village) Nassau County
133	0.3	**Carthage** (village) Jefferson County
133	0.3	**Champlain** (town) Clinton County
133	0.3	**Chesterfield** (town) Essex County
133	0.3	**Clarkson** (town) Monroe County
133	0.3	**Cornwall** (town) Orange County
133	0.3	**East Quogue** (CDP) Suffolk County
133	0.3	**Fenton** (town) Broome County
133	0.3	**Fulton** (city) Oswego County
133	0.3	**Grandyle Village** (CDP) Erie County
133	0.3	**Greenville** (town) Orange County
133	0.3	**Jay** (town) Essex County
133	0.3	**Laurens** (town) Otsego County
133	0.3	**Lima** (town) Livingston County
133	0.3	**Livonia** (town) Livingston County
133	0.3	**Lloyd Harbor** (village) Suffolk County
133	0.3	**Lowville** (village) Lewis County
133	0.3	**Massapequa Park** (village) Nassau County

Note: This section ranks incorporated places and CDPs (Census Designated Places) with populations of 2,500 or more. Unincorporated postal areas were not considered. Please refer to the User Guide for additional information.

Asian Population

Top 150 Places Ranked in *Descending* Order

State Rank	Percent	Place
1	44.0	**Searingtown** (CDP) Nassau County
2	43.5	**Stony Brook University** (CDP) Suffolk County
3	41.8	**Herricks** (CDP) Nassau County
4	40.6	**Manhasset Hills** (CDP) Nassau County
5	37.5	**Lake Success** (village) Nassau County
6	37.2	**University Gardens** (CDP) Nassau County
7	36.5	**Garden City Park** (CDP) Nassau County
8	32.6	**North New Hyde Park** (CDP) Nassau County
9	32.5	**Northeast Ithaca** (CDP) Tompkins County
10	31.6	**New Hyde Park** (village) Nassau County
11	31.5	**Jericho** (CDP) Nassau County
12	26.1	**Lansing** (village) Tompkins County
13	25.7	**University at Buffalo** (CDP) Erie County
14	24.8	**North Hills** (village) Nassau County
15	24.4	**Queens** (borough) Queens County
15	24.4	**Syosset** (CDP) Nassau County
15	24.4	**Thomaston** (village) Nassau County
18	22.9	**Binghamton University** (CDP) Broome County
19	22.7	**Albertson** (CDP) Nassau County
19	22.7	**Roslyn Heights** (CDP) Nassau County
21	22.3	**Muttontown** (village) Nassau County
22	21.5	**Hicksville** (CDP) Nassau County
23	20.1	**Cayuga Heights** (village) Tompkins County
24	19.8	**Greenville** (CDP) Westchester County
25	19.3	**Ardsley** (village) Westchester County
26	19.1	**Gang Mills** (CDP) Steuben County
27	18.9	**Hartsdale** (CDP) Westchester County
28	18.8	**Tappan** (CDP) Rockland County
29	18.2	**Old Westbury** (village) Nassau County
30	17.0	**Ithaca** (city) Tompkins County
31	16.6	**North Hempstead** (town) Nassau County
32	16.4	**Ithaca** (town) Tompkins County
32	16.4	**Manorhaven** (village) Nassau County
34	15.7	**Salisbury** (CDP) Nassau County
35	15.3	**South Valley Stream** (CDP) Nassau County
36	15.2	**Orangeburg** (CDP) Rockland County
37	14.3	**Elmont** (CDP) Nassau County
37	14.3	**Flower Hill** (village) Nassau County
37	14.3	**Nanuet** (CDP) Rockland County
37	14.3	**Valley Stream** (village) Nassau County
41	13.9	**Plainview** (CDP) Nassau County
42	13.6	**Scarsdale** (town/village) Westchester County
43	13.5	**New York** (city)
44	13.2	**Valley Cottage** (CDP) Rockland County
45	12.6	**Dix Hills** (CDP) Suffolk County
46	12.3	**Lansing** (town) Tompkins County
47	12.2	**Northwest Harbor** (CDP) Suffolk County
48	12.0	**Arlington** (CDP) Dutchess County
48	12.0	**Great Neck Plaza** (village) Nassau County
48	12.0	**North Valley Stream** (CDP) Nassau County
51	11.7	**Manhattan** (borough) New York County
52	11.6	**Vestal** (town) Broome County
53	11.5	**Brooklyn** (borough) Kings County
53	11.5	**Menands** (village) Albany County
53	11.5	**Williston Park** (village) Nassau County
56	11.4	**East Meadow** (CDP) Nassau County
56	11.4	**Westmere** (CDP) Albany County
58	11.3	**Clarkstown** (town) Rockland County
58	11.3	**Elwood** (CDP) Suffolk County
58	11.3	**New City** (CDP) Rockland County
61	11.2	**Brookville** (village) Nassau County
61	11.2	**Mineola** (village) Nassau County
61	11.2	**Myers Corner** (CDP) Dutchess County
64	11.1	**Carle Place** (CDP) Nassau County
65	11.0	**Briarcliff Manor** (village) Westchester County
65	11.0	**Vails Gate** (CDP) Orange County
67	10.9	**Congers** (CDP) Rockland County
67	10.9	**Stony Brook** (CDP) Suffolk County
69	10.8	**Brighton** (CDP) Monroe County
70	10.6	**East Williston** (village) Nassau County
70	10.6	**Erwin** (town) Steuben County
70	10.6	**Garden City South** (CDP) Nassau County
70	10.6	**Wappingers Falls** (village) Dutchess County
74	10.5	**Webster** (village) Monroe County
75	10.3	**Franklin Square** (CDP) Nassau County
75	10.3	**Oyster Bay** (town) Nassau County
77	10.2	**Bardonia** (CDP) Rockland County
78	10.1	**Manhasset** (CDP) Nassau County
79	10.0	**West Nyack** (CDP) Rockland County
80	9.9	**Utica** (city) Oneida County
81	9.8	**Irvington** (village) Westchester County
81	9.8	**Islandia** (village) Suffolk County
81	9.8	**Sands Point** (village) Nassau County
84	9.7	**Greenburgh** (town) Westchester County
84	9.7	**Roslyn** (village) Nassau County
86	9.6	**Woodbury** (CDP) Nassau County
87	9.5	**Great Neck Estates** (village) Nassau County
87	9.5	**North Great River** (CDP) Suffolk County
89	9.4	**Hewlett** (CDP) Nassau County
89	9.4	**Hillcrest** (CDP) Rockland County
91	9.3	**Elmsford** (village) Westchester County
92	9.1	**Great Neck** (village) Nassau County
93	9.0	**Farmingdale** (village) Nassau County
93	9.0	**Port Jefferson Station** (CDP) Suffolk County
93	9.0	**Spackenkill** (CDP) Dutchess County
96	8.9	**Pelham** (village) Westchester County
96	8.9	**Valhalla** (CDP) Westchester County
98	8.7	**Setauket-East Setauket** (CDP) Suffolk County
99	8.6	**Johnson City** (village) Broome County
100	8.5	**Galeville** (CDP) Onondaga County
100	8.5	**Orangetown** (town) Rockland County
100	8.5	**Piermont** (village) Rockland County
103	8.4	**Amherst** (town) Erie County
104	8.3	**Port Washington North** (village) Nassau County
105	8.1	**Eastchester** (CDP) Westchester County
106	8.0	**Staten Island** (borough) Richmond County
107	7.8	**Dobbs Ferry** (village) Westchester County
107	7.8	**New Paltz** (village) Ulster County
107	7.8	**Tuckahoe** (village) Westchester County
110	7.7	**Westbury** (village) Nassau County
111	7.6	**Eastchester** (town) Westchester County
111	7.6	**Niskayuna** (town) Schenectady County
111	7.6	**West Hempstead** (CDP) Nassau County
114	7.5	**Melville** (CDP) Suffolk County
114	7.5	**Pittsford** (town) Monroe County
116	7.4	**Deer Park** (CDP) Suffolk County
117	7.3	**Henrietta** (town) Monroe County
117	7.3	**Highland Falls** (village) Orange County
117	7.3	**Hudson** (city) Columbia County
117	7.3	**Pelham** (town) Westchester County
117	7.3	**South Huntington** (CDP) Suffolk County
122	7.2	**Colonie** (town) Albany County
122	7.2	**White Plains** (city) Westchester County
124	7.1	**Fishkill** (town) Dutchess County
124	7.1	**Guilderland** (town) Albany County
126	7.0	**Albany** (city) Albany County
126	7.0	**Harrison** (town/village) Westchester County
126	7.0	**New Castle** (town) Westchester County
126	7.0	**New Hempstead** (village) Rockland County
130	6.9	**Halfmoon** (town) Saratoga County
131	6.8	**Chester** (village) Orange County
131	6.8	**Wappinger** (town) Dutchess County
131	6.8	**Yonkers** (city) Westchester County
134	6.7	**East Garden City** (CDP) Nassau County
134	6.7	**Wheatley Heights** (CDP) Suffolk County
136	6.6	**Colonie** (village) Albany County
136	6.6	**Levittown** (CDP) Nassau County
136	6.6	**Pomona** (village) Rockland County
136	6.6	**Poughkeepsie** (town) Dutchess County
136	6.6	**Syracuse** (city) Onondaga County
141	6.5	**East Hills** (village) Nassau County
141	6.5	**Eggertsville** (CDP) Erie County
141	6.5	**North Bellmore** (CDP) Nassau County
144	6.4	**East Farmingdale** (CDP) Suffolk County
144	6.4	**Hamptonburgh** (town) Orange County
144	6.4	**Port Washington** (CDP) Nassau County
144	6.4	**South Nyack** (village) Rockland County
148	6.3	**Hamilton** (village) Madison County
148	6.3	**Pearl River** (CDP) Rockland County
150	6.2	**Coram** (CDP) Suffolk County

Note: *This section ranks incorporated places and CDPs (Census Designated Places) with populations of 2,500 or more. Unincorporated postal areas were not considered. Please refer to the User Guide for additional information.*

Asian Population

Top 150 Places Ranked in *Ascending* Order

State Rank	Percent	Place
1	0.0	**Alden** (village) Erie County
1	0.0	**Argyle** (town) Washington County
1	0.0	**Aurelius** (town) Cayuga County
1	0.0	**Bangor** (town) Franklin County
1	0.0	**Benton** (town) Yates County
1	0.0	**Blasdell** (village) Erie County
1	0.0	**Boston** (town) Erie County
1	0.0	**Brookfield** (town) Madison County
1	0.0	**Cambria** (town) Niagara County
1	0.0	**Campbell** (town) Steuben County
1	0.0	**Canastota** (village) Madison County
1	0.0	**Candor** (town) Tioga County
1	0.0	**Carroll** (town) Chautauqua County
1	0.0	**Catskill** (village) Greene County
1	0.0	**Charlton** (town) Saratoga County
1	0.0	**Chester** (town) Warren County
1	0.0	**Clarendon** (town) Orleans County
1	0.0	**Clayton** (town) Jefferson County
1	0.0	**Cohocton** (town) Steuben County
1	0.0	**Colesville** (town) Broome County
1	0.0	**Conesus** (town) Livingston County
1	0.0	**Conklin** (town) Broome County
1	0.0	**Croghan** (town) Lewis County
1	0.0	**Dannemora** (town) Clinton County
1	0.0	**Dannemora** (village) Clinton County
1	0.0	**Dansville** (village) Livingston County
1	0.0	**Darien** (town) Genesee County
1	0.0	**Dunkirk** (city) Chautauqua County
1	0.0	**East Bloomfield** (town) Ontario County
1	0.0	**East Hampton North** (CDP) Suffolk County
1	0.0	**East Syracuse** (village) Onondaga County
1	0.0	**Eden** (CDP) Erie County
1	0.0	**Eden** (town) Erie County
1	0.0	**Ellenville** (village) Ulster County
1	0.0	**Ellery** (town) Chautauqua County
1	0.0	**Ellisburg** (town) Jefferson County
1	0.0	**Enfield** (town) Tompkins County
1	0.0	**Fort Edward** (town) Washington County
1	0.0	**Fort Edward** (village) Washington County
1	0.0	**Galway** (town) Saratoga County
1	0.0	**Gardiner** (town) Ulster County
1	0.0	**Gouverneur** (town) Saint Lawrence County
1	0.0	**Granby** (town) Oswego County
1	0.0	**Greenwood Lake** (village) Orange County
1	0.0	**Guilford** (town) Chenango County
1	0.0	**Hanover** (town) Chautauqua County
1	0.0	**Haviland** (CDP) Dutchess County
1	0.0	**Holland** (town) Erie County
1	0.0	**Honeoye Falls** (village) Monroe County
1	0.0	**Hoosick** (town) Rensselaer County
1	0.0	**Hoosick Falls** (village) Rensselaer County
1	0.0	**Hopewell** (town) Ontario County
1	0.0	**Hudson Falls** (village) Washington County
1	0.0	**Kendall** (town) Orleans County
1	0.0	**Kingsbury** (town) Washington County
1	0.0	**Le Roy** (village) Genesee County
1	0.0	**Lisle** (town) Broome County
1	0.0	**Malone** (village) Franklin County
1	0.0	**Manchester** (town) Ontario County
1	0.0	**Manheim** (town) Herkimer County
1	0.0	**Marilla** (town) Erie County
1	0.0	**Mayfield** (town) Fulton County
1	0.0	**Middleburgh** (town) Schoharie County
1	0.0	**Minoa** (village) Onondaga County
1	0.0	**Mohawk** (village) Herkimer County
1	0.0	**Moira** (town) Franklin County
1	0.0	**Moriah** (town) Essex County
1	0.0	**Mount Morris** (village) Livingston County
1	0.0	**Neversink** (town) Sullivan County
1	0.0	**New Baltimore** (town) Greene County
1	0.0	**New Square** (village) Rockland County
1	0.0	**Newark Valley** (town) Tioga County
1	0.0	**Newfane** (CDP) Niagara County
1	0.0	**Newfane** (town) Niagara County
1	0.0	**Niagara** (town) Niagara County
1	0.0	**North Boston** (CDP) Erie County
1	0.0	**North Dansville** (town) Livingston County
1	0.0	**North Syracuse** (village) Onondaga County
1	0.0	**Northampton** (town) Fulton County
1	0.0	**Northumberland** (town) Saratoga County
1	0.0	**Norwich** (town) Chenango County
1	0.0	**Oneonta** (town) Otsego County
1	0.0	**Orchard Park** (village) Erie County
1	0.0	**Orleans** (town) Jefferson County
1	0.0	**Otisco** (town) Onondaga County
1	0.0	**Oxford** (town) Chenango County
1	0.0	**Palatine** (town) Montgomery County
1	0.0	**Palmyra** (village) Wayne County
1	0.0	**Pavilion** (town) Genesee County
1	0.0	**Pendleton** (town) Niagara County
1	0.0	**Perry** (town) Wyoming County
1	0.0	**Perry** (village) Wyoming County
1	0.0	**Pittstown** (town) Rensselaer County
1	0.0	**Poestenkill** (town) Rensselaer County
1	0.0	**Porter** (town) Niagara County
1	0.0	**Portville** (town) Cattaraugus County
1	0.0	**Richmond** (town) Ontario County
1	0.0	**Rose** (town) Wayne County
1	0.0	**Russia** (town) Herkimer County
1	0.0	**Saint Johnsville** (town) Montgomery County
1	0.0	**Sangerfield** (town) Oneida County
1	0.0	**Sardinia** (town) Erie County
1	0.0	**Saugerties** (village) Ulster County
1	0.0	**Schoharie** (town) Schoharie County
1	0.0	**Silver Creek** (village) Chautauqua County
1	0.0	**Sloan** (village) Erie County
1	0.0	**Somerset** (town) Niagara County
1	0.0	**Springs** (CDP) Suffolk County
1	0.0	**Springville** (village) Erie County
1	0.0	**Stanford** (town) Dutchess County
1	0.0	**Stockholm** (town) Saint Lawrence County
1	0.0	**Stockport** (town) Columbia County
1	0.0	**Unadilla** (town) Otsego County
1	0.0	**Verona** (town) Oneida County
1	0.0	**Vienna** (town) Oneida County
1	0.0	**Virgil** (town) Cortland County
1	0.0	**Volney** (town) Oswego County
1	0.0	**Walton** (town) Delaware County
1	0.0	**Walton** (village) Delaware County
1	0.0	**Warrensburg** (CDP) Warren County
1	0.0	**Warrensburg** (town) Warren County
1	0.0	**Warsaw** (town) Wyoming County
1	0.0	**Warsaw** (village) Wyoming County
1	0.0	**Warwick** (village) Orange County
1	0.0	**Waterloo** (town) Seneca County
1	0.0	**Waterloo** (village) Seneca County
1	0.0	**Wayland** (town) Steuben County
1	0.0	**Wellsville** (village) Allegany County
1	0.0	**West Monroe** (town) Oswego County
1	0.0	**Westfield** (town) Chautauqua County
1	0.0	**Westfield** (village) Chautauqua County
1	0.0	**Whitehall** (town) Washington County
1	0.0	**Whitehall** (village) Washington County
1	0.0	**Whitesboro** (village) Oneida County
1	0.0	**Wolcott** (town) Wayne County
136	0.1	**Alden** (town) Erie County
136	0.1	**Alexander** (town) Genesee County
136	0.1	**Altona** (town) Clinton County
136	0.1	**Amsterdam** (town) Montgomery County
136	0.1	**Barker** (town) Broome County
136	0.1	**Cape Vincent** (town) Jefferson County
136	0.1	**Carlton** (town) Orleans County
136	0.1	**Champlain** (town) Clinton County
136	0.1	**Denmark** (town) Lewis County
136	0.1	**East Aurora** (village) Erie County
136	0.1	**Elbridge** (town) Onondaga County
136	0.1	**Gouverneur** (village) Saint Lawrence County
136	0.1	**Groveland** (town) Livingston County
136	0.1	**Harrietstown** (town) Franklin County
136	0.1	**Hurley** (town) Ulster County

Note: *This section ranks incorporated places and CDPs (Census Designated Places) with populations of 2,500 or more. Unincorporated postal areas were not considered. Please refer to the User Guide for additional information.*

American Indian/Alaska Native Population

Top 150 Places Ranked in *Descending* Order

State Rank	Percent	Place	State Rank	Percent	Place
1	87.6	Saint Regis Mohawk Reservation (reservation) Franklin County	75	0.9	Beacon (city) Dutchess County
2	17.8	Salamanca (city) Cattaraugus County	75	0.9	Beekman (town) Dutchess County
3	6.2	Lakeview (CDP) Nassau County	75	0.9	Conesus (town) Livingston County
4	5.3	Louisville (town) Saint Lawrence County	75	0.9	Elbridge (town) Onondaga County
5	3.9	Southport (CDP) Chemung County	75	0.9	Geneva (city) Ontario County
6	3.8	Springs (CDP) Suffolk County	75	0.9	Greene (town) Chenango County
7	3.3	Gowanda (village) Cattaraugus County	75	0.9	Hastings (town) Oswego County
8	3.2	Wappingers Falls (village) Dutchess County	75	0.9	Manlius (village) Onondaga County
9	2.7	Mattituck (CDP) Suffolk County	75	0.9	North Bay Shore (CDP) Suffolk County
9	2.7	Southport (CDP) Chemung County	75	0.9	Pearl River (CDP) Rockland County
11	2.6	Ossining (village) Westchester County	75	0.9	Rochester (city) Monroe County
12	2.5	Fairview (CDP) Dutchess County	75	0.9	Solvay (village) Onondaga County
13	2.3	Fairview (CDP) Westchester County	75	0.9	Ulysses (town) Tompkins County
13	2.3	Scotchtown (CDP) Orange County	75	0.9	Wallkill (town) Orange County
15	2.2	Akron (village) Erie County	75	0.9	Wanakah (CDP) Erie County
15	2.2	Williston Park (village) Nassau County	91	0.8	Canton (village) Saint Lawrence County
17	2.1	Oneida (city) Madison County	91	0.8	Carmel (town) Putnam County
18	2.0	Freeport (village) Nassau County	91	0.8	Concord (town) Erie County
19	1.9	Floyd (town) Oneida County	91	0.8	Jamestown (city) Chautauqua County
20	1.8	Hanover (town) Chautauqua County	91	0.8	Lansing (village) Tompkins County
20	1.8	LaFayette (town) Onondaga County	91	0.8	Murray (town) Orleans County
22	1.7	Fort Drum (CDP) Jefferson County	91	0.8	North Bellmore (CDP) Nassau County
22	1.7	Galen (town) Wayne County	91	0.8	North Collins (town) Erie County
22	1.7	Ossining (town) Westchester County	91	0.8	North East (town) Dutchess County
25	1.6	Hartland (town) Niagara County	91	0.8	Olean (city) Cattaraugus County
25	1.6	Niagara (town) Niagara County	91	0.8	Red Hook (town) Dutchess County
27	1.5	Fenton (town) Broome County	91	0.8	Vernon (town) Oneida County
27	1.5	Great Neck Plaza (village) Nassau County	91	0.8	Wappinger (town) Dutchess County
27	1.5	Massena (town) Saint Lawrence County	91	0.8	Wellsville (town) Allegany County
27	1.5	Minisink (town) Orange County	105	0.7	Frankfort (village) Herkimer County
27	1.5	Springville (village) Erie County	105	0.7	Lake Carmel (CDP) Putnam County
32	1.4	Clarendon (town) Orleans County	105	0.7	Lisbon (town) Saint Lawrence County
32	1.4	Moira (town) Franklin County	105	0.7	Milton (town) Saratoga County
32	1.4	West Glens Falls (CDP) Warren County	105	0.7	Newstead (town) Erie County
32	1.4	Whitehall (town) Washington County	105	0.7	Potsdam (town) Saint Lawrence County
36	1.3	Cayuga Heights (village) Tompkins County	105	0.7	Potsdam (village) Saint Lawrence County
36	1.3	Mooers (town) Clinton County	105	0.7	Rye (town) Westchester County
36	1.3	Moriches (CDP) Suffolk County	105	0.7	Tonawanda (city) Erie County
36	1.3	Niagara Falls (city) Niagara County	105	0.7	Wyandanch (CDP) Suffolk County
36	1.3	North Syracuse (village) Onondaga County	115	0.6	Alfred (village) Allegany County
36	1.3	Richmond (town) Ontario County	115	0.6	Auburn (city) Cayuga County
36	1.3	Russia (town) Herkimer County	115	0.6	Bronx (borough) Bronx County
36	1.3	South Nyack (village) Rockland County	115	0.6	Conesus Lake (CDP) Livingston County
44	1.2	Collins (town) Erie County	115	0.6	East Meadow (CDP) Nassau County
44	1.2	Galway (town) Saratoga County	115	0.6	East Quogue (CDP) Suffolk County
44	1.2	Marcellus (town) Onondaga County	115	0.6	Ellisburg (town) Jefferson County
44	1.2	Norfolk (town) Saint Lawrence County	115	0.6	Elmira Heights (village) Chemung County
44	1.2	Porter (town) Niagara County	115	0.6	Geddes (town) Onondaga County
44	1.2	Riverhead (CDP) Suffolk County	115	0.6	Groton (village) Tompkins County
44	1.2	Romulus (town) Seneca County	115	0.6	Hancock (town) Delaware County
51	1.1	Attica (town) Wyoming County	115	0.6	Haverstraw (village) Rockland County
51	1.1	East Hampton (town) Suffolk County	115	0.6	Herricks (CDP) Nassau County
51	1.1	Greenwich (town) Washington County	115	0.6	Honeoye Falls (village) Monroe County
51	1.1	Kendall (town) Orleans County	115	0.6	Malone (town) Franklin County
51	1.1	Le Ray (town) Jefferson County	115	0.6	Middletown (city) Orange County
51	1.1	Lewiston (village) Niagara County	115	0.6	Middletown (town) Delaware County
51	1.1	Monroe (village) Orange County	115	0.6	Nanuet (CDP) Rockland County
51	1.1	Sleepy Hollow (village) Westchester County	115	0.6	Newark Valley (town) Tioga County
51	1.1	Syracuse (city) Onondaga County	115	0.6	Old Westbury (village) Nassau County
60	1.0	Blasdell (village) Erie County	115	0.6	Patchogue (village) Suffolk County
60	1.0	Carlton (town) Orleans County	115	0.6	Sheridan (town) Chautauqua County
60	1.0	Danby (town) Tompkins County	115	0.6	Silver Creek (village) Chautauqua County
60	1.0	Eaton (town) Madison County	115	0.6	Southold (town) Suffolk County
60	1.0	Heritage Hills (CDP) Westchester County	115	0.6	Village Green (CDP) Onondaga County
60	1.0	Massena (village) Saint Lawrence County	115	0.6	Watertown (town) Jefferson County
60	1.0	Mattydale (CDP) Onondaga County	115	0.6	Wayland (town) Steuben County
60	1.0	Newburgh (city) Orange County	115	0.6	West Hills (CDP) Suffolk County
60	1.0	Onondaga (town) Onondaga County	115	0.6	Westvale (CDP) Onondaga County
60	1.0	Port Chester (village) Westchester County	115	0.6	Williamson (town) Wayne County
60	1.0	Somerset (town) Niagara County	115	0.6	Yaphank (CDP) Suffolk County
60	1.0	Tully (town) Onondaga County	146	0.5	Albion (town) Orleans County
60	1.0	Volney (town) Oswego County	146	0.5	Alfred (town) Allegany County
60	1.0	Washington (town) Dutchess County	146	0.5	Batavia (town) Genesee County
60	1.0	White Plains (city) Westchester County	146	0.5	Brockport (village) Monroe County
75	0.9	Ballston Spa (village) Saratoga County	146	0.5	Cambria (town) Niagara County

Note: *This section ranks incorporated places and CDPs (Census Designated Places) with populations of 2,500 or more. Unincorporated postal areas were not considered. Please refer to the User Guide for additional information.*

Native Hawaiian/Other Pacific Islander Population

Top 150 Places Ranked in *Descending* Order

State Rank	Percent	Place
1	2.3	Fairview (CDP) Westchester County
2	1.9	Olive (town) Ulster County
3	1.6	Ilion (village) Herkimer County
4	1.5	Fort Drum (CDP) Jefferson County
5	1.3	Little Falls (city) Herkimer County
6	1.0	German Flatts (town) Herkimer County
6	1.0	Le Ray (town) Jefferson County
8	0.9	Royalton (town) Niagara County
9	0.8	Williamson (town) Wayne County
10	0.7	Riverhead (CDP) Suffolk County
11	0.6	Berne (town) Albany County
12	0.5	Canton (village) Saint Lawrence County
12	0.5	Montgomery (village) Orange County
12	0.5	Westbury (village) Nassau County
15	0.4	Cutchogue (CDP) Suffolk County
15	0.4	Oswegatchie (town) Saint Lawrence County
15	0.4	Shelby (town) Orleans County
18	0.3	Candor (town) Tioga County
18	0.3	Canton (town) Saint Lawrence County
18	0.3	Cobleskill (village) Schoharie County
18	0.3	Hudson (city) Columbia County
18	0.3	Lowville (village) Lewis County
18	0.3	Manorhaven (village) Nassau County
18	0.3	Mechanicstown (CDP) Orange County
18	0.3	Pomfret (town) Chautauqua County
18	0.3	Riverhead (town) Suffolk County
18	0.3	South Nyack (village) Rockland County
18	0.3	Watertown (town) Jefferson County
29	0.2	Briarcliff Manor (village) Westchester County
29	0.2	Canandaigua (city) Ontario County
29	0.2	Chautauqua (town) Chautauqua County
29	0.2	Clarence (town) Erie County
29	0.2	Cobleskill (town) Schoharie County
29	0.2	Dix Hills (CDP) Suffolk County
29	0.2	Holbrook (CDP) Suffolk County
29	0.2	Johnson City (village) Broome County
29	0.2	Lowville (town) Lewis County
29	0.2	Middletown (town) Delaware County
29	0.2	Newark (village) Wayne County
29	0.2	North Gates (CDP) Monroe County
29	0.2	North Valley Stream (CDP) Nassau County
29	0.2	Northampton (town) Fulton County
29	0.2	Potsdam (town) Saint Lawrence County
29	0.2	Potsdam (village) Saint Lawrence County
29	0.2	Rutland (town) Jefferson County
29	0.2	Sayville (CDP) Suffolk County
29	0.2	Seneca Falls (CDP) Seneca County
29	0.2	Triangle (town) Broome County
29	0.2	Watertown (city) Jefferson County
50	0.1	Albany (city) Albany County
50	0.1	Altona (town) Clinton County
50	0.1	Amsterdam (city) Montgomery County
50	0.1	Arcadia (town) Wayne County
50	0.1	Ballston (town) Saratoga County
50	0.1	Binghamton (city) Broome County
50	0.1	Camillus (town) Onondaga County
50	0.1	Canandaigua (town) Ontario County
50	0.1	Centereach (CDP) Suffolk County
50	0.1	Central Islip (CDP) Suffolk County
50	0.1	Champlain (town) Clinton County
50	0.1	Cheektowaga (CDP) Erie County
50	0.1	Cheektowaga (town) Erie County
50	0.1	Clifton Park (town) Saratoga County
50	0.1	Colonie (town) Albany County
50	0.1	East Northport (CDP) Suffolk County
50	0.1	East Patchogue (CDP) Suffolk County
50	0.1	Eaton (town) Madison County
50	0.1	Endwell (CDP) Broome County
50	0.1	Fishkill (town) Dutchess County
50	0.1	Fredonia (village) Chautauqua County
50	0.1	Gates (town) Monroe County
50	0.1	Glens Falls (city) Warren County
50	0.1	Gloversville (city) Fulton County
50	0.1	Greenburgh (town) Westchester County
50	0.1	Guilderland (town) Albany County
50	0.1	Jamestown (city) Chautauqua County
50	0.1	Jericho (CDP) Nassau County
50	0.1	Kings Point (village) Nassau County
50	0.1	Lima (town) Livingston County
50	0.1	Lysander (town) Onondaga County
50	0.1	Manhattan (borough) New York County
50	0.1	Maybrook (village) Orange County
50	0.1	Montgomery (town) Orange County
50	0.1	Murray (town) Orleans County
50	0.1	New Cassel (CDP) Nassau County
50	0.1	North Bellport (CDP) Suffolk County
50	0.1	North Hempstead (town) Nassau County
50	0.1	Oswego (city) Oswego County
50	0.1	Penfield (town) Monroe County
50	0.1	Port Chester (village) Westchester County
50	0.1	Poughkeepsie (town) Dutchess County
50	0.1	Seneca Falls (town) Seneca County
50	0.1	Somers (town) Westchester County
50	0.1	Southold (town) Suffolk County
50	0.1	Union (town) Broome County
50	0.1	Utica (city) Oneida County
50	0.1	Wallkill (town) Orange County
50	0.1	Wantagh (CDP) Nassau County
50	0.1	Westmoreland (town) Oneida County
50	0.1	Yates (town) Orleans County
101	0.0	Adams (town) Jefferson County
101	0.0	Addison (town) Steuben County
101	0.0	Afton (town) Chenango County
101	0.0	Airmont (village) Rockland County
101	0.0	Akron (village) Erie County
101	0.0	Albertson (CDP) Nassau County
101	0.0	Albion (town) Orleans County
101	0.0	Albion (village) Orleans County
101	0.0	Alden (town) Erie County
101	0.0	Alden (village) Erie County
101	0.0	Alexander (town) Genesee County
101	0.0	Alexandria (town) Jefferson County
101	0.0	Alfred (town) Allegany County
101	0.0	Alfred (village) Allegany County
101	0.0	Allegany (town) Cattaraugus County
101	0.0	Amenia (town) Dutchess County
101	0.0	Amherst (town) Erie County
101	0.0	Amityville (village) Suffolk County
101	0.0	Amsterdam (town) Montgomery County
101	0.0	Annsville (town) Oneida County
101	0.0	Arcade (town) Wyoming County
101	0.0	Ardsley (village) Westchester County
101	0.0	Argyle (town) Washington County
101	0.0	Arlington (CDP) Dutchess County
101	0.0	Armonk (CDP) Westchester County
101	0.0	Athens (town) Greene County
101	0.0	Attica (town) Wyoming County
101	0.0	Attica (village) Wyoming County
101	0.0	Au Sable (town) Clinton County
101	0.0	Auburn (city) Cayuga County
101	0.0	Aurelius (town) Cayuga County
101	0.0	Aurora (town) Erie County
101	0.0	Avon (town) Livingston County
101	0.0	Avon (village) Livingston County
101	0.0	Babylon (town) Suffolk County
101	0.0	Babylon (village) Suffolk County
101	0.0	Bainbridge (town) Chenango County
101	0.0	Baldwin (CDP) Nassau County
101	0.0	Baldwin Harbor (CDP) Nassau County
101	0.0	Baldwinsville (village) Onondaga County
101	0.0	Ballston Spa (village) Saratoga County
101	0.0	Balmville (CDP) Orange County
101	0.0	Bangor (town) Franklin County
101	0.0	Bardonia (CDP) Rockland County
101	0.0	Barker (town) Broome County
101	0.0	Barton (town) Tioga County
101	0.0	Batavia (city) Genesee County
101	0.0	Batavia (town) Genesee County
101	0.0	Bath (town) Steuben County
101	0.0	Bath (village) Steuben County

Note: This section ranks incorporated places and CDPs (Census Designated Places) with populations of 2,500 or more. Unincorporated postal areas were not considered. Please refer to the User Guide for additional information.

Two or More Races

Top 150 Places Ranked in *Descending* Order

State Rank	Percent	Place	State Rank	Percent	Place
1	13.4	**Uniondale** (CDP) Nassau County	72	4.8	**North Syracuse** (village) Onondaga County
2	12.6	**Monticello** (village) Sullivan County	72	4.8	**Pelham** (village) Westchester County
3	12.0	**Freeport** (village) Nassau County	72	4.8	**Randolph** (town) Cattaraugus County
4	11.9	**Roosevelt** (CDP) Nassau County	79	4.7	**Gardnertown** (CDP) Orange County
5	11.1	**Calcium** (CDP) Jefferson County	79	4.7	**Ithaca** (city) Tompkins County
5	11.1	**North Bay Shore** (CDP) Suffolk County	81	4.6	**Baldwinsville** (village) Onondaga County
7	10.8	**Ellenville** (village) Ulster County	81	4.6	**Briarcliff Manor** (village) Westchester County
8	10.3	**Hudson** (city) Columbia County	81	4.6	**Homer** (village) Cortland County
9	9.4	**Baldwin** (CDP) Nassau County	81	4.6	**Solvay** (village) Onondaga County
10	8.6	**Flanders** (CDP) Suffolk County	81	4.6	**Southport** (CDP) Chemung County
10	8.6	**Riverside** (CDP) Suffolk County	81	4.6	**Wappingers Falls** (village) Dutchess County
12	8.5	**Port Jervis** (city) Orange County	81	4.6	**West Bay Shore** (CDP) Suffolk County
13	8.4	**Balmville** (CDP) Orange County	81	4.6	**White Plains** (city) Westchester County
13	8.4	**Le Ray** (town) Jefferson County	89	4.5	**Larchmont** (village) Westchester County
15	8.1	**Greenwood Lake** (village) Orange County	89	4.5	**Rochester** (city) Monroe County
15	8.1	**Rensselaer** (city) Rensselaer County	89	4.5	**South Nyack** (village) Rockland County
17	8.0	**Kingston** (city) Ulster County	89	4.5	**Theresa** (town) Jefferson County
18	7.4	**Fort Drum** (CDP) Jefferson County	89	4.5	**Wallkill** (town) Orange County
19	7.3	**Enfield** (town) Tompkins County	89	4.5	**Watertown** (town) Jefferson County
20	7.1	**New Cassel** (CDP) Nassau County	95	4.4	**Chester** (village) Orange County
20	7.1	**Pamelia** (town) Jefferson County	95	4.4	**Putnam Lake** (CDP) Putnam County
22	7.0	**Fairview** (CDP) Westchester County	95	4.4	**South Blooming Grove** (village) Orange County
23	6.9	**Central Islip** (CDP) Suffolk County	95	4.4	**Stony Brook University** (CDP) Suffolk County
23	6.9	**Wawarsing** (town) Ulster County	99	4.3	**Geneseo** (village) Livingston County
25	6.7	**Troy** (city) Rensselaer County	99	4.3	**Mastic Beach** (village) Suffolk County
25	6.7	**West Point** (CDP) Orange County	99	4.3	**Moriches** (CDP) Suffolk County
27	6.6	**Salamanca** (city) Cattaraugus County	99	4.3	**Rutland** (town) Jefferson County
28	6.4	**Brentwood** (CDP) Suffolk County	99	4.3	**Watervliet** (city) Albany County
28	6.4	**Westbury** (village) Nassau County	104	4.2	**Croton-on-Hudson** (village) Westchester County
30	6.3	**Elmira** (city) Chemung County	104	4.2	**Lakeview** (CDP) Nassau County
30	6.3	**Greenport** (town) Columbia County	104	4.2	**Marbletown** (town) Ulster County
30	6.3	**Valhalla** (CDP) Westchester County	104	4.2	**SUNY Oswego** (CDP) Oswego County
33	6.1	**East Farmingdale** (CDP) Suffolk County	104	4.2	**Warwick** (town) Orange County
33	6.1	**East Greenbush** (CDP) Rensselaer County	104	4.2	**West Elmira** (CDP) Chemung County
33	6.1	**Mechanicstown** (CDP) Orange County	110	4.1	**Bethel** (town) Sullivan County
33	6.1	**New Windsor** (CDP) Orange County	110	4.1	**Brookhaven** (CDP) Suffolk County
37	6.0	**Poughkeepsie** (city) Dutchess County	110	4.1	**Cornwall** (town) Orange County
37	6.0	**Thompson** (town) Sullivan County	110	4.1	**Elmira** (town) Chemung County
39	5.9	**Crown Heights** (CDP) Dutchess County	110	4.1	**Hempstead** (town) Nassau County
39	5.9	**Highlands** (town) Orange County	110	4.1	**Hunter** (town) Greene County
39	5.9	**Inwood** (CDP) Nassau County	110	4.1	**Manhattan** (borough) New York County
39	5.9	**Maybrook** (village) Orange County	110	4.1	**Roslyn Heights** (CDP) Nassau County
39	5.9	**Wyandanch** (CDP) Suffolk County	110	4.1	**Scotchtown** (CDP) Orange County
44	5.7	**Lyncourt** (CDP) Onondaga County	110	4.1	**Watchtower** (CDP) Ulster County
44	5.7	**Mount Ivy** (CDP) Rockland County	120	4.0	**Catskill** (village) Greene County
44	5.7	**Rochester** (town) Ulster County	120	4.0	**Deerpark** (town) Orange County
44	5.7	**Sleepy Hollow** (village) Westchester County	120	4.0	**Gordon Heights** (CDP) Suffolk County
48	5.6	**Highland Falls** (village) Orange County	120	4.0	**Great Neck Plaza** (village) Nassau County
48	5.6	**West Hempstead** (CDP) Nassau County	120	4.0	**Lake Placid** (village) Essex County
50	5.5	**Beacon** (city) Dutchess County	120	4.0	**Mattydale** (CDP) Onondaga County
50	5.5	**Peekskill** (city) Westchester County	120	4.0	**Middletown** (city) Orange County
50	5.5	**Webster** (village) Monroe County	120	4.0	**Newburgh** (town) Orange County
53	5.4	**Elmont** (CDP) Nassau County	120	4.0	**Niagara Falls** (city) Niagara County
53	5.4	**Schenectady** (city) Schenectady County	120	4.0	**Nyack** (village) Rockland County
53	5.4	**South Fallsburg** (CDP) Sullivan County	130	3.9	**Amityville** (village) Suffolk County
53	5.4	**Syracuse** (city) Onondaga County	130	3.9	**Bergen** (town) Genesee County
57	5.3	**Catskill** (town) Greene County	130	3.9	**Brockport** (village) Monroe County
57	5.3	**Marcy** (town) Oneida County	130	3.9	**Delaware** (town) Sullivan County
59	5.2	**Cape Vincent** (town) Jefferson County	130	3.9	**Dover** (town) Dutchess County
59	5.2	**Florida** (village) Orange County	130	3.9	**Greenville** (CDP) Westchester County
61	5.1	**Baldwin Harbor** (CDP) Nassau County	130	3.9	**Hamilton** (town) Madison County
61	5.1	**Bay Shore** (CDP) Suffolk County	130	3.9	**Hempstead** (town) Nassau County
61	5.1	**Fallsburg** (town) Sullivan County	130	3.9	**Islip** (town) Suffolk County
61	5.1	**Waterloo** (village) Seneca County	130	3.9	**Lansing** (town) Tompkins County
61	5.1	**Watertown** (city) Jefferson County	130	3.9	**Manhasset Hills** (CDP) Nassau County
66	5.0	**Albany** (city) Albany County	130	3.9	**New Paltz** (village) Ulster County
66	5.0	**Amsterdam** (city) Montgomery County	130	3.9	**Otego** (town) Otsego County
66	5.0	**Avon** (village) Livingston County	130	3.9	**Pelham** (town) Westchester County
66	5.0	**Utica** (city) Oneida County	130	3.9	**Vails Gate** (CDP) Orange County
70	4.9	**Cohoes** (city) Albany County	130	3.9	**York** (town) Livingston County
70	4.9	**Hamilton** (village) Madison County	146	3.8	**Buffalo** (city) Erie County
72	4.8	**Calverton** (CDP) Suffolk County	146	3.8	**Cornwall-on-Hudson** (village) Orange County
72	4.8	**Goshen** (village) Orange County	146	3.8	**Liberty** (village) Sullivan County
72	4.8	**Gowanda** (village) Cattaraugus County	146	3.8	**Mamakating** (town) Sullivan County
72	4.8	**New Windsor** (town) Orange County	146	3.8	**New City** (CDP) Rockland County

Note: *This section ranks incorporated places and CDPs (Census Designated Places) with populations of 2,500 or more. Unincorporated postal areas were not considered. Please refer to the User Guide for additional information.*

Two or More Races

Top 150 Places Ranked in *Ascending* Order

State Rank	Percent	Place	State Rank	Percent	Place
1	0.0	**Alexander** (town) Genesee County	62	0.3	**Thomaston** (village) Nassau County
1	0.0	**Bedford Hills** (CDP) Westchester County	62	0.3	**Viola** (CDP) Rockland County
1	0.0	**Big Flats** (CDP) Chemung County	62	0.3	**Warrensburg** (CDP) Warren County
1	0.0	**Canisteo** (town) Steuben County	62	0.3	**Warrensburg** (town) Warren County
1	0.0	**Cutchogue** (CDP) Suffolk County	62	0.3	**Whitehall** (town) Washington County
1	0.0	**Durham** (town) Greene County	81	0.4	**Amsterdam** (town) Montgomery County
1	0.0	**Eden** (CDP) Erie County	81	0.4	**Barton** (town) Tioga County
1	0.0	**Eden** (town) Erie County	81	0.4	**Blue Point** (CDP) Suffolk County
1	0.0	**Elma** (town) Erie County	81	0.4	**Brookfield** (town) Madison County
1	0.0	**Elma Center** (CDP) Erie County	81	0.4	**Cairo** (town) Greene County
1	0.0	**Greenville** (town) Greene County	81	0.4	**Campbell** (town) Steuben County
1	0.0	**Heritage Hills** (CDP) Westchester County	81	0.4	**Cedarhurst** (village) Nassau County
1	0.0	**Horseheads North** (CDP) Chemung County	81	0.4	**Center Moriches** (CDP) Suffolk County
1	0.0	**Kiryas Joel** (village) Orange County	81	0.4	**Darien** (town) Genesee County
1	0.0	**Lake Luzerne** (town) Warren County	81	0.4	**East Hampton North** (CDP) Suffolk County
1	0.0	**Lakewood** (village) Chautauqua County	81	0.4	**Halesite** (CDP) Suffolk County
1	0.0	**Lawrence** (village) Nassau County	81	0.4	**Manheim** (town) Herkimer County
1	0.0	**Lewiston** (village) Niagara County	81	0.4	**Monsey** (CDP) Rockland County
1	0.0	**Lido Beach** (CDP) Nassau County	81	0.4	**Northampton** (town) Fulton County
1	0.0	**Marilla** (town) Erie County	81	0.4	**Oakfield** (town) Genesee County
1	0.0	**Milton** (CDP) Saratoga County	81	0.4	**Palermo** (town) Oswego County
1	0.0	**Mooers** (town) Clinton County	81	0.4	**Poestenkill** (town) Rensselaer County
1	0.0	**North Sea** (CDP) Suffolk County	81	0.4	**Royalton** (town) Niagara County
1	0.0	**Perry** (town) Wyoming County	81	0.4	**Rush** (town) Monroe County
1	0.0	**Pittstown** (town) Rensselaer County	81	0.4	**Skaneateles** (village) Onondaga County
1	0.0	**Schuyler** (town) Herkimer County	81	0.4	**Stephentown** (town) Rensselaer County
1	0.0	**Sherrill** (city) Oneida County	81	0.4	**Whitehall** (village) Washington County
1	0.0	**South Glens Falls** (village) Saratoga County	81	0.4	**Whitestown** (town) Oneida County
1	0.0	**Stockport** (town) Columbia County	104	0.5	**Aurelius** (town) Cayuga County
1	0.0	**Wanakah** (CDP) Erie County	104	0.5	**Batavia** (town) Genesee County
1	0.0	**West Glens Falls** (CDP) Warren County	104	0.5	**Boonville** (town) Oneida County
1	0.0	**Westerlo** (town) Albany County	104	0.5	**Cazenovia** (village) Madison County
1	0.0	**Westfield** (town) Chautauqua County	104	0.5	**Centerport** (CDP) Suffolk County
1	0.0	**Westfield** (village) Chautauqua County	104	0.5	**Croghan** (town) Lewis County
1	0.0	**Whitesboro** (village) Oneida County	104	0.5	**Dannemora** (village) Clinton County
36	0.1	**Boston** (town) Erie County	104	0.5	**East Rockaway** (village) Nassau County
36	0.1	**Chazy** (town) Clinton County	104	0.5	**Gates** (CDP) Monroe County
36	0.1	**Chester** (town) Warren County	104	0.5	**Ghent** (town) Columbia County
36	0.1	**Clayton** (town) Jefferson County	104	0.5	**Hewlett** (CDP) Nassau County
36	0.1	**Colesville** (town) Broome County	104	0.5	**Wappingers Falls** (village) Dutchess County
36	0.1	**Greenwich** (town) Washington County	104	0.5	**Marion** (town) Wayne County
36	0.1	**Haviland** (CDP) Dutchess County	104	0.5	**Marlboro** (CDP) Ulster County
36	0.1	**Locust Valley** (CDP) Nassau County	104	0.5	**Milford** (town) Otsego County
36	0.1	**Middleburgh** (town) Schoharie County	104	0.5	**Moira** (town) Franklin County
36	0.1	**Oswegatchie** (town) Saint Lawrence County	104	0.5	**Moreau** (town) Saratoga County
36	0.1	**Pound Ridge** (town) Westchester County	104	0.5	**Newfane** (CDP) Niagara County
36	0.1	**Stillwater** (town) Saratoga County	104	0.5	**North Dansville** (town) Livingston County
48	0.2	**Benton** (town) Yates County	104	0.5	**North Massapequa** (CDP) Nassau County
48	0.2	**Big Flats** (town) Chemung County	104	0.5	**Noyack** (CDP) Suffolk County
48	0.2	**Catlin** (town) Chemung County	104	0.5	**Owasco** (town) Cayuga County
48	0.2	**East Bloomfield** (town) Ontario County	104	0.5	**Pavilion** (town) Genesee County
48	0.2	**Fayetteville** (village) Onondaga County	104	0.5	**Perry** (village) Wyoming County
48	0.2	**Garden City South** (CDP) Nassau County	104	0.5	**Sand Lake** (town) Rensselaer County
48	0.2	**Gouverneur** (village) Saint Lawrence County	104	0.5	**Sangerfield** (town) Oneida County
48	0.2	**Kaser** (village) Rockland County	104	0.5	**Sardinia** (town) Erie County
48	0.2	**Lakeland** (CDP) Onondaga County	104	0.5	**Sound Beach** (CDP) Suffolk County
48	0.2	**Laurens** (town) Otsego County	104	0.5	**Springs** (CDP) Suffolk County
48	0.2	**Pendleton** (town) Niagara County	104	0.5	**Sterling** (town) Cayuga County
48	0.2	**Pierrepont** (town) Saint Lawrence County	104	0.5	**Ticonderoga** (town) Essex County
48	0.2	**Saranac** (town) Clinton County	104	0.5	**Vernon** (town) Oneida County
48	0.2	**Yorkville** (village) Oneida County	104	0.5	**Victor** (town) Ontario County
62	0.3	**Addison** (town) Steuben County	104	0.5	**West Bloomfield** (town) Ontario County
62	0.3	**Albion** (village) Orleans County	137	0.6	**Argyle** (town) Washington County
62	0.3	**Chenango Bridge** (CDP) Broome County	137	0.6	**Barker** (town) Broome County
62	0.3	**Conklin** (town) Broome County	137	0.6	**Bohemia** (CDP) Suffolk County
62	0.3	**East Moriches** (CDP) Suffolk County	137	0.6	**Callicoon** (town) Sullivan County
62	0.3	**Hancock** (town) Delaware County	137	0.6	**Cato** (town) Cayuga County
62	0.3	**Hawthorne** (CDP) Westchester County	137	0.6	**Chittenango** (village) Madison County
62	0.3	**North Boston** (CDP) Erie County	137	0.6	**Dannemora** (town) Clinton County
62	0.3	**North Great River** (CDP) Suffolk County	137	0.6	**Dansville** (village) Livingston County
62	0.3	**Orchard Park** (village) Erie County	137	0.6	**Davenport** (town) Delaware County
62	0.3	**Southampton** (village) Suffolk County	137	0.6	**East Islip** (CDP) Suffolk County
62	0.3	**Southold** (CDP) Suffolk County	137	0.6	**East Williston** (village) Nassau County
62	0.3	**Sullivan** (town) Madison County	137	0.6	**Fleming** (town) Cayuga County
62	0.3	**Tappan** (CDP) Rockland County	137	0.6	**Fort Salonga** (CDP) Suffolk County
			137	0.6	**Hamlin** (CDP) Monroe County

Note: *This section ranks incorporated places and CDPs (Census Designated Places) with populations of 2,500 or more. Unincorporated postal areas were not considered. Please refer to the User Guide for additional information.*

Hispanic Population

Top 150 Places Ranked in *Descending* Order

State Rank	Percent	Place
1	66.3	**Brentwood** (CDP) Suffolk County
2	64.6	**Haverstraw** (village) Rockland County
3	63.8	**Port Chester** (village) Westchester County
4	57.4	**North Bay Shore** (CDP) Suffolk County
5	54.6	**Bronx** (borough) Bronx County
6	52.2	**West Haverstraw** (village) Rockland County
7	51.7	**Newburgh** (city) Orange County
8	51.0	**Flanders** (CDP) Suffolk County
9	49.3	**Central Islip** (CDP) Suffolk County
10	48.8	**New Cassel** (CDP) Nassau County
11	48.1	**Sleepy Hollow** (village) Westchester County
12	47.5	**Ossining** (village) Westchester County
13	47.3	**Inwood** (CDP) Nassau County
14	46.8	**Bedford Hills** (CDP) Westchester County
15	44.9	**Mount Kisco** (town/village) Westchester County
16	44.8	**Haverstraw** (town) Rockland County
17	44.4	**Rye** (town) Westchester County
18	43.3	**Hempstead** (village) Nassau County
19	42.5	**Freeport** (village) Nassau County
20	39.8	**Uniondale** (CDP) Nassau County
21	38.4	**Middletown** (city) Orange County
22	37.7	**Huntington Station** (CDP) Suffolk County
23	36.9	**Peekskill** (city) Westchester County
24	36.8	**North Bellport** (CDP) Suffolk County
25	36.6	**North Amityville** (CDP) Suffolk County
26	36.4	**South Fallsburg** (CDP) Sullivan County
27	36.2	**Bay Shore** (CDP) Suffolk County
27	36.2	**Elmsford** (village) Westchester County
29	35.7	**Copiague** (CDP) Suffolk County
30	35.5	**Yonkers** (city) Westchester County
31	35.1	**Roosevelt** (CDP) Nassau County
32	34.4	**White Plains** (city) Westchester County
33	34.3	**Ossining** (town) Westchester County
34	32.9	**Ellenville** (village) Ulster County
35	32.8	**Patchogue** (village) Suffolk County
36	32.4	**Monticello** (village) Sullivan County
37	32.1	**Liberty** (village) Sullivan County
38	31.9	**Baywood** (CDP) Suffolk County
39	30.5	**Wappingers Falls** (village) Dutchess County
40	30.2	**Wyandanch** (CDP) Suffolk County
41	29.7	**Hampton Bays** (CDP) Suffolk County
42	29.6	**Mount Ivy** (CDP) Rockland County
43	29.5	**Islip** (town) Suffolk County
44	29.3	**Spring Valley** (village) Rockland County
44	29.3	**Valley Stream** (village) Nassau County
46	29.1	**Islandia** (village) Suffolk County
47	28.9	**Amsterdam** (city) Montgomery County
47	28.9	**New York** (city)
49	28.8	**Harriman** (village) Orange County
50	28.7	**New Windsor** (CDP) Orange County
51	28.3	**New Rochelle** (city) Westchester County
52	28.2	**Balmville** (CDP) Orange County
53	28.1	**Gordon Heights** (CDP) Suffolk County
54	27.9	**Queens** (borough) Queens County
55	27.8	**Glen Cove** (city) Nassau County
56	27.6	**Westbury** (village) Nassau County
57	26.8	**Manorhaven** (village) Nassau County
58	26.6	**Dunkirk** (city) Chautauqua County
59	26.5	**Island Park** (village) Nassau County
60	26.2	**East Hampton North** (CDP) Suffolk County
61	25.9	**Calcium** (CDP) Jefferson County
61	25.9	**Mechanicstown** (CDP) Orange County
63	25.8	**Manhattan** (borough) New York County
64	25.4	**Baldwin** (CDP) Nassau County
65	25.2	**Washingtonville** (village) Orange County
66	24.3	**Lake Mohegan** (CDP) Westchester County
67	24.2	**East Farmingdale** (CDP) Suffolk County
68	23.9	**Fallsburg** (town) Sullivan County
69	23.5	**North Patchogue** (CDP) Suffolk County
69	23.5	**Scotchtown** (CDP) Orange County
71	23.1	**Medford** (CDP) Suffolk County
71	23.1	**Noyack** (CDP) Suffolk County
73	22.7	**Thiells** (CDP) Rockland County
74	22.6	**Chester** (village) Orange County
75	22.5	**Tarrytown** (village) Westchester County
76	22.4	**Terryville** (CDP) Suffolk County
76	22.4	**Vails Gate** (CDP) Orange County
78	22.2	**Fairview** (CDP) Westchester County
78	22.2	**Orange Lake** (CDP) Orange County
80	22.0	**Liberty** (town) Sullivan County
81	21.7	**Thompson** (town) Sullivan County
82	21.6	**Wawarsing** (town) Ulster County
83	21.5	**Mastic** (CDP) Suffolk County
83	21.5	**Mineola** (village) Nassau County
83	21.5	**New Windsor** (town) Orange County
83	21.5	**Walden** (village) Orange County
83	21.5	**Wallkill** (town) Orange County
88	21.4	**East Patchogue** (CDP) Suffolk County
89	21.3	**Poughkeepsie** (city) Dutchess County
89	21.3	**Watchtower** (CDP) Ulster County
91	21.1	**Port Jefferson Station** (CDP) Suffolk County
92	21.0	**Elmont** (CDP) Nassau County
93	20.9	**Lakeview** (CDP) Nassau County
93	20.9	**Springs** (CDP) Suffolk County
95	20.6	**Mamaroneck** (village) Westchester County
95	20.6	**South Hempstead** (CDP) Nassau County
97	20.5	**Babylon** (town) Suffolk County
98	20.4	**Selden** (CDP) Suffolk County
99	20.2	**Riverhead** (CDP) Suffolk County
100	19.8	**West Hempstead** (CDP) Nassau County
101	19.7	**Beacon** (city) Dutchess County
102	19.6	**Brooklyn** (borough) Kings County
102	19.6	**Southampton** (town) Suffolk County
104	19.5	**Amityville** (village) Suffolk County
104	19.5	**North Lindenhurst** (CDP) Suffolk County
106	19.4	**North East** (town) Dutchess County
107	19.3	**Fort Drum** (CDP) Jefferson County
107	19.3	**Monroe** (village) Orange County
109	18.9	**East Massapequa** (CDP) Nassau County
109	18.9	**Hempstead** (town) Nassau County
109	18.9	**Mount Pleasant** (town) Westchester County
109	18.9	**Valhalla** (CDP) Westchester County
113	18.8	**Shirley** (CDP) Suffolk County
113	18.8	**Suffern** (village) Rockland County
113	18.8	**West Bay Shore** (CDP) Suffolk County
116	18.7	**Cedarhurst** (village) Nassau County
117	18.6	**Newburgh** (town) Orange County
118	18.5	**Dannemora** (village) Clinton County
118	18.5	**Stony Point** (CDP) Rockland County
120	18.4	**Montgomery** (village) Orange County
121	18.3	**Le Ray** (town) Jefferson County
122	18.2	**Lake Carmel** (CDP) Putnam County
123	18.0	**Chester** (town) Orange County
123	18.0	**South Blooming Grove** (village) Orange County
125	17.9	**Woodbury** (town) Orange County
126	17.8	**Staten Island** (borough) Richmond County
127	17.7	**Hillcrest** (CDP) Rockland County
128	17.6	**Blooming Grove** (town) Orange County
129	17.5	**Mastic Beach** (village) Suffolk County
130	17.4	**Rochester** (city) Monroe County
131	17.3	**Garden City Park** (CDP) Nassau County
131	17.3	**Harrison** (town/village) Westchester County
133	17.2	**New Hempstead** (village) Rockland County
134	17.0	**Islip** (CDP) Suffolk County
135	16.9	**Nyack** (village) Rockland County
135	16.9	**Woodbury** (village) Orange County
137	16.8	**Stony Point** (town) Rockland County
138	16.7	**Plattekill** (town) Ulster County
138	16.7	**Riverside** (CDP) Suffolk County
140	16.5	**Franklin Square** (CDP) Nassau County
140	16.5	**Maybrook** (village) Orange County
140	16.5	**Patterson** (town) Putnam County
143	16.4	**West Babylon** (CDP) Suffolk County
144	16.3	**Goshen** (village) Orange County
144	16.3	**Mount Morris** (town) Livingston County
146	16.2	**Cortlandt** (town) Westchester County
146	16.2	**Firthcliffe** (CDP) Orange County
146	16.2	**Southeast** (town) Putnam County
149	16.1	**Putnam Lake** (CDP) Putnam County
150	16.0	**Dannemora** (town) Clinton County

Note: *This section ranks incorporated places and CDPs (Census Designated Places) with populations of 2,500 or more. Unincorporated postal areas were not considered. Please refer to the User Guide for additional information.*

Hispanic Population

Top 150 Places Ranked in *Ascending* Order

State Rank	Percent	Place
1	0.0	**Argyle** (town) Washington County
1	0.0	**Aurelius** (town) Cayuga County
1	0.0	**Brookfield** (town) Madison County
1	0.0	**Canastota** (village) Madison County
1	0.0	**Colden** (town) Erie County
1	0.0	**Durham** (town) Greene County
1	0.0	**Elma Center** (CDP) Erie County
1	0.0	**Elmira** (town) Chemung County
1	0.0	**Elmira Heights** (village) Chemung County
1	0.0	**Fenton** (town) Broome County
1	0.0	**Gaines** (town) Orleans County
1	0.0	**Gowanda** (village) Cattaraugus County
1	0.0	**LaFayette** (town) Onondaga County
1	0.0	**Lowville** (village) Lewis County
1	0.0	**New Haven** (town) Oswego County
1	0.0	**New York Mills** (village) Oneida County
1	0.0	**Newfane** (CDP) Niagara County
1	0.0	**North Boston** (CDP) Erie County
1	0.0	**North Hills** (village) Nassau County
1	0.0	**Pavilion** (town) Genesee County
1	0.0	**Pendleton** (town) Niagara County
1	0.0	**Vienna** (town) Oneida County
1	0.0	**Village Green** (CDP) Onondaga County
1	0.0	**Wanakah** (CDP) Erie County
1	0.0	**West Elmira** (CDP) Chemung County
26	0.1	**Chester** (town) Warren County
26	0.1	**Lenox** (town) Madison County
26	0.1	**Maine** (town) Broome County
26	0.1	**Royalton** (town) Niagara County
26	0.1	**Saranac Lake** (village) Franklin County
26	0.1	**Tupper Lake** (village) Franklin County
26	0.1	**Veteran** (town) Chemung County
26	0.1	**Whitesboro** (village) Oneida County
34	0.2	**Alexander** (town) Genesee County
34	0.2	**Beekmantown** (town) Clinton County
34	0.2	**Cambria** (town) Niagara County
34	0.2	**Clayton** (town) Jefferson County
34	0.2	**Ellery** (town) Chautauqua County
34	0.2	**Kaser** (village) Rockland County
34	0.2	**Lowville** (town) Lewis County
34	0.2	**Otego** (town) Otsego County
34	0.2	**Palermo** (town) Oswego County
34	0.2	**Ticonderoga** (town) Essex County
34	0.2	**West Monroe** (town) Oswego County
45	0.3	**Cato** (town) Cayuga County
45	0.3	**Colesville** (town) Broome County
45	0.3	**Fayette** (town) Seneca County
45	0.3	**Lisbon** (town) Saint Lawrence County
45	0.3	**New Square** (village) Rockland County
45	0.3	**North Collins** (town) Erie County
45	0.3	**Oswegatchie** (town) Saint Lawrence County
45	0.3	**Owasco** (town) Cayuga County
45	0.3	**Shandaken** (town) Ulster County
54	0.4	**Benton** (town) Yates County
54	0.4	**Brewerton** (CDP) Onondaga County
54	0.4	**Chenango Bridge** (CDP) Broome County
54	0.4	**Elbridge** (town) Onondaga County
54	0.4	**Greenfield** (town) Saratoga County
54	0.4	**Jay** (town) Essex County
54	0.4	**Pittstown** (town) Rensselaer County
54	0.4	**Ticonderoga** (CDP) Essex County
54	0.4	**Verona** (town) Oneida County
54	0.4	**Wayland** (town) Steuben County
54	0.4	**West Sand Lake** (CDP) Rensselaer County
65	0.5	**Berne** (town) Albany County
65	0.5	**Chazy** (town) Clinton County
65	0.5	**Gouverneur** (village) Saint Lawrence County
65	0.5	**Harrietstown** (town) Franklin County
65	0.5	**Hastings** (town) Oswego County
65	0.5	**Livonia** (town) Livingston County
65	0.5	**Milford** (town) Otsego County
65	0.5	**Minden** (town) Montgomery County
65	0.5	**Newark Valley** (town) Tioga County
65	0.5	**Newstead** (town) Erie County
65	0.5	**Norfolk** (town) Saint Lawrence County
65	0.5	**Norwich** (town) Chenango County
65	0.5	**Nunda** (town) Livingston County
65	0.5	**Perry** (town) Wyoming County
65	0.5	**Poestenkill** (town) Rensselaer County
65	0.5	**Sterling** (town) Cayuga County
65	0.5	**Trenton** (town) Oneida County
65	0.5	**White Creek** (town) Washington County
83	0.6	**Charlton** (town) Saratoga County
83	0.6	**Deerfield** (town) Oneida County
83	0.6	**Newfane** (town) Niagara County
83	0.6	**Phelps** (town) Ontario County
83	0.6	**Sandy Creek** (town) Oswego County
83	0.6	**York** (town) Livingston County
89	0.7	**Attica** (village) Wyoming County
89	0.7	**Bangor** (town) Franklin County
89	0.7	**Barton** (town) Tioga County
89	0.7	**Champlain** (town) Clinton County
89	0.7	**Conklin** (town) Broome County
89	0.7	**Corning** (town) Steuben County
89	0.7	**Eden** (CDP) Erie County
89	0.7	**Elma** (town) Erie County
89	0.7	**Lake George** (town) Warren County
89	0.7	**Lancaster** (village) Erie County
89	0.7	**Massena** (village) Saint Lawrence County
89	0.7	**Perry** (village) Wyoming County
89	0.7	**Sangerfield** (town) Oneida County
89	0.7	**West Bloomfield** (town) Ontario County
89	0.7	**Whitehall** (town) Washington County
89	0.7	**Windsor** (town) Broome County
105	0.8	**Akron** (village) Erie County
105	0.8	**Caledonia** (town) Livingston County
105	0.8	**Davenport** (town) Delaware County
105	0.8	**Lawrence** (village) Nassau County
105	0.8	**Lisle** (town) Broome County
105	0.8	**Marion** (town) Wayne County
105	0.8	**Massena** (town) Saint Lawrence County
105	0.8	**Mexico** (town) Oswego County
105	0.8	**Northampton** (town) Fulton County
105	0.8	**Pompey** (town) Onondaga County
115	0.9	**Avon** (town) Livingston County
115	0.9	**Big Flats** (town) Chemung County
115	0.9	**Boonville** (town) Oneida County
115	0.9	**Boston** (town) Erie County
115	0.9	**Brunswick** (town) Rensselaer County
115	0.9	**Carroll** (town) Chautauqua County
115	0.9	**Centerport** (CDP) Suffolk County
115	0.9	**East Bloomfield** (town) Ontario County
115	0.9	**Granby** (town) Oswego County
115	0.9	**Greene** (town) Chenango County
115	0.9	**Hartland** (town) Niagara County
115	0.9	**Jerusalem** (town) Yates County
115	0.9	**Le Roy** (town) Genesee County
115	0.9	**Lewiston** (village) Niagara County
115	0.9	**Little Falls** (city) Herkimer County
115	0.9	**Milo** (town) Yates County
115	0.9	**Olean** (city) Cattaraugus County
115	0.9	**Saranac** (town) Clinton County
115	0.9	**Schodack** (town) Rensselaer County
115	0.9	**Stockholm** (town) Saint Lawrence County
115	0.9	**Tupper Lake** (town) Franklin County
115	0.9	**Waterloo** (village) Seneca County
115	0.9	**West Glens Falls** (CDP) Warren County
115	0.9	**Yates** (town) Orleans County
139	1.0	**Addison** (town) Steuben County
139	1.0	**Afton** (town) Chenango County
139	1.0	**Binghamton** (town) Broome County
139	1.0	**Galeville** (CDP) Onondaga County
139	1.0	**Gorham** (town) Ontario County
139	1.0	**Honeoye Falls** (village) Monroe County
139	1.0	**Knox** (town) Albany County
139	1.0	**Marilla** (town) Erie County
139	1.0	**Mooers** (town) Clinton County
139	1.0	**Moriah** (town) Essex County
139	1.0	**Sand Lake** (town) Rensselaer County
139	1.0	**Schoharie** (town) Schoharie County

Note: *This section ranks incorporated places and CDPs (Census Designated Places) with populations of 2,500 or more. Unincorporated postal areas were not considered. Please refer to the User Guide for additional information.*

Average Household Size

Top 150 Places Ranked in *Descending* Order

State Rank	Persons	Place
1	5.90	**New Square** (village) Rockland County
2	5.62	**Kiryas Joel** (village) Orange County
3	5.36	**Monsey** (CDP) Rockland County
4	5.20	**Kaser** (village) Rockland County
5	4.40	**New Hempstead** (village) Rockland County
6	4.37	**New Cassel** (CDP) Nassau County
7	4.36	**Brentwood** (CDP) Suffolk County
8	4.30	**North Bay Shore** (CDP) Suffolk County
9	4.29	**Lakeview** (CDP) Nassau County
10	4.11	**Uniondale** (CDP) Nassau County
11	3.99	**Monroe** (town) Orange County
12	3.94	**South Fallsburg** (CDP) Sullivan County
13	3.91	**West Point** (CDP) Orange County
14	3.83	**Roosevelt** (CDP) Nassau County
14	3.83	**Wyandanch** (CDP) Suffolk County
16	3.79	**Elmont** (CDP) Nassau County
17	3.78	**Viola** (CDP) Rockland County
18	3.74	**Ramapo** (town) Rockland County
19	3.72	**Spring Valley** (village) Rockland County
19	3.72	**Wesley Hills** (village) Rockland County
21	3.71	**Hillcrest** (CDP) Rockland County
22	3.68	**Wheatley Heights** (CDP) Suffolk County
23	3.65	**North Amityville** (CDP) Suffolk County
24	3.63	**Central Islip** (CDP) Suffolk County
25	3.45	**Gordon Heights** (CDP) Suffolk County
26	3.43	**North Valley Stream** (CDP) Nassau County
26	3.43	**West Haverstraw** (village) Rockland County
28	3.42	**Hempstead** (village) Nassau County
29	3.39	**Munsey Park** (village) Nassau County
30	3.38	**Lloyd Harbor** (village) Suffolk County
30	3.38	**Mastic** (CDP) Suffolk County
32	3.37	**Flanders** (CDP) Suffolk County
32	3.37	**Islandia** (village) Suffolk County
34	3.36	**Herricks** (CDP) Nassau County
34	3.36	**Inwood** (CDP) Nassau County
34	3.36	**Shirley** (CDP) Suffolk County
37	3.35	**Cedarhurst** (village) Nassau County
37	3.35	**Kings Point** (village) Nassau County
37	3.35	**Thiells** (CDP) Rockland County
40	3.32	**New Hyde Park** (village) Nassau County
40	3.32	**Pomona** (village) Rockland County
42	3.31	**Hamptonburgh** (town) Orange County
42	3.31	**Huntington Station** (CDP) Suffolk County
42	3.31	**Woodmere** (CDP) Nassau County
45	3.30	**Brookville** (village) Nassau County
45	3.30	**North Great River** (CDP) Suffolk County
45	3.30	**Roslyn Heights** (CDP) Nassau County
48	3.29	**Armonk** (CDP) Westchester County
48	3.29	**Centereach** (CDP) Suffolk County
48	3.29	**Farmingville** (CDP) Suffolk County
48	3.29	**Flower Hill** (village) Nassau County
48	3.29	**Terryville** (CDP) Suffolk County
53	3.28	**Islip** (town) Suffolk County
53	3.28	**Valley Stream** (village) Nassau County
55	3.27	**Searingtown** (CDP) Nassau County
56	3.26	**Old Westbury** (village) Nassau County
57	3.25	**Dix Hills** (CDP) Suffolk County
57	3.25	**North Bellport** (CDP) Suffolk County
59	3.24	**Franklin Square** (CDP) Nassau County
59	3.24	**Haverstraw** (village) Rockland County
59	3.24	**Lake Success** (village) Nassau County
59	3.24	**North New Hyde Park** (CDP) Nassau County
63	3.23	**Baywood** (CDP) Suffolk County
63	3.23	**Selden** (CDP) Suffolk County
63	3.23	**South Valley Stream** (CDP) Nassau County
66	3.22	**Pelham Manor** (village) Westchester County
66	3.22	**West Hempstead** (CDP) Nassau County
68	3.21	**Garden City Park** (CDP) Nassau County
68	3.21	**Monroe** (village) Orange County
68	3.21	**Pelham** (town) Westchester County
68	3.21	**Port Chester** (village) Westchester County
68	3.21	**Scarsdale** (town/village) Westchester County
73	3.20	**Freeport** (village) Nassau County
73	3.20	**Pelham** (village) Westchester County
73	3.20	**Wantagh** (CDP) Nassau County
73	3.20	**Woodbury** (town) Orange County
73	3.20	**Woodbury** (village) Orange County
78	3.19	**Garden City South** (CDP) Nassau County
79	3.18	**Duanesburg** (town) Schenectady County
79	3.18	**East Shoreham** (CDP) Suffolk County
79	3.18	**Newburgh** (city) Orange County
79	3.18	**Plainedge** (CDP) Nassau County
83	3.17	**Hicksville** (CDP) Nassau County
83	3.17	**Salisbury** (CDP) Nassau County
85	3.16	**Baldwin** (CDP) Nassau County
85	3.16	**North Merrick** (CDP) Nassau County
87	3.15	**Chestnut Ridge** (village) Rockland County
87	3.15	**Great Neck** (village) Nassau County
87	3.15	**Great Neck Estates** (village) Nassau County
87	3.15	**Muttontown** (village) Nassau County
87	3.15	**North Lindenhurst** (CDP) Suffolk County
87	3.15	**South Farmingdale** (CDP) Nassau County
93	3.14	**East Williston** (village) Nassau County
93	3.14	**Thornwood** (CDP) Westchester County
93	3.14	**Westbury** (village) Nassau County
96	3.13	**Center Moriches** (CDP) Suffolk County
96	3.13	**Haverstraw** (town) Rockland County
96	3.13	**Hempstead** (town) Nassau County
96	3.13	**Levittown** (CDP) Nassau County
96	3.13	**Massapequa** (CDP) Nassau County
96	3.13	**Medford** (CDP) Suffolk County
96	3.13	**Minisink** (town) Orange County
103	3.12	**Bay Shore** (CDP) Suffolk County
103	3.12	**North Castle** (town) Westchester County
105	3.11	**Airmont** (village) Rockland County
105	3.11	**East Farmingdale** (CDP) Suffolk County
105	3.11	**East Islip** (CDP) Suffolk County
105	3.11	**Greenville** (CDP) Westchester County
105	3.11	**Port Jefferson Station** (CDP) Suffolk County
110	3.10	**Baldwin Harbor** (CDP) Nassau County
110	3.10	**East Hills** (village) Nassau County
110	3.10	**Islip Terrace** (CDP) Suffolk County
113	3.09	**Elmsford** (village) Westchester County
113	3.09	**Greenlawn** (CDP) Suffolk County
113	3.09	**Massapequa Park** (village) Nassau County
113	3.09	**North Bellmore** (CDP) Nassau County
117	3.08	**Babylon** (town) Suffolk County
117	3.08	**Greenville** (town) Orange County
117	3.08	**Walden** (village) Orange County
117	3.08	**West Islip** (CDP) Suffolk County
121	3.07	**New Castle** (town) Westchester County
122	3.06	**East Fishkill** (town) Dutchess County
122	3.06	**South Hempstead** (CDP) Nassau County
122	3.06	**Stony Brook University** (CDP) Suffolk County
125	3.05	**Manhasset Hills** (CDP) Nassau County
125	3.05	**Mastic Beach** (village) Suffolk County
127	3.04	**Blauvelt** (CDP) Rockland County
127	3.04	**Syosset** (CDP) Nassau County
127	3.04	**West Babylon** (CDP) Suffolk County
130	3.03	**Elwood** (CDP) Suffolk County
130	3.03	**Holbrook** (CDP) Suffolk County
130	3.03	**Nesconset** (CDP) Suffolk County
133	3.02	**Copiague** (CDP) Suffolk County
133	3.02	**Lake Grove** (village) Suffolk County
133	3.02	**Montebello** (village) Rockland County
133	3.02	**New City** (CDP) Rockland County
133	3.02	**North Massapequa** (CDP) Nassau County
133	3.02	**Rye** (town) Westchester County
139	3.01	**Commack** (CDP) Suffolk County
139	3.01	**Congers** (CDP) Rockland County
139	3.01	**East Massapequa** (CDP) Nassau County
139	3.01	**Mount Hope** (town) Orange County
139	3.01	**Seaford** (CDP) Nassau County
139	3.01	**Sound Beach** (CDP) Suffolk County
139	3.01	**Stony Point** (CDP) Rockland County
139	3.01	**Valhalla** (CDP) Westchester County
139	3.01	**Wawayanda** (town) Orange County
148	3.00	**Deer Park** (CDP) Suffolk County
148	3.00	**Lindenhurst** (village) Suffolk County
148	3.00	**Manorville** (CDP) Suffolk County

Note: This section ranks incorporated places and CDPs (Census Designated Places) with populations of 2,500 or more. Unincorporated postal areas were not considered. Please refer to the User Guide for additional information.

Average Household Size

Top 150 Places Ranked in *Ascending* Order

State Rank	Persons	Place	State Rank	Persons	Place
1	1.76	**Heritage Hills** (CDP) Westchester County	71	2.19	**Johnstown** (city) Fulton County
2	1.83	**Great Neck Plaza** (village) Nassau County	71	2.19	**Skaneateles** (village) Onondaga County
3	1.91	**East Garden City** (CDP) Nassau County	71	2.19	**White Creek** (town) Washington County
4	1.92	**Village Green** (CDP) Onondaga County	79	2.20	**Delhi** (town) Delaware County
5	1.94	**Shandaken** (town) Ulster County	79	2.20	**Dickinson** (town) Broome County
6	1.95	**Lake Placid** (village) Essex County	79	2.20	**Ellery** (town) Chautauqua County
7	1.96	**Montauk** (CDP) Suffolk County	79	2.20	**Gowanda** (village) Cattaraugus County
8	1.97	**Williamsville** (village) Erie County	79	2.20	**Medina** (village) Orleans County
9	1.99	**Woodstock** (town) Ulster County	79	2.20	**Monticello** (village) Sullivan County
10	2.00	**Lansing** (village) Tompkins County	79	2.20	**Mount Morris** (village) Livingston County
11	2.02	**Piermont** (village) Rockland County	79	2.20	**Otsego** (town) Otsego County
12	2.03	**Cayuga Heights** (village) Tompkins County	87	2.21	**Amsterdam** (town) Montgomery County
12	2.03	**New York Mills** (village) Oneida County	87	2.21	**Ballston Spa** (village) Saratoga County
14	2.04	**Middletown** (town) Delaware County	87	2.21	**Cheektowaga** (CDP) Erie County
14	2.04	**Rhinebeck** (village) Dutchess County	87	2.21	**Dannemora** (village) Clinton County
16	2.05	**Hartsdale** (CDP) Westchester County	87	2.21	**Ithaca** (town) Tompkins County
16	2.05	**Potsdam** (village) Saint Lawrence County	87	2.21	**Johnson City** (village) Broome County
16	2.05	**South Glens Falls** (village) Saratoga County	87	2.21	**Lewiston** (village) Niagara County
19	2.06	**University at Buffalo** (CDP) Erie County	87	2.21	**Lowville** (village) Lewis County
20	2.08	**Bath** (village) Steuben County	87	2.21	**North Dansville** (town) Livingston County
20	2.08	**North Syracuse** (village) Onondaga County	87	2.21	**Owego** (village) Tioga County
22	2.09	**Cazenovia** (village) Madison County	87	2.21	**Southampton** (village) Suffolk County
22	2.09	**Conesus Lake** (CDP) Livingston County	87	2.21	**Walton** (town) Delaware County
22	2.09	**Manhattan** (borough) New York County	99	2.22	**Bath** (town) Steuben County
22	2.09	**New Paltz** (village) Ulster County	99	2.22	**Cheektowaga** (town) Erie County
22	2.09	**North Elba** (town) Essex County	99	2.22	**Cohoes** (city) Albany County
22	2.09	**Rhinebeck** (town) Dutchess County	99	2.22	**Glens Falls** (city) Warren County
28	2.10	**Delhi** (village) Delaware County	99	2.22	**Greenport** (town) Columbia County
28	2.10	**Fairport** (village) Monroe County	99	2.22	**Hector** (town) Schuyler County
28	2.10	**Geneva** (town) Ontario County	99	2.22	**Milford** (town) Otsego County
28	2.10	**Southport** (CDP) Chemung County	99	2.22	**New Berlin** (town) Chenango County
28	2.10	**Warsaw** (village) Wyoming County	99	2.22	**Roslyn** (village) Nassau County
33	2.11	**Herkimer** (village) Herkimer County	99	2.22	**Tupper Lake** (village) Franklin County
33	2.11	**Penn Yan** (village) Yates County	99	2.22	**Wellsville** (village) Allegany County
33	2.11	**Plattsburgh** (city) Clinton County	110	2.23	**Auburn** (city) Cayuga County
33	2.11	**Riverside** (CDP) Suffolk County	110	2.23	**Long Beach** (city) Nassau County
33	2.11	**Saratoga Springs** (city) Saratoga County	110	2.23	**Massena** (town) Saint Lawrence County
38	2.12	**Hornellsville** (town) Steuben County	110	2.23	**Milo** (town) Yates County
38	2.12	**Moriches** (CDP) Suffolk County	110	2.23	**Solvay** (village) Onondaga County
40	2.13	**Calverton** (CDP) Suffolk County	110	2.23	**Tonawanda** (town) Erie County
40	2.13	**Canandaigua** (city) Ontario County	116	2.24	**Batavia** (town) Genesee County
40	2.13	**Hudson** (city) Columbia County	116	2.24	**Callicoon** (town) Sullivan County
40	2.13	**Olive** (town) Ulster County	116	2.24	**Cobleskill** (village) Schoharie County
44	2.14	**Canton** (village) Saint Lawrence County	116	2.24	**East Syracuse** (village) Onondaga County
44	2.14	**Corning** (city) Steuben County	116	2.24	**Little Falls** (city) Herkimer County
44	2.14	**Nyack** (village) Rockland County	116	2.24	**Lyons** (village) Wayne County
47	2.15	**Honeoye Falls** (village) Monroe County	116	2.24	**Pomfret** (town) Chautauqua County
47	2.15	**North Hills** (village) Nassau County	116	2.24	**Rensselaer** (city) Rensselaer County
47	2.15	**Sidney** (town) Delaware County	116	2.24	**Salina** (town) Onondaga County
47	2.15	**Sloan** (village) Erie County	116	2.24	**South Lockport** (CDP) Niagara County
47	2.15	**Warsaw** (town) Wyoming County	116	2.24	**Southport** (town) Chemung County
47	2.15	**Watervliet** (city) Albany County	116	2.24	**Tonawanda** (CDP) Erie County
47	2.15	**Westmere** (CDP) Albany County	128	2.25	**Akron** (village) Erie County
47	2.15	**Whitesboro** (village) Oneida County	128	2.25	**Binghamton** (city) Broome County
55	2.16	**Alden** (village) Erie County	128	2.25	**Carlton** (town) Orleans County
55	2.16	**Alfred** (town) Allegany County	128	2.25	**Chautauqua** (town) Chautauqua County
55	2.16	**Brighton** (CDP) Monroe County	128	2.25	**Concord** (town) Erie County
55	2.16	**Saranac Lake** (village) Franklin County	128	2.25	**Dansville** (village) Livingston County
55	2.16	**Wellsville** (town) Allegany County	128	2.25	**Fayetteville** (village) Onondaga County
60	2.17	**Arlington** (CDP) Dutchess County	128	2.25	**Galeville** (CDP) Onondaga County
60	2.17	**Harrietstown** (town) Franklin County	128	2.25	**Highland** (CDP) Ulster County
60	2.17	**Highland Falls** (village) Orange County	128	2.25	**Hunter** (town) Greene County
60	2.17	**Horseheads** (village) Chemung County	128	2.25	**Lyncourt** (CDP) Onondaga County
60	2.17	**Kenmore** (village) Erie County	128	2.25	**North Tonawanda** (city) Niagara County
60	2.17	**Waverly** (village) Tioga County	128	2.25	**Seneca Falls** (town) Seneca County
66	2.18	**Fredonia** (village) Chautauqua County	128	2.25	**Vienna** (town) Oneida County
66	2.18	**Guilford** (town) Chenango County	142	2.26	**Canastota** (village) Madison County
66	2.18	**Lakewood** (village) Chautauqua County	142	2.26	**Cape Vincent** (town) Jefferson County
66	2.18	**Springville** (village) Erie County	142	2.26	**Ellicott** (town) Chautauqua County
66	2.18	**Tonawanda** (city) Erie County	142	2.26	**Kirkland** (town) Oneida County
71	2.19	**Albany** (city) Albany County	142	2.26	**Lackawanna** (city) Erie County
71	2.19	**Alfred** (village) Allegany County	142	2.26	**Ogdensburg** (city) Saint Lawrence County
71	2.19	**Dannemora** (town) Clinton County	142	2.26	**Olean** (city) Cattaraugus County
71	2.19	**Endicott** (village) Broome County	142	2.26	**Oneonta** (city) Otsego County
71	2.19	**Herkimer** (town) Herkimer County	142	2.26	**Saugerties** (village) Ulster County

Note: *This section ranks incorporated places and CDPs (Census Designated Places) with populations of 2,500 or more. Unincorporated postal areas were not considered. Please refer to the User Guide for additional information.*

Median Age

Top 150 Places Ranked in *Descending* Order

State Rank	Years	Place	State Rank	Years	Place
1	70.5	**Heritage Hills** (CDP) Westchester County	73	48.3	**North Dansville** (town) Livingston County
2	61.4	**North Hills** (village) Nassau County	73	48.3	**Shelter Island** (town) Suffolk County
3	58.2	**Shandaken** (town) Ulster County	73	48.3	**Southport** (CDP) Chemung County
4	56.5	**Woodstock** (town) Ulster County	73	48.3	**Wanakah** (CDP) Erie County
5	56.2	**Conesus Lake** (CDP) Livingston County	80	48.2	**Bennington** (town) Wyoming County
6	55.2	**Southampton** (village) Suffolk County	80	48.2	**Fairport** (village) Monroe County
7	54.6	**Southold** (CDP) Suffolk County	80	48.2	**Lakeland** (CDP) Onondaga County
8	54.4	**Montauk** (CDP) Suffolk County	80	48.2	**North Boston** (CDP) Erie County
9	54.3	**Calverton** (CDP) Suffolk County	80	48.2	**Otego** (town) Otsego County
10	54.1	**Hunter** (town) Greene County	85	48.1	**Kinderhook** (town) Columbia County
11	53.5	**Rhinebeck** (town) Dutchess County	85	48.1	**Sidney** (town) Delaware County
12	53.2	**Southold** (town) Suffolk County	87	48.0	**Berne** (town) Albany County
13	52.9	**Lido Beach** (CDP) Nassau County	87	48.0	**Florida** (town) Montgomery County
14	52.7	**Elma Center** (CDP) Erie County	87	48.0	**Union Vale** (town) Dutchess County
14	52.7	**New Berlin** (town) Chenango County	87	48.0	**Washington** (town) Dutchess County
16	52.5	**Skaneateles** (village) Onondaga County	91	47.9	**Canandaigua** (town) Ontario County
17	51.9	**Middletown** (town) Delaware County	91	47.9	**Carroll** (town) Chautauqua County
17	51.9	**Otsego** (town) Otsego County	91	47.9	**Copake** (town) Columbia County
19	51.6	**Cutchogue** (CDP) Suffolk County	91	47.9	**Danby** (town) Tompkins County
19	51.6	**Madison** (town) Madison County	91	47.9	**Greenville** (town) Greene County
21	51.5	**Great Neck Plaza** (village) Nassau County	91	47.9	**Hartsdale** (CDP) Westchester County
21	51.5	**Hurley** (town) Ulster County	91	47.9	**Niagara** (town) Niagara County
21	51.5	**Olive** (town) Ulster County	91	47.9	**Pound Ridge** (town) Westchester County
24	51.1	**Woodbury** (CDP) Nassau County	91	47.9	**Westerlo** (town) Albany County
25	51.0	**Richmond** (town) Ontario County	100	47.8	**Middleburgh** (town) Schoharie County
26	50.9	**Fleming** (town) Cayuga County	100	47.8	**West Hills** (CDP) Suffolk County
26	50.9	**Lake Success** (village) Nassau County	102	47.7	**Porter** (town) Niagara County
28	50.8	**Springs** (CDP) Suffolk County	103	47.6	**Montrose** (CDP) Westchester County
29	50.7	**Geneva** (town) Ontario County	103	47.6	**Valley Cottage** (CDP) Rockland County
29	50.7	**Piermont** (village) Rockland County	105	47.5	**Athens** (town) Greene County
29	50.7	**Schoharie** (town) Schoharie County	106	47.4	**Aurelius** (town) Cayuga County
29	50.7	**Williamsville** (village) Erie County	106	47.4	**Lakewood** (village) Chautauqua County
33	50.6	**Bardonia** (CDP) Rockland County	106	47.4	**Port Jefferson** (village) Suffolk County
33	50.6	**Elma** (town) Erie County	109	47.3	**Bethel** (town) Sullivan County
35	50.5	**Brookhaven** (CDP) Suffolk County	109	47.3	**Durham** (town) Greene County
35	50.5	**East Hampton** (town) Suffolk County	109	47.3	**Louisville** (town) Saint Lawrence County
35	50.5	**Oxford** (town) Chenango County	109	47.3	**New Hartford** (town) Oneida County
38	50.4	**Guilford** (town) Chenango County	109	47.3	**Searingtown** (CDP) Nassau County
38	50.4	**Lake George** (town) Warren County	109	47.3	**Somers** (town) Westchester County
40	50.3	**Amsterdam** (town) Montgomery County	115	47.2	**Batavia** (town) Genesee County
40	50.3	**North Sea** (CDP) Suffolk County	115	47.2	**Farmingdale** (village) Nassau County
42	50.2	**North Salem** (town) Westchester County	115	47.2	**Laurens** (town) Otsego County
43	50.1	**Callicoon** (town) Sullivan County	115	47.2	**Malverne** (village) Nassau County
44	49.9	**Galway** (town) Saratoga County	115	47.2	**Southport** (town) Chemung County
44	49.9	**Gorham** (town) Ontario County	120	47.1	**Chesterfield** (town) Essex County
44	49.9	**Rhinebeck** (village) Dutchess County	120	47.1	**Fort Salonga** (CDP) Suffolk County
47	49.8	**Carlton** (town) Orleans County	120	47.1	**Riga** (town) Monroe County
47	49.8	**Tioga** (town) Tioga County	120	47.1	**Stamford** (town) Delaware County
47	49.8	**Veteran** (town) Chemung County	120	47.1	**Ulster** (town) Ulster County
50	49.7	**Afton** (town) Chenango County	120	47.1	**West Elmira** (CDP) Chemung County
50	49.7	**Northwest Harbor** (CDP) Suffolk County	126	47.0	**Argyle** (town) Washington County
52	49.5	**Halesite** (CDP) Suffolk County	126	47.0	**Haviland** (CDP) Dutchess County
52	49.5	**Hurley** (CDP) Ulster County	126	47.0	**Island Park** (village) Nassau County
52	49.5	**Mattituck** (CDP) Suffolk County	126	47.0	**Marilla** (town) Erie County
55	49.4	**Ridge** (CDP) Suffolk County	130	46.9	**Sea Cliff** (village) Nassau County
55	49.4	**Skaneateles** (town) Onondaga County	130	46.9	**Village Green** (CDP) Onondaga County
57	49.1	**Melville** (CDP) Suffolk County	132	46.8	**Busti** (town) Chautauqua County
57	49.1	**Owasco** (town) Cayuga County	132	46.8	**Castile** (town) Wyoming County
57	49.1	**Sands Point** (village) Nassau County	132	46.8	**Davenport** (town) Delaware County
60	49.0	**Brinckerhoff** (CDP) Dutchess County	132	46.8	**Greenport** (town) Columbia County
60	49.0	**Ellery** (town) Chautauqua County	132	46.8	**Westmoreland** (town) Oneida County
62	48.8	**Brunswick** (town) Rensselaer County	137	46.7	**Charlton** (town) Saratoga County
62	48.8	**Muttontown** (village) Nassau County	137	46.7	**Port Ewen** (CDP) Ulster County
62	48.8	**Sangerfield** (town) Oneida County	137	46.7	**Wellsville** (town) Allegany County
65	48.6	**Eden** (town) Erie County	140	46.6	**Conesus** (town) Livingston County
65	48.6	**Northampton** (town) Fulton County	140	46.6	**Greenfield** (town) Saratoga County
65	48.6	**Sheridan** (town) Chautauqua County	140	46.6	**Mayfield** (town) Fulton County
65	48.6	**Westhampton** (CDP) Suffolk County	140	46.6	**Tuxedo** (town) Orange County
69	48.5	**Claverack** (town) Columbia County	144	46.5	**Concord** (town) Erie County
69	48.5	**Hornellsville** (town) Steuben County	144	46.5	**Eden** (CDP) Erie County
71	48.4	**Hector** (town) Schuyler County	144	46.5	**Manhasset Hills** (CDP) Nassau County
71	48.4	**Rush** (town) Monroe County	144	46.5	**Marcellus** (town) Onondaga County
73	48.3	**Ghent** (town) Columbia County	148	46.4	**Amityville** (village) Suffolk County
73	48.3	**Hancock** (town) Delaware County	148	46.4	**Bayville** (village) Nassau County
73	48.3	**Hartland** (town) Niagara County	148	46.4	**Elmira** (town) Chemung County

Note: This section ranks incorporated places and CDPs (Census Designated Places) with populations of 2,500 or more. Unincorporated postal areas were not considered. Please refer to the User Guide for additional information.

Median Age

Top 150 Places Ranked in *Ascending* Order

State Rank	Years	Place
1	12.9	**Kiryas Joel** (village) Orange County
2	14.1	**New Square** (village) Rockland County
3	14.2	**Kaser** (village) Rockland County
4	16.7	**Monsey** (CDP) Rockland County
5	19.6	**SUNY Oswego** (CDP) Oswego County
6	19.7	**Binghamton University** (CDP) Broome County
7	19.8	**University at Buffalo** (CDP) Erie County
8	20.0	**South Hill** (CDP) Tompkins County
9	20.2	**Alfred** (village) Allegany County
10	20.4	**Alfred** (town) Allegany County
11	20.6	**Delhi** (village) Delaware County
11	20.6	**Stony Brook University** (CDP) Suffolk County
13	20.8	**Geneseo** (village) Livingston County
13	20.8	**Oswego** (town) Oswego County
13	20.8	**West Point** (CDP) Orange County
16	21.1	**Hamilton** (village) Madison County
17	21.3	**Potsdam** (village) Saint Lawrence County
18	21.5	**New Paltz** (village) Ulster County
19	21.6	**Geneseo** (town) Livingston County
20	21.7	**Canton** (village) Saint Lawrence County
20	21.7	**Monroe** (town) Orange County
22	21.8	**Caneadea** (town) Allegany County
22	21.8	**Ithaca** (city) Tompkins County
22	21.8	**Oneonta** (city) Otsego County
25	21.9	**Brookville** (village) Nassau County
26	22.0	**Brockport** (village) Monroe County
27	22.2	**Fort Drum** (CDP) Jefferson County
27	22.2	**Hamilton** (town) Madison County
29	22.4	**East Garden City** (CDP) Nassau County
30	22.9	**Old Westbury** (village) Nassau County
31	23.1	**Highlands** (town) Orange County
32	23.4	**Le Ray** (town) Jefferson County
33	24.0	**Potsdam** (town) Saint Lawrence County
33	24.0	**South Fallsburg** (CDP) Sullivan County
35	24.4	**Eaton** (town) Madison County
36	24.7	**Delhi** (town) Delaware County
37	25.0	**Calcium** (CDP) Jefferson County
38	25.3	**Cobleskill** (village) Schoharie County
39	25.5	**Fredonia** (village) Chautauqua County
40	26.0	**New Paltz** (town) Ulster County
41	26.7	**Viola** (CDP) Rockland County
42	26.8	**Arlington** (CDP) Dutchess County
43	26.9	**Sweden** (town) Monroe County
44	27.2	**Ithaca** (town) Tompkins County
45	27.3	**Newburgh** (city) Orange County
46	27.5	**Cortland** (city) Cortland County
47	27.6	**Canton** (town) Saint Lawrence County
48	27.7	**Geneva** (city) Ontario County
49	28.4	**Ramapo** (town) Rockland County
50	28.6	**Fairview** (CDP) Dutchess County
50	28.6	**Wesley Hills** (village) Rockland County
52	28.8	**Spring Valley** (village) Rockland County
53	28.9	**Carthage** (village) Jefferson County
53	28.9	**Plattsburgh** (city) Clinton County
55	29.4	**Cedarhurst** (village) Nassau County
56	29.9	**Syracuse** (city) Onondaga County
57	30.3	**Wilna** (town) Jefferson County
58	30.5	**Vestal** (town) Broome County
59	30.6	**Troy** (city) Rensselaer County
59	30.6	**Watertown** (city) Jefferson County
61	30.8	**North Bellport** (CDP) Suffolk County
61	30.8	**Pomfret** (town) Chautauqua County
63	30.9	**New Hempstead** (village) Rockland County
64	31.0	**Rochester** (city) Monroe County
65	31.2	**Albany** (city) Albany County
66	31.5	**Attica** (village) Wyoming County
67	31.6	**Northeast Ithaca** (CDP) Tompkins County
67	31.6	**Saint Regis Mohawk Reservation** (reservation) Franklin County
69	31.7	**Cayuga Heights** (village) Tompkins County
69	31.7	**North Bay Shore** (CDP) Suffolk County
71	32.0	**New Cassel** (CDP) Nassau County
71	32.0	**Wyandanch** (CDP) Suffolk County
73	32.2	**Cobleskill** (town) Schoharie County
74	32.4	**Rutland** (town) Jefferson County
75	32.5	**Brentwood** (CDP) Suffolk County
76	32.7	**Gordon Heights** (CDP) Suffolk County
76	32.7	**North Amityville** (CDP) Suffolk County
78	32.8	**Watchtower** (CDP) Ulster County
79	33.0	**Brewerton** (CDP) Onondaga County
79	33.0	**New Bremen** (town) Lewis County
81	33.1	**Buffalo** (city) Erie County
81	33.1	**Elmira Heights** (village) Chemung County
83	33.2	**Bronx** (borough) Bronx County
83	33.2	**Haverstraw** (village) Rockland County
85	33.4	**Denmark** (town) Lewis County
85	33.4	**Elmira** (city) Chemung County
85	33.4	**Mount Ivy** (CDP) Rockland County
85	33.4	**Roosevelt** (CDP) Nassau County
89	33.6	**Central Islip** (CDP) Suffolk County
90	33.7	**Inwood** (CDP) Nassau County
91	33.8	**Catskill** (village) Greene County
91	33.8	**Oswego** (city) Oswego County
93	33.9	**Henrietta** (town) Monroe County
93	33.9	**Lansing** (village) Tompkins County
93	33.9	**Middletown** (city) Orange County
93	33.9	**Minoa** (village) Onondaga County
93	33.9	**West Haverstraw** (village) Rockland County
98	34.0	**East Farmingdale** (CDP) Suffolk County
98	34.0	**Menands** (village) Albany County
98	34.0	**Salamanca** (city) Cattaraugus County
98	34.0	**Utica** (city) Oneida County
102	34.1	**Bay Shore** (CDP) Suffolk County
102	34.1	**Walden** (village) Orange County
104	34.2	**Hempstead** (village) Nassau County
104	34.2	**Starkey** (town) Yates County
106	34.4	**Brooklyn** (borough) Kings County
106	34.4	**Uniondale** (CDP) Nassau County
106	34.4	**Whitehall** (village) Washington County
109	34.5	**Ellenville** (village) Ulster County
109	34.5	**Webster** (village) Monroe County
111	34.6	**Galen** (town) Wayne County
111	34.6	**Tupper Lake** (village) Franklin County
113	34.7	**Bangor** (town) Franklin County
114	34.8	**Bedford Hills** (CDP) Westchester County
114	34.8	**Flanders** (CDP) Suffolk County
116	35.0	**East Syracuse** (village) Onondaga County
116	35.0	**Lakeview** (CDP) Nassau County
118	35.1	**Patchogue** (village) Suffolk County
118	35.1	**Schenectady** (city) Schenectady County
120	35.2	**Norfolk** (town) Saint Lawrence County
120	35.2	**Norwich** (city) Chenango County
122	35.3	**Allegany** (town) Cattaraugus County
122	35.3	**Yorkville** (village) Oneida County
124	35.4	**Perry** (village) Wyoming County
125	35.5	**Canastota** (village) Madison County
125	35.5	**Fairview** (CDP) Westchester County
127	35.6	**Hamlin** (CDP) Monroe County
127	35.6	**Hounsfield** (town) Jefferson County
127	35.6	**Mastic** (CDP) Suffolk County
127	35.6	**Monroe** (village) Orange County
127	35.6	**Poughkeepsie** (town) Dutchess County
127	35.6	**Victor** (village) Ontario County
133	35.7	**Groveland** (town) Livingston County
133	35.7	**Wappingers Falls** (village) Dutchess County
135	35.8	**New York** (city)
135	35.8	**Romulus** (town) Seneca County
137	35.9	**Hornell** (city) Steuben County
137	35.9	**Mastic Beach** (village) Suffolk County
137	35.9	**Port Chester** (village) Westchester County
140	36.0	**Elmsford** (village) Westchester County
140	36.0	**Haverstraw** (town) Rockland County
140	36.0	**Hudson Falls** (village) Washington County
143	36.1	**Attica** (town) Wyoming County
143	36.1	**Harrison** (town/village) Westchester County
143	36.1	**Milton** (CDP) Saratoga County
146	36.2	**Adams** (town) Jefferson County
146	36.2	**Binghamton** (city) Broome County
146	36.2	**Harriman** (village) Orange County
146	36.2	**Monticello** (village) Sullivan County
146	36.2	**Ridgeway** (town) Orleans County

Note: This section ranks incorporated places and CDPs (Census Designated Places) with populations of 2,500 or more. Unincorporated postal areas were not considered. Please refer to the User Guide for additional information.

Population Under Age 18

Top 150 Places Ranked in *Descending* Order

State Rank	Percent	Place
1	61.2	**Kiryas Joel** (village) Orange County
2	60.9	**New Square** (village) Rockland County
3	57.8	**Kaser** (village) Rockland County
4	53.1	**Monsey** (CDP) Rockland County
5	44.1	**Monroe** (town) Orange County
6	43.4	**South Fallsburg** (CDP) Sullivan County
7	41.1	**Wesley Hills** (village) Rockland County
8	36.5	**Viola** (CDP) Rockland County
9	35.8	**Ramapo** (town) Rockland County
10	33.7	**Newburgh** (city) Orange County
11	33.3	**Spring Valley** (village) Rockland County
12	32.8	**Lloyd Harbor** (village) Suffolk County
13	32.7	**Armonk** (CDP) Westchester County
14	32.3	**Larchmont** (village) Westchester County
15	32.1	**Carthage** (village) Jefferson County
15	32.1	**New Hempstead** (village) Rockland County
15	32.1	**Scarsdale** (town/village) Westchester County
18	32.0	**Gordon Heights** (CDP) Suffolk County
18	32.0	**Wilna** (town) Jefferson County
20	31.9	**New Bremen** (town) Lewis County
21	31.6	**Woodmere** (CDP) Nassau County
22	31.5	**East Hills** (village) Nassau County
23	31.1	**Ellenville** (village) Ulster County
23	31.1	**Saint Regis Mohawk Reservation** (reservation) Franklin County
25	31.0	**Victor** (village) Ontario County
26	30.9	**Flower Hill** (village) Nassau County
26	30.9	**Fort Drum** (CDP) Jefferson County
28	30.8	**Rye** (city) Westchester County
29	30.7	**Munsey Park** (village) Nassau County
30	30.2	**Galen** (town) Wayne County
31	29.9	**Bedford Hills** (CDP) Westchester County
31	29.9	**North Bellport** (CDP) Suffolk County
33	29.6	**Great Neck** (village) Nassau County
34	29.5	**Bronxville** (village) Westchester County
34	29.5	**Minisink** (town) Orange County
34	29.5	**Salamanca** (city) Cattaraugus County
37	29.4	**Attica** (village) Wyoming County
37	29.4	**Greenville** (CDP) Westchester County
37	29.4	**North Castle** (town) Westchester County
40	29.1	**New Castle** (town) Westchester County
40	29.1	**Randolph** (town) Cattaraugus County
42	29.0	**Le Ray** (town) Jefferson County
42	29.0	**Richland** (town) Oswego County
44	28.9	**Pelham Manor** (village) Westchester County
44	28.9	**Scottsville** (village) Monroe County
46	28.8	**Cedarhurst** (village) Nassau County
46	28.8	**Inwood** (CDP) Nassau County
46	28.8	**Miller Place** (CDP) Suffolk County
46	28.8	**New Cassel** (CDP) Nassau County
46	28.8	**Starkey** (town) Yates County
51	28.7	**Great Neck Estates** (village) Nassau County
51	28.7	**North Bay Shore** (CDP) Suffolk County
53	28.6	**Farmington** (town) Ontario County
54	28.0	**Flanders** (CDP) Suffolk County
54	28.0	**Hounsfield** (town) Jefferson County
56	27.9	**Rutland** (town) Jefferson County
57	27.8	**Marlboro** (CDP) Ulster County
58	27.7	**Brewerton** (CDP) Onondaga County
58	27.7	**Pelham** (town) Westchester County
60	27.6	**Thomaston** (village) Nassau County
61	27.5	**Bainbridge** (town) Chenango County
61	27.5	**Calcium** (CDP) Jefferson County
63	27.4	**Candor** (town) Tioga County
64	27.2	**Mastic Beach** (village) Suffolk County
65	27.1	**Lawrence** (village) Nassau County
65	27.1	**Walworth** (town) Wayne County
67	27.0	**Huntington Station** (CDP) Suffolk County
68	26.9	**Croton-on-Hudson** (village) Westchester County
68	26.9	**Sidney** (village) Delaware County
68	26.9	**Silver Creek** (village) Chautauqua County
68	26.9	**West Nyack** (CDP) Rockland County
72	26.8	**Brookfield** (town) Madison County
72	26.8	**East Williston** (village) Nassau County
72	26.8	**Mamaroneck** (town) Westchester County
72	26.8	**Mendon** (town) Monroe County
76	26.7	**Irvington** (village) Westchester County
76	26.7	**Monroe** (village) Orange County
76	26.7	**New York Mills** (village) Oneida County
76	26.7	**Pelham** (village) Westchester County
76	26.7	**Wyandanch** (CDP) Suffolk County
81	26.6	**Annsville** (town) Oneida County
81	26.6	**Chittenango** (village) Madison County
81	26.6	**Clarkson** (CDP) Monroe County
84	26.5	**Bedford** (town) Westchester County
84	26.5	**Brentwood** (CDP) Suffolk County
84	26.5	**Manheim** (town) Herkimer County
84	26.5	**Mastic** (CDP) Suffolk County
84	26.5	**Roosevelt** (CDP) Nassau County
84	26.5	**Saint Johnsville** (town) Montgomery County
90	26.4	**Addison** (town) Steuben County
90	26.4	**Corinth** (village) Saratoga County
90	26.4	**East Shoreham** (CDP) Suffolk County
90	26.4	**Grandyle Village** (CDP) Erie County
90	26.4	**Hamlin** (town) Monroe County
95	26.3	**Manorville** (CDP) Suffolk County
96	26.2	**Mattydale** (CDP) Onondaga County
96	26.2	**Mount Sinai** (CDP) Suffolk County
96	26.2	**Stillwater** (town) Saratoga County
99	26.1	**Benton** (town) Yates County
99	26.1	**Cornwall** (town) Orange County
99	26.1	**Greenlawn** (CDP) Suffolk County
99	26.1	**Lakeview** (CDP) Nassau County
99	26.1	**Minden** (town) Montgomery County
99	26.1	**Ridgeway** (town) Orleans County
99	26.1	**Rocky Point** (CDP) Suffolk County
99	26.1	**South Hempstead** (CDP) Nassau County
99	26.1	**Theresa** (town) Jefferson County
99	26.1	**Walton** (village) Delaware County
99	26.1	**Woodbury** (town) Orange County
110	26.0	**Bangor** (town) Franklin County
110	26.0	**Elmira Heights** (village) Chemung County
110	26.0	**Norfolk** (town) Saint Lawrence County
110	26.0	**Verona** (town) Oneida County
110	26.0	**Victor** (town) Ontario County
110	26.0	**Whitehall** (village) Washington County
116	25.9	**Fallsburg** (town) Sullivan County
116	25.9	**Livonia** (town) Livingston County
116	25.9	**North Amityville** (CDP) Suffolk County
116	25.9	**Palatine** (town) Montgomery County
116	25.9	**Woodbury** (village) Orange County
121	25.8	**Camden** (town) Oneida County
121	25.8	**Hastings-on-Hudson** (village) Westchester County
121	25.8	**Manlius** (village) Onondaga County
121	25.8	**Sound Beach** (CDP) Suffolk County
125	25.7	**Bronx** (borough) Bronx County
125	25.7	**Central Islip** (CDP) Suffolk County
125	25.7	**Garden City** (village) Nassau County
125	25.7	**Kings Point** (village) Nassau County
125	25.7	**North Lindenhurst** (CDP) Suffolk County
125	25.7	**Roslyn Heights** (CDP) Nassau County
125	25.7	**Somerset** (town) Niagara County
125	25.7	**Syosset** (CDP) Nassau County
125	25.7	**West Glens Falls** (CDP) Warren County
125	25.7	**West Haverstraw** (village) Rockland County
135	25.6	**Clayton** (town) Jefferson County
135	25.6	**East Quogue** (CDP) Suffolk County
135	25.6	**Fulton** (city) Oswego County
135	25.6	**Norwich** (city) Chenango County
135	25.6	**Tupper Lake** (village) Franklin County
140	25.5	**Cohocton** (town) Steuben County
140	25.5	**Elwood** (CDP) Suffolk County
140	25.5	**Frankfort** (village) Herkimer County
140	25.5	**Utica** (city) Oneida County
140	25.5	**Walden** (village) Orange County
140	25.5	**Webster** (village) Monroe County
146	25.4	**Airmont** (village) Rockland County
146	25.4	**Fort Salonga** (CDP) Suffolk County
146	25.4	**Oswegatchie** (town) Saint Lawrence County
146	25.4	**Perry** (village) Wyoming County
146	25.4	**Saranac** (town) Clinton County

Note: *This section ranks incorporated places and CDPs (Census Designated Places) with populations of 2,500 or more. Unincorporated postal areas were not considered. Please refer to the User Guide for additional information.*

Population Under Age 18

Top 150 Places Ranked in *Ascending* Order

State Rank	Percent	Place
1	1.3	**University at Buffalo** (CDP) Erie County
2	1.4	**SUNY Oswego** (CDP) Oswego County
3	1.5	**Binghamton University** (CDP) Broome County
4	2.8	**Stony Brook University** (CDP) Suffolk County
5	3.0	**Watchtower** (CDP) Ulster County
6	4.2	**Riverside** (CDP) Suffolk County
7	4.5	**East Garden City** (CDP) Nassau County
8	5.0	**Dannemora** (town) Clinton County
9	5.2	**Alfred** (village) Allegany County
9	5.2	**Dannemora** (village) Clinton County
11	5.9	**Heritage Hills** (CDP) Westchester County
12	6.8	**South Hill** (CDP) Tompkins County
13	7.8	**Alfred** (town) Allegany County
14	7.9	**Potsdam** (village) Saint Lawrence County
15	8.1	**Geneseo** (village) Livingston County
15	8.1	**New Paltz** (village) Ulster County
17	8.9	**Ithaca** (city) Tompkins County
18	9.1	**Delhi** (village) Delaware County
18	9.1	**Groveland** (town) Livingston County
20	9.2	**Geneseo** (town) Livingston County
21	9.3	**Montauk** (CDP) Suffolk County
22	9.9	**Shandaken** (town) Ulster County
23	10.3	**Hamilton** (village) Madison County
24	10.4	**Canton** (village) Saint Lawrence County
24	10.4	**Cazenovia** (village) Madison County
26	10.7	**Delhi** (town) Delaware County
27	10.8	**Oneonta** (city) Otsego County
28	11.2	**Brockport** (village) Monroe County
29	11.4	**Romulus** (town) Seneca County
30	11.7	**Conesus Lake** (CDP) Livingston County
31	11.8	**Richmond** (town) Ontario County
32	12.1	**Collins** (town) Erie County
32	12.1	**Fort Ann** (town) Washington County
34	12.4	**Calverton** (CDP) Suffolk County
35	12.6	**Attica** (town) Wyoming County
36	12.7	**Oswego** (town) Oswego County
37	12.8	**Chautauqua** (town) Chautauqua County
37	12.8	**Madison** (town) Madison County
39	13.0	**Brinckerhoff** (CDP) Dutchess County
40	13.1	**Fredonia** (village) Chautauqua County
41	13.3	**New Paltz** (town) Ulster County
41	13.3	**North Elba** (town) Essex County
41	13.3	**Woodstock** (town) Ulster County
44	13.4	**Ithaca** (town) Tompkins County
44	13.4	**North Hills** (village) Nassau County
46	13.5	**Hector** (town) Schuyler County
47	13.8	**Cayuga Heights** (village) Tompkins County
47	13.8	**Great Neck Plaza** (village) Nassau County
47	13.8	**Middletown** (town) Delaware County
50	13.9	**Cape Vincent** (town) Jefferson County
50	13.9	**Wanakah** (CDP) Erie County
52	14.0	**Caneadea** (town) Allegany County
53	14.1	**Plattsburgh** (city) Clinton County
53	14.1	**Southampton** (village) Suffolk County
55	14.4	**Potsdam** (town) Saint Lawrence County
56	14.5	**Eaton** (town) Madison County
56	14.5	**Middleburgh** (town) Schoharie County
58	14.6	**Bethel** (town) Sullivan County
58	14.6	**Florida** (town) Montgomery County
58	14.6	**Manhattan** (borough) New York County
61	14.8	**Allegany** (town) Cattaraugus County
61	14.8	**Canton** (town) Saint Lawrence County
63	14.9	**Cobleskill** (village) Schoharie County
63	14.9	**Southold** (CDP) Suffolk County
65	15.0	**Elma Center** (CDP) Erie County
65	15.0	**Kirkland** (town) Oneida County
65	15.0	**Lake George** (town) Warren County
65	15.0	**Otsego** (town) Otsego County
65	15.0	**Village Green** (CDP) Onondaga County
65	15.0	**Williamsville** (village) Erie County
71	15.1	**Fairport** (village) Monroe County
71	15.1	**Guilford** (town) Chenango County
71	15.1	**Pomfret** (town) Chautauqua County
71	15.1	**Rhinebeck** (town) Dutchess County
75	15.2	**Amsterdam** (town) Montgomery County
76	15.3	**Sweden** (town) Monroe County
77	15.4	**Jerusalem** (town) Yates County
78	15.5	**Brunswick** (town) Rensselaer County
78	15.5	**Long Beach** (city) Nassau County
80	15.6	**Highland Falls** (village) Orange County
80	15.6	**Tioga** (town) Tioga County
82	15.7	**Davenport** (town) Delaware County
82	15.7	**New Berlin** (town) Chenango County
82	15.7	**Port Ewen** (CDP) Ulster County
85	15.8	**Stamford** (town) Delaware County
85	15.8	**Vestal** (town) Broome County
87	15.9	**Saratoga Springs** (city) Saratoga County
87	15.9	**Vails Gate** (CDP) Orange County
89	16.0	**Southold** (town) Suffolk County
90	16.1	**Danby** (town) Tompkins County
90	16.1	**Niagara** (town) Niagara County
92	16.2	**Island Park** (village) Nassau County
92	16.2	**Lakeland** (CDP) Onondaga County
92	16.2	**North Boston** (CDP) Erie County
92	16.2	**Piermont** (village) Rockland County
96	16.3	**Argyle** (town) Washington County
96	16.3	**Caroline** (town) Tompkins County
96	16.3	**Cortland** (city) Cortland County
96	16.3	**Otego** (town) Otsego County
96	16.3	**Stanford** (town) Dutchess County
101	16.4	**Carroll** (town) Chautauqua County
101	16.4	**Clarendon** (town) Orleans County
101	16.4	**Geneva** (town) Ontario County
101	16.4	**Hamilton** (town) Madison County
101	16.4	**Malone** (town) Franklin County
101	16.4	**New Baltimore** (town) Greene County
101	16.4	**North East** (town) Dutchess County
101	16.4	**Portland** (town) Chautauqua County
109	16.5	**Afton** (town) Chenango County
109	16.5	**Arlington** (CDP) Dutchess County
109	16.5	**Athens** (town) Greene County
109	16.5	**Cobleskill** (town) Schoharie County
109	16.5	**Elma** (town) Erie County
109	16.5	**Herkimer** (village) Herkimer County
109	16.5	**Lake Luzerne** (town) Warren County
109	16.5	**Olive** (town) Ulster County
117	16.6	**Marcy** (town) Oneida County
118	16.7	**Copake** (town) Columbia County
118	16.7	**Ghent** (town) Columbia County
118	16.7	**Roslyn** (village) Nassau County
118	16.7	**South Nyack** (village) Rockland County
122	16.8	**Albion** (town) Orleans County
122	16.8	**Enfield** (town) Tompkins County
122	16.8	**Hartsdale** (CDP) Westchester County
122	16.8	**Herkimer** (town) Herkimer County
126	16.9	**Dickinson** (town) Broome County
126	16.9	**Orangeburg** (CDP) Rockland County
126	16.9	**Oxford** (town) Chenango County
126	16.9	**Ulster** (town) Ulster County
130	17.0	**Cutchogue** (CDP) Suffolk County
130	17.0	**Gorham** (town) Ontario County
130	17.0	**Lewiston** (town) Niagara County
133	17.1	**Albany** (city) Albany County
133	17.1	**East Hampton** (town) Suffolk County
133	17.1	**Farmingdale** (village) Nassau County
133	17.1	**Livingston** (town) Columbia County
137	17.2	**Carlton** (town) Orleans County
137	17.2	**Coxsackie** (town) Greene County
137	17.2	**Tonawanda** (city) Erie County
140	17.3	**Bardonia** (CDP) Rockland County
140	17.3	**Durham** (town) Greene County
140	17.3	**North Sea** (CDP) Suffolk County
143	17.4	**Mount Hope** (town) Orange County
143	17.4	**Yorkville** (village) Oneida County
145	17.5	**Haviland** (CDP) Dutchess County
145	17.5	**Owego** (village) Tioga County
147	17.6	**Hurley** (town) Ulster County
148	17.7	**Old Westbury** (village) Nassau County
148	17.7	**Sangerfield** (town) Oneida County
150	17.8	**Alden** (town) Erie County

Note: *This section ranks incorporated places and CDPs (Census Designated Places) with populations of 2,500 or more. Unincorporated postal areas were not considered. Please refer to the User Guide for additional information.*

Population Age 65 and Over

Top 150 Places Ranked in *Descending* Order

State Rank	Percent	Place	State Rank	Percent	Place
1	66.7	**Heritage Hills** (CDP) Westchester County	76	22.0	**Claverack** (town) Columbia County
2	41.8	**North Hills** (village) Nassau County	76	22.0	**Wanakah** (CDP) Erie County
3	35.7	**Calverton** (CDP) Suffolk County	78	21.9	**Davenport** (town) Delaware County
4	32.3	**Southampton** (village) Suffolk County	78	21.9	**Fleming** (town) Cayuga County
5	31.5	**Lake Success** (village) Nassau County	78	21.9	**Milford** (town) Otsego County
6	31.3	**Great Neck Plaza** (village) Nassau County	78	21.9	**North Syracuse** (village) Onondaga County
6	31.3	**New Berlin** (town) Chenango County	78	21.9	**West Elmira** (CDP) Chemung County
8	30.1	**Southold** (CDP) Suffolk County	83	21.8	**Baldwinsville** (village) Onondaga County
9	29.7	**Woodstock** (town) Ulster County	83	21.8	**Lewiston** (town) Niagara County
10	29.5	**Rhinebeck** (town) Dutchess County	83	21.8	**Orleans** (town) Jefferson County
11	28.9	**Shelter Island** (town) Suffolk County	83	21.8	**Tuxedo** (town) Orange County
11	28.9	**Southold** (town) Suffolk County	87	21.7	**Copake** (town) Columbia County
13	28.3	**Ridge** (CDP) Suffolk County	87	21.7	**Greenport** (town) Columbia County
13	28.3	**Skaneateles** (village) Onondaga County	87	21.7	**Lakewood** (village) Chautauqua County
15	28.2	**Elma Center** (CDP) Erie County	87	21.7	**Port Jefferson** (village) Suffolk County
16	27.8	**Montauk** (CDP) Suffolk County	87	21.7	**Riverhead** (town) Suffolk County
17	27.6	**Hunter** (town) Greene County	92	21.6	**White Creek** (town) Washington County
17	27.6	**Woodbury** (CDP) Nassau County	93	21.5	**Bethel** (town) Sullivan County
19	27.4	**Roslyn** (village) Nassau County	93	21.5	**Cortlandville** (town) Cortland County
20	27.3	**Cutchogue** (CDP) Suffolk County	93	21.5	**Fairport** (village) Monroe County
21	27.2	**Conesus Lake** (CDP) Livingston County	93	21.5	**Guilford** (town) Chenango County
21	27.2	**Melville** (CDP) Suffolk County	93	21.5	**Laurens** (town) Otsego County
23	27.1	**Rhinebeck** (village) Dutchess County	93	21.5	**Schuyler** (town) Herkimer County
24	26.8	**Orangeburg** (CDP) Rockland County	93	21.5	**West Bay Shore** (CDP) Suffolk County
24	26.8	**Shandaken** (town) Ulster County	100	21.4	**Castile** (town) Wyoming County
26	26.6	**Lido Beach** (CDP) Nassau County	100	21.4	**Herkimer** (village) Herkimer County
27	26.4	**Westhampton** (CDP) Suffolk County	102	21.3	**Canandaigua** (town) Ontario County
28	26.2	**North Boston** (CDP) Erie County	102	21.3	**Chatham** (town) Columbia County
29	26.1	**Geneva** (town) Ontario County	102	21.3	**Stamford** (town) Delaware County
30	25.9	**Port Washington North** (village) Nassau County	102	21.3	**Ulster** (town) Ulster County
31	25.6	**North Sea** (CDP) Suffolk County	106	21.2	**Glens Falls North** (CDP) Warren County
32	25.5	**Schoharie** (town) Schoharie County	106	21.2	**Lewiston** (village) Niagara County
33	25.1	**Bardonia** (CDP) Rockland County	106	21.2	**Tioga** (town) Tioga County
33	25.1	**New Hartford** (town) Oneida County	109	21.1	**Herkimer** (town) Herkimer County
35	25.0	**Warwick** (village) Orange County	109	21.1	**Livingston** (town) Columbia County
36	24.9	**Afton** (town) Chenango County	109	21.1	**Mount Morris** (town) Livingston County
37	24.7	**Manhasset Hills** (CDP) Nassau County	109	21.1	**Tappan** (CDP) Rockland County
38	24.5	**Otsego** (town) Otsego County	109	21.1	**Walton** (village) Delaware County
39	24.4	**Clarence** (CDP) Erie County	109	21.1	**Washington** (town) Dutchess County
39	24.4	**Hornellsville** (town) Steuben County	109	21.1	**Wellsville** (town) Allegany County
41	24.3	**Galeville** (CDP) Onondaga County	109	21.1	**Westfield** (village) Chautauqua County
41	24.3	**Hartsdale** (CDP) Westchester County	117	21.0	**Brookhaven** (CDP) Suffolk County
41	24.3	**New York Mills** (village) Oneida County	117	21.0	**Rye Brook** (village) Westchester County
44	24.1	**Horseheads** (village) Chemung County	119	20.9	**Durham** (town) Greene County
44	24.1	**Williamsville** (village) Erie County	119	20.9	**Madison** (town) Madison County
46	24.0	**Ellery** (town) Chautauqua County	121	20.8	**Greenville** (town) Greene County
46	24.0	**Piermont** (village) Rockland County	122	20.7	**Bath** (village) Steuben County
48	23.9	**Amsterdam** (town) Montgomery County	122	20.7	**East Garden City** (CDP) Nassau County
48	23.9	**Benton** (town) Yates County	124	20.6	**Gates** (CDP) Monroe County
48	23.9	**Callicoon** (town) Sullivan County	124	20.6	**Gorham** (town) Ontario County
48	23.9	**Somers** (town) Westchester County	124	20.6	**Horseheads** (town) Chemung County
52	23.8	**East Hampton** (town) Suffolk County	124	20.6	**Lee** (town) Oneida County
53	23.5	**Westfield** (town) Chautauqua County	124	20.6	**Lyons** (town) Wayne County
54	23.4	**Ghent** (town) Columbia County	124	20.6	**Shelby** (town) Orleans County
55	23.2	**Middletown** (town) Delaware County	130	20.5	**Kings Park** (CDP) Suffolk County
55	23.2	**Otego** (town) Otsego County	130	20.5	**Lakeland** (CDP) Onondaga County
55	23.2	**Skaneateles** (town) Onondaga County	130	20.5	**Lawrence** (village) Nassau County
58	22.8	**Springs** (CDP) Suffolk County	130	20.5	**Middleburgh** (town) Schoharie County
58	22.8	**Village Green** (CDP) Onondaga County	130	20.5	**Olive** (town) Ulster County
60	22.7	**Port Ewen** (CDP) Ulster County	130	20.5	**Sanford** (town) Broome County
61	22.6	**Newfane** (CDP) Niagara County	136	20.4	**Penn Yan** (village) Yates County
62	22.5	**Carroll** (town) Chautauqua County	136	20.4	**Sherrill** (city) Oneida County
62	22.5	**Sidney** (town) Delaware County	136	20.4	**West Seneca** (CDP) Erie County
64	22.4	**Hurley** (town) Ulster County	139	20.3	**Charlton** (town) Saratoga County
64	22.4	**Portville** (town) Cattaraugus County	139	20.3	**Greece** (CDP) Monroe County
66	22.3	**Chautauqua** (town) Chautauqua County	139	20.3	**North Wantagh** (CDP) Nassau County
66	22.3	**Galway** (town) Saratoga County	142	20.2	**Argyle** (town) Washington County
66	22.3	**Sands Point** (village) Nassau County	142	20.2	**Boston** (town) Erie County
69	22.2	**Bethpage** (CDP) Nassau County	142	20.2	**Little Falls** (city) Herkimer County
69	22.2	**Danby** (town) Tompkins County	142	20.2	**Lowville** (town) Lewis County
69	22.2	**Oxford** (town) Chenango County	142	20.2	**Mechanicstown** (CDP) Orange County
72	22.1	**Elma** (town) Erie County	142	20.2	**Middle Island** (CDP) Suffolk County
72	22.1	**Lake George** (town) Warren County	142	20.2	**Northampton** (town) Fulton County
72	22.1	**Moriches** (CDP) Suffolk County	142	20.2	**Nunda** (town) Livingston County
72	22.1	**North Salem** (town) Westchester County	142	20.2	**Southport** (CDP) Chemung County

Note: This section ranks incorporated places and CDPs (Census Designated Places) with populations of 2,500 or more. Unincorporated postal areas were not considered. Please refer to the User Guide for additional information.

Population Age 65 and Over

Top 150 Places Ranked in *Ascending* Order

State Rank	Percent	Place
1	0.0	**Binghamton University** (CDP) Broome County
1	0.0	**SUNY Oswego** (CDP) Oswego County
1	0.0	**University at Buffalo** (CDP) Erie County
4	0.1	**Fort Drum** (CDP) Jefferson County
5	0.4	**West Point** (CDP) Orange County
6	0.5	**New Square** (village) Rockland County
7	1.0	**Kaser** (village) Rockland County
8	1.4	**Kiryas Joel** (village) Orange County
9	2.1	**Alfred** (village) Allegany County
10	2.5	**Le Ray** (town) Jefferson County
11	3.6	**Dannemora** (village) Clinton County
12	3.9	**Calcium** (CDP) Jefferson County
13	4.2	**Stony Brook University** (CDP) Suffolk County
14	4.6	**Alfred** (town) Allegany County
15	5.3	**Ithaca** (city) Tompkins County
16	5.6	**Monsey** (CDP) Rockland County
17	5.8	**Monroe** (town) Orange County
17	5.8	**South Hill** (CDP) Tompkins County
19	6.6	**Watchtower** (CDP) Ulster County
20	6.7	**Highlands** (town) Orange County
20	6.7	**North Bellport** (CDP) Suffolk County
22	6.8	**North Bay Shore** (CDP) Suffolk County
23	7.1	**Geneseo** (village) Livingston County
24	7.2	**Dannemora** (town) Clinton County
25	7.5	**Groveland** (town) Livingston County
26	7.6	**Attica** (town) Wyoming County
27	7.8	**Newburgh** (city) Orange County
27	7.8	**Spring Valley** (village) Rockland County
29	7.9	**Mastic** (CDP) Suffolk County
30	8.0	**Gordon Heights** (CDP) Suffolk County
30	8.0	**Mastic Beach** (village) Suffolk County
30	8.0	**Minisink** (town) Orange County
33	8.2	**Potsdam** (village) Saint Lawrence County
33	8.2	**South Fallsburg** (CDP) Sullivan County
35	8.4	**Brentwood** (CDP) Suffolk County
35	8.4	**Riverside** (CDP) Suffolk County
37	8.5	**Wyandanch** (CDP) Suffolk County
38	8.6	**Oswego** (town) Oswego County
38	8.6	**Sound Beach** (CDP) Suffolk County
40	8.7	**Shirley** (CDP) Suffolk County
41	8.9	**Greenwood Lake** (village) Orange County
41	8.9	**Hamilton** (village) Madison County
41	8.9	**Mount Hope** (town) Orange County
44	9.0	**Walden** (village) Orange County
44	9.0	**Wawayanda** (town) Orange County
44	9.0	**West Haverstraw** (village) Rockland County
47	9.2	**Brookville** (village) Nassau County
47	9.2	**New Hempstead** (village) Rockland County
49	9.4	**Delhi** (village) Delaware County
49	9.4	**New Paltz** (village) Ulster County
49	9.4	**Northeast Ithaca** (CDP) Tompkins County
52	9.5	**Brewerton** (CDP) Onondaga County
52	9.5	**Fairview** (CDP) Dutchess County
52	9.5	**Hamlin** (CDP) Monroe County
52	9.5	**Harriman** (village) Orange County
56	9.7	**Elmsford** (village) Westchester County
56	9.7	**Mount Ivy** (CDP) Rockland County
56	9.7	**Potsdam** (town) Saint Lawrence County
59	9.8	**Duanesburg** (town) Schenectady County
59	9.8	**Maybrook** (village) Orange County
59	9.8	**New Cassel** (CDP) Nassau County
59	9.8	**Rochester** (city) Monroe County
63	9.9	**Central Islip** (CDP) Suffolk County
64	10.0	**Hempstead** (village) Nassau County
64	10.0	**Menands** (village) Albany County
64	10.0	**Romulus** (town) Seneca County
67	10.1	**Ossining** (village) Westchester County
67	10.1	**Patchogue** (village) Suffolk County
67	10.1	**Roosevelt** (CDP) Nassau County
67	10.1	**Wheatley Heights** (CDP) Suffolk County
71	10.2	**Marcy** (town) Oneida County
72	10.3	**Northumberland** (town) Saratoga County
73	10.4	**Monroe** (village) Orange County
73	10.4	**Rocky Point** (CDP) Suffolk County
75	10.5	**Attica** (village) Wyoming County
75	10.5	**East Syracuse** (village) Onondaga County
77	10.6	**Mooers** (town) Clinton County
77	10.6	**Oneonta** (city) Otsego County
77	10.6	**Port Chester** (village) Westchester County
80	10.7	**Canton** (village) Saint Lawrence County
80	10.7	**Ellenville** (village) Ulster County
80	10.7	**Flanders** (CDP) Suffolk County
83	10.8	**Gouverneur** (town) Saint Lawrence County
83	10.8	**Rutland** (town) Jefferson County
83	10.8	**Watertown** (town) Jefferson County
86	10.9	**Shawangunk** (town) Ulster County
86	10.9	**Wilna** (town) Jefferson County
88	11.0	**Center Moriches** (CDP) Suffolk County
88	11.0	**Hamilton** (town) Madison County
88	11.0	**Old Westbury** (village) Nassau County
91	11.1	**Altona** (town) Clinton County
91	11.1	**Baywood** (CDP) Suffolk County
91	11.1	**Brockport** (village) Monroe County
91	11.1	**Bronx** (borough) Bronx County
91	11.1	**Ramapo** (town) Rockland County
96	11.2	**Scottsville** (village) Monroe County
96	11.2	**Theresa** (town) Jefferson County
98	11.3	**Annsville** (town) Oneida County
98	11.3	**Farmingville** (CDP) Suffolk County
98	11.3	**Huntington Station** (CDP) Suffolk County
98	11.3	**Patterson** (town) Putnam County
98	11.3	**Syracuse** (city) Onondaga County
98	11.3	**Troy** (city) Rensselaer County
104	11.4	**Elmira** (city) Chemung County
104	11.4	**Greenville** (town) Orange County
104	11.4	**Hannibal** (town) Oswego County
104	11.4	**Manorhaven** (village) Nassau County
104	11.4	**New Haven** (town) Oswego County
109	11.5	**Bedford Hills** (CDP) Westchester County
109	11.5	**Beekman** (town) Dutchess County
109	11.5	**Catlin** (town) Chemung County
109	11.5	**Chester** (village) Orange County
109	11.5	**Collins** (town) Erie County
109	11.5	**Dover** (town) Dutchess County
109	11.5	**Eaton** (town) Madison County
109	11.5	**Malone** (town) Franklin County
109	11.5	**Middletown** (city) Orange County
109	11.5	**Milton** (town) Saratoga County
109	11.5	**North Amityville** (CDP) Suffolk County
109	11.5	**Sweden** (town) Monroe County
121	11.6	**Manorville** (CDP) Suffolk County
121	11.6	**West Sand Lake** (CDP) Rensselaer County
123	11.7	**Bay Shore** (CDP) Suffolk County
123	11.7	**Elmont** (CDP) Nassau County
123	11.7	**Farmington** (town) Ontario County
123	11.7	**North Lindenhurst** (CDP) Suffolk County
123	11.7	**Somerset** (town) Niagara County
128	11.8	**Buffalo** (city) Erie County
128	11.8	**Lakeview** (CDP) Nassau County
128	11.8	**Walworth** (town) Wayne County
131	11.9	**Brooklyn** (borough) Kings County
131	11.9	**Fort Ann** (town) Washington County
131	11.9	**Hudson** (city) Columbia County
131	11.9	**Larchmont** (village) Westchester County
131	11.9	**New Castle** (town) Westchester County
131	11.9	**Saint Regis Mohawk Reservation** (reservation) Franklin County
137	12.0	**Brownville** (town) Jefferson County
137	12.0	**Haverstraw** (town) Rockland County
137	12.0	**Haverstraw** (village) Rockland County
137	12.0	**Sloatsburg** (village) Rockland County
137	12.0	**Southeast** (town) Putnam County
142	12.1	**Baldwin** (CDP) Nassau County
142	12.1	**Bangor** (town) Franklin County
142	12.1	**Coxsackie** (town) Greene County
142	12.1	**East Farmingdale** (CDP) Suffolk County
142	12.1	**East Shoreham** (CDP) Suffolk County
142	12.1	**Hamptonburgh** (town) Orange County
142	12.1	**Pavilion** (town) Genesee County
142	12.1	**Saranac** (town) Clinton County
142	12.1	**Selden** (CDP) Suffolk County

Note: This section ranks incorporated places and CDPs (Census Designated Places) with populations of 2,500 or more. Unincorporated postal areas were not considered. Please refer to the User Guide for additional information.

Males per 100 Females

Top 150 Places Ranked in *Descending* Order

State Rank	Ratio	Place	State Rank	Ratio	Place
1	578.6	Dannemora (village) Clinton County	76	105.6	Rome (city) Oneida County
2	380.2	Dannemora (town) Clinton County	77	105.5	Kaser (village) Rockland County
3	334.9	Groveland (town) Livingston County	78	105.4	Croghan (town) Lewis County
4	283.4	Attica (town) Wyoming County	79	105.3	Galway (town) Saratoga County
5	264.2	Romulus (town) Seneca County	79	105.3	Moriah (town) Essex County
6	261.1	West Point (CDP) Orange County	81	105.2	Conesus Lake (CDP) Livingston County
7	237.1	Fort Ann (town) Washington County	82	105.1	Richmond (town) Ontario County
8	228.6	Collins (town) Erie County	83	105.0	Cohocton (town) Steuben County
9	208.9	Marcy (town) Oneida County	84	104.9	Stockholm (town) Saint Lawrence County
10	184.3	Coxsackie (town) Greene County	85	104.7	Granby (town) Oswego County
11	183.5	Watchtower (CDP) Ulster County	86	104.6	Barker (town) Broome County
12	178.0	Riverside (CDP) Suffolk County	86	104.6	Southampton (town) Suffolk County
13	177.1	Cape Vincent (town) Jefferson County	88	104.4	Huntington Station (CDP) Suffolk County
14	175.8	Malone (town) Franklin County	89	104.3	Cato (town) Cayuga County
15	173.7	Moravia (town) Cayuga County	89	104.3	Ossining (town) Westchester County
16	165.2	Mount Hope (town) Orange County	91	104.2	Sloatsburg (village) Rockland County
17	163.2	Highlands (town) Orange County	92	104.1	University at Buffalo (CDP) Erie County
18	154.7	Alfred (village) Allegany County	92	104.1	Whitehall (village) Washington County
19	143.2	Alfred (town) Allegany County	94	103.9	Harrietstown (town) Franklin County
20	139.9	North Elba (town) Essex County	94	103.9	Sardinia (town) Erie County
21	135.8	Alden (town) Erie County	94	103.9	Whitehall (town) Washington County
22	135.5	Fort Drum (CDP) Jefferson County	94	103.9	Yates (town) Orleans County
23	134.7	Altona (town) Clinton County	98	103.8	Dickinson (town) Broome County
24	131.2	Shawangunk (town) Ulster County	98	103.8	Elmsford (village) Westchester County
25	131.0	Beekman (town) Dutchess County	100	103.7	Hartland (town) Niagara County
26	128.4	Watertown (town) Jefferson County	100	103.7	North Bay Shore (CDP) Suffolk County
27	128.3	Wawarsing (town) Ulster County	100	103.7	North Sea (CDP) Suffolk County
28	127.8	Gouverneur (town) Saint Lawrence County	103	103.6	Brentwood (CDP) Suffolk County
29	126.6	Portland (town) Chautauqua County	103	103.6	Randolph (town) Cattaraugus County
30	124.0	Fallsburg (town) Sullivan County	105	103.5	Fishkill (town) Dutchess County
31	123.9	Kings Point (village) Nassau County	105	103.5	New Cassel (CDP) Nassau County
32	123.5	Le Ray (town) Jefferson County	105	103.5	Northumberland (town) Saratoga County
33	120.6	Ogdensburg (city) Saint Lawrence County	105	103.5	Riverhead (CDP) Suffolk County
34	119.4	Yaphank (CDP) Suffolk County	109	103.4	Bath (town) Steuben County
35	119.1	Delhi (village) Delaware County	109	103.4	Russia (town) Herkimer County
36	114.6	Flanders (CDP) Suffolk County	111	103.3	North East (town) Dutchess County
37	113.9	Potsdam (village) Saint Lawrence County	111	103.3	Norwich (town) Chenango County
38	113.5	Beacon (city) Dutchess County	113	103.2	Clinton (town) Dutchess County
39	113.0	Ossining (village) Westchester County	113	103.2	Knox (town) Albany County
40	112.8	Hopewell (town) Ontario County	113	103.2	Monroe (town) Orange County
41	112.0	Batavia (town) Genesee County	113	103.2	Pierrepont (town) Saint Lawrence County
42	111.5	Southport (town) Chemung County	117	103.1	Greenville (town) Orange County
43	111.3	Johnstown (town) Fulton County	117	103.1	Spring Valley (village) Rockland County
44	111.2	Tupper Lake (town) Franklin County	119	103.0	Rush (town) Monroe County
45	110.7	Henrietta (town) Monroe County	119	103.0	Virgil (town) Cortland County
46	110.6	Bethel (town) Sullivan County	121	102.9	Auburn (city) Cayuga County
47	110.3	Hancock (town) Delaware County	121	102.9	Rye (town) Westchester County
47	110.3	Port Chester (village) Westchester County	121	102.9	Sandy Creek (town) Oswego County
49	110.1	Seneca (town) Ontario County	121	102.9	Sterling (town) Cayuga County
50	110.0	Stony Brook University (CDP) Suffolk County	125	102.8	Dover (town) Dutchess County
51	109.8	Delhi (town) Delaware County	125	102.8	Sennett (town) Cayuga County
52	109.4	Wolcott (town) Wayne County	125	102.8	Windsor (town) Broome County
53	109.3	Constantia (town) Oswego County	128	102.7	Westerlo (town) Albany County
54	109.1	Binghamton University (CDP) Broome County	129	102.6	Bangor (town) Franklin County
55	108.5	Springs (CDP) Suffolk County	129	102.6	Fleming (town) Cayuga County
56	108.3	Chautauqua (town) Chautauqua County	129	102.6	Floyd (town) Oneida County
56	108.3	Pamelia (town) Jefferson County	132	102.5	Calcium (CDP) Jefferson County
58	108.1	Pavilion (town) Genesee County	132	102.5	Eaton (town) Madison County
59	107.9	Potsdam (town) Saint Lawrence County	132	102.5	Hannibal (town) Oswego County
59	107.9	York (town) Livingston County	132	102.5	Southeast (town) Putnam County
61	107.5	New Square (village) Rockland County	136	102.4	Annsville (town) Oneida County
62	107.4	Mount Kisco (town/village) Westchester County	136	102.4	Conesus (town) Livingston County
63	107.3	Colesville (town) Broome County	136	102.4	Elmira (city) Chemung County
63	107.3	Kiryas Joel (village) Orange County	136	102.4	Fairview (CDP) Dutchess County
65	107.0	Bennington (town) Wyoming County	136	102.4	Hunter (town) Greene County
66	106.7	Hudson (city) Columbia County	136	102.4	Patterson (town) Putnam County
67	106.4	West Monroe (town) Oswego County	136	102.4	Putnam Lake (CDP) Putnam County
68	106.2	Stockport (town) Columbia County	136	102.4	Verona (town) Oneida County
69	106.0	Hampton Bays (CDP) Suffolk County	144	102.3	Berne (town) Albany County
69	106.0	Monsey (CDP) Rockland County	144	102.3	Carlton (town) Orleans County
71	105.9	Pawling (town) Dutchess County	146	102.2	Goshen (town) Orange County
71	105.9	Theresa (town) Jefferson County	146	102.2	Hector (town) Schuyler County
73	105.7	Darien (town) Genesee County	146	102.2	Mamakating (town) Sullivan County
73	105.7	Otisco (town) Onondaga County	149	102.1	Monroe (village) Orange County
73	105.7	Oxford (town) Chenango County	149	102.1	New Haven (town) Oswego County

Note: *This section ranks incorporated places and CDPs (Census Designated Places) with populations of 2,500 or more. Unincorporated postal areas were not considered. Please refer to the User Guide for additional information.*

Males per 100 Females

Top 150 Places Ranked in *Ascending* Order

State Rank	Ratio	Place	State Rank	Ratio	Place
1	65.0	**Heritage Hills** (CDP) Westchester County	74	88.3	**Little Falls** (city) Herkimer County
2	67.4	**Cazenovia** (village) Madison County	77	88.4	**Ardsley** (village) Westchester County
3	71.5	**New Paltz** (village) Ulster County	77	88.4	**Groton** (village) Tompkins County
4	73.8	**Orangeburg** (CDP) Rockland County	77	88.4	**Rye Brook** (village) Westchester County
5	75.4	**Great Neck Plaza** (village) Nassau County	80	88.5	**Cheektowaga** (CDP) Erie County
6	77.7	**Williamsville** (village) Erie County	80	88.5	**Fairmount** (CDP) Onondaga County
7	78.8	**Lake Success** (village) Nassau County	80	88.5	**Harrison** (town/village) Westchester County
8	79.4	**Clarence** (CDP) Erie County	80	88.5	**Manhattan** (borough) New York County
9	79.6	**Caneadea** (town) Allegany County	84	88.6	**Herkimer** (village) Herkimer County
10	80.0	**South Hill** (CDP) Tompkins County	84	88.6	**Honeoye Falls** (village) Monroe County
11	80.5	**Lewiston** (village) Niagara County	86	88.7	**Bronxville** (village) Westchester County
11	80.5	**Rhinebeck** (village) Dutchess County	86	88.7	**Eastchester** (town) Westchester County
13	80.9	**Hartsdale** (CDP) Westchester County	86	88.7	**Highland** (CDP) Ulster County
14	81.5	**Geneseo** (village) Livingston County	86	88.7	**Lewiston** (town) Niagara County
15	81.9	**Skaneateles** (village) Onondaga County	90	88.8	**Canandaigua** (city) Ontario County
16	82.1	**Jerusalem** (town) Yates County	90	88.8	**Greece** (CDP) Monroe County
17	82.3	**East Garden City** (CDP) Nassau County	90	88.8	**North Greenbush** (town) Rensselaer County
18	82.4	**Galeville** (CDP) Onondaga County	90	88.8	**Tonawanda** (town) Erie County
19	82.7	**Roslyn** (village) Nassau County	94	88.9	**Cheektowaga** (town) Erie County
20	82.8	**Horseheads** (village) Chemung County	94	88.9	**Sidney** (village) Delaware County
20	82.8	**Warwick** (village) Orange County	94	88.9	**Wellsville** (village) Allegany County
22	83.3	**Arlington** (CDP) Dutchess County	97	89.0	**Chittenango** (village) Madison County
22	83.3	**Mount Vernon** (city) Westchester County	97	89.0	**Manhasset** (CDP) Nassau County
22	83.3	**Rhinebeck** (town) Dutchess County	99	89.1	**Glenwood Landing** (CDP) Nassau County
25	83.7	**Hamilton** (village) Madison County	99	89.1	**Ithaca** (town) Tompkins County
26	83.9	**New Paltz** (town) Ulster County	99	89.1	**Plattsburgh** (city) Clinton County
26	83.9	**Oneonta** (city) Otsego County	99	89.1	**Tonawanda** (CDP) Erie County
28	84.0	**Geneseo** (town) Livingston County	103	89.2	**Dansville** (village) Livingston County
29	84.1	**Brookville** (village) Nassau County	104	89.3	**Brighton** (CDP) Monroe County
30	84.3	**Bedford** (town) Westchester County	104	89.3	**Brooklyn** (borough) Kings County
31	84.5	**Norwich** (city) Chenango County	104	89.3	**Carthage** (village) Jefferson County
32	84.7	**Mechanicstown** (CDP) Orange County	104	89.3	**East Rockaway** (village) Nassau County
33	85.0	**Malone** (village) Franklin County	104	89.3	**Horseheads North** (CDP) Chemung County
33	85.0	**Ridge** (CDP) Suffolk County	104	89.3	**Westfield** (village) Chautauqua County
35	85.6	**Otsego** (town) Otsego County	110	89.4	**Blasdell** (village) Erie County
36	85.7	**East Aurora** (village) Erie County	110	89.4	**Eastchester** (CDP) Westchester County
36	85.7	**North Amityville** (CDP) Suffolk County	110	89.4	**Hastings-on-Hudson** (village) Westchester County
38	85.8	**Westvale** (CDP) Onondaga County	110	89.4	**Johnstown** (city) Fulton County
39	85.9	**Cazenovia** (town) Madison County	110	89.4	**Nanuet** (CDP) Rockland County
40	86.0	**Maybrook** (village) Orange County	110	89.4	**Webster** (village) Monroe County
40	86.0	**Waverly** (village) Tioga County	110	89.4	**West Elmira** (CDP) Chemung County
42	86.1	**Homer** (village) Cortland County	117	89.5	**Bethpage** (CDP) Nassau County
43	86.3	**Nyack** (village) Rockland County	117	89.5	**Greenburgh** (town) Westchester County
44	86.5	**Waterloo** (village) Seneca County	117	89.5	**North Dansville** (town) Livingston County
45	86.6	**Irondequoit** (CDP) Monroe County	117	89.5	**Sayville** (CDP) Suffolk County
45	86.6	**New Hartford** (town) Oneida County	121	89.6	**Newfane** (CDP) Niagara County
45	86.6	**Tuckahoe** (village) Westchester County	122	89.7	**Cohoes** (city) Albany County
48	86.7	**Penn Yan** (village) Yates County	122	89.7	**Green Island** (town/village) Albany County
48	86.7	**Pittsford** (town) Monroe County	122	89.7	**Hornellsville** (town) Steuben County
48	86.7	**Whitesboro** (village) Oneida County	125	89.8	**Baldwinsville** (village) Onondaga County
51	86.8	**Port Ewen** (CDP) Ulster County	125	89.8	**Saint Johnsville** (town) Montgomery County
52	87.0	**Lakeview** (CDP) Nassau County	125	89.8	**Ulysses** (town) Tompkins County
52	87.0	**Mechanicville** (city) Saratoga County	125	89.8	**Wellsville** (town) Allegany County
52	87.0	**Vails Gate** (CDP) Orange County	129	89.9	**Amherst** (town) Erie County
55	87.1	**South Nyack** (village) Rockland County	129	89.9	**Batavia** (city) Genesee County
56	87.4	**Firthcliffe** (CDP) Orange County	129	89.9	**Coxsackie** (village) Greene County
56	87.4	**Geddes** (town) Onondaga County	129	89.9	**Melville** (CDP) Suffolk County
56	87.4	**Kenmore** (village) Erie County	129	89.9	**Piermont** (village) Rockland County
56	87.4	**Manlius** (village) Onondaga County	129	89.9	**Thomaston** (village) Nassau County
56	87.4	**Woodbury** (CDP) Nassau County	135	90.0	**Amsterdam** (city) Montgomery County
61	87.5	**Hoosick Falls** (village) Rensselaer County	135	90.0	**Elmira** (town) Chemung County
62	87.6	**Goshen** (village) Orange County	135	90.0	**Hamilton** (town) Madison County
62	87.6	**North Hills** (village) Nassau County	135	90.0	**Yonkers** (city) Westchester County
62	87.6	**North Valley Stream** (CDP) Nassau County	139	90.1	**Garden City** (village) Nassau County
65	87.7	**Tarrytown** (village) Westchester County	139	90.1	**Hamburg** (village) Erie County
66	87.8	**Geneva** (city) Ontario County	141	90.2	**Lowville** (village) Lewis County
66	87.8	**Glens Falls North** (CDP) Warren County	141	90.2	**Lynbrook** (village) Nassau County
66	87.8	**Medina** (village) Orleans County	141	90.2	**Mount Ivy** (CDP) Rockland County
69	88.0	**Fairview** (CDP) Westchester County	141	90.2	**South Glens Falls** (village) Saratoga County
69	88.0	**Minoa** (village) Onondaga County	141	90.2	**Wynantskill** (CDP) Rensselaer County
71	88.1	**Fredonia** (village) Chautauqua County	146	90.3	**Horseheads** (town) Chemung County
71	88.1	**Islandia** (village) Suffolk County	147	90.4	**Great Neck Estates** (village) Nassau County
73	88.2	**Rockville Centre** (village) Nassau County	147	90.4	**Greece** (town) Monroe County
74	88.3	**Brockport** (village) Monroe County	147	90.4	**New York** (city)
74	88.3	**Bronx** (borough) Bronx County	147	90.4	**Salina** (town) Onondaga County

Note: This section ranks incorporated places and CDPs (Census Designated Places) with populations of 2,500 or more. Unincorporated postal areas were not considered. Please refer to the User Guide for additional information.

Marriage Status: Never Married

Top 150 Places Ranked in *Descending* Order

State Rank	Percent	Place
1	99.7	**SUNY Oswego** (CDP) Oswego County
2	99.6	**Binghamton University** (CDP) Broome County
3	98.9	**University at Buffalo** (CDP) Erie County
4	94.2	**Stony Brook University** (CDP) Suffolk County
5	93.3	**Alfred** (village) Allegany County
6	84.3	**Alfred** (town) Allegany County
7	78.3	**South Hill** (CDP) Tompkins County
8	77.1	**Ithaca** (city) Tompkins County
9	76.9	**Geneseo** (village) Livingston County
10	76.3	**Hamilton** (village) Madison County
11	75.2	**New Paltz** (village) Ulster County
12	72.9	**Potsdam** (village) Saint Lawrence County
13	71.7	**Delhi** (village) Delaware County
13	71.7	**West Point** (CDP) Orange County
15	69.0	**Canton** (village) Saint Lawrence County
16	67.1	**Riverside** (CDP) Suffolk County
17	66.2	**Oneonta** (city) Otsego County
18	65.5	**Brockport** (village) Monroe County
19	63.6	**East Garden City** (CDP) Nassau County
20	63.5	**Geneseo** (town) Livingston County
21	60.7	**Albany** (city) Albany County
21	60.7	**Oswego** (town) Oswego County
23	59.2	**Hamilton** (town) Madison County
24	59.0	**Arlington** (CDP) Dutchess County
25	57.8	**Dannemora** (village) Clinton County
26	56.9	**Potsdam** (town) Saint Lawrence County
27	56.1	**Delhi** (town) Delaware County
28	56.0	**Cobleskill** (village) Schoharie County
28	56.0	**Eaton** (town) Madison County
30	55.3	**Fairview** (CDP) Westchester County
30	55.3	**Rochester** (city) Monroe County
32	55.2	**Cortland** (city) Cortland County
32	55.2	**Troy** (city) Rensselaer County
34	54.9	**Caneadea** (town) Allegany County
34	54.9	**New Paltz** (town) Ulster County
36	54.4	**Syracuse** (city) Onondaga County
37	53.7	**Highlands** (town) Orange County
37	53.7	**Plattsburgh** (city) Clinton County
39	53.6	**Canton** (town) Saint Lawrence County
39	53.6	**Geneva** (city) Ontario County
41	53.4	**Brookville** (village) Nassau County
42	53.2	**Ithaca** (town) Tompkins County
42	53.2	**Wyandanch** (CDP) Suffolk County
44	52.4	**Old Westbury** (village) Nassau County
45	51.6	**Sweden** (town) Monroe County
46	51.5	**Dannemora** (town) Clinton County
47	51.2	**Buffalo** (city) Erie County
48	50.8	**Fredonia** (village) Chautauqua County
49	50.7	**Manhattan** (borough) New York County
49	50.7	**Romulus** (town) Seneca County
51	49.9	**Hempstead** (village) Nassau County
52	49.7	**Cazenovia** (village) Madison County
52	49.7	**Newburgh** (city) Orange County
54	49.4	**New Cassel** (CDP) Nassau County
55	48.9	**Coxsackie** (town) Greene County
56	48.8	**Bronx** (borough) Bronx County
57	48.0	**Attica** (town) Wyoming County
58	47.6	**Binghamton** (city) Broome County
58	47.6	**Fairview** (CDP) Dutchess County
60	47.3	**North Amityville** (CDP) Suffolk County
60	47.3	**Watervliet** (city) Albany County
62	46.9	**Watchtower** (CDP) Ulster County
63	46.5	**Yorkville** (village) Oneida County
64	46.4	**Poughkeepsie** (city) Dutchess County
65	46.3	**Cayuga Heights** (village) Tompkins County
66	46.2	**Elmira** (city) Chemung County
67	45.8	**Cobleskill** (town) Schoharie County
68	45.5	**Brentwood** (CDP) Suffolk County
69	45.4	**Pomfret** (town) Chautauqua County
70	45.3	**South Nyack** (village) Rockland County
71	45.2	**Catskill** (village) Greene County
72	45.1	**Lakeview** (CDP) Nassau County
72	45.1	**Roosevelt** (CDP) Nassau County
74	45.0	**Groveland** (town) Livingston County
74	45.0	**Schenectady** (city) Schenectady County
76	44.8	**Hudson** (city) Columbia County
76	44.8	**Monticello** (village) Sullivan County
76	44.8	**Vestal** (town) Broome County
79	44.7	**Mount Vernon** (city) Westchester County
80	44.2	**Central Islip** (CDP) Suffolk County
80	44.2	**Utica** (city) Oneida County
82	44.0	**New York** (city)
83	43.9	**Brooklyn** (borough) Kings County
84	43.5	**South Fallsburg** (CDP) Sullivan County
85	43.3	**Uniondale** (CDP) Nassau County
86	43.1	**Collins** (town) Erie County
87	43.0	**Beacon** (city) Dutchess County
87	43.0	**Middletown** (city) Orange County
89	42.9	**Fort Ann** (town) Washington County
89	42.9	**Marcy** (town) Oneida County
91	42.6	**Orangeburg** (CDP) Rockland County
91	42.6	**Red Hook** (town) Dutchess County
93	42.4	**Flanders** (CDP) Suffolk County
93	42.4	**Freeport** (village) Nassau County
95	42.2	**Gordon Heights** (CDP) Suffolk County
96	42.1	**Glens Falls** (city) Warren County
97	41.9	**Kirkland** (town) Oneida County
98	41.8	**Allegany** (town) Cattaraugus County
98	41.8	**Spring Valley** (village) Rockland County
100	41.7	**Albion** (town) Orleans County
101	41.6	**Malone** (town) Franklin County
102	41.4	**Henrietta** (town) Monroe County
102	41.4	**Port Chester** (village) Westchester County
102	41.4	**Saint Regis Mohawk Reservation** (reservation) Franklin County
102	41.4	**Walden** (village) Orange County
106	41.3	**North Bellport** (CDP) Suffolk County
107	41.2	**Blasdell** (village) Erie County
108	41.1	**Fort Drum** (CDP) Jefferson County
108	41.1	**North Bay Shore** (CDP) Suffolk County
110	41.0	**Haverstraw** (village) Rockland County
111	40.9	**West Haverstraw** (village) Rockland County
112	40.8	**Harrison** (town/village) Westchester County
112	40.8	**Menands** (village) Albany County
114	40.7	**Niagara Falls** (city) Niagara County
115	40.4	**East Rochester** (town/village) Monroe County
116	40.3	**Lackawanna** (city) Erie County
116	40.3	**Mattydale** (CDP) Onondaga County
118	40.2	**Mount Ivy** (CDP) Rockland County
119	40.1	**Amsterdam** (city) Montgomery County
119	40.1	**Oswego** (city) Oswego County
119	40.1	**Thompson** (town) Sullivan County
122	40.0	**Poughkeepsie** (town) Dutchess County
123	39.9	**Fallsburg** (town) Sullivan County
123	39.9	**Mastic Beach** (village) Suffolk County
125	39.8	**Maybrook** (village) Orange County
125	39.8	**North Elba** (town) Essex County
127	39.7	**Dickinson** (town) Broome County
127	39.7	**Elmont** (CDP) Nassau County
127	39.7	**Yonkers** (city) Westchester County
130	39.6	**Bay Shore** (CDP) Suffolk County
130	39.6	**Riverhead** (CDP) Suffolk County
132	39.3	**Haverstraw** (town) Rockland County
132	39.3	**New Hempstead** (village) Rockland County
132	39.3	**Rensselaer** (city) Rensselaer County
135	39.1	**Saratoga Springs** (city) Saratoga County
135	39.1	**Saugerties** (village) Ulster County
137	39.0	**Mohawk** (village) Herkimer County
137	39.0	**Wheatley Heights** (CDP) Suffolk County
139	38.9	**Cohoes** (city) Albany County
139	38.9	**East Syracuse** (village) Onondaga County
139	38.9	**Johnson City** (village) Broome County
139	38.9	**Mechanicville** (city) Saratoga County
143	38.8	**Coxsackie** (village) Greene County
143	38.8	**Ogdensburg** (city) Saint Lawrence County
145	38.6	**Elmsford** (village) Westchester County
145	38.6	**Kingston** (city) Ulster County
145	38.6	**Patchogue** (village) Suffolk County
148	38.5	**Dunkirk** (city) Chautauqua County
148	38.5	**Owego** (village) Tioga County
150	38.4	**Mount Kisco** (town/village) Westchester County

Note: *This section ranks incorporated places and CDPs (Census Designated Places) with populations of 2,500 or more. Unincorporated postal areas were not considered. Please refer to the User Guide for additional information.*

Marriage Status: Never Married

Top 150 Places Ranked in *Ascending* Order

State Rank	Percent	Place	State Rank	Percent	Place
1	11.1	**Heritage Hills** (CDP) Westchester County	75	22.5	**Pound Ridge** (town) Westchester County
2	12.1	**North Hills** (village) Nassau County	75	22.5	**Sand Lake** (town) Rensselaer County
3	15.7	**Colesville** (town) Broome County	75	22.5	**Westerlo** (town) Albany County
4	16.6	**Halesite** (CDP) Suffolk County	79	22.6	**Haviland** (CDP) Dutchess County
5	16.7	**Callicoon** (town) Sullivan County	79	22.6	**Lawrence** (village) Nassau County
6	17.2	**Wales** (town) Erie County	79	22.6	**Port Washington** (CDP) Nassau County
7	17.3	**Woodbury** (CDP) Nassau County	82	22.7	**Benton** (town) Yates County
8	17.8	**Larchmont** (village) Westchester County	82	22.7	**Hurley** (CDP) Ulster County
8	17.8	**Richmond** (town) Ontario County	82	22.7	**Oxford** (town) Chenango County
10	18.0	**Skaneateles** (village) Onondaga County	82	22.7	**Wading River** (CDP) Suffolk County
11	18.7	**Vienna** (town) Oneida County	82	22.7	**White Creek** (town) Washington County
12	18.9	**West Elmira** (CDP) Chemung County	87	22.8	**Charlton** (town) Saratoga County
13	19.0	**Northwest Harbor** (CDP) Suffolk County	87	22.8	**Milford** (town) Otsego County
13	19.0	**Rush** (town) Monroe County	87	22.8	**Northumberland** (town) Saratoga County
13	19.0	**Veteran** (town) Chemung County	90	22.9	**Richland** (town) Oswego County
16	19.1	**Manhasset Hills** (CDP) Nassau County	91	23.0	**East Quogue** (CDP) Suffolk County
17	19.2	**Elma Center** (CDP) Erie County	91	23.0	**Pavilion** (town) Genesee County
18	19.6	**Hurley** (town) Ulster County	91	23.0	**Pierrepont** (town) Saint Lawrence County
19	19.9	**Peru** (town) Clinton County	91	23.0	**Schoharie** (town) Schoharie County
19	19.9	**Sterling** (town) Cayuga County	91	23.0	**Warrensburg** (CDP) Warren County
19	19.9	**West Bay Shore** (CDP) Suffolk County	91	23.0	**Warwick** (village) Orange County
19	19.9	**Windsor** (town) Broome County	97	23.1	**Concord** (town) Erie County
23	20.0	**Campbell** (town) Steuben County	97	23.1	**Lee** (town) Oneida County
23	20.0	**Castile** (town) Wyoming County	97	23.1	**Lysander** (town) Onondaga County
23	20.0	**Louisville** (town) Saint Lawrence County	97	23.1	**North Salem** (town) Westchester County
26	20.2	**Calcium** (CDP) Jefferson County	97	23.1	**Walworth** (town) Wayne County
26	20.2	**Scarsdale** (town/village) Westchester County	102	23.2	**Croton-on-Hudson** (village) Westchester County
28	20.4	**Greenfield** (town) Saratoga County	102	23.2	**Gorham** (town) Ontario County
28	20.4	**Mendon** (town) Monroe County	102	23.2	**Searingtown** (CDP) Nassau County
28	20.4	**Newfane** (CDP) Niagara County	102	23.2	**Victor** (town) Ontario County
31	20.5	**Wilton** (town) Saratoga County	106	23.3	**Chesterfield** (town) Essex County
32	20.6	**Irvington** (village) Westchester County	106	23.3	**Clifton Park** (town) Saratoga County
33	20.7	**East Hills** (village) Nassau County	106	23.3	**New Castle** (town) Westchester County
33	20.7	**Lido Beach** (CDP) Nassau County	106	23.3	**North Collins** (town) Erie County
33	20.7	**Otsego** (town) Otsego County	106	23.3	**Tioga** (town) Tioga County
33	20.7	**Southold** (CDP) Suffolk County	111	23.4	**Kinderhook** (town) Columbia County
37	20.8	**Fairport** (village) Monroe County	111	23.4	**Sands Point** (village) Nassau County
37	20.8	**Fleming** (town) Cayuga County	111	23.4	**Shelter Island** (town) Suffolk County
37	20.8	**Rye** (city) Westchester County	111	23.4	**Thomaston** (village) Nassau County
37	20.8	**Skaneateles** (town) Onondaga County	115	23.5	**Champion** (town) Jefferson County
37	20.8	**Yates** (town) Orleans County	115	23.5	**Croghan** (town) Lewis County
42	20.9	**Montgomery** (village) Orange County	115	23.5	**Kiryas Joel** (village) Orange County
43	21.0	**Nunda** (town) Livingston County	118	23.6	**Clarendon** (town) Orleans County
44	21.1	**Flower Hill** (village) Nassau County	118	23.6	**Great Neck Plaza** (village) Nassau County
44	21.1	**New Berlin** (town) Chenango County	118	23.6	**Manlius** (town) Onondaga County
46	21.3	**Ellisburg** (town) Jefferson County	118	23.6	**Setauket-East Setauket** (CDP) Suffolk County
46	21.3	**Somers** (town) Westchester County	118	23.6	**Sheridan** (town) Chautauqua County
48	21.4	**Melville** (CDP) Suffolk County	123	23.7	**Galway** (town) Saratoga County
49	21.5	**Elmira** (town) Chemung County	123	23.7	**Horseheads North** (CDP) Chemung County
49	21.5	**Westhampton** (CDP) Suffolk County	123	23.7	**Lisbon** (town) Saint Lawrence County
51	21.6	**Hartland** (town) Niagara County	123	23.7	**Malta** (town) Saratoga County
51	21.6	**Pittstown** (town) Rensselaer County	123	23.7	**Syosset** (CDP) Nassau County
51	21.6	**Stockholm** (town) Saint Lawrence County	123	23.7	**Webster** (town) Monroe County
51	21.6	**Wanakah** (CDP) Erie County	129	23.8	**Brownville** (town) Jefferson County
55	21.7	**Catlin** (town) Chemung County	129	23.8	**North Sea** (CDP) Suffolk County
56	21.8	**Aurelius** (town) Cayuga County	129	23.8	**Ontario** (town) Wayne County
56	21.8	**Palatine** (town) Montgomery County	129	23.8	**Pine Plains** (town) Dutchess County
58	21.9	**Canandaigua** (town) Ontario County	129	23.8	**Ridge** (CDP) Suffolk County
58	21.9	**Plainview** (CDP) Nassau County	129	23.8	**Stillwater** (town) Saratoga County
60	22.0	**Kaser** (village) Rockland County	129	23.8	**Tuxedo** (town) Orange County
60	22.0	**Lake Success** (village) Nassau County	136	23.9	**Big Flats** (CDP) Chemung County
60	22.0	**Montrose** (CDP) Westchester County	136	23.9	**Brunswick** (town) Rensselaer County
60	22.0	**Northport** (village) Suffolk County	136	23.9	**Lakeland** (CDP) Onondaga County
64	22.1	**Fayette** (town) Seneca County	136	23.9	**Port Washington North** (village) Nassau County
64	22.1	**Orleans** (town) Jefferson County	136	23.9	**Sherburne** (town) Chenango County
66	22.3	**Albertson** (CDP) Nassau County	136	23.9	**Triangle** (town) Broome County
66	22.3	**Bennington** (town) Wyoming County	136	23.9	**West Nyack** (CDP) Rockland County
66	22.3	**Ellery** (town) Chautauqua County	143	24.0	**Bainbridge** (town) Chenango County
66	22.3	**Marion** (town) Wayne County	143	24.0	**Bellmore** (CDP) Nassau County
66	22.3	**Northampton** (town) Fulton County	143	24.0	**Colden** (town) Erie County
66	22.3	**Springville** (village) Erie County	143	24.0	**Mount Sinai** (CDP) Suffolk County
66	22.3	**West Hills** (CDP) Suffolk County	143	24.0	**Sidney** (town) Delaware County
73	22.4	**Batavia** (town) Genesee County	143	24.0	**Warrensburg** (town) Warren County
73	22.4	**Elma** (town) Erie County	149	24.1	**Calverton** (CDP) Suffolk County
75	22.5	**Kendall** (town) Orleans County	149	24.1	**Carlton** (town) Orleans County

Note: This section ranks incorporated places and CDPs (Census Designated Places) with populations of 2,500 or more. Unincorporated postal areas were not considered. Please refer to the User Guide for additional information.

Marriage Status: Now Married

Top 150 Places Ranked in *Descending* Order

State Rank	Percent	Place	State Rank	Percent	Place
1	76.7	**Kaser** (village) Rockland County	74	63.4	**Port Washington** (CDP) Nassau County
2	75.0	**Kiryas Joel** (village) Orange County	77	63.3	**Northport** (village) Suffolk County
3	74.3	**Calcium** (CDP) Jefferson County	78	63.2	**Southold** (CDP) Suffolk County
4	74.1	**Scarsdale** (town/village) Westchester County	79	63.1	**Clifton Park** (town) Saratoga County
5	72.3	**East Hills** (village) Nassau County	79	63.1	**Conesus** (town) Livingston County
6	72.2	**Larchmont** (village) Westchester County	79	63.1	**Monroe** (town) Orange County
7	70.5	**New Castle** (town) Westchester County	79	63.1	**Skaneateles** (town) Onondaga County
8	69.9	**North Hills** (village) Nassau County	83	63.0	**North Collins** (town) Erie County
9	69.6	**New Square** (village) Rockland County	83	63.0	**Rye Brook** (village) Westchester County
10	69.2	**Irvington** (village) Westchester County	83	63.0	**Sand Lake** (town) Rensselaer County
11	68.9	**Manhasset Hills** (CDP) Nassau County	86	62.9	**Chemung** (town) Chemung County
12	68.8	**Lawrence** (village) Nassau County	86	62.9	**Montgomery** (village) Orange County
13	68.7	**Veteran** (town) Chemung County	86	62.9	**Northwest Harbor** (CDP) Suffolk County
14	68.1	**Halesite** (CDP) Suffolk County	86	62.9	**Philipstown** (town) Putnam County
15	67.5	**Rye** (city) Westchester County	90	62.8	**West Bay Shore** (CDP) Suffolk County
15	67.5	**Wading River** (CDP) Suffolk County	91	62.7	**Argyle** (town) Washington County
17	67.4	**Lloyd Harbor** (village) Suffolk County	91	62.7	**Elwood** (CDP) Suffolk County
18	67.3	**Wales** (town) Erie County	93	62.6	**Elmira** (town) Chemung County
18	67.3	**Wesley Hills** (village) Rockland County	93	62.6	**Kendall** (town) Orleans County
20	67.1	**West Hills** (CDP) Suffolk County	93	62.6	**Lewisboro** (town) Westchester County
21	67.0	**Horseheads North** (CDP) Chemung County	93	62.6	**Marion** (town) Wayne County
21	67.0	**Rush** (town) Monroe County	97	62.5	**Dix Hills** (CDP) Suffolk County
23	66.8	**Flower Hill** (village) Nassau County	97	62.5	**Monsey** (CDP) Rockland County
24	66.7	**Munsey Park** (village) Nassau County	97	62.5	**New Baltimore** (town) Greene County
25	66.6	**North Castle** (town) Westchester County	100	62.4	**Darien** (town) Genesee County
26	66.5	**Syosset** (CDP) Nassau County	100	62.4	**Putnam Valley** (town) Putnam County
27	66.4	**Walworth** (town) Wayne County	102	62.2	**Colden** (town) Erie County
28	66.3	**West Elmira** (CDP) Chemung County	102	62.2	**Croton-on-Hudson** (village) Westchester County
29	66.2	**Hartland** (town) Niagara County	102	62.2	**East Fishkill** (town) Dutchess County
30	66.0	**Armonk** (CDP) Westchester County	102	62.2	**Merrick** (CDP) Nassau County
30	66.0	**Pound Ridge** (town) Westchester County	102	62.2	**Wilton** (town) Saratoga County
32	65.9	**Fleming** (town) Cayuga County	102	62.2	**Windsor** (town) Broome County
32	65.9	**Plainview** (CDP) Nassau County	108	62.1	**Corning** (town) Steuben County
34	65.8	**Great Neck Estates** (village) Nassau County	108	62.1	**Hurley** (town) Ulster County
35	65.7	**Lido Beach** (CDP) Nassau County	110	62.0	**Clarence** (town) Erie County
36	65.6	**Mount Sinai** (CDP) Suffolk County	110	62.0	**Elma** (town) Erie County
36	65.6	**Northumberland** (town) Saratoga County	110	62.0	**Hewlett** (CDP) Nassau County
38	65.5	**Spackenkill** (CDP) Dutchess County	113	61.9	**Shelter Island** (town) Suffolk County
39	65.3	**Croghan** (town) Lewis County	114	61.8	**Aurelius** (town) Cayuga County
39	65.3	**Sands Point** (village) Nassau County	114	61.8	**Charlton** (town) Saratoga County
39	65.3	**Thomaston** (village) Nassau County	114	61.8	**Pittstown** (town) Rensselaer County
42	65.2	**Catlin** (town) Chemung County	117	61.7	**Bronxville** (village) Westchester County
42	65.2	**East Shoreham** (CDP) Suffolk County	117	61.7	**Garden City** (village) Nassau County
44	65.1	**Callicoon** (town) Sullivan County	117	61.7	**Hurley** (CDP) Ulster County
44	65.1	**Jericho** (CDP) Nassau County	117	61.7	**Kings Point** (village) Nassau County
44	65.1	**Louisville** (town) Saint Lawrence County	117	61.7	**Seneca** (town) Ontario County
44	65.1	**Searingtown** (CDP) Nassau County	122	61.6	**Clayton** (town) Jefferson County
48	64.7	**Albertson** (CDP) Nassau County	122	61.6	**Commack** (CDP) Suffolk County
48	64.7	**Bennington** (town) Wyoming County	122	61.6	**Haviland** (CDP) Dutchess County
48	64.7	**Cold Spring Harbor** (CDP) Suffolk County	122	61.6	**Lysander** (town) Onondaga County
48	64.7	**Peru** (town) Clinton County	122	61.6	**Owego** (town) Tioga County
52	64.6	**Ellisburg** (town) Jefferson County	122	61.6	**Pompey** (town) Onondaga County
52	64.6	**Mendon** (town) Monroe County	122	61.6	**Woodmere** (CDP) Nassau County
52	64.6	**Muttontown** (village) Nassau County	129	61.5	**Fayette** (town) Seneca County
55	64.5	**East Quogue** (CDP) Suffolk County	129	61.5	**Melville** (CDP) Suffolk County
56	64.4	**Richmond** (town) Ontario County	129	61.5	**Newark Valley** (town) Tioga County
57	64.3	**Victor** (town) Ontario County	129	61.5	**Pendleton** (town) Niagara County
58	64.2	**Greenfield** (town) Saratoga County	133	61.4	**Mamaroneck** (town) Westchester County
58	64.2	**Myers Corner** (CDP) Dutchess County	133	61.4	**Schuyler Falls** (town) Clinton County
58	64.2	**West Sand Lake** (CDP) Rensselaer County	133	61.4	**Woodbury** (CDP) Nassau County
61	64.1	**Mattituck** (CDP) Suffolk County	136	61.3	**East Williston** (village) Nassau County
62	63.9	**Greenville** (CDP) Westchester County	136	61.3	**Great Neck** (village) Nassau County
62	63.9	**Setauket-East Setauket** (CDP) Suffolk County	136	61.3	**North New Hyde Park** (CDP) Nassau County
64	63.8	**Heritage Hills** (CDP) Westchester County	136	61.3	**North Sea** (CDP) Suffolk County
64	63.8	**Somers** (town) Westchester County	136	61.3	**Pierrepont** (town) Saint Lawrence County
66	63.7	**North Salem** (town) Westchester County	141	61.2	**Brightwaters** (village) Suffolk County
66	63.7	**Old Bethpage** (CDP) Nassau County	141	61.2	**Chenango Bridge** (CDP) Broome County
66	63.7	**Stony Brook** (CDP) Suffolk County	141	61.2	**Orleans** (town) Jefferson County
69	63.6	**Castile** (town) Wyoming County	141	61.2	**Wynantskill** (CDP) Rensselaer County
69	63.6	**Fort Salonga** (CDP) Suffolk County	145	61.1	**Cutchogue** (CDP) Suffolk County
69	63.6	**La Grange** (town) Dutchess County	145	61.1	**Port Washington North** (village) Nassau County
69	63.6	**Marilla** (town) Erie County	145	61.1	**Wantagh** (CDP) Nassau County
69	63.6	**Wanakah** (CDP) Erie County	148	61.0	**Niskayuna** (town) Schenectady County
74	63.4	**Bellmore** (CDP) Nassau County	148	61.0	**Otisco** (town) Onondaga County
74	63.4	**New City** (CDP) Rockland County	148	61.0	**West Nyack** (CDP) Rockland County

Note: This section ranks incorporated places and CDPs (Census Designated Places) with populations of 2,500 or more. Unincorporated postal areas were not considered. Please refer to the User Guide for additional information.

Marriage Status: Now Married

Top 150 Places Ranked in *Ascending* Order

State Rank	Percent	Place
1	0.0	**SUNY Oswego** (CDP) Oswego County
2	0.4	**Binghamton University** (CDP) Broome County
3	0.9	**University at Buffalo** (CDP) Erie County
4	3.5	**Stony Brook University** (CDP) Suffolk County
5	5.7	**Alfred** (village) Allegany County
6	12.4	**Alfred** (town) Allegany County
7	15.2	**New Paltz** (village) Ulster County
8	16.7	**Delhi** (village) Delaware County
9	17.1	**South Hill** (CDP) Tompkins County
10	17.2	**Ithaca** (city) Tompkins County
11	17.6	**Hamilton** (village) Madison County
12	18.1	**Geneseo** (village) Livingston County
12	18.1	**Potsdam** (village) Saint Lawrence County
14	20.2	**Riverside** (CDP) Suffolk County
15	21.4	**Canton** (village) Saint Lawrence County
16	23.9	**Oneonta** (city) Otsego County
17	24.0	**Arlington** (CDP) Dutchess County
18	24.2	**Brockport** (village) Monroe County
19	25.7	**Albany** (city) Albany County
19	25.7	**West Point** (CDP) Orange County
21	25.9	**East Garden City** (CDP) Nassau County
22	26.4	**Geneseo** (town) Livingston County
23	28.6	**Delhi** (town) Delaware County
23	28.6	**Rochester** (city) Monroe County
25	29.1	**Cobleskill** (village) Schoharie County
26	29.5	**Cortland** (city) Cortland County
27	29.7	**Syracuse** (city) Onondaga County
28	30.0	**Fairview** (CDP) Westchester County
29	30.3	**Eaton** (town) Madison County
30	30.5	**Dannemora** (village) Clinton County
31	30.6	**Troy** (city) Rensselaer County
32	30.8	**Plattsburgh** (city) Clinton County
33	31.0	**Potsdam** (town) Saint Lawrence County
34	31.4	**Oswego** (town) Oswego County
35	31.5	**Buffalo** (city) Erie County
36	31.7	**Hamilton** (town) Madison County
37	31.9	**Binghamton** (city) Broome County
38	32.1	**Geneva** (city) Ontario County
39	32.3	**Canton** (town) Saint Lawrence County
40	32.9	**New Paltz** (town) Ulster County
41	33.2	**Cazenovia** (village) Madison County
42	33.3	**Hudson** (city) Columbia County
43	34.7	**South Fallsburg** (CDP) Sullivan County
44	35.1	**Elmira** (city) Chemung County
45	35.2	**Blasdell** (village) Erie County
46	35.5	**Wyandanch** (CDP) Suffolk County
47	35.7	**Cobleskill** (town) Schoharie County
47	35.7	**Whitesboro** (village) Oneida County
49	35.8	**Manhattan** (borough) New York County
49	35.8	**North Amityville** (CDP) Suffolk County
49	35.8	**Utica** (city) Oneida County
52	35.9	**Yorkville** (village) Oneida County
53	36.1	**Poughkeepsie** (city) Dutchess County
54	36.4	**Bronx** (borough) Bronx County
55	36.5	**Caneadea** (town) Allegany County
56	36.7	**Hempstead** (village) Nassau County
56	36.7	**Schenectady** (city) Schenectady County
58	36.8	**Romulus** (town) Seneca County
59	36.9	**Fredonia** (village) Chautauqua County
60	37.1	**New York Mills** (village) Oneida County
61	37.2	**Monticello** (village) Sullivan County
62	37.3	**Ithaca** (town) Tompkins County
63	37.4	**Groveland** (town) Livingston County
64	37.5	**South Glens Falls** (village) Saratoga County
65	37.6	**Glens Falls** (city) Warren County
65	37.6	**Mattydale** (CDP) Onondaga County
65	37.6	**Watervliet** (city) Albany County
68	37.7	**Dannemora** (town) Clinton County
68	37.7	**Newburgh** (city) Orange County
70	37.8	**Saint Regis Mohawk Reservation** (reservation) Franklin County
71	38.0	**Collins** (town) Erie County
71	38.0	**Sweden** (town) Monroe County
73	38.1	**Coxsackie** (town) Greene County
73	38.1	**Mount Vernon** (city) Westchester County
73	38.1	**Penn Yan** (village) Yates County
76	38.3	**Lackawanna** (city) Erie County
77	38.6	**Gowanda** (village) Cattaraugus County
78	38.8	**Highlands** (town) Orange County
79	39.1	**Niagara Falls** (city) Niagara County
80	39.3	**Attica** (town) Wyoming County
81	39.4	**Auburn** (city) Cayuga County
82	39.5	**Albion** (town) Orleans County
82	39.5	**Gordon Heights** (CDP) Suffolk County
84	39.7	**Rensselaer** (city) Rensselaer County
84	39.7	**Salamanca** (city) Cattaraugus County
86	39.8	**East Rochester** (town/village) Monroe County
86	39.8	**Johnson City** (village) Broome County
86	39.8	**Mechanicville** (city) Saratoga County
89	39.9	**Cohoes** (city) Albany County
89	39.9	**East Syracuse** (village) Onondaga County
91	40.0	**Endicott** (village) Broome County
91	40.0	**Fort Ann** (town) Washington County
93	40.2	**Dickinson** (town) Broome County
93	40.2	**Waterloo** (village) Seneca County
95	40.3	**Amsterdam** (city) Montgomery County
95	40.3	**Central Islip** (CDP) Suffolk County
95	40.3	**Saugerties** (village) Ulster County
98	40.4	**Lyncourt** (CDP) Onondaga County
98	40.4	**South Nyack** (village) Rockland County
100	40.6	**Fairview** (CDP) Dutchess County
100	40.6	**Portland** (town) Chautauqua County
102	40.7	**Rome** (city) Oneida County
103	41.0	**Beacon** (city) Dutchess County
103	41.0	**New Cassel** (CDP) Nassau County
105	41.1	**Palmyra** (village) Wayne County
106	41.2	**Oswego** (city) Oswego County
107	41.3	**Malone** (town) Franklin County
107	41.3	**Orangeburg** (CDP) Rockland County
109	41.4	**Pomfret** (town) Chautauqua County
110	41.5	**Kingston** (city) Ulster County
110	41.5	**Kirkland** (town) Oneida County
110	41.5	**Lyons** (village) Wayne County
113	41.8	**Maybrook** (village) Orange County
113	41.8	**Norwich** (city) Chenango County
113	41.8	**Ogdensburg** (city) Saint Lawrence County
116	41.9	**Brentwood** (CDP) Suffolk County
116	41.9	**Coxsackie** (village) Greene County
116	41.9	**Old Westbury** (village) Nassau County
116	41.9	**Olean** (city) Cattaraugus County
120	42.0	**Warsaw** (village) Wyoming County
121	42.1	**Freeport** (village) Nassau County
121	42.1	**Patchogue** (village) Suffolk County
123	42.2	**Uniondale** (CDP) Nassau County
124	42.3	**Frankfort** (village) Herkimer County
124	42.3	**Long Beach** (city) Nassau County
124	42.3	**Moravia** (town) Cayuga County
124	42.3	**Sloan** (village) Erie County
128	42.4	**Gouverneur** (village) Saint Lawrence County
128	42.4	**Thompson** (town) Sullivan County
130	42.5	**Brookville** (village) Nassau County
130	42.5	**Marcy** (town) Oneida County
130	42.5	**Mohawk** (village) Herkimer County
130	42.5	**New York** (city)
130	42.5	**Vails Gate** (CDP) Orange County
135	42.6	**Gouverneur** (town) Saint Lawrence County
135	42.6	**North Elba** (town) Essex County
135	42.6	**Owego** (village) Tioga County
138	42.7	**Dunkirk** (city) Chautauqua County
139	42.8	**Port Jervis** (city) Orange County
140	42.9	**Bethel** (town) Sullivan County
140	42.9	**Hudson Falls** (village) Washington County
142	43.0	**West Glens Falls** (CDP) Warren County
143	43.1	**Riverhead** (CDP) Suffolk County
143	43.1	**Vestal** (town) Broome County
145	43.2	**North Syracuse** (village) Onondaga County
146	43.3	**Brooklyn** (borough) Kings County
146	43.3	**Little Falls** (city) Herkimer County
146	43.3	**Roosevelt** (CDP) Nassau County
149	43.4	**Island Park** (village) Nassau County
149	43.4	**Middletown** (city) Orange County

Note: This section ranks incorporated places and CDPs (Census Designated Places) with populations of 2,500 or more. Unincorporated postal areas were not considered. Please refer to the User Guide for additional information.

Marriage Status: Separated

Top 150 Places Ranked in *Descending* Order

State Rank	Percent	Place	State Rank	Percent	Place
1	7.3	**Rockland** (town) Sullivan County	74	3.9	**Fort Edward** (village) Washington County
2	7.2	**Moriches** (CDP) Suffolk County	74	3.9	**Gardnertown** (CDP) Orange County
3	6.7	**Johnstown** (city) Fulton County	74	3.9	**Mechanicville** (city) Saratoga County
4	6.5	**Lakeview** (CDP) Nassau County	74	3.9	**Milo** (town) Yates County
5	6.3	**Waverly** (village) Tioga County	74	3.9	**Moravia** (town) Cayuga County
6	6.1	**Hoosick Falls** (village) Rensselaer County	74	3.9	**Mount Morris** (village) Livingston County
6	6.1	**Sidney** (village) Delaware County	74	3.9	**New Berlin** (town) Chenango County
8	5.9	**Haverstraw** (village) Rockland County	74	3.9	**Port Ewen** (CDP) Ulster County
9	5.8	**Chester** (village) Orange County	74	3.9	**Richland** (town) Oswego County
9	5.8	**Dannemora** (village) Clinton County	74	3.9	**Spring Valley** (village) Rockland County
9	5.8	**Middletown** (town) Delaware County	74	3.9	**Walton** (town) Delaware County
12	5.7	**Rutland** (town) Jefferson County	74	3.9	**Watertown** (town) Jefferson County
13	5.6	**Walton** (village) Delaware County	74	3.9	**West Haverstraw** (village) Rockland County
14	5.5	**Bronx** (borough) Bronx County	89	3.8	**Adams** (town) Jefferson County
14	5.5	**Dannemora** (town) Clinton County	89	3.8	**Athens** (town) Greene County
16	5.4	**Le Roy** (village) Genesee County	89	3.8	**Dix** (town) Schuyler County
17	5.3	**Dunkirk** (city) Chautauqua County	89	3.8	**East Syracuse** (village) Onondaga County
17	5.3	**Louisville** (town) Saint Lawrence County	89	3.8	**Gowanda** (village) Cattaraugus County
17	5.3	**Malone** (village) Franklin County	89	3.8	**Harrietstown** (town) Franklin County
17	5.3	**Nyack** (village) Rockland County	89	3.8	**Lake Placid** (village) Essex County
21	5.2	**Sidney** (town) Delaware County	89	3.8	**Minden** (town) Montgomery County
22	5.1	**Chazy** (town) Clinton County	89	3.8	**Saranac Lake** (village) Franklin County
22	5.1	**Lake Luzerne** (town) Warren County	98	3.7	**Amsterdam** (city) Montgomery County
24	5.0	**Liberty** (village) Sullivan County	98	3.7	**Calcium** (CDP) Jefferson County
24	5.0	**Watervliet** (city) Albany County	98	3.7	**Elmira** (city) Chemung County
26	4.9	**Lyons** (village) Wayne County	98	3.7	**Esopus** (town) Ulster County
27	4.8	**Davenport** (town) Delaware County	98	3.7	**Florida** (village) Orange County
27	4.8	**Gordon Heights** (CDP) Suffolk County	98	3.7	**Haverstraw** (town) Rockland County
27	4.8	**Wayland** (town) Steuben County	98	3.7	**Kirkwood** (town) Broome County
30	4.7	**Green Island** (town/village) Albany County	98	3.7	**Mechanicstown** (CDP) Orange County
30	4.7	**Monticello** (village) Sullivan County	98	3.7	**Roosevelt** (CDP) Nassau County
30	4.7	**Newburgh** (city) Orange County	98	3.7	**Saint Johnsville** (town) Montgomery County
30	4.7	**Ogdensburg** (city) Saint Lawrence County	98	3.7	**Sheridan** (town) Chautauqua County
30	4.7	**Schroeppel** (town) Oswego County	98	3.7	**Tupper Lake** (village) Franklin County
35	4.5	**Addison** (town) Steuben County	98	3.7	**Washington** (town) Dutchess County
35	4.5	**Amenia** (town) Dutchess County	98	3.7	**Wellsville** (village) Allegany County
35	4.5	**Batavia** (town) Genesee County	112	3.6	**Arlington** (CDP) Dutchess County
35	4.5	**Elbridge** (town) Onondaga County	112	3.6	**Canandaigua** (city) Ontario County
35	4.5	**Hudson** (city) Columbia County	112	3.6	**Cape Vincent** (town) Jefferson County
35	4.5	**Silver Creek** (village) Chautauqua County	112	3.6	**Catskill** (village) Greene County
41	4.4	**Bangor** (town) Franklin County	112	3.6	**Collins** (town) Erie County
41	4.4	**Castile** (town) Wyoming County	112	3.6	**Corning** (city) Steuben County
41	4.4	**Whitesboro** (village) Oneida County	112	3.6	**Ellenville** (village) Ulster County
41	4.4	**Wyandanch** (CDP) Suffolk County	112	3.6	**Fallsburg** (town) Sullivan County
45	4.3	**Bath** (town) Steuben County	112	3.6	**Islip Terrace** (CDP) Suffolk County
45	4.3	**Constantia** (town) Oswego County	112	3.6	**Livonia** (town) Livingston County
45	4.3	**Kingston** (city) Ulster County	112	3.6	**Malone** (town) Franklin County
45	4.3	**Liberty** (town) Sullivan County	112	3.6	**Mount Hope** (town) Orange County
45	4.3	**Norwich** (city) Chenango County	112	3.6	**Mount Vernon** (city) Westchester County
45	4.3	**Port Chester** (village) Westchester County	112	3.6	**Newark** (village) Wayne County
45	4.3	**Rochester** (city) Monroe County	112	3.6	**Pierrepont** (town) Saint Lawrence County
52	4.2	**Endicott** (village) Broome County	112	3.6	**Schodack** (town) Rensselaer County
52	4.2	**Fort Edward** (town) Washington County	112	3.6	**Westfield** (town) Chautauqua County
52	4.2	**Gaines** (town) Orleans County	129	3.5	**Champion** (town) Jefferson County
52	4.2	**Homer** (town) Cortland County	129	3.5	**Corinth** (village) Saratoga County
52	4.2	**Hoosick** (town) Rensselaer County	129	3.5	**Geneva** (town) Ontario County
52	4.2	**Mamakating** (town) Sullivan County	129	3.5	**Hempstead** (village) Nassau County
52	4.2	**New Haven** (town) Oswego County	129	3.5	**Hurley** (town) Ulster County
52	4.2	**Rosendale** (town) Ulster County	129	3.5	**Lakewood** (village) Chautauqua County
52	4.2	**Watertown** (city) Jefferson County	129	3.5	**Milford** (town) Otsego County
61	4.1	**Auburn** (city) Cayuga County	129	3.5	**North Bay Shore** (CDP) Suffolk County
61	4.1	**Barton** (town) Tioga County	129	3.5	**Oswego** (city) Oswego County
61	4.1	**Bath** (village) Steuben County	129	3.5	**Pavilion** (town) Genesee County
61	4.1	**Canisteo** (town) Steuben County	129	3.5	**Penn Yan** (village) Yates County
61	4.1	**Inwood** (CDP) Nassau County	129	3.5	**Plattsburgh** (town) Clinton County
61	4.1	**Middletown** (city) Orange County	129	3.5	**Stanford** (town) Dutchess County
61	4.1	**Pine Plains** (town) Dutchess County	129	3.5	**West Glens Falls** (CDP) Warren County
68	4.0	**Bainbridge** (town) Chenango County	143	3.4	**Barker** (town) Broome County
68	4.0	**Catlin** (town) Chemung County	143	3.4	**Brownville** (town) Jefferson County
68	4.0	**Hanover** (town) Chautauqua County	143	3.4	**Durham** (town) Greene County
68	4.0	**Ilion** (village) Herkimer County	143	3.4	**Galen** (town) Wayne County
68	4.0	**Warwick** (village) Orange County	143	3.4	**Groveland** (town) Livingston County
68	4.0	**Whitehall** (village) Washington County	143	3.4	**Hornellsville** (town) Steuben County
74	3.9	**Brutus** (town) Cayuga County	143	3.4	**Lackawanna** (city) Erie County
74	3.9	**Carthage** (village) Jefferson County	143	3.4	**Massena** (village) Saint Lawrence County

Note: *This section ranks incorporated places and CDPs (Census Designated Places) with populations of 2,500 or more. Unincorporated postal areas were not considered. Please refer to the User Guide for additional information.*

Marriage Status: Separated

Top 150 Places Ranked in *Ascending* Order

State Rank	Percent	Place	State Rank	Percent	Place
1	0.0	**Akron** (village) Erie County	57	0.5	**West Monroe** (town) Oswego County
1	0.0	**Alfred** (village) Allegany County	77	0.6	**Binghamton** (town) Broome County
1	0.0	**Binghamton University** (CDP) Broome County	77	0.6	**Duanesburg** (town) Schenectady County
1	0.0	**Chenango Bridge** (CDP) Broome County	77	0.6	**East Norwich** (CDP) Nassau County
1	0.0	**Montauk** (CDP) Suffolk County	77	0.6	**Hamptonburgh** (town) Orange County
1	0.0	**North Hills** (village) Nassau County	77	0.6	**Hilton** (village) Monroe County
1	0.0	**SUNY Oswego** (CDP) Oswego County	77	0.6	**Ithaca** (town) Tompkins County
1	0.0	**Searingtown** (CDP) Nassau County	77	0.6	**Lisbon** (town) Saint Lawrence County
1	0.0	**Stony Brook University** (CDP) Suffolk County	77	0.6	**Lyncourt** (CDP) Onondaga County
1	0.0	**Union Vale** (town) Dutchess County	77	0.6	**Mattituck** (CDP) Suffolk County
1	0.0	**University at Buffalo** (CDP) Erie County	77	0.6	**Mohawk** (village) Herkimer County
1	0.0	**Village Green** (CDP) Onondaga County	77	0.6	**Monroe** (village) Orange County
13	0.1	**Alfred** (town) Allegany County	77	0.6	**Newfane** (CDP) Niagara County
13	0.1	**Herricks** (CDP) Nassau County	77	0.6	**North Great River** (CDP) Suffolk County
13	0.1	**Montrose** (CDP) Westchester County	77	0.6	**Northeast Ithaca** (CDP) Tompkins County
13	0.1	**Old Westbury** (village) Nassau County	77	0.6	**Piermont** (village) Rockland County
13	0.1	**Pelham Manor** (village) Westchester County	77	0.6	**Seneca** (town) Ontario County
13	0.1	**West Point** (CDP) Orange County	77	0.6	**Wading River** (CDP) Suffolk County
13	0.1	**Yorkville** (village) Oneida County	94	0.7	**Allegany** (town) Cattaraugus County
20	0.2	**Ardsley** (village) Westchester County	94	0.7	**Canton** (town) Saint Lawrence County
20	0.2	**Argyle** (town) Washington County	94	0.7	**Danby** (town) Tompkins County
20	0.2	**Center Moriches** (CDP) Suffolk County	94	0.7	**Delhi** (village) Delaware County
20	0.2	**Garden City South** (CDP) Nassau County	94	0.7	**Dix Hills** (CDP) Suffolk County
20	0.2	**Manhasset Hills** (CDP) Nassau County	94	0.7	**East Shoreham** (CDP) Suffolk County
20	0.2	**North East** (town) Dutchess County	94	0.7	**Ellisburg** (town) Jefferson County
20	0.2	**Norwich** (town) Chenango County	94	0.7	**Elma Center** (CDP) Erie County
20	0.2	**Poestenkill** (town) Rensselaer County	94	0.7	**Garden City** (village) Nassau County
20	0.2	**Rye Brook** (village) Westchester County	94	0.7	**Gates** (CDP) Monroe County
20	0.2	**Wesley Hills** (village) Rockland County	94	0.7	**Lansing** (village) Tompkins County
20	0.2	**West Sand Lake** (CDP) Rensselaer County	94	0.7	**Lewisboro** (town) Westchester County
31	0.3	**Benton** (town) Yates County	94	0.7	**Mount Sinai** (CDP) Suffolk County
31	0.3	**Canton** (village) Saint Lawrence County	94	0.7	**Orangeburg** (CDP) Rockland County
31	0.3	**Colden** (town) Erie County	94	0.7	**Oswego** (town) Oswego County
31	0.3	**Conesus Lake** (CDP) Livingston County	94	0.7	**South Nyack** (village) Rockland County
31	0.3	**Fort Salonga** (CDP) Suffolk County	94	0.7	**South Valley Stream** (CDP) Nassau County
31	0.3	**Guilford** (town) Chenango County	94	0.7	**Tappan** (CDP) Rockland County
31	0.3	**Lloyd Harbor** (village) Suffolk County	94	0.7	**Vestal** (town) Broome County
31	0.3	**Montebello** (village) Rockland County	94	0.7	**Williston Park** (village) Nassau County
31	0.3	**New Square** (village) Rockland County	94	0.7	**Woodmere** (CDP) Nassau County
31	0.3	**Port Washington North** (village) Nassau County	115	0.8	**Brookville** (village) Nassau County
31	0.3	**Watchtower** (CDP) Ulster County	115	0.8	**Carmel** (town) Putnam County
31	0.3	**Westerlo** (town) Albany County	115	0.8	**Clarkson** (town) Monroe County
43	0.4	**Albertson** (CDP) Nassau County	115	0.8	**Coxsackie** (village) Greene County
43	0.4	**Bethpage** (CDP) Nassau County	115	0.8	**East Quogue** (CDP) Suffolk County
43	0.4	**Fayetteville** (village) Onondaga County	115	0.8	**East Williston** (village) Nassau County
43	0.4	**Grandyle Village** (CDP) Erie County	115	0.8	**Elwood** (CDP) Suffolk County
43	0.4	**Kiryas Joel** (village) Orange County	115	0.8	**Fairview** (CDP) Dutchess County
43	0.4	**Lansing** (village) Tompkins County	115	0.8	**Firthcliffe** (CDP) Orange County
43	0.4	**Manorville** (CDP) Suffolk County	115	0.8	**Nichols** (town) Tioga County
43	0.4	**Marilla** (town) Erie County	115	0.8	**North Patchogue** (CDP) Suffolk County
43	0.4	**Menands** (village) Albany County	115	0.8	**Patterson** (town) Putnam County
43	0.4	**Muttontown** (village) Nassau County	115	0.8	**Pawling** (town) Dutchess County
43	0.4	**New Bremen** (town) Lewis County	115	0.8	**Salem** (town) Washington County
43	0.4	**Old Bethpage** (CDP) Nassau County	115	0.8	**Sea Cliff** (village) Nassau County
43	0.4	**Pomona** (village) Rockland County	115	0.8	**Trenton** (town) Oneida County
43	0.4	**South Hill** (CDP) Tompkins County	115	0.8	**Van Buren** (town) Onondaga County
57	0.5	**Ballston Spa** (village) Saratoga County	115	0.8	**Virgil** (town) Cortland County
57	0.5	**Blauvelt** (CDP) Rockland County	115	0.8	**Westvale** (CDP) Onondaga County
57	0.5	**Carmel Hamlet** (CDP) Putnam County	134	0.9	**Bethlehem** (town) Albany County
57	0.5	**Deerfield** (town) Oneida County	134	0.9	**Briarcliff Manor** (village) Westchester County
57	0.5	**Elma** (town) Erie County	134	0.9	**Brightwaters** (village) Suffolk County
57	0.5	**Fairview** (CDP) Westchester County	134	0.9	**Crown Heights** (CDP) Dutchess County
57	0.5	**Greenwood Lake** (village) Orange County	134	0.9	**East Greenbush** (CDP) Rensselaer County
57	0.5	**Haviland** (CDP) Dutchess County	134	0.9	**East Hampton** (town) Suffolk County
57	0.5	**Kaser** (village) Rockland County	134	0.9	**Fleming** (town) Cayuga County
57	0.5	**Kings Point** (village) Nassau County	134	0.9	**Gardiner** (town) Ulster County
57	0.5	**Manhasset** (CDP) Nassau County	134	0.9	**Greenville** (CDP) Westchester County
57	0.5	**Monsey** (CDP) Rockland County	134	0.9	**Halesite** (CDP) Suffolk County
57	0.5	**New Castle** (town) Westchester County	134	0.9	**Highlands** (town) Orange County
57	0.5	**Newstead** (town) Erie County	134	0.9	**Hunter** (town) Greene County
57	0.5	**North Boston** (CDP) Erie County	134	0.9	**Lake Mohegan** (CDP) Westchester County
57	0.5	**Parma** (town) Monroe County	134	0.9	**Lee** (town) Oneida County
57	0.5	**Pendleton** (town) Niagara County	134	0.9	**Malta** (town) Saratoga County
57	0.5	**Roslyn** (village) Nassau County	134	0.9	**Munsey Park** (village) Nassau County
57	0.5	**Valhalla** (CDP) Westchester County	134	0.9	**New Baltimore** (town) Greene County

Note: This section ranks incorporated places and CDPs (Census Designated Places) with populations of 2,500 or more. Unincorporated postal areas were not considered. Please refer to the User Guide for additional information.

Marriage Status: Widowed

Top 150 Places Ranked in *Descending* Order

State Rank	Percent	Place	State Rank	Percent	Place
1	15.5	**Calverton** (CDP) Suffolk County	75	9.6	**Bath** (town) Steuben County
1	15.5	**Heritage Hills** (CDP) Westchester County	75	9.6	**Canandaigua** (town) Ontario County
3	15.0	**Lake Success** (village) Nassau County	75	9.6	**Greece** (CDP) Monroe County
4	14.8	**Great Neck Plaza** (village) Nassau County	75	9.6	**Mechanicstown** (CDP) Orange County
5	14.7	**Hornellsville** (town) Steuben County	75	9.6	**Sayville** (CDP) Suffolk County
6	13.9	**Woodbury** (CDP) Nassau County	75	9.6	**Vails Gate** (CDP) Orange County
7	13.5	**Montauk** (CDP) Suffolk County	82	9.5	**Baldwinsville** (village) Onondaga County
8	13.4	**Roslyn** (village) Nassau County	82	9.5	**Cobleskill** (town) Schoharie County
9	12.7	**Oswegatchie** (town) Saint Lawrence County	82	9.5	**Cortlandville** (town) Cortland County
10	12.5	**Newfane** (CDP) Niagara County	82	9.5	**Herkimer** (village) Herkimer County
11	12.4	**Otsego** (town) Otsego County	82	9.5	**Massena** (town) Saint Lawrence County
12	12.3	**Bath** (village) Steuben County	82	9.5	**Port Washington North** (village) Nassau County
13	11.9	**Ridge** (CDP) Suffolk County	82	9.5	**Warwick** (village) Orange County
13	11.9	**Southampton** (village) Suffolk County	89	9.4	**Amsterdam** (town) Montgomery County
15	11.8	**Lewiston** (village) Niagara County	89	9.4	**Elmira Heights** (village) Chemung County
16	11.7	**Galeville** (CDP) Onondaga County	89	9.4	**Mohawk** (town) Montgomery County
16	11.7	**New York Mills** (village) Oneida County	89	9.4	**Rotterdam** (CDP) Schenectady County
18	11.6	**Benton** (town) Yates County	89	9.4	**Saint Johnsville** (town) Montgomery County
18	11.6	**Lake Luzerne** (town) Warren County	89	9.4	**West Seneca** (CDP) Erie County
20	11.4	**Geneva** (town) Ontario County	95	9.3	**Liberty** (town) Sullivan County
20	11.4	**Wellsville** (town) Allegany County	95	9.3	**Medina** (village) Orleans County
22	11.3	**New Hartford** (town) Oneida County	95	9.3	**Middle Island** (CDP) Suffolk County
22	11.3	**Port Jervis** (city) Orange County	95	9.3	**Minoa** (village) Onondaga County
22	11.3	**Sangerfield** (town) Oneida County	95	9.3	**Palmyra** (village) Wayne County
25	11.1	**Tuxedo** (town) Orange County	95	9.3	**West Glens Falls** (CDP) Warren County
26	11.0	**Honeoye Falls** (village) Monroe County	101	9.2	**Alden** (village) Erie County
26	11.0	**Westfield** (village) Chautauqua County	101	9.2	**Auburn** (city) Cayuga County
28	10.9	**Lyncourt** (CDP) Onondaga County	101	9.2	**Greenport** (town) Columbia County
28	10.9	**Warsaw** (village) Wyoming County	101	9.2	**Horseheads** (town) Chemung County
30	10.8	**Copake** (town) Columbia County	101	9.2	**Lackawanna** (city) Erie County
30	10.8	**Franklinville** (town) Cattaraugus County	101	9.2	**Lakewood** (village) Chautauqua County
30	10.8	**Horseheads** (village) Chemung County	101	9.2	**Malverne** (village) Nassau County
30	10.8	**North Syracuse** (village) Onondaga County	101	9.2	**North Hills** (village) Nassau County
34	10.7	**Jay** (town) Essex County	101	9.2	**Ticonderoga** (town) Essex County
34	10.7	**Waterloo** (village) Seneca County	110	9.1	**Albion** (village) Orleans County
34	10.7	**Waverly** (village) Tioga County	110	9.1	**Coxsackie** (village) Greene County
34	10.7	**Westhampton** (CDP) Suffolk County	110	9.1	**Falconer** (village) Chautauqua County
38	10.6	**North Wantagh** (CDP) Nassau County	110	9.1	**Mount Morris** (town) Livingston County
39	10.5	**Elma Center** (CDP) Erie County	110	9.1	**Niagara** (town) Niagara County
39	10.5	**Middleburgh** (town) Schoharie County	110	9.1	**Rensselaer** (city) Rensselaer County
39	10.5	**Sennett** (town) Cayuga County	110	9.1	**Stockholm** (town) Saint Lawrence County
42	10.4	**Ballston Spa** (village) Saratoga County	110	9.1	**Whitestown** (town) Oneida County
42	10.4	**Skaneateles** (village) Onondaga County	118	9.0	**Balmville** (CDP) Orange County
42	10.4	**Valhalla** (CDP) Westchester County	118	9.0	**Carthage** (village) Jefferson County
45	10.3	**East Meadow** (CDP) Nassau County	118	9.0	**Highland** (CDP) Ulster County
45	10.3	**Little Falls** (city) Herkimer County	118	9.0	**Johnstown** (town) Fulton County
45	10.3	**New Berlin** (town) Chenango County	118	9.0	**Palatine** (town) Montgomery County
45	10.3	**South Fallsburg** (CDP) Sullivan County	118	9.0	**Richmondville** (town) Schoharie County
49	10.2	**East Glenville** (CDP) Schenectady County	118	9.0	**Rome** (city) Oneida County
49	10.2	**Lowville** (town) Lewis County	118	9.0	**Saint James** (CDP) Suffolk County
49	10.2	**Melville** (CDP) Suffolk County	118	9.0	**Solvay** (village) Onondaga County
49	10.2	**Wappingers Falls** (village) Dutchess County	118	9.0	**Waterloo** (town) Seneca County
53	10.1	**Blasdell** (village) Erie County	128	8.9	**Batavia** (city) Genesee County
53	10.1	**Glens Falls North** (CDP) Warren County	128	8.9	**Bayport** (CDP) Suffolk County
53	10.1	**Goshen** (village) Orange County	128	8.9	**Colesville** (town) Broome County
53	10.1	**Hunter** (town) Greene County	128	8.9	**Geddes** (town) Onondaga County
53	10.1	**Liberty** (village) Sullivan County	128	8.9	**Manhasset Hills** (CDP) Nassau County
53	10.1	**Middletown** (town) Delaware County	128	8.9	**Tonawanda** (town) Erie County
53	10.1	**Springville** (village) Erie County	128	8.9	**Viola** (CDP) Rockland County
53	10.1	**Ulster** (town) Ulster County	135	8.8	**Airmont** (village) Rockland County
61	10.0	**Guilford** (town) Chenango County	135	8.8	**Gowanda** (village) Cattaraugus County
61	10.0	**Orangeburg** (CDP) Rockland County	135	8.8	**Massena** (village) Saint Lawrence County
61	10.0	**Oxford** (town) Chenango County	135	8.8	**Moriches** (CDP) Suffolk County
61	10.0	**Westfield** (town) Chautauqua County	135	8.8	**Rochester** (town) Ulster County
65	9.9	**Montrose** (CDP) Westchester County	135	8.8	**Sterling** (town) Cayuga County
65	9.9	**Oyster Bay** (CDP) Nassau County	141	8.7	**Baywood** (CDP) Suffolk County
65	9.9	**Webster** (village) Monroe County	141	8.7	**Bethpage** (CDP) Nassau County
68	9.8	**Brookhaven** (CDP) Suffolk County	141	8.7	**Clarence** (CDP) Erie County
68	9.8	**Livingston** (town) Columbia County	141	8.7	**Gates** (CDP) Monroe County
68	9.8	**Penn Yan** (village) Yates County	141	8.7	**Gouverneur** (village) Saint Lawrence County
68	9.8	**Port Ewen** (CDP) Ulster County	141	8.7	**Greenlawn** (CDP) Suffolk County
68	9.8	**Rhinebeck** (town) Dutchess County	141	8.7	**Lenox** (town) Madison County
73	9.7	**Arcade** (town) Wyoming County	141	8.7	**Shelby** (town) Orleans County
73	9.7	**Warsaw** (town) Wyoming County	141	8.7	**Vienna** (town) Oneida County
75	9.6	**Arlington** (CDP) Dutchess County	150	8.6	**Amsterdam** (city) Montgomery County

Note: *This section ranks incorporated places and CDPs (Census Designated Places) with populations of 2,500 or more. Unincorporated postal areas were not considered. Please refer to the User Guide for additional information.*

Marriage Status: Widowed

Top 150 Places Ranked in *Ascending* Order

State Rank	Percent	Place	State Rank	Percent	Place
1	0.0	**Binghamton University** (CDP) Broome County	74	3.5	**Pomona** (village) Rockland County
1	0.0	**SUNY Oswego** (CDP) Oswego County	74	3.5	**Shirley** (CDP) Suffolk County
1	0.0	**University at Buffalo** (CDP) Erie County	78	3.6	**Barker** (town) Broome County
4	0.2	**Watchtower** (CDP) Ulster County	78	3.6	**Cornwall-on-Hudson** (village) Orange County
5	0.4	**Fort Drum** (CDP) Jefferson County	78	3.6	**Dover** (town) Dutchess County
5	0.4	**West Point** (CDP) Orange County	78	3.6	**Gardiner** (town) Ulster County
7	0.5	**Alfred** (village) Allegany County	78	3.6	**Madison** (town) Madison County
7	0.5	**Kaser** (village) Rockland County	78	3.6	**Scottsville** (village) Monroe County
9	0.8	**New Square** (village) Rockland County	78	3.6	**Stockport** (town) Columbia County
10	1.0	**Calcium** (CDP) Jefferson County	85	3.7	**Gordon Heights** (CDP) Suffolk County
11	1.1	**Kiryas Joel** (village) Orange County	85	3.7	**Great Neck Estates** (village) Nassau County
12	1.2	**Alfred** (town) Allegany County	85	3.7	**Hamilton** (village) Madison County
12	1.2	**Wesley Hills** (village) Rockland County	85	3.7	**Hamlin** (town) Monroe County
14	1.4	**Ithaca** (city) Tompkins County	85	3.7	**Mount Kisco** (town/village) Westchester County
14	1.4	**Jerusalem** (town) Yates County	85	3.7	**North Bay Shore** (CDP) Suffolk County
14	1.4	**Le Ray** (town) Jefferson County	85	3.7	**Sweden** (town) Monroe County
17	1.7	**Menands** (village) Albany County	92	3.8	**Baldwin Harbor** (CDP) Nassau County
18	1.8	**Monsey** (CDP) Rockland County	92	3.8	**Beekman** (town) Dutchess County
19	2.0	**Highlands** (town) Orange County	92	3.8	**Chester** (town) Orange County
20	2.1	**Groveland** (town) Livingston County	92	3.8	**Crawford** (town) Orange County
21	2.2	**Conklin** (town) Broome County	92	3.8	**Delhi** (village) Delaware County
21	2.2	**Stony Brook University** (CDP) Suffolk County	92	3.8	**Hawthorne** (CDP) Westchester County
23	2.3	**Dannemora** (town) Clinton County	92	3.8	**Hewlett** (CDP) Nassau County
23	2.3	**Geneseo** (village) Livingston County	92	3.8	**Mount Ivy** (CDP) Rockland County
23	2.3	**Greenville** (town) Orange County	100	3.9	**Batavia** (town) Genesee County
23	2.3	**Mattituck** (CDP) Suffolk County	100	3.9	**Elwood** (CDP) Suffolk County
23	2.3	**Oswego** (town) Oswego County	100	3.9	**Enfield** (town) Tompkins County
28	2.4	**Dannemora** (village) Clinton County	100	3.9	**Harriman** (village) Orange County
29	2.6	**Catskill** (village) Greene County	100	3.9	**Henrietta** (town) Monroe County
29	2.6	**Saint Regis Mohawk Reservation** (reservation) Franklin County	100	3.9	**Knox** (town) Albany County
31	2.7	**Brookville** (village) Nassau County	100	3.9	**Milton** (CDP) Saratoga County
31	2.7	**Darien** (town) Genesee County	100	3.9	**Pelham** (village) Westchester County
31	2.7	**Hamlin** (CDP) Monroe County	108	4.0	**Caroline** (town) Tompkins County
31	2.7	**Munsey Park** (village) Nassau County	108	4.0	**Cedarhurst** (village) Nassau County
31	2.7	**Pamelia** (town) Jefferson County	108	4.0	**Danby** (town) Tompkins County
36	2.8	**Mount Hope** (town) Orange County	108	4.0	**East Hills** (village) Nassau County
36	2.8	**Scarsdale** (town/village) Westchester County	108	4.0	**Fredonia** (village) Chautauqua County
38	2.9	**Lloyd Harbor** (village) Suffolk County	108	4.0	**Mastic** (CDP) Suffolk County
39	3.0	**Canton** (village) Saint Lawrence County	108	4.0	**Sound Beach** (CDP) Suffolk County
39	3.0	**Flanders** (CDP) Suffolk County	108	4.0	**Ulysses** (town) Tompkins County
39	3.0	**Fort Edward** (village) Washington County	108	4.0	**Yaphank** (CDP) Suffolk County
39	3.0	**Monroe** (town) Orange County	117	4.1	**Bedford** (town) Westchester County
39	3.0	**New Castle** (town) Westchester County	117	4.1	**Conesus Lake** (CDP) Livingston County
44	3.1	**Bangor** (town) Franklin County	117	4.1	**East Greenbush** (CDP) Rensselaer County
44	3.1	**East Shoreham** (CDP) Suffolk County	117	4.1	**Mahopac** (CDP) Putnam County
44	3.1	**Green Island** (town/village) Albany County	117	4.1	**Pembroke** (town) Genesee County
44	3.1	**Kings Point** (village) Nassau County	117	4.1	**Port Chester** (village) Westchester County
44	3.1	**North Castle** (town) Westchester County	117	4.1	**Potsdam** (village) Saint Lawrence County
44	3.1	**Pompey** (town) Onondaga County	117	4.1	**Red Oaks Mill** (CDP) Dutchess County
44	3.1	**South Hill** (CDP) Tompkins County	125	4.2	**Chautauqua** (town) Chautauqua County
44	3.1	**Stanford** (town) Dutchess County	125	4.2	**Chemung** (town) Chemung County
52	3.2	**Attica** (town) Wyoming County	125	4.2	**Denmark** (town) Lewis County
52	3.2	**Bedford Hills** (CDP) Westchester County	125	4.2	**Hounsfield** (town) Jefferson County
52	3.2	**Clarendon** (town) Orleans County	125	4.2	**Macedon** (town) Wayne County
52	3.2	**Greenville** (CDP) Westchester County	125	4.2	**Monroe** (village) Orange County
52	3.2	**Larchmont** (village) Westchester County	125	4.2	**New Haven** (town) Oswego County
52	3.2	**Romulus** (town) Seneca County	125	4.2	**Somerset** (town) Niagara County
52	3.2	**Wading River** (CDP) Suffolk County	125	4.2	**Spring Valley** (village) Rockland County
59	3.3	**Conesus** (town) Livingston County	125	4.2	**University Gardens** (CDP) Nassau County
59	3.3	**Duanesburg** (town) Schenectady County	125	4.2	**Wheatley Heights** (CDP) Suffolk County
59	3.3	**Horseheads North** (CDP) Chemung County	136	4.3	**Binghamton** (town) Broome County
59	3.3	**Northeast Ithaca** (CDP) Tompkins County	136	4.3	**Cold Spring Harbor** (CDP) Suffolk County
59	3.3	**Old Westbury** (village) Nassau County	136	4.3	**Grand Island** (town) Erie County
59	3.3	**Scriba** (town) Oswego County	136	4.3	**Hamilton** (town) Madison County
59	3.3	**Wawayanda** (town) Orange County	136	4.3	**Highland Falls** (village) Orange County
59	3.3	**West Haverstraw** (village) Rockland County	136	4.3	**Lansing** (town) Tompkins County
67	3.4	**Chester** (village) Orange County	136	4.3	**Marilla** (town) Erie County
67	3.4	**Clinton** (town) Dutchess County	136	4.3	**Oneonta** (city) Otsego County
67	3.4	**Colden** (town) Erie County	136	4.3	**Pomfret** (town) Chautauqua County
67	3.4	**East Bloomfield** (town) Ontario County	136	4.3	**Potsdam** (town) Saint Lawrence County
67	3.4	**Hartsdale** (CDP) Westchester County	146	4.4	**Brentwood** (CDP) Suffolk County
67	3.4	**Lansing** (village) Tompkins County	146	4.4	**Cazenovia** (town) Madison County
67	3.4	**Rush** (town) Monroe County	146	4.4	**Dix Hills** (CDP) Suffolk County
74	3.5	**Armonk** (CDP) Westchester County	146	4.4	**East Hampton North** (CDP) Suffolk County
74	3.5	**Ellisburg** (town) Jefferson County	146	4.4	**Elmsford** (village) Westchester County

Note: *This section ranks incorporated places and CDPs (Census Designated Places) with populations of 2,500 or more. Unincorporated postal areas were not considered. Please refer to the User Guide for additional information.*

Marriage Status: Divorced

Top 150 Places Ranked in *Descending* Order

State Rank	Percent	Place	State Rank	Percent	Place
1	21.6	**Afton** (town) Chenango County	73	14.3	**Vernon** (town) Oneida County
2	19.9	**Greenwood Lake** (village) Orange County	77	14.2	**Canastota** (village) Madison County
3	19.7	**Warsaw** (village) Wyoming County	77	14.2	**Floyd** (town) Oneida County
4	19.6	**New York Mills** (village) Oneida County	77	14.2	**Laurens** (town) Otsego County
5	19.5	**Whitesboro** (village) Oneida County	77	14.2	**Mattydale** (CDP) Onondaga County
6	18.3	**Carroll** (town) Chautauqua County	77	14.2	**North East** (town) Dutchess County
7	18.2	**Firthcliffe** (CDP) Orange County	77	14.2	**Stockport** (town) Columbia County
7	18.2	**Saint Regis Mohawk Reservation** (reservation) Franklin County	83	14.1	**Fulton** (city) Oswego County
9	18.0	**South Glens Falls** (village) Saratoga County	83	14.1	**Lockport** (city) Niagara County
10	17.8	**Conklin** (town) Broome County	83	14.1	**Sloan** (village) Erie County
10	17.8	**Walton** (village) Delaware County	86	14.0	**Palatine** (town) Montgomery County
10	17.8	**Williamsville** (village) Erie County	86	14.0	**Patchogue** (village) Suffolk County
13	17.6	**Little Falls** (city) Herkimer County	86	14.0	**Saratoga** (town) Saratoga County
14	17.4	**Granville** (town) Washington County	89	13.9	**Alden** (village) Erie County
14	17.4	**Malone** (village) Franklin County	89	13.9	**Concord** (town) Erie County
14	17.4	**Village Green** (CDP) Onondaga County	89	13.9	**East Aurora** (village) Erie County
17	17.2	**Waterloo** (town) Seneca County	89	13.9	**Lewiston** (village) Niagara County
18	17.0	**Frankfort** (village) Herkimer County	89	13.9	**Mechanicville** (city) Saratoga County
18	17.0	**Penn Yan** (village) Yates County	89	13.9	**Rome** (city) Oneida County
18	17.0	**Waterloo** (village) Seneca County	89	13.9	**Sidney** (town) Delaware County
21	16.9	**Dix** (town) Schuyler County	96	13.8	**Chittenango** (village) Madison County
21	16.9	**Lyons** (village) Wayne County	96	13.8	**Fairport** (village) Monroe County
21	16.9	**Springville** (village) Erie County	96	13.8	**North Syracuse** (village) Onondaga County
24	16.6	**Sheridan** (town) Chautauqua County	99	13.7	**Bath** (village) Steuben County
25	16.5	**Gowanda** (village) Cattaraugus County	99	13.7	**Brewerton** (CDP) Onondaga County
25	16.5	**Southampton** (village) Suffolk County	99	13.7	**Franklinville** (town) Cattaraugus County
25	16.5	**Wellsville** (village) Allegany County	99	13.7	**Gouverneur** (village) Saint Lawrence County
28	16.4	**Murray** (town) Orleans County	99	13.7	**Manchester** (town) Ontario County
29	16.3	**Olean** (city) Cattaraugus County	99	13.7	**Scotia** (village) Schenectady County
30	16.0	**Bath** (town) Steuben County	99	13.7	**Van Buren** (town) Onondaga County
30	16.0	**Warsaw** (town) Wyoming County	106	13.6	**Auburn** (city) Cayuga County
32	15.9	**Akron** (village) Erie County	106	13.6	**Carthage** (village) Jefferson County
32	15.9	**Colesville** (town) Broome County	106	13.6	**Hartsdale** (CDP) Westchester County
32	15.9	**Norwich** (city) Chenango County	106	13.6	**Johnstown** (city) Fulton County
32	15.9	**Norwich** (town) Chenango County	106	13.6	**Lansing** (village) Tompkins County
36	15.7	**Davenport** (town) Delaware County	106	13.6	**Palmyra** (town) Wayne County
36	15.7	**Sidney** (village) Delaware County	106	13.6	**Shandaken** (town) Ulster County
38	15.6	**Groveland** (town) Livingston County	113	13.5	**Blasdell** (village) Erie County
39	15.5	**Sterling** (town) Cayuga County	113	13.5	**Danby** (town) Tompkins County
39	15.5	**Vienna** (town) Oneida County	113	13.5	**Dunkirk** (city) Chautauqua County
41	15.4	**Caroline** (town) Tompkins County	113	13.5	**Green Island** (town/village) Albany County
41	15.4	**Marlboro** (CDP) Ulster County	113	13.5	**Island Park** (village) Nassau County
41	15.4	**Niagara** (town) Niagara County	113	13.5	**Marlborough** (town) Ulster County
44	15.3	**Hamlin** (CDP) Monroe County	113	13.5	**Newfane** (CDP) Niagara County
44	15.3	**Hannibal** (town) Oswego County	113	13.5	**Saint Johnsville** (town) Montgomery County
44	15.3	**Hudson** (city) Columbia County	113	13.5	**Skaneateles** (village) Onondaga County
44	15.3	**Milo** (town) Yates County	113	13.5	**Southport** (CDP) Chemung County
44	15.3	**Palmyra** (village) Wayne County	113	13.5	**Warwick** (village) Orange County
44	15.3	**Salamanca** (city) Cattaraugus County	113	13.5	**Wellsville** (town) Allegany County
44	15.3	**Scriba** (town) Oswego County	113	13.5	**Woodstock** (town) Ulster County
51	15.2	**Baldwinsville** (village) Onondaga County	126	13.4	**Brutus** (town) Cayuga County
51	15.2	**Clarendon** (town) Orleans County	126	13.4	**Corinth** (village) Saratoga County
51	15.2	**New Haven** (town) Oswego County	126	13.4	**East Rochester** (town/village) Monroe County
51	15.2	**South Lockport** (CDP) Niagara County	126	13.4	**Middletown** (town) Delaware County
55	15.1	**Portland** (town) Chautauqua County	126	13.4	**Schroeppel** (town) Oswego County
56	15.0	**Moravia** (town) Cayuga County	126	13.4	**Seneca Falls** (CDP) Seneca County
57	14.9	**Canandaigua** (city) Ontario County	126	13.4	**Spencerport** (village) Monroe County
57	14.9	**Endicott** (village) Broome County	133	13.3	**Broadalbin** (town) Fulton County
57	14.9	**Milford** (town) Otsego County	133	13.3	**Collins** (town) Erie County
60	14.8	**Jamestown** (city) Chautauqua County	133	13.3	**Fort Edward** (town) Washington County
60	14.8	**Mount Morris** (village) Livingston County	133	13.3	**Mohawk** (village) Herkimer County
60	14.8	**West Glens Falls** (CDP) Warren County	133	13.3	**Tioga** (town) Tioga County
63	14.7	**Corning** (city) Steuben County	133	13.3	**West Monroe** (town) Oswego County
63	14.7	**East Syracuse** (village) Onondaga County	133	13.3	**Windsor** (town) Broome County
63	14.7	**Gordon Heights** (CDP) Suffolk County	140	13.2	**Batavia** (town) Genesee County
63	14.7	**Homer** (village) Cortland County	140	13.2	**Gaines** (town) Orleans County
67	14.6	**Glens Falls** (city) Warren County	140	13.2	**Hanover** (town) Chautauqua County
67	14.6	**Tuckahoe** (village) Westchester County	140	13.2	**Hector** (town) Schuyler County
67	14.6	**Wilson** (town) Niagara County	140	13.2	**Hopewell** (town) Ontario County
70	14.5	**Stockholm** (town) Saint Lawrence County	140	13.2	**Johnson City** (village) Broome County
71	14.4	**Elbridge** (town) Onondaga County	140	13.2	**Seneca Falls** (town) Seneca County
71	14.4	**White Creek** (town) Washington County	140	13.2	**Whitehall** (village) Washington County
73	14.3	**Hudson Falls** (village) Washington County	148	13.1	**Hancock** (town) Delaware County
73	14.3	**Medina** (village) Orleans County	148	13.1	**Homer** (town) Cortland County
73	14.3	**Richland** (town) Oswego County	148	13.1	**Yates** (town) Orleans County

Note: This section ranks incorporated places and CDPs (Census Designated Places) with populations of 2,500 or more. Unincorporated postal areas were not considered. Please refer to the User Guide for additional information.

Marriage Status: Divorced

Top 150 Places Ranked in *Ascending* Order

State Rank	Percent	Place	State Rank	Percent	Place
1	0.1	**Binghamton University** (CDP) Broome County	74	5.1	**Syosset** (CDP) Nassau County
1	0.1	**University at Buffalo** (CDP) Erie County	77	5.2	**Lake Success** (village) Nassau County
3	0.2	**Stony Brook University** (CDP) Suffolk County	77	5.2	**Lido Beach** (CDP) Nassau County
4	0.3	**Kiryas Joel** (village) Orange County	77	5.2	**New Hyde Park** (village) Nassau County
4	0.3	**New Square** (village) Rockland County	77	5.2	**Paris** (town) Oneida County
4	0.3	**SUNY Oswego** (CDP) Oswego County	77	5.2	**Spackenkill** (CDP) Dutchess County
7	0.5	**Alfred** (village) Allegany County	77	5.2	**West Hills** (CDP) Suffolk County
8	0.8	**Kaser** (village) Rockland County	83	5.3	**Fort Salonga** (CDP) Suffolk County
9	1.3	**Brookville** (village) Nassau County	83	5.3	**Great Neck Estates** (village) Nassau County
10	1.5	**South Hill** (CDP) Tompkins County	83	5.3	**Hartland** (town) Niagara County
11	1.7	**Monsey** (CDP) Rockland County	83	5.3	**Milton** (CDP) Saratoga County
12	1.8	**Kings Point** (village) Nassau County	83	5.3	**Thiells** (CDP) Rockland County
13	2.1	**Alfred** (town) Allegany County	88	5.4	**Jericho** (CDP) Nassau County
14	2.2	**Lloyd Harbor** (village) Suffolk County	88	5.4	**Massapequa Park** (village) Nassau County
15	2.3	**West Point** (CDP) Orange County	88	5.4	**Port Washington North** (village) Nassau County
16	2.4	**Caneadea** (town) Allegany County	88	5.4	**Stony Point** (town) Rockland County
16	2.4	**Hamilton** (village) Madison County	88	5.4	**Wesley Hills** (village) Rockland County
18	2.5	**Old Westbury** (village) Nassau County	93	5.5	**Bellmore** (CDP) Nassau County
18	2.5	**Watchtower** (CDP) Ulster County	93	5.5	**Cambria** (town) Niagara County
20	2.7	**Geneseo** (village) Livingston County	93	5.5	**Clarence** (CDP) Erie County
21	2.8	**Lawrence** (village) Nassau County	93	5.5	**East Williston** (village) Nassau County
21	2.8	**Muttontown** (village) Nassau County	97	5.6	**Duanesburg** (town) Schenectady County
23	2.9	**Blauvelt** (CDP) Rockland County	97	5.6	**Great Neck** (village) Nassau County
23	2.9	**Scarsdale** (town/village) Westchester County	97	5.6	**Herricks** (CDP) Nassau County
25	3.0	**East Hills** (village) Nassau County	97	5.6	**Highlands** (town) Orange County
26	3.1	**Manhasset Hills** (CDP) Nassau County	97	5.6	**Montauk** (CDP) Suffolk County
26	3.1	**Pomona** (village) Rockland County	97	5.6	**Oneonta** (city) Otsego County
28	3.2	**New Castle** (town) Westchester County	97	5.6	**Oswego** (town) Oswego County
29	3.3	**Garden City** (village) Nassau County	97	5.6	**Pittsford** (town) Monroe County
30	3.4	**North New Hyde Park** (CDP) Nassau County	97	5.6	**Rye** (city) Westchester County
31	3.5	**Armonk** (CDP) Westchester County	97	5.6	**Tappan** (CDP) Rockland County
31	3.5	**Fort Drum** (CDP) Jefferson County	97	5.6	**University Gardens** (CDP) Nassau County
33	3.6	**Bedford Hills** (CDP) Westchester County	97	5.6	**Walworth** (town) Wayne County
33	3.6	**Cayuga Heights** (village) Tompkins County	97	5.6	**West Sayville** (CDP) Suffolk County
33	3.6	**Munsey Park** (village) Nassau County	110	5.7	**Albertson** (CDP) Nassau County
33	3.6	**New Hempstead** (village) Rockland County	110	5.7	**Ardsley** (village) Westchester County
37	3.7	**Dix Hills** (CDP) Suffolk County	110	5.7	**Commack** (CDP) Suffolk County
37	3.7	**Woodmere** (CDP) Nassau County	110	5.7	**Massapequa** (CDP) Nassau County
39	3.9	**Garden City Park** (CDP) Nassau County	110	5.7	**Seaford** (CDP) Nassau County
40	4.0	**East Garden City** (CDP) Nassau County	110	5.7	**Victor** (town) Ontario County
41	4.1	**Le Ray** (town) Jefferson County	110	5.7	**Wheatley Heights** (CDP) Suffolk County
42	4.2	**Valhalla** (CDP) Westchester County	117	5.8	**Brockport** (village) Monroe County
43	4.3	**Ithaca** (city) Tompkins County	117	5.8	**Flower Hill** (village) Nassau County
43	4.3	**Lakeview** (CDP) Nassau County	117	5.8	**Rye Brook** (village) Westchester County
43	4.3	**Old Bethpage** (CDP) Nassau County	120	5.9	**Farmingville** (CDP) Suffolk County
43	4.3	**Pelham Manor** (village) Westchester County	120	5.9	**Franklin Square** (CDP) Nassau County
43	4.3	**Searingtown** (CDP) Nassau County	120	5.9	**Ramapo** (town) Rockland County
43	4.3	**Viola** (CDP) Rockland County	120	5.9	**Wyandanch** (CDP) Suffolk County
49	4.4	**Monroe** (town) Orange County	124	6.0	**Bethpage** (CDP) Nassau County
49	4.4	**Northeast Ithaca** (CDP) Tompkins County	124	6.0	**East Rockaway** (village) Nassau County
51	4.5	**Brightwaters** (village) Suffolk County	124	6.0	**East Shoreham** (CDP) Suffolk County
51	4.5	**Calcium** (CDP) Jefferson County	124	6.0	**Horseheads North** (CDP) Chemung County
53	4.6	**Argyle** (town) Washington County	124	6.0	**North Massapequa** (CDP) Nassau County
53	4.6	**New Cassel** (CDP) Nassau County	124	6.0	**Oyster Bay** (town) Nassau County
53	4.6	**New Paltz** (village) Ulster County	124	6.0	**Philipstown** (town) Putnam County
53	4.6	**Salisbury** (CDP) Nassau County	131	6.1	**Cold Spring Harbor** (CDP) Suffolk County
57	4.7	**Hamptonburgh** (town) Orange County	131	6.1	**Croghan** (town) Lewis County
57	4.7	**Plainview** (CDP) Nassau County	131	6.1	**Glen Head** (CDP) Nassau County
57	4.7	**Wantagh** (CDP) Nassau County	131	6.1	**North Great River** (CDP) Suffolk County
57	4.7	**West Sand Lake** (CDP) Rensselaer County	131	6.1	**Orangeburg** (CDP) Rockland County
61	4.8	**Cedarhurst** (village) Nassau County	131	6.1	**Pelham** (town) Westchester County
61	4.8	**Hamilton** (town) Madison County	131	6.1	**Sands Point** (village) Nassau County
61	4.8	**Mount Sinai** (CDP) Suffolk County	138	6.2	**Airmont** (village) Rockland County
61	4.8	**South Farmingdale** (CDP) Nassau County	138	6.2	**Bardonia** (CDP) Rockland County
65	4.9	**Briarcliff Manor** (village) Westchester County	138	6.2	**Center Moriches** (CDP) Suffolk County
65	4.9	**Geneseo** (town) Livingston County	138	6.2	**Durham** (town) Greene County
65	4.9	**Stony Point** (CDP) Rockland County	138	6.2	**Monroe** (village) Orange County
68	5.0	**Hicksville** (CDP) Nassau County	138	6.2	**North Castle** (town) Westchester County
68	5.0	**Irvington** (village) Westchester County	138	6.2	**Roslyn Heights** (CDP) Nassau County
68	5.0	**Ithaca** (town) Tompkins County	145	6.3	**Babylon** (village) Suffolk County
68	5.0	**Merrick** (CDP) Nassau County	145	6.3	**Bronxville** (village) Westchester County
68	5.0	**Potsdam** (village) Saint Lawrence County	145	6.3	**East Farmingdale** (CDP) Suffolk County
68	5.0	**Stony Brook** (CDP) Suffolk County	145	6.3	**Floral Park** (village) Nassau County
74	5.1	**New City** (CDP) Rockland County	145	6.3	**Mount Pleasant** (town) Westchester County
74	5.1	**Oceanside** (CDP) Nassau County	145	6.3	**Myers Corner** (CDP) Dutchess County

Note: This section ranks incorporated places and CDPs (Census Designated Places) with populations of 2,500 or more. Unincorporated postal areas were not considered. Please refer to the User Guide for additional information.

Foreign Born

Top 150 Places Ranked in *Descending* Order

State Rank	Percent	Place	State Rank	Percent	Place
1	47.8	**Queens** (borough) Queens County	76	25.4	**Islandia** (village) Suffolk County
2	45.6	**Port Chester** (village) Westchester County	77	25.1	**Wyandanch** (CDP) Suffolk County
3	45.2	**Northeast Ithaca** (CDP) Tompkins County	78	25.0	**Baldwin** (CDP) Nassau County
4	43.5	**New Cassel** (CDP) Nassau County	78	25.0	**Harrison** (town/village) Westchester County
5	43.4	**Elmont** (CDP) Nassau County	78	25.0	**North Hills** (village) Nassau County
6	42.9	**Hillcrest** (CDP) Rockland County	81	24.9	**Jericho** (CDP) Nassau County
7	42.1	**Brentwood** (CDP) Suffolk County	82	24.8	**Carle Place** (CDP) Nassau County
8	41.9	**Spring Valley** (village) Rockland County	82	24.8	**Newburgh** (city) Orange County
9	41.1	**Elmsford** (village) Westchester County	84	24.7	**East Farmingdale** (CDP) Suffolk County
9	41.1	**Uniondale** (CDP) Nassau County	85	24.6	**North Lindenhurst** (CDP) Suffolk County
11	40.6	**University Gardens** (CDP) Nassau County	86	24.5	**Vails Gate** (CDP) Orange County
12	40.5	**Manhasset Hills** (CDP) Nassau County	87	24.4	**East Hampton North** (CDP) Suffolk County
13	39.9	**Hempstead** (village) Nassau County	88	23.9	**Wappingers Falls** (village) Dutchess County
14	39.8	**Sleepy Hollow** (village) Westchester County	89	23.7	**Bay Shore** (CDP) Suffolk County
15	39.5	**Ossining** (village) Westchester County	89	23.7	**Ithaca** (town) Tompkins County
16	39.3	**Flanders** (CDP) Suffolk County	89	23.7	**Muttontown** (village) Nassau County
17	39.2	**Garden City Park** (CDP) Nassau County	89	23.7	**Valhalla** (CDP) Westchester County
18	38.3	**Mount Kisco** (town/village) Westchester County	93	23.4	**Salisbury** (CDP) Nassau County
19	38.0	**North Valley Stream** (CDP) Nassau County	94	23.1	**Mount Ivy** (CDP) Rockland County
20	37.5	**Brooklyn** (borough) Kings County	95	22.9	**Greenburgh** (town) Westchester County
20	37.5	**Great Neck** (village) Nassau County	96	22.8	**Flower Hill** (village) Nassau County
20	37.5	**Haverstraw** (village) Rockland County	97	22.7	**Franklin Square** (CDP) Nassau County
23	37.2	**New York** (city)	97	22.7	**Tuckahoe** (village) Westchester County
24	36.5	**Inwood** (CDP) Nassau County	99	22.6	**Syosset** (CDP) Nassau County
25	36.4	**Searingtown** (CDP) Nassau County	100	22.5	**Greenville** (CDP) Westchester County
26	36.3	**Manorhaven** (village) Nassau County	100	22.5	**Old Westbury** (village) Nassau County
27	35.9	**Lansing** (village) Tompkins County	102	22.4	**University at Buffalo** (CDP) Erie County
28	35.7	**Rye** (town) Westchester County	103	22.2	**Ramapo** (town) Rockland County
29	35.5	**North Bay Shore** (CDP) Suffolk County	103	22.2	**Scarsdale** (town/village) Westchester County
30	35.3	**Bedford Hills** (CDP) Westchester County	105	22.1	**Clarkstown** (town) Rockland County
31	34.4	**Bronx** (borough) Bronx County	105	22.1	**Tappan** (CDP) Rockland County
32	34.2	**Herricks** (CDP) Nassau County	107	22.0	**Pomona** (village) Rockland County
32	34.2	**Valley Stream** (village) Nassau County	108	21.8	**Hempstead** (town) Nassau County
34	34.1	**New Hyde Park** (village) Nassau County	109	21.6	**Riverhead** (CDP) Suffolk County
35	33.9	**Central Islip** (CDP) Suffolk County	109	21.6	**Staten Island** (borough) Richmond County
35	33.9	**Mount Vernon** (city) Westchester County	111	21.3	**Valley Cottage** (CDP) Rockland County
35	33.9	**South Valley Stream** (CDP) Nassau County	112	21.0	**Mamaroneck** (town) Westchester County
38	33.4	**Kings Point** (village) Nassau County	113	20.9	**Harriman** (village) Orange County
39	33.3	**Westbury** (village) Nassau County	114	20.8	**West Hempstead** (CDP) Nassau County
40	33.2	**Fairview** (CDP) Westchester County	114	20.8	**Wheatley Heights** (CDP) Suffolk County
41	33.1	**Hartsdale** (CDP) Westchester County	116	20.7	**North Bellport** (CDP) Suffolk County
42	32.6	**White Plains** (city) Westchester County	117	20.6	**Chestnut Ridge** (village) Rockland County
43	32.2	**Roosevelt** (CDP) Nassau County	117	20.6	**South Fallsburg** (CDP) Sullivan County
44	31.5	**Mineola** (village) Nassau County	119	20.5	**Tarrytown** (village) Westchester County
45	31.4	**Copiague** (CDP) Suffolk County	120	20.4	**Baldwin Harbor** (CDP) Nassau County
45	31.4	**Stony Brook University** (CDP) Suffolk County	121	20.3	**Mount Pleasant** (town) Westchester County
47	31.3	**Freeport** (village) Nassau County	121	20.3	**Port Jefferson Station** (CDP) Suffolk County
48	31.1	**Glen Cove** (city) Nassau County	121	20.3	**Southampton** (town) Suffolk County
48	31.1	**North Amityville** (CDP) Suffolk County	124	20.2	**New Hempstead** (village) Rockland County
50	30.6	**Ossining** (town) Westchester County	125	19.7	**Chester** (village) Orange County
50	30.6	**Yonkers** (city) Westchester County	125	19.7	**Mahopac** (CDP) Putnam County
52	30.5	**Great Neck Plaza** (village) Nassau County	127	19.6	**Babylon** (town) Suffolk County
53	30.0	**Thomaston** (village) Nassau County	127	19.6	**Poughkeepsie** (city) Dutchess County
54	29.5	**Ardsley** (village) Westchester County	127	19.6	**Springs** (CDP) Suffolk County
55	29.4	**Albertson** (CDP) Nassau County	130	19.5	**Islip** (town) Suffolk County
56	29.2	**Lake Success** (village) Nassau County	130	19.5	**Pelham** (village) Westchester County
57	29.1	**Nanuet** (CDP) Rockland County	132	19.2	**Manhasset** (CDP) Nassau County
57	29.1	**New Rochelle** (city) Westchester County	132	19.2	**New City** (CDP) Rockland County
57	29.1	**North New Hyde Park** (CDP) Nassau County	134	19.1	**Locust Valley** (CDP) Nassau County
60	29.0	**Arlington** (CDP) Dutchess County	134	19.1	**Port Washington** (CDP) Nassau County
60	29.0	**North Hempstead** (town) Nassau County	134	19.1	**Webster** (village) Monroe County
62	28.9	**Manhattan** (borough) New York County	137	18.9	**Utica** (city) Oneida County
63	28.7	**Lakeview** (CDP) Nassau County	137	18.9	**Woodbury** (town) Orange County
64	28.6	**Roslyn Heights** (CDP) Nassau County	139	18.8	**East Meadow** (CDP) Nassau County
65	28.5	**Peekskill** (city) Westchester County	139	18.8	**Orangeburg** (CDP) Rockland County
66	27.8	**Haverstraw** (town) Rockland County	139	18.8	**Williston Park** (village) Nassau County
67	27.6	**Hicksville** (CDP) Nassau County	142	18.6	**Garden City South** (CDP) Nassau County
68	27.5	**Hampton Bays** (CDP) Suffolk County	142	18.6	**Roslyn** (village) Nassau County
69	27.3	**Noyack** (CDP) Suffolk County	144	18.5	**Congers** (CDP) Rockland County
70	26.6	**West Haverstraw** (village) Rockland County	144	18.5	**East Hampton** (town) Suffolk County
71	26.5	**Cedarhurst** (village) Nassau County	144	18.5	**Hewlett** (CDP) Nassau County
72	26.4	**Cayuga Heights** (village) Tompkins County	144	18.5	**Woodbury** (village) Orange County
73	26.2	**Great Neck Estates** (village) Nassau County	148	18.4	**Dobbs Ferry** (village) Westchester County
74	26.1	**Mamaroneck** (village) Westchester County	148	18.4	**Middletown** (city) Orange County
75	25.7	**Huntington Station** (CDP) Suffolk County	150	18.2	**Suffern** (village) Rockland County

Note: This section ranks incorporated places and CDPs (Census Designated Places) with populations of 2,500 or more. Unincorporated postal areas were not considered. Please refer to the User Guide for additional information.

Foreign Born

Top 150 Places Ranked in *Ascending* Order

State Rank	Percent	Place	State Rank	Percent	Place
1	0.0	**Canastota** (village) Madison County	74	1.2	**Hannibal** (town) Oswego County
1	0.0	**Otisco** (town) Onondaga County	74	1.2	**Hornell** (city) Steuben County
3	0.1	**Brookfield** (town) Madison County	74	1.2	**Hudson Falls** (village) Washington County
3	0.1	**Westfield** (town) Chautauqua County	74	1.2	**Ilion** (village) Herkimer County
5	0.2	**Cuba** (town) Allegany County	74	1.2	**Mayfield** (town) Fulton County
5	0.2	**Lisle** (town) Broome County	74	1.2	**Nichols** (town) Tioga County
5	0.2	**Palmyra** (village) Wayne County	74	1.2	**Oxford** (town) Chenango County
5	0.2	**Verona** (town) Oneida County	74	1.2	**Pembroke** (town) Genesee County
5	0.2	**Westfield** (village) Chautauqua County	74	1.2	**Saint Johnsville** (town) Montgomery County
5	0.2	**Whitesboro** (village) Oneida County	74	1.2	**Stephentown** (town) Rensselaer County
11	0.3	**Lenox** (town) Madison County	74	1.2	**Triangle** (town) Broome County
12	0.4	**Cohocton** (town) Steuben County	74	1.2	**Vienna** (town) Oneida County
12	0.4	**Colesville** (town) Broome County	74	1.2	**Walton** (town) Delaware County
12	0.4	**Fort Edward** (village) Washington County	74	1.2	**Waterloo** (town) Seneca County
12	0.4	**Jay** (town) Essex County	74	1.2	**Wolcott** (town) Wayne County
12	0.4	**Newark Valley** (town) Tioga County	91	1.3	**Amsterdam** (town) Montgomery County
12	0.4	**Pavilion** (town) Genesee County	91	1.3	**Arcade** (town) Wyoming County
12	0.4	**Sangerfield** (town) Oneida County	91	1.3	**Gaines** (town) Orleans County
12	0.4	**York** (town) Livingston County	91	1.3	**Livonia** (town) Livingston County
20	0.5	**Mooers** (town) Clinton County	91	1.3	**Malone** (village) Franklin County
20	0.5	**Moriah** (town) Essex County	91	1.3	**North Dansville** (town) Livingston County
20	0.5	**New Haven** (town) Oswego County	91	1.3	**Nunda** (town) Livingston County
20	0.5	**Norwich** (town) Chenango County	91	1.3	**Sterling** (town) Cayuga County
20	0.5	**Sardinia** (town) Erie County	91	1.3	**Ticonderoga** (town) Essex County
20	0.5	**Ticonderoga** (CDP) Essex County	91	1.3	**Warsaw** (village) Wyoming County
20	0.5	**Wayland** (town) Steuben County	91	1.3	**West Monroe** (town) Oswego County
20	0.5	**Whitehall** (town) Washington County	102	1.4	**Alden** (village) Erie County
20	0.5	**Yorkshire** (town) Cattaraugus County	102	1.4	**Barton** (town) Tioga County
29	0.6	**Holland** (town) Erie County	102	1.4	**Bennington** (town) Wyoming County
29	0.6	**Southport** (CDP) Chemung County	102	1.4	**Honeoye Falls** (village) Monroe County
29	0.6	**Waterloo** (village) Seneca County	102	1.4	**Kendall** (town) Orleans County
32	0.7	**Canisteo** (town) Steuben County	102	1.4	**Le Roy** (town) Genesee County
32	0.7	**Chittenango** (village) Madison County	102	1.4	**Mohawk** (village) Herkimer County
32	0.7	**Conklin** (town) Broome County	102	1.4	**Rose** (town) Wayne County
32	0.7	**Northumberland** (town) Saratoga County	110	1.5	**Argyle** (town) Washington County
32	0.7	**Seneca** (town) Ontario County	110	1.5	**Boonville** (town) Oneida County
32	0.7	**South Glens Falls** (village) Saratoga County	110	1.5	**Dansville** (village) Livingston County
38	0.8	**Alexander** (town) Genesee County	110	1.5	**Deerpark** (town) Orange County
38	0.8	**Attica** (village) Wyoming County	110	1.5	**Ellisburg** (town) Jefferson County
38	0.8	**Candor** (town) Tioga County	110	1.5	**Granby** (town) Oswego County
38	0.8	**Ellery** (town) Chautauqua County	110	1.5	**Greene** (town) Chenango County
38	0.8	**Fort Edward** (town) Washington County	110	1.5	**Hanover** (town) Chautauqua County
38	0.8	**Lake Luzerne** (town) Warren County	110	1.5	**Marilla** (town) Erie County
38	0.8	**Middleburgh** (town) Schoharie County	110	1.5	**Mexico** (town) Oswego County
38	0.8	**Portville** (town) Cattaraugus County	110	1.5	**Minoa** (village) Onondaga County
38	0.8	**Sherburne** (town) Chenango County	110	1.5	**Mount Morris** (town) Livingston County
38	0.8	**Walton** (village) Delaware County	110	1.5	**Newfane** (town) Niagara County
38	0.8	**Whitehall** (village) Washington County	110	1.5	**Palmyra** (town) Wayne County
38	0.8	**Windsor** (town) Broome County	110	1.5	**Pittstown** (town) Rensselaer County
50	0.9	**Altona** (town) Clinton County	125	1.6	**Alexandria** (town) Jefferson County
50	0.9	**Broadalbin** (town) Fulton County	125	1.6	**Catlin** (town) Chemung County
50	0.9	**Campbell** (town) Steuben County	125	1.6	**Elmira Heights** (village) Chemung County
50	0.9	**Clarendon** (town) Orleans County	125	1.6	**Fenton** (town) Broome County
50	0.9	**Constantia** (town) Oswego County	125	1.6	**Hamburg** (village) Erie County
50	0.9	**Denmark** (town) Lewis County	125	1.6	**Jamestown** (city) Chautauqua County
50	0.9	**Floyd** (town) Oneida County	125	1.6	**Palatine** (town) Montgomery County
50	0.9	**Lyons** (village) Wayne County	125	1.6	**Pamelia** (town) Jefferson County
50	0.9	**Moravia** (town) Cayuga County	125	1.6	**Richland** (town) Oswego County
50	0.9	**New Bremen** (town) Lewis County	125	1.6	**Starkey** (town) Yates County
50	0.9	**Perry** (town) Wyoming County	125	1.6	**White Creek** (town) Washington County
50	0.9	**Perry** (village) Wyoming County	125	1.6	**Wilson** (town) Niagara County
50	0.9	**Phelps** (town) Ontario County	125	1.6	**Yates** (town) Orleans County
50	0.9	**Poestenkill** (town) Rensselaer County	138	1.7	**Baldwinsville** (village) Onondaga County
50	0.9	**Southport** (town) Chemung County	138	1.7	**Carthage** (village) Jefferson County
50	0.9	**Vernon** (town) Oneida County	138	1.7	**Croghan** (town) Lewis County
50	0.9	**Warsaw** (town) Wyoming County	138	1.7	**East Bloomfield** (town) Ontario County
67	1.0	**Aurelius** (town) Cayuga County	138	1.7	**Falconer** (village) Chautauqua County
67	1.0	**Darien** (town) Genesee County	138	1.7	**Groton** (town) Tompkins County
67	1.0	**Le Roy** (village) Genesee County	138	1.7	**Hamlin** (town) Monroe County
67	1.0	**Milo** (town) Yates County	138	1.7	**Homer** (town) Cortland County
67	1.0	**Randolph** (town) Cattaraugus County	138	1.7	**Hoosick** (town) Rensselaer County
67	1.0	**Sandy Creek** (town) Oswego County	138	1.7	**Hoosick Falls** (village) Rensselaer County
67	1.0	**Schroeppel** (town) Oswego County	138	1.7	**Lisbon** (town) Saint Lawrence County
74	1.2	**Camden** (town) Oneida County	138	1.7	**North Boston** (CDP) Erie County
74	1.2	**Enfield** (town) Tompkins County	138	1.7	**Palermo** (town) Oswego County

Note: *This section ranks incorporated places and CDPs (Census Designated Places) with populations of 2,500 or more. Unincorporated postal areas were not considered. Please refer to the User Guide for additional information.*

Speak English Only at Home

Top 150 Places Ranked in *Descending* Order

State Rank	Percent	Place	State Rank	Percent	Place
1	99.7	**Newark Valley** (town) Tioga County	71	98.1	**Nunda** (town) Livingston County
1	99.7	**Newfane** (CDP) Niagara County	71	98.1	**Sterling** (town) Cayuga County
3	99.6	**Pavilion** (town) Genesee County	71	98.1	**Whitehall** (town) Washington County
4	99.5	**Chemung** (town) Chemung County	79	98.0	**Broadalbin** (town) Fulton County
4	99.5	**Otisco** (town) Onondaga County	79	98.0	**Canajoharie** (town) Montgomery County
4	99.5	**Whitesboro** (village) Oneida County	79	98.0	**Otego** (town) Otsego County
7	99.4	**Carroll** (town) Chautauqua County	79	98.0	**Portville** (town) Cattaraugus County
7	99.4	**Jay** (town) Essex County	79	98.0	**Wilna** (town) Jefferson County
7	99.4	**Walton** (village) Delaware County	84	97.9	**Cohocton** (town) Steuben County
10	99.3	**Cambria** (town) Niagara County	84	97.9	**Dansville** (village) Livingston County
10	99.3	**Lyons** (village) Wayne County	84	97.9	**Davenport** (town) Delaware County
12	99.2	**Orchard Park** (village) Erie County	84	97.9	**Fenton** (town) Broome County
12	99.2	**Pierrepont** (town) Saint Lawrence County	84	97.9	**Lyons** (town) Wayne County
14	99.1	**Candor** (town) Tioga County	84	97.9	**Pittstown** (town) Rensselaer County
14	99.1	**Hudson Falls** (village) Washington County	84	97.9	**Poestenkill** (town) Rensselaer County
14	99.1	**Pendleton** (town) Niagara County	84	97.9	**Randolph** (town) Cattaraugus County
14	99.1	**Saranac** (town) Clinton County	92	97.8	**Baldwinsville** (village) Onondaga County
18	99.0	**Caroline** (town) Tompkins County	92	97.8	**Barton** (town) Tioga County
18	99.0	**Croghan** (town) Lewis County	92	97.8	**Camden** (town) Oneida County
18	99.0	**Newfane** (town) Niagara County	92	97.8	**East Bloomfield** (town) Ontario County
18	99.0	**Stockport** (town) Columbia County	92	97.8	**Floyd** (town) Oneida County
18	99.0	**Vienna** (town) Oneida County	92	97.8	**Kingsbury** (town) Washington County
18	99.0	**White Creek** (town) Washington County	92	97.8	**Northampton** (town) Fulton County
24	98.9	**Argyle** (town) Washington County	92	97.8	**Orleans** (town) Jefferson County
24	98.9	**Fort Edward** (village) Washington County	92	97.8	**Pembroke** (town) Genesee County
24	98.9	**Le Roy** (town) Genesee County	92	97.8	**Royalton** (town) Niagara County
24	98.9	**Southport** (CDP) Chemung County	92	97.8	**West Elmira** (CDP) Chemung County
24	98.9	**Whitehall** (village) Washington County	103	97.7	**Catlin** (town) Chemung County
29	98.8	**Alden** (village) Erie County	103	97.7	**Chenango Bridge** (CDP) Broome County
29	98.8	**Chittenango** (village) Madison County	103	97.7	**Constantia** (town) Oswego County
31	98.7	**Canisteo** (town) Steuben County	103	97.7	**Greene** (town) Chenango County
31	98.7	**Gaines** (town) Orleans County	103	97.7	**Honeoye Falls** (village) Monroe County
31	98.7	**Sangerfield** (town) Oneida County	103	97.7	**Lake Erie Beach** (CDP) Erie County
31	98.7	**Southport** (town) Chemung County	103	97.7	**Oakfield** (town) Genesee County
31	98.7	**Veteran** (town) Chemung County	103	97.7	**Rosendale** (town) Ulster County
31	98.7	**Wayland** (town) Steuben County	103	97.7	**Schaghticoke** (town) Rensselaer County
37	98.6	**Conklin** (town) Broome County	103	97.7	**Sennett** (town) Cayuga County
37	98.6	**Denmark** (town) Lewis County	103	97.7	**Unadilla** (town) Otsego County
37	98.6	**Elbridge** (town) Onondaga County	114	97.6	**Aurora** (town) Erie County
37	98.6	**Lake Luzerne** (town) Warren County	114	97.6	**Bennington** (town) Wyoming County
37	98.6	**South Glens Falls** (village) Saratoga County	114	97.6	**Boston** (town) Erie County
37	98.6	**Sullivan** (town) Madison County	114	97.6	**Brutus** (town) Cayuga County
37	98.6	**Volney** (town) Oswego County	114	97.6	**Canastota** (village) Madison County
44	98.5	**Carthage** (village) Jefferson County	114	97.6	**Clayton** (town) Jefferson County
44	98.5	**Coxsackie** (village) Greene County	114	97.6	**Eden** (town) Erie County
44	98.5	**Mohawk** (village) Herkimer County	114	97.6	**Elmira** (town) Chemung County
44	98.5	**New Bremen** (town) Lewis County	114	97.6	**Hector** (town) Schuyler County
44	98.5	**Norwich** (town) Chenango County	114	97.6	**Ilion** (village) Herkimer County
44	98.5	**Sandy Creek** (town) Oswego County	114	97.6	**Norfolk** (town) Saint Lawrence County
44	98.5	**Waterloo** (village) Seneca County	114	97.6	**North Collins** (town) Erie County
44	98.5	**Yorkshire** (town) Cattaraugus County	114	97.6	**Sardinia** (town) Erie County
52	98.4	**Ellery** (town) Chautauqua County	114	97.6	**Warsaw** (village) Wyoming County
52	98.4	**Fort Edward** (town) Washington County	128	97.5	**Caledonia** (town) Livingston County
52	98.4	**Kendall** (town) Orleans County	128	97.5	**Groton** (town) Tompkins County
52	98.4	**Nichols** (town) Tioga County	128	97.5	**Lakewood** (village) Chautauqua County
52	98.4	**North Boston** (CDP) Erie County	128	97.5	**Moriah** (town) Essex County
52	98.4	**Tully** (town) Onondaga County	128	97.5	**Porter** (town) Niagara County
52	98.4	**Walton** (town) Delaware County	128	97.5	**Saranac Lake** (village) Franklin County
59	98.3	**Bangor** (town) Franklin County	128	97.5	**Tupper Lake** (village) Franklin County
59	98.3	**Hartland** (town) Niagara County	135	97.4	**Alexandria** (town) Jefferson County
59	98.3	**Lisle** (town) Broome County	135	97.4	**Attica** (village) Wyoming County
59	98.3	**Mexico** (town) Oswego County	135	97.4	**Clarendon** (town) Orleans County
59	98.3	**Palmyra** (village) Wayne County	135	97.4	**Colden** (town) Erie County
59	98.3	**Silver Creek** (village) Chautauqua County	135	97.4	**Eden** (CDP) Erie County
59	98.3	**Warsaw** (town) Wyoming County	135	97.4	**Gouverneur** (village) Saint Lawrence County
59	98.3	**Wilson** (town) Niagara County	135	97.4	**Granville** (town) Washington County
59	98.3	**York** (town) Livingston County	135	97.4	**Hanover** (town) Chautauqua County
68	98.2	**Madison** (town) Madison County	135	97.4	**LaFayette** (town) Onondaga County
68	98.2	**Malone** (village) Franklin County	135	97.4	**Macedon** (town) Wayne County
68	98.2	**Mooers** (town) Clinton County	135	97.4	**Mechanicville** (city) Saratoga County
71	98.1	**Alexander** (town) Genesee County	135	97.4	**Minoa** (village) Onondaga County
71	98.1	**Hannibal** (town) Oswego County	135	97.4	**Nassau** (town) Rensselaer County
71	98.1	**Holland** (town) Erie County	135	97.4	**West Monroe** (town) Oswego County
71	98.1	**Le Roy** (village) Genesee County	149	97.3	**Guilford** (town) Chenango County
71	98.1	**North Dansville** (town) Livingston County	149	97.3	**New Berlin** (town) Chenango County

Note: *This section ranks incorporated places and CDPs (Census Designated Places) with populations of 2,500 or more. Unincorporated postal areas were not considered. Please refer to the User Guide for additional information.*

Speak English Only at Home

Top 150 Places Ranked in *Ascending* Order

State Rank	Percent	Place
1	5.5	**Kiryas Joel** (village) Orange County
2	5.7	**New Square** (village) Rockland County
3	7.3	**Kaser** (village) Rockland County
4	22.6	**Monsey** (CDP) Rockland County
5	30.7	**Brentwood** (CDP) Suffolk County
6	34.7	**Port Chester** (village) Westchester County
6	34.7	**Spring Valley** (village) Rockland County
8	36.7	**New Cassel** (CDP) Nassau County
9	37.7	**Haverstraw** (village) Rockland County
10	41.1	**Flanders** (CDP) Suffolk County
11	41.7	**Bronx** (borough) Bronx County
12	42.0	**North Bay Shore** (CDP) Suffolk County
13	42.6	**Monroe** (town) Orange County
14	43.4	**Stony Brook University** (CDP) Suffolk County
15	43.7	**Queens** (borough) Queens County
16	43.8	**Sleepy Hollow** (village) Westchester County
17	44.9	**Searingtown** (CDP) Nassau County
18	45.4	**Manhasset Hills** (CDP) Nassau County
19	45.7	**Ossining** (village) Westchester County
20	46.1	**Central Islip** (CDP) Suffolk County
21	46.7	**Great Neck** (village) Nassau County
22	48.8	**Ramapo** (town) Rockland County
23	49.6	**Rye** (town) Westchester County
24	50.1	**Garden City Park** (CDP) Nassau County
25	50.4	**West Haverstraw** (village) Rockland County
26	50.5	**Hillcrest** (CDP) Rockland County
27	50.6	**Inwood** (CDP) Nassau County
28	50.8	**Uniondale** (CDP) Nassau County
29	50.9	**New York** (city)
30	51.0	**Mount Kisco** (town/village) Westchester County
31	51.5	**Manorhaven** (village) Nassau County
32	51.8	**Elmont** (CDP) Nassau County
32	51.8	**Kings Point** (village) Nassau County
34	52.2	**Bedford Hills** (CDP) Westchester County
35	52.4	**Newburgh** (city) Orange County
36	53.0	**Hempstead** (village) Nassau County
37	53.1	**Herricks** (CDP) Nassau County
38	53.4	**Brooklyn** (borough) Kings County
38	53.4	**Yonkers** (city) Westchester County
40	53.7	**Elmsford** (village) Westchester County
41	54.3	**Haverstraw** (town) Rockland County
42	54.9	**White Plains** (city) Westchester County
43	56.0	**North New Hyde Park** (CDP) Nassau County
44	56.6	**Westbury** (village) Nassau County
45	56.7	**Freeport** (village) Nassau County
46	56.8	**University Gardens** (CDP) Nassau County
47	57.6	**New Hyde Park** (village) Nassau County
48	57.8	**Ossining** (town) Westchester County
49	57.9	**Mineola** (village) Nassau County
50	58.0	**South Fallsburg** (CDP) Sullivan County
50	58.0	**Valley Stream** (village) Nassau County
52	58.4	**Glen Cove** (city) Nassau County
53	58.7	**Northeast Ithaca** (CDP) Tompkins County
54	59.1	**Viola** (CDP) Rockland County
55	59.4	**Lake Success** (village) Nassau County
56	59.7	**Huntington Station** (CDP) Suffolk County
56	59.7	**Manhattan** (borough) New York County
58	60.3	**New Rochelle** (city) Westchester County
58	60.3	**North Bellport** (CDP) Suffolk County
60	60.4	**Copiague** (CDP) Suffolk County
61	61.3	**Cedarhurst** (village) Nassau County
62	61.4	**Wappingers Falls** (village) Dutchess County
63	61.7	**Islandia** (village) Suffolk County
63	61.7	**North Amityville** (CDP) Suffolk County
63	61.7	**North Hempstead** (town) Nassau County
63	61.7	**Thomaston** (village) Nassau County
67	62.1	**Harriman** (village) Orange County
68	62.8	**Roslyn Heights** (CDP) Nassau County
69	63.2	**Nanuet** (CDP) Rockland County
70	63.5	**Valhalla** (CDP) Westchester County
71	63.7	**Franklin Square** (CDP) Nassau County
72	63.8	**Great Neck Estates** (village) Nassau County
72	63.8	**Great Neck Plaza** (village) Nassau County
74	63.9	**Peekskill** (city) Westchester County
75	64.1	**Harrison** (town/village) Westchester County
76	64.2	**Hartsdale** (CDP) Westchester County
76	64.2	**Middletown** (city) Orange County
78	64.5	**Airmont** (village) Rockland County
79	64.6	**Roosevelt** (CDP) Nassau County
80	64.7	**Mamaroneck** (village) Westchester County
81	65.2	**Bay Shore** (CDP) Suffolk County
81	65.2	**Lansing** (village) Tompkins County
81	65.2	**University at Buffalo** (CDP) Erie County
84	65.3	**Hampton Bays** (CDP) Suffolk County
85	65.5	**South Valley Stream** (CDP) Nassau County
86	65.6	**Ardsley** (village) Westchester County
87	65.8	**Hicksville** (CDP) Nassau County
88	66.1	**Albertson** (CDP) Nassau County
88	66.1	**Jericho** (CDP) Nassau County
88	66.1	**Salisbury** (CDP) Nassau County
91	66.3	**Fairview** (CDP) Westchester County
91	66.3	**Vails Gate** (CDP) Orange County
93	66.7	**North Lindenhurst** (CDP) Suffolk County
94	67.1	**Wyandanch** (CDP) Suffolk County
95	67.3	**Mount Ivy** (CDP) Rockland County
95	67.3	**Muttontown** (village) Nassau County
97	67.7	**Carle Place** (CDP) Nassau County
98	68.4	**East Hampton North** (CDP) Suffolk County
99	68.5	**Syosset** (CDP) Nassau County
100	68.7	**North Valley Stream** (CDP) Nassau County
101	69.0	**New Hempstead** (village) Rockland County
102	69.1	**Islip** (town) Suffolk County
103	69.2	**Garden City South** (CDP) Nassau County
104	69.4	**Old Westbury** (village) Nassau County
104	69.4	**Saint Regis Mohawk Reservation** (reservation) Franklin County
106	69.6	**Staten Island** (borough) Richmond County
107	70.1	**Baldwin** (CDP) Nassau County
107	70.1	**Balmville** (CDP) Orange County
107	70.1	**Pomona** (village) Rockland County
110	70.2	**Tuckahoe** (village) Westchester County
111	70.5	**Patchogue** (village) Suffolk County
112	70.6	**Clarkstown** (town) Rockland County
112	70.6	**Lakeview** (CDP) Nassau County
112	70.6	**West Hempstead** (CDP) Nassau County
115	70.7	**Noyack** (CDP) Suffolk County
116	71.1	**East Farmingdale** (CDP) Suffolk County
117	71.2	**Binghamton University** (CDP) Broome County
117	71.2	**Mechanicstown** (CDP) Orange County
119	71.3	**Greenville** (CDP) Westchester County
120	71.4	**Mamaroneck** (town) Westchester County
121	71.7	**Tarrytown** (village) Westchester County
122	71.8	**Fallsburg** (town) Sullivan County
122	71.8	**Mount Pleasant** (town) Westchester County
124	71.9	**Port Jefferson Station** (CDP) Suffolk County
125	72.1	**Greenburgh** (town) Westchester County
126	72.3	**Baywood** (CDP) Suffolk County
126	72.3	**Manhasset** (CDP) Nassau County
126	72.3	**Utica** (city) Oneida County
126	72.3	**Valley Cottage** (CDP) Rockland County
126	72.3	**Williston Park** (village) Nassau County
131	72.5	**Hempstead** (town) Nassau County
132	72.7	**Locust Valley** (CDP) Nassau County
133	72.8	**Chestnut Ridge** (village) Rockland County
134	73.2	**Gordon Heights** (CDP) Suffolk County
134	73.2	**Roslyn** (village) Nassau County
134	73.2	**Woodbury** (town) Orange County
137	73.3	**Arlington** (CDP) Dutchess County
137	73.3	**Island Park** (village) Nassau County
139	73.4	**Amsterdam** (city) Montgomery County
140	73.6	**East Meadow** (CDP) Nassau County
140	73.6	**Tappan** (CDP) Rockland County
142	73.8	**Benton** (town) Yates County
142	73.8	**New Windsor** (CDP) Orange County
142	73.8	**Northwest Harbor** (CDP) Suffolk County
145	73.9	**Orangeburg** (CDP) Rockland County
145	73.9	**Pelham** (village) Westchester County
145	73.9	**Watchtower** (CDP) Ulster County
148	74.0	**Mahopac** (CDP) Putnam County
149	74.2	**Riverhead** (CDP) Suffolk County
150	74.3	**Brookville** (village) Nassau County

Note: This section ranks incorporated places and CDPs (Census Designated Places) with populations of 2,500 or more. Unincorporated postal areas were not considered. Please refer to the User Guide for additional information.

Individuals with a Disability

Top 150 Places Ranked in *Descending* Order

State Rank	Percent	Place
1	26.3	**Middleburgh** (town) Schoharie County
2	25.6	**New Berlin** (town) Chenango County
3	24.9	**Newark** (village) Wayne County
4	23.9	**Albion** (village) Orleans County
4	23.9	**Claverack** (town) Columbia County
4	23.9	**Wellsville** (village) Allegany County
7	23.2	**Liberty** (village) Sullivan County
8	22.7	**Oxford** (town) Chenango County
9	22.3	**Medina** (village) Orleans County
10	21.9	**Fort Edward** (town) Washington County
11	21.8	**Dannemora** (village) Clinton County
11	21.8	**Monticello** (village) Sullivan County
13	21.6	**Walton** (village) Delaware County
14	21.4	**Wellsville** (town) Allegany County
15	21.3	**Lake Luzerne** (town) Warren County
15	21.3	**Norwich** (town) Chenango County
17	21.1	**Gaines** (town) Orleans County
17	21.1	**Mooers** (town) Clinton County
17	21.1	**Stamford** (town) Delaware County
20	20.6	**Mount Morris** (village) Livingston County
21	20.4	**Albion** (town) Orleans County
22	20.2	**Massena** (town) Saint Lawrence County
22	20.2	**Penn Yan** (village) Yates County
24	20.1	**Kirkwood** (town) Broome County
25	20.0	**Fort Edward** (village) Washington County
26	19.9	**Arcadia** (town) Wayne County
26	19.9	**Dover** (town) Dutchess County
26	19.9	**Yorkshire** (town) Cattaraugus County
29	19.8	**Deerpark** (town) Orange County
29	19.8	**Stockholm** (town) Saint Lawrence County
29	19.8	**Utica** (city) Oneida County
32	19.7	**Athens** (town) Greene County
32	19.7	**Collins** (town) Erie County
32	19.7	**Wayland** (town) Steuben County
35	19.6	**Hornell** (city) Steuben County
35	19.6	**Louisville** (town) Saint Lawrence County
37	19.5	**Dickinson** (town) Broome County
37	19.5	**Gouverneur** (village) Saint Lawrence County
37	19.5	**Hancock** (town) Delaware County
37	19.5	**Waverly** (village) Tioga County
41	19.4	**Catskill** (town) Greene County
41	19.4	**Lyons** (village) Wayne County
43	19.3	**Catskill** (village) Greene County
43	19.3	**Malone** (village) Franklin County
43	19.3	**Putnam Lake** (CDP) Putnam County
46	19.2	**Bath** (town) Steuben County
46	19.2	**Portland** (town) Chautauqua County
48	19.1	**Heritage Hills** (CDP) Westchester County
48	19.1	**Hornellsville** (town) Steuben County
48	19.1	**Mohawk** (village) Herkimer County
51	19.0	**Castile** (town) Wyoming County
51	19.0	**Gowanda** (village) Cattaraugus County
51	19.0	**Southport** (CDP) Chemung County
51	19.0	**Waterloo** (town) Seneca County
55	18.9	**Amsterdam** (city) Montgomery County
55	18.9	**Plattekill** (town) Ulster County
55	18.9	**Sandy Creek** (town) Oswego County
55	18.9	**Shelby** (town) Orleans County
59	18.8	**Au Sable** (town) Clinton County
59	18.8	**Mount Morris** (town) Livingston County
61	18.7	**Corinth** (village) Saratoga County
61	18.7	**Liberty** (town) Sullivan County
61	18.7	**Little Falls** (city) Herkimer County
64	18.6	**Colesville** (town) Broome County
64	18.6	**Jamestown** (city) Chautauqua County
64	18.6	**Lackawanna** (city) Erie County
67	18.4	**Cohocton** (town) Steuben County
67	18.4	**Port Jervis** (city) Orange County
69	18.3	**Binghamton** (city) Broome County
69	18.3	**Dannemora** (town) Clinton County
69	18.3	**Gloversville** (city) Fulton County
69	18.3	**Massena** (village) Saint Lawrence County
73	18.2	**Altona** (town) Clinton County
73	18.2	**Bath** (village) Steuben County
73	18.2	**Kingston** (city) Ulster County
76	18.1	**Endicott** (village) Broome County
76	18.1	**Mechanicville** (city) Saratoga County
76	18.1	**Milo** (town) Yates County
76	18.1	**Portville** (town) Cattaraugus County
76	18.1	**Stockport** (town) Columbia County
81	18.0	**Dunkirk** (city) Chautauqua County
81	18.0	**Ellenville** (village) Ulster County
81	18.0	**Wawarsing** (town) Ulster County
84	17.9	**Annsville** (town) Oneida County
84	17.9	**Chester** (village) Orange County
84	17.9	**Hudson** (city) Columbia County
84	17.9	**Minden** (town) Montgomery County
88	17.8	**Calverton** (CDP) Suffolk County
88	17.8	**Canisteo** (town) Steuben County
88	17.8	**Kendall** (town) Orleans County
88	17.8	**Mexico** (town) Oswego County
88	17.8	**Moriah** (town) Essex County
88	17.8	**Norwich** (city) Chenango County
88	17.8	**Sanford** (town) Broome County
95	17.7	**Carthage** (village) Jefferson County
95	17.7	**Floyd** (town) Oneida County
95	17.7	**Gouverneur** (town) Saint Lawrence County
95	17.7	**Guilford** (town) Chenango County
95	17.7	**Schoharie** (town) Schoharie County
95	17.7	**Thompson** (town) Sullivan County
101	17.6	**Amenia** (town) Dutchess County
101	17.6	**Dansville** (village) Livingston County
101	17.6	**Middletown** (town) Delaware County
101	17.6	**Rome** (city) Oneida County
105	17.5	**Barton** (town) Tioga County
105	17.5	**Batavia** (town) Genesee County
105	17.5	**North Dansville** (town) Livingston County
108	17.4	**Addison** (town) Steuben County
108	17.4	**Brownville** (town) Jefferson County
108	17.4	**Cohoes** (city) Albany County
108	17.4	**Hanover** (town) Chautauqua County
108	17.4	**Lyons** (town) Wayne County
108	17.4	**Saranac Lake** (village) Franklin County
114	17.3	**Caroline** (town) Tompkins County
114	17.3	**Rochester** (city) Monroe County
114	17.3	**Schroeppel** (town) Oswego County
114	17.3	**Warsaw** (village) Wyoming County
118	17.2	**Chemung** (town) Chemung County
118	17.2	**Johnstown** (city) Fulton County
118	17.2	**Ridgeway** (town) Orleans County
118	17.2	**Rose** (town) Wayne County
122	17.1	**Enfield** (town) Tompkins County
122	17.1	**Livingston** (town) Columbia County
122	17.1	**Walton** (town) Delaware County
125	17.0	**Camden** (town) Oneida County
125	17.0	**Galeville** (CDP) Onondaga County
125	17.0	**Pine Plains** (town) Dutchess County
125	17.0	**Seneca Falls** (CDP) Seneca County
125	17.0	**Warwick** (village) Orange County
130	16.9	**Canandaigua** (town) Ontario County
130	16.9	**Spencerport** (village) Monroe County
130	16.9	**Whitehall** (town) Washington County
130	16.9	**Wolcott** (town) Wayne County
134	16.8	**Alden** (village) Erie County
134	16.8	**Bainbridge** (town) Chenango County
134	16.8	**Champion** (town) Jefferson County
134	16.8	**Clinton** (town) Dutchess County
134	16.8	**Milford** (town) Otsego County
134	16.8	**Niagara Falls** (city) Niagara County
134	16.8	**Shandaken** (town) Ulster County
134	16.8	**White Creek** (town) Washington County
142	16.7	**Franklinville** (town) Cattaraugus County
142	16.7	**Haviland** (CDP) Dutchess County
142	16.7	**Herkimer** (town) Herkimer County
142	16.7	**Herkimer** (village) Herkimer County
142	16.7	**Hoosick Falls** (village) Rensselaer County
142	16.7	**Ridge** (CDP) Suffolk County
142	16.7	**Seneca Falls** (town) Seneca County
149	16.6	**Copake** (town) Columbia County
149	16.6	**Corinth** (town) Saratoga County

Note: *This section ranks incorporated places and CDPs (Census Designated Places) with populations of 2,500 or more. Unincorporated postal areas were not considered. Please refer to the User Guide for additional information.*

Individuals with a Disability

Top 150 Places Ranked in *Ascending* Order

State Rank	Percent	Place	State Rank	Percent	Place
1	1.2	Flanders (CDP) Suffolk County	72	6.8	West Point (CDP) Orange County
2	1.7	Watchtower (CDP) Ulster County	77	6.9	Baldwin (CDP) Nassau County
3	2.3	Pelham Manor (village) Westchester County	77	6.9	Cold Spring Harbor (CDP) Suffolk County
4	2.7	New Square (village) Rockland County	77	6.9	Elmsford (village) Westchester County
4	2.7	SUNY Oswego (CDP) Oswego County	77	6.9	Merrick (CDP) Nassau County
4	2.7	University at Buffalo (CDP) Erie County	77	6.9	Miller Place (CDP) Suffolk County
7	2.9	Kiryas Joel (village) Orange County	77	6.9	Woodmere (CDP) Nassau County
8	3.0	Lansing (village) Tompkins County	83	7.0	Cedarhurst (village) Nassau County
8	3.0	Larchmont (village) Westchester County	83	7.0	Irvington (village) Westchester County
10	3.2	West Sand Lake (CDP) Rensselaer County	83	7.0	Manorville (CDP) Suffolk County
11	3.8	Alfred (village) Allegany County	83	7.0	Newfane (CDP) Niagara County
12	4.0	Kaser (village) Rockland County	83	7.0	Ossining (village) Westchester County
12	4.0	Pelham (town) Westchester County	83	7.0	Pleasantville (village) Westchester County
14	4.1	Alfred (town) Allegany County	83	7.0	Sea Cliff (village) Nassau County
15	4.3	Old Westbury (village) Nassau County	90	7.1	Islip Terrace (CDP) Suffolk County
16	4.5	Bedford Hills (CDP) Westchester County	90	7.1	Sands Point (village) Nassau County
17	4.6	Bronxville (village) Westchester County	90	7.1	Wantagh (CDP) Nassau County
17	4.6	East Williston (village) Nassau County	93	7.2	Brightwaters (village) Suffolk County
17	4.6	Halesite (CDP) Suffolk County	93	7.2	East Norwich (CDP) Nassau County
17	4.6	Munsey Park (village) Nassau County	93	7.2	Hamilton (village) Madison County
17	4.6	New Cassel (CDP) Nassau County	93	7.2	Jericho (CDP) Nassau County
22	4.8	Stony Brook University (CDP) Suffolk County	93	7.2	Pompey (town) Onondaga County
23	4.9	Binghamton University (CDP) Broome County	93	7.2	Shelter Island (town) Suffolk County
24	5.0	New Castle (town) Westchester County	93	7.2	Sound Beach (CDP) Suffolk County
25	5.2	Bedford (town) Westchester County	100	7.3	Dobbs Ferry (village) Westchester County
25	5.2	Lansing (town) Tompkins County	100	7.3	East Garden City (CDP) Nassau County
27	5.3	Greenville (CDP) Westchester County	100	7.3	Stony Brook (CDP) Suffolk County
27	5.3	Lewisboro (town) Westchester County	100	7.3	Williston Park (village) Nassau County
27	5.3	Thornwood (CDP) Westchester County	104	7.4	Cambria (town) Niagara County
30	5.4	Pelham (village) Westchester County	104	7.4	Canton (village) Saint Lawrence County
30	5.4	Scarsdale (town/village) Westchester County	104	7.4	Manhasset (CDP) Nassau County
32	5.5	Great Neck Estates (village) Nassau County	104	7.4	Mendon (town) Monroe County
33	5.6	Brookville (village) Nassau County	104	7.4	Ramapo (town) Rockland County
34	5.7	Flower Hill (village) Nassau County	104	7.4	Tarrytown (village) Westchester County
34	5.7	Lawrence (village) Nassau County	110	7.5	Clifton Park (town) Saratoga County
34	5.7	Monsey (CDP) Rockland County	110	7.5	Elmont (CDP) Nassau County
34	5.7	South Hempstead (CDP) Nassau County	110	7.5	Hamilton (town) Madison County
38	5.8	Orchard Park (village) Erie County	110	7.5	Mount Ivy (CDP) Rockland County
38	5.8	Pound Ridge (town) Westchester County	110	7.5	Pittsford (town) Monroe County
40	5.9	Bardonia (CDP) Rockland County	110	7.5	Southampton (village) Suffolk County
40	5.9	Lloyd Harbor (village) Suffolk County	110	7.5	Uniondale (CDP) Nassau County
40	5.9	Northwest Harbor (CDP) Suffolk County	110	7.5	Victor (village) Ontario County
40	5.9	Wesley Hills (village) Rockland County	110	7.5	Wales (town) Erie County
44	6.0	Croton-on-Hudson (village) Westchester County	119	7.6	Bellmore (CDP) Nassau County
44	6.0	Northeast Ithaca (CDP) Tompkins County	119	7.6	East Aurora (village) Erie County
44	6.0	Setauket-East Setauket (CDP) Suffolk County	119	7.6	Fairview (CDP) Westchester County
47	6.1	Fort Drum (CDP) Jefferson County	119	7.6	Greenburgh (town) Westchester County
48	6.2	Dix Hills (CDP) Suffolk County	119	7.6	Hastings-on-Hudson (village) Westchester County
48	6.2	Lake Success (village) Nassau County	119	7.6	Islandia (village) Suffolk County
48	6.2	Manorhaven (village) Nassau County	125	7.7	Blauvelt (CDP) Rockland County
48	6.2	Nesconset (CDP) Suffolk County	125	7.7	Cazenovia (town) Madison County
48	6.2	North Castle (town) Westchester County	125	7.7	Center Moriches (CDP) Suffolk County
48	6.2	Northport (village) Suffolk County	125	7.7	Eastchester (town) Westchester County
48	6.2	Port Washington North (village) Nassau County	125	7.7	Hewlett (CDP) Nassau County
55	6.3	Muttontown (village) Nassau County	125	7.7	Huntington (town) Suffolk County
56	6.4	LaFayette (town) Onondaga County	125	7.7	Kings Point (village) Nassau County
56	6.4	Monroe (town) Orange County	125	7.7	Lewiston (village) Niagara County
56	6.4	Thomaston (village) Nassau County	125	7.7	Mamaroneck (town) Westchester County
59	6.5	East Farmingdale (CDP) Suffolk County	125	7.7	Mount Pleasant (town) Westchester County
59	6.5	North Merrick (CDP) Nassau County	125	7.7	North Great River (CDP) Suffolk County
59	6.5	Port Washington (CDP) Nassau County	125	7.7	Valley Cottage (CDP) Rockland County
59	6.5	South Valley Stream (CDP) Nassau County	125	7.7	Walworth (town) Wayne County
63	6.6	East Shoreham (CDP) Suffolk County	125	7.7	West Hills (CDP) Suffolk County
63	6.6	Glenwood Landing (CDP) Nassau County	139	7.8	Attica (town) Wyoming County
63	6.6	Hartsdale (CDP) Westchester County	139	7.8	East Quogue (CDP) Suffolk County
63	6.6	Hempstead (village) Nassau County	139	7.8	Great Neck (village) Nassau County
63	6.6	New Hempstead (village) Rockland County	139	7.8	Guilderland (town) Albany County
63	6.6	Spring Valley (village) Rockland County	139	7.8	Huntington Station (CDP) Suffolk County
69	6.7	Armonk (CDP) Westchester County	139	7.8	Lake Mohegan (CDP) Westchester County
69	6.7	Attica (village) Wyoming County	139	7.8	North Bellmore (CDP) Nassau County
69	6.7	Sand Lake (town) Rensselaer County	139	7.8	Port Jefferson (village) Suffolk County
72	6.8	Blue Point (CDP) Suffolk County	139	7.8	West Hempstead (CDP) Nassau County
72	6.8	Garden City (village) Nassau County	148	7.9	East Hills (village) Nassau County
72	6.8	Huntington (CDP) Suffolk County	148	7.9	Lake Grove (village) Suffolk County
72	6.8	Voorheesville (village) Albany County	148	7.9	New Scotland (town) Albany County

Note: *This section ranks incorporated places and CDPs (Census Designated Places) with populations of 2,500 or more. Unincorporated postal areas were not considered. Please refer to the User Guide for additional information.*

Veterans

Top 150 Places Ranked in *Descending* Order

State Rank	Percent	Place
1	45.8	**West Point** (CDP) Orange County
2	24.1	**Calcium** (CDP) Jefferson County
3	22.5	**Highlands** (town) Orange County
4	21.7	**Champion** (town) Jefferson County
5	20.7	**Pamelia** (town) Jefferson County
6	20.3	**Le Ray** (town) Jefferson County
7	18.9	**Ticonderoga** (CDP) Essex County
8	18.7	**Theresa** (town) Jefferson County
9	18.3	**Fort Drum** (CDP) Jefferson County
9	18.3	**Heritage Hills** (CDP) Westchester County
11	18.0	**Rutland** (town) Jefferson County
12	17.1	**Ticonderoga** (town) Essex County
13	16.1	**Whitesboro** (village) Oneida County
14	16.0	**Shelter Island** (town) Suffolk County
15	15.9	**Beekmantown** (town) Clinton County
15	15.9	**Milford** (town) Otsego County
17	15.8	**Hounsfield** (town) Jefferson County
17	15.8	**New York Mills** (village) Oneida County
19	15.7	**Orleans** (town) Jefferson County
20	15.4	**Rockland** (town) Sullivan County
21	15.3	**Carthage** (village) Jefferson County
21	15.3	**Peru** (town) Clinton County
23	14.9	**Highland Falls** (village) Orange County
24	14.8	**Chesterfield** (town) Essex County
24	14.8	**Galway** (town) Saratoga County
24	14.8	**Phelps** (town) Ontario County
27	14.7	**Wellsville** (village) Allegany County
28	14.6	**Granville** (town) Washington County
28	14.6	**Hornellsville** (town) Steuben County
30	14.5	**Calverton** (CDP) Suffolk County
30	14.5	**Wellsville** (town) Allegany County
32	14.4	**Dix** (town) Schuyler County
32	14.4	**New Berlin** (town) Chenango County
32	14.4	**Perry** (village) Wyoming County
32	14.4	**Portville** (town) Cattaraugus County
32	14.4	**Sterling** (town) Cayuga County
37	14.3	**Elma Center** (CDP) Erie County
38	14.2	**Oxford** (town) Chenango County
38	14.2	**West Bloomfield** (town) Ontario County
40	14.1	**Bath** (town) Steuben County
40	14.1	**Nunda** (town) Livingston County
42	14.0	**Cornwall-on-Hudson** (village) Orange County
43	13.9	**Vienna** (town) Oneida County
43	13.9	**Wanakah** (CDP) Erie County
43	13.9	**Warwick** (village) Orange County
46	13.7	**Sandy Creek** (town) Oswego County
47	13.5	**Dansville** (village) Livingston County
47	13.5	**Fort Edward** (village) Washington County
49	13.4	**Au Sable** (town) Clinton County
50	13.2	**Haviland** (CDP) Dutchess County
50	13.2	**Southport** (CDP) Chemung County
52	13.1	**Brutus** (town) Cayuga County
53	13.0	**Coxsackie** (village) Greene County
53	13.0	**Neversink** (town) Sullivan County
53	13.0	**Sanford** (town) Broome County
53	13.0	**Sloan** (village) Erie County
53	13.0	**Verona** (town) Oneida County
53	13.0	**Waverly** (village) Tioga County
59	12.9	**Bath** (village) Steuben County
59	12.9	**Canisteo** (town) Steuben County
59	12.9	**Dickinson** (town) Broome County
59	12.9	**Franklinville** (town) Cattaraugus County
59	12.9	**Northampton** (town) Fulton County
64	12.8	**Annsville** (town) Oneida County
64	12.8	**Barton** (town) Tioga County
64	12.8	**Groveland** (town) Livingston County
64	12.8	**Stockholm** (town) Saint Lawrence County
64	12.8	**Volney** (town) Oswego County
64	12.8	**Watertown** (city) Jefferson County
70	12.7	**Boonville** (town) Oneida County
70	12.7	**Corinth** (town) Saratoga County
70	12.7	**Greenwich** (town) Washington County
70	12.7	**North Dansville** (town) Livingston County
70	12.7	**Perry** (town) Wyoming County
75	12.6	**Brookfield** (town) Madison County
75	12.6	**East Greenbush** (CDP) Rensselaer County
75	12.6	**Ridgeway** (town) Orleans County
78	12.5	**Delaware** (town) Sullivan County
78	12.5	**Elmira Heights** (village) Chemung County
78	12.5	**Whitestown** (town) Oneida County
81	12.4	**Afton** (town) Chenango County
81	12.4	**Candor** (town) Tioga County
81	12.4	**Oneonta** (town) Otsego County
81	12.4	**Oswegatchie** (town) Saint Lawrence County
85	12.3	**Adams** (town) Jefferson County
85	12.3	**Cuba** (town) Allegany County
85	12.3	**Olean** (city) Cattaraugus County
85	12.3	**Wilna** (town) Jefferson County
85	12.3	**Yorkshire** (town) Cattaraugus County
90	12.2	**Hornell** (city) Steuben County
90	12.2	**Middleburgh** (town) Schoharie County
90	12.2	**Rome** (city) Oneida County
90	12.2	**Somerset** (town) Niagara County
94	12.1	**Brownville** (town) Jefferson County
94	12.1	**Campbell** (town) Steuben County
94	12.1	**Perth** (town) Fulton County
94	12.1	**Skaneateles** (village) Onondaga County
98	12.0	**Broadalbin** (town) Fulton County
98	12.0	**Greenwood Lake** (village) Orange County
98	12.0	**Herkimer** (town) Herkimer County
98	12.0	**Lowville** (village) Lewis County
98	12.0	**Springville** (village) Erie County
103	11.9	**Castile** (town) Wyoming County
103	11.9	**Clarendon** (town) Orleans County
103	11.9	**Corinth** (village) Saratoga County
103	11.9	**Harrietstown** (town) Franklin County
103	11.9	**Lee** (town) Oneida County
103	11.9	**Milton** (CDP) Saratoga County
103	11.9	**Palatine** (town) Montgomery County
103	11.9	**Pierrepont** (town) Saint Lawrence County
103	11.9	**Schuyler Falls** (town) Clinton County
103	11.9	**Tioga** (town) Tioga County
103	11.9	**Wayland** (town) Steuben County
114	11.8	**Ballston Spa** (village) Saratoga County
114	11.8	**Camden** (town) Oneida County
114	11.8	**Concord** (town) Erie County
114	11.8	**Elma** (town) Erie County
114	11.8	**Little Falls** (city) Herkimer County
114	11.8	**Oneida** (city) Madison County
114	11.8	**Watertown** (town) Jefferson County
121	11.7	**Bennington** (town) Wyoming County
121	11.7	**Gaines** (town) Orleans County
121	11.7	**Geneva** (town) Ontario County
121	11.7	**Hartland** (town) Niagara County
121	11.7	**Lowville** (town) Lewis County
121	11.7	**Seneca Falls** (CDP) Seneca County
121	11.7	**Southport** (town) Chemung County
128	11.6	**Fleming** (town) Cayuga County
128	11.6	**Saint Johnsville** (town) Montgomery County
128	11.6	**Westmoreland** (town) Oneida County
131	11.5	**Elmira** (town) Chemung County
131	11.5	**Scriba** (town) Oswego County
133	11.4	**Chemung** (town) Chemung County
133	11.4	**Cornwall** (town) Orange County
133	11.4	**Floyd** (town) Oneida County
133	11.4	**Madison** (town) Madison County
133	11.4	**Pembroke** (town) Genesee County
133	11.4	**Schoharie** (town) Schoharie County
139	11.3	**Canandaigua** (town) Ontario County
139	11.3	**Chazy** (town) Clinton County
139	11.3	**Kingsbury** (town) Washington County
139	11.3	**Oakfield** (town) Genesee County
139	11.3	**Randolph** (town) Cattaraugus County
144	11.2	**Charlton** (town) Saratoga County
144	11.2	**Colesville** (town) Broome County
144	11.2	**Conesus Lake** (CDP) Livingston County
144	11.2	**Eden** (town) Erie County
144	11.2	**Fayette** (town) Seneca County
144	11.2	**Hancock** (town) Delaware County
144	11.2	**Waterloo** (town) Seneca County

Note: *This section ranks incorporated places and CDPs (Census Designated Places) with populations of 2,500 or more. Unincorporated postal areas were not considered. Please refer to the User Guide for additional information.*

Veterans

Top 150 Places Ranked in *Ascending* Order

State Rank	Percent	Place	State Rank	Percent	Place
1	0.0	**Kaser** (village) Rockland County	76	3.9	**Oswego** (town) Oswego County
1	0.0	**SUNY Oswego** (CDP) Oswego County	76	3.9	**Pomona** (village) Rockland County
1	0.0	**Watchtower** (CDP) Ulster County	76	3.9	**Rye** (town) Westchester County
4	0.1	**Binghamton University** (CDP) Broome County	76	3.9	**Wyandanch** (CDP) Suffolk County
4	0.1	**University at Buffalo** (CDP) Erie County	80	4.0	**Ithaca** (town) Tompkins County
6	0.4	**Flanders** (CDP) Suffolk County	80	4.0	**Manhasset** (CDP) Nassau County
6	0.4	**New Square** (village) Rockland County	80	4.0	**Mount Kisco** (town/village) Westchester County
8	0.5	**Kiryas Joel** (village) Orange County	80	4.0	**New Paltz** (town) Ulster County
9	0.6	**Alfred** (village) Allegany County	80	4.0	**North Bellport** (CDP) Suffolk County
10	1.0	**Monsey** (CDP) Rockland County	85	4.1	**Glenwood Landing** (CDP) Nassau County
11	1.6	**Ithaca** (city) Tompkins County	85	4.1	**Larchmont** (village) Westchester County
12	1.7	**Great Neck Estates** (village) Nassau County	85	4.1	**Westbury** (village) Nassau County
13	1.8	**Viola** (CDP) Rockland County	85	4.1	**Yonkers** (city) Westchester County
14	1.9	**Brookville** (village) Nassau County	89	4.2	**Freeport** (village) Nassau County
14	1.9	**Old Westbury** (village) Nassau County	89	4.2	**Kings Point** (village) Nassau County
16	2.0	**New Paltz** (village) Ulster County	89	4.2	**Sands Point** (village) Nassau County
17	2.1	**Alfred** (town) Allegany County	89	4.2	**Scarsdale** (town/village) Westchester County
17	2.1	**Hartsdale** (CDP) Westchester County	89	4.2	**Sea Cliff** (village) Nassau County
17	2.1	**Roosevelt** (CDP) Nassau County	94	4.3	**Albany** (city) Albany County
20	2.2	**Spring Valley** (village) Rockland County	94	4.3	**Great Neck Plaza** (village) Nassau County
21	2.3	**Brooklyn** (borough) Kings County	94	4.3	**Jericho** (CDP) Nassau County
21	2.3	**Elmont** (CDP) Nassau County	94	4.3	**Lawrence** (village) Nassau County
23	2.4	**Cedarhurst** (village) Nassau County	94	4.3	**Newburgh** (city) Orange County
23	2.4	**New Cassel** (CDP) Nassau County	94	4.3	**Spackenkill** (CDP) Dutchess County
25	2.5	**Hamilton** (village) Madison County	94	4.3	**Tarrytown** (village) Westchester County
25	2.5	**Manhattan** (borough) New York County	94	4.3	**Tuckahoe** (village) Westchester County
25	2.5	**South Fallsburg** (CDP) Sullivan County	102	4.4	**Caroline** (town) Tompkins County
28	2.6	**Geneseo** (village) Livingston County	102	4.4	**Central Islip** (CDP) Suffolk County
29	2.7	**New York** (city)	102	4.4	**Lakeview** (CDP) Nassau County
29	2.7	**Queens** (borough) Queens County	102	4.4	**Monroe** (town) Orange County
29	2.7	**South Hill** (CDP) Tompkins County	102	4.4	**Sleepy Hollow** (village) Westchester County
32	2.8	**Flower Hill** (village) Nassau County	102	4.4	**West Sand Lake** (CDP) Rensselaer County
32	2.8	**North Bay Shore** (CDP) Suffolk County	108	4.5	**Baldwin** (CDP) Nassau County
34	2.9	**Bronx** (borough) Bronx County	108	4.5	**Canton** (village) Saint Lawrence County
34	2.9	**Inwood** (CDP) Nassau County	108	4.5	**Harris Hill** (CDP) Erie County
34	2.9	**Manorhaven** (village) Nassau County	108	4.5	**Irvington** (village) Westchester County
34	2.9	**New Hempstead** (village) Rockland County	108	4.5	**Mamaroneck** (town) Westchester County
34	2.9	**Valhalla** (CDP) Westchester County	108	4.5	**Mamaroneck** (village) Westchester County
39	3.0	**Port Chester** (village) Westchester County	108	4.5	**Mount Pleasant** (town) Westchester County
40	3.1	**Muttontown** (village) Nassau County	108	4.5	**New Rochelle** (city) Westchester County
40	3.1	**Potsdam** (village) Saint Lawrence County	108	4.5	**North Hempstead** (town) Nassau County
40	3.1	**Uniondale** (CDP) Nassau County	108	4.5	**Ossining** (town) Westchester County
40	3.1	**Wesley Hills** (village) Rockland County	108	4.5	**South Valley Stream** (CDP) Nassau County
44	3.2	**Hempstead** (village) Nassau County	108	4.5	**Thornwood** (CDP) Westchester County
44	3.2	**Mount Ivy** (CDP) Rockland County	120	4.6	**Bardonia** (CDP) Rockland County
44	3.2	**New Castle** (town) Westchester County	120	4.6	**Dannemora** (village) Clinton County
44	3.2	**South Nyack** (village) Rockland County	120	4.6	**East Syracuse** (village) Onondaga County
48	3.3	**Elmsford** (village) Westchester County	120	4.6	**Hamilton** (town) Madison County
48	3.3	**Ramapo** (town) Rockland County	120	4.6	**Merrick** (CDP) Nassau County
48	3.3	**University Gardens** (CDP) Nassau County	120	4.6	**Mineola** (village) Nassau County
48	3.3	**Woodmere** (CDP) Nassau County	120	4.6	**Nanuet** (CDP) Rockland County
52	3.4	**Bronxville** (village) Westchester County	120	4.6	**New Hyde Park** (village) Nassau County
52	3.4	**Carle Place** (CDP) Nassau County	120	4.6	**North Valley Stream** (CDP) Nassau County
52	3.4	**Dix Hills** (CDP) Suffolk County	129	4.7	**Bedford Hills** (CDP) Westchester County
52	3.4	**Wheatley Heights** (CDP) Suffolk County	129	4.7	**Carmel Hamlet** (CDP) Putnam County
56	3.5	**Brentwood** (CDP) Suffolk County	129	4.7	**Coram** (CDP) Suffolk County
56	3.5	**Cayuga Heights** (village) Tompkins County	129	4.7	**Greenburgh** (town) Westchester County
56	3.5	**Great Neck** (village) Nassau County	129	4.7	**North Amityville** (CDP) Suffolk County
56	3.5	**Harrison** (town/village) Westchester County	129	4.7	**North Castle** (town) Westchester County
56	3.5	**Hillcrest** (CDP) Rockland County	129	4.7	**Pelham** (village) Westchester County
56	3.5	**Stony Brook University** (CDP) Suffolk County	129	4.7	**Plainedge** (CDP) Nassau County
56	3.5	**White Plains** (city) Westchester County	129	4.7	**Rochester** (city) Monroe County
63	3.6	**Greenville** (CDP) Westchester County	129	4.7	**Searingtown** (CDP) Nassau County
63	3.6	**Northeast Ithaca** (CDP) Tompkins County	139	4.8	**Garden City Park** (CDP) Nassau County
63	3.6	**Roslyn Heights** (CDP) Nassau County	139	4.8	**Haverstraw** (village) Rockland County
66	3.7	**Ardsley** (village) Westchester County	139	4.8	**Lake Mohegan** (CDP) Westchester County
66	3.7	**Delhi** (village) Delaware County	139	4.8	**Lewisboro** (town) Westchester County
66	3.7	**Fairview** (CDP) Westchester County	139	4.8	**Montebello** (village) Rockland County
66	3.7	**Manhasset Hills** (CDP) Nassau County	139	4.8	**Patchogue** (village) Suffolk County
66	3.7	**Ossining** (village) Westchester County	139	4.8	**Port Washington North** (village) Nassau County
66	3.7	**Salisbury** (CDP) Nassau County	139	4.8	**Suffern** (village) Rockland County
72	3.8	**East Farmingdale** (CDP) Suffolk County	139	4.8	**West Hempstead** (CDP) Nassau County
72	3.8	**East Hampton North** (CDP) Suffolk County	139	4.8	**Woodbury** (CDP) Nassau County
72	3.8	**Mount Vernon** (city) Westchester County	149	4.9	**Bedford** (town) Westchester County
72	3.8	**Thomaston** (village) Nassau County	149	4.9	**Brewerton** (CDP) Onondaga County

Note: This section ranks incorporated places and CDPs (Census Designated Places) with populations of 2,500 or more. Unincorporated postal areas were not considered. Please refer to the User Guide for additional information.

Ancestry: German

Top 150 Places Ranked in *Descending* Order

State Rank	Percent	Place	State Rank	Percent	Place
1	73.3	**Addison** (town) Washington County	76	56.3	**Delphos** (city) Allen County
2	71.0	**Jackson** (town) Washington County	76	56.3	**New Holstein** (city) Calumet County
3	70.1	**Dyersville** (city) Dubuque County	78	56.2	**Alsace** (township) Berks County
4	69.9	**Howards Grove** (village) Sheboygan County	78	56.2	**Mack** (CDP) Hamilton County
5	69.4	**Chilton** (city) Calumet County	80	56.1	**Horace** (city) Cass County
6	69.3	**Polk** (town) Washington County	80	56.1	**Monticello** (city) Jones County
7	69.1	**Kiel** (city) Manitowoc County	80	56.1	**Sleepy Eye** (city) Brown County
8	67.9	**Harrison** (town) Calumet County	83	56.0	**Milbank** (city) Grant County
8	67.9	**Saint Henry** (village) Mercer County	83	56.0	**Sauk City** (village) Sauk County
10	67.1	**Minster** (village) Auglaize County	83	56.0	**Washington** (township) Schuylkill County
11	66.8	**Trenton** (town) Washington County	86	55.9	**Jordan** (city) Scott County
12	66.1	**Wakefield** (township) Stearns County	86	55.9	**Oregon** (town) Dane County
13	65.8	**Empire** (town) Fond du Lac County	86	55.9	**Sussex** (village) Waukesha County
14	65.6	**Medford** (town) Taylor County	89	55.8	**Centre** (township) Berks County
15	65.4	**Mayville** (city) Dodge County	90	55.7	**Johnson Creek** (village) Jefferson County
15	65.4	**New Bremen** (village) Auglaize County	90	55.7	**Sauk Centre** (city) Stearns County
17	65.0	**Hartford** (town) Washington County	92	55.4	**Belle Plaine** (city) Scott County
18	64.9	**Sheboygan** (town) Sheboygan County	93	55.3	**Norwood Young America** (city) Carver County
19	64.6	**Coldwater** (village) Mercer County	94	55.2	**Lisbon** (town) Waukesha County
20	64.3	**Springfield** (town) Dane County	95	55.1	**Harrison** (city) Hamilton County
21	64.2	**Barton** (town) Washington County	95	55.1	**Oak Harbor** (village) Ottawa County
22	64.0	**Albany** (city) Stearns County	97	55.0	**Hegins** (township) Schuylkill County
22	64.0	**Plymouth** (town) Sheboygan County	98	54.9	**Fond du Lac** (town) Fond du Lac County
24	63.9	**Kewaskum** (village) Washington County	98	54.9	**Stettin** (town) Marathon County
25	63.3	**Taycheedah** (town) Fond du Lac County	100	54.8	**Bismarck** (city) Burleigh County
26	63.1	**Brillion** (city) Calumet County	100	54.8	**Brockway** (township) Stearns County
27	63.0	**New Ulm** (city) Brown County	100	54.8	**Wayne** (city) Wayne County
28	62.5	**Auburn** (town) Fond du Lac County	103	54.7	**Beulah** (city) Mercer County
29	62.4	**Cold Spring** (city) Stearns County	103	54.7	**Muskego** (city) Waukesha County
30	62.3	**Plymouth** (city) Sheboygan County	105	54.6	**Jamestown** (city) Stutsman County
31	61.9	**Mandan** (city) Morton County	106	54.3	**Lake Wazeecha** (CDP) Wood County
32	61.8	**Center** (town) Outagamie County	106	54.3	**Merton** (town) Waukesha County
33	61.5	**Miami Heights** (CDP) Hamilton County	108	54.1	**Cottage Grove** (town) Dane County
34	61.4	**Breese** (city) Clinton County	109	54.0	**Hays** (city) Ellis County
34	61.4	**Hortonville** (village) Outagamie County	109	54.0	**Kronenwetter** (village) Marathon County
36	61.2	**Merrill** (town) Lincoln County	109	54.0	**Menasha** (town) Winnebago County
37	61.1	**Farmington** (town) Washington County	112	53.8	**De Witt** (city) Clinton County
38	60.7	**Lodi** (town) Columbia County	113	53.7	**Denmark** (township) Tuscola County
39	59.6	**Fayette** (township) Juniata County	113	53.7	**Millstadt** (village) Saint Clair County
40	59.5	**Friendship** (town) Fond du Lac County	113	53.7	**New Prague** (city) Scott County
41	59.3	**Columbus** (city) Columbia County	116	53.6	**Marshfield** (city) Wood County
41	59.3	**Sheboygan Falls** (city) Sheboygan County	117	53.5	**Lincoln** (city) Burleigh County
43	59.2	**Carroll** (city) Carroll County	117	53.5	**North Mankato** (city) Nicollet County
44	59.1	**Dale** (town) Outagamie County	117	53.5	**Watertown** (city) Jefferson County
44	59.1	**Saint Augusta** (city) Stearns County	120	53.5	**Hallam** (borough) York County
46	58.9	**Caledonia** (city) Houston County	120	53.4	**Spring Valley** (city) Fillmore County
46	58.9	**Shelby** (town) La Crosse County	122	53.3	**Glencoe** (city) McLeod County
48	58.8	**Mukwa** (town) Waupaca County	122	53.3	**Oconomowoc** (town) Waukesha County
49	58.7	**Merrill** (city) Lincoln County	122	53.3	**Reedsburg** (city) Sauk County
50	58.6	**Germantown** (village) Washington County	125	53.2	**Poynette** (village) Columbia County
51	58.5	**Lake Crystal** (city) Blue Earth County	126	53.1	**Beaver Dam** (city) Dodge County
51	58.5	**Oakland** (town) Jefferson County	126	53.1	**Dent** (CDP) Hamilton County
53	58.4	**Clintonville** (city) Waupaca County	126	53.1	**Winneconne** (village) Winnebago County
54	58.3	**Pelican** (town) Oneida County	129	53.0	**Aberdeen** (city) Brown County
54	58.3	**Saint Marys** (city) Elk County	129	53.0	**Hartford** (city) Washington County
56	58.1	**Horicon** (city) Dodge County	129	53.0	**Menasha** (city) Winnebago County
56	58.1	**Jackson** (village) Washington County	129	53.0	**Oshkosh** (city) Winnebago County
56	58.1	**Wausau** (town) Marathon County	129	53.0	**Vernon** (town) Waukesha County
59	58.0	**Beaver Dam** (town) Dodge County	134	52.9	**Brookfield** (town) Waukesha County
60	57.9	**West Bend** (town) Washington County	134	52.9	**Frankenmuth** (city) Saginaw County
61	57.7	**Richfield** (village) Washington County	134	52.9	**Marysville** (city) Marshall County
61	57.7	**Saukville** (village) Ozaukee County	134	52.9	**Pewaukee** (city) Waukesha County
63	57.5	**Delhi Hills** (CDP) Hamilton County	134	52.9	**Rockland** (township) Berks County
64	57.4	**Grundy Center** (city) Grundy County	139	52.8	**Algoma** (city) Kewaunee County
64	57.4	**Ripon** (city) Fond du Lac County	139	52.8	**West Union** (city) Fayette County
64	57.4	**West Bend** (city) Washington County	141	52.7	**Halifax** (township) Dauphin County
67	57.2	**Sherwood** (village) Calumet County	141	52.7	**Sparta** (city) Monroe County
67	57.2	**Wescott** (town) Shawano County	143	52.6	**Cross Plains** (village) Dane County
69	57.0	**Merton** (village) Waukesha County	144	52.5	**Alexandria** (township) Douglas County
70	56.9	**Grafton** (town) Ozaukee County	144	52.5	**Rock Rapids** (city) Lyon County
70	56.9	**Lake Wisconsin** (CDP) Columbia County	144	52.5	**Wheatland** (town) Kenosha County
72	56.8	**Ixonia** (town) Jefferson County	147	52.4	**North Fond du Lac** (village) Fond du Lac County
73	56.5	**Wales** (village) Waukesha County	147	52.4	**Rothsville** (CDP) Lancaster County
74	56.4	**Ashippun** (town) Dodge County	149	52.3	**Reserve** (township) Allegheny County
74	56.4	**Sebewaing** (township) Huron County	150	52.2	**Covedale** (CDP) Hamilton County

Note: This section ranks incorporated places and CDPs (Census Designated Places) with populations of 2,500 or more. Unincorporated postal areas were not considered. Please refer to the User Guide for additional information.

Ancestry: English

Top 150 Places Ranked in *Descending* Order

State Rank	Percent	Place
1	77.3	**Hildale** (city) Washington County
2	66.0	**Colorado City** (town) Mohave County
3	47.8	**Monroe** (city) Sevier County
4	42.4	**McCall** (city) Valley County
5	42.3	**Manti** (city) Sanpete County
6	40.9	**Beaver** (city) Beaver County
6	40.9	**Highland** (city) Utah County
8	39.3	**Indian Springs** (CDP) Catoosa County
9	38.7	**Sheridan** (city) Grant County
10	38.0	**Alpine** (city) Utah County
11	37.9	**Hopkinton** (town) Merrimack County
12	37.7	**Mapleton** (city) Utah County
13	37.6	**Centerville** (city) Davis County
14	37.2	**Fruit Heights** (city) Davis County
15	36.4	**Cedar Hills** (city) Utah County
15	36.4	**Elk Ridge** (city) Utah County
17	36.3	**Hyde Park** (city) Cache County
18	36.1	**Boothbay** (town) Lincoln County
19	36.0	**Farr West** (city) Weber County
20	35.3	**Rockport** (town) Knox County
20	35.3	**Wellsville** (city) Cache County
22	34.5	**Mountain Green** (CDP) Morgan County
23	34.4	**Hooper** (city) Weber County
23	34.4	**South Beach** (CDP) Indian River County
25	34.2	**Tamworth** (town) Carroll County
26	34.1	**Providence** (city) Cache County
27	33.8	**Midway** (city) Wasatch County
28	33.6	**Bountiful** (city) Davis County
28	33.6	**Wolfeboro** (CDP) Carroll County
30	33.5	**Farmingdale** (town) Kennebec County
31	33.4	**Pleasant View** (city) Weber County
31	33.4	**Salem** (city) Utah County
33	33.2	**White Hall** (city) Jefferson County
34	33.1	**Poland** (town) Androscoggin County
35	33.0	**Freeport** (town) Cumberland County
35	33.0	**Hyrum** (city) Cache County
37	32.9	**Kaysville** (city) Davis County
37	32.9	**North Logan** (city) Cache County
39	32.4	**West Bountiful** (city) Davis County
40	32.3	**Morgan** (city) Morgan County
41	32.0	**Trent Woods** (town) Craven County
42	31.9	**Rexburg** (city) Madison County
43	31.8	**Bristol** (town) Lincoln County
44	31.6	**Yarmouth** (town) Cumberland County
45	31.5	**Harrison** (town) Cumberland County
46	31.4	**Holladay** (city) Salt Lake County
47	31.3	**Parowan** (city) Iron County
48	31.2	**Farmington** (city) Davis County
49	31.1	**Kennebunkport** (town) York County
50	30.6	**Oakland** (CDP) Kennebec County
51	30.5	**Herriman** (city) Salt Lake County
51	30.5	**Woolwich** (town) Sagadahoc County
51	30.5	**Yarmouth** (CDP) Cumberland County
54	30.4	**Charlestown** (town) Sullivan County
54	30.4	**South Jordan** (city) Salt Lake County
56	30.1	**American Fork** (city) Utah County
56	30.1	**Harpswell** (town) Cumberland County
56	30.1	**Oxford** (town) Oxford County
59	30.0	**Fryeburg** (town) Oxford County
59	30.0	**Saint George** (town) Knox County
61	29.9	**Chichester** (town) Merrimack County
62	29.8	**Santa Clara** (city) Washington County
62	29.8	**Woodstock** (town) Windsor County
64	29.7	**Monmouth** (town) Kennebec County
64	29.7	**Saint George** (city) Washington County
66	29.6	**Alamo** (town) Wheeler County
66	29.6	**Eagle Mountain** (city) Utah County
66	29.6	**Santaquin** (city) Utah County
69	29.5	**Bridgton** (town) Cumberland County
69	29.5	**Indian River Shores** (town) Indian River County
69	29.5	**Lehi** (city) Utah County
69	29.5	**Manchester** (town) Kennebec County
69	29.5	**Smithfield** (city) Cache County
74	29.4	**Wolfeboro** (town) Carroll County
75	29.3	**Kanab** (city) Kane County
76	29.2	**Camden** (town) Knox County
76	29.2	**Delta** (city) Millard County
76	29.2	**Spanish Fork** (city) Utah County
79	29.1	**Bluffdale** (city) Salt Lake County
79	29.1	**Richmond** (city) Cache County
81	29.0	**Lindon** (city) Utah County
81	29.0	**Preston** (city) Franklin County
81	29.0	**Waldoboro** (town) Lincoln County
84	28.8	**Grantsville** (city) Tooele County
84	28.8	**Madison** (town) Carroll County
84	28.8	**Oneida** (town) Scott County
87	28.7	**Springville** (city) Utah County
88	28.5	**Draper** (city) Salt Lake County
88	28.5	**Ivins** (city) Washington County
88	28.5	**Nephi** (city) Juab County
88	28.5	**North Ogden** (city) Weber County
92	28.4	**Riverton** (city) Salt Lake County
92	28.4	**White City** (CDP) Salt Lake County
94	28.2	**Lake San Marcos** (CDP) San Diego County
94	28.2	**Maeser** (CDP) Uintah County
96	28.1	**Hanover** (township) Jackson County
96	28.1	**Nibley** (city) Cache County
96	28.1	**Somerset** (township) Hillsdale County
99	28.0	**Saratoga Springs** (city) Utah County
99	28.0	**Snowflake** (town) Navajo County
99	28.0	**Thetford** (town) Orange County
99	28.0	**Woods Cross** (city) Davis County
103	27.9	**Cedar City** (city) Iron County
103	27.9	**Helena** (city) Telfair County
105	27.8	**Spring Arbor** (township) Jackson County
106	27.7	**East Bloomfield** (town) Ontario County
107	27.6	**Bethel** (town) Oxford County
107	27.6	**Nicholls** (city) Coffee County
107	27.6	**Syracuse** (city) Davis County
110	27.5	**Bradford** (town) Orange County
110	27.5	**Orem** (city) Utah County
110	27.5	**Sandy** (city) Salt Lake County
113	27.4	**Hillsborough** (town) Hillsborough County
113	27.4	**New Durham** (town) Strafford County
113	27.4	**Washington Terrace** (city) Weber County
116	27.3	**Bartlett** (town) Carroll County
116	27.3	**Pleasant Grove** (city) Utah County
118	27.2	**Hope** (township) Barry County
118	27.2	**North Yarmouth** (town) Cumberland County
118	27.2	**Plainfield** (town) Sullivan County
121	27.1	**Ammon** (city) Bonneville County
122	27.0	**Anson** (town) Somerset County
123	26.9	**Northfield** (town) Franklin County
124	26.8	**Harrisville** (city) Weber County
124	26.8	**South Eliot** (CDP) York County
124	26.8	**Walpole** (town) Cheshire County
127	26.7	**China** (town) Kennebec County
127	26.7	**Fillmore** (city) Millard County
127	26.7	**Jefferson** (town) Lincoln County
130	26.6	**Holden** (town) Penobscot County
131	26.5	**Lake Monticello** (CDP) Fluvanna County
132	26.4	**Strafford** (town) Strafford County
133	26.3	**Cottonwood Heights** (city) Salt Lake County
133	26.3	**Plain City** (city) Weber County
133	26.3	**Richmond** (town) Sagadahoc County
136	26.2	**Enoch** (city) Iron County
136	26.2	**Hartland** (town) Windsor County
136	26.2	**Horse Shoe** (CDP) Henderson County
136	26.2	**Pavilion** (town) Genesee County
140	26.1	**Arundel** (town) York County
140	26.1	**Bowdoin** (town) Sagadahoc County
140	26.1	**Fairfield** (town) Somerset County
140	26.1	**Little Compton** (town) Newport County
140	26.1	**Washington** (city) Washington County
145	26.0	**Cordova** (city) Valdez-Cordova Census Area
145	26.0	**Millcreek** (CDP) Salt Lake County
145	26.0	**West Haven** (city) Weber County
148	25.9	**Buxton** (town) York County
148	25.9	**McRae** (city) Telfair County
150	25.8	**Concord** (township) Jackson County

Note: *This section ranks incorporated places and CDPs (Census Designated Places) with populations of 2,500 or more. Unincorporated postal areas were not considered. Please refer to the User Guide for additional information.*

Ancestry: American

Top 150 Places Ranked in *Descending* Order

State Rank	Percent	Place	State Rank	Percent	Place
1	63.6	La Follette (city) Campbell County	75	33.6	Harriman (city) Roane County
2	61.6	Gloverville (CDP) Aiken County	75	33.6	Rogersville (town) Hawkins County
3	58.6	Healdton (city) Carter County	78	33.5	Canton (town) Haywood County
4	57.7	Caryville (town) Campbell County	78	33.5	Galena (city) Cherokee County
5	48.2	Bonifay (city) Holmes County	80	33.4	LaFayette (city) Walker County
6	47.0	Dresden (town) Weakley County	81	33.3	Ball (town) Rapides Parish
6	47.0	Summerville (city) Chattooga County	82	33.2	Amelia (village) Clermont County
8	46.2	Clearwater (CDP) Aiken County	82	33.2	Dundee (town) Polk County
9	45.9	Pell City (city) Saint Clair County	82	33.2	Oak Grove (CDP) Washington County
10	45.5	New Tazewell (town) Claiborne County	85	33.1	Park City (CDP) Lincoln County
11	45.0	Hartford (city) Ohio County	86	33.0	England (city) Lonoke County
12	44.7	North Wilkesboro (town) Wilkes County	86	33.0	Tallapoosa (city) Haralson County
13	44.5	Treasure Lake (CDP) Clearfield County	88	32.7	Fairview (CDP) Walker County
14	44.4	Eaton (town) Madison County	88	32.7	Honea Path (town) Anderson County
15	44.3	Harrogate (city) Claiborne County	90	32.6	Miramar Beach (CDP) Walton County
16	43.8	Rockwood (city) Roane County	91	32.5	Crab Orchard (CDP) Raleigh County
17	43.5	Atkins (city) Pope County	92	32.4	Edgartown (town) Dukes County
18	42.9	Nassau Village-Ratliff (CDP) Nassau County	93	32.3	Flemingsburg (city) Fleming County
19	42.7	Wrightsville Beach (town) New Hanover County	94	32.1	Ward (city) Lonoke County
20	42.6	Temple (city) Carroll County	94	32.1	West Liberty (city) Morgan County
21	42.3	Church Hill (city) Hawkins County	96	32.0	Mountain City (town) Johnson County
21	42.3	De Funiak Springs (city) Walton County	96	32.0	Pittsburg (city) Crawford County
23	41.5	Morehead (city) Rowan County	96	32.0	Robertsdale (city) Baldwin County
24	41.1	Mascot (CDP) Knox County	96	32.0	Sandy (township) Clearfield County
25	40.9	Bremen (city) Haralson County	100	31.9	Jena (town) La Salle Parish
26	40.8	Junction City (city) Boyle County	100	31.9	Suncoast Estates (CDP) Lee County
27	40.7	Taylor (town) Houston County	102	31.8	Chelan (city) Chelan County
28	40.5	Wilkesboro (town) Wilkes County	102	31.8	Mary Esther (city) Okaloosa County
29	40.1	Margaret (town) Saint Clair County	102	31.8	Sullivan (city) Franklin County
30	40.0	Stanton (city) Powell County	105	31.7	North Terre Haute (CDP) Vigo County
31	39.8	Bean Station (city) Grainger County	106	31.6	Unicoi (town) Unicoi County
32	39.4	Eagle Lake (city) Polk County	107	31.5	Mills (town) Natrona County
33	39.3	Weyers Cave (CDP) Augusta County	108	31.4	Haynesville (town) Claiborne Parish
34	39.1	Bloomingdale (CDP) Sullivan County	108	31.4	Richlands (town) Tazewell County
35	39.0	Chincoteague (town) Accomack County	110	31.3	Hamilton (town) Madison County
36	38.7	Jan Phyl Village (CDP) Polk County	111	31.2	Mount Carmel (town) Hawkins County
37	38.2	Georgetown (city) Vermilion County	111	31.2	Moyock (CDP) Currituck County
38	38.1	Oliver Springs (town) Anderson County	113	31.1	Cypress Gardens (CDP) Polk County
39	38.0	Algood (city) Putnam County	113	31.1	Pigeon Forge (city) Sevier County
40	37.8	Hilliard (town) Nassau County	115	30.9	Beacon Square (CDP) Pasco County
41	37.4	Mount Carmel (CDP) Clermont County	116	30.8	Bayshore (CDP) New Hanover County
41	37.4	West Tisbury (town) Dukes County	116	30.8	Hannahs Mill (CDP) Upson County
41	37.4	Williamsburg (village) Clermont County	116	30.8	Odenville (town) Saint Clair County
44	37.3	Somerset (city) Pulaski County	119	30.7	Crestview (city) Okaloosa County
45	37.2	Bethel (village) Clermont County	119	30.7	Westville (village) Vermilion County
45	37.2	Dawson Springs (city) Hopkins County	121	30.6	Chipley (city) Washington County
45	37.2	Harlem (CDP) Hendry County	121	30.6	Greenville (city) Muhlenberg County
45	37.2	Stanford (city) Lincoln County	123	30.4	Wellsville (village) Columbiana County
49	37.0	Gray Summit (CDP) Franklin County	124	30.3	Bradford (township) Clearfield County
50	36.7	Hooks (city) Bowie County	125	30.2	Red Bay (city) Franklin County
51	36.6	Cullowhee (CDP) Jackson County	126	30.1	Inwood (CDP) Polk County
52	36.3	Lancaster (city) Garrard County	127	30.0	Byron (city) Peach County
53	36.2	Brooks (CDP) Bullitt County	127	30.0	Destin (city) Okaloosa County
53	36.2	Livingston (town) Overton County	129	29.9	Central City (city) Muhlenberg County
55	35.8	Blue Hill (town) Hancock County	130	29.8	Owensboro (city) Daviess County
56	35.7	Bayou Vista (CDP) Saint Mary Parish	131	29.7	Clinton (city) Anderson County
56	35.7	Waynesville (town) Haywood County	131	29.7	Hamilton (city) Marion County
58	35.6	Blennerhassett (CDP) Wood County	131	29.7	Monterey (town) Putnam County
59	35.4	Beaver Dam (city) Ohio County	131	29.7	Timberville (town) Rockingham County
59	35.4	Colonial Heights (CDP) Sullivan County	131	29.7	Yulee (CDP) Nassau County
61	35.3	Lake of the Woods (CDP) Champaign County	136	29.6	Hillview (city) Bullitt County
62	35.0	Mount Vernon (city) Rockcastle County	136	29.6	Moody (city) Saint Clair County
63	34.7	Broadway (town) Rockingham County	136	29.6	Niceville (city) Okaloosa County
63	34.7	Middlesborough (city) Bell County	136	29.6	Peru (city) Miami County
65	34.6	Cookeville (city) Putnam County	136	29.6	Salem (city) Washington County
66	34.5	Madison (town) Madison County	141	29.5	Bawcomville (CDP) Ouachita Parish
66	34.5	Sylva (town) Jackson County	141	29.5	Bessemer City (city) Gaston County
68	34.4	Inverness Highlands North (CDP) Citrus County	141	29.5	Selmer (town) McNairy County
68	34.4	Pearisburg (town) Giles County	144	29.4	Fort Scott (city) Bourbon County
70	34.3	Shepherdsville (city) Bullitt County	144	29.4	Lake Lorraine (CDP) Okaloosa County
71	34.2	Lone Grove (city) Carter County	144	29.4	Lynchburg-Moore County (metropolitan government) Moore County
72	34.0	Pike Road (town) Montgomery County	144	29.4	Malabar (town) Brevard County
73	33.9	Withamsville (CDP) Clermont County	144	29.4	Mount Orab (village) Brown County
74	33.8	Grantville (city) Coweta County	149	29.3	Winchester (city) Clark County
75	33.6	Burnettown (town) Aiken County	150	29.2	Fort Valley (city) Peach County

Note: *This section ranks incorporated places and CDPs (Census Designated Places) with populations of 2,500 or more. Unincorporated postal areas were not considered. Please refer to the User Guide for additional information.*

Ancestry: Irish

Top 150 Places Ranked in *Descending* Order

State Rank	Percent	Place
1	49.2	**Pearl River** (CDP) Rockland County
2	48.5	**Walpole** (CDP) Norfolk County
3	47.9	**Spring Lake Heights** (borough) Monmouth County
4	47.4	**Ocean Bluff-Brant Rock** (CDP) Plymouth County
4	47.4	**Rockledge** (borough) Montgomery County
6	46.8	**Green Harbor-Cedar Crest** (CDP) Plymouth County
7	46.7	**Scituate** (town) Plymouth County
8	46.0	**Scituate** (CDP) Plymouth County
9	45.7	**Hanover** (town) Plymouth County
10	45.5	**North Scituate** (CDP) Plymouth County
11	45.1	**Marshfield** (town) Plymouth County
12	44.3	**Ridley Park** (borough) Delaware County
13	44.0	**North Wildwood** (city) Cape May County
13	44.0	**Norwell** (town) Plymouth County
15	43.6	**Glenside** (CDP) Montgomery County
16	43.1	**North Middletown** (CDP) Monmouth County
17	42.8	**Littleton Common** (CDP) Middlesex County
18	42.4	**Oak Valley** (CDP) Gloucester County
19	42.3	**Braintree Town** (city) Norfolk County
20	42.2	**Whitman** (town) Plymouth County
21	41.9	**East Sandwich** (CDP) Barnstable County
22	41.8	**Walpole** (town) Norfolk County
23	41.7	**Brielle** (borough) Monmouth County
23	41.7	**Manasquan** (borough) Monmouth County
25	41.6	**Churchville** (CDP) Bucks County
26	41.3	**Spring Lake** (borough) Monmouth County
27	41.2	**Marshfield** (CDP) Plymouth County
27	41.2	**Springfield** (township) Delaware County
29	41.1	**Glenolden** (borough) Delaware County
30	41.0	**Abington** (cdp/town) Plymouth County
31	40.9	**Eddystone** (borough) Delaware County
31	40.9	**National Park** (borough) Gloucester County
33	40.5	**Cohasset** (town) Norfolk County
34	40.4	**Norwood** (borough) Delaware County
35	40.3	**Hingham** (town) Plymouth County
36	40.2	**Weymouth Town** (city) Norfolk County
37	40.1	**Wynantskill** (CDP) Rensselaer County
38	39.9	**Sayville** (CDP) Suffolk County
39	39.8	**Fairview** (CDP) Monmouth County
40	39.7	**East Bridgewater** (town) Plymouth County
40	39.7	**Folsom** (CDP) Delaware County
40	39.7	**Nahant** (cdp/town) Essex County
43	39.6	**Foxborough** (town) Norfolk County
44	39.4	**Bridgewater** (CDP) Plymouth County
44	39.4	**Mystic Island** (CDP) Ocean County
44	39.4	**Tinicum** (township) Delaware County
47	39.0	**Notre Dame** (CDP) Saint Joseph County
48	38.6	**Barrington** (borough) Camden County
48	38.6	**Gloucester City** (city) Camden County
48	38.6	**Rockland** (town) Plymouth County
51	38.3	**East Douglas** (CDP) Worcester County
51	38.3	**Hull** (cdp/town) Plymouth County
53	38.2	**Haverford** (township) Delaware County
54	38.1	**North Reading** (town) Middlesex County
55	37.9	**Haddon Heights** (borough) Camden County
55	37.9	**Hanson** (town) Plymouth County
55	37.9	**Woodbury Heights** (borough) Gloucester County
58	37.8	**Milton** (cdp/town) Norfolk County
59	37.6	**Highlands** (borough) Monmouth County
60	37.5	**Hingham** (CDP) Plymouth County
61	37.3	**Buzzards Bay** (CDP) Barnstable County
62	37.2	**Ridley** (township) Delaware County
63	37.1	**Canton** (town) Norfolk County
64	37.0	**Holbrook** (cdp/town) Norfolk County
65	36.9	**Garden City** (village) Nassau County
66	36.8	**Foxborough** (CDP) Norfolk County
67	36.6	**Kingston** (town) Plymouth County
68	36.5	**Drexel Hill** (CDP) Delaware County
69	36.4	**Ramtown** (CDP) Monmouth County
70	36.2	**Bridgewater** (town) Plymouth County
70	36.2	**West Brandywine** (township) Chester County
72	36.1	**Atkinson** (town) Rockingham County
72	36.1	**Wanamassa** (CDP) Monmouth County
74	36.0	**Norwood** (cdp/town) Norfolk County
75	35.9	**Western Springs** (village) Cook County
76	35.8	**Upton** (CDP) Worcester County
76	35.8	**Westvale** (CDP) Onondaga County
78	35.7	**East Greenbush** (CDP) Rensselaer County
79	35.6	**Avon** (town) Norfolk County
79	35.6	**Chester** (city) Hancock County
79	35.6	**Medfield** (CDP) Norfolk County
79	35.6	**Wakefield** (cdp/town) Middlesex County
83	35.5	**Aston** (township) Delaware County
84	35.4	**Green Island** (town/village) Albany County
85	35.3	**Duxbury** (town) Plymouth County
85	35.3	**Fair Haven** (borough) Monmouth County
87	35.2	**Connerton** (CDP) Pasco County
87	35.2	**Hopedale** (CDP) Worcester County
87	35.2	**Mansfield Center** (CDP) Bristol County
90	35.1	**Shrewsbury** (borough) Monmouth County
90	35.1	**Wilmington** (cdp/town) Middlesex County
92	35.0	**North Hampton** (town) Rockingham County
92	35.0	**Turnersville** (CDP) Gloucester County
94	34.9	**Aldan** (borough) Delaware County
94	34.9	**Audubon** (borough) Camden County
94	34.9	**Blue Point** (CDP) Suffolk County
94	34.9	**North Cape May** (CDP) Cape May County
94	34.9	**North Plymouth** (CDP) Plymouth County
99	34.8	**Wrentham** (town) Norfolk County
100	34.7	**Skaneateles** (village) Onondaga County
100	34.7	**West Bridgewater** (town) Plymouth County
102	34.6	**Little Egg Harbor** (township) Ocean County
102	34.6	**Prospect Park** (borough) Delaware County
104	34.5	**East Islip** (CDP) Suffolk County
104	34.5	**Plainville** (town) Norfolk County
104	34.5	**Washington** (town) Dutchess County
107	34.4	**Glendora** (CDP) Camden County
107	34.4	**Newtown** (township) Delaware County
107	34.4	**Tyngsborough** (town) Middlesex County
107	34.4	**Wall** (township) Monmouth County
111	34.3	**Port Monmouth** (CDP) Monmouth County
111	34.3	**Tewksbury** (town) Middlesex County
113	34.2	**Mansfield** (town) Bristol County
114	34.1	**North Wales** (borough) Montgomery County
114	34.1	**Pembroke** (town) Plymouth County
114	34.1	**Rockville Centre** (village) Nassau County
114	34.1	**Seabrook** (town) Rockingham County
118	34.0	**Cape Neddick** (CDP) York County
118	34.0	**Village Green-Green Ridge** (CDP) Delaware County
118	34.0	**Wanakah** (CDP) Erie County
118	34.0	**West Sayville** (CDP) Suffolk County
122	33.9	**Bellingham** (town) Norfolk County
122	33.9	**Clinton** (town) Dutchess County
124	33.8	**Haddon** (township) Camden County
124	33.8	**Marcellus** (town) Onondaga County
126	33.7	**Roseland** (borough) Essex County
127	33.6	**Bellingham** (CDP) Norfolk County
127	33.6	**Plymouth** (town) Plymouth County
129	33.5	**Bethel** (township) Delaware County
129	33.5	**Centreville** (town) Queen Anne's County
129	33.5	**East Bradford** (township) Chester County
129	33.5	**Gilford** (town) Belknap County
129	33.5	**Haddonfield** (borough) Camden County
129	33.5	**Medford Lakes** (borough) Burlington County
129	33.5	**Norton** (town) Bristol County
136	33.4	**Williston Park** (village) Nassau County
137	33.3	**Atlantic Highlands** (borough) Monmouth County
137	33.3	**Clementon** (borough) Camden County
137	33.3	**Hopkinton** (CDP) Middlesex County
137	33.3	**Melrose** (city) Middlesex County
137	33.3	**Trevose** (CDP) Bucks County
142	33.2	**Brightwaters** (village) Suffolk County
142	33.2	**Clinton** (town) Worcester County
142	33.2	**Horsham** (CDP) Montgomery County
142	33.2	**Massapequa Park** (village) Nassau County
142	33.2	**Medfield** (town) Norfolk County
142	33.2	**Rumson** (borough) Monmouth County
148	33.1	**Blauvelt** (CDP) Rockland County
148	33.1	**Clinton** (CDP) Worcester County
148	33.1	**New Britain** (borough) Bucks County

Note: This section ranks incorporated places and CDPs (Census Designated Places) with populations of 2,500 or more. Unincorporated postal areas were not considered. Please refer to the User Guide for additional information.

Ancestry: Italian

Top 150 Places Ranked in *Descending* Order

State Rank	Percent	Place
1	50.3	**Fairfield** (township) Essex County
2	49.5	**Johnston** (town) Providence County
3	47.8	**North Massapequa** (CDP) Nassau County
4	46.9	**Thornwood** (CDP) Westchester County
5	46.7	**Halesite** (CDP) Suffolk County
6	46.3	**Beach Haven West** (CDP) Ocean County
7	45.8	**Eastchester** (CDP) Westchester County
8	45.6	**Massapequa** (CDP) Nassau County
9	44.4	**Massapequa Park** (village) Nassau County
10	43.9	**North Branford** (town) New Haven County
11	43.7	**Hawthorne** (CDP) Westchester County
12	43.6	**East Haven** (cdp/town) New Haven County
13	43.2	**Hammonton** (town) Atlantic County
14	43.1	**Watertown** (CDP) Litchfield County
15	43.0	**Turnersville** (CDP) Gloucester County
16	42.3	**West Islip** (CDP) Suffolk County
17	42.1	**Frankfort** (village) Herkimer County
18	41.3	**East Hanover** (township) Morris County
18	41.3	**East Norwich** (CDP) Nassau County
20	41.2	**Islip Terrace** (CDP) Suffolk County
20	41.2	**North Haven** (cdp/town) New Haven County
22	41.1	**Glendora** (CDP) Camden County
23	40.8	**Cedar Grove** (township) Essex County
23	40.8	**Jefferson Valley-Yorktown** (CDP) Westchester County
23	40.8	**Miller Place** (CDP) Suffolk County
26	40.7	**Marlboro** (CDP) Ulster County
27	40.6	**Wood-Ridge** (borough) Bergen County
28	40.4	**Franklin Square** (CDP) Nassau County
29	40.3	**Nesconset** (CDP) Suffolk County
30	40.1	**Gibbstown** (CDP) Gloucester County
31	40.0	**Bayville** (village) Nassau County
32	39.7	**Richwood** (CDP) Gloucester County
33	39.6	**Saint James** (CDP) Suffolk County
34	39.1	**Lake Grove** (village) Suffolk County
35	38.9	**Dunmore** (borough) Lackawanna County
35	38.9	**North Providence** (town) Providence County
37	38.5	**Saugus** (cdp/town) Essex County
38	38.4	**Blackwood** (CDP) Camden County
38	38.4	**Jenkins** (township) Luzerne County
40	38.3	**South Farmingdale** (CDP) Nassau County
41	38.0	**East Islip** (CDP) Suffolk County
41	38.0	**Seaford** (CDP) Nassau County
43	37.9	**West Pittston** (borough) Luzerne County
44	37.8	**Old Forge** (borough) Lackawanna County
44	37.8	**Smithtown** (CDP) Suffolk County
46	37.5	**Prospect** (town) New Haven County
47	37.4	**Plainedge** (CDP) Nassau County
48	37.3	**Greenwich** (township) Gloucester County
48	37.3	**Manorville** (CDP) Suffolk County
50	37.0	**Watertown** (town) Litchfield County
51	36.4	**Smithtown** (town) Suffolk County
52	36.3	**Nutley** (township) Essex County
52	36.3	**Pittston** (city) Luzerne County
54	36.1	**Hauppauge** (CDP) Suffolk County
54	36.1	**Ronkonkoma** (CDP) Suffolk County
56	36.0	**Jessup** (borough) Lackawanna County
56	36.0	**Lyncourt** (CDP) Onondaga County
56	36.0	**Washington** (township) Gloucester County
59	35.9	**Eastchester** (town) Westchester County
59	35.9	**Frankfort** (town) Herkimer County
59	35.9	**Verona** (township) Essex County
62	35.8	**Barnegat** (CDP) Ocean County
62	35.8	**Centerport** (CDP) Suffolk County
64	35.7	**North Great River** (CDP) Suffolk County
64	35.7	**Oakdale** (CDP) Suffolk County
66	35.4	**North Babylon** (CDP) Suffolk County
66	35.4	**Pelham Manor** (village) Westchester County
68	35.2	**Bohemia** (CDP) Suffolk County
68	35.2	**Union Vale** (town) Dutchess County
68	35.2	**Yorktown** (town) Westchester County
71	35.1	**Center Moriches** (CDP) Suffolk County
71	35.1	**Selden** (CDP) Suffolk County
73	35.0	**Caldwell** (borough) Essex County
74	34.8	**Holbrook** (CDP) Suffolk County
74	34.8	**Holtsville** (CDP) Suffolk County
74	34.8	**Port Jefferson Station** (CDP) Suffolk County
77	34.7	**Holiday City-Berkeley** (CDP) Ocean County
77	34.7	**Oyster Bay** (CDP) Nassau County
77	34.7	**Stoneham** (cdp/town) Middlesex County
80	34.6	**Malverne** (village) Nassau County
81	34.5	**Brightwaters** (village) Suffolk County
81	34.5	**Hasbrouck Heights** (borough) Bergen County
81	34.5	**Lynnfield** (cdp/town) Essex County
84	34.4	**Bethpage** (CDP) Nassau County
84	34.4	**East Fishkill** (town) Dutchess County
84	34.4	**East Freehold** (CDP) Monmouth County
84	34.4	**Hazlet** (township) Monmouth County
84	34.4	**Kenmore** (village) Erie County
89	34.2	**Farmingville** (CDP) Suffolk County
89	34.2	**Moonachie** (borough) Bergen County
89	34.2	**Oceanport** (borough) Monmouth County
92	34.1	**Glen Head** (CDP) Nassau County
92	34.1	**Lacey** (township) Ocean County
94	33.9	**Bayport** (CDP) Suffolk County
94	33.9	**Deer Park** (CDP) Suffolk County
94	33.9	**Garden City South** (CDP) Nassau County
94	33.9	**Ocean Acres** (CDP) Ocean County
94	33.9	**West Babylon** (CDP) Suffolk County
99	33.8	**Carmel** (town) Putnam County
99	33.8	**Commack** (CDP) Suffolk County
99	33.8	**Neshannock** (township) Lawrence County
99	33.8	**Old Brookville** (village) Nassau County
103	33.7	**Blue Point** (CDP) Suffolk County
103	33.7	**Centereach** (CDP) Suffolk County
103	33.7	**Fort Salonga** (CDP) Suffolk County
103	33.7	**Kings Park** (CDP) Suffolk County
103	33.7	**Oakland** (borough) Bergen County
103	33.7	**Putnam Lake** (CDP) Putnam County
109	33.6	**Kensington** (CDP) Hartford County
109	33.6	**Lindenhurst** (village) Suffolk County
109	33.6	**Mechanicville** (city) Saratoga County
109	33.6	**Shirley** (CDP) Suffolk County
109	33.6	**Woodland Park** (borough) Passaic County
114	33.5	**Netcong** (borough) Morris County
115	33.3	**Elwood** (CDP) Suffolk County
115	33.3	**Mount Arlington** (borough) Morris County
115	33.3	**Somers** (town) Westchester County
115	33.3	**South Hackensack** (township) Bergen County
119	33.2	**Marlborough** (town) Ulster County
120	33.1	**Babylon** (village) Suffolk County
120	33.1	**Pine Lake Park** (CDP) Ocean County
120	33.1	**West Caldwell** (township) Essex County
123	33.0	**Lake Ronkonkoma** (CDP) Suffolk County
123	33.0	**Rotterdam** (CDP) Schenectady County
123	33.0	**Toms River** (township) Ocean County
126	32.9	**East Massapequa** (CDP) Nassau County
127	32.8	**Branford** (town) New Haven County
127	32.8	**North Patchogue** (CDP) Suffolk County
127	32.8	**Oakville** (CDP) Litchfield County
130	32.7	**Berkeley** (township) Ocean County
130	32.7	**Toms River** (CDP) Ocean County
130	32.7	**Washington** (township) Bergen County
133	32.6	**Greece** (town) Monroe County
133	32.6	**Mount Sinai** (CDP) Suffolk County
133	32.6	**Terryville** (CDP) Suffolk County
133	32.6	**Yaphank** (CDP) Suffolk County
137	32.5	**Emerson** (borough) Bergen County
137	32.5	**Point Pleasant** (borough) Ocean County
137	32.5	**West Long Branch** (borough) Monmouth County
140	32.4	**Cranston** (city) Providence County
140	32.4	**Fairview** (CDP) Monmouth County
140	32.4	**Lincroft** (CDP) Monmouth County
140	32.4	**Stafford** (township) Ocean County
140	32.4	**Totowa** (borough) Passaic County
140	32.4	**Wolcott** (town) New Haven County
146	32.3	**Middletown** (township) Monmouth County
147	32.2	**Berlin** (town) Hartford County
147	32.2	**Branford Center** (CDP) New Haven County
147	32.2	**Garden City** (village) Nassau County
147	32.2	**Highland Lakes** (CDP) Sussex County

Note: *This section ranks incorporated places and CDPs (Census Designated Places) with populations of 2,500 or more. Unincorporated postal areas were not considered. Please refer to the User Guide for additional information.*

Employment: Management, Business, and Financial Occupations

Top 150 Places Ranked in *Descending* Order

State Rank	Percent	Place	State Rank	Percent	Place
1	36.3	**Bronxville** (village) Westchester County	76	22.5	**Southampton** (village) Suffolk County
2	35.9	**Pelham Manor** (village) Westchester County	77	22.4	**Copake** (town) Columbia County
2	35.9	**Pound Ridge** (town) Westchester County	77	22.4	**Kinderhook** (town) Columbia County
4	34.8	**Larchmont** (village) Westchester County	77	22.4	**Spackenkill** (CDP) Dutchess County
5	33.9	**Sands Point** (village) Nassau County	77	22.4	**Victor** (town) Ontario County
6	33.6	**Munsey Park** (village) Nassau County	81	22.2	**Greenburgh** (town) Westchester County
7	33.5	**Scarsdale** (town/village) Westchester County	81	22.2	**LaFayette** (town) Onondaga County
8	33.4	**Armonk** (CDP) Westchester County	81	22.2	**Mendon** (town) Monroe County
9	32.7	**New Castle** (town) Westchester County	81	22.2	**Muttontown** (village) Nassau County
10	32.1	**Cold Spring Harbor** (CDP) Suffolk County	85	22.1	**Lakewood** (village) Chautauqua County
11	31.6	**North Hills** (village) Nassau County	85	22.1	**Northwest Harbor** (CDP) Suffolk County
12	31.5	**Pleasantville** (village) Westchester County	85	22.1	**Southold** (CDP) Suffolk County
13	31.4	**Woodbury** (CDP) Nassau County	88	22.0	**Clifton Park** (town) Saratoga County
14	31.2	**Pelham** (town) Westchester County	89	21.9	**Elma Center** (CDP) Erie County
15	29.9	**Montebello** (village) Rockland County	89	21.9	**Lake Success** (village) Nassau County
16	29.7	**Mamaroneck** (town) Westchester County	91	21.8	**Woodmere** (CDP) Nassau County
16	29.7	**Rye** (city) Westchester County	92	21.7	**Airmont** (village) Rockland County
18	28.7	**North Castle** (town) Westchester County	92	21.7	**Fayette** (town) Seneca County
19	28.6	**Garden City** (village) Nassau County	92	21.7	**Wales** (town) Erie County
20	28.4	**Searingtown** (CDP) Nassau County	95	21.6	**Lansing** (town) Tompkins County
21	28.0	**Lloyd Harbor** (village) Suffolk County	95	21.6	**North Greenbush** (town) Rensselaer County
22	27.8	**North Salem** (town) Westchester County	95	21.6	**Plainview** (CDP) Nassau County
23	27.7	**Bedford** (town) Westchester County	95	21.6	**Port Washington North** (village) Nassau County
23	27.7	**Skaneateles** (village) Onondaga County	95	21.6	**Skaneateles** (town) Onondaga County
23	27.7	**West Hills** (CDP) Suffolk County	100	21.5	**Clarkson** (town) Monroe County
26	27.6	**Syosset** (CDP) Nassau County	100	21.5	**Pittsford** (town) Monroe County
27	27.5	**Pelham** (village) Westchester County	100	21.5	**Saint Regis Mohawk Reservation** (reservation) Franklin County
28	27.4	**University Gardens** (CDP) Nassau County	100	21.5	**West Bay Shore** (CDP) Suffolk County
29	27.2	**Briarcliff Manor** (village) Westchester County	104	21.4	**East Greenbush** (CDP) Rensselaer County
30	27.1	**Rye Brook** (village) Westchester County	104	21.4	**Melville** (CDP) Suffolk County
31	27.0	**Glen Head** (CDP) Nassau County	104	21.4	**South Valley Stream** (CDP) Nassau County
32	26.8	**Lewisboro** (town) Westchester County	104	21.4	**Woodstock** (town) Ulster County
33	26.6	**Menands** (village) Albany County	108	21.3	**Lansing** (village) Tompkins County
34	26.5	**Sennett** (town) Cayuga County	109	21.2	**Goshen** (village) Orange County
35	26.4	**East Williston** (village) Nassau County	109	21.2	**La Grange** (town) Dutchess County
35	26.4	**Hartsdale** (CDP) Westchester County	109	21.2	**Mount Pleasant** (town) Westchester County
35	26.4	**Irvington** (village) Westchester County	109	21.2	**Westerlo** (town) Albany County
35	26.4	**Lido Beach** (CDP) Nassau County	113	21.1	**Babylon** (village) Suffolk County
39	26.3	**Northport** (village) Suffolk County	113	21.1	**Great Neck Plaza** (village) Nassau County
40	26.2	**Flower Hill** (village) Nassau County	113	21.1	**Malverne** (village) Nassau County
40	26.2	**Manhattan** (borough) New York County	116	21.0	**Benton** (town) Yates County
40	26.2	**Somers** (town) Westchester County	116	21.0	**Herricks** (CDP) Nassau County
43	25.9	**Manhasset Hills** (CDP) Nassau County	116	21.0	**Wantagh** (CDP) Nassau County
43	25.9	**Old Bethpage** (CDP) Nassau County	119	20.9	**Dix Hills** (CDP) Suffolk County
45	25.6	**Port Washington** (CDP) Nassau County	119	20.9	**Livonia** (town) Livingston County
46	25.5	**Greenville** (CDP) Westchester County	119	20.9	**Noyack** (CDP) Suffolk County
47	25.2	**Jericho** (CDP) Nassau County	122	20.8	**Halesite** (CDP) Suffolk County
48	25.0	**Hastings-on-Hudson** (village) Westchester County	123	20.7	**East Norwich** (CDP) Nassau County
49	24.9	**Glenwood Landing** (CDP) Nassau County	123	20.7	**Elwood** (CDP) Suffolk County
50	24.7	**Centerport** (CDP) Suffolk County	123	20.7	**Saratoga Springs** (city) Saratoga County
51	24.6	**Harrison** (town/village) Westchester County	126	20.6	**Amsterdam** (town) Montgomery County
52	24.4	**Marcellus** (town) Onondaga County	126	20.6	**East Fishkill** (town) Dutchess County
53	24.1	**Eastchester** (town) Westchester County	126	20.6	**Oyster Bay** (CDP) Nassau County
54	24.0	**Clarence** (CDP) Erie County	129	20.5	**Pomona** (village) Rockland County
55	23.9	**Manhasset** (CDP) Nassau County	130	20.4	**Balmville** (CDP) Orange County
55	23.9	**Red Oaks Mill** (CDP) Dutchess County	130	20.4	**Manorville** (CDP) Suffolk County
55	23.9	**Tarrytown** (village) Westchester County	130	20.4	**Marbletown** (town) Ulster County
58	23.8	**Rockville Centre** (village) Nassau County	130	20.4	**Mount Sinai** (CDP) Suffolk County
59	23.6	**Brookville** (village) Nassau County	130	20.4	**New City** (CDP) Rockland County
60	23.5	**Kings Point** (village) Nassau County	130	20.4	**Penfield** (town) Monroe County
61	23.4	**Albertson** (CDP) Nassau County	130	20.4	**Perinton** (town) Monroe County
62	23.3	**East Hills** (village) Nassau County	137	20.3	**Cornwall-on-Hudson** (village) Orange County
62	23.3	**Mamaroneck** (village) Westchester County	137	20.3	**Guilford** (town) Chenango County
62	23.3	**Tuxedo** (town) Orange County	137	20.3	**Pompey** (town) Onondaga County
65	23.2	**Ardsley** (village) Westchester County	140	20.2	**Big Flats** (CDP) Chemung County
66	23.1	**Croton-on-Hudson** (village) Westchester County	140	20.2	**Commack** (CDP) Suffolk County
67	23.0	**Clarence** (town) Erie County	140	20.2	**Hawthorne** (CDP) Westchester County
67	23.0	**Roslyn Heights** (CDP) Nassau County	140	20.2	**Merrick** (CDP) Nassau County
69	22.9	**Huntington** (CDP) Suffolk County	140	20.2	**Rush** (town) Monroe County
70	22.8	**Eastchester** (CDP) Westchester County	145	20.0	**Orchard Park** (town) Erie County
70	22.8	**South Nyack** (village) Rockland County	145	20.0	**Roslyn** (village) Nassau County
72	22.7	**Niskayuna** (town) Schenectady County	145	20.0	**West Nyack** (CDP) Rockland County
73	22.6	**Dobbs Ferry** (village) Westchester County	148	19.9	**Greenlawn** (CDP) Suffolk County
73	22.6	**Fort Salonga** (CDP) Suffolk County	148	19.9	**Nyack** (village) Rockland County
73	22.6	**Locust Valley** (CDP) Nassau County	148	19.9	**Yorktown** (town) Westchester County

Note: This section ranks incorporated places and CDPs (Census Designated Places) with populations of 2,500 or more. Unincorporated postal areas were not considered. Please refer to the User Guide for additional information.

Employment: Management, Business, and Financial Occupations

Top 150 Places Ranked in *Ascending* Order

State Rank	Percent	Place
1	0.0	**Watchtower** (CDP) Ulster County
2	2.3	**SUNY Oswego** (CDP) Oswego County
3	2.9	**Fort Edward** (village) Washington County
4	3.1	**Moira** (town) Franklin County
5	3.2	**Monticello** (village) Sullivan County
6	3.4	**Alfred** (village) Allegany County
7	3.7	**University at Buffalo** (CDP) Erie County
8	3.8	**Galeville** (CDP) Onondaga County
9	4.0	**Fort Edward** (town) Washington County
10	4.5	**Attica** (village) Wyoming County
11	4.6	**Lyons** (village) Wayne County
11	4.6	**Riverhead** (CDP) Suffolk County
13	4.8	**Flanders** (CDP) Suffolk County
14	5.0	**Vails Gate** (CDP) Orange County
15	5.2	**Tupper Lake** (village) Franklin County
15	5.2	**Wyandanch** (CDP) Suffolk County
17	5.3	**Saranac** (town) Clinton County
18	5.4	**Dannemora** (village) Clinton County
18	5.4	**Norfolk** (town) Saint Lawrence County
20	5.6	**Alfred** (town) Allegany County
20	5.6	**Haverstraw** (village) Rockland County
20	5.6	**New Paltz** (village) Ulster County
20	5.6	**Wayland** (town) Steuben County
24	5.7	**Kaser** (village) Rockland County
25	5.8	**Conesus** (town) Livingston County
25	5.8	**Dix** (town) Schuyler County
27	5.9	**Yorkshire** (town) Cattaraugus County
28	6.0	**Hillcrest** (CDP) Rockland County
29	6.1	**Binghamton University** (CDP) Broome County
29	6.1	**Pembroke** (town) Genesee County
31	6.2	**Albion** (village) Orleans County
31	6.2	**Brentwood** (CDP) Suffolk County
31	6.2	**Inwood** (CDP) Nassau County
31	6.2	**South Fallsburg** (CDP) Sullivan County
31	6.2	**Thompson** (town) Sullivan County
36	6.3	**Central Islip** (CDP) Suffolk County
36	6.3	**Liberty** (village) Sullivan County
36	6.3	**Roosevelt** (CDP) Nassau County
39	6.4	**Sanford** (town) Broome County
40	6.5	**Albion** (town) Orleans County
40	6.5	**Caneadea** (town) Allegany County
42	6.6	**Corinth** (town) Saratoga County
42	6.6	**Greenville** (town) Greene County
42	6.6	**Johnson City** (village) Broome County
42	6.6	**Nunda** (town) Livingston County
42	6.6	**Otego** (town) Otsego County
42	6.6	**Rutland** (town) Jefferson County
42	6.6	**West Point** (CDP) Orange County
49	6.7	**Hornell** (city) Steuben County
49	6.7	**Liberty** (town) Sullivan County
51	6.8	**Herkimer** (village) Herkimer County
51	6.8	**Hudson Falls** (village) Washington County
51	6.8	**Riverside** (CDP) Suffolk County
54	6.9	**Carroll** (town) Chautauqua County
54	6.9	**Hopewell** (town) Ontario County
54	6.9	**Waterloo** (town) Seneca County
54	6.9	**Whitehall** (town) Washington County
58	7.0	**Delhi** (village) Delaware County
58	7.0	**Rose** (town) Wayne County
60	7.1	**Dannemora** (town) Clinton County
60	7.1	**Elmira Heights** (village) Chemung County
60	7.1	**Plattsburgh** (city) Clinton County
63	7.2	**Elmira** (city) Chemung County
63	7.2	**Hannibal** (town) Oswego County
63	7.2	**Sloan** (village) Erie County
66	7.3	**Bergen** (town) Genesee County
66	7.3	**Wappingers Falls** (village) Dutchess County
68	7.4	**Canisteo** (town) Steuben County
68	7.4	**Gloversville** (city) Fulton County
68	7.4	**Kirkwood** (town) Broome County
68	7.4	**Malone** (village) Franklin County
68	7.4	**North Amityville** (CDP) Suffolk County
73	7.5	**Brockport** (village) Monroe County
73	7.5	**Catlin** (town) Chemung County
73	7.5	**Conklin** (town) Broome County
73	7.5	**Herkimer** (town) Herkimer County
73	7.5	**West Haverstraw** (village) Rockland County
78	7.6	**Durham** (town) Greene County
78	7.6	**Lyons** (town) Wayne County
78	7.6	**Pierrepont** (town) Saint Lawrence County
78	7.6	**Scottsville** (village) Monroe County
78	7.6	**Southport** (CDP) Chemung County
78	7.6	**Watertown** (town) Jefferson County
84	7.7	**North Lindenhurst** (CDP) Suffolk County
84	7.7	**Portland** (town) Chautauqua County
86	7.8	**New Cassel** (CDP) Nassau County
86	7.8	**Rockland** (town) Sullivan County
86	7.8	**Uniondale** (CDP) Nassau County
86	7.8	**Whitesboro** (village) Oneida County
90	7.9	**Colesville** (town) Broome County
90	7.9	**Granby** (town) Oswego County
90	7.9	**Manheim** (town) Herkimer County
90	7.9	**Scriba** (town) Oswego County
90	7.9	**Spring Valley** (village) Rockland County
90	7.9	**Ticonderoga** (CDP) Essex County
90	7.9	**Whitehall** (village) Washington County
97	8.0	**Calverton** (CDP) Suffolk County
97	8.0	**Delaware** (town) Sullivan County
97	8.0	**Stockholm** (town) Saint Lawrence County
97	8.0	**West Sand Lake** (CDP) Rensselaer County
101	8.1	**Bronx** (borough) Bronx County
101	8.1	**Mechanicville** (city) Saratoga County
101	8.1	**Southport** (town) Chemung County
104	8.2	**Arcade** (town) Wyoming County
104	8.2	**Bangor** (town) Franklin County
104	8.2	**Candor** (town) Tioga County
104	8.2	**Fairview** (CDP) Westchester County
104	8.2	**Falconer** (village) Chautauqua County
104	8.2	**Geneseo** (village) Livingston County
104	8.2	**Greenville** (town) Orange County
104	8.2	**Hempstead** (village) Nassau County
104	8.2	**Lake Luzerne** (town) Warren County
104	8.2	**Orleans** (town) Jefferson County
104	8.2	**Port Chester** (village) Westchester County
104	8.2	**Port Jervis** (city) Orange County
104	8.2	**Schuyler Falls** (town) Clinton County
104	8.2	**Stony Brook University** (CDP) Suffolk County
104	8.2	**Walton** (town) Delaware County
119	8.3	**Canton** (village) Saint Lawrence County
119	8.3	**Clayton** (town) Jefferson County
119	8.3	**Deerpark** (town) Orange County
119	8.3	**Dunkirk** (city) Chautauqua County
119	8.3	**Lake Erie Beach** (CDP) Erie County
119	8.3	**North Bay Shore** (CDP) Suffolk County
119	8.3	**Saint Johnsville** (town) Montgomery County
126	8.4	**Alexandria** (town) Jefferson County
126	8.4	**Canton** (town) Saint Lawrence County
126	8.4	**Corinth** (village) Saratoga County
126	8.4	**Fenton** (town) Broome County
126	8.4	**Hoosick Falls** (village) Rensselaer County
126	8.4	**Johnstown** (city) Fulton County
126	8.4	**Mastic** (CDP) Suffolk County
126	8.4	**Mooers** (town) Clinton County
126	8.4	**Oswego** (town) Oswego County
126	8.4	**Tupper Lake** (town) Franklin County
126	8.4	**Utica** (city) Oneida County
126	8.4	**Wawarsing** (town) Ulster County
138	8.5	**Endicott** (village) Broome County
138	8.5	**Galen** (town) Wayne County
138	8.5	**Mount Morris** (town) Livingston County
138	8.5	**Palatine** (town) Montgomery County
138	8.5	**Spencer** (town) Tioga County
138	8.5	**Ticonderoga** (town) Essex County
138	8.5	**Wellsville** (village) Allegany County
145	8.6	**Au Sable** (town) Clinton County
145	8.6	**Carlton** (town) Orleans County
145	8.6	**Cortland** (city) Cortland County
145	8.6	**Delhi** (town) Delaware County
145	8.6	**Greenwich** (town) Washington County
145	8.6	**Hilton** (village) Monroe County

Note: *This section ranks incorporated places and CDPs (Census Designated Places) with populations of 2,500 or more. Unincorporated postal areas were not considered. Please refer to the User Guide for additional information.*

Employment: Computer, Engineering, and Science Occupations

Top 150 Places Ranked in *Descending* Order

State Rank	Percent	Place	State Rank	Percent	Place
1	19.3	**Gang Mills** (CDP) Steuben County	75	8.4	**Manorhaven** (village) Nassau County
2	16.9	**Northeast Ithaca** (CDP) Tompkins County	75	8.4	**Nyack** (village) Rockland County
3	16.1	**Cayuga Heights** (village) Tompkins County	78	8.3	**Ardsley** (village) Westchester County
4	15.8	**Lansing** (village) Tompkins County	78	8.3	**Brinckerhoff** (CDP) Dutchess County
5	15.3	**Erwin** (town) Steuben County	78	8.3	**Homer** (town) Cortland County
6	15.2	**Spackenkill** (CDP) Dutchess County	78	8.3	**Wappingers Falls** (village) Dutchess County
7	14.1	**Ithaca** (city) Tompkins County	82	8.2	**Duanesburg** (town) Schenectady County
8	13.1	**Niskayuna** (town) Schenectady County	82	8.2	**Lloyd** (town) Ulster County
9	13.0	**Mendon** (town) Monroe County	82	8.2	**Ravena** (village) Albany County
10	12.8	**Clifton Park** (town) Saratoga County	85	8.0	**Corning** (town) Steuben County
11	12.6	**Brighton** (CDP) Monroe County	85	8.0	**Haviland** (CDP) Dutchess County
12	12.5	**Greenville** (CDP) Westchester County	85	8.0	**Union** (town) Broome County
13	12.4	**Menands** (village) Albany County	88	7.9	**Charlton** (town) Saratoga County
14	12.3	**Honeoye Falls** (village) Monroe County	88	7.9	**Colonie** (village) Albany County
15	12.2	**Malta** (town) Saratoga County	88	7.9	**Hartsdale** (CDP) Westchester County
15	12.2	**Webster** (village) Monroe County	88	7.9	**Tuxedo** (town) Orange County
17	12.1	**Veteran** (town) Chemung County	88	7.9	**Wilton** (town) Saratoga County
18	11.7	**West Sand Lake** (CDP) Rensselaer County	93	7.8	**Albertson** (CDP) Nassau County
19	11.6	**Ithaca** (town) Tompkins County	93	7.8	**Brunswick** (town) Rensselaer County
20	11.5	**Caroline** (town) Tompkins County	93	7.8	**Colonie** (town) Albany County
20	11.5	**East Glenville** (CDP) Schenectady County	93	7.8	**East Hills** (village) Nassau County
22	11.4	**Stony Brook** (CDP) Suffolk County	97	7.7	**East Greenbush** (town) Rensselaer County
23	11.1	**Riverside** (CDP) Suffolk County	97	7.7	**Irvington** (village) Westchester County
24	11.0	**Ballston Spa** (village) Saratoga County	97	7.7	**New Paltz** (town) Ulster County
24	11.0	**Fairport** (village) Monroe County	97	7.7	**Pompey** (town) Onondaga County
24	11.0	**Westmere** (CDP) Albany County	97	7.7	**Searingtown** (CDP) Nassau County
27	10.8	**East Greenbush** (CDP) Rensselaer County	97	7.7	**Williamsville** (village) Erie County
28	10.7	**Lansing** (town) Tompkins County	103	7.6	**Dryden** (town) Tompkins County
28	10.7	**Sand Lake** (town) Rensselaer County	103	7.6	**Northumberland** (town) Saratoga County
30	10.4	**Fishkill** (town) Dutchess County	103	7.6	**Pittsford** (town) Monroe County
31	10.3	**Guilderland** (town) Albany County	106	7.5	**Centerport** (CDP) Suffolk County
31	10.3	**Halfmoon** (town) Saratoga County	106	7.5	**Macedon** (town) Wayne County
31	10.3	**Henrietta** (town) Monroe County	106	7.5	**South Hill** (CDP) Tompkins County
34	10.2	**Bardonia** (CDP) Rockland County	109	7.4	**Conesus** (town) Livingston County
34	10.2	**Greenwood Lake** (village) Orange County	109	7.4	**Great Neck** (village) Nassau County
34	10.2	**Walworth** (town) Wayne County	109	7.4	**Poestenkill** (town) Rensselaer County
37	10.1	**Hastings-on-Hudson** (village) Westchester County	112	7.3	**Coeymans** (town) Albany County
37	10.1	**Stony Brook University** (CDP) Suffolk County	112	7.3	**Danby** (town) Tompkins County
39	10.0	**Penfield** (town) Monroe County	112	7.3	**Elwood** (CDP) Suffolk County
40	9.9	**Flower Hill** (village) Nassau County	112	7.3	**Kaser** (village) Rockland County
40	9.9	**Herricks** (CDP) Nassau County	112	7.3	**Larchmont** (village) Westchester County
40	9.9	**Owego** (town) Tioga County	112	7.3	**Livonia** (town) Livingston County
43	9.8	**Bethlehem** (town) Albany County	118	7.2	**Armonk** (CDP) Westchester County
43	9.8	**Endwell** (CDP) Broome County	118	7.2	**Catlin** (town) Chemung County
43	9.8	**Perinton** (town) Monroe County	118	7.2	**Elmsford** (village) Westchester County
43	9.8	**University Gardens** (CDP) Nassau County	118	7.2	**Poughkeepsie** (town) Dutchess County
47	9.7	**Corning** (city) Steuben County	118	7.2	**Syosset** (CDP) Nassau County
47	9.7	**Newark Valley** (town) Tioga County	118	7.2	**West Sayville** (CDP) Suffolk County
47	9.7	**Ogden** (town) Monroe County	124	7.1	**Albany** (city) Albany County
47	9.7	**Woodstock** (town) Ulster County	124	7.1	**Hounsfield** (town) Jefferson County
51	9.6	**Piermont** (village) Rockland County	124	7.1	**Hyde Park** (town) Dutchess County
52	9.5	**Putnam Valley** (town) Putnam County	124	7.1	**Olive** (town) Ulster County
53	9.4	**Great Neck Estates** (village) Nassau County	124	7.1	**Schoharie** (town) Schoharie County
54	9.3	**Ballston** (town) Saratoga County	124	7.1	**Warrensburg** (CDP) Warren County
54	9.3	**Bayville** (village) Nassau County	130	7.0	**Irondequoit** (CDP) Monroe County
54	9.3	**Voorheesville** (village) Albany County	130	7.0	**La Grange** (town) Dutchess County
57	9.1	**Port Jefferson Station** (CDP) Suffolk County	130	7.0	**Neversink** (town) Sullivan County
57	9.1	**Setauket-East Setauket** (CDP) Suffolk County	130	7.0	**Saratoga** (town) Saratoga County
57	9.1	**Webster** (town) Monroe County	134	6.9	**Crown Heights** (CDP) Dutchess County
60	9.0	**Highland** (CDP) Ulster County	134	6.9	**Farmingdale** (village) Nassau County
60	9.0	**Rush** (town) Monroe County	134	6.9	**Greenburgh** (town) Westchester County
60	9.0	**Union Vale** (town) Dutchess County	134	6.9	**Lake Grove** (village) Suffolk County
60	9.0	**Village Green** (CDP) Onondaga County	134	6.9	**Schodack** (town) Rensselaer County
64	8.9	**Farmington** (town) Ontario County	134	6.9	**Troy** (city) Rensselaer County
64	8.9	**South Nyack** (village) Rockland County	134	6.9	**University at Buffalo** (CDP) Erie County
66	8.8	**Chili** (town) Monroe County	141	6.8	**Amherst** (town) Erie County
67	8.6	**Eaton** (town) Madison County	141	6.8	**Avon** (village) Livingston County
67	8.6	**Washingtonville** (village) Orange County	141	6.8	**Binghamton University** (CDP) Broome County
69	8.5	**Brewerton** (CDP) Onondaga County	141	6.8	**East Norwich** (CDP) Nassau County
69	8.5	**Montrose** (CDP) Westchester County	141	6.8	**Eggertsville** (CDP) Erie County
69	8.5	**Port Jefferson** (village) Suffolk County	141	6.8	**Gardiner** (town) Ulster County
69	8.5	**Saint Regis Mohawk Reservation** (reservation) Franklin County	141	6.8	**Glenville** (town) Schenectady County
69	8.5	**Saratoga Springs** (city) Saratoga County	141	6.8	**Hamilton** (village) Madison County
69	8.5	**Vestal** (town) Broome County	141	6.8	**Stockholm** (town) Saint Lawrence County
75	8.4	**Amityville** (village) Suffolk County	141	6.8	**Victor** (village) Ontario County

Note: This section ranks incorporated places and CDPs (Census Designated Places) with populations of 2,500 or more. Unincorporated postal areas were not considered. Please refer to the User Guide for additional information.

Employment: Computer, Engineering, and Science Occupations

Top 150 Places Ranked in *Ascending* Order

State Rank	Percent	Place	State Rank	Percent	Place
1	0.0	**Carthage** (village) Jefferson County	71	1.4	**Saint Johnsville** (town) Montgomery County
1	0.0	**Ellenville** (village) Ulster County	71	1.4	**Starkey** (town) Yates County
1	0.0	**Fairview** (CDP) Westchester County	71	1.4	**Tupper Lake** (town) Franklin County
1	0.0	**South Fallsburg** (CDP) Sullivan County	71	1.4	**Tupper Lake** (village) Franklin County
1	0.0	**Watchtower** (CDP) Ulster County	71	1.4	**Westfield** (town) Chautauqua County
6	0.5	**Camden** (town) Oneida County	81	1.5	**Beekmantown** (town) Clinton County
6	0.5	**Dansville** (village) Livingston County	81	1.5	**Boonville** (town) Oneida County
6	0.5	**Hoosick Falls** (village) Rensselaer County	81	1.5	**Caneadea** (town) Allegany County
6	0.5	**Norfolk** (town) Saint Lawrence County	81	1.5	**Chesterfield** (town) Essex County
6	0.5	**Rockland** (town) Sullivan County	81	1.5	**Cohocton** (town) Steuben County
11	0.6	**Albion** (town) Orleans County	81	1.5	**Flanders** (CDP) Suffolk County
11	0.6	**Amenia** (town) Dutchess County	81	1.5	**Kings Point** (village) Nassau County
11	0.6	**Bainbridge** (town) Chenango County	81	1.5	**Moriah** (town) Essex County
11	0.6	**Inwood** (CDP) Nassau County	81	1.5	**Mount Morris** (village) Livingston County
11	0.6	**Monticello** (village) Sullivan County	90	1.6	**Center Moriches** (CDP) Suffolk County
11	0.6	**Ogdensburg** (city) Saint Lawrence County	90	1.6	**Delaware** (town) Sullivan County
17	0.7	**Croghan** (town) Lewis County	90	1.6	**Ellisburg** (town) Jefferson County
17	0.7	**Gloversville** (city) Fulton County	90	1.6	**Jerusalem** (town) Yates County
17	0.7	**Moira** (town) Franklin County	90	1.6	**Malone** (town) Franklin County
17	0.7	**Roosevelt** (CDP) Nassau County	90	1.6	**Port Chester** (village) Westchester County
21	0.8	**Copake** (town) Columbia County	90	1.6	**Romulus** (town) Seneca County
21	0.8	**Elma Center** (CDP) Erie County	97	1.7	**Arcade** (town) Wyoming County
21	0.8	**Greenport** (town) Columbia County	97	1.7	**Aurelius** (town) Cayuga County
21	0.8	**Hancock** (town) Delaware County	97	1.7	**Catskill** (town) Greene County
21	0.8	**Liberty** (town) Sullivan County	97	1.7	**Conklin** (town) Broome County
21	0.8	**North East** (town) Dutchess County	97	1.7	**Franklinville** (town) Cattaraugus County
21	0.8	**Oneonta** (town) Otsego County	97	1.7	**Spring Valley** (village) Rockland County
28	0.9	**Brownville** (town) Jefferson County	97	1.7	**Springs** (CDP) Suffolk County
28	0.9	**Gouverneur** (village) Saint Lawrence County	97	1.7	**Verona** (town) Oneida County
28	0.9	**Lakeview** (CDP) Nassau County	97	1.7	**Whitehall** (town) Washington County
28	0.9	**Louisville** (town) Saint Lawrence County	106	1.8	**Bay Shore** (CDP) Suffolk County
28	0.9	**Mount Morris** (town) Livingston County	106	1.8	**Hamptonburgh** (town) Orange County
28	0.9	**Thompson** (town) Sullivan County	106	1.8	**Hempstead** (village) Nassau County
28	0.9	**Yorkshire** (town) Cattaraugus County	106	1.8	**Lake Luzerne** (town) Warren County
35	1.0	**Carroll** (town) Chautauqua County	106	1.8	**Liberty** (village) Sullivan County
35	1.0	**Davenport** (town) Delaware County	106	1.8	**New Windsor** (CDP) Orange County
35	1.0	**Fort Ann** (town) Washington County	106	1.8	**Red Oaks Mill** (CDP) Dutchess County
35	1.0	**Hudson** (city) Columbia County	106	1.8	**Rye** (town) Westchester County
35	1.0	**Hudson Falls** (village) Washington County	106	1.8	**Salamanca** (city) Cattaraugus County
35	1.0	**Island Park** (village) Nassau County	106	1.8	**Schuyler** (town) Herkimer County
35	1.0	**Minden** (town) Montgomery County	106	1.8	**Seneca** (town) Ontario County
35	1.0	**Moriches** (CDP) Suffolk County	117	1.9	**Amsterdam** (city) Montgomery County
35	1.0	**North Dansville** (town) Livingston County	117	1.9	**Brentwood** (CDP) Suffolk County
35	1.0	**Westfield** (village) Chautauqua County	117	1.9	**Frankfort** (town) Herkimer County
45	1.1	**Albion** (village) Orleans County	117	1.9	**Middletown** (city) Orange County
45	1.1	**Castile** (town) Wyoming County	117	1.9	**Rhinebeck** (village) Dutchess County
45	1.1	**Dannemora** (town) Clinton County	117	1.9	**Shandaken** (town) Ulster County
45	1.1	**Malone** (village) Franklin County	117	1.9	**Wyandanch** (CDP) Suffolk County
45	1.1	**Oswegatchie** (town) Saint Lawrence County	124	2.0	**Bronx** (borough) Bronx County
45	1.1	**Southampton** (village) Suffolk County	124	2.0	**Firthcliffe** (CDP) Orange County
51	1.2	**Alexandria** (town) Jefferson County	124	2.0	**Fort Edward** (village) Washington County
51	1.2	**Canisteo** (town) Steuben County	124	2.0	**Kingsbury** (town) Washington County
51	1.2	**Catskill** (village) Greene County	124	2.0	**Lake Erie Beach** (CDP) Erie County
51	1.2	**Falconer** (village) Chautauqua County	124	2.0	**Lisbon** (town) Saint Lawrence County
51	1.2	**Frankfort** (village) Herkimer County	124	2.0	**Marcy** (town) Oneida County
51	1.2	**Sherburne** (town) Chenango County	124	2.0	**Norwich** (town) Chenango County
57	1.3	**Afton** (town) Chenango County	124	2.0	**Saugerties** (village) Ulster County
57	1.3	**Cairo** (town) Greene County	124	2.0	**Sidney** (village) Delaware County
57	1.3	**Colesville** (town) Broome County	134	2.1	**Baywood** (CDP) Suffolk County
57	1.3	**Deerpark** (town) Orange County	134	2.1	**Candor** (town) Tioga County
57	1.3	**Dunkirk** (city) Chautauqua County	134	2.1	**Freeport** (village) Nassau County
57	1.3	**Gouverneur** (town) Saint Lawrence County	134	2.1	**Hornellsville** (town) Steuben County
57	1.3	**Hanover** (town) Chautauqua County	134	2.1	**New Cassel** (CDP) Nassau County
57	1.3	**Livingston** (town) Columbia County	134	2.1	**Newburgh** (city) Orange County
57	1.3	**Orange Lake** (CDP) Orange County	134	2.1	**Northampton** (town) Fulton County
57	1.3	**Orleans** (town) Jefferson County	134	2.1	**Peru** (town) Clinton County
57	1.3	**Salem** (town) Washington County	134	2.1	**Ridgeway** (town) Orleans County
57	1.3	**Skaneateles** (village) Onondaga County	134	2.1	**Sidney** (town) Delaware County
57	1.3	**Ticonderoga** (town) Essex County	134	2.1	**Sodus** (town) Wayne County
57	1.3	**Waterloo** (town) Seneca County	134	2.1	**Ticonderoga** (CDP) Essex County
71	1.4	**Callicoon** (town) Sullivan County	134	2.1	**Wales** (town) Erie County
71	1.4	**Mooers** (town) Clinton County	134	2.1	**Waterloo** (village) Seneca County
71	1.4	**New York Mills** (village) Oneida County	134	2.1	**West Elmira** (CDP) Chemung County
71	1.4	**Portland** (town) Chautauqua County	134	2.1	**Wilna** (town) Jefferson County
71	1.4	**Rye Brook** (village) Westchester County	134	2.1	**Wolcott** (town) Wayne County

Note: *This section ranks incorporated places and CDPs (Census Designated Places) with populations of 2,500 or more. Unincorporated postal areas were not considered. Please refer to the User Guide for additional information.*

Employment: Education, Legal, Community Service, Arts, and Media Occupations

Top 150 Places Ranked in *Descending* Order

State Rank	Percent	Place	State Rank	Percent	Place
1	46.8	Kaser (village) Rockland County	76	21.6	Croton-on-Hudson (village) Westchester County
2	45.2	Cayuga Heights (village) Tompkins County	77	21.5	Alfred (village) Allegany County
3	37.5	New Square (village) Rockland County	77	21.5	Blauvelt (CDP) Rockland County
4	35.5	Hamilton (village) Madison County	77	21.5	Dobbs Ferry (village) Westchester County
5	35.3	Canton (village) Saint Lawrence County	80	21.4	Merrick (CDP) Nassau County
6	32.8	Northeast Ithaca (CDP) Tompkins County	81	21.2	Jefferson Valley-Yorktown (CDP) Westchester County
7	32.7	Monsey (CDP) Rockland County	81	21.2	Oneonta (city) Otsego County
8	32.6	Ithaca (town) Tompkins County	83	21.1	Briarcliff Manor (village) Westchester County
9	31.7	Callicoon (town) Sullivan County	83	21.1	Mamaroneck (town) Westchester County
10	29.3	Ithaca (city) Tompkins County	83	21.1	Pittsford (town) Monroe County
10	29.3	Potsdam (village) Saint Lawrence County	83	21.1	Saranac (town) Clinton County
12	28.9	Lido Beach (CDP) Nassau County	87	21.0	Plainview (CDP) Nassau County
13	28.4	Hastings-on-Hudson (village) Westchester County	87	21.0	Rye Brook (village) Westchester County
14	27.5	Caneadea (town) Allegany County	89	20.9	Cold Spring Harbor (CDP) Suffolk County
14	27.5	Halesite (CDP) Suffolk County	89	20.9	Manlius (town) Onondaga County
16	27.3	Port Washington North (village) Nassau County	91	20.8	Greenburgh (town) Westchester County
17	27.2	Irvington (village) Westchester County	92	20.7	Northport (village) Suffolk County
17	27.2	Tuckahoe (village) Westchester County	92	20.7	Piermont (village) Rockland County
19	26.9	Lansing (village) Tompkins County	92	20.7	Skaneateles (town) Onondaga County
20	26.8	Greenville (CDP) Westchester County	92	20.7	West Elmira (CDP) Chemung County
20	26.8	Hamilton (town) Madison County	96	20.6	Cazenovia (village) Madison County
22	26.7	Sea Cliff (village) Nassau County	96	20.6	Rockville Centre (village) Nassau County
23	26.2	Canton (town) Saint Lawrence County	96	20.6	Yorktown (town) Westchester County
24	25.9	Scarsdale (town/village) Westchester County	99	20.5	Cortlandt (town) Westchester County
25	25.3	West Hills (CDP) Suffolk County	100	20.4	Catskill (village) Greene County
26	25.2	Minoa (village) Onondaga County	100	20.4	Great Neck Estates (village) Nassau County
27	25.0	Pelham Manor (village) Westchester County	100	20.4	Port Jefferson (village) Suffolk County
27	25.0	Skaneateles (village) Onondaga County	100	20.4	Red Hook (town) Dutchess County
27	25.0	Woodstock (town) Ulster County	104	20.3	Centerport (CDP) Suffolk County
30	24.8	Lansing (town) Tompkins County	104	20.3	Honeoye Falls (village) Monroe County
30	24.8	South Nyack (village) Rockland County	104	20.3	Lowville (village) Lewis County
32	24.5	Ardsley (village) Westchester County	104	20.3	Mendon (town) Monroe County
32	24.5	Williamsville (village) Erie County	104	20.3	Stony Brook (CDP) Suffolk County
34	24.4	Calcium (CDP) Jefferson County	109	20.2	Babylon (village) Suffolk County
34	24.4	Manlius (village) Onondaga County	109	20.2	Bedford (town) Westchester County
36	24.1	New Castle (town) Westchester County	109	20.2	Tarrytown (village) Westchester County
37	24.0	Bronxville (village) Westchester County	109	20.2	University Gardens (CDP) Nassau County
37	24.0	Gardiner (town) Ulster County	113	20.0	Pelham (village) Westchester County
39	23.8	Geneseo (village) Livingston County	114	19.9	Eggertsville (CDP) Erie County
39	23.8	Woodmere (CDP) Nassau County	114	19.9	Great Neck Plaza (village) Nassau County
41	23.7	Alfred (town) Allegany County	114	19.9	Lawrence (village) Nassau County
41	23.7	Kiryas Joel (village) Orange County	117	19.7	East Aurora (village) Erie County
41	23.7	West Point (CDP) Orange County	117	19.7	Otsego (town) Otsego County
44	23.6	Old Bethpage (CDP) Nassau County	117	19.7	South Fallsburg (CDP) Sullivan County
45	23.5	Marbletown (town) Ulster County	120	19.6	East Rockaway (village) Nassau County
45	23.5	New Paltz (village) Ulster County	121	19.5	Lowville (town) Lewis County
47	23.4	Flower Hill (village) Nassau County	122	19.4	Eastchester (CDP) Westchester County
48	23.3	Blue Point (CDP) Suffolk County	122	19.4	Philipstown (town) Putnam County
49	23.2	Potsdam (town) Saint Lawrence County	124	19.3	East Norwich (CDP) Nassau County
50	23.1	Brighton (CDP) Monroe County	124	19.3	Saint James (CDP) Suffolk County
50	23.1	Huntington (CDP) Suffolk County	126	19.2	Homer (village) Cortland County
50	23.1	Port Washington (CDP) Nassau County	126	19.2	Orchard Park (village) Erie County
50	23.1	South Hill (CDP) Tompkins County	126	19.2	Victor (village) Ontario County
54	23.0	Pleasantville (village) Westchester County	129	19.1	Heritage Hills (CDP) Westchester County
55	22.7	Pound Ridge (town) Westchester County	129	19.1	Watchtower (CDP) Ulster County
56	22.6	Sayville (CDP) Suffolk County	131	19.0	Rhinebeck (town) Dutchess County
57	22.5	Fayetteville (village) Onondaga County	132	18.9	Bethlehem (town) Albany County
57	22.5	Hartsdale (CDP) Westchester County	132	18.9	Elmira (town) Chemung County
57	22.5	Larchmont (village) Westchester County	134	18.8	Baldwin Harbor (CDP) Nassau County
57	22.5	Roslyn (village) Nassau County	134	18.8	Cornwall (town) Orange County
61	22.4	Thomaston (village) Nassau County	134	18.8	East Islip (CDP) Suffolk County
62	22.2	New Paltz (town) Ulster County	134	18.8	Orangetown (town) Rockland County
62	22.2	Nyack (village) Rockland County	138	18.7	Bellmore (CDP) Nassau County
62	22.2	Pelham (town) Westchester County	138	18.7	Commack (CDP) Suffolk County
65	22.0	Geneseo (town) Livingston County	138	18.7	Cuba (town) Allegany County
65	22.0	Hewlett (CDP) Nassau County	138	18.7	Dryden (town) Tompkins County
65	22.0	Lewisboro (town) Westchester County	138	18.7	East Williston (village) Nassau County
65	22.0	Manhattan (borough) New York County	138	18.7	Haviland (CDP) Dutchess County
65	22.0	Rhinebeck (village) Dutchess County	144	18.6	East Greenbush (CDP) Rensselaer County
70	21.9	Lloyd Harbor (village) Suffolk County	144	18.6	East Hampton North (CDP) Suffolk County
70	21.9	Setauket-East Setauket (CDP) Suffolk County	144	18.6	Garden City (village) Nassau County
72	21.8	Cornwall-on-Hudson (village) Orange County	147	18.5	East Shoreham (CDP) Suffolk County
72	21.8	Eastchester (town) Westchester County	147	18.5	Long Beach (city) Nassau County
74	21.7	Hurley (town) Ulster County	147	18.5	Sloatsburg (village) Rockland County
74	21.7	Stony Brook University (CDP) Suffolk County	150	18.4	Bayville (village) Nassau County

Note: This section ranks incorporated places and CDPs (Census Designated Places) with populations of 2,500 or more. Unincorporated postal areas were not considered. Please refer to the User Guide for additional information.

Employment: Education, Legal, Community Service, Arts, and Media Occupations

Top 150 Places Ranked in *Ascending* Order

State Rank	Percent	Place	State Rank	Percent	Place
1	2.4	**Warsaw** (town) Wyoming County	74	7.4	**Oakfield** (town) Genesee County
2	2.6	**Niagara** (town) Niagara County	74	7.4	**South Lockport** (CDP) Niagara County
3	3.5	**Warsaw** (village) Wyoming County	74	7.4	**Southport** (town) Chemung County
4	3.9	**Wilna** (town) Jefferson County	74	7.4	**Verona** (town) Oneida County
5	4.1	**Brentwood** (CDP) Suffolk County	80	7.5	**Evans** (town) Erie County
5	4.1	**Pavilion** (town) Genesee County	81	7.6	**Harriman** (village) Orange County
7	4.4	**Altona** (town) Clinton County	81	7.6	**Haverstraw** (village) Rockland County
7	4.4	**Lyncourt** (CDP) Onondaga County	81	7.6	**Lake Luzerne** (town) Warren County
9	4.5	**Lake Placid** (village) Essex County	81	7.6	**Manchester** (town) Ontario County
9	4.5	**North Bay Shore** (CDP) Suffolk County	81	7.6	**Marlboro** (CDP) Ulster County
11	4.6	**Vails Gate** (CDP) Orange County	81	7.6	**Pembroke** (town) Genesee County
12	4.7	**Mattydale** (CDP) Onondaga County	81	7.6	**Salamanca** (city) Cattaraugus County
12	4.7	**Riverside** (CDP) Suffolk County	81	7.6	**Schaghticoke** (town) Rensselaer County
14	5.0	**Maybrook** (village) Orange County	81	7.6	**Westfield** (town) Chautauqua County
15	5.1	**Granby** (town) Oswego County	90	7.7	**Canajoharie** (town) Montgomery County
15	5.1	**Southport** (CDP) Chemung County	90	7.7	**Hartland** (town) Niagara County
17	5.2	**Granville** (town) Washington County	90	7.7	**Livingston** (town) Columbia County
17	5.2	**Holland** (town) Erie County	90	7.7	**Mamakating** (town) Sullivan County
19	5.4	**Milford** (town) Otsego County	90	7.7	**Vienna** (town) Oneida County
20	5.6	**Clarendon** (town) Orleans County	95	7.8	**Boonville** (town) Oneida County
20	5.6	**Mohawk** (town) Montgomery County	95	7.8	**Depew** (village) Erie County
22	5.7	**Cambria** (town) Niagara County	95	7.8	**Inwood** (CDP) Nassau County
23	5.8	**Oswegatchie** (town) Saint Lawrence County	95	7.8	**Jerusalem** (town) Yates County
24	5.9	**Brewerton** (CDP) Onondaga County	95	7.8	**Lackawanna** (city) Erie County
24	5.9	**Broadalbin** (town) Fulton County	95	7.8	**Lakewood** (village) Chautauqua County
26	6.0	**Murray** (town) Orleans County	95	7.8	**North Bellport** (CDP) Suffolk County
26	6.0	**West Bloomfield** (town) Ontario County	95	7.8	**Pendleton** (town) Niagara County
26	6.0	**Whitehall** (town) Washington County	103	7.9	**Farmingville** (CDP) Suffolk County
29	6.1	**Brookfield** (town) Madison County	103	7.9	**Russia** (town) Herkimer County
29	6.1	**Campbell** (town) Steuben County	103	7.9	**Shirley** (CDP) Suffolk County
29	6.1	**East Syracuse** (village) Onondaga County	103	7.9	**Westfield** (village) Chautauqua County
29	6.1	**Newfane** (town) Niagara County	107	8.0	**Dix** (town) Schuyler County
29	6.1	**Port Jervis** (city) Orange County	107	8.0	**Mount Morris** (town) Livingston County
34	6.2	**Attica** (town) Wyoming County	107	8.0	**Newfane** (CDP) Niagara County
34	6.2	**East Bloomfield** (town) Ontario County	107	8.0	**Palmyra** (town) Wayne County
34	6.2	**Palermo** (town) Oswego County	107	8.0	**Richmondville** (town) Schoharie County
37	6.3	**Central Islip** (CDP) Suffolk County	107	8.0	**Roosevelt** (CDP) Nassau County
37	6.3	**Hampton Bays** (CDP) Suffolk County	107	8.0	**Sodus** (town) Wayne County
37	6.3	**Hempstead** (village) Nassau County	107	8.0	**South Glens Falls** (village) Saratoga County
40	6.4	**Attica** (village) Wyoming County	115	8.1	**Alden** (village) Erie County
40	6.4	**Newburgh** (city) Orange County	115	8.1	**Amsterdam** (city) Montgomery County
42	6.5	**Blasdell** (village) Erie County	115	8.1	**Arcadia** (town) Wayne County
42	6.5	**West Haverstraw** (village) Rockland County	115	8.1	**Catlin** (town) Chemung County
42	6.5	**Wyandanch** (CDP) Suffolk County	115	8.1	**Eden** (town) Erie County
45	6.6	**Conklin** (town) Broome County	115	8.1	**Galeville** (CDP) Onondaga County
45	6.6	**Constantia** (town) Oswego County	115	8.1	**Hamlin** (CDP) Monroe County
45	6.6	**Hannibal** (town) Oswego County	115	8.1	**Highland** (CDP) Ulster County
45	6.6	**Liberty** (village) Sullivan County	115	8.1	**Moreau** (town) Saratoga County
45	6.6	**Palmyra** (village) Wayne County	115	8.1	**North Gates** (CDP) Monroe County
50	6.7	**Carthage** (village) Jefferson County	115	8.1	**Saratoga** (town) Saratoga County
50	6.7	**Port Chester** (village) Westchester County	115	8.1	**Sardinia** (town) Erie County
50	6.7	**Whitesboro** (village) Oneida County	115	8.1	**Sloan** (village) Erie County
53	6.8	**Barker** (town) Broome County	115	8.1	**South Blooming Grove** (village) Orange County
53	6.8	**Carlton** (town) Orleans County	115	8.1	**Windsor** (town) Broome County
53	6.8	**Copiague** (CDP) Suffolk County	130	8.2	**Champlain** (town) Clinton County
53	6.8	**Mastic** (CDP) Suffolk County	130	8.2	**East Farmingdale** (CDP) Suffolk County
57	6.9	**Alexander** (town) Genesee County	130	8.2	**Hanover** (town) Chautauqua County
57	6.9	**Annsville** (town) Oneida County	130	8.2	**Pine Plains** (town) Dutchess County
57	6.9	**Kingsbury** (town) Washington County	134	8.3	**Brutus** (town) Cayuga County
57	6.9	**Pittstown** (town) Rensselaer County	134	8.3	**Cohoes** (city) Albany County
61	7.0	**Chazy** (town) Clinton County	134	8.3	**Darien** (town) Genesee County
62	7.1	**Corinth** (village) Saratoga County	134	8.3	**Herricks** (CDP) Nassau County
62	7.1	**Monticello** (village) Sullivan County	134	8.3	**Middletown** (city) Orange County
64	7.2	**Cohocton** (town) Steuben County	134	8.3	**New Cassel** (CDP) Nassau County
64	7.2	**Hastings** (town) Oswego County	134	8.3	**Newstead** (town) Erie County
64	7.2	**Hudson Falls** (village) Washington County	134	8.3	**North Lindenhurst** (CDP) Suffolk County
64	7.2	**Westmoreland** (town) Oneida County	134	8.3	**Schoharie** (town) Schoharie County
64	7.2	**Yorkshire** (town) Cattaraugus County	134	8.3	**Somerset** (town) Niagara County
69	7.3	**Lewiston** (village) Niagara County	134	8.3	**Tupper Lake** (village) Franklin County
69	7.3	**Moriches** (CDP) Suffolk County	134	8.3	**Unadilla** (town) Otsego County
69	7.3	**Mount Morris** (village) Livingston County	134	8.3	**West Monroe** (town) Oswego County
69	7.3	**North Amityville** (CDP) Suffolk County	147	8.4	**Fayette** (town) Seneca County
69	7.3	**Watervliet** (city) Albany County	147	8.4	**Groveland** (town) Livingston County
74	7.4	**Kirkwood** (town) Broome County	147	8.4	**Hopewell** (town) Ontario County
74	7.4	**Nichols** (town) Tioga County	147	8.4	**Lakeland** (CDP) Onondaga County

Note: *This section ranks incorporated places and CDPs (Census Designated Places) with populations of 2,500 or more. Unincorporated postal areas were not considered. Please refer to the User Guide for additional information.*

Employment: Healthcare Practitioners

Top 150 Places Ranked in *Descending* Order

State Rank	Percent	Place	State Rank	Percent	Place
1	23.8	Great Neck Estates (village) Nassau County	72	10.7	Tappan (CDP) Rockland County
2	23.6	Manhasset Hills (CDP) Nassau County	72	10.7	Waverly (village) Tioga County
3	23.2	Lake Success (village) Nassau County	78	10.6	Mineola (village) Nassau County
4	18.9	North Hills (village) Nassau County	78	10.6	Williamsville (village) Erie County
5	18.4	Herricks (CDP) Nassau County	80	10.5	Fort Salonga (CDP) Suffolk County
6	18.2	Muttontown (village) Nassau County	80	10.5	Lysander (town) Onondaga County
7	17.8	Otsego (town) Otsego County	80	10.5	Ogdensburg (city) Saint Lawrence County
8	16.8	Old Westbury (village) Nassau County	80	10.5	Pomona (village) Rockland County
9	16.5	Lawrence (village) Nassau County	80	10.5	Syosset (CDP) Nassau County
10	16.2	Rhinebeck (village) Dutchess County	85	10.4	Hoosick (town) Rensselaer County
10	16.2	Woodbury (CDP) Nassau County	85	10.4	Lowville (town) Lewis County
12	15.3	Garden City Park (CDP) Nassau County	85	10.4	Lowville (village) Lewis County
13	14.9	Clarence (CDP) Erie County	85	10.4	Manlius (town) Onondaga County
14	14.7	Harris Hill (CDP) Erie County	89	10.3	Oneonta (town) Otsego County
14	14.7	Montebello (village) Rockland County	89	10.3	Spackenkill (CDP) Dutchess County
16	14.5	West Nyack (CDP) Rockland County	91	10.2	Conesus (town) Livingston County
17	14.4	Searingtown (CDP) Nassau County	91	10.2	Livingston (town) Columbia County
18	14.3	North New Hyde Park (CDP) Nassau County	91	10.2	Rutland (town) Jefferson County
19	14.2	East Hills (village) Nassau County	94	10.1	Armonk (CDP) Westchester County
20	13.6	Dix Hills (CDP) Suffolk County	94	10.1	Baldwin Harbor (CDP) Nassau County
21	13.5	East Williston (village) Nassau County	94	10.1	Greenville (CDP) Westchester County
21	13.5	Wesley Hills (village) Rockland County	94	10.1	Wading River (CDP) Suffolk County
23	13.4	Port Jefferson (village) Suffolk County	98	10.0	Camillus (town) Onondaga County
23	13.4	Ticonderoga (CDP) Essex County	98	10.0	Elma (town) Erie County
25	13.3	Stony Brook (CDP) Suffolk County	98	10.0	Florida (town) Montgomery County
26	13.1	Great Neck Plaza (village) Nassau County	98	10.0	Hastings-on-Hudson (village) Westchester County
26	13.1	Ticonderoga (town) Essex County	98	10.0	Lakeland (CDP) Onondaga County
28	13.0	Skaneateles (village) Onondaga County	98	10.0	Lloyd Harbor (village) Suffolk County
29	12.9	Hewlett (CDP) Nassau County	104	9.9	Baldwin (CDP) Nassau County
29	12.9	Rhinebeck (town) Dutchess County	104	9.9	Barton (town) Tioga County
31	12.7	Hillcrest (CDP) Rockland County	104	9.9	Clarkstown (town) Rockland County
32	12.6	Pittstown (town) Rensselaer County	104	9.9	Eden (CDP) Erie County
33	12.5	Great Neck (village) Nassau County	104	9.9	Onondaga (town) Onondaga County
33	12.5	Kings Point (village) Nassau County	104	9.9	Valley Cottage (CDP) Rockland County
35	12.3	Cambria (town) Niagara County	110	9.8	Canandaigua (city) Ontario County
36	12.2	Russia (town) Herkimer County	110	9.8	Chestnut Ridge (village) Rockland County
37	12.1	Brighton (CDP) Monroe County	110	9.8	Clarence (town) Erie County
37	12.1	Geneva (town) Ontario County	110	9.8	Dix (town) Schuyler County
37	12.1	New Hyde Park (village) Nassau County	110	9.8	Elmont (CDP) Nassau County
37	12.1	Roslyn Heights (CDP) Nassau County	110	9.8	Glenwood Landing (CDP) Nassau County
37	12.1	Viola (CDP) Rockland County	110	9.8	Lewiston (village) Niagara County
37	12.1	Watertown (town) Jefferson County	110	9.8	Owasco (town) Cayuga County
37	12.1	Woodmere (CDP) Nassau County	110	9.8	Village Green (CDP) Onondaga County
44	11.7	Boston (town) Erie County	110	9.8	Woodbury (village) Orange County
44	11.7	Floyd (town) Oneida County	120	9.7	Boonville (town) Oneida County
44	11.7	Jericho (CDP) Nassau County	120	9.7	Horseheads (village) Chemung County
44	11.7	New City (CDP) Rockland County	120	9.7	Irvington (village) Westchester County
44	11.7	North Valley Stream (CDP) Nassau County	120	9.7	Ulysses (town) Tompkins County
49	11.6	Johnson City (village) Broome County	120	9.7	Wheatley Heights (CDP) Suffolk County
50	11.5	Highland (CDP) Ulster County	125	9.6	Farmington (town) Ontario County
50	11.5	Sherrill (city) Oneida County	125	9.6	Galway (town) Saratoga County
52	11.4	Briarcliff Manor (village) Westchester County	125	9.6	Glen Head (CDP) Nassau County
52	11.4	Fairmount (CDP) Onondaga County	125	9.6	Lakeview (CDP) Nassau County
52	11.4	Haviland (CDP) Dutchess County	125	9.6	Monroe (village) Orange County
52	11.4	Manhasset (CDP) Nassau County	125	9.6	Oswegatchie (town) Saint Lawrence County
52	11.4	Warsaw (town) Wyoming County	125	9.6	Rush (town) Monroe County
52	11.4	Warsaw (village) Wyoming County	125	9.6	Sardinia (town) Erie County
58	11.3	Fayetteville (village) Onondaga County	133	9.5	Scarsdale (town/village) Westchester County
59	11.2	East Norwich (CDP) Nassau County	133	9.5	Thomaston (village) Nassau County
59	11.2	Hoosick Falls (village) Rensselaer County	133	9.5	Victor (town) Ontario County
61	11.1	Bardonia (CDP) Rockland County	136	9.4	Bellmore (CDP) Nassau County
61	11.1	Bethel (town) Sullivan County	136	9.4	Deerfield (town) Oneida County
61	11.1	Setauket-East Setauket (CDP) Suffolk County	136	9.4	Port Ewen (CDP) Ulster County
64	11.0	East Shoreham (CDP) Suffolk County	136	9.4	South Valley Stream (CDP) Nassau County
64	11.0	North Hempstead (town) Nassau County	136	9.4	Victor (village) Ontario County
66	10.9	Brightwaters (village) Suffolk County	136	9.4	Wales (town) Erie County
66	10.9	Carthage (village) Jefferson County	136	9.4	Woodbury (town) Orange County
68	10.8	Granby (town) Oswego County	143	9.3	Dickinson (town) Broome County
68	10.8	Maine (town) Broome County	143	9.3	Maybrook (village) Orange County
68	10.8	Manlius (village) Onondaga County	145	9.2	Bronxville (village) Westchester County
68	10.8	Pittsford (town) Monroe County	145	9.2	Elma Center (CDP) Erie County
72	10.7	Carle Place (CDP) Nassau County	145	9.2	Gouverneur (town) Saint Lawrence County
72	10.7	Marlboro (CDP) Ulster County	145	9.2	Hamburg (village) Erie County
72	10.7	North Patchogue (CDP) Suffolk County	145	9.2	Malverne (village) Nassau County
72	10.7	Roslyn (village) Nassau County	145	9.2	Mohawk (town) Montgomery County

Note: This section ranks incorporated places and CDPs (Census Designated Places) with populations of 2,500 or more. Unincorporated postal areas were not considered. Please refer to the User Guide for additional information.

Employment: Healthcare Practitioners

Top 150 Places Ranked in *Ascending* Order

State Rank	Percent	Place	State Rank	Percent	Place
1	0.0	**Binghamton University** (CDP) Broome County	69	3.0	**Sidney** (village) Delaware County
1	0.0	**Colesville** (town) Broome County	69	3.0	**Tupper Lake** (village) Franklin County
1	0.0	**Kaser** (village) Rockland County	78	3.1	**Annsville** (town) Oneida County
1	0.0	**Riverside** (CDP) Suffolk County	78	3.1	**Chester** (village) Orange County
1	0.0	**SUNY Oswego** (CDP) Oswego County	78	3.1	**Fairview** (CDP) Dutchess County
1	0.0	**South Fallsburg** (CDP) Sullivan County	78	3.1	**Hamilton** (village) Madison County
1	0.0	**Watchtower** (CDP) Ulster County	78	3.1	**Jerusalem** (town) Yates County
8	0.2	**Calcium** (CDP) Jefferson County	78	3.1	**Mechanicville** (city) Saratoga County
9	0.4	**Ellenville** (village) Ulster County	78	3.1	**New Paltz** (village) Ulster County
10	0.5	**Kiryas Joel** (village) Orange County	78	3.1	**Voorheesville** (village) Albany County
10	0.5	**New Square** (village) Rockland County	86	3.2	**Caneadea** (town) Allegany County
12	0.6	**Alfred** (village) Allegany County	86	3.2	**Mattydale** (CDP) Onondaga County
13	0.7	**Gardnertown** (CDP) Orange County	86	3.2	**Mount Morris** (village) Livingston County
14	0.8	**Stony Brook University** (CDP) Suffolk County	86	3.2	**Patchogue** (village) Suffolk County
15	0.9	**Richmond** (town) Ontario County	90	3.3	**Brentwood** (CDP) Suffolk County
16	1.1	**Southampton** (village) Suffolk County	90	3.3	**Deerpark** (town) Orange County
17	1.2	**Alfred** (town) Allegany County	90	3.3	**Enfield** (town) Tompkins County
17	1.2	**Saugerties** (village) Ulster County	90	3.3	**Gaines** (town) Orleans County
19	1.3	**Benton** (town) Yates County	90	3.3	**North Great River** (CDP) Suffolk County
20	1.4	**Potsdam** (village) Saint Lawrence County	90	3.3	**Webster** (village) Monroe County
21	1.5	**Carlton** (town) Orleans County	96	3.4	**Davenport** (town) Delaware County
22	1.6	**Monsey** (CDP) Rockland County	96	3.4	**Fayette** (town) Seneca County
22	1.6	**Palermo** (town) Oswego County	96	3.4	**Hanover** (town) Chautauqua County
24	1.7	**Rockland** (town) Sullivan County	96	3.4	**Islip Terrace** (CDP) Suffolk County
24	1.7	**University at Buffalo** (CDP) Erie County	100	3.5	**Bay Shore** (CDP) Suffolk County
26	1.8	**Norfolk** (town) Saint Lawrence County	100	3.5	**Bergen** (town) Genesee County
27	1.9	**Northwest Harbor** (CDP) Suffolk County	100	3.5	**Denmark** (town) Lewis County
27	1.9	**Riverhead** (CDP) Suffolk County	100	3.5	**Fairport** (village) Monroe County
29	2.1	**Locust Valley** (CDP) Nassau County	100	3.5	**Homer** (town) Cortland County
29	2.1	**Wanakah** (CDP) Erie County	100	3.5	**Kirkwood** (town) Broome County
31	2.2	**Greenwood Lake** (village) Orange County	100	3.5	**Noyack** (CDP) Suffolk County
31	2.2	**Norwich** (town) Chenango County	100	3.5	**Terryville** (CDP) Suffolk County
33	2.3	**Camden** (town) Oneida County	108	3.6	**Amenia** (town) Dutchess County
33	2.3	**Flanders** (CDP) Suffolk County	108	3.6	**Au Sable** (town) Clinton County
33	2.3	**Neversink** (town) Sullivan County	108	3.6	**Callicoon** (town) Sullivan County
33	2.3	**Somerset** (town) Niagara County	108	3.6	**Hamilton** (town) Madison County
37	2.4	**Brewerton** (CDP) Onondaga County	108	3.6	**Harriman** (village) Orange County
37	2.4	**Ithaca** (city) Tompkins County	108	3.6	**Moravia** (town) Cayuga County
39	2.5	**Chester** (town) Warren County	108	3.6	**Romulus** (town) Seneca County
39	2.5	**Elmsford** (village) Westchester County	108	3.6	**Sloan** (village) Erie County
39	2.5	**Fredonia** (village) Chautauqua County	108	3.6	**Wappingers Falls** (village) Dutchess County
39	2.5	**Liberty** (village) Sullivan County	108	3.6	**Wolcott** (town) Wayne County
39	2.5	**New Haven** (town) Oswego County	118	3.7	**Cayuga Heights** (village) Tompkins County
39	2.5	**Portland** (town) Chautauqua County	118	3.7	**Clarendon** (town) Orleans County
39	2.5	**Saint Regis Mohawk Reservation** (reservation) Franklin County	118	3.7	**Clarkson** (town) Monroe County
39	2.5	**Walton** (village) Delaware County	118	3.7	**Cohocton** (town) Steuben County
47	2.6	**Erwin** (town) Steuben County	118	3.7	**Dover** (town) Dutchess County
47	2.6	**Hunter** (town) Greene County	118	3.7	**Elmira Heights** (village) Chemung County
47	2.6	**Newburgh** (city) Orange County	118	3.7	**Kendall** (town) Orleans County
47	2.6	**Theresa** (town) Jefferson County	118	3.7	**Ravena** (village) Albany County
47	2.6	**Walden** (village) Orange County	118	3.7	**Sterling** (town) Cayuga County
52	2.7	**Cobleskill** (village) Schoharie County	127	3.8	**Beacon** (city) Dutchess County
52	2.7	**Fallsburg** (town) Sullivan County	127	3.8	**Copake** (town) Columbia County
52	2.7	**Gorham** (town) Ontario County	127	3.8	**Copiague** (CDP) Suffolk County
52	2.7	**Johnstown** (city) Fulton County	127	3.8	**Delhi** (town) Delaware County
52	2.7	**New Berlin** (town) Chenango County	127	3.8	**East Hampton** (town) Suffolk County
52	2.7	**New Cassel** (CDP) Nassau County	127	3.8	**Hempstead** (village) Nassau County
52	2.7	**North Bay Shore** (CDP) Suffolk County	127	3.8	**Kingsbury** (town) Washington County
52	2.7	**Oswego** (town) Oswego County	127	3.8	**Lake Ronkonkoma** (CDP) Suffolk County
52	2.7	**Otego** (town) Otsego County	127	3.8	**Palmyra** (town) Wayne County
52	2.7	**Port Chester** (village) Westchester County	127	3.8	**Ridge** (CDP) Suffolk County
62	2.8	**Castile** (town) Wyoming County	127	3.8	**Rye** (town) Westchester County
62	2.8	**Hancock** (town) Delaware County	127	3.8	**Salamanca** (city) Cattaraugus County
64	2.9	**Alexandria** (town) Jefferson County	127	3.8	**Westhampton** (CDP) Suffolk County
64	2.9	**East Syracuse** (village) Onondaga County	127	3.8	**Yates** (town) Orleans County
64	2.9	**Sanford** (town) Broome County	141	3.9	**Blasdell** (village) Erie County
64	2.9	**Shandaken** (town) Ulster County	141	3.9	**Brinckerhoff** (CDP) Dutchess County
64	2.9	**South Glens Falls** (village) Saratoga County	141	3.9	**Brownville** (town) Jefferson County
69	3.0	**Albion** (village) Orleans County	141	3.9	**Canastota** (village) Madison County
69	3.0	**Clarkson** (CDP) Monroe County	141	3.9	**Florida** (village) Orange County
69	3.0	**East Hampton North** (CDP) Suffolk County	141	3.9	**Livonia** (town) Livingston County
69	3.0	**Ghent** (town) Columbia County	141	3.9	**Minden** (town) Montgomery County
69	3.0	**Hastings** (town) Oswego County	141	3.9	**North East** (town) Dutchess County
69	3.0	**Mooers** (town) Clinton County	141	3.9	**North Gates** (CDP) Monroe County
69	3.0	**Schroeppel** (town) Oswego County	141	3.9	**Palmyra** (village) Wayne County

Note: *This section ranks incorporated places and CDPs (Census Designated Places) with populations of 2,500 or more. Unincorporated postal areas were not considered. Please refer to the User Guide for additional information.*

Employment: Service Occupations

Top 150 Places Ranked in *Descending* Order

State Rank	Percent	Place
1	46.1	**SUNY Oswego** (CDP) Oswego County
2	38.6	**Tupper Lake** (village) Franklin County
3	38.2	**Port Chester** (village) Westchester County
4	36.8	**Fairview** (CDP) Westchester County
5	36.6	**Bedford Hills** (CDP) Westchester County
5	36.6	**Mount Kisco** (town/village) Westchester County
7	35.8	**Delhi** (village) Delaware County
8	35.7	**Monticello** (village) Sullivan County
9	34.6	**Spring Valley** (village) Rockland County
10	34.3	**Elmsford** (village) Westchester County
11	34.2	**Alfred** (village) Allegany County
12	33.8	**Inwood** (CDP) Nassau County
13	33.7	**Cobleskill** (village) Schoharie County
14	33.3	**Bronx** (borough) Bronx County
14	33.3	**Oswego** (town) Oswego County
16	33.1	**Southport** (CDP) Chemung County
17	33.0	**Tupper Lake** (town) Franklin County
18	32.7	**Mount Morris** (village) Livingston County
19	32.4	**Caneadea** (town) Allegany County
19	32.4	**Norfolk** (town) Saint Lawrence County
21	32.3	**Carthage** (village) Jefferson County
22	32.2	**Wyandanch** (CDP) Suffolk County
23	32.0	**Hempstead** (village) Nassau County
24	31.9	**West Haverstraw** (village) Rockland County
25	31.7	**Flanders** (CDP) Suffolk County
25	31.7	**Hudson Falls** (village) Washington County
25	31.7	**Watchtower** (CDP) Ulster County
28	31.5	**Dannemora** (village) Clinton County
29	31.3	**Alfred** (town) Allegany County
29	31.3	**Harriman** (village) Orange County
31	31.2	**Hudson** (city) Columbia County
32	30.9	**Whitehall** (town) Washington County
33	30.8	**Whitehall** (village) Washington County
34	30.7	**Lakeview** (CDP) Nassau County
34	30.7	**North East** (town) Dutchess County
36	30.3	**Gowanda** (village) Cattaraugus County
37	29.9	**Herkimer** (village) Herkimer County
37	29.9	**Malone** (village) Franklin County
37	29.9	**Moira** (town) Franklin County
37	29.9	**Poughkeepsie** (city) Dutchess County
41	29.8	**Wanakah** (CDP) Erie County
42	29.7	**Enfield** (town) Tompkins County
42	29.7	**Moriah** (town) Essex County
42	29.7	**Salamanca** (city) Cattaraugus County
42	29.7	**South Fallsburg** (CDP) Sullivan County
46	29.6	**Binghamton University** (CDP) Broome County
46	29.6	**Vails Gate** (CDP) Orange County
48	29.5	**Rye** (city) Westchester County
49	29.4	**North Elba** (town) Essex County
49	29.4	**Rockland** (town) Sullivan County
51	29.3	**Delhi** (town) Delaware County
51	29.3	**Southport** (town) Chemung County
53	29.2	**North Amityville** (CDP) Suffolk County
54	29.0	**Haverstraw** (village) Rockland County
55	28.9	**Dix** (town) Schuyler County
55	28.9	**Penn Yan** (village) Yates County
55	28.9	**Roosevelt** (CDP) Nassau County
58	28.7	**Lisbon** (town) Saint Lawrence County
58	28.7	**Montauk** (CDP) Suffolk County
60	28.6	**Jay** (town) Essex County
61	28.5	**Geneseo** (village) Livingston County
61	28.5	**University at Buffalo** (CDP) Erie County
63	28.1	**Peekskill** (city) Westchester County
64	27.9	**Hillcrest** (CDP) Rockland County
64	27.9	**Wilna** (town) Jefferson County
66	27.8	**Beekmantown** (town) Clinton County
66	27.8	**Glen Cove** (city) Nassau County
66	27.8	**Neversink** (town) Sullivan County
69	27.7	**Cobleskill** (town) Schoharie County
70	27.6	**Fort Drum** (CDP) Jefferson County
70	27.6	**Owego** (village) Tioga County
72	27.4	**Blasdell** (village) Erie County
72	27.4	**Utica** (city) Oneida County
74	27.3	**New Cassel** (CDP) Nassau County
75	27.2	**Haverstraw** (town) Rockland County
75	27.2	**Malone** (town) Franklin County
75	27.2	**Niagara** (town) Niagara County
75	27.2	**Ossining** (village) Westchester County
75	27.2	**Portland** (town) Chautauqua County
80	27.1	**Saranac Lake** (village) Franklin County
81	27.0	**Elmira** (city) Chemung County
81	27.0	**Frankfort** (village) Herkimer County
81	27.0	**Ghent** (town) Columbia County
81	27.0	**Greenport** (town) Columbia County
85	26.9	**Hampton Bays** (CDP) Suffolk County
85	26.9	**Mount Vernon** (city) Westchester County
87	26.8	**Corinth** (village) Saratoga County
87	26.8	**Stockholm** (town) Saint Lawrence County
89	26.7	**Dannemora** (town) Clinton County
89	26.7	**Mount Ivy** (CDP) Rockland County
89	26.7	**Stamford** (town) Delaware County
92	26.6	**Lake Placid** (village) Essex County
93	26.5	**Milford** (town) Otsego County
94	26.3	**Bangor** (town) Franklin County
94	26.3	**Davenport** (town) Delaware County
94	26.3	**Newburgh** (city) Orange County
97	26.2	**Port Jervis** (city) Orange County
98	26.1	**Laurens** (town) Otsego County
98	26.1	**Mount Hope** (town) Orange County
98	26.1	**Mount Morris** (town) Livingston County
98	26.1	**Washington** (town) Dutchess County
102	26.0	**Herkimer** (town) Herkimer County
102	26.0	**Saranac** (town) Clinton County
102	26.0	**South Blooming Grove** (village) Orange County
102	26.0	**Thompson** (town) Sullivan County
106	25.9	**Hanover** (town) Chautauqua County
107	25.8	**Brentwood** (CDP) Suffolk County
108	25.7	**Gloversville** (city) Fulton County
108	25.7	**Kingsbury** (town) Washington County
110	25.6	**Rochester** (city) Monroe County
110	25.6	**Sleepy Hollow** (village) Westchester County
112	25.5	**Plattsburgh** (city) Clinton County
112	25.5	**Riverhead** (CDP) Suffolk County
114	25.4	**Fredonia** (village) Chautauqua County
114	25.4	**Hamlin** (CDP) Monroe County
116	25.3	**Corinth** (town) Saratoga County
116	25.3	**Greenville** (town) Orange County
116	25.3	**Lackawanna** (city) Erie County
116	25.3	**Uniondale** (CDP) Nassau County
116	25.3	**Wellsville** (village) Allegany County
121	25.2	**Mastic** (CDP) Suffolk County
121	25.2	**Niagara Falls** (city) Niagara County
121	25.2	**Schenectady** (city) Schenectady County
121	25.2	**Wappingers Falls** (village) Dutchess County
125	25.1	**Arlington** (CDP) Dutchess County
125	25.1	**Buffalo** (city) Erie County
125	25.1	**Huntington Station** (CDP) Suffolk County
125	25.1	**Louisville** (town) Saint Lawrence County
125	25.1	**Minden** (town) Montgomery County
130	25.0	**Gardnertown** (CDP) Orange County
131	24.9	**Hancock** (town) Delaware County
132	24.8	**Attica** (village) Wyoming County
132	24.8	**Brockport** (village) Monroe County
132	24.8	**Elmira Heights** (village) Chemung County
132	24.8	**Le Roy** (village) Genesee County
132	24.8	**Middletown** (city) Orange County
132	24.8	**New Paltz** (village) Ulster County
132	24.8	**Queens** (borough) Queens County
132	24.8	**Schuyler Falls** (town) Clinton County
140	24.7	**Elmont** (CDP) Nassau County
140	24.7	**Hopewell** (town) Ontario County
142	24.6	**Dover** (town) Dutchess County
142	24.6	**Geneseo** (town) Livingston County
142	24.6	**Locust Valley** (CDP) Nassau County
142	24.6	**Mohawk** (village) Herkimer County
146	24.5	**Central Islip** (CDP) Suffolk County
146	24.5	**Cortland** (city) Cortland County
146	24.5	**Geneva** (city) Ontario County
146	24.5	**Newfield** (town) Tompkins County
146	24.5	**South Hill** (CDP) Tompkins County

Note: *This section ranks incorporated places and CDPs (Census Designated Places) with populations of 2,500 or more. Unincorporated postal areas were not considered. Please refer to the User Guide for additional information.*

Employment: Service Occupations

Top 150 Places Ranked in *Ascending* Order

State Rank	Percent	Place	State Rank	Percent	Place
1	2.9	**Munsey Park** (village) Nassau County	76	9.6	**Tuxedo** (town) Orange County
2	3.3	**East Hills** (village) Nassau County	77	9.7	**Rye** (city) Westchester County
3	3.9	**Great Neck Estates** (village) Nassau County	78	9.8	**Lewisboro** (town) Westchester County
3	3.9	**Scarsdale** (town/village) Westchester County	78	9.8	**Pleasantville** (village) Westchester County
5	4.1	**Lawrence** (village) Nassau County	78	9.8	**Pound Ridge** (town) Westchester County
6	4.6	**Kaser** (village) Rockland County	78	9.8	**Rye Brook** (village) Westchester County
7	4.8	**Cold Spring Harbor** (CDP) Suffolk County	82	9.9	**East Norwich** (CDP) Nassau County
7	4.8	**Greenville** (CDP) Westchester County	82	9.9	**North Salem** (town) Westchester County
7	4.8	**Heritage Hills** (CDP) Westchester County	84	10.0	**Cayuga Heights** (village) Tompkins County
10	4.9	**Kings Point** (village) Nassau County	84	10.0	**Garden City** (village) Nassau County
11	5.2	**Elma Center** (CDP) Erie County	84	10.0	**Plainedge** (CDP) Nassau County
12	5.3	**Manhasset Hills** (CDP) Nassau County	87	10.1	**Malta** (town) Saratoga County
13	5.7	**Bronxville** (village) Westchester County	87	10.1	**Northport** (village) Suffolk County
13	5.7	**University Gardens** (CDP) Nassau County	89	10.2	**Mendon** (town) Monroe County
13	5.7	**West Elmira** (CDP) Chemung County	89	10.2	**Milton** (CDP) Saratoga County
16	5.8	**New Castle** (town) Westchester County	89	10.2	**West Nyack** (CDP) Rockland County
17	5.9	**Flower Hill** (village) Nassau County	92	10.3	**Fayetteville** (village) Onondaga County
17	5.9	**Glenwood Landing** (CDP) Nassau County	92	10.3	**Gardiner** (town) Ulster County
17	5.9	**North Hills** (village) Nassau County	92	10.3	**Great Neck Plaza** (village) Nassau County
17	5.9	**Viola** (CDP) Rockland County	95	10.4	**Dix Hills** (CDP) Suffolk County
21	6.0	**Centerport** (CDP) Suffolk County	95	10.4	**Haviland** (CDP) Dutchess County
22	6.2	**Woodbury** (CDP) Nassau County	97	10.5	**Manhasset** (CDP) Nassau County
23	6.3	**Port Washington North** (village) Nassau County	97	10.5	**Roslyn** (village) Nassau County
24	6.4	**Sands Point** (village) Nassau County	99	10.6	**Setauket-East Setauket** (CDP) Suffolk County
24	6.4	**Syosset** (CDP) Nassau County	100	10.7	**Eastchester** (town) Westchester County
24	6.4	**Woodmere** (CDP) Nassau County	101	10.8	**South Nyack** (village) Rockland County
27	6.7	**West Hills** (CDP) Suffolk County	101	10.8	**Stony Brook** (CDP) Suffolk County
28	6.8	**Armonk** (CDP) Westchester County	103	10.9	**Florida** (town) Montgomery County
29	7.0	**Larchmont** (village) Westchester County	104	11.0	**Eastchester** (CDP) Westchester County
29	7.0	**Searingtown** (CDP) Nassau County	104	11.0	**New Square** (village) Rockland County
31	7.1	**Montebello** (village) Rockland County	106	11.1	**Brighton** (CDP) Monroe County
31	7.1	**Muttontown** (village) Nassau County	106	11.1	**Goshen** (village) Orange County
33	7.2	**Briarcliff Manor** (village) Westchester County	106	11.1	**Woodstock** (town) Ulster County
33	7.2	**East Williston** (village) Nassau County	109	11.2	**Bethlehem** (town) Albany County
35	7.3	**Halesite** (CDP) Suffolk County	109	11.2	**Schoharie** (town) Schoharie County
35	7.3	**Skaneateles** (village) Onondaga County	109	11.2	**Victor** (town) Ontario County
37	7.4	**Elmira** (town) Chemung County	112	11.3	**Cedarhurst** (village) Nassau County
38	7.5	**Melville** (CDP) Suffolk County	112	11.3	**Rose** (town) Wayne County
38	7.5	**Old Bethpage** (CDP) Nassau County	112	11.3	**Thomaston** (village) Nassau County
40	7.6	**Somers** (town) Westchester County	115	11.4	**Avon** (village) Livingston County
41	7.8	**Village Green** (CDP) Onondaga County	115	11.4	**Carmel Hamlet** (CDP) Putnam County
42	7.9	**Great Neck** (village) Nassau County	115	11.4	**Falconer** (village) Chautauqua County
42	7.9	**Menands** (village) Albany County	115	11.4	**Manlius** (town) Onondaga County
44	8.0	**Niskayuna** (town) Schenectady County	115	11.4	**North Castle** (town) Westchester County
44	8.0	**West Sand Lake** (CDP) Rensselaer County	115	11.4	**Port Washington** (CDP) Nassau County
46	8.1	**Lake Success** (village) Nassau County	121	11.5	**Jefferson Valley-Yorktown** (CDP) Westchester County
46	8.1	**Lansing** (village) Tompkins County	121	11.5	**Moriches** (CDP) Suffolk County
48	8.2	**Hewlett** (CDP) Nassau County	121	11.5	**North New Hyde Park** (CDP) Nassau County
49	8.4	**Irvington** (village) Westchester County	121	11.5	**Otisco** (town) Onondaga County
49	8.4	**Pelham Manor** (village) Westchester County	125	11.6	**Honeoye Falls** (village) Monroe County
49	8.4	**Pompey** (town) Onondaga County	125	11.6	**Pittsford** (town) Monroe County
49	8.4	**Riverside** (CDP) Suffolk County	125	11.6	**Woodbury** (village) Orange County
53	8.5	**Lloyd Harbor** (village) Suffolk County	125	11.6	**Yates** (town) Orleans County
54	8.6	**Lido Beach** (CDP) Nassau County	129	11.7	**Holland** (town) Erie County
54	8.6	**Rush** (town) Monroe County	129	11.7	**Lysander** (town) Onondaga County
54	8.6	**Spackenkill** (CDP) Dutchess County	129	11.7	**Pelham** (town) Westchester County
57	8.7	**Veteran** (town) Chemung County	129	11.7	**Sea Cliff** (village) Nassau County
58	8.8	**Brightwaters** (village) Suffolk County	133	11.8	**Baldwin Harbor** (CDP) Nassau County
58	8.8	**Skaneateles** (town) Onondaga County	133	11.8	**Brunswick** (town) Rensselaer County
60	8.9	**Hastings-on-Hudson** (village) Westchester County	133	11.8	**Farmington** (town) Ontario County
60	8.9	**Monsey** (CDP) Rockland County	133	11.8	**Marion** (town) Wayne County
60	8.9	**Wesley Hills** (village) Rockland County	133	11.8	**North Merrick** (CDP) Nassau County
63	9.0	**Huntington** (CDP) Suffolk County	138	11.9	**East Greenbush** (town) Rensselaer County
63	9.0	**Marbletown** (town) Ulster County	138	11.9	**North Bellmore** (CDP) Nassau County
65	9.2	**East Greenbush** (CDP) Rensselaer County	140	12.0	**East Islip** (CDP) Suffolk County
65	9.2	**Hartsdale** (CDP) Westchester County	140	12.0	**Guilford** (town) Chenango County
65	9.2	**Jericho** (CDP) Nassau County	140	12.0	**Manlius** (village) Onondaga County
65	9.2	**Malverne** (village) Nassau County	140	12.0	**New City** (CDP) Rockland County
65	9.2	**Merrick** (CDP) Nassau County	144	12.1	**Bayport** (CDP) Suffolk County
65	9.2	**West Bay Shore** (CDP) Suffolk County	144	12.1	**Lansing** (town) Tompkins County
71	9.3	**Airmont** (village) Rockland County	144	12.1	**Williamsville** (village) Erie County
72	9.4	**Afton** (town) Chenango County	147	12.2	**Chittenango** (village) Madison County
72	9.4	**Albertson** (CDP) Nassau County	147	12.2	**Mamaroneck** (town) Westchester County
72	9.4	**Clifton Park** (town) Saratoga County	149	12.3	**Westerlo** (town) Albany County
75	9.5	**Plainview** (CDP) Nassau County	150	12.4	**Balmville** (CDP) Orange County

Note: *This section ranks incorporated places and CDPs (Census Designated Places) with populations of 2,500 or more. Unincorporated postal areas were not considered. Please refer to the User Guide for additional information.*

Employment: Sales and Office Occupations
Top 150 Places Ranked in *Descending* Order

State Rank	Percent	Place
1	41.5	**University at Buffalo** (CDP) Erie County
2	40.2	**Moriches** (CDP) Suffolk County
3	39.4	**Stony Brook University** (CDP) Suffolk County
4	38.2	**Kings Point** (village) Nassau County
5	38.1	**East Garden City** (CDP) Nassau County
6	38.0	**North Syracuse** (village) Onondaga County
7	37.7	**Galeville** (CDP) Onondaga County
8	36.1	**Melville** (CDP) Suffolk County
9	35.6	**Binghamton University** (CDP) Broome County
10	35.3	**Colonie** (village) Albany County
11	35.1	**East Farmingdale** (CDP) Suffolk County
12	34.7	**Crown Heights** (CDP) Dutchess County
12	34.7	**Vails Gate** (CDP) Orange County
14	34.1	**Carmel Hamlet** (CDP) Putnam County
15	33.9	**North Lindenhurst** (CDP) Suffolk County
16	33.5	**Heritage Hills** (CDP) Westchester County
17	33.4	**Brookville** (village) Nassau County
18	33.3	**SUNY Oswego** (CDP) Oswego County
18	33.3	**Selden** (CDP) Suffolk County
20	33.2	**Lawrence** (village) Nassau County
20	33.2	**Plainedge** (CDP) Nassau County
22	33.1	**Kiryas Joel** (village) Orange County
23	33.0	**Islip Terrace** (CDP) Suffolk County
23	33.0	**Red Oaks Mill** (CDP) Dutchess County
23	33.0	**Scotia** (village) Schenectady County
26	32.7	**Gates** (CDP) Monroe County
26	32.7	**Mattydale** (CDP) Onondaga County
26	32.7	**West Elmira** (CDP) Chemung County
29	32.6	**Milton** (CDP) Saratoga County
30	32.5	**Garden City Park** (CDP) Nassau County
30	32.5	**North Patchogue** (CDP) Suffolk County
32	32.2	**Jerusalem** (town) Yates County
33	31.8	**Watervliet** (city) Albany County
34	31.7	**Perth** (town) Fulton County
34	31.7	**Richmond** (town) Ontario County
36	31.6	**Great Neck** (village) Nassau County
36	31.6	**Westhampton** (CDP) Suffolk County
38	31.5	**Johnstown** (city) Fulton County
38	31.5	**South Lockport** (CDP) Niagara County
38	31.5	**Woodbury** (village) Orange County
41	31.3	**Hurley** (CDP) Ulster County
42	31.2	**Green Island** (town/village) Albany County
42	31.2	**Island Park** (village) Nassau County
42	31.2	**Kenmore** (village) Erie County
42	31.2	**Milford** (town) Otsego County
42	31.2	**Tonawanda** (city) Erie County
47	31.1	**Menands** (village) Albany County
48	31.0	**Woodbury** (town) Orange County
49	30.9	**Viola** (CDP) Rockland County
50	30.8	**Cheektowaga** (CDP) Erie County
51	30.7	**Old Westbury** (village) Nassau County
51	30.7	**Olean** (city) Cattaraugus County
53	30.6	**Cheektowaga** (town) Erie County
53	30.6	**Mechanicstown** (CDP) Orange County
55	30.5	**Tuxedo** (town) Orange County
55	30.5	**Wesley Hills** (village) Rockland County
55	30.5	**West Babylon** (CDP) Suffolk County
58	30.4	**Marilla** (town) Erie County
58	30.4	**Whitesboro** (village) Oneida County
60	30.3	**Balmville** (CDP) Orange County
60	30.3	**Lewiston** (village) Niagara County
62	30.2	**Depew** (village) Erie County
62	30.2	**Lake Carmel** (CDP) Putnam County
64	30.1	**Holland** (town) Erie County
64	30.1	**Kaser** (village) Rockland County
64	30.1	**Ronkonkoma** (CDP) Suffolk County
67	30.0	**Hewlett** (CDP) Nassau County
67	30.0	**Yorkville** (village) Oneida County
69	29.9	**Holbrook** (CDP) Suffolk County
69	29.9	**Mechanicville** (city) Saratoga County
69	29.9	**Minisink** (town) Orange County
69	29.9	**North Massapequa** (CDP) Nassau County
73	29.8	**Allegany** (town) Cattaraugus County
73	29.8	**Brunswick** (town) Rensselaer County
73	29.8	**Calverton** (CDP) Suffolk County
73	29.8	**Elmira** (town) Chemung County
73	29.8	**Pendleton** (town) Niagara County
73	29.8	**Wheatley Heights** (CDP) Suffolk County
79	29.7	**Monsey** (CDP) Rockland County
79	29.7	**Randolph** (town) Cattaraugus County
79	29.7	**Riverhead** (CDP) Suffolk County
79	29.7	**Thiells** (CDP) Rockland County
79	29.7	**Warwick** (village) Orange County
84	29.6	**Addison** (town) Steuben County
84	29.6	**Clayton** (town) Jefferson County
84	29.6	**East Syracuse** (village) Onondaga County
84	29.6	**Franklin Square** (CDP) Nassau County
88	29.5	**Brockport** (village) Monroe County
88	29.5	**Canandaigua** (town) Ontario County
88	29.5	**Levittown** (CDP) Nassau County
88	29.5	**Massena** (village) Saint Lawrence County
88	29.5	**Rutland** (town) Jefferson County
88	29.5	**Walden** (village) Orange County
94	29.4	**Fort Drum** (CDP) Jefferson County
94	29.4	**Lindenhurst** (village) Suffolk County
94	29.4	**Oswegatchie** (town) Saint Lawrence County
94	29.4	**Plattekill** (town) Ulster County
94	29.4	**Sidney** (town) Delaware County
94	29.4	**Tonawanda** (town) Erie County
100	29.3	**Firthcliffe** (CDP) Orange County
100	29.3	**Oceanside** (CDP) Nassau County
100	29.3	**Seaford** (CDP) Nassau County
103	29.2	**Centereach** (CDP) Suffolk County
103	29.2	**Mastic Beach** (village) Suffolk County
103	29.2	**Niagara Falls** (city) Niagara County
103	29.2	**North Merrick** (CDP) Nassau County
103	29.2	**Stillwater** (town) Saratoga County
108	29.1	**Massena** (town) Saint Lawrence County
108	29.1	**Sloan** (village) Erie County
108	29.1	**South Farmingdale** (CDP) Nassau County
108	29.1	**Wallkill** (town) Orange County
112	29.0	**Chester** (village) Orange County
112	29.0	**Hicksville** (CDP) Nassau County
112	29.0	**West Glens Falls** (CDP) Warren County
112	29.0	**West Sand Lake** (CDP) Rensselaer County
116	28.9	**Brewerton** (CDP) Onondaga County
116	28.9	**East Hills** (village) Nassau County
116	28.9	**Hamptonburgh** (town) Orange County
116	28.9	**Marcy** (town) Oneida County
116	28.9	**Monroe** (town) Orange County
116	28.9	**Saugerties** (village) Ulster County
116	28.9	**Tonawanda** (CDP) Erie County
116	28.9	**Triangle** (town) Broome County
124	28.8	**Bethpage** (CDP) Nassau County
124	28.8	**Brutus** (town) Cayuga County
124	28.8	**Clay** (town) Onondaga County
124	28.8	**East Meadow** (CDP) Nassau County
124	28.8	**Springs** (CDP) Suffolk County
124	28.8	**Watertown** (town) Jefferson County
124	28.8	**West Islip** (CDP) Suffolk County
131	28.7	**Massapequa Park** (village) Nassau County
131	28.7	**Plattsburgh** (city) Clinton County
133	28.6	**Garden City** (village) Nassau County
133	28.6	**Garden City South** (CDP) Nassau County
133	28.6	**Maybrook** (village) Orange County
133	28.6	**Myers Corner** (CDP) Dutchess County
137	28.5	**Cazenovia** (village) Madison County
137	28.5	**Chittenango** (village) Madison County
137	28.5	**New Paltz** (village) Ulster County
137	28.5	**Salina** (town) Onondaga County
137	28.5	**West Seneca** (CDP) Erie County
137	28.5	**Williston Park** (village) Nassau County
143	28.4	**Attica** (village) Wyoming County
143	28.4	**Warsaw** (town) Wyoming County
145	28.3	**Massapequa** (CDP) Nassau County
145	28.3	**Oakfield** (town) Genesee County
145	28.3	**Sands Point** (village) Nassau County
145	28.3	**Washingtonville** (village) Orange County
149	28.2	**Broadalbin** (town) Fulton County
149	28.2	**Canajoharie** (town) Montgomery County

Note: This section ranks incorporated places and CDPs (Census Designated Places) with populations of 2,500 or more. Unincorporated postal areas were not considered. Please refer to the User Guide for additional information.

Employment: Sales and Office Occupations

Top 150 Places Ranked in *Ascending* Order

State Rank	Percent	Place	State Rank	Percent	Place
1	0.0	**Watchtower** (CDP) Ulster County	72	17.3	**Williamsville** (village) Erie County
2	8.2	**Cayuga Heights** (village) Tompkins County	77	17.4	**Brighton** (CDP) Monroe County
3	9.6	**Walton** (village) Delaware County	77	17.4	**Corning** (town) Steuben County
4	10.3	**Gowanda** (village) Cattaraugus County	77	17.4	**Rhinebeck** (village) Dutchess County
5	11.9	**Madison** (town) Madison County	80	17.5	**Dobbs Ferry** (village) Westchester County
6	12.0	**North East** (town) Dutchess County	80	17.5	**Newark Valley** (town) Tioga County
7	12.2	**Pound Ridge** (town) Westchester County	80	17.5	**West Point** (CDP) Orange County
8	12.7	**Hastings-on-Hudson** (village) Westchester County	83	17.6	**Cape Vincent** (town) Jefferson County
9	12.9	**Callicoon** (town) Sullivan County	83	17.6	**Milo** (town) Yates County
10	13.4	**Gardiner** (town) Ulster County	83	17.6	**New Bremen** (town) Lewis County
11	13.8	**East Hampton North** (CDP) Suffolk County	83	17.6	**Sodus** (town) Wayne County
12	14.1	**White Creek** (town) Washington County	83	17.6	**Virgil** (town) Cortland County
13	14.2	**Colden** (town) Erie County	88	17.7	**Chatham** (town) Columbia County
13	14.2	**Flanders** (CDP) Suffolk County	88	17.7	**Gang Mills** (CDP) Steuben County
15	14.5	**Chautauqua** (town) Chautauqua County	88	17.7	**Shandaken** (town) Ulster County
16	14.7	**Bedford Hills** (CDP) Westchester County	91	17.8	**Ardsley** (village) Westchester County
16	14.7	**Greenville** (CDP) Westchester County	91	17.8	**Carthage** (village) Jefferson County
16	14.7	**Guilford** (town) Chenango County	91	17.8	**Hamilton** (town) Madison County
19	14.8	**Ithaca** (town) Tompkins County	91	17.8	**Pierrepont** (town) Saint Lawrence County
20	14.9	**Washington** (town) Dutchess County	95	17.9	**Horseheads North** (CDP) Chemung County
21	15.0	**Croghan** (town) Lewis County	95	17.9	**Lakewood** (village) Chautauqua County
21	15.0	**Lowville** (village) Lewis County	95	17.9	**Pleasantville** (village) Westchester County
21	15.0	**Pamelia** (town) Jefferson County	98	18.0	**Galen** (town) Wayne County
24	15.2	**Moriah** (town) Essex County	99	18.1	**Somerset** (town) Niagara County
25	15.3	**Hamilton** (village) Madison County	99	18.1	**Spackenkill** (CDP) Dutchess County
25	15.3	**Nyack** (village) Rockland County	99	18.1	**Spencerport** (village) Monroe County
25	15.3	**Stockholm** (town) Saint Lawrence County	102	18.2	**Beekmantown** (town) Clinton County
28	15.4	**Hillcrest** (CDP) Rockland County	103	18.3	**Brookfield** (town) Madison County
28	15.4	**Irvington** (village) Westchester County	103	18.3	**Cairo** (town) Greene County
30	15.5	**Northeast Ithaca** (CDP) Tompkins County	103	18.3	**Clarence** (CDP) Erie County
31	15.7	**Skaneateles** (village) Onondaga County	103	18.3	**Riverside** (CDP) Suffolk County
31	15.7	**Wanakah** (CDP) Erie County	107	18.4	**Greenwood Lake** (village) Orange County
33	15.8	**Lowville** (town) Lewis County	107	18.4	**Schuyler Falls** (town) Clinton County
33	15.8	**Shelter Island** (town) Suffolk County	107	18.4	**Shelby** (town) Orleans County
35	15.9	**Mount Kisco** (town/village) Westchester County	107	18.4	**Volney** (town) Oswego County
36	16.0	**Waverly** (village) Tioga County	111	18.5	**Collins** (town) Erie County
37	16.1	**Caneadea** (town) Allegany County	111	18.5	**Greenwich** (town) Washington County
37	16.1	**Lima** (town) Livingston County	113	18.6	**Barton** (town) Tioga County
37	16.1	**Pelham Manor** (village) Westchester County	113	18.6	**Groton** (town) Tompkins County
40	16.2	**Bangor** (town) Franklin County	113	18.6	**Newfane** (CDP) Niagara County
40	16.2	**Phelps** (town) Ontario County	113	18.6	**Stamford** (town) Delaware County
40	16.2	**Springville** (village) Erie County	113	18.6	**Tupper Lake** (town) Franklin County
40	16.2	**Windsor** (town) Broome County	113	18.6	**Vernon** (town) Oneida County
44	16.3	**Bethel** (town) Sullivan County	119	18.7	**Erwin** (town) Steuben County
44	16.3	**Galway** (town) Saratoga County	119	18.7	**Lisbon** (town) Saint Lawrence County
44	16.3	**Ithaca** (city) Tompkins County	119	18.7	**Montgomery** (village) Orange County
44	16.3	**Royalton** (town) Niagara County	119	18.7	**Oyster Bay** (CDP) Nassau County
44	16.3	**South Fallsburg** (CDP) Sullivan County	119	18.7	**Sleepy Hollow** (village) Westchester County
49	16.4	**Whitehall** (village) Washington County	119	18.7	**Wales** (town) Erie County
50	16.6	**Mendon** (town) Monroe County	125	18.8	**Bedford** (town) Westchester County
50	16.6	**Pelham** (town) Westchester County	125	18.8	**Flower Hill** (village) Nassau County
50	16.6	**Perry** (village) Wyoming County	125	18.8	**Palermo** (town) Oswego County
50	16.6	**Verona** (town) Oneida County	128	18.9	**Aurora** (town) Erie County
54	16.7	**Medina** (village) Orleans County	128	18.9	**Hoosick** (town) Rensselaer County
54	16.7	**Wolcott** (town) Wayne County	128	18.9	**Wellsville** (town) Allegany County
56	16.8	**Coxsackie** (village) Greene County	128	18.9	**Whitehall** (town) Washington County
56	16.8	**Norwich** (town) Chenango County	132	19.0	**Chester** (town) Warren County
58	16.9	**Durham** (town) Greene County	132	19.0	**Hector** (town) Schuyler County
58	16.9	**Lansing** (town) Tompkins County	132	19.0	**Inwood** (CDP) Nassau County
58	16.9	**Larchmont** (village) Westchester County	132	19.0	**Silver Creek** (village) Chautauqua County
58	16.9	**Pelham** (village) Westchester County	136	19.1	**Ridgeway** (town) Orleans County
58	16.9	**Saranac** (town) Clinton County	136	19.1	**Westerlo** (town) Albany County
58	16.9	**Woodstock** (town) Ulster County	138	19.2	**Macedon** (town) Wayne County
64	17.0	**Colesville** (town) Broome County	138	19.2	**Mamaroneck** (town) Westchester County
64	17.0	**Croton-on-Hudson** (village) Westchester County	138	19.2	**South Nyack** (village) Rockland County
64	17.0	**Peru** (town) Clinton County	138	19.2	**Unadilla** (town) Otsego County
64	17.0	**Rosendale** (town) Ulster County	142	19.3	**Le Roy** (town) Genesee County
68	17.1	**Perry** (town) Wyoming County	142	19.3	**Mohawk** (village) Herkimer County
69	17.2	**Delaware** (town) Sullivan County	142	19.3	**Pittstown** (town) Rensselaer County
69	17.2	**Lansing** (village) Tompkins County	145	19.4	**Bronxville** (village) Westchester County
69	17.2	**Wyandanch** (CDP) Suffolk County	145	19.4	**Dix** (town) Schuyler County
72	17.3	**Eaton** (town) Madison County	145	19.4	**Fleming** (town) Cayuga County
72	17.3	**Mattituck** (CDP) Suffolk County	145	19.4	**Greenburgh** (town) Westchester County
72	17.3	**Moira** (town) Franklin County	149	19.5	**Champlain** (town) Clinton County
72	17.3	**Otsego** (town) Otsego County	149	19.5	**Cortlandt** (town) Westchester County

Note: This section ranks incorporated places and CDPs (Census Designated Places) with populations of 2,500 or more. Unincorporated postal areas were not considered. Please refer to the User Guide for additional information.

Employment: Natural Resources, Construction, and Maintenance Occupations

Top 150 Places Ranked in *Descending* Order

State Rank	Percent	Place	State Rank	Percent	Place
1	42.0	**Riverside** (CDP) Suffolk County	74	14.9	**Otisco** (town) Onondaga County
2	30.9	**Flanders** (CDP) Suffolk County	74	14.9	**Oxford** (town) Chenango County
3	27.7	**East Hampton North** (CDP) Suffolk County	74	14.9	**Shandaken** (town) Ulster County
4	25.0	**Delaware** (town) Sullivan County	79	14.8	**Akron** (village) Erie County
5	22.8	**Carlton** (town) Orleans County	79	14.8	**North Bellport** (CDP) Suffolk County
5	22.8	**New Bremen** (town) Lewis County	79	14.8	**Orleans** (town) Jefferson County
7	21.3	**New Haven** (town) Oswego County	82	14.7	**Clarkson** (town) Monroe County
8	21.2	**Croghan** (town) Lewis County	82	14.7	**Medina** (village) Orleans County
9	20.8	**Yates** (town) Orleans County	82	14.7	**Rose** (town) Wayne County
10	20.2	**Gouverneur** (village) Saint Lawrence County	82	14.7	**Saugerties** (village) Ulster County
11	19.7	**Lake Luzerne** (town) Warren County	86	14.6	**Colesville** (town) Broome County
12	19.6	**Ellisburg** (town) Jefferson County	86	14.6	**Gorham** (town) Ontario County
13	19.5	**Albion** (village) Orleans County	86	14.6	**Murray** (town) Orleans County
14	19.0	**Nunda** (town) Livingston County	86	14.6	**Wayland** (town) Steuben County
15	18.9	**Mattituck** (CDP) Suffolk County	90	14.5	**Bainbridge** (town) Chenango County
16	18.3	**Elma Center** (CDP) Erie County	90	14.5	**Calverton** (CDP) Suffolk County
16	18.3	**Groveland** (town) Livingston County	90	14.5	**Cambria** (town) Niagara County
18	18.1	**Callicoon** (town) Sullivan County	90	14.5	**Oakfield** (town) Genesee County
18	18.1	**West Bloomfield** (town) Ontario County	94	14.4	**Cutchogue** (CDP) Suffolk County
20	17.9	**Cape Vincent** (town) Jefferson County	94	14.4	**Warsaw** (town) Wyoming County
20	17.9	**Chautauqua** (town) Chautauqua County	94	14.4	**Wilna** (town) Jefferson County
22	17.6	**Noyack** (CDP) Suffolk County	97	14.3	**Copake** (town) Columbia County
23	17.5	**Denmark** (town) Lewis County	97	14.3	**Crawford** (town) Orange County
23	17.5	**Palermo** (town) Oswego County	97	14.3	**Gardiner** (town) Ulster County
25	17.4	**Castile** (town) Wyoming County	97	14.3	**Mamakating** (town) Sullivan County
26	17.3	**Galen** (town) Wayne County	97	14.3	**Pembroke** (town) Genesee County
26	17.3	**Gouverneur** (town) Saint Lawrence County	97	14.3	**Seneca** (town) Ontario County
28	17.2	**Cedarhurst** (village) Nassau County	97	14.3	**Tupper Lake** (village) Franklin County
29	17.0	**Alexandria** (town) Jefferson County	104	14.2	**Ridgeway** (town) Orleans County
30	16.9	**Alexander** (town) Genesee County	104	14.2	**Southold** (town) Suffolk County
30	16.9	**North East** (town) Dutchess County	104	14.2	**Volney** (town) Oswego County
32	16.8	**Chesterfield** (town) Essex County	107	14.1	**Fort Edward** (town) Washington County
32	16.8	**Constantia** (town) Oswego County	107	14.1	**Spencer** (town) Tioga County
32	16.8	**Darien** (town) Genesee County	107	14.1	**Williamson** (town) Wayne County
35	16.7	**Pavilion** (town) Genesee County	110	14.0	**East Hampton** (town) Suffolk County
35	16.7	**Sterling** (town) Cayuga County	110	14.0	**East Moriches** (CDP) Suffolk County
35	16.7	**West Monroe** (town) Oswego County	110	14.0	**Somerset** (town) Niagara County
38	16.6	**Perry** (town) Wyoming County	113	13.9	**Benton** (town) Yates County
38	16.6	**Windsor** (town) Broome County	113	13.9	**Florida** (town) Montgomery County
38	16.6	**Wolcott** (town) Wayne County	113	13.9	**Gaines** (town) Orleans County
41	16.5	**Southampton** (town) Suffolk County	113	13.9	**Middleburgh** (town) Schoharie County
42	16.4	**Hector** (town) Schuyler County	113	13.9	**Pamelia** (town) Jefferson County
43	16.3	**Chemung** (town) Chemung County	118	13.8	**Beekman** (town) Dutchess County
44	16.2	**Mastic Beach** (village) Suffolk County	118	13.8	**Dover** (town) Dutchess County
44	16.2	**Sanford** (town) Broome County	118	13.8	**Pierrepont** (town) Saint Lawrence County
46	16.1	**Brookfield** (town) Madison County	118	13.8	**Springs** (CDP) Suffolk County
46	16.1	**Hampton Bays** (CDP) Suffolk County	122	13.7	**Madison** (town) Madison County
46	16.1	**Holland** (town) Erie County	122	13.7	**Neversink** (town) Sullivan County
46	16.1	**Manheim** (town) Herkimer County	122	13.7	**Ossining** (village) Westchester County
46	16.1	**Schroeppel** (town) Oswego County	122	13.7	**Richmondville** (town) Schoharie County
46	16.1	**Vienna** (town) Oneida County	126	13.6	**North Sea** (CDP) Suffolk County
52	15.9	**Albion** (town) Orleans County	126	13.6	**Sandy Creek** (town) Oswego County
52	15.9	**Argyle** (town) Washington County	128	13.5	**Lyons** (town) Wayne County
52	15.9	**Nichols** (town) Tioga County	129	13.4	**Amenia** (town) Dutchess County
52	15.9	**Pompey** (town) Onondaga County	129	13.4	**Beekmantown** (town) Clinton County
56	15.7	**Bergen** (town) Genesee County	129	13.4	**Mount Hope** (town) Orange County
56	15.7	**Kendall** (town) Orleans County	129	13.4	**Newstead** (town) Erie County
56	15.7	**North Collins** (town) Erie County	129	13.4	**Sardinia** (town) Erie County
59	15.6	**Berne** (town) Albany County	129	13.4	**Theresa** (town) Jefferson County
59	15.6	**Middletown** (town) Delaware County	129	13.4	**Warsaw** (village) Wyoming County
59	15.6	**Newfield** (town) Tompkins County	129	13.4	**Yorkshire** (town) Cattaraugus County
62	15.5	**Campbell** (town) Steuben County	137	13.3	**Center Moriches** (CDP) Suffolk County
63	15.4	**Fort Ann** (town) Washington County	137	13.3	**Champion** (town) Jefferson County
63	15.4	**Salem** (town) Washington County	137	13.3	**Duanesburg** (town) Schenectady County
63	15.4	**Stockport** (town) Columbia County	137	13.3	**Saugerties** (town) Ulster County
66	15.3	**Canisteo** (town) Steuben County	141	13.2	**Eden** (town) Erie County
66	15.3	**Carthage** (village) Jefferson County	141	13.2	**Kirkwood** (town) Broome County
68	15.2	**Triangle** (town) Broome County	143	13.1	**Altona** (town) Clinton County
69	15.1	**Charlton** (town) Saratoga County	143	13.1	**Cato** (town) Cayuga County
69	15.1	**Fort Edward** (village) Washington County	143	13.1	**Sheridan** (town) Chautauqua County
69	15.1	**Mooers** (town) Clinton County	143	13.1	**Shirley** (CDP) Suffolk County
72	15.0	**Hartland** (town) Niagara County	147	13.0	**East Patchogue** (CDP) Suffolk County
72	15.0	**Sodus** (town) Wayne County	147	13.0	**Groton** (town) Tompkins County
74	14.9	**Bennington** (town) Wyoming County	147	13.0	**Inwood** (CDP) Nassau County
74	14.9	**Bethel** (town) Sullivan County	147	13.0	**Tupper Lake** (town) Franklin County

Note: This section ranks incorporated places and CDPs (Census Designated Places) with populations of 2,500 or more. Unincorporated postal areas were not considered. Please refer to the User Guide for additional information.

Employment: Natural Resources, Construction, and Maintenance Occupations

Top 150 Places Ranked in *Ascending* Order

State Rank	Percent	Place
1	0.0	Binghamton University (CDP) Broome County
1	0.0	Lake Success (village) Nassau County
1	0.0	Lansing (village) Tompkins County
1	0.0	Watchtower (CDP) Ulster County
5	0.4	Hewlett (CDP) Nassau County
5	0.4	Thomaston (village) Nassau County
7	0.5	Cayuga Heights (village) Tompkins County
8	0.6	Northeast Ithaca (CDP) Tompkins County
8	0.6	Port Washington North (village) Nassau County
10	0.7	Lido Beach (CDP) Nassau County
10	0.7	Scarsdale (town/village) Westchester County
12	0.8	Lawrence (village) Nassau County
12	0.8	University Gardens (CDP) Nassau County
14	1.0	University at Buffalo (CDP) Erie County
15	1.1	New Castle (town) Westchester County
16	1.2	Ardsley (village) Westchester County
16	1.2	Arlington (CDP) Dutchess County
16	1.2	Woodbury (CDP) Nassau County
19	1.4	Brookville (village) Nassau County
19	1.4	Melville (CDP) Suffolk County
19	1.4	Old Westbury (village) Nassau County
22	1.5	Calcium (CDP) Jefferson County
23	1.6	North Hills (village) Nassau County
24	1.8	Briarcliff Manor (village) Westchester County
24	1.8	Montebello (village) Rockland County
24	1.8	Pittsford (town) Monroe County
27	1.9	Bronxville (village) Westchester County
27	1.9	Manhasset (CDP) Nassau County
27	1.9	SUNY Oswego (CDP) Oswego County
30	2.1	Armonk (CDP) Westchester County
30	2.1	Kings Point (village) Nassau County
30	2.1	Manhattan (borough) New York County
33	2.2	East Norwich (CDP) Nassau County
33	2.2	Stony Brook (CDP) Suffolk County
33	2.2	Victor (village) Ontario County
36	2.3	Garden City (village) Nassau County
36	2.3	Menands (village) Albany County
36	2.3	Pelham Manor (village) Westchester County
36	2.3	Stony Brook University (CDP) Suffolk County
40	2.4	Afton (town) Chenango County
40	2.4	Fairport (village) Monroe County
40	2.4	North Salem (town) Westchester County
43	2.5	Cold Spring Harbor (CDP) Suffolk County
43	2.5	Great Neck Plaza (village) Nassau County
43	2.5	Larchmont (village) Westchester County
43	2.5	Old Bethpage (CDP) Nassau County
43	2.5	South Nyack (village) Rockland County
48	2.6	Kaser (village) Rockland County
49	2.7	Dobbs Ferry (village) Westchester County
49	2.7	Geneseo (village) Livingston County
49	2.7	Glenwood Landing (CDP) Nassau County
49	2.7	Roslyn Heights (CDP) Nassau County
49	2.7	Viola (CDP) Rockland County
54	2.8	Bath (village) Steuben County
54	2.8	Ithaca (town) Tompkins County
54	2.8	Pleasantville (village) Westchester County
57	2.9	Brighton (CDP) Monroe County
57	2.9	Centerport (CDP) Suffolk County
57	2.9	East Hills (village) Nassau County
57	2.9	Greenville (CDP) Westchester County
57	2.9	Hartsdale (CDP) Westchester County
57	2.9	Manorhaven (village) Nassau County
57	2.9	Munsey Park (village) Nassau County
57	2.9	Pound Ridge (town) Westchester County
57	2.9	Wheatley Heights (CDP) Suffolk County
66	3.0	Dix Hills (CDP) Suffolk County
66	3.0	Halesite (CDP) Suffolk County
66	3.0	Hastings-on-Hudson (village) Westchester County
66	3.0	Manlius (village) Onondaga County
66	3.0	Potsdam (village) Saint Lawrence County
71	3.1	Port Jefferson (village) Suffolk County
71	3.1	Rye (city) Westchester County
71	3.1	Tappan (CDP) Rockland County
74	3.2	Great Neck Estates (village) Nassau County
74	3.2	Sands Point (village) Nassau County
74	3.2	Searingtown (CDP) Nassau County
77	3.3	Harris Hill (CDP) Erie County
77	3.3	Herkimer (village) Herkimer County
77	3.3	Valhalla (CDP) Westchester County
77	3.3	West Nyack (CDP) Rockland County
81	3.4	Canton (village) Saint Lawrence County
81	3.4	East Williston (village) Nassau County
83	3.5	Jericho (CDP) Nassau County
83	3.5	New Paltz (village) Ulster County
83	3.5	North Castle (town) Westchester County
83	3.5	Saratoga Springs (city) Saratoga County
83	3.5	Waverly (village) Tioga County
88	3.6	East Garden City (CDP) Nassau County
88	3.6	Milford (town) Otsego County
88	3.6	Otsego (town) Otsego County
91	3.7	Bedford (town) Westchester County
91	3.7	Greenburgh (town) Westchester County
91	3.7	Ithaca (city) Tompkins County
91	3.7	Penfield (town) Monroe County
91	3.7	Syosset (CDP) Nassau County
96	3.8	Goshen (village) Orange County
96	3.8	Herricks (CDP) Nassau County
96	3.8	Hudson (city) Columbia County
96	3.8	Lloyd Harbor (village) Suffolk County
96	3.8	Manhasset Hills (CDP) Nassau County
96	3.8	Muttontown (village) Nassau County
96	3.8	Orchard Park (village) Erie County
96	3.8	Plainview (CDP) Nassau County
96	3.8	West Elmira (CDP) Chemung County
96	3.8	Williamsville (village) Erie County
106	3.9	Amherst (town) Erie County
106	3.9	Garden City Park (CDP) Nassau County
106	3.9	Lansing (town) Tompkins County
106	3.9	Plattsburgh (city) Clinton County
110	4.0	Albertson (CDP) Nassau County
110	4.0	Bardonia (CDP) Rockland County
110	4.0	Guilderland (town) Albany County
110	4.0	Rye Brook (village) Westchester County
110	4.0	West Point (CDP) Orange County
115	4.1	Cairo (town) Greene County
115	4.1	De Witt (town) Onondaga County
115	4.1	Gang Mills (CDP) Steuben County
115	4.1	Lewiston (village) Niagara County
115	4.1	North Valley Stream (CDP) Nassau County
115	4.1	Victor (town) Ontario County
121	4.2	Croton-on-Hudson (village) Westchester County
121	4.2	Lakeview (CDP) Nassau County
121	4.2	Woodmere (CDP) Nassau County
124	4.3	Elmira Heights (village) Chemung County
124	4.3	Elwood (CDP) Suffolk County
124	4.3	Fredonia (village) Chautauqua County
124	4.3	Haviland (CDP) Dutchess County
124	4.3	Minoa (village) Onondaga County
124	4.3	Orchard Park (town) Erie County
124	4.3	Roslyn (village) Nassau County
124	4.3	Saint Regis Mohawk Reservation (reservation) Franklin County
124	4.3	Wading River (CDP) Suffolk County
133	4.4	Albany (city) Albany County
133	4.4	Mamaroneck (town) Westchester County
133	4.4	Monroe (village) Orange County
133	4.4	New Square (village) Rockland County
133	4.4	Northport (village) Suffolk County
133	4.4	Olean (city) Cattaraugus County
133	4.4	Rockville Centre (village) Nassau County
133	4.4	Setauket-East Setauket (CDP) Suffolk County
141	4.5	Cortland (city) Cortland County
141	4.5	Lewisboro (town) Westchester County
141	4.5	Pelham (town) Westchester County
141	4.5	Rochester (city) Monroe County
145	4.6	Colonie (village) Albany County
145	4.6	Eggertsville (CDP) Erie County
145	4.6	Falconer (village) Chautauqua County
145	4.6	Huntington (CDP) Suffolk County
145	4.6	Kenmore (village) Erie County
145	4.6	Malone (village) Franklin County

Note: *This section ranks incorporated places and CDPs (Census Designated Places) with populations of 2,500 or more. Unincorporated postal areas were not considered. Please refer to the User Guide for additional information.*

Employment: Production, Transportation, and Material Moving Occupations

Top 150 Places Ranked in *Descending* Order

State Rank	Percent	Place
1	49.2	**Watchtower** (CDP) Ulster County
2	33.7	**Liberty** (village) Sullivan County
3	33.5	**Afton** (town) Chenango County
4	31.7	**Falconer** (village) Chautauqua County
5	29.8	**Westfield** (village) Chautauqua County
6	28.9	**Cohocton** (town) Steuben County
7	28.2	**Westfield** (town) Chautauqua County
8	27.1	**Walton** (village) Delaware County
8	27.1	**White Creek** (town) Washington County
10	26.6	**Rose** (town) Wayne County
11	26.2	**Royalton** (town) Niagara County
12	25.9	**Yorkshire** (town) Cattaraugus County
13	25.7	**Colesville** (town) Broome County
14	24.7	**Au Sable** (town) Clinton County
15	24.4	**Guilford** (town) Chenango County
16	24.3	**Brentwood** (CDP) Suffolk County
17	23.9	**Phelps** (town) Ontario County
17	23.9	**Windsor** (town) Broome County
19	23.5	**Unadilla** (town) Otsego County
20	23.4	**Central Islip** (CDP) Suffolk County
21	23.2	**Portland** (town) Chautauqua County
22	23.1	**Verona** (town) Oneida County
23	22.9	**Ellicott** (town) Chautauqua County
24	22.8	**Dunkirk** (city) Chautauqua County
25	22.5	**Galen** (town) Wayne County
25	22.5	**North Bay Shore** (CDP) Suffolk County
27	22.3	**Bainbridge** (town) Chenango County
28	22.2	**Gloversville** (city) Fulton County
29	22.1	**Pavilion** (town) Genesee County
30	22.0	**Catlin** (town) Chemung County
30	22.0	**Newark** (village) Wayne County
32	21.9	**Brookfield** (town) Madison County
32	21.9	**Shelby** (town) Orleans County
34	21.8	**Arcade** (town) Wyoming County
34	21.8	**Croghan** (town) Lewis County
34	21.8	**Walton** (town) Delaware County
37	21.7	**Norwich** (town) Chenango County
38	21.6	**Wyandanch** (CDP) Suffolk County
39	21.4	**Hoosick Falls** (village) Rensselaer County
40	21.2	**Sloan** (village) Erie County
41	21.0	**Fort Edward** (village) Washington County
41	21.0	**Kirkwood** (town) Broome County
41	21.0	**Sheridan** (town) Chautauqua County
41	21.0	**Whitehall** (town) Washington County
45	20.9	**Hilton** (village) Monroe County
46	20.8	**Barton** (town) Tioga County
47	20.6	**Somerset** (town) Niagara County
48	20.5	**Hannibal** (town) Oswego County
48	20.5	**Mattydale** (CDP) Onondaga County
50	20.4	**South Glens Falls** (village) Saratoga County
50	20.4	**Wayland** (town) Steuben County
52	20.3	**Caledonia** (town) Livingston County
52	20.3	**Medina** (village) Orleans County
52	20.3	**Minden** (town) Montgomery County
52	20.3	**Perry** (town) Wyoming County
52	20.3	**Perry** (village) Wyoming County
57	20.2	**Granville** (town) Washington County
57	20.2	**Newburgh** (city) Orange County
57	20.2	**Whitehall** (village) Washington County
57	20.2	**York** (town) Livingston County
61	20.1	**Pembroke** (town) Genesee County
61	20.1	**South Fallsburg** (CDP) Sullivan County
61	20.1	**Virgil** (town) Cortland County
64	20.0	**Boonville** (town) Oneida County
64	20.0	**Clarendon** (town) Orleans County
64	20.0	**Granby** (town) Oswego County
67	19.9	**Le Roy** (village) Genesee County
67	19.9	**Newfane** (CDP) Niagara County
69	19.8	**Moravia** (town) Cayuga County
70	19.7	**Arcadia** (town) Wayne County
70	19.7	**Lockport** (city) Niagara County
70	19.7	**Vernon** (town) Oneida County
73	19.6	**Argyle** (town) Washington County
73	19.6	**Greenwich** (town) Washington County
73	19.6	**Ridgeway** (town) Orleans County

State Rank	Percent	Place
76	19.5	**Carroll** (town) Chautauqua County
76	19.5	**Newark Valley** (town) Tioga County
78	19.3	**Conklin** (town) Broome County
78	19.3	**Fulton** (city) Oswego County
78	19.3	**Jamestown** (city) Chautauqua County
78	19.3	**New Berlin** (town) Chenango County
78	19.3	**Randolph** (town) Cattaraugus County
78	19.3	**Vienna** (town) Oneida County
78	19.3	**Yates** (town) Orleans County
85	19.2	**Darien** (town) Genesee County
85	19.2	**Tioga** (town) Tioga County
87	19.1	**Coxsackie** (village) Greene County
87	19.1	**Hastings** (town) Oswego County
89	19.0	**Annsville** (town) Oneida County
89	19.0	**Palmyra** (town) Wayne County
89	19.0	**Silver Creek** (village) Chautauqua County
92	18.9	**Madison** (town) Madison County
93	18.8	**Amsterdam** (city) Montgomery County
93	18.8	**Hanover** (town) Chautauqua County
95	18.7	**Le Roy** (town) Genesee County
95	18.7	**Lyons** (village) Wayne County
97	18.6	**Johnstown** (city) Fulton County
97	18.6	**Moira** (town) Franklin County
97	18.6	**New Cassel** (CDP) Nassau County
97	18.6	**Newfane** (town) Niagara County
97	18.6	**Palatine** (town) Montgomery County
97	18.6	**Scriba** (town) Oswego County
97	18.6	**Waterloo** (town) Seneca County
97	18.6	**West Monroe** (town) Oswego County
105	18.5	**Barker** (town) Broome County
105	18.5	**Haverstraw** (village) Rockland County
105	18.5	**Little Falls** (city) Herkimer County
105	18.5	**Marion** (town) Wayne County
105	18.5	**Murray** (town) Orleans County
105	18.5	**Ontario** (town) Wayne County
105	18.5	**Roosevelt** (CDP) Nassau County
105	18.5	**Stamford** (town) Delaware County
113	18.4	**Blasdell** (village) Erie County
113	18.4	**Sodus** (town) Wayne County
115	18.2	**Cairo** (town) Greene County
115	18.2	**Champlain** (town) Clinton County
117	18.0	**Camden** (town) Oneida County
117	18.0	**Sidney** (village) Delaware County
117	18.0	**Starkey** (town) Yates County
120	17.9	**Bergen** (town) Genesee County
120	17.9	**Sangerfield** (town) Oneida County
122	17.8	**Coxsackie** (town) Greene County
122	17.8	**Fayette** (town) Seneca County
122	17.8	**Hancock** (town) Delaware County
122	17.8	**Lake Erie Beach** (CDP) Erie County
122	17.8	**Port Jervis** (city) Orange County
122	17.8	**Scottsville** (village) Monroe County
122	17.8	**Volney** (town) Oswego County
129	17.7	**Gowanda** (village) Cattaraugus County
129	17.7	**Hamlin** (CDP) Monroe County
129	17.7	**Liberty** (town) Sullivan County
129	17.7	**Mount Morris** (town) Livingston County
133	17.6	**Altona** (town) Clinton County
133	17.6	**Lackawanna** (city) Erie County
133	17.6	**North Boston** (CDP) Erie County
136	17.5	**Hoosick** (town) Rensselaer County
137	17.4	**Elmira Heights** (village) Chemung County
137	17.4	**Fort Edward** (town) Washington County
137	17.4	**New York Mills** (village) Oneida County
137	17.4	**Richland** (town) Oswego County
141	17.3	**Copiague** (CDP) Suffolk County
141	17.3	**Lowville** (town) Lewis County
141	17.3	**Schuyler Falls** (town) Clinton County
141	17.3	**Wolcott** (town) Wayne County
145	17.2	**Kendall** (town) Orleans County
146	17.1	**Canajoharie** (town) Montgomery County
146	17.1	**West Bloomfield** (town) Ontario County
148	17.0	**Lowville** (village) Lewis County
148	17.0	**Palermo** (town) Oswego County
148	17.0	**Patchogue** (village) Suffolk County

Note: This section ranks incorporated places and CDPs (Census Designated Places) with populations of 2,500 or more. Unincorporated postal areas were not considered. Please refer to the User Guide for additional information.

Employment: Production, Transportation, and Material Moving Occupations

Top 150 Places Ranked in *Ascending* Order

State Rank	Percent	Place	State Rank	Percent	Place
1	0.4	Irvington (village) Westchester County	76	3.6	Pearl River (CDP) Rockland County
2	0.6	Bronxville (village) Westchester County	76	3.6	Port Washington (CDP) Nassau County
2	0.6	Cayuga Heights (village) Tompkins County	76	3.6	Port Washington North (village) Nassau County
2	0.6	Pelham Manor (village) Westchester County	76	3.6	Somers (town) Westchester County
5	0.7	North Hills (village) Nassau County	76	3.6	Tuckahoe (village) Westchester County
6	0.8	Roslyn (village) Nassau County	76	3.6	Woodstock (town) Ulster County
6	0.8	Scarsdale (town/village) Westchester County	82	3.7	East Hampton (town) Suffolk County
8	0.9	Armonk (CDP) Westchester County	82	3.7	Mamaroneck (town) Westchester County
9	1.0	Lloyd Harbor (village) Suffolk County	82	3.7	Putnam Valley (town) Putnam County
9	1.0	Menands (village) Albany County	85	3.8	Albertson (CDP) Nassau County
9	1.0	Woodbury (CDP) Nassau County	85	3.8	Ardsley (village) Westchester County
12	1.2	Piermont (village) Rockland County	85	3.8	Blauvelt (CDP) Rockland County
12	1.2	Springs (CDP) Suffolk County	85	3.8	Croton-on-Hudson (village) Westchester County
14	1.3	Bedford Hills (CDP) Westchester County	85	3.8	Danby (town) Tompkins County
14	1.3	Manhasset Hills (CDP) Nassau County	85	3.8	Greenburgh (town) Westchester County
14	1.3	Sands Point (village) Nassau County	85	3.8	Pelham (town) Westchester County
17	1.4	Bedford (town) Westchester County	92	3.9	Hamilton (village) Madison County
17	1.4	Great Neck Estates (village) Nassau County	92	3.9	Montebello (village) Rockland County
19	1.6	Wesley Hills (village) Rockland County	92	3.9	South Hempstead (CDP) Nassau County
20	1.7	Nyack (village) Rockland County	92	3.9	Woodmere (CDP) Nassau County
20	1.7	West Hills (CDP) Suffolk County	96	4.0	Herricks (CDP) Nassau County
22	1.8	East Williston (village) Nassau County	96	4.0	Mineola (village) Nassau County
22	1.8	SUNY Oswego (CDP) Oswego County	96	4.0	Pleasantville (village) Westchester County
24	1.9	Garden City (village) Nassau County	96	4.0	Rochester (town) Ulster County
24	1.9	Stony Brook University (CDP) Suffolk County	96	4.0	Syosset (CDP) Nassau County
24	1.9	Valley Cottage (CDP) Rockland County	101	4.1	Carle Place (CDP) Nassau County
27	2.0	Cold Spring Harbor (CDP) Suffolk County	101	4.1	Manhattan (borough) New York County
27	2.0	Hastings-on-Hudson (village) Westchester County	101	4.1	Miller Place (CDP) Suffolk County
27	2.0	Lido Beach (CDP) Nassau County	101	4.1	Thomaston (village) Nassau County
30	2.1	Briarcliff Manor (village) Westchester County	105	4.2	Alfred (town) Allegany County
30	2.1	Flower Hill (village) Nassau County	105	4.2	North Sea (CDP) Suffolk County
30	2.1	Muttontown (village) Nassau County	105	4.2	Northport (village) Suffolk County
33	2.2	Great Neck Plaza (village) Nassau County	105	4.2	Pomona (village) Rockland County
33	2.2	Hartsdale (CDP) Westchester County	105	4.2	Pound Ridge (town) Westchester County
33	2.2	North Castle (town) Westchester County	110	4.3	Clarence (CDP) Erie County
33	2.2	Searingtown (CDP) Nassau County	110	4.3	Massapequa Park (village) Nassau County
37	2.3	Munsey Park (village) Nassau County	110	4.3	Monsey (CDP) Rockland County
37	2.3	New Castle (town) Westchester County	110	4.3	Montauk (CDP) Suffolk County
39	2.4	Alfred (village) Allegany County	110	4.3	Orangetown (town) Rockland County
39	2.4	Highland (CDP) Ulster County	110	4.3	Plainview (CDP) Nassau County
39	2.4	Northeast Ithaca (CDP) Tompkins County	110	4.3	South Nyack (village) Rockland County
42	2.5	Sea Cliff (village) Nassau County	110	4.3	Spackenkill (CDP) Dutchess County
43	2.6	Airmont (village) Rockland County	118	4.4	Melville (CDP) Suffolk County
43	2.6	Harrison (town/village) Westchester County	118	4.4	South Huntington (CDP) Suffolk County
43	2.6	Larchmont (village) Westchester County	118	4.4	Southeast (town) Putnam County
46	2.8	East Hills (village) Nassau County	121	4.5	Cazenovia (village) Madison County
46	2.8	Greenville (CDP) Westchester County	121	4.5	Dobbs Ferry (village) Westchester County
48	2.9	Fayetteville (village) Onondaga County	121	4.5	Oneonta (city) Otsego County
48	2.9	Flanders (CDP) Suffolk County	121	4.5	Tuxedo (town) Orange County
48	2.9	Fort Salonga (CDP) Suffolk County	121	4.5	University Gardens (CDP) Nassau County
48	2.9	Glen Head (CDP) Nassau County	126	4.6	Jericho (CDP) Nassau County
48	2.9	Kaser (village) Rockland County	126	4.6	New Paltz (village) Ulster County
48	2.9	Lake Success (village) Nassau County	126	4.6	North Elba (town) Essex County
48	2.9	Old Bethpage (CDP) Nassau County	129	4.7	East Garden City (CDP) Nassau County
48	2.9	Rye Brook (village) Westchester County	129	4.7	East Norwich (CDP) Nassau County
48	2.9	Tarrytown (village) Westchester County	129	4.7	Geneseo (village) Livingston County
57	3.0	Brookville (village) Nassau County	129	4.7	Huntington (CDP) Suffolk County
57	3.0	Eastchester (town) Westchester County	129	4.7	Montrose (CDP) Westchester County
57	3.0	Pittsford (town) Monroe County	129	4.7	Niskayuna (town) Schenectady County
60	3.1	Ithaca (town) Tompkins County	129	4.7	Northwest Harbor (CDP) Suffolk County
60	3.1	Lewisboro (town) Westchester County	136	4.8	East Rockaway (village) Nassau County
60	3.1	Noyack (CDP) Suffolk County	136	4.8	Harris Hill (CDP) Erie County
60	3.1	Old Westbury (village) Nassau County	136	4.8	Mount Sinai (CDP) Suffolk County
60	3.1	Setauket-East Setauket (CDP) Suffolk County	136	4.8	Stony Brook (CDP) Suffolk County
65	3.2	Lawrence (village) Nassau County	140	4.9	Brighton (CDP) Monroe County
65	3.2	Port Jefferson Station (CDP) Suffolk County	140	4.9	Brightwaters (village) Suffolk County
65	3.2	Rockville Centre (village) Nassau County	140	4.9	Callicoon (town) Sullivan County
68	3.3	Lansing (village) Tompkins County	140	4.9	Charlton (town) Saratoga County
69	3.4	Caroline (town) Tompkins County	140	4.9	East Greenbush (CDP) Rensselaer County
69	3.4	Centerport (CDP) Suffolk County	140	4.9	Long Beach (city) Nassau County
69	3.4	Eastchester (CDP) Westchester County	140	4.9	Merrick (CDP) Nassau County
69	3.4	Heritage Hills (CDP) Westchester County	140	4.9	Orchard Park (village) Erie County
69	3.4	Rye (city) Westchester County	140	4.9	Suffern (village) Rockland County
74	3.5	Malverne (village) Nassau County	140	4.9	Williston Park (village) Nassau County
74	3.5	Port Jefferson (village) Suffolk County	150	5.0	East Quogue (CDP) Suffolk County

Note: *This section ranks incorporated places and CDPs (Census Designated Places) with populations of 2,500 or more. Unincorporated postal areas were not considered. Please refer to the User Guide for additional information.*

Per Capita Income

Top 150 Places Ranked in *Descending* Order

State Rank	Dollars	Place	State Rank	Dollars	Place
1	116,486	Sands Point (village) Nassau County	76	54,858	Northport (village) Suffolk County
2	116,456	Scarsdale (town/village) Westchester County	77	54,844	Woodstock (town) Ulster County
3	111,339	Muttontown (village) Nassau County	78	54,831	Merrick (CDP) Nassau County
4	108,627	Bronxville (village) Westchester County	79	54,185	Setauket-East Setauket (CDP) Suffolk County
5	107,333	Pound Ridge (town) Westchester County	80	53,997	Heritage Hills (CDP) Westchester County
6	98,260	Lloyd Harbor (village) Suffolk County	81	53,980	Kings Point (village) Nassau County
7	94,458	North Castle (town) Westchester County	82	53,926	Stony Brook (CDP) Suffolk County
8	94,278	Armonk (CDP) Westchester County	83	53,892	Tuxedo (town) Orange County
9	90,548	Rye (city) Westchester County	84	53,820	Dobbs Ferry (village) Westchester County
10	90,345	New Castle (town) Westchester County	85	53,619	Glenwood Landing (CDP) Nassau County
11	89,556	Greenville (CDP) Westchester County	86	53,451	Shelter Island (town) Suffolk County
12	89,101	Larchmont (village) Westchester County	87	53,278	Pleasantville (village) Westchester County
13	88,701	Pelham Manor (village) Westchester County	88	53,152	Bardonia (CDP) Rockland County
14	86,651	North Hills (village) Nassau County	89	53,131	Skaneateles (town) Onondaga County
15	86,287	Munsey Park (village) Nassau County	90	52,946	Southold (CDP) Suffolk County
16	85,540	Irvington (village) Westchester County	91	52,710	West Nyack (CDP) Rockland County
17	84,066	Woodbury (CDP) Nassau County	92	52,348	Tuckahoe (village) Westchester County
18	83,979	Lido Beach (CDP) Nassau County	93	52,317	Pittsford (town) Monroe County
19	83,536	Flower Hill (village) Nassau County	94	52,202	Locust Valley (CDP) Nassau County
20	79,693	Lawrence (village) Nassau County	95	51,999	North Hempstead (town) Nassau County
21	76,495	Pelham (town) Westchester County	96	51,881	Springs (CDP) Suffolk County
22	76,256	Briarcliff Manor (village) Westchester County	97	51,485	Oyster Bay (CDP) Nassau County
23	76,032	Cold Spring Harbor (CDP) Suffolk County	98	51,318	West Elmira (CDP) Chemung County
24	73,499	Mamaroneck (town) Westchester County	99	51,107	Tarrytown (village) Westchester County
25	73,400	Piermont (village) Rockland County	100	51,057	Manhasset Hills (CDP) Nassau County
26	73,279	East Hills (village) Nassau County	101	50,942	Halesite (CDP) Suffolk County
27	72,907	Old Westbury (village) Nassau County	102	50,748	Great Neck Plaza (village) Nassau County
28	72,602	Rye Brook (village) Westchester County	103	50,497	Philipstown (town) Putnam County
29	72,593	Lake Success (village) Nassau County	104	50,304	Old Bethpage (CDP) Nassau County
30	72,240	Great Neck Estates (village) Nassau County	105	50,293	Plainview (CDP) Nassau County
31	71,544	Bedford (town) Westchester County	106	49,993	Glen Head (CDP) Nassau County
32	70,387	Lewisboro (town) Westchester County	107	49,793	Wantagh (CDP) Nassau County
33	69,870	Brookville (village) Nassau County	108	49,790	Roslyn Heights (CDP) Nassau County
34	69,450	Southampton (village) Suffolk County	109	49,697	Oyster Bay (town) Nassau County
35	68,771	Montebello (village) Rockland County	110	49,420	Tappan (CDP) Rockland County
36	68,466	North Salem (town) Westchester County	111	49,293	Pompey (town) Onondaga County
37	67,545	Roslyn (village) Nassau County	112	49,067	Huntington (town) Suffolk County
38	66,778	Pelham (village) Westchester County	113	48,827	Woodmere (CDP) Nassau County
39	66,592	Eastchester (town) Westchester County	114	48,794	West Bay Shore (CDP) Suffolk County
40	65,725	Garden City (village) Nassau County	115	48,697	Yorktown (town) Westchester County
41	65,176	Ardsley (village) Westchester County	116	48,389	New City (CDP) Rockland County
42	64,993	Manhattan (borough) New York County	117	48,259	Victor (town) Ontario County
43	64,622	Northwest Harbor (CDP) Suffolk County	118	48,075	East Hampton North (CDP) Suffolk County
44	64,491	Melville (CDP) Suffolk County	119	47,882	Cortlandt (town) Westchester County
45	63,899	Port Washington North (village) Nassau County	120	47,685	Montauk (CDP) Suffolk County
46	63,877	Hastings-on-Hudson (village) Westchester County	121	47,656	Elmira (town) Chemung County
47	63,075	Jericho (CDP) Nassau County	122	47,484	Mount Pleasant (town) Westchester County
48	62,595	East Williston (village) Nassau County	123	47,397	Bellmore (CDP) Nassau County
49	62,052	East Norwich (CDP) Nassau County	124	47,239	Rhinebeck (town) Dutchess County
50	61,619	Hartsdale (CDP) Westchester County	125	47,223	East Rockaway (village) Nassau County
51	61,089	Thomaston (village) Nassau County	126	47,126	Southold (town) Suffolk County
52	60,742	Manhasset (CDP) Nassau County	127	47,041	Noyack (CDP) Suffolk County
53	60,675	University Gardens (CDP) Nassau County	128	46,925	Long Beach (city) Nassau County
54	60,654	Syosset (CDP) Nassau County	129	46,787	Malverne (village) Nassau County
55	60,458	Huntington (CDP) Suffolk County	130	46,767	Massapequa (CDP) Nassau County
56	60,248	Greenburgh (town) Westchester County	131	46,506	Valhalla (CDP) Westchester County
57	60,166	Harrison (town/village) Westchester County	132	46,327	Herricks (CDP) Nassau County
58	59,483	Port Washington (CDP) Nassau County	133	46,299	Lansing (town) Tompkins County
59	57,762	Eastchester (CDP) Westchester County	134	46,228	Pomona (village) Rockland County
60	57,476	West Hills (CDP) Suffolk County	135	46,227	Wading River (CDP) Suffolk County
61	57,344	Sea Cliff (village) Nassau County	136	46,161	Lansing (village) Tompkins County
62	57,165	Croton-on-Hudson (village) Westchester County	137	45,909	White Plains (city) Westchester County
63	57,158	Dix Hills (CDP) Suffolk County	138	45,869	Smithtown (CDP) Suffolk County
64	56,542	Somers (town) Westchester County	139	45,863	Cornwall-on-Hudson (village) Orange County
65	56,464	Fort Salonga (CDP) Suffolk County	140	45,726	Westhampton (CDP) Suffolk County
66	56,379	Brightwaters (village) Suffolk County	141	45,614	Babylon (village) Suffolk County
67	56,135	East Hampton (town) Suffolk County	142	45,518	Smithtown (town) Suffolk County
68	56,048	Skaneateles (village) Onondaga County	143	45,356	South Nyack (village) Rockland County
69	55,735	Mendon (town) Monroe County	144	45,270	Floral Park (village) Nassau County
70	55,500	North Sea (CDP) Suffolk County	145	45,251	Bayville (village) Nassau County
71	55,294	Port Jefferson (village) Suffolk County	146	45,215	Bethlehem (town) Albany County
72	55,282	Rockville Centre (village) Nassau County	147	45,197	Washington (town) Dutchess County
73	55,194	Searingtown (CDP) Nassau County	148	45,190	Blauvelt (CDP) Rockland County
74	55,085	Centerport (CDP) Suffolk County	149	45,188	Southampton (town) Suffolk County
75	55,008	Mamaroneck (village) Westchester County	150	45,149	Hewlett (CDP) Nassau County

Note: This section ranks incorporated places and CDPs (Census Designated Places) with populations of 2,500 or more. Unincorporated postal areas were not considered. Please refer to the User Guide for additional information.

Per Capita Income

Top 150 Places Ranked in *Ascending* Order

State Rank	Dollars	Place	State Rank	Dollars	Place
1	2,936	**Binghamton University** (CDP) Broome County	76	19,964	**Niagara Falls** (city) Niagara County
2	3,673	**University at Buffalo** (CDP) Erie County	77	20,076	**Randolph** (town) Cattaraugus County
3	4,550	**Watchtower** (CDP) Ulster County	78	20,168	**Dunkirk** (city) Chautauqua County
4	5,426	**Stony Brook University** (CDP) Suffolk County	79	20,243	**Endicott** (village) Broome County
5	5,514	**New Square** (village) Rockland County	80	20,337	**Galen** (town) Wayne County
6	5,685	**Dannemora** (village) Clinton County	81	20,358	**Altona** (town) Clinton County
7	5,912	**Kaser** (village) Rockland County	82	20,369	**Le Ray** (town) Jefferson County
8	6,510	**SUNY Oswego** (CDP) Oswego County	83	20,393	**Sidney** (village) Delaware County
9	7,658	**Kiryas Joel** (village) Orange County	84	20,463	**Brentwood** (CDP) Suffolk County
10	7,780	**Alfred** (village) Allegany County	85	20,480	**Lackawanna** (city) Erie County
11	9,773	**Dannemora** (town) Clinton County	86	20,554	**Cape Vincent** (town) Jefferson County
12	11,287	**Alfred** (town) Allegany County	87	20,586	**Cobleskill** (village) Schoharie County
13	11,552	**Monsey** (CDP) Rockland County	88	20,610	**Moravia** (town) Cayuga County
14	12,236	**South Fallsburg** (CDP) Sullivan County	89	20,638	**Calcium** (CDP) Jefferson County
15	12,356	**Groveland** (town) Livingston County	90	20,697	**Corinth** (village) Saratoga County
16	13,174	**Delhi** (village) Delaware County	91	20,702	**Lyons** (village) Wayne County
17	13,403	**Riverside** (CDP) Suffolk County	92	20,704	**Mohawk** (village) Herkimer County
18	13,522	**Geneseo** (village) Livingston County	93	20,749	**Wyandanch** (CDP) Suffolk County
19	13,620	**Attica** (town) Wyoming County	94	20,751	**Buffalo** (city) Erie County
20	13,722	**Romulus** (town) Seneca County	95	20,768	**Wolcott** (town) Wayne County
21	14,264	**Albion** (town) Orleans County	96	20,779	**Elmira Heights** (village) Chemung County
22	14,826	**South Hill** (CDP) Tompkins County	97	20,793	**Frankfort** (village) Herkimer County
23	14,842	**Caneadea** (town) Allegany County	98	20,827	**Franklinville** (town) Cattaraugus County
24	16,126	**Newburgh** (city) Orange County	99	20,855	**Shelby** (town) Orleans County
25	16,152	**Salamanca** (city) Cattaraugus County	100	20,865	**Penn Yan** (village) Yates County
26	16,171	**Potsdam** (village) Saint Lawrence County	101	20,873	**Norwich** (city) Chenango County
27	16,326	**Elmira** (city) Chemung County	102	20,881	**Canisteo** (town) Steuben County
28	16,715	**Fort Ann** (town) Washington County	103	20,898	**Amsterdam** (city) Montgomery County
29	17,066	**Brockport** (village) Monroe County	104	20,910	**Auburn** (city) Cayuga County
30	17,233	**Ithaca** (city) Tompkins County	105	20,961	**Canton** (town) Saint Lawrence County
31	17,253	**Saint Regis Mohawk Reservation** (reservation) Franklin County	106	20,969	**Mattydale** (CDP) Onondaga County
32	17,535	**Eaton** (town) Madison County	107	20,988	**Mount Morris** (village) Livingston County
33	17,593	**Monticello** (village) Sullivan County	108	21,062	**Annsville** (town) Oneida County
34	17,813	**Collins** (town) Erie County	109	21,120	**Spencer** (town) Tioga County
35	17,879	**Utica** (city) Oneida County	110	21,153	**Malone** (village) Franklin County
36	17,968	**New Paltz** (village) Ulster County	111	21,159	**Herkimer** (village) Herkimer County
37	17,975	**Albion** (village) Orleans County	112	21,173	**Massena** (town) Saint Lawrence County
38	18,040	**Malone** (town) Franklin County	113	21,200	**Potsdam** (town) Saint Lawrence County
39	18,050	**Saint Johnsville** (town) Montgomery County	114	21,219	**Palermo** (town) Oswego County
40	18,137	**Walton** (village) Delaware County	115	21,257	**Schenectady** (city) Schenectady County
41	18,301	**Minden** (town) Montgomery County	116	21,285	**Norfolk** (town) Saint Lawrence County
42	18,315	**Fulton** (city) Oswego County	117	21,299	**Massena** (village) Saint Lawrence County
43	18,435	**Oneonta** (city) Otsego County	118	21,345	**Silver Creek** (village) Chautauqua County
44	18,456	**Bronx** (borough) Bronx County	119	21,385	**Laurens** (town) Otsego County
45	18,509	**Fallsburg** (town) Sullivan County	120	21,426	**Richland** (town) Oswego County
46	18,602	**Gouverneur** (town) Saint Lawrence County	121	21,445	**Troy** (city) Rensselaer County
47	18,658	**Fort Drum** (CDP) Jefferson County	122	21,510	**Hamlin** (CDP) Monroe County
48	18,732	**Canton** (village) Saint Lawrence County	123	21,532	**New York Mills** (village) Oneida County
49	18,762	**Bangor** (town) Franklin County	124	21,549	**Lyons** (town) Wayne County
50	18,796	**Jamestown** (city) Chautauqua County	125	21,560	**East Syracuse** (village) Onondaga County
51	18,876	**Gloversville** (city) Fulton County	126	21,619	**Westfield** (village) Chautauqua County
52	18,886	**Gouverneur** (village) Saint Lawrence County	127	21,646	**New Cassel** (CDP) Nassau County
53	18,999	**Cortland** (city) Cortland County	128	21,652	**Little Falls** (city) Herkimer County
54	19,034	**Hornell** (city) Steuben County	129	21,659	**Coxsackie** (town) Greene County
55	19,094	**Mount Morris** (town) Livingston County	130	21,682	**Plattsburgh** (city) Clinton County
56	19,103	**Spring Valley** (village) Rockland County	131	21,718	**Ilion** (village) Herkimer County
57	19,158	**Rochester** (city) Monroe County	132	21,740	**Rose** (town) Wayne County
58	19,236	**Newark** (village) Wayne County	133	21,750	**Medina** (village) Orleans County
59	19,380	**Arlington** (CDP) Dutchess County	134	21,764	**Walton** (town) Delaware County
60	19,400	**Geneseo** (town) Livingston County	135	21,766	**Watertown** (city) Jefferson County
61	19,483	**Portland** (town) Chautauqua County	136	21,786	**Allegany** (town) Cattaraugus County
62	19,558	**Syracuse** (city) Onondaga County	137	21,797	**Attica** (village) Wyoming County
63	19,618	**Hudson Falls** (village) Washington County	138	21,818	**Roosevelt** (CDP) Nassau County
64	19,622	**Falconer** (village) Chautauqua County	139	21,823	**New Bremen** (town) Lewis County
65	19,647	**Inwood** (CDP) Nassau County	140	21,850	**Colesville** (town) Broome County
66	19,723	**Yorkshire** (town) Cattaraugus County	141	21,879	**Hempstead** (village) Nassau County
67	19,738	**Whitehall** (village) Washington County	142	21,910	**Sidney** (town) Delaware County
68	19,754	**Hamilton** (village) Madison County	143	21,911	**North Amityville** (CDP) Suffolk County
69	19,763	**West Point** (CDP) Orange County	144	21,921	**Ellenville** (village) Ulster County
70	19,773	**Carthage** (village) Jefferson County	145	21,930	**Stamford** (town) Delaware County
71	19,839	**Geneva** (city) Ontario County	146	21,969	**Hudson** (city) Columbia County
72	19,865	**Wilna** (town) Jefferson County	147	21,978	**Westfield** (town) Chautauqua County
73	19,891	**Binghamton** (city) Broome County	148	22,034	**Granville** (town) Washington County
74	19,915	**Manheim** (town) Herkimer County	149	22,046	**Webster** (village) Monroe County
75	19,920	**Oswego** (town) Oswego County	150	22,073	**Whitehall** (town) Washington County

Note: *This section ranks incorporated places and CDPs (Census Designated Places) with populations of 2,500 or more. Unincorporated postal areas were not considered. Please refer to the User Guide for additional information.*

Median Household Income

Top 150 Places Ranked in *Descending* Order

State Rank	Dollars	Place
1	242,782	Scarsdale (town/village) Westchester County
2	230,179	Muttontown (village) Nassau County
3	214,167	Brookville (village) Nassau County
4	209,063	Munsey Park (village) Nassau County
5	208,424	Flower Hill (village) Nassau County
6	202,292	Lloyd Harbor (village) Suffolk County
7	200,952	Greenville (CDP) Westchester County
8	199,426	New Castle (town) Westchester County
9	198,834	Bronxville (village) Westchester County
10	188,659	Pelham Manor (village) Westchester County
11	185,119	Sands Point (village) Nassau County
12	183,036	Armonk (CDP) Westchester County
13	176,591	Pound Ridge (town) Westchester County
14	176,250	Great Neck Estates (village) Nassau County
15	173,533	Lake Success (village) Nassau County
16	172,167	North Castle (town) Westchester County
17	168,750	Old Westbury (village) Nassau County
18	163,710	East Hills (village) Nassau County
19	158,679	Woodbury (CDP) Nassau County
20	157,143	Cold Spring Harbor (CDP) Suffolk County
21	156,875	Searingtown (CDP) Nassau County
22	155,273	Rye (city) Westchester County
23	153,506	Garden City (village) Nassau County
24	152,284	Larchmont (village) Westchester County
25	151,607	Pelham (town) Westchester County
26	145,879	Syosset (CDP) Nassau County
27	143,333	Lido Beach (CDP) Nassau County
28	142,692	Stony Brook University (CDP) Suffolk County
29	141,447	Ardsley (village) Westchester County
30	141,250	Dix Hills (CDP) Suffolk County
31	141,170	Briarcliff Manor (village) Westchester County
32	140,391	Lawrence (village) Nassau County
33	140,242	Jericho (CDP) Nassau County
34	138,051	Irvington (village) Westchester County
35	136,250	East Williston (village) Nassau County
36	135,478	Lewisboro (town) Westchester County
37	134,309	East Norwich (CDP) Nassau County
38	132,839	Stony Brook (CDP) Suffolk County
39	132,614	Montebello (village) Rockland County
40	132,225	Merrick (CDP) Nassau County
41	131,488	Rye Brook (village) Westchester County
42	131,475	Croton-on-Hudson (village) Westchester County
43	128,661	Pomona (village) Rockland County
44	127,734	Herricks (CDP) Nassau County
45	127,660	Woodbury (village) Orange County
46	127,644	Bedford (town) Westchester County
47	127,407	Wantagh (CDP) Nassau County
48	126,968	Woodmere (CDP) Nassau County
49	125,370	Setauket-East Setauket (CDP) Suffolk County
50	124,868	North Salem (town) Westchester County
51	124,615	Glenwood Landing (CDP) Nassau County
52	124,276	Hastings-on-Hudson (village) Westchester County
53	123,856	Plainview (CDP) Nassau County
54	123,672	Pelham (village) Westchester County
55	122,692	Brightwaters (village) Suffolk County
56	122,554	Fort Salonga (CDP) Suffolk County
57	122,232	Woodbury (town) Orange County
58	121,759	Manhasset Hills (CDP) Nassau County
59	121,376	Melville (CDP) Suffolk County
60	120,318	Halesite (CDP) Suffolk County
61	120,114	West Nyack (CDP) Rockland County
62	119,703	Massapequa (CDP) Nassau County
63	119,628	East Shoreham (CDP) Suffolk County
64	119,528	New City (CDP) Rockland County
65	119,327	Thornwood (CDP) Westchester County
66	118,929	Blauvelt (CDP) Rockland County
67	117,946	Nesconset (CDP) Suffolk County
68	117,600	Old Bethpage (CDP) Nassau County
69	117,150	North Merrick (CDP) Nassau County
70	117,059	Tappan (CDP) Rockland County
71	116,671	Dobbs Ferry (village) Westchester County
72	115,927	Bardonia (CDP) Rockland County
73	115,754	Greenburgh (town) Westchester County
74	115,696	Somers (town) Westchester County
75	115,625	Thomaston (village) Nassau County
76	115,432	East Islip (CDP) Suffolk County
77	114,716	North Hills (village) Nassau County
78	114,474	Bellmore (CDP) Nassau County
79	114,463	Commack (CDP) Suffolk County
80	114,297	Spackenkill (CDP) Dutchess County
81	114,273	Mamaroneck (town) Westchester County
82	114,141	West Hills (CDP) Suffolk County
83	113,372	Smithtown (CDP) Suffolk County
84	113,160	Kings Point (village) Nassau County
85	112,693	Smithtown (town) Suffolk County
86	112,390	Northport (village) Suffolk County
87	112,250	South Hempstead (CDP) Nassau County
88	112,162	Oyster Bay (town) Nassau County
89	111,319	Lakeview (CDP) Nassau County
90	111,189	South Valley Stream (CDP) Nassau County
91	110,997	Sea Cliff (village) Nassau County
92	110,901	Huntington (CDP) Suffolk County
93	110,845	Massapequa Park (village) Nassau County
94	110,681	Port Jefferson (village) Suffolk County
95	110,655	Jefferson Valley-Yorktown (CDP) Westchester County
96	110,435	Thiells (CDP) Rockland County
97	110,417	Wading River (CDP) Suffolk County
98	110,340	West Islip (CDP) Suffolk County
99	109,935	Congers (CDP) Rockland County
100	109,264	North New Hyde Park (CDP) Nassau County
101	108,750	Albertson (CDP) Nassau County
102	108,704	Blue Point (CDP) Suffolk County
103	108,642	Mount Sinai (CDP) Suffolk County
104	108,333	Glen Head (CDP) Nassau County
105	108,287	Plainedge (CDP) Nassau County
106	107,906	Yorktown (town) Westchester County
107	107,875	New Hempstead (village) Rockland County
108	107,660	Wesley Hills (village) Rockland County
109	107,283	Manhasset (CDP) Nassau County
110	106,954	South Farmingdale (CDP) Nassau County
111	106,935	Garden City South (CDP) Nassau County
112	106,902	Port Washington North (village) Nassau County
113	106,795	Malverne (village) Nassau County
113	106,795	Seaford (CDP) Nassau County
115	106,654	Miller Place (CDP) Suffolk County
116	106,415	Rockville Centre (village) Nassau County
117	106,413	Valhalla (CDP) Westchester County
118	106,235	Hewlett (CDP) Nassau County
119	106,005	Port Washington (CDP) Nassau County
120	106,000	Monroe (village) Orange County
121	105,712	Sayville (CDP) Suffolk County
122	105,625	Pleasantville (village) Westchester County
123	105,451	Huntington (town) Suffolk County
124	105,391	North Great River (CDP) Suffolk County
125	105,318	Eastchester (town) Westchester County
126	105,305	Hauppauge (CDP) Suffolk County
127	105,227	Hawthorne (CDP) Westchester County
128	105,078	University Gardens (CDP) Nassau County
129	104,806	North Bellmore (CDP) Nassau County
130	104,698	North Hempstead (town) Nassau County
131	104,531	Lake Mohegan (CDP) Westchester County
132	104,519	Manorville (CDP) Suffolk County
133	104,476	Elwood (CDP) Suffolk County
134	104,469	Harrison (town/village) Westchester County
135	104,330	West Sayville (CDP) Suffolk County
136	104,293	Eastchester (CDP) Westchester County
137	104,250	East Garden City (CDP) Nassau County
138	104,050	Clarkstown (town) Rockland County
139	103,945	Centerport (CDP) Suffolk County
140	103,828	West Bay Shore (CDP) Suffolk County
141	103,811	New Hyde Park (village) Nassau County
142	103,546	Pittsford (town) Monroe County
143	103,438	Carmel (town) Putnam County
144	103,105	Roslyn Heights (CDP) Nassau County
145	102,750	Tarrytown (village) Westchester County
146	102,670	Philipstown (town) Putnam County
147	102,500	Valley Cottage (CDP) Rockland County
148	102,469	Baldwin Harbor (CDP) Nassau County
149	102,321	Hamptonburgh (town) Orange County
150	102,292	North Massapequa (CDP) Nassau County

Note: This section ranks incorporated places and CDPs (Census Designated Places) with populations of 2,500 or more. Unincorporated postal areas were not considered. Please refer to the User Guide for additional information.

Median Household Income

Top 150 Places Ranked in *Ascending* Order

State Rank	Dollars	Place
1	20,048	**Kaser** (village) Rockland County
2	22,470	**New Square** (village) Rockland County
3	24,205	**Albion** (village) Orleans County
4	25,469	**Alfred** (village) Allegany County
5	26,099	**Kiryas Joel** (village) Orange County
6	26,376	**Monticello** (village) Sullivan County
7	26,520	**Albion** (town) Orleans County
8	28,068	**Walton** (village) Delaware County
9	29,295	**Elmira** (city) Chemung County
10	29,824	**Binghamton** (city) Broome County
11	30,436	**Ithaca** (city) Tompkins County
12	30,504	**Utica** (city) Oneida County
13	30,557	**Salamanca** (city) Cattaraugus County
14	30,950	**Jamestown** (city) Chautauqua County
15	30,960	**Rochester** (city) Monroe County
16	31,121	**Newark** (village) Wayne County
17	31,484	**Sidney** (village) Delaware County
18	31,560	**Niagara Falls** (city) Niagara County
19	31,881	**Syracuse** (city) Onondaga County
20	31,918	**Buffalo** (city) Erie County
21	32,022	**South Fallsburg** (CDP) Sullivan County
22	32,383	**New York Mills** (village) Oneida County
23	32,726	**Endicott** (village) Broome County
24	32,917	**Saint Regis Mohawk Reservation** (reservation) Franklin County
25	33,503	**Gouverneur** (town) Saint Lawrence County
26	33,586	**Penn Yan** (village) Yates County
27	33,719	**Sidney** (town) Delaware County
28	33,917	**Amsterdam** (city) Montgomery County
29	34,088	**Liberty** (village) Sullivan County
30	34,194	**Walton** (town) Delaware County
31	34,299	**Bronx** (borough) Bronx County
32	34,313	**Hudson** (city) Columbia County
33	34,348	**Newburgh** (city) Orange County
34	35,044	**Gloversville** (city) Fulton County
35	35,175	**Gouverneur** (village) Saint Lawrence County
36	35,318	**Lyons** (village) Wayne County
37	35,352	**Lackawanna** (city) Erie County
38	35,566	**East Syracuse** (village) Onondaga County
39	35,708	**Webster** (village) Monroe County
40	36,126	**Fulton** (city) Oswego County
41	36,135	**Ogdensburg** (city) Saint Lawrence County
42	36,300	**Potsdam** (village) Saint Lawrence County
43	36,369	**Yorkshire** (town) Cattaraugus County
44	36,442	**Catskill** (village) Greene County
45	36,667	**Malone** (village) Franklin County
46	36,700	**Saint Johnsville** (town) Montgomery County
47	36,824	**Cobleskill** (village) Schoharie County
48	36,875	**Mount Morris** (village) Livingston County
49	36,887	**Minden** (town) Montgomery County
50	37,346	**Plattsburgh** (city) Clinton County
51	37,422	**Alfred** (town) Allegany County
52	37,426	**Monsey** (CDP) Rockland County
53	37,566	**Falconer** (village) Chautauqua County
54	37,813	**Delhi** (village) Delaware County
55	37,830	**Massena** (town) Saint Lawrence County
56	37,931	**Whitehall** (village) Washington County
57	37,967	**Massena** (village) Saint Lawrence County
58	38,051	**Geneseo** (village) Livingston County
59	38,113	**Oswego** (city) Oswego County
60	38,168	**Arcadia** (town) Wayne County
61	38,200	**New Berlin** (town) Chenango County
62	38,266	**Bath** (village) Steuben County
63	38,371	**Johnson City** (village) Broome County
64	38,450	**Olean** (city) Cattaraugus County
65	38,577	**Palmyra** (village) Wayne County
66	38,598	**Hornell** (city) Steuben County
67	38,738	**Herkimer** (village) Herkimer County
68	38,825	**Norwich** (city) Chenango County
69	38,897	**Little Falls** (city) Herkimer County
70	38,919	**Poughkeepsie** (city) Dutchess County
71	38,937	**Dunkirk** (city) Chautauqua County
72	38,954	**Troy** (city) Rensselaer County
73	38,968	**North Gates** (CDP) Monroe County
74	39,043	**Thompson** (town) Sullivan County
75	39,068	**Wellsville** (village) Allegany County
76	39,438	**Auburn** (city) Cayuga County
77	39,525	**Ilion** (village) Herkimer County
78	39,567	**Warsaw** (village) Wyoming County
79	39,571	**Riverside** (CDP) Suffolk County
80	40,000	**Geneva** (city) Ontario County
81	40,025	**Cortland** (city) Cortland County
82	40,142	**Portland** (town) Chautauqua County
83	40,186	**Oneonta** (city) Otsego County
84	40,246	**North Dansville** (town) Livingston County
85	40,386	**Gowanda** (village) Cattaraugus County
86	40,464	**Shelby** (town) Orleans County
87	40,467	**Vails Gate** (CDP) Orange County
88	40,588	**Randolph** (town) Cattaraugus County
89	40,755	**Schenectady** (city) Schenectady County
90	40,757	**Kingston** (city) Ulster County
91	40,841	**Dansville** (village) Livingston County
92	40,855	**Davenport** (town) Delaware County
93	40,931	**Bath** (town) Steuben County
94	40,949	**Albany** (city) Albany County
95	41,042	**Mechanicville** (city) Saratoga County
96	41,067	**Wellsville** (town) Allegany County
97	41,146	**Waverly** (village) Tioga County
98	41,298	**Lockport** (city) Niagara County
99	41,299	**Elmira Heights** (village) Chemung County
100	41,322	**Laurens** (town) Otsego County
101	41,384	**Arcade** (town) Wyoming County
102	41,414	**Watertown** (city) Jefferson County
103	41,421	**New Paltz** (village) Ulster County
104	41,452	**Mooers** (town) Clinton County
105	41,454	**Whitehall** (town) Washington County
106	41,493	**Brockport** (village) Monroe County
107	41,520	**Blasdell** (village) Erie County
108	41,538	**Medina** (village) Orleans County
109	41,584	**Batavia** (city) Genesee County
110	41,682	**Port Jervis** (city) Orange County
111	41,830	**Hornellsville** (town) Steuben County
112	41,863	**Sloan** (village) Erie County
113	41,875	**Richland** (town) Oswego County
114	41,944	**Solvay** (village) Onondaga County
115	41,952	**Geneseo** (town) Livingston County
116	41,958	**Manheim** (town) Herkimer County
117	41,966	**Fort Drum** (CDP) Jefferson County
118	41,971	**Bangor** (town) Franklin County
119	42,078	**Durham** (town) Greene County
120	42,097	**Galeville** (CDP) Onondaga County
121	42,103	**Middletown** (town) Delaware County
122	42,155	**Bedford Hills** (CDP) Westchester County
123	42,183	**Corinth** (town) Saratoga County
124	42,208	**Arlington** (CDP) Dutchess County
125	42,287	**Southport** (CDP) Chemung County
126	42,304	**Palmyra** (town) Wayne County
127	42,318	**Dix** (town) Schuyler County
128	42,338	**Vienna** (town) Oneida County
129	42,392	**Hudson Falls** (village) Washington County
130	42,421	**German Flatts** (town) Herkimer County
131	42,583	**Milo** (town) Yates County
132	42,587	**Carthage** (village) Jefferson County
133	42,672	**Wayland** (town) Steuben County
134	42,679	**Middleburgh** (town) Schoharie County
135	42,878	**Liberty** (town) Sullivan County
136	42,941	**Mohawk** (village) Herkimer County
137	42,950	**Johnstown** (city) Fulton County
138	42,958	**Colesville** (town) Broome County
139	43,182	**Richmondville** (town) Schoharie County
140	43,185	**Canandaigua** (city) Ontario County
141	43,199	**Wolcott** (town) Wayne County
142	43,208	**Frankfort** (village) Herkimer County
143	43,229	**Sherburne** (town) Chenango County
144	43,280	**Murray** (town) Orleans County
145	43,323	**Rome** (city) Oneida County
146	43,333	**Caneadea** (town) Allegany County
147	43,340	**Fallsburg** (town) Sullivan County
148	43,411	**North Syracuse** (village) Onondaga County
149	43,441	**South Lockport** (CDP) Niagara County
150	43,512	**Fairview** (CDP) Westchester County

Note: This section ranks incorporated places and CDPs (Census Designated Places) with populations of 2,500 or more. Unincorporated postal areas were not considered. Please refer to the User Guide for additional information.

Average Household Income

Top 150 Places Ranked in *Descending* Order

State Rank	Dollars	Place	State Rank	Dollars	Place
1	371,194	**Scarsdale** (town/village) Westchester County	76	149,158	**Piermont** (village) Rockland County
2	349,570	**Brookville** (village) Nassau County	77	148,492	**Sea Cliff** (village) Nassau County
3	345,142	**Muttontown** (village) Nassau County	78	148,370	**Northwest Harbor** (CDP) Suffolk County
4	335,953	**Sands Point** (village) Nassau County	79	147,754	**Pittsford** (town) Monroe County
5	332,442	**Lloyd Harbor** (village) Suffolk County	80	146,554	**Wesley Hills** (village) Rockland County
6	330,208	**Old Westbury** (village) Nassau County	81	146,535	**Mamaroneck** (village) Westchester County
7	317,063	**Bronxville** (village) Westchester County	82	146,462	**Oyster Bay** (town) Nassau County
8	303,240	**Armonk** (CDP) Westchester County	83	146,251	**Blauvelt** (CDP) Rockland County
9	291,216	**Pound Ridge** (town) Westchester County	84	146,173	**Plainview** (CDP) Nassau County
10	289,988	**Munsey Park** (village) Nassau County	85	145,586	**Tappan** (CDP) Rockland County
11	289,857	**North Castle** (town) Westchester County	86	145,336	**New City** (CDP) Rockland County
12	280,081	**Pelham Manor** (village) Westchester County	87	145,097	**Rockville Centre** (village) Nassau County
13	278,501	**Greenville** (CDP) Westchester County	88	144,070	**West Nyack** (CDP) Rockland County
14	277,541	**New Castle** (town) Westchester County	89	144,059	**Eastchester** (CDP) Westchester County
15	274,724	**Lake Success** (village) Nassau County	90	143,857	**Glenwood Landing** (CDP) Nassau County
16	273,321	**Flower Hill** (village) Nassau County	91	143,688	**Mount Pleasant** (town) Westchester County
17	257,949	**Rye** (city) Westchester County	92	143,122	**Old Bethpage** (CDP) Nassau County
18	257,534	**Larchmont** (village) Westchester County	93	142,563	**Massapequa** (CDP) Nassau County
19	240,089	**Pelham** (town) Westchester County	94	142,000	**Huntington** (town) Suffolk County
20	235,306	**Lawrence** (village) Nassau County	95	141,320	**Pleasantville** (village) Westchester County
21	235,064	**Woodbury** (CDP) Nassau County	96	140,420	**Bardonia** (CDP) Rockland County
22	232,353	**Irvington** (village) Westchester County	97	138,888	**Locust Valley** (CDP) Nassau County
23	226,076	**Bedford** (town) Westchester County	98	138,401	**Mendon** (town) Monroe County
24	225,957	**East Hills** (village) Nassau County	99	137,622	**Northport** (village) Suffolk County
25	225,194	**Great Neck Estates** (village) Nassau County	100	137,377	**Glen Head** (CDP) Nassau County
26	220,241	**Briarcliff Manor** (village) Westchester County	101	136,556	**Bellmore** (CDP) Nassau County
27	218,923	**Cold Spring Harbor** (CDP) Suffolk County	102	136,146	**Philipstown** (town) Putnam County
28	208,521	**Pelham** (village) Westchester County	103	135,915	**Valhalla** (CDP) Westchester County
29	203,664	**Montebello** (village) Rockland County	104	135,687	**Manhattan** (borough) New York County
30	202,414	**Kings Point** (village) Nassau County	105	134,958	**Elwood** (CDP) Suffolk County
31	200,593	**Mamaroneck** (town) Westchester County	106	134,936	**Tarrytown** (village) Westchester County
32	200,266	**Lido Beach** (CDP) Nassau County	107	134,615	**Smithtown** (CDP) Suffolk County
33	198,972	**Harrison** (town/village) Westchester County	108	134,591	**Yorktown** (town) Westchester County
34	198,884	**Garden City** (village) Nassau County	109	134,315	**Garden City South** (CDP) Nassau County
35	196,905	**Rye Brook** (village) Westchester County	110	133,694	**Shelter Island** (town) Suffolk County
36	192,353	**East Williston** (village) Nassau County	111	133,477	**West Bay Shore** (CDP) Suffolk County
37	191,959	**Lewisboro** (town) Westchester County	112	133,319	**Pompey** (town) Onondaga County
38	187,037	**Ardsley** (village) Westchester County	113	133,239	**Port Jefferson** (village) Suffolk County
39	186,684	**North Salem** (town) Westchester County	114	133,009	**Smithtown** (town) Suffolk County
40	186,404	**North Hills** (village) Nassau County	115	132,790	**Nesconset** (CDP) Suffolk County
41	184,220	**Dix Hills** (CDP) Suffolk County	116	132,268	**Halesite** (CDP) Suffolk County
42	183,728	**Syosset** (CDP) Nassau County	117	131,247	**Cortlandt** (town) Westchester County
43	183,522	**Jericho** (CDP) Nassau County	118	131,208	**North Merrick** (CDP) Nassau County
44	181,630	**Manhasset** (CDP) Nassau County	119	130,758	**Commack** (CDP) Suffolk County
45	178,346	**East Norwich** (CDP) Nassau County	120	130,432	**Monroe** (village) Orange County
46	177,796	**Searingtown** (CDP) Nassau County	121	130,139	**East Islip** (CDP) Suffolk County
47	173,385	**Thomaston** (village) Nassau County	122	129,520	**North New Hyde Park** (CDP) Nassau County
48	172,801	**Melville** (CDP) Suffolk County	123	129,095	**Woodbury** (village) Orange County
49	170,681	**Hastings-on-Hudson** (village) Westchester County	124	128,449	**Brookhaven** (CDP) Suffolk County
50	167,976	**Eastchester** (town) Westchester County	125	128,130	**East Hampton** (town) Suffolk County
51	165,789	**Port Washington** (CDP) Nassau County	126	128,087	**Mount Sinai** (CDP) Suffolk County
52	163,819	**Fort Salonga** (CDP) Suffolk County	127	128,083	**Springs** (CDP) Suffolk County
53	163,030	**Greenburgh** (town) Westchester County	128	128,074	**North Sea** (CDP) Suffolk County
54	162,663	**Southampton** (village) Suffolk County	129	127,899	**Spackenkill** (CDP) Dutchess County
55	162,277	**Woodmere** (CDP) Nassau County	130	127,752	**Congers** (CDP) Rockland County
56	161,684	**Roslyn** (village) Nassau County	131	127,739	**Clarkstown** (town) Rockland County
57	160,729	**Merrick** (CDP) Nassau County	132	127,109	**Woodbury** (town) Orange County
58	160,551	**Roslyn Heights** (CDP) Nassau County	133	126,764	**Hartsdale** (CDP) Westchester County
59	159,812	**Croton-on-Hudson** (village) Westchester County	134	126,705	**Thornwood** (CDP) Westchester County
60	159,211	**Brightwaters** (village) Suffolk County	135	126,439	**New Hempstead** (village) Rockland County
61	157,244	**University Gardens** (CDP) Nassau County	136	126,262	**Miller Place** (CDP) Suffolk County
62	156,983	**Wantagh** (CDP) Nassau County	137	126,205	**Wading River** (CDP) Suffolk County
63	156,335	**Dobbs Ferry** (village) Westchester County	138	125,780	**East Shoreham** (CDP) Suffolk County
64	155,611	**Port Washington North** (village) Nassau County	139	125,733	**Skaneateles** (town) Onondaga County
65	154,685	**Stony Brook** (CDP) Suffolk County	140	125,576	**Sayville** (CDP) Suffolk County
66	154,247	**Manhasset Hills** (CDP) Nassau County	141	125,229	**West Elmira** (CDP) Chemung County
67	153,736	**East Garden City** (CDP) Nassau County	142	125,195	**East Rockaway** (village) Nassau County
68	152,986	**Somers** (town) Westchester County	143	124,505	**Oyster Bay** (CDP) Nassau County
69	152,374	**North Hempstead** (town) Nassau County	144	124,467	**Floral Park** (village) Nassau County
70	152,363	**West Hills** (CDP) Suffolk County	145	124,176	**South Valley Stream** (CDP) Nassau County
71	151,663	**Herricks** (CDP) Nassau County	146	124,059	**Malverne** (village) Nassau County
72	151,435	**Setauket-East Setauket** (CDP) Suffolk County	147	123,972	**South Hempstead** (CDP) Nassau County
73	151,381	**Huntington** (CDP) Suffolk County	148	123,967	**Hewlett** (CDP) Nassau County
74	150,564	**Pomona** (village) Rockland County	149	123,907	**West Islip** (CDP) Suffolk County
75	149,192	**Centerport** (CDP) Suffolk County	150	123,671	**Bayville** (village) Nassau County

Note: *This section ranks incorporated places and CDPs (Census Designated Places) with populations of 2,500 or more. Unincorporated postal areas were not considered. Please refer to the User Guide for additional information.*

Average Household Income

Top 150 Places Ranked in *Ascending* Order

State Rank	Dollars	Place
1	8,562	**University at Buffalo** (CDP) Erie County
2	30,675	**Kaser** (village) Rockland County
3	32,432	**New Square** (village) Rockland County
4	38,272	**Monticello** (village) Sullivan County
5	39,208	**Salamanca** (city) Cattaraugus County
6	39,567	**Walton** (village) Delaware County
7	41,452	**Albion** (village) Orleans County
8	42,405	**New York Mills** (village) Oneida County
9	42,676	**Newark** (village) Wayne County
10	42,880	**Kiryas Joel** (village) Orange County
11	42,948	**Jamestown** (city) Chautauqua County
12	43,642	**Falconer** (village) Chautauqua County
13	43,682	**Rochester** (city) Monroe County
14	43,762	**Elmira** (city) Chemung County
15	44,062	**Utica** (city) Oneida County
16	44,388	**Niagara Falls** (city) Niagara County
17	44,448	**Endicott** (village) Broome County
18	44,614	**Binghamton** (city) Broome County
19	45,332	**Gouverneur** (village) Saint Lawrence County
20	45,399	**Lackawanna** (city) Erie County
21	45,418	**Lyons** (village) Wayne County
22	45,481	**Gloversville** (city) Fulton County
23	45,512	**Sidney** (village) Delaware County
24	45,516	**Mount Morris** (village) Livingston County
25	45,591	**Dunkirk** (city) Chautauqua County
26	45,784	**Yorkshire** (town) Cattaraugus County
27	45,797	**Hornell** (city) Steuben County
28	45,885	**South Fallsburg** (CDP) Sullivan County
29	45,964	**Penn Yan** (village) Yates County
30	46,040	**Saint Johnsville** (town) Montgomery County
31	46,595	**Fulton** (city) Oswego County
32	46,614	**Albion** (town) Orleans County
33	46,658	**Sidney** (town) Delaware County
34	46,918	**Buffalo** (city) Erie County
35	46,924	**East Syracuse** (village) Onondaga County
36	47,058	**Webster** (village) Monroe County
37	47,146	**Walton** (town) Delaware County
38	47,208	**Herkimer** (village) Herkimer County
39	47,223	**Alfred** (village) Allegany County
40	47,262	**Massena** (town) Saint Lawrence County
41	47,432	**Saint Regis Mohawk Reservation** (reservation) Franklin County
42	47,469	**Minden** (town) Montgomery County
43	47,502	**Whitehall** (village) Washington County
44	47,578	**Syracuse** (city) Onondaga County
45	47,940	**Mount Morris** (town) Livingston County
46	48,005	**Shelby** (town) Orleans County
47	48,280	**Massena** (village) Saint Lawrence County
48	48,282	**Riverside** (CDP) Suffolk County
49	48,554	**Bangor** (town) Franklin County
50	48,624	**Medina** (village) Orleans County
51	48,705	**Hudson** (city) Columbia County
52	48,887	**Warsaw** (village) Wyoming County
53	48,957	**Auburn** (city) Cayuga County
54	48,999	**Manheim** (town) Herkimer County
55	49,096	**Little Falls** (city) Herkimer County
56	49,145	**Malone** (village) Franklin County
57	49,391	**Galeville** (CDP) Onondaga County
58	49,504	**Cortland** (city) Cortland County
59	49,697	**Hudson Falls** (village) Washington County
60	49,751	**Amsterdam** (city) Montgomery County
61	49,774	**Calcium** (CDP) Jefferson County
62	49,856	**Lyncourt** (CDP) Onondaga County
63	49,870	**Elmira Heights** (village) Chemung County
64	49,879	**Watertown** (city) Jefferson County
65	49,892	**Tupper Lake** (village) Franklin County
66	49,899	**Newburgh** (city) Orange County
67	49,937	**South Glens Falls** (village) Saratoga County
68	50,097	**Arcadia** (town) Wayne County
69	50,123	**Ilion** (village) Herkimer County
70	50,179	**Mohawk** (village) Herkimer County
71	50,180	**Bath** (village) Steuben County
72	50,191	**Bronx** (borough) Bronx County
73	50,280	**Sloan** (village) Erie County
74	50,489	**Wellsville** (village) Allegany County
75	50,595	**Bath** (town) Steuben County
76	50,740	**Schenectady** (city) Schenectady County
77	50,775	**Ithaca** (city) Tompkins County
78	50,804	**Westfield** (town) Chautauqua County
79	50,857	**Norwich** (city) Chenango County
80	50,894	**Wolcott** (town) Wayne County
81	50,915	**Mattydale** (CDP) Onondaga County
82	50,932	**Afton** (town) Chenango County
83	51,019	**Palmyra** (village) Wayne County
84	51,028	**Delhi** (village) Delaware County
85	51,065	**Herkimer** (town) Herkimer County
86	51,073	**Laurens** (town) Otsego County
87	51,119	**Franklinville** (town) Cattaraugus County
88	51,170	**Johnson City** (village) Broome County
89	51,326	**Randolph** (town) Cattaraugus County
90	51,399	**Vienna** (town) Oneida County
91	51,451	**Gouverneur** (town) Saint Lawrence County
92	51,502	**New Berlin** (town) Chenango County
93	51,553	**Troy** (city) Rensselaer County
94	51,624	**Fort Drum** (CDP) Jefferson County
95	51,646	**Frankfort** (village) Herkimer County
96	51,824	**Spencer** (town) Tioga County
97	51,835	**Portland** (town) Chautauqua County
98	51,881	**Blasdell** (village) Erie County
99	51,884	**North Gates** (CDP) Monroe County
100	51,947	**Lyons** (town) Wayne County
101	52,043	**Sangerfield** (town) Oneida County
102	52,053	**Dansville** (village) Livingston County
103	52,169	**Whitehall** (town) Washington County
104	52,203	**Canisteo** (town) Steuben County
105	52,236	**Brockport** (village) Monroe County
106	52,638	**Caneadea** (town) Allegany County
107	52,646	**Mechanicville** (city) Saratoga County
108	52,658	**Arcade** (town) Wyoming County
109	52,668	**Geneseo** (village) Livingston County
110	52,847	**Corinth** (village) Saratoga County
111	52,879	**Wayland** (town) Steuben County
112	52,906	**Silver Creek** (village) Chautauqua County
113	52,916	**Carthage** (village) Jefferson County
114	53,006	**Westfield** (village) Chautauqua County
115	53,013	**Stamford** (town) Delaware County
116	53,022	**Oswego** (city) Oswego County
117	53,023	**Geneva** (city) Ontario County
118	53,062	**Wellsville** (town) Allegany County
119	53,148	**Plattsburgh** (city) Clinton County
120	53,322	**Southport** (CDP) Chemung County
121	53,434	**Batavia** (city) Genesee County
122	53,516	**Norfolk** (town) Saint Lawrence County
123	53,565	**Arlington** (CDP) Dutchess County
124	53,594	**Gowanda** (village) Cattaraugus County
125	53,768	**Dannemora** (village) Clinton County
126	53,777	**Fort Edward** (village) Washington County
127	53,802	**White Creek** (town) Washington County
128	53,815	**Watervliet** (city) Albany County
129	53,902	**Milo** (town) Yates County
129	53,902	**South Lockport** (CDP) Niagara County
131	54,000	**Sherburne** (town) Chenango County
132	54,220	**North Syracuse** (village) Onondaga County
133	54,317	**Le Ray** (town) Jefferson County
134	54,322	**Cohoes** (city) Albany County
135	54,512	**Nunda** (town) Livingston County
136	54,733	**German Flatts** (town) Herkimer County
137	54,809	**East Rochester** (town/village) Monroe County
138	54,820	**Davenport** (town) Delaware County
139	54,906	**Waterloo** (town) Seneca County
140	55,027	**Granville** (town) Washington County
141	55,123	**Solvay** (village) Onondaga County
142	55,169	**Hannibal** (town) Oswego County
142	55,169	**Olean** (city) Cattaraugus County
144	55,376	**Liberty** (village) Sullivan County
145	55,431	**Vails Gate** (CDP) Orange County
146	55,473	**Ravena** (village) Albany County
147	55,488	**Mooers** (town) Clinton County
148	55,493	**Richland** (town) Oswego County
149	55,498	**Kingston** (city) Ulster County
150	55,512	**Tonawanda** (city) Erie County

Note: *This section ranks incorporated places and CDPs (Census Designated Places) with populations of 2,500 or more. Unincorporated postal areas were not considered. Please refer to the User Guide for additional information.*

Households with Income of $100,000 or More

Top 150 Places Ranked in *Descending* Order

State Rank	Percent	Place
1	83.0	Scarsdale (town/village) Westchester County
2	82.6	Muttontown (village) Nassau County
3	78.4	Lloyd Harbor (village) Suffolk County
3	78.4	New Castle (town) Westchester County
5	77.9	Brookville (village) Nassau County
6	77.0	Greenville (CDP) Westchester County
7	76.4	Lake Success (village) Nassau County
8	76.2	Sands Point (village) Nassau County
9	75.7	Munsey Park (village) Nassau County
10	74.0	Pound Ridge (town) Westchester County
11	73.5	Pelham Manor (village) Westchester County
12	73.4	Cold Spring Harbor (CDP) Suffolk County
13	73.2	East Hills (village) Nassau County
14	72.8	Great Neck Estates (village) Nassau County
15	72.7	Armonk (CDP) Westchester County
15	72.7	Bronxville (village) Westchester County
17	72.3	Old Westbury (village) Nassau County
18	71.8	East Williston (village) Nassau County
19	71.7	North Castle (town) Westchester County
20	70.0	Larchmont (village) Westchester County
21	69.2	Flower Hill (village) Nassau County
22	69.1	Garden City (village) Nassau County
23	67.5	Briarcliff Manor (village) Westchester County
24	67.4	Irvington (village) Westchester County
25	67.1	Pelham (town) Westchester County
25	67.1	Syosset (CDP) Nassau County
27	66.9	Jericho (CDP) Nassau County
28	66.5	Rye (city) Westchester County
28	66.5	Searingtown (CDP) Nassau County
30	66.4	Woodbury (CDP) Nassau County
31	66.2	Lawrence (village) Nassau County
32	66.1	Merrick (CDP) Nassau County
33	65.7	Dix Hills (CDP) Suffolk County
34	65.6	Stony Brook University (CDP) Suffolk County
35	65.4	East Shoreham (CDP) Suffolk County
35	65.4	Pomona (village) Rockland County
37	65.3	Stony Brook (CDP) Suffolk County
38	65.1	Lewisboro (town) Westchester County
39	64.0	Spackenkill (CDP) Dutchess County
40	63.2	Glenwood Landing (CDP) Nassau County
41	62.9	North Salem (town) Westchester County
42	62.4	Ardsley (village) Westchester County
43	62.3	Halesite (CDP) Suffolk County
43	62.3	Setauket-East Setauket (CDP) Suffolk County
45	62.1	Pelham (village) Westchester County
46	61.9	Brightwaters (village) Suffolk County
46	61.9	Woodmere (CDP) Nassau County
48	61.4	Montebello (village) Rockland County
49	61.3	Lido Beach (CDP) Nassau County
49	61.3	Nesconset (CDP) Suffolk County
51	61.2	Herricks (CDP) Nassau County
52	61.1	Wantagh (CDP) Nassau County
53	60.9	East Norwich (CDP) Nassau County
54	60.7	New City (CDP) Rockland County
55	60.5	Manhasset Hills (CDP) Nassau County
55	60.5	Woodbury (village) Orange County
57	60.3	Plainview (CDP) Nassau County
58	60.2	Thomaston (village) Nassau County
59	60.0	Fort Salonga (CDP) Suffolk County
60	59.9	Tappan (CDP) Rockland County
61	59.8	Hastings-on-Hudson (village) Westchester County
62	59.7	Wading River (CDP) Suffolk County
63	59.4	Bedford (town) Westchester County
64	59.3	West Nyack (CDP) Rockland County
65	58.9	Smithtown (CDP) Suffolk County
65	58.9	Thiells (CDP) Rockland County
65	58.9	Woodbury (town) Orange County
68	58.7	Sea Cliff (village) Nassau County
69	58.6	Dobbs Ferry (village) Westchester County
69	58.6	North Merrick (CDP) Nassau County
69	58.6	Somers (town) Westchester County
72	58.4	Rye Brook (village) Westchester County
73	58.3	Croton-on-Hudson (village) Westchester County
74	58.1	North New Hyde Park (CDP) Nassau County
75	58.0	Massapequa (CDP) Nassau County
76	57.9	Blauvelt (CDP) Rockland County
77	57.8	Bardonia (CDP) Rockland County
78	57.6	Melville (CDP) Suffolk County
79	57.3	Old Bethpage (CDP) Nassau County
80	57.2	East Islip (CDP) Suffolk County
81	57.1	West Hills (CDP) Suffolk County
82	56.9	Greenburgh (town) Westchester County
82	56.9	Northport (village) Suffolk County
84	56.8	Commack (CDP) Suffolk County
84	56.8	Congers (CDP) Rockland County
86	56.5	Smithtown (town) Suffolk County
86	56.5	Thornwood (CDP) Westchester County
88	56.1	Valhalla (CDP) Westchester County
89	56.0	Kings Point (village) Nassau County
90	55.9	Oyster Bay (town) Nassau County
91	55.8	West Islip (CDP) Suffolk County
92	55.6	Bellmore (CDP) Nassau County
93	55.5	North Hills (village) Nassau County
94	55.4	South Hempstead (CDP) Nassau County
95	55.0	Jefferson Valley-Yorktown (CDP) Westchester County
95	55.0	Mamaroneck (town) Westchester County
97	54.9	North Bellmore (CDP) Nassau County
97	54.9	Seaford (CDP) Nassau County
97	54.9	South Farmingdale (CDP) Nassau County
97	54.9	Wesley Hills (village) Rockland County
101	54.8	Huntington (CDP) Suffolk County
101	54.8	Massapequa Park (village) Nassau County
101	54.8	Mount Sinai (CDP) Suffolk County
104	54.7	Hewlett (CDP) Nassau County
105	54.6	Glen Head (CDP) Nassau County
105	54.6	Monroe (village) Orange County
107	54.3	Pleasantville (village) Westchester County
108	54.2	Harrison (town/village) Westchester County
108	54.2	Lakeview (CDP) Nassau County
110	54.1	Centerport (CDP) Suffolk County
110	54.1	University Gardens (CDP) Nassau County
112	53.9	Port Washington (CDP) Nassau County
113	53.8	Plainedge (CDP) Nassau County
113	53.8	Yorktown (town) Westchester County
115	53.7	New Hempstead (village) Rockland County
115	53.7	Port Jefferson (village) Suffolk County
117	53.6	Manhasset (CDP) Nassau County
118	53.4	Roslyn Heights (CDP) Nassau County
119	53.3	New Hyde Park (village) Nassau County
119	53.3	Sayville (CDP) Suffolk County
119	53.3	West Bay Shore (CDP) Suffolk County
122	52.9	Lake Mohegan (CDP) Westchester County
123	52.7	Elwood (CDP) Suffolk County
124	52.6	Clarkstown (town) Rockland County
124	52.6	Huntington (town) Suffolk County
124	52.6	Malverne (village) Nassau County
124	52.6	Port Washington North (village) Nassau County
128	52.5	North Hempstead (town) Nassau County
128	52.5	South Valley Stream (CDP) Nassau County
130	52.4	Miller Place (CDP) Suffolk County
130	52.4	North Great River (CDP) Suffolk County
132	52.3	Pittsford (town) Monroe County
132	52.3	West Sayville (CDP) Suffolk County
134	52.2	Albertson (CDP) Nassau County
134	52.2	Rockville Centre (village) Nassau County
136	52.1	Blue Point (CDP) Suffolk County
137	52.0	Valley Cottage (CDP) Rockland County
138	51.9	East Garden City (CDP) Nassau County
138	51.9	Eastchester (town) Westchester County
140	51.8	Garden City South (CDP) Nassau County
141	51.7	Hauppauge (CDP) Suffolk County
142	51.6	Baldwin Harbor (CDP) Nassau County
142	51.6	Williston Park (village) Nassau County
144	51.4	Carmel (town) Putnam County
144	51.4	Eastchester (CDP) Westchester County
144	51.4	Hawthorne (CDP) Westchester County
144	51.4	Tarrytown (village) Westchester County
148	51.2	Hamptonburgh (town) Orange County
148	51.2	Mount Pleasant (town) Westchester County
148	51.2	North Massapequa (CDP) Nassau County

Note: This section ranks incorporated places and CDPs (Census Designated Places) with populations of 2,500 or more. Unincorporated postal areas were not considered. Please refer to the User Guide for additional information.

Households with Income of $100,000 or More

Top 150 Places Ranked in *Ascending* Order

State Rank	Percent	Place
1	0.0	**Binghamton University** (CDP) Broome County
1	0.0	**SUNY Oswego** (CDP) Oswego County
1	0.0	**University at Buffalo** (CDP) Erie County
1	0.0	**Watchtower** (CDP) Ulster County
5	3.7	**New Square** (village) Rockland County
6	4.4	**Kaser** (village) Rockland County
6	4.4	**Monticello** (village) Sullivan County
8	4.8	**Fort Edward** (village) Washington County
9	5.5	**Salamanca** (city) Cattaraugus County
10	6.2	**Newark** (village) Wayne County
11	6.3	**Sloan** (village) Erie County
12	6.8	**Calcium** (CDP) Jefferson County
12	6.8	**Wolcott** (town) Wayne County
14	7.2	**Perry** (village) Wyoming County
14	7.2	**Westfield** (town) Chautauqua County
16	7.3	**Mount Morris** (village) Livingston County
17	7.4	**Hornell** (city) Steuben County
17	7.4	**Jamestown** (city) Chautauqua County
19	7.5	**East Syracuse** (village) Onondaga County
19	7.5	**Mount Morris** (town) Livingston County
19	7.5	**Yorkshire** (town) Cattaraugus County
22	7.6	**Bangor** (town) Franklin County
22	7.6	**Corinth** (village) Saratoga County
22	7.6	**Mohawk** (village) Herkimer County
22	7.6	**Whitehall** (village) Washington County
26	7.8	**Carthage** (village) Jefferson County
26	7.8	**Elmira** (city) Chemung County
28	7.9	**Falconer** (village) Chautauqua County
29	8.0	**Bath** (village) Steuben County
29	8.0	**Medina** (village) Orleans County
29	8.0	**Minden** (town) Montgomery County
32	8.1	**Albion** (village) Orleans County
33	8.2	**Elmira Heights** (village) Chemung County
33	8.2	**Niagara Falls** (city) Niagara County
35	8.3	**Dunkirk** (city) Chautauqua County
36	8.4	**New York Mills** (village) Oneida County
36	8.4	**Rochester** (city) Monroe County
36	8.4	**Saint Johnsville** (town) Montgomery County
36	8.4	**Utica** (city) Oneida County
40	8.5	**Fort Edward** (town) Washington County
40	8.5	**Hannibal** (town) Oswego County
40	8.5	**Westfield** (village) Chautauqua County
43	8.6	**Galeville** (CDP) Onondaga County
43	8.6	**Tupper Lake** (village) Franklin County
45	8.7	**Fulton** (city) Oswego County
45	8.7	**Penn Yan** (village) Yates County
47	8.8	**Cortland** (city) Cortland County
47	8.8	**Fort Drum** (CDP) Jefferson County
47	8.8	**South Glens Falls** (village) Saratoga County
50	8.9	**Gowanda** (village) Cattaraugus County
50	8.9	**Lackawanna** (city) Erie County
50	8.9	**Little Falls** (city) Herkimer County
50	8.9	**Massena** (town) Saint Lawrence County
54	9.0	**Vienna** (town) Oneida County
54	9.0	**Walton** (village) Delaware County
56	9.1	**Blasdell** (village) Erie County
56	9.1	**Hudson Falls** (village) Washington County
58	9.2	**Dannemora** (village) Clinton County
58	9.2	**Gloversville** (city) Fulton County
58	9.2	**Mattydale** (CDP) Onondaga County
61	9.3	**Gouverneur** (village) Saint Lawrence County
61	9.3	**Yorkville** (village) Oneida County
63	9.4	**Gouverneur** (town) Saint Lawrence County
63	9.4	**Massena** (village) Saint Lawrence County
65	9.5	**Norfolk** (town) Saint Lawrence County
65	9.5	**Shelby** (town) Orleans County
65	9.5	**Whitesboro** (village) Oneida County
68	9.6	**Binghamton** (city) Broome County
68	9.6	**Saint Regis Mohawk Reservation** (reservation) Franklin County
68	9.6	**Southport** (CDP) Chemung County
68	9.6	**Watertown** (city) Jefferson County
72	9.7	**Afton** (town) Chenango County
72	9.7	**Attica** (village) Wyoming County
72	9.7	**Endicott** (village) Broome County
72	9.7	**Hudson** (city) Columbia County
72	9.7	**Silver Creek** (village) Chautauqua County
77	9.8	**Buffalo** (city) Erie County
77	9.8	**Canisteo** (town) Steuben County
77	9.8	**Manheim** (town) Herkimer County
80	9.9	**Hanover** (town) Chautauqua County
80	9.9	**Palmyra** (village) Wayne County
82	10.1	**Sherburne** (town) Chenango County
82	10.1	**Watervliet** (city) Albany County
84	10.2	**Webster** (village) Monroe County
85	10.3	**Bath** (town) Steuben County
85	10.3	**Herkimer** (village) Herkimer County
85	10.3	**Lyncourt** (CDP) Onondaga County
85	10.3	**Portland** (town) Chautauqua County
85	10.3	**Whitehall** (town) Washington County
90	10.6	**Franklinville** (town) Cattaraugus County
90	10.6	**Liberty** (village) Sullivan County
92	10.7	**Kiryas Joel** (village) Orange County
92	10.7	**Palermo** (town) Oswego County
92	10.7	**Rose** (town) Wayne County
95	10.8	**Caneadea** (town) Allegany County
95	10.8	**Hancock** (town) Delaware County
95	10.8	**Ravena** (village) Albany County
95	10.8	**South Fallsburg** (CDP) Sullivan County
99	10.9	**Arcadia** (town) Wayne County
99	10.9	**Perry** (town) Wyoming County
99	10.9	**Wilna** (town) Jefferson County
102	11.0	**Laurens** (town) Otsego County
102	11.0	**Lyons** (town) Wayne County
102	11.0	**Sidney** (town) Delaware County
102	11.0	**Syracuse** (city) Onondaga County
106	11.1	**Depew** (village) Erie County
106	11.1	**Galen** (town) Wayne County
106	11.1	**Johnson City** (village) Broome County
106	11.1	**Schenectady** (city) Schenectady County
110	11.2	**Davenport** (town) Delaware County
110	11.2	**Herkimer** (town) Herkimer County
110	11.2	**Milo** (town) Yates County
110	11.2	**Wellsville** (village) Allegany County
114	11.3	**Albion** (town) Orleans County
114	11.3	**Arcade** (town) Wyoming County
114	11.3	**Ilion** (village) Herkimer County
114	11.3	**Le Ray** (town) Jefferson County
114	11.3	**Lyons** (village) Wayne County
119	11.5	**Auburn** (city) Cayuga County
120	11.6	**New Berlin** (town) Chenango County
121	11.7	**Frankfort** (village) Herkimer County
121	11.7	**Rutland** (town) Jefferson County
121	11.7	**Sangerfield** (town) Oneida County
121	11.7	**Tupper Lake** (town) Franklin County
125	11.8	**Riverside** (CDP) Suffolk County
126	11.9	**Waterloo** (town) Seneca County
127	12.1	**Cohoes** (city) Albany County
127	12.1	**Stamford** (town) Delaware County
127	12.1	**Wellsville** (town) Allegany County
130	12.2	**Amsterdam** (city) Montgomery County
130	12.2	**South Lockport** (CDP) Niagara County
130	12.2	**Stockport** (town) Columbia County
130	12.2	**White Creek** (town) Washington County
134	12.3	**Verona** (town) Oneida County
134	12.3	**Warrensburg** (CDP) Warren County
136	12.4	**Bainbridge** (town) Chenango County
136	12.4	**Bronx** (borough) Bronx County
136	12.4	**Catskill** (village) Greene County
136	12.4	**Ogdensburg** (city) Saint Lawrence County
136	12.4	**Salem** (town) Washington County
136	12.4	**Sidney** (village) Delaware County
142	12.6	**Geneva** (city) Ontario County
142	12.6	**Kingsbury** (town) Washington County
142	12.6	**Niagara** (town) Niagara County
142	12.6	**North Gates** (CDP) Monroe County
142	12.6	**Walton** (town) Delaware County
147	12.7	**Olean** (city) Cattaraugus County
148	12.8	**Hornellsville** (town) Steuben County
148	12.8	**Malone** (village) Franklin County
148	12.8	**Norwich** (city) Chenango County

Note: *This section ranks incorporated places and CDPs (Census Designated Places) with populations of 2,500 or more. Unincorporated postal areas were not considered. Please refer to the User Guide for additional information.*

Poverty Rate

Top 150 Places Ranked in *Descending* Order

State Rank	Percent	Place	State Rank	Percent	Place
1	88.7	Watchtower (CDP) Ulster County	76	23.1	Endicott (village) Broome County
2	87.1	University at Buffalo (CDP) Erie County	76	23.1	Watertown (city) Jefferson County
3	73.7	Kaser (village) Rockland County	78	22.8	Batavia (city) Genesee County
4	70.5	New Square (village) Rockland County	78	22.8	Chester (town) Warren County
5	56.6	Kiryas Joel (village) Orange County	78	22.8	Schenectady (city) Schenectady County
6	46.9	Monsey (CDP) Rockland County	81	22.6	Altona (town) Clinton County
7	45.3	South Fallsburg (CDP) Sullivan County	81	22.6	Palatine (town) Montgomery County
8	44.8	Ithaca (city) Tompkins County	83	22.4	Shawangunk (town) Ulster County
9	41.5	Geneseo (village) Livingston County	84	22.1	Palmyra (village) Wayne County
10	41.2	SUNY Oswego (CDP) Oswego County	85	22.0	Massena (town) Saint Lawrence County
11	40.5	Alfred (village) Allegany County	86	21.8	Malone (town) Franklin County
12	37.7	Saint Regis Mohawk Reservation (reservation) Franklin County	86	21.8	Newark (village) Wayne County
13	35.1	Monticello (village) Sullivan County	86	21.8	Shelby (town) Orleans County
14	34.8	Syracuse (city) Onondaga County	89	21.6	Frankfort (village) Herkimer County
15	34.2	Newburgh (city) Orange County	89	21.6	Massena (village) Saint Lawrence County
16	33.9	Binghamton (city) Broome County	89	21.6	Stamford (town) Delaware County
17	33.5	Rochester (city) Monroe County	92	21.5	Lyons (town) Wayne County
18	32.7	Monroe (town) Orange County	93	21.4	Mount Morris (village) Livingston County
19	32.2	Utica (city) Oneida County	94	21.3	Dansville (village) Livingston County
20	32.1	Elmira (city) Chemung County	95	21.2	Bath (town) Steuben County
21	31.5	New Paltz (village) Ulster County	95	21.2	Cobleskill (village) Schoharie County
22	31.4	Buffalo (city) Erie County	95	21.2	Ilion (village) Herkimer County
23	31.1	Fulton (city) Oswego County	98	21.1	Wellsville (village) Allegany County
23	31.1	Malone (village) Franklin County	99	21.0	Brewerton (CDP) Onondaga County
25	30.9	Walton (village) Delaware County	99	21.0	Gowanda (village) Cattaraugus County
26	30.7	Bronx (borough) Bronx County	99	21.0	North Dansville (town) Livingston County
27	30.5	Bangor (town) Franklin County	99	21.0	Oneonta (town) Otsego County
28	30.2	Geneseo (town) Livingston County	103	20.8	Annsville (town) Oneida County
29	30.1	Whitehall (village) Washington County	104	20.7	Hempstead (village) Nassau County
30	29.7	Albion (village) Orleans County	104	20.7	Warsaw (town) Wyoming County
31	29.5	Oneonta (city) Otsego County	106	20.6	New York (city)
32	29.3	Jamestown (city) Chautauqua County	106	20.6	Newfield (town) Tompkins County
32	29.3	Webster (village) Monroe County	106	20.6	Richland (town) Oswego County
34	29.1	Gloversville (city) Fulton County	109	20.4	Mount Morris (town) Livingston County
34	29.1	Oswego (city) Oswego County	109	20.4	North Bellport (CDP) Suffolk County
36	28.9	Brockport (village) Monroe County	109	20.4	Silver Creek (village) Chautauqua County
36	28.9	Fallsburg (town) Sullivan County	112	20.3	Moira (town) Franklin County
38	28.8	Potsdam (village) Saint Lawrence County	112	20.3	Northeast Ithaca (CDP) Tompkins County
39	28.1	Salamanca (city) Cattaraugus County	114	20.2	Little Falls (city) Herkimer County
40	28.0	Amsterdam (city) Montgomery County	115	19.9	Colesville (town) Broome County
41	27.8	Albion (town) Orleans County	116	19.8	Viola (CDP) Rockland County
42	27.7	Carthage (village) Jefferson County	117	19.7	Herkimer (village) Herkimer County
42	27.7	Gouverneur (village) Saint Lawrence County	117	19.7	Lyncourt (CDP) Onondaga County
44	27.2	Alfred (town) Allegany County	117	19.7	Potsdam (town) Saint Lawrence County
45	27.0	Oswegatchie (town) Saint Lawrence County	120	19.6	Canton (village) Saint Lawrence County
46	26.8	Albany (city) Albany County	120	19.6	Corinth (village) Saratoga County
47	26.7	Niagara Falls (city) Niagara County	120	19.6	Middletown (city) Orange County
48	26.5	Saint Johnsville (town) Montgomery County	120	19.6	Rensselaer (city) Rensselaer County
49	26.3	Penn Yan (village) Yates County	124	19.4	Catskill (village) Greene County
50	26.1	Troy (city) Rensselaer County	124	19.4	Hunter (town) Greene County
51	25.9	Hornell (city) Steuben County	126	19.2	Fairview (CDP) Dutchess County
52	25.8	Gouverneur (town) Saint Lawrence County	126	19.2	Sodus (town) Wayne County
52	25.8	Laurens (town) Otsego County	128	19.1	Arcadia (town) Wayne County
54	25.7	Spring Valley (village) Rockland County	128	19.1	Arlington (CDP) Dutchess County
55	25.6	Norwich (city) Chenango County	128	19.1	Delhi (village) Delaware County
56	25.5	Wilna (town) Jefferson County	128	19.1	Fredonia (village) Chautauqua County
57	25.3	Plattsburgh (city) Clinton County	132	19.0	Arcade (town) Wyoming County
58	25.2	Minden (town) Montgomery County	132	19.0	Milo (town) Yates County
59	25.1	Hudson (city) Columbia County	134	18.9	Canton (town) Saint Lawrence County
60	25.0	Dunkirk (city) Chautauqua County	134	18.9	East Rochester (town/village) Monroe County
61	24.9	Hudson Falls (village) Washington County	134	18.9	Pomfret (town) Chautauqua County
61	24.9	Ramapo (town) Rockland County	137	18.8	German Flatts (town) Herkimer County
61	24.9	Whitehall (town) Washington County	137	18.8	Johnson City (village) Broome County
64	24.5	Walton (town) Delaware County	137	18.8	Sweden (town) Monroe County
65	24.4	Lackawanna (city) Erie County	140	18.7	Bath (village) Steuben County
66	24.2	Thompson (town) Sullivan County	140	18.7	Norfolk (town) Saint Lawrence County
67	24.1	Geneva (city) Ontario County	140	18.7	Portland (town) Chautauqua County
67	24.1	Poughkeepsie (city) Dutchess County	143	18.6	Kingston (city) Ulster County
67	24.1	Warsaw (village) Wyoming County	143	18.6	Rome (city) Oneida County
70	24.0	Cortland (city) Cortland County	143	18.6	Sleepy Hollow (village) Westchester County
71	23.7	Olean (city) Cattaraugus County	143	18.6	Waverly (village) Tioga County
72	23.5	Ogdensburg (city) Saint Lawrence County	147	18.5	Kingsbury (town) Washington County
73	23.4	Liberty (village) Sullivan County	148	18.4	Franklinville (town) Cattaraugus County
74	23.2	Brooklyn (borough) Kings County	149	18.3	Hannibal (town) Oswego County
74	23.2	Lyons (village) Wayne County	150	18.2	New York Mills (village) Oneida County

Note: This section ranks incorporated places and CDPs (Census Designated Places) with populations of 2,500 or more. Unincorporated postal areas were not considered. Please refer to the User Guide for additional information.

Poverty Rate

Top 150 Places Ranked in *Ascending* Order

State Rank	Percent	Place
1	0.0	**Stony Brook University** (CDP) Suffolk County
2	0.4	**Herricks** (CDP) Nassau County
3	0.5	**Wanakah** (CDP) Erie County
4	0.6	**Great Neck Estates** (village) Nassau County
5	0.8	**Searingtown** (CDP) Nassau County
6	0.9	**Manhasset Hills** (CDP) Nassau County
6	0.9	**Sands Point** (village) Nassau County
6	0.9	**Spackenkill** (CDP) Dutchess County
9	1.1	**Jefferson Valley-Yorktown** (CDP) Westchester County
9	1.1	**Shelter Island** (town) Suffolk County
11	1.3	**Glenwood Landing** (CDP) Nassau County
12	1.4	**Tappan** (CDP) Rockland County
13	1.5	**Massapequa** (CDP) Nassau County
13	1.5	**North Hills** (village) Nassau County
15	1.6	**Ardsley** (village) Westchester County
15	1.6	**Cold Spring Harbor** (CDP) Suffolk County
15	1.6	**Lawrence** (village) Nassau County
15	1.6	**Tuxedo** (town) Orange County
15	1.6	**Valhalla** (CDP) Westchester County
15	1.6	**West Hills** (CDP) Suffolk County
21	1.7	**Brightwaters** (village) Suffolk County
21	1.7	**Halesite** (CDP) Suffolk County
21	1.7	**Montebello** (village) Rockland County
21	1.7	**North Boston** (CDP) Erie County
25	1.9	**Armonk** (CDP) Westchester County
25	1.9	**Bellmore** (CDP) Nassau County
25	1.9	**Glen Head** (CDP) Nassau County
25	1.9	**Poestenkill** (town) Rensselaer County
29	2.0	**North Castle** (town) Westchester County
30	2.1	**Bardonia** (CDP) Rockland County
30	2.1	**Brookville** (village) Nassau County
30	2.1	**Brunswick** (town) Rensselaer County
30	2.1	**East Williston** (village) Nassau County
30	2.1	**Fleming** (town) Cayuga County
30	2.1	**Lido Beach** (CDP) Nassau County
30	2.1	**Pleasantville** (village) Westchester County
30	2.1	**Union Vale** (town) Dutchess County
38	2.2	**Briarcliff Manor** (village) Westchester County
38	2.2	**Malverne** (village) Nassau County
38	2.2	**West Elmira** (CDP) Chemung County
38	2.2	**Yorktown** (town) Westchester County
42	2.3	**Lewisboro** (town) Westchester County
42	2.3	**Richmond** (town) Ontario County
42	2.3	**Scarsdale** (town/village) Westchester County
42	2.3	**Somers** (town) Westchester County
42	2.3	**Victor** (town) Ontario County
47	2.4	**Gardnertown** (CDP) Orange County
47	2.4	**Massapequa Park** (village) Nassau County
47	2.4	**North Merrick** (CDP) Nassau County
47	2.4	**North Wantagh** (CDP) Nassau County
47	2.4	**Orchard Park** (town) Erie County
47	2.4	**Port Washington North** (village) Nassau County
47	2.4	**Sand Lake** (town) Rensselaer County
47	2.4	**Sayville** (CDP) Suffolk County
47	2.4	**South Hempstead** (CDP) Nassau County
47	2.4	**West Bay Shore** (CDP) Suffolk County
47	2.4	**West Sand Lake** (CDP) Rensselaer County
58	2.5	**Center Moriches** (CDP) Suffolk County
58	2.5	**Clifton Park** (town) Saratoga County
58	2.5	**New Castle** (town) Westchester County
58	2.5	**Orchard Park** (village) Erie County
58	2.5	**Setauket-East Setauket** (CDP) Suffolk County
58	2.5	**Wantagh** (CDP) Nassau County
64	2.6	**Dix Hills** (CDP) Suffolk County
64	2.6	**Florida** (village) Orange County
64	2.6	**Munsey Park** (village) Nassau County
64	2.6	**Owasco** (town) Cayuga County
64	2.6	**Walworth** (town) Wayne County
69	2.7	**East Greenbush** (CDP) Rensselaer County
69	2.7	**Floral Park** (village) Nassau County
69	2.7	**Holbrook** (CDP) Suffolk County
69	2.7	**Irvington** (village) Westchester County
69	2.7	**Minoa** (village) Onondaga County
69	2.7	**Northport** (village) Suffolk County
69	2.7	**Plainedge** (CDP) Nassau County
69	2.7	**West Sayville** (CDP) Suffolk County
77	2.8	**Albertson** (CDP) Nassau County
77	2.8	**Bethpage** (CDP) Nassau County
77	2.8	**Eastchester** (CDP) Westchester County
77	2.8	**Old Bethpage** (CDP) Nassau County
77	2.8	**Pelham** (town) Westchester County
77	2.8	**Pelham Manor** (village) Westchester County
77	2.8	**Plainview** (CDP) Nassau County
77	2.8	**Sennett** (town) Cayuga County
77	2.8	**West Nyack** (CDP) Rockland County
86	2.9	**Charlton** (town) Saratoga County
86	2.9	**Elma** (town) Erie County
86	2.9	**Fairport** (village) Monroe County
86	2.9	**Greenwood Lake** (village) Orange County
86	2.9	**Pelham** (village) Westchester County
86	2.9	**Putnam Lake** (CDP) Putnam County
86	2.9	**Seaford** (CDP) Nassau County
93	3.0	**Bronxville** (village) Westchester County
93	3.0	**Hawthorne** (CDP) Westchester County
93	3.0	**Levittown** (CDP) Nassau County
93	3.0	**Nesconset** (CDP) Suffolk County
97	3.1	**Croton-on-Hudson** (village) Westchester County
97	3.1	**East Quogue** (CDP) Suffolk County
97	3.1	**East Shoreham** (CDP) Suffolk County
97	3.1	**Garden City Park** (CDP) Nassau County
97	3.1	**Milton** (CDP) Saratoga County
97	3.1	**Pompey** (town) Onondaga County
97	3.1	**Thornwood** (CDP) Westchester County
97	3.1	**Wynantskill** (CDP) Rensselaer County
105	3.2	**Carmel** (town) Putnam County
105	3.2	**Centerport** (CDP) Suffolk County
105	3.2	**East Fishkill** (town) Dutchess County
105	3.2	**East Rockaway** (village) Nassau County
105	3.2	**Eastchester** (town) Westchester County
105	3.2	**Lakeland** (CDP) Onondaga County
105	3.2	**New Hempstead** (village) Rockland County
105	3.2	**Old Westbury** (village) Nassau County
113	3.3	**Cutchogue** (CDP) Suffolk County
113	3.3	**Elma Center** (CDP) Erie County
113	3.3	**Harris Hill** (CDP) Erie County
113	3.3	**Lloyd Harbor** (village) Suffolk County
113	3.3	**Malta** (town) Saratoga County
113	3.3	**Mattituck** (CDP) Suffolk County
113	3.3	**Merrick** (CDP) Nassau County
113	3.3	**Oakdale** (CDP) Suffolk County
113	3.3	**Pendleton** (town) Niagara County
113	3.3	**Voorheesville** (village) Albany County
123	3.4	**Elmira** (town) Chemung County
123	3.4	**Muttontown** (village) Nassau County
123	3.4	**Pound Ridge** (town) Westchester County
126	3.5	**Cambria** (town) Niagara County
126	3.5	**Commack** (CDP) Suffolk County
126	3.5	**Cornwall-on-Hudson** (village) Orange County
126	3.5	**Hauppauge** (CDP) Suffolk County
126	3.5	**Port Washington** (CDP) Nassau County
126	3.5	**South Farmingdale** (CDP) Nassau County
132	3.6	**Boston** (town) Erie County
132	3.6	**Islandia** (village) Suffolk County
132	3.6	**Locust Valley** (CDP) Nassau County
132	3.6	**Myers Corner** (CDP) Dutchess County
132	3.6	**Oyster Bay** (CDP) Nassau County
132	3.6	**Rye** (city) Westchester County
132	3.6	**Skaneateles** (town) Onondaga County
132	3.6	**Smithtown** (CDP) Suffolk County
140	3.7	**New Hyde Park** (village) Nassau County
140	3.7	**Oyster Bay** (town) Nassau County
142	3.8	**North New Hyde Park** (CDP) Nassau County
142	3.8	**Smithtown** (town) Suffolk County
142	3.8	**Wading River** (CDP) Suffolk County
145	3.9	**Garden City** (village) Nassau County
145	3.9	**Newstead** (town) Erie County
145	3.9	**Pittsford** (village) Monroe County
145	3.9	**Village Green** (CDP) Onondaga County
145	3.9	**West Point** (CDP) Orange County
145	3.9	**Williston Park** (village) Nassau County

Note: *This section ranks incorporated places and CDPs (Census Designated Places) with populations of 2,500 or more. Unincorporated postal areas were not considered. Please refer to the User Guide for additional information.*

Educational Attainment: High School Diploma or Higher

Top 150 Places Ranked in *Descending* Order

State Rank	Percent	Place	State Rank	Percent	Place
1	100.0	**Binghamton University** (CDP) Broome County	75	96.8	**Clifton Park** (town) Saratoga County
1	100.0	**University at Buffalo** (CDP) Erie County	75	96.8	**Conesus Lake** (CDP) Livingston County
3	99.5	**Watchtower** (CDP) Ulster County	75	96.8	**Guilderland** (town) Albany County
4	99.4	**Alfred** (village) Allegany County	75	96.8	**Lewiston** (village) Niagara County
4	99.4	**Halesite** (CDP) Suffolk County	75	96.8	**Massapequa Park** (village) Nassau County
6	99.3	**North Boston** (CDP) Erie County	75	96.8	**Merrick** (CDP) Nassau County
7	99.2	**Horseheads North** (CDP) Chemung County	75	96.8	**Port Washington North** (village) Nassau County
7	99.2	**Milton** (CDP) Saratoga County	75	96.8	**Walworth** (town) Wayne County
9	99.1	**West Elmira** (CDP) Chemung County	84	96.7	**Bethlehem** (town) Albany County
10	99.0	**East Williston** (village) Nassau County	84	96.7	**Big Flats** (CDP) Chemung County
10	99.0	**Shelter Island** (town) Suffolk County	84	96.7	**Elma** (town) Erie County
12	98.9	**West Point** (CDP) Orange County	84	96.7	**Ithaca** (town) Tompkins County
13	98.8	**Scarsdale** (town/village) Westchester County	84	96.7	**Lake Erie Beach** (CDP) Erie County
14	98.7	**Bronxville** (village) Westchester County	84	96.7	**Manlius** (village) Onondaga County
14	98.7	**North Hills** (village) Nassau County	84	96.7	**Montrose** (CDP) Westchester County
16	98.6	**Brightwaters** (village) Suffolk County	84	96.7	**West Nyack** (CDP) Rockland County
16	98.6	**Lansing** (village) Tompkins County	92	96.6	**East Quogue** (CDP) Suffolk County
18	98.5	**Orchard Park** (village) Erie County	92	96.6	**Hewlett** (CDP) Nassau County
18	98.5	**Skaneateles** (village) Onondaga County	92	96.6	**Huntington** (CDP) Suffolk County
20	98.4	**East Hills** (village) Nassau County	92	96.6	**Roslyn** (village) Nassau County
21	98.3	**Great Neck Estates** (village) Nassau County	96	96.5	**Berne** (town) Albany County
21	98.3	**Lloyd Harbor** (village) Suffolk County	96	96.5	**Cambria** (town) Niagara County
21	98.3	**Minoa** (village) Onondaga County	96	96.5	**Cornwall** (town) Orange County
21	98.3	**Port Jefferson** (village) Suffolk County	96	96.5	**North Castle** (town) Westchester County
21	98.3	**Pound Ridge** (town) Westchester County	96	96.5	**Spackenkill** (CDP) Dutchess County
21	98.3	**Skaneateles** (town) Onondaga County	96	96.5	**West Bay Shore** (CDP) Suffolk County
27	98.2	**Glenwood Landing** (CDP) Nassau County	102	96.4	**East Glenville** (CDP) Schenectady County
27	98.2	**Larchmont** (village) Westchester County	102	96.4	**East Norwich** (CDP) Nassau County
29	98.1	**Lewisboro** (town) Westchester County	102	96.4	**Honeoye Falls** (village) Monroe County
30	98.0	**Cold Spring Harbor** (CDP) Suffolk County	102	96.4	**Lido Beach** (CDP) Nassau County
30	98.0	**Fort Salonga** (CDP) Suffolk County	102	96.4	**Marilla** (town) Erie County
30	98.0	**Munsey Park** (village) Nassau County	102	96.4	**Philipstown** (town) Putnam County
30	98.0	**Northwest Harbor** (CDP) Suffolk County	108	96.3	**Ballston** (town) Saratoga County
30	98.0	**Pittsford** (town) Monroe County	108	96.3	**Clarence** (town) Erie County
30	98.0	**South Hill** (CDP) Tompkins County	108	96.3	**Elma Center** (CDP) Erie County
36	97.9	**Brookville** (village) Nassau County	108	96.3	**Greenville** (CDP) Westchester County
36	97.9	**Harris Hill** (CDP) Erie County	108	96.3	**Woodstock** (town) Ulster County
36	97.9	**Northeast Ithaca** (CDP) Tompkins County	113	96.2	**Alden** (village) Erie County
36	97.9	**Voorheesville** (village) Albany County	113	96.2	**Ballston Spa** (village) Saratoga County
40	97.8	**Marcellus** (town) Onondaga County	113	96.2	**Catskill** (village) Greene County
40	97.8	**New Castle** (town) Westchester County	113	96.2	**Danby** (town) Tompkins County
42	97.6	**Centerport** (CDP) Suffolk County	113	96.2	**East Rockaway** (village) Nassau County
42	97.6	**Lawrence** (village) Nassau County	113	96.2	**Fredonia** (village) Chautauqua County
42	97.6	**Pelham Manor** (village) Westchester County	113	96.2	**LaFayette** (town) Onondaga County
42	97.6	**Stony Brook** (CDP) Suffolk County	113	96.2	**Old Bethpage** (CDP) Nassau County
46	97.5	**Armonk** (CDP) Westchester County	113	96.2	**West Hills** (CDP) Suffolk County
46	97.5	**Blue Point** (CDP) Suffolk County	122	96.1	**Hauppauge** (CDP) Suffolk County
46	97.5	**Cayuga Heights** (village) Tompkins County	122	96.1	**Lansing** (town) Tompkins County
49	97.4	**Alfred** (town) Allegany County	122	96.1	**Niskayuna** (town) Schenectady County
49	97.4	**Garden City** (village) Nassau County	122	96.1	**Rockville Centre** (village) Nassau County
49	97.4	**Mendon** (town) Monroe County	126	96.0	**East Greenbush** (town) Rensselaer County
49	97.4	**Miller Place** (CDP) Suffolk County	126	96.0	**Manorville** (CDP) Suffolk County
49	97.4	**Old Westbury** (village) Nassau County	126	96.0	**Melville** (CDP) Suffolk County
49	97.4	**Ulysses** (town) Tompkins County	126	96.0	**Wantagh** (CDP) Nassau County
55	97.2	**Red Oaks Mill** (CDP) Dutchess County	126	96.0	**Westmere** (CDP) Albany County
56	97.1	**Elmira** (town) Chemung County	131	95.9	**Firthcliffe** (CDP) Orange County
56	97.1	**Fayetteville** (village) Onondaga County	131	95.9	**Massapequa** (CDP) Nassau County
56	97.1	**Hastings-on-Hudson** (village) Westchester County	131	95.9	**Orchard Park** (town) Erie County
56	97.1	**Northport** (village) Suffolk County	131	95.9	**Sweden** (town) Monroe County
56	97.1	**Rush** (town) Monroe County	131	95.9	**Thomaston** (village) Nassau County
56	97.1	**Sea Cliff** (village) Nassau County	131	95.9	**Victor** (village) Ontario County
56	97.1	**Williamsville** (village) Erie County	137	95.8	**Babylon** (village) Suffolk County
63	97.0	**Boston** (town) Erie County	137	95.8	**Floral Park** (village) Nassau County
63	97.0	**East Greenbush** (CDP) Rensselaer County	137	95.8	**Hamburg** (village) Erie County
63	97.0	**Pompey** (town) Onondaga County	140	95.7	**Commack** (CDP) Suffolk County
63	97.0	**Rye** (city) Westchester County	140	95.7	**Irvington** (village) Westchester County
63	97.0	**Setauket-East Setauket** (CDP) Suffolk County	140	95.7	**Plainview** (CDP) Nassau County
63	97.0	**Southold** (CDP) Suffolk County	140	95.7	**Somers** (town) Westchester County
63	97.0	**Westvale** (CDP) Onondaga County	144	95.6	**Bardonia** (CDP) Rockland County
70	96.9	**Malta** (town) Saratoga County	144	95.6	**Delaware** (town) Sullivan County
70	96.9	**Manlius** (town) Onondaga County	144	95.6	**East Moriches** (CDP) Suffolk County
70	96.9	**Perinton** (town) Monroe County	144	95.6	**Fort Drum** (CDP) Jefferson County
70	96.9	**South Nyack** (village) Rockland County	144	95.6	**Grand Island** (town) Erie County
70	96.9	**Victor** (town) Ontario County	144	95.6	**Malverne** (village) Nassau County
75	96.8	**Cazenovia** (town) Madison County	144	95.6	**Scotia** (village) Schenectady County

Note: *This section ranks incorporated places and CDPs (Census Designated Places) with populations of 2,500 or more. Unincorporated postal areas were not considered. Please refer to the User Guide for additional information.*

Educational Attainment: High School Diploma or Higher

Top 150 Places Ranked in *Ascending* Order

State Rank	Percent	Place
1	41.2	**SUNY Oswego** (CDP) Oswego County
2	61.9	**Flanders** (CDP) Suffolk County
3	63.2	**South Fallsburg** (CDP) Sullivan County
4	64.0	**Kiryas Joel** (village) Orange County
5	65.7	**Romulus** (town) Seneca County
6	68.3	**Port Chester** (village) Westchester County
7	69.3	**Spring Valley** (village) Rockland County
8	70.0	**New Cassel** (CDP) Nassau County
9	70.1	**Newburgh** (city) Orange County
10	70.6	**Bronx** (borough) Bronx County
10	70.6	**Dannemora** (village) Clinton County
10	70.6	**New Square** (village) Rockland County
13	70.8	**Brentwood** (CDP) Suffolk County
14	70.9	**Riverside** (CDP) Suffolk County
15	71.0	**Central Islip** (CDP) Suffolk County
16	71.2	**Hempstead** (village) Nassau County
17	72.1	**Ossining** (village) Westchester County
18	72.2	**North Bay Shore** (CDP) Suffolk County
19	73.0	**Dannemora** (town) Clinton County
20	73.1	**Bedford Hills** (CDP) Westchester County
21	74.0	**Haverstraw** (village) Rockland County
22	74.5	**Coxsackie** (town) Greene County
23	74.6	**Mount Morris** (town) Livingston County
24	74.8	**Albion** (town) Orleans County
25	75.2	**Albion** (village) Orleans County
26	75.4	**Inwood** (CDP) Nassau County
27	75.8	**Sleepy Hollow** (village) Westchester County
28	76.0	**Altona** (town) Clinton County
28	76.0	**Roosevelt** (CDP) Nassau County
30	76.1	**North Amityville** (CDP) Suffolk County
31	76.3	**Walton** (village) Delaware County
32	76.4	**Kaser** (village) Rockland County
33	76.7	**Minden** (town) Montgomery County
33	76.7	**Rye** (town) Westchester County
35	77.2	**Wyandanch** (CDP) Suffolk County
36	77.3	**Benton** (town) Yates County
37	77.6	**Huntington Station** (CDP) Suffolk County
38	78.0	**Malone** (town) Franklin County
39	78.5	**Monsey** (CDP) Rockland County
40	78.6	**Uniondale** (CDP) Nassau County
41	79.1	**Utica** (city) Oneida County
42	79.3	**Brooklyn** (borough) Kings County
42	79.3	**Walton** (town) Delaware County
42	79.3	**Warsaw** (village) Wyoming County
45	79.4	**North Bellport** (CDP) Suffolk County
46	79.6	**Attica** (town) Wyoming County
46	79.6	**Poughkeepsie** (city) Dutchess County
48	79.7	**New Berlin** (town) Chenango County
49	79.8	**Copiague** (CDP) Suffolk County
49	79.8	**Ellenville** (village) Ulster County
49	79.8	**Fallsburg** (town) Sullivan County
52	79.9	**Liberty** (village) Sullivan County
53	80.0	**Monticello** (village) Sullivan County
53	80.0	**Ossining** (town) Westchester County
53	80.0	**West Haverstraw** (village) Rockland County
56	80.1	**Amsterdam** (city) Montgomery County
56	80.1	**Collins** (town) Erie County
56	80.1	**Groveland** (town) Livingston County
59	80.2	**Syracuse** (city) Onondaga County
60	80.3	**Glen Cove** (city) Nassau County
60	80.3	**New York** (city)
62	80.4	**Portland** (town) Chautauqua County
62	80.4	**Queens** (borough) Queens County
64	80.5	**Rochester** (city) Monroe County
65	80.7	**Gloversville** (city) Fulton County
65	80.7	**Hudson** (city) Columbia County
67	80.8	**Peekskill** (city) Westchester County
68	81.1	**Dansville** (village) Livingston County
69	81.2	**Fort Ann** (town) Washington County
69	81.2	**Freeport** (village) Nassau County
69	81.2	**Malone** (village) Franklin County
72	81.6	**Claverack** (town) Columbia County
72	81.6	**Colesville** (town) Broome County
74	81.7	**Gouverneur** (town) Saint Lawrence County
75	82.0	**Gordon Heights** (CDP) Suffolk County
75	82.0	**Liberty** (town) Sullivan County
75	82.0	**Wappingers Falls** (village) Dutchess County
78	82.1	**Annsville** (town) Oneida County
78	82.1	**Galen** (town) Wayne County
78	82.1	**Yorkshire** (town) Cattaraugus County
81	82.2	**Mount Kisco** (town/village) Westchester County
82	82.4	**Lakeview** (CDP) Nassau County
83	82.6	**Galeville** (CDP) Onondaga County
83	82.6	**Haverstraw** (town) Rockland County
83	82.6	**North Dansville** (town) Livingston County
86	82.7	**Buffalo** (city) Erie County
86	82.7	**Marcy** (town) Oneida County
88	82.8	**Elmira** (city) Chemung County
88	82.8	**Fairview** (CDP) Westchester County
88	82.8	**Scriba** (town) Oswego County
91	82.9	**New Rochelle** (city) Westchester County
92	83.0	**Middletown** (city) Orange County
92	83.0	**Yonkers** (city) Westchester County
94	83.1	**Bay Shore** (CDP) Suffolk County
94	83.1	**Coxsackie** (village) Greene County
94	83.1	**Ramapo** (town) Rockland County
94	83.1	**Warrensburg** (CDP) Warren County
98	83.2	**Gowanda** (village) Cattaraugus County
98	83.2	**Lackawanna** (city) Erie County
98	83.2	**Palatine** (town) Montgomery County
98	83.2	**Port Jervis** (city) Orange County
102	83.3	**Elmsford** (village) Westchester County
102	83.3	**Warsaw** (town) Wyoming County
104	83.5	**Livingston** (town) Columbia County
104	83.5	**Saint Johnsville** (town) Montgomery County
106	83.7	**Au Sable** (town) Clinton County
106	83.7	**Granby** (town) Oswego County
106	83.7	**Moravia** (town) Cayuga County
109	83.8	**Fulton** (city) Oswego County
109	83.8	**Wawarsing** (town) Ulster County
111	83.9	**Bethel** (town) Sullivan County
111	83.9	**Kirkwood** (town) Broome County
111	83.9	**Monroe** (town) Orange County
111	83.9	**Salamanca** (city) Cattaraugus County
115	84.0	**Cape Vincent** (town) Jefferson County
115	84.0	**Ogdensburg** (city) Saint Lawrence County
117	84.1	**Oswegatchie** (town) Saint Lawrence County
118	84.2	**Hillcrest** (CDP) Rockland County
118	84.2	**Wilna** (town) Jefferson County
120	84.3	**Schenectady** (city) Schenectady County
120	84.3	**Yates** (town) Orleans County
122	84.4	**Auburn** (city) Cayuga County
122	84.4	**Binghamton** (city) Broome County
122	84.4	**Richland** (town) Oswego County
125	84.5	**Athens** (town) Greene County
125	84.5	**Kingston** (city) Ulster County
125	84.5	**Mount Morris** (village) Livingston County
125	84.5	**Riverhead** (CDP) Suffolk County
125	84.5	**Rose** (town) Wayne County
130	84.6	**Gates** (CDP) Monroe County
130	84.6	**Lyons** (village) Wayne County
130	84.6	**Mount Vernon** (city) Westchester County
130	84.6	**Newark** (village) Wayne County
130	84.6	**Oakfield** (town) Genesee County
135	84.7	**Manchester** (town) Ontario County
135	84.7	**North Gates** (CDP) Monroe County
135	84.7	**Thompson** (town) Sullivan County
135	84.7	**Troy** (city) Rensselaer County
139	84.8	**Mooers** (town) Clinton County
139	84.8	**Schuyler Falls** (town) Clinton County
141	84.9	**Vienna** (town) Oneida County
142	85.0	**Afton** (town) Chenango County
142	85.0	**Middleburgh** (town) Schoharie County
142	85.0	**Wolcott** (town) Wayne County
145	85.1	**Champlain** (town) Clinton County
145	85.1	**Norwich** (city) Chenango County
145	85.1	**Tupper Lake** (town) Franklin County
148	85.2	**Otego** (town) Otsego County
148	85.2	**Saint Regis Mohawk Reservation** (reservation) Franklin County
150	85.3	**Carthage** (village) Jefferson County

Note: *This section ranks incorporated places and CDPs (Census Designated Places) with populations of 2,500 or more. Unincorporated postal areas were not considered. Please refer to the User Guide for additional information.*

Educational Attainment: Bachelor's Degree or Higher

Top 150 Places Ranked in *Descending* Order

State Rank	Percent	Place
1	87.3	**Cayuga Heights** (village) Tompkins County
2	87.0	**Scarsdale** (town/village) Westchester County
3	84.0	**New Castle** (town) Westchester County
4	83.9	**Larchmont** (village) Westchester County
5	81.5	**Munsey Park** (village) Nassau County
6	81.4	**Alfred** (village) Allegany County
7	81.3	**Bronxville** (village) Westchester County
8	80.9	**Greenville** (CDP) Westchester County
9	79.6	**Northeast Ithaca** (CDP) Tompkins County
10	77.2	**East Hills** (village) Nassau County
11	77.0	**Lawrence** (village) Nassau County
12	76.7	**University at Buffalo** (CDP) Erie County
13	76.2	**Brookville** (village) Nassau County
14	76.0	**Lloyd Harbor** (village) Suffolk County
14	76.0	**Sands Point** (village) Nassau County
16	75.0	**Armonk** (CDP) Westchester County
17	74.4	**Lewisboro** (town) Westchester County
18	74.3	**Great Neck Estates** (village) Nassau County
18	74.3	**Hastings-on-Hudson** (village) Westchester County
20	74.0	**Rye** (city) Westchester County
21	73.7	**Flower Hill** (village) Nassau County
22	73.3	**Pound Ridge** (town) Westchester County
23	73.1	**Pittsford** (town) Monroe County
24	72.3	**Pelham Manor** (village) Westchester County
25	72.1	**Old Westbury** (village) Nassau County
26	71.3	**Irvington** (village) Westchester County
27	71.0	**Cold Spring Harbor** (CDP) Suffolk County
28	70.5	**Lansing** (village) Tompkins County
29	70.4	**Briarcliff Manor** (village) Westchester County
30	70.0	**Ithaca** (town) Tompkins County
31	69.8	**Muttontown** (village) Nassau County
31	69.8	**University Gardens** (CDP) Nassau County
33	69.3	**North Castle** (town) Westchester County
34	68.6	**West Point** (CDP) Orange County
35	68.5	**Garden City** (village) Nassau County
36	68.2	**Ardsley** (village) Westchester County
37	67.9	**Roslyn** (village) Nassau County
38	67.6	**Piermont** (village) Rockland County
39	67.3	**Jericho** (CDP) Nassau County
39	67.3	**New Paltz** (village) Ulster County
41	67.2	**Rye Brook** (village) Westchester County
41	67.2	**Thomaston** (village) Nassau County
43	67.1	**Skaneateles** (village) Onondaga County
44	67.0	**East Williston** (village) Nassau County
44	67.0	**Port Washington North** (village) Nassau County
46	66.5	**Mamaroneck** (town) Westchester County
46	66.5	**Sea Cliff** (village) Nassau County
48	66.3	**Lido Beach** (CDP) Nassau County
49	66.0	**Northport** (village) Suffolk County
50	65.7	**North Hills** (village) Nassau County
51	64.8	**Glenwood Landing** (CDP) Nassau County
52	64.6	**Stony Brook** (CDP) Suffolk County
53	64.1	**Port Washington** (CDP) Nassau County
54	63.7	**Syosset** (CDP) Nassau County
54	63.7	**Woodmere** (CDP) Nassau County
56	63.5	**Woodbury** (CDP) Nassau County
57	63.1	**Huntington** (CDP) Suffolk County
58	62.9	**Ithaca** (city) Tompkins County
59	62.8	**Lake Success** (village) Nassau County
59	62.8	**Pelham** (town) Westchester County
61	62.4	**Manhasset Hills** (CDP) Nassau County
62	62.3	**Alfred** (village) Allegany County
63	62.2	**Montebello** (village) Rockland County
64	62.0	**Hartsdale** (CDP) Westchester County
65	61.9	**Brighton** (CDP) Monroe County
66	61.8	**Hamilton** (village) Madison County
66	61.8	**Roslyn Heights** (CDP) Nassau County
68	61.3	**Port Jefferson** (village) Suffolk County
69	61.2	**Greenburgh** (town) Westchester County
70	61.1	**Lansing** (town) Tompkins County
71	61.0	**Plainview** (CDP) Nassau County
71	61.0	**Searingtown** (CDP) Nassau County
73	60.9	**Croton-on-Hudson** (village) Westchester County
74	60.5	**Centerport** (CDP) Suffolk County
74	60.5	**Mendon** (town) Monroe County
76	60.0	**South Nyack** (village) Rockland County
77	59.9	**Manhattan** (borough) New York County
78	59.7	**Great Neck Plaza** (village) Nassau County
78	59.7	**Manlius** (village) Onondaga County
80	59.6	**Old Bethpage** (CDP) Nassau County
81	59.5	**Rockville Centre** (village) Nassau County
82	59.3	**Setauket-East Setauket** (CDP) Suffolk County
83	59.2	**Orchard Park** (village) Erie County
84	59.1	**Eastchester** (town) Westchester County
85	58.9	**Wesley Hills** (village) Rockland County
86	58.7	**Niskayuna** (town) Schenectady County
86	58.7	**North Salem** (town) Westchester County
88	58.6	**Dix Hills** (CDP) Suffolk County
89	58.3	**East Norwich** (CDP) Nassau County
90	58.1	**Woodstock** (town) Ulster County
91	57.9	**Bedford** (town) Westchester County
91	57.9	**Merrick** (CDP) Nassau County
93	57.7	**New City** (CDP) Rockland County
93	57.7	**Pleasantville** (village) Westchester County
95	57.5	**Bardonia** (CDP) Rockland County
96	57.4	**South Hill** (CDP) Tompkins County
97	57.3	**Brightwaters** (village) Suffolk County
97	57.3	**New Paltz** (town) Ulster County
99	57.1	**Williamsville** (village) Erie County
100	56.9	**Dobbs Ferry** (village) Westchester County
100	56.9	**West Hills** (CDP) Suffolk County
102	56.6	**Clifton Park** (town) Saratoga County
102	56.6	**Manhasset** (CDP) Nassau County
104	56.4	**Shelter Island** (town) Suffolk County
105	56.3	**Bethlehem** (town) Albany County
105	56.3	**Fayetteville** (village) Onondaga County
105	56.3	**Northwest Harbor** (CDP) Suffolk County
105	56.3	**Skaneateles** (town) Onondaga County
109	55.8	**Somers** (town) Westchester County
110	55.7	**Spackenkill** (CDP) Dutchess County
110	55.7	**Tarrytown** (village) Westchester County
112	55.6	**Stony Brook University** (CDP) Suffolk County
113	55.4	**Eastchester** (CDP) Westchester County
113	55.4	**Pelham** (village) Westchester County
115	55.0	**Great Neck** (village) Nassau County
116	54.9	**Perinton** (town) Monroe County
117	54.8	**Melville** (CDP) Suffolk County
118	54.7	**Hewlett** (CDP) Nassau County
119	54.6	**Potsdam** (village) Saint Lawrence County
120	54.4	**Herricks** (CDP) Nassau County
121	54.2	**East Garden City** (CDP) Nassau County
122	54.0	**Tappan** (CDP) Rockland County
123	53.7	**Halesite** (CDP) Suffolk County
124	53.5	**Menands** (village) Albany County
125	53.4	**Amherst** (town) Erie County
126	53.3	**Blauvelt** (CDP) Rockland County
127	53.1	**North Hempstead** (town) Nassau County
128	53.0	**Tuxedo** (town) Orange County
129	52.7	**Manlius** (town) Onondaga County
130	52.6	**Victor** (town) Ontario County
130	52.6	**Voorheesville** (village) Albany County
132	52.3	**Kings Point** (village) Nassau County
132	52.3	**Tuckahoe** (village) Westchester County
134	52.2	**Noyack** (CDP) Suffolk County
135	52.1	**Pomona** (village) Rockland County
136	52.0	**Caroline** (town) Tompkins County
137	51.9	**Eggertsville** (CDP) Erie County
137	51.9	**West Elmira** (CDP) Chemung County
139	51.5	**Glen Head** (CDP) Nassau County
140	51.3	**West Nyack** (CDP) Rockland County
141	51.2	**Penfield** (town) Monroe County
142	51.1	**Cornwall-on-Hudson** (village) Orange County
142	51.1	**Fairport** (village) Monroe County
144	51.0	**Gang Mills** (CDP) Steuben County
145	50.7	**Mount Pleasant** (town) Westchester County
145	50.7	**Valhalla** (CDP) Westchester County
147	50.6	**Orangetown** (town) Rockland County
148	50.5	**Heritage Hills** (CDP) Westchester County
148	50.5	**Yorktown** (town) Westchester County
150	50.4	**Nyack** (village) Rockland County

Note: *This section ranks incorporated places and CDPs (Census Designated Places) with populations of 2,500 or more. Unincorporated postal areas were not considered. Please refer to the User Guide for additional information.*

Educational Attainment: Bachelor's Degree or Higher

Top 150 Places Ranked in *Ascending* Order

State Rank	Percent	Place		State Rank	Percent	Place
1	2.5	**Kaser** (village) Rockland County		74	14.0	**Granville** (town) Washington County
2	4.1	**New Square** (village) Rockland County		74	14.0	**Manchester** (town) Ontario County
3	4.4	**Dannemora** (village) Clinton County		78	14.1	**Alexander** (town) Genesee County
4	4.9	**Riverside** (CDP) Suffolk County		78	14.1	**Lisle** (town) Broome County
5	6.9	**Dannemora** (town) Clinton County		78	14.1	**New York Mills** (village) Oneida County
6	7.9	**Kiryas Joel** (village) Orange County		78	14.1	**Nichols** (town) Tioga County
7	8.1	**Altona** (town) Clinton County		82	14.2	**Gloversville** (city) Fulton County
8	8.2	**Carthage** (village) Jefferson County		82	14.2	**Portland** (town) Chautauqua County
9	8.3	**Wilna** (town) Jefferson County		84	14.3	**Au Sable** (town) Clinton County
10	8.6	**Hannibal** (town) Oswego County		84	14.3	**Campbell** (town) Steuben County
11	8.9	**Palermo** (town) Oswego County		86	14.4	**Amsterdam** (city) Montgomery County
12	9.1	**Albion** (village) Orleans County		86	14.4	**Brookfield** (town) Madison County
13	9.3	**Attica** (town) Wyoming County		86	14.4	**Elmira Heights** (village) Chemung County
14	9.4	**Mount Morris** (town) Livingston County		86	14.4	**Galeville** (CDP) Onondaga County
14	9.4	**Romulus** (town) Seneca County		86	14.4	**Moriah** (town) Essex County
16	9.6	**Wolcott** (town) Wayne County		86	14.4	**South Glens Falls** (village) Saratoga County
17	9.9	**Sloan** (village) Erie County		92	14.5	**Wyandanch** (CDP) Suffolk County
18	10.3	**Albion** (town) Orleans County		93	14.6	**Fort Edward** (village) Washington County
18	10.3	**Vienna** (town) Oneida County		93	14.6	**Fulton** (city) Oswego County
20	10.7	**Cohocton** (town) Steuben County		95	14.7	**Constantia** (town) Oswego County
20	10.7	**Wayland** (town) Steuben County		95	14.7	**Corinth** (village) Saratoga County
22	10.8	**Watchtower** (CDP) Ulster County		97	14.8	**Benton** (town) Yates County
23	11.0	**Galen** (town) Wayne County		97	14.8	**Norfolk** (town) Saint Lawrence County
23	11.0	**Gouverneur** (town) Saint Lawrence County		99	14.9	**Hopewell** (town) Ontario County
25	11.1	**Afton** (town) Chenango County		100	15.0	**Colesville** (town) Broome County
26	11.2	**Lyons** (village) Wayne County		100	15.0	**Fort Edward** (town) Washington County
26	11.2	**Southport** (CDP) Chemung County		100	15.0	**Stockport** (town) Columbia County
28	11.3	**Warsaw** (village) Wyoming County		103	15.1	**Canisteo** (town) Steuben County
29	11.4	**Annsville** (town) Oneida County		103	15.1	**Lackawanna** (city) Erie County
29	11.4	**Hastings** (town) Oswego County		103	15.1	**Unadilla** (town) Otsego County
29	11.4	**Mattydale** (CDP) Onondaga County		106	15.2	**Cape Vincent** (town) Jefferson County
29	11.4	**North Bay Shore** (CDP) Suffolk County		106	15.2	**Clarendon** (town) Orleans County
33	11.5	**Blasdell** (village) Erie County		106	15.2	**Sandy Creek** (town) Oswego County
33	11.5	**Liberty** (village) Sullivan County		109	15.3	**Central Islip** (CDP) Suffolk County
33	11.5	**Mount Morris** (village) Livingston County		109	15.3	**Chemung** (town) Chemung County
33	11.5	**Whitehall** (town) Washington County		109	15.3	**Lyons** (town) Wayne County
37	11.6	**Warsaw** (town) Wyoming County		109	15.3	**New Haven** (town) Oswego County
38	11.7	**Newburgh** (city) Orange County		109	15.3	**Richland** (town) Oswego County
39	11.8	**Croghan** (town) Lewis County		109	15.3	**Somerset** (town) Niagara County
40	12.0	**Fort Ann** (town) Washington County		115	15.4	**Dunkirk** (city) Chautauqua County
40	12.0	**Tupper Lake** (village) Franklin County		115	15.4	**Monticello** (village) Sullivan County
40	12.0	**Walton** (village) Delaware County		115	15.4	**Newark** (village) Wayne County
43	12.2	**Denmark** (town) Lewis County		118	15.5	**Arcadia** (town) Wayne County
43	12.2	**Hancock** (town) Delaware County		118	15.5	**Rose** (town) Wayne County
43	12.2	**Niagara** (town) Niagara County		120	15.6	**Mexico** (town) Oswego County
46	12.3	**Gouverneur** (village) Saint Lawrence County		120	15.6	**Norwich** (town) Chenango County
46	12.3	**Waterloo** (town) Seneca County		120	15.6	**Oakfield** (town) Genesee County
48	12.5	**Groveland** (town) Livingston County		120	15.6	**Pembroke** (town) Genesee County
49	12.6	**Hudson Falls** (village) Washington County		124	15.7	**Malone** (town) Franklin County
49	12.6	**Moravia** (town) Cayuga County		125	15.8	**Barton** (town) Tioga County
51	12.7	**Roosevelt** (CDP) Nassau County		125	15.8	**Palatine** (town) Montgomery County
51	12.7	**Saint Johnsville** (town) Montgomery County		125	15.8	**Schoharie** (town) Schoharie County
53	12.8	**Collins** (town) Erie County		125	15.8	**Sheridan** (town) Chautauqua County
54	12.9	**Brentwood** (CDP) Suffolk County		129	15.9	**Kendall** (town) Orleans County
54	12.9	**Broadalbin** (town) Fulton County		129	15.9	**Ogdensburg** (city) Saint Lawrence County
54	12.9	**Whitehall** (village) Washington County		131	16.0	**Bath** (town) Steuben County
54	12.9	**Yorkshire** (town) Cattaraugus County		131	16.0	**Falconer** (village) Chautauqua County
58	13.0	**Salamanca** (city) Cattaraugus County		131	16.0	**Manheim** (town) Herkimer County
59	13.1	**Minden** (town) Montgomery County		131	16.0	**Ravena** (village) Albany County
59	13.1	**West Monroe** (town) Oswego County		135	16.1	**Coxsackie** (town) Greene County
61	13.3	**Hartland** (town) Niagara County		135	16.1	**Kingsbury** (town) Washington County
61	13.3	**Randolph** (town) Cattaraugus County		135	16.1	**Kirkwood** (town) Broome County
61	13.3	**Verona** (town) Oneida County		138	16.2	**Bath** (village) Steuben County
64	13.4	**New Berlin** (town) Chenango County		138	16.2	**Middleburgh** (town) Schoharie County
64	13.4	**New Bremen** (town) Lewis County		138	16.2	**Oxford** (town) Chenango County
66	13.5	**Mooers** (town) Clinton County		138	16.2	**Southport** (town) Chemung County
67	13.7	**Deerpark** (town) Orange County		142	16.3	**Canajoharie** (town) Montgomery County
67	13.7	**Murray** (town) Orleans County		142	16.3	**Gowanda** (village) Cattaraugus County
67	13.7	**Yates** (town) Orleans County		142	16.3	**Lake Luzerne** (town) Warren County
70	13.8	**Bangor** (town) Franklin County		142	16.3	**Mayfield** (town) Fulton County
70	13.8	**Mastic** (CDP) Suffolk County		142	16.3	**Shirley** (CDP) Suffolk County
72	13.9	**Mastic Beach** (village) Suffolk County		142	16.3	**Walton** (town) Delaware County
72	13.9	**South Fallsburg** (CDP) Sullivan County		148	16.4	**Palmyra** (village) Wayne County
74	14.0	**Dix** (town) Schuyler County		148	16.4	**Saint Regis Mohawk Reservation** (reservation) Franklin County
74	14.0	**Elmira** (city) Chemung County		148	16.4	**Sodus** (town) Wayne County

Note: *This section ranks incorporated places and CDPs (Census Designated Places) with populations of 2,500 or more. Unincorporated postal areas were not considered. Please refer to the User Guide for additional information.*

Educational Attainment: Graduate/Professional Degree or Higher

Top 150 Places Ranked in *Descending* Order

State Rank	Percent	Place	State Rank	Percent	Place
1	60.8	**Cayuga Heights** (village) Tompkins County	76	31.2	**Tarrytown** (village) Westchester County
2	56.5	**Scarsdale** (town/village) Westchester County	77	31.1	**Flower Hill** (village) Nassau County
3	54.1	**Greenville** (CDP) Westchester County	78	30.9	**Canton** (village) Saint Lawrence County
4	53.9	**Northeast Ithaca** (CDP) Tompkins County	78	30.9	**Plainview** (CDP) Nassau County
5	48.6	**Alfred** (village) Allegany County	80	30.8	**Glenwood Landing** (CDP) Nassau County
6	48.0	**New Castle** (town) Westchester County	81	30.7	**Dobbs Ferry** (village) Westchester County
7	47.8	**Bronxville** (village) Westchester County	82	30.6	**Huntington** (CDP) Suffolk County
8	47.3	**Great Neck Estates** (village) Nassau County	83	30.5	**Cornwall-on-Hudson** (village) Orange County
9	47.1	**Lansing** (village) Tompkins County	84	30.4	**Mendon** (town) Monroe County
10	45.0	**Hastings-on-Hudson** (village) Westchester County	85	30.3	**Halesite** (CDP) Suffolk County
11	44.2	**Ithaca** (town) Tompkins County	86	30.2	**Eastchester** (town) Westchester County
11	44.2	**Larchmont** (village) Westchester County	87	30.1	**Pelham** (village) Westchester County
13	44.0	**Lawrence** (village) Nassau County	88	30.0	**Gang Mills** (CDP) Steuben County
14	42.7	**Lloyd Harbor** (village) Suffolk County	88	30.0	**Rockville Centre** (village) Nassau County
15	42.4	**East Hills** (village) Nassau County	90	29.9	**Great Neck Plaza** (village) Nassau County
16	42.3	**Port Jefferson** (village) Suffolk County	90	29.9	**Manhasset** (CDP) Nassau County
17	41.8	**Hamilton** (village) Madison County	90	29.9	**Syosset** (CDP) Nassau County
17	41.8	**Sands Point** (village) Nassau County	93	29.8	**New Paltz** (town) Ulster County
19	41.5	**Old Westbury** (village) Nassau County	94	29.7	**East Norwich** (CDP) Nassau County
20	41.0	**Irvington** (village) Westchester County	95	29.3	**Old Bethpage** (CDP) Nassau County
21	40.8	**Thomaston** (village) Nassau County	96	29.1	**Hamilton** (town) Madison County
22	40.4	**Alfred** (town) Allegany County	96	29.1	**Port Washington** (CDP) Nassau County
23	40.2	**Brookville** (village) Nassau County	98	29.0	**Woodstock** (town) Ulster County
24	39.9	**Munsey Park** (village) Nassau County	99	28.8	**Dix Hills** (CDP) Suffolk County
24	39.9	**Pittsford** (town) Monroe County	99	28.8	**West Hills** (CDP) Suffolk County
26	39.7	**Muttontown** (village) Nassau County	101	28.7	**Merrick** (CDP) Nassau County
27	39.4	**Pound Ridge** (town) Westchester County	102	28.6	**Shelter Island** (town) Suffolk County
28	39.1	**Briarcliff Manor** (village) Westchester County	103	28.4	**Manhattan** (borough) New York County
29	39.0	**West Point** (CDP) Orange County	104	28.3	**Hewlett** (CDP) Nassau County
30	38.1	**Stony Brook** (CDP) Suffolk County	105	28.2	**Caroline** (town) Tompkins County
31	38.0	**Ithaca** (city) Tompkins County	106	28.1	**Otsego** (town) Otsego County
32	37.8	**East Williston** (village) Nassau County	106	28.1	**Roslyn** (village) Nassau County
32	37.8	**Lewisboro** (town) Westchester County	106	28.1	**Williamsville** (village) Erie County
34	37.6	**Rye** (city) Westchester County	109	28.0	**Roslyn Heights** (CDP) Nassau County
35	37.3	**South Hill** (CDP) Tompkins County	110	27.9	**Eggertsville** (CDP) Erie County
36	37.1	**Pelham Manor** (village) Westchester County	111	27.8	**Amherst** (town) Erie County
37	36.6	**Ardsley** (village) Westchester County	111	27.8	**Bedford** (town) Westchester County
37	36.6	**Cold Spring Harbor** (CDP) Suffolk County	113	27.7	**Centerport** (CDP) Suffolk County
37	36.6	**Lido Beach** (CDP) Nassau County	114	27.6	**East Garden City** (CDP) Nassau County
40	36.5	**Armonk** (CDP) Westchester County	114	27.6	**Geneseo** (village) Livingston County
40	36.5	**New Paltz** (village) Ulster County	114	27.6	**Melville** (CDP) Suffolk County
42	36.0	**North Castle** (town) Westchester County	114	27.6	**New City** (CDP) Rockland County
43	35.8	**Woodmere** (CDP) Nassau County	114	27.6	**Tuckahoe** (village) Westchester County
44	35.5	**Lansing** (town) Tompkins County	119	27.4	**Manlius** (town) Onondaga County
45	35.3	**Setauket-East Setauket** (CDP) Suffolk County	120	27.2	**Skaneateles** (town) Onondaga County
46	35.2	**Brighton** (CDP) Monroe County	121	26.7	**East Shoreham** (CDP) Suffolk County
47	35.1	**Jericho** (CDP) Nassau County	122	26.6	**Rhinebeck** (village) Dutchess County
47	35.1	**Sea Cliff** (village) Nassau County	123	26.5	**Pleasantville** (village) Westchester County
49	35.0	**Wesley Hills** (village) Rockland County	124	26.4	**Albertson** (CDP) Nassau County
50	34.5	**Mamaroneck** (town) Westchester County	124	26.4	**Brightwaters** (village) Suffolk County
50	34.5	**Piermont** (village) Rockland County	126	26.2	**Bardonia** (CDP) Rockland County
52	34.2	**Greenburgh** (town) Westchester County	126	26.2	**Eastchester** (CDP) Westchester County
53	33.9	**North Hills** (village) Nassau County	126	26.2	**Red Hook** (town) Dutchess County
53	33.9	**University Gardens** (CDP) Nassau County	129	26.1	**Westmere** (CDP) Albany County
55	33.7	**University at Buffalo** (CDP) Erie County	130	26.0	**Fairport** (village) Monroe County
56	33.3	**Manhasset Hills** (CDP) Nassau County	130	26.0	**Great Neck** (village) Nassau County
56	33.3	**Niskayuna** (town) Schenectady County	130	26.0	**Perinton** (town) Monroe County
58	33.2	**Hartsdale** (CDP) Westchester County	133	25.9	**Somers** (town) Westchester County
59	33.1	**Pelham** (town) Westchester County	134	25.8	**Pomona** (village) Rockland County
60	32.8	**Searingtown** (CDP) Nassau County	135	25.7	**Clifton Park** (town) Saratoga County
61	32.7	**Garden City** (village) Nassau County	135	25.7	**Guilderland** (town) Albany County
62	32.5	**Croton-on-Hudson** (village) Westchester County	137	25.6	**East Aurora** (village) Erie County
62	32.5	**Woodbury** (CDP) Nassau County	137	25.6	**North Hempstead** (town) Nassau County
64	32.4	**Bethlehem** (town) Albany County	139	25.4	**East Greenbush** (CDP) Rensselaer County
64	32.4	**Montebello** (village) Rockland County	140	25.3	**West Elmira** (CDP) Chemung County
64	32.4	**Port Washington North** (village) Nassau County	141	25.2	**Clarence** (town) Erie County
64	32.4	**South Nyack** (village) Rockland County	141	25.2	**Valhalla** (CDP) Westchester County
68	32.3	**Lake Success** (village) Nassau County	143	25.1	**Mamaroneck** (village) Westchester County
68	32.3	**Rye Brook** (village) Westchester County	144	25.0	**Blauvelt** (CDP) Rockland County
70	32.2	**Orchard Park** (village) Erie County	144	25.0	**Manlius** (village) Onondaga County
71	31.9	**Skaneateles** (village) Onondaga County	144	25.0	**Mount Pleasant** (town) Westchester County
72	31.8	**Potsdam** (village) Saint Lawrence County	147	24.9	**Cornwall** (town) Orange County
73	31.6	**Spackenkill** (CDP) Dutchess County	147	24.9	**Gardiner** (town) Ulster County
74	31.5	**Northport** (village) Suffolk County	147	24.9	**Nyack** (village) Rockland County
75	31.3	**Fayetteville** (village) Onondaga County	150	24.8	**Caneadea** (town) Allegany County

Note: This section ranks incorporated places and CDPs (Census Designated Places) with populations of 2,500 or more. Unincorporated postal areas were not considered. Please refer to the User Guide for additional information.

Educational Attainment: Graduate/Professional Degree or Higher

Top 150 Places Ranked in *Ascending* Order

State Rank	Percent	Place	State Rank	Percent	Place
1	0.0	**SUNY Oswego** (CDP) Oswego County	73	4.9	**Vernon** (town) Oneida County
2	0.4	**Riverside** (CDP) Suffolk County	77	5.0	**Carthage** (village) Jefferson County
3	0.9	**Sloan** (village) Erie County	77	5.0	**Corinth** (village) Saratoga County
4	1.1	**New Square** (village) Rockland County	77	5.0	**Green Island** (town/village) Albany County
5	1.5	**Kiryas Joel** (village) Orange County	77	5.0	**Walton** (village) Delaware County
6	1.6	**Kaser** (village) Rockland County	81	5.1	**Afton** (town) Chenango County
7	1.7	**Dannemora** (village) Clinton County	81	5.1	**Clarendon** (town) Orleans County
8	2.1	**Fort Edward** (village) Washington County	81	5.1	**Port Jervis** (city) Orange County
9	2.3	**Whitehall** (town) Washington County	81	5.1	**Yates** (town) Orleans County
10	2.4	**Watchtower** (CDP) Ulster County	85	5.2	**Gouverneur** (town) Saint Lawrence County
11	2.6	**Whitehall** (village) Washington County	85	5.2	**Hamlin** (CDP) Monroe County
12	2.7	**Dannemora** (town) Clinton County	85	5.2	**Lackawanna** (city) Erie County
13	2.8	**Fort Edward** (town) Washington County	88	5.3	**Alexander** (town) Genesee County
13	2.8	**Hannibal** (town) Oswego County	88	5.3	**Benton** (town) Yates County
15	2.9	**Albion** (village) Orleans County	88	5.3	**Enfield** (town) Tompkins County
15	2.9	**Palermo** (town) Oswego County	88	5.3	**Galen** (town) Wayne County
17	3.0	**Lyncourt** (CDP) Onondaga County	88	5.3	**Palmyra** (village) Wayne County
18	3.1	**Stockport** (town) Columbia County	93	5.4	**Manchester** (town) Ontario County
19	3.2	**Southport** (CDP) Chemung County	93	5.4	**Minden** (town) Montgomery County
20	3.3	**Murray** (town) Orleans County	93	5.4	**Watervliet** (city) Albany County
20	3.3	**Vienna** (town) Oneida County	96	5.5	**Annsville** (town) Oneida County
20	3.3	**Wilna** (town) Jefferson County	96	5.5	**Cambria** (town) Niagara County
23	3.4	**Blasdell** (village) Erie County	96	5.5	**Candor** (town) Tioga County
23	3.4	**New York Mills** (village) Oneida County	96	5.5	**Ellisburg** (town) Jefferson County
23	3.4	**North Bay Shore** (CDP) Suffolk County	96	5.5	**Mastic Beach** (village) Suffolk County
26	3.5	**Denmark** (town) Lewis County	96	5.5	**Palmyra** (town) Wayne County
27	3.6	**Altona** (town) Clinton County	102	5.6	**Oakfield** (town) Genesee County
27	3.6	**Campbell** (town) Steuben County	102	5.6	**Perry** (village) Wyoming County
27	3.6	**Liberty** (village) Sullivan County	102	5.6	**Spring Valley** (village) Rockland County
30	3.7	**Broadalbin** (town) Fulton County	102	5.6	**Waterloo** (village) Seneca County
31	3.8	**Mattydale** (CDP) Onondaga County	106	5.7	**Alden** (town) Erie County
32	3.9	**Albion** (town) Orleans County	106	5.7	**Granville** (town) Washington County
32	3.9	**Attica** (town) Wyoming County	106	5.7	**New Berlin** (town) Chenango County
32	3.9	**Baywood** (CDP) Suffolk County	106	5.7	**Utica** (city) Oneida County
32	3.9	**Groveland** (town) Livingston County	106	5.7	**Wayland** (town) Steuben County
32	3.9	**Salamanca** (city) Cattaraugus County	111	5.8	**Bennington** (town) Wyoming County
32	3.9	**Warsaw** (town) Wyoming County	111	5.8	**Gaines** (town) Orleans County
32	3.9	**Warsaw** (village) Wyoming County	111	5.8	**Gates** (CDP) Monroe County
39	4.0	**Brentwood** (CDP) Suffolk County	111	5.8	**Monticello** (village) Sullivan County
39	4.0	**Hopewell** (town) Ontario County	111	5.8	**Mooers** (town) Clinton County
41	4.1	**Cohocton** (town) Steuben County	111	5.8	**Unadilla** (town) Otsego County
41	4.1	**Niagara** (town) Niagara County	111	5.8	**Vails Gate** (CDP) Orange County
41	4.1	**Roosevelt** (CDP) Nassau County	118	5.9	**Elmira Heights** (village) Chemung County
41	4.1	**Whitesboro** (village) Oneida County	118	5.9	**Hamlin** (town) Monroe County
45	4.2	**Brookfield** (town) Madison County	118	5.9	**Lyons** (village) Wayne County
45	4.2	**Romulus** (town) Seneca County	118	5.9	**Mayfield** (town) Fulton County
45	4.2	**Wyandanch** (CDP) Suffolk County	118	5.9	**Randolph** (town) Cattaraugus County
48	4.4	**Amsterdam** (city) Montgomery County	123	6.0	**Elmira** (city) Chemung County
48	4.4	**West Monroe** (town) Oswego County	123	6.0	**Floyd** (town) Oneida County
50	4.5	**Collins** (town) Erie County	123	6.0	**Fulton** (city) Oswego County
50	4.5	**Mechanicville** (city) Saratoga County	123	6.0	**Perry** (town) Wyoming County
50	4.5	**Moriah** (town) Essex County	127	6.1	**Corinth** (town) Saratoga County
50	4.5	**Ravena** (village) Albany County	127	6.1	**Hoosick Falls** (village) Rensselaer County
50	4.5	**Waterloo** (town) Seneca County	127	6.1	**Kingsbury** (town) Washington County
55	4.6	**Hudson Falls** (village) Washington County	127	6.1	**Spencer** (town) Tioga County
55	4.6	**Mastic** (CDP) Suffolk County	131	6.2	**Cape Vincent** (town) Jefferson County
55	4.6	**Nichols** (town) Tioga County	131	6.2	**Dix** (town) Schuyler County
55	4.6	**Wappingers Falls** (village) Dutchess County	131	6.2	**Moravia** (town) Cayuga County
55	4.6	**Yorkshire** (town) Cattaraugus County	131	6.2	**New Bremen** (town) Lewis County
60	4.7	**Fairview** (CDP) Westchester County	131	6.2	**New Haven** (town) Oswego County
60	4.7	**Fort Ann** (town) Washington County	131	6.2	**Schoharie** (town) Schoharie County
60	4.7	**Hoosick** (town) Rensselaer County	131	6.2	**Volney** (town) Oswego County
60	4.7	**Newburgh** (city) Orange County	138	6.3	**Central Islip** (CDP) Suffolk County
60	4.7	**Somerset** (town) Niagara County	138	6.3	**Depew** (village) Erie County
60	4.7	**Wolcott** (town) Wayne County	138	6.3	**Gouverneur** (village) Saint Lawrence County
66	4.8	**Deerpark** (town) Orange County	138	6.3	**Rutland** (town) Jefferson County
66	4.8	**East Syracuse** (village) Onondaga County	138	6.3	**Stillwater** (town) Saratoga County
66	4.8	**Hastings** (town) Oswego County	138	6.3	**Tioga** (town) Tioga County
66	4.8	**Newfane** (CDP) Niagara County	144	6.4	**Coxsackie** (town) Greene County
66	4.8	**North Gates** (CDP) Monroe County	144	6.4	**Lenox** (town) Madison County
66	4.8	**Tupper Lake** (village) Franklin County	144	6.4	**Newark** (village) Wayne County
66	4.8	**Verona** (town) Oneida County	144	6.4	**Sodus** (town) Wayne County
73	4.9	**Lisle** (town) Broome County	144	6.4	**South Glens Falls** (village) Saratoga County
73	4.9	**Mount Morris** (town) Livingston County	149	6.5	**Canisteo** (town) Steuben County
73	4.9	**Newfane** (town) Niagara County	149	6.5	**Champlain** (town) Clinton County

Note: *This section ranks incorporated places and CDPs (Census Designated Places) with populations of 2,500 or more. Unincorporated postal areas were not considered. Please refer to the User Guide for additional information.*

Homeownership Rate

Top 150 Places Ranked in *Descending* Order

State Rank	Percent	Place
1	100.0	**Munsey Park** (village) Nassau County
2	98.5	**East Hills** (village) Nassau County
3	98.4	**Searingtown** (CDP) Nassau County
4	98.0	**West Bay Shore** (CDP) Suffolk County
5	97.6	**Lake Success** (village) Nassau County
6	97.1	**Massapequa Park** (village) Nassau County
7	97.0	**Blauvelt** (CDP) Rockland County
8	96.2	**Herricks** (CDP) Nassau County
8	96.2	**Muttontown** (village) Nassau County
10	96.0	**North New Hyde Park** (CDP) Nassau County
11	95.9	**New Baltimore** (town) Greene County
12	95.5	**Elma Center** (CDP) Erie County
13	95.3	**East Norwich** (CDP) Nassau County
14	95.1	**Myers Corner** (CDP) Dutchess County
14	95.1	**North Merrick** (CDP) Nassau County
16	94.9	**Spackenkill** (CDP) Dutchess County
16	94.9	**Wantagh** (CDP) Nassau County
18	94.6	**Albertson** (CDP) Nassau County
19	94.5	**East Williston** (village) Nassau County
19	94.5	**West Islip** (CDP) Suffolk County
21	94.4	**Charlton** (town) Saratoga County
21	94.4	**Lloyd Harbor** (village) Suffolk County
21	94.4	**Miller Place** (CDP) Suffolk County
21	94.4	**New Hempstead** (village) Rockland County
25	94.3	**Merrick** (CDP) Nassau County
25	94.3	**Tappan** (CDP) Rockland County
25	94.3	**Westerlo** (town) Albany County
25	94.3	**Westvale** (CDP) Onondaga County
29	94.2	**Sands Point** (village) Nassau County
30	94.1	**Brookville** (village) Nassau County
30	94.1	**Pendleton** (town) Niagara County
32	93.9	**Kings Point** (village) Nassau County
32	93.9	**Marilla** (town) Erie County
32	93.9	**Setauket-East Setauket** (CDP) Suffolk County
35	93.8	**East Shoreham** (CDP) Suffolk County
35	93.8	**Garden City** (village) Nassau County
35	93.8	**Owasco** (town) Cayuga County
35	93.8	**Richmond** (town) Ontario County
39	93.6	**La Grange** (town) Dutchess County
39	93.6	**West Nyack** (CDP) Rockland County
41	93.5	**North Wantagh** (CDP) Nassau County
42	93.4	**Dix Hills** (CDP) Suffolk County
42	93.4	**Pelham Manor** (village) Westchester County
42	93.4	**Wading River** (CDP) Suffolk County
45	93.2	**Walworth** (town) Wayne County
46	93.1	**Malverne** (village) Nassau County
46	93.1	**Mount Sinai** (CDP) Suffolk County
48	93.0	**New Castle** (town) Westchester County
49	92.9	**Manhasset Hills** (CDP) Nassau County
49	92.9	**Plainview** (CDP) Nassau County
51	92.8	**Lido Beach** (CDP) Nassau County
51	92.8	**Wesley Hills** (village) Rockland County
53	92.7	**Massapequa** (CDP) Nassau County
53	92.7	**North Massapequa** (CDP) Nassau County
55	92.5	**Berne** (town) Albany County
56	92.4	**Greenville** (CDP) Westchester County
57	92.3	**Greenville** (town) Orange County
58	92.2	**Barker** (town) Broome County
58	92.2	**Salisbury** (CDP) Nassau County
60	92.1	**Cambria** (town) Niagara County
61	92.0	**Baldwin Harbor** (CDP) Nassau County
61	92.0	**Elwood** (CDP) Suffolk County
61	92.0	**Wales** (town) Erie County
64	91.9	**Veteran** (town) Chemung County
65	91.8	**Old Westbury** (village) Nassau County
66	91.7	**Danby** (town) Tompkins County
66	91.7	**Johnstown** (town) Fulton County
66	91.7	**Riga** (town) Monroe County
69	91.6	**Elma** (town) Erie County
69	91.6	**Gates** (CDP) Monroe County
69	91.6	**Hamptonburgh** (town) Orange County
69	91.6	**Rush** (town) Monroe County
73	91.5	**Cutchogue** (CDP) Suffolk County
74	91.4	**Carlton** (town) Orleans County
74	91.4	**Chenango Bridge** (CDP) Broome County
76	91.3	**Floyd** (town) Oneida County
76	91.3	**Lewisboro** (town) Westchester County
76	91.3	**South Farmingdale** (CDP) Nassau County
79	91.2	**Beekman** (town) Dutchess County
79	91.2	**Binghamton** (town) Broome County
81	91.1	**Centerport** (CDP) Suffolk County
81	91.1	**Commack** (CDP) Suffolk County
81	91.1	**Oswegatchie** (town) Saint Lawrence County
84	91.0	**Brightwaters** (village) Suffolk County
84	91.0	**Yaphank** (CDP) Suffolk County
86	90.9	**Old Bethpage** (CDP) Nassau County
86	90.9	**West Hills** (CDP) Suffolk County
88	90.8	**East Fishkill** (town) Dutchess County
88	90.8	**Levittown** (CDP) Nassau County
88	90.8	**Wanakah** (CDP) Erie County
91	90.7	**Scarsdale** (town/village) Westchester County
92	90.6	**Armonk** (CDP) Westchester County
92	90.6	**Great Neck Estates** (village) Nassau County
92	90.6	**Stony Brook University** (CDP) Suffolk County
92	90.6	**Syosset** (CDP) Nassau County
96	90.4	**Bethpage** (CDP) Nassau County
97	90.3	**Hopewell** (town) Ontario County
97	90.3	**North Hills** (village) Nassau County
99	90.2	**Flower Hill** (village) Nassau County
99	90.2	**Montebello** (village) Rockland County
101	90.1	**East Islip** (CDP) Suffolk County
101	90.1	**Halesite** (CDP) Suffolk County
101	90.1	**Hurley** (town) Ulster County
101	90.1	**New City** (CDP) Rockland County
101	90.1	**North Valley Stream** (CDP) Nassau County
106	90.0	**Crown Heights** (CDP) Dutchess County
106	90.0	**Plainedge** (CDP) Nassau County
106	90.0	**Wynantskill** (CDP) Rensselaer County
109	89.9	**Galway** (town) Saratoga County
109	89.9	**North Patchogue** (CDP) Suffolk County
111	89.8	**Conesus** (town) Livingston County
111	89.8	**Jefferson Valley-Yorktown** (CDP) Westchester County
111	89.8	**Pomona** (village) Rockland County
111	89.8	**Springs** (CDP) Suffolk County
111	89.8	**Sterling** (town) Cayuga County
111	89.8	**Stony Brook** (CDP) Suffolk County
117	89.7	**Fort Salonga** (CDP) Suffolk County
117	89.7	**Somers** (town) Westchester County
119	89.6	**Islip Terrace** (CDP) Suffolk County
120	89.5	**Saint James** (CDP) Suffolk County
120	89.5	**Sennett** (town) Cayuga County
122	89.4	**North Bellmore** (CDP) Nassau County
123	89.3	**Deerfield** (town) Oneida County
124	89.2	**Woodmere** (CDP) Nassau County
124	89.2	**Yates** (town) Orleans County
126	89.1	**Garden City South** (CDP) Nassau County
127	88.9	**Thiells** (CDP) Rockland County
127	88.9	**West Sayville** (CDP) Suffolk County
129	88.8	**Catlin** (town) Chemung County
130	88.6	**Cold Spring Harbor** (CDP) Suffolk County
130	88.6	**Oswego** (town) Oswego County
130	88.6	**Putnam Valley** (town) Putnam County
130	88.6	**Sound Beach** (CDP) Suffolk County
134	88.5	**Pompey** (town) Onondaga County
135	88.4	**Conklin** (town) Broome County
135	88.4	**West Sand Lake** (CDP) Rensselaer County
137	88.3	**Bellmore** (CDP) Nassau County
137	88.3	**Clarendon** (town) Orleans County
137	88.3	**Lake Erie Beach** (CDP) Erie County
137	88.3	**Pittstown** (town) Rensselaer County
141	88.2	**Glen Head** (CDP) Nassau County
142	88.1	**Farmingville** (CDP) Suffolk County
142	88.1	**Smithtown** (town) Suffolk County
142	88.1	**West Monroe** (town) Oswego County
145	88.0	**Cato** (town) Cayuga County
145	88.0	**Haviland** (CDP) Dutchess County
145	88.0	**Hurley** (CDP) Ulster County
145	88.0	**Minisink** (town) Orange County
149	87.9	**Aurelius** (town) Cayuga County
149	87.9	**Big Flats** (town) Chemung County

Note: This section ranks incorporated places and CDPs (Census Designated Places) with populations of 2,500 or more. Unincorporated postal areas were not considered. Please refer to the User Guide for additional information.

Homeownership Rate

Top 150 Places Ranked in *Ascending* Order

State Rank	Percent	Place
1	0.0	**Binghamton University** (CDP) Broome County
1	0.0	**SUNY Oswego** (CDP) Oswego County
1	0.0	**University at Buffalo** (CDP) Erie County
1	0.0	**Watchtower** (CDP) Ulster County
5	0.5	**West Point** (CDP) Orange County
6	0.6	**Fort Drum** (CDP) Jefferson County
7	3.8	**Kaser** (village) Rockland County
8	14.1	**New Square** (village) Rockland County
9	14.7	**Calcium** (CDP) Jefferson County
10	17.9	**Le Ray** (town) Jefferson County
11	19.0	**Bronx** (borough) Bronx County
12	22.9	**Manhattan** (borough) New York County
13	25.5	**Monticello** (village) Sullivan County
14	26.4	**Ithaca** (city) Tompkins County
15	26.9	**Alfred** (village) Allegany County
16	28.1	**South Fallsburg** (CDP) Sullivan County
17	29.3	**Brooklyn** (borough) Kings County
18	29.7	**Arlington** (CDP) Dutchess County
19	30.0	**New Paltz** (village) Ulster County
20	30.6	**Kiryas Joel** (village) Orange County
21	30.8	**Lansing** (village) Tompkins County
22	31.0	**Spring Valley** (village) Rockland County
23	31.4	**Nyack** (village) Rockland County
24	31.8	**New York** (city)
25	32.3	**Newburgh** (city) Orange County
26	32.7	**Wappingers Falls** (village) Dutchess County
27	33.3	**Green Island** (town/village) Albany County
28	34.0	**Hudson** (city) Columbia County
29	35.5	**Liberty** (village) Sullivan County
30	35.8	**Lake Placid** (village) Essex County
31	36.0	**Manorhaven** (village) Nassau County
31	36.0	**Menands** (village) Albany County
33	36.2	**Fairview** (CDP) Westchester County
33	36.2	**Poughkeepsie** (city) Dutchess County
35	36.9	**Rochester** (city) Monroe County
36	37.2	**Plattsburgh** (city) Clinton County
37	37.5	**Albany** (city) Albany County
38	38.2	**Troy** (city) Rensselaer County
39	38.4	**Potsdam** (village) Saint Lawrence County
40	38.5	**Sleepy Hollow** (village) Westchester County
41	38.6	**Syracuse** (city) Onondaga County
42	39.1	**Mechanicville** (city) Saratoga County
42	39.1	**Mount Vernon** (city) Westchester County
44	39.5	**Monsey** (CDP) Rockland County
45	39.6	**Highlands** (town) Orange County
46	39.8	**Watertown** (city) Jefferson County
47	40.1	**Webster** (village) Monroe County
48	40.5	**Watervliet** (city) Albany County
49	41.5	**Buffalo** (city) Erie County
50	41.8	**Cobleskill** (village) Schoharie County
51	41.9	**Bedford Hills** (CDP) Westchester County
52	42.1	**Endicott** (village) Broome County
53	42.2	**New York Mills** (village) Oneida County
54	42.6	**Geneseo** (village) Livingston County
55	42.7	**Port Chester** (village) Westchester County
56	42.9	**Cohoes** (city) Albany County
57	43.5	**Hempstead** (village) Nassau County
58	43.6	**Haverstraw** (village) Rockland County
58	43.6	**Queens** (borough) Queens County
60	43.7	**Mechanicstown** (CDP) Orange County
61	44.1	**Herkimer** (village) Herkimer County
61	44.1	**Rensselaer** (city) Rensselaer County
63	44.2	**Elmira** (city) Chemung County
64	44.3	**Kingston** (city) Ulster County
64	44.3	**Vails Gate** (CDP) Orange County
66	44.6	**Highland Falls** (village) Orange County
66	44.6	**Northeast Ithaca** (CDP) Tompkins County
68	44.8	**Brockport** (village) Monroe County
69	45.2	**Saugerties** (village) Ulster County
70	45.4	**Carthage** (village) Jefferson County
71	45.5	**Binghamton** (city) Broome County
72	45.6	**Cayuga Heights** (village) Tompkins County
73	45.8	**Canton** (village) Saint Lawrence County
74	46.1	**Cortland** (city) Cortland County
75	46.3	**Ossining** (village) Westchester County
76	46.4	**Oneonta** (city) Otsego County
76	46.4	**Utica** (city) Oneida County
78	46.5	**East Syracuse** (village) Onondaga County
79	46.6	**Auburn** (city) Cayuga County
80	46.8	**Walton** (village) Delaware County
81	47.2	**Ithaca** (town) Tompkins County
82	47.5	**Yonkers** (city) Westchester County
83	47.6	**Alfred** (town) Allegany County
83	47.6	**Gouverneur** (village) Saint Lawrence County
85	48.3	**Inwood** (CDP) Nassau County
85	48.3	**Saranac Lake** (village) Franklin County
87	48.4	**Schenectady** (city) Schenectady County
88	48.5	**Mount Morris** (village) Livingston County
89	48.7	**Thompson** (town) Sullivan County
90	49.4	**Amsterdam** (city) Montgomery County
91	49.6	**New Rochelle** (city) Westchester County
91	49.6	**Peekskill** (city) Westchester County
93	49.7	**Corning** (city) Steuben County
93	49.7	**Elmsford** (village) Westchester County
95	49.8	**Catskill** (village) Greene County
95	49.8	**Tuckahoe** (village) Westchester County
97	49.9	**Ballston Spa** (village) Saratoga County
97	49.9	**Gloversville** (city) Fulton County
99	50.1	**Geneva** (city) Ontario County
100	50.2	**Palmyra** (village) Wayne County
101	50.3	**Glens Falls** (city) Warren County
101	50.3	**Penn Yan** (village) Yates County
103	50.5	**Geneseo** (town) Livingston County
103	50.5	**Newark** (village) Wayne County
105	50.6	**Norwich** (city) Chenango County
106	50.7	**Port Jervis** (city) Orange County
107	50.8	**Wellsville** (village) Allegany County
108	50.9	**Great Neck Plaza** (village) Nassau County
108	50.9	**White Plains** (city) Westchester County
110	51.0	**Whitehall** (village) Washington County
111	51.1	**Jamestown** (city) Chautauqua County
112	51.2	**Harriman** (village) Orange County
112	51.2	**Oswego** (city) Oswego County
114	51.3	**Glen Cove** (city) Nassau County
115	51.5	**Bath** (village) Steuben County
115	51.5	**South Glens Falls** (village) Saratoga County
117	51.7	**Goshen** (village) Orange County
118	51.8	**Moriches** (CDP) Suffolk County
119	51.9	**Salamanca** (city) Cattaraugus County
120	52.0	**Olean** (city) Cattaraugus County
121	52.4	**Falconer** (village) Chautauqua County
121	52.4	**Middletown** (city) Orange County
123	52.6	**Sidney** (village) Delaware County
124	52.7	**Gang Mills** (CDP) Steuben County
125	52.9	**Hornell** (city) Steuben County
126	53.0	**Batavia** (city) Genesee County
127	53.1	**Beacon** (city) Dutchess County
127	53.1	**Blasdell** (village) Erie County
127	53.1	**Johnson City** (village) Broome County
127	53.1	**Mount Kisco** (town/village) Westchester County
131	53.2	**Fulton** (city) Oswego County
131	53.2	**Lowville** (village) Lewis County
133	53.3	**Little Falls** (city) Herkimer County
134	53.5	**Elmira Heights** (village) Chemung County
135	53.6	**Canandaigua** (city) Ontario County
135	53.6	**Malone** (village) Franklin County
137	53.7	**Herkimer** (town) Herkimer County
137	53.7	**Patchogue** (village) Suffolk County
139	53.8	**Albion** (village) Orleans County
139	53.8	**Whitesboro** (village) Oneida County
141	53.9	**Wilna** (town) Jefferson County
142	54.1	**Cobleskill** (town) Schoharie County
142	54.1	**Hudson Falls** (village) Washington County
144	54.3	**Fallsburg** (town) Sullivan County
144	54.3	**Lackawanna** (city) Erie County
146	54.4	**Rome** (city) Oneida County
146	54.4	**Rye** (town) Westchester County
148	54.5	**Ellenville** (village) Ulster County
148	54.5	**Saratoga Springs** (city) Saratoga County
150	55.0	**New Paltz** (town) Ulster County

Note: *This section ranks incorporated places and CDPs (Census Designated Places) with populations of 2,500 or more. Unincorporated postal areas were not considered. Please refer to the User Guide for additional information.*

Median Home Value

Top 150 Places Ranked in *Descending* Order

State Rank	Dollars	Place	State Rank	Dollars	Place
1	2 million+	**Sands Point** (village) Nassau County	76	591,600	**Mamaroneck** (village) Westchester County
2	1,814,700	**Brookville** (village) Nassau County	77	587,000	**Herricks** (CDP) Nassau County
3	1,692,500	**Kings Point** (village) Nassau County	78	582,900	**Dobbs Ferry** (village) Westchester County
4	1,687,500	**Old Westbury** (village) Nassau County	79	579,700	**Glen Head** (CDP) Nassau County
5	1,561,700	**Muttontown** (village) Nassau County	80	579,200	**Eastchester** (town) Westchester County
6	1,447,400	**Lloyd Harbor** (village) Suffolk County	81	578,800	**Pleasantville** (village) Westchester County
7	1,266,800	**Southampton** (village) Suffolk County	82	578,200	**North Salem** (town) Westchester County
8	1,266,400	**Great Neck Estates** (village) Nassau County	83	575,900	**Thornwood** (CDP) Westchester County
9	1,241,000	**Munsey Park** (village) Nassau County	84	575,100	**Sleepy Hollow** (village) Westchester County
10	1,230,600	**Scarsdale** (town/village) Westchester County	85	572,700	**Woodmere** (CDP) Nassau County
11	1,181,800	**Lake Success** (village) Nassau County	86	570,200	**Brooklyn** (borough) Kings County
12	1,068,500	**Flower Hill** (village) Nassau County	87	569,300	**Monsey** (CDP) Rockland County
13	1,055,100	**Rye** (city) Westchester County	88	562,400	**Valhalla** (CDP) Westchester County
14	1,044,800	**Larchmont** (village) Westchester County	89	562,300	**Oyster Bay** (CDP) Nassau County
15	937,900	**Northwest Harbor** (CDP) Suffolk County	90	560,900	**Wesley Hills** (village) Rockland County
16	927,300	**Pound Ridge** (town) Westchester County	91	559,000	**Huntington** (CDP) Suffolk County
17	924,500	**North Hills** (village) Nassau County	92	555,900	**Eastchester** (CDP) Westchester County
18	916,700	**Bronxville** (village) Westchester County	93	552,600	**New Rochelle** (city) Westchester County
19	916,600	**Manhasset** (CDP) Nassau County	94	550,400	**Viola** (CDP) Rockland County
20	907,600	**North Castle** (town) Westchester County	95	547,900	**West Hills** (CDP) Suffolk County
21	907,400	**Armonk** (CDP) Westchester County	96	547,800	**Garden City Park** (CDP) Nassau County
22	896,200	**East Hills** (village) Nassau County	97	545,300	**Locust Valley** (CDP) Nassau County
23	879,700	**Lawrence** (village) Nassau County	98	544,600	**Old Bethpage** (CDP) Nassau County
24	872,100	**New Castle** (town) Westchester County	99	540,500	**Northport** (village) Suffolk County
25	862,200	**Woodbury** (CDP) Nassau County	100	539,600	**Bayville** (village) Nassau County
26	848,700	**Manhattan** (borough) New York County	101	538,700	**Greenburgh** (town) Westchester County
27	848,300	**Greenville** (CDP) Westchester County	102	538,400	**Tarrytown** (village) Westchester County
28	821,400	**Pelham Manor** (village) Westchester County	103	536,700	**Rye** (town) Westchester County
29	816,300	**Mamaroneck** (town) Westchester County	104	527,200	**Merrick** (CDP) Nassau County
30	812,700	**East Hampton** (town) Suffolk County	105	524,200	**Halesite** (CDP) Suffolk County
31	805,900	**Manhasset Hills** (CDP) Nassau County	106	517,900	**Cedarhurst** (village) Nassau County
32	792,400	**Montauk** (CDP) Suffolk County	107	517,300	**North New Hyde Park** (CDP) Nassau County
33	778,100	**East Williston** (village) Nassau County	108	514,700	**Southold** (CDP) Suffolk County
34	774,100	**Cold Spring Harbor** (CDP) Suffolk County	109	514,600	**Manorhaven** (village) Nassau County
35	771,000	**Bedford** (town) Westchester County	110	514,000	**Albertson** (CDP) Nassau County
36	761,200	**Harrison** (town/village) Westchester County	111	513,100	**Southold** (town) Suffolk County
37	760,700	**Port Washington North** (village) Nassau County	112	511,600	**White Plains** (city) Westchester County
38	760,100	**North Sea** (CDP) Suffolk County	113	511,300	**Roslyn** (village) Nassau County
39	757,900	**Garden City** (village) Nassau County	114	505,000	**Bardonia** (CDP) Rockland County
40	753,700	**Thomaston** (village) Nassau County	115	503,600	**Croton-on-Hudson** (village) Westchester County
41	751,400	**Searingtown** (CDP) Nassau County	116	500,400	**Blauvelt** (CDP) Rockland County
42	742,300	**East Hampton North** (CDP) Suffolk County	117	498,200	**Brightwaters** (village) Suffolk County
43	734,500	**Pelham** (town) Westchester County	118	497,900	**Mattituck** (CDP) Suffolk County
44	730,100	**Rye Brook** (village) Westchester County	119	497,500	**Huntington** (town) Suffolk County
45	728,400	**Shelter Island** (town) Suffolk County	120	495,100	**Port Jefferson** (village) Suffolk County
46	721,200	**Port Washington** (CDP) Nassau County	121	494,800	**New York** (city)
47	716,700	**Noyack** (CDP) Suffolk County	122	494,500	**Hawthorne** (CDP) Westchester County
48	692,200	**Great Neck** (village) Nassau County	123	493,800	**Somers** (town) Westchester County
49	692,100	**Roslyn Heights** (CDP) Nassau County	124	492,300	**Plainview** (CDP) Nassau County
50	686,700	**Fort Salonga** (CDP) Suffolk County	125	492,000	**Floral Park** (village) Nassau County
51	682,400	**Dix Hills** (CDP) Suffolk County	126	490,000	**Cutchogue** (CDP) Suffolk County
52	673,700	**Jericho** (CDP) Nassau County	127	487,100	**Elwood** (CDP) Suffolk County
53	670,300	**Lido Beach** (CDP) Nassau County	128	486,200	**Tuckahoe** (village) Westchester County
54	669,000	**Westhampton** (CDP) Suffolk County	129	486,000	**New Hyde Park** (village) Nassau County
55	666,700	**Briarcliff Manor** (village) Westchester County	130	485,500	**Massapequa** (CDP) Nassau County
56	660,700	**Springs** (CDP) Suffolk County	131	477,600	**Carle Place** (CDP) Nassau County
57	658,200	**East Garden City** (CDP) Nassau County	132	473,700	**West Nyack** (CDP) Rockland County
58	649,200	**Sea Cliff** (village) Nassau County	133	473,600	**East Quogue** (CDP) Suffolk County
59	649,000	**Lewisboro** (town) Westchester County	134	473,200	**Glen Cove** (city) Nassau County
60	648,400	**Hastings-on-Hudson** (village) Westchester County	135	473,100	**New City** (CDP) Rockland County
61	639,300	**Pelham** (village) Westchester County	136	472,500	**Pomona** (village) Rockland County
62	633,900	**Irvington** (village) Westchester County	137	472,200	**Smithtown** (CDP) Suffolk County
63	630,400	**Montebello** (village) Rockland County	138	471,400	**Williston Park** (village) Nassau County
64	626,300	**Piermont** (village) Rockland County	139	470,800	**Oyster Bay** (town) Nassau County
65	623,700	**Melville** (CDP) Suffolk County	140	470,700	**Bedford Hills** (CDP) Westchester County
66	623,400	**North Hempstead** (town) Nassau County	141	470,100	**Tappan** (CDP) Rockland County
67	622,600	**East Norwich** (CDP) Nassau County	142	467,400	**Wantagh** (CDP) Nassau County
68	616,600	**Ardsley** (village) Westchester County	143	466,200	**Commack** (CDP) Suffolk County
69	611,400	**Syosset** (CDP) Nassau County	144	464,400	**Nesconset** (CDP) Suffolk County
70	610,900	**Mount Pleasant** (town) Westchester County	145	464,100	**Orangetown** (town) Rockland County
71	608,200	**University Gardens** (CDP) Nassau County	146	462,300	**Setauket-East Setauket** (CDP) Suffolk County
72	605,100	**Glenwood Landing** (CDP) Nassau County	147	460,800	**Smithtown** (town) Suffolk County
73	603,100	**Centerport** (CDP) Suffolk County	148	460,500	**Garden City South** (CDP) Nassau County
74	600,600	**Rockville Centre** (village) Nassau County	149	459,600	**Hauppauge** (CDP) Suffolk County
75	598,100	**Southampton** (town) Suffolk County	150	459,300	**Orangeburg** (CDP) Rockland County

Note: This section ranks incorporated places and CDPs (Census Designated Places) with populations of 2,500 or more. Unincorporated postal areas were not considered. Please refer to the User Guide for additional information.

Median Home Value

Top 150 Places Ranked in *Ascending* Order

State Rank	Dollars	Place	State Rank	Dollars	Place
1	62,400	**Lyons** (village) Wayne County	74	85,300	**Mohawk** (village) Herkimer County
2	63,600	**Jamestown** (city) Chautauqua County	77	85,700	**Dansville** (village) Livingston County
3	64,500	**Salamanca** (city) Cattaraugus County	78	85,800	**Moira** (town) Franklin County
4	64,700	**Dunkirk** (city) Chautauqua County	79	86,100	**Campbell** (town) Steuben County
5	64,900	**Hornell** (city) Steuben County	79	86,100	**Guilford** (town) Chenango County
6	65,800	**Mount Morris** (village) Livingston County	81	86,300	**New Haven** (town) Oswego County
7	66,500	**Falconer** (village) Chautauqua County	82	86,400	**Newfane** (CDP) Niagara County
8	67,400	**Niagara Falls** (city) Niagara County	83	86,500	**Herkimer** (village) Herkimer County
9	67,900	**Ogdensburg** (city) Saint Lawrence County	84	86,600	**Monticello** (village) Sullivan County
9	67,900	**Wellsville** (village) Allegany County	85	86,800	**New Berlin** (town) Chenango County
11	68,800	**Buffalo** (city) Erie County	86	86,900	**Seneca Falls** (CDP) Seneca County
11	68,800	**Elmira** (city) Chemung County	87	87,000	**Gouverneur** (town) Saint Lawrence County
13	69,100	**Lyons** (town) Wayne County	88	87,200	**Gaines** (town) Orleans County
14	69,300	**Medina** (village) Orleans County	88	87,200	**Westfield** (village) Chautauqua County
15	69,800	**Wellsville** (town) Allegany County	88	87,200	**Yorkville** (village) Oneida County
16	70,200	**Franklinville** (town) Cattaraugus County	91	87,400	**Ellicott** (town) Chautauqua County
17	70,400	**Olean** (city) Cattaraugus County	92	87,600	**Schuyler** (town) Herkimer County
17	70,400	**Riverside** (CDP) Suffolk County	92	87,600	**Southport** (town) Chemung County
19	71,500	**Brookfield** (town) Madison County	94	87,800	**Ridgeway** (town) Orleans County
20	71,600	**Albion** (village) Orleans County	94	87,800	**Warsaw** (village) Wyoming County
21	72,000	**Cuba** (town) Allegany County	96	88,000	**Castile** (town) Wyoming County
22	72,900	**Sloan** (village) Erie County	97	88,400	**Frankfort** (village) Herkimer County
23	74,500	**Gowanda** (village) Cattaraugus County	97	88,400	**Le Roy** (village) Genesee County
24	75,300	**Silver Creek** (village) Chautauqua County	99	88,500	**Portville** (town) Cattaraugus County
25	75,400	**Norfolk** (town) Saint Lawrence County	100	88,800	**Granby** (town) Oswego County
26	76,000	**Stockholm** (town) Saint Lawrence County	100	88,800	**Sterling** (town) Cayuga County
27	76,100	**Southport** (CDP) Chemung County	100	88,800	**Syracuse** (city) Onondaga County
28	76,200	**Bangor** (town) Franklin County	103	89,200	**Utica** (city) Oneida County
28	76,200	**Gloversville** (city) Fulton County	104	89,300	**Endicott** (village) Broome County
28	76,200	**Rochester** (city) Monroe County	104	89,300	**Lisle** (town) Broome County
31	76,500	**Perry** (village) Wyoming County	106	89,400	**Albion** (town) Orleans County
32	76,600	**Fulton** (city) Oswego County	106	89,400	**Wayland** (town) Steuben County
33	77,000	**Elmira Heights** (village) Chemung County	108	89,700	**East Syracuse** (village) Onondaga County
34	77,500	**Massena** (town) Saint Lawrence County	108	89,700	**Murray** (town) Orleans County
35	77,900	**Massena** (village) Saint Lawrence County	110	89,800	**Annsville** (town) Oneida County
36	78,400	**Bath** (town) Steuben County	110	89,800	**Attica** (village) Wyoming County
36	78,400	**Saint Johnsville** (town) Montgomery County	110	89,800	**Oswegatchie** (town) Saint Lawrence County
38	78,500	**Cohocton** (town) Steuben County	113	89,900	**Westfield** (town) Chautauqua County
38	78,500	**Waterloo** (town) Seneca County	114	90,000	**Candor** (town) Tioga County
40	78,800	**Bath** (village) Steuben County	114	90,000	**Sodus** (town) Wayne County
40	78,800	**Randolph** (town) Cattaraugus County	116	90,500	**Rome** (city) Oneida County
42	79,500	**Mount Morris** (town) Livingston County	117	90,600	**Palermo** (town) Oswego County
43	79,700	**Carroll** (town) Chautauqua County	118	90,700	**Geneva** (city) Ontario County
44	79,800	**Little Falls** (city) Herkimer County	118	90,700	**Whitehall** (town) Washington County
45	80,500	**Sidney** (town) Delaware County	120	91,000	**Palmyra** (village) Wayne County
46	80,700	**Oswego** (city) Oswego County	121	91,200	**Amsterdam** (city) Montgomery County
46	80,700	**Shelby** (town) Orleans County	121	91,200	**Herkimer** (town) Herkimer County
48	81,400	**Ilion** (village) Herkimer County	123	91,300	**Lyncourt** (CDP) Onondaga County
48	81,400	**Whitehall** (village) Washington County	124	92,000	**Gouverneur** (village) Saint Lawrence County
50	81,600	**Sidney** (village) Delaware County	125	92,100	**Hanover** (town) Chautauqua County
51	81,700	**Wolcott** (town) Wayne County	125	92,100	**Yates** (town) Orleans County
52	81,800	**Manheim** (town) Herkimer County	127	92,500	**Arcadia** (town) Wayne County
53	81,900	**Norwich** (town) Chenango County	128	92,800	**Tonawanda** (city) Erie County
54	82,600	**Niagara** (town) Niagara County	129	92,900	**Manchester** (town) Ontario County
55	82,700	**Lackawanna** (city) Erie County	130	93,000	**Blasdell** (village) Erie County
56	82,800	**Perry** (town) Wyoming County	131	93,200	**Hornellsville** (town) Steuben County
56	82,800	**Waterloo** (village) Seneca County	132	93,300	**Barton** (town) Tioga County
58	82,900	**Canisteo** (town) Steuben County	132	93,300	**South Lockport** (CDP) Niagara County
58	82,900	**Minden** (town) Montgomery County	134	93,600	**Whitesboro** (village) Oneida County
58	82,900	**Portland** (town) Chautauqua County	135	94,000	**East Rochester** (town/village) Monroe County
61	83,400	**Malone** (village) Franklin County	135	94,000	**Lakewood** (village) Chautauqua County
62	83,500	**Rose** (town) Wayne County	135	94,000	**Waverly** (village) Tioga County
63	83,600	**Norwich** (city) Chenango County	138	94,100	**Batavia** (city) Genesee County
64	83,700	**Galen** (town) Wayne County	139	94,200	**Cortland** (city) Cortland County
65	83,900	**Lockport** (city) Niagara County	140	94,300	**Colesville** (town) Broome County
66	84,100	**Johnson City** (village) Broome County	141	94,600	**Nunda** (town) Livingston County
66	84,100	**Newark** (village) Wayne County	142	95,000	**Bainbridge** (town) Chenango County
68	84,200	**Addison** (town) Steuben County	143	95,100	**Village Green** (CDP) Onondaga County
68	84,200	**Hannibal** (town) Oswego County	144	95,200	**Volney** (town) Oswego County
70	84,400	**Mattydale** (CDP) Onondaga County	145	95,300	**Hamlin** (CDP) Monroe County
71	84,900	**Yorkshire** (town) Cattaraugus County	146	95,400	**Nichols** (town) Tioga County
72	85,100	**German Flatts** (town) Herkimer County	147	95,700	**Fort Edward** (village) Washington County
72	85,100	**North Dansville** (town) Livingston County	147	95,700	**Moriah** (town) Essex County
74	85,300	**Altona** (town) Clinton County	149	95,800	**Lisbon** (town) Saint Lawrence County
74	85,300	**Binghamton** (city) Broome County	150	95,900	**Oakfield** (town) Genesee County

Note: *This section ranks incorporated places and CDPs (Census Designated Places) with populations of 2,500 or more. Unincorporated postal areas were not considered. Please refer to the User Guide for additional information.*

Median Year Structure Built

Top 150 Places Ranked in *Descending* Order

State Rank	Year	Place
1	2004	**East Garden City** (CDP) Nassau County
2	2000	**Calcium** (CDP) Jefferson County
3	1997	**Fort Drum** (CDP) Jefferson County
3	1997	**Kiryas Joel** (village) Orange County
5	1996	**Kaser** (village) Rockland County
5	1996	**New Square** (village) Rockland County
5	1996	**University at Buffalo** (CDP) Erie County
8	1993	**Le Ray** (town) Jefferson County
8	1993	**Saint Regis Mohawk Reservation** (reservation) Franklin County
10	1992	**Manorville** (CDP) Suffolk County
10	1992	**Milton** (CDP) Saratoga County
10	1992	**Victor** (town) Ontario County
10	1992	**Wilton** (town) Saratoga County
14	1989	**Canandaigua** (town) Ontario County
15	1988	**Brewerton** (CDP) Onondaga County
15	1988	**Halfmoon** (town) Saratoga County
15	1988	**Wheatfield** (town) Niagara County
18	1987	**Greenville** (town) Orange County
18	1987	**Monsey** (CDP) Rockland County
18	1987	**Newfield** (town) Tompkins County
21	1986	**Enfield** (town) Tompkins County
21	1986	**Gordon Heights** (CDP) Suffolk County
21	1986	**Moriches** (CDP) Suffolk County
21	1986	**North Hills** (village) Nassau County
21	1986	**South Lockport** (CDP) Niagara County
26	1985	**Calverton** (CDP) Suffolk County
26	1985	**Heritage Hills** (CDP) Westchester County
26	1985	**Malta** (town) Saratoga County
26	1985	**Northumberland** (town) Saratoga County
26	1985	**Northwest Harbor** (CDP) Suffolk County
31	1984	**Beekman** (town) Dutchess County
31	1984	**Beekmantown** (town) Clinton County
31	1984	**Greenfield** (town) Saratoga County
31	1984	**Monroe** (town) Orange County
31	1984	**Schuyler** (town) Herkimer County
36	1983	**East Moriches** (CDP) Suffolk County
36	1983	**Harriman** (village) Orange County
36	1983	**Milton** (town) Saratoga County
36	1983	**Montgomery** (village) Orange County
36	1983	**West Monroe** (town) Oswego County
41	1982	**Chester** (village) Orange County
41	1982	**Clifton Park** (town) Saratoga County
41	1982	**Davenport** (town) Delaware County
41	1982	**East Hampton North** (CDP) Suffolk County
41	1982	**Fallsburg** (town) Sullivan County
41	1982	**Gang Mills** (CDP) Steuben County
41	1982	**Hastings** (town) Oswego County
41	1982	**Hopewell** (town) Ontario County
41	1982	**Peru** (town) Clinton County
41	1982	**Scriba** (town) Oswego County
41	1982	**Walworth** (town) Wayne County
41	1982	**Washingtonville** (village) Orange County
53	1981	**Annsville** (town) Oneida County
53	1981	**Chester** (town) Orange County
53	1981	**Clarence** (town) Erie County
53	1981	**Hamptonburgh** (town) Orange County
53	1981	**Lockport** (town) Niagara County
53	1981	**Melville** (CDP) Suffolk County
53	1981	**Perth** (town) Fulton County
53	1981	**Queensbury** (town) Warren County
53	1981	**Riverhead** (town) Suffolk County
53	1981	**South Fallsburg** (CDP) Sullivan County
53	1981	**Union Vale** (town) Dutchess County
53	1981	**West Glens Falls** (CDP) Warren County
53	1981	**Yaphank** (CDP) Suffolk County
66	1980	**Altona** (town) Clinton County
66	1980	**Conesus** (town) Livingston County
66	1980	**Farmington** (town) Ontario County
66	1980	**Hannibal** (town) Oswego County
66	1980	**Hounsfield** (town) Jefferson County
66	1980	**Lysander** (town) Onondaga County
66	1980	**Macedon** (town) Wayne County
66	1980	**Pompey** (town) Onondaga County
66	1980	**Stephentown** (town) Rensselaer County
66	1980	**Warwick** (village) Orange County
66	1980	**Webster** (town) Monroe County
66	1980	**Woodbury** (CDP) Nassau County
78	1979	**Cicero** (town) Onondaga County
78	1979	**Clinton** (town) Dutchess County
78	1979	**Coram** (CDP) Suffolk County
78	1979	**Crawford** (town) Orange County
78	1979	**East Fishkill** (town) Dutchess County
78	1979	**Gaines** (town) Orleans County
78	1979	**Hamlin** (CDP) Monroe County
78	1979	**Livingston** (town) Columbia County
78	1979	**Mechanicstown** (CDP) Orange County
78	1979	**Middle Island** (CDP) Suffolk County
78	1979	**Mooers** (town) Clinton County
78	1979	**Mount Sinai** (CDP) Suffolk County
78	1979	**North Bellport** (CDP) Suffolk County
78	1979	**Pamelia** (town) Jefferson County
78	1979	**Springs** (CDP) Suffolk County
78	1979	**Stillwater** (town) Saratoga County
94	1978	**Clarendon** (town) Orleans County
94	1978	**Colesville** (town) Broome County
94	1978	**Dover** (town) Dutchess County
94	1978	**East Greenbush** (CDP) Rensselaer County
94	1978	**East Hampton** (town) Suffolk County
94	1978	**Fishkill** (town) Dutchess County
94	1978	**Gardiner** (town) Ulster County
94	1978	**Hilton** (village) Monroe County
94	1978	**Lansing** (town) Tompkins County
94	1978	**Louisville** (town) Saint Lawrence County
94	1978	**Mount Ivy** (CDP) Rockland County
94	1978	**Neversink** (town) Sullivan County
94	1978	**Otisco** (town) Onondaga County
94	1978	**Pomona** (village) Rockland County
94	1978	**Ridge** (CDP) Suffolk County
94	1978	**Theresa** (town) Jefferson County
94	1978	**Volney** (town) Oswego County
94	1978	**Westerlo** (town) Albany County
94	1978	**Woodbury** (town) Orange County
94	1978	**Yorkshire** (town) Cattaraugus County
114	1977	**Argyle** (town) Washington County
114	1977	**Clarkson** (CDP) Monroe County
114	1977	**Floyd** (town) Oneida County
114	1977	**Greenville** (town) Greene County
114	1977	**Holtsville** (CDP) Suffolk County
114	1977	**Lake Luzerne** (town) Warren County
114	1977	**Lansing** (village) Tompkins County
114	1977	**Minisink** (town) Orange County
114	1977	**Montauk** (CDP) Suffolk County
114	1977	**New Haven** (town) Oswego County
114	1977	**North Sea** (CDP) Suffolk County
114	1977	**Ontario** (town) Wayne County
114	1977	**Plattekill** (town) Ulster County
114	1977	**Riverhead** (CDP) Suffolk County
114	1977	**Rochester** (town) Ulster County
114	1977	**Shirley** (CDP) Suffolk County
114	1977	**Somers** (town) Westchester County
114	1977	**Southeast** (town) Putnam County
114	1977	**Wallkill** (town) Orange County
114	1977	**Westhampton** (CDP) Suffolk County
134	1976	**Bangor** (town) Franklin County
134	1976	**Brownville** (town) Jefferson County
134	1976	**Campbell** (town) Steuben County
134	1976	**Lisle** (town) Broome County
134	1976	**Mendon** (town) Monroe County
134	1976	**Mexico** (town) Oswego County
134	1976	**Miller Place** (CDP) Suffolk County
134	1976	**Montebello** (village) Rockland County
134	1976	**Palermo** (town) Oswego County
134	1976	**Penfield** (town) Monroe County
134	1976	**Scotchtown** (CDP) Orange County
134	1976	**Shelter Island** (town) Suffolk County
134	1976	**Tioga** (town) Tioga County
134	1976	**Village Green** (CDP) Onondaga County
134	1976	**Viola** (CDP) Rockland County
134	1976	**Wading River** (CDP) Suffolk County
134	1976	**Woodbury** (village) Orange County

Note: This section ranks incorporated places and CDPs (Census Designated Places) with populations of 2,500 or more. Unincorporated postal areas were not considered. Please refer to the User Guide for additional information.

Median Year Structure Built

Top 150 Places Ranked in *Ascending* Order

State Rank	Year	Place	State Rank	Year	Place
1	<1940	**Albany** (city) Albany County	1	<1940	**Norwich** (city) Chenango County
1	<1940	**Albion** (town) Orleans County	1	<1940	**Ogdensburg** (city) Saint Lawrence County
1	<1940	**Albion** (village) Orleans County	1	<1940	**Olean** (city) Cattaraugus County
1	<1940	**Amsterdam** (city) Montgomery County	1	<1940	**Oneida** (city) Madison County
1	<1940	**Attica** (town) Wyoming County	1	<1940	**Oneonta** (city) Otsego County
1	<1940	**Attica** (village) Wyoming County	1	<1940	**Oswego** (city) Oswego County
1	<1940	**Auburn** (city) Cayuga County	1	<1940	**Otsego** (town) Otsego County
1	<1940	**Ballston Spa** (village) Saratoga County	1	<1940	**Owego** (village) Tioga County
1	<1940	**Batavia** (city) Genesee County	1	<1940	**Pelham** (town) Westchester County
1	<1940	**Benton** (town) Yates County	1	<1940	**Pelham** (village) Westchester County
1	<1940	**Bronxville** (village) Westchester County	1	<1940	**Pelham Manor** (village) Westchester County
1	<1940	**Brooklyn** (borough) Kings County	1	<1940	**Penn Yan** (village) Yates County
1	<1940	**Buffalo** (city) Erie County	1	<1940	**Perry** (town) Wyoming County
1	<1940	**Canajoharie** (town) Montgomery County	1	<1940	**Perry** (village) Wyoming County
1	<1940	**Carthage** (village) Jefferson County	1	<1940	**Port Jervis** (city) Orange County
1	<1940	**Catskill** (village) Greene County	1	<1940	**Rensselaer** (city) Rensselaer County
1	<1940	**Cazenovia** (village) Madison County	1	<1940	**Ridgeway** (town) Orleans County
1	<1940	**Corinth** (village) Saratoga County	1	<1940	**Rochester** (city) Monroe County
1	<1940	**Corning** (city) Steuben County	1	<1940	**Saint Johnsville** (town) Montgomery County
1	<1940	**Cortland** (city) Cortland County	1	<1940	**Salamanca** (city) Cattaraugus County
1	<1940	**Coxsackie** (village) Greene County	1	<1940	**Sangerfield** (town) Oneida County
1	<1940	**Dannemora** (village) Clinton County	1	<1940	**Saranac Lake** (village) Franklin County
1	<1940	**Dansville** (village) Livingston County	1	<1940	**Schenectady** (city) Schenectady County
1	<1940	**Delhi** (village) Delaware County	1	<1940	**Sea Cliff** (village) Nassau County
1	<1940	**Dunkirk** (city) Chautauqua County	1	<1940	**Seneca Falls** (CDP) Seneca County
1	<1940	**East Aurora** (village) Erie County	1	<1940	**Shelby** (town) Orleans County
1	<1940	**East Syracuse** (village) Onondaga County	1	<1940	**Silver Creek** (village) Chautauqua County
1	<1940	**Elmira** (city) Chemung County	1	<1940	**Skaneateles** (village) Onondaga County
1	<1940	**Falconer** (village) Chautauqua County	1	<1940	**Somerset** (town) Niagara County
1	<1940	**Floral Park** (village) Nassau County	1	<1940	**South Nyack** (village) Rockland County
1	<1940	**Fort Edward** (village) Washington County	1	<1940	**Troy** (city) Rensselaer County
1	<1940	**Frankfort** (village) Herkimer County	1	<1940	**Utica** (city) Oneida County
1	<1940	**Franklinville** (town) Cattaraugus County	1	<1940	**Walton** (village) Delaware County
1	<1940	**Geneva** (city) Ontario County	1	<1940	**Warsaw** (town) Wyoming County
1	<1940	**Glens Falls** (city) Warren County	1	<1940	**Warsaw** (village) Wyoming County
1	<1940	**Gloversville** (city) Fulton County	1	<1940	**Watertown** (city) Jefferson County
1	<1940	**Gouverneur** (village) Saint Lawrence County	1	<1940	**Watervliet** (city) Albany County
1	<1940	**Gowanda** (village) Cattaraugus County	1	<1940	**Waverly** (village) Tioga County
1	<1940	**Green Island** (town/village) Albany County	1	<1940	**Wellsville** (village) Allegany County
1	<1940	**Groton** (village) Tompkins County	1	<1940	**Westfield** (town) Chautauqua County
1	<1940	**Hamilton** (town) Madison County	1	<1940	**Westfield** (village) Chautauqua County
1	<1940	**Hamilton** (village) Madison County	1	<1940	**Whitehall** (town) Washington County
1	<1940	**Harrietstown** (town) Franklin County	1	<1940	**Whitehall** (village) Washington County
1	<1940	**Hastings-on-Hudson** (village) Westchester County	1	<1940	**Williston Park** (village) Nassau County
1	<1940	**Herkimer** (village) Herkimer County	1	<1940	**Wilna** (town) Jefferson County
1	<1940	**Highland Falls** (village) Orange County	121	1940	**Binghamton** (city) Broome County
1	<1940	**Homer** (town) Cortland County	121	1940	**Fairport** (village) Monroe County
1	<1940	**Homer** (village) Cortland County	121	1940	**Manhasset** (CDP) Nassau County
1	<1940	**Hoosick** (town) Rensselaer County	121	1940	**North Dansville** (town) Livingston County
1	<1940	**Hoosick Falls** (village) Rensselaer County	121	1940	**Randolph** (town) Cattaraugus County
1	<1940	**Hornell** (city) Steuben County	121	1940	**Saugerties** (village) Ulster County
1	<1940	**Hudson** (city) Columbia County	127	1941	**Cohoes** (city) Albany County
1	<1940	**Hudson Falls** (village) Washington County	127	1941	**Endicott** (village) Broome County
1	<1940	**Ithaca** (city) Tompkins County	127	1941	**Fulton** (city) Oswego County
1	<1940	**Jamestown** (city) Chautauqua County	127	1941	**New Berlin** (town) Chenango County
1	<1940	**Johnstown** (city) Fulton County	127	1941	**Niagara Falls** (city) Niagara County
1	<1940	**Kenmore** (village) Erie County	127	1941	**Scarsdale** (town/village) Westchester County
1	<1940	**Kingston** (city) Ulster County	127	1941	**Scotia** (village) Schenectady County
1	<1940	**Larchmont** (village) Westchester County	127	1941	**Seneca** (town) Ontario County
1	<1940	**Le Roy** (village) Genesee County	135	1942	**Great Neck Estates** (village) Nassau County
1	<1940	**Little Falls** (city) Herkimer County	135	1942	**Ilion** (village) Herkimer County
1	<1940	**Lockport** (city) Niagara County	135	1942	**Malverne** (village) Nassau County
1	<1940	**Lowville** (town) Lewis County	135	1942	**Mamaroneck** (town) Westchester County
1	<1940	**Lowville** (village) Lewis County	135	1942	**Munsey Park** (village) Nassau County
1	<1940	**Lyons** (town) Wayne County	135	1942	**Murray** (town) Orleans County
1	<1940	**Lyons** (village) Wayne County	135	1942	**Nunda** (town) Livingston County
1	<1940	**Malone** (village) Franklin County	135	1942	**Oakfield** (town) Genesee County
1	<1940	**Manheim** (town) Herkimer County	135	1942	**Ticonderoga** (CDP) Essex County
1	<1940	**Mechanicville** (city) Saratoga County	144	1943	**Akron** (village) Erie County
1	<1940	**Medina** (village) Orleans County	144	1943	**Castile** (town) Wyoming County
1	<1940	**Minden** (town) Montgomery County	144	1943	**Elmira Heights** (village) Chemung County
1	<1940	**Mohawk** (village) Herkimer County	144	1943	**German Flatts** (town) Herkimer County
1	<1940	**Mount Morris** (town) Livingston County	144	1943	**Inwood** (CDP) Nassau County
1	<1940	**Mount Morris** (village) Livingston County	144	1943	**Moriah** (town) Essex County
1	<1940	**Newburgh** (city) Orange County	144	1943	**Palmyra** (village) Wayne County

Note: *This section ranks incorporated places and CDPs (Census Designated Places) with populations of 2,500 or more. Unincorporated postal areas were not considered. Please refer to the User Guide for additional information.*

Homeowner Vacancy Rate

Top 150 Places Ranked in *Descending* Order

State Rank	Percent	Place		State Rank	Percent	Place
1	12.3	**Lake Placid** (village) Essex County		72	4.6	**Lewiston** (village) Niagara County
2	11.2	**Copake** (town) Columbia County		72	4.6	**Watertown** (city) Jefferson County
3	10.7	**Niagara Falls** (city) Niagara County		72	4.6	**Whitehall** (village) Washington County
4	9.8	**Ticonderoga** (CDP) Essex County		79	4.5	**Armonk** (CDP) Westchester County
5	9.5	**Riverside** (CDP) Suffolk County		79	4.5	**Cazenovia** (town) Madison County
6	9.3	**Lakewood** (village) Chautauqua County		79	4.5	**Greenwood Lake** (village) Orange County
6	9.3	**Wilson** (town) Niagara County		79	4.5	**Liberty** (village) Sullivan County
8	9.2	**Bethel** (town) Sullivan County		79	4.5	**Pleasantville** (village) Westchester County
9	8.4	**Afton** (town) Chenango County		84	4.4	**Mexico** (town) Oswego County
10	8.3	**Lockport** (city) Niagara County		84	4.4	**North Gates** (CDP) Monroe County
10	8.3	**Shandaken** (town) Ulster County		84	4.4	**Rotterdam** (CDP) Schenectady County
12	7.7	**Gloversville** (city) Fulton County		87	4.3	**Big Flats** (CDP) Chemung County
12	7.7	**Newburgh** (city) Orange County		87	4.3	**Carroll** (town) Chautauqua County
14	7.4	**Alfred** (village) Allegany County		87	4.3	**Jay** (town) Essex County
15	7.1	**Chittenango** (village) Madison County		87	4.3	**New Baltimore** (town) Greene County
15	7.1	**Westhampton** (CDP) Suffolk County		87	4.3	**Sangerfield** (town) Oneida County
17	7.0	**Ticonderoga** (town) Essex County		87	4.3	**Scotia** (village) Schenectady County
18	6.9	**Cairo** (town) Greene County		87	4.3	**Shirley** (CDP) Suffolk County
18	6.9	**Rhinebeck** (village) Dutchess County		94	4.2	**Deerpark** (town) Orange County
18	6.9	**Rockland** (town) Sullivan County		94	4.2	**Fallsburg** (town) Sullivan County
21	6.7	**Hudson Falls** (village) Washington County		94	4.2	**Manorhaven** (village) Nassau County
21	6.7	**Richland** (town) Oswego County		94	4.2	**Mastic Beach** (village) Suffolk County
21	6.7	**Somerset** (town) Niagara County		94	4.2	**Mount Vernon** (city) Westchester County
21	6.7	**Washington** (town) Dutchess County		94	4.2	**Southold** (CDP) Suffolk County
25	6.6	**Groton** (village) Tompkins County		100	4.1	**Catskill** (town) Greene County
25	6.6	**Sterling** (town) Cayuga County		100	4.1	**Galen** (town) Wayne County
27	6.4	**Monticello** (village) Sullivan County		100	4.1	**Middleburgh** (town) Schoharie County
27	6.4	**Saint Johnsville** (town) Montgomery County		100	4.1	**North Elba** (town) Essex County
27	6.4	**West Sand Lake** (CDP) Rensselaer County		100	4.1	**Northwest Harbor** (CDP) Suffolk County
30	6.3	**Alexandria** (town) Jefferson County		105	4.0	**Coxsackie** (village) Greene County
30	6.3	**Amityville** (village) Suffolk County		105	4.0	**Esopus** (town) Ulster County
30	6.3	**Marlboro** (CDP) Ulster County		105	4.0	**Garden City South** (CDP) Nassau County
30	6.3	**North Salem** (town) Westchester County		105	4.0	**Long Beach** (city) Nassau County
34	6.2	**Richmond** (town) Ontario County		105	4.0	**Northampton** (town) Fulton County
35	6.1	**Bainbridge** (town) Chenango County		110	3.9	**Bedford** (town) Westchester County
35	6.1	**Center Moriches** (CDP) Suffolk County		110	3.9	**Brinckerhoff** (CDP) Dutchess County
37	6.0	**Nyack** (village) Rockland County		110	3.9	**East Rochester** (town/village) Monroe County
37	6.0	**Thompson** (town) Sullivan County		110	3.9	**Franklinville** (town) Cattaraugus County
39	5.9	**Lido Beach** (CDP) Nassau County		110	3.9	**Horseheads North** (CDP) Chemung County
40	5.7	**Davenport** (town) Delaware County		110	3.9	**New Windsor** (town) Orange County
40	5.7	**Hewlett** (CDP) Nassau County		110	3.9	**Pleasant Valley** (town) Dutchess County
40	5.7	**New York Mills** (village) Oneida County		110	3.9	**Roosevelt** (CDP) Nassau County
43	5.5	**Durham** (town) Greene County		118	3.8	**East Quogue** (CDP) Suffolk County
44	5.4	**Sanford** (town) Broome County		118	3.8	**Great Neck Plaza** (village) Nassau County
44	5.4	**Saranac Lake** (village) Franklin County		118	3.8	**Honeoye Falls** (village) Monroe County
46	5.3	**East Massapequa** (CDP) Nassau County		118	3.8	**Mastic** (CDP) Suffolk County
46	5.3	**Gouverneur** (village) Saint Lawrence County		118	3.8	**Ridge** (CDP) Suffolk County
46	5.3	**South Fallsburg** (CDP) Sullivan County		118	3.8	**Sidney** (village) Delaware County
49	5.2	**Palmyra** (village) Wayne County		124	3.7	**Endicott** (village) Broome County
49	5.2	**Poughkeepsie** (city) Dutchess County		124	3.7	**Grandyle Village** (CDP) Erie County
49	5.2	**Sullivan** (town) Madison County		124	3.7	**Kingsbury** (town) Washington County
52	5.1	**Amsterdam** (city) Montgomery County		124	3.7	**Le Ray** (town) Jefferson County
52	5.1	**Catskill** (village) Greene County		124	3.7	**Lewiston** (town) Niagara County
52	5.1	**Moriah** (town) Essex County		124	3.7	**Maybrook** (village) Orange County
52	5.1	**Rochester** (town) Ulster County		124	3.7	**Rotterdam** (town) Schenectady County
52	5.1	**Searingtown** (CDP) Nassau County		124	3.7	**Skaneateles** (village) Onondaga County
57	5.0	**Milton** (CDP) Saratoga County		124	3.7	**Warrensburg** (town) Warren County
57	5.0	**Olean** (city) Cattaraugus County		133	3.6	**Alfred** (town) Allegany County
57	5.0	**Palmyra** (town) Wayne County		133	3.6	**Busti** (town) Chautauqua County
57	5.0	**Walden** (village) Orange County		133	3.6	**Cazenovia** (village) Madison County
57	5.0	**Wawarsing** (town) Ulster County		133	3.6	**Moravia** (town) Cayuga County
62	4.9	**Delhi** (village) Delaware County		133	3.6	**Newfane** (town) Niagara County
62	4.9	**Warrensburg** (CDP) Warren County		133	3.6	**Niagara** (town) Niagara County
64	4.8	**Dunkirk** (city) Chautauqua County		133	3.6	**Porter** (town) Niagara County
64	4.8	**Harrietstown** (town) Franklin County		133	3.6	**Saratoga** (town) Saratoga County
64	4.8	**Mount Ivy** (CDP) Rockland County		133	3.6	**Saugerties** (village) Ulster County
64	4.8	**New Windsor** (CDP) Orange County		133	3.6	**Southampton** (village) Suffolk County
68	4.7	**Binghamton** (city) Broome County		133	3.6	**Wellsville** (village) Allegany County
68	4.7	**Granby** (town) Oswego County		144	3.5	**Cambria** (town) Niagara County
68	4.7	**Tupper Lake** (village) Franklin County		144	3.5	**Cohocton** (town) Steuben County
68	4.7	**Webster** (village) Monroe County		144	3.5	**East Norwich** (CDP) Nassau County
72	4.6	**Callicoon** (town) Sullivan County		144	3.5	**East Syracuse** (village) Onondaga County
72	4.6	**Chautauqua** (town) Chautauqua County		144	3.5	**Hartland** (town) Niagara County
72	4.6	**Firthcliffe** (CDP) Orange County		144	3.5	**Hartsdale** (CDP) Westchester County
72	4.6	**Fort Ann** (town) Washington County		144	3.5	**Mamakating** (town) Sullivan County

Note: *This section ranks incorporated places and CDPs (Census Designated Places) with populations of 2,500 or more. Unincorporated postal areas were not considered. Please refer to the User Guide for additional information.*

Median Selected Monthly Owner Costs: With Mortgage

Top 150 Places Ranked in *Descending* Order

State Rank	Dollars	Place	State Rank	Dollars	Place
1	4,000+	**Armonk** (CDP) Westchester County	76	3,391	**East Garden City** (CDP) Nassau County
1	4,000+	**Bedford** (town) Westchester County	77	3,381	**Pomona** (village) Rockland County
1	4,000+	**Briarcliff Manor** (village) Westchester County	78	3,375	**Elwood** (CDP) Suffolk County
1	4,000+	**Bronxville** (village) Westchester County	79	3,374	**South Nyack** (village) Rockland County
1	4,000+	**Brookville** (village) Nassau County	80	3,359	**Dobbs Ferry** (village) Westchester County
1	4,000+	**East Hills** (village) Nassau County	81	3,353	**Eastchester** (town) Westchester County
1	4,000+	**Flower Hill** (village) Nassau County	82	3,352	**Garden City Park** (CDP) Nassau County
1	4,000+	**Garden City** (village) Nassau County	83	3,331	**Centerport** (CDP) Suffolk County
1	4,000+	**Great Neck Estates** (village) Nassau County	84	3,313	**Monsey** (CDP) Rockland County
1	4,000+	**Greenville** (CDP) Westchester County	85	3,310	**Bardonia** (CDP) Rockland County
1	4,000+	**Irvington** (village) Westchester County	86	3,296	**Wesley Hills** (village) Rockland County
1	4,000+	**Kings Point** (village) Nassau County	87	3,290	**Stony Brook** (CDP) Suffolk County
1	4,000+	**Lake Success** (village) Nassau County	88	3,288	**Halesite** (CDP) Suffolk County
1	4,000+	**Larchmont** (village) Westchester County	89	3,287	**Ossining** (town) Westchester County
1	4,000+	**Lawrence** (village) Nassau County	90	3,285	**Mount Sinai** (CDP) Suffolk County
1	4,000+	**Lloyd Harbor** (village) Suffolk County	91	3,283	**Locust Valley** (CDP) Nassau County
1	4,000+	**Mamaroneck** (town) Westchester County	92	3,280	**Thomaston** (village) Nassau County
1	4,000+	**Manhasset** (CDP) Nassau County	93	3,261	**Croton-on-Hudson** (village) Westchester County
1	4,000+	**Manhasset Hills** (CDP) Nassau County	94	3,255	**Eastchester** (CDP) Westchester County
1	4,000+	**Montebello** (village) Rockland County	95	3,252	**West Nyack** (CDP) Rockland County
1	4,000+	**Munsey Park** (village) Nassau County	96	3,232	**Congers** (CDP) Rockland County
1	4,000+	**Muttontown** (village) Nassau County	97	3,228	**Glen Head** (CDP) Nassau County
1	4,000+	**New Castle** (town) Westchester County	97	3,228	**Hawthorne** (CDP) Westchester County
1	4,000+	**North Castle** (town) Westchester County	97	3,228	**Manorville** (CDP) Suffolk County
1	4,000+	**North Hills** (village) Nassau County	100	3,226	**Wantagh** (CDP) Nassau County
1	4,000+	**Old Westbury** (village) Nassau County	101	3,215	**Tarrytown** (village) Westchester County
1	4,000+	**Pelham** (town) Westchester County	102	3,207	**West Hills** (CDP) Suffolk County
1	4,000+	**Pelham** (village) Westchester County	103	3,203	**Huntington** (town) Suffolk County
1	4,000+	**Pelham Manor** (village) Westchester County	104	3,190	**Hewlett** (CDP) Nassau County
1	4,000+	**Pound Ridge** (town) Westchester County	105	3,186	**Plainview** (CDP) Nassau County
1	4,000+	**Rye** (city) Westchester County	106	3,185	**Thornwood** (CDP) Westchester County
1	4,000+	**Rye Brook** (village) Westchester County	107	3,181	**Bellmore** (CDP) Nassau County
1	4,000+	**Sands Point** (village) Nassau County	107	3,181	**South Valley Stream** (CDP) Nassau County
1	4,000+	**Scarsdale** (town/village) Westchester County	109	3,176	**East Rockaway** (village) Nassau County
1	4,000+	**Searingtown** (CDP) Nassau County	109	3,176	**Glenwood Landing** (CDP) Nassau County
1	4,000+	**Woodbury** (CDP) Nassau County	111	3,170	**Airmont** (village) Rockland County
37	3,965	**Sleepy Hollow** (village) Westchester County	112	3,169	**Baldwin Harbor** (CDP) Nassau County
38	3,935	**Cold Spring Harbor** (CDP) Suffolk County	113	3,166	**Massapequa** (CDP) Nassau County
39	3,925	**Jericho** (CDP) Nassau County	114	3,162	**Bayville** (village) Nassau County
40	3,919	**Dix Hills** (CDP) Suffolk County	115	3,154	**Babylon** (village) Suffolk County
41	3,903	**East Williston** (village) Nassau County	116	3,131	**Carmel Hamlet** (CDP) Putnam County
42	3,847	**Fort Salonga** (CDP) Suffolk County	117	3,129	**Jefferson Valley-Yorktown** (CDP) Westchester County
43	3,809	**Lewisboro** (town) Westchester County	118	3,127	**Roslyn** (village) Nassau County
44	3,780	**Hastings-on-Hudson** (village) Westchester County	119	3,125	**Oyster Bay** (town) Nassau County
44	3,780	**Roslyn Heights** (CDP) Nassau County	120	3,120	**Floral Park** (village) Nassau County
46	3,779	**Southampton** (village) Suffolk County	121	3,119	**Commack** (CDP) Suffolk County
47	3,771	**Harrison** (town/village) Westchester County	122	3,117	**Herricks** (CDP) Nassau County
48	3,745	**Port Washington** (CDP) Nassau County	123	3,116	**North New Hyde Park** (CDP) Nassau County
49	3,732	**Ardsley** (village) Westchester County	124	3,115	**New Hyde Park** (village) Nassau County
50	3,727	**Old Bethpage** (CDP) Nassau County	125	3,107	**Orangetown** (town) Rockland County
51	3,706	**Port Washington North** (village) Nassau County	126	3,102	**Smithtown** (CDP) Suffolk County
52	3,700	**Kaser** (village) Rockland County	127	3,101	**Chestnut Ridge** (village) Rockland County
53	3,692	**Mount Pleasant** (town) Westchester County	128	3,098	**Pearl River** (CDP) Rockland County
53	3,692	**Syosset** (CDP) Nassau County	129	3,094	**White Plains** (city) Westchester County
55	3,643	**Woodmere** (CDP) Nassau County	130	3,093	**Blauvelt** (CDP) Rockland County
56	3,601	**Great Neck** (village) Nassau County	131	3,092	**Westbury** (village) Nassau County
57	3,580	**Mamaroneck** (village) Westchester County	132	3,088	**New City** (CDP) Rockland County
58	3,545	**Lido Beach** (CDP) Nassau County	133	3,087	**Yorktown** (town) Westchester County
59	3,543	**Viola** (CDP) Rockland County	134	3,085	**Port Chester** (village) Westchester County
60	3,542	**Piermont** (village) Rockland County	135	3,082	**Clarkstown** (town) Rockland County
61	3,535	**North Salem** (town) Westchester County	136	3,077	**Setauket-East Setauket** (CDP) Suffolk County
62	3,521	**Melville** (CDP) Suffolk County	137	3,074	**Franklin Square** (CDP) Nassau County
63	3,519	**Rye** (town) Westchester County	138	3,071	**Sayville** (CDP) Suffolk County
64	3,518	**Rockville Centre** (village) Nassau County	139	3,070	**Smithtown** (town) Suffolk County
65	3,510	**Sea Cliff** (village) Nassau County	140	3,067	**North Merrick** (CDP) Nassau County
66	3,490	**Brightwaters** (village) Suffolk County	141	3,065	**Nanuet** (CDP) Rockland County
67	3,473	**Bayport** (CDP) Suffolk County	142	3,059	**Albertson** (CDP) Nassau County
68	3,465	**Huntington** (CDP) Suffolk County	143	3,055	**Tappan** (CDP) Rockland County
69	3,462	**Valhalla** (CDP) Westchester County	144	3,050	**Lynbrook** (village) Nassau County
70	3,453	**Pleasantville** (village) Westchester County	145	3,040	**Seaford** (CDP) Nassau County
71	3,452	**New Rochelle** (city) Westchester County	146	3,037	**Bethpage** (CDP) Nassau County
72	3,445	**North Hempstead** (town) Nassau County	146	3,037	**Wheatley Heights** (CDP) Suffolk County
73	3,430	**Merrick** (CDP) Nassau County	148	3,036	**Somers** (town) Westchester County
74	3,422	**East Norwich** (CDP) Nassau County	149	3,032	**Fairview** (CDP) Westchester County
75	3,397	**Greenburgh** (town) Westchester County	150	3,030	**Northwest Harbor** (CDP) Suffolk County

Note: This section ranks incorporated places and CDPs (Census Designated Places) with populations of 2,500 or more. Unincorporated postal areas were not considered. Please refer to the User Guide for additional information.

Median Selected Monthly Owner Costs: With Mortgage

Top 150 Places Ranked in *Ascending* Order

State Rank	Dollars	Place	State Rank	Dollars	Place
1	782	**Salamanca** (city) Cattaraugus County	76	1,038	**Barton** (town) Tioga County
2	783	**Saint Regis Mohawk Reservation** (reservation) Franklin County	77	1,039	**Collins** (town) Erie County
3	843	**Dunkirk** (city) Chautauqua County	77	1,039	**Geneva** (city) Ontario County
4	868	**Southport** (CDP) Chemung County	79	1,045	**Au Sable** (town) Clinton County
5	876	**Jamestown** (city) Chautauqua County	79	1,045	**Carroll** (town) Chautauqua County
6	878	**Stockholm** (town) Saint Lawrence County	79	1,045	**Kirkwood** (town) Broome County
7	879	**Hornell** (city) Steuben County	82	1,051	**Guilford** (town) Chenango County
8	887	**Wellsville** (village) Allegany County	83	1,053	**Somerset** (town) Niagara County
9	898	**Westfield** (village) Chautauqua County	84	1,054	**Mooers** (town) Clinton County
10	908	**Gowanda** (village) Cattaraugus County	85	1,055	**Portville** (town) Cattaraugus County
11	909	**Falconer** (village) Chautauqua County	86	1,056	**Fulton** (city) Oswego County
12	913	**Westfield** (town) Chautauqua County	87	1,057	**Newfane** (CDP) Niagara County
13	926	**Elmira** (city) Chemung County	88	1,060	**Silver Creek** (village) Chautauqua County
13	926	**Sloan** (village) Erie County	89	1,061	**Endicott** (village) Broome County
15	932	**Ilion** (village) Herkimer County	90	1,062	**Volney** (town) Oswego County
16	944	**Niagara Falls** (city) Niagara County	91	1,063	**New Berlin** (town) Chenango County
17	947	**Lyons** (village) Wayne County	91	1,063	**Nichols** (town) Tioga County
17	947	**Starkey** (town) Yates County	93	1,064	**Manheim** (town) Herkimer County
19	949	**Buffalo** (city) Erie County	93	1,064	**Perry** (town) Wyoming County
20	952	**Sidney** (town) Delaware County	93	1,064	**Watertown** (city) Jefferson County
21	953	**Chautauqua** (town) Chautauqua County	96	1,065	**Hornellsville** (town) Steuben County
22	956	**Elmira Heights** (village) Chemung County	97	1,068	**New York Mills** (village) Oneida County
23	961	**Franklinville** (town) Cattaraugus County	98	1,069	**Attica** (town) Wyoming County
23	961	**Lackawanna** (city) Erie County	98	1,069	**Newark** (village) Wayne County
23	961	**Tupper Lake** (village) Franklin County	98	1,069	**Waterloo** (town) Seneca County
26	966	**Boonville** (town) Oneida County	101	1,071	**Caneadea** (town) Allegany County
26	966	**Wellsville** (town) Allegany County	101	1,071	**Champion** (town) Jefferson County
28	970	**Massena** (town) Saint Lawrence County	101	1,071	**Croghan** (town) Lewis County
29	972	**Southport** (town) Chemung County	101	1,071	**Dansville** (village) Livingston County
30	974	**Village Green** (CDP) Onondaga County	105	1,074	**Portland** (town) Chautauqua County
31	975	**Gouverneur** (village) Saint Lawrence County	106	1,076	**Norfolk** (town) Saint Lawrence County
32	976	**Galen** (town) Wayne County	106	1,076	**Syracuse** (city) Onondaga County
33	977	**Ogdensburg** (city) Saint Lawrence County	106	1,076	**Tonawanda** (city) Erie County
34	979	**Olean** (city) Cattaraugus County	109	1,077	**Lockport** (city) Niagara County
35	980	**Massena** (village) Saint Lawrence County	109	1,077	**North Dansville** (town) Livingston County
36	982	**Sidney** (village) Delaware County	111	1,079	**Dix** (town) Schuyler County
37	983	**Brookfield** (town) Madison County	111	1,079	**Manchester** (town) Ontario County
38	984	**Cohocton** (town) Steuben County	113	1,082	**Binghamton** (city) Broome County
39	987	**Randolph** (town) Cattaraugus County	114	1,083	**Dannemora** (village) Clinton County
40	989	**Mattydale** (CDP) Onondaga County	114	1,083	**Norwich** (city) Chenango County
40	989	**Moira** (town) Franklin County	116	1,084	**Blasdell** (village) Erie County
42	991	**Altona** (town) Clinton County	116	1,084	**Mount Morris** (village) Livingston County
42	991	**Perry** (village) Wyoming County	118	1,085	**Frankfort** (village) Herkimer County
44	993	**Canisteo** (town) Steuben County	118	1,085	**Yorkshire** (town) Cattaraugus County
45	995	**Niagara** (town) Niagara County	120	1,086	**Waterloo** (village) Seneca County
46	1,000	**Attica** (village) Wyoming County	121	1,089	**Oswegatchie** (town) Saint Lawrence County
46	1,000	**Oxford** (town) Chenango County	122	1,092	**Akron** (village) Erie County
48	1,001	**Hanover** (town) Chautauqua County	123	1,094	**Cheektowaga** (town) Erie County
49	1,007	**Horseheads** (village) Chemung County	123	1,094	**Murray** (town) Orleans County
49	1,007	**Penn Yan** (village) Yates County	125	1,098	**Batavia** (city) Genesee County
51	1,008	**Bath** (village) Steuben County	125	1,098	**Lakewood** (village) Chautauqua County
51	1,008	**Wolcott** (town) Wayne County	127	1,099	**Cheektowaga** (CDP) Erie County
53	1,009	**Warsaw** (village) Wyoming County	127	1,099	**Louisville** (town) Saint Lawrence County
54	1,014	**Saint Johnsville** (town) Montgomery County	127	1,099	**Tupper Lake** (town) Franklin County
55	1,017	**Castile** (town) Wyoming County	130	1,100	**Cuba** (town) Allegany County
56	1,018	**Ellicott** (town) Chautauqua County	130	1,100	**Eaton** (town) Madison County
56	1,018	**Rochester** (city) Monroe County	130	1,100	**Moriah** (town) Essex County
58	1,019	**Galeville** (CDP) Onondaga County	133	1,101	**Bangor** (town) Franklin County
58	1,019	**Yorkville** (village) Oneida County	133	1,101	**Utica** (city) Oneida County
60	1,021	**Lyons** (town) Wayne County	135	1,104	**Lake Erie Beach** (CDP) Erie County
61	1,022	**Johnson City** (village) Broome County	136	1,105	**Herkimer** (town) Herkimer County
62	1,023	**Warsaw** (town) Wyoming County	136	1,105	**Lakeland** (CDP) Onondaga County
63	1,024	**Gloversville** (city) Fulton County	138	1,106	**Gates** (CDP) Monroe County
64	1,027	**Wayland** (town) Steuben County	138	1,106	**Johnstown** (city) Fulton County
65	1,028	**German Flatts** (town) Herkimer County	140	1,107	**Herkimer** (village) Herkimer County
65	1,028	**Little Falls** (city) Herkimer County	140	1,107	**Moravia** (town) Cayuga County
65	1,028	**Milo** (town) Yates County	142	1,108	**Arcade** (town) Wyoming County
68	1,029	**Sterling** (town) Cayuga County	143	1,109	**Solvay** (village) Onondaga County
69	1,032	**Bath** (town) Steuben County	144	1,111	**Albion** (village) Orleans County
69	1,032	**Medina** (village) Orleans County	145	1,112	**Rose** (town) Wayne County
71	1,033	**Seneca Falls** (CDP) Seneca County	146	1,113	**Chemung** (town) Chemung County
72	1,034	**Waverly** (village) Tioga County	146	1,113	**Groton** (village) Tompkins County
73	1,035	**Gouverneur** (town) Saint Lawrence County	146	1,113	**Nunda** (town) Livingston County
73	1,035	**Oswego** (city) Oswego County	149	1,117	**Lyncourt** (CDP) Onondaga County
75	1,037	**Mohawk** (village) Herkimer County	149	1,117	**Union** (town) Broome County

Note: This section ranks incorporated places and CDPs (Census Designated Places) with populations of 2,500 or more. Unincorporated postal areas were not considered. Please refer to the User Guide for additional information.

Median Selected Monthly Owner Costs: Without Mortgage

Top 150 Places Ranked in *Descending* Order

State Rank	Dollars	Place	State Rank	Dollars	Place
1	1,500+	**Ardsley** (village) Westchester County	76	1,445	**Wesley Hills** (village) Rockland County
1	1,500+	**Armonk** (CDP) Westchester County	77	1,435	**Nesconset** (CDP) Suffolk County
1	1,500+	**Bedford** (town) Westchester County	78	1,434	**North Hempstead** (town) Nassau County
1	1,500+	**Briarcliff Manor** (village) Westchester County	79	1,430	**Plainview** (CDP) Nassau County
1	1,500+	**Brightwaters** (village) Suffolk County	79	1,430	**Rye** (town) Westchester County
1	1,500+	**Bronxville** (village) Westchester County	81	1,426	**Pleasantville** (village) Westchester County
1	1,500+	**Brookville** (village) Nassau County	81	1,426	**Thomaston** (village) Nassau County
1	1,500+	**Cold Spring Harbor** (CDP) Suffolk County	83	1,424	**East Shoreham** (CDP) Suffolk County
1	1,500+	**Dix Hills** (CDP) Suffolk County	84	1,423	**Massapequa** (CDP) Nassau County
1	1,500+	**Dobbs Ferry** (village) Westchester County	85	1,422	**West Bay Shore** (CDP) Suffolk County
1	1,500+	**East Garden City** (CDP) Nassau County	86	1,420	**Eastchester** (CDP) Westchester County
1	1,500+	**East Hills** (village) Nassau County	87	1,418	**Valhalla** (CDP) Westchester County
1	1,500+	**East Williston** (village) Nassau County	88	1,411	**Hewlett** (CDP) Nassau County
1	1,500+	**Flower Hill** (village) Nassau County	89	1,404	**Bayport** (CDP) Suffolk County
1	1,500+	**Fort Salonga** (CDP) Suffolk County	90	1,402	**Setauket-East Setauket** (CDP) Suffolk County
1	1,500+	**Garden City** (village) Nassau County	91	1,395	**North Salem** (town) Westchester County
1	1,500+	**Great Neck** (village) Nassau County	92	1,394	**Herricks** (CDP) Nassau County
1	1,500+	**Great Neck Estates** (village) Nassau County	93	1,374	**Centerport** (CDP) Suffolk County
1	1,500+	**Greenburgh** (town) Westchester County	94	1,369	**Elwood** (CDP) Suffolk County
1	1,500+	**Greenville** (CDP) Westchester County	95	1,367	**Nyack** (village) Rockland County
1	1,500+	**Harrison** (town/village) Westchester County	96	1,359	**Port Chester** (village) Westchester County
1	1,500+	**Hastings-on-Hudson** (village) Westchester County	97	1,354	**Glen Head** (CDP) Nassau County
1	1,500+	**Huntington** (CDP) Suffolk County	98	1,351	**Floral Park** (village) Nassau County
1	1,500+	**Irvington** (village) Westchester County	99	1,350	**Bardonia** (CDP) Rockland County
1	1,500+	**Jericho** (CDP) Nassau County	99	1,350	**Stony Brook** (CDP) Suffolk County
1	1,500+	**Kings Point** (village) Nassau County	101	1,340	**New City** (CDP) Rockland County
1	1,500+	**Lake Success** (village) Nassau County	102	1,336	**Bellmore** (CDP) Nassau County
1	1,500+	**Larchmont** (village) Westchester County	103	1,330	**Huntington** (town) Suffolk County
1	1,500+	**Lawrence** (village) Nassau County	104	1,328	**Tuxedo** (town) Orange County
1	1,500+	**Lewisboro** (town) Westchester County	105	1,327	**Miller Place** (CDP) Suffolk County
1	1,500+	**Lido Beach** (CDP) Nassau County	106	1,323	**Babylon** (village) Suffolk County
1	1,500+	**Lloyd Harbor** (village) Suffolk County	106	1,323	**Glenwood Landing** (CDP) Nassau County
1	1,500+	**Mamaroneck** (town) Westchester County	108	1,322	**South Hempstead** (CDP) Nassau County
1	1,500+	**Manhasset** (CDP) Nassau County	109	1,321	**Thornwood** (CDP) Westchester County
1	1,500+	**Manhasset Hills** (CDP) Nassau County	110	1,320	**Amityville** (village) Suffolk County
1	1,500+	**Merrick** (CDP) Nassau County	110	1,320	**Malverne** (village) Nassau County
1	1,500+	**Montebello** (village) Rockland County	112	1,319	**North Bellmore** (CDP) Nassau County
1	1,500+	**Mount Pleasant** (town) Westchester County	112	1,319	**Oakdale** (CDP) Suffolk County
1	1,500+	**Munsey Park** (village) Nassau County	114	1,315	**Croton-on-Hudson** (village) Westchester County
1	1,500+	**Muttontown** (village) Nassau County	115	1,312	**West Islip** (CDP) Suffolk County
1	1,500+	**New Castle** (town) Westchester County	116	1,307	**University Gardens** (CDP) Nassau County
1	1,500+	**New Rochelle** (city) Westchester County	117	1,306	**White Plains** (city) Westchester County
1	1,500+	**North Castle** (town) Westchester County	118	1,305	**Airmont** (village) Rockland County
1	1,500+	**North Hills** (village) Nassau County	119	1,302	**Hawthorne** (CDP) Westchester County
1	1,500+	**Old Bethpage** (CDP) Nassau County	120	1,301	**Commack** (CDP) Suffolk County
1	1,500+	**Old Westbury** (village) Nassau County	121	1,297	**Halesite** (CDP) Suffolk County
1	1,500+	**Pelham** (town) Westchester County	122	1,296	**Roslyn** (village) Nassau County
1	1,500+	**Pelham** (village) Westchester County	123	1,293	**Wantagh** (CDP) Nassau County
1	1,500+	**Pelham Manor** (village) Westchester County	124	1,292	**North Wantagh** (CDP) Nassau County
1	1,500+	**Piermont** (village) Rockland County	125	1,291	**Glen Cove** (city) Nassau County
1	1,500+	**Port Washington** (CDP) Nassau County	126	1,284	**Oyster Bay** (town) Nassau County
1	1,500+	**Port Washington North** (village) Nassau County	126	1,284	**Smithtown** (CDP) Suffolk County
1	1,500+	**Pound Ridge** (town) Westchester County	126	1,284	**Wading River** (CDP) Suffolk County
1	1,500+	**Roslyn Heights** (CDP) Nassau County	129	1,280	**Blue Point** (CDP) Suffolk County
1	1,500+	**Rye** (city) Westchester County	130	1,276	**North Merrick** (CDP) Nassau County
1	1,500+	**Rye Brook** (village) Westchester County	131	1,273	**Smithtown** (town) Suffolk County
1	1,500+	**Sands Point** (village) Nassau County	132	1,269	**Lynbrook** (village) Nassau County
1	1,500+	**Scarsdale** (town/village) Westchester County	133	1,267	**Plainedge** (CDP) Nassau County
1	1,500+	**Sea Cliff** (village) Nassau County	134	1,265	**Seaford** (CDP) Nassau County
1	1,500+	**Searingtown** (CDP) Nassau County	135	1,263	**East Islip** (CDP) Suffolk County
1	1,500+	**Sleepy Hollow** (village) Westchester County	136	1,262	**Cortlandt** (town) Westchester County
1	1,500+	**South Nyack** (village) Rockland County	136	1,262	**Garden City Park** (CDP) Nassau County
1	1,500+	**Syosset** (CDP) Nassau County	138	1,261	**Brookville** (CDP) Suffolk County
1	1,500+	**Tarrytown** (village) Westchester County	139	1,260	**East Moriches** (CDP) Suffolk County
1	1,500+	**Viola** (CDP) Rockland County	139	1,260	**Hempstead** (village) Nassau County
1	1,500+	**Woodbury** (CDP) Nassau County	141	1,259	**Oyster Bay** (CDP) Nassau County
1	1,500+	**Woodmere** (CDP) Nassau County	142	1,258	**Pomona** (village) Rockland County
68	1,496	**Rockville Centre** (village) Nassau County	143	1,257	**Mount Sinai** (CDP) Suffolk County
69	1,477	**South Valley Stream** (CDP) Nassau County	143	1,257	**North Massapequa** (CDP) Nassau County
70	1,460	**Tuckahoe** (village) Westchester County	143	1,257	**Northport** (village) Suffolk County
70	1,460	**West Hills** (CDP) Suffolk County	146	1,255	**Thiells** (CDP) Rockland County
72	1,455	**Monsey** (CDP) Rockland County	147	1,252	**Hempstead** (town) Nassau County
73	1,452	**Eastchester** (town) Westchester County	147	1,252	**Salisbury** (CDP) Nassau County
74	1,451	**Mamaroneck** (village) Westchester County	149	1,248	**Oceanside** (CDP) Nassau County
75	1,447	**Ossining** (town) Westchester County	150	1,245	**Sayville** (CDP) Suffolk County

Note: *This section ranks incorporated places and CDPs (Census Designated Places) with populations of 2,500 or more. Unincorporated postal areas were not considered. Please refer to the User Guide for additional information.*

Median Selected Monthly Owner Costs: Without Mortgage

Top 150 Places Ranked in *Ascending* Order

State Rank	Dollars	Place
1	292	**Saint Regis Mohawk Reservation** (reservation) Franklin County
2	347	**Arcade** (town) Wyoming County
3	353	**Salamanca** (city) Cattaraugus County
4	356	**Altona** (town) Clinton County
5	362	**Yorkshire** (town) Cattaraugus County
6	365	**Falconer** (village) Chautauqua County
7	368	**Canisteo** (town) Steuben County
7	368	**Norwich** (town) Chenango County
9	371	**Galeville** (CDP) Onondaga County
10	372	**Calcium** (CDP) Jefferson County
11	373	**Southport** (CDP) Chemung County
12	376	**Colesville** (town) Broome County
12	376	**Mattydale** (CDP) Onondaga County
14	381	**Sloan** (village) Erie County
15	382	**Buffalo** (city) Erie County
16	386	**Manheim** (town) Herkimer County
17	387	**Southport** (town) Chemung County
18	389	**Louisville** (town) Saint Lawrence County
18	389	**Sherburne** (town) Chenango County
20	391	**New York Mills** (village) Oneida County
21	393	**Ellisburg** (town) Jefferson County
21	393	**Jamestown** (city) Chautauqua County
23	394	**Brookfield** (town) Madison County
23	394	**Pavilion** (town) Genesee County
25	395	**Croghan** (town) Lewis County
25	395	**Lisbon** (town) Saint Lawrence County
25	395	**Stockholm** (town) Saint Lawrence County
28	398	**Gowanda** (village) Cattaraugus County
29	399	**Boonville** (town) Oneida County
29	399	**Hornell** (city) Steuben County
31	400	**Mohawk** (town) Montgomery County
32	403	**Campbell** (town) Steuben County
33	404	**Castile** (town) Wyoming County
34	406	**Horseheads** (village) Chemung County
35	411	**Theresa** (town) Jefferson County
36	412	**Bangor** (town) Franklin County
37	414	**Mohawk** (village) Herkimer County
37	414	**New Square** (village) Rockland County
39	415	**New Berlin** (town) Chenango County
40	416	**Hannibal** (town) Oswego County
41	417	**Au Sable** (town) Clinton County
41	417	**Chemung** (town) Chemung County
41	417	**Cohocton** (town) Steuben County
41	417	**Unadilla** (town) Otsego County
45	418	**Ellicott** (town) Chautauqua County
46	419	**Norfolk** (town) Saint Lawrence County
47	420	**Dickinson** (town) Broome County
47	420	**Perry** (village) Wyoming County
49	421	**Wayland** (town) Steuben County
50	424	**Collins** (town) Erie County
51	425	**Frankfort** (village) Herkimer County
51	425	**Lackawanna** (city) Erie County
51	425	**Lyncourt** (CDP) Onondaga County
51	425	**North Dansville** (town) Livingston County
51	425	**Vienna** (town) Oneida County
56	427	**Barton** (town) Tioga County
56	427	**Chesterfield** (town) Essex County
56	427	**Elmira** (city) Chemung County
56	427	**Horseheads** (town) Chemung County
56	427	**Le Ray** (town) Jefferson County
56	427	**Randolph** (town) Cattaraugus County
62	428	**Lakewood** (village) Chautauqua County
62	428	**Moira** (town) Franklin County
62	428	**Perry** (town) Wyoming County
62	428	**Pierrepont** (town) Saint Lawrence County
66	429	**Portland** (town) Chautauqua County
67	431	**Niagara Falls** (city) Niagara County
67	431	**Oswegatchie** (town) Saint Lawrence County
69	433	**Sidney** (town) Delaware County
70	434	**Cape Vincent** (town) Jefferson County
70	434	**Dunkirk** (city) Chautauqua County
72	435	**German Flatts** (town) Herkimer County
72	435	**Westfield** (village) Chautauqua County
74	437	**Dix** (town) Schuyler County
74	437	**Fenton** (town) Broome County
74	437	**Saranac** (town) Clinton County
77	438	**Barker** (town) Broome County
77	438	**Rose** (town) Wayne County
79	439	**Busti** (town) Chautauqua County
79	439	**Canastota** (village) Madison County
79	439	**Windsor** (town) Broome County
82	441	**Bath** (village) Steuben County
82	441	**East Syracuse** (village) Onondaga County
82	441	**Massena** (town) Saint Lawrence County
85	443	**Chenango Bridge** (CDP) Broome County
85	443	**Nichols** (town) Tioga County
85	443	**Pamelia** (town) Jefferson County
88	445	**Annsville** (town) Oneida County
88	445	**Bath** (town) Steuben County
88	445	**Romulus** (town) Seneca County
88	445	**Westfield** (town) Chautauqua County
92	446	**Blasdell** (village) Erie County
92	446	**Wellsville** (town) Allegany County
94	447	**Champion** (town) Jefferson County
95	448	**Dansville** (village) Livingston County
95	448	**Plattsburgh** (city) Clinton County
95	448	**Waverly** (village) Tioga County
98	449	**Tioga** (town) Tioga County
99	451	**Akron** (village) Erie County
99	451	**Endicott** (village) Broome County
99	451	**Ilion** (village) Herkimer County
99	451	**Johnstown** (town) Fulton County
103	452	**Clarkson** (CDP) Monroe County
103	452	**Tupper Lake** (village) Franklin County
105	453	**Hector** (town) Schuyler County
105	453	**Orleans** (town) Jefferson County
105	453	**Yorkville** (village) Oneida County
108	454	**Corinth** (town) Saratoga County
108	454	**Lenox** (town) Madison County
108	454	**New Bremen** (town) Lewis County
108	454	**Sangerfield** (town) Oneida County
112	455	**Ogdensburg** (city) Saint Lawrence County
113	456	**Chautauqua** (town) Chautauqua County
113	456	**Horseheads North** (CDP) Chemung County
113	456	**Newfane** (CDP) Niagara County
113	456	**Rochester** (city) Monroe County
113	456	**Tupper Lake** (town) Franklin County
118	457	**Granby** (town) Oswego County
118	457	**Springville** (village) Erie County
120	459	**Hartland** (town) Niagara County
120	459	**Seneca** (town) Ontario County
122	461	**Candor** (town) Tioga County
122	461	**Davenport** (town) Delaware County
122	461	**Sherrill** (city) Oneida County
125	462	**Brownville** (town) Jefferson County
125	462	**Corning** (town) Steuben County
125	462	**Groton** (village) Tompkins County
125	462	**Lowville** (village) Lewis County
129	463	**Afton** (town) Chenango County
129	463	**Hudson Falls** (village) Washington County
129	463	**Kingsbury** (town) Washington County
129	463	**Niagara** (town) Niagara County
129	463	**Walton** (town) Delaware County
134	464	**Lake Erie Beach** (CDP) Erie County
134	464	**Walton** (village) Delaware County
136	465	**Guilford** (town) Chenango County
136	465	**Scriba** (town) Oswego County
136	465	**Verona** (town) Oneida County
139	466	**Milford** (town) Otsego County
140	467	**Plattsburgh** (town) Clinton County
140	467	**Warsaw** (village) Wyoming County
142	468	**Lowville** (town) Lewis County
142	468	**Moravia** (town) Cayuga County
142	468	**Sardinia** (town) Erie County
145	469	**Sandy Creek** (town) Oswego County
146	470	**Ellery** (town) Chautauqua County
146	470	**Syracuse** (city) Onondaga County
146	470	**Wolcott** (town) Wayne County
149	471	**Cheektowaga** (CDP) Erie County
149	471	**Cheektowaga** (town) Erie County

Note: *This section ranks incorporated places and CDPs (Census Designated Places) with populations of 2,500 or more. Unincorporated postal areas were not considered. Please refer to the User Guide for additional information.*

Median Gross Rent

Top 150 Places Ranked in *Descending* Order

State Rank	Dollars	Place	State Rank	Dollars	Place
1	3,500+	Armonk (CDP) Westchester County	76	1,786	Irvington (village) Westchester County
1	3,500+	East Williston (village) Nassau County	76	1,786	Lake Grove (village) Suffolk County
1	3,500+	Great Neck Estates (village) Nassau County	78	1,785	Cutchogue (CDP) Suffolk County
1	3,500+	Lake Success (village) Nassau County	79	1,781	Huntington (CDP) Suffolk County
1	3,500+	Scarsdale (town/village) Westchester County	79	1,781	Spackenkill (CDP) Dutchess County
6	3,400	Brookville (village) Nassau County	81	1,777	North Salem (town) Westchester County
7	3,133	Northwest Harbor (CDP) Suffolk County	82	1,771	Westhampton (CDP) Suffolk County
8	3,119	West Point (CDP) Orange County	83	1,768	Yaphank (CDP) Suffolk County
9	3,045	Cold Spring Harbor (CDP) Suffolk County	84	1,762	East Moriches (CDP) Suffolk County
10	2,821	East Norwich (CDP) Nassau County	85	1,758	Pelham Manor (village) Westchester County
11	2,758	East Garden City (CDP) Nassau County	86	1,756	Great Neck Plaza (village) Nassau County
12	2,691	Lakeview (CDP) Nassau County	87	1,755	Fort Salonga (CDP) Suffolk County
13	2,660	Muttontown (village) Nassau County	88	1,751	Holbrook (CDP) Suffolk County
14	2,641	Pomona (village) Rockland County	89	1,750	Eastchester (town) Westchester County
15	2,512	Bronxville (village) Westchester County	90	1,747	Flanders (CDP) Suffolk County
16	2,500	Heritage Hills (CDP) Westchester County	91	1,745	North Babylon (CDP) Suffolk County
17	2,428	Melville (CDP) Suffolk County	92	1,743	Wyandanch (CDP) Suffolk County
18	2,375	Greenville (CDP) Westchester County	93	1,736	Sayville (CDP) Suffolk County
19	2,344	Thomaston (village) Nassau County	94	1,733	Massapequa (CDP) Nassau County
20	2,301	Stony Brook (CDP) Suffolk County	95	1,732	Medford (CDP) Suffolk County
21	2,223	Manorhaven (village) Nassau County	96	1,728	Pelham (town) Westchester County
22	2,209	Woodbury (CDP) Nassau County	97	1,726	Pound Ridge (town) Westchester County
23	2,170	Baldwin Harbor (CDP) Nassau County	98	1,725	North Great River (CDP) Suffolk County
24	2,160	Tappan (CDP) Rockland County	99	1,723	Tuckahoe (village) Westchester County
25	2,136	Massapequa Park (village) Nassau County	100	1,722	Larchmont (village) Westchester County
25	2,136	Somers (town) Westchester County	100	1,722	Oyster Bay (town) Nassau County
27	2,134	Centereach (CDP) Suffolk County	102	1,720	Pelham (village) Westchester County
28	2,123	North Merrick (CDP) Nassau County	103	1,714	East Northport (CDP) Suffolk County
29	2,113	Merrick (CDP) Nassau County	104	1,700	Coram (CDP) Suffolk County
30	2,101	North Castle (town) Westchester County	105	1,699	Mount Sinai (CDP) Suffolk County
31	2,082	West Hills (CDP) Suffolk County	106	1,698	Hicksville (CDP) Nassau County
32	2,075	North Bellport (CDP) Suffolk County	107	1,694	Rye Brook (village) Westchester County
33	2,059	Elwood (CDP) Suffolk County	108	1,692	North Hempstead (town) Nassau County
34	2,056	Roslyn (village) Nassau County	109	1,691	North Bellmore (CDP) Nassau County
35	2,041	North Sea (CDP) Suffolk County	110	1,688	North Massapequa (CDP) Nassau County
36	2,040	Red Oaks Mill (CDP) Dutchess County	111	1,687	Gordon Heights (CDP) Suffolk County
37	2,032	Lewisboro (town) Westchester County	112	1,684	Flower Hill (village) Nassau County
38	2,031	Sands Point (village) Nassau County	113	1,683	Glen Cove (city) Nassau County
39	2,021	South Farmingdale (CDP) Nassau County	114	1,682	Blue Point (CDP) Suffolk County
40	2,019	East Shoreham (CDP) Suffolk County	114	1,682	Setauket-East Setauket (CDP) Suffolk County
41	2,013	North New Hyde Park (CDP) Nassau County	116	1,679	Syosset (CDP) Nassau County
42	2,000	Plainview (CDP) Nassau County	116	1,679	Williston Park (village) Nassau County
43	1,989	Valhalla (CDP) Westchester County	118	1,677	Southampton (town) Suffolk County
44	1,984	Lido Beach (CDP) Nassau County	119	1,676	Hampton Bays (CDP) Suffolk County
45	1,978	Plainedge (CDP) Nassau County	119	1,676	Huntington (town) Suffolk County
46	1,969	Hamptonburgh (town) Orange County	121	1,672	Moriches (CDP) Suffolk County
47	1,959	Garden City (village) Nassau County	122	1,668	Babylon (village) Suffolk County
48	1,950	Shirley (CDP) Suffolk County	123	1,664	Locust Valley (CDP) Nassau County
49	1,946	Port Washington North (village) Nassau County	124	1,660	Wheatley Heights (CDP) Suffolk County
50	1,941	Terryville (CDP) Suffolk County	125	1,657	Greenburgh (town) Westchester County
51	1,940	Farmingville (CDP) Suffolk County	126	1,653	Hastings-on-Hudson (village) Westchester County
52	1,934	New Hempstead (village) Rockland County	127	1,650	Lynbrook (village) Nassau County
53	1,921	North Valley Stream (CDP) Nassau County	128	1,648	Elmsford (village) Westchester County
54	1,914	Bellmore (CDP) Nassau County	129	1,646	Eastchester (CDP) Westchester County
55	1,908	Albertson (CDP) Nassau County	129	1,646	Mamaroneck (village) Westchester County
56	1,901	East Meadow (CDP) Nassau County	131	1,645	Sea Cliff (village) Nassau County
57	1,878	Rye (city) Westchester County	132	1,642	Holtsville (CDP) Suffolk County
58	1,875	Shelter Island (town) Suffolk County	133	1,640	Centerport (CDP) Suffolk County
59	1,871	Woodmere (CDP) Nassau County	134	1,637	Long Beach (city) Nassau County
60	1,870	Noyack (CDP) Suffolk County	134	1,637	Wantagh (CDP) Nassau County
61	1,865	Hauppauge (CDP) Suffolk County	136	1,631	Dobbs Ferry (village) Westchester County
62	1,860	Harrison (town/village) Westchester County	137	1,627	Mount Ivy (CDP) Rockland County
63	1,852	Levittown (CDP) Nassau County	137	1,627	Valley Cottage (CDP) Rockland County
64	1,850	Herricks (CDP) Nassau County	139	1,626	West Hempstead (CDP) Nassau County
65	1,844	Dix Hills (CDP) Suffolk County	140	1,622	Hartsdale (CDP) Westchester County
66	1,843	Great Neck (village) Nassau County	140	1,622	Mastic Beach (village) Suffolk County
66	1,843	Jericho (CDP) Nassau County	140	1,622	Riverside (CDP) Suffolk County
68	1,833	East Rockaway (village) Nassau County	143	1,621	Bethpage (CDP) Nassau County
69	1,830	Oyster Bay (CDP) Nassau County	144	1,617	Mastic (CDP) Suffolk County
70	1,820	Seaford (CDP) Nassau County	145	1,616	South Nyack (village) Rockland County
71	1,816	Glenwood Landing (CDP) Nassau County	146	1,615	Bohemia (CDP) Suffolk County
72	1,815	Islandia (village) Suffolk County	147	1,612	Lawrence (village) Nassau County
73	1,809	Springs (CDP) Suffolk County	148	1,609	Carle Place (CDP) Nassau County
74	1,793	East Quogue (CDP) Suffolk County	148	1,609	Commack (CDP) Suffolk County
75	1,787	Port Washington (CDP) Nassau County	148	1,609	Port Jefferson (village) Suffolk County

Note: This section ranks incorporated places and CDPs (Census Designated Places) with populations of 2,500 or more. Unincorporated postal areas were not considered. Please refer to the User Guide for additional information.

Median Gross Rent

Top 150 Places Ranked in *Ascending* Order

State Rank	Dollars	Place	State Rank	Dollars	Place
1	298	**Old Bethpage** (CDP) Nassau County	73	611	**Tupper Lake** (town) Franklin County
2	478	**Saint Regis Mohawk Reservation** (reservation) Franklin County	77	612	**Hornellsville** (town) Steuben County
3	495	**Mooers** (town) Clinton County	77	612	**Moravia** (town) Cayuga County
4	504	**Clarence** (CDP) Erie County	79	613	**Dix** (town) Schuyler County
5	508	**Carroll** (town) Chautauqua County	80	614	**Dunkirk** (city) Chautauqua County
6	514	**Oswegatchie** (town) Saint Lawrence County	80	614	**Lyons** (village) Wayne County
7	516	**Floyd** (town) Oneida County	82	616	**Fredonia** (village) Chautauqua County
8	524	**Eaton** (town) Madison County	83	617	**Westfield** (town) Chautauqua County
9	525	**Randolph** (town) Cattaraugus County	84	618	**Hornell** (city) Steuben County
10	531	**Manheim** (town) Herkimer County	84	618	**Nichols** (town) Tioga County
11	535	**Nunda** (town) Livingston County	86	619	**Sherburne** (town) Chenango County
12	536	**Gaines** (town) Orleans County	86	619	**Unadilla** (town) Otsego County
12	536	**Holland** (town) Erie County	88	620	**Ellicott** (town) Chautauqua County
14	537	**Palatine** (town) Montgomery County	88	620	**Solvay** (village) Onondaga County
15	538	**Newark Valley** (town) Tioga County	90	623	**Olean** (city) Cattaraugus County
16	540	**Guilford** (town) Chenango County	90	623	**Westfield** (village) Chautauqua County
17	541	**Caneadea** (town) Allegany County	92	624	**Lowville** (village) Lewis County
18	552	**Lockport** (town) Niagara County	93	625	**Afton** (town) Chenango County
18	552	**Stamford** (town) Delaware County	93	625	**Cambria** (town) Niagara County
20	553	**Eden** (CDP) Erie County	95	626	**Groton** (village) Tompkins County
21	554	**Falconer** (village) Chautauqua County	96	627	**Greene** (town) Chenango County
22	556	**Portland** (town) Chautauqua County	96	627	**Minden** (town) Montgomery County
23	557	**Frankfort** (village) Herkimer County	96	627	**Norwich** (city) Chenango County
24	558	**Boonville** (town) Oneida County	99	628	**Newfane** (town) Niagara County
24	558	**Mohawk** (village) Herkimer County	100	629	**Cuba** (town) Allegany County
26	559	**Warsaw** (town) Wyoming County	100	629	**Saint Johnsville** (town) Montgomery County
27	560	**Bath** (village) Steuben County	100	629	**Shelby** (town) Orleans County
28	562	**Warsaw** (village) Wyoming County	100	629	**Waterloo** (village) Seneca County
29	564	**Eden** (town) Erie County	104	630	**Barton** (town) Tioga County
30	569	**South Lockport** (CDP) Niagara County	104	630	**Elmira Heights** (village) Chemung County
30	569	**Walton** (village) Delaware County	104	630	**Medina** (village) Orleans County
30	569	**Wellsville** (village) Allegany County	104	630	**Mexico** (town) Oswego County
33	573	**Newfane** (CDP) Niagara County	108	631	**Catlin** (town) Chemung County
34	574	**Stockholm** (town) Saint Lawrence County	109	632	**Frankfort** (town) Herkimer County
35	576	**Bennington** (town) Wyoming County	110	633	**Au Sable** (town) Clinton County
36	577	**Wolcott** (town) Wayne County	110	633	**Lowville** (town) Lewis County
37	579	**Tupper Lake** (village) Franklin County	110	633	**Lyons** (town) Wayne County
37	579	**Wellsville** (town) Allegany County	110	633	**Sloan** (village) Erie County
39	580	**Bath** (town) Steuben County	110	633	**Somerset** (town) Niagara County
39	580	**Ilion** (village) Herkimer County	115	634	**Champlain** (town) Clinton County
41	582	**German Flatts** (town) Herkimer County	115	634	**Dannemora** (village) Clinton County
42	583	**Concord** (town) Erie County	117	635	**Mohawk** (town) Montgomery County
43	584	**Croghan** (town) Lewis County	118	637	**Canastota** (village) Madison County
44	585	**Hancock** (town) Delaware County	118	637	**Waverly** (village) Tioga County
44	585	**Oakfield** (town) Genesee County	120	638	**Allegany** (town) Cattaraugus County
44	585	**Portville** (town) Cattaraugus County	120	638	**Conklin** (town) Broome County
44	585	**Sangerfield** (town) Oneida County	120	638	**Niagara Falls** (city) Niagara County
48	586	**Little Falls** (city) Herkimer County	120	638	**North Collins** (town) Erie County
48	586	**Owego** (village) Tioga County	120	638	**Owego** (town) Tioga County
50	587	**Collins** (town) Erie County	120	638	**Sidney** (village) Delaware County
50	587	**Jamestown** (city) Chautauqua County	126	639	**Candor** (town) Tioga County
50	587	**Yorkshire** (town) Cattaraugus County	127	640	**Gowanda** (village) Cattaraugus County
53	588	**Gorham** (town) Ontario County	127	640	**Mount Morris** (village) Livingston County
54	589	**Perry** (town) Wyoming County	127	640	**North Wantagh** (CDP) Nassau County
54	589	**Springville** (village) Erie County	130	642	**Castile** (town) Wyoming County
56	590	**Perry** (village) Wyoming County	131	643	**Pomfret** (town) Chautauqua County
56	590	**Windsor** (town) Broome County	132	644	**Chenango Bridge** (CDP) Broome County
58	592	**Walton** (town) Delaware County	132	644	**Schoharie** (town) Schoharie County
59	593	**Addison** (town) Steuben County	134	645	**Murray** (town) Orleans County
60	594	**Colden** (town) Erie County	134	645	**Sidney** (town) Delaware County
60	594	**Lackawanna** (city) Erie County	134	645	**Sterling** (town) Cayuga County
62	597	**Attica** (town) Wyoming County	137	646	**Camden** (town) Oneida County
62	597	**Whitesboro** (village) Oneida County	137	646	**Herkimer** (village) Herkimer County
64	599	**Albion** (village) Orleans County	137	646	**Williamson** (town) Wayne County
64	599	**Arcade** (town) Wyoming County	140	647	**Verona** (town) Oneida County
66	600	**Attica** (village) Wyoming County	141	649	**Newark** (village) Wayne County
66	600	**Wheatfield** (town) Niagara County	142	651	**Harrietstown** (town) Franklin County
68	601	**Sherrill** (city) Oneida County	142	651	**Herkimer** (town) Herkimer County
69	602	**Hartland** (town) Niagara County	142	651	**Milo** (town) Yates County
69	602	**Madison** (town) Madison County	142	651	**Oxford** (town) Chenango County
71	603	**Ogdensburg** (city) Saint Lawrence County	146	652	**Dansville** (village) Livingston County
72	606	**Norwich** (town) Chenango County	146	652	**North Dansville** (town) Livingston County
73	611	**Albion** (town) Orleans County	148	654	**Akron** (village) Erie County
73	611	**Aurelius** (town) Cayuga County	148	654	**Auburn** (city) Cayuga County
73	611	**Salamanca** (city) Cattaraugus County	150	655	**Canisteo** (town) Steuben County

Note: *This section ranks incorporated places and CDPs (Census Designated Places) with populations of 2,500 or more. Unincorporated postal areas were not considered. Please refer to the User Guide for additional information.*

Rental Vacancy Rate

Top 150 Places Ranked in *Descending* Order

State Rank	Percent	Place	State Rank	Percent	Place
1	33.9	**Montauk** (CDP) Suffolk County	76	12.4	**East Islip** (CDP) Suffolk County
2	29.3	**Galen** (town) Wayne County	77	12.3	**Lakeland** (CDP) Onondaga County
3	26.4	**Eaton** (town) Madison County	77	12.3	**New Haven** (town) Oswego County
4	25.1	**Catskill** (village) Greene County	77	12.3	**Warrensburg** (CDP) Warren County
5	24.6	**Oneonta** (town) Otsego County	77	12.3	**Whitesboro** (village) Oneida County
6	24.1	**Muttontown** (village) Nassau County	81	12.2	**Marlboro** (CDP) Ulster County
7	23.4	**Durham** (town) Greene County	81	12.2	**Ravena** (village) Albany County
8	23.1	**Lloyd Harbor** (village) Suffolk County	83	12.0	**Busti** (town) Chautauqua County
9	23.0	**Hewlett** (CDP) Nassau County	83	12.0	**Delhi** (town) Delaware County
10	22.4	**Wilson** (town) Niagara County	83	12.0	**Firthcliffe** (CDP) Orange County
11	22.1	**Kings Point** (village) Nassau County	83	12.0	**Gouverneur** (village) Saint Lawrence County
12	21.8	**Marilla** (town) Erie County	83	12.0	**Lloyd** (town) Ulster County
13	21.4	**Lakeview** (CDP) Nassau County	88	11.9	**Fallsburg** (town) Sullivan County
14	21.3	**Rocky Point** (CDP) Suffolk County	89	11.8	**Clinton** (town) Dutchess County
15	21.1	**Chester** (town) Warren County	89	11.8	**Monticello** (village) Sullivan County
16	20.9	**Montrose** (CDP) Westchester County	89	11.8	**Orange Lake** (CDP) Orange County
17	20.4	**Ghent** (town) Columbia County	89	11.8	**Penfield** (town) Monroe County
18	20.0	**East Shoreham** (CDP) Suffolk County	89	11.8	**Yonkers** (city) Westchester County
19	19.9	**Oswego** (town) Oswego County	94	11.7	**Seneca Falls** (CDP) Seneca County
20	19.8	**Hunter** (town) Greene County	94	11.7	**Williamson** (town) Wayne County
20	19.8	**Tappan** (CDP) Rockland County	96	11.6	**Brewerton** (CDP) Onondaga County
22	18.8	**Thornwood** (CDP) Westchester County	96	11.6	**Sennett** (town) Cayuga County
23	18.6	**Bethpage** (CDP) Nassau County	98	11.5	**Gordon Heights** (CDP) Suffolk County
23	18.6	**South Fallsburg** (CDP) Sullivan County	98	11.5	**Guilford** (town) Chenango County
25	18.5	**Minden** (town) Montgomery County	98	11.5	**Hector** (town) Schuyler County
26	18.2	**Catskill** (town) Greene County	98	11.5	**Mamakating** (town) Sullivan County
26	18.2	**Niagara Falls** (city) Niagara County	98	11.5	**Nesconset** (CDP) Suffolk County
28	18.0	**Ridge** (CDP) Suffolk County	98	11.5	**Pomfret** (town) Chautauqua County
29	17.9	**Milton** (CDP) Saratoga County	104	11.4	**Cuba** (town) Allegany County
29	17.9	**North Great River** (CDP) Suffolk County	104	11.4	**Myers Corner** (CDP) Dutchess County
31	17.7	**Setauket-East Setauket** (CDP) Suffolk County	104	11.4	**Port Ewen** (CDP) Ulster County
31	17.7	**Southold** (CDP) Suffolk County	104	11.4	**Southold** (town) Suffolk County
33	17.6	**Perth** (town) Fulton County	108	11.3	**Camden** (town) Oneida County
34	17.1	**South Lockport** (CDP) Niagara County	108	11.3	**Little Falls** (city) Herkimer County
35	17.0	**Knox** (town) Albany County	108	11.3	**New Hartford** (town) Oneida County
36	16.7	**Walworth** (town) Wayne County	108	11.3	**Sandy Creek** (town) Oswego County
37	16.5	**Newfane** (town) Niagara County	112	11.2	**Canandaigua** (town) Ontario County
38	16.3	**Highland** (CDP) Ulster County	112	11.2	**Dix Hills** (CDP) Suffolk County
38	16.3	**Old Westbury** (village) Nassau County	112	11.2	**Williston Park** (village) Nassau County
40	16.2	**Lockport** (city) Niagara County	115	11.1	**Berne** (town) Albany County
41	16.1	**Lakewood** (village) Chautauqua County	115	11.1	**Northport** (village) Suffolk County
42	15.9	**Lockport** (town) Niagara County	117	11.0	**Big Flats** (town) Chemung County
42	15.9	**Vernon** (town) Oneida County	117	11.0	**Middletown** (town) Delaware County
44	15.8	**Constantia** (town) Oswego County	117	11.0	**Southport** (CDP) Chemung County
45	15.7	**Shandaken** (town) Ulster County	120	10.9	**Sodus** (town) Wayne County
46	15.4	**Cedarhurst** (village) Nassau County	120	10.9	**Trenton** (town) Oneida County
47	15.3	**Colden** (town) Erie County	122	10.8	**Rockland** (town) Sullivan County
47	15.3	**Stony Point** (CDP) Rockland County	123	10.7	**Canajoharie** (town) Montgomery County
47	15.3	**Wappingers Falls** (village) Dutchess County	123	10.7	**East Quogue** (CDP) Suffolk County
50	15.0	**Floyd** (town) Oneida County	125	10.6	**Harris Hill** (CDP) Erie County
51	14.6	**Orchard Park** (town) Erie County	125	10.6	**Peru** (town) Clinton County
52	14.4	**Warrensburg** (town) Warren County	127	10.5	**Jamestown** (city) Chautauqua County
53	14.3	**Pelham Manor** (village) Westchester County	127	10.5	**Nassau** (town) Rensselaer County
53	14.3	**Somerset** (town) Niagara County	129	10.4	**East Hampton** (town) Suffolk County
53	14.3	**South Farmingdale** (CDP) Nassau County	129	10.4	**Vienna** (town) Oneida County
56	14.0	**Denmark** (town) Lewis County	131	10.3	**Geneseo** (town) Livingston County
56	14.0	**Geneseo** (village) Livingston County	132	10.2	**Chittenango** (village) Madison County
56	14.0	**Hartland** (town) Niagara County	132	10.2	**Niagara** (town) Niagara County
59	13.9	**Dover** (town) Dutchess County	134	10.1	**Gouverneur** (town) Saint Lawrence County
59	13.9	**Stony Point** (town) Rockland County	134	10.1	**Seneca Falls** (town) Seneca County
61	13.8	**Merrick** (CDP) Nassau County	134	10.1	**Southport** (town) Chemung County
62	13.6	**Lisle** (town) Broome County	137	10.0	**Centereach** (CDP) Suffolk County
62	13.6	**Northampton** (town) Fulton County	137	10.0	**Chesterfield** (town) Essex County
64	13.5	**Theresa** (town) Jefferson County	137	10.0	**Heritage Hills** (CDP) Westchester County
64	13.5	**Ulysses** (town) Tompkins County	140	9.9	**Delhi** (village) Delaware County
66	13.4	**Greenfield** (town) Saratoga County	140	9.9	**Farmingville** (CDP) Suffolk County
67	13.0	**Cato** (town) Cayuga County	140	9.9	**Otego** (town) Otsego County
68	12.9	**Fredonia** (village) Chautauqua County	140	9.9	**Otsego** (town) Otsego County
68	12.9	**Oakdale** (CDP) Suffolk County	140	9.9	**Paris** (town) Oneida County
68	12.9	**Wheatfield** (town) Niagara County	140	9.9	**Tuxedo** (town) Orange County
71	12.8	**Thompson** (town) Sullivan County	146	9.8	**Blooming Grove** (town) Orange County
72	12.7	**Roslyn Heights** (CDP) Nassau County	146	9.8	**Newfane** (CDP) Niagara County
72	12.7	**Royalton** (town) Niagara County	146	9.8	**Piermont** (village) Rockland County
72	12.7	**Union Vale** (town) Dutchess County	149	9.7	**Brunswick** (town) Rensselaer County
75	12.5	**Rochester** (town) Ulster County	149	9.7	**Cornwall** (town) Orange County

Note: *This section ranks incorporated places and CDPs (Census Designated Places) with populations of 2,500 or more. Unincorporated postal areas were not considered. Please refer to the User Guide for additional information.*

Population with Health Insurance

Top 150 Places Ranked in *Descending* Order

State Rank	Percent	Place
1	99.9	**West Point** (CDP) Orange County
2	99.7	**Minoa** (village) Onondaga County
3	99.5	**University at Buffalo** (CDP) Erie County
4	99.0	**New York Mills** (village) Oneida County
5	98.9	**East Greenbush** (CDP) Rensselaer County
6	98.8	**Kiryas Joel** (village) Orange County
7	98.7	**Clarkson** (CDP) Monroe County
7	98.7	**Woodbury** (CDP) Nassau County
9	98.6	**Port Washington North** (village) Nassau County
9	98.6	**Walworth** (town) Wayne County
11	98.5	**Briarcliff Manor** (village) Westchester County
11	98.5	**Bronxville** (village) Westchester County
11	98.5	**Lewiston** (village) Niagara County
11	98.5	**Miller Place** (CDP) Suffolk County
11	98.5	**Munsey Park** (village) Nassau County
11	98.5	**New Square** (village) Rockland County
11	98.5	**North Hills** (village) Nassau County
11	98.5	**Pittsford** (town) Monroe County
11	98.5	**Sands Point** (village) Nassau County
20	98.4	**Larchmont** (village) Westchester County
20	98.4	**Melville** (CDP) Suffolk County
20	98.4	**Owasco** (town) Cayuga County
20	98.4	**Westerlo** (town) Albany County
24	98.3	**Elma Center** (CDP) Erie County
24	98.3	**Garden City** (village) Nassau County
24	98.3	**Rush** (town) Monroe County
24	98.3	**Scarsdale** (town/village) Westchester County
24	98.3	**Spackenkill** (CDP) Dutchess County
24	98.3	**West Nyack** (CDP) Rockland County
24	98.3	**Westvale** (CDP) Onondaga County
31	98.2	**Poestenkill** (town) Rensselaer County
32	98.0	**Carroll** (town) Chautauqua County
32	98.0	**Manlius** (village) Onondaga County
32	98.0	**Orchard Park** (town) Erie County
32	98.0	**South Hill** (CDP) Tompkins County
32	98.0	**Wanakah** (CDP) Erie County
37	97.9	**Ballston** (town) Saratoga County
37	97.9	**Glenwood Landing** (CDP) Nassau County
37	97.9	**Horseheads North** (CDP) Chemung County
37	97.9	**Lido Beach** (CDP) Nassau County
37	97.9	**North Salem** (town) Westchester County
42	97.8	**Heritage Hills** (CDP) Westchester County
42	97.8	**Lawrence** (village) Nassau County
42	97.8	**Manhasset Hills** (CDP) Nassau County
42	97.8	**SUNY Oswego** (CDP) Oswego County
42	97.8	**Setauket-East Setauket** (CDP) Suffolk County
47	97.7	**Bellmore** (CDP) Nassau County
47	97.7	**East Williston** (village) Nassau County
47	97.7	**Jefferson Valley-Yorktown** (CDP) Westchester County
47	97.7	**North Great River** (CDP) Suffolk County
51	97.6	**Amsterdam** (town) Montgomery County
51	97.6	**Clifton Park** (town) Saratoga County
51	97.6	**Gang Mills** (CDP) Steuben County
51	97.6	**Marlboro** (CDP) Ulster County
55	97.5	**Fort Drum** (CDP) Jefferson County
55	97.5	**Lake Success** (village) Nassau County
55	97.5	**Menands** (village) Albany County
55	97.5	**Ridge** (CDP) Suffolk County
55	97.5	**Rockville Centre** (village) Nassau County
55	97.5	**Stony Brook University** (CDP) Suffolk County
61	97.4	**East Norwich** (CDP) Nassau County
61	97.4	**East Shoreham** (CDP) Suffolk County
61	97.4	**Massapequa** (CDP) Nassau County
61	97.4	**Montebello** (village) Rockland County
61	97.4	**North Wantagh** (CDP) Nassau County
61	97.4	**Northport** (village) Suffolk County
61	97.4	**Voorheesville** (village) Albany County
61	97.4	**Wantagh** (CDP) Nassau County
69	97.3	**Bethlehem** (town) Albany County
69	97.3	**Centerport** (CDP) Suffolk County
69	97.3	**Cold Spring Harbor** (CDP) Suffolk County
69	97.3	**Hawthorne** (CDP) Westchester County
69	97.3	**New Castle** (town) Westchester County
69	97.3	**Plainview** (CDP) Nassau County
69	97.3	**Richmond** (town) Ontario County
69	97.3	**Union Vale** (town) Dutchess County
77	97.2	**Great Neck Estates** (village) Nassau County
77	97.2	**Searingtown** (CDP) Nassau County
77	97.2	**Williamsville** (village) Erie County
80	97.1	**Greenville** (CDP) Westchester County
80	97.1	**Kaser** (village) Rockland County
80	97.1	**Mount Sinai** (CDP) Suffolk County
80	97.1	**North Massapequa** (CDP) Nassau County
80	97.1	**Penfield** (town) Monroe County
80	97.1	**Sand Lake** (town) Rensselaer County
80	97.1	**Schuyler Falls** (town) Clinton County
80	97.1	**Skaneateles** (village) Onondaga County
80	97.1	**West Sand Lake** (CDP) Rensselaer County
80	97.1	**Woodmere** (CDP) Nassau County
90	97.0	**Dannemora** (village) Clinton County
90	97.0	**Erwin** (town) Steuben County
90	97.0	**Fort Salonga** (CDP) Suffolk County
90	97.0	**Geneseo** (town) Livingston County
90	97.0	**Hamilton** (village) Madison County
90	97.0	**Harris Hill** (CDP) Erie County
90	97.0	**Merrick** (CDP) Nassau County
90	97.0	**Mooers** (town) Clinton County
90	97.0	**New Hartford** (town) Oneida County
90	97.0	**West Hills** (CDP) Suffolk County
90	97.0	**Westmere** (CDP) Albany County
101	96.9	**Airmont** (village) Rockland County
101	96.9	**Bayport** (CDP) Suffolk County
101	96.9	**Bohemia** (CDP) Suffolk County
101	96.9	**Brookville** (village) Nassau County
101	96.9	**East Greenbush** (town) Rensselaer County
101	96.9	**Gaines** (town) Orleans County
101	96.9	**Hilton** (village) Monroe County
101	96.9	**Huntington** (CDP) Suffolk County
101	96.9	**Nesconset** (CDP) Suffolk County
101	96.9	**Northumberland** (town) Saratoga County
101	96.9	**Rye** (city) Westchester County
101	96.9	**Sardinia** (town) Erie County
101	96.9	**Southold** (CDP) Suffolk County
101	96.9	**Spencerport** (village) Monroe County
101	96.9	**Tappan** (CDP) Rockland County
116	96.8	**Charlton** (town) Saratoga County
116	96.8	**Conesus Lake** (CDP) Livingston County
116	96.8	**Eastchester** (CDP) Westchester County
116	96.8	**Geneva** (town) Ontario County
116	96.8	**Halesite** (CDP) Suffolk County
116	96.8	**Kenmore** (village) Erie County
116	96.8	**Pendleton** (town) Niagara County
116	96.8	**Perinton** (town) Monroe County
116	96.8	**Scotia** (village) Schenectady County
116	96.8	**Wynantskill** (CDP) Rensselaer County
126	96.7	**Castile** (town) Wyoming County
126	96.7	**Catlin** (town) Chemung County
126	96.7	**Commack** (CDP) Suffolk County
126	96.7	**Hauppauge** (CDP) Suffolk County
126	96.7	**Malta** (town) Saratoga County
126	96.7	**Marilla** (town) Erie County
126	96.7	**Muttontown** (village) Nassau County
126	96.7	**Niskayuna** (town) Schenectady County
126	96.7	**Onondaga** (town) Onondaga County
126	96.7	**Plainedge** (CDP) Nassau County
126	96.7	**Sayville** (CDP) Suffolk County
126	96.7	**Seaford** (CDP) Nassau County
126	96.7	**Smithtown** (town) Suffolk County
126	96.7	**Stony Brook** (CDP) Suffolk County
126	96.7	**West Bay Shore** (CDP) Suffolk County
141	96.6	**Amherst** (town) Erie County
141	96.6	**Canandaigua** (town) Ontario County
141	96.6	**East Islip** (CDP) Suffolk County
141	96.6	**Irvington** (village) Westchester County
141	96.6	**Jericho** (CDP) Nassau County
141	96.6	**Manhasset** (CDP) Nassau County
141	96.6	**Pelham Manor** (village) Westchester County
141	96.6	**Schoharie** (town) Schoharie County
141	96.6	**Smithtown** (CDP) Suffolk County
141	96.6	**Wading River** (CDP) Suffolk County

Note: This section ranks incorporated places and CDPs (Census Designated Places) with populations of 2,500 or more. Unincorporated postal areas were not considered. Please refer to the User Guide for additional information.

Population with Health Insurance

Top 150 Places Ranked in *Ascending* Order

State Rank	Percent	Place
1	34.9	**Watchtower** (CDP) Ulster County
2	61.5	**Riverside** (CDP) Suffolk County
2	61.5	**Saint Regis Mohawk Reservation** (reservation) Franklin County
4	68.7	**Benton** (town) Yates County
5	69.3	**Bedford Hills** (CDP) Westchester County
6	71.6	**Flanders** (CDP) Suffolk County
7	72.0	**Port Chester** (village) Westchester County
8	75.6	**New Cassel** (CDP) Nassau County
9	76.6	**Oswegatchie** (town) Saint Lawrence County
9	76.6	**Riverhead** (CDP) Suffolk County
11	76.9	**Spring Valley** (village) Rockland County
12	77.5	**Hempstead** (village) Nassau County
13	77.9	**Galen** (town) Wayne County
14	78.0	**Noyack** (CDP) Suffolk County
15	79.0	**Brentwood** (CDP) Suffolk County
15	79.0	**Ossining** (village) Westchester County
17	79.4	**Mount Kisco** (town/village) Westchester County
17	79.4	**Romulus** (town) Seneca County
19	79.5	**Inwood** (CDP) Nassau County
20	79.7	**Milo** (town) Yates County
21	79.9	**Newburgh** (city) Orange County
21	79.9	**Rye** (town) Westchester County
23	80.1	**Starkey** (town) Yates County
24	80.4	**Bainbridge** (town) Chenango County
24	80.4	**Central Islip** (CDP) Suffolk County
26	80.5	**Hampton Bays** (CDP) Suffolk County
27	81.0	**Wyandanch** (CDP) Suffolk County
28	81.2	**Uniondale** (CDP) Nassau County
29	81.4	**Palatine** (town) Montgomery County
30	81.9	**Shawangunk** (town) Ulster County
31	82.5	**North Amityville** (CDP) Suffolk County
32	82.8	**East Hampton North** (CDP) Suffolk County
32	82.8	**Huntington Station** (CDP) Suffolk County
32	82.8	**Minden** (town) Montgomery County
32	82.8	**Roosevelt** (CDP) Nassau County
36	82.9	**North East** (town) Dutchess County
37	83.0	**Patchogue** (village) Suffolk County
38	83.2	**Westbury** (village) Nassau County
39	83.3	**Elmsford** (village) Westchester County
39	83.3	**Manorhaven** (village) Nassau County
41	83.8	**Pamelia** (town) Jefferson County
42	84.4	**Freeport** (village) Nassau County
42	84.4	**Palmyra** (village) Wayne County
42	84.4	**Queens** (borough) Queens County
45	84.5	**Mount Ivy** (CDP) Rockland County
45	84.5	**Southampton** (town) Suffolk County
47	84.7	**Afton** (town) Chenango County
47	84.7	**Liberty** (village) Sullivan County
49	84.8	**Haverstraw** (village) Rockland County
50	85.0	**Vails Gate** (CDP) Orange County
51	85.2	**Yates** (town) Orleans County
52	85.3	**Ossining** (town) Westchester County
52	85.3	**Wappingers Falls** (village) Dutchess County
54	85.5	**Fairview** (CDP) Westchester County
54	85.5	**Poughkeepsie** (city) Dutchess County
54	85.5	**Rose** (town) Wayne County
57	85.6	**Shandaken** (town) Ulster County
57	85.6	**White Plains** (city) Westchester County
59	85.8	**Hector** (town) Schuyler County
60	86.0	**Monticello** (village) Sullivan County
61	86.2	**Copiague** (CDP) Suffolk County
61	86.2	**Richland** (town) Oswego County
63	86.3	**Bronx** (borough) Bronx County
63	86.3	**Saint Johnsville** (town) Montgomery County
65	86.4	**Glen Cove** (city) Nassau County
65	86.4	**Peekskill** (city) Westchester County
67	86.5	**Sleepy Hollow** (village) Westchester County
68	86.6	**Hillcrest** (CDP) Rockland County
68	86.6	**Mount Morris** (town) Livingston County
68	86.6	**New Bremen** (town) Lewis County
68	86.6	**North Bellport** (CDP) Suffolk County
72	86.7	**Colesville** (town) Broome County
73	86.8	**Middletown** (city) Orange County
73	86.8	**North Bay Shore** (CDP) Suffolk County
75	86.9	**Fayette** (town) Seneca County
75	86.9	**New Berlin** (town) Chenango County
75	86.9	**New Hempstead** (village) Rockland County
75	86.9	**Penn Yan** (village) Yates County
79	87.0	**Gouverneur** (village) Saint Lawrence County
79	87.0	**Riverhead** (town) Suffolk County
81	87.1	**Ellisburg** (town) Jefferson County
82	87.2	**Bay Shore** (CDP) Suffolk County
82	87.2	**Northwest Harbor** (CDP) Suffolk County
84	87.3	**East Patchogue** (CDP) Suffolk County
84	87.3	**Mastic** (CDP) Suffolk County
84	87.3	**Middletown** (town) Delaware County
84	87.3	**Sanford** (town) Broome County
84	87.3	**South Fallsburg** (CDP) Sullivan County
89	87.4	**Lake Luzerne** (town) Warren County
89	87.4	**Mount Vernon** (city) Westchester County
89	87.4	**Whitehall** (village) Washington County
92	87.5	**Alexandria** (town) Jefferson County
92	87.5	**Gowanda** (village) Cattaraugus County
92	87.5	**Haverstraw** (town) Rockland County
92	87.5	**Salamanca** (city) Cattaraugus County
92	87.5	**Saugerties** (village) Ulster County
92	87.5	**West Haverstraw** (village) Rockland County
98	87.6	**Garden City South** (CDP) Nassau County
98	87.6	**Gouverneur** (town) Saint Lawrence County
98	87.6	**New York** (city)
101	87.7	**Albion** (town) Orleans County
101	87.7	**Albion** (village) Orleans County
101	87.7	**Ravena** (village) Albany County
101	87.7	**West Bloomfield** (town) Ontario County
101	87.7	**Yorkshire** (town) Cattaraugus County
106	87.8	**Franklinville** (town) Cattaraugus County
106	87.8	**Hudson Falls** (village) Washington County
108	87.9	**Carthage** (village) Jefferson County
108	87.9	**Palmyra** (town) Wayne County
110	88.0	**Brooklyn** (borough) Kings County
110	88.0	**Chautauqua** (town) Chautauqua County
110	88.0	**Croghan** (town) Lewis County
110	88.0	**Esopus** (town) Ulster County
110	88.0	**Newfane** (CDP) Niagara County
110	88.0	**Thompson** (town) Sullivan County
116	88.1	**Bethel** (town) Sullivan County
116	88.1	**Harriman** (village) Orange County
118	88.2	**Conklin** (town) Broome County
118	88.2	**Elmont** (CDP) Nassau County
118	88.2	**Gloversville** (city) Fulton County
118	88.2	**Yonkers** (city) Westchester County
122	88.3	**Rosendale** (town) Ulster County
123	88.4	**Addison** (town) Steuben County
123	88.4	**Croton-on-Hudson** (village) Westchester County
123	88.4	**Perry** (town) Wyoming County
123	88.4	**Walton** (town) Delaware County
127	88.5	**Fallsburg** (town) Sullivan County
127	88.5	**Livingston** (town) Columbia County
129	88.6	**Locust Valley** (CDP) Nassau County
129	88.6	**New Rochelle** (city) Westchester County
131	88.7	**Batavia** (town) Genesee County
131	88.7	**East Farmingdale** (CDP) Suffolk County
131	88.7	**Granville** (town) Washington County
131	88.7	**Mamakating** (town) Sullivan County
135	88.8	**Blasdell** (village) Erie County
135	88.8	**Endicott** (village) Broome County
135	88.8	**Gorham** (town) Ontario County
135	88.8	**Ilion** (village) Herkimer County
135	88.8	**Ticonderoga** (CDP) Essex County
140	88.9	**Amityville** (village) Suffolk County
140	88.9	**Corning** (town) Steuben County
140	88.9	**Kingsbury** (town) Washington County
140	88.9	**Palermo** (town) Oswego County
144	89.0	**Cape Vincent** (town) Jefferson County
144	89.0	**Lake George** (town) Warren County
144	89.0	**Owego** (village) Tioga County
144	89.0	**Whitehall** (town) Washington County
148	89.1	**Montauk** (CDP) Suffolk County
148	89.1	**Port Jervis** (city) Orange County
150	89.2	**Brookfield** (town) Madison County

Note: This section ranks incorporated places and CDPs (Census Designated Places) with populations of 2,500 or more. Unincorporated postal areas were not considered. Please refer to the User Guide for additional information.

Population with Private Health Insurance

Top 150 Places Ranked in *Descending* Order

State Rank	Percent	Place
1	94.1	**West Point** (CDP) Orange County
2	92.9	**New Castle** (town) Westchester County
2	92.9	**Sands Point** (village) Nassau County
4	92.8	**Armonk** (CDP) Westchester County
5	92.7	**Pittsford** (town) Monroe County
6	92.5	**Bronxville** (village) Westchester County
6	92.5	**Greenville** (CDP) Westchester County
8	92.4	**Larchmont** (village) Westchester County
9	92.3	**Briarcliff Manor** (village) Westchester County
9	92.3	**Garden City** (village) Nassau County
11	92.2	**East Shoreham** (CDP) Suffolk County
11	92.2	**South Hill** (CDP) Tompkins County
11	92.2	**University at Buffalo** (CDP) Erie County
14	92.1	**Scarsdale** (town/village) Westchester County
15	91.9	**Glenwood Landing** (CDP) Nassau County
15	91.9	**Lawrence** (village) Nassau County
15	91.9	**North Great River** (CDP) Suffolk County
15	91.9	**Woodbury** (CDP) Nassau County
19	91.7	**Munsey Park** (village) Nassau County
20	91.6	**Brightwaters** (village) Suffolk County
20	91.6	**East Norwich** (CDP) Nassau County
22	91.3	**Brookville** (village) Nassau County
23	91.2	**East Williston** (village) Nassau County
23	91.2	**Minoa** (village) Onondaga County
23	91.2	**Stony Brook** (CDP) Suffolk County
23	91.2	**Union Vale** (town) Dutchess County
23	91.2	**Wantagh** (CDP) Nassau County
28	91.1	**West Sand Lake** (CDP) Rensselaer County
29	90.8	**Clifton Park** (town) Saratoga County
30	90.7	**East Hills** (village) Nassau County
30	90.7	**Halesite** (CDP) Suffolk County
30	90.7	**North Castle** (town) Westchester County
30	90.7	**Setauket-East Setauket** (CDP) Suffolk County
34	90.6	**East Islip** (CDP) Suffolk County
35	90.5	**Bellmore** (CDP) Nassau County
35	90.5	**Fort Drum** (CDP) Jefferson County
35	90.5	**Irvington** (village) Westchester County
35	90.5	**Lake Success** (village) Nassau County
35	90.5	**Manhasset Hills** (CDP) Nassau County
35	90.5	**Montebello** (village) Rockland County
41	90.4	**Great Neck Estates** (village) Nassau County
41	90.4	**North Merrick** (CDP) Nassau County
41	90.4	**Thornwood** (CDP) Westchester County
44	90.3	**Orchard Park** (town) Erie County
44	90.3	**Southold** (CDP) Suffolk County
44	90.3	**Wanakah** (CDP) Erie County
47	90.2	**Mendon** (town) Monroe County
47	90.2	**Sand Lake** (town) Rensselaer County
47	90.2	**Westerlo** (town) Albany County
50	90.1	**Plainedge** (CDP) Nassau County
50	90.1	**Wading River** (CDP) Suffolk County
50	90.1	**Williamsville** (village) Erie County
53	90.0	**Centerport** (CDP) Suffolk County
53	90.0	**Charlton** (town) Saratoga County
53	90.0	**Sayville** (CDP) Suffolk County
56	89.9	**East Greenbush** (CDP) Rensselaer County
56	89.9	**Skaneateles** (village) Onondaga County
58	89.8	**Bardonia** (CDP) Rockland County
58	89.8	**Cayuga Heights** (village) Tompkins County
58	89.8	**Northport** (village) Suffolk County
61	89.7	**Alfred** (village) Allegany County
61	89.7	**Owasco** (town) Cayuga County
61	89.7	**Westmere** (CDP) Albany County
64	89.6	**Floral Park** (village) Nassau County
64	89.6	**Seaford** (CDP) Nassau County
66	89.5	**Bethlehem** (town) Albany County
66	89.5	**Nesconset** (CDP) Suffolk County
66	89.5	**Saint James** (CDP) Suffolk County
69	89.4	**Cold Spring Harbor** (CDP) Suffolk County
69	89.4	**Huntington** (CDP) Suffolk County
69	89.4	**Jefferson Valley-Yorktown** (CDP) Westchester County
69	89.4	**West Nyack** (CDP) Rockland County
73	89.2	**Pelham Manor** (village) Westchester County
73	89.2	**Pound Ridge** (town) Westchester County
73	89.2	**Smithtown** (CDP) Suffolk County
76	89.1	**Merrick** (CDP) Nassau County
77	89.0	**Elma Center** (CDP) Erie County
77	89.0	**Pleasantville** (village) Westchester County
77	89.0	**SUNY Oswego** (CDP) Oswego County
80	88.8	**Lloyd Harbor** (village) Suffolk County
80	88.8	**Malta** (town) Saratoga County
82	88.7	**East Greenbush** (town) Rensselaer County
82	88.7	**Massapequa Park** (village) Nassau County
82	88.7	**West Hills** (CDP) Suffolk County
85	88.6	**Eastchester** (CDP) Westchester County
85	88.6	**Malverne** (village) Nassau County
85	88.6	**Miller Place** (CDP) Suffolk County
85	88.6	**North Wantagh** (CDP) Nassau County
85	88.6	**Smithtown** (town) Suffolk County
90	88.5	**Poestenkill** (town) Rensselaer County
91	88.4	**Syosset** (CDP) Nassau County
91	88.4	**Walworth** (town) Wayne County
93	88.3	**Commack** (CDP) Suffolk County
93	88.3	**Sea Cliff** (village) Nassau County
93	88.3	**Spackenkill** (CDP) Dutchess County
96	88.2	**Lewiston** (town) Niagara County
96	88.2	**Victor** (town) Ontario County
98	88.1	**Blue Point** (CDP) Suffolk County
98	88.1	**Eastchester** (town) Westchester County
98	88.1	**Hamilton** (village) Madison County
98	88.1	**Hauppauge** (CDP) Suffolk County
98	88.1	**Rush** (town) Monroe County
98	88.1	**Rye** (city) Westchester County
104	88.0	**Orchard Park** (village) Erie County
104	88.0	**Woodbury** (town) Orange County
106	87.9	**Babylon** (village) Suffolk County
106	87.9	**Harris Hill** (CDP) Erie County
106	87.9	**Jericho** (CDP) Nassau County
106	87.9	**Pelham** (town) Westchester County
106	87.9	**Voorheesville** (village) Albany County
111	87.8	**Muttontown** (village) Nassau County
111	87.8	**Somers** (town) Westchester County
111	87.8	**West Islip** (CDP) Suffolk County
114	87.7	**Marilla** (town) Erie County
114	87.7	**Woodbury** (village) Orange County
116	87.6	**Dix Hills** (CDP) Suffolk County
116	87.6	**Flower Hill** (village) Nassau County
116	87.6	**Guilderland** (town) Albany County
116	87.6	**Haviland** (CDP) Dutchess County
116	87.6	**Lansing** (village) Tompkins County
116	87.6	**Port Jefferson** (village) Suffolk County
122	87.5	**Geneseo** (town) Livingston County
122	87.5	**Horseheads North** (CDP) Chemung County
122	87.5	**Kings Point** (village) Nassau County
122	87.5	**Massapequa** (CDP) Nassau County
122	87.5	**Plainview** (CDP) Nassau County
127	87.4	**Chenango Bridge** (CDP) Broome County
127	87.4	**Lansing** (town) Tompkins County
127	87.4	**Skaneateles** (town) Onondaga County
130	87.3	**Brunswick** (town) Rensselaer County
130	87.3	**Mount Sinai** (CDP) Suffolk County
130	87.3	**Rockville Centre** (village) Nassau County
133	87.2	**Bayport** (CDP) Suffolk County
133	87.2	**Yorktown** (town) Westchester County
135	87.1	**Cambria** (town) Niagara County
135	87.1	**Hawthorne** (CDP) Westchester County
135	87.1	**Highlands** (town) Orange County
135	87.1	**West Elmira** (CDP) Chemung County
139	87.0	**Clarence** (CDP) Erie County
139	87.0	**Clarence** (town) Erie County
139	87.0	**Lido Beach** (CDP) Nassau County
139	87.0	**Melville** (CDP) Suffolk County
139	87.0	**North Salem** (town) Westchester County
139	87.0	**Williston Park** (village) Nassau County
145	86.9	**North Massapequa** (CDP) Nassau County
146	86.8	**Binghamton University** (CDP) Broome County
146	86.8	**East Moriches** (CDP) Suffolk County
146	86.8	**Fort Salonga** (CDP) Suffolk County
146	86.8	**New Scotland** (town) Albany County
146	86.8	**Pelham** (village) Westchester County

Note: This section ranks incorporated places and CDPs (Census Designated Places) with populations of 2,500 or more. Unincorporated postal areas were not considered. Please refer to the User Guide for additional information.

Population with Private Health Insurance

Top 150 Places Ranked in *Ascending* Order

State Rank	Percent	Place
1	8.6	**Kaser** (village) Rockland County
2	15.4	**New Square** (village) Rockland County
3	20.8	**Watchtower** (CDP) Ulster County
4	24.0	**Kiryas Joel** (village) Orange County
5	26.1	**South Fallsburg** (CDP) Sullivan County
6	28.9	**Saint Regis Mohawk Reservation** (reservation) Franklin County
7	32.6	**Monsey** (CDP) Rockland County
8	35.5	**Spring Valley** (village) Rockland County
9	35.6	**Monticello** (village) Sullivan County
10	39.0	**Liberty** (village) Sullivan County
11	42.8	**Newburgh** (city) Orange County
12	42.9	**Bedford Hills** (CDP) Westchester County
13	43.1	**Bronx** (borough) Bronx County
14	45.0	**Hempstead** (village) Nassau County
15	45.5	**Utica** (city) Oneida County
16	47.0	**Haverstraw** (village) Rockland County
17	47.3	**Inwood** (CDP) Nassau County
18	47.7	**Whitehall** (village) Washington County
19	47.8	**Fairview** (CDP) Westchester County
20	47.9	**Elmira** (city) Chemung County
21	49.3	**Port Chester** (village) Westchester County
22	49.7	**Riverside** (CDP) Suffolk County
22	49.7	**Thompson** (town) Sullivan County
24	49.8	**Buffalo** (city) Erie County
25	49.9	**Fallsburg** (town) Sullivan County
26	50.0	**Gloversville** (city) Fulton County
26	50.0	**Rochester** (city) Monroe County
28	50.3	**Gouverneur** (village) Saint Lawrence County
29	50.6	**Endicott** (village) Broome County
30	50.7	**Riverhead** (CDP) Suffolk County
31	51.1	**Minden** (town) Montgomery County
31	51.1	**Ramapo** (town) Rockland County
33	51.2	**Wellsville** (village) Allegany County
34	51.4	**Brooklyn** (borough) Kings County
34	51.4	**Monroe** (town) Orange County
36	51.6	**Saint Johnsville** (town) Montgomery County
37	51.8	**Albion** (village) Orleans County
37	51.8	**Hudson** (city) Columbia County
39	51.9	**Poughkeepsie** (city) Dutchess County
40	52.0	**Amsterdam** (city) Montgomery County
41	52.2	**Gouverneur** (town) Saint Lawrence County
41	52.2	**Kingston** (city) Ulster County
43	52.5	**Fulton** (city) Oswego County
44	53.1	**Albion** (town) Orleans County
45	53.2	**Wyandanch** (CDP) Suffolk County
46	53.3	**Hornell** (city) Steuben County
46	53.3	**Salamanca** (city) Cattaraugus County
48	53.7	**Flanders** (CDP) Suffolk County
49	54.0	**Sidney** (village) Delaware County
50	54.1	**Penn Yan** (village) Yates County
51	54.2	**Viola** (CDP) Rockland County
52	54.4	**Binghamton** (city) Broome County
53	54.5	**Queens** (borough) Queens County
54	54.6	**Walton** (village) Delaware County
55	54.8	**Jamestown** (city) Chautauqua County
56	55.0	**Mount Morris** (town) Livingston County
56	55.0	**New York** (city)
58	55.3	**Bainbridge** (town) Chenango County
59	55.4	**Starkey** (town) Yates County
59	55.4	**Syracuse** (city) Onondaga County
61	55.5	**Newfield** (town) Tompkins County
62	55.6	**Milo** (town) Yates County
63	55.7	**Schenectady** (city) Schenectady County
64	55.9	**Carthage** (village) Jefferson County
65	56.1	**Wilna** (town) Jefferson County
66	56.2	**Liberty** (town) Sullivan County
67	56.3	**Brentwood** (CDP) Suffolk County
68	56.5	**Vails Gate** (CDP) Orange County
69	56.6	**Whitehall** (town) Washington County
70	56.7	**Malone** (village) Franklin County
71	56.8	**Benton** (town) Yates County
71	56.8	**Ilion** (village) Herkimer County
73	56.9	**Central Islip** (CDP) Suffolk County
74	57.3	**Newark** (village) Wayne County
74	57.3	**Roosevelt** (CDP) Nassau County
76	57.4	**Manheim** (town) Herkimer County
77	57.6	**Galen** (town) Wayne County
77	57.6	**Webster** (village) Monroe County
79	57.7	**Hudson Falls** (village) Washington County
80	57.8	**New Berlin** (town) Chenango County
81	57.9	**Uniondale** (CDP) Nassau County
82	58.1	**Niagara Falls** (city) Niagara County
82	58.1	**Oswegatchie** (town) Saint Lawrence County
82	58.1	**Sanford** (town) Broome County
85	58.3	**Ossining** (village) Westchester County
85	58.3	**Palermo** (town) Oswego County
87	58.4	**Lackawanna** (city) Erie County
87	58.4	**Palmyra** (village) Wayne County
89	58.5	**Colesville** (town) Broome County
89	58.5	**Mount Kisco** (town/village) Westchester County
89	58.5	**Stamford** (town) Delaware County
92	58.6	**Laurens** (town) Otsego County
92	58.6	**Sidney** (town) Delaware County
94	59.0	**Hannibal** (town) Oswego County
94	59.0	**New Cassel** (CDP) Nassau County
96	59.1	**Sleepy Hollow** (village) Westchester County
97	59.2	**North Bay Shore** (CDP) Suffolk County
98	59.3	**Hunter** (town) Greene County
98	59.3	**Port Jervis** (city) Orange County
100	59.4	**Wolcott** (town) Wayne County
101	59.5	**North East** (town) Dutchess County
101	59.5	**Warrensburg** (CDP) Warren County
103	59.6	**Little Falls** (city) Herkimer County
103	59.6	**Ticonderoga** (CDP) Essex County
105	59.7	**Ellenville** (village) Ulster County
105	59.7	**Herkimer** (village) Herkimer County
105	59.7	**Palatine** (town) Montgomery County
108	59.9	**Dix** (town) Schuyler County
109	60.0	**Annsville** (town) Oneida County
110	60.2	**Mount Morris** (village) Livingston County
110	60.2	**North Amityville** (CDP) Suffolk County
112	60.3	**Mount Vernon** (city) Westchester County
112	60.3	**Wellsville** (town) Allegany County
114	60.4	**Walton** (town) Delaware County
115	60.5	**Gordon Heights** (CDP) Suffolk County
115	60.5	**Peekskill** (city) Westchester County
117	60.7	**Watertown** (city) Jefferson County
118	60.9	**Franklinville** (town) Cattaraugus County
119	61.1	**Bath** (village) Steuben County
119	61.1	**Dunkirk** (city) Chautauqua County
121	61.2	**Richland** (town) Oswego County
122	61.4	**German Flatts** (town) Herkimer County
122	61.4	**Rye** (town) Westchester County
124	61.5	**Verona** (town) Oneida County
125	61.7	**Sandy Creek** (town) Oswego County
126	62.0	**Middletown** (city) Orange County
126	62.0	**Portland** (town) Chautauqua County
126	62.0	**Rose** (town) Wayne County
129	62.1	**Haverstraw** (town) Rockland County
130	62.3	**Afton** (town) Chenango County
130	62.3	**Norwich** (city) Chenango County
132	62.4	**Middletown** (town) Delaware County
132	62.4	**Palmyra** (town) Wayne County
134	62.6	**Noyack** (CDP) Suffolk County
134	62.6	**Yonkers** (city) Westchester County
136	62.8	**Addison** (town) Steuben County
136	62.8	**Bath** (town) Steuben County
136	62.8	**Granby** (town) Oswego County
136	62.8	**Hampton Bays** (CDP) Suffolk County
136	62.8	**Herkimer** (town) Herkimer County
136	62.8	**Wawarsing** (town) Ulster County
142	62.9	**Yorkshire** (town) Cattaraugus County
143	63.0	**Arcadia** (town) Wayne County
143	63.0	**Fort Edward** (town) Washington County
143	63.0	**Vienna** (town) Oneida County
143	63.0	**Warsaw** (village) Wyoming County
147	63.1	**Ticonderoga** (town) Essex County
148	63.2	**Lyons** (village) Wayne County
148	63.2	**Richmondville** (town) Schoharie County
150	63.4	**Massena** (town) Saint Lawrence County

Note: This section ranks incorporated places and CDPs (Census Designated Places) with populations of 2,500 or more. Unincorporated postal areas were not considered. Please refer to the User Guide for additional information.

Population with Public Health Insurance

Top 150 Places Ranked in *Descending* Order

State Rank	Percent	Place
1	90.9	**Kaser** (village) Rockland County
2	87.2	**New Square** (village) Rockland County
3	80.8	**Kiryas Joel** (village) Orange County
4	71.9	**Heritage Hills** (CDP) Westchester County
5	69.2	**South Fallsburg** (CDP) Sullivan County
6	68.9	**Monsey** (CDP) Rockland County
7	60.7	**Monticello** (village) Sullivan County
8	58.8	**Walton** (village) Delaware County
9	57.7	**Utica** (city) Oneida County
10	57.4	**Liberty** (village) Sullivan County
11	56.8	**New York Mills** (village) Oneida County
12	54.3	**Amsterdam** (city) Montgomery County
13	54.1	**Hornell** (city) Steuben County
13	54.1	**Wellsville** (village) Allegany County
15	53.9	**Whitehall** (village) Washington County
16	53.2	**Elmira** (city) Chemung County
17	52.9	**Malone** (village) Franklin County
18	52.5	**Albion** (village) Orleans County
18	52.5	**Monroe** (village) Orange County
20	52.4	**Medina** (village) Orleans County
21	52.2	**Hudson** (city) Columbia County
22	52.0	**Bronx** (borough) Bronx County
22	52.0	**Buffalo** (city) Erie County
24	51.8	**Ellenville** (village) Ulster County
25	51.6	**Fulton** (city) Oswego County
26	51.5	**Gloversville** (city) Fulton County
27	51.3	**Jamestown** (city) Chautauqua County
27	51.3	**Niagara Falls** (city) Niagara County
29	51.1	**Sidney** (village) Delaware County
30	51.0	**Thompson** (town) Sullivan County
31	50.9	**Fallsburg** (town) Sullivan County
32	50.5	**Endicott** (village) Broome County
32	50.5	**New Berlin** (town) Chenango County
34	50.4	**Laurens** (town) Otsego County
35	50.2	**Rochester** (city) Monroe County
36	50.1	**Sidney** (town) Delaware County
36	50.1	**Webster** (village) Monroe County
38	49.7	**Binghamton** (city) Broome County
38	49.7	**Fort Edward** (town) Washington County
38	49.7	**Kingston** (city) Ulster County
41	49.4	**Stamford** (town) Delaware County
42	49.3	**Bath** (village) Steuben County
42	49.3	**Whitehall** (town) Washington County
44	49.2	**Penn Yan** (village) Yates County
45	49.1	**Albion** (town) Orleans County
45	49.1	**Gouverneur** (village) Saint Lawrence County
45	49.1	**Newark** (village) Wayne County
48	48.8	**Bangor** (town) Franklin County
48	48.8	**Middleburgh** (town) Schoharie County
50	48.7	**Wellsville** (town) Allegany County
51	48.6	**Lackawanna** (city) Erie County
52	48.4	**Bath** (town) Steuben County
52	48.4	**Little Falls** (city) Herkimer County
54	48.3	**Minden** (town) Montgomery County
54	48.3	**Warrensburg** (CDP) Warren County
56	47.4	**Shelby** (town) Orleans County
57	47.3	**Dunkirk** (city) Chautauqua County
57	47.3	**Salamanca** (city) Cattaraugus County
59	47.1	**Mount Morris** (village) Livingston County
59	47.1	**Sandy Creek** (town) Oswego County
61	46.9	**Ramapo** (town) Rockland County
61	46.9	**Spring Valley** (village) Rockland County
61	46.9	**Syracuse** (city) Onondaga County
64	46.8	**Hannibal** (town) Oswego County
64	46.8	**Olean** (city) Cattaraugus County
66	46.6	**Poughkeepsie** (city) Dutchess County
67	46.5	**Herkimer** (village) Herkimer County
67	46.5	**Hoosick Falls** (village) Rensselaer County
69	46.3	**Gordon Heights** (CDP) Suffolk County
69	46.3	**Warrensburg** (town) Warren County
71	46.2	**Herkimer** (town) Herkimer County
71	46.2	**Hunter** (town) Greene County
71	46.2	**Mount Morris** (town) Livingston County
74	46.1	**Newfield** (town) Tompkins County
75	45.8	**Calverton** (CDP) Suffolk County
75	45.8	**Warsaw** (village) Wyoming County
75	45.8	**Watertown** (city) Jefferson County
75	45.8	**Wilna** (town) Jefferson County
79	45.7	**Galeville** (CDP) Onondaga County
80	45.6	**Dansville** (village) Livingston County
80	45.6	**Davenport** (town) Delaware County
80	45.6	**Gouverneur** (town) Saint Lawrence County
80	45.6	**Schenectady** (city) Schenectady County
84	45.5	**Ilion** (village) Herkimer County
85	45.4	**Arcadia** (town) Wayne County
85	45.4	**Lyons** (village) Wayne County
85	45.4	**Verona** (town) Oneida County
88	45.3	**Haverstraw** (village) Rockland County
88	45.3	**Moira** (town) Franklin County
88	45.3	**Saint Johnsville** (town) Montgomery County
91	45.2	**Annsville** (town) Oneida County
91	45.2	**Malone** (town) Franklin County
93	45.1	**North Dansville** (town) Livingston County
93	45.1	**Viola** (CDP) Rockland County
95	45.0	**Cohocton** (town) Steuben County
95	45.0	**Manheim** (town) Herkimer County
95	45.0	**Ogdensburg** (city) Saint Lawrence County
98	44.7	**Rome** (city) Oneida County
98	44.7	**Sanford** (town) Broome County
100	44.5	**Carthage** (village) Jefferson County
100	44.5	**Hudson Falls** (village) Washington County
102	44.4	**Newburgh** (city) Orange County
103	44.3	**Liberty** (town) Sullivan County
104	44.2	**Fort Edward** (village) Washington County
104	44.2	**Wawarsing** (town) Ulster County
106	44.1	**Vienna** (town) Oneida County
107	43.9	**Walton** (town) Delaware County
108	43.8	**Canajoharie** (town) Montgomery County
108	43.8	**White Creek** (town) Washington County
110	43.7	**Norwich** (city) Chenango County
111	43.5	**German Flatts** (town) Herkimer County
112	43.4	**Brooklyn** (borough) Kings County
112	43.4	**Claverack** (town) Columbia County
112	43.4	**Massena** (town) Saint Lawrence County
112	43.4	**Sodus** (town) Wayne County
116	43.2	**Groveland** (town) Livingston County
116	43.2	**West Monroe** (town) Oswego County
118	43.1	**Fairview** (CDP) Westchester County
118	43.1	**Southport** (CDP) Chemung County
120	43.0	**Rensselaer** (city) Rensselaer County
121	42.9	**Ballston Spa** (village) Saratoga County
121	42.9	**Carlton** (town) Orleans County
121	42.9	**Granby** (town) Oswego County
121	42.9	**Johnson City** (village) Broome County
121	42.9	**Randolph** (town) Cattaraugus County
126	42.8	**Batavia** (city) Genesee County
126	42.8	**Mexico** (town) Oswego County
126	42.8	**Moriah** (town) Essex County
129	42.7	**Dannemora** (town) Clinton County
129	42.7	**Schoharie** (town) Schoharie County
131	42.6	**Mohawk** (village) Herkimer County
131	42.6	**South Lockport** (CDP) Niagara County
133	42.5	**Lyons** (town) Wayne County
133	42.5	**Waterloo** (town) Seneca County
133	42.5	**Wolcott** (town) Wayne County
136	42.4	**Brewerton** (CDP) Onondaga County
136	42.4	**Colesville** (town) Broome County
136	42.4	**Collins** (town) Erie County
136	42.4	**Mooers** (town) Clinton County
140	42.3	**Middletown** (town) Delaware County
140	42.3	**Palermo** (town) Oswego County
140	42.3	**Richmondville** (town) Schoharie County
143	42.2	**Au Sable** (town) Clinton County
143	42.2	**Franklinville** (town) Cattaraugus County
145	42.1	**North Hills** (village) Nassau County
146	42.0	**Altona** (town) Clinton County
146	42.0	**Madison** (town) Madison County
148	41.9	**Cape Vincent** (town) Jefferson County
148	41.9	**Hastings** (town) Oswego County
148	41.9	**Hornellsville** (town) Steuben County

Note: *This section ranks incorporated places and CDPs (Census Designated Places) with populations of 2,500 or more. Unincorporated postal areas were not considered. Please refer to the User Guide for additional information.*

Population with Public Health Insurance

Top 150 Places Ranked in *Ascending* Order

State Rank	Percent	Place
1	9.0	University at Buffalo (CDP) Erie County
2	9.2	West Point (CDP) Orange County
3	10.9	Binghamton University (CDP) Broome County
4	11.1	SUNY Oswego (CDP) Oswego County
5	11.5	Brookville (village) Nassau County
6	11.7	Alfred (village) Allegany County
7	12.2	South Hill (CDP) Tompkins County
8	13.1	New Castle (town) Westchester County
9	13.4	Armonk (CDP) Westchester County
10	14.0	Fort Drum (CDP) Jefferson County
11	14.8	Watchtower (CDP) Ulster County
12	14.9	Greenville (CDP) Westchester County
13	15.3	North Castle (town) Westchester County
14	15.5	Scarsdale (town/village) Westchester County
15	15.7	Old Westbury (village) Nassau County
16	15.8	East Islip (CDP) Suffolk County
16	15.8	Lloyd Harbor (village) Suffolk County
16	15.8	Thornwood (CDP) Westchester County
19	15.9	Alfred (town) Allegany County
19	15.9	East Hills (village) Nassau County
19	15.9	Pelham Manor (village) Westchester County
19	15.9	Stony Brook University (CDP) Suffolk County
23	16.0	Larchmont (village) Westchester County
23	16.0	West Sand Lake (CDP) Rensselaer County
25	16.1	Northeast Ithaca (CDP) Tompkins County
26	16.4	Munsey Park (village) Nassau County
27	16.7	Bronxville (village) Westchester County
27	16.7	Flower Hill (village) Nassau County
27	16.7	Lansing (village) Tompkins County
30	16.9	Brightwaters (village) Suffolk County
30	16.9	Pelham (town) Westchester County
32	17.0	Woodbury (town) Orange County
33	17.1	Mendon (town) Monroe County
34	17.2	Minisink (town) Orange County
35	17.3	East Shoreham (CDP) Suffolk County
35	17.3	Hamilton (village) Madison County
35	17.3	Ithaca (city) Tompkins County
38	17.4	Irvington (village) Westchester County
39	17.5	Cold Spring Harbor (CDP) Suffolk County
39	17.5	Woodbury (village) Orange County
41	17.6	Wading River (CDP) Suffolk County
42	17.7	Pelham (village) Westchester County
43	18.1	East Norwich (CDP) Nassau County
44	18.2	East Moriches (CDP) Suffolk County
44	18.2	Geneseo (village) Livingston County
46	18.3	North Merrick (CDP) Nassau County
47	18.6	Manorville (CDP) Suffolk County
47	18.6	Nesconset (CDP) Suffolk County
49	18.7	Great Neck Estates (village) Nassau County
50	18.8	Halesite (CDP) Suffolk County
50	18.8	Lewisboro (town) Westchester County
52	18.9	Muttontown (village) Nassau County
53	19.1	Pound Ridge (town) Westchester County
54	19.2	Dix Hills (CDP) Suffolk County
54	19.2	East Williston (village) Nassau County
56	19.3	West Islip (CDP) Suffolk County
57	19.4	Babylon (village) Suffolk County
57	19.4	Wantagh (CDP) Nassau County
59	19.6	East Greenbush (CDP) Rensselaer County
59	19.6	Merrick (CDP) Nassau County
61	19.8	Blue Point (CDP) Suffolk County
61	19.8	University Gardens (CDP) Nassau County
63	20.0	Highlands (town) Orange County
63	20.0	Rye (city) Westchester County
63	20.0	Syosset (CDP) Nassau County
63	20.0	Thomaston (village) Nassau County
67	20.1	Briarcliff Manor (village) Westchester County
67	20.1	Pompey (town) Onondaga County
67	20.1	Tarrytown (village) Westchester County
70	20.2	Huntington (CDP) Suffolk County
70	20.2	Seaford (CDP) Nassau County
72	20.3	Cayuga Heights (village) Tompkins County
72	20.3	West Hills (CDP) Suffolk County
74	20.4	Croton-on-Hudson (village) Westchester County
74	20.4	Glenwood Landing (CDP) Nassau County
74	20.4	Setauket-East Setauket (CDP) Suffolk County
77	20.5	Le Ray (town) Jefferson County
77	20.5	New Paltz (village) Ulster County
77	20.5	Plainedge (CDP) Nassau County
80	20.6	Bellmore (CDP) Nassau County
80	20.6	Clifton Park (town) Saratoga County
80	20.6	Ithaca (town) Tompkins County
80	20.6	Montebello (village) Rockland County
84	20.7	Dobbs Ferry (village) Westchester County
84	20.7	Holbrook (CDP) Suffolk County
84	20.7	Massapequa Park (village) Nassau County
84	20.7	Red Hook (town) Dutchess County
84	20.7	Sloatsburg (village) Rockland County
89	20.8	Harriman (village) Orange County
89	20.8	Islip Terrace (CDP) Suffolk County
89	20.8	Lake Grove (village) Suffolk County
89	20.8	Lansing (town) Tompkins County
89	20.8	Smithtown (CDP) Suffolk County
94	20.9	Pleasantville (village) Westchester County
94	20.9	Sayville (CDP) Suffolk County
96	21.0	Carmel (town) Putnam County
96	21.0	Duanesburg (town) Schenectady County
96	21.0	Floral Park (village) Nassau County
96	21.0	Garden City (village) Nassau County
96	21.0	Sands Point (village) Nassau County
101	21.2	Centerport (CDP) Suffolk County
101	21.2	Jericho (CDP) Nassau County
101	21.2	Malta (town) Saratoga County
101	21.2	Sea Cliff (village) Nassau County
105	21.3	Canton (village) Saint Lawrence County
105	21.3	Eastchester (town) Westchester County
105	21.3	Southeast (town) Putnam County
105	21.3	Stony Brook (CDP) Suffolk County
109	21.4	Baldwin (CDP) Nassau County
109	21.4	Baldwin Harbor (CDP) Nassau County
109	21.4	Miller Place (CDP) Suffolk County
112	21.5	Cornwall (town) Orange County
112	21.5	Lake Mohegan (CDP) Westchester County
112	21.5	Milton (CDP) Saratoga County
112	21.5	North Bellmore (CDP) Nassau County
112	21.5	Sand Lake (town) Rensselaer County
117	21.6	Blauvelt (CDP) Rockland County
117	21.6	East Fishkill (town) Dutchess County
117	21.6	Geneseo (town) Livingston County
117	21.6	Harrison (town/village) Westchester County
117	21.6	Wheatley Heights (CDP) Suffolk County
122	21.7	Carle Place (CDP) Nassau County
122	21.7	Shawangunk (town) Ulster County
122	21.7	Walworth (town) Wayne County
125	21.8	Smithtown (town) Suffolk County
125	21.8	South Farmingdale (CDP) Nassau County
125	21.8	Washingtonville (village) Orange County
128	21.9	Eastchester (CDP) Westchester County
128	21.9	Menands (village) Albany County
128	21.9	North Patchogue (CDP) Suffolk County
128	21.9	Pearl River (CDP) Rockland County
132	22.0	Garden City South (CDP) Nassau County
132	22.0	Greenville (town) Orange County
132	22.0	Hauppauge (CDP) Suffolk County
132	22.0	North Great River (CDP) Suffolk County
132	22.0	Salisbury (CDP) Nassau County
132	22.0	Union Vale (town) Dutchess County
138	22.1	Brockport (village) Monroe County
138	22.1	Greenburgh (town) Westchester County
138	22.1	Myers Corner (CDP) Dutchess County
141	22.2	Mahopac (CDP) Putnam County
141	22.2	Ogden (town) Monroe County
141	22.2	Pittsford (town) Monroe County
144	22.3	Clarence (town) Erie County
144	22.3	Commack (CDP) Suffolk County
144	22.3	East Hampton North (CDP) Suffolk County
147	22.4	Congers (CDP) Rockland County
147	22.4	Farmingville (CDP) Suffolk County
147	22.4	Victor (town) Ontario County
147	22.4	Williston Park (village) Nassau County

Note: *This section ranks incorporated places and CDPs (Census Designated Places) with populations of 2,500 or more. Unincorporated postal areas were not considered. Please refer to the User Guide for additional information.*

Population with No Health Insurance

Top 150 Places Ranked in *Descending* Order

State Rank	Percent	Place
1	65.1	**Watchtower** (CDP) Ulster County
2	38.5	**Riverside** (CDP) Suffolk County
2	38.5	**Saint Regis Mohawk Reservation** (reservation) Franklin County
4	31.3	**Benton** (town) Yates County
5	30.7	**Bedford Hills** (CDP) Westchester County
6	28.4	**Flanders** (CDP) Suffolk County
7	28.0	**Port Chester** (village) Westchester County
8	24.4	**New Cassel** (CDP) Nassau County
9	23.4	**Oswegatchie** (town) Saint Lawrence County
9	23.4	**Riverhead** (CDP) Suffolk County
11	23.1	**Spring Valley** (village) Rockland County
12	22.5	**Hempstead** (village) Nassau County
13	22.1	**Galen** (town) Wayne County
14	22.0	**Noyack** (CDP) Suffolk County
15	21.0	**Brentwood** (CDP) Suffolk County
15	21.0	**Ossining** (village) Westchester County
17	20.6	**Mount Kisco** (town/village) Westchester County
17	20.6	**Romulus** (town) Seneca County
19	20.5	**Inwood** (CDP) Nassau County
20	20.3	**Milo** (town) Yates County
21	20.1	**Newburgh** (city) Orange County
21	20.1	**Rye** (town) Westchester County
23	19.9	**Starkey** (town) Yates County
24	19.6	**Bainbridge** (town) Chenango County
24	19.6	**Central Islip** (CDP) Suffolk County
26	19.5	**Hampton Bays** (CDP) Suffolk County
27	19.0	**Wyandanch** (CDP) Suffolk County
28	18.8	**Uniondale** (CDP) Nassau County
29	18.6	**Palatine** (town) Montgomery County
30	18.1	**Shawangunk** (town) Ulster County
31	17.5	**North Amityville** (CDP) Suffolk County
32	17.2	**East Hampton North** (CDP) Suffolk County
32	17.2	**Huntington Station** (CDP) Suffolk County
32	17.2	**Minden** (town) Montgomery County
32	17.2	**Roosevelt** (CDP) Nassau County
36	17.1	**North East** (town) Dutchess County
37	17.0	**Patchogue** (village) Suffolk County
38	16.8	**Westbury** (village) Nassau County
39	16.7	**Elmsford** (village) Westchester County
39	16.7	**Manorhaven** (village) Nassau County
41	16.2	**Pamelia** (town) Jefferson County
42	15.6	**Freeport** (village) Nassau County
42	15.6	**Palmyra** (village) Wayne County
42	15.6	**Queens** (borough) Queens County
45	15.5	**Mount Ivy** (CDP) Rockland County
45	15.5	**Southampton** (town) Suffolk County
47	15.3	**Afton** (town) Chenango County
47	15.3	**Liberty** (village) Sullivan County
49	15.2	**Haverstraw** (village) Rockland County
50	15.0	**Vails Gate** (CDP) Orange County
51	14.8	**Yates** (town) Orleans County
52	14.7	**Ossining** (town) Westchester County
52	14.7	**Wappingers Falls** (village) Dutchess County
54	14.5	**Fairview** (CDP) Westchester County
54	14.5	**Poughkeepsie** (city) Dutchess County
54	14.5	**Rose** (town) Wayne County
57	14.4	**Shandaken** (town) Ulster County
57	14.4	**White Plains** (city) Westchester County
59	14.2	**Hector** (town) Schuyler County
60	14.0	**Monticello** (village) Sullivan County
61	13.8	**Copiague** (CDP) Suffolk County
61	13.8	**Richland** (town) Oswego County
63	13.7	**Bronx** (borough) Bronx County
63	13.7	**Saint Johnsville** (town) Montgomery County
65	13.6	**Glen Cove** (city) Nassau County
65	13.6	**Peekskill** (city) Westchester County
67	13.5	**Sleepy Hollow** (village) Westchester County
68	13.4	**Hillcrest** (CDP) Rockland County
68	13.4	**Mount Morris** (town) Livingston County
68	13.4	**New Bremen** (town) Lewis County
68	13.4	**North Bellport** (CDP) Suffolk County
72	13.3	**Colesville** (town) Broome County
73	13.2	**Middletown** (city) Orange County
73	13.2	**North Bay Shore** (CDP) Suffolk County
75	13.1	**Fayette** (town) Seneca County
75	13.1	**New Berlin** (town) Chenango County
75	13.1	**New Hempstead** (village) Rockland County
75	13.1	**Penn Yan** (village) Yates County
79	13.0	**Gouverneur** (village) Saint Lawrence County
79	13.0	**Riverhead** (town) Suffolk County
81	12.9	**Ellisburg** (town) Jefferson County
82	12.8	**Bay Shore** (CDP) Suffolk County
82	12.8	**Northwest Harbor** (CDP) Suffolk County
84	12.7	**East Patchogue** (CDP) Suffolk County
84	12.7	**Mastic** (CDP) Suffolk County
84	12.7	**Middletown** (town) Delaware County
84	12.7	**Sanford** (town) Broome County
84	12.7	**South Fallsburg** (CDP) Sullivan County
89	12.6	**Lake Luzerne** (town) Warren County
89	12.6	**Mount Vernon** (city) Westchester County
89	12.6	**Whitehall** (village) Washington County
92	12.5	**Alexandria** (town) Jefferson County
92	12.5	**Gowanda** (village) Cattaraugus County
92	12.5	**Haverstraw** (town) Rockland County
92	12.5	**Salamanca** (city) Cattaraugus County
92	12.5	**Saugerties** (village) Ulster County
92	12.5	**West Haverstraw** (village) Rockland County
98	12.4	**Garden City South** (CDP) Nassau County
98	12.4	**Gouverneur** (town) Saint Lawrence County
98	12.4	**New York** (city)
101	12.3	**Albion** (town) Orleans County
101	12.3	**Albion** (village) Orleans County
101	12.3	**Ravena** (village) Albany County
101	12.3	**West Bloomfield** (town) Ontario County
101	12.3	**Yorkshire** (town) Cattaraugus County
106	12.2	**Franklinville** (town) Cattaraugus County
106	12.2	**Hudson Falls** (village) Washington County
108	12.1	**Carthage** (village) Jefferson County
108	12.1	**Palmyra** (town) Wayne County
110	12.0	**Brooklyn** (borough) Kings County
110	12.0	**Chautauqua** (town) Chautauqua County
110	12.0	**Croghan** (town) Lewis County
110	12.0	**Esopus** (town) Ulster County
110	12.0	**Newfane** (CDP) Niagara County
110	12.0	**Thompson** (town) Sullivan County
116	11.9	**Bethel** (town) Sullivan County
116	11.9	**Harriman** (village) Orange County
118	11.8	**Conklin** (town) Broome County
118	11.8	**Elmont** (CDP) Nassau County
118	11.8	**Gloversville** (city) Fulton County
118	11.8	**Yonkers** (city) Westchester County
122	11.7	**Rosendale** (town) Ulster County
123	11.6	**Addison** (town) Steuben County
123	11.6	**Croton-on-Hudson** (village) Westchester County
123	11.6	**Perry** (town) Wyoming County
123	11.6	**Walton** (town) Delaware County
127	11.5	**Fallsburg** (town) Sullivan County
127	11.5	**Livingston** (town) Columbia County
129	11.4	**Locust Valley** (CDP) Nassau County
129	11.4	**New Rochelle** (city) Westchester County
131	11.3	**Batavia** (town) Genesee County
131	11.3	**East Farmingdale** (CDP) Suffolk County
131	11.3	**Granville** (town) Washington County
131	11.3	**Mamakating** (town) Sullivan County
135	11.2	**Blasdell** (village) Erie County
135	11.2	**Endicott** (village) Broome County
135	11.2	**Gorham** (town) Ontario County
135	11.2	**Ilion** (village) Herkimer County
135	11.2	**Ticonderoga** (CDP) Essex County
140	11.1	**Amityville** (village) Suffolk County
140	11.1	**Corning** (town) Steuben County
140	11.1	**Kingsbury** (town) Washington County
140	11.1	**Palermo** (town) Oswego County
144	11.0	**Cape Vincent** (town) Jefferson County
144	11.0	**Lake George** (town) Warren County
144	11.0	**Owego** (village) Tioga County
144	11.0	**Whitehall** (town) Washington County
148	10.9	**Montauk** (CDP) Suffolk County
148	10.9	**Port Jervis** (city) Orange County
150	10.8	**Brookfield** (town) Madison County

Note: *This section ranks incorporated places and CDPs (Census Designated Places) with populations of 2,500 or more. Unincorporated postal areas were not considered. Please refer to the User Guide for additional information.*

Population with No Health Insurance

Top 150 Places Ranked in *Ascending* Order

State Rank	Percent	Place	State Rank	Percent	Place
1	0.1	**West Point** (CDP) Orange County	69	2.7	**Union Vale** (town) Dutchess County
2	0.3	**Minoa** (village) Onondaga County	77	2.8	**Great Neck Estates** (village) Nassau County
3	0.5	**University at Buffalo** (CDP) Erie County	77	2.8	**Searingtown** (CDP) Nassau County
4	1.0	**New York Mills** (village) Oneida County	77	2.8	**Williamsville** (village) Erie County
5	1.1	**East Greenbush** (CDP) Rensselaer County	80	2.9	**Greenville** (CDP) Westchester County
6	1.2	**Kiryas Joel** (village) Orange County	80	2.9	**Kaser** (village) Rockland County
7	1.3	**Clarkson** (CDP) Monroe County	80	2.9	**Mount Sinai** (CDP) Suffolk County
7	1.3	**Woodbury** (CDP) Nassau County	80	2.9	**North Massapequa** (CDP) Nassau County
9	1.4	**Port Washington North** (village) Nassau County	80	2.9	**Penfield** (town) Monroe County
9	1.4	**Walworth** (town) Wayne County	80	2.9	**Sand Lake** (town) Rensselaer County
11	1.5	**Briarcliff Manor** (village) Westchester County	80	2.9	**Schuyler Falls** (town) Clinton County
11	1.5	**Bronxville** (village) Westchester County	80	2.9	**Skaneateles** (village) Onondaga County
11	1.5	**Lewiston** (village) Niagara County	80	2.9	**West Sand Lake** (CDP) Rensselaer County
11	1.5	**Miller Place** (CDP) Suffolk County	80	2.9	**Woodmere** (CDP) Nassau County
11	1.5	**Munsey Park** (village) Nassau County	90	3.0	**Dannemora** (village) Clinton County
11	1.5	**New Square** (village) Rockland County	90	3.0	**Erwin** (town) Steuben County
11	1.5	**North Hills** (village) Nassau County	90	3.0	**Fort Salonga** (CDP) Suffolk County
11	1.5	**Pittsford** (town) Monroe County	90	3.0	**Geneseo** (town) Livingston County
11	1.5	**Sands Point** (village) Nassau County	90	3.0	**Hamilton** (village) Madison County
20	1.6	**Larchmont** (village) Westchester County	90	3.0	**Harris Hill** (CDP) Erie County
20	1.6	**Melville** (CDP) Suffolk County	90	3.0	**Merrick** (CDP) Nassau County
20	1.6	**Owasco** (town) Cayuga County	90	3.0	**Mooers** (town) Clinton County
20	1.6	**Westerlo** (town) Albany County	90	3.0	**New Hartford** (town) Oneida County
24	1.7	**Elma Center** (CDP) Erie County	90	3.0	**West Hills** (CDP) Suffolk County
24	1.7	**Garden City** (village) Nassau County	90	3.0	**Westmere** (CDP) Albany County
24	1.7	**Rush** (town) Monroe County	101	3.1	**Airmont** (village) Rockland County
24	1.7	**Scarsdale** (town/village) Westchester County	101	3.1	**Bayport** (CDP) Suffolk County
24	1.7	**Spackenkill** (CDP) Dutchess County	101	3.1	**Bohemia** (CDP) Suffolk County
24	1.7	**West Nyack** (CDP) Rockland County	101	3.1	**Brookville** (village) Nassau County
24	1.7	**Westvale** (CDP) Onondaga County	101	3.1	**East Greenbush** (town) Rensselaer County
31	1.8	**Poestenkill** (town) Rensselaer County	101	3.1	**Gaines** (town) Orleans County
32	2.0	**Carroll** (town) Chautauqua County	101	3.1	**Hilton** (village) Monroe County
32	2.0	**Manlius** (village) Onondaga County	101	3.1	**Huntington** (CDP) Suffolk County
32	2.0	**Orchard Park** (town) Erie County	101	3.1	**Nesconset** (CDP) Suffolk County
32	2.0	**South Hill** (CDP) Tompkins County	101	3.1	**Northumberland** (town) Saratoga County
32	2.0	**Wanakah** (CDP) Erie County	101	3.1	**Rye** (city) Westchester County
37	2.1	**Ballston** (town) Saratoga County	101	3.1	**Sardinia** (town) Erie County
37	2.1	**Glenwood Landing** (CDP) Nassau County	101	3.1	**Southold** (CDP) Suffolk County
37	2.1	**Horseheads North** (CDP) Chemung County	101	3.1	**Spencerport** (village) Monroe County
37	2.1	**Lido Beach** (CDP) Nassau County	101	3.1	**Tappan** (CDP) Rockland County
37	2.1	**North Salem** (town) Westchester County	116	3.2	**Charlton** (town) Saratoga County
42	2.2	**Heritage Hills** (CDP) Westchester County	116	3.2	**Conesus Lake** (CDP) Livingston County
42	2.2	**Lawrence** (village) Nassau County	116	3.2	**Eastchester** (CDP) Westchester County
42	2.2	**Manhasset Hills** (CDP) Nassau County	116	3.2	**Geneva** (town) Ontario County
42	2.2	**SUNY Oswego** (CDP) Oswego County	116	3.2	**Halesite** (CDP) Suffolk County
42	2.2	**Setauket-East Setauket** (CDP) Suffolk County	116	3.2	**Kenmore** (village) Erie County
47	2.3	**Bellmore** (CDP) Nassau County	116	3.2	**Pendleton** (town) Niagara County
47	2.3	**East Williston** (village) Nassau County	116	3.2	**Perinton** (town) Monroe County
47	2.3	**Jefferson Valley-Yorktown** (CDP) Westchester County	116	3.2	**Scotia** (village) Schenectady County
47	2.3	**North Great River** (CDP) Suffolk County	116	3.2	**Wynantskill** (CDP) Rensselaer County
51	2.4	**Amsterdam** (town) Montgomery County	126	3.3	**Castile** (town) Wyoming County
51	2.4	**Clifton Park** (town) Saratoga County	126	3.3	**Catlin** (town) Chemung County
51	2.4	**Gang Mills** (CDP) Steuben County	126	3.3	**Commack** (CDP) Suffolk County
51	2.4	**Marlboro** (CDP) Ulster County	126	3.3	**Hauppauge** (CDP) Suffolk County
55	2.5	**Fort Drum** (CDP) Jefferson County	126	3.3	**Malta** (town) Saratoga County
55	2.5	**Lake Success** (village) Nassau County	126	3.3	**Marilla** (town) Erie County
55	2.5	**Menands** (village) Albany County	126	3.3	**Muttontown** (village) Nassau County
55	2.5	**Ridge** (CDP) Suffolk County	126	3.3	**Niskayuna** (town) Schenectady County
55	2.5	**Rockville Centre** (village) Nassau County	126	3.3	**Onondaga** (town) Onondaga County
55	2.5	**Stony Brook University** (CDP) Suffolk County	126	3.3	**Plainedge** (CDP) Nassau County
61	2.6	**East Norwich** (CDP) Nassau County	126	3.3	**Sayville** (CDP) Suffolk County
61	2.6	**East Shoreham** (CDP) Suffolk County	126	3.3	**Seaford** (CDP) Nassau County
61	2.6	**Massapequa** (CDP) Nassau County	126	3.3	**Smithtown** (town) Suffolk County
61	2.6	**Montebello** (village) Rockland County	126	3.3	**Stony Brook** (CDP) Suffolk County
61	2.6	**North Wantagh** (CDP) Nassau County	126	3.3	**West Bay Shore** (CDP) Suffolk County
61	2.6	**Northport** (village) Suffolk County	141	3.4	**Amherst** (town) Erie County
61	2.6	**Voorheesville** (village) Albany County	141	3.4	**Canandaigua** (town) Ontario County
61	2.6	**Wantagh** (CDP) Nassau County	141	3.4	**East Islip** (CDP) Suffolk County
69	2.7	**Bethlehem** (town) Albany County	141	3.4	**Irvington** (village) Westchester County
69	2.7	**Centerport** (CDP) Suffolk County	141	3.4	**Jericho** (CDP) Nassau County
69	2.7	**Cold Spring Harbor** (CDP) Suffolk County	141	3.4	**Manhasset** (CDP) Nassau County
69	2.7	**Hawthorne** (CDP) Westchester County	141	3.4	**Pelham Manor** (village) Westchester County
69	2.7	**New Castle** (town) Westchester County	141	3.4	**Schoharie** (town) Schoharie County
69	2.7	**Plainview** (CDP) Nassau County	141	3.4	**Smithtown** (CDP) Suffolk County
69	2.7	**Richmond** (town) Ontario County	141	3.4	**Wading River** (CDP) Suffolk County

Note: *This section ranks incorporated places and CDPs (Census Designated Places) with populations of 2,500 or more. Unincorporated postal areas were not considered. Please refer to the User Guide for additional information.*

Population Under 18 Years Old with No Health Insurance

Top 150 Places Ranked in *Descending* Order

State Rank	Percent	Place	State Rank	Percent	Place
1	74.7	**Watchtower** (CDP) Ulster County	76	9.4	**Gouverneur** (town) Saint Lawrence County
2	61.2	**Benton** (town) Yates County	76	9.4	**Ithaca** (city) Tompkins County
3	51.6	**Saint Regis Mohawk Reservation** (reservation) Franklin County	76	9.4	**Lake Erie Beach** (CDP) Erie County
4	42.2	**Oswegatchie** (town) Saint Lawrence County	79	9.3	**Campbell** (town) Steuben County
5	30.5	**Milo** (town) Yates County	79	9.3	**Manchester** (town) Ontario County
5	30.5	**Minden** (town) Montgomery County	81	9.1	**Brownville** (town) Jefferson County
7	30.4	**Northwest Harbor** (CDP) Suffolk County	81	9.1	**Lake Luzerne** (town) Warren County
8	29.9	**Starkey** (town) Yates County	81	9.1	**Liberty** (village) Sullivan County
9	29.0	**Conklin** (town) Broome County	81	9.1	**Virgil** (town) Cortland County
10	27.5	**Bainbridge** (town) Chenango County	81	9.1	**Waterford** (town) Saratoga County
10	27.5	**Lakeland** (CDP) Onondaga County	81	9.1	**Wilna** (town) Jefferson County
12	26.9	**Jerusalem** (town) Yates County	87	9.0	**East Bloomfield** (town) Ontario County
13	26.5	**Galen** (town) Wayne County	88	8.9	**Colesville** (town) Broome County
14	25.7	**Palatine** (town) Montgomery County	88	8.9	**Ellisburg** (town) Jefferson County
15	25.5	**Chautauqua** (town) Chautauqua County	90	8.8	**Canisteo** (town) Steuben County
16	24.9	**Richland** (town) Oswego County	90	8.8	**Flanders** (CDP) Suffolk County
17	24.6	**Pamelia** (town) Jefferson County	90	8.8	**Flower Hill** (village) Nassau County
18	23.7	**Romulus** (town) Seneca County	93	8.7	**Manheim** (town) Herkimer County
19	22.4	**Gorham** (town) Ontario County	94	8.6	**Corning** (town) Steuben County
20	21.9	**Rose** (town) Wayne County	94	8.6	**Esopus** (town) Ulster County
21	18.8	**Hunter** (town) Greene County	96	8.5	**Brookfield** (town) Madison County
22	18.1	**Afton** (town) Chenango County	96	8.5	**Floyd** (town) Oneida County
23	18.0	**Saint Johnsville** (town) Montgomery County	98	8.3	**Marcellus** (town) Onondaga County
24	17.2	**Ticonderoga** (CDP) Essex County	99	8.2	**Cato** (town) Cayuga County
25	16.7	**Fayette** (town) Seneca County	99	8.2	**Shelby** (town) Orleans County
25	16.7	**Yates** (town) Orleans County	101	8.1	**Walton** (town) Delaware County
27	16.3	**Moriches** (CDP) Suffolk County	102	8.0	**Addison** (town) Steuben County
28	15.9	**New Bremen** (town) Lewis County	102	8.0	**Blasdell** (village) Erie County
29	15.8	**Riverside** (CDP) Suffolk County	104	7.9	**Phelps** (town) Ontario County
30	15.7	**Shandaken** (town) Ulster County	104	7.9	**Wolcott** (town) Wayne County
31	15.5	**Lisbon** (town) Saint Lawrence County	106	7.8	**North Sea** (CDP) Suffolk County
32	15.3	**Carthage** (village) Jefferson County	107	7.7	**Copiague** (CDP) Suffolk County
33	15.0	**Seneca** (town) Ontario County	107	7.7	**Durham** (town) Greene County
34	14.9	**Bedford Hills** (CDP) Westchester County	107	7.7	**Pearl River** (CDP) Rockland County
35	14.8	**Lyncourt** (CDP) Onondaga County	107	7.7	**Spencer** (town) Tioga County
35	14.8	**Penn Yan** (village) Yates County	111	7.5	**Gowanda** (village) Cattaraugus County
37	14.7	**New Cassel** (CDP) Nassau County	111	7.5	**Kingsbury** (town) Washington County
38	14.5	**Alden** (village) Erie County	111	7.5	**Saranac Lake** (village) Franklin County
39	14.4	**Mount Ivy** (CDP) Rockland County	111	7.5	**Waverly** (village) Tioga County
40	14.0	**Yorkshire** (town) Cattaraugus County	115	7.4	**Bay Shore** (CDP) Suffolk County
41	13.9	**Viola** (CDP) Rockland County	115	7.4	**Huntington Station** (CDP) Suffolk County
42	13.5	**Blauvelt** (CDP) Rockland County	115	7.4	**Moira** (town) Franklin County
43	12.9	**Croghan** (town) Lewis County	115	7.4	**New Hempstead** (village) Rockland County
43	12.9	**Westbury** (village) Nassau County	115	7.4	**Ridgeway** (town) Orleans County
45	12.7	**Carmel Hamlet** (CDP) Putnam County	115	7.4	**Saratoga** (town) Saratoga County
46	12.1	**Ticonderoga** (town) Essex County	115	7.4	**Wellsville** (town) Allegany County
47	12.0	**SUNY Oswego** (CDP) Oswego County	122	7.3	**Davenport** (town) Delaware County
48	11.9	**Batavia** (town) Genesee County	122	7.3	**Halesite** (CDP) Suffolk County
49	11.8	**Warsaw** (town) Wyoming County	122	7.3	**Lakewood** (village) Chautauqua County
50	11.6	**Uniondale** (CDP) Nassau County	122	7.3	**Newburgh** (city) Orange County
51	11.4	**Hillcrest** (CDP) Rockland County	122	7.3	**Roosevelt** (CDP) Nassau County
52	11.3	**Orchard Park** (village) Erie County	127	7.2	**Brentwood** (CDP) Suffolk County
53	11.2	**LaFayette** (town) Onondaga County	127	7.2	**East Garden City** (CDP) Nassau County
53	11.2	**New Berlin** (town) Chenango County	127	7.2	**Gloversville** (city) Fulton County
55	11.0	**Chester** (town) Warren County	127	7.2	**Granville** (town) Washington County
55	11.0	**Glens Falls North** (CDP) Warren County	127	7.2	**Inwood** (CDP) Nassau County
57	10.8	**Clarendon** (town) Orleans County	127	7.2	**Jay** (town) Essex County
58	10.7	**Evans** (town) Erie County	127	7.2	**Johnstown** (town) Fulton County
58	10.7	**Red Oaks Mill** (CDP) Dutchess County	134	7.1	**Dansville** (village) Livingston County
58	10.7	**Riverhead** (CDP) Suffolk County	134	7.1	**East Hampton** (town) Suffolk County
61	10.6	**Cornwall-on-Hudson** (village) Orange County	134	7.1	**Massena** (village) Saint Lawrence County
62	10.5	**Williamson** (town) Wayne County	134	7.1	**Mattituck** (CDP) Suffolk County
63	10.2	**Lake Placid** (village) Essex County	134	7.1	**Sidney** (village) Delaware County
64	10.1	**Chesterfield** (town) Essex County	139	7.0	**Hampton Bays** (CDP) Suffolk County
64	10.1	**Clinton** (town) Dutchess County	139	7.0	**Palmyra** (village) Wayne County
64	10.1	**Freeport** (village) Nassau County	139	7.0	**Wellsville** (village) Allegany County
64	10.1	**Homer** (town) Cortland County	139	7.0	**Whitehall** (town) Washington County
64	10.1	**Northampton** (town) Fulton County	143	6.9	**Constantia** (town) Oswego County
69	9.9	**Granby** (town) Oswego County	143	6.9	**Hudson Falls** (village) Washington County
69	9.9	**Harriman** (village) Orange County	143	6.9	**Plattekill** (town) Ulster County
69	9.9	**Salamanca** (city) Cattaraugus County	143	6.9	**Shelter Island** (town) Suffolk County
72	9.7	**Salem** (town) Washington County	147	6.8	**Kirkwood** (town) Broome County
72	9.7	**Wyandanch** (CDP) Suffolk County	147	6.8	**Port Jefferson Station** (CDP) Suffolk County
74	9.6	**Portland** (town) Chautauqua County	147	6.8	**Sidney** (town) Delaware County
75	9.5	**Perry** (town) Wyoming County	150	6.7	**Candor** (town) Tioga County

Note: This section ranks incorporated places and CDPs (Census Designated Places) with populations of 2,500 or more. Unincorporated postal areas were not considered. Please refer to the User Guide for additional information.

Population Under 18 Years Old with No Health Insurance

Top 150 Places Ranked in *Ascending* Order

State Rank	Percent	Place	State Rank	Percent	Place
1	0.0	**Alexandria** (town) Jefferson County	1	0.0	**Hartsdale** (CDP) Westchester County
1	0.0	**Alfred** (town) Allegany County	1	0.0	**Haviland** (CDP) Dutchess County
1	0.0	**Alfred** (village) Allegany County	1	0.0	**Hawthorne** (CDP) Westchester County
1	0.0	**Allegany** (town) Cattaraugus County	1	0.0	**Heritage Hills** (CDP) Westchester County
1	0.0	**Au Sable** (town) Clinton County	1	0.0	**Herricks** (CDP) Nassau County
1	0.0	**Avon** (town) Livingston County	1	0.0	**Highland** (CDP) Ulster County
1	0.0	**Avon** (village) Livingston County	1	0.0	**Hilton** (village) Monroe County
1	0.0	**Ballston** (town) Saratoga County	1	0.0	**Honeoye Falls** (village) Monroe County
1	0.0	**Bangor** (town) Franklin County	1	0.0	**Hoosick Falls** (village) Rensselaer County
1	0.0	**Barker** (town) Broome County	1	0.0	**Horseheads North** (CDP) Chemung County
1	0.0	**Beekmantown** (town) Clinton County	1	0.0	**Irvington** (village) Westchester County
1	0.0	**Bellmore** (CDP) Nassau County	1	0.0	**Islandia** (village) Suffolk County
1	0.0	**Bethel** (town) Sullivan County	1	0.0	**Lake George** (town) Warren County
1	0.0	**Binghamton University** (CDP) Broome County	1	0.0	**Lansing** (town) Tompkins County
1	0.0	**Boston** (town) Erie County	1	0.0	**Lansing** (village) Tompkins County
1	0.0	**Brightwaters** (village) Suffolk County	1	0.0	**Larchmont** (village) Westchester County
1	0.0	**Bronxville** (village) Westchester County	1	0.0	**Lawrence** (village) Nassau County
1	0.0	**Brookville** (village) Nassau County	1	0.0	**Lenox** (town) Madison County
1	0.0	**Brunswick** (town) Rensselaer County	1	0.0	**Lewiston** (village) Niagara County
1	0.0	**Brutus** (town) Cayuga County	1	0.0	**Livingston** (town) Columbia County
1	0.0	**Cairo** (town) Greene County	1	0.0	**Louisville** (town) Saint Lawrence County
1	0.0	**Caledonia** (town) Livingston County	1	0.0	**Madison** (town) Madison County
1	0.0	**Calverton** (CDP) Suffolk County	1	0.0	**Maine** (town) Broome County
1	0.0	**Canandaigua** (town) Ontario County	1	0.0	**Malone** (village) Franklin County
1	0.0	**Canastota** (village) Madison County	1	0.0	**Manlius** (village) Onondaga County
1	0.0	**Caroline** (town) Tompkins County	1	0.0	**Mechanicstown** (CDP) Orange County
1	0.0	**Carroll** (town) Chautauqua County	1	0.0	**Medina** (village) Orleans County
1	0.0	**Catlin** (town) Chemung County	1	0.0	**Melville** (CDP) Suffolk County
1	0.0	**Cayuga Heights** (village) Tompkins County	1	0.0	**Menands** (village) Albany County
1	0.0	**Centerport** (CDP) Suffolk County	1	0.0	**Minoa** (village) Onondaga County
1	0.0	**Charlton** (town) Saratoga County	1	0.0	**Mohawk** (town) Montgomery County
1	0.0	**Clarkson** (CDP) Monroe County	1	0.0	**Mohawk** (village) Herkimer County
1	0.0	**Clarkson** (town) Monroe County	1	0.0	**Montgomery** (village) Orange County
1	0.0	**Cobleskill** (town) Schoharie County	1	0.0	**Monticello** (village) Sullivan County
1	0.0	**Cobleskill** (village) Schoharie County	1	0.0	**Mount Morris** (village) Livingston County
1	0.0	**Collins** (town) Erie County	1	0.0	**Neversink** (town) Sullivan County
1	0.0	**Conesus** (town) Livingston County	1	0.0	**New Baltimore** (town) Greene County
1	0.0	**Conesus Lake** (CDP) Livingston County	1	0.0	**New Windsor** (town) Orange County
1	0.0	**Copake** (town) Columbia County	1	0.0	**New York Mills** (village) Oneida County
1	0.0	**Coxsackie** (village) Greene County	1	0.0	**North Boston** (CDP) Erie County
1	0.0	**Cutchogue** (CDP) Suffolk County	1	0.0	**North Great River** (CDP) Suffolk County
1	0.0	**Dannemora** (town) Clinton County	1	0.0	**North Hills** (village) Nassau County
1	0.0	**Dannemora** (village) Clinton County	1	0.0	**North Patchogue** (CDP) Suffolk County
1	0.0	**Delaware** (town) Sullivan County	1	0.0	**North Salem** (town) Westchester County
1	0.0	**Delhi** (town) Delaware County	1	0.0	**Olive** (town) Ulster County
1	0.0	**Delhi** (village) Delaware County	1	0.0	**Orange Lake** (CDP) Orange County
1	0.0	**East Greenbush** (CDP) Rensselaer County	1	0.0	**Otego** (town) Otsego County
1	0.0	**East Moriches** (CDP) Suffolk County	1	0.0	**Owasco** (town) Cayuga County
1	0.0	**East Northport** (CDP) Suffolk County	1	0.0	**Oyster Bay** (CDP) Nassau County
1	0.0	**East Rochester** (town/village) Monroe County	1	0.0	**Pembroke** (town) Genesee County
1	0.0	**East Rockaway** (village) Nassau County	1	0.0	**Piermont** (village) Rockland County
1	0.0	**East Williston** (village) Nassau County	1	0.0	**Pierrepont** (town) Saint Lawrence County
1	0.0	**Elma Center** (CDP) Erie County	1	0.0	**Poestenkill** (town) Rensselaer County
1	0.0	**Elmira Heights** (village) Chemung County	1	0.0	**Pompey** (town) Onondaga County
1	0.0	**Fairport** (village) Monroe County	1	0.0	**Port Ewen** (CDP) Ulster County
1	0.0	**Fairview** (CDP) Westchester County	1	0.0	**Port Washington North** (village) Nassau County
1	0.0	**Falconer** (village) Chautauqua County	1	0.0	**Richmond** (town) Ontario County
1	0.0	**Fenton** (town) Broome County	1	0.0	**Richmondville** (town) Schoharie County
1	0.0	**Florida** (town) Montgomery County	1	0.0	**Rockville Centre** (village) Nassau County
1	0.0	**Florida** (village) Orange County	1	0.0	**Rush** (town) Monroe County
1	0.0	**Frankfort** (town) Herkimer County	1	0.0	**Sands Point** (village) Nassau County
1	0.0	**Frankfort** (village) Herkimer County	1	0.0	**Saranac** (town) Clinton County
1	0.0	**Fredonia** (village) Chautauqua County	1	0.0	**Sardinia** (town) Erie County
1	0.0	**Gaines** (town) Orleans County	1	0.0	**Saugerties** (village) Ulster County
1	0.0	**Garden City Park** (CDP) Nassau County	1	0.0	**Schroeppel** (town) Oswego County
1	0.0	**Garden City South** (CDP) Nassau County	1	0.0	**Schuyler** (town) Herkimer County
1	0.0	**Gates** (CDP) Monroe County	1	0.0	**Scriba** (town) Oswego County
1	0.0	**Geneva** (town) Ontario County	1	0.0	**Sennett** (town) Cayuga County
1	0.0	**Glen Head** (CDP) Nassau County	1	0.0	**Sheridan** (town) Chautauqua County
1	0.0	**Gordon Heights** (CDP) Suffolk County	1	0.0	**Solvay** (village) Onondaga County
1	0.0	**Great Neck Estates** (village) Nassau County	1	0.0	**Sound Beach** (CDP) Suffolk County
1	0.0	**Greenville** (CDP) Westchester County	1	0.0	**South Fallsburg** (CDP) Sullivan County
1	0.0	**Greenville** (town) Greene County	1	0.0	**Southold** (CDP) Suffolk County
1	0.0	**Greenwood Lake** (village) Orange County	1	0.0	**Spackenkill** (CDP) Dutchess County
1	0.0	**Hamptonburgh** (town) Orange County	1	0.0	**Spencerport** (village) Monroe County

Note: This section ranks incorporated places and CDPs (Census Designated Places) with populations of 2,500 or more. Unincorporated postal areas were not considered. Please refer to the User Guide for additional information.

Commute to Work: Car

Top 150 Places Ranked in *Descending* Order

State Rank	Percent	Place	State Rank	Percent	Place
1	100.0	**Wanakah** (CDP) Erie County	76	95.5	**Minoa** (village) Onondaga County
2	99.6	**North Boston** (CDP) Erie County	76	95.5	**Norwich** (town) Chenango County
3	99.0	**Carroll** (town) Chautauqua County	78	95.4	**Maine** (town) Broome County
4	98.9	**Lakeland** (CDP) Onondaga County	78	95.4	**Neversink** (town) Sullivan County
5	98.7	**Newfane** (CDP) Niagara County	78	95.4	**Pembroke** (town) Genesee County
6	98.2	**Lake Erie Beach** (CDP) Erie County	78	95.4	**Schodack** (town) Rensselaer County
7	98.1	**Windsor** (town) Broome County	82	95.3	**Chenango Bridge** (CDP) Broome County
8	98.0	**Schuyler** (town) Herkimer County	82	95.3	**Depew** (village) Erie County
9	97.9	**Elma Center** (CDP) Erie County	82	95.3	**Pittstown** (town) Rensselaer County
9	97.9	**Newark Valley** (town) Tioga County	82	95.3	**South Glens Falls** (village) Saratoga County
11	97.8	**Horseheads North** (CDP) Chemung County	86	95.2	**Binghamton** (town) Broome County
11	97.8	**Saranac** (town) Clinton County	86	95.2	**Greece** (CDP) Monroe County
13	97.7	**Fenton** (town) Broome County	86	95.2	**Parma** (town) Monroe County
14	97.6	**Aurelius** (town) Cayuga County	86	95.2	**West Monroe** (town) Oswego County
14	97.6	**Clarkson** (CDP) Monroe County	90	95.1	**Broadalbin** (town) Fulton County
14	97.6	**Spencerport** (village) Monroe County	90	95.1	**Brookfield** (town) Madison County
17	97.5	**Alden** (town) Erie County	90	95.1	**Charlton** (town) Saratoga County
17	97.5	**Paris** (town) Oneida County	90	95.1	**Cheektowaga** (town) Erie County
19	97.3	**Milton** (CDP) Saratoga County	90	95.1	**Gates** (town) Monroe County
20	97.2	**Lancaster** (village) Erie County	90	95.1	**Gouverneur** (village) Saint Lawrence County
20	97.2	**Mount Morris** (village) Livingston County	90	95.1	**Palermo** (town) Oswego County
20	97.2	**Portville** (town) Cattaraugus County	90	95.1	**Royalton** (town) Niagara County
20	97.2	**West Sand Lake** (CDP) Rensselaer County	98	95.0	**Cheektowaga** (CDP) Erie County
24	97.1	**Johnstown** (city) Fulton County	98	95.0	**Colesville** (town) Broome County
24	97.1	**Oakfield** (town) Genesee County	98	95.0	**Grandyle Village** (CDP) Erie County
26	97.0	**Catlin** (town) Chemung County	98	95.0	**Walworth** (town) Wayne County
26	97.0	**Conesus** (town) Livingston County	102	94.9	**Brownville** (town) Jefferson County
26	97.0	**Ontario** (town) Wayne County	102	94.9	**Brutus** (town) Cayuga County
29	96.9	**Schaghticoke** (town) Rensselaer County	102	94.9	**Canandaigua** (town) Ontario County
30	96.7	**Norfolk** (town) Saint Lawrence County	102	94.9	**East Shoreham** (CDP) Suffolk County
30	96.7	**Sloan** (village) Erie County	102	94.9	**Mooers** (town) Clinton County
32	96.6	**Gates** (CDP) Monroe County	102	94.9	**Victor** (village) Ontario County
32	96.6	**Lakewood** (village) Chautauqua County	108	94.8	**Chittenango** (village) Madison County
32	96.6	**New York Mills** (village) Oneida County	108	94.8	**Colonie** (village) Albany County
35	96.4	**Altona** (town) Clinton County	108	94.8	**Wheatfield** (town) Niagara County
35	96.4	**Manorville** (CDP) Suffolk County	108	94.8	**Yorkville** (village) Oneida County
35	96.4	**Murray** (town) Orleans County	112	94.7	**Cambria** (town) Niagara County
35	96.4	**Sterling** (town) Cayuga County	112	94.7	**Conesus Lake** (CDP) Livingston County
35	96.4	**Wawayanda** (town) Orange County	112	94.7	**Deerfield** (town) Oneida County
40	96.3	**Boston** (town) Erie County	112	94.7	**Grand Island** (town) Erie County
40	96.3	**Busti** (town) Chautauqua County	112	94.7	**Greece** (town) Monroe County
40	96.3	**Livonia** (town) Livingston County	112	94.7	**West Seneca** (CDP) Erie County
40	96.3	**Moreau** (town) Saratoga County	112	94.7	**Wilson** (town) Niagara County
40	96.3	**Poestenkill** (town) Rensselaer County	119	94.6	**Alexander** (town) Genesee County
40	96.3	**Seneca** (town) Ontario County	119	94.6	**Big Flats** (CDP) Chemung County
46	96.2	**Madison** (town) Madison County	119	94.6	**Caledonia** (town) Livingston County
46	96.2	**Marilla** (town) Erie County	119	94.6	**Lockport** (town) Niagara County
48	96.1	**Adams** (town) Jefferson County	119	94.6	**North Tonawanda** (city) Niagara County
48	96.1	**Canastota** (village) Madison County	119	94.6	**West Bloomfield** (town) Ontario County
48	96.1	**Veteran** (town) Chemung County	119	94.6	**Wheatland** (town) Monroe County
48	96.1	**West Elmira** (CDP) Chemung County	126	94.5	**Addison** (town) Steuben County
52	96.0	**Amsterdam** (town) Montgomery County	126	94.5	**Barton** (town) Tioga County
52	96.0	**Colden** (town) Erie County	126	94.5	**Chazy** (town) Clinton County
52	96.0	**Conklin** (town) Broome County	126	94.5	**Elbridge** (town) Onondaga County
52	96.0	**Corning** (town) Steuben County	126	94.5	**Hamlin** (town) Monroe County
52	96.0	**Eden** (town) Erie County	126	94.5	**Mastic Beach** (village) Suffolk County
52	96.0	**Gaines** (town) Orleans County	126	94.5	**Nassau** (town) Rensselaer County
52	96.0	**Gang Mills** (CDP) Steuben County	126	94.5	**Orchard Park** (town) Erie County
59	95.9	**Clarendon** (town) Orleans County	126	94.5	**Plattsburgh** (town) Clinton County
59	95.9	**East Greenbush** (CDP) Rensselaer County	126	94.5	**Trenton** (town) Oneida County
59	95.9	**Evans** (town) Erie County	126	94.5	**Vernon** (town) Oneida County
59	95.9	**Hamlin** (CDP) Monroe County	126	94.5	**Warrensburg** (town) Warren County
59	95.9	**Lancaster** (town) Erie County	138	94.4	**Hilton** (village) Monroe County
59	95.9	**Newfane** (town) Niagara County	138	94.4	**Kendall** (town) Orleans County
59	95.9	**Riga** (town) Monroe County	138	94.4	**North Collins** (town) Erie County
59	95.9	**Sand Lake** (town) Rensselaer County	138	94.4	**Putnam Lake** (CDP) Putnam County
67	95.8	**Berne** (town) Albany County	138	94.4	**Ridge** (CDP) Suffolk County
67	95.8	**Lenox** (town) Madison County	138	94.4	**Rose** (town) Wayne County
69	95.7	**Alden** (village) Erie County	138	94.4	**Tioga** (town) Tioga County
69	95.7	**Eden** (CDP) Erie County	145	94.3	**Avon** (town) Livingston County
69	95.7	**Floyd** (town) Oneida County	145	94.3	**Cicero** (town) Onondaga County
69	95.7	**Mayfield** (town) Fulton County	145	94.3	**Deerpark** (town) Orange County
73	95.6	**Moravia** (town) Cayuga County	145	94.3	**New Hartford** (town) Oneida County
73	95.6	**Rutland** (town) Jefferson County	145	94.3	**Pendleton** (town) Niagara County
73	95.6	**Sandy Creek** (town) Oswego County	145	94.3	**Rotterdam** (CDP) Schenectady County

Note: *This section ranks incorporated places and CDPs (Census Designated Places) with populations of 2,500 or more. Unincorporated postal areas were not considered. Please refer to the User Guide for additional information.*

Commute to Work: Car

Top 150 Places Ranked in *Ascending* Order

State Rank	Percent	Place
1	2.9	**Watchtower** (CDP) Ulster County
2	8.0	**Manhattan** (borough) New York County
3	22.9	**Binghamton University** (CDP) Broome County
4	23.0	**Brooklyn** (borough) Kings County
5	23.7	**Stony Brook University** (CDP) Suffolk County
6	24.1	**West Point** (CDP) Orange County
7	26.7	**New York** (city)
8	27.3	**Bronx** (borough) Bronx County
9	28.5	**Alfred** (village) Allegany County
10	30.5	**SUNY Oswego** (CDP) Oswego County
11	33.1	**New Square** (village) Rockland County
12	37.4	**Larchmont** (village) Westchester County
13	37.6	**Kaser** (village) Rockland County
14	38.0	**Queens** (borough) Queens County
15	39.1	**Alfred** (town) Allegany County
16	40.2	**Ithaca** (city) Tompkins County
17	41.4	**Bronxville** (village) Westchester County
18	42.0	**Scarsdale** (town/village) Westchester County
19	42.1	**University at Buffalo** (CDP) Erie County
20	44.2	**Kiryas Joel** (village) Orange County
21	47.1	**Tuckahoe** (village) Westchester County
22	47.2	**Hamilton** (village) Madison County
23	47.4	**Munsey Park** (village) Nassau County
24	47.9	**Mamaroneck** (town) Westchester County
25	48.7	**Potsdam** (village) Saint Lawrence County
26	51.5	**Greenville** (CDP) Westchester County
27	52.7	**Great Neck Plaza** (village) Nassau County
27	52.7	**Highlands** (town) Orange County
29	53.4	**Canton** (village) Saint Lawrence County
30	53.6	**South Hill** (CDP) Tompkins County
31	53.7	**East Garden City** (CDP) Nassau County
32	54.1	**Port Washington** (CDP) Nassau County
33	54.8	**Hartsdale** (CDP) Westchester County
34	54.9	**Briarcliff Manor** (village) Westchester County
35	55.2	**New Paltz** (village) Ulster County
36	55.4	**Rye** (city) Westchester County
37	55.5	**Caneadea** (town) Allegany County
38	55.6	**Geneseo** (village) Livingston County
39	56.1	**Sleepy Hollow** (village) Westchester County
40	57.1	**Kings Point** (village) Nassau County
41	57.5	**Hastings-on-Hudson** (village) Westchester County
41	57.5	**New Castle** (town) Westchester County
43	58.1	**Thomaston** (village) Nassau County
44	59.3	**Manhasset** (CDP) Nassau County
45	59.7	**Pelham** (village) Westchester County
46	60.5	**Arlington** (CDP) Dutchess County
47	60.7	**Port Chester** (village) Westchester County
48	61.4	**Cayuga Heights** (village) Tompkins County
48	61.4	**Sands Point** (village) Nassau County
50	61.6	**Eastchester** (town) Westchester County
50	61.6	**Flower Hill** (village) Nassau County
52	61.7	**Mamaroneck** (village) Westchester County
53	62.2	**Mount Vernon** (city) Westchester County
54	62.3	**Oneonta** (city) Otsego County
55	62.6	**Ithaca** (town) Tompkins County
55	62.6	**Monsey** (CDP) Rockland County
57	63.3	**Great Neck** (village) Nassau County
57	63.3	**Rye** (town) Westchester County
59	63.6	**Brookville** (village) Nassau County
59	63.6	**New Rochelle** (city) Westchester County
61	63.9	**Harrison** (town/village) Westchester County
62	64.0	**Rockville Centre** (village) Nassau County
62	64.0	**Rye Brook** (village) Westchester County
64	64.3	**Pelham** (town) Westchester County
64	64.3	**Port Washington North** (village) Nassau County
66	64.4	**Bedford** (town) Westchester County
67	64.5	**Staten Island** (borough) Richmond County
68	64.6	**Delhi** (village) Delaware County
68	64.6	**Inwood** (CDP) Nassau County
70	64.8	**Croton-on-Hudson** (village) Westchester County
71	65.0	**Brockport** (village) Monroe County
71	65.0	**Fort Drum** (CDP) Jefferson County
71	65.0	**Hamilton** (town) Madison County
74	65.1	**Great Neck Estates** (village) Nassau County
74	65.1	**Pound Ridge** (town) Westchester County
74	65.1	**Yonkers** (city) Westchester County
77	65.4	**Garden City** (village) Nassau County
78	65.5	**White Plains** (city) Westchester County
79	65.7	**Old Westbury** (village) Nassau County
79	65.7	**Tarrytown** (village) Westchester County
81	66.4	**Hempstead** (village) Nassau County
82	66.6	**Dobbs Ferry** (village) Westchester County
83	66.7	**Geneseo** (town) Livingston County
84	66.9	**Hudson** (city) Columbia County
84	66.9	**Woodmere** (CDP) Nassau County
86	67.0	**Lido Beach** (CDP) Nassau County
87	67.2	**Lakeview** (CDP) Nassau County
87	67.2	**University Gardens** (CDP) Nassau County
87	67.2	**Woodstock** (town) Ulster County
90	67.6	**Southampton** (village) Suffolk County
91	67.7	**South Valley Stream** (CDP) Nassau County
92	67.8	**Cobleskill** (village) Schoharie County
92	67.8	**Philipstown** (town) Putnam County
94	68.1	**Irvington** (village) Westchester County
95	68.3	**Greenburgh** (town) Westchester County
96	68.5	**Lansing** (village) Tompkins County
96	68.5	**Ossining** (town) Westchester County
98	69.0	**South Fallsburg** (CDP) Sullivan County
99	69.2	**Cazenovia** (village) Madison County
99	69.2	**Lynbrook** (village) Nassau County
101	69.3	**Fairview** (CDP) Westchester County
102	70.0	**Canton** (town) Saint Lawrence County
103	70.1	**Long Beach** (city) Nassau County
103	70.1	**Roslyn Heights** (CDP) Nassau County
105	70.2	**Centerport** (CDP) Suffolk County
105	70.2	**Pelham Manor** (village) Westchester County
107	70.3	**Monroe** (town) Orange County
107	70.3	**Potsdam** (town) Saint Lawrence County
109	70.7	**Ossining** (village) Westchester County
109	70.7	**Viola** (CDP) Rockland County
111	71.0	**Otsego** (town) Otsego County
112	71.1	**Albany** (city) Albany County
112	71.1	**Newburgh** (city) Orange County
114	71.3	**Mount Pleasant** (town) Westchester County
115	71.5	**Cold Spring Harbor** (CDP) Suffolk County
116	71.7	**Lloyd Harbor** (village) Suffolk County
117	71.9	**North Hempstead** (town) Nassau County
118	72.0	**East Hills** (village) Nassau County
118	72.0	**New Paltz** (town) Ulster County
120	72.1	**Mount Kisco** (town/village) Westchester County
120	72.1	**Spring Valley** (village) Rockland County
122	72.2	**Eastchester** (CDP) Westchester County
123	72.3	**Peekskill** (city) Westchester County
124	72.4	**Ardsley** (village) Westchester County
125	72.6	**Elmont** (CDP) Nassau County
125	72.6	**Manorhaven** (village) Nassau County
127	72.7	**Lawrence** (village) Nassau County
127	72.7	**Oswego** (town) Oswego County
129	72.8	**Merrick** (CDP) Nassau County
130	72.9	**Syosset** (CDP) Nassau County
131	73.0	**Hunter** (town) Greene County
132	73.1	**Poughkeepsie** (city) Dutchess County
133	73.2	**East Williston** (village) Nassau County
134	73.4	**Eaton** (town) Madison County
134	73.4	**Rhinebeck** (village) Dutchess County
136	73.5	**Sea Cliff** (village) Nassau County
137	73.6	**Le Ray** (town) Jefferson County
137	73.6	**Valhalla** (CDP) Westchester County
139	73.8	**Syracuse** (city) Onondaga County
140	74.0	**North Castle** (town) Westchester County
140	74.0	**Valley Stream** (village) Nassau County
142	74.2	**Stanford** (town) Dutchess County
143	74.4	**Red Hook** (town) Dutchess County
143	74.4	**South Nyack** (village) Rockland County
145	74.5	**Muttontown** (village) Nassau County
145	74.5	**North Valley Stream** (CDP) Nassau County
147	74.6	**Pleasantville** (village) Westchester County
148	74.8	**Hewlett** (CDP) Nassau County
149	75.0	**Geneva** (city) Ontario County
149	75.0	**North Salem** (town) Westchester County

Note: *This section ranks incorporated places and CDPs (Census Designated Places) with populations of 2,500 or more. Unincorporated postal areas were not considered. Please refer to the User Guide for additional information.*

Commute to Work: Public Transportation

Top 150 Places Ranked in *Descending* Order

State Rank	Percent	Place	State Rank	Percent	Place
1	61.7	**Brooklyn** (borough) Kings County	75	18.8	**Harrison** (town/village) Westchester County
2	59.7	**Bronx** (borough) Bronx County	75	18.8	**Herricks** (CDP) Nassau County
3	59.2	**Manhattan** (borough) New York County	78	18.7	**Cold Spring Harbor** (CDP) Suffolk County
4	56.5	**New York** (city)	79	18.3	**Syosset** (CDP) Nassau County
5	52.5	**Larchmont** (village) Westchester County	80	18.1	**Baldwin** (CDP) Nassau County
6	52.3	**Queens** (borough) Queens County	81	18.0	**Peekskill** (city) Westchester County
7	48.0	**Munsey Park** (village) Nassau County	82	17.8	**Lawrence** (village) Nassau County
8	45.2	**Bronxville** (village) Westchester County	83	17.7	**Philipstown** (town) Putnam County
9	44.8	**Scarsdale** (town/village) Westchester County	84	17.6	**Pleasantville** (village) Westchester County
10	38.1	**Greenville** (CDP) Westchester County	85	17.4	**Glenwood Landing** (CDP) Nassau County
11	37.9	**Tuckahoe** (village) Westchester County	86	17.1	**Rye** (town) Westchester County
12	36.4	**Mamaroneck** (town) Westchester County	87	17.0	**Centerport** (CDP) Suffolk County
13	34.4	**Thomaston** (village) Nassau County	87	17.0	**Lloyd Harbor** (village) Suffolk County
14	33.4	**Rye** (city) Westchester County	87	17.0	**Viola** (CDP) Rockland County
15	29.8	**Port Washington North** (village) Nassau County	90	16.9	**Hempstead** (town) Nassau County
15	29.8	**Staten Island** (borough) Richmond County	90	16.9	**Searingtown** (CDP) Nassau County
17	29.6	**New Castle** (town) Westchester County	92	16.8	**Muttontown** (village) Nassau County
18	29.4	**Port Washington** (CDP) Nassau County	92	16.8	**Spring Valley** (village) Rockland County
19	29.0	**University Gardens** (CDP) Nassau County	94	16.7	**Bellmore** (CDP) Nassau County
20	28.7	**Hastings-on-Hudson** (village) Westchester County	95	16.5	**East Hills** (village) Nassau County
21	28.6	**Eastchester** (town) Westchester County	96	16.4	**North New Hyde Park** (CDP) Nassau County
21	28.6	**Pelham** (village) Westchester County	97	16.3	**Mount Pleasant** (town) Westchester County
23	28.3	**Hartsdale** (CDP) Westchester County	98	16.2	**East Rockaway** (village) Nassau County
24	27.7	**Briarcliff Manor** (village) Westchester County	98	16.2	**Sea Cliff** (village) Nassau County
25	27.5	**Great Neck Plaza** (village) Nassau County	100	16.0	**North Castle** (town) Westchester County
26	27.3	**Lakeview** (CDP) Nassau County	101	15.9	**Ossining** (town) Westchester County
27	26.6	**Pelham** (town) Westchester County	102	15.7	**Armonk** (CDP) Westchester County
28	26.5	**Manhasset** (CDP) Nassau County	103	15.4	**Jericho** (CDP) Nassau County
28	26.5	**Mount Vernon** (city) Westchester County	103	15.4	**Roosevelt** (CDP) Nassau County
28	26.5	**Rye Brook** (village) Westchester County	105	15.2	**Garden City South** (CDP) Nassau County
31	26.4	**Yonkers** (city) Westchester County	106	15.1	**Roslyn** (village) Nassau County
32	26.0	**Rockville Centre** (village) Nassau County	107	15.0	**Farmingdale** (village) Nassau County
33	25.0	**Croton-on-Hudson** (village) Westchester County	107	15.0	**Island Park** (village) Nassau County
33	25.0	**Garden City** (village) Nassau County	107	15.0	**Manhasset Hills** (CDP) Nassau County
33	25.0	**Lansing** (village) Tompkins County	107	15.0	**Plainview** (CDP) Nassau County
36	24.5	**Hempstead** (village) Nassau County	111	14.8	**Amityville** (village) Suffolk County
37	24.3	**South Valley Stream** (CDP) Nassau County	112	14.7	**Fairview** (CDP) Westchester County
38	24.2	**Mamaroneck** (village) Westchester County	112	14.7	**Massapequa** (CDP) Nassau County
39	23.9	**Great Neck** (village) Nassau County	114	14.4	**Albany** (city) Albany County
39	23.9	**Pelham Manor** (village) Westchester County	114	14.4	**Cortlandt** (town) Westchester County
41	23.8	**Kings Point** (village) Nassau County	114	14.4	**Port Chester** (village) Westchester County
42	23.5	**Tarrytown** (village) Westchester County	114	14.4	**South Hempstead** (CDP) Nassau County
43	23.4	**Flower Hill** (village) Nassau County	118	14.3	**Mineola** (village) Nassau County
44	23.3	**Woodmere** (CDP) Nassau County	118	14.3	**Northport** (village) Suffolk County
45	23.0	**East Williston** (village) Nassau County	118	14.3	**Wantagh** (CDP) Nassau County
46	22.9	**Inwood** (CDP) Nassau County	121	14.2	**Freeport** (village) Nassau County
46	22.9	**Sands Point** (village) Nassau County	122	14.1	**Malverne** (village) Nassau County
48	22.5	**Dobbs Ferry** (village) Westchester County	122	14.1	**Pound Ridge** (town) Westchester County
48	22.5	**Irvington** (village) Westchester County	124	14.0	**Williston Park** (village) Nassau County
50	22.0	**Bedford** (town) Westchester County	125	13.9	**North Merrick** (CDP) Nassau County
50	22.0	**Lynbrook** (village) Nassau County	125	13.9	**Stony Brook University** (CDP) Suffolk County
50	22.0	**Roslyn Heights** (CDP) Nassau County	127	13.7	**Westbury** (village) Nassau County
53	21.8	**New Rochelle** (city) Westchester County	128	13.6	**Haverstraw** (village) Rockland County
54	21.5	**Elmont** (CDP) Nassau County	129	13.5	**Cayuga Heights** (village) Tompkins County
54	21.5	**Greenburgh** (town) Westchester County	130	13.4	**Babylon** (village) Suffolk County
54	21.5	**Sleepy Hollow** (village) Westchester County	130	13.4	**Elmsford** (village) Westchester County
57	21.2	**Valley Stream** (village) Nassau County	130	13.4	**Wheatley Heights** (CDP) Suffolk County
58	21.1	**Hewlett** (CDP) Nassau County	133	13.3	**West Hempstead** (CDP) Nassau County
59	20.8	**New Hyde Park** (village) Nassau County	134	13.2	**Kaser** (village) Rockland County
60	20.7	**Eastchester** (CDP) Westchester County	134	13.2	**Ossining** (village) Westchester County
60	20.7	**Manorhaven** (village) Nassau County	136	13.1	**Oceanside** (CDP) Nassau County
62	20.6	**North Valley Stream** (CDP) Nassau County	137	13.0	**Lake Success** (village) Nassau County
63	20.4	**Merrick** (CDP) Nassau County	137	13.0	**Montrose** (CDP) Westchester County
64	20.0	**Lido Beach** (CDP) Nassau County	139	12.9	**Oyster Bay** (town) Nassau County
65	19.9	**Valhalla** (CDP) Westchester County	139	12.9	**Springs** (CDP) Suffolk County
66	19.6	**Kiryas Joel** (village) Orange County	141	12.7	**Monroe** (town) Orange County
67	19.5	**White Plains** (city) Westchester County	141	12.7	**South Nyack** (village) Rockland County
68	19.4	**Woodbury** (CDP) Nassau County	143	12.6	**Lewisboro** (town) Westchester County
69	19.3	**Baldwin Harbor** (CDP) Nassau County	143	12.6	**Old Bethpage** (CDP) Nassau County
69	19.3	**Great Neck Estates** (village) Nassau County	145	12.5	**Massapequa Park** (village) Nassau County
71	19.2	**North Hempstead** (town) Nassau County	146	12.4	**Huntington** (CDP) Suffolk County
72	19.0	**Ardsley** (village) Westchester County	147	12.3	**Albertson** (CDP) Nassau County
72	19.0	**Floral Park** (village) Nassau County	147	12.3	**Cedarhurst** (village) Nassau County
72	19.0	**Long Beach** (city) Nassau County	147	12.3	**University at Buffalo** (CDP) Erie County
75	18.8	**Garden City Park** (CDP) Nassau County	147	12.3	**West Bay Shore** (CDP) Suffolk County

Note: *This section ranks incorporated places and CDPs (Census Designated Places) with populations of 2,500 or more. Unincorporated postal areas were not considered. Please refer to the User Guide for additional information.*

Commute to Work: Walk

Top 150 Places Ranked in *Descending* Order

State Rank	Percent	Place
1	67.3	**Alfred** (village) Allegany County
2	58.4	**Binghamton University** (CDP) Broome County
3	58.3	**SUNY Oswego** (CDP) Oswego County
4	57.3	**Alfred** (town) Allegany County
5	55.3	**Stony Brook University** (CDP) Suffolk County
6	48.2	**New Square** (village) Rockland County
7	40.2	**Ithaca** (city) Tompkins County
8	40.0	**Kaser** (village) Rockland County
9	38.0	**Potsdam** (village) Saint Lawrence County
10	37.9	**Caneadea** (town) Allegany County
11	37.5	**University at Buffalo** (CDP) Erie County
12	37.0	**Geneseo** (village) Livingston County
13	36.2	**West Point** (CDP) Orange County
14	36.0	**Hamilton** (village) Madison County
15	34.6	**New Paltz** (village) Ulster County
16	34.4	**South Hill** (CDP) Tompkins County
17	30.9	**Canton** (village) Saint Lawrence County
18	28.8	**East Garden City** (CDP) Nassau County
18	28.8	**Kiryas Joel** (village) Orange County
20	28.0	**Brockport** (village) Monroe County
21	26.5	**Geneseo** (town) Livingston County
22	26.1	**Oneonta** (city) Otsego County
23	25.6	**Arlington** (CDP) Dutchess County
23	25.6	**Watchtower** (CDP) Ulster County
25	24.8	**Fort Drum** (CDP) Jefferson County
26	24.7	**Cobleskill** (village) Schoharie County
27	22.7	**Delhi** (village) Delaware County
27	22.7	**Hamilton** (town) Madison County
29	22.1	**Highlands** (town) Orange County
30	21.0	**Hudson** (city) Columbia County
31	20.7	**Manhattan** (borough) New York County
32	20.5	**Oswego** (town) Oswego County
33	20.3	**Potsdam** (town) Saint Lawrence County
34	19.8	**South Fallsburg** (CDP) Sullivan County
35	19.1	**Cazenovia** (village) Madison County
36	19.0	**Otsego** (town) Otsego County
37	18.9	**Ithaca** (town) Tompkins County
38	18.6	**Eaton** (town) Madison County
39	17.9	**Cayuga Heights** (village) Tompkins County
39	17.9	**New Paltz** (town) Ulster County
41	17.8	**Geneva** (city) Ontario County
42	17.6	**Brookville** (village) Nassau County
43	17.5	**Le Ray** (town) Jefferson County
44	17.0	**Canton** (town) Saint Lawrence County
44	17.0	**Cobleskill** (town) Schoharie County
46	16.9	**Lowville** (village) Lewis County
47	16.8	**Penn Yan** (village) Yates County
48	16.5	**Sweden** (town) Monroe County
49	16.3	**Delhi** (town) Delaware County
50	15.7	**Sleepy Hollow** (village) Westchester County
51	15.2	**Monsey** (CDP) Rockland County
52	15.0	**Cortland** (city) Cortland County
53	14.9	**Old Westbury** (village) Nassau County
54	14.7	**Riverside** (CDP) Suffolk County
55	14.6	**Vails Gate** (CDP) Orange County
56	14.2	**Fredonia** (village) Chautauqua County
57	13.9	**Saranac Lake** (village) Franklin County
58	13.5	**Norwich** (city) Chenango County
59	13.4	**Ellenville** (village) Ulster County
60	13.3	**Plattsburgh** (city) Clinton County
61	13.2	**Sidney** (village) Delaware County
62	12.9	**Port Chester** (village) Westchester County
63	12.5	**Jerusalem** (town) Yates County
64	12.4	**Lowville** (town) Lewis County
65	12.1	**Herkimer** (village) Herkimer County
66	11.9	**Troy** (city) Rensselaer County
67	11.8	**Dansville** (village) Livingston County
68	11.6	**Dix** (town) Schuyler County
69	11.5	**Milo** (town) Yates County
70	11.4	**Poughkeepsie** (town) Dutchess County
70	11.4	**Rhinebeck** (village) Dutchess County
72	11.3	**Pomfret** (town) Chautauqua County
73	11.1	**Syracuse** (city) Onondaga County
74	11.0	**Lake Placid** (village) Essex County
75	10.9	**Poughkeepsie** (city) Dutchess County
76	10.8	**Hunter** (town) Greene County
76	10.8	**Saint Johnsville** (town) Montgomery County
78	10.7	**Harrietstown** (town) Franklin County
78	10.7	**Kirkland** (town) Oneida County
80	10.5	**Allegany** (town) Cattaraugus County
80	10.5	**Herkimer** (town) Herkimer County
82	10.4	**Fairview** (CDP) Dutchess County
82	10.4	**Great Neck Plaza** (village) Nassau County
84	10.3	**Albany** (city) Albany County
85	10.2	**New York** (city)
85	10.2	**Stanford** (town) Dutchess County
87	10.1	**Endicott** (village) Broome County
88	10.0	**Ossining** (village) Westchester County
89	9.9	**Franklinville** (town) Cattaraugus County
90	9.7	**Fairview** (CDP) Westchester County
90	9.7	**Harrison** (town/village) Westchester County
90	9.7	**Monroe** (town) Orange County
90	9.7	**Red Hook** (town) Dutchess County
90	9.7	**Washington** (town) Dutchess County
95	9.6	**Falconer** (village) Chautauqua County
95	9.6	**Newburgh** (city) Orange County
95	9.6	**Sidney** (town) Delaware County
98	9.5	**North Dansville** (town) Livingston County
99	9.4	**Saratoga Springs** (city) Saratoga County
100	9.3	**Hancock** (town) Delaware County
100	9.3	**Olean** (city) Cattaraugus County
102	9.2	**Dannemora** (village) Clinton County
102	9.2	**Monticello** (village) Sullivan County
102	9.2	**Rye** (town) Westchester County
105	8.8	**Brooklyn** (borough) Kings County
105	8.8	**Fallsburg** (town) Sullivan County
107	8.7	**Benton** (town) Yates County
107	8.7	**Orangeburg** (CDP) Rockland County
109	8.6	**Inwood** (CDP) Nassau County
109	8.6	**North Elba** (town) Essex County
109	8.6	**Port Jervis** (city) Orange County
112	8.4	**Delaware** (town) Sullivan County
112	8.4	**North East** (town) Dutchess County
114	8.3	**Chester** (town) Warren County
114	8.3	**Mount Kisco** (town/village) Westchester County
116	8.2	**Bath** (village) Steuben County
116	8.2	**Vestal** (town) Broome County
116	8.2	**White Creek** (town) Washington County
116	8.2	**White Plains** (city) Westchester County
120	8.1	**Corning** (city) Steuben County
121	8.0	**Bronx** (borough) Bronx County
122	7.9	**Glens Falls** (city) Warren County
123	7.8	**Mineola** (village) Nassau County
123	7.8	**Newark** (village) Wayne County
123	7.8	**Ossining** (town) Westchester County
126	7.7	**Saugerties** (village) Ulster County
127	7.5	**Boonville** (town) Oneida County
127	7.5	**Kingston** (city) Ulster County
127	7.5	**Manhasset** (CDP) Nassau County
127	7.5	**New Rochelle** (city) Westchester County
127	7.5	**Oswego** (city) Oswego County
127	7.5	**Tuckahoe** (village) Westchester County
133	7.3	**Whitehall** (town) Washington County
134	7.2	**Elmira** (city) Chemung County
134	7.2	**Little Falls** (city) Herkimer County
134	7.2	**Port Washington** (CDP) Nassau County
134	7.2	**Romulus** (town) Seneca County
134	7.2	**Wappingers Falls** (village) Dutchess County
134	7.2	**Westfield** (village) Chautauqua County
140	7.1	**Binghamton** (city) Broome County
140	7.1	**Cazenovia** (town) Madison County
140	7.1	**Johnson City** (village) Broome County
143	7.0	**Lima** (town) Livingston County
144	6.9	**Cedarhurst** (village) Nassau County
144	6.9	**Hornell** (city) Steuben County
144	6.9	**Wellsville** (village) Allegany County
147	6.8	**Gowanda** (village) Cattaraugus County
147	6.8	**Owego** (village) Tioga County
147	6.8	**Rhinebeck** (town) Dutchess County
150	6.7	**Nyack** (village) Rockland County

Note: *This section ranks incorporated places and CDPs (Census Designated Places) with populations of 2,500 or more. Unincorporated postal areas were not considered. Please refer to the User Guide for additional information.*

Commute to Work: Walk

Top 150 Places Ranked in *Ascending* Order

State Rank	Percent	Place
1	0.0	**Altona** (town) Clinton County
1	0.0	**Bethel** (town) Sullivan County
1	0.0	**Binghamton** (town) Broome County
1	0.0	**Carthage** (village) Jefferson County
1	0.0	**Catlin** (town) Chemung County
1	0.0	**Charlton** (town) Saratoga County
1	0.0	**Clarendon** (town) Orleans County
1	0.0	**Clarkson** (CDP) Monroe County
1	0.0	**Colden** (town) Erie County
1	0.0	**Conesus** (town) Livingston County
1	0.0	**Conesus Lake** (CDP) Livingston County
1	0.0	**Coxsackie** (village) Greene County
1	0.0	**Elma Center** (CDP) Erie County
1	0.0	**Elwood** (CDP) Suffolk County
1	0.0	**Fenton** (town) Broome County
1	0.0	**Fleming** (town) Cayuga County
1	0.0	**Fort Salonga** (CDP) Suffolk County
1	0.0	**Gardnertown** (CDP) Orange County
1	0.0	**Greenfield** (town) Saratoga County
1	0.0	**Greenville** (town) Orange County
1	0.0	**Hawthorne** (CDP) Westchester County
1	0.0	**Heritage Hills** (CDP) Westchester County
1	0.0	**Highland** (CDP) Ulster County
1	0.0	**Horseheads North** (CDP) Chemung County
1	0.0	**Hurley** (CDP) Ulster County
1	0.0	**Islandia** (village) Suffolk County
1	0.0	**Kirkwood** (town) Broome County
1	0.0	**Lake Carmel** (CDP) Putnam County
1	0.0	**Lake Erie Beach** (CDP) Erie County
1	0.0	**Lakeland** (CDP) Onondaga County
1	0.0	**Louisville** (town) Saint Lawrence County
1	0.0	**Manhasset Hills** (CDP) Nassau County
1	0.0	**Milton** (CDP) Saratoga County
1	0.0	**Minisink** (town) Orange County
1	0.0	**Montrose** (CDP) Westchester County
1	0.0	**Moriches** (CDP) Suffolk County
1	0.0	**Munsey Park** (village) Nassau County
1	0.0	**New Baltimore** (town) Greene County
1	0.0	**New Hempstead** (village) Rockland County
1	0.0	**North Boston** (CDP) Erie County
1	0.0	**Orange Lake** (CDP) Orange County
1	0.0	**Pierrepont** (town) Saint Lawrence County
1	0.0	**Port Washington North** (village) Nassau County
1	0.0	**Rush** (town) Monroe County
1	0.0	**Saint Regis Mohawk Reservation** (reservation) Franklin County
1	0.0	**Schuyler** (town) Herkimer County
1	0.0	**Schuyler Falls** (town) Clinton County
1	0.0	**Shandaken** (town) Ulster County
1	0.0	**South Blooming Grove** (village) Orange County
1	0.0	**Spencerport** (village) Monroe County
1	0.0	**Tappan** (CDP) Rockland County
1	0.0	**Tioga** (town) Tioga County
1	0.0	**Village Green** (CDP) Onondaga County
1	0.0	**Volney** (town) Oswego County
1	0.0	**Wading River** (CDP) Suffolk County
1	0.0	**Walworth** (town) Wayne County
1	0.0	**Wanakah** (CDP) Erie County
1	0.0	**West Monroe** (town) Oswego County
1	0.0	**West Nyack** (CDP) Rockland County
1	0.0	**Wheatley Heights** (CDP) Suffolk County
1	0.0	**Wilton** (town) Saratoga County
1	0.0	**Yorkville** (village) Oneida County
63	0.1	**Broadalbin** (town) Fulton County
63	0.1	**East Greenbush** (CDP) Rensselaer County
63	0.1	**Farmingville** (CDP) Suffolk County
63	0.1	**Mount Hope** (town) Orange County
63	0.1	**Nichols** (town) Tioga County
63	0.1	**Pittstown** (town) Rensselaer County
69	0.2	**Albertson** (CDP) Nassau County
69	0.2	**Bayport** (CDP) Suffolk County
69	0.2	**Centereach** (CDP) Suffolk County
69	0.2	**Hartland** (town) Niagara County
69	0.2	**Hector** (town) Schuyler County
69	0.2	**Johnstown** (town) Fulton County
69	0.2	**Lancaster** (village) Erie County
69	0.2	**Medford** (CDP) Suffolk County
69	0.2	**Pembroke** (town) Genesee County
69	0.2	**Schodack** (town) Rensselaer County
69	0.2	**Scotchtown** (CDP) Orange County
69	0.2	**Woodbury** (CDP) Nassau County
81	0.3	**Airmont** (village) Rockland County
81	0.3	**East Fishkill** (town) Dutchess County
81	0.3	**Gaines** (town) Orleans County
81	0.3	**Ghent** (town) Columbia County
81	0.3	**Hamlin** (CDP) Monroe County
81	0.3	**Islip Terrace** (CDP) Suffolk County
81	0.3	**Macedon** (town) Wayne County
81	0.3	**Montebello** (village) Rockland County
81	0.3	**North Hills** (village) Nassau County
81	0.3	**Otisco** (town) Onondaga County
81	0.3	**Paris** (town) Oneida County
81	0.3	**Plainedge** (CDP) Nassau County
81	0.3	**Ridge** (CDP) Suffolk County
81	0.3	**Rochester** (town) Ulster County
81	0.3	**Scriba** (town) Oswego County
81	0.3	**Seneca** (town) Ontario County
81	0.3	**Shelter Island** (town) Suffolk County
81	0.3	**West Sayville** (CDP) Suffolk County
81	0.3	**Yaphank** (CDP) Suffolk County
100	0.4	**Alden** (town) Erie County
100	0.4	**Amsterdam** (town) Montgomery County
100	0.4	**Blooming Grove** (town) Orange County
100	0.4	**Blue Point** (CDP) Suffolk County
100	0.4	**Carmel Hamlet** (CDP) Putnam County
100	0.4	**Clarkson** (town) Monroe County
100	0.4	**Congers** (CDP) Rockland County
100	0.4	**Coram** (CDP) Suffolk County
100	0.4	**Coxsackie** (town) Greene County
100	0.4	**East Norwich** (CDP) Nassau County
100	0.4	**Glenwood Landing** (CDP) Nassau County
100	0.4	**Grand Island** (town) Erie County
100	0.4	**Holbrook** (CDP) Suffolk County
100	0.4	**Lake Mohegan** (CDP) Westchester County
100	0.4	**Livingston** (town) Columbia County
100	0.4	**Locust Valley** (CDP) Nassau County
100	0.4	**Manorville** (CDP) Suffolk County
100	0.4	**Marilla** (town) Erie County
100	0.4	**Mastic Beach** (village) Suffolk County
100	0.4	**Miller Place** (CDP) Suffolk County
100	0.4	**Newark Valley** (town) Tioga County
100	0.4	**North Gates** (CDP) Monroe County
100	0.4	**Noyack** (CDP) Suffolk County
100	0.4	**Poestenkill** (town) Rensselaer County
100	0.4	**Putnam Lake** (CDP) Putnam County
100	0.4	**Putnam Valley** (town) Putnam County
100	0.4	**Salisbury** (CDP) Nassau County
100	0.4	**Schaghticoke** (town) Rensselaer County
100	0.4	**South Huntington** (CDP) Suffolk County
100	0.4	**Terryville** (CDP) Suffolk County
100	0.4	**Union Vale** (town) Dutchess County
100	0.4	**Victor** (town) Ontario County
132	0.5	**Baywood** (CDP) Suffolk County
132	0.5	**Carlton** (town) Orleans County
132	0.5	**Clifton Park** (town) Saratoga County
132	0.5	**Cold Spring Harbor** (CDP) Suffolk County
132	0.5	**East Northport** (CDP) Suffolk County
132	0.5	**East Shoreham** (CDP) Suffolk County
132	0.5	**Gang Mills** (CDP) Steuben County
132	0.5	**Greenlawn** (CDP) Suffolk County
132	0.5	**Hauppauge** (CDP) Suffolk County
132	0.5	**Holtsville** (CDP) Suffolk County
132	0.5	**Islip** (CDP) Suffolk County
132	0.5	**Lancaster** (town) Erie County
132	0.5	**Livonia** (town) Livingston County
132	0.5	**Malta** (town) Saratoga County
132	0.5	**Marcy** (town) Oneida County
132	0.5	**Moira** (town) Franklin County
132	0.5	**Moreau** (town) Saratoga County
132	0.5	**New Windsor** (CDP) Orange County
132	0.5	**Newburgh** (town) Orange County

Note: *This section ranks incorporated places and CDPs (Census Designated Places) with populations of 2,500 or more. Unincorporated postal areas were not considered. Please refer to the User Guide for additional information.*

Commute to Work: Work from Home

Top 150 Places Ranked in *Descending* Order

State Rank	Percent	Place	State Rank	Percent	Place
1	71.5	**Watchtower** (CDP) Ulster County	76	8.5	**Hastings-on-Hudson** (village) Westchester County
2	37.6	**West Point** (CDP) Orange County	76	8.5	**Lake Success** (village) Nassau County
3	22.8	**Woodstock** (town) Ulster County	76	8.5	**Lewisboro** (town) Westchester County
4	21.9	**Highlands** (town) Orange County	76	8.5	**Milford** (town) Otsego County
5	17.4	**Southampton** (village) Suffolk County	76	8.5	**Pittsford** (town) Monroe County
6	15.7	**Pound Ridge** (town) Westchester County	81	8.4	**Arlington** (CDP) Dutchess County
7	14.6	**Wesley Hills** (village) Rockland County	81	8.4	**East Hampton** (town) Suffolk County
8	14.1	**Hunter** (town) Greene County	81	8.4	**Goshen** (town) Orange County
9	13.7	**Rhinebeck** (town) Dutchess County	81	8.4	**Honeoye Falls** (village) Monroe County
10	13.6	**Great Neck Estates** (village) Nassau County	81	8.4	**Mamaroneck** (town) Westchester County
11	13.5	**Noyack** (CDP) Suffolk County	81	8.4	**Oxford** (town) Chenango County
12	13.1	**Binghamton University** (CDP) Broome County	81	8.4	**Shelter Island** (town) Suffolk County
12	13.1	**Briarcliff Manor** (village) Westchester County	88	8.3	**Rye Brook** (village) Westchester County
14	12.5	**Flower Hill** (village) Nassau County	89	8.2	**Ghent** (town) Columbia County
15	12.3	**Kings Point** (village) Nassau County	89	8.2	**Ithaca** (town) Tompkins County
16	12.2	**Chatham** (town) Columbia County	89	8.2	**Marcy** (town) Oneida County
17	11.9	**Middletown** (town) Delaware County	89	8.2	**Pine Plains** (town) Dutchess County
17	11.9	**North Salem** (town) Westchester County	93	8.1	**Ballston Spa** (village) Saratoga County
19	11.5	**Red Oaks Mill** (CDP) Dutchess County	93	8.1	**Russia** (town) Herkimer County
19	11.5	**Rhinebeck** (village) Dutchess County	93	8.1	**Shawangunk** (town) Ulster County
21	11.4	**Scarsdale** (town/village) Westchester County	96	8.0	**Huntington** (CDP) Suffolk County
22	11.1	**Afton** (town) Chenango County	96	8.0	**New Berlin** (town) Chenango County
22	11.1	**Centerport** (CDP) Suffolk County	98	7.9	**Argyle** (town) Washington County
24	11.0	**Delhi** (village) Delaware County	98	7.9	**Clinton** (town) Dutchess County
24	11.0	**Philipstown** (town) Putnam County	98	7.9	**Glen Head** (CDP) Nassau County
26	10.9	**Mendon** (town) Monroe County	98	7.9	**Romulus** (town) Seneca County
27	10.8	**Tully** (town) Onondaga County	98	7.9	**Sanford** (town) Broome County
28	10.7	**Red Hook** (town) Dutchess County	98	7.9	**Skaneateles** (village) Onondaga County
28	10.7	**Shandaken** (town) Ulster County	104	7.8	**Greene** (town) Chenango County
30	10.6	**Lido Beach** (CDP) Nassau County	104	7.8	**Hamilton** (town) Madison County
30	10.6	**Montauk** (CDP) Suffolk County	104	7.8	**Jerusalem** (town) Yates County
32	10.5	**Callicoon** (town) Sullivan County	104	7.8	**North Castle** (town) Westchester County
32	10.5	**Schroeppel** (town) Oswego County	104	7.8	**Port Washington** (CDP) Nassau County
32	10.5	**South Hill** (CDP) Tompkins County	109	7.7	**Chautauqua** (town) Chautauqua County
35	10.4	**Brookville** (village) Nassau County	109	7.7	**New Square** (village) Rockland County
35	10.4	**Chester** (town) Warren County	111	7.6	**Larchmont** (village) Westchester County
35	10.4	**New Castle** (town) Westchester County	111	7.6	**Tappan** (CDP) Rockland County
38	10.3	**Bedford** (town) Westchester County	113	7.5	**Canton** (town) Saint Lawrence County
38	10.3	**Cazenovia** (village) Madison County	113	7.5	**Chesterfield** (town) Essex County
40	10.2	**Cape Vincent** (town) Jefferson County	113	7.5	**Cold Spring Harbor** (CDP) Suffolk County
40	10.2	**Cazenovia** (town) Madison County	113	7.5	**Esopus** (town) Ulster County
40	10.2	**East Syracuse** (village) Onondaga County	113	7.5	**Orchard Park** (village) Erie County
40	10.2	**Johnstown** (town) Fulton County	113	7.5	**Thornwood** (CDP) Westchester County
40	10.2	**Sands Point** (village) Nassau County	119	7.4	**Greenfield** (town) Saratoga County
45	10.0	**Moira** (town) Franklin County	119	7.4	**Monsey** (CDP) Rockland County
46	9.9	**East Hills** (village) Nassau County	119	7.4	**Otsego** (town) Otsego County
46	9.9	**Salem** (town) Washington County	119	7.4	**Palatine** (town) Montgomery County
48	9.8	**Stanford** (town) Dutchess County	119	7.4	**Port Jervis** (city) Orange County
49	9.6	**Marcellus** (town) Onondaga County	119	7.4	**Tupper Lake** (town) Franklin County
50	9.5	**Duanesburg** (town) Schenectady County	119	7.4	**Walton** (town) Delaware County
50	9.5	**Otisco** (town) Onondaga County	126	7.3	**Delaware** (town) Sullivan County
50	9.5	**Potsdam** (village) Saint Lawrence County	126	7.3	**Halesite** (CDP) Suffolk County
53	9.4	**Manhasset Hills** (CDP) Nassau County	126	7.3	**Minden** (town) Montgomery County
53	9.4	**North Hills** (village) Nassau County	126	7.3	**Muttontown** (village) Nassau County
53	9.4	**Stony Brook** (CDP) Suffolk County	130	7.2	**Lloyd Harbor** (village) Suffolk County
56	9.3	**Cutchogue** (CDP) Suffolk County	130	7.2	**Northwest Harbor** (CDP) Suffolk County
56	9.3	**North East** (town) Dutchess County	130	7.2	**Somers** (town) Westchester County
56	9.3	**Pomona** (village) Rockland County	130	7.2	**Southold** (town) Suffolk County
59	9.2	**Oneonta** (town) Otsego County	134	7.1	**Fleming** (town) Cayuga County
60	9.1	**Starkey** (town) Yates County	134	7.1	**Gardiner** (town) Ulster County
61	9.0	**Benton** (town) Yates County	134	7.1	**Unadilla** (town) Otsego County
61	9.0	**Ellery** (town) Chautauqua County	137	7.0	**Annsville** (town) Oneida County
61	9.0	**Enfield** (town) Tompkins County	137	7.0	**Chester** (town) Orange County
61	9.0	**Hamilton** (village) Madison County	137	7.0	**Goshen** (village) Orange County
65	8.9	**Olive** (town) Ulster County	137	7.0	**Lawrence** (village) Nassau County
65	8.9	**Westhampton** (CDP) Suffolk County	141	6.9	**Canton** (village) Saint Lawrence County
67	8.8	**Greenville** (CDP) Westchester County	141	6.9	**La Grange** (town) Dutchess County
67	8.8	**Saratoga Springs** (city) Saratoga County	141	6.9	**Westmoreland** (town) Oneida County
67	8.8	**Washington** (town) Dutchess County	144	6.8	**Bardonia** (CDP) Rockland County
70	8.7	**Mount Ivy** (CDP) Rockland County	144	6.8	**Irvington** (village) Westchester County
70	8.7	**New Baltimore** (town) Greene County	144	6.8	**Lake Placid** (village) Essex County
70	8.7	**Pompey** (town) Onondaga County	144	6.8	**Manhattan** (borough) New York County
70	8.7	**Viola** (CDP) Rockland County	144	6.8	**Manheim** (town) Herkimer County
74	8.6	**Hartsdale** (CDP) Westchester County	144	6.8	**Montebello** (village) Rockland County
74	8.6	**Virgil** (town) Cortland County	144	6.8	**North Greenbush** (town) Rensselaer County

Note: This section ranks incorporated places and CDPs (Census Designated Places) with populations of 2,500 or more. Unincorporated postal areas were not considered. Please refer to the User Guide for additional information.

Commute to Work: Work from Home

Top 150 Places Ranked in *Ascending* Order

State Rank	Percent	Place	State Rank	Percent	Place
1	0.0	**Carroll** (town) Chautauqua County	73	1.2	**Lakewood** (village) Chautauqua County
1	0.0	**Flanders** (CDP) Suffolk County	73	1.2	**North Collins** (town) Erie County
1	0.0	**Lyons** (village) Wayne County	73	1.2	**Solvay** (village) Onondaga County
1	0.0	**New York Mills** (village) Oneida County	73	1.2	**University Gardens** (CDP) Nassau County
1	0.0	**North Boston** (CDP) Erie County	73	1.2	**Walden** (village) Orange County
1	0.0	**Port Jefferson Station** (CDP) Suffolk County	73	1.2	**Williston Park** (village) Nassau County
1	0.0	**Portville** (town) Cattaraugus County	82	1.3	**Alden** (town) Erie County
1	0.0	**Riverside** (CDP) Suffolk County	82	1.3	**East Rochester** (town/village) Monroe County
1	0.0	**Saint Regis Mohawk Reservation** (reservation) Franklin County	82	1.3	**Eden** (CDP) Erie County
1	0.0	**Sidney** (village) Delaware County	82	1.3	**Miller Place** (CDP) Suffolk County
1	0.0	**Wanakah** (CDP) Erie County	82	1.3	**Niagara Falls** (city) Niagara County
12	0.2	**Amsterdam** (town) Montgomery County	82	1.3	**North Lindenhurst** (CDP) Suffolk County
12	0.2	**Canastota** (village) Madison County	82	1.3	**North New Hyde Park** (CDP) Nassau County
14	0.3	**Mount Morris** (town) Livingston County	82	1.3	**Southport** (town) Chemung County
14	0.3	**Perry** (village) Wyoming County	82	1.3	**Tonawanda** (CDP) Erie County
14	0.3	**Putnam Lake** (CDP) Putnam County	82	1.3	**Warrensburg** (CDP) Warren County
17	0.4	**Johnstown** (city) Fulton County	82	1.3	**Warrensburg** (town) Warren County
17	0.4	**Lakeview** (CDP) Nassau County	93	1.4	**Depew** (village) Erie County
17	0.4	**Madison** (town) Madison County	93	1.4	**Liberty** (village) Sullivan County
17	0.4	**Mount Morris** (village) Livingston County	93	1.4	**Lowville** (town) Lewis County
17	0.4	**New Cassel** (CDP) Nassau County	93	1.4	**Lowville** (village) Lewis County
22	0.5	**Island Park** (village) Nassau County	93	1.4	**Mohawk** (village) Herkimer County
22	0.5	**Lackawanna** (city) Erie County	93	1.4	**Owego** (village) Tioga County
22	0.5	**Newark** (village) Wayne County	93	1.4	**Paris** (town) Oneida County
22	0.5	**Sloan** (village) Erie County	93	1.4	**Ravena** (village) Albany County
22	0.5	**Warsaw** (town) Wyoming County	93	1.4	**Ronkonkoma** (CDP) Suffolk County
27	0.6	**Blasdell** (village) Erie County	93	1.4	**Saranac** (town) Clinton County
27	0.6	**Mattydale** (CDP) Onondaga County	93	1.4	**Scotchtown** (CDP) Orange County
27	0.6	**Newark Valley** (town) Tioga County	93	1.4	**South Blooming Grove** (village) Orange County
27	0.6	**Pamelia** (town) Jefferson County	93	1.4	**Tonawanda** (city) Erie County
27	0.6	**Perry** (town) Wyoming County	93	1.4	**Wappingers Falls** (village) Dutchess County
27	0.6	**Wellsville** (town) Allegany County	93	1.4	**Wheatland** (town) Monroe County
27	0.6	**West Sand Lake** (CDP) Rensselaer County	108	1.5	**Arcade** (town) Wyoming County
34	0.7	**Fort Edward** (village) Washington County	108	1.5	**Chittenango** (village) Madison County
34	0.7	**Hilton** (village) Monroe County	108	1.5	**Conesus** (town) Livingston County
34	0.7	**Hornell** (city) Steuben County	108	1.5	**Elmira** (town) Chemung County
34	0.7	**Newfane** (CDP) Niagara County	108	1.5	**Greenport** (town) Columbia County
34	0.7	**Oswego** (city) Oswego County	108	1.5	**Lenox** (town) Madison County
34	0.7	**Vails Gate** (CDP) Orange County	108	1.5	**Silver Creek** (village) Chautauqua County
34	0.7	**Wellsville** (village) Allegany County	108	1.5	**Verona** (town) Oneida County
41	0.8	**Aurelius** (town) Cayuga County	116	1.6	**Au Sable** (town) Clinton County
41	0.8	**Vienna** (town) Oneida County	116	1.6	**Bennington** (town) Wyoming County
41	0.8	**Warsaw** (village) Wyoming County	116	1.6	**Catskill** (village) Greene County
44	0.9	**Attica** (village) Wyoming County	116	1.6	**Centereach** (CDP) Suffolk County
44	0.9	**Bohemia** (CDP) Suffolk County	116	1.6	**Clarkson** (CDP) Monroe County
44	0.9	**Central Islip** (CDP) Suffolk County	116	1.6	**Cohoes** (city) Albany County
44	0.9	**Horseheads** (village) Chemung County	116	1.6	**Corning** (town) Steuben County
44	0.9	**Lyons** (town) Wayne County	116	1.6	**Dannemora** (village) Clinton County
44	0.9	**Mechanicstown** (CDP) Orange County	116	1.6	**Ellenville** (village) Ulster County
44	0.9	**Minoa** (village) Onondaga County	116	1.6	**Gloversville** (city) Fulton County
44	0.9	**Oakfield** (town) Genesee County	116	1.6	**Holbrook** (CDP) Suffolk County
44	0.9	**West Elmira** (CDP) Chemung County	116	1.6	**Plattsburgh** (city) Clinton County
53	1.0	**Bath** (village) Steuben County	116	1.6	**Southport** (CDP) Chemung County
53	1.0	**Boston** (town) Erie County	116	1.6	**Sterling** (town) Cayuga County
53	1.0	**Dunkirk** (city) Chautauqua County	116	1.6	**Tonawanda** (town) Erie County
53	1.0	**Hillcrest** (CDP) Rockland County	116	1.6	**Valley Stream** (village) Nassau County
53	1.0	**Ontario** (town) Wayne County	132	1.7	**Corning** (city) Steuben County
53	1.0	**Webster** (village) Monroe County	132	1.7	**Elmira Heights** (village) Chemung County
53	1.0	**Westfield** (village) Chautauqua County	132	1.7	**Garden City Park** (CDP) Nassau County
53	1.0	**Windsor** (town) Broome County	132	1.7	**Haviland** (CDP) Dutchess County
61	1.1	**Berne** (town) Albany County	132	1.7	**Johnson City** (village) Broome County
61	1.1	**Brentwood** (CDP) Suffolk County	132	1.7	**Levittown** (CDP) Nassau County
61	1.1	**Clarendon** (town) Orleans County	132	1.7	**Mohawk** (town) Montgomery County
61	1.1	**Colonie** (village) Albany County	132	1.7	**Montgomery** (village) Orange County
61	1.1	**Falconer** (village) Chautauqua County	132	1.7	**North Tonawanda** (city) Niagara County
61	1.1	**Gouverneur** (village) Saint Lawrence County	132	1.7	**Pleasantville** (village) Westchester County
61	1.1	**Lakeland** (CDP) Onondaga County	132	1.7	**West Haverstraw** (village) Rockland County
61	1.1	**Lindenhurst** (village) Suffolk County	132	1.7	**Yorkville** (village) Oneida County
61	1.1	**Neversink** (town) Sullivan County	144	1.8	**Adams** (town) Jefferson County
61	1.1	**North Amityville** (CDP) Suffolk County	144	1.8	**Campbell** (town) Steuben County
61	1.1	**Uniondale** (CDP) Nassau County	144	1.8	**Darien** (town) Genesee County
61	1.1	**Wawayanda** (town) Orange County	144	1.8	**Dix** (town) Schuyler County
73	1.2	**Albion** (town) Orleans County	144	1.8	**Eden** (town) Erie County
73	1.2	**Cheektowaga** (CDP) Erie County	144	1.8	**Evans** (town) Erie County
73	1.2	**Cheektowaga** (town) Erie County	144	1.8	**Hamburg** (village) Erie County

Note: *This section ranks incorporated places and CDPs (Census Designated Places) with populations of 2,500 or more. Unincorporated postal areas were not considered. Please refer to the User Guide for additional information.*

Mean Travel Time to Work

Top 150 Places Ranked in *Descending* Order

State Rank	Minutes	Place		State Rank	Minutes	Place
1	49.7	**Greenwood Lake** (village) Orange County		76	37.4	**East Fishkill** (town) Dutchess County
2	48.3	**Lloyd Harbor** (village) Suffolk County		76	37.4	**Mamaroneck** (town) Westchester County
3	47.5	**Larchmont** (village) Westchester County		76	37.4	**Manhasset Hills** (CDP) Nassau County
4	44.9	**Munsey Park** (village) Nassau County		79	37.3	**Mamakating** (town) Sullivan County
5	44.6	**Manorhaven** (village) Nassau County		79	37.3	**Pomona** (village) Rockland County
6	44.5	**Putnam Valley** (town) Putnam County		79	37.3	**Woodbury** (town) Orange County
7	44.0	**Scarsdale** (town/village) Westchester County		82	37.2	**Baldwin** (CDP) Nassau County
8	43.1	**Woodmere** (CDP) Nassau County		82	37.2	**Hartsdale** (CDP) Westchester County
9	43.0	**Bronx** (borough) Bronx County		84	37.1	**Northport** (village) Suffolk County
10	42.8	**Philipstown** (town) Putnam County		85	37.0	**Coram** (CDP) Suffolk County
11	42.6	**Queens** (borough) Queens County		85	37.0	**Woodbury** (village) Orange County
11	42.6	**Staten Island** (borough) Richmond County		87	36.9	**Carmel** (town) Putnam County
13	42.2	**South Valley Stream** (CDP) Nassau County		87	36.9	**Massapequa Park** (village) Nassau County
14	41.8	**Kings Point** (village) Nassau County		87	36.9	**Miller Place** (CDP) Suffolk County
14	41.8	**Shandaken** (town) Ulster County		87	36.9	**West Sayville** (CDP) Suffolk County
16	41.7	**Brooklyn** (borough) Kings County		91	36.8	**East Norwich** (CDP) Nassau County
16	41.7	**New Castle** (town) Westchester County		91	36.8	**Roslyn** (village) Nassau County
18	41.6	**Pound Ridge** (town) Westchester County		91	36.8	**Russia** (town) Herkimer County
18	41.6	**Sands Point** (village) Nassau County		94	36.7	**Balmville** (CDP) Orange County
20	41.3	**Glenwood Landing** (CDP) Nassau County		94	36.7	**Mahopac** (CDP) Putnam County
21	41.2	**Kent** (town) Putnam County		96	36.6	**Bayville** (village) Nassau County
22	41.1	**Greenville** (CDP) Westchester County		96	36.6	**Cedarhurst** (village) Nassau County
22	41.1	**Putnam Lake** (CDP) Putnam County		96	36.6	**Chester** (town) Orange County
24	40.9	**Lake Carmel** (CDP) Putnam County		96	36.6	**Middle Island** (CDP) Suffolk County
24	40.9	**Mount Hope** (town) Orange County		96	36.6	**Montebello** (village) Rockland County
26	40.8	**University Gardens** (CDP) Nassau County		96	36.6	**New Windsor** (town) Orange County
27	40.7	**Lido Beach** (CDP) Nassau County		96	36.6	**Nunda** (town) Livingston County
28	40.6	**Florida** (village) Orange County		103	36.5	**Cold Spring Harbor** (CDP) Suffolk County
29	40.4	**Warwick** (town) Orange County		103	36.5	**East Shoreham** (CDP) Suffolk County
30	40.3	**Long Beach** (city) Nassau County		105	36.4	**Massapequa** (CDP) Nassau County
30	40.3	**Valley Stream** (village) Nassau County		105	36.4	**Mount Sinai** (CDP) Suffolk County
32	40.2	**Roslyn Heights** (CDP) Nassau County		107	36.2	**New Hyde Park** (village) Nassau County
32	40.2	**South Blooming Grove** (village) Orange County		107	36.2	**Plainview** (CDP) Nassau County
34	40.0	**Baldwin Harbor** (CDP) Nassau County		107	36.2	**Somers** (town) Westchester County
34	40.0	**North Valley Stream** (CDP) Nassau County		107	36.2	**Yorktown** (town) Westchester County
34	40.0	**Port Washington** (CDP) Nassau County		111	36.1	**Greenville** (town) Orange County
37	39.9	**Croton-on-Hudson** (village) Westchester County		111	36.1	**Malverne** (village) Nassau County
37	39.9	**Lewisboro** (town) Westchester County		111	36.1	**Rye** (city) Westchester County
37	39.9	**New York** (city)		111	36.1	**West Hempstead** (CDP) Nassau County
40	39.8	**Minisink** (town) Orange County		115	36.0	**Garden City** (village) Nassau County
41	39.6	**Port Washington North** (village) Nassau County		116	35.9	**Bellmore** (CDP) Nassau County
42	39.5	**Elmont** (CDP) Nassau County		116	35.9	**Dix Hills** (CDP) Suffolk County
42	39.5	**Searingtown** (CDP) Nassau County		116	35.9	**East Hills** (village) Nassau County
44	39.4	**Beekman** (town) Dutchess County		116	35.9	**Southold** (CDP) Suffolk County
44	39.4	**Patterson** (town) Putnam County		120	35.8	**Montgomery** (village) Orange County
46	39.3	**Blooming Grove** (town) Orange County		121	35.7	**Hewlett** (CDP) Nassau County
46	39.3	**Briarcliff Manor** (village) Westchester County		122	35.6	**Nesconset** (CDP) Suffolk County
48	39.2	**Bedford** (town) Westchester County		122	35.6	**North New Hyde Park** (CDP) Nassau County
48	39.2	**Washingtonville** (village) Orange County		124	35.5	**Jericho** (CDP) Nassau County
50	39.1	**Bronxville** (village) Westchester County		124	35.5	**Union Vale** (town) Dutchess County
50	39.1	**Lake Mohegan** (CDP) Westchester County		126	35.4	**Huntington** (CDP) Suffolk County
50	39.1	**Rocky Point** (CDP) Suffolk County		126	35.4	**Warwick** (village) Orange County
50	39.1	**Sound Beach** (CDP) Suffolk County		128	35.3	**Dover** (town) Dutchess County
50	39.1	**Tuxedo** (town) Orange County		128	35.3	**Middleburgh** (town) Schoharie County
50	39.1	**Woodbury** (CDP) Nassau County		128	35.3	**New Hempstead** (village) Rockland County
56	39.0	**Lynbrook** (village) Nassau County		131	35.2	**Fishkill** (town) Dutchess County
56	39.0	**Muttontown** (village) Nassau County		132	35.1	**Constantia** (town) Oswego County
58	38.9	**Jefferson Valley-Yorktown** (CDP) Westchester County		132	35.1	**Hempstead** (town) Nassau County
58	38.9	**Pawling** (town) Dutchess County		132	35.1	**Southeast** (town) Putnam County
60	38.8	**Cortlandt** (town) Westchester County		132	35.1	**West Bay Shore** (CDP) Suffolk County
60	38.8	**Herricks** (CDP) Nassau County		136	35.0	**Great Neck** (village) Nassau County
60	38.8	**Mastic Beach** (village) Suffolk County		136	35.0	**Pelham** (village) Westchester County
60	38.8	**Thomaston** (village) Nassau County		138	34.9	**Floral Park** (village) Nassau County
64	38.7	**Merrick** (CDP) Nassau County		138	34.9	**Garden City Park** (CDP) Nassau County
65	38.6	**Syosset** (CDP) Nassau County		138	34.9	**Heritage Hills** (CDP) Westchester County
66	38.1	**Rockville Centre** (village) Nassau County		138	34.9	**Mechanicstown** (CDP) Orange County
67	38.0	**Flower Hill** (village) Nassau County		138	34.9	**Monroe** (village) Orange County
67	38.0	**Hastings-on-Hudson** (village) Westchester County		143	34.8	**Durham** (town) Greene County
67	38.0	**Viola** (CDP) Rockland County		143	34.8	**Lake Grove** (village) Suffolk County
70	37.9	**Centerport** (CDP) Suffolk County		143	34.8	**North Hempstead** (town) Nassau County
70	37.9	**Red Oaks Mill** (CDP) Dutchess County		146	34.7	**East Williston** (village) Nassau County
72	37.8	**North Salem** (town) Westchester County		146	34.7	**La Grange** (town) Dutchess County
73	37.7	**Carmel Hamlet** (CDP) Putnam County		148	34.6	**Myers Corner** (CDP) Dutchess County
74	37.6	**Lawrence** (village) Nassau County		148	34.6	**North Massapequa** (CDP) Nassau County
75	37.5	**Lakeview** (CDP) Nassau County		148	34.6	**Pelham** (town) Westchester County

Note: *This section ranks incorporated places and CDPs (Census Designated Places) with populations of 2,500 or more. Unincorporated postal areas were not considered. Please refer to the User Guide for additional information.*

Mean Travel Time to Work

Top 150 Places Ranked in *Ascending* Order

State Rank	Minutes	Place
1	0.0	**Watchtower** (CDP) Ulster County
2	9.0	**West Point** (CDP) Orange County
3	9.2	**SUNY Oswego** (CDP) Oswego County
4	9.3	**Fort Drum** (CDP) Jefferson County
5	10.7	**Alfred** (village) Allegany County
6	11.2	**Le Ray** (town) Jefferson County
7	11.5	**Alfred** (town) Allegany County
8	11.6	**Binghamton University** (CDP) Broome County
9	11.8	**Hamilton** (village) Madison County
10	12.2	**Potsdam** (village) Saint Lawrence County
11	12.3	**University at Buffalo** (CDP) Erie County
12	12.4	**South Fallsburg** (CDP) Sullivan County
13	12.7	**South Hill** (CDP) Tompkins County
14	13.4	**Delhi** (village) Delaware County
14	13.4	**Whitesboro** (village) Oneida County
16	13.5	**Cayuga Heights** (village) Tompkins County
17	13.6	**Tupper Lake** (village) Franklin County
18	13.7	**Plattsburgh** (city) Clinton County
19	13.8	**Falconer** (village) Chautauqua County
19	13.8	**Pamelia** (town) Jefferson County
21	13.9	**Fredonia** (village) Chautauqua County
21	13.9	**New York Mills** (village) Oneida County
21	13.9	**Ogdensburg** (city) Saint Lawrence County
24	14.0	**Dunkirk** (city) Chautauqua County
24	14.0	**Ellicott** (town) Chautauqua County
26	14.3	**Norwich** (city) Chenango County
27	14.4	**Caneadea** (town) Allegany County
28	14.5	**Gang Mills** (CDP) Steuben County
29	14.7	**Calcium** (CDP) Jefferson County
29	14.7	**Jamestown** (city) Chautauqua County
29	14.7	**Tupper Lake** (town) Franklin County
32	14.8	**Lyncourt** (CDP) Onondaga County
32	14.8	**Olean** (city) Cattaraugus County
34	14.9	**Watertown** (city) Jefferson County
35	15.1	**Erwin** (town) Steuben County
35	15.1	**Kaser** (village) Rockland County
35	15.1	**North Elba** (town) Essex County
38	15.3	**Corning** (city) Steuben County
38	15.3	**Dickinson** (town) Broome County
40	15.4	**Hamilton** (town) Madison County
40	15.4	**Ithaca** (city) Tompkins County
40	15.4	**Ithaca** (town) Tompkins County
40	15.4	**Lake Placid** (village) Essex County
40	15.4	**Oneonta** (city) Otsego County
40	15.4	**Pomfret** (town) Chautauqua County
46	15.5	**Galeville** (CDP) Onondaga County
47	15.6	**Gates** (CDP) Monroe County
47	15.6	**Lakewood** (village) Chautauqua County
49	15.8	**Canton** (village) Saint Lawrence County
49	15.8	**Geneseo** (village) Livingston County
49	15.8	**Otsego** (town) Otsego County
52	15.9	**Colonie** (village) Albany County
52	15.9	**Cortland** (city) Cortland County
52	15.9	**East Syracuse** (village) Onondaga County
52	15.9	**Potsdam** (town) Saint Lawrence County
56	16.0	**Brighton** (CDP) Monroe County
56	16.0	**Kirkland** (town) Oneida County
58	16.1	**Eggertsville** (CDP) Erie County
58	16.1	**Menands** (village) Albany County
58	16.1	**Penn Yan** (village) Yates County
61	16.2	**Johnson City** (village) Broome County
62	16.3	**Geneva** (town) Ontario County
62	16.3	**Horseheads** (village) Chemung County
62	16.3	**Ticonderoga** (CDP) Essex County
62	16.3	**Whitestown** (town) Oneida County
66	16.4	**Big Flats** (CDP) Chemung County
66	16.4	**Waverly** (village) Tioga County
68	16.5	**Mattydale** (CDP) Onondaga County
69	16.6	**Bath** (village) Steuben County
70	16.7	**De Witt** (town) Onondaga County
70	16.7	**New Hartford** (town) Oneida County
70	16.7	**Northeast Ithaca** (CDP) Tompkins County
70	16.7	**Plattsburgh** (town) Clinton County
74	16.8	**Elmira** (town) Chemung County
74	16.8	**Saranac Lake** (village) Franklin County
74	16.8	**West Elmira** (CDP) Chemung County
77	16.9	**Geneva** (city) Ontario County
77	16.9	**Highlands** (town) Orange County
77	16.9	**Louisville** (town) Saint Lawrence County
77	16.9	**Rutland** (town) Jefferson County
77	16.9	**Salamanca** (city) Cattaraugus County
82	17.0	**Allegany** (town) Cattaraugus County
82	17.0	**Green Island** (town/village) Albany County
82	17.0	**Oswego** (city) Oswego County
85	17.1	**Lakeland** (CDP) Onondaga County
86	17.2	**Gaines** (town) Orleans County
87	17.3	**East Rochester** (town/village) Monroe County
87	17.3	**Massena** (village) Saint Lawrence County
87	17.3	**Union** (town) Broome County
90	17.4	**Auburn** (city) Cayuga County
90	17.4	**Yorkville** (village) Oneida County
92	17.5	**Carroll** (town) Chautauqua County
92	17.5	**New Square** (village) Rockland County
92	17.5	**Utica** (city) Oneida County
95	17.6	**Big Flats** (town) Chemung County
95	17.6	**Endwell** (CDP) Broome County
95	17.6	**Glens Falls** (city) Warren County
95	17.6	**Massena** (town) Saint Lawrence County
95	17.6	**North Gates** (CDP) Monroe County
95	17.6	**Ticonderoga** (town) Essex County
101	17.7	**Delhi** (town) Delaware County
101	17.7	**Gates** (town) Monroe County
101	17.7	**Sidney** (village) Delaware County
101	17.7	**Webster** (village) Monroe County
101	17.7	**Wellsville** (town) Allegany County
106	17.8	**Canton** (town) Saint Lawrence County
106	17.8	**Henrietta** (town) Monroe County
106	17.8	**Malone** (town) Franklin County
106	17.8	**Minoa** (village) Onondaga County
106	17.8	**Niagara Falls** (city) Niagara County
106	17.8	**Rome** (city) Oneida County
106	17.8	**Wellsville** (village) Allegany County
113	17.9	**Albion** (village) Orleans County
113	17.9	**Pittsford** (town) Monroe County
113	17.9	**Sidney** (town) Delaware County
113	17.9	**Watertown** (town) Jefferson County
117	18.0	**Binghamton** (city) Broome County
117	18.0	**Endicott** (village) Broome County
117	18.0	**Hornellsville** (town) Steuben County
117	18.0	**Horseheads North** (CDP) Chemung County
117	18.0	**Malone** (village) Franklin County
117	18.0	**Mount Morris** (village) Livingston County
117	18.0	**Newark** (village) Wayne County
117	18.0	**Oswegatchie** (town) Saint Lawrence County
117	18.0	**Salina** (town) Onondaga County
126	18.1	**Chenango Bridge** (CDP) Broome County
126	18.1	**East Hampton North** (CDP) Suffolk County
126	18.1	**Elmira Heights** (village) Chemung County
126	18.1	**Lansing** (town) Tompkins County
130	18.2	**Batavia** (city) Genesee County
130	18.2	**Grandyle Village** (CDP) Erie County
132	18.3	**Busti** (town) Chautauqua County
132	18.3	**Fayette** (town) Seneca County
132	18.3	**Jerusalem** (town) Yates County
132	18.3	**North Syracuse** (village) Onondaga County
132	18.3	**Oneida** (city) Madison County
132	18.3	**Syracuse** (city) Onondaga County
132	18.3	**Watervliet** (city) Albany County
139	18.4	**Cortlandville** (town) Cortland County
139	18.4	**Fallsburg** (town) Sullivan County
141	18.5	**Corning** (town) Steuben County
141	18.5	**Elmira** (city) Chemung County
141	18.5	**Mount Morris** (town) Livingston County
144	18.6	**Bath** (town) Steuben County
144	18.6	**Chemung** (town) Chemung County
144	18.6	**Cuba** (town) Allegany County
144	18.6	**Eaton** (town) Madison County
144	18.6	**Greece** (CDP) Monroe County
144	18.6	**Horseheads** (town) Chemung County
144	18.6	**Rensselaer** (city) Rensselaer County

Note: *This section ranks incorporated places and CDPs (Census Designated Places) with populations of 2,500 or more. Unincorporated postal areas were not considered. Please refer to the User Guide for additional information.*

Violent Crime Rate per 10,000 Population

Top 150 Places Ranked in *Descending* Order

State Rank	Rate	Place	State Rank	Rate	Place
1	146.7	**Newburgh** (city) Orange County	76	19.4	**Mechanicville** (city) Saratoga County
2	113.3	**Niagara Falls** (city) Niagara County	77	19.3	**Irondequoit** (CDP) Monroe County
3	111.9	**Buffalo** (city) Erie County	78	19.0	**Fulton** (city) Oswego County
4	87.6	**Rochester** (city) Monroe County	79	18.8	**Oneida** (city) Madison County
5	85.8	**Troy** (city) Rensselaer County	80	18.7	**Little Falls** (city) Herkimer County
6	80.3	**Albany** (city) Albany County	81	18.6	**Olean** (city) Cattaraugus County
7	79.3	**Syracuse** (city) Onondaga County	82	18.4	**Sidney** (village) Delaware County
8	79.2	**Poughkeepsie** (city) Dutchess County	83	17.9	**Chester** (village) Orange County
9	78.3	**Jamestown** (city) Chautauqua County	84	17.8	**Warsaw** (village) Wyoming County
10	72.1	**Hempstead** (village) Nassau County	85	17.7	**Wellsville** (village) Allegany County
11	69.3	**Mount Vernon** (city) Westchester County	86	17.5	**White Plains** (city) Westchester County
12	67.3	**Binghamton** (city) Broome County	87	17.4	**Greece** (town) Monroe County
13	62.2	**Herkimer** (village) Herkimer County	87	17.4	**Oneonta** (city) Otsego County
14	59.4	**Corning** (city) Steuben County	87	17.4	**Tonawanda** (city) Erie County
15	58.6	**New York** (city)	90	16.9	**Massena** (village) Saint Lawrence County
16	57.7	**Liberty** (village) Sullivan County	91	16.7	**Amsterdam** (city) Montgomery County
17	57.1	**Utica** (city) Oneida County	92	16.6	**Scotia** (village) Schenectady County
18	55.3	**Lackawanna** (city) Erie County	93	16.4	**Carthage** (village) Jefferson County
19	54.7	**Gloversville** (city) Fulton County	93	16.4	**East Rochester** (town/village) Monroe County
20	52.3	**Watertown** (city) Jefferson County	95	16.1	**Harriman** (village) Orange County
21	51.5	**Endicott** (village) Broome County	95	16.1	**Peekskill** (city) Westchester County
22	50.7	**Batavia** (city) Genesee County	97	16.0	**Niagara** (town) Niagara County
23	49.5	**Auburn** (city) Cayuga County	98	15.7	**Cortland** (city) Cortland County
24	48.1	**Johnson City** (village) Broome County	99	15.6	**Ellicott** (town) Chautauqua County
25	47.3	**Spring Valley** (village) Rockland County	100	14.8	**Wallkill** (town) Orange County
26	47.1	**Yonkers** (city) Westchester County	101	14.7	**Ellenville** (village) Ulster County
27	43.9	**Monticello** (village) Sullivan County	101	14.7	**Walden** (village) Orange County
28	40.9	**Middletown** (city) Orange County	103	14.6	**Ossining** (village) Westchester County
29	39.6	**Malone** (village) Franklin County	104	14.1	**Bath** (village) Steuben County
29	39.6	**Port Jervis** (city) Orange County	104	14.1	**Fallsburg** (town) Sullivan County
31	39.2	**Salamanca** (city) Cattaraugus County	106	13.9	**South Nyack** (village) Rockland County
32	38.9	**Beacon** (city) Dutchess County	107	13.7	**Medina** (village) Orleans County
32	38.9	**Cazenovia** (village) Madison County	108	13.6	**North Tonawanda** (city) Niagara County
32	38.9	**South Glens Falls** (village) Saratoga County	109	13.3	**Clarkstown** (town) Rockland County
35	38.8	**Whitehall** (village) Washington County	110	13.2	**New Windsor** (town) Orange County
36	37.3	**Newark** (village) Wayne County	111	13.0	**Haverstraw** (town) Rockland County
37	36.7	**Hudson** (city) Columbia County	111	13.0	**Long Beach** (city) Nassau County
38	34.9	**Lockport** (city) Niagara County	111	13.0	**Sherrill** (city) Oneida County
39	34.4	**Canandaigua** (city) Ontario County	114	12.8	**Canastota** (village) Madison County
40	34.0	**Oswego** (city) Oswego County	115	12.7	**Ilion** (village) Herkimer County
41	32.0	**Freeport** (village) Nassau County	116	12.5	**Depew** (village) Erie County
41	32.0	**Owego** (village) Tioga County	116	12.5	**Pelham Manor** (village) Westchester County
43	31.9	**Lowville** (village) Lewis County	118	12.4	**Groton** (village) Tompkins County
44	31.4	**Ogdensburg** (city) Saint Lawrence County	118	12.4	**Rome** (city) Oneida County
45	31.3	**Dunkirk** (city) Chautauqua County	120	12.3	**Evans** (town) Erie County
46	30.7	**Fort Edward** (village) Washington County	121	12.2	**Lake Placid** (village) Essex County
47	30.2	**Kingston** (city) Ulster County	122	11.6	**East Greenbush** (town) Rensselaer County
48	30.1	**Norwich** (city) Chenango County	123	11.5	**Marlborough** (town) Ulster County
49	29.8	**Brockport** (village) Monroe County	124	11.3	**Saranac Lake** (village) Franklin County
50	29.5	**Elmira** (city) Chemung County	125	11.1	**Camillus** (town) Onondaga County
51	29.3	**Gates** (town) Monroe County	125	11.1	**Montgomery** (town) Orange County
52	29.1	**Hudson Falls** (village) Washington County	127	10.6	**Greenburgh** (town) Westchester County
53	28.0	**Solvay** (village) Onondaga County	128	10.5	**Kenmore** (village) Erie County
54	27.7	**Mount Morris** (village) Livingston County	129	10.4	**Elmsford** (village) Westchester County
55	26.4	**Hoosick Falls** (village) Rensselaer County	130	10.3	**Deerpark** (town) Orange County
56	25.9	**Catskill** (village) Greene County	130	10.3	**Poughkeepsie** (town) Dutchess County
57	25.3	**Port Chester** (village) Westchester County	132	10.1	**Chester** (town) Orange County
58	25.1	**Glens Falls** (city) Warren County	132	10.1	**North Syracuse** (village) Onondaga County
59	24.9	**Tupper Lake** (village) Franklin County	132	10.1	**Nunda** (town) Livingston County
60	24.8	**New Paltz** (town) Ulster County	135	10.0	**Alfred** (village) Allegany County
61	24.4	**Cheektowaga** (town) Erie County	135	10.0	**Menands** (village) Albany County
61	24.4	**Watervliet** (city) Albany County	135	10.0	**Shandaken** (town) Ulster County
63	24.3	**Tonawanda** (town) Erie County	135	10.0	**Southold** (town) Suffolk County
64	23.4	**Albion** (village) Orleans County	139	9.9	**Ogden** (town) Monroe County
64	23.4	**Cohoes** (city) Albany County	139	9.9	**West Seneca** (CDP) Erie County
66	22.8	**Gowanda** (village) Cattaraugus County	141	9.7	**Amherst** (town) Erie County
67	22.1	**Geneva** (city) Ontario County	141	9.7	**Greenwood Lake** (village) Orange County
68	21.9	**Plattsburgh** (city) Clinton County	141	9.7	**Newburgh** (town) Orange County
68	21.9	**Waterloo** (village) Seneca County	141	9.7	**Plattekill** (town) Ulster County
70	21.3	**New Rochelle** (city) Westchester County	145	9.5	**Rotterdam** (town) Schenectady County
71	21.1	**Rensselaer** (city) Rensselaer County	146	9.4	**Cuba** (town) Allegany County
72	21.0	**Saratoga Springs** (city) Saratoga County	146	9.4	**Waverly** (village) Tioga County
73	20.4	**Seneca Falls** (town) Seneca County	148	9.3	**Ballston Spa** (village) Saratoga County
74	19.9	**Perry** (village) Wyoming County	148	9.3	**Colonie** (town) Albany County
75	19.5	**Delhi** (village) Delaware County	148	9.3	**Southampton** (village) Suffolk County

Note: *This section ranks incorporated places and CDPs (Census Designated Places) with populations of 2,500 or more. Unincorporated postal areas were not considered. Please refer to the User Guide for additional information.*

Violent Crime Rate per 10,000 Population

Top 150 Places Ranked in *Ascending* Order

State Rank	Rate	Place	State Rank	Rate	Place
1	0.0	**Ardsley** (village) Westchester County	76	4.6	**Monroe** (village) Orange County
1	0.0	**Briarcliff Manor** (village) Westchester County	77	4.8	**Croton-on-Hudson** (village) Westchester County
1	0.0	**Carroll** (town) Chautauqua County	77	4.8	**Hamilton** (village) Madison County
1	0.0	**Cayuga Heights** (village) Tompkins County	77	4.8	**Johnstown** (city) Fulton County
1	0.0	**Durham** (town) Greene County	80	4.9	**Niskayuna** (town) Schenectady County
1	0.0	**Elmira** (town) Chemung County	81	5.0	**Glenville** (town) Schenectady County
1	0.0	**Great Neck Estates** (village) Nassau County	81	5.0	**Rockville Centre** (village) Nassau County
1	0.0	**Horseheads** (village) Chemung County	83	5.1	**Cicero** (town) Onondaga County
1	0.0	**Kirkland** (town) Oneida County	84	5.2	**Hamburg** (village) Erie County
1	0.0	**Lake Success** (village) Nassau County	84	5.2	**Washingtonville** (village) Orange County
1	0.0	**Lewisboro** (town) Westchester County	86	5.3	**Amityville** (village) Suffolk County
1	0.0	**Lloyd Harbor** (village) Suffolk County	86	5.3	**Cornwall** (town) Orange County
1	0.0	**Malverne** (village) Nassau County	88	5.4	**Northport** (village) Suffolk County
1	0.0	**New Berlin** (town) Chenango County	88	5.4	**Orchard Park** (town) Erie County
1	0.0	**Olive** (town) Ulster County	88	5.4	**Webster** (town) Monroe County
1	0.0	**Pine Plains** (town) Dutchess County	91	5.5	**Glen Cove** (city) Nassau County
1	0.0	**Rhinebeck** (village) Dutchess County	91	5.5	**Warwick** (town) Orange County
1	0.0	**Sands Point** (village) Nassau County	91	5.5	**Woodbury** (town) Orange County
1	0.0	**Skaneateles** (village) Onondaga County	94	5.6	**Fairport** (village) Monroe County
1	0.0	**Stillwater** (town) Saratoga County	94	5.6	**Fredonia** (village) Chautauqua County
1	0.0	**Stockport** (town) Columbia County	94	5.6	**Goshen** (village) Orange County
1	0.0	**Tuxedo** (town) Orange County	94	5.6	**Lynbrook** (village) Nassau County
1	0.0	**Whitestown** (town) Oneida County	94	5.6	**Moriah** (town) Essex County
24	0.6	**Rye** (city) Westchester County	94	5.6	**Pleasantville** (village) Westchester County
25	1.1	**New Castle** (town) Westchester County	100	5.7	**Pelham** (village) Westchester County
26	1.3	**Baldwinsville** (village) Onondaga County	101	5.9	**Brighton** (CDP) Monroe County
26	1.3	**Eden** (town) Erie County	101	5.9	**Hamburg** (town) Erie County
26	1.3	**Garden City** (village) Nassau County	101	5.9	**New Hartford** (town) Oneida County
29	1.4	**Harrison** (town/village) Westchester County	104	6.0	**Penn Yan** (village) Yates County
29	1.4	**Mount Hope** (town) Orange County	105	6.1	**Avon** (village) Livingston County
31	1.5	**Irvington** (village) Westchester County	106	6.2	**Hastings-on-Hudson** (village) Westchester County
31	1.5	**Kent** (town) Putnam County	106	6.2	**Montgomery** (village) Orange County
31	1.5	**Tuckahoe** (village) Westchester County	106	6.2	**Port Washington** (CDP) Nassau County
34	1.7	**Rosendale** (town) Ulster County	109	6.4	**Mount Pleasant** (town) Westchester County
34	1.7	**Scarsdale** (town/village) Westchester County	109	6.4	**Westfield** (village) Chautauqua County
36	1.9	**Floral Park** (village) Nassau County	111	6.5	**Larchmont** (village) Westchester County
36	1.9	**Kings Point** (village) Nassau County	111	6.5	**Mamaroneck** (town) Westchester County
38	2.0	**Carmel** (town) Putnam County	111	6.5	**Old Westbury** (village) Nassau County
39	2.1	**Rye Brook** (village) Westchester County	114	6.6	**Norfolk** (town) Saint Lawrence County
40	2.2	**Bedford** (town) Westchester County	115	6.7	**Cobleskill** (village) Schoharie County
40	2.2	**Macedon** (town) Wayne County	115	6.7	**Coeymans** (town) Albany County
42	2.4	**Greenport** (town) Columbia County	115	6.7	**Geddes** (town) Onondaga County
42	2.4	**Hornell** (city) Steuben County	115	6.7	**Lancaster** (town) Erie County
44	2.9	**Guilderland** (town) Albany County	119	6.8	**Walton** (village) Delaware County
45	3.0	**Canton** (village) Saint Lawrence County	119	6.8	**Woodstock** (town) Ulster County
45	3.0	**Eastchester** (town) Westchester County	121	6.9	**Bethlehem** (town) Albany County
47	3.1	**Cairo** (town) Greene County	122	7.0	**Le Roy** (village) Genesee County
47	3.1	**Lewiston** (town) Niagara County	123	7.1	**Vestal** (town) Broome County
47	3.1	**Mamaroneck** (village) Westchester County	124	7.4	**Coxsackie** (village) Greene County
47	3.1	**Potsdam** (village) Saint Lawrence County	124	7.4	**Geneseo** (village) Livingston County
51	3.2	**Fishkill** (town) Dutchess County	124	7.4	**Ulster** (town) Ulster County
51	3.2	**Maybrook** (village) Orange County	127	7.5	**Elmira Heights** (village) Chemung County
51	3.2	**North Castle** (town) Westchester County	128	7.6	**Crawford** (town) Orange County
54	3.4	**Blooming Grove** (town) Orange County	128	7.6	**Green Island** (town/village) Albany County
54	3.4	**Cornwall-on-Hudson** (village) Orange County	130	7.7	**Schodack** (town) Rensselaer County
54	3.4	**East Fishkill** (town) Dutchess County	131	7.8	**Sleepy Hollow** (village) Westchester County
54	3.4	**Florida** (village) Orange County	131	7.8	**Tarrytown** (village) Westchester County
58	3.5	**Akron** (village) Erie County	133	7.9	**Frankfort** (village) Herkimer County
59	3.6	**Highlands** (town) Orange County	133	7.9	**Orangetown** (town) Rockland County
59	3.6	**Wappingers Falls** (village) Dutchess County	135	8.0	**Ticonderoga** (town) Essex County
59	3.6	**Waterford** (town) Saratoga County	136	8.1	**Dobbs Ferry** (village) Westchester County
62	3.8	**Hyde Park** (town) Dutchess County	136	8.1	**Whitesboro** (village) Oneida County
62	3.8	**Pound Ridge** (town) Westchester County	138	8.2	**North Greenbush** (town) Rensselaer County
62	3.8	**Yorktown** (town) Westchester County	139	8.5	**Lloyd** (town) Ulster County
65	3.9	**Addison** (town) Steuben County	140	8.6	**Ramapo** (town) Rockland County
65	3.9	**Piermont** (village) Rockland County	141	8.8	**Palmyra** (village) Wayne County
67	4.0	**Chittenango** (village) Madison County	142	9.0	**Suffern** (village) Rockland County
67	4.0	**Frankfort** (town) Herkimer County	143	9.3	**Ballston Spa** (village) Saratoga County
69	4.1	**Shelter Island** (town) Suffolk County	143	9.3	**Colonie** (town) Albany County
70	4.2	**Saugerties** (town) Ulster County	143	9.3	**Southampton** (village) Suffolk County
70	4.2	**Shawangunk** (town) Ulster County	146	9.4	**Cuba** (town) Allegany County
72	4.4	**Dansville** (village) Livingston County	146	9.4	**Waverly** (village) Tioga County
73	4.5	**East Hampton** (town) Suffolk County	148	9.5	**Rotterdam** (town) Schenectady County
73	4.5	**Manlius** (town) Onondaga County	149	9.7	**Amherst** (town) Erie County
73	4.5	**Stony Point** (town) Rockland County	149	9.7	**Greenwood Lake** (village) Orange County

Note: This section ranks incorporated places and CDPs (Census Designated Places) with populations of 2,500 or more. Unincorporated postal areas were not considered. Please refer to the User Guide for additional information.

Property Crime Rate per 10,000 Population

Top 150 Places Ranked in *Descending* Order

State Rank	Rate	Place	State Rank	Rate	Place
1	715.2	**Johnson City** (village) Broome County	76	220.0	**Medina** (village) Orleans County
2	583.2	**Niagara** (town) Niagara County	77	217.3	**Scotia** (village) Schenectady County
3	515.6	**Niagara Falls** (city) Niagara County	78	214.3	**Fredonia** (village) Chautauqua County
4	478.4	**Watertown** (city) Jefferson County	79	214.2	**Vestal** (town) Broome County
5	477.6	**Herkimer** (village) Herkimer County	80	210.6	**Kenmore** (village) Erie County
6	454.3	**Binghamton** (city) Broome County	81	209.6	**Brighton** (CDP) Monroe County
7	450.0	**Woodbury** (town) Orange County	82	205.3	**Watervliet** (city) Albany County
8	434.1	**Sidney** (village) Delaware County	83	203.0	**Lowville** (village) Lewis County
9	433.2	**Ellicott** (town) Chautauqua County	84	202.5	**Dansville** (village) Livingston County
10	433.0	**Buffalo** (city) Erie County	85	202.4	**Canandaigua** (city) Ontario County
11	425.0	**Endicott** (village) Broome County	86	200.7	**Glenville** (town) Schenectady County
12	415.9	**Gloversville** (city) Fulton County	87	197.9	**Groton** (village) Tompkins County
13	406.2	**New Hartford** (town) Oneida County	88	197.8	**Saratoga Springs** (city) Saratoga County
14	403.6	**Troy** (city) Rensselaer County	89	197.6	**Hamburg** (town) Erie County
15	393.8	**Rochester** (city) Monroe County	90	196.1	**Tonawanda** (city) Erie County
16	391.2	**Cobleskill** (village) Schoharie County	91	195.4	**Wallkill** (town) Orange County
17	384.6	**Liberty** (village) Sullivan County	92	190.9	**Rome** (city) Oneida County
18	379.5	**Massena** (village) Saint Lawrence County	93	190.3	**Depew** (village) Erie County
19	379.1	**Malone** (village) Franklin County	93	190.3	**Tonawanda** (town) Erie County
20	368.5	**Fulton** (city) Oswego County	95	190.2	**Oneonta** (city) Otsego County
21	368.1	**Auburn** (city) Cayuga County	96	189.7	**Chester** (village) Orange County
22	364.0	**Greenport** (town) Columbia County	97	185.5	**North Greenbush** (town) Rensselaer County
23	359.4	**Utica** (city) Oneida County	98	183.6	**Monroe** (village) Orange County
24	353.6	**Oneida** (city) Madison County	99	183.3	**Green Island** (town/village) Albany County
25	353.2	**Syracuse** (city) Onondaga County	100	181.7	**Salamanca** (city) Cattaraugus County
26	352.9	**Seneca Falls** (town) Seneca County	101	175.7	**Port Chester** (village) Westchester County
27	344.3	**Norwich** (city) Chenango County	102	174.4	**Solvay** (village) Onondaga County
28	340.1	**Gates** (town) Monroe County	102	174.4	**White Plains** (city) Westchester County
29	337.0	**Newburgh** (town) Orange County	104	173.3	**Beacon** (city) Dutchess County
30	334.4	**Jamestown** (city) Chautauqua County	105	172.7	**Hudson** (city) Columbia County
31	327.0	**Corning** (city) Steuben County	106	172.5	**Carthage** (village) Jefferson County
32	325.4	**Batavia** (city) Genesee County	106	172.5	**Clarkstown** (town) Rockland County
33	325.1	**Albany** (city) Albany County	108	170.6	**Perry** (village) Wyoming County
34	316.9	**Menands** (village) Albany County	109	168.7	**Camillus** (town) Onondaga County
34	316.9	**Olean** (city) Cattaraugus County	110	168.1	**Ilion** (village) Herkimer County
36	316.1	**Catskill** (village) Greene County	111	167.7	**Guilderland** (town) Albany County
37	315.0	**Owego** (village) Tioga County	112	167.2	**Lake Placid** (village) Essex County
38	310.5	**Waterloo** (village) Seneca County	113	166.4	**New Windsor** (town) Orange County
39	310.4	**Ulster** (town) Ulster County	114	165.4	**Manlius** (town) Onondaga County
40	310.3	**Rotterdam** (town) Schenectady County	115	164.1	**Mount Vernon** (city) Westchester County
41	307.5	**Monticello** (village) Sullivan County	116	163.8	**Wappingers Falls** (village) Dutchess County
42	306.1	**Elmira** (city) Chemung County	117	163.6	**Glens Falls** (city) Warren County
43	302.9	**Cheektowaga** (town) Erie County	118	161.3	**Freeport** (village) Nassau County
44	301.5	**Ogdensburg** (city) Saint Lawrence County	119	159.9	**Brockport** (village) Monroe County
45	300.7	**Newark** (village) Wayne County	120	159.8	**New Rochelle** (city) Westchester County
46	297.6	**Poughkeepsie** (town) Dutchess County	121	159.4	**Amherst** (town) Erie County
47	294.5	**Port Jervis** (city) Orange County	122	159.2	**East Rochester** (town/village) Monroe County
48	294.3	**Southampton** (village) Suffolk County	123	158.8	**Pelham Manor** (village) Westchester County
49	292.1	**Geneva** (city) Ontario County	124	158.6	**Saranac Lake** (village) Franklin County
50	282.0	**Newburgh** (city) Orange County	125	158.2	**Southold** (town) Suffolk County
51	281.0	**Kingston** (city) Ulster County	126	154.1	**Ballston Spa** (village) Saratoga County
52	278.6	**Albion** (village) Orleans County	127	151.9	**New York** (city)
53	275.9	**Amsterdam** (city) Montgomery County	128	150.8	**North Tonawanda** (city) Niagara County
54	272.0	**Oswego** (city) Oswego County	129	150.5	**Elmira Heights** (village) Chemung County
55	265.4	**Little Falls** (city) Herkimer County	130	150.0	**Potsdam** (village) Saint Lawrence County
56	261.8	**Irondequoit** (CDP) Monroe County	131	147.5	**Geneseo** (village) Livingston County
57	254.8	**Lockport** (city) Niagara County	132	147.4	**East Hampton** (town) Suffolk County
58	252.5	**Bath** (village) Steuben County	133	145.3	**Harriman** (village) Orange County
59	251.0	**Greece** (town) Monroe County	134	142.9	**West Seneca** (CDP) Erie County
60	249.8	**Colonie** (town) Albany County	135	142.2	**Skaneateles** (village) Onondaga County
61	247.4	**Johnstown** (city) Fulton County	136	141.8	**Cohoes** (city) Albany County
62	247.2	**Middletown** (city) Orange County	136	141.8	**South Glens Falls** (village) Saratoga County
63	244.7	**Ellenville** (village) Ulster County	138	141.1	**Rensselaer** (city) Rensselaer County
64	235.4	**Gowanda** (village) Cattaraugus County	139	140.7	**Niskayuna** (town) Schenectady County
65	233.8	**Walton** (village) Delaware County	140	140.6	**Evans** (town) Erie County
66	232.8	**Tupper Lake** (village) Franklin County	141	138.6	**Hornell** (city) Steuben County
67	232.1	**Mount Morris** (village) Livingston County	142	138.4	**Greenburgh** (town) Westchester County
68	231.9	**Warsaw** (village) Wyoming County	143	137.6	**Amityville** (village) Suffolk County
69	231.0	**Geddes** (town) Onondaga County	144	137.3	**Rhinebeck** (village) Dutchess County
70	229.3	**Cuba** (town) Allegany County	145	134.6	**Cortland** (city) Cortland County
71	228.3	**Dunkirk** (city) Chautauqua County	146	132.4	**New Paltz** (town) Ulster County
72	227.5	**Wellsville** (village) Allegany County	147	132.2	**Horseheads** (village) Chemung County
73	227.2	**Lackawanna** (city) Erie County	148	131.7	**Mechanicville** (city) Saratoga County
74	225.9	**East Greenbush** (town) Rensselaer County	149	131.6	**Bethlehem** (town) Albany County
75	224.2	**Poughkeepsie** (city) Dutchess County	150	131.0	**Penn Yan** (village) Yates County

Note: *This section ranks incorporated places and CDPs (Census Designated Places) with populations of 2,500 or more. Unincorporated postal areas were not considered. Please refer to the User Guide for additional information.*

Property Crime Rate per 10,000 Population

Top 150 Places Ranked in *Ascending* Order

State Rank	Rate	Place	State Rank	Rate	Place
1	0.8	**Lewisboro** (town) Westchester County	76	68.7	**Hastings-on-Hudson** (village) Westchester County
2	1.7	**Elmira** (town) Chemung County	77	69.3	**Schodack** (town) Rensselaer County
3	2.8	**Moriah** (town) Essex County	78	69.9	**Whitehall** (village) Washington County
4	3.2	**Maybrook** (village) Orange County	79	70.3	**Palmyra** (village) Wayne County
5	3.4	**Tuxedo** (town) Orange County	80	70.7	**Mamaroneck** (village) Westchester County
6	6.6	**Norfolk** (town) Saint Lawrence County	81	71.8	**Old Westbury** (village) Nassau County
7	11.0	**Stockport** (town) Columbia County	82	72.7	**Mount Pleasant** (town) Westchester County
8	14.5	**Highlands** (town) Orange County	83	73.1	**Fishkill** (town) Dutchess County
9	15.3	**Fort Edward** (village) Washington County	84	75.5	**Northport** (village) Suffolk County
10	16.1	**Westfield** (village) Chautauqua County	85	75.6	**Lynbrook** (village) Nassau County
11	16.3	**Pine Plains** (town) Dutchess County	86	75.7	**Whitesboro** (village) Oneida County
12	17.7	**Great Neck Estates** (village) Nassau County	87	78.3	**Orangetown** (town) Rockland County
13	20.2	**Chester** (town) Orange County	88	79.1	**Mamaroneck** (town) Westchester County
14	20.4	**Carroll** (town) Chautauqua County	89	79.3	**Yorktown** (town) Westchester County
15	21.1	**Waverly** (village) Tioga County	90	79.8	**Ossining** (village) Westchester County
16	25.1	**Kirkland** (town) Oneida County	91	80.1	**Rockville Centre** (village) Nassau County
17	25.4	**Stillwater** (town) Saratoga County	92	80.2	**Alfred** (village) Allegany County
18	26.9	**Nunda** (town) Livingston County	93	80.3	**Lewiston** (town) Niagara County
19	27.0	**Cornwall-on-Hudson** (village) Orange County	94	80.7	**Dobbs Ferry** (village) Westchester County
20	28.6	**Hamilton** (village) Madison County	95	80.8	**Warwick** (town) Orange County
21	29.1	**Malverne** (village) Nassau County	96	81.7	**Scarsdale** (town/village) Westchester County
22	29.9	**Rye** (city) Westchester County	97	82.6	**Macedon** (town) Wayne County
23	31.1	**Kings Point** (village) Nassau County	98	84.1	**Ticonderoga** (town) Essex County
24	31.6	**New Castle** (town) Westchester County	99	84.9	**Plattsburgh** (city) Clinton County
25	32.4	**Eden** (town) Erie County	100	85.1	**Eastchester** (town) Westchester County
26	32.6	**Croton-on-Hudson** (village) Westchester County	101	86.1	**Saugerties** (town) Ulster County
27	33.0	**Sleepy Hollow** (village) Westchester County	102	87.1	**Lloyd** (town) Ulster County
28	33.3	**Coxsackie** (village) Greene County	103	87.6	**Orchard Park** (town) Erie County
29	33.7	**Durham** (town) Greene County	104	88.3	**Baldwinsville** (village) Onondaga County
30	34.4	**Kent** (town) Putnam County	105	89.7	**Whitestown** (town) Oneida County
31	34.6	**Olive** (town) Ulster County	106	90.3	**Greenwood Lake** (village) Orange County
32	36.0	**Waterford** (town) Saratoga County	107	90.9	**Marlborough** (town) Ulster County
33	36.2	**Frankfort** (town) Herkimer County	108	91.1	**Delhi** (village) Delaware County
34	36.3	**Irvington** (village) Westchester County	109	91.2	**Haverstraw** (town) Rockland County
35	36.8	**Cornwall** (town) Orange County	110	92.1	**Fallsburg** (town) Sullivan County
36	36.9	**Floral Park** (village) Nassau County	111	93.3	**Long Beach** (city) Nassau County
37	37.9	**Lloyd Harbor** (village) Suffolk County	112	93.6	**Ogden** (town) Monroe County
38	39.2	**Harrison** (town/village) Westchester County	113	94.0	**Larchmont** (village) Westchester County
39	39.9	**Briarcliff Manor** (village) Westchester County	114	94.8	**New Berlin** (town) Chenango County
40	41.8	**Pound Ridge** (town) Westchester County	115	95.7	**Le Roy** (village) Genesee County
41	43.4	**Montgomery** (village) Orange County	116	96.6	**Crawford** (town) Orange County
42	44.9	**Bedford** (town) Westchester County	117	99.5	**Yonkers** (city) Westchester County
43	45.4	**Avon** (village) Livingston County	118	102.4	**Canastota** (village) Madison County
44	45.5	**Sherrill** (city) Oneida County	119	102.6	**Hoosick Falls** (village) Rensselaer County
45	45.6	**Akron** (village) Erie County	120	104.3	**Pleasantville** (village) Westchester County
45	45.6	**Carmel** (town) Putnam County	121	104.4	**Goshen** (village) Orange County
47	46.4	**Cairo** (town) Greene County	122	104.9	**Pelham** (village) Westchester County
48	47.2	**Sands Point** (village) Nassau County	123	105.8	**North Syracuse** (village) Onondaga County
49	47.4	**Tarrytown** (village) Westchester County	124	107.2	**Woodstock** (town) Ulster County
50	47.9	**Canton** (village) Saint Lawrence County	125	109.7	**Cazenovia** (village) Madison County
50	47.9	**North Castle** (town) Westchester County	126	109.9	**Cicero** (town) Onondaga County
52	49.5	**Stony Point** (town) Rockland County	127	110.3	**Florida** (village) Orange County
53	50.7	**Glen Cove** (city) Nassau County	128	111.1	**Lake Success** (village) Nassau County
54	54.6	**Hyde Park** (town) Dutchess County	129	111.6	**Shelter Island** (town) Suffolk County
55	55.2	**Cayuga Heights** (village) Tompkins County	130	112.2	**Spring Valley** (village) Rockland County
56	55.4	**Rosendale** (town) Ulster County	131	113.3	**Garden City** (village) Nassau County
57	55.6	**Frankfort** (village) Herkimer County	132	113.6	**Addison** (town) Steuben County
58	57.8	**Port Washington** (CDP) Nassau County	133	114.0	**Webster** (town) Monroe County
59	58.0	**Chittenango** (village) Madison County	134	116.7	**Shandaken** (town) Ulster County
59	58.0	**Shawangunk** (town) Ulster County	135	117.1	**Peekskill** (city) Westchester County
61	58.3	**Elmsford** (village) Westchester County	136	117.4	**Lancaster** (town) Erie County
62	58.5	**East Fishkill** (town) Dutchess County	137	121.6	**Walden** (village) Orange County
63	59.2	**Plattekill** (town) Ulster County	138	123.5	**Coeymans** (town) Albany County
64	59.7	**Suffern** (village) Rockland County	139	124.9	**Hudson Falls** (village) Washington County
65	60.4	**Rye Brook** (village) Westchester County	140	125.0	**Deerpark** (town) Orange County
66	61.2	**South Nyack** (village) Rockland County	141	128.1	**Hamburg** (village) Erie County
67	61.3	**Blooming Grove** (town) Orange County	142	128.2	**Hempstead** (village) Nassau County
67	61.3	**Montgomery** (town) Orange County	143	131.0	**Penn Yan** (village) Yates County
69	62.0	**Mount Hope** (town) Orange County	144	131.6	**Bethlehem** (town) Albany County
70	63.2	**Fairport** (village) Monroe County	145	131.7	**Mechanicville** (city) Saratoga County
71	64.2	**Washingtonville** (village) Orange County	146	132.2	**Horseheads** (village) Chemung County
72	65.8	**Piermont** (village) Rockland County	147	132.4	**New Paltz** (town) Ulster County
73	66.1	**Tuckahoe** (village) Westchester County	148	134.6	**Cortland** (city) Cortland County
74	67.7	**Ardsley** (village) Westchester County	149	137.3	**Rhinebeck** (village) Dutchess County
75	68.4	**Ramapo** (town) Rockland County	150	137.6	**Amityville** (village) Suffolk County

Note: *This section ranks incorporated places and CDPs (Census Designated Places) with populations of 2,500 or more. Unincorporated postal areas were not considered. Please refer to the User Guide for additional information.*

Education

New York Public School Educational Profile

Category	Value	Category	Value
Schools *(2013-2014)*	4,800	**Averaged Freshman Graduation Rate** (%) *(2011-2012)*	
Instructional Level		All Students	78
Primary	2,559	Female	79
Middle	837	Male	76
High	1,001	**Event Dropout Rate** (%) *(2011-2012)*	
Other/Not Reported	403	All Students	3.8
Curriculum		**Staff** *(2013-2014)*	
Regular	4,617	Teachers (FTE)	206,665.0
Special Education	128	Salary[1] ($)	77,957
Vocational	25	Librarians/Media Specialists (FTE)	2,511.5
Alternative	30	Guidance Counselors (FTE)	4,374.9
Type		**Ratios** *(2013-2014)*	
Magnet	103	Number of Students per Teacher	13.2 to 1
Charter	233	Number of Students per Librarian	1,088.1 to 1
Title I Eligible	4,651	Number of Students per Guidance Counselor	624.6 to 1
School-wide Title I	3,132	**Finances** *(2012-2013)*	
Students *(2013-2014)*	2,732,689	Expenditures ($ per student)	
Gender (%)		Total Expenditures	21,489
Male	51.4	Current Expenditures	19,529
Female	48.6	Instruction	13,540
Race/Ethnicity (%)		Support Services	5,589
White, Non-Hispanic	46.5	Non-Instruction	401
Black, Non-Hispanic	18.2	Net Current per Attendance for Title I	20,604
Asian, Non-Hispanic	8.8	Revenue ($ per student)	
American Indian/Alaska Native, Non-Hispanic	0.6	Total Revenue	21,768
Hawaiian Native/Pacific Islander, Non-Hispanic	n/a	From Federal Sources	1,193
Two or More Races, Non-Hispanic	1.5	From State Sources	8,731
Hispanic of Any Race	24.5	From Local Sources	11,844
Special Programs (%)		From Intermediate Sources	126
Individual Education Program (IEP)	16.6	**College Entrance Exam Scores**	
English Language Learner (ELL)	2.5	SAT Reasoning Test™ *(2015)*	
Eligible for Free Lunch Program	43.7	Test Takers	153,543
Eligible for Reduced-Price Lunch Program	5.9	Mean Combined Score	1,469
Adjusted Cohort Graduation Rate (%) *(2013-2014)*		Mean Critical Reading Score	489
All Students	78	Mean Math Score	502
White, Non-Hispanic	88	Mean Writing Score	478
Black, Non-Hispanic	65	ACT *(2015)*	
Asian/Pacific Islander, Non-Hispanic	84	Participation Rate (%)	28
American Indian/Alaska Native, Non-Hispanic	65	Mean Composite Score	23.7
Hispanic of Any Race	n/a	Mean English Score	23.0
Students with Disabilities	52	Mean Math Score	23.8
Limited English Proficient	37	Mean Reading Score	23.9
Economically Disadvantaged	69	Mean Science Score	23.5

Note: For an explanation of data, please refer to the User Guide in the front of the book; (1) Average salary for classroom teachers in 2015-16

Number of Schools

Rank	Number	District Name	City
1	1,816	New York City Public Schools	New York
2	116	NYC Geographic District # 2	New York
3	86	NYC Geographic District #10	Bronx
4	74	NYC Geographic District #9	Bronx
5	69	NYC Geographic District #31	Staten Island
6	66	NYC Geographic District #11	Bronx
7	61	NYC Geographic District #27	Ozone Park
8	59	NYC Geographic District # 8	Bronx
9	57	NYC Geographic District #17	Brooklyn
9	57	NYC Special Schools - District 75	New York
11	56	Buffalo City SD	Buffalo
12	55	NYC Geographic District #24	Corona
13	54	NYC Geographic District #12	Bronx
14	53	Rochester City SD	Rochester
15	51	NYC Geographic District #19	Brooklyn
16	48	NYC Geographic District #28	Jamaica
17	47	NYC Geographic District #6	New York
17	47	NYC Geographic District #15	Brooklyn
19	46	NYC Geographic District # 7	Bronx
19	46	NYC Geographic District #29	Queens Village
19	46	NYC Geographic District #30	Long Isl City
22	45	NYC Geographic District # 3	New York
22	45	NYC Geographic District #25	Flushing
24	43	NYC Geographic District #13	Brooklyn
24	43	NYC Geographic District #20	Brooklyn
26	42	NYC Geographic District #14	Brooklyn
27	40	NYC Geographic District #21	Brooklyn
27	40	NYC Geographic District #22	Brooklyn
29	39	Yonkers City SD	Yonkers
30	34	NYC Geographic District # 4	New York
30	34	NYC Geographic District #18	Brooklyn
32	33	NYC Geographic District #23	Brooklyn
33	32	NYC Geographic District # 5	New York
34	31	NYC Geographic District # 1	New York
34	31	NYC Geographic District #26	Bayside
36	30	Syracuse City SD	Syracuse
37	28	NYC Geographic District #32	Brooklyn
38	27	NYC Geographic District #16	Brooklyn
39	18	Sachem Central SD	Lake Ronkonkoma
40	17	Brentwood UFSD	Brentwood
40	17	Greece Central SD	Rochester
40	17	Schenectady City SD	Schenectady
43	16	Clarkstown Central SD	New City
43	16	Mount Vernon SD	Mount Vernon
45	15	Albany City SD	Albany
45	15	Wappingers Central SD	Wappingers Fls
47	14	East Ramapo CSD (Spring Valley)	Spring Valley
47	14	Middle Country Central SD	Centereach
49	13	Liverpool Central SD	Liverpool
49	13	Smithtown Central SD	Smithtown
49	13	Utica City SD	Utica
49	13	Williamsville Central SD	East Amherst
53	12	Arlington Central SD	Lagrangeville
53	12	Elmira City SD	Elmira
53	12	Ithaca City SD	Ithaca
53	12	Kenmore-Tonawanda UFSD	Buffalo
53	12	Newburgh City SD	Newburgh
53	12	Shenendehowa Central SD	Clifton Park
53	12	West Seneca Central SD	West Seneca
60	11	Connetquot Central SD	Bohemia
60	11	Corning City SD	Painted Post
60	11	Half Hollow Hills Central SD	Dix Hills
60	11	Niagara Falls City SD	Niagara Falls
60	11	North Syracuse Central SD	North Syracuse
60	11	Patchogue-Medford UFSD	Patchogue
60	11	Webster Central SD	Webster
67	10	Binghamton City SD	Binghamton
67	10	Great Neck UFSD	Great Neck
67	10	Hempstead UFSD	Hempstead
67	10	Kingston City SD	Kingston
67	10	Levittown UFSD	Levittown
67	10	New Rochelle City SD	New Rochelle
67	10	Oceanside UFSD	Oceanside
67	10	Rome City SD	Rome
67	10	Syosset Central SD	Syosset
67	10	West Irondequoit Central SD	Rochester
77	9	East Meadow UFSD	Westbury
77	9	Hicksville UFSD	Hicksville
77	9	Jamestown City SD	Jamestown
77	9	Massapequa UFSD	Massapequa
77	9	Northport-East Northport UFSD	Northport
77	9	Pittsford Central SD	Pittsford
77	9	Rush-Henrietta Central SD	Henrietta
84	8	Baldwinsville Central SD	Baldwinsville
84	8	Central Islip UFSD	Central Islip
84	8	Central Square Central SD	Central Square
84	8	Commack UFSD	East Northport
84	8	Fairport Central SD	Fairport
84	8	Freeport UFSD	Freeport
84	8	Haverstraw-Stony Point CSD	Garnerville
84	8	Huntington UFSD	Huntington Stn
84	8	Indian River Central SD	Philadelphia
84	8	Lakeland Central SD	Shrub Oak
84	8	Lindenhurst UFSD	Lindenhurst
84	8	Lockport City SD	Lockport
84	8	Niskayuna Central SD	Schenectady
84	8	North Colonie CSD	Latham
84	8	Oswego City SD	Oswego
84	8	Plainview-Old Bethpage Central SD	Plainview
84	8	Saratoga Spgs City SD	Saratoga Spgs
84	8	South Colonie Central SD	Albany
84	8	Three Village Central SD	Stony Brook
84	8	Uniondale UFSD	Uniondale
84	8	Watertown City SD	Watertown
84	8	William Floyd UFSD	Mastic Beach
106	7	Auburn City SD	Auburn
106	7	Baldwin UFSD	Baldwin
106	7	Bay Shore UFSD	Bay Shore
106	7	Bedford Central SD	Bedford
106	7	Bethlehem Central SD	Delmar
106	7	East Greenbush Central SD	East Greenbush
106	7	East Syracuse-Minoa Central SD	East Syracuse
106	7	Garden City UFSD	Garden City
106	7	Guilderland Central SD	Guilderland Center
106	7	Horseheads Central SD	Horseheads
106	7	Lancaster Central SD	Lancaster
106	7	Longwood Central SD	Middle Island
106	7	Lynbrook UFSD	Lynbrook
106	7	Middletown City SD	Middletown
106	7	Monroe-Woodbury Central SD	Central Valley
106	7	North Babylon UFSD	North Babylon
106	7	Pine Bush Central SD	Pine Bush
106	7	Port Washington UFSD	Port Washington
106	7	Poughkeepsie City SD	Poughkeepsie
106	7	Ramapo Central SD (Suffern)	Hillburn
106	7	Riverhead Central SD	Riverhead
106	7	Rockville Ctr UFSD	Rockville Ctr
106	7	Scarsdale UFSD	Scarsdale
106	7	South Huntington UFSD	Huntington Stn
106	7	Troy City SD	Troy
106	7	Vestal Central SD	Vestal
106	7	West Babylon UFSD	West Babylon
106	7	West Genesee Central SD	Camillus
106	7	West Islip UFSD	West Islip
106	7	White Plains City SD	White Plains
106	7	Whitesboro Central SD	Yorkville
137	6	Amsterdam City SD	Amsterdam
137	6	Ballston Spa Central SD	Ballston Spa
137	6	Beacon City SD	Beacon
137	6	Brookhaven-Comsewogue UFSD	Port Jefferson Sta
137	6	Camden Central SD	Camden
137	6	Chappaqua Central SD	Chappaqua
137	6	Clarence Central SD	Clarence
137	6	Copiague UFSD	Copiague
137	6	Cortland City SD	Cortland
137	6	Dunkirk City SD	Dunkirk
137	6	East Irondequoit Central SD	Rochester
137	6	East Islip UFSD	Islip Terrace
137	6	Elmont UFSD	Elmont
137	6	Farmingdale UFSD	Farmingdale
137	6	Fayetteville-Manlius Central SD	Manlius
137	6	Frontier Central SD	Hamburg
137	6	Fulton City SD	Fulton
137	6	Gates-Chili Central SD	Rochester
137	6	Glen Cove City SD	Glen Cove
137	6	Gloversville City SD	Gloversville
137	6	Greenburgh Central SD	Hartsdale
137	6	Hamburg Central SD	Hamburg
137	6	Harrison Central SD	Harrison
137	6	Hyde Park Central SD	Hyde Park
137	6	Iroquois Central SD	Elma
137	6	Katonah-Lewisboro UFSD	Goldens Bridge
137	6	Long Beach City SD	Long Beach
137	6	Mamaroneck UFSD	Mamaroneck
137	6	Niagara-Wheatfield Central SD	Niagara Falls
137	6	North Tonawanda City SD	North Tonawanda
137	6	Oneida City SD	Oneida
137	6	Orchard Park Central SD	West Seneca
137	6	Ossining UFSD	Ossining
137	6	Peekskill City SD	Peekskill
137	6	Pelham UFSD	Pelham
137	6	Penfield Central SD	Rochester
137	6	Port Chester-Rye UFSD	Port Chester
137	6	Saugerties Central SD	Saugerties
137	6	Scotia-Glenville Central SD	Scotia
137	6	South Country Central SD	East Patchogue
137	6	S Glens Fls Central SD	S Glens Fls
137	6	Spencerport Central SD	Spencerport
137	6	Sweet Home Central SD	Amherst
137	6	Union-Endicott Central SD	Endicott
137	6	Valley Central SD (Montgomery)	Montgomery
137	6	Westbury UFSD	Old Westbury
183	5	Amityville UFSD	Amityville
183	5	Averill Park Central SD	Averill Park
183	5	Bayport-Blue Point UFSD	Bayport
183	5	Bellmore-Merrick Central High SD	North Merrick
183	5	Bethpage UFSD	Bethpage
183	5	Brockport Central SD	Brockport
183	5	Burnt Hills-Ballston Lake Central SD	Scotia
183	5	Carmel Central SD	Patterson
183	5	Carthage Central SD	Carthage
183	5	Chittenango Central SD	Chittenango
183	5	Churchville-Chili Central SD	Churchville
183	5	Cohoes City SD	Cohoes
183	5	Cornwall Central SD	Cornwall on Hdsn
183	5	Deer Park UFSD	Deer Park
183	5	Dryden Central SD	Dryden
183	5	Eastchester UFSD	Eastchester
183	5	Evans-Brant Central SD (Lake Shore)	Angola
183	5	Glens Falls City SD	Glens Falls
183	5	Grand Island Central SD	Grand Island
183	5	Hauppauge UFSD	Hauppauge
183	5	Hendrick Hudson Central SD	Montrose
183	5	Herricks UFSD	New Hyde Park
183	5	Hewlett-Woodmere UFSD	Woodmere
183	5	Hilton Central SD	Hilton
183	5	Homer Central SD	Homer
183	5	Hornell City SD	Hornell
183	5	Hudson Falls Central SD	Fort Edward
183	5	Islip UFSD	Islip
183	5	Jamesville-Dewitt Central SD	Dewitt
183	5	Jericho UFSD	Jericho
183	5	Johnstown City SD	Johnstown
183	5	Kings Park Central SD	Kings Park
183	5	Lawrence UFSD	Lawrence
183	5	Mahopac Central SD	Mahopac
183	5	Malone Central SD	Malone
183	5	Massena Central SD	Massena
183	5	Mexico Central SD	Mexico
183	5	Mineola UFSD	Mineola
183	5	Minisink Valley Central SD	Slate Hill
183	5	Monticello Central SD	Monticello
183	5	New Hartford Central SD	New Hartford
183	5	Newark Central SD	Newark
183	5	North Bellmore UFSD	Bellmore
183	5	North Shore Central SD	Sea Cliff
183	5	Nyack UFSD	Nyack
183	5	Oneonta City SD	Oneonta
183	5	Pearl River UFSD	Pearl River
183	5	Plainedge UFSD	N Massapequa
183	5	Plattsburgh City SD	Plattsburgh
183	5	Rondout Valley Central SD	Accord
183	5	Roosevelt UFSD	Roosevelt
183	5	Roslyn UFSD	Roslyn
183	5	Rye City SD	Rye
183	5	Sayville UFSD	Sayville
183	5	Sewanhaka Central High SD	Floral Park
183	5	Sherrill City SD	Verona
183	5	Shoreham-Wading River Central SD	Shoreham
183	5	South Orangetown Central SD	Blauvelt
183	5	UFSD of the Tarrytowns	Sleepy Hollow
183	5	Victor Central SD	Victor
183	5	Wallkill Central SD	Wallkill
183	5	Wantagh UFSD	Wantagh
183	5	Washingtonville Central SD	Washingtonville
183	5	Waverly Central SD	Waverly
183	5	Wayne Central SD	Ontario Center
183	5	West Hempstead UFSD	West Hempstead
183	5	Yorktown Central SD	Yorktown Hgts

Note: This section only includes districts with 1,500 or more students; All categories are ranked from high to low

250	4	Amherst Central SD	Amherst
250	4	Batavia City SD	Batavia
250	4	Beekmantown Central SD	West Chazy
250	4	Brewster Central SD	Brewster
250	4	Brighton Central SD	Rochester
250	4	Broadalbin-Perth Central SD	Broadalbin
250	4	Byram Hills Central SD	Armonk
250	4	Canandaigua City SD	Canandaigua
250	4	Central Valley CSD At Ilion-Mohawk	Ilion
250	4	Cheektowaga Central SD	Cheektowaga
250	4	Cheektowaga-Maryvale UFSD	Cheektowaga
250	4	Chenango Valley Central SD	Binghamton
250	4	Cobleskill-Richmondville Central SD	Cobleskill
250	4	Cold Spring Hrbr Central SD	Cold Spring Hrbr
250	4	Eastport-South Manor CSD	Manorville
250	4	Elwood UFSD	Greenlawn
250	4	Geneva City SD	Geneva
250	4	Goshen Central SD	Goshen
250	4	Harborfields Central SD	Greenlawn
250	4	Honeoye Falls-Lima Central SD	Honeoye Falls
250	4	Irvington UFSD	Irvington
250	4	Island Trees UFSD	Levittown
250	4	Johnson City Central SD	Johnson City
250	4	Kinderhook Central SD	Valatie
250	4	Lackawanna City SD	Lackawanna
250	4	Lansingburgh Central SD	Troy
250	4	Lewiston-Porter Central SD	Youngstown
250	4	Locust Valley Central SD	Locust Valley
250	4	Maine-Endwell Central SD	Endwell
250	4	Malverne UFSD	Malverne
250	4	Manhasset UFSD	Manhasset
250	4	Miller Place UFSD	Miller Place
250	4	Mount Pleasant Central SD	Thornwood
250	4	Nanuet UFSD	Nanuet
250	4	New Hyde Pk-Garden City Pk UFSD	New Hyde Park
250	4	New Paltz Central SD	New Paltz
250	4	Newfane Central SD	Burt
250	4	Norwich City SD	Norwich
250	4	Ogdensburg City SD	Ogdensburg
250	4	Olean City SD	Olean
250	4	Owego-Apalachin Central SD	Owego
250	4	Palmyra-Macedon Central SD	Palmyra
250	4	Phelps-Clifton Springs Central SD	Clifton Springs
250	4	Port Jervis City SD	Port Jervis
250	4	Queensbury UFSD	Queensbury
250	4	Ravena-Coeymans-Selkirk Ctrl SD	Ravena
250	4	Red Hook Central SD	Red Hook
250	4	Rocky Point UFSD	Rocky Point
250	4	Rotterdam-Mohonasen Central SD	Schenectady
250	4	Rye Neck UFSD	Mamaroneck
250	4	Salmon River Central SD	Fort Covington
250	4	Seaford UFSD	Seaford
250	4	Somers Central SD	Somers
250	4	South Jefferson Central SD	Adams Center
250	4	Spackenkill UFSD	Poughkeepsie
250	4	Springville-Griffith Institute CSD	Springville
250	4	Starpoint Central SD	Lockport
250	4	Susquehanna Valley Central SD	Conklin
250	4	Tonawanda City SD	Tonawanda
250	4	Valhalla UFSD	Valhalla
250	4	Valley Stream 13 UFSD	Valley Stream
250	4	Valley Stream Central High SD	Valley Stream
250	4	Warwick Valley Central SD	Warwick
250	4	Waterloo Central SD	Waterloo
250	4	Westhill Central SD	Syracuse
250	4	Windsor Central SD	Windsor
250	4	Wyandanch UFSD	Wyandanch
250	4	Yorkshire-Pioneer Central SD	Yorkshire
318	3	Albion Central SD	Albion
318	3	Alden Central SD	Alden
318	3	Ardsley UFSD	Ardsley
318	3	Babylon UFSD	Babylon
318	3	Bath Central SD	Bath
318	3	Briarcliff Mnr UFSD	Briarcliff Mnr
318	3	Bronxville UFSD	Bronxville
318	3	Catskill Central SD	Catskill
318	3	Cazenovia Central SD	Cazenovia
318	3	Center Moriches UFSD	Center Moriches
318	3	Chenango Forks Central SD	Binghamton
318	3	Croton-Harmon UFSD	Croton on Hdsn
318	3	Dansville Central SD	Dansville
318	3	Depew UFSD	Depew
318	3	East Aurora UFSD	East Aurora
318	3	East Hampton UFSD	East Hampton
318	3	East Williston UFSD	Old Westbury
318	3	Eden Central SD	Eden
318	3	Edgemont UFSD	Scarsdale
318	3	Ellenville Central SD	Ellenville
318	3	Franklin Square UFSD	Franklin Square
318	3	Fredonia Central SD	Fredonia
318	3	General Brown Central SD	Dexter
318	3	Gouverneur Central SD	Gouverneur
318	3	Hampton Bays UFSD	Hampton Bays
318	3	Hastings-On-Hudson UFSD	Hastings on Hdsn
318	3	Highland Central SD	Highland
318	3	Hudson City SD	Hudson
318	3	Livonia Central SD	Livonia
318	3	Marcellus Central SD	Marcellus
318	3	Marlboro Central SD	Milton
318	3	Medina Central SD	Medina
318	3	Merrick UFSD	Merrick
318	3	Mount Sinai UFSD	Mount Sinai
318	3	Oyster Bay-East Norwich Central SD	Oyster Bay
318	3	Penn Yan Central SD	Penn Yan
318	3	Phoenix Central SD	Phoenix
318	3	Pleasantville UFSD	Pleasantville
318	3	Putnam Valley Central SD	Putnam Valley
318	3	Schalmont Central SD	Schenectady
318	3	Schuylerville Central SD	Schuylerville
318	3	Solvay UFSD	Solvay
318	3	Southampton UFSD	Southampton
318	3	Westhampton Bch UFSD	Westhampton Bch
362	2	Liberty Central SD	Liberty
362	2	Peru Central SD	Peru
364	1	Charter School for Applied Tech	Buffalo
364	1	Orange-Ulster Boces	Goshen

Number of Teachers

Rank	Number	District Name	City
1	71,635.0	New York City Public Schools	New York
2	4,627.6	NYC Special Schools - District 75	New York
3	3,805.2	NYC Geographic District # 2	New York
4	3,629.4	NYC Geographic District #31	Staten Island
5	3,628.6	NYC Geographic District #10	Bronx
6	3,402.3	NYC Geographic District #24	Corona
7	2,881.3	NYC Geographic District #20	Brooklyn
8	2,858.8	Buffalo City SD	Buffalo
9	2,821.1	NYC Geographic District #27	Ozone Park
10	2,543.1	Rochester City SD	Rochester
11	2,464.0	NYC Geographic District # 9	Bronx
12	2,430.1	NYC Geographic District #30	Long Isl City
13	2,412.4	NYC Geographic District #11	Bronx
14	2,259.2	NYC Geographic District #28	Jamaica
15	2,162.0	NYC Geographic District #25	Flushing
16	2,078.6	NYC Geographic District #21	Brooklyn
17	2,045.9	NYC Geographic District #22	Brooklyn
18	2,043.3	NYC Geographic District #15	Brooklyn
19	2,021.5	NYC Geographic District # 8	Bronx
20	1,675.9	NYC Geographic District #12	Bronx
21	1,669.1	NYC Geographic District #26	Bayside
22	1,620.9	NYC Geographic District # 6	New York
23	1,600.7	NYC Geographic District #29	Queens Village
24	1,567.8	Syracuse City SD	Syracuse
25	1,567.6	NYC Geographic District #17	Brooklyn
26	1,549.7	NYC Geographic District #19	Brooklyn
27	1,534.3	Yonkers City SD	Yonkers
28	1,453.2	NYC Geographic District # 3	New York
29	1,387.6	NYC Geographic District # 7	Bronx
30	1,366.0	NYC Geographic District #13	Brooklyn
31	1,345.3	NYC Geographic District #14	Brooklyn
32	1,156.1	NYC Geographic District #18	Brooklyn
33	1,045.2	Brentwood UFSD	Brentwood
34	1,033.7	NYC Geographic District # 4	New York
35	937.0	Greece Central SD	Rochester
36	916.6	NYC Geographic District #32	Brooklyn
37	913.3	Sachem Central SD	Lake Ronkonkoma
38	887.2	NYC Geographic District # 5	New York
39	856.4	NYC Geographic District # 1	New York
40	846.7	Newburgh City SD	Newburgh
41	780.0	Wappingers Central SD	Wappingers Fls
42	743.5	Williamsville Central SD	East Amherst
43	720.2	NYC Geographic District #23	Brooklyn
44	711.3	Schenectady City SD	Schenectady
45	706.2	New Rochelle City SD	New Rochelle
46	684.2	Half Hollow Hills Central SD	Dix Hills
47	682.6	Smithtown Central SD	Smithtown
48	681.4	Middle Country Central SD	Centereach
49	674.8	Clarkstown Central SD	New City
50	658.2	Webster Central SD	Webster
51	650.4	Arlington Central SD	Lagrangeville
52	633.1	Albany City SD	Albany
53	631.9	North Syracuse Central SD	North Syracuse
54	627.4	Shenendehowa Central SD	Clifton Park
55	626.2	Utica City SD	Utica
56	614.4	Mount Vernon SD	Mount Vernon
57	614.1	Kenmore-Tonawanda UFSD	Buffalo
58	611.5	Levittown UFSD	Levittown
59	610.9	NYC Geographic District #16	Brooklyn
60	607.0	Massapequa UFSD	Massapequa
61	604.1	Great Neck UFSD	Great Neck
62	597.1	Syosset Central SD	Syosset
63	591.8	Longwood Central SD	Middle Island
64	587.0	William Floyd UFSD	Mastic Beach
65	567.7	East Meadow UFSD	Westbury
66	564.5	Sewanhaka Central High SD	Floral Park
67	559.7	Haverstraw-Stony Point CSD	Garnerville
68	542.3	Liverpool Central SD	Liverpool
69	541.3	East Ramapo CSD (Spring Valley)	Spring Valley
70	538.4	Uniondale UFSD	Uniondale
71	532.4	White Plains City SD	White Plains
72	526.2	Connetquot Central SD	Bohemia
73	514.7	Middletown City SD	Middletown
74	513.4	Commack UFSD	East Northport
75	510.1	Patchogue-Medford UFSD	Patchogue
76	508.1	Northport-East Northport UFSD	Northport
77	503.2	Fairport Central SD	Fairport
78	501.4	Monroe-Woodbury Central SD	Central Valley
79	497.2	Freeport UFSD	Freeport
80	497.0	West Seneca Central SD	West Seneca
81	493.3	Kingston City SD	Kingston
82	489.7	Three Village Central SD	Stony Brook
83	489.1	Binghamton City SD	Binghamton
84	487.8	Lindenhurst UFSD	Lindenhurst
85	484.0	Ithaca City SD	Ithaca
86	483.6	Farmingdale UFSD	Farmingdale
87	481.1	Rush-Henrietta Central SD	Henrietta
88	470.1	Pittsford Central SD	Pittsford
89	470.0	Saratoga Spgs City SD	Saratoga Spgs
90	467.0	Central Islip UFSD	Central Islip
91	458.2	Lakeland Central SD	Shrub Oak
92	455.7	Hempstead UFSD	Hempstead
93	454.9	Rome City SD	Rome
94	448.4	Plainview-Old Bethpage Central SD	Plainview
95	442.0	South Huntington UFSD	Huntington Stn
96	436.8	Oceanside UFSD	Oceanside
97	436.5	Bay Shore UFSD	Bay Shore
98	429.0	North Colonie CSD	Latham
99	425.0	Niagara Falls City SD	Niagara Falls
100	421.8	Port Washington UFSD	Port Washington
101	421.3	Jamestown City SD	Jamestown
102	419.3	Bellmore-Merrick Central High SD	North Merrick
103	418.2	Lancaster Central SD	Lancaster
104	417.9	Corning City SD	Painted Post
105	417.0	Elmira City SD	Elmira
106	392.6	Guilderland Central SD	Guilderland Center
107	390.9	Hicksville UFSD	Hicksville
108	390.8	Mamaroneck UFSD	Mamaroneck
109	386.1	Lockport City SD	Lockport
110	384.2	Scarsdale UFSD	Scarsdale
111	381.2	Orchard Park Central SD	West Seneca
112	380.9	South Colonie Central SD	Albany
113	376.6	Baldwin UFSD	Baldwin
113	376.6	Penfield Central SD	Rochester
115	375.2	Pine Bush Central SD	Pine Bush
116	374.4	West Islip UFSD	West Islip
117	371.2	Ramapo Central SD (Suffern)	Hillburn
118	370.2	Baldwinsville Central SD	Baldwinsville
119	367.6	South Country Central SD	East Patchogue
120	363.3	West Genesee Central SD	Camillus
121	362.3	Frontier Central SD	Hamburg
122	359.7	Bedford Central SD	Bedford
123	347.6	Deer Park UFSD	Deer Park
124	346.1	Mahopac Central SD	Mahopac
125	345.4	Gates-Chili Central SD	Rochester
126	343.3	Hilton Central SD	Hilton
127	343.1	West Babylon UFSD	West Babylon
128	338.5	East Islip UFSD	Islip Terrace
129	337.1	Long Beach City SD	Long Beach
130	334.9	Riverhead Central SD	Riverhead
131	330.3	Bethlehem Central SD	Delmar

Note: This section only includes districts with 1,500 or more students; All categories are ranked from high to low

132	329.7	Huntington UFSD	Huntington Stn
133	327.0	Ballston Spa Central SD	Ballston Spa
134	326.2	Ossining UFSD	Ossining
135	325.8	North Babylon UFSD	North Babylon
136	325.3	Westbury UFSD	Old Westbury
137	324.0	Auburn City SD	Auburn
138	322.4	Chappaqua Central SD	Chappaqua
139	322.0	Rockville Ctr UFSD	Rockville Ctr
140	320.3	Oswego City SD	Oswego
141	320.0	Clarence Central SD	Clarence
142	319.7	Fayetteville-Manlius Central SD	Manlius
143	319.6	Harrison Central SD	Harrison
144	318.6	Poughkeepsie City SD	Poughkeepsie
145	315.4	Valley Stream Central High SD	Valley Stream
146	315.1	Spencerport Central SD	Spencerport
147	314.6	Elmont UFSD	Elmont
148	314.5	Victor Central SD	Victor
149	314.2	East Greenbush Central SD	East Greenbush
150	313.1	Herricks UFSD	New Hyde Park
151	312.1	Union-Endicott Central SD	Endicott
152	309.3	Troy City SD	Troy
153	307.7	Garden City UFSD	Garden City
153	307.7	Jericho UFSD	Jericho
155	305.7	Copiague UFSD	Copiague
156	305.1	Churchville-Chili Central SD	Churchville
157	304.5	Brighton Central SD	Rochester
158	304.3	Carmel Central SD	Patterson
159	304.1	Indian River Central SD	Philadelphia
160	302.5	Valley Central SD (Montgomery)	Montgomery
161	302.0	East Syracuse-Minoa Central SD	East Syracuse
162	300.2	Central Square Central SD	Central Square
163	299.1	Port Chester-Rye UFSD	Port Chester
164	298.5	Washingtonville Central SD	Washingtonville
165	296.4	Brockport Central SD	Brockport
166	295.5	Canandaigua City SD	Canandaigua
167	293.4	Hauppauge UFSD	Hauppauge
168	293.0	Hyde Park Central SD	Hyde Park
169	291.1	Watertown City SD	Watertown
170	290.4	Niskayuna Central SD	Schenectady
171	285.7	Hamburg Central SD	Hamburg
172	285.5	Eastport-South Manor CSD	Manorville
173	284.4	North Shore Central SD	Sea Cliff
174	282.8	Amsterdam City SD	Amsterdam
175	282.7	Horseheads Central SD	Horseheads
176	278.3	Orange-Ulster Boces	Goshen
177	277.2	North Tonawanda City SD	North Tonawanda
178	275.0	Sweet Home Central SD	Amherst
179	274.9	Yorktown Central SD	Yorktown Hgts
180	274.4	Fulton City SD	Fulton
180	274.4	Katonah-Lewisboro UFSD	Goldens Bridge
182	271.1	Minisink Valley Central SD	Slate Hill
183	267.8	East Irondequoit Central SD	Rochester
184	263.7	Kings Park Central SD	Kings Park
185	263.6	Roslyn UFSD	Roslyn
186	263.5	Vestal Central SD	Vestal
187	262.9	Warwick Valley Central SD	Warwick
188	262.7	Amherst Central SD	Amherst
189	261.6	Monticello Central SD	Monticello
190	259.3	Bethpage UFSD	Bethpage
191	258.3	Brookhaven-Comsewogue UFSD	Port Jefferson Sta
192	257.6	South Orangetown Central SD	Blauvelt
193	257.5	Niagara-Wheatfield Central SD	Niagara Falls
194	257.4	Hewlett-Woodmere UFSD	Woodmere
195	257.0	Wantagh UFSD	Wantagh
196	256.1	Lawrence UFSD	Lawrence
197	254.2	Queensbury UFSD	Queensbury
198	253.6	Carthage Central SD	Carthage
199	252.5	Glen Cove City SD	Glen Cove
200	249.5	Lynbrook UFSD	Lynbrook
201	248.7	Burnt Hills-Ballston Lake Central SD	Scotia
202	246.4	Whitesboro Central SD	Yorkville
203	245.8	Plainedge UFSD	N Massapequa
204	245.0	West Irondequoit Central SD	Rochester
205	244.8	Somers Central SD	Somers
206	242.6	Nyack UFSD	Nyack
207	242.5	Manhasset UFSD	Manhasset
208	242.3	Rocky Point UFSD	Rocky Point
209	241.5	Mineola UFSD	Mineola
210	241.2	Brewster Central SD	Brewster
211	240.9	Islip UFSD	Islip
212	240.8	S Glens Fls Central SD	S Glens Fls
213	239.9	Rye City SD	Rye
214	239.6	Wallkill Central SD	Wallkill
215	237.6	Harborfields Central SD	Greenlawn
216	235.1	Amityville UFSD	Amityville
217	235.0	Sayville UFSD	Sayville
218	234.9	Beacon City SD	Beacon
219	231.0	Eastchester UFSD	Eastchester
220	229.3	Gloversville City SD	Gloversville
221	228.4	Bayport-Blue Point UFSD	Bayport
222	223.5	Grand Island Central SD	Grand Island
223	223.3	Jamesville-Dewitt Central SD	Dewitt
224	222.6	Byram Hills Central SD	Armonk
225	222.0	Roosevelt UFSD	Roosevelt
226	221.1	Port Jervis City SD	Port Jervis
227	220.8	Wayne Central SD	Ontario Center
228	220.3	Pelham UFSD	Pelham
229	217.6	Cornwall Central SD	Cornwall on Hdsn
230	217.2	Cortland City SD	Cortland
231	216.2	Peekskill City SD	Peekskill
232	213.2	Goshen Central SD	Goshen
233	212.4	Averill Park Central SD	Averill Park
234	212.3	Evans-Brant Central SD (Lake Shore)	Angola
235	207.9	New Hartford Central SD	New Hartford
236	207.0	UFSD of the Tarrytowns	Sleepy Hollow
237	206.0	Hendrick Hudson Central SD	Montrose
238	205.4	Saugerties Central SD	Saugerties
239	205.3	Johnson City Central SD	Johnson City
240	204.7	Batavia City SD	Batavia
241	202.0	Yorkshire-Pioneer Central SD	Yorkshire
242	201.9	Geneva City SD	Geneva
243	200.8	Miller Place UFSD	Miller Place
244	200.1	Camden Central SD	Camden
245	200.0	Starpoint Central SD	Lockport
246	197.7	Seaford UFSD	Seaford
247	196.0	Scotia-Glenville Central SD	Scotia
248	195.2	Dunkirk City SD	Dunkirk
249	193.6	Malone Central SD	Malone
250	192.9	Shoreham-Wading River Central SD	Shoreham
251	192.3	Rotterdam-Mohonasen Central SD	Schenectady
252	192.0	Mexico Central SD	Mexico
253	190.8	Locust Valley Central SD	Locust Valley
254	188.7	Lansingburgh Central SD	Troy
255	188.2	Honeoye Falls-Lima Central SD	Honeoye Falls
255	188.2	Iroquois Central SD	Elma
257	187.7	Rondout Valley Central SD	Accord
258	187.4	Massena Central SD	Massena
259	186.6	Island Trees UFSD	Levittown
260	185.5	Ravena-Coeymans-Selkirk Ctrl SD	Ravena
261	184.6	Plattsburgh City SD	Plattsburgh
262	183.9	Pearl River UFSD	Pearl River
263	183.2	Newark Central SD	Newark
264	180.1	Cheektowaga Central SD	Cheektowaga
265	179.9	Nanuet UFSD	Nanuet
266	179.1	Ardsley UFSD	Ardsley
267	178.2	North Bellmore UFSD	Bellmore
268	177.8	Homer Central SD	Homer
268	177.8	Maine-Endwell Central SD	Endwell
270	172.5	East Hampton UFSD	East Hampton
271	172.1	Palmyra-Macedon Central SD	Palmyra
272	171.5	New Paltz Central SD	New Paltz
273	171.3	Mount Sinai UFSD	Mount Sinai
274	171.1	Mount Pleasant Central SD	Thornwood
275	170.5	Olean City SD	Olean
276	169.1	Oneida City SD	Oneida
277	168.1	Central Valley CSD At Ilion-Mohawk	Ilion
278	167.0	Glens Falls City SD	Glens Falls
279	166.7	Red Hook Central SD	Red Hook
280	166.6	Owego-Apalachin Central SD	Owego
281	166.3	Westhampton Bch UFSD	Westhampton Bch
282	166.2	Hudson Falls Central SD	Fort Edward
283	165.7	Lewiston-Porter Central SD	Youngstown
284	165.2	Elwood UFSD	Greenlawn
285	164.6	Valley Stream 13 UFSD	Valley Stream
286	163.9	Phoenix Central SD	Phoenix
287	163.8	Greenburgh Central SD	Hartsdale
288	163.4	Dryden Central SD	Dryden
289	162.5	Norwich City SD	Norwich
290	162.0	West Hempstead UFSD	West Hempstead
291	161.2	Beekmantown Central SD	West Chazy
292	159.9	Chittenango Central SD	Chittenango
293	159.2	Southampton UFSD	Southampton
294	158.5	Irvington UFSD	Irvington
295	158.0	Cohoes City SD	Cohoes
296	157.9	Wyandanch UFSD	Wyandanch
297	157.4	Malverne UFSD	Malverne
298	156.7	Hampton Bays UFSD	Hampton Bays
299	156.2	Cold Spring Hrbr Central SD	Cold Spring Hrbr
300	155.3	East Williston UFSD	Old Westbury
301	153.9	Depew UFSD	Depew
302	153.1	Edgemont UFSD	Scarsdale
303	152.8	Hudson City SD	Hudson
304	151.1	Pleasantville UFSD	Pleasantville
305	150.9	Kinderhook Central SD	Valatie
305	150.9	Peru Central SD	Peru
307	150.8	Cobleskill-Richmondville Central SD	Cobleskill
308	149.8	Cheektowaga-Maryvale UFSD	Cheektowaga
309	149.3	Susquehanna Valley Central SD	Conklin
310	149.2	Oyster Bay-East Norwich Central SD	Oyster Bay
311	148.6	Oneonta City SD	Oneonta
312	148.1	Lackawanna City SD	Lackawanna
312	148.1	Merrick UFSD	Merrick
314	146.5	Albion Central SD	Albion
315	146.1	Tonawanda City SD	Tonawanda
316	144.3	Windsor Central SD	Windsor
317	144.2	Penn Yan Central SD	Penn Yan
318	144.0	Spackenkill UFSD	Poughkeepsie
319	143.8	Sherrill City SD	Verona
320	143.1	Livonia Central SD	Livonia
321	142.7	Marlboro Central SD	Milton
322	142.6	Schalmont Central SD	Schenectady
323	141.5	Springville-Griffith Institute CSD	Springville
324	141.2	Hastings-On-Hudson UFSD	Hastings on Hdsn
325	141.1	Franklin Square UFSD	Franklin Square
325	141.1	Waterloo Central SD	Waterloo
327	141.0	Hornell City SD	Hornell
328	139.8	Phelps-Clifton Springs Central SD	Clifton Springs
329	139.0	Catskill Central SD	Catskill
330	137.5	Liberty Central SD	Liberty
331	136.7	Salmon River Central SD	Fort Covington
332	135.8	Marcellus Central SD	Marcellus
333	135.4	Ogdensburg City SD	Ogdensburg
334	134.4	South Jefferson Central SD	Adams Center
335	133.6	Westhill Central SD	Syracuse
336	133.5	Bath Central SD	Bath
337	132.9	Briarcliff Mnr UFSD	Briarcliff Mnr
338	132.7	Highland Central SD	Highland
339	132.4	Medina Central SD	Medina
340	132.1	Bronxville UFSD	Bronxville
341	131.8	Broadalbin-Perth Central SD	Broadalbin
341	131.8	Dansville Central SD	Dansville
341	131.8	Fredonia Central SD	Fredonia
344	131.7	Newfane Central SD	Burt
344	131.7	Valhalla UFSD	Valhalla
346	131.6	Solvay UFSD	Solvay
347	131.3	New Hyde Pk-Garden City Pk UFSD	New Hyde Park
348	131.1	Putnam Valley Central SD	Putnam Valley
349	130.5	Alden Central SD	Alden
350	130.3	Schuylerville Central SD	Schuylerville
351	129.9	Croton-Harmon UFSD	Croton on Hdsn
352	129.0	East Aurora UFSD	East Aurora
353	128.8	Chenango Valley Central SD	Binghamton
354	126.6	Babylon UFSD	Babylon
355	126.0	Ellenville Central SD	Ellenville
356	125.6	Cazenovia Central SD	Cazenovia
356	125.6	Johnstown City SD	Johnstown
358	123.9	Waverly Central SD	Waverly
359	120.6	Center Moriches UFSD	Center Moriches
360	118.3	Eden Central SD	Eden
361	117.1	Rye Neck UFSD	Mamaroneck
362	116.5	Gouverneur Central SD	Gouverneur
363	112.4	Charter School for Applied Tech	Buffalo
364	98.7	Chenango Forks Central SD	Binghamton
365	90.9	General Brown Central SD	Dexter

Number of Students

Rank	Number	District Name	City
	11,060,521	New York City Public Schools	New York
2	62,120	NYC Geographic District # 2	New York
3	59,836	NYC Geographic District #31	Staten Island
4	56,150	NYC Geographic District #24	Corona
5	55,059	NYC Geographic District #10	Bronx
6	47,623	NYC Geographic District #20	Brooklyn
7	44,106	NYC Geographic District #27	Ozone Park
8	39,824	NYC Geographic District #30	Long Isl City
9	39,018	NYC Geographic District #28	Jamaica
10	38,373	NYC Geographic District #11	Bronx
11	35,810	NYC Geographic District #25	Flushing
12	35,525	NYC Geographic District # 9	Bronx

Note: This section only includes districts with 1,500 or more students; All categories are ranked from high to low

13	34,977	NYC Geographic District #22	Brooklyn
14	34,854	Buffalo City SD	Buffalo
15	33,641	NYC Geographic District #21	Brooklyn
16	31,357	NYC Geographic District #26	Bayside
17	30,295	Rochester City SD	Rochester
18	29,504	NYC Geographic District #15	Brooklyn
19	28,923	NYC Geographic District # 8	Bronx
20	26,680	NYC Geographic District #29	Queens Village
21	26,516	Yonkers City SD	Yonkers
22	24,358	NYC Geographic District #17	Brooklyn
23	24,210	NYC Geographic District #6	New York
24	23,659	NYC Geographic District #12	Bronx
25	23,447	NYC Geographic District #19	Brooklyn
26	22,844	NYC Geographic District #3	New York
27	22,599	NYC Special Schools - District 75	New York
28	22,101	NYC Geographic District #13	Brooklyn
29	21,212	Syracuse City SD	Syracuse
30	20,153	NYC Geographic District #14	Brooklyn
31	19,488	NYC Geographic District # 7	Bronx
32	17,963	Brentwood UFSD	Brentwood
33	17,096	NYC Geographic District #18	Brooklyn
34	14,061	Sachem Central SD	Lake Ronkonkoma
35	13,762	NYC Geographic District #4	New York
36	13,750	NYC Geographic District #32	Brooklyn
37	12,511	NYC Geographic District # 5	New York
38	11,958	NYC Geographic District # 1	New York
39	11,703	Wappingers Central SD	Wappingers Fls
40	11,495	Newburgh City SD	Newburgh
41	11,434	Greece Central SD	Rochester
42	10,922	New Rochelle City SD	New Rochelle
43	10,320	Williamsville Central SD	East Amherst
44	10,299	Middle Country Central SD	Centereach
45	10,268	NYC Geographic District #23	Brooklyn
46	10,062	Smithtown Central SD	Smithtown
47	9,921	Schenectady City SD	Schenectady
48	9,758	Shenendehowa Central SD	Clifton Park
49	9,717	Utica City SD	Utica
50	9,177	Half Hollow Hills Central SD	Dix Hills
51	9,089	Arlington Central SD	Lagrangeville
52	9,064	North Syracuse Central SD	North Syracuse
53	9,038	Longwood Central SD	Middle Island
54	8,825	William Floyd UFSD	Mastic Beach
55	8,660	Webster Central SD	Webster
56	8,602	Clarkstown Central SD	New City
57	8,595	Albany City SD	Albany
58	8,456	Mount Vernon SD	Mount Vernon
59	8,234	East Ramapo CSD (Spring Valley)	Spring Valley
60	8,202	Sewanhaka Central High SD	Floral Park
61	8,201	NYC Geographic District #16	Brooklyn
62	7,915	Haverstraw-Stony Point CSD	Garnerville
63	7,886	Patchogue-Medford UFSD	Patchogue
64	7,481	Massapequa UFSD	Massapequa
65	7,331	Levittown UFSD	Levittown
66	7,227	Liverpool Central SD	Liverpool
67	7,193	Kenmore-Tonawanda UFSD	Buffalo
68	7,141	Middletown City SD	Middletown
69	7,129	East Meadow UFSD	Westbury
70	7,110	Niagara Falls City SD	Niagara Falls
71	7,098	White Plains City SD	White Plains
72	7,059	Hempstead UFSD	Hempstead
73	6,999	West Seneca Central SD	West Seneca
74	6,993	Monroe-Woodbury Central SD	Central Valley
75	6,992	Commack UFSD	East Northport
76	6,949	Three Village Central SD	Stony Brook
77	6,785	Central Islip UFSD	Central Islip
78	6,639	Great Neck UFSD	Great Neck
79	6,582	Saratoga Spgs City SD	Saratoga Spgs
80	6,576	Kingston City SD	Kingston
81	6,567	Elmira City SD	Elmira
82	6,558	Freeport UFSD	Freeport
83	6,456	Uniondale UFSD	Uniondale
84	6,404	Syosset Central SD	Syosset
85	6,282	Lindenhurst UFSD	Lindenhurst
86	6,269	Connetquot Central SD	Bohemia
87	6,222	Fairport Central SD	Fairport
88	6,105	Bay Shore UFSD	Bay Shore
89	6,036	Lakeland Central SD	Shrub Oak
90	6,018	South Huntington UFSD	Huntington Stn
91	5,911	Farmingdale UFSD	Farmingdale
92	5,901	Northport-East Northport UFSD	Northport
93	5,858	Pittsford Central SD	Pittsford
94	5,789	Lancaster Central SD	Lancaster
95	5,786	Binghamton City SD	Binghamton
96	5,698	Bellmore-Merrick Central High SD	North Merrick
97	5,678	Oceanside UFSD	Oceanside
98	5,590	Pine Bush Central SD	Pine Bush
99	5,543	Baldwinsville Central SD	Baldwinsville
100	5,463	Rome City SD	Rome
101	5,354	North Colonie CSD	Latham
102	5,348	Rush-Henrietta Central SD	Henrietta
103	5,337	Ithaca City SD	Ithaca
104	5,244	Mamaroneck UFSD	Mamaroneck
105	5,238	Port Washington UFSD	Port Washington
106	5,210	Hicksville UFSD	Hicksville
107	5,127	Jamestown City SD	Jamestown
108	5,043	Riverhead Central SD	Riverhead
109	5,042	Frontier Central SD	Hamburg
110	5,025	South Colonie Central SD	Albany
111	4,964	Orchard Park Central SD	West Seneca
112	4,944	Guilderland Central SD	Guilderland Center
113	4,914	Lockport City SD	Lockport
114	4,908	Corning City SD	Painted Post
115	4,889	Copiague UFSD	Copiague
116	4,879	Plainview-Old Bethpage Central SD	Plainview
117	4,843	West Genesee Central SD	Camillus
118	4,832	West Islip UFSD	West Islip
119	4,814	Baldwin UFSD	Baldwin
120	4,801	Scarsdale UFSD	Scarsdale
121	4,761	Clarence Central SD	Clarence
122	4,742	Ossining UFSD	Ossining
123	4,731	Westbury UFSD	Old Westbury
124	4,722	Bethlehem Central SD	Delmar
125	4,699	North Babylon UFSD	North Babylon
126	4,667	Mahopac Central SD	Mahopac
127	4,593	Valley Stream Central High SD	Valley Stream
128	4,550	South Country Central SD	East Patchogue
129	4,522	Hilton Central SD	Hilton
130	4,489	Ramapo Central SD (Suffern)	Hillburn
131	4,475	Penfield Central SD	Rochester
132	4,442	Poughkeepsie City SD	Poughkeepsie
133	4,428	Port Chester-Rye UFSD	Port Chester
134	4,425	Bedford Central SD	Bedford
135	4,393	Victor Central SD	Victor
136	4,392	Huntington UFSD	Huntington Stn
137	4,374	Valley Central SD (Montgomery)	Montgomery
138	4,372	Carmel Central SD	Patterson
139	4,350	Deer Park UFSD	Deer Park
140	4,319	Washingtonville Central SD	Washingtonville
141	4,244	Auburn City SD	Auburn
142	4,236	Fayetteville-Manlius Central SD	Manlius
143	4,230	Indian River Central SD	Philadelphia
144	4,221	Ballston Spa Central SD	Ballston Spa
145	4,151	East Greenbush Central SD	East Greenbush
146	4,147	Central Square Central SD	Central Square
147	4,140	Horseheads Central SD	Horseheads
148	4,123	West Babylon UFSD	West Babylon
149	4,106	Gates-Chili Central SD	Rochester
150	4,100	Niskayuna Central SD	Schenectady
151	4,097	East Islip UFSD	Islip Terrace
152	4,021	Minisink Valley Central SD	Slate Hill
153	4,005	Oswego City SD	Oswego
154	3,987	Chappaqua Central SD	Chappaqua
155	3,969	Watertown City SD	Watertown
156	3,941	Elmont UFSD	Elmont
157	3,934	Garden City UFSD	Garden City
158	3,930	Troy City SD	Troy
159	3,924	Churchville-Chili Central SD	Churchville
160	3,916	Hauppauge UFSD	Hauppauge
161	3,914	Herricks UFSD	New Hyde Park
162	3,842	Brookhaven-Comsewogue UFSD	Port Jefferson Sta
163	3,816	Niagara-Wheatfield Central SD	Niagara Falls
164	3,800	Union-Endicott Central SD	Endicott
165	3,770	Amsterdam City SD	Amsterdam
166	3,743	Warwick Valley Central SD	Warwick
167	3,729	Canandaigua City SD	Canandaigua
168	3,725	Hamburg Central SD	Hamburg
169	3,717	Spencerport Central SD	Spencerport
170	3,710	North Tonawanda City SD	North Tonawanda
171	3,705	Hyde Park Central SD	Hyde Park
172	3,680	Brockport Central SD	Brockport
173	3,676	Kings Park Central SD	Kings Park
174	3,670	Eastport-South Manor CSD	Manorville
175	3,608	West Irondequoit Central SD	Rochester
176	3,595	Fulton City SD	Fulton
177	3,583	Long Beach City SD	Long Beach
178	3,566	Rockville Ctr UFSD	Rockville Ctr
179	3,545	Harrison Central SD	Harrison
180	3,538	Brighton Central SD	Rochester
181	3,533	East Syracuse-Minoa Central SD	East Syracuse
182	3,528	Yorktown Central SD	Yorktown Hgts
183	3,449	Queensbury UFSD	Queensbury
184	3,429	Carthage Central SD	Carthage
185	3,394	Vestal Central SD	Vestal
186	3,388	Katonah-Lewisboro UFSD	Goldens Bridge
187	3,385	Harborfields Central SD	Greenlawn
188	3,329	Cornwall Central SD	Cornwall on Hdsn
189	3,321	Somers Central SD	Somers
190	3,303	Rye City SD	Rye
191	3,298	Manhasset UFSD	Manhasset
192	3,284	Sweet Home Central SD	Amherst
193	3,281	South Orangetown Central SD	Blauvelt
194	3,280	Rocky Point UFSD	Rocky Point
195	3,275	Brewster Central SD	Brewster
196	3,263	Glen Cove City SD	Glen Cove
197	3,239	Wantagh UFSD	Wantagh
198	3,231	Peekskill City SD	Peekskill
199	3,227	Whitesboro Central SD	Yorkville
200	3,211	Beacon City SD	Beacon
201	3,195	Burnt Hills-Ballston Lake Central SD	Scotia
202	3,193	Amityville UFSD	Amityville
203	3,185	Plainedge UFSD	N Massapequa
204	3,179	Roslyn UFSD	Roslyn
205	3,173	Eastchester UFSD	Eastchester
206	3,146	Wallkill Central SD	Wallkill
207	3,140	S Glens Fls Central SD	S Glens Fls
208	3,095	Sayville UFSD	Sayville
209	3,092	Hewlett-Woodmere UFSD	Woodmere
210	3,087	Islip UFSD	Islip
210	3,087	Roosevelt UFSD	Roosevelt
212	3,084	Grand Island Central SD	Grand Island
213	3,076	Averill Park Central SD	Averill Park
214	3,034	Monticello Central SD	Monticello
215	2,999	Jericho UFSD	Jericho
216	2,986	East Irondequoit Central SD	Rochester
217	2,945	Nyack UFSD	Nyack
218	2,944	Amherst Central SD	Amherst
219	2,925	Goshen Central SD	Goshen
220	2,924	Massena Central SD	Massena
221	2,916	Bethpage UFSD	Bethpage
222	2,904	Lawrence UFSD	Lawrence
223	2,896	Gloversville City SD	Gloversville
224	2,891	Jamesville-Dewitt Central SD	Dewitt
225	2,871	Rotterdam-Mohonasen Central SD	Schenectady
226	2,842	Miller Place UFSD	Miller Place
227	2,828	Lynbrook UFSD	Lynbrook
228	2,817	Pelham UFSD	Pelham
229	2,785	Port Jervis City SD	Port Jervis
229	2,785	Saugerties Central SD	Saugerties
231	2,778	Mineola UFSD	Mineola
232	2,751	UFSD of the Tarrytowns	Sleepy Hollow
233	2,739	North Shore Central SD	Sea Cliff
234	2,684	Orange-Ulster Boces	Goshen
235	2,644	Starpoint Central SD	Lockport
236	2,613	Cortland City SD	Cortland
237	2,606	New Hartford Central SD	New Hartford
238	2,594	Byram Hills Central SD	Armonk
239	2,577	Pearl River UFSD	Pearl River
240	2,574	Johnson City Central SD	Johnson City
241	2,547	Scotia-Glenville Central SD	Scotia
242	2,541	Yorkshire-Pioneer Central SD	Yorkshire
243	2,527	Evans-Brant Central SD (Lake Shore)	Angola
244	2,473	Shoreham-Wading River Central SD	Shoreham
245	2,443	Mount Sinai UFSD	Mount Sinai
246	2,442	Maine-Endwell Central SD	Endwell
247	2,440	Hudson Falls Central SD	Fort Edward
248	2,424	Hendrick Hudson Central SD	Montrose
249	2,415	Lansingburgh Central SD	Troy
250	2,414	Bayport-Blue Point UFSD	Bayport
251	2,413	Elwood UFSD	Greenlawn
252	2,412	Central Valley CSD At Ilion-Mohawk	Ilion
253	2,391	Iroquois Central SD	Elma
254	2,383	Seaford UFSD	Seaford
255	2,366	Batavia City SD	Batavia
256	2,356	Honeoye Falls-Lima Central SD	Honeoye Falls
257	2,354	Wayne Central SD	Ontario Center
258	2,350	Island Trees UFSD	Levittown
259	2,282	Malone Central SD	Malone
260	2,279	Camden Central SD	Camden
261	2,261	New Paltz Central SD	New Paltz
262	2,255	Oneida City SD	Oneida
263	2,244	Nanuet UFSD	Nanuet
264	2,227	Cheektowaga-Maryvale UFSD	Cheektowaga

Note: This section only includes districts with 1,500 or more students; All categories are ranked from high to low

264	2,227	Wyandanch UFSD	Wyandanch
266	2,226	Olean City SD	Olean
267	2,215	Cheektowaga Central SD	Cheektowaga
268	2,191	Owego-Apalachin Central SD	Owego
269	2,190	Geneva City SD	Geneva
270	2,169	Locust Valley Central SD	Locust Valley
271	2,161	Mexico Central SD	Mexico
272	2,160	Newark Central SD	Newark
273	2,144	Valley Stream 13 UFSD	Valley Stream
274	2,122	West Hempstead UFSD	West Hempstead
275	2,114	North Bellmore UFSD	Bellmore
276	2,088	Lewiston-Porter Central SD	Youngstown
277	2,079	Hampton Bays UFSD	Hampton Bays
278	2,072	Glens Falls City SD	Glens Falls
279	2,071	Chittenango Central SD	Chittenango
280	2,060	Homer Central SD	Homer
281	2,051	Sherrill City SD	Verona
282	2,041	Dunkirk City SD	Dunkirk
283	2,033	Ardsley UFSD	Ardsley
284	2,031	Rondout Valley Central SD	Accord
285	2,016	Albion Central SD	Albion
286	2,014	Franklin Square UFSD	Franklin Square
287	1,995	South Jefferson Central SD	Adams Center
288	1,981	Red Hook Central SD	Red Hook
289	1,970	Palmyra-Macedon Central SD	Palmyra
290	1,962	Ravena-Coeymans-Selkirk Ctrl SD	Ravena
291	1,961	Marlboro Central SD	Milton
292	1,953	Mount Pleasant Central SD	Thornwood
293	1,949	Peru Central SD	Peru
294	1,948	Beekmantown Central SD	West Chazy
295	1,911	Cohoes City SD	Cohoes
296	1,907	Edgemont UFSD	Scarsdale
297	1,895	Norwich City SD	Norwich
298	1,889	Kinderhook Central SD	Valatie
299	1,879	Phoenix Central SD	Phoenix
300	1,878	Cold Spring Hrbr Central SD	Cold Spring Hrbr
301	1,876	Hudson City SD	Hudson
302	1,864	Cobleskill-Richmondville Central SD	Cobleskill
303	1,860	East Hampton UFSD	East Hampton
304	1,857	Depew UFSD	Depew
305	1,854	Plattsburgh City SD	Plattsburgh
306	1,846	Springville-Griffith Institute CSD	Springville
307	1,845	Schalmont Central SD	Schenectady
308	1,839	Highland Central SD	Highland
309	1,838	Greenburgh Central SD	Hartsdale
310	1,830	Westhampton Bch UFSD	Westhampton Bch
311	1,821	East Aurora UFSD	East Aurora
312	1,820	Tonawanda City SD	Tonawanda
313	1,798	Chenango Valley Central SD	Binghamton
314	1,797	Johnstown City SD	Johnstown
315	1,793	Westhill Central SD	Syracuse
316	1,792	Irvington UFSD	Irvington
317	1,790	Broadalbin-Perth Central SD	Broadalbin
318	1,782	Oneonta City SD	Oneonta
319	1,781	Pleasantville UFSD	Pleasantville
320	1,776	Putnam Valley Central SD	Putnam Valley
321	1,769	East Williston UFSD	Old Westbury
322	1,754	Marcellus Central SD	Marcellus
323	1,751	Schuylerville Central SD	Schuylerville
324	1,748	Ellenville Central SD	Ellenville
325	1,747	Windsor Central SD	Windsor
326	1,741	Hornell City SD	Hornell
327	1,740	Lackawanna City SD	Lackawanna
328	1,730	Medina Central SD	Medina
329	1,728	Alden Central SD	Alden
330	1,724	Waterloo Central SD	Waterloo
331	1,714	Livonia Central SD	Livonia
332	1,711	Bronxville UFSD	Bronxville
332	1,711	Croton-Harmon UFSD	Croton on Hdsn
334	1,682	Center Moriches UFSD	Center Moriches
335	1,678	Newfane Central SD	Burt
336	1,674	Charter School for Applied Tech	Buffalo
336	1,674	Malverne UFSD	Malverne
338	1,670	New Hyde Pk-Garden City Pk UFSD	New Hyde Park
339	1,667	Oyster Bay-East Norwich Central SD	Oyster Bay
340	1,658	Babylon UFSD	Babylon
340	1,658	Ogdensburg City SD	Ogdensburg
342	1,646	Gouverneur Central SD	Gouverneur
343	1,640	Dryden Central SD	Dryden
344	1,635	Waverly Central SD	Waverly
345	1,632	Liberty Central SD	Liberty
346	1,631	Phelps-Clifton Springs Central SD	Clifton Springs
347	1,617	Catskill Central SD	Catskill
348	1,613	Southampton UFSD	Southampton
349	1,594	Hastings-On-Hudson UFSD	Hastings on Hdsn
350	1,584	Susquehanna Valley Central SD	Conklin
351	1,583	Bath Central SD	Bath
352	1,578	Rye Neck UFSD	Mamaroneck
353	1,568	Dansville Central SD	Dansville
354	1,567	Fredonia Central SD	Fredonia
355	1,560	Chenango Forks Central SD	Binghamton
356	1,555	Salmon River Central SD	Fort Covington
357	1,552	General Brown Central SD	Dexter
358	1,551	Briarcliff Mnr UFSD	Briarcliff Mnr
359	1,544	Solvay UFSD	Solvay
360	1,543	Eden Central SD	Eden
361	1,531	Valhalla UFSD	Valhalla
362	1,528	Cazenovia Central SD	Cazenovia
363	1,514	Merrick UFSD	Merrick
364	1,509	Penn Yan Central SD	Penn Yan
365	1,505	Spackenkill UFSD	Poughkeepsie

Male Students

Rank	Percent	District Name	City
1	73.2	NYC Special Schools - District 75	New York
2	59.0	Orange-Ulster Boces	Goshen
3	54.7	Chenango Forks Central SD	Binghamton
4	54.4	Roosevelt UFSD	Roosevelt
5	54.1	Susquehanna Valley Central SD	Conklin
6	53.7	Lansingburgh Central SD	Troy
7	53.6	West Hempstead UFSD	West Hempstead
8	53.5	Mineola UFSD	Mineola
8	53.5	NYC Geographic District # 7	Bronx
8	53.5	Southampton UFSD	Southampton
8	53.5	Wallkill Central SD	Wallkill
12	53.4	Kinderhook Central SD	Valatie
13	53.3	Amityville UFSD	Amityville
14	53.2	Deer Park UFSD	Deer Park
14	53.2	Lackawanna City SD	Lackawanna
16	53.1	Ballston Spa Central SD	Ballston Spa
16	53.1	Eden Central SD	Eden
16	53.1	Farmingdale UFSD	Farmingdale
16	53.1	Jericho UFSD	Jericho
16	53.1	Malone Central SD	Malone
16	53.1	Westhampton Bch UFSD	Westhampton Bch
22	53.0	Hewlett-Woodmere UFSD	Woodmere
22	53.0	Owego-Apalachin Central SD	Owego
22	53.0	Shoreham-Wading River Central SD	Shoreham
25	52.9	NYC Geographic District #11	Bronx
25	52.9	NYC Geographic District #24	Corona
27	52.8	Fredonia Central SD	Fredonia
27	52.8	NYC Geographic District #23	Brooklyn
27	52.8	Pleasantville UFSD	Pleasantville
30	52.7	Ardsley UFSD	Ardsley
30	52.7	Briarcliff Mnr UFSD	Briarcliff Mnr
30	52.7	Hornell City SD	Hornell
30	52.7	Miller Place UFSD	Miller Place
30	52.7	NYC Geographic District #14	Brooklyn
30	52.7	NYC Geographic District #20	Brooklyn
30	52.7	Syosset Central SD	Syosset
30	52.7	Windsor Central SD	Windsor
38	52.6	Cobleskill-Richmondville Central SD	Cobleskill
38	52.6	Lawrence UFSD	Lawrence
40	52.5	Chappaqua Central SD	Chappaqua
40	52.5	Cheektowaga Central SD	Cheektowaga
40	52.5	Lewiston-Porter Central SD	Youngstown
40	52.5	NYC Geographic District #16	Brooklyn
40	52.5	NYC Geographic District #19	Brooklyn
40	52.5	Northport-East Northport UFSD	Northport
40	52.5	Ravena-Coeymans-Selkirk Ctrl SD	Ravena
40	52.5	Roslyn UFSD	Roslyn
48	52.4	Beekmantown Central SD	West Chazy
48	52.4	East Islip UFSD	Islip Terrace
48	52.4	Hampton Bays UFSD	Hampton Bays
48	52.4	Malverne UFSD	Malverne
48	52.4	Pine Bush Central SD	Pine Bush
53	52.3	Brockport Central SD	Brockport
53	52.3	Center Moriches UFSD	Center Moriches
53	52.3	Dunkirk City SD	Dunkirk
53	52.3	Homer Central SD	Homer
53	52.3	Irvington UFSD	Irvington
53	52.3	NYC Geographic District #27	Ozone Park
53	52.3	Scotia-Glenville Central SD	Scotia
53	52.3	South Huntington UFSD	Huntington Stn
61	52.2	Cortland City SD	Cortland
61	52.2	Fulton City SD	Fulton
61	52.2	Hempstead UFSD	Hempstead
61	52.2	Hicksville UFSD	Hicksville
61	52.2	Lynbrook UFSD	Lynbrook
61	52.2	Ossining UFSD	Ossining
61	52.2	Schenectady City SD	Schenectady
61	52.2	Sherrill City SD	Verona
61	52.2	Spencerport Central SD	Spencerport
70	52.1	Brentwood UFSD	Brentwood
70	52.1	East Williston UFSD	Old Westbury
70	52.1	General Brown Central SD	Dexter
70	52.1	Half Hollow Hills Central SD	Dix Hills
70	52.1	Huntington UFSD	Huntington Stn
70	52.1	NYC Geographic District # 5	New York
70	52.1	Ogdensburg City SD	Ogdensburg
70	52.1	Port Jervis City SD	Port Jervis
70	52.1	Rondout Valley Central SD	Accord
70	52.1	Rye City SD	Rye
80	52.0	Bay Shore UFSD	Bay Shore
80	52.0	Cazenovia Central SD	Cazenovia
80	52.0	Clarkstown Central SD	New City
80	52.0	Connetquot Central SD	Bohemia
80	52.0	Freeport UFSD	Freeport
80	52.0	Hauppauge UFSD	Hauppauge
80	52.0	Ithaca City SD	Ithaca
80	52.0	Marcellus Central SD	Marcellus
80	52.0	Mount Vernon SD	Mount Vernon
80	52.0	Plattsburgh City SD	Plattsburgh
80	52.0	West Islip UFSD	West Islip
91	51.9	Baldwinsville Central SD	Baldwinsville
91	51.9	Jamestown City SD	Jamestown
91	51.9	Middle Country Central SD	Centereach
91	51.9	New Rochelle City SD	New Rochelle
91	51.9	NYC Geographic District # 6	New York
91	51.9	Niagara-Wheatfield Central SD	Niagara Falls
91	51.9	Pelham UFSD	Pelham
91	51.9	Rome City SD	Rome
91	51.9	Valley Stream Central High SD	Valley Stream
91	51.9	Yonkers City SD	Yonkers
101	51.8	Bath Central SD	Bath
101	51.8	East Ramapo CSD (Spring Valley)	Spring Valley
101	51.8	Elmira City SD	Elmira
101	51.8	Johnstown City SD	Johnstown
101	51.8	Manhasset UFSD	Manhasset
101	51.8	Marlboro Central SD	Milton
101	51.8	Newburgh City SD	Newburgh
101	51.8	Newfane Central SD	Burt
101	51.8	Olean City SD	Olean
101	51.8	Oswego City SD	Oswego
101	51.8	Phoenix Central SD	Phoenix
101	51.8	Plainview-Old Bethpage Central SD	Plainview
101	51.8	Starpoint Central SD	Lockport
101	51.8	Syracuse City SD	Syracuse
115	51.7	Batavia City SD	Batavia
115	51.7	Bedford Central SD	Bedford
115	51.7	Binghamton City SD	Binghamton
115	51.7	Cohoes City SD	Cohoes
115	51.7	Eastchester UFSD	Eastchester
115	51.7	Jamesville-Dewitt Central SD	Dewitt
115	51.7	North Colonie CSD	Latham
115	51.7	Poughkeepsie City SD	Poughkeepsie
115	51.7	Putnam Valley Central SD	Putnam Valley
115	51.7	Schalmont Central SD	Schenectady
115	51.7	Wappingers Central SD	Wappingers Fls
126	51.6	Bronxville UFSD	Bronxville
126	51.6	Fairport Central SD	Fairport
126	51.6	Glen Cove City SD	Glen Cove
126	51.6	Gouverneur Central SD	Gouverneur
126	51.6	Great Neck UFSD	Great Neck
126	51.6	Hyde Park Central SD	Hyde Park
126	51.6	Mount Pleasant Central SD	Thornwood
126	51.6	Mount Sinai UFSD	Mount Sinai
126	51.6	North Syracuse Central SD	North Syracuse
126	51.6	Queensbury UFSD	Queensbury
126	51.6	Riverhead Central SD	Riverhead
126	51.6	West Genesee Central SD	Camillus
126	51.6	West Seneca Central SD	West Seneca
139	51.5	Canandaigua City SD	Canandaigua
139	51.5	Catskill Central SD	Catskill
139	51.5	Cold Spring Hrbr Central SD	Cold Spring Hrbr
139	51.5	Edgemont UFSD	Scarsdale
139	51.5	Hastings-On-Hudson UFSD	Hastings on Hdsn
139	51.5	Haverstraw-Stony Point CSD	Garnerville
139	51.5	Herricks UFSD	New Hyde Park
139	51.5	Honeoye Falls-Lima Central SD	Honeoye Falls

Note: This section only includes districts with 1,500 or more students; All categories are ranked from high to low

139	51.5	New Hartford Central SD	New Hartford
139	51.5	NYC Geographic District #31	Staten Island
139	51.5	North Tonawanda City SD	North Tonawanda
139	51.5	Norwich City SD	Norwich
139	51.5	Oceanside UFSD	Oceanside
139	51.5	Rye Neck UFSD	Mamaroneck
139	51.5	Schuylerville Central SD	Schuylerville
139	51.5	S Glens Fls Central SD	S Glens Fls
139	51.5	Uniondale UFSD	Uniondale
139	51.5	New York City Public Schools	New York
157	51.4	Albany City SD	Albany
157	51.4	Central Islip UFSD	Central Islip
157	51.4	Central Square Central SD	Central Square
157	51.4	Depew UFSD	Depew
157	51.4	Eastport-South Manor CSD	Manorville
157	51.4	Elwood UFSD	Greenlawn
157	51.4	Hamburg Central SD	Hamburg
157	51.4	Hilton Central SD	Hilton
157	51.4	Middletown City SD	Middletown
157	51.4	NYC Geographic District #13	Brooklyn
157	51.4	NYC Geographic District #21	Brooklyn
157	51.4	North Babylon UFSD	North Babylon
157	51.4	Peru Central SD	Peru
157	51.4	Red Hook Central SD	Red Hook
157	51.4	Rochester City SD	Rochester
157	51.4	Vestal Central SD	Vestal
157	51.4	Waverly Central SD	Waverly
174	51.3	Amherst Central SD	Amherst
174	51.3	Bethlehem Central SD	Delmar
174	51.3	Carmel Central SD	Patterson
174	51.3	East Irondequoit Central SD	Rochester
174	51.3	Hudson City SD	Hudson
174	51.3	Iroquois Central SD	Elma
174	51.3	Kenmore-Tonawanda UFSD	Buffalo
174	51.3	Merrick UFSD	Merrick
174	51.3	NYC Geographic District #26	Bayside
174	51.3	Peekskill City SD	Peekskill
174	51.3	Rockville Ctr UFSD	Rockville Ctr
174	51.3	Shenendehowa Central SD	Clifton Park
174	51.3	Somers Central SD	Somers
174	51.3	South Country Central SD	East Patchogue
174	51.3	Sweet Home Central SD	Amherst
189	51.2	Alden Central SD	Alden
189	51.2	Amsterdam City SD	Amsterdam
189	51.2	Auburn City SD	Auburn
189	51.2	Bayport-Blue Point UFSD	Bayport
189	51.2	Brewster Central SD	Brewster
189	51.2	Broadalbin-Perth Central SD	Broadalbin
189	51.2	Carthage Central SD	Carthage
189	51.2	Churchville-Chili Central SD	Churchville
189	51.2	Levittown UFSD	Levittown
189	51.2	Lindenhurst UFSD	Lindenhurst
189	51.2	Longwood Central SD	Middle Island
189	51.2	Medina Central SD	Medina
189	51.2	Monroe-Woodbury Central SD	Central Valley
189	51.2	Monticello Central SD	Monticello
189	51.2	NYC Geographic District # 9	Bronx
189	51.2	NYC Geographic District #10	Bronx
189	51.2	NYC Geographic District #29	Queens Village
189	51.2	Seaford UFSD	Seaford
189	51.2	Sewanhaka Central High SD	Floral Park
189	51.2	Springville-Griffith Institute CSD	Springville
189	51.2	Wayne Central SD	Ontario Center
210	51.1	Buffalo City SD	Buffalo
210	51.1	East Syracuse-Minoa Central SD	East Syracuse
210	51.1	Frontier Central SD	Hamburg
210	51.1	Glens Falls City SD	Glens Falls
210	51.1	Goshen Central SD	Goshen
210	51.1	Horseheads Central SD	Horseheads
210	51.1	New Paltz Central SD	New Paltz
210	51.1	NYC Geographic District # 8	Bronx
210	51.1	NYC Geographic District #25	Flushing
210	51.1	Phelps-Clifton Springs Central SD	Clifton Springs
210	51.1	Warwick Valley Central SD	Warwick
210	51.1	Washingtonville Central SD	Washingtonville
210	51.1	West Irondequoit Central SD	Rochester
223	51.0	Baldwin UFSD	Baldwin
223	51.0	Camden Central SD	Camden
223	51.0	Dryden Central SD	Dryden
223	51.0	Gloversville City SD	Gloversville
223	51.0	Lockport City SD	Lockport
223	51.0	Mahopac Central SD	Mahopac
223	51.0	NYC Geographic District # 1	New York
223	51.0	NYC Geographic District #22	Brooklyn
223	51.0	Palmyra-Macedon Central SD	Palmyra
223	51.0	Saugerties Central SD	Saugerties
223	51.0	Yorkshire-Pioneer Central SD	Yorkshire
223	51.0	Yorktown Central SD	Yorktown Hgts
235	50.9	Chittenango Central SD	Chittenango
235	50.9	Copiague UFSD	Copiague
235	50.9	Corning City SD	Painted Post
235	50.9	Elmont UFSD	Elmont
235	50.9	Greenburgh Central SD	Hartsdale
235	50.9	Indian River Central SD	Philadelphia
235	50.9	Lakeland Central SD	Shrub Oak
235	50.9	Minisink Valley Central SD	Slate Hill
235	50.9	NYC Geographic District #12	Bronx
235	50.9	Plainedge UFSD	N Massapequa
235	50.9	Salmon River Central SD	Fort Covington
235	50.9	Three Village Central SD	Stony Brook
235	50.9	Valley Stream 13 UFSD	Valley Stream
235	50.9	Webster Central SD	Webster
235	50.9	William Floyd UFSD	Mastic Beach
250	50.8	Central Valley CSD At Ilion-Mohawk	Ilion
250	50.8	Commack UFSD	East Northport
250	50.8	East Meadow UFSD	Westbury
250	50.8	Ellenville Central SD	Ellenville
250	50.8	Greece Central SD	Rochester
250	50.8	Kingston City SD	Kingston
250	50.8	Liverpool Central SD	Liverpool
250	50.8	Locust Valley Central SD	Locust Valley
250	50.8	Long Beach City SD	Long Beach
250	50.8	Mamaroneck UFSD	Mamaroneck
250	50.8	Massena Central SD	Massena
250	50.8	NYC Geographic District #30	Long Isl City
250	50.8	Nyack UFSD	Nyack
250	50.8	Orchard Park Central SD	West Seneca
250	50.8	Penn Yan Central SD	Penn Yan
250	50.8	Sayville UFSD	Sayville
250	50.8	South Colonie Central SD	Albany
250	50.8	Watertown City SD	Watertown
268	50.7	Arlington Central SD	Lagrangeville
268	50.7	Dansville Central SD	Dansville
268	50.7	Garden City UFSD	Garden City
268	50.7	Geneva City SD	Geneva
268	50.7	Islip UFSD	Islip
268	50.7	Kings Park Central SD	Kings Park
268	50.7	Oyster Bay-East Norwich Central SD	Oyster Bay
268	50.7	Troy City SD	Troy
268	50.7	Whitesboro Central SD	Yorkville
268	50.7	Williamsville Central SD	East Amherst
268	50.7	Wyandanch UFSD	Wyandanch
279	50.6	Clarence Central SD	Clarence
279	50.6	East Aurora UFSD	East Aurora
279	50.6	Fayetteville-Manlius Central SD	Manlius
279	50.6	Lancaster Central SD	Lancaster
279	50.6	Livonia Central SD	Livonia
279	50.6	Niagara Falls City SD	Niagara Falls
279	50.6	Port Chester-Rye UFSD	Port Chester
279	50.6	Port Washington UFSD	Port Washington
279	50.6	Smithtown Central SD	Smithtown
279	50.6	Waterloo Central SD	Waterloo
289	50.5	Bellmore-Merrick Central High SD	North Merrick
289	50.5	Bethpage UFSD	Bethpage
289	50.5	Grand Island Central SD	Grand Island
289	50.5	Hudson Falls Central SD	Fort Edward
289	50.5	NYC Geographic District #18	Brooklyn
289	50.5	Pearl River UFSD	Pearl River
289	50.5	Valley Central SD (Montgomery)	Montgomery
289	50.5	Victor Central SD	Victor
289	50.5	Westbury UFSD	Old Westbury
298	50.4	Albion Central SD	Albion
298	50.4	Averill Park Central SD	Averill Park
298	50.4	Massapequa UFSD	Massapequa
298	50.4	Mexico Central SD	Mexico
298	50.4	NYC Geographic District #28	Jamaica
298	50.4	Niskayuna Central SD	Schenectady
298	50.4	Penfield Central SD	Rochester
298	50.4	Saratoga Spgs City SD	Saratoga Spgs
298	50.4	Union-Endicott Central SD	Endicott
298	50.4	Utica City SD	Utica
308	50.3	Babylon UFSD	Babylon
308	50.3	Byram Hills Central SD	Armonk
308	50.3	Evans-Brant Central SD (Lake Shore)	Angola
308	50.3	Guilderland Central SD	Guilderland Center
308	50.3	Liberty Central SD	Liberty
308	50.3	Patchogue-Medford UFSD	Patchogue
308	50.3	Rotterdam-Mohonasen Central SD	Schenectady
308	50.3	Tonawanda City SD	Tonawanda
316	50.2	Chenango Valley Central SD	Binghamton
316	50.2	NYC Geographic District #32	Brooklyn
316	50.2	Rush-Henrietta Central SD	Henrietta
316	50.2	Sachem Central SD	Lake Ronkonkoma
316	50.2	Spackenkill UFSD	Poughkeepsie
316	50.2	West Babylon UFSD	West Babylon
322	50.1	East Greenbush Central SD	East Greenbush
322	50.1	Franklin Square UFSD	Franklin Square
322	50.1	Hendrick Hudson Central SD	Montrose
322	50.1	North Shore Central SD	Sea Cliff
322	50.1	Solvay UFSD	Solvay
327	50.0	Brookhaven-Comsewogue UFSD	Port Jefferson Sta
327	50.0	Burnt Hills-Ballston Lake Central SD	Scotia
327	50.0	Cheektowaga-Maryvale UFSD	Cheektowaga
327	50.0	Gates-Chili Central SD	Rochester
327	50.0	Island Trees UFSD	Levittown
332	49.9	Maine-Endwell Central SD	Endwell
332	49.9	NYC Geographic District #15	Brooklyn
332	49.9	Newark Central SD	Newark
332	49.9	Oneonta City SD	Oneonta
332	49.9	Scarsdale UFSD	Scarsdale
332	49.9	South Orangetown Central SD	Blauvelt
332	49.9	UFSD of the Tarrytowns	Sleepy Hollow
339	49.8	Harborfields Central SD	Greenlawn
339	49.8	Highland Central SD	Highland
339	49.8	Oneida City SD	Oneida
339	49.8	South Jefferson Central SD	Adams Center
339	49.8	White Plains City SD	White Plains
344	49.7	Rocky Point UFSD	Rocky Point
345	49.6	Harrison Central SD	Harrison
345	49.6	Pittsford Central SD	Pittsford
345	49.6	Wantagh UFSD	Wantagh
348	49.5	Cornwall Central SD	Cornwall on Hdsn
348	49.5	Westhill Central SD	Syracuse
350	49.4	Beacon City SD	Beacon
350	49.4	NYC Geographic District #17	Brooklyn
352	49.3	New Hyde Pk-Garden City Pk UFSD	New Hyde Park
352	49.3	North Bellmore UFSD	Bellmore
354	49.2	East Hampton UFSD	East Hampton
354	49.2	Nanuet UFSD	Nanuet
356	49.1	Brighton Central SD	Rochester
356	49.1	Johnson City Central SD	Johnson City
358	49.0	Valhalla UFSD	Valhalla
359	48.8	Croton-Harmon UFSD	Croton on Hdsn
359	48.8	Katonah-Lewisboro UFSD	Goldens Bridge
359	48.8	NYC Geographic District # 4	New York
362	48.7	Ramapo Central SD (Suffern)	Hillburn
363	47.7	Charter School for Applied Tech	Buffalo
363	47.7	NYC Geographic District # 2	New York
365	46.9	NYC Geographic District # 3	New York

Female Students

Rank	Percent	District Name	City
1	53.1	NYC Geographic District # 3	New York
2	52.3	Charter School for Applied Tech	Buffalo
2	52.3	NYC Geographic District # 2	New York
4	51.3	Ramapo Central SD (Suffern)	Hillburn
5	51.2	Croton-Harmon UFSD	Croton on Hdsn
5	51.2	Katonah-Lewisboro UFSD	Goldens Bridge
5	51.2	NYC Geographic District # 4	New York
8	51.0	Valhalla UFSD	Valhalla
9	50.9	Brighton Central SD	Rochester
9	50.9	Johnson City Central SD	Johnson City
11	50.8	East Hampton UFSD	East Hampton
11	50.8	Nanuet UFSD	Nanuet
13	50.7	New Hyde Pk-Garden City Pk UFSD	New Hyde Park
13	50.7	North Bellmore UFSD	Bellmore
15	50.6	Beacon City SD	Beacon
15	50.6	NYC Geographic District #17	Brooklyn
17	50.5	Cornwall Central SD	Cornwall on Hdsn
17	50.5	Westhill Central SD	Syracuse
19	50.4	Harrison Central SD	Harrison
19	50.4	Pittsford Central SD	Pittsford
19	50.4	Wantagh UFSD	Wantagh
22	50.3	Rocky Point UFSD	Rocky Point
23	50.2	Harborfields Central SD	Greenlawn
23	50.2	Highland Central SD	Highland
23	50.2	Oneida City SD	Oneida
23	50.2	South Jefferson Central SD	Adams Center
23	50.2	White Plains City SD	White Plains
28	50.1	Maine-Endwell Central SD	Endwell

Note: This section only includes districts with 1,500 or more students; All categories are ranked from high to low

28	50.1	NYC Geographic District #15	Brooklyn
28	50.1	Newark Central SD	Newark
28	50.1	Oneonta City SD	Oneonta
28	50.1	Scarsdale UFSD	Scarsdale
28	50.1	South Orangetown Central SD	Blauvelt
28	50.1	UFSD of the Tarrytowns	Sleepy Hollow
35	50.0	Brookhaven-Comsewogue UFSD	Port Jefferson Sta
35	50.0	Burnt Hills-Ballston Lake Central SD	Scotia
35	50.0	Cheektowaga-Maryvale UFSD	Cheektowaga
35	50.0	Gates-Chili Central SD	Rochester
35	50.0	Island Trees UFSD	Levittown
40	49.9	East Greenbush Central SD	East Greenbush
40	49.9	Franklin Square UFSD	Franklin Square
40	49.9	Hendrick Hudson Central SD	Montrose
40	49.9	North Shore Central SD	Sea Cliff
40	49.9	Solvay UFSD	Solvay
45	49.8	Chenango Valley Central SD	Binghamton
45	49.8	NYC Geographic District #32	Brooklyn
45	49.8	Rush-Henrietta Central SD	Henrietta
45	49.8	Sachem Central SD	Lake Ronkonkoma
45	49.8	Spackenkill UFSD	Poughkeepsie
45	49.8	West Babylon UFSD	West Babylon
51	49.7	Babylon UFSD	Babylon
51	49.7	Byram Hills Central SD	Armonk
51	49.7	Evans-Brant Central SD (Lake Shore)	Angola
51	49.7	Guilderland Central SD	Guilderland Center
51	49.7	Liberty Central SD	Liberty
51	49.7	Patchogue-Medford UFSD	Patchogue
51	49.7	Rotterdam-Mohonasen Central SD	Schenectady
51	49.7	Tonawanda City SD	Tonawanda
59	49.6	Albion Central SD	Albion
59	49.6	Averill Park Central SD	Averill Park
59	49.6	Massapequa UFSD	Massapequa
59	49.6	Mexico Central SD	Mexico
59	49.6	NYC Geographic District #28	Jamaica
59	49.6	Niskayuna Central SD	Schenectady
59	49.6	Penfield Central SD	Rochester
59	49.6	Saratoga Spgs City SD	Saratoga Spgs
59	49.6	Union-Endicott Central SD	Endicott
59	49.6	Utica City SD	Utica
69	49.5	Bellmore-Merrick Central High SD	North Merrick
69	49.5	Bethpage UFSD	Bethpage
69	49.5	Grand Island Central SD	Grand Island
69	49.5	Hudson Falls Central SD	Fort Edward
69	49.5	NYC Geographic District #18	Brooklyn
69	49.5	Pearl River UFSD	Pearl River
69	49.5	Valley Central SD (Montgomery)	Montgomery
69	49.5	Victor Central SD	Victor
69	49.5	Westbury UFSD	Old Westbury
78	49.4	Clarence Central SD	Clarence
78	49.4	East Aurora UFSD	East Aurora
78	49.4	Fayetteville-Manlius Central SD	Manlius
78	49.4	Lancaster Central SD	Lancaster
78	49.4	Livonia Central SD	Livonia
78	49.4	Niagara Falls City SD	Niagara Falls
78	49.4	Port Chester-Rye UFSD	Port Chester
78	49.4	Port Washington UFSD	Port Washington
78	49.4	Smithtown Central SD	Smithtown
78	49.4	Waterloo Central SD	Waterloo
88	49.3	Arlington Central SD	Lagrangeville
88	49.3	Dansville Central SD	Dansville
88	49.3	Garden City UFSD	Garden City
88	49.3	Geneva City SD	Geneva
88	49.3	Islip UFSD	Islip
88	49.3	Kings Park Central SD	Kings Park
88	49.3	Oyster Bay-East Norwich Central SD	Oyster Bay
88	49.3	Troy City SD	Troy
88	49.3	Whitesboro Central SD	Yorkville
88	49.3	Williamsville Central SD	East Amherst
88	49.3	Wyandanch UFSD	Wyandanch
99	49.2	Central Valley CSD At Ilion-Mohawk	Ilion
99	49.2	Commack UFSD	East Northport
99	49.2	East Meadow UFSD	Westbury
99	49.2	Ellenville Central SD	Ellenville
99	49.2	Elmont UFSD	Elmont
99	49.2	Greece Central SD	Rochester
99	49.2	Kingston City SD	Kingston
99	49.2	Liverpool Central SD	Liverpool
99	49.2	Locust Valley Central SD	Locust Valley
99	49.2	Long Beach City SD	Long Beach
99	49.2	Mamaroneck UFSD	Mamaroneck
99	49.2	Massena Central SD	Massena
99	49.2	NYC Geographic District #30	Long Isl City
99	49.2	Nyack UFSD	Nyack
99	49.2	Orchard Park Central SD	West Seneca
99	49.2	Penn Yan Central SD	Penn Yan
99	49.2	Sayville UFSD	Sayville
99	49.2	South Colonie Central SD	Albany
99	49.2	Watertown City SD	Watertown
118	49.1	Chittenango Central SD	Chittenango
118	49.1	Copiague UFSD	Copiague
118	49.1	Corning City SD	Painted Post
118	49.1	Greenburgh Central SD	Hartsdale
118	49.1	Indian River Central SD	Philadelphia
118	49.1	Lakeland Central SD	Shrub Oak
118	49.1	Minisink Valley Central SD	Slate Hill
118	49.1	NYC Geographic District #12	Bronx
118	49.1	Plainedge UFSD	N Massapequa
118	49.1	Salmon River Central SD	Fort Covington
118	49.1	Three Village Central SD	Stony Brook
118	49.1	Valley Stream 13 UFSD	Valley Stream
118	49.1	Webster Central SD	Webster
118	49.1	William Floyd UFSD	Mastic Beach
132	49.0	Baldwin UFSD	Baldwin
132	49.0	Camden Central SD	Camden
132	49.0	Dryden Central SD	Dryden
132	49.0	Gloversville City SD	Gloversville
132	49.0	Lockport City SD	Lockport
132	49.0	Mahopac Central SD	Mahopac
132	49.0	NYC Geographic District # 1	New York
132	49.0	NYC Geographic District #22	Brooklyn
132	49.0	Palmyra-Macedon Central SD	Palmyra
132	49.0	Saugerties Central SD	Saugerties
132	49.0	Yorkshire-Pioneer Central SD	Yorkshire
132	49.0	Yorktown Central SD	Yorktown Hgts
144	48.9	Buffalo City SD	Buffalo
144	48.9	East Syracuse-Minoa Central SD	East Syracuse
144	48.9	Frontier Central SD	Hamburg
144	48.9	Glens Falls City SD	Glens Falls
144	48.9	Goshen Central SD	Goshen
144	48.9	Horseheads Central SD	Horseheads
144	48.9	New Paltz Central SD	New Paltz
144	48.9	NYC Geographic District # 8	Bronx
144	48.9	NYC Geographic District #25	Flushing
144	48.9	Phelps-Clifton Springs Central SD	Clifton Springs
144	48.9	Warwick Valley Central SD	Warwick
144	48.9	Washingtonville Central SD	Washingtonville
144	48.9	West Irondequoit Central SD	Rochester
157	48.8	Alden Central SD	Alden
157	48.8	Amsterdam City SD	Amsterdam
157	48.8	Auburn City SD	Auburn
157	48.8	Bayport-Blue Point UFSD	Bayport
157	48.8	Brewster Central SD	Brewster
157	48.8	Broadalbin-Perth Central SD	Broadalbin
157	48.8	Carthage Central SD	Carthage
157	48.8	Churchville-Chili Central SD	Churchville
157	48.8	Levittown UFSD	Levittown
157	48.8	Lindenhurst UFSD	Lindenhurst
157	48.8	Longwood Central SD	Middle Island
157	48.8	Medina Central SD	Medina
157	48.8	Monroe-Woodbury Central SD	Central Valley
157	48.8	Monticello Central SD	Monticello
157	48.8	NYC Geographic District # 9	Bronx
157	48.8	NYC Geographic District #10	Bronx
157	48.8	NYC Geographic District #29	Queens Village
157	48.8	Seaford UFSD	Seaford
157	48.8	Sewanhaka Central High SD	Floral Park
157	48.8	Springville-Griffith Institute CSD	Springville
157	48.8	Wayne Central SD	Ontario Center
178	48.7	Amherst Central SD	Amherst
178	48.7	Bethlehem Central SD	Delmar
178	48.7	Carmel Central SD	Patterson
178	48.7	East Irondequoit Central SD	Rochester
178	48.7	Hudson City SD	Hudson
178	48.7	Iroquois Central SD	Elma
178	48.7	Kenmore-Tonawanda UFSD	Buffalo
178	48.7	Merrick UFSD	Merrick
178	48.7	NYC Geographic District #26	Bayside
178	48.7	Peekskill City SD	Peekskill
178	48.7	Rockville Ctr UFSD	Rockville Ctr
178	48.7	Shenendehowa Central SD	Clifton Park
178	48.7	Somers Central SD	Somers
178	48.7	South Country Central SD	East Patchogue
178	48.7	Sweet Home Central SD	Amherst
193	48.6	Albany City SD	Albany
193	48.6	Central Islip UFSD	Central Islip
193	48.6	Central Square Central SD	Central Square
193	48.6	Depew UFSD	Depew
193	48.6	Eastport-South Manor CSD	Manorville
193	48.6	Elwood UFSD	Greenlawn
193	48.6	Hamburg Central SD	Hamburg
193	48.6	Hilton Central SD	Hilton
193	48.6	Middletown City SD	Middletown
193	48.6	NYC Geographic District #13	Brooklyn
193	48.6	NYC Geographic District #21	Brooklyn
193	48.6	North Babylon UFSD	North Babylon
193	48.6	Peru Central SD	Peru
193	48.6	Red Hook Central SD	Red Hook
193	48.6	Rochester City SD	Rochester
193	48.6	Vestal Central SD	Vestal
193	48.6	Waverly Central SD	Waverly
210	48.5	Canandaigua City SD	Canandaigua
210	48.5	Catskill Central SD	Catskill
210	48.5	Cold Spring Hrbr Central SD	Cold Spring Hrbr
210	48.5	Edgemont UFSD	Scarsdale
210	48.5	Hastings-On-Hudson UFSD	Hastings on Hdsn
210	48.5	Haverstraw-Stony Point CSD	Garnerville
210	48.5	Herricks UFSD	New Hyde Park
210	48.5	Honeoye Falls-Lima Central SD	Honeoye Falls
210	48.5	New Hartford Central SD	New Hartford
210	48.5	NYC Geographic District #31	Staten Island
210	48.5	North Tonawanda City SD	North Tonawanda
210	48.5	Norwich City SD	Norwich
210	48.5	Oceanside UFSD	Oceanside
210	48.5	Rye Neck UFSD	Mamaroneck
210	48.5	Schuylerville Central SD	Schuylerville
210	48.5	S Glens Fls Central SD	S Glens Fls
210	48.5	Uniondale UFSD	Uniondale
210	48.5	New York City Public Schools	New York
228	48.4	Bronxville UFSD	Bronxville
228	48.4	Fairport Central SD	Fairport
228	48.4	Glen Cove City SD	Glen Cove
228	48.4	Gouverneur Central SD	Gouverneur
228	48.4	Great Neck UFSD	Great Neck
228	48.4	Hyde Park Central SD	Hyde Park
228	48.4	Mount Pleasant Central SD	Thornwood
228	48.4	Mount Sinai UFSD	Mount Sinai
228	48.4	North Syracuse Central SD	North Syracuse
228	48.4	Queensbury UFSD	Queensbury
228	48.4	Riverhead Central SD	Riverhead
228	48.4	West Genesee Central SD	Camillus
228	48.4	West Seneca Central SD	West Seneca
241	48.3	Batavia City SD	Batavia
241	48.3	Bedford Central SD	Bedford
241	48.3	Binghamton City SD	Binghamton
241	48.3	Cohoes City SD	Cohoes
241	48.3	Eastchester UFSD	Eastchester
241	48.3	Jamesville-Dewitt Central SD	Dewitt
241	48.3	North Colonie CSD	Latham
241	48.3	Poughkeepsie City SD	Poughkeepsie
241	48.3	Putnam Valley Central SD	Putnam Valley
241	48.3	Schalmont Central SD	Schenectady
241	48.3	Wappingers Central SD	Wappingers Fls
252	48.2	Bath Central SD	Bath
252	48.2	East Ramapo CSD (Spring Valley)	Spring Valley
252	48.2	Elmira City SD	Elmira
252	48.2	Johnstown City SD	Johnstown
252	48.2	Manhasset UFSD	Manhasset
252	48.2	Marlboro Central SD	Milton
252	48.2	Newburgh City SD	Newburgh
252	48.2	Newfane Central SD	Burt
252	48.2	Olean City SD	Olean
252	48.2	Oswego City SD	Oswego
252	48.2	Phoenix Central SD	Phoenix
252	48.2	Plainview-Old Bethpage Central SD	Plainview
252	48.2	Starpoint Central SD	Lockport
252	48.2	Syracuse City SD	Syracuse
266	48.1	Baldwinsville Central SD	Baldwinsville
266	48.1	Jamestown City SD	Jamestown
266	48.1	Middle Country Central SD	Centereach
266	48.1	New Rochelle City SD	New Rochelle
266	48.1	NYC Geographic District # 6	New York
266	48.1	Niagara-Wheatfield Central SD	Niagara Falls
266	48.1	Pelham UFSD	Pelham
266	48.1	Rome City SD	Rome
266	48.1	Valley Stream Central High SD	Valley Stream
266	48.1	Yonkers City SD	Yonkers
276	48.0	Bay Shore UFSD	Bay Shore
276	48.0	Cazenovia Central SD	Cazenovia
276	48.0	Clarkstown Central SD	New City
276	48.0	Connetquot Central SD	Bohemia
276	48.0	Freeport UFSD	Freeport

Note: This section only includes districts with 1,500 or more students; All categories are ranked from high to low

Rank	Percent	District Name	City
276	48.0	Hauppauge UFSD	Hauppauge
276	48.0	Ithaca City SD	Ithaca
276	48.0	Marcellus Central SD	Marcellus
276	48.0	Mount Vernon SD	Mount Vernon
276	48.0	Plattsburgh City SD	Plattsburgh
276	48.0	West Islip UFSD	West Islip
287	47.9	Brentwood UFSD	Brentwood
287	47.9	East Williston UFSD	Old Westbury
287	47.9	General Brown Central SD	Dexter
287	47.9	Half Hollow Hills Central SD	Dix Hills
287	47.9	Huntington UFSD	Huntington Stn
287	47.9	NYC Geographic District # 5	New York
287	47.9	Ogdensburg City SD	Ogdensburg
287	47.9	Port Jervis City SD	Port Jervis
287	47.9	Rondout Valley Central SD	Accord
287	47.9	Rye City SD	Rye
297	47.8	Cortland City SD	Cortland
297	47.8	Fulton City SD	Fulton
297	47.8	Hempstead UFSD	Hempstead
297	47.8	Hicksville UFSD	Hicksville
297	47.8	Lynbrook UFSD	Lynbrook
297	47.8	Ossining UFSD	Ossining
297	47.8	Schenectady City SD	Schenectady
297	47.8	Sherrill City SD	Verona
297	47.8	Spencerport Central SD	Spencerport
306	47.7	Brockport Central SD	Brockport
306	47.7	Center Moriches UFSD	Center Moriches
306	47.7	Dunkirk City SD	Dunkirk
306	47.7	Homer Central SD	Homer
306	47.7	Irvington UFSD	Irvington
306	47.7	NYC Geographic District #27	Ozone Park
306	47.7	Scotia-Glenville Central SD	Scotia
306	47.7	South Huntington UFSD	Huntington Stn
314	47.6	Beekmantown Central SD	West Chazy
314	47.6	East Islip UFSD	Islip Terrace
314	47.6	Hampton Bays UFSD	Hampton Bays
314	47.6	Malverne UFSD	Malverne
314	47.6	Pine Bush Central SD	Pine Bush
319	47.5	Chappaqua Central SD	Chappaqua
319	47.5	Cheektowaga Central SD	Cheektowaga
319	47.5	Lewiston-Porter Central SD	Youngstown
319	47.5	NYC Geographic District #16	Brooklyn
319	47.5	NYC Geographic District #19	Brooklyn
319	47.5	Northport-East Northport UFSD	Northport
319	47.5	Ravena-Coeymans-Selkirk Ctrl SD	Ravena
319	47.5	Roslyn UFSD	Roslyn
327	47.4	Cobleskill-Richmondville Central SD	Cobleskill
327	47.4	Lawrence UFSD	Lawrence
329	47.3	Ardsley UFSD	Ardsley
329	47.3	Briarcliff Mnr UFSD	Briarcliff Mnr
329	47.3	Hornell City SD	Hornell
329	47.3	Miller Place UFSD	Miller Place
329	47.3	NYC Geographic District #14	Brooklyn
329	47.3	NYC Geographic District #20	Brooklyn
329	47.3	Syosset Central SD	Syosset
329	47.3	Windsor Central SD	Windsor
337	47.2	Fredonia Central SD	Fredonia
337	47.2	NYC Geographic District #23	Brooklyn
337	47.2	Pleasantville UFSD	Pleasantville
340	47.1	NYC Geographic District #11	Bronx
340	47.1	NYC Geographic District #24	Corona
342	47.0	Hewlett-Woodmere UFSD	Woodmere
342	47.0	Owego-Apalachin Central SD	Owego
342	47.0	Shoreham-Wading River Central SD	Shoreham
345	46.9	Ballston Spa Central SD	Ballston Spa
345	46.9	Eden Central SD	Eden
345	46.9	Farmingdale UFSD	Farmingdale
345	46.9	Jericho UFSD	Jericho
345	46.9	Malone Central SD	Malone
345	46.9	Westhampton Bch UFSD	Westhampton Bch
351	46.8	Deer Park UFSD	Deer Park
351	46.8	Lackawanna City SD	Lackawanna
353	46.7	Amityville UFSD	Amityville
354	46.6	Kinderhook Central SD	Valatie
355	46.5	Mineola UFSD	Mineola
355	46.5	NYC Geographic District # 7	Bronx
355	46.5	Southampton UFSD	Southampton
355	46.5	Wallkill Central SD	Wallkill
359	46.4	West Hempstead UFSD	West Hempstead
360	46.3	Lansingburgh Central SD	Troy
361	45.9	Susquehanna Valley Central SD	Conklin
362	45.6	Roosevelt UFSD	Roosevelt
363	45.3	Chenango Forks Central SD	Binghamton
364	41.0	Orange-Ulster Boces	Goshen
365	26.8	NYC Special Schools - District 75	New York

White Students

Rank	Percent	District Name	City
1	97.5	Ogdensburg City SD	Ogdensburg
2	97.1	South Jefferson Central SD	Adams Center
3	97.0	Bath Central SD	Bath
4	96.8	Marcellus Central SD	Marcellus
5	96.7	Eden Central SD	Eden
6	96.6	Malone Central SD	Malone
6	96.6	Waverly Central SD	Waverly
8	96.5	Gouverneur Central SD	Gouverneur
9	96.3	Alden Central SD	Alden
9	96.3	Beekmantown Central SD	West Chazy
11	96.2	Camden Central SD	Camden
11	96.2	East Aurora UFSD	East Aurora
11	96.2	Sherrill City SD	Verona
14	96.0	Yorkshire-Pioneer Central SD	Yorkshire
15	95.9	Homer Central SD	Homer
16	95.8	Ballston Spa Central SD	Ballston Spa
17	95.6	Livonia Central SD	Livonia
18	95.5	Phoenix Central SD	Phoenix
18	95.5	S Glens Fls Central SD	S Glens Fls
20	95.3	Mexico Central SD	Mexico
21	95.2	Central Square Central SD	Central Square
21	95.2	Hamburg Central SD	Hamburg
23	95.1	Iroquois Central SD	Elma
24	95.0	Cazenovia Central SD	Cazenovia
24	95.0	Starpoint Central SD	Lockport
26	94.9	Massapequa UFSD	Massapequa
27	94.7	Central Valley CSD At Ilion-Mohawk	Ilion
28	94.5	Burnt Hills-Ballston Lake Central SD	Scotia
28	94.5	General Brown Central SD	Dexter
28	94.5	Owego-Apalachin Central SD	Owego
31	94.4	Averill Park Central SD	Averill Park
32	94.3	Springville-Griffith Institute CSD	Springville
33	94.2	Newfane Central SD	Burt
33	94.2	Orchard Park Central SD	West Seneca
33	94.2	Queensbury UFSD	Queensbury
33	94.2	Schuylerville Central SD	Schuylerville
37	94.1	Kinderhook Central SD	Valatie
38	94.0	Peru Central SD	Peru
39	93.9	Broadalbin-Perth Central SD	Broadalbin
39	93.9	Cobleskill-Richmondville Central SD	Cobleskill
41	93.8	Dansville Central SD	Dansville
41	93.8	Lancaster Central SD	Lancaster
43	93.7	Chittenango Central SD	Chittenango
44	93.6	Whitesboro Central SD	Yorkville
45	93.5	Chenango Forks Central SD	Binghamton
45	93.5	Windsor Central SD	Windsor
47	93.4	Wayne Central SD	Ontario Center
48	93.1	Johnstown City SD	Johnstown
49	92.8	Honeoye Falls-Lima Central SD	Honeoye Falls
50	92.7	Garden City UFSD	Garden City
50	92.7	Lewiston-Porter Central SD	Youngstown
52	92.6	Eastport-South Manor CSD	Manorville
53	92.4	Cold Spring Hrbr Central SD	Cold Spring Hrbr
54	92.3	Hudson Falls Central SD	Fort Edward
55	92.2	Frontier Central SD	Hamburg
55	92.2	Phelps-Clifton Springs Central SD	Clifton Springs
57	92.1	Maine-Endwell Central SD	Endwell
57	92.1	Plainedge UFSD	N Massapequa
59	92.0	Fulton City SD	Fulton
59	92.0	Oneida City SD	Oneida
59	92.0	Scotia-Glenville Central SD	Scotia
62	91.9	Kings Park Central SD	Kings Park
62	91.9	Penn Yan Central SD	Penn Yan
62	91.9	Wantagh UFSD	Wantagh
65	91.8	Dryden Central SD	Dryden
65	91.8	North Tonawanda City SD	North Tonawanda
65	91.8	Norwich City SD	Norwich
68	91.7	Susquehanna Valley Central SD	Conklin
69	91.6	West Genesee Central SD	Camillus
70	91.5	Clarence Central SD	Clarence
71	91.3	West Seneca Central SD	West Seneca
72	91.2	Saratoga Spgs City SD	Saratoga Spgs
73	91.1	Sayville UFSD	Sayville
73	91.1	Seaford UFSD	Seaford
73	91.1	Tonawanda City SD	Tonawanda
76	91.0	Hilton Central SD	Hilton
76	91.0	Somers Central SD	Somers
78	90.9	Palmyra-Macedon Central SD	Palmyra
79	90.8	Hornell City SD	Hornell
80	90.7	Oswego City SD	Oswego
81	90.6	Schalmont Central SD	Schenectady
82	90.5	Chenango Valley Central SD	Binghamton
82	90.5	Shoreham-Wading River Central SD	Shoreham
82	90.5	Westhill Central SD	Syracuse
85	90.4	Waterloo Central SD	Waterloo
86	90.2	Bayport-Blue Point UFSD	Bayport
87	90.1	Baldwinsville Central SD	Baldwinsville
87	90.1	Canandaigua City SD	Canandaigua
89	90.0	Byram Hills Central SD	Armonk
89	90.0	Horseheads Central SD	Horseheads
91	89.8	Depew UFSD	Depew
91	89.8	Plattsburgh City SD	Plattsburgh
91	89.8	Victor Central SD	Victor
94	89.3	Red Hook Central SD	Red Hook
95	89.1	Grand Island Central SD	Grand Island
96	89.0	East Syracuse-Minoa Central SD	East Syracuse
97	88.8	Smithtown Central SD	Smithtown
97	88.8	West Islip UFSD	West Islip
99	88.7	Northport-East Northport UFSD	Northport
100	88.5	Rondout Valley Central SD	Accord
101	88.3	Gloversville City SD	Gloversville
101	88.3	Rocky Point UFSD	Rocky Point
103	88.2	Bethlehem Central SD	Delmar
103	88.2	Corning City SD	Painted Post
103	88.2	Miller Place UFSD	Miller Place
106	87.9	Fairport Central SD	Fairport
106	87.9	Merrick UFSD	Merrick
108	87.8	Cortland City SD	Cortland
108	87.8	Rotterdam-Mohonasen Central SD	Schenectady
110	87.7	Glens Falls City SD	Glens Falls
111	87.6	Bellmore-Merrick Central High SD	North Merrick
112	87.1	Webster Central SD	Webster
113	86.5	Mount Sinai UFSD	Mount Sinai
113	86.5	North Syracuse Central SD	North Syracuse
115	86.0	Mount Pleasant Central SD	Thornwood
116	85.7	Bronxville UFSD	Bronxville
117	85.3	Commack UFSD	East Northport
117	85.3	New Hartford Central SD	New Hartford
119	85.2	Fayetteville-Manlius Central SD	Manlius
119	85.2	Penfield Central SD	Rochester
121	85.1	North Shore Central SD	Sea Cliff
121	85.1	Ravena-Coeymans-Selkirk Ctrl SD	Ravena
123	84.7	Pearl River UFSD	Pearl River
123	84.7	Rye City SD	Rye
125	84.6	Massena Central SD	Massena
126	84.5	Katonah-Lewisboro UFSD	Goldens Bridge
127	84.4	Brockport Central SD	Brockport
127	84.4	Spencerport Central SD	Spencerport
127	84.4	Three Village Central SD	Stony Brook
130	84.0	Vestal Central SD	Vestal
131	83.9	Fredonia Central SD	Fredonia
132	83.8	Connetquot Central SD	Bohemia
133	83.7	Churchville-Chili Central SD	Churchville
133	83.7	East Greenbush Central SD	East Greenbush
135	83.5	Rome City SD	Rome
136	83.3	Saugerties Central SD	Saugerties
137	83.2	Pleasantville UFSD	Pleasantville
138	82.8	Kenmore-Tonawanda UFSD	Buffalo
139	82.7	Niagara-Wheatfield Central SD	Niagara Falls
139	82.7	Solvay UFSD	Solvay
141	82.3	Shenendehowa Central SD	Clifton Park
142	82.1	Putnam Valley Central SD	Putnam Valley
143	82.0	Babylon UFSD	Babylon
143	82.0	Evans-Brant Central SD (Lake Shore)	Angola
143	82.0	Harborfields Central SD	Greenlawn
143	82.0	Hauppauge UFSD	Hauppauge
147	81.8	Warwick Valley Central SD	Warwick
148	81.6	Olean City SD	Olean
149	81.5	Auburn City SD	Auburn
149	81.5	Cheektowaga-Maryvale UFSD	Cheektowaga
151	81.3	Mahopac Central SD	Mahopac
151	81.3	Oneonta City SD	Oneonta
153	81.2	East Islip UFSD	Islip Terrace
154	81.1	Chappaqua Central SD	Chappaqua
155	80.6	Guilderland Central SD	Guilderland Center
155	80.6	Sachem Central SD	Lake Ronkonkoma
157	80.3	Briarcliff Mnr UFSD	Briarcliff Mnr
158	80.2	Cohoes City SD	Cohoes
158	80.2	Pittsford Central SD	Pittsford
160	79.4	Orange-Ulster Boces	Goshen
161	79.3	Locust Valley Central SD	Locust Valley
162	79.2	Medina Central SD	Medina

Note: This section only includes districts with 1,500 or more students; All categories are ranked from high to low

163	79.1	Minisink Valley Central SD	Slate Hill
163	79.1	Oceanside UFSD	Oceanside
165	79.0	Liverpool Central SD	Liverpool
165	79.0	New Paltz Central SD	New Paltz
167	78.8	Plainview-Old Bethpage Central SD	Plainview
168	78.6	Williamsville Central SD	East Amherst
169	78.5	Center Moriches UFSD	Center Moriches
170	78.4	Yorktown Central SD	Yorktown Hgts
171	78.1	Rockville Ctr UFSD	Rockville Ctr
172	78.0	East Williston UFSD	Old Westbury
172	78.0	North Bellmore UFSD	Bellmore
174	77.8	Niskayuna Central SD	Schenectady
175	77.7	Lynbrook UFSD	Lynbrook
176	77.5	Bethpage UFSD	Bethpage
177	77.1	Albion Central SD	Albion
177	77.1	South Orangetown Central SD	Blauvelt
179	77.0	Jamesville-Dewitt Central SD	Dewitt
180	76.7	Marlboro Central SD	Milton
180	76.7	Union-Endicott Central SD	Endicott
182	76.5	Batavia City SD	Batavia
183	76.0	Arlington Central SD	Lagrangeville
184	75.7	Croton-Harmon UFSD	Croton on Hdsn
184	75.7	Lindenhurst UFSD	Lindenhurst
186	75.6	West Irondequoit Central SD	Rochester
187	75.5	Lockport City SD	Lockport
188	75.4	Island Trees UFSD	Levittown
189	75.2	Levittown UFSD	Levittown
190	75.1	Manhasset UFSD	Manhasset
190	75.1	Newark Central SD	Newark
190	75.1	Roslyn UFSD	Roslyn
193	75.0	Wappingers Central SD	Wappingers Fls
194	74.8	Elmira City SD	Elmira
194	74.8	Hastings-On-Hudson UFSD	Hastings on Hdsn
196	74.7	Carthage Central SD	Carthage
196	74.7	Irvington UFSD	Irvington
198	74.6	North Colonie CSD	Latham
199	74.4	Port Jervis City SD	Port Jervis
200	74.2	Highland Central SD	Highland
201	74.0	Watertown City SD	Watertown
202	73.9	Westhampton Bch UFSD	Westhampton Bch
203	73.7	Middle Country Central SD	Centereach
204	73.5	Cornwall Central SD	Cornwall on Hdsn
205	73.4	Carmel Central SD	Patterson
206	73.2	South Colonie Central SD	Albany
207	73.1	Goshen Central SD	Goshen
208	73.0	Oyster Bay-East Norwich Central SD	Oyster Bay
209	72.7	Eastchester UFSD	Eastchester
210	72.5	Lakeland Central SD	Shrub Oak
211	72.4	Catskill Central SD	Catskill
212	71.7	Mamaroneck UFSD	Mamaroneck
213	71.4	Scarsdale UFSD	Scarsdale
214	71.3	West Babylon UFSD	West Babylon
215	71.0	Franklin Square UFSD	Franklin Square
216	70.9	Hyde Park Central SD	Hyde Park
216	70.9	Wallkill Central SD	Wallkill
218	70.8	Amherst Central SD	Amherst
219	70.7	Brighton Central SD	Rochester
220	70.4	Brookhaven-Comsewogue UFSD	Port Jefferson Sta
221	70.2	Harrison Central SD	Harrison
222	70.1	Pelham UFSD	Pelham
222	70.1	Washingtonville Central SD	Washingtonville
224	69.9	Farmingdale UFSD	Farmingdale
225	69.8	Elwood UFSD	Greenlawn
226	69.4	Greece Central SD	Rochester
227	68.3	Islip UFSD	Islip
228	68.1	Ramapo Central SD (Suffern)	Hillburn
229	67.9	Brewster Central SD	Brewster
230	67.8	Clarkstown Central SD	New City
230	67.8	Sweet Home Central SD	Amherst
232	67.6	Rye Neck UFSD	Mamaroneck
233	67.5	Ardsley UFSD	Ardsley
234	67.4	Pine Bush Central SD	Pine Bush
235	67.3	Syosset Central SD	Syosset
236	66.9	Valley Central SD (Montgomery)	Montgomery
237	66.8	Jamestown City SD	Jamestown
237	66.8	Lackawanna City SD	Lackawanna
239	66.7	Lansingburgh Central SD	Troy
240	66.6	Hewlett-Woodmere UFSD	Woodmere
241	66.4	Johnson City Central SD	Johnson City
242	66.2	Port Washington UFSD	Port Washington
243	66.0	Hendrick Hudson Central SD	Montrose
244	65.7	Ithaca City SD	Ithaca
245	65.5	Monroe-Woodbury Central SD	Central Valley
246	64.3	Rush-Henrietta Central SD	Henrietta
247	64.2	Gates-Chili Central SD	Rochester
248	64.1	Nanuet UFSD	Nanuet
249	63.6	Half Hollow Hills Central SD	Dix Hills
250	63.5	Spackenkill UFSD	Poughkeepsie
251	63.3	Indian River Central SD	Philadelphia
252	63.0	Mineola UFSD	Mineola
253	61.9	Bedford Central SD	Bedford
254	60.2	Long Beach City SD	Long Beach
254	60.2	Valhalla UFSD	Valhalla
256	60.1	Kingston City SD	Kingston
257	58.7	East Meadow UFSD	Westbury
258	57.1	Patchogue-Medford UFSD	Patchogue
259	56.9	Great Neck UFSD	Great Neck
260	56.8	East Irondequoit Central SD	Rochester
261	56.7	Edgemont UFSD	Scarsdale
262	55.9	William Floyd UFSD	Mastic Beach
263	53.9	Longwood Central SD	Middle Island
264	53.7	Cheektowaga Central SD	Cheektowaga
265	52.6	Southampton UFSD	Southampton
266	52.2	Ellenville Central SD	Ellenville
267	51.9	Jericho UFSD	Jericho
268	51.7	Geneva City SD	Geneva
269	51.5	Liberty Central SD	Liberty
270	50.8	NYC Geographic District #31	Staten Island
271	50.7	Deer Park UFSD	Deer Park
272	50.6	Amsterdam City SD	Amsterdam
273	49.8	Nyack UFSD	Nyack
274	49.7	South Huntington UFSD	Huntington Stn
275	49.5	North Babylon UFSD	North Babylon
276	49.2	Binghamton City SD	Binghamton
277	48.6	Monticello Central SD	Monticello
278	48.0	Hudson City SD	Hudson
279	47.9	Riverhead Central SD	Riverhead
280	47.7	Niagara Falls City SD	Niagara Falls
281	47.6	Troy City SD	Troy
282	46.6	Hampton Bays UFSD	Hampton Bays
283	46.5	Beacon City SD	Beacon
284	46.3	South Country Central SD	East Patchogue
285	46.1	East Hampton UFSD	East Hampton
286	45.6	Huntington UFSD	Huntington Stn
287	41.2	Dunkirk City SD	Dunkirk
288	40.5	Hicksville UFSD	Hicksville
289	39.5	New Hyde Pk-Garden City Pk UFSD	New Hyde Park
290	38.3	Sewanhaka Central High SD	Floral Park
291	37.2	Herricks UFSD	New Hyde Park
292	37.1	West Hempstead UFSD	West Hempstead
293	36.7	Utica City SD	Utica
294	35.3	Bay Shore UFSD	Bay Shore
295	34.8	Valley Stream 13 UFSD	Valley Stream
296	33.8	Salmon River Central SD	Fort Covington
297	33.2	UFSD of the Tarrytowns	Sleepy Hollow
298	32.7	Haverstraw-Stony Point CSD	Garnerville
299	32.3	Glen Cove City SD	Glen Cove
300	32.2	NYC Geographic District #21	Brooklyn
301	30.9	Charter School for Applied Tech	Buffalo
302	30.4	Schenectady City SD	Schenectady
303	29.8	NYC Geographic District # 3	New York
304	29.0	New Rochelle City SD	New Rochelle
305	28.9	NYC Geographic District #22	Brooklyn
306	27.4	NYC Geographic District #20	Brooklyn
307	27.0	Ossining UFSD	Ossining
308	25.7	White Plains City SD	White Plains
309	25.6	NYC Geographic District #15	Brooklyn
310	25.5	Valley Stream Central High SD	Valley Stream
311	24.3	Syracuse City SD	Syracuse
312	23.3	NYC Geographic District # 2	New York
313	22.8	Lawrence UFSD	Lawrence
314	22.7	Newburgh City SD	Newburgh
315	22.0	Baldwin UFSD	Baldwin
316	21.5	Buffalo City SD	Buffalo
317	21.4	Albany City SD	Albany
318	20.0	Malverne UFSD	Malverne
319	19.7	Middletown City SD	Middletown
320	18.0	NYC Geographic District #26	Bayside
321	17.8	Yonkers City SD	Yonkers
322	17.2	Copiague UFSD	Copiague
322	17.2	NYC Geographic District # 1	New York
324	16.8	Port Chester-Rye UFSD	Port Chester
325	15.8	NYC Geographic District #28	Jamaica
326	15.4	NYC Geographic District #30	Long Isl City
327	14.6	NYC Geographic District #25	Flushing
328	14.5	New York City Public Schools	New York
329	14.2	NYC Geographic District #24	Corona
330	13.8	NYC Special Schools - District 75	New York
331	13.3	Greenburgh Central SD	Hartsdale
332	11.2	NYC Geographic District #13	Brooklyn
333	11.1	NYC Geographic District #14	Brooklyn
334	10.4	Poughkeepsie City SD	Poughkeepsie
334	10.4	Rochester City SD	Rochester
336	10.2	NYC Geographic District #27	Ozone Park
337	9.8	Peekskill City SD	Peekskill
338	8.5	Elmont UFSD	Elmont
339	7.5	NYC Geographic District #11	Bronx
340	7.0	Amityville UFSD	Amityville
341	6.7	Freeport UFSD	Freeport
342	6.1	Central Islip UFSD	Central Islip
343	6.0	NYC Geographic District # 8	Bronx
344	5.8	NYC Geographic District #10	Bronx
345	5.7	Brentwood UFSD	Brentwood
346	5.4	East Ramapo CSD (Spring Valley)	Spring Valley
347	5.1	Mount Vernon SD	Mount Vernon
348	3.7	NYC Geographic District # 4	New York
348	3.7	NYC Geographic District # 5	New York
348	3.7	NYC Geographic District # 6	New York
351	3.2	Hempstead UFSD	Hempstead
352	2.0	Westbury UFSD	Old Westbury
353	1.9	NYC Geographic District #17	Brooklyn
353	1.9	NYC Geographic District #29	Queens Village
355	1.7	NYC Geographic District #18	Brooklyn
356	1.5	NYC Geographic District #32	Brooklyn
357	1.4	NYC Geographic District #19	Brooklyn
358	1.2	NYC Geographic District #12	Bronx
358	1.2	NYC Geographic District #16	Brooklyn
360	1.0	NYC Geographic District # 7	Bronx
360	1.0	NYC Geographic District #23	Brooklyn
362	0.9	Wyandanch UFSD	Wyandanch
363	0.8	NYC Geographic District # 9	Bronx
364	0.6	Uniondale UFSD	Uniondale
365	0.1	Roosevelt UFSD	Roosevelt

Black Students

Rank	Percent	District Name	City
1	89.7	NYC Geographic District #18	Brooklyn
2	80.6	NYC Geographic District #17	Brooklyn
3	79.1	NYC Geographic District #16	Brooklyn
4	77.4	NYC Geographic District #23	Brooklyn
5	75.3	Mount Vernon SD	Mount Vernon
6	67.8	NYC Geographic District #29	Queens Village
7	60.2	Rochester City SD	Rochester
8	58.6	Roosevelt UFSD	Roosevelt
9	56.2	Wyandanch UFSD	Wyandanch
10	54.6	Malverne UFSD	Malverne
11	54.4	Poughkeepsie City SD	Poughkeepsie
12	52.1	NYC Geographic District # 5	New York
13	51.8	NYC Geographic District #13	Brooklyn
14	50.3	Buffalo City SD	Buffalo
15	50.1	Albany City SD	Albany
15	50.1	NYC Geographic District #19	Brooklyn
17	49.6	Syracuse City SD	Syracuse
18	48.0	Elmont UFSD	Elmont
19	46.8	Uniondale UFSD	Uniondale
20	46.1	Amityville UFSD	Amityville
21	45.8	Baldwin UFSD	Baldwin
22	43.0	East Ramapo CSD (Spring Valley)	Spring Valley
23	42.9	Greenburgh Central SD	Hartsdale
24	42.4	NYC Geographic District #11	Bronx
25	39.2	NYC Special Schools - District 75	New York
26	37.4	NYC Geographic District #22	Brooklyn
27	34.6	Niagara Falls City SD	Niagara Falls
28	34.1	Hempstead UFSD	Hempstead
29	33.8	Schenectady City SD	Schenectady
30	32.5	Troy City SD	Troy
31	31.9	Valley Stream Central High SD	Valley Stream
32	31.5	Cheektowaga Central SD	Cheektowaga
33	30.8	Charter School for Applied Tech	Buffalo
34	30.5	NYC Geographic District # 9	Bronx
35	29.3	Westbury UFSD	Old Westbury
36	29.2	Freeport UFSD	Freeport
37	28.8	Peekskill City SD	Peekskill
38	28.4	New York City Public Schools	New York
39	27.2	NYC Geographic District # 7	Bronx
39	27.2	Sewanhaka Central High SD	Floral Park
41	26.9	NYC Geographic District #12	Bronx
42	26.6	NYC Geographic District # 4	New York
43	26.3	NYC Geographic District #27	Ozone Park
44	26.2	Binghamton City SD	Binghamton

Note: This section only includes districts with 1,500 or more students; All categories are ranked from high to low

45	26.0	Newburgh City SD	Newburgh
46	25.8	Copiague UFSD	Copiague
47	25.6	Utica City SD	Utica
48	25.0	NYC Geographic District # 3	New York
48	25.0	NYC Geographic District #28	Jamaica
50	24.8	Middletown City SD	Middletown
50	24.8	NYC Geographic District #14	Brooklyn
52	24.2	NYC Geographic District # 8	Bronx
53	23.8	Hudson City SD	Hudson
54	23.2	North Babylon UFSD	North Babylon
55	22.9	New Rochelle City SD	New Rochelle
55	22.9	Valley Stream 13 UFSD	Valley Stream
57	22.8	Lawrence UFSD	Lawrence
58	22.5	Central Islip UFSD	Central Islip
59	21.3	Monticello Central SD	Monticello
60	20.8	Bay Shore UFSD	Bay Shore
61	20.7	South Country Central SD	East Patchogue
62	20.5	Yonkers City SD	Yonkers
63	19.9	NYC Geographic District #32	Brooklyn
64	19.8	Sweet Home Central SD	Amherst
65	19.3	Nyack UFSD	Nyack
66	19.2	Beacon City SD	Beacon
67	19.1	East Irondequoit Central SD	Rochester
68	18.9	West Hempstead UFSD	West Hempstead
69	17.8	Lackawanna City SD	Lackawanna
69	17.8	Longwood Central SD	Middle Island
69	17.8	NYC Geographic District # 1	New York
72	17.7	NYC Geographic District #10	Bronx
73	17.5	Deer Park UFSD	Deer Park
74	17.4	Lansingburgh Central SD	Troy
75	17.1	NYC Geographic District # 2	New York
76	16.8	Gates-Chili Central SD	Rochester
77	16.5	NYC Geographic District #21	Brooklyn
78	16.1	Kingston City SD	Kingston
79	16.0	NYC Geographic District #15	Brooklyn
80	15.6	Elmira City SD	Elmira
81	15.5	Riverhead Central SD	Riverhead
82	15.4	Rush-Henrietta Central SD	Henrietta
83	15.1	White Plains City SD	White Plains
84	14.8	Amherst Central SD	Amherst
85	14.3	William Floyd UFSD	Mastic Beach
86	13.7	Geneva City SD	Geneva
87	13.3	Greece Central SD	Rochester
87	13.3	Lockport City SD	Lockport
89	13.2	NYC Geographic District #31	Staten Island
90	13.1	Johnson City Central SD	Johnson City
91	12.8	NYC Geographic District #26	Bayside
92	12.6	Orange-Ulster Boces	Goshen
93	12.5	Ossining UFSD	Ossining
94	12.4	Brentwood UFSD	Brentwood
95	12.2	Catskill Central SD	Catskill
95	12.2	Haverstraw-Stony Point CSD	Garnerville
97	12.1	Hyde Park Central SD	Hyde Park
98	12.0	Half Hollow Hills Central SD	Dix Hills
99	11.2	Long Beach City SD	Long Beach
100	11.1	Indian River Central SD	Philadelphia
101	10.5	Ellenville Central SD	Ellenville
101	10.5	Glen Cove City SD	Glen Cove
101	10.5	Pine Bush Central SD	Pine Bush
104	10.4	Albion Central SD	Albion
105	10.2	Liberty Central SD	Liberty
106	10.0	Ithaca City SD	Ithaca
107	9.9	Valley Central SD (Montgomery)	Montgomery
108	9.4	NYC Geographic District #25	Flushing
109	9.3	Rome City SD	Rome
110	9.1	South Huntington UFSD	Huntington Stn
111	9.0	Spackenkill UFSD	Poughkeepsie
111	9.0	Watertown City SD	Watertown
111	9.0	West Irondequoit Central SD	Rochester
114	8.9	Huntington UFSD	Huntington Stn
114	8.9	Port Jervis City SD	Port Jervis
116	8.8	Cohoes City SD	Cohoes
117	8.4	Jamesville-Dewitt Central SD	Dewitt
118	8.2	Auburn City SD	Auburn
118	8.2	Cheektowaga-Maryvale UFSD	Cheektowaga
120	8.1	Valhalla UFSD	Valhalla
121	8.0	Liverpool Central SD	Liverpool
122	7.7	Elwood UFSD	Greenlawn
122	7.7	Newark Central SD	Newark
124	7.6	Dunkirk City SD	Dunkirk
124	7.6	NYC Geographic District # 6	New York
126	7.4	Oneonta City SD	Oneonta
127	7.3	Carthage Central SD	Carthage
127	7.3	NYC Geographic District #30	Long Isl City
127	7.3	Washingtonville Central SD	Washingtonville
130	7.2	Highland Central SD	Highland
130	7.2	South Colonie Central SD	Albany
132	7.1	Churchville-Chili Central SD	Churchville
133	7.0	Union-Endicott Central SD	Endicott
134	6.9	Arlington Central SD	Lagrangeville
134	6.9	Batavia City SD	Batavia
134	6.9	Marlboro Central SD	Milton
137	6.8	Monroe-Woodbury Central SD	Central Valley
137	6.8	Olean City SD	Olean
139	6.7	Brighton Central SD	Rochester
140	6.6	Plattsburgh City SD	Plattsburgh
141	6.5	Hewlett-Woodmere UFSD	Woodmere
142	6.4	Wallkill Central SD	Wallkill
143	6.3	Cornwall Central SD	Cornwall on Hdsn
143	6.3	Kenmore-Tonawanda UFSD	Buffalo
143	6.3	Port Chester-Rye UFSD	Port Chester
146	6.2	West Babylon UFSD	West Babylon
147	6.1	Lakeland Central SD	Shrub Oak
148	6.0	Rockville Ctr UFSD	Rockville Ctr
149	5.9	Farmingdale UFSD	Farmingdale
150	5.7	Islip UFSD	Islip
150	5.7	Pelham UFSD	Pelham
150	5.7	Wappingers Central SD	Wappingers Fls
153	5.5	Medina Central SD	Medina
154	5.3	North Colonie CSD	Latham
155	5.2	Amsterdam City SD	Amsterdam
156	5.1	Ramapo Central SD (Suffern)	Hillburn
157	5.0	New Paltz Central SD	New Paltz
158	4.9	Center Moriches UFSD	Center Moriches
158	4.9	Spencerport Central SD	Spencerport
158	4.9	Warwick Valley Central SD	Warwick
161	4.7	Hendrick Hudson Central SD	Montrose
161	4.7	Minisink Valley Central SD	Slate Hill
161	4.7	UFSD of the Tarrytowns	Sleepy Hollow
164	4.6	Patchogue-Medford UFSD	Patchogue
165	4.5	Fairport Central SD	Fairport
165	4.5	Gloversville City SD	Gloversville
165	4.5	Irvington UFSD	Irvington
165	4.5	Nanuet UFSD	Nanuet
165	4.5	Southampton UFSD	Southampton
170	4.4	Brockport Central SD	Brockport
170	4.4	East Syracuse-Minoa Central SD	East Syracuse
170	4.4	Goshen Central SD	Goshen
173	4.3	East Hampton UFSD	East Hampton
174	4.1	Ardsley UFSD	Ardsley
174	4.1	Cortland City SD	Cortland
174	4.1	Harborfields Central SD	Greenlawn
174	4.1	Jamestown City SD	Jamestown
178	4.0	Hornell City SD	Hornell
179	3.9	Glens Falls City SD	Glens Falls
180	3.8	Clarkstown Central SD	New City
180	3.8	North Syracuse Central SD	North Syracuse
182	3.7	Middle Country Central SD	Centereach
182	3.7	NYC Geographic District #20	Brooklyn
182	3.7	Niskayuna Central SD	Schenectady
182	3.7	Ravena-Coeymans-Selkirk Ctrl SD	Ravena
182	3.7	Williamsville Central SD	East Amherst
187	3.6	Babylon UFSD	Babylon
187	3.6	Bedford Central SD	Bedford
189	3.5	Central Valley CSD At Ilion-Mohawk	Ilion
189	3.5	East Meadow UFSD	Westbury
189	3.5	Scotia-Glenville Central SD	Scotia
189	3.5	Waterloo Central SD	Waterloo
193	3.4	Guilderland Central SD	Guilderland Center
193	3.4	Penfield Central SD	Rochester
193	3.4	Rotterdam-Mohonasen Central SD	Schenectady
193	3.4	Webster Central SD	Webster
193	3.4	Westhill Central SD	Syracuse
198	3.3	Roslyn UFSD	Roslyn
199	3.2	Croton-Harmon UFSD	Croton on Hdsn
199	3.2	Depew UFSD	Depew
199	3.2	Oyster Bay-East Norwich Central SD	Oyster Bay
202	3.1	Corning City SD	Painted Post
202	3.1	NYC Geographic District #24	Corona
202	3.1	Rye Neck UFSD	Mamaroneck
205	3.0	Rondout Valley Central SD	Accord
205	3.0	Solvay UFSD	Solvay
207	2.8	Brewster Central SD	Brewster
207	2.8	Fayetteville-Manlius Central SD	Manlius
207	2.8	Lindenhurst UFSD	Lindenhurst
207	2.8	Pittsford Central SD	Pittsford
211	2.7	Hastings-On-Hudson UFSD	Hastings on Hdsn
211	2.7	Hauppauge UFSD	Hauppauge
211	2.7	Hicksville UFSD	Hicksville
211	2.7	Lynbrook UFSD	Lynbrook
211	2.7	Norwich City SD	Norwich
211	2.7	Vestal Central SD	Vestal
217	2.6	Kinderhook Central SD	Valatie
217	2.6	Manhasset UFSD	Manhasset
217	2.6	West Genesee Central SD	Camillus
217	2.6	Westhampton Bch UFSD	Westhampton Bch
221	2.5	East Greenbush Central SD	East Greenbush
221	2.5	Mamaroneck UFSD	Mamaroneck
221	2.5	Mineola UFSD	Mineola
221	2.5	Niagara-Wheatfield Central SD	Niagara Falls
221	2.5	Putnam Valley Central SD	Putnam Valley
221	2.5	Shenendehowa Central SD	Clifton Park
221	2.5	West Seneca Central SD	West Seneca
228	2.4	Bethlehem Central SD	Delmar
228	2.4	Carmel Central SD	Patterson
228	2.4	Sachem Central SD	Lake Ronkonkoma
228	2.4	Victor Central SD	Victor
232	2.3	Red Hook Central SD	Red Hook
232	2.3	Susquehanna Valley Central SD	Conklin
234	2.2	Broadalbin-Perth Central SD	Broadalbin
234	2.2	Jericho UFSD	Jericho
234	2.2	North Bellmore UFSD	Bellmore
234	2.2	Saratoga Spgs City SD	Saratoga Spgs
234	2.2	Saugerties Central SD	Saugerties
239	2.1	Briarcliff Mnr UFSD	Briarcliff Mnr
239	2.1	Chenango Valley Central SD	Binghamton
239	2.1	Maine-Endwell Central SD	Endwell
239	2.1	Mount Sinai UFSD	Mount Sinai
239	2.1	Peru Central SD	Peru
239	2.1	Windsor Central SD	Windsor
239	2.1	Yorktown Central SD	Yorktown Hgts
246	2.0	Canandaigua City SD	Canandaigua
246	2.0	Evans-Brant Central SD (Lake Shore)	Angola
246	2.0	New Hartford Central SD	New Hartford
249	1.9	Owego-Apalachin Central SD	Owego
249	1.9	Schuylerville Central SD	Schuylerville
251	1.8	Brookhaven-Comsewogue UFSD	Port Jefferson Sta
251	1.8	Dansville Central SD	Dansville
251	1.8	Grand Island Central SD	Grand Island
251	1.8	Horseheads Central SD	Horseheads
251	1.8	Oswego City SD	Oswego
251	1.8	Schalmont Central SD	Schenectady
257	1.7	Ballston Spa Central SD	Ballston Spa
257	1.7	Bellmore-Merrick Central High SD	North Merrick
257	1.7	Chenango Forks Central SD	Binghamton
257	1.7	Eastchester UFSD	Eastchester
257	1.7	Franklin Square UFSD	Franklin Square
257	1.7	Harrison Central SD	Harrison
257	1.7	Miller Place UFSD	Miller Place
257	1.7	North Tonawanda City SD	North Tonawanda
257	1.7	Phelps-Clifton Springs Central SD	Clifton Springs
257	1.7	Pleasantville UFSD	Pleasantville
257	1.7	Port Washington UFSD	Port Washington
268	1.6	Eastport-South Manor CSD	Manorville
268	1.6	Edgemont UFSD	Scarsdale
268	1.6	Fulton City SD	Fulton
268	1.6	Johnstown City SD	Johnstown
268	1.6	Lewiston-Porter Central SD	Youngstown
268	1.6	Oceanside UFSD	Oceanside
268	1.6	South Orangetown Central SD	Blauvelt
268	1.6	Tonawanda City SD	Tonawanda
276	1.5	Bath Central SD	Bath
276	1.5	Beekmantown Central SD	West Chazy
276	1.5	Connetquot Central SD	Bohemia
276	1.5	East Islip UFSD	Islip Terrace
276	1.5	Fredonia Central SD	Fredonia
276	1.5	Rye City SD	Rye
276	1.5	Shoreham-Wading River Central SD	Shoreham
276	1.5	Three Village Central SD	Stony Brook
276	1.5	Wayne Central SD	Ontario Center
285	1.4	Baldwinsville Central SD	Baldwinsville
285	1.4	General Brown Central SD	Dexter
285	1.4	Hilton Central SD	Hilton
285	1.4	Mahopac Central SD	Mahopac
285	1.4	Starpoint Central SD	Lockport
290	1.3	Bayport-Blue Point UFSD	Bayport
290	1.3	Cobleskill-Richmondville Central SD	Cobleskill
290	1.3	Hampton Bays UFSD	Hampton Bays
290	1.3	Island Trees UFSD	Levittown
290	1.3	Massena Central SD	Massena
290	1.3	Oneida City SD	Oneida
296	1.2	Great Neck UFSD	Great Neck

Note: This section only includes districts with 1,500 or more students; All categories are ranked from high to low

296	1.2	Hudson Falls Central SD	Fort Edward
296	1.2	Merrick UFSD	Merrick
296	1.2	Ogdensburg City SD	Ogdensburg
296	1.2	Orchard Park Central SD	West Seneca
296	1.2	Pearl River UFSD	Pearl River
296	1.2	Queensbury UFSD	Queensbury
296	1.2	Scarsdale UFSD	Scarsdale
304	1.1	Chittenango Central SD	Chittenango
304	1.1	Commack UFSD	East Northport
304	1.1	Frontier Central SD	Hamburg
304	1.1	Lancaster Central SD	Lancaster
304	1.1	Somers Central SD	Somers
304	1.1	S Glens Fls Central SD	S Glens Fls
304	1.1	Whitesboro Central SD	Yorkville
311	1.0	Alden Central SD	Alden
311	1.0	Burnt Hills-Ballston Lake Central SD	Scotia
311	1.0	Cazenovia Central SD	Cazenovia
311	1.0	Clarence Central SD	Clarence
311	1.0	Dryden Central SD	Dryden
311	1.0	Gouverneur Central SD	Gouverneur
311	1.0	Levittown UFSD	Levittown
311	1.0	Locust Valley Central SD	Locust Valley
311	1.0	North Shore Central SD	Sea Cliff
320	0.9	Chappaqua Central SD	Chappaqua
320	0.9	Mount Pleasant Central SD	Thornwood
320	0.9	Smithtown Central SD	Smithtown
320	0.9	Yorkshire-Pioneer Central SD	Yorkshire
324	0.8	Honeoye Falls-Lima Central SD	Honeoye Falls
324	0.8	Livonia Central SD	Livonia
324	0.8	Mexico Central SD	Mexico
324	0.8	Palmyra-Macedon Central SD	Palmyra
324	0.8	Penn Yan Central SD	Penn Yan
324	0.8	Rocky Point UFSD	Rocky Point
324	0.8	Seaford UFSD	Seaford
324	0.8	Sherrill City SD	Verona
332	0.7	Camden Central SD	Camden
332	0.7	Central Square Central SD	Central Square
332	0.7	East Aurora UFSD	East Aurora
332	0.7	East Williston UFSD	Old Westbury
332	0.7	Homer Central SD	Homer
332	0.7	Katonah-Lewisboro UFSD	Goldens Bridge
332	0.7	Malone Central SD	Malone
332	0.7	New Hyde Pk-Garden City Pk UFSD	New Hyde Park
332	0.7	Northport-East Northport UFSD	Northport
332	0.7	Waverly Central SD	Waverly
342	0.6	Averill Park Central SD	Averill Park
342	0.6	Byram Hills Central SD	Armonk
342	0.6	Cold Spring Hrbr Central SD	Cold Spring Hrbr
342	0.6	Garden City UFSD	Garden City
342	0.6	Herricks UFSD	New Hyde Park
342	0.6	Sayville UFSD	Sayville
342	0.6	South Jefferson Central SD	Adams Center
349	0.5	Hamburg Central SD	Hamburg
349	0.5	Iroquois Central SD	Elma
349	0.5	Kings Park Central SD	Kings Park
349	0.5	Newfane Central SD	Burt
349	0.5	Syosset Central SD	Syosset
354	0.4	Bethpage UFSD	Bethpage
354	0.4	Bronxville UFSD	Bronxville
354	0.4	Eden Central SD	Eden
354	0.4	Phoenix Central SD	Phoenix
354	0.4	Springville-Griffith Institute CSD	Springville
359	0.3	Massapequa UFSD	Massapequa
359	0.3	Plainedge UFSD	N Massapequa
359	0.3	Plainview-Old Bethpage Central SD	Plainview
359	0.3	West Islip UFSD	West Islip
363	0.2	Marcellus Central SD	Marcellus
364	0.1	Salmon River Central SD	Fort Covington
364	0.1	Wantagh UFSD	Wantagh

Asian Students

Rank	Percent	District Name	City
1	55.7	Herricks UFSD	New Hyde Park
2	51.0	NYC Geographic District #26	Bayside
3	46.5	NYC Geographic District #25	Flushing
4	43.0	Jericho UFSD	Jericho
5	41.8	New Hyde Pk-Garden City Pk UFSD	New Hyde Park
5	41.8	NYC Geographic District #20	Brooklyn
7	32.6	Great Neck UFSD	Great Neck
8	30.4	Edgemont UFSD	Scarsdale
9	29.3	Hicksville UFSD	Hicksville
9	29.3	NYC Geographic District #28	Jamaica
11	27.9	Syosset Central SD	Syosset
12	25.5	NYC Geographic District #21	Brooklyn
13	23.4	NYC Geographic District # 2	New York
14	23.3	NYC Geographic District #27	Ozone Park
15	22.3	NYC Geographic District #30	Long Isl City
16	21.6	NYC Geographic District # 1	New York
17	19.7	NYC Geographic District #24	Corona
18	18.9	NYC Geographic District #13	Brooklyn
19	18.4	Sewanhaka Central High SD	Floral Park
20	18.2	NYC Geographic District #22	Brooklyn
21	17.6	Valley Stream Central High SD	Valley Stream
22	17.5	East Meadow UFSD	Westbury
23	16.9	Ardsley UFSD	Ardsley
24	16.4	East Williston UFSD	Old Westbury
25	16.1	Scarsdale UFSD	Scarsdale
26	15.9	Manhasset UFSD	Manhasset
27	15.6	Plainview-Old Bethpage Central SD	Plainview
28	15.5	Utica City SD	Utica
29	15.4	Nanuet UFSD	Nanuet
29	15.4	New York City Public Schools	New York
31	15.3	NYC Geographic District #15	Brooklyn
31	15.3	Valley Stream 13 UFSD	Valley Stream
33	15.2	Schenectady City SD	Schenectady
34	15.1	Elmont UFSD	Elmont
35	14.9	Roslyn UFSD	Roslyn
36	14.8	Niskayuna Central SD	Schenectady
37	14.7	NYC Geographic District #29	Queens Village
38	14.0	Spackenkill UFSD	Poughkeepsie
39	13.6	Clarkstown Central SD	New City
40	13.2	North Colonie CSD	Latham
41	12.8	Brighton Central SD	Rochester
42	12.7	Ithaca City SD	Ithaca
43	12.4	Half Hollow Hills Central SD	Dix Hills
44	11.8	Mineola UFSD	Mineola
45	11.7	Eastchester UFSD	Eastchester
46	11.6	Port Washington UFSD	Port Washington
47	11.2	Rush-Henrietta Central SD	Henrietta
48	11.0	Briarcliff Mnr UFSD	Briarcliff Mnr
48	11.0	Hewlett-Woodmere UFSD	Woodmere
50	10.9	Irvington UFSD	Irvington
51	10.7	Harrison Central SD	Harrison
52	10.5	Deer Park UFSD	Deer Park
52	10.5	Williamsville Central SD	East Amherst
54	10.4	Guilderland Central SD	Guilderland Center
55	10.0	Hudson City SD	Hudson
56	9.8	Chappaqua Central SD	Chappaqua
57	9.5	Pittsford Central SD	Pittsford
58	9.3	Valhalla UFSD	Valhalla
59	9.1	Bethpage UFSD	Bethpage
60	8.9	Three Village Central SD	Stony Brook
61	8.7	Albany City SD	Albany
61	8.7	South Orangetown Central SD	Blauvelt
63	8.6	Island Trees UFSD	Levittown
64	8.5	Greenburgh Central SD	Hartsdale
65	8.4	Fayetteville-Manlius Central SD	Manlius
65	8.4	Ramapo Central SD (Suffern)	Hillburn
65	8.4	South Colonie Central SD	Albany
65	8.4	Vestal Central SD	Vestal
69	8.3	Franklin Square UFSD	Franklin Square
69	8.3	NYC Geographic District #31	Staten Island
71	8.2	Jamesville-Dewitt Central SD	Dewitt
72	8.1	Nyack UFSD	Nyack
73	8.0	Rye Neck UFSD	Mamaroneck
73	8.0	Shenendehowa Central SD	Clifton Park
75	7.9	Elwood UFSD	Greenlawn
76	7.8	NYC Geographic District # 3	New York
76	7.8	NYC Geographic District #10	Bronx
78	7.7	West Hempstead UFSD	West Hempstead
79	7.4	Levittown UFSD	Levittown
79	7.4	Rye City SD	Rye
79	7.4	Syracuse City SD	Syracuse
82	7.1	Buffalo City SD	Buffalo
82	7.1	Hauppauge UFSD	Hauppauge
82	7.1	NYC Geographic District #11	Bronx
85	6.9	Commack UFSD	East Northport
85	6.9	North Bellmore UFSD	Bellmore
87	6.8	Hastings-On-Hudson UFSD	Hastings on Hdsn
88	6.7	Monroe-Woodbury Central SD	Central Valley
89	6.6	NYC Special Schools - District 75	New York
90	6.5	NYC Geographic District # 4	New York
90	6.5	Yorktown Central SD	Yorktown Hgts
92	6.3	NYC Geographic District #19	Brooklyn
92	6.3	South Huntington UFSD	Huntington Stn
94	6.2	Bronxville UFSD	Bronxville
94	6.2	Lawrence UFSD	Lawrence
96	6.1	New Hartford Central SD	New Hartford
96	6.1	Pleasantville UFSD	Pleasantville
98	5.9	Bethlehem Central SD	Delmar
99	5.7	Amherst Central SD	Amherst
99	5.7	Middle Country Central SD	Centereach
99	5.7	Sweet Home Central SD	Amherst
102	5.6	Johnson City Central SD	Johnson City
102	5.6	Sachem Central SD	Lake Ronkonkoma
104	5.5	Mount Sinai UFSD	Mount Sinai
104	5.5	Wappingers Central SD	Wappingers Fls
106	5.4	Gates-Chili Central SD	Rochester
106	5.4	Yonkers City SD	Yonkers
108	5.3	Croton-Harmon UFSD	Croton on Hdsn
108	5.3	East Ramapo CSD (Spring Valley)	Spring Valley
108	5.3	North Babylon UFSD	North Babylon
111	5.2	Byram Hills Central SD	Armonk
111	5.2	Farmingdale UFSD	Farmingdale
113	5.1	Cheektowaga Central SD	Cheektowaga
114	5.0	Bellmore-Merrick Central High SD	North Merrick
114	5.0	Merrick UFSD	Merrick
114	5.0	Pearl River UFSD	Pearl River
117	4.9	Cornwall Central SD	Cornwall on Hdsn
117	4.9	NYC Geographic District # 8	Bronx
117	4.9	Ossining UFSD	Ossining
120	4.8	Connetquot Central SD	Bohemia
120	4.8	Pelham UFSD	Pelham
122	4.7	Liverpool Central SD	Liverpool
122	4.7	Lynbrook UFSD	Lynbrook
122	4.7	Mamaroneck UFSD	Mamaroneck
125	4.6	North Shore Central SD	Sea Cliff
125	4.6	West Babylon UFSD	West Babylon
127	4.4	Bay Shore UFSD	Bay Shore
127	4.4	Hendrick Hudson Central SD	Montrose
127	4.4	Highland Central SD	Highland
127	4.4	Lakeland Central SD	Shrub Oak
131	4.3	Arlington Central SD	Lagrangeville
131	4.3	Malverne UFSD	Malverne
131	4.3	New Rochelle City SD	New Rochelle
134	4.2	Baldwin UFSD	Baldwin
134	4.2	East Greenbush Central SD	East Greenbush
134	4.2	Glen Cove City SD	Glen Cove
134	4.2	NYC Geographic District #14	Brooklyn
138	4.1	Bedford Central SD	Bedford
138	4.1	Mount Pleasant Central SD	Thornwood
140	4.0	Goshen Central SD	Goshen
140	4.0	Long Beach City SD	Long Beach
140	4.0	Smithtown Central SD	Smithtown
143	3.9	Haverstraw-Stony Point CSD	Garnerville
144	3.8	Locust Valley Central SD	Locust Valley
144	3.8	Somers Central SD	Somers
146	3.7	Brookhaven-Comsewogue UFSD	Port Jefferson Sta
146	3.7	Harborfields Central SD	Greenlawn
146	3.7	Oyster Bay-East Norwich Central SD	Oyster Bay
146	3.7	Rochester City SD	Rochester
150	3.6	Longwood Central SD	Middle Island
150	3.6	White Plains City SD	White Plains
152	3.5	Clarence Central SD	Clarence
152	3.5	Fairport Central SD	Fairport
154	3.4	Binghamton City SD	Binghamton
154	3.4	Cold Spring Hrbr Central SD	Cold Spring Hrbr
154	3.4	Garden City UFSD	Garden City
154	3.4	Oneonta City SD	Oneonta
154	3.4	Webster Central SD	Webster
159	3.3	Babylon UFSD	Babylon
159	3.3	Corning City SD	Painted Post
159	3.3	Horseheads Central SD	Horseheads
159	3.3	Penfield Central SD	Rochester
163	3.2	Lindenhurst UFSD	Lindenhurst
163	3.2	New Paltz Central SD	New Paltz
163	3.2	Oceanside UFSD	Oceanside
163	3.2	UFSD of the Tarrytowns	Sleepy Hollow
167	3.1	Greece Central SD	Rochester
167	3.1	Indian River Central SD	Philadelphia
167	3.1	NYC Geographic District # 5	New York
170	3.0	Southampton UFSD	Southampton
170	3.0	Victor Central SD	Victor
172	2.9	Cheektowaga-Maryvale UFSD	Cheektowaga
172	2.9	Islip UFSD	Islip
172	2.9	Katonah-Lewisboro UFSD	Goldens Bridge
172	2.9	Miller Place UFSD	Miller Place
172	2.9	Northport-East Northport UFSD	Northport
172	2.9	Washingtonville Central SD	Washingtonville
178	2.8	Grand Island Central SD	Grand Island

Note: This section only includes districts with 1,500 or more students; All categories are ranked from high to low

178	2.8	Plainedge UFSD	N Massapequa
180	2.7	Brewster Central SD	Brewster
180	2.7	Kings Park Central SD	Kings Park
180	2.7	Pine Bush Central SD	Pine Bush
180	2.7	West Irondequoit Central SD	Rochester
180	2.7	William Floyd UFSD	Mastic Beach
185	2.6	Carmel Central SD	Patterson
185	2.6	Churchville-Chili Central SD	Churchville
185	2.6	Olean City SD	Olean
188	2.5	Beacon City SD	Beacon
188	2.5	Newburgh City SD	Newburgh
188	2.5	Patchogue-Medford UFSD	Patchogue
188	2.5	Plattsburgh City SD	Plattsburgh
188	2.5	Rockville Ctr UFSD	Rockville Ctr
193	2.4	Middletown City SD	Middletown
193	2.4	Rotterdam-Mohonasen Central SD	Schenectady
193	2.4	Union-Endicott Central SD	Endicott
196	2.3	Central Islip UFSD	Central Islip
196	2.3	NYC Geographic District #17	Brooklyn
196	2.3	Niagara Wheatfield Central SD	Niagara Falls
196	2.3	Red Hook Central SD	Red Hook
200	2.2	Brentwood UFSD	Brentwood
200	2.2	Kingston City SD	Kingston
200	2.2	Shoreham-Wading River Central SD	Shoreham
203	2.1	East Hampton UFSD	East Hampton
203	2.1	East Syracuse-Minoa Central SD	East Syracuse
203	2.1	Mahopac Central SD	Mahopac
203	2.1	Putnam Valley Central SD	Putnam Valley
203	2.1	Seaford UFSD	Seaford
203	2.1	South Country Central SD	East Patchogue
203	2.1	Spencerport Central SD	Spencerport
203	2.1	Valley Central SD (Montgomery)	Montgomery
203	2.1	Wantagh UFSD	Wantagh
203	2.1	Watertown City SD	Watertown
213	2.0	Bayport-Blue Point UFSD	Bayport
213	2.0	Depew UFSD	Depew
213	2.0	Ellenville Central SD	Ellenville
213	2.0	Fredonia Central SD	Fredonia
213	2.0	Huntington UFSD	Huntington Stn
213	2.0	Hyde Park Central SD	Hyde Park
213	2.0	NYC Geographic District #12	Bronx
213	2.0	Schalmont Central SD	Schenectady
213	2.0	Troy City SD	Troy
222	1.9	Carthage Central SD	Carthage
222	1.9	Honeoye Falls-Lima Central SD	Honeoye Falls
222	1.9	Minisink Valley Central SD	Slate Hill
222	1.9	Peekskill City SD	Peekskill
222	1.9	Sayville UFSD	Sayville
222	1.9	Scotia-Glenville Central SD	Scotia
228	1.8	East Irondequoit Central SD	Rochester
228	1.8	East Islip UFSD	Islip Terrace
228	1.8	Geneva City SD	Geneva
228	1.8	Glens Falls City SD	Glens Falls
228	1.8	Kenmore-Tonawanda UFSD	Buffalo
228	1.8	NYC Geographic District #32	Brooklyn
228	1.8	North Syracuse Central SD	North Syracuse
228	1.8	Riverhead Central SD	Riverhead
228	1.8	Rondout Valley Central SD	Accord
228	1.8	Saratoga Spgs City SD	Saratoga Spgs
228	1.8	Saugerties Central SD	Saugerties
228	1.8	Westhill Central SD	Syracuse
240	1.7	Copiague UFSD	Copiague
240	1.7	Lewiston-Porter Central SD	Youngstown
240	1.7	Maine-Endwell Central SD	Endwell
240	1.7	Orchard Park Central SD	West Seneca
240	1.7	Rocky Point UFSD	Rocky Point
240	1.7	Warwick Valley Central SD	Warwick
246	1.6	Baldwinsville Central SD	Baldwinsville
246	1.6	Brockport Central SD	Brockport
246	1.6	Chenango Valley Central SD	Binghamton
246	1.6	Monticello Central SD	Monticello
246	1.6	Niagara Falls City SD	Niagara Falls
246	1.6	Port Chester-Rye UFSD	Port Chester
246	1.6	West Islip UFSD	West Islip
253	1.5	Averill Park Central SD	Averill Park
253	1.5	Burnt Hills-Ballston Lake Central SD	Scotia
253	1.5	Center Moriches UFSD	Center Moriches
253	1.5	Freeport UFSD	Freeport
253	1.5	Marcellus Central SD	Marcellus
253	1.5	Massapequa UFSD	Massapequa
253	1.5	Mount Vernon SD	Mount Vernon
253	1.5	NYC Geographic District #16	Brooklyn
253	1.5	Wallkill Central SD	Wallkill
253	1.5	Windsor Central SD	Windsor
263	1.4	Canandaigua City SD	Canandaigua
263	1.4	Cazenovia Central SD	Cazenovia
263	1.4	Port Jervis City SD	Port Jervis
263	1.4	Rome City SD	Rome
263	1.4	West Genesee Central SD	Camillus
268	1.3	Johnstown City SD	Johnstown
268	1.3	Kinderhook Central SD	Valatie
268	1.3	Marlboro Central SD	Milton
268	1.3	NYC Geographic District # 9	Bronx
268	1.3	Norwich City SD	Norwich
268	1.3	Oneida City SD	Oneida
268	1.3	Queensbury UFSD	Queensbury
268	1.3	West Seneca Central SD	West Seneca
268	1.3	Westhampton Bch UFSD	Westhampton Bch
268	1.3	Whitesboro Central SD	Yorkville
278	1.2	Ballston Spa Central SD	Ballston Spa
278	1.2	Cohoes City SD	Cohoes
278	1.2	Hilton Central SD	Hilton
278	1.2	NYC Geographic District # 6	New York
278	1.2	NYC Geographic District # 7	Bronx
278	1.2	Poughkeepsie City SD	Poughkeepsie
284	1.1	Broadalbin-Perth Central SD	Broadalbin
284	1.1	Catskill Central SD	Catskill
284	1.1	Eastport-South Manor CSD	Manorville
284	1.1	Lancaster Central SD	Lancaster
284	1.1	NYC Geographic District #18	Brooklyn
284	1.1	North Tonawanda City SD	North Tonawanda
284	1.1	Oswego City SD	Oswego
284	1.1	Ravena-Coeymans-Selkirk Ctrl SD	Ravena
284	1.1	Starpoint Central SD	Lockport
284	1.1	Uniondale UFSD	Uniondale
284	1.1	Wayne Central SD	Ontario Center
284	1.1	Westbury UFSD	Old Westbury
296	1.0	Amsterdam City SD	Amsterdam
296	1.0	Auburn City SD	Auburn
296	1.0	Batavia City SD	Batavia
296	1.0	Central Valley CSD At Ilion-Mohawk	Ilion
296	1.0	Cortland City SD	Cortland
296	1.0	East Aurora UFSD	East Aurora
296	1.0	Iroquois Central SD	Elma
296	1.0	Malone Central SD	Malone
296	1.0	Orange-Ulster Boces	Goshen
296	1.0	S Glens Fls Central SD	S Glens Fls
306	0.9	Amityville UFSD	Amityville
306	0.9	Dansville Central SD	Dansville
306	0.9	Hampton Bays UFSD	Hampton Bays
306	0.9	Homer Central SD	Homer
306	0.9	Hornell City SD	Hornell
306	0.9	Lackawanna City SD	Lackawanna
306	0.9	Lockport City SD	Lockport
306	0.9	NYC Geographic District #23	Brooklyn
306	0.9	Peru Central SD	Peru
306	0.9	Phelps-Clifton Springs Central SD	Clifton Springs
306	0.9	Solvay UFSD	Solvay
306	0.9	Susquehanna Valley Central SD	Conklin
306	0.9	Waverly Central SD	Waverly
319	0.8	Albion Central SD	Albion
319	0.8	Charter School for Applied Tech	Buffalo
319	0.8	Chittenango Central SD	Chittenango
319	0.8	Cobleskill-Richmondville Central SD	Cobleskill
319	0.8	Frontier Central SD	Hamburg
319	0.8	Fulton City SD	Fulton
319	0.8	Gloversville City SD	Gloversville
319	0.8	Hamburg Central SD	Hamburg
319	0.8	Ogdensburg City SD	Ogdensburg
319	0.8	Palmyra-Macedon Central SD	Palmyra
319	0.8	Schuylerville Central SD	Schuylerville
319	0.8	Springville-Griffith Institute CSD	Springville
331	0.7	Alden Central SD	Alden
331	0.7	Central Square Central SD	Central Square
331	0.7	Dryden Central SD	Dryden
331	0.7	Evans-Brant Central SD (Lake Shore)	Angola
331	0.7	Massena Central SD	Massena
331	0.7	Newark Central SD	Newark
331	0.7	Waterloo Central SD	Waterloo
338	0.6	Beekmantown Central SD	West Chazy
338	0.6	Elmira City SD	Elmira
338	0.6	General Brown Central SD	Dexter
338	0.6	Hempstead UFSD	Hempstead
338	0.6	Lansingburgh Central SD	Troy
338	0.6	Liberty Central SD	Liberty
338	0.6	Owego-Apalachin Central SD	Owego
338	0.6	Penn Yan Central SD	Penn Yan
338	0.6	Sherrill City SD	Verona
338	0.6	Tonawanda City SD	Tonawanda
338	0.6	Yorkshire-Pioneer Central SD	Yorkshire
349	0.5	Eden Central SD	Eden
349	0.5	Hudson Falls Central SD	Fort Edward
349	0.5	South Jefferson Central SD	Adams Center
352	0.4	Chenango Forks Central SD	Binghamton
352	0.4	Dunkirk City SD	Dunkirk
352	0.4	Jamestown City SD	Jamestown
352	0.4	Medina Central SD	Medina
352	0.4	Mexico Central SD	Mexico
352	0.4	Wyandanch UFSD	Wyandanch
358	0.3	Camden Central SD	Camden
358	0.3	Gouverneur Central SD	Gouverneur
358	0.3	Newfane Central SD	Burt
358	0.3	Phoenix Central SD	Phoenix
362	0.2	Bath Central SD	Bath
362	0.2	Livonia Central SD	Livonia
362	0.2	Salmon River Central SD	Fort Covington
365	0.0	Roosevelt UFSD	Roosevelt

American Indian/Alaska Native Students

Rank	Percent	District Name	City
1	64.5	Salmon River Central SD	Fort Covington
2	12.2	Evans-Brant Central SD (Lake Shore)	Angola
3	10.9	Massena Central SD	Massena
4	8.1	Southampton UFSD	Southampton
5	7.3	Niagara-Wheatfield Central SD	Niagara Falls
6	3.4	Center Moriches UFSD	Center Moriches
7	3.2	Niagara Falls City SD	Niagara Falls
8	2.7	NYC Geographic District #27	Ozone Park
9	2.6	NYC Geographic District #28	Jamaica
10	2.2	Oneida City SD	Oneida
11	1.9	North Tonawanda City SD	North Tonawanda
12	1.7	NYC Geographic District #29	Queens Village
13	1.3	Olean City SD	Olean
13	1.3	Syracuse City SD	Syracuse
15	1.1	Albion Central SD	Albion
15	1.1	Buffalo City SD	Buffalo
15	1.1	Freeport UFSD	Freeport
15	1.1	NYC Geographic District #11	Bronx
15	1.1	Solvay UFSD	Solvay
20	1.0	NYC Geographic District #17	Brooklyn
20	1.0	NYC Geographic District #19	Brooklyn
20	1.0	NYC Special Schools - District 75	New York
20	1.0	West Genesee Central SD	Camillus
24	0.9	Glen Cove City SD	Glen Cove
24	0.9	NYC Geographic District #12	Bronx
26	0.8	East Syracuse-Minoa Central SD	East Syracuse
26	0.8	Malone Central SD	Malone
26	0.8	NYC Geographic District # 1	New York
26	0.8	NYC Geographic District #23	Brooklyn
26	0.8	South Country Central SD	East Patchogue
26	0.8	Springville-Griffith Institute CSD	Springville
32	0.7	Carthage Central SD	Carthage
32	0.7	Kenmore-Tonawanda UFSD	Buffalo
32	0.7	NYC Geographic District # 5	New York
32	0.7	NYC Geographic District # 8	Bronx
32	0.7	New York City Public Schools	New York
37	0.6	Central Square Central SD	Central Square
37	0.6	Lackawanna City SD	Lackawanna
37	0.6	Lawrence UFSD	Lawrence
37	0.6	Lewiston-Porter Central SD	Youngstown
37	0.6	NYC Geographic District # 2	New York
37	0.6	NYC Geographic District # 3	New York
37	0.6	NYC Geographic District # 4	New York
37	0.6	NYC Geographic District #13	Brooklyn
37	0.6	NYC Geographic District #16	Brooklyn
37	0.6	North Syracuse Central SD	North Syracuse
37	0.6	Rotterdam-Mohonasen Central SD	Schenectady
37	0.6	Sherrill City SD	Verona
37	0.6	Tonawanda City SD	Tonawanda
50	0.5	Alden Central SD	Alden
50	0.5	Cheektowaga Central SD	Cheektowaga
50	0.5	Dunkirk City SD	Dunkirk
50	0.5	General Brown Central SD	Dexter
50	0.5	Iroquois Central SD	Elma
50	0.5	Jamesville-Dewitt Central SD	Dewitt
50	0.5	Johnson City Central SD	Johnson City
50	0.5	Lockport City SD	Lockport
50	0.5	NYC Geographic District # 7	Bronx
50	0.5	NYC Geographic District #10	Bronx
50	0.5	NYC Geographic District #18	Brooklyn

Note: This section only includes districts with 1,500 or more students; All categories are ranked from high to low

50	0.5	NYC Geographic District #22	Brooklyn
50	0.5	NYC Geographic District #26	Bayside
50	0.5	NYC Geographic District #30	Long Isl City
50	0.5	NYC Geographic District #32	Brooklyn
50	0.5	Newfane Central SD	Burt
50	0.5	Phoenix Central SD	Phoenix
50	0.5	Plattsburgh City SD	Plattsburgh
50	0.5	Ramapo Central SD (Suffern)	Hillburn
50	0.5	Riverhead Central SD	Riverhead
50	0.5	Watertown City SD	Watertown
50	0.5	William Floyd UFSD	Mastic Beach
72	0.4	Amityville UFSD	Amityville
72	0.4	Baldwinsville Central SD	Baldwinsville
72	0.4	Bayport-Blue Point UFSD	Bayport
72	0.4	Bellmore-Merrick Central High SD	North Merrick
72	0.4	Binghamton City SD	Binghamton
72	0.4	Cheektowaga-Maryvale UFSD	Cheektowaga
72	0.4	Chittenango Central SD	Chittenango
72	0.4	Corning City SD	Painted Post
72	0.4	Depew UFSD	Depew
72	0.4	Dryden Central SD	Dryden
72	0.4	Franklin Square UFSD	Franklin Square
72	0.4	Frontier Central SD	Hamburg
72	0.4	Grand Island Central SD	Grand Island
72	0.4	Indian River Central SD	Philadelphia
72	0.4	Jamestown City SD	Jamestown
72	0.4	Kingston City SD	Kingston
72	0.4	Liverpool Central SD	Liverpool
72	0.4	Medina Central SD	Medina
72	0.4	Minisink Valley Central SD	Slate Hill
72	0.4	NYC Geographic District # 9	Bronx
72	0.4	NYC Geographic District #14	Brooklyn
72	0.4	NYC Geographic District #21	Brooklyn
72	0.4	NYC Geographic District #25	Flushing
72	0.4	NYC Geographic District #31	Staten Island
72	0.4	Orchard Park Central SD	West Seneca
72	0.4	Palmyra-Macedon Central SD	Palmyra
72	0.4	Port Jervis City SD	Port Jervis
72	0.4	Rome City SD	Rome
72	0.4	Rush-Henrietta Central SD	Henrietta
72	0.4	Valley Stream 13 UFSD	Valley Stream
72	0.4	Victor Central SD	Victor
72	0.4	West Seneca Central SD	West Seneca
104	0.3	Albany City SD	Albany
104	0.3	Amherst Central SD	Amherst
104	0.3	Brentwood UFSD	Brentwood
104	0.3	Canandaigua City SD	Canandaigua
104	0.3	Cazenovia Central SD	Cazenovia
104	0.3	Central Valley CSD At Ilion-Mohawk	Ilion
104	0.3	Chenango Forks Central SD	Binghamton
104	0.3	Chenango Valley Central SD	Binghamton
104	0.3	Clarence Central SD	Clarence
104	0.3	Cornwall Central SD	Cornwall on Hdsn
104	0.3	Eden Central SD	Eden
104	0.3	Fredonia Central SD	Fredonia
104	0.3	Fulton City SD	Fulton
104	0.3	Gates-Chili Central SD	Rochester
104	0.3	Hempstead UFSD	Hempstead
104	0.3	Hewlett-Woodmere UFSD	Woodmere
104	0.3	Honeoye Falls-Lima Central SD	Honeoye Falls
104	0.3	Ithaca City SD	Ithaca
104	0.3	Lancaster Central SD	Lancaster
104	0.3	Longwood Central SD	Middle Island
104	0.3	Lynbrook UFSD	Lynbrook
104	0.3	Maine-Endwell Central SD	Endwell
104	0.3	NYC Geographic District #24	Corona
104	0.3	North Babylon UFSD	North Babylon
104	0.3	North Shore Central SD	Sea Cliff
104	0.3	Nyack UFSD	Nyack
104	0.3	Orange-Ulster Boces	Goshen
104	0.3	Red Hook Central SD	Red Hook
104	0.3	Rondout Valley Central SD	Accord
104	0.3	South Jefferson Central SD	Adams Center
104	0.3	Spackenkill UFSD	Poughkeepsie
104	0.3	Susquehanna Valley Central SD	Conklin
104	0.3	Valhalla UFSD	Valhalla
104	0.3	Washingtonville Central SD	Washingtonville
104	0.3	Williamsville Central SD	East Amherst
104	0.3	Yonkers City SD	Yonkers
104	0.3	Yorkshire-Pioneer Central SD	Yorkshire
141	0.2	Auburn City SD	Auburn
141	0.2	Batavia City SD	Batavia
141	0.2	Beekmantown Central SD	West Chazy
141	0.2	Brookhaven-Comsewogue UFSD	Port Jefferson Sta
141	0.2	Catskill Central SD	Catskill
141	0.2	Charter School for Applied Tech	Buffalo
141	0.2	Cohoes City SD	Cohoes
141	0.2	Connetquot Central SD	Bohemia
141	0.2	East Greenbush Central SD	East Greenbush
141	0.2	Eastchester UFSD	Eastchester
141	0.2	Ellenville Central SD	Ellenville
141	0.2	Elmira City SD	Elmira
141	0.2	Elmont UFSD	Elmont
141	0.2	Fayetteville-Manlius Central SD	Manlius
141	0.2	Goshen Central SD	Goshen
141	0.2	Greece Central SD	Rochester
141	0.2	Half Hollow Hills Central SD	Dix Hills
141	0.2	Hamburg Central SD	Hamburg
141	0.2	Haverstraw-Stony Point CSD	Garnerville
141	0.2	Highland Central SD	Highland
141	0.2	Hilton Central SD	Hilton
141	0.2	Hornell City SD	Hornell
141	0.2	Horseheads Central SD	Horseheads
141	0.2	Hudson Falls Central SD	Fort Edward
141	0.2	Livonia Central SD	Livonia
141	0.2	Marcellus Central SD	Marcellus
141	0.2	Marlboro Central SD	Milton
141	0.2	Massapequa UFSD	Massapequa
141	0.2	Mexico Central SD	Mexico
141	0.2	Monroe-Woodbury Central SD	Central Valley
141	0.2	Mount Vernon SD	Mount Vernon
141	0.2	New Hyde Pk-Garden City Pk UFSD	New Hyde Park
141	0.2	New Paltz Central SD	New Paltz
141	0.2	NYC Geographic District # 6	New York
141	0.2	NYC Geographic District #15	Brooklyn
141	0.2	NYC Geographic District #20	Brooklyn
141	0.2	Newark Central SD	Newark
141	0.2	Newburgh City SD	Newburgh
141	0.2	North Bellmore UFSD	Bellmore
141	0.2	Oswego City SD	Oswego
141	0.2	Oyster Bay-East Norwich Central SD	Oyster Bay
141	0.2	Patchogue-Medford UFSD	Patchogue
141	0.2	Peru Central SD	Peru
141	0.2	Pine Bush Central SD	Pine Bush
141	0.2	Plainedge UFSD	N Massapequa
141	0.2	Port Chester-Rye UFSD	Port Chester
141	0.2	Queensbury UFSD	Queensbury
141	0.2	Rochester City SD	Rochester
141	0.2	Rocky Point UFSD	Rocky Point
141	0.2	Rye City SD	Rye
141	0.2	Sachem Central SD	Lake Ronkonkoma
141	0.2	Saugerties Central SD	Saugerties
141	0.2	Smithtown Central SD	Smithtown
141	0.2	Spencerport Central SD	Spencerport
141	0.2	Starpoint Central SD	Lockport
141	0.2	Sweet Home Central SD	Amherst
141	0.2	Troy City SD	Troy
141	0.2	Union-Endicott Central SD	Endicott
141	0.2	Uniondale UFSD	Uniondale
141	0.2	Valley Central SD (Montgomery)	Montgomery
141	0.2	Vestal Central SD	Vestal
141	0.2	Wallkill Central SD	Wallkill
141	0.2	Wayne Central SD	Ontario Center
141	0.2	West Irondequoit Central SD	Rochester
141	0.2	Westhill Central SD	Syracuse
206	0.1	Amsterdam City SD	Amsterdam
206	0.1	Baldwin UFSD	Baldwin
206	0.1	Bath Central SD	Bath
206	0.1	Bay Shore UFSD	Bay Shore
206	0.1	Beacon City SD	Beacon
206	0.1	Bethpage UFSD	Bethpage
206	0.1	Brewster Central SD	Brewster
206	0.1	Brighton Central SD	Rochester
206	0.1	Broadalbin-Perth Central SD	Broadalbin
206	0.1	Brockport Central SD	Brockport
206	0.1	Burnt Hills-Ballston Lake Central SD	Scotia
206	0.1	Camden Central SD	Camden
206	0.1	Carmel Central SD	Patterson
206	0.1	Central Islip UFSD	Central Islip
206	0.1	Chappaqua Central SD	Chappaqua
206	0.1	Churchville-Chili Central SD	Churchville
206	0.1	Clarkstown Central SD	New City
206	0.1	Cold Spring Hrbr Central SD	Cold Spring Hrbr
206	0.1	Commack UFSD	East Northport
206	0.1	Copiague UFSD	Copiague
206	0.1	Croton-Harmon UFSD	Croton on Hdsn
206	0.1	Dansville Central SD	Dansville
206	0.1	Deer Park UFSD	Deer Park
206	0.1	East Aurora UFSD	East Aurora
206	0.1	East Hampton UFSD	East Hampton
206	0.1	East Irondequoit Central SD	Rochester
206	0.1	East Meadow UFSD	Westbury
206	0.1	Eastport-South Manor CSD	Manorville
206	0.1	Edgemont UFSD	Scarsdale
206	0.1	Fairport Central SD	Fairport
206	0.1	Farmingdale UFSD	Farmingdale
206	0.1	Geneva City SD	Geneva
206	0.1	Glens Falls City SD	Glens Falls
206	0.1	Gouverneur Central SD	Gouverneur
206	0.1	Greenburgh Central SD	Hartsdale
206	0.1	Guilderland Central SD	Guilderland Center
206	0.1	Hampton Bays UFSD	Hampton Bays
206	0.1	Harborfields Central SD	Greenlawn
206	0.1	Hauppauge UFSD	Hauppauge
206	0.1	Hendrick Hudson Central SD	Montrose
206	0.1	Hicksville UFSD	Hicksville
206	0.1	Hudson City SD	Hudson
206	0.1	Hyde Park Central SD	Hyde Park
206	0.1	Irvington UFSD	Irvington
206	0.1	Johnstown City SD	Johnstown
206	0.1	Katonah-Lewisboro UFSD	Goldens Bridge
206	0.1	Kinderhook Central SD	Valatie
206	0.1	Lakeland Central SD	Shrub Oak
206	0.1	Lansingburgh Central SD	Troy
206	0.1	Levittown UFSD	Levittown
206	0.1	Liberty Central SD	Liberty
206	0.1	Lindenhurst UFSD	Lindenhurst
206	0.1	Merrick UFSD	Merrick
206	0.1	Middletown City SD	Middletown
206	0.1	Miller Place UFSD	Miller Place
206	0.1	Mineola UFSD	Mineola
206	0.1	Monticello Central SD	Monticello
206	0.1	New Rochelle City SD	New Rochelle
206	0.1	North Colonie CSD	Latham
206	0.1	Northport-East Northport UFSD	Northport
206	0.1	Norwich City SD	Norwich
206	0.1	Oceanside UFSD	Oceanside
206	0.1	Ogdensburg City SD	Ogdensburg
206	0.1	Peekskill City SD	Peekskill
206	0.1	Pelham UFSD	Pelham
206	0.1	Penfield Central SD	Rochester
206	0.1	Penn Yan Central SD	Penn Yan
206	0.1	Phelps-Clifton Springs Central SD	Clifton Springs
206	0.1	Port Washington UFSD	Port Washington
206	0.1	Poughkeepsie City SD	Poughkeepsie
206	0.1	Putnam Valley Central SD	Putnam Valley
206	0.1	Ravena-Coeymans-Selkirk Ctrl SD	Ravena
206	0.1	Saratoga Spgs City SD	Saratoga Spgs
206	0.1	Sayville UFSD	Sayville
206	0.1	Schalmont Central SD	Schenectady
206	0.1	Schenectady City SD	Schenectady
206	0.1	Scotia-Glenville Central SD	Scotia
206	0.1	Shenendehowa Central SD	Clifton Park
206	0.1	South Colonie Central SD	Albany
206	0.1	South Huntington UFSD	Huntington Stn
206	0.1	South Orangetown Central SD	Blauvelt
206	0.1	Syosset Central SD	Syosset
206	0.1	Three Village Central SD	Stony Brook
206	0.1	Utica City SD	Utica
206	0.1	Valley Stream Central High SD	Valley Stream
206	0.1	Wappingers Central SD	Wappingers Fls
206	0.1	Waterloo Central SD	Waterloo
206	0.1	Webster Central SD	Webster
206	0.1	West Hempstead UFSD	West Hempstead
206	0.1	Westbury UFSD	Old Westbury
206	0.1	Westhampton Bch UFSD	Westhampton Bch
206	0.1	Whitesboro Central SD	Yorkville
206	0.1	Windsor Central SD	Windsor
206	0.1	Yorktown Central SD	Yorktown Hgts
300	0.0	Ardsley UFSD	Ardsley
300	0.0	Arlington Central SD	Lagrangeville
300	0.0	Averill Park Central SD	Averill Park
300	0.0	Babylon UFSD	Babylon
300	0.0	Ballston Spa Central SD	Ballston Spa
300	0.0	Bedford Central SD	Bedford
300	0.0	Bethlehem Central SD	Delmar
300	0.0	Briarcliff Mnr UFSD	Briarcliff Mnr
300	0.0	Bronxville UFSD	Bronxville
300	0.0	Byram Hills Central SD	Armonk
300	0.0	Cobleskill-Richmondville Central SD	Cobleskill
300	0.0	Cortland City SD	Cortland
300	0.0	East Islip UFSD	Islip Terrace

Note: This section only includes districts with 1,500 or more students; All categories are ranked from high to low

300	0.0	East Ramapo CSD (Spring Valley)	Spring Valley
300	0.0	East Williston UFSD	Old Westbury
300	0.0	Elwood UFSD	Greenlawn
300	0.0	Garden City UFSD	Garden City
300	0.0	Gloversville City SD	Gloversville
300	0.0	Great Neck UFSD	Great Neck
300	0.0	Harrison Central SD	Harrison
300	0.0	Hastings-On-Hudson UFSD	Hastings on Hdsn
300	0.0	Herricks UFSD	New Hyde Park
300	0.0	Homer Central SD	Homer
300	0.0	Huntington UFSD	Huntington Stn
300	0.0	Island Trees UFSD	Levittown
300	0.0	Islip UFSD	Islip
300	0.0	Jericho UFSD	Jericho
300	0.0	Kings Park Central SD	Kings Park
300	0.0	Locust Valley Central SD	Locust Valley
300	0.0	Long Beach City SD	Long Beach
300	0.0	Mahopac Central SD	Mahopac
300	0.0	Malverne UFSD	Malverne
300	0.0	Mamaroneck UFSD	Mamaroneck
300	0.0	Manhasset UFSD	Manhasset
300	0.0	Middle Country Central SD	Centereach
300	0.0	Mount Pleasant Central SD	Thornwood
300	0.0	Mount Sinai UFSD	Mount Sinai
300	0.0	Nanuet UFSD	Nanuet
300	0.0	New Hartford Central SD	New Hartford
300	0.0	Niskayuna Central SD	Schenectady
300	0.0	Oneonta City SD	Oneonta
300	0.0	Ossining UFSD	Ossining
300	0.0	Owego-Apalachin Central SD	Owego
300	0.0	Pearl River UFSD	Pearl River
300	0.0	Pittsford Central SD	Pittsford
300	0.0	Plainview-Old Bethpage Central SD	Plainview
300	0.0	Pleasantville UFSD	Pleasantville
300	0.0	Rockville Ctr UFSD	Rockville Ctr
300	0.0	Roosevelt UFSD	Roosevelt
300	0.0	Roslyn UFSD	Roslyn
300	0.0	Rye Neck UFSD	Mamaroneck
300	0.0	Scarsdale UFSD	Scarsdale
300	0.0	Schuylerville Central SD	Schuylerville
300	0.0	Seaford UFSD	Seaford
300	0.0	Sewanhaka Central High SD	Floral Park
300	0.0	Shoreham-Wading River Central SD	Shoreham
300	0.0	Somers Central SD	Somers
300	0.0	S Glens Fls Central SD	S Glens Fls
300	0.0	UFSD of the Tarrytowns	Sleepy Hollow
300	0.0	Wantagh UFSD	Wantagh
300	0.0	Warwick Valley Central SD	Warwick
300	0.0	Waverly Central SD	Waverly
300	0.0	West Babylon UFSD	West Babylon
300	0.0	West Islip UFSD	West Islip
300	0.0	White Plains City SD	White Plains
300	0.0	Wyandanch UFSD	Wyandanch

Native Hawaiian/Pacific Islander Students

Rank	Percent	District Name	City
n/a	n/a	Albany City SD	Albany
n/a	n/a	Albion Central SD	Albion
n/a	n/a	Alden Central SD	Alden
n/a	n/a	Amherst Central SD	Amherst
n/a	n/a	Amityville UFSD	Amityville
n/a	n/a	Amsterdam City SD	Amsterdam
n/a	n/a	Ardsley UFSD	Ardsley
n/a	n/a	Arlington Central SD	Lagrangeville
n/a	n/a	Auburn City SD	Auburn
n/a	n/a	Averill Park Central SD	Averill Park
n/a	n/a	Babylon UFSD	Babylon
n/a	n/a	Baldwin UFSD	Baldwin
n/a	n/a	Baldwinsville Central SD	Baldwinsville
n/a	n/a	Ballston Spa Central SD	Ballston Spa
n/a	n/a	Batavia City SD	Batavia
n/a	n/a	Bath Central SD	Bath
n/a	n/a	Bay Shore UFSD	Bay Shore
n/a	n/a	Bayport-Blue Point UFSD	Bayport
n/a	n/a	Beacon City SD	Beacon
n/a	n/a	Bedford Central SD	Bedford
n/a	n/a	Beekmantown Central SD	West Chazy
n/a	n/a	Bellmore-Merrick Central High SD	North Merrick
n/a	n/a	Bethlehem Central SD	Delmar
n/a	n/a	Bethpage UFSD	Bethpage
n/a	n/a	Binghamton City SD	Binghamton
n/a	n/a	Brentwood UFSD	Brentwood
n/a	n/a	Brewster Central SD	Brewster
n/a	n/a	Briarcliff Mnr UFSD	Briarcliff Mnr
n/a	n/a	Brighton Central SD	Rochester
n/a	n/a	Broadalbin-Perth Central SD	Broadalbin
n/a	n/a	Brockport Central SD	Brockport
n/a	n/a	Bronxville UFSD	Bronxville
n/a	n/a	Brookhaven-Comsewogue UFSD	Port Jefferson Sta
n/a	n/a	Buffalo City SD	Buffalo
n/a	n/a	Burnt Hills-Ballston Lake Central SD	Scotia
n/a	n/a	Byram Hills Central SD	Armonk
n/a	n/a	Camden Central SD	Camden
n/a	n/a	Canandaigua City SD	Canandaigua
n/a	n/a	Carmel Central SD	Patterson
n/a	n/a	Carthage Central SD	Carthage
n/a	n/a	Catskill Central SD	Catskill
n/a	n/a	Cazenovia Central SD	Cazenovia
n/a	n/a	Center Moriches UFSD	Center Moriches
n/a	n/a	Central Islip UFSD	Central Islip
n/a	n/a	Central Square Central SD	Central Square
n/a	n/a	Central Valley CSD At Ilion-Mohawk	Ilion
n/a	n/a	Chappaqua Central SD	Chappaqua
n/a	n/a	Charter School for Applied Tech	Buffalo
n/a	n/a	Cheektowaga Central SD	Cheektowaga
n/a	n/a	Cheektowaga-Maryvale UFSD	Cheektowaga
n/a	n/a	Chenango Forks Central SD	Binghamton
n/a	n/a	Chenango Valley Central SD	Binghamton
n/a	n/a	Chittenango Central SD	Chittenango
n/a	n/a	Churchville-Chili Central SD	Churchville
n/a	n/a	Clarence Central SD	Clarence
n/a	n/a	Clarkstown Central SD	New City
n/a	n/a	Cobleskill-Richmondville Central SD	Cobleskill
n/a	n/a	Cohoes City SD	Cohoes
n/a	n/a	Cold Spring Hrbr Central SD	Cold Spring Hrbr
n/a	n/a	Commack UFSD	East Northport
n/a	n/a	Connetquot Central SD	Bohemia
n/a	n/a	Copiague UFSD	Copiague
n/a	n/a	Corning City SD	Painted Post
n/a	n/a	Cornwall Central SD	Cornwall on Hudson
n/a	n/a	Cortland City SD	Cortland
n/a	n/a	Croton-Harmon UFSD	Croton on Hdsn
n/a	n/a	Dansville Central SD	Dansville
n/a	n/a	Deer Park UFSD	Deer Park
n/a	n/a	Depew UFSD	Depew
n/a	n/a	Dryden Central SD	Dryden
n/a	n/a	Dunkirk City SD	Dunkirk
n/a	n/a	East Aurora UFSD	East Aurora
n/a	n/a	East Greenbush Central SD	East Greenbush
n/a	n/a	East Hampton UFSD	East Hampton
n/a	n/a	East Irondequoit Central SD	Rochester
n/a	n/a	East Islip UFSD	Islip Terrace
n/a	n/a	East Meadow UFSD	Westbury
n/a	n/a	East Ramapo CSD (Spring Valley)	Spring Valley
n/a	n/a	East Syracuse-Minoa Central SD	East Syracuse
n/a	n/a	East Williston UFSD	Old Westbury
n/a	n/a	Eastchester UFSD	Eastchester
n/a	n/a	Eastport-South Manor CSD	Manorville
n/a	n/a	Eden Central SD	Eden
n/a	n/a	Edgemont UFSD	Scarsdale
n/a	n/a	Ellenville Central SD	Ellenville
n/a	n/a	Elmira City SD	Elmira
n/a	n/a	Elmont UFSD	Elmont
n/a	n/a	Elwood UFSD	Greenlawn
n/a	n/a	Evans-Brant Central SD (Lake Shore)	Angola
n/a	n/a	Fairport Central SD	Fairport
n/a	n/a	Farmingdale UFSD	Farmingdale
n/a	n/a	Fayetteville-Manlius Central SD	Manlius
n/a	n/a	Franklin Square UFSD	Franklin Square
n/a	n/a	Fredonia Central SD	Fredonia
n/a	n/a	Freeport UFSD	Freeport
n/a	n/a	Frontier Central SD	Hamburg
n/a	n/a	Fulton City SD	Fulton
n/a	n/a	Garden City UFSD	Garden City
n/a	n/a	Gates-Chili Central SD	Rochester
n/a	n/a	General Brown Central SD	Dexter
n/a	n/a	Geneva City SD	Geneva
n/a	n/a	Glen Cove City SD	Glen Cove
n/a	n/a	Glens Falls City SD	Glens Falls
n/a	n/a	Gloversville City SD	Gloversville
n/a	n/a	Goshen Central SD	Goshen
n/a	n/a	Gouverneur Central SD	Gouverneur
n/a	n/a	Grand Island Central SD	Grand Island
n/a	n/a	Great Neck UFSD	Great Neck
n/a	n/a	Greece Central SD	Rochester
n/a	n/a	Greenburgh Central SD	Hartsdale
n/a	n/a	Guilderland Central SD	Guilderland Center
n/a	n/a	Half Hollow Hills Central SD	Dix Hills
n/a	n/a	Hamburg Central SD	Hamburg
n/a	n/a	Hampton Bays UFSD	Hampton Bays
n/a	n/a	Harborfields Central SD	Greenlawn
n/a	n/a	Harrison Central SD	Harrison
n/a	n/a	Hastings-On-Hudson UFSD	Hastings on Hdsn
n/a	n/a	Hauppauge UFSD	Hauppauge
n/a	n/a	Haverstraw-Stony Point CSD	Garnerville
n/a	n/a	Hempstead UFSD	Hempstead
n/a	n/a	Hendrick Hudson Central SD	Montrose
n/a	n/a	Herricks UFSD	New Hyde Park
n/a	n/a	Hewlett-Woodmere UFSD	Woodmere
n/a	n/a	Hicksville UFSD	Hicksville
n/a	n/a	Highland Central SD	Highland
n/a	n/a	Hilton Central SD	Hilton
n/a	n/a	Homer Central SD	Homer
n/a	n/a	Honeoye Falls-Lima Central SD	Honeoye Falls
n/a	n/a	Hornell City SD	Hornell
n/a	n/a	Horseheads Central SD	Horseheads
n/a	n/a	Hudson City SD	Hudson
n/a	n/a	Hudson Falls Central SD	Fort Edward
n/a	n/a	Huntington UFSD	Huntington Stn
n/a	n/a	Hyde Park Central SD	Hyde Park
n/a	n/a	Indian River Central SD	Philadelphia
n/a	n/a	Iroquois Central SD	Elma
n/a	n/a	Irvington UFSD	Irvington
n/a	n/a	Island Trees UFSD	Levittown
n/a	n/a	Islip UFSD	Islip
n/a	n/a	Ithaca City SD	Ithaca
n/a	n/a	Jamestown City SD	Jamestown
n/a	n/a	Jamesville-Dewitt Central SD	Dewitt
n/a	n/a	Jericho UFSD	Jericho
n/a	n/a	Johnson City Central SD	Johnson City
n/a	n/a	Johnstown City SD	Johnstown
n/a	n/a	Katonah-Lewisboro UFSD	Goldens Bridge
n/a	n/a	Kenmore-Tonawanda UFSD	Buffalo
n/a	n/a	Kinderhook Central SD	Valatie
n/a	n/a	Kings Park Central SD	Kings Park
n/a	n/a	Kingston City SD	Kingston
n/a	n/a	Lackawanna City SD	Lackawanna
n/a	n/a	Lakeland Central SD	Shrub Oak
n/a	n/a	Lancaster Central SD	Lancaster
n/a	n/a	Lansingburgh Central SD	Troy
n/a	n/a	Lawrence UFSD	Lawrence
n/a	n/a	Levittown UFSD	Levittown
n/a	n/a	Lewiston-Porter Central SD	Youngstown
n/a	n/a	Liberty Central SD	Liberty
n/a	n/a	Lindenhurst UFSD	Lindenhurst
n/a	n/a	Liverpool Central SD	Liverpool
n/a	n/a	Livonia Central SD	Livonia
n/a	n/a	Lockport City SD	Lockport
n/a	n/a	Locust Valley Central SD	Locust Valley
n/a	n/a	Long Beach City SD	Long Beach
n/a	n/a	Longwood Central SD	Middle Island
n/a	n/a	Lynbrook UFSD	Lynbrook
n/a	n/a	Mahopac Central SD	Mahopac
n/a	n/a	Maine-Endwell Central SD	Endwell
n/a	n/a	Malone Central SD	Malone
n/a	n/a	Malverne UFSD	Malverne
n/a	n/a	Mamaroneck UFSD	Mamaroneck
n/a	n/a	Manhasset UFSD	Manhasset
n/a	n/a	Marcellus Central SD	Marcellus
n/a	n/a	Marlboro Central SD	Milton
n/a	n/a	Massapequa UFSD	Massapequa
n/a	n/a	Massena Central SD	Massena
n/a	n/a	Medina Central SD	Medina
n/a	n/a	Merrick UFSD	Merrick
n/a	n/a	Mexico Central SD	Mexico
n/a	n/a	Middle Country Central SD	Centereach
n/a	n/a	Middletown City SD	Middletown
n/a	n/a	Miller Place UFSD	Miller Place
n/a	n/a	Mineola UFSD	Mineola
n/a	n/a	Minisink Valley Central SD	Slate Hill
n/a	n/a	Monroe-Woodbury Central SD	Central Valley
n/a	n/a	Monticello Central SD	Monticello
n/a	n/a	Mount Pleasant Central SD	Thornwood
n/a	n/a	Mount Sinai UFSD	Mount Sinai
n/a	n/a	Mount Vernon SD	Mount Vernon
n/a	n/a	Nanuet UFSD	Nanuet
n/a	n/a	New Hartford Central SD	New Hartford
n/a	n/a	New Hyde Pk-Garden City Pk UFSD	New Hyde Park
n/a	n/a	New Paltz Central SD	New Paltz

Note: This section only includes districts with 1,500 or more students; All categories are ranked from high to low

n/a	n/a	New Rochelle City SD	New Rochelle
n/a	n/a	NYC Geographic District # 1	New York
n/a	n/a	NYC Geographic District # 2	New York
n/a	n/a	NYC Geographic District # 3	New York
n/a	n/a	NYC Geographic District # 4	New York
n/a	n/a	NYC Geographic District # 5	New York
n/a	n/a	NYC Geographic District # 6	New York
n/a	n/a	NYC Geographic District # 7	Bronx
n/a	n/a	NYC Geographic District # 8	Bronx
n/a	n/a	NYC Geographic District # 9	Bronx
n/a	n/a	NYC Geographic District #10	Bronx
n/a	n/a	NYC Geographic District #11	Bronx
n/a	n/a	NYC Geographic District #12	Bronx
n/a	n/a	NYC Geographic District #13	Brooklyn
n/a	n/a	NYC Geographic District #14	Brooklyn
n/a	n/a	NYC Geographic District #15	Brooklyn
n/a	n/a	NYC Geographic District #16	Brooklyn
n/a	n/a	NYC Geographic District #17	Brooklyn
n/a	n/a	NYC Geographic District #18	Brooklyn
n/a	n/a	NYC Geographic District #19	Brooklyn
n/a	n/a	NYC Geographic District #20	Brooklyn
n/a	n/a	NYC Geographic District #21	Brooklyn
n/a	n/a	NYC Geographic District #22	Brooklyn
n/a	n/a	NYC Geographic District #23	Brooklyn
n/a	n/a	NYC Geographic District #24	Corona
n/a	n/a	NYC Geographic District #25	Flushing
n/a	n/a	NYC Geographic District #26	Bayside
n/a	n/a	NYC Geographic District #27	Ozone Park
n/a	n/a	NYC Geographic District #28	Jamaica
n/a	n/a	NYC Geographic District #29	Queens Village
n/a	n/a	NYC Geographic District #30	Long Isl City
n/a	n/a	NYC Geographic District #31	Staten Island
n/a	n/a	NYC Geographic District #32	Brooklyn
n/a	n/a	Newark Central SD	Newark
n/a	n/a	Newburgh City SD	Newburgh
n/a	n/a	Newfane Central SD	Burt
n/a	n/a	Niagara Falls City SD	Niagara Falls
n/a	n/a	Niagara-Wheatfield Central SD	Niagara Falls
n/a	n/a	Niskayuna Central SD	Schenectady
n/a	n/a	North Babylon UFSD	North Babylon
n/a	n/a	North Bellmore UFSD	Bellmore
n/a	n/a	North Colonie CSD	Latham
n/a	n/a	North Shore Central SD	Sea Cliff
n/a	n/a	North Syracuse Central SD	North Syracuse
n/a	n/a	North Tonawanda City SD	North Tonawanda
n/a	n/a	Northport-East Northport UFSD	Northport
n/a	n/a	Norwich City SD	Norwich
n/a	n/a	Nyack UFSD	Nyack
n/a	n/a	NYC Special Schools - District 75	New York
n/a	n/a	Oceanside UFSD	Oceanside
n/a	n/a	Ogdensburg City SD	Ogdensburg
n/a	n/a	Olean City SD	Olean
n/a	n/a	Oneida City SD	Oneida
n/a	n/a	Oneonta City SD	Oneonta
n/a	n/a	Orange-Ulster Boces	Goshen
n/a	n/a	Orchard Park Central SD	West Seneca
n/a	n/a	Ossining UFSD	Ossining
n/a	n/a	Oswego City SD	Oswego
n/a	n/a	Owego-Apalachin Central SD	Owego
n/a	n/a	Oyster Bay-East Norwich Central SD	Oyster Bay
n/a	n/a	Palmyra-Macedon Central SD	Palmyra
n/a	n/a	Patchogue-Medford UFSD	Patchogue
n/a	n/a	Pearl River UFSD	Pearl River
n/a	n/a	Peekskill City SD	Peekskill
n/a	n/a	Pelham UFSD	Pelham
n/a	n/a	Penfield Central SD	Rochester
n/a	n/a	Penn Yan Central SD	Penn Yan
n/a	n/a	Peru Central SD	Peru
n/a	n/a	Phelps-Clifton Springs Central SD	Clifton Springs
n/a	n/a	Phoenix Central SD	Phoenix
n/a	n/a	Pine Bush Central SD	Pine Bush
n/a	n/a	Pittsford Central SD	Pittsford
n/a	n/a	Plainedge UFSD	N Massapequa
n/a	n/a	Plainview-Old Bethpage Central SD	Plainview
n/a	n/a	Plattsburgh City SD	Plattsburgh
n/a	n/a	Pleasantville UFSD	Pleasantville
n/a	n/a	Port Chester-Rye UFSD	Port Chester
n/a	n/a	Port Jervis City SD	Port Jervis
n/a	n/a	Port Washington UFSD	Port Washington
n/a	n/a	Poughkeepsie City SD	Poughkeepsie
n/a	n/a	Putnam Valley Central SD	Putnam Valley
n/a	n/a	Queensbury UFSD	Queensbury
n/a	n/a	Ramapo Central SD (Suffern)	Hillburn
n/a	n/a	Ravena-Coeymans-Selkirk Ctrl SD	Ravena
n/a	n/a	Red Hook Central SD	Red Hook
n/a	n/a	Riverhead Central SD	Riverhead
n/a	n/a	Rochester City SD	Rochester
n/a	n/a	Rockville Ctr UFSD	Rockville Ctr
n/a	n/a	Rocky Point UFSD	Rocky Point
n/a	n/a	Rome City SD	Rome
n/a	n/a	Rondout Valley Central SD	Accord
n/a	n/a	Roosevelt UFSD	Roosevelt
n/a	n/a	Roslyn UFSD	Roslyn
n/a	n/a	Rotterdam-Mohonasen Central SD	Schenectady
n/a	n/a	Rush-Henrietta Central SD	Henrietta
n/a	n/a	Rye City SD	Rye
n/a	n/a	Rye Neck UFSD	Mamaroneck
n/a	n/a	Sachem Central SD	Lake Ronkonkoma
n/a	n/a	Salmon River Central SD	Fort Covington
n/a	n/a	Saratoga Spgs City SD	Saratoga Spgs
n/a	n/a	Saugerties Central SD	Saugerties
n/a	n/a	Sayville UFSD	Sayville
n/a	n/a	Scarsdale UFSD	Scarsdale
n/a	n/a	Schalmont Central SD	Schenectady
n/a	n/a	Schenectady City SD	Schenectady
n/a	n/a	Schuylerville Central SD	Schuylerville
n/a	n/a	Scotia-Glenville Central SD	Scotia
n/a	n/a	Seaford UFSD	Seaford
n/a	n/a	Sewanhaka Central High SD	Floral Park
n/a	n/a	Shenendehowa Central SD	Clifton Park
n/a	n/a	Sherrill City SD	Verona
n/a	n/a	Shoreham-Wading River Central SD	Shoreham
n/a	n/a	Smithtown Central SD	Smithtown
n/a	n/a	Solvay UFSD	Solvay
n/a	n/a	Somers Central SD	Somers
n/a	n/a	South Colonie Central SD	Albany
n/a	n/a	South Country Central SD	East Patchogue
n/a	n/a	S Glens Fls Central SD	S Glens Fls
n/a	n/a	South Huntington UFSD	Huntington Stn
n/a	n/a	South Jefferson Central SD	Adams Center
n/a	n/a	South Orangetown Central SD	Blauvelt
n/a	n/a	Southampton UFSD	Southampton
n/a	n/a	Spackenkill UFSD	Poughkeepsie
n/a	n/a	Spencerport Central SD	Spencerport
n/a	n/a	Springville-Griffith Institute CSD	Springville
n/a	n/a	Starpoint Central SD	Lockport
n/a	n/a	Susquehanna Valley Central SD	Conklin
n/a	n/a	Sweet Home Central SD	Amherst
n/a	n/a	Syosset Central SD	Syosset
n/a	n/a	Syracuse City SD	Syracuse
n/a	n/a	Three Village Central SD	Stony Brook
n/a	n/a	Tonawanda City SD	Tonawanda
n/a	n/a	Troy City SD	Troy
n/a	n/a	UFSD of the Tarrytowns	Sleepy Hollow
n/a	n/a	Union-Endicott Central SD	Endicott
n/a	n/a	Uniondale UFSD	Uniondale
n/a	n/a	Utica City SD	Utica
n/a	n/a	Valhalla UFSD	Valhalla
n/a	n/a	Valley Central SD (Montgomery)	Montgomery
n/a	n/a	Valley Stream 13 UFSD	Valley Stream
n/a	n/a	Valley Stream Central High SD	Valley Stream
n/a	n/a	Vestal Central SD	Vestal
n/a	n/a	Victor Central SD	Victor
n/a	n/a	Wallkill Central SD	Wallkill
n/a	n/a	Wantagh UFSD	Wantagh
n/a	n/a	Wappingers Central SD	Wappingers Fls
n/a	n/a	Warwick Valley Central SD	Warwick
n/a	n/a	Washingtonville Central SD	Washingtonville
n/a	n/a	Waterloo Central SD	Waterloo
n/a	n/a	Watertown City SD	Watertown
n/a	n/a	Waverly Central SD	Waverly
n/a	n/a	Wayne Central SD	Ontario Center
n/a	n/a	Webster Central SD	Webster
n/a	n/a	West Babylon UFSD	West Babylon
n/a	n/a	West Genesee Central SD	Camillus
n/a	n/a	West Hempstead UFSD	West Hempstead
n/a	n/a	West Irondequoit Central SD	Rochester
n/a	n/a	West Islip UFSD	West Islip
n/a	n/a	West Seneca Central SD	West Seneca
n/a	n/a	Westbury UFSD	Old Westbury
n/a	n/a	Westhampton Bch UFSD	Westhampton Bch
n/a	n/a	Westhill Central SD	Syracuse
n/a	n/a	White Plains City SD	White Plains
n/a	n/a	Whitesboro Central SD	Yorkville
n/a	n/a	William Floyd UFSD	Mastic Beach
n/a	n/a	Williamsville Central SD	East Amherst
n/a	n/a	Windsor Central SD	Windsor
n/a	n/a	Wyandanch UFSD	Wyandanch
n/a	n/a	Yonkers City SD	Yonkers
n/a	n/a	Yorkshire-Pioneer Central SD	Yorkshire
n/a	n/a	Yorktown Central SD	Yorktown Hgts
n/a	n/a	New York City Public Schools	New York

Students who are Two or More Races

Rank	Percent	District Name	City
1	9.4	Jamestown City SD	Jamestown
2	9.2	Geneva City SD	Geneva
3	9.1	Batavia City SD	Batavia
4	8.4	Binghamton City SD	Binghamton
5	7.5	Niagara Falls City SD	Niagara Falls
6	7.4	Union-Endicott Central SD	Endicott
7	7.3	Charter School for Applied Tech	Buffalo
7	7.3	Medina Central SD	Medina
9	6.6	Indian River Central SD	Philadelphia
10	6.5	Elmira City SD	Elmira
10	6.5	Solvay UFSD	Solvay
12	5.9	Carthage Central SD	Carthage
12	5.9	Johnson City Central SD	Johnson City
14	5.7	Ithaca City SD	Ithaca
14	5.7	Kingston City SD	Kingston
16	5.6	Auburn City SD	Auburn
16	5.6	Watertown City SD	Watertown
18	5.5	Scarsdale UFSD	Scarsdale
19	5.3	East Irondequoit Central SD	Rochester
19	5.3	Hudson City SD	Hudson
19	5.3	Lansingburgh Central SD	Troy
22	5.0	Olean City SD	Olean
23	4.9	Edgemont UFSD	Scarsdale
24	4.8	East Greenbush Central SD	East Greenbush
24	4.8	Gates-Chili Central SD	Rochester
26	4.6	Catskill Central SD	Catskill
26	4.6	South Colonie Central SD	Albany
28	4.5	Brighton Central SD	Rochester
28	4.5	Hastings-On-Hudson UFSD	Hastings on Hdsn
28	4.5	Pelham UFSD	Pelham
31	4.4	Newark Central SD	Newark
32	4.3	Beacon City SD	Beacon
33	4.2	Poughkeepsie City SD	Poughkeepsie
33	4.2	Syracuse City SD	Syracuse
35	4.1	Katonah-Lewisboro UFSD	Goldens Bridge
35	4.1	North Syracuse Central SD	North Syracuse
35	4.1	Utica City SD	Utica
38	4.0	Hendrick Hudson Central SD	Montrose
38	4.0	Lockport City SD	Lockport
40	3.9	Albany City SD	Albany
40	3.9	Rye Neck UFSD	Mamaroneck
42	3.8	Brockport Central SD	Brockport
42	3.8	Cheektowaga Central SD	Cheektowaga
42	3.8	Ravena-Coeymans-Selkirk Ctrl SD	Ravena
42	3.8	Troy City SD	Troy
46	3.7	Chappaqua Central SD	Chappaqua
46	3.7	Westhampton Bch UFSD	Westhampton Bch
48	3.6	Cohoes City SD	Cohoes
48	3.6	Liverpool Central SD	Liverpool
48	3.6	Williamsville Central SD	East Amherst
51	3.5	Dryden Central SD	Dryden
51	3.5	Nyack UFSD	Nyack
53	3.4	Amherst Central SD	Amherst
53	3.4	Longwood Central SD	Middle Island
53	3.4	Saugerties Central SD	Saugerties
53	3.4	Spencerport Central SD	Spencerport
57	3.3	Baldwinsville Central SD	Baldwinsville
57	3.3	Chenango Valley Central SD	Binghamton
57	3.3	Cortland City SD	Cortland
57	3.3	Monticello Central SD	Monticello
61	3.2	Cheektowaga-Maryvale UFSD	Cheektowaga
61	3.2	Eastchester UFSD	Eastchester
61	3.2	Hudson Falls Central SD	Fort Edward
61	3.2	Pittsford Central SD	Pittsford
65	3.1	Glens Falls City SD	Glens Falls
65	3.1	Greece Central SD	Rochester
65	3.1	Highland Central SD	Highland
68	3.0	Baldwin UFSD	Baldwin
68	3.0	Half Hollow Hills Central SD	Dix Hills
68	3.0	Kenmore-Tonawanda UFSD	Buffalo
68	3.0	Niagara-Wheatfield Central SD	Niagara Falls
68	3.0	Palmyra-Macedon Central SD	Palmyra
68	3.0	Schenectady City SD	Schenectady
74	2.9	Corning City SD	Painted Post
74	2.9	Hyde Park Central SD	Hyde Park

Note: This section only includes districts with 1,500 or more students; All categories are ranked from high to low

74	2.9	Irvington UFSD	Irvington
74	2.9	William Floyd UFSD	Mastic Beach
78	2.8	Bronxville UFSD	Bronxville
78	2.8	Buffalo City SD	Buffalo
78	2.8	Gloversville City SD	Gloversville
78	2.8	North Colonie CSD	Latham
78	2.8	Penfield Central SD	Rochester
78	2.8	Rush-Henrietta Central SD	Henrietta
84	2.7	Fredonia Central SD	Fredonia
84	2.7	Susquehanna Valley Central SD	Conklin
84	2.7	West Irondequoit Central SD	Rochester
87	2.6	Bedford Central SD	Bedford
87	2.6	Brewster Central SD	Brewster
87	2.6	Canandaigua City SD	Canandaigua
87	2.6	Huntington UFSD	Huntington Stn
87	2.6	New Hartford Central SD	New Hartford
92	2.5	Dunkirk City SD	Dunkirk
92	2.5	Ossining UFSD	Ossining
92	2.5	Pine Bush Central SD	Pine Bush
92	2.5	Port Jervis City SD	Port Jervis
92	2.5	Tonawanda City SD	Tonawanda
92	2.5	West Hempstead UFSD	West Hempstead
98	2.4	Frontier Central SD	Hamburg
98	2.4	Grand Island Central SD	Grand Island
98	2.4	Guilderland Central SD	Guilderland Center
98	2.4	Islip UFSD	Islip
98	2.4	Shenendehowa Central SD	Clifton Park
103	2.3	Amityville UFSD	Amityville
103	2.3	Hornell City SD	Hornell
103	2.3	Penn Yan Central SD	Penn Yan
103	2.3	Spackenkill UFSD	Poughkeepsie
107	2.2	Amsterdam City SD	Amsterdam
107	2.2	Carmel Central SD	Patterson
107	2.2	Harborfields Central SD	Greenlawn
107	2.2	Horseheads Central SD	Horseheads
107	2.2	Jamesville-Dewitt Central SD	Dewitt
107	2.2	Newfane Central SD	Burt
107	2.2	Oyster Bay-East Norwich Central SD	Oyster Bay
107	2.2	Port Washington UFSD	Port Washington
107	2.2	Rockville Ctr UFSD	Rockville Ctr
107	2.2	UFSD of the Tarrytowns	Sleepy Hollow
107	2.2	Yorktown Central SD	Yorktown Hgts
118	2.1	Arlington Central SD	Lagrangeville
118	2.1	Deer Park UFSD	Deer Park
118	2.1	East Islip UFSD	Islip Terrace
118	2.1	Ellenville Central SD	Ellenville
118	2.1	Hilton Central SD	Hilton
118	2.1	Middletown City SD	Middletown
118	2.1	New Hyde Pk-Garden City Pk UFSD	New Hyde Park
118	2.1	NYC Geographic District # 3	New York
118	2.1	North Bellmore UFSD	Bellmore
118	2.1	South Huntington UFSD	Huntington Stn
118	2.1	Whitesboro Central SD	Yorkville
129	2.0	Liberty Central SD	Liberty
129	2.0	Mamaroneck UFSD	Mamaroneck
129	2.0	NYC Geographic District # 2	New York
129	2.0	Oceanside UFSD	Oceanside
129	2.0	Oneida City SD	Oneida
129	2.0	Phoenix Central SD	Phoenix
129	2.0	Rotterdam-Mohonasen Central SD	Schenectady
129	2.0	Schalmont Central SD	Schenectady
129	2.0	Springville-Griffith Institute CSD	Springville
138	1.9	Churchville-Chili Central SD	Churchville
138	1.9	East Syracuse-Minoa Central SD	East Syracuse
138	1.9	Hewlett-Woodmere UFSD	Woodmere
138	1.9	Marlboro Central SD	Milton
138	1.9	New Paltz Central SD	New Paltz
138	1.9	Newburgh City SD	Newburgh
138	1.9	Ramapo Central SD (Suffern)	Hillburn
138	1.9	Saratoga Spgs City SD	Saratoga Spgs
138	1.9	Vestal Central SD	Vestal
138	1.9	Waterloo Central SD	Waterloo
148	1.8	East Hampton UFSD	East Hampton
148	1.8	Honeoye Falls-Lima Central SD	Honeoye Falls
148	1.8	NYC Geographic District #15	Brooklyn
148	1.8	South Country Central SD	East Patchogue
148	1.8	Valhalla UFSD	Valhalla
148	1.8	Valley Central SD (Montgomery)	Montgomery
148	1.8	West Islip UFSD	West Islip
155	1.7	Chittenango Central SD	Chittenango
155	1.7	Clarence Central SD	Clarence
155	1.7	Elwood UFSD	Greenlawn
155	1.7	Mahopac Central SD	Mahopac
155	1.7	NYC Geographic District #13	Brooklyn

155	1.7	Peru Central SD	Peru
155	1.7	White Plains City SD	White Plains
162	1.6	Bay Shore UFSD	Bay Shore
162	1.6	Depew UFSD	Depew
162	1.6	Elmont UFSD	Elmont
162	1.6	Iroquois Central SD	Elma
162	1.6	Maine-Endwell Central SD	Endwell
162	1.6	Middle Country Central SD	Centereach
162	1.6	North Shore Central SD	Sea Cliff
162	1.6	Oswego City SD	Oswego
162	1.6	South Orangetown Central SD	Blauvelt
162	1.6	Westhill Central SD	Syracuse
172	1.5	Babylon UFSD	Babylon
172	1.5	Central Square Central SD	Central Square
172	1.5	Clarkstown Central SD	New City
172	1.5	Lancaster Central SD	Lancaster
172	1.5	Livonia Central SD	Livonia
172	1.5	Long Beach City SD	Long Beach
172	1.5	Mexico Central SD	Mexico
172	1.5	Oneonta City SD	Oneonta
180	1.4	Averill Park Central SD	Averill Park
180	1.4	Franklin Square UFSD	Franklin Square
180	1.4	Hicksville UFSD	Hicksville
180	1.4	Miller Place UFSD	Miller Place
180	1.4	NYC Geographic District # 1	New York
180	1.4	Northport-East Northport UFSD	Northport
180	1.4	Patchogue-Medford UFSD	Patchogue
180	1.4	West Seneca Central SD	West Seneca
188	1.3	Bethlehem Central SD	Delmar
188	1.3	Burnt Hills-Ballston Lake Central SD	Scotia
188	1.3	Chenango Forks Central SD	Binghamton
188	1.3	Cornwall Central SD	Cornwall on Hdsn
188	1.3	Croton-Harmon UFSD	Croton on Hdsn
188	1.3	Great Neck UFSD	Great Neck
188	1.3	NYC Geographic District #28	Jamaica
188	1.3	Niskayuna Central SD	Schenectady
188	1.3	Peekskill City SD	Peekskill
188	1.3	Queensbury UFSD	Queensbury
188	1.3	Valley Stream 13 UFSD	Valley Stream
188	1.3	Webster Central SD	Webster
200	1.2	Brookhaven-Comsewogue UFSD	Port Jefferson Sta
200	1.2	Fairport Central SD	Fairport
200	1.2	Freeport UFSD	Freeport
200	1.2	Fulton City SD	Fulton
200	1.2	Hamburg Central SD	Hamburg
200	1.2	Lackawanna City SD	Lackawanna
200	1.2	Lewiston-Porter Central SD	Youngstown
200	1.2	Locust Valley Central SD	Locust Valley
200	1.2	North Babylon UFSD	North Babylon
200	1.2	Rocky Point UFSD	Rocky Point
200	1.2	Sayville UFSD	Sayville
200	1.2	Victor Central SD	Victor
200	1.2	Wantagh UFSD	Wantagh
200	1.2	Wayne Central SD	Ontario Center
200	1.2	West Genesee Central SD	Camillus
200	1.2	Yonkers City SD	Yonkers
216	1.1	Byram Hills Central SD	Armonk
216	1.1	Camden Central SD	Camden
216	1.1	Commack UFSD	East Northport
216	1.1	Copiague UFSD	Copiague
216	1.1	Fayetteville-Manlius Central SD	Manlius
216	1.1	Haverstraw-Stony Point CSD	Garnerville
216	1.1	Lynbrook UFSD	Lynbrook
216	1.1	Malverne UFSD	Malverne
216	1.1	Manhasset UFSD	Manhasset
216	1.1	Riverhead Central SD	Riverhead
216	1.1	Sachem Central SD	Lake Ronkonkoma
216	1.1	Sherrill City SD	Verona
216	1.1	Sweet Home Central SD	Amherst
216	1.1	Syosset Central SD	Syosset
216	1.1	Washingtonville Central SD	Washingtonville
216	1.1	Windsor Central SD	Windsor
232	1.0	Bayport-Blue Point UFSD	Bayport
232	1.0	Goshen Central SD	Goshen
232	1.0	Hauppauge UFSD	Hauppauge
232	1.0	Owego-Apalachin Central SD	Owego
232	1.0	Pleasantville UFSD	Pleasantville
232	1.0	Salmon River Central SD	Fort Covington
232	1.0	South Jefferson Central SD	Adams Center
232	1.0	Wallkill Central SD	Wallkill
232	1.0	West Babylon UFSD	West Babylon
241	0.9	Evans-Brant Central SD (Lake Shore)	Angola
241	0.9	Greenburgh Central SD	Hartsdale
241	0.9	Harrison Central SD	Harrison

241	0.9	Johnstown City SD	Johnstown
241	0.9	Lakeland Central SD	Shrub Oak
241	0.9	Merrick UFSD	Merrick
241	0.9	Nanuet UFSD	Nanuet
241	0.9	NYC Geographic District #31	Staten Island
241	0.9	North Tonawanda City SD	North Tonawanda
241	0.9	Norwich City SD	Norwich
241	0.9	Plainview-Old Bethpage Central SD	Plainview
241	0.9	Shoreham-Wading River Central SD	Shoreham
241	0.9	Wappingers Central SD	Wappingers Fls
241	0.9	Waverly Central SD	Waverly
255	0.8	Bethpage UFSD	Bethpage
255	0.8	Briarcliff Mnr UFSD	Briarcliff Mnr
255	0.8	East Ramapo CSD (Spring Valley)	Spring Valley
255	0.8	Farmingdale UFSD	Farmingdale
255	0.8	Garden City UFSD	Garden City
255	0.8	General Brown Central SD	Dexter
255	0.8	Homer Central SD	Homer
255	0.8	Malone Central SD	Malone
255	0.8	Massena Central SD	Massena
255	0.8	NYC Geographic District # 4	New York
255	0.8	NYC Geographic District # 5	New York
255	0.8	NYC Geographic District #26	Bayside
255	0.8	Orchard Park Central SD	West Seneca
255	0.8	Seaford UFSD	Seaford
255	0.8	S Glens Fls Central SD	S Glens Fls
255	0.8	Starpoint Central SD	Lockport
255	0.8	Three Village Central SD	Stony Brook
255	0.8	Warwick Valley Central SD	Warwick
273	0.7	Lawrence UFSD	Lawrence
273	0.7	Levittown UFSD	Levittown
273	0.7	Lindenhurst UFSD	Lindenhurst
273	0.7	Orange-Ulster Boces	Goshen
273	0.7	Putnam Valley Central SD	Putnam Valley
273	0.7	Rye City SD	Rye
273	0.7	Smithtown Central SD	Smithtown
273	0.7	New York City Public Schools	New York
281	0.6	Ardsley UFSD	Ardsley
281	0.6	Cobleskill-Richmondville Central SD	Cobleskill
281	0.6	Connetquot Central SD	Bohemia
281	0.6	Eden Central SD	Eden
281	0.6	Hampton Bays UFSD	Hampton Bays
281	0.6	Kings Park Central SD	Kings Park
281	0.6	Marcellus Central SD	Marcellus
281	0.6	Mineola UFSD	Mineola
281	0.6	Monroe-Woodbury Central SD	Central Valley
281	0.6	NYC Geographic District #17	Brooklyn
281	0.6	NYC Geographic District #22	Brooklyn
281	0.6	NYC Geographic District #25	Flushing
281	0.6	NYC Geographic District #30	Long Isl City
281	0.6	NYC Special Schools - District 75	New York
281	0.6	Rondout Valley Central SD	Accord
296	0.5	Broadalbin-Perth Central SD	Broadalbin
296	0.5	East Meadow UFSD	Westbury
296	0.5	New Rochelle City SD	New Rochelle
296	0.5	NYC Geographic District #10	Bronx
296	0.5	NYC Geographic District #14	Brooklyn
296	0.5	NYC Geographic District #21	Brooklyn
296	0.5	NYC Geographic District #27	Ozone Park
296	0.5	NYC Geographic District #29	Queens Village
296	0.5	Uniondale UFSD	Uniondale
296	0.5	Yorkshire-Pioneer Central SD	Yorkshire
306	0.4	Bath Central SD	Bath
306	0.4	Cazenovia Central SD	Cazenovia
306	0.4	Cold Spring Hrbr Central SD	Cold Spring Hrbr
306	0.4	East Aurora UFSD	East Aurora
306	0.4	East Williston UFSD	Old Westbury
306	0.4	Glen Cove City SD	Glen Cove
306	0.4	Herricks UFSD	New Hyde Park
306	0.4	Mount Pleasant Central SD	Thornwood
306	0.4	Mount Vernon SD	Mount Vernon
306	0.4	NYC Geographic District # 6	New York
306	0.4	NYC Geographic District #11	Bronx
306	0.4	NYC Geographic District #18	Brooklyn
306	0.4	NYC Geographic District #20	Brooklyn
306	0.4	Rome City SD	Rome
306	0.4	Wyandanch UFSD	Wyandanch
321	0.3	Alden Central SD	Alden
321	0.3	Brentwood UFSD	Brentwood
321	0.3	Dansville Central SD	Dansville
321	0.3	Eastport-South Manor CSD	Manorville
321	0.3	Kinderhook Central SD	Valatie
321	0.3	NYC Geographic District # 7	Bronx
321	0.3	NYC Geographic District # 8	Bronx

Note: This section only includes districts with 1,500 or more students; All categories are ranked from high to low

321	0.3	NYC Geographic District #16	Brooklyn
321	0.3	NYC Geographic District #24	Corona
321	0.3	Plattsburgh City SD	Plattsburgh
321	0.3	Roslyn UFSD	Roslyn
321	0.3	Scotia-Glenville Central SD	Scotia
333	0.2	Ballston Spa Central SD	Ballston Spa
333	0.2	Central Valley CSD At Ilion-Mohawk	Ilion
333	0.2	Gouverneur Central SD	Gouverneur
333	0.2	Hempstead UFSD	Hempstead
333	0.2	Island Trees UFSD	Levittown
333	0.2	Jericho UFSD	Jericho
333	0.2	Mount Sinai UFSD	Mount Sinai
333	0.2	NYC Geographic District # 9	Bronx
333	0.2	NYC Geographic District #12	Bronx
333	0.2	NYC Geographic District #19	Brooklyn
333	0.2	NYC Geographic District #23	Brooklyn
333	0.2	Ogdensburg City SD	Ogdensburg
333	0.2	Phelps-Clifton Springs Central SD	Clifton Springs
333	0.2	Port Chester-Rye UFSD	Port Chester
333	0.2	Red Hook Central SD	Red Hook
333	0.2	Schuylerville Central SD	Schuylerville
333	0.2	Southampton UFSD	Southampton
333	0.2	Valley Stream Central High SD	Valley Stream
351	0.1	Beekmantown Central SD	West Chazy
351	0.1	Bellmore-Merrick Central High SD	North Merrick
351	0.1	Central Islip UFSD	Central Islip
351	0.1	Massapequa UFSD	Massapequa
351	0.1	NYC Geographic District #32	Brooklyn
351	0.1	Rochester City SD	Rochester
351	0.1	Sewanhaka Central High SD	Floral Park
351	0.1	Somers Central SD	Somers
351	0.1	Westbury UFSD	Old Westbury
360	0.0	Albion Central SD	Albion
360	0.0	Center Moriches UFSD	Center Moriches
360	0.0	Minisink Valley Central SD	Slate Hill
360	0.0	Pearl River UFSD	Pearl River
360	0.0	Plainedge UFSD	N Massapequa
360	0.0	Roosevelt UFSD	Roosevelt

Hispanic Students

Rank	Percent	District Name	City
1	86.9	NYC Geographic District # 6	New York
2	79.2	Brentwood UFSD	Brentwood
3	76.2	NYC Geographic District #32	Brooklyn
4	74.8	Port Chester-Rye UFSD	Port Chester
5	69.7	NYC Geographic District # 7	Bronx
6	68.8	Central Islip UFSD	Central Islip
6	68.8	NYC Geographic District #12	Bronx
8	67.7	NYC Geographic District #10	Bronx
9	67.3	Westbury UFSD	Old Westbury
10	66.8	NYC Geographic District # 9	Bronx
11	64.0	NYC Geographic District # 8	Bronx
12	62.3	NYC Geographic District #24	Corona
13	61.9	NYC Geographic District # 4	New York
14	61.5	Hempstead UFSD	Hempstead
15	60.3	Freeport UFSD	Freeport
16	59.0	NYC Geographic District #14	Brooklyn
17	58.1	Peekskill City SD	Peekskill
18	56.7	UFSD of the Tarrytowns	Sleepy Hollow
19	54.9	Yonkers City SD	Yonkers
20	54.1	Copiague UFSD	Copiague
21	53.9	NYC Geographic District #30	Long Isl City
22	53.8	White Plains City SD	White Plains
23	53.1	Ossining UFSD	Ossining
24	51.6	Glen Cove City SD	Glen Cove
25	50.8	Middletown City SD	Middletown
25	50.8	Uniondale UFSD	Uniondale
27	50.5	Hampton Bays UFSD	Hampton Bays
28	49.8	Haverstraw-Stony Point CSD	Garnerville
29	47.8	Dunkirk City SD	Dunkirk
30	47.0	Lawrence UFSD	Lawrence
31	46.7	Newburgh City SD	Newburgh
32	45.6	East Hampton UFSD	East Hampton
33	45.5	East Ramapo CSD (Spring Valley)	Spring Valley
34	43.3	Amityville UFSD	Amityville
35	43.2	New Rochelle City SD	New Rochelle
36	42.1	Wyandanch UFSD	Wyandanch
37	41.6	NYC Geographic District #11	Bronx
38	41.3	Roosevelt UFSD	Roosevelt
39	41.1	NYC Geographic District # 1	New York
39	41.1	NYC Geographic District #15	Brooklyn
41	41.0	NYC Geographic District #19	Brooklyn
42	40.9	Huntington UFSD	Huntington Stn
43	40.8	Amsterdam City SD	Amsterdam
44	40.2	New York City Public Schools	New York
45	39.6	NYC Geographic District # 5	New York
46	38.8	NYC Special Schools - District 75	New York
47	37.8	Bay Shore UFSD	Bay Shore
48	36.8	NYC Geographic District #27	Ozone Park
49	35.7	Liberty Central SD	Liberty
50	34.6	NYC Geographic District # 3	New York
51	34.4	Greenburgh Central SD	Hartsdale
52	34.3	Patchogue-Medford UFSD	Patchogue
53	33.8	West Hempstead UFSD	West Hempstead
54	33.5	NYC Geographic District # 2	New York
55	33.1	Riverhead Central SD	Riverhead
56	33.0	Ellenville Central SD	Ellenville
57	32.7	South Huntington UFSD	Huntington Stn
58	31.6	Southampton UFSD	Southampton
59	30.0	Charter School for Applied Tech	Buffalo
60	29.7	Poughkeepsie City SD	Poughkeepsie
61	28.5	NYC Geographic District #25	Flushing
62	28.4	South Country Central SD	East Patchogue
63	27.8	Bedford Central SD	Bedford
64	27.4	Beacon City SD	Beacon
65	26.7	Elmont UFSD	Elmont
66	26.5	NYC Geographic District #20	Brooklyn
67	26.3	NYC Geographic District #31	Staten Island
68	26.0	Hicksville UFSD	Hicksville
68	26.0	NYC Geographic District #28	Jamaica
70	25.5	Rochester City SD	Rochester
71	25.3	Valley Stream 13 UFSD	Valley Stream
72	25.1	Monticello Central SD	Monticello
73	25.0	Baldwin UFSD	Baldwin
73	25.0	NYC Geographic District #21	Brooklyn
75	24.8	Valley Stream Central High SD	Valley Stream
76	23.9	Brewster Central SD	Brewster
77	23.8	William Floyd UFSD	Mastic Beach
78	23.5	Geneva City SD	Geneva
79	23.1	Long Beach City SD	Long Beach
80	22.7	Brookhaven-Comsewogue UFSD	Port Jefferson Sta
81	22.0	Mineola UFSD	Mineola
82	20.9	Hendrick Hudson Central SD	Montrose
82	20.9	Longwood Central SD	Middle Island
84	20.6	Islip UFSD	Islip
85	20.5	North Babylon UFSD	North Babylon
86	20.3	Monroe-Woodbury Central SD	Central Valley
86	20.3	Valhalla UFSD	Valhalla
88	20.1	Wallkill Central SD	Wallkill
89	20.0	Malverne UFSD	Malverne
90	19.7	East Meadow UFSD	Westbury
90	19.7	NYC Geographic District #23	Brooklyn
92	19.4	Carmel Central SD	Patterson
93	19.3	Valley Central SD (Montgomery)	Montgomery
94	19.1	Deer Park UFSD	Deer Park
94	19.1	Mamaroneck UFSD	Mamaroneck
94	19.1	Nyack UFSD	Nyack
97	18.9	Jamestown City SD	Jamestown
98	18.4	Westhampton Bch UFSD	Westhampton Bch
99	18.3	Washingtonville Central SD	Washingtonville
100	18.2	Farmingdale UFSD	Farmingdale
100	18.2	Port Washington UFSD	Port Washington
102	17.9	Utica City SD	Utica
103	17.8	Oyster Bay-East Norwich Central SD	Oyster Bay
104	17.6	Mount Vernon SD	Mount Vernon
105	17.5	Schenectady City SD	Schenectady
106	17.4	Lindenhurst UFSD	Lindenhurst
106	17.4	NYC Geographic District #16	Brooklyn
108	17.3	Goshen Central SD	Goshen
108	17.3	Rye Neck UFSD	Mamaroneck
110	17.2	Buffalo City SD	Buffalo
110	17.2	Franklin Square UFSD	Franklin Square
112	16.9	East Irondequoit Central SD	Rochester
112	16.9	NYC Geographic District #26	Bayside
112	16.9	West Babylon UFSD	West Babylon
115	16.7	Pine Bush Central SD	Pine Bush
116	16.5	Harrison Central SD	Harrison
117	16.1	Lakeland Central SD	Shrub Oak
117	16.1	Sewanhaka Central High SD	Floral Park
119	15.9	Ramapo Central SD (Suffern)	Hillburn
120	15.8	NYC Geographic District #13	Brooklyn
121	15.7	Levittown UFSD	Levittown
121	15.7	New Hyde Pk-Garden City Pk UFSD	New Hyde Park
123	15.6	Albany City SD	Albany
123	15.6	Kingston City SD	Kingston
125	15.5	Indian River Central SD	Philadelphia
126	15.2	Middle Country Central SD	Centereach
127	15.1	Nanuet UFSD	Nanuet
128	14.9	Pelham UFSD	Pelham
129	14.6	Locust Valley Central SD	Locust Valley
130	14.5	Croton-Harmon UFSD	Croton on Hdsn
130	14.5	Island Trees UFSD	Levittown
130	14.5	NYC Geographic District #22	Brooklyn
133	13.9	Minisink Valley Central SD	Slate Hill
133	13.9	Oceanside UFSD	Oceanside
133	13.9	Troy City SD	Troy
136	13.7	Cornwall Central SD	Cornwall on Hdsn
136	13.7	Hewlett-Woodmere UFSD	Woodmere
136	13.7	NYC Geographic District #17	Brooklyn
139	13.5	Lynbrook UFSD	Lynbrook
139	13.5	Mahopac Central SD	Mahopac
139	13.5	NYC Geographic District #29	Queens Village
142	13.4	East Islip UFSD	Islip Terrace
143	13.3	Clarkstown Central SD	New City
144	13.2	Syracuse City SD	Syracuse
145	13.1	Marlboro Central SD	Milton
146	12.9	Elwood UFSD	Greenlawn
147	12.8	Hudson City SD	Hudson
148	12.7	Lackawanna City SD	Lackawanna
148	12.7	Wappingers Central SD	Wappingers Fls
150	12.5	Putnam Valley Central SD	Putnam Valley
151	12.4	Binghamton City SD	Binghamton
152	12.3	Port Jervis City SD	Port Jervis
153	12.1	Bethpage UFSD	Bethpage
154	11.9	Hyde Park Central SD	Hyde Park
154	11.9	Newark Central SD	Newark
156	11.7	Center Moriches UFSD	Center Moriches
157	11.3	Hastings-On-Hudson UFSD	Hastings on Hdsn
158	11.1	Rockville Ctr UFSD	Rockville Ctr
159	11.0	Spackenkill UFSD	Poughkeepsie
160	10.9	Ardsley UFSD	Ardsley
160	10.9	Greece Central SD	Rochester
160	10.9	Highland Central SD	Highland
160	10.9	South Orangetown Central SD	Blauvelt
164	10.7	Arlington Central SD	Lagrangeville
164	10.7	New Paltz Central SD	New Paltz
164	10.7	Warwick Valley Central SD	Warwick
164	10.7	Yorktown Central SD	Yorktown Hgts
168	10.6	Albion Central SD	Albion
168	10.6	Eastchester UFSD	Eastchester
170	10.5	North Bellmore UFSD	Bellmore
171	10.2	Sachem Central SD	Lake Ronkonkoma
172	10.0	Lansingburgh Central SD	Troy
173	9.8	West Irondequoit Central SD	Rochester
174	9.6	Babylon UFSD	Babylon
174	9.6	Catskill Central SD	Catskill
174	9.6	Fredonia Central SD	Fredonia
177	9.4	Carthage Central SD	Carthage
178	9.2	Saugerties Central SD	Saugerties
179	9.1	Connetquot Central SD	Bohemia
180	9.0	Pearl River UFSD	Pearl River
181	8.8	Half Hollow Hills Central SD	Dix Hills
181	8.8	Watertown City SD	Watertown
183	8.6	Johnson City Central SD	Johnson City
183	8.6	Mount Pleasant Central SD	Thornwood
185	8.5	Gates-Chili Central SD	Rochester
186	8.0	Pleasantville UFSD	Pleasantville
187	7.9	Great Neck UFSD	Great Neck
187	7.9	Harborfields Central SD	Greenlawn
187	7.9	Rocky Point UFSD	Rocky Point
190	7.8	Katonah-Lewisboro UFSD	Goldens Bridge
191	7.4	North Shore Central SD	Sea Cliff
191	7.4	West Islip UFSD	West Islip
193	7.2	Medina Central SD	Medina
194	7.1	Hauppauge UFSD	Hauppauge
195	6.9	Irvington UFSD	Irvington
196	6.6	NYC Geographic District #18	Brooklyn
197	6.5	South Colonie Central SD	Albany
198	6.4	Oneonta City SD	Oneonta
198	6.4	Roslyn UFSD	Roslyn
198	6.4	Union-Endicott Central SD	Endicott
201	6.3	Batavia City SD	Batavia
201	6.3	Edgemont UFSD	Scarsdale
201	6.3	Northport-East Northport UFSD	Northport
201	6.3	Ravena-Coeymans-Selkirk Ctrl SD	Ravena
205	6.0	Cohoes City SD	Cohoes
205	6.0	Herricks UFSD	New Hyde Park
205	6.0	Orange-Ulster Boces	Goshen
208	5.9	Briarcliff Mnr UFSD	Briarcliff Mnr
208	5.9	Rush-Henrietta Central SD	Henrietta

Note: This section only includes districts with 1,500 or more students; All categories are ranked from high to low

208	5.9	Scarsdale UFSD	Scarsdale
211	5.8	Lockport City SD	Lockport
211	5.8	Miller Place UFSD	Miller Place
211	5.8	Solvay UFSD	Solvay
214	5.7	Brockport Central SD	Brockport
214	5.7	Ithaca City SD	Ithaca
214	5.7	Rondout Valley Central SD	Accord
217	5.6	Commack UFSD	East Northport
217	5.6	Mount Sinai UFSD	Mount Sinai
217	5.6	Red Hook Central SD	Red Hook
217	5.6	Rye City SD	Rye
221	5.5	Smithtown Central SD	Smithtown
222	5.4	Cheektowaga Central SD	Cheektowaga
222	5.4	Kenmore-Tonawanda UFSD	Buffalo
222	5.4	Niagara Falls City SD	Niagara Falls
222	5.4	Sweet Home Central SD	Amherst
226	5.3	Bellmore-Merrick Central High SD	North Merrick
226	5.3	Manhasset UFSD	Manhasset
228	5.2	Brighton Central SD	Rochester
228	5.2	Penfield Central SD	Rochester
228	5.2	Sayville UFSD	Sayville
228	5.2	Seaford UFSD	Seaford
232	5.1	Bayport-Blue Point UFSD	Bayport
233	5.0	Amherst Central SD	Amherst
233	5.0	Bronxville UFSD	Bronxville
233	5.0	Merrick UFSD	Merrick
233	5.0	Spencerport Central SD	Spencerport
237	4.9	Phelps-Clifton Springs Central SD	Clifton Springs
237	4.9	Rome City SD	Rome
239	4.8	Shoreham-Wading River Central SD	Shoreham
240	4.7	Wantagh UFSD	Wantagh
240	4.7	Webster Central SD	Webster
242	4.6	Churchville-Chili Central SD	Churchville
242	4.6	East Greenbush Central SD	East Greenbush
242	4.6	Oswego City SD	Oswego
242	4.6	Plainedge UFSD	N Massapequa
242	4.6	Shenendehowa Central SD	Clifton Park
247	4.5	East Williston UFSD	Old Westbury
248	4.4	Chappaqua Central SD	Chappaqua
248	4.4	Penn Yan Central SD	Penn Yan
250	4.3	Kings Park Central SD	Kings Park
250	4.3	Liverpool Central SD	Liverpool
250	4.3	Pittsford Central SD	Pittsford
250	4.3	Plainview-Old Bethpage Central SD	Plainview
250	4.3	Three Village Central SD	Stony Brook
255	4.2	Eastport-South Manor CSD	Manorville
256	4.1	Fulton City SD	Fulton
256	4.1	Hilton Central SD	Hilton
256	4.1	Somers Central SD	Somers
259	4.0	New Hartford Central SD	New Hartford
259	4.0	North Colonie CSD	Latham
259	4.0	Palmyra-Macedon Central SD	Palmyra
262	3.9	Cortland City SD	Cortland
263	3.8	Rotterdam-Mohonasen Central SD	Schenectady
264	3.7	Cheektowaga-Maryvale UFSD	Cheektowaga
264	3.7	Jamesville-Dewitt Central SD	Dewitt
266	3.6	Auburn City SD	Auburn
266	3.6	Gloversville City SD	Gloversville
266	3.6	Tonawanda City SD	Tonawanda
269	3.5	Canandaigua City SD	Canandaigua
269	3.5	Grand Island Central SD	Grand Island
269	3.5	Schalmont Central SD	Schenectady
272	3.4	Cobleskill-Richmondville Central SD	Cobleskill
272	3.4	Glens Falls City SD	Glens Falls
272	3.4	Waterloo Central SD	Waterloo
275	3.3	Williamsville Central SD	East Amherst
276	3.2	Baldwinsville Central SD	Baldwinsville
276	3.2	Norwich City SD	Norwich
276	3.2	Victor Central SD	Victor
279	3.1	Byram Hills Central SD	Armonk
279	3.1	Cold Spring Hrbr Central SD	Cold Spring Hrbr
279	3.1	Dansville Central SD	Dansville
279	3.1	Depew UFSD	Depew
279	3.1	Frontier Central SD	Hamburg
279	3.1	Massapequa UFSD	Massapequa
279	3.1	North Syracuse Central SD	North Syracuse
279	3.1	Syosset Central SD	Syosset
279	3.1	West Seneca Central SD	West Seneca
288	3.0	Guilderland Central SD	Guilderland Center
288	3.0	Johnstown City SD	Johnstown
290	2.8	Chenango Forks Central SD	Binghamton
290	2.8	Fairport Central SD	Fairport
290	2.8	Saratoga Spgs City SD	Saratoga Spgs
290	2.8	Schuylerville Central SD	Schuylerville
290	2.8	Vestal Central SD	Vestal
295	2.7	Dryden Central SD	Dryden
295	2.7	Olean City SD	Olean
297	2.6	Garden City UFSD	Garden City
297	2.6	Horseheads Central SD	Horseheads
297	2.6	Hudson Falls Central SD	Fort Edward
297	2.6	Jericho UFSD	Jericho
297	2.6	North Tonawanda City SD	North Tonawanda
297	2.6	Wayne Central SD	Ontario Center
297	2.6	Westhill Central SD	Syracuse
304	2.5	Honeoye Falls-Lima Central SD	Honeoye Falls
305	2.4	Niskayuna Central SD	Schenectady
306	2.3	Broadalbin-Perth Central SD	Broadalbin
306	2.3	Chittenango Central SD	Chittenango
306	2.3	Elmira City SD	Elmira
306	2.3	Evans-Brant Central SD (Lake Shore)	Angola
306	2.3	Fayetteville-Manlius Central SD	Manlius
306	2.3	General Brown Central SD	Dexter
306	2.3	Newfane Central SD	Burt
306	2.3	Niagara-Wheatfield Central SD	Niagara Falls
314	2.2	Bethlehem Central SD	Delmar
314	2.2	Chenango Valley Central SD	Binghamton
314	2.2	Lancaster Central SD	Lancaster
314	2.2	Maine-Endwell Central SD	Endwell
314	2.2	Scotia-Glenville Central SD	Scotia
314	2.2	West Genesee Central SD	Camillus
320	2.1	Averill Park Central SD	Averill Park
320	2.1	Lewiston-Porter Central SD	Youngstown
320	2.1	Susquehanna Valley Central SD	Conklin
323	2.0	Cazenovia Central SD	Cazenovia
323	2.0	Clarence Central SD	Clarence
323	2.0	Corning City SD	Painted Post
323	2.0	Hamburg Central SD	Hamburg
327	1.9	East Syracuse-Minoa Central SD	East Syracuse
327	1.9	Owego-Apalachin Central SD	Owego
329	1.8	East Aurora UFSD	East Aurora
329	1.8	Gouverneur Central SD	Gouverneur
329	1.8	Hornell City SD	Hornell
329	1.8	Livonia Central SD	Livonia
329	1.8	Mexico Central SD	Mexico
329	1.8	Queensbury UFSD	Queensbury
329	1.8	Windsor Central SD	Windsor
336	1.7	Homer Central SD	Homer
336	1.7	Massena Central SD	Massena
336	1.7	Orchard Park Central SD	West Seneca
336	1.7	Springville-Griffith Institute CSD	Springville
336	1.7	Whitesboro Central SD	Yorkville
336	1.7	Yorkshire-Pioneer Central SD	Yorkshire
342	1.6	Burnt Hills-Ballston Lake Central SD	Scotia
342	1.6	Camden Central SD	Camden
342	1.6	Eden Central SD	Eden
342	1.6	Kinderhook Central SD	Valatie
342	1.6	S Glens Fls Central SD	S Glens Fls
347	1.4	Beekmantown Central SD	West Chazy
347	1.4	Iroquois Central SD	Elma
347	1.4	Starpoint Central SD	Lockport
350	1.3	Central Square Central SD	Central Square
350	1.3	Phoenix Central SD	Phoenix
352	1.2	Alden Central SD	Alden
352	1.2	Oneida City SD	Oneida
354	1.1	Peru Central SD	Peru
355	1.0	Ballston Spa Central SD	Ballston Spa
356	0.9	Waverly Central SD	Waverly
357	0.7	Bath Central SD	Bath
357	0.7	Marcellus Central SD	Marcellus
359	0.6	Sherrill City SD	Verona
359	0.6	South Jefferson Central SD	Adams Center
361	0.5	Salmon River Central SD	Fort Covington
362	0.4	Plattsburgh City SD	Plattsburgh
363	0.3	Central Valley CSD At Ilion-Mohawk	Ilion
364	0.2	Malone Central SD	Malone
365	0.1	Ogdensburg City SD	Ogdensburg

Individual Education Program Students

Rank	Percent	District Name	City
1	31.5	East Ramapo CSD (Spring Valley)	Spring Valley
2	31.4	NYC Geographic District #16	Brooklyn
3	30.7	Lawrence UFSD	Lawrence
4	29.0	Lackawanna City SD	Lackawanna
5	27.9	NYC Geographic District # 5	New York
6	27.8	NYC Geographic District #23	Brooklyn
7	27.1	NYC Geographic District # 8	Bronx
8	26.8	NYC Geographic District # 7	Bronx
9	25.4	NYC Geographic District # 4	New York
10	25.3	NYC Geographic District # 9	Bronx
11	25.1	Buffalo City SD	Buffalo
12	24.8	NYC Geographic District #31	Staten Island
13	24.0	Kingston City SD	Kingston
14	23.8	NYC Geographic District #12	Bronx
15	23.6	NYC Geographic District #19	Brooklyn
16	23.2	Kenmore-Tonawanda UFSD	Buffalo
16	23.2	NYC Geographic District #11	Bronx
18	23.0	NYC Geographic District #17	Brooklyn
19	22.7	Wyandanch UFSD	Wyandanch
20	22.4	Troy City SD	Troy
21	21.8	North Tonawanda City SD	North Tonawanda
22	21.7	Peekskill City SD	Peekskill
23	21.5	NYC Geographic District #10	Bronx
23	21.5	NYC Geographic District #32	Brooklyn
25	21.4	Lansingburgh Central SD	Troy
26	21.3	Mount Vernon SD	Mount Vernon
26	21.3	Plattsburgh City SD	Plattsburgh
26	21.3	Rochester City SD	Rochester
29	21.2	Hudson City SD	Hudson
30	21.0	NYC Geographic District # 1	New York
30	21.0	NYC Geographic District #21	Brooklyn
30	21.0	NYC Geographic District #22	Brooklyn
30	21.0	Valley Central SD (Montgomery)	Montgomery
34	20.9	NYC Geographic District #18	Brooklyn
35	20.8	Syracuse City SD	Syracuse
36	20.7	Schenectady City SD	Schenectady
37	20.6	Catskill Central SD	Catskill
37	20.6	Port Jervis City SD	Port Jervis
39	20.5	Ellenville Central SD	Ellenville
40	20.3	Hyde Park Central SD	Hyde Park
40	20.3	NYC Geographic District #27	Ozone Park
40	20.3	West Islip UFSD	West Islip
43	20.1	NYC Geographic District #14	Brooklyn
44	19.9	Gouverneur Central SD	Gouverneur
44	19.9	Rondout Valley Central SD	Accord
46	19.8	Long Beach City SD	Long Beach
46	19.8	Malverne UFSD	Malverne
48	19.7	Beekmantown Central SD	West Chazy
48	19.7	NYC Geographic District #29	Queens Village
50	19.6	Hewlett-Woodmere UFSD	Woodmere
50	19.6	NYC Geographic District #15	Brooklyn
52	19.5	Dryden Central SD	Dryden
53	19.4	Beacon City SD	Beacon
54	19.3	NYC Geographic District # 6	New York
55	19.2	Gloversville City SD	Gloversville
55	19.2	Malone Central SD	Malone
55	19.2	Oneonta City SD	Oneonta
58	19.1	Locust Valley Central SD	Locust Valley
58	19.1	Saugerties Central SD	Saugerties
60	18.9	Poughkeepsie City SD	Poughkeepsie
61	18.8	Albany City SD	Albany
62	18.7	Gates-Chili Central SD	Rochester
62	18.7	Hornell City SD	Hornell
62	18.7	Niagara Falls City SD	Niagara Falls
62	18.7	Utica City SD	Utica
66	18.6	Averill Park Central SD	Averill Park
66	18.6	Olean City SD	Olean
68	18.5	East Greenbush Central SD	East Greenbush
69	18.4	Amityville UFSD	Amityville
69	18.4	Frontier Central SD	Hamburg
69	18.4	Greenburgh Central SD	Hartsdale
69	18.4	Liverpool Central SD	Liverpool
69	18.4	New York City Public Schools	New York
74	18.3	Lewiston-Porter Central SD	Youngstown
74	18.3	NYC Geographic District #20	Brooklyn
74	18.3	Owego-Apalachin Central SD	Owego
77	18.2	Maine-Endwell Central SD	Endwell
78	18.1	Huntington UFSD	Huntington Stn
79	18.0	Evans-Brant Central SD (Lake Shore)	Angola
79	18.0	Lockport City SD	Lockport
81	17.9	Longwood Central SD	Middle Island
81	17.9	Rocky Point UFSD	Rocky Point
81	17.9	Scotia-Glenville Central SD	Scotia
84	17.8	Mahopac Central SD	Mahopac
84	17.8	Merrick UFSD	Merrick
84	17.8	Mexico Central SD	Mexico
84	17.8	North Bellmore UFSD	Bellmore
88	17.7	Bath Central SD	Bath
88	17.7	Cheektowaga Central SD	Cheektowaga
88	17.7	Glen Cove City SD	Glen Cove
88	17.7	Half Hollow Hills Central SD	Dix Hills

Note: This section only includes districts with 1,500 or more students; All categories are ranked from high to low

92	17.6	Baldwin UFSD	Baldwin
92	17.6	North Shore Central SD	Sea Cliff
92	17.6	Union-Endicott Central SD	Endicott
95	17.4	Marlboro Central SD	Milton
95	17.4	Minisink Valley Central SD	Slate Hill
95	17.4	Norwich City SD	Norwich
98	17.3	East Syracuse-Minoa Central SD	East Syracuse
98	17.3	Hudson Falls Central SD	Fort Edward
98	17.3	Lakeland Central SD	Shrub Oak
101	17.2	Glens Falls City SD	Glens Falls
101	17.2	North Babylon UFSD	North Babylon
101	17.2	Penn Yan Central SD	Penn Yan
101	17.2	West Hempstead UFSD	West Hempstead
101	17.2	Yonkers City SD	Yonkers
106	17.1	Corning City SD	Painted Post
106	17.1	Dansville Central SD	Dansville
106	17.1	Fulton City SD	Fulton
106	17.1	Lindenhurst UFSD	Lindenhurst
106	17.1	Monticello Central SD	Monticello
106	17.1	Port Washington UFSD	Port Washington
106	17.1	Shoreham-Wading River Central SD	Shoreham
106	17.1	Wappingers Central SD	Wappingers Fls
114	17.0	Central Valley CSD At Ilion-Mohawk	Ilion
114	17.0	South Jefferson Central SD	Adams Center
116	16.9	Kinderhook Central SD	Valatie
116	16.9	Kings Park Central SD	Kings Park
116	16.9	NYC Geographic District #24	Corona
116	16.9	Ogdensburg City SD	Ogdensburg
116	16.9	Oneida City SD	Oneida
116	16.9	Watertown City SD	Watertown
122	16.8	Mount Pleasant Central SD	Thornwood
122	16.8	New Paltz Central SD	New Paltz
122	16.8	Newburgh City SD	Newburgh
122	16.8	Waterloo Central SD	Waterloo
122	16.8	Yorkshire-Pioneer Central SD	Yorkshire
127	16.7	Commack UFSD	East Northport
127	16.7	NYC Geographic District #28	Jamaica
129	16.5	Binghamton City SD	Binghamton
129	16.5	Depew UFSD	Depew
129	16.5	Lancaster Central SD	Lancaster
129	16.5	NYC Geographic District # 3	New York
129	16.5	Orchard Park Central SD	West Seneca
129	16.5	Oswego City SD	Oswego
129	16.5	Phelps-Clifton Springs Central SD	Clifton Springs
129	16.5	Ramapo Central SD (Suffern)	Hillburn
129	16.5	Seaford UFSD	Seaford
138	16.4	Riverhead Central SD	Riverhead
138	16.4	Rome City SD	Rome
138	16.4	Somers Central SD	Somers
138	16.4	South Huntington UFSD	Huntington Stn
138	16.4	Yorktown Central SD	Yorktown Hgts
143	16.3	Middletown City SD	Middletown
143	16.3	Plainview-Old Bethpage Central SD	Plainview
145	16.2	Arlington Central SD	Lagrangeville
145	16.2	Babylon UFSD	Babylon
145	16.2	Connetquot Central SD	Bohemia
145	16.2	Deer Park UFSD	Deer Park
149	16.1	Mineola UFSD	Mineola
149	16.1	Monroe-Woodbury Central SD	Central Valley
151	16.0	Carthage Central SD	Carthage
151	16.0	Cohoes City SD	Cohoes
151	16.0	Harborfields Central SD	Greenlawn
151	16.0	Johnson City Central SD	Johnson City
151	16.0	NYC Geographic District #30	Long Isl City
156	15.9	Brighton Central SD	Rochester
156	15.9	Levittown UFSD	Levittown
158	15.8	Hamburg Central SD	Hamburg
159	15.7	Bay Shore UFSD	Bay Shore
159	15.7	Bayport-Blue Point UFSD	Bayport
159	15.7	Central Square Central SD	Central Square
159	15.7	Chenango Forks Central SD	Binghamton
159	15.7	Whitesboro Central SD	Yorkville
164	15.6	Brookhaven-Comsewogue UFSD	Port Jefferson Sta
164	15.6	Clarkstown Central SD	New City
164	15.6	Eden Central SD	Eden
164	15.6	North Colonie CSD	Latham
164	15.6	Southampton UFSD	Southampton
169	15.5	Guilderland Central SD	Guilderland Center
169	15.5	Newfane Central SD	Burt
169	15.5	Salmon River Central SD	Fort Covington
169	15.5	Westhill Central SD	Syracuse
169	15.5	White Plains City SD	White Plains
174	15.4	Alden Central SD	Alden
174	15.4	Auburn City SD	Auburn
174	15.4	Chenango Valley Central SD	Binghamton
174	15.4	Goshen Central SD	Goshen
174	15.4	Hempstead UFSD	Hempstead
179	15.3	Carmel Central SD	Patterson
179	15.3	Farmingdale UFSD	Farmingdale
179	15.3	Pine Bush Central SD	Pine Bush
179	15.3	South Country Central SD	East Patchogue
179	15.3	Warwick Valley Central SD	Warwick
184	15.2	Copiague UFSD	Copiague
184	15.2	Geneva City SD	Geneva
184	15.2	Putnam Valley Central SD	Putnam Valley
187	15.1	East Islip UFSD	Islip Terrace
187	15.1	Eastport-South Manor CSD	Manorville
189	15.0	Amsterdam City SD	Amsterdam
189	15.0	Ballston Spa Central SD	Ballston Spa
189	15.0	Elmira City SD	Elmira
189	15.0	Jamesville-Dewitt Central SD	Dewitt
189	15.0	Middle Country Central SD	Centereach
189	15.0	Northport-East Northport UFSD	Northport
189	15.0	South Colonie Central SD	Albany
189	15.0	Vestal Central SD	Vestal
197	14.9	Canandaigua City SD	Canandaigua
197	14.9	Chittenango Central SD	Chittenango
197	14.9	Jericho UFSD	Jericho
197	14.9	Katonah-Lewisboro UFSD	Goldens Bridge
197	14.9	Miller Place UFSD	Miller Place
197	14.9	NYC Geographic District # 2	New York
197	14.9	North Syracuse Central SD	North Syracuse
197	14.9	Oyster Bay-East Norwich Central SD	Oyster Bay
205	14.8	Brockport Central SD	Brockport
205	14.8	Freeport UFSD	Freeport
205	14.8	Manhasset UFSD	Manhasset
205	14.8	NYC Geographic District #25	Flushing
205	14.8	Ravena-Coeymans-Selkirk Ctrl SD	Ravena
205	14.8	Susquehanna Valley Central SD	Conklin
205	14.8	Wantagh UFSD	Wantagh
212	14.7	Center Moriches UFSD	Center Moriches
212	14.7	Herricks UFSD	New Hyde Park
212	14.7	Homer Central SD	Homer
212	14.7	Rotterdam-Mohonasen Central SD	Schenectady
212	14.7	Smithtown Central SD	Smithtown
212	14.7	Wallkill Central SD	Wallkill
218	14.6	Fairport Central SD	Fairport
218	14.6	General Brown Central SD	Dexter
218	14.6	Great Neck UFSD	Great Neck
218	14.6	Highland Central SD	Highland
218	14.6	Nyack UFSD	Nyack
218	14.6	Solvay UFSD	Solvay
218	14.6	Valhalla UFSD	Valhalla
225	14.5	Baldwinsville Central SD	Baldwinsville
225	14.5	Brentwood UFSD	Brentwood
225	14.5	East Irondequoit Central SD	Rochester
225	14.5	Sayville UFSD	Sayville
225	14.5	Valley Stream Central High SD	Valley Stream
225	14.5	West Babylon UFSD	West Babylon
231	14.4	Cheektowaga-Maryvale UFSD	Cheektowaga
231	14.4	Iroquois Central SD	Elma
231	14.4	Islip UFSD	Islip
231	14.4	Rockville Ctr UFSD	Rockville Ctr
231	14.4	Three Village Central SD	Stony Brook
236	14.3	Amherst Central SD	Amherst
236	14.3	Ardsley UFSD	Ardsley
236	14.3	Brewster Central SD	Brewster
236	14.3	Irvington UFSD	Irvington
236	14.3	Ithaca City SD	Ithaca
236	14.3	Patchogue-Medford UFSD	Patchogue
236	14.3	Roosevelt UFSD	Roosevelt
236	14.3	William Floyd UFSD	Mastic Beach
244	14.2	Massena Central SD	Massena
244	14.2	Pleasantville UFSD	Pleasantville
244	14.2	Port Chester-Rye UFSD	Port Chester
244	14.2	Tonawanda City SD	Tonawanda
248	14.1	Burnt Hills-Ballston Lake Central SD	Scotia
248	14.1	Hendrick Hudson Central SD	Montrose
248	14.1	Hicksville UFSD	Hicksville
248	14.1	Palmyra-Macedon Central SD	Palmyra
248	14.1	Red Hook Central SD	Red Hook
248	14.1	Sachem Central SD	Lake Ronkonkoma
248	14.1	S Glens Fls Central SD	S Glens Fls
255	14.0	Indian River Central SD	Philadelphia
255	14.0	NYC Geographic District #13	Brooklyn
255	14.0	West Genesee Central SD	Camillus
258	13.9	Edgemont UFSD	Scarsdale
258	13.9	Hauppauge UFSD	Hauppauge
258	13.9	Mamaroneck UFSD	Mamaroneck
258	13.9	New Rochelle City SD	New Rochelle
258	13.9	Queensbury UFSD	Queensbury
258	13.9	Westbury UFSD	Old Westbury
264	13.8	Byram Hills Central SD	Armonk
264	13.8	Camden Central SD	Camden
264	13.8	Clarence Central SD	Clarence
264	13.8	Pearl River UFSD	Pearl River
264	13.8	UFSD of the Tarrytowns	Sleepy Hollow
269	13.7	Haverstraw-Stony Point CSD	Garnerville
269	13.7	Lynbrook UFSD	Lynbrook
269	13.7	Newark Central SD	Newark
269	13.7	Spencerport Central SD	Spencerport
269	13.7	Valley Stream 13 UFSD	Valley Stream
269	13.7	Waverly Central SD	Waverly
269	13.7	Windsor Central SD	Windsor
276	13.5	Greece Central SD	Rochester
276	13.5	Honeoye Falls-Lima Central SD	Honeoye Falls
278	13.4	Bethpage UFSD	Bethpage
278	13.4	Churchville-Chili Central SD	Churchville
278	13.4	Grand Island Central SD	Grand Island
278	13.4	NYC Geographic District #26	Bayside
282	13.3	Bellmore-Merrick Central High SD	North Merrick
282	13.3	Central Islip UFSD	Central Islip
282	13.3	East Meadow UFSD	Westbury
282	13.3	Eastchester UFSD	Eastchester
282	13.3	Garden City UFSD	Garden City
282	13.3	Washingtonville Central SD	Washingtonville
288	13.2	Elmont UFSD	Elmont
288	13.2	Horseheads Central SD	Horseheads
288	13.2	Jamestown City SD	Jamestown
288	13.2	Ossining UFSD	Ossining
292	13.1	Cortland City SD	Cortland
292	13.1	Oceanside UFSD	Oceanside
292	13.1	West Seneca Central SD	West Seneca
295	12.9	Batavia City SD	Batavia
295	12.9	Cornwall Central SD	Cornwall on Hdsn
295	12.9	Croton-Harmon UFSD	Croton on Hdsn
295	12.9	Sewanhaka Central High SD	Floral Park
295	12.9	South Orangetown Central SD	Blauvelt
300	12.8	Cazenovia Central SD	Cazenovia
300	12.8	Medina Central SD	Medina
302	12.7	Bethlehem Central SD	Delmar
302	12.7	Hastings-On-Hudson UFSD	Hastings on Hdsn
302	12.7	Liberty Central SD	Liberty
302	12.7	Plainedge UFSD	N Massapequa
306	12.6	New Hyde Pk-Garden City Pk UFSD	New Hyde Park
306	12.6	Schalmont Central SD	Schenectady
308	12.4	Hampton Bays UFSD	Hampton Bays
308	12.4	Harrison Central SD	Harrison
308	12.4	Spackenkill UFSD	Poughkeepsie
311	12.3	East Williston UFSD	Old Westbury
311	12.3	Island Trees UFSD	Levittown
311	12.3	Nanuet UFSD	Nanuet
311	12.3	Wayne Central SD	Ontario Center
315	12.2	Mount Sinai UFSD	Mount Sinai
315	12.2	Syosset Central SD	Syosset
317	12.1	Elwood UFSD	Greenlawn
318	12.0	Bedford Central SD	Bedford
318	12.0	Pelham UFSD	Pelham
318	12.0	Springville-Griffith Institute CSD	Springville
321	11.9	Niagara-Wheatfield Central SD	Niagara Falls
322	11.8	Johnstown City SD	Johnstown
323	11.7	Franklin Square UFSD	Franklin Square
323	11.7	Starpoint Central SD	Lockport
323	11.7	Uniondale UFSD	Uniondale
323	11.7	Westhampton Bch UFSD	Westhampton Bch
327	11.6	East Hampton UFSD	East Hampton
328	11.5	Williamsville Central SD	East Amherst
329	11.3	Albion Central SD	Albion
329	11.3	Marcellus Central SD	Marcellus
329	11.3	Phoenix Central SD	Phoenix
329	11.3	Shenendehowa Central SD	Clifton Park
333	11.2	Chappaqua Central SD	Chappaqua
334	11.1	Rush-Henrietta Central SD	Henrietta
335	11.0	Fayetteville-Manlius Central SD	Manlius
335	11.0	Niskayuna Central SD	Schenectady
337	10.9	Fredonia Central SD	Fredonia
338	10.8	Rye Neck UFSD	Mamaroneck
339	10.7	Broadalbin-Perth Central SD	Broadalbin
339	10.7	Massapequa UFSD	Massapequa
341	10.6	Saratoga Spgs City SD	Saratoga Spgs
341	10.6	Sherrill City SD	Verona
341	10.6	West Irondequoit Central SD	Rochester

Note: This section only includes districts with 1,500 or more students; All categories are ranked from high to low

344	10.4	Cobleskill-Richmondville Central SD	Cobleskill
344	10.4	East Aurora UFSD	East Aurora
344	10.4	Pittsford Central SD	Pittsford
344	10.4	Webster Central SD	Webster
348	10.3	Dunkirk City SD	Dunkirk
349	10.2	Cold Spring Hrbr Central SD	Cold Spring Hrbr
350	10.0	New Hartford Central SD	New Hartford
351	9.9	Penfield Central SD	Rochester
351	9.9	Schuylerville Central SD	Schuylerville
353	9.8	Hilton Central SD	Hilton
354	9.7	Livonia Central SD	Livonia
355	9.6	Roslyn UFSD	Roslyn
355	9.6	Victor Central SD	Victor
357	9.5	Scarsdale UFSD	Scarsdale
358	9.2	Briarcliff Mnr UFSD	Briarcliff Mnr
358	9.2	Bronxville UFSD	Bronxville
360	8.8	Sweet Home Central SD	Amherst
361	8.4	Rye City SD	Rye
362	0.0	Charter School for Applied Tech	Buffalo
362	0.0	NYC Special Schools - District 75	New York
362	0.0	Orange-Ulster Boces	Goshen
n/a	n/a	Peru Central SD	Peru

English Language Learner Students

Rank	Percent	District Name	City
1	32.2	Brentwood UFSD	Brentwood
2	30.1	Westbury UFSD	Old Westbury
3	28.2	East Ramapo CSD (Spring Valley)	Spring Valley
4	26.7	Central Islip UFSD	Central Islip
5	25.4	Port Chester-Rye UFSD	Port Chester
6	23.8	Hempstead UFSD	Hempstead
7	19.5	Roosevelt UFSD	Roosevelt
8	18.1	Peekskill City SD	Peekskill
9	16.5	Hampton Bays UFSD	Hampton Bays
10	16.2	Freeport UFSD	Freeport
11	16.1	Wyandanch UFSD	Wyandanch
12	15.5	Utica City SD	Utica
13	14.9	White Plains City SD	White Plains
14	14.8	Riverhead Central SD	Riverhead
15	14.4	Amityville UFSD	Amityville
16	14.2	Copiague UFSD	Copiague
17	13.8	UFSD of the Tarrytowns	Sleepy Hollow
18	13.6	Huntington UFSD	Huntington Stn
19	13.0	Newburgh City SD	Newburgh
20	12.9	Uniondale UFSD	Uniondale
21	12.7	East Hampton UFSD	East Hampton
22	12.6	Lackawanna City SD	Lackawanna
23	12.3	Syracuse City SD	Syracuse
24	12.2	Haverstraw-Stony Point CSD	Garnerville
25	12.1	Buffalo City SD	Buffalo
26	12.0	Middletown City SD	Middletown
27	11.8	Glen Cove City SD	Glen Cove
27	11.8	Yonkers City SD	Yonkers
29	11.4	Dunkirk City SD	Dunkirk
30	11.2	South Huntington UFSD	Huntington Stn
31	11.0	Southampton UFSD	Southampton
32	10.6	Patchogue-Medford UFSD	Patchogue
33	9.8	Rochester City SD	Rochester
34	9.6	New Rochelle City SD	New Rochelle
35	9.4	Bedford Central SD	Bedford
36	9.2	Poughkeepsie City SD	Poughkeepsie
37	8.9	Ossining UFSD	Ossining
38	8.8	Lawrence UFSD	Lawrence
39	8.3	Hicksville UFSD	Hicksville
40	8.1	Albany City SD	Albany
41	7.8	Harrison Central SD	Harrison
42	7.5	Mineola UFSD	Mineola
42	7.5	Mount Vernon SD	Mount Vernon
44	7.2	Hudson City SD	Hudson
45	7.1	Port Washington UFSD	Port Washington
46	6.4	Greenburgh Central SD	Hartsdale
47	6.3	Geneva City SD	Geneva
47	6.3	South Country Central SD	East Patchogue
49	6.2	West Hempstead UFSD	West Hempstead
50	6.1	Liberty Central SD	Liberty
51	5.7	Valley Stream 13 UFSD	Valley Stream
52	5.5	New Hyde Pk-Garden City Pk UFSD	New Hyde Park
53	5.3	Nyack UFSD	Nyack
54	5.2	Eastchester UFSD	Eastchester
55	5.1	Oyster Bay-East Norwich Central SD	Oyster Bay
56	5.0	Bay Shore UFSD	Bay Shore
57	4.9	Herricks UFSD	New Hyde Park
58	4.7	Brewster Central SD	Brewster
58	4.7	Great Neck UFSD	Great Neck
60	4.5	Westhampton Bch UFSD	Westhampton Bch
61	4.4	Brookhaven-Comsewogue UFSD	Port Jefferson Sta
61	4.4	Ithaca City SD	Ithaca
61	4.4	Jamestown City SD	Jamestown
61	4.4	Nanuet UFSD	Nanuet
65	4.1	Baldwin UFSD	Baldwin
65	4.1	Elmont UFSD	Elmont
65	4.1	Rush-Henrietta Central SD	Henrietta
68	4.0	Binghamton City SD	Binghamton
69	3.9	Long Beach City SD	Long Beach
69	3.9	Longwood Central SD	Middle Island
71	3.8	Deer Park UFSD	Deer Park
71	3.8	Lindenhurst UFSD	Lindenhurst
71	3.8	Locust Valley Central SD	Locust Valley
74	3.7	Schenectady City SD	Schenectady
74	3.7	Sweet Home Central SD	Amherst
76	3.6	East Meadow UFSD	Westbury
76	3.6	Islip UFSD	Islip
78	3.5	Mamaroneck UFSD	Mamaroneck
78	3.5	West Babylon UFSD	West Babylon
80	3.4	Rye Neck UFSD	Mamaroneck
81	3.3	Kingston City SD	Kingston
81	3.3	Monticello Central SD	Monticello
81	3.3	William Floyd UFSD	Mastic Beach
84	3.2	Amsterdam City SD	Amsterdam
84	3.2	Hewlett-Woodmere UFSD	Woodmere
84	3.2	North Babylon UFSD	North Babylon
84	3.2	Ramapo Central SD (Suffern)	Hillburn
88	3.1	Guilderland Central SD	Guilderland Center
88	3.1	Indian River Central SD	Philadelphia
88	3.1	Kinderhook Central SD	Valatie
88	3.1	Oceanside UFSD	Oceanside
92	3.0	Ellenville Central SD	Ellenville
92	3.0	Middle Country Central SD	Centereach
94	2.9	Center Moriches UFSD	Center Moriches
94	2.9	Elwood UFSD	Greenlawn
94	2.9	Island Trees UFSD	Levittown
94	2.9	Malverne UFSD	Malverne
94	2.9	Monroe-Woodbury Central SD	Central Valley
99	2.8	Farmingdale UFSD	Farmingdale
99	2.8	Fredonia Central SD	Fredonia
99	2.8	Rye City SD	Rye
99	2.8	Solvay UFSD	Solvay
99	2.8	Valhalla UFSD	Valhalla
104	2.7	Gates-Chili Central SD	Rochester
104	2.7	North Colonie CSD	Latham
104	2.7	South Orangetown Central SD	Blauvelt
107	2.6	Goshen Central SD	Goshen
107	2.6	Roslyn UFSD	Roslyn
109	2.5	Charter School for Applied Tech	Buffalo
109	2.5	East Irondequoit Central SD	Rochester
109	2.5	Hyde Park Central SD	Hyde Park
109	2.5	Johnson City Central SD	Johnson City
109	2.5	Sewanhaka Central High SD	Floral Park
114	2.4	Brighton Central SD	Rochester
114	2.4	Cheektowaga-Maryvale UFSD	Cheektowaga
116	2.3	Amherst Central SD	Amherst
116	2.3	Carmel Central SD	Patterson
116	2.3	Rocky Point UFSD	Rocky Point
116	2.3	Spackenkill UFSD	Poughkeepsie
120	2.2	Bethpage UFSD	Bethpage
120	2.2	Franklin Square UFSD	Franklin Square
120	2.2	Jericho UFSD	Jericho
120	2.2	Scarsdale UFSD	Scarsdale
120	2.2	Williamsville Central SD	East Amherst
125	2.1	Irvington UFSD	Irvington
125	2.1	Kenmore-Tonawanda UFSD	Buffalo
127	2.0	Cheektowaga Central SD	Cheektowaga
127	2.0	Clarkstown Central SD	New City
127	2.0	Manhasset UFSD	Manhasset
127	2.0	New Paltz Central SD	New Paltz
127	2.0	Red Hook Central SD	Red Hook
127	2.0	Spencerport Central SD	Spencerport
127	2.0	Valley Stream Central High SD	Valley Stream
134	1.9	East Williston UFSD	Old Westbury
134	1.9	Greece Central SD	Rochester
134	1.9	Half Hollow Hills Central SD	Dix Hills
134	1.9	Hendrick Hudson Central SD	Montrose
134	1.9	Levittown UFSD	Levittown
134	1.9	Pleasantville UFSD	Pleasantville
140	1.8	Albion Central SD	Albion
140	1.8	Beacon City SD	Beacon
140	1.8	Cohoes City SD	Cohoes
140	1.8	Lansingburgh Central SD	Troy
140	1.8	Newark Central SD	Newark
140	1.8	Syosset Central SD	Syosset
146	1.7	Croton-Harmon UFSD	Croton on Hdsn
146	1.7	East Syracuse-Minoa Central SD	East Syracuse
146	1.7	Liverpool Central SD	Liverpool
146	1.7	Mahopac Central SD	Mahopac
146	1.7	North Bellmore UFSD	Bellmore
146	1.7	South Colonie Central SD	Albany
152	1.6	Ardsley UFSD	Ardsley
152	1.6	Jamesville-Dewitt Central SD	Dewitt
152	1.6	Marlboro Central SD	Milton
152	1.6	Watertown City SD	Watertown
152	1.6	Yorktown Central SD	Yorktown Hgts
157	1.5	Edgemont UFSD	Scarsdale
157	1.5	Grand Island Central SD	Grand Island
157	1.5	Lynbrook UFSD	Lynbrook
157	1.5	Northport-East Northport UFSD	Northport
157	1.5	Pine Bush Central SD	Pine Bush
157	1.5	Troy City SD	Troy
157	1.5	Webster Central SD	Webster
164	1.4	Niskayuna Central SD	Schenectady
164	1.4	Phelps-Clifton Springs Central SD	Clifton Springs
164	1.4	Rockville Ctr UFSD	Rockville Ctr
164	1.4	Sachem Central SD	Lake Ronkonkoma
164	1.4	Saugerties Central SD	Saugerties
164	1.4	Wallkill Central SD	Wallkill
164	1.4	West Irondequoit Central SD	Rochester
171	1.3	Arlington Central SD	Lagrangeville
171	1.3	Connetquot Central SD	Bohemia
171	1.3	Fairport Central SD	Fairport
171	1.3	Hauppauge UFSD	Hauppauge
171	1.3	Mount Pleasant Central SD	Thornwood
171	1.3	Pearl River UFSD	Pearl River
171	1.3	Warwick Valley Central SD	Warwick
178	1.2	East Islip UFSD	Islip Terrace
178	1.2	Harborfields Central SD	Greenlawn
178	1.2	Lakeland Central SD	Shrub Oak
178	1.2	Penfield Central SD	Rochester
178	1.2	Rome City SD	Rome
178	1.2	Vestal Central SD	Vestal
184	1.1	Babylon UFSD	Babylon
184	1.1	Churchville-Chili Central SD	Churchville
184	1.1	Hastings-On-Hudson UFSD	Hastings on Hdsn
184	1.1	Katonah-Lewisboro UFSD	Goldens Bridge
184	1.1	North Syracuse Central SD	North Syracuse
184	1.1	Pelham UFSD	Pelham
184	1.1	Shenendehowa Central SD	Clifton Park
191	1.0	Carthage Central SD	Carthage
191	1.0	Dansville Central SD	Dansville
191	1.0	Eastport-South Manor CSD	Manorville
191	1.0	Kings Park Central SD	Kings Park
191	1.0	Lockport City SD	Lockport
191	1.0	New Hartford Central SD	New Hartford
191	1.0	Niagara Falls City SD	Niagara Falls
191	1.0	North Tonawanda City SD	North Tonawanda
191	1.0	Oswego City SD	Oswego
191	1.0	Somers Central SD	Somers
201	0.9	Catskill Central SD	Catskill
201	0.9	Medina Central SD	Medina
201	0.9	Merrick UFSD	Merrick
201	0.9	Penn Yan Central SD	Penn Yan
201	0.9	Plainedge UFSD	N Massapequa
201	0.9	Port Jervis City SD	Port Jervis
201	0.9	Valley Central SD (Montgomery)	Montgomery
201	0.9	West Genesee Central SD	Camillus
209	0.8	Bethlehem Central SD	Delmar
209	0.8	Brockport Central SD	Brockport
209	0.8	Chappaqua Central SD	Chappaqua
209	0.8	Depew UFSD	Depew
209	0.8	Minisink Valley Central SD	Slate Hill
209	0.8	Putnam Valley Central SD	Putnam Valley
209	0.8	Ravena-Coeymans-Selkirk Ctrl SD	Ravena
209	0.8	Rondout Valley Central SD	Accord
209	0.8	Rotterdam-Mohonasen Central SD	Schenectady
209	0.8	Victor Central SD	Victor
209	0.8	Wappingers Central SD	Wappingers Fls
220	0.7	Bronxville UFSD	Bronxville
220	0.7	Commack UFSD	East Northport
220	0.7	Cornwall Central SD	Cornwall on Hdsn
220	0.7	Miller Place UFSD	Miller Place
220	0.7	Niagara-Wheatfield Central SD	Niagara Falls
220	0.7	North Shore Central SD	Sea Cliff

Note: This section only includes districts with 1,500 or more students; All categories are ranked from high to low

220	0.7	Plattsburgh City SD	Plattsburgh
220	0.7	Schuylerville Central SD	Schuylerville
220	0.7	Seaford UFSD	Seaford
220	0.7	Smithtown Central SD	Smithtown
220	0.7	Three Village Central SD	Stony Brook
220	0.7	Washingtonville Central SD	Washingtonville
220	0.7	Wayne Central SD	Ontario Center
220	0.7	Westhill Central SD	Syracuse
234	0.6	Canandaigua City SD	Canandaigua
234	0.6	Cazenovia Central SD	Cazenovia
234	0.6	Chenango Valley Central SD	Binghamton
234	0.6	Cold Spring Hrbr Central SD	Cold Spring Hrbr
234	0.6	Corning City SD	Painted Post
234	0.6	East Greenbush Central SD	East Greenbush
234	0.6	Fayetteville-Manlius Central SD	Manlius
234	0.6	Highland Central SD	Highland
234	0.6	Hilton Central SD	Hilton
234	0.6	Plainview-Old Bethpage Central SD	Plainview
234	0.6	Shoreham-Wading River Central SD	Shoreham
234	0.6	Whitesboro Central SD	Yorkville
246	0.5	Ballston Spa Central SD	Ballston Spa
246	0.5	Batavia City SD	Batavia
246	0.5	Bellmore-Merrick Central High SD	North Merrick
246	0.5	Dryden Central SD	Dryden
246	0.5	Homer Central SD	Homer
246	0.5	Pittsford Central SD	Pittsford
246	0.5	Queensbury UFSD	Queensbury
246	0.5	Saratoga Spgs City SD	Saratoga Spgs
246	0.5	Union-Endicott Central SD	Endicott
246	0.5	West Islip UFSD	West Islip
256	0.4	Auburn City SD	Auburn
256	0.4	Averill Park Central SD	Averill Park
256	0.4	Baldwinsville Central SD	Baldwinsville
256	0.4	Clarence Central SD	Clarence
256	0.4	Honeoye Falls-Lima Central SD	Honeoye Falls
256	0.4	Horseheads Central SD	Horseheads
256	0.4	Hudson Falls Central SD	Fort Edward
256	0.4	Johnstown City SD	Johnstown
256	0.4	Mount Sinai UFSD	Mount Sinai
256	0.4	Oneonta City SD	Oneonta
256	0.4	Owego-Apalachin Central SD	Owego
256	0.4	Starpoint Central SD	Lockport
256	0.4	Tonawanda City SD	Tonawanda
256	0.4	Wantagh UFSD	Wantagh
256	0.4	West Seneca Central SD	West Seneca
271	0.3	Bayport-Blue Point UFSD	Bayport
271	0.3	Briarcliff Mnr UFSD	Briarcliff Mnr
271	0.3	Byram Hills Central SD	Armonk
271	0.3	Central Valley CSD At Ilion-Mohawk	Ilion
271	0.3	Fulton City SD	Fulton
271	0.3	General Brown Central SD	Dexter
271	0.3	Gouverneur Central SD	Gouverneur
271	0.3	Livonia Central SD	Livonia
271	0.3	Maine-Endwell Central SD	Endwell
271	0.3	Marcellus Central SD	Marcellus
271	0.3	Norwich City SD	Norwich
271	0.3	Orchard Park Central SD	West Seneca
271	0.3	Sayville UFSD	Sayville
271	0.3	Windsor Central SD	Windsor
285	0.2	Alden Central SD	Alden
285	0.2	Chittenango Central SD	Chittenango
285	0.2	Cortland City SD	Cortland
285	0.2	Eden Central SD	Eden
285	0.2	Elmira City SD	Elmira
285	0.2	Frontier Central SD	Hamburg
285	0.2	Garden City UFSD	Garden City
285	0.2	Gloversville City SD	Gloversville
285	0.2	Lewiston-Porter Central SD	Youngstown
285	0.2	Massapequa UFSD	Massapequa
285	0.2	Oneida City SD	Oneida
285	0.2	Palmyra-Macedon Central SD	Palmyra
285	0.2	Schalmont Central SD	Schenectady
285	0.2	Scotia-Glenville Central SD	Scotia
285	0.2	Sherrill City SD	Verona
285	0.2	South Jefferson Central SD	Adams Center
301	0.1	Bath Central SD	Bath
301	0.1	Broadalbin-Perth Central SD	Broadalbin
301	0.1	Burnt Hills-Ballston Lake Central SD	Scotia
301	0.1	Chenango Forks Central SD	Binghamton
301	0.1	Cobleskill-Richmondville Central SD	Cobleskill
301	0.1	East Aurora UFSD	East Aurora
301	0.1	Evans-Brant Central SD (Lake Shore)	Angola
301	0.1	Glens Falls City SD	Glens Falls
301	0.1	Hamburg Central SD	Hamburg
301	0.1	Iroquois Central SD	Elma
301	0.1	Lancaster Central SD	Lancaster
301	0.1	S Glens Fls Central SD	S Glens Fls
301	0.1	Springville-Griffith Institute CSD	Springville
301	0.1	Susquehanna Valley Central SD	Conklin
301	0.1	Waterloo Central SD	Waterloo
301	0.1	Waverly Central SD	Waverly
301	0.1	Yorkshire-Pioneer Central SD	Yorkshire
318	0.0	Massena Central SD	Massena
318	0.0	Olean City SD	Olean
n/a	n/a	Beekmantown Central SD	West Chazy
n/a	n/a	Camden Central SD	Camden
n/a	n/a	Central Square Central SD	Central Square
n/a	n/a	Hornell City SD	Hornell
n/a	n/a	Malone Central SD	Malone
n/a	n/a	Mexico Central SD	Mexico
n/a	n/a	NYC Geographic District # 1	New York
n/a	n/a	NYC Geographic District # 2	New York
n/a	n/a	NYC Geographic District # 3	New York
n/a	n/a	NYC Geographic District # 4	New York
n/a	n/a	NYC Geographic District # 5	New York
n/a	n/a	NYC Geographic District # 6	New York
n/a	n/a	NYC Geographic District # 7	Bronx
n/a	n/a	NYC Geographic District # 8	Bronx
n/a	n/a	NYC Geographic District # 9	Bronx
n/a	n/a	NYC Geographic District #10	Bronx
n/a	n/a	NYC Geographic District #11	Bronx
n/a	n/a	NYC Geographic District #12	Bronx
n/a	n/a	NYC Geographic District #13	Brooklyn
n/a	n/a	NYC Geographic District #14	Brooklyn
n/a	n/a	NYC Geographic District #15	Brooklyn
n/a	n/a	NYC Geographic District #16	Brooklyn
n/a	n/a	NYC Geographic District #17	Brooklyn
n/a	n/a	NYC Geographic District #18	Brooklyn
n/a	n/a	NYC Geographic District #19	Brooklyn
n/a	n/a	NYC Geographic District #20	Brooklyn
n/a	n/a	NYC Geographic District #21	Brooklyn
n/a	n/a	NYC Geographic District #22	Brooklyn
n/a	n/a	NYC Geographic District #23	Brooklyn
n/a	n/a	NYC Geographic District #24	Corona
n/a	n/a	NYC Geographic District #25	Flushing
n/a	n/a	NYC Geographic District #26	Bayside
n/a	n/a	NYC Geographic District #27	Ozone Park
n/a	n/a	NYC Geographic District #28	Jamaica
n/a	n/a	NYC Geographic District #29	Queens Village
n/a	n/a	NYC Geographic District #30	Long Isl City
n/a	n/a	NYC Geographic District #31	Staten Island
n/a	n/a	NYC Geographic District #32	Brooklyn
n/a	n/a	Newfane Central SD	Burt
n/a	n/a	NYC Special Schools - District 75	New York
n/a	n/a	Ogdensburg City SD	Ogdensburg
n/a	n/a	Orange-Ulster Boces	Goshen
n/a	n/a	Peru Central SD	Peru
n/a	n/a	Phoenix Central SD	Phoenix
n/a	n/a	Salmon River Central SD	Fort Covington
n/a	n/a	New York City Public Schools	New York

Students Eligible for Free Lunch

Rank	Percent	District Name	City
1	87.8	NYC Geographic District # 9	Bronx
2	86.5	NYC Geographic District # 7	Bronx
3	84.8	NYC Geographic District #12	Bronx
4	83.1	NYC Geographic District #32	Brooklyn
5	81.5	NYC Geographic District #23	Brooklyn
6	80.7	NYC Geographic District #19	Brooklyn
7	80.6	NYC Geographic District # 6	New York
8	79.1	NYC Geographic District #16	Brooklyn
9	78.7	NYC Geographic District #10	Bronx
10	78.5	Rochester City SD	Rochester
11	77.1	NYC Geographic District # 5	New York
11	77.1	Westbury UFSD	Old Westbury
13	76.8	NYC Geographic District #17	Brooklyn
14	75.9	Poughkeepsie City SD	Poughkeepsie
15	75.0	NYC Geographic District # 4	New York
16	74.2	NYC Geographic District # 8	Bronx
17	72.3	East Ramapo CSD (Spring Valley)	Spring Valley
18	71.7	New York City Public Schools	New York
19	71.3	NYC Geographic District #18	Brooklyn
19	71.3	Utica City SD	Utica
21	71.1	Schenectady City SD	Schenectady
22	70.5	NYC Geographic District #11	Bronx
23	70.3	Charter School for Applied Tech	Buffalo
24	69.5	NYC Geographic District #27	Ozone Park
25	69.2	Wyandanch UFSD	Wyandanch
26	69.1	NYC Geographic District #20	Brooklyn
27	68.8	Syracuse City SD	Syracuse
28	68.7	Buffalo City SD	Buffalo
29	68.3	NYC Geographic District #24	Corona
30	67.9	NYC Geographic District #14	Brooklyn
31	67.8	Albany City SD	Albany
32	66.3	NYC Geographic District #29	Queens Village
33	65.1	NYC Special Schools - District 75	New York
33	65.1	Yonkers City SD	Yonkers
35	64.9	NYC Geographic District #30	Long Isl City
36	64.8	Peekskill City SD	Peekskill
37	64.6	Troy City SD	Troy
38	64.3	Dunkirk City SD	Dunkirk
39	64.2	Lackawanna City SD	Lackawanna
40	63.6	Brentwood UFSD	Brentwood
41	63.0	Salmon River Central SD	Fort Covington
42	62.5	NYC Geographic District #21	Brooklyn
43	62.0	Mount Vernon SD	Mount Vernon
44	61.8	NYC Geographic District #13	Brooklyn
45	61.4	NYC Geographic District #28	Jamaica
46	61.0	Central Islip UFSD	Central Islip
47	59.9	Middletown City SD	Middletown
48	59.8	Binghamton City SD	Binghamton
49	59.4	Niagara Falls City SD	Niagara Falls
50	57.6	NYC Geographic District #22	Brooklyn
51	57.5	NYC Geographic District # 1	New York
51	57.5	NYC Geographic District #25	Flushing
53	57.2	Hempstead UFSD	Hempstead
54	56.7	Newburgh City SD	Newburgh
55	55.4	Johnson City Central SD	Johnson City
55	55.4	NYC Geographic District #15	Brooklyn
57	55.2	Jamestown City SD	Jamestown
58	54.0	Elmira City SD	Elmira
59	53.8	Freeport UFSD	Freeport
60	53.5	Amsterdam City SD	Amsterdam
61	52.7	Cohoes City SD	Cohoes
62	52.3	Amityville UFSD	Amityville
63	51.9	Lansingburgh Central SD	Troy
63	51.9	Monticello Central SD	Monticello
65	51.8	Port Jervis City SD	Port Jervis
66	51.2	Hudson City SD	Hudson
67	50.9	Port Chester-Rye UFSD	Port Chester
68	50.8	Lawrence UFSD	Lawrence
69	50.5	Gloversville City SD	Gloversville
69	50.5	NYC Geographic District # 2	New York
71	49.2	Copiague UFSD	Copiague
72	49.1	Liberty Central SD	Liberty
73	48.0	Fulton City SD	Fulton
74	47.4	William Floyd UFSD	Mastic Beach
75	47.3	NYC Geographic District # 3	New York
76	47.2	Geneva City SD	Geneva
77	46.7	NYC Geographic District #31	Staten Island
78	46.4	Cheektowaga Central SD	Cheektowaga
79	45.7	Hornell City SD	Hornell
79	45.7	Norwich City SD	Norwich
81	45.4	NYC Geographic District #26	Bayside
82	45.2	Uniondale UFSD	Uniondale
83	45.1	Ellenville Central SD	Ellenville
84	44.5	Batavia City SD	Batavia
85	44.3	Kingston City SD	Kingston
86	43.6	UFSD of the Tarrytowns	Sleepy Hollow
87	43.3	Rome City SD	Rome
88	42.3	Massena Central SD	Massena
89	42.1	Cortland City SD	Cortland
89	42.1	Watertown City SD	Watertown
91	41.5	Glen Cove City SD	Glen Cove
91	41.5	Waverly Central SD	Waverly
93	41.2	East Irondequoit Central SD	Rochester
93	41.2	Olean City SD	Olean
95	41.0	Ogdensburg City SD	Ogdensburg
96	40.9	Greenburgh Central SD	Hartsdale
97	40.8	Bath Central SD	Bath
98	40.7	Auburn City SD	Auburn
99	40.6	Oswego City SD	Oswego
99	40.6	Riverhead Central SD	Riverhead
101	40.5	Haverstraw-Stony Point CSD	Garnerville
102	40.2	Central Valley CSD At Ilion-Mohawk	Ilion
103	40.0	Beekmantown Central SD	West Chazy
104	39.8	Catskill Central SD	Catskill
104	39.8	Lockport City SD	Lockport
106	39.6	Elmont UFSD	Elmont
106	39.6	Penn Yan Central SD	Penn Yan

Note: This section only includes districts with 1,500 or more students; All categories are ranked from high to low

108	39.5	Albion Central SD	Albion
108	39.5	Gouverneur Central SD	Gouverneur
110	39.4	Newark Central SD	Newark
111	38.9	Phoenix Central SD	Phoenix
112	38.8	Solvay UFSD	Solvay
112	38.8	Union-Endicott Central SD	Endicott
114	37.8	Bay Shore UFSD	Bay Shore
114	37.8	Plattsburgh City SD	Plattsburgh
116	37.4	Malone Central SD	Malone
117	37.3	Oneida City SD	Oneida
118	36.7	Dryden Central SD	Dryden
119	36.6	Camden Central SD	Camden
120	36.5	Dansville Central SD	Dansville
121	36.2	Mexico Central SD	Mexico
121	36.2	Patchogue-Medford UFSD	Patchogue
123	35.7	New Rochelle City SD	New Rochelle
124	35.6	Sweet Home Central SD	Amherst
125	35.3	Evans-Brant Central SD (Lake Shore)	Angola
126	35.2	Medina Central SD	Medina
127	35.1	Glens Falls City SD	Glens Falls
128	34.3	Longwood Central SD	Middle Island
128	34.3	White Plains City SD	White Plains
130	34.1	Beacon City SD	Beacon
131	33.8	Cheektowaga-Maryvale UFSD	Cheektowaga
132	33.5	Yorkshire-Pioneer Central SD	Yorkshire
133	33.4	Owego-Apalachin Central SD	Owego
134	32.0	Johnstown City SD	Johnstown
135	31.3	Kenmore-Tonawanda UFSD	Buffalo
136	31.2	Rondout Valley Central SD	Accord
137	30.9	Corning City SD	Painted Post
138	30.8	Huntington UFSD	Huntington Stn
138	30.8	South Jefferson Central SD	Adams Center
140	30.3	Hyde Park Central SD	Hyde Park
140	30.3	Ossining UFSD	Ossining
142	30.2	Broadalbin-Perth Central SD	Broadalbin
143	30.1	Ravena-Coeymans-Selkirk Ctrl SD	Ravena
144	29.9	Central Square Central SD	Central Square
144	29.9	Waterloo Central SD	Waterloo
146	29.7	Windsor Central SD	Windsor
147	29.4	Cobleskill-Richmondville Central SD	Cobleskill
147	29.4	Gates-Chili Central SD	Rochester
147	29.4	Susquehanna Valley Central SD	Conklin
150	29.3	North Tonawanda City SD	North Tonawanda
150	29.3	Peru Central SD	Peru
152	28.9	Saugerties Central SD	Saugerties
153	28.7	South Country Central SD	East Patchogue
153	28.7	South Huntington UFSD	Huntington Stn
155	28.3	Brockport Central SD	Brockport
155	28.3	Rush-Henrietta Central SD	Henrietta
157	28.2	Oneonta City SD	Oneonta
158	27.9	Depew UFSD	Depew
159	27.8	Chittenango Central SD	Chittenango
159	27.8	Southampton UFSD	Southampton
161	27.7	Carthage Central SD	Carthage
161	27.7	Homer Central SD	Homer
161	27.7	Pine Bush Central SD	Pine Bush
164	26.9	Chenango Valley Central SD	Binghamton
165	26.8	Malverne UFSD	Malverne
165	26.8	Phelps-Clifton Springs Central SD	Clifton Springs
167	26.7	Indian River Central SD	Philadelphia
168	26.5	Tonawanda City SD	Tonawanda
169	26.4	Deer Park UFSD	Deer Park
170	26.2	Chenango Forks Central SD	Binghamton
171	25.6	East Syracuse-Minoa Central SD	East Syracuse
172	25.5	General Brown Central SD	Dexter
172	25.5	Liverpool Central SD	Liverpool
174	25.4	Highland Central SD	Highland
175	25.2	Valley Central SD (Montgomery)	Montgomery
176	25.1	Sherrill City SD	Verona
177	24.8	Newfane Central SD	Burt
178	24.7	Ithaca City SD	Ithaca
178	24.7	West Babylon UFSD	West Babylon
180	24.6	Hudson Falls Central SD	Fort Edward
180	24.6	Palmyra-Macedon Central SD	Palmyra
182	24.4	Hampton Bays UFSD	Hampton Bays
183	24.2	Fredonia Central SD	Fredonia
184	24.1	North Syracuse Central SD	North Syracuse
185	24.0	Maine-Endwell Central SD	Endwell
186	23.7	Greece Central SD	Rochester
187	23.6	Marlboro Central SD	Milton
188	23.5	Kinderhook Central SD	Valatie
189	22.8	Canandaigua City SD	Canandaigua
190	22.5	Amherst Central SD	Amherst
191	22.3	West Seneca Central SD	West Seneca
192	22.2	Horseheads Central SD	Horseheads
193	21.9	Roosevelt UFSD	Roosevelt
194	21.8	Rotterdam-Mohonasen Central SD	Schenectady
195	21.7	Livonia Central SD	Livonia
195	21.7	Nyack UFSD	Nyack
197	21.4	Niagara-Wheatfield Central SD	Niagara Falls
198	21.3	North Babylon UFSD	North Babylon
199	20.8	Hicksville UFSD	Hicksville
200	20.4	Ballston Spa Central SD	Ballston Spa
201	20.3	Springville-Griffith Institute CSD	Springville
202	19.5	Lindenhurst UFSD	Lindenhurst
202	19.5	Wallkill Central SD	Wallkill
202	19.5	Wayne Central SD	Ontario Center
205	19.4	Schuylerville Central SD	Schuylerville
206	18.9	Schalmont Central SD	Schenectady
207	18.8	Queensbury UFSD	Queensbury
207	18.8	S Glens Fls Central SD	S Glens Fls
209	18.6	West Hempstead UFSD	West Hempstead
210	18.2	Long Beach City SD	Long Beach
211	18.1	Frontier Central SD	Hamburg
212	17.9	Islip UFSD	Islip
213	17.8	Goshen Central SD	Goshen
213	17.8	Whitesboro Central SD	Yorkville
215	17.5	Churchville-Chili Central SD	Churchville
216	17.2	New Paltz Central SD	New Paltz
216	17.2	Spencerport Central SD	Spencerport
218	16.9	South Colonie Central SD	Albany
219	16.7	Baldwinsville Central SD	Baldwinsville
219	16.7	Middle Country Central SD	Centereach
221	16.6	Brookhaven-Comsewogue UFSD	Port Jefferson Sta
221	16.6	Ramapo Central SD (Suffern)	Hillburn
223	16.3	Sachem Central SD	Lake Ronkonkoma
224	16.2	Alden Central SD	Alden
224	16.2	Scotia-Glenville Central SD	Scotia
226	16.0	Valley Stream Central High SD	Valley Stream
227	15.9	Westhampton Bch UFSD	Westhampton Bch
228	15.7	Rocky Point UFSD	Rocky Point
229	15.4	Washingtonville Central SD	Washingtonville
230	15.1	Farmingdale UFSD	Farmingdale
231	15.0	Oyster Bay-East Norwich Central SD	Oyster Bay
232	14.9	Spackenkill UFSD	Poughkeepsie
233	14.5	Monroe-Woodbury Central SD	Central Valley
234	14.4	Connetquot Central SD	Bohemia
235	14.3	Brewster Central SD	Brewster
235	14.3	Mineola UFSD	Mineola
237	14.1	East Hampton UFSD	East Hampton
238	13.8	West Genesee Central SD	Camillus
239	13.6	Elwood UFSD	Greenlawn
239	13.6	Hendrick Hudson Central SD	Montrose
239	13.6	Minisink Valley Central SD	Slate Hill
239	13.6	Vestal Central SD	Vestal
243	13.5	Averill Park Central SD	Averill Park
243	13.5	Valley Stream 13 UFSD	Valley Stream
245	13.4	Jamesville-Dewitt Central SD	Dewitt
246	13.3	Grand Island Central SD	Grand Island
247	13.1	Arlington Central SD	Lagrangeville
247	13.1	Saratoga Spgs City SD	Saratoga Spgs
249	12.9	Carmel Central SD	Patterson
249	12.9	Sewanhaka Central High SD	Floral Park
251	12.8	Center Moriches UFSD	Center Moriches
251	12.8	Eden Central SD	Eden
251	12.8	Lewiston-Porter Central SD	Youngstown
254	12.6	Mamaroneck UFSD	Mamaroneck
255	12.3	Wappingers Central SD	Wappingers Fls
256	12.2	Red Hook Central SD	Red Hook
257	12.1	Hilton Central SD	Hilton
257	12.1	Lakeland Central SD	Shrub Oak
259	12.0	Marcellus Central SD	Marcellus
260	11.8	Cazenovia Central SD	Cazenovia
261	11.5	Babylon UFSD	Babylon
262	11.2	Putnam Valley Central SD	Putnam Valley
263	11.1	Levittown UFSD	Levittown
264	11.0	Fairport Central SD	Fairport
265	10.9	East Meadow UFSD	Westbury
265	10.9	Starpoint Central SD	Lockport
267	10.8	New Hyde Pk-Garden City Pk UFSD	New Hyde Park
268	10.7	Hamburg Central SD	Hamburg
268	10.7	Hewlett-Woodmere UFSD	Woodmere
270	10.5	East Greenbush Central SD	East Greenbush
271	10.3	Port Washington UFSD	Port Washington
272	9.9	Half Hollow Hills Central SD	Dix Hills
273	9.7	Nanuet UFSD	Nanuet
274	9.6	Cornwall Central SD	Cornwall on Hdsn
275	9.4	East Islip UFSD	Islip Terrace
275	9.4	Lancaster Central SD	Lancaster
277	9.3	Rockville Ctr UFSD	Rockville Ctr
277	9.3	Victor Central SD	Victor
279	9.2	Bedford Central SD	Bedford
279	9.2	Locust Valley Central SD	Locust Valley
281	9.0	Brighton Central SD	Rochester
281	9.0	Guilderland Central SD	Guilderland Center
281	9.0	North Colonie CSD	Latham
281	9.0	Shenendehowa Central SD	Clifton Park
281	9.0	West Irondequoit Central SD	Rochester
286	8.9	Valhalla UFSD	Valhalla
286	8.9	Westhill Central SD	Syracuse
288	8.8	Eastport-South Manor CSD	Manorville
288	8.8	Webster Central SD	Webster
290	8.7	Baldwin UFSD	Baldwin
290	8.7	Island Trees UFSD	Levittown
290	8.7	Penfield Central SD	Rochester
290	8.7	Rye Neck UFSD	Mamaroneck
294	8.5	Williamsville Central SD	East Amherst
295	8.1	Bethpage UFSD	Bethpage
296	7.9	New Hartford Central SD	New Hartford
297	7.8	North Bellmore UFSD	Bellmore
297	7.8	Oceanside UFSD	Oceanside
299	7.7	Harrison Central SD	Harrison
300	7.6	Burnt Hills-Ballston Lake Central SD	Scotia
300	7.6	Honeoye Falls-Lima Central SD	Honeoye Falls
300	7.6	Warwick Valley Central SD	Warwick
303	7.5	Franklin Square UFSD	Franklin Square
304	7.4	Iroquois Central SD	Elma
304	7.4	Orchard Park Central SD	West Seneca
306	7.3	Great Neck UFSD	Great Neck
307	7.2	South Orangetown Central SD	Blauvelt
308	7.1	Massapequa UFSD	Massapequa
309	6.8	Bayport-Blue Point UFSD	Bayport
309	6.8	East Aurora UFSD	East Aurora
311	6.7	Niskayuna Central SD	Schenectady
312	6.4	Fayetteville-Manlius Central SD	Manlius
312	6.4	Miller Place UFSD	Miller Place
314	6.3	Roslyn UFSD	Roslyn
315	6.2	Plainedge UFSD	N Massapequa
316	6.1	Clarkstown Central SD	New City
317	6.0	Mount Pleasant Central SD	Thornwood
317	6.0	Sayville UFSD	Sayville
319	5.9	West Islip UFSD	West Islip
320	5.8	Bethlehem Central SD	Delmar
320	5.8	Hauppauge UFSD	Hauppauge
320	5.8	Lynbrook UFSD	Lynbrook
323	5.7	Mahopac Central SD	Mahopac
324	5.6	Pelham UFSD	Pelham
325	5.4	Somers Central SD	Somers
326	5.3	Clarence Central SD	Clarence
326	5.3	Harborfields Central SD	Greenlawn
328	5.2	Three Village Central SD	Stony Brook
329	4.5	Pearl River UFSD	Pearl River
330	4.4	Irvington UFSD	Irvington
330	4.4	Mount Sinai UFSD	Mount Sinai
330	4.4	Seaford UFSD	Seaford
333	4.3	Manhasset UFSD	Manhasset
333	4.3	North Shore Central SD	Sea Cliff
333	4.3	Northport-East Northport UFSD	Northport
336	4.0	Bellmore-Merrick Central High SD	North Merrick
336	4.0	Commack UFSD	East Northport
338	3.9	Pleasantville UFSD	Pleasantville
338	3.9	Smithtown Central SD	Smithtown
340	3.8	Hastings-On-Hudson UFSD	Hastings on Hdsn
341	3.6	Plainview-Old Bethpage Central SD	Plainview
342	3.5	Wantagh UFSD	Wantagh
343	3.4	Kings Park Central SD	Kings Park
344	3.3	Ardsley UFSD	Ardsley
345	3.0	Herricks UFSD	New Hyde Park
345	3.0	Shoreham-Wading River Central SD	Shoreham
345	3.0	Yorktown Central SD	Yorktown Hgts
348	2.9	Pittsford Central SD	Pittsford
349	2.3	Katonah-Lewisboro UFSD	Goldens Bridge
350	1.9	Rye City SD	Rye
351	1.6	East Williston UFSD	Old Westbury
352	1.3	Syosset Central SD	Syosset
353	1.2	Chappaqua Central SD	Chappaqua
354	1.1	Briarcliff Mnr UFSD	Briarcliff Mnr
354	1.1	Merrick UFSD	Merrick
356	0.9	Byram Hills Central SD	Armonk
357	0.8	Garden City UFSD	Garden City
358	0.7	Cold Spring Hrbr Central SD	Cold Spring Hrbr
359	0.1	Bronxville UFSD	Bronxville

Note: This section only includes districts with 1,500 or more students; All categories are ranked from high to low

360	0.0	Croton-Harmon UFSD	Croton on Hdsn
360	0.0	Eastchester UFSD	Eastchester
360	0.0	Edgemont UFSD	Scarsdale
360	0.0	Jericho UFSD	Jericho
360	0.0	Orange-Ulster Boces	Goshen
360	0.0	Scarsdale UFSD	Scarsdale

Students Eligible for Reduced-Price Lunch

Rank	Percent	District Name	City
1	22.3	Indian River Central SD	Philadelphia
2	15.3	Middletown City SD	Middletown
3	15.1	Charter School for Applied Tech	Buffalo
4	14.3	Bedford Central SD	Bedford
4	14.3	Yorkshire-Pioneer Central SD	Yorkshire
6	13.8	Ogdensburg City SD	Ogdensburg
7	13.4	Camden Central SD	Camden
8	13.3	Gates-Chili Central SD	Rochester
9	12.9	Carthage Central SD	Carthage
10	12.7	Depew UFSD	Depew
11	12.6	Elmont UFSD	Elmont
12	12.2	Johnstown City SD	Johnstown
13	11.6	NYC Geographic District #26	Bayside
14	11.5	Hyde Park Central SD	Hyde Park
15	11.4	Saugerties Central SD	Saugerties
16	11.3	Solvay UFSD	Solvay
17	11.2	East Irondequoit Central SD	Rochester
18	11.1	Cheektowaga Central SD	Cheektowaga
18	11.1	Newark Central SD	Newark
20	11.0	Hornell City SD	Hornell
21	10.9	Cheektowaga-Maryvale UFSD	Cheektowaga
21	10.9	Glen Cove City SD	Glen Cove
21	10.9	Kenmore-Tonawanda UFSD	Buffalo
21	10.9	UFSD of the Tarrytowns	Sleepy Hollow
25	10.8	Mexico Central SD	Mexico
26	10.5	Liberty Central SD	Liberty
27	10.4	Brockport Central SD	Brockport
27	10.4	Patchogue-Medford UFSD	Patchogue
27	10.4	Salmon River Central SD	Fort Covington
30	10.3	Central Valley CSD At Ilion-Mohawk	Ilion
31	10.2	Albion Central SD	Albion
31	10.2	Port Chester-Rye UFSD	Port Chester
33	10.1	Windsor Central SD	Windsor
34	10.0	Beacon City SD	Beacon
34	10.0	NYC Geographic District #25	Flushing
34	10.0	Penn Yan Central SD	Penn Yan
34	10.0	Peru Central SD	Peru
34	10.0	Pine Bush Central SD	Pine Bush
39	9.9	Greece Central SD	Rochester
39	9.9	Newfane Central SD	Burt
41	9.8	Highland Central SD	Highland
42	9.7	Brentwood UFSD	Brentwood
42	9.7	Hudson City SD	Hudson
44	9.6	Freeport UFSD	Freeport
44	9.6	Lackawanna City SD	Lackawanna
44	9.6	Malone Central SD	Malone
44	9.6	Watertown City SD	Watertown
48	9.5	Uniondale UFSD	Uniondale
49	9.4	Deer Park UFSD	Deer Park
49	9.4	East Syracuse-Minoa Central SD	East Syracuse
49	9.4	William Floyd UFSD	Mastic Beach
52	9.3	Cortland City SD	Cortland
52	9.3	Dansville Central SD	Dansville
52	9.3	Lockport City SD	Lockport
52	9.3	North Babylon UFSD	North Babylon
52	9.3	Ossining UFSD	Ossining
52	9.3	Springville-Griffith Institute CSD	Springville
58	9.2	Beekmantown Central SD	West Chazy
58	9.2	Evans-Brant Central SD (Lake Shore)	Angola
58	9.2	Homer Central SD	Homer
61	9.1	Massena Central SD	Massena
62	9.0	Central Islip UFSD	Central Islip
62	9.0	Central Square Central SD	Central Square
62	9.0	Chenango Forks Central SD	Binghamton
62	9.0	NYC Geographic District #29	Queens Village
62	9.0	Wayne Central SD	Ontario Center
67	8.9	Longwood Central SD	Middle Island
67	8.9	Valley Central SD (Montgomery)	Montgomery
69	8.8	General Brown Central SD	Dexter
70	8.6	Frontier Central SD	Hamburg
70	8.6	Greenburgh Central SD	Hartsdale
70	8.6	Lindenhurst UFSD	Lindenhurst

70	8.6	Port Jervis City SD	Port Jervis
74	8.5	Lawrence UFSD	Lawrence
74	8.5	Palmyra-Macedon Central SD	Palmyra
74	8.5	Rush-Henrietta Central SD	Henrietta
77	8.4	Bath Central SD	Bath
77	8.4	East Ramapo CSD (Spring Valley)	Spring Valley
77	8.4	Liverpool Central SD	Liverpool
77	8.4	North Tonawanda City SD	North Tonawanda
77	8.4	Olean City SD	Olean
77	8.4	Schuylerville Central SD	Schuylerville
77	8.4	Susquehanna Valley Central SD	Conklin
77	8.4	West Seneca Central SD	West Seneca
85	8.3	Fulton City SD	Fulton
85	8.3	Kingston City SD	Kingston
85	8.3	Lansingburgh Central SD	Troy
85	8.3	Sherrill City SD	Verona
89	8.2	Cohoes City SD	Cohoes
89	8.2	Mount Vernon SD	Mount Vernon
89	8.2	NYC Geographic District #28	Jamaica
89	8.2	Owego-Apalachin Central SD	Owego
89	8.2	Rondout Valley Central SD	Accord
89	8.2	Spencerport Central SD	Spencerport
95	8.1	Copiague UFSD	Copiague
95	8.1	Newburgh City SD	Newburgh
97	8.0	Bay Shore UFSD	Bay Shore
97	8.0	Dryden Central SD	Dryden
97	8.0	Fredonia Central SD	Fredonia
97	8.0	Geneva City SD	Geneva
97	8.0	Malverne UFSD	Malverne
97	8.0	Peekskill City SD	Peekskill
97	8.0	Phoenix Central SD	Phoenix
97	8.0	Washingtonville Central SD	Washingtonville
105	7.9	Catskill Central SD	Catskill
105	7.9	Chittenango Central SD	Chittenango
105	7.9	NYC Geographic District #31	Staten Island
105	7.9	Rome City SD	Rome
105	7.9	Rotterdam-Mohonasen Central SD	Schenectady
105	7.9	Southampton UFSD	Southampton
105	7.9	Tonawanda City SD	Tonawanda
112	7.8	Johnson City Central SD	Johnson City
112	7.8	Middle Country Central SD	Centereach
114	7.7	Amityville UFSD	Amityville
114	7.7	Poughkeepsie City SD	Poughkeepsie
116	7.6	Oneida City SD	Oneida
116	7.6	Waterloo Central SD	Waterloo
118	7.5	Hampton Bays UFSD	Hampton Bays
118	7.5	NYC Geographic District #13	Brooklyn
120	7.4	Gloversville City SD	Gloversville
120	7.4	Gouverneur Central SD	Gouverneur
120	7.4	New Rochelle City SD	New Rochelle
120	7.4	North Syracuse Central SD	North Syracuse
120	7.4	South Jefferson Central SD	Adams Center
125	7.3	Batavia City SD	Batavia
125	7.3	Chenango Valley Central SD	Binghamton
125	7.3	Sweet Home Central SD	Amherst
128	7.2	Churchville-Chili Central SD	Churchville
128	7.2	NYC Geographic District #27	Ozone Park
128	7.2	Phelps-Clifton Springs Central SD	Clifton Springs
131	7.1	Corning City SD	Painted Post
131	7.1	Hicksville UFSD	Hicksville
131	7.1	Plattsburgh City SD	Plattsburgh
131	7.1	S Glens Fls Central SD	S Glens Fls
131	7.1	Union-Endicott Central SD	Endicott
136	7.0	Alden Central SD	Alden
137	6.9	Haverstraw-Stony Point CSD	Garnerville
137	6.9	Hudson Falls Central SD	Fort Edward
139	6.7	Broadalbin-Perth Central SD	Broadalbin
139	6.7	Schenectady City SD	Schenectady
139	6.7	Westbury UFSD	Old Westbury
142	6.6	Oneonta City SD	Oneonta
143	6.5	Amherst Central SD	Amherst
143	6.5	Auburn City SD	Auburn
143	6.5	Dunkirk City SD	Dunkirk
143	6.5	Glens Falls City SD	Glens Falls
143	6.5	Marlboro Central SD	Milton
148	6.4	Islip UFSD	Islip
148	6.4	Maine-Endwell Central SD	Endwell
148	6.4	Monticello Central SD	Monticello
148	6.4	NYC Geographic District #22	Brooklyn
148	6.4	Rocky Point UFSD	Rocky Point
148	6.4	West Genesee Central SD	Camillus
154	6.3	Niagara-Wheatfield Central SD	Niagara Falls
155	6.2	Hendrick Hudson Central SD	Montrose
155	6.2	Minisink Valley Central SD	Slate Hill

155	6.2	NYC Geographic District #18	Brooklyn
158	6.1	Hilton Central SD	Hilton
158	6.1	Horseheads Central SD	Horseheads
158	6.1	Waverly Central SD	Waverly
161	6.0	East Hampton UFSD	East Hampton
162	5.9	Medina Central SD	Medina
162	5.9	NYC Geographic District #30	Long Isl City
162	5.9	Norwich City SD	Norwich
162	5.9	White Plains City SD	White Plains
166	5.8	Great Neck UFSD	Great Neck
166	5.8	Niagara Falls City SD	Niagara Falls
166	5.8	Oswego City SD	Oswego
166	5.8	Yonkers City SD	Yonkers
170	5.7	NYC Geographic District #24	Corona
170	5.7	Riverhead Central SD	Riverhead
172	5.6	Cobleskill-Richmondville Central SD	Cobleskill
172	5.6	East Meadow UFSD	Westbury
172	5.6	Hewlett-Woodmere UFSD	Woodmere
172	5.6	Levittown UFSD	Levittown
172	5.6	Troy City SD	Troy
172	5.6	Wallkill Central SD	Wallkill
178	5.5	Ravena-Coeymans-Selkirk Ctrl SD	Ravena
178	5.5	West Babylon UFSD	West Babylon
178	5.5	West Hempstead UFSD	West Hempstead
181	5.4	Binghamton City SD	Binghamton
181	5.4	NYC Geographic District #20	Brooklyn
181	5.4	Valley Stream Central High SD	Valley Stream
181	5.4	Wappingers Central SD	Wappingers Fls
185	5.3	Lakeland Central SD	Shrub Oak
185	5.3	New York City Public Schools	New York
187	5.2	Canandaigua City SD	Canandaigua
187	5.2	Elmira City SD	Elmira
187	5.2	Livonia Central SD	Livonia
187	5.2	Scotia-Glenville Central SD	Scotia
187	5.2	South Colonie Central SD	Albany
187	5.2	Whitesboro Central SD	Yorkville
193	5.1	Baldwinsville Central SD	Baldwinsville
193	5.1	Mineola UFSD	Mineola
193	5.1	NYC Geographic District # 2	New York
193	5.1	NYC Geographic District #21	Brooklyn
193	5.1	Westhampton Bch UFSD	Westhampton Bch
198	5.0	Connetquot Central SD	Bohemia
198	5.0	Kinderhook Central SD	Valatie
198	5.0	NYC Geographic District # 1	New York
201	4.9	Ellenville Central SD	Ellenville
202	4.8	Lewiston-Porter Central SD	Youngstown
202	4.8	NYC Geographic District #11	Bronx
202	4.8	Sachem Central SD	Lake Ronkonkoma
202	4.8	Utica City SD	Utica
206	4.7	Carmel Central SD	Patterson
206	4.7	NYC Geographic District #17	Brooklyn
206	4.7	Queensbury UFSD	Queensbury
206	4.7	Schalmont Central SD	Schenectady
210	4.6	Grand Island Central SD	Grand Island
210	4.6	Putnam Valley Central SD	Putnam Valley
210	4.6	Vestal Central SD	Vestal
213	4.5	Red Hook Central SD	Red Hook
213	4.5	South Country Central SD	East Patchogue
213	4.5	Valley Stream 13 UFSD	Valley Stream
216	4.4	Amsterdam City SD	Amsterdam
216	4.4	Brookhaven-Comsewogue UFSD	Port Jefferson Sta
216	4.4	New Hyde Pk-Garden City Pk UFSD	New Hyde Park
219	4.3	Averill Park Central SD	Averill Park
219	4.3	Ballston Spa Central SD	Ballston Spa
219	4.3	Jamestown City SD	Jamestown
219	4.3	Roslyn UFSD	Roslyn
219	4.3	Spackenkill UFSD	Poughkeepsie
224	4.2	Hempstead UFSD	Hempstead
224	4.2	NYC Geographic District # 3	New York
224	4.2	NYC Geographic District # 8	Bronx
227	4.1	Albany City SD	Albany
227	4.1	Cornwall Central SD	Cornwall on Hdsn
227	4.1	Farmingdale UFSD	Farmingdale
227	4.1	Port Washington UFSD	Port Washington
227	4.1	Sewanhaka Central High SD	Floral Park
227	4.1	Starpoint Central SD	Lockport
233	4.0	Bethpage UFSD	Bethpage
233	4.0	Brewster Central SD	Brewster
233	4.0	Iroquois Central SD	Elma
233	4.0	New Hartford Central SD	New Hartford
233	4.0	NYC Geographic District # 5	New York
233	4.0	Nyack UFSD	Nyack
233	4.0	South Huntington UFSD	Huntington Stn
233	4.0	Wyandanch UFSD	Wyandanch

Note: This section only includes districts with 1,500 or more students; All categories are ranked from high to low

241	3.9	Goshen Central SD	Goshen
241	3.9	Huntington UFSD	Huntington Stn
241	3.9	NYC Geographic District # 4	New York
244	3.8	Arlington Central SD	Lagrangeville
244	3.8	Oyster Bay-East Norwich Central SD	Oyster Bay
246	3.7	Franklin Square UFSD	Franklin Square
246	3.7	Island Trees UFSD	Levittown
246	3.7	Long Beach City SD	Long Beach
246	3.7	New Paltz Central SD	New Paltz
246	3.7	NYC Geographic District #10	Bronx
246	3.7	Rochester City SD	Rochester
246	3.7	Syracuse City SD	Syracuse
246	3.7	West Irondequoit Central SD	Rochester
254	3.6	Elwood UFSD	Greenlawn
254	3.6	Locust Valley Central SD	Locust Valley
254	3.6	NYC Geographic District # 6	New York
257	3.5	Harrison Central SD	Harrison
257	3.5	Ithaca City SD	Ithaca
257	3.5	Lancaster Central SD	Lancaster
257	3.5	NYC Geographic District #14	Brooklyn
257	3.5	Penfield Central SD	Rochester
257	3.5	Ramapo Central SD (Suffern)	Hillburn
257	3.5	Roosevelt UFSD	Roosevelt
257	3.5	Victor Central SD	Victor
265	3.4	Eden Central SD	Eden
265	3.4	Monroe-Woodbury Central SD	Central Valley
267	3.3	Center Moriches UFSD	Center Moriches
267	3.3	Half Hollow Hills Central SD	Dix Hills
267	3.3	Hamburg Central SD	Hamburg
267	3.3	NYC Geographic District #15	Brooklyn
267	3.3	NYC Geographic District #23	Brooklyn
272	3.2	East Aurora UFSD	East Aurora
272	3.2	East Greenbush Central SD	East Greenbush
272	3.2	East Islip UFSD	Islip Terrace
272	3.2	NYC Geographic District #19	Brooklyn
272	3.2	North Bellmore UFSD	Bellmore
277	3.1	Fairport Central SD	Fairport
277	3.1	NYC Geographic District # 7	Bronx
277	3.1	Warwick Valley Central SD	Warwick
280	3.0	Brighton Central SD	Rochester
280	3.0	Buffalo City SD	Buffalo
280	3.0	NYC Geographic District #16	Brooklyn
280	3.0	NYC Geographic District #32	Brooklyn
280	3.0	North Shore Central SD	Sea Cliff
285	2.9	Guilderland Central SD	Guilderland Center
285	2.9	Mahopac Central SD	Mahopac
285	2.9	Miller Place UFSD	Miller Place
285	2.9	Nanuet UFSD	Nanuet
285	2.9	NYC Geographic District #12	Bronx
285	2.9	Webster Central SD	Webster
291	2.8	Burnt Hills-Ballston Lake Central SD	Scotia
291	2.8	Cazenovia Central SD	Cazenovia
291	2.8	Jamesville-Dewitt Central SD	Dewitt
291	2.8	Williamsville Central SD	East Amherst
295	2.7	Eastport-South Manor CSD	Manorville
295	2.7	Fayetteville-Manlius Central SD	Manlius
295	2.7	NYC Geographic District # 9	Bronx
295	2.7	North Colonie CSD	Latham
295	2.7	Saratoga Spgs City SD	Saratoga Spgs
300	2.6	Hauppauge UFSD	Hauppauge
300	2.6	Pelham UFSD	Pelham
302	2.5	Oceanside UFSD	Oceanside
302	2.5	Sayville UFSD	Sayville
302	2.5	West Islip UFSD	West Islip
305	2.4	Babylon UFSD	Babylon
305	2.4	Mamaroneck UFSD	Mamaroneck
305	2.4	Rockville Ctr UFSD	Rockville Ctr
305	2.4	Shenendehowa Central SD	Clifton Park
309	2.3	Clarkstown Central SD	New City
309	2.3	Herricks UFSD	New Hyde Park
309	2.3	Honeoye Falls-Lima Central SD	Honeoye Falls
309	2.3	Westhill Central SD	Syracuse
313	2.2	South Orangetown Central SD	Blauvelt
314	2.1	Mount Pleasant Central SD	Thornwood
314	2.1	Orchard Park Central SD	West Seneca
314	2.1	Seaford UFSD	Seaford
317	2.0	Irvington UFSD	Irvington
317	2.0	Plainedge UFSD	N Massapequa
317	2.0	Rye Neck UFSD	Mamaroneck
320	1.9	Marcellus Central SD	Marcellus
320	1.9	Massapequa UFSD	Massapequa
320	1.9	Niskayuna Central SD	Schenectady
320	1.9	Pleasantville UFSD	Pleasantville
324	1.8	Plainview-Old Bethpage Central SD	Plainview
324	1.8	Three Village Central SD	Stony Brook
326	1.7	Bayport-Blue Point UFSD	Bayport
327	1.6	Bellmore-Merrick Central High SD	North Merrick
327	1.6	Clarence Central SD	Clarence
327	1.6	Valhalla UFSD	Valhalla
330	1.5	Bethlehem Central SD	Delmar
331	1.4	Northport-East Northport UFSD	Northport
331	1.4	Pittsford Central SD	Pittsford
331	1.4	Smithtown Central SD	Smithtown
334	1.3	Commack UFSD	East Northport
335	1.2	Ardsley UFSD	Ardsley
335	1.2	Yorktown Central SD	Yorktown Hgts
337	1.1	Hastings-On-Hudson UFSD	Hastings on Hdsn
337	1.1	Pearl River UFSD	Pearl River
339	1.0	Harborfields Central SD	Greenlawn
339	1.0	NYC Special Schools - District 75	New York
341	0.9	Kings Park Central SD	Kings Park
341	0.9	Lynbrook UFSD	Lynbrook
341	0.9	Mount Sinai UFSD	Mount Sinai
344	0.8	Manhasset UFSD	Manhasset
345	0.7	Katonah-Lewisboro UFSD	Goldens Bridge
345	0.7	Wantagh UFSD	Wantagh
347	0.6	Byram Hills Central SD	Armonk
348	0.5	Briarcliff Mnr UFSD	Briarcliff Mnr
348	0.5	Chappaqua Central SD	Chappaqua
348	0.5	Somers Central SD	Somers
348	0.5	Syosset Central SD	Syosset
352	0.4	East Williston UFSD	Old Westbury
352	0.4	Shoreham-Wading River Central SD	Shoreham
354	0.3	Rye City SD	Rye
355	0.2	Garden City UFSD	Garden City
356	0.0	Baldwin UFSD	Baldwin
356	0.0	Bronxville UFSD	Bronxville
356	0.0	Cold Spring Hrbr Central SD	Cold Spring Hrbr
356	0.0	Croton-Harmon UFSD	Croton on Hdsn
356	0.0	Eastchester UFSD	Eastchester
356	0.0	Edgemont UFSD	Scarsdale
356	0.0	Jericho UFSD	Jericho
356	0.0	Merrick UFSD	Merrick
356	0.0	Orange-Ulster Boces	Goshen
356	0.0	Scarsdale UFSD	Scarsdale

Student/Teacher Ratio

(number of students per teacher)

Rank	Number	District Name	City
1	4.9	NYC Special Schools - District 75	New York
2	9.6	North Shore Central SD	Sea Cliff
2	9.6	Orange-Ulster Boces	Goshen
4	9.7	Jericho UFSD	Jericho
5	10.0	Dryden Central SD	Dryden
5	10.0	Plattsburgh City SD	Plattsburgh
7	10.1	Southampton UFSD	Southampton
8	10.2	Merrick UFSD	Merrick
9	10.4	Spackenkill UFSD	Poughkeepsie
10	10.5	Dunkirk City SD	Dunkirk
10	10.5	Penn Yan Central SD	Penn Yan
12	10.6	Bayport-Blue Point UFSD	Bayport
12	10.6	Long Beach City SD	Long Beach
12	10.6	Malverne UFSD	Malverne
12	10.6	Ravena-Coeymans-Selkirk Ctrl SD	Ravena
12	10.6	Susquehanna Valley Central SD	Conklin
17	10.7	Syosset Central SD	Syosset
17	10.7	Wayne Central SD	Ontario Center
19	10.8	East Hampton UFSD	East Hampton
19	10.8	Geneva City SD	Geneva
19	10.8	Rondout Valley Central SD	Accord
22	10.9	Plainview-Old Bethpage Central SD	Plainview
23	11.0	Great Neck UFSD	Great Neck
23	11.0	Ithaca City SD	Ithaca
23	11.0	Westhampton Bch UFSD	Westhampton Bch
26	11.1	Harrison Central SD	Harrison
26	11.1	Rockville Ctr UFSD	Rockville Ctr
26	11.1	Rush-Henrietta Central SD	Henrietta
29	11.2	Amherst Central SD	Amherst
29	11.2	Bethpage UFSD	Bethpage
29	11.2	East Irondequoit Central SD	Rochester
29	11.2	Greenburgh Central SD	Hartsdale
29	11.2	Oyster Bay-East Norwich Central SD	Oyster Bay
34	11.3	Ardsley UFSD	Ardsley
34	11.3	Hastings-On-Hudson UFSD	Hastings on Hdsn
34	11.3	Irvington UFSD	Irvington
34	11.3	Lawrence UFSD	Lawrence
34	11.3	Lynbrook UFSD	Lynbrook
34	11.3	Mexico Central SD	Mexico
40	11.4	Camden Central SD	Camden
40	11.4	East Williston UFSD	Old Westbury
40	11.4	Locust Valley Central SD	Locust Valley
40	11.4	Mount Pleasant Central SD	Thornwood
40	11.4	Palmyra-Macedon Central SD	Palmyra
40	11.4	Salmon River Central SD	Fort Covington
46	11.5	Mineola UFSD	Mineola
46	11.5	Phoenix Central SD	Phoenix
48	11.6	Batavia City SD	Batavia
48	11.6	Brighton Central SD	Rochester
48	11.6	Catskill Central SD	Catskill
48	11.6	Homer Central SD	Homer
48	11.6	Monticello Central SD	Monticello
48	11.6	Northport-East Northport UFSD	Northport
48	11.6	Valhalla UFSD	Valhalla
55	11.7	Briarcliff Mnr UFSD	Briarcliff Mnr
55	11.7	Byram Hills Central SD	Armonk
55	11.7	Corning City SD	Painted Post
55	11.7	East Syracuse-Minoa Central SD	East Syracuse
55	11.7	Kenmore-Tonawanda UFSD	Buffalo
55	11.7	Norwich City SD	Norwich
55	11.7	Phelps-Clifton Springs Central SD	Clifton Springs
55	11.7	Solvay UFSD	Solvay
63	11.8	Binghamton City SD	Binghamton
63	11.8	Hendrick Hudson Central SD	Montrose
63	11.8	Lackawanna City SD	Lackawanna
63	11.8	Malone Central SD	Malone
63	11.8	Newark Central SD	Newark
63	11.8	Pleasantville UFSD	Pleasantville
63	11.8	Spencerport Central SD	Spencerport
70	11.9	Bath Central SD	Bath
70	11.9	Connetquot Central SD	Bohemia
70	11.9	Dansville Central SD	Dansville
70	11.9	Evans-Brant Central SD (Lake Shore)	Angola
70	11.9	Fredonia Central SD	Fredonia
70	11.9	Gates-Chili Central SD	Rochester
70	11.9	Liberty Central SD	Liberty
70	11.9	North Bellmore UFSD	Bellmore
70	11.9	Penfield Central SD	Rochester
70	11.9	Red Hook Central SD	Red Hook
70	11.9	Rochester City SD	Rochester
70	11.9	Sweet Home Central SD	Amherst
82	12.0	Cold Spring Hrbr Central SD	Cold Spring Hrbr
82	12.0	Cortland City SD	Cortland
82	12.0	Hewlett-Woodmere UFSD	Woodmere
82	12.0	Levittown UFSD	Levittown
82	12.0	Livonia Central SD	Livonia
82	12.0	Oneonta City SD	Oneonta
82	12.0	Rome City SD	Rome
82	12.0	Uniondale UFSD	Uniondale
82	12.0	West Babylon UFSD	West Babylon
91	12.1	Beekmantown Central SD	West Chazy
91	12.1	Cohoes City SD	Cohoes
91	12.1	Depew UFSD	Depew
91	12.1	East Islip UFSD	Islip Terrace
91	12.1	Nyack UFSD	Nyack
91	12.1	Ramapo Central SD (Suffern)	Hillburn
91	12.1	Roslyn UFSD	Roslyn
91	12.1	Seaford UFSD	Seaford
91	12.1	Windsor Central SD	Windsor
100	12.2	Buffalo City SD	Buffalo
100	12.2	Cazenovia Central SD	Cazenovia
100	12.2	Farmingdale UFSD	Farmingdale
100	12.2	Greece Central SD	Rochester
100	12.2	Jamestown City SD	Jamestown
100	12.2	Ogdensburg City SD	Ogdensburg
100	12.2	Union-Endicott Central SD	Endicott
100	12.2	Waterloo Central SD	Waterloo
108	12.3	Bedford Central SD	Bedford
108	12.3	Cheektowaga Central SD	Cheektowaga
108	12.3	Hornell City SD	Hornell
108	12.3	Hudson City SD	Hudson
108	12.3	Katonah-Lewisboro UFSD	Goldens Bridge
108	12.3	Massapequa UFSD	Massapequa
114	12.4	Brockport Central SD	Brockport
114	12.4	Chappaqua Central SD	Chappaqua
114	12.4	Cobleskill-Richmondville Central SD	Cobleskill
114	12.4	Fairport Central SD	Fairport
114	12.4	Glens Falls City SD	Glens Falls
114	12.4	Port Washington UFSD	Port Washington
114	12.4	South Country Central SD	East Patchogue
121	12.5	Deer Park UFSD	Deer Park

Note: This section only includes districts with 1,500 or more students; All categories are ranked from high to low

121	12.5	Edgemont UFSD	Scarsdale
121	12.5	Elmont UFSD	Elmont
121	12.5	Herricks UFSD	New Hyde Park
121	12.5	Honeoye Falls-Lima Central SD	Honeoye Falls
121	12.5	Johnson City Central SD	Johnson City
121	12.5	Kinderhook Central SD	Valatie
121	12.5	Nanuet UFSD	Nanuet
121	12.5	New Hartford Central SD	New Hartford
121	12.5	North Colonie CSD	Latham
121	12.5	Oswego City SD	Oswego
121	12.5	Pittsford Central SD	Pittsford
121	12.5	Scarsdale UFSD	Scarsdale
121	12.5	Tonawanda City SD	Tonawanda
135	12.6	Canandaigua City SD	Canandaigua
135	12.6	East Meadow UFSD	Westbury
135	12.6	Gloversville City SD	Gloversville
135	12.6	Guilderland Central SD	Guilderland Center
135	12.6	Hyde Park Central SD	Hyde Park
135	12.6	Island Trees UFSD	Levittown
135	12.6	Lewiston-Porter Central SD	Youngstown
135	12.6	Port Jervis City SD	Port Jervis
135	12.6	Wantagh UFSD	Wantagh
135	12.6	Yorkshire-Pioneer Central SD	Yorkshire
145	12.7	Clarkstown Central SD	New City
145	12.7	Iroquois Central SD	Elma
145	12.7	Lockport City SD	Lockport
145	12.7	New Hyde Pk-Garden City Pk UFSD	New Hyde Park
145	12.7	Newfane Central SD	Burt
145	12.7	South Orangetown Central SD	Blauvelt
145	12.7	Troy City SD	Troy
152	12.8	Baldwin UFSD	Baldwin
152	12.8	Burnt Hills-Ballston Lake Central SD	Scotia
152	12.8	Garden City UFSD	Garden City
152	12.8	Islip UFSD	Islip
152	12.8	Lansingburgh Central SD	Troy
152	12.8	Pelham UFSD	Pelham
152	12.8	Shoreham-Wading River Central SD	Shoreham
152	12.8	Yorktown Central SD	Yorktown Hgts
160	12.9	Ballston Spa Central SD	Ballston Spa
160	12.9	Churchville-Chili Central SD	Churchville
160	12.9	Eastport-South Manor CSD	Manorville
160	12.9	Glen Cove City SD	Glen Cove
160	12.9	Jamesville-Dewitt Central SD	Dewitt
160	12.9	Lindenhurst UFSD	Lindenhurst
160	12.9	Marcellus Central SD	Marcellus
160	12.9	Peru Central SD	Peru
160	12.9	Schalmont Central SD	Schenectady
160	12.9	Vestal Central SD	Vestal
160	12.9	West Islip UFSD	West Islip
171	13.0	Bronxville UFSD	Bronxville
171	13.0	Chittenango Central SD	Chittenango
171	13.0	Eden Central SD	Eden
171	13.0	Hamburg Central SD	Hamburg
171	13.0	Oceanside UFSD	Oceanside
171	13.0	Orchard Park Central SD	West Seneca
171	13.0	Plainedge UFSD	N Massapequa
171	13.0	Scotia-Glenville Central SD	Scotia
171	13.0	S Glens Fls Central SD	S Glens Fls
171	13.0	Valley Stream 13 UFSD	Valley Stream
181	13.1	Auburn City SD	Auburn
181	13.1	Babylon UFSD	Babylon
181	13.1	Fulton City SD	Fulton
181	13.1	Medina Central SD	Medina
181	13.1	Olean City SD	Olean
181	13.1	Springville-Griffith Institute CSD	Springville
181	13.1	Wallkill Central SD	Wallkill
181	13.1	West Hempstead UFSD	West Hempstead
181	13.1	Whitesboro Central SD	Yorkville
190	13.2	Alden Central SD	Alden
190	13.2	Croton-Harmon UFSD	Croton on Hdsn
190	13.2	East Greenbush Central SD	East Greenbush
190	13.2	Fayetteville-Manlius Central SD	Manlius
190	13.2	Freeport UFSD	Freeport
190	13.2	Hilton Central SD	Hilton
190	13.2	Lakeland Central SD	Shrub Oak
190	13.2	New Paltz Central SD	New Paltz
190	13.2	Owego-Apalachin Central SD	Owego
190	13.2	Sayville UFSD	Sayville
190	13.2	South Colonie Central SD	Albany
190	13.2	Starpoint Central SD	Lockport
190	13.2	Waverly Central SD	Waverly
190	13.2	Webster Central SD	Webster
204	13.3	Amsterdam City SD	Amsterdam
204	13.3	Hampton Bays UFSD	Hampton Bays
204	13.3	Hauppauge UFSD	Hauppauge
204	13.3	Hicksville UFSD	Hicksville
204	13.3	Huntington UFSD	Huntington Stn
204	13.3	Kingston City SD	Kingston
204	13.3	Liverpool Central SD	Liverpool
204	13.3	NYC Geographic District # 4	New York
204	13.3	Oneida City SD	Oneida
204	13.3	UFSD of the Tarrytowns	Sleepy Hollow
204	13.3	West Genesee Central SD	Camillus
204	13.3	White Plains City SD	White Plains
216	13.4	Half Hollow Hills Central SD	Dix Hills
216	13.4	Mamaroneck UFSD	Mamaroneck
216	13.4	NYC Geographic District #16	Brooklyn
216	13.4	North Tonawanda City SD	North Tonawanda
216	13.4	Schuylerville Central SD	Schuylerville
216	13.4	Westhill Central SD	Syracuse
222	13.5	Carthage Central SD	Carthage
222	13.5	Mahopac Central SD	Mahopac
222	13.5	Putnam Valley Central SD	Putnam Valley
222	13.5	Rocky Point UFSD	Rocky Point
222	13.5	Rye Neck UFSD	Mamaroneck
222	13.5	Syracuse City SD	Syracuse
228	13.6	Albany City SD	Albany
228	13.6	Amityville UFSD	Amityville
228	13.6	Bellmore-Merrick Central High SD	North Merrick
228	13.6	Brewster Central SD	Brewster
228	13.6	Broadalbin-Perth Central SD	Broadalbin
228	13.6	Commack UFSD	East Northport
228	13.6	Manhasset UFSD	Manhasset
228	13.6	Newburgh City SD	Newburgh
228	13.6	Queensbury UFSD	Queensbury
228	13.6	Saugerties Central SD	Saugerties
228	13.6	Somers Central SD	Somers
228	13.6	South Huntington UFSD	Huntington Stn
228	13.6	Watertown City SD	Watertown
241	13.7	Beacon City SD	Beacon
241	13.7	Eastchester UFSD	Eastchester
241	13.7	Goshen Central SD	Goshen
241	13.7	Maine-Endwell Central SD	Endwell
241	13.7	Marlboro Central SD	Milton
246	13.8	Albion Central SD	Albion
246	13.8	Central Square Central SD	Central Square
246	13.8	Grand Island Central SD	Grand Island
246	13.8	Lancaster Central SD	Lancaster
246	13.8	Mount Vernon SD	Mount Vernon
246	13.8	Rye City SD	Rye
252	13.9	Center Moriches UFSD	Center Moriches
252	13.9	Ellenville Central SD	Ellenville
252	13.9	Frontier Central SD	Hamburg
252	13.9	Highland Central SD	Highland
252	13.9	Indian River Central SD	Philadelphia
252	13.9	Kings Park Central SD	Kings Park
252	13.9	Middletown City SD	Middletown
252	13.9	Monroe-Woodbury Central SD	Central Valley
252	13.9	Poughkeepsie City SD	Poughkeepsie
252	13.9	Roosevelt UFSD	Roosevelt
252	13.9	Schenectady City SD	Schenectady
252	13.9	Williamsville Central SD	East Amherst
264	14.0	Arlington Central SD	Lagrangeville
264	14.0	Bay Shore UFSD	Bay Shore
264	14.0	Chenango Valley Central SD	Binghamton
264	14.0	NYC Geographic District # 1	New York
264	14.0	NYC Geographic District # 7	Bronx
264	14.0	Pearl River UFSD	Pearl River
264	14.0	Saratoga Spgs City SD	Saratoga Spgs
264	14.0	Victor Central SD	Victor
272	14.1	East Aurora UFSD	East Aurora
272	14.1	Gouverneur Central SD	Gouverneur
272	14.1	Haverstraw-Stony Point CSD	Garnerville
272	14.1	NYC Geographic District # 5	New York
272	14.1	NYC Geographic District #12	Bronx
272	14.1	Niskayuna Central SD	Schenectady
272	14.1	West Seneca Central SD	West Seneca
272	14.1	Wyandanch UFSD	Wyandanch
280	14.2	Harborfields Central SD	Greenlawn
280	14.2	Miller Place UFSD	Miller Place
280	14.2	Three Village Central SD	Stony Brook
280	14.2	Warwick Valley Central SD	Warwick
284	14.3	Bethlehem Central SD	Delmar
284	14.3	Franklin Square UFSD	Franklin Square
284	14.3	Johnstown City SD	Johnstown
284	14.3	Mount Sinai UFSD	Mount Sinai
284	14.3	NYC Geographic District # 8	Bronx
284	14.3	NYC Geographic District #23	Brooklyn
284	14.3	North Syracuse Central SD	North Syracuse
284	14.3	Sherrill City SD	Verona
292	14.4	Carmel Central SD	Patterson
292	14.4	Central Valley CSD At Ilion-Mohawk	Ilion
292	14.4	NYC Geographic District # 9	Bronx
292	14.4	NYC Geographic District #15	Brooklyn
292	14.4	North Babylon UFSD	North Babylon
297	14.5	Averill Park Central SD	Averill Park
297	14.5	Central Islip UFSD	Central Islip
297	14.5	Ossining UFSD	Ossining
297	14.5	Sewanhaka Central High SD	Floral Park
297	14.5	Valley Central SD (Montgomery)	Montgomery
297	14.5	Washingtonville Central SD	Washingtonville
297	14.5	Westbury UFSD	Old Westbury
304	14.6	Elwood UFSD	Greenlawn
304	14.6	Horseheads Central SD	Horseheads
304	14.6	Valley Stream Central High SD	Valley Stream
307	14.7	Hudson Falls Central SD	Fort Edward
307	14.7	Smithtown Central SD	Smithtown
307	14.7	West Irondequoit Central SD	Rochester
310	14.8	Minisink Valley Central SD	Slate Hill
310	14.8	NYC Geographic District #18	Brooklyn
310	14.8	Niagara-Wheatfield Central SD	Niagara Falls
310	14.8	Port Chester-Rye UFSD	Port Chester
310	14.8	South Jefferson Central SD	Adams Center
310	14.8	New York City Public Schools	New York
316	14.9	Brookhaven-Comsewogue UFSD	Port Jefferson Sta
316	14.9	Charter School for Applied Tech	Buffalo
316	14.9	Cheektowaga-Maryvale UFSD	Cheektowaga
316	14.9	Clarence Central SD	Clarence
316	14.9	NYC Geographic District # 6	New York
316	14.9	Peekskill City SD	Peekskill
316	14.9	Pine Bush Central SD	Pine Bush
316	14.9	Rotterdam-Mohonasen Central SD	Schenectady
324	15.0	Baldwinsville Central SD	Baldwinsville
324	15.0	NYC Geographic District #14	Brooklyn
324	15.0	NYC Geographic District #32	Brooklyn
324	15.0	Wappingers Central SD	Wappingers Fls
324	15.0	William Floyd UFSD	Mastic Beach
329	15.1	Middle Country Central SD	Centereach
329	15.1	NYC Geographic District #19	Brooklyn
329	15.1	Riverhead Central SD	Riverhead
332	15.2	East Ramapo CSD (Spring Valley)	Spring Valley
332	15.2	NYC Geographic District #10	Bronx
334	15.3	Cornwall Central SD	Cornwall on Hdsn
334	15.3	Longwood Central SD	Middle Island
336	15.4	Sachem Central SD	Lake Ronkonkoma
337	15.5	Hempstead UFSD	Hempstead
337	15.5	New Rochelle City SD	New Rochelle
337	15.5	NYC Geographic District #17	Brooklyn
337	15.5	Patchogue-Medford UFSD	Patchogue
337	15.5	Utica City SD	Utica
342	15.6	Massena Central SD	Massena
342	15.6	NYC Geographic District #27	Ozone Park
342	15.6	Shenendehowa Central SD	Clifton Park
345	15.7	Elmira City SD	Elmira
345	15.7	NYC Geographic District # 3	New York
347	15.8	Chenango Forks Central SD	Binghamton
348	15.9	NYC Geographic District #11	Bronx
349	16.0	Copiague UFSD	Copiague
350	16.2	NYC Geographic District #13	Brooklyn
350	16.2	NYC Geographic District #21	Brooklyn
352	16.3	NYC Geographic District # 2	New York
353	16.4	NYC Geographic District #30	Long Isl City
354	16.5	NYC Geographic District #20	Brooklyn
354	16.5	NYC Geographic District #24	Corona
354	16.5	NYC Geographic District #31	Staten Island
357	16.6	NYC Geographic District #25	Flushing
358	16.7	NYC Geographic District #29	Queens Village
358	16.7	Niagara Falls City SD	Niagara Falls
360	17.1	General Brown Central SD	Dexter
360	17.1	NYC Geographic District #22	Brooklyn
362	17.2	Brentwood UFSD	Brentwood
363	17.3	NYC Geographic District #28	Jamaica
363	17.3	Yonkers City SD	Yonkers
365	18.8	NYC Geographic District #26	Bayside

Student/Librarian Ratio

(number of students per librarian)

Rank	Number	District Name	City
1	361.5	Locust Valley Central SD	Locust Valley
2	372.7	Oneida City SD	Oneida

Note: This section only includes districts with 1,500 or more students; All categories are ranked from high to low

3	398.5	Iroquois Central SD	Elma
4	410.2	Sherrill City SD	Verona
5	410.5	Ithaca City SD	Ithaca
6	445.5	Oneonta City SD	Oneonta
7	448.3	Westhill Central SD	Syracuse
8	459.5	Greenburgh Central SD	Hartsdale
9	463.5	Plattsburgh City SD	Plattsburgh
10	466.0	Cobleskill-Richmondville Central SD	Cobleskill
11	475.1	Cortland City SD	Cortland
12	481.2	Peru Central SD	Peru
13	491.2	New Hyde Pk-Garden City Pk UFSD	New Hyde Park
14	495.3	Red Hook Central SD	Red Hook
15	504.4	Evans-Brant Central SD (Lake Shore)	Angola
16	504.7	Merrick UFSD	Merrick
17	506.4	Camden Central SD	Camden
18	507.8	Rondout Valley Central SD	Accord
19	510.3	Valhalla UFSD	Valhalla
20	515.0	Homer Central SD	Homer
21	518.8	Byram Hills Central SD	Armonk
22	519.8	Scotia-Glenville Central SD	Scotia
23	522.7	Dansville Central SD	Dansville
24	534.8	Rush-Henrietta Central SD	Henrietta
25	535.4	North Colonie CSD	Latham
26	535.8	S Glens Fls Central SD	S Glens Fls
27	536.0	Valley Stream 13 UFSD	Valley Stream
28	537.5	Spackenkill UFSD	Poughkeepsie
29	537.7	Southampton UFSD	Southampton
30	541.9	East Irondequoit Central SD	Rochester
31	547.8	North Shore Central SD	Sea Cliff
31	547.8	Owego-Apalachin Central SD	Owego
33	553.1	Bedford Central SD	Bedford
34	556.8	Wyandanch UFSD	Wyandanch
35	558.3	South Colonie Central SD	Albany
36	559.4	Penfield Central SD	Rochester
37	564.7	Katonah-Lewisboro UFSD	Goldens Bridge
38	565.3	New Paltz Central SD	New Paltz
39	569.6	Chappaqua Central SD	Chappaqua
40	570.5	Malone Central SD	Malone
41	571.3	Livonia Central SD	Livonia
42	571.6	Guilderland Central SD	Guilderland Center
43	571.9	Massapequa UFSD	Massapequa
44	572.1	Oswego City SD	Oswego
45	574.0	Plainview-Old Bethpage Central SD	Plainview
46	576.0	Alden Central SD	Alden
47	576.7	Medina Central SD	Medina
48	578.9	Hicksville UFSD	Hicksville
49	579.1	New Hartford Central SD	New Hartford
50	582.3	Windsor Central SD	Windsor
51	583.2	Bethpage UFSD	Bethpage
52	585.7	Niskayuna Central SD	Schenectady
53	586.6	Gates-Chili Central SD	Rochester
54	586.9	Uniondale UFSD	Uniondale
55	588.5	Wayne Central SD	Ontario Center
56	589.0	Honeoye Falls-Lima Central SD	Honeoye Falls
56	589.0	Nyack UFSD	Nyack
56	589.0	West Babylon UFSD	West Babylon
59	591.5	Batavia City SD	Batavia
60	592.0	Glens Falls City SD	Glens Falls
61	595.8	Seaford UFSD	Seaford
62	596.4	Roslyn UFSD	Roslyn
63	597.3	Irvington UFSD	Irvington
64	599.2	Fulton City SD	Fulton
64	599.2	Lynbrook UFSD	Lynbrook
66	599.8	Jericho UFSD	Jericho
67	602.3	Liverpool Central SD	Liverpool
68	603.5	Bayport-Blue Point UFSD	Bayport
69	606.3	Auburn City SD	Auburn
70	606.7	Tonawanda City SD	Tonawanda
71	607.0	East Aurora UFSD	East Aurora
72	607.1	Clarkstown Central SD	New City
73	610.2	Pittsford Central SD	Pittsford
74	613.0	Highland Central SD	Highland
75	614.4	Burnt Hills-Ballston Lake Central SD	Scotia
76	615.0	Schalmont Central SD	Schenectady
77	617.4	Roosevelt UFSD	Roosevelt
78	617.5	Hyde Park Central SD	Hyde Park
79	619.0	Depew UFSD	Depew
80	620.0	East Hampton UFSD	East Hampton
81	622.1	Indian River Central SD	Philadelphia
82	625.5	Kenmore-Tonawanda UFSD	Buffalo
83	629.2	Corning City SD	Painted Post
84	629.7	Kinderhook Central SD	Valatie
85	635.3	Yorkshire-Pioneer Central SD	Yorkshire
86	635.7	Edgemont UFSD	Scarsdale
87	637.0	Plainedge UFSD	N Massapequa
88	642.2	Beacon City SD	Beacon
89	643.3	Solvay UFSD	Solvay
90	646.4	Spencerport Central SD	Spencerport
91	654.0	Churchville-Chili Central SD	Churchville
92	655.6	Rochester City SD	Rochester
93	655.7	Northport-East Northport UFSD	Northport
94	656.6	Cold Spring Hrbr Central SD	Cold Spring Hrbr
95	656.7	Palmyra-Macedon Central SD	Palmyra
96	656.8	Elmont UFSD	Elmont
97	658.1	Croton-Harmon UFSD	Croton on Hdsn
98	663.2	Babylon UFSD	Babylon
99	664.8	Greece Central SD	Rochester
100	665.5	Westhampton Bch UFSD	Westhampton Bch
101	669.6	Malverne UFSD	Malverne
102	672.0	Albion Central SD	Albion
103	677.7	Ardsley UFSD	Ardsley
104	679.0	East Meadow UFSD	Westbury
105	680.4	East Williston UFSD	Old Westbury
106	680.8	West Irondequoit Central SD	Rochester
107	682.9	Rome City SD	Rome
108	685.4	Garden City UFSD	Garden City
109	685.9	Scarsdale UFSD	Scarsdale
110	692.9	Baldwinsville Central SD	Baldwinsville
111	693.0	Hampton Bays UFSD	Hampton Bays
112	694.5	Mineola UFSD	Mineola
113	695.2	Rye Neck UFSD	Mamaroneck
114	695.4	Farmingdale UFSD	Farmingdale
115	696.3	Saugerties Central SD	Saugerties
116	696.6	Connetquot Central SD	Bohemia
117	703.4	Sayville UFSD	Sayville
118	703.5	Ballston Spa Central SD	Ballston Spa
119	704.6	Whitesboro Central SD	Yorkville
120	704.7	North Bellmore UFSD	Bellmore
121	705.5	Saratoga Spgs City SD	Saratoga Spgs
122	705.6	Yorktown Central SD	Yorktown Hgts
123	706.0	Fayetteville-Manlius Central SD	Manlius
124	706.9	Bethlehem Central SD	Delmar
125	707.3	West Hempstead UFSD	West Hempstead
126	709.7	Elwood UFSD	Greenlawn
127	711.6	Syosset Central SD	Syosset
128	712.4	Pleasantville UFSD	Pleasantville
129	717.0	Great Neck UFSD	Great Neck
130	718.6	Penn Yan Central SD	Penn Yan
131	720.0	Newark Central SD	Newark
132	722.8	Jamesville-Dewitt Central SD	Dewitt
133	723.6	Lancaster Central SD	Lancaster
134	730.0	Geneva City SD	Geneva
135	730.7	Kingston City SD	Kingston
136	731.4	Central Square Central SD	Central Square
137	736.0	Amherst Central SD	Amherst
138	736.2	Hewlett-Woodmere UFSD	Woodmere
139	740.3	Poughkeepsie City SD	Poughkeepsie
140	742.3	Cheektowaga-Maryvale UFSD	Cheektowaga
141	743.9	Monroe-Woodbury Central SD	Central Valley
142	745.0	Hamburg Central SD	Hamburg
143	746.3	Harrison Central SD	Harrison
144	748.0	Nanuet UFSD	Nanuet
145	748.5	East Ramapo CSD (Spring Valley)	Spring Valley
145	748.5	Syracuse City SD	Syracuse
147	751.6	Phoenix Central SD	Phoenix
148	753.1	Hauppauge UFSD	Hauppauge
149	753.2	Lindenhurst UFSD	Lindenhurst
150	754.5	Lakeland Central SD	Shrub Oak
151	758.3	South Country Central SD	East Patchogue
152	758.5	Monticello Central SD	Monticello
153	758.8	Glen Cove City SD	Glen Cove
154	764.0	Cazenovia Central SD	Cazenovia
155	768.4	Brookhaven-Comsewogue UFSD	Port Jefferson Sta
156	769.0	Averill Park Central SD	Averill Park
157	769.8	Hempstead UFSD	Hempstead
158	771.0	Grand Island Central SD	Grand Island
159	771.2	Wantagh UFSD	Wantagh
160	771.5	Binghamton City SD	Binghamton
161	774.7	Brockport Central SD	Brockport
162	775.5	Briarcliff Mnr UFSD	Briarcliff Mnr
163	775.6	Orchard Park Central SD	West Seneca
164	776.7	Webster Central SD	Webster
165	777.5	Salmon River Central SD	Fort Covington
166	777.7	West Seneca Central SD	West Seneca
167	777.8	Fairport Central SD	Fairport
168	780.0	Chenango Forks Central SD	Binghamton
169	783.5	Arlington Central SD	Lagrangeville
170	784.8	Ravena-Coeymans-Selkirk Ctrl SD	Ravena
171	791.5	Bath Central SD	Bath
172	792.0	Susquehanna Valley Central SD	Conklin
173	792.8	Newburgh City SD	Newburgh
174	793.8	Williamsville Central SD	East Amherst
175	796.2	Long Beach City SD	Long Beach
176	797.0	Hastings-On-Hudson UFSD	Hastings on Hdsn
177	798.6	Pine Bush Central SD	Pine Bush
178	800.2	Sewanhaka Central High SD	Floral Park
179	804.2	Minisink Valley Central SD	Slate Hill
180	805.8	Port Washington UFSD	Port Washington
181	808.0	Hendrick Hudson Central SD	Montrose
182	808.5	Catskill Central SD	Catskill
183	808.7	Herricks UFSD	New Hyde Park
184	813.0	Commack UFSD	East Northport
185	815.5	Phelps-Clifton Springs Central SD	Clifton Springs
186	815.7	Half Hollow Hills Central SD	Dix Hills
187	816.0	Liberty Central SD	Liberty
188	818.8	Brewster Central SD	Brewster
189	819.0	Lockport City SD	Lockport
190	819.3	Utica City SD	Utica
191	821.0	Sweet Home Central SD	Amherst
192	821.6	Jamestown City SD	Jamestown
192	821.6	Longwood Central SD	Middle Island
194	823.0	Gouverneur Central SD	Gouverneur
195	824.0	North Syracuse Central SD	North Syracuse
196	824.2	Wappingers Central SD	Wappingers Fls
197	824.5	Manhasset UFSD	Manhasset
198	826.3	Starpoint Central SD	Lockport
199	829.0	Ogdensburg City SD	Ogdensburg
200	830.3	Somers Central SD	Somers
201	832.3	Cornwall Central SD	Cornwall on Hdsn
202	835.0	West Genesee Central SD	Camillus
203	840.3	Frontier Central SD	Hamburg
204	840.5	Riverhead Central SD	Riverhead
205	845.6	Mount Vernon SD	Mount Vernon
206	847.4	Three Village Central SD	Stony Brook
207	855.5	Bronxville UFSD	Bronxville
208	857.3	Carthage Central SD	Carthage
209	862.0	Waterloo Central SD	Waterloo
210	862.3	Queensbury UFSD	Queensbury
211	866.6	Patchogue-Medford UFSD	Patchogue
212	866.7	Springville-Griffith Institute CSD	Springville
213	867.7	White Plains City SD	White Plains
214	871.6	Horseheads Central SD	Horseheads
215	874.0	Ellenville Central SD	Ellenville
216	875.5	Schuylerville Central SD	Schuylerville
217	877.0	Marcellus Central SD	Marcellus
218	878.6	Victor Central SD	Victor
219	879.4	Haverstraw-Stony Point CSD	Garnerville
220	883.3	East Syracuse-Minoa Central SD	East Syracuse
221	883.4	Schenectady City SD	Schenectady
222	884.5	Brighton Central SD	Rochester
223	887.1	Shenendehowa Central SD	Clifton Park
224	887.3	Hudson Falls Central SD	Fort Edward
225	890.0	Oceanside UFSD	Oceanside
226	892.7	Rye City SD	Rye
227	898.4	Smithtown Central SD	Smithtown
228	898.5	Johnstown City SD	Johnstown
229	902.4	East Greenbush Central SD	East Greenbush
230	903.7	North Babylon UFSD	North Babylon
231	903.8	Island Trees UFSD	Levittown
232	904.4	Hilton Central SD	Hilton
233	907.6	Eden Central SD	Eden
234	914.1	Center Moriches UFSD	Center Moriches
235	917.5	Eastport-South Manor CSD	Manorville
236	928.3	Port Jervis City SD	Port Jervis
237	935.8	Warwick Valley Central SD	Warwick
238	936.9	Freeport UFSD	Freeport
239	938.0	Hudson City SD	Hudson
240	939.0	Pelham UFSD	Pelham
241	939.2	Bay Shore UFSD	Bay Shore
242	942.0	Buffalo City SD	Buffalo
243	942.5	Amsterdam City SD	Amsterdam
244	944.5	Albany City SD	Albany
245	946.2	Westbury UFSD	Old Westbury
246	947.5	Norwich City SD	Norwich
247	950.0	Union-Endicott Central SD	Endicott
248	957.0	Rotterdam-Mohonasen Central SD	Schenectady
249	964.7	Rocky Point UFSD	Rocky Point
250	968.0	Lawrence UFSD	Lawrence
251	969.3	Central Islip UFSD	Central Islip
252	974.7	Massena Central SD	Massena
253	976.5	Mount Pleasant Central SD	Thornwood
254	980.5	Marlboro Central SD	Milton

Note: This section only includes districts with 1,500 or more students; All categories are ranked from high to low

255	980.6	William Floyd UFSD	Mastic Beach
256	981.6	Washingtonville Central SD	Washingtonville
257	982.0	Dryden Central SD	Dryden
258	992.3	Watertown City SD	Watertown
259	1,003.0	South Huntington UFSD	Huntington Stn
260	1,004.4	Sachem Central SD	Lake Ronkonkoma
261	1,007.0	Franklin Square UFSD	Franklin Square
262	1,036.2	Beekmantown Central SD	West Chazy
263	1,044.0	Lewiston-Porter Central SD	Youngstown
264	1,048.1	Maine-Endwell Central SD	Endwell
265	1,048.8	Mamaroneck UFSD	Mamaroneck
266	1,057.7	Eastchester UFSD	Eastchester
267	1,064.3	Amityville UFSD	Amityville
268	1,071.2	Huntington UFSD	Huntington Stn
269	1,077.0	Peekskill City SD	Peekskill
270	1,086.4	Copiague UFSD	Copiague
271	1,107.5	Cheektowaga Central SD	Cheektowaga
272	1,111.3	Oyster Bay-East Norwich Central SD	Oyster Bay
273	1,123.7	West Islip UFSD	West Islip
274	1,131.3	Vestal Central SD	Vestal
275	1,139.6	Bellmore-Merrick Central High SD	North Merrick
276	1,148.3	Valley Stream Central High SD	Valley Stream
277	1,190.3	Clarence Central SD	Clarence
278	1,206.0	Central Valley CSD At Ilion-Mohawk	Ilion
279	1,231.2	Middletown City SD	Middletown
280	1,236.5	Shoreham-Wading River Central SD	Shoreham
281	1,243.0	Canandaigua City SD	Canandaigua
282	1,274.0	Cohoes City SD	Cohoes
283	1,287.0	Johnson City Central SD	Johnson City
284	1,342.0	Orange-Ulster Boces	Goshen
285	1,365.3	New Rochelle City SD	New Rochelle
286	1,380.7	Chittenango Central SD	Chittenango
287	1,403.6	Troy City SD	Troy
288	1,421.0	Miller Place UFSD	Miller Place
289	1,440.7	Mexico Central SD	Mexico
290	1,472.6	Pearl River UFSD	Pearl River
291	1,543.5	Islip UFSD	Islip
292	1,552.0	General Brown Central SD	Dexter
293	1,567.0	Fredonia Central SD	Fredonia
294	1,573.0	Wallkill Central SD	Wallkill
295	1,594.2	East Islip UFSD	Islip Terrace
296	1,604.7	Baldwin UFSD	Baldwin
297	1,635.0	Waverly Central SD	Waverly
298	1,640.5	South Orangetown Central SD	Blauvelt
299	1,678.0	Newfane Central SD	Burt
300	1,740.0	Deer Park UFSD	Deer Park
300	1,740.0	Lackawanna City SD	Lackawanna
302	1,741.0	Hornell City SD	Hornell
303	1,762.8	NYC Geographic District #32	Brooklyn
304	1,776.0	Putnam Valley Central SD	Putnam Valley
305	1,783.0	Rockville Ctr UFSD	Rockville Ctr
306	1,790.0	Broadalbin-Perth Central SD	Broadalbin
307	1,798.0	Chenango Valley Central SD	Binghamton
308	1,832.8	Levittown UFSD	Levittown
309	1,838.0	Kings Park Central SD	Kings Park
310	1,839.4	NYC Geographic District #30	Long Isl City
311	1,855.0	North Tonawanda City SD	North Tonawanda
312	1,896.0	Niagara Falls City SD	Niagara Falls
313	1,995.0	South Jefferson Central SD	Adams Center
314	2,017.5	NYC Geographic District # 6	New York
315	2,041.0	Dunkirk City SD	Dunkirk
316	2,053.6	NYC Geographic District #23	Brooklyn
317	2,059.8	Middle Country Central SD	Centereach
318	2,085.2	NYC Geographic District # 5	New York
319	2,186.0	Carmel Central SD	Patterson
320	2,186.1	NYC Geographic District #22	Brooklyn
321	2,187.0	Valley Central SD (Montgomery)	Montgomery
322	2,189.0	Elmira City SD	Elmira
323	2,210.1	NYC Geographic District #13	Brooklyn
324	2,214.0	Port Chester-Rye UFSD	Port Chester
325	2,226.0	Olean City SD	Olean
326	2,239.8	NYC Geographic District #26	Bayside
327	2,244.5	Ramapo Central SD (Suffern)	Hillburn
328	2,245.4	Brentwood UFSD	Brentwood
329	2,256.7	Harborfields Central SD	Greenlawn
330	2,344.7	NYC Geographic District #19	Brooklyn
331	2,360.3	NYC Geographic District #15	Brooklyn
332	2,371.0	Ossining UFSD	Ossining
333	2,391.6	NYC Geographic District # 1	New York
334	2,404.6	NYC Geographic District # 3	New York
335	2,415.0	Lansingburgh Central SD	Troy
336	2,443.0	Mount Sinai UFSD	Mount Sinai
337	2,564.5	NYC Geographic District #20	Brooklyn
338	2,608.2	NYC Geographic District #25	Flushing
339	2,683.2	NYC Geographic District #31	Staten Island
340	2,733.7	NYC Geographic District #16	Brooklyn
341	2,751.0	UFSD of the Tarrytowns	Sleepy Hollow
342	2,753.0	NYC Geographic District #10	Bronx
343	2,790.0	Charter School for Applied Tech	Buffalo
344	2,840.8	NYC Geographic District # 7	Bronx
345	2,841.3	NYC Geographic District #21	Brooklyn
346	2,892.3	NYC Geographic District # 8	Bronx
347	2,892.9	NYC Geographic District #17	Brooklyn
348	2,896.0	Gloversville City SD	Gloversville
349	2,925.0	Goshen Central SD	Goshen
350	2,991.6	New York City Public Schools	New York
351	3,058.2	NYC Geographic District # 4	New York
352	3,255.8	NYC Geographic District # 2	New York
353	3,335.0	NYC Geographic District #29	Queens Village
354	3,500.0	NYC Geographic District # 9	Bronx
355	3,515.1	NYC Geographic District #28	Jamaica
356	3,535.5	Yonkers City SD	Yonkers
357	3,639.8	NYC Geographic District #12	Bronx
358	3,816.0	Niagara-Wheatfield Central SD	Niagara Falls
359	4,030.6	NYC Geographic District #14	Brooklyn
360	4,090.9	NYC Geographic District #11	Bronx
361	4,319.2	NYC Geographic District #24	Corona
362	4,354.0	NYC Geographic District #27	Ozone Park
363	4,667.0	Mahopac Central SD	Mahopac
364	5,136.1	NYC Special Schools - District 75	New York
365	8,548.0	NYC Geographic District #18	Brooklyn

Student/Counselor Ratio

(number of students per counselor)

Rank	Number	District Name	City
1	206.0	Plattsburgh City SD	Plattsburgh
2	210.6	Norwich City SD	Norwich
3	214.0	Wayne Central SD	Ontario Center
4	215.8	Sewanhaka Central High SD	Floral Park
5	221.1	East Williston UFSD	Old Westbury
6	222.8	Oneonta City SD	Oneonta
7	223.7	Orange-Ulster Boces	Goshen
8	224.0	Dansville Central SD	Dansville
9	225.7	Rondout Valley Central SD	Accord
10	230.1	Chittenango Central SD	Chittenango
11	230.4	Southampton UFSD	Southampton
12	232.0	Batavia City SD	Batavia
13	232.1	Depew UFSD	Depew
14	232.5	East Hampton UFSD	East Hampton
15	232.8	Salmon River Central SD	Fort Covington
16	235.5	Bellmore-Merrick Central High SD	North Merrick
16	235.5	Valley Stream Central High SD	Valley Stream
18	246.3	Waterloo Central SD	Waterloo
19	247.3	Olean City SD	Olean
20	248.6	Penfield Central SD	Rochester
21	249.6	Windsor Central SD	Windsor
22	250.1	Schuylerville Central SD	Schuylerville
23	251.5	Penn Yan Central SD	Penn Yan
24	253.6	Malone Central SD	Malone
25	254.1	Ardsley UFSD	Ardsley
26	256.0	Irvington UFSD	Irvington
27	262.1	Brighton Central SD	Rochester
28	263.0	Rye Neck UFSD	Mamaroneck
29	263.4	West Irondequoit Central SD	Rochester
30	263.8	Bath Central SD	Bath
31	265.7	Hastings-On-Hudson UFSD	Hastings on Hdsn
32	267.7	North Colonie CSD	Latham
33	271.8	East Syracuse-Minoa Central SD	East Syracuse
34	273.7	Sweet Home Central SD	Amherst
35	274.3	Gouverneur Central SD	Gouverneur
36	278.3	Beekmantown Central SD	West Chazy
36	278.3	Geneva City SD	Geneva
38	279.7	Newfane Central SD	Burt
39	280.3	Ravena-Coeymans-Selkirk Ctrl SD	Ravena
40	280.8	Evans-Brant Central SD (Lake Shore)	Angola
41	281.4	Palmyra-Macedon Central SD	Palmyra
42	284.8	Chappaqua Central SD	Chappaqua
42	284.8	Jamestown City SD	Jamestown
44	285.2	Bronxville UFSD	Bronxville
45	285.9	Greece Central SD	Rochester
45	285.9	Spencerport Central SD	Spencerport
47	287.0	Plainview-Old Bethpage Central SD	Plainview
48	287.9	Washingtonville Central SD	Washingtonville
49	288.0	Albion Central SD	Albion
50	288.2	Byram Hills Central SD	Armonk
51	289.0	Roslyn UFSD	Roslyn
52	290.2	Hornell City SD	Hornell
53	290.5	Troy City SD	Troy
54	293.5	Niagara-Wheatfield Central SD	Niagara Falls
55	293.8	Island Trees UFSD	Levittown
56	294.5	Honeoye Falls-Lima Central SD	Honeoye Falls
57	295.3	Rome City SD	Rome
58	296.3	Niagara Falls City SD	Niagara Falls
59	299.3	Port Washington UFSD	Port Washington
60	301.0	Spackenkill UFSD	Poughkeepsie
61	302.6	Fayetteville-Manlius Central SD	Manlius
62	303.0	Hendrick Hudson Central SD	Montrose
63	305.0	Westhampton Bch UFSD	Westhampton Bch
64	306.2	Valhalla UFSD	Valhalla
65	306.7	Brockport Central SD	Brockport
66	307.7	Springville-Griffith Institute CSD	Springville
67	309.4	Port Jervis City SD	Port Jervis
68	310.7	Cobleskill-Richmondville Central SD	Cobleskill
69	310.8	Canandaigua City SD	Canandaigua
70	313.0	Cold Spring Hrbr Central SD	Cold Spring Hrbr
71	313.5	Queensbury UFSD	Queensbury
72	314.2	Lynbrook UFSD	Lynbrook
73	314.5	Medina Central SD	Medina
74	314.8	Kinderhook Central SD	Valatie
75	315.0	Mount Pleasant Central SD	Thornwood
76	317.3	Eastchester UFSD	Eastchester
77	317.8	Edgemont UFSD	Scarsdale
78	319.0	Rotterdam-Mohonasen Central SD	Schenectady
79	320.6	Nanuet UFSD	Nanuet
80	321.0	Pittsford Central SD	Pittsford
81	321.8	Gloversville City SD	Gloversville
82	322.6	Kenmore-Tonawanda UFSD	Buffalo
83	322.9	West Genesee Central SD	Camillus
84	324.8	Peru Central SD	Peru
85	325.6	Camden Central SD	Camden
86	325.7	Long Beach City SD	Long Beach
87	325.8	Katonah-Lewisboro UFSD	Goldens Bridge
88	326.4	Liberty Central SD	Liberty
89	327.0	Churchville-Chili Central SD	Churchville
90	327.9	Bethlehem Central SD	Delmar
91	328.0	Dryden Central SD	Dryden
92	329.8	Manhasset UFSD	Manhasset
93	330.2	Red Hook Central SD	Red Hook
94	331.6	Babylon UFSD	Babylon
95	331.8	East Irondequoit Central SD	Rochester
96	332.0	Great Neck UFSD	Great Neck
97	332.1	Somers Central SD	Somers
98	333.2	Jericho UFSD	Jericho
99	333.4	Oyster Bay-East Norwich Central SD	Oyster Bay
100	335.3	Lakeland Central SD	Shrub Oak
101	336.3	Locust Valley Central SD	Locust Valley
102	337.9	Westbury UFSD	Old Westbury
103	338.6	Hamburg Central SD	Hamburg
104	339.4	Vestal Central SD	Vestal
105	340.2	Dunkirk City SD	Dunkirk
106	340.3	Warwick Valley Central SD	Warwick
107	342.4	North Shore Central SD	Sea Cliff
108	343.1	Solvay UFSD	Solvay
109	343.6	Hewlett-Woodmere UFSD	Woodmere
110	344.0	Massena Central SD	Massena
111	345.3	Glens Falls City SD	Glens Falls
112	348.0	Lewiston-Porter Central SD	Youngstown
113	348.5	Shenendehowa Central SD	Clifton Park
114	349.6	Ellenville Central SD	Ellenville
115	350.8	Marcellus Central SD	Marcellus
116	352.1	Pelham UFSD	Pelham
117	353.0	Half Hollow Hills Central SD	Dix Hills
118	353.7	West Hempstead UFSD	West Hempstead
119	354.5	Harrison Central SD	Harrison
120	356.0	Hauppauge UFSD	Hauppauge
121	356.2	Pleasantville UFSD	Pleasantville
122	358.6	Westhill Central SD	Syracuse
123	358.7	Liverpool Central SD	Liverpool
124	360.0	Newark Central SD	Newark
125	360.2	Mexico Central SD	Mexico
126	361.4	Jamesville-Dewitt Central SD	Dewitt
127	361.8	Hilton Central SD	Hilton
128	362.1	Williamsville Central SD	East Amherst
129	363.2	Roosevelt UFSD	Roosevelt
130	363.9	Wantagh UFSD	Wantagh
131	364.0	Tonawanda City SD	Tonawanda
132	364.1	Oswego City SD	Oswego
133	369.2	Cheektowaga Central SD	Cheektowaga
134	369.3	Ithaca City SD	Ithaca
134	369.3	Scarsdale UFSD	Scarsdale

Note: This section only includes districts with 1,500 or more students; All categories are ranked from high to low

136	373.6	White Plains City SD	White Plains
137	374.7	Corning City SD	Painted Post
138	375.2	East Meadow UFSD	Westbury
139	375.8	Mount Sinai UFSD	Mount Sinai
139	375.8	Phoenix Central SD	Phoenix
141	376.1	Copiague UFSD	Copiague
141	376.1	Harborfields Central SD	Greenlawn
143	376.3	Herricks UFSD	New Hyde Park
144	377.7	Starpoint Central SD	Lockport
145	378.7	Arlington Central SD	Lagrangeville
146	380.9	Livonia Central SD	Livonia
147	382.0	Cazenovia Central SD	Cazenovia
148	384.5	Indian River Central SD	Philadelphia
149	385.8	Eden Central SD	Eden
150	385.9	Islip UFSD	Islip
151	388.1	Syosset Central SD	Syosset
152	388.9	Croton-Harmon UFSD	Croton on Hdsn
153	390.0	Chenango Forks Central SD	Binghamton
154	391.8	Fredonia Central SD	Fredonia
155	392.0	Yorktown Central SD	Yorktown Hgts
156	392.2	Marlboro Central SD	Milton
157	393.0	UFSD of the Tarrytowns	Sleepy Hollow
158	393.4	Garden City UFSD	Garden City
158	393.4	Northport-East Northport UFSD	Northport
160	395.9	East Aurora UFSD	East Aurora
161	396.0	Susquehanna Valley Central SD	Conklin
162	396.2	Rockville Ctr UFSD	Rockville Ctr
163	396.9	Mineola UFSD	Mineola
164	397.1	Three Village Central SD	Stony Brook
165	398.1	Plainedge UFSD	N Massapequa
166	399.0	South Jefferson Central SD	Adams Center
167	399.4	Fulton City SD	Fulton
168	400.1	Clarkstown Central SD	New City
169	402.3	Bayport-Blue Point UFSD	Bayport
169	402.3	Bedford Central SD	Bedford
171	403.7	Carmel Central SD	Patterson
172	404.3	Catskill Central SD	Catskill
173	404.4	Massapequa UFSD	Massapequa
174	405.6	Oceanside UFSD	Oceanside
175	407.3	Levittown UFSD	Levittown
176	407.6	Buffalo City SD	Buffalo
177	407.8	Phelps-Clifton Springs Central SD	Clifton Springs
178	407.9	Glen Cove City SD	Glen Cove
179	408.1	Ramapo Central SD (Suffern)	Hillburn
180	409.4	Brewster Central SD	Brewster
181	410.0	Niskayuna Central SD	Schenectady
182	410.1	South Orangetown Central SD	Blauvelt
183	411.4	Rush-Henrietta Central SD	Henrietta
184	412.4	Webster Central SD	Webster
185	412.9	Rye City SD	Rye
186	413.7	Orchard Park Central SD	West Seneca
187	414.5	Ogdensburg City SD	Ogdensburg
188	414.8	Fairport Central SD	Fairport
189	414.9	Lawrence UFSD	Lawrence
190	416.0	Bethpage UFSD	Bethpage
191	416.5	Uniondale UFSD	Uniondale
192	417.9	Goshen Central SD	Goshen
193	420.5	Center Moriches UFSD	Center Moriches
194	420.7	Nyack UFSD	Nyack
195	422.1	Ballston Spa Central SD	Ballston Spa
196	422.6	Briarcliff Mnr UFSD	Briarcliff Mnr
197	424.5	Scotia-Glenville Central SD	Scotia
198	430.4	Longwood Central SD	Middle Island
199	432.0	Alden Central SD	Alden
200	432.1	Mahopac Central SD	Mahopac
201	432.7	Rochester City SD	Rochester
202	436.1	Bay Shore UFSD	Bay Shore
203	436.5	Schenectady City SD	Schenectady
204	437.0	Commack UFSD	East Northport
204	437.0	Mamaroneck UFSD	Mamaroneck
206	437.2	Miller Place UFSD	Miller Place
207	437.8	Elmira City SD	Elmira
208	437.9	Farmingdale UFSD	Farmingdale
209	438.4	Kingston City SD	Kingston
210	439.3	West Islip UFSD	West Islip
211	439.4	Averill Park Central SD	Averill Park
212	439.7	Haverstraw-Stony Point CSD	Garnerville
213	440.6	Grand Island Central SD	Grand Island
214	442.9	East Islip UFSD	Islip Terrace
215	444.0	Putnam Valley Central SD	Putnam Valley
216	445.4	Cheektowaga-Maryvale UFSD	Cheektowaga
217	446.8	Minisink Valley Central SD	Slate Hill
218	447.5	Broadalbin-Perth Central SD	Broadalbin
219	448.6	S Glens Fls Central SD	S Glens Fls
220	448.7	Lindenhurst UFSD	Lindenhurst
221	449.3	Johnstown City SD	Johnstown
221	449.3	New Hartford Central SD	New Hartford
223	449.5	Chenango Valley Central SD	Binghamton
224	449.9	Cornwall Central SD	Cornwall on Hdsn
225	451.9	Lackawanna City SD	Lackawanna
226	452.2	New Paltz Central SD	New Paltz
227	456.1	Amityville UFSD	Amityville
228	456.2	Gates-Chili Central SD	Rochester
229	456.4	Burnt Hills-Ballston Lake Central SD	Scotia
230	457.8	North Syracuse Central SD	North Syracuse
231	458.5	Baldwin UFSD	Baldwin
232	458.7	Beacon City SD	Beacon
233	458.8	Eastport-South Manor CSD	Manorville
234	459.5	Greenburgh Central SD	Hartsdale
235	461.0	Whitesboro Central SD	Yorkville
236	461.3	Schalmont Central SD	Schenectady
237	462.9	South Huntington UFSD	Huntington Stn
238	463.1	Hyde Park Central SD	Hyde Park
239	464.8	New Rochelle City SD	New Rochelle
240	465.8	Pine Bush Central SD	Pine Bush
241	468.6	Rocky Point UFSD	Rocky Point
242	469.0	Hudson City SD	Hudson
243	469.8	Mount Vernon SD	Mount Vernon
244	473.6	Hicksville UFSD	Hicksville
245	474.2	Ossining UFSD	Ossining
246	475.4	Guilderland Central SD	Guilderland Center
247	476.6	Seaford UFSD	Seaford
248	477.8	Cohoes City SD	Cohoes
249	478.2	Iroquois Central SD	Elma
250	479.1	Smithtown Central SD	Smithtown
251	482.2	Binghamton City SD	Binghamton
252	482.6	Elwood UFSD	Greenlawn
253	483.0	Lansingburgh Central SD	Troy
254	483.3	Deer Park UFSD	Deer Park
255	488.0	Hudson Falls Central SD	Fort Edward
255	488.0	Huntington UFSD	Huntington Stn
257	488.4	Maine-Endwell Central SD	Endwell
258	490.8	West Babylon UFSD	West Babylon
259	492.0	Port Chester-Rye UFSD	Port Chester
260	494.6	Shoreham-Wading River Central SD	Shoreham
261	497.3	Saugerties Central SD	Saugerties
262	499.5	Monroe-Woodbury Central SD	Central Valley
263	500.6	General Brown Central SD	Dexter
264	503.2	East Greenbush Central SD	East Greenbush
265	504.5	Freeport UFSD	Freeport
266	505.7	Monticello Central SD	Monticello
267	508.2	Yorkshire-Pioneer Central SD	Yorkshire
268	512.8	Sherrill City SD	Verona
269	515.0	Homer Central SD	Homer
270	515.4	Pearl River UFSD	Pearl River
271	515.8	Sayville UFSD	Sayville
272	518.4	Central Square Central SD	Central Square
273	519.2	Amherst Central SD	Amherst
274	519.8	Hampton Bays UFSD	Hampton Bays
275	520.1	Wappingers Central SD	Wappingers Fls
276	520.8	Sachem Central SD	Lake Ronkonkoma
277	524.3	Wallkill Central SD	Wallkill
278	525.1	Kings Park Central SD	Kings Park
279	537.2	Albany City SD	Albany
280	540.0	Malverne UFSD	Malverne
281	542.9	Union-Endicott Central SD	Endicott
282	543.9	Syracuse City SD	Syracuse
283	544.9	Middle Country Central SD	Centereach
284	545.4	Lockport City SD	Lockport
285	546.8	Valley Central SD (Montgomery)	Montgomery
286	547.8	Owego-Apalachin Central SD	Owego
287	548.5	Saratoga Spgs City SD	Saratoga Spgs
288	548.9	Brookhaven-Comsewogue UFSD	Port Jefferson Sta
289	549.3	Middletown City SD	Middletown
290	554.3	Baldwinsville Central SD	Baldwinsville
291	556.8	Wyandanch UFSD	Wyandanch
292	560.3	Riverhead Central SD	Riverhead
293	563.8	Oneida City SD	Oneida
294	565.9	Auburn City SD	Auburn
295	567.0	Watertown City SD	Watertown
296	567.8	Frontier Central SD	Hamburg
297	569.9	Connetquot Central SD	Bohemia
298	570.5	Carthage Central SD	Carthage
299	570.8	North Tonawanda City SD	North Tonawanda
300	577.0	Peekskill City SD	Peekskill
301	578.9	Lancaster Central SD	Lancaster
302	583.3	West Seneca Central SD	West Seneca
303	587.4	North Babylon UFSD	North Babylon
304	588.1	East Ramapo CSD (Spring Valley)	Spring Valley
305	591.4	Horseheads Central SD	Horseheads
306	603.0	Central Valley CSD At Ilion-Mohawk	Ilion
307	606.6	Patchogue-Medford UFSD	Patchogue
308	607.7	Cortland City SD	Cortland
309	608.0	Clarence Central SD	Clarence
310	613.0	Highland Central SD	Highland
311	627.3	South Colonie Central SD	Albany
312	627.6	Victor Central SD	Victor
313	634.6	Poughkeepsie City SD	Poughkeepsie
314	638.6	Newburgh City SD	Newburgh
315	641.7	Hempstead UFSD	Hempstead
316	643.5	Johnson City Central SD	Johnson City
317	650.0	South Country Central SD	East Patchogue
318	678.8	William Floyd UFSD	Mastic Beach
319	707.3	Amsterdam City SD	Amsterdam
320	747.5	Utica City SD	Utica
321	748.5	Brentwood UFSD	Brentwood
322	753.9	Central Islip UFSD	Central Islip
323	817.5	Waverly Central SD	Waverly
324	856.7	Yonkers City SD	Yonkers
n/a	n/a	Charter School for Applied Tech	Buffalo
n/a	n/a	Elmont UFSD	Elmont
n/a	n/a	Franklin Square UFSD	Franklin Square
n/a	n/a	Merrick UFSD	Merrick
n/a	n/a	New Hyde Pk-Garden City Pk UFSD	New Hyde Park
n/a	n/a	NYC Geographic District # 1	New York
n/a	n/a	NYC Geographic District # 2	New York
n/a	n/a	NYC Geographic District # 3	New York
n/a	n/a	NYC Geographic District # 4	New York
n/a	n/a	NYC Geographic District # 5	New York
n/a	n/a	NYC Geographic District # 6	New York
n/a	n/a	NYC Geographic District # 7	Bronx
n/a	n/a	NYC Geographic District # 8	Bronx
n/a	n/a	NYC Geographic District # 9	Bronx
n/a	n/a	NYC Geographic District #10	Bronx
n/a	n/a	NYC Geographic District #11	Bronx
n/a	n/a	NYC Geographic District #12	Bronx
n/a	n/a	NYC Geographic District #13	Brooklyn
n/a	n/a	NYC Geographic District #14	Brooklyn
n/a	n/a	NYC Geographic District #15	Brooklyn
n/a	n/a	NYC Geographic District #16	Brooklyn
n/a	n/a	NYC Geographic District #17	Brooklyn
n/a	n/a	NYC Geographic District #18	Brooklyn
n/a	n/a	NYC Geographic District #19	Brooklyn
n/a	n/a	NYC Geographic District #20	Brooklyn
n/a	n/a	NYC Geographic District #21	Brooklyn
n/a	n/a	NYC Geographic District #22	Brooklyn
n/a	n/a	NYC Geographic District #23	Brooklyn
n/a	n/a	NYC Geographic District #24	Corona
n/a	n/a	NYC Geographic District #25	Flushing
n/a	n/a	NYC Geographic District #26	Bayside
n/a	n/a	NYC Geographic District #27	Ozone Park
n/a	n/a	NYC Geographic District #28	Jamaica
n/a	n/a	NYC Geographic District #29	Queens Village
n/a	n/a	NYC Geographic District #30	Long Isl City
n/a	n/a	NYC Geographic District #31	Staten Island
n/a	n/a	NYC Geographic District #32	Brooklyn
n/a	n/a	North Bellmore UFSD	Bellmore
n/a	n/a	NYC Special Schools - District 75	New York
n/a	n/a	Valley Stream 13 UFSD	Valley Stream
n/a	n/a	New York City Public Schools	New York

Current Expenditures per Student

Rank	Dollars	District Name	City
1	33,474	Southampton UFSD	Southampton
2	32,587	Jericho UFSD	Jericho
3	32,467	Greenburgh Central SD	Hartsdale
4	31,866	Locust Valley Central SD	Locust Valley
5	31,612	Lawrence UFSD	Lawrence
6	30,248	North Shore Central SD	Sea Cliff
7	29,678	Hewlett-Woodmere UFSD	Woodmere
8	29,605	East Hampton UFSD	East Hampton
9	29,507	Long Beach City SD	Long Beach
10	29,214	Briarcliff Mnr UFSD	Briarcliff Mnr
11	28,820	Katonah-Lewisboro UFSD	Goldens Bridge
12	28,661	East Williston UFSD	Old Westbury
13	28,628	Great Neck UFSD	Great Neck
14	28,513	Mineola UFSD	Mineola
15	28,260	Syosset Central SD	Syosset
16	28,225	Cold Spring Hrbr Central SD	Cold Spring Hrbr
17	28,203	Roslyn UFSD	Roslyn

Note: This section only includes districts with 1,500 or more students; All categories are ranked from high to low

18	28,106	Oyster Bay-East Norwich Central SD	Oyster Bay
19	28,047	Chappaqua Central SD	Chappaqua
20	27,466	Harrison Central SD	Harrison
21	27,258	East Ramapo CSD (Spring Valley)	Spring Valley
22	27,053	Byram Hills Central SD	Armonk
23	26,936	Scarsdale UFSD	Scarsdale
24	26,641	Malverne UFSD	Malverne
25	26,561	Plainview-Old Bethpage Central SD	Plainview
26	26,349	Garden City UFSD	Garden City
27	26,327	Wyandanch UFSD	Wyandanch
28	26,109	Rockville Ctr UFSD	Rockville Ctr
29	25,980	Irvington UFSD	Irvington
30	25,883	Nanuet UFSD	Nanuet
31	25,813	Hastings-On-Hudson UFSD	Hastings on Hdsn
32	25,686	Bedford Central SD	Bedford
33	25,614	Hendrick Hudson Central SD	Montrose
34	25,405	Central Islip UFSD	Central Islip
35	25,242	Manhasset UFSD	Manhasset
36	25,226	Hempstead UFSD	Hempstead
37	25,120	Babylon UFSD	Babylon
38	25,090	Roosevelt UFSD	Roosevelt
39	25,064	Valhalla UFSD	Valhalla
40	24,971	Herricks UFSD	New Hyde Park
41	24,970	Merrick UFSD	Merrick
42	24,882	Rondout Valley Central SD	Accord
43	24,871	Ardsley UFSD	Ardsley
44	24,785	Eastchester UFSD	Eastchester
45	24,721	White Plains City SD	White Plains
46	24,669	Port Washington UFSD	Port Washington
47	24,534	Uniondale UFSD	Uniondale
48	24,474	Bayport-Blue Point UFSD	Bayport
49	24,466	West Hempstead UFSD	West Hempstead
50	24,435	Westhampton Bch UFSD	Westhampton Bch
51	24,398	Ramapo Central SD (Suffern)	Hillburn
52	24,364	Bethpage UFSD	Bethpage
53	24,254	Bronxville UFSD	Bronxville
54	24,195	Levittown UFSD	Levittown
55	24,164	Northport-East Northport UFSD	Northport
56	24,107	Lynbrook UFSD	Lynbrook
57	24,011	Amityville UFSD	Amityville
58	23,879	Liberty Central SD	Liberty
59	23,869	Sayville UFSD	Sayville
60	23,802	Spackenkill UFSD	Poughkeepsie
61	23,792	Huntington UFSD	Huntington Stn
62	23,775	Brewster Central SD	Brewster
63	23,675	Peekskill City SD	Peekskill
64	23,665	Farmingdale UFSD	Farmingdale
65	23,658	Mount Pleasant Central SD	Thornwood
66	23,631	Connetquot Central SD	Bohemia
67	23,519	Monticello Central SD	Monticello
68	23,466	Edgemont UFSD	Scarsdale
69	23,434	Nyack UFSD	Nyack
70	23,347	East Meadow UFSD	Westbury
71	23,264	Mount Vernon SD	Mount Vernon
72	23,243	Haverstraw-Stony Point CSD	Garnerville
73	23,214	Oceanside UFSD	Oceanside
74	23,187	Carmel Central SD	Patterson
75	23,138	Shoreham-Wading River Central SD	Shoreham
76	23,079	Lakeland Central SD	Shrub Oak
77	23,013	Yorktown Central SD	Yorktown Hgts
78	22,974	Seaford UFSD	Seaford
79	22,959	South Orangetown Central SD	Blauvelt
80	22,881	Putnam Valley Central SD	Putnam Valley
81	22,668	Bay Shore UFSD	Bay Shore
82	22,655	Three Village Central SD	Stony Brook
83	22,533	Marlboro Central SD	Milton
84	22,448	Pleasantville UFSD	Pleasantville
85	22,334	Mahopac Central SD	Mahopac
86	22,332	Westbury UFSD	Old Westbury
87	22,260	East Islip UFSD	Islip Terrace
88	22,211	South Huntington UFSD	Huntington Stn
89	22,188	Glen Cove City SD	Glen Cove
90	22,179	West Babylon UFSD	West Babylon
91	22,178	Massapequa UFSD	Massapequa
92	22,143	Baldwin UFSD	Baldwin
93	22,105	Island Trees UFSD	Levittown
94	22,085	South Country Central SD	East Patchogue
95	22,063	Copiague UFSD	Copiague
96	22,056	Hauppauge UFSD	Hauppauge
97	22,017	Mamaroneck UFSD	Mamaroneck
98	22,005	Longwood Central SD	Middle Island
99	21,955	Half Hollow Hills Central SD	Dix Hills
100	21,880	Ellenville Central SD	Ellenville
101	21,825	North Bellmore UFSD	Bellmore
102	21,765	Center Moriches UFSD	Center Moriches
103	21,737	Rye Neck UFSD	Mamaroneck
104	21,733	Rye City SD	Rye
105	21,682	Pearl River UFSD	Pearl River
106	21,663	Commack UFSD	East Northport
107	21,647	Plainedge UFSD	N Massapequa
108	21,617	Somers Central SD	Somers
109	21,585	UFSD of the Tarrytowns	Sleepy Hollow
110	21,529	Pelham UFSD	Pelham
111	21,470	Bellmore-Merrick Central High SD	North Merrick
112	21,432	Riverhead Central SD	Riverhead
113	21,399	Islip UFSD	Islip
114	21,337	Ossining UFSD	Ossining
115	21,234	Kingston City SD	Kingston
116	21,176	Lindenhurst UFSD	Lindenhurst
117	21,167	Deer Park UFSD	Deer Park
118	21,053	Croton-Harmon UFSD	Croton on Hdsn
119	21,052	New Paltz Central SD	New Paltz
120	21,031	Hicksville UFSD	Hicksville
121	20,988	Elwood UFSD	Greenlawn
122	20,986	Salmon River Central SD	Fort Covington
123	20,904	Freeport UFSD	Freeport
124	20,880	New Hyde Pk-Garden City Pk UFSD	New Hyde Park
125	20,727	West Islip UFSD	West Islip
126	20,715	Red Hook Central SD	Red Hook
127	20,658	New Rochelle City SD	New Rochelle
128	20,437	Monroe-Woodbury Central SD	Central Valley
129	20,417	Port Jervis City SD	Port Jervis
130	20,394	Albany City SD	Albany
131	20,388	Valley Stream Central High SD	Valley Stream
132	20,333	Rochester City SD	Rochester
133	20,331	New York City Public Schools	New York
134	20,269	Geneva City SD	Geneva
135	20,259	Lackawanna City SD	Lackawanna
136	20,117	North Babylon UFSD	North Babylon
137	20,064	Kings Park Central SD	Kings Park
138	20,052	Eastport-South Manor CSD	Manorville
139	20,040	Newburgh City SD	Newburgh
140	20,027	Hampton Bays UFSD	Hampton Bays
141	19,936	William Floyd UFSD	Mastic Beach
142	19,847	Gates-Chili Central SD	Rochester
143	19,813	Rocky Point UFSD	Rocky Point
144	19,705	Hudson City SD	Hudson
145	19,703	Mount Sinai UFSD	Mount Sinai
146	19,694	Smithtown Central SD	Smithtown
147	19,664	Mexico Central SD	Mexico
148	19,656	Miller Place UFSD	Miller Place
149	19,652	Harborfields Central SD	Greenlawn
150	19,602	Hyde Park Central SD	Hyde Park
151	19,574	Ogdensburg City SD	Ogdensburg
152	19,564	Catskill Central SD	Catskill
153	19,560	Schalmont Central SD	Schenectady
154	19,559	Susquehanna Valley Central SD	Conklin
154	19,559	Wantagh UFSD	Wantagh
156	19,529	Poughkeepsie City SD	Poughkeepsie
157	19,518	Ithaca City SD	Ithaca
158	19,389	Clarkstown Central SD	New City
159	19,342	Sewanhaka Central High SD	Floral Park
160	19,291	Patchogue-Medford UFSD	Patchogue
161	19,169	Goshen Central SD	Goshen
162	19,157	Plattsburgh City SD	Plattsburgh
163	19,118	East Irondequoit Central SD	Rochester
164	19,107	Valley Stream 13 UFSD	Valley Stream
165	19,100	Sachem Central SD	Lake Ronkonkoma
166	19,015	Middle Country Central SD	Centereach
167	18,940	Warwick Valley Central SD	Warwick
168	18,934	Yonkers City SD	Yonkers
169	18,905	East Syracuse-Minoa Central SD	East Syracuse
170	18,900	Dunkirk City SD	Dunkirk
171	18,852	Valley Central SD (Montgomery)	Montgomery
172	18,840	Troy City SD	Troy
173	18,828	Brookhaven-Comsewogue UFSD	Port Jefferson Sta
174	18,819	Evans-Brant Central SD (Lake Shore)	Angola
175	18,814	Elmont UFSD	Elmont
176	18,773	Buffalo City SD	Buffalo
177	18,379	Oswego City SD	Oswego
178	18,374	Brentwood UFSD	Brentwood
179	18,350	Ravena-Coeymans-Selkirk Ctrl SD	Ravena
180	18,259	Dryden Central SD	Dryden
181	18,239	Rush-Henrietta Central SD	Henrietta
182	18,221	Phoenix Central SD	Phoenix
183	18,176	Arlington Central SD	Lagrangeville
184	18,102	Middletown City SD	Middletown
185	18,097	Sweet Home Central SD	Amherst
186	17,998	Highland Central SD	Highland
187	17,982	Penn Yan Central SD	Penn Yan
187	17,982	Peru Central SD	Peru
189	17,972	Wallkill Central SD	Wallkill
190	17,966	Kenmore-Tonawanda UFSD	Buffalo
191	17,911	Rome City SD	Rome
192	17,906	Port Chester-Rye UFSD	Port Chester
193	17,895	Saugerties Central SD	Saugerties
194	17,875	Lewiston-Porter Central SD	Youngstown
195	17,752	Vestal Central SD	Vestal
196	17,689	Syracuse City SD	Syracuse
197	17,635	Malone Central SD	Malone
198	17,536	Glens Falls City SD	Glens Falls
199	17,447	East Greenbush Central SD	East Greenbush
200	17,308	Newark Central SD	Newark
201	17,282	Washingtonville Central SD	Washingtonville
202	17,251	Minisink Valley Central SD	Slate Hill
203	17,239	Palmyra-Macedon Central SD	Palmyra
204	17,190	Brighton Central SD	Rochester
205	17,184	Yorkshire-Pioneer Central SD	Yorkshire
206	17,167	Pittsford Central SD	Pittsford
207	17,117	Fulton City SD	Fulton
208	17,074	Pine Bush Central SD	Pine Bush
209	17,039	Phelps-Clifton Springs Central SD	Clifton Springs
210	17,008	Penfield Central SD	Rochester
211	16,994	Ballston Spa Central SD	Ballston Spa
212	16,975	Johnson City Central SD	Johnson City
213	16,939	Bath Central SD	Bath
213	16,939	South Colonie Central SD	Albany
215	16,920	Depew UFSD	Depew
216	16,878	Beekmantown Central SD	West Chazy
217	16,871	Cohoes City SD	Cohoes
218	16,864	Norwich City SD	Norwich
219	16,848	Binghamton City SD	Binghamton
220	16,809	Franklin Square UFSD	Franklin Square
221	16,787	Maine-Endwell Central SD	Endwell
222	16,761	Owego-Apalachin Central SD	Owego
223	16,694	Beacon City SD	Beacon
224	16,659	Wayne Central SD	Ontario Center
225	16,639	Oneonta City SD	Oneonta
226	16,636	Spencerport Central SD	Spencerport
227	16,633	Windsor Central SD	Windsor
228	16,609	Gouverneur Central SD	Gouverneur
229	16,605	Cobleskill-Richmondville Central SD	Cobleskill
230	16,598	Kinderhook Central SD	Valatie
231	16,591	Camden Central SD	Camden
232	16,496	Cornwall Central SD	Cornwall on Hdsn
233	16,481	Springville-Griffith Institute CSD	Springville
234	16,435	Liverpool Central SD	Liverpool
235	16,424	Chenango Valley Central SD	Binghamton
236	16,410	Wappingers Central SD	Wappingers Fls
237	16,382	Union-Endicott Central SD	Endicott
238	16,380	Guilderland Central SD	Guilderland Center
239	16,354	Waterloo Central SD	Waterloo
240	16,353	Homer Central SD	Homer
241	16,345	Scotia-Glenville Central SD	Scotia
242	16,295	Chenango Forks Central SD	Binghamton
243	16,288	Batavia City SD	Batavia
244	16,281	Schuylerville Central SD	Schuylerville
245	16,260	Newfane Central SD	Burt
246	16,235	Indian River Central SD	Philadelphia
247	16,153	Brockport Central SD	Brockport
248	16,138	Fairport Central SD	Fairport
249	16,119	Burnt Hills-Ballston Lake Central SD	Scotia
250	16,114	Greece Central SD	Rochester
251	16,113	West Irondequoit Central SD	Rochester
252	16,105	Hornell City SD	Hornell
253	16,096	North Colonie CSD	Latham
254	16,090	Iroquois Central SD	Elma
255	16,085	Schenectady City SD	Schenectady
256	16,015	Corning City SD	Painted Post
257	15,966	Fredonia Central SD	Fredonia
258	15,947	New Hartford Central SD	New Hartford
259	15,873	Gloversville City SD	Gloversville
260	15,824	Niagara Falls City SD	Niagara Falls
261	15,793	Fayetteville-Manlius Central SD	Manlius
262	15,748	North Tonawanda City SD	North Tonawanda
262	15,748	Solvay UFSD	Solvay
264	15,718	Jamesville-Dewitt Central SD	Dewitt
265	15,691	Webster Central SD	Webster
266	15,675	Cheektowaga Central SD	Cheektowaga
267	15,624	Lockport City SD	Lockport
268	15,621	Churchville-Chili Central SD	Churchville
269	15,468	Westhill Central SD	Syracuse

Note: This section only includes districts with 1,500 or more students; All categories are ranked from high to low

270	15,457	Orchard Park Central SD	West Seneca
271	15,436	Olean City SD	Olean
272	15,412	Oneida City SD	Oneida
273	15,376	Medina Central SD	Medina
274	15,286	Cortland City SD	Cortland
275	15,279	Canandaigua City SD	Canandaigua
276	15,210	Honeoye Falls-Lima Central SD	Honeoye Falls
277	15,199	Averill Park Central SD	Averill Park
278	15,196	Chittenango Central SD	Chittenango
279	15,192	Bethlehem Central SD	Delmar
280	15,111	Dansville Central SD	Dansville
281	15,108	Horseheads Central SD	Horseheads
282	15,100	Grand Island Central SD	Grand Island
283	15,060	Livonia Central SD	Livonia
284	15,052	Niskayuna Central SD	Schenectady
285	15,021	Cazenovia Central SD	Cazenovia
286	14,983	Starpoint Central SD	Lockport
287	14,894	North Syracuse Central SD	North Syracuse
288	14,874	Central Square Central SD	Central Square
289	14,854	Waverly Central SD	Waverly
290	14,831	Baldwinsville Central SD	Baldwinsville
291	14,763	West Seneca Central SD	West Seneca
292	14,747	Amsterdam City SD	Amsterdam
293	14,726	Lansingburgh Central SD	Troy
294	14,672	S Glens Fls Central SD	S Glens Fls
295	14,642	Williamsville Central SD	East Amherst
296	14,618	Saratoga Spgs City SD	Saratoga Spgs
297	14,604	Hilton Central SD	Hilton
298	14,579	Niagara-Wheatfield Central SD	Niagara Falls
299	14,570	Auburn City SD	Auburn
300	14,567	Amherst Central SD	Amherst
301	14,541	Whitesboro Central SD	Yorkville
302	14,534	Cheektowaga-Maryvale UFSD	Cheektowaga
303	14,481	Elmira City SD	Elmira
304	14,463	Alden Central SD	Alden
305	14,410	Johnstown City SD	Johnstown
306	14,401	Hudson Falls Central SD	Fort Edward
307	14,395	Massena Central SD	Massena
308	14,364	Utica City SD	Utica
309	14,358	Tonawanda City SD	Tonawanda
310	14,351	East Aurora UFSD	East Aurora
311	14,286	Eden Central SD	Eden
312	14,186	Carthage Central SD	Carthage
313	14,155	Sherrill City SD	Verona
314	14,100	Hamburg Central SD	Hamburg
315	13,994	Shenendehowa Central SD	Clifton Park
316	13,984	Marcellus Central SD	Marcellus
317	13,970	Broadalbin-Perth Central SD	Broadalbin
318	13,797	Watertown City SD	Watertown
319	13,784	West Genesee Central SD	Camillus
320	13,571	Jamestown City SD	Jamestown
321	13,567	Rotterdam-Mohonasen Central SD	Schenectady
322	13,503	Frontier Central SD	Hamburg
323	13,423	Albion Central SD	Albion
324	13,380	Lancaster Central SD	Lancaster
325	13,363	Queensbury UFSD	Queensbury
326	13,030	General Brown Central SD	Dexter
327	12,872	Clarence Central SD	Clarence
328	12,870	South Jefferson Central SD	Adams Center
329	11,801	Victor Central SD	Victor
n/a	n/a	Central Valley CSD At Ilion-Mohawk	Ilion
n/a	n/a	Charter School for Applied Tech	Buffalo
n/a	n/a	NYC Geographic District # 1	New York
n/a	n/a	NYC Geographic District # 2	New York
n/a	n/a	NYC Geographic District # 3	New York
n/a	n/a	NYC Geographic District # 4	New York
n/a	n/a	NYC Geographic District # 5	New York
n/a	n/a	NYC Geographic District # 6	New York
n/a	n/a	NYC Geographic District # 7	Bronx
n/a	n/a	NYC Geographic District # 8	Bronx
n/a	n/a	NYC Geographic District # 9	Bronx
n/a	n/a	NYC Geographic District #10	Bronx
n/a	n/a	NYC Geographic District #11	Bronx
n/a	n/a	NYC Geographic District #12	Bronx
n/a	n/a	NYC Geographic District #13	Brooklyn
n/a	n/a	NYC Geographic District #14	Brooklyn
n/a	n/a	NYC Geographic District #15	Brooklyn
n/a	n/a	NYC Geographic District #16	Brooklyn
n/a	n/a	NYC Geographic District #17	Brooklyn
n/a	n/a	NYC Geographic District #18	Brooklyn
n/a	n/a	NYC Geographic District #19	Brooklyn
n/a	n/a	NYC Geographic District #20	Brooklyn
n/a	n/a	NYC Geographic District #21	Brooklyn
n/a	n/a	NYC Geographic District #22	Brooklyn
n/a	n/a	NYC Geographic District #23	Brooklyn
n/a	n/a	NYC Geographic District #24	Corona
n/a	n/a	NYC Geographic District #25	Flushing
n/a	n/a	NYC Geographic District #26	Bayside
n/a	n/a	NYC Geographic District #27	Ozone Park
n/a	n/a	NYC Geographic District #28	Jamaica
n/a	n/a	NYC Geographic District #29	Queens Village
n/a	n/a	NYC Geographic District #30	Long Isl City
n/a	n/a	NYC Geographic District #31	Staten Island
n/a	n/a	NYC Geographic District #32	Brooklyn
n/a	n/a	NYC Special Schools - District 75	New York
n/a	n/a	Orange-Ulster Boces	Goshen

Total General Revenue per Student

Rank	Dollars	District Name	City
1	37,631	Southampton UFSD	Southampton
2	37,107	Jericho UFSD	Jericho
3	36,219	Locust Valley Central SD	Locust Valley
4	35,758	Greenburgh Central SD	Hartsdale
5	35,155	Hewlett-Woodmere UFSD	Woodmere
6	34,377	North Shore Central SD	Sea Cliff
7	33,854	East Hampton UFSD	East Hampton
8	33,561	Roosevelt UFSD	Roosevelt
9	32,845	Long Beach City SD	Long Beach
10	32,713	Katonah-Lewisboro UFSD	Goldens Bridge
11	31,982	Lawrence UFSD	Lawrence
12	31,917	Oyster Bay-East Norwich Central SD	Oyster Bay
13	31,776	Byram Hills Central SD	Armonk
14	31,765	Great Neck UFSD	Great Neck
15	31,687	Roslyn UFSD	Roslyn
16	31,586	Mineola UFSD	Mineola
17	31,364	Irvington UFSD	Irvington
18	31,198	East Williston UFSD	Old Westbury
19	31,109	Cold Spring Hrbr Central SD	Cold Spring Hrbr
20	31,046	Syosset Central SD	Syosset
21	29,710	Malverne UFSD	Malverne
22	29,526	Briarcliff Mnr UFSD	Briarcliff Mnr
23	29,492	Valhalla UFSD	Valhalla
24	29,330	Harrison Central SD	Harrison
25	29,107	Scarsdale UFSD	Scarsdale
26	29,105	Ardsley UFSD	Ardsley
27	28,779	Hendrick Hudson Central SD	Montrose
28	28,773	Chappaqua Central SD	Chappaqua
29	28,666	Wyandanch UFSD	Wyandanch
30	28,312	Hempstead UFSD	Hempstead
31	28,262	Plainview-Old Bethpage Central SD	Plainview
32	28,189	Bronxville UFSD	Bronxville
33	28,111	Westhampton Bch UFSD	Westhampton Bch
34	28,089	Rondout Valley Central SD	Accord
35	27,967	White Plains City SD	White Plains
36	27,896	Rockville Ctr UFSD	Rockville Ctr
37	27,882	Albany City SD	Albany
38	27,881	East Ramapo CSD (Spring Valley)	Spring Valley
39	27,779	Buffalo City SD	Buffalo
40	27,767	Central Islip UFSD	Central Islip
41	27,758	Merrick UFSD	Merrick
42	27,547	Nanuet UFSD	Nanuet
43	27,531	Ramapo Central SD (Suffern)	Hillburn
44	27,520	Marlboro Central SD	Milton
45	27,350	Bedford Central SD	Bedford
46	27,291	Herricks UFSD	New Hyde Park
47	27,171	Babylon UFSD	Babylon
48	27,164	Sayville UFSD	Sayville
49	27,119	Mount Pleasant Central SD	Thornwood
50	27,111	Port Washington UFSD	Port Washington
51	27,109	Bethpage UFSD	Bethpage
52	27,018	Manhasset UFSD	Manhasset
53	26,935	Uniondale UFSD	Uniondale
54	26,766	Lynbrook UFSD	Lynbrook
55	26,755	West Hempstead UFSD	West Hempstead
56	26,742	Hastings-On-Hudson UFSD	Hastings on Hdsn
57	26,670	Edgemont UFSD	Scarsdale
58	26,660	Plainedge UFSD	N Massapequa
59	26,633	Shoreham-Wading River Central SD	Shoreham
60	26,440	Liberty Central SD	Liberty
61	26,309	Levittown UFSD	Levittown
62	26,288	Connetquot Central SD	Bohemia
63	26,257	Mount Vernon SD	Mount Vernon
64	26,205	Garden City UFSD	Garden City
65	26,166	Huntington UFSD	Huntington Stn
66	26,121	Bayport-Blue Point UFSD	Bayport
67	26,097	Nyack UFSD	Nyack
68	26,072	Monticello Central SD	Monticello
69	26,057	Yorktown Central SD	Yorktown Hgts
70	25,933	Brewster Central SD	Brewster
71	25,727	Putnam Valley Central SD	Putnam Valley
72	25,726	Spackenkill UFSD	Poughkeepsie
73	25,707	Northport-East Northport UFSD	Northport
74	25,368	South Orangetown Central SD	Blauvelt
75	25,340	Lackawanna City SD	Lackawanna
76	25,278	Pleasantville UFSD	Pleasantville
77	25,237	Lakeland Central SD	Shrub Oak
78	25,234	Amityville UFSD	Amityville
79	25,201	Carmel Central SD	Patterson
80	25,084	Farmingdale UFSD	Farmingdale
81	25,049	South Country Central SD	East Patchogue
82	24,950	Peekskill City SD	Peekskill
83	24,902	Croton-Harmon UFSD	Croton on Hdsn
83	24,902	Mahopac Central SD	Mahopac
85	24,883	East Meadow UFSD	Westbury
86	24,872	Somers Central SD	Somers
87	24,813	Three Village Central SD	Stony Brook
88	24,804	Mamaroneck UFSD	Mamaroneck
89	24,708	UFSD of the Tarrytowns	Sleepy Hollow
89	24,708	Westbury UFSD	Old Westbury
91	24,638	Commack UFSD	East Northport
92	24,546	Salmon River Central SD	Fort Covington
93	24,481	Ossining UFSD	Ossining
94	24,474	Island Trees UFSD	Levittown
95	24,448	South Huntington UFSD	Huntington Stn
96	24,443	Oceanside UFSD	Oceanside
97	24,331	Massapequa UFSD	Massapequa
98	24,314	Seaford UFSD	Seaford
99	24,305	Ellenville Central SD	Ellenville
100	24,301	Hauppauge UFSD	Hauppauge
101	24,296	Troy City SD	Troy
102	24,096	Catskill Central SD	Catskill
103	24,093	Glen Cove City SD	Glen Cove
104	24,064	Haverstraw-Stony Point CSD	Garnerville
105	24,028	East Islip UFSD	Islip Terrace
106	24,023	Half Hollow Hills Central SD	Dix Hills
107	23,961	Hudson City SD	Hudson
108	23,943	Rye Neck UFSD	Mamaroneck
109	23,882	Rye City SD	Rye
110	23,800	Hicksville UFSD	Hicksville
111	23,703	Rochester City SD	Rochester
112	23,699	Eastchester UFSD	Eastchester
113	23,690	New York City Public Schools	New York
114	23,678	Riverhead Central SD	Riverhead
115	23,645	Baldwin UFSD	Baldwin
116	23,638	Red Hook Central SD	Red Hook
117	23,617	Eastport-South Manor CSD	Manorville
118	23,604	East Irondequoit Central SD	Rochester
119	23,420	William Floyd UFSD	Mastic Beach
120	23,378	Pearl River UFSD	Pearl River
121	23,283	Longwood Central SD	Middle Island
122	23,282	New Paltz Central SD	New Paltz
123	23,245	Center Moriches UFSD	Center Moriches
124	23,130	Islip UFSD	Islip
125	23,105	Mexico Central SD	Mexico
126	23,083	Schalmont Central SD	Schenectady
127	23,015	West Babylon UFSD	West Babylon
128	23,012	Hampton Bays UFSD	Hampton Bays
129	22,982	Kingston City SD	Kingston
130	22,898	Pelham UFSD	Pelham
131	22,890	Port Jervis City SD	Port Jervis
132	22,672	Geneva City SD	Geneva
133	22,648	Deer Park UFSD	Deer Park
134	22,632	Bay Shore UFSD	Bay Shore
135	22,617	Freeport UFSD	Freeport
136	22,539	West Islip UFSD	West Islip
137	22,501	Lindenhurst UFSD	Lindenhurst
138	22,470	Monroe-Woodbury Central SD	Central Valley
138	22,470	North Bellmore UFSD	Bellmore
140	22,442	Elwood UFSD	Greenlawn
141	22,405	Dunkirk City SD	Dunkirk
142	22,394	Newburgh City SD	Newburgh
143	22,370	Valley Stream Central High SD	Valley Stream
144	22,335	Gates-Chili Central SD	Rochester
145	22,256	Goshen Central SD	Goshen
146	22,153	Smithtown Central SD	Smithtown
147	22,100	Bellmore-Merrick Central High SD	North Merrick
148	22,056	New Rochelle City SD	New Rochelle
149	21,989	Susquehanna Valley Central SD	Conklin
150	21,913	Copiague UFSD	Copiague
151	21,895	Poughkeepsie City SD	Poughkeepsie

Note: This section only includes districts with 1,500 or more students; All categories are ranked from high to low

152	21,883	Mount Sinai UFSD	Mount Sinai
153	21,860	Rocky Point UFSD	Rocky Point
154	21,758	New Hyde Pk-Garden City Pk UFSD	New Hyde Park
155	21,740	Harborfields Central SD	Greenlawn
156	21,671	Hyde Park Central SD	Hyde Park
157	21,667	Ravena-Coeymans-Selkirk Ctrl SD	Ravena
158	21,653	Indian River Central SD	Philadelphia
159	21,643	Patchogue-Medford UFSD	Patchogue
160	21,620	Wantagh UFSD	Wantagh
161	21,556	Phoenix Central SD	Phoenix
162	21,518	North Babylon UFSD	North Babylon
163	21,463	Waterloo Central SD	Waterloo
164	21,435	Miller Place UFSD	Miller Place
165	21,402	Syracuse City SD	Syracuse
166	21,398	Minisink Valley Central SD	Slate Hill
167	21,388	Cohoes City SD	Cohoes
168	21,337	Middletown City SD	Middletown
169	21,137	Dryden Central SD	Dryden
170	21,111	Owego-Apalachin Central SD	Owego
171	21,053	Clarkstown Central SD	New City
172	21,028	Penn Yan Central SD	Penn Yan
173	20,989	Plattsburgh City SD	Plattsburgh
174	20,891	Bath Central SD	Bath
175	20,861	Sweet Home Central SD	Amherst
176	20,755	Warwick Valley Central SD	Warwick
177	20,736	Rush-Henrietta Central SD	Henrietta
178	20,716	Middle Country Central SD	Centereach
179	20,707	Rome City SD	Rome
180	20,704	Kings Park Central SD	Kings Park
181	20,701	Ithaca City SD	Ithaca
182	20,693	Phelps-Clifton Springs Central SD	Clifton Springs
183	20,691	Evans-Brant Central SD (Lake Shore)	Angola
184	20,563	Ogdensburg City SD	Ogdensburg
185	20,537	Newark Central SD	Newark
186	20,467	Pittsford Central SD	Pittsford
187	20,393	Westhill Central SD	Syracuse
188	20,350	Johnson City Central SD	Johnson City
189	20,331	Hornell City SD	Hornell
190	20,316	Saugerties Central SD	Saugerties
191	20,315	Malone Central SD	Malone
192	20,306	Medina Central SD	Medina
193	20,296	Vestal Central SD	Vestal
194	20,264	Sachem Central SD	Lake Ronkonkoma
195	20,211	Penfield Central SD	Rochester
196	20,161	Arlington Central SD	Lagrangeville
197	19,975	Brookhaven-Comsewogue UFSD	Port Jefferson Sta
198	19,966	Valley Stream 13 UFSD	Valley Stream
199	19,947	Highland Central SD	Highland
200	19,922	Wallkill Central SD	Wallkill
201	19,920	Binghamton City SD	Binghamton
202	19,917	East Greenbush Central SD	East Greenbush
203	19,876	Sewanhaka Central High SD	Floral Park
204	19,861	East Syracuse-Minoa Central SD	East Syracuse
205	19,829	Yonkers City SD	Yonkers
206	19,824	Oswego City SD	Oswego
207	19,816	Beacon City SD	Beacon
208	19,807	Elmont UFSD	Elmont
209	19,782	Peru Central SD	Peru
210	19,761	Camden Central SD	Camden
211	19,754	Solvay UFSD	Solvay
212	19,749	Port Chester-Rye UFSD	Port Chester
213	19,707	Valley Central SD (Montgomery)	Montgomery
214	19,579	Kenmore-Tonawanda UFSD	Buffalo
215	19,523	Livonia Central SD	Livonia
216	19,473	Beekmantown Central SD	West Chazy
217	19,392	Brentwood UFSD	Brentwood
218	19,333	Yorkshire-Pioneer Central SD	Yorkshire
219	19,332	Cobleskill-Richmondville Central SD	Cobleskill
220	19,301	Oneonta City SD	Oneonta
221	19,278	Depew UFSD	Depew
222	19,251	Churchville-Chili Central SD	Churchville
223	19,232	Gloversville City SD	Gloversville
224	19,220	Norwich City SD	Norwich
225	19,082	Windsor Central SD	Windsor
226	19,076	Union-Endicott Central SD	Endicott
227	19,069	Chenango Valley Central SD	Binghamton
228	19,018	Brighton Central SD	Rochester
229	19,016	Kinderhook Central SD	Valatie
230	18,910	Spencerport Central SD	Spencerport
231	18,866	Niagara-Wheatfield Central SD	Niagara Falls
232	18,830	Lewiston-Porter Central SD	Youngstown
233	18,824	Pine Bush Central SD	Pine Bush
234	18,820	Ballston Spa Central SD	Ballston Spa
235	18,803	Glens Falls City SD	Glens Falls
236	18,800	Washingtonville Central SD	Washingtonville
237	18,711	Niagara Falls City SD	Niagara Falls
238	18,691	Palmyra-Macedon Central SD	Palmyra
239	18,683	Dansville Central SD	Dansville
240	18,675	Fulton City SD	Fulton
241	18,669	Brockport Central SD	Brockport
242	18,514	Maine-Endwell Central SD	Endwell
243	18,432	Gouverneur Central SD	Gouverneur
244	18,398	Greece Central SD	Rochester
245	18,390	Schuylerville Central SD	Schuylerville
246	18,362	Newfane Central SD	Burt
247	18,354	Corning City SD	Painted Post
248	18,336	Bethlehem Central SD	Delmar
249	18,320	Honeoye Falls-Lima Central SD	Honeoye Falls
250	18,294	Springville-Griffith Institute CSD	Springville
251	18,273	Cheektowaga-Maryvale UFSD	Cheektowaga
252	18,272	Niskayuna Central SD	Schenectady
253	18,263	Chenango Forks Central SD	Binghamton
254	18,262	Liverpool Central SD	Liverpool
255	18,253	Wayne Central SD	Ontario Center
256	18,251	Cornwall Central SD	Cornwall on Hdsn
257	18,249	Homer Central SD	Homer
258	18,238	Franklin Square UFSD	Franklin Square
259	18,227	Schenectady City SD	Schenectady
260	18,223	Scotia-Glenville Central SD	Scotia
261	18,194	West Irondequoit Central SD	Rochester
262	18,188	Broadalbin-Perth Central SD	Broadalbin
263	18,165	Guilderland Central SD	Guilderland Center
264	18,154	Cheektowaga Central SD	Cheektowaga
265	18,095	Cortland City SD	Cortland
266	18,079	Burnt Hills-Ballston Lake Central SD	Scotia
267	18,021	South Colonie Central SD	Albany
268	18,020	Fredonia Central SD	Fredonia
269	17,988	Carthage Central SD	Carthage
270	17,878	Olean City SD	Olean
271	17,873	Canandaigua City SD	Canandaigua
272	17,815	Elmira City SD	Elmira
273	17,770	New Hartford Central SD	New Hartford
274	17,679	North Colonie CSD	Latham
275	17,623	Alden Central SD	Alden
276	17,542	North Tonawanda City SD	North Tonawanda
277	17,519	Chittenango Central SD	Chittenango
278	17,493	Averill Park Central SD	Averill Park
279	17,487	Lansingburgh Central SD	Troy
280	17,414	Iroquois Central SD	Elma
281	17,374	Fayetteville-Manlius Central SD	Manlius
282	17,345	Batavia City SD	Batavia
283	17,254	Fairport Central SD	Fairport
284	17,214	Wappingers Central SD	Wappingers Fls
285	17,198	Starpoint Central SD	Lockport
286	17,197	Jamesville-Dewitt Central SD	Dewitt
287	17,124	Amsterdam City SD	Amsterdam
288	17,115	Oneida City SD	Oneida
289	16,917	Webster Central SD	Webster
290	16,916	Whitesboro Central SD	Yorkville
291	16,892	Albion Central SD	Albion
292	16,830	Tonawanda City SD	Tonawanda
293	16,827	Hilton Central SD	Hilton
294	16,742	Orchard Park Central SD	West Seneca
295	16,716	Lockport City SD	Lockport
296	16,688	Marcellus Central SD	Marcellus
297	16,686	Auburn City SD	Auburn
298	16,651	Hudson Falls Central SD	Fort Edward
299	16,650	Rotterdam-Mohonasen Central SD	Schenectady
300	16,641	Grand Island Central SD	Grand Island
301	16,526	Amherst Central SD	Amherst
302	16,524	Utica City SD	Utica
303	16,500	Eden Central SD	Eden
304	16,484	S Glens Fls Central SD	S Glens Fls
305	16,458	Saratoga Spgs City SD	Saratoga Spgs
306	16,300	North Syracuse Central SD	North Syracuse
307	16,271	Cazenovia Central SD	Cazenovia
308	16,245	Horseheads Central SD	Horseheads
309	16,200	Baldwinsville Central SD	Baldwinsville
310	16,131	Williamsville Central SD	East Amherst
311	16,126	Central Square Central SD	Central Square
312	16,069	Hamburg Central SD	Hamburg
313	16,040	Waverly Central SD	Waverly
314	16,018	Jamestown City SD	Jamestown
315	15,975	Queensbury UFSD	Queensbury
316	15,863	East Aurora UFSD	East Aurora
317	15,790	West Seneca Central SD	West Seneca
318	15,773	Shenendehowa Central SD	Clifton Park
319	15,752	Massena Central SD	Massena
320	15,641	Sherrill City SD	Verona
321	15,633	West Genesee Central SD	Camillus
322	15,104	Lancaster Central SD	Lancaster
323	14,895	Clarence Central SD	Clarence
324	14,816	Johnstown City SD	Johnstown
325	14,749	Watertown City SD	Watertown
326	14,504	South Jefferson Central SD	Adams Center
327	14,442	Frontier Central SD	Hamburg
328	13,727	Victor Central SD	Victor
329	13,213	General Brown Central SD	Dexter
n/a	n/a	Central Valley CSD At Ilion-Mohawk	Ilion
n/a	n/a	Charter School for Applied Tech	Buffalo
n/a	n/a	NYC Geographic District # 1	New York
n/a	n/a	NYC Geographic District # 2	New York
n/a	n/a	NYC Geographic District # 3	New York
n/a	n/a	NYC Geographic District # 4	New York
n/a	n/a	NYC Geographic District # 5	New York
n/a	n/a	NYC Geographic District # 6	New York
n/a	n/a	NYC Geographic District # 7	Bronx
n/a	n/a	NYC Geographic District # 8	Bronx
n/a	n/a	NYC Geographic District # 9	Bronx
n/a	n/a	NYC Geographic District #10	Bronx
n/a	n/a	NYC Geographic District #11	Bronx
n/a	n/a	NYC Geographic District #12	Bronx
n/a	n/a	NYC Geographic District #13	Brooklyn
n/a	n/a	NYC Geographic District #14	Brooklyn
n/a	n/a	NYC Geographic District #15	Brooklyn
n/a	n/a	NYC Geographic District #16	Brooklyn
n/a	n/a	NYC Geographic District #17	Brooklyn
n/a	n/a	NYC Geographic District #18	Brooklyn
n/a	n/a	NYC Geographic District #19	Brooklyn
n/a	n/a	NYC Geographic District #20	Brooklyn
n/a	n/a	NYC Geographic District #21	Brooklyn
n/a	n/a	NYC Geographic District #22	Brooklyn
n/a	n/a	NYC Geographic District #23	Brooklyn
n/a	n/a	NYC Geographic District #24	Corona
n/a	n/a	NYC Geographic District #25	Flushing
n/a	n/a	NYC Geographic District #26	Bayside
n/a	n/a	NYC Geographic District #27	Ozone Park
n/a	n/a	NYC Geographic District #28	Jamaica
n/a	n/a	NYC Geographic District #29	Queens Village
n/a	n/a	NYC Geographic District #30	Long Isl City
n/a	n/a	NYC Geographic District #31	Staten Island
n/a	n/a	NYC Geographic District #32	Brooklyn
n/a	n/a	NYC Special Schools - District 75	New York
n/a	n/a	Orange-Ulster Boces	Goshen

Long-Term Debt per Student (end of FY)

Rank	Dollars	District Name	City
1	43,141	Roosevelt UFSD	Roosevelt
2	35,155	Buffalo City SD	Buffalo
3	34,887	East Hampton UFSD	East Hampton
4	34,784	Eastport-South Manor CSD	Manorville
5	32,183	Pleasantville UFSD	Pleasantville
6	30,660	Southampton UFSD	Southampton
7	30,019	Waterloo Central SD	Waterloo
8	29,998	Marlboro Central SD	Milton
9	29,102	Haverstraw-Stony Point CSD	Garnerville
10	28,032	Hornell City SD	Hornell
11	25,765	East Irondequoit Central SD	Rochester
12	24,488	Irvington UFSD	Irvington
13	24,272	Catskill Central SD	Catskill
14	24,159	Penn Yan Central SD	Penn Yan
15	23,798	Hudson City SD	Hudson
16	22,702	Long Beach City SD	Long Beach
17	22,316	Phoenix Central SD	Phoenix
18	22,135	South Country Central SD	East Patchogue
19	21,810	Peekskill City SD	Peekskill
20	21,385	Westhampton Bch UFSD	Westhampton Bch
21	20,578	Westhill Central SD	Syracuse
22	20,441	Niskayuna Central SD	Schenectady
23	20,182	Cohoes City SD	Cohoes
24	20,028	Gloversville City SD	Gloversville
25	19,985	Camden Central SD	Camden
26	19,436	Minisink Valley Central SD	Slate Hill
27	19,313	Bath Central SD	Bath
28	18,960	Byram Hills Central SD	Armonk
29	18,942	Hudson Falls Central SD	Fort Edward
30	18,856	Albany City SD	Albany
31	18,619	Salmon River Central SD	Fort Covington
32	18,518	Johnson City Central SD	Johnson City
33	18,492	Nanuet UFSD	Nanuet

Note: This section only includes districts with 1,500 or more students; All categories are ranked from high to low

34	18,360	Hampton Bays UFSD	Hampton Bays
35	17,818	Maine-Endwell Central SD	Endwell
36	17,713	Newark Central SD	Newark
37	17,618	Susquehanna Valley Central SD	Conklin
38	17,200	Malone Central SD	Malone
39	17,149	Bayport-Blue Point UFSD	Bayport
40	16,692	Geneva City SD	Geneva
41	16,640	Liberty Central SD	Liberty
42	16,274	Medina Central SD	Medina
43	15,855	Dunkirk City SD	Dunkirk
44	15,749	Phelps-Clifton Springs Central SD	Clifton Springs
45	15,521	Ithaca City SD	Ithaca
46	15,441	Arlington Central SD	Lagrangeville
47	15,320	Pelham UFSD	Pelham
48	15,287	Cobleskill-Richmondville Central SD	Cobleskill
49	15,168	Niagara Falls City SD	Niagara Falls
50	14,951	Bethlehem Central SD	Delmar
51	14,842	Somers Central SD	Somers
52	14,763	Garden City UFSD	Garden City
53	14,692	Schuylerville Central SD	Schuylerville
54	14,676	Gates-Chili Central SD	Rochester
55	14,660	Cheektowaga-Maryvale UFSD	Cheektowaga
56	14,552	Solvay UFSD	Solvay
57	14,524	Norwich City SD	Norwich
58	14,285	Ardsley UFSD	Ardsley
59	14,170	UFSD of the Tarrytowns	Sleepy Hollow
60	14,153	Three Village Central SD	Stony Brook
61	14,137	Patchogue-Medford UFSD	Patchogue
62	14,085	Beacon City SD	Beacon
63	14,066	Sweet Home Central SD	Amherst
64	14,007	Sachem Central SD	Lake Ronkonkoma
65	13,937	Hendrick Hudson Central SD	Montrose
66	13,835	Broadalbin-Perth Central SD	Broadalbin
67	13,777	Homer Central SD	Homer
68	13,733	Rondout Valley Central SD	Accord
69	13,659	Oneida City SD	Oneida
70	13,649	Croton-Harmon UFSD	Croton on Hdsn
70	13,649	New York City Public Schools	New York
72	13,585	Niagara-Wheatfield Central SD	Niagara Falls
73	13,450	Waverly Central SD	Waverly
74	13,345	Pittsford Central SD	Pittsford
75	13,270	Cold Spring Hrbr Central SD	Cold Spring Hrbr
76	13,260	Chappaqua Central SD	Chappaqua
77	13,234	Churchville-Chili Central SD	Churchville
78	13,219	Depew UFSD	Depew
79	13,194	Wyandanch UFSD	Wyandanch
80	13,147	Eastchester UFSD	Eastchester
81	13,061	Mount Pleasant Central SD	Thornwood
82	13,058	Peru Central SD	Peru
83	12,986	Bedford Central SD	Bedford
84	12,879	Miller Place UFSD	Miller Place
85	12,803	Starpoint Central SD	Lockport
86	12,772	Ramapo Central SD (Suffern)	Hillburn
87	12,748	Honeoye Falls-Lima Central SD	Honeoye Falls
88	12,741	Lewiston-Porter Central SD	Youngstown
89	12,713	Rye City SD	Rye
90	12,680	Mount Vernon SD	Mount Vernon
91	12,644	Spencerport Central SD	Spencerport
92	12,528	Rochester City SD	Rochester
93	12,388	Oswego City SD	Oswego
94	12,380	Indian River Central SD	Philadelphia
95	12,362	Yorktown Central SD	Yorktown Hgts
96	12,291	Vestal Central SD	Vestal
97	12,258	Owego-Apalachin Central SD	Owego
98	12,219	Marcellus Central SD	Marcellus
99	12,198	Briarcliff Mnr UFSD	Briarcliff Mnr
100	12,079	White Plains City SD	White Plains
101	12,028	Hewlett-Woodmere UFSD	Woodmere
102	11,929	Valhalla UFSD	Valhalla
103	11,915	Dansville Central SD	Dansville
104	11,908	Olean City SD	Olean
105	11,810	Sayville UFSD	Sayville
106	11,805	Cornwall Central SD	Cornwall on Hdsn
107	11,697	Whitesboro Central SD	Yorkville
108	11,647	Windsor Central SD	Windsor
109	11,632	New Hyde Pk-Garden City Pk UFSD	New Hyde Park
110	11,620	Elmira City SD	Elmira
111	11,571	Connetquot Central SD	Bohemia
112	11,529	Canandaigua City SD	Canandaigua
112	11,529	Chenango Forks Central SD	Binghamton
114	11,369	Mamaroneck UFSD	Mamaroneck
115	11,249	Schalmont Central SD	Schenectady
116	11,234	William Floyd UFSD	Mastic Beach
117	11,175	Commack UFSD	East Northport
118	11,168	Lackawanna City SD	Lackawanna
119	11,140	Jamestown City SD	Jamestown
120	11,108	Cazenovia Central SD	Cazenovia
121	11,090	Warwick Valley Central SD	Warwick
122	11,044	Oyster Bay-East Norwich Central SD	Oyster Bay
123	10,999	Chenango Valley Central SD	Binghamton
124	10,779	Red Hook Central SD	Red Hook
125	10,693	Oneonta City SD	Oneonta
126	10,608	New Hartford Central SD	New Hartford
127	10,546	Rome City SD	Rome
128	10,498	Tonawanda City SD	Tonawanda
129	10,476	Yorkshire-Pioneer Central SD	Yorkshire
130	10,431	South Huntington UFSD	Huntington Stn
131	10,367	Putnam Valley Central SD	Putnam Valley
132	10,242	Spackenkill UFSD	Poughkeepsie
133	10,232	Carthage Central SD	Carthage
134	10,225	Bay Shore UFSD	Bay Shore
135	10,203	Scarsdale UFSD	Scarsdale
136	10,143	Monticello Central SD	Monticello
137	10,127	Queensbury UFSD	Queensbury
138	10,063	West Islip UFSD	West Islip
139	10,011	Mexico Central SD	Mexico
140	9,986	Newfane Central SD	Burt
141	9,980	Center Moriches UFSD	Center Moriches
142	9,962	Harborfields Central SD	Greenlawn
143	9,952	Dryden Central SD	Dryden
144	9,939	Middletown City SD	Middletown
145	9,804	Binghamton City SD	Binghamton
146	9,785	Amsterdam City SD	Amsterdam
147	9,738	East Islip UFSD	Islip Terrace
148	9,701	Batavia City SD	Batavia
149	9,668	Bronxville UFSD	Bronxville
150	9,642	Union-Endicott Central SD	Endicott
151	9,631	East Syracuse-Minoa Central SD	East Syracuse
152	9,491	Jamesville-Dewitt Central SD	Dewitt
153	9,486	Hauppauge UFSD	Hauppauge
154	9,437	East Williston UFSD	Old Westbury
155	9,409	Burnt Hills-Ballston Lake Central SD	Scotia
156	9,370	Malverne UFSD	Malverne
157	9,341	Smithtown Central SD	Smithtown
158	9,224	Babylon UFSD	Babylon
159	9,220	North Shore Central SD	Sea Cliff
160	9,199	Longwood Central SD	Middle Island
161	9,161	Lansingburgh Central SD	Troy
162	9,142	Clarence Central SD	Clarence
163	9,065	Port Jervis City SD	Port Jervis
164	9,037	Syracuse City SD	Syracuse
165	9,003	Rotterdam-Mohonasen Central SD	Schenectady
166	8,966	Springville-Griffith Institute CSD	Springville
167	8,907	Fredonia Central SD	Fredonia
167	8,907	Watertown City SD	Watertown
169	8,877	Port Washington UFSD	Port Washington
170	8,865	Massena Central SD	Massena
171	8,842	Plainedge UFSD	N Massapequa
172	8,771	Troy City SD	Troy
173	8,730	Guilderland Central SD	Guilderland Center
174	8,681	Glens Falls City SD	Glens Falls
175	8,666	Auburn City SD	Auburn
176	8,612	South Orangetown Central SD	Blauvelt
177	8,540	Monroe-Woodbury Central SD	Central Valley
178	8,517	Manhasset UFSD	Manhasset
179	8,509	Webster Central SD	Webster
180	8,422	Katonah-Lewisboro UFSD	Goldens Bridge
181	8,340	Hilton Central SD	Hilton
182	8,336	Chittenango Central SD	Chittenango
183	8,259	Bethpage UFSD	Bethpage
184	8,253	Penfield Central SD	Rochester
185	8,232	Plattsburgh City SD	Plattsburgh
186	8,180	North Babylon UFSD	North Babylon
187	8,115	Merrick UFSD	Merrick
188	8,078	Poughkeepsie City SD	Poughkeepsie
189	8,048	General Brown Central SD	Dexter
190	8,040	Greece Central SD	Rochester
191	8,012	Livonia Central SD	Livonia
192	8,010	West Irondequoit Central SD	Rochester
193	7,927	Brentwood UFSD	Brentwood
194	7,714	Lakeland Central SD	Shrub Oak
195	7,686	Averill Park Central SD	Averill Park
196	7,657	Central Islip UFSD	Central Islip
197	7,643	East Greenbush Central SD	East Greenbush
198	7,513	Island Trees UFSD	Levittown
199	7,497	Seaford UFSD	Seaford
200	7,456	Gouverneur Central SD	Gouverneur
201	7,455	Evans-Brant Central SD (Lake Shore)	Angola
202	7,453	Fulton City SD	Fulton
203	7,424	Newburgh City SD	Newburgh
204	7,412	Sherrill City SD	Verona
205	7,405	Shenendehowa Central SD	Clifton Park
206	7,379	Half Hollow Hills Central SD	Dix Hills
207	7,313	Locust Valley Central SD	Locust Valley
208	7,307	Islip UFSD	Islip
209	7,262	Edgemont UFSD	Scarsdale
210	7,234	Ravena-Coeymans-Selkirk Ctrl SD	Ravena
211	7,191	Brockport Central SD	Brockport
212	7,126	Mount Sinai UFSD	Mount Sinai
213	7,114	Carmel Central SD	Patterson
214	7,041	S Glens Fls Central SD	S Glens Fls
215	6,981	West Babylon UFSD	West Babylon
216	6,950	Middle Country Central SD	Centereach
217	6,943	Highland Central SD	Highland
218	6,928	Victor Central SD	Victor
219	6,875	Freeport UFSD	Freeport
220	6,874	Mineola UFSD	Mineola
221	6,852	Yonkers City SD	Yonkers
222	6,812	Utica City SD	Utica
223	6,781	New Paltz Central SD	New Paltz
224	6,760	Amherst Central SD	Amherst
225	6,649	Pearl River UFSD	Pearl River
226	6,593	Central Square Central SD	Central Square
227	6,552	West Genesee Central SD	Camillus
228	6,532	Saugerties Central SD	Saugerties
229	6,490	Saratoga Spgs City SD	Saratoga Spgs
230	6,449	Kenmore-Tonawanda UFSD	Buffalo
230	6,449	South Jefferson Central SD	Adams Center
232	6,341	Eden Central SD	Eden
233	6,333	Palmyra-Macedon Central SD	Palmyra
234	6,290	Wantagh UFSD	Wantagh
235	6,083	Kings Park Central SD	Kings Park
236	6,066	Fayetteville-Manlius Central SD	Manlius
237	6,065	Alden Central SD	Alden
238	6,050	New Rochelle City SD	New Rochelle
239	6,021	Rocky Point UFSD	Rocky Point
240	6,004	Fairport Central SD	Fairport
241	5,995	Albion Central SD	Albion
242	5,987	Lancaster Central SD	Lancaster
243	5,970	Clarkstown Central SD	New City
244	5,954	Roslyn UFSD	Roslyn
245	5,936	Syosset Central SD	Syosset
246	5,906	Brookhaven-Comsewogue UFSD	Port Jefferson Sta
247	5,854	Orchard Park Central SD	West Seneca
248	5,711	North Bellmore UFSD	Bellmore
249	5,659	Brewster Central SD	Brewster
250	5,584	Washingtonville Central SD	Washingtonville
251	5,524	Hyde Park Central SD	Hyde Park
252	5,503	North Syracuse Central SD	North Syracuse
253	5,491	Lockport City SD	Lockport
254	5,479	Liverpool Central SD	Liverpool
255	5,414	Riverhead Central SD	Riverhead
256	5,413	Iroquois Central SD	Elma
257	5,389	Beekmantown Central SD	West Chazy
258	5,382	West Hempstead UFSD	West Hempstead
259	5,359	Elwood UFSD	Greenlawn
260	5,322	Port Chester-Rye UFSD	Port Chester
261	5,277	Massapequa UFSD	Massapequa
262	5,255	Pine Bush Central SD	Pine Bush
263	5,223	North Colonie CSD	Latham
264	5,185	Johnstown City SD	Johnstown
265	5,110	Rye Neck UFSD	Mamaroneck
266	4,990	Baldwinsville Central SD	Baldwinsville
267	4,950	Lindenhurst UFSD	Lindenhurst
268	4,911	Scotia-Glenville Central SD	Scotia
269	4,870	Ballston Spa Central SD	Ballston Spa
270	4,864	Ogdensburg City SD	Ogdensburg
271	4,846	South Colonie Central SD	Albany
272	4,710	Cheektowaga Central SD	Cheektowaga
273	4,674	Franklin Square UFSD	Franklin Square
274	4,665	Wallkill Central SD	Wallkill
275	4,653	East Meadow UFSD	Westbury
276	4,634	Baldwin UFSD	Baldwin
277	4,243	Herricks UFSD	New Hyde Park
278	4,168	Rockville Ctr UFSD	Rockville Ctr
279	4,154	Horseheads Central SD	Horseheads
280	4,139	Elmont UFSD	Elmont
281	4,059	Oceanside UFSD	Oceanside
282	4,015	Kinderhook Central SD	Valatie
283	4,003	Hamburg Central SD	Hamburg
284	3,982	West Seneca Central SD	West Seneca
285	3,922	Grand Island Central SD	Grand Island

Note: This section only includes districts with 1,500 or more students; All categories are ranked from high to low

Rank	Students	District	Location
286	3,874	Wayne Central SD	Ontario Center
287	3,867	Mahopac Central SD	Mahopac
288	3,758	Ellenville Central SD	Ellenville
289	3,734	Westbury UFSD	Old Westbury
290	3,700	Rush-Henrietta Central SD	Henrietta
291	3,691	Plainview-Old Bethpage Central SD	Plainview
292	3,639	Hastings-On-Hudson UFSD	Hastings on Hdsn
293	3,541	Frontier Central SD	Hamburg
294	3,487	Northport-East Northport UFSD	Northport
295	3,473	Hempstead UFSD	Hempstead
296	3,415	Kingston City SD	Kingston
297	3,360	Deer Park UFSD	Deer Park
298	3,272	Amityville UFSD	Amityville
299	3,201	Ossining UFSD	Ossining
300	3,175	Goshen Central SD	Goshen
301	3,144	Nyack UFSD	Nyack
302	3,089	East Ramapo CSD (Spring Valley)	Spring Valley
303	3,035	Great Neck UFSD	Great Neck
304	3,029	Jericho UFSD	Jericho
305	2,986	Schenectady City SD	Schenectady
306	2,944	Levittown UFSD	Levittown
307	2,942	Hicksville UFSD	Hicksville
307	2,942	Valley Central SD (Montgomery)	Montgomery
309	2,910	Farmingdale UFSD	Farmingdale
310	2,826	Brighton Central SD	Rochester
311	2,741	Williamsville Central SD	East Amherst
312	2,638	Copiague UFSD	Copiague
313	2,323	Glen Cove City SD	Glen Cove
314	2,311	Wappingers Central SD	Wappingers Fls
315	1,992	Greenburgh Central SD	Hartsdale
316	1,819	Corning City SD	Painted Post
317	1,417	North Tonawanda City SD	North Tonawanda
318	1,413	Shoreham-Wading River Central SD	Shoreham
319	1,412	Uniondale UFSD	Uniondale
320	1,321	East Aurora UFSD	East Aurora
321	982	Harrison Central SD	Harrison
322	895	Huntington UFSD	Huntington Stn
323	644	Lawrence UFSD	Lawrence
324	639	Valley Stream Central High SD	Valley Stream
325	254	Cortland City SD	Cortland
326	169	Lynbrook UFSD	Lynbrook
327	136	Valley Stream 13 UFSD	Valley Stream
328	15	Bellmore-Merrick Central High SD	North Merrick
329	0	Sewanhaka Central High SD	Floral Park
n/a	n/a	Central Valley CSD At Ilion-Mohawk	Ilion
n/a	n/a	Charter School for Applied Tech	Buffalo
n/a	n/a	NYC Geographic District # 1	New York
n/a	n/a	NYC Geographic District # 2	New York
n/a	n/a	NYC Geographic District # 3	New York
n/a	n/a	NYC Geographic District # 4	New York
n/a	n/a	NYC Geographic District # 5	New York
n/a	n/a	NYC Geographic District # 6	New York
n/a	n/a	NYC Geographic District # 7	Bronx
n/a	n/a	NYC Geographic District # 8	Bronx
n/a	n/a	NYC Geographic District # 9	Bronx
n/a	n/a	NYC Geographic District #10	Bronx
n/a	n/a	NYC Geographic District #11	Bronx
n/a	n/a	NYC Geographic District #12	Bronx
n/a	n/a	NYC Geographic District #13	Brooklyn
n/a	n/a	NYC Geographic District #14	Brooklyn
n/a	n/a	NYC Geographic District #15	Brooklyn
n/a	n/a	NYC Geographic District #16	Brooklyn
n/a	n/a	NYC Geographic District #17	Brooklyn
n/a	n/a	NYC Geographic District #18	Brooklyn
n/a	n/a	NYC Geographic District #19	Brooklyn
n/a	n/a	NYC Geographic District #20	Brooklyn
n/a	n/a	NYC Geographic District #21	Brooklyn
n/a	n/a	NYC Geographic District #22	Brooklyn
n/a	n/a	NYC Geographic District #23	Brooklyn
n/a	n/a	NYC Geographic District #24	Corona
n/a	n/a	NYC Geographic District #25	Flushing
n/a	n/a	NYC Geographic District #26	Bayside
n/a	n/a	NYC Geographic District #27	Ozone Park
n/a	n/a	NYC Geographic District #28	Jamaica
n/a	n/a	NYC Geographic District #29	Queens Village
n/a	n/a	NYC Geographic District #30	Long Isl City
n/a	n/a	NYC Geographic District #31	Staten Island
n/a	n/a	NYC Geographic District #32	Brooklyn
n/a	n/a	NYC Special Schools - District 75	New York
n/a	n/a	Orange-Ulster Boces	Goshen

Note: This section only includes districts with 1,500 or more students; All categories are ranked from high to low

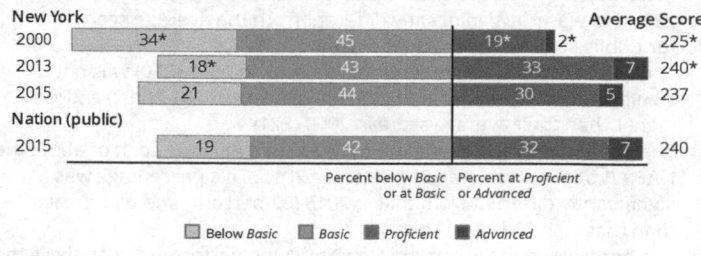

2015 Mathematics State Snapshot Report
New York · Grade 4 · Public Schools

Overall Results

- In 2015, the average score of fourth-grade students in New York was 237. This was lower than the average score of 240 for public school students in the nation.
- The average score for students in New York in 2015 (237) was lower than their average score in 2013 (240) and was higher than their average score in 2000 (225).
- The percentage of students in New York who performed at or above the NAEP *Proficient* level was 35 percent in 2015. This percentage was smaller than that in 2013 (40 percent) and was greater than that in 2000 (21 percent).
- The percentage of students in New York who performed at or above the NAEP *Basic* level was 79 percent in 2015. This percentage was smaller than that in 2013 (82 percent) and was greater than that in 2000 (66 percent).

Achievement-Level Percentages and Average Score Results

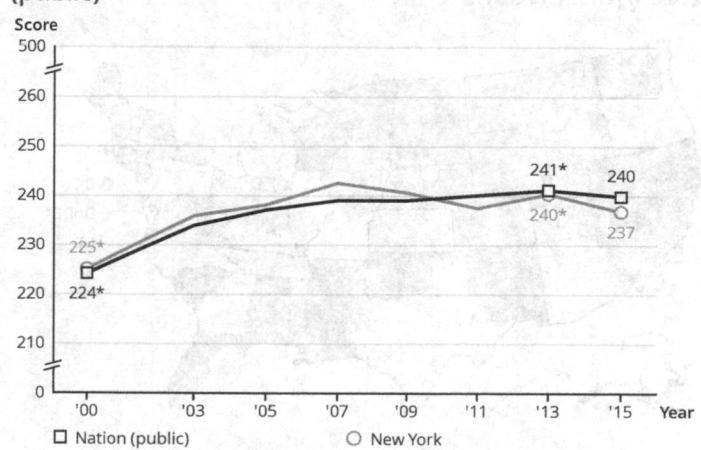

* Significantly different (*p* < .05) from state's results in 2015. Significance tests were performed using unrounded numbers.
NOTE: Detail may not sum to totals because of rounding.

Compare the Average Score in 2015 to Other States/Jurisdictions

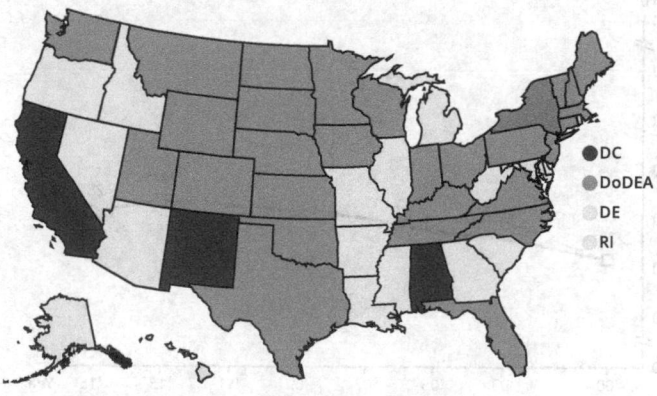

In 2015, the average score in New York (237) was

- ▓ lower than those in 29 states/jurisdictions
- ■ higher than those in 4 states/jurisdictions
- ░ not significantly different from those in 18 states/jurisdictions

DoDEA = Department of Defense Education Activity (overseas and domestic schools)

Average Scores for State/Jurisdiction and Nation (public)

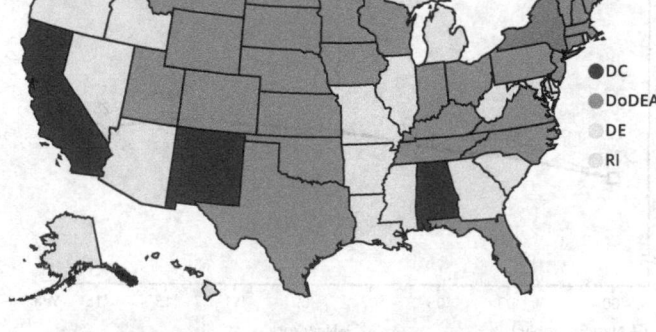

* Significantly different (*p* < .05) from 2015. Significance tests were performed using unrounded numbers.

Results for Student Groups in 2015

Reporting Groups	Percentage of students	Avg. score	Percentage at or above Basic	Percentage at or above Proficient	Percentage at Advanced
Race/Ethnicity					
White	45	245	88	47	7
Black	19	221	60	14	1
Hispanic	26	228	72	21	1
Asian	8	253	89	59	16
American Indian/Alaska Native	#	‡	‡	‡	‡
Native Hawaiian/Pacific Islander	#	‡	‡	‡	‡
Two or more races	1	‡	‡	‡	‡
Gender					
Male	52	238	79	36	6
Female	48	236	79	34	4
National School Lunch Program					
Eligible	58	228	71	23	2
Not eligible	39	248	90	51	9

\# Rounds to zero.
‡ Reporting standards not met.
NOTE: Detail may not sum to totals because of rounding, and because the "Information not available" category for the National School Lunch Program, which provides free/reduced-price lunches, is not displayed. Black includes African American and Hispanic includes Latino. Race categories exclude Hispanic origin.

Score Gaps for Student Groups

- In 2015, Black students had an average score that was 25 points lower than that for White students. This performance gap was not significantly different from that in 2000 (27 points).
- In 2015, Hispanic students had an average score that was 17 points lower than that for White students. This performance gap was narrower than that in 2000 (30 points).
- In 2015, male students in New York had an average score that was not significantly different from that for female students.
- In 2015, students who were eligible for free/reduced-price school lunch, an indicator of low family income, had an average score that was 20 points lower than that for students who were not eligible. This performance gap was narrower than that in 2000 (26 points).

NATIONAL CENTER FOR EDUCATION STATISTICS
Institute of Education Sciences

NOTE: Statistical comparisons are calculated on the basis of unrounded scale scores or percentages.
SOURCE: U.S. Department of Education, Institute of Education Sciences, National Center for Education Statistics, National Assessment of Educational Progress (NAEP), various years, 2000-2015 Mathematics Assessments.

The Nation's Report Card

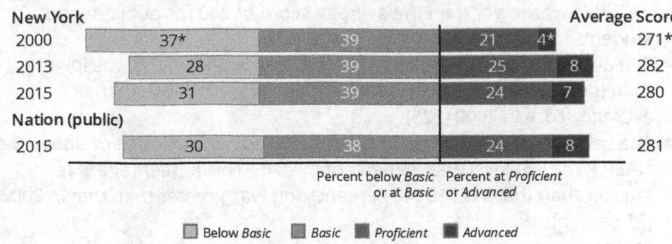

2015 Mathematics State Snapshot Report
New York • Grade 8 • Public Schools

Overall Results

- In 2015, the average score of eighth-grade students in New York was 280. This was not significantly different from the average score of 281 for public school students in the nation.
- The average score for students in New York in 2015 (280) was not significantly different from their average score in 2013 (282) and was higher than their average score in 2000 (271).
- The percentage of students in New York who performed at or above the NAEP *Proficient* level was 31 percent in 2015. This percentage was not significantly different from that in 2013 (32 percent) and was greater than that in 2000 (24 percent).
- The percentage of students in New York who performed at or above the NAEP *Basic* level was 69 percent in 2015. This percentage was not significantly different from that in 2013 (72 percent) and was greater than that in 2000 (63 percent).

Achievement-Level Percentages and Average Score Results

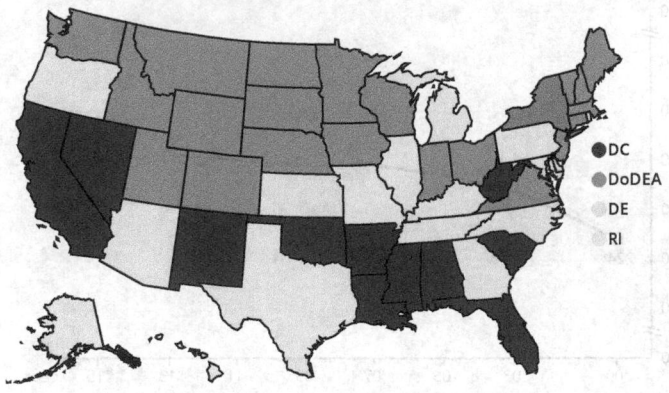

* Significantly different (*p* < .05) from state's results in 2015. Significance tests were performed using unrounded numbers.
NOTE: Detail may not sum to totals because of rounding.

Compare the Average Score in 2015 to Other States/Jurisdictions

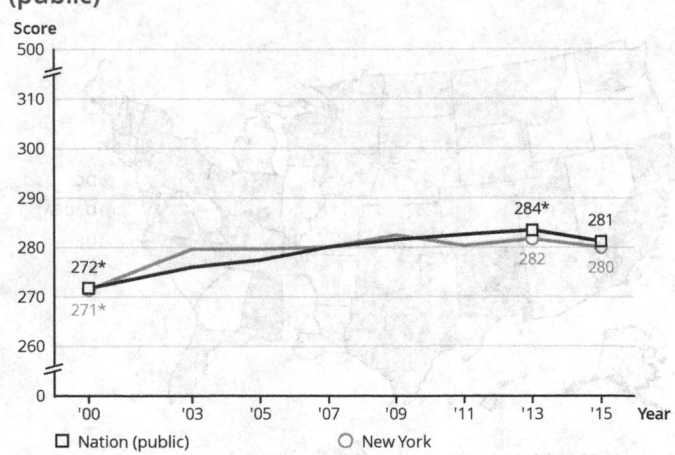

In 2015, the average score in New York (280) was

- ▨ lower than those in 22 states/jurisdictions
- ■ higher than those in 12 states/jurisdictions
- ▫ not significantly different from those in 17 states/jurisdictions

DoDEA = Department of Defense Education Activity (overseas and domestic schools)

Average Scores for State/Jurisdiction and Nation (public)

* Significantly different (*p* < .05) from 2015. Significance tests were performed using unrounded numbers.

Results for Student Groups in 2015

Reporting Groups	Percentage of students	Avg. score	Percentage at or above Basic	Percentage at or above Proficient	Percentage at Advanced
Race/Ethnicity					
White	47	290	80	40	9
Black	20	264	52	15	2
Hispanic	23	268	59	19	3
Asian	9	298	82	52	20
American Indian/Alaska Native	#	‡	‡	‡	‡
Native Hawaiian/Pacific Islander	#	‡	‡	‡	‡
Two or more races	1	‡	‡	‡	‡
Gender					
Male	51	280	70	32	7
Female	49	280	69	30	7
National School Lunch Program					
Eligible	57	271	60	21	4
Not eligible	41	292	81	44	11

\# Rounds to zero.
‡ Reporting standards not met.
NOTE: Detail may not sum to totals because of rounding, and because the "Information not available" category for the National School Lunch Program, which provides free/reduced-price lunches, is not displayed. Black includes African American and Hispanic includes Latino. Race categories exclude Hispanic origin.

Score Gaps for Student Groups

- In 2015, Black students had an average score that was 25 points lower than that for White students. This performance gap was not significantly different from that in 2000 (33 points).
- In 2015, Hispanic students had an average score that was 21 points lower than that for White students. This performance gap was narrower than that in 2000 (34 points).
- In 2015, male students in New York had an average score that was not significantly different from that for female students.
- In 2015, students who were eligible for free/reduced-price school lunch, an indicator of low family income, had an average score that was 21 points lower than that for students who were not eligible. This performance gap was not significantly different from that in 2000 (29 points).

ies NATIONAL CENTER FOR EDUCATION STATISTICS
Institute of Education Sciences

NOTE: Statistical comparisons are calculated on the basis of unrounded scale scores or percentages.
SOURCE: U.S. Department of Education, Institute of Education Sciences, National Center for Education Statistics, National Assessment of Educational Progress (NAEP), various years, 2000-2015 Mathematics Assessments.

The Nation's Report Card

Overall Results

- In 2015, the average score of fourth-grade students in New York was 223. This was not significantly different from the average score of 221 for public school students in the nation.
- The average score for students in New York in 2015 (223) was not significantly different from their average score in 2013 (224) and was higher than their average score in 1998 (215).
- The percentage of students in New York who performed at or above the NAEP *Proficient* level was 36 percent in 2015. This percentage was not significantly different from that in 2013 (37 percent) and was greater than that in 1998 (29 percent).
- The percentage of students in New York who performed at or above the NAEP *Basic* level was 68 percent in 2015. This percentage was not significantly different from that in 2013 (70 percent) and was greater than that in 1998 (62 percent).

Achievement-Level Percentages and Average Score Results

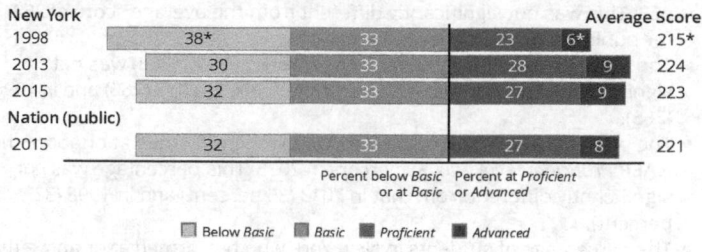

* Significantly different (*p* < .05) from state's results in 2015. Significance tests were performed using unrounded numbers.
NOTE: Detail may not sum to totals because of rounding.

Compare the Average Score in 2015 to Other States/Jurisdictions

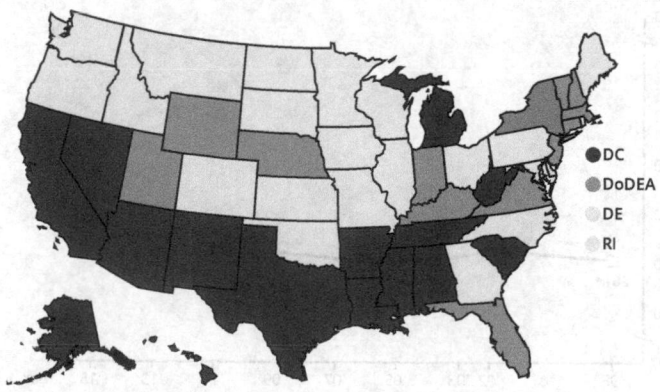

In 2015, the average score in New York (223) was

- ▨ lower than those in 13 states/jurisdictions
- ■ higher than those in 16 states/jurisdictions
- ▫ not significantly different from those in 22 states/jurisdictions

DoDEA = Department of Defense Education Activity (overseas and domestic schools)

Average Scores for State/Jurisdiction and Nation (public)

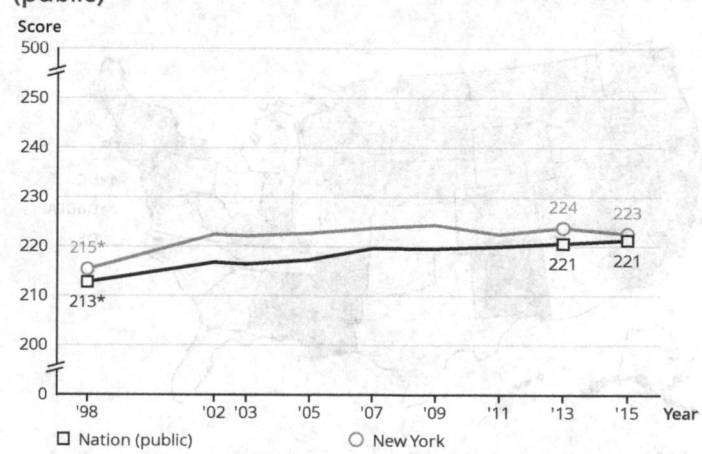

* Significantly different (*p* < .05) from 2015. Significance tests were performed using unrounded numbers.

Results for Student Groups in 2015

Reporting Groups	Percentage of students	Avg. score	Percentage at or above Basic	Percentage at or above Proficient	Percentage at Advanced
Race/Ethnicity					
White	45	234	80	49	14
Black	19	208	52	18	3
Hispanic	26	209	56	19	2
Asian	8	236	80	51	18
American Indian/Alaska Native	1	‡	‡	‡	‡
Native Hawaiian/Pacific Islander	#	‡	‡	‡	‡
Two or more races	1	‡	‡	‡	‡
Gender					
Male	51	219	65	33	7
Female	49	226	72	39	10
National School Lunch Program					
Eligible	57	211	57	21	3
Not eligible	40	238	84	53	15

Rounds to zero.
‡ Reporting standards not met.
NOTE: Detail may not sum to totals because of rounding, and because the "Information not available" category for the National School Lunch Program, which provides free/reduced-price lunches, is not displayed. Black includes African American and Hispanic includes Latino. Race categories exclude Hispanic origin.

Score Gaps for Student Groups

- In 2015, Black students had an average score that was 26 points lower than that for White students. This performance gap was narrower than that in 1998 (37 points).
- In 2015, Hispanic students had an average score that was 25 points lower than that for White students. This performance gap was narrower than that in 1998 (40 points).
- In 2015, female students in New York had an average score that was higher than that for male students by 7 points.
- In 2015, students who were eligible for free/reduced-price school lunch, an indicator of low family income, had an average score that was 27 points lower than that for students who were not eligible. This performance gap was narrower than that in 1998 (35 points).

NATIONAL CENTER FOR EDUCATION STATISTICS
Institute of Education Sciences

NOTE: Statistical comparisons are calculated on the basis of unrounded scale scores or percentages.
SOURCE: U.S. Department of Education, Institute of Education Sciences, National Center for Education Statistics, National Assessment of Educational Progress (NAEP), various years, 1998-2015 Reading Assessments.

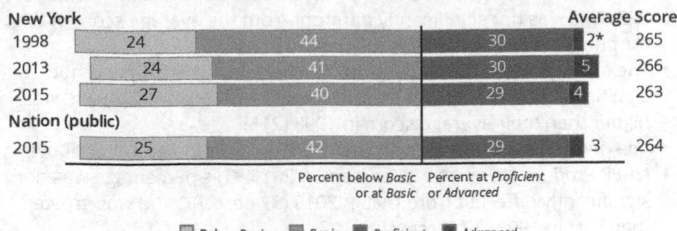

2015 Reading State Snapshot Report
New York • Grade 8 • Public Schools

Overall Results

- In 2015, the average score of eighth-grade students in New York was 263. This was not significantly different from the average score of 264 for public school students in the nation.
- The average score for students in New York in 2015 (263) was not significantly different from their average score in 2013 (266) and in 1998 (265).
- The percentage of students in New York who performed at or above the NAEP *Proficient* level was 33 percent in 2015. This percentage was not significantly different from that in 2013 (35 percent) and in 1998 (32 percent).
- The percentage of students in New York who performed at or above the NAEP *Basic* level was 73 percent in 2015. This percentage was not significantly different from that in 2013 (76 percent) and in 1998 (76 percent).

Achievement-Level Percentages and Average Score Results

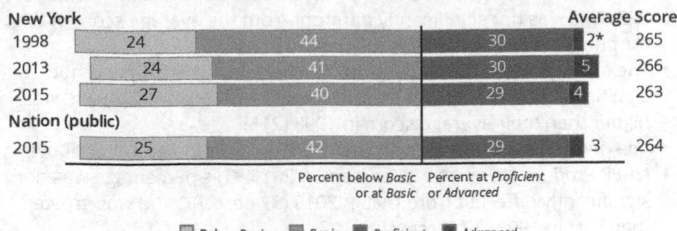

New York	Below Basic	Basic	Proficient	Advanced	Average Score
1998	24	44	30	2*	265
2013	24	41	30	5	266
2015	27	40	29	4	263
Nation (public)					
2015	25	42	29	3	264

Percent below *Basic*   Percent at *Proficient*
or at *Basic*   or *Advanced*

■ Below *Basic*   ■ *Basic*   ■ *Proficient*   ■ *Advanced*

* Significantly different (*p* < .05) from state's results in 2015. Significance tests were performed using unrounded numbers.
NOTE: Detail may not sum to totals because of rounding.

Compare the Average Score in 2015 to Other States/Jurisdictions

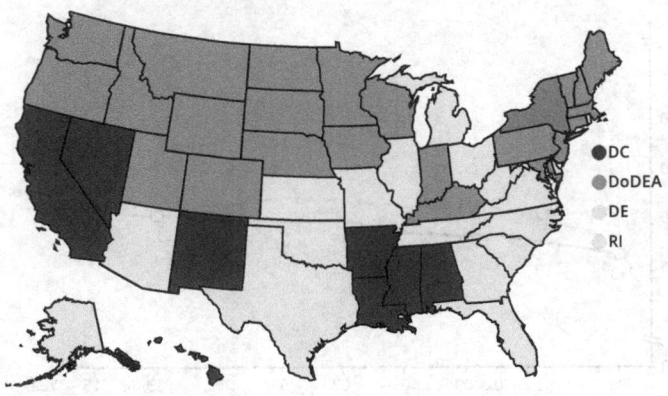

● DC
● DoDEA
○ DE
○ RI

In 2015, the average score in New York (263) was

■ lower than those in 24 states/jurisdictions
■ higher than those in 9 states/jurisdictions
□ not significantly different from those in 18 states/jurisdictions

DoDEA = Department of Defense Education Activity (overseas and domestic schools)

Average Scores for State/Jurisdiction and Nation (public)

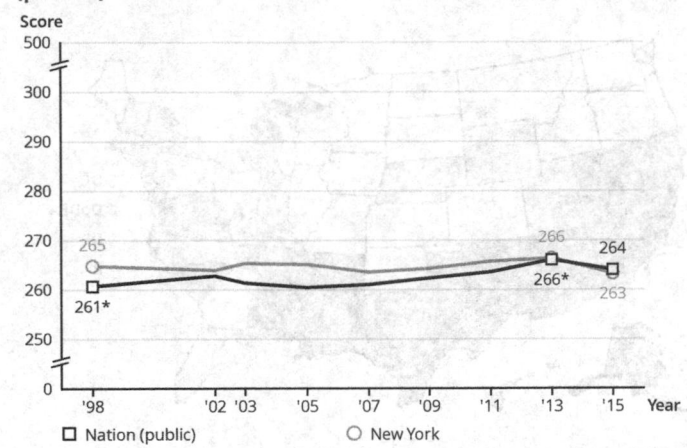

□ Nation (public)   ○ New York

* Significantly different (*p* < .05) from 2015. Significance tests were performed using unrounded numbers.

Results for Student Groups in 2015

Reporting Groups	Percentage of students	Avg. score	Percentage at or above Basic	Percentage at or above Proficient	Percentage at Advanced
Race/Ethnicity					
White	46	273	82	43	5
Black	20	248	58	17	1
Hispanic	23	254	65	22	2
Asian	9	272	80	42	7
American Indian/Alaska Native	#	‡	‡	‡	‡
Native Hawaiian/Pacific Islander	#	‡	‡	‡	‡
Two or more races	1	‡	‡	‡	‡
Gender					
Male	51	259	69	28	3
Female	49	268	77	37	5
National School Lunch Program					
Eligible	55	254	64	22	1
Not eligible	43	275	84	46	6

\# Rounds to zero.
‡ Reporting standards not met.
NOTE: Detail may not sum to totals because of rounding, and because the "Information not available" category for the National School Lunch Program, which provides free/reduced-price lunches, is not displayed. Black includes African American and Hispanic includes Latino. Race categories exclude Hispanic origin.

Score Gaps for Student Groups

- In 2015, Black students had an average score that was 25 points lower than that for White students. This performance gap was not significantly different from that in 1998 (28 points).
- In 2015, Hispanic students had an average score that was 19 points lower than that for White students. This performance gap was narrower than that in 1998 (28 points).
- In 2015, female students in New York had an average score that was higher than that for male students by 9 points.
- In 2015, students who were eligible for free/reduced-price school lunch, an indicator of low family income, had an average score that was 22 points lower than that for students who were not eligible. This performance gap was not significantly different from that in 1998 (25 points).

NATIONAL CENTER FOR EDUCATION STATISTICS
Institute of Education Sciences

NOTE: Statistical comparisons are calculated on the basis of unrounded scale scores or percentages.
SOURCE: U.S. Department of Education, Institute of Education Sciences, National Center for Education Statistics, National Assessment of Educational Progress (NAEP), various years, 1998-2015 Reading Assessments.

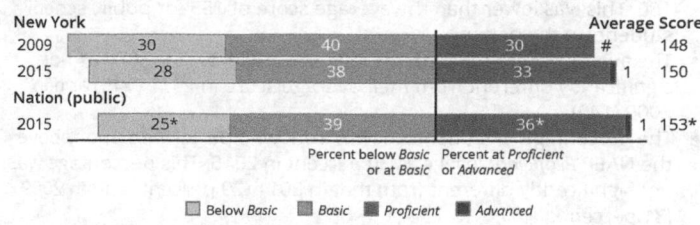

Overall Results

- In 2015, the average score of fourth-grade students in New York was 150. This was lower than the average score of 153 for public school students in the nation.
- The average score for students in New York in 2015 (150) was not significantly different from their average score in 2009 (148).
- The percentage of students in New York who performed at or above the NAEP *Proficient* level was 33 percent in 2015. This percentage was not significantly different from that in 2009 (30 percent).
- The percentage of students in New York who performed at or above the NAEP *Basic* level was 72 percent in 2015. This percentage was not significantly different from that in 2009 (70 percent).

Achievement-Level Percentages and Average Score Results

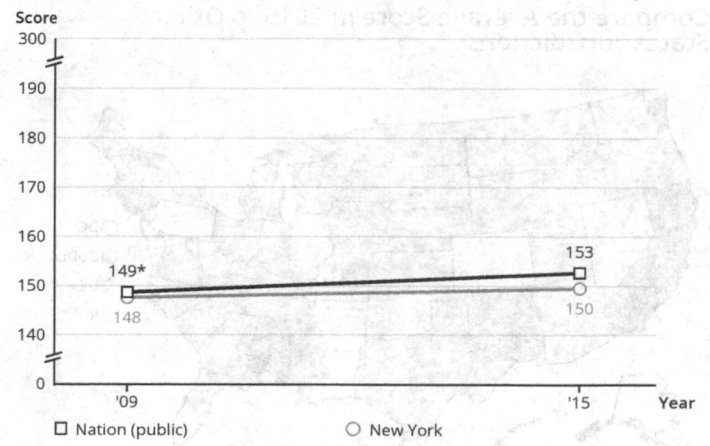

\# Rounds to zero.
* Significantly different (*p* < .05) from state's results in 2015. Significance tests were performed using unrounded numbers.
NOTE: Detail may not sum to totals because of rounding.

Compare the Average Score in 2015 to Other States/Jurisdictions

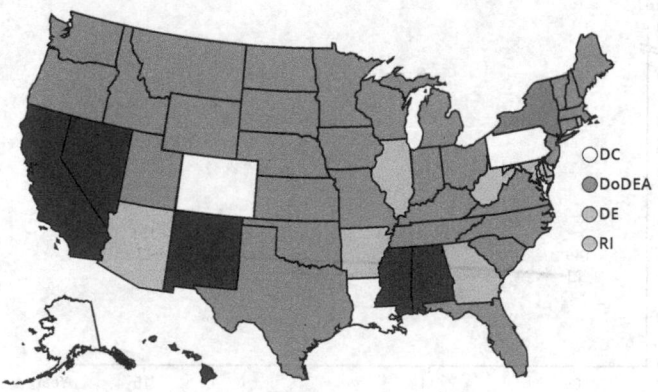

In 2015, the average score in New York (150) was
- lower than those in 32 states/jurisdictions
- higher than those in 6 states/jurisdictions
- not significantly different from those in 8 states/jurisdictions

☐ 5 states/jurisdictions did not participate in 2015

DoDEA = Department of Defense Education Activity (overseas and domestic schools)

Average Scores for State/Jurisdiction and Nation (public)

* Significantly different (*p* < .05) from 2015. Significance tests were performed using unrounded numbers.

Results for Student Groups in 2015

Reporting Groups	Percentage of students	Avg. score	Percentage at or above Basic	Percentage at or above Proficient	Percentage at Advanced
Race/Ethnicity					
White	45	164	87	49	1
Black	19	130	49	12	#
Hispanic	26	135	58	16	#
Asian	8	159	81	46	1
American Indian/Alaska Native	1	‡	‡	‡	‡
Native Hawaiian/Pacific Islander	#	‡	‡	‡	‡
Two or more races	1	‡	‡	‡	‡
Gender					
Male	52	150	72	35	1
Female	48	149	71	32	1
National School Lunch Program					
Eligible	56	138	59	20	#
Not eligible	41	164	87	49	1

\# Rounds to zero.
‡ Reporting standards not met.
NOTE: Detail may not sum to totals because of rounding, and because the "Information not available" category for the National School Lunch Program, which provides free/reduced-price lunches, is not displayed. Black includes African American and Hispanic includes Latino. Race categories exclude Hispanic origin.

Score Gaps for Student Groups

- In 2015, Black students had an average score that was 34 points lower than that for White students. This performance gap was not significantly different from that in 2009 (34 points).
- In 2015, Hispanic students had an average score that was 28 points lower than that for White students. This performance gap was not significantly different from that in 2009 (31 points).
- In 2015, male students in New York had an average score that was not significantly different from that for female students.
- In 2015, students who were eligible for free/reduced-price school lunch, an indicator of low family income, had an average score that was 26 points lower than that for students who were not eligible. This performance gap was not significantly different from that in 2009 (27 points).

NOTE: The NAEP science scale ranges from 0 to 300. Statistical comparisons are calculated on the basis of unrounded scale scores or percentages.
SOURCE: U.S. Department of Education, Institute of Education Sciences, National Center for Education Statistics, National Assessment of Educational Progress (NAEP), 2009 and 2015 Science Assessments.

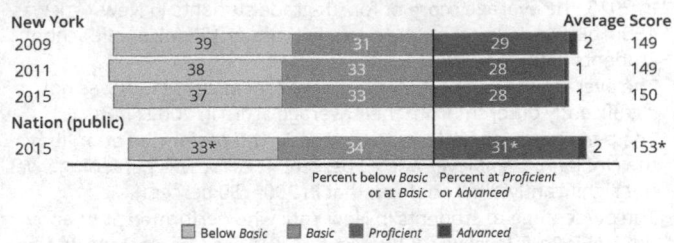

The Nation's Report Card

2015 Science State Snapshot Report
New York • Grade 8 • Public Schools

Overall Results

- In 2015, the average score of eighth-grade students in New York was 150. This was lower than the average score of 153 for public school students in the nation.
- The average score for students in New York in 2015 (150) was not significantly different from their average score in 2011 (149) and in 2009 (149).
- The percentage of students in New York who performed at or above the NAEP *Proficient* level was 30 percent in 2015. This percentage was not significantly different from that in 2011 (29 percent) and in 2009 (31 percent).
- The percentage of students in New York who performed at or above the NAEP *Basic* level was 63 percent in 2015. This percentage was not significantly different from that in 2011 (62 percent) and in 2009 (61 percent).

Achievement-Level Percentages and Average Score Results

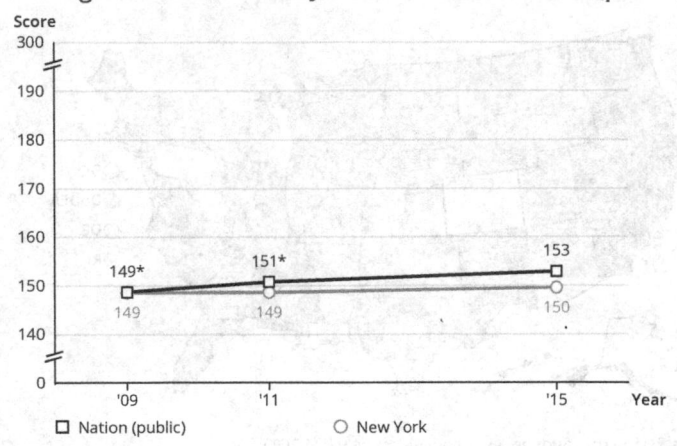

* Significantly different (*p* < .05) from state's results in 2015. Significance tests were performed using unrounded numbers.
NOTE: Detail may not sum to totals because of rounding.

Compare the Average Score in 2015 to Other States/Jurisdictions

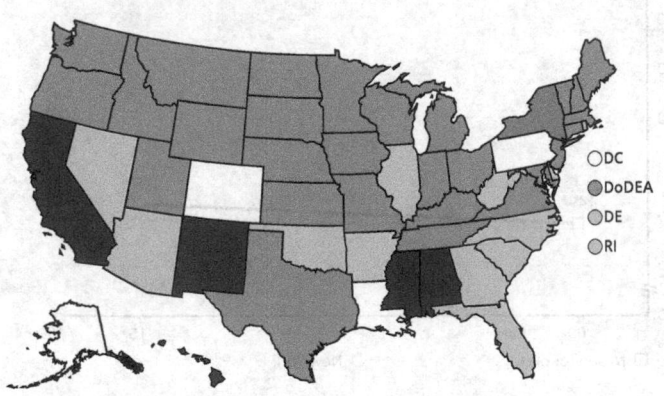

In 2015, the average score in New York (150) was
- ▨ lower than those in 29 states/jurisdictions
- ■ higher than those in 5 states/jurisdictions
- ▦ not significantly different from those in 12 states/jurisdictions

☐ 5 states/jurisdictions did not participate in 2015

DoDEA = Department of Defense Education Activity (overseas and domestic schools)

Average Scores for State/Jurisdiction and Nation (public)

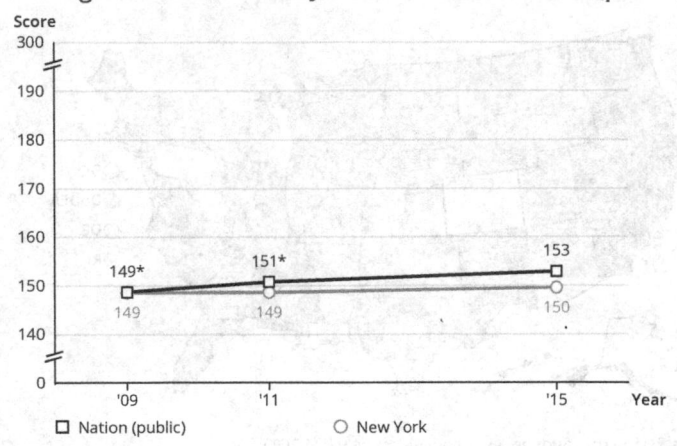

* Significantly different (*p* < .05) from 2015. Significance tests were performed using unrounded numbers.

Results for Student Groups in 2015

Reporting Groups	Percentage of students	Avg. score	Percentage at or above Basic	Percentage at or above Proficient	Percentage at Advanced
Race/Ethnicity					
White	47	164	79	45	2
Black	20	129	38	9	#
Hispanic	23	134	46	13	#
Asian	9	158	73	39	3
American Indian/Alaska Native	#	‡	‡	‡	‡
Native Hawaiian/Pacific Islander	#	‡	‡	‡	‡
Two or more races	1	‡	‡	‡	‡
Gender					
Male	51	150	63	32	2
Female	49	149	62	28	1
National School Lunch Program					
Eligible	56	139	50	17	#
Not eligible	42	163	78	45	3

Rounds to zero.
‡ Reporting standards not met.
NOTE: Detail may not sum to totals because of rounding, and because the "Information not available" category for the National School Lunch Program, which provides free/reduced-price lunches, is not displayed. Black includes African American and Hispanic includes Latino. Race categories exclude Hispanic origin.

Score Gaps for Student Groups

- In 2015, Black students had an average score that was 35 points lower than that for White students. This performance gap was not significantly different from that in 2009 (41 points).
- In 2015, Hispanic students had an average score that was 30 points lower than that for White students. This performance gap was narrower than that in 2009 (39 points).
- In 2015, male students in New York had an average score that was not significantly different from that for female students.
- In 2015, students who were eligible for free/reduced-price school lunch, an indicator of low family income, had an average score that was 24 points lower than that for students who were not eligible. This performance gap was narrower than that in 2009 (33 points).

NATIONAL CENTER FOR EDUCATION STATISTICS
Institute of Education Sciences

NOTE: The NAEP science scale ranges from 0 to 300. Statistical comparisons are calculated on the basis of unrounded scale scores or percentages.
SOURCE: U.S. Department of Education, Institute of Education Sciences, National Center for Education Statistics, National Assessment of Educational Progress (NAEP), various years, 2009-2015 Science Assessments.

NCES
National Center for
Education Statistics

Nation's Report Card **NAEP**

The Nation's Report Card
State **Writing** 2002
Snapshot Report

New York
Grade 4
Public School

NCES 2003-532NY4

The writing assessment of the National Assessment of Educational Progress (NAEP) measures narrative, informative, and persuasive writing–three purposes identified in the NAEP framework. The NAEP writing scale ranges from 0 to 300.

Overall Writing Results for New York

- The average scale score for fourth-grade students in New York was 163.

- New York's average score (163) was higher[1] than that of the nation's public schools (153).

- Students' average scale scores in New York were higher than those in 42 jurisdictions[2], not significantly different from those in 3 jurisdictions, and lower than those in 2 jurisdictions.

- The percentage of students who performed at or above the NAEP *Proficient* level was 37 percent. The percentage of students who performed at or above the *Basic* level was 91 percent.

Student Percentage at Each Achievement Level

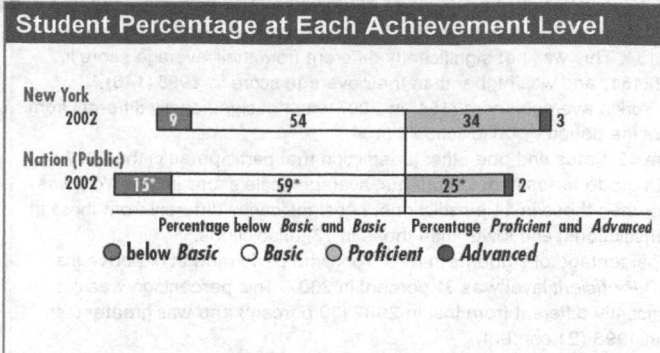

Percentage below *Basic* and *Basic*   Percentage *Proficient* and *Advanced*

● below *Basic*   ○ *Basic*   ◐ *Proficient* ● *Advanced*

Performance of NAEP Reporting Groups in New York

Reporting groups	Percentage of students	Average Score	Percentage of students at			
			Below *Basic*	*Basic*	*Proficient*	*Advanced*
Male	51	156 ↑	12 ↓	58	28 ↑	2
Female	49	170 ↑	6 ↓	50 ↓	40 ↑	4
White	54	172 ↑	4 ↓	49 ↓	42 ↑	4
Black	19	148 ↑	16 ↓	63	20 ↑	1
Hispanic	21	149	16	61	22	1
Asian/Pacific Islander	6	176	4	44	47	5
American Indian/Alaska Native	#	---	---	---	---	---
Free/reduced-priced school lunch						
Eligible	44	150 ↑	16 ↓	61	22 ↑	1
Not eligible	49	172 ↑	4 ↓	49 ↓	43 ↑	4
Information not available	7	175 ↑	5 ↓	43	46 ↑	6

Average Score Gaps Between Selected Groups

- Female students in New York had an average score that was higher than that of male students (14 points). This performance gap was not significantly different from that of the Nation (18 points).

- White students had an average score that was higher than that of Black students (24 points). This performance gap was not significantly different from that of the Nation (20 points).

- White students had an average score that was higher than that of Hispanic students (23 points). This performance gap was not significantly different from that of the Nation (19 points).

- Students who were not eligible for free/reduced-price school lunch had an average score that was higher than that of students who were eligible (22 points). This performance gap was not significantly different from that of the Nation (22 points).

Writing Scale Scores at Selected Percentiles

Scale Score Distribution

	25th Percentile	50th Percentile	75th Percentile
New York	139 ↑	164 ↑	187 ↑
Nation (Public)	128	153	178

An examination of scores at different percentiles on the 0-300 NAEP writing scale at each grade indicates how well students at lower, middle, and higher levels of the distribution performed. For example, the data above shows that 75 percent of students in public schools nationally scored below *178*, while 75 percent of students in New York scored below *187*.

Percentage rounds to zero.   --- Reporting standards not met; sample size insufficient to permit a reliable estimate.
* Significantly different from New York.   ↑ Significantly higher than, ↓ lower than appropriate subgroup in the nation (public).
[1] Comparisons (higher/lower/not different) are based on statistical tests. The .05 level was used for testing statistical significance.
[2] "Jurisdictions" includes participating states and other jurisdictions (such as Guam or the District of Columbia).
NOTE: Detail may not sum to totals because of rounding. Score gaps are calculated based on differences between unrounded average scale scores.
Visit http://nces.ed.gov/nationsreportcard/states/ for additional results and detailed information.
SOURCE: U.S. Department of Education, Institute of Education Sciences, National Center for Education Statistics, National Assessment of Educational Progress (NAEP), 2002 Writing Assessment.

The National Assessment of Educational Progress (NAEP) assesses writing for three purposes identified in the NAEP framework: narrative, informative, and persuasive. The NAEP writing scale ranges from 0 to 300.

Overall Writing Results for New York

- In 2007, the average scale score for eighth-grade students in New York was 154. This was not significantly different from their average score in 2002 (151) and was higher than their average score in 1998 (146).[1]
- New York's average score (154) in 2007 was not significantly different from that of the nation's public schools (154).
- Of the 45 states and one other jurisdiction that participated in the 2007 eighth-grade assessment, students' average scale score in New York was higher than those in 11 jurisdictions, not significantly different from those in 21 jurisdictions, and lower than those in 13 jurisdictions.[2]
- The percentage of students in New York who performed at or above the NAEP Proficient level was 31 percent in 2007. This percentage was not significantly different from that in 2002 (30 percent) and was greater than that in 1998 (21 percent).
- The percentage of students in New York who performed at or above the NAEP Basic level was 87 percent in 2007. This percentage was not significantly different from that in 2002 (84 percent) and was not significantly different from that in 1998 (84 percent).

Percentages at NAEP Achievement Levels and Average Score

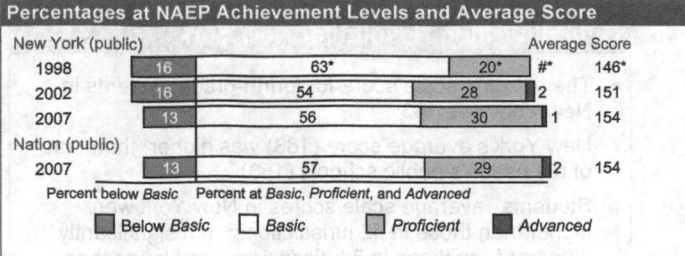

NOTE: The NAEP grade 8 writing achievement levels correspond to the following scale points: Below Basic, 113 or lower; Basic, 114–172; Proficient, 173–223; Advanced, 224 or above.

Performance of NAEP Reporting Groups in New York: 2007

Reporting groups	Percent of students	Average score	Percent below Basic	Percent of students at or above Basic	Proficient	Percent Advanced
Male	50	145	19	81	22	1
Female	50	163	8	92	41	2
White	56	161	8	92	38	2
Black	19	140	20	80	15	#
Hispanic	18	140	25	75	20	1
Asian/Pacific Islander	7	170	9	91	52	5
American Indian/Alaska Native	#	‡	‡	‡	‡	‡
Eligible for National School Lunch Program	47↑	145↑	20	80	22↑	1
Not eligible for National School Lunch Program	51	164	7	93	40	2

Average Score Gaps Between Selected Groups

- In 2007, male students in New York had an average score that was lower than that of female students by 18 points. This performance gap was not significantly different from that of 1998 (15 points).
- In 2007, Black students had an average score that was lower than that of White students by 21 points. This performance gap was not significantly different from that of 1998 (25 points).
- In 2007, Hispanic students had an average score that was lower than that of White students by 21 points. This performance gap was narrower than that of 1998 (31 points).
- In 2007, students who were eligible for free/reduced-price school lunch, an indicator of poverty, had an average score that was lower than that of students who were not eligible for free/reduced-price school lunch by 19 points. This performance gap was not significantly different from that of 1998 (26 points).
- In 2007, the score gap between students at the 75th percentile and students at the 25th percentile was 47 points. This performance gap was not significantly different from that of 1998 (44 points).

Writing Scores at Selected Percentiles in New York

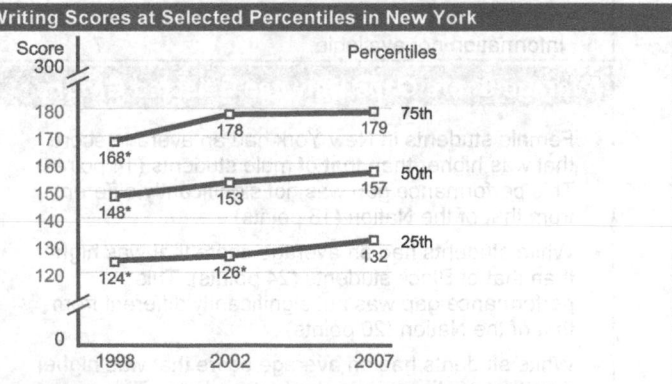

NOTE: Scores at selected percentiles on the NAEP writing scale indicate how well students at lower, middle, and higher levels performed.

Rounds to zero.   ‡ Reporting standards not met.
* Significantly different from 2007.   ↑ Significantly higher than 2002. ↓ Significantly lower than 2002.
[1] Comparisons (higher/lower/narrower/wider/not different) are based on statistical tests. The .05 level with appropriate adjustments for multiple comparisons was used for testing statistical significance. Statistical comparisons are calculated on the basis of unrounded scale scores or percentages. Comparisons across jurisdictions and comparisons with the nation or within a jurisdiction across years may be affected by differences in exclusion rates for students with disabilities (SD) and English language learners (ELL). The exclusion rates for SD and ELL in New York were 2 percent and 1 percent in 2007, respectively. For more information on NAEP significance testing, see http://nces.ed.gov/nationsreportcard/writing/interpret-results.asp#statistical.
[2] "Jurisdiction" refers to states, the District of Columbia, and the Department of Defense Education Activity schools.
NOTE: Detail may not sum to totals because of rounding and because the "Information not available" category for the National School Lunch Program, which provides free and reduced-price lunches, and the "Unclassified" category for race/ethnicity are not displayed. Visit http://nces.ed.gov/nationsreportcard/states/ for additional results and detailed information.
SOURCE: U.S. Department of Education, Institute of Education Sciences, National Center for Education Statistics, National Assessment of Educational Progress (NAEP), 1998, 2002, and 2007 Writing Assessments.

These enrollment data are collected as part of NYSED's Student Information Repository System (SIRS). These counts are as of "BEDS Day" which is typically the first Wednesday in October. Available are enrollment counts for public and charter school students by various demographics for the 2015 - 16 school year. For nonpublic school enrollment data please see the Non-Public School Enrollment and Staff information on our Information and Reporting Services webpage.

NY STATE PUBLIC SCHOOL ENROLLMENT (2015 - 16)

K-12 Enrollment: 2,640,250

ENROLLMENT BY GENDER

MALE	
1,354,055	51%

FEMALE	
1,286,195	49%

ENROLLMENT BY ETHNICITY

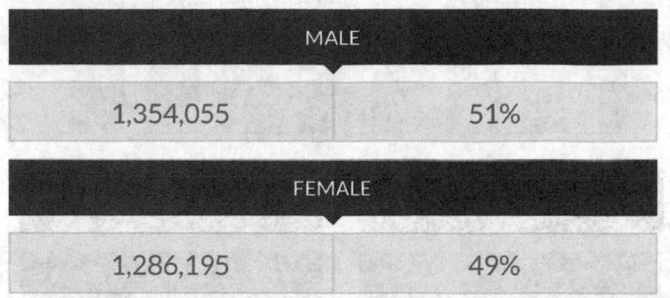

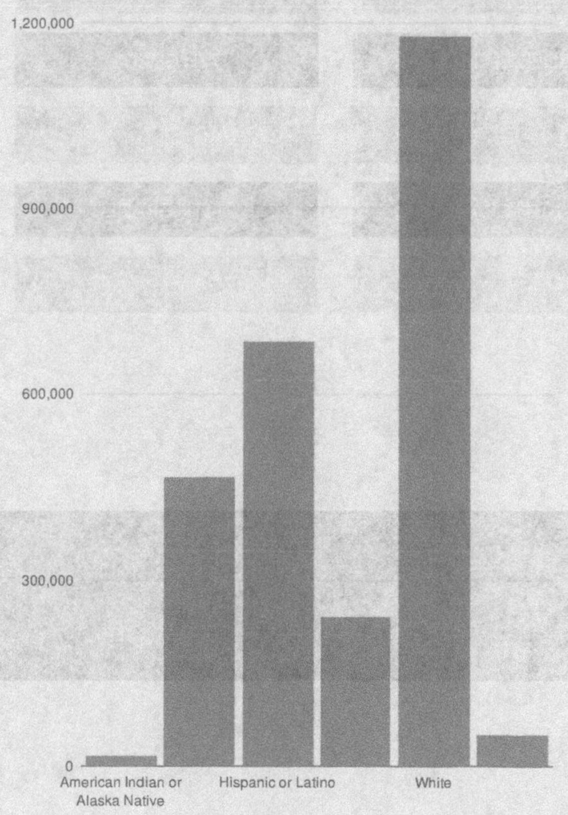

AMERICAN INDIAN OR ALASKA NATIVE	
16,921	1%

BLACK OR AFRICAN AMERICAN	
465,157	18%

HISPANIC OR LATINO	
685,149	26%

ASIAN OR NATIVE HAWAIIAN/OTHER PACIFIC ISLANDER	
241,670	9%

WHITE	
1,179,331	45%

MULTIRACIAL	
52,022	2%

OTHER GROUPS

ENGLISH LANGUAGE LEARNERS		STUDENTS WITH DISABILITIES		ECONOMICALLY DISADVANTAGED	
217,198	8%	456,388	17%	1,431,076	54%

ENROLLMENT BY GRADE

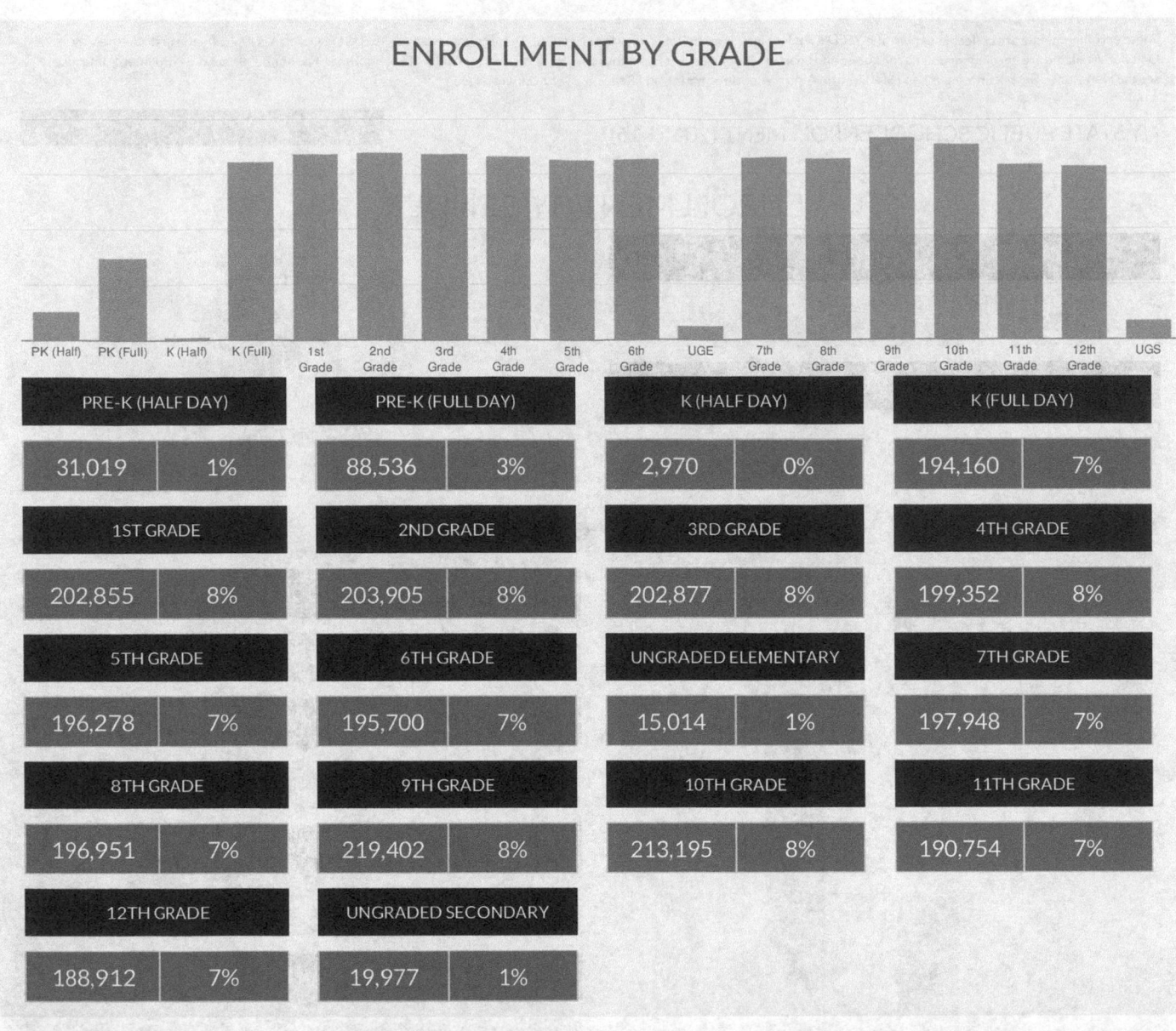

PRE-K (HALF DAY)		PRE-K (FULL DAY)		K (HALF DAY)		K (FULL DAY)	
31,019	1%	88,536	3%	2,970	0%	194,160	7%

1ST GRADE		2ND GRADE		3RD GRADE		4TH GRADE	
202,855	8%	203,905	8%	202,877	8%	199,352	8%

5TH GRADE		6TH GRADE		UNGRADED ELEMENTARY		7TH GRADE	
196,278	7%	195,700	7%	15,014	1%	197,948	7%

8TH GRADE		9TH GRADE		10TH GRADE		11TH GRADE	
196,951	7%	219,402	8%	213,195	8%	190,754	7%

12TH GRADE		UNGRADED SECONDARY	
188,912	7%	19,977	1%

NY STATE - SCHOOL REPORT CARD DATA [2015 - 16]

AVERAGE CLASS SIZE (2015 - 16)

GROUP	CLASS SIZE
COMMON BRANCH	22
GRADE 8 ENGLISH	22
GRADE 8 MATHEMATICS	23
GRADE 8 SCIENCE	23
GRADE 8 SOCIAL STUDIES	23
GRADE 10 ENGLISH	21
GRADE 10 MATHEMATICS	20
GRADE 10 SCIENCE	20
GRADE 10 SOCIAL STUDIES	21

NY STATE GRADES 3-8 ELA ASSESSMENT DATA

The grades 3-8 English Language Arts (ELA) and mathematics assessments measure the higher learning standards that were adopted by the State Board of Regents in 2010, which more accurately reflect students' progress toward college and career readiness. Data are available statewide and at the county, district, and school level.

Data available on this site are based on those reported by schools and districts to the State as of July 18, 2016 via the Student Information Repository System (SIRS). The New York State School Report Card 3-8 English Language Arts (ELA) and mathematics assessment data will be based on those data reported as of the final school year reporting deadline.

For more information and additional files, please view the NYSED press release

Due to changes in the 2016 exams, the proficiency rates from exams prior to 2016 are not directly comparable to the 2016 proficiency rates.

Assessment Data - Glossary of Terms | Assessment Data - Business Rules

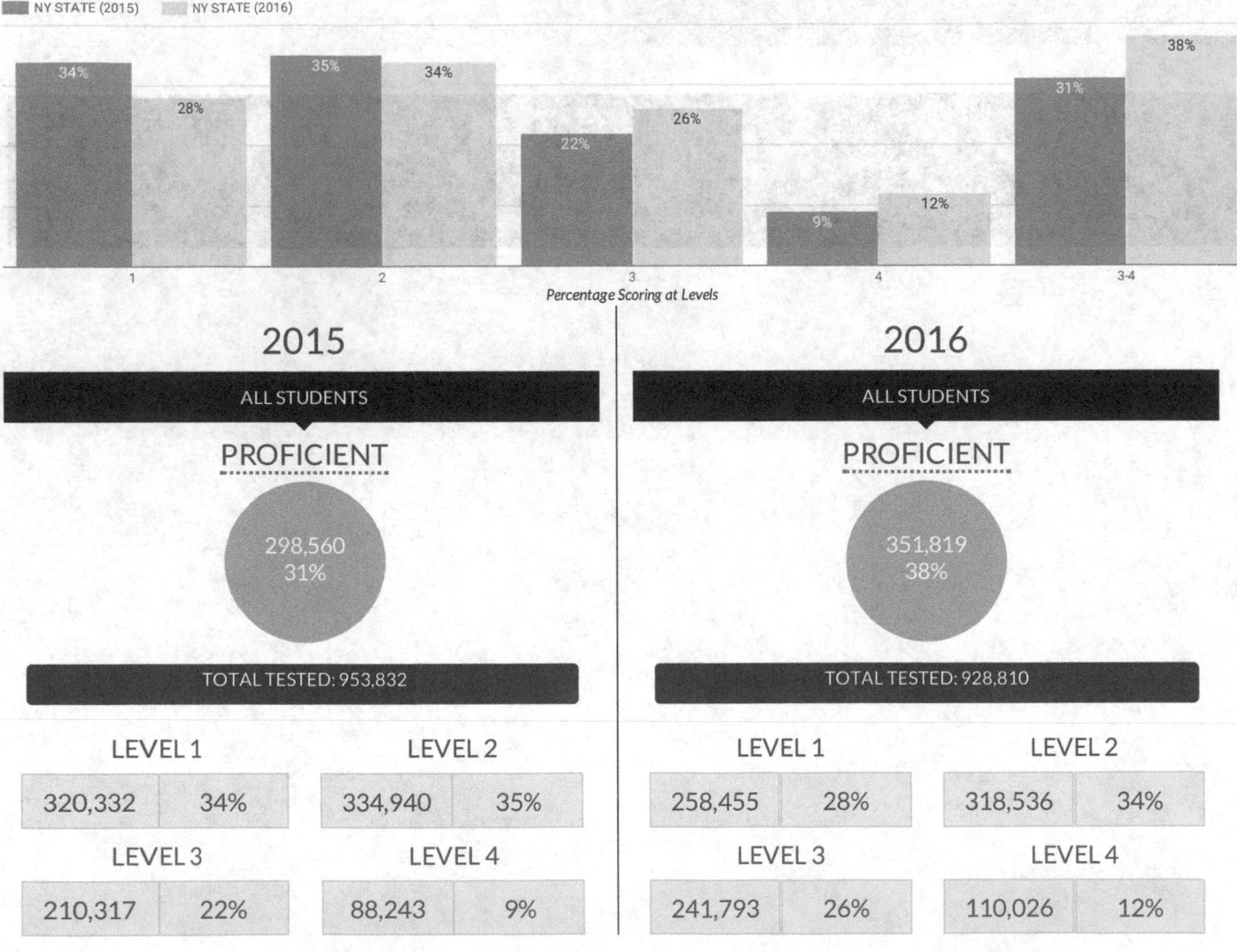

NY STATE (2015)   NY STATE (2016)

Percentage Scoring at Levels

	1	2	3	4	3-4
NY STATE (2015)	34%	35%	22%	9%	31%
NY STATE (2016)	28%	34%	26%	12%	38%

2015

ALL STUDENTS

PROFICIENT

298,560
31%

TOTAL TESTED: 953,832

LEVEL 1		LEVEL 2	
320,332	34%	334,940	35%

LEVEL 3		LEVEL 4	
210,317	22%	88,243	9%

2016

ALL STUDENTS

PROFICIENT

351,819
38%

TOTAL TESTED: 928,810

LEVEL 1		LEVEL 2	
258,455	28%	318,536	34%

LEVEL 3		LEVEL 4	
241,793	26%	110,026	12%

BY GENDER

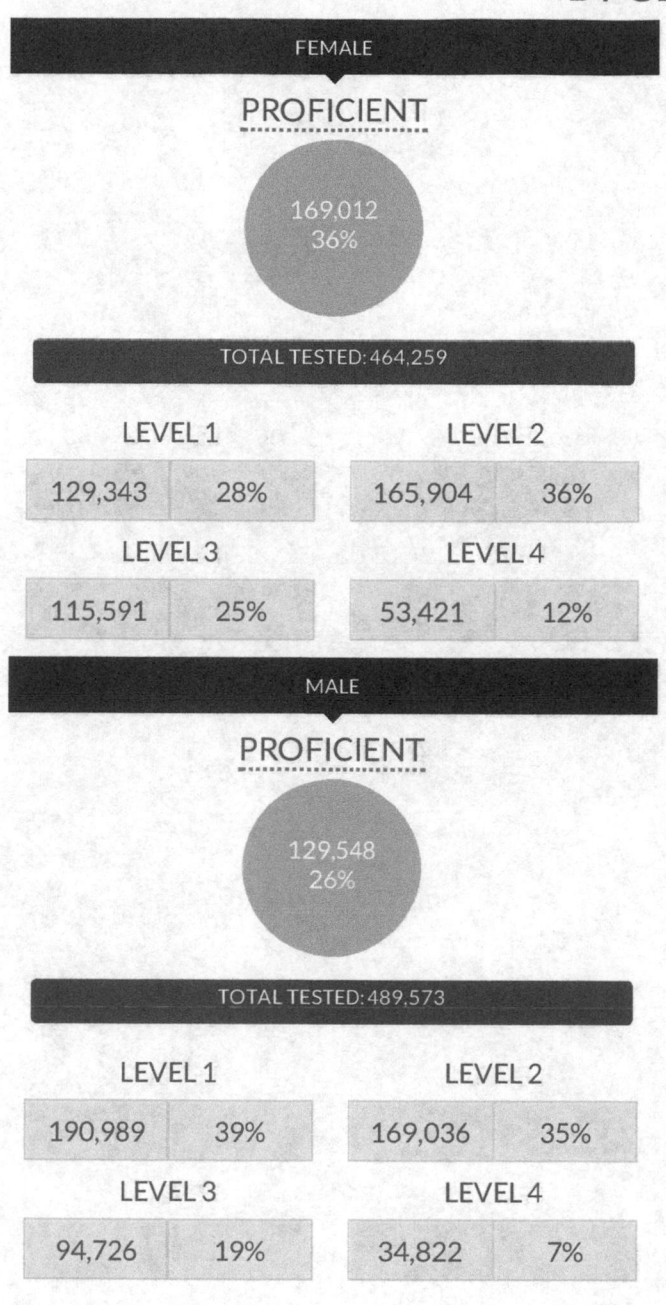

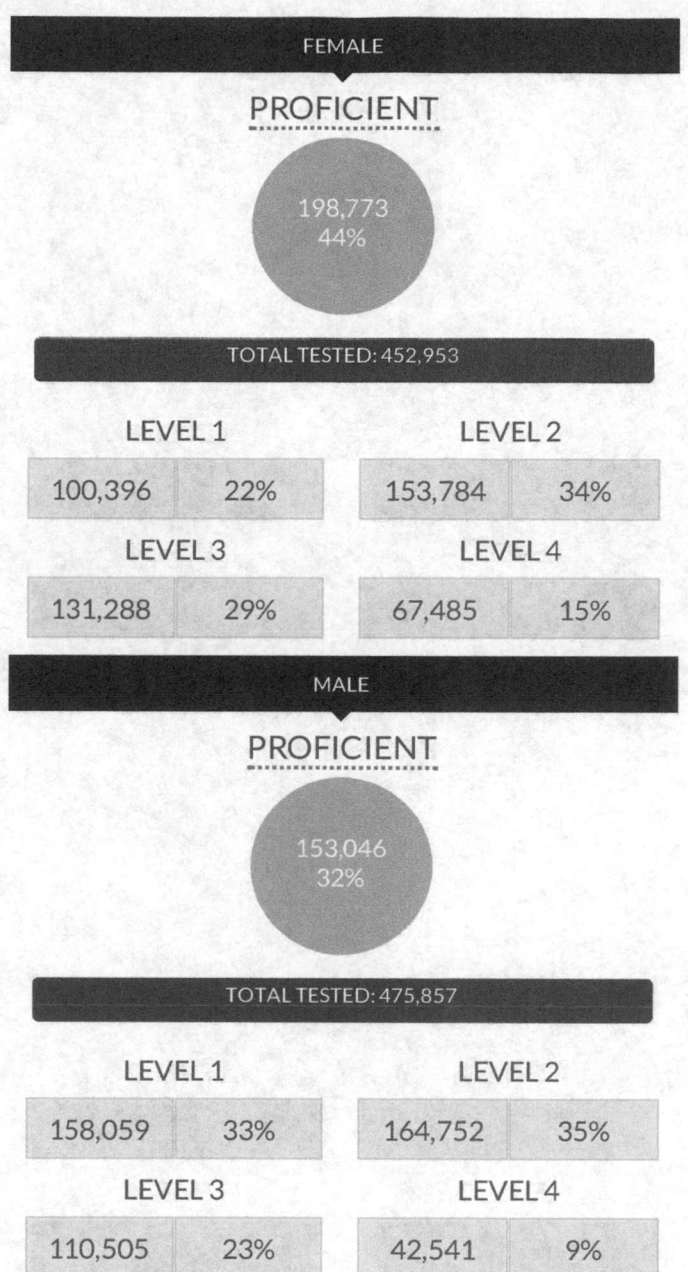

BY ETHNICITY

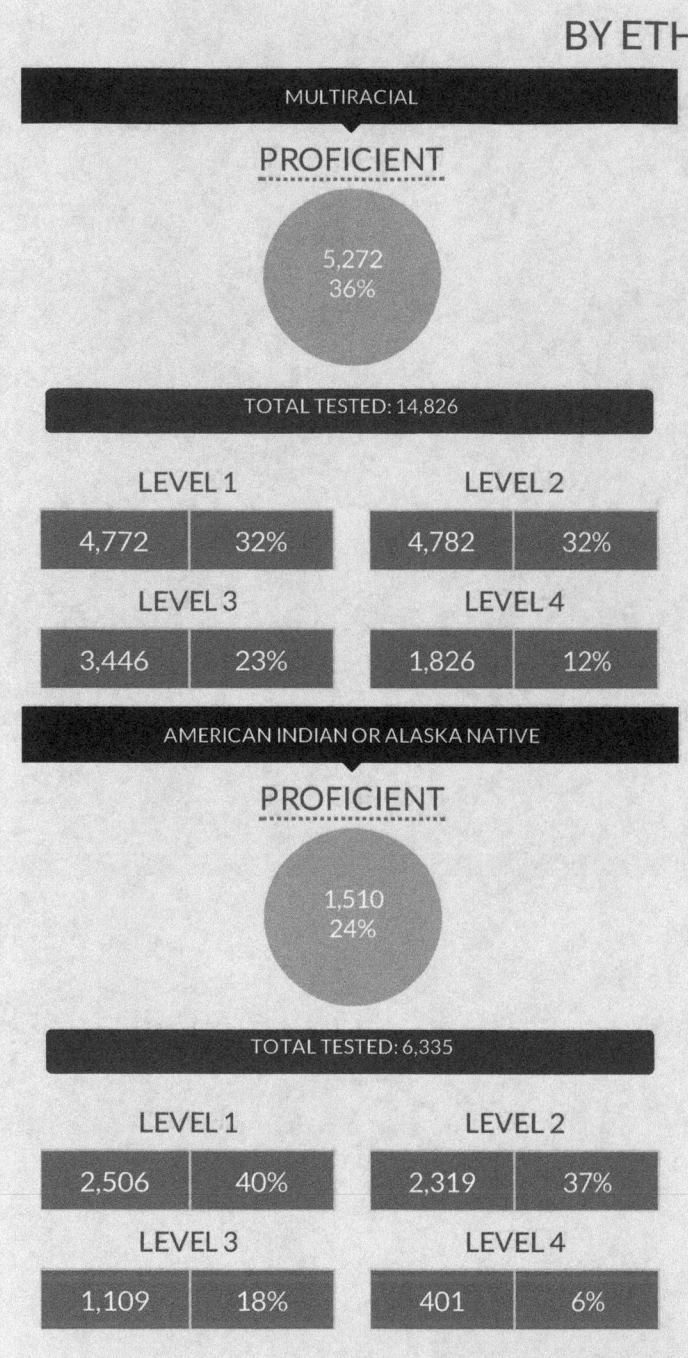

MULTIRACIAL

PROFICIENT

5,272
36%

TOTAL TESTED: 14,826

LEVEL 1		LEVEL 2	
4,772	32%	4,782	32%

LEVEL 3		LEVEL 4	
3,446	23%	1,826	12%

AMERICAN INDIAN OR ALASKA NATIVE

PROFICIENT

1,510
24%

TOTAL TESTED: 6,335

LEVEL 1		LEVEL 2	
2,506	40%	2,319	37%

LEVEL 3		LEVEL 4	
1,109	18%	401	6%

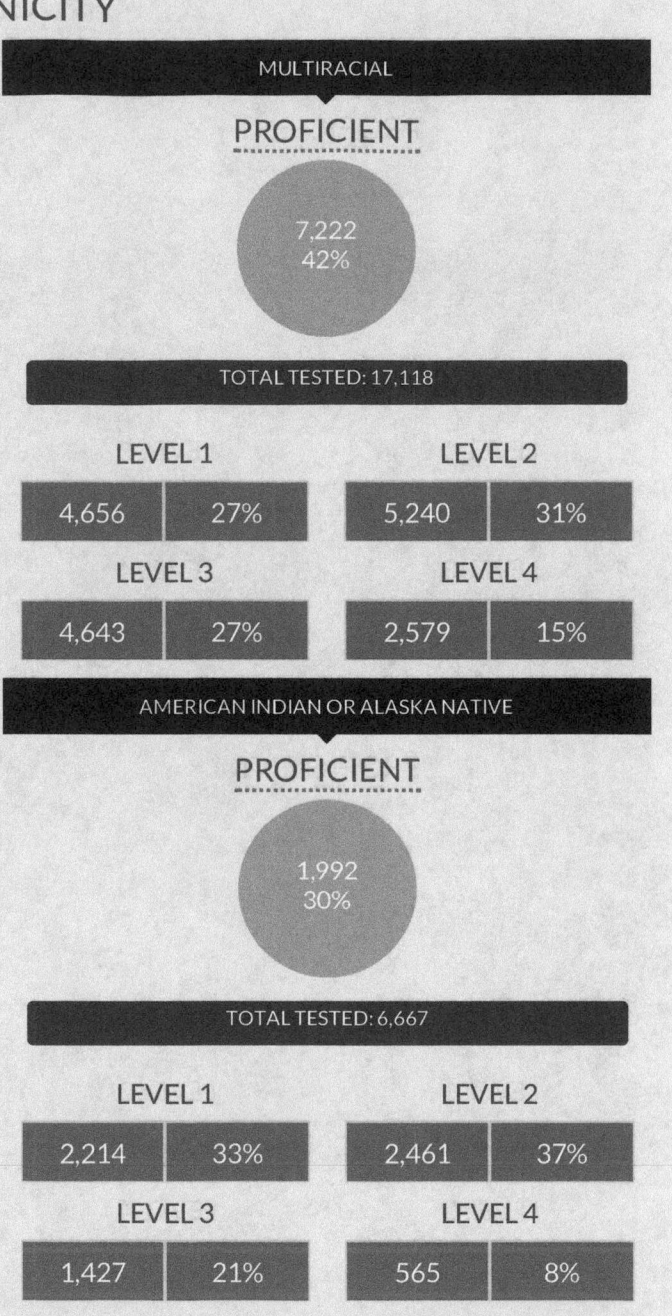

MULTIRACIAL

PROFICIENT

7,222
42%

TOTAL TESTED: 17,118

LEVEL 1		LEVEL 2	
4,656	27%	5,240	31%

LEVEL 3		LEVEL 4	
4,643	27%	2,579	15%

AMERICAN INDIAN OR ALASKA NATIVE

PROFICIENT

1,992
30%

TOTAL TESTED: 6,667

LEVEL 1		LEVEL 2	
2,214	33%	2,461	37%

LEVEL 3		LEVEL 4	
1,427	21%	565	8%

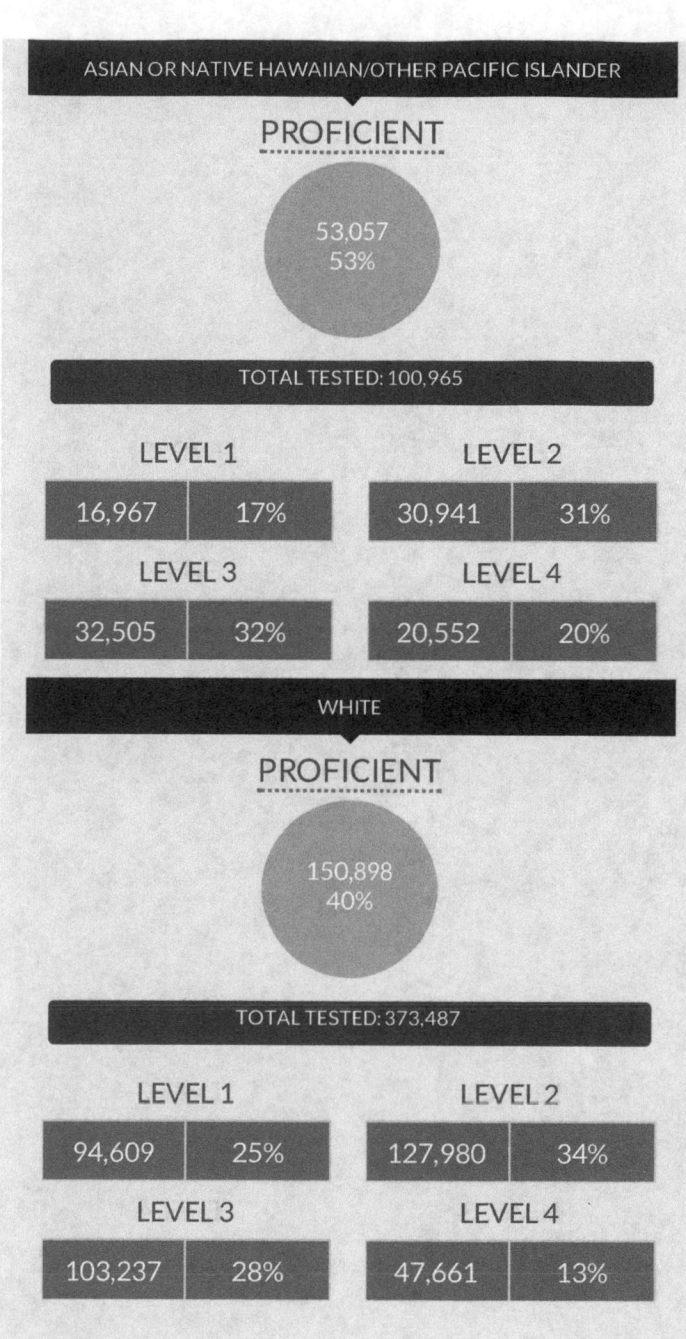

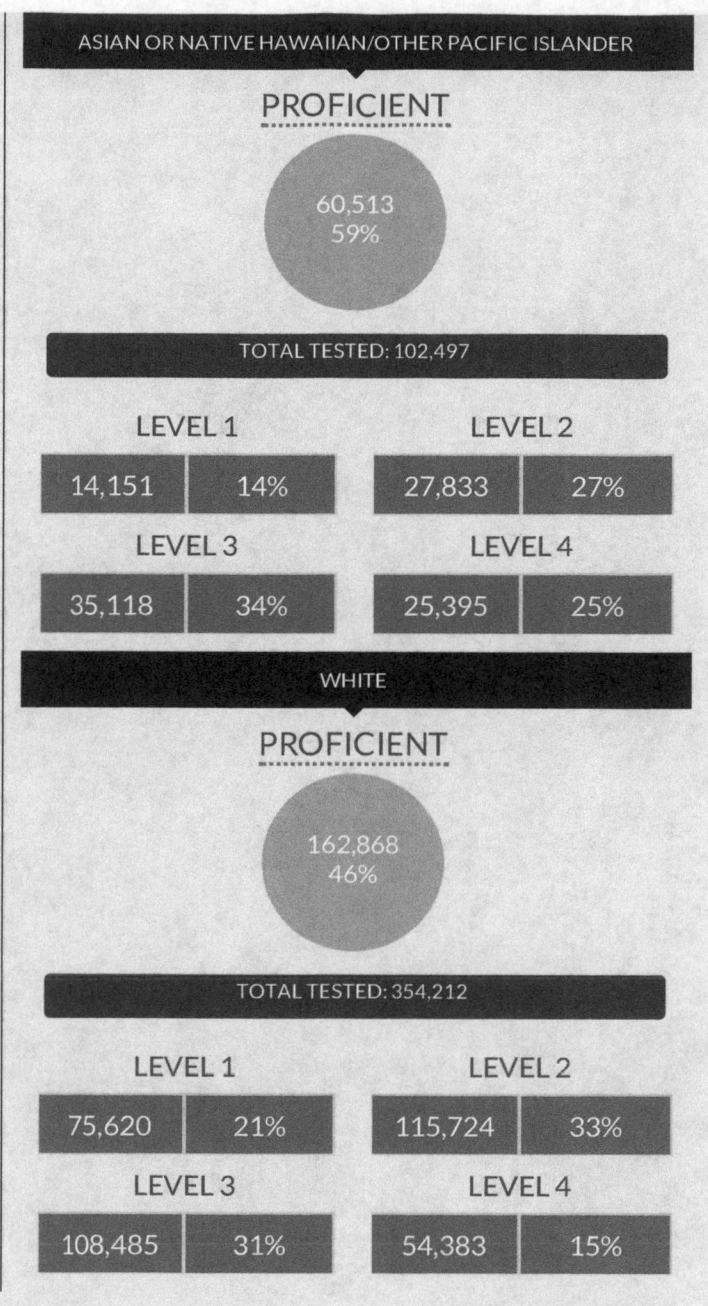

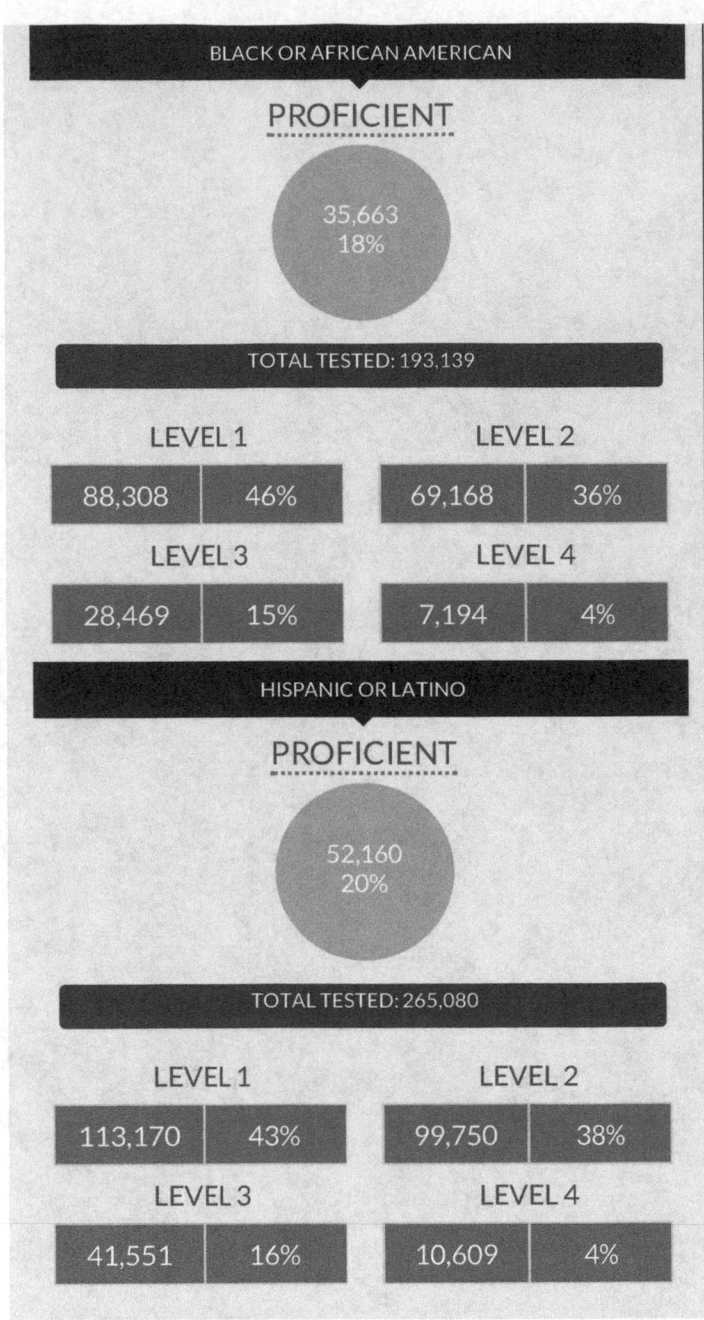

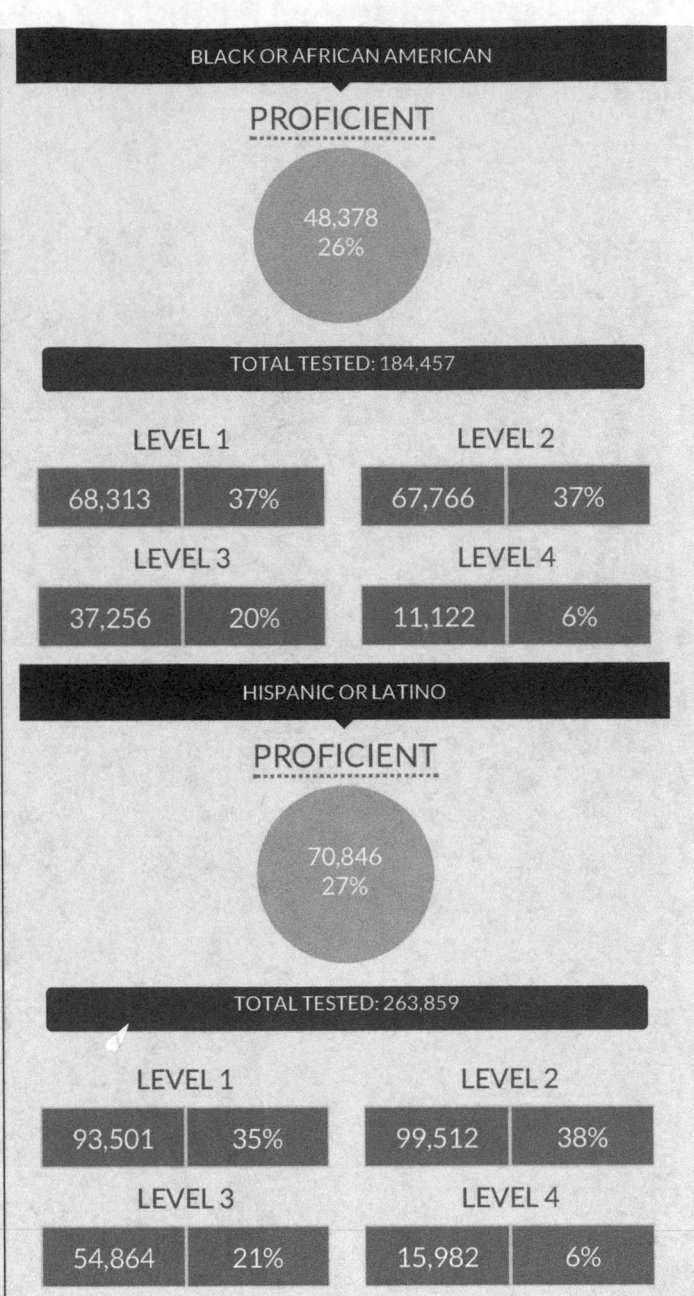

BLACK OR AFRICAN AMERICAN

PROFICIENT

35,663
18%

TOTAL TESTED: 193,139

LEVEL 1		LEVEL 2	
88,308	46%	69,168	36%

LEVEL 3		LEVEL 4	
28,469	15%	7,194	4%

BLACK OR AFRICAN AMERICAN

PROFICIENT

48,378
26%

TOTAL TESTED: 184,457

LEVEL 1		LEVEL 2	
68,313	37%	67,766	37%

LEVEL 3		LEVEL 4	
37,256	20%	11,122	6%

HISPANIC OR LATINO

PROFICIENT

52,160
20%

TOTAL TESTED: 265,080

LEVEL 1		LEVEL 2	
113,170	43%	99,750	38%

LEVEL 3		LEVEL 4	
41,551	16%	10,609	4%

HISPANIC OR LATINO

PROFICIENT

70,846
27%

TOTAL TESTED: 263,859

LEVEL 1		LEVEL 2	
93,501	35%	99,512	38%

LEVEL 3		LEVEL 4	
54,864	21%	15,982	6%

OTHER GROUPS

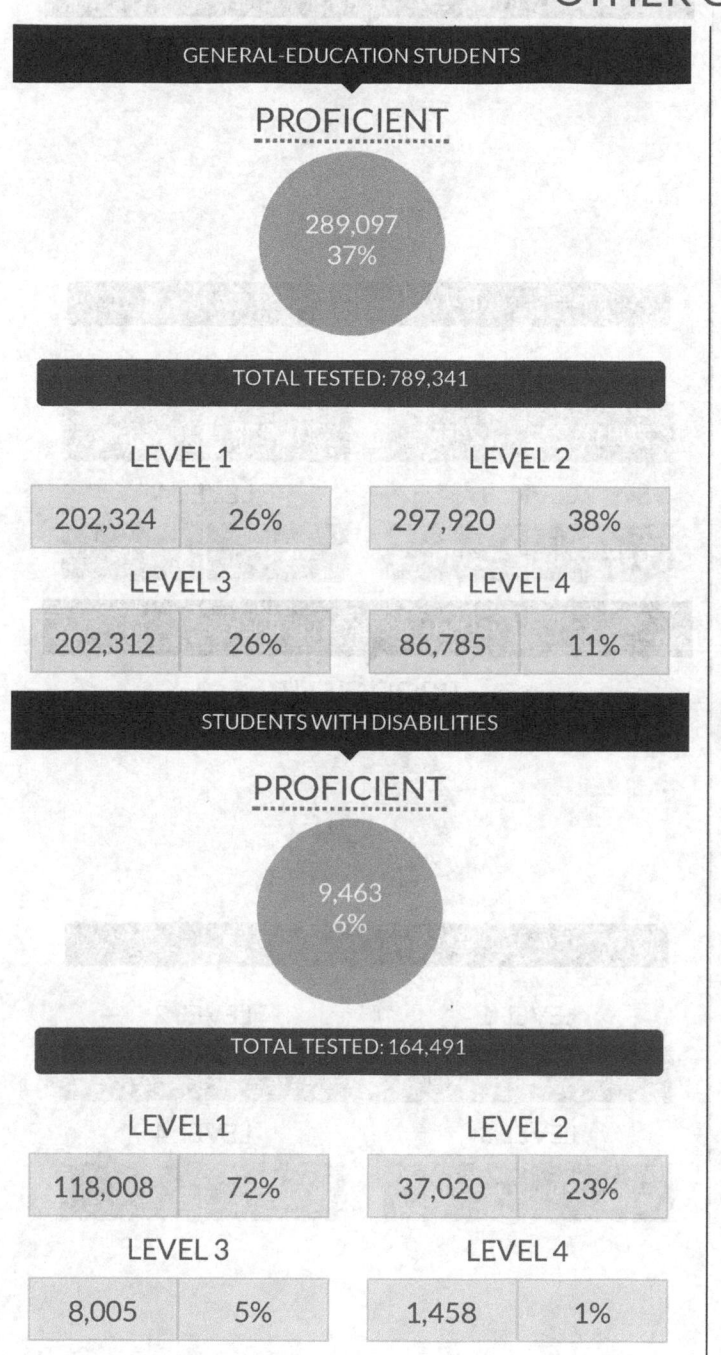

GENERAL-EDUCATION STUDENTS

PROFICIENT

289,097
37%

TOTAL TESTED: 789,341

LEVEL 1		LEVEL 2	
202,324	26%	297,920	38%
LEVEL 3		LEVEL 4	
202,312	26%	86,785	11%

STUDENTS WITH DISABILITIES

PROFICIENT

9,463
6%

TOTAL TESTED: 164,491

LEVEL 1		LEVEL 2	
118,008	72%	37,020	23%
LEVEL 3		LEVEL 4	
8,005	5%	1,458	1%

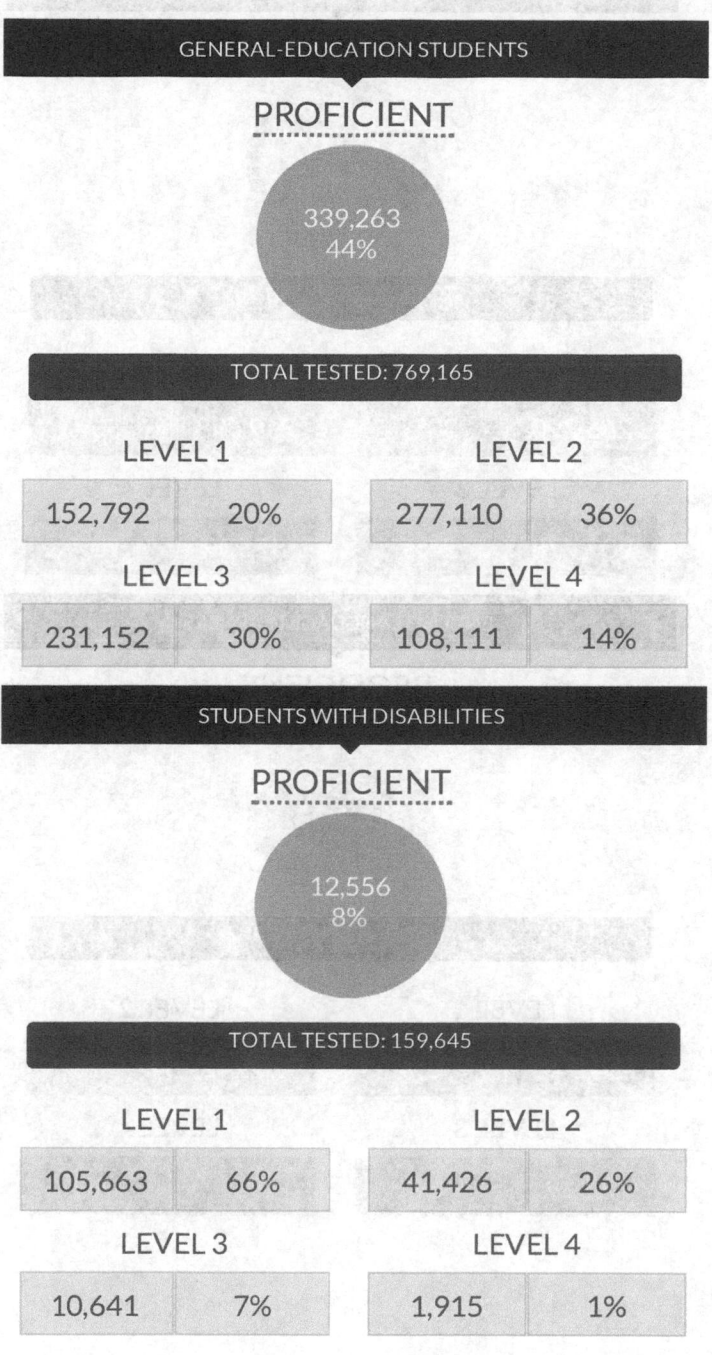

GENERAL-EDUCATION STUDENTS

PROFICIENT

339,263
44%

TOTAL TESTED: 769,165

LEVEL 1		LEVEL 2	
152,792	20%	277,110	36%
LEVEL 3		LEVEL 4	
231,152	30%	108,111	14%

STUDENTS WITH DISABILITIES

PROFICIENT

12,556
8%

TOTAL TESTED: 159,645

LEVEL 1		LEVEL 2	
105,663	66%	41,426	26%
LEVEL 3		LEVEL 4	
10,641	7%	1,915	1%

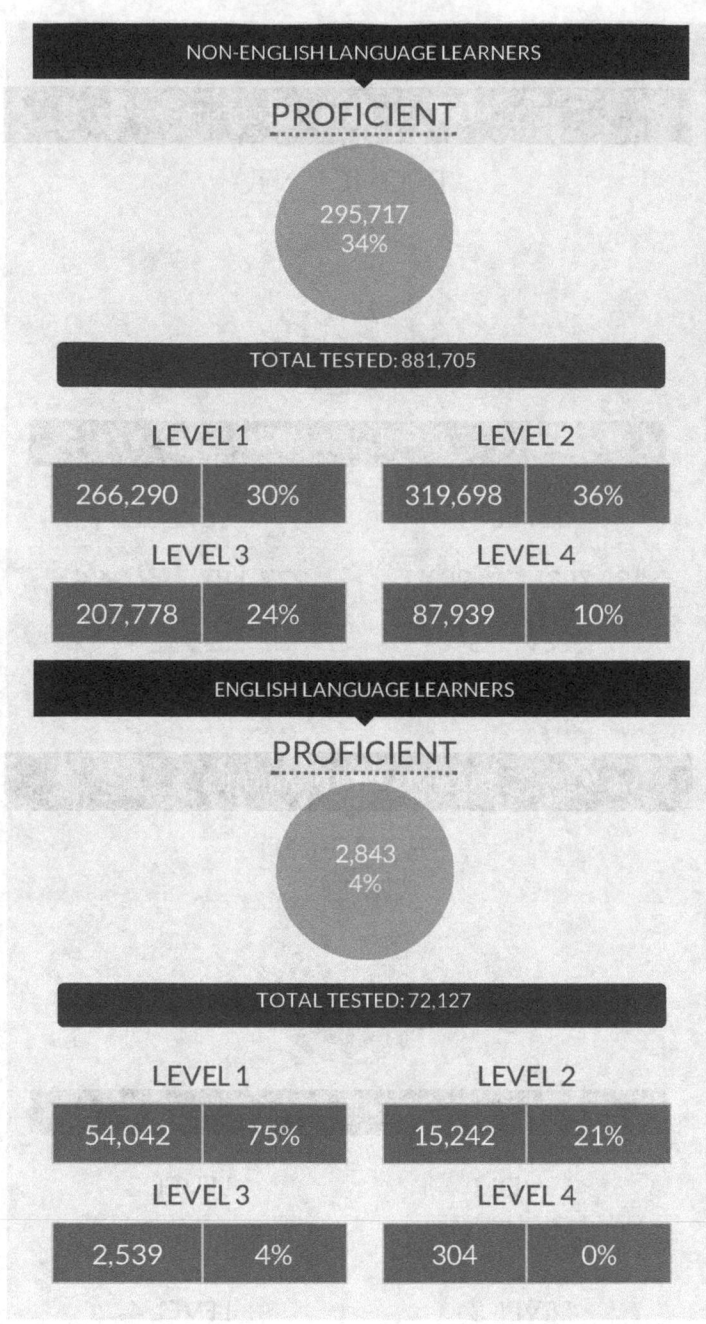

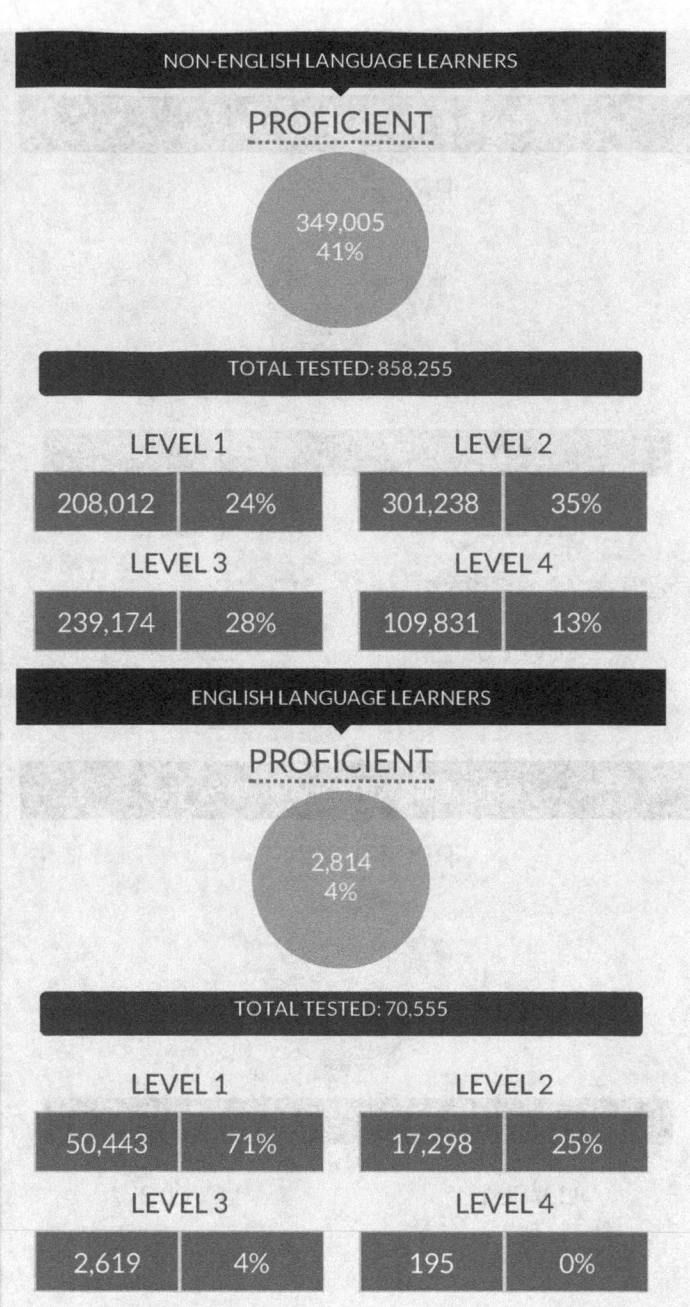

NON-ENGLISH LANGUAGE LEARNERS

PROFICIENT

295,717
34%

TOTAL TESTED: 881,705

LEVEL 1		LEVEL 2	
266,290	30%	319,698	36%

LEVEL 3		LEVEL 4	
207,778	24%	87,939	10%

ENGLISH LANGUAGE LEARNERS

PROFICIENT

2,843
4%

TOTAL TESTED: 72,127

LEVEL 1		LEVEL 2	
54,042	75%	15,242	21%

LEVEL 3		LEVEL 4	
2,539	4%	304	0%

NON-ENGLISH LANGUAGE LEARNERS

PROFICIENT

349,005
41%

TOTAL TESTED: 858,255

LEVEL 1		LEVEL 2	
208,012	24%	301,238	35%

LEVEL 3		LEVEL 4	
239,174	28%	109,831	13%

ENGLISH LANGUAGE LEARNERS

PROFICIENT

2,814
4%

TOTAL TESTED: 70,555

LEVEL 1		LEVEL 2	
50,443	71%	17,298	25%

LEVEL 3		LEVEL 4	
2,619	4%	195	0%

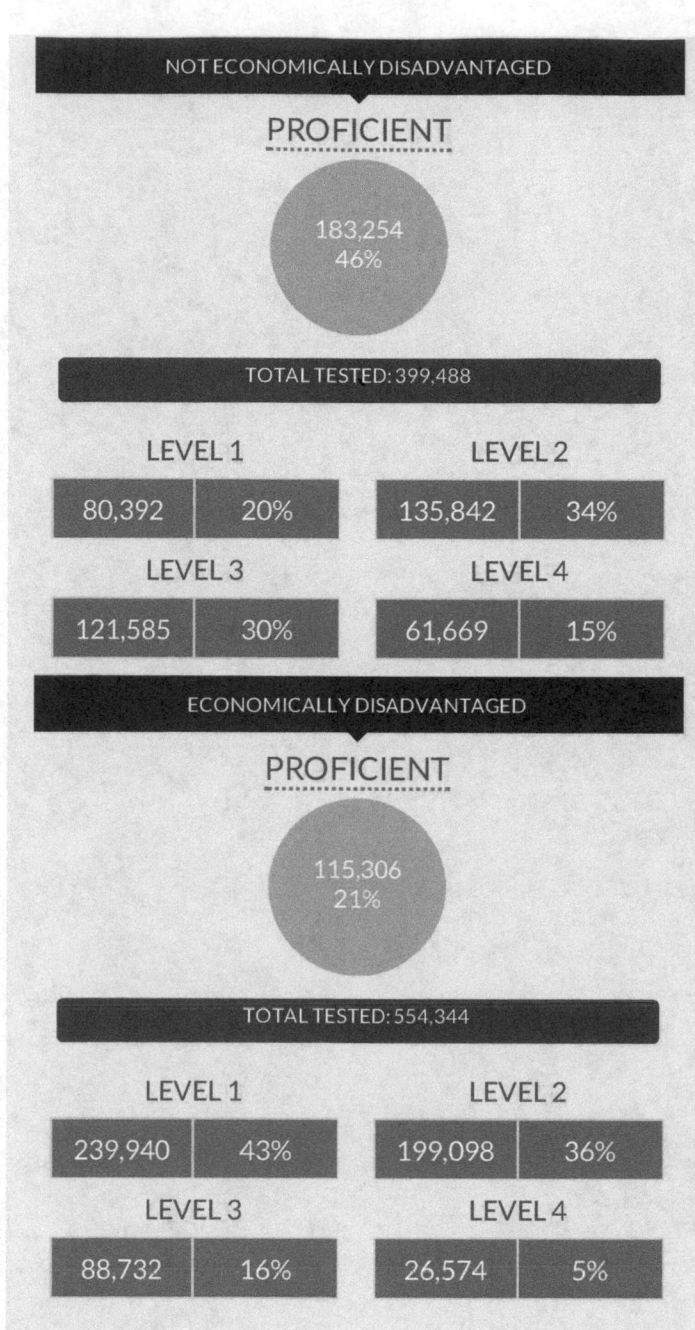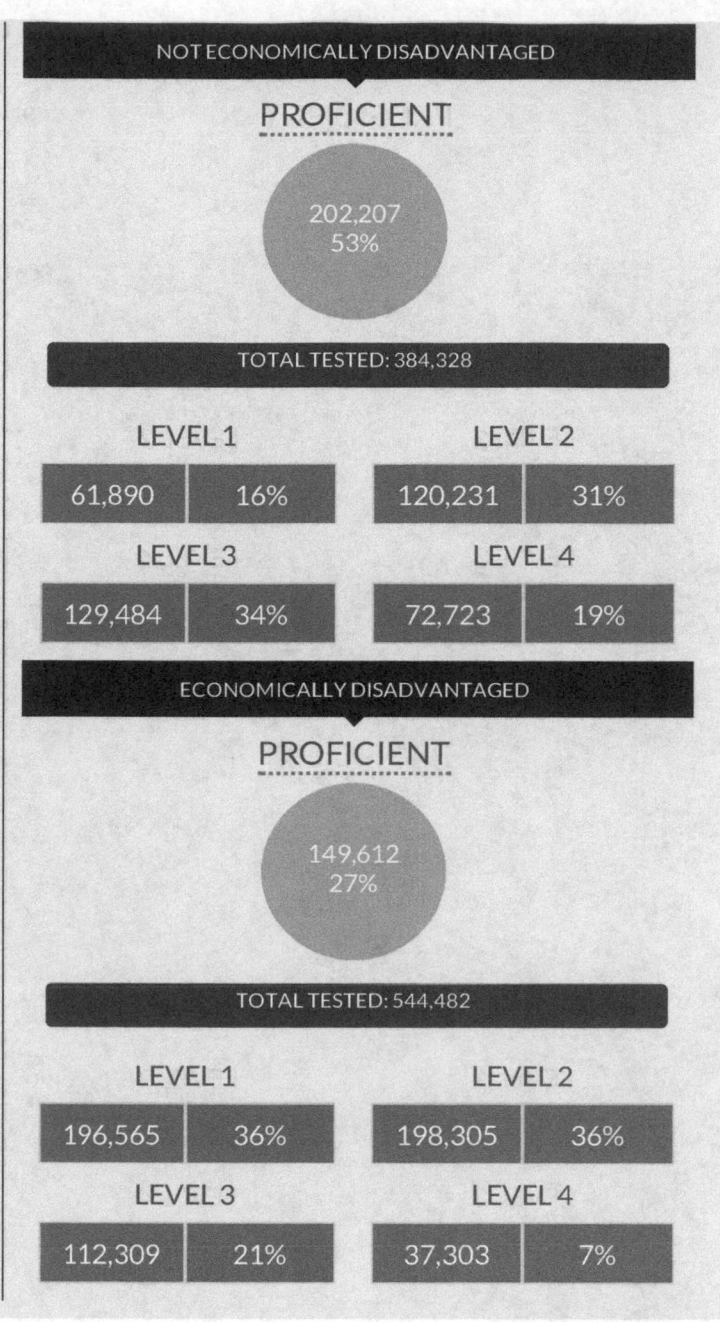

NOT ECONOMICALLY DISADVANTAGED

PROFICIENT

183,254
46%

TOTAL TESTED: 399,488

LEVEL 1		LEVEL 2	
80,392	20%	135,842	34%

LEVEL 3		LEVEL 4	
121,585	30%	61,669	15%

NOT ECONOMICALLY DISADVANTAGED

PROFICIENT

202,207
53%

TOTAL TESTED: 384,328

LEVEL 1		LEVEL 2	
61,890	16%	120,231	31%

LEVEL 3		LEVEL 4	
129,484	34%	72,723	19%

ECONOMICALLY DISADVANTAGED

PROFICIENT

115,306
21%

TOTAL TESTED: 554,344

LEVEL 1		LEVEL 2	
239,940	43%	199,098	36%

LEVEL 3		LEVEL 4	
88,732	16%	26,574	5%

ECONOMICALLY DISADVANTAGED

PROFICIENT

149,612
27%

TOTAL TESTED: 544,482

LEVEL 1		LEVEL 2	
196,565	36%	198,305	36%

LEVEL 3		LEVEL 4	
112,309	21%	37,303	7%

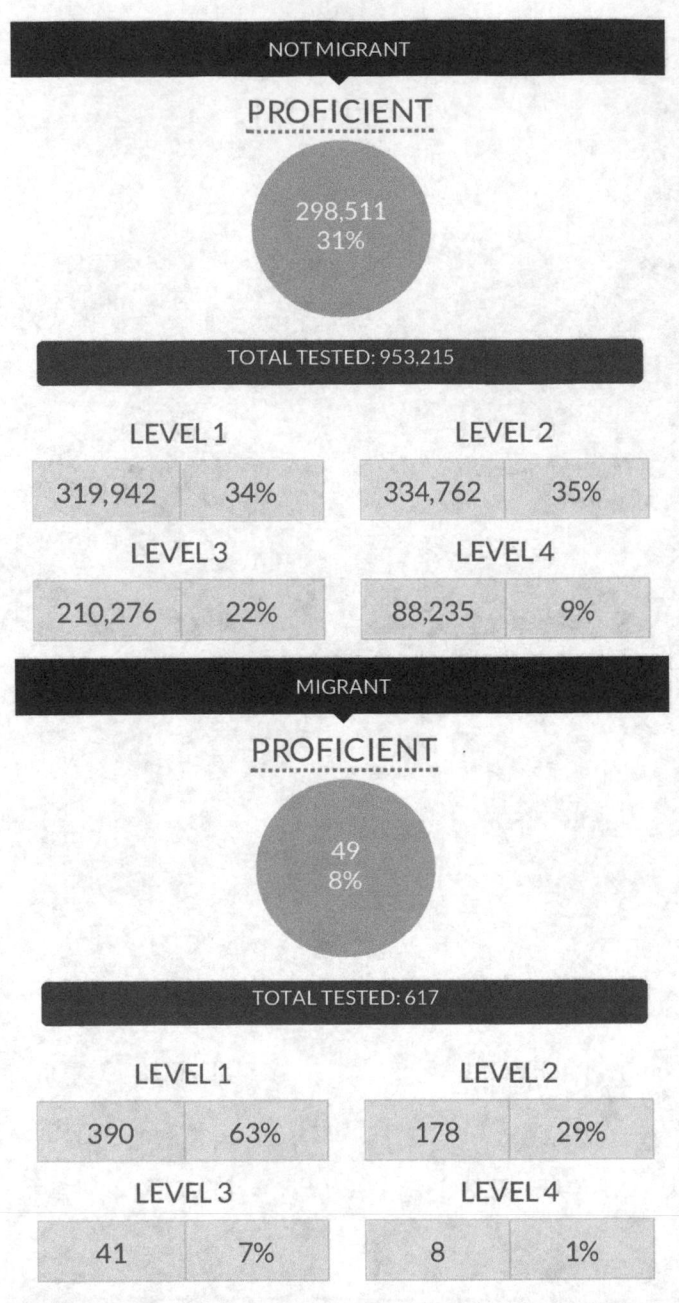

NOT MIGRANT

PROFICIENT

298,511
31%

TOTAL TESTED: 953,215

LEVEL 1		LEVEL 2	
319,942	34%	334,762	35%

LEVEL 3		LEVEL 4	
210,276	22%	88,235	9%

MIGRANT

PROFICIENT

49
8%

TOTAL TESTED: 617

LEVEL 1		LEVEL 2	
390	63%	178	29%

LEVEL 3		LEVEL 4	
41	7%	8	1%

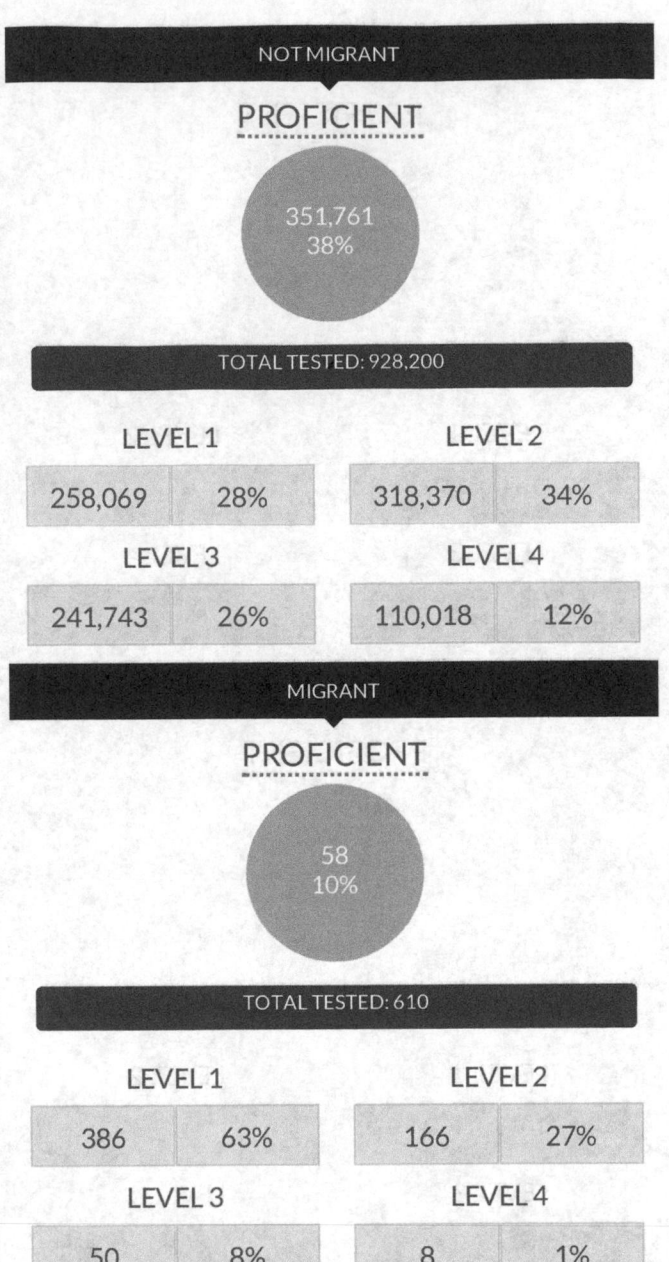

NOT MIGRANT

PROFICIENT

351,761
38%

TOTAL TESTED: 928,200

LEVEL 1		LEVEL 2	
258,069	28%	318,370	34%

LEVEL 3		LEVEL 4	
241,743	26%	110,018	12%

MIGRANT

PROFICIENT

58
10%

TOTAL TESTED: 610

LEVEL 1		LEVEL 2	
386	63%	166	27%

LEVEL 3		LEVEL 4	
50	8%	8	1%

NY STATE - SCHOOL REPORT CARD DATA [2015 - 16]

GRADE 3 MATHEMATICS

Due to changes in the 2015-16 grades 3-8 ELA and math exams, the proficiency rates from exams prior to 2015-16 are not directly comparable to the 2015-16 proficiency rates.

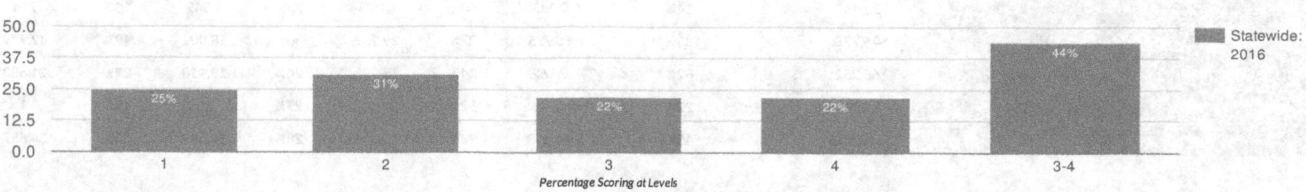

Percentage Scoring at Levels

MEAN SCORE: 306

GROUP	TOTAL TESTED	PROFICIENT	LEVEL 1		LEVEL 2		LEVEL 3		LEVEL 4	
ALL STUDENTS	170,617	44%	43,035	25%	52,392	31%	37,665	22%	37,525	22%
GENERAL EDUCATION	142,957	49%	27,627	19%	44,754	31%	34,761	24%	35,815	25%
STUDENTS WITH DISABILITIES	27,660	17%	15,408	56%	7,638	28%	2,904	10%	1,710	6%
AMERICAN INDIAN OR ALASKA NATIVE	1,245	35%	379	30%	425	34%	247	20%	194	16%
ASIAN OR NATIVE HAWAIIAN/OTHER PACIFIC...	18,901	68%	1,885	10%	4,201	22%	4,820	26%	7,995	42%
BLACK OR AFRICAN AMERICAN	31,818	30%	12,010	38%	10,369	33%	5,296	17%	4,143	13%
HISPANIC OR LATINO	50,367	31%	17,200	34%	17,729	35%	9,418	19%	6,020	12%
WHITE	64,029	55%	10,580	17%	18,429	29%	16,911	26%	18,109	28%
MULTIRACIAL	4,257	48%	981	23%	1,239	29%	973	23%	1,064	25%
FEMALE	83,903	44%	20,476	24%	26,651	32%	18,867	22%	17,909	21%
MALE	86,714	44%	22,559	26%	25,741	30%	18,798	22%	19,616	23%
NON-ENGLISH LANGUAGE LEARNERS	153,004	47%	33,750	22%	46,948	31%	35,747	23%	36,559	24%
ENGLISH LANGUAGE LEARNERS	17,613	16%	9,285	53%	5,444	31%	1,918	11%	966	5%
ECONOMICALLY DISADVANTAGED	102,341	33%	34,310	34%	34,401	34%	19,143	19%	14,487	14%
NOT ECONOMICALLY DISADVANTAGED	68,276	61%	8,725	13%	17,991	26%	18,522	27%	23,038	34%
MIGRANT	144	17%	69	48%	51	35%	19	13%	5	3%
NOT MIGRANT	170,473	44%	42,966	25%	52,341	31%	37,646	22%	37,520	22%

GRADE 4 MATHEMATICS

Due to changes in the 2015-16 grades 3-8 ELA and math exams, the proficiency rates from exams prior to 2015-16 are not directly comparable to the 2015-16 proficiency rates.

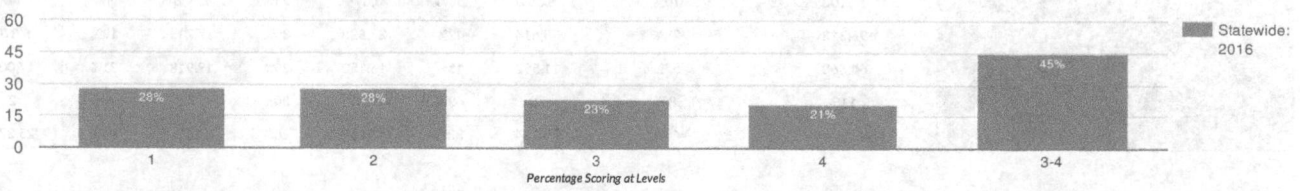

Percentage Scoring at Levels

MEAN SCORE: 305

GROUP	TOTAL TESTED	PROFICIENT	LEVEL 1		LEVEL 2		LEVEL 3		LEVEL 4	
ALL STUDENTS	163,027	45%	44,887	28%	45,267	28%	38,212	23%	34,661	21%
GENERAL EDUCATION	135,165	51%	27,775	21%	38,623	29%	35,490	26%	33,277	25%
STUDENTS WITH DISABILITIES	27,862	15%	17,112	61%	6,644	24%	2,722	10%	1,384	5%
AMERICAN INDIAN OR ALASKA NATIVE	1,103	38%	352	32%	336	30%	215	19%	200	18%
ASIAN OR NATIVE HAWAIIAN/OTHER PACIFIC...	18,163	70%	1,999	11%	3,402	19%	4,662	26%	8,100	45%
BLACK OR AFRICAN AMERICAN	31,066	28%	13,201	42%	9,183	30%	5,236	17%	3,446	11%
HISPANIC OR LATINO	47,636	31%	17,990	38%	14,957	31%	9,205	19%	5,484	12%

WHITE	61,519	56%	10,452	17%	16,461	27%	18,035	29%	16,571	27%
MULTIRACIAL	3,540	49%	893	25%	928	26%	859	24%	860	24%
FEMALE	79,695	45%	21,558	27%	22,657	28%	18,874	24%	16,606	21%
MALE	83,332	45%	23,329	28%	22,610	27%	19,338	23%	18,055	22%
NON-ENGLISH LANGUAGE LEARNERS	147,285	48%	35,502	24%	41,173	28%	36,663	25%	33,947	23%
ENGLISH LANGUAGE LEARNERS	15,742	14%	9,385	60%	4,094	26%	1,549	10%	714	5%
ECONOMICALLY DISADVANTAGED	96,775	33%	35,725	37%	29,269	30%	18,802	19%	12,979	13%
NOT ECONOMICALLY DISADVANTAGED	66,252	62%	9,162	14%	15,998	24%	19,410	29%	21,682	33%
MIGRANT	124	22%	64	52%	33	27%	23	19%	4	3%
NOT MIGRANT	162,903	45%	44,823	28%	45,234	28%	38,189	23%	34,657	21%

GRADE 5 MATHEMATICS

Due to changes in the 2015-16 grades 3-8 ELA and math exams, the proficiency rates from exams prior to 2015-16 are not directly comparable to the 2015-16 proficiency rates.

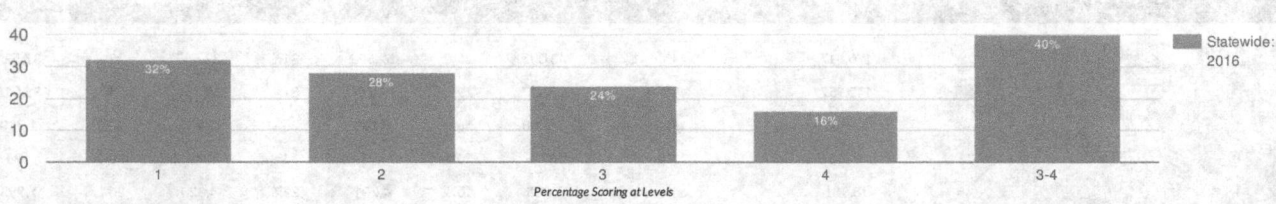

Percentage Scoring at Levels

MEAN SCORE: 307

GROUP	TOTAL TESTED	PROFICIENT	LEVEL 1		LEVEL 2		LEVEL 3		LEVEL 4	
ALL STUDENTS	156,990	40%	50,206	32%	43,773	28%	37,633	24%	25,378	16%
GENERAL EDUCATION	129,084	46%	31,621	24%	37,728	29%	35,164	27%	24,571	19%
STUDENTS WITH DISABILITIES	27,906	12%	18,585	67%	6,045	22%	2,469	9%	807	3%
AMERICAN INDIAN OR ALASKA NATIVE	1,109	31%	463	42%	304	27%	222	20%	120	11%
ASIAN OR NATIVE HAWAIIAN/OTHER PACIFIC...	17,580	67%	2,171	12%	3,544	20%	5,253	30%	6,612	38%
BLACK OR AFRICAN AMERICAN	30,857	23%	14,854	48%	9,017	29%	5,165	17%	1,821	6%
HISPANIC OR LATINO	45,600	26%	19,148	42%	14,484	32%	8,562	19%	3,406	7%
WHITE	58,913	52%	12,637	21%	15,696	27%	17,751	30%	12,829	22%
MULTIRACIAL	2,931	43%	933	32%	728	25%	680	23%	590	20%
FEMALE	76,331	39%	23,645	31%	22,570	30%	18,804	25%	11,312	15%
MALE	80,659	41%	26,561	33%	21,203	26%	18,829	23%	14,066	17%
NON-ENGLISH LANGUAGE LEARNERS	143,882	43%	41,547	29%	40,677	28%	36,627	25%	25,031	17%
ENGLISH LANGUAGE LEARNERS	13,108	10%	8,659	66%	3,096	24%	1,006	8%	347	3%
ECONOMICALLY DISADVANTAGED	92,322	28%	38,614	42%	27,623	30%	17,715	19%	8,370	9%
NOT ECONOMICALLY DISADVANTAGED	64,668	57%	11,592	18%	16,150	25%	19,918	31%	17,008	26%
MIGRANT	115	8%	72	63%	34	30%	7	6%	2	2%
NOT MIGRANT	156,875	40%	50,134	32%	43,739	28%	37,626	24%	25,376	16%

GRADE 6 MATHEMATICS

Due to changes in the 2015-16 grades 3-8 ELA and math exams, the proficiency rates from exams prior to 2015-16 are not directly comparable to the 2015-16 proficiency rates.

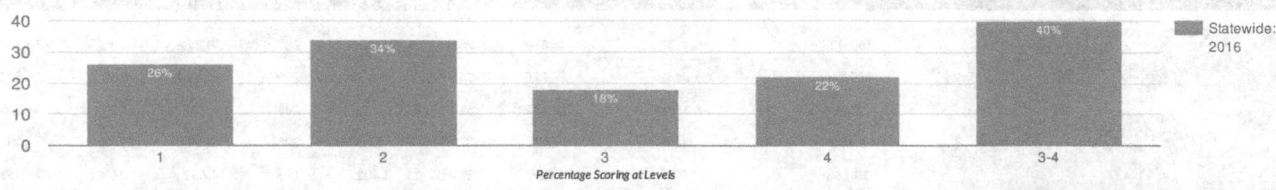

Percentage Scoring at Levels

MEAN SCORE: 305

GROUP	TOTAL TESTED	PROFICIENT	LEVEL 1		LEVEL 2		LEVEL 3		LEVEL 4	
ALL STUDENTS	150,325	40%	38,897	26%	51,109	34%	27,736	18%	32,583	22%
GENERAL EDUCATION	123,872	47%	22,846	18%	43,322	35%	26,052	21%	31,652	26%
STUDENTS WITH DISABILITIES	26,453	10%	16,051	61%	7,787	29%	1,684	6%	931	4%
AMERICAN INDIAN OR ALASKA NATIVE	1,076	28%	332	31%	442	41%	173	16%	129	12%
ASIAN OR NATIVE HAWAIIAN/OTHER PACIFIC...	17,561	69%	1,703	10%	3,826	22%	3,590	20%	8,442	48%
BLACK OR AFRICAN AMERICAN	29,770	23%	12,034	40%	11,010	37%	3,946	13%	2,780	9%
HISPANIC OR LATINO	42,290	25%	15,335	36%	16,418	39%	6,172	15%	4,365	10%
WHITE	57,255	52%	8,967	16%	18,671	33%	13,426	23%	16,191	28%
MULTIRACIAL	2,373	47%	526	22%	742	31%	429	18%	676	28%
FEMALE	73,067	41%	17,139	23%	25,673	35%	14,309	20%	15,946	22%
MALE	77,258	39%	21,758	28%	25,436	33%	13,427	17%	16,637	22%
NON-ENGLISH LANGUAGE LEARNERS	137,497	43%	31,147	23%	47,245	34%	26,996	20%	32,109	23%
ENGLISH LANGUAGE LEARNERS	12,828	9%	7,750	60%	3,864	30%	740	6%	474	4%
ECONOMICALLY DISADVANTAGED	87,627	28%	30,413	35%	32,429	37%	13,108	15%	11,677	13%
NOT ECONOMICALLY DISADVANTAGED	62,698	57%	8,484	14%	18,680	30%	14,628	23%	20,906	33%
MIGRANT	100	13%	59	59%	28	28%	11	11%	2	2%
NOT MIGRANT	150,225	40%	38,838	26%	51,081	34%	27,725	18%	32,581	22%

GRADE 7 MATHEMATICS

Due to changes in the 2015-16 grades 3-8 ELA and math exams, the proficiency rates from exams prior to 2015-16 are not directly comparable to the 2015-16 proficiency rates.

Mean scores and data in the table for grade 7 math include only those for grade 7 students who took the Grade 7 New York State Testing Program Assessment (NYSTP) in Mathematics. For 2015 and forward, data in the bar charts include those for grade 7 students who took the Grade 7 NYSTP in Mathematics and grade 7 students who took a Regents math test in lieu of the NYSTP. For 2014 and earlier, data in the bar charts include only those for grade 7 students who took the Grade 7 NYSTP.

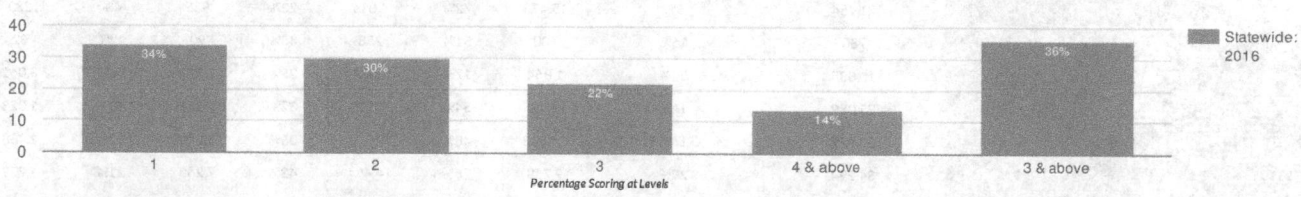

Percentage Scoring at Levels

Statewide: 2016

MEAN SCORE: 305

GROUP	TOTAL TESTED	PROFICIENT	LEVEL 1		LEVEL 2		LEVEL 3		LEVEL 4	
ALL STUDENTS	142,051	36%	47,888	34%	43,159	30%	31,275	22%	19,729	14%
GENERAL EDUCATION	117,709	42%	30,419	26%	37,992	32%	29,944	25%	19,354	16%
STUDENTS WITH DISABILITIES	24,342	7%	17,469	72%	5,167	21%	1,331	5%	375	2%
AMERICAN INDIAN OR ALASKA NATIVE	1,094	25%	459	42%	363	33%	186	17%	86	8%
ASIAN OR NATIVE HAWAIIAN/OTHER PACIFIC...	16,664	66%	2,176	13%	3,498	21%	4,758	29%	6,232	37%
BLACK OR AFRICAN AMERICAN	28,984	19%	14,830	51%	8,704	30%	4,016	14%	1,434	5%
HISPANIC OR LATINO	40,394	22%	18,434	46%	13,191	33%	6,409	16%	2,360	6%
WHITE	53,046	47%	11,434	22%	16,878	32%	15,465	29%	9,269	17%
MULTIRACIAL	1,869	42%	555	30%	525	28%	441	24%	348	19%
FEMALE	68,418	38%	21,304	31%	21,434	31%	15,769	23%	9,911	14%
MALE	73,633	34%	26,584	36%	21,725	30%	15,506	21%	9,818	13%
NON-ENGLISH LANGUAGE LEARNERS	130,720	38%	39,632	30%	40,948	31%	30,621	23%	19,519	15%
ENGLISH LANGUAGE LEARNERS	11,331	8%	8,256	73%	2,211	20%	654	6%	210	2%
ECONOMICALLY DISADVANTAGED	82,096	25%	36,100	44%	25,558	31%	13,363	16%	7,075	9%
NOT ECONOMICALLY DISADVANTAGED	59,955	51%	11,788	20%	17,601	29%	17,912	30%	12,654	21%
MIGRANT	71	13%	36	51%	26	37%	7	10%	2	3%
NOT MIGRANT	141,980	36%	47,852	34%	43,133	30%	31,268	22%	19,727	14%

GRADE 7 STUDENTS TAKING A REGENTS MATH TEST

Accelerated grade 7 students who took a Regents math test in lieu of the Grade 7 NYSTP in Mathematics.

GROUP	TOTAL TESTED	LEVEL 1		LEVEL 2		LEVEL 3		4 & ABOVE		3 & ABOVE	
ALL STUDENTS	736	2	0%	5	1%	97	13%	632	86%	729	99%

GRADE 8 MATHEMATICS

Due to changes in the 2015-16 grades 3-8 ELA and math exams, the proficiency rates from exams prior to 2015-16 are not directly comparable to the 2015-16 proficiency rates.

Mean scores and data in the table for grade 8 math include only those for grade 8 students who took the Grade 8 New York State Testing Program Assessment (NYSTP) in Mathematics. For 2015 and forward, data in the bar charts include those for grade 8 students who took the Grade 8 NYSTP in Mathematics and grade 8 students who took a Regents math test in lieu of the NYSTP. For 2014 and earlier, data in the bar charts include only those for grade 8 students who took the Grade 8 NYSTP.

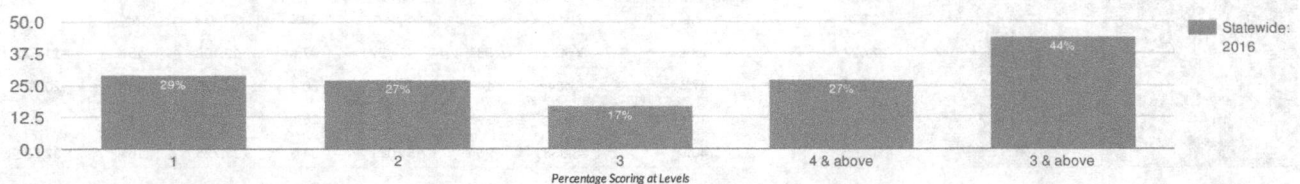

Percentage Scoring at Levels

MEAN SCORE: 292

GROUP	TOTAL TESTED	PROFICIENT	LEVEL 1		LEVEL 2		LEVEL 3		LEVEL 4	
ALL STUDENTS	106,058	24%	42,329	40%	38,523	36%	16,779	16%	8,427	8%
GENERAL EDUCATION	84,604	28%	26,856	32%	33,707	40%	15,844	19%	8,197	10%
STUDENTS WITH DISABILITIES	21,454	5%	15,473	72%	4,816	22%	935	4%	230	1%
AMERICAN INDIAN OR ALASKA NATIVE	780	16%	400	51%	258	33%	90	12%	32	4%
ASIAN OR NATIVE HAWAIIAN/OTHER PACIFIC...	10,835	54%	1,864	17%	3,138	29%	2,772	26%	3,061	28%
BLACK OR AFRICAN AMERICAN	25,089	14%	13,425	54%	8,125	32%	2,516	10%	1,023	4%
HISPANIC OR LATINO	33,979	16%	16,438	48%	12,113	36%	3,970	12%	1,458	4%
WHITE	34,294	29%	9,758	28%	14,494	42%	7,263	21%	2,779	8%
MULTIRACIAL	1,081	22%	444	41%	395	37%	168	16%	74	7%
FEMALE	49,955	25%	18,487	37%	18,949	38%	8,253	17%	4,266	9%
MALE	56,103	23%	23,842	42%	19,574	35%	8,526	15%	4,161	7%
NON-ENGLISH LANGUAGE LEARNERS	95,163	26%	34,753	37%	36,011	38%	16,207	17%	8,192	9%
ENGLISH LANGUAGE LEARNERS	10,895	7%	7,576	70%	2,512	23%	572	5%	235	2%
ECONOMICALLY DISADVANTAGED	67,573	19%	31,663	47%	23,287	34%	8,313	12%	4,310	6%
NOT ECONOMICALLY DISADVANTAGED	38,485	33%	10,666	28%	15,236	40%	8,466	22%	4,117	11%
MIGRANT	77	4%	52	68%	22	29%	2	3%	1	1%
NOT MIGRANT	105,981	24%	42,277	40%	38,501	36%	16,777	16%	8,426	8%

GRADE 8 STUDENTS TAKING A REGENTS MATH TEST

Accelerated grade 8 students who took a Regents math test in lieu of the Grade 8 NYSTP in Mathematics.

GROUP	TOTAL TESTED	LEVEL 1		LEVEL 2		LEVEL 3		4 & ABOVE		3 & ABOVE	
ALL STUDENTS	42,161	801	2%	1,219	3%	8,174	19%	31,967	76%	40,141	95%

NY STATE - SCHOOL REPORT CARD DATA [2015 - 16]

GRADE 4 SCIENCE

Due to changes in the 2015-16 grades 3-8 ELA and math exams, the proficiency rates from exams prior to 2015-16 are not directly comparable to the 2015-16 proficiency rates.

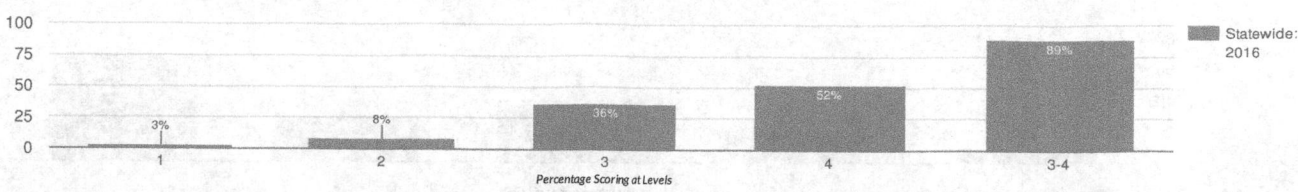

Percentage Scoring at Levels

MEAN SCORE: 81

GROUP	TOTAL TESTED	PROFICIENT	LEVEL 1		LEVEL 2		LEVEL 3		LEVEL 4	
ALL STUDENTS	173,260	89%	5,274	3%	14,588	8%	62,979	36%	90,419	52%
GENERAL EDUCATION	143,927	92%	2,968	2%	8,910	6%	48,822	34%	83,227	58%
STUDENTS WITH DISABILITIES	29,333	73%	2,306	8%	5,678	19%	14,157	48%	7,192	25%
AMERICAN INDIAN OR ALASKA NATIVE	1,150	87%	41	4%	114	10%	466	41%	529	46%
ASIAN OR NATIVE HAWAIIAN/OTHER PACIFIC...	18,154	94%	373	2%	793	4%	4,578	25%	12,410	68%
BLACK OR AFRICAN AMERICAN	31,464	81%	1,646	5%	4,291	14%	14,434	46%	11,093	35%
HISPANIC OR LATINO	48,719	83%	2,118	4%	6,202	13%	21,875	45%	18,524	38%
WHITE	69,938	94%	1,010	1%	2,923	4%	20,339	29%	45,666	65%
MULTIRACIAL	3,835	91%	86	2%	265	7%	1,287	34%	2,197	57%
FEMALE	84,937	89%	2,290	3%	6,945	8%	31,673	37%	44,029	52%
MALE	88,323	88%	2,984	3%	7,643	9%	31,306	35%	46,390	53%
NON-ENGLISH LANGUAGE LEARNERS	157,290	91%	3,097	2%	10,619	7%	55,635	35%	87,939	56%
ENGLISH LANGUAGE LEARNERS	15,970	62%	2,177	14%	3,969	25%	7,344	46%	2,480	16%
ECONOMICALLY DISADVANTAGED	99,778	84%	4,383	4%	12,015	12%	44,023	44%	39,357	39%
NOT ECONOMICALLY DISADVANTAGED	73,482	95%	891	1%	2,573	4%	18,956	26%	51,062	69%
MIGRANT	135	75%	13	10%	21	16%	64	47%	37	27%
NOT MIGRANT	173,125	89%	5,261	3%	14,567	8%	62,915	36%	90,382	52%

GRADE 8 SCIENCE

Due to changes in the 2015-16 grades 3-8 ELA and math exams, the proficiency rates from exams prior to 2015-16 are not directly comparable to the 2015-16 proficiency rates.

Data in the bar charts include those for grade 8 students who took the New York State Grade 8 Science Test and grade 8 students who took a Regents science test in lieu of this test. Mean scores and data in the table for grade 8 science include only those for grade 8 students who took the New York State Grade 8 Science Test.

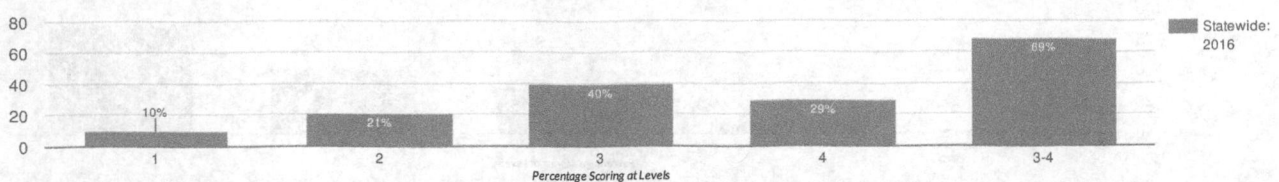

Percentage Scoring at Levels

MEAN SCORE: 67

GROUP	TOTAL TESTED	PROFICIENT	LEVEL 1		LEVEL 2		LEVEL 3		LEVEL 4	
ALL STUDENTS	115,173	60%	14,193	12%	31,644	27%	50,536	44%	18,800	16%
GENERAL EDUCATION	93,065	67%	8,219	9%	22,198	24%	44,579	48%	18,069	19%
STUDENTS WITH DISABILITIES	22,108	30%	5,974	27%	9,446	43%	5,957	27%	731	3%
AMERICAN INDIAN OR ALASKA NATIVE	868	52%	124	14%	295	34%	356	41%	93	11%
ASIAN OR NATIVE HAWAIIAN/OTHER PACIFIC...	10,885	76%	736	7%	1,917	18%	5,092	47%	3,140	29%
BLACK OR AFRICAN AMERICAN	24,555	41%	5,269	21%	9,201	37%	8,619	35%	1,466	6%
HISPANIC OR LATINO	33,407	47%	5,709	17%	12,112	36%	13,212	40%	2,374	7%
WHITE	44,124	77%	2,227	5%	7,809	18%	22,620	51%	11,468	26%
MULTIRACIAL	1,334	67%	128	10%	310	23%	637	48%	259	19%
FEMALE	54,490	61%	5,986	11%	15,537	29%	24,539	45%	8,428	15%
MALE	60,683	60%	8,207	14%	16,107	27%	25,997	43%	10,372	17%
NON-ENGLISH LANGUAGE LEARNERS	104,775	65%	9,728	9%	27,353	26%	48,982	47%	18,712	18%
ENGLISH LANGUAGE LEARNERS	10,398	16%	4,465	43%	4,291	41%	1,554	15%	88	1%
ECONOMICALLY DISADVANTAGED	70,568	50%	11,385	16%	23,581	33%	28,764	41%	6,838	10%
NOT ECONOMICALLY DISADVANTAGED	44,605	76%	2,808	6%	8,063	18%	21,772	49%	11,962	27%
MIGRANT	95	38%	25	26%	34	36%	33	35%	3	3%
NOT MIGRANT	115,078	60%	14,168	12%	31,610	27%	50,503	44%	18,797	16%

GRADE 8 STUDENTS TAKING A REGENTS SCIENCE TEST

Accelerated grade 8 students who take a Regents science test in lieu of the New York State Grade 8 Science Test.

GROUP	TOTAL TESTED	PROFICIENT	LEVEL 1		LEVEL 2		LEVEL 3		LEVEL 4	
ALL STUDENTS	45,208	92%	1,606	4%	1,812	4%	13,600	30%	28,190	62%

NY STATE - SCHOOL REPORT CARD DATA [2015 - 16]

Regents Examination Results (2015 - 16)

COMPREHENSIVE ENGLISH

REGENTS COMPREHENSIVE ENGLISH

GROUP	TOTAL TESTED	55		65		85	
ALL STUDENTS	26,902	20,071	75%	14,370	53%	2,306	9%
GENERAL EDUCATION	19,412	15,380	79%	11,766	61%	2,146	11%
STUDENTS WITH DISABILITIES	7,490	4,691	63%	2,604	35%	160	2%
AMERICAN INDIAN OR ALASKA NATIVE	192	149	78%	96	50%	7	4%
ASIAN OR NATIVE HAWAIIAN/OTHER PACIFIC...	2,571	1,884	73%	1,322	51%	193	8%
BLACK OR AFRICAN AMERICAN	7,548	5,516	73%	3,767	50%	328	4%
HISPANIC OR LATINO	9,644	6,786	70%	4,713	49%	396	4%
WHITE	6,740	5,553	82%	4,338	64%	1,353	20%
MULTIRACIAL	207	183	88%	134	65%	29	14%
FEMALE	11,612	9,129	79%	6,787	58%	1,259	11%
MALE	15,290	10,942	72%	7,583	50%	1,047	7%
NON-ENGLISH LANGUAGE LEARNERS	21,362	17,149	80%	12,652	59%	2,280	11%
ENGLISH LANGUAGE LEARNERS	5,540	2,922	53%	1,718	31%	26	0%
ECONOMICALLY DISADVANTAGED	18,218	13,145	72%	9,037	50%	919	5%
NOT ECONOMICALLY DISADVANTAGED	8,684	6,926	80%	5,333	61%	1,387	16%
MIGRANT	26	16	62%	11	42%	0	0%
NOT MIGRANT	26,876	20,055	75%	14,359	53%	2,306	9%

ENGLISH LANGUAGE ARTS (COMMON CORE)

ENGLISH LANGUAGE ARTS (COMMON CORE)

GROUP	TOTAL TESTED	LEVEL 1		LEVEL 2		LEVEL 3		LEVEL 4		LEVEL 5	
ALL STUDENTS	207,161	16,178	8%	12,581	6%	42,755	21%	32,857	16%	102,790	50%
GENERAL EDUCATION	177,748	9,200	5%	7,858	4%	33,162	19%	28,809	16%	98,719	56%
STUDENTS WITH DISABILITIES	29,413	6,978	24%	4,723	16%	9,593	33%	4,048	14%	4,071	14%
AMERICAN INDIAN OR ALASKA NATIVE	1,164	115	10%	107	9%	300	26%	217	19%	425	37%
ASIAN OR NATIVE HAWAIIAN/OTHER PACIFIC...	20,292	1,412	7%	939	5%	3,293	16%	2,670	13%	11,978	59%
BLACK OR AFRICAN AMERICAN	39,788	5,044	13%	3,902	10%	11,661	29%	7,196	18%	11,985	30%
HISPANIC OR LATINO	48,366	6,269	13%	4,350	9%	12,959	27%	8,630	18%	16,158	33%
WHITE	94,852	3,233	3%	3,162	3%	14,056	15%	13,715	14%	60,686	64%
MULTIRACIAL	2,699	105	4%	121	4%	486	18%	429	16%	1,558	58%
FEMALE	102,205	5,786	6%	5,122	5%	18,926	19%	15,666	15%	56,705	55%
MALE	104,956	10,392	10%	7,459	7%	23,829	23%	17,191	16%	46,085	44%
NON-ENGLISH LANGUAGE LEARNERS	194,640	10,927	6%	10,343	5%	39,051	20%	31,956	16%	102,363	53%
ENGLISH LANGUAGE LEARNERS	12,521	5,251	42%	2,238	18%	3,704	30%	901	7%	427	3%
ECONOMICALLY DISADVANTAGED	105,302	12,373	12%	9,213	9%	28,211	27%	18,642	18%	36,863	35%
NOT ECONOMICALLY DISADVANTAGED	101,859	3,805	4%	3,368	3%	14,544	14%	14,215	14%	65,927	65%
MIGRANT	78	23	29%	9	12%	27	35%	7	9%	12	15%
NOT MIGRANT	207,083	16,155	8%	12,572	6%	42,728	21%	32,850	16%	102,778	50%

INTEGRATED ALGEBRA

REGENTS INTEGRATED ALGEBRA

GROUP	TOTAL TESTED	55		65		85	
ALL STUDENTS	17,585	13,749	78%	10,275	58%	689	4%
GENERAL EDUCATION	13,052	11,076	85%	8,744	67%	661	5%
STUDENTS WITH DISABILITIES	4,533	2,673	59%	1,531	34%	28	1%
AMERICAN INDIAN OR ALASKA NATIVE	115	85	74%	65	57%	1	1%
ASIAN OR NATIVE HAWAIIAN/OTHER PACIFIC...	1,226	1,039	85%	846	69%	116	9%
BLACK OR AFRICAN AMERICAN	5,753	4,361	76%	3,138	55%	67	1%
HISPANIC OR LATINO	7,289	5,647	77%	4,155	57%	115	2%
WHITE	3,069	2,513	82%	1,989	65%	387	13%
MULTIRACIAL	133	104	78%	82	62%	3	2%
FEMALE	8,212	6,628	81%	5,093	62%	351	4%
MALE	9,373	7,121	76%	5,182	55%	338	4%
NON-ENGLISH LANGUAGE LEARNERS	14,755	11,862	80%	9,030	61%	664	5%
ENGLISH LANGUAGE LEARNERS	2,830	1,887	67%	1,245	44%	25	1%
ECONOMICALLY DISADVANTAGED	12,869	9,961	77%	7,336	57%	279	2%
NOT ECONOMICALLY DISADVANTAGED	4,716	3,788	80%	2,939	62%	410	9%
MIGRANT	9	6	67%	5	56%	0	0%
NOT MIGRANT	17,576	13,743	78%	10,270	58%	689	4%

GEOMETRY

REGENTS GEOMETRY

GROUP	TOTAL TESTED	55		65		85	
ALL STUDENTS	19,059	12,762	67%	7,157	38%	677	4%
GENERAL EDUCATION	16,991	11,746	69%	6,721	40%	673	4%
STUDENTS WITH DISABILITIES	2,068	1,016	49%	436	21%	4	0%
AMERICAN INDIAN OR ALASKA NATIVE	136	107	79%	58	43%	5	4%
ASIAN OR NATIVE HAWAIIAN/OTHER PACIFIC...	1,832	1,397	76%	955	52%	217	12%
BLACK OR AFRICAN AMERICAN	5,500	3,176	58%	1,540	28%	47	1%
HISPANIC OR LATINO	5,686	3,436	60%	1,653	29%	55	1%
WHITE	5,680	4,489	79%	2,864	50%	347	6%
MULTIRACIAL	225	157	70%	87	39%	6	3%
FEMALE	10,143	6,848	68%	3,815	38%	372	4%
MALE	8,916	5,914	66%	3,342	37%	305	3%
NON-ENGLISH LANGUAGE LEARNERS	18,038	12,245	68%	6,838	38%	621	3%
ENGLISH LANGUAGE LEARNERS	1,021	517	51%	319	31%	56	5%
ECONOMICALLY DISADVANTAGED	11,539	7,249	63%	3,797	33%	253	2%
NOT ECONOMICALLY DISADVANTAGED	7,520	5,513	73%	3,360	45%	424	6%
MIGRANT	8	6	75%	2	25%	0	0%
NOT MIGRANT	19,051	12,756	67%	7,155	38%	677	4%

ALGEBRA 2/TRIGONOMETRY

REGENTS ALGEBRA 2/TRIGONOMETRY

GROUP	TOTAL TESTED	55		65		85	
ALL STUDENTS	98,248	70,875	72%	53,841	55%	19,006	19%
GENERAL EDUCATION	94,984	69,100	73%	52,661	55%	18,749	20%
STUDENTS WITH DISABILITIES	3,264	1,775	54%	1,180	36%	257	8%
AMERICAN INDIAN OR ALASKA NATIVE	481	315	65%	222	46%	67	14%
ASIAN OR NATIVE HAWAIIAN/OTHER PACIFIC...	14,628	12,060	82%	10,094	69%	5,200	36%
BLACK OR AFRICAN AMERICAN	12,620	6,786	54%	4,406	35%	821	7%
HISPANIC OR LATINO	16,943	9,724	57%	6,653	39%	1,614	10%
WHITE	52,220	41,013	79%	31,701	61%	10,990	21%
MULTIRACIAL	1,356	977	72%	765	56%	314	23%
FEMALE	52,533	38,127	73%	29,030	55%	10,342	20%
MALE	45,715	32,748	72%	24,811	54%	8,664	19%
NON-ENGLISH LANGUAGE LEARNERS	97,100	70,223	72%	53,364	55%	18,813	19%
ENGLISH LANGUAGE LEARNERS	1,148	652	57%	477	42%	193	17%
ECONOMICALLY DISADVANTAGED	39,486	24,889	63%	17,944	45%	5,686	14%
NOT ECONOMICALLY DISADVANTAGED	58,762	45,986	78%	35,897	61%	13,320	23%
MIGRANT	19	11	58%	8	42%	3	16%
NOT MIGRANT	98,229	70,864	72%	53,833	55%	19,003	19%

ALGEBRA I (COMMON CORE)

ALGEBRA I (COMMON CORE)

GROUP	TOTAL TESTED	LEVEL 1		LEVEL 2		LEVEL 3		LEVEL 4		LEVEL 5	
ALL STUDENTS	277,410	34,542	12%	44,016	16%	113,361	41%	48,555	18%	36,936	13%
GENERAL EDUCATION	230,996	19,894	9%	31,224	14%	97,547	42%	46,101	20%	36,230	16%
STUDENTS WITH DISABILITIES	46,414	14,648	32%	12,792	28%	15,814	34%	2,454	5%	706	2%
AMERICAN INDIAN OR ALASKA NATIVE	1,787	277	16%	329	18%	825	46%	254	14%	102	6%
ASIAN OR NATIVE HAWAIIAN/OTHER PACIFIC...	25,413	1,351	5%	2,078	8%	7,937	31%	6,028	24%	8,019	32%
BLACK OR AFRICAN AMERICAN	58,709	12,392	21%	14,338	24%	25,739	44%	4,685	8%	1,555	3%
HISPANIC OR LATINO	74,998	13,930	19%	16,772	22%	33,220	44%	7,878	11%	3,198	4%
WHITE	112,343	6,225	6%	9,893	9%	43,830	39%	28,911	26%	23,484	21%
MULTIRACIAL	4,160	367	9%	606	15%	1,810	44%	799	19%	578	14%
FEMALE	135,958	14,556	11%	20,169	15%	56,274	41%	25,522	19%	19,437	14%
MALE	141,452	19,986	14%	23,847	17%	57,087	40%	23,033	16%	17,499	12%
NON-ENGLISH LANGUAGE LEARNERS	254,281	27,510	11%	37,828	15%	105,320	41%	47,275	19%	36,348	14%
ENGLISH LANGUAGE LEARNERS	23,129	7,032	30%	6,188	27%	8,041	35%	1,280	6%	588	3%
ECONOMICALLY DISADVANTAGED	155,945	26,281	17%	32,163	21%	69,268	44%	18,918	12%	9,315	6%
NOT ECONOMICALLY DISADVANTAGED	121,465	8,261	7%	11,853	10%	44,093	36%	29,637	24%	27,621	23%
MIGRANT	181	39	22%	43	24%	80	44%	15	8%	4	2%
NOT MIGRANT	277,229	34,503	12%	43,973	16%	113,281	41%	48,540	18%	36,932	13%

GEOMETRY (COMMON CORE)

GEOMETRY (COMMON CORE)

GROUP	TOTAL TESTED	LEVEL 1		LEVEL 2		LEVEL 3		LEVEL 4		LEVEL 5	
ALL STUDENTS	138,138	27,795	20%	23,573	17%	57,545	42%	13,247	10%	15,978	12%
GENERAL EDUCATION	127,733	22,467	18%	21,448	17%	54,999	43%	13,011	10%	15,808	12%
STUDENTS WITH DISABILITIES	10,405	5,328	51%	2,125	20%	2,546	24%	236	2%	170	2%
AMERICAN INDIAN OR ALASKA NATIVE	671	178	27%	127	19%	275	41%	55	8%	36	5%
ASIAN OR NATIVE HAWAIIAN/OTHER PACIFIC...	16,128	1,692	10%	1,837	11%	6,239	39%	2,329	14%	4,031	25%
BLACK OR AFRICAN AMERICAN	20,366	8,772	43%	4,954	24%	5,785	28%	536	3%	319	2%
HISPANIC OR LATINO	27,019	9,710	36%	6,174	23%	9,099	34%	1,188	4%	848	3%
WHITE	71,877	7,049	10%	10,112	14%	35,312	49%	8,940	12%	10,464	15%
MULTIRACIAL	2,077	394	19%	369	18%	835	40%	199	10%	280	13%
FEMALE	72,069	14,423	20%	12,425	17%	30,312	42%	6,819	9%	8,090	11%
MALE	66,069	13,372	20%	11,148	17%	27,233	41%	6,428	10%	7,888	12%
NON-ENGLISH LANGUAGE LEARNERS	133,927	25,602	19%	22,877	17%	56,570	42%	13,083	10%	15,795	12%
ENGLISH LANGUAGE LEARNERS	4,211	2,193	52%	696	17%	975	23%	164	4%	183	4%
ECONOMICALLY DISADVANTAGED	60,468	18,704	31%	13,017	22%	21,935	36%	3,501	6%	3,311	5%
NOT ECONOMICALLY DISADVANTAGED	77,670	9,091	12%	10,556	14%	35,610	46%	9,746	13%	12,667	16%
MIGRANT	41	15	37%	12	29%	11	27%	2	5%	1	2%
NOT MIGRANT	138,097	27,780	20%	23,561	17%	57,534	42%	13,245	10%	15,977	12%

ALGEBRA II (COMMON CORE)

ALGEBRA II (COMMON CORE)

GROUP	TOTAL TESTED	LEVEL 1		LEVEL 2		LEVEL 3		LEVEL 4		LEVEL 5	
ALL STUDENTS	86,897	11,459	13%	10,910	13%	34,520	40%	21,079	24%	8,929	10%
GENERAL EDUCATION	84,287	10,667	13%	10,447	12%	33,615	40%	20,702	25%	8,856	11%
STUDENTS WITH DISABILITIES	2,610	792	30%	463	18%	905	35%	377	14%	73	3%
AMERICAN INDIAN OR ALASKA NATIVE	396	71	18%	73	18%	186	47%	50	13%	16	4%
ASIAN OR NATIVE HAWAIIAN/OTHER PACIFIC...	12,965	1,219	9%	1,270	10%	4,583	35%	3,622	28%	2,271	18%
BLACK OR AFRICAN AMERICAN	8,709	2,683	31%	1,785	20%	3,189	37%	887	10%	165	2%
HISPANIC OR LATINO	12,692	3,345	26%	2,483	20%	4,968	39%	1,520	12%	376	3%
WHITE	50,854	3,979	8%	5,148	10%	21,110	42%	14,671	29%	5,946	12%
MULTIRACIAL	1,281	162	13%	151	12%	484	38%	329	26%	155	12%
FEMALE	46,357	6,399	14%	5,951	13%	18,847	41%	10,959	24%	4,201	9%
MALE	40,540	5,060	12%	4,959	12%	15,673	39%	10,120	25%	4,728	12%
NON-ENGLISH LANGUAGE LEARNERS	85,877	11,114	13%	10,719	12%	34,211	40%	20,954	24%	8,879	10%
ENGLISH LANGUAGE LEARNERS	1,020	345	34%	191	19%	309	30%	125	12%	50	5%
ECONOMICALLY DISADVANTAGED	31,078	6,647	21%	5,306	17%	12,332	40%	5,156	17%	1,637	5%
NOT ECONOMICALLY DISADVANTAGED	55,819	4,812	9%	5,604	10%	22,188	40%	15,923	29%	7,292	13%
MIGRANT	16	1	6%	2	13%	9	56%	3	19%	1	6%
NOT MIGRANT	86,881	11,458	13%	10,908	13%	34,511	40%	21,076	24%	8,928	10%

GLOBAL HISTORY AND GEOGRAPHY

REGENTS GLOBAL HISTORY AND GEOGRAPHY

GROUP	TOTAL TESTED	55		65		85	
ALL STUDENTS	254,340	209,152	82%	173,128	68%	71,849	28%
GENERAL EDUCATION	208,993	182,914	88%	156,803	75%	69,244	33%
STUDENTS WITH DISABILITIES	45,347	26,238	58%	16,325	36%	2,605	6%
AMERICAN INDIAN OR ALASKA NATIVE	1,588	1,219	77%	931	59%	251	16%
ASIAN OR NATIVE HAWAIIAN/OTHER PACIFIC...	21,715	19,682	91%	17,952	83%	10,237	47%
BLACK OR AFRICAN AMERICAN	53,839	37,860	70%	26,938	50%	5,347	10%
HISPANIC OR LATINO	64,556	48,410	75%	36,319	56%	8,890	14%
WHITE	109,056	98,836	91%	88,288	81%	45,869	42%
MULTIRACIAL	3,586	3,145	88%	2,700	75%	1,255	35%
FEMALE	126,197	105,293	83%	86,742	69%	35,403	28%
MALE	128,143	103,859	81%	86,386	67%	36,446	28%
NON-ENGLISH LANGUAGE LEARNERS	237,864	200,505	84%	167,732	71%	71,123	30%
ENGLISH LANGUAGE LEARNERS	16,476	8,647	52%	5,396	33%	726	4%
ECONOMICALLY DISADVANTAGED	138,056	104,351	76%	79,355	57%	21,686	16%
NOT ECONOMICALLY DISADVANTAGED	116,284	104,801	90%	93,773	81%	50,163	43%
MIGRANT	153	107	70%	76	50%	14	9%
NOT MIGRANT	254,187	209,045	82%	173,052	68%	71,835	28%

U.S. HISTORY & GOVERNMENT

REGENTS U.S. HISTORY & GOVERNMENT

GROUP	TOTAL TESTED	55		65		85	
ALL STUDENTS	210,761	190,450	90%	173,437	82%	102,190	48%
GENERAL EDUCATION	179,503	167,945	94%	156,456	87%	97,121	54%
STUDENTS WITH DISABILITIES	31,258	22,505	72%	16,981	54%	5,069	16%
AMERICAN INDIAN OR ALASKA NATIVE	1,246	1,087	87%	938	75%	416	33%
ASIAN OR NATIVE HAWAIIAN/OTHER PACIFIC...	19,675	18,624	95%	17,668	90%	12,550	64%
BLACK OR AFRICAN AMERICAN	41,094	33,444	81%	27,791	68%	9,866	24%
HISPANIC OR LATINO	49,393	41,726	84%	35,701	72%	14,780	30%
WHITE	96,735	93,097	96%	89,049	92%	63,121	65%
MULTIRACIAL	2,618	2,472	94%	2,290	87%	1,457	56%
FEMALE	104,477	95,376	91%	86,535	83%	50,340	48%
MALE	106,284	95,074	89%	86,902	82%	51,850	49%
NON-ENGLISH LANGUAGE LEARNERS	199,675	183,220	92%	168,100	84%	101,065	51%
ENGLISH LANGUAGE LEARNERS	11,086	7,230	65%	5,337	48%	1,125	10%
ECONOMICALLY DISADVANTAGED	106,546	91,367	86%	79,272	74%	35,313	33%
NOT ECONOMICALLY DISADVANTAGED	104,215	99,083	95%	94,165	90%	66,877	64%
MIGRANT	86	68	79%	57	66%	13	15%
NOT MIGRANT	210,675	190,382	90%	173,380	82%	102,177	48%

LIVING ENVIRONMENT

REGENTS LIVING ENVIRONMENT

GROUP	TOTAL TESTED	55		65		85	
ALL STUDENTS	239,540	216,016	90%	186,083	78%	71,587	30%
GENERAL EDUCATION	197,769	185,716	94%	166,014	84%	69,040	35%
STUDENTS WITH DISABILITIES	41,771	30,300	73%	20,069	48%	2,547	6%
AMERICAN INDIAN OR ALASKA NATIVE	1,527	1,341	88%	1,088	71%	254	17%
ASIAN OR NATIVE HAWAIIAN/OTHER PACIFIC...	22,315	20,859	93%	19,224	86%	10,234	46%
BLACK OR AFRICAN AMERICAN	48,862	40,045	82%	29,694	61%	4,591	9%
HISPANIC OR LATINO	61,472	52,201	85%	40,714	66%	7,756	13%
WHITE	101,820	98,234	96%	92,375	91%	47,518	47%
MULTIRACIAL	3,544	3,336	94%	2,988	84%	1,234	35%
FEMALE	120,262	109,388	91%	93,785	78%	35,339	29%
MALE	119,278	106,628	89%	92,298	77%	36,248	30%
NON-ENGLISH LANGUAGE LEARNERS	219,930	202,891	92%	177,894	81%	70,889	32%
ENGLISH LANGUAGE LEARNERS	19,610	13,125	67%	8,189	42%	698	4%
ECONOMICALLY DISADVANTAGED	131,440	112,864	86%	90,285	69%	21,157	16%
NOT ECONOMICALLY DISADVANTAGED	108,100	103,152	95%	95,798	89%	50,430	47%
MIGRANT	162	128	79%	92	57%	13	8%
NOT MIGRANT	239,378	215,888	90%	185,991	78%	71,574	30%

PHYSICAL SETTING/EARTH SCIENCE

REGENTS PHYSICAL SETTING/EARTH SCIENCE

GROUP	TOTAL TESTED	55		65		85	
ALL STUDENTS	155,283	130,803	84%	110,055	71%	50,746	33%
GENERAL EDUCATION	135,588	118,849	88%	102,140	75%	49,111	36%
STUDENTS WITH DISABILITIES	19,695	11,954	61%	7,915	40%	1,635	8%
AMERICAN INDIAN OR ALASKA NATIVE	879	665	76%	510	58%	161	18%
ASIAN OR NATIVE HAWAIIAN/OTHER PACIFIC...	12,997	11,633	90%	10,375	80%	5,800	45%
BLACK OR AFRICAN AMERICAN	24,004	16,173	67%	11,087	46%	2,403	10%
HISPANIC OR LATINO	32,831	24,338	74%	17,982	55%	4,978	15%
WHITE	82,262	76,003	92%	68,438	83%	36,697	45%
MULTIRACIAL	2,310	1,991	86%	1,663	72%	707	31%
FEMALE	79,206	66,699	84%	55,420	70%	24,889	31%
MALE	76,077	64,104	84%	54,635	72%	25,857	34%
NON-ENGLISH LANGUAGE LEARNERS	149,420	127,942	86%	108,384	73%	50,469	34%
ENGLISH LANGUAGE LEARNERS	5,863	2,861	49%	1,671	29%	277	5%
ECONOMICALLY DISADVANTAGED	72,520	54,857	76%	41,469	57%	12,363	17%
NOT ECONOMICALLY DISADVANTAGED	82,763	75,946	92%	68,586	83%	38,383	46%
MIGRANT	78	53	68%	42	54%	4	5%
NOT MIGRANT	155,205	130,750	84%	110,013	71%	50,742	33%

PHYSICAL SETTING/CHEMISTRY

REGENTS PHYSICAL SETTING/CHEMISTRY

GROUP	TOTAL TESTED	55		65		85	
ALL STUDENTS	106,408	98,733	93%	80,792	76%	25,499	24%
GENERAL EDUCATION	103,008	96,136	93%	79,035	77%	25,190	24%
STUDENTS WITH DISABILITIES	3,400	2,597	76%	1,757	52%	309	9%
AMERICAN INDIAN OR ALASKA NATIVE	414	364	88%	276	67%	69	17%
ASIAN OR NATIVE HAWAIIAN/OTHER PACIFIC...	14,574	13,932	96%	12,149	83%	5,069	35%
BLACK OR AFRICAN AMERICAN	11,573	9,374	81%	6,031	52%	923	8%
HISPANIC OR LATINO	16,173	13,557	84%	9,363	58%	1,694	10%
WHITE	62,075	60,012	97%	51,761	83%	17,340	28%
MULTIRACIAL	1,599	1,494	93%	1,212	76%	404	25%
FEMALE	57,305	53,250	93%	43,193	75%	13,425	23%
MALE	49,103	45,483	93%	37,599	77%	12,074	25%
NON-ENGLISH LANGUAGE LEARNERS	105,509	98,147	93%	80,427	76%	25,430	24%
ENGLISH LANGUAGE LEARNERS	899	586	65%	365	41%	69	8%
ECONOMICALLY DISADVANTAGED	37,744	32,736	87%	23,840	63%	5,373	14%
NOT ECONOMICALLY DISADVANTAGED	68,664	65,997	96%	56,952	83%	20,126	29%
MIGRANT	13	13	100%	10	77%	3	23%
NOT MIGRANT	106,395	98,720	93%	80,782	76%	25,496	24%

PHYSICAL SETTING/PHYSICS

REGENTS PHYSICAL SETTING/PHYSICS

GROUP	TOTAL TESTED	55		65		85	
ALL STUDENTS	47,917	43,258	90%	37,858	79%	15,156	32%
GENERAL EDUCATION	47,059	42,615	91%	37,335	79%	14,981	32%
STUDENTS WITH DISABILITIES	858	643	75%	523	61%	175	20%
AMERICAN INDIAN OR ALASKA NATIVE	145	121	83%	107	74%	34	23%
ASIAN OR NATIVE HAWAIIAN/OTHER PACIFIC...	8,781	8,133	93%	7,311	83%	3,462	39%
BLACK OR AFRICAN AMERICAN	3,452	2,569	74%	1,974	57%	407	12%
HISPANIC OR LATINO	5,378	4,315	80%	3,394	63%	910	17%
WHITE	29,522	27,550	93%	24,549	83%	10,109	34%
MULTIRACIAL	639	570	89%	523	82%	234	37%
FEMALE	23,114	20,813	90%	17,984	78%	6,453	28%
MALE	24,803	22,445	90%	19,874	80%	8,703	35%
NON-ENGLISH LANGUAGE LEARNERS	47,767	43,155	90%	37,767	79%	15,124	32%
ENGLISH LANGUAGE LEARNERS	150	103	69%	91	61%	32	21%
ECONOMICALLY DISADVANTAGED	14,430	12,110	84%	10,085	70%	3,328	23%
NOT ECONOMICALLY DISADVANTAGED	33,487	31,148	93%	27,773	83%	11,828	35%
MIGRANT	2	–	–	–	–	–	–
NOT MIGRANT	47,915	–	–	–	–	–	–

NY STATE - SCHOOL REPORT CARD DATA [2015 - 16]

REGENTS COMPETENCY TEST RESULTS (2015 - 16)

GROUP	READING		WRITING		MATH		GLOBAL STUDIES		US HIST & GOV'T		SCIENCE	
ALL STUDENTS	164	63%	77	88%	98	50%	244	44%	255	51%	139	61%
GENERAL EDUCATION	11	82%	2	_	7	86%	30	50%	28	54%	15	67%
STUDENTS WITH DISABILITIES	153	62%	75	_	91	47%	214	43%	227	51%	124	60%
AMERICAN INDIAN OR ALASKA NATIVE	1	_	2	_	2	_		1		_	1	_
ASIAN OR NATIVE HAWAIIAN/OTHER PACIFIC...	8	_	2	_	4	_		10		_	2	_
BLACK OR AFRICAN AMERICAN	66	67%	38	84%	47	47%	123	46%	123	47%	74	54%
HISPANIC OR LATINO	64	64%	27	93%	33	55%	66	41%	84	60%	45	67%
WHITE	25	56%	10	_	16	_	46	50%	36	47%	17	_
MULTIRACIAL		3				_		1			_	
SMALL GROUP TOTAL	9	56%	12	92%	18	50%	9	11%	12	50%	20	75%
FEMALE	47	62%	21	86%	31	45%	93	43%	108	45%	60	58%
MALE	117	64%	56	89%	67	52%	151	45%	147	56%	79	63%
NON-ENGLISH LANGUAGE LEARNERS	140	64%	68	90%	86	50%	220	44%	223	50%	120	63%
ENGLISH LANGUAGE LEARNERS	24	58%	9	78%	12	50%	24	46%	32	63%	19	53%
ECONOMICALLY DISADVANTAGED	106	69%	45	87%	59	42%	144	38%	150	52%	86	56%
NOT ECONOMICALLY DISADVANTAGED	58	53%	32	91%	39	62%	100	53%	105	50%	53	70%
NOT MIGRANT	164	63%	77	88%	98	50%	244	44%	255	51%	139	61%

NY STATE - SCHOOL REPORT CARD DATA [2015 - 16]

HIGH SCHOOL COMPLETERS (2015 - 16)

GROUP	COMPLETERS (GRADUATES + COMMENCEMENT CREDENTIALS)	GRADUATES (REGENTS + LOCAL DIPLOMAS)	REGENTS DIPLOMA	
ALL STUDENTS	184639	181270	168365	93%
GENERAL EDUCATION	160876	160856	157306	98%
STUDENTS WITH DISABILITIES	23763	20414	11059	54%

GROUP	REGENTS WITH ADVANCED DESIGNATION		REGENTS WITH CTE ENDORSEMENT		LOCAL DIPLOMAS		COMMENCEMENT CREDENTIALS	
ALL STUDENTS	65182	36%	10379	6%	12905	7%	3369	2%
GENERAL EDUCATION	64190	40%	9256	6%	3550	2%	20	0%
STUDENTS WITH DISABILITIES	992	5%	1123	6%	9355	46%	3349	14%

HIGH SCHOOL NON-COMPLETERS (2015 - 16)

GROUP	DROPPED OUT		ENTERED APPROVED HIGH SCHOOL EQUIVALENCY PREPARATION PROGRAM		TOTAL NONCOMPLETERS	
ALL STUDENTS	23659	3%	2722	0%	26381	3%
GENERAL EDUCATION	17073	2%	1910	0%	18983	3%
STUDENTS WITH DISABILITIES	6586	5%	812	1%	7398	5%

NY STATE - SCHOOL REPORT CARD DATA [2015 - 16]

OVERALL GRADUATION RATE FOR ACCOUNTABILITY

ALL ACCOUNTABILITY GROUPS MADE AYP: NO

GROUP	MADE AYP
ALL STUDENTS	YES
AMERICAN INDIAN OR ALASKA NATIVE	YES
BLACK OR AFRICAN AMERICAN	YES
HISPANIC OR LATINO	YES
ASIAN OR NATIVE HAWAIIAN/OTHER PACIFIC ISLANDER	YES
WHITE	YES
MULTIRACIAL	YES
STUDENTS WITH DISABILITIES	NO
LIMITED ENGLISH PROFICIENT	NO
ECONOMICALLY DISADVANTAGED	YES

— There were not enough students to make an AYP determination.

FOUR-YEAR GRADUATION-RATE TOTAL COHORT FOR ACCOUNTABILITY

GROUP	MET GRADUATION-RATE CRITERION:	2011 FOUR-YEAR GRADUATION-RATE TOTAL COHORT	GRADUATION RATE	STATE STANDARD	PROGRESS TARGET
ALL STUDENTS	YES	208,389	80%	80%	79%
AMERICAN INDIAN OR ALASKA NATIVE	YES	1,175	68%	80%	67%
BLACK OR AFRICAN AMERICAN	YES	38,525	68%	80%	68%
HISPANIC OR LATINO	YES	46,127	68%	80%	67%
ASIAN OR NATIVE HAWAIIAN/OTHER PACIFIC...	YES	18,924	87%	80%	80%
WHITE	YES	102,045	89%	80%	80%
MULTIRACIAL	YES	1,593	82%	80%	80%
STUDENTS WITH DISABILITIES	NO	32,951†	54%†	80%	57%
LIMITED ENGLISH PROFICIENT	NO	13,588‡	48%‡	80%	49%
ECONOMICALLY DISADVANTAGED	YES	98,409	73%	80%	72%

YES Graduation rate is equal to or greater than the State Standard or the group's Progress Target.
NO Graduation rate is less than the State Standard and the group's Progress Target.
— There were fewer than 30 students in the cohort.
† Includes former students with disabilities because the number of students with disabilities in the current year is equal to or greater than 30.
‡ Includes former english language learner students because the number of english language learner students in the current year is equal to or greater than 30.

FIVE-YEAR GRADUATION-RATE TOTAL COHORT FOR ACCOUNTABILITY

GROUP	MET GRADUATION-RATE CRITERION:	2010 FIVE-YEAR GRADUATION-RATE TOTAL COHORT	GRADUATION RATE	STATE STANDARD	PROGRESS TARGET
ALL STUDENTS	YES	211,355	83%	80%	80%
AMERICAN INDIAN OR ALASKA NATIVE	NO	1,114	69%	80%	71%
BLACK OR AFRICAN AMERICAN	YES	38,533	73%	80%	73%
HISPANIC OR LATINO	NO	45,606	72%	80%	73%
ASIAN OR NATIVE HAWAIIAN/OTHER PACIFIC...	YES	18,901	88%	80%	80%
WHITE	YES	105,854	91%	80%	80%
MULTIRACIAL	YES	1,347	82%	80%	80%
STUDENTS WITH DISABILITIES	NO	32,765†	60%†	80%	63%
LIMITED ENGLISH PROFICIENT	NO	14,178‡	54%‡	80%	59%
ECONOMICALLY DISADVANTAGED	YES	91,628	77%	80%	76%

YES Graduation rate is equal to or greater than the State Standard or the group's Progress Target.
NO Graduation rate is less than the State Standard and the group's Progress Target.
— There were fewer than 30 students in the cohort.
† Includes former students with disabilities because the number of students with disabilities in the current year is equal to or greater than 30.
‡ Includes former english language learner students because the number of english language learner students in the current year is equal to or greater than 30.

GRADUATION RATES FOR NON-AYP GROUPS FOR ACCOUNTABILITY

GROUP	FOUR-YEAR GRADUATION-RATE TOTAL COHORT		FIVE-YEAR GRADUATION-RATE TOTAL COHORT	
	2011 FOUR-YEAR GRADUATION-RATE TOTAL COHORT	GRADUATION RATE	2010 FOUR-YEAR GRADUATION-RATE TOTAL COHORT	GRADUATION RATE
NOT AMERICAN INDIAN OR ALASKA NATIVE	207,214	80%	210,241	83%
NOT BLACK OR AFRICAN AMERICAN	169,864	83%	172,822	85%
NOT HISPANIC OR LATINO	162,262	84%	165,749	86%
NOT ASIAN OR NATIVE HAWAIIAN/OTHER PA...	189,465	80%	192,454	83%
NOT WHITE	106,344	72%	105,501	75%
NOT MULTIRACIAL	206,796	80%	210,008	83%
GENERAL EDUCATION	176,097	85%	180,122	87%
ENGLISH PROFICIENT	198,244	83%	200,478	85%
NOT ECONOMICALLY DISADVANTAGED	109,980	87%	119,727	87%
MALE	106,615	77%	108,257	80%
FEMALE	101,774	84%	103,098	86%
MIGRANT	82	61%	84	68%
NOT MIGRANT	208,307	80%	211,271	83%

— There were fewer than 30 students in the cohort.

Ancestry and Ethnicity

New York State Profile

Population: 19,378,102

Ancestry	Population	%
Afghan (9,904)	10,755	0.06
African, Sub-Saharan (178,451)	240,909	1.25
African (90,390)	142,623	0.74
Cape Verdean (463)	844	<0.01
Ethiopian (4,371)	5,107	0.03
Ghanaian (22,113)	23,006	0.12
Kenyan (1,138)	1,324	0.01
Liberian (2,675)	3,006	0.02
Nigerian (25,852)	28,991	0.15
Senegalese (2,893)	3,166	0.02
Sierra Leonean (1,672)	1,711	0.01
Somalian (2,764)	3,053	0.02
South African (2,838)	3,993	0.02
Sudanese (1,819)	2,137	0.01
Ugandan (388)	464	<0.01
Zimbabwean (607)	646	<0.01
Other Sub-Saharan African (18,468)	20,838	0.11
Albanian (41,939)	46,223	0.24
Alsatian (202)	882	<0.01
American (689,298)	689,298	3.58
Arab (103,238)	145,746	0.76
Arab (20,874)	25,231	0.13
Egyptian (21,344)	25,478	0.13
Iraqi (1,882)	3,013	0.02
Jordanian (3,956)	4,623	0.02
Lebanese (16,431)	32,642	0.17
Moroccan (9,220)	12,364	0.06
Palestinian (4,397)	5,501	0.03
Syrian (7,544)	14,535	0.08
Other Arab (17,590)	22,359	0.12
Armenian (15,331)	24,803	0.13
Assyrian/Chaldean/Syriac (384)	644	<0.01
Australian (4,252)	7,418	0.04
Austrian (22,923)	91,260	0.47
Basque (570)	1,514	0.01
Belgian (4,380)	13,929	0.07
Brazilian (19,433)	26,401	0.14
British (29,032)	58,548	0.30
Bulgarian (6,409)	8,210	0.04
Cajun (295)	897	<0.01
Canadian (23,228)	50,059	0.26
Carpatho Rusyn (474)	741	<0.01
Celtic (1,106)	2,324	0.01
Croatian (15,221)	26,607	0.14
Cypriot (1,402)	1,721	0.01
Czech (13,656)	57,264	0.30
Czechoslovakian (9,727)	22,547	0.12
Danish (8,961)	35,247	0.18
Dutch (50,011)	277,731	1.44
Eastern European (82,212)	89,540	0.47
English (307,176)	1,180,365	6.14
Estonian (1,710)	3,462	0.02
European (142,136)	157,939	0.82
Finnish (5,117)	16,941	0.09
French, ex. Basque (93,941)	505,680	2.63
French Canadian (52,040)	134,420	0.70
German (532,432)	2,238,521	11.64
German Russian (196)	587	<0.01
Greek (102,342)	163,796	0.85
Guyanese (109,285)	123,809	0.64
Hungarian (61,925)	154,481	0.80
Icelander (753)	1,528	0.01
Iranian (23,356)	27,773	0.14
Irish (763,450)	2,565,928	13.34
Israeli (25,337)	36,808	0.19
Italian (1,405,357)	2,731,316	14.20
Latvian (4,261)	9,194	0.05
Lithuanian (15,565)	48,825	0.25
Luxemburger (158)	582	<0.01
Macedonian (6,414)	7,783	0.04
Maltese (3,431)	7,645	0.04
New Zealander (484)	1,002	0.01
Northern European (8,610)	10,116	0.05
Norwegian (23,292)	85,859	0.45
Pennsylvania German (8,537)	13,519	0.07
Polish (396,502)	1,007,597	5.24
Portuguese (28,735)	52,967	0.28
Romanian (28,352)	56,605	0.29
Russian (241,898)	474,184	2.47
Scandinavian (4,984)	12,891	0.07
Scotch-Irish (58,045)	164,725	0.86
Scottish (53,369)	227,255	1.18
Serbian (5,585)	8,499	0.04
Slavic (3,865)	9,898	0.05
Slovak (14,038)	35,389	0.18
Slovene (1,922)	4,802	0.02
Soviet Union (317)	458	<0.01
Swedish (29,980)	132,781	0.69
Swiss (9,956)	39,241	0.20
Turkish (22,814)	29,907	0.16
Ukrainian (73,876)	133,633	0.69
Welsh (15,842)	88,255	0.46
West Indian, ex. Hispanic (665,395)	790,170	4.11
Bahamian (1,110)	1,796	0.01
Barbadian (22,928)	27,200	0.14
Belizean (5,612)	7,037	0.04
Bermudan (433)	672	<0.01
British West Indian (42,984)	49,916	0.26
Dutch West Indian (1,177)	1,887	0.01
Haitian (164,815)	179,024	0.93
Jamaican (265,516)	300,094	1.56
Trinidadian/Tobagonian (76,788)	89,490	0.47
U.S. Virgin Islander (2,037)	2,873	0.01
West Indian (80,923)	128,763	0.67
Other West Indian (1,072)	1,418	0.01
Yugoslavian (20,521)	28,253	0.15

Hispanic Origin	Population	%
Hispanic or Latino (of any race)	3,416,922	17.63
Central American, ex. Mexican	353,589	1.82
Costa Rican	11,576	0.06
Guatemalan	73,806	0.38
Honduran	71,919	0.37
Nicaraguan	13,006	0.07
Panamanian	28,200	0.15
Salvadoran	152,130	0.79
Other Central American	2,952	0.02
Cuban	70,803	0.37
Dominican Republic	674,787	3.48
Mexican	457,288	2.36
Puerto Rican	1,070,558	5.52
South American	513,417	2.65
Argentinean	24,969	0.13
Bolivian	7,122	0.04
Chilean	15,050	0.08
Colombian	141,879	0.73
Ecuadorian	228,216	1.18
Paraguayan	5,940	0.03
Peruvian	66,318	0.34
Uruguayan	6,021	0.03
Venezuelan	13,910	0.07
Other South American	3,992	0.02
Other Hispanic or Latino	276,480	1.43

Race*	Population	%
African-American/Black (3,073,800)	3,334,550	17.21
Not Hispanic (2,783,857)	2,946,880	15.21
Hispanic (289,943)	387,670	2.00
American Indian/Alaska Native (106,906)	221,058	1.14
Not Hispanic (53,908)	128,049	0.66
Hispanic (52,998)	93,009	0.48
Alaska Athabascan (Ala. Nat.) (57)	116	<0.01
Aleut (Alaska Native) (48)	82	<0.01
Apache (337)	1,080	0.01
Arapaho (24)	65	<0.01
Blackfeet (606)	4,496	0.02
Canadian/French Am. Ind. (530)	1,022	0.01
Central American Ind. (4,475)	8,602	0.04
Cherokee (2,714)	16,947	0.09
Cheyenne (47)	163	<0.01
Chickasaw (68)	215	<0.01
Chippewa (548)	1,125	0.01
Choctaw (263)	1,052	0.01
Colville (11)	22	<0.01
Comanche (69)	199	<0.01
Cree (50)	263	<0.01
Creek (155)	624	<0.01
Crow (52)	181	<0.01
Delaware (598)	1,384	0.01
Hopi (39)	115	<0.01
Houma (35)	48	<0.01
Inupiat (Alaska Native) (91)	169	<0.01
Iroquois (16,957)	26,567	0.14
Kiowa (24)	44	<0.01
Lumbee (127)	304	<0.01
Menominee (19)	41	<0.01
Mexican American Ind. (5,344)	7,439	0.04
Navajo (347)	788	<0.01
Osage (31)	86	<0.01
Ottawa (24)	52	<0.01
Paiute (25)	49	<0.01
Pima (13)	40	<0.01
Potawatomi (83)	166	<0.01
Pueblo (556)	1,096	0.01
Puget Sound Salish (14)	33	<0.01
Seminole (107)	848	<0.01
Shoshone (22)	96	<0.01
Sioux (628)	1,758	0.01
South American Ind. (6,294)	13,078	0.07
Spanish American Ind. (2,563)	3,506	0.02
Tlingit-Haida (Alaska Native) (60)	169	<0.01
Tohono O'Odham (59)	103	<0.01
Tsimshian (Alaska Native) (4)	5	<0.01
Ute (13)	36	<0.01
Yakama (8)	18	<0.01
Yaqui (48)	104	<0.01
Yuman (24)	45	<0.01
Yup'ik (Alaska Native) (20)	39	<0.01
Asian (1,420,244)	1,579,494	8.15
Not Hispanic (1,406,194)	1,545,106	7.97
Hispanic (14,050)	34,388	0.18
Bangladeshi (57,761)	67,063	0.35
Bhutanese (1,534)	1,824	0.01
Burmese (11,214)	12,174	0.06
Cambodian (4,212)	5,114	0.03
Chinese, ex. Taiwanese (559,516)	598,597	3.09
Filipino (104,287)	126,129	0.65
Hmong (227)	296	<0.01
Indian (313,620)	368,767	1.90
Indonesian (4,568)	6,122	0.03
Japanese (37,780)	51,781	0.27
Korean (140,994)	153,609	0.79
Laotian (3,420)	4,471	0.02
Malaysian (2,537)	3,908	0.02
Nepalese (6,844)	7,625	0.04
Pakistani (63,696)	70,622	0.36
Sri Lankan (5,196)	6,153	0.03
Taiwanese (16,023)	18,868	0.10
Thai (9,258)	11,763	0.06
Vietnamese (28,764)	34,510	0.18
Hawaii Native/Pacific Islander (8,766)	36,423	0.19
Not Hispanic (5,320)	21,768	0.11
Hispanic (3,446)	14,655	0.08
Fijian (157)	321	<0.01
Guamanian/Chamorro (2,235)	3,407	0.02
Marshallese (32)	37	<0.01
Native Hawaiian (1,802)	5,108	0.03
Samoan (685)	1,654	0.01
Tongan (80)	138	<0.01
White (12,740,974)	13,155,274	67.89
Not Hispanic (11,304,247)	11,534,988	59.53
Hispanic (1,436,727)	1,620,286	8.36

*Notes: † The Census 2010 population figure is used to calculate the percentages in the Hispanic Origin and Race categories. Ancestry percentages are based on the 2006-2010 American Community Survey population (not shown); ‡ Numbers in parentheses indicate the number of people reporting a single ancestry; * Numbers in parentheses indicate the number of persons reporting this race alone, not in combination with any other race; Please refer to the Explanation of Data for more information.*

County Profiles

Albany County
Population: 304,204

Ancestry	Population	%
Afghan (14)	14	<0.01
African, Sub-Saharan (1,796)	2,330	0.77
African (1,075)	1,506	0.50
Cape Verdean (0)	13	<0.01
Ethiopian (34)	34	0.01
Ghanaian (167)	167	0.05
Kenyan (101)	101	0.03
Liberian (0)	0	<0.01
Nigerian (241)	300	0.10
Senegalese (0)	0	<0.01
Sierra Leonean (0)	0	<0.01
Somalian (0)	0	<0.01
South African (9)	32	0.01
Sudanese (25)	25	0.01
Ugandan (0)	0	<0.01
Zimbabwean (0)	8	<0.01
Other Sub-Saharan African (144)	144	0.05
Albanian (934)	1,000	0.33
Alsatian (19)	61	0.02
American (8,399)	8,399	2.76
Arab (1,379)	2,384	0.78
Arab (329)	357	0.12
Egyptian (190)	273	0.09
Iraqi (0)	0	<0.01
Jordanian (76)	76	0.02
Lebanese (222)	571	0.19
Moroccan (64)	111	0.04
Palestinian (207)	312	0.10
Syrian (102)	451	0.15
Other Arab (189)	233	0.08
Armenian (309)	621	0.20
Assyrian/Chaldean/Syriac (0)	0	<0.01
Australian (68)	126	0.04
Austrian (202)	1,353	0.45
Basque (0)	38	0.01
Belgian (59)	109	0.04
Brazilian (195)	249	0.08
British (584)	1,052	0.35
Bulgarian (22)	31	0.01
Cajun (0)	0	<0.01
Canadian (471)	996	0.33
Carpatho Rusyn (12)	26	0.01
Celtic (15)	15	<0.01
Croatian (48)	163	0.05
Cypriot (0)	0	<0.01
Czech (334)	1,289	0.42
Czechoslovakian (52)	232	0.08
Danish (187)	869	0.29
Dutch (1,770)	11,451	3.77
Eastern European (648)	757	0.25
English (5,861)	28,025	9.22
Estonian (0)	0	<0.01
European (3,073)	3,521	1.16
Finnish (55)	316	0.10
French, ex. Basque (3,090)	19,696	6.48
French Canadian (2,042)	5,377	1.77
German (10,142)	50,507	16.61
German Russian (0)	0	<0.01
Greek (1,010)	2,365	0.78
Guyanese (716)	764	0.25
Hungarian (553)	2,084	0.69
Icelander (10)	10	<0.01
Iranian (186)	219	0.07
Irish (20,997)	72,953	24.00
Israeli (84)	117	0.04
Italian (20,747)	52,353	17.22
Latvian (111)	198	0.07
Lithuanian (160)	1,067	0.35
Luxemburger (9)	22	0.01
Macedonian (0)	0	<0.01
Maltese (11)	24	0.01
New Zealander (0)	0	<0.01

Ancestry	Population	%
Northern European (252)	356	0.12
Norwegian (574)	1,786	0.59
Pennsylvania German (52)	88	0.03
Polish (6,313)	20,711	6.81
Portuguese (208)	613	0.20
Romanian (81)	470	0.15
Russian (2,189)	5,714	1.88
Scandinavian (132)	581	0.19
Scotch-Irish (1,469)	4,121	1.36
Scottish (1,196)	5,513	1.81
Serbian (19)	19	0.01
Slavic (81)	189	0.06
Slovak (245)	780	0.26
Slovene (40)	133	0.04
Soviet Union (0)	0	<0.01
Swedish (521)	2,885	0.95
Swiss (190)	646	0.21
Turkish (35)	84	0.03
Ukrainian (1,078)	2,985	0.98
Welsh (221)	2,282	0.75
West Indian, ex. Hispanic (3,212)	4,660	1.53
Bahamian (0)	0	<0.01
Barbadian (14)	45	0.01
Belizean (0)	0	<0.01
Bermudan (36)	49	0.02
British West Indian (133)	210	0.07
Dutch West Indian (39)	90	0.03
Haitian (669)	825	0.27
Jamaican (1,592)	2,172	0.71
Trinidadian/Tobagonian (215)	329	0.11
U.S. Virgin Islander (0)	0	<0.01
West Indian (447)	873	0.29
Other West Indian (67)	67	0.02
Yugoslavian (245)	282	0.09

Hispanic Origin	Population	%
Hispanic or Latino (of any race)	14,917	4.90
Central American, ex. Mexican	735	0.24
Costa Rican	84	0.03
Guatemalan	117	0.04
Honduran	114	0.04
Nicaraguan	57	0.02
Panamanian	137	0.05
Salvadoran	208	0.07
Other Central American	18	0.01
Cuban	548	0.18
Dominican Republic	1,622	0.53
Mexican	1,540	0.51
Puerto Rican	7,633	2.51
South American	1,278	0.42
Argentinean	119	0.04
Bolivian	25	0.01
Chilean	72	0.02
Colombian	431	0.14
Ecuadorian	256	0.08
Paraguayan	12	<0.01
Peruvian	228	0.07
Uruguayan	21	0.01
Venezuelan	84	0.03
Other South American	30	0.01
Other Hispanic or Latino	1,561	0.51

Race*	Population	%
African-American/Black (38,609)	43,076	14.16
Not Hispanic (36,396)	40,017	13.15
Hispanic (2,213)	3,059	1.01
American Indian/Alaska Native (654)	2,326	0.76
Not Hispanic (453)	1,830	0.60
Hispanic (201)	496	0.16
Alaska Athabascan (Ala. Nat.) (1)	2	<0.01
Aleut (Alaska Native) (0)	0	<0.01
Apache (1)	13	<0.01
Arapaho (0)	1	<0.01
Blackfeet (11)	103	0.03
Canadian/French Am. Ind. (11)	23	0.01
Central American Ind. (13)	22	0.01

Race*	Population	%
Cherokee (39)	312	0.10
Cheyenne (0)	1	<0.01
Chickasaw (5)	5	<0.01
Chippewa (2)	6	<0.01
Choctaw (3)	15	<0.01
Colville (0)	0	<0.01
Comanche (0)	5	<0.01
Cree (1)	9	<0.01
Creek (0)	7	<0.01
Crow (2)	2	<0.01
Delaware (2)	12	<0.01
Hopi (1)	1	<0.01
Houma (0)	0	<0.01
Inupiat (Alaska Native) (1)	1	<0.01
Iroquois (80)	278	0.09
Kiowa (0)	0	<0.01
Lumbee (0)	0	<0.01
Menominee (0)	0	<0.01
Mexican American Ind. (43)	54	0.02
Navajo (2)	9	<0.01
Osage (0)	1	<0.01
Ottawa (0)	1	<0.01
Paiute (0)	0	<0.01
Pima (0)	0	<0.01
Potawatomi (1)	3	<0.01
Pueblo (1)	1	<0.01
Puget Sound Salish (0)	0	<0.01
Seminole (4)	17	0.01
Shoshone (0)	3	<0.01
Sioux (15)	32	0.01
South American Ind. (37)	85	0.03
Spanish American Ind. (8)	14	<0.01
Tlingit-Haida (Alaska Native) (2)	4	<0.01
Tohono O'Odham (0)	0	<0.01
Tsimshian (Alaska Native) (0)	0	<0.01
Ute (0)	0	<0.01
Yakama (1)	1	<0.01
Yaqui (0)	0	<0.01
Yuman (0)	0	<0.01
Yup'ik (Alaska Native) (2)	2	<0.01
Asian (14,579)	16,511	5.43
Not Hispanic (14,500)	16,300	5.36
Hispanic (79)	211	0.07
Bangladeshi (273)	305	0.10
Bhutanese (62)	62	0.02
Burmese (313)	342	0.11
Cambodian (21)	30	0.01
Chinese, ex. Taiwanese (3,552)	3,908	1.28
Filipino (1,147)	1,460	0.48
Hmong (0)	0	<0.01
Indian (4,600)	5,085	1.67
Indonesian (32)	43	0.01
Japanese (315)	520	0.17
Korean (1,329)	1,531	0.50
Laotian (5)	14	<0.01
Malaysian (11)	23	0.01
Nepalese (70)	78	0.03
Pakistani (1,377)	1,520	0.50
Sri Lankan (68)	75	0.02
Taiwanese (160)	189	0.06
Thai (93)	125	0.04
Vietnamese (610)	717	0.24
Hawaii Native/Pacific Islander (98)	333	0.11
Not Hispanic (88)	270	0.09
Hispanic (10)	63	0.02
Fijian (3)	4	<0.01
Guamanian/Chamorro (13)	31	0.01
Marshallese (0)	0	<0.01
Native Hawaiian (16)	71	0.02
Samoan (16)	29	0.01
Tongan (1)	6	<0.01
White (237,873)	244,245	80.29
Not Hispanic (231,152)	236,400	77.71
Hispanic (6,721)	7,845	2.58

Notes: † The Census 2010 population figure is used to calculate the percentages in the Hispanic Origin and Race categories. Ancestry percentages are based on the 2006-2010 American Community Survey population (not shown); ‡ Numbers in parentheses indicate the number of people reporting a single ancestry; * Numbers in parentheses indicate the number of persons reporting this race alone, not in combination with any other race; Please refer to the Explanation of Data for more information.

Allegany County

Population: 48,946

Ancestry	Population	%
Afghan (0)	0	<0.01
African, Sub-Saharan (22)	37	0.08
African (0)	15	0.03
Cape Verdean (0)	0	<0.01
Ethiopian (0)	0	<0.01
Ghanaian (0)	0	<0.01
Kenyan (22)	22	0.04
Liberian (0)	0	<0.01
Nigerian (0)	0	<0.01
Senegalese (0)	0	<0.01
Sierra Leonean (0)	0	<0.01
Somalian (0)	0	<0.01
South African (0)	0	<0.01
Sudanese (0)	0	<0.01
Ugandan (0)	0	<0.01
Zimbabwean (0)	0	<0.01
Other Sub-Saharan African (0)	0	<0.01
Albanian (0)	0	<0.01
Alsatian (4)	4	0.01
American (2,579)	2,579	5.25
Arab (59)	104	0.21
Arab (0)	0	<0.01
Egyptian (2)	2	<0.01
Iraqi (0)	0	<0.01
Jordanian (0)	0	<0.01
Lebanese (54)	83	0.17
Moroccan (0)	0	<0.01
Palestinian (0)	0	<0.01
Syrian (0)	13	0.03
Other Arab (3)	6	0.01
Armenian (3)	3	0.01
Assyrian/Chaldean/Syriac (0)	0	<0.01
Australian (0)	4	0.01
Austrian (16)	132	0.27
Basque (0)	0	<0.01
Belgian (8)	15	0.03
Brazilian (0)	10	0.02
British (101)	249	0.51
Bulgarian (0)	0	<0.01
Cajun (0)	2	<0.01
Canadian (23)	135	0.27
Carpatho Rusyn (0)	0	<0.01
Celtic (19)	19	0.04
Croatian (0)	39	0.08
Cypriot (0)	0	<0.01
Czech (34)	138	0.28
Czechoslovakian (34)	63	0.13
Danish (18)	87	0.18
Dutch (292)	1,775	3.61
Eastern European (8)	8	0.02
English (3,179)	8,971	18.27
Estonian (0)	0	<0.01
European (191)	255	0.52
Finnish (0)	59	0.12
French, ex. Basque (258)	1,883	3.83
French Canadian (212)	508	1.03
German (3,788)	14,728	29.99
German Russian (0)	0	<0.01
Greek (29)	74	0.15
Guyanese (0)	18	0.04
Hungarian (71)	224	0.46
Icelander (0)	0	<0.01
Iranian (0)	0	<0.01
Irish (2,480)	9,350	19.04
Israeli (0)	9	0.02
Italian (1,381)	3,451	7.03
Latvian (0)	0	<0.01
Lithuanian (42)	108	0.22
Luxemburger (0)	0	<0.01
Macedonian (0)	0	<0.01
Maltese (12)	27	0.05
New Zealander (0)	0	<0.01
Northern European (23)	23	0.05
Norwegian (64)	214	0.44
Pennsylvania German (320)	409	0.83

Ancestry (cont.)	Population	%
Polish (892)	2,591	5.28
Portuguese (0)	38	0.08
Romanian (11)	45	0.09
Russian (48)	234	0.48
Scandinavian (29)	69	0.14
Scotch-Irish (332)	1,044	2.13
Scottish (411)	1,397	2.84
Serbian (0)	6	0.01
Slavic (8)	87	0.18
Slovak (7)	41	0.08
Slovene (20)	30	0.06
Soviet Union (0)	0	<0.01
Swedish (178)	789	1.61
Swiss (55)	225	0.46
Turkish (0)	0	<0.01
Ukrainian (49)	123	0.25
Welsh (116)	581	1.18
West Indian, ex. Hispanic (26)	68	0.14
Bahamian (0)	0	<0.01
Barbadian (0)	0	<0.01
Belizean (0)	0	<0.01
Bermudan (0)	0	<0.01
British West Indian (7)	19	0.04
Dutch West Indian (0)	0	<0.01
Haitian (0)	12	0.02
Jamaican (0)	12	0.02
Trinidadian/Tobagonian (14)	20	0.04
U.S. Virgin Islander (0)	0	<0.01
West Indian (5)	5	0.01
Other West Indian (0)	0	<0.01
Yugoslavian (0)	7	0.01

Hispanic Origin	Population	%
Hispanic or Latino (of any race)	670	1.37
Central American, ex. Mexican	47	0.10
Costa Rican	1	<0.01
Guatemalan	15	0.03
Honduran	5	0.01
Nicaraguan	4	0.01
Panamanian	8	0.02
Salvadoran	14	0.03
Other Central American	0	<0.01
Cuban	17	0.03
Dominican Republic	58	0.12
Mexican	182	0.37
Puerto Rican	203	0.41
South American	78	0.16
Argentinean	1	<0.01
Bolivian	6	0.01
Chilean	5	0.01
Colombian	28	0.06
Ecuadorian	13	0.03
Paraguayan	1	<0.01
Peruvian	13	0.03
Uruguayan	0	<0.01
Venezuelan	4	0.01
Other South American	7	0.01
Other Hispanic or Latino	85	0.17

Race*	Population	%
African-American/Black (524)	732	1.50
Not Hispanic (494)	677	1.38
Hispanic (30)	55	0.11
American Indian/Alaska Native (113)	332	0.68
Not Hispanic (97)	295	0.60
Hispanic (16)	37	0.08
Alaska Athabascan (Ala. Nat.) (0)	0	<0.01
Aleut (Alaska Native) (0)	0	<0.01
Apache (2)	5	0.01
Arapaho (0)	0	<0.01
Blackfeet (0)	7	0.01
Canadian/French Am. Ind. (2)	3	0.01
Central American Ind. (0)	0	<0.01
Cherokee (11)	32	0.07
Cheyenne (0)	0	<0.01
Chickasaw (0)	0	<0.01
Chippewa (2)	4	0.01
Choctaw (0)	3	0.01
Colville (0)	0	<0.01

Race* (cont.)	Population	%
Comanche (0)	0	<0.01
Cree (0)	0	<0.01
Creek (1)	1	<0.01
Crow (1)	2	<0.01
Delaware (0)	3	0.01
Hopi (0)	0	<0.01
Houma (1)	1	<0.01
Inupiat (Alaska Native) (0)	0	<0.01
Iroquois (38)	84	0.17
Kiowa (0)	0	<0.01
Lumbee (1)	1	<0.01
Menominee (1)	1	<0.01
Mexican American Ind. (2)	3	0.01
Navajo (0)	3	0.01
Osage (0)	0	<0.01
Ottawa (0)	0	<0.01
Paiute (0)	0	<0.01
Pima (0)	0	<0.01
Potawatomi (0)	0	<0.01
Pueblo (0)	0	<0.01
Puget Sound Salish (0)	0	<0.01
Seminole (0)	0	<0.01
Shoshone (0)	0	<0.01
Sioux (0)	1	<0.01
South American Ind. (2)	7	0.01
Spanish American Ind. (0)	0	<0.01
Tlingit-Haida (Alaska Native) (0)	0	<0.01
Tohono O'Odham (0)	0	<0.01
Tsimshian (Alaska Native) (0)	0	<0.01
Ute (0)	0	<0.01
Yakama (0)	0	<0.01
Yaqui (0)	0	<0.01
Yuman (0)	0	<0.01
Yup'ik (Alaska Native) (0)	0	<0.01
Asian (452)	603	1.23
Not Hispanic (451)	591	1.21
Hispanic (1)	12	0.02
Bangladeshi (0)	0	<0.01
Bhutanese (0)	0	<0.01
Burmese (0)	0	<0.01
Cambodian (2)	3	0.01
Chinese, ex. Taiwanese (172)	205	0.42
Filipino (22)	58	0.12
Hmong (0)	0	<0.01
Indian (52)	71	0.15
Indonesian (3)	3	0.01
Japanese (59)	88	0.18
Korean (82)	111	0.23
Laotian (3)	3	0.01
Malaysian (0)	0	<0.01
Nepalese (0)	0	<0.01
Pakistani (3)	3	0.01
Sri Lankan (3)	3	0.01
Taiwanese (9)	11	0.02
Thai (9)	12	0.02
Vietnamese (12)	22	0.04
Hawaii Native/Pacific Islander (9)	20	0.04
Not Hispanic (7)	16	0.03
Hispanic (2)	4	0.01
Fijian (0)	0	<0.01
Guamanian/Chamorro (1)	2	<0.01
Marshallese (0)	0	<0.01
Native Hawaiian (7)	15	0.03
Samoan (1)	4	0.01
Tongan (0)	0	<0.01
White (47,085)	47,605	97.26
Not Hispanic (46,701)	47,175	96.38
Hispanic (384)	430	0.88

Notes: † The Census 2010 population figure is used to calculate the percentages in the Hispanic Origin and Race categories. Ancestry percentages are based on the 2006-2010 American Community Survey population (not shown); ‡ Numbers in parentheses indicate the number of people reporting a single ancestry; * Numbers in parentheses indicate the number of persons reporting this race alone, not in combination with any other race; Please refer to the Explanation of Data for more information.

Bronx County

Population: 1,385,108

Ancestry	Population	%
Afghan (14)	14	<0.01
African, Sub-Saharan (50,131)	55,928	4.10
African (19,345)	22,647	1.66
Cape Verdean (49)	108	0.01
Ethiopian (790)	945	0.07
Ghanaian (13,163)	13,490	0.99
Kenyan (12)	24	<0.01
Liberian (365)	450	0.03
Nigerian (4,896)	5,538	0.41
Senegalese (956)	1,068	0.08
Sierra Leonean (759)	759	0.06
Somalian (11)	35	<0.01
South African (29)	68	<0.01
Sudanese (88)	149	0.01
Ugandan (0)	0	<0.01
Zimbabwean (108)	108	0.01
Other Sub-Saharan African (9,560)	10,539	0.77
Albanian (7,460)	7,835	0.57
Alsatian (0)	0	<0.01
American (16,297)	16,297	1.19
Arab (4,063)	5,008	0.37
Arab (1,481)	1,719	0.13
Egyptian (495)	718	0.05
Iraqi (64)	73	0.01
Jordanian (8)	8	<0.01
Lebanese (229)	347	0.03
Moroccan (526)	667	0.05
Palestinian (28)	28	<0.01
Syrian (44)	192	0.01
Other Arab (1,188)	1,256	0.09
Armenian (128)	237	0.02
Assyrian/Chaldean/Syriac (0)	18	<0.01
Australian (8)	21	<0.01
Austrian (539)	1,868	0.14
Basque (66)	109	0.01
Belgian (52)	131	0.01
Brazilian (276)	397	0.03
British (517)	1,115	0.08
Bulgarian (506)	521	0.04
Cajun (0)	0	<0.01
Canadian (197)	375	0.03
Carpatho Rusyn (0)	12	<0.01
Celtic (1)	13	<0.01
Croatian (91)	219	0.02
Cypriot (12)	38	<0.01
Czech (99)	388	0.03
Czechoslovakian (90)	226	0.02
Danish (17)	385	0.03
Dutch (314)	1,920	0.14
Eastern European (1,425)	1,646	0.12
English (1,821)	7,038	0.52
Estonian (70)	85	0.01
European (1,845)	2,270	0.17
Finnish (89)	291	0.02
French, ex. Basque (909)	4,971	0.36
French Canadian (102)	403	0.03
German (3,729)	16,487	1.21
German Russian (7)	30	<0.01
Greek (2,499)	3,607	0.26
Guyanese (10,276)	11,837	0.87
Hungarian (966)	2,427	0.18
Icelander (6)	6	<0.01
Iranian (187)	248	0.02
Irish (18,712)	38,479	2.82
Israeli (427)	618	0.05
Italian (38,592)	57,527	4.21
Latvian (92)	103	0.01
Lithuanian (167)	547	0.04
Luxemburger (0)	0	<0.01
Macedonian (628)	628	0.05
Maltese (16)	45	<0.01
New Zealander (23)	23	<0.01
Northern European (25)	25	<0.01
Norwegian (260)	773	0.06
Pennsylvania German (0)	0	<0.01

Ancestry	Population	%
Polish (3,429)	7,834	0.57
Portuguese (474)	1,113	0.08
Romanian (691)	1,164	0.09
Russian (4,351)	8,064	0.59
Scandinavian (102)	155	0.01
Scotch-Irish (516)	1,601	0.12
Scottish (388)	1,570	0.11
Serbian (154)	187	0.01
Slavic (15)	90	0.01
Slovak (87)	226	0.02
Slovene (10)	45	<0.01
Soviet Union (12)	12	<0.01
Swedish (119)	549	0.04
Swiss (24)	166	0.01
Turkish (589)	686	0.05
Ukrainian (970)	1,608	0.12
Welsh (101)	530	0.04
West Indian, ex. Hispanic (93,323)	107,527	7.87
Bahamian (165)	208	0.02
Barbadian (1,285)	1,612	0.12
Belizean (1,253)	1,493	0.11
Bermudan (101)	198	0.01
British West Indian (5,959)	7,136	0.52
Dutch West Indian (127)	172	0.01
Haitian (3,891)	4,652	0.34
Jamaican (58,387)	64,222	4.70
Trinidadian/Tobagonian (3,695)	4,811	0.35
U.S. Virgin Islander (737)	952	0.07
West Indian (17,683)	21,941	1.61
Other West Indian (40)	130	0.01
Yugoslavian (1,275)	1,480	0.11

Hispanic Origin	Population	%
Hispanic or Latino (of any race)	741,413	53.53
Central American, ex. Mexican	34,492	2.49
Costa Rican	1,095	0.08
Guatemalan	4,645	0.34
Honduran	17,990	1.30
Nicaraguan	2,342	0.17
Panamanian	2,372	0.17
Salvadoran	5,469	0.39
Other Central American	579	0.04
Cuban	8,785	0.63
Dominican Republic	240,987	17.40
Mexican	71,194	5.14
Puerto Rican	298,921	21.58
South American	35,463	2.56
Argentinean	1,117	0.08
Bolivian	227	0.02
Chilean	646	0.05
Colombian	4,635	0.33
Ecuadorian	23,206	1.68
Paraguayan	223	0.02
Peruvian	3,596	0.26
Uruguayan	148	0.01
Venezuelan	1,296	0.09
Other South American	369	0.03
Other Hispanic or Latino	51,571	3.72

Race*	Population	%
African-American/Black (505,200)	541,622	39.10
Not Hispanic (416,695)	427,134	30.84
Hispanic (88,505)	114,488	8.27
American Indian/Alaska Native (18,260)	32,011	2.31
Not Hispanic (3,460)	7,638	0.55
Hispanic (14,800)	24,373	1.76
Alaska Athabascan (Ala. Nat.) (4)	8	<0.01
Aleut (Alaska Native) (0)	3	<0.01
Apache (30)	99	0.01
Arapaho (2)	3	<0.01
Blackfeet (43)	310	0.02
Canadian/French Am. Ind. (13)	25	<0.01
Central American Ind. (2,274)	4,520	0.33
Cherokee (247)	1,312	0.09
Cheyenne (2)	5	<0.01
Chickasaw (6)	16	<0.01
Chippewa (25)	38	<0.01
Choctaw (4)	43	<0.01
Colville (0)	2	<0.01

	Population	%
Comanche (8)	26	<0.01
Cree (1)	16	<0.01
Creek (7)	47	<0.01
Crow (1)	16	<0.01
Delaware (1)	10	<0.01
Hopi (0)	2	<0.01
Houma (12)	12	<0.01
Inupiat (Alaska Native) (11)	15	<0.01
Iroquois (81)	170	0.01
Kiowa (1)	1	<0.01
Lumbee (3)	6	<0.01
Menominee (1)	3	<0.01
Mexican American Ind. (714)	963	0.07
Navajo (24)	42	<0.01
Osage (2)	3	<0.01
Ottawa (0)	1	<0.01
Paiute (0)	5	<0.01
Pima (1)	1	<0.01
Potawatomi (1)	2	<0.01
Pueblo (177)	382	0.03
Puget Sound Salish (0)	0	<0.01
Seminole (6)	50	<0.01
Shoshone (0)	8	<0.01
Sioux (46)	82	0.01
South American Ind. (1,568)	2,938	0.21
Spanish American Ind. (709)	992	0.07
Tlingit-Haida (Alaska Native) (1)	11	<0.01
Tohono O'Odham (4)	9	<0.01
Tsimshian (Alaska Native) (0)	0	<0.01
Ute (2)	5	<0.01
Yakama (3)	3	<0.01
Yaqui (4)	5	<0.01
Yuman (1)	2	<0.01
Yup'ik (Alaska Native) (1)	6	<0.01
Asian (49,609)	59,085	4.27
Not Hispanic (47,335)	53,458	3.86
Hispanic (2,274)	5,627	0.41
Bangladeshi (7,323)	8,623	0.62
Bhutanese (74)	104	0.01
Burmese (71)	81	0.01
Cambodian (1,055)	1,188	0.09
Chinese, ex. Taiwanese (6,644)	8,112	0.59
Filipino (5,576)	6,456	0.47
Hmong (1)	3	<0.01
Indian (15,865)	20,357	1.47
Indonesian (50)	96	0.01
Japanese (562)	1,027	0.07
Korean (2,840)	3,101	0.22
Laotian (99)	148	0.01
Malaysian (11)	30	<0.01
Nepalese (129)	159	0.01
Pakistani (2,399)	2,728	0.20
Sri Lankan (174)	234	0.02
Taiwanese (98)	130	0.01
Thai (326)	414	0.03
Vietnamese (3,215)	3,526	0.25
Hawaii Native/Pacific Islander (1,288)	6,213	0.45
Not Hispanic (398)	1,854	0.13
Hispanic (890)	4,359	0.31
Fijian (13)	13	<0.01
Guamanian/Chamorro (251)	376	0.03
Marshallese (3)	3	<0.01
Native Hawaiian (371)	669	0.05
Samoan (70)	160	0.01
Tongan (5)	7	<0.01
White (386,497)	427,659	30.88
Not Hispanic (151,209)	158,245	11.42
Hispanic (235,288)	269,414	19.45

*Notes: † The Census 2010 population figure is used to calculate the percentages in the Hispanic Origin and Race categories. Ancestry percentages are based on the 2006-2010 American Community Survey population (not shown); ‡ Numbers in parentheses indicate the number of people reporting a single ancestry; * Numbers in parentheses indicate the number of persons reporting this race alone, not in combination with any other race; Please refer to the Explanation of Data for more information.*

Broome County

Population: 200,600

Ancestry	Population	%
Afghan (0)	0	<0.01
African, Sub-Saharan (397)	646	0.32
African (262)	488	0.24
Cape Verdean (11)	11	0.01
Ethiopian (0)	0	<0.01
Ghanaian (43)	43	0.02
Kenyan (6)	6	<0.01
Liberian (0)	0	<0.01
Nigerian (17)	17	0.01
Senegalese (0)	0	<0.01
Sierra Leonean (0)	0	<0.01
Somalian (0)	0	<0.01
South African (9)	32	0.02
Sudanese (0)	0	<0.01
Ugandan (0)	0	<0.01
Zimbabwean (0)	0	<0.01
Other Sub-Saharan African (49)	49	0.02
Albanian (13)	20	0.01
Alsatian (0)	13	0.01
American (8,398)	8,398	4.18
Arab (1,042)	1,422	0.71
Arab (115)	132	0.07
Egyptian (106)	155	0.08
Iraqi (6)	6	<0.01
Jordanian (12)	12	0.01
Lebanese (255)	459	0.23
Moroccan (0)	8	<0.01
Palestinian (13)	25	0.01
Syrian (19)	20	0.01
Other Arab (516)	605	0.30
Armenian (139)	329	0.16
Assyrian/Chaldean/Syriac (0)	0	<0.01
Australian (39)	39	0.02
Austrian (155)	882	0.44
Basque (0)	0	<0.01
Belgian (15)	133	0.07
Brazilian (13)	13	0.01
British (355)	1,018	0.51
Bulgarian (62)	62	0.03
Cajun (3)	12	0.01
Canadian (134)	338	0.17
Carpatho Rusyn (64)	126	0.06
Celtic (30)	67	0.03
Croatian (21)	68	0.03
Cypriot (0)	0	<0.01
Czech (788)	2,348	1.17
Czechoslovakian (509)	872	0.43
Danish (163)	449	0.22
Dutch (1,265)	6,844	3.41
Eastern European (314)	386	0.19
English (7,900)	26,062	12.98
Estonian (21)	42	0.02
European (1,586)	1,795	0.89
Finnish (10)	181	0.09
French, ex. Basque (644)	6,871	3.42
French Canadian (488)	1,377	0.69
German (9,379)	36,306	18.08
German Russian (0)	0	<0.01
Greek (606)	1,245	0.62
Guyanese (171)	251	0.12
Hungarian (238)	903	0.45
Icelander (46)	46	0.02
Iranian (36)	70	0.03
Irish (12,853)	43,809	21.82
Israeli (0)	26	0.01
Italian (10,921)	27,706	13.80
Latvian (35)	125	0.06
Lithuanian (314)	1,211	0.60
Luxemburger (0)	0	<0.01
Macedonian (55)	55	0.03
Maltese (0)	24	0.01
New Zealander (0)	0	<0.01
Northern European (59)	59	0.03
Norwegian (303)	987	0.49
Pennsylvania German (541)	938	0.47

Ancestry (cont.)	Population	%
Polish (4,815)	14,217	7.08
Portuguese (77)	128	0.06
Romanian (214)	387	0.19
Russian (1,876)	5,545	2.76
Scandinavian (32)	187	0.09
Scotch-Irish (1,024)	2,833	1.41
Scottish (1,085)	4,355	2.17
Serbian (10)	65	0.03
Slavic (439)	618	0.31
Slovak (2,653)	6,570	3.27
Slovene (51)	137	0.07
Soviet Union (0)	0	<0.01
Swedish (473)	1,729	0.86
Swiss (119)	522	0.26
Turkish (189)	212	0.11
Ukrainian (1,127)	2,148	1.07
Welsh (762)	4,482	2.23
West Indian, ex. Hispanic (716)	973	0.48
Bahamian (0)	0	<0.01
Barbadian (0)	0	<0.01
Belizean (5)	5	<0.01
Bermudan (0)	0	<0.01
British West Indian (29)	55	0.03
Dutch West Indian (0)	0	<0.01
Haitian (210)	222	0.11
Jamaican (338)	478	0.24
Trinidadian/Tobagonian (54)	54	0.03
U.S. Virgin Islander (0)	0	<0.01
West Indian (80)	159	0.08
Other West Indian (0)	0	<0.01
Yugoslavian (273)	310	0.15

Hispanic Origin	Population	%
Hispanic or Latino (of any race)	6,778	3.38
Central American, ex. Mexican	420	0.21
Costa Rican	44	0.02
Guatemalan	112	0.06
Honduran	87	0.04
Nicaraguan	31	0.02
Panamanian	65	0.03
Salvadoran	81	0.04
Other Central American	0	<0.01
Cuban	322	0.16
Dominican Republic	505	0.25
Mexican	765	0.38
Puerto Rican	3,442	1.72
South American	606	0.30
Argentinean	92	0.05
Bolivian	14	0.01
Chilean	45	0.02
Colombian	181	0.09
Ecuadorian	128	0.06
Paraguayan	5	<0.01
Peruvian	94	0.05
Uruguayan	9	<0.01
Venezuelan	33	0.02
Other South American	5	<0.01
Other Hispanic or Latino	718	0.36

Race*	Population	%
African-American/Black (9,614)	12,499	6.23
Not Hispanic (8,850)	11,278	5.62
Hispanic (764)	1,221	0.61
American Indian/Alaska Native (396)	1,664	0.83
Not Hispanic (328)	1,445	0.72
Hispanic (68)	219	0.11
Alaska Athabascan (Ala. Nat.) (1)	4	<0.01
Aleut (Alaska Native) (0)	0	<0.01
Apache (7)	34	0.02
Arapaho (0)	0	<0.01
Blackfeet (8)	75	0.04
Canadian/French Am. Ind. (4)	10	<0.01
Central American Ind. (1)	1	<0.01
Cherokee (37)	248	0.12
Cheyenne (0)	0	<0.01
Chickasaw (0)	1	<0.01
Chippewa (7)	15	0.01
Choctaw (3)	14	0.01
Colville (0)	1	<0.01

Race* (cont.)	Population	%
Comanche (0)	3	<0.01
Cree (2)	6	<0.01
Creek (2)	7	<0.01
Crow (0)	5	<0.01
Delaware (2)	29	0.01
Hopi (0)	0	<0.01
Houma (0)	1	<0.01
Inupiat (Alaska Native) (0)	0	<0.01
Iroquois (74)	254	0.13
Kiowa (0)	1	<0.01
Lumbee (0)	1	<0.01
Menominee (0)	0	<0.01
Mexican American Ind. (7)	21	0.01
Navajo (0)	11	0.01
Osage (0)	1	<0.01
Ottawa (0)	0	<0.01
Paiute (0)	2	<0.01
Pima (0)	1	<0.01
Potawatomi (1)	3	<0.01
Pueblo (0)	2	<0.01
Puget Sound Salish (0)	0	<0.01
Seminole (0)	5	<0.01
Shoshone (0)	0	<0.01
Sioux (12)	39	0.02
South American Ind. (15)	31	0.02
Spanish American Ind. (4)	5	<0.01
Tlingit-Haida (Alaska Native) (0)	0	<0.01
Tohono O'Odham (0)	0	<0.01
Tsimshian (Alaska Native) (0)	0	<0.01
Ute (0)	0	<0.01
Yakama (0)	0	<0.01
Yaqui (2)	2	<0.01
Yuman (0)	0	<0.01
Yup'ik (Alaska Native) (0)	0	<0.01
Asian (7,065)	8,193	4.08
Not Hispanic (7,019)	8,072	4.02
Hispanic (46)	121	0.06
Bangladeshi (56)	67	0.03
Bhutanese (0)	0	<0.01
Burmese (12)	14	0.01
Cambodian (9)	16	0.01
Chinese, ex. Taiwanese (2,135)	2,397	1.19
Filipino (329)	515	0.26
Hmong (0)	0	<0.01
Indian (1,487)	1,683	0.84
Indonesian (24)	34	0.02
Japanese (127)	227	0.11
Korean (980)	1,117	0.56
Laotian (541)	667	0.33
Malaysian (8)	17	0.01
Nepalese (15)	18	0.01
Pakistani (233)	241	0.12
Sri Lankan (14)	22	0.01
Taiwanese (82)	103	0.05
Thai (42)	69	0.03
Vietnamese (716)	838	0.42
Hawaii Native/Pacific Islander (82)	243	0.12
Not Hispanic (60)	191	0.10
Hispanic (22)	52	0.03
Fijian (0)	3	<0.01
Guamanian/Chamorro (25)	43	0.02
Marshallese (0)	0	<0.01
Native Hawaiian (16)	48	0.02
Samoan (6)	12	0.01
Tongan (1)	1	<0.01
White (176,444)	181,009	90.23
Not Hispanic (173,074)	176,969	88.22
Hispanic (3,370)	4,040	2.01

Notes: † The Census 2010 population figure is used to calculate the percentages in the Hispanic Origin and Race categories. Ancestry percentages are based on the 2006-2010 American Community Survey population (not shown); ‡ Numbers in parentheses indicate the number of people reporting a single ancestry; * Numbers in parentheses indicate the number of persons reporting this race alone, not in combination with any other race; Please refer to the Explanation of Data for more information.

Cattaraugus County
Population: 80,317

Ancestry	Population	%
Afghan (0)	0	<0.01
African, Sub-Saharan (11)	52	0.06
African (11)	52	0.06
Cape Verdean (0)	0	<0.01
Ethiopian (0)	0	<0.01
Ghanaian (0)	0	<0.01
Kenyan (0)	0	<0.01
Liberian (0)	0	<0.01
Nigerian (0)	0	<0.01
Senegalese (0)	0	<0.01
Sierra Leonean (0)	0	<0.01
Somalian (0)	0	<0.01
South African (0)	0	<0.01
Sudanese (0)	0	<0.01
Ugandan (0)	0	<0.01
Zimbabwean (0)	0	<0.01
Other Sub-Saharan African (0)	0	<0.01
Albanian (0)	0	<0.01
Alsatian (0)	7	0.01
American (3,710)	3,710	4.59
Arab (161)	452	0.56
Arab (23)	23	0.03
Egyptian (0)	0	<0.01
Iraqi (0)	0	<0.01
Jordanian (0)	0	<0.01
Lebanese (138)	429	0.53
Moroccan (0)	0	<0.01
Palestinian (0)	0	<0.01
Syrian (0)	0	<0.01
Other Arab (0)	0	<0.01
Armenian (2)	6	0.01
Assyrian/Chaldean/Syriac (0)	0	<0.01
Australian (0)	0	<0.01
Austrian (28)	215	0.27
Basque (0)	4	<0.01
Belgian (51)	95	0.12
Brazilian (6)	6	0.01
British (90)	213	0.26
Bulgarian (3)	13	0.02
Cajun (0)	0	<0.01
Canadian (99)	253	0.31
Carpatho Rusyn (0)	5	0.01
Celtic (0)	0	<0.01
Croatian (39)	61	0.08
Cypriot (0)	0	<0.01
Czech (29)	225	0.28
Czechoslovakian (59)	251	0.31
Danish (37)	157	0.19
Dutch (265)	2,195	2.72
Eastern European (51)	51	0.06
English (2,780)	10,168	12.59
Estonian (3)	3	<0.01
European (246)	375	0.46
Finnish (9)	40	0.05
French, ex. Basque (257)	2,353	2.91
French Canadian (241)	614	0.76
German (8,573)	25,659	31.77
German Russian (0)	0	<0.01
Greek (60)	178	0.22
Guyanese (0)	13	0.02
Hungarian (111)	421	0.52
Icelander (0)	0	<0.01
Iranian (0)	0	<0.01
Irish (4,105)	16,140	19.98
Israeli (6)	6	0.01
Italian (3,226)	8,276	10.25
Latvian (0)	0	<0.01
Lithuanian (44)	117	0.14
Luxemburger (0)	4	<0.01
Macedonian (8)	26	0.03
Maltese (0)	0	<0.01
New Zealander (0)	0	<0.01
Northern European (107)	107	0.13
Norwegian (102)	302	0.37
Pennsylvania German (745)	922	1.14

Ancestry (cont.)	Population	%
Polish (3,395)	9,202	11.39
Portuguese (24)	72	0.09
Romanian (38)	88	0.11
Russian (56)	311	0.39
Scandinavian (44)	87	0.11
Scotch-Irish (498)	1,255	1.55
Scottish (474)	1,632	2.02
Serbian (6)	22	0.03
Slavic (10)	78	0.10
Slovak (22)	62	0.08
Slovene (80)	102	0.13
Soviet Union (0)	0	<0.01
Swedish (581)	2,178	2.70
Swiss (52)	379	0.47
Turkish (0)	8	0.01
Ukrainian (51)	270	0.33
Welsh (171)	821	1.02
West Indian, ex. Hispanic (45)	73	0.09
Bahamian (0)	0	<0.01
Barbadian (0)	0	<0.01
Belizean (0)	0	<0.01
Bermudan (0)	0	<0.01
British West Indian (0)	0	<0.01
Dutch West Indian (0)	0	<0.01
Haitian (11)	11	0.01
Jamaican (11)	17	0.02
Trinidadian/Tobagonian (0)	0	<0.01
U.S. Virgin Islander (0)	0	<0.01
West Indian (23)	45	0.06
Other West Indian (0)	0	<0.01
Yugoslavian (37)	56	0.07

Hispanic Origin	Population	%
Hispanic or Latino (of any race)	1,345	1.67
Central American, ex. Mexican	44	0.05
Costa Rican	3	<0.01
Guatemalan	12	0.01
Honduran	9	0.01
Nicaraguan	2	<0.01
Panamanian	5	0.01
Salvadoran	13	0.02
Other Central American	0	<0.01
Cuban	37	0.05
Dominican Republic	30	0.04
Mexican	308	0.38
Puerto Rican	690	0.86
South American	70	0.09
Argentinean	8	0.01
Bolivian	2	<0.01
Chilean	5	0.01
Colombian	21	0.03
Ecuadorian	12	0.01
Paraguayan	0	<0.01
Peruvian	9	0.01
Uruguayan	1	<0.01
Venezuelan	12	0.01
Other South American	0	<0.01
Other Hispanic or Latino	166	0.21

Race*	Population	%
African-American/Black (1,024)	1,619	2.02
Not Hispanic (966)	1,519	1.89
Hispanic (58)	100	0.12
American Indian/Alaska Native (2,443)	3,079	3.83
Not Hispanic (2,361)	2,945	3.67
Hispanic (82)	134	0.17
Alaska Athabascan (Ala. Nat.) (10)	15	0.02
Aleut (Alaska Native) (1)	1	<0.01
Apache (1)	4	<0.01
Arapaho (0)	1	<0.01
Blackfeet (4)	17	0.02
Canadian/French Am. Ind. (9)	15	0.02
Central American Ind. (7)	7	0.01
Cherokee (17)	46	0.06
Cheyenne (1)	5	0.01
Chickasaw (0)	0	<0.01
Chippewa (5)	11	0.01
Choctaw (3)	4	<0.01
Colville (0)	0	<0.01

Race* (cont.)	Population	%
Comanche (0)	0	<0.01
Cree (0)	0	<0.01
Creek (7)	7	0.01
Crow (3)	4	0.01
Delaware (8)	10	0.01
Hopi (0)	0	<0.01
Houma (0)	0	<0.01
Inupiat (Alaska Native) (1)	1	<0.01
Iroquois (1,961)	2,291	2.85
Kiowa (2)	2	<0.01
Lumbee (4)	7	0.01
Menominee (2)	2	<0.01
Mexican American Ind. (2)	3	<0.01
Navajo (4)	6	0.01
Osage (0)	0	<0.01
Ottawa (0)	0	<0.01
Paiute (6)	9	0.01
Pima (0)	0	<0.01
Potawatomi (0)	0	<0.01
Pueblo (0)	0	<0.01
Puget Sound Salish (0)	0	<0.01
Seminole (0)	5	0.01
Shoshone (2)	2	<0.01
Sioux (19)	25	0.03
South American Ind. (12)	14	0.02
Spanish American Ind. (0)	0	<0.01
Tlingit-Haida (Alaska Native) (0)	0	<0.01
Tohono O'Odham (1)	1	<0.01
Tsimshian (Alaska Native) (0)	0	<0.01
Ute (0)	0	<0.01
Yakama (0)	0	<0.01
Yaqui (1)	1	<0.01
Yuman (0)	0	<0.01
Yup'ik (Alaska Native) (0)	0	<0.01
Asian (528)	688	0.86
Not Hispanic (524)	675	0.84
Hispanic (4)	13	0.02
Bangladeshi (1)	1	<0.01
Bhutanese (0)	0	<0.01
Burmese (0)	0	<0.01
Cambodian (2)	4	<0.01
Chinese, ex. Taiwanese (109)	138	0.17
Filipino (61)	92	0.11
Hmong (0)	0	<0.01
Indian (171)	205	0.26
Indonesian (0)	5	0.01
Japanese (23)	46	0.06
Korean (42)	61	0.08
Laotian (13)	21	0.03
Malaysian (2)	2	<0.01
Nepalese (4)	4	<0.01
Pakistani (50)	50	0.06
Sri Lankan (8)	8	0.01
Taiwanese (2)	2	<0.01
Thai (3)	8	0.01
Vietnamese (27)	31	0.04
Hawaii Native/Pacific Islander (15)	36	0.04
Not Hispanic (14)	35	0.04
Hispanic (1)	1	<0.01
Fijian (0)	5	0.01
Guamanian/Chamorro (0)	0	<0.01
Marshallese (0)	0	<0.01
Native Hawaiian (7)	18	0.02
Samoan (0)	1	<0.01
Tongan (0)	0	<0.01
White (74,639)	75,918	94.52
Not Hispanic (73,849)	75,003	93.38
Hispanic (790)	915	1.14

Notes: † The Census 2010 population figure is used to calculate the percentages in the Hispanic Origin and Race categories. Ancestry percentages are based on the 2006-2010 American Community Survey population (not shown); ‡ Numbers in parentheses indicate the number of people reporting a single ancestry; * Numbers in parentheses indicate the number of persons reporting this race alone, not in combination with any other race; Please refer to the Explanation of Data for more information.

Cayuga County

Population: 80,026

Ancestry	Population	%
Afghan (0)	0	<0.01
African, Sub-Saharan (110)	224	0.28
African (110)	206	0.26
Cape Verdean (0)	0	<0.01
Ethiopian (0)	0	<0.01
Ghanaian (0)	0	<0.01
Kenyan (0)	0	<0.01
Liberian (0)	0	<0.01
Nigerian (0)	0	<0.01
Senegalese (0)	0	<0.01
Sierra Leonean (0)	0	<0.01
Somalian (0)	0	<0.01
South African (0)	0	<0.01
Sudanese (0)	0	<0.01
Ugandan (0)	0	<0.01
Zimbabwean (0)	0	<0.01
Other Sub-Saharan African (0)	18	0.02
Albanian (36)	36	0.04
Alsatian (0)	7	0.01
American (3,805)	3,805	4.73
Arab (39)	115	0.14
Arab (2)	5	0.01
Egyptian (0)	0	<0.01
Iraqi (0)	0	<0.01
Jordanian (0)	0	<0.01
Lebanese (20)	65	0.08
Moroccan (0)	0	<0.01
Palestinian (0)	0	<0.01
Syrian (7)	35	0.04
Other Arab (10)	10	0.01
Armenian (0)	11	0.01
Assyrian/Chaldean/Syriac (0)	0	<0.01
Australian (0)	10	0.01
Austrian (57)	197	0.24
Basque (0)	0	<0.01
Belgian (2)	41	0.05
Brazilian (37)	40	0.05
British (120)	275	0.34
Bulgarian (0)	0	<0.01
Cajun (0)	0	<0.01
Canadian (92)	175	0.22
Carpatho Rusyn (0)	0	<0.01
Celtic (6)	6	0.01
Croatian (0)	0	<0.01
Cypriot (0)	0	<0.01
Czech (49)	207	0.26
Czechoslovakian (72)	117	0.15
Danish (65)	201	0.25
Dutch (736)	3,758	4.67
Eastern European (24)	26	0.03
English (4,214)	14,572	18.12
Estonian (0)	0	<0.01
European (439)	513	0.64
Finnish (25)	62	0.08
French, ex. Basque (604)	3,973	4.94
French Canadian (555)	1,669	2.08
German (3,317)	14,518	18.05
German Russian (0)	0	<0.01
Greek (39)	204	0.25
Guyanese (20)	20	0.02
Hungarian (39)	187	0.23
Icelander (0)	3	<0.01
Iranian (0)	0	<0.01
Irish (5,999)	19,589	24.36
Israeli (0)	0	<0.01
Italian (4,906)	11,827	14.70
Latvian (3)	6	0.01
Lithuanian (30)	71	0.09
Luxemburger (0)	0	<0.01
Macedonian (0)	0	<0.01
Maltese (0)	0	<0.01
New Zealander (0)	0	<0.01
Northern European (42)	42	0.05
Norwegian (86)	467	0.58
Pennsylvania German (77)	112	0.14

Ancestry	Population	%
Polish (1,970)	5,462	6.79
Portuguese (8)	74	0.09
Romanian (0)	37	0.05
Russian (179)	482	0.60
Scandinavian (30)	50	0.06
Scotch-Irish (477)	1,048	1.30
Scottish (433)	1,739	2.16
Serbian (0)	4	<0.01
Slavic (37)	37	0.05
Slovak (8)	120	0.15
Slovene (0)	0	<0.01
Soviet Union (0)	0	<0.01
Swedish (100)	712	0.89
Swiss (53)	429	0.53
Turkish (0)	20	0.02
Ukrainian (910)	2,400	2.98
Welsh (214)	839	1.04
West Indian, ex. Hispanic (140)	413	0.51
Bahamian (0)	0	<0.01
Barbadian (0)	8	0.01
Belizean (0)	0	<0.01
Bermudan (0)	0	<0.01
British West Indian (0)	1	<0.01
Dutch West Indian (8)	8	0.01
Haitian (26)	38	0.05
Jamaican (37)	118	0.15
Trinidadian/Tobagonian (34)	45	0.06
U.S. Virgin Islander (0)	0	<0.01
West Indian (35)	195	0.24
Other West Indian (0)	0	<0.01
Yugoslavian (13)	18	0.02

Hispanic Origin	Population	%
Hispanic or Latino (of any race)	1,896	2.37
Central American, ex. Mexican	331	0.41
Costa Rican	6	0.01
Guatemalan	249	0.31
Honduran	17	0.02
Nicaraguan	12	0.01
Panamanian	36	0.04
Salvadoran	10	0.01
Other Central American	1	<0.01
Cuban	75	0.09
Dominican Republic	87	0.11
Mexican	340	0.42
Puerto Rican	799	1.00
South American	85	0.11
Argentinean	2	<0.01
Bolivian	2	<0.01
Chilean	6	0.01
Colombian	29	0.04
Ecuadorian	23	0.03
Paraguayan	1	<0.01
Peruvian	10	0.01
Uruguayan	1	<0.01
Venezuelan	9	0.01
Other South American	2	<0.01
Other Hispanic or Latino	179	0.22

Race*	Population	%
African-American/Black (3,195)	4,052	5.06
Not Hispanic (3,009)	3,782	4.73
Hispanic (186)	270	0.34
American Indian/Alaska Native (283)	703	0.88
Not Hispanic (252)	636	0.79
Hispanic (31)	67	0.08
Alaska Athabascan (Ala. Nat.) (0)	0	<0.01
Aleut (Alaska Native) (1)	1	<0.01
Apache (2)	8	0.01
Arapaho (0)	1	<0.01
Blackfeet (2)	21	0.03
Canadian/French Am. Ind. (5)	6	0.01
Central American Ind. (1)	3	<0.01
Cherokee (13)	62	0.08
Cheyenne (0)	1	<0.01
Chickasaw (0)	0	<0.01
Chippewa (3)	13	0.02
Choctaw (9)	11	0.01
Colville (0)	0	<0.01

Race*	Population	%
Comanche (0)	3	<0.01
Cree (0)	0	<0.01
Creek (1)	1	<0.01
Crow (0)	1	<0.01
Delaware (0)	0	<0.01
Hopi (0)	0	<0.01
Houma (0)	0	<0.01
Inupiat (Alaska Native) (0)	0	<0.01
Iroquois (107)	224	0.28
Kiowa (0)	0	<0.01
Lumbee (5)	5	0.01
Menominee (0)	0	<0.01
Mexican American Ind. (8)	15	0.02
Navajo (4)	5	0.01
Osage (0)	3	<0.01
Ottawa (5)	5	0.01
Paiute (0)	0	<0.01
Pima (0)	0	<0.01
Potawatomi (0)	0	<0.01
Pueblo (2)	2	<0.01
Puget Sound Salish (0)	0	<0.01
Seminole (0)	0	<0.01
Shoshone (0)	0	<0.01
Sioux (6)	13	0.02
South American Ind. (1)	7	0.01
Spanish American Ind. (1)	1	<0.01
Tlingit-Haida (Alaska Native) (0)	0	<0.01
Tohono O'Odham (0)	0	<0.01
Tsimshian (Alaska Native) (0)	0	<0.01
Ute (0)	0	<0.01
Yakama (0)	0	<0.01
Yaqui (0)	0	<0.01
Yuman (0)	0	<0.01
Yup'ik (Alaska Native) (0)	0	<0.01
Asian (390)	544	0.68
Not Hispanic (387)	531	0.66
Hispanic (3)	13	0.02
Bangladeshi (0)	0	<0.01
Bhutanese (0)	0	<0.01
Burmese (10)	10	0.01
Cambodian (3)	4	<0.01
Chinese, ex. Taiwanese (87)	99	0.12
Filipino (55)	98	0.12
Hmong (0)	0	<0.01
Indian (70)	92	0.11
Indonesian (1)	1	<0.01
Japanese (18)	42	0.05
Korean (51)	64	0.08
Laotian (14)	15	0.02
Malaysian (0)	0	<0.01
Nepalese (0)	0	<0.01
Pakistani (13)	13	0.02
Sri Lankan (0)	0	<0.01
Taiwanese (1)	2	<0.01
Thai (13)	20	0.02
Vietnamese (29)	59	0.07
Hawaii Native/Pacific Islander (31)	67	0.08
Not Hispanic (26)	53	0.07
Hispanic (5)	14	0.02
Fijian (1)	1	<0.01
Guamanian/Chamorro (8)	10	0.01
Marshallese (0)	0	<0.01
Native Hawaiian (10)	22	0.03
Samoan (11)	21	0.03
Tongan (0)	0	<0.01
White (74,042)	75,378	94.19
Not Hispanic (73,098)	74,281	92.82
Hispanic (944)	1,097	1.37

*Notes: † The Census 2010 population figure is used to calculate the percentages in the Hispanic Origin and Race categories. Ancestry percentages are based on the 2006-2010 American Community Survey population (not shown); ‡ Numbers in parentheses indicate the number of people reporting a single ancestry; * Numbers in parentheses indicate the number of persons reporting this race alone, not in combination with any other race; Please refer to the Explanation of Data for more information.*

Chautauqua County
Population: 134,905

Ancestry	Population	%
Afghan (0)	0	<0.01
African, Sub-Saharan (28)	147	0.11
African (13)	129	0.10
Cape Verdean (0)	0	<0.01
Ethiopian (0)	0	<0.01
Ghanaian (0)	0	<0.01
Kenyan (0)	0	<0.01
Liberian (0)	0	<0.01
Nigerian (8)	11	0.01
Senegalese (0)	0	<0.01
Sierra Leonean (0)	0	<0.01
Somalian (0)	0	<0.01
South African (0)	0	<0.01
Sudanese (7)	7	0.01
Ugandan (0)	0	<0.01
Zimbabwean (0)	0	<0.01
Other Sub-Saharan African (0)	0	<0.01
Albanian (107)	158	0.12
Alsatian (0)	0	<0.01
American (4,291)	4,291	3.17
Arab (100)	450	0.33
Arab (0)	44	0.03
Egyptian (11)	36	0.03
Iraqi (0)	0	<0.01
Jordanian (0)	0	<0.01
Lebanese (55)	212	0.16
Moroccan (0)	0	<0.01
Palestinian (7)	23	0.02
Syrian (27)	135	0.10
Other Arab (0)	0	<0.01
Armenian (23)	32	0.02
Assyrian/Chaldean/Syriac (0)	0	<0.01
Australian (0)	3	<0.01
Austrian (62)	422	0.31
Basque (0)	0	<0.01
Belgian (33)	45	0.03
Brazilian (19)	28	0.02
British (140)	373	0.28
Bulgarian (13)	13	0.01
Cajun (0)	0	<0.01
Canadian (98)	277	0.20
Carpatho Rusyn (0)	0	<0.01
Celtic (0)	31	0.02
Croatian (97)	210	0.16
Cypriot (0)	0	<0.01
Czech (88)	400	0.30
Czechoslovakian (43)	151	0.11
Danish (203)	649	0.48
Dutch (960)	4,144	3.06
Eastern European (31)	31	0.02
English (6,689)	21,635	15.99
Estonian (3)	3	<0.01
European (588)	620	0.46
Finnish (16)	163	0.12
French, ex. Basque (460)	3,331	2.46
French Canadian (337)	870	0.64
German (10,307)	33,780	24.97
German Russian (0)	0	<0.01
Greek (75)	159	0.12
Guyanese (0)	0	<0.01
Hungarian (273)	948	0.70
Icelander (0)	0	<0.01
Iranian (4)	4	<0.01
Irish (5,085)	20,147	14.89
Israeli (0)	16	0.01
Italian (9,579)	21,679	16.03
Latvian (5)	21	0.02
Lithuanian (11)	59	0.04
Luxemburger (0)	0	<0.01
Macedonian (50)	50	0.04
Maltese (0)	0	<0.01
New Zealander (0)	6	<0.01
Northern European (72)	80	0.06
Norwegian (298)	684	0.51
Pennsylvania German (636)	967	0.71

Ancestry	Population	%
Polish (5,698)	14,377	10.63
Portuguese (0)	28	0.02
Romanian (1)	88	0.07
Russian (127)	667	0.49
Scandinavian (88)	145	0.11
Scotch-Irish (567)	2,235	1.65
Scottish (497)	2,598	1.92
Serbian (0)	0	<0.01
Slavic (95)	169	0.12
Slovak (110)	254	0.19
Slovene (10)	38	0.03
Soviet Union (0)	0	<0.01
Swedish (6,798)	17,330	12.81
Swiss (191)	536	0.40
Turkish (0)	5	<0.01
Ukrainian (171)	372	0.28
Welsh (176)	1,038	0.77
West Indian, ex. Hispanic (99)	225	0.17
Bahamian (0)	0	<0.01
Barbadian (0)	3	<0.01
Belizean (0)	6	<0.01
Bermudan (0)	0	<0.01
British West Indian (3)	3	<0.01
Dutch West Indian (0)	3	<0.01
Haitian (36)	67	0.05
Jamaican (12)	85	0.06
Trinidadian/Tobagonian (23)	31	0.02
U.S. Virgin Islander (0)	0	<0.01
West Indian (25)	27	0.02
Other West Indian (0)	0	<0.01
Yugoslavian (28)	79	0.06

Hispanic Origin	Population	%
Hispanic or Latino (of any race)	8,241	6.11
Central American, ex. Mexican	148	0.11
Costa Rican	14	0.01
Guatemalan	56	0.04
Honduran	20	0.01
Nicaraguan	7	0.01
Panamanian	7	0.01
Salvadoran	44	0.03
Other Central American	0	<0.01
Cuban	101	0.07
Dominican Republic	167	0.12
Mexican	851	0.63
Puerto Rican	6,401	4.74
South American	180	0.13
Argentinean	26	0.02
Bolivian	5	<0.01
Chilean	5	<0.01
Colombian	70	0.05
Ecuadorian	30	0.02
Paraguayan	1	<0.01
Peruvian	22	0.02
Uruguayan	3	<0.01
Venezuelan	18	0.01
Other South American	0	<0.01
Other Hispanic or Latino	393	0.29

Race*	Population	%
African-American/Black (3,197)	4,710	3.49
Not Hispanic (2,763)	4,006	2.97
Hispanic (434)	704	0.52
American Indian/Alaska Native (689)	1,462	1.08
Not Hispanic (576)	1,258	0.93
Hispanic (113)	204	0.15
Alaska Athabascan (Ala. Nat.) (1)	1	<0.01
Aleut (Alaska Native) (0)	0	<0.01
Apache (2)	2	<0.01
Arapaho (1)	1	<0.01
Blackfeet (7)	46	0.03
Canadian/French Am. Ind. (4)	9	0.01
Central American Ind. (1)	1	<0.01
Cherokee (26)	116	0.09
Cheyenne (0)	2	<0.01
Chickasaw (0)	0	<0.01
Chippewa (5)	20	0.01
Choctaw (1)	1	<0.01
Colville (0)	0	<0.01

Race*	Population	%
Comanche (0)	0	<0.01
Cree (0)	0	<0.01
Creek (2)	2	<0.01
Crow (1)	1	<0.01
Delaware (4)	5	<0.01
Hopi (0)	0	<0.01
Houma (1)	1	<0.01
Inupiat (Alaska Native) (5)	6	<0.01
Iroquois (365)	615	0.46
Kiowa (0)	0	<0.01
Lumbee (0)	0	<0.01
Menominee (0)	0	<0.01
Mexican American Ind. (22)	27	0.02
Navajo (3)	3	<0.01
Osage (0)	0	<0.01
Ottawa (0)	0	<0.01
Paiute (0)	0	<0.01
Pima (0)	0	<0.01
Potawatomi (0)	2	<0.01
Pueblo (3)	4	<0.01
Puget Sound Salish (0)	0	<0.01
Seminole (0)	2	<0.01
Shoshone (0)	0	<0.01
Sioux (3)	6	<0.01
South American Ind. (6)	18	0.01
Spanish American Ind. (0)	0	<0.01
Tlingit-Haida (Alaska Native) (0)	0	<0.01
Tohono O'Odham (0)	0	<0.01
Tsimshian (Alaska Native) (0)	0	<0.01
Ute (0)	0	<0.01
Yakama (0)	0	<0.01
Yaqui (0)	0	<0.01
Yuman (0)	0	<0.01
Yup'ik (Alaska Native) (0)	1	<0.01
Asian (688)	945	0.70
Not Hispanic (676)	892	0.66
Hispanic (12)	53	0.04
Bangladeshi (1)	1	<0.01
Bhutanese (0)	0	<0.01
Burmese (5)	5	<0.01
Cambodian (5)	6	<0.01
Chinese, ex. Taiwanese (169)	203	0.15
Filipino (105)	176	0.13
Hmong (1)	1	<0.01
Indian (130)	152	0.11
Indonesian (5)	15	0.01
Japanese (33)	71	0.05
Korean (105)	142	0.11
Laotian (1)	9	0.01
Malaysian (0)	3	<0.01
Nepalese (0)	0	<0.01
Pakistani (41)	42	0.03
Sri Lankan (3)	5	<0.01
Taiwanese (4)	7	0.01
Thai (22)	29	0.02
Vietnamese (36)	49	0.04
Hawaii Native/Pacific Islander (36)	100	0.07
Not Hispanic (31)	73	0.05
Hispanic (5)	27	0.02
Fijian (2)	2	<0.01
Guamanian/Chamorro (8)	16	0.01
Marshallese (0)	0	<0.01
Native Hawaiian (8)	24	0.02
Samoan (5)	8	0.01
Tongan (0)	0	<0.01
White (124,875)	127,434	94.46
Not Hispanic (120,463)	122,474	90.79
Hispanic (4,412)	4,960	3.68

Notes: † The Census 2010 population figure is used to calculate the percentages in the Hispanic Origin and Race categories. Ancestry percentages are based on the 2006-2010 American Community Survey population (not shown); ‡ Numbers in parentheses indicate the number of people reporting a single ancestry; * Numbers in parentheses indicate the number of persons reporting this race alone, not in combination with any other race; Please refer to the Explanation of Data for more information.

Chemung County

Population: 88,830

Ancestry	Population	%
Afghan (0)	0	<0.01
African, Sub-Saharan (234)	248	0.28
African (172)	186	0.21
Cape Verdean (0)	0	<0.01
Ethiopian (11)	11	0.01
Ghanaian (11)	11	0.01
Kenyan (39)	39	0.04
Liberian (0)	0	<0.01
Nigerian (1)	1	<0.01
Senegalese (0)	0	<0.01
Sierra Leonean (0)	0	<0.01
Somalian (0)	0	<0.01
South African (0)	0	<0.01
Sudanese (0)	0	<0.01
Ugandan (0)	0	<0.01
Zimbabwean (0)	0	<0.01
Other Sub-Saharan African (0)	0	<0.01
Albanian (0)	0	<0.01
Alsatian (0)	10	0.01
American (7,001)	7,001	7.89
Arab (185)	293	0.33
Arab (0)	0	<0.01
Egyptian (4)	4	<0.01
Iraqi (0)	0	<0.01
Jordanian (0)	0	<0.01
Lebanese (151)	245	0.28
Moroccan (0)	0	<0.01
Palestinian (18)	18	0.02
Syrian (0)	14	0.02
Other Arab (12)	12	0.01
Armenian (0)	37	0.04
Assyrian/Chaldean/Syriac (0)	0	<0.01
Australian (0)	0	<0.01
Austrian (60)	214	0.24
Basque (0)	0	<0.01
Belgian (37)	62	0.07
Brazilian (0)	0	<0.01
British (82)	151	0.17
Bulgarian (12)	12	0.01
Cajun (0)	0	<0.01
Canadian (175)	269	0.30
Carpatho Rusyn (0)	0	<0.01
Celtic (2)	12	0.01
Croatian (15)	62	0.07
Cypriot (0)	0	<0.01
Czech (142)	369	0.42
Czechoslovakian (104)	259	0.29
Danish (78)	202	0.23
Dutch (764)	3,692	4.16
Eastern European (32)	32	0.04
English (3,931)	12,489	14.08
Estonian (12)	12	0.01
European (260)	282	0.32
Finnish (144)	475	0.54
French, ex. Basque (455)	2,813	3.17
French Canadian (291)	894	1.01
German (5,023)	18,529	20.89
German Russian (0)	0	<0.01
Greek (134)	312	0.35
Guyanese (0)	0	<0.01
Hungarian (110)	267	0.30
Icelander (0)	0	<0.01
Iranian (12)	12	0.01
Irish (5,564)	17,907	20.19
Israeli (0)	20	0.02
Italian (3,852)	10,020	11.30
Latvian (0)	55	0.06
Lithuanian (78)	183	0.21
Luxemburger (0)	0	<0.01
Macedonian (0)	0	<0.01
Maltese (9)	9	0.01
New Zealander (0)	0	<0.01
Northern European (13)	13	0.01
Norwegian (99)	591	0.67
Pennsylvania German (229)	522	0.59

Ancestry (cont.)	Population	%
Polish (2,122)	6,087	6.86
Portuguese (35)	115	0.13
Romanian (0)	43	0.05
Russian (129)	600	0.68
Scandinavian (4)	23	0.03
Scotch-Irish (616)	1,482	1.67
Scottish (456)	1,673	1.89
Serbian (11)	11	0.01
Slavic (4)	84	0.09
Slovak (44)	201	0.23
Slovene (15)	41	0.05
Soviet Union (0)	0	<0.01
Swedish (364)	1,326	1.49
Swiss (26)	166	0.19
Turkish (10)	21	0.02
Ukrainian (548)	1,369	1.54
Welsh (366)	1,410	1.59
West Indian, ex. Hispanic (228)	300	0.34
Bahamian (31)	31	0.03
Barbadian (26)	26	0.03
Belizean (0)	0	<0.01
Bermudan (0)	0	<0.01
British West Indian (14)	41	0.05
Dutch West Indian (0)	0	<0.01
Haitian (51)	51	0.06
Jamaican (72)	107	0.12
Trinidadian/Tobagonian (0)	0	<0.01
U.S. Virgin Islander (0)	0	<0.01
West Indian (23)	33	0.04
Other West Indian (11)	11	0.01
Yugoslavian (139)	193	0.22

Hispanic Origin	Population	%
Hispanic or Latino (of any race)	2,240	2.52
Central American, ex. Mexican	121	0.14
Costa Rican	18	0.02
Guatemalan	35	0.04
Honduran	15	0.02
Nicaraguan	5	0.01
Panamanian	31	0.03
Salvadoran	17	0.02
Other Central American	0	<0.01
Cuban	82	0.09
Dominican Republic	100	0.11
Mexican	404	0.45
Puerto Rican	1,156	1.30
South American	119	0.13
Argentinean	15	0.02
Bolivian	8	0.01
Chilean	2	<0.01
Colombian	26	0.03
Ecuadorian	23	0.03
Paraguayan	0	<0.01
Peruvian	27	0.03
Uruguayan	3	<0.01
Venezuelan	6	0.01
Other South American	9	0.01
Other Hispanic or Latino	258	0.29

Race*	Population	%
African-American/Black (5,828)	7,391	8.32
Not Hispanic (5,528)	6,946	7.82
Hispanic (300)	445	0.50
American Indian/Alaska Native (233)	812	0.91
Not Hispanic (206)	713	0.80
Hispanic (27)	99	0.11
Alaska Athabascan (Ala. Nat.) (0)	0	<0.01
Aleut (Alaska Native) (0)	0	<0.01
Apache (6)	8	0.01
Arapaho (0)	0	<0.01
Blackfeet (6)	44	0.05
Canadian/French Am. Ind. (0)	5	0.01
Central American Ind. (0)	1	<0.01
Cherokee (21)	121	0.14
Cheyenne (0)	0	<0.01
Chickasaw (0)	1	<0.01
Chippewa (2)	3	<0.01
Choctaw (0)	0	<0.01
Colville (0)	0	<0.01

Race* (cont.)	Population	%
Comanche (0)	0	<0.01
Cree (0)	3	<0.01
Creek (0)	1	<0.01
Crow (0)	0	<0.01
Delaware (0)	1	<0.01
Hopi (0)	0	<0.01
Houma (2)	2	<0.01
Inupiat (Alaska Native) (0)	0	<0.01
Iroquois (74)	153	0.17
Kiowa (1)	1	<0.01
Lumbee (0)	0	<0.01
Menominee (0)	0	<0.01
Mexican American Ind. (2)	8	0.01
Navajo (0)	11	0.01
Osage (0)	0	<0.01
Ottawa (0)	0	<0.01
Paiute (0)	0	<0.01
Pima (0)	0	<0.01
Potawatomi (0)	1	<0.01
Pueblo (1)	1	<0.01
Puget Sound Salish (0)	2	<0.01
Seminole (0)	6	0.01
Shoshone (0)	0	<0.01
Sioux (1)	16	0.02
South American Ind. (3)	7	0.01
Spanish American Ind. (0)	1	<0.01
Tlingit-Haida (Alaska Native) (3)	3	<0.01
Tohono O'Odham (0)	1	<0.01
Tsimshian (Alaska Native) (0)	0	<0.01
Ute (0)	0	<0.01
Yakama (0)	1	<0.01
Yaqui (0)	0	<0.01
Yuman (0)	0	<0.01
Yup'ik (Alaska Native) (0)	0	<0.01
Asian (1,057)	1,334	1.50
Not Hispanic (1,041)	1,296	1.46
Hispanic (16)	38	0.04
Bangladeshi (20)	20	0.02
Bhutanese (0)	0	<0.01
Burmese (0)	0	<0.01
Cambodian (2)	2	<0.01
Chinese, ex. Taiwanese (279)	312	0.35
Filipino (95)	164	0.18
Hmong (0)	0	<0.01
Indian (261)	310	0.35
Indonesian (4)	5	<0.01
Japanese (53)	100	0.11
Korean (79)	128	0.14
Laotian (12)	32	0.04
Malaysian (2)	3	<0.01
Nepalese (3)	3	<0.01
Pakistani (97)	108	0.12
Sri Lankan (11)	12	0.01
Taiwanese (15)	21	0.02
Thai (9)	18	0.02
Vietnamese (63)	68	0.08
Hawaii Native/Pacific Islander (20)	56	0.06
Not Hispanic (14)	44	0.05
Hispanic (6)	12	0.01
Fijian (0)	0	<0.01
Guamanian/Chamorro (5)	12	0.01
Marshallese (0)	0	<0.01
Native Hawaiian (8)	17	0.02
Samoan (6)	11	0.01
Tongan (0)	1	<0.01
White (78,771)	81,009	91.20
Not Hispanic (77,643)	79,627	89.64
Hispanic (1,128)	1,382	1.56

Notes: † The Census 2010 population figure is used to calculate the percentages in the Hispanic Origin and Race categories. Ancestry percentages are based on the 2006-2010 American Community Survey population (not shown); ‡ Numbers in parentheses indicate the number of people reporting a single ancestry; * Numbers in parentheses indicate the number of persons reporting this race alone, not in combination with any other race; Please refer to the Explanation of Data for more information.

Chenango County
Population: 50,477

Ancestry	Population	%
Afghan (0)	0	<0.01
African, Sub-Saharan (11)	53	0.10
African (2)	31	0.06
Cape Verdean (0)	0	<0.01
Ethiopian (0)	0	<0.01
Ghanaian (5)	5	0.01
Kenyan (0)	0	<0.01
Liberian (4)	4	0.01
Nigerian (0)	13	0.03
Senegalese (0)	0	<0.01
Sierra Leonean (0)	0	<0.01
Somalian (0)	0	<0.01
South African (0)	0	<0.01
Sudanese (0)	0	<0.01
Ugandan (0)	0	<0.01
Zimbabwean (0)	0	<0.01
Other Sub-Saharan African (0)	0	<0.01
Albanian (0)	0	<0.01
Alsatian (0)	13	0.03
American (3,611)	3,611	7.07
Arab (39)	94	0.18
Arab (0)	0	<0.01
Egyptian (2)	2	<0.01
Iraqi (0)	0	<0.01
Jordanian (0)	0	<0.01
Lebanese (33)	88	0.17
Moroccan (0)	0	<0.01
Palestinian (0)	0	<0.01
Syrian (4)	4	0.01
Other Arab (0)	0	<0.01
Armenian (3)	5	0.01
Assyrian/Chaldean/Syriac (0)	0	<0.01
Australian (0)	12	0.02
Austrian (37)	147	0.29
Basque (0)	0	<0.01
Belgian (0)	7	0.01
Brazilian (3)	3	0.01
British (91)	185	0.36
Bulgarian (0)	0	<0.01
Cajun (0)	0	<0.01
Canadian (47)	133	0.26
Carpatho Rusyn (0)	0	<0.01
Celtic (3)	3	<0.01
Croatian (0)	0	<0.01
Cypriot (0)	0	<0.01
Czech (43)	169	0.33
Czechoslovakian (36)	60	0.12
Danish (89)	225	0.44
Dutch (506)	2,167	4.25
Eastern European (109)	109	0.21
English (3,435)	9,260	18.14
Estonian (9)	14	0.03
European (423)	486	0.95
Finnish (7)	41	0.08
French, ex. Basque (426)	2,237	4.38
French Canadian (225)	653	1.28
German (2,635)	8,972	17.58
German Russian (0)	0	<0.01
Greek (27)	71	0.14
Guyanese (0)	0	<0.01
Hungarian (103)	456	0.89
Icelander (0)	0	<0.01
Iranian (48)	48	0.09
Irish (2,193)	8,509	16.67
Israeli (0)	0	<0.01
Italian (1,990)	4,673	9.15
Latvian (0)	0	<0.01
Lithuanian (116)	196	0.38
Luxemburger (0)	0	<0.01
Macedonian (0)	0	<0.01
Maltese (0)	0	<0.01
New Zealander (0)	0	<0.01
Northern European (173)	173	0.34
Norwegian (108)	432	0.85
Pennsylvania German (24)	86	0.17

Ancestry (cont.)	Population	%
Polish (664)	1,903	3.73
Portuguese (56)	98	0.19
Romanian (2)	18	0.04
Russian (204)	337	0.66
Scandinavian (21)	75	0.15
Scotch-Irish (337)	1,126	2.21
Scottish (250)	1,081	2.12
Serbian (0)	0	<0.01
Slavic (0)	11	0.02
Slovak (80)	166	0.33
Slovene (0)	0	<0.01
Soviet Union (0)	0	<0.01
Swedish (120)	522	1.02
Swiss (182)	301	0.59
Turkish (7)	7	0.01
Ukrainian (40)	117	0.23
Welsh (230)	1,011	1.98
West Indian, ex. Hispanic (39)	50	0.10
Bahamian (0)	0	<0.01
Barbadian (0)	0	<0.01
Belizean (0)	0	<0.01
Bermudan (0)	0	<0.01
British West Indian (0)	0	<0.01
Dutch West Indian (3)	6	0.01
Haitian (0)	3	0.01
Jamaican (36)	41	0.08
Trinidadian/Tobagonian (0)	0	<0.01
U.S. Virgin Islander (0)	0	<0.01
West Indian (0)	0	<0.01
Other West Indian (0)	0	<0.01
Yugoslavian (10)	51	0.10

Hispanic Origin	Population	%
Hispanic or Latino (of any race)	929	1.84
Central American, ex. Mexican	43	0.09
Costa Rican	6	0.01
Guatemalan	23	0.05
Honduran	7	0.01
Nicaraguan	0	<0.01
Panamanian	4	0.01
Salvadoran	3	0.01
Other Central American	0	<0.01
Cuban	44	0.09
Dominican Republic	27	0.05
Mexican	175	0.35
Puerto Rican	450	0.89
South American	55	0.11
Argentinean	2	<0.01
Bolivian	0	<0.01
Chilean	4	0.01
Colombian	26	0.05
Ecuadorian	17	0.03
Paraguayan	4	0.01
Peruvian	2	<0.01
Uruguayan	0	<0.01
Venezuelan	0	<0.01
Other South American	0	<0.01
Other Hispanic or Latino	135	0.27

Race*	Population	%
African-American/Black (345)	562	1.11
Not Hispanic (323)	527	1.04
Hispanic (22)	35	0.07
American Indian/Alaska Native (172)	453	0.90
Not Hispanic (151)	426	0.84
Hispanic (21)	27	0.05
Alaska Athabascan (Ala. Nat.) (0)	0	<0.01
Aleut (Alaska Native) (1)	1	<0.01
Apache (1)	5	0.01
Arapaho (0)	0	<0.01
Blackfeet (3)	25	0.05
Canadian/French Am. Ind. (0)	0	<0.01
Central American Ind. (3)	3	0.01
Cherokee (12)	43	0.09
Cheyenne (1)	1	<0.01
Chickasaw (0)	0	<0.01
Chippewa (1)	1	<0.01
Choctaw (4)	6	0.01
Colville (0)	0	<0.01

Race* (cont.)	Population	%
Comanche (0)	1	<0.01
Cree (1)	1	<0.01
Creek (0)	0	<0.01
Crow (0)	0	<0.01
Delaware (5)	6	0.01
Hopi (0)	0	<0.01
Houma (1)	1	<0.01
Inupiat (Alaska Native) (0)	0	<0.01
Iroquois (40)	85	0.17
Kiowa (0)	0	<0.01
Lumbee (3)	3	0.01
Menominee (0)	0	<0.01
Mexican American Ind. (2)	3	0.01
Navajo (1)	1	<0.01
Osage (0)	0	<0.01
Ottawa (0)	0	<0.01
Paiute (0)	0	<0.01
Pima (0)	0	<0.01
Potawatomi (0)	0	<0.01
Pueblo (1)	2	<0.01
Puget Sound Salish (0)	0	<0.01
Seminole (0)	0	<0.01
Shoshone (0)	2	<0.01
Sioux (4)	12	0.02
South American Ind. (0)	3	0.01
Spanish American Ind. (2)	2	<0.01
Tlingit-Haida (Alaska Native) (2)	2	<0.01
Tohono O'Odham (0)	0	<0.01
Tsimshian (Alaska Native) (0)	0	<0.01
Ute (0)	0	<0.01
Yakama (0)	0	<0.01
Yaqui (0)	0	<0.01
Yuman (0)	0	<0.01
Yup'ik (Alaska Native) (0)	0	<0.01
Asian (204)	315	0.62
Not Hispanic (200)	306	0.61
Hispanic (4)	9	0.02
Bangladeshi (0)	0	<0.01
Bhutanese (0)	0	<0.01
Burmese (0)	0	<0.01
Cambodian (0)	0	<0.01
Chinese, ex. Taiwanese (58)	65	0.13
Filipino (40)	82	0.16
Hmong (0)	0	<0.01
Indian (33)	43	0.09
Indonesian (3)	3	0.01
Japanese (13)	22	0.04
Korean (29)	47	0.09
Laotian (2)	5	0.01
Malaysian (2)	5	0.01
Nepalese (0)	0	<0.01
Pakistani (0)	0	<0.01
Sri Lankan (0)	0	<0.01
Taiwanese (7)	10	0.02
Thai (3)	6	0.01
Vietnamese (10)	17	0.03
Hawaii Native/Pacific Islander (6)	27	0.05
Not Hispanic (4)	24	0.05
Hispanic (2)	3	<0.01
Fijian (0)	0	<0.01
Guamanian/Chamorro (0)	3	0.01
Marshallese (0)	0	<0.01
Native Hawaiian (4)	12	0.02
Samoan (1)	1	<0.01
Tongan (0)	0	<0.01
White (48,896)	49,525	98.11
Not Hispanic (48,265)	48,823	96.72
Hispanic (631)	702	1.39

Notes: † The Census 2010 population figure is used to calculate the percentages in the Hispanic Origin and Race categories. Ancestry percentages are based on the 2006-2010 American Community Survey population (not shown); ‡ Numbers in parentheses indicate the number of people reporting a single ancestry; * Numbers in parentheses indicate the number of persons reporting this race alone, not in combination with any other race; Please refer to the Explanation of Data for more information.

Clinton County
Population: 82,128

Ancestry	Population	%
Afghan (0)	0	<0.01
African, Sub-Saharan (153)	172	0.21
African (85)	104	0.13
Cape Verdean (0)	0	<0.01
Ethiopian (8)	8	0.01
Ghanaian (13)	13	0.02
Kenyan (0)	0	<0.01
Liberian (0)	0	<0.01
Nigerian (0)	0	<0.01
Senegalese (0)	0	<0.01
Sierra Leonean (0)	0	<0.01
Somalian (0)	0	<0.01
South African (0)	0	<0.01
Sudanese (0)	0	<0.01
Ugandan (0)	0	<0.01
Zimbabwean (0)	0	<0.01
Other Sub-Saharan African (47)	47	0.06
Albanian (70)	70	0.08
Alsatian (0)	0	<0.01
American (7,652)	7,652	9.29
Arab (114)	350	0.42
Arab (12)	18	0.02
Egyptian (13)	19	0.02
Iraqi (0)	0	<0.01
Jordanian (0)	2	<0.01
Lebanese (59)	257	0.31
Moroccan (10)	10	0.01
Palestinian (0)	0	<0.01
Syrian (19)	43	0.05
Other Arab (1)	1	<0.01
Armenian (25)	130	0.16
Assyrian/Chaldean/Syriac (0)	0	<0.01
Australian (0)	27	0.03
Austrian (5)	234	0.28
Basque (0)	0	<0.01
Belgian (0)	39	0.05
Brazilian (22)	22	0.03
British (97)	286	0.35
Bulgarian (0)	0	<0.01
Cajun (21)	21	0.03
Canadian (602)	893	1.08
Carpatho Rusyn (0)	0	<0.01
Celtic (0)	10	0.01
Croatian (0)	48	0.06
Cypriot (0)	0	<0.01
Czech (48)	189	0.23
Czechoslovakian (0)	19	0.02
Danish (42)	149	0.18
Dutch (124)	1,267	1.54
Eastern European (39)	58	0.07
English (3,020)	9,045	10.98
Estonian (14)	31	0.04
European (370)	388	0.47
Finnish (54)	150	0.18
French, ex. Basque (7,155)	20,474	24.85
French Canadian (4,464)	6,631	8.05
German (1,440)	7,220	8.76
German Russian (0)	0	<0.01
Greek (76)	174	0.21
Guyanese (5)	19	0.02
Hungarian (30)	225	0.27
Icelander (7)	23	0.03
Iranian (167)	167	0.20
Irish (3,162)	13,491	16.38
Israeli (0)	0	<0.01
Italian (2,215)	6,104	7.41
Latvian (0)	2	<0.01
Lithuanian (61)	362	0.44
Luxemburger (0)	0	<0.01
Macedonian (0)	0	<0.01
Maltese (28)	28	0.03
New Zealander (0)	0	<0.01
Northern European (17)	17	0.02
Norwegian (77)	411	0.50
Pennsylvania German (4)	27	0.03

Ancestry	Population	%
Polish (720)	2,685	3.26
Portuguese (74)	164	0.20
Romanian (0)	80	0.10
Russian (266)	688	0.84
Scandinavian (9)	33	0.04
Scotch-Irish (620)	1,300	1.58
Scottish (519)	1,860	2.26
Serbian (0)	14	0.02
Slavic (0)	27	0.03
Slovak (32)	118	0.14
Slovene (0)	47	0.06
Soviet Union (0)	0	<0.01
Swedish (83)	585	0.71
Swiss (39)	106	0.13
Turkish (34)	34	0.04
Ukrainian (140)	255	0.31
Welsh (80)	406	0.49
West Indian, ex. Hispanic (140)	248	0.30
Bahamian (0)	0	<0.01
Barbadian (0)	4	<0.01
Belizean (0)	0	<0.01
Bermudan (0)	0	<0.01
British West Indian (43)	56	0.07
Dutch West Indian (0)	0	<0.01
Haitian (0)	14	0.02
Jamaican (35)	39	0.05
Trinidadian/Tobagonian (26)	48	0.06
U.S. Virgin Islander (0)	0	<0.01
West Indian (36)	87	0.11
Other West Indian (0)	0	<0.01
Yugoslavian (0)	10	0.01

Hispanic Origin	Population	%
Hispanic or Latino (of any race)	2,054	2.50
Central American, ex. Mexican	155	0.19
Costa Rican	12	0.01
Guatemalan	27	0.03
Honduran	31	0.04
Nicaraguan	15	0.02
Panamanian	25	0.03
Salvadoran	44	0.05
Other Central American	1	<0.01
Cuban	95	0.12
Dominican Republic	207	0.25
Mexican	302	0.37
Puerto Rican	928	1.13
South American	151	0.18
Argentinean	10	0.01
Bolivian	2	<0.01
Chilean	11	0.01
Colombian	58	0.07
Ecuadorian	24	0.03
Paraguayan	8	0.01
Peruvian	24	0.03
Uruguayan	2	<0.01
Venezuelan	10	0.01
Other South American	2	<0.01
Other Hispanic or Latino	216	0.26

Race*	Population	%
African-American/Black (3,209)	3,704	4.51
Not Hispanic (2,953)	3,383	4.12
Hispanic (256)	321	0.39
American Indian/Alaska Native (286)	747	0.91
Not Hispanic (266)	685	0.83
Hispanic (20)	62	0.08
Alaska Athabascan (Ala. Nat.) (2)	2	<0.01
Aleut (Alaska Native) (0)	1	<0.01
Apache (0)	10	0.01
Arapaho (1)	1	<0.01
Blackfeet (6)	29	0.04
Canadian/French Am. Ind. (11)	22	0.03
Central American Ind. (1)	3	<0.01
Cherokee (13)	79	0.10
Cheyenne (0)	1	<0.01
Chickasaw (0)	2	<0.01
Chippewa (5)	9	0.01
Choctaw (2)	2	<0.01
Colville (0)	0	<0.01

Race* (cont.)	Population	%
Comanche (1)	3	<0.01
Cree (2)	2	<0.01
Creek (0)	1	<0.01
Crow (1)	3	<0.01
Delaware (0)	0	<0.01
Hopi (0)	0	<0.01
Houma (0)	0	<0.01
Inupiat (Alaska Native) (2)	2	<0.01
Iroquois (73)	136	0.17
Kiowa (0)	0	<0.01
Lumbee (0)	0	<0.01
Menominee (0)	0	<0.01
Mexican American Ind. (2)	4	<0.01
Navajo (0)	1	<0.01
Osage (0)	0	<0.01
Ottawa (0)	0	<0.01
Paiute (0)	0	<0.01
Pima (0)	0	<0.01
Potawatomi (1)	2	<0.01
Pueblo (1)	1	<0.01
Puget Sound Salish (0)	1	<0.01
Seminole (0)	0	<0.01
Shoshone (0)	0	<0.01
Sioux (12)	22	0.03
South American Ind. (1)	7	0.01
Spanish American Ind. (0)	0	<0.01
Tlingit-Haida (Alaska Native) (0)	0	<0.01
Tohono O'Odham (0)	0	<0.01
Tsimshian (Alaska Native) (0)	0	<0.01
Ute (0)	0	<0.01
Yakama (0)	0	<0.01
Yaqui (0)	0	<0.01
Yuman (0)	0	<0.01
Yup'ik (Alaska Native) (1)	1	<0.01
Asian (898)	1,147	1.40
Not Hispanic (890)	1,121	1.36
Hispanic (8)	26	0.03
Bangladeshi (2)	2	<0.01
Bhutanese (0)	0	<0.01
Burmese (1)	2	<0.01
Cambodian (2)	3	<0.01
Chinese, ex. Taiwanese (238)	273	0.33
Filipino (114)	185	0.23
Hmong (0)	0	<0.01
Indian (160)	182	0.22
Indonesian (0)	3	<0.01
Japanese (91)	125	0.15
Korean (96)	139	0.17
Laotian (0)	5	0.01
Malaysian (2)	4	<0.01
Nepalese (9)	9	0.01
Pakistani (30)	35	0.04
Sri Lankan (8)	13	0.02
Taiwanese (10)	11	0.01
Thai (20)	38	0.05
Vietnamese (66)	74	0.09
Hawaii Native/Pacific Islander (19)	58	0.07
Not Hispanic (15)	42	0.05
Hispanic (4)	16	0.02
Fijian (0)	0	<0.01
Guamanian/Chamorro (6)	9	0.01
Marshallese (0)	0	<0.01
Native Hawaiian (5)	17	0.02
Samoan (2)	7	0.01
Tongan (0)	0	<0.01
White (75,997)	77,099	93.88
Not Hispanic (74,832)	75,785	92.28
Hispanic (1,165)	1,314	1.60

Notes: † The Census 2010 population figure is used to calculate the percentages in the Hispanic Origin and Race categories. Ancestry percentages are based on the 2006-2010 American Community Survey population (not shown); ‡ Numbers in parentheses indicate the number of people reporting a single ancestry; * Numbers in parentheses indicate the number of persons reporting this race alone, not in combination with any other race; Please refer to the Explanation of Data for more information.

Columbia County
Population: 63,096

Ancestry	Population	%
Afghan (0)	0	<0.01
African, Sub-Saharan (171)	200	0.32
African (102)	130	0.21
Cape Verdean (0)	0	<0.01
Ethiopian (0)	0	<0.01
Ghanaian (0)	0	<0.01
Kenyan (0)	0	<0.01
Liberian (16)	16	0.03
Nigerian (29)	29	0.05
Senegalese (0)	0	<0.01
Sierra Leonean (0)	0	<0.01
Somalian (0)	0	<0.01
South African (24)	25	0.04
Sudanese (0)	0	<0.01
Ugandan (0)	0	<0.01
Zimbabwean (0)	0	<0.01
Other Sub-Saharan African (0)	0	<0.01
Albanian (0)	0	<0.01
Alsatian (0)	0	<0.01
American (5,649)	5,649	8.93
Arab (200)	246	0.39
Arab (127)	127	0.20
Egyptian (0)	3	<0.01
Iraqi (0)	0	<0.01
Jordanian (0)	0	<0.01
Lebanese (17)	32	0.05
Moroccan (43)	43	0.07
Palestinian (0)	24	0.04
Syrian (2)	6	0.01
Other Arab (11)	11	0.02
Armenian (39)	60	0.09
Assyrian/Chaldean/Syriac (0)	0	<0.01
Australian (4)	11	0.02
Austrian (60)	369	0.58
Basque (0)	4	0.01
Belgian (3)	46	0.07
Brazilian (72)	74	0.12
British (174)	400	0.63
Bulgarian (0)	0	<0.01
Cajun (0)	14	0.02
Canadian (25)	166	0.26
Carpatho Rusyn (0)	0	<0.01
Celtic (21)	21	0.03
Croatian (7)	14	0.02
Cypriot (0)	0	<0.01
Czech (52)	291	0.46
Czechoslovakian (41)	99	0.16
Danish (57)	236	0.37
Dutch (631)	4,629	7.32
Eastern European (176)	176	0.28
English (1,608)	6,951	10.99
Estonian (4)	4	0.01
European (411)	498	0.79
Finnish (68)	92	0.15
French, ex. Basque (285)	3,225	5.10
French Canadian (304)	695	1.10
German (3,377)	14,502	22.93
German Russian (0)	0	<0.01
Greek (62)	410	0.65
Guyanese (0)	0	<0.01
Hungarian (217)	681	1.08
Icelander (0)	0	<0.01
Iranian (18)	44	0.07
Irish (3,234)	12,327	19.49
Israeli (2)	2	<0.01
Italian (3,909)	10,205	16.14
Latvian (3)	55	0.09
Lithuanian (123)	309	0.49
Luxemburger (0)	0	<0.01
Macedonian (0)	0	<0.01
Maltese (0)	3	<0.01
New Zealander (0)	0	<0.01
Northern European (20)	20	0.03
Norwegian (130)	496	0.78
Pennsylvania German (9)	11	0.02
Polish (1,145)	3,588	5.67
Portuguese (20)	46	0.07
Romanian (67)	185	0.29
Russian (312)	1,220	1.93
Scandinavian (54)	78	0.12
Scotch-Irish (308)	1,127	1.78
Scottish (333)	1,672	2.64
Serbian (10)	14	0.02
Slavic (24)	89	0.14
Slovak (74)	131	0.21
Slovene (8)	16	0.03
Soviet Union (0)	0	<0.01
Swedish (112)	872	1.38
Swiss (44)	227	0.36
Turkish (20)	26	0.04
Ukrainian (304)	720	1.14
Welsh (49)	424	0.67
West Indian, ex. Hispanic (372)	418	0.66
Bahamian (0)	0	<0.01
Barbadian (0)	0	<0.01
Belizean (0)	0	<0.01
Bermudan (0)	3	<0.01
British West Indian (11)	11	0.02
Dutch West Indian (0)	0	<0.01
Haitian (93)	100	0.16
Jamaican (256)	277	0.44
Trinidadian/Tobagonian (12)	24	0.04
U.S. Virgin Islander (0)	0	<0.01
West Indian (0)	3	<0.01
Other West Indian (0)	0	<0.01
Yugoslavian (0)	11	0.02

Hispanic Origin	Population	%
Hispanic or Latino (of any race)	2,454	3.89
Central American, ex. Mexican	253	0.40
Costa Rican	11	0.02
Guatemalan	112	0.18
Honduran	34	0.05
Nicaraguan	25	0.04
Panamanian	16	0.03
Salvadoran	55	0.09
Other Central American	0	<0.01
Cuban	93	0.15
Dominican Republic	77	0.12
Mexican	732	1.16
Puerto Rican	931	1.48
South American	162	0.26
Argentinean	12	0.02
Bolivian	0	<0.01
Chilean	17	0.03
Colombian	70	0.11
Ecuadorian	41	0.06
Paraguayan	0	<0.01
Peruvian	9	0.01
Uruguayan	4	0.01
Venezuelan	8	0.01
Other South American	1	<0.01
Other Hispanic or Latino	206	0.33

Race*	Population	%
African-American/Black (2,855)	3,570	5.66
Not Hispanic (2,691)	3,327	5.27
Hispanic (164)	243	0.39
American Indian/Alaska Native (123)	476	0.75
Not Hispanic (85)	401	0.64
Hispanic (38)	75	0.12
Alaska Athabascan (Ala. Nat.) (0)	0	<0.01
Aleut (Alaska Native) (0)	0	<0.01
Apache (0)	7	0.01
Arapaho (0)	0	<0.01
Blackfeet (0)	25	0.04
Canadian/French Am. Ind. (2)	3	<0.01
Central American Ind. (0)	0	<0.01
Cherokee (10)	76	0.12
Cheyenne (0)	0	<0.01
Chickasaw (0)	5	0.01
Chippewa (1)	9	0.01
Choctaw (0)	1	<0.01
Colville (0)	0	<0.01
Comanche (0)	0	<0.01
Cree (0)	3	<0.01
Creek (0)	1	<0.01
Crow (0)	0	<0.01
Delaware (1)	1	<0.01
Hopi (0)	0	<0.01
Houma (0)	0	<0.01
Inupiat (Alaska Native) (0)	1	<0.01
Iroquois (21)	61	0.10
Kiowa (0)	0	<0.01
Lumbee (0)	2	<0.01
Menominee (0)	0	<0.01
Mexican American Ind. (8)	8	0.01
Navajo (0)	0	<0.01
Osage (0)	0	<0.01
Ottawa (0)	0	<0.01
Paiute (0)	0	<0.01
Pima (0)	0	<0.01
Potawatomi (1)	3	<0.01
Pueblo (0)	0	<0.01
Puget Sound Salish (0)	0	<0.01
Seminole (1)	5	0.01
Shoshone (0)	0	<0.01
Sioux (4)	11	0.02
South American Ind. (12)	17	0.03
Spanish American Ind. (0)	0	<0.01
Tlingit-Haida (Alaska Native) (0)	0	<0.01
Tohono O'Odham (0)	0	<0.01
Tsimshian (Alaska Native) (0)	0	<0.01
Ute (0)	0	<0.01
Yakama (0)	1	<0.01
Yaqui (0)	0	<0.01
Yuman (0)	0	<0.01
Yup'ik (Alaska Native) (0)	0	<0.01
Asian (1,002)	1,220	1.93
Not Hispanic (998)	1,192	1.89
Hispanic (4)	28	0.04
Bangladeshi (248)	279	0.44
Bhutanese (0)	0	<0.01
Burmese (0)	0	<0.01
Cambodian (3)	3	<0.01
Chinese, ex. Taiwanese (152)	198	0.31
Filipino (72)	105	0.17
Hmong (0)	0	<0.01
Indian (256)	315	0.50
Indonesian (4)	4	0.01
Japanese (59)	97	0.15
Korean (65)	82	0.13
Laotian (0)	1	<0.01
Malaysian (0)	0	<0.01
Nepalese (11)	11	0.02
Pakistani (28)	30	0.05
Sri Lankan (2)	2	<0.01
Taiwanese (2)	2	<0.01
Thai (7)	8	0.01
Vietnamese (33)	48	0.08
Hawaii Native/Pacific Islander (18)	45	0.07
Not Hispanic (15)	39	0.06
Hispanic (3)	6	0.01
Fijian (1)	1	<0.01
Guamanian/Chamorro (2)	3	<0.01
Marshallese (0)	0	<0.01
Native Hawaiian (2)	12	0.02
Samoan (3)	8	0.01
Tongan (0)	0	<0.01
White (57,136)	58,319	92.43
Not Hispanic (55,672)	56,690	89.85
Hispanic (1,464)	1,629	2.58

*Notes: † The Census 2010 population figure is used to calculate the percentages in the Hispanic Origin and Race categories. Ancestry percentages are based on the 2006-2010 American Community Survey population (not shown); ‡ Numbers in parentheses indicate the number of people reporting a single ancestry; * Numbers in parentheses indicate the number of persons reporting this race alone, not in combination with any other race; Please refer to the Explanation of Data for more information.*

Cortland County

Population: 49,336

Ancestry	Population	%
Afghan (0)	0	<0.01
African, Sub-Saharan (0)	0	<0.01
African (0)	0	<0.01
Cape Verdean (0)	0	<0.01
Ethiopian (0)	0	<0.01
Ghanaian (0)	0	<0.01
Kenyan (0)	0	<0.01
Liberian (0)	0	<0.01
Nigerian (0)	0	<0.01
Senegalese (0)	0	<0.01
Sierra Leonean (0)	0	<0.01
Somalian (0)	0	<0.01
South African (0)	0	<0.01
Sudanese (0)	0	<0.01
Ugandan (0)	0	<0.01
Zimbabwean (0)	0	<0.01
Other Sub-Saharan African (0)	0	<0.01
Albanian (0)	0	<0.01
Alsatian (0)	0	<0.01
American (2,591)	2,591	5.24
Arab (86)	252	0.51
Arab (5)	18	0.04
Egyptian (0)	0	<0.01
Iraqi (0)	0	<0.01
Jordanian (0)	0	<0.01
Lebanese (81)	207	0.42
Moroccan (0)	0	<0.01
Palestinian (0)	0	<0.01
Syrian (0)	27	0.05
Other Arab (0)	0	<0.01
Armenian (0)	0	<0.01
Assyrian/Chaldean/Syriac (3)	3	0.01
Australian (0)	0	<0.01
Austrian (9)	124	0.25
Basque (0)	0	<0.01
Belgian (16)	19	0.04
Brazilian (0)	13	0.03
British (49)	93	0.19
Bulgarian (0)	0	<0.01
Cajun (0)	0	<0.01
Canadian (72)	149	0.30
Carpatho Rusyn (0)	0	<0.01
Celtic (8)	19	0.04
Croatian (0)	39	0.08
Cypriot (0)	0	<0.01
Czech (15)	111	0.22
Czechoslovakian (4)	34	0.07
Danish (21)	78	0.16
Dutch (304)	1,860	3.76
Eastern European (30)	30	0.06
English (3,066)	7,856	15.89
Estonian (7)	7	0.01
European (795)	812	1.64
Finnish (0)	92	0.19
French, ex. Basque (326)	1,886	3.81
French Canadian (226)	647	1.31
German (2,599)	8,405	17.00
German Russian (0)	0	<0.01
Greek (49)	190	0.38
Guyanese (0)	0	<0.01
Hungarian (39)	146	0.30
Icelander (10)	10	0.02
Iranian (0)	2	<0.01
Irish (2,679)	8,790	17.77
Israeli (0)	0	<0.01
Italian (2,049)	5,160	10.43
Latvian (0)	2	<0.01
Lithuanian (8)	55	0.11
Luxemburger (6)	6	0.01
Macedonian (0)	0	<0.01
Maltese (3)	25	0.05
New Zealander (0)	0	<0.01
Northern European (176)	239	0.48
Norwegian (51)	265	0.54
Pennsylvania German (70)	97	0.20

Ancestry	Population	%
Polish (615)	1,744	3.53
Portuguese (15)	28	0.06
Romanian (35)	75	0.15
Russian (75)	434	0.88
Scandinavian (25)	39	0.08
Scotch-Irish (176)	635	1.28
Scottish (356)	1,046	2.12
Serbian (0)	6	0.01
Slavic (18)	36	0.07
Slovak (13)	54	0.11
Slovene (0)	0	<0.01
Soviet Union (0)	0	<0.01
Swedish (71)	327	0.66
Swiss (24)	126	0.25
Turkish (50)	77	0.16
Ukrainian (151)	231	0.47
Welsh (95)	464	0.94
West Indian, ex. Hispanic (12)	34	0.07
Bahamian (0)	0	<0.01
Barbadian (0)	0	<0.01
Belizean (0)	0	<0.01
Bermudan (0)	0	<0.01
British West Indian (0)	0	<0.01
Dutch West Indian (0)	0	<0.01
Haitian (12)	25	0.05
Jamaican (0)	0	<0.01
Trinidadian/Tobagonian (0)	9	0.02
U.S. Virgin Islander (0)	0	<0.01
West Indian (0)	0	<0.01
Other West Indian (0)	0	<0.01
Yugoslavian (6)	13	0.03

Hispanic Origin	Population	%
Hispanic or Latino (of any race)	1,094	2.22
Central American, ex. Mexican	64	0.13
Costa Rican	3	0.01
Guatemalan	40	0.08
Honduran	4	0.01
Nicaraguan	1	<0.01
Panamanian	4	0.01
Salvadoran	11	0.02
Other Central American	1	<0.01
Cuban	60	0.12
Dominican Republic	66	0.13
Mexican	207	0.42
Puerto Rican	458	0.93
South American	94	0.19
Argentinean	3	0.01
Bolivian	4	0.01
Chilean	6	0.01
Colombian	40	0.08
Ecuadorian	23	0.05
Paraguayan	0	<0.01
Peruvian	11	0.02
Uruguayan	4	0.01
Venezuelan	3	0.01
Other South American	0	<0.01
Other Hispanic or Latino	145	0.29

Race*	Population	%
African-American/Black (760)	1,131	2.29
Not Hispanic (705)	1,033	2.09
Hispanic (55)	98	0.20
American Indian/Alaska Native (137)	454	0.92
Not Hispanic (126)	405	0.82
Hispanic (11)	49	0.10
Alaska Athabascan (Ala. Nat.) (0)	0	<0.01
Aleut (Alaska Native) (0)	0	<0.01
Apache (1)	1	<0.01
Arapaho (0)	0	<0.01
Blackfeet (2)	15	0.03
Canadian/French Am. Ind. (2)	10	0.02
Central American Ind. (0)	0	<0.01
Cherokee (4)	47	0.10
Cheyenne (1)	1	<0.01
Chickasaw (0)	0	<0.01
Chippewa (0)	0	<0.01
Choctaw (0)	2	<0.01
Colville (0)	0	<0.01

Race* (cont.)	Population	%
Comanche (0)	0	<0.01
Cree (1)	2	<0.01
Creek (0)	0	<0.01
Crow (0)	0	<0.01
Delaware (0)	4	0.01
Hopi (0)	0	<0.01
Houma (0)	0	<0.01
Inupiat (Alaska Native) (0)	0	<0.01
Iroquois (43)	118	0.24
Kiowa (0)	0	<0.01
Lumbee (1)	1	<0.01
Menominee (0)	0	<0.01
Mexican American Ind. (2)	4	0.01
Navajo (2)	4	0.01
Osage (0)	0	<0.01
Ottawa (0)	0	<0.01
Paiute (0)	0	<0.01
Pima (0)	0	<0.01
Potawatomi (1)	2	<0.01
Pueblo (0)	0	<0.01
Puget Sound Salish (0)	0	<0.01
Seminole (0)	0	<0.01
Shoshone (0)	0	<0.01
Sioux (3)	8	0.02
South American Ind. (1)	1	<0.01
Spanish American Ind. (0)	0	<0.01
Tlingit-Haida (Alaska Native) (0)	0	<0.01
Tohono O'Odham (0)	0	<0.01
Tsimshian (Alaska Native) (0)	0	<0.01
Ute (0)	0	<0.01
Yakama (0)	0	<0.01
Yaqui (0)	0	<0.01
Yuman (0)	0	<0.01
Yup'ik (Alaska Native) (0)	0	<0.01
Asian (416)	575	1.17
Not Hispanic (412)	558	1.13
Hispanic (4)	17	0.03
Bangladeshi (7)	13	0.03
Bhutanese (0)	0	<0.01
Burmese (0)	0	<0.01
Cambodian (1)	1	<0.01
Chinese, ex. Taiwanese (104)	136	0.28
Filipino (40)	84	0.17
Hmong (0)	0	<0.01
Indian (109)	126	0.26
Indonesian (5)	9	0.02
Japanese (26)	60	0.12
Korean (61)	83	0.17
Laotian (9)	11	0.02
Malaysian (0)	1	<0.01
Nepalese (0)	0	<0.01
Pakistani (6)	6	0.01
Sri Lankan (2)	2	<0.01
Taiwanese (2)	3	0.01
Thai (1)	3	0.01
Vietnamese (22)	24	0.05
Hawaii Native/Pacific Islander (5)	30	0.06
Not Hispanic (3)	23	0.05
Hispanic (2)	7	0.01
Fijian (0)	0	<0.01
Guamanian/Chamorro (2)	2	<0.01
Marshallese (0)	0	<0.01
Native Hawaiian (0)	12	0.02
Samoan (0)	1	<0.01
Tongan (0)	1	<0.01
White (46,901)	47,697	96.68
Not Hispanic (46,252)	46,953	95.17
Hispanic (649)	744	1.51

*Notes: † The Census 2010 population figure is used to calculate the percentages in the Hispanic Origin and Race categories. Ancestry percentages are based on the 2006-2010 American Community Survey population (not shown); ‡ Numbers in parentheses indicate the number of people reporting a single ancestry; * Numbers in parentheses indicate the number of persons reporting this race alone, not in combination with any other race; Please refer to the Explanation of Data for more information.*

Delaware County
Population: 47,980

Ancestry	Population	%
Afghan (0)	0	<0.01
African, Sub-Saharan (16)	45	0.09
African (16)	45	0.09
Cape Verdean (0)	0	<0.01
Ethiopian (0)	0	<0.01
Ghanaian (0)	0	<0.01
Kenyan (0)	0	<0.01
Liberian (0)	0	<0.01
Nigerian (0)	0	<0.01
Senegalese (0)	0	<0.01
Sierra Leonean (0)	0	<0.01
Somalian (0)	0	<0.01
South African (0)	0	<0.01
Sudanese (0)	0	<0.01
Ugandan (0)	0	<0.01
Zimbabwean (0)	0	<0.01
Other Sub-Saharan African (0)	0	<0.01
Albanian (0)	0	<0.01
Alsatian (0)	0	<0.01
American (1,873)	1,873	3.88
Arab (15)	15	0.03
Arab (0)	0	<0.01
Egyptian (0)	0	<0.01
Iraqi (0)	0	<0.01
Jordanian (0)	0	<0.01
Lebanese (5)	5	0.01
Moroccan (0)	0	<0.01
Palestinian (0)	0	<0.01
Syrian (8)	8	0.02
Other Arab (2)	2	<0.01
Armenian (0)	24	0.05
Assyrian/Chaldean/Syriac (0)	0	<0.01
Australian (18)	23	0.05
Austrian (30)	217	0.45
Basque (0)	0	<0.01
Belgian (5)	19	0.04
Brazilian (9)	9	0.02
British (84)	152	0.32
Bulgarian (0)	3	0.01
Cajun (0)	0	<0.01
Canadian (40)	139	0.29
Carpatho Rusyn (0)	0	<0.01
Celtic (0)	0	<0.01
Croatian (11)	11	0.02
Cypriot (0)	0	<0.01
Czech (49)	235	0.49
Czechoslovakian (46)	88	0.18
Danish (93)	274	0.57
Dutch (498)	2,859	5.93
Eastern European (53)	69	0.14
English (2,101)	7,882	16.35
Estonian (16)	16	0.03
European (124)	124	0.26
Finnish (12)	76	0.16
French, ex. Basque (281)	2,275	4.72
French Canadian (73)	414	0.86
German (3,517)	13,135	27.24
German Russian (0)	0	<0.01
Greek (82)	197	0.41
Guyanese (0)	0	<0.01
Hungarian (61)	507	1.05
Icelander (0)	8	0.02
Iranian (10)	10	0.02
Irish (2,940)	10,183	21.12
Israeli (0)	0	<0.01
Italian (2,129)	5,867	12.17
Latvian (4)	16	0.03
Lithuanian (27)	117	0.24
Luxemburger (0)	0	<0.01
Macedonian (4)	7	0.01
Maltese (5)	5	0.01
New Zealander (0)	0	<0.01
Northern European (61)	61	0.13
Norwegian (144)	542	1.12
Pennsylvania German (6)	43	0.09

Ancestry	Population	%
Polish (605)	2,189	4.54
Portuguese (22)	108	0.22
Romanian (77)	113	0.23
Russian (143)	490	1.02
Scandinavian (26)	87	0.18
Scotch-Irish (505)	1,432	2.97
Scottish (756)	2,831	5.87
Serbian (0)	0	<0.01
Slavic (13)	65	0.13
Slovak (63)	285	0.59
Slovene (20)	26	0.05
Soviet Union (0)	0	<0.01
Swedish (94)	1,011	2.10
Swiss (28)	176	0.36
Turkish (73)	78	0.16
Ukrainian (49)	124	0.26
Welsh (112)	628	1.30
West Indian, ex. Hispanic (113)	189	0.39
Bahamian (0)	0	<0.01
Barbadian (0)	9	0.02
Belizean (0)	0	<0.01
Bermudan (0)	0	<0.01
British West Indian (0)	29	0.06
Dutch West Indian (0)	0	<0.01
Haitian (30)	33	0.07
Jamaican (40)	65	0.13
Trinidadian/Tobagonian (0)	0	<0.01
U.S. Virgin Islander (28)	28	0.06
West Indian (15)	25	0.05
Other West Indian (0)	0	<0.01
Yugoslavian (53)	103	0.21

Hispanic Origin	Population	%
Hispanic or Latino (of any race)	1,560	3.25
Central American, ex. Mexican	66	0.14
Costa Rican	7	0.01
Guatemalan	19	0.04
Honduran	11	0.02
Nicaraguan	2	<0.01
Panamanian	9	0.02
Salvadoran	18	0.04
Other Central American	0	<0.01
Cuban	70	0.15
Dominican Republic	95	0.20
Mexican	381	0.79
Puerto Rican	659	1.37
South American	104	0.22
Argentinean	18	0.04
Bolivian	0	<0.01
Chilean	15	0.03
Colombian	38	0.08
Ecuadorian	14	0.03
Paraguayan	0	<0.01
Peruvian	9	0.02
Uruguayan	4	0.01
Venezuelan	6	0.01
Other South American	0	<0.01
Other Hispanic or Latino	185	0.39

Race*	Population	%
African-American/Black (779)	1,040	2.17
Not Hispanic (691)	923	1.92
Hispanic (88)	117	0.24
American Indian/Alaska Native (131)	366	0.76
Not Hispanic (102)	314	0.65
Hispanic (29)	52	0.11
Alaska Athabascan (Ala. Nat.) (0)	0	<0.01
Aleut (Alaska Native) (0)	0	<0.01
Apache (0)	0	<0.01
Arapaho (0)	0	<0.01
Blackfeet (1)	14	0.03
Canadian/French Am. Ind. (0)	0	<0.01
Central American Ind. (3)	3	0.01
Cherokee (7)	49	0.10
Cheyenne (1)	1	<0.01
Chickasaw (0)	0	<0.01
Chippewa (8)	8	0.02
Choctaw (0)	4	0.01
Colville (0)	1	<0.01

Race*	Population	%
Comanche (0)	0	<0.01
Cree (0)	1	<0.01
Creek (0)	1	<0.01
Crow (0)	1	<0.01
Delaware (2)	8	0.02
Hopi (0)	0	<0.01
Houma (0)	0	<0.01
Inupiat (Alaska Native) (0)	1	<0.01
Iroquois (18)	41	0.09
Kiowa (0)	2	<0.01
Lumbee (0)	0	<0.01
Menominee (0)	0	<0.01
Mexican American Ind. (1)	4	0.01
Navajo (3)	5	0.01
Osage (0)	0	<0.01
Ottawa (0)	0	<0.01
Paiute (0)	0	<0.01
Pima (0)	0	<0.01
Potawatomi (0)	1	<0.01
Pueblo (0)	0	<0.01
Puget Sound Salish (0)	0	<0.01
Seminole (2)	2	<0.01
Shoshone (1)	2	<0.01
Sioux (4)	7	0.01
South American Ind. (4)	7	0.01
Spanish American Ind. (0)	0	<0.01
Tlingit-Haida (Alaska Native) (1)	1	<0.01
Tohono O'Odham (0)	0	<0.01
Tsimshian (Alaska Native) (0)	0	<0.01
Ute (0)	0	<0.01
Yakama (0)	0	<0.01
Yaqui (0)	1	<0.01
Yuman (0)	0	<0.01
Yup'ik (Alaska Native) (0)	1	<0.01
Asian (367)	500	1.04
Not Hispanic (363)	483	1.01
Hispanic (4)	17	0.04
Bangladeshi (2)	2	<0.01
Bhutanese (3)	3	0.01
Burmese (2)	2	<0.01
Cambodian (2)	2	<0.01
Chinese, ex. Taiwanese (104)	136	0.28
Filipino (70)	101	0.21
Hmong (0)	0	<0.01
Indian (74)	101	0.21
Indonesian (1)	4	0.01
Japanese (45)	69	0.14
Korean (24)	29	0.06
Laotian (2)	8	0.02
Malaysian (0)	0	<0.01
Nepalese (1)	1	<0.01
Pakistani (9)	9	0.02
Sri Lankan (3)	3	0.01
Taiwanese (6)	6	0.01
Thai (0)	1	<0.01
Vietnamese (5)	11	0.02
Hawaii Native/Pacific Islander (12)	35	0.07
Not Hispanic (6)	24	0.05
Hispanic (6)	11	0.02
Fijian (0)	0	<0.01
Guamanian/Chamorro (6)	8	0.02
Marshallese (0)	0	<0.01
Native Hawaiian (2)	6	0.01
Samoan (0)	5	0.01
Tongan (0)	0	<0.01
White (45,675)	46,241	96.38
Not Hispanic (44,706)	45,191	94.19
Hispanic (969)	1,050	2.19

*Notes: † The Census 2010 population figure is used to calculate the percentages in the Hispanic Origin and Race categories. Ancestry percentages are based on the 2006-2010 American Community Survey population (not shown); ‡ Numbers in parentheses indicate the number of people reporting a single ancestry; * Numbers in parentheses indicate the number of persons reporting this race alone, not in combination with any other race; Please refer to the Explanation of Data for more information.*

Dutchess County

Population: 297,488

Ancestry	Population	%
Afghan (18)	18	0.01
African, Sub-Saharan (1,645)	2,652	0.90
African (874)	1,553	0.52
Cape Verdean (0)	0	<0.01
Ethiopian (0)	0	<0.01
Ghanaian (121)	121	0.04
Kenyan (32)	32	0.01
Liberian (0)	0	<0.01
Nigerian (383)	632	0.21
Senegalese (0)	12	<0.01
Sierra Leonean (0)	0	<0.01
Somalian (0)	0	<0.01
South African (50)	84	0.03
Sudanese (0)	0	<0.01
Ugandan (0)	0	<0.01
Zimbabwean (0)	0	<0.01
Other Sub-Saharan African (185)	218	0.07
Albanian (700)	799	0.27
Alsatian (0)	10	<0.01
American (7,260)	7,260	2.45
Arab (1,145)	2,373	0.80
Arab (118)	335	0.11
Egyptian (43)	131	0.04
Iraqi (0)	0	<0.01
Jordanian (552)	808	0.27
Lebanese (257)	562	0.19
Moroccan (65)	65	0.02
Palestinian (0)	183	0.06
Syrian (11)	53	0.02
Other Arab (99)	236	0.08
Armenian (116)	253	0.09
Assyrian/Chaldean/Syriac (0)	0	<0.01
Australian (40)	134	0.05
Austrian (398)	1,727	0.58
Basque (19)	32	0.01
Belgian (53)	345	0.12
Brazilian (93)	184	0.06
British (511)	1,357	0.46
Bulgarian (106)	139	0.05
Cajun (30)	61	0.02
Canadian (222)	656	0.22
Carpatho Rusyn (27)	38	0.01
Celtic (8)	46	0.02
Croatian (57)	338	0.11
Cypriot (9)	9	<0.01
Czech (443)	1,985	0.67
Czechoslovakian (129)	515	0.17
Danish (110)	914	0.31
Dutch (1,356)	8,775	2.96
Eastern European (414)	596	0.20
English (5,208)	28,099	9.49
Estonian (32)	50	0.02
European (1,482)	1,666	0.56
Finnish (113)	488	0.16
French, ex. Basque (1,230)	9,725	3.28
French Canadian (1,021)	2,977	1.01
German (9,511)	51,637	17.44
German Russian (0)	0	<0.01
Greek (1,086)	2,738	0.92
Guyanese (233)	263	0.09
Hungarian (969)	3,435	1.16
Icelander (7)	32	0.01
Iranian (97)	203	0.07
Irish (18,790)	70,744	23.89
Israeli (127)	217	0.07
Italian (29,305)	69,349	23.42
Latvian (212)	328	0.11
Lithuanian (335)	957	0.32
Luxemburger (0)	0	<0.01
Macedonian (57)	57	0.02
Maltese (53)	92	0.03
New Zealander (21)	53	0.02
Northern European (137)	198	0.07
Norwegian (521)	2,307	0.78
Pennsylvania German (16)	188	0.06

Ancestry (cont.)	Population	%
Polish (3,538)	14,799	5.00
Portuguese (589)	1,539	0.52
Romanian (130)	592	0.20
Russian (1,673)	5,793	1.96
Scandinavian (100)	252	0.09
Scotch-Irish (1,448)	4,218	1.42
Scottish (1,334)	5,831	1.97
Serbian (45)	132	0.04
Slavic (128)	319	0.11
Slovak (349)	888	0.30
Slovene (36)	94	0.03
Soviet Union (0)	0	<0.01
Swedish (627)	3,518	1.19
Swiss (289)	1,231	0.42
Turkish (67)	226	0.08
Ukrainian (470)	1,586	0.54
Welsh (180)	1,432	0.48
West Indian, ex. Hispanic (5,456)	7,721	2.61
Bahamian (0)	0	<0.01
Barbadian (0)	36	0.01
Belizean (53)	83	0.03
Bermudan (0)	0	<0.01
British West Indian (89)	117	0.04
Dutch West Indian (0)	0	<0.01
Haitian (257)	507	0.17
Jamaican (4,473)	5,581	1.88
Trinidadian/Tobagonian (250)	356	0.12
U.S. Virgin Islander (7)	55	0.02
West Indian (327)	986	0.33
Other West Indian (0)	0	<0.01
Yugoslavian (315)	617	0.21

Hispanic Origin	Population	%
Hispanic or Latino (of any race)	31,267	10.51
Central American, ex. Mexican	2,115	0.71
Costa Rican	135	0.05
Guatemalan	1,032	0.35
Honduran	333	0.11
Nicaraguan	86	0.03
Panamanian	159	0.05
Salvadoran	361	0.12
Other Central American	9	<0.01
Cuban	1,069	0.36
Dominican Republic	1,860	0.63
Mexican	7,575	2.55
Puerto Rican	11,984	4.03
South American	4,140	1.39
Argentinean	293	0.10
Bolivian	55	0.02
Chilean	179	0.06
Colombian	1,096	0.37
Ecuadorian	1,531	0.51
Paraguayan	48	0.02
Peruvian	576	0.19
Uruguayan	163	0.05
Venezuelan	149	0.05
Other South American	50	0.02
Other Hispanic or Latino	2,524	0.85

Race*	Population	%
African-American/Black (29,518)	33,599	11.29
Not Hispanic (27,395)	30,458	10.24
Hispanic (2,123)	3,141	1.06
American Indian/Alaska Native (893)	2,648	0.89
Not Hispanic (465)	1,829	0.61
Hispanic (428)	819	0.28
Alaska Athabascan (Ala. Nat.) (0)	0	<0.01
Aleut (Alaska Native) (3)	4	<0.01
Apache (4)	24	0.01
Arapaho (0)	0	<0.01
Blackfeet (20)	109	0.04
Canadian/French Am. Ind. (4)	7	<0.01
Central American Ind. (9)	32	0.01
Cherokee (43)	401	0.13
Cheyenne (2)	3	<0.01
Chickasaw (1)	4	<0.01
Chippewa (9)	18	0.01
Choctaw (4)	13	<0.01
Colville (1)	1	<0.01

Race* (cont.)	Population	%
Comanche (1)	2	<0.01
Cree (0)	3	<0.01
Creek (4)	13	<0.01
Crow (0)	5	<0.01
Delaware (1)	5	<0.01
Hopi (0)	2	<0.01
Houma (0)	0	<0.01
Inupiat (Alaska Native) (3)	3	<0.01
Iroquois (72)	215	0.07
Kiowa (0)	0	<0.01
Lumbee (5)	12	<0.01
Menominee (3)	4	<0.01
Mexican American Ind. (157)	200	0.07
Navajo (4)	17	0.01
Osage (3)	3	<0.01
Ottawa (2)	2	<0.01
Paiute (0)	1	<0.01
Pima (0)	0	<0.01
Potawatomi (0)	2	<0.01
Pueblo (0)	8	<0.01
Puget Sound Salish (0)	0	<0.01
Seminole (3)	24	0.01
Shoshone (0)	3	<0.01
Sioux (11)	45	0.02
South American Ind. (53)	115	0.04
Spanish American Ind. (3)	8	<0.01
Tlingit-Haida (Alaska Native) (0)	1	<0.01
Tohono O'Odham (2)	4	<0.01
Tsimshian (Alaska Native) (0)	0	<0.01
Ute (1)	2	<0.01
Yakama (2)	2	<0.01
Yaqui (0)	0	<0.01
Yuman (0)	0	<0.01
Yup'ik (Alaska Native) (0)	0	<0.01
Asian (10,437)	12,220	4.11
Not Hispanic (10,330)	11,925	4.01
Hispanic (107)	295	0.10
Bangladeshi (166)	190	0.06
Bhutanese (0)	0	<0.01
Burmese (51)	54	0.02
Cambodian (34)	49	0.02
Chinese, ex. Taiwanese (2,733)	3,188	1.07
Filipino (869)	1,215	0.41
Hmong (0)	0	<0.01
Indian (3,531)	3,939	1.32
Indonesian (26)	53	0.02
Japanese (367)	560	0.19
Korean (1,167)	1,331	0.45
Laotian (37)	44	0.01
Malaysian (14)	25	0.01
Nepalese (42)	43	0.01
Pakistani (370)	429	0.14
Sri Lankan (43)	59	0.02
Taiwanese (127)	144	0.05
Thai (74)	115	0.04
Vietnamese (450)	527	0.18
Hawaii Native/Pacific Islander (108)	356	0.12
Not Hispanic (80)	253	0.09
Hispanic (28)	103	0.03
Fijian (0)	1	<0.01
Guamanian/Chamorro (23)	44	0.01
Marshallese (0)	1	<0.01
Native Hawaiian (26)	79	0.03
Samoan (7)	17	0.01
Tongan (3)	8	<0.01
White (238,387)	244,919	82.33
Not Hispanic (221,812)	226,434	76.12
Hispanic (16,575)	18,485	6.21

Notes: † The Census 2010 population figure is used to calculate the percentages in the Hispanic Origin and Race categories. Ancestry percentages are based on the 2006-2010 American Community Survey population (not shown); ‡ Numbers in parentheses indicate the number of people reporting a single ancestry; * Numbers in parentheses indicate the number of persons reporting this race alone, not in combination with any other race; Please refer to the Explanation of Data for more information.

Erie County
Population: 919,040

Ancestry	Population	%
Afghan (430)	430	0.05
African, Sub-Saharan (6,954)	7,909	0.86
African (4,615)	5,206	0.57
Cape Verdean (95)	95	0.01
Ethiopian (307)	307	0.03
Ghanaian (83)	83	0.01
Kenyan (74)	136	0.01
Liberian (92)	107	0.01
Nigerian (302)	313	0.03
Senegalese (0)	18	<0.01
Sierra Leonean (17)	17	<0.01
Somalian (706)	858	0.09
South African (79)	92	0.01
Sudanese (259)	268	0.03
Ugandan (24)	33	<0.01
Zimbabwean (45)	45	<0.01
Other Sub-Saharan African (256)	331	0.04
Albanian (515)	763	0.08
Alsatian (50)	188	0.02
American (23,171)	23,171	2.52
Arab (5,684)	8,086	0.88
Arab (2,321)	2,545	0.28
Egyptian (73)	158	0.02
Iraqi (316)	318	0.03
Jordanian (95)	108	0.01
Lebanese (1,316)	3,012	0.33
Moroccan (34)	96	0.01
Palestinian (42)	42	<0.01
Syrian (116)	306	0.03
Other Arab (1,371)	1,501	0.16
Armenian (282)	517	0.06
Assyrian/Chaldean/Syriac (0)	0	<0.01
Australian (57)	153	0.02
Austrian (952)	4,008	0.44
Basque (9)	9	<0.01
Belgian (77)	354	0.04
Brazilian (323)	370	0.04
British (1,012)	2,544	0.28
Bulgarian (530)	715	0.08
Cajun (15)	26	<0.01
Canadian (1,587)	3,446	0.37
Carpatho Rusyn (6)	19	<0.01
Celtic (80)	132	0.01
Croatian (914)	2,803	0.30
Cypriot (17)	17	<0.01
Czech (414)	2,207	0.24
Czechoslovakian (396)	1,048	0.11
Danish (250)	1,162	0.13
Dutch (1,341)	9,750	1.06
Eastern European (1,072)	1,169	0.13
English (16,244)	70,914	7.70
Estonian (110)	316	0.03
European (3,832)	4,225	0.46
Finnish (213)	883	0.10
French, ex. Basque (2,539)	25,048	2.72
French Canadian (1,843)	6,635	0.72
German (68,487)	245,605	26.66
German Russian (61)	86	0.01
Greek (1,933)	4,465	0.48
Guyanese (616)	628	0.07
Hungarian (2,785)	9,692	1.05
Icelander (25)	37	<0.01
Iranian (318)	403	0.04
Irish (39,231)	163,985	17.80
Israeli (179)	302	0.03
Italian (65,466)	152,676	16.57
Latvian (130)	237	0.03
Lithuanian (369)	1,275	0.14
Luxemburger (0)	45	<0.01
Macedonian (326)	486	0.05
Maltese (21)	58	0.01
New Zealander (11)	37	<0.01
Northern European (318)	441	0.05
Norwegian (767)	2,897	0.31
Pennsylvania German (296)	680	0.07

Ancestry (cont.)	Population	%
Polish (80,210)	174,651	18.96
Portuguese (349)	1,172	0.13
Romanian (392)	909	0.10
Russian (3,531)	8,992	0.98
Scandinavian (71)	489	0.05
Scotch-Irish (3,515)	10,370	1.13
Scottish (2,997)	14,392	1.56
Serbian (785)	1,550	0.17
Slavic (286)	741	0.08
Slovak (407)	1,584	0.17
Slovene (86)	261	0.03
Soviet Union (0)	0	<0.01
Swedish (1,594)	8,485	0.92
Swiss (267)	1,342	0.15
Turkish (457)	687	0.07
Ukrainian (3,183)	7,778	0.84
Welsh (957)	5,167	0.56
West Indian, ex. Hispanic (3,504)	4,339	0.47
Bahamian (34)	34	<0.01
Barbadian (38)	64	0.01
Belizean (0)	50	0.01
Bermudan (0)	0	<0.01
British West Indian (128)	141	0.02
Dutch West Indian (0)	17	<0.01
Haitian (679)	864	0.09
Jamaican (1,863)	2,179	0.24
Trinidadian/Tobagonian (299)	349	0.04
U.S. Virgin Islander (0)	0	<0.01
West Indian (463)	641	0.07
Other West Indian (0)	0	<0.01
Yugoslavian (890)	1,263	0.14

Hispanic Origin	Population	%
Hispanic or Latino (of any race)	41,731	4.54
Central American, ex. Mexican	1,034	0.11
Costa Rican	89	0.01
Guatemalan	305	0.03
Honduran	140	0.02
Nicaraguan	58	0.01
Panamanian	200	0.02
Salvadoran	224	0.02
Other Central American	18	<0.01
Cuban	1,214	0.13
Dominican Republic	1,179	0.13
Mexican	3,992	0.43
Puerto Rican	29,400	3.20
South American	1,831	0.20
Argentinean	229	0.02
Bolivian	77	0.01
Chilean	113	0.01
Colombian	684	0.07
Ecuadorian	282	0.03
Paraguayan	27	<0.01
Peruvian	245	0.03
Uruguayan	13	<0.01
Venezuelan	136	0.01
Other South American	25	<0.01
Other Hispanic or Latino	3,081	0.34

Race*	Population	%
African-American/Black (123,931)	133,049	14.48
Not Hispanic (119,916)	127,397	13.86
Hispanic (4,015)	5,652	0.61
American Indian/Alaska Native (5,908)	10,110	1.10
Not Hispanic (5,199)	8,799	0.96
Hispanic (709)	1,311	0.14
Alaska Athabascan (Ala. Nat.) (1)	3	<0.01
Aleut (Alaska Native) (0)	0	<0.01
Apache (7)	26	<0.01
Arapaho (1)	2	<0.01
Blackfeet (22)	188	0.02
Canadian/French Am. Ind. (84)	141	0.02
Central American Ind. (14)	24	<0.01
Cherokee (87)	579	0.06
Cheyenne (0)	5	<0.01
Chickasaw (2)	3	<0.01
Chippewa (60)	105	0.01
Choctaw (12)	44	<0.01
Colville (0)	0	<0.01

Race* (cont.)	Population	%
Comanche (2)	6	<0.01
Cree (2)	9	<0.01
Creek (8)	23	<0.01
Crow (4)	12	<0.01
Delaware (13)	24	<0.01
Hopi (4)	9	<0.01
Houma (1)	2	<0.01
Inupiat (Alaska Native) (3)	9	<0.01
Iroquois (3,416)	4,481	0.49
Kiowa (1)	1	<0.01
Lumbee (3)	10	<0.01
Menominee (3)	8	<0.01
Mexican American Ind. (63)	90	0.01
Navajo (25)	43	<0.01
Osage (6)	6	<0.01
Ottawa (1)	4	<0.01
Paiute (7)	9	<0.01
Pima (1)	4	<0.01
Potawatomi (8)	16	<0.01
Pueblo (5)	12	<0.01
Puget Sound Salish (1)	2	<0.01
Seminole (3)	40	<0.01
Shoshone (0)	0	<0.01
Sioux (39)	78	0.01
South American Ind. (41)	110	0.01
Spanish American Ind. (20)	27	<0.01
Tlingit-Haida (Alaska Native) (3)	6	<0.01
Tohono O'Odham (3)	5	<0.01
Tsimshian (Alaska Native) (0)	0	<0.01
Ute (0)	0	<0.01
Yakama (0)	0	<0.01
Yaqui (3)	3	<0.01
Yuman (2)	2	<0.01
Yup'ik (Alaska Native) (1)	3	<0.01
Asian (23,789)	27,624	3.01
Not Hispanic (23,621)	27,176	2.96
Hispanic (168)	448	0.05
Bangladeshi (217)	260	0.03
Bhutanese (298)	370	0.04
Burmese (2,313)	2,414	0.26
Cambodian (88)	102	0.01
Chinese, ex. Taiwanese (4,978)	5,566	0.61
Filipino (928)	1,490	0.16
Hmong (6)	8	<0.01
Indian (6,796)	7,576	0.82
Indonesian (65)	103	0.01
Japanese (490)	838	0.09
Korean (2,356)	2,775	0.30
Laotian (369)	445	0.05
Malaysian (82)	97	0.01
Nepalese (140)	185	0.02
Pakistani (1,014)	1,159	0.13
Sri Lankan (198)	219	0.02
Taiwanese (241)	285	0.03
Thai (176)	281	0.03
Vietnamese (2,037)	2,256	0.25
Hawaii Native/Pacific Islander (219)	714	0.08
Not Hispanic (165)	552	0.06
Hispanic (54)	162	0.02
Fijian (6)	6	<0.01
Guamanian/Chamorro (40)	88	0.01
Marshallese (1)	1	<0.01
Native Hawaiian (46)	185	0.02
Samoan (45)	112	0.01
Tongan (3)	4	<0.01
White (735,244)	749,229	81.52
Not Hispanic (714,156)	725,671	78.96
Hispanic (21,088)	23,558	2.56

*Notes: † The Census 2010 population figure is used to calculate the percentages in the Hispanic Origin and Race categories. Ancestry percentages are based on the 2006-2010 American Community Survey population (not shown); ‡ Numbers in parentheses indicate the number of people reporting a single ancestry; * Numbers in parentheses indicate the number of persons reporting this race alone, not in combination with any other race; Please refer to the Explanation of Data for more information.*

Essex County

Population: 39,370

Ancestry	Population	%
Afghan (0)	0	<0.01
African, Sub-Saharan (83)	96	0.24
African (55)	67	0.17
Cape Verdean (17)	18	0.05
Ethiopian (11)	11	0.03
Ghanaian (0)	0	<0.01
Kenyan (0)	0	<0.01
Liberian (0)	0	<0.01
Nigerian (0)	0	<0.01
Senegalese (0)	0	<0.01
Sierra Leonean (0)	0	<0.01
Somalian (0)	0	<0.01
South African (0)	0	<0.01
Sudanese (0)	0	<0.01
Ugandan (0)	0	<0.01
Zimbabwean (0)	0	<0.01
Other Sub-Saharan African (0)	0	<0.01
Albanian (35)	35	0.09
Alsatian (0)	0	<0.01
American (1,715)	1,715	4.35
Arab (110)	330	0.84
Arab (0)	0	<0.01
Egyptian (0)	0	<0.01
Iraqi (0)	0	<0.01
Jordanian (0)	0	<0.01
Lebanese (83)	157	0.40
Moroccan (21)	56	0.14
Palestinian (0)	74	0.19
Syrian (3)	22	0.06
Other Arab (3)	21	0.05
Armenian (35)	43	0.11
Assyrian/Chaldean/Syriac (0)	0	<0.01
Australian (0)	0	<0.01
Austrian (19)	86	0.22
Basque (0)	0	<0.01
Belgian (0)	18	0.05
Brazilian (0)	0	<0.01
British (94)	137	0.35
Bulgarian (0)	0	<0.01
Cajun (0)	0	<0.01
Canadian (156)	231	0.59
Carpatho Rusyn (0)	0	<0.01
Celtic (44)	60	0.15
Croatian (0)	0	<0.01
Cypriot (0)	0	<0.01
Czech (95)	225	0.57
Czechoslovakian (5)	28	0.07
Danish (34)	93	0.24
Dutch (213)	940	2.38
Eastern European (64)	82	0.21
English (1,732)	5,580	14.16
Estonian (0)	0	<0.01
European (206)	216	0.55
Finnish (4)	15	0.04
French, ex. Basque (2,335)	8,236	20.90
French Canadian (573)	921	2.34
German (1,511)	5,372	13.63
German Russian (0)	0	<0.01
Greek (83)	199	0.50
Guyanese (0)	10	0.03
Hungarian (171)	308	0.78
Icelander (0)	0	<0.01
Iranian (0)	0	<0.01
Irish (2,945)	8,753	22.21
Israeli (0)	40	0.10
Italian (1,513)	3,545	8.99
Latvian (5)	5	0.01
Lithuanian (17)	44	0.11
Luxemburger (0)	0	<0.01
Macedonian (0)	0	<0.01
Maltese (0)	0	<0.01
New Zealander (0)	0	<0.01
Northern European (4)	4	0.01
Norwegian (33)	268	0.68
Pennsylvania German (0)	11	0.03

Ancestry	Population	%
Polish (383)	1,483	3.76
Portuguese (23)	27	0.07
Romanian (126)	183	0.46
Russian (310)	688	1.75
Scandinavian (9)	41	0.10
Scotch-Irish (249)	998	2.53
Scottish (340)	1,350	3.43
Serbian (9)	29	0.07
Slavic (0)	14	0.04
Slovak (75)	106	0.27
Slovene (0)	0	<0.01
Soviet Union (0)	0	<0.01
Swedish (112)	634	1.61
Swiss (13)	108	0.27
Turkish (0)	0	<0.01
Ukrainian (11)	53	0.13
Welsh (37)	424	1.08
West Indian, ex. Hispanic (75)	114	0.29
Bahamian (0)	0	<0.01
Barbadian (0)	0	<0.01
Belizean (0)	0	<0.01
Bermudan (0)	0	<0.01
British West Indian (0)	10	0.03
Dutch West Indian (0)	0	<0.01
Haitian (0)	0	<0.01
Jamaican (17)	17	0.04
Trinidadian/Tobagonian (11)	11	0.03
U.S. Virgin Islander (0)	0	<0.01
West Indian (47)	76	0.19
Other West Indian (0)	0	<0.01
Yugoslavian (0)	0	<0.01

Hispanic Origin	Population	%
Hispanic or Latino (of any race)	993	2.52
Central American, ex. Mexican	92	0.23
Costa Rican	7	0.02
Guatemalan	29	0.07
Honduran	15	0.04
Nicaraguan	3	0.01
Panamanian	7	0.02
Salvadoran	31	0.08
Other Central American	0	<0.01
Cuban	25	0.06
Dominican Republic	83	0.21
Mexican	355	0.90
Puerto Rican	296	0.75
South American	42	0.11
Argentinean	3	0.01
Bolivian	0	<0.01
Chilean	4	0.01
Colombian	16	0.04
Ecuadorian	0	<0.01
Paraguayan	0	<0.01
Peruvian	8	0.02
Uruguayan	4	0.01
Venezuelan	7	0.02
Other South American	0	<0.01
Other Hispanic or Latino	100	0.25

Race*	Population	%
African-American/Black (1,073)	1,213	3.08
Not Hispanic (982)	1,101	2.80
Hispanic (91)	112	0.28
American Indian/Alaska Native (126)	370	0.94
Not Hispanic (99)	327	0.83
Hispanic (27)	43	0.11
Alaska Athabascan (Ala. Nat.) (1)	3	0.01
Aleut (Alaska Native) (0)	0	<0.01
Apache (1)	2	0.01
Arapaho (0)	0	<0.01
Blackfeet (4)	19	0.05
Canadian/French Am. Ind. (3)	8	0.02
Central American Ind. (0)	1	<0.01
Cherokee (2)	22	0.06
Cheyenne (0)	1	<0.01
Chickasaw (0)	0	<0.01
Chippewa (1)	1	<0.01
Choctaw (2)	2	0.01
Colville (0)	0	<0.01

Race*	Population	%
Comanche (0)	6	0.02
Cree (0)	6	0.02
Creek (0)	0	<0.01
Crow (0)	0	<0.01
Delaware (0)	1	<0.01
Hopi (0)	1	<0.01
Houma (0)	0	<0.01
Inupiat (Alaska Native) (1)	1	<0.01
Iroquois (33)	101	0.26
Kiowa (0)	0	<0.01
Lumbee (2)	7	0.02
Menominee (0)	0	<0.01
Mexican American Ind. (13)	14	0.04
Navajo (3)	3	<0.01
Osage (0)	0	<0.01
Ottawa (0)	0	<0.01
Paiute (0)	0	<0.01
Pima (0)	0	<0.01
Potawatomi (0)	0	<0.01
Pueblo (0)	1	<0.01
Puget Sound Salish (0)	0	<0.01
Seminole (0)	0	<0.01
Shoshone (0)	0	<0.01
Sioux (1)	8	0.02
South American Ind. (0)	1	<0.01
Spanish American Ind. (0)	0	<0.01
Tlingit-Haida (Alaska Native) (0)	0	<0.01
Tohono O'Odham (0)	0	<0.01
Tsimshian (Alaska Native) (0)	0	<0.01
Ute (0)	0	<0.01
Yakama (0)	0	<0.01
Yaqui (0)	1	<0.01
Yuman (0)	0	<0.01
Yup'ik (Alaska Native) (0)	0	<0.01
Asian (263)	324	0.82
Not Hispanic (260)	316	0.80
Hispanic (3)	8	0.02
Bangladeshi (0)	0	<0.01
Bhutanese (0)	0	<0.01
Burmese (0)	0	<0.01
Cambodian (5)	5	0.01
Chinese, ex. Taiwanese (63)	73	0.19
Filipino (36)	54	0.14
Hmong (0)	0	<0.01
Indian (33)	41	0.10
Indonesian (0)	0	<0.01
Japanese (21)	31	0.08
Korean (38)	46	0.12
Laotian (1)	1	<0.01
Malaysian (1)	1	<0.01
Nepalese (0)	0	<0.01
Pakistani (29)	30	0.08
Sri Lankan (0)	0	<0.01
Taiwanese (0)	0	<0.01
Thai (3)	6	0.02
Vietnamese (17)	19	0.05
Hawaii Native/Pacific Islander (9)	31	0.08
Not Hispanic (8)	28	0.07
Hispanic (1)	3	0.01
Fijian (0)	0	<0.01
Guamanian/Chamorro (1)	3	0.01
Marshallese (0)	0	<0.01
Native Hawaiian (5)	15	0.04
Samoan (0)	1	<0.01
Tongan (3)	3	0.01
White (37,100)	37,536	95.34
Not Hispanic (36,588)	36,969	93.90
Hispanic (512)	567	1.44

Notes: † The Census 2010 population figure is used to calculate the percentages in the Hispanic Origin and Race categories. Ancestry percentages are based on the 2006-2010 American Community Survey population (not shown); ‡ Numbers in parentheses indicate the number of people reporting a single ancestry; * Numbers in parentheses indicate the number of persons reporting this race alone, not in combination with any other race; Please refer to the Explanation of Data for more information.

Franklin County

Population: 51,599

Ancestry	Population	%
Afghan (0)	0	<0.01
African, Sub-Saharan (46)	191	0.37
African (46)	182	0.35
Cape Verdean (0)	0	<0.01
Ethiopian (0)	0	<0.01
Ghanaian (0)	0	<0.01
Kenyan (0)	0	<0.01
Liberian (0)	0	<0.01
Nigerian (0)	0	<0.01
Senegalese (0)	0	<0.01
Sierra Leonean (0)	0	<0.01
Somalian (0)	0	<0.01
South African (0)	9	0.02
Sudanese (0)	0	<0.01
Ugandan (0)	0	<0.01
Zimbabwean (0)	0	<0.01
Other Sub-Saharan African (0)	0	<0.01
Albanian (74)	74	0.14
Alsatian (0)	0	<0.01
American (3,069)	3,069	5.94
Arab (243)	285	0.55
Arab (12)	12	0.02
Egyptian (0)	0	<0.01
Iraqi (0)	0	<0.01
Jordanian (0)	0	<0.01
Lebanese (59)	82	0.16
Moroccan (80)	80	0.15
Palestinian (0)	0	<0.01
Syrian (13)	22	0.04
Other Arab (79)	89	0.17
Armenian (8)	8	0.02
Assyrian/Chaldean/Syriac (0)	0	<0.01
Australian (0)	14	0.03
Austrian (21)	143	0.28
Basque (0)	0	<0.01
Belgian (5)	22	0.04
Brazilian (5)	5	0.01
British (82)	128	0.25
Bulgarian (15)	15	0.03
Cajun (0)	0	<0.01
Canadian (249)	431	0.83
Carpatho Rusyn (0)	0	<0.01
Celtic (0)	7	0.01
Croatian (0)	14	0.03
Cypriot (0)	0	<0.01
Czech (10)	73	0.14
Czechoslovakian (0)	6	0.01
Danish (23)	138	0.27
Dutch (163)	1,095	2.12
Eastern European (13)	20	0.04
English (1,709)	5,133	9.93
Estonian (0)	0	<0.01
European (179)	191	0.37
Finnish (6)	18	0.03
French, ex. Basque (3,834)	11,336	21.93
French Canadian (1,852)	2,810	5.44
German (937)	4,795	9.28
German Russian (0)	0	<0.01
Greek (63)	144	0.28
Guyanese (99)	187	0.36
Hungarian (32)	205	0.40
Icelander (0)	0	<0.01
Iranian (0)	0	<0.01
Irish (2,541)	9,398	18.18
Israeli (0)	21	0.04
Italian (794)	2,508	4.85
Latvian (0)	0	<0.01
Lithuanian (12)	94	0.18
Luxemburger (0)	6	0.01
Macedonian (0)	0	<0.01
Maltese (0)	0	<0.01
New Zealander (0)	0	<0.01
Northern European (23)	38	0.07
Norwegian (35)	145	0.28
Pennsylvania German (58)	115	0.22

	Population	%
Polish (407)	1,135	2.20
Portuguese (30)	60	0.12
Romanian (2)	18	0.03
Russian (101)	306	0.59
Scandinavian (22)	38	0.07
Scotch-Irish (293)	865	1.67
Scottish (326)	1,124	2.17
Serbian (0)	0	<0.01
Slavic (0)	0	<0.01
Slovak (18)	37	0.07
Slovene (9)	15	0.03
Soviet Union (0)	0	<0.01
Swedish (40)	285	0.55
Swiss (59)	159	0.31
Turkish (16)	22	0.04
Ukrainian (85)	200	0.39
Welsh (41)	336	0.65
West Indian, ex. Hispanic (27)	65	0.13
Bahamian (0)	0	<0.01
Barbadian (0)	0	<0.01
Belizean (0)	0	<0.01
Bermudan (0)	0	<0.01
British West Indian (0)	0	<0.01
Dutch West Indian (0)	0	<0.01
Haitian (0)	14	0.03
Jamaican (19)	35	0.07
Trinidadian/Tobagonian (8)	8	0.02
U.S. Virgin Islander (0)	0	<0.01
West Indian (0)	8	0.02
Other West Indian (0)	0	<0.01
Yugoslavian (0)	25	0.05

Hispanic Origin	Population	%
Hispanic or Latino (of any race)	1,506	2.92
Central American, ex. Mexican	123	0.24
Costa Rican	7	0.01
Guatemalan	25	0.05
Honduran	37	0.07
Nicaraguan	1	<0.01
Panamanian	26	0.05
Salvadoran	27	0.05
Other Central American	0	<0.01
Cuban	55	0.11
Dominican Republic	209	0.41
Mexican	211	0.41
Puerto Rican	730	1.41
South American	79	0.15
Argentinean	2	<0.01
Bolivian	0	<0.01
Chilean	2	<0.01
Colombian	24	0.05
Ecuadorian	24	0.05
Paraguayan	0	<0.01
Peruvian	18	0.03
Uruguayan	1	<0.01
Venezuelan	8	0.02
Other South American	0	<0.01
Other Hispanic or Latino	99	0.19

Race*	Population	%
African-American/Black (3,127)	3,262	6.32
Not Hispanic (2,834)	2,957	5.73
Hispanic (293)	305	0.59
American Indian/Alaska Native (3,797)	4,187	8.11
Not Hispanic (3,753)	4,124	7.99
Hispanic (44)	63	0.12
Alaska Athabascan (Ala. Nat.) (0)	0	<0.01
Aleut (Alaska Native) (0)	0	<0.01
Apache (3)	4	0.01
Arapaho (0)	1	<0.01
Blackfeet (2)	6	0.01
Canadian/French Am. Ind. (5)	10	0.02
Central American Ind. (0)	0	<0.01
Cherokee (17)	36	0.07
Cheyenne (0)	0	<0.01
Chickasaw (0)	0	<0.01
Chippewa (8)	10	0.02
Choctaw (0)	0	<0.01
Colville (1)	1	<0.01

	Population	%
Comanche (0)	0	<0.01
Cree (4)	4	0.01
Creek (1)	2	<0.01
Crow (0)	6	0.01
Delaware (7)	11	0.02
Hopi (0)	0	<0.01
Houma (0)	0	<0.01
Inupiat (Alaska Native) (0)	0	<0.01
Iroquois (2,928)	3,130	6.07
Kiowa (0)	0	<0.01
Lumbee (1)	1	<0.01
Menominee (0)	0	<0.01
Mexican American Ind. (8)	9	0.02
Navajo (6)	6	0.01
Osage (0)	0	<0.01
Ottawa (0)	0	<0.01
Paiute (1)	1	<0.01
Pima (0)	0	<0.01
Potawatorni (0)	0	<0.01
Pueblo (1)	1	<0.01
Puget Sound Salish (0)	0	<0.01
Seminole (0)	0	<0.01
Shoshone (1)	1	<0.01
Sioux (1)	1	<0.01
South American Ind. (13)	17	0.03
Spanish American Ind. (8)	8	0.02
Tlingit-Haida (Alaska Native) (0)	1	<0.01
Tohono O'Odham (0)	0	<0.01
Tsimshian (Alaska Native) (0)	0	<0.01
Ute (0)	0	<0.01
Yakama (0)	0	<0.01
Yaqui (1)	1	<0.01
Yuman (0)	0	<0.01
Yup'ik (Alaska Native) (1)	1	<0.01
Asian (219)	323	0.63
Not Hispanic (215)	307	0.59
Hispanic (4)	16	0.03
Bangladeshi (2)	2	<0.01
Bhutanese (0)	0	<0.01
Burmese (0)	0	<0.01
Cambodian (2)	2	<0.01
Chinese, ex. Taiwanese (61)	70	0.14
Filipino (36)	83	0.16
Hmong (0)	0	<0.01
Indian (51)	64	0.12
Indonesian (0)	8	0.02
Japanese (6)	11	0.02
Korean (18)	34	0.07
Laotian (0)	3	0.01
Malaysian (0)	0	<0.01
Nepalese (0)	0	<0.01
Pakistani (2)	2	<0.01
Sri Lankan (0)	0	<0.01
Taiwanese (0)	0	<0.01
Thai (3)	6	0.01
Vietnamese (4)	13	0.03
Hawaii Native/Pacific Islander (10)	23	0.04
Not Hispanic (8)	19	0.04
Hispanic (2)	4	0.01
Fijian (0)	0	<0.01
Guamanian/Chamorro (1)	5	0.01
Marshallese (0)	0	<0.01
Native Hawaiian (0)	3	0.01
Samoan (1)	2	<0.01
Tongan (7)	7	0.01
White (43,437)	44,021	85.31
Not Hispanic (42,640)	43,177	83.68
Hispanic (797)	844	1.64

Notes: † *The Census 2010 population figure is used to calculate the percentages in the Hispanic Origin and Race categories. Ancestry percentages are based on the 2006-2010 American Community Survey population (not shown);* ‡ *Numbers in parentheses indicate the number of people reporting a single ancestry;* * *Numbers in parentheses indicate the number of persons reporting this race alone, not in combination with any other race; Please refer to the Explanation of Data for more information.*

Fulton County
Population: 55,531.

Ancestry	Population	%
Afghan (0)	0	<0.01
African, Sub-Saharan (23)	23	0.04
African (23)	23	0.04
Cape Verdean (0)	0	<0.01
Ethiopian (0)	0	<0.01
Ghanaian (0)	0	<0.01
Kenyan (0)	0	<0.01
Liberian (0)	0	<0.01
Nigerian (0)	0	<0.01
Senegalese (0)	0	<0.01
Sierra Leonean (0)	0	<0.01
Somalian (0)	0	<0.01
South African (0)	0	<0.01
Sudanese (0)	0	<0.01
Ugandan (0)	0	<0.01
Zimbabwean (0)	0	<0.01
Other Sub-Saharan African (0)	0	<0.01
Albanian (0)	0	<0.01
Alsatian (0)	0	<0.01
American (5,287)	5,287	9.53
Arab (38)	86	0.15
Arab (0)	0	<0.01
Egyptian (0)	0	<0.01
Iraqi (0)	0	<0.01
Jordanian (0)	0	<0.01
Lebanese (18)	57	0.10
Moroccan (0)	0	<0.01
Palestinian (0)	9	0.02
Syrian (0)	0	<0.01
Other Arab (20)	20	0.04
Armenian (37)	88	0.16
Assyrian/Chaldean/Syriac (0)	0	<0.01
Australian (0)	0	<0.01
Austrian (21)	81	0.15
Basque (0)	0	<0.01
Belgian (11)	35	0.06
Brazilian (2)	8	0.01
British (61)	162	0.29
Bulgarian (0)	15	0.03
Cajun (0)	0	<0.01
Canadian (162)	220	0.40
Carpatho Rusyn (0)	0	<0.01
Celtic (0)	0	<0.01
Croatian (0)	0	<0.01
Cypriot (0)	0	<0.01
Czech (67)	239	0.43
Czechoslovakian (74)	146	0.26
Danish (36)	125	0.23
Dutch (358)	3,774	6.80
Eastern European (32)	32	0.06
English (2,859)	7,912	14.26
Estonian (13)	13	0.02
European (146)	153	0.28
Finnish (13)	26	0.05
French, ex. Basque (486)	3,837	6.91
French Canadian (261)	694	1.25
German (2,540)	12,273	22.11
German Russian (0)	0	<0.01
Greek (34)	142	0.26
Guyanese (0)	0	<0.01
Hungarian (47)	284	0.51
Icelander (0)	0	<0.01
Iranian (142)	145	0.26
Irish (2,348)	10,129	18.25
Israeli (0)	0	<0.01
Italian (3,386)	8,675	15.63
Latvian (0)	25	0.05
Lithuanian (187)	469	0.85
Luxemburger (0)	0	<0.01
Macedonian (0)	0	<0.01
Maltese (0)	0	<0.01
New Zealander (0)	0	<0.01
Northern European (36)	36	0.06
Norwegian (33)	279	0.50
Pennsylvania German (15)	46	0.08

Ancestry (cont.)	Population	%
Polish (1,314)	4,092	7.37
Portuguese (17)	101	0.18
Romanian (0)	0	<0.01
Russian (78)	190	0.34
Scandinavian (0)	6	0.01
Scotch-Irish (155)	653	1.18
Scottish (226)	1,178	2.12
Serbian (0)	0	<0.01
Slavic (3)	40	0.07
Slovak (328)	666	1.20
Slovene (0)	4	0.01
Soviet Union (0)	0	<0.01
Swedish (84)	410	0.74
Swiss (0)	131	0.24
Turkish (0)	15	0.03
Ukrainian (248)	510	0.92
Welsh (55)	422	0.76
West Indian, ex. Hispanic (36)	72	0.13
Bahamian (0)	0	<0.01
Barbadian (0)	0	<0.01
Belizean (0)	0	<0.01
Bermudan (0)	0	<0.01
British West Indian (0)	0	<0.01
Dutch West Indian (0)	0	<0.01
Haitian (0)	0	<0.01
Jamaican (27)	36	0.06
Trinidadian/Tobagonian (0)	27	0.05
U.S. Virgin Islander (0)	0	<0.01
West Indian (9)	9	0.02
Other West Indian (0)	0	<0.01
Yugoslavian (98)	109	0.20

Hispanic Origin	Population	%
Hispanic or Latino (of any race)	1,263	2.27
Central American, ex. Mexican	51	0.09
Costa Rican	22	0.04
Guatemalan	5	0.01
Honduran	9	0.02
Nicaraguan	2	<0.01
Panamanian	11	0.02
Salvadoran	2	<0.01
Other Central American	0	<0.01
Cuban	30	0.05
Dominican Republic	68	0.12
Mexican	138	0.25
Puerto Rican	782	1.41
South American	54	0.10
Argentinean	8	0.01
Bolivian	1	<0.01
Chilean	1	<0.01
Colombian	19	0.03
Ecuadorian	13	0.02
Paraguayan	0	<0.01
Peruvian	11	0.02
Uruguayan	0	<0.01
Venezuelan	1	<0.01
Other South American	0	<0.01
Other Hispanic or Latino	140	0.25

Race*	Population	%
African-American/Black (1,060)	1,433	2.58
Not Hispanic (981)	1,315	2.37
Hispanic (79)	118	0.21
American Indian/Alaska Native (116)	356	0.64
Not Hispanic (104)	331	0.60
Hispanic (12)	25	0.05
Alaska Athabascan (Ala. Nat.) (0)	0	<0.01
Aleut (Alaska Native) (0)	0	<0.01
Apache (4)	7	0.01
Arapaho (0)	0	<0.01
Blackfeet (3)	18	0.03
Canadian/French Am. Ind. (3)	7	0.01
Central American Ind. (0)	0	<0.01
Cherokee (5)	29	0.05
Cheyenne (0)	0	<0.01
Chickasaw (1)	1	<0.01
Chippewa (0)	4	0.01
Choctaw (0)	0	<0.01
Colville (0)	0	<0.01

Race* (cont.)	Population	%
Comanche (0)	1	<0.01
Cree (0)	1	<0.01
Creek (1)	1	<0.01
Crow (0)	0	<0.01
Delaware (1)	2	<0.01
Hopi (0)	0	<0.01
Houma (0)	0	<0.01
Inupiat (Alaska Native) (0)	0	<0.01
Iroquois (37)	86	0.15
Kiowa (0)	0	<0.01
Lumbee (0)	0	<0.01
Menominee (0)	0	<0.01
Mexican American Ind. (3)	3	0.01
Navajo (3)	6	0.01
Osage (0)	0	<0.01
Ottawa (0)	0	<0.01
Paiute (0)	0	<0.01
Pima (0)	0	<0.01
Potawatomi (0)	0	<0.01
Pueblo (0)	0	<0.01
Puget Sound Salish (0)	0	<0.01
Seminole (0)	4	0.01
Shoshone (0)	0	<0.01
Sioux (0)	5	0.01
South American Ind. (0)	0	<0.01
Spanish American Ind. (0)	0	<0.01
Tlingit-Haida (Alaska Native) (0)	0	<0.01
Tohono O'Odham (0)	0	<0.01
Tsimshian (Alaska Native) (0)	0	<0.01
Ute (0)	0	<0.01
Yakama (0)	0	<0.01
Yaqui (0)	0	<0.01
Yuman (0)	0	<0.01
Yup'ik (Alaska Native) (0)	0	<0.01
Asian (321)	454	0.82
Not Hispanic (320)	444	0.80
Hispanic (1)	10	0.02
Bangladeshi (0)	0	<0.01
Bhutanese (0)	0	<0.01
Burmese (0)	0	<0.01
Cambodian (0)	1	<0.01
Chinese, ex. Taiwanese (71)	88	0.16
Filipino (44)	80	0.14
Hmong (0)	0	<0.01
Indian (82)	100	0.18
Indonesian (3)	7	0.01
Japanese (32)	47	0.08
Korean (45)	65	0.12
Laotian (0)	0	<0.01
Malaysian (1)	2	<0.01
Nepalese (0)	0	<0.01
Pakistani (3)	5	0.01
Sri Lankan (0)	0	<0.01
Taiwanese (2)	6	0.01
Thai (2)	2	<0.01
Vietnamese (20)	29	0.05
Hawaii Native/Pacific Islander (13)	61	0.11
Not Hispanic (11)	46	0.08
Hispanic (2)	15	0.03
Fijian (0)	0	<0.01
Guamanian/Chamorro (0)	0	<0.01
Marshallese (0)	0	<0.01
Native Hawaiian (4)	34	0.06
Samoan (0)	7	0.01
Tongan (0)	0	<0.01
White (52,948)	53,684	96.67
Not Hispanic (52,110)	52,773	95.03
Hispanic (838)	911	1.64

Notes: † The Census 2010 population figure is used to calculate the percentages in the Hispanic Origin and Race categories. Ancestry percentages are based on the 2006-2010 American Community Survey population (not shown); ‡ Numbers in parentheses indicate the number of people reporting a single ancestry; * Numbers in parentheses indicate the number of persons reporting this race alone, not in combination with any other race; Please refer to the Explanation of Data for more information.

Genesee County

Population: 60,079

Ancestry	Population	%
Afghan (0)	0	<0.01
African, Sub-Saharan (46)	142	0.24
African (46)	142	0.24
Cape Verdean (0)	0	<0.01
Ethiopian (0)	0	<0.01
Ghanaian (0)	0	<0.01
Kenyan (0)	0	<0.01
Liberian (0)	0	<0.01
Nigerian (0)	0	<0.01
Senegalese (0)	0	<0.01
Sierra Leonean (0)	0	<0.01
Somalian (0)	0	<0.01
South African (0)	0	<0.01
Sudanese (0)	0	<0.01
Ugandan (0)	0	<0.01
Zimbabwean (0)	0	<0.01
Other Sub-Saharan African (0)	0	<0.01
Albanian (0)	0	<0.01
Alsatian (0)	0	<0.01
American (2,398)	2,398	4.00
Arab (49)	75	0.13
Arab (17)	36	0.06
Egyptian (0)	0	<0.01
Iraqi (0)	0	<0.01
Jordanian (0)	0	<0.01
Lebanese (0)	0	<0.01
Moroccan (0)	0	<0.01
Palestinian (22)	22	0.04
Syrian (0)	0	<0.01
Other Arab (10)	17	0.03
Armenian (0)	0	<0.01
Assyrian/Chaldean/Syriac (0)	0	<0.01
Australian (0)	0	<0.01
Austrian (53)	141	0.24
Basque (0)	0	<0.01
Belgian (22)	55	0.09
Brazilian (0)	0	<0.01
British (84)	183	0.31
Bulgarian (0)	83	0.14
Cajun (0)	0	<0.01
Canadian (128)	244	0.41
Carpatho Rusyn (0)	0	<0.01
Celtic (0)	0	<0.01
Croatian (10)	61	0.10
Cypriot (0)	0	<0.01
Czech (36)	194	0.32
Czechoslovakian (38)	63	0.11
Danish (47)	85	0.14
Dutch (172)	1,821	3.04
Eastern European (7)	32	0.05
English (2,539)	10,461	17.45
Estonian (0)	0	<0.01
European (240)	272	0.45
Finnish (32)	56	0.09
French, ex. Basque (314)	2,447	4.08
French Canadian (213)	453	0.76
German (5,537)	19,568	32.64
German Russian (0)	0	<0.01
Greek (151)	285	0.48
Guyanese (172)	229	0.38
Hungarian (55)	370	0.62
Icelander (0)	2	<0.01
Iranian (0)	0	<0.01
Irish (2,577)	11,417	19.04
Israeli (0)	0	<0.01
Italian (4,677)	10,953	18.27
Latvian (0)	0	<0.01
Lithuanian (12)	71	0.12
Luxemburger (0)	0	<0.01
Macedonian (0)	0	<0.01
Maltese (0)	0	<0.01
New Zealander (0)	0	<0.01
Northern European (32)	32	0.05
Norwegian (46)	168	0.28
Pennsylvania German (6)	33	0.06

Ancestry	Population	%
Polish (2,200)	6,848	11.42
Portuguese (26)	33	0.06
Romanian (26)	35	0.06
Russian (39)	181	0.30
Scandinavian (7)	14	0.02
Scotch-Irish (365)	1,105	1.84
Scottish (446)	1,321	2.20
Serbian (0)	19	0.03
Slavic (9)	30	0.05
Slovak (73)	123	0.21
Slovene (0)	9	0.02
Soviet Union (0)	0	<0.01
Swedish (135)	398	0.66
Swiss (37)	114	0.19
Turkish (21)	29	0.05
Ukrainian (75)	230	0.38
Welsh (81)	480	0.80
West Indian, ex. Hispanic (62)	94	0.16
Bahamian (0)	0	<0.01
Barbadian (0)	0	<0.01
Belizean (0)	0	<0.01
Bermudan (0)	0	<0.01
British West Indian (0)	0	<0.01
Dutch West Indian (0)	0	<0.01
Haitian (0)	16	0.03
Jamaican (17)	17	0.03
Trinidadian/Tobagonian (0)	16	0.03
U.S. Virgin Islander (0)	0	<0.01
West Indian (45)	45	0.08
Other West Indian (0)	0	<0.01
Yugoslavian (0)	11	0.02

Hispanic Origin	Population	%
Hispanic or Latino (of any race)	1,616	2.69
Central American, ex. Mexican	66	0.11
Costa Rican	0	<0.01
Guatemalan	36	0.06
Honduran	10	0.02
Nicaraguan	5	0.01
Panamanian	6	0.01
Salvadoran	9	0.01
Other Central American	0	<0.01
Cuban	24	0.04
Dominican Republic	49	0.08
Mexican	683	1.14
Puerto Rican	620	1.03
South American	65	0.11
Argentinean	6	0.01
Bolivian	7	0.01
Chilean	5	0.01
Colombian	21	0.03
Ecuadorian	14	0.02
Paraguayan	0	<0.01
Peruvian	5	0.01
Uruguayan	0	<0.01
Venezuelan	7	0.01
Other South American	0	<0.01
Other Hispanic or Latino	109	0.18

Race*	Population	%
African-American/Black (1,612)	2,243	3.73
Not Hispanic (1,491)	2,053	3.42
Hispanic (121)	190	0.32
American Indian/Alaska Native (679)	997	1.66
Not Hispanic (661)	949	1.58
Hispanic (18)	48	0.08
Alaska Athabascan (Ala. Nat.) (0)	0	<0.01
Aleut (Alaska Native) (0)	0	<0.01
Apache (1)	5	0.01
Arapaho (0)	0	<0.01
Blackfeet (0)	19	0.03
Canadian/French Am. Ind. (7)	9	0.01
Central American Ind. (1)	1	<0.01
Cherokee (10)	42	0.07
Cheyenne (0)	0	<0.01
Chickasaw (0)	0	<0.01
Chippewa (5)	8	0.01
Choctaw (3)	7	0.01
Colville (0)	0	<0.01

Race*	Population	%
Comanche (1)	1	<0.01
Cree (0)	5	0.01
Creek (4)	4	0.01
Crow (0)	0	<0.01
Delaware (1)	2	<0.01
Hopi (1)	1	<0.01
Houma (0)	0	<0.01
Inupiat (Alaska Native) (0)	0	<0.01
Iroquois (267)	344	0.57
Kiowa (0)	0	<0.01
Lumbee (0)	0	<0.01
Menominee (0)	0	<0.01
Mexican American Ind. (1)	2	<0.01
Navajo (3)	4	0.01
Osage (0)	4	0.01
Ottawa (0)	0	<0.01
Paiute (0)	0	<0.01
Pima (0)	0	<0.01
Potawatomi (0)	0	<0.01
Pueblo (0)	0	<0.01
Puget Sound Salish (0)	0	<0.01
Seminole (0)	10	0.02
Shoshone (0)	0	<0.01
Sioux (3)	5	0.01
South American Ind. (2)	2	<0.01
Spanish American Ind. (0)	0	<0.01
Tlingit-Haida (Alaska Native) (0)	0	<0.01
Tohono O'Odham (0)	0	<0.01
Tsimshian (Alaska Native) (0)	0	<0.01
Ute (0)	0	<0.01
Yakama (0)	0	<0.01
Yaqui (0)	5	0.01
Yuman (0)	0	<0.01
Yup'ik (Alaska Native) (0)	0	<0.01
Asian (357)	494	0.82
Not Hispanic (355)	481	0.80
Hispanic (2)	13	0.02
Bangladeshi (2)	4	0.01
Bhutanese (0)	0	<0.01
Burmese (0)	0	<0.01
Cambodian (0)	1	<0.01
Chinese, ex. Taiwanese (72)	95	0.16
Filipino (50)	83	0.14
Hmong (0)	0	<0.01
Indian (84)	103	0.17
Indonesian (1)	3	<0.01
Japanese (43)	57	0.09
Korean (52)	76	0.13
Laotian (14)	17	0.03
Malaysian (0)	0	<0.01
Nepalese (0)	0	<0.01
Pakistani (10)	10	0.02
Sri Lankan (0)	0	<0.01
Taiwanese (0)	0	<0.01
Thai (5)	12	0.02
Vietnamese (6)	10	0.02
Hawaii Native/Pacific Islander (4)	27	0.04
Not Hispanic (2)	17	0.03
Hispanic (2)	10	0.02
Fijian (0)	0	<0.01
Guamanian/Chamorro (2)	4	0.01
Marshallese (0)	0	<0.01
Native Hawaiian (2)	12	0.02
Samoan (0)	1	<0.01
Tongan (0)	0	<0.01
White (55,787)	56,763	94.48
Not Hispanic (54,990)	55,842	92.95
Hispanic (797)	921	1.53

Notes: † The Census 2010 population figure is used to calculate the percentages in the Hispanic Origin and Race categories. Ancestry percentages are based on the 2006-2010 American Community Survey population (not shown); ‡ Numbers in parentheses indicate the number of people reporting a single ancestry; * Numbers in parentheses indicate the number of persons reporting this race alone, not in combination with any other race; Please refer to the Explanation of Data for more information.

Greene County

Population: 49,221

Ancestry	Population	%
Afghan (0)	0	<0.01
African, Sub-Saharan (114)	121	0.24
African (57)	64	0.13
Cape Verdean (5)	5	0.01
Ethiopian (8)	8	0.02
Ghanaian (44)	44	0.09
Kenyan (0)	0	<0.01
Liberian (0)	0	<0.01
Nigerian (0)	0	<0.01
Senegalese (0)	0	<0.01
Sierra Leonean (0)	0	<0.01
Somalian (0)	0	<0.01
South African (0)	0	<0.01
Sudanese (0)	0	<0.01
Ugandan (0)	0	<0.01
Zimbabwean (0)	0	<0.01
Other Sub-Saharan African (0)	0	<0.01
Albanian (80)	85	0.17
Alsatian (0)	0	<0.01
American (5,920)	5,920	11.98
Arab (66)	96	0.19
Arab (0)	0	<0.01
Egyptian (0)	0	<0.01
Iraqi (0)	0	<0.01
Jordanian (0)	0	<0.01
Lebanese (11)	30	0.06
Moroccan (0)	0	<0.01
Palestinian (0)	0	<0.01
Syrian (55)	66	0.13
Other Arab (0)	0	<0.01
Armenian (26)	46	0.09
Assyrian/Chaldean/Syriac (0)	0	<0.01
Australian (25)	25	0.05
Austrian (150)	313	0.63
Basque (0)	0	<0.01
Belgian (6)	6	0.01
Brazilian (10)	10	0.02
British (176)	231	0.47
Bulgarian (0)	0	<0.01
Cajun (0)	62	0.13
Canadian (123)	223	0.45
Carpatho Rusyn (0)	0	<0.01
Celtic (0)	0	<0.01
Croatian (41)	125	0.25
Cypriot (0)	0	<0.01
Czech (31)	170	0.34
Czechoslovakian (130)	181	0.37
Danish (75)	163	0.33
Dutch (675)	2,970	6.01
Eastern European (125)	134	0.27
English (1,220)	4,245	8.59
Estonian (0)	0	<0.01
European (695)	806	1.63
Finnish (1)	84	0.17
French, ex. Basque (341)	1,780	3.60
French Canadian (221)	536	1.08
German (2,656)	8,675	17.56
German Russian (0)	0	<0.01
Greek (180)	294	0.60
Guyanese (8)	8	0.02
Hungarian (183)	448	0.91
Icelander (0)	0	<0.01
Iranian (15)	15	0.03
Irish (3,244)	9,113	18.44
Israeli (9)	9	0.02
Italian (4,020)	8,909	18.03
Latvian (0)	31	0.06
Lithuanian (48)	98	0.20
Luxemburger (0)	3	0.01
Macedonian (0)	0	<0.01
Maltese (0)	0	<0.01
New Zealander (0)	0	<0.01
Northern European (10)	16	0.03
Norwegian (206)	423	0.86
Pennsylvania German (5)	18	0.04

Ancestry	Population	%
Polish (718)	2,469	5.00
Portuguese (32)	148	0.30
Romanian (67)	83	0.17
Russian (160)	484	0.98
Scandinavian (54)	87	0.18
Scotch-Irish (163)	554	1.12
Scottish (153)	674	1.36
Serbian (68)	86	0.17
Slavic (8)	79	0.16
Slovak (110)	155	0.31
Slovene (0)	0	<0.01
Soviet Union (0)	0	<0.01
Swedish (74)	340	0.69
Swiss (31)	103	0.21
Turkish (0)	0	<0.01
Ukrainian (279)	465	0.94
Welsh (19)	225	0.46
West Indian, ex. Hispanic (82)	118	0.24
Bahamian (0)	0	<0.01
Barbadian (0)	0	<0.01
Belizean (0)	0	<0.01
Bermudan (0)	0	<0.01
British West Indian (0)	0	<0.01
Dutch West Indian (0)	0	<0.01
Haitian (8)	8	0.02
Jamaican (57)	70	0.14
Trinidadian/Tobagonian (17)	17	0.03
U.S. Virgin Islander (0)	0	<0.01
West Indian (0)	23	0.05
Other West Indian (0)	0	<0.01
Yugoslavian (36)	106	0.21

Hispanic Origin	Population	%
Hispanic or Latino (of any race)	2,419	4.91
Central American, ex. Mexican	162	0.33
Costa Rican	10	0.02
Guatemalan	30	0.06
Honduran	22	0.04
Nicaraguan	5	0.01
Panamanian	12	0.02
Salvadoran	83	0.17
Other Central American	0	<0.01
Cuban	74	0.15
Dominican Republic	148	0.30
Mexican	343	0.70
Puerto Rican	1,298	2.64
South American	189	0.38
Argentinean	17	0.03
Bolivian	0	<0.01
Chilean	22	0.04
Colombian	72	0.15
Ecuadorian	28	0.06
Paraguayan	1	<0.01
Peruvian	26	0.05
Uruguayan	4	0.01
Venezuelan	17	0.03
Other South American	2	<0.01
Other Hispanic or Latino	205	0.42

Race*	Population	%
African-American/Black (2,826)	3,272	6.65
Not Hispanic (2,606)	3,010	6.12
Hispanic (220)	262	0.53
American Indian/Alaska Native (145)	406	0.82
Not Hispanic (122)	360	0.73
Hispanic (23)	46	0.09
Alaska Athabascan (Ala. Nat.) (0)	0	<0.01
Aleut (Alaska Native) (0)	0	<0.01
Apache (2)	10	0.02
Arapaho (0)	2	<0.01
Blackfeet (0)	5	0.01
Canadian/French Am. Ind. (0)	0	<0.01
Central American Ind. (1)	2	<0.01
Cherokee (5)	45	0.09
Cheyenne (0)	0	<0.01
Chickasaw (0)	0	<0.01
Chippewa (4)	6	0.01
Choctaw (2)	6	0.01
Colville (0)	0	<0.01

Race*	Population	%
Comanche (0)	1	<0.01
Cree (0)	0	<0.01
Creek (0)	2	<0.01
Crow (0)	0	<0.01
Delaware (1)	4	0.01
Hopi (0)	0	<0.01
Houma (0)	0	<0.01
Inupiat (Alaska Native) (1)	2	<0.01
Iroquois (19)	46	0.09
Kiowa (0)	0	<0.01
Lumbee (1)	2	<0.01
Menominee (0)	0	<0.01
Mexican American Ind. (8)	8	0.02
Navajo (1)	1	<0.01
Osage (0)	0	<0.01
Ottawa (0)	0	<0.01
Paiute (0)	0	<0.01
Pima (0)	0	<0.01
Potawatomi (0)	0	<0.01
Pueblo (0)	0	<0.01
Puget Sound Salish (0)	0	<0.01
Seminole (1)	1	<0.01
Shoshone (0)	0	<0.01
Sioux (4)	14	0.03
South American Ind. (0)	1	<0.01
Spanish American Ind. (0)	0	<0.01
Tlingit-Haida (Alaska Native) (0)	0	<0.01
Tohono O'Odham (1)	2	<0.01
Tsimshian (Alaska Native) (0)	0	<0.01
Ute (0)	0	<0.01
Yakama (0)	1	<0.01
Yaqui (0)	0	<0.01
Yuman (0)	0	<0.01
Yup'ik (Alaska Native) (0)	0	<0.01
Asian (391)	523	1.06
Not Hispanic (382)	507	1.03
Hispanic (9)	16	0.03
Bangladeshi (0)	0	<0.01
Bhutanese (0)	0	<0.01
Burmese (5)	5	0.01
Cambodian (0)	0	<0.01
Chinese, ex. Taiwanese (127)	143	0.29
Filipino (45)	78	0.16
Hmong (0)	0	<0.01
Indian (72)	106	0.22
Indonesian (0)	0	<0.01
Japanese (23)	39	0.08
Korean (20)	27	0.05
Laotian (1)	1	<0.01
Malaysian (0)	0	<0.01
Nepalese (6)	6	0.01
Pakistani (25)	31	0.06
Sri Lankan (0)	3	0.01
Taiwanese (3)	3	0.01
Thai (6)	13	0.03
Vietnamese (20)	25	0.05
Hawaii Native/Pacific Islander (19)	43	0.09
Not Hispanic (15)	39	0.08
Hispanic (4)	4	0.01
Fijian (0)	0	<0.01
Guamanian/Chamorro (6)	8	0.02
Marshallese (0)	0	<0.01
Native Hawaiian (3)	11	0.02
Samoan (1)	2	<0.01
Tongan (0)	0	<0.01
White (44,440)	45,212	91.86
Not Hispanic (42,857)	43,514	88.41
Hispanic (1,583)	1,698	3.45

Notes: † The Census 2010 population figure is used to calculate the percentages in the Hispanic Origin and Race categories. Ancestry percentages are based on the 2006-2010 American Community Survey population (not shown); ‡ Numbers in parentheses indicate the number of people reporting a single ancestry; * Numbers in parentheses indicate the number of persons reporting this race alone, not in combination with any other race; Please refer to the Explanation of Data for more information.

Hamilton County

Population: 4,836

Ancestry	Population	%
Afghan (0)	0	<0.01
African, Sub-Saharan (5)	5	0.10
African (5)	5	0.10
Cape Verdean (0)	0	<0.01
Ethiopian (0)	0	<0.01
Ghanaian (0)	0	<0.01
Kenyan (0)	0	<0.01
Liberian (0)	0	<0.01
Nigerian (0)	0	<0.01
Senegalese (0)	0	<0.01
Sierra Leonean (0)	0	<0.01
Somalian (0)	0	<0.01
South African (0)	0	<0.01
Sudanese (0)	0	<0.01
Ugandan (0)	0	<0.01
Zimbabwean (0)	0	<0.01
Other Sub-Saharan African (0)	0	<0.01
Albanian (10)	10	0.20
Alsatian (0)	0	<0.01
American (263)	263	5.36
Arab (7)	25	0.51
Arab (0)	11	0.22
Egyptian (0)	0	<0.01
Iraqi (0)	0	<0.01
Jordanian (0)	0	<0.01
Lebanese (3)	6	0.12
Moroccan (0)	0	<0.01
Palestinian (0)	0	<0.01
Syrian (4)	8	0.16
Other Arab (0)	0	<0.01
Armenian (0)	0	<0.01
Assyrian/Chaldean/Syriac (0)	0	<0.01
Australian (5)	10	0.20
Austrian (0)	18	0.37
Basque (0)	0	<0.01
Belgian (0)	0	<0.01
Brazilian (0)	0	<0.01
British (0)	5	0.10
Bulgarian (0)	0	<0.01
Cajun (0)	0	<0.01
Canadian (15)	30	0.61
Carpatho Rusyn (0)	0	<0.01
Celtic (0)	0	<0.01
Croatian (5)	5	0.10
Cypriot (0)	0	<0.01
Czech (5)	5	0.10
Czechoslovakian (2)	3	0.06
Danish (0)	5	0.10
Dutch (64)	275	5.60
Eastern European (3)	3	0.06
English (246)	1,011	20.60
Estonian (0)	0	<0.01
European (13)	13	0.26
Finnish (7)	7	0.14
French, ex. Basque (144)	524	10.68
French Canadian (77)	133	2.71
German (276)	1,057	21.54
German Russian (0)	0	<0.01
Greek (4)	9	0.18
Guyanese (21)	21	0.43
Hungarian (10)	14	0.29
Icelander (0)	0	<0.01
Iranian (0)	0	<0.01
Irish (506)	1,117	22.76
Israeli (0)	0	<0.01
Italian (176)	421	8.58
Latvian (3)	3	0.06
Lithuanian (2)	10	0.20
Luxemburger (0)	0	<0.01
Macedonian (0)	0	<0.01
Maltese (0)	0	<0.01
New Zealander (0)	0	<0.01
Northern European (21)	21	0.43
Norwegian (32)	79	1.61
Pennsylvania German (0)	4	0.08

Ancestry	Population	%
Polish (118)	274	5.58
Portuguese (6)	6	0.12
Romanian (11)	11	0.22
Russian (18)	53	1.08
Scandinavian (0)	2	0.04
Scotch-Irish (50)	114	2.32
Scottish (70)	286	5.83
Serbian (0)	0	<0.01
Slavic (6)	6	0.12
Slovak (7)	7	0.14
Slovene (0)	0	<0.01
Soviet Union (0)	0	<0.01
Swedish (12)	64	1.30
Swiss (12)	19	0.39
Turkish (0)	0	<0.01
Ukrainian (2)	13	0.26
Welsh (19)	57	1.16
West Indian, ex. Hispanic (0)	0	<0.01
Bahamian (0)	0	<0.01
Barbadian (0)	0	<0.01
Belizean (0)	0	<0.01
Bermudan (0)	0	<0.01
British West Indian (0)	0	<0.01
Dutch West Indian (0)	0	<0.01
Haitian (0)	0	<0.01
Jamaican (0)	0	<0.01
Trinidadian/Tobagonian (0)	0	<0.01
U.S. Virgin Islander (0)	0	<0.01
West Indian (0)	0	<0.01
Other West Indian (0)	0	<0.01
Yugoslavian (0)	0	<0.01

Hispanic Origin	Population	%
Hispanic or Latino (of any race)	51	1.05
Central American, ex. Mexican	0	<0.01
Costa Rican	0	<0.01
Guatemalan	0	<0.01
Honduran	0	<0.01
Nicaraguan	0	<0.01
Panamanian	0	<0.01
Salvadoran	0	<0.01
Other Central American	0	<0.01
Cuban	2	0.04
Dominican Republic	3	0.06
Mexican	5	0.10
Puerto Rican	30	0.62
South American	5	0.10
Argentinean	0	<0.01
Bolivian	0	<0.01
Chilean	0	<0.01
Colombian	3	0.06
Ecuadorian	0	<0.01
Paraguayan	0	<0.01
Peruvian	0	<0.01
Uruguayan	0	<0.01
Venezuelan	0	<0.01
Other South American	2	0.04
Other Hispanic or Latino	6	0.12

Race*	Population	%
African-American/Black (35)	40	0.83
Not Hispanic (33)	38	0.79
Hispanic (2)	2	0.04
American Indian/Alaska Native (11)	58	1.20
Not Hispanic (11)	53	1.10
Hispanic (0)	5	0.10
Alaska Athabascan (Ala. Nat.) (0)	0	<0.01
Aleut (Alaska Native) (0)	0	<0.01
Apache (0)	1	0.02
Arapaho (0)	0	<0.01
Blackfeet (0)	2	0.04
Canadian/French Am. Ind. (0)	0	<0.01
Central American Ind. (0)	0	<0.01
Cherokee (1)	6	0.12
Cheyenne (0)	0	<0.01
Chickasaw (0)	0	<0.01
Chippewa (0)	0	<0.01
Choctaw (0)	1	0.02
Colville (0)	0	<0.01

Race* (continued)	Population	%
Comanche (0)	0	<0.01
Cree (0)	0	<0.01
Creek (0)	0	<0.01
Crow (0)	1	0.02
Delaware (0)	0	<0.01
Hopi (0)	0	<0.01
Houma (0)	0	<0.01
Inupiat (Alaska Native) (0)	0	<0.01
Iroquois (5)	17	0.35
Kiowa (0)	0	<0.01
Lumbee (0)	0	<0.01
Menominee (0)	0	<0.01
Mexican American Ind. (0)	0	<0.01
Navajo (0)	0	<0.01
Osage (0)	0	<0.01
Ottawa (0)	0	<0.01
Paiute (0)	0	<0.01
Pima (0)	0	<0.01
Potawatomi (0)	0	<0.01
Pueblo (0)	0	<0.01
Puget Sound Salish (0)	0	<0.01
Seminole (0)	0	<0.01
Shoshone (0)	0	<0.01
Sioux (0)	1	0.02
South American Ind. (0)	2	0.04
Spanish American Ind. (0)	0	<0.01
Tlingit-Haida (Alaska Native) (0)	0	<0.01
Tohono O'Odham (0)	0	<0.01
Tsimshian (Alaska Native) (0)	0	<0.01
Ute (0)	0	<0.01
Yakama (0)	0	<0.01
Yaqui (0)	0	<0.01
Yuman (0)	0	<0.01
Yup'ik (Alaska Native) (0)	0	<0.01
Asian (24)	29	0.60
Not Hispanic (24)	27	0.56
Hispanic (0)	2	0.04
Bangladeshi (0)	0	<0.01
Bhutanese (0)	0	<0.01
Burmese (0)	0	<0.01
Cambodian (0)	0	<0.01
Chinese, ex. Taiwanese (4)	5	0.10
Filipino (7)	11	0.23
Hmong (0)	0	<0.01
Indian (3)	3	0.06
Indonesian (0)	0	<0.01
Japanese (1)	1	0.02
Korean (3)	3	0.06
Laotian (0)	0	<0.01
Malaysian (0)	0	<0.01
Nepalese (0)	0	<0.01
Pakistani (6)	6	0.12
Sri Lankan (0)	0	<0.01
Taiwanese (0)	0	<0.01
Thai (0)	0	<0.01
Vietnamese (0)	0	<0.01
Hawaii Native/Pacific Islander (4)	4	0.08
Not Hispanic (4)	4	0.08
Hispanic (0)	0	<0.01
Fijian (0)	0	<0.01
Guamanian/Chamorro (0)	0	<0.01
Marshallese (0)	0	<0.01
Native Hawaiian (4)	4	0.08
Samoan (0)	0	<0.01
Tongan (0)	0	<0.01
White (4,705)	4,755	98.33
Not Hispanic (4,664)	4,711	97.42
Hispanic (41)	44	0.91

*Notes: † The Census 2010 population figure is used to calculate the percentages in the Hispanic Origin and Race categories. Ancestry percentages are based on the 2006-2010 American Community Survey population (not shown); ‡ Numbers in parentheses indicate the number of people reporting a single ancestry; * Numbers in parentheses indicate the number of persons reporting this race alone, not in combination with any other race; Please refer to the Explanation of Data for more information.*

Herkimer County

Population: 64,519

Ancestry	Population	%
Afghan (0)	0	<0.01
African, Sub-Saharan (42)	131	0.20
African (42)	131	0.20
Cape Verdean (0)	0	<0.01
Ethiopian (0)	0	<0.01
Ghanaian (0)	0	<0.01
Kenyan (0)	0	<0.01
Liberian (0)	0	<0.01
Nigerian (0)	0	<0.01
Senegalese (0)	0	<0.01
Sierra Leonean (0)	0	<0.01
Somalian (0)	0	<0.01
South African (0)	0	<0.01
Sudanese (0)	0	<0.01
Ugandan (0)	0	<0.01
Zimbabwean (0)	0	<0.01
Other Sub-Saharan African (0)	0	<0.01
Albanian (0)	4	0.01
Alsatian (0)	11	0.02
American (3,518)	3,518	5.47
Arab (112)	348	0.54
Arab (53)	53	0.08
Egyptian (0)	0	<0.01
Iraqi (0)	0	<0.01
Jordanian (0)	0	<0.01
Lebanese (59)	276	0.43
Moroccan (0)	0	<0.01
Palestinian (0)	0	<0.01
Syrian (0)	19	0.03
Other Arab (0)	0	<0.01
Armenian (5)	12	0.02
Assyrian/Chaldean/Syriac (0)	5	0.01
Australian (0)	26	0.04
Austrian (66)	243	0.38
Basque (0)	0	<0.01
Belgian (4)	26	0.04
Brazilian (0)	0	<0.01
British (77)	170	0.26
Bulgarian (5)	42	0.07
Cajun (0)	0	<0.01
Canadian (49)	189	0.29
Carpatho Rusyn (8)	8	0.01
Celtic (0)	19	0.03
Croatian (0)	0	<0.01
Cypriot (0)	0	<0.01
Czech (165)	257	0.40
Czechoslovakian (70)	167	0.26
Danish (103)	365	0.57
Dutch (443)	2,912	4.53
Eastern European (38)	56	0.09
English (2,785)	8,608	13.38
Estonian (36)	36	0.06
European (176)	209	0.32
Finnish (3)	32	0.05
French, ex. Basque (681)	4,581	7.12
French Canadian (802)	1,567	2.44
German (3,471)	14,484	22.51
German Russian (0)	0	<0.01
Greek (99)	160	0.25
Guyanese (0)	0	<0.01
Hungarian (47)	187	0.29
Icelander (0)	6	0.01
Iranian (0)	0	<0.01
Irish (3,812)	14,052	21.84
Israeli (0)	7	0.01
Italian (5,689)	11,059	17.19
Latvian (0)	3	<0.01
Lithuanian (102)	219	0.34
Luxemburger (0)	0	<0.01
Macedonian (0)	6	0.01
Maltese (0)	0	<0.01
New Zealander (0)	0	<0.01
Northern European (27)	27	0.04
Norwegian (23)	152	0.24
Pennsylvania German (138)	141	0.22

Ancestry	Population	%
Polish (1,884)	5,302	8.24
Portuguese (12)	36	0.06
Romanian (17)	51	0.08
Russian (242)	562	0.87
Scandinavian (9)	13	0.02
Scotch-Irish (171)	559	0.87
Scottish (231)	970	1.51
Serbian (0)	0	<0.01
Slavic (17)	48	0.07
Slovak (105)	255	0.40
Slovene (87)	165	0.26
Soviet Union (0)	0	<0.01
Swedish (89)	356	0.55
Swiss (155)	302	0.47
Turkish (0)	0	<0.01
Ukrainian (534)	990	1.54
Welsh (496)	2,032	3.16
West Indian, ex. Hispanic (3)	137	0.21
Bahamian (0)	0	<0.01
Barbadian (0)	0	<0.01
Belizean (0)	0	<0.01
Bermudan (0)	0	<0.01
British West Indian (0)	0	<0.01
Dutch West Indian (0)	0	<0.01
Haitian (0)	20	0.03
Jamaican (0)	108	0.17
Trinidadian/Tobagonian (3)	9	0.01
U.S. Virgin Islander (0)	0	<0.01
West Indian (0)	0	<0.01
Other West Indian (0)	0	<0.01
Yugoslavian (81)	129	0.20

Hispanic Origin	Population	%
Hispanic or Latino (of any race)	1,040	1.61
Central American, ex. Mexican	51	0.08
Costa Rican	12	0.02
Guatemalan	17	0.03
Honduran	4	0.01
Nicaraguan	2	<0.01
Panamanian	8	0.01
Salvadoran	8	0.01
Other Central American	0	<0.01
Cuban	32	0.05
Dominican Republic	48	0.07
Mexican	180	0.28
Puerto Rican	514	0.80
South American	76	0.12
Argentinean	9	0.01
Bolivian	9	0.01
Chilean	7	0.01
Colombian	12	0.02
Ecuadorian	10	0.02
Paraguayan	0	<0.01
Peruvian	15	0.02
Uruguayan	6	0.01
Venezuelan	3	<0.01
Other South American	5	0.01
Other Hispanic or Latino	139	0.22

Race*	Population	%
African-American/Black (700)	1,079	1.67
Not Hispanic (640)	976	1.51
Hispanic (60)	103	0.16
American Indian/Alaska Native (157)	398	0.62
Not Hispanic (137)	340	0.53
Hispanic (20)	58	0.09
Alaska Athabascan (Ala. Nat.) (0)	0	<0.01
Aleut (Alaska Native) (0)	0	<0.01
Apache (0)	1	<0.01
Arapaho (0)	0	<0.01
Blackfeet (2)	6	0.01
Canadian/French Am. Ind. (0)	2	<0.01
Central American Ind. (1)	1	<0.01
Cherokee (3)	33	0.05
Cheyenne (0)	0	<0.01
Chickasaw (0)	0	<0.01
Chippewa (2)	3	<0.01
Choctaw (0)	0	<0.01
Colville (0)	0	<0.01

	Population	%
Comanche (0)	0	<0.01
Cree (0)	0	<0.01
Creek (2)	2	<0.01
Crow (0)	1	<0.01
Delaware (1)	6	0.01
Hopi (0)	0	<0.01
Houma (0)	0	<0.01
Inupiat (Alaska Native) (4)	4	0.01
Iroquois (40)	89	0.14
Kiowa (0)	1	<0.01
Lumbee (0)	1	<0.01
Menominee (0)	0	<0.01
Mexican American Ind. (7)	7	0.01
Navajo (3)	3	<0.01
Osage (0)	0	<0.01
Ottawa (0)	0	<0.01
Paiute (0)	0	<0.01
Pima (0)	0	<0.01
Potawatomi (3)	3	<0.01
Pueblo (0)	0	<0.01
Puget Sound Salish (0)	0	<0.01
Seminole (0)	0	<0.01
Shoshone (0)	0	<0.01
Sioux (2)	13	0.02
South American Ind. (5)	6	0.01
Spanish American Ind. (0)	1	<0.01
Tlingit-Haida (Alaska Native) (3)	3	<0.01
Tohono O'Odham (1)	1	<0.01
Tsimshian (Alaska Native) (0)	0	<0.01
Ute (0)	1	<0.01
Yakama (0)	0	<0.01
Yaqui (4)	4	0.01
Yuman (0)	0	<0.01
Yup'ik (Alaska Native) (0)	0	<0.01
Asian (332)	445	0.69
Not Hispanic (325)	433	0.67
Hispanic (7)	12	0.02
Bangladeshi (0)	0	<0.01
Bhutanese (0)	0	<0.01
Burmese (0)	0	<0.01
Cambodian (3)	8	0.01
Chinese, ex. Taiwanese (68)	77	0.12
Filipino (73)	108	0.17
Hmong (0)	0	<0.01
Indian (76)	98	0.15
Indonesian (1)	1	<0.01
Japanese (35)	54	0.08
Korean (29)	40	0.06
Laotian (4)	6	0.01
Malaysian (0)	0	<0.01
Nepalese (0)	0	<0.01
Pakistani (1)	1	<0.01
Sri Lankan (0)	0	<0.01
Taiwanese (0)	0	<0.01
Thai (10)	13	0.02
Vietnamese (13)	18	0.03
Hawaii Native/Pacific Islander (11)	23	0.04
Not Hispanic (8)	18	0.03
Hispanic (3)	5	0.01
Fijian (0)	0	<0.01
Guamanian/Chamorro (4)	5	0.01
Marshallese (0)	0	<0.01
Native Hawaiian (4)	9	0.01
Samoan (1)	3	<0.01
Tongan (0)	0	<0.01
White (62,320)	63,066	97.75
Not Hispanic (61,690)	62,311	96.58
Hispanic (630)	755	1.17

*Notes: † The Census 2010 population figure is used to calculate the percentages in the Hispanic Origin and Race categories. Ancestry percentages are based on the 2006-2010 American Community Survey population (not shown); ‡ Numbers in parentheses indicate the number of people reporting a single ancestry; * Numbers in parentheses indicate the number of persons reporting this race alone, not in combination with any other race; Please refer to the Explanation of Data for more information.*

Jefferson County

Population: 116,229

Ancestry	Population	%
Afghan (0)	0	<0.01
African, Sub-Saharan (367)	470	0.41
African (316)	409	0.36
Cape Verdean (0)	0	<0.01
Ethiopian (7)	7	0.01
Ghanaian (15)	15	0.01
Kenyan (0)	0	<0.01
Liberian (0)	0	<0.01
Nigerian (0)	0	<0.01
Senegalese (14)	23	0.02
Sierra Leonean (0)	0	<0.01
Somalian (0)	0	<0.01
South African (15)	16	0.01
Sudanese (0)	0	<0.01
Ugandan (0)	0	<0.01
Zimbabwean (0)	0	<0.01
Other Sub-Saharan African (0)	0	<0.01
Albanian (0)	3	<0.01
Alsatian (0)	0	<0.01
American (6,079)	6,079	5.28
Arab (229)	384	0.33
Arab (0)	0	<0.01
Egyptian (80)	80	0.07
Iraqi (6)	6	0.01
Jordanian (6)	6	0.01
Lebanese (18)	129	0.11
Moroccan (99)	99	0.09
Palestinian (14)	14	0.01
Syrian (6)	50	0.04
Other Arab (0)	0	<0.01
Armenian (15)	50	0.04
Assyrian/Chaldean/Syriac (0)	0	<0.01
Australian (52)	56	0.05
Austrian (37)	208	0.18
Basque (0)	0	<0.01
Belgian (67)	246	0.21
Brazilian (31)	99	0.09
British (177)	345	0.30
Bulgarian (0)	0	<0.01
Cajun (8)	8	0.01
Canadian (624)	1,138	0.99
Carpatho Rusyn (0)	0	<0.01
Celtic (0)	11	0.01
Croatian (25)	94	0.08
Cypriot (0)	0	<0.01
Czech (40)	199	0.17
Czechoslovakian (84)	122	0.11
Danish (54)	172	0.15
Dutch (642)	3,044	2.65
Eastern European (60)	76	0.07
English (4,695)	14,861	12.91
Estonian (0)	0	<0.01
European (540)	609	0.53
Finnish (20)	51	0.04
French, ex. Basque (2,381)	12,941	11.25
French Canadian (1,909)	4,176	3.63
German (5,792)	22,170	19.27
German Russian (17)	17	0.01
Greek (191)	351	0.31
Guyanese (205)	228	0.20
Hungarian (305)	700	0.61
Icelander (0)	0	<0.01
Iranian (9)	9	0.01
Irish (7,451)	23,186	20.15
Israeli (0)	9	0.01
Italian (4,621)	12,267	10.66
Latvian (0)	0	<0.01
Lithuanian (18)	114	0.10
Luxemburger (0)	0	<0.01
Macedonian (7)	9	0.01
Maltese (0)	0	<0.01
New Zealander (0)	0	<0.01
Northern European (64)	73	0.06
Norwegian (299)	657	0.57
Pennsylvania German (42)	75	0.07

Ancestry	Population	%
Polish (1,233)	3,949	3.43
Portuguese (111)	356	0.31
Romanian (60)	107	0.09
Russian (277)	600	0.52
Scandinavian (51)	77	0.07
Scotch-Irish (698)	1,943	1.69
Scottish (1,255)	3,937	3.42
Serbian (7)	7	0.01
Slavic (35)	58	0.05
Slovak (22)	90	0.08
Slovene (0)	0	<0.01
Soviet Union (0)	0	<0.01
Swedish (200)	883	0.77
Swiss (32)	371	0.32
Turkish (94)	104	0.09
Ukrainian (205)	366	0.32
Welsh (99)	860	0.75
West Indian, ex. Hispanic (927)	1,171	1.02
Bahamian (0)	0	<0.01
Barbadian (197)	220	0.19
Belizean (35)	40	0.03
Bermudan (0)	0	<0.01
British West Indian (2)	2	<0.01
Dutch West Indian (0)	74	0.06
Haitian (154)	158	0.14
Jamaican (349)	401	0.35
Trinidadian/Tobagonian (30)	76	0.07
U.S. Virgin Islander (7)	7	0.01
West Indian (153)	193	0.17
Other West Indian (0)	0	<0.01
Yugoslavian (26)	31	0.03

Hispanic Origin	Population	%
Hispanic or Latino (of any race)	6,143	5.29
Central American, ex. Mexican	421	0.36
Costa Rican	20	0.02
Guatemalan	84	0.07
Honduran	56	0.05
Nicaraguan	43	0.04
Panamanian	143	0.12
Salvadoran	75	0.06
Other Central American	0	<0.01
Cuban	186	0.16
Dominican Republic	252	0.22
Mexican	2,211	1.90
Puerto Rican	2,202	1.89
South American	339	0.29
Argentinean	17	0.01
Bolivian	5	<0.01
Chilean	20	0.02
Colombian	115	0.10
Ecuadorian	84	0.07
Paraguayan	9	0.01
Peruvian	60	0.05
Uruguayan	1	<0.01
Venezuelan	24	0.02
Other South American	4	<0.01
Other Hispanic or Latino	532	0.46

Race*	Population	%
African-American/Black (5,876)	7,366	6.34
Not Hispanic (5,475)	6,724	5.79
Hispanic (401)	642	0.55
American Indian/Alaska Native (586)	1,483	1.28
Not Hispanic (500)	1,288	1.11
Hispanic (86)	195	0.17
Alaska Athabascan (Ala. Nat.) (5)	11	0.01
Aleut (Alaska Native) (6)	6	0.01
Apache (8)	29	0.02
Arapaho (0)	0	<0.01
Blackfeet (14)	49	0.04
Canadian/French Am. Ind. (5)	11	0.01
Central American Ind. (2)	4	<0.01
Cherokee (47)	201	0.17
Cheyenne (0)	1	<0.01
Chickasaw (3)	3	<0.01
Chippewa (9)	19	0.02
Choctaw (15)	34	0.03
Colville (0)	0	<0.01

Race*	Population	%
Comanche (1)	1	<0.01
Cree (1)	5	<0.01
Creek (5)	10	0.01
Crow (0)	1	<0.01
Delaware (2)	7	0.01
Hopi (0)	1	<0.01
Houma (0)	0	<0.01
Inupiat (Alaska Native) (6)	8	0.01
Iroquois (154)	320	0.28
Kiowa (0)	0	<0.01
Lumbee (3)	3	<0.01
Menominee (1)	1	<0.01
Mexican American Ind. (11)	23	0.02
Navajo (25)	42	0.04
Osage (0)	3	<0.01
Ottawa (0)	0	<0.01
Paiute (0)	0	<0.01
Pima (0)	0	<0.01
Potawatomi (6)	6	0.01
Pueblo (9)	14	0.01
Puget Sound Salish (0)	1	<0.01
Seminole (2)	2	<0.01
Shoshone (0)	0	<0.01
Sioux (15)	40	0.03
South American Ind. (3)	14	0.01
Spanish American Ind. (2)	4	<0.01
Tlingit-Haida (Alaska Native) (0)	2	<0.01
Tohono O'Odham (0)	0	<0.01
Tsimshian (Alaska Native) (0)	0	<0.01
Ute (0)	1	<0.01
Yakama (0)	0	<0.01
Yaqui (0)	1	<0.01
Yuman (0)	0	<0.01
Yup'ik (Alaska Native) (4)	4	<0.01
Asian (1,518)	2,253	1.94
Not Hispanic (1,464)	2,110	1.82
Hispanic (54)	143	0.12
Bangladeshi (10)	10	0.01
Bhutanese (1)	4	<0.01
Burmese (1)	1	<0.01
Cambodian (17)	27	0.02
Chinese, ex. Taiwanese (171)	242	0.21
Filipino (496)	777	0.67
Hmong (2)	4	<0.01
Indian (133)	179	0.15
Indonesian (3)	11	0.01
Japanese (71)	190	0.16
Korean (357)	558	0.48
Laotian (7)	16	0.01
Malaysian (0)	0	<0.01
Nepalese (0)	0	<0.01
Pakistani (25)	31	0.03
Sri Lankan (1)	1	<0.01
Taiwanese (3)	3	<0.01
Thai (32)	69	0.06
Vietnamese (82)	125	0.11
Hawaii Native/Pacific Islander (298)	529	0.46
Not Hispanic (273)	464	0.40
Hispanic (25)	65	0.06
Fijian (3)	4	<0.01
Guamanian/Chamorro (103)	133	0.11
Marshallese (15)	15	0.01
Native Hawaiian (52)	157	0.14
Samoan (68)	99	0.09
Tongan (2)	2	<0.01
White (103,047)	105,977	91.18
Not Hispanic (99,682)	102,062	87.81
Hispanic (3,365)	3,915	3.37

Kings County

Population: 2,504,700

Ancestry	Population	%
Afghan (335)	344	0.01
African, Sub-Saharan (30,768)	63,004	2.55
African (17,256)	48,168	1.95
Cape Verdean (106)	153	0.01
Ethiopian (283)	330	0.01
Ghanaian (3,692)	3,898	0.16
Kenyan (65)	77	<0.01
Liberian (392)	452	0.02
Nigerian (5,499)	6,033	0.24
Senegalese (401)	401	0.02
Sierra Leonean (147)	147	0.01
Somalian (234)	260	0.01
South African (204)	320	0.01
Sudanese (693)	731	0.03
Ugandan (29)	54	<0.01
Zimbabwean (99)	99	<0.01
Other Sub-Saharan African (1,668)	1,881	0.08
Albanian (6,490)	6,871	0.28
Alsatian (0)	27	<0.01
American (78,858)	78,858	3.20
Arab (29,346)	34,840	1.41
Arab (6,779)	7,609	0.31
Egyptian (4,705)	5,231	0.21
Iraqi (71)	134	0.01
Jordanian (714)	752	0.03
Lebanese (3,425)	4,757	0.19
Moroccan (2,156)	2,648	0.11
Palestinian (1,372)	1,482	0.06
Syrian (4,854)	5,890	0.24
Other Arab (5,270)	6,337	0.26
Armenian (1,798)	2,300	0.09
Assyrian/Chaldean/Syriac (22)	44	<0.01
Australian (539)	832	0.03
Austrian (1,677)	5,123	0.21
Basque (69)	129	0.01
Belgian (498)	1,012	0.04
Brazilian (1,257)	1,719	0.07
British (2,002)	4,749	0.19
Bulgarian (970)	1,128	0.05
Cajun (99)	175	0.01
Canadian (1,814)	3,116	0.13
Carpatho Rusyn (46)	53	<0.01
Celtic (16)	32	<0.01
Croatian (488)	998	0.04
Cypriot (37)	62	<0.01
Czech (759)	3,393	0.14
Czechoslovakian (793)	1,684	0.07
Danish (380)	1,267	0.05
Dutch (1,616)	5,664	0.23
Eastern European (11,912)	12,941	0.52
English (9,927)	32,407	1.31
Estonian (209)	340	0.01
European (25,194)	27,499	1.11
Finnish (303)	692	0.03
French, ex. Basque (3,484)	14,137	0.57
French Canadian (1,082)	2,974	0.12
German (12,299)	52,798	2.14
German Russian (29)	55	<0.01
Greek (10,688)	14,075	0.57
Guyanese (36,322)	38,963	1.58
Hungarian (17,858)	26,607	1.08
Icelander (69)	103	<0.01
Iranian (1,520)	1,822	0.07
Irish (32,255)	84,945	3.44
Israeli (7,062)	9,707	0.39
Italian (108,743)	152,814	6.19
Latvian (418)	667	0.03
Lithuanian (938)	2,676	0.11
Luxemburger (41)	58	<0.01
Macedonian (389)	498	0.02
Maltese (197)	362	0.01
New Zealander (71)	140	0.01
Northern European (905)	961	0.04
Norwegian (2,042)	5,982	0.24
Pennsylvania German (19)	59	<0.01

Ancestry	Population	%
Polish (41,882)	66,792	2.71
Portuguese (1,106)	2,882	0.12
Romanian (4,537)	8,046	0.33
Russian (69,188)	88,579	3.59
Scandinavian (512)	882	0.04
Scotch-Irish (1,997)	6,090	0.25
Scottish (2,407)	8,809	0.36
Serbian (288)	520	0.02
Slavic (289)	564	0.02
Slovak (1,164)	1,826	0.07
Slovene (55)	160	0.01
Soviet Union (185)	219	0.01
Swedish (1,240)	5,185	0.21
Swiss (473)	1,491	0.06
Turkish (4,449)	5,164	0.21
Ukrainian (21,703)	25,046	1.02
Welsh (345)	2,606	0.11
West Indian, ex. Hispanic (257,579)	306,541	12.43
Bahamian (195)	266	0.01
Barbadian (13,358)	14,916	0.60
Belizean (1,610)	2,026	0.08
Bermudan (16)	16	<0.01
British West Indian (28,123)	30,607	1.24
Dutch West Indian (289)	424	0.02
Haitian (67,083)	69,941	2.84
Jamaican (74,216)	80,999	3.28
Trinidadian/Tobagonian (42,450)	46,490	1.88
U.S. Virgin Islander (470)	558	0.02
West Indian (29,404)	59,844	2.43
Other West Indian (365)	454	0.02
Yugoslavian (2,305)	2,800	0.11

Hispanic Origin	Population	%
Hispanic or Latino (of any race)	496,285	19.81
Central American, ex. Mexican	46,119	1.84
Costa Rican	2,576	0.10
Guatemalan	9,160	0.37
Honduran	10,071	0.40
Nicaraguan	2,407	0.10
Panamanian	13,681	0.55
Salvadoran	7,737	0.31
Other Central American	487	0.02
Cuban	7,581	0.30
Dominican Republic	86,764	3.46
Mexican	94,585	3.78
Puerto Rican	176,528	7.05
South American	49,003	1.96
Argentinean	2,760	0.11
Bolivian	310	0.01
Chilean	1,026	0.04
Colombian	8,861	0.35
Ecuadorian	28,684	1.15
Paraguayan	230	0.01
Peruvian	4,222	0.17
Uruguayan	488	0.02
Venezuelan	1,916	0.08
Other South American	506	0.02
Other Hispanic or Latino	35,705	1.43

Race*	Population	%
African-American/Black (860,083)	896,165	35.78
Not Hispanic (799,066)	820,437	32.76
Hispanic (61,017)	75,728	3.02
American Indian/Alaska Native (13,524)	26,571	1.06
Not Hispanic (4,638)	12,062	0.48
Hispanic (8,886)	14,509	0.58
Alaska Athabascan (Ala. Nat.) (1)	5	<0.01
Aleut (Alaska Native) (4)	8	<0.01
Apache (46)	122	<0.01
Arapaho (2)	10	<0.01
Blackfeet (89)	531	0.02
Canadian/French Am. Ind. (42)	62	<0.01
Central American Ind. (616)	1,263	0.05
Cherokee (289)	1,903	0.08
Cheyenne (0)	10	<0.01
Chickasaw (9)	30	<0.01
Chippewa (23)	65	<0.01
Choctaw (30)	104	<0.01
Colville (1)	1	<0.01

	Population	%
Comanche (5)	19	<0.01
Cree (3)	15	<0.01
Creek (20)	81	<0.01
Crow (5)	19	<0.01
Delaware (5)	35	<0.01
Hopi (7)	12	<0.01
Houma (1)	3	<0.01
Inupiat (Alaska Native) (7)	21	<0.01
Iroquois (194)	381	0.02
Kiowa (1)	2	<0.01
Lumbee (6)	24	<0.01
Menominee (1)	4	<0.01
Mexican American Ind. (1,022)	1,363	0.05
Navajo (41)	93	<0.01
Osage (1)	3	<0.01
Ottawa (2)	5	<0.01
Paiute (0)	1	<0.01
Pima (0)	2	<0.01
Potawatomi (3)	11	<0.01
Pueblo (93)	169	0.01
Puget Sound Salish (1)	1	<0.01
Seminole (18)	92	<0.01
Shoshone (6)	23	<0.01
Sioux (29)	121	<0.01
South American Ind. (874)	1,855	0.07
Spanish American Ind. (290)	382	0.02
Tlingit-Haida (Alaska Native) (4)	28	<0.01
Tohono O'Odham (9)	10	<0.01
Tsimshian (Alaska Native) (0)	0	<0.01
Ute (0)	4	<0.01
Yakama (1)	3	<0.01
Yaqui (11)	19	<0.01
Yuman (5)	8	<0.01
Yup'ik (Alaska Native) (0)	1	<0.01
Asian (262,276)	284,489	11.36
Not Hispanic (260,129)	279,499	11.16
Hispanic (2,147)	4,990	0.20
Bangladeshi (10,667)	12,408	0.50
Bhutanese (5)	8	<0.01
Burmese (1,055)	1,260	0.05
Cambodian (613)	751	0.03
Chinese, ex. Taiwanese (171,214)	178,214	7.12
Filipino (7,930)	10,208	0.41
Hmong (14)	22	<0.01
Indian (26,144)	33,490	1.34
Indonesian (383)	564	0.02
Japanese (3,938)	5,917	0.24
Korean (6,904)	8,201	0.33
Laotian (82)	131	0.01
Malaysian (478)	708	0.03
Nepalese (355)	393	0.02
Pakistani (18,296)	19,840	0.79
Sri Lankan (219)	270	0.01
Taiwanese (857)	1,075	0.04
Thai (636)	883	0.04
Vietnamese (3,944)	5,041	0.20
Hawaii Native/Pacific Islander (1,243)	5,784	0.23
Not Hispanic (633)	3,463	0.14
Hispanic (610)	2,321	0.09
Fijian (20)	45	<0.01
Guamanian/Chamorro (386)	568	0.02
Marshallese (1)	2	<0.01
Native Hawaiian (208)	564	0.02
Samoan (72)	216	0.01
Tongan (5)	10	<0.01
White (1,072,041)	1,120,592	44.74
Not Hispanic (893,306)	917,717	36.64
Hispanic (178,735)	202,875	8.10

*Notes: † The Census 2010 population figure is used to calculate the percentages in the Hispanic Origin and Race categories. Ancestry percentages are based on the 2006-2010 American Community Survey population (not shown); ‡ Numbers in parentheses indicate the number of people reporting a single ancestry; * Numbers in parentheses indicate the number of persons reporting this race alone, not in combination with any other race; Please refer to the Explanation of Data for more information.*

Lewis County

Population: 27,087

Ancestry	Population	%
Afghan (0)	0	<0.01
African, Sub-Saharan (17)	30	0.11
African (17)	26	0.10
Cape Verdean (0)	0	<0.01
Ethiopian (0)	0	<0.01
Ghanaian (0)	0	<0.01
Kenyan (0)	0	<0.01
Liberian (0)	0	<0.01
Nigerian (0)	0	<0.01
Senegalese (0)	0	<0.01
Sierra Leonean (0)	0	<0.01
Somalian (0)	0	<0.01
South African (0)	4	0.01
Sudanese (0)	0	<0.01
Ugandan (0)	0	<0.01
Zimbabwean (0)	0	<0.01
Other Sub-Saharan African (0)	0	<0.01
Albanian (25)	25	0.09
Alsatian (13)	50	0.19
American (1,155)	1,155	4.28
Arab (79)	83	0.31
Arab (0)	0	<0.01
Egyptian (45)	45	0.17
Iraqi (0)	0	<0.01
Jordanian (0)	0	<0.01
Lebanese (13)	13	0.05
Moroccan (0)	0	<0.01
Palestinian (0)	0	<0.01
Syrian (0)	4	0.01
Other Arab (21)	21	0.08
Armenian (7)	7	0.03
Assyrian/Chaldean/Syriac (0)	0	<0.01
Australian (0)	0	<0.01
Austrian (5)	61	0.23
Basque (0)	0	<0.01
Belgian (0)	2	0.01
Brazilian (0)	0	<0.01
British (20)	58	0.21
Bulgarian (0)	0	<0.01
Cajun (4)	4	0.01
Canadian (61)	140	0.52
Carpatho Rusyn (0)	0	<0.01
Celtic (0)	0	<0.01
Croatian (24)	24	0.09
Cypriot (0)	0	<0.01
Czech (3)	14	0.05
Czechoslovakian (6)	8	0.03
Danish (30)	71	0.26
Dutch (146)	882	3.26
Eastern European (37)	37	0.14
English (757)	2,702	10.00
Estonian (0)	0	<0.01
European (62)	71	0.26
Finnish (0)	10	0.04
French, ex. Basque (708)	3,633	13.45
French Canadian (484)	788	2.92
German (2,964)	8,378	31.01
German Russian (0)	0	<0.01
Greek (7)	12	0.04
Guyanese (39)	39	0.14
Hungarian (212)	307	1.14
Icelander (0)	0	<0.01
Iranian (9)	9	0.03
Irish (1,034)	4,543	16.82
Israeli (0)	0	<0.01
Italian (617)	1,963	7.27
Latvian (0)	0	<0.01
Lithuanian (23)	26	0.10
Luxemburger (0)	0	<0.01
Macedonian (0)	0	<0.01
Maltese (0)	0	<0.01
New Zealander (0)	0	<0.01
Northern European (22)	22	0.08
Norwegian (51)	93	0.34
Pennsylvania German (0)	0	<0.01

	Population	%
Polish (623)	1,338	4.95
Portuguese (0)	31	0.11
Romanian (5)	5	0.02
Russian (44)	98	0.36
Scandinavian (0)	0	<0.01
Scotch-Irish (205)	396	1.47
Scottish (161)	521	1.93
Serbian (0)	0	<0.01
Slavic (0)	0	<0.01
Slovak (5)	5	0.02
Slovene (0)	20	0.07
Soviet Union (0)	0	<0.01
Swedish (52)	137	0.51
Swiss (202)	630	2.33
Turkish (0)	0	<0.01
Ukrainian (6)	29	0.11
Welsh (128)	377	1.40
West Indian, ex. Hispanic (6)	41	0.15
Bahamian (0)	0	<0.01
Barbadian (0)	0	<0.01
Belizean (0)	0	<0.01
Bermudan (0)	0	<0.01
British West Indian (0)	0	<0.01
Dutch West Indian (0)	0	<0.01
Haitian (0)	0	<0.01
Jamaican (0)	35	0.13
Trinidadian/Tobagonian (0)	0	<0.01
U.S. Virgin Islander (0)	0	<0.01
West Indian (6)	6	0.02
Other West Indian (0)	0	<0.01
Yugoslavian (15)	18	0.07

Hispanic Origin	Population	%
Hispanic or Latino (of any race)	357	1.32
Central American, ex. Mexican	22	0.08
Costa Rican	1	<0.01
Guatemalan	8	0.03
Honduran	8	0.03
Nicaraguan	2	0.01
Panamanian	3	0.01
Salvadoran	0	<0.01
Other Central American	0	<0.01
Cuban	5	0.02
Dominican Republic	5	0.02
Mexican	171	0.63
Puerto Rican	98	0.36
South American	10	0.04
Argentinean	2	0.01
Bolivian	0	<0.01
Chilean	1	<0.01
Colombian	4	0.01
Ecuadorian	3	0.01
Paraguayan	0	<0.01
Peruvian	0	<0.01
Uruguayan	0	<0.01
Venezuelan	0	<0.01
Other South American	0	<0.01
Other Hispanic or Latino	46	0.17

Race*	Population	%
African-American/Black (184)	265	0.98
Not Hispanic (170)	230	0.85
Hispanic (14)	35	0.13
American Indian/Alaska Native (53)	157	0.58
Not Hispanic (44)	146	0.54
Hispanic (9)	11	0.04
Alaska Athabascan (Ala. Nat.) (0)	0	<0.01
Aleut (Alaska Native) (4)	4	0.01
Apache (2)	3	0.01
Arapaho (0)	0	<0.01
Blackfeet (1)	9	0.03
Canadian/French Am. Ind. (0)	2	0.01
Central American Ind. (2)	3	0.01
Cherokee (2)	17	0.06
Cheyenne (0)	0	<0.01
Chickasaw (0)	0	<0.01
Chippewa (0)	2	0.01
Choctaw (0)	0	<0.01
Colville (0)	0	<0.01

	Population	%
Comanche (0)	0	<0.01
Cree (0)	1	<0.01
Creek (0)	0	<0.01
Crow (0)	0	<0.01
Delaware (0)	0	<0.01
Hopi (0)	0	<0.01
Houma (0)	0	<0.01
Inupiat (Alaska Native) (0)	0	<0.01
Iroquois (19)	37	0.14
Kiowa (0)	0	<0.01
Lumbee (0)	2	0.01
Menominee (0)	0	<0.01
Mexican American Ind. (0)	0	<0.01
Navajo (0)	1	<0.01
Osage (0)	0	<0.01
Ottawa (0)	0	<0.01
Paiute (0)	0	<0.01
Pima (0)	0	<0.01
Potawatomi (0)	0	<0.01
Pueblo (0)	0	<0.01
Puget Sound Salish (0)	0	<0.01
Seminole (0)	1	<0.01
Shoshone (0)	0	<0.01
Sioux (0)	3	0.01
South American Ind. (0)	0	<0.01
Spanish American Ind. (0)	0	<0.01
Tlingit-Haida (Alaska Native) (0)	0	<0.01
Tohono O'Odham (0)	0	<0.01
Tsimshian (Alaska Native) (0)	0	<0.01
Ute (0)	0	<0.01
Yakama (0)	0	<0.01
Yaqui (0)	0	<0.01
Yuman (0)	0	<0.01
Yup'ik (Alaska Native) (0)	0	<0.01
Asian (75)	114	0.42
Not Hispanic (72)	107	0.40
Hispanic (3)	7	0.03
Bangladeshi (0)	0	<0.01
Bhutanese (0)	0	<0.01
Burmese (0)	0	<0.01
Cambodian (3)	5	0.02
Chinese, ex. Taiwanese (14)	16	0.06
Filipino (25)	38	0.14
Hmong (0)	0	<0.01
Indian (8)	13	0.05
Indonesian (0)	0	<0.01
Japanese (3)	11	0.04
Korean (14)	22	0.08
Laotian (0)	0	<0.01
Malaysian (0)	0	<0.01
Nepalese (0)	0	<0.01
Pakistani (3)	4	0.01
Sri Lankan (1)	1	<0.01
Taiwanese (0)	0	<0.01
Thai (2)	5	0.02
Vietnamese (0)	1	<0.01
Hawaii Native/Pacific Islander (16)	30	0.11
Not Hispanic (16)	27	0.10
Hispanic (0)	3	0.01
Fijian (0)	0	<0.01
Guamanian/Chamorro (4)	4	0.01
Marshallese (0)	0	<0.01
Native Hawaiian (0)	7	0.03
Samoan (1)	3	0.01
Tongan (0)	0	<0.01
White (26,465)	26,686	98.52
Not Hispanic (26,225)	26,416	97.52
Hispanic (240)	270	1.00

Notes: † The Census 2010 population figure is used to calculate the percentages in the Hispanic Origin and Race categories. Ancestry percentages are based on the 2006-2010 American Community Survey population (not shown); ‡ Numbers in parentheses indicate the number of people reporting a single ancestry; * Numbers in parentheses indicate the number of persons reporting this race alone, not in combination with any other race; Please refer to the Explanation of Data for more information.

Livingston County
Population: 65,393

Ancestry	Population	%
Afghan (0)	0	<0.01
African, Sub-Saharan (206)	240	0.37
African (99)	132	0.20
Cape Verdean (0)	0	<0.01
Ethiopian (27)	27	0.04
Ghanaian (0)	0	<0.01
Kenyan (0)	0	<0.01
Liberian (0)	0	<0.01
Nigerian (0)	0	<0.01
Senegalese (12)	12	0.02
Sierra Leonean (0)	0	<0.01
Somalian (0)	0	<0.01
South African (64)	64	0.10
Sudanese (0)	0	<0.01
Ugandan (0)	0	<0.01
Zimbabwean (0)	0	<0.01
Other Sub-Saharan African (4)	5	0.01
Albanian (9)	9	0.01
Alsatian (0)	0	<0.01
American (3,367)	3,367	5.15
Arab (33)	163	0.25
Arab (3)	3	<0.01
Egyptian (0)	0	<0.01
Iraqi (0)	0	<0.01
Jordanian (0)	0	<0.01
Lebanese (17)	90	0.14
Moroccan (0)	0	<0.01
Palestinian (0)	0	<0.01
Syrian (13)	70	0.11
Other Arab (0)	0	<0.01
Armenian (0)	0	<0.01
Assyrian/Chaldean/Syriac (0)	0	<0.01
Australian (21)	24	0.04
Austrian (54)	201	0.31
Basque (0)	0	<0.01
Belgian (65)	105	0.16
Brazilian (0)	88	0.13
British (86)	243	0.37
Bulgarian (0)	0	<0.01
Cajun (0)	0	<0.01
Canadian (135)	235	0.36
Carpatho Rusyn (0)	0	<0.01
Celtic (0)	0	<0.01
Croatian (0)	6	0.01
Cypriot (0)	0	<0.01
Czech (46)	179	0.27
Czechoslovakian (10)	15	0.02
Danish (11)	137	0.21
Dutch (415)	2,843	4.34
Eastern European (71)	71	0.11
English (2,964)	11,436	17.48
Estonian (0)	0	<0.01
European (506)	606	0.93
Finnish (4)	28	0.04
French, ex. Basque (318)	2,864	4.38
French Canadian (260)	668	1.02
German (5,115)	19,312	29.51
German Russian (0)	0	<0.01
Greek (41)	112	0.17
Guyanese (14)	14	0.02
Hungarian (113)	436	0.67
Icelander (0)	2	<0.01
Iranian (6)	6	0.01
Irish (3,826)	15,027	22.96
Israeli (0)	0	<0.01
Italian (3,398)	8,851	13.53
Latvian (21)	32	0.05
Lithuanian (26)	190	0.29
Luxemburger (0)	0	<0.01
Macedonian (5)	5	0.01
Maltese (0)	13	0.02
New Zealander (0)	0	<0.01
Northern European (19)	37	0.06
Norwegian (60)	173	0.26
Pennsylvania German (103)	162	0.25

Ancestry (cont.)	Population	%
Polish (973)	3,039	4.64
Portuguese (12)	189	0.29
Romanian (23)	64	0.10
Russian (65)	403	0.62
Scandinavian (44)	124	0.19
Scotch-Irish (465)	1,278	1.95
Scottish (497)	1,873	2.86
Serbian (0)	20	0.03
Slavic (0)	2	<0.01
Slovak (48)	168	0.26
Slovene (0)	12	0.02
Soviet Union (0)	0	<0.01
Swedish (160)	678	1.04
Swiss (13)	253	0.39
Turkish (0)	0	<0.01
Ukrainian (198)	491	0.75
Welsh (97)	523	0.80
West Indian, ex. Hispanic (107)	154	0.24
Bahamian (0)	0	<0.01
Barbadian (0)	0	<0.01
Belizean (0)	0	<0.01
Bermudan (0)	0	<0.01
British West Indian (8)	8	0.01
Dutch West Indian (0)	0	<0.01
Haitian (13)	14	0.02
Jamaican (52)	80	0.12
Trinidadian/Tobagonian (17)	17	0.03
U.S. Virgin Islander (0)	0	<0.01
West Indian (17)	35	0.05
Other West Indian (0)	0	<0.01
Yugoslavian (19)	43	0.07

Hispanic Origin	Population	%
Hispanic or Latino (of any race)	1,802	2.76
Central American, ex. Mexican	86	0.13
Costa Rican	8	0.01
Guatemalan	19	0.03
Honduran	17	0.03
Nicaraguan	8	0.01
Panamanian	15	0.02
Salvadoran	19	0.03
Other Central American	0	<0.01
Cuban	82	0.13
Dominican Republic	76	0.12
Mexican	327	0.50
Puerto Rican	1,006	1.54
South American	102	0.16
Argentinean	7	0.01
Bolivian	1	<0.01
Chilean	23	0.04
Colombian	36	0.06
Ecuadorian	12	0.02
Paraguayan	4	0.01
Peruvian	13	0.02
Uruguayan	2	<0.01
Venezuelan	3	<0.01
Other South American	1	<0.01
Other Hispanic or Latino	123	0.19

Race*	Population	%
African-American/Black (1,598)	1,932	2.95
Not Hispanic (1,491)	1,786	2.73
Hispanic (107)	146	0.22
American Indian/Alaska Native (187)	527	0.81
Not Hispanic (158)	474	0.72
Hispanic (29)	53	0.08
Alaska Athabascan (Ala. Nat.) (0)	0	<0.01
Aleut (Alaska Native) (0)	0	<0.01
Apache (0)	2	<0.01
Arapaho (0)	0	<0.01
Blackfeet (3)	17	0.03
Canadian/French Am. Ind. (2)	8	0.01
Central American Ind. (0)	0	<0.01
Cherokee (5)	33	0.05
Cheyenne (0)	0	<0.01
Chickasaw (0)	1	<0.01
Chippewa (4)	9	0.01
Choctaw (1)	3	<0.01
Colville (0)	0	<0.01

Race* (cont.)	Population	%
Comanche (0)	3	<0.01
Cree (0)	1	<0.01
Creek (0)	1	<0.01
Crow (0)	1	<0.01
Delaware (0)	0	<0.01
Hopi (0)	0	<0.01
Houma (0)	0	<0.01
Inupiat (Alaska Native) (0)	1	<0.01
Iroquois (66)	166	0.25
Kiowa (0)	0	<0.01
Lumbee (0)	0	<0.01
Menominee (0)	0	<0.01
Mexican American Ind. (3)	4	0.01
Navajo (2)	6	0.01
Osage (0)	0	<0.01
Ottawa (0)	0	<0.01
Paiute (0)	0	<0.01
Pima (0)	0	<0.01
Potawatomi (0)	0	<0.01
Pueblo (0)	0	<0.01
Puget Sound Salish (0)	0	<0.01
Seminole (0)	6	0.01
Shoshone (0)	0	<0.01
Sioux (0)	5	0.01
South American Ind. (4)	10	0.02
Spanish American Ind. (0)	0	<0.01
Tlingit-Haida (Alaska Native) (0)	1	<0.01
Tohono O'Odham (0)	0	<0.01
Tsimshian (Alaska Native) (0)	0	<0.01
Ute (0)	0	<0.01
Yakama (0)	0	<0.01
Yaqui (0)	0	<0.01
Yuman (0)	0	<0.01
Yup'ik (Alaska Native) (0)	0	<0.01
Asian (785)	1,019	1.56
Not Hispanic (780)	991	1.52
Hispanic (5)	28	0.04
Bangladeshi (1)	1	<0.01
Bhutanese (0)	0	<0.01
Burmese (7)	7	0.01
Cambodian (7)	9	0.01
Chinese, ex. Taiwanese (207)	254	0.39
Filipino (77)	127	0.19
Hmong (1)	1	<0.01
Indian (84)	115	0.18
Indonesian (0)	2	<0.01
Japanese (47)	71	0.11
Korean (170)	226	0.35
Laotian (16)	31	0.05
Malaysian (1)	4	0.01
Nepalese (3)	4	0.01
Pakistani (41)	53	0.08
Sri Lankan (9)	9	0.01
Taiwanese (6)	7	0.01
Thai (5)	6	0.01
Vietnamese (56)	71	0.11
Hawaii Native/Pacific Islander (18)	53	0.08
Not Hispanic (11)	37	0.06
Hispanic (7)	16	0.02
Fijian (0)	1	<0.01
Guamanian/Chamorro (4)	9	0.01
Marshallese (0)	0	<0.01
Native Hawaiian (7)	25	0.04
Samoan (0)	3	<0.01
Tongan (0)	0	<0.01
White (61,363)	62,245	95.19
Not Hispanic (60,296)	61,067	93.38
Hispanic (1,067)	1,178	1.80

Notes: † The Census 2010 population figure is used to calculate the percentages in the Hispanic Origin and Race categories. Ancestry percentages are based on the 2006-2010 American Community Survey population (not shown); ‡ Numbers in parentheses indicate the number of people reporting a single ancestry; * Numbers in parentheses indicate the number of persons reporting this race alone, not in combination with any other race; Please refer to the Explanation of Data for more information.

Madison County

Population: 73,442

Ancestry	Population	%
Afghan (9)	27	0.04
African, Sub-Saharan (154)	214	0.29
African (65)	89	0.12
Cape Verdean (0)	0	<0.01
Ethiopian (0)	0	<0.01
Ghanaian (12)	22	0.03
Kenyan (10)	10	0.01
Liberian (0)	0	<0.01
Nigerian (33)	48	0.07
Senegalese (0)	0	<0.01
Sierra Leonean (12)	12	0.02
Somalian (0)	0	<0.01
South African (0)	11	0.02
Sudanese (11)	11	0.02
Ugandan (11)	11	0.02
Zimbabwean (0)	0	<0.01
Other Sub-Saharan African (0)	0	<0.01
Albanian (0)	28	0.04
Alsatian (0)	0	<0.01
American (10,024)	10,024	13.75
Arab (98)	173	0.24
Arab (70)	88	0.12
Egyptian (0)	0	<0.01
Iraqi (0)	0	<0.01
Jordanian (0)	0	<0.01
Lebanese (15)	49	0.07
Moroccan (0)	0	<0.01
Palestinian (0)	0	<0.01
Syrian (13)	28	0.04
Other Arab (0)	8	0.01
Armenian (12)	28	0.04
Assyrian/Chaldean/Syriac (0)	0	<0.01
Australian (8)	19	0.03
Austrian (10)	266	0.36
Basque (0)	0	<0.01
Belgian (42)	106	0.15
Brazilian (0)	0	<0.01
British (169)	338	0.46
Bulgarian (0)	0	<0.01
Cajun (0)	0	<0.01
Canadian (234)	460	0.63
Carpatho Rusyn (0)	0	<0.01
Celtic (0)	3	<0.01
Croatian (7)	70	0.10
Cypriot (0)	0	<0.01
Czech (7)	221	0.30
Czechoslovakian (19)	106	0.15
Danish (57)	298	0.41
Dutch (520)	2,648	3.63
Eastern European (82)	89	0.12
English (3,594)	11,718	16.08
Estonian (9)	9	0.01
European (647)	668	0.92
Finnish (4)	48	0.07
French, ex. Basque (628)	4,501	6.18
French Canadian (573)	1,461	2.00
German (3,834)	15,853	21.75
German Russian (0)	0	<0.01
Greek (78)	260	0.36
Guyanese (0)	0	<0.01
Hungarian (117)	282	0.39
Icelander (0)	0	<0.01
Iranian (0)	0	<0.01
Irish (3,752)	13,797	18.93
Israeli (0)	0	<0.01
Italian (3,492)	8,141	11.17
Latvian (9)	20	0.03
Lithuanian (64)	201	0.28
Luxemburger (9)	27	0.04
Macedonian (12)	12	0.02
Maltese (0)	0	<0.01
New Zealander (0)	0	<0.01
Northern European (69)	69	0.09
Norwegian (80)	305	0.42
Pennsylvania German (112)	126	0.17

Ancestry (cont.)	Population	%
Polish (1,425)	4,350	5.97
Portuguese (26)	137	0.19
Romanian (3)	43	0.06
Russian (181)	521	0.71
Scandinavian (27)	99	0.14
Scotch-Irish (372)	1,148	1.58
Scottish (549)	1,988	2.73
Serbian (0)	0	<0.01
Slavic (33)	113	0.16
Slovak (21)	110	0.15
Slovene (13)	29	0.04
Soviet Union (0)	0	<0.01
Swedish (103)	512	0.70
Swiss (14)	368	0.50
Turkish (0)	0	<0.01
Ukrainian (160)	482	0.66
Welsh (500)	1,628	2.23
West Indian, ex. Hispanic (248)	371	0.51
Bahamian (0)	0	<0.01
Barbadian (0)	0	<0.01
Belizean (0)	0	<0.01
Bermudan (0)	0	<0.01
British West Indian (8)	8	0.01
Dutch West Indian (0)	0	<0.01
Haitian (74)	90	0.12
Jamaican (148)	212	0.29
Trinidadian/Tobagonian (0)	43	0.06
U.S. Virgin Islander (0)	0	<0.01
West Indian (18)	18	0.02
Other West Indian (0)	0	<0.01
Yugoslavian (116)	192	0.26

Hispanic Origin	Population	%
Hispanic or Latino (of any race)	1,316	1.79
Central American, ex. Mexican	90	0.12
Costa Rican	11	0.01
Guatemalan	44	0.06
Honduran	1	<0.01
Nicaraguan	4	0.01
Panamanian	6	0.01
Salvadoran	24	0.03
Other Central American	0	<0.01
Cuban	92	0.13
Dominican Republic	88	0.12
Mexican	279	0.38
Puerto Rican	469	0.64
South American	132	0.18
Argentinean	12	0.02
Bolivian	1	<0.01
Chilean	16	0.02
Colombian	42	0.06
Ecuadorian	16	0.02
Paraguayan	1	<0.01
Peruvian	30	0.04
Uruguayan	2	<0.01
Venezuelan	11	0.01
Other South American	1	<0.01
Other Hispanic or Latino	166	0.23

Race*	Population	%
African-American/Black (1,350)	1,763	2.40
Not Hispanic (1,260)	1,624	2.21
Hispanic (90)	139	0.19
American Indian/Alaska Native (524)	878	1.20
Not Hispanic (473)	800	1.09
Hispanic (51)	78	0.11
Alaska Athabascan (Ala. Nat.) (1)	1	<0.01
Aleut (Alaska Native) (0)	0	<0.01
Apache (0)	0	<0.01
Arapaho (0)	0	<0.01
Blackfeet (4)	5	0.01
Canadian/French Am. Ind. (4)	5	0.01
Central American Ind. (1)	1	<0.01
Cherokee (13)	55	0.07
Cheyenne (0)	2	<0.01
Chickasaw (0)	0	<0.01
Chippewa (8)	11	0.01
Choctaw (1)	4	0.01
Colville (2)	3	<0.01

Race* (cont.)	Population	%
Comanche (0)	0	<0.01
Cree (0)	1	<0.01
Creek (0)	0	<0.01
Crow (0)	0	<0.01
Delaware (0)	3	<0.01
Hopi (0)	0	<0.01
Houma (1)	1	<0.01
Inupiat (Alaska Native) (0)	0	<0.01
Iroquois (298)	414	0.56
Kiowa (0)	1	<0.01
Lumbee (0)	0	<0.01
Menominee (0)	0	<0.01
Mexican American Ind. (2)	6	0.01
Navajo (0)	4	0.01
Osage (0)	2	<0.01
Ottawa (0)	0	<0.01
Paiute (1)	1	<0.01
Pima (0)	0	<0.01
Potawatomi (0)	1	<0.01
Pueblo (0)	1	<0.01
Puget Sound Salish (0)	0	<0.01
Seminole (0)	0	<0.01
Shoshone (0)	0	<0.01
Sioux (10)	15	0.02
South American Ind. (12)	14	0.01
Spanish American Ind. (4)	4	0.01
Tlingit-Haida (Alaska Native) (2)	2	<0.01
Tohono O'Odham (0)	0	<0.01
Tsimshian (Alaska Native) (0)	0	<0.01
Ute (0)	0	<0.01
Yakama (0)	0	<0.01
Yaqui (0)	0	<0.01
Yuman (0)	1	<0.01
Yup'ik (Alaska Native) (3)	3	<0.01
Asian (583)	793	1.08
Not Hispanic (576)	779	1.06
Hispanic (7)	14	0.02
Bangladeshi (6)	6	0.01
Bhutanese (7)	7	0.01
Burmese (5)	5	0.01
Cambodian (6)	9	0.01
Chinese, ex. Taiwanese (178)	224	0.31
Filipino (48)	90	0.12
Hmong (1)	1	<0.01
Indian (105)	138	0.19
Indonesian (1)	2	<0.01
Japanese (38)	83	0.11
Korean (72)	95	0.13
Laotian (7)	7	0.01
Malaysian (0)	1	<0.01
Nepalese (6)	6	0.01
Pakistani (5)	8	0.01
Sri Lankan (12)	12	0.02
Taiwanese (7)	9	0.01
Thai (8)	15	0.02
Vietnamese (34)	45	0.06
Hawaii Native/Pacific Islander (17)	43	0.06
Not Hispanic (11)	32	0.04
Hispanic (6)	11	0.01
Fijian (0)	0	<0.01
Guamanian/Chamorro (7)	12	0.02
Marshallese (0)	0	<0.01
Native Hawaiian (9)	23	0.03
Samoan (0)	2	<0.01
Tongan (0)	1	<0.01
White (69,740)	70,644	96.19
Not Hispanic (68,916)	69,724	94.94
Hispanic (824)	920	1.25

Notes: † The Census 2010 population figure is used to calculate the percentages in the Hispanic Origin and Race categories. Ancestry percentages are based on the 2006-2010 American Community Survey population (not shown); ‡ Numbers in parentheses indicate the number of people reporting a single ancestry; * Numbers in parentheses indicate the number of persons reporting this race alone, not in combination with any other race; Please refer to the Explanation of Data for more information.

Monroe County

Population: 744,344

Ancestry	Population	%
Afghan (593)	593	0.08
African, Sub-Saharan (9,510)	10,853	1.46
African (6,140)	7,288	0.98
Cape Verdean (0)	0	<0.01
Ethiopian (734)	734	0.10
Ghanaian (49)	49	0.01
Kenyan (9)	9	<0.01
Liberian (89)	109	0.01
Nigerian (503)	603	0.08
Senegalese (26)	26	<0.01
Sierra Leonean (0)	0	<0.01
Somalian (1,018)	1,018	0.14
South African (156)	179	0.02
Sudanese (181)	205	0.03
Ugandan (0)	0	<0.01
Zimbabwean (76)	76	0.01
Other Sub-Saharan African (529)	557	0.08
Albanian (375)	445	0.06
Alsatian (3)	34	<0.01
American (20,394)	20,394	2.75
Arab (2,460)	3,916	0.53
Arab (591)	865	0.12
Egyptian (314)	339	0.05
Iraqi (111)	167	0.02
Jordanian (0)	0	<0.01
Lebanese (539)	1,243	0.17
Moroccan (171)	221	0.03
Palestinian (80)	140	0.02
Syrian (126)	231	0.03
Other Arab (528)	710	0.10
Armenian (338)	695	0.09
Assyrian/Chaldean/Syriac (0)	0	<0.01
Australian (161)	304	0.04
Austrian (484)	2,334	0.31
Basque (13)	13	<0.01
Belgian (346)	1,318	0.18
Brazilian (223)	312	0.04
British (1,603)	3,430	0.46
Bulgarian (95)	224	0.03
Cajun (0)	0	<0.01
Canadian (1,638)	3,828	0.52
Carpatho Rusyn (0)	16	<0.01
Celtic (69)	119	0.02
Croatian (67)	308	0.04
Cypriot (0)	0	<0.01
Czech (445)	2,461	0.33
Czechoslovakian (230)	589	0.08
Danish (406)	1,719	0.23
Dutch (3,397)	19,639	2.65
Eastern European (1,085)	1,267	0.17
English (25,417)	94,030	12.68
Estonian (26)	186	0.03
European (5,777)	6,513	0.88
Finnish (177)	774	0.10
French, ex. Basque (2,904)	23,189	3.13
French Canadian (2,803)	8,059	1.09
German (37,495)	156,984	21.18
German Russian (7)	35	<0.01
Greek (2,336)	4,548	0.61
Guyanese (586)	694	0.09
Hungarian (1,031)	3,581	0.48
Icelander (75)	75	0.01
Iranian (234)	257	0.03
Irish (28,758)	123,123	16.61
Israeli (254)	436	0.06
Italian (71,014)	140,596	18.97
Latvian (208)	456	0.06
Lithuanian (1,049)	2,950	0.40
Luxemburger (43)	101	0.01
Macedonian (564)	754	0.10
Maltese (37)	123	0.02
New Zealander (0)	0	<0.01
Northern European (328)	433	0.06
Norwegian (662)	2,890	0.39
Pennsylvania German (218)	469	0.06

Ancestry	Population	%
Polish (11,957)	40,211	5.42
Portuguese (453)	1,455	0.20
Romanian (555)	1,117	0.15
Russian (3,981)	8,944	1.21
Scandinavian (166)	486	0.07
Scotch-Irish (3,160)	9,722	1.31
Scottish (3,214)	15,779	2.13
Serbian (52)	164	0.02
Slavic (236)	599	0.08
Slovak (329)	893	0.12
Slovene (86)	226	0.03
Soviet Union (0)	0	<0.01
Swedish (1,498)	6,462	0.87
Swiss (294)	2,029	0.27
Turkish (2,064)	2,586	0.35
Ukrainian (5,827)	10,628	1.43
Welsh (841)	5,288	0.71
West Indian, ex. Hispanic (5,376)	8,191	1.10
Bahamian (58)	218	0.03
Barbadian (318)	379	0.05
Belizean (185)	275	0.04
Bermudan (0)	0	<0.01
British West Indian (99)	223	0.03
Dutch West Indian (0)	13	<0.01
Haitian (917)	1,040	0.14
Jamaican (2,942)	4,448	0.60
Trinidadian/Tobagonian (268)	413	0.06
U.S. Virgin Islander (0)	0	<0.01
West Indian (589)	1,182	0.16
Other West Indian (0)	0	<0.01
Yugoslavian (551)	813	0.11

Hispanic Origin	Population	%
Hispanic or Latino (of any race)	54,005	7.26
Central American, ex. Mexican	1,513	0.20
Costa Rican	156	0.02
Guatemalan	353	0.05
Honduran	242	0.03
Nicaraguan	192	0.03
Panamanian	241	0.03
Salvadoran	320	0.04
Other Central American	9	<0.01
Cuban	2,913	0.39
Dominican Republic	2,160	0.29
Mexican	3,364	0.45
Puerto Rican	38,907	5.23
South American	2,258	0.30
Argentinean	225	0.03
Bolivian	62	0.01
Chilean	321	0.04
Colombian	753	0.10
Ecuadorian	267	0.04
Paraguayan	55	0.01
Peruvian	358	0.05
Uruguayan	29	<0.01
Venezuelan	153	0.02
Other South American	35	<0.01
Other Hispanic or Latino	2,890	0.39

Race*	Population	%
African-American/Black (113,171)	124,305	16.70
Not Hispanic (107,448)	115,820	15.56
Hispanic (5,723)	8,485	1.14
American Indian/Alaska Native (2,136)	6,360	0.85
Not Hispanic (1,589)	4,952	0.67
Hispanic (547)	1,408	0.19
Alaska Athabascan (Ala. Nat.) (2)	7	<0.01
Aleut (Alaska Native) (1)	2	<0.01
Apache (11)	34	<0.01
Arapaho (0)	4	<0.01
Blackfeet (21)	184	0.02
Canadian/French Am. Ind. (27)	52	0.01
Central American Ind. (23)	41	0.01
Cherokee (88)	754	0.10
Cheyenne (3)	4	<0.01
Chickasaw (4)	12	<0.01
Chippewa (46)	70	0.01
Choctaw (8)	57	0.01
Colville (0)	2	<0.01

	Population	%
Comanche (0)	3	<0.01
Cree (6)	15	<0.01
Creek (7)	28	<0.01
Crow (1)	5	<0.01
Delaware (8)	28	<0.01
Hopi (1)	1	<0.01
Houma (2)	2	<0.01
Inupiat (Alaska Native) (4)	7	<0.01
Iroquois (686)	1,325	0.18
Kiowa (0)	0	<0.01
Lumbee (1)	5	<0.01
Menominee (0)	0	<0.01
Mexican American Ind. (53)	95	0.01
Navajo (20)	49	0.01
Osage (1)	5	<0.01
Ottawa (1)	1	<0.01
Paiute (1)	2	<0.01
Pima (0)	3	<0.01
Potawatomi (11)	17	<0.01
Pueblo (1)	6	<0.01
Puget Sound Salish (1)	1	<0.01
Seminole (3)	63	0.01
Shoshone (0)	3	<0.01
Sioux (26)	72	0.01
South American Ind. (70)	235	0.03
Spanish American Ind. (18)	22	<0.01
Tlingit-Haida (Alaska Native) (4)	12	<0.01
Tohono O'Odham (1)	1	<0.01
Tsimshian (Alaska Native) (0)	0	<0.01
Ute (1)	6	<0.01
Yakama (0)	0	<0.01
Yaqui (0)	0	<0.01
Yuman (3)	3	<0.01
Yup'ik (Alaska Native) (0)	0	<0.01
Asian (24,281)	28,675	3.85
Not Hispanic (24,023)	28,047	3.77
Hispanic (258)	628	0.08
Bangladeshi (79)	98	0.01
Bhutanese (369)	411	0.06
Burmese (559)	599	0.08
Cambodian (485)	580	0.08
Chinese, ex. Taiwanese (5,587)	6,499	0.87
Filipino (954)	1,567	0.21
Hmong (2)	3	<0.01
Indian (6,146)	6,938	0.93
Indonesian (45)	106	0.01
Japanese (586)	1,157	0.16
Korean (2,387)	2,997	0.40
Laotian (1,301)	1,551	0.21
Malaysian (98)	108	0.01
Nepalese (196)	246	0.03
Pakistani (845)	951	0.13
Sri Lankan (149)	173	0.02
Taiwanese (340)	438	0.06
Thai (196)	296	0.04
Vietnamese (2,824)	3,205	0.43
Hawaii Native/Pacific Islander (227)	874	0.12
Not Hispanic (182)	622	0.08
Hispanic (45)	252	0.03
Fijian (1)	9	<0.01
Guamanian/Chamorro (45)	77	0.01
Marshallese (0)	1	<0.01
Native Hawaiian (62)	208	0.03
Samoan (44)	88	0.01
Tongan (5)	6	<0.01
White (566,535)	582,035	78.19
Not Hispanic (542,034)	553,986	74.43
Hispanic (24,501)	28,049	3.77

*Notes: † The Census 2010 population figure is used to calculate the percentages in the Hispanic Origin and Race categories. Ancestry percentages are based on the 2006-2010 American Community Survey population (not shown); ‡ Numbers in parentheses indicate the number of people reporting a single ancestry; * Numbers in parentheses indicate the number of persons reporting this race alone, not in combination with any other race; Please refer to the Explanation of Data for more information.*

Montgomery County

Population: 50,219

Ancestry	Population	%
Afghan (0)	0	<0.01
African, Sub-Saharan (64)	64	0.13
African (49)	49	0.10
Cape Verdean (0)	0	<0.01
Ethiopian (0)	0	<0.01
Ghanaian (0)	0	<0.01
Kenyan (0)	0	<0.01
Liberian (0)	0	<0.01
Nigerian (4)	4	0.01
Senegalese (0)	0	<0.01
Sierra Leonean (0)	0	<0.01
Somalian (0)	0	<0.01
South African (11)	11	0.02
Sudanese (0)	0	<0.01
Ugandan (0)	0	<0.01
Zimbabwean (0)	0	<0.01
Other Sub-Saharan African (0)	0	<0.01
Albanian (11)	25	0.05
Alsatian (0)	0	<0.01
American (4,301)	4,301	8.61
Arab (22)	105	0.21
Arab (0)	18	0.04
Egyptian (0)	0	<0.01
Iraqi (0)	0	<0.01
Jordanian (0)	0	<0.01
Lebanese (22)	67	0.13
Moroccan (0)	0	<0.01
Palestinian (0)	9	0.02
Syrian (0)	11	0.02
Other Arab (0)	0	<0.01
Armenian (0)	66	0.13
Assyrian/Chaldean/Syriac (0)	0	<0.01
Australian (0)	11	0.02
Austrian (55)	127	0.25
Basque (0)	0	<0.01
Belgian (0)	21	0.04
Brazilian (5)	5	0.01
British (65)	85	0.17
Bulgarian (0)	0	<0.01
Cajun (0)	0	<0.01
Canadian (60)	136	0.27
Carpatho Rusyn (0)	0	<0.01
Celtic (0)	0	<0.01
Croatian (2)	12	0.02
Cypriot (0)	0	<0.01
Czech (54)	168	0.34
Czechoslovakian (0)	15	0.03
Danish (32)	199	0.40
Dutch (296)	2,858	5.72
Eastern European (98)	98	0.20
English (2,674)	6,458	12.93
Estonian (0)	0	<0.01
European (188)	207	0.41
Finnish (0)	13	0.03
French, ex. Basque (218)	2,400	4.81
French Canadian (155)	753	1.51
German (2,515)	8,912	17.84
German Russian (0)	0	<0.01
Greek (41)	218	0.44
Guyanese (0)	0	<0.01
Hungarian (30)	95	0.19
Icelander (0)	0	<0.01
Iranian (0)	0	<0.01
Irish (1,526)	8,038	16.09
Israeli (0)	0	<0.01
Italian (4,249)	9,234	18.49
Latvian (18)	32	0.06
Lithuanian (336)	636	1.27
Luxemburger (0)	0	<0.01
Macedonian (0)	0	<0.01
Maltese (0)	0	<0.01
New Zealander (0)	0	<0.01
Northern European (13)	13	0.03
Norwegian (25)	86	0.17
Pennsylvania German (283)	293	0.59

Ancestry (cont.)	Population	%
Polish (2,668)	5,283	10.58
Portuguese (8)	40	0.08
Romanian (8)	22	0.04
Russian (25)	172	0.34
Scandinavian (12)	12	0.02
Scotch-Irish (173)	422	0.84
Scottish (192)	772	1.55
Serbian (0)	2	<0.01
Slavic (0)	4	0.01
Slovak (58)	129	0.26
Slovene (4)	11	0.02
Soviet Union (0)	0	<0.01
Swedish (28)	252	0.50
Swiss (17)	86	0.17
Turkish (0)	0	<0.01
Ukrainian (103)	376	0.75
Welsh (16)	108	0.22
West Indian, ex. Hispanic (65)	149	0.30
Bahamian (0)	0	<0.01
Barbadian (0)	0	<0.01
Belizean (0)	0	<0.01
Bermudan (0)	0	<0.01
British West Indian (0)	0	<0.01
Dutch West Indian (0)	0	<0.01
Haitian (5)	5	0.01
Jamaican (56)	140	0.28
Trinidadian/Tobagonian (4)	4	0.01
U.S. Virgin Islander (0)	0	<0.01
West Indian (0)	0	<0.01
Other West Indian (0)	0	<0.01
Yugoslavian (10)	10	0.02

Hispanic Origin	Population	%
Hispanic or Latino (of any race)	5,654	11.26
Central American, ex. Mexican	245	0.49
Costa Rican	131	0.26
Guatemalan	47	0.09
Honduran	11	0.02
Nicaraguan	11	0.02
Panamanian	10	0.02
Salvadoran	35	0.07
Other Central American	0	<0.01
Cuban	90	0.18
Dominican Republic	259	0.52
Mexican	218	0.43
Puerto Rican	4,330	8.62
South American	160	0.32
Argentinean	6	0.01
Bolivian	1	<0.01
Chilean	12	0.02
Colombian	41	0.08
Ecuadorian	76	0.15
Paraguayan	0	<0.01
Peruvian	19	0.04
Uruguayan	1	<0.01
Venezuelan	3	0.01
Other South American	1	<0.01
Other Hispanic or Latino	352	0.70

Race*	Population	%
African-American/Black (951)	1,447	2.88
Not Hispanic (712)	1,067	2.12
Hispanic (239)	380	0.76
American Indian/Alaska Native (169)	408	0.81
Not Hispanic (103)	298	0.59
Hispanic (66)	110	0.22
Alaska Athabascan (Ala. Nat.) (0)	0	<0.01
Aleut (Alaska Native) (0)	0	<0.01
Apache (0)	3	0.01
Arapaho (0)	0	<0.01
Blackfeet (1)	13	0.03
Canadian/French Am. Ind. (0)	1	<0.01
Central American Ind. (2)	4	0.01
Cherokee (7)	37	0.07
Cheyenne (1)	1	<0.01
Chickasaw (0)	0	<0.01
Chippewa (1)	1	<0.01
Choctaw (2)	4	0.01
Colville (0)	0	<0.01

Race* (cont.)	Population	%
Comanche (0)	0	<0.01
Cree (1)	3	0.01
Creek (0)	0	<0.01
Crow (0)	0	<0.01
Delaware (4)	8	0.02
Hopi (0)	0	<0.01
Houma (0)	0	<0.01
Inupiat (Alaska Native) (0)	0	<0.01
Iroquois (22)	89	0.18
Kiowa (0)	0	<0.01
Lumbee (1)	3	0.01
Menominee (0)	0	<0.01
Mexican American Ind. (3)	6	0.01
Navajo (0)	2	<0.01
Osage (0)	1	<0.01
Ottawa (0)	1	<0.01
Paiute (0)	0	<0.01
Pima (0)	0	<0.01
Potawatomi (0)	0	<0.01
Pueblo (0)	0	<0.01
Puget Sound Salish (0)	0	<0.01
Seminole (0)	1	<0.01
Shoshone (0)	0	<0.01
Sioux (2)	7	0.01
South American Ind. (12)	20	0.04
Spanish American Ind. (2)	5	0.01
Tlingit-Haida (Alaska Native) (2)	3	0.01
Tohono O'Odham (0)	0	<0.01
Tsimshian (Alaska Native) (0)	0	<0.01
Ute (0)	0	<0.01
Yakama (0)	0	<0.01
Yaqui (0)	0	<0.01
Yuman (0)	0	<0.01
Yup'ik (Alaska Native) (0)	0	<0.01
Asian (369)	468	0.93
Not Hispanic (356)	435	0.87
Hispanic (13)	33	0.07
Bangladeshi (0)	0	<0.01
Bhutanese (0)	0	<0.01
Burmese (0)	0	<0.01
Cambodian (0)	0	<0.01
Chinese, ex. Taiwanese (65)	84	0.17
Filipino (42)	58	0.12
Hmong (0)	0	<0.01
Indian (136)	149	0.30
Indonesian (4)	4	0.01
Japanese (12)	30	0.06
Korean (45)	61	0.12
Laotian (0)	0	<0.01
Malaysian (0)	0	<0.01
Nepalese (1)	2	<0.01
Pakistani (16)	21	0.04
Sri Lankan (0)	0	<0.01
Taiwanese (1)	1	<0.01
Thai (7)	15	0.03
Vietnamese (4)	13	0.03
Hawaii Native/Pacific Islander (19)	56	0.11
Not Hispanic (11)	23	0.05
Hispanic (8)	33	0.07
Fijian (0)	0	<0.01
Guamanian/Chamorro (9)	12	0.02
Marshallese (0)	0	<0.01
Native Hawaiian (4)	9	0.02
Samoan (3)	3	0.01
Tongan (2)	2	<0.01
White (45,519)	46,382	92.36
Not Hispanic (42,732)	43,292	86.21
Hispanic (2,787)	3,090	6.15

Notes: † The Census 2010 population figure is used to calculate the percentages in the Hispanic Origin and Race categories. Ancestry percentages are based on the 2006-2010 American Community Survey population (not shown); ‡ Numbers in parentheses indicate the number of people reporting a single ancestry; * Numbers in parentheses indicate the number of persons reporting this race alone, not in combination with any other race; Please refer to the Explanation of Data for more information.

Nassau County
Population: 1,339,532

Ancestry	Population	%
Afghan (938)	1,420	0.11
African, Sub-Saharan (5,338)	7,241	0.54
African (3,221)	4,618	0.35
Cape Verdean (12)	12	<0.01
Ethiopian (87)	155	0.01
Ghanaian (356)	423	0.03
Kenyan (0)	0	<0.01
Liberian (0)	3	<0.01
Nigerian (1,144)	1,356	0.10
Senegalese (0)	0	<0.01
Sierra Leonean (24)	24	<0.01
Somalian (15)	15	<0.01
South African (190)	225	0.02
Sudanese (33)	50	<0.01
Ugandan (0)	0	<0.01
Zimbabwean (0)	0	<0.01
Other Sub-Saharan African (256)	360	0.03
Albanian (1,157)	1,726	0.13
Alsatian (9)	46	<0.01
American (42,503)	42,503	3.20
Arab (4,560)	7,635	0.57
Arab (502)	692	0.05
Egyptian (1,361)	1,995	0.15
Iraqi (528)	793	0.06
Jordanian (66)	66	<0.01
Lebanese (426)	995	0.07
Moroccan (244)	618	0.05
Palestinian (154)	232	0.02
Syrian (165)	754	0.06
Other Arab (1,114)	1,490	0.11
Armenian (2,406)	3,535	0.27
Assyrian/Chaldean/Syriac (7)	40	<0.01
Australian (154)	388	0.03
Austrian (3,200)	11,903	0.90
Basque (2)	167	0.01
Belgian (311)	821	0.06
Brazilian (1,025)	1,516	0.11
British (1,099)	2,526	0.19
Bulgarian (230)	299	0.02
Cajun (0)	59	<0.01
Canadian (632)	1,951	0.15
Carpatho Rusyn (4)	36	<0.01
Celtic (84)	143	0.01
Croatian (1,742)	2,842	0.21
Cypriot (306)	381	0.03
Czech (1,112)	4,825	0.36
Czechoslovakian (735)	2,195	0.17
Danish (453)	2,201	0.17
Dutch (815)	5,539	0.42
Eastern European (13,083)	13,843	1.04
English (6,821)	42,066	3.17
Estonian (213)	360	0.03
European (10,190)	11,073	0.83
Finnish (197)	1,079	0.08
French, ex. Basque (1,972)	15,598	1.17
French Canadian (907)	3,222	0.24
German (29,737)	143,597	10.80
German Russian (0)	43	<0.01
Greek (13,704)	21,516	1.62
Guyanese (3,463)	4,442	0.33
Hungarian (4,774)	13,637	1.03
Icelander (50)	144	0.01
Iranian (10,076)	11,333	0.85
Irish (73,529)	224,843	16.92
Israeli (4,093)	5,327	0.40
Italian (170,115)	305,805	23.01
Latvian (463)	965	0.07
Lithuanian (1,501)	4,623	0.35
Luxemburger (0)	16	<0.01
Macedonian (41)	51	<0.01
Maltese (496)	1,367	0.10
New Zealander (0)	0	<0.01
Northern European (619)	717	0.05
Norwegian (1,502)	6,174	0.46
Pennsylvania German (121)	182	0.01

Ancestry	Population	%
Polish (24,310)	72,081	5.42
Portuguese (5,557)	7,340	0.55
Romanian (2,430)	5,933	0.45
Russian (26,109)	59,061	4.44
Scandinavian (274)	647	0.05
Scotch-Irish (3,219)	8,938	0.67
Scottish (1,993)	8,512	0.64
Serbian (144)	294	0.02
Slavic (100)	549	0.04
Slovak (491)	1,528	0.11
Slovene (98)	277	0.02
Soviet Union (0)	10	<0.01
Swedish (1,026)	7,946	0.60
Swiss (395)	2,316	0.17
Turkish (1,731)	2,980	0.22
Ukrainian (2,820)	5,868	0.44
Welsh (224)	1,755	0.13
West Indian, ex. Hispanic (43,896)	52,648	3.96
Bahamian (5)	51	<0.01
Barbadian (1,197)	1,489	0.11
Belizean (145)	228	0.02
Bermudan (52)	65	<0.01
British West Indian (813)	1,182	0.09
Dutch West Indian (217)	285	0.02
Haitian (18,556)	20,810	1.57
Jamaican (16,745)	19,674	1.48
Trinidadian/Tobagonian (2,369)	3,518	0.26
U.S. Virgin Islander (15)	45	<0.01
West Indian (3,765)	5,269	0.40
Other West Indian (17)	32	<0.01
Yugoslavian (357)	1,166	0.09

Hispanic Origin	Population	%
Hispanic or Latino (of any race)	195,355	14.58
Central American, ex. Mexican	69,816	5.21
Costa Rican	992	0.07
Guatemalan	7,853	0.59
Honduran	11,051	0.82
Nicaraguan	925	0.07
Panamanian	1,360	0.10
Salvadoran	47,180	3.52
Other Central American	455	0.03
Cuban	5,430	0.41
Dominican Republic	20,216	1.51
Mexican	10,535	0.79
Puerto Rican	29,965	2.24
South American	38,719	2.89
Argentinean	2,533	0.19
Bolivian	696	0.05
Chilean	2,945	0.22
Colombian	13,257	0.99
Ecuadorian	9,239	0.69
Paraguayan	406	0.03
Peruvian	7,853	0.59
Uruguayan	628	0.05
Venezuelan	825	0.06
Other South American	337	0.03
Other Hispanic or Latino	20,674	1.54

Race*	Population	%
African-American/Black (149,049)	159,230	11.89
Not Hispanic (141,305)	148,211	11.06
Hispanic (7,744)	11,019	0.82
American Indian/Alaska Native (3,185)	8,027	0.60
Not Hispanic (1,379)	4,240	0.32
Hispanic (1,806)	3,787	0.28
Alaska Athabascan (Ala. Nat.) (0)	1	<0.01
Aleut (Alaska Native) (2)	3	<0.01
Apache (8)	26	<0.01
Arapaho (0)	0	<0.01
Blackfeet (17)	151	0.01
Canadian/French Am. Ind. (10)	18	<0.01
Central American Ind. (73)	138	0.01
Cherokee (83)	783	0.06
Cheyenne (5)	7	<0.01
Chickasaw (0)	7	<0.01
Chippewa (14)	28	<0.01
Choctaw (15)	49	<0.01
Colville (1)	1	<0.01

	Population	%
Comanche (7)	11	<0.01
Cree (0)	5	<0.01
Creek (7)	37	<0.01
Crow (0)	3	<0.01
Delaware (9)	24	<0.01
Hopi (1)	5	<0.01
Houma (0)	0	<0.01
Inupiat (Alaska Native) (2)	5	<0.01
Iroquois (102)	240	0.02
Kiowa (1)	1	<0.01
Lumbee (9)	23	<0.01
Menominee (0)	0	<0.01
Mexican American Ind. (157)	239	0.02
Navajo (4)	16	<0.01
Osage (0)	3	<0.01
Ottawa (1)	1	<0.01
Paiute (0)	0	<0.01
Pima (0)	0	<0.01
Potawatomi (2)	4	<0.01
Pueblo (13)	18	<0.01
Puget Sound Salish (0)	0	<0.01
Seminole (2)	29	<0.01
Shoshone (2)	5	<0.01
Sioux (22)	57	<0.01
South American Ind. (210)	450	0.03
Spanish American Ind. (178)	217	0.02
Tlingit-Haida (Alaska Native) (3)	6	<0.01
Tohono O'Odham (7)	7	<0.01
Tsimshian (Alaska Native) (0)	0	<0.01
Ute (2)	2	<0.01
Yakama (0)	0	<0.01
Yaqui (1)	1	<0.01
Yuman (0)	0	<0.01
Yup'ik (Alaska Native) (0)	0	<0.01
Asian (102,266)	113,831	8.50
Not Hispanic (101,558)	111,861	8.35
Hispanic (708)	1,970	0.15
Bangladeshi (1,269)	1,408	0.11
Bhutanese (1)	1	<0.01
Burmese (147)	179	0.01
Cambodian (89)	120	0.01
Chinese, ex. Taiwanese (23,026)	25,716	1.92
Filipino (9,881)	11,622	0.87
Hmong (0)	2	<0.01
Indian (39,572)	43,171	3.22
Indonesian (93)	157	0.01
Japanese (1,967)	2,587	0.19
Korean (13,558)	14,338	1.07
Laotian (30)	42	<0.01
Malaysian (60)	97	0.01
Nepalese (106)	111	0.01
Pakistani (6,737)	7,382	0.55
Sri Lankan (281)	330	0.02
Taiwanese (1,448)	1,673	0.12
Thai (436)	555	0.04
Vietnamese (809)	1,071	0.08
Hawaii Native/Pacific Islander (336)	1,557	0.12
Not Hispanic (197)	1,015	0.08
Hispanic (139)	542	0.04
Fijian (10)	13	<0.01
Guamanian/Chamorro (128)	164	0.01
Marshallese (2)	2	<0.01
Native Hawaiian (48)	193	0.01
Samoan (27)	71	0.01
Tongan (2)	2	<0.01
White (977,577)	1,000,818	74.71
Not Hispanic (877,309)	889,240	66.38
Hispanic (100,268)	111,578	8.33

New York County

Population: 1,585,873

Ancestry	Population	%
Afghan (59)	85	0.01
African, Sub-Saharan (19,667)	24,146	1.52
African (10,054)	12,839	0.81
Cape Verdean (81)	206	0.01
Ethiopian (932)	1,043	0.07
Ghanaian (714)	818	0.05
Kenyan (43)	69	<0.01
Liberian (169)	176	0.01
Nigerian (1,650)	1,953	0.12
Senegalese (1,118)	1,216	0.08
Sierra Leonean (422)	422	0.03
Somalian (125)	125	0.01
South African (991)	1,372	0.09
Sudanese (137)	137	0.01
Ugandan (95)	125	0.01
Zimbabwean (80)	100	0.01
Other Sub-Saharan African (3,056)	3,545	0.22
Albanian (1,385)	1,618	0.10
Alsatian (5)	129	0.01
American (54,694)	54,694	3.45
Arab (8,584)	13,828	0.87
Arab (1,250)	1,720	0.11
Egyptian (1,374)	1,906	0.12
Iraqi (275)	583	0.04
Jordanian (0)	48	<0.01
Lebanese (1,838)	3,331	0.21
Moroccan (914)	1,592	0.10
Palestinian (626)	794	0.05
Syrian (518)	1,112	0.07
Other Arab (1,789)	2,742	0.17
Armenian (1,520)	2,653	0.17
Assyrian/Chaldean/Syriac (94)	137	0.01
Australian (1,965)	2,719	0.17
Austrian (4,202)	14,656	0.93
Basque (191)	428	0.03
Belgian (928)	2,470	0.16
Brazilian (2,870)	4,541	0.29
British (6,950)	12,129	0.77
Bulgarian (927)	1,272	0.08
Cajun (22)	224	0.01
Canadian (3,037)	5,646	0.36
Carpatho Rusyn (89)	112	0.01
Celtic (129)	304	0.02
Croatian (1,299)	2,164	0.14
Cypriot (139)	216	0.01
Czech (1,439)	4,820	0.30
Czechoslovakian (619)	1,256	0.08
Danish (1,444)	4,095	0.26
Dutch (2,847)	10,414	0.66
Eastern European (23,269)	25,277	1.60
English (22,270)	77,799	4.91
Estonian (190)	424	0.03
European (25,127)	27,846	1.76
Finnish (666)	1,658	0.10
French, ex. Basque (10,278)	31,783	2.01
French Canadian (1,692)	5,246	0.33
German (27,493)	107,666	6.80
German Russian (0)	41	<0.01
Greek (7,557)	13,078	0.83
Guyanese (1,802)	2,259	0.14
Hungarian (4,686)	14,667	0.93
Icelander (246)	382	0.02
Iranian (3,458)	4,256	0.27
Irish (40,008)	117,355	7.41
Israeli (4,839)	6,624	0.42
Italian (44,498)	98,563	6.22
Latvian (713)	1,822	0.12
Lithuanian (1,597)	5,775	0.36
Luxemburger (23)	68	<0.01
Macedonian (973)	1,086	0.07
Maltese (548)	840	0.05
New Zealander (243)	405	0.03
Northern European (1,296)	1,485	0.09
Norwegian (1,552)	7,445	0.47
Pennsylvania German (123)	327	0.02

Ancestry	Population	%
Polish (20,565)	64,078	4.05
Portuguese (1,436)	3,862	0.24
Romanian (3,035)	7,692	0.49
Russian (36,296)	82,983	5.24
Scandinavian (753)	1,731	0.11
Scotch-Irish (4,283)	13,158	0.83
Scottish (4,846)	19,553	1.23
Serbian (1,160)	1,526	0.10
Slavic (177)	400	0.03
Slovak (812)	2,298	0.15
Slovene (271)	695	0.04
Soviet Union (28)	54	<0.01
Swedish (3,045)	10,408	0.66
Swiss (1,381)	4,962	0.31
Turkish (2,708)	3,703	0.23
Ukrainian (4,361)	8,849	0.56
Welsh (944)	6,000	0.38
West Indian, ex. Hispanic (22,411)	30,009	1.90
Bahamian (303)	457	0.03
Barbadian (738)	907	0.06
Belizean (654)	735	0.05
Bermudan (86)	127	0.01
British West Indian (1,308)	1,658	0.10
Dutch West Indian (212)	276	0.02
Haitian (5,308)	6,500	0.41
Jamaican (7,099)	9,242	0.58
Trinidadian/Tobagonian (3,010)	3,877	0.24
U.S. Virgin Islander (343)	487	0.03
West Indian (3,296)	5,618	0.35
Other West Indian (54)	125	0.01
Yugoslavian (1,478)	1,876	0.12

Hispanic Origin	Population	%
Hispanic or Latino (of any race)	403,577	25.45
Central American, ex. Mexican	13,948	0.88
Costa Rican	987	0.06
Guatemalan	2,051	0.13
Honduran	4,058	0.26
Nicaraguan	1,556	0.10
Panamanian	1,716	0.11
Salvadoran	3,419	0.22
Other Central American	161	0.01
Cuban	11,623	0.73
Dominican Republic	155,971	9.84
Mexican	41,965	2.65
Puerto Rican	107,774	6.80
South American	36,748	2.32
Argentinean	4,339	0.27
Bolivian	522	0.03
Chilean	1,824	0.12
Colombian	8,411	0.53
Ecuadorian	14,132	0.89
Paraguayan	268	0.02
Peruvian	3,852	0.24
Uruguayan	549	0.03
Venezuelan	2,573	0.16
Other South American	278	0.02
Other Hispanic or Latino	35,548	2.24

Race*	Population	%
African-American/Black (246,687)	272,993	17.21
Not Hispanic (205,340)	217,102	13.69
Hispanic (41,347)	55,891	3.52
American Indian/Alaska Native (8,669)	19,415	1.22
Not Hispanic (2,144)	7,395	0.47
Hispanic (6,525)	12,020	0.76
Alaska Athabascan (Ala. Nat.) (11)	18	<0.01
Aleut (Alaska Native) (4)	7	<0.01
Apache (28)	92	0.01
Arapaho (3)	5	<0.01
Blackfeet (41)	356	0.02
Canadian/French Am. Ind. (29)	62	<0.01
Central American Ind. (610)	1,090	0.07
Cherokee (288)	1,845	0.12
Cheyenne (4)	9	<0.01
Chickasaw (15)	43	<0.01
Chippewa (36)	99	0.01
Choctaw (41)	179	0.01
Colville (4)	5	<0.01

	Population	%
Comanche (13)	22	<0.01
Cree (4)	22	<0.01
Creek (12)	61	<0.01
Crow (4)	11	<0.01
Delaware (14)	54	<0.01
Hopi (8)	15	<0.01
Houma (0)	3	<0.01
Inupiat (Alaska Native) (2)	8	<0.01
Iroquois (97)	265	0.02
Kiowa (9)	11	<0.01
Lumbee (10)	21	<0.01
Menominee (2)	3	<0.01
Mexican American Ind. (479)	752	0.05
Navajo (38)	83	0.01
Osage (7)	12	<0.01
Ottawa (0)	3	<0.01
Paiute (2)	8	<0.01
Pima (2)	4	<0.01
Potawatomi (10)	20	<0.01
Pueblo (70)	175	0.01
Puget Sound Salish (2)	5	<0.01
Seminole (6)	110	0.01
Shoshone (3)	6	<0.01
Sioux (38)	133	0.01
South American Ind. (813)	1,935	0.12
Spanish American Ind. (373)	514	0.03
Tlingit-Haida (Alaska Native) (2)	15	<0.01
Tohono O'Odham (11)	15	<0.01
Tsimshian (Alaska Native) (3)	3	<0.01
Ute (1)	2	<0.01
Yakama (1)	2	<0.01
Yaqui (8)	22	<0.01
Yuman (4)	6	<0.01
Yup'ik (Alaska Native) (0)	2	<0.01
Asian (179,552)	199,722	12.59
Not Hispanic (177,624)	194,929	12.29
Hispanic (1,928)	4,793	0.30
Bangladeshi (1,672)	2,029	0.13
Bhutanese (26)	26	<0.01
Burmese (240)	317	0.02
Cambodian (168)	220	0.01
Chinese, ex. Taiwanese (92,088)	99,287	6.26
Filipino (10,399)	13,388	0.84
Hmong (16)	20	<0.01
Indian (25,857)	29,979	1.89
Indonesian (470)	693	0.04
Japanese (13,201)	16,600	1.05
Korean (19,683)	21,996	1.39
Laotian (109)	157	0.01
Malaysian (524)	766	0.05
Nepalese (240)	281	0.02
Pakistani (2,482)	2,940	0.19
Sri Lankan (450)	563	0.04
Taiwanese (2,789)	3,318	0.21
Thai (1,282)	1,657	0.10
Vietnamese (2,194)	2,919	0.18
Hawaii Native/Pacific Islander (873)	3,727	0.24
Not Hispanic (533)	1,776	0.11
Hispanic (340)	1,951	0.12
Fijian (29)	73	<0.01
Guamanian/Chamorro (132)	242	0.02
Marshallese (3)	4	<0.01
Native Hawaiian (185)	608	0.04
Samoan (87)	183	0.01
Tongan (18)	33	<0.01
White (911,073)	956,864	60.34
Not Hispanic (761,493)	785,299	49.52
Hispanic (149,580)	171,565	10.82

Notes: † The Census 2010 population figure is used to calculate the percentages in the Hispanic Origin and Race categories. Ancestry percentages are based on the 2006-2010 American Community Survey population (not shown); ‡ Numbers in parentheses indicate the number of people reporting a single ancestry; * Numbers in parentheses indicate the number of persons reporting this race alone, not in combination with any other race; Please refer to the Explanation of Data for more information.

Niagara County
Population: 216,469

Ancestry	Population	%
Afghan (0)	0	<0.01
African, Sub-Saharan (371)	625	0.29
African (339)	577	0.27
Cape Verdean (0)	0	<0.01
Ethiopian (24)	32	0.01
Ghanaian (0)	0	<0.01
Kenyan (0)	8	<0.01
Liberian (0)	0	<0.01
Nigerian (0)	0	<0.01
Senegalese (0)	0	<0.01
Sierra Leonean (0)	0	<0.01
Somalian (0)	0	<0.01
South African (8)	8	<0.01
Sudanese (0)	0	<0.01
Ugandan (0)	0	<0.01
Zimbabwean (0)	0	<0.01
Other Sub-Saharan African (0)	0	<0.01
Albanian (0)	0	<0.01
Alsatian (0)	14	0.01
American (7,216)	7,216	3.34
Arab (916)	1,832	0.85
Arab (144)	175	0.08
Egyptian (24)	61	0.03
Iraqi (0)	13	0.01
Jordanian (282)	282	0.13
Lebanese (388)	1,098	0.51
Moroccan (0)	0	<0.01
Palestinian (28)	28	0.01
Syrian (9)	83	0.04
Other Arab (41)	92	0.04
Armenian (164)	269	0.12
Assyrian/Chaldean/Syriac (0)	0	<0.01
Australian (31)	60	0.03
Austrian (255)	1,001	0.46
Basque (0)	0	<0.01
Belgian (38)	97	0.04
Brazilian (18)	18	0.01
British (270)	512	0.24
Bulgarian (0)	10	<0.01
Cajun (0)	0	<0.01
Canadian (707)	1,755	0.81
Carpatho Rusyn (14)	14	0.01
Celtic (0)	27	0.01
Croatian (196)	353	0.16
Cypriot (0)	0	<0.01
Czech (63)	422	0.20
Czechoslovakian (86)	245	0.11
Danish (77)	408	0.19
Dutch (548)	3,738	1.73
Eastern European (60)	60	0.03
English (9,005)	29,036	13.44
Estonian (8)	8	<0.01
European (960)	978	0.45
Finnish (0)	44	0.02
French, ex. Basque (1,222)	9,233	4.27
French Canadian (898)	2,590	1.20
German (18,960)	62,469	28.91
German Russian (16)	16	0.01
Greek (348)	969	0.45
Guyanese (43)	43	0.02
Hungarian (708)	2,506	1.16
Icelander (10)	68	0.03
Iranian (15)	24	0.01
Irish (9,618)	39,511	18.29
Israeli (12)	12	0.01
Italian (19,116)	41,083	19.01
Latvian (12)	28	0.01
Lithuanian (191)	455	0.21
Luxemburger (0)	0	<0.01
Macedonian (0)	0	<0.01
Maltese (0)	0	<0.01
New Zealander (0)	0	<0.01
Northern European (50)	50	0.02
Norwegian (257)	1,008	0.47
Pennsylvania German (178)	315	0.15

Ancestry	Population	%
Polish (10,633)	26,701	12.36
Portuguese (135)	258	0.12
Romanian (15)	107	0.05
Russian (777)	1,533	0.71
Scandinavian (86)	178	0.08
Scotch-Irish (964)	2,795	1.29
Scottish (1,335)	4,977	2.30
Serbian (0)	27	0.01
Slavic (129)	382	0.18
Slovak (142)	461	0.21
Slovene (28)	65	0.03
Soviet Union (0)	0	<0.01
Swedish (250)	1,940	0.90
Swiss (67)	236	0.11
Turkish (10)	41	0.02
Ukrainian (438)	1,138	0.53
Welsh (301)	1,779	0.82
West Indian, ex. Hispanic (431)	666	0.31
Bahamian (0)	0	<0.01
Barbadian (0)	0	<0.01
Belizean (29)	29	0.01
Bermudan (0)	0	<0.01
British West Indian (9)	9	<0.01
Dutch West Indian (0)	0	<0.01
Haitian (9)	9	<0.01
Jamaican (346)	409	0.19
Trinidadian/Tobagonian (15)	15	0.01
U.S. Virgin Islander (0)	0	<0.01
West Indian (23)	195	0.09
Other West Indian (0)	0	<0.01
Yugoslavian (28)	123	0.06

Hispanic Origin	Population	%
Hispanic or Latino (of any race)	4,694	2.17
Central American, ex. Mexican	165	0.08
Costa Rican	19	0.01
Guatemalan	50	0.02
Honduran	25	0.01
Nicaraguan	4	<0.01
Panamanian	47	0.02
Salvadoran	19	0.01
Other Central American	1	<0.01
Cuban	164	0.08
Dominican Republic	118	0.05
Mexican	1,107	0.51
Puerto Rican	2,263	1.05
South American	230	0.11
Argentinean	22	0.01
Bolivian	1	<0.01
Chilean	11	0.01
Colombian	104	0.05
Ecuadorian	33	0.02
Paraguayan	6	<0.01
Peruvian	31	0.01
Uruguayan	0	<0.01
Venezuelan	18	0.01
Other South American	4	<0.01
Other Hispanic or Latino	647	0.30

Race*	Population	%
African-American/Black (14,851)	17,632	8.15
Not Hispanic (14,511)	17,058	7.88
Hispanic (340)	574	0.27
American Indian/Alaska Native (2,285)	3,859	1.78
Not Hispanic (2,135)	3,589	1.66
Hispanic (150)	270	0.12
Alaska Athabascan (Ala. Nat.) (0)	1	<0.01
Aleut (Alaska Native) (0)	0	<0.01
Apache (2)	5	<0.01
Arapaho (0)	0	<0.01
Blackfeet (6)	49	0.02
Canadian/French Am. Ind. (39)	53	0.02
Central American Ind. (9)	13	0.01
Cherokee (34)	165	0.08
Cheyenne (1)	3	<0.01
Chickasaw (1)	1	<0.01
Chippewa (39)	64	0.03
Choctaw (1)	13	0.01
Colville (0)	0	<0.01

Race*	Population	%
Comanche (1)	1	<0.01
Cree (2)	5	<0.01
Creek (0)	6	<0.01
Crow (2)	2	<0.01
Delaware (5)	7	<0.01
Hopi (0)	0	<0.01
Houma (0)	0	<0.01
Inupiat (Alaska Native) (1)	2	<0.01
Iroquois (1,163)	1,751	0.81
Kiowa (1)	1	<0.01
Lumbee (4)	8	<0.01
Menominee (0)	2	<0.01
Mexican American Ind. (20)	21	0.01
Navajo (9)	9	<0.01
Osage (3)	4	<0.01
Ottawa (1)	2	<0.01
Paiute (0)	0	<0.01
Pima (0)	0	<0.01
Potawatomi (0)	0	<0.01
Pueblo (0)	0	<0.01
Puget Sound Salish (0)	0	<0.01
Seminole (0)	11	0.01
Shoshone (0)	0	<0.01
Sioux (13)	36	0.02
South American Ind. (10)	18	0.01
Spanish American Ind. (5)	5	<0.01
Tlingit-Haida (Alaska Native) (0)	1	<0.01
Tohono O'Odham (0)	0	<0.01
Tsimshian (Alaska Native) (0)	0	<0.01
Ute (1)	1	<0.01
Yakama (0)	1	<0.01
Yaqui (2)	2	<0.01
Yuman (0)	0	<0.01
Yup'ik (Alaska Native) (0)	0	<0.01
Asian (1,823)	2,407	1.11
Not Hispanic (1,807)	2,354	1.09
Hispanic (16)	53	0.02
Bangladeshi (2)	2	<0.01
Bhutanese (0)	0	<0.01
Burmese (13)	13	0.01
Cambodian (3)	8	<0.01
Chinese, ex. Taiwanese (347)	425	0.20
Filipino (133)	262	0.12
Hmong (4)	10	<0.01
Indian (671)	789	0.36
Indonesian (14)	18	0.01
Japanese (66)	135	0.06
Korean (210)	295	0.14
Laotian (18)	25	0.01
Malaysian (2)	2	<0.01
Nepalese (0)	0	<0.01
Pakistani (113)	127	0.06
Sri Lankan (6)	16	0.01
Taiwanese (19)	20	0.01
Thai (21)	38	0.02
Vietnamese (107)	135	0.06
Hawaii Native/Pacific Islander (62)	158	0.07
Not Hispanic (55)	141	0.07
Hispanic (7)	17	0.01
Fijian (1)	2	<0.01
Guamanian/Chamorro (8)	12	0.01
Marshallese (1)	1	<0.01
Native Hawaiian (14)	39	0.02
Samoan (5)	17	0.01
Tongan (4)	4	<0.01
White (191,673)	195,911	90.50
Not Hispanic (188,907)	192,737	89.04
Hispanic (2,766)	3,174	1.47

Notes: † The Census 2010 population figure is used to calculate the percentages in the Hispanic Origin and Race categories. Ancestry percentages are based on the 2006-2010 American Community Survey population (not shown); ‡ Numbers in parentheses indicate the number of people reporting a single ancestry; * Numbers in parentheses indicate the number of persons reporting this race alone, not in combination with any other race; Please refer to the Explanation of Data for more information.

Oneida County

Population: 234,878

Ancestry	Population	%
Afghan (42)	42	0.02
African, Sub-Saharan (699)	998	0.43
African (446)	671	0.29
Cape Verdean (0)	0	<0.01
Ethiopian (20)	79	0.03
Ghanaian (14)	14	0.01
Kenyan (12)	27	0.01
Liberian (88)	88	0.04
Nigerian (2)	2	<0.01
Senegalese (0)	0	<0.01
Sierra Leonean (0)	0	<0.01
Somalian (99)	99	0.04
South African (0)	0	<0.01
Sudanese (0)	0	<0.01
Ugandan (0)	0	<0.01
Zimbabwean (0)	0	<0.01
Other Sub-Saharan African (18)	18	0.01
Albanian (22)	55	0.02
Alsatian (0)	29	0.01
American (9,419)	9,419	4.02
Arab (2,006)	4,287	1.83
Arab (181)	267	0.11
Egyptian (149)	189	0.08
Iraqi (0)	6	<0.01
Jordanian (28)	28	0.01
Lebanese (1,246)	2,742	1.17
Moroccan (41)	50	0.02
Palestinian (10)	10	<0.01
Syrian (155)	742	0.32
Other Arab (196)	253	0.11
Armenian (130)	196	0.08
Assyrian/Chaldean/Syriac (0)	0	<0.01
Australian (32)	92	0.04
Austrian (69)	587	0.25
Basque (0)	0	<0.01
Belgian (8)	75	0.03
Brazilian (33)	86	0.04
British (394)	620	0.26
Bulgarian (0)	5	<0.01
Cajun (0)	0	<0.01
Canadian (288)	644	0.27
Carpatho Rusyn (8)	15	0.01
Celtic (8)	16	0.01
Croatian (24)	106	0.05
Cypriot (0)	0	<0.01
Czech (45)	576	0.25
Czechoslovakian (91)	233	0.10
Danish (99)	560	0.24
Dutch (908)	6,105	2.60
Eastern European (180)	200	0.09
English (6,403)	26,141	11.15
Estonian (0)	9	<0.01
European (1,134)	1,173	0.50
Finnish (30)	198	0.08
French, ex. Basque (1,786)	13,375	5.70
French Canadian (1,392)	3,834	1.63
German (9,284)	44,884	19.14
German Russian (0)	0	<0.01
Greek (145)	490	0.21
Guyanese (54)	68	0.03
Hungarian (203)	964	0.41
Icelander (0)	14	0.01
Iranian (35)	35	0.01
Irish (11,623)	45,802	19.53
Israeli (0)	0	<0.01
Italian (24,027)	47,602	20.30
Latvian (11)	14	0.01
Lithuanian (145)	683	0.29
Luxemburger (0)	0	<0.01
Macedonian (21)	21	0.01
Maltese (0)	0	<0.01
New Zealander (4)	4	<0.01
Northern European (195)	198	0.08
Norwegian (169)	709	0.30
Pennsylvania German (63)	159	0.07
Polish (10,228)	26,014	11.09
Portuguese (110)	488	0.21
Romanian (148)	239	0.10
Russian (1,169)	2,226	0.95
Scandinavian (32)	161	0.07
Scotch-Irish (737)	2,747	1.17
Scottish (732)	3,742	1.60
Serbian (0)	82	0.03
Slavic (13)	30	0.01
Slovak (135)	249	0.11
Slovene (9)	11	<0.01
Soviet Union (0)	0	<0.01
Swedish (266)	1,098	0.47
Swiss (294)	1,595	0.68
Turkish (0)	7	<0.01
Ukrainian (1,187)	2,419	1.03
Welsh (1,540)	7,279	3.10
West Indian, ex. Hispanic (1,119)	1,537	0.66
Bahamian (0)	0	<0.01
Barbadian (30)	34	0.01
Belizean (0)	10	<0.01
Bermudan (0)	0	<0.01
British West Indian (68)	96	0.04
Dutch West Indian (0)	0	<0.01
Haitian (241)	376	0.16
Jamaican (504)	675	0.29
Trinidadian/Tobagonian (139)	169	0.07
U.S. Virgin Islander (9)	9	<0.01
West Indian (128)	168	0.07
Other West Indian (0)	0	<0.01
Yugoslavian (3,270)	3,482	1.48

Hispanic Origin	Population	%
Hispanic or Latino (of any race)	10,819	4.61
Central American, ex. Mexican	551	0.23
Costa Rican	19	0.01
Guatemalan	88	0.04
Honduran	88	0.04
Nicaraguan	38	0.02
Panamanian	87	0.04
Salvadoran	221	0.09
Other Central American	10	<0.01
Cuban	187	0.08
Dominican Republic	1,211	0.52
Mexican	872	0.37
Puerto Rican	6,538	2.78
South American	448	0.19
Argentinean	25	0.01
Bolivian	12	0.01
Chilean	20	0.01
Colombian	109	0.05
Ecuadorian	154	0.07
Paraguayan	3	<0.01
Peruvian	66	0.03
Uruguayan	4	<0.01
Venezuelan	49	0.02
Other South American	6	<0.01
Other Hispanic or Latino	1,012	0.43

Race*	Population	%
African-American/Black (14,688)	17,445	7.43
Not Hispanic (13,682)	15,969	6.80
Hispanic (1,006)	1,476	0.63
American Indian/Alaska Native (605)	1,692	0.72
Not Hispanic (499)	1,393	0.59
Hispanic (106)	299	0.13
Alaska Athabascan (Ala. Nat.) (0)	0	<0.01
Aleut (Alaska Native) (3)	3	<0.01
Apache (9)	20	0.01
Arapaho (2)	2	<0.01
Blackfeet (3)	41	0.02
Canadian/French Am. Ind. (3)	17	0.01
Central American Ind. (9)	13	0.01
Cherokee (24)	158	0.07
Cheyenne (1)	10	<0.01
Chickasaw (1)	5	<0.01
Chippewa (12)	25	0.01
Choctaw (0)	7	<0.01
Colville (0)	0	<0.01
Comanche (0)	0	<0.01
Cree (2)	8	<0.01
Creek (0)	3	<0.01
Crow (0)	3	<0.01
Delaware (2)	4	<0.01
Hopi (0)	1	<0.01
Houma (0)	0	<0.01
Inupiat (Alaska Native) (1)	2	<0.01
Iroquois (190)	419	0.18
Kiowa (1)	3	<0.01
Lumbee (4)	4	<0.01
Menominee (0)	0	<0.01
Mexican American Ind. (6)	12	0.01
Navajo (4)	12	0.01
Osage (0)	0	<0.01
Ottawa (1)	1	<0.01
Paiute (1)	1	<0.01
Pima (0)	1	<0.01
Potawatomi (5)	5	<0.01
Pueblo (3)	5	<0.01
Puget Sound Salish (0)	0	<0.01
Seminole (0)	4	<0.01
Shoshone (0)	1	<0.01
Sioux (22)	60	0.03
South American Ind. (8)	28	0.01
Spanish American Ind. (0)	1	<0.01
Tlingit-Haida (Alaska Native) (1)	4	<0.01
Tohono O'Odham (1)	1	<0.01
Tsimshian (Alaska Native) (0)	0	<0.01
Ute (0)	0	<0.01
Yakama (0)	0	<0.01
Yaqui (0)	5	<0.01
Yuman (0)	0	<0.01
Yup'ik (Alaska Native) (0)	0	<0.01
Asian (6,565)	7,434	3.17
Not Hispanic (6,522)	7,310	3.11
Hispanic (43)	124	0.05
Bangladeshi (18)	18	0.01
Bhutanese (30)	36	0.02
Burmese (2,270)	2,394	1.02
Cambodian (435)	513	0.22
Chinese, ex. Taiwanese (537)	672	0.29
Filipino (219)	379	0.16
Hmong (2)	2	<0.01
Indian (806)	975	0.42
Indonesian (7)	7	<0.01
Japanese (106)	181	0.08
Korean (311)	386	0.16
Laotian (77)	117	0.05
Malaysian (6)	20	0.01
Nepalese (11)	17	0.01
Pakistani (137)	152	0.06
Sri Lankan (18)	23	0.01
Taiwanese (19)	26	0.01
Thai (104)	149	0.06
Vietnamese (1,032)	1,147	0.49
Hawaii Native/Pacific Islander (69)	258	0.11
Not Hispanic (49)	194	0.08
Hispanic (20)	64	0.03
Fijian (0)	0	<0.01
Guamanian/Chamorro (12)	30	0.01
Marshallese (0)	0	<0.01
Native Hawaiian (30)	69	0.03
Samoan (12)	26	0.01
Tongan (2)	4	<0.01
White (204,679)	208,959	88.96
Not Hispanic (199,254)	202,734	86.31
Hispanic (5,425)	6,225	2.65

Notes: † The Census 2010 population figure is used to calculate the percentages in the Hispanic Origin and Race categories. Ancestry percentages are based on the 2006-2010 American Community Survey population (not shown); ‡ Numbers in parentheses indicate the number of people reporting a single ancestry; * Numbers in parentheses indicate the number of persons reporting this race alone, not in combination with any other race; Please refer to the Explanation of Data for more information.

Onondaga County
Population: 467,026

Ancestry	Population	%
Afghan (19)	19	<0.01
African, Sub-Saharan (2,607)	3,016	0.65
African (1,156)	1,474	0.32
Cape Verdean (0)	23	<0.01
Ethiopian (12)	12	<0.01
Ghanaian (187)	187	0.04
Kenyan (0)	17	<0.01
Liberian (246)	246	0.05
Nigerian (246)	280	0.06
Senegalese (0)	0	<0.01
Sierra Leonean (13)	13	<0.01
Somalian (478)	478	0.10
South African (10)	10	<0.01
Sudanese (160)	177	0.04
Ugandan (26)	26	<0.01
Zimbabwean (0)	0	<0.01
Other Sub-Saharan African (73)	73	0.02
Albanian (472)	537	0.12
Alsatian (39)	39	0.01
American (14,013)	14,013	3.02
Arab (1,701)	3,500	0.75
Arab (580)	951	0.21
Egyptian (164)	228	0.05
Iraqi (0)	0	<0.01
Jordanian (28)	28	0.01
Lebanese (430)	1,493	0.32
Moroccan (60)	86	0.02
Palestinian (154)	184	0.04
Syrian (126)	343	0.07
Other Arab (159)	187	0.04
Armenian (254)	861	0.19
Assyrian/Chaldean/Syriac (19)	29	0.01
Australian (42)	96	0.02
Austrian (469)	2,236	0.48
Basque (0)	0	<0.01
Belgian (130)	347	0.07
Brazilian (103)	120	0.03
British (664)	1,397	0.30
Bulgarian (34)	56	0.01
Cajun (24)	34	0.01
Canadian (872)	1,837	0.40
Carpatho Rusyn (0)	0	<0.01
Celtic (18)	91	0.02
Croatian (60)	239	0.05
Cypriot (0)	0	<0.01
Czech (311)	1,294	0.28
Czechoslovakian (208)	456	0.10
Danish (258)	914	0.20
Dutch (1,303)	10,861	2.34
Eastern European (523)	644	0.14
English (14,320)	60,136	12.97
Estonian (7)	26	0.01
European (2,482)	2,761	0.60
Finnish (235)	699	0.15
French, ex. Basque (3,327)	25,406	5.48
French Canadian (2,708)	8,589	1.85
German (17,906)	90,839	19.59
German Russian (0)	0	<0.01
Greek (1,634)	3,322	0.72
Guyanese (151)	209	0.05
Hungarian (627)	2,113	0.46
Icelander (13)	32	0.01
Iranian (303)	364	0.08
Irish (28,391)	107,847	23.26
Israeli (145)	184	0.04
Italian (35,847)	82,484	17.79
Latvian (116)	280	0.06
Lithuanian (317)	1,064	0.23
Luxemburger (0)	40	0.01
Macedonian (375)	498	0.11
Maltese (33)	53	0.01
New Zealander (2)	17	<0.01
Northern European (315)	333	0.07
Norwegian (417)	1,540	0.33
Pennsylvania German (85)	173	0.04

Ancestry (cont.)	Population	%
Polish (11,929)	35,362	7.63
Portuguese (374)	943	0.20
Romanian (118)	408	0.09
Russian (2,120)	5,700	1.23
Scandinavian (175)	394	0.08
Scotch-Irish (2,597)	7,595	1.64
Scottish (2,048)	9,589	2.07
Serbian (76)	144	0.03
Slavic (64)	322	0.07
Slovak (287)	948	0.20
Slovene (53)	229	0.05
Soviet Union (0)	0	<0.01
Swedish (822)	3,763	0.81
Swiss (401)	1,724	0.37
Turkish (377)	537	0.12
Ukrainian (3,319)	6,832	1.47
Welsh (699)	4,566	0.98
West Indian, ex. Hispanic (2,495)	3,224	0.70
Bahamian (0)	0	<0.01
Barbadian (105)	136	0.03
Belizean (9)	9	<0.01
Bermudan (0)	0	<0.01
British West Indian (39)	67	0.01
Dutch West Indian (0)	0	<0.01
Haitian (351)	415	0.09
Jamaican (1,406)	1,928	0.42
Trinidadian/Tobagonian (187)	187	0.04
U.S. Virgin Islander (0)	0	<0.01
West Indian (398)	482	0.10
Other West Indian (0)	0	<0.01
Yugoslavian (1,565)	1,698	0.37

Hispanic Origin	Population	%
Hispanic or Latino (of any race)	18,829	4.03
Central American, ex. Mexican	802	0.17
Costa Rican	64	0.01
Guatemalan	346	0.07
Honduran	106	0.02
Nicaraguan	53	0.01
Panamanian	126	0.03
Salvadoran	102	0.02
Other Central American	5	<0.01
Cuban	1,766	0.38
Dominican Republic	944	0.20
Mexican	2,338	0.50
Puerto Rican	10,246	2.19
South American	1,190	0.25
Argentinean	108	0.02
Bolivian	26	0.01
Chilean	89	0.02
Colombian	398	0.09
Ecuadorian	195	0.04
Paraguayan	19	<0.01
Peruvian	204	0.04
Uruguayan	33	0.01
Venezuelan	103	0.02
Other South American	15	<0.01
Other Hispanic or Latino	1,543	0.33

Race*	Population	%
African-American/Black (51,220)	58,984	12.63
Not Hispanic (48,696)	55,309	11.84
Hispanic (2,524)	3,675	0.79
American Indian/Alaska Native (3,818)	7,490	1.60
Not Hispanic (3,432)	6,695	1.43
Hispanic (386)	795	0.17
Alaska Athabascan (Ala. Nat.) (0)	5	<0.01
Aleut (Alaska Native) (1)	2	<0.01
Apache (16)	42	0.01
Arapaho (2)	2	<0.01
Blackfeet (10)	156	0.03
Canadian/French Am. Ind. (59)	102	0.02
Central American Ind. (5)	18	<0.01
Cherokee (49)	434	0.09
Cheyenne (0)	3	<0.01
Chickasaw (0)	5	<0.01
Chippewa (32)	53	0.01
Choctaw (9)	49	0.01
Colville (0)	1	<0.01

Race* (cont.)	Population	%
Comanche (7)	14	<0.01
Cree (3)	11	<0.01
Creek (4)	15	<0.01
Crow (0)	2	<0.01
Delaware (8)	14	<0.01
Hopi (0)	5	<0.01
Houma (1)	1	<0.01
Inupiat (Alaska Native) (5)	9	<0.01
Iroquois (1,942)	3,255	0.70
Kiowa (1)	2	<0.01
Lumbee (5)	9	<0.01
Menominee (1)	1	<0.01
Mexican American Ind. (53)	75	0.02
Navajo (8)	12	<0.01
Osage (2)	6	<0.01
Ottawa (1)	4	<0.01
Paiute (0)	0	<0.01
Pima (1)	2	<0.01
Potawatomi (6)	9	<0.01
Pueblo (0)	0	<0.01
Puget Sound Salish (0)	0	<0.01
Seminole (5)	27	0.01
Shoshone (1)	3	<0.01
Sioux (29)	64	0.01
South American Ind. (50)	94	0.02
Spanish American Ind. (9)	9	<0.01
Tlingit-Haida (Alaska Native) (1)	2	<0.01
Tohono O'Odham (1)	1	<0.01
Tsimshian (Alaska Native) (0)	0	<0.01
Ute (0)	0	<0.01
Yakama (0)	0	<0.01
Yaqui (0)	1	<0.01
Yuman (1)	4	<0.01
Yup'ik (Alaska Native) (0)	1	<0.01
Asian (14,454)	16,875	3.61
Not Hispanic (14,370)	16,607	3.56
Hispanic (84)	268	0.06
Bangladeshi (86)	101	0.02
Bhutanese (392)	516	0.11
Burmese (1,202)	1,242	0.27
Cambodian (204)	255	0.05
Chinese, ex. Taiwanese (2,955)	3,411	0.73
Filipino (703)	1,094	0.23
Hmong (112)	134	0.03
Indian (2,910)	3,295	0.71
Indonesian (30)	58	0.01
Japanese (251)	559	0.12
Korean (1,788)	2,125	0.46
Laotian (133)	169	0.04
Malaysian (8)	18	<0.01
Nepalese (177)	280	0.06
Pakistani (343)	388	0.08
Sri Lankan (51)	62	0.01
Taiwanese (144)	178	0.04
Thai (134)	195	0.04
Vietnamese (2,133)	2,393	0.51
Hawaii Native/Pacific Islander (148)	534	0.11
Not Hispanic (120)	432	0.09
Hispanic (28)	102	0.02
Fijian (0)	4	<0.01
Guamanian/Chamorro (41)	53	0.01
Marshallese (0)	1	<0.01
Native Hawaiian (42)	156	0.03
Samoan (14)	44	0.01
Tongan (1)	2	<0.01
White (378,885)	390,050	83.52
Not Hispanic (370,040)	379,663	81.29
Hispanic (8,845)	10,387	2.22

*Notes: † The Census 2010 population figure is used to calculate the percentages in the Hispanic Origin and Race categories. Ancestry percentages are based on the 2006-2010 American Community Survey population (not shown); ‡ Numbers in parentheses indicate the number of people reporting a single ancestry; * Numbers in parentheses indicate the number of persons reporting this race alone, not in combination with any other race; Please refer to the Explanation of Data for more information.*

Ontario County

Population: 107,931

Ancestry	Population	%
Afghan (0)	0	<0.01
African, Sub-Saharan (31)	105	0.10
African (31)	105	0.10
Cape Verdean (0)	0	<0.01
Ethiopian (0)	0	<0.01
Ghanaian (0)	0	<0.01
Kenyan (0)	0	<0.01
Liberian (0)	0	<0.01
Nigerian (0)	0	<0.01
Senegalese (0)	0	<0.01
Sierra Leonean (0)	0	<0.01
Somalian (0)	0	<0.01
South African (0)	0	<0.01
Sudanese (0)	0	<0.01
Ugandan (0)	0	<0.01
Zimbabwean (0)	0	<0.01
Other Sub-Saharan African (0)	0	<0.01
Albanian (436)	436	0.41
Alsatian (0)	0	<0.01
American (5,011)	5,011	4.71
Arab (106)	390	0.37
Arab (6)	6	0.01
Egyptian (0)	0	<0.01
Iraqi (0)	0	<0.01
Jordanian (0)	0	<0.01
Lebanese (23)	63	0.06
Moroccan (0)	3	<0.01
Palestinian (0)	14	0.01
Syrian (77)	304	0.29
Other Arab (0)	0	<0.01
Armenian (14)	24	0.02
Assyrian/Chaldean/Syriac (0)	0	<0.01
Australian (0)	5	<0.01
Austrian (78)	251	0.24
Basque (0)	0	<0.01
Belgian (54)	160	0.15
Brazilian (0)	11	0.01
British (275)	630	0.59
Bulgarian (11)	83	0.08
Cajun (0)	0	<0.01
Canadian (312)	525	0.49
Carpatho Rusyn (0)	0	<0.01
Celtic (3)	6	0.01
Croatian (13)	13	0.01
Cypriot (0)	0	<0.01
Czech (44)	381	0.36
Czechoslovakian (67)	147	0.14
Danish (237)	1,121	1.05
Dutch (1,459)	7,090	6.67
Eastern European (95)	135	0.13
English (5,898)	22,292	20.97
Estonian (0)	0	<0.01
European (1,060)	1,131	1.06
Finnish (85)	136	0.13
French, ex. Basque (635)	4,770	4.49
French Canadian (419)	1,770	1.67
German (6,907)	29,630	27.87
German Russian (0)	0	<0.01
Greek (115)	382	0.36
Guyanese (102)	102	0.10
Hungarian (213)	399	0.38
Icelander (0)	10	0.01
Iranian (0)	0	<0.01
Irish (5,165)	22,198	20.88
Israeli (0)	0	<0.01
Italian (6,590)	16,105	15.15
Latvian (0)	0	<0.01
Lithuanian (109)	270	0.25
Luxemburger (0)	0	<0.01
Macedonian (10)	35	0.03
Maltese (20)	20	0.02
New Zealander (0)	0	<0.01
Northern European (92)	98	0.09
Norwegian (168)	644	0.61
Pennsylvania German (263)	366	0.34

Ancestry	Population	%
Polish (1,315)	5,470	5.15
Portuguese (40)	117	0.11
Romanian (87)	142	0.13
Russian (121)	465	0.44
Scandinavian (145)	381	0.36
Scotch-Irish (620)	1,768	1.66
Scottish (735)	2,962	2.79
Serbian (21)	66	0.06
Slavic (0)	51	0.05
Slovak (101)	273	0.26
Slovene (0)	5	<0.01
Soviet Union (0)	0	<0.01
Swedish (453)	1,399	1.32
Swiss (105)	371	0.35
Turkish (3)	20	0.02
Ukrainian (180)	827	0.78
Welsh (251)	1,231	1.16
West Indian, ex. Hispanic (374)	459	0.43
Bahamian (0)	0	<0.01
Barbadian (0)	0	<0.01
Belizean (0)	0	<0.01
Bermudan (0)	0	<0.01
British West Indian (0)	27	0.03
Dutch West Indian (0)	0	<0.01
Haitian (0)	28	0.03
Jamaican (311)	324	0.30
Trinidadian/Tobagonian (29)	46	0.04
U.S. Virgin Islander (0)	0	<0.01
West Indian (34)	34	0.03
Other West Indian (0)	0	<0.01
Yugoslavian (57)	133	0.13

Hispanic Origin	Population	%
Hispanic or Latino (of any race)	3,679	3.41
Central American, ex. Mexican	180	0.17
Costa Rican	22	0.02
Guatemalan	60	0.06
Honduran	30	0.03
Nicaraguan	15	0.01
Panamanian	33	0.03
Salvadoran	20	0.02
Other Central American	0	<0.01
Cuban	105	0.10
Dominican Republic	110	0.10
Mexican	837	0.78
Puerto Rican	2,078	1.93
South American	182	0.17
Argentinean	27	0.03
Bolivian	4	<0.01
Chilean	8	0.01
Colombian	63	0.06
Ecuadorian	26	0.02
Paraguayan	0	<0.01
Peruvian	35	0.03
Uruguayan	0	<0.01
Venezuelan	19	0.02
Other South American	0	<0.01
Other Hispanic or Latino	187	0.17

Race*	Population	%
African-American/Black (2,432)	3,342	3.10
Not Hispanic (2,226)	3,001	2.78
Hispanic (206)	341	0.32
American Indian/Alaska Native (276)	776	0.72
Not Hispanic (244)	688	0.64
Hispanic (32)	88	0.08
Alaska Athabascan (Ala. Nat.) (1)	1	<0.01
Aleut (Alaska Native) (0)	1	<0.01
Apache (5)	14	0.01
Arapaho (0)	0	<0.01
Blackfeet (3)	19	0.02
Canadian/French Am. Ind. (4)	7	0.01
Central American Ind. (1)	1	<0.01
Cherokee (19)	105	0.10
Cheyenne (0)	5	<0.01
Chickasaw (1)	2	<0.01
Chippewa (16)	20	0.02
Choctaw (2)	8	0.01
Colville (0)	0	<0.01

	Population	%
Comanche (0)	1	<0.01
Cree (0)	1	<0.01
Creek (0)	0	<0.01
Crow (0)	7	0.01
Delaware (5)	6	0.01
Hopi (2)	2	<0.01
Houma (1)	1	<0.01
Inupiat (Alaska Native) (0)	1	<0.01
Iroquois (84)	190	0.18
Kiowa (1)	1	<0.01
Lumbee (1)	1	<0.01
Menominee (0)	0	<0.01
Mexican American Ind. (2)	2	<0.01
Navajo (1)	2	<0.01
Osage (0)	0	<0.01
Ottawa (1)	1	<0.01
Paiute (0)	0	<0.01
Pima (0)	0	<0.01
Potawatomi (0)	0	<0.01
Pueblo (0)	3	<0.01
Puget Sound Salish (0)	0	<0.01
Seminole (0)	6	0.01
Shoshone (0)	0	<0.01
Sioux (9)	25	0.02
South American Ind. (2)	8	0.01
Spanish American Ind. (0)	0	<0.01
Tlingit-Haida (Alaska Native) (0)	0	<0.01
Tohono O'Odham (0)	0	<0.01
Tsimshian (Alaska Native) (0)	0	<0.01
Ute (0)	2	<0.01
Yakama (0)	0	<0.01
Yaqui (0)	0	<0.01
Yuman (0)	0	<0.01
Yup'ik (Alaska Native) (1)	1	<0.01
Asian (1,126)	1,486	1.38
Not Hispanic (1,111)	1,455	1.35
Hispanic (15)	31	0.03
Bangladeshi (3)	3	<0.01
Bhutanese (0)	0	<0.01
Burmese (7)	7	0.01
Cambodian (18)	18	0.02
Chinese, ex. Taiwanese (318)	391	0.36
Filipino (113)	202	0.19
Hmong (0)	0	<0.01
Indian (231)	271	0.25
Indonesian (7)	16	0.01
Japanese (53)	95	0.09
Korean (144)	205	0.19
Laotian (35)	42	0.04
Malaysian (3)	4	<0.01
Nepalese (3)	4	<0.01
Pakistani (29)	33	0.03
Sri Lankan (5)	5	<0.01
Taiwanese (14)	16	0.01
Thai (23)	27	0.03
Vietnamese (70)	86	0.08
Hawaii Native/Pacific Islander (24)	83	0.08
Not Hispanic (16)	65	0.06
Hispanic (8)	18	0.02
Fijian (0)	0	<0.01
Guamanian/Chamorro (6)	23	0.02
Marshallese (0)	0	<0.01
Native Hawaiian (11)	25	0.02
Samoan (0)	0	<0.01
Tongan (0)	0	<0.01
White (101,078)	102,741	95.19
Not Hispanic (99,119)	100,508	93.12
Hispanic (1,959)	2,233	2.07

Notes: † The Census 2010 population figure is used to calculate the percentages in the Hispanic Origin and Race categories. Ancestry percentages are based on the 2006-2010 American Community Survey population (not shown); ‡ Numbers in parentheses indicate the number of people reporting a single ancestry; * Numbers in parentheses indicate the number of persons reporting this race alone, not in combination with any other race; Please refer to the Explanation of Data for more information.

Orange County

Population: 372,813

Ancestry	Population	%
Afghan (25)	25	0.01
African, Sub-Saharan (2,270)	2,998	0.81
African (1,369)	1,938	0.52
Cape Verdean (0)	0	<0.01
Ethiopian (23)	23	0.01
Ghanaian (140)	140	0.04
Kenyan (0)	0	<0.01
Liberian (0)	22	0.01
Nigerian (581)	647	0.17
Senegalese (0)	12	<0.01
Sierra Leonean (0)	0	<0.01
Somalian (20)	61	0.02
South African (14)	22	0.01
Sudanese (0)	0	<0.01
Ugandan (0)	0	<0.01
Zimbabwean (0)	0	<0.01
Other Sub-Saharan African (123)	133	0.04
Albanian (231)	545	0.15
Alsatian (0)	8	<0.01
American (23,068)	23,068	6.23
Arab (828)	1,606	0.43
Arab (16)	38	0.01
Egyptian (387)	508	0.14
Iraqi (0)	15	<0.01
Jordanian (156)	156	0.04
Lebanese (82)	315	0.09
Moroccan (19)	66	0.02
Palestinian (0)	0	<0.01
Syrian (20)	330	0.09
Other Arab (148)	178	0.05
Armenian (177)	407	0.11
Assyrian/Chaldean/Syriac (3)	3	<0.01
Australian (42)	182	0.05
Austrian (528)	2,246	0.61
Basque (0)	40	0.01
Belgian (49)	272	0.07
Brazilian (86)	151	0.04
British (591)	1,408	0.38
Bulgarian (190)	198	0.05
Cajun (52)	67	0.02
Canadian (394)	1,325	0.36
Carpatho Rusyn (0)	0	<0.01
Celtic (59)	82	0.02
Croatian (128)	430	0.12
Cypriot (13)	13	<0.01
Czech (306)	1,641	0.44
Czechoslovakian (325)	773	0.21
Danish (89)	596	0.16
Dutch (2,181)	9,116	2.46
Eastern European (906)	925	0.25
English (4,565)	24,564	6.64
Estonian (58)	125	0.03
European (3,404)	3,842	1.04
Finnish (154)	546	0.15
French, ex. Basque (821)	6,903	1.86
French Canadian (540)	2,032	0.55
German (11,282)	54,956	14.84
German Russian (0)	0	<0.01
Greek (825)	2,583	0.70
Guyanese (206)	432	0.12
Hungarian (3,947)	8,222	2.22
Icelander (23)	124	0.03
Iranian (50)	108	0.03
Irish (23,448)	75,052	20.27
Israeli (302)	1,042	0.28
Italian (26,639)	67,312	18.18
Latvian (107)	332	0.09
Lithuanian (300)	1,081	0.29
Luxemburger (0)	0	<0.01
Macedonian (0)	0	<0.01
Maltese (203)	302	0.08
New Zealander (0)	35	0.01
Northern European (67)	95	0.03
Norwegian (783)	3,015	0.81
Pennsylvania German (31)	128	0.03

Ancestry	Population	%
Polish (6,061)	20,649	5.58
Portuguese (473)	1,228	0.33
Romanian (758)	3,000	0.81
Russian (2,107)	6,133	1.66
Scandinavian (132)	412	0.11
Scotch-Irish (1,373)	4,366	1.18
Scottish (1,032)	4,871	1.32
Serbian (62)	96	0.03
Slavic (59)	201	0.05
Slovak (396)	1,031	0.28
Slovene (33)	103	0.03
Soviet Union (0)	0	<0.01
Swedish (599)	3,116	0.84
Swiss (270)	900	0.24
Turkish (126)	255	0.07
Ukrainian (1,049)	2,847	0.77
Welsh (264)	1,567	0.42
West Indian, ex. Hispanic (4,550)	6,861	1.85
Bahamian (0)	13	<0.01
Barbadian (69)	191	0.05
Belizean (0)	80	0.02
Bermudan (0)	0	<0.01
British West Indian (395)	708	0.19
Dutch West Indian (10)	48	0.01
Haitian (1,324)	1,665	0.45
Jamaican (1,855)	2,353	0.64
Trinidadian/Tobagonian (291)	585	0.16
U.S. Virgin Islander (0)	48	0.01
West Indian (566)	1,128	0.30
Other West Indian (40)	42	0.01
Yugoslavian (75)	369	0.10

Hispanic Origin	Population	%
Hispanic or Latino (of any race)	67,185	18.02
Central American, ex. Mexican	5,302	1.42
Costa Rican	159	0.04
Guatemalan	988	0.27
Honduran	2,659	0.71
Nicaraguan	112	0.03
Panamanian	376	0.10
Salvadoran	965	0.26
Other Central American	43	0.01
Cuban	1,489	0.40
Dominican Republic	4,293	1.15
Mexican	16,480	4.42
Puerto Rican	29,210	7.84
South American	6,144	1.65
Argentinean	654	0.18
Bolivian	81	0.02
Chilean	223	0.06
Colombian	1,772	0.48
Ecuadorian	1,426	0.38
Paraguayan	28	0.01
Peruvian	1,662	0.45
Uruguayan	91	0.02
Venezuelan	152	0.04
Other South American	55	0.01
Other Hispanic or Latino	4,267	1.14

Race*	Population	%
African-American/Black (37,946)	44,056	11.82
Not Hispanic (33,895)	37,986	10.19
Hispanic (4,051)	6,070	1.63
American Indian/Alaska Native (1,748)	4,451	1.19
Not Hispanic (908)	2,843	0.76
Hispanic (840)	1,608	0.43
Alaska Athabascan (Ala. Nat.) (0)	0	<0.01
Aleut (Alaska Native) (1)	2	<0.01
Apache (1)	31	0.01
Arapaho (1)	3	<0.01
Blackfeet (13)	113	0.03
Canadian/French Am. Ind. (3)	9	<0.01
Central American Ind. (23)	38	0.01
Cherokee (65)	477	0.13
Cheyenne (1)	3	<0.01
Chickasaw (0)	3	<0.01
Chippewa (14)	33	0.01
Choctaw (8)	13	<0.01
Colville (0)	0	<0.01

Race*	Population	%
Comanche (2)	3	<0.01
Cree (1)	7	<0.01
Creek (2)	10	<0.01
Crow (1)	7	<0.01
Delaware (214)	428	0.11
Hopi (0)	3	<0.01
Houma (2)	2	<0.01
Inupiat (Alaska Native) (3)	7	<0.01
Iroquois (144)	302	0.08
Kiowa (1)	2	<0.01
Lumbee (4)	7	<0.01
Menominee (0)	0	<0.01
Mexican American Ind. (116)	156	0.04
Navajo (9)	28	0.01
Osage (0)	1	<0.01
Ottawa (1)	1	<0.01
Paiute (0)	0	<0.01
Pima (0)	4	<0.01
Potawatomi (2)	6	<0.01
Pueblo (1)	5	<0.01
Puget Sound Salish (0)	2	<0.01
Seminole (0)	21	0.01
Shoshone (5)	7	<0.01
Sioux (9)	55	0.01
South American Ind. (136)	291	0.08
Spanish American Ind. (101)	113	0.03
Tlingit-Haida (Alaska Native) (2)	2	<0.01
Tohono O'Odham (1)	15	<0.01
Tsimshian (Alaska Native) (0)	0	<0.01
Ute (0)	0	<0.01
Yakama (0)	0	<0.01
Yaqui (0)	0	<0.01
Yuman (1)	5	<0.01
Yup'ik (Alaska Native) (1)	1	<0.01
Asian (8,895)	11,280	3.03
Not Hispanic (8,685)	10,687	2.87
Hispanic (210)	593	0.16
Bangladeshi (136)	154	0.04
Bhutanese (2)	2	<0.01
Burmese (26)	28	0.01
Cambodian (83)	106	0.03
Chinese, ex. Taiwanese (1,718)	2,206	0.59
Filipino (1,601)	2,144	0.58
Hmong (1)	1	<0.01
Indian (2,621)	3,050	0.82
Indonesian (40)	62	0.02
Japanese (196)	486	0.13
Korean (1,005)	1,333	0.36
Laotian (7)	14	<0.01
Malaysian (3)	4	<0.01
Nepalese (7)	10	<0.01
Pakistani (542)	614	0.16
Sri Lankan (47)	56	0.02
Taiwanese (44)	51	0.01
Thai (91)	152	0.04
Vietnamese (374)	481	0.13
Hawaii Native/Pacific Islander (125)	434	0.12
Not Hispanic (80)	266	0.07
Hispanic (45)	168	0.05
Fijian (1)	2	<0.01
Guamanian/Chamorro (44)	63	0.02
Marshallese (0)	0	<0.01
Native Hawaiian (15)	93	0.02
Samoan (13)	29	0.01
Tongan (1)	1	<0.01
White (287,802)	297,221	79.72
Not Hispanic (254,259)	260,102	69.77
Hispanic (33,543)	37,119	9.96

*Notes: † The Census 2010 population figure is used to calculate the percentages in the Hispanic Origin and Race categories. Ancestry percentages are based on the 2006-2010 American Community Survey population (not shown); ‡ Numbers in parentheses indicate the number of people reporting a single ancestry; * Numbers in parentheses indicate the number of persons reporting this race alone, not in combination with any other race; Please refer to the Explanation of Data for more information.*

Orleans County
Population: 42,883

Ancestry	Population	%
Afghan (0)	0	<0.01
African, Sub-Saharan (8)	37	0.09
African (0)	29	0.07
Cape Verdean (0)	0	<0.01
Ethiopian (0)	0	<0.01
Ghanaian (0)	0	<0.01
Kenyan (0)	0	<0.01
Liberian (0)	0	<0.01
Nigerian (8)	8	0.02
Senegalese (0)	0	<0.01
Sierra Leonean (0)	0	<0.01
Somalian (0)	0	<0.01
South African (0)	0	<0.01
Sudanese (0)	0	<0.01
Ugandan (0)	0	<0.01
Zimbabwean (0)	0	<0.01
Other Sub-Saharan African (0)	0	<0.01
Albanian (0)	9	0.02
Alsatian (0)	0	<0.01
American (2,445)	2,445	5.66
Arab (15)	47	0.11
Arab (0)	0	<0.01
Egyptian (0)	11	0.03
Iraqi (0)	0	<0.01
Jordanian (0)	0	<0.01
Lebanese (15)	36	0.08
Moroccan (0)	0	<0.01
Palestinian (0)	0	<0.01
Syrian (0)	0	<0.01
Other Arab (0)	0	<0.01
Armenian (0)	0	<0.01
Assyrian/Chaldean/Syriac (0)	0	<0.01
Australian (0)	0	<0.01
Austrian (0)	18	0.04
Basque (0)	0	<0.01
Belgian (0)	18	0.04
Brazilian (15)	15	0.03
British (59)	114	0.26
Bulgarian (0)	0	<0.01
Cajun (0)	0	<0.01
Canadian (92)	211	0.49
Carpatho Rusyn (0)	0	<0.01
Celtic (0)	0	<0.01
Croatian (0)	69	0.16
Cypriot (0)	0	<0.01
Czech (4)	52	0.12
Czechoslovakian (0)	0	<0.01
Danish (0)	32	0.07
Dutch (129)	1,314	3.04
Eastern European (39)	39	0.09
English (2,770)	9,383	21.74
Estonian (0)	0	<0.01
European (123)	128	0.30
Finnish (0)	0	<0.01
French, ex. Basque (198)	2,092	4.85
French Canadian (140)	489	1.13
German (3,260)	11,665	27.02
German Russian (0)	0	<0.01
Greek (33)	71	0.16
Guyanese (0)	0	<0.01
Hungarian (13)	144	0.33
Icelander (0)	0	<0.01
Iranian (0)	0	<0.01
Irish (1,230)	7,575	17.55
Israeli (0)	0	<0.01
Italian (2,135)	5,503	12.75
Latvian (0)	0	<0.01
Lithuanian (64)	99	0.23
Luxemburger (0)	0	<0.01
Macedonian (0)	0	<0.01
Maltese (0)	0	<0.01
New Zealander (0)	0	<0.01
Northern European (6)	6	0.01
Norwegian (50)	82	0.19
Pennsylvania German (42)	86	0.20

Ancestry	Population	%
Polish (1,595)	3,934	9.11
Portuguese (0)	29	0.07
Romanian (0)	0	<0.01
Russian (57)	150	0.35
Scandinavian (0)	0	<0.01
Scotch-Irish (158)	509	1.18
Scottish (103)	950	2.20
Serbian (0)	0	<0.01
Slavic (0)	17	0.04
Slovak (8)	28	0.06
Slovene (19)	19	0.04
Soviet Union (0)	0	<0.01
Swedish (56)	157	0.36
Swiss (11)	62	0.14
Turkish (0)	0	<0.01
Ukrainian (101)	573	1.33
Welsh (61)	357	0.83
West Indian, ex. Hispanic (158)	207	0.48
Bahamian (0)	0	<0.01
Barbadian (5)	5	0.01
Belizean (0)	0	<0.01
Bermudan (0)	0	<0.01
British West Indian (0)	0	<0.01
Dutch West Indian (0)	0	<0.01
Haitian (13)	19	0.04
Jamaican (120)	163	0.38
Trinidadian/Tobagonian (14)	14	0.03
U.S. Virgin Islander (0)	0	<0.01
West Indian (6)	6	0.01
Other West Indian (0)	0	<0.01
Yugoslavian (21)	29	0.07

Hispanic Origin	Population	%
Hispanic or Latino (of any race)	1,757	4.10
Central American, ex. Mexican	79	0.18
Costa Rican	1	<0.01
Guatemalan	21	0.05
Honduran	7	0.02
Nicaraguan	4	0.01
Panamanian	31	0.07
Salvadoran	15	0.03
Other Central American	0	<0.01
Cuban	53	0.12
Dominican Republic	46	0.11
Mexican	741	1.73
Puerto Rican	663	1.55
South American	38	0.09
Argentinean	0	<0.01
Bolivian	0	<0.01
Chilean	1	<0.01
Colombian	19	0.04
Ecuadorian	8	0.02
Paraguayan	0	<0.01
Peruvian	8	0.02
Uruguayan	1	<0.01
Venezuelan	1	<0.01
Other South American	0	<0.01
Other Hispanic or Latino	137	0.32

Race*	Population	%
African-American/Black (2,523)	2,965	6.91
Not Hispanic (2,368)	2,771	6.46
Hispanic (155)	194	0.45
American Indian/Alaska Native (247)	527	1.23
Not Hispanic (199)	449	1.05
Hispanic (48)	78	0.18
Alaska Athabascan (Ala. Nat.) (0)	1	<0.01
Aleut (Alaska Native) (1)	3	0.01
Apache (6)	17	0.04
Arapaho (0)	0	<0.01
Blackfeet (1)	17	0.04
Canadian/French Am. Ind. (1)	3	0.01
Central American Ind. (5)	5	0.01
Cherokee (8)	48	0.11
Cheyenne (0)	1	<0.01
Chickasaw (0)	0	<0.01
Chippewa (0)	11	0.03
Choctaw (1)	5	0.01
Colville (0)	0	<0.01

	Population	%
Comanche (0)	0	<0.01
Cree (0)	0	<0.01
Creek (0)	1	<0.01
Crow (0)	1	<0.01
Delaware (10)	14	0.03
Hopi (0)	0	<0.01
Houma (1)	1	<0.01
Inupiat (Alaska Native) (0)	0	<0.01
Iroquois (87)	134	0.31
Kiowa (0)	0	<0.01
Lumbee (0)	0	<0.01
Menominee (0)	0	<0.01
Mexican American Ind. (9)	21	0.05
Navajo (1)	2	<0.01
Osage (0)	0	<0.01
Ottawa (0)	0	<0.01
Paiute (0)	0	<0.01
Pima (0)	0	<0.01
Potawatomi (0)	0	<0.01
Pueblo (0)	1	<0.01
Puget Sound Salish (0)	0	<0.01
Seminole (0)	0	<0.01
Shoshone (0)	8	0.02
Sioux (2)	4	0.01
South American Ind. (3)	5	0.01
Spanish American Ind. (3)	3	0.01
Tlingit-Haida (Alaska Native) (0)	0	<0.01
Tohono O'Odham (0)	0	<0.01
Tsimshian (Alaska Native) (0)	0	<0.01
Ute (0)	0	<0.01
Yakama (0)	0	<0.01
Yaqui (0)	0	<0.01
Yuman (0)	0	<0.01
Yup'ik (Alaska Native) (0)	0	<0.01
Asian (179)	259	0.60
Not Hispanic (173)	250	0.58
Hispanic (6)	9	0.02
Bangladeshi (0)	0	<0.01
Bhutanese (0)	0	<0.01
Burmese (1)	1	<0.01
Cambodian (0)	0	<0.01
Chinese, ex. Taiwanese (31)	41	0.10
Filipino (39)	63	0.15
Hmong (0)	0	<0.01
Indian (17)	40	0.09
Indonesian (0)	0	<0.01
Japanese (6)	17	0.04
Korean (21)	23	0.05
Laotian (0)	0	<0.01
Malaysian (0)	0	<0.01
Nepalese (0)	0	<0.01
Pakistani (15)	15	0.03
Sri Lankan (1)	3	0.01
Taiwanese (0)	5	0.01
Thai (5)	8	0.02
Vietnamese (2)	5	0.01
Hawaii Native/Pacific Islander (9)	35	0.08
Not Hispanic (7)	25	0.06
Hispanic (2)	10	0.02
Fijian (0)	0	<0.01
Guamanian/Chamorro (1)	2	<0.01
Marshallese (0)	0	<0.01
Native Hawaiian (6)	11	0.03
Samoan (2)	3	0.01
Tongan (0)	0	<0.01
White (38,528)	39,297	91.64
Not Hispanic (37,658)	38,305	89.32
Hispanic (870)	992	2.31

Notes: † The Census 2010 population figure is used to calculate the percentages in the Hispanic Origin and Race categories. Ancestry percentages are based on the 2006-2010 American Community Survey population (not shown); ‡ Numbers in parentheses indicate the number of people reporting a single ancestry; * Numbers in parentheses indicate the number of persons reporting this race alone, not in combination with any other race; Please refer to the Explanation of Data for more information.

Oswego County
Population: 122,109

Ancestry	Population	%
Afghan (50)	50	0.04
African, Sub-Saharan (105)	109	0.09
African (22)	26	0.02
Cape Verdean (0)	0	<0.01
Ethiopian (0)	0	<0.01
Ghanaian (30)	30	0.02
Kenyan (6)	6	<0.01
Liberian (0)	0	<0.01
Nigerian (0)	0	<0.01
Senegalese (19)	19	0.02
Sierra Leonean (0)	0	<0.01
Somalian (0)	0	<0.01
South African (16)	16	0.01
Sudanese (0)	0	<0.01
Ugandan (0)	0	<0.01
Zimbabwean (0)	0	<0.01
Other Sub-Saharan African (12)	12	0.01
Albanian (0)	3	<0.01
Alsatian (0)	0	<0.01
American (6,704)	6,704	5.49
Arab (63)	291	0.24
Arab (0)	0	<0.01
Egyptian (10)	10	0.01
Iraqi (0)	0	<0.01
Jordanian (0)	0	<0.01
Lebanese (40)	195	0.16
Moroccan (0)	0	<0.01
Palestinian (0)	0	<0.01
Syrian (13)	74	0.06
Other Arab (0)	12	0.01
Armenian (34)	92	0.08
Assyrian/Chaldean/Syriac (0)	0	<0.01
Australian (0)	0	<0.01
Austrian (62)	235	0.19
Basque (0)	0	<0.01
Belgian (12)	94	0.08
Brazilian (17)	17	0.01
British (200)	394	0.32
Bulgarian (0)	0	<0.01
Cajun (0)	15	0.01
Canadian (347)	837	0.68
Carpatho Rusyn (0)	28	0.02
Celtic (15)	15	0.01
Croatian (31)	254	0.21
Cypriot (0)	0	<0.01
Czech (72)	356	0.29
Czechoslovakian (62)	112	0.09
Danish (82)	255	0.21
Dutch (661)	4,758	3.89
Eastern European (42)	65	0.05
English (5,611)	18,945	15.50
Estonian (0)	0	<0.01
European (840)	848	0.69
Finnish (65)	315	0.26
French, ex. Basque (2,417)	12,503	10.23
French Canadian (1,857)	4,004	3.28
German (5,985)	25,630	20.97
German Russian (0)	0	<0.01
Greek (152)	437	0.36
Guyanese (0)	0	<0.01
Hungarian (139)	441	0.36
Icelander (20)	20	0.02
Iranian (0)	0	<0.01
Irish (8,045)	27,954	22.87
Israeli (39)	39	0.03
Italian (6,436)	17,452	14.28
Latvian (0)	10	0.01
Lithuanian (148)	359	0.29
Luxemburger (0)	0	<0.01
Macedonian (19)	40	0.03
Maltese (12)	27	0.02
New Zealander (0)	0	<0.01
Northern European (94)	94	0.08
Norwegian (179)	506	0.41
Pennsylvania German (36)	83	0.07

Ancestry (cont.)	Population	%
Polish (2,367)	7,803	6.38
Portuguese (79)	149	0.12
Romanian (0)	39	0.03
Russian (323)	984	0.81
Scandinavian (20)	46	0.04
Scotch-Irish (714)	1,948	1.59
Scottish (710)	2,653	2.17
Serbian (0)	22	0.02
Slavic (2)	13	0.01
Slovak (50)	114	0.09
Slovene (0)	24	0.02
Soviet Union (0)	0	<0.01
Swedish (164)	837	0.68
Swiss (92)	340	0.28
Turkish (0)	23	0.02
Ukrainian (393)	1,111	0.91
Welsh (167)	1,232	1.01
West Indian, ex. Hispanic (98)	226	0.18
Bahamian (0)	0	<0.01
Barbadian (12)	12	0.01
Belizean (0)	12	0.01
Bermudan (0)	0	<0.01
British West Indian (0)	15	0.01
Dutch West Indian (0)	0	<0.01
Haitian (73)	73	0.06
Jamaican (13)	72	0.06
Trinidadian/Tobagonian (0)	42	0.03
U.S. Virgin Islander (0)	0	<0.01
West Indian (0)	0	<0.01
Other West Indian (0)	0	<0.01
Yugoslavian (0)	42	0.03

Hispanic Origin	Population	%
Hispanic or Latino (of any race)	2,552	2.09
Central American, ex. Mexican	140	0.11
Costa Rican	8	0.01
Guatemalan	66	0.05
Honduran	17	0.01
Nicaraguan	4	<0.01
Panamanian	18	0.01
Salvadoran	27	0.02
Other Central American	0	<0.01
Cuban	65	0.05
Dominican Republic	97	0.08
Mexican	641	0.52
Puerto Rican	1,193	0.98
South American	155	0.13
Argentinean	19	0.02
Bolivian	3	<0.01
Chilean	11	0.01
Colombian	49	0.04
Ecuadorian	37	0.03
Paraguayan	2	<0.01
Peruvian	25	0.02
Uruguayan	2	<0.01
Venezuelan	5	<0.01
Other South American	2	<0.01
Other Hispanic or Latino	261	0.21

Race*	Population	%
African-American/Black (972)	1,531	1.25
Not Hispanic (862)	1,367	1.12
Hispanic (110)	164	0.13
American Indian/Alaska Native (520)	1,200	0.98
Not Hispanic (465)	1,097	0.90
Hispanic (55)	103	0.08
Alaska Athabascan (Ala. Nat.) (1)	1	<0.01
Aleut (Alaska Native) (0)	0	<0.01
Apache (1)	9	0.01
Arapaho (0)	0	<0.01
Blackfeet (14)	41	0.03
Canadian/French Am. Ind. (18)	26	0.02
Central American Ind. (2)	4	<0.01
Cherokee (19)	77	0.06
Cheyenne (2)	5	<0.01
Chickasaw (1)	2	<0.01
Chippewa (5)	12	0.01
Choctaw (2)	6	<0.01
Colville (0)	0	<0.01

Race* (cont.)	Population	%
Comanche (0)	0	<0.01
Cree (0)	3	<0.01
Creek (1)	2	<0.01
Crow (1)	2	<0.01
Delaware (1)	5	<0.01
Hopi (0)	0	<0.01
Houma (0)	0	<0.01
Inupiat (Alaska Native) (0)	0	<0.01
Iroquois (212)	430	0.35
Kiowa (0)	0	<0.01
Lumbee (0)	0	<0.01
Menominee (0)	0	<0.01
Mexican American Ind. (6)	9	<0.01
Navajo (2)	5	<0.01
Osage (0)	0	<0.01
Ottawa (0)	0	<0.01
Paiute (0)	0	<0.01
Pima (0)	0	<0.01
Potawatomi (0)	0	<0.01
Pueblo (0)	1	<0.01
Puget Sound Salish (0)	0	<0.01
Seminole (0)	2	<0.01
Shoshone (0)	0	<0.01
Sioux (13)	31	0.03
South American Ind. (6)	16	0.01
Spanish American Ind. (2)	2	<0.01
Tlingit-Haida (Alaska Native) (0)	0	<0.01
Tohono O'Odham (0)	0	<0.01
Tsimshian (Alaska Native) (0)	0	<0.01
Ute (0)	1	<0.01
Yakama (0)	1	<0.01
Yaqui (0)	0	<0.01
Yuman (0)	0	<0.01
Yup'ik (Alaska Native) (0)	0	<0.01
Asian (723)	986	0.81
Not Hispanic (709)	947	0.78
Hispanic (14)	39	0.03
Bangladeshi (2)	2	<0.01
Bhutanese (0)	0	<0.01
Burmese (1)	1	<0.01
Cambodian (0)	1	<0.01
Chinese, ex. Taiwanese (234)	269	0.22
Filipino (139)	222	0.18
Hmong (0)	0	<0.01
Indian (100)	137	0.11
Indonesian (1)	4	<0.01
Japanese (46)	82	0.07
Korean (104)	134	0.11
Laotian (0)	0	<0.01
Malaysian (1)	1	<0.01
Nepalese (0)	0	<0.01
Pakistani (16)	16	0.01
Sri Lankan (4)	4	<0.01
Taiwanese (1)	6	<0.01
Thai (14)	32	0.03
Vietnamese (38)	52	0.04
Hawaii Native/Pacific Islander (16)	65	0.05
Not Hispanic (14)	51	0.04
Hispanic (2)	14	0.01
Fijian (0)	0	<0.01
Guamanian/Chamorro (3)	7	0.01
Marshallese (0)	0	<0.01
Native Hawaiian (5)	18	0.01
Samoan (0)	4	<0.01
Tongan (0)	0	<0.01
White (117,632)	119,116	97.55
Not Hispanic (116,091)	117,378	96.13
Hispanic (1,541)	1,738	1.42

Notes: † The Census 2010 population figure is used to calculate the percentages in the Hispanic Origin and Race categories. Ancestry percentages are based on the 2006-2010 American Community Survey population (not shown); ‡ Numbers in parentheses indicate the number of people reporting a single ancestry; * Numbers in parentheses indicate the number of persons reporting this race alone, not in combination with any other race; Please refer to the Explanation of Data for more information.

Otsego County
Population: 62,259

Ancestry	Population	%
Afghan (0)	0	<0.01
African, Sub-Saharan (131)	151	0.24
African (24)	24	0.04
Cape Verdean (0)	0	<0.01
Ethiopian (0)	0	<0.01
Ghanaian (0)	0	<0.01
Kenyan (81)	81	0.13
Liberian (0)	0	<0.01
Nigerian (0)	0	<0.01
Senegalese (0)	0	<0.01
Sierra Leonean (0)	0	<0.01
Somalian (0)	0	<0.01
South African (0)	20	0.03
Sudanese (0)	0	<0.01
Ugandan (0)	0	<0.01
Zimbabwean (26)	26	0.04
Other Sub-Saharan African (0)	0	<0.01
Albanian (6)	60	0.10
Alsatian (0)	0	<0.01
American (6,461)	6,461	10.32
Arab (110)	207	0.33
Arab (10)	10	0.02
Egyptian (0)	0	<0.01
Iraqi (0)	0	<0.01
Jordanian (0)	0	<0.01
Lebanese (78)	155	0.25
Moroccan (0)	0	<0.01
Palestinian (5)	5	0.01
Syrian (17)	37	0.06
Other Arab (0)	0	<0.01
Armenian (59)	62	0.10
Assyrian/Chaldean/Syriac (0)	0	<0.01
Australian (0)	0	<0.01
Austrian (52)	414	0.66
Basque (0)	0	<0.01
Belgian (0)	33	0.05
Brazilian (0)	0	<0.01
British (163)	234	0.37
Bulgarian (0)	0	<0.01
Cajun (0)	0	<0.01
Canadian (100)	297	0.47
Carpatho Rusyn (0)	0	<0.01
Celtic (0)	5	0.01
Croatian (27)	82	0.13
Cypriot (0)	0	<0.01
Czech (31)	230	0.37
Czechoslovakian (31)	37	0.06
Danish (133)	376	0.60
Dutch (610)	3,421	5.46
Eastern European (109)	157	0.25
English (2,928)	9,969	15.92
Estonian (3)	5	0.01
European (511)	543	0.87
Finnish (32)	94	0.15
French, ex. Basque (345)	3,084	4.93
French Canadian (314)	842	1.34
German (2,872)	13,660	21.82
German Russian (0)	0	<0.01
Greek (84)	239	0.38
Guyanese (12)	12	0.02
Hungarian (165)	678	1.08
Icelander (0)	7	0.01
Iranian (0)	19	0.03
Irish (3,032)	11,787	18.83
Israeli (13)	13	0.02
Italian (2,804)	7,612	12.16
Latvian (16)	22	0.04
Lithuanian (12)	154	0.25
Luxemburger (0)	0	<0.01
Macedonian (0)	0	<0.01
Maltese (0)	0	<0.01
New Zealander (0)	5	0.01
Northern European (42)	42	0.07
Norwegian (243)	784	1.25
Pennsylvania German (79)	144	0.23

Ancestry (cont.)	Population	%
Polish (784)	2,833	4.53
Portuguese (56)	95	0.15
Romanian (21)	41	0.07
Russian (299)	1,047	1.67
Scandinavian (51)	115	0.18
Scotch-Irish (366)	1,232	1.97
Scottish (492)	2,493	3.98
Serbian (11)	15	0.02
Slavic (55)	118	0.19
Slovak (78)	143	0.23
Slovene (57)	146	0.23
Soviet Union (0)	0	<0.01
Swedish (153)	1,004	1.60
Swiss (30)	206	0.33
Turkish (0)	0	<0.01
Ukrainian (116)	249	0.40
Welsh (237)	1,116	1.78
West Indian, ex. Hispanic (283)	321	0.51
Bahamian (0)	0	<0.01
Barbadian (0)	0	<0.01
Belizean (0)	0	<0.01
Bermudan (0)	0	<0.01
British West Indian (12)	12	0.02
Dutch West Indian (20)	20	0.03
Haitian (75)	79	0.13
Jamaican (160)	194	0.31
Trinidadian/Tobagonian (15)	15	0.02
U.S. Virgin Islander (0)	0	<0.01
West Indian (1)	1	<0.01
Other West Indian (0)	0	<0.01
Yugoslavian (36)	107	0.17

Hispanic Origin	Population	%
Hispanic or Latino (of any race)	1,921	3.09
Central American, ex. Mexican	122	0.20
Costa Rican	7	0.01
Guatemalan	29	0.05
Honduran	12	0.02
Nicaraguan	2	<0.01
Panamanian	18	0.03
Salvadoran	53	0.09
Other Central American	1	<0.01
Cuban	90	0.14
Dominican Republic	86	0.14
Mexican	306	0.49
Puerto Rican	798	1.28
South American	216	0.35
Argentinean	14	0.02
Bolivian	6	0.01
Chilean	22	0.04
Colombian	67	0.11
Ecuadorian	45	0.07
Paraguayan	1	<0.01
Peruvian	42	0.07
Uruguayan	11	0.02
Venezuelan	6	0.01
Other South American	2	<0.01
Other Hispanic or Latino	303	0.49

Race*	Population	%
African-American/Black (1,066)	1,506	2.42
Not Hispanic (958)	1,309	2.10
Hispanic (108)	197	0.32
American Indian/Alaska Native (121)	497	0.80
Not Hispanic (103)	429	0.69
Hispanic (18)	68	0.11
Alaska Athabascan (Ala. Nat.) (0)	0	<0.01
Aleut (Alaska Native) (0)	0	<0.01
Apache (0)	2	<0.01
Arapaho (0)	0	<0.01
Blackfeet (1)	16	0.03
Canadian/French Am. Ind. (1)	3	<0.01
Central American Ind. (0)	0	<0.01
Cherokee (13)	57	0.09
Cheyenne (0)	0	<0.01
Chickasaw (0)	2	<0.01
Chippewa (3)	11	0.02
Choctaw (1)	11	0.02
Colville (0)	0	<0.01

Race* (cont.)	Population	%
Comanche (0)	0	<0.01
Cree (0)	0	<0.01
Creek (0)	1	<0.01
Crow (0)	0	<0.01
Delaware (8)	13	0.02
Hopi (0)	1	<0.01
Houma (0)	0	<0.01
Inupiat (Alaska Native) (0)	1	<0.01
Iroquois (14)	63	0.10
Kiowa (0)	2	<0.01
Lumbee (1)	1	<0.01
Menominee (0)	0	<0.01
Mexican American Ind. (1)	6	0.01
Navajo (2)	3	<0.01
Osage (0)	0	<0.01
Ottawa (0)	0	<0.01
Paiute (0)	0	<0.01
Pima (0)	0	<0.01
Potawatomi (0)	0	<0.01
Pueblo (0)	0	<0.01
Puget Sound Salish (0)	0	<0.01
Seminole (0)	0	<0.01
Shoshone (0)	0	<0.01
Sioux (2)	10	0.02
South American Ind. (3)	8	0.01
Spanish American Ind. (1)	2	<0.01
Tlingit-Haida (Alaska Native) (0)	0	<0.01
Tohono O'Odham (0)	0	<0.01
Tsimshian (Alaska Native) (0)	0	<0.01
Ute (0)	0	<0.01
Yakama (0)	0	<0.01
Yaqui (0)	0	<0.01
Yuman (0)	0	<0.01
Yup'ik (Alaska Native) (0)	0	<0.01
Asian (674)	894	1.44
Not Hispanic (660)	856	1.37
Hispanic (14)	38	0.06
Bangladeshi (0)	0	<0.01
Bhutanese (0)	0	<0.01
Burmese (0)	0	<0.01
Cambodian (0)	0	<0.01
Chinese, ex. Taiwanese (196)	240	0.39
Filipino (59)	122	0.20
Hmong (0)	0	<0.01
Indian (134)	162	0.26
Indonesian (1)	5	0.01
Japanese (56)	87	0.14
Korean (120)	159	0.26
Laotian (1)	1	<0.01
Malaysian (0)	0	<0.01
Nepalese (5)	5	0.01
Pakistani (31)	34	0.05
Sri Lankan (3)	3	<0.01
Taiwanese (12)	16	0.03
Thai (15)	21	0.03
Vietnamese (15)	21	0.03
Hawaii Native/Pacific Islander (18)	50	0.08
Not Hispanic (16)	40	0.06
Hispanic (2)	10	0.02
Fijian (1)	1	<0.01
Guamanian/Chamorro (2)	3	<0.01
Marshallese (0)	0	<0.01
Native Hawaiian (7)	18	0.03
Samoan (4)	5	<0.01
Tongan (0)	0	<0.01
White (58,935)	59,860	96.15
Not Hispanic (57,734)	58,502	93.97
Hispanic (1,201)	1,358	2.18

Notes: † The Census 2010 population figure is used to calculate the percentages in the Hispanic Origin and Race categories. Ancestry percentages are based on the 2006-2010 American Community Survey population (not shown); ‡ Numbers in parentheses indicate the number of people reporting a single ancestry; * Numbers in parentheses indicate the number of persons reporting this race alone, not in combination with any other race; Please refer to the Explanation of Data for more information.

Putnam County

Population: 99,710

Ancestry	Population	%
Afghan (0)	0	<0.01
African, Sub-Saharan (180)	263	0.26
African (90)	137	0.14
Cape Verdean (0)	0	<0.01
Ethiopian (26)	26	0.03
Ghanaian (0)	0	<0.01
Kenyan (0)	0	<0.01
Liberian (0)	0	<0.01
Nigerian (0)	20	0.02
Senegalese (64)	64	0.06
Sierra Leonean (0)	0	<0.01
Somalian (0)	0	<0.01
South African (0)	16	0.02
Sudanese (0)	0	<0.01
Ugandan (0)	0	<0.01
Zimbabwean (0)	0	<0.01
Other Sub-Saharan African (0)	0	<0.01
Albanian (924)	980	0.98
Alsatian (0)	0	<0.01
American (2,598)	2,598	2.61
Arab (212)	448	0.45
Arab (0)	61	0.06
Egyptian (103)	117	0.12
Iraqi (0)	0	<0.01
Jordanian (71)	71	0.07
Lebanese (38)	138	0.14
Moroccan (0)	0	<0.01
Palestinian (0)	21	0.02
Syrian (0)	33	0.03
Other Arab (0)	7	0.01
Armenian (10)	42	0.04
Assyrian/Chaldean/Syriac (0)	0	<0.01
Australian (54)	144	0.14
Austrian (174)	879	0.88
Basque (0)	14	0.01
Belgian (21)	135	0.14
Brazilian (49)	143	0.14
British (185)	301	0.30
Bulgarian (35)	35	0.04
Cajun (0)	0	<0.01
Canadian (191)	392	0.39
Carpatho Rusyn (0)	0	<0.01
Celtic (0)	6	0.01
Croatian (140)	200	0.20
Cypriot (0)	0	<0.01
Czech (119)	541	0.54
Czechoslovakian (134)	263	0.26
Danish (114)	298	0.30
Dutch (288)	1,529	1.54
Eastern European (154)	186	0.19
English (1,140)	7,439	7.47
Estonian (0)	64	0.06
European (710)	787	0.79
Finnish (82)	197	0.20
French, ex. Basque (282)	2,532	2.54
French Canadian (251)	680	0.68
German (2,967)	17,556	17.64
German Russian (0)	0	<0.01
Greek (382)	1,015	1.02
Guyanese (0)	0	<0.01
Hungarian (311)	1,309	1.31
Icelander (0)	0	<0.01
Iranian (125)	125	0.13
Irish (8,053)	27,534	27.66
Israeli (0)	32	0.03
Italian (14,946)	31,433	31.58
Latvian (9)	32	0.03
Lithuanian (57)	546	0.55
Luxemburger (0)	0	<0.01
Macedonian (0)	0	<0.01
Maltese (38)	50	0.05
New Zealander (0)	0	<0.01
Northern European (85)	125	0.13
Norwegian (159)	677	0.68
Pennsylvania German (11)	11	0.01

Ancestry	Population	%
Polish (1,827)	5,597	5.62
Portuguese (415)	830	0.83
Romanian (115)	324	0.33
Russian (793)	2,712	2.72
Scandinavian (107)	193	0.19
Scotch-Irish (506)	1,769	1.78
Scottish (297)	1,829	1.84
Serbian (0)	13	0.01
Slavic (27)	66	0.07
Slovak (183)	439	0.44
Slovene (13)	45	0.05
Soviet Union (0)	0	<0.01
Swedish (133)	1,061	1.07
Swiss (16)	140	0.14
Turkish (16)	31	0.03
Ukrainian (368)	959	0.96
Welsh (73)	490	0.49
West Indian, ex. Hispanic (280)	467	0.47
Bahamian (0)	0	<0.01
Barbadian (0)	0	<0.01
Belizean (0)	0	<0.01
Bermudan (0)	0	<0.01
British West Indian (0)	0	<0.01
Dutch West Indian (0)	0	<0.01
Haitian (50)	84	0.08
Jamaican (56)	160	0.16
Trinidadian/Tobagonian (165)	205	0.21
U.S. Virgin Islander (0)	0	<0.01
West Indian (9)	18	0.02
Other West Indian (0)	0	<0.01
Yugoslavian (99)	198	0.20

Hispanic Origin	Population	%
Hispanic or Latino (of any race)	11,661	11.69
Central American, ex. Mexican	2,565	2.57
Costa Rican	62	0.06
Guatemalan	1,909	1.91
Honduran	125	0.13
Nicaraguan	43	0.04
Panamanian	43	0.04
Salvadoran	374	0.38
Other Central American	9	0.01
Cuban	349	0.35
Dominican Republic	605	0.61
Mexican	1,023	1.03
Puerto Rican	3,850	3.86
South American	2,106	2.11
Argentinean	158	0.16
Bolivian	34	0.03
Chilean	89	0.09
Colombian	457	0.46
Ecuadorian	897	0.90
Paraguayan	53	0.05
Peruvian	301	0.30
Uruguayan	63	0.06
Venezuelan	43	0.04
Other South American	11	0.01
Other Hispanic or Latino	1,163	1.17

Race*	Population	%
African-American/Black (2,350)	2,967	2.98
Not Hispanic (2,047)	2,437	2.44
Hispanic (303)	530	0.53
American Indian/Alaska Native (175)	607	0.61
Not Hispanic (121)	452	0.45
Hispanic (54)	155	0.16
Alaska Athabascan (Ala. Nat.) (0)	0	<0.01
Aleut (Alaska Native) (1)	1	<0.01
Apache (1)	3	<0.01
Arapaho (2)	2	<0.01
Blackfeet (2)	31	0.03
Canadian/French Am. Ind. (6)	12	0.01
Central American Ind. (14)	19	0.02
Cherokee (7)	75	0.08
Cheyenne (0)	6	0.01
Chickasaw (0)	0	<0.01
Chippewa (2)	10	0.01
Choctaw (2)	9	0.01
Colville (0)	0	<0.01

Race*	Population	%
Comanche (0)	0	<0.01
Cree (0)	0	<0.01
Creek (1)	5	0.01
Crow (0)	0	<0.01
Delaware (0)	0	<0.01
Hopi (0)	0	<0.01
Houma (0)	0	<0.01
Inupiat (Alaska Native) (1)	1	<0.01
Iroquois (18)	37	0.04
Kiowa (0)	1	<0.01
Lumbee (0)	0	<0.01
Menominee (0)	0	<0.01
Mexican American Ind. (7)	25	0.03
Navajo (1)	1	<0.01
Osage (0)	0	<0.01
Ottawa (0)	0	<0.01
Paiute (0)	0	<0.01
Pima (0)	0	<0.01
Potawatomi (0)	1	<0.01
Pueblo (0)	0	<0.01
Puget Sound Salish (0)	0	<0.01
Seminole (0)	8	0.01
Shoshone (0)	0	<0.01
Sioux (4)	16	0.02
South American Ind. (13)	25	0.03
Spanish American Ind. (2)	3	<0.01
Tlingit-Haida (Alaska Native) (0)	0	<0.01
Tohono O'Odham (0)	0	<0.01
Tsimshian (Alaska Native) (0)	0	<0.01
Ute (0)	0	<0.01
Yakama (0)	0	<0.01
Yaqui (0)	0	<0.01
Yuman (1)	1	<0.01
Yup'ik (Alaska Native) (0)	0	<0.01
Asian (1,882)	2,442	2.45
Not Hispanic (1,832)	2,324	2.33
Hispanic (50)	118	0.12
Bangladeshi (12)	13	0.01
Bhutanese (0)	0	<0.01
Burmese (1)	1	<0.01
Cambodian (6)	7	0.01
Chinese, ex. Taiwanese (530)	691	0.69
Filipino (259)	377	0.38
Hmong (0)	0	<0.01
Indian (573)	666	0.67
Indonesian (0)	3	<0.01
Japanese (122)	189	0.19
Korean (184)	228	0.23
Laotian (1)	5	0.01
Malaysian (6)	12	0.01
Nepalese (13)	16	0.02
Pakistani (35)	45	0.05
Sri Lankan (4)	6	0.01
Taiwanese (11)	15	0.02
Thai (21)	33	0.03
Vietnamese (38)	55	0.06
Hawaii Native/Pacific Islander (35)	118	0.12
Not Hispanic (14)	61	0.06
Hispanic (21)	57	0.06
Fijian (0)	0	<0.01
Guamanian/Chamorro (19)	40	0.04
Marshallese (0)	0	<0.01
Native Hawaiian (2)	18	0.02
Samoan (3)	5	0.01
Tongan (0)	0	<0.01
White (90,470)	92,223	92.49
Not Hispanic (82,709)	83,747	83.99
Hispanic (7,761)	8,476	8.50

*Notes: † The Census 2010 population figure is used to calculate the percentages in the Hispanic Origin and Race categories. Ancestry percentages are based on the 2006-2010 American Community Survey population (not shown); ‡ Numbers in parentheses indicate the number of people reporting a single ancestry; * Numbers in parentheses indicate the number of persons reporting this race alone, not in combination with any other race; Please refer to the Explanation of Data for more information.*

Queens County

Population: 2,230,722

Ancestry	Population	%
Afghan (5,842)	6,027	0.27
African, Sub-Saharan (19,754)	25,166	1.14
African (9,764)	14,083	0.64
Cape Verdean (46)	117	0.01
Ethiopian (478)	505	0.02
Ghanaian (1,269)	1,326	0.06
Kenyan (96)	96	<0.01
Liberian (297)	381	0.02
Nigerian (5,989)	6,304	0.29
Senegalese (84)	84	<0.01
Sierra Leonean (127)	127	0.01
Somalian (52)	98	<0.01
South African (230)	356	0.02
Sudanese (161)	286	0.01
Ugandan (65)	77	<0.01
Zimbabwean (107)	107	<0.01
Other Sub-Saharan African (989)	1,219	0.06
Albanian (6,264)	6,624	0.30
Alsatian (26)	37	<0.01
American (45,604)	45,604	2.07
Arab (16,286)	19,669	0.89
Arab (1,921)	2,283	0.10
Egyptian (5,905)	6,551	0.30
Iraqi (224)	315	0.01
Jordanian (260)	307	0.01
Lebanese (1,548)	2,228	0.10
Moroccan (2,945)	3,459	0.16
Palestinian (582)	638	0.03
Syrian (193)	420	0.02
Other Arab (2,708)	3,468	0.16
Armenian (4,083)	4,658	0.21
Assyrian/Chaldean/Syriac (13)	13	<0.01
Australian (163)	285	0.01
Austrian (2,702)	7,523	0.34
Basque (29)	159	0.01
Belgian (289)	593	0.03
Brazilian (4,871)	6,175	0.28
British (1,346)	2,457	0.11
Bulgarian (1,928)	2,090	0.10
Cajun (0)	33	<0.01
Canadian (604)	1,308	0.06
Carpatho Rusyn (0)	9	<0.01
Celtic (92)	169	0.01
Croatian (5,621)	7,054	0.32
Cypriot (556)	644	0.03
Czech (1,116)	3,464	0.16
Czechoslovakian (816)	1,467	0.07
Danish (171)	792	0.04
Dutch (727)	3,516	0.16
Eastern European (4,442)	4,673	0.21
English (4,389)	20,267	0.92
Estonian (164)	198	0.01
European (5,335)	6,584	0.30
Finnish (269)	693	0.03
French, ex. Basque (3,945)	12,532	0.57
French Canadian (552)	2,020	0.09
German (20,566)	70,399	3.20
German Russian (33)	78	<0.01
Greek (35,368)	41,654	1.89
Guyanese (47,132)	53,961	2.45
Hungarian (4,718)	9,470	0.43
Icelander (10)	26	<0.01
Iranian (3,162)	3,707	0.17
Irish (43,033)	105,348	4.79
Israeli (3,355)	4,164	0.19
Italian (104,251)	159,812	7.27
Latvian (342)	568	0.03
Lithuanian (1,463)	3,131	0.14
Luxemburger (0)	13	<0.01
Macedonian (938)	1,109	0.05
Maltese (952)	1,565	0.07
New Zealander (0)	16	<0.01
Northern European (370)	512	0.02
Norwegian (670)	2,559	0.12
Pennsylvania German (9)	38	<0.01

Ancestry	Population	%
Polish (37,726)	59,757	2.72
Portuguese (2,784)	4,727	0.21
Romanian (9,232)	11,686	0.53
Russian (29,779)	44,676	2.03
Scandinavian (131)	545	0.02
Scotch-Irish (2,079)	4,602	0.21
Scottish (1,567)	5,718	0.26
Serbian (2,176)	2,438	0.11
Slavic (370)	765	0.03
Slovak (1,161)	1,882	0.09
Slovene (171)	468	0.02
Soviet Union (12)	71	<0.01
Swedish (511)	2,862	0.13
Swiss (381)	1,260	0.06
Turkish (3,054)	3,767	0.17
Ukrainian (5,770)	8,375	0.38
Welsh (201)	1,666	0.08
West Indian, ex. Hispanic (131,014)	147,460	6.71
Bahamian (134)	185	0.01
Barbadian (4,074)	5,021	0.23
Belizean (1,106)	1,344	0.06
Bermudan (142)	177	0.01
British West Indian (3,765)	4,689	0.21
Dutch West Indian (122)	206	0.01
Haitian (35,439)	38,368	1.74
Jamaican (55,278)	59,999	2.73
Trinidadian/Tobagonian (16,227)	19,255	0.88
U.S. Virgin Islander (234)	364	0.02
West Indian (14,052)	17,400	0.79
Other West Indian (441)	452	0.02
Yugoslavian (3,824)	4,516	0.21

Hispanic Origin	Population	%
Hispanic or Latino (of any race)	613,750	27.51
Central American, ex. Mexican	52,509	2.35
Costa Rican	1,749	0.08
Guatemalan	13,700	0.61
Honduran	8,546	0.38
Nicaraguan	2,842	0.13
Panamanian	3,977	0.18
Salvadoran	21,342	0.96
Other Central American	353	0.02
Cuban	11,020	0.49
Dominican Republic	88,061	3.95
Mexican	92,835	4.16
Puerto Rican	102,881	4.61
South American	214,022	9.59
Argentinean	6,345	0.28
Bolivian	3,268	0.15
Chilean	3,184	0.14
Colombian	70,290	3.15
Ecuadorian	98,512	4.42
Paraguayan	2,775	0.12
Peruvian	22,886	1.03
Uruguayan	1,743	0.08
Venezuelan	3,580	0.16
Other South American	1,439	0.06
Other Hispanic or Latino	52,422	2.35

Race*	Population	%
African-American/Black (426,683)	462,351	20.73
Not Hispanic (395,881)	419,695	18.81
Hispanic (30,802)	42,656	1.91
American Indian/Alaska Native (15,364)	30,033	1.35
Not Hispanic (6,490)	15,412	0.69
Hispanic (8,874)	14,621	0.66
Alaska Athabascan (Ala. Nat.) (2)	3	<0.01
Aleut (Alaska Native) (4)	6	<0.01
Apache (15)	53	<0.01
Arapaho (0)	2	<0.01
Blackfeet (45)	342	0.02
Canadian/French Am. Ind. (20)	38	<0.01
Central American Ind. (419)	733	0.03
Cherokee (267)	1,425	0.06
Cheyenne (13)	20	<0.01
Chickasaw (9)	21	<0.01
Chippewa (14)	37	<0.01
Choctaw (16)	68	<0.01
Colville (1)	1	<0.01

Race*	Population	%
Comanche (3)	6	<0.01
Cree (6)	24	<0.01
Creek (23)	73	<0.01
Crow (1)	4	<0.01
Delaware (14)	35	<0.01
Hopi (1)	15	<0.01
Houma (0)	4	<0.01
Inupiat (Alaska Native) (6)	13	<0.01
Iroquois (140)	308	0.01
Kiowa (0)	0	<0.01
Lumbee (7)	30	<0.01
Menominee (0)	0	<0.01
Mexican American Ind. (1,270)	1,640	0.07
Navajo (13)	37	<0.01
Osage (5)	5	<0.01
Ottawa (0)	2	<0.01
Paiute (3)	4	<0.01
Pima (0)	0	<0.01
Potawatomi (6)	7	<0.01
Pueblo (102)	161	0.01
Puget Sound Salish (2)	5	<0.01
Seminole (15)	79	<0.01
Shoshone (0)	6	<0.01
Sioux (35)	104	<0.01
South American Ind. (1,281)	2,448	0.11
Spanish American Ind. (468)	659	0.03
Tlingit-Haida (Alaska Native) (8)	20	<0.01
Tohono O'Odham (4)	6	<0.01
Tsimshian (Alaska Native) (0)	1	<0.01
Ute (4)	5	<0.01
Yakama (0)	0	<0.01
Yaqui (3)	7	<0.01
Yuman (2)	5	<0.01
Yup'ik (Alaska Native) (1)	1	<0.01
Asian (511,787)	552,867	24.78
Not Hispanic (508,334)	545,389	24.45
Hispanic (3,453)	7,478	0.34
Bangladeshi (33,152)	38,341	1.72
Bhutanese (240)	250	0.01
Burmese (2,132)	2,344	0.11
Cambodian (230)	303	0.01
Chinese, ex. Taiwanese (191,693)	200,714	9.00
Filipino (38,163)	41,773	1.87
Hmong (24)	30	<0.01
Indian (117,550)	141,147	6.33
Indonesian (2,860)	3,386	0.15
Japanese (6,375)	7,790	0.35
Korean (64,107)	66,124	2.96
Laotian (137)	210	0.01
Malaysian (1,029)	1,620	0.07
Nepalese (4,930)	5,319	0.24
Pakistani (16,215)	18,084	0.81
Sri Lankan (1,293)	1,536	0.07
Taiwanese (7,776)	8,962	0.40
Thai (3,677)	4,124	0.18
Vietnamese (3,566)	4,322	0.19
Hawaii Native/Pacific Islander (1,530)	7,691	0.34
Not Hispanic (1,094)	5,685	0.25
Hispanic (436)	2,006	0.09
Fijian (36)	76	<0.01
Guamanian/Chamorro (337)	483	0.02
Marshallese (0)	0	<0.01
Native Hawaiian (191)	486	0.02
Samoan (62)	179	0.01
Tongan (7)	14	<0.01
White (886,053)	941,608	42.21
Not Hispanic (616,727)	638,051	28.60
Hispanic (269,326)	303,557	13.61

Notes: † The Census 2010 population figure is used to calculate the percentages in the Hispanic Origin and Race categories. Ancestry percentages are based on the 2006-2010 American Community Survey population (not shown); ‡ Numbers in parentheses indicate the number of people reporting a single ancestry; * Numbers in parentheses indicate the number of persons reporting this race alone, not in combination with any other race; Please refer to the Explanation of Data for more information.

Rensselaer County
Population: 159,429

Ancestry	Population	%
Afghan (0)	0	<0.01
African, Sub-Saharan (697)	883	0.56
African (405)	565	0.36
Cape Verdean (0)	11	0.01
Ethiopian (0)	0	<0.01
Ghanaian (103)	103	0.06
Kenyan (0)	0	<0.01
Liberian (0)	0	<0.01
Nigerian (8)	8	0.01
Senegalese (0)	0	<0.01
Sierra Leonean (0)	0	<0.01
Somalian (0)	0	<0.01
South African (0)	0	<0.01
Sudanese (28)	28	0.02
Ugandan (0)	0	<0.01
Zimbabwean (0)	0	<0.01
Other Sub-Saharan African (153)	168	0.11
Albanian (80)	82	0.05
Alsatian (13)	13	0.01
American (6,888)	6,888	4.34
Arab (537)	1,052	0.66
Arab (72)	91	0.06
Egyptian (90)	210	0.13
Iraqi (0)	0	<0.01
Jordanian (0)	0	<0.01
Lebanese (284)	572	0.36
Moroccan (0)	0	<0.01
Palestinian (0)	0	<0.01
Syrian (16)	65	0.04
Other Arab (75)	114	0.07
Armenian (412)	992	0.63
Assyrian/Chaldean/Syriac (0)	0	<0.01
Australian (17)	17	0.01
Austrian (117)	580	0.37
Basque (0)	0	<0.01
Belgian (0)	125	0.08
Brazilian (126)	143	0.09
British (258)	500	0.32
Bulgarian (0)	0	<0.01
Cajun (0)	0	<0.01
Canadian (317)	787	0.50
Carpatho Rusyn (0)	0	<0.01
Celtic (0)	40	0.03
Croatian (89)	113	0.07
Cypriot (0)	0	<0.01
Czech (115)	607	0.38
Czechoslovakian (116)	305	0.19
Danish (172)	977	0.62
Dutch (850)	7,465	4.71
Eastern European (126)	171	0.11
English (3,787)	18,308	11.54
Estonian (15)	32	0.02
European (1,054)	1,508	0.95
Finnish (32)	195	0.12
French, ex. Basque (2,073)	16,113	10.16
French Canadian (1,505)	4,489	2.83
German (6,342)	31,702	19.98
German Russian (0)	65	0.04
Greek (301)	959	0.60
Guyanese (138)	217	0.14
Hungarian (161)	744	0.47
Icelander (0)	0	<0.01
Iranian (57)	57	0.04
Irish (11,871)	43,414	27.37
Israeli (13)	13	0.01
Italian (7,939)	24,089	15.19
Latvian (29)	77	0.05
Lithuanian (214)	1,079	0.68
Luxemburger (0)	0	<0.01
Macedonian (0)	0	<0.01
Maltese (0)	3	<0.01
New Zealander (0)	0	<0.01
Northern European (88)	88	0.06
Norwegian (140)	672	0.42
Pennsylvania German (40)	53	0.03

Ancestry	Population	%
Polish (2,632)	10,494	6.62
Portuguese (135)	465	0.29
Romanian (11)	88	0.06
Russian (484)	1,724	1.09
Scandinavian (41)	180	0.11
Scotch-Irish (754)	2,400	1.51
Scottish (872)	3,489	2.20
Serbian (0)	10	0.01
Slavic (18)	107	0.07
Slovak (44)	188	0.12
Slovene (8)	23	0.01
Soviet Union (0)	0	<0.01
Swedish (342)	1,747	1.10
Swiss (37)	467	0.29
Turkish (170)	223	0.14
Ukrainian (746)	2,107	1.33
Welsh (289)	1,378	0.87
West Indian, ex. Hispanic (954)	1,304	0.82
Bahamian (0)	0	<0.01
Barbadian (15)	55	0.03
Belizean (0)	10	0.01
Bermudan (0)	0	<0.01
British West Indian (23)	30	0.02
Dutch West Indian (0)	0	<0.01
Haitian (176)	232	0.15
Jamaican (316)	440	0.28
Trinidadian/Tobagonian (274)	320	0.20
U.S. Virgin Islander (0)	0	<0.01
West Indian (150)	204	0.13
Other West Indian (0)	13	0.01
Yugoslavian (21)	51	0.03

Hispanic Origin	Population	%
Hispanic or Latino (of any race)	6,080	3.81
Central American, ex. Mexican	275	0.17
Costa Rican	37	0.02
Guatemalan	58	0.04
Honduran	21	0.01
Nicaraguan	20	0.01
Panamanian	73	0.05
Salvadoran	63	0.04
Other Central American	3	<0.01
Cuban	179	0.11
Dominican Republic	312	0.20
Mexican	806	0.51
Puerto Rican	3,498	2.19
South American	362	0.23
Argentinean	40	0.03
Bolivian	6	<0.01
Chilean	31	0.02
Colombian	104	0.07
Ecuadorian	79	0.05
Paraguayan	7	<0.01
Peruvian	47	0.03
Uruguayan	4	<0.01
Venezuelan	39	0.02
Other South American	5	<0.01
Other Hispanic or Latino	648	0.41

Race*	Population	%
African-American/Black (10,338)	12,620	7.92
Not Hispanic (9,592)	11,487	7.21
Hispanic (746)	1,133	0.71
American Indian/Alaska Native (385)	1,273	0.80
Not Hispanic (283)	1,058	0.66
Hispanic (102)	215	0.13
Alaska Athabascan (Ala. Nat.) (0)	0	<0.01
Aleut (Alaska Native) (0)	0	<0.01
Apache (4)	14	0.01
Arapaho (0)	0	<0.01
Blackfeet (5)	74	0.05
Canadian/French Am. Ind. (6)	26	0.02
Central American Ind. (1)	3	<0.01
Cherokee (29)	149	0.09
Cheyenne (0)	1	<0.01
Chickasaw (0)	0	<0.01
Chippewa (2)	12	0.01
Choctaw (4)	7	<0.01
Colville (0)	0	<0.01

Race*	Population	%
Comanche (0)	2	<0.01
Cree (2)	4	<0.01
Creek (0)	3	<0.01
Crow (0)	3	<0.01
Delaware (3)	6	<0.01
Hopi (0)	0	<0.01
Houma (0)	0	<0.01
Inupiat (Alaska Native) (0)	2	<0.01
Iroquois (51)	173	0.11
Kiowa (0)	0	<0.01
Lumbee (2)	5	<0.01
Menominee (3)	3	<0.01
Mexican American Ind. (4)	7	<0.01
Navajo (2)	6	<0.01
Osage (0)	0	<0.01
Ottawa (0)	1	<0.01
Paiute (0)	0	<0.01
Pima (1)	1	<0.01
Potawatomi (0)	0	<0.01
Pueblo (0)	0	<0.01
Puget Sound Salish (0)	0	<0.01
Seminole (1)	4	<0.01
Shoshone (0)	0	<0.01
Sioux (4)	13	0.01
South American Ind. (19)	30	0.02
Spanish American Ind. (4)	5	<0.01
Tlingit-Haida (Alaska Native) (1)	2	<0.01
Tohono O'Odham (0)	0	<0.01
Tsimshian (Alaska Native) (0)	0	<0.01
Ute (0)	0	<0.01
Yakama (0)	0	<0.01
Yaqui (0)	0	<0.01
Yuman (0)	0	<0.01
Yup'ik (Alaska Native) (0)	2	<0.01
Asian (3,517)	4,293	2.69
Not Hispanic (3,469)	4,205	2.64
Hispanic (48)	88	0.06
Bangladeshi (43)	52	0.03
Bhutanese (0)	0	<0.01
Burmese (327)	348	0.22
Cambodian (6)	19	0.01
Chinese, ex. Taiwanese (976)	1,120	0.70
Filipino (228)	380	0.24
Hmong (2)	5	<0.01
Indian (924)	1,075	0.67
Indonesian (9)	15	0.01
Japanese (99)	207	0.13
Korean (315)	413	0.26
Laotian (2)	6	<0.01
Malaysian (12)	14	0.01
Nepalese (16)	22	0.01
Pakistani (193)	217	0.14
Sri Lankan (4)	8	0.01
Taiwanese (46)	52	0.03
Thai (32)	49	0.03
Vietnamese (121)	160	0.10
Hawaii Native/Pacific Islander (34)	123	0.08
Not Hispanic (25)	100	0.06
Hispanic (9)	23	0.01
Fijian (1)	1	<0.01
Guamanian/Chamorro (7)	13	0.01
Marshallese (0)	0	<0.01
Native Hawaiian (12)	43	0.03
Samoan (0)	6	<0.01
Tongan (0)	0	<0.01
White (139,529)	143,012	89.70
Not Hispanic (136,555)	139,499	87.50
Hispanic (2,974)	3,513	2.20

Notes: † The Census 2010 population figure is used to calculate the percentages in the Hispanic Origin and Race categories. Ancestry percentages are based on the 2006-2010 American Community Survey population (not shown); ‡ Numbers in parentheses indicate the number of people reporting a single ancestry; * Numbers in parentheses indicate the number of persons reporting this race alone, not in combination with any other race; Please refer to the Explanation of Data for more information.

Richmond County

Population: 468,730

Ancestry	Population	%
Afghan (0)	0	<0.01
African, Sub-Saharan (6,533)	7,234	1.56
African (3,732)	4,164	0.90
Cape Verdean (0)	11	<0.01
Ethiopian (41)	46	0.01
Ghanaian (239)	250	0.05
Kenyan (78)	78	0.02
Liberian (515)	532	0.11
Nigerian (1,509)	1,679	0.36
Senegalese (126)	126	0.03
Sierra Leonean (90)	117	0.03
Somalian (0)	0	<0.01
South African (0)	0	<0.01
Sudanese (0)	0	<0.01
Ugandan (0)	0	<0.01
Zimbabwean (0)	0	<0.01
Other Sub-Saharan African (203)	231	0.05
Albanian (7,700)	8,108	1.75
Alsatian (0)	24	0.01
American (13,977)	13,977	3.02
Arab (7,711)	8,820	1.90
Arab (1,694)	1,829	0.39
Egyptian (3,200)	3,292	0.71
Iraqi (11)	32	0.01
Jordanian (159)	183	0.04
Lebanese (784)	1,019	0.22
Moroccan (502)	621	0.13
Palestinian (443)	479	0.10
Syrian (209)	584	0.13
Other Arab (709)	781	0.17
Armenian (83)	311	0.07
Assyrian/Chaldean/Syriac (15)	15	<0.01
Australian (24)	49	0.01
Austrian (343)	1,542	0.33
Basque (15)	77	0.02
Belgian (36)	266	0.06
Brazilian (183)	287	0.06
British (231)	615	0.13
Bulgarian (0)	0	<0.01
Cajun (0)	0	<0.01
Canadian (290)	544	0.12
Carpatho Rusyn (63)	63	0.01
Celtic (37)	46	0.01
Croatian (598)	869	0.19
Cypriot (0)	0	<0.01
Czech (146)	735	0.16
Czechoslovakian (93)	237	0.05
Danish (90)	479	0.10
Dutch (137)	1,637	0.35
Eastern European (433)	433	0.09
English (1,973)	9,014	1.94
Estonian (10)	10	<0.01
European (1,914)	2,068	0.45
Finnish (48)	185	0.04
French, ex. Basque (800)	3,772	0.81
French Canadian (248)	750	0.16
German (4,111)	25,477	5.50
German Russian (0)	0	<0.01
Greek (2,403)	4,183	0.90
Guyanese (767)	952	0.21
Hungarian (1,024)	2,288	0.49
Icelander (55)	55	0.01
Iranian (121)	171	0.04
Irish (20,064)	64,762	13.97
Israeli (542)	759	0.16
Italian (107,263)	156,288	33.72
Latvian (98)	142	0.03
Lithuanian (178)	645	0.14
Luxemburger (12)	54	0.01
Macedonian (1,368)	1,590	0.34
Maltese (104)	290	0.06
New Zealander (0)	0	<0.01
Northern European (60)	60	0.01
Norwegian (1,617)	5,135	1.11
Pennsylvania German (9)	41	0.01

Ancestry	Population	%
Polish (9,167)	18,430	3.98
Portuguese (180)	617	0.13
Romanian (530)	964	0.21
Russian (11,315)	16,388	3.54
Scandinavian (35)	121	0.03
Scotch-Irish (759)	1,886	0.41
Scottish (718)	2,350	0.51
Serbian (219)	240	0.05
Slavic (68)	143	0.03
Slovak (233)	553	0.12
Slovene (86)	108	0.02
Soviet Union (51)	63	0.01
Swedish (253)	1,936	0.42
Swiss (76)	256	0.06
Turkish (1,267)	1,607	0.35
Ukrainian (3,759)	4,836	1.04
Welsh (68)	417	0.09
West Indian, ex. Hispanic (5,348)	6,967	1.50
Bahamian (31)	31	0.01
Barbadian (94)	94	0.02
Belizean (76)	76	0.02
Bermudan (0)	0	<0.01
British West Indian (113)	236	0.05
Dutch West Indian (39)	89	0.02
Haitian (676)	791	0.17
Jamaican (1,463)	2,033	0.44
Trinidadian/Tobagonian (1,412)	1,807	0.39
U.S. Virgin Islander (22)	22	<0.01
West Indian (1,392)	1,745	0.38
Other West Indian (30)	43	0.01
Yugoslavian (1,237)	1,738	0.38

Hispanic Origin	Population	%
Hispanic or Latino (of any race)	81,051	17.29
Central American, ex. Mexican	4,310	0.92
Costa Rican	266	0.06
Guatemalan	864	0.18
Honduran	1,735	0.37
Nicaraguan	199	0.04
Panamanian	607	0.13
Salvadoran	592	0.13
Other Central American	47	0.01
Cuban	1,831	0.39
Dominican Republic	4,918	1.05
Mexican	18,684	3.99
Puerto Rican	37,517	8.00
South American	8,232	1.76
Argentinean	608	0.13
Bolivian	161	0.03
Chilean	346	0.07
Colombian	2,526	0.54
Ecuadorian	2,675	0.57
Paraguayan	38	0.01
Peruvian	1,462	0.31
Uruguayan	76	0.02
Venezuelan	254	0.05
Other South American	86	0.02
Other Hispanic or Latino	5,559	1.19

Race*	Population	%
African-American/Black (49,857)	55,014	11.74
Not Hispanic (44,313)	47,521	10.14
Hispanic (5,544)	7,493	1.60
American Indian/Alaska Native (1,695)	3,719	0.79
Not Hispanic (695)	2,034	0.43
Hispanic (1,000)	1,685	0.36
Alaska Athabascan (Ala. Nat.) (1)	3	<0.01
Aleut (Alaska Native) (0)	2	<0.01
Apache (16)	35	0.01
Arapaho (1)	1	<0.01
Blackfeet (17)	88	0.02
Canadian/French Am. Ind. (7)	10	<0.01
Central American Ind. (29)	56	0.01
Cherokee (104)	467	0.10
Cheyenne (0)	2	<0.01
Chickasaw (1)	3	<0.01
Chippewa (7)	13	<0.01
Choctaw (3)	11	<0.01
Colville (0)	0	<0.01

	Population	%
Comanche (2)	3	<0.01
Cree (0)	4	<0.01
Creek (3)	29	0.01
Crow (0)	0	<0.01
Delaware (16)	43	0.01
Hopi (1)	5	<0.01
Houma (1)	1	<0.01
Inupiat (Alaska Native) (0)	1	<0.01
Iroquois (61)	152	0.03
Kiowa (0)	1	<0.01
Lumbee (1)	8	<0.01
Menominee (0)	0	<0.01
Mexican American Ind. (161)	204	0.04
Navajo (10)	17	<0.01
Osage (0)	0	<0.01
Ottawa (0)	0	<0.01
Paiute (0)	0	<0.01
Pima (2)	2	<0.01
Potawatomi (0)	0	<0.01
Pueblo (4)	5	<0.01
Puget Sound Salish (0)	0	<0.01
Seminole (7)	26	0.01
Shoshone (1)	3	<0.01
Sioux (11)	24	0.01
South American Ind. (146)	288	0.06
Spanish American Ind. (31)	47	0.01
Tlingit-Haida (Alaska Native) (0)	1	<0.01
Tohono O'Odham (4)	8	<0.01
Tsimshian (Alaska Native) (0)	0	<0.01
Ute (1)	1	<0.01
Yakama (0)	0	<0.01
Yaqui (1)	1	<0.01
Yuman (0)	1	<0.01
Yup'ik (Alaska Native) (0)	0	<0.01
Asian (35,164)	38,756	8.27
Not Hispanic (34,697)	37,689	8.04
Hispanic (467)	1,067	0.23
Bangladeshi (360)	387	0.08
Bhutanese (0)	0	<0.01
Burmese (116)	130	0.03
Cambodian (100)	129	0.03
Chinese, ex. Taiwanese (13,144)	14,107	3.01
Filipino (5,224)	6,205	1.32
Hmong (4)	8	<0.01
Indian (6,793)	7,723	1.65
Indonesian (22)	52	0.01
Japanese (201)	408	0.09
Korean (3,207)	3,398	0.72
Laotian (13)	18	<0.01
Malaysian (58)	96	0.02
Nepalese (27)	35	0.01
Pakistani (2,495)	2,777	0.59
Sri Lankan (1,560)	1,766	0.38
Taiwanese (160)	197	0.04
Thai (135)	166	0.04
Vietnamese (468)	570	0.12
Hawaii Native/Pacific Islander (213)	683	0.15
Not Hispanic (137)	439	0.09
Hispanic (76)	244	0.05
Fijian (6)	6	<0.01
Guamanian/Chamorro (88)	115	0.02
Marshallese (1)	1	<0.01
Native Hawaiian (46)	121	0.03
Samoan (5)	26	0.01
Tongan (2)	2	<0.01
White (341,677)	350,679	74.81
Not Hispanic (300,169)	305,118	65.09
Hispanic (41,508)	45,561	9.72

Notes: † The Census 2010 population figure is used to calculate the percentages in the Hispanic Origin and Race categories. Ancestry percentages are based on the 2006-2010 American Community Survey population (not shown); ‡ Numbers in parentheses indicate the number of people reporting a single ancestry; * Numbers in parentheses indicate the number of persons reporting this race alone, not in combination with any other race; Please refer to the Explanation of Data for more information.

Rockland County
Population: 311,687

Ancestry	Population	%
Afghan (172)	172	0.06
African, Sub-Saharan (1,590)	2,071	0.68
African (567)	971	0.32
Cape Verdean (0)	0	<0.01
Ethiopian (27)	44	0.01
Ghanaian (339)	339	0.11
Kenyan (92)	92	0.03
Liberian (0)	0	<0.01
Nigerian (207)	262	0.09
Senegalese (52)	52	0.02
Sierra Leonean (0)	0	<0.01
Somalian (0)	0	<0.01
South African (89)	89	0.03
Sudanese (0)	0	<0.01
Ugandan (86)	86	0.03
Zimbabwean (0)	0	<0.01
Other Sub-Saharan African (131)	136	0.04
Albanian (501)	569	0.19
Alsatian (0)	3	<0.01
American (13,566)	13,566	4.44
Arab (1,299)	1,848	0.60
Arab (330)	351	0.11
Egyptian (344)	377	0.12
Iraqi (19)	72	0.02
Jordanian (87)	87	0.03
Lebanese (161)	338	0.11
Moroccan (216)	301	0.10
Palestinian (0)	25	0.01
Syrian (24)	156	0.05
Other Arab (118)	141	0.05
Armenian (239)	332	0.11
Assyrian/Chaldean/Syriac (11)	51	0.02
Australian (40)	125	0.04
Austrian (667)	2,856	0.93
Basque (0)	0	<0.01
Belgian (270)	922	0.30
Brazilian (215)	476	0.16
British (457)	879	0.29
Bulgarian (8)	24	0.01
Cajun (0)	0	<0.01
Canadian (470)	1,139	0.37
Carpatho Rusyn (4)	4	<0.01
Celtic (19)	19	0.01
Croatian (78)	264	0.09
Cypriot (0)	0	<0.01
Czech (310)	1,346	0.44
Czechoslovakian (489)	955	0.31
Danish (107)	402	0.13
Dutch (469)	2,665	0.87
Eastern European (2,769)	3,036	0.99
English (2,442)	10,647	3.49
Estonian (24)	50	0.02
European (9,157)	10,292	3.37
Finnish (50)	191	0.06
French, ex. Basque (590)	3,512	1.15
French Canadian (318)	795	0.26
German (5,904)	24,634	8.06
German Russian (12)	12	<0.01
Greek (1,370)	2,748	0.90
Guyanese (387)	482	0.16
Hungarian (4,329)	8,874	2.91
Icelander (0)	0	<0.01
Iranian (381)	626	0.20
Irish (22,489)	47,471	15.54
Israeli (1,696)	3,753	1.23
Italian (22,741)	44,310	14.51
Latvian (227)	349	0.11
Lithuanian (439)	1,258	0.41
Luxemburger (0)	0	<0.01
Macedonian (24)	24	0.01
Maltese (38)	85	0.03
New Zealander (0)	58	0.02
Northern European (20)	71	0.02
Norwegian (405)	962	0.31
Pennsylvania German (20)	38	0.01

Ancestry (cont.)	Population	%
Polish (5,690)	16,940	5.55
Portuguese (692)	1,011	0.33
Romanian (800)	2,551	0.84
Russian (6,114)	13,933	4.56
Scandinavian (38)	88	0.03
Scotch-Irish (611)	1,605	0.53
Scottish (672)	2,422	0.79
Serbian (51)	76	0.02
Slavic (29)	159	0.05
Slovak (362)	801	0.26
Slovene (31)	54	0.02
Soviet Union (0)	0	<0.01
Swedish (298)	1,500	0.49
Swiss (73)	267	0.09
Turkish (139)	282	0.09
Ukrainian (1,524)	2,602	0.85
Welsh (78)	620	0.20
West Indian, ex. Hispanic (17,509)	18,661	6.11
Bahamian (0)	0	<0.01
Barbadian (125)	149	0.05
Belizean (141)	164	0.05
Bermudan (0)	3	<0.01
British West Indian (323)	347	0.11
Dutch West Indian (0)	0	<0.01
Haitian (12,516)	13,086	4.28
Jamaican (3,254)	3,514	1.15
Trinidadian/Tobagonian (738)	819	0.27
U.S. Virgin Islander (0)	19	0.01
West Indian (412)	560	0.18
Other West Indian (0)	0	<0.01
Yugoslavian (110)	207	0.07

Hispanic Origin	Population	%
Hispanic or Latino (of any race)	48,783	15.65
Central American, ex. Mexican	9,272	2.97
Costa Rican	205	0.07
Guatemalan	5,356	1.72
Honduran	383	0.12
Nicaraguan	101	0.03
Panamanian	145	0.05
Salvadoran	3,012	0.97
Other Central American	70	0.02
Cuban	1,191	0.38
Dominican Republic	9,105	2.92
Mexican	5,358	1.72
Puerto Rican	12,650	4.06
South American	7,348	2.36
Argentinean	379	0.12
Bolivian	55	0.02
Chilean	203	0.07
Colombian	982	0.32
Ecuadorian	4,926	1.58
Paraguayan	26	0.01
Peruvian	562	0.18
Uruguayan	63	0.02
Venezuelan	119	0.04
Other South American	33	0.01
Other Hispanic or Latino	3,859	1.24

Race*	Population	%
African-American/Black (37,058)	40,486	12.99
Not Hispanic (34,623)	36,893	11.84
Hispanic (2,435)	3,593	1.15
American Indian/Alaska Native (911)	2,250	0.72
Not Hispanic (487)	1,366	0.44
Hispanic (424)	884	0.28
Alaska Athabascan (Ala. Nat.) (1)	1	<0.01
Aleut (Alaska Native) (1)	1	<0.01
Apache (3)	8	<0.01
Arapaho (0)	0	<0.01
Blackfeet (3)	34	0.01
Canadian/French Am. Ind. (0)	3	<0.01
Central American Ind. (28)	46	0.01
Cherokee (18)	192	0.06
Cheyenne (0)	2	<0.01
Chickasaw (0)	0	<0.01
Chippewa (1)	2	<0.01
Choctaw (3)	12	<0.01
Colville (0)	0	<0.01

Race* (cont.)	Population	%
Comanche (3)	7	<0.01
Cree (0)	2	<0.01
Creek (0)	3	<0.01
Crow (1)	1	<0.01
Delaware (113)	236	0.08
Hopi (0)	0	<0.01
Houma (0)	0	<0.01
Inupiat (Alaska Native) (0)	0	<0.01
Iroquois (44)	85	0.03
Kiowa (0)	0	<0.01
Lumbee (4)	7	<0.01
Menominee (0)	0	<0.01
Mexican American Ind. (72)	107	0.03
Navajo (0)	5	<0.01
Osage (0)	1	<0.01
Ottawa (0)	0	<0.01
Paiute (1)	1	<0.01
Pima (0)	0	<0.01
Potawatomi (1)	1	<0.01
Pueblo (5)	9	<0.01
Puget Sound Salish (0)	0	<0.01
Seminole (0)	8	<0.01
Shoshone (0)	0	<0.01
Sioux (4)	18	0.01
South American Ind. (62)	185	0.06
Spanish American Ind. (9)	16	0.01
Tlingit-Haida (Alaska Native) (2)	8	<0.01
Tohono O'Odham (2)	4	<0.01
Tsimshian (Alaska Native) (0)	0	<0.01
Ute (0)	0	<0.01
Yakama (0)	1	<0.01
Yaqui (1)	1	<0.01
Yuman (0)	0	<0.01
Yup'ik (Alaska Native) (0)	0	<0.01
Asian (19,293)	21,506	6.90
Not Hispanic (19,099)	21,015	6.74
Hispanic (194)	491	0.16
Bangladeshi (144)	166	0.05
Bhutanese (0)	0	<0.01
Burmese (10)	14	<0.01
Cambodian (147)	166	0.05
Chinese, ex. Taiwanese (2,686)	3,154	1.01
Filipino (4,482)	5,049	1.62
Hmong (30)	32	0.01
Indian (7,028)	7,759	2.49
Indonesian (30)	52	0.02
Japanese (277)	410	0.13
Korean (2,199)	2,340	0.75
Laotian (9)	14	<0.01
Malaysian (5)	16	0.01
Nepalese (14)	16	0.01
Pakistani (961)	1,080	0.35
Sri Lankan (78)	93	0.03
Taiwanese (86)	101	0.03
Thai (185)	220	0.07
Vietnamese (402)	503	0.16
Hawaii Native/Pacific Islander (130)	538	0.17
Not Hispanic (43)	295	0.09
Hispanic (87)	243	0.08
Fijian (0)	2	<0.01
Guamanian/Chamorro (48)	65	0.02
Marshallese (0)	0	<0.01
Native Hawaiian (15)	42	0.01
Samoan (10)	17	0.01
Tongan (2)	2	<0.01
White (228,295)	234,099	75.11
Not Hispanic (203,670)	206,768	66.34
Hispanic (24,625)	27,331	8.77

Notes: † The Census 2010 population figure is used to calculate the percentages in the Hispanic Origin and Race categories. Ancestry percentages are based on the 2006-2010 American Community Survey population (not shown); ‡ Numbers in parentheses indicate the number of people reporting a single ancestry; * Numbers in parentheses indicate the number of persons reporting this race alone, not in combination with any other race; Please refer to the Explanation of Data for more information.

Saratoga County

Population: 219,607

Ancestry	Population	%
Afghan (215)	256	0.12
African, Sub-Saharan (91)	164	0.08
African (5)	78	0.04
Cape Verdean (0)	0	<0.01
Ethiopian (0)	0	<0.01
Ghanaian (61)	61	0.03
Kenyan (0)	0	<0.01
Liberian (0)	0	<0.01
Nigerian (25)	25	0.01
Senegalese (0)	0	<0.01
Sierra Leonean (0)	0	<0.01
Somalian (0)	0	<0.01
South African (0)	0	<0.01
Sudanese (0)	0	<0.01
Ugandan (0)	0	<0.01
Zimbabwean (0)	0	<0.01
Other Sub-Saharan African (0)	0	<0.01
Albanian (101)	148	0.07
Alsatian (0)	0	<0.01
American (26,948)	26,948	12.40
Arab (305)	939	0.43
Arab (0)	13	0.01
Egyptian (146)	156	0.07
Iraqi (0)	10	<0.01
Jordanian (0)	0	<0.01
Lebanese (71)	460	0.21
Moroccan (60)	72	0.03
Palestinian (0)	0	<0.01
Syrian (22)	205	0.09
Other Arab (6)	23	0.01
Armenian (142)	458	0.21
Assyrian/Chaldean/Syriac (13)	13	0.01
Australian (55)	115	0.05
Austrian (318)	966	0.44
Basque (7)	11	0.01
Belgian (46)	222	0.10
Brazilian (179)	214	0.10
British (535)	886	0.41
Bulgarian (20)	39	0.02
Cajun (0)	0	<0.01
Canadian (422)	937	0.43
Carpatho Rusyn (0)	0	<0.01
Celtic (11)	19	0.01
Croatian (112)	198	0.09
Cypriot (0)	0	<0.01
Czech (190)	848	0.39
Czechoslovakian (167)	387	0.18
Danish (117)	964	0.44
Dutch (1,294)	6,872	3.16
Eastern European (261)	287	0.13
English (7,312)	27,103	12.47
Estonian (20)	71	0.03
European (1,477)	1,634	0.75
Finnish (154)	433	0.20
French, ex. Basque (3,190)	21,115	9.72
French Canadian (2,301)	5,476	2.52
German (7,897)	35,201	16.20
German Russian (0)	26	0.01
Greek (552)	1,127	0.52
Guyanese (193)	200	0.09
Hungarian (249)	1,427	0.66
Icelander (0)	14	0.01
Iranian (85)	113	0.05
Irish (15,092)	52,194	24.02
Israeli (113)	127	0.06
Italian (13,634)	34,416	15.84
Latvian (59)	189	0.09
Lithuanian (325)	1,033	0.48
Luxemburger (0)	0	<0.01
Macedonian (11)	11	0.01
Maltese (12)	78	0.04
New Zealander (0)	0	<0.01
Northern European (63)	106	0.05
Norwegian (591)	1,971	0.91
Pennsylvania German (32)	45	0.02

Ancestry (cont.)	Population	%
Polish (4,777)	16,507	7.60
Portuguese (106)	360	0.17
Romanian (49)	227	0.10
Russian (1,235)	3,548	1.63
Scandinavian (100)	250	0.12
Scotch-Irish (1,288)	3,641	1.68
Scottish (1,088)	4,810	2.21
Serbian (42)	63	0.03
Slavic (72)	236	0.11
Slovak (219)	911	0.42
Slovene (44)	63	0.03
Soviet Union (0)	0	<0.01
Swedish (319)	1,884	0.87
Swiss (95)	442	0.20
Turkish (99)	113	0.05
Ukrainian (697)	1,955	0.90
Welsh (285)	1,941	0.89
West Indian, ex. Hispanic (265)	558	0.26
Bahamian (0)	13	0.01
Barbadian (24)	24	0.01
Belizean (0)	0	<0.01
Bermudan (0)	0	<0.01
British West Indian (0)	0	<0.01
Dutch West Indian (0)	0	<0.01
Haitian (2)	25	0.01
Jamaican (132)	353	0.16
Trinidadian/Tobagonian (40)	40	0.02
U.S. Virgin Islander (9)	9	<0.01
West Indian (58)	94	0.04
Other West Indian (0)	0	<0.01
Yugoslavian (116)	216	0.10

Hispanic Origin	Population	%
Hispanic or Latino (of any race)	5,279	2.40
Central American, ex. Mexican	336	0.15
Costa Rican	32	0.01
Guatemalan	90	0.04
Honduran	46	0.02
Nicaraguan	14	0.01
Panamanian	41	0.02
Salvadoran	110	0.05
Other Central American	3	<0.01
Cuban	225	0.10
Dominican Republic	271	0.12
Mexican	1,331	0.61
Puerto Rican	1,920	0.87
South American	540	0.25
Argentinean	57	0.03
Bolivian	18	0.01
Chilean	61	0.03
Colombian	159	0.07
Ecuadorian	84	0.04
Paraguayan	6	<0.01
Peruvian	80	0.04
Uruguayan	9	<0.01
Venezuelan	54	0.02
Other South American	12	0.01
Other Hispanic or Latino	656	0.30

Race*	Population	%
African-American/Black (3,269)	4,700	2.14
Not Hispanic (3,053)	4,314	1.96
Hispanic (216)	386	0.18
American Indian/Alaska Native (388)	1,377	0.63
Not Hispanic (325)	1,211	0.55
Hispanic (63)	166	0.08
Alaska Athabascan (Ala. Nat.) (1)	1	<0.01
Aleut (Alaska Native) (1)	5	<0.01
Apache (7)	20	0.01
Arapaho (0)	3	<0.01
Blackfeet (8)	56	0.03
Canadian/French Am. Ind. (3)	13	0.01
Central American Ind. (2)	7	<0.01
Cherokee (23)	168	0.08
Cheyenne (0)	1	<0.01
Chickasaw (3)	3	<0.01
Chippewa (3)	13	0.01
Choctaw (4)	9	<0.01
Colville (0)	0	<0.01

Race* (cont.)	Population	%
Comanche (2)	5	<0.01
Cree (1)	8	<0.01
Creek (0)	2	<0.01
Crow (1)	1	<0.01
Delaware (2)	6	<0.01
Hopi (0)	0	<0.01
Houma (0)	0	<0.01
Inupiat (Alaska Native) (0)	1	<0.01
Iroquois (64)	186	0.08
Kiowa (0)	1	<0.01
Lumbee (1)	4	<0.01
Menominee (1)	3	<0.01
Mexican American Ind. (17)	22	0.01
Navajo (16)	28	0.01
Osage (0)	0	<0.01
Ottawa (0)	0	<0.01
Paiute (0)	0	<0.01
Pima (0)	0	<0.01
Potawatomi (0)	5	<0.01
Pueblo (2)	3	<0.01
Puget Sound Salish (0)	0	<0.01
Seminole (1)	6	<0.01
Shoshone (0)	0	<0.01
Sioux (4)	20	0.01
South American Ind. (8)	23	0.01
Spanish American Ind. (0)	0	<0.01
Tlingit-Haida (Alaska Native) (0)	2	<0.01
Tohono O'Odham (0)	0	<0.01
Tsimshian (Alaska Native) (0)	0	<0.01
Ute (0)	0	<0.01
Yakama (0)	0	<0.01
Yaqui (2)	2	<0.01
Yuman (0)	0	<0.01
Yup'ik (Alaska Native) (0)	0	<0.01
Asian (3,919)	5,079	2.31
Not Hispanic (3,880)	4,981	2.27
Hispanic (39)	98	0.04
Bangladeshi (24)	24	0.01
Bhutanese (0)	0	<0.01
Burmese (2)	3	<0.01
Cambodian (12)	13	0.01
Chinese, ex. Taiwanese (1,059)	1,280	0.58
Filipino (275)	500	0.23
Hmong (0)	0	<0.01
Indian (1,164)	1,338	0.61
Indonesian (6)	20	0.01
Japanese (184)	346	0.16
Korean (430)	605	0.28
Laotian (5)	13	0.01
Malaysian (7)	9	<0.01
Nepalese (11)	11	0.01
Pakistani (276)	319	0.15
Sri Lankan (12)	17	0.01
Taiwanese (45)	53	0.02
Thai (54)	97	0.04
Vietnamese (187)	223	0.10
Hawaii Native/Pacific Islander (44)	162	0.07
Not Hispanic (35)	132	0.06
Hispanic (9)	30	0.01
Fijian (0)	0	<0.01
Guamanian/Chamorro (10)	16	0.01
Marshallese (0)	0	<0.01
Native Hawaiian (18)	75	0.03
Samoan (4)	16	0.01
Tongan (0)	0	<0.01
White (207,181)	210,587	95.89
Not Hispanic (203,647)	206,635	94.09
Hispanic (3,534)	3,952	1.80

Notes: † The Census 2010 population figure is used to calculate the percentages in the Hispanic Origin and Race categories. Ancestry percentages are based on the 2006-2010 American Community Survey population (not shown); ‡ Numbers in parentheses indicate the number of people reporting a single ancestry; * Numbers in parentheses indicate the number of persons reporting this race alone, not in combination with any other race; Please refer to the Explanation of Data for more information.

Schenectady County

Population: 154,727

Ancestry	Population	%
Afghan (318)	318	0.21
African, Sub-Saharan (639)	860	0.56
African (286)	424	0.28
Cape Verdean (0)	0	<0.01
Ethiopian (0)	0	<0.01
Ghanaian (24)	24	0.02
Kenyan (69)	69	0.05
Liberian (24)	24	0.02
Nigerian (131)	186	0.12
Senegalese (0)	0	<0.01
Sierra Leonean (0)	0	<0.01
Somalian (0)	0	<0.01
South African (0)	0	<0.01
Sudanese (0)	0	<0.01
Ugandan (0)	0	<0.01
Zimbabwean (0)	0	<0.01
Other Sub-Saharan African (105)	133	0.09
Albanian (38)	80	0.05
Alsatian (0)	0	<0.01
American (8,939)	8,939	5.83
Arab (231)	473	0.31
Arab (81)	131	0.09
Egyptian (13)	13	0.01
Iraqi (0)	0	<0.01
Jordanian (0)	0	<0.01
Lebanese (106)	213	0.14
Moroccan (0)	0	<0.01
Palestinian (0)	0	<0.01
Syrian (0)	58	0.04
Other Arab (31)	58	0.04
Armenian (70)	92	0.06
Assyrian/Chaldean/Syriac (0)	0	<0.01
Australian (0)	51	0.03
Austrian (111)	467	0.30
Basque (0)	0	<0.01
Belgian (7)	28	0.02
Brazilian (156)	206	0.13
British (292)	611	0.40
Bulgarian (0)	0	<0.01
Cajun (0)	6	<0.01
Canadian (206)	511	0.33
Carpatho Rusyn (0)	0	<0.01
Celtic (35)	35	0.02
Croatian (15)	40	0.03
Cypriot (54)	54	0.04
Czech (130)	778	0.51
Czechoslovakian (174)	314	0.20
Danish (244)	681	0.44
Dutch (1,069)	5,702	3.72
Eastern European (326)	338	0.22
English (3,915)	14,772	9.64
Estonian (39)	39	0.03
European (1,101)	1,173	0.77
Finnish (15)	32	0.02
French, ex. Basque (1,638)	9,023	5.89
French Canadian (964)	2,716	1.77
German (4,964)	22,454	14.65
German Russian (0)	0	<0.01
Greek (305)	613	0.40
Guyanese (1,867)	1,999	1.30
Hungarian (286)	1,109	0.72
Icelander (0)	0	<0.01
Iranian (8)	8	0.01
Irish (8,174)	26,759	17.46
Israeli (0)	9	0.01
Italian (16,081)	30,411	19.84
Latvian (15)	94	0.06
Lithuanian (210)	708	0.46
Luxemburger (0)	0	<0.01
Macedonian (0)	0	<0.01
Maltese (0)	9	0.01
New Zealander (0)	18	0.01
Northern European (283)	297	0.19
Norwegian (149)	570	0.37
Pennsylvania German (10)	35	0.02

Ancestry (cont.)	Population	%
Polish (5,392)	12,827	8.37
Portuguese (125)	198	0.13
Romanian (25)	127	0.08
Russian (561)	1,487	0.97
Scandinavian (35)	108	0.07
Scotch-Irish (666)	1,949	1.27
Scottish (906)	3,064	2.00
Serbian (0)	24	0.02
Slavic (54)	84	0.05
Slovak (198)	543	0.35
Slovene (0)	9	0.01
Soviet Union (0)	0	<0.01
Swedish (273)	1,002	0.65
Swiss (204)	517	0.34
Turkish (94)	123	0.08
Ukrainian (335)	808	0.53
Welsh (237)	989	0.65
West Indian, ex. Hispanic (1,560)	1,804	1.18
Bahamian (0)	0	<0.01
Barbadian (43)	94	0.06
Belizean (0)	0	<0.01
Bermudan (0)	0	<0.01
British West Indian (75)	75	0.05
Dutch West Indian (0)	10	0.01
Haitian (24)	61	0.04
Jamaican (766)	817	0.53
Trinidadian/Tobagonian (24)	106	0.07
U.S. Virgin Islander (0)	0	<0.01
West Indian (628)	641	0.42
Other West Indian (0)	0	<0.01
Yugoslavian (48)	73	0.05

Hispanic Origin	Population	%
Hispanic or Latino (of any race)	8,827	5.70
Central American, ex. Mexican	481	0.31
Costa Rican	52	0.03
Guatemalan	101	0.07
Honduran	64	0.04
Nicaraguan	30	0.02
Panamanian	49	0.03
Salvadoran	170	0.11
Other Central American	15	0.01
Cuban	229	0.15
Dominican Republic	582	0.38
Mexican	702	0.45
Puerto Rican	5,442	3.52
South American	661	0.43
Argentinean	65	0.04
Bolivian	21	0.01
Chilean	35	0.02
Colombian	184	0.12
Ecuadorian	115	0.07
Paraguayan	10	0.01
Peruvian	118	0.08
Uruguayan	15	0.01
Venezuelan	55	0.04
Other South American	43	0.03
Other Hispanic or Latino	730	0.47

Race*	Population	%
African-American/Black (14,710)	17,992	11.63
Not Hispanic (13,528)	16,273	10.52
Hispanic (1,182)	1,719	1.11
American Indian/Alaska Native (575)	1,769	1.14
Not Hispanic (445)	1,465	0.95
Hispanic (130)	304	0.20
Alaska Athabascan (Ala. Nat.) (1)	1	<0.01
Aleut (Alaska Native) (0)	0	<0.01
Apache (6)	9	0.01
Arapaho (1)	1	<0.01
Blackfeet (3)	65	0.04
Canadian/French Am. Ind. (5)	12	0.01
Central American Ind. (6)	7	<0.01
Cherokee (14)	174	0.11
Cheyenne (1)	2	<0.01
Chickasaw (0)	1	<0.01
Chippewa (6)	17	0.01
Choctaw (1)	2	<0.01
Colville (0)	0	<0.01

Race* (cont.)	Population	%
Comanche (0)	0	<0.01
Cree (0)	5	<0.01
Creek (1)	5	<0.01
Crow (0)	6	<0.01
Delaware (4)	12	0.01
Hopi (0)	1	<0.01
Houma (0)	0	<0.01
Inupiat (Alaska Native) (4)	4	<0.01
Iroquois (37)	159	0.10
Kiowa (0)	1	<0.01
Lumbee (2)	4	<0.01
Menominee (0)	0	<0.01
Mexican American Ind. (16)	20	0.01
Navajo (1)	4	<0.01
Osage (0)	0	<0.01
Ottawa (0)	0	<0.01
Paiute (0)	0	<0.01
Pima (1)	5	<0.01
Potawatomi (2)	7	<0.01
Pueblo (0)	1	<0.01
Puget Sound Salish (0)	0	<0.01
Seminole (2)	11	0.01
Shoshone (0)	0	<0.01
Sioux (6)	24	0.02
South American Ind. (18)	39	0.03
Spanish American Ind. (1)	7	<0.01
Tlingit-Haida (Alaska Native) (0)	0	<0.01
Tohono O'Odham (0)	0	<0.01
Tsimshian (Alaska Native) (0)	0	<0.01
Ute (0)	0	<0.01
Yakama (0)	0	<0.01
Yaqui (0)	0	<0.01
Yuman (0)	0	<0.01
Yup'ik (Alaska Native) (0)	0	<0.01
Asian (4,960)	6,587	4.26
Not Hispanic (4,917)	6,436	4.16
Hispanic (43)	151	0.10
Bangladeshi (13)	20	0.01
Bhutanese (1)	1	<0.01
Burmese (6)	9	0.01
Cambodian (9)	13	0.01
Chinese, ex. Taiwanese (938)	1,093	0.71
Filipino (257)	368	0.24
Hmong (0)	0	<0.01
Indian (2,597)	3,182	2.06
Indonesian (16)	22	0.01
Japanese (76)	160	0.10
Korean (325)	451	0.29
Laotian (2)	12	0.01
Malaysian (3)	9	0.01
Nepalese (12)	17	0.01
Pakistani (279)	316	0.20
Sri Lankan (21)	26	0.02
Taiwanese (25)	33	0.02
Thai (31)	53	0.03
Vietnamese (181)	214	0.14
Hawaii Native/Pacific Islander (105)	391	0.25
Not Hispanic (81)	327	0.21
Hispanic (24)	64	0.04
Fijian (1)	1	<0.01
Guamanian/Chamorro (6)	14	0.01
Marshallese (0)	0	<0.01
Native Hawaiian (19)	48	0.03
Samoan (4)	10	0.01
Tongan (1)	1	<0.01
White (123,211)	127,516	82.41
Not Hispanic (119,409)	123,004	79.50
Hispanic (3,802)	4,512	2.92

Notes: † The Census 2010 population figure is used to calculate the percentages in the Hispanic Origin and Race categories. Ancestry percentages are based on the 2006-2010 American Community Survey population (not shown); ‡ Numbers in parentheses indicate the number of people reporting a single ancestry; * Numbers in parentheses indicate the number of persons reporting this race alone, not in combination with any other race; Please refer to the Explanation of Data for more information.

Schoharie County
Population: 32,749

Ancestry	Population	%
Afghan (0)	0	<0.01
African, Sub-Saharan (66)	102	0.31
African (51)	87	0.27
Cape Verdean (0)	0	<0.01
Ethiopian (5)	5	0.02
Ghanaian (0)	0	<0.01
Kenyan (0)	0	<0.01
Liberian (0)	0	<0.01
Nigerian (10)	10	0.03
Senegalese (0)	0	<0.01
Sierra Leonean (0)	0	<0.01
Somalian (0)	0	<0.01
South African (0)	0	<0.01
Sudanese (0)	0	<0.01
Ugandan (0)	0	<0.01
Zimbabwean (0)	0	<0.01
Other Sub-Saharan African (0)	0	<0.01
Albanian (0)	0	<0.01
Alsatian (0)	0	<0.01
American (3,401)	3,401	10.37
Arab (73)	143	0.44
Arab (0)	0	<0.01
Egyptian (0)	40	0.12
Iraqi (46)	46	0.14
Jordanian (0)	0	<0.01
Lebanese (15)	36	0.11
Moroccan (0)	0	<0.01
Palestinian (0)	0	<0.01
Syrian (12)	21	0.06
Other Arab (0)	0	<0.01
Armenian (0)	30	0.09
Assyrian/Chaldean/Syriac (0)	0	<0.01
Australian (0)	20	0.06
Austrian (31)	187	0.57
Basque (0)	0	<0.01
Belgian (5)	33	0.10
Brazilian (0)	10	0.03
British (53)	135	0.41
Bulgarian (3)	3	0.01
Cajun (0)	0	<0.01
Canadian (72)	127	0.39
Carpatho Rusyn (0)	0	<0.01
Celtic (3)	3	0.01
Croatian (21)	34	0.10
Cypriot (0)	0	<0.01
Czech (21)	169	0.52
Czechoslovakian (44)	83	0.25
Danish (29)	118	0.36
Dutch (510)	2,676	8.16
Eastern European (30)	30	0.09
English (1,129)	4,576	13.96
Estonian (0)	24	0.07
European (402)	442	1.35
Finnish (7)	50	0.15
French, ex. Basque (194)	1,670	5.09
French Canadian (152)	546	1.67
German (2,500)	10,082	30.75
German Russian (0)	0	<0.01
Greek (44)	95	0.29
Guyanese (0)	0	<0.01
Hungarian (37)	242	0.74
Icelander (0)	0	<0.01
Iranian (3)	3	0.01
Irish (1,597)	7,351	22.42
Israeli (0)	0	<0.01
Italian (1,592)	4,233	12.91
Latvian (6)	6	0.02
Lithuanian (6)	46	0.14
Luxemburger (0)	0	<0.01
Macedonian (0)	0	<0.01
Maltese (0)	21	0.06
New Zealander (0)	0	<0.01
Northern European (4)	8	0.02
Norwegian (180)	461	1.41
Pennsylvania German (8)	11	0.03

Ancestry (cont.)	Population	%
Polish (442)	1,690	5.15
Portuguese (0)	50	0.15
Romanian (20)	26	0.08
Russian (72)	336	1.02
Scandinavian (17)	63	0.19
Scotch-Irish (199)	464	1.42
Scottish (146)	1,033	3.15
Serbian (0)	0	<0.01
Slavic (0)	20	0.06
Slovak (13)	34	0.10
Slovene (0)	4	0.01
Soviet Union (0)	0	<0.01
Swedish (29)	271	0.83
Swiss (14)	158	0.48
Turkish (0)	0	<0.01
Ukrainian (53)	151	0.46
Welsh (55)	384	1.17
West Indian, ex. Hispanic (92)	115	0.35
Bahamian (0)	0	<0.01
Barbadian (0)	0	<0.01
Belizean (0)	0	<0.01
Bermudan (0)	0	<0.01
British West Indian (0)	0	<0.01
Dutch West Indian (0)	0	<0.01
Haitian (19)	22	0.07
Jamaican (47)	67	0.20
Trinidadian/Tobagonian (14)	14	0.04
U.S. Virgin Islander (0)	0	<0.01
West Indian (12)	12	0.04
Other West Indian (0)	0	<0.01
Yugoslavian (0)	13	0.04

Hispanic Origin	Population	%
Hispanic or Latino (of any race)	924	2.82
Central American, ex. Mexican	58	0.18
Costa Rican	2	0.01
Guatemalan	26	0.08
Honduran	6	0.02
Nicaraguan	9	0.03
Panamanian	5	0.02
Salvadoran	10	0.03
Other Central American	0	<0.01
Cuban	60	0.18
Dominican Republic	37	0.11
Mexican	87	0.27
Puerto Rican	449	1.37
South American	96	0.29
Argentinean	9	0.03
Bolivian	0	<0.01
Chilean	3	0.01
Colombian	38	0.12
Ecuadorian	20	0.06
Paraguayan	2	0.01
Peruvian	19	0.06
Uruguayan	1	<0.01
Venezuelan	4	0.01
Other South American	0	<0.01
Other Hispanic or Latino	137	0.42

Race*	Population	%
African-American/Black (435)	603	1.84
Not Hispanic (394)	541	1.65
Hispanic (41)	62	0.19
American Indian/Alaska Native (70)	273	0.83
Not Hispanic (54)	238	0.73
Hispanic (16)	35	0.11
Alaska Athabascan (Ala. Nat.) (0)	0	<0.01
Aleut (Alaska Native) (2)	2	0.01
Apache (2)	7	0.02
Arapaho (1)	2	0.01
Blackfeet (0)	4	0.01
Canadian/French Am. Ind. (0)	0	<0.01
Central American Ind. (0)	1	<0.01
Cherokee (4)	32	0.10
Cheyenne (0)	1	<0.01
Chickasaw (0)	0	<0.01
Chippewa (1)	2	0.01
Choctaw (0)	0	<0.01
Colville (0)	0	<0.01

Race* (cont.)	Population	%
Comanche (0)	0	<0.01
Cree (0)	0	<0.01
Creek (0)	0	<0.01
Crow (0)	1	<0.01
Delaware (3)	3	0.01
Hopi (0)	0	<0.01
Houma (0)	0	<0.01
Inupiat (Alaska Native) (0)	0	<0.01
Iroquois (11)	42	0.13
Kiowa (1)	1	<0.01
Lumbee (0)	0	<0.01
Menominee (0)	0	<0.01
Mexican American Ind. (0)	0	<0.01
Navajo (1)	1	<0.01
Osage (0)	1	<0.01
Ottawa (0)	0	<0.01
Paiute (0)	0	<0.01
Pima (0)	0	<0.01
Potawatomi (0)	0	<0.01
Pueblo (0)	0	<0.01
Puget Sound Salish (0)	0	<0.01
Seminole (0)	1	<0.01
Shoshone (0)	0	<0.01
Sioux (1)	3	0.01
South American Ind. (5)	9	0.03
Spanish American Ind. (0)	0	<0.01
Tlingit-Haida (Alaska Native) (0)	0	<0.01
Tohono O'Odham (0)	0	<0.01
Tsimshian (Alaska Native) (0)	0	<0.01
Ute (0)	1	<0.01
Yakama (0)	0	<0.01
Yaqui (0)	0	<0.01
Yuman (0)	0	<0.01
Yup'ik (Alaska Native) (0)	0	<0.01
Asian (217)	288	0.88
Not Hispanic (217)	279	0.85
Hispanic (0)	9	0.03
Bangladeshi (0)	0	<0.01
Bhutanese (0)	0	<0.01
Burmese (0)	0	<0.01
Cambodian (0)	0	<0.01
Chinese, ex. Taiwanese (40)	48	0.15
Filipino (26)	45	0.14
Hmong (0)	0	<0.01
Indian (52)	64	0.20
Indonesian (0)	0	<0.01
Japanese (32)	37	0.11
Korean (26)	42	0.13
Laotian (0)	0	<0.01
Malaysian (0)	1	<0.01
Nepalese (3)	4	0.01
Pakistani (17)	17	0.05
Sri Lankan (3)	4	0.01
Taiwanese (0)	0	<0.01
Thai (3)	4	0.01
Vietnamese (7)	9	0.03
Hawaii Native/Pacific Islander (6)	27	0.08
Not Hispanic (3)	21	0.06
Hispanic (3)	6	0.02
Fijian (0)	0	<0.01
Guamanian/Chamorro (3)	4	0.01
Marshallese (0)	0	<0.01
Native Hawaiian (1)	10	0.03
Samoan (0)	2	0.01
Tongan (0)	0	<0.01
White (31,402)	31,818	97.16
Not Hispanic (30,742)	31,106	94.98
Hispanic (660)	712	2.17

*Notes: † The Census 2010 population figure is used to calculate the percentages in the Hispanic Origin and Race categories. Ancestry percentages are based on the 2006-2010 American Community Survey population (not shown); ‡ Numbers in parentheses indicate the number of people reporting a single ancestry; * Numbers in parentheses indicate the number of persons reporting this race alone, not in combination with any other race; Please refer to the Explanation of Data for more information.*

Schuyler County
Population: 18,343

Ancestry	Population	%
Afghan (0)	0	<0.01
African, Sub-Saharan (0)	0	<0.01
African (0)	0	<0.01
Cape Verdean (0)	0	<0.01
Ethiopian (0)	0	<0.01
Ghanaian (0)	0	<0.01
Kenyan (0)	0	<0.01
Liberian (0)	0	<0.01
Nigerian (0)	0	<0.01
Senegalese (0)	0	<0.01
Sierra Leonean (0)	0	<0.01
Somalian (0)	0	<0.01
South African (0)	0	<0.01
Sudanese (0)	0	<0.01
Ugandan (0)	0	<0.01
Zimbabwean (0)	0	<0.01
Other Sub-Saharan African (0)	0	<0.01
Albanian (107)	126	0.68
Alsatian (0)	0	<0.01
American (2,366)	2,366	12.74
Arab (43)	45	0.24
Arab (43)	43	0.23
Egyptian (0)	0	<0.01
Iraqi (0)	0	<0.01
Jordanian (0)	0	<0.01
Lebanese (0)	2	0.01
Moroccan (0)	0	<0.01
Palestinian (0)	0	<0.01
Syrian (0)	0	<0.01
Other Arab (0)	0	<0.01
Armenian (0)	0	<0.01
Assyrian/Chaldean/Syriac (0)	0	<0.01
Australian (7)	7	0.04
Austrian (11)	34	0.18
Basque (0)	0	<0.01
Belgian (10)	39	0.21
Brazilian (0)	0	<0.01
British (87)	122	0.66
Bulgarian (0)	0	<0.01
Cajun (0)	0	<0.01
Canadian (33)	50	0.27
Carpatho Rusyn (0)	0	<0.01
Celtic (0)	3	0.02
Croatian (0)	0	<0.01
Cypriot (0)	0	<0.01
Czech (95)	183	0.99
Czechoslovakian (7)	42	0.23
Danish (6)	43	0.23
Dutch (178)	942	5.07
Eastern European (11)	46	0.25
English (1,136)	3,077	16.57
Estonian (0)	0	<0.01
European (74)	85	0.46
Finnish (12)	101	0.54
French, ex. Basque (110)	694	3.74
French Canadian (64)	134	0.72
German (1,125)	3,444	18.55
German Russian (0)	0	<0.01
Greek (6)	21	0.11
Guyanese (0)	0	<0.01
Hungarian (7)	47	0.25
Icelander (0)	0	<0.01
Iranian (0)	0	<0.01
Irish (981)	3,340	17.99
Israeli (0)	0	<0.01
Italian (864)	1,984	10.69
Latvian (0)	0	<0.01
Lithuanian (16)	20	0.11
Luxemburger (0)	0	<0.01
Macedonian (0)	19	0.10
Maltese (0)	0	<0.01
New Zealander (0)	0	<0.01
Northern European (0)	0	<0.01
Norwegian (50)	119	0.64
Pennsylvania German (38)	83	0.45

Ancestry (cont.)	Population	%
Polish (337)	1,027	5.53
Portuguese (0)	19	0.10
Romanian (0)	11	0.06
Russian (11)	130	0.70
Scandinavian (0)	0	<0.01
Scotch-Irish (192)	314	1.69
Scottish (198)	699	3.76
Serbian (0)	0	<0.01
Slavic (0)	3	0.02
Slovak (11)	17	0.09
Slovene (3)	3	0.02
Soviet Union (0)	0	<0.01
Swedish (51)	216	1.16
Swiss (76)	148	0.80
Turkish (0)	0	<0.01
Ukrainian (29)	85	0.46
Welsh (74)	205	1.10
West Indian, ex. Hispanic (39)	39	0.21
Bahamian (0)	0	<0.01
Barbadian (0)	0	<0.01
Belizean (0)	0	<0.01
Bermudan (0)	0	<0.01
British West Indian (0)	0	<0.01
Dutch West Indian (0)	0	<0.01
Haitian (28)	28	0.15
Jamaican (11)	11	0.06
Trinidadian/Tobagonian (0)	0	<0.01
U.S. Virgin Islander (0)	0	<0.01
West Indian (0)	0	<0.01
Other West Indian (0)	0	<0.01
Yugoslavian (0)	7	0.04

Hispanic Origin	Population	%
Hispanic or Latino (of any race)	234	1.28
Central American, ex. Mexican	10	0.05
Costa Rican	1	0.01
Guatemalan	3	0.02
Honduran	1	0.01
Nicaraguan	2	0.01
Panamanian	0	<0.01
Salvadoran	3	0.02
Other Central American	0	<0.01
Cuban	2	0.01
Dominican Republic	14	0.08
Mexican	64	0.35
Puerto Rican	99	0.54
South American	17	0.09
Argentinean	5	0.03
Bolivian	0	<0.01
Chilean	0	<0.01
Colombian	3	0.02
Ecuadorian	1	0.01
Paraguayan	1	0.01
Peruvian	5	0.03
Uruguayan	0	<0.01
Venezuelan	2	0.01
Other South American	0	<0.01
Other Hispanic or Latino	28	0.15

Race*	Population	%
African-American/Black (159)	244	1.33
Not Hispanic (143)	216	1.18
Hispanic (16)	28	0.15
American Indian/Alaska Native (47)	161	0.88
Not Hispanic (44)	152	0.83
Hispanic (3)	9	0.05
Alaska Athabascan (Ala. Nat.) (1)	1	0.01
Aleut (Alaska Native) (0)	0	<0.01
Apache (0)	0	<0.01
Arapaho (0)	0	<0.01
Blackfeet (2)	11	0.06
Canadian/French Am. Ind. (1)	2	0.01
Central American Ind. (0)	0	<0.01
Cherokee (3)	23	0.13
Cheyenne (0)	0	<0.01
Chickasaw (0)	0	<0.01
Chippewa (0)	0	<0.01
Choctaw (0)	2	0.01
Colville (0)	1	0.01

Race* (cont.)	Population	%
Comanche (0)	0	<0.01
Cree (1)	1	0.01
Creek (0)	0	<0.01
Crow (0)	0	<0.01
Delaware (1)	2	0.01
Hopi (1)	2	0.01
Houma (0)	0	<0.01
Inupiat (Alaska Native) (0)	0	<0.01
Iroquois (12)	41	0.22
Kiowa (0)	0	<0.01
Lumbee (0)	0	<0.01
Menominee (0)	0	<0.01
Mexican American Ind. (0)	0	<0.01
Navajo (0)	4	0.02
Osage (0)	0	<0.01
Ottawa (0)	0	<0.01
Paiute (0)	0	<0.01
Pima (0)	0	<0.01
Potawatomi (0)	0	<0.01
Pueblo (1)	1	0.01
Puget Sound Salish (0)	0	<0.01
Seminole (0)	3	0.02
Shoshone (0)	0	<0.01
Sioux (1)	2	0.01
South American Ind. (0)	1	0.01
Spanish American Ind. (0)	0	<0.01
Tlingit-Haida (Alaska Native) (0)	0	<0.01
Tohono O'Odham (0)	0	<0.01
Tsimshian (Alaska Native) (0)	0	<0.01
Ute (0)	0	<0.01
Yakama (0)	0	<0.01
Yaqui (0)	0	<0.01
Yuman (0)	0	<0.01
Yup'ik (Alaska Native) (0)	0	<0.01
Asian (53)	88	0.48
Not Hispanic (51)	82	0.45
Hispanic (2)	6	0.03
Bangladeshi (0)	0	<0.01
Bhutanese (0)	0	<0.01
Burmese (0)	0	<0.01
Cambodian (1)	1	0.01
Chinese, ex. Taiwanese (9)	12	0.07
Filipino (6)	15	0.08
Hmong (0)	0	<0.01
Indian (14)	23	0.13
Indonesian (1)	2	0.01
Japanese (7)	11	0.06
Korean (5)	8	0.04
Laotian (1)	3	0.02
Malaysian (0)	0	<0.01
Nepalese (0)	0	<0.01
Pakistani (1)	1	0.01
Sri Lankan (0)	0	<0.01
Taiwanese (1)	3	0.02
Thai (3)	6	0.03
Vietnamese (0)	1	0.01
Hawaii Native/Pacific Islander (4)	5	0.03
Not Hispanic (4)	5	0.03
Hispanic (0)	0	<0.01
Fijian (0)	0	<0.01
Guamanian/Chamorro (1)	1	0.01
Marshallese (0)	0	<0.01
Native Hawaiian (0)	0	<0.01
Samoan (1)	1	0.01
Tongan (0)	0	<0.01
White (17,803)	18,035	98.32
Not Hispanic (17,646)	17,851	97.32
Hispanic (157)	184	1.00

Notes: † *The Census 2010 population figure is used to calculate the percentages in the Hispanic Origin and Race categories. Ancestry percentages are based on the 2006-2010 American Community Survey population (not shown); ‡ Numbers in parentheses indicate the number of people reporting a single ancestry; * Numbers in parentheses indicate the number of persons reporting this race alone, not in combination with any other race; Please refer to the Explanation of Data for more information.*

Seneca County
Population: 35,251

Ancestry	Population	%
Afghan (0)	0	<0.01
African, Sub-Saharan (54)	82	0.23
African (54)	82	0.23
Cape Verdean (0)	0	<0.01
Ethiopian (0)	0	<0.01
Ghanaian (0)	0	<0.01
Kenyan (0)	0	<0.01
Liberian (0)	0	<0.01
Nigerian (0)	0	<0.01
Senegalese (0)	0	<0.01
Sierra Leonean (0)	0	<0.01
Somalian (0)	0	<0.01
South African (0)	0	<0.01
Sudanese (0)	0	<0.01
Ugandan (0)	0	<0.01
Zimbabwean (0)	0	<0.01
Other Sub-Saharan African (0)	0	<0.01
Albanian (9)	9	0.03
Alsatian (2)	6	0.02
American (2,242)	2,242	6.35
Arab (13)	31	0.09
Arab (0)	0	<0.01
Egyptian (0)	0	<0.01
Iraqi (0)	0	<0.01
Jordanian (0)	0	<0.01
Lebanese (13)	31	0.09
Moroccan (0)	0	<0.01
Palestinian (0)	0	<0.01
Syrian (0)	0	<0.01
Other Arab (0)	0	<0.01
Armenian (0)	0	<0.01
Assyrian/Chaldean/Syriac (0)	0	<0.01
Australian (3)	7	0.02
Austrian (10)	76	0.22
Basque (0)	0	<0.01
Belgian (2)	8	0.02
Brazilian (18)	18	0.05
British (43)	121	0.34
Bulgarian (0)	0	<0.01
Cajun (0)	0	<0.01
Canadian (19)	49	0.14
Carpatho Rusyn (0)	0	<0.01
Celtic (0)	0	<0.01
Croatian (39)	43	0.12
Cypriot (0)	0	<0.01
Czech (10)	99	0.28
Czechoslovakian (28)	53	0.15
Danish (44)	170	0.48
Dutch (390)	1,725	4.89
Eastern European (9)	9	0.03
English (2,254)	6,403	18.13
Estonian (0)	0	<0.01
European (129)	155	0.44
Finnish (49)	65	0.18
French, ex. Basque (391)	1,487	4.21
French Canadian (139)	348	0.99
German (2,464)	8,012	22.69
German Russian (0)	0	<0.01
Greek (21)	44	0.12
Guyanese (8)	8	0.02
Hungarian (37)	149	0.42
Icelander (0)	0	<0.01
Iranian (3)	3	0.01
Irish (1,800)	6,509	18.43
Israeli (0)	0	<0.01
Italian (2,972)	6,175	17.49
Latvian (0)	0	<0.01
Lithuanian (21)	100	0.28
Luxemburger (0)	0	<0.01
Macedonian (0)	0	<0.01
Maltese (0)	0	<0.01
New Zealander (0)	0	<0.01
Northern European (0)	0	<0.01
Norwegian (29)	131	0.37
Pennsylvania German (299)	353	1.00

	Population	%
Polish (330)	1,065	3.02
Portuguese (7)	12	0.03
Romanian (11)	46	0.13
Russian (84)	155	0.44
Scandinavian (0)	13	0.04
Scotch-Irish (128)	496	1.40
Scottish (232)	782	2.21
Serbian (0)	0	<0.01
Slavic (2)	6	0.02
Slovak (14)	35	0.10
Slovene (0)	2	0.01
Soviet Union (0)	0	<0.01
Swedish (79)	213	0.60
Swiss (151)	371	1.05
Turkish (0)	0	<0.01
Ukrainian (84)	208	0.59
Welsh (42)	242	0.69
West Indian, ex. Hispanic (50)	97	0.27
Bahamian (0)	0	<0.01
Barbadian (0)	0	<0.01
Belizean (0)	0	<0.01
Bermudan (0)	0	<0.01
British West Indian (0)	0	<0.01
Dutch West Indian (0)	0	<0.01
Haitian (8)	17	0.05
Jamaican (25)	55	0.16
Trinidadian/Tobagonian (9)	17	0.05
U.S. Virgin Islander (0)	0	<0.01
West Indian (8)	8	0.02
Other West Indian (0)	0	<0.01
Yugoslavian (0)	0	<0.01

Hispanic Origin	Population	%
Hispanic or Latino (of any race)	952	2.70
Central American, ex. Mexican	68	0.19
Costa Rican	2	0.01
Guatemalan	13	0.04
Honduran	13	0.04
Nicaraguan	1	<0.01
Panamanian	15	0.04
Salvadoran	21	0.06
Other Central American	3	0.01
Cuban	30	0.09
Dominican Republic	61	0.17
Mexican	154	0.44
Puerto Rican	527	1.49
South American	24	0.07
Argentinean	1	<0.01
Bolivian	0	<0.01
Chilean	0	<0.01
Colombian	14	0.04
Ecuadorian	0	<0.01
Paraguayan	1	<0.01
Peruvian	6	0.02
Uruguayan	0	<0.01
Venezuelan	2	0.01
Other South American	0	<0.01
Other Hispanic or Latino	88	0.25

Race*	Population	%
African-American/Black (1,607)	1,812	5.14
Not Hispanic (1,513)	1,705	4.84
Hispanic (94)	107	0.30
American Indian/Alaska Native (104)	281	0.80
Not Hispanic (96)	269	0.76
Hispanic (8)	12	0.03
Alaska Athabascan (Ala. Nat.) (0)	0	<0.01
Aleut (Alaska Native) (0)	0	<0.01
Apache (0)	1	<0.01
Arapaho (0)	2	0.01
Blackfeet (0)	17	0.05
Canadian/French Am. Ind. (0)	0	<0.01
Central American Ind. (0)	0	<0.01
Cherokee (7)	34	0.10
Cheyenne (0)	0	<0.01
Chickasaw (0)	0	<0.01
Chippewa (2)	5	0.01
Choctaw (0)	0	<0.01
Colville (0)	0	<0.01

	Population	%
Comanche (0)	1	<0.01
Cree (1)	1	<0.01
Creek (0)	2	0.01
Crow (0)	0	<0.01
Delaware (0)	3	0.01
Hopi (0)	0	<0.01
Houma (0)	0	<0.01
Inupiat (Alaska Native) (0)	0	<0.01
Iroquois (12)	53	0.15
Kiowa (0)	0	<0.01
Lumbee (3)	3	0.01
Menominee (0)	1	<0.01
Mexican American Ind. (5)	7	0.02
Navajo (0)	0	<0.01
Osage (0)	0	<0.01
Ottawa (0)	2	0.01
Paiute (0)	0	<0.01
Pima (0)	0	<0.01
Potawatomi (0)	0	<0.01
Pueblo (0)	0	<0.01
Puget Sound Salish (0)	0	<0.01
Seminole (0)	0	<0.01
Shoshone (0)	1	<0.01
Sioux (7)	9	0.03
South American Ind. (1)	2	0.01
Spanish American Ind. (0)	0	<0.01
Tlingit-Haida (Alaska Native) (0)	0	<0.01
Tohono O'Odham (0)	0	<0.01
Tsimshian (Alaska Native) (0)	0	<0.01
Ute (0)	0	<0.01
Yakama (0)	0	<0.01
Yaqui (0)	0	<0.01
Yuman (0)	0	<0.01
Yup'ik (Alaska Native) (0)	0	<0.01
Asian (244)	291	0.83
Not Hispanic (238)	285	0.81
Hispanic (6)	6	0.02
Bangladeshi (0)	0	<0.01
Bhutanese (0)	0	<0.01
Burmese (0)	0	<0.01
Cambodian (0)	0	<0.01
Chinese, ex. Taiwanese (42)	49	0.14
Filipino (20)	31	0.09
Hmong (0)	0	<0.01
Indian (49)	67	0.19
Indonesian (0)	0	<0.01
Japanese (12)	19	0.05
Korean (38)	44	0.12
Laotian (18)	20	0.06
Malaysian (0)	0	<0.01
Nepalese (0)	0	<0.01
Pakistani (11)	14	0.04
Sri Lankan (6)	6	0.02
Taiwanese (7)	7	0.02
Thai (5)	5	0.01
Vietnamese (15)	15	0.04
Hawaii Native/Pacific Islander (2)	8	0.02
Not Hispanic (2)	8	0.02
Hispanic (0)	0	<0.01
Fijian (0)	0	<0.01
Guamanian/Chamorro (1)	1	<0.01
Marshallese (0)	0	<0.01
Native Hawaiian (0)	3	0.01
Samoan (1)	3	0.01
Tongan (0)	0	<0.01
White (32,591)	33,034	93.71
Not Hispanic (31,999)	32,386	91.87
Hispanic (592)	648	1.84

*Notes: † The Census 2010 population figure is used to calculate the percentages in the Hispanic Origin and Race categories. Ancestry percentages are based on the 2006-2010 American Community Survey population (not shown); ‡ Numbers in parentheses indicate the number of people reporting a single ancestry; * Numbers in parentheses indicate the number of persons reporting this race alone, not in combination with any other race; Please refer to the Explanation of Data for more information.*

St. Lawrence County

Population: 111,944

Ancestry	Population	%
Afghan (13)	13	0.01
African, Sub-Saharan (105)	182	0.16
African (54)	113	0.10
Cape Verdean (0)	0	<0.01
Ethiopian (4)	13	0.01
Ghanaian (0)	0	<0.01
Kenyan (15)	15	0.01
Liberian (0)	0	<0.01
Nigerian (17)	26	0.02
Senegalese (0)	0	<0.01
Sierra Leonean (0)	0	<0.01
Somalian (0)	0	<0.01
South African (0)	0	<0.01
Sudanese (2)	2	<0.01
Ugandan (0)	0	<0.01
Zimbabwean (13)	13	0.01
Other Sub-Saharan African (0)	0	<0.01
Albanian (43)	43	0.04
Alsatian (0)	0	<0.01
American (10,121)	10,121	9.05
Arab (162)	284	0.25
Arab (81)	100	0.09
Egyptian (11)	13	0.01
Iraqi (0)	0	<0.01
Jordanian (21)	21	0.02
Lebanese (44)	75	0.07
Moroccan (5)	44	0.04
Palestinian (0)	0	<0.01
Syrian (0)	0	<0.01
Other Arab (0)	31	0.03
Armenian (13)	22	0.02
Assyrian/Chaldean/Syriac (0)	0	<0.01
Australian (17)	17	0.02
Austrian (41)	114	0.10
Basque (0)	0	<0.01
Belgian (3)	64	0.06
Brazilian (4)	5	<0.01
British (289)	476	0.43
Bulgarian (73)	85	0.08
Cajun (0)	6	0.01
Canadian (862)	1,468	1.31
Carpatho Rusyn (0)	0	<0.01
Celtic (0)	0	<0.01
Croatian (23)	35	0.03
Cypriot (0)	0	<0.01
Czech (26)	167	0.15
Czechoslovakian (16)	54	0.05
Danish (22)	147	0.13
Dutch (594)	3,189	2.85
Eastern European (26)	71	0.06
English (7,608)	16,754	14.99
Estonian (13)	13	0.01
European (654)	676	0.60
Finnish (37)	158	0.14
French, ex. Basque (6,347)	18,278	16.35
French Canadian (3,623)	6,370	5.70
German (2,911)	11,355	10.16
German Russian (0)	0	<0.01
Greek (126)	286	0.26
Guyanese (19)	19	0.02
Hungarian (420)	956	0.86
Icelander (0)	13	0.01
Iranian (24)	49	0.04
Irish (6,686)	19,743	17.66
Israeli (30)	34	0.03
Italian (2,977)	8,006	7.16
Latvian (0)	14	0.01
Lithuanian (43)	175	0.16
Luxemburger (0)	9	0.01
Macedonian (0)	7	0.01
Maltese (0)	14	0.01
New Zealander (0)	0	<0.01
Northern European (15)	15	0.01
Norwegian (102)	470	0.42
Pennsylvania German (967)	994	0.89

Ancestry	Population	%
Polish (980)	3,024	2.71
Portuguese (40)	126	0.11
Romanian (63)	108	0.10
Russian (285)	713	0.64
Scandinavian (52)	184	0.16
Scotch-Irish (932)	2,320	2.08
Scottish (1,251)	4,260	3.81
Serbian (0)	0	<0.01
Slavic (0)	10	0.01
Slovak (69)	117	0.10
Slovene (4)	4	<0.01
Soviet Union (0)	0	<0.01
Swedish (93)	651	0.58
Swiss (42)	138	0.12
Turkish (49)	58	0.05
Ukrainian (139)	464	0.42
Welsh (212)	802	0.72
West Indian, ex. Hispanic (319)	387	0.35
Bahamian (14)	20	0.02
Barbadian (7)	13	0.01
Belizean (0)	0	<0.01
Bermudan (0)	0	<0.01
British West Indian (0)	14	0.01
Dutch West Indian (0)	0	<0.01
Haitian (88)	91	0.08
Jamaican (169)	207	0.19
Trinidadian/Tobagonian (0)	0	<0.01
U.S. Virgin Islander (0)	0	<0.01
West Indian (41)	42	0.04
Other West Indian (0)	0	<0.01
Yugoslavian (24)	83	0.07

Hispanic Origin	Population	%
Hispanic or Latino (of any race)	2,146	1.92
Central American, ex. Mexican	199	0.18
Costa Rican	21	0.02
Guatemalan	65	0.06
Honduran	27	0.02
Nicaraguan	3	<0.01
Panamanian	32	0.03
Salvadoran	49	0.04
Other Central American	2	<0.01
Cuban	67	0.06
Dominican Republic	205	0.18
Mexican	437	0.39
Puerto Rican	845	0.75
South American	137	0.12
Argentinean	13	0.01
Bolivian	2	<0.01
Chilean	6	0.01
Colombian	39	0.03
Ecuadorian	39	0.03
Paraguayan	4	<0.01
Peruvian	16	0.01
Uruguayan	9	0.01
Venezuelan	6	0.01
Other South American	3	<0.01
Other Hispanic or Latino	256	0.23

Race*	Population	%
African-American/Black (2,420)	2,895	2.59
Not Hispanic (2,259)	2,688	2.40
Hispanic (161)	207	0.18
American Indian/Alaska Native (1,135)	1,901	1.70
Not Hispanic (1,051)	1,756	1.57
Hispanic (84)	145	0.13
Alaska Athabascan (Ala. Nat.) (0)	3	<0.01
Aleut (Alaska Native) (0)	0	<0.01
Apache (2)	3	<0.01
Arapaho (1)	1	<0.01
Blackfeet (5)	25	0.02
Canadian/French Am. Ind. (12)	32	0.03
Central American Ind. (4)	4	<0.01
Cherokee (15)	88	0.08
Cheyenne (0)	0	<0.01
Chickasaw (0)	1	<0.01
Chippewa (8)	10	0.01
Choctaw (3)	13	0.01
Colville (0)	0	<0.01

Race*	Population	%
Comanche (0)	0	<0.01
Cree (0)	3	<0.01
Creek (2)	2	<0.01
Crow (0)	1	<0.01
Delaware (14)	19	0.02
Hopi (2)	4	<0.01
Houma (0)	0	<0.01
Inupiat (Alaska Native) (0)	1	<0.01
Iroquois (694)	979	0.87
Kiowa (1)	1	<0.01
Lumbee (1)	1	<0.01
Menominee (0)	0	<0.01
Mexican American Ind. (9)	11	0.01
Navajo (4)	7	0.01
Osage (0)	0	<0.01
Ottawa (1)	1	<0.01
Paiute (0)	0	<0.01
Pima (0)	0	<0.01
Potawatomi (0)	0	<0.01
Pueblo (0)	4	<0.01
Puget Sound Salish (0)	0	<0.01
Seminole (0)	4	<0.01
Shoshone (0)	0	<0.01
Sioux (4)	10	0.01
South American Ind. (13)	19	0.02
Spanish American Ind. (0)	1	<0.01
Tlingit-Haida (Alaska Native) (0)	0	<0.01
Tohono O'Odham (0)	0	<0.01
Tsimshian (Alaska Native) (0)	0	<0.01
Ute (0)	0	<0.01
Yakama (0)	0	<0.01
Yaqui (0)	0	<0.01
Yuman (0)	0	<0.01
Yup'ik (Alaska Native) (0)	3	<0.01
Asian (1,085)	1,366	1.22
Not Hispanic (1,074)	1,343	1.20
Hispanic (11)	23	0.02
Bangladeshi (6)	11	0.01
Bhutanese (0)	0	<0.01
Burmese (0)	1	<0.01
Cambodian (5)	5	<0.01
Chinese, ex. Taiwanese (331)	391	0.35
Filipino (89)	163	0.15
Hmong (2)	3	<0.01
Indian (283)	336	0.30
Indonesian (4)	10	0.01
Japanese (33)	62	0.06
Korean (152)	176	0.16
Laotian (4)	7	0.01
Malaysian (1)	7	0.01
Nepalese (5)	5	<0.01
Pakistani (39)	42	0.04
Sri Lankan (14)	14	0.01
Taiwanese (12)	19	0.02
Thai (13)	15	0.01
Vietnamese (42)	60	0.05
Hawaii Native/Pacific Islander (36)	95	0.08
Not Hispanic (26)	65	0.06
Hispanic (10)	30	0.03
Fijian (0)	0	<0.01
Guamanian/Chamorro (4)	8	0.01
Marshallese (0)	0	<0.01
Native Hawaiian (26)	50	0.04
Samoan (1)	5	<0.01
Tongan (0)	0	<0.01
White (105,064)	106,470	95.11
Not Hispanic (103,943)	105,195	93.97
Hispanic (1,121)	1,275	1.14

*Notes: † The Census 2010 population figure is used to calculate the percentages in the Hispanic Origin and Race categories. Ancestry percentages are based on the 2006-2010 American Community Survey population (not shown); ‡ Numbers in parentheses indicate the number of people reporting a single ancestry; * Numbers in parentheses indicate the number of persons reporting this race alone, not in combination with any other race; Please refer to the Explanation of Data for more information.*

Steuben County

Population: 98,990

Ancestry	Population	%
Afghan (0)	0	<0.01
African, Sub-Saharan (102)	115	0.12
African (79)	92	0.09
Cape Verdean (0)	0	<0.01
Ethiopian (23)	23	0.02
Ghanaian (0)	0	<0.01
Kenyan (0)	0	<0.01
Liberian (0)	0	<0.01
Nigerian (0)	0	<0.01
Senegalese (0)	0	<0.01
Sierra Leonean (0)	0	<0.01
Somalian (0)	0	<0.01
South African (0)	0	<0.01
Sudanese (0)	0	<0.01
Ugandan (0)	0	<0.01
Zimbabwean (0)	0	<0.01
Other Sub-Saharan African (0)	0	<0.01
Albanian (0)	0	<0.01
Alsatian (0)	12	0.01
American (8,840)	8,840	8.95
Arab (73)	105	0.11
Arab (0)	0	<0.01
Egyptian (0)	0	<0.01
Iraqi (0)	0	<0.01
Jordanian (0)	0	<0.01
Lebanese (41)	61	0.06
Moroccan (14)	14	0.01
Palestinian (0)	0	<0.01
Syrian (18)	30	0.03
Other Arab (0)	0	<0.01
Armenian (7)	19	0.02
Assyrian/Chaldean/Syriac (0)	0	<0.01
Australian (0)	4	<0.01
Austrian (28)	211	0.21
Basque (0)	13	0.01
Belgian (17)	74	0.07
Brazilian (11)	19	0.02
British (250)	488	0.49
Bulgarian (5)	9	0.01
Cajun (0)	0	<0.01
Canadian (81)	184	0.19
Carpatho Rusyn (23)	23	0.02
Celtic (0)	102	0.10
Croatian (0)	31	0.03
Cypriot (0)	0	<0.01
Czech (95)	366	0.37
Czechoslovakian (62)	83	0.08
Danish (106)	229	0.23
Dutch (886)	4,824	4.89
Eastern European (94)	96	0.10
English (5,831)	17,210	17.43
Estonian (5)	5	0.01
European (685)	701	0.71
Finnish (30)	118	0.12
French, ex. Basque (745)	3,810	3.86
French Canadian (323)	859	0.87
German (6,305)	22,942	23.24
German Russian (0)	0	<0.01
Greek (115)	200	0.20
Guyanese (31)	31	0.03
Hungarian (119)	343	0.35
Icelander (0)	0	<0.01
Iranian (0)	0	<0.01
Irish (6,137)	19,859	20.12
Israeli (23)	30	0.03
Italian (2,932)	8,609	8.72
Latvian (6)	42	0.04
Lithuanian (22)	94	0.10
Luxemburger (5)	5	0.01
Macedonian (0)	0	<0.01
Maltese (0)	0	<0.01
New Zealander (0)	0	<0.01
Northern European (70)	80	0.08
Norwegian (184)	541	0.55
Pennsylvania German (772)	1,134	1.15

Ancestry	Population	%
Polish (1,810)	5,161	5.23
Portuguese (54)	165	0.17
Romanian (24)	79	0.08
Russian (120)	456	0.46
Scandinavian (37)	82	0.08
Scotch-Irish (681)	1,744	1.77
Scottish (550)	2,433	2.46
Serbian (3)	13	0.01
Slavic (9)	21	0.02
Slovak (60)	161	0.16
Slovene (0)	18	0.02
Soviet Union (12)	12	0.01
Swedish (423)	1,367	1.38
Swiss (122)	317	0.32
Turkish (25)	46	0.05
Ukrainian (194)	456	0.46
Welsh (262)	1,328	1.35
West Indian, ex. Hispanic (120)	142	0.14
Bahamian (0)	0	<0.01
Barbadian (93)	93	0.09
Belizean (0)	0	<0.01
Bermudan (0)	0	<0.01
British West Indian (0)	0	<0.01
Dutch West Indian (0)	0	<0.01
Haitian (6)	6	0.01
Jamaican (21)	32	0.03
Trinidadian/Tobagonian (0)	0	<0.01
U.S. Virgin Islander (0)	0	<0.01
West Indian (0)	11	0.01
Other West Indian (0)	0	<0.01
Yugoslavian (0)	7	0.01

Hispanic Origin	Population	%
Hispanic or Latino (of any race)	1,371	1.38
Central American, ex. Mexican	109	0.11
Costa Rican	1	<0.01
Guatemalan	14	0.01
Honduran	43	0.04
Nicaraguan	10	0.01
Panamanian	13	0.01
Salvadoran	28	0.03
Other Central American	0	<0.01
Cuban	31	0.03
Dominican Republic	44	0.04
Mexican	432	0.44
Puerto Rican	500	0.51
South American	89	0.09
Argentinean	1	<0.01
Bolivian	3	<0.01
Chilean	8	0.01
Colombian	21	0.02
Ecuadorian	19	0.02
Paraguayan	7	0.01
Peruvian	20	0.02
Uruguayan	1	<0.01
Venezuelan	5	0.01
Other South American	4	<0.01
Other Hispanic or Latino	166	0.17

Race*	Population	%
African-American/Black (1,540)	2,158	2.18
Not Hispanic (1,487)	2,074	2.10
Hispanic (53)	84	0.08
American Indian/Alaska Native (230)	765	0.77
Not Hispanic (193)	683	0.69
Hispanic (37)	82	0.08
Alaska Athabascan (Ala. Nat.) (0)	0	<0.01
Aleut (Alaska Native) (0)	0	<0.01
Apache (1)	6	0.01
Arapaho (0)	0	<0.01
Blackfeet (11)	60	0.06
Canadian/French Am. Ind. (1)	4	<0.01
Central American Ind. (0)	0	<0.01
Cherokee (20)	100	0.10
Cheyenne (0)	2	<0.01
Chickasaw (0)	0	<0.01
Chippewa (2)	4	<0.01
Choctaw (3)	10	0.01
Colville (0)	0	<0.01

Race*	Population	%
Comanche (0)	0	<0.01
Cree (0)	1	<0.01
Creek (0)	4	<0.01
Crow (3)	4	<0.01
Delaware (1)	9	0.01
Hopi (0)	0	<0.01
Houma (0)	0	<0.01
Inupiat (Alaska Native) (3)	5	0.01
Iroquois (48)	144	0.15
Kiowa (0)	0	<0.01
Lumbee (0)	0	<0.01
Menominee (0)	0	<0.01
Mexican American Ind. (7)	7	0.01
Navajo (1)	3	<0.01
Osage (0)	0	<0.01
Ottawa (0)	0	<0.01
Paiute (0)	0	<0.01
Pima (0)	0	<0.01
Potawatomi (0)	0	<0.01
Pueblo (1)	1	<0.01
Puget Sound Salish (0)	0	<0.01
Seminole (0)	3	<0.01
Shoshone (0)	1	<0.01
Sioux (4)	19	0.02
South American Ind. (2)	7	0.01
Spanish American Ind. (1)	4	<0.01
Tlingit-Haida (Alaska Native) (5)	5	0.01
Tohono O'Odham (0)	0	<0.01
Tsimshian (Alaska Native) (0)	0	<0.01
Ute (0)	0	<0.01
Yakama (0)	0	<0.01
Yaqui (0)	0	<0.01
Yuman (0)	0	<0.01
Yup'ik (Alaska Native) (2)	2	<0.01
Asian (1,161)	1,352	1.37
Not Hispanic (1,151)	1,332	1.35
Hispanic (10)	20	0.02
Bangladeshi (12)	12	0.01
Bhutanese (0)	0	<0.01
Burmese (1)	1	<0.01
Cambodian (5)	5	0.01
Chinese, ex. Taiwanese (336)	382	0.39
Filipino (111)	161	0.16
Hmong (0)	0	<0.01
Indian (392)	438	0.44
Indonesian (6)	6	0.01
Japanese (43)	70	0.07
Korean (82)	108	0.11
Laotian (12)	14	0.01
Malaysian (2)	2	<0.01
Nepalese (12)	12	0.01
Pakistani (45)	49	0.05
Sri Lankan (4)	4	<0.01
Taiwanese (28)	28	0.03
Thai (12)	15	0.02
Vietnamese (25)	30	0.03
Hawaii Native/Pacific Islander (17)	48	0.05
Not Hispanic (14)	42	0.04
Hispanic (3)	6	0.01
Fijian (2)	2	<0.01
Guamanian/Chamorro (3)	6	0.01
Marshallese (2)	2	<0.01
Native Hawaiian (8)	24	0.02
Samoan (0)	1	<0.01
Tongan (0)	0	<0.01
White (94,315)	95,643	96.62
Not Hispanic (93,476)	94,659	95.62
Hispanic (839)	984	0.99

Notes: † The Census 2010 population figure is used to calculate the percentages in the Hispanic Origin and Race categories. Ancestry percentages are based on the 2006-2010 American Community Survey population (not shown); ‡ Numbers in parentheses indicate the number of people reporting a single ancestry; * Numbers in parentheses indicate the number of persons reporting this race alone, not in combination with any other race; Please refer to the Explanation of Data for more information.

Suffolk County

Population: 1,493,350

Ancestry	Population	%
Afghan (742)	823	0.06
African, Sub-Saharan (5,702)	7,192	0.49
African (3,798)	4,984	0.34
Cape Verdean (0)	9	<0.01
Ethiopian (21)	136	0.01
Ghanaian (192)	192	0.01
Kenyan (0)	0	<0.01
Liberian (309)	318	0.02
Nigerian (1,092)	1,220	0.08
Senegalese (0)	0	<0.01
Sierra Leonean (0)	0	<0.01
Somalian (0)	0	<0.01
South African (84)	102	0.01
Sudanese (0)	14	<0.01
Ugandan (0)	0	<0.01
Zimbabwean (0)	0	<0.01
Other Sub-Saharan African (206)	217	0.01
Albanian (614)	824	0.06
Alsatian (0)	39	<0.01
American (31,772)	31,772	2.14
Arab (3,411)	5,631	0.38
Arab (547)	751	0.05
Egyptian (1,042)	1,355	0.09
Iraqi (94)	283	0.02
Jordanian (233)	365	0.02
Lebanese (210)	787	0.05
Moroccan (426)	579	0.04
Palestinian (280)	302	0.02
Syrian (151)	574	0.04
Other Arab (428)	635	0.04
Armenian (1,000)	2,005	0.14
Assyrian/Chaldean/Syriac (0)	0	<0.01
Australian (165)	361	0.02
Austrian (1,961)	9,897	0.67
Basque (48)	76	0.01
Belgian (219)	1,025	0.07
Brazilian (1,446)	2,033	0.14
British (1,885)	3,939	0.27
Bulgarian (199)	296	0.02
Cajun (0)	42	<0.01
Canadian (1,220)	3,384	0.23
Carpatho Rusyn (46)	46	<0.01
Celtic (126)	220	0.01
Croatian (1,176)	2,492	0.17
Cypriot (146)	158	0.01
Czech (1,747)	8,389	0.57
Czechoslovakian (1,155)	2,893	0.20
Danish (865)	3,979	0.27
Dutch (2,110)	12,986	0.88
Eastern European (4,046)	4,484	0.30
English (15,317)	86,937	5.86
Estonian (193)	470	0.03
European (6,998)	7,658	0.52
Finnish (437)	1,833	0.12
French, ex. Basque (2,763)	25,117	1.69
French Canadian (2,013)	6,822	0.46
German (45,404)	248,603	16.77
German Russian (0)	40	<0.01
Greek (8,977)	19,268	1.30
Guyanese (1,567)	1,875	0.13
Hungarian (2,826)	12,736	0.86
Icelander (54)	150	0.01
Iranian (1,181)	1,367	0.09
Irish (87,385)	340,599	22.97
Israeli (740)	1,266	0.09
Italian (202,824)	427,711	28.85
Latvian (251)	567	0.04
Lithuanian (1,966)	5,680	0.38
Luxemburger (0)	36	<0.01
Macedonian (22)	44	<0.01
Maltese (405)	1,698	0.11
New Zealander (44)	57	<0.01
Northern European (525)	590	0.04
Norwegian (3,647)	14,773	1.00
Pennsylvania German (69)	107	0.01

Ancestry	Population	%
Polish (28,723)	89,379	6.03
Portuguese (4,698)	7,670	0.52
Romanian (1,746)	4,330	0.29
Russian (12,970)	39,198	2.64
Scandinavian (395)	1,115	0.08
Scotch-Irish (5,695)	15,856	1.07
Scottish (2,865)	16,692	1.13
Serbian (64)	237	0.02
Slavic (137)	601	0.04
Slovak (803)	1,936	0.13
Slovene (220)	324	0.02
Soviet Union (3)	3	<0.01
Swedish (1,863)	13,486	0.91
Swiss (672)	3,707	0.25
Turkish (3,736)	4,401	0.30
Ukrainian (2,645)	7,707	0.52
Welsh (687)	3,742	0.25
West Indian, ex. Hispanic (25,884)	31,391	2.12
Bahamian (66)	188	0.01
Barbadian (189)	308	0.02
Belizean (35)	47	<0.01
Bermudan (0)	34	<0.01
British West Indian (378)	665	0.04
Dutch West Indian (49)	49	<0.01
Haitian (11,652)	12,903	0.87
Jamaican (8,020)	10,122	0.68
Trinidadian/Tobagonian (2,485)	2,971	0.20
U.S. Virgin Islander (91)	154	0.01
West Indian (2,912)	3,916	0.26
Other West Indian (7)	34	<0.01
Yugoslavian (475)	1,653	0.11

Hispanic Origin	Population	%
Hispanic or Latino (of any race)	246,239	16.49
Central American, ex. Mexican	77,117	5.16
Costa Rican	1,656	0.11
Guatemalan	11,229	0.75
Honduran	9,563	0.64
Nicaraguan	683	0.05
Panamanian	1,203	0.08
Salvadoran	52,315	3.50
Other Central American	468	0.03
Cuban	4,310	0.29
Dominican Republic	21,751	1.46
Mexican	15,663	1.05
Puerto Rican	58,549	3.92
South American	44,731	3.00
Argentinean	2,260	0.15
Bolivian	565	0.04
Chilean	1,507	0.10
Colombian	13,846	0.93
Ecuadorian	17,638	1.18
Paraguayan	282	0.02
Peruvian	6,962	0.47
Uruguayan	474	0.03
Venezuelan	919	0.06
Other South American	278	0.02
Other Hispanic or Latino	24,118	1.62

Race*	Population	%
African-American/Black (111,224)	125,571	8.41
Not Hispanic (102,117)	112,207	7.51
Hispanic (9,107)	13,364	0.89
American Indian/Alaska Native (5,366)	12,535	0.84
Not Hispanic (2,906)	7,986	0.53
Hispanic (2,460)	4,549	0.30
Alaska Athabascan (Ala. Nat.) (1)	6	<0.01
Aleut (Alaska Native) (5)	7	<0.01
Apache (24)	65	<0.01
Arapaho (0)	3	<0.01
Blackfeet (44)	364	0.02
Canadian/French Am. Ind. (20)	43	<0.01
Central American Ind. (128)	195	0.01
Cherokee (246)	1,501	0.10
Cheyenne (2)	12	<0.01
Chickasaw (2)	11	<0.01
Chippewa (31)	63	<0.01
Choctaw (13)	90	0.01
Colville (0)	0	<0.01

	Population	%
Comanche (6)	24	<0.01
Cree (2)	9	<0.01
Creek (5)	58	<0.01
Crow (13)	23	<0.01
Delaware (7)	35	<0.01
Hopi (5)	11	<0.01
Houma (1)	3	<0.01
Inupiat (Alaska Native) (2)	5	<0.01
Iroquois (160)	388	0.03
Kiowa (1)	1	<0.01
Lumbee (14)	40	<0.01
Menominee (0)	0	<0.01
Mexican American Ind. (264)	376	0.03
Navajo (15)	45	<0.01
Osage (0)	5	<0.01
Ottawa (0)	5	<0.01
Paiute (2)	4	<0.01
Pima (1)	1	<0.01
Potawatomi (9)	13	<0.01
Pueblo (20)	29	<0.01
Puget Sound Salish (5)	7	<0.01
Seminole (12)	63	<0.01
Shoshone (0)	7	<0.01
Sioux (36)	109	0.01
South American Ind. (332)	629	0.04
Spanish American Ind. (133)	182	0.01
Tlingit-Haida (Alaska Native) (5)	14	<0.01
Tohono O'Odham (0)	1	<0.01
Tsimshian (Alaska Native) (0)	0	<0.01
Ute (0)	2	<0.01
Yakama (0)	1	<0.01
Yaqui (2)	7	<0.01
Yuman (1)	2	<0.01
Yup'ik (Alaska Native) (0)	0	<0.01
Asian (50,972)	59,859	4.01
Not Hispanic (50,295)	57,980	3.88
Hispanic (677)	1,879	0.13
Bangladeshi (1,243)	1,469	0.10
Bhutanese (3)	3	<0.01
Burmese (61)	80	0.01
Cambodian (53)	71	<0.01
Chinese, ex. Taiwanese (11,537)	13,502	0.90
Filipino (5,202)	6,881	0.46
Hmong (1)	4	<0.01
Indian (15,975)	18,167	1.22
Indonesian (117)	174	0.01
Japanese (904)	1,673	0.11
Korean (5,627)	6,461	0.43
Laotian (84)	107	0.01
Malaysian (25)	55	<0.01
Nepalese (69)	72	<0.01
Pakistani (5,426)	5,997	0.40
Sri Lankan (149)	183	0.01
Taiwanese (470)	550	0.04
Thai (401)	553	0.04
Vietnamese (1,565)	1,835	0.12
Hawaii Native/Pacific Islander (495)	1,606	0.11
Not Hispanic (275)	939	0.06
Hispanic (220)	667	0.04
Fijian (3)	16	<0.01
Guamanian/Chamorro (208)	263	0.02
Marshallese (1)	1	<0.01
Native Hawaiian (105)	331	0.02
Samoan (25)	59	<0.01
Tongan (1)	5	<0.01
White (1,206,297)	1,234,863	82.69
Not Hispanic (1,068,728)	1,083,973	72.59
Hispanic (137,569)	150,890	10.10

Notes: † The Census 2010 population figure is used to calculate the percentages in the Hispanic Origin and Race categories. Ancestry percentages are based on the 2006-2010 American Community Survey population (not shown); ‡ Numbers in parentheses indicate the number of people reporting a single ancestry; * Numbers in parentheses indicate the number of persons reporting this race alone, not in combination with any other race; Please refer to the Explanation of Data for more information.

Sullivan County

Population: 77,547

Ancestry	Population	%
Afghan (0)	0	<0.01
African, Sub-Saharan (208)	232	0.30
African (84)	108	0.14
Cape Verdean (0)	0	<0.01
Ethiopian (0)	0	<0.01
Ghanaian (16)	16	0.02
Kenyan (9)	9	0.01
Liberian (18)	18	0.02
Nigerian (34)	34	0.04
Senegalese (0)	0	<0.01
Sierra Leonean (0)	0	<0.01
Somalian (0)	0	<0.01
South African (0)	0	<0.01
Sudanese (0)	0	<0.01
Ugandan (0)	0	<0.01
Zimbabwean (40)	40	0.05
Other Sub-Saharan African (7)	7	0.01
Albanian (59)	71	0.09
Alsatian (0)	0	<0.01
American (4,050)	4,050	5.22
Arab (251)	350	0.45
Arab (5)	9	0.01
Egyptian (102)	145	0.19
Iraqi (0)	0	<0.01
Jordanian (117)	137	0.18
Lebanese (2)	21	0.03
Moroccan (0)	0	<0.01
Palestinian (0)	0	<0.01
Syrian (12)	25	0.03
Other Arab (13)	13	0.02
Armenian (24)	26	0.03
Assyrian/Chaldean/Syriac (0)	0	<0.01
Australian (17)	81	0.10
Austrian (130)	374	0.48
Basque (0)	0	<0.01
Belgian (18)	18	0.02
Brazilian (53)	86	0.11
British (84)	183	0.24
Bulgarian (0)	0	<0.01
Cajun (0)	0	<0.01
Canadian (131)	386	0.50
Carpatho Rusyn (0)	0	<0.01
Celtic (14)	38	0.05
Croatian (65)	154	0.20
Cypriot (0)	0	<0.01
Czech (84)	390	0.50
Czechoslovakian (127)	308	0.40
Danish (65)	251	0.32
Dutch (428)	2,234	2.88
Eastern European (227)	299	0.39
English (1,413)	5,957	7.67
Estonian (8)	16	0.02
European (325)	410	0.53
Finnish (35)	64	0.08
French, ex. Basque (450)	2,130	2.74
French Canadian (120)	393	0.51
German (4,582)	14,760	19.01
German Russian (0)	0	<0.01
Greek (285)	449	0.58
Guyanese (35)	35	0.05
Hungarian (318)	1,183	1.52
Icelander (0)	0	<0.01
Iranian (94)	100	0.13
Irish (4,513)	15,183	19.56
Israeli (30)	58	0.07
Italian (4,173)	10,325	13.30
Latvian (34)	60	0.08
Lithuanian (158)	381	0.49
Luxemburger (0)	0	<0.01
Macedonian (53)	64	0.08
Maltese (0)	0	<0.01
New Zealander (0)	18	0.02
Northern European (33)	66	0.09
Norwegian (355)	918	1.18
Pennsylvania German (26)	35	0.05

Ancestry (cont.)	Population	%
Polish (1,384)	4,248	5.47
Portuguese (100)	280	0.36
Romanian (110)	221	0.28
Russian (1,015)	2,172	2.80
Scandinavian (49)	115	0.15
Scotch-Irish (296)	812	1.05
Scottish (291)	1,158	1.49
Serbian (24)	24	0.03
Slavic (0)	22	0.03
Slovak (92)	181	0.23
Slovene (0)	10	0.01
Soviet Union (0)	0	<0.01
Swedish (219)	595	0.77
Swiss (186)	430	0.55
Turkish (39)	86	0.11
Ukrainian (453)	989	1.27
Welsh (128)	600	0.77
West Indian, ex. Hispanic (723)	1,131	1.46
Bahamian (0)	0	<0.01
Barbadian (77)	149	0.19
Belizean (0)	0	<0.01
Bermudan (0)	0	<0.01
British West Indian (16)	16	0.02
Dutch West Indian (0)	55	0.07
Haitian (73)	73	0.09
Jamaican (298)	415	0.53
Trinidadian/Tobagonian (176)	287	0.37
U.S. Virgin Islander (0)	0	<0.01
West Indian (83)	136	0.18
Other West Indian (0)	0	<0.01
Yugoslavian (107)	152	0.20

Hispanic Origin	Population	%
Hispanic or Latino (of any race)	10,554	13.61
Central American, ex. Mexican	1,461	1.88
Costa Rican	46	0.06
Guatemalan	223	0.29
Honduran	575	0.74
Nicaraguan	45	0.06
Panamanian	50	0.06
Salvadoran	516	0.67
Other Central American	6	0.01
Cuban	297	0.38
Dominican Republic	448	0.58
Mexican	1,385	1.79
Puerto Rican	5,309	6.85
South American	866	1.12
Argentinean	68	0.09
Bolivian	9	0.01
Chilean	46	0.06
Colombian	398	0.51
Ecuadorian	144	0.19
Paraguayan	8	0.01
Peruvian	153	0.20
Uruguayan	14	0.02
Venezuelan	13	0.02
Other South American	13	0.02
Other Hispanic or Latino	788	1.02

Race*	Population	%
African-American/Black (7,039)	8,207	10.58
Not Hispanic (6,349)	7,180	9.26
Hispanic (690)	1,027	1.32
American Indian/Alaska Native (354)	950	1.23
Not Hispanic (228)	653	0.84
Hispanic (126)	297	0.38
Alaska Athabascan (Ala. Nat.) (0)	0	<0.01
Aleut (Alaska Native) (0)	0	<0.01
Apache (5)	12	0.02
Arapaho (0)	0	<0.01
Blackfeet (10)	51	0.07
Canadian/French Am. Ind. (1)	3	<0.01
Central American Ind. (3)	4	0.01
Cherokee (24)	147	0.19
Cheyenne (0)	0	<0.01
Chickasaw (0)	0	<0.01
Chippewa (3)	8	0.01
Choctaw (1)	7	0.01
Colville (0)	0	<0.01

Race* (cont.)	Population	%
Comanche (0)	0	<0.01
Cree (0)	3	<0.01
Creek (3)	4	0.01
Crow (1)	3	<0.01
Delaware (30)	60	0.08
Hopi (0)	0	<0.01
Houma (2)	2	<0.01
Inupiat (Alaska Native) (1)	1	<0.01
Iroquois (21)	47	0.06
Kiowa (0)	0	<0.01
Lumbee (0)	0	<0.01
Menominee (0)	0	<0.01
Mexican American Ind. (24)	35	0.05
Navajo (2)	4	0.01
Osage (0)	0	<0.01
Ottawa (0)	0	<0.01
Paiute (0)	0	<0.01
Pima (2)	2	<0.01
Potawatomi (0)	0	<0.01
Pueblo (0)	0	<0.01
Puget Sound Salish (0)	0	<0.01
Seminole (0)	1	<0.01
Shoshone (0)	0	<0.01
Sioux (1)	4	0.01
South American Ind. (16)	25	0.03
Spanish American Ind. (5)	11	0.01
Tlingit-Haida (Alaska Native) (0)	0	<0.01
Tohono O'Odham (1)	2	<0.01
Tsimshian (Alaska Native) (0)	0	<0.01
Ute (0)	0	<0.01
Yakama (0)	0	<0.01
Yaqui (0)	0	<0.01
Yuman (0)	0	<0.01
Yup'ik (Alaska Native) (0)	0	<0.01
Asian (1,075)	1,395	1.80
Not Hispanic (1,033)	1,311	1.69
Hispanic (42)	84	0.11
Bangladeshi (10)	16	0.02
Bhutanese (0)	0	<0.01
Burmese (3)	3	<0.01
Cambodian (3)	3	<0.01
Chinese, ex. Taiwanese (223)	278	0.36
Filipino (142)	212	0.27
Hmong (0)	0	<0.01
Indian (346)	409	0.53
Indonesian (5)	8	0.01
Japanese (34)	66	0.09
Korean (166)	207	0.27
Laotian (4)	5	0.01
Malaysian (0)	0	<0.01
Nepalese (1)	1	<0.01
Pakistani (48)	58	0.07
Sri Lankan (1)	3	<0.01
Taiwanese (6)	8	0.01
Thai (3)	9	0.01
Vietnamese (24)	35	0.05
Hawaii Native/Pacific Islander (24)	87	0.11
Not Hispanic (14)	55	0.07
Hispanic (10)	32	0.04
Fijian (0)	0	<0.01
Guamanian/Chamorro (13)	19	0.02
Marshallese (0)	0	<0.01
Native Hawaiian (2)	11	0.01
Samoan (6)	15	0.02
Tongan (0)	0	<0.01
White (63,560)	65,476	84.43
Not Hispanic (57,780)	59,010	76.10
Hispanic (5,780)	6,466	8.34

Notes: † The Census 2010 population figure is used to calculate the percentages in the Hispanic Origin and Race categories. Ancestry percentages are based on the 2006-2010 American Community Survey population (not shown); ‡ Numbers in parentheses indicate the number of people reporting a single ancestry; * Numbers in parentheses indicate the number of persons reporting this race alone, not in combination with any other race; Please refer to the Explanation of Data for more information.

Tioga County
Population: 51,125

Ancestry	Population	%
Afghan (0)	0	<0.01
African, Sub-Saharan (36)	40	0.08
African (11)	15	0.03
Cape Verdean (0)	0	<0.01
Ethiopian (0)	0	<0.01
Ghanaian (0)	0	<0.01
Kenyan (0)	0	<0.01
Liberian (0)	0	<0.01
Nigerian (0)	0	<0.01
Senegalese (0)	0	<0.01
Sierra Leonean (0)	0	<0.01
Somalian (0)	0	<0.01
South African (25)	25	0.05
Sudanese (0)	0	<0.01
Ugandan (0)	0	<0.01
Zimbabwean (0)	0	<0.01
Other Sub-Saharan African (0)	0	<0.01
Albanian (0)	0	<0.01
Alsatian (19)	22	0.04
American (4,114)	4,114	8.01
Arab (76)	115	0.22
Arab (0)	0	<0.01
Egyptian (16)	16	0.03
Iraqi (0)	0	<0.01
Jordanian (0)	0	<0.01
Lebanese (60)	99	0.19
Moroccan (0)	0	<0.01
Palestinian (0)	0	<0.01
Syrian (0)	0	<0.01
Other Arab (0)	0	<0.01
Armenian (0)	28	0.05
Assyrian/Chaldean/Syriac (0)	0	<0.01
Australian (0)	0	<0.01
Austrian (43)	129	0.25
Basque (0)	34	0.07
Belgian (0)	20	0.04
Brazilian (34)	34	0.07
British (86)	123	0.24
Bulgarian (0)	0	<0.01
Cajun (0)	0	<0.01
Canadian (72)	170	0.33
Carpatho Rusyn (0)	0	<0.01
Celtic (0)	16	0.03
Croatian (20)	20	0.04
Cypriot (0)	0	<0.01
Czech (148)	382	0.74
Czechoslovakian (27)	122	0.24
Danish (31)	123	0.24
Dutch (419)	2,091	4.07
Eastern European (0)	0	<0.01
English (3,529)	9,618	18.72
Estonian (0)	0	<0.01
European (598)	624	1.21
Finnish (208)	305	0.59
French, ex. Basque (306)	1,803	3.51
French Canadian (143)	395	0.77
German (3,822)	12,009	23.37
German Russian (0)	0	<0.01
Greek (67)	198	0.39
Guyanese (0)	0	<0.01
Hungarian (241)	430	0.84
Icelander (0)	0	<0.01
Iranian (0)	0	<0.01
Irish (2,587)	9,130	17.77
Israeli (0)	0	<0.01
Italian (1,844)	4,941	9.62
Latvian (28)	61	0.12
Lithuanian (35)	235	0.46
Luxemburger (0)	0	<0.01
Macedonian (0)	0	<0.01
Maltese (0)	16	0.03
New Zealander (0)	0	<0.01
Northern European (110)	110	0.21
Norwegian (120)	344	0.67
Pennsylvania German (242)	441	0.86

Ancestry	Population	%
Polish (881)	2,677	5.21
Portuguese (26)	67	0.13
Romanian (20)	50	0.10
Russian (365)	838	1.63
Scandinavian (17)	45	0.09
Scotch-Irish (338)	858	1.67
Scottish (304)	1,298	2.53
Serbian (0)	0	<0.01
Slavic (22)	81	0.16
Slovak (202)	549	1.07
Slovene (47)	50	0.10
Soviet Union (0)	0	<0.01
Swedish (196)	882	1.72
Swiss (56)	163	0.32
Turkish (10)	18	0.04
Ukrainian (203)	422	0.82
Welsh (156)	1,226	2.39
West Indian, ex. Hispanic (8)	17	0.03
Bahamian (0)	0	<0.01
Barbadian (0)	0	<0.01
Belizean (0)	0	<0.01
Bermudan (0)	0	<0.01
British West Indian (0)	0	<0.01
Dutch West Indian (0)	0	<0.01
Haitian (0)	0	<0.01
Jamaican (8)	8	0.02
Trinidadian/Tobagonian (0)	0	<0.01
U.S. Virgin Islander (0)	0	<0.01
West Indian (0)	9	0.02
Other West Indian (0)	0	<0.01
Yugoslavian (0)	13	0.03

Hispanic Origin	Population	%
Hispanic or Latino (of any race)	694	1.36
Central American, ex. Mexican	53	0.10
Costa Rican	3	0.01
Guatemalan	7	0.01
Honduran	1	<0.01
Nicaraguan	4	0.01
Panamanian	11	0.02
Salvadoran	27	0.05
Other Central American	0	<0.01
Cuban	28	0.05
Dominican Republic	22	0.04
Mexican	169	0.33
Puerto Rican	271	0.53
South American	73	0.14
Argentinean	4	0.01
Bolivian	1	<0.01
Chilean	6	0.01
Colombian	19	0.04
Ecuadorian	24	0.05
Paraguayan	1	<0.01
Peruvian	8	0.02
Uruguayan	4	0.01
Venezuelan	3	0.01
Other South American	3	0.01
Other Hispanic or Latino	78	0.15

Race*	Population	%
African-American/Black (375)	581	1.14
Not Hispanic (349)	532	1.04
Hispanic (26)	49	0.10
American Indian/Alaska Native (86)	306	0.60
Not Hispanic (73)	274	0.54
Hispanic (13)	32	0.06
Alaska Athabascan (Ala. Nat.) (0)	0	<0.01
Aleut (Alaska Native) (0)	0	<0.01
Apache (0)	0	<0.01
Arapaho (0)	0	<0.01
Blackfeet (2)	16	0.03
Canadian/French Am. Ind. (1)	5	0.01
Central American Ind. (0)	0	<0.01
Cherokee (5)	42	0.08
Cheyenne (0)	2	<0.01
Chickasaw (0)	0	<0.01
Chippewa (0)	1	<0.01
Choctaw (0)	1	<0.01
Colville (0)	0	<0.01

Race*	Population	%
Comanche (1)	1	<0.01
Cree (0)	0	<0.01
Creek (0)	4	0.01
Crow (1)	1	<0.01
Delaware (3)	7	0.01
Hopi (1)	1	<0.01
Houma (0)	0	<0.01
Inupiat (Alaska Native) (0)	0	<0.01
Iroquois (15)	61	0.12
Kiowa (0)	0	<0.01
Lumbee (0)	1	<0.01
Menominee (0)	0	<0.01
Mexican American Ind. (3)	5	0.01
Navajo (6)	15	0.03
Osage (0)	0	<0.01
Ottawa (0)	0	<0.01
Paiute (0)	0	<0.01
Pima (0)	0	<0.01
Potawatomi (0)	0	<0.01
Pueblo (0)	0	<0.01
Puget Sound Salish (0)	0	<0.01
Seminole (0)	0	<0.01
Shoshone (0)	0	<0.01
Sioux (2)	11	0.02
South American Ind. (1)	3	0.01
Spanish American Ind. (0)	0	<0.01
Tlingit-Haida (Alaska Native) (0)	0	<0.01
Tohono O'Odham (1)	1	<0.01
Tsimshian (Alaska Native) (0)	0	<0.01
Ute (0)	0	<0.01
Yakama (0)	0	<0.01
Yaqui (0)	0	<0.01
Yuman (0)	0	<0.01
Yup'ik (Alaska Native) (0)	0	<0.01
Asian (372)	475	0.93
Not Hispanic (371)	465	0.91
Hispanic (1)	10	0.02
Bangladeshi (0)	0	<0.01
Bhutanese (0)	0	<0.01
Burmese (0)	0	<0.01
Cambodian (0)	0	<0.01
Chinese, ex. Taiwanese (107)	119	0.23
Filipino (35)	67	0.13
Hmong (0)	0	<0.01
Indian (83)	93	0.18
Indonesian (0)	0	<0.01
Japanese (25)	47	0.09
Korean (35)	46	0.09
Laotian (0)	2	<0.01
Malaysian (0)	0	<0.01
Nepalese (0)	0	<0.01
Pakistani (33)	33	0.06
Sri Lankan (0)	0	<0.01
Taiwanese (9)	11	0.02
Thai (3)	4	0.01
Vietnamese (35)	43	0.08
Hawaii Native/Pacific Islander (15)	40	0.08
Not Hispanic (12)	35	0.07
Hispanic (3)	5	0.01
Fijian (1)	1	<0.01
Guamanian/Chamorro (6)	9	0.02
Marshallese (0)	0	<0.01
Native Hawaiian (6)	11	0.02
Samoan (0)	1	<0.01
Tongan (0)	0	<0.01
White (49,556)	50,101	98.00
Not Hispanic (49,105)	49,578	96.97
Hispanic (451)	523	1.02

Tompkins County

Population: 101,564

Ancestry	Population	%
Afghan (15)	15	0.01
African, Sub-Saharan (546)	631	0.63
African (254)	301	0.30
Cape Verdean (0)	0	<0.01
Ethiopian (0)	0	<0.01
Ghanaian (59)	59	0.06
Kenyan (20)	20	0.02
Liberian (44)	44	0.04
Nigerian (56)	56	0.06
Senegalese (0)	0	<0.01
Sierra Leonean (22)	22	0.02
Somalian (0)	0	<0.01
South African (31)	35	0.03
Sudanese (0)	13	0.01
Ugandan (24)	24	0.02
Zimbabwean (13)	24	0.02
Other Sub-Saharan African (23)	33	0.03
Albanian (0)	0	<0.01
Alsatian (0)	0	<0.01
American (4,786)	4,786	4.76
Arab (429)	571	0.57
Arab (85)	85	0.08
Egyptian (88)	88	0.09
Iraqi (0)	0	<0.01
Jordanian (14)	14	0.01
Lebanese (39)	113	0.11
Moroccan (79)	79	0.08
Palestinian (72)	72	0.07
Syrian (52)	92	0.09
Other Arab (0)	28	0.03
Armenian (138)	280	0.28
Assyrian/Chaldean/Syriac (0)	0	<0.01
Australian (24)	30	0.03
Austrian (53)	496	0.49
Basque (0)	0	<0.01
Belgian (41)	81	0.08
Brazilian (58)	116	0.12
British (381)	1,040	1.03
Bulgarian (81)	129	0.13
Cajun (14)	14	0.01
Canadian (309)	594	0.59
Carpatho Rusyn (0)	0	<0.01
Celtic (6)	22	0.02
Croatian (77)	205	0.20
Cypriot (0)	16	0.02
Czech (206)	714	0.71
Czechoslovakian (83)	191	0.19
Danish (43)	266	0.26
Dutch (586)	2,655	2.64
Eastern European (429)	525	0.52
English (3,791)	13,741	13.66
Estonian (36)	50	0.05
European (1,537)	1,682	1.67
Finnish (248)	687	0.68
French, ex. Basque (512)	3,128	3.11
French Canadian (330)	799	0.79
German (3,464)	16,093	16.00
German Russian (0)	0	<0.01
Greek (211)	512	0.51
Guyanese (97)	119	0.12
Hungarian (383)	1,004	1.00
Icelander (14)	29	0.03
Iranian (99)	216	0.21
Irish (3,221)	14,348	14.26
Israeli (145)	194	0.19
Italian (3,055)	8,635	8.58
Latvian (0)	70	0.07
Lithuanian (202)	486	0.48
Luxemburger (10)	24	0.02
Macedonian (0)	0	<0.01
Maltese (0)	0	<0.01
New Zealander (0)	45	0.04
Northern European (163)	210	0.21
Norwegian (215)	873	0.87
Pennsylvania German (124)	377	0.37

Ancestry	Population	%
Polish (1,003)	3,827	3.80
Portuguese (0)	103	0.10
Romanian (43)	148	0.15
Russian (1,015)	2,382	2.37
Scandinavian (88)	225	0.22
Scotch-Irish (635)	1,729	1.72
Scottish (505)	2,480	2.46
Serbian (16)	71	0.07
Slavic (55)	106	0.11
Slovak (94)	252	0.25
Slovene (6)	24	0.02
Soviet Union (0)	0	<0.01
Swedish (245)	1,517	1.51
Swiss (159)	559	0.56
Turkish (98)	137	0.14
Ukrainian (291)	595	0.59
Welsh (183)	1,158	1.15
West Indian, ex. Hispanic (211)	328	0.33
Bahamian (0)	0	<0.01
Barbadian (0)	10	0.01
Belizean (0)	0	<0.01
Bermudan (0)	0	<0.01
British West Indian (12)	21	0.02
Dutch West Indian (32)	32	0.03
Haitian (103)	135	0.13
Jamaican (27)	72	0.07
Trinidadian/Tobagonian (0)	9	0.01
U.S. Virgin Islander (0)	0	<0.01
West Indian (37)	49	0.05
Other West Indian (0)	0	<0.01
Yugoslavian (64)	87	0.09

Hispanic Origin	Population	%
Hispanic or Latino (of any race)	4,264	4.20
Central American, ex. Mexican	314	0.31
Costa Rican	43	0.04
Guatemalan	115	0.11
Honduran	27	0.03
Nicaraguan	40	0.04
Panamanian	27	0.03
Salvadoran	61	0.06
Other Central American	1	<0.01
Cuban	253	0.25
Dominican Republic	264	0.26
Mexican	909	0.90
Puerto Rican	1,167	1.15
South American	824	0.81
Argentinean	105	0.10
Bolivian	29	0.03
Chilean	88	0.09
Colombian	230	0.23
Ecuadorian	98	0.10
Paraguayan	8	0.01
Peruvian	144	0.14
Uruguayan	17	0.02
Venezuelan	94	0.09
Other South American	11	0.01
Other Hispanic or Latino	533	0.52

Race*	Population	%
African-American/Black (4,020)	5,411	5.33
Not Hispanic (3,773)	4,969	4.89
Hispanic (247)	442	0.44
American Indian/Alaska Native (360)	1,159	1.14
Not Hispanic (270)	952	0.94
Hispanic (90)	207	0.20
Alaska Athabascan (Ala. Nat.) (1)	2	<0.01
Aleut (Alaska Native) (0)	0	<0.01
Apache (6)	16	0.02
Arapaho (0)	0	<0.01
Blackfeet (7)	53	0.05
Canadian/French Am. Ind. (2)	8	0.01
Central American Ind. (4)	9	0.01
Cherokee (37)	167	0.16
Cheyenne (0)	2	<0.01
Chickasaw (0)	4	<0.01
Chippewa (5)	20	0.02
Choctaw (1)	15	0.01
Colville (0)	0	<0.01

	Population	%
Comanche (0)	1	<0.01
Cree (0)	3	<0.01
Creek (3)	11	0.01
Crow (1)	1	<0.01
Delaware (5)	20	0.02
Hopi (0)	1	<0.01
Houma (0)	0	<0.01
Inupiat (Alaska Native) (0)	0	<0.01
Iroquois (52)	159	0.16
Kiowa (0)	1	<0.01
Lumbee (5)	5	<0.01
Menominee (0)	1	<0.01
Mexican American Ind. (18)	30	0.03
Navajo (4)	14	0.01
Osage (1)	2	<0.01
Ottawa (4)	4	<0.01
Paiute (0)	0	<0.01
Pima (0)	1	<0.01
Potawatomi (1)	1	<0.01
Pueblo (1)	1	<0.01
Puget Sound Salish (2)	2	<0.01
Seminole (7)	15	0.01
Shoshone (0)	0	<0.01
Sioux (14)	28	0.03
South American Ind. (29)	51	0.05
Spanish American Ind. (0)	1	<0.01
Tlingit-Haida (Alaska Native) (0)	0	<0.01
Tohono O'Odham (0)	0	<0.01
Tsimshian (Alaska Native) (0)	0	<0.01
Ute (0)	0	<0.01
Yakama (0)	0	<0.01
Yaqui (2)	7	0.01
Yuman (0)	0	<0.01
Yup'ik (Alaska Native) (0)	1	<0.01
Asian (8,737)	9,963	9.81
Not Hispanic (8,680)	9,848	9.70
Hispanic (57)	115	0.11
Bangladeshi (32)	34	0.03
Bhutanese (0)	0	<0.01
Burmese (126)	133	0.13
Cambodian (120)	137	0.13
Chinese, ex. Taiwanese (3,581)	4,058	4.00
Filipino (154)	314	0.31
Hmong (0)	0	<0.01
Indian (1,435)	1,610	1.59
Indonesian (54)	81	0.08
Japanese (285)	535	0.53
Korean (1,722)	1,861	1.83
Laotian (52)	80	0.08
Malaysian (17)	34	0.03
Nepalese (34)	39	0.04
Pakistani (117)	135	0.13
Sri Lankan (24)	32	0.03
Taiwanese (319)	382	0.38
Thai (123)	158	0.16
Vietnamese (236)	297	0.29
Hawaii Native/Pacific Islander (45)	160	0.16
Not Hispanic (40)	141	0.14
Hispanic (5)	19	0.02
Fijian (1)	7	0.01
Guamanian/Chamorro (8)	23	0.02
Marshallese (0)	0	<0.01
Native Hawaiian (14)	43	0.04
Samoan (9)	28	0.03
Tongan (3)	3	<0.01
White (83,941)	86,872	85.53
Not Hispanic (81,490)	84,038	82.74
Hispanic (2,451)	2,834	2.79

Notes: † The Census 2010 population figure is used to calculate the percentages in the Hispanic Origin and Race categories. Ancestry percentages are based on the 2006-2010 American Community Survey population (not shown); ‡ Numbers in parentheses indicate the number of people reporting a single ancestry; * Numbers in parentheses indicate the number of persons reporting this race alone, not in combination with any other race; Please refer to the Explanation of Data for more information.

Ulster County
Population: 182,493

Ancestry	Population	%
Afghan (29)	29	0.02
African, Sub-Saharan (309)	450	0.25
African (186)	291	0.16
Cape Verdean (0)	0	<0.01
Ethiopian (37)	73	0.04
Ghanaian (0)	0	<0.01
Kenyan (0)	0	<0.01
Liberian (0)	0	<0.01
Nigerian (75)	75	0.04
Senegalese (0)	0	<0.01
Sierra Leonean (0)	0	<0.01
Somalian (0)	0	<0.01
South African (0)	0	<0.01
Sudanese (0)	0	<0.01
Ugandan (0)	0	<0.01
Zimbabwean (0)	0	<0.01
Other Sub-Saharan African (11)	11	0.01
Albanian (180)	180	0.10
Alsatian (0)	20	0.01
American (12,589)	12,589	6.89
Arab (209)	460	0.25
Arab (0)	22	0.01
Egyptian (96)	165	0.09
Iraqi (0)	0	<0.01
Jordanian (0)	0	<0.01
Lebanese (75)	180	0.10
Moroccan (0)	0	<0.01
Palestinian (11)	41	0.02
Syrian (0)	25	0.01
Other Arab (27)	27	0.01
Armenian (71)	127	0.07
Assyrian/Chaldean/Syriac (8)	8	<0.01
Australian (18)	87	0.05
Austrian (169)	1,512	0.83
Basque (27)	50	0.03
Belgian (62)	279	0.15
Brazilian (178)	263	0.14
British (319)	898	0.49
Bulgarian (0)	78	0.04
Cajun (0)	0	<0.01
Canadian (192)	523	0.29
Carpatho Rusyn (0)	10	0.01
Celtic (25)	50	0.03
Croatian (147)	234	0.13
Cypriot (8)	8	<0.01
Czech (213)	801	0.44
Czechoslovakian (98)	286	0.16
Danish (119)	734	0.40
Dutch (1,775)	9,680	5.30
Eastern European (808)	877	0.48
English (3,859)	18,135	9.92
Estonian (0)	0	<0.01
European (3,396)	3,517	1.92
Finnish (112)	409	0.22
French, ex. Basque (1,080)	7,193	3.94
French Canadian (413)	1,291	0.71
German (7,795)	35,911	19.65
German Russian (0)	0	<0.01
Greek (429)	1,460	0.80
Guyanese (185)	185	0.10
Hungarian (486)	1,824	1.00
Icelander (0)	15	0.01
Iranian (58)	70	0.04
Irish (9,720)	38,535	21.08
Israeli (53)	114	0.06
Italian (14,757)	35,905	19.64
Latvian (40)	123	0.07
Lithuanian (59)	527	0.29
Luxemburger (0)	0	<0.01
Macedonian (0)	0	<0.01
Maltese (9)	39	0.02
New Zealander (0)	0	<0.01
Northern European (281)	291	0.16
Norwegian (683)	2,848	1.56
Pennsylvania German (67)	148	0.08
Polish (2,603)	9,470	5.18
Portuguese (145)	604	0.33
Romanian (259)	440	0.24
Russian (1,337)	4,045	2.21
Scandinavian (89)	248	0.14
Scotch-Irish (907)	2,805	1.53
Scottish (759)	3,592	1.97
Serbian (10)	10	0.01
Slavic (100)	224	0.12
Slovak (145)	540	0.30
Slovene (0)	12	0.01
Soviet Union (0)	0	<0.01
Swedish (539)	2,391	1.31
Swiss (63)	283	0.15
Turkish (109)	156	0.09
Ukrainian (806)	1,416	0.77
Welsh (317)	1,117	0.61
West Indian, ex. Hispanic (1,151)	1,576	0.86
Bahamian (0)	0	<0.01
Barbadian (61)	99	0.05
Belizean (0)	0	<0.01
Bermudan (0)	0	<0.01
British West Indian (30)	62	0.03
Dutch West Indian (0)	0	<0.01
Haitian (69)	219	0.12
Jamaican (666)	738	0.40
Trinidadian/Tobagonian (85)	111	0.06
U.S. Virgin Islander (0)	0	<0.01
West Indian (240)	347	0.19
Other West Indian (0)	0	<0.01
Yugoslavian (162)	237	0.13

Hispanic Origin	Population	%
Hispanic or Latino (of any race)	15,909	8.72
Central American, ex. Mexican	1,464	0.80
Costa Rican	34	0.02
Guatemalan	331	0.18
Honduran	228	0.12
Nicaraguan	17	0.01
Panamanian	106	0.06
Salvadoran	735	0.40
Other Central American	13	0.01
Cuban	438	0.24
Dominican Republic	813	0.45
Mexican	2,945	1.61
Puerto Rican	7,191	3.94
South American	1,449	0.79
Argentinean	142	0.08
Bolivian	13	0.01
Chilean	124	0.07
Colombian	520	0.28
Ecuadorian	267	0.15
Paraguayan	16	0.01
Peruvian	263	0.14
Uruguayan	34	0.02
Venezuelan	46	0.03
Other South American	24	0.01
Other Hispanic or Latino	1,609	0.88

Race*	Population	%
African-American/Black (10,982)	13,644	7.48
Not Hispanic (9,982)	12,055	6.61
Hispanic (1,000)	1,589	0.87
American Indian/Alaska Native (597)	1,975	1.08
Not Hispanic (414)	1,572	0.86
Hispanic (183)	403	0.22
Alaska Athabascan (Ala. Nat.) (0)	0	<0.01
Aleut (Alaska Native) (0)	0	<0.01
Apache (6)	26	0.01
Arapaho (3)	6	<0.01
Blackfeet (6)	61	0.03
Canadian/French Am. Ind. (5)	13	0.01
Central American Ind. (12)	19	0.01
Cherokee (59)	321	0.18
Cheyenne (1)	2	<0.01
Chickasaw (1)	2	<0.01
Chippewa (4)	12	0.01
Choctaw (2)	10	0.01
Colville (0)	0	<0.01
Comanche (1)	3	<0.01
Cree (0)	5	<0.01
Creek (12)	22	0.01
Crow (1)	1	<0.01
Delaware (27)	62	0.03
Hopi (1)	2	<0.01
Houma (0)	0	<0.01
Inupiat (Alaska Native) (1)	4	<0.01
Iroquois (52)	188	0.10
Kiowa (0)	0	<0.01
Lumbee (5)	13	0.01
Menominee (0)	1	<0.01
Mexican American Ind. (28)	44	0.02
Navajo (1)	11	0.01
Osage (0)	3	<0.01
Ottawa (0)	0	<0.01
Paiute (0)	0	<0.01
Pima (1)	1	<0.01
Potawatomi (1)	1	<0.01
Pueblo (6)	6	<0.01
Puget Sound Salish (0)	1	<0.01
Seminole (1)	13	0.01
Shoshone (0)	0	<0.01
Sioux (27)	49	0.03
South American Ind. (26)	57	0.03
Spanish American Ind. (1)	7	<0.01
Tlingit-Haida (Alaska Native) (0)	0	<0.01
Tohono O'Odham (0)	0	<0.01
Tsimshian (Alaska Native) (1)	1	<0.01
Ute (0)	0	<0.01
Yakama (0)	0	<0.01
Yaqui (0)	0	<0.01
Yuman (0)	0	<0.01
Yup'ik (Alaska Native) (2)	2	<0.01
Asian (3,106)	4,029	2.21
Not Hispanic (3,060)	3,892	2.13
Hispanic (46)	137	0.08
Bangladeshi (85)	95	0.05
Bhutanese (1)	1	<0.01
Burmese (6)	8	<0.01
Cambodian (10)	16	0.01
Chinese, ex. Taiwanese (838)	1,039	0.57
Filipino (277)	456	0.25
Hmong (0)	0	<0.01
Indian (709)	926	0.51
Indonesian (15)	27	0.01
Japanese (197)	344	0.19
Korean (302)	402	0.22
Laotian (2)	4	<0.01
Malaysian (5)	16	0.01
Nepalese (19)	24	0.01
Pakistani (175)	211	0.12
Sri Lankan (21)	30	0.02
Taiwanese (41)	45	0.02
Thai (52)	78	0.04
Vietnamese (118)	163	0.09
Hawaii Native/Pacific Islander (34)	165	0.09
Not Hispanic (29)	122	0.07
Hispanic (5)	43	0.02
Fijian (2)	3	<0.01
Guamanian/Chamorro (7)	21	0.01
Marshallese (0)	0	<0.01
Native Hawaiian (8)	40	0.02
Samoan (3)	16	0.01
Tongan (2)	5	<0.01
White (158,184)	162,629	89.12
Not Hispanic (149,099)	152,405	83.51
Hispanic (9,085)	10,224	5.60

Notes: † The Census 2010 population figure is used to calculate the percentages in the Hispanic Origin and Race categories. Ancestry percentages are based on the 2006-2010 American Community Survey population (not shown); ‡ Numbers in parentheses indicate the number of people reporting a single ancestry; * Numbers in parentheses indicate the number of persons reporting this race alone, not in combination with any other race; Please refer to the Explanation of Data for more information.

Warren County

Population: 65,707

Ancestry	Population	%
Afghan (0)	9	0.01
African, Sub-Saharan (9)	36	0.05
African (9)	36	0.05
Cape Verdean (0)	0	<0.01
Ethiopian (0)	0	<0.01
Ghanaian (0)	0	<0.01
Kenyan (0)	0	<0.01
Liberian (0)	0	<0.01
Nigerian (0)	0	<0.01
Senegalese (0)	0	<0.01
Sierra Leonean (0)	0	<0.01
Somalian (0)	0	<0.01
South African (0)	0	<0.01
Sudanese (0)	0	<0.01
Ugandan (0)	0	<0.01
Zimbabwean (0)	0	<0.01
Other Sub-Saharan African (0)	0	<0.01
Albanian (0)	0	<0.01
Alsatian (0)	0	<0.01
American (5,380)	5,380	8.19
Arab (174)	318	0.48
Arab (0)	16	0.02
Egyptian (0)	0	<0.01
Iraqi (0)	0	<0.01
Jordanian (0)	0	<0.01
Lebanese (17)	61	0.09
Moroccan (0)	0	<0.01
Palestinian (0)	0	<0.01
Syrian (150)	230	0.35
Other Arab (7)	11	0.02
Armenian (23)	70	0.11
Assyrian/Chaldean/Syriac (0)	0	<0.01
Australian (9)	9	0.01
Austrian (41)	199	0.30
Basque (0)	0	<0.01
Belgian (7)	24	0.04
Brazilian (8)	8	0.01
British (82)	183	0.28
Bulgarian (20)	32	0.05
Cajun (0)	0	<0.01
Canadian (419)	607	0.92
Carpatho Rusyn (0)	0	<0.01
Celtic (14)	43	0.07
Croatian (0)	9	0.01
Cypriot (0)	0	<0.01
Czech (45)	195	0.30
Czechoslovakian (12)	54	0.08
Danish (31)	142	0.22
Dutch (259)	2,232	3.40
Eastern European (149)	149	0.23
English (2,731)	9,825	14.95
Estonian (18)	18	0.03
European (357)	379	0.58
Finnish (0)	43	0.07
French, ex. Basque (1,964)	8,502	12.94
French Canadian (1,045)	2,407	3.66
German (2,352)	9,279	14.12
German Russian (0)	16	0.02
Greek (34)	92	0.14
Guyanese (17)	17	0.03
Hungarian (93)	439	0.67
Icelander (0)	7	0.01
Iranian (5)	30	0.05
Irish (4,734)	15,493	23.58
Israeli (0)	15	0.02
Italian (3,791)	8,622	13.12
Latvian (28)	59	0.09
Lithuanian (54)	314	0.48
Luxemburger (0)	0	<0.01
Macedonian (0)	0	<0.01
Maltese (0)	0	<0.01
New Zealander (0)	0	<0.01
Northern European (42)	42	0.06
Norwegian (75)	324	0.49
Pennsylvania German (14)	48	0.07

Ancestry (cont.)	Population	%
Polish (718)	2,771	4.22
Portuguese (17)	113	0.17
Romanian (51)	51	0.08
Russian (212)	669	1.02
Scandinavian (58)	66	0.10
Scotch-Irish (752)	1,489	2.27
Scottish (585)	1,966	2.99
Serbian (17)	17	0.03
Slavic (14)	55	0.08
Slovak (39)	148	0.23
Slovene (0)	0	<0.01
Soviet Union (0)	0	<0.01
Swedish (258)	910	1.38
Swiss (19)	137	0.21
Turkish (0)	4	0.01
Ukrainian (137)	315	0.48
Welsh (206)	986	1.50
West Indian, ex. Hispanic (80)	97	0.15
Bahamian (0)	0	<0.01
Barbadian (0)	0	<0.01
Belizean (0)	0	<0.01
Bermudan (0)	0	<0.01
British West Indian (5)	5	0.01
Dutch West Indian (0)	0	<0.01
Haitian (0)	0	<0.01
Jamaican (70)	70	0.11
Trinidadian/Tobagonian (0)	0	<0.01
U.S. Virgin Islander (0)	0	<0.01
West Indian (5)	22	0.03
Other West Indian (0)	0	<0.01
Yugoslavian (15)	24	0.04

Hispanic Origin	Population	%
Hispanic or Latino (of any race)	1,178	1.79
Central American, ex. Mexican	66	0.10
Costa Rican	5	0.01
Guatemalan	15	0.02
Honduran	9	0.01
Nicaraguan	5	0.01
Panamanian	12	0.02
Salvadoran	20	0.03
Other Central American	0	<0.01
Cuban	45	0.07
Dominican Republic	32	0.05
Mexican	239	0.36
Puerto Rican	528	0.80
South American	92	0.14
Argentinean	9	0.01
Bolivian	3	<0.01
Chilean	5	0.01
Colombian	31	0.05
Ecuadorian	7	0.01
Paraguayan	1	<0.01
Peruvian	23	0.04
Uruguayan	3	<0.01
Venezuelan	10	0.02
Other South American	0	<0.01
Other Hispanic or Latino	176	0.27

Race*	Population	%
African-American/Black (590)	949	1.44
Not Hispanic (556)	861	1.31
Hispanic (34)	88	0.13
American Indian/Alaska Native (144)	531	0.81
Not Hispanic (117)	470	0.72
Hispanic (27)	61	0.09
Alaska Athabascan (Ala. Nat.) (1)	1	<0.01
Aleut (Alaska Native) (0)	0	<0.01
Apache (0)	6	0.01
Arapaho (0)	0	<0.01
Blackfeet (6)	26	0.04
Canadian/French Am. Ind. (6)	8	0.01
Central American Ind. (1)	1	<0.01
Cherokee (16)	45	0.07
Cheyenne (0)	2	<0.01
Chickasaw (0)	0	<0.01
Chippewa (3)	6	0.01
Choctaw (0)	1	<0.01
Colville (0)	0	<0.01

Race* (cont.)	Population	%
Comanche (0)	0	<0.01
Cree (0)	2	<0.01
Creek (0)	0	<0.01
Crow (0)	1	<0.01
Delaware (1)	1	<0.01
Hopi (0)	0	<0.01
Houma (0)	0	<0.01
Inupiat (Alaska Native) (0)	0	<0.01
Iroquois (17)	77	0.12
Kiowa (0)	0	<0.01
Lumbee (0)	0	<0.01
Menominee (0)	3	<0.01
Mexican American Ind. (5)	6	0.01
Navajo (0)	0	<0.01
Osage (0)	0	<0.01
Ottawa (1)	1	<0.01
Paiute (0)	0	<0.01
Pima (0)	0	<0.01
Potawatomi (0)	1	<0.01
Pueblo (0)	0	<0.01
Puget Sound Salish (0)	0	<0.01
Seminole (1)	5	0.01
Shoshone (0)	0	<0.01
Sioux (2)	15	0.02
South American Ind. (4)	5	0.01
Spanish American Ind. (1)	2	<0.01
Tlingit-Haida (Alaska Native) (1)	4	0.01
Tohono O'Odham (0)	0	<0.01
Tsimshian (Alaska Native) (0)	0	<0.01
Ute (0)	0	<0.01
Yakama (0)	0	<0.01
Yaqui (0)	2	<0.01
Yuman (0)	0	<0.01
Yup'ik (Alaska Native) (0)	0	<0.01
Asian (456)	615	0.94
Not Hispanic (449)	596	0.91
Hispanic (7)	19	0.03
Bangladeshi (1)	2	<0.01
Bhutanese (0)	0	<0.01
Burmese (0)	0	<0.01
Cambodian (0)	1	<0.01
Chinese, ex. Taiwanese (116)	140	0.21
Filipino (75)	118	0.18
Hmong (0)	1	<0.01
Indian (69)	97	0.15
Indonesian (2)	2	<0.01
Japanese (15)	30	0.05
Korean (65)	101	0.15
Laotian (3)	4	0.01
Malaysian (1)	2	<0.01
Nepalese (0)	0	<0.01
Pakistani (27)	34	0.05
Sri Lankan (1)	1	<0.01
Taiwanese (7)	7	0.01
Thai (13)	16	0.02
Vietnamese (41)	47	0.07
Hawaii Native/Pacific Islander (8)	34	0.05
Not Hispanic (5)	25	0.04
Hispanic (3)	9	0.01
Fijian (0)	0	<0.01
Guamanian/Chamorro (1)	6	0.01
Marshallese (0)	0	<0.01
Native Hawaiian (4)	10	0.02
Samoan (2)	3	<0.01
Tongan (0)	0	<0.01
White (63,391)	64,255	97.79
Not Hispanic (62,585)	63,331	96.38
Hispanic (806)	924	1.41

Notes: † The Census 2010 population figure is used to calculate the percentages in the Hispanic Origin and Race categories. Ancestry percentages are based on the 2006-2010 American Community Survey population (not shown); ‡ Numbers in parentheses indicate the number of people reporting a single ancestry; * Numbers in parentheses indicate the number of persons reporting this race alone, not in combination with any other race; Please refer to the Explanation of Data for more information.

Washington County

Population: 63,216

Ancestry	Population	%
Afghan (0)	0	<0.01
African, Sub-Saharan (40)	66	0.10
African (28)	54	0.09
Cape Verdean (0)	0	<0.01
Ethiopian (0)	0	<0.01
Ghanaian (0)	0	<0.01
Kenyan (0)	0	<0.01
Liberian (0)	0	<0.01
Nigerian (8)	8	0.01
Senegalese (0)	0	<0.01
Sierra Leonean (0)	0	<0.01
Somalian (0)	0	<0.01
South African (0)	0	<0.01
Sudanese (0)	0	<0.01
Ugandan (0)	0	<0.01
Zimbabwean (0)	0	<0.01
Other Sub-Saharan African (4)	4	0.01
Albanian (17)	17	0.03
Alsatian (0)	4	0.01
American (6,527)	6,527	10.35
Arab (40)	175	0.28
Arab (0)	0	<0.01
Egyptian (0)	0	<0.01
Iraqi (0)	0	<0.01
Jordanian (0)	0	<0.01
Lebanese (13)	83	0.13
Moroccan (0)	0	<0.01
Palestinian (0)	0	<0.01
Syrian (18)	83	0.13
Other Arab (9)	9	0.01
Armenian (29)	113	0.18
Assyrian/Chaldean/Syriac (0)	0	<0.01
Australian (9)	14	0.02
Austrian (59)	200	0.32
Basque (0)	13	0.02
Belgian (0)	23	0.04
Brazilian (0)	19	0.03
British (106)	174	0.28
Bulgarian (0)	4	0.01
Cajun (0)	0	<0.01
Canadian (204)	341	0.54
Carpatho Rusyn (0)	0	<0.01
Celtic (7)	7	0.01
Croatian (0)	0	<0.01
Cypriot (0)	0	<0.01
Czech (65)	117	0.19
Czechoslovakian (118)	258	0.41
Danish (34)	183	0.29
Dutch (254)	1,822	2.89
Eastern European (84)	84	0.13
English (2,389)	9,121	14.46
Estonian (0)	0	<0.01
European (209)	209	0.33
Finnish (25)	47	0.07
French, ex. Basque (1,714)	9,148	14.50
French Canadian (1,192)	2,416	3.83
German (1,476)	7,658	12.14
German Russian (0)	0	<0.01
Greek (35)	117	0.19
Guyanese (31)	47	0.07
Hungarian (205)	325	0.52
Icelander (0)	0	<0.01
Iranian (0)	0	<0.01
Irish (4,128)	13,852	21.96
Israeli (39)	39	0.06
Italian (1,842)	5,717	9.06
Latvian (23)	42	0.07
Lithuanian (95)	300	0.48
Luxemburger (0)	0	<0.01
Macedonian (0)	0	<0.01
Maltese (5)	9	0.01
New Zealander (5)	5	0.01
Northern European (7)	29	0.05
Norwegian (79)	279	0.44
Pennsylvania German (5)	8	0.01

Ancestry	Population	%
Polish (811)	2,342	3.71
Portuguese (93)	251	0.40
Romanian (12)	69	0.11
Russian (144)	686	1.09
Scandinavian (15)	21	0.03
Scotch-Irish (983)	1,767	2.80
Scottish (694)	2,905	4.60
Serbian (0)	13	0.02
Slavic (8)	20	0.03
Slovak (74)	201	0.32
Slovene (9)	18	0.03
Soviet Union (0)	0	<0.01
Swedish (289)	843	1.34
Swiss (12)	132	0.21
Turkish (0)	0	<0.01
Ukrainian (88)	299	0.47
Welsh (336)	1,157	1.83
West Indian, ex. Hispanic (218)	272	0.43
Bahamian (9)	9	0.01
Barbadian (16)	16	0.03
Belizean (0)	0	<0.01
Bermudan (0)	0	<0.01
British West Indian (9)	9	0.01
Dutch West Indian (0)	0	<0.01
Haitian (87)	110	0.17
Jamaican (33)	60	0.10
Trinidadian/Tobagonian (26)	26	0.04
U.S. Virgin Islander (0)	0	<0.01
West Indian (38)	42	0.07
Other West Indian (0)	0	<0.01
Yugoslavian (0)	0	<0.01

Hispanic Origin	Population	%
Hispanic or Latino (of any race)	1,446	2.29
Central American, ex. Mexican	115	0.18
Costa Rican	2	<0.01
Guatemalan	53	0.08
Honduran	7	0.01
Nicaraguan	2	<0.01
Panamanian	19	0.03
Salvadoran	32	0.05
Other Central American	0	<0.01
Cuban	55	0.09
Dominican Republic	112	0.18
Mexican	452	0.72
Puerto Rican	522	0.83
South American	75	0.12
Argentinean	3	<0.01
Bolivian	6	0.01
Chilean	6	0.01
Colombian	18	0.03
Ecuadorian	18	0.03
Paraguayan	0	<0.01
Peruvian	12	0.02
Uruguayan	6	0.01
Venezuelan	5	0.01
Other South American	1	<0.01
Other Hispanic or Latino	115	0.18

Race*	Population	%
African-American/Black (1,893)	2,149	3.40
Not Hispanic (1,734)	1,966	3.11
Hispanic (159)	183	0.29
American Indian/Alaska Native (128)	420	0.66
Not Hispanic (109)	375	0.59
Hispanic (19)	45	0.07
Alaska Athabascan (Ala. Nat.) (0)	0	<0.01
Aleut (Alaska Native) (1)	1	<0.01
Apache (2)	5	0.01
Arapaho (0)	0	<0.01
Blackfeet (2)	29	0.05
Canadian/French Am. Ind. (2)	3	<0.01
Central American Ind. (1)	1	<0.01
Cherokee (7)	39	0.06
Cheyenne (0)	0	<0.01
Chickasaw (0)	0	<0.01
Chippewa (0)	0	<0.01
Choctaw (1)	2	<0.01
Colville (0)	0	<0.01

Race*	Population	%
Comanche (0)	1	<0.01
Cree (0)	3	<0.01
Creek (0)	0	<0.01
Crow (0)	1	<0.01
Delaware (0)	1	<0.01
Hopi (1)	3	<0.01
Houma (0)	0	<0.01
Inupiat (Alaska Native) (1)	1	<0.01
Iroquois (11)	39	0.06
Kiowa (0)	0	<0.01
Lumbee (0)	0	<0.01
Menominee (0)	0	<0.01
Mexican American Ind. (4)	12	0.02
Navajo (1)	1	<0.01
Osage (0)	0	<0.01
Ottawa (0)	0	<0.01
Paiute (0)	0	<0.01
Pima (0)	0	<0.01
Potawatomi (0)	0	<0.01
Pueblo (0)	0	<0.01
Puget Sound Salish (0)	0	<0.01
Seminole (0)	2	<0.01
Shoshone (0)	0	<0.01
Sioux (2)	4	0.01
South American Ind. (0)	0	<0.01
Spanish American Ind. (0)	0	<0.01
Tlingit-Haida (Alaska Native) (1)	1	<0.01
Tohono O'Odham (0)	0	<0.01
Tsimshian (Alaska Native) (0)	0	<0.01
Ute (0)	0	<0.01
Yakama (0)	0	<0.01
Yaqui (0)	0	<0.01
Yuman (1)	1	<0.01
Yup'ik (Alaska Native) (0)	0	<0.01
Asian (266)	371	0.59
Not Hispanic (260)	359	0.57
Hispanic (6)	12	0.02
Bangladeshi (0)	0	<0.01
Bhutanese (0)	0	<0.01
Burmese (0)	0	<0.01
Cambodian (11)	14	0.02
Chinese, ex. Taiwanese (67)	83	0.13
Filipino (60)	96	0.15
Hmong (0)	0	<0.01
Indian (29)	44	0.07
Indonesian (0)	1	<0.01
Japanese (14)	30	0.05
Korean (46)	62	0.10
Laotian (0)	0	<0.01
Malaysian (1)	1	<0.01
Nepalese (1)	3	<0.01
Pakistani (0)	1	<0.01
Sri Lankan (0)	0	<0.01
Taiwanese (4)	4	0.01
Thai (7)	10	0.02
Vietnamese (5)	6	0.01
Hawaii Native/Pacific Islander (13)	37	0.06
Not Hispanic (11)	32	0.05
Hispanic (2)	5	0.01
Fijian (0)	0	<0.01
Guamanian/Chamorro (0)	4	0.01
Marshallese (0)	0	<0.01
Native Hawaiian (2)	20	0.03
Samoan (2)	2	<0.01
Tongan (0)	0	<0.01
White (59,815)	60,458	95.64
Not Hispanic (58,996)	59,556	94.21
Hispanic (819)	902	1.43

*Notes: † The Census 2010 population figure is used to calculate the percentages in the Hispanic Origin and Race categories. Ancestry percentages are based on the 2006-2010 American Community Survey population (not shown); ‡ Numbers in parentheses indicate the number of people reporting a single ancestry; * Numbers in parentheses indicate the number of persons reporting this race alone, not in combination with any other race; Please refer to the Explanation of Data for more information.*

Wayne County

Population: 93,772

Ancestry	Population	%
Afghan (0)	0	<0.01
African, Sub-Saharan (145)	156	0.17
African (124)	135	0.14
Cape Verdean (0)	0	<0.01
Ethiopian (0)	0	<0.01
Ghanaian (0)	0	<0.01
Kenyan (0)	0	<0.01
Liberian (0)	0	<0.01
Nigerian (0)	0	<0.01
Senegalese (0)	0	<0.01
Sierra Leonean (0)	0	<0.01
Somalian (0)	0	<0.01
South African (0)	0	<0.01
Sudanese (21)	21	0.02
Ugandan (0)	0	<0.01
Zimbabwean (0)	0	<0.01
Other Sub-Saharan African (0)	0	<0.01
Albanian (155)	202	0.22
Alsatian (0)	0	<0.01
American (5,150)	5,150	5.50
Arab (64)	115	0.12
Arab (0)	0	<0.01
Egyptian (0)	0	<0.01
Iraqi (0)	0	<0.01
Jordanian (0)	0	<0.01
Lebanese (45)	87	0.09
Moroccan (19)	19	0.02
Palestinian (0)	0	<0.01
Syrian (0)	0	<0.01
Other Arab (0)	9	0.01
Armenian (0)	13	0.01
Assyrian/Chaldean/Syriac (0)	0	<0.01
Australian (0)	57	0.06
Austrian (52)	174	0.19
Basque (0)	0	<0.01
Belgian (86)	225	0.24
Brazilian (0)	24	0.03
British (161)	396	0.42
Bulgarian (0)	6	0.01
Cajun (3)	3	<0.01
Canadian (231)	527	0.56
Carpatho Rusyn (0)	0	<0.01
Celtic (0)	0	<0.01
Croatian (35)	44	0.05
Cypriot (0)	0	<0.01
Czech (83)	274	0.29
Czechoslovakian (25)	69	0.07
Danish (133)	267	0.29
Dutch (3,364)	12,028	12.84
Eastern European (21)	21	0.02
English (3,997)	15,284	16.32
Estonian (0)	0	<0.01
European (556)	652	0.70
Finnish (68)	167	0.18
French, ex. Basque (462)	4,569	4.88
French Canadian (553)	1,649	1.76
German (6,047)	24,173	25.81
German Russian (0)	0	<0.01
Greek (350)	402	0.43
Guyanese (33)	33	0.04
Hungarian (88)	331	0.35
Icelander (3)	3	<0.01
Iranian (0)	0	<0.01
Irish (2,837)	15,277	16.31
Israeli (0)	0	<0.01
Italian (5,298)	13,414	14.32
Latvian (7)	81	0.09
Lithuanian (121)	258	0.28
Luxemburger (0)	0	<0.01
Macedonian (11)	28	0.03
Maltese (0)	58	0.06
New Zealander (0)	0	<0.01
Northern European (12)	15	0.02
Norwegian (81)	387	0.41
Pennsylvania German (183)	213	0.23

Ancestry	Population	%
Polish (1,063)	4,302	4.59
Portuguese (62)	149	0.16
Romanian (24)	43	0.05
Russian (113)	392	0.42
Scandinavian (14)	68	0.07
Scotch-Irish (626)	1,703	1.82
Scottish (528)	2,308	2.46
Serbian (0)	0	<0.01
Slavic (47)	72	0.08
Slovak (16)	99	0.11
Slovene (0)	73	0.08
Soviet Union (0)	0	<0.01
Swedish (112)	536	0.57
Swiss (387)	863	0.92
Turkish (0)	0	<0.01
Ukrainian (335)	978	1.04
Welsh (173)	996	1.06
West Indian, ex. Hispanic (248)	285	0.30
Bahamian (0)	0	<0.01
Barbadian (0)	0	<0.01
Belizean (0)	0	<0.01
Bermudan (0)	0	<0.01
British West Indian (0)	0	<0.01
Dutch West Indian (7)	7	0.01
Haitian (124)	156	0.17
Jamaican (68)	68	0.07
Trinidadian/Tobagonian (0)	0	<0.01
U.S. Virgin Islander (0)	0	<0.01
West Indian (49)	49	0.05
Other West Indian (0)	5	0.01
Yugoslavian (45)	96	0.10

Hispanic Origin	Population	%
Hispanic or Latino (of any race)	3,476	3.71
Central American, ex. Mexican	144	0.15
Costa Rican	5	0.01
Guatemalan	53	0.06
Honduran	57	0.06
Nicaraguan	3	<0.01
Panamanian	10	0.01
Salvadoran	16	0.02
Other Central American	0	<0.01
Cuban	51	0.05
Dominican Republic	85	0.09
Mexican	1,219	1.30
Puerto Rican	1,729	1.84
South American	64	0.07
Argentinean	10	0.01
Bolivian	4	<0.01
Chilean	1	<0.01
Colombian	22	0.02
Ecuadorian	10	0.01
Paraguayan	0	<0.01
Peruvian	11	0.01
Uruguayan	0	<0.01
Venezuelan	6	0.01
Other South American	0	<0.01
Other Hispanic or Latino	184	0.20

Race*	Population	%
African-American/Black (2,887)	3,853	4.11
Not Hispanic (2,743)	3,600	3.84
Hispanic (144)	253	0.27
American Indian/Alaska Native (258)	770	0.82
Not Hispanic (201)	661	0.70
Hispanic (57)	109	0.12
Alaska Athabascan (Ala. Nat.) (0)	0	<0.01
Aleut (Alaska Native) (0)	0	<0.01
Apache (2)	6	0.01
Arapaho (0)	0	<0.01
Blackfeet (4)	12	0.01
Canadian/French Am. Ind. (3)	9	0.01
Central American Ind. (3)	3	<0.01
Cherokee (16)	102	0.11
Cheyenne (0)	0	<0.01
Chickasaw (0)	0	<0.01
Chippewa (16)	18	0.02
Choctaw (6)	12	0.01
Colville (0)	0	<0.01

Race*	Population	%
Comanche (2)	2	<0.01
Cree (0)	5	0.01
Creek (1)	1	<0.01
Crow (0)	0	<0.01
Delaware (1)	1	<0.01
Hopi (0)	0	<0.01
Houma (0)	0	<0.01
Inupiat (Alaska Native) (0)	0	<0.01
Iroquois (60)	164	0.17
Kiowa (0)	0	<0.01
Lumbee (1)	8	0.01
Menominee (0)	0	<0.01
Mexican American Ind. (12)	15	0.02
Navajo (1)	2	<0.01
Osage (0)	1	<0.01
Ottawa (0)	0	<0.01
Paiute (0)	0	<0.01
Pima (2)	2	<0.01
Potawatomi (0)	0	<0.01
Pueblo (0)	1	<0.01
Puget Sound Salish (0)	0	<0.01
Seminole (0)	7	0.01
Shoshone (0)	0	<0.01
Sioux (2)	11	0.01
South American Ind. (4)	5	0.01
Spanish American Ind. (1)	2	<0.01
Tlingit-Haida (Alaska Native) (0)	0	<0.01
Tohono O'Odham (0)	0	<0.01
Tsimshian (Alaska Native) (0)	0	<0.01
Ute (0)	0	<0.01
Yakama (0)	0	<0.01
Yaqui (0)	0	<0.01
Yuman (0)	0	<0.01
Yup'ik (Alaska Native) (0)	0	<0.01
Asian (473)	704	0.75
Not Hispanic (465)	685	0.73
Hispanic (8)	19	0.02
Bangladeshi (1)	1	<0.01
Bhutanese (0)	0	<0.01
Burmese (0)	0	<0.01
Cambodian (16)	20	0.02
Chinese, ex. Taiwanese (104)	142	0.15
Filipino (60)	97	0.10
Hmong (0)	0	<0.01
Indian (51)	93	0.10
Indonesian (2)	5	0.01
Japanese (25)	57	0.06
Korean (74)	110	0.12
Laotian (47)	53	0.06
Malaysian (1)	1	<0.01
Nepalese (0)	0	<0.01
Pakistani (6)	6	0.01
Sri Lankan (1)	1	<0.01
Taiwanese (0)	0	<0.01
Thai (12)	25	0.03
Vietnamese (50)	71	0.08
Hawaii Native/Pacific Islander (24)	59	0.06
Not Hispanic (24)	54	0.06
Hispanic (0)	5	0.01
Fijian (0)	0	<0.01
Guamanian/Chamorro (4)	7	0.01
Marshallese (1)	1	<0.01
Native Hawaiian (3)	25	0.03
Samoan (1)	4	<0.01
Tongan (0)	1	<0.01
White (87,148)	88,857	94.76
Not Hispanic (85,318)	86,736	92.50
Hispanic (1,830)	2,121	2.26

*Notes: † The Census 2010 population figure is used to calculate the percentages in the Hispanic Origin and Race categories. Ancestry percentages are based on the 2006-2010 American Community Survey population (not shown); ‡ Numbers in parentheses indicate the number of people reporting a single ancestry; * Numbers in parentheses indicate the number of persons reporting this race alone, not in combination with any other race; Please refer to the Explanation of Data for more information.*

Westchester County
Population: 949,113

Ancestry	Population	%
Afghan (12)	12	<0.01
African, Sub-Saharan (7,149)	9,172	0.98
African (3,123)	4,390	0.47
Cape Verdean (41)	52	0.01
Ethiopian (391)	470	0.05
Ghanaian (952)	1,063	0.11
Kenyan (237)	271	0.03
Liberian (7)	16	<0.01
Nigerian (1,135)	1,280	0.14
Senegalese (21)	33	<0.01
Sierra Leonean (39)	51	0.01
Somalian (6)	6	<0.01
South African (500)	750	0.08
Sudanese (13)	13	<0.01
Ugandan (28)	28	<0.01
Zimbabwean (0)	0	<0.01
Other Sub-Saharan African (656)	749	0.08
Albanian (4,494)	4,876	0.52
Alsatian (0)	0	<0.01
American (41,120)	41,120	4.38
Arab (5,524)	7,908	0.84
Arab (1,268)	1,569	0.17
Egyptian (636)	827	0.09
Iraqi (111)	141	0.02
Jordanian (971)	1,058	0.11
Lebanese (1,105)	2,033	0.22
Moroccan (407)	657	0.07
Palestinian (229)	251	0.03
Syrian (118)	418	0.04
Other Arab (679)	954	0.10
Armenian (879)	1,450	0.15
Assyrian/Chaldean/Syriac (176)	265	0.03
Australian (283)	472	0.05
Austrian (1,636)	7,685	0.82
Basque (75)	94	0.01
Belgian (202)	717	0.08
Brazilian (5,072)	5,979	0.64
British (2,417)	4,054	0.43
Bulgarian (306)	425	0.05
Cajun (0)	0	<0.01
Canadian (723)	1,750	0.19
Carpatho Rusyn (60)	78	0.01
Celtic (66)	120	0.01
Croatian (1,470)	2,181	0.23
Cypriot (105)	105	0.01
Czech (857)	3,626	0.39
Czechoslovakian (610)	1,412	0.15
Danish (413)	1,707	0.18
Dutch (1,314)	5,907	0.63
Eastern European (11,389)	12,279	1.31
English (8,923)	38,197	4.07
Estonian (92)	278	0.03
European (8,977)	10,052	1.07
Finnish (346)	849	0.09
French, ex. Basque (3,407)	15,245	1.62
French Canadian (1,046)	3,477	0.37
German (15,113)	70,010	7.45
German Russian (14)	27	<0.01
Greek (4,560)	7,851	0.84
Guyanese (1,434)	1,848	0.20
Hungarian (3,232)	8,762	0.93
Icelander (0)	52	0.01
Iranian (986)	1,275	0.14
Irish (46,713)	124,206	13.22
Israeli (965)	1,392	0.15
Italian (112,477)	183,819	19.57
Latvian (344)	723	0.08
Lithuanian (778)	2,739	0.29
Luxemburger (0)	33	<0.01
Macedonian (443)	563	0.06
Maltese (164)	263	0.03
New Zealander (60)	60	0.01
Northern European (525)	637	0.07
Norwegian (1,179)	3,840	0.41
Pennsylvania German (33)	67	0.01

Ancestry	Population	%
Polish (12,575)	37,394	3.98
Portuguese (6,819)	9,618	1.02
Romanian (1,381)	3,301	0.35
Russian (14,440)	35,555	3.78
Scandinavian (290)	778	0.08
Scotch-Irish (2,663)	6,751	0.72
Scottish (2,357)	10,201	1.09
Serbian (32)	82	0.01
Slavic (440)	806	0.09
Slovak (899)	2,547	0.27
Slovene (64)	250	0.03
Soviet Union (14)	14	<0.01
Swedish (863)	5,211	0.55
Swiss (576)	2,042	0.22
Turkish (779)	1,198	0.13
Ukrainian (2,421)	4,931	0.52
Welsh (384)	2,296	0.24
West Indian, ex. Hispanic (31,329)	36,267	3.86
Bahamian (65)	72	0.01
Barbadian (718)	979	0.10
Belizean (267)	306	0.03
Bermudan (0)	0	<0.01
British West Indian (935)	1,296	0.14
Dutch West Indian (3)	3	<0.01
Haitian (3,480)	3,878	0.41
Jamaican (21,122)	23,768	2.53
Trinidadian/Tobagonian (1,606)	1,812	0.19
U.S. Virgin Islander (55)	106	0.01
West Indian (3,078)	4,037	0.43
Other West Indian (0)	10	<0.01
Yugoslavian (717)	977	0.10

Hispanic Origin	Population	%
Hispanic or Latino (of any race)	207,032	21.81
Central American, ex. Mexican	22,365	2.36
Costa Rican	584	0.06
Guatemalan	11,337	1.19
Honduran	3,055	0.32
Nicaraguan	885	0.09
Panamanian	686	0.07
Salvadoran	5,658	0.60
Other Central American	160	0.02
Cuban	5,287	0.56
Dominican Republic	26,573	2.80
Mexican	44,060	4.64
Puerto Rican	41,836	4.41
South American	50,521	5.32
Argentinean	1,922	0.20
Bolivian	749	0.08
Chilean	1,551	0.16
Colombian	10,245	1.08
Ecuadorian	22,460	2.37
Paraguayan	1,328	0.14
Peruvian	9,774	1.03
Uruguayan	1,251	0.13
Venezuelan	971	0.10
Other South American	270	0.03
Other Hispanic or Latino	16,390	1.73

Race*	Population	%
African-American/Black (138,118)	149,710	15.77
Not Hispanic (126,585)	133,406	14.06
Hispanic (11,533)	16,304	1.72
American Indian/Alaska Native (3,965)	8,854	0.93
Not Hispanic (1,141)	3,720	0.39
Hispanic (2,824)	5,134	0.54
Alaska Athabascan (Ala. Nat.) (3)	3	<0.01
Aleut (Alaska Native) (0)	5	<0.01
Apache (17)	56	0.01
Arapaho (0)	2	<0.01
Blackfeet (36)	196	0.02
Canadian/French Am. Ind. (11)	19	<0.01
Central American Ind. (106)	232	0.02
Cherokee (104)	742	0.08
Cheyenne (4)	15	<0.01
Chickasaw (2)	15	<0.01
Chippewa (16)	38	<0.01
Choctaw (11)	45	<0.01
Colville (0)	1	<0.01

	Population	%
Comanche (0)	7	<0.01
Cree (0)	6	<0.01
Creek (3)	17	<0.01
Crow (2)	5	<0.01
Delaware (8)	28	<0.01
Hopi (1)	8	<0.01
Houma (4)	4	<0.01
Inupiat (Alaska Native) (8)	11	<0.01
Iroquois (68)	178	0.02
Kiowa (0)	1	<0.01
Lumbee (3)	5	<0.01
Menominee (0)	0	<0.01
Mexican American Ind. (396)	619	0.07
Navajo (11)	28	<0.01
Osage (5)	7	<0.01
Ottawa (1)	3	<0.01
Paiute (0)	0	<0.01
Pima (2)	2	<0.01
Potawatomi (1)	10	<0.01
Pueblo (31)	58	0.01
Puget Sound Salish (0)	3	<0.01
Seminole (4)	43	<0.01
Shoshone (0)	1	<0.01
Sioux (24)	75	0.01
South American Ind. (315)	820	0.09
Spanish American Ind. (162)	216	0.02
Tlingit-Haida (Alaska Native) (1)	2	<0.01
Tohono O'Odham (1)	5	<0.01
Tsimshian (Alaska Native) (0)	0	<0.01
Ute (0)	0	<0.01
Yakama (0)	0	<0.01
Yaqui (0)	2	<0.01
Yuman (2)	4	<0.01
Yup'ik (Alaska Native) (0)	0	<0.01
Asian (51,716)	59,734	6.29
Not Hispanic (51,123)	57,958	6.11
Hispanic (593)	1,776	0.19
Bangladeshi (349)	408	0.04
Bhutanese (19)	19	<0.01
Burmese (106)	116	0.01
Cambodian (104)	135	0.01
Chinese, ex. Taiwanese (10,224)	12,423	1.31
Filipino (6,441)	7,629	0.80
Hmong (1)	1	<0.01
Indian (17,798)	19,819	2.09
Indonesian (92)	146	0.02
Japanese (5,719)	6,828	0.72
Korean (5,440)	6,184	0.65
Laotian (60)	115	0.01
Malaysian (44)	67	0.01
Nepalese (137)	153	0.02
Pakistani (1,868)	2,111	0.22
Sri Lankan (206)	232	0.02
Taiwanese (496)	613	0.06
Thai (633)	796	0.08
Vietnamese (501)	646	0.07
Hawaii Native/Pacific Islander (387)	1,501	0.16
Not Hispanic (218)	825	0.09
Hispanic (169)	676	0.07
Fijian (12)	16	<0.01
Guamanian/Chamorro (121)	196	0.02
Marshallese (1)	1	<0.01
Native Hawaiian (64)	173	0.02
Samoan (15)	43	<0.01
Tongan (0)	0	<0.01
White (646,471)	669,460	70.54
Not Hispanic (544,563)	555,692	58.55
Hispanic (101,908)	113,768	11.99

*Notes: † The Census 2010 population figure is used to calculate the percentages in the Hispanic Origin and Race categories. Ancestry percentages are based on the 2006-2010 American Community Survey population (not shown); ‡ Numbers in parentheses indicate the number of people reporting a single ancestry; * Numbers in parentheses indicate the number of persons reporting this race alone, not in combination with any other race; Please refer to the Explanation of Data for more information.*

Wyoming County
Population: 42,155

Ancestry	Population	%
Afghan (0)	0	<0.01
African, Sub-Saharan (135)	145	0.34
African (126)	135	0.32
Cape Verdean (0)	0	<0.01
Ethiopian (0)	0	<0.01
Ghanaian (0)	0	<0.01
Kenyan (0)	0	<0.01
Liberian (0)	0	<0.01
Nigerian (9)	10	0.02
Senegalese (0)	0	<0.01
Sierra Leonean (0)	0	<0.01
Somalian (0)	0	<0.01
South African (0)	0	<0.01
Sudanese (0)	0	<0.01
Ugandan (0)	0	<0.01
Zimbabwean (0)	0	<0.01
Other Sub-Saharan African (0)	0	<0.01
Albanian (0)	0	<0.01
Alsatian (0)	2	<0.01
American (1,695)	1,695	4.00
Arab (20)	53	0.13
Arab (0)	0	<0.01
Egyptian (0)	9	0.02
Iraqi (0)	0	<0.01
Jordanian (0)	0	<0.01
Lebanese (20)	44	0.10
Moroccan (0)	0	<0.01
Palestinian (0)	0	<0.01
Syrian (0)	0	<0.01
Other Arab (0)	0	<0.01
Armenian (0)	0	<0.01
Assyrian/Chaldean/Syriac (0)	0	<0.01
Australian (32)	32	0.08
Austrian (37)	102	0.24
Basque (0)	0	<0.01
Belgian (29)	174	0.41
Brazilian (4)	4	0.01
British (65)	125	0.30
Bulgarian (0)	16	0.04
Cajun (0)	9	0.02
Canadian (18)	144	0.34
Carpatho Rusyn (0)	0	<0.01
Celtic (16)	32	0.08
Croatian (6)	43	0.10
Cypriot (0)	0	<0.01
Czech (15)	61	0.14
Czechoslovakian (23)	87	0.21
Danish (22)	62	0.15
Dutch (203)	1,260	2.97
Eastern European (0)	0	<0.01
English (1,993)	7,557	17.84
Estonian (0)	0	<0.01
European (351)	383	0.90
Finnish (0)	12	0.03
French, ex. Basque (177)	1,615	3.81
French Canadian (133)	389	0.92
German (5,087)	14,749	34.81
German Russian (0)	0	<0.01
Greek (14)	96	0.23
Guyanese (8)	8	0.02
Hungarian (56)	163	0.38
Icelander (0)	0	<0.01
Iranian (0)	0	<0.01
Irish (1,451)	6,765	15.97
Israeli (0)	0	<0.01
Italian (1,447)	3,971	9.37
Latvian (0)	0	<0.01
Lithuanian (0)	59	0.14
Luxemburger (0)	12	0.03
Macedonian (0)	0	<0.01
Maltese (0)	0	<0.01
New Zealander (0)	0	<0.01
Northern European (0)	0	<0.01
Norwegian (32)	138	0.33
Pennsylvania German (106)	163	0.38

	Population	%
Polish (1,672)	4,223	9.97
Portuguese (151)	173	0.41
Romanian (31)	31	0.07
Russian (138)	232	0.55
Scandinavian (28)	48	0.11
Scotch-Irish (226)	617	1.46
Scottish (187)	922	2.18
Serbian (0)	19	0.04
Slavic (0)	8	0.02
Slovak (8)	66	0.16
Slovene (8)	32	0.08
Soviet Union (0)	0	<0.01
Swedish (38)	411	0.97
Swiss (57)	271	0.64
Turkish (0)	0	<0.01
Ukrainian (129)	198	0.47
Welsh (45)	486	1.15
West Indian, ex. Hispanic (108)	139	0.33
Bahamian (0)	0	<0.01
Barbadian (0)	0	<0.01
Belizean (9)	9	0.02
Bermudan (0)	0	<0.01
British West Indian (0)	0	<0.01
Dutch West Indian (0)	0	<0.01
Haitian (26)	35	0.08
Jamaican (47)	52	0.12
Trinidadian/Tobagonian (8)	16	0.04
U.S. Virgin Islander (10)	10	0.02
West Indian (8)	17	0.04
Other West Indian (0)	0	<0.01
Yugoslavian (19)	79	0.19

Hispanic Origin	Population	%
Hispanic or Latino (of any race)	1,244	2.95
Central American, ex. Mexican	69	0.16
Costa Rican	1	<0.01
Guatemalan	29	0.07
Honduran	9	0.02
Nicaraguan	3	0.01
Panamanian	14	0.03
Salvadoran	13	0.03
Other Central American	0	<0.01
Cuban	40	0.09
Dominican Republic	94	0.22
Mexican	342	0.81
Puerto Rican	526	1.25
South American	65	0.15
Argentinean	2	<0.01
Bolivian	0	<0.01
Chilean	2	<0.01
Colombian	24	0.06
Ecuadorian	27	0.06
Paraguayan	0	<0.01
Peruvian	7	0.02
Uruguayan	1	<0.01
Venezuelan	2	<0.01
Other South American	0	<0.01
Other Hispanic or Latino	108	0.26

Race*	Population	%
African-American/Black (2,375)	2,492	5.91
Not Hispanic (2,233)	2,337	5.54
Hispanic (142)	155	0.37
American Indian/Alaska Native (126)	272	0.65
Not Hispanic (103)	222	0.53
Hispanic (23)	50	0.12
Alaska Athabascan (Ala. Nat.) (1)	1	<0.01
Aleut (Alaska Native) (0)	0	<0.01
Apache (1)	1	<0.01
Arapaho (0)	0	<0.01
Blackfeet (0)	5	0.01
Canadian/French Am. Ind. (1)	1	<0.01
Central American Ind. (1)	1	<0.01
Cherokee (5)	15	0.04
Cheyenne (0)	0	<0.01
Chickasaw (0)	0	<0.01
Chippewa (5)	5	0.01
Choctaw (0)	1	<0.01
Colville (0)	0	<0.01

	Population	%
Comanche (0)	0	<0.01
Cree (0)	0	<0.01
Creek (0)	0	<0.01
Crow (0)	0	<0.01
Delaware (0)	1	<0.01
Hopi (0)	0	<0.01
Houma (0)	0	<0.01
Inupiat (Alaska Native) (1)	1	<0.01
Iroquois (35)	75	0.18
Kiowa (0)	0	<0.01
Lumbee (0)	0	<0.01
Menominee (0)	0	<0.01
Mexican American Ind. (4)	7	0.02
Navajo (0)	2	<0.01
Osage (0)	0	<0.01
Ottawa (0)	0	<0.01
Paiute (0)	0	<0.01
Pima (0)	0	<0.01
Potawatomi (0)	0	<0.01
Pueblo (0)	0	<0.01
Puget Sound Salish (0)	0	<0.01
Seminole (0)	0	<0.01
Shoshone (0)	0	<0.01
Sioux (1)	3	0.01
South American Ind. (6)	6	0.01
Spanish American Ind. (1)	1	<0.01
Tlingit-Haida (Alaska Native) (0)	0	<0.01
Tohono O'Odham (3)	3	0.01
Tsimshian (Alaska Native) (0)	0	<0.01
Ute (0)	0	<0.01
Yakama (0)	0	<0.01
Yaqui (0)	0	<0.01
Yuman (0)	0	<0.01
Yup'ik (Alaska Native) (0)	0	<0.01
Asian (160)	229	0.54
Not Hispanic (156)	217	0.51
Hispanic (4)	12	0.03
Bangladeshi (3)	3	0.01
Bhutanese (0)	0	<0.01
Burmese (0)	0	<0.01
Cambodian (1)	1	<0.01
Chinese, ex. Taiwanese (39)	52	0.12
Filipino (21)	41	0.10
Hmong (0)	0	<0.01
Indian (24)	32	0.08
Indonesian (0)	1	<0.01
Japanese (7)	16	0.04
Korean (21)	27	0.06
Laotian (10)	14	0.03
Malaysian (0)	0	<0.01
Nepalese (0)	0	<0.01
Pakistani (7)	8	0.02
Sri Lankan (0)	0	<0.01
Taiwanese (1)	1	<0.01
Thai (2)	5	0.01
Vietnamese (7)	11	0.03
Hawaii Native/Pacific Islander (7)	14	0.03
Not Hispanic (7)	12	0.03
Hispanic (0)	2	<0.01
Fijian (0)	0	<0.01
Guamanian/Chamorro (0)	0	<0.01
Marshallese (0)	0	<0.01
Native Hawaiian (1)	3	0.01
Samoan (0)	0	<0.01
Tongan (0)	0	<0.01
White (38,602)	38,955	92.41
Not Hispanic (38,042)	38,323	90.91
Hispanic (560)	632	1.50

Notes: † The Census 2010 population figure is used to calculate the percentages in the Hispanic Origin and Race categories. Ancestry percentages are based on the 2006-2010 American Community Survey population (not shown); ‡ Numbers in parentheses indicate the number of people reporting a single ancestry; * Numbers in parentheses indicate the number of persons reporting this race alone, not in combination with any other race; Please refer to the Explanation of Data for more information.

Yates County

Population: 25,348

Ancestry	Population	%
Afghan (0)	0	<0.01
African, Sub-Saharan (10)	14	0.06
African (0)	4	0.02
Cape Verdean (0)	0	<0.01
Ethiopian (0)	0	<0.01
Ghanaian (0)	0	<0.01
Kenyan (10)	10	0.04
Liberian (0)	0	<0.01
Nigerian (0)	0	<0.01
Senegalese (0)	0	<0.01
Sierra Leonean (0)	0	<0.01
Somalian (0)	0	<0.01
South African (0)	0	<0.01
Sudanese (0)	0	<0.01
Ugandan (0)	0	<0.01
Zimbabwean (0)	0	<0.01
Other Sub-Saharan African (0)	0	<0.01
Albanian (0)	0	<0.01
Alsatian (0)	0	<0.01
American (2,456)	2,456	9.73
Arab (3)	17	0.07
Arab (0)	0	<0.01
Egyptian (0)	0	<0.01
Iraqi (0)	0	<0.01
Jordanian (0)	0	<0.01
Lebanese (8)	8	0.03
Moroccan (0)	0	<0.01
Palestinian (0)	0	<0.01
Syrian (3)	9	0.04
Other Arab (0)	0	<0.01
Armenian (0)	28	0.11
Assyrian/Chaldean/Syriac (0)	0	<0.01
Australian (4)	8	0.03
Austrian (12)	56	0.22
Basque (0)	0	<0.01
Belgian (3)	15	0.06
Brazilian (0)	0	<0.01
British (52)	151	0.60
Bulgarian (0)	0	<0.01
Cajun (0)	0	<0.01
Canadian (29)	88	0.35
Carpatho Rusyn (0)	0	<0.01
Celtic (0)	0	<0.01
Croatian (0)	0	<0.01
Cypriot (0)	0	<0.01
Czech (3)	66	0.26
Czechoslovakian (3)	3	0.01
Danish (393)	801	3.17
Dutch (200)	1,287	5.10
Eastern European (19)	19	0.08
English (1,552)	4,563	18.07
Estonian (0)	0	<0.01
European (75)	82	0.32
Finnish (0)	75	0.30
French, ex. Basque (105)	778	3.08
French Canadian (56)	224	0.89
German (2,782)	6,401	25.35
German Russian (0)	0	<0.01
Greek (27)	121	0.48
Guyanese (0)	0	<0.01
Hungarian (48)	128	0.51
Icelander (0)	0	<0.01
Iranian (9)	21	0.08
Irish (1,496)	5,291	20.95
Israeli (0)	6	0.02
Italian (794)	2,160	8.55
Latvian (0)	0	<0.01
Lithuanian (0)	16	0.06
Luxemburger (0)	0	<0.01
Macedonian (0)	0	<0.01
Maltese (0)	0	<0.01
New Zealander (0)	0	<0.01
Northern European (10)	10	0.04
Norwegian (19)	106	0.42
Pennsylvania German (408)	471	1.87

Ancestry (cont.)	Population	%
Polish (256)	915	3.62
Portuguese (13)	13	0.05
Romanian (4)	4	0.02
Russian (50)	123	0.49
Scandinavian (0)	39	0.15
Scotch-Irish (174)	418	1.66
Scottish (219)	770	3.05
Serbian (0)	0	<0.01
Slavic (0)	3	0.01
Slovak (42)	66	0.26
Slovene (10)	13	0.05
Soviet Union (0)	0	<0.01
Swedish (58)	207	0.82
Swiss (501)	719	2.85
Turkish (0)	0	<0.01
Ukrainian (29)	99	0.39
Welsh (59)	266	1.05
West Indian, ex. Hispanic (52)	52	0.21
Bahamian (0)	0	<0.01
Barbadian (0)	0	<0.01
Belizean (0)	0	<0.01
Bermudan (0)	0	<0.01
British West Indian (0)	0	<0.01
Dutch West Indian (0)	0	<0.01
Haitian (0)	0	<0.01
Jamaican (8)	8	0.03
Trinidadian/Tobagonian (0)	0	<0.01
U.S. Virgin Islander (0)	0	<0.01
West Indian (44)	44	0.17
Other West Indian (0)	0	<0.01
Yugoslavian (10)	21	0.08

Hispanic Origin	Population	%
Hispanic or Latino (of any race)	421	1.66
Central American, ex. Mexican	15	0.06
Costa Rican	0	<0.01
Guatemalan	7	0.03
Honduran	5	0.02
Nicaraguan	0	<0.01
Panamanian	3	0.01
Salvadoran	0	<0.01
Other Central American	0	<0.01
Cuban	10	0.04
Dominican Republic	7	0.03
Mexican	152	0.60
Puerto Rican	159	0.63
South American	23	0.09
Argentinean	1	<0.01
Bolivian	0	<0.01
Chilean	3	0.01
Colombian	8	0.03
Ecuadorian	7	0.03
Paraguayan	3	0.01
Peruvian	1	<0.01
Uruguayan	0	<0.01
Venezuelan	3	0.01
Other South American	0	<0.01
Other Hispanic or Latino	55	0.22

Race*	Population	%
African-American/Black (203)	316	1.25
Not Hispanic (196)	295	1.16
Hispanic (7)	21	0.08
American Indian/Alaska Native (38)	144	0.57
Not Hispanic (35)	127	0.50
Hispanic (3)	17	0.07
Alaska Athabascan (Ala. Nat.) (0)	0	<0.01
Aleut (Alaska Native) (0)	0	<0.01
Apache (0)	1	<0.01
Arapaho (0)	1	<0.01
Blackfeet (0)	6	0.02
Canadian/French Am. Ind. (1)	2	0.01
Central American Ind. (0)	0	<0.01
Cherokee (1)	14	0.06
Cheyenne (0)	0	<0.01
Chickasaw (0)	0	<0.01
Chippewa (0)	4	0.02
Choctaw (0)	0	<0.01
Colville (0)	0	<0.01

Race* (cont.)	Population	%
Comanche (0)	0	<0.01
Cree (0)	0	<0.01
Creek (0)	0	<0.01
Crow (0)	0	<0.01
Delaware (0)	0	<0.01
Hopi (0)	0	<0.01
Houma (0)	0	<0.01
Inupiat (Alaska Native) (0)	0	<0.01
Iroquois (8)	32	0.13
Kiowa (0)	0	<0.01
Lumbee (0)	0	<0.01
Menominee (0)	0	<0.01
Mexican American Ind. (0)	0	<0.01
Navajo (0)	0	<0.01
Osage (0)	0	<0.01
Ottawa (0)	0	<0.01
Paiute (0)	0	<0.01
Pima (0)	1	<0.01
Potawatomi (0)	0	<0.01
Pueblo (1)	1	<0.01
Puget Sound Salish (0)	0	<0.01
Seminole (0)	0	<0.01
Shoshone (0)	0	<0.01
Sioux (1)	5	0.02
South American Ind. (1)	4	0.02
Spanish American Ind. (0)	0	<0.01
Tlingit-Haida (Alaska Native) (0)	0	<0.01
Tohono O'Odham (0)	0	<0.01
Tsimshian (Alaska Native) (0)	0	<0.01
Ute (0)	0	<0.01
Yakama (0)	0	<0.01
Yaqui (0)	1	<0.01
Yuman (0)	0	<0.01
Yup'ik (Alaska Native) (0)	0	<0.01
Asian (97)	124	0.49
Not Hispanic (96)	120	0.47
Hispanic (1)	4	0.02
Bangladeshi (0)	0	<0.01
Bhutanese (0)	0	<0.01
Burmese (0)	0	<0.01
Cambodian (3)	3	0.01
Chinese, ex. Taiwanese (30)	42	0.17
Filipino (8)	10	0.04
Hmong (0)	0	<0.01
Indian (11)	16	0.06
Indonesian (0)	0	<0.01
Japanese (9)	26	0.10
Korean (22)	25	0.10
Laotian (4)	6	0.02
Malaysian (0)	0	<0.01
Nepalese (0)	0	<0.01
Pakistani (0)	0	<0.01
Sri Lankan (0)	0	<0.01
Taiwanese (0)	0	<0.01
Thai (0)	0	<0.01
Vietnamese (1)	2	0.01
Hawaii Native/Pacific Islander (4)	16	0.06
Not Hispanic (1)	11	0.04
Hispanic (3)	5	0.02
Fijian (0)	0	<0.01
Guamanian/Chamorro (1)	7	0.03
Marshallese (0)	0	<0.01
Native Hawaiian (0)	3	0.01
Samoan (3)	3	0.01
Tongan (0)	0	<0.01
White (24,647)	24,903	98.24
Not Hispanic (24,371)	24,577	96.96
Hispanic (276)	326	1.29

*Notes: † The Census 2010 population figure is used to calculate the percentages in the Hispanic Origin and Race categories. Ancestry percentages are based on the 2006-2010 American Community Survey population (not shown); ‡ Numbers in parentheses indicate the number of people reporting a single ancestry; * Numbers in parentheses indicate the number of persons reporting this race alone, not in combination with any other race; Please refer to the Explanation of Data for more information.*

Place Profiles

Albany

Place Type: City
County: Albany
Population: 97,856

Ancestry	Population	%
Afghan (0)	0	<0.01
African, Sub-Saharan (1,142)	1,533	1.57
African (656)	975	1.00
Cape Verdean (0)	13	0.01
Ethiopian (21)	21	0.02
Ghanaian (143)	143	0.15
Kenyan (101)	101	0.10
Liberian (0)	0	<0.01
Nigerian (132)	191	0.19
Senegalese (0)	0	<0.01
Sierra Leonean (0)	0	<0.01
Somalian (0)	0	<0.01
South African (0)	0	<0.01
Sudanese (25)	25	0.03
Ugandan (0)	0	<0.01
Zimbabwean (0)	0	<0.01
Other Sub-Saharan African (64)	64	0.07
Albanian (318)	384	0.39
Alsatian (19)	51	0.05
American (1,531)	1,531	1.56
Arab (181)	525	0.54
Arab (105)	116	0.12
Egyptian (41)	124	0.13
Iraqi (0)	0	<0.01
Jordanian (0)	0	<0.01
Lebanese (23)	138	0.14
Moroccan (0)	0	<0.01
Palestinian (12)	25	0.03
Syrian (0)	104	0.11
Other Arab (0)	18	0.02
Armenian (26)	75	0.08
Assyrian/Chaldean/Syriac (0)	0	<0.01
Australian (30)	88	0.09
Austrian (31)	247	0.25
Basque (0)	0	<0.01
Belgian (53)	78	0.08
Brazilian (45)	45	0.05
British (132)	255	0.26
Bulgarian (0)	9	0.01
Cajun (0)	0	<0.01
Canadian (80)	128	0.13
Carpatho Rusyn (12)	12	0.01
Celtic (0)	0	<0.01
Croatian (32)	54	0.06
Cypriot (0)	0	<0.01
Czech (153)	392	0.40
Czechoslovakian (11)	35	0.04
Danish (89)	303	0.31
Dutch (321)	1,664	1.70
Eastern European (220)	253	0.26
English (1,100)	5,315	5.43
Estonian (0)	0	<0.01
European (1,163)	1,362	1.39
Finnish (0)	35	0.04
French, ex. Basque (458)	3,690	3.77
French Canadian (329)	1,061	1.08
German (1,888)	10,150	10.36
German Russian (0)	0	<0.01
Greek (368)	755	0.77
Guyanese (466)	483	0.49
Hungarian (183)	405	0.41
Icelander (0)	0	<0.01
Iranian (50)	60	0.06
Irish (5,251)	17,818	18.19
Israeli (0)	0	<0.01
Italian (4,932)	12,860	13.13
Latvian (15)	24	0.02
Lithuanian (38)	217	0.22
Luxemburger (9)	9	0.01
Macedonian (0)	0	<0.01

Ancestry	Population	%
Maltese (11)	24	0.02
New Zealander (0)	0	<0.01
Northern European (56)	160	0.16
Norwegian (146)	406	0.41
Pennsylvania German (0)	12	0.01
Polish (1,282)	4,476	4.57
Portuguese (116)	266	0.27
Romanian (0)	182	0.19
Russian (483)	1,487	1.52
Scandinavian (31)	313	0.32
Scotch-Irish (229)	842	0.86
Scottish (311)	1,162	1.19
Serbian (19)	19	0.02
Slavic (28)	94	0.10
Slovak (110)	351	0.36
Slovene (12)	70	0.07
Soviet Union (0)	0	<0.01
Swedish (57)	444	0.45
Swiss (15)	125	0.13
Turkish (14)	39	0.04
Ukrainian (85)	496	0.51
Welsh (103)	597	0.61
West Indian, ex. Hispanic (2,407)	3,298	3.37
Bahamian (0)	0	<0.01
Barbadian (14)	29	0.03
Belizean (0)	0	<0.01
Bermudan (36)	36	0.04
British West Indian (133)	210	0.21
Dutch West Indian (39)	79	0.08
Haitian (421)	446	0.46
Jamaican (1,228)	1,636	1.67
Trinidadian/Tobagonian (193)	219	0.22
U.S. Virgin Islander (0)	0	<0.01
West Indian (276)	576	0.59
Other West Indian (67)	67	0.07
Yugoslavian (36)	48	0.05

Hispanic Origin	Population	%
Hispanic or Latino (of any race)	8,396	8.58
Central American, ex. Mexican	343	0.35
Costa Rican	35	0.04
Guatemalan	54	0.06
Honduran	70	0.07
Nicaraguan	28	0.03
Panamanian	81	0.08
Salvadoran	65	0.07
Other Central American	10	0.01
Cuban	298	0.30
Dominican Republic	1,095	1.12
Mexican	616	0.63
Puerto Rican	4,654	4.76
South American	626	0.64
Argentinean	38	0.04
Bolivian	5	0.01
Chilean	38	0.04
Colombian	196	0.20
Ecuadorian	184	0.19
Paraguayan	6	0.01
Peruvian	89	0.09
Uruguayan	15	0.02
Venezuelan	39	0.04
Other South American	16	0.02
Other Hispanic or Latino	764	0.78

Race*	Population	%
African-American/Black (30,110)	32,569	33.28
Not Hispanic (28,479)	30,376	31.04
Hispanic (1,631)	2,193	2.24
American Indian/Alaska Native (295)	1,120	1.14
Not Hispanic (191)	856	0.87
Hispanic (104)	264	0.27
Alaska Athabascan (Ala. Nat.) (0)	1	<0.01
Aleut (Alaska Native) (0)	0	<0.01
Apache (0)	5	0.01
Arapaho (0)	0	<0.01
Blackfeet (6)	57	0.06

Race*	Population	%
Canadian/French Am. Ind. (0)	5	0.01
Central American Ind. (5)	10	0.01
Cherokee (23)	205	0.21
Cheyenne (0)	0	<0.01
Chickasaw (2)	2	<0.01
Chippewa (0)	3	<0.01
Choctaw (2)	8	0.01
Colville (0)	0	<0.01
Comanche (0)	0	<0.01
Cree (1)	4	<0.01
Creek (0)	6	0.01
Crow (0)	0	<0.01
Delaware (2)	11	0.01
Hopi (0)	0	<0.01
Houma (0)	0	<0.01
Inupiat (Alaska Native) (1)	1	<0.01
Iroquois (26)	102	0.10
Kiowa (0)	0	<0.01
Lumbee (0)	0	<0.01
Menominee (0)	0	<0.01
Mexican American Ind. (10)	13	0.01
Navajo (1)	2	<0.01
Osage (0)	0	<0.01
Ottawa (0)	1	<0.01
Paiute (0)	0	<0.01
Pima (0)	0	<0.01
Potawatomi (1)	2	<0.01
Pueblo (1)	1	<0.01
Puget Sound Salish (0)	0	<0.01
Seminole (1)	7	0.01
Shoshone (0)	1	<0.01
Sioux (5)	11	0.01
South American Ind. (24)	49	0.05
Spanish American Ind. (6)	10	0.01
Tlingit-Haida (Alaska Native) (1)	3	<0.01
Tohono O'Odham (0)	0	<0.01
Tsimshian (Alaska Native) (0)	0	<0.01
Ute (0)	0	<0.01
Yakama (1)	1	<0.01
Yaqui (0)	0	<0.01
Yuman (0)	0	<0.01
Yup'ik (Alaska Native) (1)	1	<0.01
Asian (4,890)	5,588	5.71
Not Hispanic (4,850)	5,482	5.60
Hispanic (40)	106	0.11
Bangladeshi (148)	171	0.17
Bhutanese (62)	62	0.06
Burmese (294)	322	0.33
Cambodian (8)	12	0.01
Chinese, ex. Taiwanese (1,219)	1,349	1.38
Filipino (645)	746	0.76
Hmong (0)	0	<0.01
Indian (1,009)	1,198	1.22
Indonesian (10)	12	0.01
Japanese (109)	200	0.20
Korean (368)	426	0.44
Laotian (0)	3	<0.01
Malaysian (2)	8	0.01
Nepalese (48)	55	0.06
Pakistani (425)	483	0.49
Sri Lankan (13)	13	0.01
Taiwanese (61)	69	0.07
Thai (35)	46	0.05
Vietnamese (197)	231	0.24
Hawaii Native/Pacific Islander (55)	180	0.18
Not Hispanic (47)	158	0.16
Hispanic (8)	22	0.02
Fijian (0)	1	<0.01
Guamanian/Chamorro (7)	15	0.02
Marshallese (0)	0	<0.01
Native Hawaiian (8)	38	0.04
Samoan (9)	15	0.02
Tongan (0)	1	<0.01
White (55,783)	58,605	59.89
Not Hispanic (52,857)	55,044	56.25
Hispanic (2,926)	3,561	3.64

Notes: † The Census 2010 population figure is used to calculate the percentages in the Hispanic Origin and Race categories. Ancestry percentages are based on the 2006-2010 American Community Survey population (not shown); ‡ Numbers in parentheses indicate the number of people reporting a single ancestry; * Numbers in parentheses indicate the number of persons reporting this race alone, not in combination with any other race; Please refer to the Explanation of Data for more information.

Amherst

Place Type: Town
County: Erie
Population: 122,366

Ancestry	Population	%
Afghan (144)	144	0.12
African, Sub-Saharan (897)	1,095	0.91
African (481)	625	0.52
Cape Verdean (0)	0	<0.01
Ethiopian (71)	71	0.06
Ghanaian (15)	15	0.01
Kenyan (12)	12	0.01
Liberian (0)	0	<0.01
Nigerian (167)	167	0.14
Senegalese (0)	0	<0.01
Sierra Leonean (0)	0	<0.01
Somalian (0)	0	<0.01
South African (22)	35	0.03
Sudanese (0)	0	<0.01
Ugandan (0)	0	<0.01
Zimbabwean (0)	0	<0.01
Other Sub-Saharan African (129)	170	0.14
Albanian (26)	114	0.09
Alsatian (9)	32	0.03
American (3,077)	3,077	2.54
Arab (818)	1,530	1.27
Arab (46)	90	0.07
Egyptian (8)	8	0.01
Iraqi (0)	0	<0.01
Jordanian (84)	84	0.07
Lebanese (342)	985	0.81
Moroccan (13)	13	0.01
Palestinian (18)	18	0.01
Syrian (48)	62	0.05
Other Arab (259)	270	0.22
Armenian (157)	203	0.17
Assyrian/Chaldean/Syriac (0)	0	<0.01
Australian (29)	47	0.04
Austrian (367)	1,014	0.84
Basque (0)	0	<0.01
Belgian (11)	38	0.03
Brazilian (223)	223	0.18
British (194)	438	0.36
Bulgarian (68)	98	0.08
Cajun (0)	0	<0.01
Canadian (282)	589	0.49
Carpatho Rusyn (0)	0	<0.01
Celtic (10)	10	0.01
Croatian (114)	393	0.32
Cypriot (0)	0	<0.01
Czech (105)	255	0.21
Czechoslovakian (46)	82	0.07
Danish (55)	199	0.16
Dutch (148)	1,690	1.40
Eastern European (507)	575	0.48
English (3,188)	11,840	9.79
Estonian (10)	25	0.02
European (915)	981	0.81
Finnish (35)	196	0.16
French, ex. Basque (438)	3,549	2.93
French Canadian (283)	983	0.81
German (8,678)	30,579	25.28
German Russian (0)	0	<0.01
Greek (323)	802	0.66
Guyanese (43)	43	0.04
Hungarian (420)	1,194	0.99
Icelander (0)	0	<0.01
Iranian (174)	188	0.16
Irish (5,285)	22,106	18.28
Israeli (75)	122	0.10
Italian (11,256)	23,615	19.53
Latvian (26)	64	0.05
Lithuanian (82)	182	0.15
Luxemburger (0)	0	<0.01
Macedonian (0)	14	0.01
Maltese (0)	0	<0.01
New Zealander (0)	26	0.02
Northern European (29)	101	0.08

Norwegian (114)	400	0.33
Pennsylvania German (0)	43	0.04
Polish (6,777)	17,104	14.14
Portuguese (90)	144	0.12
Romanian (169)	324	0.27
Russian (1,684)	3,468	2.87
Scandinavian (11)	116	0.10
Scotch-Irish (504)	1,527	1.26
Scottish (333)	1,736	1.44
Serbian (81)	158	0.13
Slavic (25)	153	0.13
Slovak (40)	141	0.12
Slovene (40)	53	0.04
Soviet Union (0)	0	<0.01
Swedish (139)	902	0.75
Swiss (67)	222	0.18
Turkish (138)	164	0.14
Ukrainian (545)	1,074	0.89
Welsh (218)	798	0.66
West Indian, ex. Hispanic (282)	440	0.36
Bahamian (0)	0	<0.01
Barbadian (12)	12	0.01
Belizean (0)	0	<0.01
Bermudan (0)	0	<0.01
British West Indian (13)	13	0.01
Dutch West Indian (0)	0	<0.01
Haitian (45)	45	0.04
Jamaican (169)	226	0.19
Trinidadian/Tobagonian (5)	19	0.02
U.S. Virgin Islander (0)	0	<0.01
West Indian (38)	125	0.10
Other West Indian (0)	0	<0.01
Yugoslavian (52)	52	0.04

Hispanic Origin	Population	%
Hispanic or Latino (of any race)	2,870	2.35
Central American, ex. Mexican	189	0.15
Costa Rican	20	0.02
Guatemalan	49	0.04
Honduran	23	0.02
Nicaraguan	8	0.01
Panamanian	39	0.03
Salvadoran	49	0.04
Other Central American	1	<0.01
Cuban	120	0.10
Dominican Republic	194	0.16
Mexican	478	0.39
Puerto Rican	1,108	0.91
South American	436	0.36
Argentinean	57	0.05
Bolivian	14	0.01
Chilean	40	0.03
Colombian	163	0.13
Ecuadorian	63	0.05
Paraguayan	5	<0.01
Peruvian	52	0.04
Uruguayan	7	0.01
Venezuelan	33	0.03
Other South American	2	<0.01
Other Hispanic or Latino	345	0.28

Race*	Population	%
African-American/Black (7,009)	7,946	6.49
Not Hispanic (6,765)	7,563	6.18
Hispanic (244)	383	0.31
American Indian/Alaska Native (220)	616	0.50
Not Hispanic (196)	531	0.43
Hispanic (24)	85	0.07
Alaska Athabascan (Ala. Nat.) (0)	1	<0.01
Aleut (Alaska Native) (0)	0	<0.01
Apache (0)	0	<0.01
Arapaho (0)	0	<0.01
Blackfeet (2)	14	0.01
Canadian/French Am. Ind. (9)	11	0.01
Central American Ind. (0)	1	<0.01
Cherokee (7)	67	0.05
Cheyenne (0)	0	<0.01
Chickasaw (0)	0	<0.01
Chippewa (1)	7	0.01

Choctaw (1)	3	<0.01
Colville (0)	0	<0.01
Comanche (0)	0	<0.01
Cree (0)	0	<0.01
Creek (0)	2	<0.01
Crow (2)	2	<0.01
Delaware (1)	2	<0.01
Hopi (0)	0	<0.01
Houma (0)	0	<0.01
Inupiat (Alaska Native) (0)	3	<0.01
Iroquois (84)	155	0.13
Kiowa (0)	0	<0.01
Lumbee (1)	1	<0.01
Menominee (0)	0	<0.01
Mexican American Ind. (11)	22	0.02
Navajo (0)	1	<0.01
Osage (1)	1	<0.01
Ottawa (0)	0	<0.01
Paiute (0)	0	<0.01
Pima (0)	0	<0.01
Potawatomi (0)	0	<0.01
Pueblo (2)	5	<0.01
Puget Sound Salish (0)	0	<0.01
Seminole (0)	10	0.01
Shoshone (0)	0	<0.01
Sioux (0)	1	<0.01
South American Ind. (4)	13	0.01
Spanish American Ind. (0)	0	<0.01
Tlingit-Haida (Alaska Native) (0)	1	<0.01
Tohono O'Odham (1)	1	<0.01
Tsimshian (Alaska Native) (0)	0	<0.01
Ute (0)	0	<0.01
Yakama (0)	0	<0.01
Yaqui (0)	0	<0.01
Yuman (0)	0	<0.01
Yup'ik (Alaska Native) (0)	1	<0.01
Asian (9,675)	10,683	8.73
Not Hispanic (9,643)	10,590	8.65
Hispanic (32)	93	0.08
Bangladeshi (42)	45	0.04
Bhutanese (0)	0	<0.01
Burmese (28)	32	0.03
Cambodian (16)	17	0.01
Chinese, ex. Taiwanese (2,925)	3,146	2.57
Filipino (273)	396	0.32
Hmong (0)	0	<0.01
Indian (3,263)	3,491	2.85
Indonesian (26)	42	0.03
Japanese (215)	294	0.24
Korean (1,377)	1,493	1.22
Laotian (19)	25	0.02
Malaysian (41)	47	0.04
Nepalese (12)	12	0.01
Pakistani (515)	592	0.48
Sri Lankan (122)	130	0.11
Taiwanese (180)	202	0.17
Thai (36)	52	0.04
Vietnamese (307)	362	0.30
Hawaii Native/Pacific Islander (26)	94	0.08
Not Hispanic (26)	86	0.07
Hispanic (0)	8	0.01
Fijian (3)	3	<0.01
Guamanian/Chamorro (8)	10	0.01
Marshallese (1)	1	<0.01
Native Hawaiian (9)	24	0.02
Samoan (3)	12	0.01
Tongan (0)	0	<0.01
White (102,558)	104,439	85.35
Not Hispanic (100,778)	102,429	83.71
Hispanic (1,780)	2,010	1.64

Notes: † The Census 2010 population figure is used to calculate the percentages in the Hispanic Origin and Race categories. Ancestry percentages are based on the 2006-2010 American Community Survey population (not shown); ‡ Numbers in parentheses indicate the number of people reporting a single ancestry; * Numbers in parentheses indicate the number of persons reporting this race alone, not in combination with any other race; Please refer to the Explanation of Data for more information.

Babylon

Place Type: Town
County: Suffolk
Population: 213,603

Ancestry	Population	%
Afghan (219)	219	0.10
African, Sub-Saharan (1,803)	2,217	1.04
African (734)	1,071	0.50
Cape Verdean (0)	9	<0.01
Ethiopian (0)	11	0.01
Ghanaian (64)	64	0.03
Kenyan (0)	0	<0.01
Liberian (300)	309	0.14
Nigerian (670)	707	0.33
Senegalese (0)	0	<0.01
Sierra Leonean (0)	0	<0.01
Somalian (0)	0	<0.01
South African (0)	0	<0.01
Sudanese (0)	0	<0.01
Ugandan (0)	0	<0.01
Zimbabwean (0)	0	<0.01
Other Sub-Saharan African (35)	46	0.02
Albanian (139)	210	0.10
Alsatian (0)	0	<0.01
American (3,343)	3,343	1.56
Arab (595)	842	0.39
Arab (236)	259	0.12
Egyptian (30)	79	0.04
Iraqi (0)	0	<0.01
Jordanian (0)	0	<0.01
Lebanese (20)	79	0.04
Moroccan (142)	209	0.10
Palestinian (114)	114	0.05
Syrian (0)	49	0.02
Other Arab (53)	53	0.02
Armenian (69)	188	0.09
Assyrian/Chaldean/Syriac (0)	0	<0.01
Australian (0)	20	0.01
Austrian (149)	808	0.38
Basque (15)	15	0.01
Belgian (22)	41	0.02
Brazilian (30)	166	0.08
British (149)	348	0.16
Bulgarian (8)	20	0.01
Cajun (0)	0	<0.01
Canadian (80)	581	0.27
Carpatho Rusyn (0)	0	<0.01
Celtic (33)	64	0.03
Croatian (144)	207	0.10
Cypriot (0)	0	<0.01
Czech (61)	578	0.27
Czechoslovakian (296)	438	0.21
Danish (107)	384	0.18
Dutch (218)	1,653	0.77
Eastern European (253)	270	0.13
English (1,368)	8,596	4.02
Estonian (10)	33	0.02
European (342)	416	0.19
Finnish (26)	190	0.09
French, ex. Basque (203)	2,679	1.25
French Canadian (445)	939	0.44
German (5,375)	31,578	14.78
German Russian (0)	0	<0.01
Greek (964)	2,182	1.02
Guyanese (602)	747	0.35
Hungarian (188)	989	0.46
Icelander (22)	22	0.01
Iranian (53)	69	0.03
Irish (10,079)	42,364	19.83
Israeli (28)	172	0.08
Italian (32,274)	61,852	28.95
Latvian (11)	35	0.02
Lithuanian (287)	642	0.30
Luxemburger (0)	0	<0.01
Macedonian (11)	33	0.02
Maltese (61)	378	0.18
New Zealander (0)	0	<0.01
Northern European (45)	61	0.03

Ancestry	Population	%
Norwegian (303)	1,701	0.80
Pennsylvania German (18)	18	0.01
Polish (5,564)	12,444	5.82
Portuguese (168)	676	0.32
Romanian (230)	316	0.15
Russian (845)	3,774	1.77
Scandinavian (17)	48	0.02
Scotch-Irish (570)	1,863	0.87
Scottish (225)	1,548	0.72
Serbian (16)	19	0.01
Slavic (6)	64	0.03
Slovak (134)	367	0.17
Slovene (14)	14	0.01
Soviet Union (0)	0	<0.01
Swedish (205)	1,400	0.66
Swiss (57)	361	0.17
Turkish (826)	939	0.44
Ukrainian (329)	905	0.42
Welsh (103)	423	0.20
West Indian, ex. Hispanic (9,910)	11,187	5.24
Bahamian (35)	88	0.04
Barbadian (105)	183	0.09
Belizean (0)	12	0.01
Bermudan (0)	0	<0.01
British West Indian (64)	119	0.06
Dutch West Indian (6)	6	<0.01
Haitian (3,585)	3,789	1.77
Jamaican (4,141)	4,758	2.23
Trinidadian/Tobagonian (842)	854	0.40
U.S. Virgin Islander (0)	0	<0.01
West Indian (1,132)	1,378	0.64
Other West Indian (0)	0	<0.01
Yugoslavian (14)	156	0.07

Hispanic Origin	Population	%
Hispanic or Latino (of any race)	35,793	16.76
Central American, ex. Mexican	11,096	5.19
Costa Rican	146	0.07
Guatemalan	884	0.41
Honduran	1,756	0.82
Nicaraguan	112	0.05
Panamanian	305	0.14
Salvadoran	7,805	3.65
Other Central American	88	0.04
Cuban	550	0.26
Dominican Republic	6,543	3.06
Mexican	1,145	0.54
Puerto Rican	7,562	3.54
South American	5,576	2.61
Argentinean	336	0.16
Bolivian	78	0.04
Chilean	226	0.11
Colombian	2,036	0.95
Ecuadorian	1,348	0.63
Paraguayan	37	0.02
Peruvian	1,313	0.61
Uruguayan	64	0.03
Venezuelan	104	0.05
Other South American	34	0.02
Other Hispanic or Latino	3,321	1.55

Race*	Population	%
African-American/Black (34,881)	37,421	17.52
Not Hispanic (33,147)	34,993	16.38
Hispanic (1,734)	2,428	1.14
American Indian/Alaska Native (719)	1,894	0.89
Not Hispanic (447)	1,351	0.63
Hispanic (272)	543	0.25
Alaska Athabascan (Ala. Nat.) (0)	0	<0.01
Aleut (Alaska Native) (2)	2	<0.01
Apache (1)	11	0.01
Arapaho (0)	0	<0.01
Blackfeet (4)	44	0.02
Canadian/French Am. Ind. (7)	10	<0.01
Central American Ind. (14)	22	0.01
Cherokee (51)	250	0.12
Cheyenne (1)	1	<0.01
Chickasaw (0)	0	<0.01
Chippewa (6)	7	<0.01

Race*	Population	%
Choctaw (1)	5	<0.01
Colville (0)	0	<0.01
Comanche (1)	2	<0.01
Cree (1)	2	<0.01
Creek (0)	13	0.01
Crow (0)	1	<0.01
Delaware (2)	2	<0.01
Hopi (3)	5	<0.01
Houma (0)	0	<0.01
Inupiat (Alaska Native) (0)	1	<0.01
Iroquois (34)	65	0.03
Kiowa (0)	0	<0.01
Lumbee (3)	12	0.01
Menominee (0)	0	<0.01
Mexican American Ind. (15)	25	0.01
Navajo (1)	6	<0.01
Osage (0)	0	<0.01
Ottawa (0)	0	<0.01
Paiute (0)	0	<0.01
Pima (0)	0	<0.01
Potawatomi (0)	0	<0.01
Pueblo (9)	9	<0.01
Puget Sound Salish (0)	0	<0.01
Seminole (2)	13	0.01
Shoshone (0)	0	<0.01
Sioux (8)	16	0.01
South American Ind. (47)	82	0.04
Spanish American Ind. (8)	17	0.01
Tlingit-Haida (Alaska Native) (0)	1	<0.01
Tohono O'Odham (0)	1	<0.01
Tsimshian (Alaska Native) (0)	0	<0.01
Ute (0)	0	<0.01
Yakama (0)	0	<0.01
Yaqui (0)	0	<0.01
Yuman (0)	0	<0.01
Yup'ik (Alaska Native) (0)	0	<0.01
Asian (6,524)	7,919	3.71
Not Hispanic (6,411)	7,577	3.55
Hispanic (113)	342	0.16
Bangladeshi (271)	341	0.16
Bhutanese (0)	0	<0.01
Burmese (4)	7	<0.01
Cambodian (3)	5	<0.01
Chinese, ex. Taiwanese (1,108)	1,357	0.64
Filipino (765)	1,046	0.49
Hmong (0)	0	<0.01
Indian (2,582)	2,940	1.38
Indonesian (16)	22	0.01
Japanese (88)	186	0.09
Korean (388)	477	0.22
Laotian (6)	9	<0.01
Malaysian (2)	3	<0.01
Nepalese (4)	4	<0.01
Pakistani (678)	739	0.35
Sri Lankan (25)	32	0.01
Taiwanese (24)	26	0.01
Thai (41)	67	0.03
Vietnamese (257)	297	0.14
Hawaii Native/Pacific Islander (51)	272	0.13
Not Hispanic (31)	153	0.07
Hispanic (20)	119	0.06
Fijian (0)	0	<0.01
Guamanian/Chamorro (11)	22	0.01
Marshallese (0)	0	<0.01
Native Hawaiian (13)	45	0.02
Samoan (3)	10	<0.01
Tongan (0)	0	<0.01
White (153,067)	157,336	73.66
Not Hispanic (133,961)	136,259	63.79
Hispanic (19,106)	21,077	9.87

Notes: † The Census 2010 population figure is used to calculate the percentages in the Hispanic Origin and Race categories. Ancestry percentages are based on the 2006-2010 American Community Survey population (not shown); ‡ Numbers in parentheses indicate the number of people reporting a single ancestry; * Numbers in parentheses indicate the number of persons reporting this race alone, not in combination with any other race; Please refer to the Explanation of Data for more information.

Brentwood

Place Type: CDP
County: Suffolk
Population: 60,664

Ancestry	Population	%
Afghan (50)	68	0.12
African, Sub-Saharan (301)	336	0.61
African (86)	106	0.19
Cape Verdean (0)	0	<0.01
Ethiopian (0)	0	<0.01
Ghanaian (45)	45	0.08
Kenyan (0)	0	<0.01
Liberian (0)	0	<0.01
Nigerian (90)	105	0.19
Senegalese (0)	0	<0.01
Sierra Leonean (0)	0	<0.01
Somalian (0)	0	<0.01
South African (0)	0	<0.01
Sudanese (0)	0	<0.01
Ugandan (0)	0	<0.01
Zimbabwean (0)	0	<0.01
Other Sub-Saharan African (80)	80	0.15
Albanian (0)	0	<0.01
Alsatian (0)	0	<0.01
American (588)	588	1.07
Arab (82)	92	0.17
Arab (25)	25	0.05
Egyptian (20)	20	0.04
Iraqi (0)	0	<0.01
Jordanian (0)	0	<0.01
Lebanese (0)	10	0.02
Moroccan (0)	0	<0.01
Palestinian (0)	0	<0.01
Syrian (0)	0	<0.01
Other Arab (37)	37	0.07
Armenian (0)	0	<0.01
Assyrian/Chaldean/Syriac (0)	0	<0.01
Australian (0)	8	0.01
Austrian (19)	80	0.15
Basque (0)	0	<0.01
Belgian (0)	9	0.02
Brazilian (418)	418	0.76
British (46)	78	0.14
Bulgarian (0)	0	<0.01
Cajun (0)	0	<0.01
Canadian (0)	8	0.01
Carpatho Rusyn (0)	0	<0.01
Celtic (0)	0	<0.01
Croatian (0)	0	<0.01
Cypriot (0)	0	<0.01
Czech (0)	38	0.07
Czechoslovakian (8)	25	0.05
Danish (0)	0	<0.01
Dutch (0)	96	0.18
Eastern European (0)	0	<0.01
English (338)	850	1.55
Estonian (0)	17	0.03
European (32)	43	0.08
Finnish (8)	11	0.02
French, ex. Basque (57)	181	0.33
French Canadian (10)	48	0.09
German (310)	1,994	3.64
German Russian (0)	0	<0.01
Greek (37)	59	0.11
Guyanese (126)	138	0.25
Hungarian (16)	42	0.08
Icelander (0)	0	<0.01
Iranian (0)	0	<0.01
Irish (934)	2,578	4.70
Israeli (0)	0	<0.01
Italian (1,517)	3,236	5.90
Latvian (0)	0	<0.01
Lithuanian (9)	25	0.05
Luxemburger (0)	0	<0.01
Macedonian (0)	0	<0.01
Maltese (17)	17	0.03
New Zealander (0)	0	<0.01
Northern European (0)	0	<0.01
Norwegian (24)	72	0.13
Pennsylvania German (0)	0	<0.01
Polish (164)	623	1.14
Portuguese (504)	524	0.96
Romanian (0)	0	<0.01
Russian (61)	180	0.33
Scandinavian (7)	29	0.05
Scotch-Irish (39)	161	0.29
Scottish (20)	92	0.17
Serbian (0)	10	0.02
Slavic (0)	0	<0.01
Slovak (8)	8	0.01
Slovene (0)	0	<0.01
Soviet Union (0)	0	<0.01
Swedish (39)	210	0.38
Swiss (0)	14	0.03
Turkish (0)	5	0.01
Ukrainian (0)	10	0.02
Welsh (0)	0	<0.01
West Indian, ex. Hispanic (3,143)	3,472	6.33
Bahamian (0)	0	<0.01
Barbadian (5)	5	0.01
Belizean (0)	0	<0.01
Bermudan (0)	0	<0.01
British West Indian (37)	58	0.11
Dutch West Indian (0)	0	<0.01
Haitian (2,072)	2,162	3.94
Jamaican (622)	771	1.41
Trinidadian/Tobagonian (104)	152	0.28
U.S. Virgin Islander (0)	0	<0.01
West Indian (303)	324	0.59
Other West Indian (0)	0	<0.01
Yugoslavian (0)	10	0.02

Hispanic Origin	Population	%
Hispanic or Latino (of any race)	41,529	68.46
Central American, ex. Mexican	19,957	32.90
Costa Rican	85	0.14
Guatemalan	1,553	2.56
Honduran	2,062	3.40
Nicaraguan	87	0.14
Panamanian	148	0.24
Salvadoran	15,946	26.29
Other Central American	76	0.13
Cuban	223	0.37
Dominican Republic	4,205	6.93
Mexican	1,193	1.97
Puerto Rican	6,125	10.10
South American	6,350	10.47
Argentinean	203	0.33
Bolivian	79	0.13
Chilean	153	0.25
Colombian	2,083	3.43
Ecuadorian	1,985	3.27
Paraguayan	36	0.06
Peruvian	1,610	2.65
Uruguayan	80	0.13
Venezuelan	113	0.19
Other South American	8	0.01
Other Hispanic or Latino	3,476	5.73

Race*	Population	%
African-American/Black (9,934)	11,026	18.18
Not Hispanic (8,344)	8,888	14.65
Hispanic (1,590)	2,138	3.52
American Indian/Alaska Native (710)	1,135	1.87
Not Hispanic (132)	326	0.54
Hispanic (578)	809	1.33
Alaska Athabascan (Ala. Nat.) (0)	1	<0.01
Aleut (Alaska Native) (0)	0	<0.01
Apache (0)	0	<0.01
Arapaho (0)	0	<0.01
Blackfeet (5)	6	0.01
Canadian/French Am. Ind. (0)	0	<0.01
Central American Ind. (27)	36	0.06
Cherokee (16)	76	0.13
Cheyenne (0)	0	<0.01
Chickasaw (0)	0	<0.01
Chippewa (4)	5	0.01
Choctaw (0)	0	<0.01
Colville (0)	0	<0.01
Comanche (0)	7	0.01
Cree (0)	0	<0.01
Creek (0)	0	<0.01
Crow (11)	11	0.02
Delaware (0)	0	<0.01
Hopi (0)	0	<0.01
Houma (0)	0	<0.01
Inupiat (Alaska Native) (0)	0	<0.01
Iroquois (14)	17	0.03
Kiowa (0)	0	<0.01
Lumbee (2)	2	<0.01
Menominee (0)	0	<0.01
Mexican American Ind. (48)	72	0.12
Navajo (3)	4	0.01
Osage (0)	1	<0.01
Ottawa (0)	0	<0.01
Paiute (0)	0	<0.01
Pima (1)	1	<0.01
Potawatomi (0)	0	<0.01
Pueblo (4)	5	0.01
Puget Sound Salish (0)	0	<0.01
Seminole (0)	0	<0.01
Shoshone (0)	0	<0.01
Sioux (2)	2	<0.01
South American Ind. (63)	87	0.14
Spanish American Ind. (41)	52	0.09
Tlingit-Haida (Alaska Native) (3)	3	<0.01
Tohono O'Odham (0)	0	<0.01
Tsimshian (Alaska Native) (0)	0	<0.01
Ute (0)	0	<0.01
Yakama (0)	0	<0.01
Yaqui (1)	1	<0.01
Yuman (0)	0	<0.01
Yup'ik (Alaska Native) (0)	0	<0.01
Asian (1,193)	1,544	2.55
Not Hispanic (1,101)	1,349	2.22
Hispanic (92)	195	0.32
Bangladeshi (33)	37	0.06
Bhutanese (0)	0	<0.01
Burmese (1)	1	<0.01
Cambodian (5)	5	0.01
Chinese, ex. Taiwanese (95)	141	0.23
Filipino (120)	163	0.27
Hmong (0)	0	<0.01
Indian (516)	647	1.07
Indonesian (10)	12	0.02
Japanese (3)	15	0.02
Korean (11)	17	0.03
Laotian (8)	8	0.01
Malaysian (1)	3	<0.01
Nepalese (0)	0	<0.01
Pakistani (246)	268	0.44
Sri Lankan (6)	10	0.02
Taiwanese (4)	4	0.01
Thai (30)	38	0.06
Vietnamese (47)	57	0.09
Hawaii Native/Pacific Islander (29)	134	0.22
Not Hispanic (11)	59	0.10
Hispanic (18)	75	0.12
Fijian (0)	1	<0.01
Guamanian/Chamorro (8)	8	0.01
Marshallese (0)	0	<0.01
Native Hawaiian (8)	17	0.03
Samoan (1)	4	0.01
Tongan (0)	2	<0.01
White (29,344)	31,986	52.73
Not Hispanic (8,554)	8,973	14.79
Hispanic (20,790)	23,013	37.94

Notes: † The Census 2010 population figure is used to calculate the percentages in the Hispanic Origin and Race categories. Ancestry percentages are based on the 2006-2010 American Community Survey population (not shown); ‡ Numbers in parentheses indicate the number of people reporting a single ancestry; * Numbers in parentheses indicate the number of persons reporting this race alone, not in combination with any other race; Please refer to the Explanation of Data for more information.

Bronx

Place Type: Borough
County: Bronx
Population: 1,385,108

Ancestry	Population	%
Afghan (14)	14	<0.01
African, Sub-Saharan (50,131)	55,928	4.10
African (19,345)	22,647	1.66
Cape Verdean (49)	108	0.01
Ethiopian (790)	945	0.07
Ghanaian (13,163)	13,490	0.99
Kenyan (12)	24	<0.01
Liberian (365)	450	0.03
Nigerian (4,896)	5,538	0.41
Senegalese (956)	1,068	0.08
Sierra Leonean (759)	759	0.06
Somalian (11)	35	<0.01
South African (29)	68	<0.01
Sudanese (88)	149	0.01
Ugandan (0)	0	<0.01
Zimbabwean (108)	108	0.01
Other Sub-Saharan African (9,560)	10,539	0.77
Albanian (7,460)	7,835	0.57
Alsatian (0)	0	<0.01
American (16,297)	16,297	1.19
Arab (4,063)	5,008	0.37
Arab (1,481)	1,719	0.13
Egyptian (495)	718	0.05
Iraqi (64)	73	<0.01
Jordanian (8)	8	<0.01
Lebanese (229)	347	0.03
Moroccan (526)	667	0.05
Palestinian (28)	28	<0.01
Syrian (44)	192	0.01
Other Arab (1,188)	1,256	0.09
Armenian (128)	237	0.02
Assyrian/Chaldean/Syriac (0)	18	<0.01
Australian (8)	21	<0.01
Austrian (539)	1,868	0.14
Basque (66)	109	0.01
Belgian (52)	131	0.01
Brazilian (276)	397	0.03
British (517)	1,115	0.08
Bulgarian (506)	521	0.04
Cajun (0)	0	<0.01
Canadian (197)	375	0.03
Carpatho Rusyn (0)	12	<0.01
Celtic (1)	13	<0.01
Croatian (91)	219	0.02
Cypriot (12)	38	<0.01
Czech (99)	388	0.03
Czechoslovakian (90)	226	0.02
Danish (17)	385	0.03
Dutch (314)	1,920	0.14
Eastern European (1,425)	1,646	0.12
English (1,821)	7,038	0.52
Estonian (70)	85	0.01
European (1,845)	2,270	0.17
Finnish (89)	291	0.02
French, ex. Basque (909)	4,971	0.36
French Canadian (102)	403	0.03
German (3,729)	16,487	1.21
German Russian (7)	30	<0.01
Greek (2,499)	3,607	0.26
Guyanese (10,276)	11,837	0.87
Hungarian (966)	2,427	0.18
Icelander (6)	6	<0.01
Iranian (187)	248	0.02
Irish (18,712)	38,479	2.82
Israeli (427)	618	0.05
Italian (38,592)	57,527	4.21
Latvian (92)	103	0.01
Lithuanian (167)	547	0.04
Luxemburger (0)	0	<0.01
Macedonian (628)	628	0.05
Maltese (16)	45	<0.01
New Zealander (23)	23	<0.01
Northern European (25)	25	<0.01

Ancestry	Population	%
Norwegian (260)	773	0.06
Pennsylvania German (0)	0	<0.01
Polish (3,429)	7,834	0.57
Portuguese (474)	1,113	0.08
Romanian (691)	1,164	0.09
Russian (4,351)	8,064	0.59
Scandinavian (102)	155	0.01
Scotch-Irish (516)	1,601	0.12
Scottish (388)	1,570	0.11
Serbian (154)	187	0.01
Slavic (15)	90	0.01
Slovak (87)	226	0.02
Slovene (10)	45	<0.01
Soviet Union (12)	12	<0.01
Swedish (119)	549	0.04
Swiss (24)	166	0.01
Turkish (589)	686	0.05
Ukrainian (970)	1,608	0.12
Welsh (101)	530	0.04
West Indian, ex. Hispanic (93,323)	107,527	7.87
Bahamian (165)	208	0.02
Barbadian (1,285)	1,612	0.12
Belizean (1,253)	1,493	0.11
Bermudan (101)	198	0.01
British West Indian (5,959)	7,136	0.52
Dutch West Indian (127)	172	0.01
Haitian (3,891)	4,652	0.34
Jamaican (58,387)	64,222	4.70
Trinidadian/Tobagonian (3,695)	4,811	0.35
U.S. Virgin Islander (737)	952	0.07
West Indian (17,683)	21,941	1.61
Other West Indian (40)	130	0.01
Yugoslavian (1,275)	1,480	0.11

Hispanic Origin	Population	%
Hispanic or Latino (of any race)	741,413	53.53
Central American, ex. Mexican	34,492	2.49
Costa Rican	1,095	0.08
Guatemalan	4,645	0.34
Honduran	17,990	1.30
Nicaraguan	2,342	0.17
Panamanian	2,372	0.17
Salvadoran	5,469	0.39
Other Central American	579	0.04
Cuban	8,785	0.63
Dominican Republic	240,987	17.40
Mexican	71,194	5.14
Puerto Rican	298,921	21.58
South American	35,463	2.56
Argentinean	1,117	0.08
Bolivian	227	0.02
Chilean	646	0.05
Colombian	4,635	0.33
Ecuadorian	23,206	1.68
Paraguayan	223	0.02
Peruvian	3,596	0.26
Uruguayan	148	0.01
Venezuelan	1,296	0.09
Other South American	369	0.03
Other Hispanic or Latino	51,571	3.72

Race*	Population	%
African-American/Black (505,200)	541,622	39.10
Not Hispanic (416,695)	427,134	30.84
Hispanic (88,505)	114,488	8.27
American Indian/Alaska Native (18,260)	32,011	2.31
Not Hispanic (3,460)	7,638	0.55
Hispanic (14,800)	24,373	1.76
Alaska Athabascan (Ala. Nat.) (4)	8	<0.01
Aleut (Alaska Native) (0)	3	<0.01
Apache (30)	99	0.01
Arapaho (2)	3	<0.01
Blackfeet (43)	310	0.02
Canadian/French Am. Ind. (13)	25	<0.01
Central American Ind. (2,274)	4,520	0.33
Cherokee (247)	1,312	0.09
Cheyenne (2)	5	<0.01
Chickasaw (6)	16	<0.01
Chippewa (25)	38	<0.01

Race*	Population	%
Choctaw (4)	43	<0.01
Colville (0)	2	<0.01
Comanche (8)	26	<0.01
Cree (1)	16	<0.01
Creek (7)	47	<0.01
Crow (1)	16	<0.01
Delaware (1)	10	<0.01
Hopi (0)	2	<0.01
Houma (12)	12	<0.01
Inupiat (Alaska Native) (11)	15	<0.01
Iroquois (81)	170	0.01
Kiowa (1)	1	<0.01
Lumbee (3)	6	<0.01
Menominee (1)	3	<0.01
Mexican American Ind. (714)	963	0.07
Navajo (24)	42	<0.01
Osage (2)	3	<0.01
Ottawa (0)	1	<0.01
Paiute (0)	5	<0.01
Pima (0)	1	<0.01
Potawatomi (1)	2	<0.01
Pueblo (177)	382	0.03
Puget Sound Salish (0)	0	<0.01
Seminole (6)	50	<0.01
Shoshone (0)	8	<0.01
Sioux (46)	82	0.01
South American Ind. (1,568)	2,938	0.21
Spanish American Ind. (709)	992	0.07
Tlingit-Haida (Alaska Native) (1)	11	<0.01
Tohono O'Odham (4)	9	<0.01
Tsimshian (Alaska Native) (0)	0	<0.01
Ute (2)	5	<0.01
Yakama (3)	3	<0.01
Yaqui (4)	5	<0.01
Yuman (1)	2	<0.01
Yup'ik (Alaska Native) (1)	6	<0.01
Asian (49,609)	59,085	4.27
Not Hispanic (47,335)	53,458	3.86
Hispanic (2,274)	5,627	0.41
Bangladeshi (7,323)	8,623	0.62
Bhutanese (74)	104	0.01
Burmese (71)	81	0.01
Cambodian (1,055)	1,188	0.09
Chinese, ex. Taiwanese (6,644)	8,112	0.59
Filipino (5,576)	6,456	0.47
Hmong (1)	3	<0.01
Indian (15,865)	20,357	1.47
Indonesian (50)	96	0.01
Japanese (562)	1,027	0.07
Korean (2,840)	3,101	0.22
Laotian (99)	148	0.01
Malaysian (11)	30	<0.01
Nepalese (129)	159	0.01
Pakistani (2,399)	2,728	0.20
Sri Lankan (174)	234	0.02
Taiwanese (98)	130	0.01
Thai (326)	414	0.03
Vietnamese (3,215)	3,526	0.25
Hawaii Native/Pacific Islander (1,288)	6,213	0.45
Not Hispanic (398)	1,854	0.13
Hispanic (890)	4,359	0.31
Fijian (13)	13	<0.01
Guamanian/Chamorro (251)	376	0.03
Marshallese (3)	3	<0.01
Native Hawaiian (371)	669	0.05
Samoan (70)	160	0.01
Tongan (5)	7	<0.01
White (386,497)	427,659	30.88
Not Hispanic (151,209)	158,245	11.42
Hispanic (235,288)	269,414	19.45

Notes: † The Census 2010 population figure is used to calculate the percentages in the Hispanic Origin and Race categories. Ancestry percentages are based on the 2006-2010 American Community Survey population (not shown); ‡ Numbers in parentheses indicate the number of people reporting a single ancestry; * Numbers in parentheses indicate the number of persons reporting this race alone, not in combination with any other race; Please refer to the Explanation of Data for more information.

Brookhaven

Place Type: Town
County: Suffolk
Population: 486,040

Ancestry	Population	%
Afghan (0)	0	<0.01
African, Sub-Saharan (2,475)	2,832	0.59
African (2,224)	2,533	0.53
Cape Verdean (0)	0	<0.01
Ethiopian (0)	0	<0.01
Ghanaian (57)	57	0.01
Kenyan (0)	0	<0.01
Liberian (9)	9	<0.01
Nigerian (163)	179	0.04
Senegalese (0)	0	<0.01
Sierra Leonean (0)	0	<0.01
Somalian (0)	0	<0.01
South African (6)	24	<0.01
Sudanese (0)	14	<0.01
Ugandan (0)	0	<0.01
Zimbabwean (0)	0	<0.01
Other Sub-Saharan African (16)	16	<0.01
Albanian (59)	133	0.03
Alsatian (0)	12	<0.01
American (10,016)	10,016	2.09
Arab (797)	1,321	0.28
Arab (164)	191	0.04
Egyptian (317)	435	0.09
Iraqi (0)	0	<0.01
Jordanian (100)	178	0.04
Lebanese (29)	98	0.02
Moroccan (15)	15	<0.01
Palestinian (0)	13	<0.01
Syrian (12)	220	0.05
Other Arab (160)	171	0.04
Armenian (254)	643	0.13
Assyrian/Chaldean/Syriac (0)	0	<0.01
Australian (31)	79	0.02
Austrian (603)	2,867	0.60
Basque (9)	23	<0.01
Belgian (61)	401	0.08
Brazilian (314)	436	0.09
British (605)	1,235	0.26
Bulgarian (101)	128	0.03
Cajun (0)	0	<0.01
Canadian (432)	999	0.21
Carpatho Rusyn (0)	0	<0.01
Celtic (0)	31	0.01
Croatian (317)	588	0.12
Cypriot (51)	51	0.01
Czech (697)	3,121	0.65
Czechoslovakian (344)	917	0.19
Danish (180)	1,229	0.26
Dutch (554)	4,038	0.84
Eastern European (604)	728	0.15
English (4,862)	30,089	6.27
Estonian (14)	102	0.02
European (1,893)	2,098	0.44
Finnish (144)	706	0.15
French, ex. Basque (933)	8,961	1.87
French Canadian (665)	2,478	0.52
German (16,000)	89,711	18.69
German Russian (0)	40	0.01
Greek (2,196)	5,703	1.19
Guyanese (373)	441	0.09
Hungarian (814)	4,390	0.91
Icelander (18)	45	0.01
Iranian (353)	398	0.08
Irish (29,544)	122,200	25.45
Israeli (355)	545	0.11
Italian (72,814)	155,749	32.44
Latvian (120)	182	0.04
Lithuanian (674)	1,898	0.40
Luxemburger (0)	36	0.01
Macedonian (0)	0	<0.01
Maltese (235)	686	0.14
New Zealander (10)	23	<0.01
Northern European (233)	249	0.05

Ancestry	Population	%
Norwegian (1,381)	5,078	1.06
Pennsylvania German (45)	66	0.01
Polish (7,478)	27,233	5.67
Portuguese (2,684)	3,802	0.79
Romanian (472)	1,216	0.25
Russian (4,331)	12,073	2.51
Scandinavian (127)	388	0.08
Scotch-Irish (1,789)	5,102	1.06
Scottish (1,051)	5,703	1.19
Serbian (0)	0	<0.01
Slavic (22)	91	0.02
Slovak (304)	690	0.14
Slovene (5)	76	0.02
Soviet Union (0)	0	<0.01
Swedish (519)	4,045	0.84
Swiss (319)	1,356	0.28
Turkish (1,572)	1,935	0.40
Ukrainian (779)	2,350	0.49
Welsh (195)	1,189	0.25
West Indian, ex. Hispanic (4,567)	6,377	1.33
Bahamian (0)	47	0.01
Barbadian (44)	44	0.01
Belizean (0)	0	<0.01
Bermudan (0)	34	0.01
British West Indian (59)	59	0.01
Dutch West Indian (20)	20	<0.01
Haitian (1,544)	2,077	0.43
Jamaican (998)	1,546	0.32
Trinidadian/Tobagonian (922)	1,200	0.25
U.S. Virgin Islander (0)	0	<0.01
West Indian (980)	1,323	0.28
Other West Indian (0)	27	0.01
Yugoslavian (145)	518	0.11

Hispanic Origin	Population	%
Hispanic or Latino (of any race)	60,270	12.40
Central American, ex. Mexican	9,259	1.90
Costa Rican	198	0.04
Guatemalan	1,411	0.29
Honduran	1,195	0.25
Nicaraguan	159	0.03
Panamanian	291	0.06
Salvadoran	5,899	1.21
Other Central American	106	0.02
Cuban	1,500	0.31
Dominican Republic	4,781	0.98
Mexican	4,926	1.01
Puerto Rican	21,429	4.41
South American	12,182	2.51
Argentinean	653	0.13
Bolivian	148	0.03
Chilean	363	0.07
Colombian	2,970	0.61
Ecuadorian	6,437	1.32
Paraguayan	50	0.01
Peruvian	1,074	0.22
Uruguayan	87	0.02
Venezuelan	302	0.06
Other South American	98	0.02
Other Hispanic or Latino	6,193	1.27

Race*	Population	%
African-American/Black (26,639)	31,615	6.50
Not Hispanic (24,428)	28,098	5.78
Hispanic (2,211)	3,517	0.72
American Indian/Alaska Native (1,368)	3,782	0.78
Not Hispanic (847)	2,586	0.53
Hispanic (521)	1,196	0.25
Alaska Athabascan (Ala. Nat.) (1)	4	<0.01
Aleut (Alaska Native) (2)	3	<0.01
Apache (4)	18	<0.01
Arapaho (0)	1	<0.01
Blackfeet (12)	164	0.03
Canadian/French Am. Ind. (4)	15	<0.01
Central American Ind. (27)	53	0.01
Cherokee (82)	546	0.11
Cheyenne (1)	6	<0.01
Chickasaw (0)	3	<0.01
Chippewa (8)	19	<0.01

Race*	Population	%
Choctaw (7)	34	0.01
Colville (0)	0	<0.01
Comanche (0)	4	<0.01
Cree (1)	4	<0.01
Creek (1)	12	<0.01
Crow (0)	1	<0.01
Delaware (3)	12	<0.01
Hopi (0)	1	<0.01
Houma (0)	0	<0.01
Inupiat (Alaska Native) (1)	2	<0.01
Iroquois (39)	116	0.02
Kiowa (0)	0	<0.01
Lumbee (2)	7	<0.01
Menominee (0)	0	<0.01
Mexican American Ind. (37)	64	0.01
Navajo (3)	15	<0.01
Osage (0)	2	<0.01
Ottawa (0)	3	<0.01
Paiute (2)	4	<0.01
Pima (0)	0	<0.01
Potawatomi (6)	6	<0.01
Pueblo (2)	2	<0.01
Puget Sound Salish (5)	6	<0.01
Seminole (7)	33	0.01
Shoshone (0)	4	<0.01
Sioux (16)	42	0.01
South American Ind. (47)	136	0.03
Spanish American Ind. (26)	34	0.01
Tlingit-Haida (Alaska Native) (0)	5	<0.01
Tohono O'Odham (0)	0	<0.01
Tsimshian (Alaska Native) (0)	0	<0.01
Ute (0)	1	<0.01
Yakama (0)	1	<0.01
Yaqui (1)	5	<0.01
Yuman (1)	1	<0.01
Yup'ik (Alaska Native) (0)	0	<0.01
Asian (19,082)	21,849	4.50
Not Hispanic (18,880)	21,257	4.37
Hispanic (202)	592	0.12
Bangladeshi (528)	621	0.13
Bhutanese (0)	0	<0.01
Burmese (36)	40	<0.01
Cambodian (14)	29	0.01
Chinese, ex. Taiwanese (5,433)	6,107	1.26
Filipino (2,117)	2,705	0.56
Hmong (1)	4	<0.01
Indian (5,078)	5,745	1.18
Indonesian (38)	63	0.01
Japanese (339)	605	0.12
Korean (1,728)	2,025	0.42
Laotian (42)	54	0.01
Malaysian (9)	18	<0.01
Nepalese (43)	44	0.01
Pakistani (1,867)	2,081	0.43
Sri Lankan (85)	100	0.02
Taiwanese (181)	213	0.04
Thai (150)	211	0.04
Vietnamese (544)	620	0.13
Hawaii Native/Pacific Islander (152)	447	0.09
Not Hispanic (98)	306	0.06
Hispanic (54)	141	0.03
Fijian (3)	10	<0.01
Guamanian/Chamorro (40)	51	0.01
Marshallese (0)	0	<0.01
Native Hawaiian (31)	100	0.02
Samoan (6)	15	<0.01
Tongan (0)	2	<0.01
White (410,649)	419,725	86.36
Not Hispanic (373,782)	379,158	78.01
Hispanic (36,867)	40,567	8.35

Notes: † The Census 2010 population figure is used to calculate the percentages in the Hispanic Origin and Race categories. Ancestry percentages are based on the 2006-2010 American Community Survey population (not shown); ‡ Numbers in parentheses indicate the number of people reporting a single ancestry; * Numbers in parentheses indicate the number of persons reporting this race alone, not in combination with any other race; Please refer to the Explanation of Data for more information.

Brooklyn

Place Type: Borough
County: Kings
Population: 2,504,700

Ancestry	Population	%
Afghan (335)	344	0.01
African, Sub-Saharan (30,768)	63,004	2.55
African (17,256)	48,168	1.95
Cape Verdean (106)	153	0.01
Ethiopian (283)	330	0.01
Ghanaian (3,692)	3,898	0.16
Kenyan (65)	77	<0.01
Liberian (392)	452	0.02
Nigerian (5,499)	6,033	0.24
Senegalese (401)	401	0.02
Sierra Leonean (147)	147	0.01
Somalian (234)	260	0.01
South African (204)	320	0.01
Sudanese (693)	731	0.03
Ugandan (29)	54	<0.01
Zimbabwean (99)	99	<0.01
Other Sub-Saharan African (1,668)	1,881	0.08
Albanian (6,490)	6,871	0.28
Alsatian (0)	27	<0.01
American (78,858)	78,858	3.20
Arab (29,346)	34,840	1.41
Arab (6,779)	7,609	0.31
Egyptian (4,705)	5,231	0.21
Iraqi (71)	134	0.01
Jordanian (714)	752	0.03
Lebanese (3,425)	4,757	0.19
Moroccan (2,156)	2,648	0.11
Palestinian (1,372)	1,482	0.06
Syrian (4,854)	5,890	0.24
Other Arab (5,270)	6,337	0.26
Armenian (1,798)	2,300	0.09
Assyrian/Chaldean/Syriac (22)	44	<0.01
Australian (539)	832	0.03
Austrian (1,677)	5,123	0.21
Basque (69)	129	0.01
Belgian (498)	1,012	0.04
Brazilian (1,257)	1,719	0.07
British (2,002)	4,749	0.19
Bulgarian (970)	1,128	0.05
Cajun (99)	175	0.01
Canadian (1,814)	3,116	0.13
Carpatho Rusyn (46)	53	<0.01
Celtic (16)	32	<0.01
Croatian (488)	998	0.04
Cypriot (37)	62	<0.01
Czech (759)	3,393	0.14
Czechoslovakian (793)	1,684	0.07
Danish (380)	1,267	0.05
Dutch (1,616)	5,664	0.23
Eastern European (11,912)	12,941	0.52
English (9,927)	32,407	1.31
Estonian (209)	340	0.01
European (25,194)	27,499	1.11
Finnish (303)	692	0.03
French, ex. Basque (3,484)	14,137	0.57
French Canadian (1,082)	2,974	0.12
German (12,299)	52,798	2.14
German Russian (29)	55	<0.01
Greek (10,688)	14,075	0.57
Guyanese (36,322)	38,963	1.58
Hungarian (17,858)	26,607	1.08
Icelander (69)	103	<0.01
Iranian (1,520)	1,822	0.07
Irish (32,255)	84,945	3.44
Israeli (7,062)	9,707	0.39
Italian (108,743)	152,814	6.19
Latvian (418)	667	0.03
Lithuanian (938)	2,676	0.11
Luxemburger (41)	58	<0.01
Macedonian (389)	498	0.02
Maltese (197)	362	0.01
New Zealander (71)	140	0.01
Northern European (905)	961	0.04

Ancestry (cont.)	Population	%
Norwegian (2,042)	5,982	0.24
Pennsylvania German (19)	59	<0.01
Polish (41,882)	66,792	2.71
Portuguese (1,106)	2,882	0.12
Romanian (4,537)	8,046	0.33
Russian (69,188)	88,579	3.59
Scandinavian (512)	882	0.04
Scotch-Irish (1,997)	6,090	0.25
Scottish (2,407)	8,809	0.36
Serbian (288)	520	0.02
Slavic (289)	564	0.02
Slovak (1,164)	1,826	0.07
Slovene (55)	160	0.01
Soviet Union (185)	219	0.01
Swedish (1,240)	5,185	0.21
Swiss (473)	1,491	0.06
Turkish (4,449)	5,164	0.21
Ukrainian (21,703)	25,046	1.02
Welsh (345)	2,606	0.11
West Indian, ex. Hispanic (257,579)	306,541	12.43
Bahamian (195)	266	0.01
Barbadian (13,358)	14,916	0.60
Belizean (1,610)	2,026	0.08
Bermudan (16)	16	<0.01
British West Indian (28,123)	30,607	1.24
Dutch West Indian (289)	424	0.02
Haitian (67,083)	69,941	2.84
Jamaican (74,216)	80,999	3.28
Trinidadian/Tobagonian (42,450)	46,490	1.88
U.S. Virgin Islander (470)	558	0.02
West Indian (29,404)	59,844	2.43
Other West Indian (365)	454	0.02
Yugoslavian (2,305)	2,800	0.11

Hispanic Origin	Population	%
Hispanic or Latino (of any race)	496,285	19.81
Central American, ex. Mexican	46,119	1.84
Costa Rican	2,576	0.10
Guatemalan	9,160	0.37
Honduran	10,071	0.40
Nicaraguan	2,407	0.10
Panamanian	13,681	0.55
Salvadoran	7,737	0.31
Other Central American	487	0.02
Cuban	7,581	0.30
Dominican Republic	86,764	3.46
Mexican	94,585	3.78
Puerto Rican	176,528	7.05
South American	49,003	1.96
Argentinean	2,760	0.11
Bolivian	310	0.01
Chilean	1,026	0.04
Colombian	8,861	0.35
Ecuadorian	28,684	1.15
Paraguayan	230	0.01
Peruvian	4,222	0.17
Uruguayan	488	0.02
Venezuelan	1,916	0.08
Other South American	506	0.02
Other Hispanic or Latino	35,705	1.43

Race*	Population	%
African-American/Black (860,083)	896,165	35.78
Not Hispanic (799,066)	820,437	32.76
Hispanic (61,017)	75,728	3.02
American Indian/Alaska Native (13,524)	26,571	1.06
Not Hispanic (4,638)	12,062	0.48
Hispanic (8,886)	14,509	0.58
Alaska Athabascan (Ala. Nat.) (1)	5	<0.01
Aleut (Alaska Native) (4)	8	<0.01
Apache (46)	122	<0.01
Arapaho (2)	10	<0.01
Blackfeet (89)	531	0.02
Canadian/French Am. Ind. (42)	62	<0.01
Central American Ind. (616)	1,263	0.05
Cherokee (289)	1,903	0.08
Cheyenne (0)	10	<0.01
Chickasaw (9)	30	<0.01
Chippewa (23)	65	<0.01

Race* (cont.)	Population	%
Choctaw (30)	104	<0.01
Colville (1)	1	<0.01
Comanche (5)	19	<0.01
Cree (3)	15	<0.01
Creek (20)	81	<0.01
Crow (5)	19	<0.01
Delaware (5)	35	<0.01
Hopi (7)	12	<0.01
Houma (1)	3	<0.01
Inupiat (Alaska Native) (7)	21	<0.01
Iroquois (194)	381	0.02
Kiowa (1)	2	<0.01
Lumbee (6)	24	<0.01
Menominee (1)	4	<0.01
Mexican American Ind. (1,022)	1,363	0.05
Navajo (41)	93	<0.01
Osage (1)	3	<0.01
Ottawa (2)	5	<0.01
Paiute (0)	1	<0.01
Pima (0)	2	<0.01
Potawatomi (3)	11	<0.01
Pueblo (93)	169	0.01
Puget Sound Salish (1)	1	<0.01
Seminole (18)	92	<0.01
Shoshone (6)	23	<0.01
Sioux (29)	121	<0.01
South American Ind. (874)	1,855	0.07
Spanish American Ind. (290)	382	0.02
Tlingit-Haida (Alaska Native) (4)	28	<0.01
Tohono O'Odham (9)	10	<0.01
Tsimshian (Alaska Native) (0)	0	<0.01
Ute (0)	4	<0.01
Yakama (1)	3	<0.01
Yaqui (11)	19	<0.01
Yuman (5)	8	<0.01
Yup'ik (Alaska Native) (0)	1	<0.01
Asian (262,276)	284,489	11.36
Not Hispanic (260,129)	279,499	11.16
Hispanic (2,147)	4,990	0.20
Bangladeshi (10,667)	12,408	0.50
Bhutanese (5)	8	<0.01
Burmese (1,055)	1,260	0.05
Cambodian (613)	751	0.03
Chinese, ex. Taiwanese (171,214)	178,214	7.12
Filipino (7,930)	10,208	0.41
Hmong (14)	22	<0.01
Indian (26,144)	33,490	1.34
Indonesian (383)	564	0.02
Japanese (3,938)	5,917	0.24
Korean (6,904)	8,201	0.33
Laotian (82)	131	0.01
Malaysian (478)	708	0.03
Nepalese (355)	393	0.02
Pakistani (18,296)	19,840	0.79
Sri Lankan (219)	270	0.01
Taiwanese (857)	1,075	0.04
Thai (636)	883	0.04
Vietnamese (3,944)	5,041	0.20
Hawaii Native/Pacific Islander (1,243)	5,784	0.23
Not Hispanic (633)	3,463	0.14
Hispanic (610)	2,321	0.09
Fijian (20)	45	<0.01
Guamanian/Chamorro (386)	568	0.02
Marshallese (1)	2	<0.01
Native Hawaiian (208)	564	0.02
Samoan (72)	216	0.01
Tongan (5)	10	<0.01
White (1,072,041)	1,120,592	44.74
Not Hispanic (893,306)	917,717	36.64
Hispanic (178,735)	202,875	8.10

*Notes: † The Census 2010 population figure is used to calculate the percentages in the Hispanic Origin and Race categories. Ancestry percentages are based on the 2006-2010 American Community Survey population (not shown); ‡ Numbers in parentheses indicate the number of people reporting a single ancestry; * Numbers in parentheses indicate the number of persons reporting this race alone, not in combination with any other race; Please refer to the Explanation of Data for more information.*

Buffalo

Place Type: City
County: Erie
Population: 261,310

Ancestry	Population	%
Afghan (178)	178	0.07
African, Sub-Saharan (5,618)	6,085	2.29
African (3,925)	4,177	1.57
Cape Verdean (95)	95	0.04
Ethiopian (223)	223	0.08
Ghanaian (43)	43	0.02
Kenyan (38)	38	0.01
Liberian (74)	74	0.03
Nigerian (94)	105	0.04
Senegalese (0)	0	<0.01
Sierra Leonean (17)	17	0.01
Somalian (706)	858	0.32
South African (0)	0	<0.01
Sudanese (259)	268	0.10
Ugandan (24)	33	0.01
Zimbabwean (45)	45	0.02
Other Sub-Saharan African (75)	109	0.04
Albanian (360)	369	0.14
Alsatian (12)	12	<0.01
American (6,386)	6,386	2.40
Arab (1,374)	1,815	0.68
Arab (586)	644	0.24
Egyptian (27)	39	0.01
Iraqi (286)	288	0.11
Jordanian (2)	4	<0.01
Lebanese (165)	481	0.18
Moroccan (21)	57	0.02
Palestinian (0)	0	<0.01
Syrian (17)	32	0.01
Other Arab (270)	270	0.10
Armenian (39)	67	0.03
Assyrian/Chaldean/Syriac (0)	0	<0.01
Australian (0)	14	0.01
Austrian (244)	799	0.30
Basque (9)	9	<0.01
Belgian (21)	21	0.01
Brazilian (25)	25	0.01
British (306)	722	0.27
Bulgarian (114)	201	0.08
Cajun (0)	11	<0.01
Canadian (264)	558	0.21
Carpatho Rusyn (0)	0	<0.01
Celtic (0)	13	<0.01
Croatian (249)	487	0.18
Cypriot (0)	0	<0.01
Czech (13)	310	0.12
Czechoslovakian (76)	231	0.09
Danish (41)	152	0.06
Dutch (224)	1,451	0.55
Eastern European (189)	198	0.07
English (2,703)	11,203	4.21
Estonian (0)	11	<0.01
European (884)	1,016	0.38
Finnish (56)	248	0.09
French, ex. Basque (446)	4,110	1.55
French Canadian (420)	1,376	0.52
German (7,601)	35,760	13.44
German Russian (16)	41	0.02
Greek (305)	769	0.29
Guyanese (517)	529	0.20
Hungarian (748)	2,201	0.83
Icelander (0)	0	<0.01
Iranian (82)	125	0.05
Irish (9,009)	34,103	12.82
Israeli (104)	180	0.07
Italian (13,524)	30,606	11.51
Latvian (13)	22	0.01
Lithuanian (121)	358	0.13
Luxemburger (0)	24	0.01
Macedonian (40)	52	0.02
Maltese (0)	8	<0.01
New Zealander (0)	0	<0.01
Northern European (31)	31	0.01
Norwegian (78)	586	0.22
Pennsylvania German (0)	159	0.06
Polish (12,089)	28,108	10.57
Portuguese (169)	474	0.18
Romanian (30)	122	0.05
Russian (616)	1,883	0.71
Scandinavian (0)	76	0.03
Scotch-Irish (902)	2,324	0.87
Scottish (437)	2,816	1.06
Serbian (115)	291	0.11
Slavic (15)	35	0.01
Slovak (27)	174	0.07
Slovene (23)	100	0.04
Soviet Union (0)	0	<0.01
Swedish (309)	1,596	0.60
Swiss (41)	308	0.12
Turkish (251)	350	0.13
Ukrainian (899)	1,739	0.65
Welsh (90)	729	0.27
West Indian, ex. Hispanic (2,330)	2,773	1.04
Bahamian (13)	13	<0.01
Barbadian (18)	44	0.02
Belizean (0)	0	<0.01
Bermudan (0)	0	<0.01
British West Indian (102)	115	0.04
Dutch West Indian (0)	17	0.01
Haitian (480)	626	0.24
Jamaican (1,260)	1,420	0.53
Trinidadian/Tobagonian (196)	200	0.08
U.S. Virgin Islander (0)	0	<0.01
West Indian (261)	338	0.13
Other West Indian (0)	0	<0.01
Yugoslavian (187)	282	0.11

Hispanic Origin	Population	%
Hispanic or Latino (of any race)	27,519	10.53
Central American, ex. Mexican	386	0.15
Costa Rican	27	0.01
Guatemalan	72	0.03
Honduran	76	0.03
Nicaraguan	25	0.01
Panamanian	89	0.03
Salvadoran	92	0.04
Other Central American	5	<0.01
Cuban	795	0.30
Dominican Republic	707	0.27
Mexican	1,382	0.53
Puerto Rican	22,076	8.45
South American	679	0.26
Argentinean	117	0.04
Bolivian	35	0.01
Chilean	35	0.01
Colombian	215	0.08
Ecuadorian	106	0.04
Paraguayan	8	<0.01
Peruvian	105	0.04
Uruguayan	2	<0.01
Venezuelan	44	0.02
Other South American	12	<0.01
Other Hispanic or Latino	1,494	0.57

Race*	Population	%
African-American/Black (100,774)	106,107	40.61
Not Hispanic (97,637)	101,817	38.96
Hispanic (3,137)	4,290	1.64
American Indian/Alaska Native (2,009)	4,019	1.54
Not Hispanic (1,597)	3,229	1.24
Hispanic (412)	790	0.30
Alaska Athabascan (Ala. Nat.) (1)	1	<0.01
Aleut (Alaska Native) (0)	0	<0.01
Apache (5)	11	<0.01
Arapaho (0)	1	<0.01
Blackfeet (10)	104	0.04
Canadian/French Am. Ind. (29)	57	0.02
Central American Ind. (9)	17	0.01
Cherokee (37)	294	0.11
Cheyenne (0)	0	<0.01
Chickasaw (2)	2	<0.01
Chippewa (24)	42	0.02

	Population	%
Choctaw (3)	21	0.01
Colville (0)	0	<0.01
Comanche (1)	4	<0.01
Cree (1)	4	<0.01
Creek (0)	7	<0.01
Crow (0)	1	<0.01
Delaware (6)	10	<0.01
Hopi (0)	5	<0.01
Houma (1)	2	<0.01
Inupiat (Alaska Native) (2)	4	<0.01
Iroquois (935)	1,316	0.50
Kiowa (1)	1	<0.01
Lumbee (1)	1	<0.01
Menominee (2)	2	<0.01
Mexican American Ind. (19)	27	0.01
Navajo (8)	16	0.01
Osage (0)	0	<0.01
Ottawa (0)	0	<0.01
Paiute (0)	0	<0.01
Pima (1)	1	<0.01
Potawatomi (0)	0	<0.01
Pueblo (3)	4	<0.01
Puget Sound Salish (0)	0	<0.01
Seminole (3)	23	0.01
Shoshone (0)	0	<0.01
Sioux (24)	46	0.02
South American Ind. (24)	60	0.02
Spanish American Ind. (11)	14	0.01
Tlingit-Haida (Alaska Native) (2)	3	<0.01
Tohono O'Odham (1)	3	<0.01
Tsimshian (Alaska Native) (0)	0	<0.01
Ute (0)	0	<0.01
Yakama (0)	0	<0.01
Yaqui (2)	2	<0.01
Yuman (1)	1	<0.01
Yup'ik (Alaska Native) (0)	0	<0.01
Asian (8,409)	9,698	3.71
Not Hispanic (8,313)	9,459	3.62
Hispanic (96)	239	0.09
Bangladeshi (167)	206	0.08
Bhutanese (298)	370	0.14
Burmese (2,267)	2,361	0.90
Cambodian (43)	48	0.02
Chinese, ex. Taiwanese (919)	1,065	0.41
Filipino (214)	417	0.16
Hmong (5)	6	<0.01
Indian (1,576)	1,889	0.72
Indonesian (17)	22	0.01
Japanese (128)	243	0.09
Korean (350)	447	0.17
Laotian (248)	288	0.11
Malaysian (19)	21	0.01
Nepalese (115)	160	0.06
Pakistani (320)	362	0.14
Sri Lankan (45)	54	0.02
Taiwanese (31)	43	0.02
Thai (59)	107	0.04
Vietnamese (1,128)	1,220	0.47
Hawaii Native/Pacific Islander (119)	357	0.14
Not Hispanic (79)	252	0.10
Hispanic (40)	105	0.04
Fijian (0)	0	<0.01
Guamanian/Chamorro (10)	30	0.01
Marshallese (0)	0	<0.01
Native Hawaiian (21)	75	0.03
Samoan (32)	63	0.02
Tongan (3)	3	<0.01
White (131,753)	138,013	52.82
Not Hispanic (119,801)	124,612	47.69
Hispanic (11,952)	13,401	5.13

Notes: † The Census 2010 population figure is used to calculate the percentages in the Hispanic Origin and Race categories. Ancestry percentages are based on the 2006-2010 American Community Survey population (not shown); ‡ Numbers in parentheses indicate the number of people reporting a single ancestry; * Numbers in parentheses indicate the number of persons reporting this race alone, not in combination with any other race; Please refer to the Explanation of Data for more information.

Cheektowaga

Place Type: CDP
County: Erie
Population: 75,178

Ancestry	Population	%
Afghan (0)	0	<0.01
African, Sub-Saharan (178)	178	0.23
African (145)	145	0.19
Cape Verdean (0)	0	<0.01
Ethiopian (0)	0	<0.01
Ghanaian (0)	0	<0.01
Kenyan (0)	0	<0.01
Liberian (0)	0	<0.01
Nigerian (0)	0	<0.01
Senegalese (0)	0	<0.01
Sierra Leonean (0)	0	<0.01
Somalian (0)	0	<0.01
South African (0)	0	<0.01
Sudanese (0)	0	<0.01
Ugandan (0)	0	<0.01
Zimbabwean (0)	0	<0.01
Other Sub-Saharan African (33)	33	0.04
Albanian (15)	21	0.03
Alsatian (0)	0	<0.01
American (1,642)	1,642	2.17
Arab (498)	611	0.81
Arab (208)	224	0.30
Egyptian (0)	0	<0.01
Iraqi (30)	30	0.04
Jordanian (0)	0	<0.01
Lebanese (260)	338	0.45
Moroccan (0)	0	<0.01
Palestinian (0)	0	<0.01
Syrian (0)	13	0.02
Other Arab (0)	6	0.01
Armenian (0)	13	0.02
Assyrian/Chaldean/Syriac (0)	0	<0.01
Australian (0)	0	<0.01
Austrian (33)	202	0.27
Basque (0)	0	<0.01
Belgian (0)	29	0.04
Brazilian (0)	0	<0.01
British (51)	217	0.29
Bulgarian (30)	30	0.04
Cajun (0)	0	<0.01
Canadian (63)	193	0.25
Carpatho Rusyn (6)	6	0.01
Celtic (0)	0	<0.01
Croatian (21)	90	0.12
Cypriot (0)	0	<0.01
Czech (0)	249	0.33
Czechoslovakian (10)	10	0.01
Danish (0)	53	0.07
Dutch (59)	763	1.01
Eastern European (0)	0	<0.01
English (753)	4,258	5.62
Estonian (78)	78	0.10
European (101)	122	0.16
Finnish (12)	28	0.04
French, ex. Basque (123)	2,246	2.96
French Canadian (122)	608	0.80
German (6,860)	21,843	28.83
German Russian (12)	12	0.02
Greek (116)	188	0.25
Guyanese (23)	23	0.03
Hungarian (132)	542	0.72
Icelander (0)	0	<0.01
Iranian (0)	0	<0.01
Irish (2,376)	11,306	14.92
Israeli (0)	0	<0.01
Italian (5,350)	12,314	16.26
Latvian (16)	16	0.02
Lithuanian (12)	84	0.11
Luxemburger (0)	0	<0.01
Macedonian (21)	35	0.05
Maltese (0)	0	<0.01
New Zealander (11)	11	0.01
Northern European (0)	0	<0.01

Ancestry	Population	%
Norwegian (15)	247	0.33
Pennsylvania German (15)	24	0.03
Polish (15,029)	26,237	34.63
Portuguese (11)	75	0.10
Romanian (38)	51	0.07
Russian (173)	411	0.54
Scandinavian (0)	15	0.02
Scotch-Irish (268)	861	1.14
Scottish (183)	788	1.04
Serbian (82)	100	0.13
Slavic (11)	45	0.06
Slovak (71)	229	0.30
Slovene (0)	16	0.02
Soviet Union (0)	0	<0.01
Swedish (143)	418	0.55
Swiss (14)	63	0.08
Turkish (0)	42	0.06
Ukrainian (268)	499	0.66
Welsh (8)	327	0.43
West Indian, ex. Hispanic (240)	315	0.42
Bahamian (0)	0	<0.01
Barbadian (8)	8	0.01
Belizean (0)	0	<0.01
Bermudan (0)	0	<0.01
British West Indian (13)	13	0.02
Dutch West Indian (0)	0	<0.01
Haitian (7)	7	0.01
Jamaican (129)	182	0.24
Trinidadian/Tobagonian (33)	55	0.07
U.S. Virgin Islander (0)	0	<0.01
West Indian (50)	50	0.07
Other West Indian (0)	0	<0.01
Yugoslavian (69)	69	0.09

Hispanic Origin	Population	%
Hispanic or Latino (of any race)	1,672	2.22
Central American, ex. Mexican	55	0.07
Costa Rican	5	0.01
Guatemalan	11	0.01
Honduran	6	0.01
Nicaraguan	1	<0.01
Panamanian	13	0.02
Salvadoran	14	0.02
Other Central American	5	0.01
Cuban	47	0.06
Dominican Republic	55	0.07
Mexican	244	0.32
Puerto Rican	1,011	1.34
South American	105	0.14
Argentinean	7	0.01
Bolivian	6	0.01
Chilean	4	0.01
Colombian	39	0.05
Ecuadorian	22	0.03
Paraguayan	2	<0.01
Peruvian	10	0.01
Uruguayan	2	<0.01
Venezuelan	11	0.01
Other South American	2	<0.01
Other Hispanic or Latino	155	0.21

Race*	Population	%
African-American/Black (6,881)	7,619	10.13
Not Hispanic (6,716)	7,368	9.80
Hispanic (165)	251	0.33
American Indian/Alaska Native (189)	469	0.62
Not Hispanic (171)	416	0.55
Hispanic (18)	53	0.07
Alaska Athabascan (Ala. Nat.) (0)	0	<0.01
Aleut (Alaska Native) (0)	0	<0.01
Apache (1)	6	0.01
Arapaho (0)	0	<0.01
Blackfeet (0)	12	0.02
Canadian/French Am. Ind. (5)	5	0.01
Central American Ind. (1)	1	<0.01
Cherokee (6)	45	0.06
Cheyenne (0)	1	<0.01
Chickasaw (0)	0	<0.01
Chippewa (5)	6	0.01

Race*	Population	%
Choctaw (2)	3	<0.01
Colville (0)	0	<0.01
Comanche (0)	0	<0.01
Cree (0)	1	<0.01
Creek (1)	1	<0.01
Crow (0)	0	<0.01
Delaware (2)	2	<0.01
Hopi (2)	2	<0.01
Houma (0)	0	<0.01
Inupiat (Alaska Native) (0)	0	<0.01
Iroquois (95)	179	0.24
Kiowa (0)	0	<0.01
Lumbee (0)	0	<0.01
Menominee (0)	0	<0.01
Mexican American Ind. (5)	7	0.01
Navajo (1)	3	<0.01
Osage (0)	0	<0.01
Ottawa (0)	0	<0.01
Paiute (0)	0	<0.01
Pima (0)	0	<0.01
Potawatomi (0)	0	<0.01
Pueblo (0)	3	<0.01
Puget Sound Salish (0)	0	<0.01
Seminole (0)	0	<0.01
Shoshone (0)	0	<0.01
Sioux (1)	6	0.01
South American Ind. (0)	4	0.01
Spanish American Ind. (0)	0	<0.01
Tlingit-Haida (Alaska Native) (0)	0	<0.01
Tohono O'Odham (0)	0	<0.01
Tsimshian (Alaska Native) (0)	0	<0.01
Ute (0)	0	<0.01
Yakama (0)	0	<0.01
Yaqui (0)	0	<0.01
Yuman (0)	0	<0.01
Yup'ik (Alaska Native) (0)	0	<0.01
Asian (1,252)	1,476	1.96
Not Hispanic (1,249)	1,455	1.94
Hispanic (3)	21	0.03
Bangladeshi (2)	2	<0.01
Bhutanese (0)	0	<0.01
Burmese (6)	8	0.01
Cambodian (9)	11	0.01
Chinese, ex. Taiwanese (100)	134	0.18
Filipino (68)	112	0.15
Hmong (0)	1	<0.01
Indian (499)	529	0.70
Indonesian (6)	10	0.01
Japanese (16)	37	0.05
Korean (61)	89	0.12
Laotian (58)	65	0.09
Malaysian (12)	12	0.02
Nepalese (5)	5	0.01
Pakistani (37)	52	0.07
Sri Lankan (0)	2	<0.01
Taiwanese (4)	4	0.01
Thai (5)	10	0.01
Vietnamese (297)	326	0.43
Hawaii Native/Pacific Islander (12)	39	0.05
Not Hispanic (9)	30	0.04
Hispanic (3)	9	0.01
Fijian (2)	2	<0.01
Guamanian/Chamorro (2)	7	0.01
Marshallese (0)	0	<0.01
Native Hawaiian (5)	14	0.02
Samoan (1)	2	<0.01
Tongan (0)	0	<0.01
White (65,225)	66,265	88.14
Not Hispanic (64,288)	65,180	86.70
Hispanic (937)	1,085	1.44

Notes: † The Census 2010 population figure is used to calculate the percentages in the Hispanic Origin and Race categories. Ancestry percentages are based on the 2006-2010 American Community Survey population (not shown); ‡ Numbers in parentheses indicate the number of people reporting a single ancestry; * Numbers in parentheses indicate the number of persons reporting this race alone, not in combination with any other race; Please refer to the Explanation of Data for more information.

Cheektowaga

Place Type: Town
County: Erie
Population: 88,226

Ancestry	Population	%
Afghan (0)	0	<0.01
African, Sub-Saharan (178)	178	0.20
African (145)	145	0.16
Cape Verdean (0)	0	<0.01
Ethiopian (0)	0	<0.01
Ghanaian (0)	0	<0.01
Kenyan (0)	0	<0.01
Liberian (0)	0	<0.01
Nigerian (0)	0	<0.01
Senegalese (0)	0	<0.01
Sierra Leonean (0)	0	<0.01
Somalian (0)	0	<0.01
South African (0)	0	<0.01
Sudanese (0)	0	<0.01
Ugandan (0)	0	<0.01
Zimbabwean (0)	0	<0.01
Other Sub-Saharan African (33)	33	0.04
Albanian (15)	30	0.03
Alsatian (0)	0	<0.01
American (1,927)	1,927	2.17
Arab (768)	905	1.02
Arab (231)	247	0.28
Egyptian (0)	0	<0.01
Iraqi (30)	30	0.03
Jordanian (0)	0	<0.01
Lebanese (260)	350	0.39
Moroccan (0)	0	<0.01
Palestinian (9)	9	0.01
Syrian (0)	25	0.03
Other Arab (238)	244	0.27
Armenian (0)	13	0.01
Assyrian/Chaldean/Syriac (0)	0	<0.01
Australian (0)	0	<0.01
Austrian (33)	225	0.25
Basque (0)	0	<0.01
Belgian (0)	29	0.03
Brazilian (0)	0	<0.01
British (84)	277	0.31
Bulgarian (73)	73	0.08
Cajun (0)	0	<0.01
Canadian (72)	202	0.23
Carpatho Rusyn (6)	6	0.01
Celtic (0)	0	<0.01
Croatian (21)	90	0.10
Cypriot (0)	0	<0.01
Czech (29)	312	0.35
Czechoslovakian (48)	60	0.07
Danish (0)	53	0.06
Dutch (125)	935	1.05
Eastern European (0)	0	<0.01
English (852)	4,818	5.42
Estonian (78)	78	0.09
European (123)	144	0.16
Finnish (12)	28	0.03
French, ex. Basque (132)	2,577	2.90
French Canadian (122)	701	0.79
German (7,899)	26,125	29.39
German Russian (12)	12	0.01
Greek (169)	249	0.28
Guyanese (23)	23	0.03
Hungarian (132)	575	0.65
Icelander (0)	0	<0.01
Iranian (0)	0	<0.01
Irish (2,677)	13,325	14.99
Israeli (0)	0	<0.01
Italian (6,376)	14,630	16.46
Latvian (16)	16	0.02
Lithuanian (12)	99	0.11
Luxemburger (0)	0	<0.01
Macedonian (21)	35	0.04
Maltese (0)	0	<0.01
New Zealander (11)	11	0.01
Northern European (130)	130	0.15

Ancestry (cont.)	Population	%
Norwegian (15)	256	0.29
Pennsylvania German (24)	33	0.04
Polish (18,227)	31,456	35.39
Portuguese (11)	84	0.09
Romanian (38)	61	0.07
Russian (182)	430	0.48
Scandinavian (0)	44	0.05
Scotch-Irish (291)	969	1.09
Scottish (232)	954	1.07
Serbian (82)	100	0.11
Slavic (11)	45	0.05
Slovak (71)	229	0.26
Slovene (0)	16	0.02
Soviet Union (0)	0	<0.01
Swedish (228)	542	0.61
Swiss (26)	85	0.10
Turkish (0)	42	0.05
Ukrainian (295)	556	0.63
Welsh (8)	383	0.43
West Indian, ex. Hispanic (240)	315	0.35
Bahamian (0)	0	<0.01
Barbadian (8)	8	0.01
Belizean (0)	0	<0.01
Bermudan (0)	0	<0.01
British West Indian (13)	13	0.01
Dutch West Indian (0)	0	<0.01
Haitian (7)	7	0.01
Jamaican (129)	182	0.20
Trinidadian/Tobagonian (33)	55	0.06
U.S. Virgin Islander (0)	0	<0.01
West Indian (50)	50	0.06
Other West Indian (0)	0	<0.01
Yugoslavian (69)	69	0.08

Hispanic Origin	Population	%
Hispanic or Latino (of any race)	1,900	2.15
Central American, ex. Mexican	78	0.09
Costa Rican	5	0.01
Guatemalan	21	0.02
Honduran	6	0.01
Nicaraguan	4	<0.01
Panamanian	13	0.01
Salvadoran	21	0.02
Other Central American	8	0.01
Cuban	51	0.06
Dominican Republic	59	0.07
Mexican	285	0.32
Puerto Rican	1,138	1.29
South American	112	0.13
Argentinean	7	0.01
Bolivian	6	0.01
Chilean	4	<0.01
Colombian	41	0.05
Ecuadorian	26	0.03
Paraguayan	2	<0.01
Peruvian	10	0.01
Uruguayan	2	<0.01
Venezuelan	12	0.01
Other South American	2	<0.01
Other Hispanic or Latino	177	0.20

Race*	Population	%
African-American/Black (7,069)	7,879	8.93
Not Hispanic (6,898)	7,611	8.63
Hispanic (171)	268	0.30
American Indian/Alaska Native (223)	546	0.62
Not Hispanic (200)	482	0.55
Hispanic (23)	64	0.07
Alaska Athabascan (Ala. Nat.) (0)	0	<0.01
Aleut (Alaska Native) (0)	0	<0.01
Apache (1)	6	0.01
Arapaho (1)	1	<0.01
Blackfeet (0)	15	0.02
Canadian/French Am. Ind. (5)	5	0.01
Central American Ind. (3)	4	<0.01
Cherokee (6)	52	0.06
Cheyenne (0)	1	<0.01
Chickasaw (0)	0	<0.01
Chippewa (5)	6	0.01

Race* (cont.)	Population	%
Choctaw (2)	3	<0.01
Colville (0)	0	<0.01
Comanche (0)	0	<0.01
Cree (0)	1	<0.01
Creek (1)	2	<0.01
Crow (0)	0	<0.01
Delaware (2)	2	<0.01
Hopi (2)	2	<0.01
Houma (0)	0	<0.01
Inupiat (Alaska Native) (0)	0	<0.01
Iroquois (110)	194	0.22
Kiowa (0)	0	<0.01
Lumbee (0)	4	<0.01
Menominee (0)	0	<0.01
Mexican American Ind. (7)	9	0.01
Navajo (1)	3	<0.01
Osage (0)	0	<0.01
Ottawa (0)	0	<0.01
Paiute (0)	0	<0.01
Pima (0)	0	<0.01
Potawatomi (0)	0	<0.01
Pueblo (0)	3	<0.01
Puget Sound Salish (0)	0	<0.01
Seminole (0)	0	<0.01
Shoshone (0)	0	<0.01
Sioux (1)	6	0.01
South American Ind. (0)	4	<0.01
Spanish American Ind. (0)	0	<0.01
Tlingit-Haida (Alaska Native) (0)	0	<0.01
Tohono O'Odham (0)	0	<0.01
Tsimshian (Alaska Native) (0)	0	<0.01
Ute (0)	0	<0.01
Yakama (0)	0	<0.01
Yaqui (0)	0	<0.01
Yuman (0)	0	<0.01
Yup'ik (Alaska Native) (0)	0	<0.01
Asian (1,336)	1,598	1.81
Not Hispanic (1,333)	1,576	1.79
Hispanic (3)	22	0.02
Bangladeshi (4)	4	<0.01
Bhutanese (0)	0	<0.01
Burmese (6)	8	0.01
Cambodian (10)	15	0.02
Chinese, ex. Taiwanese (111)	146	0.17
Filipino (77)	128	0.15
Hmong (0)	1	<0.01
Indian (530)	568	0.64
Indonesian (6)	10	0.01
Japanese (17)	38	0.04
Korean (69)	106	0.12
Laotian (58)	65	0.07
Malaysian (13)	13	0.01
Nepalese (5)	5	0.01
Pakistani (37)	52	0.06
Sri Lankan (0)	2	<0.01
Taiwanese (4)	4	<0.01
Thai (5)	10	0.01
Vietnamese (315)	344	0.39
Hawaii Native/Pacific Islander (14)	43	0.05
Not Hispanic (10)	33	0.04
Hispanic (4)	10	0.01
Fijian (2)	2	<0.01
Guamanian/Chamorro (3)	8	0.01
Marshallese (0)	0	<0.01
Native Hawaiian (5)	16	0.02
Samoan (1)	5	0.01
Tongan (0)	0	<0.01
White (77,769)	78,958	89.50
Not Hispanic (76,673)	77,687	88.05
Hispanic (1,096)	1,271	1.44

Notes: † The Census 2010 population figure is used to calculate the percentages in the Hispanic Origin and Race categories. Ancestry percentages are based on the 2006-2010 American Community Survey population (not shown); ‡ Numbers in parentheses indicate the number of people reporting a single ancestry; * Numbers in parentheses indicate the number of persons reporting this race alone, not in combination with any other race; Please refer to the Explanation of Data for more information.

Clarkstown

Place Type: Town
County: Rockland
Population: 84,187

Ancestry	Population	%
Afghan (0)	0	<0.01
African, Sub-Saharan (248)	283	0.34
African (149)	184	0.22
Cape Verdean (0)	0	<0.01
Ethiopian (0)	0	<0.01
Ghanaian (99)	99	0.12
Kenyan (0)	0	<0.01
Liberian (0)	0	<0.01
Nigerian (0)	0	<0.01
Senegalese (0)	0	<0.01
Sierra Leonean (0)	0	<0.01
Somalian (0)	0	<0.01
South African (0)	0	<0.01
Sudanese (0)	0	<0.01
Ugandan (0)	0	<0.01
Zimbabwean (0)	0	<0.01
Other Sub-Saharan African (0)	0	<0.01
Albanian (317)	328	0.39
Alsatian (0)	3	<0.01
American (4,138)	4,138	4.96
Arab (440)	705	0.85
Arab (8)	29	0.03
Egyptian (229)	254	0.30
Iraqi (7)	24	0.03
Jordanian (9)	9	0.01
Lebanese (138)	252	0.30
Moroccan (0)	0	<0.01
Palestinian (0)	0	<0.01
Syrian (0)	88	0.11
Other Arab (49)	49	0.06
Armenian (84)	99	0.12
Assyrian/Chaldean/Syriac (11)	51	0.06
Australian (12)	18	0.02
Austrian (199)	827	0.99
Basque (0)	0	<0.01
Belgian (0)	42	0.05
Brazilian (69)	203	0.24
British (105)	190	0.23
Bulgarian (0)	0	<0.01
Cajun (0)	0	<0.01
Canadian (78)	112	0.13
Carpatho Rusyn (0)	0	<0.01
Celtic (0)	0	<0.01
Croatian (54)	111	0.13
Cypriot (0)	0	<0.01
Czech (65)	292	0.35
Czechoslovakian (75)	123	0.15
Danish (20)	91	0.11
Dutch (130)	487	0.58
Eastern European (1,163)	1,282	1.54
English (620)	2,751	3.30
Estonian (0)	0	<0.01
European (659)	690	0.83
Finnish (50)	119	0.14
French, ex. Basque (154)	874	1.05
French Canadian (98)	288	0.35
German (1,752)	7,742	9.28
German Russian (0)	0	<0.01
Greek (204)	613	0.74
Guyanese (77)	95	0.11
Hungarian (301)	1,008	1.21
Icelander (0)	0	<0.01
Iranian (100)	146	0.18
Irish (7,258)	15,823	18.97
Israeli (99)	247	0.30
Italian (9,086)	16,766	20.10
Latvian (64)	87	0.10
Lithuanian (129)	286	0.34
Luxemburger (0)	0	<0.01
Macedonian (24)	24	0.03
Maltese (0)	8	0.01
New Zealander (0)	3	<0.01
Northern European (15)	28	0.03
Norwegian (214)	464	0.56
Pennsylvania German (0)	0	<0.01
Polish (1,491)	4,159	4.99
Portuguese (165)	216	0.26
Romanian (167)	544	0.65
Russian (2,652)	5,317	6.38
Scandinavian (12)	16	0.02
Scotch-Irish (228)	499	0.60
Scottish (102)	591	0.71
Serbian (11)	19	0.02
Slavic (11)	40	0.05
Slovak (179)	310	0.37
Slovene (0)	0	<0.01
Soviet Union (0)	0	<0.01
Swedish (65)	359	0.43
Swiss (39)	85	0.10
Turkish (66)	72	0.09
Ukrainian (387)	690	0.83
Welsh (0)	212	0.25
West Indian, ex. Hispanic (2,635)	2,834	3.40
Bahamian (0)	0	<0.01
Barbadian (10)	10	0.01
Belizean (9)	9	0.01
Bermudan (0)	3	<0.01
British West Indian (21)	45	0.05
Dutch West Indian (0)	0	<0.01
Haitian (2,003)	2,077	2.49
Jamaican (382)	432	0.52
Trinidadian/Tobagonian (90)	117	0.14
U.S. Virgin Islander (0)	0	<0.01
West Indian (120)	141	0.17
Other West Indian (0)	0	<0.01
Yugoslavian (43)	53	0.06

Hispanic Origin	Population	%
Hispanic or Latino (of any race)	9,831	11.68
Central American, ex. Mexican	1,656	1.97
Costa Rican	40	0.05
Guatemalan	802	0.95
Honduran	80	0.10
Nicaraguan	10	0.01
Panamanian	41	0.05
Salvadoran	662	0.79
Other Central American	21	0.02
Cuban	421	0.50
Dominican Republic	939	1.12
Mexican	897	1.07
Puerto Rican	3,427	4.07
South American	1,708	2.03
Argentinean	113	0.13
Bolivian	31	0.04
Chilean	73	0.09
Colombian	281	0.33
Ecuadorian	1,051	1.25
Paraguayan	5	0.01
Peruvian	119	0.14
Uruguayan	14	0.02
Venezuelan	14	0.02
Other South American	7	0.01
Other Hispanic or Latino	783	0.93

Race*	Population	%
African-American/Black (8,091)	8,965	10.65
Not Hispanic (7,598)	8,194	9.73
Hispanic (493)	771	0.92
American Indian/Alaska Native (193)	459	0.55
Not Hispanic (111)	308	0.37
Hispanic (82)	151	0.18
Alaska Athabascan (Ala. Nat.) (0)	0	<0.01
Aleut (Alaska Native) (0)	0	<0.01
Apache (0)	2	<0.01
Arapaho (0)	0	<0.01
Blackfeet (1)	8	0.01
Canadian/French Am. Ind. (0)	0	<0.01
Central American Ind. (1)	2	<0.01
Cherokee (1)	42	0.05
Cheyenne (0)	0	<0.01
Chickasaw (0)	0	<0.01
Chippewa (1)	1	<0.01

	Population	%
Choctaw (1)	6	0.01
Colville (0)	0	<0.01
Comanche (0)	0	<0.01
Cree (0)	1	<0.01
Creek (0)	3	<0.01
Crow (0)	0	<0.01
Delaware (12)	16	0.02
Hopi (0)	0	<0.01
Houma (0)	0	<0.01
Inupiat (Alaska Native) (0)	0	<0.01
Iroquois (8)	13	0.02
Kiowa (0)	0	<0.01
Lumbee (2)	2	<0.01
Menominee (0)	0	<0.01
Mexican American Ind. (6)	8	0.01
Navajo (0)	1	<0.01
Osage (0)	0	<0.01
Ottawa (0)	0	<0.01
Paiute (1)	1	<0.01
Pima (0)	0	<0.01
Potawatomi (1)	1	<0.01
Pueblo (1)	4	<0.01
Puget Sound Salish (0)	0	<0.01
Seminole (0)	4	<0.01
Shoshone (0)	0	<0.01
Sioux (1)	2	<0.01
South American Ind. (22)	38	0.05
Spanish American Ind. (0)	0	<0.01
Tlingit-Haida (Alaska Native) (0)	1	<0.01
Tohono O'Odham (0)	0	<0.01
Tsimshian (Alaska Native) (0)	0	<0.01
Ute (0)	0	<0.01
Yakama (0)	0	<0.01
Yaqui (0)	0	<0.01
Yuman (0)	0	<0.01
Yup'ik (Alaska Native) (0)	0	<0.01
Asian (8,800)	9,614	11.42
Not Hispanic (8,748)	9,462	11.24
Hispanic (52)	152	0.18
Bangladeshi (73)	85	0.10
Bhutanese (0)	0	<0.01
Burmese (4)	8	0.01
Cambodian (59)	68	0.08
Chinese, ex. Taiwanese (1,132)	1,326	1.58
Filipino (2,079)	2,320	2.76
Hmong (0)	0	<0.01
Indian (3,576)	3,874	4.60
Indonesian (5)	14	0.02
Japanese (73)	110	0.13
Korean (994)	1,026	1.22
Laotian (0)	0	<0.01
Malaysian (3)	6	0.01
Nepalese (2)	2	<0.01
Pakistani (322)	346	0.41
Sri Lankan (43)	55	0.07
Taiwanese (49)	58	0.07
Thai (109)	121	0.14
Vietnamese (129)	164	0.19
Hawaii Native/Pacific Islander (22)	106	0.13
Not Hispanic (5)	77	0.09
Hispanic (17)	29	0.03
Fijian (0)	0	<0.01
Guamanian/Chamorro (13)	21	0.02
Marshallese (0)	0	<0.01
Native Hawaiian (1)	5	0.01
Samoan (1)	2	<0.01
Tongan (0)	0	<0.01
White (62,210)	63,664	75.62
Not Hispanic (56,369)	57,290	68.05
Hispanic (5,841)	6,374	7.57

Notes: † The Census 2010 population figure is used to calculate the percentages in the Hispanic Origin and Race categories. Ancestry percentages are based on the 2006-2010 American Community Survey population (not shown); ‡ Numbers in parentheses indicate the number of people reporting a single ancestry; * Numbers in parentheses indicate the number of persons reporting this race alone, not in combination with any other race; Please refer to the Explanation of Data for more information.

Clay

Place Type: Town
County: Onondaga
Population: 58,206

Ancestry	Population	%
Afghan (0)	0	<0.01
African, Sub-Saharan (172)	216	0.37
African (107)	145	0.25
Cape Verdean (0)	6	0.01
Ethiopian (0)	0	<0.01
Ghanaian (65)	65	0.11
Kenyan (0)	0	<0.01
Liberian (0)	0	<0.01
Nigerian (0)	0	<0.01
Senegalese (0)	0	<0.01
Sierra Leonean (0)	0	<0.01
Somalian (0)	0	<0.01
South African (0)	0	<0.01
Sudanese (0)	0	<0.01
Ugandan (0)	0	<0.01
Zimbabwean (0)	0	<0.01
Other Sub-Saharan African (0)	0	<0.01
Albanian (10)	31	0.05
Alsatian (0)	0	<0.01
American (1,975)	1,975	3.40
Arab (153)	417	0.72
Arab (58)	136	0.23
Egyptian (7)	7	0.01
Iraqi (0)	0	<0.01
Jordanian (0)	0	<0.01
Lebanese (47)	213	0.37
Moroccan (0)	0	<0.01
Palestinian (0)	13	0.02
Syrian (0)	7	0.01
Other Arab (41)	41	0.07
Armenian (0)	0	<0.01
Assyrian/Chaldean/Syriac (0)	0	<0.01
Australian (0)	0	<0.01
Austrian (49)	113	0.19
Basque (0)	0	<0.01
Belgian (57)	68	0.12
Brazilian (43)	43	0.07
British (33)	118	0.20
Bulgarian (0)	0	<0.01
Cajun (0)	0	<0.01
Canadian (176)	345	0.59
Carpatho Rusyn (0)	0	<0.01
Celtic (0)	47	0.08
Croatian (0)	0	<0.01
Cypriot (0)	0	<0.01
Czech (35)	312	0.54
Czechoslovakian (0)	34	0.06
Danish (0)	68	0.12
Dutch (106)	1,704	2.93
Eastern European (25)	40	0.07
English (1,748)	8,266	14.23
Estonian (0)	0	<0.01
European (505)	550	0.95
Finnish (20)	55	0.09
French, ex. Basque (420)	3,175	5.47
French Canadian (432)	1,241	2.14
German (2,624)	14,237	24.51
German Russian (0)	0	<0.01
Greek (203)	475	0.82
Guyanese (17)	17	0.03
Hungarian (170)	353	0.61
Icelander (0)	0	<0.01
Iranian (78)	99	0.17
Irish (3,324)	14,197	24.44
Israeli (0)	0	<0.01
Italian (5,434)	13,235	22.78
Latvian (0)	0	<0.01
Lithuanian (78)	143	0.25
Luxemburger (0)	26	0.04
Macedonian (177)	185	0.32
Maltese (0)	0	<0.01
New Zealander (0)	0	<0.01
Northern European (35)	35	0.06
Norwegian (55)	221	0.38
Pennsylvania German (20)	38	0.07
Polish (1,694)	4,728	8.14
Portuguese (0)	37	0.06
Romanian (0)	29	0.05
Russian (60)	276	0.48
Scandinavian (8)	8	0.01
Scotch-Irish (380)	1,162	2.00
Scottish (302)	1,377	2.37
Serbian (0)	9	0.02
Slavic (8)	93	0.16
Slovak (78)	150	0.26
Slovene (0)	9	0.02
Soviet Union (0)	0	<0.01
Swedish (114)	625	1.08
Swiss (22)	175	0.30
Turkish (11)	11	0.02
Ukrainian (136)	650	1.12
Welsh (52)	496	0.85
West Indian, ex. Hispanic (380)	494	0.85
Bahamian (0)	0	<0.01
Barbadian (9)	40	0.07
Belizean (0)	0	<0.01
Bermudan (0)	0	<0.01
British West Indian (0)	0	<0.01
Dutch West Indian (0)	0	<0.01
Haitian (157)	157	0.27
Jamaican (162)	245	0.42
Trinidadian/Tobagonian (40)	40	0.07
U.S. Virgin Islander (0)	0	<0.01
West Indian (12)	12	0.02
Other West Indian (0)	0	<0.01
Yugoslavian (108)	132	0.23

Hispanic Origin	Population	%
Hispanic or Latino (of any race)	1,472	2.53
Central American, ex. Mexican	94	0.16
Costa Rican	3	0.01
Guatemalan	35	0.06
Honduran	16	0.03
Nicaraguan	12	0.02
Panamanian	21	0.04
Salvadoran	7	0.01
Other Central American	0	<0.01
Cuban	91	0.16
Dominican Republic	61	0.10
Mexican	283	0.49
Puerto Rican	633	1.09
South American	161	0.28
Argentinean	7	0.01
Bolivian	8	0.01
Chilean	16	0.03
Colombian	65	0.11
Ecuadorian	10	0.02
Paraguayan	6	0.01
Peruvian	29	0.05
Uruguayan	2	<0.01
Venezuelan	16	0.03
Other South American	2	<0.01
Other Hispanic or Latino	149	0.26

Race*	Population	%
African-American/Black (2,524)	3,202	5.50
Not Hispanic (2,398)	3,014	5.18
Hispanic (126)	188	0.32
American Indian/Alaska Native (266)	627	1.08
Not Hispanic (228)	557	0.96
Hispanic (38)	70	0.12
Alaska Athabascan (Ala. Nat.) (0)	0	<0.01
Aleut (Alaska Native) (0)	0	<0.01
Apache (1)	3	0.01
Arapaho (0)	0	<0.01
Blackfeet (0)	11	0.02
Canadian/French Am. Ind. (9)	16	0.03
Central American Ind. (0)	0	<0.01
Cherokee (8)	42	0.07
Cheyenne (0)	0	<0.01
Chickasaw (0)	0	<0.01
Chippewa (5)	11	0.02
Choctaw (1)	5	0.01
Colville (0)	0	<0.01
Comanche (1)	1	<0.01
Cree (1)	1	<0.01
Creek (0)	1	<0.01
Crow (0)	0	<0.01
Delaware (0)	1	<0.01
Hopi (0)	2	<0.01
Houma (1)	1	<0.01
Inupiat (Alaska Native) (0)	1	<0.01
Iroquois (130)	252	0.43
Kiowa (0)	0	<0.01
Lumbee (0)	3	0.01
Menominee (0)	0	<0.01
Mexican American Ind. (5)	9	0.02
Navajo (3)	4	0.01
Osage (1)	1	<0.01
Ottawa (1)	1	<0.01
Paiute (0)	0	<0.01
Pima (0)	0	<0.01
Potawatomi (0)	1	<0.01
Pueblo (0)	0	<0.01
Puget Sound Salish (0)	0	<0.01
Seminole (0)	3	0.01
Shoshone (0)	0	<0.01
Sioux (2)	4	0.01
South American Ind. (1)	4	0.01
Spanish American Ind. (8)	8	0.01
Tlingit-Haida (Alaska Native) (0)	0	<0.01
Tohono O'Odham (0)	0	<0.01
Tsimshian (Alaska Native) (0)	0	<0.01
Ute (0)	0	<0.01
Yakama (0)	0	<0.01
Yaqui (0)	0	<0.01
Yuman (0)	0	<0.01
Yup'ik (Alaska Native) (0)	0	<0.01
Asian (1,430)	1,754	3.01
Not Hispanic (1,426)	1,733	2.98
Hispanic (4)	21	0.04
Bangladeshi (0)	1	<0.01
Bhutanese (0)	0	<0.01
Burmese (5)	5	0.01
Cambodian (28)	29	0.05
Chinese, ex. Taiwanese (259)	299	0.51
Filipino (123)	192	0.33
Hmong (61)	75	0.13
Indian (367)	398	0.68
Indonesian (1)	2	<0.01
Japanese (21)	66	0.11
Korean (130)	190	0.33
Laotian (47)	52	0.09
Malaysian (0)	1	<0.01
Nepalese (4)	4	0.01
Pakistani (47)	52	0.09
Sri Lankan (2)	2	<0.01
Taiwanese (11)	12	0.02
Thai (14)	18	0.03
Vietnamese (246)	265	0.46
Hawaii Native/Pacific Islander (20)	44	0.08
Not Hispanic (17)	40	0.07
Hispanic (3)	4	0.01
Fijian (0)	0	<0.01
Guamanian/Chamorro (6)	7	0.01
Marshallese (0)	0	<0.01
Native Hawaiian (7)	18	0.03
Samoan (0)	1	<0.01
Tongan (0)	0	<0.01
White (52,324)	53,514	91.94
Not Hispanic (51,459)	52,515	90.22
Hispanic (865)	999	1.72

Notes: † The Census 2010 population figure is used to calculate the percentages in the Hispanic Origin and Race categories. Ancestry percentages are based on the 2006-2010 American Community Survey population (not shown); ‡ Numbers in parentheses indicate the number of people reporting a single ancestry; * Numbers in parentheses indicate the number of persons reporting this race alone, not in combination with any other race; Please refer to the Explanation of Data for more information.

Colonie

Place Type: Town
County: Albany
Population: 81,591

Ancestry	Population	%
Afghan (0)	0	<0.01
African, Sub-Saharan (408)	482	0.59
African (259)	310	0.38
Cape Verdean (0)	0	<0.01
Ethiopian (13)	13	0.02
Ghanaian (11)	11	0.01
Kenyan (0)	0	<0.01
Liberian (0)	0	<0.01
Nigerian (80)	80	0.10
Senegalese (0)	0	<0.01
Sierra Leonean (0)	0	<0.01
Somalian (0)	0	<0.01
South African (9)	32	0.04
Sudanese (0)	0	<0.01
Ugandan (0)	0	<0.01
Zimbabwean (0)	0	<0.01
Other Sub-Saharan African (36)	36	0.04
Albanian (405)	405	0.50
Alsatian (0)	0	<0.01
American (2,133)	2,133	2.62
Arab (561)	863	1.06
Arab (0)	17	0.02
Egyptian (125)	125	0.15
Iraqi (0)	0	<0.01
Jordanian (0)	0	<0.01
Lebanese (144)	267	0.33
Moroccan (64)	111	0.14
Palestinian (72)	72	0.09
Syrian (27)	116	0.14
Other Arab (129)	155	0.19
Armenian (142)	244	0.30
Assyrian/Chaldean/Syriac (0)	0	<0.01
Australian (10)	10	0.01
Austrian (112)	470	0.58
Basque (0)	0	<0.01
Belgian (0)	25	0.03
Brazilian (13)	13	0.02
British (140)	240	0.29
Bulgarian (9)	9	0.01
Cajun (0)	0	<0.01
Canadian (114)	321	0.39
Carpatho Rusyn (0)	0	<0.01
Celtic (11)	11	0.01
Croatian (16)	74	0.09
Cypriot (0)	0	<0.01
Czech (134)	453	0.56
Czechoslovakian (26)	124	0.15
Danish (35)	195	0.24
Dutch (627)	3,334	4.09
Eastern European (46)	83	0.10
English (1,400)	8,332	10.22
Estonian (0)	0	<0.01
European (492)	544	0.67
Finnish (6)	68	0.08
French, ex. Basque (786)	5,795	7.11
French Canadian (545)	1,591	1.95
German (2,908)	14,495	17.78
German Russian (0)	0	<0.01
Greek (238)	563	0.69
Guyanese (116)	137	0.17
Hungarian (124)	542	0.66
Icelander (0)	0	<0.01
Iranian (9)	9	0.01
Irish (6,490)	23,049	28.27
Israeli (42)	42	0.05
Italian (6,582)	16,393	20.11
Latvian (34)	34	0.04
Lithuanian (55)	377	0.46
Luxemburger (0)	13	0.02
Macedonian (0)	0	<0.01
Maltese (0)	0	<0.01
New Zealander (0)	0	<0.01
Northern European (39)	39	0.05

Ancestry	Population	%
Norwegian (159)	598	0.73
Pennsylvania German (17)	25	0.03
Polish (2,206)	6,915	8.48
Portuguese (0)	80	0.10
Romanian (55)	228	0.28
Russian (690)	1,626	1.99
Scandinavian (27)	39	0.05
Scotch-Irish (468)	1,261	1.55
Scottish (263)	1,526	1.87
Serbian (0)	0	<0.01
Slavic (18)	28	0.03
Slovak (72)	185	0.23
Slovene (0)	0	<0.01
Soviet Union (0)	0	<0.01
Swedish (217)	944	1.16
Swiss (17)	145	0.18
Turkish (10)	10	0.01
Ukrainian (212)	860	1.05
Welsh (41)	704	0.86
West Indian, ex. Hispanic (372)	580	0.71
Bahamian (0)	0	<0.01
Barbadian (0)	0	<0.01
Belizean (0)	0	<0.01
Bermudan (0)	0	<0.01
British West Indian (0)	0	<0.01
Dutch West Indian (0)	0	<0.01
Haitian (60)	83	0.10
Jamaican (235)	373	0.46
Trinidadian/Tobagonian (0)	4	<0.01
U.S. Virgin Islander (0)	0	<0.01
West Indian (77)	120	0.15
Other West Indian (0)	0	<0.01
Yugoslavian (143)	143	0.18

Hispanic Origin	Population	%
Hispanic or Latino (of any race)	2,526	3.10
Central American, ex. Mexican	159	0.19
Costa Rican	24	0.03
Guatemalan	25	0.03
Honduran	20	0.02
Nicaraguan	17	0.02
Panamanian	13	0.02
Salvadoran	59	0.07
Other Central American	1	<0.01
Cuban	114	0.14
Dominican Republic	224	0.27
Mexican	462	0.57
Puerto Rican	1,001	1.23
South American	278	0.34
Argentinean	26	0.03
Bolivian	9	0.01
Chilean	12	0.01
Colombian	94	0.12
Ecuadorian	35	0.04
Paraguayan	3	<0.01
Peruvian	76	0.09
Uruguayan	1	<0.01
Venezuelan	19	0.02
Other South American	3	<0.01
Other Hispanic or Latino	288	0.35

Race*	Population	%
African-American/Black (4,288)	5,091	6.24
Not Hispanic (4,061)	4,752	5.82
Hispanic (227)	339	0.42
American Indian/Alaska Native (121)	397	0.49
Not Hispanic (79)	318	0.39
Hispanic (42)	79	0.10
Alaska Athabascan (Ala. Nat.) (1)	1	<0.01
Aleut (Alaska Native) (0)	0	<0.01
Apache (0)	0	<0.01
Arapaho (0)	0	<0.01
Blackfeet (1)	11	0.01
Canadian/French Am. Ind. (6)	10	0.01
Central American Ind. (3)	3	<0.01
Cherokee (6)	32	0.04
Cheyenne (0)	0	<0.01
Chickasaw (0)	0	<0.01
Chippewa (0)	1	<0.01

Race*	Population	%
Choctaw (0)	1	<0.01
Colville (0)	0	<0.01
Comanche (0)	0	<0.01
Cree (0)	2	<0.01
Creek (0)	0	<0.01
Crow (1)	1	<0.01
Delaware (0)	0	<0.01
Hopi (0)	0	<0.01
Houma (0)	0	<0.01
Inupiat (Alaska Native) (0)	0	<0.01
Iroquois (15)	50	0.06
Kiowa (0)	0	<0.01
Lumbee (0)	0	<0.01
Menominee (0)	0	<0.01
Mexican American Ind. (28)	29	0.04
Navajo (0)	1	<0.01
Osage (0)	1	<0.01
Ottawa (0)	0	<0.01
Paiute (0)	0	<0.01
Pima (0)	0	<0.01
Potawatomi (0)	1	<0.01
Pueblo (0)	0	<0.01
Puget Sound Salish (0)	0	<0.01
Seminole (0)	3	<0.01
Shoshone (0)	0	<0.01
Sioux (3)	7	0.01
South American Ind. (5)	10	0.01
Spanish American Ind. (0)	2	<0.01
Tlingit-Haida (Alaska Native) (1)	1	<0.01
Tohono O'Odham (0)	0	<0.01
Tsimshian (Alaska Native) (0)	0	<0.01
Ute (0)	0	<0.01
Yakama (0)	0	<0.01
Yaqui (0)	0	<0.01
Yuman (0)	0	<0.01
Yup'ik (Alaska Native) (0)	0	<0.01
Asian (5,353)	5,892	7.22
Not Hispanic (5,342)	5,866	7.19
Hispanic (11)	26	0.03
Bangladeshi (78)	80	0.10
Bhutanese (0)	0	<0.01
Burmese (3)	4	<0.01
Cambodian (2)	3	<0.01
Chinese, ex. Taiwanese (1,186)	1,284	1.57
Filipino (306)	397	0.49
Hmong (0)	0	<0.01
Indian (1,969)	2,099	2.57
Indonesian (11)	13	0.02
Japanese (58)	90	0.11
Korean (471)	531	0.65
Laotian (2)	4	<0.01
Malaysian (3)	5	0.01
Nepalese (13)	13	0.02
Pakistani (680)	736	0.90
Sri Lankan (24)	30	0.04
Taiwanese (48)	60	0.07
Thai (30)	40	0.05
Vietnamese (313)	360	0.44
Hawaii Native/Pacific Islander (15)	66	0.08
Not Hispanic (14)	47	0.06
Hispanic (1)	19	0.02
Fijian (1)	1	<0.01
Guamanian/Chamorro (2)	6	0.01
Marshallese (0)	0	<0.01
Native Hawaiian (2)	10	0.01
Samoan (4)	9	0.01
Tongan (1)	5	0.01
White (69,541)	70,917	86.92
Not Hispanic (68,088)	69,290	84.92
Hispanic (1,453)	1,627	1.99

Notes: † The Census 2010 population figure is used to calculate the percentages in the Hispanic Origin and Race categories. Ancestry percentages are based on the 2006-2010 American Community Survey population (not shown); ‡ Numbers in parentheses indicate the number of people reporting a single ancestry; * Numbers in parentheses indicate the number of persons reporting this race alone, not in combination with any other race; Please refer to the Explanation of Data for more information.

Greece

Place Type: Town
County: Monroe
Population: 96,095

Ancestry	Population	%
Afghan (0)	0	<0.01
African, Sub-Saharan (373)	434	0.45
African (217)	244	0.26
Cape Verdean (0)	0	<0.01
Ethiopian (49)	49	0.05
Ghanaian (0)	0	<0.01
Kenyan (0)	0	<0.01
Liberian (0)	0	<0.01
Nigerian (0)	0	<0.01
Senegalese (0)	0	<0.01
Sierra Leonean (0)	0	<0.01
Somalian (0)	0	<0.01
South African (38)	48	0.05
Sudanese (27)	51	0.05
Ugandan (0)	0	<0.01
Zimbabwean (0)	0	<0.01
Other Sub-Saharan African (42)	42	0.04
Albanian (113)	113	0.12
Alsatian (0)	0	<0.01
American (2,361)	2,361	2.47
Arab (161)	384	0.40
Arab (0)	42	0.04
Egyptian (0)	0	<0.01
Iraqi (0)	0	<0.01
Jordanian (0)	0	<0.01
Lebanese (98)	214	0.22
Moroccan (0)	0	<0.01
Palestinian (0)	31	0.03
Syrian (63)	97	0.10
Other Arab (0)	0	<0.01
Armenian (0)	0	<0.01
Assyrian/Chaldean/Syriac (0)	0	<0.01
Australian (29)	87	0.09
Austrian (36)	225	0.24
Basque (0)	0	<0.01
Belgian (57)	254	0.27
Brazilian (23)	23	0.02
British (178)	387	0.41
Bulgarian (25)	25	0.03
Cajun (0)	0	<0.01
Canadian (228)	525	0.55
Carpatho Rusyn (0)	0	<0.01
Celtic (12)	12	0.01
Croatian (0)	13	0.01
Cypriot (0)	0	<0.01
Czech (77)	507	0.53
Czechoslovakian (55)	151	0.16
Danish (40)	144	0.15
Dutch (571)	2,890	3.03
Eastern European (81)	115	0.12
English (3,011)	12,568	13.17
Estonian (0)	40	0.04
European (406)	451	0.47
Finnish (15)	62	0.06
French, ex. Basque (553)	3,655	3.83
French Canadian (346)	1,220	1.28
German (6,357)	25,631	26.85
German Russian (0)	0	<0.01
Greek (153)	610	0.64
Guyanese (40)	40	0.04
Hungarian (85)	397	0.42
Icelander (0)	0	<0.01
Iranian (14)	14	0.01
Irish (4,177)	19,015	19.92
Israeli (0)	0	<0.01
Italian (15,156)	26,121	27.36
Latvian (12)	71	0.07
Lithuanian (183)	543	0.57
Luxemburger (0)	15	0.02
Macedonian (92)	119	0.12
Maltese (0)	0	<0.01
New Zealander (0)	0	<0.01
Northern European (0)	0	<0.01

Ancestry	Population	%
Norwegian (139)	434	0.45
Pennsylvania German (46)	145	0.15
Polish (1,797)	5,879	6.16
Portuguese (111)	314	0.33
Romanian (16)	60	0.06
Russian (229)	654	0.69
Scandinavian (10)	88	0.09
Scotch-Irish (524)	1,469	1.54
Scottish (452)	1,843	1.93
Serbian (10)	10	0.01
Slavic (156)	240	0.25
Slovak (81)	236	0.25
Slovene (31)	31	0.03
Soviet Union (0)	0	<0.01
Swedish (31)	447	0.47
Swiss (16)	116	0.12
Turkish (489)	561	0.59
Ukrainian (993)	1,758	1.84
Welsh (36)	564	0.59
West Indian, ex. Hispanic (285)	447	0.47
Bahamian (0)	0	<0.01
Barbadian (16)	16	0.02
Belizean (0)	0	<0.01
Bermudan (0)	0	<0.01
British West Indian (0)	0	<0.01
Dutch West Indian (0)	0	<0.01
Haitian (114)	114	0.12
Jamaican (144)	243	0.25
Trinidadian/Tobagonian (11)	27	0.03
U.S. Virgin Islander (0)	0	<0.01
West Indian (0)	47	0.05
Other West Indian (0)	0	<0.01
Yugoslavian (77)	91	0.10

Hispanic Origin	Population	%
Hispanic or Latino (of any race)	4,625	4.81
Central American, ex. Mexican	159	0.17
Costa Rican	11	0.01
Guatemalan	27	0.03
Honduran	12	0.01
Nicaraguan	22	0.02
Panamanian	18	0.02
Salvadoran	68	0.07
Other Central American	1	<0.01
Cuban	312	0.32
Dominican Republic	194	0.20
Mexican	338	0.35
Puerto Rican	3,072	3.20
South American	257	0.27
Argentinean	7	0.01
Bolivian	1	<0.01
Chilean	63	0.07
Colombian	89	0.09
Ecuadorian	21	0.02
Paraguayan	4	<0.01
Peruvian	33	0.03
Uruguayan	4	<0.01
Venezuelan	27	0.03
Other South American	8	0.01
Other Hispanic or Latino	293	0.30

Race*	Population	%
African-American/Black (5,743)	6,728	7.00
Not Hispanic (5,446)	6,227	6.48
Hispanic (297)	501	0.52
American Indian/Alaska Native (263)	658	0.68
Not Hispanic (212)	545	0.57
Hispanic (51)	113	0.12
Alaska Athabascan (Ala. Nat.) (0)	0	<0.01
Aleut (Alaska Native) (0)	0	<0.01
Apache (1)	3	<0.01
Arapaho (0)	4	<0.01
Blackfeet (1)	9	0.01
Canadian/French Am. Ind. (8)	14	0.01
Central American Ind. (5)	6	0.01
Cherokee (7)	75	0.08
Cheyenne (0)	0	<0.01
Chickasaw (0)	0	<0.01
Chippewa (10)	13	0.01

	Population	%
Choctaw (3)	8	0.01
Colville (0)	0	<0.01
Comanche (0)	1	<0.01
Cree (3)	4	<0.01
Creek (2)	2	<0.01
Crow (0)	0	<0.01
Delaware (0)	1	<0.01
Hopi (0)	0	<0.01
Houma (2)	2	<0.01
Inupiat (Alaska Native) (0)	1	<0.01
Iroquois (114)	181	0.19
Kiowa (0)	0	<0.01
Lumbee (0)	0	<0.01
Menominee (0)	0	<0.01
Mexican American Ind. (4)	7	0.01
Navajo (2)	2	<0.01
Osage (0)	0	<0.01
Ottawa (0)	0	<0.01
Paiute (0)	0	<0.01
Pima (0)	0	<0.01
Potawatomi (0)	0	<0.01
Pueblo (0)	0	<0.01
Puget Sound Salish (0)	0	<0.01
Seminole (1)	4	<0.01
Shoshone (0)	1	<0.01
Sioux (3)	11	0.01
South American Ind. (7)	16	0.02
Spanish American Ind. (1)	5	0.01
Tlingit-Haida (Alaska Native) (0)	1	<0.01
Tohono O'Odham (0)	0	<0.01
Tsimshian (Alaska Native) (0)	0	<0.01
Ute (0)	0	<0.01
Yakama (0)	0	<0.01
Yaqui (0)	0	<0.01
Yuman (1)	1	<0.01
Yup'ik (Alaska Native) (0)	0	<0.01
Asian (1,664)	2,054	2.14
Not Hispanic (1,643)	2,014	2.10
Hispanic (21)	40	0.04
Bangladeshi (6)	9	0.01
Bhutanese (0)	0	<0.01
Burmese (0)	0	<0.01
Cambodian (33)	47	0.05
Chinese, ex. Taiwanese (294)	351	0.37
Filipino (141)	213	0.22
Hmong (0)	0	<0.01
Indian (283)	330	0.34
Indonesian (3)	5	0.01
Japanese (28)	71	0.07
Korean (209)	261	0.27
Laotian (112)	139	0.14
Malaysian (0)	0	<0.01
Nepalese (3)	3	<0.01
Pakistani (25)	32	0.03
Sri Lankan (5)	5	0.01
Taiwanese (10)	11	0.01
Thai (21)	24	0.02
Vietnamese (433)	473	0.49
Hawaii Native/Pacific Islander (14)	59	0.06
Not Hispanic (12)	40	0.04
Hispanic (2)	19	0.02
Fijian (0)	0	<0.01
Guamanian/Chamorro (4)	7	0.01
Marshallese (0)	0	<0.01
Native Hawaiian (5)	18	0.02
Samoan (2)	5	0.01
Tongan (0)	0	<0.01
White (85,220)	86,829	90.36
Not Hispanic (82,634)	83,902	87.31
Hispanic (2,586)	2,927	3.05

Notes: † The Census 2010 population figure is used to calculate the percentages in the Hispanic Origin and Race categories. Ancestry percentages are based on the 2006-2010 American Community Survey population (not shown); ‡ Numbers in parentheses indicate the number of people reporting a single ancestry; * Numbers in parentheses indicate the number of persons reporting this race alone, not in combination with any other race; Please refer to the Explanation of Data for more information.

Greenburgh

Place Type: Town
County: Westchester
Population: 88,400

Ancestry	Population	%
Afghan (0)	0	<0.01
African, Sub-Saharan (642)	914	1.04
African (287)	536	0.61
Cape Verdean (0)	0	<0.01
Ethiopian (39)	39	0.04
Ghanaian (16)	16	0.02
Kenyan (55)	55	0.06
Liberian (0)	0	<0.01
Nigerian (231)	231	0.26
Senegalese (0)	0	<0.01
Sierra Leonean (14)	14	0.02
Somalian (0)	0	<0.01
South African (0)	23	0.03
Sudanese (0)	0	<0.01
Ugandan (0)	0	<0.01
Zimbabwean (0)	0	<0.01
Other Sub-Saharan African (0)	0	<0.01
Albanian (80)	80	0.09
Alsatian (0)	0	<0.01
American (3,324)	3,324	3.79
Arab (306)	485	0.55
Arab (0)	22	0.03
Egyptian (9)	37	0.04
Iraqi (0)	0	<0.01
Jordanian (45)	45	0.05
Lebanese (213)	224	0.26
Moroccan (0)	35	0.04
Palestinian (0)	8	0.01
Syrian (32)	107	0.12
Other Arab (7)	7	0.01
Armenian (109)	175	0.20
Assyrian/Chaldean/Syriac (15)	29	0.03
Australian (0)	24	0.03
Austrian (267)	1,117	1.27
Basque (0)	8	0.01
Belgian (21)	93	0.11
Brazilian (74)	123	0.14
British (358)	519	0.59
Bulgarian (54)	54	0.06
Cajun (0)	0	<0.01
Canadian (53)	282	0.32
Carpatho Rusyn (0)	0	<0.01
Celtic (0)	7	0.01
Croatian (384)	609	0.69
Cypriot (0)	0	<0.01
Czech (40)	415	0.47
Czechoslovakian (72)	172	0.20
Danish (10)	130	0.15
Dutch (174)	580	0.66
Eastern European (1,840)	2,009	2.29
English (1,185)	4,118	4.70
Estonian (15)	57	0.07
European (1,275)	1,360	1.55
Finnish (34)	85	0.10
French, ex. Basque (225)	1,496	1.71
French Canadian (166)	483	0.55
German (1,568)	7,526	8.58
German Russian (0)	13	0.01
Greek (762)	1,202	1.37
Guyanese (52)	226	0.26
Hungarian (520)	1,242	1.42
Icelander (0)	0	<0.01
Iranian (248)	267	0.30
Irish (4,736)	11,358	12.95
Israeli (172)	225	0.26
Italian (9,180)	16,339	18.64
Latvian (48)	153	0.17
Lithuanian (51)	328	0.37
Luxemburger (0)	0	<0.01
Macedonian (24)	24	0.03
Maltese (0)	11	0.01
New Zealander (0)	0	<0.01
Northern European (47)	65	0.07
Norwegian (204)	530	0.60
Pennsylvania German (0)	0	<0.01
Polish (1,541)	4,636	5.29
Portuguese (534)	718	0.82
Romanian (234)	489	0.56
Russian (2,209)	5,042	5.75
Scandinavian (46)	79	0.09
Scotch-Irish (336)	741	0.85
Scottish (258)	987	1.13
Serbian (8)	8	0.01
Slavic (6)	6	0.01
Slovak (117)	388	0.44
Slovene (0)	0	<0.01
Soviet Union (0)	0	<0.01
Swedish (33)	374	0.43
Swiss (46)	211	0.24
Turkish (85)	172	0.20
Ukrainian (263)	652	0.74
Welsh (0)	81	0.09
West Indian, ex. Hispanic (2,889)	3,562	4.06
Bahamian (0)	0	<0.01
Barbadian (143)	155	0.18
Belizean (10)	19	0.02
Bermudan (0)	0	<0.01
British West Indian (65)	76	0.09
Dutch West Indian (0)	0	<0.01
Haitian (469)	516	0.59
Jamaican (1,753)	2,150	2.45
Trinidadian/Tobagonian (159)	201	0.23
U.S. Virgin Islander (0)	0	<0.01
West Indian (290)	445	0.51
Other West Indian (0)	0	<0.01
Yugoslavian (123)	130	0.15

Hispanic Origin	Population	%
Hispanic or Latino (of any race)	12,366	13.99
Central American, ex. Mexican	878	0.99
Costa Rican	34	0.04
Guatemalan	434	0.49
Honduran	90	0.10
Nicaraguan	50	0.06
Panamanian	73	0.08
Salvadoran	185	0.21
Other Central American	12	0.01
Cuban	565	0.64
Dominican Republic	1,400	1.58
Mexican	1,711	1.94
Puerto Rican	2,629	2.97
South American	4,004	4.53
Argentinean	188	0.21
Bolivian	48	0.05
Chilean	192	0.22
Colombian	845	0.96
Ecuadorian	1,434	1.62
Paraguayan	144	0.16
Peruvian	962	1.09
Uruguayan	65	0.07
Venezuelan	94	0.11
Other South American	32	0.04
Other Hispanic or Latino	1,179	1.33

Race*	Population	%
African-American/Black (11,103)	12,045	13.63
Not Hispanic (10,377)	11,022	12.47
Hispanic (726)	1,023	1.16
American Indian/Alaska Native (201)	630	0.71
Not Hispanic (64)	334	0.38
Hispanic (137)	296	0.33
Alaska Athabascan (Ala. Nat.) (0)	0	<0.01
Aleut (Alaska Native) (0)	1	<0.01
Apache (1)	6	0.01
Arapaho (0)	0	<0.01
Blackfeet (0)	7	0.01
Canadian/French Am. Ind. (0)	2	<0.01
Central American Ind. (1)	4	<0.01
Cherokee (5)	90	0.10
Cheyenne (0)	5	0.01
Chickasaw (0)	1	<0.01
Chippewa (0)	4	<0.01
Choctaw (0)	3	<0.01
Colville (0)	0	<0.01
Comanche (0)	5	0.01
Cree (0)	3	<0.01
Creek (0)	0	<0.01
Crow (0)	0	<0.01
Delaware (3)	5	0.01
Hopi (0)	0	<0.01
Houma (0)	0	<0.01
Inupiat (Alaska Native) (1)	1	<0.01
Iroquois (6)	19	0.02
Kiowa (0)	0	<0.01
Lumbee (1)	1	<0.01
Menominee (0)	0	<0.01
Mexican American Ind. (10)	25	0.03
Navajo (0)	3	<0.01
Osage (0)	0	<0.01
Ottawa (0)	0	<0.01
Paiute (0)	0	<0.01
Pima (0)	0	<0.01
Potawatomi (0)	0	<0.01
Pueblo (0)	0	<0.01
Puget Sound Salish (0)	0	<0.01
Seminole (0)	3	<0.01
Shoshone (0)	0	<0.01
Sioux (1)	8	0.01
South American Ind. (30)	72	0.08
Spanish American Ind. (14)	23	0.03
Tlingit-Haida (Alaska Native) (0)	0	<0.01
Tohono O'Odham (0)	0	<0.01
Tsimshian (Alaska Native) (0)	0	<0.01
Ute (0)	0	<0.01
Yakama (0)	0	<0.01
Yaqui (0)	0	<0.01
Yuman (0)	0	<0.01
Yup'ik (Alaska Native) (0)	0	<0.01
Asian (9,210)	10,180	11.52
Not Hispanic (9,155)	10,025	11.34
Hispanic (55)	155	0.18
Bangladeshi (37)	44	0.05
Bhutanese (8)	8	0.01
Burmese (28)	28	0.03
Cambodian (4)	4	<0.01
Chinese, ex. Taiwanese (1,910)	2,225	2.52
Filipino (826)	959	1.08
Hmong (0)	0	<0.01
Indian (3,241)	3,518	3.98
Indonesian (18)	24	0.03
Japanese (1,018)	1,230	1.39
Korean (1,328)	1,452	1.64
Laotian (3)	5	0.01
Malaysian (6)	11	0.01
Nepalese (48)	55	0.06
Pakistani (212)	244	0.28
Sri Lankan (14)	20	0.02
Taiwanese (113)	142	0.16
Thai (62)	77	0.09
Vietnamese (81)	95	0.11
Hawaii Native/Pacific Islander (33)	116	0.13
Not Hispanic (23)	88	0.10
Hispanic (10)	28	0.03
Fijian (0)	0	<0.01
Guamanian/Chamorro (11)	16	0.02
Marshallese (1)	1	<0.01
Native Hawaiian (1)	10	0.01
Samoan (1)	5	0.01
Tongan (0)	0	<0.01
White (61,185)	63,005	71.27
Not Hispanic (54,539)	55,731	63.04
Hispanic (6,646)	7,274	8.23

Notes: † The Census 2010 population figure is used to calculate the percentages in the Hispanic Origin and Race categories. Ancestry percentages are based on the 2006-2010 American Community Survey population (not shown); ‡ Numbers in parentheses indicate the number of people reporting a single ancestry; * Numbers in parentheses indicate the number of persons reporting this race alone, not in combination with any other race; Please refer to the Explanation of Data for more information.

Hamburg

Place Type: Town
County: Erie
Population: 56,936

Ancestry	Population	%
Afghan (0)	0	<0.01
African, Sub-Saharan (57)	57	0.10
African (0)	0	<0.01
Cape Verdean (0)	0	<0.01
Ethiopian (0)	0	<0.01
Ghanaian (0)	0	<0.01
Kenyan (0)	0	<0.01
Liberian (0)	0	<0.01
Nigerian (0)	0	<0.01
Senegalese (0)	0	<0.01
Sierra Leonean (0)	0	<0.01
Somalian (0)	0	<0.01
South African (57)	57	0.10
Sudanese (0)	0	<0.01
Ugandan (0)	0	<0.01
Zimbabwean (0)	0	<0.01
Other Sub-Saharan African (0)	0	<0.01
Albanian (0)	0	<0.01
Alsatian (9)	27	0.05
American (1,835)	1,835	3.24
Arab (93)	325	0.57
Arab (23)	70	0.12
Egyptian (38)	38	0.07
Iraqi (0)	0	<0.01
Jordanian (0)	11	0.02
Lebanese (17)	136	0.24
Moroccan (0)	26	0.05
Palestinian (15)	15	0.03
Syrian (0)	0	<0.01
Other Arab (0)	29	0.05
Armenian (0)	0	<0.01
Assyrian/Chaldean/Syriac (0)	0	<0.01
Australian (0)	0	<0.01
Austrian (35)	216	0.38
Basque (0)	0	<0.01
Belgian (0)	25	0.04
Brazilian (0)	0	<0.01
British (66)	154	0.27
Bulgarian (183)	192	0.34
Cajun (0)	0	<0.01
Canadian (180)	368	0.65
Carpatho Rusyn (0)	0	<0.01
Celtic (43)	43	0.08
Croatian (37)	246	0.43
Cypriot (0)	0	<0.01
Czech (45)	144	0.25
Czechoslovakian (27)	57	0.10
Danish (32)	66	0.12
Dutch (69)	660	1.17
Eastern European (37)	45	0.08
English (1,093)	5,284	9.34
Estonian (0)	0	<0.01
European (223)	250	0.44
Finnish (0)	9	0.02
French, ex. Basque (199)	2,079	3.67
French Canadian (153)	586	1.04
German (5,209)	19,590	34.62
German Russian (0)	0	<0.01
Greek (61)	186	0.33
Guyanese (33)	33	0.06
Hungarian (200)	761	1.34
Icelander (0)	0	<0.01
Iranian (44)	44	0.08
Irish (3,944)	15,679	27.71
Israeli (0)	0	<0.01
Italian (3,775)	10,185	18.00
Latvian (0)	11	0.02
Lithuanian (26)	63	0.11
Luxemburger (0)	0	<0.01
Macedonian (119)	149	0.26
Maltese (0)	0	<0.01
New Zealander (0)	0	<0.01
Northern European (0)	0	<0.01

Ancestry (cont.)	Population	%
Norwegian (9)	52	0.09
Pennsylvania German (39)	103	0.18
Polish (5,175)	13,189	23.31
Portuguese (0)	45	0.08
Romanian (0)	0	<0.01
Russian (39)	385	0.68
Scandinavian (0)	8	0.01
Scotch-Irish (164)	542	0.96
Scottish (159)	836	1.48
Serbian (55)	279	0.49
Slavic (0)	57	0.10
Slovak (24)	182	0.32
Slovene (0)	16	0.03
Soviet Union (0)	0	<0.01
Swedish (188)	948	1.68
Swiss (17)	57	0.10
Turkish (0)	0	<0.01
Ukrainian (185)	664	1.17
Welsh (105)	292	0.52
West Indian, ex. Hispanic (200)	230	0.41
Bahamian (21)	21	0.04
Barbadian (0)	0	<0.01
Belizean (0)	30	0.05
Bermudan (0)	0	<0.01
British West Indian (0)	0	<0.01
Dutch West Indian (0)	0	<0.01
Haitian (0)	0	<0.01
Jamaican (144)	144	0.25
Trinidadian/Tobagonian (13)	13	0.02
U.S. Virgin Islander (0)	0	<0.01
West Indian (22)	22	0.04
Other West Indian (0)	0	<0.01
Yugoslavian (43)	70	0.12

Hispanic Origin	Population	%
Hispanic or Latino (of any race)	1,214	2.13
Central American, ex. Mexican	38	0.07
Costa Rican	7	0.01
Guatemalan	20	0.04
Honduran	2	<0.01
Nicaraguan	4	0.01
Panamanian	0	<0.01
Salvadoran	5	0.01
Other Central American	0	<0.01
Cuban	29	0.05
Dominican Republic	32	0.06
Mexican	296	0.52
Puerto Rican	551	0.97
South American	72	0.13
Argentinean	4	0.01
Bolivian	7	0.01
Chilean	8	0.01
Colombian	37	0.06
Ecuadorian	2	<0.01
Paraguayan	2	<0.01
Peruvian	10	0.02
Uruguayan	0	<0.01
Venezuelan	2	<0.01
Other South American	0	<0.01
Other Hispanic or Latino	196	0.34

Race*	Population	%
African-American/Black (433)	664	1.17
Not Hispanic (404)	608	1.07
Hispanic (29)	56	0.10
American Indian/Alaska Native (179)	319	0.56
Not Hispanic (158)	290	0.51
Hispanic (21)	29	0.05
Alaska Athabascan (Ala. Nat.) (0)	0	<0.01
Aleut (Alaska Native) (0)	0	<0.01
Apache (1)	1	<0.01
Arapaho (0)	0	<0.01
Blackfeet (1)	2	<0.01
Canadian/French Am. Ind. (8)	12	0.02
Central American Ind. (0)	0	<0.01
Cherokee (9)	19	0.03
Cheyenne (0)	0	<0.01
Chickasaw (0)	0	<0.01
Chippewa (2)	7	0.01

Race* (cont.)	Population	%
Choctaw (0)	0	<0.01
Colville (0)	0	<0.01
Comanche (1)	1	<0.01
Cree (0)	0	<0.01
Creek (0)	0	<0.01
Crow (0)	2	<0.01
Delaware (0)	1	<0.01
Hopi (0)	0	<0.01
Houma (0)	0	<0.01
Inupiat (Alaska Native) (0)	0	<0.01
Iroquois (100)	159	0.28
Kiowa (0)	0	<0.01
Lumbee (0)	1	<0.01
Menominee (0)	0	<0.01
Mexican American Ind. (4)	5	0.01
Navajo (0)	0	<0.01
Osage (0)	0	<0.01
Ottawa (0)	0	<0.01
Paiute (0)	2	<0.01
Pima (0)	0	<0.01
Potawatomi (0)	0	<0.01
Pueblo (0)	0	<0.01
Puget Sound Salish (0)	0	<0.01
Seminole (0)	1	<0.01
Shoshone (0)	0	<0.01
Sioux (1)	3	0.01
South American Ind. (1)	1	<0.01
Spanish American Ind. (2)	2	<0.01
Tlingit-Haida (Alaska Native) (0)	0	<0.01
Tohono O'Odham (0)	0	<0.01
Tsimshian (Alaska Native) (0)	0	<0.01
Ute (0)	0	<0.01
Yakama (0)	0	<0.01
Yaqui (0)	0	<0.01
Yuman (0)	0	<0.01
Yup'ik (Alaska Native) (0)	0	<0.01
Asian (325)	431	0.76
Not Hispanic (322)	423	0.74
Hispanic (3)	8	0.01
Bangladeshi (0)	0	<0.01
Bhutanese (0)	0	<0.01
Burmese (0)	0	<0.01
Cambodian (3)	3	0.01
Chinese, ex. Taiwanese (63)	80	0.14
Filipino (31)	52	0.09
Hmong (0)	0	<0.01
Indian (72)	85	0.15
Indonesian (3)	5	0.01
Japanese (7)	19	0.03
Korean (43)	61	0.11
Laotian (3)	9	0.02
Malaysian (0)	0	<0.01
Nepalese (0)	0	<0.01
Pakistani (11)	11	0.02
Sri Lankan (0)	0	<0.01
Taiwanese (2)	2	<0.01
Thai (26)	32	0.06
Vietnamese (31)	35	0.06
Hawaii Native/Pacific Islander (6)	18	0.03
Not Hispanic (4)	14	0.02
Hispanic (2)	4	0.01
Fijian (0)	0	<0.01
Guamanian/Chamorro (4)	8	0.01
Marshallese (0)	0	<0.01
Native Hawaiian (0)	4	0.01
Samoan (0)	0	<0.01
Tongan (0)	0	<0.01
White (55,242)	55,749	97.92
Not Hispanic (54,366)	54,789	96.23
Hispanic (876)	960	1.69

Notes: † The Census 2010 population figure is used to calculate the percentages in the Hispanic Origin and Race categories. Ancestry percentages are based on the 2006-2010 American Community Survey population (not shown); ‡ Numbers in parentheses indicate the number of people reporting a single ancestry; * Numbers in parentheses indicate the number of persons reporting this race alone, not in combination with any other race; Please refer to the Explanation of Data for more information.

Hempstead

Place Type: Town
County: Nassau
Population: 759,757

Ancestry	Population	%
Afghan (260)	399	0.05
African, Sub-Saharan (4,323)	5,844	0.78
African (2,716)	3,879	0.51
Cape Verdean (0)	0	<0.01
Ethiopian (38)	106	0.01
Ghanaian (239)	306	0.04
Kenyan (0)	0	<0.01
Liberian (0)	0	<0.01
Nigerian (952)	1,115	0.15
Senegalese (0)	0	<0.01
Sierra Leonean (11)	11	<0.01
Somalian (15)	15	<0.01
South African (72)	104	0.01
Sudanese (33)	33	<0.01
Ugandan (0)	0	<0.01
Zimbabwean (0)	0	<0.01
Other Sub-Saharan African (247)	275	0.04
Albanian (733)	1,052	0.14
Alsatian (0)	30	<0.01
American (23,869)	23,869	3.17
Arab (2,403)	4,218	0.56
Arab (232)	319	0.04
Egyptian (787)	1,227	0.16
Iraqi (149)	284	0.04
Jordanian (66)	66	0.01
Lebanese (270)	657	0.09
Moroccan (163)	376	0.05
Palestinian (64)	113	0.01
Syrian (103)	512	0.07
Other Arab (569)	664	0.09
Armenian (922)	1,451	0.19
Assyrian/Chaldean/Syriac (3)	19	<0.01
Australian (98)	236	0.03
Austrian (1,518)	4,963	0.66
Basque (2)	43	0.01
Belgian (136)	405	0.05
Brazilian (208)	479	0.06
British (540)	1,197	0.16
Bulgarian (158)	181	0.02
Cajun (0)	0	<0.01
Canadian (321)	1,084	0.14
Carpatho Rusyn (4)	36	<0.01
Celtic (13)	24	<0.01
Croatian (536)	1,033	0.14
Cypriot (197)	254	0.03
Czech (615)	2,447	0.32
Czechoslovakian (357)	1,054	0.14
Danish (150)	1,023	0.14
Dutch (387)	3,142	0.42
Eastern European (5,468)	5,775	0.77
English (3,407)	21,808	2.89
Estonian (120)	175	0.02
European (5,191)	5,650	0.75
Finnish (105)	647	0.09
French, ex. Basque (1,119)	8,239	1.09
French Canadian (440)	1,779	0.24
German (15,495)	78,518	10.42
German Russian (0)	17	<0.01
Greek (6,061)	10,033	1.33
Guyanese (2,705)	3,520	0.47
Hungarian (2,954)	6,992	0.93
Icelander (19)	92	0.01
Iranian (290)	539	0.07
Irish (41,161)	125,911	16.71
Israeli (1,902)	2,558	0.34
Italian (90,988)	164,467	21.82
Latvian (193)	438	0.06
Lithuanian (826)	2,538	0.34
Luxemburger (0)	0	<0.01
Macedonian (41)	51	0.01
Maltese (254)	540	0.07
New Zealander (0)	0	<0.01
Northern European (433)	514	0.07
Norwegian (826)	3,371	0.45
Pennsylvania German (82)	143	0.02
Polish (11,210)	35,774	4.75
Portuguese (1,774)	2,805	0.37
Romanian (1,090)	2,811	0.37
Russian (11,619)	26,754	3.55
Scandinavian (171)	360	0.05
Scotch-Irish (1,797)	4,788	0.64
Scottish (822)	3,831	0.51
Serbian (23)	38	0.01
Slavic (62)	166	0.02
Slovak (182)	702	0.09
Slovene (6)	89	0.01
Soviet Union (0)	10	<0.01
Swedish (601)	3,930	0.52
Swiss (173)	1,183	0.16
Turkish (820)	1,202	0.16
Ukrainian (1,249)	2,806	0.37
Welsh (84)	865	0.11
West Indian, ex. Hispanic (37,978)	45,733	6.07
Bahamian (5)	51	0.01
Barbadian (1,031)	1,279	0.17
Belizean (85)	118	0.02
Bermudan (52)	52	0.01
British West Indian (635)	972	0.13
Dutch West Indian (165)	199	0.03
Haitian (15,396)	17,422	2.31
Jamaican (15,060)	17,690	2.35
Trinidadian/Tobagonian (2,092)	3,155	0.42
U.S. Virgin Islander (0)	30	<0.01
West Indian (3,440)	4,748	0.63
Other West Indian (17)	17	<0.01
Yugoslavian (227)	649	0.09

Hispanic Origin	Population	%
Hispanic or Latino (of any race)	132,154	17.39
Central American, ex. Mexican	49,236	6.48
Costa Rican	664	0.09
Guatemalan	5,948	0.78
Honduran	7,842	1.03
Nicaraguan	656	0.09
Panamanian	1,163	0.15
Salvadoran	32,681	4.30
Other Central American	282	0.04
Cuban	3,597	0.47
Dominican Republic	16,914	2.23
Mexican	5,000	0.66
Puerto Rican	20,508	2.70
South American	23,626	3.11
Argentinean	1,500	0.20
Bolivian	494	0.07
Chilean	1,415	0.19
Colombian	8,522	1.12
Ecuadorian	5,881	0.77
Paraguayan	185	0.02
Peruvian	4,510	0.59
Uruguayan	359	0.05
Venezuelan	517	0.07
Other South American	243	0.03
Other Hispanic or Latino	13,273	1.75

Race*	Population	%
African-American/Black (125,724)	133,280	17.54
Not Hispanic (119,480)	124,525	16.39
Hispanic (6,244)	8,755	1.15
American Indian/Alaska Native (2,092)	5,363	0.71
Not Hispanic (913)	2,835	0.37
Hispanic (1,179)	2,528	0.33
Alaska Athabascan (Ala. Nat.) (0)	0	<0.01
Aleut (Alaska Native) (1)	2	<0.01
Apache (5)	21	<0.01
Arapaho (0)	0	<0.01
Blackfeet (16)	117	0.02
Canadian/French Am. Ind. (5)	9	<0.01
Central American Ind. (36)	87	0.01
Cherokee (59)	572	0.08
Cheyenne (0)	2	<0.01
Chickasaw (0)	5	<0.01
Chippewa (4)	7	<0.01

	Population	%
Choctaw (10)	36	<0.01
Colville (1)	1	<0.01
Comanche (7)	11	<0.01
Cree (0)	2	<0.01
Creek (6)	29	<0.01
Crow (0)	2	<0.01
Delaware (4)	11	<0.01
Hopi (0)	2	<0.01
Houma (0)	0	<0.01
Inupiat (Alaska Native) (0)	3	<0.01
Iroquois (66)	145	0.02
Kiowa (0)	0	<0.01
Lumbee (9)	22	<0.01
Menominee (0)	0	<0.01
Mexican American Ind. (85)	143	0.02
Navajo (2)	13	<0.01
Osage (0)	2	<0.01
Ottawa (1)	1	<0.01
Paiute (0)	0	<0.01
Pima (0)	0	<0.01
Potawatomi (0)	0	<0.01
Pueblo (9)	13	<0.01
Puget Sound Salish (0)	0	<0.01
Seminole (2)	28	<0.01
Shoshone (1)	3	<0.01
Sioux (12)	33	<0.01
South American Ind. (147)	294	0.04
Spanish American Ind. (111)	137	0.02
Tlingit-Haida (Alaska Native) (3)	6	<0.01
Tohono O'Odham (7)	7	<0.01
Tsimshian (Alaska Native) (0)	0	<0.01
Ute (1)	1	<0.01
Yakama (0)	0	<0.01
Yaqui (0)	0	<0.01
Yuman (0)	0	<0.01
Yup'ik (Alaska Native) (0)	0	<0.01
Asian (39,495)	45,112	5.94
Not Hispanic (39,084)	43,880	5.78
Hispanic (411)	1,232	0.16
Bangladeshi (530)	582	0.08
Bhutanese (0)	0	<0.01
Burmese (37)	61	0.01
Cambodian (46)	65	0.01
Chinese, ex. Taiwanese (6,491)	7,849	1.03
Filipino (6,252)	7,212	0.95
Hmong (0)	2	<0.01
Indian (15,861)	17,802	2.34
Indonesian (37)	66	0.01
Japanese (360)	657	0.09
Korean (2,720)	3,074	0.40
Laotian (21)	32	<0.01
Malaysian (12)	29	<0.01
Nepalese (41)	45	0.01
Pakistani (4,581)	4,976	0.65
Sri Lankan (180)	201	0.03
Taiwanese (367)	438	0.06
Thai (213)	278	0.04
Vietnamese (492)	617	0.08
Hawaii Native/Pacific Islander (229)	1,001	0.13
Not Hispanic (117)	599	0.08
Hispanic (112)	402	0.05
Fijian (9)	10	<0.01
Guamanian/Chamorro (88)	110	0.01
Marshallese (1)	1	<0.01
Native Hawaiian (34)	114	0.02
Samoan (12)	36	<0.01
Tongan (0)	0	<0.01
White (518,756)	532,650	70.11
Not Hispanic (454,883)	460,994	60.68
Hispanic (63,873)	71,656	9.43

Notes: † The Census 2010 population figure is used to calculate the percentages in the Hispanic Origin and Race categories. Ancestry percentages are based on the 2006-2010 American Community Survey population (not shown); ‡ Numbers in parentheses indicate the number of people reporting a single ancestry; * Numbers in parentheses indicate the number of persons reporting this race alone, not in combination with any other race; Please refer to the Explanation of Data for more information.

Hempstead

Place Type: Village
County: Nassau
Population: 53,891

Ancestry	Population	%
Afghan (0)	0	<0.01
African, Sub-Saharan (1,102)	1,285	2.41
African (682)	850	1.59
Cape Verdean (0)	0	<0.01
Ethiopian (0)	0	<0.01
Ghanaian (8)	8	0.01
Kenyan (0)	0	<0.01
Liberian (0)	0	<0.01
Nigerian (412)	427	0.80
Senegalese (0)	0	<0.01
Sierra Leonean (0)	0	<0.01
Somalian (0)	0	<0.01
South African (0)	0	<0.01
Sudanese (0)	0	<0.01
Ugandan (0)	0	<0.01
Zimbabwean (0)	0	<0.01
Other Sub-Saharan African (0)	0	<0.01
Albanian (0)	0	<0.01
Alsatian (0)	0	<0.01
American (471)	471	0.88
Arab (54)	54	0.10
Arab (12)	12	0.02
Egyptian (0)	0	<0.01
Iraqi (0)	0	<0.01
Jordanian (0)	0	<0.01
Lebanese (0)	0	<0.01
Moroccan (42)	42	0.08
Palestinian (0)	0	<0.01
Syrian (0)	0	<0.01
Other Arab (0)	0	<0.01
Armenian (0)	0	<0.01
Assyrian/Chaldean/Syriac (0)	0	<0.01
Australian (9)	9	0.02
Austrian (28)	64	0.12
Basque (0)	0	<0.01
Belgian (0)	0	<0.01
Brazilian (0)	41	0.08
British (0)	90	0.17
Bulgarian (0)	0	<0.01
Cajun (0)	0	<0.01
Canadian (0)	143	0.27
Carpatho Rusyn (0)	0	<0.01
Celtic (0)	0	<0.01
Croatian (0)	0	<0.01
Cypriot (0)	9	0.02
Czech (7)	7	0.01
Czechoslovakian (0)	0	<0.01
Danish (0)	0	<0.01
Dutch (6)	6	0.01
Eastern European (34)	34	0.06
English (47)	124	0.23
Estonian (0)	0	<0.01
European (0)	0	<0.01
Finnish (0)	0	<0.01
French, ex. Basque (0)	82	0.15
French Canadian (0)	9	0.02
German (130)	594	1.11
German Russian (0)	0	<0.01
Greek (203)	231	0.43
Guyanese (259)	307	0.58
Hungarian (32)	41	0.08
Icelander (0)	0	<0.01
Iranian (0)	0	<0.01
Irish (278)	659	1.23
Israeli (0)	0	<0.01
Italian (333)	641	1.20
Latvian (0)	6	0.01
Lithuanian (28)	36	0.07
Luxemburger (0)	0	<0.01
Macedonian (0)	0	<0.01
Maltese (0)	0	<0.01
New Zealander (0)	0	<0.01
Northern European (0)	0	<0.01

Ancestry (cont.)	Population	%
Norwegian (0)	0	<0.01
Pennsylvania German (0)	0	<0.01
Polish (203)	351	0.66
Portuguese (13)	69	0.13
Romanian (0)	0	<0.01
Russian (44)	129	0.24
Scandinavian (0)	0	<0.01
Scotch-Irish (17)	47	0.09
Scottish (21)	103	0.19
Serbian (0)	0	<0.01
Slavic (0)	0	<0.01
Slovak (0)	9	0.02
Slovene (0)	0	<0.01
Soviet Union (0)	0	<0.01
Swedish (23)	102	0.19
Swiss (9)	47	0.09
Turkish (0)	0	<0.01
Ukrainian (62)	90	0.17
Welsh (0)	71	0.13
West Indian, ex. Hispanic (5,489)	6,463	12.11
Bahamian (0)	0	<0.01
Barbadian (153)	153	0.29
Belizean (0)	0	<0.01
Bermudan (9)	9	0.02
British West Indian (228)	250	0.47
Dutch West Indian (31)	31	0.06
Haitian (1,796)	2,104	3.94
Jamaican (2,500)	2,809	5.26
Trinidadian/Tobagonian (203)	322	0.60
U.S. Virgin Islander (0)	0	<0.01
West Indian (569)	785	1.47
Other West Indian (0)	0	<0.01
Yugoslavian (0)	0	<0.01

Hispanic Origin	Population	%
Hispanic or Latino (of any race)	23,823	44.21
Central American, ex. Mexican	16,171	30.01
Costa Rican	44	0.08
Guatemalan	1,402	2.60
Honduran	3,758	6.97
Nicaraguan	56	0.10
Panamanian	138	0.26
Salvadoran	10,707	19.87
Other Central American	66	0.12
Cuban	174	0.32
Dominican Republic	1,398	2.59
Mexican	752	1.40
Puerto Rican	1,144	2.12
South American	1,575	2.92
Argentinean	25	0.05
Bolivian	23	0.04
Chilean	21	0.04
Colombian	506	0.94
Ecuadorian	641	1.19
Paraguayan	16	0.03
Peruvian	279	0.52
Uruguayan	4	0.01
Venezuelan	37	0.07
Other South American	23	0.04
Other Hispanic or Latino	2,609	4.84

Race*	Population	%
African-American/Black (26,016)	27,076	50.24
Not Hispanic (24,724)	25,388	47.11
Hispanic (1,292)	1,688	3.13
American Indian/Alaska Native (316)	997	1.85
Not Hispanic (96)	404	0.75
Hispanic (220)	593	1.10
Alaska Athabascan (Ala. Nat.) (0)	0	<0.01
Aleut (Alaska Native) (0)	0	<0.01
Apache (2)	5	0.01
Arapaho (0)	0	<0.01
Blackfeet (1)	27	0.05
Canadian/French Am. Ind. (0)	0	<0.01
Central American Ind. (5)	15	0.03
Cherokee (17)	109	0.20
Cheyenne (0)	1	<0.01
Chickasaw (0)	0	<0.01
Chippewa (1)	1	<0.01

Race* (cont.)	Population	%
Choctaw (0)	3	0.01
Colville (0)	0	<0.01
Comanche (0)	1	<0.01
Cree (0)	0	<0.01
Creek (1)	2	<0.01
Crow (0)	0	<0.01
Delaware (0)	4	0.01
Hopi (0)	2	<0.01
Houma (0)	0	<0.01
Inupiat (Alaska Native) (0)	0	<0.01
Iroquois (13)	19	0.04
Kiowa (0)	0	<0.01
Lumbee (0)	1	<0.01
Menominee (0)	0	<0.01
Mexican American Ind. (17)	27	0.05
Navajo (1)	2	<0.01
Osage (0)	0	<0.01
Ottawa (0)	0	<0.01
Paiute (0)	0	<0.01
Pima (0)	0	<0.01
Potawatomi (0)	0	<0.01
Pueblo (4)	6	0.01
Puget Sound Salish (0)	0	<0.01
Seminole (0)	5	0.01
Shoshone (0)	0	<0.01
Sioux (1)	6	0.01
South American Ind. (9)	18	0.03
Spanish American Ind. (42)	47	0.09
Tlingit-Haida (Alaska Native) (0)	2	<0.01
Tohono O'Odham (0)	0	<0.01
Tsimshian (Alaska Native) (0)	0	<0.01
Ute (0)	0	<0.01
Yakama (0)	0	<0.01
Yaqui (0)	0	<0.01
Yuman (0)	0	<0.01
Yup'ik (Alaska Native) (0)	0	<0.01
Asian (751)	977	1.81
Not Hispanic (704)	842	1.56
Hispanic (47)	135	0.25
Bangladeshi (11)	11	0.02
Bhutanese (0)	0	<0.01
Burmese (0)	0	<0.01
Cambodian (0)	0	<0.01
Chinese, ex. Taiwanese (135)	177	0.33
Filipino (150)	171	0.32
Hmong (0)	0	<0.01
Indian (282)	383	0.71
Indonesian (3)	5	0.01
Japanese (6)	14	0.03
Korean (24)	29	0.05
Laotian (3)	4	0.01
Malaysian (1)	1	<0.01
Nepalese (7)	9	0.02
Pakistani (48)	60	0.11
Sri Lankan (15)	15	0.03
Taiwanese (1)	1	<0.01
Thai (5)	10	0.02
Vietnamese (6)	9	0.02
Hawaii Native/Pacific Islander (23)	117	0.22
Not Hispanic (13)	57	0.11
Hispanic (10)	60	0.11
Fijian (1)	1	<0.01
Guamanian/Chamorro (9)	13	0.02
Marshallese (0)	0	<0.01
Native Hawaiian (1)	9	0.02
Samoan (0)	3	0.01
Tongan (0)	0	<0.01
White (11,788)	13,665	25.36
Not Hispanic (3,548)	3,892	7.22
Hispanic (8,240)	9,773	18.13

Notes: † The Census 2010 population figure is used to calculate the percentages in the Hispanic Origin and Race categories. Ancestry percentages are based on the 2006-2010 American Community Survey population (not shown); ‡ Numbers in parentheses indicate the number of people reporting a single ancestry; * Numbers in parentheses indicate the number of persons reporting this race alone, not in combination with any other race; Please refer to the Explanation of Data for more information.

Huntington

Place Type: Town
County: Suffolk
Population: 203,264

Ancestry	Population	%
Afghan (314)	314	0.16
African, Sub-Saharan (317)	481	0.24
African (146)	206	0.10
Cape Verdean (0)	0	<0.01
Ethiopian (21)	125	0.06
Ghanaian (0)	0	<0.01
Kenyan (0)	0	<0.01
Liberian (0)	0	<0.01
Nigerian (87)	87	0.04
Senegalese (0)	0	<0.01
Sierra Leonean (0)	0	<0.01
Somalian (0)	0	<0.01
South African (63)	63	0.03
Sudanese (0)	0	<0.01
Ugandan (0)	0	<0.01
Zimbabwean (0)	0	<0.01
Other Sub-Saharan African (0)	0	<0.01
Albanian (216)	237	0.12
Alsatian (0)	9	<0.01
American (5,873)	5,873	2.90
Arab (721)	1,231	0.61
Arab (65)	73	0.04
Egyptian (318)	425	0.21
Iraqi (42)	166	0.08
Jordanian (11)	11	0.01
Lebanese (46)	184	0.09
Moroccan (142)	192	0.09
Palestinian (0)	9	<0.01
Syrian (15)	35	0.02
Other Arab (82)	136	0.07
Armenian (368)	525	0.26
Assyrian/Chaldean/Syriac (0)	0	<0.01
Australian (59)	101	0.05
Austrian (454)	2,004	0.99
Basque (6)	20	0.01
Belgian (30)	115	0.06
Brazilian (142)	195	0.10
British (515)	840	0.42
Bulgarian (44)	65	0.03
Cajun (0)	19	0.01
Canadian (356)	743	0.37
Carpatho Rusyn (20)	20	0.01
Celtic (65)	65	0.03
Croatian (337)	781	0.39
Cypriot (70)	82	0.04
Czech (275)	1,271	0.63
Czechoslovakian (89)	435	0.22
Danish (359)	809	0.40
Dutch (427)	2,168	1.07
Eastern European (1,918)	2,012	1.00
English (2,429)	13,038	6.45
Estonian (77)	140	0.07
European (1,982)	2,177	1.08
Finnish (21)	178	0.09
French, ex. Basque (400)	3,023	1.50
French Canadian (214)	772	0.38
German (6,140)	33,758	16.70
German Russian (0)	0	<0.01
Greek (1,839)	3,284	1.62
Guyanese (124)	180	0.09
Hungarian (784)	3,005	1.49
Icelander (9)	38	0.02
Iranian (443)	471	0.23
Irish (12,700)	45,750	22.63
Israeli (217)	285	0.14
Italian (26,684)	56,013	27.70
Latvian (75)	193	0.10
Lithuanian (269)	956	0.47
Luxemburger (0)	0	<0.01
Macedonian (0)	0	<0.01
Maltese (30)	88	0.04
New Zealander (26)	26	0.01
Northern European (57)	63	0.03

Ancestry	Population	%
Norwegian (538)	1,833	0.91
Pennsylvania German (0)	17	0.01
Polish (3,447)	13,208	6.53
Portuguese (198)	526	0.26
Romanian (503)	1,364	0.67
Russian (3,393)	9,499	4.70
Scandinavian (107)	292	0.14
Scotch-Irish (1,045)	2,325	1.15
Scottish (588)	2,306	1.14
Serbian (17)	80	0.04
Slavic (28)	97	0.05
Slovak (109)	225	0.11
Slovene (27)	37	0.02
Soviet Union (0)	0	<0.01
Swedish (322)	2,237	1.11
Swiss (118)	632	0.31
Turkish (438)	502	0.25
Ukrainian (668)	1,742	0.86
Welsh (126)	533	0.26
West Indian, ex. Hispanic (2,499)	2,882	1.43
Bahamian (31)	31	0.02
Barbadian (18)	18	0.01
Belizean (0)	0	<0.01
Bermudan (0)	0	<0.01
British West Indian (0)	0	<0.01
Dutch West Indian (7)	7	<0.01
Haitian (1,223)	1,277	0.63
Jamaican (733)	893	0.44
Trinidadian/Tobagonian (128)	170	0.08
U.S. Virgin Islander (91)	147	0.07
West Indian (261)	332	0.16
Other West Indian (7)	7	<0.01
Yugoslavian (161)	467	0.23

Hispanic Origin	Population	%
Hispanic or Latino (of any race)	22,362	11.00
Central American, ex. Mexican	9,599	4.72
Costa Rican	118	0.06
Guatemalan	1,080	0.53
Honduran	1,651	0.81
Nicaraguan	58	0.03
Panamanian	77	0.04
Salvadoran	6,563	3.23
Other Central American	52	0.03
Cuban	603	0.30
Dominican Republic	1,011	0.50
Mexican	1,440	0.71
Puerto Rican	4,187	2.06
South American	3,043	1.50
Argentinean	329	0.16
Bolivian	60	0.03
Chilean	252	0.12
Colombian	957	0.47
Ecuadorian	637	0.31
Paraguayan	91	0.04
Peruvian	538	0.26
Uruguayan	57	0.03
Venezuelan	87	0.04
Other South American	35	0.02
Other Hispanic or Latino	2,479	1.22

Race*	Population	%
African-American/Black (9,515)	10,864	5.34
Not Hispanic (8,933)	9,917	4.88
Hispanic (582)	947	0.47
American Indian/Alaska Native (398)	1,197	0.59
Not Hispanic (187)	785	0.39
Hispanic (211)	412	0.20
Alaska Athabascan (Ala. Nat.) (0)	0	<0.01
Aleut (Alaska Native) (0)	0	<0.01
Apache (10)	14	0.01
Arapaho (0)	0	<0.01
Blackfeet (2)	36	0.02
Canadian/French Am. Ind. (6)	10	<0.01
Central American Ind. (11)	20	0.01
Cherokee (15)	150	0.07
Cheyenne (0)	4	<0.01
Chickasaw (0)	3	<0.01
Chippewa (2)	10	<0.01

Race*	Population	%
Choctaw (0)	13	0.01
Colville (0)	0	<0.01
Comanche (5)	8	<0.01
Cree (0)	3	<0.01
Creek (1)	15	0.01
Crow (2)	5	<0.01
Delaware (1)	12	0.01
Hopi (0)	0	<0.01
Houma (0)	0	<0.01
Inupiat (Alaska Native) (0)	0	<0.01
Iroquois (18)	42	0.02
Kiowa (0)	0	<0.01
Lumbee (2)	5	<0.01
Menominee (0)	0	<0.01
Mexican American Ind. (18)	26	0.01
Navajo (3)	8	<0.01
Osage (0)	1	<0.01
Ottawa (0)	2	<0.01
Paiute (0)	0	<0.01
Pima (0)	0	<0.01
Potawatomi (0)	0	<0.01
Pueblo (0)	0	<0.01
Puget Sound Salish (0)	0	<0.01
Seminole (1)	4	<0.01
Shoshone (0)	0	<0.01
Sioux (1)	9	<0.01
South American Ind. (22)	69	0.03
Spanish American Ind. (8)	16	0.01
Tlingit-Haida (Alaska Native) (0)	1	<0.01
Tohono O'Odham (0)	0	<0.01
Tsimshian (Alaska Native) (0)	0	<0.01
Ute (0)	0	<0.01
Yakama (0)	0	<0.01
Yaqui (0)	0	<0.01
Yuman (0)	0	<0.01
Yup'ik (Alaska Native) (0)	0	<0.01
Asian (10,089)	11,684	5.75
Not Hispanic (10,009)	11,463	5.64
Hispanic (80)	221	0.11
Bangladeshi (108)	120	0.06
Bhutanese (1)	1	<0.01
Burmese (8)	13	0.01
Cambodian (10)	10	<0.01
Chinese, ex. Taiwanese (2,144)	2,546	1.25
Filipino (637)	905	0.45
Hmong (0)	0	<0.01
Indian (3,166)	3,529	1.74
Indonesian (11)	18	0.01
Japanese (218)	338	0.17
Korean (1,952)	2,122	1.04
Laotian (5)	5	<0.01
Malaysian (6)	13	0.01
Nepalese (3)	3	<0.01
Pakistani (1,149)	1,264	0.62
Sri Lankan (20)	22	0.01
Taiwanese (140)	157	0.08
Thai (58)	75	0.04
Vietnamese (151)	186	0.09
Hawaii Native/Pacific Islander (48)	159	0.08
Not Hispanic (32)	93	0.05
Hispanic (16)	66	0.03
Fijian (0)	0	<0.01
Guamanian/Chamorro (18)	25	0.01
Marshallese (0)	0	<0.01
Native Hawaiian (16)	40	0.02
Samoan (6)	7	<0.01
Tongan (0)	0	<0.01
White (171,048)	174,612	85.90
Not Hispanic (158,690)	160,914	79.17
Hispanic (12,358)	13,698	6.74

Notes: † The Census 2010 population figure is used to calculate the percentages in the Hispanic Origin and Race categories. Ancestry percentages are based on the 2006-2010 American Community Survey population (not shown); ‡ Numbers in parentheses indicate the number of people reporting a single ancestry; * Numbers in parentheses indicate the number of persons reporting this race alone, not in combination with any other race; Please refer to the Explanation of Data for more information.

Irondequoit

Place Type: CDP/Town
County: Monroe
Population: 51,692

Ancestry	Population	%
Afghan (145)	145	0.28
African, Sub-Saharan (653)	763	1.48
African (344)	454	0.88
Cape Verdean (0)	0	<0.01
Ethiopian (192)	192	0.37
Ghanaian (0)	0	<0.01
Kenyan (0)	0	<0.01
Liberian (0)	0	<0.01
Nigerian (85)	85	0.16
Senegalese (0)	0	<0.01
Sierra Leonean (0)	0	<0.01
Somalian (0)	0	<0.01
South African (0)	0	<0.01
Sudanese (0)	0	<0.01
Ugandan (0)	0	<0.01
Zimbabwean (0)	0	<0.01
Other Sub-Saharan African (32)	32	0.06
Albanian (41)	41	0.08
Alsatian (0)	0	<0.01
American (1,362)	1,362	2.64
Arab (107)	120	0.23
Arab (59)	59	0.11
Egyptian (11)	11	0.02
Iraqi (0)	0	<0.01
Jordanian (0)	0	<0.01
Lebanese (37)	50	0.10
Moroccan (0)	0	<0.01
Palestinian (0)	0	<0.01
Syrian (0)	0	<0.01
Other Arab (0)	0	<0.01
Armenian (54)	72	0.14
Assyrian/Chaldean/Syriac (0)	0	<0.01
Australian (0)	12	0.02
Austrian (25)	176	0.34
Basque (0)	0	<0.01
Belgian (23)	93	0.18
Brazilian (52)	71	0.14
British (94)	189	0.37
Bulgarian (0)	0	<0.01
Cajun (0)	0	<0.01
Canadian (208)	419	0.81
Carpatho Rusyn (0)	0	<0.01
Celtic (14)	14	0.03
Croatian (0)	43	0.08
Cypriot (0)	0	<0.01
Czech (32)	153	0.30
Czechoslovakian (23)	42	0.08
Danish (14)	111	0.22
Dutch (161)	1,310	2.54
Eastern European (35)	35	0.07
English (2,071)	7,215	13.98
Estonian (0)	0	<0.01
European (385)	424	0.82
Finnish (22)	30	0.06
French, ex. Basque (121)	1,636	3.17
French Canadian (191)	465	0.90
German (2,967)	11,815	22.89
German Russian (0)	28	0.05
Greek (199)	335	0.65
Guyanese (0)	0	<0.01
Hungarian (74)	172	0.33
Icelander (0)	0	<0.01
Iranian (12)	12	0.02
Irish (1,901)	9,070	17.57
Israeli (0)	0	<0.01
Italian (8,322)	14,566	28.22
Latvian (12)	26	0.05
Lithuanian (142)	267	0.52
Luxemburger (24)	24	0.05
Macedonian (212)	266	0.52
Maltese (0)	0	<0.01
New Zealander (0)	0	<0.01
Northern European (0)	10	0.02

Ancestry (cont.)	Population	%
Norwegian (33)	157	0.30
Pennsylvania German (7)	32	0.06
Polish (1,257)	3,828	7.42
Portuguese (34)	113	0.22
Romanian (59)	71	0.14
Russian (120)	491	0.95
Scandinavian (0)	7	0.01
Scotch-Irish (132)	396	0.77
Scottish (153)	935	1.81
Serbian (0)	16	0.03
Slavic (17)	24	0.05
Slovak (10)	43	0.08
Slovene (13)	13	0.03
Soviet Union (0)	0	<0.01
Swedish (86)	482	0.93
Swiss (34)	255	0.49
Turkish (238)	245	0.47
Ukrainian (617)	1,169	2.27
Welsh (21)	352	0.68
West Indian, ex. Hispanic (97)	143	0.28
Bahamian (0)	0	<0.01
Barbadian (29)	29	0.06
Belizean (0)	0	<0.01
Bermudan (0)	0	<0.01
British West Indian (0)	0	<0.01
Dutch West Indian (0)	0	<0.01
Haitian (58)	58	0.11
Jamaican (10)	56	0.11
Trinidadian/Tobagonian (0)	0	<0.01
U.S. Virgin Islander (0)	0	<0.01
West Indian (0)	0	<0.01
Other West Indian (0)	0	<0.01
Yugoslavian (58)	69	0.13

Hispanic Origin	Population	%
Hispanic or Latino (of any race)	3,220	6.23
Central American, ex. Mexican	88	0.17
Costa Rican	19	0.04
Guatemalan	28	0.05
Honduran	4	0.01
Nicaraguan	11	0.02
Panamanian	7	0.01
Salvadoran	19	0.04
Other Central American	0	<0.01
Cuban	167	0.32
Dominican Republic	94	0.18
Mexican	145	0.28
Puerto Rican	2,436	4.71
South American	146	0.28
Argentinean	20	0.04
Bolivian	0	<0.01
Chilean	23	0.04
Colombian	53	0.10
Ecuadorian	18	0.03
Paraguayan	3	0.01
Peruvian	10	0.02
Uruguayan	0	<0.01
Venezuelan	15	0.03
Other South American	4	0.01
Other Hispanic or Latino	144	0.28

Race*	Population	%
African-American/Black (3,996)	4,577	8.85
Not Hispanic (3,741)	4,168	8.06
Hispanic (255)	409	0.79
American Indian/Alaska Native (112)	313	0.61
Not Hispanic (81)	240	0.46
Hispanic (31)	73	0.14
Alaska Athabascan (Ala. Nat.) (0)	0	<0.01
Aleut (Alaska Native) (0)	0	<0.01
Apache (1)	3	0.01
Arapaho (0)	0	<0.01
Blackfeet (3)	4	0.01
Canadian/French Am. Ind. (2)	6	0.01
Central American Ind. (1)	1	<0.01
Cherokee (0)	16	0.03
Cheyenne (0)	0	<0.01
Chickasaw (0)	0	<0.01
Chippewa (6)	7	0.01

Race* (cont.)	Population	%
Choctaw (0)	0	<0.01
Colville (0)	1	<0.01
Comanche (0)	0	<0.01
Cree (0)	0	<0.01
Creek (0)	1	<0.01
Crow (0)	0	<0.01
Delaware (3)	7	0.01
Hopi (0)	0	<0.01
Houma (0)	0	<0.01
Inupiat (Alaska Native) (0)	0	<0.01
Iroquois (36)	98	0.19
Kiowa (0)	0	<0.01
Lumbee (0)	0	<0.01
Menominee (0)	0	<0.01
Mexican American Ind. (5)	5	0.01
Navajo (0)	0	<0.01
Osage (0)	0	<0.01
Ottawa (0)	0	<0.01
Paiute (0)	0	<0.01
Pima (0)	1	<0.01
Potawatomi (0)	0	<0.01
Pueblo (0)	1	<0.01
Puget Sound Salish (0)	0	<0.01
Seminole (0)	2	<0.01
Shoshone (0)	0	<0.01
Sioux (0)	0	<0.01
South American Ind. (2)	6	0.01
Spanish American Ind. (7)	7	0.01
Tlingit-Haida (Alaska Native) (0)	0	<0.01
Tohono O'Odham (0)	0	<0.01
Tsimshian (Alaska Native) (0)	0	<0.01
Ute (0)	0	<0.01
Yakama (0)	0	<0.01
Yaqui (0)	0	<0.01
Yuman (0)	0	<0.01
Yup'ik (Alaska Native) (0)	0	<0.01
Asian (662)	888	1.72
Not Hispanic (648)	851	1.65
Hispanic (14)	37	0.07
Bangladeshi (0)	1	<0.01
Bhutanese (0)	0	<0.01
Burmese (3)	3	0.01
Cambodian (29)	31	0.06
Chinese, ex. Taiwanese (120)	146	0.28
Filipino (101)	155	0.30
Hmong (0)	0	<0.01
Indian (78)	100	0.19
Indonesian (1)	5	0.01
Japanese (12)	37	0.07
Korean (73)	107	0.21
Laotian (94)	109	0.21
Malaysian (0)	1	<0.01
Nepalese (1)	1	<0.01
Pakistani (28)	30	0.06
Sri Lankan (0)	0	<0.01
Taiwanese (3)	3	0.01
Thai (7)	15	0.03
Vietnamese (88)	98	0.19
Hawaii Native/Pacific Islander (12)	42	0.08
Not Hispanic (10)	34	0.07
Hispanic (2)	8	0.02
Fijian (1)	1	<0.01
Guamanian/Chamorro (2)	2	<0.01
Marshallese (0)	0	<0.01
Native Hawaiian (5)	11	0.02
Samoan (0)	0	<0.01
Tongan (1)	1	<0.01
White (44,883)	45,826	88.65
Not Hispanic (43,125)	43,832	84.79
Hispanic (1,758)	1,994	3.86

*Notes: † The Census 2010 population figure is used to calculate the percentages in the Hispanic Origin and Race categories. Ancestry percentages are based on the 2006-2010 American Community Survey population (not shown); ‡ Numbers in parentheses indicate the number of people reporting a single ancestry; * Numbers in parentheses indicate the number of persons reporting this race alone, not in combination with any other race; Please refer to the Explanation of Data for more information.*

Islip

Place Type: Town
County: Suffolk
Population: 335,543

Ancestry	Population	%
Afghan (182)	263	0.08
African, Sub-Saharan (854)	1,222	0.37
African (464)	793	0.24
Cape Verdean (0)	0	<0.01
Ethiopian (0)	0	<0.01
Ghanaian (71)	71	0.02
Kenyan (0)	0	<0.01
Liberian (0)	0	<0.01
Nigerian (164)	203	0.06
Senegalese (0)	0	<0.01
Sierra Leonean (0)	0	<0.01
Somalian (0)	0	<0.01
South African (0)	0	<0.01
Sudanese (0)	0	<0.01
Ugandan (0)	0	<0.01
Zimbabwean (0)	0	<0.01
Other Sub-Saharan African (155)	155	0.05
Albanian (16)	51	0.02
Alsatian (0)	18	0.01
American (5,894)	5,894	1.77
Arab (986)	1,453	0.44
Arab (51)	177	0.05
Egyptian (339)	364	0.11
Iraqi (0)	0	<0.01
Jordanian (68)	122	0.04
Lebanese (86)	185	0.06
Moroccan (123)	141	0.04
Palestinian (166)	166	0.05
Syrian (69)	144	0.04
Other Arab (84)	154	0.05
Armenian (174)	272	0.08
Assyrian/Chaldean/Syriac (0)	0	<0.01
Australian (32)	100	0.03
Austrian (335)	2,019	0.61
Basque (18)	18	0.01
Belgian (68)	328	0.10
Brazilian (683)	895	0.27
British (132)	453	0.14
Bulgarian (0)	0	<0.01
Cajun (0)	23	0.01
Canadian (111)	405	0.12
Carpatho Rusyn (0)	0	<0.01
Celtic (28)	53	0.02
Croatian (88)	291	0.09
Cypriot (25)	25	0.01
Czech (409)	2,026	0.61
Czechoslovakian (224)	596	0.18
Danish (39)	761	0.23
Dutch (310)	2,191	0.66
Eastern European (337)	433	0.13
English (2,211)	13,963	4.18
Estonian (86)	175	0.05
European (772)	811	0.24
Finnish (59)	271	0.08
French, ex. Basque (403)	4,451	1.33
French Canadian (223)	1,160	0.35
German (7,849)	48,335	14.48
German Russian (0)	0	<0.01
Greek (1,129)	3,126	0.94
Guyanese (460)	499	0.15
Hungarian (433)	2,067	0.62
Icelander (0)	29	0.01
Iranian (111)	170	0.05
Irish (17,586)	68,763	20.61
Israeli (36)	56	0.02
Italian (38,447)	84,360	25.28
Latvian (21)	49	0.01
Lithuanian (294)	799	0.24
Luxemburger (0)	0	<0.01
Macedonian (0)	0	<0.01
Maltese (54)	292	0.09
New Zealander (8)	8	<0.01
Northern European (63)	63	0.02

Ancestry	Population	%
Norwegian (661)	2,978	0.89
Pennsylvania German (0)	0	<0.01
Polish (3,602)	14,896	4.46
Portuguese (1,434)	1,977	0.59
Romanian (213)	467	0.14
Russian (1,589)	5,019	1.50
Scandinavian (55)	183	0.05
Scotch-Irish (960)	3,159	0.95
Scottish (329)	2,852	0.85
Serbian (0)	46	0.01
Slavic (29)	109	0.03
Slovak (46)	280	0.08
Slovene (27)	27	0.01
Soviet Union (0)	0	<0.01
Swedish (401)	2,528	0.76
Swiss (81)	619	0.19
Turkish (281)	384	0.12
Ukrainian (343)	1,272	0.38
Welsh (102)	552	0.17
West Indian, ex. Hispanic (8,546)	10,274	3.08
Bahamian (0)	22	0.01
Barbadian (22)	63	0.02
Belizean (35)	35	0.01
Bermudan (0)	0	<0.01
British West Indian (255)	470	0.14
Dutch West Indian (16)	16	<0.01
Haitian (5,195)	5,636	1.69
Jamaican (1,961)	2,690	0.81
Trinidadian/Tobagonian (530)	665	0.20
U.S. Virgin Islander (0)	0	<0.01
West Indian (532)	677	0.20
Other West Indian (0)	0	<0.01
Yugoslavian (70)	202	0.06

Hispanic Origin	Population	%
Hispanic or Latino (of any race)	97,371	29.02
Central American, ex. Mexican	38,530	11.48
Costa Rican	297	0.09
Guatemalan	3,256	0.97
Honduran	4,232	1.26
Nicaraguan	253	0.08
Panamanian	466	0.14
Salvadoran	29,849	8.90
Other Central American	177	0.05
Cuban	1,113	0.33
Dominican Republic	8,547	2.55
Mexican	3,139	0.94
Puerto Rican	21,506	6.41
South American	16,012	4.77
Argentinean	616	0.18
Bolivian	220	0.07
Chilean	448	0.13
Colombian	5,156	1.54
Ecuadorian	5,323	1.59
Paraguayan	58	0.02
Peruvian	3,599	1.07
Uruguayan	216	0.06
Venezuelan	322	0.10
Other South American	54	0.02
Other Hispanic or Latino	8,524	2.54

Race*	Population	%
African-American/Black (32,024)	35,995	10.73
Not Hispanic (27,898)	30,295	9.03
Hispanic (4,126)	5,700	1.70
American Indian/Alaska Native (1,586)	3,396	1.01
Not Hispanic (520)	1,565	0.47
Hispanic (1,066)	1,831	0.55
Alaska Athabascan (Ala. Nat.) (0)	1	<0.01
Aleut (Alaska Native) (1)	1	<0.01
Apache (5)	12	<0.01
Arapaho (0)	1	<0.01
Blackfeet (12)	77	0.02
Canadian/French Am. Ind. (0)	0	<0.01
Central American Ind. (52)	73	0.02
Cherokee (44)	316	0.09
Cheyenne (0)	1	<0.01
Chickasaw (1)	3	<0.01
Chippewa (6)	13	<0.01

Race*	Population	%
Choctaw (3)	17	0.01
Colville (0)	0	<0.01
Comanche (0)	8	<0.01
Cree (0)	0	<0.01
Creek (1)	7	<0.01
Crow (11)	16	<0.01
Delaware (1)	7	<0.01
Hopi (1)	3	<0.01
Houma (1)	3	<0.01
Inupiat (Alaska Native) (1)	2	<0.01
Iroquois (36)	92	0.03
Kiowa (0)	0	<0.01
Lumbee (6)	8	<0.01
Menominee (0)	0	<0.01
Mexican American Ind. (83)	135	0.04
Navajo (7)	14	<0.01
Osage (0)	1	<0.01
Ottawa (0)	0	<0.01
Paiute (0)	0	<0.01
Pima (1)	1	<0.01
Potawatomi (1)	1	<0.01
Pueblo (4)	7	<0.01
Puget Sound Salish (0)	0	<0.01
Seminole (2)	4	<0.01
Shoshone (0)	3	<0.01
Sioux (6)	27	0.01
South American Ind. (143)	249	0.07
Spanish American Ind. (67)	91	0.03
Tlingit-Haida (Alaska Native) (5)	6	<0.01
Tohono O'Odham (0)	0	<0.01
Tsimshian (Alaska Native) (0)	0	<0.01
Ute (0)	0	<0.01
Yakama (0)	0	<0.01
Yaqui (1)	1	<0.01
Yuman (0)	1	<0.01
Yup'ik (Alaska Native) (0)	0	<0.01
Asian (9,572)	11,510	3.43
Not Hispanic (9,358)	10,957	3.27
Hispanic (214)	553	0.16
Bangladeshi (305)	356	0.11
Bhutanese (0)	0	<0.01
Burmese (9)	15	<0.01
Cambodian (23)	24	0.01
Chinese, ex. Taiwanese (1,424)	1,766	0.53
Filipino (1,012)	1,301	0.39
Hmong (0)	0	<0.01
Indian (3,680)	4,276	1.27
Indonesian (29)	37	0.01
Japanese (91)	216	0.06
Korean (573)	700	0.21
Laotian (21)	25	0.01
Malaysian (5)	12	<0.01
Nepalese (13)	13	<0.01
Pakistani (1,368)	1,520	0.45
Sri Lankan (13)	21	0.01
Taiwanese (49)	54	0.02
Thai (80)	106	0.03
Vietnamese (433)	518	0.15
Hawaii Native/Pacific Islander (101)	471	0.14
Not Hispanic (52)	244	0.07
Hispanic (49)	227	0.07
Fijian (0)	4	<0.01
Guamanian/Chamorro (28)	44	0.01
Marshallese (1)	1	<0.01
Native Hawaiian (26)	75	0.02
Samoan (6)	15	<0.01
Tongan (0)	2	<0.01
White (245,918)	254,235	75.77
Not Hispanic (195,283)	198,326	59.11
Hispanic (50,635)	55,909	16.66

*Notes: † The Census 2010 population figure is used to calculate the percentages in the Hispanic Origin and Race categories. Ancestry percentages are based on the 2006-2010 American Community Survey population (not shown); ‡ Numbers in parentheses indicate the number of people reporting a single ancestry; * Numbers in parentheses indicate the number of persons reporting this race alone, not in combination with any other race; Please refer to the Explanation of Data for more information.*

Levittown

Place Type: CDP
County: Nassau
Population: 51,881

Ancestry	Population	%
Afghan (0)	0	<0.01
African, Sub-Saharan (0)	20	0.04
African (0)	20	0.04
Cape Verdean (0)	0	<0.01
Ethiopian (0)	0	<0.01
Ghanaian (0)	0	<0.01
Kenyan (0)	0	<0.01
Liberian (0)	0	<0.01
Nigerian (0)	0	<0.01
Senegalese (0)	0	<0.01
Sierra Leonean (0)	0	<0.01
Somalian (0)	0	<0.01
South African (0)	0	<0.01
Sudanese (0)	0	<0.01
Ugandan (0)	0	<0.01
Zimbabwean (0)	0	<0.01
Other Sub-Saharan African (0)	0	<0.01
Albanian (49)	49	0.09
Alsatian (0)	0	<0.01
American (1,347)	1,347	2.52
Arab (190)	271	0.51
Arab (0)	0	<0.01
Egyptian (136)	136	0.25
Iraqi (0)	0	<0.01
Jordanian (0)	0	<0.01
Lebanese (22)	68	0.13
Moroccan (10)	10	0.02
Palestinian (0)	0	<0.01
Syrian (0)	35	0.07
Other Arab (22)	22	0.04
Armenian (21)	80	0.15
Assyrian/Chaldean/Syriac (0)	0	<0.01
Australian (14)	14	0.03
Austrian (66)	307	0.57
Basque (0)	16	0.03
Belgian (10)	18	0.03
Brazilian (8)	8	0.01
British (92)	121	0.23
Bulgarian (0)	0	<0.01
Cajun (0)	0	<0.01
Canadian (11)	74	0.14
Carpatho Rusyn (0)	0	<0.01
Celtic (0)	0	<0.01
Croatian (24)	67	0.13
Cypriot (0)	0	<0.01
Czech (44)	215	0.40
Czechoslovakian (25)	47	0.09
Danish (10)	110	0.21
Dutch (11)	340	0.64
Eastern European (107)	107	0.20
English (316)	2,076	3.88
Estonian (0)	0	<0.01
European (276)	321	0.60
Finnish (0)	36	0.07
French, ex. Basque (239)	1,242	2.32
French Canadian (74)	206	0.39
German (1,428)	9,190	17.18
German Russian (0)	0	<0.01
Greek (630)	1,100	2.06
Guyanese (0)	0	<0.01
Hungarian (158)	781	1.46
Icelander (9)	52	0.10
Iranian (23)	79	0.15
Irish (4,151)	14,886	27.84
Israeli (32)	72	0.13
Italian (8,524)	17,446	32.62
Latvian (0)	31	0.06
Lithuanian (73)	314	0.59
Luxemburger (0)	0	<0.01
Macedonian (0)	0	<0.01
Maltese (45)	96	0.18
New Zealander (0)	0	<0.01
Northern European (0)	0	<0.01
Norwegian (49)	274	0.51
Pennsylvania German (0)	54	0.10
Polish (535)	2,652	4.96
Portuguese (189)	243	0.45
Romanian (27)	98	0.18
Russian (640)	1,993	3.73
Scandinavian (0)	33	0.06
Scotch-Irish (261)	722	1.35
Scottish (53)	303	0.57
Serbian (0)	0	<0.01
Slavic (0)	0	<0.01
Slovak (6)	6	0.01
Slovene (0)	0	<0.01
Soviet Union (0)	0	<0.01
Swedish (13)	287	0.54
Swiss (55)	105	0.20
Turkish (112)	181	0.34
Ukrainian (83)	249	0.47
Welsh (0)	43	0.08
West Indian, ex. Hispanic (89)	117	0.22
Bahamian (0)	0	<0.01
Barbadian (0)	0	<0.01
Belizean (0)	0	<0.01
Bermudan (0)	0	<0.01
British West Indian (0)	0	<0.01
Dutch West Indian (0)	0	<0.01
Haitian (0)	0	<0.01
Jamaican (20)	36	0.07
Trinidadian/Tobagonian (69)	69	0.13
U.S. Virgin Islander (0)	0	<0.01
West Indian (0)	12	0.02
Other West Indian (0)	0	<0.01
Yugoslavian (41)	52	0.10

Hispanic Origin	Population	%
Hispanic or Latino (of any race)	5,979	11.52
Central American, ex. Mexican	1,200	2.31
Costa Rican	41	0.08
Guatemalan	132	0.25
Honduran	103	0.20
Nicaraguan	26	0.05
Panamanian	12	0.02
Salvadoran	876	1.69
Other Central American	10	0.02
Cuban	274	0.53
Dominican Republic	260	0.50
Mexican	214	0.41
Puerto Rican	1,716	3.31
South American	1,746	3.37
Argentinean	82	0.16
Bolivian	18	0.03
Chilean	112	0.22
Colombian	733	1.41
Ecuadorian	400	0.77
Paraguayan	19	0.04
Peruvian	285	0.55
Uruguayan	47	0.09
Venezuelan	23	0.04
Other South American	27	0.05
Other Hispanic or Latino	569	1.10

Race*	Population	%
African-American/Black (470)	667	1.29
Not Hispanic (403)	539	1.04
Hispanic (67)	128	0.25
American Indian/Alaska Native (55)	185	0.36
Not Hispanic (43)	134	0.26
Hispanic (12)	51	0.10
Alaska Athabascan (Ala. Nat.) (0)	0	<0.01
Aleut (Alaska Native) (0)	0	<0.01
Apache (0)	0	<0.01
Arapaho (0)	0	<0.01
Blackfeet (0)	4	0.01
Canadian/French Am. Ind. (0)	0	<0.01
Central American Ind. (0)	0	<0.01
Cherokee (2)	26	0.05
Cheyenne (0)	0	<0.01
Chickasaw (0)	0	<0.01
Chippewa (1)	1	<0.01
Choctaw (0)	1	<0.01
Colville (0)	0	<0.01
Comanche (7)	7	0.01
Cree (0)	0	<0.01
Creek (0)	1	<0.01
Crow (0)	0	<0.01
Delaware (0)	0	<0.01
Hopi (0)	0	<0.01
Houma (0)	0	<0.01
Inupiat (Alaska Native) (0)	0	<0.01
Iroquois (4)	13	0.03
Kiowa (0)	0	<0.01
Lumbee (3)	6	<0.01
Menominee (0)	0	<0.01
Mexican American Ind. (0)	5	<0.01
Navajo (0)	0	<0.01
Osage (0)	1	<0.01
Ottawa (0)	0	<0.01
Paiute (0)	0	<0.01
Pima (0)	0	<0.01
Potawatomi (0)	0	<0.01
Pueblo (0)	0	<0.01
Puget Sound Salish (0)	0	<0.01
Seminole (1)	3	0.01
Shoshone (1)	1	<0.01
Sioux (0)	1	<0.01
South American Ind. (9)	12	0.02
Spanish American Ind. (0)	1	<0.01
Tlingit-Haida (Alaska Native) (0)	0	<0.01
Tohono O'Odham (0)	0	<0.01
Tsimshian (Alaska Native) (0)	0	<0.01
Ute (0)	0	<0.01
Yakama (0)	0	<0.01
Yaqui (0)	0	<0.01
Yuman (0)	0	<0.01
Yup'ik (Alaska Native) (0)	0	<0.01
Asian (2,956)	3,352	6.46
Not Hispanic (2,937)	3,298	6.36
Hispanic (19)	54	0.10
Bangladeshi (65)	70	0.13
Bhutanese (0)	0	<0.01
Burmese (1)	6	0.01
Cambodian (10)	14	0.03
Chinese, ex. Taiwanese (467)	589	1.14
Filipino (446)	525	1.01
Hmong (0)	0	<0.01
Indian (1,110)	1,212	2.34
Indonesian (4)	6	0.01
Japanese (26)	44	0.08
Korean (358)	380	0.73
Laotian (3)	3	0.01
Malaysian (0)	7	0.01
Nepalese (2)	2	<0.01
Pakistani (226)	239	0.46
Sri Lankan (1)	1	<0.01
Taiwanese (22)	25	0.05
Thai (26)	40	0.08
Vietnamese (103)	107	0.21
Hawaii Native/Pacific Islander (10)	47	0.09
Not Hispanic (6)	21	0.04
Hispanic (4)	26	0.05
Fijian (0)	0	<0.01
Guamanian/Chamorro (2)	3	0.01
Marshallese (0)	0	<0.01
Native Hawaiian (0)	3	0.01
Samoan (5)	7	0.01
Tongan (0)	0	<0.01
White (46,137)	46,970	90.53
Not Hispanic (41,814)	42,268	81.47
Hispanic (4,323)	4,702	9.06

Notes: † The Census 2010 population figure is used to calculate the percentages in the Hispanic Origin and Race categories. Ancestry percentages are based on the 2006-2010 American Community Survey population (not shown); ‡ Numbers in parentheses indicate the number of people reporting a single ancestry; * Numbers in parentheses indicate the number of persons reporting this race alone, not in combination with any other race; Please refer to the Explanation of Data for more information.

Manhattan

Place Type: Borough
County: New York
Population: 1,585,873

Ancestry	Population	%
Afghan (59)	85	0.01
African, Sub-Saharan (19,667)	24,146	1.52
African (10,054)	12,839	0.81
Cape Verdean (81)	206	0.01
Ethiopian (932)	1,043	0.07
Ghanaian (714)	818	0.05
Kenyan (43)	69	<0.01
Liberian (169)	176	0.01
Nigerian (1,650)	1,953	0.12
Senegalese (1,118)	1,216	0.08
Sierra Leonean (422)	422	0.03
Somalian (125)	125	0.01
South African (991)	1,372	0.09
Sudanese (137)	137	0.01
Ugandan (95)	125	0.01
Zimbabwean (80)	100	0.01
Other Sub-Saharan African (3,056)	3,545	0.22
Albanian (1,385)	1,618	0.10
Alsatian (5)	129	0.01
American (54,694)	54,694	3.45
Arab (8,584)	13,828	0.87
Arab (1,250)	1,720	0.11
Egyptian (1,374)	1,906	0.12
Iraqi (275)	583	0.04
Jordanian (0)	48	<0.01
Lebanese (1,838)	3,331	0.21
Moroccan (914)	1,592	0.10
Palestinian (626)	794	0.05
Syrian (518)	1,112	0.07
Other Arab (1,789)	2,742	0.17
Armenian (1,520)	2,653	0.17
Assyrian/Chaldean/Syriac (94)	137	0.01
Australian (1,965)	2,719	0.17
Austrian (4,202)	14,656	0.93
Basque (191)	428	0.03
Belgian (928)	2,470	0.16
Brazilian (2,870)	4,541	0.29
British (6,950)	12,129	0.77
Bulgarian (927)	1,272	0.08
Cajun (22)	224	0.01
Canadian (3,037)	5,646	0.36
Carpatho Rusyn (89)	112	0.01
Celtic (129)	304	0.02
Croatian (1,299)	2,164	0.14
Cypriot (139)	216	0.01
Czech (1,439)	4,820	0.30
Czechoslovakian (619)	1,256	0.08
Danish (1,444)	4,095	0.26
Dutch (2,847)	10,414	0.66
Eastern European (23,269)	25,277	1.60
English (22,270)	77,799	4.91
Estonian (190)	424	0.03
European (25,127)	27,846	1.76
Finnish (666)	1,658	0.10
French, ex. Basque (10,278)	31,783	2.01
French Canadian (1,692)	5,246	0.33
German (27,493)	107,666	6.80
German Russian (0)	41	<0.01
Greek (7,557)	13,078	0.83
Guyanese (1,802)	2,259	0.14
Hungarian (4,686)	14,667	0.93
Icelander (246)	382	0.02
Iranian (3,458)	4,256	0.27
Irish (40,008)	117,355	7.41
Israeli (4,839)	6,624	0.42
Italian (44,498)	98,563	6.22
Latvian (713)	1,822	0.12
Lithuanian (1,597)	5,775	0.36
Luxemburger (23)	68	<0.01
Macedonian (973)	1,086	0.07
Maltese (548)	840	0.05
New Zealander (243)	405	0.03
Northern European (1,296)	1,485	0.09
Norwegian (1,552)	7,445	0.47
Pennsylvania German (123)	327	0.02
Polish (20,565)	64,078	4.05
Portuguese (1,436)	3,862	0.24
Romanian (3,035)	7,692	0.49
Russian (36,296)	82,983	5.24
Scandinavian (753)	1,731	0.11
Scotch-Irish (4,283)	13,158	0.83
Scottish (4,846)	19,553	1.23
Serbian (1,160)	1,526	0.10
Slavic (177)	400	0.03
Slovak (812)	2,298	0.15
Slovene (271)	695	0.04
Soviet Union (28)	54	<0.01
Swedish (3,045)	10,408	0.66
Swiss (1,381)	4,962	0.31
Turkish (2,708)	3,703	0.23
Ukrainian (4,361)	8,849	0.56
Welsh (944)	6,000	0.38
West Indian, ex. Hispanic (22,411)	30,009	1.90
Bahamian (303)	457	0.03
Barbadian (738)	907	0.06
Belizean (654)	735	0.05
Bermudan (86)	127	0.01
British West Indian (1,308)	1,658	0.10
Dutch West Indian (212)	276	0.02
Haitian (5,308)	6,500	0.41
Jamaican (7,099)	9,242	0.58
Trinidadian/Tobagonian (3,010)	3,877	0.24
U.S. Virgin Islander (343)	487	0.03
West Indian (3,296)	5,618	0.35
Other West Indian (54)	125	0.01
Yugoslavian (1,478)	1,876	0.12

Hispanic Origin	Population	%
Hispanic or Latino (of any race)	403,577	25.45
Central American, ex. Mexican	13,948	0.88
Costa Rican	987	0.06
Guatemalan	2,051	0.13
Honduran	4,058	0.26
Nicaraguan	1,556	0.10
Panamanian	1,716	0.11
Salvadoran	3,419	0.22
Other Central American	161	0.01
Cuban	11,623	0.73
Dominican Republic	155,971	9.84
Mexican	41,965	2.65
Puerto Rican	107,774	6.80
South American	36,748	2.32
Argentinean	4,339	0.27
Bolivian	522	0.03
Chilean	1,824	0.12
Colombian	8,411	0.53
Ecuadorian	14,132	0.89
Paraguayan	268	0.02
Peruvian	3,852	0.24
Uruguayan	549	0.03
Venezuelan	2,573	0.16
Other South American	278	0.02
Other Hispanic or Latino	35,548	2.24

Race*	Population	%
African-American/Black (246,687)	272,993	17.21
Not Hispanic (205,340)	217,102	13.69
Hispanic (41,347)	55,891	3.52
American Indian/Alaska Native (8,669)	19,415	1.22
Not Hispanic (2,144)	7,395	0.47
Hispanic (6,525)	12,020	0.76
Alaska Athabascan (Ala. Nat.) (11)	18	<0.01
Aleut (Alaska Native) (4)	7	<0.01
Apache (28)	92	0.01
Arapaho (3)	5	<0.01
Blackfeet (41)	356	0.02
Canadian/French Am. Ind. (29)	62	<0.01
Central American Ind. (610)	1,090	0.07
Cherokee (288)	1,845	0.12
Cheyenne (4)	9	<0.01
Chickasaw (15)	43	<0.01
Chippewa (36)	99	0.01

	Population	%
Choctaw (41)	179	0.01
Colville (4)	5	<0.01
Comanche (13)	22	<0.01
Cree (4)	22	<0.01
Creek (12)	61	<0.01
Crow (4)	11	<0.01
Delaware (14)	54	<0.01
Hopi (8)	15	<0.01
Houma (0)	3	<0.01
Inupiat (Alaska Native) (2)	8	<0.01
Iroquois (97)	265	0.02
Kiowa (9)	11	<0.01
Lumbee (10)	21	<0.01
Menominee (2)	3	<0.01
Mexican American Ind. (479)	752	0.05
Navajo (38)	83	0.01
Osage (7)	12	<0.01
Ottawa (0)	3	<0.01
Paiute (2)	8	<0.01
Pima (2)	4	<0.01
Potawatomi (10)	20	<0.01
Pueblo (70)	175	0.01
Puget Sound Salish (2)	5	<0.01
Seminole (6)	110	0.01
Shoshone (3)	6	<0.01
Sioux (38)	133	0.01
South American Ind. (813)	1,935	0.12
Spanish American Ind. (373)	514	0.03
Tlingit-Haida (Alaska Native) (2)	15	<0.01
Tohono O'Odham (11)	15	<0.01
Tsimshian (Alaska Native) (3)	3	<0.01
Ute (1)	2	<0.01
Yakama (1)	2	<0.01
Yaqui (8)	22	<0.01
Yuman (4)	6	<0.01
Yup'ik (Alaska Native) (0)	2	<0.01
Asian (179,552)	199,722	12.59
Not Hispanic (177,624)	194,929	12.29
Hispanic (1,928)	4,793	0.30
Bangladeshi (1,672)	2,029	0.13
Bhutanese (26)	26	<0.01
Burmese (240)	317	0.02
Cambodian (168)	220	0.01
Chinese, ex. Taiwanese (92,088)	99,287	6.26
Filipino (10,399)	13,388	0.84
Hmong (16)	20	<0.01
Indian (25,857)	29,979	1.89
Indonesian (470)	693	0.04
Japanese (13,201)	16,600	1.05
Korean (19,683)	21,996	1.39
Laotian (109)	157	0.01
Malaysian (524)	766	0.05
Nepalese (240)	281	0.02
Pakistani (2,482)	2,940	0.19
Sri Lankan (450)	563	0.04
Taiwanese (2,789)	3,318	0.21
Thai (1,282)	1,657	0.10
Vietnamese (2,194)	2,919	0.18
Hawaii Native/Pacific Islander (873)	3,727	0.24
Not Hispanic (533)	1,776	0.11
Hispanic (340)	1,951	0.12
Fijian (29)	73	<0.01
Guamanian/Chamorro (132)	242	0.02
Marshallese (3)	4	<0.01
Native Hawaiian (185)	608	0.04
Samoan (87)	183	0.01
Tongan (18)	33	<0.01
White (911,073)	956,864	60.34
Not Hispanic (761,493)	785,299	49.52
Hispanic (149,580)	171,565	10.82

Notes: † The Census 2010 population figure is used to calculate the percentages in the Hispanic Origin and Race categories. Ancestry percentages are based on the 2006-2010 American Community Survey population (not shown); ‡ Numbers in parentheses indicate the number of people reporting a single ancestry; * Numbers in parentheses indicate the number of persons reporting this race alone, not in combination with any other race; Please refer to the Explanation of Data for more information.

Mount Vernon

Place Type: City
County: Westchester
Population: 67,292

Ancestry	Population	%
Afghan (0)	0	<0.01
African, Sub-Saharan (1,490)	1,910	2.85
African (786)	1,162	1.73
Cape Verdean (0)	11	0.02
Ethiopian (0)	0	<0.01
Ghanaian (347)	347	0.52
Kenyan (0)	0	<0.01
Liberian (0)	9	0.01
Nigerian (148)	148	0.22
Senegalese (0)	12	0.02
Sierra Leonean (10)	22	0.03
Somalian (0)	0	<0.01
South African (0)	0	<0.01
Sudanese (0)	0	<0.01
Ugandan (19)	19	0.03
Zimbabwean (0)	0	<0.01
Other Sub-Saharan African (180)	180	0.27
Albanian (303)	303	0.45
Alsatian (0)	0	<0.01
American (2,069)	2,069	3.08
Arab (217)	305	0.45
Arab (0)	0	<0.01
Egyptian (56)	68	0.10
Iraqi (0)	0	<0.01
Jordanian (0)	0	<0.01
Lebanese (0)	12	0.02
Moroccan (0)	64	0.10
Palestinian (13)	13	0.02
Syrian (0)	0	<0.01
Other Arab (148)	148	0.22
Armenian (0)	0	<0.01
Assyrian/Chaldean/Syriac (0)	0	<0.01
Australian (0)	13	0.02
Austrian (60)	150	0.22
Basque (0)	0	<0.01
Belgian (0)	0	<0.01
Brazilian (1,938)	2,013	3.00
British (45)	146	0.22
Bulgarian (0)	0	<0.01
Cajun (0)	0	<0.01
Canadian (0)	61	0.09
Carpatho Rusyn (0)	0	<0.01
Celtic (0)	0	<0.01
Croatian (0)	0	<0.01
Cypriot (0)	0	<0.01
Czech (47)	70	0.10
Czechoslovakian (11)	11	0.02
Danish (10)	21	0.03
Dutch (22)	191	0.28
Eastern European (93)	127	0.19
English (260)	843	1.26
Estonian (21)	45	0.07
European (145)	145	0.22
Finnish (12)	12	0.02
French, ex. Basque (129)	377	0.56
French Canadian (14)	62	0.09
German (373)	1,326	1.98
German Russian (0)	0	<0.01
Greek (100)	185	0.28
Guyanese (326)	360	0.54
Hungarian (74)	129	0.19
Icelander (0)	0	<0.01
Iranian (0)	21	0.03
Irish (950)	2,889	4.31
Israeli (116)	174	0.26
Italian (3,462)	5,281	7.87
Latvian (0)	10	0.01
Lithuanian (13)	57	0.08
Luxemburger (0)	0	<0.01
Macedonian (0)	0	<0.01
Maltese (24)	24	0.04
New Zealander (0)	0	<0.01
Northern European (0)	0	<0.01
Norwegian (10)	21	0.03
Pennsylvania German (0)	0	<0.01
Polish (283)	651	0.97
Portuguese (979)	1,149	1.71
Romanian (123)	123	0.18
Russian (143)	433	0.65
Scandinavian (15)	15	0.02
Scotch-Irish (60)	127	0.19
Scottish (46)	150	0.22
Serbian (8)	8	0.01
Slavic (9)	9	0.01
Slovak (0)	0	<0.01
Slovene (0)	0	<0.01
Soviet Union (0)	0	<0.01
Swedish (0)	46	0.07
Swiss (0)	0	<0.01
Turkish (0)	0	<0.01
Ukrainian (0)	69	0.10
Welsh (0)	63	0.09
West Indian, ex. Hispanic (12,148)	13,279	19.80
Bahamian (11)	11	0.02
Barbadian (190)	208	0.31
Belizean (118)	118	0.18
Bermudan (0)	0	<0.01
British West Indian (315)	348	0.52
Dutch West Indian (0)	0	<0.01
Haitian (324)	465	0.69
Jamaican (9,769)	10,445	15.57
Trinidadian/Tobagonian (370)	397	0.59
U.S. Virgin Islander (0)	0	<0.01
West Indian (1,051)	1,287	1.92
Other West Indian (0)	0	<0.01
Yugoslavian (9)	9	0.01

Hispanic Origin	Population	%
Hispanic or Latino (of any race)	9,592	14.25
Central American, ex. Mexican	754	1.12
Costa Rican	64	0.10
Guatemalan	141	0.21
Honduran	233	0.35
Nicaraguan	35	0.05
Panamanian	131	0.19
Salvadoran	137	0.20
Other Central American	13	0.02
Cuban	231	0.34
Dominican Republic	1,611	2.39
Mexican	2,454	3.65
Puerto Rican	2,582	3.84
South American	1,205	1.79
Argentinean	91	0.14
Bolivian	18	0.03
Chilean	29	0.04
Colombian	407	0.60
Ecuadorian	268	0.40
Paraguayan	68	0.10
Peruvian	219	0.33
Uruguayan	16	0.02
Venezuelan	56	0.08
Other South American	33	0.05
Other Hispanic or Latino	755	1.12

Race*	Population	%
African-American/Black (42,667)	44,244	65.75
Not Hispanic (41,226)	42,361	62.95
Hispanic (1,441)	1,883	2.80
American Indian/Alaska Native (312)	820	1.22
Not Hispanic (200)	585	0.87
Hispanic (112)	235	0.35
Alaska Athabascan (Ala. Nat.) (0)	0	<0.01
Aleut (Alaska Native) (0)	0	<0.01
Apache (0)	0	<0.01
Arapaho (0)	0	<0.01
Blackfeet (1)	38	0.06
Canadian/French Am. Ind. (0)	0	<0.01
Central American Ind. (7)	19	0.03
Cherokee (27)	116	0.17
Cheyenne (0)	0	<0.01
Chickasaw (2)	4	0.01
Chippewa (0)	0	<0.01
Choctaw (4)	4	0.01
Colville (0)	0	<0.01
Comanche (0)	0	<0.01
Cree (0)	2	<0.01
Creek (0)	0	<0.01
Crow (0)	0	<0.01
Delaware (1)	1	<0.01
Hopi (0)	0	<0.01
Houma (0)	0	<0.01
Inupiat (Alaska Native) (0)	0	<0.01
Iroquois (2)	8	<0.01
Kiowa (0)	0	<0.01
Lumbee (0)	0	<0.01
Menominee (0)	0	<0.01
Mexican American Ind. (13)	14	0.02
Navajo (1)	2	<0.01
Osage (0)	0	<0.01
Ottawa (0)	0	<0.01
Paiute (0)	0	<0.01
Pima (0)	0	<0.01
Potawatomi (0)	0	<0.01
Pueblo (4)	7	0.01
Puget Sound Salish (0)	0	<0.01
Seminole (0)	9	0.01
Shoshone (0)	0	<0.01
Sioux (1)	6	0.01
South American Ind. (15)	36	0.05
Spanish American Ind. (0)	4	0.01
Tlingit-Haida (Alaska Native) (0)	0	<0.01
Tohono O'Odham (0)	0	<0.01
Tsimshian (Alaska Native) (0)	0	<0.01
Ute (0)	0	<0.01
Yakama (0)	0	<0.01
Yaqui (0)	0	<0.01
Yuman (0)	0	<0.01
Yup'ik (Alaska Native) (0)	0	<0.01
Asian (1,236)	1,672	2.48
Not Hispanic (1,206)	1,587	2.36
Hispanic (30)	85	0.13
Bangladeshi (7)	11	0.02
Bhutanese (0)	0	<0.01
Burmese (2)	2	<0.01
Cambodian (7)	9	0.01
Chinese, ex. Taiwanese (187)	264	0.39
Filipino (220)	281	0.42
Hmong (0)	0	<0.01
Indian (529)	711	1.06
Indonesian (0)	11	0.02
Japanese (55)	88	0.13
Korean (72)	92	0.14
Laotian (5)	12	0.02
Malaysian (0)	1	<0.01
Nepalese (4)	4	0.01
Pakistani (26)	38	0.06
Sri Lankan (1)	1	<0.01
Taiwanese (10)	10	0.01
Thai (67)	73	0.11
Vietnamese (7)	12	0.02
Hawaii Native/Pacific Islander (36)	156	0.23
Not Hispanic (27)	130	0.19
Hispanic (9)	26	0.04
Fijian (0)	1	<0.01
Guamanian/Chamorro (1)	4	0.01
Marshallese (0)	0	<0.01
Native Hawaiian (5)	13	0.02
Samoan (1)	3	<0.01
Tongan (0)	0	<0.01
White (16,371)	17,846	26.52
Not Hispanic (12,449)	13,354	19.84
Hispanic (3,922)	4,492	6.68

Notes: † The Census 2010 population figure is used to calculate the percentages in the Hispanic Origin and Race categories. Ancestry percentages are based on the 2006-2010 American Community Survey population (not shown); ‡ Numbers in parentheses indicate the number of people reporting a single ancestry; * Numbers in parentheses indicate the number of persons reporting this race alone, not in combination with any other race; Please refer to the Explanation of Data for more information.

New Rochelle

Place Type: City
County: Westchester
Population: 77,062

Ancestry	Population	%
Afghan (0)	0	<0.01
African, Sub-Saharan (850)	1,030	1.36
African (253)	309	0.41
Cape Verdean (0)	0	<0.01
Ethiopian (0)	0	<0.01
Ghanaian (18)	18	0.02
Kenyan (19)	19	0.03
Liberian (0)	0	<0.01
Nigerian (125)	125	0.16
Senegalese (0)	0	<0.01
Sierra Leonean (15)	15	0.02
Somalian (0)	0	<0.01
South African (92)	179	0.24
Sudanese (0)	0	<0.01
Ugandan (0)	0	<0.01
Zimbabwean (0)	0	<0.01
Other Sub-Saharan African (328)	365	0.48
Albanian (324)	370	0.49
Alsatian (0)	0	<0.01
American (2,542)	2,542	3.35
Arab (338)	413	0.54
Arab (177)	187	0.25
Egyptian (13)	13	0.02
Iraqi (0)	0	<0.01
Jordanian (11)	46	0.06
Lebanese (102)	132	0.17
Moroccan (8)	8	0.01
Palestinian (0)	0	<0.01
Syrian (0)	0	<0.01
Other Arab (27)	27	0.04
Armenian (31)	75	0.10
Assyrian/Chaldean/Syriac (0)	0	<0.01
Australian (33)	33	0.04
Austrian (104)	547	0.72
Basque (12)	12	0.02
Belgian (27)	118	0.16
Brazilian (580)	728	0.96
British (145)	208	0.27
Bulgarian (9)	9	0.01
Cajun (0)	0	<0.01
Canadian (13)	41	0.05
Carpatho Rusyn (0)	0	<0.01
Celtic (0)	0	<0.01
Croatian (103)	167	0.22
Cypriot (0)	0	<0.01
Czech (78)	402	0.53
Czechoslovakian (32)	108	0.14
Danish (0)	55	0.07
Dutch (38)	257	0.34
Eastern European (870)	870	1.15
English (493)	1,832	2.42
Estonian (9)	16	0.02
European (773)	808	1.07
Finnish (36)	60	0.08
French, ex. Basque (342)	1,322	1.74
French Canadian (62)	152	0.20
German (734)	3,942	5.20
German Russian (0)	0	<0.01
Greek (377)	573	0.76
Guyanese (104)	125	0.16
Hungarian (231)	684	0.90
Icelander (0)	0	<0.01
Iranian (12)	33	0.04
Irish (2,797)	7,400	9.76
Israeli (26)	93	0.12
Italian (9,697)	14,355	18.93
Latvian (28)	74	0.10
Lithuanian (130)	228	0.30
Luxemburger (0)	9	0.01
Macedonian (154)	177	0.23
Maltese (0)	16	0.02
New Zealander (0)	0	<0.01
Northern European (25)	25	0.03

Norwegian (18)	72	0.09
Pennsylvania German (0)	0	<0.01
Polish (1,042)	2,744	3.62
Portuguese (615)	830	1.09
Romanian (83)	272	0.36
Russian (917)	3,102	4.09
Scandinavian (0)	0	<0.01
Scotch-Irish (92)	326	0.43
Scottish (166)	563	0.74
Serbian (0)	0	<0.01
Slavic (116)	171	0.23
Slovak (0)	116	0.15
Slovene (0)	0	<0.01
Soviet Union (0)	0	<0.01
Swedish (84)	428	0.56
Swiss (35)	56	0.07
Turkish (48)	137	0.18
Ukrainian (13)	146	0.19
Welsh (17)	129	0.17
West Indian, ex. Hispanic (3,998)	4,597	6.06
Bahamian (0)	0	<0.01
Barbadian (241)	316	0.42
Belizean (0)	0	<0.01
Bermudan (0)	0	<0.01
British West Indian (80)	153	0.20
Dutch West Indian (0)	0	<0.01
Haitian (926)	951	1.25
Jamaican (2,245)	2,635	3.48
Trinidadian/Tobagonian (295)	317	0.42
U.S. Virgin Islander (0)	0	<0.01
West Indian (211)	225	0.30
Other West Indian (0)	0	<0.01
Yugoslavian (23)	47	0.06

Hispanic Origin	Population	%
Hispanic or Latino (of any race)	21,452	27.84
Central American, ex. Mexican	2,017	2.62
Costa Rican	65	0.08
Guatemalan	1,232	1.60
Honduran	242	0.31
Nicaraguan	74	0.10
Panamanian	67	0.09
Salvadoran	330	0.43
Other Central American	7	0.01
Cuban	371	0.48
Dominican Republic	960	1.25
Mexican	10,363	13.45
Puerto Rican	2,779	3.61
South American	3,697	4.80
Argentinean	170	0.22
Bolivian	50	0.06
Chilean	76	0.10
Colombian	1,451	1.88
Ecuadorian	378	0.49
Paraguayan	49	0.06
Peruvian	1,297	1.68
Uruguayan	88	0.11
Venezuelan	131	0.17
Other South American	7	0.01
Other Hispanic or Latino	1,265	1.64

Race*	Population	%
African-American/Black (14,847)	15,858	20.58
Not Hispanic (13,956)	14,611	18.96
Hispanic (891)	1,247	1.62
American Indian/Alaska Native (398)	770	1.00
Not Hispanic (94)	308	0.40
Hispanic (304)	462	0.60
Alaska Athabascan (Ala. Nat.) (0)	0	<0.01
Aleut (Alaska Native) (0)	0	<0.01
Apache (0)	6	0.01
Arapaho (0)	0	<0.01
Blackfeet (5)	25	0.03
Canadian/French Am. Ind. (0)	2	<0.01
Central American Ind. (7)	20	0.03
Cherokee (5)	65	0.08
Cheyenne (1)	1	<0.01
Chickasaw (0)	1	<0.01
Chippewa (0)	3	<0.01

Choctaw (0)	2	<0.01
Colville (0)	0	<0.01
Comanche (0)	0	<0.01
Cree (0)	0	<0.01
Creek (0)	1	<0.01
Crow (0)	0	<0.01
Delaware (0)	2	<0.01
Hopi (0)	0	<0.01
Houma (0)	0	<0.01
Inupiat (Alaska Native) (0)	0	<0.01
Iroquois (5)	11	0.01
Kiowa (0)	0	<0.01
Lumbee (0)	0	<0.01
Menominee (0)	0	<0.01
Mexican American Ind. (47)	72	0.09
Navajo (0)	1	<0.01
Osage (0)	0	<0.01
Ottawa (0)	0	<0.01
Paiute (0)	0	<0.01
Pima (0)	0	<0.01
Potawatomi (0)	0	<0.01
Pueblo (0)	0	<0.01
Puget Sound Salish (0)	0	<0.01
Seminole (0)	1	<0.01
Shoshone (0)	0	<0.01
Sioux (1)	2	<0.01
South American Ind. (29)	56	0.07
Spanish American Ind. (1)	1	<0.01
Tlingit-Haida (Alaska Native) (0)	0	<0.01
Tohono O'Odham (0)	0	<0.01
Tsimshian (Alaska Native) (0)	0	<0.01
Ute (0)	0	<0.01
Yakama (0)	0	<0.01
Yaqui (0)	0	<0.01
Yuman (0)	0	<0.01
Yup'ik (Alaska Native) (0)	0	<0.01
Asian (3,262)	3,798	4.93
Not Hispanic (3,212)	3,631	4.71
Hispanic (50)	167	0.22
Bangladeshi (48)	55	0.07
Bhutanese (2)	2	<0.01
Burmese (6)	8	0.01
Cambodian (8)	9	0.01
Chinese, ex. Taiwanese (547)	715	0.93
Filipino (471)	543	0.70
Hmong (0)	0	<0.01
Indian (1,352)	1,508	1.96
Indonesian (6)	6	0.01
Japanese (106)	158	0.21
Korean (276)	319	0.41
Laotian (2)	14	0.02
Malaysian (5)	5	0.01
Nepalese (5)	5	0.01
Pakistani (147)	164	0.21
Sri Lankan (75)	83	0.11
Taiwanese (18)	32	0.04
Thai (25)	39	0.05
Vietnamese (19)	31	0.04
Hawaii Native/Pacific Islander (48)	123	0.16
Not Hispanic (20)	65	0.08
Hispanic (28)	58	0.08
Fijian (0)	0	<0.01
Guamanian/Chamorro (32)	43	0.06
Marshallese (0)	0	<0.01
Native Hawaiian (1)	12	0.02
Samoan (5)	7	0.01
Tongan (0)	0	<0.01
White (50,231)	52,208	67.75
Not Hispanic (36,948)	37,786	49.03
Hispanic (13,283)	14,422	18.71

Notes: † The Census 2010 population figure is used to calculate the percentages in the Hispanic Origin and Race categories. Ancestry percentages are based on the 2006-2010 American Community Survey population (not shown); ‡ Numbers in parentheses indicate the number of people reporting a single ancestry; * Numbers in parentheses indicate the number of persons reporting this race alone, not in combination with any other race; Please refer to the Explanation of Data for more information.

New York

Place Type: City
Counties: Bronx, Kings, New York, Queens, and Richmond
Population: 8,175,133

Ancestry	Population	%
Afghan (6,250)	6,470	0.08
African, Sub-Saharan (126,853)	175,478	2.17
African (60,151)	101,901	1.26
Cape Verdean (282)	595	0.01
Ethiopian (2,524)	2,869	0.04
Ghanaian (19,077)	19,782	0.24
Kenyan (294)	344	<0.01
Liberian (1,738)	1,991	0.02
Nigerian (19,543)	21,507	0.27
Senegalese (2,685)	2,895	0.04
Sierra Leonean (1,545)	1,572	0.02
Somalian (422)	518	0.01
South African (1,454)	2,116	0.03
Sudanese (1,079)	1,303	0.02
Ugandan (189)	256	<0.01
Zimbabwean (394)	414	0.01
Other Sub-Saharan African (15,476)	17,415	0.22
Albanian (29,299)	31,056	0.38
Alsatian (31)	217	<0.01
American (209,430)	209,430	2.59
Arab (65,990)	82,165	1.02
Arab (13,125)	15,160	0.19
Egyptian (15,679)	17,698	0.22
Iraqi (645)	1,137	0.01
Jordanian (1,141)	1,298	0.02
Lebanese (7,824)	11,682	0.14
Moroccan (7,043)	8,987	0.11
Palestinian (3,051)	3,421	0.04
Syrian (5,818)	8,198	0.10
Other Arab (11,664)	14,584	0.18
Armenian (7,612)	10,159	0.13
Assyrian/Chaldean/Syriac (144)	227	<0.01
Australian (2,699)	3,906	0.05
Austrian (9,463)	30,712	0.38
Basque (370)	902	0.01
Belgian (1,803)	4,472	0.06
Brazilian (9,457)	13,119	0.16
British (11,046)	21,065	0.26
Bulgarian (4,331)	5,011	0.06
Cajun (121)	432	0.01
Canadian (5,942)	10,989	0.14
Carpatho Rusyn (198)	249	<0.01
Celtic (275)	564	0.01
Croatian (8,097)	11,304	0.14
Cypriot (744)	960	0.01
Czech (3,559)	12,800	0.16
Czechoslovakian (2,411)	4,870	0.06
Danish (2,102)	7,018	0.09
Dutch (5,641)	23,151	0.29
Eastern European (41,481)	44,970	0.56
English (40,380)	146,525	1.81
Estonian (643)	1,057	0.01
European (59,415)	66,267	0.82
Finnish (1,375)	3,519	0.04
French, ex. Basque (19,416)	67,195	0.83
French Canadian (3,676)	11,393	0.14
German (68,198)	272,827	3.38
German Russian (69)	204	<0.01
Greek (58,515)	76,597	0.95
Guyanese (96,299)	107,972	1.34
Hungarian (29,252)	55,459	0.69
Icelander (386)	572	0.01
Iranian (8,448)	10,204	0.13
Irish (154,072)	410,889	5.09
Israeli (16,225)	21,872	0.27
Italian (403,347)	625,004	7.74
Latvian (1,663)	3,302	0.04
Lithuanian (4,343)	12,774	0.16
Luxemburger (76)	193	<0.01
Macedonian (4,296)	4,911	0.06
Maltese (1,817)	3,102	0.04
New Zealander (337)	584	0.01
Northern European (2,656)	3,043	0.04

Ancestry (cont.)	Population	%
Norwegian (6,141)	21,894	0.27
Pennsylvania German (160)	465	0.01
Polish (112,769)	216,891	2.68
Portuguese (5,980)	13,201	0.16
Romanian (18,025)	29,552	0.37
Russian (150,929)	240,690	2.98
Scandinavian (1,533)	3,434	0.04
Scotch-Irish (9,634)	27,337	0.34
Scottish (9,926)	38,000	0.47
Serbian (3,997)	4,911	0.06
Slavic (919)	1,962	0.02
Slovak (3,457)	6,785	0.08
Slovene (593)	1,476	0.02
Soviet Union (288)	419	0.01
Swedish (5,168)	20,940	0.26
Swiss (2,335)	8,135	0.10
Turkish (12,067)	14,927	0.18
Ukrainian (36,563)	48,714	0.60
Welsh (1,659)	11,219	0.14
West Indian, ex. Hispanic (509,675)	598,504	7.41
Bahamian (828)	1,147	0.01
Barbadian (19,549)	22,550	0.28
Belizean (4,699)	5,674	0.07
Bermudan (345)	518	0.01
British West Indian (39,268)	44,326	0.55
Dutch West Indian (789)	1,167	0.01
Haitian (112,397)	120,252	1.49
Jamaican (196,443)	216,495	2.68
Trinidadian/Tobagonian (66,794)	76,240	0.94
U.S. Virgin Islander (1,806)	2,383	0.03
West Indian (65,827)	106,548	1.32
Other West Indian (930)	1,204	0.01
Yugoslavian (10,119)	12,410	0.15

Hispanic Origin	Population	%
Hispanic or Latino (of any race)	2,336,076	28.58
Central American, ex. Mexican	151,378	1.85
Costa Rican	6,673	0.08
Guatemalan	30,420	0.37
Honduran	42,400	0.52
Nicaraguan	9,346	0.11
Panamanian	22,353	0.27
Salvadoran	38,559	0.47
Other Central American	1,627	0.02
Cuban	40,840	0.50
Dominican Republic	576,701	7.05
Mexican	319,263	3.91
Puerto Rican	723,621	8.85
South American	343,468	4.20
Argentinean	15,169	0.19
Bolivian	4,488	0.05
Chilean	7,026	0.09
Colombian	94,723	1.16
Ecuadorian	167,209	2.05
Paraguayan	3,534	0.04
Peruvian	36,018	0.44
Uruguayan	3,004	0.04
Venezuelan	9,619	0.12
Other South American	2,678	0.03
Other Hispanic or Latino	180,805	2.21

Race*	Population	%
African-American/Black (2,088,510)	2,228,145	27.26
Not Hispanic (1,861,295)	1,931,889	23.63
Hispanic (227,215)	296,256	3.62
American Indian/Alaska Native (57,512)	111,749	1.37
Not Hispanic (17,427)	44,541	0.54
Hispanic (40,085)	67,208	0.82
Alaska Athabascan (Ala. Nat.) (19)	37	<0.01
Aleut (Alaska Native) (12)	26	<0.01
Apache (135)	401	<0.01
Arapaho (8)	21	<0.01
Blackfeet (235)	1,627	0.02
Canadian/French Am. Ind. (111)	197	<0.01
Central American Ind. (3,948)	7,662	0.09
Cherokee (1,195)	6,952	0.09
Cheyenne (19)	46	<0.01
Chickasaw (40)	113	<0.01
Chippewa (105)	252	<0.01

Race* (cont.)	Population	%
Choctaw (94)	405	<0.01
Colville (6)	9	<0.01
Comanche (31)	76	<0.01
Cree (14)	81	<0.01
Creek (65)	291	<0.01
Crow (11)	50	<0.01
Delaware (50)	177	<0.01
Hopi (17)	49	<0.01
Houma (14)	23	<0.01
Inupiat (Alaska Native) (26)	58	<0.01
Iroquois (573)	1,276	0.02
Kiowa (11)	15	<0.01
Lumbee (27)	89	<0.01
Menominee (4)	10	<0.01
Mexican American Ind. (3,646)	4,922	0.06
Navajo (126)	272	<0.01
Osage (10)	23	<0.01
Ottawa (2)	11	<0.01
Paiute (5)	18	<0.01
Pima (4)	9	<0.01
Potawatomi (20)	40	<0.01
Pueblo (446)	892	0.01
Puget Sound Salish (5)	11	<0.01
Seminole (52)	357	<0.01
Shoshone (10)	46	<0.01
Sioux (159)	464	0.01
South American Ind. (4,682)	9,464	0.12
Spanish American Ind. (1,871)	2,594	0.03
Tlingit-Haida (Alaska Native) (15)	75	<0.01
Tohono O'Odham (32)	48	<0.01
Tsimshian (Alaska Native) (3)	4	<0.01
Ute (8)	17	<0.01
Yakama (5)	8	<0.01
Yaqui (27)	54	<0.01
Yuman (12)	22	<0.01
Yup'ik (Alaska Native) (2)	10	<0.01
Asian (1,038,388)	1,134,919	13.88
Not Hispanic (1,028,119)	1,110,964	13.59
Hispanic (10,269)	23,955	0.29
Bangladeshi (53,174)	61,788	0.76
Bhutanese (345)	388	<0.01
Burmese (3,614)	4,132	0.05
Cambodian (2,166)	2,591	0.03
Chinese, ex. Taiwanese (474,783)	500,434	6.12
Filipino (67,292)	78,030	0.95
Hmong (59)	83	<0.01
Indian (192,209)	232,696	2.85
Indonesian (3,785)	4,791	0.06
Japanese (24,277)	31,742	0.39
Korean (96,741)	102,820	1.26
Laotian (440)	664	0.01
Malaysian (2,100)	3,220	0.04
Nepalese (5,681)	6,187	0.08
Pakistani (41,887)	46,369	0.57
Sri Lankan (3,696)	4,369	0.05
Taiwanese (11,680)	13,682	0.17
Thai (6,056)	7,244	0.09
Vietnamese (13,387)	16,378	0.20
Hawaii Native/Pacific Islander (5,147)	24,098	0.29
Not Hispanic (2,795)	13,217	0.16
Hispanic (2,352)	10,881	0.13
Fijian (104)	213	<0.01
Guamanian/Chamorro (1,194)	1,784	0.02
Marshallese (8)	10	<0.01
Native Hawaiian (1,001)	2,448	0.03
Samoan (296)	764	0.01
Tongan (37)	66	<0.01
White (3,597,341)	3,797,402	46.45
Not Hispanic (2,722,904)	2,804,430	34.30
Hispanic (874,437)	992,972	12.15

Notes: † The Census 2010 population figure is used to calculate the percentages in the Hispanic Origin and Race categories. Ancestry percentages are based on the 2006-2010 American Community Survey population (not shown); ‡ Numbers in parentheses indicate the number of people reporting a single ancestry; * Numbers in parentheses indicate the number of persons reporting this race alone, not in combination with any other race; Please refer to the Explanation of Data for more information.

Niagara Falls

Place Type: City
County: Niagara
Population: 50,193

Ancestry	Population	%
Afghan (0)	0	<0.01
African, Sub-Saharan (318)	520	1.02
African (286)	488	0.96
Cape Verdean (0)	0	<0.01
Ethiopian (24)	24	0.05
Ghanaian (0)	0	<0.01
Kenyan (0)	0	<0.01
Liberian (0)	0	<0.01
Nigerian (0)	0	<0.01
Senegalese (0)	0	<0.01
Sierra Leonean (0)	0	<0.01
Somalian (0)	0	<0.01
South African (8)	8	0.02
Sudanese (0)	0	<0.01
Ugandan (0)	0	<0.01
Zimbabwean (0)	0	<0.01
Other Sub-Saharan African (0)	0	<0.01
Albanian (0)	0	<0.01
Alsatian (0)	0	<0.01
American (1,655)	1,655	3.25
Arab (204)	411	0.81
Arab (72)	103	0.20
Egyptian (0)	29	0.06
Iraqi (0)	0	<0.01
Jordanian (0)	0	<0.01
Lebanese (116)	228	0.45
Moroccan (0)	0	<0.01
Palestinian (0)	0	<0.01
Syrian (9)	44	0.09
Other Arab (7)	7	0.01
Armenian (96)	156	0.31
Assyrian/Chaldean/Syriac (0)	0	<0.01
Australian (31)	49	0.10
Austrian (38)	115	0.23
Basque (0)	0	<0.01
Belgian (0)	0	<0.01
Brazilian (0)	0	<0.01
British (29)	64	0.13
Bulgarian (0)	0	<0.01
Cajun (0)	0	<0.01
Canadian (210)	442	0.87
Carpatho Rusyn (14)	14	0.03
Celtic (0)	0	<0.01
Croatian (73)	85	0.17
Cypriot (0)	0	<0.01
Czech (37)	92	0.18
Czechoslovakian (0)	6	0.01
Danish (12)	134	0.26
Dutch (62)	498	0.98
Eastern European (0)	0	<0.01
English (2,722)	6,055	11.90
Estonian (0)	0	<0.01
European (44)	44	0.09
Finnish (0)	31	0.06
French, ex. Basque (256)	1,555	3.06
French Canadian (125)	493	0.97
German (2,324)	8,658	17.01
German Russian (16)	16	0.03
Greek (121)	318	0.62
Guyanese (0)	0	<0.01
Hungarian (68)	191	0.38
Icelander (0)	0	<0.01
Iranian (0)	0	<0.01
Irish (1,933)	7,048	13.85
Israeli (12)	12	0.02
Italian (6,763)	11,524	22.64
Latvian (0)	0	<0.01
Lithuanian (71)	128	0.25
Luxemburger (0)	0	<0.01
Macedonian (0)	0	<0.01
Maltese (0)	0	<0.01
New Zealander (0)	0	<0.01
Northern European (11)	11	0.02

Ancestry (cont.)	Population	%
Norwegian (9)	72	0.14
Pennsylvania German (61)	130	0.26
Polish (1,934)	4,962	9.75
Portuguese (135)	151	0.30
Romanian (15)	44	0.09
Russian (140)	312	0.61
Scandinavian (0)	9	0.02
Scotch-Irish (163)	522	1.03
Scottish (257)	747	1.47
Serbian (0)	0	<0.01
Slavic (28)	33	0.06
Slovak (39)	88	0.17
Slovene (0)	0	<0.01
Soviet Union (0)	0	<0.01
Swedish (51)	395	0.78
Swiss (6)	19	0.04
Turkish (0)	18	0.04
Ukrainian (59)	114	0.22
Welsh (93)	346	0.68
West Indian, ex. Hispanic (174)	366	0.72
Bahamian (0)	0	<0.01
Barbadian (0)	0	<0.01
Belizean (29)	29	0.06
Bermudan (0)	0	<0.01
British West Indian (9)	9	0.02
Dutch West Indian (0)	0	<0.01
Haitian (0)	0	<0.01
Jamaican (121)	167	0.33
Trinidadian/Tobagonian (15)	15	0.03
U.S. Virgin Islander (0)	0	<0.01
West Indian (0)	146	0.29
Other West Indian (0)	0	<0.01
Yugoslavian (0)	33	0.06

Hispanic Origin	Population	%
Hispanic or Latino (of any race)	1,508	3.00
Central American, ex. Mexican	39	0.08
Costa Rican	3	0.01
Guatemalan	15	0.03
Honduran	9	0.02
Nicaraguan	0	<0.01
Panamanian	8	0.02
Salvadoran	4	0.01
Other Central American	0	<0.01
Cuban	61	0.12
Dominican Republic	35	0.07
Mexican	228	0.45
Puerto Rican	797	1.59
South American	50	0.10
Argentinean	8	0.02
Bolivian	0	<0.01
Chilean	5	0.01
Colombian	23	0.05
Ecuadorian	3	0.01
Paraguayan	0	<0.01
Peruvian	4	0.01
Uruguayan	0	<0.01
Venezuelan	7	0.01
Other South American	0	<0.01
Other Hispanic or Latino	298	0.59

Race*	Population	%
African-American/Black (10,835)	12,203	24.31
Not Hispanic (10,643)	11,905	23.72
Hispanic (192)	298	0.59
American Indian/Alaska Native (977)	1,624	3.24
Not Hispanic (930)	1,524	3.04
Hispanic (47)	100	0.20
Alaska Athabascan (Ala. Nat.) (0)	0	<0.01
Aleut (Alaska Native) (0)	0	<0.01
Apache (0)	2	<0.01
Arapaho (0)	0	<0.01
Blackfeet (1)	16	0.03
Canadian/French Am. Ind. (18)	20	0.04
Central American Ind. (8)	11	0.02
Cherokee (8)	48	0.10
Cheyenne (1)	1	<0.01
Chickasaw (0)	0	<0.01
Chippewa (16)	23	0.05

Race* (cont.)	Population	%
Choctaw (1)	1	<0.01
Colville (0)	0	<0.01
Comanche (0)	0	<0.01
Cree (2)	3	0.01
Creek (0)	0	<0.01
Crow (0)	0	<0.01
Delaware (0)	0	<0.01
Hopi (0)	0	<0.01
Houma (0)	0	<0.01
Inupiat (Alaska Native) (0)	0	<0.01
Iroquois (542)	801	1.60
Kiowa (0)	0	<0.01
Lumbee (4)	6	<0.01
Menominee (0)	2	<0.01
Mexican American Ind. (4)	4	0.01
Navajo (1)	1	<0.01
Osage (0)	0	<0.01
Ottawa (1)	1	<0.01
Paiute (0)	0	<0.01
Pima (0)	0	<0.01
Potawatomi (0)	0	<0.01
Pueblo (0)	0	<0.01
Puget Sound Salish (0)	0	<0.01
Seminole (0)	5	0.01
Shoshone (0)	0	<0.01
Sioux (5)	8	0.02
South American Ind. (1)	2	<0.01
Spanish American Ind. (0)	0	<0.01
Tlingit-Haida (Alaska Native) (0)	0	<0.01
Tohono O'Odham (0)	0	<0.01
Tsimshian (Alaska Native) (0)	0	<0.01
Ute (0)	0	<0.01
Yakama (0)	1	<0.01
Yaqui (1)	1	<0.01
Yuman (0)	0	<0.01
Yup'ik (Alaska Native) (0)	0	<0.01
Asian (609)	751	1.50
Not Hispanic (599)	732	1.46
Hispanic (10)	19	0.04
Bangladeshi (0)	0	<0.01
Bhutanese (0)	0	<0.01
Burmese (1)	1	<0.01
Cambodian (1)	1	<0.01
Chinese, ex. Taiwanese (97)	106	0.21
Filipino (45)	81	0.16
Hmong (0)	0	<0.01
Indian (286)	327	0.65
Indonesian (0)	0	<0.01
Japanese (14)	26	0.05
Korean (36)	48	0.10
Laotian (12)	16	0.03
Malaysian (0)	0	<0.01
Nepalese (0)	0	<0.01
Pakistani (58)	64	0.13
Sri Lankan (0)	5	0.01
Taiwanese (5)	5	0.01
Thai (4)	15	0.03
Vietnamese (19)	22	0.04
Hawaii Native/Pacific Islander (15)	51	0.10
Not Hispanic (10)	43	0.09
Hispanic (5)	8	0.02
Fijian (0)	1	<0.01
Guamanian/Chamorro (5)	5	0.01
Marshallese (0)	0	<0.01
Native Hawaiian (6)	10	0.02
Samoan (2)	2	<0.01
Tongan (0)	0	<0.01
White (35,394)	37,102	73.92
Not Hispanic (34,663)	36,227	72.18
Hispanic (731)	875	1.74

*Notes: † The Census 2010 population figure is used to calculate the percentages in the Hispanic Origin and Race categories. Ancestry percentages are based on the 2006-2010 American Community Survey population (not shown); ‡ Numbers in parentheses indicate the number of people reporting a single ancestry; * Numbers in parentheses indicate the number of persons reporting this race alone, not in combination with any other race; Please refer to the Explanation of Data for more information.*

North Hempstead

Place Type: Town
County: Nassau
Population: 226,322

Ancestry	Population	%
Afghan (88)	203	0.09
African, Sub-Saharan (670)	862	0.39
African (277)	437	0.20
Cape Verdean (0)	0	<0.01
Ethiopian (49)	49	0.02
Ghanaian (117)	117	0.05
Kenyan (0)	0	<0.01
Liberian (0)	3	<0.01
Nigerian (145)	154	0.07
Senegalese (0)	0	<0.01
Sierra Leonean (13)	13	0.01
Somalian (0)	0	<0.01
South African (60)	63	0.03
Sudanese (0)	17	0.01
Ugandan (0)	0	<0.01
Zimbabwean (0)	0	<0.01
Other Sub-Saharan African (9)	9	<0.01
Albanian (156)	296	0.13
Alsatian (9)	9	<0.01
American (7,110)	7,110	3.18
Arab (1,529)	2,078	0.93
Arab (82)	103	0.05
Egyptian (404)	529	0.24
Iraqi (370)	500	0.22
Jordanian (0)	0	<0.01
Lebanese (105)	147	0.07
Moroccan (34)	85	0.04
Palestinian (59)	59	0.03
Syrian (10)	84	0.04
Other Arab (465)	571	0.26
Armenian (391)	631	0.28
Assyrian/Chaldean/Syriac (4)	21	0.01
Australian (22)	80	0.04
Austrian (661)	2,782	1.24
Basque (0)	121	0.05
Belgian (93)	166	0.07
Brazilian (489)	613	0.27
British (233)	705	0.32
Bulgarian (56)	73	0.03
Cajun (0)	22	0.01
Canadian (182)	307	0.14
Carpatho Rusyn (0)	0	<0.01
Celtic (0)	48	0.02
Croatian (478)	672	0.30
Cypriot (46)	64	0.03
Czech (150)	636	0.28
Czechoslovakian (205)	493	0.22
Danish (141)	419	0.19
Dutch (110)	784	0.35
Eastern European (3,518)	3,769	1.69
English (1,073)	6,017	2.69
Estonian (18)	48	0.02
European (1,809)	2,051	0.92
Finnish (38)	128	0.06
French, ex. Basque (273)	2,191	0.98
French Canadian (207)	490	0.22
German (4,524)	18,322	8.19
German Russian (0)	26	0.01
Greek (2,635)	3,568	1.60
Guyanese (324)	405	0.18
Hungarian (894)	2,628	1.18
Icelander (0)	0	<0.01
Iranian (8,611)	9,262	4.14
Irish (10,304)	27,339	12.22
Israeli (1,537)	1,853	0.83
Italian (23,753)	40,182	17.97
Latvian (122)	254	0.11
Lithuanian (197)	718	0.32
Luxemburger (0)	16	0.01
Macedonian (0)	0	<0.01
Maltese (125)	248	0.11
New Zealander (0)	0	<0.01
Northern European (82)	91	0.04
Norwegian (129)	715	0.32
Pennsylvania German (15)	15	0.01
Polish (5,076)	13,352	5.97
Portuguese (3,596)	3,978	1.78
Romanian (662)	1,434	0.64
Russian (6,882)	14,712	6.58
Scandinavian (67)	122	0.05
Scotch-Irish (405)	1,188	0.53
Scottish (369)	1,567	0.70
Serbian (109)	153	0.07
Slavic (11)	195	0.09
Slovak (122)	312	0.14
Slovene (59)	79	0.04
Soviet Union (0)	0	<0.01
Swedish (179)	1,391	0.62
Swiss (77)	362	0.16
Turkish (308)	408	0.18
Ukrainian (488)	1,005	0.45
Welsh (46)	328	0.15
West Indian, ex. Hispanic (3,572)	4,095	1.83
Bahamian (0)	0	<0.01
Barbadian (152)	184	0.08
Belizean (44)	81	0.04
Bermudan (0)	0	<0.01
British West Indian (46)	46	0.02
Dutch West Indian (45)	65	0.03
Haitian (2,247)	2,394	1.07
Jamaican (723)	868	0.39
Trinidadian/Tobagonian (87)	94	0.04
U.S. Virgin Islander (0)	0	<0.01
West Indian (228)	363	0.16
Other West Indian (0)	0	<0.01
Yugoslavian (65)	170	0.08

Hispanic Origin	Population	%
Hispanic or Latino (of any race)	29,074	12.85
Central American, ex. Mexican	11,455	5.06
Costa Rican	124	0.05
Guatemalan	1,193	0.53
Honduran	1,572	0.69
Nicaraguan	110	0.05
Panamanian	84	0.04
Salvadoran	8,262	3.65
Other Central American	110	0.05
Cuban	660	0.29
Dominican Republic	1,362	0.60
Mexican	3,488	1.54
Puerto Rican	2,705	1.20
South American	6,333	2.80
Argentinean	435	0.19
Bolivian	62	0.03
Chilean	664	0.29
Colombian	1,914	0.85
Ecuadorian	1,966	0.87
Paraguayan	140	0.06
Peruvian	925	0.41
Uruguayan	84	0.04
Venezuelan	97	0.04
Other South American	46	0.02
Other Hispanic or Latino	3,071	1.36

Race*	Population	%
African-American/Black (12,587)	13,593	6.01
Not Hispanic (11,971)	12,707	5.61
Hispanic (616)	886	0.39
American Indian/Alaska Native (461)	1,149	0.51
Not Hispanic (183)	566	0.25
Hispanic (278)	583	0.26
Alaska Athabascan (Ala. Nat.) (0)	0	<0.01
Aleut (Alaska Native) (0)	0	<0.01
Apache (1)	3	<0.01
Arapaho (0)	0	<0.01
Blackfeet (0)	0	<0.01
Canadian/French Am. Ind. (0)	0	<0.01
Central American Ind. (9)	16	0.01
Cherokee (14)	86	0.04
Cheyenne (3)	3	<0.01
Chickasaw (0)	0	<0.01
Chippewa (0)	4	<0.01
Choctaw (3)	8	<0.01
Colville (0)	0	<0.01
Comanche (0)	0	<0.01
Cree (0)	0	<0.01
Creek (0)	3	<0.01
Crow (0)	0	<0.01
Delaware (2)	5	<0.01
Hopi (1)	3	<0.01
Houma (0)	0	<0.01
Inupiat (Alaska Native) (2)	2	<0.01
Iroquois (17)	37	0.02
Kiowa (0)	0	<0.01
Lumbee (0)	1	<0.01
Menominee (0)	0	<0.01
Mexican American Ind. (36)	48	0.02
Navajo (0)	0	<0.01
Osage (0)	0	<0.01
Ottawa (0)	0	<0.01
Paiute (0)	0	<0.01
Pima (0)	0	<0.01
Potawatomi (1)	1	<0.01
Pueblo (0)	0	<0.01
Puget Sound Salish (0)	0	<0.01
Seminole (0)	0	<0.01
Shoshone (0)	0	<0.01
Sioux (8)	17	0.01
South American Ind. (32)	79	0.03
Spanish American Ind. (39)	40	0.02
Tlingit-Haida (Alaska Native) (0)	0	<0.01
Tohono O'Odham (0)	0	<0.01
Tsimshian (Alaska Native) (0)	0	<0.01
Ute (0)	0	<0.01
Yakama (0)	0	<0.01
Yaqui (1)	1	<0.01
Yuman (0)	0	<0.01
Yup'ik (Alaska Native) (0)	0	<0.01
Asian (33,889)	36,973	16.34
Not Hispanic (33,747)	36,641	16.19
Hispanic (142)	332	0.15
Bangladeshi (392)	441	0.19
Bhutanese (1)	1	<0.01
Burmese (83)	88	0.04
Cambodian (11)	14	0.01
Chinese, ex. Taiwanese (9,631)	10,292	4.55
Filipino (1,567)	1,899	0.84
Hmong (0)	0	<0.01
Indian (12,549)	13,427	5.93
Indonesian (30)	53	0.02
Japanese (1,094)	1,266	0.56
Korean (5,820)	6,015	2.66
Laotian (7)	8	<0.01
Malaysian (24)	35	0.02
Nepalese (17)	17	0.01
Pakistani (904)	1,029	0.45
Sri Lankan (52)	59	0.03
Taiwanese (717)	809	0.36
Thai (103)	126	0.06
Vietnamese (132)	186	0.08
Hawaii Native/Pacific Islander (31)	275	0.12
Not Hispanic (24)	224	0.10
Hispanic (7)	51	0.02
Fijian (0)	0	<0.01
Guamanian/Chamorro (14)	20	0.01
Marshallese (0)	0	<0.01
Native Hawaiian (0)	34	0.02
Samoan (7)	14	0.01
Tongan (0)	0	<0.01
White (161,955)	166,538	73.58
Not Hispanic (146,760)	149,607	66.10
Hispanic (15,195)	16,931	7.48

*Notes: † The Census 2010 population figure is used to calculate the percentages in the Hispanic Origin and Race categories. Ancestry percentages are based on the 2006-2010 American Community Survey population (not shown); ‡ Numbers in parentheses indicate the number of people reporting a single ancestry; * Numbers in parentheses indicate the number of persons reporting this race alone, not in combination with any other race; Please refer to the Explanation of Data for more information.*

Oyster Bay

Place Type: Town
County: Nassau
Population: 293,214

Ancestry	Population	%
Afghan (580)	808	0.28
African, Sub-Saharan (294)	484	0.17
African (215)	289	0.10
Cape Verdean (12)	12	<0.01
Ethiopian (0)	0	<0.01
Ghanaian (0)	0	<0.01
Kenyan (0)	0	<0.01
Liberian (0)	0	<0.01
Nigerian (37)	77	0.03
Senegalese (0)	0	<0.01
Sierra Leonean (0)	0	<0.01
Somalian (0)	0	<0.01
South African (30)	30	0.01
Sudanese (0)	0	<0.01
Ugandan (0)	0	<0.01
Zimbabwean (0)	0	<0.01
Other Sub-Saharan African (0)	76	0.03
Albanian (268)	368	0.13
Alsatian (0)	0	<0.01
American (9,798)	9,798	3.36
Arab (597)	1,227	0.42
Arab (177)	245	0.08
Egyptian (153)	222	0.08
Iraqi (9)	9	<0.01
Jordanian (0)	0	<0.01
Lebanese (51)	191	0.07
Moroccan (47)	131	0.04
Palestinian (31)	60	0.02
Syrian (49)	114	0.04
Other Arab (80)	255	0.09
Armenian (1,034)	1,383	0.47
Assyrian/Chaldean/Syriac (0)	0	<0.01
Australian (3)	41	0.01
Austrian (879)	3,412	1.17
Basque (0)	3	<0.01
Belgian (53)	201	0.07
Brazilian (328)	370	0.13
British (208)	476	0.16
Bulgarian (16)	45	0.02
Cajun (0)	37	0.01
Canadian (107)	441	0.15
Carpatho Rusyn (0)	0	<0.01
Celtic (55)	55	0.02
Croatian (623)	1,002	0.34
Cypriot (63)	63	0.02
Czech (223)	1,379	0.47
Czechoslovakian (163)	618	0.21
Danish (126)	573	0.20
Dutch (288)	1,343	0.46
Eastern European (3,693)	3,841	1.32
English (1,832)	11,799	4.05
Estonian (68)	130	0.04
European (2,787)	2,919	1.00
Finnish (39)	265	0.09
French, ex. Basque (422)	4,302	1.48
French Canadian (238)	807	0.28
German (8,307)	41,381	14.19
German Russian (0)	0	<0.01
Greek (4,277)	6,908	2.37
Guyanese (134)	187	0.06
Hungarian (705)	3,138	1.08
Icelander (31)	52	0.02
Iranian (1,115)	1,464	0.50
Irish (17,041)	59,765	20.49
Israeli (422)	663	0.23
Italian (48,450)	88,723	30.43
Latvian (110)	235	0.08
Lithuanian (378)	1,079	0.37
Luxemburger (0)	0	<0.01
Macedonian (0)	0	<0.01
Maltese (117)	579	0.20
New Zealander (0)	0	<0.01
Northern European (97)	105	0.04

Ancestry (cont.)	Population	%
Norwegian (469)	1,882	0.65
Pennsylvania German (24)	24	0.01
Polish (6,380)	19,395	6.65
Portuguese (145)	445	0.15
Romanian (609)	1,492	0.51
Russian (5,986)	14,554	4.99
Scandinavian (24)	144	0.05
Scotch-Irish (832)	2,523	0.87
Scottish (646)	2,493	0.85
Serbian (12)	103	0.04
Slavic (27)	173	0.06
Slovak (164)	442	0.15
Slovene (10)	55	0.02
Soviet Union (0)	0	<0.01
Swedish (191)	2,325	0.80
Swiss (114)	686	0.24
Turkish (520)	1,232	0.42
Ukrainian (859)	1,774	0.61
Welsh (83)	515	0.18
West Indian, ex. Hispanic (1,924)	2,311	0.79
Bahamian (0)	0	<0.01
Barbadian (14)	26	0.01
Belizean (16)	29	0.01
Bermudan (0)	13	<0.01
British West Indian (125)	157	0.05
Dutch West Indian (7)	21	0.01
Haitian (732)	813	0.28
Jamaican (818)	972	0.33
Trinidadian/Tobagonian (111)	148	0.05
U.S. Virgin Islander (15)	15	0.01
West Indian (86)	102	0.03
Other West Indian (0)	15	0.01
Yugoslavian (65)	334	0.11

Hispanic Origin	Population	%
Hispanic or Latino (of any race)	21,923	7.48
Central American, ex. Mexican	4,958	1.69
Costa Rican	101	0.03
Guatemalan	397	0.14
Honduran	952	0.32
Nicaraguan	78	0.03
Panamanian	88	0.03
Salvadoran	3,297	1.12
Other Central American	45	0.02
Cuban	906	0.31
Dominican Republic	1,429	0.49
Mexican	1,550	0.53
Puerto Rican	4,810	1.64
South American	5,752	1.96
Argentinean	441	0.15
Bolivian	110	0.04
Chilean	569	0.19
Colombian	2,035	0.69
Ecuadorian	1,082	0.37
Paraguayan	64	0.02
Peruvian	1,156	0.39
Uruguayan	134	0.05
Venezuelan	129	0.04
Other South American	32	0.01
Other Hispanic or Latino	2,518	0.86

Race*	Population	%
African-American/Black (6,657)	7,671	2.62
Not Hispanic (6,168)	6,908	2.36
Hispanic (489)	763	0.26
American Indian/Alaska Native (442)	1,035	0.35
Not Hispanic (210)	646	0.22
Hispanic (232)	389	0.13
Alaska Athabascan (Ala. Nat.) (0)	1	<0.01
Aleut (Alaska Native) (1)	1	<0.01
Apache (2)	2	<0.01
Arapaho (0)	0	<0.01
Blackfeet (0)	17	0.01
Canadian/French Am. Ind. (4)	6	<0.01
Central American Ind. (13)	16	0.01
Cherokee (6)	86	0.03
Cheyenne (0)	0	<0.01
Chickasaw (0)	2	<0.01
Chippewa (9)	14	<0.01

Race* (cont.)	Population	%
Choctaw (2)	5	<0.01
Colville (0)	0	<0.01
Comanche (0)	0	<0.01
Cree (0)	3	<0.01
Creek (1)	5	<0.01
Crow (0)	1	<0.01
Delaware (3)	6	<0.01
Hopi (0)	0	<0.01
Houma (0)	0	<0.01
Inupiat (Alaska Native) (0)	0	<0.01
Iroquois (13)	47	0.02
Kiowa (1)	1	<0.01
Lumbee (0)	0	<0.01
Menominee (0)	0	<0.01
Mexican American Ind. (26)	34	0.01
Navajo (2)	3	<0.01
Osage (0)	1	<0.01
Ottawa (0)	0	<0.01
Paiute (0)	0	<0.01
Pima (0)	0	<0.01
Potawatomi (1)	2	<0.01
Pueblo (2)	3	<0.01
Puget Sound Salish (0)	0	<0.01
Seminole (0)	0	<0.01
Shoshone (1)	1	<0.01
Sioux (2)	7	<0.01
South American Ind. (24)	57	0.02
Spanish American Ind. (21)	25	0.01
Tlingit-Haida (Alaska Native) (0)	0	<0.01
Tohono O'Odham (0)	0	<0.01
Tsimshian (Alaska Native) (0)	0	<0.01
Ute (0)	0	<0.01
Yakama (0)	0	<0.01
Yaqui (0)	0	<0.01
Yuman (0)	0	<0.01
Yup'ik (Alaska Native) (0)	0	<0.01
Asian (26,723)	29,203	9.96
Not Hispanic (26,611)	28,910	9.86
Hispanic (112)	293	0.10
Bangladeshi (331)	365	0.12
Bhutanese (0)	0	<0.01
Burmese (23)	26	0.01
Cambodian (29)	38	0.01
Chinese, ex. Taiwanese (6,454)	7,054	2.41
Filipino (1,445)	1,803	0.61
Hmong (0)	0	<0.01
Indian (10,593)	11,289	3.85
Indonesian (24)	33	0.01
Japanese (431)	554	0.19
Korean (4,774)	4,977	1.70
Laotian (2)	2	<0.01
Malaysian (21)	30	0.01
Nepalese (48)	49	0.02
Pakistani (1,212)	1,330	0.45
Sri Lankan (39)	59	0.02
Taiwanese (346)	401	0.14
Thai (90)	110	0.04
Vietnamese (165)	237	0.08
Hawaii Native/Pacific Islander (34)	174	0.06
Not Hispanic (24)	124	0.04
Hispanic (10)	50	0.02
Fijian (0)	2	<0.01
Guamanian/Chamorro (7)	15	0.01
Marshallese (0)	0	<0.01
Native Hawaiian (9)	29	0.01
Samoan (3)	10	<0.01
Tongan (1)	1	<0.01
White (249,159)	252,713	86.19
Not Hispanic (234,536)	236,944	80.81
Hispanic (14,623)	15,769	5.38

Notes: † The Census 2010 population figure is used to calculate the percentages in the Hispanic Origin and Race categories. Ancestry percentages are based on the 2006-2010 American Community Survey population (not shown); ‡ Numbers in parentheses indicate the number of people reporting a single ancestry; * Numbers in parentheses indicate the number of persons reporting this race alone, not in combination with any other race; Please refer to the Explanation of Data for more information.

Queens

Place Type: Borough
County: Queens
Population: 2,230,722

Ancestry	Population	%
Afghan (5,842)	6,027	0.27
African, Sub-Saharan (19,754)	25,166	1.14
African (9,764)	14,083	0.64
Cape Verdean (46)	117	0.01
Ethiopian (478)	505	0.02
Ghanaian (1,269)	1,326	0.06
Kenyan (96)	96	<0.01
Liberian (297)	381	0.02
Nigerian (5,989)	6,304	0.29
Senegalese (84)	84	<0.01
Sierra Leonean (127)	127	0.01
Somalian (52)	98	<0.01
South African (230)	356	0.02
Sudanese (161)	286	0.01
Ugandan (65)	77	<0.01
Zimbabwean (107)	107	<0.01
Other Sub-Saharan African (989)	1,219	0.06
Albanian (6,264)	6,624	0.30
Alsatian (26)	37	<0.01
American (45,604)	45,604	2.07
Arab (16,286)	19,669	0.89
Arab (1,921)	2,283	0.10
Egyptian (5,905)	6,551	0.30
Iraqi (224)	315	0.01
Jordanian (260)	307	0.01
Lebanese (1,548)	2,228	0.10
Moroccan (2,945)	3,459	0.16
Palestinian (582)	638	0.03
Syrian (193)	420	0.02
Other Arab (2,708)	3,468	0.16
Armenian (4,083)	4,658	0.21
Assyrian/Chaldean/Syriac (13)	13	<0.01
Australian (163)	285	0.01
Austrian (2,702)	7,523	0.34
Basque (29)	159	0.01
Belgian (289)	593	0.03
Brazilian (4,871)	6,175	0.28
British (1,346)	2,457	0.11
Bulgarian (1,928)	2,090	0.10
Cajun (0)	33	<0.01
Canadian (604)	1,308	0.06
Carpatho Rusyn (0)	9	<0.01
Celtic (92)	169	0.01
Croatian (5,621)	7,054	0.32
Cypriot (556)	644	0.03
Czech (1,116)	3,464	0.16
Czechoslovakian (816)	1,467	0.07
Danish (171)	792	0.04
Dutch (727)	3,516	0.16
Eastern European (4,442)	4,673	0.21
English (4,389)	20,267	0.92
Estonian (164)	198	0.01
European (5,335)	6,584	0.30
Finnish (269)	693	0.03
French, ex. Basque (3,945)	12,532	0.57
French Canadian (552)	2,020	0.09
German (20,566)	70,399	3.20
German Russian (33)	78	<0.01
Greek (35,368)	41,654	1.89
Guyanese (47,132)	53,961	2.45
Hungarian (4,718)	9,470	0.43
Icelander (10)	26	<0.01
Iranian (3,162)	3,707	0.17
Irish (43,033)	105,348	4.79
Israeli (3,355)	4,164	0.19
Italian (104,251)	159,812	7.27
Latvian (342)	568	0.03
Lithuanian (1,463)	3,131	0.14
Luxemburger (0)	13	<0.01
Macedonian (938)	1,109	0.05
Maltese (952)	1,565	0.07
New Zealander (0)	16	<0.01
Northern European (370)	512	0.02

	Population	%
Norwegian (670)	2,559	0.12
Pennsylvania German (9)	38	<0.01
Polish (37,726)	59,757	2.72
Portuguese (2,784)	4,727	0.21
Romanian (9,232)	11,686	0.53
Russian (29,779)	44,676	2.03
Scandinavian (131)	545	0.02
Scotch-Irish (2,079)	4,602	0.21
Scottish (1,567)	5,718	0.26
Serbian (2,176)	2,438	0.11
Slavic (370)	765	0.03
Slovak (1,161)	1,882	0.09
Slovene (171)	468	0.02
Soviet Union (12)	71	<0.01
Swedish (511)	2,862	0.13
Swiss (381)	1,260	0.06
Turkish (3,054)	3,767	0.17
Ukrainian (5,770)	8,375	0.38
Welsh (201)	1,666	0.08
West Indian, ex. Hispanic (131,014)	147,460	6.71
Bahamian (134)	185	0.01
Barbadian (4,074)	5,021	0.23
Belizean (1,106)	1,344	0.06
Bermudan (142)	177	0.01
British West Indian (3,765)	4,689	0.21
Dutch West Indian (122)	206	0.01
Haitian (35,439)	38,368	1.74
Jamaican (55,278)	59,999	2.73
Trinidadian/Tobagonian (16,227)	19,255	0.88
U.S. Virgin Islander (234)	364	0.02
West Indian (14,052)	17,400	0.79
Other West Indian (441)	452	0.02
Yugoslavian (3,824)	4,516	0.21

Hispanic Origin	Population	%
Hispanic or Latino (of any race)	613,750	27.51
Central American, ex. Mexican	52,509	2.35
Costa Rican	1,749	0.08
Guatemalan	13,700	0.61
Honduran	8,546	0.38
Nicaraguan	2,842	0.13
Panamanian	3,977	0.18
Salvadoran	21,342	0.96
Other Central American	353	0.02
Cuban	11,020	0.49
Dominican Republic	88,061	3.95
Mexican	92,835	4.16
Puerto Rican	102,881	4.61
South American	214,022	9.59
Argentinean	6,345	0.28
Bolivian	3,268	0.15
Chilean	3,184	0.14
Colombian	70,290	3.15
Ecuadorian	98,512	4.42
Paraguayan	2,775	0.12
Peruvian	22,886	1.03
Uruguayan	1,743	0.08
Venezuelan	3,580	0.16
Other South American	1,439	0.06
Other Hispanic or Latino	52,422	2.35

Race*	Population	%
African-American/Black (426,683)	462,351	20.73
Not Hispanic (395,881)	419,695	18.81
Hispanic (30,802)	42,656	1.91
American Indian/Alaska Native (15,364)	30,033	1.35
Not Hispanic (6,490)	15,412	0.69
Hispanic (8,874)	14,621	0.66
Alaska Athabascan (Ala. Nat.) (2)	3	<0.01
Aleut (Alaska Native) (4)	6	<0.01
Apache (15)	53	<0.01
Arapaho (0)	2	<0.01
Blackfeet (45)	342	0.02
Canadian/French Am. Ind. (20)	38	<0.01
Central American Ind. (419)	733	0.03
Cherokee (267)	1,425	0.06
Cheyenne (13)	20	<0.01
Chickasaw (9)	21	<0.01
Chippewa (14)	37	<0.01

	Population	%
Choctaw (16)	68	<0.01
Colville (1)	1	<0.01
Comanche (3)	6	<0.01
Cree (6)	24	<0.01
Creek (23)	73	<0.01
Crow (1)	4	<0.01
Delaware (14)	35	<0.01
Hopi (1)	15	<0.01
Houma (0)	4	<0.01
Inupiat (Alaska Native) (6)	13	<0.01
Iroquois (140)	308	0.01
Kiowa (0)	0	<0.01
Lumbee (7)	30	<0.01
Menominee (0)	0	<0.01
Mexican American Ind. (1,270)	1,640	0.07
Navajo (13)	37	<0.01
Osage (0)	5	<0.01
Ottawa (0)	2	<0.01
Paiute (3)	4	<0.01
Pima (0)	0	<0.01
Potawatomi (6)	7	<0.01
Pueblo (102)	161	0.01
Puget Sound Salish (2)	5	<0.01
Seminole (15)	79	<0.01
Shoshone (0)	6	<0.01
Sioux (35)	104	<0.01
South American Ind. (1,281)	2,448	0.11
Spanish American Ind. (468)	659	0.03
Tlingit-Haida (Alaska Native) (8)	20	<0.01
Tohono O'Odham (4)	6	<0.01
Tsimshian (Alaska Native) (0)	1	<0.01
Ute (4)	5	<0.01
Yakama (0)	0	<0.01
Yaqui (3)	7	<0.01
Yuman (2)	5	<0.01
Yup'ik (Alaska Native) (1)	1	<0.01
Asian (511,787)	552,867	24.78
Not Hispanic (508,334)	545,389	24.45
Hispanic (3,453)	7,478	0.34
Bangladeshi (33,152)	38,341	1.72
Bhutanese (240)	250	0.01
Burmese (2,132)	2,344	0.11
Cambodian (230)	303	0.01
Chinese, ex. Taiwanese (191,693)	200,714	9.00
Filipino (38,163)	41,773	1.87
Hmong (24)	30	<0.01
Indian (117,550)	141,147	6.33
Indonesian (2,860)	3,386	0.15
Japanese (6,375)	7,790	0.35
Korean (64,107)	66,124	2.96
Laotian (137)	210	0.01
Malaysian (1,029)	1,620	0.07
Nepalese (4,930)	5,319	0.24
Pakistani (16,215)	18,084	0.81
Sri Lankan (1,293)	1,536	0.07
Taiwanese (7,776)	8,962	0.40
Thai (3,677)	4,124	0.18
Vietnamese (3,566)	4,322	0.19
Hawaii Native/Pacific Islander (1,530)	7,691	0.34
Not Hispanic (1,094)	5,685	0.25
Hispanic (436)	2,006	0.09
Fijian (36)	76	<0.01
Guamanian/Chamorro (337)	483	0.02
Marshallese (0)	0	<0.01
Native Hawaiian (191)	486	0.02
Samoan (62)	179	0.01
Tongan (7)	14	<0.01
White (886,053)	941,608	42.21
Not Hispanic (616,727)	638,051	28.60
Hispanic (269,326)	303,557	13.61

Notes: † The Census 2010 population figure is used to calculate the percentages in the Hispanic Origin and Race categories. Ancestry percentages are based on the 2006-2010 American Community Survey population (not shown); ‡ Numbers in parentheses indicate the number of people reporting a single ancestry; * Numbers in parentheses indicate the number of persons reporting this race alone, not in combination with any other race; Please refer to the Explanation of Data for more information.

Ramapo

Place Type: Town
County: Rockland
Population: 126,595

Ancestry	Population	%
Afghan (111)	111	0.09
African, Sub-Saharan (718)	858	0.70
African (292)	427	0.35
Cape Verdean (0)	0	<0.01
Ethiopian (0)	0	<0.01
Ghanaian (77)	77	0.06
Kenyan (0)	0	<0.01
Liberian (0)	0	<0.01
Nigerian (207)	207	0.17
Senegalese (0)	0	<0.01
Sierra Leonean (0)	0	<0.01
Somalian (0)	0	<0.01
South African (56)	56	0.05
Sudanese (0)	0	<0.01
Ugandan (86)	86	0.07
Zimbabwean (0)	0	<0.01
Other Sub-Saharan African (0)	5	<0.01
Albanian (0)	0	<0.01
Alsatian (0)	0	<0.01
American (5,092)	5,092	4.15
Arab (608)	781	0.64
Arab (245)	245	0.20
Egyptian (16)	24	0.02
Iraqi (12)	48	0.04
Jordanian (10)	10	0.01
Lebanese (23)	37	0.03
Moroccan (216)	291	0.24
Palestinian (0)	25	0.02
Syrian (17)	17	0.01
Other Arab (69)	84	0.07
Armenian (33)	63	0.05
Assyrian/Chaldean/Syriac (0)	0	<0.01
Australian (19)	86	0.07
Austrian (328)	1,328	1.08
Basque (0)	0	<0.01
Belgian (218)	751	0.61
Brazilian (101)	228	0.19
British (179)	396	0.32
Bulgarian (8)	24	0.02
Cajun (0)	0	<0.01
Canadian (309)	680	0.55
Carpatho Rusyn (0)	0	<0.01
Celtic (19)	19	0.02
Croatian (0)	16	0.01
Cypriot (0)	0	<0.01
Czech (174)	565	0.46
Czechoslovakian (355)	654	0.53
Danish (56)	129	0.11
Dutch (208)	772	0.63
Eastern European (1,057)	1,144	0.93
English (863)	3,171	2.58
Estonian (24)	48	0.04
European (7,822)	8,814	7.18
Finnish (0)	17	0.01
French, ex. Basque (183)	954	0.78
French Canadian (53)	174	0.14
German (2,191)	7,630	6.22
German Russian (0)	0	<0.01
Greek (402)	653	0.53
Guyanese (294)	371	0.30
Hungarian (3,672)	6,804	5.54
Icelander (0)	0	<0.01
Iranian (181)	314	0.26
Irish (3,209)	8,081	6.59
Israeli (1,511)	3,342	2.72
Italian (4,569)	8,664	7.06
Latvian (87)	174	0.14
Lithuanian (98)	538	0.44
Luxemburger (0)	0	<0.01
Macedonian (0)	0	<0.01
Maltese (0)	0	<0.01
New Zealander (0)	55	0.04
Northern European (0)	38	0.03

Ancestry (cont.)	Population	%
Norwegian (64)	140	0.11
Pennsylvania German (10)	17	0.01
Polish (3,146)	9,453	7.70
Portuguese (120)	252	0.21
Romanian (524)	1,695	1.38
Russian (2,367)	6,069	4.95
Scandinavian (15)	52	0.04
Scotch-Irish (119)	424	0.35
Scottish (193)	640	0.52
Serbian (0)	0	<0.01
Slavic (18)	63	0.05
Slovak (69)	114	0.09
Slovene (31)	46	0.04
Soviet Union (0)	0	<0.01
Swedish (28)	316	0.26
Swiss (34)	85	0.07
Turkish (28)	114	0.09
Ukrainian (949)	1,403	1.14
Welsh (10)	182	0.15
West Indian, ex. Hispanic (12,117)	12,710	10.36
Bahamian (0)	0	<0.01
Barbadian (10)	34	0.03
Belizean (12)	35	0.03
Bermudan (0)	0	<0.01
British West Indian (253)	253	0.21
Dutch West Indian (0)	0	<0.01
Haitian (8,747)	8,948	7.29
Jamaican (2,336)	2,509	2.04
Trinidadian/Tobagonian (550)	604	0.49
U.S. Virgin Islander (0)	19	0.02
West Indian (209)	308	0.25
Other West Indian (0)	0	<0.01
Yugoslavian (42)	78	0.06

Hispanic Origin	Population	%
Hispanic or Latino (of any race)	17,223	13.60
Central American, ex. Mexican	5,319	4.20
Costa Rican	103	0.08
Guatemalan	4,050	3.20
Honduran	182	0.14
Nicaraguan	29	0.02
Panamanian	54	0.04
Salvadoran	872	0.69
Other Central American	29	0.02
Cuban	279	0.22
Dominican Republic	1,021	0.81
Mexican	2,433	1.92
Puerto Rican	2,904	2.29
South American	3,759	2.97
Argentinean	166	0.13
Bolivian	9	0.01
Chilean	66	0.05
Colombian	308	0.24
Ecuadorian	2,915	2.30
Paraguayan	8	0.01
Peruvian	204	0.16
Uruguayan	16	0.01
Venezuelan	59	0.05
Other South American	8	0.01
Other Hispanic or Latino	1,508	1.19

Race*	Population	%
African-American/Black (20,056)	21,297	16.82
Not Hispanic (19,173)	20,078	15.86
Hispanic (883)	1,219	0.96
American Indian/Alaska Native (430)	963	0.76
Not Hispanic (253)	613	0.48
Hispanic (177)	350	0.28
Alaska Athabascan (Ala. Nat.) (0)	0	<0.01
Aleut (Alaska Native) (1)	1	<0.01
Apache (2)	3	<0.01
Arapaho (0)	0	<0.01
Blackfeet (1)	11	0.01
Canadian/French Am. Ind. (0)	0	<0.01
Central American Ind. (10)	22	0.02
Cherokee (9)	69	0.05
Cheyenne (0)	1	<0.01
Chickasaw (0)	0	<0.01
Chippewa (0)	1	<0.01

Race* (cont.)	Population	%
Choctaw (1)	1	<0.01
Colville (0)	0	<0.01
Comanche (0)	2	<0.01
Cree (0)	0	<0.01
Creek (0)	0	<0.01
Crow (0)	0	<0.01
Delaware (93)	167	0.13
Hopi (0)	0	<0.01
Houma (0)	0	<0.01
Inupiat (Alaska Native) (0)	0	<0.01
Iroquois (21)	36	0.03
Kiowa (0)	0	<0.01
Lumbee (0)	2	<0.01
Menominee (0)	0	<0.01
Mexican American Ind. (52)	74	0.06
Navajo (0)	4	<0.01
Osage (0)	0	<0.01
Ottawa (0)	0	<0.01
Paiute (0)	0	<0.01
Pima (0)	0	<0.01
Potawatomi (0)	0	<0.01
Pueblo (1)	1	<0.01
Puget Sound Salish (0)	0	<0.01
Seminole (0)	2	<0.01
Shoshone (0)	0	<0.01
Sioux (0)	2	<0.01
South American Ind. (20)	68	0.05
Spanish American Ind. (3)	7	0.01
Tlingit-Haida (Alaska Native) (2)	7	0.01
Tohono O'Odham (2)	4	<0.01
Tsimshian (Alaska Native) (0)	0	<0.01
Ute (0)	0	<0.01
Yakama (0)	1	<0.01
Yaqui (0)	0	<0.01
Yuman (0)	0	<0.01
Yup'ik (Alaska Native) (0)	0	<0.01
Asian (5,082)	5,750	4.54
Not Hispanic (5,013)	5,609	4.43
Hispanic (69)	141	0.11
Bangladeshi (56)	63	0.05
Bhutanese (0)	0	<0.01
Burmese (1)	1	<0.01
Cambodian (48)	52	0.04
Chinese, ex. Taiwanese (606)	730	0.58
Filipino (1,338)	1,472	1.16
Hmong (0)	0	<0.01
Indian (1,751)	1,962	1.55
Indonesian (18)	23	0.02
Japanese (98)	136	0.11
Korean (300)	339	0.27
Laotian (4)	6	<0.01
Malaysian (2)	8	0.01
Nepalese (11)	11	0.01
Pakistani (461)	524	0.41
Sri Lankan (23)	26	0.02
Taiwanese (19)	21	0.02
Thai (30)	37	0.03
Vietnamese (112)	148	0.12
Hawaii Native/Pacific Islander (45)	237	0.19
Not Hispanic (18)	156	0.12
Hispanic (27)	81	0.06
Fijian (0)	2	<0.01
Guamanian/Chamorro (16)	19	0.02
Marshallese (0)	0	<0.01
Native Hawaiian (8)	17	0.01
Samoan (4)	9	0.01
Tongan (0)	2	<0.01
White (90,924)	92,843	73.34
Not Hispanic (83,094)	84,071	66.41
Hispanic (7,830)	8,772	6.93

Notes: † The Census 2010 population figure is used to calculate the percentages in the Hispanic Origin and Race categories. Ancestry percentages are based on the 2006-2010 American Community Survey population (not shown); ‡ Numbers in parentheses indicate the number of people reporting a single ancestry; * Numbers in parentheses indicate the number of persons reporting this race alone, not in combination with any other race; Please refer to the Explanation of Data for more information.

Rochester

Place Type: City
County: Monroe
Population: 210,565

Ancestry	Population	%
Afghan (0)	0	<0.01
African, Sub-Saharan (7,095)	7,909	3.73
African (5,087)	5,828	2.75
Cape Verdean (0)	0	<0.01
Ethiopian (227)	227	0.11
Ghanaian (49)	49	0.02
Kenyan (9)	9	<0.01
Liberian (89)	89	0.04
Nigerian (151)	203	0.10
Senegalese (0)	0	<0.01
Sierra Leonean (0)	0	<0.01
Somalian (980)	980	0.46
South African (19)	32	0.02
Sudanese (107)	107	0.05
Ugandan (0)	0	<0.01
Zimbabwean (76)	76	0.04
Other Sub-Saharan African (301)	309	0.15
Albanian (31)	42	0.02
Alsatian (0)	0	<0.01
American (3,617)	3,617	1.71
Arab (785)	1,077	0.51
Arab (245)	263	0.12
Egyptian (81)	81	0.04
Iraqi (36)	36	0.02
Jordanian (0)	0	<0.01
Lebanese (136)	196	0.09
Moroccan (17)	48	0.02
Palestinian (30)	30	0.01
Syrian (11)	33	0.02
Other Arab (229)	390	0.18
Armenian (84)	105	0.05
Assyrian/Chaldean/Syriac (0)	0	<0.01
Australian (0)	69	0.03
Austrian (103)	450	0.21
Basque (0)	0	<0.01
Belgian (27)	185	0.09
Brazilian (35)	90	0.04
British (259)	606	0.29
Bulgarian (0)	33	0.02
Cajun (0)	0	<0.01
Canadian (227)	550	0.26
Carpatho Rusyn (0)	0	<0.01
Celtic (13)	40	0.02
Croatian (12)	61	0.03
Cypriot (0)	0	<0.01
Czech (77)	484	0.23
Czechoslovakian (30)	44	0.02
Danish (51)	275	0.13
Dutch (406)	2,898	1.37
Eastern European (200)	237	0.11
English (3,972)	13,510	6.37
Estonian (0)	38	0.02
European (893)	1,150	0.54
Finnish (11)	160	0.08
French, ex. Basque (683)	4,083	1.93
French Canadian (652)	1,474	0.70
German (5,802)	22,972	10.84
German Russian (0)	0	<0.01
Greek (337)	623	0.29
Guyanese (348)	381	0.18
Hungarian (246)	783	0.37
Icelander (0)	0	<0.01
Iranian (97)	120	0.06
Irish (5,531)	19,595	9.24
Israeli (37)	57	0.03
Italian (8,976)	19,728	9.31
Latvian (33)	55	0.03
Lithuanian (236)	466	0.22
Luxemburger (19)	62	0.03
Macedonian (0)	10	<0.01
Maltese (34)	100	0.05
New Zealander (0)	0	<0.01
Northern European (23)	23	0.01

Ancestry	Population	%
Norwegian (135)	444	0.21
Pennsylvania German (8)	70	0.03
Polish (1,583)	5,614	2.65
Portuguese (47)	199	0.09
Romanian (96)	186	0.09
Russian (498)	1,342	0.63
Scandinavian (34)	111	0.05
Scotch-Irish (433)	1,614	0.76
Scottish (526)	3,002	1.42
Serbian (0)	49	0.02
Slavic (32)	78	0.04
Slovak (24)	157	0.07
Slovene (24)	37	0.02
Soviet Union (0)	0	<0.01
Swedish (403)	1,156	0.55
Swiss (36)	271	0.13
Turkish (486)	612	0.29
Ukrainian (727)	1,325	0.63
Welsh (141)	992	0.47
West Indian, ex. Hispanic (3,129)	5,230	2.47
Bahamian (58)	218	0.10
Barbadian (169)	230	0.11
Belizean (119)	171	0.08
Bermudan (0)	0	<0.01
British West Indian (99)	223	0.11
Dutch West Indian (0)	13	0.01
Haitian (352)	383	0.18
Jamaican (1,743)	2,834	1.34
Trinidadian/Tobagonian (199)	288	0.14
U.S. Virgin Islander (0)	0	<0.01
West Indian (390)	870	0.41
Other West Indian (0)	0	<0.01
Yugoslavian (117)	138	0.07

Hispanic Origin	Population	%
Hispanic or Latino (of any race)	34,456	16.36
Central American, ex. Mexican	569	0.27
Costa Rican	72	0.03
Guatemalan	85	0.04
Honduran	129	0.06
Nicaraguan	56	0.03
Panamanian	123	0.06
Salvadoran	96	0.05
Other Central American	8	<0.01
Cuban	1,616	0.77
Dominican Republic	1,373	0.65
Mexican	1,168	0.55
Puerto Rican	27,734	13.17
South American	517	0.25
Argentinean	49	0.02
Bolivian	18	0.01
Chilean	82	0.04
Colombian	182	0.09
Ecuadorian	72	0.03
Paraguayan	10	<0.01
Peruvian	68	0.03
Uruguayan	7	<0.01
Venezuelan	22	0.01
Other South American	7	<0.01
Other Hispanic or Latino	1,479	0.70

Race*	Population	%
African-American/Black (87,897)	94,587	44.92
Not Hispanic (83,346)	88,052	41.82
Hispanic (4,551)	6,535	3.10
American Indian/Alaska Native (1,013)	3,202	1.52
Not Hispanic (666)	2,330	1.11
Hispanic (347)	872	0.41
Alaska Athabascan (Ala. Nat.) (0)	1	<0.01
Aleut (Alaska Native) (1)	2	<0.01
Apache (8)	20	0.01
Arapaho (0)	0	<0.01
Blackfeet (16)	134	0.06
Canadian/French Am. Ind. (3)	9	<0.01
Central American Ind. (15)	29	0.01
Cherokee (51)	411	0.20
Cheyenne (2)	3	<0.01
Chickasaw (0)	2	<0.01
Chippewa (9)	18	0.01

Race*	Population	%
Choctaw (1)	28	0.01
Colville (0)	1	<0.01
Comanche (0)	2	<0.01
Cree (1)	2	<0.01
Creek (2)	9	<0.01
Crow (0)	1	<0.01
Delaware (1)	10	<0.01
Hopi (1)	1	<0.01
Houma (0)	0	<0.01
Inupiat (Alaska Native) (3)	4	<0.01
Iroquois (265)	483	0.23
Kiowa (0)	0	<0.01
Lumbee (0)	0	<0.01
Menominee (0)	0	<0.01
Mexican American Ind. (20)	38	0.02
Navajo (11)	30	0.01
Osage (1)	3	<0.01
Ottawa (0)	0	<0.01
Paiute (1)	1	<0.01
Pima (0)	2	<0.01
Potawatomi (3)	5	<0.01
Pueblo (0)	2	<0.01
Puget Sound Salish (0)	0	<0.01
Seminole (1)	44	0.02
Shoshone (0)	1	<0.01
Sioux (2)	22	0.01
South American Ind. (45)	144	0.07
Spanish American Ind. (9)	9	<0.01
Tlingit-Haida (Alaska Native) (0)	0	<0.01
Tohono O'Odham (1)	1	<0.01
Tsimshian (Alaska Native) (0)	0	<0.01
Ute (0)	4	<0.01
Yakama (0)	0	<0.01
Yaqui (0)	0	<0.01
Yuman (0)	0	<0.01
Yup'ik (Alaska Native) (0)	0	<0.01
Asian (6,493)	7,752	3.68
Not Hispanic (6,350)	7,397	3.51
Hispanic (143)	355	0.17
Bangladeshi (25)	27	0.01
Bhutanese (369)	411	0.20
Burmese (527)	565	0.27
Cambodian (342)	381	0.18
Chinese, ex. Taiwanese (1,195)	1,456	0.69
Filipino (215)	378	0.18
Hmong (2)	3	<0.01
Indian (780)	1,006	0.48
Indonesian (13)	27	0.01
Japanese (127)	301	0.14
Korean (578)	741	0.35
Laotian (564)	668	0.32
Malaysian (8)	10	<0.01
Nepalese (118)	165	0.08
Pakistani (53)	75	0.04
Sri Lankan (23)	27	0.01
Taiwanese (104)	132	0.06
Thai (67)	103	0.05
Vietnamese (942)	1,050	0.50
Hawaii Native/Pacific Islander (101)	449	0.21
Not Hispanic (77)	284	0.13
Hispanic (24)	165	0.08
Fijian (0)	4	<0.01
Guamanian/Chamorro (12)	26	0.01
Marshallese (0)	0	<0.01
Native Hawaiian (30)	77	0.04
Samoan (31)	63	0.03
Tongan (2)	3	<0.01
White (91,951)	98,814	46.93
Not Hispanic (79,178)	84,019	39.90
Hispanic (12,773)	14,795	7.03

Notes: † The Census 2010 population figure is used to calculate the percentages in the Hispanic Origin and Race categories. Ancestry percentages are based on the 2006-2010 American Community Survey population (not shown); ‡ Numbers in parentheses indicate the number of people reporting a single ancestry; * Numbers in parentheses indicate the number of persons reporting this race alone, not in combination with any other race; Please refer to the Explanation of Data for more information.

Schenectady

Place Type: City
County: Schenectady
Population: 66,135

Ancestry	Population	%
Afghan (318)	318	0.49
African, Sub-Saharan (554)	770	1.18
African (201)	334	0.51
Cape Verdean (0)	0	<0.01
Ethiopian (0)	0	<0.01
Ghanaian (24)	24	0.04
Kenyan (69)	69	0.11
Liberian (24)	24	0.04
Nigerian (131)	186	0.28
Senegalese (0)	0	<0.01
Sierra Leonean (0)	0	<0.01
Somalian (0)	0	<0.01
South African (0)	0	<0.01
Sudanese (0)	0	<0.01
Ugandan (0)	0	<0.01
Zimbabwean (0)	0	<0.01
Other Sub-Saharan African (105)	133	0.20
Albanian (28)	39	0.06
Alsatian (0)	0	<0.01
American (3,124)	3,124	4.78
Arab (140)	191	0.29
Arab (81)	113	0.17
Egyptian (0)	0	<0.01
Iraqi (0)	0	<0.01
Jordanian (0)	0	<0.01
Lebanese (59)	78	0.12
Moroccan (0)	0	<0.01
Palestinian (0)	0	<0.01
Syrian (0)	0	<0.01
Other Arab (0)	0	<0.01
Armenian (19)	19	0.03
Assyrian/Chaldean/Syriac (0)	0	<0.01
Australian (0)	0	<0.01
Austrian (11)	77	0.12
Basque (0)	0	<0.01
Belgian (0)	0	<0.01
Brazilian (144)	194	0.30
British (100)	187	0.29
Bulgarian (0)	0	<0.01
Cajun (0)	0	<0.01
Canadian (44)	72	0.11
Carpatho Rusyn (0)	0	<0.01
Celtic (20)	20	0.03
Croatian (0)	0	<0.01
Cypriot (0)	0	<0.01
Czech (50)	236	0.36
Czechoslovakian (68)	167	0.26
Danish (97)	121	0.19
Dutch (393)	1,521	2.33
Eastern European (76)	76	0.12
English (1,339)	3,998	6.12
Estonian (0)	0	<0.01
European (205)	263	0.40
Finnish (15)	26	0.04
French, ex. Basque (658)	2,862	4.38
French Canadian (193)	902	1.38
German (1,915)	6,846	10.47
German Russian (0)	0	<0.01
Greek (147)	224	0.34
Guyanese (1,783)	1,915	2.93
Hungarian (128)	341	0.52
Icelander (0)	0	<0.01
Iranian (0)	0	<0.01
Irish (2,754)	8,655	13.24
Israeli (0)	9	0.01
Italian (5,680)	9,882	15.12
Latvian (0)	0	<0.01
Lithuanian (42)	240	0.37
Luxemburger (0)	0	<0.01
Macedonian (0)	0	<0.01
Maltese (0)	0	<0.01
New Zealander (0)	0	<0.01
Northern European (83)	97	0.15

Ancestry	Population	%
Norwegian (0)	63	0.10
Pennsylvania German (0)	11	0.02
Polish (1,904)	3,977	6.08
Portuguese (20)	70	0.11
Romanian (10)	10	0.02
Russian (98)	430	0.66
Scandinavian (13)	13	0.02
Scotch-Irish (186)	509	0.78
Scottish (248)	656	1.00
Serbian (0)	12	0.02
Slavic (40)	40	0.06
Slovak (32)	93	0.14
Slovene (0)	0	<0.01
Soviet Union (0)	0	<0.01
Swedish (52)	177	0.27
Swiss (57)	171	0.26
Turkish (10)	10	0.02
Ukrainian (91)	236	0.36
Welsh (65)	320	0.49
West Indian, ex. Hispanic (1,255)	1,477	2.26
Bahamian (0)	0	<0.01
Barbadian (43)	94	0.14
Belizean (0)	0	<0.01
Bermudan (0)	0	<0.01
British West Indian (7)	7	0.01
Dutch West Indian (0)	10	0.02
Haitian (24)	61	0.09
Jamaican (730)	781	1.19
Trinidadian/Tobagonian (18)	78	0.12
U.S. Virgin Islander (0)	0	<0.01
West Indian (433)	446	0.68
Other West Indian (0)	0	<0.01
Yugoslavian (0)	1	<0.01

Hispanic Origin	Population	%
Hispanic or Latino (of any race)	6,922	10.47
Central American, ex. Mexican	321	0.49
Costa Rican	34	0.05
Guatemalan	61	0.09
Honduran	41	0.06
Nicaraguan	17	0.03
Panamanian	31	0.05
Salvadoran	126	0.19
Other Central American	11	0.02
Cuban	150	0.23
Dominican Republic	478	0.72
Mexican	430	0.65
Puerto Rican	4,677	7.07
South American	346	0.52
Argentinean	18	0.03
Bolivian	5	0.01
Chilean	13	0.02
Colombian	86	0.13
Ecuadorian	62	0.09
Paraguayan	9	0.01
Peruvian	74	0.11
Uruguayan	9	0.01
Venezuelan	27	0.04
Other South American	43	0.07
Other Hispanic or Latino	520	0.79

Race*	Population	%
African-American/Black (13,354)	16,103	24.35
Not Hispanic (12,258)	14,556	22.01
Hispanic (1,096)	1,547	2.34
American Indian/Alaska Native (458)	1,372	2.07
Not Hispanic (343)	1,126	1.70
Hispanic (115)	246	0.37
Alaska Athabascan (Ala. Nat.) (0)	0	<0.01
Aleut (Alaska Native) (0)	0	<0.01
Apache (2)	5	0.01
Arapaho (1)	1	<0.01
Blackfeet (2)	58	0.09
Canadian/French Am. Ind. (3)	9	0.01
Central American Ind. (5)	6	0.01
Cherokee (9)	145	0.22
Cheyenne (1)	2	<0.01
Chickasaw (0)	0	<0.01
Chippewa (2)	11	0.02

Race*	Population	%
Choctaw (0)	1	<0.01
Colville (0)	0	<0.01
Comanche (0)	0	<0.01
Cree (0)	4	0.01
Creek (1)	5	0.01
Crow (0)	6	0.01
Delaware (4)	12	0.02
Hopi (0)	0	<0.01
Houma (0)	0	<0.01
Inupiat (Alaska Native) (3)	3	<0.01
Iroquois (17)	88	0.13
Kiowa (0)	1	<0.01
Lumbee (2)	4	0.01
Menominee (0)	0	<0.01
Mexican American Ind. (16)	17	0.03
Navajo (1)	2	<0.01
Osage (0)	0	<0.01
Ottawa (0)	0	<0.01
Paiute (0)	0	<0.01
Pima (1)	5	0.01
Potawatomi (0)	5	0.01
Pueblo (0)	1	<0.01
Puget Sound Salish (0)	0	<0.01
Seminole (1)	4	0.01
Shoshone (0)	0	<0.01
Sioux (3)	14	0.02
South American Ind. (17)	33	0.05
Spanish American Ind. (1)	7	0.01
Tlingit-Haida (Alaska Native) (0)	0	<0.01
Tohono O'Odham (0)	0	<0.01
Tsimshian (Alaska Native) (0)	0	<0.01
Ute (0)	0	<0.01
Yakama (0)	0	<0.01
Yaqui (0)	0	<0.01
Yuman (0)	0	<0.01
Yup'ik (Alaska Native) (0)	0	<0.01
Asian (2,396)	3,522	5.33
Not Hispanic (2,360)	3,400	5.14
Hispanic (36)	122	0.18
Bangladeshi (12)	15	0.02
Bhutanese (1)	1	<0.01
Burmese (0)	0	<0.01
Cambodian (7)	8	0.01
Chinese, ex. Taiwanese (291)	361	0.55
Filipino (116)	157	0.24
Hmong (0)	0	<0.01
Indian (1,571)	2,050	3.10
Indonesian (4)	9	0.01
Japanese (21)	70	0.11
Korean (87)	141	0.21
Laotian (2)	6	0.01
Malaysian (0)	5	0.01
Nepalese (5)	8	0.01
Pakistani (80)	86	0.13
Sri Lankan (4)	6	0.01
Taiwanese (7)	8	0.01
Thai (6)	15	0.02
Vietnamese (75)	87	0.13
Hawaii Native/Pacific Islander (92)	333	0.50
Not Hispanic (68)	272	0.41
Hispanic (24)	61	0.09
Fijian (1)	1	<0.01
Guamanian/Chamorro (6)	14	0.02
Marshallese (0)	0	<0.01
Native Hawaiian (14)	33	0.05
Samoan (4)	10	0.02
Tongan (0)	0	<0.01
White (40,592)	43,710	66.09
Not Hispanic (38,006)	40,587	61.37
Hispanic (2,586)	3,123	4.72

Notes: † The Census 2010 population figure is used to calculate the percentages in the Hispanic Origin and Race categories. Ancestry percentages are based on the 2006-2010 American Community Survey population (not shown); ‡ Numbers in parentheses indicate the number of people reporting a single ancestry; * Numbers in parentheses indicate the number of persons reporting this race alone, not in combination with any other race; Please refer to the Explanation of Data for more information.

Smithtown

Place Type: Town
County: Suffolk
Population: 117,801

Ancestry	Population	%
Afghan (27)	27	0.02
African, Sub-Saharan (8)	150	0.13
African (0)	106	0.09
Cape Verdean (0)	0	<0.01
Ethiopian (0)	0	<0.01
Ghanaian (0)	0	<0.01
Kenyan (0)	0	<0.01
Liberian (0)	0	<0.01
Nigerian (8)	44	0.04
Senegalese (0)	0	<0.01
Sierra Leonean (0)	0	<0.01
Somalian (0)	0	<0.01
South African (0)	0	<0.01
Sudanese (0)	0	<0.01
Ugandan (0)	0	<0.01
Zimbabwean (0)	0	<0.01
Other Sub-Saharan African (0)	0	<0.01
Albanian (121)	130	0.11
Alsatian (0)	0	<0.01
American (3,187)	3,187	2.71
Arab (248)	537	0.46
Arab (11)	16	0.01
Egyptian (38)	52	0.04
Iraqi (52)	89	0.08
Jordanian (54)	54	0.05
Lebanese (24)	150	0.13
Moroccan (4)	4	<0.01
Palestinian (0)	0	<0.01
Syrian (39)	89	0.08
Other Arab (26)	83	0.07
Armenian (69)	210	0.18
Assyrian/Chaldean/Syriac (0)	0	<0.01
Australian (19)	23	0.02
Austrian (205)	930	0.79
Basque (0)	0	<0.01
Belgian (4)	88	0.07
Brazilian (22)	32	0.03
British (94)	242	0.21
Bulgarian (0)	22	0.02
Cajun (0)	0	<0.01
Canadian (85)	315	0.27
Carpatho Rusyn (26)	26	0.02
Celtic (0)	3	<0.01
Croatian (53)	247	0.21
Cypriot (0)	0	<0.01
Czech (151)	692	0.59
Czechoslovakian (88)	310	0.26
Danish (76)	314	0.27
Dutch (199)	983	0.84
Eastern European (651)	651	0.55
English (852)	6,551	5.57
Estonian (0)	0	<0.01
European (936)	997	0.85
Finnish (26)	120	0.10
French, ex. Basque (122)	2,352	2.00
French Canadian (233)	648	0.55
German (4,715)	23,592	20.06
German Russian (0)	0	<0.01
Greek (1,657)	3,078	2.62
Guyanese (8)	8	0.01
Hungarian (307)	1,257	1.07
Icelander (5)	16	0.01
Iranian (199)	237	0.20
Irish (8,107)	31,963	27.18
Israeli (104)	180	0.15
Italian (21,409)	45,388	38.60
Latvian (24)	81	0.07
Lithuanian (141)	627	0.53
Luxemburger (0)	0	<0.01
Macedonian (0)	0	<0.01
Maltese (10)	206	0.18
New Zealander (0)	0	<0.01
Northern European (4)	4	<0.01

Ancestry (cont.)	Population	%
Norwegian (397)	1,686	1.43
Pennsylvania German (6)	6	0.01
Polish (2,350)	8,707	7.40
Portuguese (47)	247	0.21
Romanian (196)	707	0.60
Russian (1,686)	5,319	4.52
Scandinavian (26)	64	0.05
Scotch-Irish (579)	1,732	1.47
Scottish (148)	1,517	1.29
Serbian (31)	92	0.08
Slavic (9)	116	0.10
Slovak (82)	163	0.14
Slovene (140)	147	0.13
Soviet Union (0)	0	<0.01
Swedish (160)	1,304	1.11
Swiss (34)	217	0.18
Turkish (182)	204	0.17
Ukrainian (145)	452	0.38
Welsh (8)	259	0.22
West Indian, ex. Hispanic (160)	341	0.29
Bahamian (0)	0	<0.01
Barbadian (0)	0	<0.01
Belizean (0)	0	<0.01
Bermudan (0)	0	<0.01
British West Indian (0)	0	<0.01
Dutch West Indian (0)	0	<0.01
Haitian (100)	100	0.09
Jamaican (44)	92	0.08
Trinidadian/Tobagonian (9)	28	0.02
U.S. Virgin Islander (0)	0	<0.01
West Indian (7)	121	0.10
Other West Indian (0)	0	<0.01
Yugoslavian (68)	216	0.18

Hispanic Origin	Population	%
Hispanic or Latino (of any race)	6,272	5.32
Central American, ex. Mexican	768	0.65
Costa Rican	22	0.02
Guatemalan	95	0.08
Honduran	161	0.14
Nicaraguan	9	0.01
Panamanian	37	0.03
Salvadoran	428	0.36
Other Central American	16	0.01
Cuban	298	0.25
Dominican Republic	349	0.30
Mexican	524	0.44
Puerto Rican	2,200	1.87
South American	1,376	1.17
Argentinean	159	0.13
Bolivian	41	0.03
Chilean	96	0.08
Colombian	503	0.43
Ecuadorian	258	0.22
Paraguayan	17	0.01
Peruvian	227	0.19
Uruguayan	28	0.02
Venezuelan	37	0.03
Other South American	10	0.01
Other Hispanic or Latino	757	0.64

Race*	Population	%
African-American/Black (1,238)	1,546	1.31
Not Hispanic (1,122)	1,350	1.15
Hispanic (116)	196	0.17
American Indian/Alaska Native (91)	317	0.27
Not Hispanic (53)	224	0.19
Hispanic (38)	93	0.08
Alaska Athabascan (Ala. Nat.) (0)	0	<0.01
Aleut (Alaska Native) (0)	0	<0.01
Apache (0)	0	<0.01
Arapaho (0)	0	<0.01
Blackfeet (3)	7	0.01
Canadian/French Am. Ind. (0)	2	<0.01
Central American Ind. (1)	1	<0.01
Cherokee (3)	44	0.04
Cheyenne (0)	0	<0.01
Chickasaw (0)	0	<0.01
Chippewa (0)	2	<0.01

Race* (cont.)	Population	%
Choctaw (0)	2	<0.01
Colville (0)	0	<0.01
Comanche (0)	0	<0.01
Cree (0)	0	<0.01
Creek (0)	7	0.01
Crow (0)	0	<0.01
Delaware (0)	1	<0.01
Hopi (0)	0	<0.01
Houma (0)	0	<0.01
Inupiat (Alaska Native) (0)	0	<0.01
Iroquois (19)	36	0.03
Kiowa (1)	1	<0.01
Lumbee (5)	5	<0.01
Menominee (0)	0	<0.01
Mexican American Ind. (2)	6	0.01
Navajo (0)	1	<0.01
Osage (0)	0	<0.01
Ottawa (0)	0	<0.01
Paiute (0)	0	<0.01
Pima (0)	0	<0.01
Potawatomi (0)	0	<0.01
Pueblo (0)	1	<0.01
Puget Sound Salish (0)	0	<0.01
Seminole (0)	0	<0.01
Shoshone (0)	0	<0.01
Sioux (1)	2	<0.01
South American Ind. (13)	23	0.02
Spanish American Ind. (0)	0	<0.01
Tlingit-Haida (Alaska Native) (0)	1	<0.01
Tohono O'Odham (0)	0	<0.01
Tsimshian (Alaska Native) (0)	0	<0.01
Ute (0)	1	<0.01
Yakama (0)	0	<0.01
Yaqui (0)	1	<0.01
Yuman (0)	0	<0.01
Yup'ik (Alaska Native) (0)	0	<0.01
Asian (4,224)	4,865	4.13
Not Hispanic (4,197)	4,788	4.06
Hispanic (27)	77	0.07
Bangladeshi (24)	24	0.02
Bhutanese (2)	2	<0.01
Burmese (2)	2	<0.01
Cambodian (0)	0	<0.01
Chinese, ex. Taiwanese (1,070)	1,262	1.07
Filipino (414)	562	0.48
Hmong (0)	0	<0.01
Indian (1,206)	1,322	1.12
Indonesian (14)	18	0.02
Japanese (68)	119	0.10
Korean (842)	918	0.78
Laotian (3)	3	<0.01
Malaysian (1)	2	<0.01
Nepalese (4)	4	<0.01
Pakistani (280)	299	0.25
Sri Lankan (5)	6	0.01
Taiwanese (66)	90	0.08
Thai (28)	34	0.03
Vietnamese (59)	70	0.06
Hawaii Native/Pacific Islander (10)	58	0.05
Not Hispanic (7)	41	0.03
Hispanic (3)	17	0.01
Fijian (0)	2	<0.01
Guamanian/Chamorro (3)	5	<0.01
Marshallese (0)	0	<0.01
Native Hawaiian (6)	30	0.03
Samoan (0)	0	<0.01
Tongan (0)	0	<0.01
White (109,790)	111,000	94.23
Not Hispanic (104,976)	105,870	89.87
Hispanic (4,814)	5,130	4.35

Notes: † The Census 2010 population figure is used to calculate the percentages in the Hispanic Origin and Race categories. Ancestry percentages are based on the 2006-2010 American Community Survey population (not shown); ‡ Numbers in parentheses indicate the number of people reporting a single ancestry; * Numbers in parentheses indicate the number of persons reporting this race alone, not in combination with any other race; Please refer to the Explanation of Data for more information.

Southampton

Place Type: Town
County: Suffolk
Population: 56,790

Ancestry	Population	%
Afghan (0)	0	<0.01
African, Sub-Saharan (64)	64	0.11
African (64)	64	0.11
Cape Verdean (0)	0	<0.01
Ethiopian (0)	0	<0.01
Ghanaian (0)	0	<0.01
Kenyan (0)	0	<0.01
Liberian (0)	0	<0.01
Nigerian (0)	0	<0.01
Senegalese (0)	0	<0.01
Sierra Leonean (0)	0	<0.01
Somalian (0)	0	<0.01
South African (0)	0	<0.01
Sudanese (0)	0	<0.01
Ugandan (0)	0	<0.01
Zimbabwean (0)	0	<0.01
Other Sub-Saharan African (0)	0	<0.01
Albanian (63)	63	0.11
Alsatian (0)	0	<0.01
American (1,540)	1,540	2.72
Arab (52)	130	0.23
Arab (20)	35	0.06
Egyptian (0)	0	<0.01
Iraqi (0)	28	0.05
Jordanian (0)	0	<0.01
Lebanese (5)	16	0.03
Moroccan (0)	18	0.03
Palestinian (0)	0	<0.01
Syrian (13)	13	0.02
Other Arab (14)	20	0.04
Armenian (23)	42	0.07
Assyrian/Chaldean/Syriac (0)	0	<0.01
Australian (24)	38	0.07
Austrian (113)	621	1.10
Basque (0)	0	<0.01
Belgian (34)	34	0.06
Brazilian (242)	289	0.51
British (224)	404	0.71
Bulgarian (29)	29	0.05
Cajun (0)	0	<0.01
Canadian (96)	153	0.27
Carpatho Rusyn (0)	0	<0.01
Celtic (0)	4	0.01
Croatian (174)	227	0.40
Cypriot (0)	0	<0.01
Czech (80)	198	0.35
Czechoslovakian (51)	97	0.17
Danish (54)	135	0.24
Dutch (91)	743	1.31
Eastern European (55)	118	0.21
English (1,413)	5,792	10.24
Estonian (6)	6	0.01
European (518)	523	0.93
Finnish (53)	206	0.36
French, ex. Basque (250)	1,438	2.54
French Canadian (49)	352	0.62
German (1,998)	8,313	14.70
German Russian (0)	0	<0.01
Greek (583)	995	1.76
Guyanese (0)	0	<0.01
Hungarian (164)	529	0.94
Icelander (0)	0	<0.01
Iranian (0)	0	<0.01
Irish (4,208)	12,998	22.99
Israeli (0)	28	0.05
Italian (4,376)	9,808	17.35
Latvian (0)	7	0.01
Lithuanian (137)	267	0.47
Luxemburger (0)	0	<0.01
Macedonian (11)	11	0.02
Maltese (15)	33	0.06
New Zealander (0)	0	<0.01
Northern European (42)	42	0.07

Ancestry	Population	%
Norwegian (172)	498	0.88
Pennsylvania German (0)	0	<0.01
Polish (1,918)	4,196	7.42
Portuguese (59)	145	0.26
Romanian (57)	102	0.18
Russian (514)	1,517	2.68
Scandinavian (31)	57	0.10
Scotch-Irish (251)	701	1.24
Scottish (225)	966	1.71
Serbian (0)	0	<0.01
Slavic (0)	53	0.09
Slovak (92)	134	0.24
Slovene (7)	7	0.01
Soviet Union (0)	0	<0.01
Swedish (152)	598	1.06
Swiss (37)	231	0.41
Turkish (75)	75	0.13
Ukrainian (198)	419	0.74
Welsh (43)	132	0.23
West Indian, ex. Hispanic (0)	24	0.04
Bahamian (0)	0	<0.01
Barbadian (0)	0	<0.01
Belizean (0)	0	<0.01
Bermudan (0)	0	<0.01
British West Indian (0)	0	<0.01
Dutch West Indian (0)	0	<0.01
Haitian (0)	16	0.03
Jamaican (0)	0	<0.01
Trinidadian/Tobagonian (0)	0	<0.01
U.S. Virgin Islander (0)	0	<0.01
West Indian (0)	8	0.01
Other West Indian (0)	0	<0.01
Yugoslavian (0)	0	<0.01

Hispanic Origin	Population	%
Hispanic or Latino (of any race)	11,295	19.89
Central American, ex. Mexican	3,715	6.54
Costa Rican	618	1.09
Guatemalan	2,081	3.66
Honduran	246	0.43
Nicaraguan	50	0.09
Panamanian	14	0.02
Salvadoran	689	1.21
Other Central American	17	0.03
Cuban	93	0.16
Dominican Republic	124	0.22
Mexican	2,856	5.03
Puerto Rican	593	1.04
South American	2,446	4.31
Argentinean	89	0.16
Bolivian	9	0.02
Chilean	44	0.08
Colombian	1,024	1.80
Ecuadorian	1,102	1.94
Paraguayan	26	0.05
Peruvian	97	0.17
Uruguayan	7	0.01
Venezuelan	36	0.06
Other South American	12	0.02
Other Hispanic or Latino	1,468	2.58

Race*	Population	%
African-American/Black (2,929)	3,353	5.90
Not Hispanic (2,776)	3,108	5.47
Hispanic (153)	245	0.43
American Indian/Alaska Native (292)	546	0.96
Not Hispanic (136)	344	0.61
Hispanic (156)	202	0.36
Alaska Athabascan (Ala. Nat.) (0)	0	<0.01
Aleut (Alaska Native) (0)	0	<0.01
Apache (0)	0	<0.01
Arapaho (0)	0	<0.01
Blackfeet (6)	14	0.02
Canadian/French Am. Ind. (0)	3	0.01
Central American Ind. (3)	3	0.01
Cherokee (13)	68	0.12
Cheyenne (0)	0	<0.01
Chickasaw (0)	0	<0.01
Chippewa (7)	7	0.01

	Population	%
Choctaw (1)	2	<0.01
Colville (0)	0	<0.01
Comanche (0)	0	<0.01
Cree (0)	0	<0.01
Creek (2)	2	<0.01
Crow (0)	0	<0.01
Delaware (0)	0	<0.01
Hopi (0)	1	<0.01
Houma (0)	0	<0.01
Inupiat (Alaska Native) (0)	0	<0.01
Iroquois (5)	11	0.02
Kiowa (0)	0	<0.01
Lumbee (0)	0	<0.01
Menominee (0)	0	<0.01
Mexican American Ind. (76)	83	0.15
Navajo (0)	0	<0.01
Osage (0)	0	<0.01
Ottawa (0)	0	<0.01
Paiute (0)	0	<0.01
Pima (0)	0	<0.01
Potawatomi (0)	0	<0.01
Pueblo (0)	5	0.01
Puget Sound Salish (0)	0	<0.01
Seminole (0)	1	<0.01
Shoshone (0)	0	<0.01
Sioux (2)	3	0.01
South American Ind. (23)	28	0.05
Spanish American Ind. (7)	7	0.01
Tlingit-Haida (Alaska Native) (0)	0	<0.01
Tohono O'Odham (0)	0	<0.01
Tsimshian (Alaska Native) (0)	0	<0.01
Ute (0)	0	<0.01
Yakama (0)	0	<0.01
Yaqui (0)	0	<0.01
Yuman (0)	0	<0.01
Yup'ik (Alaska Native) (0)	0	<0.01
Asian (633)	869	1.53
Not Hispanic (618)	834	1.47
Hispanic (15)	35	0.06
Bangladeshi (0)	0	<0.01
Bhutanese (0)	0	<0.01
Burmese (0)	0	<0.01
Cambodian (1)	1	<0.01
Chinese, ex. Taiwanese (133)	177	0.31
Filipino (146)	197	0.35
Hmong (0)	0	<0.01
Indian (123)	151	0.27
Indonesian (5)	6	0.01
Japanese (40)	97	0.17
Korean (69)	102	0.18
Laotian (1)	2	<0.01
Malaysian (1)	2	<0.01
Nepalese (1)	1	<0.01
Pakistani (8)	10	0.02
Sri Lankan (0)	0	<0.01
Taiwanese (3)	3	0.01
Thai (30)	37	0.07
Vietnamese (38)	51	0.09
Hawaii Native/Pacific Islander (62)	103	0.18
Not Hispanic (36)	61	0.11
Hispanic (26)	42	0.07
Fijian (0)	0	<0.01
Guamanian/Chamorro (48)	55	0.10
Marshallese (0)	0	<0.01
Native Hawaiian (10)	27	0.05
Samoan (2)	7	0.01
Tongan (0)	0	<0.01
White (47,795)	48,682	85.72
Not Hispanic (41,156)	41,727	73.48
Hispanic (6,639)	6,955	12.25

Notes: † The Census 2010 population figure is used to calculate the percentages in the Hispanic Origin and Race categories. Ancestry percentages are based on the 2006-2010 American Community Survey population (not shown); ‡ Numbers in parentheses indicate the number of people reporting a single ancestry; * Numbers in parentheses indicate the number of persons reporting this race alone, not in combination with any other race; Please refer to the Explanation of Data for more information.

Staten Island

Place Type: Borough
County: Richmond
Population: 468,730

Ancestry	Population	%
Afghan (0)	0	<0.01
African, Sub-Saharan (6,533)	7,234	1.56
African (3,732)	4,164	0.90
Cape Verdean (0)	11	<0.01
Ethiopian (41)	46	0.01
Ghanaian (239)	250	0.05
Kenyan (78)	78	0.02
Liberian (515)	532	0.11
Nigerian (1,509)	1,679	0.36
Senegalese (126)	126	0.03
Sierra Leonean (90)	117	0.03
Somalian (0)	0	<0.01
South African (0)	0	<0.01
Sudanese (0)	0	<0.01
Ugandan (0)	0	<0.01
Zimbabwean (0)	0	<0.01
Other Sub-Saharan African (203)	231	0.05
Albanian (7,700)	8,108	1.75
Alsatian (0)	24	0.01
American (13,977)	13,977	3.02
Arab (7,711)	8,820	1.90
Arab (1,694)	1,829	0.39
Egyptian (3,200)	3,292	0.71
Iraqi (11)	32	0.01
Jordanian (159)	183	0.04
Lebanese (784)	1,019	0.22
Moroccan (502)	621	0.13
Palestinian (443)	479	0.10
Syrian (209)	584	0.13
Other Arab (709)	781	0.17
Armenian (83)	311	0.07
Assyrian/Chaldean/Syriac (15)	15	<0.01
Australian (24)	49	0.01
Austrian (343)	1,542	0.33
Basque (15)	77	0.02
Belgian (36)	266	0.06
Brazilian (183)	287	0.06
British (231)	615	0.13
Bulgarian (0)	0	<0.01
Cajun (0)	0	<0.01
Canadian (290)	544	0.12
Carpatho Rusyn (63)	63	0.01
Celtic (37)	46	0.01
Croatian (598)	869	0.19
Cypriot (0)	0	<0.01
Czech (146)	735	0.16
Czechoslovakian (93)	237	0.05
Danish (90)	479	0.10
Dutch (137)	1,637	0.35
Eastern European (433)	433	0.09
English (1,973)	9,014	1.94
Estonian (10)	10	<0.01
European (1,914)	2,068	0.45
Finnish (48)	185	0.04
French, ex. Basque (800)	3,772	0.81
French Canadian (248)	750	0.16
German (4,111)	25,477	5.50
German Russian (0)	0	<0.01
Greek (2,403)	4,183	0.90
Guyanese (767)	952	0.21
Hungarian (1,024)	2,288	0.49
Icelander (55)	55	0.01
Iranian (121)	171	0.04
Irish (20,064)	64,762	13.97
Israeli (542)	759	0.16
Italian (107,263)	156,288	33.72
Latvian (98)	142	0.03
Lithuanian (178)	645	0.14
Luxemburger (12)	54	0.01
Macedonian (1,368)	1,590	0.34
Maltese (104)	290	0.06
New Zealander (0)	0	<0.01
Northern European (60)	60	0.01

Ancestry (cont.)	Population	%
Norwegian (1,617)	5,135	1.11
Pennsylvania German (9)	41	0.01
Polish (9,167)	18,430	3.98
Portuguese (180)	617	0.13
Romanian (530)	964	0.21
Russian (11,315)	16,388	3.54
Scandinavian (35)	121	0.03
Scotch-Irish (759)	1,886	0.41
Scottish (718)	2,350	0.51
Serbian (219)	240	0.05
Slavic (68)	143	0.03
Slovak (233)	553	0.12
Slovene (86)	108	0.02
Soviet Union (51)	63	0.01
Swedish (253)	1,936	0.42
Swiss (76)	256	0.06
Turkish (1,267)	1,607	0.35
Ukrainian (3,759)	4,836	1.04
Welsh (68)	417	0.09
West Indian, ex. Hispanic (5,348)	6,967	1.50
Bahamian (31)	31	0.01
Barbadian (94)	94	0.02
Belizean (76)	76	0.02
Bermudan (0)	0	<0.01
British West Indian (113)	236	0.05
Dutch West Indian (39)	89	0.02
Haitian (676)	791	0.17
Jamaican (1,463)	2,033	0.44
Trinidadian/Tobagonian (1,412)	1,807	0.39
U.S. Virgin Islander (22)	22	<0.01
West Indian (1,392)	1,745	0.38
Other West Indian (30)	43	0.01
Yugoslavian (1,237)	1,738	0.38

Hispanic Origin	Population	%
Hispanic or Latino (of any race)	81,051	17.29
Central American, ex. Mexican	4,310	0.92
Costa Rican	266	0.06
Guatemalan	864	0.18
Honduran	1,735	0.37
Nicaraguan	199	0.04
Panamanian	607	0.13
Salvadoran	592	0.13
Other Central American	47	0.01
Cuban	1,831	0.39
Dominican Republic	4,918	1.05
Mexican	18,684	3.99
Puerto Rican	37,517	8.00
South American	8,232	1.76
Argentinean	608	0.13
Bolivian	161	0.03
Chilean	346	0.07
Colombian	2,526	0.54
Ecuadorian	2,675	0.57
Paraguayan	38	0.01
Peruvian	1,462	0.31
Uruguayan	76	0.02
Venezuelan	254	0.05
Other South American	86	0.02
Other Hispanic or Latino	5,559	1.19

Race*	Population	%
African-American/Black (49,857)	55,014	11.74
Not Hispanic (44,313)	47,521	10.14
Hispanic (5,544)	7,493	1.60
American Indian/Alaska Native (1,695)	3,719	0.79
Not Hispanic (695)	2,034	0.43
Hispanic (1,000)	1,685	0.36
Alaska Athabascan (Ala. Nat.) (1)	3	<0.01
Aleut (Alaska Native) (0)	2	<0.01
Apache (16)	35	0.01
Arapaho (1)	1	<0.01
Blackfeet (17)	88	0.02
Canadian/French Am. Ind. (7)	10	<0.01
Central American Ind. (29)	56	0.01
Cherokee (104)	467	0.10
Cheyenne (0)	2	<0.01
Chickasaw (1)	3	<0.01
Chippewa (7)	13	<0.01

Race* (cont.)	Population	%
Choctaw (3)	11	<0.01
Colville (0)	0	<0.01
Comanche (2)	3	<0.01
Cree (0)	4	<0.01
Creek (3)	29	0.01
Crow (0)	0	<0.01
Delaware (16)	43	0.01
Hopi (1)	5	<0.01
Houma (1)	1	<0.01
Inupiat (Alaska Native) (0)	1	<0.01
Iroquois (61)	152	0.03
Kiowa (0)	1	<0.01
Lumbee (1)	8	<0.01
Menominee (0)	0	<0.01
Mexican American Ind. (161)	204	0.04
Navajo (10)	17	<0.01
Osage (0)	0	<0.01
Ottawa (0)	0	<0.01
Paiute (0)	0	<0.01
Pima (2)	2	<0.01
Potawatomi (0)	0	<0.01
Pueblo (4)	5	<0.01
Puget Sound Salish (0)	0	<0.01
Seminole (7)	26	0.01
Shoshone (1)	3	<0.01
Sioux (11)	24	0.01
South American Ind. (146)	288	0.06
Spanish American Ind. (31)	47	0.01
Tlingit-Haida (Alaska Native) (0)	1	<0.01
Tohono O'Odham (4)	8	<0.01
Tsimshian (Alaska Native) (0)	0	<0.01
Ute (1)	1	<0.01
Yakama (0)	0	<0.01
Yaqui (1)	1	<0.01
Yuman (0)	1	<0.01
Yup'ik (Alaska Native) (0)	0	<0.01
Asian (35,164)	38,756	8.27
Not Hispanic (34,697)	37,689	8.04
Hispanic (467)	1,067	0.23
Bangladeshi (360)	387	0.08
Bhutanese (0)	0	<0.01
Burmese (116)	130	0.03
Cambodian (100)	129	0.03
Chinese, ex. Taiwanese (13,144)	14,107	3.01
Filipino (5,224)	6,205	1.32
Hmong (4)	8	<0.01
Indian (6,793)	7,723	1.65
Indonesian (22)	52	0.01
Japanese (201)	408	0.09
Korean (3,207)	3,398	0.72
Laotian (13)	18	<0.01
Malaysian (58)	96	0.02
Nepalese (27)	35	0.01
Pakistani (2,495)	2,777	0.59
Sri Lankan (1,560)	1,766	0.38
Taiwanese (160)	197	0.04
Thai (135)	166	0.04
Vietnamese (468)	570	0.12
Hawaii Native/Pacific Islander (213)	683	0.15
Not Hispanic (137)	439	0.09
Hispanic (76)	244	0.05
Fijian (6)	6	<0.01
Guamanian/Chamorro (88)	115	0.02
Marshallese (1)	1	<0.01
Native Hawaiian (46)	121	0.03
Samoan (5)	26	0.01
Tongan (2)	2	<0.01
White (341,677)	350,679	74.81
Not Hispanic (300,169)	305,118	65.09
Hispanic (41,508)	45,561	9.72

Notes: † The Census 2010 population figure is used to calculate the percentages in the Hispanic Origin and Race categories. Ancestry percentages are based on the 2006-2010 American Community Survey population (not shown); ‡ Numbers in parentheses indicate the number of people reporting a single ancestry; * Numbers in parentheses indicate the number of persons reporting this race alone, not in combination with any other race; Please refer to the Explanation of Data for more information.

Syracuse

Place Type: City
County: Onondaga
Population: 145,170

Ancestry	Population	%
Afghan (19)	19	0.01
African, Sub-Saharan (2,165)	2,470	1.71
African (898)	1,142	0.79
Cape Verdean (0)	8	0.01
Ethiopian (0)	0	<0.01
Ghanaian (113)	113	0.08
Kenyan (0)	17	0.01
Liberian (246)	246	0.17
Nigerian (148)	167	0.12
Senegalese (0)	0	<0.01
Sierra Leonean (13)	13	0.01
Somalian (478)	478	0.33
South African (10)	10	0.01
Sudanese (160)	177	0.12
Ugandan (26)	26	0.02
Zimbabwean (0)	0	<0.01
Other Sub-Saharan African (73)	73	0.05
Albanian (429)	455	0.31
Alsatian (0)	0	<0.01
American (3,220)	3,220	2.22
Arab (571)	900	0.62
Arab (226)	267	0.18
Egyptian (13)	13	0.01
Iraqi (0)	0	<0.01
Jordanian (0)	0	<0.01
Lebanese (100)	269	0.19
Moroccan (60)	86	0.06
Palestinian (58)	66	0.05
Syrian (57)	114	0.08
Other Arab (57)	85	0.06
Armenian (24)	229	0.16
Assyrian/Chaldean/Syriac (0)	0	<0.01
Australian (42)	54	0.04
Austrian (81)	372	0.26
Basque (0)	0	<0.01
Belgian (53)	81	0.06
Brazilian (30)	42	0.03
British (199)	418	0.29
Bulgarian (18)	18	0.01
Cajun (24)	24	0.02
Canadian (96)	350	0.24
Carpatho Rusyn (0)	0	<0.01
Celtic (12)	12	0.01
Croatian (0)	46	0.03
Cypriot (0)	0	<0.01
Czech (36)	163	0.11
Czechoslovakian (44)	77	0.05
Danish (36)	109	0.08
Dutch (174)	2,128	1.47
Eastern European (153)	178	0.12
English (2,028)	10,153	7.01
Estonian (0)	12	0.01
European (440)	487	0.34
Finnish (14)	52	0.04
French, ex. Basque (735)	6,182	4.27
French Canadian (804)	1,782	1.23
German (3,496)	17,038	11.77
German Russian (0)	0	<0.01
Greek (339)	678	0.47
Guyanese (100)	158	0.11
Hungarian (88)	540	0.37
Icelander (0)	10	0.01
Iranian (65)	105	0.07
Irish (6,064)	22,387	15.47
Israeli (133)	146	0.10
Italian (8,625)	18,571	12.83
Latvian (28)	41	0.03
Lithuanian (72)	309	0.21
Luxemburger (0)	14	0.01
Macedonian (46)	67	0.05
Maltese (0)	0	<0.01
New Zealander (0)	13	0.01
Northern European (71)	71	0.05

	Population	%
Norwegian (107)	366	0.25
Pennsylvania German (14)	33	0.02
Polish (2,445)	7,273	5.03
Portuguese (34)	330	0.23
Romanian (38)	113	0.08
Russian (596)	1,831	1.27
Scandinavian (49)	98	0.07
Scotch-Irish (639)	1,546	1.07
Scottish (505)	2,233	1.54
Serbian (0)	26	0.02
Slavic (12)	45	0.03
Slovak (46)	158	0.11
Slovene (15)	85	0.06
Soviet Union (0)	0	<0.01
Swedish (288)	1,044	0.72
Swiss (91)	286	0.20
Turkish (169)	279	0.19
Ukrainian (589)	1,095	0.76
Welsh (155)	1,060	0.73
West Indian, ex. Hispanic (1,588)	1,931	1.33
Bahamian (0)	0	<0.01
Barbadian (96)	96	0.07
Belizean (0)	0	<0.01
Bermudan (0)	0	<0.01
British West Indian (22)	50	0.03
Dutch West Indian (0)	0	<0.01
Haitian (145)	145	0.10
Jamaican (908)	1,181	0.82
Trinidadian/Tobagonian (95)	95	0.07
U.S. Virgin Islander (0)	0	<0.01
West Indian (322)	364	0.25
Other West Indian (0)	0	<0.01
Yugoslavian (765)	774	0.53

Hispanic Origin	Population	%
Hispanic or Latino (of any race)	12,036	8.29
Central American, ex. Mexican	348	0.24
Costa Rican	29	0.02
Guatemalan	133	0.09
Honduran	40	0.03
Nicaraguan	30	0.02
Panamanian	54	0.04
Salvadoran	59	0.04
Other Central American	3	<0.01
Cuban	1,192	0.82
Dominican Republic	689	0.47
Mexican	958	0.66
Puerto Rican	7,594	5.23
South American	530	0.37
Argentinean	49	0.03
Bolivian	11	0.01
Chilean	35	0.02
Colombian	173	0.12
Ecuadorian	101	0.07
Paraguayan	3	<0.01
Peruvian	89	0.06
Uruguayan	27	0.02
Venezuelan	39	0.03
Other South American	3	<0.01
Other Hispanic or Latino	725	0.50

Race*	Population	%
African-American/Black (42,770)	48,029	33.08
Not Hispanic (40,672)	45,084	31.06
Hispanic (2,098)	2,945	2.03
American Indian/Alaska Native (1,606)	3,537	2.44
Not Hispanic (1,390)	3,067	2.11
Hispanic (216)	470	0.32
Alaska Athabascan (Ala. Nat.) (0)	3	<0.01
Aleut (Alaska Native) (0)	1	<0.01
Apache (8)	25	0.02
Arapaho (2)	2	<0.01
Blackfeet (7)	111	0.08
Canadian/French Am. Ind. (35)	51	0.04
Central American Ind. (4)	9	0.01
Cherokee (20)	258	0.18
Cheyenne (0)	2	<0.01
Chickasaw (0)	4	<0.01
Chippewa (11)	18	0.01

	Population	%
Choctaw (1)	28	0.02
Colville (0)	0	<0.01
Comanche (6)	12	0.01
Cree (1)	6	<0.01
Creek (4)	9	0.01
Crow (0)	1	<0.01
Delaware (3)	5	<0.01
Hopi (0)	0	<0.01
Houma (0)	0	<0.01
Inupiat (Alaska Native) (3)	6	<0.01
Iroquois (790)	1,373	0.95
Kiowa (0)	1	<0.01
Lumbee (4)	4	<0.01
Menominee (1)	1	<0.01
Mexican American Ind. (24)	34	0.02
Navajo (2)	5	<0.01
Osage (1)	1	<0.01
Ottawa (0)	2	<0.01
Paiute (0)	0	<0.01
Pima (1)	2	<0.01
Potawatomi (1)	2	<0.01
Pueblo (0)	0	<0.01
Puget Sound Salish (0)	0	<0.01
Seminole (4)	16	0.01
Shoshone (0)	0	<0.01
Sioux (13)	38	0.03
South American Ind. (25)	49	0.03
Spanish American Ind. (0)	0	<0.01
Tlingit-Haida (Alaska Native) (0)	1	<0.01
Tohono O'Odham (1)	1	<0.01
Tsimshian (Alaska Native) (0)	0	<0.01
Ute (0)	0	<0.01
Yakama (0)	0	<0.01
Yaqui (0)	0	<0.01
Yuman (0)	0	<0.01
Yup'ik (Alaska Native) (0)	1	<0.01
Asian (8,021)	9,073	6.25
Not Hispanic (7,971)	8,924	6.15
Hispanic (50)	149	0.10
Bangladeshi (47)	57	0.04
Bhutanese (392)	516	0.36
Burmese (1,178)	1,218	0.84
Cambodian (114)	149	0.10
Chinese, ex. Taiwanese (1,543)	1,749	1.20
Filipino (218)	388	0.27
Hmong (26)	34	0.02
Indian (1,216)	1,397	0.96
Indonesian (14)	26	0.02
Japanese (109)	243	0.17
Korean (861)	937	0.65
Laotian (71)	89	0.06
Malaysian (5)	13	0.01
Nepalese (160)	262	0.18
Pakistani (107)	121	0.08
Sri Lankan (13)	17	0.01
Taiwanese (80)	93	0.06
Thai (64)	89	0.06
Vietnamese (1,414)	1,554	1.07
Hawaii Native/Pacific Islander (44)	279	0.19
Not Hispanic (37)	218	0.15
Hispanic (7)	61	0.04
Fijian (0)	1	<0.01
Guamanian/Chamorro (5)	12	0.01
Marshallese (0)	1	<0.01
Native Hawaiian (15)	65	0.04
Samoan (8)	21	0.01
Tongan (0)	1	<0.01
White (81,319)	87,414	60.21
Not Hispanic (76,653)	81,787	56.34
Hispanic (4,666)	5,627	3.88

Notes: † The Census 2010 population figure is used to calculate the percentages in the Hispanic Origin and Race categories. Ancestry percentages are based on the 2006-2010 American Community Survey population (not shown); ‡ Numbers in parentheses indicate the number of people reporting a single ancestry; * Numbers in parentheses indicate the number of persons reporting this race alone, not in combination with any other race; Please refer to the Explanation of Data for more information.

Tonawanda

Place Type: CDP
County: Erie
Population: 58,144

Ancestry	Population	%
Afghan (108)	108	0.18
African, Sub-Saharan (59)	194	0.33
African (16)	89	0.15
Cape Verdean (0)	0	<0.01
Ethiopian (0)	0	<0.01
Ghanaian (19)	19	0.03
Kenyan (24)	86	0.15
Liberian (0)	0	<0.01
Nigerian (0)	0	<0.01
Senegalese (0)	0	<0.01
Sierra Leonean (0)	0	<0.01
Somalian (0)	0	<0.01
South African (0)	0	<0.01
Sudanese (0)	0	<0.01
Ugandan (0)	0	<0.01
Zimbabwean (0)	0	<0.01
Other Sub-Saharan African (0)	0	<0.01
Albanian (48)	59	0.10
Alsatian (0)	24	0.04
American (1,226)	1,226	2.09
Arab (293)	502	0.86
Arab (21)	34	0.06
Egyptian (0)	8	0.01
Iraqi (0)	0	<0.01
Jordanian (9)	9	0.02
Lebanese (223)	401	0.68
Moroccan (0)	0	<0.01
Palestinian (0)	0	<0.01
Syrian (0)	10	0.02
Other Arab (40)	40	0.07
Armenian (43)	43	0.07
Assyrian/Chaldean/Syriac (0)	0	<0.01
Australian (0)	29	0.05
Austrian (54)	415	0.71
Basque (0)	0	<0.01
Belgian (0)	13	0.02
Brazilian (0)	13	0.02
British (33)	97	0.17
Bulgarian (0)	0	<0.01
Cajun (0)	0	<0.01
Canadian (144)	288	0.49
Carpatho Rusyn (0)	0	<0.01
Celtic (0)	0	<0.01
Croatian (84)	219	0.37
Cypriot (0)	0	<0.01
Czech (22)	168	0.29
Czechoslovakian (32)	177	0.30
Danish (47)	151	0.26
Dutch (89)	716	1.22
Eastern European (23)	23	0.04
English (1,484)	6,115	10.44
Estonian (0)	0	<0.01
European (354)	354	0.60
Finnish (49)	95	0.16
French, ex. Basque (188)	2,149	3.67
French Canadian (128)	537	0.92
German (4,626)	19,292	32.95
German Russian (0)	0	<0.01
Greek (260)	424	0.72
Guyanese (0)	0	<0.01
Hungarian (220)	976	1.67
Icelander (11)	11	0.02
Iranian (0)	0	<0.01
Irish (2,820)	11,980	20.46
Israeli (0)	0	<0.01
Italian (6,780)	14,269	24.37
Latvian (0)	13	0.02
Lithuanian (29)	162	0.28
Luxemburger (0)	0	<0.01
Macedonian (0)	18	0.03
Maltese (8)	26	0.04
New Zealander (0)	0	<0.01
Northern European (18)	18	0.03

Ancestry	Population	%
Norwegian (60)	150	0.26
Pennsylvania German (40)	85	0.15
Polish (3,451)	9,014	15.40
Portuguese (10)	24	0.04
Romanian (77)	158	0.27
Russian (337)	688	1.18
Scandinavian (15)	15	0.03
Scotch-Irish (309)	989	1.69
Scottish (328)	1,430	2.44
Serbian (54)	73	0.12
Slavic (30)	59	0.10
Slovak (62)	112	0.19
Slovene (0)	0	<0.01
Soviet Union (0)	0	<0.01
Swedish (77)	584	1.00
Swiss (44)	109	0.19
Turkish (0)	0	<0.01
Ukrainian (239)	422	0.72
Welsh (57)	332	0.57
West Indian, ex. Hispanic (29)	29	0.05
Bahamian (0)	0	<0.01
Barbadian (0)	0	<0.01
Belizean (0)	0	<0.01
Bermudan (0)	0	<0.01
British West Indian (0)	0	<0.01
Dutch West Indian (0)	0	<0.01
Haitian (0)	0	<0.01
Jamaican (12)	12	0.02
Trinidadian/Tobagonian (17)	17	0.03
U.S. Virgin Islander (0)	0	<0.01
West Indian (0)	0	<0.01
Other West Indian (0)	0	<0.01
Yugoslavian (66)	124	0.21

Hispanic Origin	Population	%
Hispanic or Latino (of any race)	1,485	2.55
Central American, ex. Mexican	32	0.06
Costa Rican	2	<0.01
Guatemalan	19	0.03
Honduran	4	0.01
Nicaraguan	0	<0.01
Panamanian	5	0.01
Salvadoran	2	<0.01
Other Central American	0	<0.01
Cuban	31	0.05
Dominican Republic	43	0.07
Mexican	210	0.36
Puerto Rican	942	1.62
South American	89	0.15
Argentinean	7	0.01
Bolivian	7	0.01
Chilean	1	<0.01
Colombian	37	0.06
Ecuadorian	18	0.03
Paraguayan	0	<0.01
Peruvian	14	0.02
Uruguayan	0	<0.01
Venezuelan	1	<0.01
Other South American	4	0.01
Other Hispanic or Latino	138	0.24

Race*	Population	%
African-American/Black (1,773)	2,226	3.83
Not Hispanic (1,678)	2,088	3.59
Hispanic (95)	138	0.24
American Indian/Alaska Native (220)	409	0.70
Not Hispanic (183)	354	0.61
Hispanic (37)	55	0.09
Alaska Athabascan (Ala. Nat.) (0)	0	<0.01
Aleut (Alaska Native) (0)	0	<0.01
Apache (0)	4	0.01
Arapaho (0)	0	<0.01
Blackfeet (2)	5	0.01
Canadian/French Am. Ind. (3)	4	0.01
Central American Ind. (0)	0	<0.01
Cherokee (2)	31	0.05
Cheyenne (0)	0	<0.01
Chickasaw (0)	0	<0.01
Chippewa (2)	3	0.01

Race*	Population	%
Choctaw (0)	5	0.01
Colville (0)	0	<0.01
Comanche (0)	0	<0.01
Cree (0)	0	<0.01
Creek (0)	1	<0.01
Crow (0)	0	<0.01
Delaware (1)	1	<0.01
Hopi (0)	0	<0.01
Houma (0)	0	<0.01
Inupiat (Alaska Native) (0)	0	<0.01
Iroquois (113)	165	0.28
Kiowa (0)	0	<0.01
Lumbee (0)	0	<0.01
Menominee (0)	0	<0.01
Mexican American Ind. (2)	2	<0.01
Navajo (1)	1	<0.01
Osage (0)	0	<0.01
Ottawa (0)	0	<0.01
Paiute (0)	0	<0.01
Pima (0)	0	<0.01
Potawatomi (5)	9	0.02
Pueblo (0)	0	<0.01
Puget Sound Salish (0)	1	<0.01
Seminole (0)	1	<0.01
Shoshone (0)	0	<0.01
Sioux (1)	2	<0.01
South American Ind. (8)	14	0.02
Spanish American Ind. (2)	2	<0.01
Tlingit-Haida (Alaska Native) (0)	0	<0.01
Tohono O'Odham (0)	0	<0.01
Tsimshian (Alaska Native) (0)	0	<0.01
Ute (0)	0	<0.01
Yakama (0)	0	<0.01
Yaqui (1)	1	<0.01
Yuman (0)	0	<0.01
Yup'ik (Alaska Native) (0)	0	<0.01
Asian (831)	1,029	1.77
Not Hispanic (823)	1,011	1.74
Hispanic (8)	18	0.03
Bangladeshi (3)	4	0.01
Bhutanese (0)	0	<0.01
Burmese (2)	3	0.01
Cambodian (1)	1	<0.01
Chinese, ex. Taiwanese (210)	239	0.41
Filipino (57)	93	0.16
Hmong (0)	0	<0.01
Indian (266)	284	0.49
Indonesian (3)	8	0.01
Japanese (16)	33	0.06
Korean (135)	160	0.28
Laotian (11)	17	0.03
Malaysian (3)	4	0.01
Nepalese (1)	1	<0.01
Pakistani (5)	7	0.01
Sri Lankan (8)	8	0.01
Taiwanese (10)	16	0.03
Thai (11)	23	0.04
Vietnamese (64)	77	0.13
Hawaii Native/Pacific Islander (1)	31	0.05
Not Hispanic (1)	21	0.04
Hispanic (0)	10	0.02
Fijian (0)	0	<0.01
Guamanian/Chamorro (0)	3	0.01
Marshallese (0)	0	<0.01
Native Hawaiian (0)	12	0.02
Samoan (1)	2	<0.01
Tongan (0)	1	<0.01
White (54,151)	54,936	94.48
Not Hispanic (53,210)	53,890	92.68
Hispanic (941)	1,046	1.80

Notes: † The Census 2010 population figure is used to calculate the percentages in the Hispanic Origin and Race categories. Ancestry percentages are based on the 2006-2010 American Community Survey population (not shown); ‡ Numbers in parentheses indicate the number of people reporting a single ancestry; * Numbers in parentheses indicate the number of persons reporting this race alone, not in combination with any other race; Please refer to the Explanation of Data for more information.

Tonawanda

Place Type: Town
County: Erie
Population: 73,567

Ancestry	Population	%
Afghan (108)	108	0.15
African, Sub-Saharan (85)	220	0.30
African (16)	89	0.12
Cape Verdean (0)	0	<0.01
Ethiopian (13)	13	0.02
Ghanaian (19)	19	0.03
Kenyan (24)	86	0.12
Liberian (0)	0	<0.01
Nigerian (0)	0	<0.01
Senegalese (0)	0	<0.01
Sierra Leonean (0)	0	<0.01
Somalian (0)	0	<0.01
South African (0)	0	<0.01
Sudanese (0)	0	<0.01
Ugandan (0)	0	<0.01
Zimbabwean (0)	0	<0.01
Other Sub-Saharan African (13)	13	0.02
Albanian (48)	59	0.08
Alsatian (0)	24	0.03
American (1,511)	1,511	2.04
Arab (344)	592	0.80
Arab (21)	46	0.06
Egyptian (0)	8	0.01
Iraqi (0)	0	<0.01
Jordanian (9)	9	0.01
Lebanese (223)	428	0.58
Moroccan (0)	0	<0.01
Palestinian (0)	0	<0.01
Syrian (12)	22	0.03
Other Arab (79)	79	0.11
Armenian (68)	96	0.13
Assyrian/Chaldean/Syriac (0)	0	<0.01
Australian (0)	29	0.04
Austrian (54)	459	0.62
Basque (0)	0	<0.01
Belgian (0)	13	0.02
Brazilian (0)	13	0.02
British (33)	104	0.14
Bulgarian (0)	0	<0.01
Cajun (0)	0	<0.01
Canadian (144)	312	0.42
Carpatho Rusyn (0)	13	0.02
Celtic (0)	0	<0.01
Croatian (132)	326	0.44
Cypriot (0)	0	<0.01
Czech (42)	223	0.30
Czechoslovakian (32)	179	0.24
Danish (60)	179	0.24
Dutch (104)	872	1.18
Eastern European (44)	44	0.06
English (1,746)	7,240	9.77
Estonian (0)	0	<0.01
European (439)	439	0.59
Finnish (49)	95	0.13
French, ex. Basque (254)	2,508	3.39
French Canadian (188)	881	1.19
German (5,590)	24,085	32.51
German Russian (0)	0	<0.01
Greek (260)	493	0.67
Guyanese (0)	0	<0.01
Hungarian (294)	1,188	1.60
Icelander (11)	11	0.01
Iranian (0)	0	<0.01
Irish (3,462)	15,685	21.17
Israeli (0)	0	<0.01
Italian (9,140)	19,213	25.93
Latvian (15)	28	0.04
Lithuanian (41)	174	0.23
Luxemburger (0)	0	<0.01
Macedonian (0)	18	0.02
Maltese (8)	26	0.04
New Zealander (0)	0	<0.01
Northern European (18)	18	0.02

Ancestry (cont.)	Population	%
Norwegian (60)	150	0.20
Pennsylvania German (53)	98	0.13
Polish (4,057)	11,479	15.49
Portuguese (10)	24	0.03
Romanian (77)	158	0.21
Russian (347)	745	1.01
Scandinavian (15)	15	0.02
Scotch-Irish (370)	1,170	1.58
Scottish (448)	1,915	2.58
Serbian (66)	85	0.11
Slavic (62)	123	0.17
Slovak (74)	124	0.17
Slovene (0)	0	<0.01
Soviet Union (0)	0	<0.01
Swedish (144)	758	1.02
Swiss (44)	131	0.18
Turkish (0)	0	<0.01
Ukrainian (295)	535	0.72
Welsh (57)	429	0.58
West Indian, ex. Hispanic (49)	63	0.09
Bahamian (0)	0	<0.01
Barbadian (0)	0	<0.01
Belizean (0)	0	<0.01
Bermudan (0)	0	<0.01
British West Indian (0)	0	<0.01
Dutch West Indian (0)	0	<0.01
Haitian (0)	0	<0.01
Jamaican (32)	46	0.06
Trinidadian/Tobagonian (17)	17	0.02
U.S. Virgin Islander (0)	0	<0.01
West Indian (0)	0	<0.01
Other West Indian (0)	0	<0.01
Yugoslavian (75)	133	0.18

Hispanic Origin	Population	%
Hispanic or Latino (of any race)	2,003	2.72
Central American, ex. Mexican	63	0.09
Costa Rican	9	0.01
Guatemalan	33	0.04
Honduran	5	0.01
Nicaraguan	3	<0.01
Panamanian	9	0.01
Salvadoran	4	0.01
Other Central American	0	<0.01
Cuban	39	0.05
Dominican Republic	51	0.07
Mexican	261	0.35
Puerto Rican	1,277	1.74
South American	130	0.18
Argentinean	12	0.02
Bolivian	8	0.01
Chilean	1	<0.01
Colombian	49	0.07
Ecuadorian	27	0.04
Paraguayan	0	<0.01
Peruvian	20	0.03
Uruguayan	1	<0.01
Venezuelan	8	0.01
Other South American	4	0.01
Other Hispanic or Latino	182	0.25

Race*	Population	%
African-American/Black (2,234)	2,842	3.86
Not Hispanic (2,114)	2,658	3.61
Hispanic (120)	184	0.25
American Indian/Alaska Native (312)	575	0.78
Not Hispanic (266)	510	0.69
Hispanic (46)	65	0.09
Alaska Athabascan (Ala. Nat.) (0)	0	<0.01
Aleut (Alaska Native) (0)	0	<0.01
Apache (0)	4	0.01
Arapaho (0)	0	<0.01
Blackfeet (2)	6	0.01
Canadian/French Am. Ind. (7)	8	0.01
Central American Ind. (0)	0	<0.01
Cherokee (3)	38	0.05
Cheyenne (0)	0	<0.01
Chickasaw (0)	0	<0.01
Chippewa (4)	5	0.01

Race* (cont.)	Population	%
Choctaw (0)	8	0.01
Colville (0)	0	<0.01
Comanche (0)	0	<0.01
Cree (0)	3	<0.01
Creek (0)	1	<0.01
Crow (0)	2	<0.01
Delaware (1)	1	<0.01
Hopi (0)	0	<0.01
Houma (0)	0	<0.01
Inupiat (Alaska Native) (0)	0	<0.01
Iroquois (164)	256	0.35
Kiowa (0)	0	<0.01
Lumbee (0)	1	<0.01
Menominee (0)	0	<0.01
Mexican American Ind. (2)	2	<0.01
Navajo (1)	1	<0.01
Osage (0)	0	<0.01
Ottawa (0)	0	<0.01
Paiute (0)	0	<0.01
Pima (0)	0	<0.01
Potawatomi (5)	9	0.01
Pueblo (0)	0	<0.01
Puget Sound Salish (0)	1	<0.01
Seminole (0)	1	<0.01
Shoshone (0)	0	<0.01
Sioux (2)	5	0.01
South American Ind. (8)	14	0.02
Spanish American Ind. (2)	2	<0.01
Tlingit-Haida (Alaska Native) (0)	0	<0.01
Tohono O'Odham (0)	0	<0.01
Tsimshian (Alaska Native) (0)	0	<0.01
Ute (0)	0	<0.01
Yakama (0)	0	<0.01
Yaqui (1)	1	<0.01
Yuman (0)	0	<0.01
Yup'ik (Alaska Native) (0)	0	<0.01
Asian (981)	1,234	1.68
Not Hispanic (972)	1,209	1.64
Hispanic (9)	25	0.03
Bangladeshi (3)	4	0.01
Bhutanese (0)	0	<0.01
Burmese (2)	3	<0.01
Cambodian (6)	6	0.01
Chinese, ex. Taiwanese (251)	290	0.39
Filipino (68)	114	0.15
Hmong (0)	0	<0.01
Indian (287)	312	0.42
Indonesian (3)	9	0.01
Japanese (27)	59	0.08
Korean (166)	198	0.27
Laotian (13)	19	0.03
Malaysian (5)	6	0.01
Nepalese (2)	2	<0.01
Pakistani (7)	10	0.01
Sri Lankan (8)	8	0.01
Taiwanese (12)	18	0.02
Thai (13)	25	0.03
Vietnamese (68)	81	0.11
Hawaii Native/Pacific Islander (2)	38	0.05
Not Hispanic (2)	25	0.03
Hispanic (0)	13	0.02
Fijian (0)	0	<0.01
Guamanian/Chamorro (0)	3	<0.01
Marshallese (0)	0	<0.01
Native Hawaiian (0)	16	0.02
Samoan (1)	2	<0.01
Tongan (0)	1	<0.01
White (68,462)	69,534	94.52
Not Hispanic (67,172)	68,098	92.57
Hispanic (1,290)	1,436	1.95

Notes: † The Census 2010 population figure is used to calculate the percentages in the Hispanic Origin and Race categories. Ancestry percentages are based on the 2006-2010 American Community Survey population (not shown); ‡ Numbers in parentheses indicate the number of people reporting a single ancestry; * Numbers in parentheses indicate the number of persons reporting this race alone, not in combination with any other race; Please refer to the Explanation of Data for more information.

Troy

Place Type: City
County: Rensselaer
Population: 50,129

Ancestry	Population	%
Afghan (0)	0	<0.01
African, Sub-Saharan (643)	773	1.55
African (372)	476	0.95
Cape Verdean (0)	11	0.02
Ethiopian (0)	0	<0.01
Ghanaian (91)	91	0.18
Kenyan (0)	0	<0.01
Liberian (0)	0	<0.01
Nigerian (8)	8	0.02
Senegalese (0)	0	<0.01
Sierra Leonean (0)	0	<0.01
Somalian (0)	0	<0.01
South African (0)	0	<0.01
Sudanese (28)	28	0.06
Ugandan (0)	0	<0.01
Zimbabwean (0)	0	<0.01
Other Sub-Saharan African (144)	159	0.32
Albanian (55)	55	0.11
Alsatian (0)	0	<0.01
American (1,657)	1,657	3.31
Arab (304)	439	0.88
Arab (72)	72	0.14
Egyptian (7)	44	0.09
Iraqi (0)	0	<0.01
Jordanian (0)	0	<0.01
Lebanese (204)	270	0.54
Moroccan (0)	0	<0.01
Palestinian (0)	0	<0.01
Syrian (0)	0	<0.01
Other Arab (21)	53	0.11
Armenian (270)	418	0.84
Assyrian/Chaldean/Syriac (0)	0	<0.01
Australian (11)	11	0.02
Austrian (42)	124	0.25
Basque (0)	0	<0.01
Belgian (0)	19	0.04
Brazilian (25)	42	0.08
British (97)	207	0.41
Bulgarian (0)	0	<0.01
Cajun (0)	0	<0.01
Canadian (60)	177	0.35
Carpatho Rusyn (0)	0	<0.01
Celtic (0)	23	0.05
Croatian (0)	0	<0.01
Cypriot (0)	0	<0.01
Czech (9)	182	0.36
Czechoslovakian (20)	38	0.08
Danish (37)	223	0.45
Dutch (117)	1,379	2.76
Eastern European (11)	24	0.05
English (888)	4,004	8.01
Estonian (15)	15	0.03
European (257)	529	1.06
Finnish (0)	74	0.15
French, ex. Basque (679)	4,862	9.72
French Canadian (445)	1,245	2.49
German (926)	6,417	12.83
German Russian (0)	65	0.13
Greek (161)	358	0.72
Guyanese (79)	79	0.16
Hungarian (14)	129	0.26
Icelander (0)	0	<0.01
Iranian (0)	0	<0.01
Irish (3,757)	12,384	24.76
Israeli (13)	13	0.03
Italian (2,238)	6,644	13.29
Latvian (19)	32	0.06
Lithuanian (30)	141	0.28
Luxemburger (0)	0	<0.01
Macedonian (0)	0	<0.01
Maltese (0)	0	<0.01
New Zealander (0)	0	<0.01
Northern European (10)	10	0.02
Norwegian (12)	134	0.27
Pennsylvania German (40)	50	0.10
Polish (733)	2,521	5.04
Portuguese (42)	81	0.16
Romanian (11)	37	0.07
Russian (74)	287	0.57
Scandinavian (8)	8	0.02
Scotch-Irish (239)	784	1.57
Scottish (304)	848	1.70
Serbian (0)	0	<0.01
Slavic (0)	38	0.08
Slovak (0)	52	0.10
Slovene (0)	0	<0.01
Soviet Union (0)	0	<0.01
Swedish (30)	279	0.56
Swiss (0)	79	0.16
Turkish (170)	207	0.41
Ukrainian (299)	819	1.64
Welsh (67)	432	0.86
West Indian, ex. Hispanic (582)	797	1.59
Bahamian (0)	0	<0.01
Barbadian (15)	55	0.11
Belizean (0)	10	0.02
Bermudan (0)	0	<0.01
British West Indian (10)	17	0.03
Dutch West Indian (0)	0	<0.01
Haitian (96)	109	0.22
Jamaican (230)	288	0.58
Trinidadian/Tobagonian (214)	243	0.49
U.S. Virgin Islander (0)	0	<0.01
West Indian (17)	62	0.12
Other West Indian (0)	13	0.03
Yugoslavian (21)	34	0.07

Hispanic Origin	Population	%
Hispanic or Latino (of any race)	3,984	7.95
Central American, ex. Mexican	153	0.31
Costa Rican	16	0.03
Guatemalan	16	0.03
Honduran	12	0.02
Nicaraguan	15	0.03
Panamanian	57	0.11
Salvadoran	37	0.07
Other Central American	0	<0.01
Cuban	96	0.19
Dominican Republic	218	0.43
Mexican	400	0.80
Puerto Rican	2,598	5.18
South American	189	0.38
Argentinean	22	0.04
Bolivian	4	0.01
Chilean	6	0.01
Colombian	61	0.12
Ecuadorian	40	0.08
Paraguayan	3	0.01
Peruvian	29	0.06
Uruguayan	3	0.01
Venezuelan	20	0.04
Other South American	1	<0.01
Other Hispanic or Latino	330	0.66

Race*	Population	%
African-American/Black (8,211)	9,646	19.24
Not Hispanic (7,587)	8,756	17.47
Hispanic (624)	890	1.78
American Indian/Alaska Native (163)	531	1.06
Not Hispanic (104)	407	0.81
Hispanic (59)	124	0.25
Alaska Athabascan (Ala. Nat.) (0)	0	<0.01
Aleut (Alaska Native) (0)	0	<0.01
Apache (4)	10	0.02
Arapaho (0)	0	<0.01
Blackfeet (3)	22	0.04
Canadian/French Am. Ind. (1)	2	<0.01
Central American Ind. (0)	1	<0.01
Cherokee (8)	80	0.16
Cheyenne (0)	1	<0.01
Chickasaw (0)	0	<0.01
Chippewa (0)	5	0.01
Choctaw (0)	1	<0.01
Colville (0)	0	<0.01
Comanche (0)	2	<0.01
Cree (0)	0	<0.01
Creek (0)	2	<0.01
Crow (0)	0	<0.01
Delaware (3)	6	0.01
Hopi (0)	0	<0.01
Houma (0)	0	<0.01
Inupiat (Alaska Native) (0)	0	<0.01
Iroquois (10)	55	0.11
Kiowa (0)	0	<0.01
Lumbee (1)	4	0.01
Menominee (3)	3	0.01
Mexican American Ind. (1)	3	0.01
Navajo (2)	5	0.01
Osage (0)	0	<0.01
Ottawa (0)	1	<0.01
Paiute (0)	0	<0.01
Pima (1)	1	<0.01
Potawatomi (0)	0	<0.01
Pueblo (0)	0	<0.01
Puget Sound Salish (0)	0	<0.01
Seminole (0)	0	<0.01
Shoshone (0)	0	<0.01
Sioux (0)	6	0.01
South American Ind. (8)	16	0.03
Spanish American Ind. (4)	5	0.01
Tlingit-Haida (Alaska Native) (0)	1	<0.01
Tohono O'Odham (0)	0	<0.01
Tsimshian (Alaska Native) (0)	0	<0.01
Ute (0)	0	<0.01
Yakama (0)	0	<0.01
Yaqui (0)	0	<0.01
Yuman (0)	0	<0.01
Yup'ik (Alaska Native) (0)	0	<0.01
Asian (1,721)	2,066	4.12
Not Hispanic (1,687)	2,012	4.01
Hispanic (34)	54	0.11
Bangladeshi (19)	23	0.05
Bhutanese (0)	0	<0.01
Burmese (28)	28	0.06
Cambodian (3)	7	0.01
Chinese, ex. Taiwanese (674)	759	1.51
Filipino (92)	157	0.31
Hmong (0)	0	<0.01
Indian (480)	546	1.09
Indonesian (4)	5	0.01
Japanese (21)	63	0.13
Korean (127)	174	0.35
Laotian (0)	1	<0.01
Malaysian (12)	14	0.03
Nepalese (12)	12	0.02
Pakistani (72)	81	0.16
Sri Lankan (2)	6	0.01
Taiwanese (34)	39	0.08
Thai (10)	15	0.03
Vietnamese (59)	78	0.16
Hawaii Native/Pacific Islander (20)	64	0.13
Not Hispanic (15)	50	0.10
Hispanic (5)	14	0.03
Fijian (0)	0	<0.01
Guamanian/Chamorro (4)	5	0.01
Marshallese (0)	0	<0.01
Native Hawaiian (9)	24	0.05
Samoan (0)	2	<0.01
Tongan (0)	0	<0.01
White (36,555)	38,385	76.57
Not Hispanic (34,953)	36,446	72.70
Hispanic (1,602)	1,939	3.87

Notes: † The Census 2010 population figure is used to calculate the percentages in the Hispanic Origin and Race categories. Ancestry percentages are based on the 2006-2010 American Community Survey population (not shown); ‡ Numbers in parentheses indicate the number of people reporting a single ancestry; * Numbers in parentheses indicate the number of persons reporting this race alone, not in combination with any other race; Please refer to the Explanation of Data for more information.

Union

Place Type: Town
County: Broome
Population: 56,346

Ancestry	Population	%
Afghan (0)	0	<0.01
African, Sub-Saharan (117)	208	0.37
African (63)	154	0.27
Cape Verdean (11)	11	0.02
Ethiopian (0)	0	<0.01
Ghanaian (30)	30	0.05
Kenyan (0)	0	<0.01
Liberian (0)	0	<0.01
Nigerian (13)	13	0.02
Senegalese (0)	0	<0.01
Sierra Leonean (0)	0	<0.01
Somalian (0)	0	<0.01
South African (0)	0	<0.01
Sudanese (0)	0	<0.01
Ugandan (0)	0	<0.01
Zimbabwean (0)	0	<0.01
Other Sub-Saharan African (0)	0	<0.01
Albanian (0)	7	0.01
Alsatian (0)	0	<0.01
American (2,180)	2,180	3.87
Arab (175)	231	0.41
Arab (73)	73	0.13
Egyptian (57)	69	0.12
Iraqi (6)	6	0.01
Jordanian (0)	0	<0.01
Lebanese (18)	38	0.07
Moroccan (0)	0	<0.01
Palestinian (13)	25	0.04
Syrian (0)	0	<0.01
Other Arab (8)	20	0.04
Armenian (0)	16	0.03
Assyrian/Chaldean/Syriac (0)	0	<0.01
Australian (0)	0	<0.01
Austrian (36)	297	0.53
Basque (0)	0	<0.01
Belgian (0)	31	0.06
Brazilian (0)	0	<0.01
British (82)	250	0.44
Bulgarian (0)	0	<0.01
Cajun (3)	12	0.02
Canadian (46)	153	0.27
Carpatho Rusyn (46)	101	0.18
Celtic (0)	27	0.05
Croatian (0)	21	0.04
Cypriot (0)	0	<0.01
Czech (289)	929	1.65
Czechoslovakian (221)	364	0.65
Danish (26)	119	0.21
Dutch (410)	1,823	3.24
Eastern European (61)	83	0.15
English (2,117)	7,072	12.56
Estonian (0)	0	<0.01
European (596)	660	1.17
Finnish (0)	10	0.02
French, ex. Basque (304)	2,044	3.63
French Canadian (268)	520	0.92
German (2,612)	10,592	18.81
German Russian (0)	0	<0.01
Greek (128)	417	0.74
Guyanese (136)	191	0.34
Hungarian (61)	266	0.47
Icelander (0)	0	<0.01
Iranian (0)	11	0.02
Irish (3,292)	12,320	21.88
Israeli (0)	0	<0.01
Italian (4,117)	9,710	17.24
Latvian (12)	12	0.02
Lithuanian (124)	452	0.80
Luxemburger (0)	0	<0.01
Macedonian (0)	0	<0.01
Maltese (0)	0	<0.01
New Zealander (0)	0	<0.01
Northern European (0)	0	<0.01
Norwegian (127)	291	0.52
Pennsylvania German (148)	197	0.35
Polish (1,489)	4,619	8.20
Portuguese (33)	59	0.10
Romanian (8)	68	0.12
Russian (582)	1,778	3.16
Scandinavian (9)	18	0.03
Scotch-Irish (171)	712	1.26
Scottish (158)	1,114	1.98
Serbian (10)	65	0.12
Slavic (250)	291	0.52
Slovak (1,272)	3,003	5.33
Slovene (18)	67	0.12
Soviet Union (0)	0	<0.01
Swedish (158)	406	0.72
Swiss (12)	76	0.13
Turkish (92)	103	0.18
Ukrainian (317)	666	1.18
Welsh (184)	1,372	2.44
West Indian, ex. Hispanic (92)	189	0.34
Bahamian (0)	0	<0.01
Barbadian (0)	0	<0.01
Belizean (0)	0	<0.01
Bermudan (0)	0	<0.01
British West Indian (0)	0	<0.01
Dutch West Indian (0)	0	<0.01
Haitian (31)	31	0.06
Jamaican (14)	60	0.11
Trinidadian/Tobagonian (0)	0	<0.01
U.S. Virgin Islander (0)	0	<0.01
West Indian (47)	98	0.17
Other West Indian (0)	0	<0.01
Yugoslavian (63)	83	0.15

Hispanic Origin	Population	%
Hispanic or Latino (of any race)	1,802	3.20
Central American, ex. Mexican	120	0.21
Costa Rican	15	0.03
Guatemalan	46	0.08
Honduran	22	0.04
Nicaraguan	15	0.03
Panamanian	11	0.02
Salvadoran	11	0.02
Other Central American	0	<0.01
Cuban	64	0.11
Dominican Republic	108	0.19
Mexican	247	0.44
Puerto Rican	928	1.65
South American	126	0.22
Argentinean	25	0.04
Bolivian	2	<0.01
Chilean	4	0.01
Colombian	48	0.09
Ecuadorian	22	0.04
Paraguayan	0	<0.01
Peruvian	10	0.02
Uruguayan	5	0.01
Venezuelan	9	0.02
Other South American	1	<0.01
Other Hispanic or Latino	209	0.37

Race*	Population	%
African-American/Black (2,499)	3,402	6.04
Not Hispanic (2,338)	3,092	5.49
Hispanic (161)	310	0.55
American Indian/Alaska Native (96)	425	0.75
Not Hispanic (75)	363	0.64
Hispanic (21)	62	0.11
Alaska Athabascan (Ala. Nat.) (0)	0	<0.01
Aleut (Alaska Native) (0)	0	<0.01
Apache (5)	11	0.02
Arapaho (0)	0	<0.01
Blackfeet (0)	13	0.02
Canadian/French Am. Ind. (3)	4	0.01
Central American Ind. (0)	0	<0.01
Cherokee (10)	56	0.10
Cheyenne (0)	0	<0.01
Chickasaw (0)	0	<0.01
Chippewa (2)	2	<0.01
Choctaw (1)	4	0.01
Colville (0)	0	<0.01
Comanche (0)	0	<0.01
Cree (0)	0	<0.01
Creek (0)	0	<0.01
Crow (0)	1	<0.01
Delaware (1)	5	0.01
Hopi (0)	0	<0.01
Houma (0)	1	<0.01
Inupiat (Alaska Native) (0)	0	<0.01
Iroquois (14)	53	0.09
Kiowa (0)	0	<0.01
Lumbee (0)	0	<0.01
Menominee (0)	0	<0.01
Mexican American Ind. (2)	6	0.01
Navajo (0)	2	<0.01
Osage (0)	0	<0.01
Ottawa (0)	0	<0.01
Paiute (0)	0	<0.01
Pima (0)	1	<0.01
Potawatomi (0)	2	<0.01
Pueblo (0)	0	<0.01
Puget Sound Salish (0)	0	<0.01
Seminole (0)	3	0.01
Shoshone (0)	0	<0.01
Sioux (3)	8	0.01
South American Ind. (1)	1	<0.01
Spanish American Ind. (3)	4	0.01
Tlingit-Haida (Alaska Native) (0)	0	<0.01
Tohono O'Odham (0)	0	<0.01
Tsimshian (Alaska Native) (0)	0	<0.01
Ute (0)	0	<0.01
Yakama (0)	0	<0.01
Yaqui (1)	1	<0.01
Yuman (0)	0	<0.01
Yup'ik (Alaska Native) (0)	0	<0.01
Asian (1,625)	1,958	3.47
Not Hispanic (1,619)	1,933	3.43
Hispanic (6)	25	0.04
Bangladeshi (3)	3	0.01
Bhutanese (0)	0	<0.01
Burmese (4)	4	<0.01
Cambodian (4)	5	0.01
Chinese, ex. Taiwanese (333)	405	0.72
Filipino (90)	143	0.25
Hmong (0)	0	<0.01
Indian (291)	342	0.61
Indonesian (10)	12	0.02
Japanese (22)	55	0.10
Korean (118)	161	0.29
Laotian (355)	406	0.72
Malaysian (2)	7	0.01
Nepalese (9)	9	0.02
Pakistani (66)	68	0.12
Sri Lankan (2)	2	<0.01
Taiwanese (11)	13	0.02
Thai (14)	19	0.03
Vietnamese (215)	248	0.44
Hawaii Native/Pacific Islander (41)	77	0.14
Not Hispanic (29)	55	0.10
Hispanic (12)	22	0.04
Fijian (0)	1	<0.01
Guamanian/Chamorro (13)	16	0.03
Marshallese (0)	0	<0.01
Native Hawaiian (4)	17	0.03
Samoan (2)	5	0.01
Tongan (0)	0	<0.01
White (50,181)	51,487	91.38
Not Hispanic (49,190)	50,317	89.30
Hispanic (991)	1,170	2.08

Utica

Place Type: City
County: Oneida
Population: 62,235

Ancestry	Population	%
Afghan (42)	42	0.07
African, Sub-Saharan (477)	594	0.96
African (272)	374	0.60
Cape Verdean (0)	0	<0.01
Ethiopian (0)	0	<0.01
Ghanaian (0)	0	<0.01
Kenyan (0)	15	0.02
Liberian (88)	88	0.14
Nigerian (0)	0	<0.01
Senegalese (0)	0	<0.01
Sierra Leonean (0)	0	<0.01
Somalian (99)	99	0.16
South African (0)	0	<0.01
Sudanese (0)	0	<0.01
Ugandan (0)	0	<0.01
Zimbabwean (0)	0	<0.01
Other Sub-Saharan African (18)	18	0.03
Albanian (22)	55	0.09
Alsatian (0)	0	<0.01
American (1,237)	1,237	2.00
Arab (875)	1,558	2.52
Arab (170)	198	0.32
Egyptian (22)	37	0.06
Iraqi (0)	0	<0.01
Jordanian (0)	0	<0.01
Lebanese (506)	947	1.53
Moroccan (11)	20	0.03
Palestinian (10)	10	0.02
Syrian (58)	248	0.40
Other Arab (98)	98	0.16
Armenian (18)	29	0.05
Assyrian/Chaldean/Syriac (0)	0	<0.01
Australian (13)	13	0.02
Austrian (0)	79	0.13
Basque (0)	0	<0.01
Belgian (8)	8	0.01
Brazilian (10)	32	0.05
British (9)	31	0.05
Bulgarian (0)	0	<0.01
Cajun (0)	0	<0.01
Canadian (32)	61	0.10
Carpatho Rusyn (0)	0	<0.01
Celtic (8)	16	0.03
Croatian (12)	86	0.14
Cypriot (0)	0	<0.01
Czech (0)	79	0.13
Czechoslovakian (22)	22	0.04
Danish (12)	45	0.07
Dutch (149)	884	1.43
Eastern European (11)	20	0.03
English (812)	3,140	5.08
Estonian (0)	0	<0.01
European (98)	108	0.17
Finnish (17)	17	0.03
French, ex. Basque (167)	2,016	3.26
French Canadian (219)	620	1.00
German (1,489)	7,355	11.89
German Russian (0)	0	<0.01
Greek (57)	225	0.36
Guyanese (8)	8	0.01
Hungarian (37)	118	0.19
Icelander (0)	14	0.02
Iranian (23)	23	0.04
Irish (2,616)	9,380	15.17
Israeli (0)	0	<0.01
Italian (7,837)	14,163	22.90
Latvian (0)	0	<0.01
Lithuanian (43)	76	0.12
Luxemburger (0)	0	<0.01
Macedonian (21)	21	0.03
Maltese (0)	0	<0.01
New Zealander (0)	0	<0.01
Northern European (0)	0	<0.01
Norwegian (9)	50	0.08
Pennsylvania German (13)	13	0.02
Polish (2,611)	5,408	8.75
Portuguese (27)	114	0.18
Romanian (51)	103	0.17
Russian (655)	862	1.39
Scandinavian (0)	48	0.08
Scotch-Irish (110)	254	0.41
Scottish (68)	351	0.57
Serbian (0)	82	0.13
Slavic (0)	0	<0.01
Slovak (51)	59	0.10
Slovene (0)	0	<0.01
Soviet Union (0)	0	<0.01
Swedish (0)	89	0.14
Swiss (32)	74	0.12
Turkish (0)	0	<0.01
Ukrainian (359)	505	0.82
Welsh (120)	775	1.25
West Indian, ex. Hispanic (681)	952	1.54
Bahamian (0)	0	<0.01
Barbadian (21)	21	0.03
Belizean (0)	0	<0.01
Bermudan (0)	0	<0.01
British West Indian (0)	28	0.05
Dutch West Indian (0)	0	<0.01
Haitian (168)	286	0.46
Jamaican (325)	420	0.68
Trinidadian/Tobagonian (81)	111	0.18
U.S. Virgin Islander (0)	0	<0.01
West Indian (86)	86	0.14
Other West Indian (0)	0	<0.01
Yugoslavian (3,075)	3,231	5.23

Hispanic Origin	Population	%
Hispanic or Latino (of any race)	6,555	10.53
Central American, ex. Mexican	272	0.44
Costa Rican	9	0.01
Guatemalan	8	0.01
Honduran	46	0.07
Nicaraguan	11	0.02
Panamanian	25	0.04
Salvadoran	163	0.26
Other Central American	10	0.02
Cuban	89	0.14
Dominican Republic	940	1.51
Mexican	243	0.39
Puerto Rican	4,220	6.78
South American	231	0.37
Argentinean	7	0.01
Bolivian	2	<0.01
Chilean	7	0.01
Colombian	43	0.07
Ecuadorian	100	0.16
Paraguayan	1	<0.01
Peruvian	35	0.06
Uruguayan	3	<0.01
Venezuelan	31	0.05
Other South American	2	<0.01
Other Hispanic or Latino	560	0.90

Race*	Population	%
African-American/Black (9,501)	11,107	17.85
Not Hispanic (8,851)	10,139	16.29
Hispanic (650)	968	1.56
American Indian/Alaska Native (180)	581	0.93
Not Hispanic (123)	432	0.69
Hispanic (57)	149	0.24
Alaska Athabascan (Ala. Nat.) (0)	0	<0.01
Aleut (Alaska Native) (1)	1	<0.01
Apache (4)	7	0.01
Arapaho (0)	0	<0.01
Blackfeet (0)	17	0.03
Canadian/French Am. Ind. (0)	6	0.01
Central American Ind. (8)	8	0.01
Cherokee (5)	56	0.09
Cheyenne (0)	4	0.01
Chickasaw (0)	1	<0.01
Chippewa (2)	8	0.01

	Population	%
Choctaw (0)	3	<0.01
Colville (0)	0	<0.01
Comanche (0)	0	<0.01
Cree (0)	0	<0.01
Creek (0)	1	<0.01
Crow (0)	3	<0.01
Delaware (0)	1	<0.01
Hopi (0)	0	<0.01
Houma (0)	0	<0.01
Inupiat (Alaska Native) (0)	0	<0.01
Iroquois (42)	94	0.15
Kiowa (0)	2	<0.01
Lumbee (1)	1	<0.01
Menominee (0)	0	<0.01
Mexican American Ind. (0)	0	<0.01
Navajo (1)	2	<0.01
Osage (0)	0	<0.01
Ottawa (0)	0	<0.01
Paiute (1)	1	<0.01
Pima (0)	1	<0.01
Potawatomi (0)	0	<0.01
Pueblo (1)	1	<0.01
Puget Sound Salish (0)	0	<0.01
Seminole (0)	0	<0.01
Shoshone (0)	1	<0.01
Sioux (10)	29	0.05
South American Ind. (4)	15	0.02
Spanish American Ind. (0)	0	<0.01
Tlingit-Haida (Alaska Native) (1)	4	0.01
Tohono O'Odham (0)	0	<0.01
Tsimshian (Alaska Native) (0)	0	<0.01
Ute (0)	0	<0.01
Yakama (0)	0	<0.01
Yaqui (0)	0	<0.01
Yuman (0)	0	<0.01
Yup'ik (Alaska Native) (0)	0	<0.01
Asian (4,626)	5,009	8.05
Not Hispanic (4,594)	4,936	7.93
Hispanic (32)	73	0.12
Bangladeshi (0)	0	<0.01
Bhutanese (30)	36	0.06
Burmese (2,198)	2,317	3.72
Cambodian (412)	480	0.77
Chinese, ex. Taiwanese (140)	200	0.32
Filipino (37)	83	0.13
Hmong (0)	0	<0.01
Indian (273)	368	0.59
Indonesian (0)	0	<0.01
Japanese (44)	66	0.11
Korean (107)	133	0.21
Laotian (42)	72	0.12
Malaysian (2)	2	<0.01
Nepalese (6)	12	0.02
Pakistani (41)	46	0.07
Sri Lankan (2)	2	<0.01
Taiwanese (1)	2	<0.01
Thai (34)	50	0.08
Vietnamese (932)	1,022	1.64
Hawaii Native/Pacific Islander (36)	137	0.22
Not Hispanic (16)	95	0.15
Hispanic (20)	42	0.07
Fijian (0)	0	<0.01
Guamanian/Chamorro (10)	18	0.03
Marshallese (0)	0	<0.01
Native Hawaiian (12)	20	0.03
Samoan (9)	18	0.03
Tongan (1)	1	<0.01
White (42,945)	45,066	72.41
Not Hispanic (40,164)	41,788	67.15
Hispanic (2,781)	3,278	5.27

*Notes: † The Census 2010 population figure is used to calculate the percentages in the Hispanic Origin and Race categories. Ancestry percentages are based on the 2006-2010 American Community Survey population (not shown); ‡ Numbers in parentheses indicate the number of people reporting a single ancestry; * Numbers in parentheses indicate the number of persons reporting this race alone, not in combination with any other race; Please refer to the Explanation of Data for more information.*

White Plains

Place Type: City
County: Westchester
Population: 56,853

Ancestry	Population	%
Afghan (0)	0	<0.01
African, Sub-Saharan (230)	331	0.59
African (97)	97	0.17
Cape Verdean (0)	0	<0.01
Ethiopian (0)	0	<0.01
Ghanaian (0)	0	<0.01
Kenyan (0)	0	<0.01
Liberian (0)	0	<0.01
Nigerian (66)	97	0.17
Senegalese (0)	0	<0.01
Sierra Leonean (0)	0	<0.01
Somalian (0)	0	<0.01
South African (43)	78	0.14
Sudanese (0)	0	<0.01
Ugandan (9)	9	0.02
Zimbabwean (0)	0	<0.01
Other Sub-Saharan African (15)	50	0.09
Albanian (58)	73	0.13
Alsatian (0)	0	<0.01
American (2,743)	2,743	4.91
Arab (162)	307	0.55
Arab (10)	64	0.11
Egyptian (44)	44	0.08
Iraqi (0)	0	<0.01
Jordanian (21)	21	0.04
Lebanese (46)	56	0.10
Moroccan (24)	71	0.13
Palestinian (7)	7	0.01
Syrian (0)	7	0.01
Other Arab (10)	37	0.07
Armenian (44)	60	0.11
Assyrian/Chaldean/Syriac (0)	8	0.01
Australian (0)	0	<0.01
Austrian (201)	572	1.02
Basque (0)	0	<0.01
Belgian (47)	94	0.17
Brazilian (409)	440	0.79
British (34)	126	0.23
Bulgarian (40)	62	0.11
Cajun (0)	0	<0.01
Canadian (69)	128	0.23
Carpatho Rusyn (0)	0	<0.01
Celtic (0)	0	<0.01
Croatian (61)	61	0.11
Cypriot (0)	0	<0.01
Czech (41)	115	0.21
Czechoslovakian (0)	20	0.04
Danish (9)	48	0.09
Dutch (64)	313	0.56
Eastern European (542)	557	1.00
English (489)	1,818	3.25
Estonian (0)	0	<0.01
European (593)	684	1.22
Finnish (15)	25	0.04
French, ex. Basque (101)	696	1.25
French Canadian (30)	155	0.28
German (754)	3,324	5.95
German Russian (0)	0	<0.01
Greek (102)	279	0.50
Guyanese (130)	175	0.31
Hungarian (148)	401	0.72
Icelander (0)	0	<0.01
Iranian (28)	48	0.09
Irish (2,251)	5,662	10.13
Israeli (153)	181	0.32
Italian (5,382)	9,116	16.31
Latvian (7)	7	0.01
Lithuanian (94)	226	0.40
Luxemburger (0)	0	<0.01
Macedonian (14)	54	0.10
Maltese (0)	0	<0.01
New Zealander (29)	29	0.05
Northern European (31)	54	0.10
Norwegian (42)	134	0.24
Pennsylvania German (0)	0	<0.01
Polish (765)	2,000	3.58
Portuguese (198)	325	0.58
Romanian (61)	183	0.33
Russian (1,095)	2,307	4.13
Scandinavian (0)	0	<0.01
Scotch-Irish (100)	241	0.43
Scottish (116)	435	0.78
Serbian (16)	16	0.03
Slavic (0)	0	<0.01
Slovak (18)	85	0.15
Slovene (0)	0	<0.01
Soviet Union (0)	0	<0.01
Swedish (30)	282	0.50
Swiss (46)	129	0.23
Turkish (96)	120	0.21
Ukrainian (228)	290	0.52
Welsh (6)	89	0.16
West Indian, ex. Hispanic (1,351)	1,555	2.78
Bahamian (26)	26	0.05
Barbadian (25)	25	0.04
Belizean (125)	155	0.28
Bermudan (0)	0	<0.01
British West Indian (34)	57	0.10
Dutch West Indian (0)	0	<0.01
Haitian (386)	397	0.71
Jamaican (596)	702	1.26
Trinidadian/Tobagonian (49)	49	0.09
U.S. Virgin Islander (23)	23	0.04
West Indian (87)	121	0.22
Other West Indian (0)	0	<0.01
Yugoslavian (24)	24	0.04

Hispanic Origin	Population	%
Hispanic or Latino (of any race)	16,839	29.62
Central American, ex. Mexican	968	1.70
Costa Rican	35	0.06
Guatemalan	551	0.97
Honduran	75	0.13
Nicaraguan	35	0.06
Panamanian	56	0.10
Salvadoran	204	0.36
Other Central American	12	0.02
Cuban	321	0.56
Dominican Republic	1,177	2.07
Mexican	5,773	10.15
Puerto Rican	1,541	2.71
South American	5,850	10.29
Argentinean	189	0.33
Bolivian	72	0.13
Chilean	67	0.12
Colombian	1,838	3.23
Ecuadorian	1,001	1.76
Paraguayan	260	0.46
Peruvian	2,260	3.98
Uruguayan	63	0.11
Venezuelan	77	0.14
Other South American	23	0.04
Other Hispanic or Latino	1,209	2.13

Race*	Population	%
African-American/Black (8,070)	8,768	15.42
Not Hispanic (7,502)	7,918	13.93
Hispanic (568)	850	1.50
American Indian/Alaska Native (394)	890	1.57
Not Hispanic (47)	193	0.34
Hispanic (347)	697	1.23
Alaska Athabascan (Ala. Nat.) (0)	0	<0.01
Aleut (Alaska Native) (0)	0	<0.01
Apache (0)	6	0.01
Arapaho (0)	0	<0.01
Blackfeet (3)	16	0.03
Canadian/French Am. Ind. (0)	0	<0.01
Central American Ind. (1)	6	0.01
Cherokee (2)	36	0.06
Cheyenne (0)	0	<0.01
Chickasaw (0)	0	<0.01
Chippewa (4)	4	0.01
Choctaw (0)	0	<0.01
Colville (0)	0	<0.01
Comanche (0)	0	<0.01
Cree (0)	0	<0.01
Creek (2)	3	0.01
Crow (0)	1	<0.01
Delaware (0)	1	<0.01
Hopi (0)	1	<0.01
Houma (3)	3	0.01
Inupiat (Alaska Native) (0)	0	<0.01
Iroquois (1)	12	0.02
Kiowa (0)	0	<0.01
Lumbee (1)	1	<0.01
Menominee (0)	0	<0.01
Mexican American Ind. (95)	162	0.28
Navajo (0)	1	<0.01
Osage (1)	2	<0.01
Ottawa (0)	0	<0.01
Paiute (0)	0	<0.01
Pima (0)	0	<0.01
Potawatomi (0)	0	<0.01
Pueblo (13)	19	0.03
Puget Sound Salish (0)	0	<0.01
Seminole (0)	1	<0.01
Shoshone (0)	1	<0.01
Sioux (0)	7	0.01
South American Ind. (42)	116	0.20
Spanish American Ind. (12)	15	0.03
Tlingit-Haida (Alaska Native) (0)	0	<0.01
Tohono O'Odham (0)	0	<0.01
Tsimshian (Alaska Native) (0)	0	<0.01
Ute (0)	0	<0.01
Yakama (0)	0	<0.01
Yaqui (0)	1	<0.01
Yuman (0)	0	<0.01
Yup'ik (Alaska Native) (0)	0	<0.01
Asian (3,623)	4,080	7.18
Not Hispanic (3,587)	3,959	6.96
Hispanic (36)	121	0.21
Bangladeshi (35)	37	0.07
Bhutanese (0)	0	<0.01
Burmese (9)	9	0.02
Cambodian (13)	13	0.02
Chinese, ex. Taiwanese (813)	934	1.64
Filipino (373)	451	0.79
Hmong (0)	0	<0.01
Indian (1,281)	1,397	2.46
Indonesian (6)	10	0.02
Japanese (372)	441	0.78
Korean (384)	431	0.76
Laotian (1)	3	0.01
Malaysian (8)	11	0.02
Nepalese (7)	7	0.01
Pakistani (70)	79	0.14
Sri Lankan (10)	17	0.03
Taiwanese (35)	44	0.08
Thai (31)	42	0.07
Vietnamese (73)	82	0.14
Hawaii Native/Pacific Islander (20)	180	0.32
Not Hispanic (14)	71	0.12
Hispanic (6)	109	0.19
Fijian (6)	6	0.01
Guamanian/Chamorro (2)	7	0.01
Marshallese (0)	0	<0.01
Native Hawaiian (4)	7	0.01
Samoan (0)	0	<0.01
Tongan (0)	0	<0.01
White (36,178)	37,846	66.57
Not Hispanic (27,805)	28,446	50.03
Hispanic (8,373)	9,400	16.53

Notes: † The Census 2010 population figure is used to calculate the percentages in the Hispanic Origin and Race categories. Ancestry percentages are based on the 2006-2010 American Community Survey population (not shown); ‡ Numbers in parentheses indicate the number of people reporting a single ancestry; * Numbers in parentheses indicate the number of persons reporting this race alone, not in combination with any other race; Please refer to the Explanation of Data for more information.

Yonkers

Place Type: City
County: Westchester
Population: 195,976

Ancestry	Population	%
Afghan (0)	0	<0.01
African, Sub-Saharan (2,404)	2,939	1.51
African (1,162)	1,496	0.77
Cape Verdean (41)	41	0.02
Ethiopian (159)	159	0.08
Ghanaian (489)	585	0.30
Kenyan (73)	107	0.05
Liberian (7)	7	<0.01
Nigerian (371)	442	0.23
Senegalese (21)	21	0.01
Sierra Leonean (0)	0	<0.01
Somalian (6)	6	<0.01
South African (59)	59	0.03
Sudanese (0)	0	<0.01
Ugandan (0)	0	<0.01
Zimbabwean (0)	0	<0.01
Other Sub-Saharan African (16)	16	0.01
Albanian (2,122)	2,270	1.16
Alsatian (0)	0	<0.01
American (5,127)	5,127	2.63
Arab (2,696)	3,210	1.65
Arab (899)	1,036	0.53
Egyptian (243)	243	0.12
Iraqi (103)	103	0.05
Jordanian (855)	907	0.47
Lebanese (44)	327	0.17
Moroccan (103)	110	0.06
Palestinian (139)	139	0.07
Syrian (13)	33	0.02
Other Arab (297)	312	0.16
Armenian (338)	411	0.21
Assyrian/Chaldean/Syriac (135)	157	0.08
Australian (0)	17	0.01
Austrian (121)	618	0.32
Basque (0)	0	<0.01
Belgian (0)	12	0.01
Brazilian (334)	422	0.22
British (168)	297	0.15
Bulgarian (10)	10	0.01
Cajun (0)	0	<0.01
Canadian (111)	182	0.09
Carpatho Rusyn (40)	40	0.02
Celtic (11)	15	0.01
Croatian (65)	121	0.06
Cypriot (0)	0	<0.01
Czech (152)	478	0.25
Czechoslovakian (185)	354	0.18
Danish (0)	62	0.03
Dutch (50)	468	0.24
Eastern European (441)	458	0.24
English (1,054)	3,968	2.04
Estonian (0)	53	0.03
European (325)	391	0.20
Finnish (50)	84	0.04
French, ex. Basque (245)	1,367	0.70
French Canadian (53)	284	0.15
German (1,666)	8,502	4.36
German Russian (14)	14	0.01
Greek (949)	1,272	0.65
Guyanese (410)	526	0.27
Hungarian (410)	920	0.47
Icelander (0)	0	<0.01
Iranian (137)	173	0.09
Irish (10,811)	22,187	11.38
Israeli (38)	77	0.04
Italian (21,697)	32,142	16.49
Latvian (33)	71	0.04
Lithuanian (111)	327	0.17
Luxemburger (0)	13	0.01
Macedonian (236)	236	0.12
Maltese (73)	73	0.04
New Zealander (8)	8	<0.01
Northern European (13)	13	0.01
Norwegian (79)	370	0.19
Pennsylvania German (0)	0	<0.01
Polish (2,602)	5,453	2.80
Portuguese (1,947)	2,670	1.37
Romanian (170)	278	0.14
Russian (1,453)	2,804	1.44
Scandinavian (10)	21	0.01
Scotch-Irish (274)	562	0.29
Scottish (293)	1,047	0.54
Serbian (0)	11	0.01
Slavic (185)	237	0.12
Slovak (274)	590	0.30
Slovene (10)	10	0.01
Soviet Union (14)	14	0.01
Swedish (115)	574	0.29
Swiss (12)	83	0.04
Turkish (112)	112	0.06
Ukrainian (943)	1,494	0.77
Welsh (20)	140	0.07
West Indian, ex. Hispanic (7,179)	8,578	4.40
Bahamian (0)	0	<0.01
Barbadian (47)	157	0.08
Belizean (0)	0	<0.01
Bermudan (0)	0	<0.01
British West Indian (313)	497	0.26
Dutch West Indian (3)	3	<0.01
Haitian (897)	1,026	0.53
Jamaican (4,479)	5,051	2.59
Trinidadian/Tobagonian (650)	689	0.35
U.S. Virgin Islander (32)	83	0.04
West Indian (758)	1,072	0.55
Other West Indian (0)	0	<0.01
Yugoslavian (38)	46	0.02

Hispanic Origin	Population	%
Hispanic or Latino (of any race)	67,927	34.66
Central American, ex. Mexican	5,822	2.97
Costa Rican	156	0.08
Guatemalan	765	0.39
Honduran	1,451	0.74
Nicaraguan	534	0.27
Panamanian	185	0.09
Salvadoran	2,691	1.37
Other Central American	40	0.02
Cuban	1,501	0.77
Dominican Republic	15,903	8.11
Mexican	13,761	7.02
Puerto Rican	19,875	10.14
South American	6,622	3.38
Argentinean	273	0.14
Bolivian	30	0.02
Chilean	215	0.11
Colombian	1,493	0.76
Ecuadorian	3,271	1.67
Paraguayan	79	0.04
Peruvian	946	0.48
Uruguayan	45	0.02
Venezuelan	207	0.11
Other South American	63	0.03
Other Hispanic or Latino	4,443	2.27

Race*	Population	%
African-American/Black (36,572)	40,198	20.51
Not Hispanic (31,297)	32,873	16.77
Hispanic (5,275)	7,325	3.74
American Indian/Alaska Native (1,463)	2,801	1.43
Not Hispanic (382)	995	0.51
Hispanic (1,081)	1,806	0.92
Alaska Athabascan (Ala. Nat.) (1)	1	<0.01
Aleut (Alaska Native) (0)	0	<0.01
Apache (3)	10	0.01
Arapaho (0)	0	<0.01
Blackfeet (17)	58	0.03
Canadian/French Am. Ind. (3)	4	<0.01
Central American Ind. (46)	103	0.05
Cherokee (28)	151	0.08
Cheyenne (1)	3	<0.01
Chickasaw (0)	1	<0.01
Chippewa (6)	8	<0.01
Choctaw (1)	12	0.01
Colville (0)	1	<0.01
Comanche (0)	0	<0.01
Cree (0)	0	<0.01
Creek (1)	3	<0.01
Crow (1)	2	<0.01
Delaware (2)	6	<0.01
Hopi (1)	5	<0.01
Houma (1)	1	<0.01
Inupiat (Alaska Native) (3)	5	<0.01
Iroquois (16)	41	0.02
Kiowa (0)	0	<0.01
Lumbee (1)	2	<0.01
Menominee (0)	0	<0.01
Mexican American Ind. (99)	171	0.09
Navajo (7)	7	<0.01
Osage (1)	1	<0.01
Ottawa (0)	0	<0.01
Paiute (0)	0	<0.01
Pima (0)	0	<0.01
Potawatomi (0)	0	<0.01
Pueblo (8)	20	0.01
Puget Sound Salish (0)	0	<0.01
Seminole (1)	11	0.01
Shoshone (0)	0	<0.01
Sioux (5)	13	0.01
South American Ind. (95)	270	0.14
Spanish American Ind. (104)	132	0.07
Tlingit-Haida (Alaska Native) (0)	1	<0.01
Tohono O'Odham (0)	3	<0.01
Tsimshian (Alaska Native) (0)	0	<0.01
Ute (0)	0	<0.01
Yakama (0)	0	<0.01
Yaqui (0)	0	<0.01
Yuman (2)	2	<0.01
Yup'ik (Alaska Native) (0)	0	<0.01
Asian (11,556)	13,253	6.76
Not Hispanic (11,370)	12,736	6.50
Hispanic (186)	517	0.26
Bangladeshi (148)	167	0.09
Bhutanese (1)	1	<0.01
Burmese (11)	11	0.01
Cambodian (26)	36	0.02
Chinese, ex. Taiwanese (872)	1,149	0.59
Filipino (2,584)	2,819	1.44
Hmong (0)	0	<0.01
Indian (5,313)	5,818	2.97
Indonesian (20)	28	0.01
Japanese (155)	251	0.13
Korean (906)	977	0.50
Laotian (16)	18	0.01
Malaysian (3)	7	<0.01
Nepalese (8)	9	<0.01
Pakistani (783)	874	0.45
Sri Lankan (36)	39	0.02
Taiwanese (41)	49	0.03
Thai (248)	268	0.14
Vietnamese (79)	95	0.05
Hawaii Native/Pacific Islander (122)	483	0.25
Not Hispanic (58)	211	0.11
Hispanic (64)	272	0.14
Fijian (5)	6	<0.01
Guamanian/Chamorro (27)	52	0.03
Marshallese (0)	0	<0.01
Native Hawaiian (35)	57	0.03
Samoan (4)	8	<0.01
Tongan (0)	0	<0.01
White (109,351)	114,948	58.65
Not Hispanic (81,163)	83,170	42.44
Hispanic (28,188)	31,778	16.22

Notes: † The Census 2010 population figure is used to calculate the percentages in the Hispanic Origin and Race categories. Ancestry percentages are based on the 2006-2010 American Community Survey population (not shown); ‡ Numbers in parentheses indicate the number of people reporting a single ancestry; * Numbers in parentheses indicate the number of persons reporting this race alone, not in combination with any other race; Please refer to the Explanation of Data for more information.

Ancestry Group Rankings

Afghan

Top 10 Places Sorted by Population
Based on all places, regardless of total population

Place	Population	%
New York (city)	6,470	0.08
Queens (borough) Queens County	6,027	0.27
Oyster Bay (town) Nassau County	808	0.28
Hempstead (town) Nassau County	399	0.05
Brooklyn (borough) Kings County	344	0.01
Hicksville (cdp) Nassau County	323	0.77
Schenectady (city) Schenectady County	318	0.49
Huntington (town) Suffolk County	314	0.16
Huntington Station (cdp) Suffolk County	268	0.85
Islip (town) Suffolk County	263	0.08

Top 10 Places Sorted by Percent of Total Population
Based on all places, regardless of total population

Place	Population	%
DeRuyter (town) Madison County	27	2.14
Pomona (village) Rockland County	61	1.73
Malverne (village) Nassau County	139	1.63
Viola (cdp) Rockland County	111	1.57
Huntington Bay (village) Suffolk County	21	1.47
Woodbury (cdp) Nassau County	125	1.38
Wyandanch (cdp) Suffolk County	123	1.13
Jericho (cdp) Nassau County	129	0.99
New Hyde Park (village) Nassau County	89	0.93
Upper Brookville (village) Nassau County	13	0.87

Top 10 Places Sorted by Percent of Total Population
Based on places with total population of 50,000 or more

Place	Population	%
Schenectady (city) Schenectady County	318	0.49
Oyster Bay (town) Nassau County	808	0.28
Irondequoit (cdp/town) Monroe County	145	0.28
Queens (borough) Queens County	6,027	0.27
Tonawanda (cdp) Erie County	108	0.18
Huntington (town) Suffolk County	314	0.16
Tonawanda (town) Erie County	108	0.15
Amherst (town) Erie County	144	0.12
Brentwood (cdp) Suffolk County	68	0.12
Babylon (town) Suffolk County	219	0.10

African, Sub-Saharan

Top 10 Places Sorted by Population
Based on all places, regardless of total population

Place	Population	%
New York (city)	175,478	2.17
Brooklyn (borough) Kings County	63,004	2.55
Bronx (borough) Bronx County	55,928	4.10
Queens (borough) Queens County	25,166	1.14
Manhattan (borough) New York County	24,146	1.52
Rochester (city) Monroe County	7,909	3.73
Staten Island (borough) Richmond County	7,234	1.56
Buffalo (city) Erie County	6,085	2.29
Hempstead (town) Nassau County	5,844	0.78
Yonkers (city) Westchester County	2,939	1.51

Top 10 Places Sorted by Percent of Total Population
Based on all places, regardless of total population

Place	Population	%
Linwood (cdp) Livingston County	64	48.85
Wheatley Heights (cdp) Suffolk County	896	14.46
North Bellport (cdp) Suffolk County	737	6.54
Gordon Heights (cdp) Suffolk County	199	6.10
Hobart (village) Delaware County	29	5.99
Pomona (village) Rockland County	207	5.86
South Blooming Grove (village) Orange County	192	5.83
Aurora (village) Cayuga County	64	5.72
Deferiet (village) Jefferson County	26	5.53
West End (cdp) Otsego County	86	5.50

Top 10 Places Sorted by Percent of Total Population
Based on places with total population of 50,000 or more

Place	Population	%
Bronx (borough) Bronx County	55,928	4.10
Rochester (city) Monroe County	7,909	3.73
Mount Vernon (city) Westchester County	1,910	2.85
Brooklyn (borough) Kings County	63,004	2.55
Hempstead (village) Nassau County	1,285	2.41
Buffalo (city) Erie County	6,085	2.29
New York (city)	175,478	2.17
Syracuse (city) Onondaga County	2,470	1.71
Albany (city) Albany County	1,533	1.57
Staten Island (borough) Richmond County	7,234	1.56

African, Sub-Saharan: African

Top 10 Places Sorted by Population
Based on all places, regardless of total population

Place	Population	%
New York (city)	101,901	1.26
Brooklyn (borough) Kings County	48,168	1.95
Bronx (borough) Bronx County	22,647	1.66
Queens (borough) Queens County	14,083	0.64
Manhattan (borough) New York County	12,839	0.81
Rochester (city) Monroe County	5,828	2.75
Buffalo (city) Erie County	4,177	1.57
Staten Island (borough) Richmond County	4,164	0.90
Hempstead (town) Nassau County	3,879	0.51
Brookhaven (town) Suffolk County	2,533	0.53

Top 10 Places Sorted by Percent of Total Population
Based on all places, regardless of total population

Place	Population	%
North Bellport (cdp) Suffolk County	728	6.46
Gordon Heights (cdp) Suffolk County	199	6.10
Hobart (village) Delaware County	29	5.99
Wheatley Heights (cdp) Suffolk County	368	5.94
Aurora (village) Cayuga County	64	5.72
Great River (cdp) Suffolk County	80	4.86
St. Regis Mohawk Reservation Franklin County	134	4.28
South Blooming Grove (village) Orange County	135	4.10
Deferiet (village) Jefferson County	19	4.04
Groveland (town) Livingston County	132	3.90

Top 10 Places Sorted by Percent of Total Population
Based on places with total population of 50,000 or more

Place	Population	%
Rochester (city) Monroe County	5,828	2.75
Brooklyn (borough) Kings County	48,168	1.95
Mount Vernon (city) Westchester County	1,162	1.73
Bronx (borough) Bronx County	22,647	1.66
Hempstead (village) Nassau County	850	1.59
Buffalo (city) Erie County	4,177	1.57
New York (city)	101,901	1.26
Albany (city) Albany County	975	1.00
Niagara Falls (city) Niagara County	488	0.96
Troy (city) Rensselaer County	476	0.95

African, Sub-Saharan: Cape Verdean

Top 10 Places Sorted by Population
Based on all places, regardless of total population

Place	Population	%
New York (city)	595	0.01
Manhattan (borough) New York County	206	0.01
Brooklyn (borough) Kings County	153	0.01
Queens (borough) Queens County	117	0.01
Bronx (borough) Bronx County	108	0.01
Buffalo (city) Erie County	95	0.04
Yonkers (city) Westchester County	41	0.02
North Elba (town) Essex County	17	0.19
Albany (city) Albany County	13	0.01
Plainview (cdp) Nassau County	12	0.05

Top 10 Places Sorted by Percent of Total Population
Based on all places, regardless of total population

Place	Population	%
Liverpool (village) Onondaga County	9	0.38
North Elba (town) Essex County	17	0.19
New Baltimore (town) Greene County	5	0.15
Endwell (cdp) Broome County	11	0.09
Plainview (cdp) Nassau County	12	0.05
Buffalo (city) Erie County	95	0.04
Copiague (cdp) Suffolk County	9	0.04
Jay (town) Essex County	1	0.04
Salina (town) Onondaga County	9	0.03
Yonkers (city) Westchester County	41	0.02

Top 10 Places Sorted by Percent of Total Population
Based on places with total population of 50,000 or more

Place	Population	%
Buffalo (city) Erie County	95	0.04
Yonkers (city) Westchester County	41	0.02
Mount Vernon (city) Westchester County	11	0.02
Troy (city) Rensselaer County	11	0.02
Union (town) Broome County	11	0.02
New York (city)	595	0.01
Manhattan (borough) New York County	206	0.01
Brooklyn (borough) Kings County	153	0.01
Queens (borough) Queens County	117	0.01
Bronx (borough) Bronx County	108	0.01

African, Sub-Saharan: Ethiopian

Top 10 Places Sorted by Population
Based on all places, regardless of total population

Place	Population	%
New York (city)	2,869	0.04
Manhattan (borough) New York County	1,043	0.07
Bronx (borough) Bronx County	945	0.07
Queens (borough) Queens County	505	0.02
Brooklyn (borough) Kings County	330	0.01
Rochester (city) Monroe County	227	0.11
Buffalo (city) Erie County	223	0.08
Irondequoit (cdp/town) Monroe County	192	0.37
Henrietta (town) Monroe County	177	0.42
Yonkers (city) Westchester County	159	0.08

Top 10 Places Sorted by Percent of Total Population
Based on all places, regardless of total population

Place	Population	%
Lloyd Harbor (village) Suffolk County	110	3.00
Jasper (town) Steuben County	23	1.84
Sparta (town) Livingston County	27	1.62
Deferiet (village) Jefferson County	7	1.49
North Salem (town) Westchester County	75	1.47
Manhasset Hills (cdp) Nassau County	38	1.03
Pomona (village) Rockland County	31	0.88
Elmsford (village) Westchester County	39	0.84
Bedford (town) Westchester County	117	0.67
Athens (village) Greene County	8	0.48

Top 10 Places Sorted by Percent of Total Population
Based on places with total population of 50,000 or more

Place	Population	%
Irondequoit (cdp/town) Monroe County	192	0.37
Rochester (city) Monroe County	227	0.11
Buffalo (city) Erie County	223	0.08
Yonkers (city) Westchester County	159	0.08
Manhattan (borough) New York County	1,043	0.07
Bronx (borough) Bronx County	945	0.07
Huntington (town) Suffolk County	125	0.06
Amherst (town) Erie County	71	0.06
Greece (town) Monroe County	49	0.05
Niagara Falls (city) Niagara County	24	0.05

African, Sub-Saharan: Ghanaian

Top 10 Places Sorted by Population
Based on all places, regardless of total population

Place	Population	%
New York (city)	19,782	0.24
Bronx (borough) Bronx County	13,490	0.99
Brooklyn (borough) Kings County	3,898	0.16
Queens (borough) Queens County	1,326	0.06
Manhattan (borough) New York County	818	0.05
Yonkers (city) Westchester County	585	0.30
Mount Vernon (city) Westchester County	347	0.52
Hempstead (town) Nassau County	306	0.04
Staten Island (borough) Richmond County	250	0.05
Lakeview (cdp) Nassau County	169	3.03

Top 10 Places Sorted by Percent of Total Population
Based on all places, regardless of total population

Place	Population	%
Lakeview (cdp) Nassau County	169	3.03
South Blooming Grove (village) Orange County	57	1.73
Coxsackie (village) Greene County	44	1.54
Katonah (cdp) Westchester County	20	1.36
West Haverstraw (village) Rockland County	108	1.07
Wheatley Heights (cdp) Suffolk County	64	1.03
Bronx (borough) Bronx County	13,490	0.99
Hillcrest (cdp) Rockland County	77	0.94
Flower Hill (village) Nassau County	39	0.85
SUNY Oswego (cdp) Oswego County	30	0.67

Top 10 Places Sorted by Percent of Total Population
Based on places with total population of 50,000 or more

Place	Population	%
Bronx (borough) Bronx County	13,490	0.99
Mount Vernon (city) Westchester County	347	0.52
Yonkers (city) Westchester County	585	0.30
New York (city)	19,782	0.24
Troy (city) Rensselaer County	91	0.18
Brooklyn (borough) Kings County	3,898	0.16
Albany (city) Albany County	143	0.15
Clarkstown (town) Rockland County	99	0.12
Clay (town) Onondaga County	65	0.11
Syracuse (city) Onondaga County	113	0.08

African, Sub-Saharan: Kenyan

Top 10 Places Sorted by Population
Based on all places, regardless of total population

Place	Population	%
New York (city)	344	<0.01
Yonkers (city) Westchester County	107	0.05
Albany (city) Albany County	101	0.10
Queens (borough) Queens County	96	<0.01
Tonawanda (cdp) Erie County	86	0.15
Tonawanda (town) Erie County	86	0.12
West End (cdp) Otsego County	81	5.18
Oneonta (town) Otsego County	81	1.56
Staten Island (borough) Richmond County	78	0.02
Brooklyn (borough) Kings County	77	<0.01

Top 10 Places Sorted by Percent of Total Population
Based on all places, regardless of total population

Place	Population	%
West End (cdp) Otsego County	81	5.18
Oneonta (town) Otsego County	81	1.56
Houghton (cdp) Allegany County	22	1.29
Piermont (village) Rockland County	32	1.27
Caneadea (town) Allegany County	22	0.86
Mount Ivy (cdp) Rockland County	50	0.76
Horseheads (village) Chemung County	39	0.61
Youngstown (village) Niagara County	8	0.42
Hamilton (village) Madison County	10	0.28
Ossining (village) Westchester County	66	0.27

Top 10 Places Sorted by Percent of Total Population
Based on places with total population of 50,000 or more

Place	Population	%
Tonawanda (cdp) Erie County	86	0.15
Tonawanda (town) Erie County	86	0.12
Schenectady (city) Schenectady County	69	0.11
Albany (city) Albany County	101	0.10

Greenburgh (town) Westchester County	55	0.06
Yonkers (city) Westchester County	107	0.05
New Rochelle (city) Westchester County	19	0.03
Staten Island (borough) Richmond County	78	0.02
Utica (city) Oneida County	15	0.02
Buffalo (city) Erie County	38	0.01

African, Sub-Saharan: Liberian

Top 10 Places Sorted by Population
Based on all places, regardless of total population

Place	Population	%
New York (city)	1,991	0.02
Staten Island (borough) Richmond County	532	0.11
Brooklyn (borough) Kings County	452	0.02
Bronx (borough) Bronx County	450	0.03
Queens (borough) Queens County	381	0.02
Babylon (town) Suffolk County	309	0.14
Wheatley Heights (cdp) Suffolk County	251	4.05
Syracuse (city) Onondaga County	246	0.17
Manhattan (borough) New York County	176	0.01
Rochester (city) Monroe County	89	0.04

Top 10 Places Sorted by Percent of Total Population
Based on all places, regardless of total population

Place	Population	%
Wheatley Heights (cdp) Suffolk County	251	4.05
Copake (town) Columbia County	16	0.45
Wyandanch (cdp) Suffolk County	33	0.30
Smithville (town) Chenango County	4	0.29
Saddle Rock (village) Nassau County	3	0.29
Danby (town) Tompkins County	9	0.28
Port Jervis (city) Orange County	22	0.25
Syracuse (city) Onondaga County	246	0.17
Babylon (town) Suffolk County	309	0.14
Utica (city) Oneida County	88	0.14

Top 10 Places Sorted by Percent of Total Population
Based on places with total population of 50,000 or more

Place	Population	%
Syracuse (city) Onondaga County	246	0.17
Babylon (town) Suffolk County	309	0.14
Utica (city) Oneida County	88	0.14
Staten Island (borough) Richmond County	532	0.11
Rochester (city) Monroe County	89	0.04
Schenectady (city) Schenectady County	24	0.04
Bronx (borough) Bronx County	450	0.03
Buffalo (city) Erie County	74	0.03
New York (city)	1,991	0.02
Brooklyn (borough) Kings County	452	0.02

African, Sub-Saharan: Nigerian

Top 10 Places Sorted by Population
Based on all places, regardless of total population

Place	Population	%
New York (city)	21,507	0.27
Queens (borough) Queens County	6,304	0.29
Brooklyn (borough) Kings County	6,033	0.24
Bronx (borough) Bronx County	5,538	0.41
Manhattan (borough) New York County	1,953	0.12
Staten Island (borough) Richmond County	1,679	0.36
Hempstead (town) Nassau County	1,115	0.15
Babylon (town) Suffolk County	707	0.33
Yonkers (city) Westchester County	442	0.23
Hempstead (village) Nassau County	427	0.80

Top 10 Places Sorted by Percent of Total Population
Based on all places, regardless of total population

Place	Population	%
Wesley Hills (village) Rockland County	180	3.30
Wheatley Heights (cdp) Suffolk County	167	2.70
Deerpark (town) Orange County	196	2.47
Myers Corner (cdp) Dutchess County	134	2.10
Chester (village) Orange County	66	1.67
Wyandanch (cdp) Suffolk County	172	1.57
North Valley Stream (cdp) Nassau County	212	1.28
Orchard Park (village) Erie County	41	1.26
Rock Hill (cdp) Sullivan County	20	1.21
New Lebanon (town) Columbia County	29	1.17

Top 10 Places Sorted by Percent of Total Population
Based on places with total population of 50,000 or more

Place	Population	%
Hempstead (village) Nassau County	427	0.80
Bronx (borough) Bronx County	5,538	0.41
Staten Island (borough) Richmond County	1,679	0.36
Babylon (town) Suffolk County	707	0.33
Queens (borough) Queens County	6,304	0.29
Schenectady (city) Schenectady County	186	0.28
New York (city)	21,507	0.27
Greenburgh (town) Westchester County	231	0.26
Brooklyn (borough) Kings County	6,033	0.24
Yonkers (city) Westchester County	442	0.23

African, Sub-Saharan: Senegalese

Top 10 Places Sorted by Population
Based on all places, regardless of total population

Place	Population	%
New York (city)	2,895	0.04
Manhattan (borough) New York County	1,216	0.08
Bronx (borough) Bronx County	1,068	0.08
Brooklyn (borough) Kings County	401	0.02
Staten Island (borough) Richmond County	126	0.03
Queens (borough) Queens County	84	<0.01
Mahopac (cdp) Putnam County	64	0.84
Carmel (town) Putnam County	64	0.19
Haverstraw (village) Rockland County	52	0.45
Haverstraw (town) Rockland County	52	0.14

Top 10 Places Sorted by Percent of Total Population
Based on all places, regardless of total population

Place	Population	%
Cattaraugus Reservation Erie County	18	0.96
Mahopac (cdp) Putnam County	64	0.84
Clayton (village) Jefferson County	17	0.83
Haverstraw (village) Rockland County	52	0.45
Sackets Harbor (village) Jefferson County	6	0.44
SUNY Oswego (cdp) Oswego County	19	0.43
Crown Heights (cdp) Dutchess County	12	0.42
Clayton (town) Jefferson County	17	0.34
Oswego (town) Oswego County	19	0.24
Carmel (town) Putnam County	64	0.19

Top 10 Places Sorted by Percent of Total Population
Based on places with total population of 50,000 or more

Place	Population	%
Manhattan (borough) New York County	1,216	0.08
Bronx (borough) Bronx County	1,068	0.08
New York (city)	2,895	0.04
Staten Island (borough) Richmond County	126	0.03
Brooklyn (borough) Kings County	401	0.02
Mount Vernon (city) Westchester County	12	0.02
Yonkers (city) Westchester County	21	0.01
Queens (borough) Queens County	84	<0.01
Albany (city) Albany County	0	0.00
Amherst (town) Erie County	0	0.00

African, Sub-Saharan: Sierra Leonean

Top 10 Places Sorted by Population
Based on all places, regardless of total population

Place	Population	%
New York (city)	1,572	0.02
Bronx (borough) Bronx County	759	0.06
Manhattan (borough) New York County	422	0.03
Brooklyn (borough) Kings County	147	0.01
Queens (borough) Queens County	127	0.01
Staten Island (borough) Richmond County	117	0.03
Dryden (town) Tompkins County	22	0.15
Mount Vernon (city) Westchester County	22	0.03
Buffalo (city) Erie County	17	0.01
New Rochelle (city) Westchester County	15	0.02

Top 10 Places Sorted by Percent of Total Population
Based on all places, regardless of total population

Place	Population	%
Hamilton (village) Madison County	12	0.34
Hamilton (town) Madison County	12	0.18
Manhasset (cdp) Nassau County	13	0.16

Place	Population	%
Dryden (town) Tompkins County	22	0.15
Bronx (borough) Bronx County	759	0.06
Baldwin (cdp) Nassau County	11	0.05
Manhattan (borough) New York County	422	0.03
Staten Island (borough) Richmond County	117	0.03
Mount Vernon (city) Westchester County	22	0.03
New York (city)	1,572	0.02

Top 10 Places Sorted by Percent of Total Population
Based on places with total population of 50,000 or more

Place	Population	%
Bronx (borough) Bronx County	759	0.06
Manhattan (borough) New York County	422	0.03
Staten Island (borough) Richmond County	117	0.03
Mount Vernon (city) Westchester County	22	0.03
New York (city)	1,572	0.02
New Rochelle (city) Westchester County	15	0.02
Greenburgh (town) Westchester County	14	0.02
Brooklyn (borough) Kings County	147	0.01
Queens (borough) Queens County	127	0.01
Buffalo (city) Erie County	17	0.01

African, Sub-Saharan: Somalian

Top 10 Places Sorted by Population
Based on all places, regardless of total population

Place	Population	%
Rochester (city) Monroe County	980	0.46
Buffalo (city) Erie County	858	0.32
New York (city)	518	0.01
Syracuse (city) Onondaga County	478	0.33
Brooklyn (borough) Kings County	260	0.01
Manhattan (borough) New York County	125	0.01
Utica (city) Oneida County	99	0.16
Queens (borough) Queens County	98	<0.01
Perinton (town) Monroe County	38	0.08
Newburgh (city) Orange County	35	0.12

Top 10 Places Sorted by Percent of Total Population
Based on all places, regardless of total population

Place	Population	%
Rochester (city) Monroe County	980	0.46
Syracuse (city) Onondaga County	478	0.33
Buffalo (city) Erie County	858	0.32
Port Jervis (city) Orange County	26	0.29
Utica (city) Oneida County	99	0.16
Newburgh (city) Orange County	35	0.12
Perinton (town) Monroe County	38	0.08
Uniondale (cdp) Nassau County	15	0.06
New York (city)	518	0.01
Brooklyn (borough) Kings County	260	0.01

Top 10 Places Sorted by Percent of Total Population
Based on places with total population of 50,000 or more

Place	Population	%
Rochester (city) Monroe County	980	0.46
Syracuse (city) Onondaga County	478	0.33
Buffalo (city) Erie County	858	0.32
Utica (city) Oneida County	99	0.16
New York (city)	518	0.01
Brooklyn (borough) Kings County	260	0.01
Manhattan (borough) New York County	125	0.01
Queens (borough) Queens County	98	<0.01
Bronx (borough) Bronx County	35	<0.01
Hempstead (town) Nassau County	15	<0.01

African, Sub-Saharan: South African

Top 10 Places Sorted by Population
Based on all places, regardless of total population

Place	Population	%
New York (city)	2,116	0.03
Manhattan (borough) New York County	1,372	0.09
Queens (borough) Queens County	356	0.02
Brooklyn (borough) Kings County	320	0.01
New Rochelle (city) Westchester County	179	0.24
Hempstead (town) Nassau County	104	0.01
Scarsdale (town/village) Westchester County	80	0.47
Cortlandt (town) Westchester County	80	0.20
White Plains (city) Westchester County	78	0.14
Mount Pleasant (town) Westchester County	77	0.18

Top 10 Places Sorted by Percent of Total Population
Based on all places, regardless of total population

Place	Population	%
Linwood (cdp) Livingston County	64	48.85
Cape Vincent (village) Jefferson County	15	2.21
York (town) Livingston County	64	1.89
Kinderhook (village) Columbia County	24	1.71
Woodsburgh (village) Nassau County	10	1.34
Rhinebeck (village) Dutchess County	29	1.05
Great Neck Estates (village) Nassau County	25	0.92
Pomona (village) Rockland County	30	0.85
Pelham Manor (village) Westchester County	43	0.79
Orangeburg (cdp) Rockland County	33	0.76

Top 10 Places Sorted by Percent of Total Population
Based on places with total population of 50,000 or more

Place	Population	%
New Rochelle (city) Westchester County	179	0.24
White Plains (city) Westchester County	78	0.14
Hamburg (town) Erie County	57	0.10
Manhattan (borough) New York County	1,372	0.09
Ramapo (town) Rockland County	56	0.05
Greece (town) Monroe County	48	0.05
Colonie (town) Albany County	32	0.04
New York (city)	2,116	0.03
Huntington (town) Suffolk County	63	0.03
North Hempstead (town) Nassau County	63	0.03

African, Sub-Saharan: Sudanese

Top 10 Places Sorted by Population
Based on all places, regardless of total population

Place	Population	%
New York (city)	1,303	0.02
Brooklyn (borough) Kings County	731	0.03
Queens (borough) Queens County	286	0.01
Buffalo (city) Erie County	268	0.10
Syracuse (city) Onondaga County	177	0.12
Bronx (borough) Bronx County	149	0.01
Manhattan (borough) New York County	137	0.01
Rochester (city) Monroe County	107	0.05
Greece (town) Monroe County	51	0.05
Brighton (cdp/town) Monroe County	47	0.13

Top 10 Places Sorted by Percent of Total Population
Based on all places, regardless of total population

Place	Population	%
Northeast Ithaca (cdp) Tompkins County	13	0.49
Morrisville (village) Madison County	11	0.43
Williamson (town) Wayne County	21	0.30
Eaton (town) Madison County	11	0.21
Portland (town) Chautauqua County	7	0.14
Brighton (cdp/town) Monroe County	47	0.13
Syracuse (city) Onondaga County	177	0.12
Russell (town) St. Lawrence County	2	0.12
Port Washington (cdp) Nassau County	17	0.11
Buffalo (city) Erie County	268	0.10

Top 10 Places Sorted by Percent of Total Population
Based on places with total population of 50,000 or more

Place	Population	%
Syracuse (city) Onondaga County	177	0.12
Buffalo (city) Erie County	268	0.10
Troy (city) Rensselaer County	28	0.06
Rochester (city) Monroe County	107	0.05
Greece (town) Monroe County	51	0.05
Brooklyn (borough) Kings County	731	0.03
Albany (city) Albany County	25	0.03
New York (city)	1,303	0.02
Queens (borough) Queens County	286	0.01
Bronx (borough) Bronx County	149	0.01

African, Sub-Saharan: Ugandan

Top 10 Places Sorted by Population
Based on all places, regardless of total population

Place	Population	%
New York (city)	256	<0.01
Manhattan (borough) New York County	125	0.01
Spring Valley (village) Rockland County	86	0.28

Place	Population	%
Ramapo (town) Rockland County	86	0.07
Queens (borough) Queens County	77	<0.01
Brooklyn (borough) Kings County	54	<0.01
Buffalo (city) Erie County	33	0.01
Syracuse (city) Onondaga County	26	0.02
Ithaca (town) Tompkins County	24	0.12
Mount Vernon (city) Westchester County	19	0.03

Top 10 Places Sorted by Percent of Total Population
Based on all places, regardless of total population

Place	Population	%
Hamilton (village) Madison County	11	0.31
Spring Valley (village) Rockland County	86	0.28
Hamilton (town) Madison County	11	0.17
Ithaca (town) Tompkins County	24	0.12
Ramapo (town) Rockland County	86	0.07
Mount Vernon (city) Westchester County	19	0.03
Syracuse (city) Onondaga County	26	0.02
White Plains (city) Westchester County	9	0.02
Manhattan (borough) New York County	125	0.01
Buffalo (city) Erie County	33	0.01

Top 10 Places Sorted by Percent of Total Population
Based on places with total population of 50,000 or more

Place	Population	%
Ramapo (town) Rockland County	86	0.07
Mount Vernon (city) Westchester County	19	0.03
Syracuse (city) Onondaga County	26	0.02
White Plains (city) Westchester County	9	0.02
Manhattan (borough) New York County	125	0.01
Buffalo (city) Erie County	33	0.01
New York (city)	256	<0.01
Queens (borough) Queens County	77	<0.01
Brooklyn (borough) Kings County	54	<0.01
Albany (city) Albany County	0	0.00

African, Sub-Saharan: Zimbabwean

Top 10 Places Sorted by Population
Based on all places, regardless of total population

Place	Population	%
New York (city)	414	0.01
Bronx (borough) Bronx County	108	0.01
Queens (borough) Queens County	107	<0.01
Manhattan (borough) New York County	100	0.01
Brooklyn (borough) Kings County	99	<0.01
Rochester (city) Monroe County	76	0.04
Buffalo (city) Erie County	45	0.02
Callicoon (town) Sullivan County	40	1.30
Oneonta (city) Otsego County	26	0.19
East Ithaca (cdp) Tompkins County	24	1.20

Top 10 Places Sorted by Percent of Total Population
Based on all places, regardless of total population

Place	Population	%
Callicoon (town) Sullivan County	40	1.30
East Ithaca (cdp) Tompkins County	24	1.20
Canton (village) St. Lawrence County	13	0.21
Oneonta (city) Otsego County	26	0.19
Ithaca (town) Tompkins County	24	0.12
Canton (town) St. Lawrence County	13	0.12
Rochester (city) Monroe County	76	0.04
Buffalo (city) Erie County	45	0.02
Bethlehem (town) Albany County	8	0.02
New York (city)	414	0.01

Top 10 Places Sorted by Percent of Total Population
Based on places with total population of 50,000 or more

Place	Population	%
Rochester (city) Monroe County	76	0.04
Buffalo (city) Erie County	45	0.02
New York (city)	414	0.01
Bronx (borough) Bronx County	108	0.01
Manhattan (borough) New York County	100	0.01
Queens (borough) Queens County	107	<0.01
Brooklyn (borough) Kings County	99	<0.01
Albany (city) Albany County	0	0.00
Amherst (town) Erie County	0	0.00
Babylon (town) Suffolk County	0	0.00

African, Sub-Saharan: Other

Top 10 Places Sorted by Population
Based on all places, regardless of total population

Place	Population	%
New York (city)	17,415	0.22
Bronx (borough) Bronx County	10,539	0.77
Manhattan (borough) New York County	3,545	0.22
Brooklyn (borough) Kings County	1,881	0.08
Queens (borough) Queens County	1,219	0.06
New Rochelle (city) Westchester County	365	0.48
Rochester (city) Monroe County	309	0.15
Hempstead (town) Nassau County	275	0.04
Staten Island (borough) Richmond County	231	0.05
Mount Vernon (city) Westchester County	180	0.27

Top 10 Places Sorted by Percent of Total Population
Based on all places, regardless of total population

Place	Population	%
South Nyack (village) Rockland County	105	1.89
Pelham (village) Westchester County	68	1.00
Menands (village) Albany County	36	0.90
Woodbury (cdp) Nassau County	76	0.84
West Hempstead (cdp) Nassau County	143	0.78
Bronx (borough) Bronx County	10,539	0.77
Wheatley Heights (cdp) Suffolk County	46	0.74
Pomona (village) Rockland County	26	0.74
Ravena (village) Albany County	23	0.69
Pelham (town) Westchester County	76	0.62

Top 10 Places Sorted by Percent of Total Population
Based on places with total population of 50,000 or more

Place	Population	%
Bronx (borough) Bronx County	10,539	0.77
New Rochelle (city) Westchester County	365	0.48
Troy (city) Rensselaer County	159	0.32
Mount Vernon (city) Westchester County	180	0.27
New York (city)	17,415	0.22
Manhattan (borough) New York County	3,545	0.22
Schenectady (city) Schenectady County	133	0.20
Rochester (city) Monroe County	309	0.15
Brentwood (cdp) Suffolk County	80	0.15
Amherst (town) Erie County	170	0.14

Albanian

Top 10 Places Sorted by Population
Based on all places, regardless of total population

Place	Population	%
New York (city)	31,056	0.38
Staten Island (borough) Richmond County	8,108	1.75
Bronx (borough) Bronx County	7,835	0.57
Brooklyn (borough) Kings County	6,871	0.28
Queens (borough) Queens County	6,624	0.30
Yonkers (city) Westchester County	2,270	1.16
Manhattan (borough) New York County	1,618	0.10
Hempstead (town) Nassau County	1,052	0.14
Yorktown (town) Westchester County	628	1.75
Syracuse (city) Onondaga County	455	0.31

Top 10 Places Sorted by Percent of Total Population
Based on all places, regardless of total population

Place	Population	%
Yorktown Heights (cdp) Westchester County	170	10.19
Milton (cdp) Ulster County	101	8.68
Shrub Oak (cdp) Westchester County	134	7.40
Brewster Hill (cdp) Putnam County	91	3.78
Monroe (village) Orange County	310	3.73
Saltaire (village) Suffolk County	2	3.45
Farmington (town) Ontario County	388	3.35
Dix (town) Schuyler County	126	3.20
Tivoli (village) Dutchess County	30	3.02
Keene (town) Essex County	23	2.63

Top 10 Places Sorted by Percent of Total Population
Based on places with total population of 50,000 or more

Place	Population	%
Staten Island (borough) Richmond County	8,108	1.75
Yonkers (city) Westchester County	2,270	1.16
Bronx (borough) Bronx County	7,835	0.57
Colonie (town) Albany County	405	0.50

New Rochelle (city) Westchester County	370	0.49
Mount Vernon (city) Westchester County	303	0.45
Albany (city) Albany County	384	0.39
Clarkstown (town) Rockland County	328	0.39
New York (city)	31,056	0.38
Syracuse (city) Onondaga County	455	0.31

Alsatian

Top 10 Places Sorted by Population
Based on all places, regardless of total population

Place	Population	%
New York (city)	217	<0.01
Manhattan (borough) New York County	129	0.01
Albany (city) Albany County	51	0.05
New Bremen (town) Lewis County	50	1.85
Orchard Park (town) Erie County	40	0.14
De Witt (town) Onondaga County	39	0.15
Queens (borough) Queens County	37	<0.01
Amherst (town) Erie County	32	0.03
Hempstead (town) Nassau County	30	<0.01
Hamburg (town) Erie County	27	0.05

Top 10 Places Sorted by Percent of Total Population
Based on all places, regardless of total population

Place	Population	%
Rifton (cdp) Ulster County	20	3.31
New Bremen (town) Lewis County	50	1.85
Pittsford (village) Monroe County	12	0.85
Gainesville (village) Wyoming County	2	0.75
Wayne (town) Steuben County	4	0.41
Tioga (town) Tioga County	19	0.39
Berne (town) Albany County	10	0.36
East Aurora (village) Erie County	21	0.33
Great Neck Estates (village) Nassau County	9	0.33
Varick (town) Seneca County	6	0.33

Top 10 Places Sorted by Percent of Total Population
Based on places with total population of 50,000 or more

Place	Population	%
Albany (city) Albany County	51	0.05
Hamburg (town) Erie County	27	0.05
Tonawanda (cdp) Erie County	24	0.04
Amherst (town) Erie County	32	0.03
Tonawanda (town) Erie County	24	0.03
Manhattan (borough) New York County	129	0.01
Staten Island (borough) Richmond County	24	0.01
Islip (town) Suffolk County	18	0.01
New York (city)	217	<0.01
Queens (borough) Queens County	37	<0.01

American

Top 10 Places Sorted by Population
Based on all places, regardless of total population

Place	Population	%
New York (city)	209,430	2.59
Brooklyn (borough) Kings County	78,858	3.20
Manhattan (borough) New York County	54,694	3.45
Queens (borough) Queens County	45,604	2.07
Hempstead (town) Nassau County	23,869	3.17
Bronx (borough) Bronx County	16,297	1.19
Staten Island (borough) Richmond County	13,977	3.02
Brookhaven (town) Suffolk County	10,016	2.09
Oyster Bay (town) Nassau County	9,798	3.36
North Hempstead (town) Nassau County	7,110	3.18

Top 10 Places Sorted by Percent of Total Population
Based on all places, regardless of total population

Place	Population	%
Cumminsville (cdp) Livingston County	59	50.86
Northumberland (town) Saratoga County	1,519	30.31
Durham (town) Greene County	815	29.96
Ashland (town) Greene County	182	29.74
Schuylerville (village) Saratoga County	441	29.72
Hadley (cdp) Saratoga County	284	29.04
Lodi (village) Seneca County	137	28.84
Victory (village) Saratoga County	154	27.21
Cranberry Lake (cdp) St. Lawrence County	51	26.84
Hadley (town) Saratoga County	462	26.81

Top 10 Places Sorted by Percent of Total Population
Based on places with total population of 50,000 or more

Place	Population	%
Clarkstown (town) Rockland County	4,138	4.96
White Plains (city) Westchester County	2,743	4.91
Schenectady (city) Schenectady County	3,124	4.78
Ramapo (town) Rockland County	5,092	4.15
Union (town) Broome County	2,180	3.87
Greenburgh (town) Westchester County	3,324	3.79
Manhattan (borough) New York County	54,694	3.45
Clay (town) Onondaga County	1,975	3.40
Oyster Bay (town) Nassau County	9,798	3.36
New Rochelle (city) Westchester County	2,542	3.35

Arab: Total

Top 10 Places Sorted by Population
Based on all places, regardless of total population

Place	Population	%
New York (city)	82,165	1.02
Brooklyn (borough) Kings County	34,840	1.41
Queens (borough) Queens County	19,669	0.89
Manhattan (borough) New York County	13,828	0.87
Staten Island (borough) Richmond County	8,820	1.90
Bronx (borough) Bronx County	5,008	0.37
Hempstead (town) Nassau County	4,218	0.56
Yonkers (city) Westchester County	3,210	1.65
North Hempstead (town) Nassau County	2,078	0.93
Buffalo (city) Erie County	1,815	0.68

Top 10 Places Sorted by Percent of Total Population
Based on all places, regardless of total population

Place	Population	%
Clark Mills (cdp) Oneida County	109	9.71
Lackawanna (city) Erie County	1,753	9.61
Crown Point (town) Essex County	167	8.06
Saddle Rock (village) Nassau County	74	7.06
Hewlett Bay Park (village) Nassau County	33	6.36
Ravena (village) Albany County	200	6.03
Deerfield (town) Oneida County	230	5.48
Tannersville (village) Greene County	22	5.07
Northwest Ithaca (cdp) Tompkins County	56	4.85
New York Mills (village) Oneida County	161	4.77

Top 10 Places Sorted by Percent of Total Population
Based on places with total population of 50,000 or more

Place	Population	%
Utica (city) Oneida County	1,558	2.52
Staten Island (borough) Richmond County	8,820	1.90
Yonkers (city) Westchester County	3,210	1.65
Brooklyn (borough) Kings County	34,840	1.41
Amherst (town) Erie County	1,530	1.27
Colonie (town) Albany County	863	1.06
New York (city)	82,165	1.02
Cheektowaga (town) Erie County	905	1.02
North Hempstead (town) Nassau County	2,078	0.93
Queens (borough) Queens County	19,669	0.89

Arab: Arab

Top 10 Places Sorted by Population
Based on all places, regardless of total population

Place	Population	%
New York (city)	15,160	0.19
Brooklyn (borough) Kings County	7,609	0.31
Queens (borough) Queens County	2,283	0.10
Staten Island (borough) Richmond County	1,829	0.39
Manhattan (borough) New York County	1,720	0.11
Bronx (borough) Bronx County	1,719	0.13
Lackawanna (city) Erie County	1,331	7.30
Yonkers (city) Westchester County	1,036	0.53
Buffalo (city) Erie County	644	0.24
Henrietta (town) Monroe County	321	0.76

Top 10 Places Sorted by Percent of Total Population
Based on all places, regardless of total population

Place	Population	%
Lackawanna (city) Erie County	1,331	7.30
Brinckerhoff (cdp) Dutchess County	101	3.13
Millbrook (village) Dutchess County	48	2.94

Place	Population	%
Clark Mills (cdp) Oneida County	32	2.85
Morristown (town) St. Lawrence County	71	2.59
New Scotland (town) Albany County	209	2.41
Orange (town) Schuyler County	43	2.41
Cherry Valley (village) Otsego County	10	2.27
Spencerport (village) Monroe County	72	2.02
Hudson (city) Columbia County	127	1.85

Top 10 Places Sorted by Percent of Total Population
Based on places with total population of 50,000 or more

Place	Population	%
Yonkers (city) Westchester County	1,036	0.53
Staten Island (borough) Richmond County	1,829	0.39
Utica (city) Oneida County	198	0.32
Brooklyn (borough) Kings County	7,609	0.31
Cheektowaga (cdp) Erie County	224	0.30
Cheektowaga (town) Erie County	247	0.28
New Rochelle (city) Westchester County	187	0.25
Buffalo (city) Erie County	644	0.24
Clay (town) Onondaga County	136	0.23
Ramapo (town) Rockland County	245	0.20

Arab: Egyptian

Top 10 Places Sorted by Population
Based on all places, regardless of total population

Place	Population	%
New York (city)	17,698	0.22
Queens (borough) Queens County	6,551	0.30
Brooklyn (borough) Kings County	5,231	0.21
Staten Island (borough) Richmond County	3,292	0.71
Manhattan (borough) New York County	1,906	0.12
Hempstead (town) Nassau County	1,227	0.16
Bronx (borough) Bronx County	718	0.05
North Hempstead (town) Nassau County	529	0.24
Brookhaven (town) Suffolk County	435	0.09
Huntington (town) Suffolk County	425	0.21

Top 10 Places Sorted by Percent of Total Population
Based on all places, regardless of total population

Place	Population	%
Callicoon (town) Sullivan County	125	4.05
Oakdale (cdp) Suffolk County	220	2.87
Orange Lake (cdp) Orange County	183	2.68
Deerfield (town) Oneida County	110	2.62
Northwest Ithaca (cdp) Tompkins County	28	2.43
Woodmere (cdp) Nassau County	418	2.39
Gordon Heights (cdp) Suffolk County	76	2.33
Woodridge (village) Sullivan County	20	2.23
Carlisle (town) Schoharie County	40	2.15
Herricks (cdp) Nassau County	75	1.91

Top 10 Places Sorted by Percent of Total Population
Based on places with total population of 50,000 or more

Place	Population	%
Staten Island (borough) Richmond County	3,292	0.71
Queens (borough) Queens County	6,551	0.30
Clarkstown (town) Rockland County	254	0.30
Levittown (cdp) Nassau County	136	0.25
North Hempstead (town) Nassau County	529	0.24
New York (city)	17,698	0.22
Brooklyn (borough) Kings County	5,231	0.21
Huntington (town) Suffolk County	425	0.21
Hempstead (town) Nassau County	1,227	0.16
Colonie (town) Albany County	125	0.15

Arab: Iraqi

Top 10 Places Sorted by Population
Based on all places, regardless of total population

Place	Population	%
New York (city)	1,137	0.01
Manhattan (borough) New York County	583	0.04
North Hempstead (town) Nassau County	500	0.22
Queens (borough) Queens County	315	0.01
Buffalo (city) Erie County	288	0.11
Hempstead (town) Nassau County	284	0.04
Dix Hills (cdp) Suffolk County	166	0.63
Huntington (town) Suffolk County	166	0.08
Brooklyn (borough) Kings County	134	0.01
West Hempstead (cdp) Nassau County	112	0.61

Top 10 Places Sorted by Percent of Total Population
Based on all places, regardless of total population

Place	Population	%
Saddle Rock (village) Nassau County	46	4.39
Kensington (village) Nassau County	28	2.32
Herricks (cdp) Nassau County	86	2.18
Water Mill (cdp) Suffolk County	28	1.83
Great Neck Gardens (cdp) Nassau County	16	1.76
Hewlett (cdp) Nassau County	94	1.40
Sands Point (village) Nassau County	33	1.24
Middleburgh (town) Schoharie County	46	1.23
Atlantic Beach (village) Nassau County	21	1.13
East Hills (village) Nassau County	71	1.04

Top 10 Places Sorted by Percent of Total Population
Based on places with total population of 50,000 or more

Place	Population	%
North Hempstead (town) Nassau County	500	0.22
Buffalo (city) Erie County	288	0.11
Huntington (town) Suffolk County	166	0.08
Smithtown (town) Suffolk County	89	0.04
Yonkers (city) Westchester County	103	0.05
Southampton (town) Suffolk County	28	0.05
Manhattan (borough) New York County	583	0.04
Hempstead (town) Nassau County	284	0.04
Ramapo (town) Rockland County	48	0.04
Cheektowaga (cdp) Erie County	30	0.04

Arab: Jordanian

Top 10 Places Sorted by Population
Based on all places, regardless of total population

Place	Population	%
New York (city)	1,298	0.02
Yonkers (city) Westchester County	907	0.47
Brooklyn (borough) Kings County	752	0.03
Queens (borough) Queens County	307	0.01
Poughkeepsie (town) Dutchess County	223	0.51
Hyde Park (town) Dutchess County	204	0.94
Staten Island (borough) Richmond County	183	0.04
Brookhaven (town) Suffolk County	178	0.04
La Grange (town) Dutchess County	175	1.12
Niagara (town) Niagara County	149	1.77

Top 10 Places Sorted by Percent of Total Population
Based on all places, regardless of total population

Place	Population	%
Fairview (cdp) Dutchess County	108	2.32
Niagara (town) Niagara County	149	1.77
Fremont (town) Sullivan County	20	1.62
Putnam Lake (cdp) Putnam County	52	1.42
Woodbury (village) Orange County	126	1.20
Liberty (town) Sullivan County	117	1.18
Woodbury (town) Orange County	126	1.14
La Grange (town) Dutchess County	175	1.12
Baywood (cdp) Suffolk County	82	1.04
Hyde Park (town) Dutchess County	204	0.94

Top 10 Places Sorted by Percent of Total Population
Based on places with total population of 50,000 or more

Place	Population	%
Yonkers (city) Westchester County	907	0.47
Amherst (town) Erie County	84	0.07
New Rochelle (city) Westchester County	46	0.06
Smithtown (town) Suffolk County	54	0.05
Greenburgh (town) Westchester County	45	0.05
Staten Island (borough) Richmond County	183	0.04
Brookhaven (town) Suffolk County	178	0.04
Islip (town) Suffolk County	122	0.04
White Plains (city) Westchester County	21	0.04
Brooklyn (borough) Kings County	752	0.03

Arab: Lebanese

Top 10 Places Sorted by Population
Based on all places, regardless of total population

Place	Population	%
New York (city)	11,682	0.14
Brooklyn (borough) Kings County	4,757	0.19
Manhattan (borough) New York County	3,331	0.21

Place	Population	%
Queens (borough) Queens County	2,228	0.10
Staten Island (borough) Richmond County	1,019	0.22
Amherst (town) Erie County	985	0.81
Utica (city) Oneida County	947	1.53
Hempstead (town) Nassau County	657	0.09
Whitestown (town) Oneida County	495	2.66
Buffalo (city) Erie County	481	0.18

Top 10 Places Sorted by Percent of Total Population
Based on all places, regardless of total population

Place	Population	%
Clark Mills (cdp) Oneida County	65	5.79
Crown Point (town) Essex County	94	4.54
New York Mills (village) Oneida County	145	4.30
Lewiston (village) Niagara County	105	3.88
Williamsville (village) Erie County	177	3.33
Yorkville (village) Oneida County	76	2.83
Vernon (town) Oneida County	144	2.68
Whitestown (town) Oneida County	495	2.66
Lacona (village) Oswego County	16	2.63
Pultneyville (cdp) Wayne County	20	2.61

Top 10 Places Sorted by Percent of Total Population
Based on places with total population of 50,000 or more

Place	Population	%
Utica (city) Oneida County	947	1.53
Amherst (town) Erie County	985	0.81
Tonawanda (cdp) Erie County	401	0.68
Tonawanda (town) Erie County	428	0.58
Troy (city) Rensselaer County	270	0.54
Cheektowaga (cdp) Erie County	338	0.45
Niagara Falls (city) Niagara County	228	0.45
Cheektowaga (town) Erie County	350	0.39
Clay (town) Onondaga County	213	0.37
Colonie (town) Albany County	267	0.33

Arab: Moroccan

Top 10 Places Sorted by Population
Based on all places, regardless of total population

Place	Population	%
New York (city)	8,987	0.11
Queens (borough) Queens County	3,459	0.16
Brooklyn (borough) Kings County	2,648	0.11
Manhattan (borough) New York County	1,592	0.10
Bronx (borough) Bronx County	667	0.05
Staten Island (borough) Richmond County	621	0.13
Hempstead (town) Nassau County	376	0.05
Ramapo (town) Rockland County	291	0.24
Lindenhurst (village) Suffolk County	209	0.76
Babylon (town) Suffolk County	209	0.10

Top 10 Places Sorted by Percent of Total Population
Based on all places, regardless of total population

Place	Population	%
Northwest Ithaca (cdp) Tompkins County	28	2.43
Philmont (village) Columbia County	24	2.07
Tupper Lake (village) Franklin County	68	1.77
South Valley Stream (cdp) Nassau County	76	1.44
Airmont (village) Rockland County	109	1.29
Brookville (village) Nassau County	43	1.24
Wheeler (town) Steuben County	14	1.19
Tupper Lake (town) Franklin County	68	1.13
Mechanicville (city) Saratoga County	58	1.12
Gouverneur (village) St. Lawrence County	44	1.10

Top 10 Places Sorted by Percent of Total Population
Based on places with total population of 50,000 or more

Place	Population	%
Ramapo (town) Rockland County	291	0.24
Queens (borough) Queens County	3,459	0.16
Colonie (town) Albany County	111	0.14
Staten Island (borough) Richmond County	621	0.13
White Plains (city) Westchester County	71	0.13
New York (city)	8,987	0.11
Brooklyn (borough) Kings County	2,648	0.11
Manhattan (borough) New York County	1,592	0.10
Babylon (town) Suffolk County	209	0.10
Mount Vernon (city) Westchester County	64	0.10

Arab: Palestinian

Top 10 Places Sorted by Population
Based on all places, regardless of total population

Place	Population	%
New York (city)	3,421	0.04
Brooklyn (borough) Kings County	1,482	0.06
Manhattan (borough) New York County	794	0.05
Queens (borough) Queens County	638	0.03
Staten Island (borough) Richmond County	479	0.10
Ravena (village) Albany County	200	6.03
Coeymans (town) Albany County	200	2.63
Poughkeepsie (town) Dutchess County	183	0.42
Islip (town) Suffolk County	166	0.05
Yonkers (city) Westchester County	139	0.07

Top 10 Places Sorted by Percent of Total Population
Based on all places, regardless of total population

Place	Population	%
Ravena (village) Albany County	200	6.03
Crown Point (town) Essex County	70	3.38
Coeymans (town) Albany County	200	2.63
Van Etten (town) Chemung County	18	1.43
Roslyn (village) Nassau County	35	1.28
Stuyvesant (town) Columbia County	24	1.19
Oakfield (village) Genesee County	22	1.07
Silver Creek (village) Chautauqua County	23	0.86
Farmingdale (village) Nassau County	58	0.71
Oakfield (town) Genesee County	22	0.68

Top 10 Places Sorted by Percent of Total Population
Based on places with total population of 50,000 or more

Place	Population	%
Staten Island (borough) Richmond County	479	0.10
Colonie (town) Albany County	72	0.09
Yonkers (city) Westchester County	139	0.07
Brooklyn (borough) Kings County	1,482	0.06
Manhattan (borough) New York County	794	0.05
Islip (town) Suffolk County	166	0.05
Babylon (town) Suffolk County	114	0.05
Syracuse (city) Onondaga County	66	0.05
New York (city)	3,421	0.04
Union (town) Broome County	25	0.04

Arab: Syrian

Top 10 Places Sorted by Population
Based on all places, regardless of total population

Place	Population	%
New York (city)	8,198	0.10
Brooklyn (borough) Kings County	5,890	0.24
Manhattan (borough) New York County	1,112	0.07
Staten Island (borough) Richmond County	584	0.13
Hempstead (town) Nassau County	512	0.07
Queens (borough) Queens County	420	0.02
New Hartford (town) Oneida County	351	1.60
Utica (city) Oneida County	248	0.40
Brookhaven (town) Suffolk County	220	0.05
Bronx (borough) Bronx County	192	0.01

Top 10 Places Sorted by Percent of Total Population
Based on all places, regardless of total population

Place	Population	%
Tannersville (village) Greene County	22	5.07
Chautauqua (cdp) Chautauqua County	12	4.55
Mountain Lodge Park (cdp) Orange County	74	3.98
Manchester (village) Ontario County	46	2.86
Beaver Dam Lake (cdp) Orange County	55	2.01
Fort Montgomery (cdp) Orange County	17	1.99
Taylor (town) Cortland County	11	1.98
West Glens Falls (cdp) Warren County	126	1.90
Chadwicks (cdp) Oneida County	22	1.84
Fillmore (cdp) Allegany County	10	1.63

Top 10 Places Sorted by Percent of Total Population
Based on places with total population of 50,000 or more

Place	Population	%
Utica (city) Oneida County	248	0.40
Brooklyn (borough) Kings County	5,890	0.24
Colonie (town) Albany County	116	0.14
Staten Island (borough) Richmond County	584	0.13

Place	Population	%
Greenburgh (town) Westchester County	107	0.12
Albany (city) Albany County	104	0.11
Clarkstown (town) Rockland County	88	0.11
New York (city)	8,198	0.10
Greece (town) Monroe County	97	0.10
Niagara Falls (city) Niagara County	44	0.09

Arab: Other

Top 10 Places Sorted by Population
Based on all places, regardless of total population

Place	Population	%
New York (city)	14,584	0.18
Brooklyn (borough) Kings County	6,337	0.26
Queens (borough) Queens County	3,468	0.16
Manhattan (borough) New York County	2,742	0.17
Bronx (borough) Bronx County	1,256	0.09
Staten Island (borough) Richmond County	781	0.17
Hempstead (town) Nassau County	664	0.09
North Hempstead (town) Nassau County	571	0.26
Binghamton (city) Broome County	521	1.10
Lackawanna (city) Erie County	402	2.20

Top 10 Places Sorted by Percent of Total Population
Based on all places, regardless of total population

Place	Population	%
Hewlett Bay Park (village) Nassau County	26	5.01
Gates (cdp) Monroe County	256	4.76
Saddle Rock (village) Nassau County	28	2.67
Lackawanna (city) Erie County	402	2.20
St. Regis Mohawk Reservation Franklin County	65	2.07
Depew (village) Erie County	303	1.96
Kings Point (village) Nassau County	92	1.85
Roslyn Heights (cdp) Nassau County	107	1.65
Mill Neck (village) Nassau County	13	1.61
Sands Point (village) Nassau County	41	1.54

Top 10 Places Sorted by Percent of Total Population
Based on places with total population of 50,000 or more

Place	Population	%
Cheektowaga (town) Erie County	244	0.27
Brooklyn (borough) Kings County	6,337	0.26
North Hempstead (town) Nassau County	571	0.26
Amherst (town) Erie County	270	0.22
Mount Vernon (city) Westchester County	148	0.22
Colonie (town) Albany County	155	0.19
New York (city)	14,584	0.18
Rochester (city) Monroe County	390	0.18
Manhattan (borough) New York County	2,742	0.17
Staten Island (borough) Richmond County	781	0.17

Armenian

Top 10 Places Sorted by Population
Based on all places, regardless of total population

Place	Population	%
New York (city)	10,159	0.13
Queens (borough) Queens County	4,658	0.21
Manhattan (borough) New York County	2,653	0.17
Brooklyn (borough) Kings County	2,300	0.09
Hempstead (town) Nassau County	1,451	0.19
Oyster Bay (town) Nassau County	1,383	0.47
Brookhaven (town) Suffolk County	643	0.13
North Hempstead (town) Nassau County	631	0.28
Huntington (town) Suffolk County	525	0.26
Troy (city) Rensselaer County	418	0.84

Top 10 Places Sorted by Percent of Total Population
Based on all places, regardless of total population

Place	Population	%
Harbor Hills (cdp) Nassau County	67	13.54
Tannersville (village) Greene County	34	7.83
Duane Lake (cdp) Schenectady County	16	6.61
Pine Hill (cdp) Ulster County	13	5.06
Pleasant Valley (cdp) Dutchess County	41	4.95
Boylston (town) Oswego County	19	3.98
Hewlett (cdp) Nassau County	264	3.92
Munsey Park (village) Nassau County	103	3.87
Pittsford (village) Monroe County	52	3.70
Chenango Bridge (cdp) Broome County	106	3.48

Top 10 Places Sorted by Percent of Total Population
Based on places with total population of 50,000 or more

Place	Population	%
Troy (city) Rensselaer County	418	0.84
Oyster Bay (town) Nassau County	1,383	0.47
Niagara Falls (city) Niagara County	156	0.31
Colonie (town) Albany County	244	0.30
North Hempstead (town) Nassau County	631	0.28
Huntington (town) Suffolk County	525	0.26
Queens (borough) Queens County	4,658	0.21
Yonkers (city) Westchester County	411	0.21
Greenburgh (town) Westchester County	175	0.20
Hempstead (town) Nassau County	1,451	0.19

Assyrian/Chaldean/Syriac

Top 10 Places Sorted by Population
Based on all places, regardless of total population

Place	Population	%
New York (city)	227	<0.01
Yonkers (city) Westchester County	157	0.08
Manhattan (borough) New York County	137	0.01
Clarkstown (town) Rockland County	51	0.06
Cortlandt (town) Westchester County	45	0.11
Brooklyn (borough) Kings County	44	<0.01
Congers (cdp) Rockland County	34	0.43
Greenburgh (town) Westchester County	29	0.03
Peekskill (city) Westchester County	26	0.11
North Hempstead (town) Nassau County	21	0.01

Top 10 Places Sorted by Percent of Total Population
Based on all places, regardless of total population

Place	Population	%
Tuxedo Park (village) Orange County	3	0.50
Congers (cdp) Rockland County	34	0.43
Plandome Heights (village) Nassau County	4	0.38
Cuyler (town) Cortland County	3	0.33
Fairfield (town) Herkimer County	5	0.30
New Paltz (village) Ulster County	8	0.12
East Williston (village) Nassau County	3	0.12
Cortlandt (town) Westchester County	45	0.11
Peekskill (city) Westchester County	26	0.11
Yonkers (city) Westchester County	157	0.08

Top 10 Places Sorted by Percent of Total Population
Based on places with total population of 50,000 or more

Place	Population	%
Yonkers (city) Westchester County	157	0.08
Clarkstown (town) Rockland County	51	0.06
Greenburgh (town) Westchester County	29	0.03
Manhattan (borough) New York County	137	0.01
North Hempstead (town) Nassau County	21	0.01
White Plains (city) Westchester County	8	0.01
New York (city)	227	<0.01
Brooklyn (borough) Kings County	44	<0.01
Hempstead (town) Nassau County	19	<0.01
Bronx (borough) Bronx County	18	<0.01

Australian

Top 10 Places Sorted by Population
Based on all places, regardless of total population

Place	Population	%
New York (city)	3,906	0.05
Manhattan (borough) New York County	2,719	0.17
Brooklyn (borough) Kings County	832	0.03
Queens (borough) Queens County	285	0.01
Hempstead (town) Nassau County	236	0.03
Huntington (town) Suffolk County	101	0.05
Islip (town) Suffolk County	100	0.03
Scarsdale (town/village) Westchester County	96	0.56
Putnam Valley (town) Putnam County	90	0.77
Albany (city) Albany County	88	0.09

Top 10 Places Sorted by Percent of Total Population
Based on all places, regardless of total population

Place	Population	%
Cape Vincent (village) Jefferson County	13	1.91
Galway (village) Saratoga County	2	1.85
Newport (village) Herkimer County	9	1.84

Place	Population	%
Andes (cdp) Delaware County	5	1.80
Bovina (town) Delaware County	9	1.76
Marlboro (cdp) Ulster County	63	1.57
Windham (town) Greene County	25	1.50
Ovid (village) Seneca County	7	1.47
Alexandria Bay (village) Jefferson County	14	1.28
Hagaman (village) Montgomery County	11	1.04

Top 10 Places Sorted by Percent of Total Population
Based on places with total population of 50,000 or more

Place	Population	%
Manhattan (borough) New York County	2,719	0.17
Niagara Falls (city) Niagara County	49	0.10
Albany (city) Albany County	88	0.09
Greece (town) Monroe County	87	0.09
Ramapo (town) Rockland County	86	0.07
Southampton (town) Suffolk County	38	0.07
New York (city)	3,906	0.05
Huntington (town) Suffolk County	101	0.05
Tonawanda (cdp) Erie County	29	0.05
North Hempstead (town) Nassau County	80	0.04

Austrian

Top 10 Places Sorted by Population
Based on all places, regardless of total population

Place	Population	%
New York (city)	30,712	0.38
Manhattan (borough) New York County	14,656	0.93
Queens (borough) Queens County	7,523	0.34
Brooklyn (borough) Kings County	5,123	0.21
Hempstead (town) Nassau County	4,963	0.66
Oyster Bay (town) Nassau County	3,412	1.17
Brookhaven (town) Suffolk County	2,867	0.60
North Hempstead (town) Nassau County	2,782	1.24
Islip (town) Suffolk County	2,019	0.61
Huntington (town) Suffolk County	2,004	0.99

Top 10 Places Sorted by Percent of Total Population
Based on all places, regardless of total population

Place	Population	%
West Hampton Dunes (village) Suffolk County	8	18.60
Harbor Hills (cdp) Nassau County	50	10.10
Great Neck Gardens (cdp) Nassau County	64	7.05
Saltaire (village) Suffolk County	4	6.90
Palenville (cdp) Greene County	70	6.17
Islip Terrace (cdp) Suffolk County	353	6.15
Cuylerville (cdp) Livingston County	25	5.76
High Falls (cdp) Ulster County	45	5.23
Ocean Beach (village) Suffolk County	6	5.22
Golden's Bridge (cdp) Westchester County	86	4.81

Top 10 Places Sorted by Percent of Total Population
Based on places with total population of 50,000 or more

Place	Population	%
Greenburgh (town) Westchester County	1,117	1.27
North Hempstead (town) Nassau County	2,782	1.24
Oyster Bay (town) Nassau County	3,412	1.17
Southampton (town) Suffolk County	621	1.10
Ramapo (town) Rockland County	1,328	1.08
White Plains (city) Westchester County	572	1.02
Huntington (town) Suffolk County	2,004	0.99
Clarkstown (town) Rockland County	827	0.99
Manhattan (borough) New York County	14,656	0.93
Amherst (town) Erie County	1,014	0.84

Basque

Top 10 Places Sorted by Population
Based on all places, regardless of total population

Place	Population	%
New York (city)	902	0.01
Manhattan (borough) New York County	428	0.03
Queens (borough) Queens County	159	0.01
Brooklyn (borough) Kings County	129	0.01
North Hempstead (town) Nassau County	121	0.05
Bronx (borough) Bronx County	109	0.01
Staten Island (borough) Richmond County	77	0.02
Mineola (village) Nassau County	54	0.29
Hempstead (town) Nassau County	43	0.01
Croton-on-Hudson (village) Westchester County	42	0.53

Top 10 Places Sorted by Percent of Total Population
Based on all places, regardless of total population

Place	Population	%
Plattekill (cdp) Ulster County	15	1.09
East Williston (village) Nassau County	17	0.67
Gardiner (town) Ulster County	35	0.62
Williston Park (village) Nassau County	39	0.54
Croton-on-Hudson (village) Westchester County	42	0.53
Fort Edward (village) Washington County	13	0.39
Mill Neck (village) Nassau County	3	0.37
Waterford (village) Saratoga County	7	0.34
Arlington (cdp) Dutchess County	13	0.31
Austerlitz (town) Columbia County	4	0.31

Top 10 Places Sorted by Percent of Total Population
Based on places with total population of 50,000 or more

Place	Population	%
North Hempstead (town) Nassau County	121	0.05
Manhattan (borough) New York County	428	0.03
Levittown (cdp) Nassau County	16	0.03
Staten Island (borough) Richmond County	77	0.02
New Rochelle (city) Westchester County	12	0.02
New York (city)	902	0.01
Queens (borough) Queens County	159	0.01
Brooklyn (borough) Kings County	129	0.01
Bronx (borough) Bronx County	109	0.01
Hempstead (town) Nassau County	43	0.01

Belgian

Top 10 Places Sorted by Population
Based on all places, regardless of total population

Place	Population	%
New York (city)	4,472	0.06
Manhattan (borough) New York County	2,470	0.16
Brooklyn (borough) Kings County	1,012	0.04
Ramapo (town) Rockland County	751	0.61
Queens (borough) Queens County	593	0.03
Hempstead (town) Nassau County	405	0.05
Brookhaven (town) Suffolk County	401	0.08
Monsey (cdp) Rockland County	400	2.66
Islip (town) Suffolk County	328	0.10
Staten Island (borough) Richmond County	266	0.06

Top 10 Places Sorted by Percent of Total Population
Based on all places, regardless of total population

Place	Population	%
DeKalb Junction (cdp) St. Lawrence County	41	12.58
Sheldon (town) Wyoming County	82	3.77
New Square (village) Rockland County	225	3.48
Odessa (village) Schuyler County	18	3.43
Wallkill (cdp) Ulster County	75	3.18
Westport (cdp) Essex County	14	3.11
Strykersville (cdp) Wyoming County	14	2.78
Cold Spring (village) Putnam County	47	2.77
Tuscarora Nation Reservation Niagara County	27	2.68
Monsey (cdp) Rockland County	400	2.66

Top 10 Places Sorted by Percent of Total Population
Based on places with total population of 50,000 or more

Place	Population	%
Ramapo (town) Rockland County	751	0.61
Greece (town) Monroe County	254	0.27
Irondequoit (cdp/town) Monroe County	93	0.18
White Plains (city) Westchester County	94	0.17
Manhattan (borough) New York County	2,470	0.16
New Rochelle (city) Westchester County	118	0.16
Clay (town) Onondaga County	68	0.12
Greenburgh (town) Westchester County	93	0.11
Islip (town) Suffolk County	328	0.10
Rochester (city) Monroe County	185	0.09

Brazilian

Top 10 Places Sorted by Population
Based on all places, regardless of total population

Place	Population	%
New York (city)	13,119	0.16
Queens (borough) Queens County	6,175	0.28
Manhattan (borough) New York County	4,541	0.29

Place	Population	%
Mount Vernon (city) Westchester County	2,013	3.00
Brooklyn (borough) Kings County	1,719	0.07
Rye (town) Westchester County	929	2.05
Islip (town) Suffolk County	895	0.27
Port Chester (village) Westchester County	803	2.81
New Rochelle (city) Westchester County	728	0.96
North Hempstead (town) Nassau County	613	0.27

Top 10 Places Sorted by Percent of Total Population
Based on all places, regardless of total population

Place	Population	%
Three Mile Bay (cdp) Jefferson County	21	9.95
Saddle Rock Estates (cdp) Nassau County	33	6.30
Sagaponack (village) Suffolk County	11	4.30
West Sand Lake (cdp) Rensselaer County	101	3.85
Mount Vernon (city) Westchester County	2,013	3.00
Port Chester (village) Westchester County	803	2.81
University at Buffalo (cdp) Erie County	156	2.77
Flanders (cdp) Suffolk County	120	2.66
Napanoch (cdp) Ulster County	24	2.26
Cragsmoor (cdp) Ulster County	8	2.22

Top 10 Places Sorted by Percent of Total Population
Based on places with total population of 50,000 or more

Place	Population	%
Mount Vernon (city) Westchester County	2,013	3.00
New Rochelle (city) Westchester County	728	0.96
White Plains (city) Westchester County	440	0.79
Brentwood (cdp) Suffolk County	418	0.76
Southampton (town) Suffolk County	289	0.51
Schenectady (city) Schenectady County	194	0.30
Manhattan (borough) New York County	4,541	0.29
Queens (borough) Queens County	6,175	0.28
Islip (town) Suffolk County	895	0.27
North Hempstead (town) Nassau County	613	0.27

British

Top 10 Places Sorted by Population
Based on all places, regardless of total population

Place	Population	%
New York (city)	21,065	0.26
Manhattan (borough) New York County	12,129	0.77
Brooklyn (borough) Kings County	4,749	0.19
Queens (borough) Queens County	2,457	0.11
Brookhaven (town) Suffolk County	1,235	0.26
Hempstead (town) Nassau County	1,197	0.16
Bronx (borough) Bronx County	1,115	0.08
Huntington (town) Suffolk County	840	0.42
Buffalo (city) Erie County	722	0.27
North Hempstead (town) Nassau County	705	0.32

Top 10 Places Sorted by Percent of Total Population
Based on all places, regardless of total population

Place	Population	%
Pierrepont Manor (cdp) Jefferson County	28	22.95
Salisbury Mills (cdp) Orange County	36	12.33
Gorham (cdp) Ontario County	47	8.08
Chazy (cdp) Clinton County	34	6.71
Montague (town) Lewis County	6	6.12
New Suffolk (cdp) Suffolk County	10	5.32
Prattsburgh (cdp) Steuben County	29	4.07
Old Forge (cdp) Herkimer County	20	3.88
Poquott (village) Suffolk County	45	3.85
Burke (village) Franklin County	7	3.85

Top 10 Places Sorted by Percent of Total Population
Based on places with total population of 50,000 or more

Place	Population	%
Manhattan (borough) New York County	12,129	0.77
Southampton (town) Suffolk County	404	0.71
Greenburgh (town) Westchester County	519	0.59
Union (town) Broome County	250	0.44
Huntington (town) Suffolk County	840	0.42
Greece (town) Monroe County	387	0.41
Troy (city) Rensselaer County	207	0.41
Irondequoit (cdp/town) Monroe County	189	0.37
Amherst (town) Erie County	438	0.36
North Hempstead (town) Nassau County	705	0.32

Bulgarian

Top 10 Places Sorted by Population
Based on all places, regardless of total population

Place	Population	%
New York (city)	5,011	0.06
Queens (borough) Queens County	2,090	0.10
Manhattan (borough) New York County	1,272	0.08
Brooklyn (borough) Kings County	1,128	0.05
Bronx (borough) Bronx County	521	0.04
Buffalo (city) Erie County	201	0.08
Hamburg (town) Erie County	192	0.34
Hempstead (town) Nassau County	181	0.02
West Hempstead (cdp) Nassau County	142	0.77
Brookhaven (town) Suffolk County	128	0.03

Top 10 Places Sorted by Percent of Total Population
Based on all places, regardless of total population

Place	Population	%
Bedford Hills (cdp) Westchester County	99	3.04
Wales (town) Erie County	81	2.72
Fairfield (town) Herkimer County	42	2.49
Pembroke (town) Genesee County	83	1.92
Maybrook (village) Orange County	44	1.48
Crompond (cdp) Westchester County	26	1.27
Walden (village) Orange County	82	1.19
Hilton (village) Monroe County	69	1.18
Glasco (cdp) Ulster County	22	0.95
Mayfield (village) Fulton County	8	0.92

Top 10 Places Sorted by Percent of Total Population
Based on places with total population of 50,000 or more

Place	Population	%
Hamburg (town) Erie County	192	0.34
White Plains (city) Westchester County	62	0.11
Queens (borough) Queens County	2,090	0.10
Manhattan (borough) New York County	1,272	0.08
Buffalo (city) Erie County	201	0.08
Amherst (town) Erie County	98	0.08
Cheektowaga (town) Erie County	73	0.08
New York (city)	5,011	0.06
Greenburgh (town) Westchester County	54	0.06
Brooklyn (borough) Kings County	1,128	0.05

Cajun

Top 10 Places Sorted by Population
Based on all places, regardless of total population

Place	Population	%
New York (city)	432	0.01
Manhattan (borough) New York County	224	0.01
Brooklyn (borough) Kings County	175	0.01
Catskill (village) Greene County	62	1.50
Catskill (town) Greene County	62	0.52
West Point (cdp) Orange County	54	0.57
Highlands (town) Orange County	54	0.43
Poughkeepsie (city) Dutchess County	41	0.13
Oyster Bay (town) Nassau County	37	0.01
Queens (borough) Queens County	33	<0.01

Top 10 Places Sorted by Percent of Total Population
Based on all places, regardless of total population

Place	Population	%
Catskill (village) Greene County	62	1.50
Madrid (cdp) St. Lawrence County	6	0.82
Brownville (village) Jefferson County	8	0.76
West Point (cdp) Orange County	54	0.57
Elma Center (cdp) Erie County	15	0.55
East Ithaca (cdp) Tompkins County	11	0.55
Catskill (town) Greene County	62	0.52
Chazy (town) Clinton County	21	0.49
West Sayville (cdp) Suffolk County	23	0.44
Kings Point (village) Nassau County	22	0.44

Top 10 Places Sorted by Percent of Total Population
Based on places with total population of 50,000 or more

Place	Population	%
Syracuse (city) Onondaga County	24	0.02
Union (town) Broome County	12	0.02
New York (city)	432	0.01
Manhattan (borough) New York County	224	0.01

Place	Population	%
Brooklyn (borough) Kings County	175	0.01
Oyster Bay (town) Nassau County	37	0.01
Islip (town) Suffolk County	23	0.01
North Hempstead (town) Nassau County	22	0.01
Huntington (town) Suffolk County	19	0.01
Queens (borough) Queens County	33	<0.01

Canadian

Top 10 Places Sorted by Population
Based on all places, regardless of total population

Place	Population	%
New York (city)	10,989	0.14
Manhattan (borough) New York County	5,646	0.36
Brooklyn (borough) Kings County	3,116	0.13
Queens (borough) Queens County	1,308	0.06
Hempstead (town) Nassau County	1,084	0.14
Brookhaven (town) Suffolk County	999	0.21
Huntington (town) Suffolk County	743	0.37
Ramapo (town) Rockland County	680	0.55
Amherst (town) Erie County	589	0.49
Babylon (town) Suffolk County	581	0.27

Top 10 Places Sorted by Percent of Total Population
Based on all places, regardless of total population

Place	Population	%
Fishers Landing (cdp) Jefferson County	10	18.87
Natural Bridge (cdp) Jefferson County	58	14.36
La Fargeville (cdp) Jefferson County	99	14.14
Cumminsville (cdp) Livingston County	9	7.76
Orleans (town) Jefferson County	164	6.09
Chateaugay (village) Franklin County	31	5.54
Birdsall (town) Allegany County	17	5.54
Waddington (village) St. Lawrence County	37	5.13
Richville (village) St. Lawrence County	15	5.12
Machias (cdp) Cattaraugus County	37	5.08

Top 10 Places Sorted by Percent of Total Population
Based on places with total population of 50,000 or more

Place	Population	%
Niagara Falls (city) Niagara County	442	0.87
Irondequoit (cdp/town) Monroe County	419	0.81
Hamburg (town) Erie County	368	0.65
Clay (town) Onondaga County	345	0.59
Ramapo (town) Rockland County	680	0.55
Greece (town) Monroe County	525	0.55
Amherst (town) Erie County	589	0.49
Tonawanda (cdp) Erie County	288	0.49
Tonawanda (town) Erie County	312	0.42
Colonie (town) Albany County	321	0.39

Carpatho Rusyn

Top 10 Places Sorted by Population
Based on all places, regardless of total population

Place	Population	%
New York (city)	249	<0.01
Manhattan (borough) New York County	112	0.01
Union (town) Broome County	101	0.18
Staten Island (borough) Richmond County	63	0.01
Brooklyn (borough) Kings County	53	<0.01
Yonkers (city) Westchester County	40	0.02
Johnson City (village) Broome County	39	0.26
Hempstead (town) Nassau County	36	<0.01
Oswego (town) Oswego County	28	0.35
Hauppauge (cdp) Suffolk County	26	0.12

Top 10 Places Sorted by Percent of Total Population
Based on all places, regardless of total population

Place	Population	%
Shenorock (cdp) Westchester County	20	1.02
New Hartford (village) Oneida County	15	0.78
Stewart Manor (village) Nassau County	13	0.60
Gang Mills (cdp) Steuben County	23	0.55
Oswego (town) Oswego County	28	0.35
North Salem (town) Westchester County	18	0.35
Erwin (town) Steuben County	23	0.29
Johnson City (village) Broome County	39	0.26
Fairview (cdp) Dutchess County	10	0.22
Persia (town) Cattaraugus County	5	0.20

Top 10 Places Sorted by Percent of Total Population
Based on places with total population of 50,000 or more

Place	Population	%
Union (town) Broome County	101	0.18
Niagara Falls (city) Niagara County	14	0.03
Yonkers (city) Westchester County	40	0.02
Smithtown (town) Suffolk County	26	0.02
Tonawanda (town) Erie County	13	0.02
Manhattan (borough) New York County	112	0.01
Staten Island (borough) Richmond County	63	0.01
Huntington (town) Suffolk County	20	0.01
Albany (city) Albany County	12	0.01
Cheektowaga (cdp) Erie County	6	0.01

Celtic

Top 10 Places Sorted by Population
Based on all places, regardless of total population

Place	Population	%
New York (city)	564	0.01
Manhattan (borough) New York County	304	0.02
Queens (borough) Queens County	169	0.01
Hornell (city) Steuben County	102	1.18
Huntington (town) Suffolk County	65	0.03
Babylon (town) Suffolk County	64	0.03
Oyster Bay (town) Nassau County	55	0.02
Islip (town) Suffolk County	53	0.02
Williston Park (village) Nassau County	48	0.66
North Hempstead (town) Nassau County	48	0.02

Top 10 Places Sorted by Percent of Total Population
Based on all places, regardless of total population

Place	Population	%
Napanoch (cdp) Ulster County	25	2.35
North Lynbrook (cdp) Nassau County	13	1.75
Katonah (cdp) Westchester County	22	1.50
Lewis (town) Essex County	18	1.41
St. Armand (town) Essex County	17	1.33
Cayuga (village) Cayuga County	6	1.32
Hornell (city) Steuben County	102	1.18
Clinton (town) Dutchess County	45	1.05
Chesterfield (town) Essex County	25	1.04
Delanson (village) Schenectady County	3	1.02

Top 10 Places Sorted by Percent of Total Population
Based on places with total population of 50,000 or more

Place	Population	%
Clay (town) Onondaga County	47	0.08
Hamburg (town) Erie County	43	0.08
Union (town) Broome County	27	0.05
Troy (city) Rensselaer County	23	0.05
Huntington (town) Suffolk County	65	0.03
Babylon (town) Suffolk County	64	0.03
Schenectady (city) Schenectady County	20	0.03
Utica (city) Oneida County	16	0.03
Irondequoit (cdp/town) Monroe County	14	0.03
Manhattan (borough) New York County	304	0.02

Croatian

Top 10 Places Sorted by Population
Based on all places, regardless of total population

Place	Population	%
New York (city)	11,304	0.14
Queens (borough) Queens County	7,054	0.32
Manhattan (borough) New York County	2,164	0.14
Hempstead (town) Nassau County	1,033	0.14
Oyster Bay (town) Nassau County	1,002	0.34
Brooklyn (borough) Kings County	998	0.04
Staten Island (borough) Richmond County	869	0.19
Huntington (town) Suffolk County	781	0.39
North Hempstead (town) Nassau County	672	0.30
Greenburgh (town) Westchester County	609	0.69

Top 10 Places Sorted by Percent of Total Population
Based on all places, regardless of total population

Place	Population	%
Castorland (village) Lewis County	21	5.44
North Lynbrook (cdp) Nassau County	30	4.04
Pleasantville (village) Westchester County	276	3.93

Place	Population	%
Irvington (village) Westchester County	245	3.82
Halesite (cdp) Suffolk County	78	3.70
Rockland (town) Sullivan County	124	3.22
Herricks (cdp) Nassau County	126	3.20
Palenville (cdp) Greene County	31	2.73
Strykersville (cdp) Wyoming County	13	2.58
North Sea (cdp) Suffolk County	133	2.57

Top 10 Places Sorted by Percent of Total Population
Based on places with total population of 50,000 or more

Place	Population	%
Greenburgh (town) Westchester County	609	0.69
Tonawanda (town) Erie County	326	0.44
Hamburg (town) Erie County	246	0.43
Southampton (town) Suffolk County	227	0.40
Huntington (town) Suffolk County	781	0.39
Tonawanda (cdp) Erie County	219	0.37
Oyster Bay (town) Nassau County	1,002	0.34
Queens (borough) Queens County	7,054	0.32
Amherst (town) Erie County	393	0.32
North Hempstead (town) Nassau County	672	0.30

Cypriot

Top 10 Places Sorted by Population
Based on all places, regardless of total population

Place	Population	%
New York (city)	960	0.01
Queens (borough) Queens County	644	0.03
Hempstead (town) Nassau County	254	0.03
Manhattan (borough) New York County	216	0.01
Oceanside (cdp) Nassau County	90	0.29
Huntington (town) Suffolk County	82	0.04
Valley Stream (village) Nassau County	68	0.18
Franklin Square (cdp) Nassau County	67	0.23
Yorktown (town) Westchester County	65	0.18
North Hempstead (town) Nassau County	64	0.03

Top 10 Places Sorted by Percent of Total Population
Based on all places, regardless of total population

Place	Population	%
Hillside (cdp) Ulster County	8	1.06
Eatons Neck (cdp) Suffolk County	12	0.89
Clarence Center (cdp) Erie County	17	0.79
Hewlett Harbor (village) Nassau County	7	0.60
Greenlawn (cdp) Suffolk County	56	0.43
Laurel Hollow (village) Nassau County	8	0.42
Balmville (cdp) Orange County	13	0.39
Muttontown (village) Nassau County	13	0.38
Lake Grove (village) Suffolk County	39	0.35
Roslyn (village) Nassau County	9	0.33

Top 10 Places Sorted by Percent of Total Population
Based on places with total population of 50,000 or more

Place	Population	%
Huntington (town) Suffolk County	82	0.04
Queens (borough) Queens County	644	0.03
Hempstead (town) Nassau County	254	0.03
North Hempstead (town) Nassau County	64	0.03
Oyster Bay (town) Nassau County	63	0.02
Hempstead (village) Nassau County	9	0.02
New York (city)	960	0.01
Manhattan (borough) New York County	216	0.01
Brookhaven (town) Suffolk County	51	0.01
Islip (town) Suffolk County	25	0.01

Czech

Top 10 Places Sorted by Population
Based on all places, regardless of total population

Place	Population	%
New York (city)	12,800	0.16
Manhattan (borough) New York County	4,820	0.30
Queens (borough) Queens County	3,464	0.16
Brooklyn (borough) Kings County	3,393	0.14
Brookhaven (town) Suffolk County	3,121	0.65
Hempstead (town) Nassau County	2,447	0.32
Islip (town) Suffolk County	2,026	0.61
Oyster Bay (town) Nassau County	1,379	0.47
Huntington (town) Suffolk County	1,271	0.63
Union (town) Broome County	929	1.65

Top 10 Places Sorted by Percent of Total Population
Based on all places, regardless of total population

Place	Population	%
West Hampton Dunes (village) Suffolk County	6	13.95
Durhamville (cdp) Oneida County	61	10.61
Pleasant Valley (cdp) Dutchess County	83	10.01
Lakeville (cdp) Livingston County	42	6.98
Shoreham (village) Suffolk County	45	6.73
Andes (cdp) Delaware County	16	5.76
Summerhill (town) Cayuga County	59	5.20
Boylston (town) Oswego County	24	5.03
Constantia (cdp) Oswego County	72	4.77
Williamson (cdp) Wayne County	103	4.33

Top 10 Places Sorted by Percent of Total Population
Based on places with total population of 50,000 or more

Place	Population	%
Union (town) Broome County	929	1.65
Brookhaven (town) Suffolk County	3,121	0.65
Huntington (town) Suffolk County	1,271	0.63
Islip (town) Suffolk County	2,026	0.61
Smithtown (town) Suffolk County	692	0.59
Colonie (town) Albany County	453	0.56
Clay (town) Onondaga County	312	0.54
Greece (town) Monroe County	507	0.53
New Rochelle (city) Westchester County	402	0.53
Oyster Bay (town) Nassau County	1,379	0.47

Czechoslovakian

Top 10 Places Sorted by Population
Based on all places, regardless of total population

Place	Population	%
New York (city)	4,870	0.06
Brooklyn (borough) Kings County	1,684	0.07
Queens (borough) Queens County	1,467	0.07
Manhattan (borough) New York County	1,256	0.08
Hempstead (town) Nassau County	1,054	0.14
Brookhaven (town) Suffolk County	917	0.19
Ramapo (town) Rockland County	654	0.53
Oyster Bay (town) Nassau County	618	0.21
Islip (town) Suffolk County	596	0.18
North Hempstead (town) Nassau County	493	0.22

Top 10 Places Sorted by Percent of Total Population
Based on all places, regardless of total population

Place	Population	%
Smallwood (cdp) Sullivan County	145	21.08
Ellisburg (village) Jefferson County	17	6.75
Yorkshire (cdp) Cattaraugus County	75	5.96
Walker Valley (cdp) Ulster County	28	5.22
Kensington (village) Nassau County	56	4.65
Greenville (cdp) Greene County	34	3.91
Bethel (town) Sullivan County	156	3.62
Preston-Potter Hollow (cdp) Albany County	9	3.30
Freedom (town) Cattaraugus County	75	3.18
Pleasant Valley (cdp) Dutchess County	26	3.14

Top 10 Places Sorted by Percent of Total Population
Based on places with total population of 50,000 or more

Place	Population	%
Union (town) Broome County	364	0.65
Ramapo (town) Rockland County	654	0.53
Tonawanda (cdp) Erie County	177	0.30
Smithtown (town) Suffolk County	310	0.26
Schenectady (city) Schenectady County	167	0.26
Tonawanda (town) Erie County	179	0.24
North Hempstead (town) Nassau County	493	0.22
Huntington (town) Suffolk County	435	0.22
Oyster Bay (town) Nassau County	618	0.21
Babylon (town) Suffolk County	438	0.21

Danish

Top 10 Places Sorted by Population
Based on all places, regardless of total population

Place	Population	%
New York (city)	7,018	0.09
Manhattan (borough) New York County	4,095	0.26
Brooklyn (borough) Kings County	1,267	0.05

Place	Population	%
Brookhaven (town) Suffolk County	1,229	0.26
Hempstead (town) Nassau County	1,023	0.14
Huntington (town) Suffolk County	809	0.40
Queens (borough) Queens County	792	0.04
Islip (town) Suffolk County	761	0.23
Oyster Bay (town) Nassau County	573	0.20
Staten Island (borough) Richmond County	479	0.10

Top 10 Places Sorted by Percent of Total Population
Based on all places, regardless of total population

Place	Population	%
Thousand Island Park (cdp) Jefferson County	16	14.41
Pine Hill (cdp) Ulster County	23	8.95
Windham (cdp) Greene County	37	8.53
Benton (town) Yates County	224	7.99
Hall (cdp) Ontario County	15	7.77
Dresden (village) Yates County	18	7.53
Shokan (cdp) Ulster County	53	6.85
Shrub Oak (cdp) Westchester County	111	6.13
Duane (town) Franklin County	10	5.65
Birdsall (town) Allegany County	17	5.54

Top 10 Places Sorted by Percent of Total Population
Based on places with total population of 50,000 or more

Place	Population	%
Troy (city) Rensselaer County	223	0.45
Huntington (town) Suffolk County	809	0.40
Albany (city) Albany County	303	0.31
Smithtown (town) Suffolk County	314	0.27
Manhattan (borough) New York County	4,095	0.26
Brookhaven (town) Suffolk County	1,229	0.26
Tonawanda (cdp) Erie County	151	0.26
Niagara Falls (city) Niagara County	134	0.26
Colonie (town) Albany County	195	0.24
Tonawanda (town) Erie County	179	0.24

Dutch

Top 10 Places Sorted by Population
Based on all places, regardless of total population

Place	Population	%
New York (city)	23,151	0.29
Manhattan (borough) New York County	10,414	0.66
Brooklyn (borough) Kings County	5,664	0.23
Brookhaven (town) Suffolk County	4,038	0.84
Queens (borough) Queens County	3,516	0.16
Colonie (town) Albany County	3,334	4.09
Hempstead (town) Nassau County	3,142	0.42
Rochester (city) Monroe County	2,898	1.37
Greece (town) Monroe County	2,890	3.03
Arcadia (town) Wayne County	2,484	17.31

Top 10 Places Sorted by Percent of Total Population
Based on all places, regardless of total population

Place	Population	%
Tuscarora (cdp) Livingston County	36	46.75
Malden-on-Hudson (cdp) Ulster County	104	32.20
Livonia Center (cdp) Livingston County	141	28.89
Hall (cdp) Ontario County	55	28.50
Clymer (town) Chautauqua County	431	24.83
Galway (village) Saratoga County	26	24.07
Pultneyville (cdp) Wayne County	183	23.92
Pierrepont Manor (cdp) Jefferson County	27	22.13
Blenheim (town) Schoharie County	64	19.39
Cattaraugus Reservation Chautauqua County	3	18.75

Top 10 Places Sorted by Percent of Total Population
Based on places with total population of 50,000 or more

Place	Population	%
Colonie (town) Albany County	3,334	4.09
Union (town) Broome County	1,823	3.24
Greece (town) Monroe County	2,890	3.03
Clay (town) Onondaga County	1,704	2.93
Troy (city) Rensselaer County	1,379	2.76
Irondequoit (cdp/town) Monroe County	1,310	2.54
Schenectady (city) Schenectady County	1,521	2.33
Albany (city) Albany County	1,664	1.70
Syracuse (city) Onondaga County	2,128	1.47
Utica (city) Oneida County	884	1.43

Eastern European

Top 10 Places Sorted by Population
Based on all places, regardless of total population

Place	Population	%
New York (city)	44,970	0.56
Manhattan (borough) New York County	25,277	1.60
Brooklyn (borough) Kings County	12,941	0.52
Hempstead (town) Nassau County	5,775	0.77
Queens (borough) Queens County	4,673	0.21
Oyster Bay (town) Nassau County	3,841	1.32
North Hempstead (town) Nassau County	3,769	1.69
Huntington (town) Suffolk County	2,012	1.00
Greenburgh (town) Westchester County	2,009	2.29
Bronx (borough) Bronx County	1,646	0.12

Top 10 Places Sorted by Percent of Total Population
Based on all places, regardless of total population

Place	Population	%
Great Neck Gardens (cdp) Nassau County	106	11.67
Saddle Rock Estates (cdp) Nassau County	60	11.45
Hewlett Harbor (village) Nassau County	109	9.29
Harbor Hills (cdp) Nassau County	44	8.89
East Hills (village) Nassau County	523	7.63
Old Westbury (village) Nassau County	297	7.54
Greenvale (cdp) Nassau County	33	7.35
Hewlett Neck (village) Nassau County	34	7.26
Scarsdale (town/village) Westchester County	1,208	7.06
Matinecock (village) Nassau County	54	7.05

Top 10 Places Sorted by Percent of Total Population
Based on places with total population of 50,000 or more

Place	Population	%
Greenburgh (town) Westchester County	2,009	2.29
North Hempstead (town) Nassau County	3,769	1.69
Manhattan (borough) New York County	25,277	1.60
Clarkstown (town) Rockland County	1,282	1.54
Oyster Bay (town) Nassau County	3,841	1.32
New Rochelle (city) Westchester County	870	1.15
Huntington (town) Suffolk County	2,012	1.00
White Plains (city) Westchester County	557	1.00
Ramapo (town) Rockland County	1,144	0.93
Hempstead (town) Nassau County	5,775	0.77

English

Top 10 Places Sorted by Population
Based on all places, regardless of total population

Place	Population	%
New York (city)	146,525	1.81
Manhattan (borough) New York County	77,799	4.91
Brooklyn (borough) Kings County	32,407	1.31
Brookhaven (town) Suffolk County	30,089	6.27
Hempstead (town) Nassau County	21,808	2.89
Queens (borough) Queens County	20,267	0.92
Islip (town) Suffolk County	13,963	4.18
Rochester (city) Monroe County	13,510	6.37
Huntington (town) Suffolk County	13,038	6.45
Greece (town) Monroe County	12,568	13.17

Top 10 Places Sorted by Percent of Total Population
Based on all places, regardless of total population

Place	Population	%
Thousand Island Park (cdp) Jefferson County	58	52.25
Dalton (cdp) Livingston County	165	51.24
Dering Harbor (village) Suffolk County	8	50.00
Redwood (cdp) Jefferson County	152	49.19
Denning (town) Ulster County	202	38.70
Davenport Center (cdp) Delaware County	113	38.18
Honeoye (cdp) Ontario County	266	37.62
Piffard (cdp) Livingston County	21	35.00
Central Bridge (cdp) Schoharie County	208	34.61
Saltaire (village) Suffolk County	20	34.48

Top 10 Places Sorted by Percent of Total Population
Based on places with total population of 50,000 or more

Place	Population	%
Clay (town) Onondaga County	8,266	14.23
Irondequoit (cdp/town) Monroe County	7,215	13.98
Greece (town) Monroe County	12,568	13.17
Union (town) Broome County	7,072	12.56

Niagara Falls (city) Niagara County	6,055	11.90
Tonawanda (cdp) Erie County	6,115	10.44
Southampton (town) Suffolk County	5,792	10.24
Colonie (town) Albany County	8,332	10.22
Amherst (town) Erie County	11,840	9.79
Tonawanda (town) Erie County	7,240	9.77

Estonian

Top 10 Places Sorted by Population
Based on all places, regardless of total population

Place	Population	%
New York (city)	1,057	0.01
Manhattan (borough) New York County	424	0.03
Brooklyn (borough) Kings County	340	0.01
Queens (borough) Queens County	198	0.01
Islip (town) Suffolk County	175	0.05
Hempstead (town) Nassau County	175	0.02
Huntington (town) Suffolk County	140	0.07
Oyster Bay (town) Nassau County	130	0.04
Brookhaven (town) Suffolk County	102	0.02
Bronx (borough) Bronx County	85	0.01

Top 10 Places Sorted by Percent of Total Population
Based on all places, regardless of total population

Place	Population	%
Redford (cdp) Clinton County	31	6.47
Fort Montgomery (cdp) Orange County	55	6.44
Warren (town) Herkimer County	36	3.18
Clarence (cdp) Erie County	78	2.64
Chenango Bridge (cdp) Broome County	32	1.05
Red Hook (village) Dutchess County	18	0.96
Preston (town) Chenango County	9	0.93
Orient (cdp) Suffolk County	5	0.83
Saranac (town) Clinton County	31	0.77
Yaphank (cdp) Suffolk County	47	0.76

Top 10 Places Sorted by Percent of Total Population
Based on places with total population of 50,000 or more

Place	Population	%
Cheektowaga (cdp) Erie County	78	0.10
Cheektowaga (town) Erie County	78	0.09
Huntington (town) Suffolk County	140	0.07
Greenburgh (town) Westchester County	57	0.07
Mount Vernon (city) Westchester County	45	0.07
Islip (town) Suffolk County	175	0.05
Oyster Bay (town) Nassau County	130	0.04
Ramapo (town) Rockland County	48	0.04
Greece (town) Monroe County	40	0.04
Manhattan (borough) New York County	424	0.03

European

Top 10 Places Sorted by Population
Based on all places, regardless of total population

Place	Population	%
New York (city)	66,267	0.82
Manhattan (borough) New York County	27,846	1.76
Brooklyn (borough) Kings County	27,499	1.11
Ramapo (town) Rockland County	8,814	7.18
Queens (borough) Queens County	6,584	0.30
Hempstead (town) Nassau County	5,650	0.75
Monsey (cdp) Rockland County	3,363	22.35
Oyster Bay (town) Nassau County	2,919	1.00
Bronx (borough) Bronx County	2,270	0.17
Huntington (town) Suffolk County	2,177	1.08

Top 10 Places Sorted by Percent of Total Population
Based on all places, regardless of total population

Place	Population	%
Kaser (village) Rockland County	1,293	29.15
Monsey (cdp) Rockland County	3,363	22.35
New Square (village) Rockland County	1,147	17.76
West Hampton Dunes (village) Suffolk County	6	13.95
Ghent (town) Columbia County	70	11.02
Adams Center (cdp) Jefferson County	179	10.45
Wesley Hills (village) Rockland County	551	10.11
Covington (town) Wyoming County	111	8.80
Claverack-Red Mills (cdp) Columbia County	72	8.56
Accord (cdp) Ulster County	50	8.40

Top 10 Places Sorted by Percent of Total Population
Based on places with total population of 50,000 or more

Place	Population	%
Ramapo (town) Rockland County	8,814	7.18
Manhattan (borough) New York County	27,846	1.76
Greenburgh (town) Westchester County	1,360	1.55
Albany (city) Albany County	1,362	1.39
White Plains (city) Westchester County	684	1.22
Union (town) Broome County	660	1.17
Brooklyn (borough) Kings County	27,499	1.11
Huntington (town) Suffolk County	2,177	1.08
New Rochelle (city) Westchester County	808	1.07
Troy (city) Rensselaer County	529	1.06

Finnish

Top 10 Places Sorted by Population
Based on all places, regardless of total population

Place	Population	%
New York (city)	3,519	0.04
Manhattan (borough) New York County	1,658	0.10
Brookhaven (town) Suffolk County	706	0.15
Queens (borough) Queens County	693	0.03
Brooklyn (borough) Kings County	692	0.03
Hempstead (town) Nassau County	647	0.09
Bronx (borough) Bronx County	291	0.02
Islip (town) Suffolk County	271	0.08
Oyster Bay (town) Nassau County	265	0.09
Dryden (town) Tompkins County	254	1.78

Top 10 Places Sorted by Percent of Total Population
Based on all places, regardless of total population

Place	Population	%
Van Etten (village) Chemung County	39	8.71
Van Etten (town) Chemung County	109	8.68
Freeville (village) Tompkins County	29	5.80
Ward (town) Allegany County	18	5.34
Spencer (town) Tioga County	151	4.80
Preston-Potter Hollow (cdp) Albany County	12	4.40
Hunter (village) Greene County	21	4.25
East Randolph (village) Cattaraugus County	21	4.07
Smyrna (village) Chenango County	6	3.51
Shelter Island (cdp) Suffolk County	45	3.45

Top 10 Places Sorted by Percent of Total Population
Based on places with total population of 50,000 or more

Place	Population	%
Southampton (town) Suffolk County	206	0.36
Amherst (town) Erie County	196	0.16
Tonawanda (cdp) Erie County	95	0.16
Brookhaven (town) Suffolk County	706	0.15
Troy (city) Rensselaer County	74	0.15
Clarkstown (town) Rockland County	119	0.14
Tonawanda (town) Erie County	95	0.13
Manhattan (borough) New York County	1,658	0.10
Smithtown (town) Suffolk County	120	0.10
Greenburgh (town) Westchester County	85	0.10

French, except Basque

Top 10 Places Sorted by Population
Based on all places, regardless of total population

Place	Population	%
New York (city)	67,195	0.83
Manhattan (borough) New York County	31,783	2.01
Brooklyn (borough) Kings County	14,137	0.57
Queens (borough) Queens County	12,532	0.57
Brookhaven (town) Suffolk County	8,961	1.87
Hempstead (town) Nassau County	8,239	1.09
Syracuse (city) Onondaga County	6,182	4.27
Colonie (town) Albany County	5,795	7.11
Bronx (borough) Bronx County	4,971	0.36
Troy (city) Rensselaer County	4,862	9.72

Top 10 Places Sorted by Percent of Total Population
Based on all places, regardless of total population

Place	Population	%
Witherbee (cdp) Essex County	175	70.56
Chazy (cdp) Clinton County	293	57.79
Redford (cdp) Clinton County	255	53.24

Place	Population	%
Redwood (cdp) Jefferson County	158	51.13
Saranac (town) Clinton County	1,685	41.73
Bellmont (town) Franklin County	720	39.80
Mooers (cdp) Clinton County	218	38.86
Three Mile Bay (cdp) Jefferson County	80	37.91
Byersville (cdp) Livingston County	23	37.70
Norfolk (cdp) St. Lawrence County	461	37.12

Top 10 Places Sorted by Percent of Total Population
Based on places with total population of 50,000 or more

Place	Population	%
Troy (city) Rensselaer County	4,862	9.72
Colonie (town) Albany County	5,795	7.11
Clay (town) Onondaga County	3,175	5.47
Schenectady (city) Schenectady County	2,862	4.38
Syracuse (city) Onondaga County	6,182	4.27
Greece (town) Monroe County	3,655	3.83
Albany (city) Albany County	3,690	3.77
Tonawanda (cdp) Erie County	2,149	3.67
Hamburg (town) Erie County	2,079	3.67
Union (town) Broome County	2,044	3.63

French Canadian

Top 10 Places Sorted by Population
Based on all places, regardless of total population

Place	Population	%
New York (city)	11,393	0.14
Manhattan (borough) New York County	5,246	0.33
Brooklyn (borough) Kings County	2,974	0.12
Brookhaven (town) Suffolk County	2,478	0.52
Queens (borough) Queens County	2,020	0.09
Syracuse (city) Onondaga County	1,782	1.23
Hempstead (town) Nassau County	1,779	0.24
Colonie (town) Albany County	1,591	1.95
Rochester (city) Monroe County	1,474	0.70
Buffalo (city) Erie County	1,376	0.52

Top 10 Places Sorted by Percent of Total Population
Based on all places, regardless of total population

Place	Population	%
Mooers (cdp) Clinton County	124	22.10
Champlain (town) Clinton County	1,079	18.59
Mooers (town) Clinton County	614	17.16
Rensselaer Falls (village) St. Lawrence County	75	15.56
Waverly (town) Franklin County	157	15.23
Tupper Lake (village) Franklin County	581	15.11
St. Regis Falls (cdp) Franklin County	57	14.73
Clinton (town) Clinton County	114	14.36
Schenevus (cdp) Otsego County	39	14.18
Salt Point (cdp) Dutchess County	46	14.11

Top 10 Places Sorted by Percent of Total Population
Based on places with total population of 50,000 or more

Place	Population	%
Troy (city) Rensselaer County	1,245	2.49
Clay (town) Onondaga County	1,241	2.14
Colonie (town) Albany County	1,591	1.95
Schenectady (city) Schenectady County	902	1.38
Greece (town) Monroe County	1,220	1.28
Syracuse (city) Onondaga County	1,782	1.23
Tonawanda (town) Erie County	881	1.19
Albany (city) Albany County	1,061	1.08
Hamburg (town) Erie County	586	1.04
Utica (city) Oneida County	620	1.00

German

Top 10 Places Sorted by Population
Based on all places, regardless of total population

Place	Population	%
New York (city)	272,827	3.38
Manhattan (borough) New York County	107,666	6.80
Brookhaven (town) Suffolk County	89,711	18.69
Hempstead (town) Nassau County	78,518	10.42
Queens (borough) Queens County	70,399	3.20
Brooklyn (borough) Kings County	52,798	2.14
Islip (town) Suffolk County	48,335	14.48
Oyster Bay (town) Nassau County	41,381	14.19
Buffalo (city) Erie County	35,760	13.44
Huntington (town) Suffolk County	33,758	16.70

Top 10 Places Sorted by Percent of Total Population
Based on all places, regardless of total population

Place	Population	%
Websters Crossing (cdp) Livingston County	42	100.00
Belleville (cdp) Jefferson County	78	66.67
South Lima (cdp) Livingston County	132	65.02
Farnham (village) Erie County	148	62.45
Corfu (village) Genesee County	453	58.83
Livonia Center (cdp) Livingston County	276	56.56
Allen (town) Allegany County	273	55.38
Java (town) Wyoming County	1,212	54.69
Machias (cdp) Cattaraugus County	393	53.91
Alexander (village) Genesee County	330	53.23

Top 10 Places Sorted by Percent of Total Population
Based on places with total population of 50,000 or more

Place	Population	%
Hamburg (town) Erie County	19,590	34.62
Tonawanda (cdp) Erie County	19,292	32.95
Tonawanda (town) Erie County	24,085	32.51
Cheektowaga (town) Erie County	26,125	29.39
Cheektowaga (cdp) Erie County	21,843	28.83
Greece (town) Monroe County	25,631	26.85
Amherst (town) Erie County	30,579	25.28
Clay (town) Onondaga County	14,237	24.51
Irondequoit (cdp/town) Monroe County	11,815	22.89
Smithtown (town) Suffolk County	23,592	20.06

German Russian

Top 10 Places Sorted by Population
Based on all places, regardless of total population

Place	Population	%
New York (city)	204	<0.01
Queens (borough) Queens County	78	<0.01
Troy (city) Rensselaer County	65	0.13
Brooklyn (borough) Kings County	55	<0.01
Buffalo (city) Erie County	41	0.02
Manhattan (borough) New York County	41	<0.01
Mastic (cdp) Suffolk County	40	0.28
Brookhaven (town) Suffolk County	40	0.01
Tonawanda (city) Erie County	33	0.22
Bronx (borough) Bronx County	30	<0.01

Top 10 Places Sorted by Percent of Total Population
Based on all places, regardless of total population

Place	Population	%
Lake George (town) Warren County	16	0.45
Garden City Park (cdp) Nassau County	26	0.33
Mastic (cdp) Suffolk County	40	0.28
Tonawanda (city) Erie County	33	0.22
Fort Drum (cdp) Jefferson County	17	0.14
Troy (city) Rensselaer County	65	0.13
Dobbs Ferry (village) Westchester County	13	0.12
Haverstraw (village) Rockland County	12	0.10
Wantagh (cdp) Nassau County	17	0.09
Le Ray (town) Jefferson County	17	0.08

Top 10 Places Sorted by Percent of Total Population
Based on places with total population of 50,000 or more

Place	Population	%
Troy (city) Rensselaer County	65	0.13
Irondequoit (cdp/town) Monroe County	28	0.05
Niagara Falls (city) Niagara County	16	0.03
Buffalo (city) Erie County	41	0.02
Cheektowaga (cdp) Erie County	12	0.02
Brookhaven (town) Suffolk County	40	0.01
North Hempstead (town) Nassau County	26	0.01
Yonkers (city) Westchester County	14	0.01
Greenburgh (town) Westchester County	13	0.01
Cheektowaga (town) Erie County	12	0.01

Greek

Top 10 Places Sorted by Population
Based on all places, regardless of total population

Place	Population	%
New York (city)	76,597	0.95
Queens (borough) Queens County	41,654	1.89
Brooklyn (borough) Kings County	14,075	0.57

Place	Population	%
Manhattan (borough) New York County	13,078	0.83
Hempstead (town) Nassau County	10,033	1.33
Oyster Bay (town) Nassau County	6,908	2.37
Brookhaven (town) Suffolk County	5,703	1.19
Staten Island (borough) Richmond County	4,183	0.90
Bronx (borough) Bronx County	3,607	0.26
North Hempstead (town) Nassau County	3,568	1.60

Top 10 Places Sorted by Percent of Total Population
Based on all places, regardless of total population

Place	Population	%
Harbor Hills (cdp) Nassau County	94	18.99
Plandome Manor (village) Nassau County	97	11.02
Manhasset Hills (cdp) Nassau County	328	8.90
Old Brookville (village) Nassau County	189	8.49
Sparkill (cdp) Rockland County	114	8.25
Halcott (town) Greene County	20	7.52
Shinnecock Hills (cdp) Suffolk County	133	7.25
High Falls (cdp) Ulster County	62	7.20
Bellerose (village) Nassau County	84	6.75
Mattituck (cdp) Suffolk County	279	6.73

Top 10 Places Sorted by Percent of Total Population
Based on places with total population of 50,000 or more

Place	Population	%
Smithtown (town) Suffolk County	3,078	2.62
Oyster Bay (town) Nassau County	6,908	2.37
Levittown (cdp) Nassau County	1,100	2.06
Queens (borough) Queens County	41,654	1.89
Southampton (town) Suffolk County	995	1.76
Huntington (town) Suffolk County	3,284	1.62
North Hempstead (town) Nassau County	3,568	1.60
Greenburgh (town) Westchester County	1,202	1.37
Hempstead (town) Nassau County	10,033	1.33
Brookhaven (town) Suffolk County	5,703	1.19

Guyanese

Top 10 Places Sorted by Population
Based on all places, regardless of total population

Place	Population	%
New York (city)	107,972	1.34
Queens (borough) Queens County	53,961	2.45
Brooklyn (borough) Kings County	38,963	1.58
Bronx (borough) Bronx County	11,837	0.87
Hempstead (town) Nassau County	3,520	0.47
Manhattan (borough) New York County	2,259	0.14
Schenectady (city) Schenectady County	1,915	2.93
Staten Island (borough) Richmond County	952	0.21
Valley Stream (village) Nassau County	840	2.27
Babylon (town) Suffolk County	747	0.35

Top 10 Places Sorted by Percent of Total Population
Based on all places, regardless of total population

Place	Population	%
St. Regis Mohawk Reservation Franklin County	162	5.17
Greenville (town) Orange County	161	3.57
Hillcrest (cdp) Rockland County	280	3.42
Schenectady (city) Schenectady County	1,915	2.93
Manhasset Hills (cdp) Nassau County	102	2.77
Highland (cdp) Ulster County	149	2.62
Batavia (town) Genesee County	172	2.60
Queens (borough) Queens County	53,961	2.45
Menands (village) Albany County	97	2.43
Valley Stream (village) Nassau County	840	2.27

Top 10 Places Sorted by Percent of Total Population
Based on places with total population of 50,000 or more

Place	Population	%
Schenectady (city) Schenectady County	1,915	2.93
Queens (borough) Queens County	53,961	2.45
Brooklyn (borough) Kings County	38,963	1.58
New York (city)	107,972	1.34
Bronx (borough) Bronx County	11,837	0.87
Hempstead (village) Nassau County	307	0.58
Mount Vernon (city) Westchester County	360	0.54
Albany (city) Albany County	483	0.49
Hempstead (town) Nassau County	3,520	0.47
Babylon (town) Suffolk County	747	0.35

Hungarian

Top 10 Places Sorted by Population
Based on all places, regardless of total population

Place	Population	%
New York (city)	55,459	0.69
Brooklyn (borough) Kings County	26,607	1.08
Manhattan (borough) New York County	14,667	0.93
Queens (borough) Queens County	9,470	0.43
Hempstead (town) Nassau County	6,992	0.93
Ramapo (town) Rockland County	6,804	5.54
Monroe (town) Orange County	5,591	14.45
Kiryas Joel (village) Orange County	5,471	28.66
Brookhaven (town) Suffolk County	4,390	0.91
Oyster Bay (town) Nassau County	3,138	1.08

Top 10 Places Sorted by Percent of Total Population
Based on all places, regardless of total population

Place	Population	%
South Lima (cdp) Livingston County	72	35.47
Natural Bridge (cdp) Jefferson County	137	33.91
Kiryas Joel (village) Orange County	5,471	28.66
New Square (village) Rockland County	1,787	27.67
Kaser (village) Rockland County	1,034	23.31
Monroe (town) Orange County	5,591	14.45
Prattsville (cdp) Greene County	41	12.85
Lawrence (village) Nassau County	746	11.57
Monsey (cdp) Rockland County	1,483	9.85
Saddle Rock Estates (cdp) Nassau County	48	9.16

Top 10 Places Sorted by Percent of Total Population
Based on places with total population of 50,000 or more

Place	Population	%
Ramapo (town) Rockland County	6,804	5.54
Tonawanda (cdp) Erie County	976	1.67
Tonawanda (town) Erie County	1,188	1.60
Huntington (town) Suffolk County	3,005	1.49
Levittown (cdp) Nassau County	781	1.46
Greenburgh (town) Westchester County	1,242	1.42
Hamburg (town) Erie County	761	1.34
Clarkstown (town) Rockland County	1,008	1.21
North Hempstead (town) Nassau County	2,628	1.18
Brooklyn (borough) Kings County	26,607	1.08

Icelander

Top 10 Places Sorted by Population
Based on all places, regardless of total population

Place	Population	%
New York (city)	572	0.01
Manhattan (borough) New York County	382	0.02
Brooklyn (borough) Kings County	103	<0.01
Hempstead (town) Nassau County	92	0.01
Pittsford (town) Monroe County	63	0.22
Blooming Grove (town) Orange County	62	0.34
Wawayanda (town) Orange County	55	0.77
Staten Island (borough) Richmond County	55	0.01
Lockport (town) Niagara County	52	0.26
Levittown (cdp) Nassau County	52	0.10

Top 10 Places Sorted by Percent of Total Population
Based on all places, regardless of total population

Place	Population	%
Northwest Ithaca (cdp) Tompkins County	14	1.21
Brewerton (cdp) Onondaga County	33	0.81
Wawayanda (town) Orange County	55	0.77
Meredith (town) Delaware County	8	0.51
West Monroe (town) Oswego County	20	0.47
Port Ewen (cdp) Ulster County	15	0.40
Sempronius (town) Cayuga County	3	0.36
Blooming Grove (town) Orange County	62	0.34
Dannemora (town) Clinton County	16	0.32
Homer (village) Cortland County	10	0.30

Top 10 Places Sorted by Percent of Total Population
Based on places with total population of 50,000 or more

Place	Population	%
Levittown (cdp) Nassau County	52	0.10
Manhattan (borough) New York County	382	0.02
Oyster Bay (town) Nassau County	52	0.02
Huntington (town) Suffolk County	38	0.02

Utica (city) Oneida County	14	0.02
Tonawanda (cdp) Erie County	11	0.02
New York (city)	572	0.01
Hempstead (town) Nassau County	92	0.01
Staten Island (borough) Richmond County	55	0.01
Brookhaven (town) Suffolk County	45	0.01

Iranian

Top 10 Places Sorted by Population
Based on all places, regardless of total population

Place	Population	%
New York (city)	10,204	0.13
North Hempstead (town) Nassau County	9,262	4.14
Manhattan (borough) New York County	4,256	0.27
Queens (borough) Queens County	3,707	0.17
Great Neck (village) Nassau County	2,382	24.20
Kings Point (village) Nassau County	2,070	41.62
Brooklyn (borough) Kings County	1,822	0.07
Oyster Bay (town) Nassau County	1,464	0.50
Great Neck Plaza (village) Nassau County	673	10.18
Great Neck Estates (village) Nassau County	566	20.72

Top 10 Places Sorted by Percent of Total Population
Based on all places, regardless of total population

Place	Population	%
Kings Point (village) Nassau County	2,070	41.62
Saddle Rock (village) Nassau County	380	36.26
Great Neck (village) Nassau County	2,382	24.20
Great Neck Estates (village) Nassau County	566	20.72
Saddle Rock Estates (cdp) Nassau County	90	17.18
Kensington (village) Nassau County	180	14.94
Great Neck Plaza (village) Nassau County	673	10.18
Roslyn Heights (cdp) Nassau County	452	6.97
North Hills (village) Nassau County	316	6.40
Flower Hill (village) Nassau County	294	6.38

Top 10 Places Sorted by Percent of Total Population
Based on places with total population of 50,000 or more

Place	Population	%
North Hempstead (town) Nassau County	9,262	4.14
Oyster Bay (town) Nassau County	1,464	0.50
Greenburgh (town) Westchester County	267	0.30
Manhattan (borough) New York County	4,256	0.27
Ramapo (town) Rockland County	314	0.26
Huntington (town) Suffolk County	471	0.23
Smithtown (town) Suffolk County	237	0.20
Clarkstown (town) Rockland County	146	0.18
Queens (borough) Queens County	3,707	0.17
Clay (town) Onondaga County	99	0.17

Irish

Top 10 Places Sorted by Population
Based on all places, regardless of total population

Place	Population	%
New York (city)	410,889	5.09
Hempstead (town) Nassau County	125,911	16.71
Brookhaven (town) Suffolk County	122,200	25.45
Manhattan (borough) New York County	117,355	7.41
Queens (borough) Queens County	105,348	4.79
Brooklyn (borough) Kings County	84,945	3.44
Islip (town) Suffolk County	68,763	20.61
Staten Island (borough) Richmond County	64,762	13.97
Oyster Bay (town) Nassau County	59,765	20.49
Huntington (town) Suffolk County	45,750	22.63

Top 10 Places Sorted by Percent of Total Population
Based on all places, regardless of total population

Place	Population	%
Oak Beach-Captree (cdp) Suffolk County	348	73.26
Hopewell Junction (cdp) Dutchess County	290	61.97
Point Lookout (cdp) Nassau County	763	59.98
Walker Valley (cdp) Ulster County	319	59.51
Pearl River (cdp) Rockland County	7,647	52.46
Staatsburg (cdp) Dutchess County	274	52.29
Bellerose (village) Nassau County	648	52.09
Palenville (cdp) Greene County	584	51.45
Winthrop (cdp) St. Lawrence County	236	50.97
Parc (cdp) Clinton County	20	47.62

Israeli

Top 10 Places Sorted by Percent of Total Population
Based on places with total population of 50,000 or more

Place	Population	%
Colonie (town) Albany County	23,049	28.27
Levittown (cdp) Nassau County	14,886	27.84
Hamburg (town) Erie County	15,679	27.71
Smithtown (town) Suffolk County	31,963	27.18
Brookhaven (town) Suffolk County	122,200	25.45
Troy (city) Rensselaer County	12,384	24.76
Clay (town) Onondaga County	14,197	24.44
Southampton (town) Suffolk County	12,998	22.99
Huntington (town) Suffolk County	45,750	22.63
Union (town) Broome County	12,320	21.88

Israeli

Top 10 Places Sorted by Population
Based on all places, regardless of total population

Place	Population	%
New York (city)	21,872	0.27
Brooklyn (borough) Kings County	9,707	0.39
Manhattan (borough) New York County	6,624	0.42
Queens (borough) Queens County	4,164	0.19
Ramapo (town) Rockland County	3,342	2.72
Hempstead (town) Nassau County	2,558	0.34
North Hempstead (town) Nassau County	1,853	0.83
Kiryas Joel (village) Orange County	949	4.97
Monroe (town) Orange County	949	2.45
Woodmere (cdp) Nassau County	879	5.04

Top 10 Places Sorted by Percent of Total Population
Based on all places, regardless of total population

Place	Population	%
Saddle Rock (village) Nassau County	153	14.60
Kaser (village) Rockland County	540	12.17
Viola (cdp) Rockland County	792	11.23
Greenvale (cdp) Nassau County	32	7.13
Lake Success (village) Nassau County	172	5.94
South Valley Stream (cdp) Nassau County	268	5.09
Woodmere (cdp) Nassau County	879	5.04
Kiryas Joel (village) Orange County	949	4.97
Wesley Hills (village) Rockland County	231	4.24
Monsey (cdp) Rockland County	608	4.04

Top 10 Places Sorted by Percent of Total Population
Based on places with total population of 50,000 or more

Place	Population	%
Ramapo (town) Rockland County	3,342	2.72
North Hempstead (town) Nassau County	1,853	0.83
Manhattan (borough) New York County	6,624	0.42
Brooklyn (borough) Kings County	9,707	0.39
Hempstead (town) Nassau County	2,558	0.34
White Plains (city) Westchester County	181	0.32
Clarkstown (town) Rockland County	247	0.30
New York (city)	21,872	0.27
Greenburgh (town) Westchester County	225	0.26
Mount Vernon (city) Westchester County	174	0.26

Italian

Top 10 Places Sorted by Population
Based on all places, regardless of total population

Place	Population	%
New York (city)	625,004	7.74
Hempstead (town) Nassau County	164,467	21.82
Queens (borough) Queens County	159,812	7.27
Staten Island (borough) Richmond County	156,288	33.72
Brookhaven (town) Suffolk County	155,749	32.44
Brooklyn (borough) Kings County	152,814	6.19
Manhattan (borough) New York County	98,563	6.22
Oyster Bay (town) Nassau County	88,723	30.43
Islip (town) Suffolk County	84,360	25.28
Babylon (town) Suffolk County	61,852	28.95

Top 10 Places Sorted by Percent of Total Population
Based on all places, regardless of total population

Place	Population	%
Witherbee (cdp) Essex County	149	60.08
Hillside Lake (cdp) Dutchess County	350	51.32
North Massapequa (cdp) Nassau County	9,384	50.28

Place	Population	%
Frankfort (village) Herkimer County	1,299	50.17
East Kingston (cdp) Ulster County	170	49.56
Great River (cdp) Suffolk County	803	48.78
Leeds (cdp) Greene County	151	47.19
Fowlerville (cdp) Livingston County	116	46.96
Moriches (cdp) Suffolk County	1,413	46.85
Franklin Square (cdp) Nassau County	13,514	45.54

Top 10 Places Sorted by Percent of Total Population
Based on places with total population of 50,000 or more

Place	Population	%
Smithtown (town) Suffolk County	45,388	38.60
Staten Island (borough) Richmond County	156,288	33.72
Levittown (cdp) Nassau County	17,446	32.62
Brookhaven (town) Suffolk County	155,749	32.44
Oyster Bay (town) Nassau County	88,723	30.43
Babylon (town) Suffolk County	61,852	28.95
Irondequoit (cdp/town) Monroe County	14,566	28.22
Huntington (town) Suffolk County	56,013	27.70
Greece (town) Monroe County	26,121	27.36
Tonawanda (town) Erie County	19,213	25.93

Latvian

Top 10 Places Sorted by Population
Based on all places, regardless of total population

Place	Population	%
New York (city)	3,302	0.04
Manhattan (borough) New York County	1,822	0.12
Brooklyn (borough) Kings County	667	0.03
Queens (borough) Queens County	568	0.03
Hempstead (town) Nassau County	438	0.06
North Hempstead (town) Nassau County	254	0.11
Oyster Bay (town) Nassau County	235	0.08
Huntington (town) Suffolk County	193	0.10
Brookhaven (town) Suffolk County	182	0.04
Ramapo (town) Rockland County	174	0.14

Top 10 Places Sorted by Percent of Total Population
Based on all places, regardless of total population

Place	Population	%
Williamson (cdp) Wayne County	62	2.61
Halesite (cdp) Suffolk County	55	2.61
Stony Creek (town) Warren County	24	2.61
Bemus Point (village) Chautauqua County	6	2.05
Airmont (village) Rockland County	132	1.57
Pleasant Valley (cdp) Dutchess County	13	1.57
Tully (village) Onondaga County	13	1.52
Esperance (village) Schoharie County	6	1.34
LaFayette (town) Onondaga County	65	1.32
North Hills (village) Nassau County	59	1.19

Top 10 Places Sorted by Percent of Total Population
Based on places with total population of 50,000 or more

Place	Population	%
Greenburgh (town) Westchester County	153	0.17
Ramapo (town) Rockland County	174	0.14
Manhattan (borough) New York County	1,822	0.12
North Hempstead (town) Nassau County	254	0.11
Huntington (town) Suffolk County	193	0.10
Clarkstown (town) Rockland County	87	0.10
New Rochelle (city) Westchester County	74	0.10
Oyster Bay (town) Nassau County	235	0.08
Smithtown (town) Suffolk County	81	0.07
Greece (town) Monroe County	71	0.07

Lithuanian

Top 10 Places Sorted by Population
Based on all places, regardless of total population

Place	Population	%
New York (city)	12,774	0.16
Manhattan (borough) New York County	5,775	0.36
Queens (borough) Queens County	3,131	0.14
Brooklyn (borough) Kings County	2,676	0.11
Hempstead (town) Nassau County	2,538	0.34
Brookhaven (town) Suffolk County	1,898	0.40
Oyster Bay (town) Nassau County	1,079	0.37
Huntington (town) Suffolk County	956	0.47
Islip (town) Suffolk County	799	0.24
North Hempstead (town) Nassau County	718	0.32

Top 10 Places Sorted by Percent of Total Population
Based on all places, regardless of total population

Place	Population	%
Lyon Mountain (cdp) Clinton County	61	16.05
Wynantskill (cdp) Rensselaer County	256	7.24
Marion (cdp) Wayne County	102	5.38
Santa Clara (town) Franklin County	21	5.33
Leeds (cdp) Greene County	16	5.00
Hagaman (village) Montgomery County	48	4.52
Webb (town) Herkimer County	68	4.38
Durhamville (cdp) Oneida County	25	4.35
Napeague (cdp) Suffolk County	9	4.31
Old Forge (cdp) Herkimer County	22	4.27

Top 10 Places Sorted by Percent of Total Population
Based on places with total population of 50,000 or more

Place	Population	%
Union (town) Broome County	452	0.80
Levittown (cdp) Nassau County	314	0.59
Greece (town) Monroe County	543	0.57
Smithtown (town) Suffolk County	627	0.53
Irondequoit (cdp/town) Monroe County	267	0.52
Huntington (town) Suffolk County	956	0.47
Southampton (town) Suffolk County	267	0.47
Colonie (town) Albany County	377	0.46
Ramapo (town) Rockland County	538	0.44
Brookhaven (town) Suffolk County	1,898	0.40

Luxemburger

Top 10 Places Sorted by Population
Based on all places, regardless of total population

Place	Population	%
New York (city)	193	<0.01
Manhattan (borough) New York County	68	<0.01
Rochester (city) Monroe County	62	0.03
Brooklyn (borough) Kings County	58	<0.01
Staten Island (borough) Richmond County	54	0.01
Brookhaven (town) Suffolk County	36	0.01
Lenox (town) Madison County	27	0.30
Clay (town) Onondaga County	26	0.04
Ithaca (city) Tompkins County	24	0.08
Irondequoit (cdp/town) Monroe County	24	0.05

Top 10 Places Sorted by Percent of Total Population
Based on all places, regardless of total population

Place	Population	%
Lyndon (town) Cattaraugus County	4	0.70
Dickinson (town) Franklin County	6	0.56
Sheldon (town) Wyoming County	7	0.32
Lenox (town) Madison County	27	0.30
Roslyn Heights (cdp) Nassau County	16	0.25
Virgil (town) Cortland County	6	0.25
Java (town) Wyoming County	5	0.23
Athens (village) Greene County	3	0.18
Caton (town) Steuben County	5	0.17
Terryville (cdp) Suffolk County	18	0.15

Top 10 Places Sorted by Percent of Total Population
Based on places with total population of 50,000 or more

Place	Population	%
Irondequoit (cdp/town) Monroe County	24	0.05
Clay (town) Onondaga County	26	0.04
Rochester (city) Monroe County	62	0.03
Greece (town) Monroe County	15	0.02
Colonie (town) Albany County	13	0.02
Staten Island (borough) Richmond County	54	0.01
Brookhaven (town) Suffolk County	36	0.01
Buffalo (city) Erie County	24	0.01
North Hempstead (town) Nassau County	16	0.01
Syracuse (city) Onondaga County	14	0.01

Macedonian

Top 10 Places Sorted by Population
Based on all places, regardless of total population

Place	Population	%
New York (city)	4,911	0.06
Staten Island (borough) Richmond County	1,590	0.34
Queens (borough) Queens County	1,109	0.05

Place	Population	%
Manhattan (borough) New York County	1,086	0.07
Bronx (borough) Bronx County	628	0.05
Brooklyn (borough) Kings County	498	0.02
Irondequoit (cdp/town) Monroe County	266	0.52
Yonkers (city) Westchester County	236	0.12
Clay (town) Onondaga County	185	0.32
New Rochelle (city) Westchester County	177	0.23

Top 10 Places Sorted by Percent of Total Population
Based on all places, regardless of total population

Place	Population	%
Sunset Bay (cdp) Chautauqua County	50	5.55
Hannibal (village) Oswego County	15	2.65
Cold Brook (village) Herkimer County	6	1.59
Village Green (cdp) Onondaga County	56	1.25
Chappaqua (cdp) Westchester County	13	1.25
Union Vale (town) Dutchess County	57	1.18
Riga (town) Monroe County	61	1.10
Angola on the Lake (cdp) Erie County	12	0.86
Pulaski (village) Oswego County	19	0.78
Hanover (town) Chautauqua County	50	0.70

Top 10 Places Sorted by Percent of Total Population
Based on places with total population of 50,000 or more

Place	Population	%
Irondequoit (cdp/town) Monroe County	266	0.52
Staten Island (borough) Richmond County	1,590	0.34
Clay (town) Onondaga County	185	0.32
Hamburg (town) Erie County	149	0.26
New Rochelle (city) Westchester County	177	0.23
Yonkers (city) Westchester County	236	0.12
Greece (town) Monroe County	119	0.12
White Plains (city) Westchester County	54	0.10
Manhattan (borough) New York County	1,086	0.07
New York (city)	4,911	0.06

Maltese

Top 10 Places Sorted by Population
Based on all places, regardless of total population

Place	Population	%
New York (city)	3,102	0.04
Queens (borough) Queens County	1,565	0.07
Manhattan (borough) New York County	840	0.05
Brookhaven (town) Suffolk County	686	0.14
Oyster Bay (town) Nassau County	579	0.20
Hempstead (town) Nassau County	540	0.07
Babylon (town) Suffolk County	378	0.18
Brooklyn (borough) Kings County	362	0.01
Islip (town) Suffolk County	292	0.09
Staten Island (borough) Richmond County	290	0.06

Top 10 Places Sorted by Percent of Total Population
Based on all places, regardless of total population

Place	Population	%
Tuxedo (town) Orange County	93	2.59
Hamptonburgh (town) Orange County	103	1.89
Plandome Heights (village) Nassau County	15	1.42
Carle Place (cdp) Nassau County	77	1.38
Hillside Lake (cdp) Dutchess County	8	1.17
Wright (town) Schoharie County	21	1.11
East Patchogue (cdp) Suffolk County	220	1.04
Milton (cdp) Ulster County	12	1.03
Sparkill (cdp) Rockland County	13	0.94
Brewerton (cdp) Onondaga County	36	0.89

Top 10 Places Sorted by Percent of Total Population
Based on places with total population of 50,000 or more

Place	Population	%
Oyster Bay (town) Nassau County	579	0.20
Babylon (town) Suffolk County	378	0.18
Smithtown (town) Suffolk County	206	0.18
Levittown (cdp) Nassau County	96	0.18
Brookhaven (town) Suffolk County	686	0.14
North Hempstead (town) Nassau County	248	0.11
Islip (town) Suffolk County	292	0.09
Queens (borough) Queens County	1,565	0.07
Hempstead (town) Nassau County	540	0.07
Staten Island (borough) Richmond County	290	0.06

New Zealander

Top 10 Places Sorted by Population
Based on all places, regardless of total population

Place	Population	%
New York (city)	584	0.01
Manhattan (borough) New York County	405	0.03
Brooklyn (borough) Kings County	140	0.01
Monsey (cdp) Rockland County	55	0.37
Ramapo (town) Rockland County	55	0.04
Ithaca (city) Tompkins County	45	0.15
Milan (town) Dutchess County	35	1.38
Deerpark (town) Orange County	35	0.44
White Plains (city) Westchester County	29	0.05
Eggertsville (cdp) Erie County	26	0.17

Top 10 Places Sorted by Percent of Total Population
Based on all places, regardless of total population

Place	Population	%
Milan (town) Dutchess County	35	1.38
Oriskany Falls (village) Oneida County	4	0.53
Deerpark (town) Orange County	35	0.44
Niskayuna (cdp) Schenectady County	18	0.39
Monsey (cdp) Rockland County	55	0.37
North Harmony (town) Chautauqua County	6	0.28
Cooperstown (village) Otsego County	5	0.28
Hartford (town) Washington County	5	0.22
Spafford (town) Onondaga County	4	0.20
Augusta (town) Oneida County	4	0.19

Top 10 Places Sorted by Percent of Total Population
Based on places with total population of 50,000 or more

Place	Population	%
White Plains (city) Westchester County	29	0.05
Ramapo (town) Rockland County	55	0.04
Manhattan (borough) New York County	405	0.03
Amherst (town) Erie County	26	0.02
New York (city)	584	0.01
Brooklyn (borough) Kings County	140	0.01
Huntington (town) Suffolk County	26	0.01
Syracuse (city) Onondaga County	13	0.01
Cheektowaga (cdp) Erie County	11	0.01
Cheektowaga (town) Erie County	11	0.01

Northern European

Top 10 Places Sorted by Population
Based on all places, regardless of total population

Place	Population	%
New York (city)	3,043	0.04
Manhattan (borough) New York County	1,485	0.09
Brooklyn (borough) Kings County	961	0.04
Hempstead (town) Nassau County	514	0.07
Queens (borough) Queens County	512	0.02
Brookhaven (town) Suffolk County	249	0.05
Oceanside (cdp) Nassau County	161	0.52
Albany (city) Albany County	160	0.16
Depew (village) Erie County	130	0.84
Cheektowaga (town) Erie County	130	0.15

Top 10 Places Sorted by Percent of Total Population
Based on all places, regardless of total population

Place	Population	%
Duanesburg (cdp) Schenectady County	21	12.00
Schenevus (cdp) Otsego County	32	11.64
West Valley (cdp) Cattaraugus County	33	7.37
Newfield Hamlet (cdp) Tompkins County	30	4.48
Long Lake (cdp) Hamilton County	21	3.92
Guilford (town) Chenango County	97	3.27
New Suffolk (cdp) Suffolk County	6	3.19
Scott (town) Cortland County	36	2.85
Long Lake (town) Hamilton County	21	2.80
Laurel (cdp) Suffolk County	30	2.79

Top 10 Places Sorted by Percent of Total Population
Based on places with total population of 50,000 or more

Place	Population	%
Albany (city) Albany County	160	0.16
Cheektowaga (town) Erie County	130	0.15
Schenectady (city) Schenectady County	97	0.15
White Plains (city) Westchester County	54	0.10

Manhattan (borough) New York County	1,485	0.09
Amherst (town) Erie County	101	0.08
Hempstead (town) Nassau County	514	0.07
Greenburgh (town) Westchester County	65	0.07
Southampton (town) Suffolk County	42	0.07
Clay (town) Onondaga County	35	0.06

Norwegian

Top 10 Places Sorted by Population
Based on all places, regardless of total population

Place	Population	%
New York (city)	21,894	0.27
Manhattan (borough) New York County	7,445	0.47
Brooklyn (borough) Kings County	5,982	0.24
Staten Island (borough) Richmond County	5,135	1.11
Brookhaven (town) Suffolk County	5,078	1.06
Hempstead (town) Nassau County	3,371	0.45
Islip (town) Suffolk County	2,978	0.89
Queens (borough) Queens County	2,559	0.12
Oyster Bay (town) Nassau County	1,882	0.65
Huntington (town) Suffolk County	1,833	0.91

Top 10 Places Sorted by Percent of Total Population
Based on all places, regardless of total population

Place	Population	%
Saltaire (village) Suffolk County	8	13.79
Stone Ridge (cdp) Ulster County	91	10.48
Margaretville (village) Delaware County	52	9.83
Great Bend (cdp) Jefferson County	86	9.50
Fishers Island (cdp) Suffolk County	21	8.40
Red House (town) Cattaraugus County	2	7.69
Northville (cdp) Suffolk County	88	7.39
Benson (town) Hamilton County	11	7.24
Pitcher (town) Chenango County	48	7.08
Shokan (cdp) Ulster County	44	5.68

Top 10 Places Sorted by Percent of Total Population
Based on places with total population of 50,000 or more

Place	Population	%
Smithtown (town) Suffolk County	1,686	1.43
Staten Island (borough) Richmond County	5,135	1.11
Brookhaven (town) Suffolk County	5,078	1.06
Huntington (town) Suffolk County	1,833	0.91
Islip (town) Suffolk County	2,978	0.89
Southampton (town) Suffolk County	498	0.88
Babylon (town) Suffolk County	1,701	0.80
Colonie (town) Albany County	598	0.73
Oyster Bay (town) Nassau County	1,882	0.65
Greenburgh (town) Westchester County	530	0.60

Pennsylvania German

Top 10 Places Sorted by Population
Based on all places, regardless of total population

Place	Population	%
New York (city)	465	0.01
Morristown (town) St. Lawrence County	433	15.79
Troupsburg (town) Steuben County	341	23.32
Manhattan (borough) New York County	327	0.02
Conewango (town) Cattaraugus County	262	18.04
Jamestown (city) Chautauqua County	245	0.79
Colesville (town) Broome County	220	4.18
Hume (town) Allegany County	219	10.74
Lisbon (town) St. Lawrence County	215	5.28
St. Johnsville (town) Montgomery County	209	7.99

Top 10 Places Sorted by Percent of Total Population
Based on all places, regardless of total population

Place	Population	%
Troupsburg (town) Steuben County	341	23.32
Conewango (town) Cattaraugus County	262	18.04
Morristown (town) St. Lawrence County	433	15.79
De Peyster (town) St. Lawrence County	147	15.34
Napoli (town) Cattaraugus County	181	11.95
Hume (town) Allegany County	219	10.74
Junius (town) Seneca County	160	10.12
Leon (town) Cattaraugus County	148	10.12
Sherman (town) Chautauqua County	166	8.96
Cherry Creek (town) Chautauqua County	108	8.52

Top 10 Places Sorted by Percent of Total Population
Based on places with total population of 50,000 or more

Place	Population	%
Union (town) Broome County	197	0.35
Niagara Falls (city) Niagara County	130	0.26
Hamburg (town) Erie County	103	0.18
Greece (town) Monroe County	145	0.15
Tonawanda (cdp) Erie County	85	0.15
Tonawanda (town) Erie County	98	0.13
Levittown (cdp) Nassau County	54	0.10
Troy (city) Rensselaer County	50	0.10
Clay (town) Onondaga County	38	0.07
Buffalo (city) Erie County	159	0.06

Polish

Top 10 Places Sorted by Population
Based on all places, regardless of total population

Place	Population	%
New York (city)	216,891	2.68
Brooklyn (borough) Kings County	66,792	2.71
Manhattan (borough) New York County	64,078	4.05
Queens (borough) Queens County	59,757	2.72
Hempstead (town) Nassau County	35,774	4.75
Cheektowaga (town) Erie County	31,456	35.39
Buffalo (city) Erie County	28,108	10.57
Brookhaven (town) Suffolk County	27,233	5.67
Cheektowaga (cdp) Erie County	26,237	34.63
Oyster Bay (town) Nassau County	19,395	6.65

Top 10 Places Sorted by Percent of Total Population
Based on all places, regardless of total population

Place	Population	%
Sloan (village) Erie County	1,831	49.88
Depew (village) Erie County	5,979	38.69
Piffard (cdp) Livingston County	22	36.67
Lancaster (town) Erie County	15,025	36.65
Cheektowaga (town) Erie County	31,456	35.39
Marilla (town) Erie County	1,884	35.06
Cheektowaga (cdp) Erie County	26,237	34.63
Darien (town) Genesee County	946	30.30
Duane Lake (cdp) Schenectady County	73	30.17
Lancaster (village) Erie County	3,134	29.99

Top 10 Places Sorted by Percent of Total Population
Based on places with total population of 50,000 or more

Place	Population	%
Cheektowaga (town) Erie County	31,456	35.39
Cheektowaga (cdp) Erie County	26,237	34.63
Hamburg (town) Erie County	13,189	23.31
Tonawanda (town) Erie County	11,479	15.49
Tonawanda (cdp) Erie County	9,014	15.40
Amherst (town) Erie County	17,104	14.14
Buffalo (city) Erie County	28,108	10.57
Niagara Falls (city) Niagara County	4,962	9.75
Utica (city) Oneida County	5,408	8.75
Colonie (town) Albany County	6,915	8.48

Portuguese

Top 10 Places Sorted by Population
Based on all places, regardless of total population

Place	Population	%
New York (city)	13,201	0.16
Queens (borough) Queens County	4,727	0.21
North Hempstead (town) Nassau County	3,978	1.78
Manhattan (borough) New York County	3,862	0.24
Brookhaven (town) Suffolk County	3,802	0.79
Brooklyn (borough) Kings County	2,882	0.12
Hempstead (town) Nassau County	2,805	0.37
Yonkers (city) Westchester County	2,670	1.37
Mineola (village) Nassau County	2,368	12.67
Islip (town) Suffolk County	1,977	0.59

Top 10 Places Sorted by Percent of Total Population
Based on all places, regardless of total population

Place	Population	%
Freedom Plains (cdp) Dutchess County	134	19.06
Mineola (village) Nassau County	2,368	12.67
Fishers Landing (cdp) Jefferson County	5	9.43

Place	Population	%
Farmingville (cdp) Suffolk County	1,109	6.92
Fishers Island (cdp) Suffolk County	16	6.40
Carle Place (cdp) Nassau County	318	5.69
Fishkill (village) Dutchess County	111	5.34
Decatur (town) Otsego County	15	4.78
Davenport Center (cdp) Delaware County	14	4.73
Phoenicia (cdp) Ulster County	17	4.66

Top 10 Places Sorted by Percent of Total Population
Based on places with total population of 50,000 or more

Place	Population	%
North Hempstead (town) Nassau County	3,978	1.78
Mount Vernon (city) Westchester County	1,149	1.71
Yonkers (city) Westchester County	2,670	1.37
New Rochelle (city) Westchester County	830	1.09
Brentwood (cdp) Suffolk County	524	0.96
Greenburgh (town) Westchester County	718	0.82
Brookhaven (town) Suffolk County	3,802	0.79
Islip (town) Suffolk County	1,977	0.59
White Plains (city) Westchester County	325	0.58
Levittown (cdp) Nassau County	243	0.45

Romanian

Top 10 Places Sorted by Population
Based on all places, regardless of total population

Place	Population	%
New York (city)	29,552	0.37
Queens (borough) Queens County	11,686	0.53
Brooklyn (borough) Kings County	8,046	0.33
Manhattan (borough) New York County	7,692	0.49
Hempstead (town) Nassau County	2,811	0.37
Monroe (town) Orange County	2,439	6.31
Kiryas Joel (village) Orange County	2,293	12.01
Ramapo (town) Rockland County	1,695	1.38
Oyster Bay (town) Nassau County	1,492	0.51
North Hempstead (town) Nassau County	1,434	0.64

Top 10 Places Sorted by Percent of Total Population
Based on all places, regardless of total population

Place	Population	%
Kiryas Joel (village) Orange County	2,293	12.01
Kaser (village) Rockland County	497	11.20
Monroe (town) Orange County	2,439	6.31
Harbor Hills (cdp) Nassau County	27	5.45
University Gardens (cdp) Nassau County	217	5.44
Smallwood (cdp) Sullivan County	32	4.65
Milford (town) Otsego County	21	4.12
Port Henry (village) Essex County	74	4.11
East Norwich (cdp) Nassau County	95	3.67
Barker (town) Broome County	95	3.48

Top 10 Places Sorted by Percent of Total Population
Based on places with total population of 50,000 or more

Place	Population	%
Ramapo (town) Rockland County	1,695	1.38
Huntington (town) Suffolk County	1,364	0.67
Clarkstown (town) Rockland County	544	0.65
North Hempstead (town) Nassau County	1,434	0.64
Smithtown (town) Suffolk County	707	0.60
Greenburgh (town) Westchester County	489	0.56
Queens (borough) Queens County	11,686	0.53
Oyster Bay (town) Nassau County	1,492	0.51
Manhattan (borough) New York County	7,692	0.49
New York (city)	29,552	0.37

Russian

Top 10 Places Sorted by Population
Based on all places, regardless of total population

Place	Population	%
New York (city)	240,690	2.98
Brooklyn (borough) Kings County	88,579	3.59
Manhattan (borough) New York County	82,983	5.24
Queens (borough) Queens County	44,676	2.03
Hempstead (town) Nassau County	26,754	3.55
Staten Island (borough) Richmond County	16,388	3.54
North Hempstead (town) Nassau County	14,712	6.58
Oyster Bay (town) Nassau County	14,554	4.99
Brookhaven (town) Suffolk County	12,073	2.51
Huntington (town) Suffolk County	9,499	4.70

Top 10 Places Sorted by Percent of Total Population
Based on all places, regardless of total population

Place	Population	%
Piffard (cdp) Livingston County	22	36.67
Hewlett Bay Park (village) Nassau County	155	29.87
Great Neck Gardens (cdp) Nassau County	258	28.41
Hewlett Harbor (village) Nassau County	331	28.22
Roslyn Estates (village) Nassau County	327	26.48
Woodsburgh (village) Nassau County	178	23.89
Grand View-on-Hudson (village) Rockland County	62	21.83
Hewlett Neck (village) Nassau County	97	20.73
Russell Gardens (village) Nassau County	199	20.66
Scotts Corners (cdp) Westchester County	102	20.28

Top 10 Places Sorted by Percent of Total Population
Based on places with total population of 50,000 or more

Place	Population	%
North Hempstead (town) Nassau County	14,712	6.58
Clarkstown (town) Rockland County	5,317	6.38
Greenburgh (town) Westchester County	5,042	5.75
Manhattan (borough) New York County	82,983	5.24
Oyster Bay (town) Nassau County	14,554	4.99
Ramapo (town) Rockland County	6,069	4.95
Huntington (town) Suffolk County	9,499	4.70
Smithtown (town) Suffolk County	5,319	4.52
White Plains (city) Westchester County	2,307	4.13
New Rochelle (city) Westchester County	3,102	4.09

Scandinavian

Top 10 Places Sorted by Population
Based on all places, regardless of total population

Place	Population	%
New York (city)	3,434	0.04
Manhattan (borough) New York County	1,731	0.11
Brooklyn (borough) Kings County	882	0.04
Queens (borough) Queens County	545	0.02
Brookhaven (town) Suffolk County	388	0.08
Hempstead (town) Nassau County	360	0.05
Albany (city) Albany County	313	0.32
Huntington (town) Suffolk County	292	0.14
Islip (town) Suffolk County	183	0.05
Bronx (borough) Bronx County	155	0.01

Top 10 Places Sorted by Percent of Total Population
Based on all places, regardless of total population

Place	Population	%
Norfolk (cdp) St. Lawrence County	85	6.84
Pine Hill (cdp) Ulster County	15	5.84
Afton (village) Chenango County	39	4.00
Gardiner (cdp) Ulster County	40	3.82
Clifton (town) St. Lawrence County	27	3.35
Shortsville (village) Ontario County	39	3.08
Cairo (cdp) Greene County	54	2.89
Springfield (town) Otsego County	41	2.85
Limestone (village) Cattaraugus County	9	2.85
Sharon Springs (village) Schoharie County	10	2.77

Top 10 Places Sorted by Percent of Total Population
Based on places with total population of 50,000 or more

Place	Population	%
Albany (city) Albany County	313	0.32
Huntington (town) Suffolk County	292	0.14
Manhattan (borough) New York County	1,731	0.11
Amherst (town) Erie County	116	0.10
Southampton (town) Suffolk County	57	0.10
Greece (town) Monroe County	88	0.09
Greenburgh (town) Westchester County	79	0.09
Brookhaven (town) Suffolk County	388	0.08
Utica (city) Oneida County	48	0.08
Syracuse (city) Onondaga County	98	0.07

Scotch-Irish

Top 10 Places Sorted by Population
Based on all places, regardless of total population

Place	Population	%
New York (city)	27,337	0.34
Manhattan (borough) New York County	13,158	0.83
Brooklyn (borough) Kings County	6,090	0.25

Place	Population	%
Brookhaven (town) Suffolk County	5,102	1.06
Hempstead (town) Nassau County	4,788	0.64
Queens (borough) Queens County	4,602	0.21
Islip (town) Suffolk County	3,159	0.95
Oyster Bay (town) Nassau County	2,523	0.87
Huntington (town) Suffolk County	2,325	1.15
Buffalo (city) Erie County	2,324	0.87

Top 10 Places Sorted by Percent of Total Population
Based on all places, regardless of total population

Place	Population	%
Onondaga Nation Reservation Onondaga County	8	53.33
Laurens (village) Otsego County	35	17.33
Port Gibson (cdp) Ontario County	80	14.98
Argyle (village) Washington County	49	13.61
Parish (village) Oswego County	63	12.91
Claverack-Red Mills (cdp) Columbia County	108	12.84
Oxbow (cdp) Jefferson County	9	12.50
Piffard (cdp) Livingston County	7	11.67
Breesport (cdp) Chemung County	85	10.81
Windham (cdp) Greene County	41	9.45

Top 10 Places Sorted by Percent of Total Population
Based on places with total population of 50,000 or more

Place	Population	%
Clay (town) Onondaga County	1,162	2.00
Tonawanda (cdp) Erie County	989	1.69
Tonawanda (town) Erie County	1,170	1.58
Troy (city) Rensselaer County	784	1.57
Colonie (town) Albany County	1,261	1.55
Greece (town) Monroe County	1,469	1.54
Smithtown (town) Suffolk County	1,732	1.47
Levittown (cdp) Nassau County	722	1.35
Amherst (town) Erie County	1,527	1.26
Union (town) Broome County	712	1.26

Scottish

Top 10 Places Sorted by Population
Based on all places, regardless of total population

Place	Population	%
New York (city)	38,000	0.47
Manhattan (borough) New York County	19,553	1.23
Brooklyn (borough) Kings County	8,809	0.36
Queens (borough) Queens County	5,718	0.26
Brookhaven (town) Suffolk County	5,703	1.19
Hempstead (town) Nassau County	3,831	0.51
Rochester (city) Monroe County	3,002	1.42
Islip (town) Suffolk County	2,852	0.85
Buffalo (city) Erie County	2,816	1.06
Oyster Bay (town) Nassau County	2,493	0.85

Top 10 Places Sorted by Percent of Total Population
Based on all places, regardless of total population

Place	Population	%
Dering Harbor (village) Suffolk County	5	31.25
Rhinecliff (cdp) Dutchess County	86	23.18
Callicoon (cdp) Sullivan County	21	18.75
Colton (cdp) St. Lawrence County	64	16.75
Andes (town) Delaware County	149	15.63
Tuscarora (cdp) Livingston County	12	15.58
Salt Point (cdp) Dutchess County	47	14.42
Thousand Island Park (cdp) Jefferson County	16	14.41
Laurel (cdp) Suffolk County	152	14.14
Walton (village) Delaware County	372	14.06

Top 10 Places Sorted by Percent of Total Population
Based on places with total population of 50,000 or more

Place	Population	%
Tonawanda (town) Erie County	1,915	2.58
Tonawanda (cdp) Erie County	1,430	2.44
Clay (town) Onondaga County	1,377	2.37
Union (town) Broome County	1,114	1.98
Greece (town) Monroe County	1,843	1.93
Colonie (town) Albany County	1,526	1.87
Irondequoit (cdp/town) Monroe County	935	1.81
Southampton (town) Suffolk County	966	1.71
Troy (city) Rensselaer County	848	1.70
Syracuse (city) Onondaga County	2,233	1.54

Serbian

Top 10 Places Sorted by Population
Based on all places, regardless of total population

Place	Population	%
New York (city)	4,911	0.06
Queens (borough) Queens County	2,438	0.11
Manhattan (borough) New York County	1,526	0.10
Brooklyn (borough) Kings County	520	0.02
Buffalo (city) Erie County	291	0.11
Hamburg (town) Erie County	279	0.49
Orchard Park (town) Erie County	247	0.86
Staten Island (borough) Richmond County	240	0.05
Bronx (borough) Bronx County	187	0.01
Amherst (town) Erie County	158	0.13

Top 10 Places Sorted by Percent of Total Population
Based on all places, regardless of total population

Place	Population	%
West Almond (town) Allegany County	6	2.08
Port Henry (village) Essex County	29	1.61
Ames (village) Montgomery County	2	1.24
Roslyn (village) Nassau County	30	1.10
South Nyack (village) Rockland County	57	1.03
Cairo (town) Greene County	68	1.02
Scottsville (village) Monroe County	20	0.96
New Albion (town) Cattaraugus County	19	0.96
Arcade (village) Wyoming County	19	0.87
Orchard Park (town) Erie County	247	0.86

Top 10 Places Sorted by Percent of Total Population
Based on places with total population of 50,000 or more

Place	Population	%
Hamburg (town) Erie County	279	0.49
Amherst (town) Erie County	158	0.13
Cheektowaga (cdp) Erie County	100	0.13
Utica (city) Oneida County	82	0.13
Tonawanda (cdp) Erie County	73	0.12
Union (town) Broome County	65	0.12
Queens (borough) Queens County	2,438	0.11
Buffalo (city) Erie County	291	0.11
Cheektowaga (town) Erie County	100	0.11
Tonawanda (town) Erie County	85	0.11

Slavic

Top 10 Places Sorted by Population
Based on all places, regardless of total population

Place	Population	%
New York (city)	1,962	0.02
Queens (borough) Queens County	765	0.03
Brooklyn (borough) Kings County	564	0.02
Manhattan (borough) New York County	400	0.03
Union (town) Broome County	291	0.52
Greece (town) Monroe County	240	0.25
Yonkers (city) Westchester County	237	0.12
North Tonawanda (city) Niagara County	209	0.66
North Hempstead (town) Nassau County	195	0.09
Oyster Bay (town) Nassau County	173	0.06

Top 10 Places Sorted by Percent of Total Population
Based on all places, regardless of total population

Place	Population	%
Tannersville (village) Greene County	15	3.46
Rhinecliff (cdp) Dutchess County	12	3.23
Depauville (cdp) Jefferson County	12	2.70
Jefferson Heights (cdp) Greene County	40	2.51
Harmony (town) Chautauqua County	44	1.96
Apalachin (cdp) Tioga County	22	1.96
Riverside (cdp) Suffolk County	53	1.89
Corfu (village) Genesee County	13	1.69
Hawthorne (cdp) Westchester County	76	1.68
Ripley (town) Chautauqua County	35	1.64

Top 10 Places Sorted by Percent of Total Population
Based on places with total population of 50,000 or more

Place	Population	%
Union (town) Broome County	291	0.52
Greece (town) Monroe County	240	0.25
New Rochelle (city) Westchester County	171	0.23
Tonawanda (town) Erie County	123	0.17

Place	Population	%
Clay (town) Onondaga County	93	0.16
Amherst (town) Erie County	153	0.13
Yonkers (city) Westchester County	237	0.12
Smithtown (town) Suffolk County	116	0.10
Albany (city) Albany County	94	0.10
Tonawanda (cdp) Erie County	59	0.10

Slovak

Top 10 Places Sorted by Population
Based on all places, regardless of total population

Place	Population	%
New York (city)	6,785	0.08
Union (town) Broome County	3,003	5.33
Manhattan (borough) New York County	2,298	0.15
Queens (borough) Queens County	1,882	0.09
Brooklyn (borough) Kings County	1,826	0.07
Binghamton (city) Broome County	1,334	2.81
Johnson City (village) Broome County	908	5.96
Endwell (cdp) Broome County	740	6.33
Hempstead (town) Nassau County	702	0.09
Brookhaven (town) Suffolk County	690	0.14

Top 10 Places Sorted by Percent of Total Population
Based on all places, regardless of total population

Place	Population	%
Fowlerville (cdp) Livingston County	42	17.00
Port Dickinson (village) Broome County	109	7.68
Endwell (cdp) Broome County	740	6.33
Maine (town) Broome County	334	6.20
Johnson City (village) Broome County	908	5.96
Apalachin (cdp) Tioga County	60	5.36
Union (town) Broome County	3,003	5.33
Endicott (village) Broome County	634	4.76
Hemlock (cdp) Livingston County	11	4.35
Lincolndale (cdp) Westchester County	58	4.33

Top 10 Places Sorted by Percent of Total Population
Based on places with total population of 50,000 or more

Place	Population	%
Union (town) Broome County	3,003	5.33
Greenburgh (town) Westchester County	388	0.44
Clarkstown (town) Rockland County	310	0.37
Albany (city) Albany County	351	0.36
Hamburg (town) Erie County	182	0.32
Yonkers (city) Westchester County	590	0.30
Cheektowaga (cdp) Erie County	229	0.30
Cheektowaga (town) Erie County	229	0.26
Clay (town) Onondaga County	150	0.26
Greece (town) Monroe County	236	0.25

Slovene

Top 10 Places Sorted by Population
Based on all places, regardless of total population

Place	Population	%
New York (city)	1,476	0.02
Manhattan (borough) New York County	695	0.04
Queens (borough) Queens County	468	0.02
Brooklyn (borough) Kings County	160	0.01
Commack (cdp) Suffolk County	150	0.41
Smithtown (town) Suffolk County	147	0.13
Staten Island (borough) Richmond County	108	0.02
Buffalo (city) Erie County	100	0.04
Bedford (town) Westchester County	96	0.55
Hempstead (town) Nassau County	89	0.01

Top 10 Places Sorted by Percent of Total Population
Based on all places, regardless of total population

Place	Population	%
Decatur (town) Otsego County	15	4.78
Bedford (cdp) Westchester County	86	4.73
Bovina (town) Delaware County	20	3.92
Worcester (cdp) Otsego County	51	3.24
Little Falls (town) Herkimer County	41	2.88
Titusville (cdp) Dutchess County	13	2.72
Worcester (town) Otsego County	57	2.22
Pavilion (cdp) Genesee County	9	1.86
Laurel Hollow (village) Nassau County	32	1.70
Horseheads North (cdp) Chemung County	41	1.56

Top 10 Places Sorted by Percent of Total Population
Based on places with total population of 50,000 or more

Place	Population	%
Smithtown (town) Suffolk County	147	0.13
Union (town) Broome County	67	0.12
Albany (city) Albany County	70	0.07
Syracuse (city) Onondaga County	85	0.06
Manhattan (borough) New York County	695	0.04
Buffalo (city) Erie County	100	0.04
North Hempstead (town) Nassau County	79	0.04
Amherst (town) Erie County	53	0.04
Ramapo (town) Rockland County	46	0.04
Greece (town) Monroe County	31	0.03

Soviet Union

Top 10 Places Sorted by Population
Based on all places, regardless of total population

Place	Population	%
New York (city)	419	0.01
Brooklyn (borough) Kings County	219	0.01
Queens (borough) Queens County	71	<0.01
Staten Island (borough) Richmond County	63	0.01
Manhattan (borough) New York County	54	<0.01
Yonkers (city) Westchester County	14	0.01
Hornell (city) Steuben County	12	0.14
Bronx (borough) Bronx County	12	<0.01
Oceanside (cdp) Nassau County	10	0.03
Hempstead (town) Nassau County	10	<0.01

Top 10 Places Sorted by Percent of Total Population
Based on all places, regardless of total population

Place	Population	%
Wainscott (cdp) Suffolk County	3	0.69
Hornell (city) Steuben County	12	0.14
Oceanside (cdp) Nassau County	10	0.03
New York (city)	419	0.01
Brooklyn (borough) Kings County	219	0.01
Staten Island (borough) Richmond County	63	0.01
Yonkers (city) Westchester County	14	0.01
East Hampton (town) Suffolk County	3	0.01
Queens (borough) Queens County	71	<0.01
Manhattan (borough) New York County	54	<0.01

Top 10 Places Sorted by Percent of Total Population
Based on places with total population of 50,000 or more

Place	Population	%
New York (city)	419	0.01
Brooklyn (borough) Kings County	219	0.01
Staten Island (borough) Richmond County	63	0.01
Yonkers (city) Westchester County	14	0.01
Queens (borough) Queens County	71	<0.01
Manhattan (borough) New York County	54	<0.01
Bronx (borough) Bronx County	12	<0.01
Hempstead (town) Nassau County	10	<0.01
Albany (city) Albany County	0	0.00
Amherst (town) Erie County	0	0.00

Swedish

Top 10 Places Sorted by Population
Based on all places, regardless of total population

Place	Population	%
New York (city)	20,940	0.26
Manhattan (borough) New York County	10,408	0.66
Jamestown (city) Chautauqua County	5,809	18.63
Brooklyn (borough) Kings County	5,185	0.21
Brookhaven (town) Suffolk County	4,045	0.84
Hempstead (town) Nassau County	3,930	0.52
Queens (borough) Queens County	2,862	0.13
Islip (town) Suffolk County	2,528	0.76
Oyster Bay (town) Nassau County	2,325	0.80
Busti (town) Chautauqua County	2,252	30.51

Top 10 Places Sorted by Percent of Total Population
Based on all places, regardless of total population

Place	Population	%
Chautauqua (cdp) Chautauqua County	119	45.08
Kiantone (town) Chautauqua County	482	32.44
Busti (town) Chautauqua County	2,252	30.51

Celoron (village) Chautauqua County	345	30.45
Busti (cdp) Chautauqua County	158	29.81
Poland (town) Chautauqua County	614	27.47
Frewsburg (cdp) Chautauqua County	531	26.14
Carroll (town) Chautauqua County	903	25.67
Ellicott (town) Chautauqua County	2,238	25.52
Lakewood (village) Chautauqua County	773	25.44

Top 10 Places Sorted by Percent of Total Population
Based on places with total population of 50,000 or more

Place	Population	%
Hamburg (town) Erie County	948	1.68
Colonie (town) Albany County	944	1.16
Huntington (town) Suffolk County	2,237	1.11
Smithtown (town) Suffolk County	1,304	1.11
Clay (town) Onondaga County	625	1.08
Southampton (town) Suffolk County	598	1.06
Tonawanda (town) Erie County	758	1.02
Tonawanda (cdp) Erie County	584	1.00
Irondequoit (cdp/town) Monroe County	482	0.93
Brookhaven (town) Suffolk County	4,045	0.84

Swiss

Top 10 Places Sorted by Population
Based on all places, regardless of total population

Place	Population	%
New York (city)	8,135	0.10
Manhattan (borough) New York County	4,962	0.31
Brooklyn (borough) Kings County	1,491	0.06
Brookhaven (town) Suffolk County	1,356	0.28
Queens (borough) Queens County	1,260	0.06
Hempstead (town) Nassau County	1,183	0.16
Oyster Bay (town) Nassau County	686	0.24
Huntington (town) Suffolk County	632	0.31
Islip (town) Suffolk County	619	0.19
Galen (town) Wayne County	390	9.04

Top 10 Places Sorted by Percent of Total Population
Based on all places, regardless of total population

Place	Population	%
Belleville (cdp) Jefferson County	79	67.52
Constableville (village) Lewis County	36	11.65
Barrington (town) Yates County	184	10.73
Jeffersonville (village) Sullivan County	31	9.63
Galen (town) Wayne County	390	9.04
Castorland (village) Lewis County	34	8.81
Leon (town) Cattaraugus County	116	7.93
Torrey (town) Yates County	100	7.69
Red House (town) Cattaraugus County	2	7.69
Benton (town) Yates County	190	6.78

Top 10 Places Sorted by Percent of Total Population
Based on places with total population of 50,000 or more

Place	Population	%
Irondequoit (cdp/town) Monroe County	255	0.49
Southampton (town) Suffolk County	231	0.41
Manhattan (borough) New York County	4,962	0.31
Huntington (town) Suffolk County	632	0.31
Clay (town) Onondaga County	175	0.30
Brookhaven (town) Suffolk County	1,356	0.28
Schenectady (city) Schenectady County	171	0.26
Oyster Bay (town) Nassau County	686	0.24
Greenburgh (town) Westchester County	211	0.24
White Plains (city) Westchester County	129	0.23

Turkish

Top 10 Places Sorted by Population
Based on all places, regardless of total population

Place	Population	%
New York (city)	14,927	0.18
Brooklyn (borough) Kings County	5,164	0.21
Queens (borough) Queens County	3,767	0.17
Manhattan (borough) New York County	3,703	0.23
Brookhaven (town) Suffolk County	1,935	0.40
Staten Island (borough) Richmond County	1,607	0.35
Oyster Bay (town) Nassau County	1,232	0.42
Hempstead (town) Nassau County	1,202	0.16
Babylon (town) Suffolk County	939	0.44
Bronx (borough) Bronx County	686	0.05

Top 10 Places Sorted by Percent of Total Population
Based on all places, regardless of total population

Place	Population	%
Dering Harbor (village) Suffolk County	5	31.25
Jeffersonville (village) Sullivan County	15	4.66
Orient (cdp) Suffolk County	20	3.33
Port Washington North (village) Nassau County	100	3.29
Walton (village) Delaware County	61	2.31
Wading River (cdp) Suffolk County	178	2.18
Northport (village) Suffolk County	161	2.16
Piermont (village) Rockland County	50	1.99
Bayville (village) Nassau County	128	1.91
East Patchogue (cdp) Suffolk County	388	1.84

Top 10 Places Sorted by Percent of Total Population
Based on places with total population of 50,000 or more

Place	Population	%
Greece (town) Monroe County	561	0.59
Irondequoit (cdp/town) Monroe County	245	0.47
Babylon (town) Suffolk County	939	0.44
Oyster Bay (town) Nassau County	1,232	0.42
Troy (city) Rensselaer County	207	0.41
Brookhaven (town) Suffolk County	1,935	0.40
Staten Island (borough) Richmond County	1,607	0.35
Levittown (cdp) Nassau County	181	0.34
Rochester (city) Monroe County	612	0.29
Huntington (town) Suffolk County	502	0.25

Ukrainian

Top 10 Places Sorted by Population
Based on all places, regardless of total population

Place	Population	%
New York (city)	48,714	0.60
Brooklyn (borough) Kings County	25,046	1.02
Manhattan (borough) New York County	8,849	0.56
Queens (borough) Queens County	8,375	0.38
Staten Island (borough) Richmond County	4,836	1.04
Hempstead (town) Nassau County	2,806	0.37
Brookhaven (town) Suffolk County	2,350	0.49
Oyster Bay (town) Nassau County	1,774	0.61
Greece (town) Monroe County	1,758	1.84
Huntington (town) Suffolk County	1,742	0.86

Top 10 Places Sorted by Percent of Total Population
Based on all places, regardless of total population

Place	Population	%
Washington Mills (cdp) Oneida County	186	17.30
Kerhonkson (cdp) Ulster County	202	15.97
Cragsmoor (cdp) Ulster County	43	11.94
Clarendon (town) Orleans County	374	10.35
Webster (village) Monroe County	531	9.90
Redwood (cdp) Jefferson County	30	9.71
Schuyler (town) Herkimer County	321	9.46
Mountain Lodge Park (cdp) Orange County	175	9.41
Cayuga (village) Cayuga County	36	7.93
Walker Valley (cdp) Ulster County	41	7.65

Top 10 Places Sorted by Percent of Total Population
Based on places with total population of 50,000 or more

Place	Population	%
Irondequoit (cdp/town) Monroe County	1,169	2.27
Greece (town) Monroe County	1,758	1.84
Troy (city) Rensselaer County	819	1.64
Union (town) Broome County	666	1.18
Hamburg (town) Erie County	664	1.17
Ramapo (town) Rockland County	1,403	1.14
Clay (town) Onondaga County	650	1.12
Colonie (town) Albany County	860	1.05
Staten Island (borough) Richmond County	4,836	1.04
Brooklyn (borough) Kings County	25,046	1.02

Welsh

Top 10 Places Sorted by Population
Based on all places, regardless of total population

Place	Population	%
New York (city)	11,219	0.14
Manhattan (borough) New York County	6,000	0.38
Brooklyn (borough) Kings County	2,606	0.11

Queens (borough) Queens County	1,666	0.08
Union (town) Broome County	1,372	2.44
Brookhaven (town) Suffolk County	1,189	0.25
Syracuse (city) Onondaga County	1,060	0.73
Rochester (city) Monroe County	992	0.47
Rome (city) Oneida County	891	2.63
Hempstead (town) Nassau County	865	0.11

Top 10 Places Sorted by Percent of Total Population
Based on all places, regardless of total population

Place	Population	%
Parc (cdp) Clinton County	22	52.38
Barneveld (village) Oneida County	74	24.10
Duanesburg (cdp) Schenectady County	28	16.00
Remsen (town) Oneida County	274	14.13
West Winfield (village) Herkimer County	112	14.11
Winfield (town) Herkimer County	268	13.96
Remsen (village) Oneida County	76	13.89
Holland Patent (village) Oneida County	75	13.54
Madison (village) Madison County	49	12.47
Thousand Island Park (cdp) Jefferson County	13	11.71

Top 10 Places Sorted by Percent of Total Population
Based on places with total population of 50,000 or more

Place	Population	%
Union (town) Broome County	1,372	2.44
Utica (city) Oneida County	775	1.25
Colonie (town) Albany County	704	0.86
Troy (city) Rensselaer County	432	0.86
Clay (town) Onondaga County	496	0.85
Syracuse (city) Onondaga County	1,060	0.73
Irondequoit (cdp/town) Monroe County	352	0.68
Niagara Falls (city) Niagara County	346	0.68
Amherst (town) Erie County	798	0.66
Albany (city) Albany County	597	0.61

West Indian, excluding Hispanic

Top 10 Places Sorted by Population
Based on all places, regardless of total population

Place	Population	%
New York (city)	598,504	7.41
Brooklyn (borough) Kings County	306,541	12.43
Queens (borough) Queens County	147,460	6.71
Bronx (borough) Bronx County	107,527	7.87
Hempstead (town) Nassau County	45,733	6.07
Manhattan (borough) New York County	30,009	1.90
Mount Vernon (city) Westchester County	13,279	19.80
Ramapo (town) Rockland County	12,710	10.36
Babylon (town) Suffolk County	11,187	5.24
Islip (town) Suffolk County	10,274	3.08

Top 10 Places Sorted by Percent of Total Population
Based on all places, regardless of total population

Place	Population	%
Hillcrest (cdp) Rockland County	2,791	34.04
Elmont (cdp) Nassau County	9,499	27.54
Spring Valley (village) Rockland County	7,957	26.24
North Valley Stream (cdp) Nassau County	4,249	25.74
North Amityville (cdp) Suffolk County	3,825	21.47
Uniondale (cdp) Nassau County	5,218	21.30
Mount Vernon (city) Westchester County	13,279	19.80
Lakeview (cdp) Nassau County	1,015	18.22
South Floral Park (village) Nassau County	271	17.35
Wheatley Heights (cdp) Suffolk County	1,036	16.72

Top 10 Places Sorted by Percent of Total Population
Based on places with total population of 50,000 or more

Place	Population	%
Mount Vernon (city) Westchester County	13,279	19.80
Brooklyn (borough) Kings County	306,541	12.43
Hempstead (village) Nassau County	6,463	12.11
Ramapo (town) Rockland County	12,710	10.36
Bronx (borough) Bronx County	107,527	7.87
New York (city)	598,504	7.41
Queens (borough) Queens County	147,460	6.71
Brentwood (cdp) Suffolk County	3,472	6.33
Hempstead (town) Nassau County	45,733	6.07
New Rochelle (city) Westchester County	4,597	6.06

West Indian: Bahamian, excluding Hispanic

Top 10 Places Sorted by Population
Based on all places, regardless of total population

Place	Population	%
New York (city)	1,147	0.01
Manhattan (borough) New York County	457	0.03
Brooklyn (borough) Kings County	266	0.01
Rochester (city) Monroe County	218	0.10
Bronx (borough) Bronx County	208	0.02
Queens (borough) Queens County	185	0.01
North Amityville (cdp) Suffolk County	88	0.49
Babylon (town) Suffolk County	88	0.04
Hempstead (town) Nassau County	51	0.01
Miller Place (cdp) Suffolk County	47	0.38

Top 10 Places Sorted by Percent of Total Population
Based on all places, regardless of total population

Place	Population	%
North Amityville (cdp) Suffolk County	88	0.49
Miller Place (cdp) Suffolk County	47	0.38
South Floral Park (village) Nassau County	5	0.32
Fowler (town) St. Lawrence County	6	0.24
Melville (cdp) Suffolk County	31	0.16
West Hempstead (cdp) Nassau County	28	0.15
Potsdam (village) St. Lawrence County	14	0.15
Fort Ann (town) Washington County	9	0.14
Peekskill (city) Westchester County	28	0.12
Elmira (city) Chemung County	31	0.11

Top 10 Places Sorted by Percent of Total Population
Based on places with total population of 50,000 or more

Place	Population	%
Rochester (city) Monroe County	218	0.10
White Plains (city) Westchester County	26	0.05
Babylon (town) Suffolk County	88	0.04
Hamburg (town) Erie County	21	0.04
Manhattan (borough) New York County	457	0.03
Bronx (borough) Bronx County	208	0.02
Huntington (town) Suffolk County	31	0.02
Mount Vernon (city) Westchester County	11	0.02
New York (city)	1,147	0.01
Brooklyn (borough) Kings County	266	0.01

West Indian: Barbadian, excluding Hispanic

Top 10 Places Sorted by Population
Based on all places, regardless of total population

Place	Population	%
New York (city)	22,550	0.28
Brooklyn (borough) Kings County	14,916	0.60
Queens (borough) Queens County	5,021	0.23
Bronx (borough) Bronx County	1,612	0.12
Hempstead (town) Nassau County	1,279	0.17
Manhattan (borough) New York County	907	0.06
Freeport (village) Nassau County	447	1.05
New Rochelle (city) Westchester County	316	0.42
Rochester (city) Monroe County	230	0.11
Mount Vernon (city) Westchester County	208	0.31

Top 10 Places Sorted by Percent of Total Population
Based on all places, regardless of total population

Place	Population	%
Carthage (village) Jefferson County	183	4.92
Wilna (town) Jefferson County	183	2.87
South Nyack (village) Rockland County	105	1.89
Harriman (village) Orange County	44	1.86
Lakeview (cdp) Nassau County	89	1.60
South Valley Stream (cdp) Nassau County	73	1.39
Hornell (city) Steuben County	93	1.08
Freeport (village) Nassau County	447	1.05
Monticello (village) Sullivan County	68	1.01
Westbury (village) Nassau County	129	0.87

Top 10 Places Sorted by Percent of Total Population
Based on places with total population of 50,000 or more

Place	Population	%
Brooklyn (borough) Kings County	14,916	0.60

Place	Population	%
New Rochelle (city) Westchester County	316	0.42
Mount Vernon (city) Westchester County	208	0.31
Hempstead (village) Nassau County	153	0.29
New York (city)	22,550	0.28
Queens (borough) Queens County	5,021	0.23
Greenburgh (town) Westchester County	155	0.18
Hempstead (town) Nassau County	1,279	0.17
Schenectady (city) Schenectady County	94	0.14
Bronx (borough) Bronx County	1,612	0.12

West Indian: Belizean, excluding Hispanic

Top 10 Places Sorted by Population
Based on all places, regardless of total population

Place	Population	%
New York (city)	5,674	0.07
Brooklyn (borough) Kings County	2,026	0.08
Bronx (borough) Bronx County	1,493	0.11
Queens (borough) Queens County	1,344	0.06
Manhattan (borough) New York County	735	0.05
Rochester (city) Monroe County	171	0.08
White Plains (city) Westchester County	155	0.28
South Nyack (village) Rockland County	120	2.16
Orangetown (town) Rockland County	120	0.25
Mount Vernon (city) Westchester County	118	0.18

Top 10 Places Sorted by Percent of Total Population
Based on all places, regardless of total population

Place	Population	%
South Nyack (village) Rockland County	120	2.16
Black River (village) Jefferson County	22	1.41
Panama (village) Chautauqua County	6	1.26
Herricks (cdp) Nassau County	37	0.94
Rutland (town) Jefferson County	22	0.73
Cattaraugus Reservation Erie County	12	0.64
Carthage (village) Jefferson County	17	0.46
Chestnut Ridge (village) Rockland County	35	0.45
Brookville (village) Nassau County	13	0.38
Chili (town) Monroe County	85	0.30

Top 10 Places Sorted by Percent of Total Population
Based on places with total population of 50,000 or more

Place	Population	%
White Plains (city) Westchester County	155	0.28
Mount Vernon (city) Westchester County	118	0.18
Bronx (borough) Bronx County	1,493	0.11
Brooklyn (borough) Kings County	2,026	0.08
Rochester (city) Monroe County	171	0.08
New York (city)	5,674	0.07
Queens (borough) Queens County	1,344	0.06
Niagara Falls (city) Niagara County	29	0.06
Manhattan (borough) New York County	735	0.05
Hamburg (town) Erie County	30	0.05

West Indian: Bermudan, excluding Hispanic

Top 10 Places Sorted by Population
Based on all places, regardless of total population

Place	Population	%
New York (city)	518	0.01
Bronx (borough) Bronx County	198	0.01
Queens (borough) Queens County	177	0.01
Manhattan (borough) New York County	127	0.01
Hempstead (town) Nassau County	52	0.01
Roosevelt (cdp) Nassau County	43	0.29
Albany (city) Albany County	36	0.04
Centereach (cdp) Suffolk County	34	0.11
Brookhaven (town) Suffolk County	34	0.01
Brooklyn (borough) Kings County	16	<0.01

Top 10 Places Sorted by Percent of Total Population
Based on all places, regardless of total population

Place	Population	%
Green Island (town/village) Albany County	13	0.51
Old Westbury (village) Nassau County	13	0.33
Roosevelt (cdp) Nassau County	43	0.29
Clermont (town) Columbia County	3	0.15
Upper Nyack (village) Rockland County	3	0.15
Centereach (cdp) Suffolk County	34	0.11
Albany (city) Albany County	36	0.04

Place	Population	%
Hempstead (village) Nassau County	9	0.02
New York (city)	518	0.01
Bronx (borough) Bronx County	198	0.01

Top 10 Places Sorted by Percent of Total Population
Based on places with total population of 50,000 or more

Place	Population	%
Albany (city) Albany County	36	0.04
Hempstead (village) Nassau County	9	0.02
New York (city)	518	0.01
Bronx (borough) Bronx County	198	0.01
Queens (borough) Queens County	177	0.01
Manhattan (borough) New York County	127	0.01
Hempstead (town) Nassau County	52	0.01
Brookhaven (town) Suffolk County	34	0.01
Brooklyn (borough) Kings County	16	<0.01
Oyster Bay (town) Nassau County	13	<0.01

West Indian: British West Indian, excluding Hispanic

Top 10 Places Sorted by Population
Based on all places, regardless of total population

Place	Population	%
New York (city)	44,326	0.55
Brooklyn (borough) Kings County	30,607	1.24
Bronx (borough) Bronx County	7,136	0.52
Queens (borough) Queens County	4,689	0.21
Manhattan (borough) New York County	1,658	0.10
Hempstead (town) Nassau County	972	0.13
Yonkers (city) Westchester County	497	0.26
Islip (town) Suffolk County	470	0.14
Mount Vernon (city) Westchester County	348	0.52
Wallkill (town) Orange County	296	1.09

Top 10 Places Sorted by Percent of Total Population
Based on all places, regardless of total population

Place	Population	%
Wawayanda (town) Orange County	271	3.79
Scotchtown (cdp) Orange County	222	2.28
Amagansett (cdp) Suffolk County	17	1.90
Cumberland Head (cdp) Clinton County	25	1.51
Brooklyn (borough) Kings County	30,607	1.24
Hillcrest (cdp) Rockland County	93	1.13
Wallkill (town) Orange County	296	1.09
Bay Shore (cdp) Suffolk County	253	0.91
Highland (cdp) Ulster County	49	0.86
Mechanicstown (cdp) Orange County	63	0.84

Top 10 Places Sorted by Percent of Total Population
Based on places with total population of 50,000 or more

Place	Population	%
Brooklyn (borough) Kings County	30,607	1.24
New York (city)	44,326	0.55
Bronx (borough) Bronx County	7,136	0.52
Mount Vernon (city) Westchester County	348	0.52
Hempstead (village) Nassau County	250	0.47
Yonkers (city) Westchester County	497	0.26
Queens (borough) Queens County	4,689	0.21
Ramapo (town) Rockland County	253	0.21
Albany (city) Albany County	210	0.21
New Rochelle (city) Westchester County	153	0.20

West Indian: Dutch West Indian, excluding Hispanic

Top 10 Places Sorted by Population
Based on all places, regardless of total population

Place	Population	%
New York (city)	1,167	0.01
Brooklyn (borough) Kings County	424	0.02
Manhattan (borough) New York County	276	0.02
Queens (borough) Queens County	206	0.01
Hempstead (town) Nassau County	199	0.03
Bronx (borough) Bronx County	172	0.01
North Valley Stream (cdp) Nassau County	134	0.81
Staten Island (borough) Richmond County	89	0.02
Albany (city) Albany County	79	0.08
Brownville (town) Jefferson County	71	1.16

Top 10 Places Sorted by Percent of Total Population
Based on all places, regardless of total population

Place	Population	%
Brownville (town) Jefferson County	71	1.16
Barnum Island (cdp) Nassau County	25	0.95
German (town) Chenango County	3	0.95
Hartwick (town) Otsego County	20	0.83
North Valley Stream (cdp) Nassau County	134	0.81
Mamakating (town) Sullivan County	55	0.46
Westbury (village) Nassau County	65	0.44
Lansing (village) Tompkins County	14	0.40
Preston (town) Chenango County	3	0.31
Lansing (town) Tompkins County	32	0.29

Top 10 Places Sorted by Percent of Total Population
Based on places with total population of 50,000 or more

Place	Population	%
Albany (city) Albany County	79	0.08
Hempstead (village) Nassau County	31	0.06
Hempstead (town) Nassau County	199	0.03
North Hempstead (town) Nassau County	65	0.03
Brooklyn (borough) Kings County	424	0.02
Manhattan (borough) New York County	276	0.02
Staten Island (borough) Richmond County	89	0.02
Schenectady (city) Schenectady County	10	0.02
New York (city)	1,167	0.01
Queens (borough) Queens County	206	0.01

West Indian: Haitian, excluding Hispanic

Top 10 Places Sorted by Population
Based on all places, regardless of total population

Place	Population	%
New York (city)	120,252	1.49
Brooklyn (borough) Kings County	69,941	2.84
Queens (borough) Queens County	38,368	1.74
Hempstead (town) Nassau County	17,422	2.31
Ramapo (town) Rockland County	8,948	7.29
Spring Valley (village) Rockland County	6,665	21.98
Manhattan (borough) New York County	6,500	0.41
Islip (town) Suffolk County	5,636	1.69
Elmont (cdp) Nassau County	5,587	16.20
Bronx (borough) Bronx County	4,652	0.34

Top 10 Places Sorted by Percent of Total Population
Based on all places, regardless of total population

Place	Population	%
Spring Valley (village) Rockland County	6,665	21.98
Elmont (cdp) Nassau County	5,587	16.20
Hillcrest (cdp) Rockland County	1,310	15.98
North Valley Stream (cdp) Nassau County	1,827	11.07
Hillburn (village) Rockland County	88	9.27
Wheatley Heights (cdp) Suffolk County	545	8.80
New Cassel (cdp) Nassau County	1,053	8.38
Nyack (village) Rockland County	577	8.29
Deferiet (village) Jefferson County	38	8.09
Uniondale (cdp) Nassau County	1,927	7.87

Top 10 Places Sorted by Percent of Total Population
Based on places with total population of 50,000 or more

Place	Population	%
Ramapo (town) Rockland County	8,948	7.29
Brentwood (cdp) Suffolk County	2,162	3.94
Hempstead (village) Nassau County	2,104	3.94
Brooklyn (borough) Kings County	69,941	2.84
Clarkstown (town) Rockland County	2,077	2.49
Hempstead (town) Nassau County	17,422	2.31
Babylon (town) Suffolk County	3,789	1.77
Queens (borough) Queens County	38,368	1.74
Islip (town) Suffolk County	5,636	1.69
New York (city)	120,252	1.49

West Indian: Jamaican, excluding Hispanic

Top 10 Places Sorted by Population
Based on all places, regardless of total population

Place	Population	%
New York (city)	216,495	2.68
Brooklyn (borough) Kings County	80,999	3.28

Place	Population	%
Bronx (borough) Bronx County	64,222	4.70
Queens (borough) Queens County	59,999	2.73
Hempstead (town) Nassau County	17,690	2.35
Mount Vernon (city) Westchester County	10,445	15.57
Manhattan (borough) New York County	9,242	0.58
Yonkers (city) Westchester County	5,051	2.59
Babylon (town) Suffolk County	4,758	2.23
Poughkeepsie (city) Dutchess County	3,093	9.53

Top 10 Places Sorted by Percent of Total Population
Based on all places, regardless of total population

Place	Population	%
Mount Vernon (city) Westchester County	10,445	15.57
Lakeview (cdp) Nassau County	791	14.20
North Amityville (cdp) Suffolk County	2,248	12.62
Hillcrest (cdp) Rockland County	854	10.42
Poughkeepsie (city) Dutchess County	3,093	9.53
South Floral Park (village) Nassau County	141	9.03
Elmont (cdp) Nassau County	2,968	8.61
Uniondale (cdp) Nassau County	1,905	7.78
North Valley Stream (cdp) Nassau County	1,257	7.62
Morrisville (village) Madison County	173	6.83

Top 10 Places Sorted by Percent of Total Population
Based on places with total population of 50,000 or more

Place	Population	%
Mount Vernon (city) Westchester County	10,445	15.57
Hempstead (village) Nassau County	2,809	5.26
Bronx (borough) Bronx County	64,222	4.70
New Rochelle (city) Westchester County	2,635	3.48
Brooklyn (borough) Kings County	80,999	3.28
Queens (borough) Queens County	59,999	2.73
New York (city)	216,495	2.68
Yonkers (city) Westchester County	5,051	2.59
Greenburgh (town) Westchester County	2,150	2.45
Hempstead (town) Nassau County	17,690	2.35

West Indian: Trinidadian and Tobagonian, excluding Hispanic

Top 10 Places Sorted by Population
Based on all places, regardless of total population

Place	Population	%
New York (city)	76,240	0.94
Brooklyn (borough) Kings County	46,490	1.88
Queens (borough) Queens County	19,255	0.88
Bronx (borough) Bronx County	4,811	0.35
Manhattan (borough) New York County	3,877	0.24
Hempstead (town) Nassau County	3,155	0.42
Staten Island (borough) Richmond County	1,807	0.39
Brookhaven (town) Suffolk County	1,200	0.25
Babylon (town) Suffolk County	854	0.40
Yonkers (city) Westchester County	689	0.35

Top 10 Places Sorted by Percent of Total Population
Based on all places, regardless of total population

Place	Population	%
Brewster (village) Putnam County	131	6.53
Hillcrest (cdp) Rockland County	367	4.48
East Marion (cdp) Suffolk County	54	4.04
South Floral Park (village) Nassau County	53	3.39
North Valley Stream (cdp) Nassau County	551	3.34
Rockland (town) Sullivan County	106	2.75
South Valley Stream (cdp) Nassau County	110	2.09
Greenwood Lake (village) Orange County	67	2.07
Goshen (village) Orange County	111	2.00
Brooklyn (borough) Kings County	46,490	1.88

Top 10 Places Sorted by Percent of Total Population
Based on places with total population of 50,000 or more

Place	Population	%
Brooklyn (borough) Kings County	46,490	1.88
New York (city)	76,240	0.94
Queens (borough) Queens County	19,255	0.88
Hempstead (village) Nassau County	322	0.60
Mount Vernon (city) Westchester County	397	0.59
Ramapo (town) Rockland County	604	0.49
Troy (city) Rensselaer County	243	0.49
Hempstead (town) Nassau County	3,155	0.42
New Rochelle (city) Westchester County	317	0.42
Babylon (town) Suffolk County	854	0.40

West Indian: U.S. Virgin Islander, excluding Hispanic

Top 10 Places Sorted by Population
Based on all places, regardless of total population

Place	Population	%
New York (city)	2,383	0.03
Bronx (borough) Bronx County	952	0.07
Brooklyn (borough) Kings County	558	0.02
Manhattan (borough) New York County	487	0.03
Queens (borough) Queens County	364	0.02
South Huntington (cdp) Suffolk County	147	1.49
Huntington (town) Suffolk County	147	0.07
Yonkers (city) Westchester County	83	0.04
Poughkeepsie (city) Dutchess County	42	0.13
Middletown (city) Orange County	33	0.12

Top 10 Places Sorted by Percent of Total Population
Based on all places, regardless of total population

Place	Population	%
South Huntington (cdp) Suffolk County	147	1.49
Roxbury (town) Delaware County	28	1.12
Brownville (village) Jefferson County	7	0.67
Brookville (village) Nassau County	15	0.43
Otisville (village) Orange County	4	0.36
New Hyde Park (village) Nassau County	30	0.31
Washingtonville (village) Orange County	11	0.18
Poughkeepsie (city) Dutchess County	42	0.13
Attica (town) Wyoming County	10	0.13
Middletown (city) Orange County	33	0.12

Top 10 Places Sorted by Percent of Total Population
Based on places with total population of 50,000 or more

Place	Population	%
Bronx (borough) Bronx County	952	0.07
Huntington (town) Suffolk County	147	0.07
Yonkers (city) Westchester County	83	0.04
White Plains (city) Westchester County	23	0.04
New York (city)	2,383	0.03
Manhattan (borough) New York County	487	0.03
Brooklyn (borough) Kings County	558	0.02
Queens (borough) Queens County	364	0.02
Ramapo (town) Rockland County	19	0.02
Oyster Bay (town) Nassau County	15	0.01

West Indian: West Indian, excluding Hispanic

Top 10 Places Sorted by Population
Based on all places, regardless of total population

Place	Population	%
New York (city)	106,548	1.32
Brooklyn (borough) Kings County	59,844	2.43
Bronx (borough) Bronx County	21,941	1.61
Queens (borough) Queens County	17,400	0.79
Manhattan (borough) New York County	5,618	0.35
Hempstead (town) Nassau County	4,748	0.63
Staten Island (borough) Richmond County	1,745	0.38
Babylon (town) Suffolk County	1,378	0.64
Brookhaven (town) Suffolk County	1,323	0.28
Mount Vernon (city) Westchester County	1,287	1.92

Top 10 Places Sorted by Percent of Total Population
Based on all places, regardless of total population

Place	Population	%
Aurora (village) Cayuga County	76	6.79
Rushville (village) Yates County	44	6.48
Fairview (cdp) Westchester County	103	4.32
Hillburn (village) Rockland County	38	4.00
Ledyard (town) Cayuga County	76	3.41
South Blooming Grove (village) Orange County	105	3.19
South Hempstead (cdp) Nassau County	90	2.82
Moravia (town) Cayuga County	102	2.75
Calcium (cdp) Jefferson County	91	2.57
North Valley Stream (cdp) Nassau County	422	2.56

Top 10 Places Sorted by Percent of Total Population
Based on places with total population of 50,000 or more

Place	Population	%
Brooklyn (borough) Kings County	59,844	2.43

Place	Population	%
Mount Vernon (city) Westchester County	1,287	1.92
Bronx (borough) Bronx County	21,941	1.61
Hempstead (village) Nassau County	785	1.47
New York (city)	106,548	1.32
Queens (borough) Queens County	17,400	0.79
Schenectady (city) Schenectady County	446	0.68
Babylon (town) Suffolk County	1,378	0.64
Hempstead (town) Nassau County	4,748	0.63
Albany (city) Albany County	576	0.59

West Indian: Other, excluding Hispanic

Top 10 Places Sorted by Population
Based on all places, regardless of total population

Place	Population	%
New York (city)	1,204	0.01
Brooklyn (borough) Kings County	454	0.02
Queens (borough) Queens County	452	0.02
Bronx (borough) Bronx County	130	0.01
Manhattan (borough) New York County	125	0.01
Albany (city) Albany County	67	0.07
Staten Island (borough) Richmond County	43	0.01
Monroe (village) Orange County	40	0.48
Monroe (town) Orange County	40	0.10
Brookhaven (town) Suffolk County	27	0.01

Top 10 Places Sorted by Percent of Total Population
Based on all places, regardless of total population

Place	Population	%
Unionville (village) Orange County	2	0.52
Monroe (village) Orange County	40	0.48
Horseheads (village) Chemung County	11	0.17
Monroe (town) Orange County	40	0.10

Place	Population	%
Stony Brook (cdp) Suffolk County	12	0.09
Albany (city) Albany County	67	0.07
Massapequa (cdp) Nassau County	15	0.07
Williamson (town) Wayne County	5	0.07
Horseheads (town) Chemung County	11	0.06
Centereach (cdp) Suffolk County	15	0.05

Top 10 Places Sorted by Percent of Total Population
Based on places with total population of 50,000 or more

Place	Population	%
Albany (city) Albany County	67	0.07
Troy (city) Rensselaer County	13	0.03
Brooklyn (borough) Kings County	454	0.02
Queens (borough) Queens County	452	0.02
New York (city)	1,204	0.01
Bronx (borough) Bronx County	130	0.01
Manhattan (borough) New York County	125	0.01
Staten Island (borough) Richmond County	43	0.01
Brookhaven (town) Suffolk County	27	0.01
Oyster Bay (town) Nassau County	15	0.01

Yugoslavian

Top 10 Places Sorted by Population
Based on all places, regardless of total population

Place	Population	%
New York (city)	12,410	0.15
Queens (borough) Queens County	4,516	0.21
Utica (city) Oneida County	3,231	5.23
Brooklyn (borough) Kings County	2,800	0.11
Manhattan (borough) New York County	1,876	0.12
Staten Island (borough) Richmond County	1,738	0.38
Bronx (borough) Bronx County	1,480	0.11

Place	Population	%
Syracuse (city) Onondaga County	774	0.53
Hempstead (town) Nassau County	649	0.09
Brookhaven (town) Suffolk County	518	0.11

Top 10 Places Sorted by Percent of Total Population
Based on all places, regardless of total population

Place	Population	%
Napeague (cdp) Suffolk County	51	24.40
Pinckney (town) Lewis County	15	6.33
Utica (city) Oneida County	3,231	5.23
Lebanon (town) Madison County	73	4.93
Hawthorne (cdp) Westchester County	211	4.66
Angola on the Lake (cdp) Erie County	55	3.92
Exeter (town) Otsego County	27	3.11
Fleischmanns (village) Delaware County	6	2.91
Masonville (town) Delaware County	38	2.81
Milan (town) Dutchess County	71	2.80

Top 10 Places Sorted by Percent of Total Population
Based on places with total population of 50,000 or more

Place	Population	%
Utica (city) Oneida County	3,231	5.23
Syracuse (city) Onondaga County	774	0.53
Staten Island (borough) Richmond County	1,738	0.38
Huntington (town) Suffolk County	467	0.23
Clay (town) Onondaga County	132	0.23
Queens (borough) Queens County	4,516	0.21
Tonawanda (cdp) Erie County	124	0.21
Smithtown (town) Suffolk County	216	0.18
Colonie (town) Albany County	143	0.18
Tonawanda (town) Erie County	133	0.18

Hispanic Origin Rankings

Hispanic or Latino (of any race)

Top 10 Places Sorted by Population
Based on all places, regardless of total population

Place	Population	%
New York (city)	2,336,076	28.58
Bronx (borough) Bronx County	741,413	53.53
Queens (borough) Queens County	613,750	27.51
Brooklyn (borough) Kings County	496,285	19.81
Manhattan (borough) New York County	403,577	25.45
Hempstead (town) Nassau County	132,154	17.39
Islip (town) Suffolk County	97,371	29.02
Staten Island (borough) Richmond County	81,051	17.29
Yonkers (city) Westchester County	67,927	34.66
Brookhaven (town) Suffolk County	60,270	12.40

Top 10 Places Sorted by Percent of Total Population
Based on all places, regardless of total population

Place	Population	%
Brentwood (cdp) Suffolk County	41,529	68.46
Haverstraw (village) Rockland County	7,993	67.11
North Bay Shore (cdp) Suffolk County	12,310	64.98
Port Chester (village) Westchester County	17,193	59.35
Brewster (village) Putnam County	1,338	55.98
New Cassel (cdp) Nassau County	7,577	53.89
Bronx (borough) Bronx County	741,413	53.53
Central Islip (cdp) Suffolk County	17,938	52.07
Sleepy Hollow (village) Westchester County	5,038	51.04
Newburgh (city) Orange County	13,814	47.86

Top 10 Places Sorted by Percent of Total Population
Based on places with total population of 50,000 or more

Place	Population	%
Brentwood (cdp) Suffolk County	41,529	68.46
Bronx (borough) Bronx County	741,413	53.53
Hempstead (village) Nassau County	23,823	44.21
Yonkers (city) Westchester County	67,927	34.66
White Plains (city) Westchester County	16,839	29.62
Islip (town) Suffolk County	97,371	29.02
New York (city)	2,336,076	28.58
New Rochelle (city) Westchester County	21,452	27.84
Queens (borough) Queens County	613,750	27.51
Manhattan (borough) New York County	403,577	25.45

Central American, excluding Mexican

Top 10 Places Sorted by Population
Based on all places, regardless of total population

Place	Population	%
New York (city)	151,378	1.85
Queens (borough) Queens County	52,509	2.35
Hempstead (town) Nassau County	49,236	6.48
Brooklyn (borough) Kings County	46,119	1.84
Islip (town) Suffolk County	38,530	11.48
Bronx (borough) Bronx County	34,492	2.49
Brentwood (cdp) Suffolk County	19,957	32.90
Hempstead (village) Nassau County	16,171	30.01
Manhattan (borough) New York County	13,948	0.88
North Hempstead (town) Nassau County	11,455	5.06

Top 10 Places Sorted by Percent of Total Population
Based on all places, regardless of total population

Place	Population	%
Brewster (village) Putnam County	967	40.46
Brentwood (cdp) Suffolk County	19,957	32.90
New Cassel (cdp) Nassau County	4,455	31.69
North Bay Shore (cdp) Suffolk County	5,763	30.42
Hempstead (village) Nassau County	16,171	30.01
Inwood (cdp) Nassau County	2,509	25.62
Uniondale (cdp) Nassau County	6,264	25.30
Central Islip (cdp) Suffolk County	8,487	24.64
Flanders (cdp) Suffolk County	1,034	23.12
Roosevelt (cdp) Nassau County	3,748	23.05

Top 10 Places Sorted by Percent of Total Population
Based on places with total population of 50,000 or more

Place	Population	%
Brentwood (cdp) Suffolk County	19,957	32.90
Hempstead (village) Nassau County	16,171	30.01
Islip (town) Suffolk County	38,530	11.48
Southampton (town) Suffolk County	3,715	6.54
Hempstead (town) Nassau County	49,236	6.48
Babylon (town) Suffolk County	11,096	5.19
North Hempstead (town) Nassau County	11,455	5.06
Huntington (town) Suffolk County	9,599	4.72
Ramapo (town) Rockland County	5,319	4.20
Yonkers (city) Westchester County	5,822	2.97

Central American: Costa Rican

Top 10 Places Sorted by Population
Based on all places, regardless of total population

Place	Population	%
New York (city)	6,673	0.08
Brooklyn (borough) Kings County	2,576	0.10
Queens (borough) Queens County	1,749	0.08
Bronx (borough) Bronx County	1,095	0.08
Manhattan (borough) New York County	987	0.06
Hempstead (town) Nassau County	664	0.09
Southampton (town) Suffolk County	618	1.09
Hampton Bays (cdp) Suffolk County	406	2.98
Islip (town) Suffolk County	297	0.09
Staten Island (borough) Richmond County	266	0.06

Top 10 Places Sorted by Percent of Total Population
Based on all places, regardless of total population

Place	Population	%
Hampton Bays (cdp) Suffolk County	406	2.98
Tuckahoe (cdp) Suffolk County	23	1.68
Springs (cdp) Suffolk County	103	1.56
East Hampton North (cdp) Suffolk County	53	1.28
Bridgehampton (cdp) Suffolk County	21	1.20
Peconic (cdp) Suffolk County	8	1.17
Southampton (town) Suffolk County	618	1.09
East Hampton (town) Suffolk County	216	1.01
Shinnecock Hills (cdp) Suffolk County	22	1.01
Woodridge (village) Sullivan County	8	0.94

Top 10 Places Sorted by Percent of Total Population
Based on places with total population of 50,000 or more

Place	Population	%
Southampton (town) Suffolk County	618	1.09
Brentwood (cdp) Suffolk County	85	0.14
Brooklyn (borough) Kings County	2,576	0.10
Mount Vernon (city) Westchester County	64	0.10
Hempstead (town) Nassau County	664	0.09
Islip (town) Suffolk County	297	0.09
New York (city)	6,673	0.08
Queens (borough) Queens County	1,749	0.08
Bronx (borough) Bronx County	1,095	0.08
Yonkers (city) Westchester County	156	0.08

Central American: Guatemalan

Top 10 Places Sorted by Population
Based on all places, regardless of total population

Place	Population	%
New York (city)	30,420	0.37
Queens (borough) Queens County	13,700	0.61
Brooklyn (borough) Kings County	9,160	0.37
Hempstead (town) Nassau County	5,948	0.78
Bronx (borough) Bronx County	4,645	0.34
Ramapo (town) Rockland County	4,050	3.20
Spring Valley (village) Rockland County	3,265	10.42
Islip (town) Suffolk County	3,256	0.97
Rye (town) Westchester County	2,654	5.78
Port Chester (village) Westchester County	2,433	8.40

Top 10 Places Sorted by Percent of Total Population
Based on all places, regardless of total population

Place	Population	%
Brewster (village) Putnam County	912	38.16
Mount Kisco (town/village) Westchester County	1,782	16.38
Flanders (cdp) Suffolk County	678	15.16
Cattaraugus Reservation Chautauqua County	5	13.16
Greenport (village) Suffolk County	287	13.06
Quiogue (cdp) Suffolk County	103	12.62
Bedford Hills (cdp) Westchester County	317	10.56
Spring Valley (village) Rockland County	3,265	10.42
Westhampton Beach (village) Suffolk County	178	10.34
Riverside (cdp) Suffolk County	273	9.38

Top 10 Places Sorted by Percent of Total Population
Based on places with total population of 50,000 or more

Place	Population	%
Southampton (town) Suffolk County	2,081	3.66
Ramapo (town) Rockland County	4,050	3.20
Hempstead (village) Nassau County	1,402	2.60
Brentwood (cdp) Suffolk County	1,553	2.56
New Rochelle (city) Westchester County	1,232	1.60
Islip (town) Suffolk County	3,256	0.97
White Plains (city) Westchester County	551	0.97
Clarkstown (town) Rockland County	802	0.95
Hempstead (town) Nassau County	5,948	0.78
Queens (borough) Queens County	13,700	0.61

Central American: Honduran

Top 10 Places Sorted by Population
Based on all places, regardless of total population

Place	Population	%
New York (city)	42,400	0.52
Bronx (borough) Bronx County	17,990	1.30
Brooklyn (borough) Kings County	10,071	0.40
Queens (borough) Queens County	8,546	0.38
Hempstead (town) Nassau County	7,842	1.03
Islip (town) Suffolk County	4,232	1.26
Manhattan (borough) New York County	4,058	0.26
Hempstead (village) Nassau County	3,758	6.97
Brentwood (cdp) Suffolk County	2,062	3.40
Babylon (town) Suffolk County	1,756	0.82

Top 10 Places Sorted by Percent of Total Population
Based on all places, regardless of total population

Place	Population	%
Woodridge (village) Sullivan County	60	7.08
Hempstead (village) Nassau County	3,758	6.97
South Fallsburg (cdp) Sullivan County	200	6.97
New Cassel (cdp) Nassau County	812	5.78
Newburgh (city) Orange County	1,545	5.35
Huntington Station (cdp) Suffolk County	1,260	3.81
Brentwood (cdp) Suffolk County	2,062	3.40
Uniondale (cdp) Nassau County	806	3.26
Central Islip (cdp) Suffolk County	1,118	3.25
Oyster Bay (cdp) Nassau County	212	3.16

Top 10 Places Sorted by Percent of Total Population
Based on places with total population of 50,000 or more

Place	Population	%
Hempstead (village) Nassau County	3,758	6.97
Brentwood (cdp) Suffolk County	2,062	3.40
Bronx (borough) Bronx County	17,990	1.30
Islip (town) Suffolk County	4,232	1.26
Hempstead (town) Nassau County	7,842	1.03
Babylon (town) Suffolk County	1,756	0.82
Huntington (town) Suffolk County	1,651	0.81
Yonkers (city) Westchester County	1,451	0.74
North Hempstead (town) Nassau County	1,572	0.69
New York (city)	42,400	0.52

Central American: Nicaraguan

Top 10 Places Sorted by Population
Based on all places, regardless of total population

Place	Population	%
New York (city)	9,346	0.11
Queens (borough) Queens County	2,842	0.13
Brooklyn (borough) Kings County	2,407	0.10
Bronx (borough) Bronx County	2,342	0.17
Manhattan (borough) New York County	1,556	0.10
Hempstead (town) Nassau County	656	0.09
Yonkers (city) Westchester County	534	0.27
Islip (town) Suffolk County	253	0.08
Staten Island (borough) Richmond County	199	0.04
Brookhaven (town) Suffolk County	159	0.03

Top 10 Places Sorted by Percent of Total Population
Based on all places, regardless of total population

Place	Population	%
Quiogue (cdp) Suffolk County	8	0.98
Inwood (cdp) Nassau County	79	0.81
Cove Neck (village) Nassau County	2	0.70
Hewlett (cdp) Nassau County	36	0.53
North Hornell (village) Steuben County	4	0.51
Woodmere (cdp) Nassau County	73	0.43
Bellerose Terrace (cdp) Nassau County	9	0.41
South Fallsburg (cdp) Sullivan County	11	0.38
Greenport (village) Suffolk County	8	0.36
Cedarhurst (village) Nassau County	23	0.35

Top 10 Places Sorted by Percent of Total Population
Based on places with total population of 50,000 or more

Place	Population	%
Yonkers (city) Westchester County	534	0.27
Bronx (borough) Bronx County	2,342	0.17
Brentwood (cdp) Suffolk County	87	0.14
Queens (borough) Queens County	2,842	0.13
New York (city)	9,346	0.11
Brooklyn (borough) Kings County	2,407	0.10
Manhattan (borough) New York County	1,556	0.10
New Rochelle (city) Westchester County	74	0.10
Hempstead (village) Nassau County	56	0.10
Hempstead (town) Nassau County	656	0.09

Central American: Panamanian

Top 10 Places Sorted by Population
Based on all places, regardless of total population

Place	Population	%
New York (city)	22,353	0.27
Brooklyn (borough) Kings County	13,681	0.55
Queens (borough) Queens County	3,977	0.18
Bronx (borough) Bronx County	2,372	0.17
Manhattan (borough) New York County	1,716	0.11
Hempstead (town) Nassau County	1,163	0.15
Staten Island (borough) Richmond County	607	0.13
Islip (town) Suffolk County	466	0.14
Babylon (town) Suffolk County	305	0.14
Brookhaven (town) Suffolk County	291	0.06

Top 10 Places Sorted by Percent of Total Population
Based on all places, regardless of total population

Place	Population	%
Lakeview (cdp) Nassau County	53	0.94
Northampton (cdp) Suffolk County	5	0.88
Evans Mills (village) Jefferson County	5	0.81
Parc (cdp) Clinton County	2	0.79
Washington Heights (cdp) Orange County	11	0.65
Otego (village) Otsego County	6	0.59
North Valley Stream (cdp) Nassau County	93	0.56
Corfu (village) Genesee County	4	0.56
Brooklyn (borough) Kings County	13,681	0.55
Wyandanch (cdp) Suffolk County	57	0.49

Top 10 Places Sorted by Percent of Total Population
Based on places with total population of 50,000 or more

Place	Population	%
Brooklyn (borough) Kings County	13,681	0.55
New York (city)	22,353	0.27
Hempstead (village) Nassau County	138	0.26
Brentwood (cdp) Suffolk County	148	0.24

Mount Vernon (city) Westchester County	131	0.19
Queens (borough) Queens County	3,977	0.18
Bronx (borough) Bronx County	2,372	0.17
Hempstead (town) Nassau County	1,163	0.15
Islip (town) Suffolk County	466	0.14
Babylon (town) Suffolk County	305	0.14

Central American: Salvadoran

Top 10 Places Sorted by Population
Based on all places, regardless of total population

Place	Population	%
New York (city)	38,559	0.47
Hempstead (town) Nassau County	32,681	4.30
Islip (town) Suffolk County	29,849	8.90
Queens (borough) Queens County	21,342	0.96
Brentwood (cdp) Suffolk County	15,946	26.29
Hempstead (village) Nassau County	10,707	19.87
North Hempstead (town) Nassau County	8,262	3.65
Babylon (town) Suffolk County	7,805	3.65
Brooklyn (borough) Kings County	7,737	0.31
Huntington (town) Suffolk County	6,563	3.23

Top 10 Places Sorted by Percent of Total Population
Based on all places, regardless of total population

Place	Population	%
Brentwood (cdp) Suffolk County	15,946	26.29
New Cassel (cdp) Nassau County	3,477	24.73
North Bay Shore (cdp) Suffolk County	4,530	23.91
Uniondale (cdp) Nassau County	4,998	20.19
Hempstead (village) Nassau County	10,707	19.87
Central Islip (cdp) Suffolk County	6,381	18.52
Roosevelt (cdp) Nassau County	2,891	17.78
Huntington Station (cdp) Suffolk County	5,233	15.84
Inwood (cdp) Nassau County	1,523	15.55
Wyandanch (cdp) Suffolk County	1,485	12.75

Top 10 Places Sorted by Percent of Total Population
Based on places with total population of 50,000 or more

Place	Population	%
Brentwood (cdp) Suffolk County	15,946	26.29
Hempstead (village) Nassau County	10,707	19.87
Islip (town) Suffolk County	29,849	8.90
Hempstead (town) Nassau County	32,681	4.30
North Hempstead (town) Nassau County	8,262	3.65
Babylon (town) Suffolk County	7,805	3.65
Huntington (town) Suffolk County	6,563	3.23
Levittown (cdp) Nassau County	876	1.69
Yonkers (city) Westchester County	2,691	1.37
Brookhaven (town) Suffolk County	5,899	1.21

Central American: Other Central American

Top 10 Places Sorted by Population
Based on all places, regardless of total population

Place	Population	%
New York (city)	1,627	0.02
Bronx (borough) Bronx County	579	0.04
Brooklyn (borough) Kings County	487	0.02
Queens (borough) Queens County	353	0.02
Hempstead (town) Nassau County	282	0.04
Islip (town) Suffolk County	177	0.05
Manhattan (borough) New York County	161	0.01
North Hempstead (town) Nassau County	110	0.05
Brookhaven (town) Suffolk County	106	0.02
Babylon (town) Suffolk County	88	0.04

Top 10 Places Sorted by Percent of Total Population
Based on all places, regardless of total population

Place	Population	%
Mount Kisco (town/village) Westchester County	31	0.29
New Cassel (cdp) Nassau County	37	0.26
Flanders (cdp) Suffolk County	10	0.22
Pawling (village) Dutchess County	5	0.21
Amityville (village) Suffolk County	19	0.20
West Nyack (cdp) Rockland County	7	0.20
Central Islip (cdp) Suffolk County	65	0.19
Berne (town) Albany County	5	0.18
Greenvale (cdp) Nassau County	2	0.18
Mattituck (cdp) Suffolk County	7	0.17

Top 10 Places Sorted by Percent of Total Population
Based on places with total population of 50,000 or more

Place	Population	%
Brentwood (cdp) Suffolk County	76	0.13
Hempstead (village) Nassau County	66	0.12
Islip (town) Suffolk County	177	0.05
North Hempstead (town) Nassau County	110	0.05
Bronx (borough) Bronx County	579	0.04
Hempstead (town) Nassau County	282	0.04
Babylon (town) Suffolk County	88	0.04
Huntington (town) Suffolk County	52	0.03
Southampton (town) Suffolk County	17	0.03
New York (city)	1,627	0.02

Cuban

Top 10 Places Sorted by Population
Based on all places, regardless of total population

Place	Population	%
New York (city)	40,840	0.50
Manhattan (borough) New York County	11,623	0.73
Queens (borough) Queens County	11,020	0.49
Bronx (borough) Bronx County	8,785	0.63
Brooklyn (borough) Kings County	7,581	0.30
Hempstead (town) Nassau County	3,597	0.47
Staten Island (borough) Richmond County	1,831	0.39
Rochester (city) Monroe County	1,616	0.77
Yonkers (city) Westchester County	1,501	0.77
Brookhaven (town) Suffolk County	1,500	0.31

Top 10 Places Sorted by Percent of Total Population
Based on all places, regardless of total population

Place	Population	%
Hunt (cdp) Livingston County	2	2.56
Hewlett Bay Park (village) Nassau County	10	2.48
East Kingston (cdp) Ulster County	6	2.17
Tarrytown (village) Westchester County	205	1.82
Bellerose (village) Nassau County	20	1.68
South Floral Park (village) Nassau County	23	1.30
Sleepy Hollow (village) Westchester County	123	1.25
North Hudson (town) Essex County	3	1.25
Port Chester (village) Westchester County	359	1.24
Plattekill (cdp) Ulster County	14	1.11

Top 10 Places Sorted by Percent of Total Population
Based on places with total population of 50,000 or more

Place	Population	%
Syracuse (city) Onondaga County	1,192	0.82
Rochester (city) Monroe County	1,616	0.77
Yonkers (city) Westchester County	1,501	0.77
Manhattan (borough) New York County	11,623	0.73
Greenburgh (town) Westchester County	565	0.64
Bronx (borough) Bronx County	8,785	0.63
White Plains (city) Westchester County	321	0.56
Levittown (cdp) Nassau County	274	0.53
New York (city)	40,840	0.50
Clarkstown (town) Rockland County	421	0.50

Dominican Republic

Top 10 Places Sorted by Population
Based on all places, regardless of total population

Place	Population	%
New York (city)	576,701	7.05
Bronx (borough) Bronx County	240,987	17.40
Manhattan (borough) New York County	155,971	9.84
Queens (borough) Queens County	88,061	3.95
Brooklyn (borough) Kings County	86,764	3.46
Hempstead (town) Nassau County	16,914	2.23
Yonkers (city) Westchester County	15,903	8.11
Islip (town) Suffolk County	8,547	2.55
Babylon (town) Suffolk County	6,543	3.06
Haverstraw (town) Rockland County	6,277	17.13

Top 10 Places Sorted by Percent of Total Population
Based on all places, regardless of total population

Place	Population	%
Haverstraw (village) Rockland County	3,847	32.30
Sleepy Hollow (village) Westchester County	1,831	18.55
Bronx (borough) Bronx County	240,987	17.40

Haverstraw (town) Rockland County	6,277	17.13
West Haverstraw (village) Rockland County	1,667	16.40
Freeport (village) Nassau County	5,539	12.92
Copiague (cdp) Suffolk County	2,846	12.38
Manhattan (borough) New York County	155,971	9.84
Yonkers (city) Westchester County	15,903	8.11
New York (city)	576,701	7.05

Top 10 Places Sorted by Percent of Total Population
Based on places with total population of 50,000 or more

Place	Population	%
Bronx (borough) Bronx County	240,987	17.40
Manhattan (borough) New York County	155,971	9.84
Yonkers (city) Westchester County	15,903	8.11
New York (city)	576,701	7.05
Brentwood (cdp) Suffolk County	4,205	6.93
Queens (borough) Queens County	88,061	3.95
Brooklyn (borough) Kings County	86,764	3.46
Babylon (town) Suffolk County	6,543	3.06
Hempstead (village) Nassau County	1,398	2.59
Islip (town) Suffolk County	8,547	2.55

Mexican

Top 10 Places Sorted by Population
Based on all places, regardless of total population

Place	Population	%
New York (city)	319,263	3.91
Brooklyn (borough) Kings County	94,585	3.78
Queens (borough) Queens County	92,835	4.16
Bronx (borough) Bronx County	71,194	5.14
Manhattan (borough) New York County	41,965	2.65
Staten Island (borough) Richmond County	18,684	3.99
Yonkers (city) Westchester County	13,761	7.02
New Rochelle (city) Westchester County	10,363	13.45
Newburgh (city) Orange County	6,181	21.41
White Plains (city) Westchester County	5,773	10.15

Top 10 Places Sorted by Percent of Total Population
Based on all places, regardless of total population

Place	Population	%
Fleischmanns (village) Delaware County	117	33.33
Newburgh (city) Orange County	6,181	21.41
Port Chester (village) Westchester County	4,864	16.79
Middletown (city) Orange County	4,208	14.98
New Rochelle (city) Westchester County	10,363	13.45
Tuckahoe (cdp) Suffolk County	181	13.18
Shinnecock Hills (cdp) Suffolk County	282	12.89
New Cassel (cdp) Nassau County	1,739	12.37
Rye (town) Westchester County	5,313	11.57
Dresden (village) Yates County	34	11.04

Top 10 Places Sorted by Percent of Total Population
Based on places with total population of 50,000 or more

Place	Population	%
New Rochelle (city) Westchester County	10,363	13.45
White Plains (city) Westchester County	5,773	10.15
Yonkers (city) Westchester County	13,761	7.02
Bronx (borough) Bronx County	71,194	5.14
Southampton (town) Suffolk County	2,856	5.03
Queens (borough) Queens County	92,835	4.16
Staten Island (borough) Richmond County	18,684	3.99
New York (city)	319,263	3.91
Brooklyn (borough) Kings County	94,585	3.78
Mount Vernon (city) Westchester County	2,454	3.65

Puerto Rican

Top 10 Places Sorted by Population
Based on all places, regardless of total population

Place	Population	%
New York (city)	723,621	8.85
Bronx (borough) Bronx County	298,921	21.58
Brooklyn (borough) Kings County	176,528	7.05
Manhattan (borough) New York County	107,774	6.80
Queens (borough) Queens County	102,881	4.61
Staten Island (borough) Richmond County	37,517	8.00
Rochester (city) Monroe County	27,734	13.17
Buffalo (city) Erie County	22,076	8.45
Islip (town) Suffolk County	21,506	6.41
Brookhaven (town) Suffolk County	21,429	4.41

Top 10 Places Sorted by Percent of Total Population
Based on all places, regardless of total population

Place	Population	%
Plattekill (cdp) Ulster County	328	26.03
Dunkirk (city) Chautauqua County	2,782	22.14
Bronx (borough) Bronx County	298,921	21.58
Amsterdam (city) Montgomery County	3,923	21.07
Ellenville (village) Ulster County	832	20.12
Middletown (city) Orange County	4,533	16.14
Monticello (village) Sullivan County	1,073	15.95
Washington Heights (cdp) Orange County	261	15.45
Scotchtown (cdp) Orange County	1,410	15.31
Mechanicstown (cdp) Orange County	996	14.52

Top 10 Places Sorted by Percent of Total Population
Based on places with total population of 50,000 or more

Place	Population	%
Bronx (borough) Bronx County	298,921	21.58
Rochester (city) Monroe County	27,734	13.17
Yonkers (city) Westchester County	19,875	10.14
Brentwood (cdp) Suffolk County	6,125	10.10
New York (city)	723,621	8.85
Buffalo (city) Erie County	22,076	8.45
Staten Island (borough) Richmond County	37,517	8.00
Schenectady (city) Schenectady County	4,677	7.07
Brooklyn (borough) Kings County	176,528	7.05
Manhattan (borough) New York County	107,774	6.80

South American

Top 10 Places Sorted by Population
Based on all places, regardless of total population

Place	Population	%
New York (city)	343,468	4.20
Queens (borough) Queens County	214,022	9.59
Brooklyn (borough) Kings County	49,003	1.96
Manhattan (borough) New York County	36,748	2.32
Bronx (borough) Bronx County	35,463	2.56
Hempstead (town) Nassau County	23,626	3.11
Islip (town) Suffolk County	16,012	4.77
Brookhaven (town) Suffolk County	12,182	2.51
Staten Island (borough) Richmond County	8,232	1.76
Ossining (town) Westchester County	6,825	18.12

Top 10 Places Sorted by Percent of Total Population
Based on all places, regardless of total population

Place	Population	%
East Hampton North (cdp) Suffolk County	1,076	25.98
Ossining (village) Westchester County	6,440	25.70
Springs (cdp) Suffolk County	1,623	24.62
Sleepy Hollow (village) Westchester County	2,098	21.26
Port Chester (village) Westchester County	5,769	19.92
Ossining (town) Westchester County	6,825	18.12
Elmsford (village) Westchester County	812	17.41
Peekskill (city) Westchester County	4,041	17.14
East Hampton (town) Suffolk County	3,513	16.37
Patchogue (village) Suffolk County	1,777	15.06

Top 10 Places Sorted by Percent of Total Population
Based on places with total population of 50,000 or more

Place	Population	%
Brentwood (cdp) Suffolk County	6,350	10.47
White Plains (city) Westchester County	5,850	10.29
Queens (borough) Queens County	214,022	9.59
New Rochelle (city) Westchester County	3,697	4.80
Islip (town) Suffolk County	16,012	4.77
Greenburgh (town) Westchester County	4,004	4.53
Southampton (town) Suffolk County	2,446	4.31
New York (city)	343,468	4.20
Yonkers (city) Westchester County	6,622	3.38
Levittown (cdp) Nassau County	1,746	3.37

South American: Argentinean

Top 10 Places Sorted by Population
Based on all places, regardless of total population

Place	Population	%
New York (city)	15,169	0.19
Queens (borough) Queens County	6,345	0.28
Manhattan (borough) New York County	4,339	0.27
Brooklyn (borough) Kings County	2,760	0.11
Hempstead (town) Nassau County	1,500	0.20
Bronx (borough) Bronx County	1,117	0.08
Brookhaven (town) Suffolk County	653	0.13
Islip (town) Suffolk County	616	0.18
Staten Island (borough) Richmond County	608	0.13
Oyster Bay (town) Nassau County	441	0.15

Top 10 Places Sorted by Percent of Total Population
Based on all places, regardless of total population

Place	Population	%
Russell Gardens (village) Nassau County	9	0.95
Kiryas Joel (village) Orange County	186	0.92
Hobart (village) Delaware County	4	0.91
Northville (cdp) Suffolk County	9	0.67
Woodsburgh (village) Nassau County	5	0.64
Asharoken (village) Suffolk County	4	0.61
Lynbrook (village) Nassau County	110	0.57
Salisbury Mills (cdp) Orange County	3	0.56
Monroe (town) Orange County	217	0.54
Harbor Hills (cdp) Nassau County	3	0.52

Top 10 Places Sorted by Percent of Total Population
Based on places with total population of 50,000 or more

Place	Population	%
Brentwood (cdp) Suffolk County	203	0.33
White Plains (city) Westchester County	189	0.33
Queens (borough) Queens County	6,345	0.28
Manhattan (borough) New York County	4,339	0.27
New Rochelle (city) Westchester County	170	0.22
Greenburgh (town) Westchester County	188	0.21
Hempstead (town) Nassau County	1,500	0.20
New York (city)	15,169	0.19
North Hempstead (town) Nassau County	435	0.19
Islip (town) Suffolk County	616	0.18

South American: Bolivian

Top 10 Places Sorted by Population
Based on all places, regardless of total population

Place	Population	%
New York (city)	4,488	0.05
Queens (borough) Queens County	3,268	0.15
Manhattan (borough) New York County	522	0.03
Hempstead (town) Nassau County	494	0.07
Rye (town) Westchester County	375	0.82
Port Chester (village) Westchester County	350	1.21
Brooklyn (borough) Kings County	310	0.01
Bronx (borough) Bronx County	227	0.02
Islip (town) Suffolk County	220	0.07
Staten Island (borough) Richmond County	161	0.03

Top 10 Places Sorted by Percent of Total Population
Based on all places, regardless of total population

Place	Population	%
Poospatuck Reservation Suffolk County	4	1.23
Port Chester (village) Westchester County	350	1.21
Rye (town) Westchester County	375	0.82
Merritt Park (cdp) Dutchess County	6	0.48
Inwood (cdp) Nassau County	43	0.44
Matinecock (village) Nassau County	3	0.37
Friendship (cdp) Allegany County	4	0.33
East Rockaway (village) Nassau County	31	0.32
Islandia (village) Suffolk County	10	0.30
Cedarhurst (village) Nassau County	18	0.27

Top 10 Places Sorted by Percent of Total Population
Based on places with total population of 50,000 or more

Place	Population	%
Queens (borough) Queens County	3,268	0.15
Brentwood (cdp) Suffolk County	79	0.13
White Plains (city) Westchester County	72	0.13
Hempstead (town) Nassau County	494	0.07
Islip (town) Suffolk County	220	0.07
New Rochelle (city) Westchester County	50	0.06
New York (city)	4,488	0.05
Greenburgh (town) Westchester County	48	0.05
Oyster Bay (town) Nassau County	110	0.04
Babylon (town) Suffolk County	78	0.04

South American: Chilean

Top 10 Places Sorted by Population
Based on all places, regardless of total population

Place	Population	%
New York (city)	7,026	0.09
Queens (borough) Queens County	3,184	0.14
Manhattan (borough) New York County	1,824	0.12
Hempstead (town) Nassau County	1,415	0.19
Brooklyn (borough) Kings County	1,026	0.04
North Hempstead (town) Nassau County	664	0.29
Bronx (borough) Bronx County	646	0.05
Oyster Bay (town) Nassau County	569	0.19
Islip (town) Suffolk County	448	0.13
Brookhaven (town) Suffolk County	363	0.07

Top 10 Places Sorted by Percent of Total Population
Based on all places, regardless of total population

Place	Population	%
Manorhaven (village) Nassau County	234	3.57
Oyster Bay (cdp) Nassau County	179	2.67
Windham (cdp) Greene County	6	1.63
Sleepy Hollow (village) Westchester County	146	1.48
Forest Home (cdp) Tompkins County	8	1.40
Ames (village) Montgomery County	2	1.38
Inwood (cdp) Nassau County	108	1.10
North Lynbrook (cdp) Nassau County	8	1.01
Cedarhurst (village) Nassau County	65	0.99
Port Washington (cdp) Nassau County	149	0.94

Top 10 Places Sorted by Percent of Total Population
Based on places with total population of 50,000 or more

Place	Population	%
North Hempstead (town) Nassau County	664	0.29
Brentwood (cdp) Suffolk County	153	0.25
Greenburgh (town) Westchester County	192	0.22
Levittown (cdp) Nassau County	112	0.22
Hempstead (town) Nassau County	1,415	0.19
Oyster Bay (town) Nassau County	569	0.19
Queens (borough) Queens County	3,184	0.14
Islip (town) Suffolk County	448	0.13
Manhattan (borough) New York County	1,824	0.12
Huntington (town) Suffolk County	252	0.12

South American: Colombian

Top 10 Places Sorted by Population
Based on all places, regardless of total population

Place	Population	%
New York (city)	94,723	1.16
Queens (borough) Queens County	70,290	3.15
Brooklyn (borough) Kings County	8,861	0.35
Hempstead (town) Nassau County	8,522	1.12
Manhattan (borough) New York County	8,411	0.53
Islip (town) Suffolk County	5,156	1.54
Bronx (borough) Bronx County	4,635	0.33
Brookhaven (town) Suffolk County	2,970	0.61
Staten Island (borough) Richmond County	2,526	0.54
Brentwood (cdp) Suffolk County	2,083	3.43

Top 10 Places Sorted by Percent of Total Population
Based on all places, regardless of total population

Place	Population	%
East Hampton North (cdp) Suffolk County	284	6.86
Springs (cdp) Suffolk County	430	6.52
Bellerose Terrace (cdp) Nassau County	124	5.64
East Hampton (town) Suffolk County	987	4.60
Hampton Bays (cdp) Suffolk County	614	4.51
Elmsford (village) Westchester County	186	3.99
Shinnecock Hills (cdp) Suffolk County	84	3.84
Montauk (cdp) Suffolk County	119	3.58
Brentwood (cdp) Suffolk County	2,083	3.43
White Plains (city) Westchester County	1,838	3.23

Top 10 Places Sorted by Percent of Total Population
Based on places with total population of 50,000 or more

Place	Population	%
Brentwood (cdp) Suffolk County	2,083	3.43
White Plains (city) Westchester County	1,838	3.23
Queens (borough) Queens County	70,290	3.15
New Rochelle (city) Westchester County	1,451	1.88

Southampton (town) Suffolk County	1,024	1.80
Islip (town) Suffolk County	5,156	1.54
Levittown (cdp) Nassau County	733	1.41
New York (city)	94,723	1.16
Hempstead (town) Nassau County	8,522	1.12
Greenburgh (town) Westchester County	845	0.96

South American: Ecuadorian

Top 10 Places Sorted by Population
Based on all places, regardless of total population

Place	Population	%
New York (city)	167,209	2.05
Queens (borough) Queens County	98,512	4.42
Brooklyn (borough) Kings County	28,684	1.15
Bronx (borough) Bronx County	23,206	1.68
Manhattan (borough) New York County	14,132	0.89
Brookhaven (town) Suffolk County	6,437	1.32
Hempstead (town) Nassau County	5,881	0.77
Islip (town) Suffolk County	5,323	1.59
Ossining (town) Westchester County	4,988	13.24
Ossining (village) Westchester County	4,840	19.31

Top 10 Places Sorted by Percent of Total Population
Based on all places, regardless of total population

Place	Population	%
Ossining (village) Westchester County	4,840	19.31
Sleepy Hollow (village) Westchester County	1,731	17.54
East Hampton North (cdp) Suffolk County	717	17.31
Springs (cdp) Suffolk County	1,137	17.25
Peekskill (city) Westchester County	3,490	14.80
Patchogue (village) Suffolk County	1,616	13.70
Ossining (town) Westchester County	4,988	13.24
East Hampton (town) Suffolk County	2,319	10.81
Port Chester (village) Westchester County	2,774	9.58
Spring Valley (village) Rockland County	2,681	8.55

Top 10 Places Sorted by Percent of Total Population
Based on places with total population of 50,000 or more

Place	Population	%
Queens (borough) Queens County	98,512	4.42
Brentwood (cdp) Suffolk County	1,985	3.27
Ramapo (town) Rockland County	2,915	2.30
New York (city)	167,209	2.05
Southampton (town) Suffolk County	1,102	1.94
White Plains (city) Westchester County	1,001	1.76
Bronx (borough) Bronx County	23,206	1.68
Yonkers (city) Westchester County	3,271	1.67
Greenburgh (town) Westchester County	1,434	1.62
Islip (town) Suffolk County	5,323	1.59

South American: Paraguayan

Top 10 Places Sorted by Population
Based on all places, regardless of total population

Place	Population	%
New York (city)	3,534	0.04
Queens (borough) Queens County	2,775	0.12
Manhattan (borough) New York County	268	0.02
White Plains (city) Westchester County	260	0.46
Harrison (town/village) Westchester County	235	0.86
Brooklyn (borough) Kings County	230	0.01
Bronx (borough) Bronx County	223	0.02
Hempstead (town) Nassau County	185	0.02
Greenburgh (town) Westchester County	144	0.16
North Hempstead (town) Nassau County	140	0.06

Top 10 Places Sorted by Percent of Total Population
Based on all places, regardless of total population

Place	Population	%
Bedford (cdp) Westchester County	28	1.53
Scotts Corners (cdp) Westchester County	10	1.41
Cove Neck (village) Nassau County	3	1.05
Fairview (cdp) Westchester County	28	0.90
Harrison (town/village) Westchester County	235	0.86
Elmsford (village) Westchester County	35	0.75
Mamaroneck (village) Westchester County	130	0.69
Hewlett Bay Park (village) Nassau County	2	0.50
Bedford Hills (cdp) Westchester County	14	0.47
White Plains (city) Westchester County	260	0.46

Top 10 Places Sorted by Percent of Total Population
Based on places with total population of 50,000 or more

Place	Population	%
White Plains (city) Westchester County	260	0.46
Greenburgh (town) Westchester County	144	0.16
Queens (borough) Queens County	2,775	0.12
Mount Vernon (city) Westchester County	68	0.10
North Hempstead (town) Nassau County	140	0.06
New Rochelle (city) Westchester County	49	0.06
Brentwood (cdp) Suffolk County	36	0.06
Southampton (town) Suffolk County	26	0.05
New York (city)	3,534	0.04
Huntington (town) Suffolk County	91	0.04

South American: Peruvian

Top 10 Places Sorted by Population
Based on all places, regardless of total population

Place	Population	%
New York (city)	36,018	0.44
Queens (borough) Queens County	22,886	1.03
Hempstead (town) Nassau County	4,510	0.59
Brooklyn (borough) Kings County	4,222	0.17
Manhattan (borough) New York County	3,852	0.24
Islip (town) Suffolk County	3,599	1.07
Bronx (borough) Bronx County	3,596	0.26
White Plains (city) Westchester County	2,260	3.98
Rye (town) Westchester County	1,734	3.78
Brentwood (cdp) Suffolk County	1,610	2.65

Top 10 Places Sorted by Percent of Total Population
Based on all places, regardless of total population

Place	Population	%
Port Chester (village) Westchester County	1,485	5.13
Island Park (village) Nassau County	234	5.03
Elmsford (village) Westchester County	189	4.05
White Plains (city) Westchester County	2,260	3.98
Rye (town) Westchester County	1,734	3.78
Glen Cove (city) Nassau County	883	3.27
Baywood (cdp) Suffolk County	222	3.02
Barnum Island (cdp) Nassau County	73	3.02
Fairview (cdp) Westchester County	89	2.87
Bellerose Terrace (cdp) Nassau County	60	2.73

Top 10 Places Sorted by Percent of Total Population
Based on places with total population of 50,000 or more

Place	Population	%
White Plains (city) Westchester County	2,260	3.98
Brentwood (cdp) Suffolk County	1,610	2.65
New Rochelle (city) Westchester County	1,297	1.68
Greenburgh (town) Westchester County	962	1.09
Islip (town) Suffolk County	3,599	1.07
Queens (borough) Queens County	22,886	1.03
Babylon (town) Suffolk County	1,313	0.61
Hempstead (town) Nassau County	4,510	0.59
Levittown (cdp) Nassau County	285	0.55
Hempstead (village) Nassau County	279	0.52

South American: Uruguayan

Top 10 Places Sorted by Population
Based on all places, regardless of total population

Place	Population	%
New York (city)	3,004	0.04
Queens (borough) Queens County	1,743	0.08
Manhattan (borough) New York County	549	0.03
Brooklyn (borough) Kings County	488	0.02
Hempstead (town) Nassau County	359	0.05
Ossining (town) Westchester County	273	0.72
Ossining (village) Westchester County	230	0.92
Islip (town) Suffolk County	216	0.06
Rye (town) Westchester County	211	0.46
Port Chester (village) Westchester County	159	0.55

Top 10 Places Sorted by Percent of Total Population
Based on all places, regardless of total population

Place	Population	%
Ossining (village) Westchester County	230	0.92
Ossining (town) Westchester County	273	0.72
Cove Neck (village) Nassau County	2	0.70

Place	Population	%
Buchanan (village) Westchester County	13	0.58
Port Chester (village) Westchester County	159	0.55
Hillside Lake (cdp) Dutchess County	6	0.55
Crugers (cdp) Westchester County	8	0.52
Rye (town) Westchester County	211	0.46
Islandia (village) Suffolk County	15	0.45
Chappaqua (cdp) Westchester County	6	0.42

Top 10 Places Sorted by Percent of Total Population
Based on places with total population of 50,000 or more

Place	Population	%
Brentwood (cdp) Suffolk County	80	0.13
New Rochelle (city) Westchester County	88	0.11
White Plains (city) Westchester County	63	0.11
Levittown (cdp) Nassau County	47	0.09
Queens (borough) Queens County	1,743	0.08
Greenburgh (town) Westchester County	65	0.07
Islip (town) Suffolk County	216	0.06
Hempstead (town) Nassau County	359	0.05
Oyster Bay (town) Nassau County	134	0.05
New York (city)	3,004	0.04

South American: Venezuelan

Top 10 Places Sorted by Population
Based on all places, regardless of total population

Place	Population	%
New York (city)	9,619	0.12
Queens (borough) Queens County	3,580	0.16
Manhattan (borough) New York County	2,573	0.16
Brooklyn (borough) Kings County	1,916	0.08
Bronx (borough) Bronx County	1,296	0.09
Hempstead (town) Nassau County	517	0.07
Islip (town) Suffolk County	322	0.10
Brookhaven (town) Suffolk County	302	0.06
Staten Island (borough) Richmond County	254	0.05
Yonkers (city) Westchester County	207	0.11

Top 10 Places Sorted by Percent of Total Population
Based on all places, regardless of total population

Place	Population	%
Westport (cdp) Essex County	6	1.16
Ward (town) Allegany County	4	1.09
Shinnecock Reservation Suffolk County	4	0.60
Scotts Corners (cdp) Westchester County	4	0.56
Shoreham (village) Suffolk County	3	0.56
Merritt Park (cdp) Dutchess County	6	0.48
Westport (town) Essex County	6	0.46
Mountain Lodge Park (cdp) Orange County	7	0.44
Jewett (town) Greene County	4	0.42
Washington Mills (cdp) Oneida County	4	0.34

Top 10 Places Sorted by Percent of Total Population
Based on places with total population of 50,000 or more

Place	Population	%
Brentwood (cdp) Suffolk County	113	0.19
New Rochelle (city) Westchester County	131	0.17
Queens (borough) Queens County	3,580	0.16
Manhattan (borough) New York County	2,573	0.16
White Plains (city) Westchester County	77	0.14
New York (city)	9,619	0.12
Yonkers (city) Westchester County	207	0.11
Greenburgh (town) Westchester County	94	0.11
Islip (town) Suffolk County	322	0.10
Bronx (borough) Bronx County	1,296	0.09

South American: Other South American

Top 10 Places Sorted by Population
Based on all places, regardless of total population

Place	Population	%
New York (city)	2,678	0.03
Queens (borough) Queens County	1,439	0.06
Brooklyn (borough) Kings County	506	0.02
Bronx (borough) Bronx County	369	0.03
Manhattan (borough) New York County	278	0.02
Hempstead (town) Nassau County	243	0.03
Brookhaven (town) Suffolk County	98	0.02
Staten Island (borough) Richmond County	86	0.02
Yonkers (city) Westchester County	63	0.03
Islip (town) Suffolk County	54	0.02

Top 10 Places Sorted by Percent of Total Population
Based on all places, regardless of total population

Place	Population	%
Woodsburgh (village) Nassau County	8	1.03
Quiogue (cdp) Suffolk County	4	0.49
East Hampton North (cdp) Suffolk County	19	0.46
Plattekill (cdp) Ulster County	5	0.40
Scio (town) Allegany County	5	0.27
Northwest Harbor (cdp) Suffolk County	8	0.24
Dolgeville (village) Herkimer County	5	0.23
Lakeview (cdp) Nassau County	12	0.21
Harriman (village) Orange County	5	0.21
Cold Spring (village) Putnam County	4	0.20

Top 10 Places Sorted by Percent of Total Population
Based on places with total population of 50,000 or more

Place	Population	%
Schenectady (city) Schenectady County	43	0.07
Queens (borough) Queens County	1,439	0.06
Mount Vernon (city) Westchester County	33	0.05

Place	Population	%
Levittown (cdp) Nassau County	27	0.05
Greenburgh (town) Westchester County	32	0.04
Hempstead (village) Nassau County	23	0.04
White Plains (city) Westchester County	23	0.04
New York (city)	2,678	0.03
Bronx (borough) Bronx County	369	0.03
Hempstead (town) Nassau County	243	0.03

Other Hispanic or Latino

Top 10 Places Sorted by Population
Based on all places, regardless of total population

Place	Population	%
New York (city)	180,805	2.21
Queens (borough) Queens County	52,422	2.35
Bronx (borough) Bronx County	51,571	3.72
Brooklyn (borough) Kings County	35,705	1.43
Manhattan (borough) New York County	35,548	2.24
Hempstead (town) Nassau County	13,273	1.75
Islip (town) Suffolk County	8,524	2.54
Brookhaven (town) Suffolk County	6,193	1.27
Staten Island (borough) Richmond County	5,559	1.19
Yonkers (city) Westchester County	4,443	2.27

Top 10 Places Sorted by Percent of Total Population
Based on all places, regardless of total population

Place	Population	%
Riverside (cdp) Suffolk County	348	11.95
Watchtower (cdp) Ulster County	171	7.18
Brentwood (cdp) Suffolk County	3,476	5.73
North Bay Shore (cdp) Suffolk County	967	5.10
Northwest Harbor (cdp) Suffolk County	168	5.06
New Cassel (cdp) Nassau County	699	4.97
Hempstead (village) Nassau County	2,609	4.84
Central Islip (cdp) Suffolk County	1,667	4.84
Inwood (cdp) Nassau County	467	4.77
Brewster (village) Putnam County	113	4.73

Top 10 Places Sorted by Percent of Total Population
Based on places with total population of 50,000 or more

Place	Population	%
Brentwood (cdp) Suffolk County	3,476	5.73
Hempstead (village) Nassau County	2,609	4.84
Bronx (borough) Bronx County	51,571	3.72
Southampton (town) Suffolk County	1,468	2.58
Islip (town) Suffolk County	8,524	2.54
Queens (borough) Queens County	52,422	2.35
Yonkers (city) Westchester County	4,443	2.27
Manhattan (borough) New York County	35,548	2.24
New York (city)	180,805	2.21
White Plains (city) Westchester County	1,209	2.13

Racial Group Rankings

African-American/Black

Top 10 Places Sorted by Population
Based on all places, regardless of total population

Place	Population	%
New York (city)	2,228,145	27.26
Brooklyn (borough) Kings County	896,165	35.78
Bronx (borough) Bronx County	541,622	39.10
Queens (borough) Queens County	462,351	20.73
Manhattan (borough) New York County	272,993	17.21
Hempstead (town) Nassau County	133,280	17.54
Buffalo (city) Erie County	106,107	40.61
Rochester (city) Monroe County	94,587	44.92
Staten Island (borough) Richmond County	55,014	11.74
Syracuse (city) Onondaga County	48,029	33.08

Top 10 Places Sorted by Percent of Total Population
Based on all places, regardless of total population

Place	Population	%
Lakeview (cdp) Nassau County	4,757	84.72
Wyandanch (cdp) Suffolk County	7,865	67.53
Mount Vernon (city) Westchester County	44,244	65.75
Roosevelt (cdp) Nassau County	10,657	65.55
North Amityville (cdp) Suffolk County	10,971	61.42
Fairview (cdp) Westchester County	1,895	61.15
South Floral Park (village) Nassau County	1,075	60.94
Wheatley Heights (cdp) Suffolk County	2,960	57.70
Hillcrest (cdp) Rockland County	4,328	57.26
Gordon Heights (cdp) Suffolk County	2,294	56.75

Top 10 Places Sorted by Percent of Total Population
Based on places with total population of 50,000 or more

Place	Population	%
Mount Vernon (city) Westchester County	44,244	65.75
Hempstead (village) Nassau County	27,076	50.24
Rochester (city) Monroe County	94,587	44.92
Buffalo (city) Erie County	106,107	40.61
Bronx (borough) Bronx County	541,622	39.10
Brooklyn (borough) Kings County	896,165	35.78
Albany (city) Albany County	32,569	33.28
Syracuse (city) Onondaga County	48,029	33.08
New York (city)	2,228,145	27.26
Schenectady (city) Schenectady County	16,103	24.35

African-American/Black: Not Hispanic

Top 10 Places Sorted by Population
Based on all places, regardless of total population

Place	Population	%
New York (city)	1,931,889	23.63
Brooklyn (borough) Kings County	820,437	32.76
Bronx (borough) Bronx County	427,134	30.84
Queens (borough) Queens County	419,695	18.81
Manhattan (borough) New York County	217,102	13.69
Hempstead (town) Nassau County	124,525	16.39
Buffalo (city) Erie County	101,817	38.96
Rochester (city) Monroe County	88,052	41.82
Staten Island (borough) Richmond County	47,521	10.14
Syracuse (city) Onondaga County	45,084	31.06

Top 10 Places Sorted by Percent of Total Population
Based on all places, regardless of total population

Place	Population	%
Lakeview (cdp) Nassau County	4,534	80.75
Wyandanch (cdp) Suffolk County	7,550	64.82
Mount Vernon (city) Westchester County	42,361	62.95
Roosevelt (cdp) Nassau County	10,138	62.36
North Amityville (cdp) Suffolk County	10,434	58.41
Fairview (cdp) Westchester County	1,800	58.08
South Floral Park (village) Nassau County	1,024	58.05
Wheatley Heights (cdp) Suffolk County	2,821	54.99
Hillcrest (cdp) Rockland County	4,140	54.78
Gordon Heights (cdp) Suffolk County	2,073	51.29

Top 10 Places Sorted by Percent of Total Population
Based on places with total population of 50,000 or more

Place	Population	%
Mount Vernon (city) Westchester County	42,361	62.95
Hempstead (village) Nassau County	25,388	47.11
Rochester (city) Monroe County	88,052	41.82
Buffalo (city) Erie County	101,817	38.96
Brooklyn (borough) Kings County	820,437	32.76
Syracuse (city) Onondaga County	45,084	31.06
Albany (city) Albany County	30,376	31.04
Bronx (borough) Bronx County	427,134	30.84
Niagara Falls (city) Niagara County	11,905	23.72
New York (city)	1,931,889	23.63

African-American/Black: Hispanic

Top 10 Places Sorted by Population
Based on all places, regardless of total population

Place	Population	%
New York (city)	296,256	3.62
Bronx (borough) Bronx County	114,488	8.27
Brooklyn (borough) Kings County	75,728	3.02
Manhattan (borough) New York County	55,891	3.52
Queens (borough) Queens County	42,656	1.91
Hempstead (town) Nassau County	8,755	1.15
Staten Island (borough) Richmond County	7,493	1.60
Yonkers (city) Westchester County	7,325	3.74
Rochester (city) Monroe County	6,535	3.10
Islip (town) Suffolk County	5,700	1.70

Top 10 Places Sorted by Percent of Total Population
Based on all places, regardless of total population

Place	Population	%
Bronx (borough) Bronx County	114,488	8.27
Gordon Heights (cdp) Suffolk County	221	5.47
Haverstraw (village) Rockland County	574	4.82
Middletown (city) Orange County	1,209	4.30
Monticello (village) Sullivan County	283	4.21
Washington Heights (cdp) Orange County	68	4.03
North Bay Shore (cdp) Suffolk County	756	3.99
Lakeview (cdp) Nassau County	223	3.97
Parc (cdp) Clinton County	10	3.94
Yonkers (city) Westchester County	7,325	3.74

Top 10 Places Sorted by Percent of Total Population
Based on places with total population of 50,000 or more

Place	Population	%
Bronx (borough) Bronx County	114,488	8.27
Yonkers (city) Westchester County	7,325	3.74
New York (city)	296,256	3.62
Manhattan (borough) New York County	55,891	3.52
Brentwood (cdp) Suffolk County	2,138	3.52
Hempstead (village) Nassau County	1,688	3.13
Rochester (city) Monroe County	6,535	3.10
Brooklyn (borough) Kings County	75,728	3.02
Mount Vernon (city) Westchester County	1,883	2.80
Schenectady (city) Schenectady County	1,547	2.34

American Indian/Alaska Native

Top 10 Places Sorted by Population
Based on all places, regardless of total population

Place	Population	%
New York (city)	111,749	1.37
Bronx (borough) Bronx County	32,011	2.31
Queens (borough) Queens County	30,033	1.35
Brooklyn (borough) Kings County	26,571	1.06
Manhattan (borough) New York County	19,415	1.22
Hempstead (town) Nassau County	5,363	0.71
Buffalo (city) Erie County	4,019	1.54
Brookhaven (town) Suffolk County	3,782	0.78
Staten Island (borough) Richmond County	3,719	0.79
Syracuse (city) Onondaga County	3,537	2.44

Top 10 Places Sorted by Percent of Total Population
Based on all places, regardless of total population

Place	Population	%
Tonawanda Reservation Erie County	34	100.00
Oil Springs Reservation Allegany County	1	100.00
Onondaga Nation Reservation Onondaga County	457	97.65
St. Regis Mohawk Reservation Franklin County	3,131	97.00
Tonawanda Reservation Genesee County	463	95.86
Cattaraugus Reservation Cattaraugus County	294	93.63
Cattaraugus Reservation Erie County	1,672	91.22
Shinnecock Reservation Suffolk County	584	88.22
Cattaraugus Reservation Chautauqua County	29	76.32
Allegany Reservation Cattaraugus County	670	65.69

Top 10 Places Sorted by Percent of Total Population
Based on places with total population of 50,000 or more

Place	Population	%
Niagara Falls (city) Niagara County	1,624	3.24
Syracuse (city) Onondaga County	3,537	2.44
Bronx (borough) Bronx County	32,011	2.31
Schenectady (city) Schenectady County	1,372	2.07
Brentwood (cdp) Suffolk County	1,135	1.87
Hempstead (village) Nassau County	997	1.85
White Plains (city) Westchester County	890	1.57
Buffalo (city) Erie County	4,019	1.54
Rochester (city) Monroe County	3,202	1.52
Yonkers (city) Westchester County	2,801	1.43

American Indian/Alaska Native: Not Hispanic

Top 10 Places Sorted by Population
Based on all places, regardless of total population

Place	Population	%
New York (city)	44,541	0.54
Queens (borough) Queens County	15,412	0.69
Brooklyn (borough) Kings County	12,062	0.48
Bronx (borough) Bronx County	7,638	0.55
Manhattan (borough) New York County	7,395	0.47
Buffalo (city) Erie County	3,229	1.24
St. Regis Mohawk Reservation Franklin County	3,116	96.53
Syracuse (city) Onondaga County	3,067	2.11
Hempstead (town) Nassau County	2,835	0.37
Brookhaven (town) Suffolk County	2,586	0.53

Top 10 Places Sorted by Percent of Total Population
Based on all places, regardless of total population

Place	Population	%
Tonawanda Reservation Erie County	34	100.00
Oil Springs Reservation Allegany County	1	100.00
St. Regis Mohawk Reservation Franklin County	3,116	96.53
Onondaga Nation Reservation Onondaga County	447	95.51
Tonawanda Reservation Genesee County	447	92.55
Cattaraugus Reservation Cattaraugus County	283	90.13
Cattaraugus Reservation Erie County	1,613	88.00
Shinnecock Reservation Suffolk County	554	83.69
Allegany Reservation Cattaraugus County	645	63.24
Cattaraugus Reservation Chautauqua County	24	63.16

Top 10 Places Sorted by Percent of Total Population
Based on places with total population of 50,000 or more

Place	Population	%
Niagara Falls (city) Niagara County	1,524	3.04
Syracuse (city) Onondaga County	3,067	2.11
Schenectady (city) Schenectady County	1,126	1.70
Buffalo (city) Erie County	3,229	1.24
Rochester (city) Monroe County	2,330	1.11
Clay (town) Onondaga County	557	0.96
Albany (city) Albany County	856	0.87
Mount Vernon (city) Westchester County	585	0.87
Troy (city) Rensselaer County	407	0.81
Hempstead (village) Nassau County	404	0.75

American Indian/Alaska Native: Hispanic

Top 10 Places Sorted by Population
Based on all places, regardless of total population

Place	Population	%
New York (city)	67,208	0.82
Bronx (borough) Bronx County	24,373	1.76
Queens (borough) Queens County	14,621	0.66
Brooklyn (borough) Kings County	14,509	0.58
Manhattan (borough) New York County	12,020	0.76
Hempstead (town) Nassau County	2,528	0.33
Islip (town) Suffolk County	1,831	0.55
Yonkers (city) Westchester County	1,806	0.92
Staten Island (borough) Richmond County	1,685	0.36
Brookhaven (town) Suffolk County	1,196	0.25

Top 10 Places Sorted by Percent of Total Population
Based on all places, regardless of total population

Place	Population	%
Cattaraugus Reservation Chautauqua County	5	13.16
Baxter Estates (village) Nassau County	51	5.11
Shinnecock Reservation Suffolk County	30	4.53
Poospatuck Reservation Suffolk County	14	4.32
Cattaraugus Reservation Cattaraugus County	11	3.50
Tonawanda Reservation Genesee County	16	3.31
Cattaraugus Reservation Erie County	59	3.22
Allegany Reservation Cattaraugus County	25	2.45
Onondaga Nation Reservation Onondaga County	10	2.14
Shinnecock Hills (cdp) Suffolk County	46	2.10

Top 10 Places Sorted by Percent of Total Population
Based on places with total population of 50,000 or more

Place	Population	%
Bronx (borough) Bronx County	24,373	1.76
Brentwood (cdp) Suffolk County	809	1.33
White Plains (city) Westchester County	697	1.23
Hempstead (village) Nassau County	593	1.10
Yonkers (city) Westchester County	1,806	0.92
New York (city)	67,208	0.82
Manhattan (borough) New York County	12,020	0.76
Queens (borough) Queens County	14,621	0.66
New Rochelle (city) Westchester County	462	0.60
Brooklyn (borough) Kings County	14,509	0.58

Alaska Native: Alaska Athabascan

Top 10 Places Sorted by Population
Based on all places, regardless of total population

Place	Population	%
New York (city)	37	<0.01
Manhattan (borough) New York County	18	<0.01
Salamanca (city) Cattaraugus County	9	0.15
Watertown (city) Jefferson County	8	0.03
Bronx (borough) Bronx County	8	<0.01
Brighton (cdp/town) Monroe County	5	0.01
Brooklyn (borough) Kings County	5	<0.01
Brookhaven (town) Suffolk County	4	<0.01
Schroon (town) Essex County	3	0.18
Gouverneur (town) St. Lawrence County	3	0.04

Top 10 Places Sorted by Percent of Total Population
Based on all places, regardless of total population

Place	Population	%
Burdett (village) Schuyler County	1	0.29
Schroon (town) Essex County	3	0.18
Salamanca (city) Cattaraugus County	9	0.15
Little Valley (town) Cattaraugus County	2	0.11
Orwell (town) Oswego County	1	0.09
Randolph (town) Cattaraugus County	2	0.08
Napoli (town) Cattaraugus County	1	0.08
Randolph (village) Cattaraugus County	1	0.08
Orleans (town) Jefferson County	2	0.07
Lattingtown (village) Nassau County	1	0.06

Top 10 Places Sorted by Percent of Total Population
Based on places with total population of 50,000 or more

Place	Population	%
New York (city)	37	<0.01
Manhattan (borough) New York County	18	<0.01
Bronx (borough) Bronx County	8	<0.01
Brooklyn (borough) Kings County	5	<0.01

Brookhaven (town) Suffolk County	4	<0.01
Queens (borough) Queens County	3	<0.01
Staten Island (borough) Richmond County	3	<0.01
Syracuse (city) Onondaga County	3	<0.01
Albany (city) Albany County	1	<0.01
Amherst (town) Erie County	1	<0.01

Alaska Native: Aleut

Top 10 Places Sorted by Population
Based on all places, regardless of total population

Place	Population	%
New York (city)	26	<0.01
Brooklyn (borough) Kings County	8	<0.01
Manhattan (borough) New York County	7	<0.01
Queens (borough) Queens County	6	<0.01
Wilton (town) Saratoga County	5	0.03
Denmark (town) Lewis County	4	0.14
Mamaroneck (town) Westchester County	4	0.01
Carlton (town) Orleans County	3	0.10
Champion (town) Jefferson County	3	0.07
Bronx (borough) Bronx County	3	<0.01

Top 10 Places Sorted by Percent of Total Population
Based on all places, regardless of total population

Place	Population	%
Denmark (town) Lewis County	4	0.14
Sempronius (town) Cayuga County	1	0.11
Carlton (town) Orleans County	3	0.10
Richmondville (town) Schoharie County	2	0.08
Champion (town) Jefferson County	3	0.07
Little Valley (town) Cattaraugus County	1	0.06
Morrisonville (cdp) Clinton County	1	0.06
Beaver Dam Lake (cdp) Orange County	1	0.04
Rhinebeck (village) Dutchess County	1	0.04
Salem (town) Washington County	1	0.04

Top 10 Places Sorted by Percent of Total Population
Based on places with total population of 50,000 or more

Place	Population	%
New York (city)	26	<0.01
Brooklyn (borough) Kings County	8	<0.01
Manhattan (borough) New York County	7	<0.01
Queens (borough) Queens County	6	<0.01
Bronx (borough) Bronx County	3	<0.01
Brookhaven (town) Suffolk County	3	<0.01
Babylon (town) Suffolk County	2	<0.01
Hempstead (town) Nassau County	2	<0.01
Rochester (city) Monroe County	2	<0.01
Staten Island (borough) Richmond County	2	<0.01

American Indian: Apache

Top 10 Places Sorted by Population
Based on all places, regardless of total population

Place	Population	%
New York (city)	401	<0.01
Brooklyn (borough) Kings County	122	<0.01
Bronx (borough) Bronx County	99	0.01
Manhattan (borough) New York County	92	0.01
Queens (borough) Queens County	53	<0.01
Staten Island (borough) Richmond County	35	0.01
Syracuse (city) Onondaga County	25	0.02
Hempstead (town) Nassau County	21	<0.01
Rochester (city) Monroe County	20	<0.01
Brookhaven (town) Suffolk County	18	<0.01

Top 10 Places Sorted by Percent of Total Population
Based on all places, regardless of total population

Place	Population	%
Breesport (cdp) Chemung County	5	0.80
Smithville Flats (cdp) Chenango County	2	0.57
Benson (town) Hamilton County	1	0.52
Waterville (village) Oneida County	6	0.38
Lyndonville (village) Orleans County	3	0.36
Ellenburg (town) Clinton County	6	0.34
Stone Ridge (cdp) Ulster County	4	0.34
Windsor (village) Broome County	3	0.33
Carlton (town) Orleans County	9	0.30
German (town) Chenango County	1	0.27

Top 10 Places Sorted by Percent of Total Population
Based on places with total population of 50,000 or more

Place	Population	%
Syracuse (city) Onondaga County	25	0.02
Union (town) Broome County	11	0.02
Troy (city) Rensselaer County	10	0.02
Bronx (borough) Bronx County	99	0.01
Manhattan (borough) New York County	92	0.01
Staten Island (borough) Richmond County	35	0.01
Rochester (city) Monroe County	20	0.01
Huntington (town) Suffolk County	14	0.01
Babylon (town) Suffolk County	11	0.01
Yonkers (city) Westchester County	10	0.01

American Indian: Arapaho

Top 10 Places Sorted by Population
Based on all places, regardless of total population

Place	Population	%
New York (city)	21	<0.01
Brooklyn (borough) Kings County	10	<0.01
Manhattan (borough) New York County	5	<0.01
Greece (town) Monroe County	4	<0.01
Malta (town) Saratoga County	3	0.02
Bronx (borough) Bronx County	3	<0.01
New Baltimore (town) Greene County	2	0.06
Waterloo (town) Seneca County	2	0.03
Philipstown (town) Putnam County	2	0.02
Kingston (city) Ulster County	2	0.01

Top 10 Places Sorted by Percent of Total Population
Based on all places, regardless of total population

Place	Population	%
Rifton (cdp) Ulster County	1	0.22
New Baltimore (town) Greene County	2	0.06
Victory (town) Cayuga County	1	0.06
Boonville (village) Oneida County	1	0.05
Carlisle (town) Schoharie County	1	0.05
Berne (town) Albany County	1	0.04
Machias (town) Cattaraugus County	1	0.04
Waterloo (town) Seneca County	2	0.03
Montauk (cdp) Suffolk County	1	0.03
Saugerties (village) Ulster County	1	0.03

Top 10 Places Sorted by Percent of Total Population
Based on places with total population of 50,000 or more

Place	Population	%
New York (city)	21	<0.01
Brooklyn (borough) Kings County	10	<0.01
Manhattan (borough) New York County	5	<0.01
Greece (town) Monroe County	4	<0.01
Bronx (borough) Bronx County	3	<0.01
Queens (borough) Queens County	2	<0.01
Syracuse (city) Onondaga County	2	<0.01
Brookhaven (town) Suffolk County	1	<0.01
Buffalo (city) Erie County	1	<0.01
Cheektowaga (town) Erie County	1	<0.01

American Indian: Blackfeet

Top 10 Places Sorted by Population
Based on all places, regardless of total population

Place	Population	%
New York (city)	1,627	0.02
Brooklyn (borough) Kings County	531	0.02
Manhattan (borough) New York County	356	0.02
Queens (borough) Queens County	342	0.02
Bronx (borough) Bronx County	310	0.02
Brookhaven (town) Suffolk County	164	0.03
Rochester (city) Monroe County	134	0.06
Hempstead (town) Nassau County	117	0.02
Syracuse (city) Onondaga County	111	0.08
Buffalo (city) Erie County	104	0.04

Top 10 Places Sorted by Percent of Total Population
Based on all places, regardless of total population

Place	Population	%
Ellisburg (village) Jefferson County	6	2.46
Cohocton (village) Steuben County	7	0.84
Nassau (village) Rensselaer County	9	0.79

Place	Population	%
Cameron (town) Steuben County	7	0.74
Cayuta (town) Schuyler County	4	0.72
Dresden (village) Yates County	2	0.65
Theresa (village) Jefferson County	5	0.58
Hemlock (cdp) Livingston County	3	0.54
Lyons Falls (village) Lewis County	3	0.53
East Avon (cdp) Livingston County	3	0.49

Top 10 Places Sorted by Percent of Total Population
Based on places with total population of 50,000 or more

Place	Population	%
Schenectady (city) Schenectady County	58	0.09
Syracuse (city) Onondaga County	111	0.08
Rochester (city) Monroe County	134	0.06
Albany (city) Albany County	57	0.06
Mount Vernon (city) Westchester County	38	0.06
Hempstead (village) Nassau County	27	0.05
Buffalo (city) Erie County	104	0.04
Troy (city) Rensselaer County	22	0.04
Brookhaven (town) Suffolk County	164	0.03
Yonkers (city) Westchester County	58	0.03

American Indian: Canadian/French American Indian

Top 10 Places Sorted by Population
Based on all places, regardless of total population

Place	Population	%
New York (city)	197	<0.01
Brooklyn (borough) Kings County	62	<0.01
Manhattan (borough) New York County	62	<0.01
Buffalo (city) Erie County	57	0.02
Syracuse (city) Onondaga County	51	0.04
Queens (borough) Queens County	38	<0.01
Bronx (borough) Bronx County	25	<0.01
Niagara Falls (city) Niagara County	20	0.04
Clay (town) Onondaga County	16	0.03
Grand Island (town) Erie County	15	0.07

Top 10 Places Sorted by Percent of Total Population
Based on all places, regardless of total population

Place	Population	%
Tonawanda Reservation Genesee County	5	1.04
Clare (town) St. Lawrence County	1	0.95
Farnham (village) Erie County	3	0.79
Orwell (town) Oswego County	6	0.51
Rifton (cdp) Ulster County	2	0.44
Verona (cdp) Oneida County	3	0.35
Sinclairville (village) Chautauqua County	2	0.34
East Avon (cdp) Livingston County	2	0.33
Bellmont (town) Franklin County	4	0.28
Decatur (town) Otsego County	1	0.28

Top 10 Places Sorted by Percent of Total Population
Based on places with total population of 50,000 or more

Place	Population	%
Syracuse (city) Onondaga County	51	0.04
Niagara Falls (city) Niagara County	20	0.04
Clay (town) Onondaga County	16	0.03
Buffalo (city) Erie County	57	0.02
Hamburg (town) Erie County	12	0.02
Greece (town) Monroe County	14	0.01
Amherst (town) Erie County	11	0.01
Colonie (town) Albany County	10	0.01
Schenectady (city) Schenectady County	9	0.01
Tonawanda (town) Erie County	8	0.01

American Indian: Central American Indian

Top 10 Places Sorted by Population
Based on all places, regardless of total population

Place	Population	%
New York (city)	7,662	0.09
Bronx (borough) Bronx County	4,520	0.33
Brooklyn (borough) Kings County	1,263	0.05
Manhattan (borough) New York County	1,090	0.07
Queens (borough) Queens County	733	0.03
Yonkers (city) Westchester County	103	0.05
Hempstead (town) Nassau County	87	0.01
Islip (town) Suffolk County	73	0.02
Staten Island (borough) Richmond County	56	0.01

Place	Population	%
Brookhaven (town) Suffolk County	53	0.01

Top 10 Places Sorted by Percent of Total Population
Based on all places, regardless of total population

Place	Population	%
Shelter Island (cdp) Suffolk County	14	1.05
Shelter Island (town) Suffolk County	16	0.67
Nelliston (village) Montgomery County	3	0.50
Mount Kisco (town/village) Westchester County	43	0.40
Washington Heights (cdp) Orange County	6	0.36
Bronx (borough) Bronx County	4,520	0.33
Copenhagen (village) Lewis County	2	0.25
Columbus (town) Chenango County	2	0.21
Shelter Island Heights (cdp) Suffolk County	2	0.19
Bolton Landing (cdp) Warren County	1	0.19

Top 10 Places Sorted by Percent of Total Population
Based on places with total population of 50,000 or more

Place	Population	%
Bronx (borough) Bronx County	4,520	0.33
New York (city)	7,662	0.09
Manhattan (borough) New York County	1,090	0.07
Brentwood (cdp) Suffolk County	36	0.06
Brooklyn (borough) Kings County	1,263	0.05
Yonkers (city) Westchester County	103	0.05
Queens (borough) Queens County	733	0.03
New Rochelle (city) Westchester County	20	0.03
Mount Vernon (city) Westchester County	19	0.03
Hempstead (village) Nassau County	15	0.03

American Indian: Cherokee

Top 10 Places Sorted by Population
Based on all places, regardless of total population

Place	Population	%
New York (city)	6,952	0.09
Brooklyn (borough) Kings County	1,903	0.08
Manhattan (borough) New York County	1,845	0.12
Queens (borough) Queens County	1,425	0.06
Bronx (borough) Bronx County	1,312	0.09
Hempstead (town) Nassau County	572	0.08
Brookhaven (town) Suffolk County	546	0.11
Staten Island (borough) Richmond County	467	0.10
Rochester (city) Monroe County	411	0.20
Islip (town) Suffolk County	316	0.09

Top 10 Places Sorted by Percent of Total Population
Based on all places, regardless of total population

Place	Population	%
Poospatuck Reservation Suffolk County	11	3.40
Shinnecock Reservation Suffolk County	16	2.42
Winthrop (cdp) St. Lawrence County	11	2.16
Bloomingburg (village) Sullivan County	9	2.14
North Rose (cdp) Wayne County	11	1.73
Phoenicia (cdp) Ulster County	5	1.62
Wainscott (cdp) Suffolk County	9	1.38
Hopewell Junction (cdp) Dutchess County	5	1.33
Morehouse (town) Hamilton County	1	1.16
Natural Bridge (cdp) Jefferson County	4	1.10

Top 10 Places Sorted by Percent of Total Population
Based on places with total population of 50,000 or more

Place	Population	%
Schenectady (city) Schenectady County	145	0.22
Albany (city) Albany County	205	0.21
Rochester (city) Monroe County	411	0.20
Hempstead (village) Nassau County	109	0.20
Syracuse (city) Onondaga County	258	0.18
Mount Vernon (city) Westchester County	116	0.17
Troy (city) Rensselaer County	80	0.16
Brentwood (cdp) Suffolk County	76	0.13
Manhattan (borough) New York County	1,845	0.12
Babylon (town) Suffolk County	250	0.12

American Indian: Cheyenne

Top 10 Places Sorted by Population
Based on all places, regardless of total population

Place	Population	%
New York (city)	46	<0.01

Place	Population	%
Queens (borough) Queens County	20	<0.01
Brooklyn (borough) Kings County	10	<0.01
Manhattan (borough) New York County	9	<0.01
Kent (town) Putnam County	6	0.04
Brookhaven (town) Suffolk County	6	<0.01
Greenburgh (town) Westchester County	5	<0.01
Bronx (borough) Bronx County	5	<0.01
Whitestown (town) Oneida County	4	0.02
Utica (city) Oneida County	4	0.01

Top 10 Places Sorted by Percent of Total Population
Based on all places, regardless of total population

Place	Population	%
Bloomville (cdp) Delaware County	1	0.47
Celoron (village) Chautauqua County	2	0.18
Hannibal (village) Oswego County	1	0.18
Conewango (town) Cattaraugus County	3	0.16
Crompond (cdp) Westchester County	3	0.13
Willsboro (cdp) Essex County	1	0.13
Yorkville (village) Oneida County	3	0.11
Cameron (town) Steuben County	1	0.11
Nelson (town) Madison County	2	0.10
Allegany Reservation Cattaraugus County	1	0.10

Top 10 Places Sorted by Percent of Total Population
Based on places with total population of 50,000 or more

Place	Population	%
Greenburgh (town) Westchester County	5	0.01
Utica (city) Oneida County	4	0.01
New York (city)	46	<0.01
Queens (borough) Queens County	20	<0.01
Brooklyn (borough) Kings County	10	<0.01
Manhattan (borough) New York County	9	<0.01
Brookhaven (town) Suffolk County	6	<0.01
Bronx (borough) Bronx County	5	<0.01
Huntington (town) Suffolk County	4	<0.01
North Hempstead (town) Nassau County	3	<0.01

American Indian: Chickasaw

Top 10 Places Sorted by Population
Based on all places, regardless of total population

Place	Population	%
New York (city)	113	<0.01
Manhattan (borough) New York County	43	<0.01
Brooklyn (borough) Kings County	30	<0.01
Queens (borough) Queens County	21	<0.01
Bronx (borough) Bronx County	16	<0.01
Mount Kisco (town/village) Westchester County	5	0.05
Hempstead (town) Nassau County	5	<0.01
Chatham (village) Columbia County	4	0.23
Chatham (town) Columbia County	4	0.10
Rockville Centre (village) Nassau County	4	0.02

Top 10 Places Sorted by Percent of Total Population
Based on all places, regardless of total population

Place	Population	%
Chatham (village) Columbia County	4	0.23
Port Gibson (cdp) Ontario County	1	0.22
Chatham (town) Columbia County	4	0.10
Gasport (cdp) Niagara County	1	0.08
Philadelphia (village) Jefferson County	1	0.08
West Sparta (town) Livingston County	1	0.08
Pittsfield (town) Otsego County	1	0.07
Austerlitz (town) Columbia County	1	0.06
Cumberland Head (cdp) Clinton County	1	0.06
Mount Kisco (town/village) Westchester County	5	0.05

Top 10 Places Sorted by Percent of Total Population
Based on places with total population of 50,000 or more

Place	Population	%
Mount Vernon (city) Westchester County	4	0.01
New York (city)	113	<0.01
Manhattan (borough) New York County	43	<0.01
Brooklyn (borough) Kings County	30	<0.01
Queens (borough) Queens County	21	<0.01
Bronx (borough) Bronx County	16	<0.01
Hempstead (town) Nassau County	5	<0.01
Syracuse (city) Onondaga County	4	<0.01
Brookhaven (town) Suffolk County	3	<0.01
Huntington (town) Suffolk County	3	<0.01

American Indian: Chippewa

Top 10 Places Sorted by Population
Based on all places, regardless of total population

Place	Population	%
New York (city)	252	<0.01
Manhattan (borough) New York County	99	0.01
Brooklyn (borough) Kings County	65	<0.01
Buffalo (city) Erie County	42	0.02
Bronx (borough) Bronx County	38	<0.01
Queens (borough) Queens County	37	<0.01
Niagara Falls (city) Niagara County	23	0.05
Brookhaven (town) Suffolk County	19	<0.01
Rochester (city) Monroe County	18	0.01
Syracuse (city) Onondaga County	18	0.01

Top 10 Places Sorted by Percent of Total Population
Based on all places, regardless of total population

Place	Population	%
Barneveld (village) Oneida County	3	1.06
Milford (village) Otsego County	3	0.72
Poospatuck Reservation Suffolk County	2	0.62
Amenia (cdp) Dutchess County	5	0.52
Morristown (village) St. Lawrence County	2	0.51
Dickinson (town) Franklin County	4	0.49
Piffard (cdp) Livingston County	1	0.45
French Creek (town) Chautauqua County	4	0.44
Greenville (cdp) Greene County	3	0.44
Wampsville (village) Madison County	2	0.37

Top 10 Places Sorted by Percent of Total Population
Based on places with total population of 50,000 or more

Place	Population	%
Niagara Falls (city) Niagara County	23	0.05
Buffalo (city) Erie County	42	0.02
Clay (town) Onondaga County	11	0.02
Schenectady (city) Schenectady County	11	0.02
Manhattan (borough) New York County	99	0.01
Rochester (city) Monroe County	18	0.01
Syracuse (city) Onondaga County	18	0.01
Greece (town) Monroe County	13	0.01
Utica (city) Oneida County	8	0.01
Amherst (town) Erie County	7	0.01

American Indian: Choctaw

Top 10 Places Sorted by Population
Based on all places, regardless of total population

Place	Population	%
New York (city)	405	<0.01
Manhattan (borough) New York County	179	<0.01
Brooklyn (borough) Kings County	104	<0.01
Queens (borough) Queens County	68	<0.01
Bronx (borough) Bronx County	43	<0.01
Hempstead (town) Nassau County	36	<0.01
Brookhaven (town) Suffolk County	34	0.01
Syracuse (city) Onondaga County	28	0.02
Rochester (city) Monroe County	28	0.01
Buffalo (city) Erie County	21	0.01

Top 10 Places Sorted by Percent of Total Population
Based on all places, regardless of total population

Place	Population	%
Winthrop (cdp) St. Lawrence County	5	0.98
Smallwood (cdp) Sullivan County	5	0.86
Schaghticoke (village) Rensselaer County	4	0.68
Cattaraugus Reservation Cattaraugus County	2	0.64
Theresa (village) Jefferson County	3	0.35
Old Field (village) Suffolk County	3	0.33
Rose (town) Wayne County	7	0.30
Worcester (cdp) Otsego County	3	0.27
Leeds (cdp) Greene County	1	0.27
Marcellus (village) Onondaga County	4	0.22

Top 10 Places Sorted by Percent of Total Population
Based on places with total population of 50,000 or more

Place	Population	%
Syracuse (city) Onondaga County	28	0.02
Manhattan (borough) New York County	179	0.01
Brookhaven (town) Suffolk County	34	0.01
Rochester (city) Monroe County	28	0.01

Buffalo (city) Erie County	21	0.01
Islip (town) Suffolk County	17	0.01
Huntington (town) Suffolk County	13	0.01
Yonkers (city) Westchester County	12	0.01
Albany (city) Albany County	8	0.01
Greece (town) Monroe County	8	0.01

American Indian: Colville

Top 10 Places Sorted by Population
Based on all places, regardless of total population

Place	Population	%
New York (city)	9	<0.01
Manhattan (borough) New York County	5	<0.01
Brookfield (town) Madison County	3	0.12
Bronx (borough) Bronx County	2	<0.01
Sidney (village) Delaware County	1	0.03
St. Regis Mohawk Reservation Franklin County	1	0.03
Triangle (town) Broome County	1	0.03
Hector (town) Schuyler County	1	0.02
LaFayette (town) Onondaga County	1	0.02
Sidney (town) Delaware County	1	0.02

Top 10 Places Sorted by Percent of Total Population
Based on all places, regardless of total population

Place	Population	%
Brookfield (town) Madison County	3	0.12
Sidney (village) Delaware County	1	0.03
St. Regis Mohawk Reservation Franklin County	1	0.03
Triangle (town) Broome County	1	0.03
Hector (town) Schuyler County	1	0.02
LaFayette (town) Onondaga County	1	0.02
Sidney (town) Delaware County	1	0.02
New York (city)	9	<0.01
Manhattan (borough) New York County	5	<0.01
Bronx (borough) Bronx County	2	<0.01

Top 10 Places Sorted by Percent of Total Population
Based on places with total population of 50,000 or more

Place	Population	%
New York (city)	9	<0.01
Manhattan (borough) New York County	5	<0.01
Bronx (borough) Bronx County	2	<0.01
Brooklyn (borough) Kings County	1	<0.01
Hempstead (town) Nassau County	1	<0.01
Irondequoit (cdp/town) Monroe County	1	<0.01
Queens (borough) Queens County	1	<0.01
Rochester (city) Monroe County	1	<0.01
Yonkers (city) Westchester County	1	<0.01
Albany (city) Albany County	0	0.00

American Indian: Comanche

Top 10 Places Sorted by Population
Based on all places, regardless of total population

Place	Population	%
New York (city)	76	<0.01
Bronx (borough) Bronx County	26	<0.01
Manhattan (borough) New York County	22	<0.01
Brooklyn (borough) Kings County	19	<0.01
Syracuse (city) Onondaga County	12	0.01
Hempstead (town) Nassau County	11	<0.01
Huntington (town) Suffolk County	8	<0.01
Islip (town) Suffolk County	8	<0.01
Brentwood (cdp) Suffolk County	7	0.01
Levittown (cdp) Nassau County	7	0.01

Top 10 Places Sorted by Percent of Total Population
Based on all places, regardless of total population

Place	Population	%
Westport (cdp) Essex County	3	0.58
Cato (village) Cayuga County	3	0.56
Westport (town) Essex County	3	0.23
Schroon (town) Essex County	3	0.18
Accord (cdp) Ulster County	1	0.18
Ira (town) Cayuga County	3	0.14
Elmsford (village) Westchester County	5	0.11
Amenia (cdp) Dutchess County	1	0.10
Tyre (town) Seneca County	1	0.10
North Dansville (town) Livingston County	3	0.05

Top 10 Places Sorted by Percent of Total Population
Based on places with total population of 50,000 or more

Place	Population	%
Syracuse (city) Onondaga County	12	0.01
Brentwood (cdp) Suffolk County	7	0.01
Levittown (cdp) Nassau County	7	0.01
Greenburgh (town) Westchester County	5	0.01
New York (city)	76	<0.01
Bronx (borough) Bronx County	26	<0.01
Manhattan (borough) New York County	22	<0.01
Brooklyn (borough) Kings County	19	<0.01
Hempstead (town) Nassau County	11	<0.01
Huntington (town) Suffolk County	8	<0.01

American Indian: Cree

Top 10 Places Sorted by Population
Based on all places, regardless of total population

Place	Population	%
New York (city)	81	<0.01
Queens (borough) Queens County	24	<0.01
Manhattan (borough) New York County	22	<0.01
Bronx (borough) Bronx County	16	<0.01
Brooklyn (borough) Kings County	15	<0.01
Syracuse (city) Onondaga County	6	<0.01
Elizabethtown (cdp) Essex County	5	0.66
Elizabethtown (town) Essex County	5	0.43
Pembroke (town) Genesee County	5	0.12
Brownville (town) Jefferson County	5	0.08

Top 10 Places Sorted by Percent of Total Population
Based on all places, regardless of total population

Place	Population	%
Elizabethtown (cdp) Essex County	5	0.66
Elizabethtown (town) Essex County	5	0.43
Fonda (village) Montgomery County	2	0.25
Germantown (cdp) Columbia County	2	0.24
Port Gibson (cdp) Ontario County	1	0.22
Denning (town) Ulster County	1	0.18
Margaretville (village) Delaware County	1	0.17
Pembroke (town) Genesee County	5	0.12
St. Regis Mohawk Reservation Franklin County	4	0.12
Triangle (town) Broome County	3	0.10

Top 10 Places Sorted by Percent of Total Population
Based on places with total population of 50,000 or more

Place	Population	%
Schenectady (city) Schenectady County	4	0.01
Niagara Falls (city) Niagara County	3	0.01
New York (city)	81	<0.01
Queens (borough) Queens County	24	<0.01
Manhattan (borough) New York County	22	<0.01
Bronx (borough) Bronx County	16	<0.01
Brooklyn (borough) Kings County	15	<0.01
Syracuse (city) Onondaga County	6	<0.01
Albany (city) Albany County	4	<0.01
Brookhaven (town) Suffolk County	4	<0.01

American Indian: Creek

Top 10 Places Sorted by Population
Based on all places, regardless of total population

Place	Population	%
New York (city)	291	<0.01
Brooklyn (borough) Kings County	81	<0.01
Queens (borough) Queens County	73	<0.01
Manhattan (borough) New York County	61	<0.01
Bronx (borough) Bronx County	47	<0.01
Staten Island (borough) Richmond County	29	0.01
Hempstead (town) Nassau County	29	<0.01
Huntington (town) Suffolk County	15	0.01
Babylon (town) Suffolk County	13	0.01
Brookhaven (town) Suffolk County	12	<0.01

Top 10 Places Sorted by Percent of Total Population
Based on all places, regardless of total population

Place	Population	%
Cattaraugus Reservation Cattaraugus County	6	1.91
Tonawanda Reservation Genesee County	4	0.83
Pamelia Center (cdp) Jefferson County	1	0.38

Place	Population	%
Milton (cdp) Ulster County	5	0.36
Apalachin (cdp) Tioga County	4	0.35
Plandome Manor (village) Nassau County	3	0.34
Avoca (village) Steuben County	3	0.32
Cattaraugus Reservation Erie County	5	0.27
Rapids (cdp) Niagara County	3	0.18
Rock Hill (cdp) Sullivan County	3	0.17

Top 10 Places Sorted by Percent of Total Population
Based on places with total population of 50,000 or more

Place	Population	%
Staten Island (borough) Richmond County	29	0.01
Huntington (town) Suffolk County	15	0.01
Babylon (town) Suffolk County	13	0.01
Syracuse (city) Onondaga County	9	0.01
Smithtown (town) Suffolk County	7	0.01
Albany (city) Albany County	6	0.01
Schenectady (city) Schenectady County	5	0.01
White Plains (city) Westchester County	3	0.01
New York (city)	291	<0.01
Brooklyn (borough) Kings County	81	<0.01

American Indian: Crow

Top 10 Places Sorted by Population
Based on all places, regardless of total population

Place	Population	%
New York (city)	50	<0.01
Brooklyn (borough) Kings County	19	<0.01
Bronx (borough) Bronx County	16	<0.01
Islip (town) Suffolk County	16	<0.01
Brentwood (cdp) Suffolk County	11	0.02
Manhattan (borough) New York County	11	<0.01
Schenectady (city) Schenectady County	6	0.01
Bombay (town) Franklin County	5	0.37
Huntington (town) Suffolk County	5	<0.01
Crown Heights (cdp) Dutchess County	4	0.14

Top 10 Places Sorted by Percent of Total Population
Based on all places, regardless of total population

Place	Population	%
Benson (town) Hamilton County	1	0.52
Bombay (town) Franklin County	5	0.37
Santa Clara (town) Franklin County	1	0.29
Valley Falls (village) Rensselaer County	1	0.21
East Avon (cdp) Livingston County	1	0.16
Crown Heights (cdp) Dutchess County	4	0.14
Cumberland Head (cdp) Clinton County	2	0.12
Manchester (village) Ontario County	2	0.12
Portville (village) Cattaraugus County	1	0.10
Gilboa (town) Schoharie County	1	0.08

Top 10 Places Sorted by Percent of Total Population
Based on places with total population of 50,000 or more

Place	Population	%
Brentwood (cdp) Suffolk County	11	0.02
Schenectady (city) Schenectady County	6	0.01
New York (city)	50	<0.01
Brooklyn (borough) Kings County	19	<0.01
Bronx (borough) Bronx County	16	<0.01
Islip (town) Suffolk County	16	<0.01
Manhattan (borough) New York County	11	<0.01
Huntington (town) Suffolk County	5	<0.01
Queens (borough) Queens County	4	<0.01
Utica (city) Oneida County	3	<0.01

American Indian: Delaware

Top 10 Places Sorted by Population
Based on all places, regardless of total population

Place	Population	%
New York (city)	177	<0.01
Ramapo (town) Rockland County	167	0.13
Hillburn (village) Rockland County	120	12.62
Warwick (town) Orange County	58	0.18
Wallkill (town) Orange County	57	0.21
Manhattan (borough) New York County	54	<0.01
Blooming Grove (town) Orange County	51	0.28
Middletown (city) Orange County	43	0.15
Staten Island (borough) Richmond County	43	0.01
Port Jervis (city) Orange County	39	0.44

Top 10 Places Sorted by Percent of Total Population
Based on all places, regardless of total population

Place	Population	%
Hillburn (village) Rockland County	120	12.62
Mountain Lodge Park (cdp) Orange County	25	1.57
Brushton (village) Franklin County	4	0.84
La Fargeville (cdp) Jefferson County	5	0.82
Wurtsboro (village) Sullivan County	8	0.64
Brandon (town) Franklin County	3	0.52
Greenwood Lake (village) Orange County	15	0.48
Port Jervis (city) Orange County	39	0.44
Chester (village) Orange County	17	0.43
Roseboom (town) Otsego County	3	0.42

Top 10 Places Sorted by Percent of Total Population
Based on places with total population of 50,000 or more

Place	Population	%
Ramapo (town) Rockland County	167	0.13
Clarkstown (town) Rockland County	16	0.02
Schenectady (city) Schenectady County	12	0.02
Staten Island (borough) Richmond County	43	0.01
Huntington (town) Suffolk County	12	0.01
Albany (city) Albany County	11	0.01
Irondequoit (cdp/town) Monroe County	7	0.01
Troy (city) Rensselaer County	6	0.01
Greenburgh (town) Westchester County	5	0.01
Union (town) Broome County	5	0.01

American Indian: Hopi

Top 10 Places Sorted by Population
Based on all places, regardless of total population

Place	Population	%
New York (city)	49	<0.01
Manhattan (borough) New York County	15	<0.01
Queens (borough) Queens County	15	<0.01
Brooklyn (borough) Kings County	12	<0.01
Babylon (town) Suffolk County	5	<0.01
Buffalo (city) Erie County	5	<0.01
Staten Island (borough) Richmond County	5	<0.01
Yonkers (city) Westchester County	5	<0.01
Village Green (cdp) Onondaga County	3	0.08
Massena (village) St. Lawrence County	3	0.03

Top 10 Places Sorted by Percent of Total Population
Based on all places, regardless of total population

Place	Population	%
Tonawanda Reservation Genesee County	1	0.21
Cayuta (town) Schuyler County	1	0.18
Shinnecock Reservation Suffolk County	1	0.15
Village Green (cdp) Onondaga County	3	0.08
North Collins (town) Erie County	2	0.06
Massena (village) St. Lawrence County	3	0.03
Shandaken (town) Ulster County	1	0.03
Theresa (town) Jefferson County	1	0.03
Cornwall (town) Orange County	3	0.02
Kingsbury (town) Washington County	3	0.02

Top 10 Places Sorted by Percent of Total Population
Based on places with total population of 50,000 or more

Place	Population	%
New York (city)	49	<0.01
Manhattan (borough) New York County	15	<0.01
Queens (borough) Queens County	15	<0.01
Brooklyn (borough) Kings County	12	<0.01
Babylon (town) Suffolk County	5	<0.01
Buffalo (city) Erie County	5	<0.01
Staten Island (borough) Richmond County	5	<0.01
Yonkers (city) Westchester County	5	<0.01
Islip (town) Suffolk County	3	<0.01
North Hempstead (town) Nassau County	3	<0.01

American Indian: Houma

Top 10 Places Sorted by Population
Based on all places, regardless of total population

Place	Population	%
New York (city)	23	<0.01
Bronx (borough) Bronx County	12	<0.01
Queens (borough) Queens County	4	<0.01

Place	Population	%
White Plains (city) Westchester County	3	0.01
Brooklyn (borough) Kings County	3	<0.01
Islip (town) Suffolk County	3	<0.01
Manhattan (borough) New York County	3	<0.01
Liberty (village) Sullivan County	2	0.05
Firthcliffe (cdp) Orange County	2	0.04
West Bay Shore (cdp) Suffolk County	2	0.04

Top 10 Places Sorted by Percent of Total Population
Based on all places, regardless of total population

Place	Population	%
Willing (town) Allegany County	1	0.08
Coventry (town) Chenango County	1	0.06
Liberty (village) Sullivan County	2	0.05
Firthcliffe (cdp) Orange County	2	0.04
West Bay Shore (cdp) Suffolk County	2	0.04
Kendall (town) Orleans County	1	0.04
Cornwall (town) Orange County	2	0.02
Liberty (town) Sullivan County	2	0.02
Elmira Heights (village) Chemung County	1	0.02
White Plains (city) Westchester County	3	0.01

Top 10 Places Sorted by Percent of Total Population
Based on places with total population of 50,000 or more

Place	Population	%
White Plains (city) Westchester County	3	0.01
New York (city)	23	<0.01
Bronx (borough) Bronx County	12	<0.01
Queens (borough) Queens County	4	<0.01
Brooklyn (borough) Kings County	3	<0.01
Islip (town) Suffolk County	3	<0.01
Manhattan (borough) New York County	3	<0.01
Buffalo (city) Erie County	2	<0.01
Greece (town) Monroe County	2	<0.01
Clay (town) Onondaga County	1	<0.01

Alaska Native: Inupiat (Eskimo)

Top 10 Places Sorted by Population
Based on all places, regardless of total population

Place	Population	%
New York (city)	58	<0.01
Brooklyn (borough) Kings County	21	<0.01
Bronx (borough) Bronx County	15	<0.01
Queens (borough) Queens County	13	<0.01
Manhattan (borough) New York County	8	<0.01
Syracuse (city) Onondaga County	6	<0.01
Port Chester (village) Westchester County	5	0.02
Rye (town) Westchester County	5	<0.01
Yonkers (city) Westchester County	5	<0.01
Frewsburg (cdp) Chautauqua County	4	0.21

Top 10 Places Sorted by Percent of Total Population
Based on all places, regardless of total population

Place	Population	%
West Winfield (village) Herkimer County	3	0.36
Frewsburg (cdp) Chautauqua County	4	0.21
Winfield (town) Herkimer County	3	0.14
Mountain Lodge Park (cdp) Orange County	2	0.13
North Hornell (village) Steuben County	1	0.13
Pine Plains (town) Dutchess County	3	0.12
Schroon Lake (cdp) Essex County	1	0.12
Carroll (town) Chautauqua County	4	0.11
Dexter (village) Jefferson County	1	0.10
Rathbone (town) Steuben County	1	0.09

Top 10 Places Sorted by Percent of Total Population
Based on places with total population of 50,000 or more

Place	Population	%
New York (city)	58	<0.01
Brooklyn (borough) Kings County	21	<0.01
Bronx (borough) Bronx County	15	<0.01
Queens (borough) Queens County	13	<0.01
Manhattan (borough) New York County	8	<0.01
Syracuse (city) Onondaga County	6	<0.01
Yonkers (city) Westchester County	5	<0.01
Buffalo (city) Erie County	4	<0.01
Rochester (city) Monroe County	4	<0.01
Amherst (town) Erie County	3	<0.01

American Indian: Iroquois

Top 10 Places Sorted by Population
Based on all places, regardless of total population

Place	Population	%
St. Regis Mohawk Reservation Franklin County	2,493	77.23
Syracuse (city) Onondaga County	1,373	0.95
Buffalo (city) Erie County	1,316	0.50
Cattaraugus Reservation Erie County	1,295	70.65
New York (city)	1,276	0.02
Salamanca (city) Cattaraugus County	951	16.35
Niagara Falls (city) Niagara County	801	1.60
Allegany Reservation Cattaraugus County	610	59.80
Rochester (city) Monroe County	483	0.23
Massena (town) St. Lawrence County	442	3.43

Top 10 Places Sorted by Percent of Total Population
Based on all places, regardless of total population

Place	Population	%
St. Regis Mohawk Reservation Franklin County	2,493	77.23
Tonawanda Reservation Erie County	26	76.47
Cattaraugus Reservation Cattaraugus County	227	72.29
Cattaraugus Reservation Erie County	1,295	70.65
Allegany Reservation Cattaraugus County	610	59.80
Cattaraugus Reservation Chautauqua County	20	52.63
Tonawanda Reservation Genesee County	168	34.78
Onondaga Nation Reservation Onondaga County	93	19.87
Salamanca (city) Cattaraugus County	951	16.35
Bombay (town) Franklin County	206	15.18

Top 10 Places Sorted by Percent of Total Population
Based on places with total population of 50,000 or more

Place	Population	%
Niagara Falls (city) Niagara County	801	1.60
Syracuse (city) Onondaga County	1,373	0.95
Buffalo (city) Erie County	1,316	0.50
Clay (town) Onondaga County	252	0.43
Tonawanda (town) Erie County	256	0.35
Tonawanda (cdp) Erie County	165	0.28
Hamburg (town) Erie County	159	0.28
Cheektowaga (cdp) Erie County	179	0.24
Rochester (city) Monroe County	483	0.23
Cheektowaga (town) Erie County	194	0.22

American Indian: Kiowa

Top 10 Places Sorted by Population
Based on all places, regardless of total population

Place	Population	%
New York (city)	15	<0.01
Manhattan (borough) New York County	11	<0.01
Middlefield (town) Otsego County	2	0.09
Roxbury (town) Delaware County	2	0.08
Brooklyn (borough) Kings County	2	<0.01
Utica (city) Oneida County	2	<0.01
Old Forge (cdp) Herkimer County	1	0.13
Tuscarora Nation Reservation Niagara County	1	0.09
Webb (town) Herkimer County	1	0.06
Carlisle (town) Schoharie County	1	0.05

Top 10 Places Sorted by Percent of Total Population
Based on all places, regardless of total population

Place	Population	%
Old Forge (cdp) Herkimer County	1	0.13
Middlefield (town) Otsego County	2	0.09
Tuscarora Nation Reservation Niagara County	1	0.09
Roxbury (town) Delaware County	2	0.08
Webb (town) Herkimer County	1	0.06
Carlisle (town) Schoharie County	1	0.05
New Hartford (village) Oneida County	1	0.05
Triangle (town) Broome County	1	0.03
Elmira Heights (village) Chemung County	1	0.02
Old Bethpage (cdp) Nassau County	1	0.02

Top 10 Places Sorted by Percent of Total Population
Based on places with total population of 50,000 or more

Place	Population	%
New York (city)	15	<0.01
Manhattan (borough) New York County	11	<0.01
Brooklyn (borough) Kings County	2	<0.01
Utica (city) Oneida County	2	<0.01

Place	Population	%
Bronx (borough) Bronx County	1	<0.01
Buffalo (city) Erie County	1	<0.01
Oyster Bay (town) Nassau County	1	<0.01
Schenectady (city) Schenectady County	1	<0.01
Smithtown (town) Suffolk County	1	<0.01
Staten Island (borough) Richmond County	1	<0.01

American Indian: Lumbee

Top 10 Places Sorted by Population
Based on all places, regardless of total population

Place	Population	%
New York (city)	89	<0.01
Queens (borough) Queens County	30	<0.01
Brooklyn (borough) Kings County	24	<0.01
Hempstead (town) Nassau County	22	<0.01
Manhattan (borough) New York County	21	<0.01
Babylon (town) Suffolk County	12	0.01
Islip (town) Suffolk County	8	<0.01
Staten Island (borough) Richmond County	8	<0.01
Rose (town) Wayne County	7	0.30
Brookhaven (town) Suffolk County	7	<0.01

Top 10 Places Sorted by Percent of Total Population
Based on all places, regardless of total population

Place	Population	%
Limestone (village) Cattaraugus County	3	0.77
Shinnecock Reservation Suffolk County	3	0.45
Newfield Hamlet (cdp) Tompkins County	3	0.40
Farmersville (town) Cattaraugus County	4	0.37
St. Armand (town) Essex County	5	0.32
Rose (town) Wayne County	7	0.30
Hermon (village) St. Lawrence County	1	0.24
Carrollton (town) Cattaraugus County	3	0.23
Brushton (village) Franklin County	1	0.21
Shandaken (town) Ulster County	6	0.19

Top 10 Places Sorted by Percent of Total Population
Based on places with total population of 50,000 or more

Place	Population	%
Babylon (town) Suffolk County	12	0.01
Levittown (cdp) Nassau County	6	0.01
Niagara Falls (city) Niagara County	6	0.01
Schenectady (city) Schenectady County	4	0.01
Troy (city) Rensselaer County	4	0.01
Clay (town) Onondaga County	3	0.01
New York (city)	89	<0.01
Queens (borough) Queens County	30	<0.01
Brooklyn (borough) Kings County	24	<0.01
Hempstead (town) Nassau County	22	<0.01

American Indian: Menominee

Top 10 Places Sorted by Population
Based on all places, regardless of total population

Place	Population	%
New York (city)	10	<0.01
Cattaraugus Reservation Erie County	5	0.27
Brooklyn (borough) Kings County	4	<0.01
Crown Heights (cdp) Dutchess County	3	0.11
Northumberland (town) Saratoga County	3	0.06
Glens Falls (city) Warren County	3	0.02
Poughkeepsie (town) Dutchess County	3	0.01
Troy (city) Rensselaer County	3	0.01
Bronx (borough) Bronx County	3	<0.01
Manhattan (borough) New York County	3	<0.01

Top 10 Places Sorted by Percent of Total Population
Based on all places, regardless of total population

Place	Population	%
Cattaraugus Reservation Erie County	5	0.27
Fillmore (cdp) Allegany County	1	0.17
Crown Heights (cdp) Dutchess County	3	0.11
Pine Plains (cdp) Dutchess County	1	0.07
Northumberland (town) Saratoga County	3	0.06
Trumansburg (village) Tompkins County	1	0.06
Angola (village) Erie County	1	0.05
Hume (town) Allegany County	1	0.05
Pine Plains (town) Dutchess County	1	0.04
Glens Falls (city) Warren County	3	0.02

American Indian: Mexican American Indian

Top 10 Places Sorted by Percent of Total Population
Based on places with total population of 50,000 or more

Place	Population	%
Troy (city) Rensselaer County	3	0.01
New York (city)	10	<0.01
Brooklyn (borough) Kings County	4	<0.01
Bronx (borough) Bronx County	3	<0.01
Manhattan (borough) New York County	3	<0.01
Buffalo (city) Erie County	2	<0.01
Niagara Falls (city) Niagara County	2	<0.01
Syracuse (city) Onondaga County	1	<0.01
Albany (city) Albany County	0	0.00
Amherst (town) Erie County	0	0.00

Top 10 Places Sorted by Population
Based on all places, regardless of total population

Place	Population	%
New York (city)	4,922	0.06
Queens (borough) Queens County	1,640	0.07
Brooklyn (borough) Kings County	1,363	0.05
Bronx (borough) Bronx County	963	0.07
Manhattan (borough) New York County	752	0.05
Staten Island (borough) Richmond County	204	0.04
Yonkers (city) Westchester County	171	0.09
White Plains (city) Westchester County	162	0.28
Poughkeepsie (city) Dutchess County	160	0.49
Hempstead (town) Nassau County	143	0.02

Top 10 Places Sorted by Percent of Total Population
Based on all places, regardless of total population

Place	Population	%
Cattaraugus Reservation Chautauqua County	5	13.16
Shinnecock Hills (cdp) Suffolk County	27	1.23
Westhampton Beach (village) Suffolk County	13	0.76
Flanders (cdp) Suffolk County	29	0.65
Phoenicia (cdp) Ulster County	2	0.65
Rensselaer Falls (village) St. Lawrence County	2	0.60
Lorraine (cdp) Jefferson County	1	0.57
Poughkeepsie (city) Dutchess County	160	0.49
Palatine Bridge (village) Montgomery County	3	0.41
Woodstock (cdp) Ulster County	8	0.38

Top 10 Places Sorted by Percent of Total Population
Based on places with total population of 50,000 or more

Place	Population	%
White Plains (city) Westchester County	162	0.28
Southampton (town) Suffolk County	83	0.15
Brentwood (cdp) Suffolk County	72	0.12
Yonkers (city) Westchester County	171	0.09
New Rochelle (city) Westchester County	72	0.09
Queens (borough) Queens County	1,640	0.07
Bronx (borough) Bronx County	963	0.07
New York (city)	4,922	0.06
Ramapo (town) Rockland County	74	0.06
Brooklyn (borough) Kings County	1,363	0.05

American Indian: Navajo

Top 10 Places Sorted by Population
Based on all places, regardless of total population

Place	Population	%
New York (city)	272	<0.01
Brooklyn (borough) Kings County	93	<0.01
Manhattan (borough) New York County	83	0.01
Bronx (borough) Bronx County	42	<0.01
Queens (borough) Queens County	37	<0.01
Rochester (city) Monroe County	30	0.01
Le Ray (town) Jefferson County	24	0.11
Fort Drum (cdp) Jefferson County	23	0.18
Staten Island (borough) Richmond County	17	<0.01
Buffalo (city) Erie County	16	0.01

Top 10 Places Sorted by Percent of Total Population
Based on all places, regardless of total population

Place	Population	%
Rodman (cdp) Jefferson County	1	0.65
Tonawanda Reservation Genesee County	3	0.62

Place	Population	%
Margaretville (village) Delaware County	3	0.50
Lakeville (cdp) Livingston County	3	0.40
Allegany Reservation Cattaraugus County	4	0.39
Baldwin (town) Chemung County	3	0.36
East Avon (cdp) Livingston County	2	0.33
Strykersville (cdp) Wyoming County	2	0.31
Brant (town) Erie County	5	0.24
Owego (village) Tioga County	9	0.23

Top 10 Places Sorted by Percent of Total Population
Based on places with total population of 50,000 or more

Place	Population	%
Manhattan (borough) New York County	83	0.01
Rochester (city) Monroe County	30	0.01
Buffalo (city) Erie County	16	0.01
Troy (city) Rensselaer County	5	0.01
Brentwood (cdp) Suffolk County	4	0.01
Clay (town) Onondaga County	4	0.01
New York (city)	272	<0.01
Brooklyn (borough) Kings County	93	<0.01
Bronx (borough) Bronx County	42	<0.01
Queens (borough) Queens County	37	<0.01

American Indian: Osage

Top 10 Places Sorted by Population
Based on all places, regardless of total population

Place	Population	%
New York (city)	23	<0.01
Manhattan (borough) New York County	12	<0.01
Queens (borough) Queens County	5	<0.01
Oakfield (village) Genesee County	4	0.22
Oakfield (town) Genesee County	4	0.12
Manlius (town) Onondaga County	4	0.01
Moravia (village) Cayuga County	3	0.23
Moravia (town) Cayuga County	3	0.08
Wheatfield (town) Niagara County	3	0.02
Le Ray (town) Jefferson County	3	0.01

Top 10 Places Sorted by Percent of Total Population
Based on all places, regardless of total population

Place	Population	%
Poospatuck Reservation Suffolk County	1	0.31
Moravia (village) Cayuga County	3	0.23
Oakfield (village) Genesee County	4	0.22
Oakfield (town) Genesee County	4	0.12
Moravia (town) Cayuga County	3	0.08
North Collins (town) Erie County	2	0.06
Wolcott (village) Wayne County	1	0.06
Woodstock (cdp) Ulster County	1	0.05
Florida (town) Montgomery County	1	0.04
Cazenovia (town) Madison County	2	0.03

Top 10 Places Sorted by Percent of Total Population
Based on places with total population of 50,000 or more

Place	Population	%
New York (city)	23	<0.01
Manhattan (borough) New York County	12	<0.01
Queens (borough) Queens County	5	<0.01
Bronx (borough) Bronx County	3	<0.01
Brooklyn (borough) Kings County	3	<0.01
Rochester (city) Monroe County	3	<0.01
Brookhaven (town) Suffolk County	2	<0.01
Hempstead (town) Nassau County	2	<0.01
White Plains (city) Westchester County	2	<0.01
Amherst (town) Erie County	1	<0.01

American Indian: Ottawa

Top 10 Places Sorted by Population
Based on all places, regardless of total population

Place	Population	%
New York (city)	11	<0.01
Auburn (city) Cayuga County	5	0.02
Brooklyn (borough) Kings County	5	0.01
Newfield Hamlet (cdp) Tompkins County	4	0.53
Newfield (town) Tompkins County	4	0.08
East Aurora (village) Erie County	3	0.05
Aurora (town) Erie County	3	0.02
Setauket-East Setauket (cdp) Suffolk County	3	0.02
Brookhaven (town) Suffolk County	3	<0.01
Manhattan (borough) New York County	3	<0.01

Top 10 Places Sorted by Percent of Total Population
Based on all places, regardless of total population

Place	Population	%
Newfield Hamlet (cdp) Tompkins County	4	0.53
Newfield (town) Tompkins County	4	0.08
East Aurora (village) Erie County	3	0.05
Cattaraugus Reservation Erie County	1	0.05
Seneca Falls (village) Seneca County	2	0.03
Mohawk (town) Montgomery County	1	0.03
Auburn (city) Cayuga County	5	0.02
Aurora (town) Erie County	3	0.02
Setauket-East Setauket (cdp) Suffolk County	3	0.02
Lewisboro (town) Westchester County	2	0.02

Top 10 Places Sorted by Percent of Total Population
Based on places with total population of 50,000 or more

Place	Population	%
New York (city)	11	<0.01
Brooklyn (borough) Kings County	5	<0.01
Brookhaven (town) Suffolk County	3	<0.01
Manhattan (borough) New York County	3	<0.01
Huntington (town) Suffolk County	2	<0.01
Queens (borough) Queens County	2	<0.01
Syracuse (city) Onondaga County	2	<0.01
Albany (city) Albany County	1	<0.01
Bronx (borough) Bronx County	1	<0.01
Clay (town) Onondaga County	1	<0.01

American Indian: Paiute

Top 10 Places Sorted by Population
Based on all places, regardless of total population

Place	Population	%
New York (city)	18	<0.01
Manhattan (borough) New York County	8	<0.01
Perrysburg (town) Cattaraugus County	6	0.37
Cattaraugus Reservation Erie County	6	0.33
Bronx (borough) Bronx County	5	<0.01
Brookhaven (town) Suffolk County	4	<0.01
Queens (borough) Queens County	4	<0.01
Olean (city) Cattaraugus County	3	0.02
Conklin (town) Broome County	2	0.04
Manorville (cdp) Suffolk County	2	0.01

Top 10 Places Sorted by Percent of Total Population
Based on all places, regardless of total population

Place	Population	%
Perrysburg (town) Cattaraugus County	6	0.37
Cattaraugus Reservation Erie County	6	0.33
Upper Nyack (village) Rockland County	1	0.05
Conklin (town) Broome County	2	0.04
Gowanda (village) Cattaraugus County	1	0.04
St. Regis Mohawk Reservation Franklin County	1	0.03
Olean (city) Cattaraugus County	3	0.02
Collins (town) Erie County	1	0.02
Manorville (cdp) Suffolk County	2	0.01
Miller Place (cdp) Suffolk County	1	0.01

Top 10 Places Sorted by Percent of Total Population
Based on places with total population of 50,000 or more

Place	Population	%
New York (city)	18	<0.01
Manhattan (borough) New York County	8	<0.01
Bronx (borough) Bronx County	5	<0.01
Brookhaven (town) Suffolk County	4	<0.01
Queens (borough) Queens County	4	<0.01
Hamburg (town) Erie County	2	<0.01
Brooklyn (borough) Kings County	1	<0.01
Clarkstown (town) Rockland County	1	<0.01
Rochester (city) Monroe County	1	<0.01
Utica (city) Oneida County	1	<0.01

American Indian: Pima

Top 10 Places Sorted by Population
Based on all places, regardless of total population

Place	Population	%
New York (city)	9	<0.01

Place	Population	%
Schenectady (city) Schenectady County	5	0.01
Manhattan (borough) New York County	4	<0.01
Fort Montgomery (cdp) Orange County	3	0.19
Gowanda (village) Cattaraugus County	3	0.11
Collins (town) Erie County	3	0.05
Highlands (town) Orange County	3	0.02
Fallsburg (town) Sullivan County	2	0.02
Ontario (town) Wayne County	2	0.02
Harrison (town/village) Westchester County	2	0.01

Top 10 Places Sorted by Percent of Total Population
Based on all places, regardless of total population

Place	Population	%
Fort Montgomery (cdp) Orange County	3	0.19
Rushville (village) Yates County	1	0.15
Gowanda (village) Cattaraugus County	3	0.11
Collins (town) Erie County	3	0.05
Potter (town) Yates County	1	0.05
Highlands (town) Orange County	3	0.02
Fallsburg (town) Sullivan County	2	0.02
Ontario (town) Wayne County	2	0.02
Minisink (town) Orange County	1	0.02
Ulysses (town) Tompkins County	1	0.02

Top 10 Places Sorted by Percent of Total Population
Based on places with total population of 50,000 or more

Place	Population	%
Schenectady (city) Schenectady County	5	0.01
New York (city)	9	<0.01
Manhattan (borough) New York County	4	<0.01
Brooklyn (borough) Kings County	2	<0.01
Rochester (city) Monroe County	2	<0.01
Staten Island (borough) Richmond County	2	<0.01
Syracuse (city) Onondaga County	2	<0.01
Brentwood (cdp) Suffolk County	1	<0.01
Bronx (borough) Bronx County	1	<0.01
Buffalo (city) Erie County	1	<0.01

American Indian: Potawatomi

Top 10 Places Sorted by Population
Based on all places, regardless of total population

Place	Population	%
New York (city)	40	<0.01
Manhattan (borough) New York County	20	<0.01
Brooklyn (borough) Kings County	11	<0.01
Tonawanda (cdp) Erie County	9	0.02
Tonawanda (town) Erie County	9	0.01
Queens (borough) Queens County	7	<0.01
Brookhaven (town) Suffolk County	6	<0.01
Fort Drum (cdp) Jefferson County	5	0.04
Le Ray (town) Jefferson County	5	0.02
Schenectady (city) Schenectady County	5	0.01

Top 10 Places Sorted by Percent of Total Population
Based on all places, regardless of total population

Place	Population	%
Onondaga Nation Reservation Onondaga County	4	0.85
Mina (town) Chautauqua County	2	0.18
Denning (town) Ulster County	1	0.18
Merritt Park (cdp) Dutchess County	2	0.16
Russia (town) Herkimer County	3	0.12
Cuyler (town) Cortland County	1	0.10
Greenport West (cdp) Suffolk County	2	0.09
Truxton (town) Cortland County	1	0.09
Lake Erie Beach (cdp) Erie County	3	0.08
Vernon (town) Oneida County	3	0.06

Top 10 Places Sorted by Percent of Total Population
Based on places with total population of 50,000 or more

Place	Population	%
Tonawanda (cdp) Erie County	9	0.02
Tonawanda (town) Erie County	9	0.01
Schenectady (city) Schenectady County	5	0.01
New York (city)	40	<0.01
Manhattan (borough) New York County	20	<0.01
Brooklyn (borough) Kings County	11	<0.01
Queens (borough) Queens County	7	<0.01
Brookhaven (town) Suffolk County	6	<0.01
Rochester (city) Monroe County	5	<0.01
Albany (city) Albany County	2	<0.01

American Indian: Pueblo

Top 10 Places Sorted by Population
Based on all places, regardless of total population

Place	Population	%
New York (city)	892	0.01
Bronx (borough) Bronx County	382	0.03
Manhattan (borough) New York County	175	0.01
Brooklyn (borough) Kings County	169	0.01
Queens (borough) Queens County	161	0.01
Yonkers (city) Westchester County	20	0.01
White Plains (city) Westchester County	19	0.03
Hempstead (town) Nassau County	13	<0.01
Le Ray (town) Jefferson County	11	0.05
Fort Drum (cdp) Jefferson County	10	0.08

Top 10 Places Sorted by Percent of Total Population
Based on all places, regardless of total population

Place	Population	%
DeKalb Junction (cdp) St. Lawrence County	4	0.77
Denning (town) Ulster County	2	0.36
Pine Hill (cdp) Ulster County	1	0.36
Natural Bridge (cdp) Jefferson County	1	0.27
De Kalb (town) St. Lawrence County	4	0.16
Northwest Harbor (cdp) Suffolk County	4	0.12
Ripley (cdp) Chautauqua County	1	0.11
Stone Ridge (cdp) Ulster County	1	0.09
Fort Drum (cdp) Jefferson County	10	0.08
Ripley (town) Chautauqua County	2	0.08

Top 10 Places Sorted by Percent of Total Population
Based on places with total population of 50,000 or more

Place	Population	%
Bronx (borough) Bronx County	382	0.03
White Plains (city) Westchester County	19	0.03
New York (city)	892	0.01
Manhattan (borough) New York County	175	0.01
Brooklyn (borough) Kings County	169	0.01
Queens (borough) Queens County	161	0.01
Yonkers (city) Westchester County	20	0.01
Mount Vernon (city) Westchester County	7	0.01
Hempstead (village) Nassau County	6	0.01
Brentwood (cdp) Suffolk County	5	0.01

American Indian: Puget Sound Salish

Top 10 Places Sorted by Population
Based on all places, regardless of total population

Place	Population	%
New York (city)	11	<0.01
Brookhaven (town) Suffolk County	6	<0.01
Gordon Heights (cdp) Suffolk County	5	0.12
Manhattan (borough) New York County	5	<0.01
Queens (borough) Queens County	5	<0.01
Bronxville (village) Westchester County	3	0.05
Eastchester (town) Westchester County	3	0.01
East Ithaca (cdp) Tompkins County	2	0.09
Horseheads (village) Chemung County	2	0.03
Orange Lake (cdp) Orange County	2	0.03

Top 10 Places Sorted by Percent of Total Population
Based on all places, regardless of total population

Place	Population	%
Gordon Heights (cdp) Suffolk County	5	0.12
East Ithaca (cdp) Tompkins County	2	0.09
Bronxville (village) Westchester County	3	0.05
Bellport (village) Suffolk County	1	0.05
Cattaraugus Reservation Erie County	1	0.05
Horseheads (village) Chemung County	2	0.03
Orange Lake (cdp) Orange County	2	0.03
Calcium (cdp) Jefferson County	1	0.03
Southold (cdp) Suffolk County	1	0.02
Eastchester (town) Westchester County	3	0.01

Top 10 Places Sorted by Percent of Total Population
Based on places with total population of 50,000 or more

Place	Population	%
New York (city)	11	<0.01
Brookhaven (town) Suffolk County	6	<0.01
Manhattan (borough) New York County	5	<0.01
Queens (borough) Queens County	5	<0.01

Place	Population	%
Brooklyn (borough) Kings County	1	<0.01
Tonawanda (cdp) Erie County	1	<0.01
Tonawanda (town) Erie County	1	<0.01
Albany (city) Albany County	0	0.00
Amherst (town) Erie County	0	0.00
Babylon (town) Suffolk County	0	0.00

American Indian: Seminole

Top 10 Places Sorted by Population
Based on all places, regardless of total population

Place	Population	%
New York (city)	357	<0.01
Manhattan (borough) New York County	110	0.01
Brooklyn (borough) Kings County	92	<0.01
Queens (borough) Queens County	79	<0.01
Bronx (borough) Bronx County	50	<0.01
Rochester (city) Monroe County	44	0.02
Brookhaven (town) Suffolk County	33	<0.01
Hempstead (town) Nassau County	28	<0.01
Staten Island (borough) Richmond County	26	0.01
Buffalo (city) Erie County	23	0.01

Top 10 Places Sorted by Percent of Total Population
Based on all places, regardless of total population

Place	Population	%
Randolph (village) Cattaraugus County	5	0.39
Cuylerville (cdp) Livingston County	1	0.34
Wainscott (cdp) Suffolk County	2	0.31
Poospatuck Reservation Suffolk County	1	0.31
West Sparta (town) Livingston County	3	0.24
Randolph (town) Cattaraugus County	5	0.19
Haviland (cdp) Dutchess County	5	0.14
Greenport (village) Suffolk County	3	0.14
Veteran (town) Chemung County	4	0.12
De Kalb (town) St. Lawrence County	3	0.12

Top 10 Places Sorted by Percent of Total Population
Based on places with total population of 50,000 or more

Place	Population	%
Rochester (city) Monroe County	44	0.02
Manhattan (borough) New York County	110	0.01
Brookhaven (town) Suffolk County	33	0.01
Staten Island (borough) Richmond County	26	0.01
Buffalo (city) Erie County	23	0.01
Syracuse (city) Onondaga County	16	0.01
Babylon (town) Suffolk County	13	0.01
Yonkers (city) Westchester County	11	0.01
Amherst (town) Erie County	10	0.01
Mount Vernon (city) Westchester County	9	0.01

American Indian: Shoshone

Top 10 Places Sorted by Population
Based on all places, regardless of total population

Place	Population	%
New York (city)	46	<0.01
Brooklyn (borough) Kings County	23	<0.01
Yates (town) Orleans County	8	0.31
Bronx (borough) Bronx County	8	<0.01
Manhattan (borough) New York County	6	<0.01
Queens (borough) Queens County	6	<0.01
Middletown (city) Orange County	4	0.01
Brookhaven (town) Suffolk County	4	<0.01
Bay Shore (cdp) Suffolk County	3	<0.01
Hempstead (town) Nassau County	3	<0.01

Top 10 Places Sorted by Percent of Total Population
Based on all places, regardless of total population

Place	Population	%
Rhinecliff (cdp) Dutchess County	2	0.47
Hobart (village) Delaware County	2	0.45
Yates (town) Orleans County	8	0.31
St. Regis Falls (cdp) Franklin County	1	0.22
Waverly (town) Franklin County	1	0.10
Stamford (town) Delaware County	2	0.09
Covert (town) Seneca County	1	0.05
Minisink (town) Orange County	2	0.04
Afton (town) Chenango County	1	0.04
Rhinebeck (town) Dutchess County	2	0.03

Top 10 Places Sorted by Percent of Total Population
Based on places with total population of 50,000 or more

Place	Population	%
New York (city)	46	<0.01
Brooklyn (borough) Kings County	23	<0.01
Bronx (borough) Bronx County	8	<0.01
Manhattan (borough) New York County	6	<0.01
Queens (borough) Queens County	6	<0.01
Brookhaven (town) Suffolk County	4	<0.01
Hempstead (town) Nassau County	3	<0.01
Islip (town) Suffolk County	3	<0.01
Staten Island (borough) Richmond County	3	<0.01
Albany (city) Albany County	1	<0.01

American Indian: Sioux

Top 10 Places Sorted by Population
Based on all places, regardless of total population

Place	Population	%
New York (city)	464	0.01
Manhattan (borough) New York County	133	0.01
Brooklyn (borough) Kings County	121	<0.01
Queens (borough) Queens County	104	<0.01
Bronx (borough) Bronx County	82	0.01
Buffalo (city) Erie County	46	0.02
Brookhaven (town) Suffolk County	42	0.01
Syracuse (city) Onondaga County	38	0.03
Hempstead (town) Nassau County	33	<0.01
Utica (city) Oneida County	29	0.05

Top 10 Places Sorted by Percent of Total Population
Based on all places, regardless of total population

Place	Population	%
Hardenburgh (town) Ulster County	10	4.20
Napeague (cdp) Suffolk County	3	1.50
Poospatuck Reservation Suffolk County	3	0.93
Windham (cdp) Greene County	3	0.82
Redfield (town) Oswego County	4	0.73
Plessis (cdp) Jefferson County	1	0.61
Allegany Reservation Cattaraugus County	6	0.59
Perrysburg (village) Cattaraugus County	2	0.50
Ashland (town) Chemung County	7	0.41
Calcium (cdp) Jefferson County	14	0.40

Top 10 Places Sorted by Percent of Total Population
Based on places with total population of 50,000 or more

Place	Population	%
Utica (city) Oneida County	29	0.05
Syracuse (city) Onondaga County	38	0.03
Buffalo (city) Erie County	46	0.02
Schenectady (city) Schenectady County	14	0.02
Niagara Falls (city) Niagara County	8	0.02
New York (city)	464	0.01
Manhattan (borough) New York County	133	0.01
Bronx (borough) Bronx County	82	0.01
Brookhaven (town) Suffolk County	42	0.01
Islip (town) Suffolk County	27	0.01

American Indian: South American Indian

Top 10 Places Sorted by Population
Based on all places, regardless of total population

Place	Population	%
New York (city)	9,464	0.12
Bronx (borough) Bronx County	2,938	0.21
Queens (borough) Queens County	2,448	0.11
Manhattan (borough) New York County	1,935	0.12
Brooklyn (borough) Kings County	1,855	0.07
Hempstead (town) Nassau County	294	0.04
Staten Island (borough) Richmond County	288	0.06
Yonkers (city) Westchester County	270	0.14
Islip (town) Suffolk County	249	0.07
Rochester (city) Monroe County	144	0.07

Top 10 Places Sorted by Percent of Total Population
Based on all places, regardless of total population

Place	Population	%
Onondaga Nation Reservation Onondaga County	9	1.92
Cattaraugus Reservation Cattaraugus County	5	1.59
Allegany Reservation Cattaraugus County	9	0.88

Shinnecock Hills (cdp) Suffolk County 18 0.82
Poospatuck Reservation Suffolk County 2 0.62
Roslyn Harbor (village) Nassau County 4 0.38
Fairview (cdp) Westchester County 11 0.35
East Hampton North (cdp) Suffolk County 13 0.31
St. Regis Mohawk Reservation Franklin County 10 0.31
Haverstraw (village) Rockland County 32 0.27

Top 10 Places Sorted by Percent of Total Population
Based on places with total population of 50,000 or more

Place	Population	%
Bronx (borough) Bronx County	2,938	0.21
White Plains (city) Westchester County	116	0.20
Yonkers (city) Westchester County	270	0.14
Brentwood (cdp) Suffolk County	87	0.14
New York (city)	9,464	0.12
Manhattan (borough) New York County	1,935	0.12
Queens (borough) Queens County	2,448	0.11
Greenburgh (town) Westchester County	72	0.08
Brooklyn (borough) Kings County	1,855	0.07
Islip (town) Suffolk County	249	0.07

American Indian: Spanish American Indian

Top 10 Places Sorted by Population
Based on all places, regardless of total population

Place	Population	%
New York (city)	2,594	0.03
Bronx (borough) Bronx County	992	0.07
Queens (borough) Queens County	659	0.03
Manhattan (borough) New York County	514	0.03
Brooklyn (borough) Kings County	382	0.02
Hempstead (town) Nassau County	137	0.02
Yonkers (city) Westchester County	132	0.07
Newburgh (city) Orange County	92	0.32
Islip (town) Suffolk County	91	0.03
Brentwood (cdp) Suffolk County	52	0.09

Top 10 Places Sorted by Percent of Total Population
Based on all places, regardless of total population

Place	Population	%
Shinnecock Reservation Suffolk County	4	0.60
Fort Covington Hamlet (cdp) Franklin County	7	0.54
Fort Covington (town) Franklin County	7	0.42
Newburgh (city) Orange County	92	0.32
Lebanon (town) Madison County	4	0.30
Westhampton Beach (village) Suffolk County	5	0.29
Greenport West (cdp) Suffolk County	6	0.28
South Floral Park (village) Nassau County	4	0.23
Woodstock (cdp) Ulster County	4	0.19
Canisteo (village) Steuben County	4	0.18

Top 10 Places Sorted by Percent of Total Population
Based on places with total population of 50,000 or more

Place	Population	%
Brentwood (cdp) Suffolk County	52	0.09
Hempstead (village) Nassau County	47	0.09
Bronx (borough) Bronx County	992	0.07
Yonkers (city) Westchester County	132	0.07
New York (city)	2,594	0.03
Queens (borough) Queens County	659	0.03
Manhattan (borough) New York County	514	0.03
Islip (town) Suffolk County	91	0.03
Greenburgh (town) Westchester County	23	0.03
White Plains (city) Westchester County	15	0.03

Alaska Native: Tlingit-Haida

Top 10 Places Sorted by Population
Based on all places, regardless of total population

Place	Population	%
New York (city)	75	<0.01
Brooklyn (borough) Kings County	28	<0.01
Queens (borough) Queens County	20	<0.01
Manhattan (borough) New York County	15	<0.01
Bronx (borough) Bronx County	11	<0.01
Ramapo (town) Rockland County	7	0.01
Hempstead (town) Nassau County	6	<0.01
Islip (town) Suffolk County	6	<0.01
Hilton (village) Monroe County	5	0.08

Parma (town) Monroe County 5 0.03

Top 10 Places Sorted by Percent of Total Population
Based on all places, regardless of total population

Place	Population	%
Wampsville (village) Madison County	1	0.18
Lake George (town) Warren County	4	0.11
Dolgeville (village) Herkimer County	2	0.09
Poestenkill (cdp) Rensselaer County	1	0.09
Hilton (village) Monroe County	5	0.08
Gordon Heights (cdp) Suffolk County	3	0.07
Bellmont (town) Franklin County	1	0.07
Manheim (town) Herkimer County	2	0.06
Hornell (city) Steuben County	4	0.05
Hillcrest (cdp) Rockland County	3	0.04

Top 10 Places Sorted by Percent of Total Population
Based on places with total population of 50,000 or more

Place	Population	%
Ramapo (town) Rockland County	7	0.01
Utica (city) Oneida County	4	0.01
New York (city)	75	<0.01
Brooklyn (borough) Kings County	28	<0.01
Queens (borough) Queens County	20	<0.01
Manhattan (borough) New York County	15	<0.01
Bronx (borough) Bronx County	11	<0.01
Hempstead (town) Nassau County	6	<0.01
Islip (town) Suffolk County	6	<0.01
Brookhaven (town) Suffolk County	5	<0.01

American Indian: Tohono O'Odham

Top 10 Places Sorted by Population
Based on all places, regardless of total population

Place	Population	%
New York (city)	48	<0.01
Manhattan (borough) New York County	15	<0.01
Brooklyn (borough) Kings County	10	<0.01
Bronx (borough) Bronx County	9	<0.01
Staten Island (borough) Richmond County	8	<0.01
Hempstead (town) Nassau County	7	<0.01
Middletown (city) Orange County	6	0.02
New Windsor (town) Orange County	6	0.02
Uniondale (cdp) Nassau County	6	0.02
Queens (borough) Queens County	6	<0.01

Top 10 Places Sorted by Percent of Total Population
Based on all places, regardless of total population

Place	Population	%
Hillburn (village) Rockland County	4	0.42
Covington (town) Wyoming County	3	0.24
Allegany Reservation Cattaraugus County	1	0.10
Chester (village) Orange County	3	0.08
Durham (town) Greene County	1	0.04
Chester (town) Orange County	3	0.03
Middletown (city) Orange County	6	0.02
New Windsor (town) Orange County	6	0.02
Uniondale (cdp) Nassau County	6	0.02
Poughkeepsie (city) Dutchess County	3	0.01

Top 10 Places Sorted by Percent of Total Population
Based on places with total population of 50,000 or more

Place	Population	%
New York (city)	48	<0.01
Manhattan (borough) New York County	15	<0.01
Brooklyn (borough) Kings County	10	<0.01
Bronx (borough) Bronx County	9	<0.01
Staten Island (borough) Richmond County	8	<0.01
Hempstead (town) Nassau County	7	<0.01
Queens (borough) Queens County	6	<0.01
Ramapo (town) Rockland County	4	<0.01
Buffalo (city) Erie County	3	<0.01
Yonkers (city) Westchester County	3	<0.01

Alaska Native: Tsimshian

Top 10 Places Sorted by Population
Based on all places, regardless of total population

Place	Population	%
New York (city)	4	<0.01

Manhattan (borough) New York County 3 <0.01
Rochester (town) Ulster County 1 0.01
Queens (borough) Queens County 1 <0.01
Accord (cdp) Ulster County 0 0.00
Adams (village) Jefferson County 0 0.00
Adams (town) Jefferson County 0 0.00
Adams Center (cdp) Jefferson County 0 0.00
Addison (village) Steuben County 0 0.00
Addison (town) Steuben County 0 0.00

Top 10 Places Sorted by Percent of Total Population
Based on all places, regardless of total population

Place	Population	%
Rochester (town) Ulster County	1	0.01
New York (city)	4	<0.01
Manhattan (borough) New York County	3	<0.01
Queens (borough) Queens County	1	<0.01
Accord (cdp) Ulster County	0	0.00
Adams (village) Jefferson County	0	0.00
Adams (town) Jefferson County	0	0.00
Adams Center (cdp) Jefferson County	0	0.00
Addison (village) Steuben County	0	0.00
Addison (town) Steuben County	0	0.00

Top 10 Places Sorted by Percent of Total Population
Based on places with total population of 50,000 or more

Place	Population	%
New York (city)	4	<0.01
Manhattan (borough) New York County	3	<0.01
Queens (borough) Queens County	1	<0.01
Albany (city) Albany County	0	0.00
Amherst (town) Erie County	0	0.00
Babylon (town) Suffolk County	0	0.00
Brentwood (cdp) Suffolk County	0	0.00
Bronx (borough) Bronx County	0	0.00
Brookhaven (town) Suffolk County	0	0.00
Brooklyn (borough) Kings County	0	0.00

American Indian: Ute

Top 10 Places Sorted by Population
Based on all places, regardless of total population

Place	Population	%
New York (city)	17	<0.01
Bronx (borough) Bronx County	5	<0.01
Queens (borough) Queens County	5	<0.01
Brooklyn (borough) Kings County	4	<0.01
Rochester (city) Monroe County	4	<0.01
Farmington (town) Ontario County	2	0.02
Manhattan (borough) New York County	2	<0.01
Jefferson (town) Schoharie County	1	0.07
Calcium (cdp) Jefferson County	1	0.03
Amenia (town) Dutchess County	1	0.02

Top 10 Places Sorted by Percent of Total Population
Based on all places, regardless of total population

Place	Population	%
Jefferson (town) Schoharie County	1	0.07
Calcium (cdp) Jefferson County	1	0.03
Farmington (town) Ontario County	2	0.02
Amenia (town) Dutchess County	1	0.02
Little Falls (city) Herkimer County	1	0.02
Wilson (town) Niagara County	1	0.02
Center Moriches (cdp) Suffolk County	1	0.01
Hastings (town) Oswego County	1	0.01
Kings Park (cdp) Suffolk County	1	0.01
Lynbrook (village) Nassau County	1	0.01

Top 10 Places Sorted by Percent of Total Population
Based on places with total population of 50,000 or more

Place	Population	%
New York (city)	17	<0.01
Bronx (borough) Bronx County	5	<0.01
Queens (borough) Queens County	5	<0.01
Brooklyn (borough) Kings County	4	<0.01
Rochester (city) Monroe County	4	<0.01
Manhattan (borough) New York County	2	<0.01
Brookhaven (town) Suffolk County	1	<0.01
Hempstead (town) Nassau County	1	<0.01
Smithtown (town) Suffolk County	1	<0.01
Staten Island (borough) Richmond County	1	<0.01

American Indian: Yakama

Top 10 Places Sorted by Population
Based on all places, regardless of total population

Place	Population	%
New York (city)	8	<0.01
Bronx (borough) Bronx County	3	<0.01
Brooklyn (borough) Kings County	3	<0.01
Poughkeepsie (city) Dutchess County	2	0.01
Manhattan (borough) New York County	2	<0.01
Austerlitz (town) Columbia County	1	0.06
Coxsackie (village) Greene County	1	0.04
Gordon Heights (cdp) Suffolk County	1	0.02
Coxsackie (town) Greene County	1	0.01
Oswego (city) Oswego County	1	0.01

Top 10 Places Sorted by Percent of Total Population
Based on all places, regardless of total population

Place	Population	%
Austerlitz (town) Columbia County	1	0.06
Coxsackie (village) Greene County	1	0.04
Gordon Heights (cdp) Suffolk County	1	0.02
Poughkeepsie (city) Dutchess County	2	0.01
Coxsackie (town) Greene County	1	0.01
Oswego (city) Oswego County	1	0.01
New York (city)	8	<0.01
Bronx (borough) Bronx County	3	<0.01
Brooklyn (borough) Kings County	3	<0.01
Manhattan (borough) New York County	2	<0.01

Top 10 Places Sorted by Percent of Total Population
Based on places with total population of 50,000 or more

Place	Population	%
New York (city)	8	<0.01
Bronx (borough) Bronx County	3	<0.01
Brooklyn (borough) Kings County	3	<0.01
Manhattan (borough) New York County	2	<0.01
Albany (city) Albany County	1	<0.01
Brookhaven (town) Suffolk County	1	<0.01
Niagara Falls (city) Niagara County	1	<0.01
Ramapo (town) Rockland County	1	<0.01
Amherst (town) Erie County	0	0.00
Babylon (town) Suffolk County	0	0.00

American Indian: Yaqui

Top 10 Places Sorted by Population
Based on all places, regardless of total population

Place	Population	%
New York (city)	54	<0.01
Manhattan (borough) New York County	22	<0.01
Brooklyn (borough) Kings County	19	<0.01
Queens (borough) Queens County	7	<0.01
Groton (village) Tompkins County	5	0.21
Pembroke (town) Genesee County	5	0.12
Groton (town) Tompkins County	5	0.08
Kirkland (town) Oneida County	5	0.05
Bronx (borough) Bronx County	5	<0.01
Brookhaven (town) Suffolk County	5	<0.01

Top 10 Places Sorted by Percent of Total Population
Based on all places, regardless of total population

Place	Population	%
Groton (village) Tompkins County	5	0.21
Lake Luzerne (cdp) Warren County	2	0.16
Rushville (village) Yates County	1	0.15
Pembroke (town) Genesee County	5	0.12
Schuyler (town) Herkimer County	4	0.12
Chateaugay (village) Franklin County	1	0.12
Allegany Reservation Cattaraugus County	1	0.10
Groton (town) Tompkins County	5	0.08
Lake Luzerne (town) Warren County	2	0.06
Kortright (town) Delaware County	1	0.06

Top 10 Places Sorted by Percent of Total Population
Based on places with total population of 50,000 or more

Place	Population	%
New York (city)	54	<0.01
Manhattan (borough) New York County	22	<0.01
Brooklyn (borough) Kings County	19	<0.01
Queens (borough) Queens County	7	<0.01

Place	Population	%
Bronx (borough) Bronx County	5	<0.01
Brookhaven (town) Suffolk County	5	<0.01
Buffalo (city) Erie County	2	<0.01
Brentwood (cdp) Suffolk County	1	<0.01
Islip (town) Suffolk County	1	<0.01
Niagara Falls (city) Niagara County	1	<0.01

American Indian: Yuman

Top 10 Places Sorted by Population
Based on all places, regardless of total population

Place	Population	%
New York (city)	22	<0.01
Brooklyn (borough) Kings County	8	<0.01
Manhattan (borough) New York County	6	<0.01
Queens (borough) Queens County	5	<0.01
Deerpark (town) Orange County	4	0.05
De Witt (town) Onondaga County	4	0.02
Webster (village) Monroe County	2	0.04
Bronx (borough) Bronx County	2	<0.01
Webster (town) Monroe County	2	<0.01
Yonkers (city) Westchester County	2	<0.01

Top 10 Places Sorted by Percent of Total Population
Based on all places, regardless of total population

Place	Population	%
Deerpark (town) Orange County	4	0.05
Webster (village) Monroe County	2	0.04
Brewster (village) Putnam County	1	0.04
De Witt (town) Onondaga County	4	0.02
Lyncourt (cdp) Onondaga County	1	0.02
Eastchester (cdp) Westchester County	1	0.01
Granville (town) Washington County	1	0.01
Greece (cdp) Monroe County	1	0.01
Highlands (town) Orange County	1	0.01
Southeast (town) Putnam County	1	0.01

Top 10 Places Sorted by Percent of Total Population
Based on places with total population of 50,000 or more

Place	Population	%
New York (city)	22	<0.01
Brooklyn (borough) Kings County	8	<0.01
Manhattan (borough) New York County	6	<0.01
Queens (borough) Queens County	5	<0.01
Bronx (borough) Bronx County	2	<0.01
Yonkers (city) Westchester County	2	<0.01
Brookhaven (town) Suffolk County	1	<0.01
Buffalo (city) Erie County	1	<0.01
Greece (town) Monroe County	1	<0.01
Islip (town) Suffolk County	1	<0.01

Alaska Native: Yup'ik

Top 10 Places Sorted by Population
Based on all places, regardless of total population

Place	Population	%
New York (city)	10	<0.01
Bronx (borough) Bronx County	6	<0.01
Cazenovia (town) Madison County	3	0.04
Canton (town) St. Lawrence County	3	0.03
Fort Drum (cdp) Jefferson County	3	0.02
Le Ray (town) Jefferson County	3	0.01
Stephentown (town) Rensselaer County	2	0.07
Colden (town) Erie County	2	0.06
New Paltz (village) Ulster County	2	0.03
New Paltz (town) Ulster County	2	0.01

Top 10 Places Sorted by Percent of Total Population
Based on all places, regardless of total population

Place	Population	%
Forest Home (cdp) Tompkins County	1	0.17
Savona (village) Steuben County	1	0.12
Ripley (cdp) Chautauqua County	1	0.11
Rathbone (town) Steuben County	1	0.09
Stephentown (town) Rensselaer County	2	0.07
Colden (town) Erie County	2	0.06
Cazenovia (town) Madison County	3	0.04
Franklin (town) Delaware County	1	0.04
Green Island (town/village) Albany County	1	0.04
Orleans (town) Jefferson County	1	0.04

Top 10 Places Sorted by Percent of Total Population
Based on places with total population of 50,000 or more

Place	Population	%
New York (city)	10	<0.01
Bronx (borough) Bronx County	6	<0.01
Manhattan (borough) New York County	2	<0.01
Albany (city) Albany County	1	<0.01
Amherst (town) Erie County	1	<0.01
Brooklyn (borough) Kings County	1	<0.01
Queens (borough) Queens County	1	<0.01
Syracuse (city) Onondaga County	1	<0.01
Babylon (town) Suffolk County	0	0.00
Brentwood (cdp) Suffolk County	0	0.00

Asian

Top 10 Places Sorted by Population
Based on all places, regardless of total population

Place	Population	%
New York (city)	1,134,919	13.88
Queens (borough) Queens County	552,867	24.78
Brooklyn (borough) Kings County	284,489	11.36
Manhattan (borough) New York County	199,722	12.59
Bronx (borough) Bronx County	59,085	4.27
Hempstead (town) Nassau County	45,112	5.94
Staten Island (borough) Richmond County	38,756	8.27
North Hempstead (town) Nassau County	36,973	16.34
Oyster Bay (town) Nassau County	29,203	9.96
Brookhaven (town) Suffolk County	21,849	4.50

Top 10 Places Sorted by Percent of Total Population
Based on all places, regardless of total population

Place	Population	%
Herricks (cdp) Nassau County	1,943	45.24
Manhasset Hills (cdp) Nassau County	1,483	41.29
Searingtown (cdp) Nassau County	2,008	40.85
Forest Home (cdp) Tompkins County	210	36.71
Merritt Park (cdp) Dutchess County	442	35.19
Garden City Park (cdp) Nassau County	2,698	34.56
University Gardens (cdp) Nassau County	1,316	31.14
North New Hyde Park (cdp) Nassau County	4,585	30.77
Bellerose Terrace (cdp) Nassau County	663	30.16
Thomaston (village) Nassau County	783	29.92

Top 10 Places Sorted by Percent of Total Population
Based on places with total population of 50,000 or more

Place	Population	%
Queens (borough) Queens County	552,867	24.78
North Hempstead (town) Nassau County	36,973	16.34
New York (city)	1,134,919	13.88
Manhattan (borough) New York County	199,722	12.59
Greenburgh (town) Westchester County	10,180	11.52
Clarkstown (town) Rockland County	9,614	11.42
Brooklyn (borough) Kings County	284,489	11.36
Oyster Bay (town) Nassau County	29,203	9.96
Amherst (town) Erie County	10,683	8.73
Staten Island (borough) Richmond County	38,756	8.27

Asian: Not Hispanic

Top 10 Places Sorted by Population
Based on all places, regardless of total population

Place	Population	%
New York (city)	1,110,964	13.59
Queens (borough) Queens County	545,389	24.45
Brooklyn (borough) Kings County	279,499	11.16
Manhattan (borough) New York County	194,929	12.29
Bronx (borough) Bronx County	53,458	3.86
Hempstead (town) Nassau County	43,880	5.78
Staten Island (borough) Richmond County	37,689	8.04
North Hempstead (town) Nassau County	36,641	16.19
Oyster Bay (town) Nassau County	28,910	9.86
Brookhaven (town) Suffolk County	21,257	4.37

Top 10 Places Sorted by Percent of Total Population
Based on all places, regardless of total population

Place	Population	%
Herricks (cdp) Nassau County	1,931	44.96
Manhasset Hills (cdp) Nassau County	1,476	41.09
Searingtown (cdp) Nassau County	2,000	40.69

Place	Population	%
Forest Home (cdp) Tompkins County	210	36.71
Merritt Park (cdp) Dutchess County	442	35.19
Garden City Park (cdp) Nassau County	2,670	34.20
University Gardens (cdp) Nassau County	1,309	30.97
North New Hyde Park (cdp) Nassau County	4,558	30.59
Bellerose Terrace (cdp) Nassau County	652	29.66
Thomaston (village) Nassau County	772	29.50

Top 10 Places Sorted by Percent of Total Population
Based on places with total population of 50,000 or more

Place	Population	%
Queens (borough) Queens County	545,389	24.45
North Hempstead (town) Nassau County	36,641	16.19
New York (city)	1,110,964	13.59
Manhattan (borough) New York County	194,929	12.29
Greenburgh (town) Westchester County	10,025	11.34
Clarkstown (town) Rockland County	9,462	11.24
Brooklyn (borough) Kings County	279,499	11.16
Oyster Bay (town) Nassau County	28,910	9.86
Amherst (town) Erie County	10,590	8.65
Staten Island (borough) Richmond County	37,689	8.04

Asian: Hispanic

Top 10 Places Sorted by Population
Based on all places, regardless of total population

Place	Population	%
New York (city)	23,955	0.29
Queens (borough) Queens County	7,478	0.34
Bronx (borough) Bronx County	5,627	0.41
Brooklyn (borough) Kings County	4,990	0.20
Manhattan (borough) New York County	4,793	0.30
Hempstead (town) Nassau County	1,232	0.16
Staten Island (borough) Richmond County	1,067	0.23
Brookhaven (town) Suffolk County	592	0.12
Islip (town) Suffolk County	553	0.16
Yonkers (city) Westchester County	517	0.26

Top 10 Places Sorted by Percent of Total Population
Based on all places, regardless of total population

Place	Population	%
Salamanca (town) Cattaraugus County	4	0.83
Nelsonville (village) Putnam County	5	0.80
North Lynbrook (cdp) Nassau County	6	0.76
Grove (town) Allegany County	4	0.73
La Fargeville (cdp) Jefferson County	4	0.66
Tonawanda Reservation Genesee County	3	0.62
Rensselaer Falls (village) St. Lawrence County	2	0.60
Tannersville (village) Greene County	3	0.56
Waterford (village) Saratoga County	11	0.55
Chautauqua (cdp) Chautauqua County	1	0.52

Top 10 Places Sorted by Percent of Total Population
Based on places with total population of 50,000 or more

Place	Population	%
Bronx (borough) Bronx County	5,627	0.41
Queens (borough) Queens County	7,478	0.34
Brentwood (cdp) Suffolk County	195	0.32
Manhattan (borough) New York County	4,793	0.30
New York (city)	23,955	0.29
Yonkers (city) Westchester County	517	0.26
Hempstead (village) Nassau County	135	0.25
Staten Island (borough) Richmond County	1,067	0.23
New Rochelle (city) Westchester County	167	0.22
White Plains (city) Westchester County	121	0.21

Asian: Bangladeshi

Top 10 Places Sorted by Population
Based on all places, regardless of total population

Place	Population	%
New York (city)	61,788	0.76
Queens (borough) Queens County	38,341	1.72
Brooklyn (borough) Kings County	12,408	0.50
Bronx (borough) Bronx County	8,623	0.62
Manhattan (borough) New York County	2,029	0.13
Brookhaven (town) Suffolk County	621	0.13
Hempstead (town) Nassau County	582	0.08
North Hempstead (town) Nassau County	441	0.19
Staten Island (borough) Richmond County	387	0.08
Oyster Bay (town) Nassau County	365	0.12

Top 10 Places Sorted by Percent of Total Population
Based on all places, regardless of total population

Place	Population	%
Hudson (city) Columbia County	271	4.04
Bellerose Terrace (cdp) Nassau County	44	2.00
Queens (borough) Queens County	38,341	1.72
Harriman (village) Orange County	40	1.65
Clintondale (cdp) Ulster County	22	1.52
Manhasset Hills (cdp) Nassau County	33	0.92
Greenvale (cdp) Nassau County	9	0.82
Deer Park (cdp) Suffolk County	224	0.81
Herricks (cdp) Nassau County	35	0.81
New York (city)	61,788	0.76

Top 10 Places Sorted by Percent of Total Population
Based on places with total population of 50,000 or more

Place	Population	%
Queens (borough) Queens County	38,341	1.72
New York (city)	61,788	0.76
Bronx (borough) Bronx County	8,623	0.62
Brooklyn (borough) Kings County	12,408	0.50
North Hempstead (town) Nassau County	441	0.19
Albany (city) Albany County	171	0.17
Babylon (town) Suffolk County	341	0.16
Manhattan (borough) New York County	2,029	0.13
Brookhaven (town) Suffolk County	621	0.13
Levittown (cdp) Nassau County	70	0.13

Asian: Bhutanese

Top 10 Places Sorted by Population
Based on all places, regardless of total population

Place	Population	%
Syracuse (city) Onondaga County	516	0.36
Rochester (city) Monroe County	411	0.20
New York (city)	388	<0.01
Buffalo (city) Erie County	370	0.14
Queens (borough) Queens County	250	0.01
Bronx (borough) Bronx County	104	0.01
Albany (city) Albany County	62	0.06
Utica (city) Oneida County	36	0.06
Manhattan (borough) New York County	26	<0.01
Greenville (cdp) Westchester County	8	0.11

Top 10 Places Sorted by Percent of Total Population
Based on all places, regardless of total population

Place	Population	%
Syracuse (city) Onondaga County	516	0.36
Rochester (city) Monroe County	411	0.20
Meredith (town) Delaware County	3	0.20
Buffalo (city) Erie County	370	0.14
Greenville (cdp) Westchester County	8	0.11
Albany (city) Albany County	62	0.06
Utica (city) Oneida County	36	0.06
Kerhonkson (cdp) Ulster County	1	0.06
Sullivan (town) Madison County	7	0.05
Harrison (town/village) Westchester County	8	0.03

Top 10 Places Sorted by Percent of Total Population
Based on places with total population of 50,000 or more

Place	Population	%
Syracuse (city) Onondaga County	516	0.36
Rochester (city) Monroe County	411	0.20
Buffalo (city) Erie County	370	0.14
Albany (city) Albany County	62	0.06
Utica (city) Oneida County	36	0.06
Queens (borough) Queens County	250	0.01
Bronx (borough) Bronx County	104	0.01
Greenburgh (town) Westchester County	8	0.01
New York (city)	388	<0.01
Manhattan (borough) New York County	26	<0.01

Asian: Burmese

Top 10 Places Sorted by Population
Based on all places, regardless of total population

Place	Population	%
New York (city)	4,132	0.05
Buffalo (city) Erie County	2,361	0.90
Queens (borough) Queens County	2,344	0.11
Utica (city) Oneida County	2,317	3.72
Brooklyn (borough) Kings County	1,260	0.05
Syracuse (city) Onondaga County	1,218	0.84
Rochester (city) Monroe County	565	0.27
Albany (city) Albany County	322	0.33
Manhattan (borough) New York County	317	0.02
Rensselaer (city) Rensselaer County	316	3.36

Top 10 Places Sorted by Percent of Total Population
Based on all places, regardless of total population

Place	Population	%
Utica (city) Oneida County	2,317	3.72
Rensselaer (city) Rensselaer County	316	3.36
East Ithaca (cdp) Tompkins County	46	2.06
Buffalo (city) Erie County	2,361	0.90
Syracuse (city) Onondaga County	1,218	0.84
Lakeville (cdp) Livingston County	4	0.53
Union Springs (village) Cayuga County	6	0.50
Northeast Ithaca (cdp) Tompkins County	12	0.45
Green Island (town/village) Albany County	11	0.42
Albany (city) Albany County	322	0.33

Top 10 Places Sorted by Percent of Total Population
Based on places with total population of 50,000 or more

Place	Population	%
Utica (city) Oneida County	2,317	3.72
Buffalo (city) Erie County	2,361	0.90
Syracuse (city) Onondaga County	1,218	0.84
Albany (city) Albany County	322	0.33
Rochester (city) Monroe County	565	0.27
Queens (borough) Queens County	2,344	0.11
Troy (city) Rensselaer County	28	0.06
New York (city)	4,132	0.05
Brooklyn (borough) Kings County	1,260	0.05
North Hempstead (town) Nassau County	88	0.04

Asian: Cambodian

Top 10 Places Sorted by Population
Based on all places, regardless of total population

Place	Population	%
New York (city)	2,591	0.03
Bronx (borough) Bronx County	1,188	0.09
Brooklyn (borough) Kings County	751	0.03
Utica (city) Oneida County	480	0.77
Rochester (city) Monroe County	381	0.18
Queens (borough) Queens County	303	0.01
Manhattan (borough) New York County	220	0.01
Syracuse (city) Onondaga County	149	0.10
Staten Island (borough) Richmond County	129	0.03
Ithaca (city) Tompkins County	68	0.23

Top 10 Places Sorted by Percent of Total Population
Based on all places, regardless of total population

Place	Population	%
Fowlerville (cdp) Livingston County	2	0.88
Utica (city) Oneida County	480	0.77
East Ithaca (cdp) Tompkins County	13	0.58
York Hamlet (cdp) Livingston County	3	0.55
East Nassau (town) Rensselaer County	3	0.51
Bloomingburg (village) Sullivan County	2	0.48
Lansing (village) Tompkins County	16	0.45
Andes (cdp) Delaware County	1	0.40
Parc (cdp) Clinton County	1	0.39
Argyle (town) Washington County	12	0.32

Top 10 Places Sorted by Percent of Total Population
Based on places with total population of 50,000 or more

Place	Population	%
Utica (city) Oneida County	480	0.77
Rochester (city) Monroe County	381	0.18
Syracuse (city) Onondaga County	149	0.10
Bronx (borough) Bronx County	1,188	0.09
Clarkstown (town) Rockland County	68	0.08
Irondequoit (cdp/town) Monroe County	31	0.06
Greece (town) Monroe County	47	0.05
Clay (town) Onondaga County	29	0.05
Ramapo (town) Rockland County	52	0.04
New York (city)	2,591	0.03

Asian: Chinese, except Taiwanese

Top 10 Places Sorted by Population
Based on all places, regardless of total population

Place	Population	%
New York (city)	500,434	6.12
Queens (borough) Queens County	200,714	9.00
Brooklyn (borough) Kings County	178,214	7.12
Manhattan (borough) New York County	99,287	6.26
Staten Island (borough) Richmond County	14,107	3.01
North Hempstead (town) Nassau County	10,292	4.55
Bronx (borough) Bronx County	8,112	0.59
Hempstead (town) Nassau County	7,849	1.03
Oyster Bay (town) Nassau County	7,054	2.41
Brookhaven (town) Suffolk County	6,107	1.26

Top 10 Places Sorted by Percent of Total Population
Based on all places, regardless of total population

Place	Population	%
University Gardens (cdp) Nassau County	711	16.82
Thomaston (village) Nassau County	398	15.21
Lake Success (village) Nassau County	382	13.02
Russell Gardens (village) Nassau County	119	12.59
Forest Home (cdp) Tompkins County	68	11.89
Manhasset Hills (cdp) Nassau County	417	11.61
Binghamton University (cdp) Broome County	694	11.24
Lansing (village) Tompkins County	375	10.63
North Hills (village) Nassau County	516	10.17
University at Buffalo (cdp) Erie County	589	9.71

Top 10 Places Sorted by Percent of Total Population
Based on places with total population of 50,000 or more

Place	Population	%
Queens (borough) Queens County	200,714	9.00
Brooklyn (borough) Kings County	178,214	7.12
Manhattan (borough) New York County	99,287	6.26
New York (city)	500,434	6.12
North Hempstead (town) Nassau County	10,292	4.55
Staten Island (borough) Richmond County	14,107	3.01
Amherst (town) Erie County	3,146	2.57
Greenburgh (town) Westchester County	2,225	2.52
Oyster Bay (town) Nassau County	7,054	2.41
White Plains (city) Westchester County	934	1.64

Asian: Filipino

Top 10 Places Sorted by Population
Based on all places, regardless of total population

Place	Population	%
New York (city)	78,030	0.95
Queens (borough) Queens County	41,773	1.87
Manhattan (borough) New York County	13,388	0.84
Brooklyn (borough) Kings County	10,208	0.41
Hempstead (town) Nassau County	7,212	0.95
Bronx (borough) Bronx County	6,456	0.47
Staten Island (borough) Richmond County	6,205	1.32
Yonkers (city) Westchester County	2,819	1.44
Brookhaven (town) Suffolk County	2,705	0.56
Clarkstown (town) Rockland County	2,320	2.76

Top 10 Places Sorted by Percent of Total Population
Based on all places, regardless of total population

Place	Population	%
Hillcrest (cdp) Rockland County	441	5.83
Bellerose Terrace (cdp) Nassau County	119	5.41
Valley Cottage (cdp) Rockland County	485	5.33
Orangeburg (cdp) Rockland County	237	5.19
Sparkill (cdp) Rockland County	56	3.58
Nanuet (cdp) Rockland County	574	3.21
Merritt Park (cdp) Dutchess County	37	2.95
South Valley Stream (cdp) Nassau County	174	2.92
New Hempstead (village) Rockland County	150	2.92
Clarkstown (town) Rockland County	2,320	2.76

Top 10 Places Sorted by Percent of Total Population
Based on places with total population of 50,000 or more

Place	Population	%
Clarkstown (town) Rockland County	2,320	2.76
Queens (borough) Queens County	41,773	1.87
Yonkers (city) Westchester County	2,819	1.44
Staten Island (borough) Richmond County	6,205	1.32

Ramapo (town) Rockland County	1,472	1.16
Greenburgh (town) Westchester County	959	1.08
Levittown (cdp) Nassau County	525	1.01
New York (city)	78,030	0.95
Hempstead (town) Nassau County	7,212	0.95
Manhattan (borough) New York County	13,388	0.84

Asian: Hmong

Top 10 Places Sorted by Population
Based on all places, regardless of total population

Place	Population	%
New York (city)	83	<0.01
Clay (town) Onondaga County	75	0.13
Syracuse (city) Onondaga County	34	0.02
Orangetown (town) Rockland County	32	0.07
South Nyack (village) Rockland County	31	0.88
Queens (borough) Queens County	30	<0.01
Brooklyn (borough) Kings County	22	<0.01
Manhattan (borough) New York County	20	<0.01
Cicero (town) Onondaga County	12	0.04
Salina (town) Onondaga County	11	0.03

Top 10 Places Sorted by Percent of Total Population
Based on all places, regardless of total population

Place	Population	%
South Nyack (village) Rockland County	31	0.88
Newfane (cdp) Niagara County	10	0.26
Clay (town) Onondaga County	75	0.13
Newfane (town) Niagara County	10	0.10
Orangetown (town) Rockland County	32	0.07
Spafford (town) Onondaga County	1	0.06
Nelson (town) Madison County	1	0.05
Cicero (town) Onondaga County	12	0.04
Galeville (cdp) Onondaga County	2	0.04
Johnsburg (town) Warren County	1	0.04

Top 10 Places Sorted by Percent of Total Population
Based on places with total population of 50,000 or more

Place	Population	%
Clay (town) Onondaga County	75	0.13
Syracuse (city) Onondaga County	34	0.02
New York (city)	83	<0.01
Queens (borough) Queens County	30	<0.01
Brooklyn (borough) Kings County	22	<0.01
Manhattan (borough) New York County	20	<0.01
Staten Island (borough) Richmond County	8	<0.01
Buffalo (city) Erie County	6	<0.01
Brookhaven (town) Suffolk County	4	<0.01
Bronx (borough) Bronx County	3	<0.01

Asian: Indian

Top 10 Places Sorted by Population
Based on all places, regardless of total population

Place	Population	%
New York (city)	232,696	2.85
Queens (borough) Queens County	141,147	6.33
Brooklyn (borough) Kings County	33,490	1.34
Manhattan (borough) New York County	29,979	1.89
Bronx (borough) Bronx County	20,357	1.47
Hempstead (town) Nassau County	17,802	2.34
North Hempstead (town) Nassau County	13,427	5.93
Oyster Bay (town) Nassau County	11,289	3.85
Staten Island (borough) Richmond County	7,723	1.65
Yonkers (city) Westchester County	5,818	2.97

Top 10 Places Sorted by Percent of Total Population
Based on all places, regardless of total population

Place	Population	%
Herricks (cdp) Nassau County	1,036	24.12
Manhasset Hills (cdp) Nassau County	690	19.21
Garden City Park (cdp) Nassau County	1,487	19.05
Searingtown (cdp) Nassau County	935	19.02
New Hyde Park (village) Nassau County	1,682	17.32
North New Hyde Park (cdp) Nassau County	2,547	17.10
Merritt Park (cdp) Dutchess County	208	16.56
Muttontown (village) Nassau County	569	16.27
Albertson (cdp) Nassau County	690	13.32
Bellerose Terrace (cdp) Nassau County	277	12.60

Top 10 Places Sorted by Percent of Total Population
Based on places with total population of 50,000 or more

Place	Population	%
Queens (borough) Queens County	141,147	6.33
North Hempstead (town) Nassau County	13,427	5.93
Clarkstown (town) Rockland County	3,874	4.60
Greenburgh (town) Westchester County	3,518	3.98
Oyster Bay (town) Nassau County	11,289	3.85
Schenectady (city) Schenectady County	2,050	3.10
Yonkers (city) Westchester County	5,818	2.97
New York (city)	232,696	2.85
Amherst (town) Erie County	3,491	2.85
Colonie (town) Albany County	2,099	2.57

Asian: Indonesian

Top 10 Places Sorted by Population
Based on all places, regardless of total population

Place	Population	%
New York (city)	4,791	0.06
Queens (borough) Queens County	3,386	0.15
Manhattan (borough) New York County	693	0.04
Brooklyn (borough) Kings County	564	0.02
Bronx (borough) Bronx County	96	0.01
Hempstead (town) Nassau County	66	0.01
Brookhaven (town) Suffolk County	63	0.01
North Hempstead (town) Nassau County	53	0.02
Staten Island (borough) Richmond County	52	0.01
Amherst (town) Erie County	42	0.03

Top 10 Places Sorted by Percent of Total Population
Based on all places, regardless of total population

Place	Population	%
Forest Home (cdp) Tompkins County	11	1.92
Grand View-on-Hudson (village) Rockland County	2	0.70
Colton (cdp) St. Lawrence County	2	0.58
Lyndon (town) Cattaraugus County	4	0.57
Lansing (village) Tompkins County	11	0.31
Adams Center (cdp) Jefferson County	4	0.26
Kensington (village) Nassau County	3	0.26
South Hempstead (cdp) Nassau County	7	0.22
Port Gibson (cdp) Ontario County	1	0.22
Hillburn (village) Rockland County	2	0.21

Top 10 Places Sorted by Percent of Total Population
Based on places with total population of 50,000 or more

Place	Population	%
Queens (borough) Queens County	3,386	0.15
New York (city)	4,791	0.06
Manhattan (borough) New York County	693	0.04
Amherst (town) Erie County	42	0.03
Greenburgh (town) Westchester County	24	0.03
Brooklyn (borough) Kings County	564	0.02
North Hempstead (town) Nassau County	53	0.02
Syracuse (city) Onondaga County	26	0.02
Ramapo (town) Rockland County	23	0.02
Smithtown (town) Suffolk County	18	0.02

Asian: Japanese

Top 10 Places Sorted by Population
Based on all places, regardless of total population

Place	Population	%
New York (city)	31,742	0.39
Manhattan (borough) New York County	16,600	1.05
Queens (borough) Queens County	7,790	0.35
Brooklyn (borough) Kings County	5,917	0.24
North Hempstead (town) Nassau County	1,266	0.56
Harrison (town/village) Westchester County	1,239	4.51
Greenburgh (town) Westchester County	1,230	1.39
Bronx (borough) Bronx County	1,027	0.07
Eastchester (town) Westchester County	903	2.79
Hempstead (town) Nassau County	657	0.09

Top 10 Places Sorted by Percent of Total Population
Based on all places, regardless of total population

Place	Population	%
Manorhaven (village) Nassau County	368	5.61
Hartsdale (cdp) Westchester County	246	4.65
Harrison (town/village) Westchester County	1,239	4.51

Place	Population	%
Tuckahoe (village) Westchester County	210	3.24
Greenville (cdp) Westchester County	223	3.13
Eastchester (cdp) Westchester County	610	3.12
Rye (city) Westchester County	482	3.07
Eastchester (town) Westchester County	903	2.79
Scarsdale (town/village) Westchester County	428	2.49
Fishkill (village) Dutchess County	52	2.40

Top 10 Places Sorted by Percent of Total Population
Based on places with total population of 50,000 or more

Place	Population	%
Greenburgh (town) Westchester County	1,230	1.39
Manhattan (borough) New York County	16,600	1.05
White Plains (city) Westchester County	441	0.78
North Hempstead (town) Nassau County	1,266	0.56
New York (city)	31,742	0.39
Queens (borough) Queens County	7,790	0.35
Brooklyn (borough) Kings County	5,917	0.24
Amherst (town) Erie County	294	0.24
New Rochelle (city) Westchester County	158	0.21
Albany (city) Albany County	200	0.20

Asian: Korean

Top 10 Places Sorted by Population
Based on all places, regardless of total population

Place	Population	%
New York (city)	102,820	1.26
Queens (borough) Queens County	66,124	2.96
Manhattan (borough) New York County	21,996	1.39
Brooklyn (borough) Kings County	8,201	0.33
North Hempstead (town) Nassau County	6,015	2.66
Oyster Bay (town) Nassau County	4,977	1.70
Staten Island (borough) Richmond County	3,398	0.72
Bronx (borough) Bronx County	3,101	0.22
Hempstead (town) Nassau County	3,074	0.40
Huntington (town) Suffolk County	2,122	1.04

Top 10 Places Sorted by Percent of Total Population
Based on all places, regardless of total population

Place	Population	%
Lake Success (village) Nassau County	290	9.88
Forest Home (cdp) Tompkins County	54	9.44
University Gardens (cdp) Nassau County	383	9.06
Fishkill (village) Dutchess County	179	8.25
Thomaston (village) Nassau County	209	7.99
Jericho (cdp) Nassau County	1,078	7.95
Searingtown (cdp) Nassau County	380	7.73
North Hills (village) Nassau County	383	7.55
Manorhaven (village) Nassau County	457	6.97
Lansing (village) Tompkins County	237	6.72

Top 10 Places Sorted by Percent of Total Population
Based on places with total population of 50,000 or more

Place	Population	%
Queens (borough) Queens County	66,124	2.96
North Hempstead (town) Nassau County	6,015	2.66
Oyster Bay (town) Nassau County	4,977	1.70
Greenburgh (town) Westchester County	1,452	1.64
Manhattan (borough) New York County	21,996	1.39
New York (city)	102,820	1.26
Amherst (town) Erie County	1,493	1.22
Clarkstown (town) Rockland County	1,026	1.22
Huntington (town) Suffolk County	2,122	1.04
Smithtown (town) Suffolk County	918	0.78

Asian: Laotian

Top 10 Places Sorted by Population
Based on all places, regardless of total population

Place	Population	%
Rochester (city) Monroe County	668	0.32
New York (city)	664	0.01
Union (town) Broome County	406	0.72
Buffalo (city) Erie County	288	0.11
Johnson City (village) Broome County	278	1.83
Henrietta (town) Monroe County	235	0.55
Binghamton (city) Broome County	211	0.45
Queens (borough) Queens County	210	0.01
Manhattan (borough) New York County	157	0.01
Bronx (borough) Bronx County	148	0.01

Top 10 Places Sorted by Percent of Total Population
Based on all places, regardless of total population

Place	Population	%
Fowlerville (cdp) Livingston County	5	2.20
Johnson City (village) Broome County	278	1.83
Union (town) Broome County	406	0.72
Interlaken (village) Seneca County	4	0.66
Henrietta (town) Monroe County	235	0.55
Smithfield (town) Madison County	7	0.54
Chautauqua (cdp) Chautauqua County	1	0.52
York (town) Livingston County	16	0.47
Binghamton (city) Broome County	211	0.45
Endicott (village) Broome County	54	0.40

Top 10 Places Sorted by Percent of Total Population
Based on places with total population of 50,000 or more

Place	Population	%
Union (town) Broome County	406	0.72
Rochester (city) Monroe County	668	0.32
Irondequoit (cdp/town) Monroe County	109	0.21
Greece (town) Monroe County	139	0.14
Utica (city) Oneida County	72	0.12
Buffalo (city) Erie County	288	0.11
Cheektowaga (cdp) Erie County	65	0.09
Clay (town) Onondaga County	52	0.09
Cheektowaga (town) Erie County	65	0.07
Syracuse (city) Onondaga County	89	0.06

Asian: Malaysian

Top 10 Places Sorted by Population
Based on all places, regardless of total population

Place	Population	%
New York (city)	3,220	0.04
Queens (borough) Queens County	1,620	0.07
Manhattan (borough) New York County	766	0.05
Brooklyn (borough) Kings County	708	0.03
Staten Island (borough) Richmond County	96	0.02
Henrietta (town) Monroe County	70	0.16
Amherst (town) Erie County	47	0.04
North Hempstead (town) Nassau County	35	0.02
Oyster Bay (town) Nassau County	30	0.01
Bronx (borough) Bronx County	30	<0.01

Top 10 Places Sorted by Percent of Total Population
Based on all places, regardless of total population

Place	Population	%
Forest Home (cdp) Tompkins County	5	0.87
Grand View-on-Hudson (village) Rockland County	1	0.35
Portage (town) Livingston County	3	0.34
University at Buffalo (cdp) Erie County	15	0.25
Brocton (village) Chautauqua County	3	0.20
Washington Mills (cdp) Oneida County	2	0.17
Henrietta (town) Monroe County	70	0.16
Breesport (cdp) Chemung County	1	0.16
New Berlin (town) Chenango County	4	0.15
Wainscott (cdp) Suffolk County	1	0.15

Top 10 Places Sorted by Percent of Total Population
Based on places with total population of 50,000 or more

Place	Population	%
Queens (borough) Queens County	1,620	0.07
Manhattan (borough) New York County	766	0.05
New York (city)	3,220	0.04
Amherst (town) Erie County	47	0.04
Brooklyn (borough) Kings County	708	0.03
Troy (city) Rensselaer County	14	0.03
Staten Island (borough) Richmond County	96	0.02
North Hempstead (town) Nassau County	35	0.02
Cheektowaga (cdp) Erie County	12	0.02
White Plains (city) Westchester County	11	0.02

Asian: Nepalese

Top 10 Places Sorted by Population
Based on all places, regardless of total population

Place	Population	%
New York (city)	6,187	0.08
Queens (borough) Queens County	5,319	0.24
Brooklyn (borough) Kings County	393	0.02

Place	Population	%
Manhattan (borough) New York County	281	0.02
Syracuse (city) Onondaga County	262	0.18
Rochester (city) Monroe County	165	0.08
Buffalo (city) Erie County	160	0.06
Bronx (borough) Bronx County	159	0.01
Albany (city) Albany County	55	0.06
Greenburgh (town) Westchester County	55	0.06

Top 10 Places Sorted by Percent of Total Population
Based on all places, regardless of total population

Place	Population	%
Windham (cdp) Greene County	6	1.63
Forest Home (cdp) Tompkins County	3	0.52
Merritt Park (cdp) Dutchess County	6	0.48
Windham (town) Greene County	6	0.35
Nelliston (village) Montgomery County	2	0.34
Argyle (village) Washington County	1	0.33
Northeast Ithaca (cdp) Tompkins County	8	0.30
Brewster (village) Putnam County	7	0.29
Elmsford (village) Westchester County	12	0.26
Queens (borough) Queens County	5,319	0.24

Top 10 Places Sorted by Percent of Total Population
Based on places with total population of 50,000 or more

Place	Population	%
Queens (borough) Queens County	5,319	0.24
Syracuse (city) Onondaga County	262	0.18
New York (city)	6,187	0.08
Rochester (city) Monroe County	165	0.08
Buffalo (city) Erie County	160	0.06
Albany (city) Albany County	55	0.06
Greenburgh (town) Westchester County	55	0.06
Brooklyn (borough) Kings County	393	0.02
Manhattan (borough) New York County	281	0.02
Oyster Bay (town) Nassau County	49	0.02

Asian: Pakistani

Top 10 Places Sorted by Population
Based on all places, regardless of total population

Place	Population	%
New York (city)	46,369	0.57
Brooklyn (borough) Kings County	19,840	0.79
Queens (borough) Queens County	18,084	0.81
Hempstead (town) Nassau County	4,976	0.65
Manhattan (borough) New York County	2,940	0.19
Staten Island (borough) Richmond County	2,777	0.59
Bronx (borough) Bronx County	2,728	0.20
Brookhaven (town) Suffolk County	2,081	0.43
Islip (town) Suffolk County	1,520	0.45
Oyster Bay (town) Nassau County	1,330	0.45

Top 10 Places Sorted by Percent of Total Population
Based on all places, regardless of total population

Place	Population	%
Bellerose Terrace (cdp) Nassau County	103	4.69
South Valley Stream (cdp) Nassau County	249	4.18
North Valley Stream (cdp) Nassau County	425	2.56
Herricks (cdp) Nassau County	85	1.98
Elmont (cdp) Nassau County	650	1.96
Valley Stream (village) Nassau County	733	1.95
East Meadow (cdp) Nassau County	708	1.86
Garden City Park (cdp) Nassau County	124	1.59
Muttontown (village) Nassau County	50	1.43
North Bellmore (cdp) Nassau County	278	1.39

Top 10 Places Sorted by Percent of Total Population
Based on places with total population of 50,000 or more

Place	Population	%
Colonie (town) Albany County	736	0.90
Queens (borough) Queens County	18,084	0.81
Brooklyn (borough) Kings County	19,840	0.79
Hempstead (town) Nassau County	4,976	0.65
Huntington (town) Suffolk County	1,264	0.62
Staten Island (borough) Richmond County	2,777	0.59
New York (city)	46,369	0.57
Albany (city) Albany County	483	0.49
Amherst (town) Erie County	592	0.48
Levittown (cdp) Nassau County	239	0.46

Asian: Sri Lankan

Top 10 Places Sorted by Population
Based on all places, regardless of total population

Place	Population	%
New York (city)	4,369	0.05
Staten Island (borough) Richmond County	1,766	0.38
Queens (borough) Queens County	1,536	0.07
Manhattan (borough) New York County	563	0.04
Brooklyn (borough) Kings County	270	0.01
Bronx (borough) Bronx County	234	0.02
Hempstead (town) Nassau County	201	0.03
Amherst (town) Erie County	130	0.11
Brookhaven (town) Suffolk County	100	0.02
New Rochelle (city) Westchester County	83	0.11

Top 10 Places Sorted by Percent of Total Population
Based on all places, regardless of total population

Place	Population	%
Poquott (village) Suffolk County	6	0.63
Bellerose Terrace (cdp) Nassau County	10	0.45
Watchtower (cdp) Ulster County	10	0.42
Fishers Island (cdp) Suffolk County	1	0.42
Staten Island (borough) Richmond County	1,766	0.38
Forestburgh (town) Sullivan County	3	0.37
South Floral Park (village) Nassau County	6	0.34
Bedford (cdp) Westchester County	6	0.33
Harbor Isle (cdp) Nassau County	4	0.31
Garden City Park (cdp) Nassau County	22	0.28

Top 10 Places Sorted by Percent of Total Population
Based on places with total population of 50,000 or more

Place	Population	%
Staten Island (borough) Richmond County	1,766	0.38
Amherst (town) Erie County	130	0.11
New Rochelle (city) Westchester County	83	0.11
Queens (borough) Queens County	1,536	0.07
Clarkstown (town) Rockland County	55	0.07
New York (city)	4,369	0.05
Manhattan (borough) New York County	563	0.04
Colonie (town) Albany County	30	0.04
Hempstead (town) Nassau County	201	0.03
North Hempstead (town) Nassau County	59	0.03

Asian: Taiwanese

Top 10 Places Sorted by Population
Based on all places, regardless of total population

Place	Population	%
New York (city)	13,682	0.17
Queens (borough) Queens County	8,962	0.40
Manhattan (borough) New York County	3,318	0.21
Brooklyn (borough) Kings County	1,075	0.04
North Hempstead (town) Nassau County	809	0.36
Hempstead (town) Nassau County	438	0.06
Oyster Bay (town) Nassau County	401	0.14
Ithaca (city) Tompkins County	214	0.71
Brookhaven (town) Suffolk County	213	0.04
Amherst (town) Erie County	202	0.17

Top 10 Places Sorted by Percent of Total Population
Based on all places, regardless of total population

Place	Population	%
Russell Gardens (village) Nassau County	23	2.43
Forest Home (cdp) Tompkins County	13	2.27
Thomaston (village) Nassau County	47	1.80
University Gardens (cdp) Nassau County	63	1.49
East Ithaca (cdp) Tompkins County	33	1.48
North Hills (village) Nassau County	56	1.10
Lansing (village) Tompkins County	36	1.02
Harbor Hills (cdp) Nassau County	5	0.87
Lake Success (village) Nassau County	25	0.85
Saddle Rock (village) Nassau County	7	0.84

Top 10 Places Sorted by Percent of Total Population
Based on places with total population of 50,000 or more

Place	Population	%
Queens (borough) Queens County	8,962	0.40
North Hempstead (town) Nassau County	809	0.36
Manhattan (borough) New York County	3,318	0.21
New York (city)	13,682	0.17

Place	Population	%
Amherst (town) Erie County	202	0.17
Greenburgh (town) Westchester County	142	0.16
Oyster Bay (town) Nassau County	401	0.14
Huntington (town) Suffolk County	157	0.08
Smithtown (town) Suffolk County	90	0.08
White Plains (city) Westchester County	44	0.08

Asian: Thai

Top 10 Places Sorted by Population
Based on all places, regardless of total population

Place	Population	%
New York (city)	7,244	0.09
Queens (borough) Queens County	4,124	0.18
Manhattan (borough) New York County	1,657	0.10
Brooklyn (borough) Kings County	883	0.04
Bronx (borough) Bronx County	414	0.03
Hempstead (town) Nassau County	278	0.04
Yonkers (city) Westchester County	268	0.14
Brookhaven (town) Suffolk County	211	0.04
Staten Island (borough) Richmond County	166	0.04
North Hempstead (town) Nassau County	126	0.06

Top 10 Places Sorted by Percent of Total Population
Based on all places, regardless of total population

Place	Population	%
Forest Home (cdp) Tompkins County	8	1.40
Watchtower (cdp) Ulster County	20	0.84
Greenvale (cdp) Nassau County	9	0.82
Lyon Mountain (cdp) Clinton County	3	0.71
Tribes Hill (cdp) Montgomery County	7	0.70
Quiogue (cdp) Suffolk County	5	0.61
Cooperstown (village) Otsego County	11	0.59
West Nyack (cdp) Rockland County	18	0.52
Middlefield (town) Otsego County	11	0.52
Lansing (village) Tompkins County	16	0.45

Top 10 Places Sorted by Percent of Total Population
Based on places with total population of 50,000 or more

Place	Population	%
Queens (borough) Queens County	4,124	0.18
Yonkers (city) Westchester County	268	0.14
Clarkstown (town) Rockland County	121	0.14
Mount Vernon (city) Westchester County	73	0.11
Manhattan (borough) New York County	1,657	0.10
New York (city)	7,244	0.09
Greenburgh (town) Westchester County	77	0.09
Utica (city) Oneida County	50	0.08
Levittown (cdp) Nassau County	40	0.08
White Plains (city) Westchester County	42	0.07

Asian: Vietnamese

Top 10 Places Sorted by Population
Based on all places, regardless of total population

Place	Population	%
New York (city)	16,378	0.20
Brooklyn (borough) Kings County	5,041	0.20
Queens (borough) Queens County	4,322	0.19
Bronx (borough) Bronx County	3,526	0.25
Manhattan (borough) New York County	2,919	0.18
Syracuse (city) Onondaga County	1,554	1.07
Buffalo (city) Erie County	1,220	0.47
Rochester (city) Monroe County	1,050	0.50
Utica (city) Oneida County	1,022	1.64
Brookhaven (town) Suffolk County	620	0.13

Top 10 Places Sorted by Percent of Total Population
Based on all places, regardless of total population

Place	Population	%
Byersville (cdp) Livingston County	2	4.26
North Gates (cdp) Monroe County	183	1.92
Utica (city) Oneida County	1,022	1.64
Salt Point (cdp) Dutchess County	3	1.58
Gates (town) Monroe County	411	1.45
Gates (cdp) Monroe County	71	1.45
Websters Crossing (cdp) Livingston County	1	1.45
Galeville (cdp) Onondaga County	62	1.34
Pamelia Center (cdp) Jefferson County	3	1.14
Syracuse (city) Onondaga County	1,554	1.07

Top 10 Places Sorted by Percent of Total Population
Based on places with total population of 50,000 or more

Place	Population	%
Utica (city) Oneida County	1,022	1.64
Syracuse (city) Onondaga County	1,554	1.07
Rochester (city) Monroe County	1,050	0.50
Greece (town) Monroe County	473	0.49
Buffalo (city) Erie County	1,220	0.47
Clay (town) Onondaga County	265	0.46
Colonie (town) Albany County	360	0.44
Union (town) Broome County	248	0.44
Cheektowaga (cdp) Erie County	326	0.43
Cheektowaga (town) Erie County	344	0.39

Hawaii Native/Pacific Islander

Top 10 Places Sorted by Population
Based on all places, regardless of total population

Place	Population	%
New York (city)	24,098	0.29
Queens (borough) Queens County	7,691	0.34
Bronx (borough) Bronx County	6,213	0.45
Brooklyn (borough) Kings County	5,784	0.23
Manhattan (borough) New York County	3,727	0.24
Hempstead (town) Nassau County	1,001	0.13
Staten Island (borough) Richmond County	683	0.15
Yonkers (city) Westchester County	483	0.25
Islip (town) Suffolk County	471	0.14
Rochester (city) Monroe County	449	0.21

Top 10 Places Sorted by Percent of Total Population
Based on all places, regardless of total population

Place	Population	%
Philadelphia (village) Jefferson County	25	2.00
Fort Drum (cdp) Jefferson County	226	1.74
Quiogue (cdp) Suffolk County	13	1.59
Burke (village) Franklin County	3	1.42
Le Ray (town) Jefferson County	286	1.31
Philadelphia (town) Jefferson County	25	1.28
Herrings (village) Jefferson County	1	1.11
Brewster (village) Putnam County	24	1.00
Speculator (village) Hamilton County	3	0.93
Calcium (cdp) Jefferson County	32	0.92

Top 10 Places Sorted by Percent of Total Population
Based on places with total population of 50,000 or more

Place	Population	%
Schenectady (city) Schenectady County	333	0.50
Bronx (borough) Bronx County	6,213	0.45
Queens (borough) Queens County	7,691	0.34
White Plains (city) Westchester County	180	0.32
New York (city)	24,098	0.29
Yonkers (city) Westchester County	483	0.25
Manhattan (borough) New York County	3,727	0.24
Brooklyn (borough) Kings County	5,784	0.23
Mount Vernon (city) Westchester County	156	0.23
Utica (city) Oneida County	137	0.22

Hawaii Native/Pacific Islander: Not Hispanic

Top 10 Places Sorted by Population
Based on all places, regardless of total population

Place	Population	%
New York (city)	13,217	0.16
Queens (borough) Queens County	5,685	0.25
Brooklyn (borough) Kings County	3,463	0.14
Bronx (borough) Bronx County	1,854	0.13
Manhattan (borough) New York County	1,776	0.11
Hempstead (town) Nassau County	599	0.08
Staten Island (borough) Richmond County	439	0.09
Brookhaven (town) Suffolk County	306	0.06
Rochester (city) Monroe County	284	0.13
Schenectady (city) Schenectady County	272	0.41

Top 10 Places Sorted by Percent of Total Population
Based on all places, regardless of total population

Place	Population	%
Quiogue (cdp) Suffolk County	13	1.59
Fort Drum (cdp) Jefferson County	196	1.51

Place		
Philadelphia (village) Jefferson County	18	1.44
Le Ray (town) Jefferson County	244	1.12
Herrings (village) Jefferson County	1	1.11
Burke (village) Franklin County	2	0.95
Speculator (village) Hamilton County	3	0.93
Philadelphia (village) Jefferson County	18	0.92
Constableville (village) Lewis County	2	0.83
La Fargeville (cdp) Jefferson County	5	0.82

Top 10 Places Sorted by Percent of Total Population
Based on places with total population of 50,000 or more

Place	Population	%
Schenectady (city) Schenectady County	272	0.41
Queens (borough) Queens County	5,685	0.25
Mount Vernon (city) Westchester County	130	0.19
New York (city)	13,217	0.16
Albany (city) Albany County	158	0.16
Syracuse (city) Onondaga County	218	0.15
Utica (city) Oneida County	95	0.15
Brooklyn (borough) Kings County	3,463	0.14
Bronx (borough) Bronx County	1,854	0.13
Rochester (city) Monroe County	284	0.13

Hawaii Native/Pacific Islander: Hispanic

Top 10 Places Sorted by Population
Based on all places, regardless of total population

Place	Population	%
New York (city)	10,881	0.13
Bronx (borough) Bronx County	4,359	0.31
Brooklyn (borough) Kings County	2,321	0.09
Queens (borough) Queens County	2,006	0.09
Manhattan (borough) New York County	1,951	0.12
Hempstead (town) Nassau County	402	0.05
Yonkers (city) Westchester County	272	0.14
Staten Island (borough) Richmond County	244	0.05
Islip (town) Suffolk County	227	0.07
Rochester (city) Monroe County	165	0.08

Top 10 Places Sorted by Percent of Total Population
Based on all places, regardless of total population

Place	Population	%
Brewster (village) Putnam County	23	0.96
Philadelphia (village) Jefferson County	7	0.56
Haverstraw (village) Rockland County	66	0.55
Aquebogue (cdp) Suffolk County	13	0.53
Woodridge (village) Sullivan County	4	0.47
Burke (village) Franklin County	1	0.47
Philadelphia (town) Jefferson County	7	0.36
Tivoli (village) Dutchess County	4	0.36
Bronx (borough) Bronx County	4,359	0.31
Sleepy Hollow (village) Westchester County	31	0.31

Top 10 Places Sorted by Percent of Total Population
Based on places with total population of 50,000 or more

Place	Population	%
Bronx (borough) Bronx County	4,359	0.31
White Plains (city) Westchester County	109	0.19
Yonkers (city) Westchester County	272	0.14
New York (city)	10,881	0.13
Manhattan (borough) New York County	1,951	0.12
Brentwood (cdp) Suffolk County	75	0.12
Hempstead (village) Nassau County	60	0.11
Brooklyn (borough) Kings County	2,321	0.09
Queens (borough) Queens County	2,006	0.09
Schenectady (city) Schenectady County	61	0.09

Hawaii Native/Pacific Islander: Fijian

Top 10 Places Sorted by Population
Based on all places, regardless of total population

Place	Population	%
New York (city)	213	<0.01
Queens (borough) Queens County	76	<0.01
Manhattan (borough) New York County	73	<0.01
Brooklyn (borough) Kings County	45	<0.01
Bronx (borough) Bronx County	13	<0.01
Brookhaven (town) Suffolk County	10	<0.01
Hempstead (town) Nassau County	10	<0.01
Sound Beach (cdp) Suffolk County	6	0.08
Woodmere (cdp) Nassau County	6	0.04

Place		
White Plains (city) Westchester County	6	0.01

Top 10 Places Sorted by Percent of Total Population
Based on all places, regardless of total population

Place	Population	%
Salamanca (city) Cattaraugus County	5	0.09
Sound Beach (cdp) Suffolk County	6	0.08
Woodmere (cdp) Nassau County	6	0.04
Florida (village) Orange County	1	0.04
Fairmount (cdp) Onondaga County	3	0.03
Pelham (village) Westchester County	2	0.03
South Hill (cdp) Tompkins County	2	0.03
Westmere (cdp) Albany County	2	0.03
Lansing (village) Tompkins County	1	0.03
Spencer (town) Tioga County	1	0.03

Top 10 Places Sorted by Percent of Total Population
Based on places with total population of 50,000 or more

Place	Population	%
White Plains (city) Westchester County	6	0.01
New York (city)	213	<0.01
Queens (borough) Queens County	76	<0.01
Manhattan (borough) New York County	73	<0.01
Brooklyn (borough) Kings County	45	<0.01
Bronx (borough) Bronx County	13	<0.01
Brookhaven (town) Suffolk County	10	<0.01
Hempstead (town) Nassau County	10	<0.01
Staten Island (borough) Richmond County	6	<0.01
Yonkers (city) Westchester County	6	<0.01

Hawaii Native/Pacific Islander: Guamanian or Chamorro

Top 10 Places Sorted by Population
Based on all places, regardless of total population

Place	Population	%
New York (city)	1,784	0.02
Brooklyn (borough) Kings County	568	0.02
Queens (borough) Queens County	483	0.02
Bronx (borough) Bronx County	376	0.03
Manhattan (borough) New York County	242	0.02
Staten Island (borough) Richmond County	115	0.02
Hempstead (town) Nassau County	110	0.01
Le Ray (town) Jefferson County	88	0.40
Fort Drum (cdp) Jefferson County	70	0.54
Southampton (town) Suffolk County	55	0.10

Top 10 Places Sorted by Percent of Total Population
Based on all places, regardless of total population

Place	Population	%
Quiogue (cdp) Suffolk County	13	1.59
Burke (village) Franklin County	2	0.95
Brewster (village) Putnam County	22	0.92
Fort Drum (cdp) Jefferson County	70	0.54
Aquebogue (cdp) Suffolk County	13	0.53
Port Gibson (cdp) Ontario County	2	0.44
Le Ray (town) Jefferson County	88	0.40
Southold (cdp) Suffolk County	22	0.38
Adams Center (cdp) Jefferson County	6	0.38
Pamelia Center (cdp) Jefferson County	1	0.38

Top 10 Places Sorted by Percent of Total Population
Based on places with total population of 50,000 or more

Place	Population	%
Southampton (town) Suffolk County	55	0.10
New Rochelle (city) Westchester County	43	0.06
Bronx (borough) Bronx County	376	0.03
Yonkers (city) Westchester County	52	0.03
Utica (city) Oneida County	18	0.03
Union (town) Broome County	16	0.03
New York (city)	1,784	0.02
Brooklyn (borough) Kings County	568	0.02
Queens (borough) Queens County	483	0.02
Manhattan (borough) New York County	242	0.02

Hawaii Native/Pacific Islander: Marshallese

Top 10 Places Sorted by Population
Based on all places, regardless of total population

Place	Population	%
New York (city)	10	<0.01
Le Ray (town) Jefferson County	6	0.03
Carthage (village) Jefferson County	5	0.13
Wilna (town) Jefferson County	5	0.08
Fort Drum (cdp) Jefferson County	5	0.04
Philadelphia (village) Jefferson County	4	0.32
Philadelphia (town) Jefferson County	4	0.21
Manhattan (borough) New York County	4	<0.01
Bronx (borough) Bronx County	3	<0.01
Hornell (city) Steuben County	2	0.02

Top 10 Places Sorted by Percent of Total Population
Based on all places, regardless of total population

Place	Population	%
Philadelphia (village) Jefferson County	4	0.32
Philadelphia (town) Jefferson County	4	0.21
Carthage (village) Jefferson County	5	0.13
Wilna (town) Jefferson County	5	0.08
Huron (town) Wayne County	1	0.05
Fort Drum (cdp) Jefferson County	5	0.04
Le Ray (town) Jefferson County	6	0.03
Hornell (city) Steuben County	2	0.02
Hartland (town) Niagara County	1	0.02
Hartsdale (cdp) Westchester County	1	0.02

Top 10 Places Sorted by Percent of Total Population
Based on places with total population of 50,000 or more

Place	Population	%
New York (city)	10	<0.01
Manhattan (borough) New York County	4	<0.01
Bronx (borough) Bronx County	3	<0.01
Brooklyn (borough) Kings County	2	<0.01
Amherst (town) Erie County	1	<0.01
Greenburgh (town) Westchester County	1	<0.01
Hempstead (town) Nassau County	1	<0.01
Islip (town) Suffolk County	1	<0.01
Staten Island (borough) Richmond County	1	<0.01
Syracuse (city) Onondaga County	1	<0.01

Hawaii Native/Pacific Islander: Native Hawaiian

Top 10 Places Sorted by Population
Based on all places, regardless of total population

Place	Population	%
New York (city)	2,448	0.03
Bronx (borough) Bronx County	669	0.05
Manhattan (borough) New York County	608	0.04
Brooklyn (borough) Kings County	564	0.02
Queens (borough) Queens County	486	0.02
Staten Island (borough) Richmond County	121	0.03
Hempstead (town) Nassau County	114	0.02
Brookhaven (town) Suffolk County	100	0.02
Rochester (city) Monroe County	77	0.04
Buffalo (city) Erie County	75	0.03

Top 10 Places Sorted by Percent of Total Population
Based on all places, regardless of total population

Place	Population	%
Speculator (village) Hamilton County	3	0.93
Felts Mills (cdp) Jefferson County	3	0.81
Hemlock (cdp) Livingston County	4	0.72
Waterville (village) Oneida County	8	0.51
Philadelphia (village) Jefferson County	6	0.48
Ischua (town) Cattaraugus County	4	0.47
Tivoli (village) Dutchess County	5	0.45
Calcium (cdp) Jefferson County	15	0.43
Plandome Heights (village) Nassau County	4	0.40
Fort Drum (cdp) Jefferson County	49	0.38

Top 10 Places Sorted by Percent of Total Population
Based on places with total population of 50,000 or more

Place	Population	%
Bronx (borough) Bronx County	669	0.05

Place	Population	%
Schenectady (city) Schenectady County	33	0.05
Southampton (town) Suffolk County	27	0.05
Troy (city) Rensselaer County	24	0.05
Manhattan (borough) New York County	608	0.04
Rochester (city) Monroe County	77	0.04
Syracuse (city) Onondaga County	65	0.04
Albany (city) Albany County	38	0.04
New York (city)	2,448	0.03
Staten Island (borough) Richmond County	121	0.03

Hawaii Native/Pacific Islander: Samoan

Top 10 Places Sorted by Population
Based on all places, regardless of total population

Place	Population	%
New York (city)	764	0.01
Brooklyn (borough) Kings County	216	0.01
Manhattan (borough) New York County	183	0.01
Queens (borough) Queens County	179	0.01
Bronx (borough) Bronx County	160	0.01
Rochester (city) Monroe County	63	0.03
Buffalo (city) Erie County	63	0.02
Le Ray (town) Jefferson County	53	0.24
Fort Drum (cdp) Jefferson County	49	0.38
Hempstead (town) Nassau County	36	<0.01

Top 10 Places Sorted by Percent of Total Population
Based on all places, regardless of total population

Place	Population	%
Philadelphia (village) Jefferson County	12	0.96
Constableville (village) Lewis County	2	0.83
La Fargeville (cdp) Jefferson County	4	0.66
Philadelphia (village) Jefferson County	12	0.62
Staatsburg (cdp) Dutchess County	2	0.53
Fremont (town) Sullivan County	6	0.43
Fort Drum (cdp) Jefferson County	49	0.38
Caroline (town) Tompkins County	12	0.37
Sagaponack (village) Suffolk County	1	0.32
Worcester (cdp) Otsego County	3	0.27

Top 10 Places Sorted by Percent of Total Population
Based on places with total population of 50,000 or more

Place	Population	%
Rochester (city) Monroe County	63	0.03
Utica (city) Oneida County	18	0.03
Buffalo (city) Erie County	63	0.02
Albany (city) Albany County	15	0.02
Schenectady (city) Schenectady County	10	0.02
New York (city)	764	0.01
Brooklyn (borough) Kings County	216	0.01
Manhattan (borough) New York County	183	0.01
Queens (borough) Queens County	179	0.01
Bronx (borough) Bronx County	160	0.01

Hawaii Native/Pacific Islander: Tongan

Top 10 Places Sorted by Population
Based on all places, regardless of total population

Place	Population	%
New York (city)	66	<0.01
Manhattan (borough) New York County	33	<0.01
Queens (borough) Queens County	14	<0.01
Brooklyn (borough) Kings County	10	<0.01
Bronx (borough) Bronx County	7	<0.01
Chateaugay (village) Franklin County	6	0.72
Chateaugay (town) Franklin County	6	0.28
Colonie (town) Albany County	5	0.01
Stone Ridge (cdp) Ulster County	4	0.34
Cambria (town) Niagara County	4	0.07

Top 10 Places Sorted by Percent of Total Population
Based on all places, regardless of total population

Place	Population	%
Chateaugay (village) Franklin County	6	0.72
Staatsburg (cdp) Dutchess County	2	0.53
Elizabethtown (cdp) Essex County	3	0.40
Stone Ridge (cdp) Ulster County	4	0.34
Chateaugay (town) Franklin County	6	0.28
Elizabethtown (town) Essex County	3	0.26
Fort Plain (village) Montgomery County	2	0.09
Franklin (town) Franklin County	1	0.09
Washington Mills (cdp) Oneida County	1	0.08
Cambria (town) Niagara County	4	0.07

Top 10 Places Sorted by Percent of Total Population
Based on places with total population of 50,000 or more

Place	Population	%
Colonie (town) Albany County	5	0.01
New York (city)	66	<0.01
Manhattan (borough) New York County	33	<0.01
Queens (borough) Queens County	14	<0.01
Brooklyn (borough) Kings County	10	<0.01
Bronx (borough) Bronx County	7	<0.01
Buffalo (city) Erie County	3	<0.01
Rochester (city) Monroe County	3	<0.01
Brentwood (cdp) Suffolk County	2	<0.01
Brookhaven (town) Suffolk County	2	<0.01

White

Top 10 Places Sorted by Population
Based on all places, regardless of total population

Place	Population	%
New York (city)	3,797,402	46.45
Brooklyn (borough) Kings County	1,120,592	44.74
Manhattan (borough) New York County	956,864	60.34
Queens (borough) Queens County	941,608	42.21
Hempstead (town) Nassau County	532,650	70.11
Bronx (borough) Bronx County	427,659	30.88
Brookhaven (town) Suffolk County	419,725	86.36
Staten Island (borough) Richmond County	350,679	74.81
Islip (town) Suffolk County	254,235	75.77
Oyster Bay (town) Nassau County	252,713	86.19

Top 10 Places Sorted by Percent of Total Population
Based on all places, regardless of total population

Place	Population	%
Putnam (town) Washington County	609	100.00
Odessa (village) Schuyler County	591	100.00
DeKalb Junction (cdp) St. Lawrence County	519	100.00
Cold Brook (village) Herkimer County	329	100.00
Pinckney (town) Lewis County	329	100.00
West Union (town) Steuben County	312	100.00
Madison (village) Madison County	305	100.00
Gainesville (village) Wyoming County	229	100.00
Osceola (town) Lewis County	229	100.00
Pierrepont Manor (cdp) Jefferson County	228	100.00

Top 10 Places Sorted by Percent of Total Population
Based on places with total population of 50,000 or more

Place	Population	%
Hamburg (town) Erie County	55,749	97.92
Tonawanda (town) Erie County	69,534	94.52
Tonawanda (cdp) Erie County	54,936	94.48
Smithtown (town) Suffolk County	111,000	94.23
Clay (town) Onondaga County	53,514	91.94
Union (town) Broome County	51,487	91.38
Levittown (cdp) Nassau County	46,970	90.53
Greece (town) Monroe County	86,829	90.36
Cheektowaga (town) Erie County	78,958	89.50
Irondequoit (cdp/town) Monroe County	45,826	88.65

White: Not Hispanic

Top 10 Places Sorted by Population
Based on all places, regardless of total population

Place	Population	%
New York (city)	2,804,430	34.30
Brooklyn (borough) Kings County	917,717	36.64
Manhattan (borough) New York County	785,299	49.52
Queens (borough) Queens County	638,051	28.60
Hempstead (town) Nassau County	460,994	60.68
Brookhaven (town) Suffolk County	379,158	78.01
Staten Island (borough) Richmond County	305,118	65.09
Oyster Bay (town) Nassau County	236,944	80.81
Islip (town) Suffolk County	198,326	59.11
Huntington (town) Suffolk County	160,914	79.17

Top 10 Places Sorted by Percent of Total Population
Based on all places, regardless of total population

Place	Population	%
Osceola (town) Lewis County	229	100.00
Birdsall (town) Allegany County	221	100.00
Oxbow (cdp) Jefferson County	108	100.00
Morehouse (town) Hamilton County	86	100.00
Woodsville (cdp) Livingston County	80	100.00
Linwood (cdp) Livingston County	74	100.00
Tuscarora (cdp) Livingston County	74	100.00
Red House (town) Cattaraugus County	38	100.00
Saltaire (village) Suffolk County	37	100.00
Thousand Island Park (cdp) Jefferson County	31	100.00

Top 10 Places Sorted by Percent of Total Population
Based on places with total population of 50,000 or more

Place	Population	%
Hamburg (town) Erie County	54,789	96.23
Tonawanda (cdp) Erie County	53,890	92.68
Tonawanda (town) Erie County	68,098	92.57
Clay (town) Onondaga County	52,515	90.22
Smithtown (town) Suffolk County	105,870	89.87
Union (town) Broome County	50,317	89.30
Cheektowaga (town) Erie County	77,687	88.05
Greece (town) Monroe County	83,902	87.31
Cheektowaga (cdp) Erie County	65,180	86.70
Colonie (town) Albany County	69,290	84.92

White: Hispanic

Top 10 Places Sorted by Population
Based on all places, regardless of total population

Place	Population	%
New York (city)	992,972	12.15
Queens (borough) Queens County	303,557	13.61
Bronx (borough) Bronx County	269,414	19.45
Brooklyn (borough) Kings County	202,875	8.10
Manhattan (borough) New York County	171,565	10.82
Hempstead (town) Nassau County	71,656	9.43
Islip (town) Suffolk County	55,909	16.66
Staten Island (borough) Richmond County	45,561	9.72
Brookhaven (town) Suffolk County	40,567	8.35
Yonkers (city) Westchester County	31,778	16.22

Top 10 Places Sorted by Percent of Total Population
Based on all places, regardless of total population

Place	Population	%
Brewster (village) Putnam County	993	41.55
Brentwood (cdp) Suffolk County	23,013	37.94
North Bay Shore (cdp) Suffolk County	6,358	33.56
Haverstraw (village) Rockland County	3,914	32.86
Port Chester (village) Westchester County	9,507	32.82
Central Islip (cdp) Suffolk County	9,372	27.20
Springs (cdp) Suffolk County	1,608	24.39
Sleepy Hollow (village) Westchester County	2,406	24.38
East Hampton North (cdp) Suffolk County	999	24.12
Rye (town) Westchester County	11,021	24.00

Top 10 Places Sorted by Percent of Total Population
Based on places with total population of 50,000 or more

Place	Population	%
Brentwood (cdp) Suffolk County	23,013	37.94
Bronx (borough) Bronx County	269,414	19.45
New Rochelle (city) Westchester County	14,422	18.71
Hempstead (village) Nassau County	9,773	18.13
Islip (town) Suffolk County	55,909	16.66
White Plains (city) Westchester County	9,400	16.53
Yonkers (city) Westchester County	31,778	16.22
Queens (borough) Queens County	303,557	13.61
Southampton (town) Suffolk County	6,955	12.25
New York (city)	992,972	12.15

Climate

New York State Physical Features and Climate Narrative

PHYSICAL FEATURES. New York State contains 49,576 square miles, inclusive of 1,637 square miles of inland water, but exclusive of the boundary-water areas of Long Island Sound, New York Harbor, Lake Ontario, and Lake Erie. The major portion of the State lies generally between latitudes 42° and 45° N. and between longitudes 73° 30' and 79° 45' W. However, in the extreme southeast, a triangular portion extends southward to about latitude 40° 30' N., while Long Island lies eastward to about longitude 72° W.

The principal highland regions of the State are the Adirondacks in the northeast and the Appalachian Plateau (Southern Plateau) in the south. A minor highland region occurs in southeastern New York where the Hudson River has cut a valley between the Palisades on the west, near the New Jersey border, and the Taconic Mountains on the east, along the Connecticut and Massachusetts border. Just west of the Adirondacks and the upper Black River Valley in Lewis County is another minor highland known as Tug Hill. Much of the eastern border of the State consists of a long, narrow lowland region which is occupied by Lake Champlain, Lake George, and the middle and lower portions of the Hudson Valley.

Approximately 40 percent of New York State has an elevation of more than 1,000 feet above sea level. In northwestern Essex County are a number of peaks with an elevation of between 4,000 to 5,000 feet. The highest point, Mount Marcy, reaches a height of 5,344 feet above sea level. The Appalachian Plateau merges variously into the Great Lakes Plain of western New York with gradual- to steep-sloping terrain. This Plateau is penetrated by the valleys of the Finger Lakes which extend southward from the Great Lakes Plain. Other prominent lakes plus innumerable smaller lakes and ponds dot the landscape, with more than 1,500 in the Adirondack region alone.

GENERAL CLIMATE. The climate of New York State is broadly representative of the humid continental type which prevails in the Northeastern United States, but its diversity is not usually encountered within an area of comparable size. The geographical position of the State and the usual course of air masses, governed by the large-scale patterns of atmospheric circulation, provide general climatic controls. Differences in latitude, character of the topography, and proximity to large bodies of water have pronounced effects on the climate.

Lengthy periods of either abnormally cold or warm weather result from the movement of great high pressure (anticyclonic) systems into and through the Eastern United States. Cold winter temperatures prevail over New York whenever Arctic air masses, under high barometric pressure, flow southward from central Canada or from Hudson Bay. High pressure systems often move just off the Atlantic coast, become more or less stagnant for several days, and then a persistent air flow from the southwest or south affects the State. This circulation brings the very warm, often humid weather of the summer season and the mild, more pleasant temperatures during the fall, winter, and spring seasons.

TEMPERATURE. Many atmospheric and physiographic controls on the climate result in a considerable variation of temperature conditions over New York State. The average annual mean temperature ranges from about 40°F. in the Adirondacks to near 55°F. in the New York City area. The winters are long and cold in the Plateau Divisions of the State. Winter temperatures are moderated considerably in the Great Lakes Plain of western New York. The moderating influence of Lakes Erie and Ontario is comparable to that produced by the Atlantic Ocean in the southern portion of the Hudson Valley.

The summer climate is cool in the Adirondacks, Catskills, and higher elevations of the Southern Plateau. The New York City area and lower portions of the Hudson Valley have rather warm summers by comparison, with some periods of high, uncomfortable humidity. The remainder of New York State enjoys pleasantly warm summers, marred by only occasional, brief intervals of sultry conditions. Summer daytime temperatures usually range from the upper 70s to mid-80s over much of the State. The moderating effect of Lakes Erie and Ontario on temperatures assumes practical importance during the spring and fall seasons. The lake waters warm slowly in the spring, the effect of which is to reduce the warming of the atmosphere over adjacent land areas. In the fall season, the lake waters cool more slowly than the land areas and thus serve as a heat source.

PRECIPITATION. Moisture for precipitation in New York State is transported primarily from the Gulf of Mexico and Atlantic Ocean through circulation patterns and storm systems of the atmosphere. Distribution of precipitation within the State is

greatly influenced by topography and proximity to the Great Lakes or Atlantic Ocean. Average annual amounts in excess of 50 inches occur in the western Adirondacks, Tug Hill area, and the Catskills, while slightly less than that amount is noted in the higher elevations of the Western Plateau southeast of Lake Erie. Areas of least rainfall, with average accumulations of about 30 inches, occur near Lake Ontario in the extreme western counties, in the lower half of the Genesee River Valley, and in the vicinity of Lake Champlain.

New York State has a fairly uniform distribution of precipitation during the year. There are no distinctly dry or wet seasons which are regularly repeated on an annual basis. Minimum precipitation occurs in the winter season. Maximum amounts are noted in the summer season throughout the State except along the Great Lakes where slight peaks of similar magnitude occur in both the spring and fall seasons.

SNOWFALL. The climate of New York State is marked by abundant snowfall. With the exception of the Coastal Division, the State receives an average seasonal amount of 40 inches or more. The average snowfall is greater than 70 inches over some 60 percent of New York's area. The moderating influence of the Atlantic Ocean reduces the snow accumulation to 25 to 35 inches in the New York City area and on Long Island. About one-third of the winter season precipitation in the Coastal Division occurs from storms which also yield at least one inch of snow. The great bulk of the winter precipitation in upstate New York comes as snow.

A durable snow cover generally begins to develop in the Adirondacks and northern lowlands by late November and remains on the ground until various times in April, depending upon late winter snowfall and early spring temperatures. The Southern Plateau, Great Lakes Plain in southern portions of western upstate New York, and the Hudson Valley experience a continuous snow cover from about mid-December to mid-March, with maximum depths usually occurring in February. Bare ground may occur briefly in the lower elevations of these regions during some winters. From late December or early January through February, the Atlantic coastal region of the State experiences alternating periods of measurable snow cover and bare ground.

FLOODS. Although major floods are relatively infrequent, the greatest potential and frequency for floods occur in the early spring when substantial rains combine with rapid snowmelting to produce a heavy runoff. Damaging floods are caused at other times of the year by prolonged periods of heavy rainfall.

WINDS AND STORMS. The prevailing wind is generally from the west in New York State. A southwest component becomes evident in winds during the warmer months while a northwest component is characteristic of the colder one-half of the year. Thunderstorms occur on an average of about 30 days in a year throughout the State. Destructive winds and lightning strikes in local areas are common with the more vigorous warm-season thunderstorms. Locally, hail occurs with more severe thunderstorms. Tornadoes are not common. About 3 or 4 of these storms strike limited, localized areas of New York State in most years. Tornadoes occur generally between late May and late August. Storms of freezing rain occur on one or more occasions during the winter season and often affect a wide area of the State in any one incident. Such storms are usually limited to a thin but dangerous coating of ice on exposed surfaces. Hurricanes and tropical storms periodically cause serious and heavy losses in the vicinity of Long Island and southeastern upstate New York. The greatest storm hazard in terms of area affected is heavy snow. Coastal northeaster storms occur with some frequency in most winters. Blizzard conditions of heavy snow, high winds, and rapidly falling temperature occur occasionally, but are much less characteristic of New York's climate than in the plains of Midwestern United States.

OTHER CLIMATIC ELEMENTS. The climate of the State features much cloudy weather during the months of November, December, and January in upstate New York. From June through September, however, about 60 to 70 percent of the possible sunshine hours is received. In the Atlantic coastal region, the sunshine hours increases from 50 percent of possible in the winter to about 65 percent of possible in the summer. The occurrence of heavy dense fog is variable over the State. The valleys and ridges of the Southern Plateau are most subject to periods of fog, with occurrences averaging about 50 days in a year. In the Great Lakes Plain and northern valleys, the frequency decreases to only 10 to 20 days annually. In those portions of the State with greater maritime influence, the frequency of dense fog in a year ranges from about 35 days on the south shore of Long Island to 25 days in the Hudson Valley.

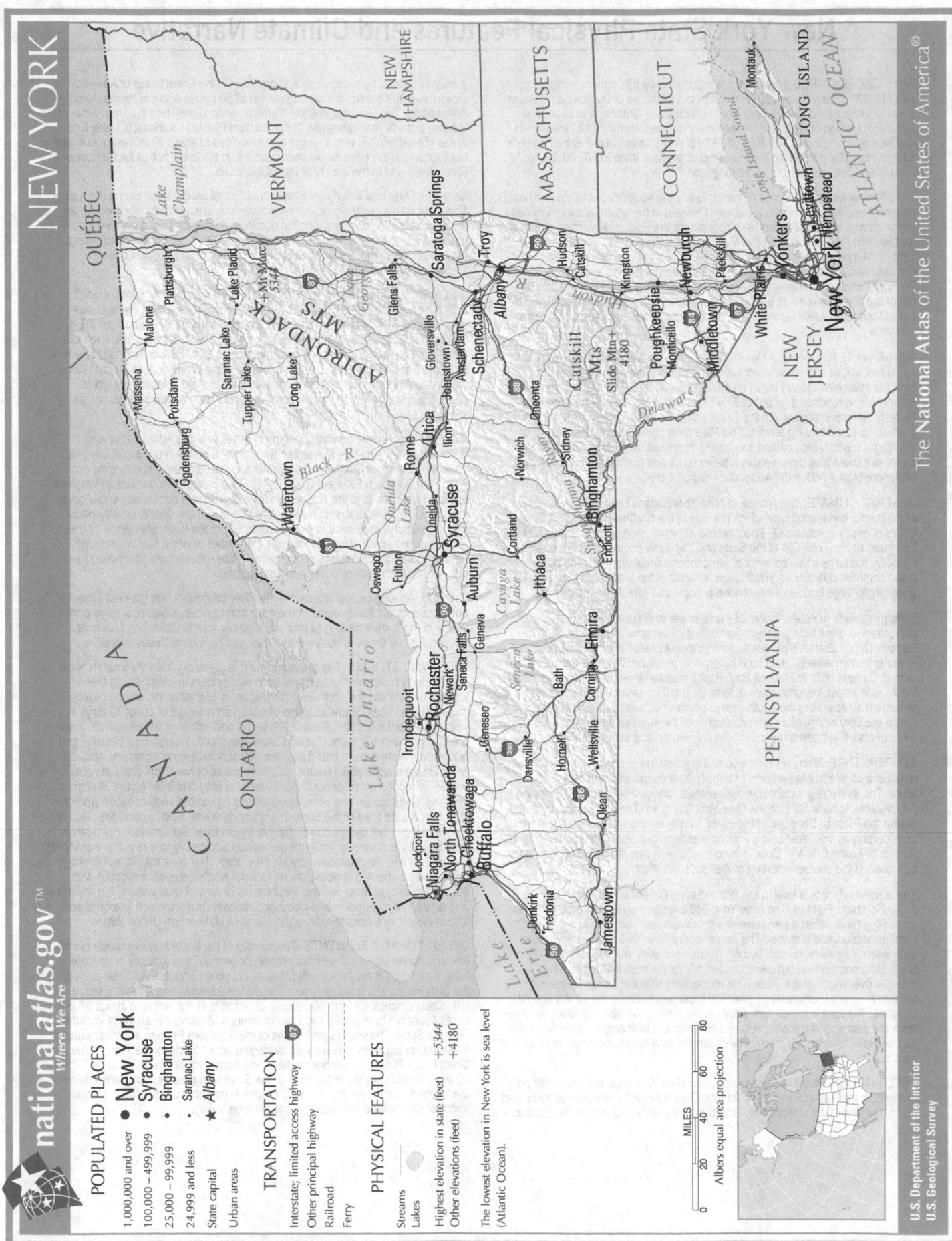

nationalatlas.gov™
Where We Are

POPULATED PLACES

● New York   1,000,000 and over
● Syracuse   100,000 – 499,999
● Binghamton 25,000 – 99,999
· Saranac Lake 24,999 and less
★ Albany   State capital
              Urban areas

TRANSPORTATION

───── Interstate; limited access highway
───── Other principal highway
───── Railroad
- - - Ferry

PHYSICAL FEATURES

───── Streams
       Lakes
+5344 Highest elevation in state (feet)
+4180 Other elevations (feet)

The lowest elevation in New York is sea level
(Atlantic Ocean).

MILES
0   20   40   60   80

Albers equal area projection

Elevation in Feet

10000 - 20320
9500 - 9999
9000 - 9499
8500 - 8999
8000 - 8499
7500 - 7999
7000 - 7499
6500 - 6999
6000 - 6499
5500 - 5999
5000 - 5499
4500 - 4999
4000 - 4499
3500 - 3999
3000 - 3499
2500 - 2999
2000 - 2499
1500 - 1999
1000 - 1499
500 - 999
250 - 499
1 - 249
-282 - 0
Water

44° 14' 27"
North

69° 47' 46" West

79° 11' 56" West

46° 23' 25"
North

Montpelier

Concord

Boston

Providence

Hartford

Albany

New York

80° 49' 45" West
Lambert Azimuthal Equal-Area
Projection

National Atlas of the United States

nationalatlas.gov

Miles   25   50   75

39° 47' 20"
North

72° 01' 07" West
http://nationalatlas.gov
02-Dec-10 01:29PM

41° 44' 33"
North

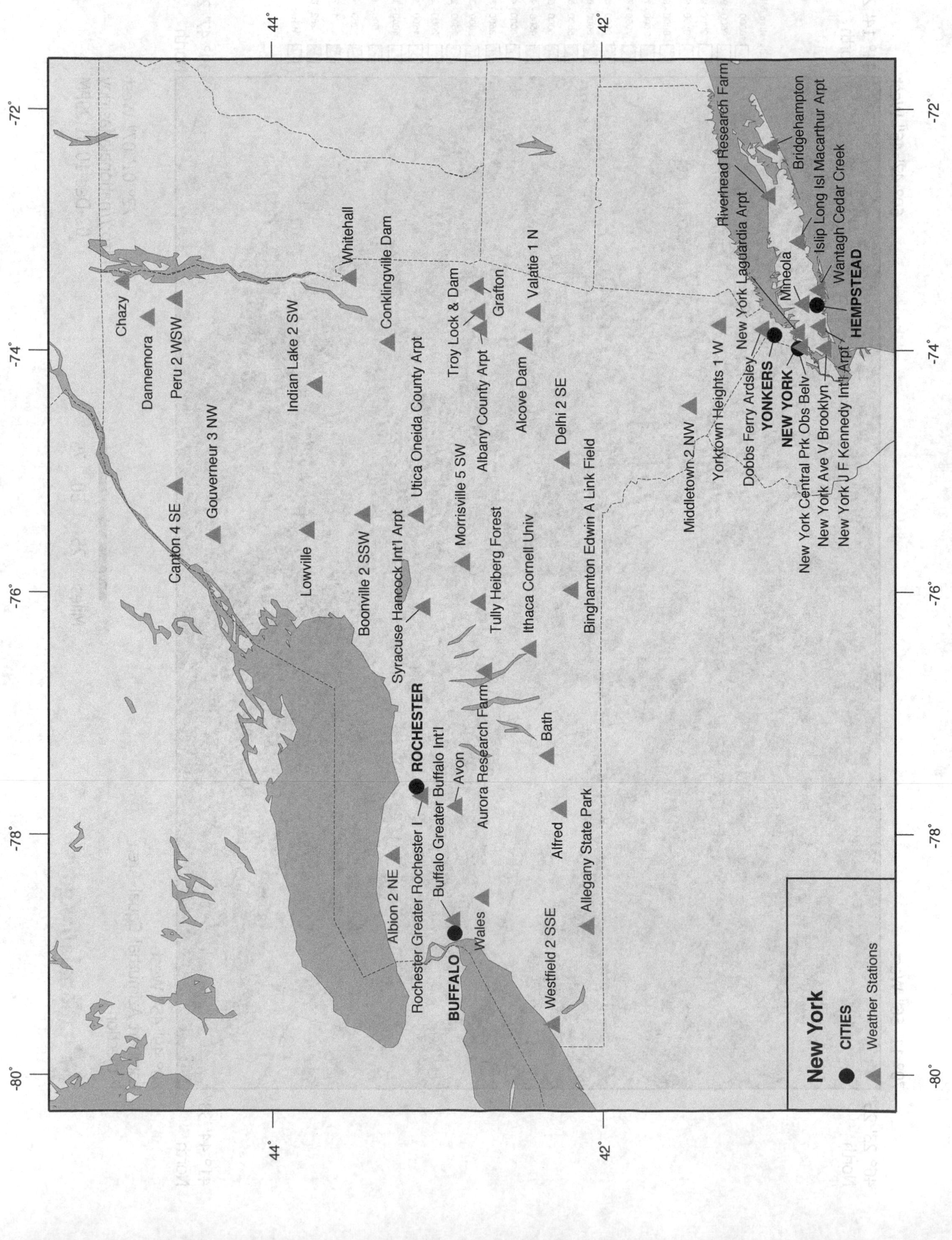

44°

42°

-72°

-72°

-74°

-74°

-76°

-76°

-78°

-78°

-80°

-80°

44°

42°

Chazy

Dannemora

Peru 2 WSW

Whitehall

Conklingville Dam

Riverhead Research Farm

Bridgehampton

Islip Long Isl Macarthur Arpt

Wantagh Cedar Creek

HEMPSTEAD

Gouverneur 3 NW

Indian Lake 2 SW

Mineola

New York Laguardia Arpt

Canton 4 SE

Troy Lock & Dam

Grafton

Valatie 1 N

Yorktown Heights 1 W

Dobbs Ferry Ardsley

YONKERS

NEW YORK

New York Central Prk Obs Belv

New York Ave V Brooklyn

New York JF Kennedy Int'l Arpt

Lowville

Boonville 2 SSW

Syracuse Hancock Int'l Arpt

Utica Oneida County Arpt

Morrisville 5 SW

Albany County Arpt

Alcove Dam

Delhi 2 SE

Middletown 2 NW

Tully Heiberg Forest

Ithaca Cornell Univ

Binghamton Edwin A Link Field

ROCHESTER

Avon

Aurora Research Farm

Bath

Rochester Greater Rochester I

Buffalo Greater Buffalo Int'l

Alfred

Allegany State Park

Albion 2 NE

Wales

BUFFALO

Westfield 2 SSE

New York

● CITIES

▲ Weather Stations

New York Weather Stations by County

County	Station Name
Albany	Albany County Arpt
	Alcove Dam
Allegany	Alfred
Broome	Binghamton Edwin A Link Field
Cattaraugus	Allegany State Park
Cayuga	Aurora Research Farm
Chautauqua	Westfield 2 SSE
Clinton	Chazy
	Dannemora
	Peru 2 WSW
Columbia	Valatie 1 N
Cortland	Tully Heiberg Forest
Delaware	Delhi 2 SE
Erie	Buffalo Greater Buffalo Int'l
	Wales
Hamilton	Indian Lake 2 SW
Kings	New York Ave V Brooklyn
Lewis	Lowville
Livingston	Avon
Madison	Morrisville 5 SW
Monroe	Rochester Intl Arpt
Nassau	Mineola
	Wantagh Cedar Creek
New York	New York Central Park Observ
Oneida	Boonville 2 SSW
	Utica Oneida County Arpt
Onondaga	Syracuse Hancock Int'l Arpt
Orange	Middletown 2 NW
Orleans	Albion 2 NE
Queens	New York J F Kennedy Int'l Arpt
	New York Laguardia Arpt
Rensselaer	Grafton
	Troy Lock and Dam
Saratoga	Conklingville Dam
St. Lawrence	Canton 4 SE
	Gouverneur 3 NW
Steuben	Bath

County	Station Name
Suffolk	Bridgehampton
	Islip-Macarthur Arpt
	Riverhead Research Farm
Tompkins	Ithaca Cornell Univ
Washington	Whitehall
Westchester	Dobbs Ferry Ardsley
	Yorktown Heights 1 W

See User Guide for station inclusion criteria.

New York Weather Stations by City

City	Station Name	Miles
Albany	Albany County Arpt	6.2
	Alcove Dam	15.4
	Grafton	18.3
	Troy Lock and Dam	8.1
	Valatie 1 N	16.5
Amherst	Buffalo Greater Buffalo Int'l	4.5
	Wales	21.1
Babylon	Islip-Macarthur Arpt	14.7
	Mineola	13.2
	New York J F Kennedy Int'l Arpt	23.2
	Wantagh Cedar Creek	8.3
Brentwood	Islip-Macarthur Arpt	7.5
	Mineola	19.8
	Wantagh Cedar Creek	16.2
Bronx	Essex Fells Serv Bldg, NJ	21.0
	Newark Intl Arpt, NJ	18.3
	Dobbs Ferry Ardsley	10.7
	Mineola	16.1
	New York Ave V Brooklyn	18.1
	New York Central Park Observ	6.4
	New York J F Kennedy Int'l Arpt	14.5
	New York Laguardia Arpt	4.6
	Wantagh Cedar Creek	24.3
Brookhaven	Bridgeport Sikorsky Memorial, CT	24.2
	Islip-Macarthur Arpt	7.6
	Riverhead Research Farm	16.3
Brooklyn	Canoe Brook, NJ	21.8
	Cranford, NJ	18.1
	Essex Fells Serv Bldg, NJ	21.4
	Newark Intl Arpt, NJ	12.8
	Plainfield, NJ	23.6
	Mineola	18.6
	New York Ave V Brooklyn	3.8
	New York Central Park Observ	9.2
	New York J F Kennedy Int'l Arpt	8.1
	New York Laguardia Arpt	9.9
	Wantagh Cedar Creek	23.8
Buffalo	Buffalo Greater Buffalo Int'l	6.0
	Wales	20.1
Cheektowaga	Buffalo Greater Buffalo Int'l	2.1
	Wales	16.1
Clarkstown	Stamford 5 N, CT	22.6
	Charlotteburg Reservoir, NJ	24.3
	Dobbs Ferry Ardsley	11.7
	New York Central Park Observ	23.7
	New York Laguardia Arpt	24.3
	Yorktown Heights 1 W	13.6
Clay	Syracuse Hancock Int'l Arpt	5.2
Colonie	Albany County Arpt	1.5
	Alcove Dam	19.7
	Grafton	16.7
	Troy Lock and Dam	5.4
	Valatie 1 N	21.2

City	Station Name	Miles
Greece	Albion 2 NE	24.6
	Avon	22.3
	Rochester Intl Arpt	8.2
Greenburgh	Stamford 5 N, CT	16.0
	Dobbs Ferry Ardsley	2.1
	Mineola	23.5
	New York Central Park Observ	18.4
	New York Laguardia Arpt	17.3
	Yorktown Heights 1 W	16.4
Hamburg	Buffalo Greater Buffalo Int'l	14.0
	Wales	16.8
Hempstead	Dobbs Ferry Ardsley	24.8
	Mineola	3.6
	New York Ave V Brooklyn	19.9
	New York Central Park Observ	19.6
	New York J F Kennedy Int'l Arpt	9.7
	New York Laguardia Arpt	15.6
	Wantagh Cedar Creek	6.6
Huntington	Stamford 5 N, CT	20.7
	Islip-Macarthur Arpt	14.9
	Mineola	15.1
	Wantagh Cedar Creek	15.4
Islip	Islip-Macarthur Arpt	5.2
	Mineola	22.1
	Wantagh Cedar Creek	17.7
Levittown	Islip-Macarthur Arpt	22.0
	Mineola	5.5
	New York Central Park Observ	24.1
	New York J F Kennedy Int'l Arpt	15.9
	New York Laguardia Arpt	19.8
	Wantagh Cedar Creek	5.2
Manhattan	Canoe Brook, NJ	20.3
	Cranford, NJ	19.7
	Essex Fells Serv Bldg, NJ	17.1
	Newark Intl Arpt, NJ	12.2
	Dobbs Ferry Ardsley	16.7
	Mineola	18.5
	New York Ave V Brooklyn	12.5
	New York Central Park Observ	0.2
	New York J F Kennedy Int'l Arpt	12.5
	New York Laguardia Arpt	4.3
Mount Vernon	Stamford 5 N, CT	20.4
	Essex Fells Serv Bldg, NJ	24.2
	Newark Intl Arpt, NJ	22.8
	Dobbs Ferry Ardsley	6.0
	Mineola	16.7
	New York Ave V Brooklyn	23.0
	New York Central Park Observ	11.4
	New York J F Kennedy Int'l Arpt	18.2
	New York Laguardia Arpt	9.3
	Yorktown Heights 1 W	24.5
New Rochelle	Stamford 5 N, CT	18.2
	Dobbs Ferry Ardsley	6.0
	Mineola	15.7

City	Station Name	Miles
New Rochelle (cont.)	New York Ave V Brooklyn	24.5
	New York Central Park Observ	13.5
	New York J F Kennedy Int'l Arpt	18.8
	New York Laguardia Arpt	10.8
	Wantagh Cedar Creek	24.0
	Yorktown Heights 1 W	23.9
New York	Canoe Brook, NJ	22.5
	Cranford, NJ	20.5
	Essex Fells Serv Bldg, NJ	20.4
	Newark Intl Arpt, NJ	13.7
	Dobbs Ferry Ardsley	19.6
	Mineola	15.9
	New York Ave V Brooklyn	9.2
	New York Central Park Observ	4.7
	New York J F Kennedy Int'l Arpt	8.2
	New York Laguardia Arpt	4.5
	Wantagh Cedar Creek	22.7
Niagara Falls	Buffalo Greater Buffalo Int'l	18.2
North Hempstead	Stamford 5 N, CT	24.1
	Dobbs Ferry Ardsley	17.6
	Mineola	4.1
	New York Ave V Brooklyn	20.7
	New York Central Park Observ	15.7
	New York J F Kennedy Int'l Arpt	11.3
	New York Laguardia Arpt	11.4
	Wantagh Cedar Creek	12.5
Oyster Bay	Stamford 5 N, CT	24.8
	Dobbs Ferry Ardsley	24.1
	Islip-Macarthur Arpt	20.8
	Mineola	6.5
	New York Central Park Observ	24.6
	New York J F Kennedy Int'l Arpt	17.6
	New York Laguardia Arpt	20.3
	Wantagh Cedar Creek	7.6
Queens	Cranford, NJ	24.9
	Essex Fells Serv Bldg, NJ	24.8
	Newark Intl Arpt, NJ	18.3
	Dobbs Ferry Ardsley	19.2
	Mineola	11.4
	New York Ave V Brooklyn	11.5
	New York Central Park Observ	8.2
	New York J F Kennedy Int'l Arpt	5.3
	New York Laguardia Arpt	5.0
	Wantagh Cedar Creek	18.2
Ramapo	Charlotteburg Reservoir, NJ	19.7
	Essex Fells Serv Bldg, NJ	22.7
	Dobbs Ferry Ardsley	15.1
	New York Central Park Observ	24.1
	Yorktown Heights 1 W	17.4
Rochester	Avon	18.5
	Rochester Intl Arpt	4.9
Schenectady	Albany County Arpt	7.5
	Alcove Dam	23.3
	Grafton	23.5
	Troy Lock and Dam	13.0
Smithtown	Bridgeport Sikorsky Memorial, CT	22.7

City	Station Name	Miles
Smithtown (cont.)	Stamford 5 N, CT	24.9
	Islip-Macarthur Arpt	8.0
	Mineola	22.7
	Wantagh Cedar Creek	20.8
Southampton	Bridgehampton	11.7
	Riverhead Research Farm	12.1
Staten Island	Canoe Brook, NJ	15.8
	Cranford, NJ	9.6
	Essex Fells Serv Bldg, NJ	18.6
	Newark Intl Arpt, NJ	9.2
	New Brunswick 3 SE, NJ	17.7
	Plainfield, NJ	13.8
	New York Ave V Brooklyn	8.1
	New York Central Park Observ	16.1
	New York J F Kennedy Int'l Arpt	18.2
	New York Laguardia Arpt	18.9
Syracuse	Syracuse Hancock Int'l Arpt	5.5
	Tully Heiberg Forest	19.3
Tonawanda	Buffalo Greater Buffalo Int'l	7.0
	Wales	23.4
Union	Binghamton Edwin A Link Field	6.2
	Montrose, PA	19.3
Utica	Utica Oneida County Arpt	8.5
White Plains	Stamford 5 N, CT	12.8
	Dobbs Ferry Ardsley	4.0
	Mineola	21.6
	New York Central Park Observ	19.8
	New York Laguardia Arpt	17.9
	Yorktown Heights 1 W	16.7
Yonkers	Stamford 5 N, CT	20.9
	Essex Fells Serv Bldg, NJ	22.6
	Newark Intl Arpt, NJ	22.2
	Dobbs Ferry Ardsley	4.8
	Mineola	19.5
	New York Ave V Brooklyn	24.0
	New York Central Park Observ	11.7
	New York J F Kennedy Int'l Arpt	20.2
	New York Laguardia Arpt	10.7
	Yorktown Heights 1 W	23.1

Note: Miles is the distance between the geographic center of the city and the weather station.

New York Weather Stations by Elevation

Feet	Station Name
1,898	Tully Heiberg Forest
1,770	Alfred
1,660	Indian Lake 2 SW
1,600	Binghamton Edwin A Link Field
1,580	Boonville 2 SSW
1,560	Grafton
1,500	Allegany State Park
1,439	Delhi 2 SE
1,339	Dannemora
1,299	Morrisville 5 SW
1,120	Bath
1,089	Wales
959	Ithaca Cornell Univ
859	Lowville
830	Aurora Research Farm
808	Conklingville Dam
711	Utica Oneida County Arpt
707	Westfield 2 SSE
705	Buffalo Greater Buffalo Int'l
700	Middletown 2 NW
669	Yorktown Heights 1 W
606	Alcove Dam
600	Rochester Intl Arpt
544	Avon
509	Peru 2 WSW
439	Albion 2 NE
439	Canton 4 SE
419	Gouverneur 3 NW
410	Syracuse Hancock Int'l Arpt
299	Valatie 1 N
274	Albany County Arpt
200	Dobbs Ferry Ardsley
169	Chazy
131	New York Central Park Observ
119	Whitehall
100	Riverhead Research Farm
96	Mineola
83	Islip-Macarthur Arpt
60	Bridgehampton
23	Troy Lock and Dam
20	New York Ave V Brooklyn
16	New York J F Kennedy Int'l Arpt
11	New York Laguardia Arpt
9	Wantagh Cedar Creek

Albany County Airport

Albany is located on the west bank of the Hudson River some 150 miles north of New York City, and 8 miles south of the confluence of the Mohawk and Hudson Rivers. The river-front portion of the city is only a few feet above sea level, and there is a tidal effect upstream to Troy. Eleven miles west of Albany the Helderberg hill range rises to 1,800 feet. Between it and the Hudson River the valley floor is gently rolling, ranging some 200 to 500 feet above sea level. East of the city there is more rugged terrain 5 or 6 miles wide with elevations of 300 to 600 feet. Farther to the east the terrain rises more sharply. It reaches a north-south range of hills 12 miles east of Albany with elevations ranging to 2,000 feet.

The climate at Albany is primarily continental in character, but is subjected to some modification by the Atlantic Ocean. The moderating effect on temperatures is more pronounced during the warmer months than in winter when outbursts of cold air sweep down from Canada. In the warmer seasons, temperatures rise rapidly in the daytime. However, temperatures also fall rapidly after sunset so that the nights are relatively cool. Occasionally there are extended periods of oppressive heat up to a week or more in duration.

Winters are usually cold and sometimes fairly severe. Maximum temperatures during the colder winters are often below freezing and nighttime lows are frequently below 10 degrees. Sub-zero readings occur about 12 times a year. Snowfall throughout the area is quite variable and snow flurries are quite frequent during the winter. Precipitation is sufficient to serve the economy of the region in most years, and only occasionally do periods of drought exist. Most of the rainfall in the summer is from thunderstorms. Tornadoes are quite rare and hail is not usually of any consequence.

Wind velocities are moderate. The north-south Hudson River Valley has a marked effect on the lighter winds and in the warm months, average wind direction is usually southerly. Destructive winds rarely occur.

The area enjoys one of the highest percentages of sunshine in the entire state. Seldom does the area experience long periods of cloudy days and long periods of smog are rare.

Based on the 1951-1980 period, the average first occurrence of 32 degrees Fahrenheit in the fall is September 29 and the average last occurrence in the spring is May 7.

Albany County Airport *Albany County*   Elevation: 274 ft.   Latitude: 42° 45' N   Longitude: 73° 48' W

	JAN	FEB	MAR	APR	MAY	JUN	JUL	AUG	SEP	OCT	NOV	DEC	YEAR
Mean Maximum Temp. (°F)	31.1	34.9	44.3	58.3	69.6	77.9	82.3	80.5	72.4	60.0	48.2	36.1	58.0
Mean Temp. (°F)	22.8	25.9	34.8	47.6	58.2	67.0	71.6	70.0	61.8	49.8	39.8	28.4	48.2
Mean Minimum Temp. (°F)	14.5	16.8	25.2	36.9	46.8	56.1	60.9	59.5	51.2	39.4	31.3	20.8	38.3
Extreme Maximum Temp. (°F)	71	68	89	92	94	96	99	97	92	86	81	71	99
Extreme Minimum Temp. (°F)	-23	-18	-6	13	28	36	44	34	28	18	6	-20	-23
Days Maximum Temp. ≥ 90°F	0	0	0	0	0	2	4	2	0	0	0	0	8
Days Maximum Temp. ≤ 32°F	17	11	4	0	0	0	0	0	0	0	1	10	43
Days Minimum Temp. ≤ 32°F	29	26	24	9	1	0	0	0	0	7	18	27	141
Days Minimum Temp. ≤ 0°F	5	2	1	0	0	0	0	0	0	0	0	1	9
Heating Degree Days (base 65°F)	1,301	1,099	929	519	231	51	6	19	138	469	749	1,127	6,638
Cooling Degree Days (base 65°F)	0	0	1	4	27	117	217	183	50	4	0	0	603
Mean Precipitation (in.)	2.54	2.09	3.26	3.22	3.58	3.80	4.11	3.62	3.26	3.52	3.27	2.87	39.14
Maximum Precipitation (in.)*	6.4	5.0	5.9	7.9	9.0	7.4	7.0	7.3	7.9	8.8	8.1	6.7	47.2
Minimum Precipitation (in.)*	0.4	0.2	0.3	1.1	1.0	0.6	0.5	0.7	0.4	0.2	0.6	0.6	21.5
Extreme Maximum Daily Precip. (in.)	1.78	1.60	2.02	2.26	2.16	3.30	3.49	2.78	5.60	2.82	2.21	2.79	5.60
Days With ≥ 0.1" Precipitation	6	5	7	7	8	8	7	7	6	6	7	7	81
Days With ≥ 0.5" Precipitation	2	1	2	2	3	3	3	2	2	2	2	2	26
Days With ≥ 1.0" Precipitation	0	0	1	1	0	1	1	1	1	1	1	0	8
Mean Snowfall (in.)	17.7	11.5	11.4	2.3	0.1	trace	trace	0.0	trace	0.3	3.2	13.7	60.2
Maximum Snowfall (in.)*	48	35	35	18	2	0	0	0	0	7	25	58	107
Maximum 24-hr. Snowfall (in.)*	13	17	22	17	2	0	0	0	0	7	22	14	22
Maximum Snow Depth (in.)	24	20	28	13	trace	trace	trace	0	trace	2	10	16	28
Days With ≥ 1.0" Snow Depth	19	16	9	1	0	0	0	0	0	0	2	12	59
Thunderstorm Days*	< 1	< 1	1	1	3	5	6	5	2	1	< 1	< 1	24
Foggy Days*	10	9	11	9	12	13	14	17	17	15	13	12	152
Predominant Sky Cover*	OVR	OVR	OVR	OVR	OVR	OVR	OVR	OVR	OVR	OVR	OVR	OVR	OVR
Mean Relative Humidity 7am (%)*	77	77	76	72	74	77	80	85	88	86	82	80	80
Mean Relative Humidity 4pm (%)*	64	59	54	48	50	53	53	55	57	56	64	67	57
Mean Dewpoint (°F)*	14	15	23	33	45	55	60	59	52	41	31	20	38
Prevailing Wind Direction*	WNW	WNW	WNW	WNW	S	S	S	S	S	S	WNW	WNW	S
Prevailing Wind Speed (mph)*	15	15	15	15	10	9	8	8	9	9	14	14	12
Maximum Wind Gust (mph)*	62	67	61	58	67	59	77	62	64	60	67	63	77

Note: (*) Period of record is 1946-1995

Binghamton Edwin A. Link Field

Binghamton, in south central New York lies in a comparatively narrow valley at the confluence of the Susquehanna and Chenango Rivers. Within a radius of 5 miles, hills rise to elevations of 1,400-1,600 feet above mean sea level. In the spring, melting snow, sometimes supplemented by rainfall, occasionally causes flooding in the city and along the streams.

The climate of Binghamton is representative of the humid area of the north-eastern United States and is primarily continental in type. The area, being adjacent to the so-called St. Lawrence Valley storm track, and also subject to cold air masses approaching from the west and north, has a variable climate, characterized by frequent and rapid changes. Furthermore, diurnal and seasonal changes assist in the production of an invigorating climate. As a rule, the temperature rises rapidly to moderate daytime levels with readings of 90 degrees or above only a few days in any month summer nights provide favorable sleeping conditions.

Winters are usually cold, but not commonly severe. Highest daytime temperatures average in the high 20s to low 30s, while the lowest nighttime readings average from the mid-teens to low 20s. Ordinarily a few sub-zero readings may be expected in January and February, with a lesser number in November, December, and March. The transitional seasons, spring and autumn, are the most variable of the year.

Most of the precipitation in the Binghamton area derives from moisture laden air transported from the Gulf of Mexico and cyclonic systems moving northward along the Atlantic coast. The annual rainfall is rather evenly distributed over the year. However, the greatest average monthly amounts occur during the growing season, April through September. As a rule, rainfall is ample for good crop growth and comes mostly in the form of thunderstorms. Annual snowfall is around 50 inches in Binghamton and above 85 inches at Edwin A. Link Field, some 10 miles to the NNW, and about 700 feet higher in elevation. Most of the snow falls during the normal winter months. However, heavy snows can occur as early as November and as late as April. Being adjacent to the track of storms that move through the St. Lawrence Valley, and being under the influence of winds that sweep across Lakes Erie and Ontario to the interior of the state, the area is subject to much cloudiness and winter snow flurries.

For the most part, the winds at Binghamton have northerly and westerly components. Tornadoes, although rare, have struck in the Binghamton area.

Based on the 1951-1980 period, the growing season averages 150 to 160 days. Usually the last spring frost occurs during early May, and the first frost in autumn during early October.

Binghamton Edwin A. Link Field *Broome County*　Elevation: 1,600 ft.　Latitude: 42° 12' N　Longitude: 75° 59' W

	JAN	FEB	MAR	APR	MAY	JUN	JUL	AUG	SEP	OCT	NOV	DEC	YEAR
Mean Maximum Temp. (°F)	29.4	32.5	41.3	54.6	66.0	74.2	78.3	77.0	69.1	57.2	45.4	33.8	54.9
Mean Temp. (°F)	22.6	25.0	33.0	45.3	56.2	64.7	69.0	67.8	59.9	48.7	38.5	27.5	46.5
Mean Minimum Temp. (°F)	15.8	17.4	24.6	36.0	46.2	55.1	59.7	58.4	50.8	40.2	31.5	21.2	38.1
Extreme Maximum Temp. (°F)	63	63	82	89	89	92	98	95	91	82	77	65	98
Extreme Minimum Temp. (°F)	-15	-10	-7	9	28	33	44	38	27	19	8	-18	-18
Days Maximum Temp. ≥ 90°F	0	0	0	0	0	0	1	1	0	0	0	0	2
Days Maximum Temp. ≤ 32°F	19	15	7	0	0	0	0	0	0	0	3	14	58
Days Minimum Temp. ≤ 32°F	29	26	24	11	1	0	0	0	0	6	18	27	142
Days Minimum Temp. ≤ 0°F	3	1	0	0	0	0	0	0	0	0	0	1	5
Heating Degree Days (base 65°F)	1,307	1,124	987	588	290	85	20	35	180	500	790	1,154	7,060
Cooling Degree Days (base 65°F)	0	0	1	4	22	82	152	128	35	2	0	0	426
Mean Precipitation (in.)	2.38	2.29	3.09	3.53	3.53	4.33	3.67	3.37	3.55	3.30	3.29	2.81	39.14
Maximum Precipitation (in.)*	6.4	4.4	6.0	8.6	6.5	9.5	7.4	7.5	9.7	9.4	7.5	6.1	48.0
Minimum Precipitation (in.)*	0.8	0.4	0.7	1.0	0.8	1.0	0.8	0.6	0.6	0.3	1.0	0.9	29.9
Extreme Maximum Daily Precip. (in.)	1.64	1.80	1.83	2.86	2.91	4.05	1.70	2.73	3.50	2.94	2.35	2.66	4.05
Days With ≥ 0.1" Precipitation	6	6	7	8	8	8	7	7	7	6	7	7	84
Days With ≥ 0.5" Precipitation	1	1	2	2	2	3	3	2	2	2	2	2	24
Days With ≥ 1.0" Precipitation	0	0	0	1	1	1	1	1	1	1	1	0	8
Mean Snowfall (in.)	21.7	15.9	15.5	4.3	0.1	trace	0.0	trace	trace	1.1	7.0	17.2	82.8
Maximum Snowfall (in.)*	44	44	38	23	3	0	0	0	trace	12	29	60	138
Maximum 24-hr. Snowfall (in.)*	18	21	19	12	3	0	0	0	trace	7	11	14	21
Maximum Snow Depth (in.)	32	19	35	9	1	trace	0	trace	trace	3	13	15	35
Days With ≥ 1.0" Snow Depth	23	20	13	2	0	0	0	0	0	0	5	16	79
Thunderstorm Days*	< 1	< 1	1	2	4	6	7	5	3	1	< 1	< 1	29
Foggy Days*	11	10	13	12	14	15	16	19	17	15	14	13	169
Predominant Sky Cover*	OVR	OVR	OVR	OVR	OVR	OVR	OVR	OVR	OVR	OVR	OVR	OVR	OVR
Mean Relative Humidity 7am (%)*	80	79	79	76	78	83	85	89	90	85	82	82	82
Mean Relative Humidity 4pm (%)*	69	65	60	54	54	57	57	59	62	60	68	72	61
Mean Dewpoint (°F)*	15	16	23	32	44	54	59	58	51	40	31	20	37
Prevailing Wind Direction*	WNW	NW	NW	NW	NW	SW	SW	SW	SW	S	SW	WNW	NW
Prevailing Wind Speed (mph)*	14	14	14	13	12	9	8	8	9	9	10	14	12
Maximum Wind Gust (mph)*	61	56	58	64	54	60	74	63	48	51	58	54	74

Note: (*) Period of record is 1948-1995

Buffalo Int'l Airport

The country surrounding Buffalo is comparatively low and level to the west. To the east and south the land is gently rolling, rising to pronounced hills within 12 to 18 miles, and to 1,000 feet above the level of Lake Erie about 35 miles south-southeast of the city. A steep slope of 50 to 100 feet lies east-west one and a half miles to the north. The eastern end of Lake Erie is nine miles to the west-southwest, while Lake Ontario lies 25 miles to the north, the two being connected by the Niagara River, which flows north-northwestward from the end of Lake Erie.

Buffalo is located near the mean position of the polar front. Its weather is varied and changeable, characteristic of the latitude. Wide seasonal swings of temperature from hot to cold are tempered appreciably by the proximity of Lakes Erie and Ontario. Lake Erie lies to the southwest, the direction of the prevailing wind. Wind flow throughout the year is somewhat higher due to this exposure. The vigorous interplay of warm and cold air masses during the winter and early spring months causes one or more windstorms. Precipitation is moderate and fairly evenly divided throughout the twelve months.

The spring season is more cloudy and cooler than points not affected by the cold lake. Spring growth of vegetation is retarded, protecting it from late spring frosts. With heavy winter ice accumulations in the lake, typical spring conditions are delayed until late May or early June.

Summer comes suddenly in mid-June. Lake breezes temper the extreme heat of the summer season. Temperatures of 90 degrees and above are infrequent. There is more summer sunshine here than in any other section of the state. Due to the stabilizing effects of Lake Erie, thunderstorms are relatively infrequent. Most of them are caused by frontal action. To the north and south of the city thunderstorms occur more often.

Autumn has long, dry periods and is frost free usually until mid-October. Cloudiness increases in November, continuing mostly cloudy throughout the winter and early spring. Snow flurries off the lake begin in mid-November or early December. Outbreaks of Arctic air in December and throughout the winter months produce locally heavy snowfalls from the lake. At the same time, temperatures of well below zero over Canada and the midwest are raised 10 to 30 degrees in crossing the lakes. Only on rare occasions do polar air masses drop southward from eastern Hudson Bay across Lake Ontario without appreciable warming.

Buffalo Int'l Airport *Erie County*   Elevation: 705 ft.   Latitude: 42° 56' N   Longitude: 78° 44' W

	JAN	FEB	MAR	APR	MAY	JUN	JUL	AUG	SEP	OCT	NOV	DEC	YEAR
Mean Maximum Temp. (°F)	31.8	33.6	42.1	55.2	66.7	75.5	80.1	78.7	71.4	59.3	47.8	36.5	56.6
Mean Temp. (°F)	25.3	26.5	34.0	46.0	57.1	66.4	71.3	69.9	62.5	51.1	41.0	30.3	48.5
Mean Minimum Temp. (°F)	18.8	19.3	25.9	36.9	47.5	57.2	62.4	61.0	53.5	42.9	34.2	24.1	40.3
Extreme Maximum Temp. (°F)	68	71	79	94	91	96	97	96	92	86	73	74	97
Extreme Minimum Temp. (°F)	-16	-6	-7	12	31	38	46	38	32	25	11	-10	-16
Days Maximum Temp. ≥ 90°F	0	0	0	0	0	1	1	1	0	0	0	0	3
Days Maximum Temp. ≤ 32°F	16	14	7	1	0	0	0	0	0	0	2	11	51
Days Minimum Temp. ≤ 32°F	27	25	23	9	0	0	0	0	0	3	13	25	125
Days Minimum Temp. ≤ 0°F	2	1	0	0	0	0	0	0	0	0	0	1	4
Heating Degree Days (base 65°F)	1,223	1,083	953	566	261	61	7	16	126	430	713	1,069	6,508
Cooling Degree Days (base 65°F)	0	0	0	3	25	109	208	175	57	5	0	0	582
Mean Precipitation (in.)	3.13	2.47	2.94	3.03	3.41	3.58	3.24	3.32	3.95	3.57	3.97	3.88	40.49
Maximum Precipitation (in.)*	6.9	5.9	6.0	5.9	7.2	8.4	8.9	10.7	9.0	9.1	9.8	8.7	53.5
Minimum Precipitation (in.)*	1.0	0.8	1.2	1.3	1.2	0.1	0.9	1.1	0.8	0.3	1.5	1.7	28.5
Extreme Maximum Daily Precip. (in.)	1.83	1.74	1.39	1.66	3.41	5.01	2.19	2.41	3.55	2.42	2.31	1.66	5.01
Days With ≥ 0.1" Precipitation	9	7	8	8	8	8	6	7	7	8	9	10	95
Days With ≥ 0.5" Precipitation	1	1	2	2	2	2	2	2	3	3	2	2	24
Days With ≥ 1.0" Precipitation	0	0	0	0	1	1	1	1	1	1	1	0	7
Mean Snowfall (in.)	24.4	17.2	13.4	2.8	0.3	trace	trace	trace	trace	0.9	8.1	26.9	94.0
Maximum Snowfall (in.)*	68	54	29	15	8	0	0	0	trace	3	31	68	176
Maximum 24-hr. Snowfall (in.)*	18	18	15	6	8	0	0	0	trace	3	19	34	34
Maximum Snow Depth (in.)	30	20	20	6	4	trace	trace	trace	trace	22	25	44	44
Days With ≥ 1.0" Snow Depth	21	19	11	1	0	0	0	0	0	0	4	15	71
Thunderstorm Days*	< 1	< 1	1	2	3	5	6	6	4	2	1	< 1	30
Foggy Days*	12	12	14	13	14	13	13	15	13	13	13	13	158
Predominant Sky Cover*	OVR	OVR	OVR	OVR	OVR	OVR	SCT	OVR	OVR	OVR	OVR	OVR	OVR
Mean Relative Humidity 7am (%)*	79	80	80	77	76	77	79	83	83	81	80	80	79
Mean Relative Humidity 4pm (%)*	73	70	65	57	55	54	54	56	59	60	69	73	62
Mean Dewpoint (°F)*	18	18	25	34	44	54	59	59	52	42	33	23	39
Prevailing Wind Direction*	WSW	WSW	SW	SW	SW	SW	SW	SW	SW	SW	W	W	SW
Prevailing Wind Speed (mph)*	18	17	16	15	14	14	13	13	13	15	15	15	15
Maximum Wind Gust (mph)*	71	82	73	74	64	79	59	81	62	63	73	69	82

Note: (*) Period of record is 1946-1995

Islip Macarthur Airport

Long Island is the terminal moraine marking the southernmost advance of the ice sheet along the Atlantic Coast during the last ice age. The terrain is generally flat, with only a gradual rise in elevation from Long Island Sound on the northern shore and from the Atlantic Ocean on the southern shore toward the middle of the island. Islip is located about half-way out Long Island on the southern coast. The airport is located about seven miles to the northeast of the city. Islip is protected from flooding during periods of high tides by Fire Island, a natural barrier located about three miles offshore. Most of the air masses affecting Islip are continental in origin, however the ocean has a pronounced influence on the climate of the area.

A cool sea breeze blowing off the ocean during the summer months helps to alleviate the afternoon heat. There are an average of 7 days between June and September when the afternoon temperature exceeds 90 degrees, while farther inland there are 10 to 15 such days.

It is uncommon for the eye of a tropical storm to pass directly over Long Island. Tropical weather systems moving along the Atlantic Coast, however, are capable of producing episodes of heavy rain and strong winds in the late summer or fall.

The winter season is relatively mild. Below zero temperatures are reported on only one or two days in about half the winters. Temperatures of 10 degrees below zero or colder are extremely rare. The seasonal snowfall averages about 29 inches. Almost all of this snow falls between December and March. Coastal low pressure systems, Northeasters, are the principle source of this snow. These weather systems will occasionally produce a heavy snowfall. There are usually extended periods during the winter when the ground is bare of snow.

Based on the 1951-1980 period, the average date of the last spring temperature of 32 degrees is April 27 and the average first fall occurrence is October 21. Inland locations would expect a shorter freeze-free season.

Islip Macarthur Airport *Suffolk County*   Elevation: 83 ft.   Latitude: 40° 47' N   Longitude: 73° 06' W

	JAN	FEB	MAR	APR	MAY	JUN	JUL	AUG	SEP	OCT	NOV	DEC	YEAR
Mean Maximum Temp. (°F)	39.5	41.0	47.8	58.0	67.9	77.2	82.0	81.1	74.2	63.5	53.8	43.9	60.8
Mean Temp. (°F)	31.9	33.0	39.5	49.3	58.8	68.7	74.1	73.3	65.9	54.6	45.5	36.2	52.6
Mean Minimum Temp. (°F)	24.4	24.9	31.2	40.6	49.6	60.2	66.1	65.4	57.6	45.5	37.2	28.5	44.3
Extreme Maximum Temp. (°F)	69	67	82	94	98	96	102	100	92	88	78	77	102
Extreme Minimum Temp. (°F)	-7	2	5	23	32	42	50	50	38	29	11	5	-7
Days Maximum Temp. ≥ 90°F	0	0	0	0	1	2	3	2	0	0	0	0	8
Days Maximum Temp. ≤ 32°F	7	5	1	0	0	0	0	0	0	0	0	4	17
Days Minimum Temp. ≤ 32°F	25	23	18	3	0	0	0	0	0	1	10	21	101
Days Minimum Temp. ≤ 0°F	0	0	0	0	0	0	0	0	0	0	0	0	0
Heating Degree Days (base 65°F)	1,017	898	782	467	211	32	1	2	59	327	579	886	5,261
Cooling Degree Days (base 65°F)	0	0	0	3	24	151	290	266	94	11	0	0	839
Mean Precipitation (in.)	3.79	2.99	4.37	4.25	3.80	4.08	3.29	4.34	3.83	4.01	3.59	4.19	46.53
Maximum Precipitation (in.)*	6.3	5.5	5.5	5.1	10.1	7.9	8.4	13.8	5.1	8.7	8.0	6.1	65.3
Minimum Precipitation (in.)*	1.3	1.1	1.3	1.3	0.7	0.6	1.2	0.5	0.8	0.3	1.3	0.9	34.4
Extreme Maximum Daily Precip. (in.)	3.61	2.32	3.25	4.63	4.01	4.87	3.34	6.74	2.85	5.38	2.63	2.65	6.74
Days With ≥ 0.1" Precipitation	7	6	7	7	7	6	6	6	6	6	6	7	77
Days With ≥ 0.5" Precipitation	3	2	3	3	2	2	2	3	3	3	3	3	32
Days With ≥ 1.0" Precipitation	1	1	1	1	1	1	1	1	1	1	1	1	12
Mean Snowfall (in.)	na	na	na	na	na	na	na	na	na	na	na	na	na
Maximum Snowfall (in.)*	14	20	13	3	0	0	0	0	0	0	8	10	34
Maximum 24-hr. Snowfall (in.)*	6	7	8	3	0	0	0	0	0	0	8	9	9
Maximum Snow Depth (in.)	na	na	na	na	na	na	na	na	na	na	na	na	na
Days With ≥ 1.0" Snow Depth	na	na	na	na	na	na	na	na	na	na	na	na	na
Thunderstorm Days*	< 1	< 1	1	2	3	5	6	4	2	1	1	< 1	25
Foggy Days*	15	14	16	16	18	16	22	19	17	15	14	14	196
Predominant Sky Cover*	OVR	OVR	OVR	OVR	OVR	SCT	OVR	SCT	OVR	CLR	OVR	OVR	OVR
Mean Relative Humidity 7am (%)*	76	76	77	76	76	77	81	84	85	85	80	76	79
Mean Relative Humidity 4pm (%)*	62	59	57	58	59	59	63	63	63	62	62	60	61
Mean Dewpoint (°F)*	22	22	28	38	48	58	65	64	57	46	36	26	43
Prevailing Wind Direction*	WNW	NW	NW	SW	SW	SW	SW	SW	SW	SW	SW	WNW	SW
Prevailing Wind Speed (mph)*	13	13	13	10	10	10	10	9	10	10	10	12	12
Maximum Wind Gust (mph)*	na	na	na	na	na	na	na	na	na	na	na	na	na

Note: (*) Period of record is 1984-1995

New York Central Park Observatory

New York City, in area exceeding 300 square miles, is located on the Atlantic coastal plain at the mouth of the Hudson River. The terrain is laced with numerous waterways, all but one of the five boroughs in the city are situated on islands. Elevations range from less than 50 feet over most of Manhattan, Brooklyn, and Queens to almost 300 feet in northern Manhattan and the Bronx, and over 400 feet in Staten Island.

The New York Metropolitan area is close to the path of most storm and frontal systems which move across the North American continent. Therefore, weather conditions affecting the city most often approach from a westerly direction, resulting in higher temperatures in summer and lower ones in winter than would otherwise be expected in a coastal area. However, the frequent passage of weather systems often helps reduce the length of extremes.

Although continental influence predominates, oceanic influence is by no means absent. During the summer local sea breezes, winds blowing onshore from the cool water surface, often moderate the afternoon heat. The effect of the sea breeze diminishes inland. On winter mornings, ocean temperatures which are warm relative to the land reinforce the effect of the city heat island and low temperatures are often 10-20 degrees lower in the inland suburbs than in the central city. The relatively warm water temperatures also delay the advent of winter snows. Conversely, the lag in warming of water temperatures keeps spring temperatures relatively cool.

Precipitation is moderate and distributed fairly evenly throughout the year. Most of the rainfall from May through October comes from thunderstorms, usually of brief duration and sometimes intense. Heavy rains of long duration associated with tropical storms occur infrequently in late summer or fall. For the other seasons precipitation is associated with widespread storm areas, producing day-long rain or snow. Coastal storms, occurring most often in the fall and winter months, produce on occasion considerable amounts of precipitation, record rains, snows, and high winds.

The average annual precipitation is reasonably uniform within the city but higher in the suburbs and less on eastern Long Island. Annual snowfall totals also show a consistent increase to the north and west of the city with lesser amounts along the south shores and the eastern end of Long Island.

Local Climatological Data is published for three locations in New York City, Central Park, La Guardia Airport, and John°F. Kennedy International Airport.

Based on the 1951-1980 period, the average first occurrence of 32 degrees Fahrenheit in the fall is November 11 and the average last occurrence in the spring is April 1.

New York Central Park Observatory *New York County*   Elevation: 131 ft.   Latitude: 40° 47' N   Longitude: 73° 58' W

	JAN	FEB	MAR	APR	MAY	JUN	JUL	AUG	SEP	OCT	NOV	DEC	YEAR
Mean Maximum Temp. (°F)	39.2	42.2	50.3	61.9	71.6	79.9	84.8	83.5	76.0	64.5	54.5	43.8	62.7
Mean Temp. (°F)	33.1	35.5	42.7	53.3	62.8	71.7	76.8	75.8	68.4	57.2	48.0	37.9	55.3
Mean Minimum Temp. (°F)	26.9	28.7	35.0	44.8	54.0	63.5	68.8	68.0	60.8	49.9	41.4	31.9	47.8
Extreme Maximum Temp. (°F)	72	75	86	96	97	98	102	103	99	87	80	75	103
Extreme Minimum Temp. (°F)	-2	4	10	21	40	47	53	50	43	31	18	-1	-2
Days Maximum Temp. ≥ 90°F	0	0	0	0	1	3	7	5	1	0	0	0	17
Days Maximum Temp. ≤ 32°F	8	4	1	0	0	0	0	0	0	0	0	4	17
Days Minimum Temp. ≤ 32°F	21	19	11	1	0	0	0	0	0	0	3	15	70
Days Minimum Temp. ≤ 0°F	0	0	0	0	0	0	0	0	0	0	0	0	0
Heating Degree Days (base 65°F)	983	829	687	355	124	15	0	1	36	254	505	833	4,622
Cooling Degree Days (base 65°F)	0	0	2	12	64	223	374	343	145	20	1	0	1,184
Mean Precipitation (in.)	3.59	2.92	4.13	4.35	4.16	4.51	4.73	4.24	4.21	4.36	4.00	3.88	49.08
Maximum Precipitation (in.)*	10.5	6.0	10.4	8.3	10.2	9.3	11.8	12.4	9.3	7.8	12.4	10.0	67.0
Minimum Precipitation (in.)*	0.6	0.5	0.9	1.3	0.6	1.2	1.3	0.2	1.3	0.1	0.3	0.6	26.1
Extreme Maximum Daily Precip. (in.)	2.73	1.94	3.10	7.56	2.40	3.07	3.75	4.64	5.02	4.35	3.60	2.41	7.56
Days With ≥ 0.1" Precipitation	6	6	7	7	7	7	7	6	6	6	6	7	78
Days With ≥ 0.5" Precipitation	3	2	3	3	3	3	3	3	3	3	3	3	35
Days With ≥ 1.0" Precipitation	1	1	1	1	1	1	1	1	1	1	1	1	12
Mean Snowfall (in.)	7.0	7.6	3.8	0.6	trace	0.0	trace	0.0	0.0	trace	0.3	4.3	23.6
Maximum Snowfall (in.)*	20	26	17	10	trace	0	0	0	0	trace	5	12	53
Maximum 24-hr. Snowfall (in.)*	12	16	10	10	trace	0	0	0	0	trace	4	7	16
Maximum Snow Depth (in.)	14	na	9	9	trace	0	trace	0	0	0	5	10	na
Days With ≥ 1.0" Snow Depth	8	na	3	0	0	0	0	0	0	0	0	2	na
Thunderstorm Days*	< 1	< 1	1	1	3	4	5	4	1	1	< 1	< 1	20
Foggy Days*	0	0	0	0	0	0	0	0	0	0	0	< 1	1
Predominant Sky Cover*	OVR	OVR	OVR	OVR	OVR	SCT	SCT	SCT	OVR	CLR	OVR	OVR	OVR
Mean Relative Humidity 7am (%)*	67	67	66	64	72	74	74	76	78	75	72	69	71
Mean Relative Humidity 4pm (%)*	55	53	50	45	52	55	53	54	56	55	58	59	54
Mean Dewpoint (°F)*	18	19	26	34	47	57	62	62	56	44	34	25	40
Prevailing Wind Direction*	NW	NW	NW	NW	NE	SW	SW	SW	SW	W	W	NW	NW
Prevailing Wind Speed (mph)*	12	12	13	12	10	8	8	8	8	9	9	12	10
Maximum Wind Gust (mph)*	52	51	63	46	44	41	46	43	52	46	58	64	64

Note: (*) Period of record is 1965-1995

New York JFK Int'l Airport

New York City, in area exceeding 300 square miles, is located on the Atlantic coastal plain at the mouth of the Hudson River. The terrain is laced with numerous waterways, all but one of the five boroughs in the city are situated on islands. Elevations range from less than 50 feet over most of Manhattan, Brooklyn, and Queens to almost 300 feet in northern Manhattan and the Bronx, and over 400 feet in Staten Island.

The New York Metropolitan area is close to the path of most storm and frontal systems which move across the North American continent. Therefore, weather conditions affecting the city most often approach from a westerly direction, resulting in higher temperatures in summer and lower ones in winter than would otherwise be expected in a coastal area. However, the frequent passage of weather systems often helps reduce the length of extremes.

Although continental influence predominates, oceanic influence is by no means absent. During the summer local sea breezes, winds blowing onshore from the cool water surface, often moderate the afternoon heat. The effect of the sea breeze diminishes inland. On winter mornings, ocean temperatures which are warm relative to the land reinforce the effect of the city heat island and low temperatures are often 10-20 degrees lower in the inland suburbs than in the central city. The relatively warm water temperatures also delay the advent of winter snows. Conversely, the lag in warming of water temperatures keeps spring temperatures relatively cool.

Precipitation is moderate and distributed fairly evenly throughout the year. Most of the rainfall from May through October comes from thunderstorms, usually of brief duration and sometimes intense. Heavy rains of long duration associated with tropical storms occur infrequently in late summer or fall. For the other seasons precipitation is associated with widespread storm areas, producing day-long rain or snow. Coastal storms, occurring most often in the fall and winter months, produce on occasion considerable amounts of precipitation, record rains, snows, and high winds.

The average annual precipitation is reasonably uniform within the city but higher in the suburbs and less on eastern Long Island. Annual snowfall totals also show a consistent increase to the north and west of the city with lesser amounts along the south shores and the eastern end of Long Island.

Local Climatological Data is published for three locations in New York City, Central Park, La Guardia Airport, and John°F. Kennedy International Airport.

Based on the 1951-1980 period, the average first occurrence of 32 degrees Fahrenheit in the fall is November 11 and the average last occurrence in the spring is April 1.

New York JFK Int'l Airport *Queens County*   Elevation: 16 ft.   Latitude: 40° 39' N   Longitude: 73° 48' W

	JAN	FEB	MAR	APR	MAY	JUN	JUL	AUG	SEP	OCT	NOV	DEC	YEAR
Mean Maximum Temp. (°F)	39.1	41.7	48.8	58.8	68.4	77.7	82.9	82.0	75.4	64.4	54.3	44.1	61.5
Mean Temp. (°F)	32.8	34.8	41.4	51.2	60.6	70.2	75.7	75.0	68.2	57.1	47.5	37.9	54.4
Mean Minimum Temp. (°F)	26.3	27.9	34.0	43.6	52.8	62.5	68.5	68.0	60.9	49.7	40.8	31.5	47.2
Extreme Maximum Temp. (°F)	71	71	85	90	95	98	102	100	98	90	77	75	102
Extreme Minimum Temp. (°F)	-2	7	8	20	37	48	56	51	43	31	19	2	-2
Days Maximum Temp. ≥ 90°F	0	0	0	0	0	2	4	3	1	0	0	0	10
Days Maximum Temp. ≤ 32°F	7	4	1	0	0	0	0	0	0	0	0	3	15
Days Minimum Temp. ≤ 32°F	22	20	12	1	0	0	0	0	0	0	3	16	74
Days Minimum Temp. ≤ 0°F	0	0	0	0	0	0	0	0	0	0	0	0	0
Heating Degree Days (base 65°F)	993	846	725	410	162	19	0	1	33	255	518	834	4,796
Cooling Degree Days (base 65°F)	0	0	0	3	33	180	341	319	135	15	0	0	1,026
Mean Precipitation (in.)	3.15	2.42	3.77	4.01	3.97	3.93	4.13	3.61	3.39	3.57	3.37	3.32	42.64
Maximum Precipitation (in.)*	8.3	4.9	8.2	9.5	10.7	8.1	8.5	8.3	9.6	6.6	9.5	6.7	59.1
Minimum Precipitation (in.)*	0.5	1.0	0.9	1.4	0.6	trace	0.5	0.2	1.0	0.9	0.3	0.6	25.4
Extreme Maximum Daily Precip. (in.)	3.78	1.62	2.56	3.15	2.70	6.27	3.51	4.10	3.42	4.66	2.45	2.55	6.27
Days With ≥ 0.1" Precipitation	6	5	7	7	7	6	6	6	5	5	6	6	72
Days With ≥ 0.5" Precipitation	2	2	3	3	3	3	3	2	2	3	3	2	31
Days With ≥ 1.0" Precipitation	1	1	1	1	1	1	1	1	1	1	1	1	12
Mean Snowfall (in.)	6.4	7.4	3.6	0.8	trace	0.0	trace	0.0	0.0	trace	0.3	4.2	22.7
Maximum Snowfall (in.)*	20	25	16	8	0	0	0	0	0	trace	4	22	49
Maximum 24-hr. Snowfall (in.)*	13	20	9	8	0	0	0	0	0	trace	3	18	20
Maximum Snow Depth (in.)	22	28	8	8	trace	0	trace	0	0	trace	4	14	28
Days With ≥ 1.0" Snow Depth	7	5	3	0	0	0	0	0	0	0	0	3	18
Thunderstorm Days*	< 1	< 1	1	2	3	4	5	5	2	1	1	< 1	24
Foggy Days*	10	9	11	11	13	12	13	13	11	10	11	10	133
Predominant Sky Cover*	OVR	OVR	OVR	OVR	OVR	OVR	SCT	SCT	OVR	CLR	OVR	OVR	OVR
Mean Relative Humidity 7am (%)*	71	71	71	70	73	74	75	78	79	78	76	73	74
Mean Relative Humidity 4pm (%)*	61	59	57	58	61	63	63	63	62	60	61	62	61
Mean Dewpoint (°F)*	21	22	28	37	48	58	64	63	57	46	36	26	42
Prevailing Wind Direction*	NW	NW	NW	S	S	S	S	S	S	WSW	NW	NW	S
Prevailing Wind Speed (mph)*	16	17	17	13	13	12	12	12	12	10	15	16	14
Maximum Wind Gust (mph)*	59	60	68	61	71	56	54	68	60	62	67	61	71

Note: (*) Period of record is 1948-1995

New York Laguardia Airport

New York City, in area exceeding 300 square miles, is located on the Atlantic coastal plain at the mouth of the Hudson River. The terrain is laced with numerous waterways, all but one of the five boroughs in the city are situated on islands. Elevations range from less than 50 feet over most of Manhattan, Brooklyn, and Queens to almost 300 feet in northern Manhattan and the Bronx, and over 400 feet in Staten Island.

The New York Metropolitan area is close to the path of most storm and frontal systems which move across the North American continent. Therefore, weather conditions affecting the city most often approach from a westerly direction, resulting in higher temperatures in summer and lower ones in winter than would otherwise be expected in a coastal area. However, the frequent passage of weather systems often helps reduce the length of extremes.

Although continental influence predominates, oceanic influence is by no means absent. During the summer local sea breezes, winds blowing onshore from the cool water surface, often moderate the afternoon heat. The effect of the sea breeze diminishes inland. On winter mornings, ocean temperatures which are warm relative to the land reinforce the effect of the city heat island and low temperatures are often 10-20 degrees lower in the inland suburbs than in the central city. The relatively warm water temperatures also delay the advent of winter snows. Conversely, the lag in warming of water temperatures keeps spring temperatures relatively cool.

Precipitation is moderate and distributed fairly evenly throughout the year. Most of the rainfall from May through October comes from thunderstorms, usually of brief duration and sometimes intense. Heavy rains of long duration associated with tropical storms occur infrequently in late summer or fall. For the other seasons precipitation is associated with widespread storm areas, producing day-long rain or snow. Coastal storms, occurring most often in the fall and winter months, produce on occasion considerable amounts of precipitation, record rains, snows, and high winds.

The average annual precipitation is reasonably uniform within the city but higher in the suburbs and less on eastern Long Island. Annual snowfall totals also show a consistent increase to the north and west of the city with lesser amounts along the south shores and the eastern end of Long Island.

Local Climatological Data is published for three locations in New York City, Central Park, La Guardia Airport, and John°F. Kennedy International Airport.

Based on the 1951-1980 period, the average first occurrence of 32 degrees Fahrenheit in the fall is November 11 and the average last occurrence in the spring is April 1.

New York Laguardia Airport *Queens County*   Elevation: 11 ft.   Latitude: 40° 47' N   Longitude: 73° 53' W

	JAN	FEB	MAR	APR	MAY	JUN	JUL	AUG	SEP	OCT	NOV	DEC	YEAR
Mean Maximum Temp. (°F)	39.1	42.0	49.4	60.5	71.0	80.1	85.0	83.5	76.1	64.9	54.4	44.2	62.5
Mean Temp. (°F)	33.3	35.6	42.3	52.8	62.8	72.3	77.6	76.6	69.4	58.3	48.4	38.4	55.6
Mean Minimum Temp. (°F)	27.4	29.1	35.1	45.1	54.6	64.4	70.1	69.6	62.6	51.6	42.4	32.6	48.7
Extreme Maximum Temp. (°F)	72	73	83	94	97	100	103	104	96	89	80	75	104
Extreme Minimum Temp. (°F)	-3	4	8	22	38	49	56	51	45	34	20	-1	-3
Days Maximum Temp. ≥ 90°F	0	0	0	0	1	4	7	5	1	0	0	0	18
Days Maximum Temp. ≤ 32°F	8	5	1	0	0	0	0	0	0	0	0	4	18
Days Minimum Temp. ≤ 32°F	21	18	10	1	0	0	0	0	0	0	3	14	67
Days Minimum Temp. ≤ 0°F	0	0	0	0	0	0	0	0	0	0	0	0	0
Heating Degree Days (base 65°F)	976	825	698	366	124	13	0	1	29	227	491	816	4,566
Cooling Degree Days (base 65°F)	0	0	1	8	62	238	395	366	166	25	1	0	1,262
Mean Precipitation (in.)	3.18	2.62	3.94	4.13	3.77	4.00	4.57	4.09	3.67	3.73	3.49	3.47	44.66
Maximum Precipitation (in.)*	8.7	5.7	8.7	11.5	9.3	8.1	12.3	16.0	9.6	7.3	9.9	7.7	60.8
Minimum Precipitation (in.)*	0.5	0.7	0.9	1.0	0.4	trace	0.7	0.1	1.0	0.1	0.3	0.3	22.2
Extreme Maximum Daily Precip. (in.)	2.60	1.63	2.83	6.69	2.57	4.00	3.53	3.54	4.63	4.39	2.91	2.74	6.69
Days With ≥ 0.1" Precipitation	6	5	7	7	7	7	7	6	5	5	6	7	75
Days With ≥ 0.5" Precipitation	2	2	3	2	3	3	3	3	2	3	3	3	32
Days With ≥ 1.0" Precipitation	1	1	1	1	1	1	1	1	1	1	1	1	12
Mean Snowfall (in.)	7.5	8.2	4.5	0.6	trace	0.0	trace	trace	0.0	trace	0.3	4.8	25.9
Maximum Snowfall (in.)*	18	26	19	8	trace	0	0	0	0	1	6	22	60
Maximum 24-hr. Snowfall (in.)*	11	17	14	8	trace	0	0	0	0	1	6	16	17
Maximum Snow Depth (in.)	25	22	9	8	trace	0	trace	trace	0	trace	6	15	25
Days With ≥ 1.0" Snow Depth	7	6	3	0	0	0	0	0	0	0	0	3	19
Thunderstorm Days*	< 1	< 1	1	2	3	4	5	5	2	1	< 1	< 1	23
Foggy Days*	10	9	10	10	11	9	8	8	8	8	9	10	110
Predominant Sky Cover*	OVR	OVR	OVR	OVR	OVR	OVR	SCT	SCT	OVR	OVR	OVR	OVR	OVR
Mean Relative Humidity 7am (%)*	67	67	67	67	71	71	73	75	76	74	71	68	71
Mean Relative Humidity 4pm (%)*	57	55	52	51	53	53	54	56	56	55	57	59	55
Mean Dewpoint (°F)*	20	21	27	36	48	57	63	62	56	45	35	25	41
Prevailing Wind Direction*	NW	WNW	NW	NW	S	S	S	S	S	SW	WNW	WNW	NW
Prevailing Wind Speed (mph)*	17	17	17	16	12	12	12	12	10	12	15	16	14
Maximum Wind Gust (mph)*	61	67	71	63	56	56	59	73	64	71	76	77	77

Note: (*) Period of record is 1947-1995

Rochester Int'l Airport

Rochester is located at the mouth of the Genesee River at about the mid point of the south shore of Lake Ontario. The river flows northward from northwest Pennsylvania and empties into Lake Ontario. The land slopes from a lakeshore elevation of 246 feet to over 1,000 feet some 20 miles south. The airport is located just south of the city.

Lake Ontario plays a major role in the Rochester weather. In the summer its cooling effect inhibits the temperature from rising much above the low to mid 90s. In the winter the modifying temperature effect prevents temperatures from falling below -15 degrees most of the time, although temperatures at locations more than 15 miles inland do drop below -30 degrees.

The lake plays a major role in winter snowfall distribution. Well inland from the lake and toward the airport, the seasonal snowfall is usually less than in the area north of the airport and toward the lakeshore where wide variations occur. This is due to what is called the lake effect. Snowfalls of one to two feet or more in 24 hours are common near the lake in winter due the lake effect alone. The lake rarely freezes over because of its depth. The area is also prone to other heavy snowstorms and blizzards because of its proximity to the paths of low pressure systems coming up the east coast, out of the Ohio Valley.

Precipitation is rather evenly distributed throughout the year. Excessive rains occur infrequently but may be caused by slowly moving thunderstorms, slowly moving or stalled major low pressure systems, or by hurricanes and tropical storms that move inland. Hail occurs occasionally and heavy fog is rare.

The growing season averages 150 to 180 days. The years first frost usually occurs in late September and the last frost typically occurs in mid-May.

Rochester Int'l Airport *Monroe County*   Elevation: 600 ft.   Latitude: 43° 07' N   Longitude: 77° 41' W

	JAN	FEB	MAR	APR	MAY	JUN	JUL	AUG	SEP	OCT	NOV	DEC	YEAR
Mean Maximum Temp. (°F)	32.0	34.2	42.8	56.0	67.8	76.8	81.2	79.4	72.0	59.8	48.2	36.8	57.3
Mean Temp. (°F)	24.9	26.4	34.2	46.4	57.2	66.4	71.0	69.6	62.1	50.8	40.7	30.2	48.3
Mean Minimum Temp. (°F)	17.8	18.6	25.6	36.7	46.5	55.9	60.8	59.7	52.1	41.7	33.2	23.5	39.3
Extreme Maximum Temp. (°F)	68	73	83	93	94	95	98	97	95	85	75	72	98
Extreme Minimum Temp. (°F)	-17	-8	-7	13	30	36	45	38	30	21	9	-12	-17
Days Maximum Temp. ≥ 90°F	0	0	0	0	0	1	3	2	0	0	0	0	6
Days Maximum Temp. ≤ 32°F	16	13	6	0	0	0	0	0	0	0	1	10	46
Days Minimum Temp. ≤ 32°F	28	25	23	10	1	0	0	0	0	4	15	25	131
Days Minimum Temp. ≤ 0°F	3	1	0	0	0	0	0	0	0	0	0	0	4
Heating Degree Days (base 65°F)	1,236	1,084	948	556	265	64	10	20	135	440	723	1,072	6,553
Cooling Degree Days (base 65°F)	0	0	0	5	29	112	204	170	55	6	0	0	581
Mean Precipitation (in.)	2.37	1.90	2.55	2.76	2.83	3.36	3.20	3.49	3.39	2.73	2.92	2.62	34.12
Maximum Precipitation (in.)*	5.8	5.1	5.0	4.1	6.6	6.8	6.0	6.0	6.3	7.8	7.0	4.6	40.5
Minimum Precipitation (in.)*	0.7	0.7	0.5	1.2	0.4	0.2	0.6	0.8	0.3	0.2	0.4	0.6	22.4
Extreme Maximum Daily Precip. (in.)	1.77	1.59	1.44	1.79	2.12	2.19	3.33	2.51	3.08	2.94	1.83	1.46	3.33
Days With ≥ 0.1" Precipitation	7	6	7	7	6	7	6	6	7	6	7	8	80
Days With ≥ 0.5" Precipitation	1	1	1	2	2	2	2	2	2	2	2	1	20
Days With ≥ 1.0" Precipitation	0	0	0	0	0	1	1	1	1	1	0	0	4
Mean Snowfall (in.)	27.0	21.3	17.0	3.9	0.4	trace	trace	0.0	trace	0.1	7.6	22.1	99.4
Maximum Snowfall (in.)*	60	65	40	20	11	0	0	0	trace	3	23	46	152
Maximum 24-hr. Snowfall (in.)*	18	18	18	10	11	0	0	0	trace	3	12	18	18
Maximum Snow Depth (in.)	28	17	34	7	4	trace	trace	0	trace	trace	10	13	34
Days With ≥ 1.0" Snow Depth	21	20	12	1	0	0	0	0	0	0	4	15	73
Thunderstorm Days*	< 1	< 1	1	2	3	5	6	6	3	1	< 1	< 1	27
Foggy Days*	8	9	10	10	10	10	11	13	12	11	11	10	125
Predominant Sky Cover*	OVR	OVR	OVR	OVR	OVR	OVR	SCT	OVR	OVR	OVR	OVR	OVR	OVR
Mean Relative Humidity 7am (%)*	79	80	80	78	77	79	82	86	88	85	82	81	81
Mean Relative Humidity 4pm (%)*	71	69	63	56	53	53	52	55	59	60	69	73	61
Mean Dewpoint (°F)*	18	18	25	35	45	55	60	59	53	42	33	23	39
Prevailing Wind Direction*	WSW	WSW	WSW	WSW	WSW	WSW	SW	SW	SW	WSW	WSW	WSW	WSW
Prevailing Wind Speed (mph)*	16	15	15	14	13	12	8	8	8	12	14	14	13
Maximum Wind Gust (mph)*	63	70	68	71	64	52	56	62	51	60	67	55	71

Note: (*) Period of record is 1948-1995

Syracuse Hancock Int'l Airport

Syracuse is located approximately at the geographical center of the state. Gently rolling terrain stretches northward for about 30 miles to the eastern end of Lake Ontario. Oneida Lake is about 8 miles northeast of Syracuse. Approximately five miles south of the city, hills rise to 1,500 feet. Immediately to the west, the terrain is gently rolling with elevations 500 to 800 feet above sea level.

The climate of Syracuse is primarily continental in character and comparatively humid. Nearly all cyclonic systems moving from the interior of the country through the St. Lawrence Valley will affect the Syracuse area. Seasonal and diurnal changes are marked and produce an invigorating climate.

In the summer and in portions of the transitional seasons, temperatures usually rise rapidly during the daytime to moderate levels and as a rule fall rapidly after sunset. The nights are relatively cool and comfortable. There are only a few days in a year when atmospheric humidity causes great personal discomfort.

Winters are usually cold and are sometimes severe in part. Daytime temperatures average in the low 30s with nighttime lows in the teens. Low winter temperatures below -25 degrees have been recorded. The autumn, winter, and spring seasons display marked variability.

Based on the 1951-1980 period, the average first occurrence of 32 degrees Fahrenheit in the fall is October 16 and the average last occurrence in the spring is April 28.

Precipitation in the Syracuse area is derived principally from cyclonic storms which pass from the interior of the country through the St. Lawrence Valley. Lake Ontario provides the source of significant winter precipitation. The lake is quite deep and never freezes so cold air flowing over the lake is quickly saturated and produces the cloudiness and snow squalls which are a well-known feature of winter weather in the Syracuse area.

The precipitation is uncommonly well distributed, averaging about 3 inches per month throughout the year. Snowfall is moderately heavy with an average just over 100 inches. There are about 30 days per year with thunderstorms.

Wind velocities are moderate, but during the winter months there are numerous days with sufficient winds to cause blowing and drifting snow.

During December, January, and February there is much cloudiness. Syracuse receives only about one-third of possible sunshine during winter months. Approximately two-thirds of possible sunshine is received during the warm months.

Syracuse Hancock Int'l Airport *Onondaga County*   Elevation: 410 ft.   Latitude: 43° 07' N   Longitude: 76° 06' W

	JAN	FEB	MAR	APR	MAY	JUN	JUL	AUG	SEP	OCT	NOV	DEC	YEAR
Mean Maximum Temp. (°F)	31.7	34.2	43.0	57.1	68.9	77.5	81.7	80.2	72.3	59.9	48.2	36.5	57.6
Mean Temp. (°F)	23.8	25.7	33.9	46.8	57.6	66.6	71.3	69.9	62.1	50.5	40.5	29.3	48.2
Mean Minimum Temp. (°F)	15.8	17.3	24.8	36.5	46.3	55.7	60.9	59.5	51.8	41.0	32.7	22.0	38.7
Extreme Maximum Temp. (°F)	70	69	87	92	93	97	98	101	95	85	76	72	101
Extreme Minimum Temp. (°F)	-25	-15	-15	12	27	36	46	42	28	22	6	-22	-25
Days Maximum Temp. ≥ 90°F	0	0	0	0	0	2	4	2	0	0	0	0	8
Days Maximum Temp. ≤ 32°F	16	13	6	0	0	0	0	0	0	0	2	11	48
Days Minimum Temp. ≤ 32°F	28	26	24	10	0	0	0	0	0	5	15	26	134
Days Minimum Temp. ≤ 0°F	4	2	1	0	0	0	0	0	0	0	0	1	8
Heating Degree Days (base 65°F)	1,272	1,103	957	543	249	59	7	19	134	446	729	1,100	6,618
Cooling Degree Days (base 65°F)	0	0	1	5	27	114	209	177	53	4	0	0	590
Mean Precipitation (in.)	2.46	2.04	3.00	3.27	3.17	3.24	3.72	3.40	3.62	3.40	3.52	3.06	37.90
Maximum Precipitation (in.)*	5.8	5.4	6.8	8.1	7.4	12.3	9.5	8.4	8.8	8.3	6.8	5.5	57.9
Minimum Precipitation (in.)*	1.0	0.6	1.0	1.2	0.8	1.0	0.9	1.3	0.8	0.2	1.3	0.8	27.1
Extreme Maximum Daily Precip. (in.)	1.41	1.62	1.33	1.60	1.69	2.86	4.29	2.98	2.59	2.98	3.56	1.48	4.29
Days With ≥ 0.1" Precipitation	7	6	8	8	8	7	7	7	7	8	9	8	90
Days With ≥ 0.5" Precipitation	1	1	2	2	2	3	2	2	2	2	2	2	23
Days With ≥ 1.0" Precipitation	0	0	0	0	0	0	1	1	1	1	0	0	4
Mean Snowfall (in.)	34.9	26.2	18.7	3.8	0.1	trace	trace	trace	trace	0.4	9.7	30.7	124.5
Maximum Snowfall (in.)*	72	73	54	16	2	0	0	trace	trace	6	34	65	208
Maximum 24-hr. Snowfall (in.)*	22	21	22	7	2	0	0	trace	trace	3	12	16	22
Maximum Snow Depth (in.)	26	33	35	6	1	trace	trace	trace	trace	trace	10	20	35
Days With ≥ 1.0" Snow Depth	23	21	13	1	0	0	0	0	0	0	4	16	78
Thunderstorm Days*	< 1	< 1	1	2	3	5	6	5	3	1	1	< 1	27
Foggy Days*	10	9	11	10	11	11	12	13	14	12	12	11	136
Predominant Sky Cover*	OVR	OVR	OVR	OVR	OVR	OVR	OVR	OVR	OVR	OVR	OVR	OVR	OVR
Mean Relative Humidity 7am (%)*	77	78	78	76	76	77	79	85	86	84	80	79	80
Mean Relative Humidity 4pm (%)*	69	67	60	52	53	54	54	57	60	60	68	72	60
Mean Dewpoint (°F)*	16	17	24	34	45	55	60	59	53	42	32	22	38
Prevailing Wind Direction*	WSW	WSW	WNW	WNW	WNW	WNW	WSW	WSW	WSW	WSW	WSW	WSW	WSW
Prevailing Wind Speed (mph)*	15	14	14	14	12	12	9	9	9	10	13	14	12
Maximum Wind Gust (mph)*	58	56	61	63	76	67	66	49	48	60	58	63	76

Note: (*) Period of record is 1945-1995

Albion 2 NE *Orleans County*   Elevation: 439 ft.   Latitude: 43° 17' N   Longitude: 78° 10' W

	JAN	FEB	MAR	APR	MAY	JUN	JUL	AUG	SEP	OCT	NOV	DEC	YEAR
Mean Maximum Temp. (°F)	32.3	34.6	43.5	57.1	68.9	78.0	82.1	80.4	73.2	60.7	48.5	37.1	58.0
Mean Temp. (°F)	25.4	26.9	34.8	47.1	57.9	67.4	72.0	70.5	63.5	51.8	41.3	30.6	49.1
Mean Minimum Temp. (°F)	18.4	19.2	26.0	36.9	46.9	56.8	61.8	60.5	53.7	42.9	33.9	24.0	40.1
Extreme Maximum Temp. (°F)	67	74	80	87	91	96	101	98	93	84	74	75	101
Extreme Minimum Temp. (°F)	-15	-6	-5	13	28	35	45	39	32	22	11	-10	-15
Days Maximum Temp. ≥ 90°F	0	0	0	0	0	2	4	2	0	0	0	0	8
Days Maximum Temp. ≤ 32°F	16	13	6	0	0	0	0	0	0	0	1	10	46
Days Minimum Temp. ≤ 32°F	28	25	23	10	1	0	0	0	0	3	14	25	129
Days Minimum Temp. ≤ 0°F	2	1	0	0	0	0	0	0	0	0	0	0	3
Heating Degree Days (base 65°F)	1,222	1,070	931	537	245	53	6	15	110	409	706	1,061	6,365
Cooling Degree Days (base 65°F)	0	0	1	5	32	132	229	192	71	7	0	0	669
Mean Precipitation (in.)	2.68	2.04	2.77	3.01	2.99	3.14	3.01	3.04	3.57	3.13	3.22	2.95	35.55
Extreme Maximum Daily Precip. (in.)	2.00	1.36	1.90	1.85	2.15	3.79	2.31	3.06	3.28	2.28	2.16	1.96	3.79
Days With ≥ 0.1" Precipitation	8	6	7	8	7	7	6	7	7	7	9	8	87
Days With ≥ 0.5" Precipitation	1	1	2	2	2	2	2	2	2	2	2	1	21
Days With ≥ 1.0" Precipitation	0	0	0	0	0	1	1	1	1	1	0	0	5
Mean Snowfall (in.)	19.5	13.6	11.1	2.1	0.3	0.0	0.0	0.0	0.0	0.2	4.5	15.1	66.4
Maximum Snow Depth (in.)	30	25	19	5	6	0	0	0	0	2	9	12	30
Days With ≥ 1.0" Snow Depth	15	11	6	1	0	0	0	0	0	0	3	11	47

Alcove Dam *Albany County*   Elevation: 606 ft.   Latitude: 42° 28' N   Longitude: 73° 56' W

	JAN	FEB	MAR	APR	MAY	JUN	JUL	AUG	SEP	OCT	NOV	DEC	YEAR
Mean Maximum Temp. (°F)	31.3	34.6	42.4	56.3	67.7	75.8	80.0	78.9	71.0	58.9	47.3	35.9	56.7
Mean Temp. (°F)	21.5	24.1	32.0	45.1	55.9	64.6	69.1	67.9	59.8	48.0	38.3	27.2	46.1
Mean Minimum Temp. (°F)	11.6	13.6	21.6	33.9	44.1	53.4	58.1	56.8	48.6	37.1	29.2	18.6	35.5
Extreme Maximum Temp. (°F)	71	70	86	91	90	96	100	96	98	83	81	73	100
Extreme Minimum Temp. (°F)	-29	-16	-13	10	26	32	39	35	28	18	6	-24	-29
Days Maximum Temp. ≥ 90°F	0	0	0	0	0	1	2	2	0	0	0	0	5
Days Maximum Temp. ≤ 32°F	16	12	6	0	0	0	0	0	0	0	2	11	47
Days Minimum Temp. ≤ 32°F	30	27	27	14	2	0	0	0	1	10	21	28	160
Days Minimum Temp. ≤ 0°F	6	3	1	0	0	0	0	0	0	0	0	2	12
Heating Degree Days (base 65°F)	1,343	1,150	1,017	592	291	83	20	36	180	521	794	1,163	7,190
Cooling Degree Days (base 65°F)	0	0	0	2	16	78	153	131	31	1	0	0	412
Mean Precipitation (in.)	2.43	2.05	3.54	3.77	3.48	4.46	3.84	3.54	3.71	3.45	3.48	2.81	40.56
Extreme Maximum Daily Precip. (in.)	2.15	1.80	5.38	3.95	2.25	4.28	3.42	2.84	6.89	3.51	3.38	2.05	6.89
Days With ≥ 0.1" Precipitation	5	5	6	7	7	8	7	7	6	6	6	6	76
Days With ≥ 0.5" Precipitation	2	1	3	3	2	3	3	2	2	2	3	2	28
Days With ≥ 1.0" Precipitation	0	0	1	1	1	1	1	1	1	1	1	1	10
Mean Snowfall (in.)	na	na	na	0.4	trace	0.0	0.0	0.0	0.0	0.1	0.4	na	na
Maximum Snow Depth (in.)	na	na	na	na	na	na	na	na	na	na	na	na	na
Days With ≥ 1.0" Snow Depth	na	na	na	0	0	0	0	0	0	0	0	0	na

Alfred *Allegany County*   Elevation: 1,770 ft.   Latitude: 42° 16' N   Longitude: 77° 47' W

	JAN	FEB	MAR	APR	MAY	JUN	JUL	AUG	SEP	OCT	NOV	DEC	YEAR
Mean Maximum Temp. (°F)	31.4	34.8	43.6	56.7	68.2	76.3	80.1	78.5	70.7	59.1	47.0	36.1	56.9
Mean Temp. (°F)	22.0	24.1	31.9	44.0	54.3	63.0	67.1	65.5	58.2	47.2	37.4	27.3	45.2
Mean Minimum Temp. (°F)	12.6	13.4	20.4	31.3	40.3	49.8	54.1	52.5	45.7	35.3	27.8	18.6	33.5
Extreme Maximum Temp. (°F)	63	65	83	91	93	93	96	98	94	84	77	68	98
Extreme Minimum Temp. (°F)	-25	-15	-16	5	22	28	37	27	20	15	4	-21	-25
Days Maximum Temp. ≥ 90°F	0	0	0	0	0	1	2	1	0	0	0	0	4
Days Maximum Temp. ≤ 32°F	17	13	5	0	0	0	0	0	0	0	2	11	48
Days Minimum Temp. ≤ 32°F	29	27	27	17	7	0	0	0	2	12	21	28	170
Days Minimum Temp. ≤ 0°F	6	5	2	0	0	0	0	0	0	0	0	2	15
Heating Degree Days (base 65°F)	1,325	1,151	1,019	624	339	114	38	60	219	545	821	1,161	7,416
Cooling Degree Days (base 65°F)	0	0	0	2	14	62	110	83	22	1	0	0	294
Mean Precipitation (in.)	2.15	1.71	2.66	2.99	3.32	4.25	3.91	3.63	3.73	3.30	3.29	2.55	37.49
Extreme Maximum Daily Precip. (in.)	1.75	1.29	1.62	1.70	2.23	3.33	2.46	1.96	2.43	2.92	2.10	1.10	3.33
Days With ≥ 0.1" Precipitation	6	6	7	8	8	8	8	7	7	8	8	7	88
Days With ≥ 0.5" Precipitation	1	1	2	2	2	3	3	2	2	2	2	1	23
Days With ≥ 1.0" Precipitation	0	0	0	0	0	1	1	1	1	1	1	0	6
Mean Snowfall (in.)	20.8	16.7	17.1	4.0	0.3	0.0	0.0	0.0	0.0	0.5	8.6	19.6	87.6
Maximum Snow Depth (in.)	na	na	na	8	trace	0	0	0	0	2	8	na	na
Days With ≥ 1.0" Snow Depth	na	na	na	1	0	0	0	0	0	0	2	na	na

Allegany State Park *Cattaraugus County*   Elevation: 1,500 ft.   Latitude: 42° 06' N   Longitude: 78° 45' W

	JAN	FEB	MAR	APR	MAY	JUN	JUL	AUG	SEP	OCT	NOV	DEC	YEAR
Mean Maximum Temp. (°F)	30.3	32.9	41.8	54.7	66.7	74.6	77.9	76.3	69.0	57.2	46.1	34.6	55.2
Mean Temp. (°F)	21.8	23.4	31.1	43.2	53.8	62.2	66.0	64.9	57.9	46.6	37.6	27.1	44.6
Mean Minimum Temp. (°F)	13.3	13.9	20.4	31.5	40.9	49.8	54.0	53.4	46.7	36.0	29.1	19.5	34.0
Extreme Maximum Temp. (°F)	63	68	80	89	90	92	97	93	89	80	75	70	97
Extreme Minimum Temp. (°F)	-22	-18	-17	11	21	24	29	31	26	14	-1	-16	-22
Days Maximum Temp. ≥ 90°F	0	0	0	0	0	0	1	0	0	0	0	0	1
Days Maximum Temp. ≤ 32°F	18	14	7	1	0	0	0	0	0	0	3	13	56
Days Minimum Temp. ≤ 32°F	28	26	26	17	6	1	0	0	1	11	20	27	163
Days Minimum Temp. ≤ 0°F	5	4	2	0	0	0	0	0	0	0	0	2	13
Heating Degree Days (base 65°F)	1,330	1,169	1,045	651	351	127	52	70	226	562	816	1,168	7,567
Cooling Degree Days (base 65°F)	0	0	0	1	11	50	89	73	19	1	0	0	244
Mean Precipitation (in.)	3.03	2.34	3.05	3.53	3.78	4.92	4.55	4.08	4.07	3.81	3.88	3.43	44.47
Extreme Maximum Daily Precip. (in.)	2.08	1.64	1.84	2.15	2.30	4.00	2.62	3.38	3.75	2.55	2.05	1.45	4.00
Days With ≥ 0.1" Precipitation	9	7	8	9	8	9	9	7	8	10	9	10	103
Days With ≥ 0.5" Precipitation	1	1	2	2	3	3	3	2	3	2	2	2	26
Days With ≥ 1.0" Precipitation	0	0	0	0	1	1	1	1	1	1	0	0	5
Mean Snowfall (in.)	na	na	10.5	2.1	trace	0.0	0.0	0.0	0.0	0.1	4.3	na	na
Maximum Snow Depth (in.)	24	21	25	9	trace	0	0	0	0	5	16	24	25
Days With ≥ 1.0" Snow Depth	26	24	18	2	0	0	0	0	0	0	6	19	95

The period of record for all cooperative weather station data is 1980 – 2009. See User Guide for detailed explanation of data.

Aurora Research Farm *Cayuga County*   Elevation: 830 ft.   Latitude: 42° 44' N   Longitude: 76° 39' W

	JAN	FEB	MAR	APR	MAY	JUN	JUL	AUG	SEP	OCT	NOV	DEC	YEAR
Mean Maximum Temp. (°F)	31.9	34.4	42.1	55.8	67.7	76.9	81.3	80.1	72.7	59.9	48.2	36.8	57.3
Mean Temp. (°F)	24.4	26.2	33.5	46.1	57.1	66.6	71.0	69.6	62.5	50.7	40.7	30.0	48.2
Mean Minimum Temp. (°F)	16.9	18.0	24.9	36.4	46.5	56.3	60.6	59.1	52.2	41.5	33.2	23.1	39.0
Extreme Maximum Temp. (°F)	67	67	85	93	94	96	101	97	98	87	81	69	101
Extreme Minimum Temp. (°F)	-21	-15	-11	10	28	34	45	40	27	23	10	-15	-21
Days Maximum Temp. ≥ 90°F	0	0	0	0	0	2	4	2	1	0	0	0	9
Days Maximum Temp. ≤ 32°F	16	12	7	0	0	0	0	0	0	0	1	10	46
Days Minimum Temp. ≤ 32°F	28	25	24	11	1	0	0	0	0	4	14	25	132
Days Minimum Temp. ≤ 0°F	3	1	0	0	0	0	0	0	0	0	0	1	5
Heating Degree Days (base 65°F)	1,252	1,091	970	566	270	70	15	24	132	442	722	1,079	6,633
Cooling Degree Days (base 65°F)	0	0	1	7	32	125	207	174	63	6	0	0	615
Mean Precipitation (in.)	1.85	1.68	2.57	3.26	3.18	3.83	3.53	3.12	4.10	3.36	3.22	2.31	36.01
Extreme Maximum Daily Precip. (in.)	1.75	1.44	1.83	1.91	1.36	*1.91*	2.85	2.98	3.03	1.85	2.73	1.34	*3.03*
Days With ≥ 0.1" Precipitation	5	5	7	8	8	8	8	6	7	7	7	6	82
Days With ≥ 0.5" Precipitation	1	1	1	2	2	2	2	2	3	2	2	1	21
Days With ≥ 1.0" Precipitation	0	0	0	0	0	1	1	1	1	1	0	0	5
Mean Snowfall (in.)	14.5	11.8	12.1	3.9	0.2	0.0	0.0	0.0	0.0	0.2	4.9	11.3	58.9
Maximum Snow Depth (in.)	25	28	43	16	4	0	0	0	0	3	17	17	43
Days With ≥ 1.0" Snow Depth	21	19	12	2	0	0	0	0	0	0	4	13	71

Avon *Livingston County*   Elevation: 544 ft.   Latitude: 42° 55' N   Longitude: 77° 45' W

	JAN	FEB	MAR	APR	MAY	JUN	JUL	AUG	SEP	OCT	NOV	DEC	YEAR
Mean Maximum Temp. (°F)	32.5	34.5	42.6	55.9	68.1	77.3	81.3	79.7	72.5	60.6	48.8	37.0	57.6
Mean Temp. (°F)	24.6	25.8	33.1	45.3	56.5	66.3	70.4	68.7	61.4	50.2	40.4	29.8	47.7
Mean Minimum Temp. (°F)	16.7	17.0	23.5	34.7	44.8	55.2	59.4	57.6	50.2	39.7	31.9	22.6	37.8
Extreme Maximum Temp. (°F)	67	72	84	91	93	95	99	97	93	87	77	71	99
Extreme Minimum Temp. (°F)	-24	-13	-9	11	28	35	45	37	28	21	9	-7	-24
Days Maximum Temp. ≥ 90°F	0	0	0	0	0	2	3	2	0	0	0	0	7
Days Maximum Temp. ≤ 32°F	16	12	7	0	0	0	0	0	0	0	1	10	46
Days Minimum Temp. ≤ 32°F	28	26	25	14	1	0	0	0	0	6	17	26	143
Days Minimum Temp. ≤ 0°F	4	2	1	0	0	0	0	0	0	0	0	1	8
Heating Degree Days (base 65°F)	1,246	1,102	982	587	284	67	13	29	150	456	733	1,083	6,732
Cooling Degree Days (base 65°F)	0	0	0	4	26	113	187	150	48	5	0	0	533
Mean Precipitation (in.)	1.79	1.56	2.42	2.72	2.78	3.25	3.31	3.35	3.35	2.65	2.72	2.09	31.99
Extreme Maximum Daily Precip. (in.)	3.04	1.91	1.95	1.35	1.71	1.85	1.92	5.20	3.12	2.60	1.57	1.23	5.20
Days With ≥ 0.1" Precipitation	5	4	5	6	7	7	7	7	7	7	7	6	75
Days With ≥ 0.5" Precipitation	1	1	1	2	2	2	2	2	2	1	2	1	19
Days With ≥ 1.0" Precipitation	0	0	0	0	0	1	1	1	1	0	0	0	4
Mean Snowfall (in.)	13.3	10.5	10.7	2.1	0.2	0.0	0.0	0.0	0.0	trace	3.7	11.4	51.9
Maximum Snow Depth (in.)	18	14	27	7	4	0	0	0	0	1	10	10	27
Days With ≥ 1.0" Snow Depth	21	19	11	1	0	0	0	0	0	0	3	15	70

Bath *Steuben County*   Elevation: 1,120 ft.   Latitude: 42° 21' N   Longitude: 77° 21' W

	JAN	FEB	MAR	APR	MAY	JUN	JUL	AUG	SEP	OCT	NOV	DEC	YEAR
Mean Maximum Temp. (°F)	31.5	*34.9*	42.7	55.9	68.2	*76.6*	80.7	*79.3*	*72.2*	59.7	47.4	36.4	*57.1*
Mean Temp. (°F)	22.1	*24.6*	31.7	44.0	54.7	*63.5*	67.8	66.5	*59.2*	47.6	38.0	27.8	*45.6*
Mean Minimum Temp. (°F)	12.7	*14.2*	20.6	32.0	41.3	*50.5*	54.9	53.7	*46.1*	35.3	28.6	19.2	*34.1*
Extreme Maximum Temp. (°F)	*64*	*69*	84	92	94	*93*	*101*	*100*	94	85	77	70	*101*
Extreme Minimum Temp. (°F)	*-24*	*-13*	-18	8	24	*28*	*39*	*28*	25	16	*1*	-16	*-24*
Days Maximum Temp. ≥ 90°F	0	*0*	0	0	0	*1*	*3*	*2*	*0*	*0*	0	0	*6*
Days Maximum Temp. ≤ 32°F	*16*	*12*	6	0	0	*0*	*0*	*0*	*0*	*0*	2	10	*46*
Days Minimum Temp. ≤ 32°F	29	*27*	27	17	5	*0*	*0*	*0*	*2*	13	21	28	*169*
Days Minimum Temp. ≤ 0°F	*5*	*4*	1	0	0	*0*	*0*	*0*	*0*	*0*	0	2	*12*
Heating Degree Days (base 65°F)	*1,314*	*1,137*	1,026	626	325	*106*	*33*	*50*	*200*	534	804	1,146	*7,301*
Cooling Degree Days (base 65°F)	*0*	*0*	0	3	14	*68*	*127*	*104*	*30*	1	0	0	*347*
Mean Precipitation (in.)	1.69	*1.48*	2.09	2.79	2.86	*3.75*	*3.19*	2.84	3.37	2.46	2.67	2.05	*31.24*
Extreme Maximum Daily Precip. (in.)	*3.00*	*1.25*	*1.55*	1.73	*2.20*	*4.67*	*2.30*	2.90	*2.40*	2.05	2.06	*1.30*	*4.67*
Days With ≥ 0.1" Precipitation	4	*4*	6	7	7	*7*	*7*	6	6	6	6	5	*71*
Days With ≥ 0.5" Precipitation	1	*1*	1	2	2	*2*	*2*	2	2	1	1	1	*18*
Days With ≥ 1.0" Precipitation	0	*0*	0	0	0	*1*	*0*	1	1	0	0	0	*3*
Mean Snowfall (in.)	*11.1*	*9.1*	*10.3*	1.5	trace	*trace*	*0.0*	*0.0*	0.0	*trace*	3.6	9.2	*44.8*
Maximum Snow Depth (in.)	23	*28*	36	9	trace	*trace*	*0*	*0*	0	*trace*	14	14	*36*
Days With ≥ 1.0" Snow Depth	*19*	*18*	12	1	0	*0*	*0*	*0*	0	*0*	4	13	*67*

Boonville 2 SSW *Oneida County*   Elevation: 1,580 ft.   Latitude: 43° 27' N   Longitude: 75° 21' W

	JAN	FEB	MAR	APR	MAY	JUN	JUL	AUG	SEP	OCT	NOV	DEC	YEAR
Mean Maximum Temp. (°F)	24.7	27.9	36.1	50.5	63.0	71.3	74.9	73.9	65.9	53.9	41.4	29.8	51.1
Mean Temp. (°F)	16.5	19.1	27.5	41.2	53.1	61.6	65.8	64.7	56.9	45.3	34.4	22.6	42.4
Mean Minimum Temp. (°F)	8.3	10.2	18.8	31.9	43.0	52.0	56.7	55.4	47.8	36.6	27.4	15.3	33.6
Extreme Maximum Temp. (°F)	57	55	77	86	88	89	94	90	89	79	68	62	94
Extreme Minimum Temp. (°F)	-31	-22	-18	0	22	29	33	38	25	17	0	-33	-33
Days Maximum Temp. ≥ 90°F	0	0	0	0	0	0	0	0	0	0	0	0	0
Days Maximum Temp. ≤ 32°F	24	19	12	2	0	0	0	0	0	0	6	19	82
Days Minimum Temp. ≤ 32°F	30	27	28	17	3	0	0	0	1	11	22	29	168
Days Minimum Temp. ≤ 0°F	9	7	3	0	0	0	0	0	0	0	0	4	23
Heating Degree Days (base 65°F)	1,498	1,291	1,157	709	373	140	53	74	253	604	910	1,307	8,369
Cooling Degree Days (base 65°F)	0	0	0	1	10	46	86	71	16	0	0	0	230
Mean Precipitation (in.)	4.99	3.95	4.48	4.49	4.52	4.69	4.37	4.69	5.50	5.57	5.37	5.46	58.08
Extreme Maximum Daily Precip. (in.)	3.11	2.65	1.90	3.18	2.66	3.11	3.67	3.01	4.86	3.08	3.15	1.97	4.86
Days With ≥ 0.1" Precipitation	12	10	10	9	9	9	8	8	9	10	11	12	116
Days With ≥ 0.5" Precipitation	3	2	3	3	3	3	3	3	4	4	3	3	37
Days With ≥ 1.0" Precipitation	1	1	1	1	1	1	1	1	2	1	1	1	13
Mean Snowfall (in.)	52.9	39.8	31.4	8.5	0.2	trace	0.0	0.0	trace	2.2	17.8	44.7	197.5
Maximum Snow Depth (in.)	51	48	57	48	2	trace	0	0	trace	9	21	35	57
Days With ≥ 1.0" Snow Depth	29	28	29	10	0	0	0	0	0	1	11	26	134

The period of record for all cooperative weather station data is 1980 – 2009. See User Guide for detailed explanation of data.

Bridgehampton *Suffolk County*   Elevation: 60 ft.   Latitude: 40° 57' N   Longitude: 72° 18' W

	JAN	FEB	MAR	APR	MAY	JUN	JUL	AUG	SEP	OCT	NOV	DEC	YEAR
Mean Maximum Temp. (°F)	38.7	40.4	46.6	56.1	65.9	75.1	80.9	80.2	73.6	63.2	53.5	43.8	59.8
Mean Temp. (°F)	31.0	32.6	38.5	47.6	56.8	66.3	72.1	71.4	64.4	53.8	45.2	35.9	51.3
Mean Minimum Temp. (°F)	23.2	24.8	30.3	39.0	47.6	57.4	63.3	62.7	55.2	44.4	36.8	27.9	42.7
Extreme Maximum Temp. (°F)	67	63	79	92	93	95	102	98	93	83	75	70	102
Extreme Minimum Temp. (°F)	-11	0	6	14	29	39	48	41	35	24	10	-5	-11
Days Maximum Temp. ≥ 90°F	0	0	0	0	0	1	2	2	0	0	0	0	5
Days Maximum Temp. ≤ 32°F	8	5	1	0	0	0	0	0	0	0	0	3	17
Days Minimum Temp. ≤ 32°F	26	23	19	5	0	0	0	0	0	3	11	22	109
Days Minimum Temp. ≤ 0°F	0	0	0	0	0	0	0	0	0	0	0	0	0
Heating Degree Days (base 65°F)	1,047	908	815	518	260	51	4	7	80	347	589	897	5,523
Cooling Degree Days (base 65°F)	0	0	0	1	11	97	232	214	70	7	0	0	632
Mean Precipitation (in.)	3.99	3.52	4.86	4.65	3.73	4.18	3.41	3.95	4.44	4.19	4.41	4.32	49.65
Extreme Maximum Daily Precip. (in.)	2.35	2.49	3.96	3.46	3.25	6.61	3.55	7.04	5.87	5.69	3.19	3.27	7.04
Days With ≥ 0.1" Precipitation	7	6	7	8	7	6	5	5	6	6	7	8	78
Days With ≥ 0.5" Precipitation	3	2	3	3	2	3	2	2	3	3	3	3	32
Days With ≥ 1.0" Precipitation	1	1	1	1	1	1	1	1	1	1	1	1	12
Mean Snowfall (in.)	7.7	7.9	5.3	0.9	0.0	0.0	0.0	0.0	0.0	trace	0.7	4.0	26.5
Maximum Snow Depth (in.)	27	24	13	8	0	0	0	0	0	trace	7	18	27
Days With ≥ 1.0" Snow Depth	8	6	3	0	0	0	0	0	0	0	0	3	20

Canton 4 SE *St. Lawrence County*   Elevation: 439 ft.   Latitude: 44° 34' N   Longitude: 75° 07' W

	JAN	FEB	MAR	APR	MAY	JUN	JUL	AUG	SEP	OCT	NOV	DEC	YEAR
Mean Maximum Temp. (°F)	26.2	29.4	38.7	53.3	65.7	74.4	79.0	77.5	69.4	56.8	44.8	32.3	54.0
Mean Temp. (°F)	15.8	18.6	28.5	43.1	54.9	64.0	68.7	66.8	58.6	46.8	36.4	23.2	43.8
Mean Minimum Temp. (°F)	5.3	7.7	18.4	32.8	44.1	53.6	58.4	56.1	47.7	36.7	27.9	14.1	33.6
Extreme Maximum Temp. (°F)	66	65	92	89	90	93	93	97	93	82	76	69	97
Extreme Minimum Temp. (°F)	-40	-37	-26	6	23	29	35	33	22	15	-5	-37	-40
Days Maximum Temp. ≥ 90°F	0	0	0	0	0	1	1	0	0	0	0	0	2
Days Maximum Temp. ≤ 32°F	20	17	10	1	0	0	0	0	0	0	3	15	66
Days Minimum Temp. ≤ 32°F	30	26	27	15	3	0	0	0	2	11	20	28	162
Days Minimum Temp. ≤ 0°F	12	10	3	0	0	0	0	0	0	0	0	6	31
Heating Degree Days (base 65°F)	1,521	1,308	1,124	653	323	102	30	59	218	559	851	1,287	8,035
Cooling Degree Days (base 65°F)	0	0	0	2	17	80	153	122	33	3	0	0	410
Mean Precipitation (in.)	2.10	1.79	2.13	2.90	3.11	3.26	3.86	3.67	4.03	3.86	3.37	2.56	36.64
Extreme Maximum Daily Precip. (in.)	1.30	1.58	1.17	1.43	1.86	1.75	4.10	2.85	3.20	2.35	2.68	1.46	4.10
Days With ≥ 0.1" Precipitation	6	5	6	7	8	7	7	7	8	8	8	6	83
Days With ≥ 0.5" Precipitation	1	1	1	2	2	2	2	2	3	2	2	1	21
Days With ≥ 1.0" Precipitation	0	0	0	0	0	0	1	1	1	1	0	0	4
Mean Snowfall (in.)	20.1	16.9	12.4	3.6	trace	0.0	0.0	0.0	trace	0.6	5.8	18.5	77.9
Maximum Snow Depth (in.)	30	33	38	11	1	0	0	0	trace	8	8	24	38
Days With ≥ 1.0" Snow Depth	25	23	17	2	0	0	0	0	0	0	6	19	92

Chazy *Clinton County*   Elevation: 169 ft.   Latitude: 44° 53' N   Longitude: 73° 26' W

	JAN	FEB	MAR	APR	MAY	JUN	JUL	AUG	SEP	OCT	NOV	DEC	YEAR
Mean Maximum Temp. (°F)	27.4	30.4	40.1	55.4	67.8	76.3	80.4	78.7	70.1	57.2	44.8	32.9	55.1
Mean Temp. (°F)	17.7	20.2	30.1	44.7	56.3	65.2	69.8	68.0	59.8	48.0	37.0	24.5	45.1
Mean Minimum Temp. (°F)	8.0	10.0	20.2	34.0	44.8	54.1	59.1	57.3	49.5	38.6	29.2	16.1	35.1
Extreme Maximum Temp. (°F)	61	60	79	91	91	97	96	100	95	85	74	66	100
Extreme Minimum Temp. (°F)	-44	-41	-28	6	27	30	38	36	22	17	-2	-26	-44
Days Maximum Temp. ≥ 90°F	0	0	0	0	0	1	1	1	0	0	0	0	3
Days Maximum Temp. ≤ 32°F	20	16	7	0	0	0	0	0	0	0	3	14	60
Days Minimum Temp. ≤ 32°F	29	26	26	14	2	0	0	0	1	9	19	27	153
Days Minimum Temp. ≤ 0°F	10	8	3	0	0	0	0	0	0	0	0	4	25
Heating Degree Days (base 65°F)	1,460	1,260	1,074	604	275	73	16	36	181	523	833	1,249	7,584
Cooling Degree Days (base 65°F)	0	0	0	3	14	84	170	136	32	2	0	0	441
Mean Precipitation (in.)	*0.78*	na	*0.85*	2.25	2.94	3.46	3.53	3.81	3.23	3.05	*2.21*	*0.81*	na
Extreme Maximum Daily Precip. (in.)	*1.30*	na	*1.80*	2.10	1.65	*2.66*	1.76	2.98	2.80	*2.85*	*4.27*	*1.30*	na
Days With ≥ 0.1" Precipitation	*2*	*2*	2	5	7	7	7	7	6	6	*4*	*2*	57
Days With ≥ 0.5" Precipitation	*0*	*0*	0	2	2	2	3	3	2	2	*1*	*1*	18
Days With ≥ 1.0" Precipitation	*0*	*0*	0	0	0	1	1	1	1	1	0	0	5
Mean Snowfall (in.)	13.7	*12.7*	11.1	2.9	0.1	0.0	0.0	0.0	0.0	0.3	*4.6*	11.2	*56.6*
Maximum Snow Depth (in.)	30	31	50	15	0	0	0	0	0	0	12	20	*50*
Days With ≥ 1.0" Snow Depth	22	21	16	2	0	0	0	0	0	0	4	16	*81*

Conklingville Dam *Saratoga County*   Elevation: 808 ft.   Latitude: 43° 19' N   Longitude: 73° 56' W

	JAN	FEB	MAR	APR	MAY	JUN	JUL	AUG	SEP	OCT	NOV	DEC	YEAR
Mean Maximum Temp. (°F)	29.4	*33.1*	*41.1*	54.3	*66.3*	*74.1*	*78.3*	76.6	69.1	57.8	*45.8*	*33.4*	*54.9*
Mean Temp. (°F)	19.4	*22.3*	*31.1*	43.7	*55.4*	64.0	*68.4*	66.9	59.3	48.1	*37.8*	25.2	45.1
Mean Minimum Temp. (°F)	9.4	*11.5*	*20.9*	33.1	*44.6*	53.7	*58.4*	57.2	49.4	38.3	*29.7*	17.0	*35.3*
Extreme Maximum Temp. (°F)	60	61	80	87	89	92	95	91	88	80	75	67	95
Extreme Minimum Temp. (°F)	-29	-22	-13	7	27	30	44	35	28	22	8	-22	-29
Days Maximum Temp. ≥ 90°F	0	0	0	0	0	0	1	1	0	0	0	0	1
Days Maximum Temp. ≤ 32°F	18	12	5	0	0	0	0	0	0	0	1	12	48
Days Minimum Temp. ≤ 32°F	29	25	26	14	1	0	0	0	0	7	18	27	147
Days Minimum Temp. ≤ 0°F	8	5	1	0	0	0	0	0	0	0	0	3	17
Heating Degree Days (base 65°F)	1,408	*1,202*	*1,046*	633	*302*	*89*	*19*	*39*	189	519	*809*	1,228	7,483
Cooling Degree Days (base 65°F)	0	*0*	*0*	1	*13*	*64*	*131*	*105*	24	1	*0*	*0*	339
Mean Precipitation (in.)	3.35	2.77	3.96	3.69	4.06	4.06	4.19	4.02	3.76	3.71	3.84	3.75	45.16
Extreme Maximum Daily Precip. (in.)	2.53	1.71	2.70	2.97	*2.67*	2.25	2.85	2.25	4.01	2.83	2.90	*2.38*	*4.01*
Days With ≥ 0.1" Precipitation	7	6	7	7	8	8	7	6	6	7	7	7	83
Days With ≥ 0.5" Precipitation	2	2	3	2	3	3	3	3	2	2	2	2	29
Days With ≥ 1.0" Precipitation	1	1	1	1	1	1	1	1	1	1	1	1	12
Mean Snowfall (in.)	19.9	13.8	13.8	2.6	trace	0.0	0.0	0.0	0.0	0.1	3.7	16.5	70.4
Maximum Snow Depth (in.)	39	37	45	20	1	0	0	0	0	trace	16	23	45
Days With ≥ 1.0" Snow Depth	24	25	20	3	0	0	0	0	0	0	3	19	94

The period of record for all cooperative weather station data is 1980 – 2009. See User Guide for detailed explanation of data.

Dannemora *Clinton County*   Elevation: 1,339 ft.   Latitude: 44° 43' N   Longitude: 73° 43' W

	JAN	FEB	MAR	APR	MAY	JUN	JUL	AUG	SEP	OCT	NOV	DEC	YEAR
Mean Maximum Temp. (°F)	25.7	29.5	38.4	52.6	65.4	74.0	78.0	76.1	68.5	55.7	42.5	31.0	53.1
Mean Temp. (°F)	16.9	20.4	29.3	43.0	55.0	64.0	68.2	66.4	58.6	46.9	35.1	23.1	43.9
Mean Minimum Temp. (°F)	8.1	11.3	20.2	33.3	44.5	53.9	58.5	56.7	48.8	38.0	27.7	15.1	34.7
Extreme Maximum Temp. (°F)	64	62	77	87	88	94	96	93	93	79	70	65	96
Extreme Minimum Temp. (°F)	-34	-23	-22	2	18	32	42	33	25	17	0	-28	-34
Days Maximum Temp. ≥ 90°F	0	0	0	0	0	1	1	0	0	0	0	0	2
Days Maximum Temp. ≤ 32°F	22	18	10	1	0	0	0	0	0	0	5	17	73
Days Minimum Temp. ≤ 32°F	30	27	27	14	2	0	0	0	1	9	21	29	160
Days Minimum Temp. ≤ 0°F	9	6	2	0	0	0	0	0	0	0	0	4	21
Heating Degree Days (base 65°F)	1,485	1,255	1,098	657	319	97	23	49	210	556	890	1,294	7,933
Cooling Degree Days (base 65°F)	0	0	0	0	2	15	73	100	25	1	0	0	347
Mean Precipitation (in.)	2.45	2.12	2.53	3.32	3.63	3.98	4.18	4.40	3.85	3.94	3.61	2.92	40.93
Extreme Maximum Daily Precip. (in.)	2.79	2.10	1.78	2.30	1.62	1.95	3.01	2.80	4.55	3.09	3.64	2.41	4.55
Days With ≥ 0.1" Precipitation	6	6	8	8	9	9	9	9	8	9	8	8	97
Days With ≥ 0.5" Precipitation	2	1	1	2	2	3	3	3	3	3	2	2	27
Days With ≥ 1.0" Precipitation	0	0	0	0	0	1	1	1	1	1	1	0	6
Mean Snowfall (in.)	na	na	na	trace	0.0	0.0	0.0	0.0	0.0	trace	1.0	na	na
Maximum Snow Depth (in.)	na	na	na	na	na	na	na	na	na	na	na	na	na
Days With ≥ 1.0" Snow Depth	na	na	na	0	0	0	0	0	0	0	0	na	na

Delhi 2 SE *Delaware County*   Elevation: 1,439 ft.   Latitude: 42° 15' N   Longitude: 74° 54' W

	JAN	FEB	MAR	APR	MAY	JUN	JUL	AUG	SEP	OCT	NOV	DEC	YEAR
Mean Maximum Temp. (°F)	31.1	34.3	42.3	55.4	66.7	75.1	79.2	78.3	70.7	59.4	47.3	35.7	56.3
Mean Temp. (°F)	20.9	23.4	31.4	43.6	53.9	62.7	66.7	65.7	58.3	47.1	37.8	26.7	44.8
Mean Minimum Temp. (°F)	10.6	12.4	20.5	31.8	41.0	50.3	54.2	53.1	45.8	34.7	28.2	17.7	33.3
Extreme Maximum Temp. (°F)	65	64	83	91	91	91	97	96	90	83	77	66	97
Extreme Minimum Temp. (°F)	-32	-24	-18	8	20	26	33	32	23	11	-1	-25	-32
Days Maximum Temp. ≥ 90°F	0	0	0	0	0	1	1	1	0	0	0	0	3
Days Maximum Temp. ≤ 32°F	16	12	6	0	0	0	0	0	0	0	2	12	48
Days Minimum Temp. ≤ 32°F	29	27	26	17	6	0	0	0	2	14	21	28	170
Days Minimum Temp. ≤ 0°F	8	5	2	0	0	0	0	0	0	0	0	3	18
Heating Degree Days (base 65°F)	1,362	1,170	1,035	637	349	121	48	60	218	551	811	1,180	7,542
Cooling Degree Days (base 65°F)	0	0	0	0	2	11	60	106	89	24	1	0	293
Mean Precipitation (in.)	3.23	2.49	3.54	3.94	4.24	4.60	4.55	3.64	4.38	4.02	3.90	3.45	45.98
Extreme Maximum Daily Precip. (in.)	2.05	2.00	2.17	2.46	2.77	4.31	2.91	3.40	4.49	3.15	3.62	2.54	4.49
Days With ≥ 0.1" Precipitation	8	6	8	8	9	9	9	7	7	8	8	8	94
Days With ≥ 0.5" Precipitation	2	1	2	2	3	3	3	3	3	3	3	2	30
Days With ≥ 1.0" Precipitation	0	0	0	1	1	1	1	1	1	1	1	0	8
Mean Snowfall (in.)	18.2	12.4	11.2	3.8	0.1	0.0	0.0	0.0	0.0	0.6	4.3	14.8	65.4
Maximum Snow Depth (in.)	25	23	28	17	3	0	0	0	0	0	7	9	31	31
Days With ≥ 1.0" Snow Depth	23	20	13	2	0	0	0	0	0	0	4	16	78

Dobbs Ferry Ardsley *Westchester County*   Elevation: 200 ft.   Latitude: 41° 00' N   Longitude: 73° 50' W

	JAN	FEB	MAR	APR	MAY	JUN	JUL	AUG	SEP	OCT	NOV	DEC	YEAR
Mean Maximum Temp. (°F)	38.7	42.3	50.5	62.4	72.4	80.6	85.2	83.6	76.4	65.3	54.3	43.3	62.9
Mean Temp. (°F)	30.9	33.5	40.7	51.4	61.1	69.8	74.8	73.6	66.2	55.1	45.4	35.6	53.2
Mean Minimum Temp. (°F)	23.1	24.6	30.8	40.4	49.6	58.9	64.3	63.5	55.9	44.9	36.4	27.8	43.4
Extreme Maximum Temp. (°F)	72	75	86	96	97	98	104	100	98	88	81	77	104
Extreme Minimum Temp. (°F)	-10	-2	2	17	29	38	49	44	34	27	12	-4	-10
Days Maximum Temp. ≥ 90°F	0	0	0	0	1	4	7	5	1	0	0	0	18
Days Maximum Temp. ≤ 32°F	8	4	1	0	0	0	0	0	0	0	0	4	17
Days Minimum Temp. ≤ 32°F	26	23	18	5	0	0	0	0	0	2	10	22	106
Days Minimum Temp. ≤ 0°F	1	0	0	0	0	0	0	0	0	0	0	0	1
Heating Degree Days (base 65°F)	1,049	884	748	408	160	24	1	3	64	312	582	905	5,140
Cooling Degree Days (base 65°F)	0	0	1	6	45	175	312	277	106	13	0	0	935
Mean Precipitation (in.)	3.78	3.03	4.45	4.74	4.47	4.39	4.64	4.23	4.64	4.48	4.39	4.25	51.49
Extreme Maximum Daily Precip. (in.)	3.11	2.85	2.97	5.34	2.80	4.49	3.22	3.30	7.62	3.27	3.25	3.07	7.62
Days With ≥ 0.1" Precipitation	7	6	7	8	7	7	7	6	6	6	7	7	81
Days With ≥ 0.5" Precipitation	3	2	3	3	3	3	3	3	3	3	3	3	35
Days With ≥ 1.0" Precipitation	1	1	1	1	1	1	2	1	1	1	1	1	13
Mean Snowfall (in.)	9.0	8.4	5.7	0.9	trace	0.0	0.0	0.0	0.0	0.1	0.7	5.8	30.6
Maximum Snow Depth (in.)	26	20	17	10	trace	0	0	0	0	2	4	14	26
Days With ≥ 1.0" Snow Depth	12	11	5	0	0	0	0	0	0	0	0	6	34

Gouverneur 3 NW *St. Lawrence County*   Elevation: 419 ft.   Latitude: 44° 21' N   Longitude: 75° 31' W

	JAN	FEB	MAR	APR	MAY	JUN	JUL	AUG	SEP	OCT	NOV	DEC	YEAR
Mean Maximum Temp. (°F)	27.3	30.6	39.8	54.8	66.9	75.8	80.1	78.8	71.0	57.7	45.4	32.9	55.1
Mean Temp. (°F)	16.5	19.3	28.9	43.6	54.6	64.0	68.3	66.7	58.8	46.9	36.6	23.6	44.0
Mean Minimum Temp. (°F)	5.7	7.9	17.9	32.3	42.1	52.1	56.5	54.6	46.5	36.0	27.7	14.2	32.8
Extreme Maximum Temp. (°F)	65	64	81	87	88	96	95	98	94	81	73	70	98
Extreme Minimum Temp. (°F)	-45	-37	-27	4	23	29	36	32	22	15	-10	-37	-45
Days Maximum Temp. ≥ 90°F	0	0	0	0	0	1	1	1	0	0	0	0	3
Days Maximum Temp. ≤ 32°F	19	16	8	1	0	0	0	0	0	0	3	14	61
Days Minimum Temp. ≤ 32°F	30	27	27	16	4	0	0	0	2	11	20	29	166
Days Minimum Temp. ≤ 0°F	12	10	4	0	0	0	0	0	0	0	0	6	32
Heating Degree Days (base 65°F)	1,498	1,288	1,114	638	327	96	29	51	209	556	846	1,278	7,930
Cooling Degree Days (base 65°F)	0	0	0	2	10	72	138	111	29	2	0	0	364
Mean Precipitation (in.)	2.30	1.97	2.24	3.00	3.09	3.26	3.60	3.44	3.94	4.04	3.72	2.72	37.32
Extreme Maximum Daily Precip. (in.)	1.56	1.45	1.68	1.95	1.72	2.48	4.18	2.50	4.51	2.06	2.70	1.72	4.51
Days With ≥ 0.1" Precipitation	6	5	6	7	7	7	7	7	8	8	9	7	84
Days With ≥ 0.5" Precipitation	1	1	1	2	2	2	3	2	3	3	2	1	22
Days With ≥ 1.0" Precipitation	0	0	0	0	0	1	1	1	1	1	1	0	6
Mean Snowfall (in.)	21.9	18.2	13.6	3.9	trace	trace	0.0	0.0	trace	1.0	6.8	19.2	84.6
Maximum Snow Depth (in.)	30	30	30	8	trace	0	0	0	trace	12	12	19	30
Days With ≥ 1.0" Snow Depth	26	25	19	2	0	0	0	0	0	0	5	20	97

The period of record for all cooperative weather station data is 1980 – 2009. See User Guide for detailed explanation of data.

Grafton *Rensselaer County*   Elevation: 1,560 ft.   Latitude: 42° 47' N   Longitude: 73° 28' W

	JAN	FEB	MAR	APR	MAY	JUN	JUL	AUG	SEP	OCT	NOV	DEC	YEAR
Mean Maximum Temp. (°F)	28.2	32.5	41.0	54.4	66.4	73.6	77.9	75.9	68.1	56.7	44.5	33.3	54.4
Mean Temp. (°F)	20.2	23.8	31.9	44.4	55.8	63.5	68.1	66.5	58.9	47.9	36.9	25.9	45.3
Mean Minimum Temp. (°F)	12.1	15.0	22.7	34.3	45.2	53.4	58.2	57.1	49.8	39.1	29.3	18.5	36.2
Extreme Maximum Temp. (°F)	61	62	83	88	86	90	93	94	89	79	76	65	94
Extreme Minimum Temp. (°F)	-26	-21	-11	5	26	32	40	32	27	18	4	-23	-26
Days Maximum Temp. ≥ 90°F	0	0	0	0	0	0	0	0	0	0	0	0	0
Days Maximum Temp. ≤ 32°F	21	15	7	0	0	0	0	0	0	0	4	15	62
Days Minimum Temp. ≤ 32°F	30	26	26	14	1	0	0	0	0	8	20	28	153
Days Minimum Temp. ≤ 0°F	6	4	1	0	0	0	0	0	0	0	0	2	13
Heating Degree Days (base 65°F)	1,383	1,161	1,020	613	293	100	24	47	201	524	835	1,205	7,406
Cooling Degree Days (base 65°F)	0	0	0	2	14	62	128	102	26	1	0	0	335
Mean Precipitation (in.)	2.88	2.57	3.56	3.87	4.53	4.15	4.51	4.46	4.19	3.98	4.00	3.21	45.91
Extreme Maximum Daily Precip. (in.)	1.50	2.60	1.95	2.14	2.06	2.52	3.75	3.50	3.58	4.75	2.65	2.56	4.75
Days With ≥ 0.1" Precipitation	7	6	9	9	9	8	8	8	7	8	9	8	96
Days With ≥ 0.5" Precipitation	2	2	3	3	3	3	3	3	3	3	3	2	33
Days With ≥ 1.0" Precipitation	0	0	1	1	1	1	1	1	1	1	1	1	10
Mean Snowfall (in.)	20.6	14.9	15.4	5.9	0.2	0.0	0.0	0.0	trace	1.2	7.2	17.8	83.2
Maximum Snow Depth (in.)	37	31	32	23	trace	0	0	0	trace	22	14	23	37
Days With ≥ 1.0" Snow Depth	24	24	18	3	0	0	0	0	0	0	5	20	94

Indian Lake 2 SW *Hamilton County*   Elevation: 1,660 ft.   Latitude: 43° 45' N   Longitude: 74° 17' W

	JAN	FEB	MAR	APR	MAY	JUN	JUL	AUG	SEP	OCT	NOV	DEC	YEAR
Mean Maximum Temp. (°F)	25.5	28.7	36.6	49.8	62.5	70.7	74.2	73.1	65.8	53.7	41.6	30.3	51.0
Mean Temp. (°F)	15.3	17.5	25.7	39.1	50.8	59.8	63.8	62.6	55.3	43.7	33.5	21.4	40.7
Mean Minimum Temp. (°F)	5.0	6.3	14.8	28.4	39.0	48.8	53.4	52.1	44.7	33.6	25.4	12.6	30.3
Extreme Maximum Temp. (°F)	55	57	74	85	85	90	91	90	89	78	68	64	91
Extreme Minimum Temp. (°F)	-35	-30	-25	-1	21	29	35	31	23	15	-2	-27	-35
Days Maximum Temp. ≥ 90°F	0	0	0	0	0	0	0	0	0	0	0	0	0
Days Maximum Temp. ≤ 32°F	22	18	11	1	0	0	0	0	0	0	5	18	75
Days Minimum Temp. ≤ 32°F	30	28	29	21	8	0	0	0	2	15	23	30	186
Days Minimum Temp. ≤ 0°F	12	11	5	0	0	0	0	0	0	0	0	6	34
Heating Degree Days (base 65°F)	1,537	1,338	1,211	770	437	178	85	111	295	653	938	1,343	8,896
Cooling Degree Days (base 65°F)	0	0	0	0	4	28	55	44	9	0	0	0	140
Mean Precipitation (in.)	2.83	2.34	2.92	3.20	3.59	3.70	3.85	3.62	3.73	4.22	3.33	2.86	40.19
Extreme Maximum Daily Precip. (in.)	1.70	2.10	2.40	2.09	2.03	3.00	2.42	2.58	3.43	3.34	2.90	1.70	3.43
Days With ≥ 0.1" Precipitation	7	6	7	7	8	8	8	8	7	8	7	7	88
Days With ≥ 0.5" Precipitation	2	1	2	2	2	2	2	3	3	2	2	2	25
Days With ≥ 1.0" Precipitation	0	0	1	1	1	1	1	1	1	1	1	0	9
Mean Snowfall (in.)	na	na	na	3.0	0.1	0.0	0.0	0.0	0.0	0.7	na	na	na
Maximum Snow Depth (in.)	na	na	na	na	na	na	na	na	na	na	na	na	na
Days With ≥ 1.0" Snow Depth	na	na	na	4	0	0	0	0	0	1	na	na	na

Ithaca Cornell Univ *Tompkins County*   Elevation: 959 ft.   Latitude: 42° 27' N   Longitude: 76° 27' W

	JAN	FEB	MAR	APR	MAY	JUN	JUL	AUG	SEP	OCT	NOV	DEC	YEAR
Mean Maximum Temp. (°F)	31.2	33.6	41.4	54.8	67.0	75.5	79.5	78.6	71.2	58.9	47.3	35.8	56.2
Mean Temp. (°F)	23.0	24.7	32.2	44.6	55.4	64.4	68.7	67.7	60.3	48.8	39.3	28.5	46.5
Mean Minimum Temp. (°F)	14.7	15.7	22.9	34.3	43.8	53.4	57.7	56.7	49.3	38.6	31.4	21.1	36.6
Extreme Maximum Temp. (°F)	66	67	83	91	93	94	98	97	92	84	78	69	98
Extreme Minimum Temp. (°F)	-24	-18	-17	11	25	31	40	34	24	18	2	-19	-24
Days Maximum Temp. ≥ 90°F	0	0	0	0	0	1	2	1	0	0	0	0	4
Days Maximum Temp. ≤ 32°F	17	13	7	1	0	0	0	0	0	0	2	12	52
Days Minimum Temp. ≤ 32°F	29	26	25	13	4	0	0	0	1	8	17	27	150
Days Minimum Temp. ≤ 0°F	5	3	1	0	0	0	0	0	0	0	0	2	11
Heating Degree Days (base 65°F)	1,297	1,132	1,011	609	309	96	30	42	175	500	763	1,126	7,090
Cooling Degree Days (base 65°F)	0	0	1	4	20	86	150	133	41	3	0	0	438
Mean Precipitation (in.)	1.99	1.83	2.76	3.27	3.16	3.91	3.86	3.54	3.69	3.29	3.16	2.32	36.78
Extreme Maximum Daily Precip. (in.)	1.87	1.52	2.06	2.13	2.25	2.04	2.08	3.30	3.90	5.08	4.02	1.87	5.08
Days With ≥ 0.1" Precipitation	6	5	6	8	8	9	8	7	7	7	7	6	84
Days With ≥ 0.5" Precipitation	1	1	1	2	2	2	3	2	2	2	2	1	21
Days With ≥ 1.0" Precipitation	0	0	0	0	0	1	1	1	1	1	0	0	5
Mean Snowfall (in.)	17.3	12.7	12.2	3.6	0.0	0.0	0.0	0.0	0.0	0.4	4.8	12.9	63.9
Maximum Snow Depth (in.)	19	20	28	14	0	0	0	0	0	5	12	11	28
Days With ≥ 1.0" Snow Depth	21	20	12	2	0	0	0	0	0	0	4	15	74

Lowville *Lewis County*   Elevation: 859 ft.   Latitude: 43° 48' N   Longitude: 75° 29' W

	JAN	FEB	MAR	APR	MAY	JUN	JUL	AUG	SEP	OCT	NOV	DEC	YEAR
Mean Maximum Temp. (°F)	26.2	29.1	37.5	52.4	65.0	73.6	77.9	76.7	68.7	56.1	43.7	31.6	53.2
Mean Temp. (°F)	16.7	19.1	28.1	42.4	53.9	62.9	67.2	65.8	57.7	46.3	35.7	23.4	43.3
Mean Minimum Temp. (°F)	7.2	9.1	18.6	32.4	42.7	52.2	56.5	54.8	46.7	36.5	27.6	15.0	33.3
Extreme Maximum Temp. (°F)	62	59	80	87	88	97	94	96	92	81	72	67	97
Extreme Minimum Temp. (°F)	-35	-28	-25	5	23	28	39	32	24	18	-1	-29	-35
Days Maximum Temp. ≥ 90°F	0	0	0	0	0	1	1	1	0	0	0	0	3
Days Maximum Temp. ≤ 32°F	21	17	10	1	0	0	0	0	0	0	4	15	68
Days Minimum Temp. ≤ 32°F	30	27	27	17	3	0	0	0	2	11	21	29	167
Days Minimum Temp. ≤ 0°F	10	9	3	0	0	0	0	0	0	0	0	5	27
Heating Degree Days (base 65°F)	1,491	1,292	1,138	673	349	119	40	65	235	573	873	1,285	8,133
Cooling Degree Days (base 65°F)	0	0	0	2	11	63	116	95	23	1	0	0	311
Mean Precipitation (in.)	3.16	2.49	2.73	3.23	3.34	3.35	3.63	3.70	3.96	4.09	3.92	3.64	41.24
Extreme Maximum Daily Precip. (in.)	2.35	2.03	2.12	2.27	2.45	2.10	2.25	3.05	4.78	2.60	3.30	2.02	4.78
Days With ≥ 0.1" Precipitation	8	7	7	7	8	7	7	7	8	9	9	10	94
Days With ≥ 0.5" Precipitation	2	1	2	2	2	2	2	2	3	3	2	2	25
Days With ≥ 1.0" Precipitation	0	0	0	1	1	1	1	1	1	1	1	0	8
Mean Snowfall (in.)	33.0	25.7	14.9	4.7	0.1	0.0	0.0	0.0	trace	0.8	9.3	32.9	121.4
Maximum Snow Depth (in.)	33	26	27	16	1	0	0	0	trace	8	11	28	33
Days With ≥ 1.0" Snow Depth	27	26	20	4	0	0	0	0	0	0	7	23	107

The period of record for all cooperative weather station data is 1980 – 2009. See User Guide for detailed explanation of data.

Middletown 2 NW *Orange County*   Elevation: 700 ft.   Latitude: 41° 28' N   Longitude: 74° 27' W

	JAN	FEB	MAR	APR	MAY	JUN	JUL	AUG	SEP	OCT	NOV	DEC	YEAR
Mean Maximum Temp. (°F)	35.4	39.2	48.1	61.1	71.5	79.4	83.4	82.1	74.9	63.4	51.4	39.7	60.8
Mean Temp. (°F)	27.0	29.8	37.9	50.2	60.4	68.9	73.2	71.9	64.6	53.2	42.9	32.1	51.0
Mean Minimum Temp. (°F)	18.5	20.4	27.7	39.3	49.2	58.3	63.0	61.6	54.3	43.0	34.3	24.5	41.2
Extreme Maximum Temp. (°F)	66	71	85	91	92	93	101	97	94	87	78	71	101
Extreme Minimum Temp. (°F)	-23	-8	-7	17	26	40	47	41	27	19	12	-10	-23
Days Maximum Temp. ≥ 90°F	0	0	0	0	0	2	4	3	1	0	0	0	10
Days Maximum Temp. ≤ 32°F	12	7	2	0	0	0	0	0	0	0	0	7	28
Days Minimum Temp. ≤ 32°F	28	25	21	5	0	0	0	0	0	3	14	25	121
Days Minimum Temp. ≤ 0°F	2	1	0	0	0	0	0	0	0	0	0	0	3
Heating Degree Days (base 65°F)	1,172	990	832	443	177	30	3	7	85	364	658	1,012	5,773
Cooling Degree Days (base 65°F)	0	0	0	6	40	153	265	227	80	7	0	0	778
Mean Precipitation (in.)	2.66	2.34	3.14	4.03	4.13	4.47	3.98	3.98	4.15	3.76	3.58	3.14	43.36
Extreme Maximum Daily Precip. (in.)	2.00	2.52	2.45	3.46	2.51	2.95	2.49	5.00	3.00	4.12	1.94	2.87	5.00
Days With ≥ 0.1" Precipitation	6	5	6	7	8	8	7	6	6	6	6	6	77
Days With ≥ 0.5" Precipitation	2	2	2	3	3	3	3	3	3	3	3	2	32
Days With ≥ 1.0" Precipitation	0	0	1	1	1	1	1	1	1	1	1	1	10
Mean Snowfall (in.)	na	na	na	trace	0.0	0.0	0.0	0.0	0.0	0.0	0.2	na	na
Maximum Snow Depth (in.)	na	na	na	na	na	na	na	na	na	na	na	na	na
Days With ≥ 1.0" Snow Depth	na	na	na	0	0	0	0	0	0	0	0	na	na

Mineola *Nassau County*   Elevation: 96 ft.   Latitude: 40° 44' N   Longitude: 73° 37' W

	JAN	FEB	MAR	APR	MAY	JUN	JUL	AUG	SEP	OCT	NOV	DEC	YEAR
Mean Maximum Temp. (°F)	39.1	42.2	49.4	59.4	69.2	78.8	83.7	82.4	75.1	64.4	55.1	44.3	61.9
Mean Temp. (°F)	32.4	34.7	41.4	50.6	59.7	69.5	74.8	73.7	66.5	56.0	47.5	37.6	53.7
Mean Minimum Temp. (°F)	25.7	27.3	33.2	41.8	50.2	60.2	65.9	64.9	57.8	47.3	39.8	30.8	45.4
Extreme Maximum Temp. (°F)	71	73	85	94	97	101	103	105	95	89	79	76	105
Extreme Minimum Temp. (°F)	-4	3	5	13	34	43	50	46	38	29	18	-1	-4
Days Maximum Temp. ≥ 90°F	0	0	0	0	1	3	6	4	1	0	0	0	15
Days Maximum Temp. ≤ 32°F	8	4	1	0	0	0	0	0	0	0	0	3	16
Days Minimum Temp. ≤ 32°F	23	20	14	2	0	0	0	0	0	0	5	18	82
Days Minimum Temp. ≤ 0°F	0	0	0	0	0	0	0	0	0	0	0	0	0
Heating Degree Days (base 65°F)	1,002	850	725	430	190	23	1	4	56	287	519	844	4,931
Cooling Degree Days (base 65°F)	0	0	0	4	34	167	313	279	107	14	0	0	918
Mean Precipitation (in.)	3.49	2.72	4.28	4.37	3.99	3.90	4.36	3.65	3.81	4.01	3.78	3.72	46.08
Extreme Maximum Daily Precip. (in.)	4.05	2.05	3.11	3.72	2.87	4.30	3.82	4.04	3.52	4.02	2.92	2.95	4.30
Days With ≥ 0.1" Precipitation	6	5	7	7	7	6	6	6	5	6	6	7	74
Days With ≥ 0.5" Precipitation	2	2	3	3	3	3	3	2	3	3	3	3	33
Days With ≥ 1.0" Precipitation	1	1	1	1	1	1	1	1	1	1	1	1	12
Mean Snowfall (in.)	4.9	6.4	3.6	0.6	0.0	0.0	0.0	0.0	0.0	0.0	0.1	4.2	19.8
Maximum Snow Depth (in.)	12	20	8	9	0	0	0	0	0	0	3	14	20
Days With ≥ 1.0" Snow Depth	7	6	2	0	0	0	0	0	0	0	0	3	18

Morrisville 5 SW *Madison County*   Elevation: 1,299 ft.   Latitude: 42° 50' N   Longitude: 75° 44' W

	JAN	FEB	MAR	APR	MAY	JUN	JUL	AUG	SEP	OCT	NOV	DEC	YEAR
Mean Maximum Temp. (°F)	28.7	32.0	39.9	53.9	65.8	73.8	77.5	76.0	69.1	56.6	44.8	33.6	54.3
Mean Temp. (°F)	20.0	22.6	30.2	43.5	54.6	63.0	67.0	65.6	58.8	47.0	37.1	26.2	44.6
Mean Minimum Temp. (°F)	11.4	13.1	20.4	33.1	43.4	52.2	56.3	55.3	48.5	37.3	29.3	18.7	34.9
Extreme Maximum Temp. (°F)	60	60	82	87	87	89	92	90	89	80	75	64	92
Extreme Minimum Temp. (°F)	-27	-25	-21	4	24	30	36	35	24	16	1	-30	-30
Days Maximum Temp. ≥ 90°F	0	0	0	0	0	0	0	0	0	0	0	0	0
Days Maximum Temp. ≤ 32°F	19	15	9	1	0	0	0	0	0	0	3	15	62
Days Minimum Temp. ≤ 32°F	29	26	26	15	3	0	0	0	1	9	20	28	157
Days Minimum Temp. ≤ 0°F	7	5	2	0	0	0	0	0	0	0	0	2	16
Heating Degree Days (base 65°F)	1,388	1,192	1,074	641	325	108	36	57	203	551	830	1,196	7,601
Cooling Degree Days (base 65°F)	0	0	0	2	10	57	104	84	25	1	0	0	283
Mean Precipitation (in.)	3.15	2.99	3.38	3.66	4.09	4.48	4.02	3.57	4.32	4.08	3.94	3.88	45.56
Extreme Maximum Daily Precip. (in.)	1.65	2.39	1.55	2.15	3.39	2.80	2.08	2.36	4.11	2.10	2.89	1.67	4.11
Days With ≥ 0.1" Precipitation	10	8	9	8	9	8	7	7	8	9	9	11	103
Days With ≥ 0.5" Precipitation	1	2	2	2	3	3	3	2	3	3	2	2	28
Days With ≥ 1.0" Precipitation	0	0	0	0	1	1	1	1	1	1	1	0	7
Mean Snowfall (in.)	30.5	25.7	21.1	5.6	0.2	0.0	0.0	0.0	trace	1.5	12.0	27.5	124.1
Maximum Snow Depth (in.)	45	51	44	29	4	0	0	0	trace	17	16	30	51
Days With ≥ 1.0" Snow Depth	27	27	22	5	0	0	0	0	0	1	9	24	115

New York Ave V Brooklyn *Kings County*   Elevation: 20 ft.   Latitude: 40° 36' N   Longitude: 73° 59' W

	JAN	FEB	MAR	APR	MAY	JUN	JUL	AUG	SEP	OCT	NOV	DEC	YEAR
Mean Maximum Temp. (°F)	39.5	42.3	49.6	60.2	70.4	79.5	84.5	83.3	76.1	64.8	54.6	43.6	62.4
Mean Temp. (°F)	33.4	35.7	42.3	52.4	62.3	71.7	77.1	76.1	68.9	57.6	48.1	37.8	55.3
Mean Minimum Temp. (°F)	27.2	29.0	34.9	44.5	54.2	63.8	69.7	68.9	61.7	50.3	41.5	31.9	48.2
Extreme Maximum Temp. (°F)	70	73	83	91	96	97	103	101	98	86	79	75	103
Extreme Minimum Temp. (°F)	-4	6	10	19	40	48	57	51	44	36	23	-1	-4
Days Maximum Temp. ≥ 90°F	0	0	0	0	1	3	6	4	1	0	0	0	15
Days Maximum Temp. ≤ 32°F	7	4	1	0	0	0	0	0	0	0	0	4	16
Days Minimum Temp. ≤ 32°F	21	18	11	1	0	0	0	0	0	0	3	15	69
Days Minimum Temp. ≤ 0°F	0	0	0	0	0	0	0	0	0	0	0	0	0
Heating Degree Days (base 65°F)	973	822	697	378	130	13	0	1	29	241	501	836	4,621
Cooling Degree Days (base 65°F)	0	0	0	6	54	220	382	353	153	18	1	0	1,187
Mean Precipitation (in.)	3.54	2.66	4.22	4.36	4.19	3.92	4.83	3.68	3.73	3.73	3.78	3.32	45.96
Extreme Maximum Daily Precip. (in.)	3.13	1.68	2.92	5.46	2.36	2.91	4.62	2.85	4.44	4.29	2.68	2.49	5.46
Days With ≥ 0.1" Precipitation	7	6	7	7	7	7	7	6	6	6	6	6	77
Days With ≥ 0.5" Precipitation	3	2	3	2	3	3	3	3	2	2	3	3	32
Days With ≥ 1.0" Precipitation	1	1	1	1	1	1	2	1	1	1	1	1	13
Mean Snowfall (in.)	6.6	7.3	3.9	0.7	0.0	0.0	0.0	0.0	0.0	trace	0.3	3.5	22.3
Maximum Snow Depth (in.)	23	20	10	9	0	0	0	0	0	trace	4	12	23
Days With ≥ 1.0" Snow Depth	7	6	3	0	0	0	0	0	0	0	0	2	18

The period of record for all cooperative weather station data is 1980 – 2009. See User Guide for detailed explanation of data.

Peru 2 WSW *Clinton County*   Elevation: 509 ft.   Latitude: 44° 34' N   Longitude: 73° 34' W

	JAN	FEB	MAR	APR	MAY	JUN	JUL	AUG	SEP	OCT	NOV	DEC	YEAR
Mean Maximum Temp. (°F)	27.9	31.7	41.0	55.7	68.4	77.2	81.4	79.4	71.0	57.9	45.4	33.3	55.8
Mean Temp. (°F)	18.6	21.9	31.1	44.7	56.5	65.7	70.2	68.0	59.9	48.0	37.3	25.1	45.6
Mean Minimum Temp. (°F)	9.2	12.1	21.2	33.8	44.6	54.2	58.9	56.5	48.7	37.9	29.1	16.8	35.3
Extreme Maximum Temp. (°F)	65	63	83	92	93	98	98	98	95	84	75	69	98
Extreme Minimum Temp. (°F)	-34	-30	-17	5	25	29	40	37	24	18	1	-26	-34
Days Maximum Temp. ≥ 90°F	0	0	0	0	0	1	3	2	0	0	0	0	6
Days Maximum Temp. ≤ 32°F	20	15	7	0	0	0	0	0	0	0	3	14	59
Days Minimum Temp. ≤ 32°F	29	26	26	14	2	0	0	0	1	9	19	28	154
Days Minimum Temp. ≤ 0°F	8	6	2	0	0	0	0	0	0	0	0	4	20
Heating Degree Days (base 65°F)	1,434	1,212	1,043	604	276	70	13	37	182	523	825	1,231	7,450
Cooling Degree Days (base 65°F)	0	0	0	3	21	98	180	136	35	2	0	0	475
Mean Precipitation (in.)	1.37	1.29	1.71	2.56	2.73	3.62	3.49	3.51	2.81	3.00	2.67	1.96	30.72
Extreme Maximum Daily Precip. (in.)	1.12	1.26	1.50	1.85	2.40	4.10	3.27	3.11	4.08	2.41	4.80	1.85	4.80
Days With ≥ 0.1" Precipitation	4	3	4	6	7	7	7	7	5	6	6	4	66
Days With ≥ 0.5" Precipitation	1	1	1	2	2	2	3	2	2	2	2	1	21
Days With ≥ 1.0" Precipitation	0	0	0	0	0	1	1	1	1	1	1	0	6
Mean Snowfall (in.)	11.3	10.4	11.1	2.9	0.0	0.0	0.0	0.0	0.0	0.5	3.2	12.6	52.0
Maximum Snow Depth (in.)	na	na	na	na	na	na	na	na	na	na	na	na	na
Days With ≥ 1.0" Snow Depth	na	na	na	0	0	0	0	0	0	0	0	na	na

Riverhead Research Farm *Suffolk County*   Elevation: 100 ft.   Latitude: 40° 58' N   Longitude: 72° 43' W

	JAN	FEB	MAR	APR	MAY	JUN	JUL	AUG	SEP	OCT	NOV	DEC	YEAR
Mean Maximum Temp. (°F)	39.6	41.5	48.6	59.8	70.5	79.3	84.0	82.5	75.7	64.8	54.5	44.5	62.1
Mean Temp. (°F)	32.3	34.0	40.3	50.3	60.3	69.5	74.8	73.7	67.1	56.3	47.1	37.3	53.6
Mean Minimum Temp. (°F)	25.0	26.4	32.0	40.8	50.0	59.7	65.5	64.8	58.4	47.8	39.5	30.1	45.0
Extreme Maximum Temp. (°F)	68	67	80	92	96	97	100	99	97	85	78	76	100
Extreme Minimum Temp. (°F)	-8	4	9	18	32	42	47	45	37	28	17	0	-8
Days Maximum Temp. ≥ 90°F	0	0	0	0	1	2	5	3	0	0	0	0	11
Days Maximum Temp. ≤ 32°F	7	4	1	0	0	0	0	0	0	0	0	3	15
Days Minimum Temp. ≤ 32°F	25	21	17	3	0	0	0	0	0	1	6	19	92
Days Minimum Temp. ≤ 0°F	0	0	0	0	0	0	0	0	0	0	0	0	0
Heating Degree Days (base 65°F)	1,006	870	758	436	172	22	0	2	42	274	532	851	4,965
Cooling Degree Days (base 65°F)	0	0	0	3	33	165	310	280	111	12	0	0	914
Mean Precipitation (in.)	3.71	3.14	4.48	4.49	3.86	4.12	3.21	3.90	3.84	4.22	4.27	4.01	47.25
Extreme Maximum Daily Precip. (in.)	3.10	2.34	3.06	3.18	3.01	5.27	3.38	6.34	3.84	5.58	2.90	3.62	6.34
Days With ≥ 0.1" Precipitation	7	6	7	7	7	7	5	6	6	6	7	7	78
Days With ≥ 0.5" Precipitation	3	2	3	3	3	3	2	3	3	3	3	3	34
Days With ≥ 1.0" Precipitation	1	1	1	1	1	1	1	1	1	1	1	1	12
Mean Snowfall (in.)	8.4	7.6	5.1	0.7	0.0	0.0	0.0	0.0	0.0	0.0	0.5	4.7	27.0
Maximum Snow Depth (in.)	20	16	14	6	0	0	0	0	0	0	7	20	20
Days With ≥ 1.0" Snow Depth	9	6	3	0	0	0	0	0	0	0	0	3	21

Troy Lock and Dam *Rensselaer County*   Elevation: 23 ft.   Latitude: 42° 45' N   Longitude: 73° 41' W

	JAN	FEB	MAR	APR	MAY	JUN	JUL	AUG	SEP	OCT	NOV	DEC	YEAR
Mean Maximum Temp. (°F)	31.7	35.3	44.3	58.6	70.4	78.7	83.5	82.2	74.3	61.6	49.4	37.1	58.9
Mean Temp. (°F)	23.2	25.9	34.7	48.0	59.2	68.2	73.1	71.6	63.5	51.3	40.9	29.6	49.1
Mean Minimum Temp. (°F)	14.6	16.5	25.0	37.4	47.9	57.7	62.6	60.9	52.6	40.9	32.4	22.1	39.2
Extreme Maximum Temp. (°F)	66	67	84	92	92	96	101	99	93	86	81	69	101
Extreme Minimum Temp. (°F)	-23	-14	-7	15	27	39	48	40	31	23	10	-15	-23
Days Maximum Temp. ≥ 90°F	0	0	0	0	0	3	5	4	1	0	0	0	13
Days Maximum Temp. ≤ 32°F	15	11	4	0	0	0	0	0	0	0	1	9	40
Days Minimum Temp. ≤ 32°F	28	26	24	8	0	0	0	0	0	5	16	26	133
Days Minimum Temp. ≤ 0°F	5	2	1	0	0	0	0	0	0	0	0	1	9
Heating Degree Days (base 65°F)	1,290	1,098	933	506	204	40	3	12	107	423	716	1,090	6,422
Cooling Degree Days (base 65°F)	0	0	0	4	30	142	260	224	68	5	0	0	733
Mean Precipitation (in.)	2.23	1.88	2.98	3.26	3.74	4.22	4.42	4.09	3.32	3.65	3.09	2.58	39.46
Extreme Maximum Daily Precip. (in.)	1.80	1.71	3.00	2.20	2.40	2.68	2.70	2.71	3.00	2.22	2.62	2.50	3.00
Days With ≥ 0.1" Precipitation	5	5	6	7	8	7	8	7	6	7	6	6	78
Days With ≥ 0.5" Precipitation	1	1	2	2	3	3	3	3	2	3	2	2	27
Days With ≥ 1.0" Precipitation	0	0	1	1	1	1	1	1	1	1	1	0	9
Mean Snowfall (in.)	12.7	8.0	7.5	1.3	0.0	0.0	0.0	0.0	0.0	0.1	1.8	7.2	38.6
Maximum Snow Depth (in.)	38	39	30	16	0	0	0	0	0	0	10	19	39
Days With ≥ 1.0" Snow Depth	19	16	8	1	0	0	0	0	0	0	1	10	55

Tully Heiberg Forest *Cortland County*   Elevation: 1,898 ft.   Latitude: 42° 46' N   Longitude: 76° 05' W

	JAN	FEB	MAR	APR	MAY	JUN	JUL	AUG	SEP	OCT	NOV	DEC	YEAR
Mean Maximum Temp. (°F)	27.2	29.8	37.5	50.6	63.0	71.6	75.9	74.7	66.9	54.9	43.1	31.9	52.3
Mean Temp. (°F)	19.5	21.3	28.9	41.5	53.1	61.9	66.4	65.2	57.6	46.1	35.7	24.7	43.5
Mean Minimum Temp. (°F)	11.6	12.8	20.3	32.2	43.2	52.2	56.9	55.7	48.2	37.2	28.2	17.5	34.7
Extreme Maximum Temp. (°F)	61	58	80	85	88	89	93	92	89	80	74	65	93
Extreme Minimum Temp. (°F)	-21	-19	-11	5	24	30	41	33	25	17	3	-29	-29
Days Maximum Temp. ≥ 90°F	0	0	0	0	0	0	0	0	0	0	0	0	0
Days Maximum Temp. ≤ 32°F	21	17	11	2	0	0	0	0	0	0	5	16	72
Days Minimum Temp. ≤ 32°F	30	27	27	16	3	0	0	0	0	10	21	29	164
Days Minimum Temp. ≤ 0°F	6	5	1	0	0	0	0	0	0	0	0	2	14
Heating Degree Days (base 65°F)	1,406	1,228	1,113	702	374	141	50	69	238	580	872	1,241	8,014
Cooling Degree Days (base 65°F)	0	0	0	2	11	53	101	83	21	1	0	0	272
Mean Precipitation (in.)	2.85	2.67	3.33	3.96	3.99	4.85	4.00	4.04	4.80	3.97	4.00	3.28	45.74
Extreme Maximum Daily Precip. (in.)	1.91	1.30	2.22	2.23	1.85	3.22	2.30	4.24	4.98	3.56	3.56	2.68	4.98
Days With ≥ 0.1" Precipitation	9	7	9	9	9	10	8	8	9	9	9	8	103
Days With ≥ 0.5" Precipitation	1	1	2	2	3	3	2	3	3	2	3	2	27
Days With ≥ 1.0" Precipitation	0	0	0	1	0	1	1	1	1	1	1	0	8
Mean Snowfall (in.)	26.3	23.3	21.1	7.6	0.4	trace	0.0	0.0	trace	1.8	11.9	23.4	115.8
Maximum Snow Depth (in.)	47	43	60	36	5	0	0	0	trace	9	17	34	60
Days With ≥ 1.0" Snow Depth	28	27	26	8	0	0	0	0	0	1	10	24	124

The period of record for all cooperative weather station data is 1980 – 2009. See User Guide for detailed explanation of data.

Utica Oneida County Arpt *Oneida County*   Elevation: 711 ft.   Latitude: 43° 09' N   Longitude: 75° 23' W

	JAN	FEB	MAR	APR	MAY	JUN	JUL	AUG	SEP	OCT	NOV	DEC	YEAR
Mean Maximum Temp. (°F)	29.4	32.3	40.9	55.0	67.6	75.9	80.4	78.7	70.6	58.1	46.0	34.0	55.7
Mean Temp. (°F)	21.9	24.1	32.4	45.3	56.8	65.4	70.2	68.6	60.8	49.0	38.8	27.0	46.7
Mean Minimum Temp. (°F)	14.3	15.9	23.9	35.6	46.0	54.9	59.9	58.4	50.9	39.9	31.5	20.1	37.6
Extreme Maximum Temp. (°F)	65	63	85	91	91	94	96	97	92	82	79	69	97
Extreme Minimum Temp. (°F)	-27	-17	-12	9	27	33	45	40	25	21	1	-23	-27
Days Maximum Temp. ≥ 90°F	0	0	0	0	0	1	2	1	0	0	0	0	4
Days Maximum Temp. ≤ 32°F	18	15	7	0	0	0	0	0	0	0	2	13	55
Days Minimum Temp. ≤ 32°F	28	26	24	11	1	0	0	0	0	6	17	27	140
Days Minimum Temp. ≤ 0°F	5	3	1	0	0	0	0	0	0	0	0	2	11
Heating Degree Days (base 65°F)	1,328	1,149	1,005	586	269	77	12	29	162	492	780	1,170	7,059
Cooling Degree Days (base 65°F)	0	0	1	3	22	95	181	148	42	2	0	0	494
Mean Precipitation (in.)	2.94	2.38	3.15	3.47	3.90	4.28	3.86	3.88	4.10	3.66	3.91	3.37	42.90
Extreme Maximum Daily Precip. (in.)	1.64	1.88	2.31	1.96	2.75	2.98	3.24	2.80	4.14	1.88	2.35	2.11	4.14
Days With ≥ 0.1" Precipitation	8	7	8	9	9	8	7	7	7	8	10	9	97
Days With ≥ 0.5" Precipitation	1	1	2	2	2	3	3	3	3	2	2	1	25
Days With ≥ 1.0" Precipitation	0	0	1	0	1	1	1	1	1	1	1	0	8
Mean Snowfall (in.)	na	na	na	na	na	na	na	na	na	na	na	na	na
Maximum Snow Depth (in.)	33	na	na	na	na	na	na	na	na	na	na	na	na
Days With ≥ 1.0" Snow Depth	24	na	na	na	na	na	na	na	na	na	na	na	na

Valatie 1 N *Columbia County*   Elevation: 299 ft.   Latitude: 42° 26' N   Longitude: 73° 41' W

	JAN	FEB	MAR	APR	MAY	JUN	JUL	AUG	SEP	OCT	NOV	DEC	YEAR
Mean Maximum Temp. (°F)	32.2	35.9	44.2	57.7	69.4	77.5	82.2	80.9	73.4	61.1	49.2	37.2	58.4
Mean Temp. (°F)	22.6	26.1	34.2	46.6	57.6	66.2	70.7	69.6	61.7	49.6	39.9	28.3	47.8
Mean Minimum Temp. (°F)	13.0	16.2	24.0	35.3	45.7	54.9	59.2	58.2	49.9	38.1	30.6	19.5	37.1
Extreme Maximum Temp. (°F)	71	69	86	93	92	97	100	97	94	87	81	69	100
Extreme Minimum Temp. (°F)	-25	-13	-9	10	27	34	43	35	28	19	2	-20	-25
Days Maximum Temp. ≥ 90°F	0	0	0	0	0	2	4	3	1	0	0	0	10
Days Maximum Temp. ≤ 32°F	15	11	4	0	0	0	0	0	0	0	1	9	40
Days Minimum Temp. ≤ 32°F	29	26	25	12	2	0	0	0	0	9	18	27	148
Days Minimum Temp. ≤ 0°F	6	2	1	0	0	0	0	0	0	0	0	2	11
Heating Degree Days (base 65°F)	1,308	1,094	950	550	250	65	13	25	142	474	747	1,129	6,747
Cooling Degree Days (base 65°F)	0	0	1	3	27	109	197	173	48	3	0	0	561
Mean Precipitation (in.)	2.05	1.90	2.82	3.74	4.07	4.50	4.06	4.14	3.96	3.91	3.29	2.55	40.99
Extreme Maximum Daily Precip. (in.)	1.28	1.15	3.89	3.65	3.00	2.68	3.87	3.51	5.10	2.94	2.16	2.25	5.10
Days With ≥ 0.1" Precipitation	5	5	6	8	8	8	7	7	7	7	6	6	80
Days With ≥ 0.5" Precipitation	2	1	2	2	3	3	3	3	3	3	2	2	29
Days With ≥ 1.0" Precipitation	0	0	1	1	1	1	1	1	1	1	1	0	9
Mean Snowfall (in.)	10.8	8.2	6.4	2.2	0.0	0.0	0.0	0.0	0.0	0.3	2.4	11.1	41.4
Maximum Snow Depth (in.)	33	24	18	14	0	0	0	0	0	6	9	17	33
Days With ≥ 1.0" Snow Depth	18	15	8	1	0	0	0	0	0	0	1	10	53

Wales *Erie County*   Elevation: 1,089 ft.   Latitude: 42° 45' N   Longitude: 78° 31' W

	JAN	FEB	MAR	APR	MAY	JUN	JUL	AUG	SEP	OCT	NOV	DEC	YEAR
Mean Maximum Temp. (°F)	31.3	32.5	41.2	54.6	65.5	74.0	77.4	76.3	69.5	57.9	46.9	35.2	55.2
Mean Temp. (°F)	23.6	23.6	31.6	44.0	54.4	63.8	67.4	66.1	59.3	48.4	38.9	28.2	45.8
Mean Minimum Temp. (°F)	15.9	14.7	22.0	33.4	43.3	53.7	57.4	55.9	48.9	38.8	30.9	21.1	36.3
Extreme Maximum Temp. (°F)	65	71	82	89	88	92	95	94	90	83	73	68	95
Extreme Minimum Temp. (°F)	-18	-14	-12	12	27	31	40	35	26	21	7	-19	-19
Days Maximum Temp. ≥ 90°F	0	0	0	0	0	0	0	0	0	0	0	0	0
Days Maximum Temp. ≤ 32°F	17	14	9	1	0	0	0	0	0	0	3	12	56
Days Minimum Temp. ≤ 32°F	28	26	26	16	3	0	0	0	1	8	18	27	153
Days Minimum Temp. ≤ 0°F	4	4	1	0	0	0	0	0	0	0	0	1	10
Heating Degree Days (base 65°F)	1,275	1,163	1,027	625	337	103	38	55	195	513	776	1,135	7,242
Cooling Degree Days (base 65°F)	0	0	1	3	17	75	120	96	29	4	0	0	345
Mean Precipitation (in.)	3.49	2.55	3.00	3.35	3.36	4.17	3.90	3.71	4.26	3.72	3.68	3.80	42.99
Extreme Maximum Daily Precip. (in.)	2.47	2.30	1.76	1.64	1.54	5.33	2.97	3.22	3.09	1.89	2.35	1.43	5.33
Days With ≥ 0.1" Precipitation	11	8	8	8	8	8	8	8	8	8	9	11	103
Days With ≥ 0.5" Precipitation	2	1	2	2	2	3	3	3	3	3	3	2	29
Days With ≥ 1.0" Precipitation	0	0	0	0	0	1	1	1	1	1	0	0	5
Mean Snowfall (in.)	32.7	19.0	15.9	4.8	0.3	0.0	0.0	0.0	0.0	0.3	10.1	27.7	110.8
Maximum Snow Depth (in.)	34	28	29	11	6	0	0	0	0	2	20	19	34
Days With ≥ 1.0" Snow Depth	25	23	16	3	0	0	0	0	0	0	6	20	93

Wantagh Cedar Creek *Nassau County*   Elevation: 9 ft.   Latitude: 40° 39' N   Longitude: 73° 30' W

	JAN	FEB	MAR	APR	MAY	JUN	JUL	AUG	SEP	OCT	NOV	DEC	YEAR
Mean Maximum Temp. (°F)	38.3	40.2	47.1	56.4	65.9	76.1	81.4	81.2	74.4	64.0	54.0	43.4	60.2
Mean Temp. (°F)	32.3	33.8	40.3	49.3	58.4	68.7	74.0	73.8	66.7	56.3	47.0	37.4	53.2
Mean Minimum Temp. (°F)	26.2	27.3	33.4	41.9	50.9	61.2	66.7	66.4	59.0	48.5	40.0	31.3	46.1
Extreme Maximum Temp. (°F)	69	67	81	89	95	97	103	103	92	90	78	77	103
Extreme Minimum Temp. (°F)	-3	0	5	19	29	34	45	48	38	28	15	3	-3
Days Maximum Temp. ≥ 90°F	0	0	0	0	0	1	3	2	0	0	0	0	6
Days Maximum Temp. ≤ 32°F	8	5	1	0	0	0	0	0	0	0	0	4	18
Days Minimum Temp. ≤ 32°F	22	21	14	2	0	0	0	0	0	0	6	18	83
Days Minimum Temp. ≤ 0°F	0	0	0	0	0	0	0	0	0	0	0	0	0
Heating Degree Days (base 65°F)	1,008	876	760	466	220	32	7	3	51	279	534	847	5,083
Cooling Degree Days (base 65°F)	0	0	0	2	23	149	295	283	109	16	1	0	878
Mean Precipitation (in.)	3.32	2.62	4.00	4.22	3.60	3.57	3.60	3.29	3.50	3.67	3.46	3.55	42.40
Extreme Maximum Daily Precip. (in.)	4.91	2.19	2.47	4.64	2.44	3.32	3.90	3.89	3.73	5.43	2.21	2.36	5.43
Days With ≥ 0.1" Precipitation	6	5	7	7	6	6	6	5	5	5	6	7	71
Days With ≥ 0.5" Precipitation	2	1	3	3	2	2	3	2	2	2	3	3	28
Days With ≥ 1.0" Precipitation	1	0	1	1	1	1	1	1	1	1	1	1	11
Mean Snowfall (in.)	na	na	na	0.0	0.0	0.0	0.0	0.0	0.0	0.0	0.0	na	na
Maximum Snow Depth (in.)	na	na	na	na	na	na	na	na	na	na	na	na	na
Days With ≥ 1.0" Snow Depth	na	na	na	0	0	0	0	0	0	0	0	na	na

The period of record for all cooperative weather station data is 1980 – 2009. See User Guide for detailed explanation of data.

Westfield 2 SSE *Chautauqua County*   Elevation: 707 ft.   Latitude: 42° 18' N   Longitude: 79° 35' W

	JAN	FEB	MAR	APR	MAY	JUN	JUL	AUG	SEP	OCT	NOV	DEC	YEAR
Mean Maximum Temp. (°F)	32.8	35.3	43.1	55.6	67.3	76.1	80.3	78.2	71.0	59.7	48.2	37.4	57.1
Mean Temp. (°F)	26.4	28.0	35.0	46.8	58.3	67.2	71.8	70.1	63.1	52.2	41.8	31.5	49.3
Mean Minimum Temp. (°F)	19.9	20.5	26.9	37.9	49.2	58.1	63.3	62.0	55.2	44.6	35.4	25.6	41.6
Extreme Maximum Temp. (°F)	66	70	82	90	91	97	96	99	92	83	74	72	99
Extreme Minimum Temp. (°F)	-16	-7	-13	14	29	37	49	41	36	27	16	-8	-16
Days Maximum Temp. ≥ 90°F	0	0	0	0	0	2	2	1	0	0	0	0	5
Days Maximum Temp. ≤ 32°F	15	12	6	0	0	0	0	0	0	0	1	10	44
Days Minimum Temp. ≤ 32°F	27	25	23	9	0	0	0	0	0	1	11	24	120
Days Minimum Temp. ≤ 0°F	1	1	0	0	0	0	0	0	0	0	0	0	2
Heating Degree Days (base 65°F)	1,191	1,041	924	546	241	60	7	14	119	398	690	1,032	6,263
Cooling Degree Days (base 65°F)	0	0	1	7	40	131	226	180	70	7	0	0	662
Mean Precipitation (in.)	2.50	2.20	2.90	3.40	3.82	4.14	4.16	3.96	4.89	4.88	4.32	3.42	44.59
Extreme Maximum Daily Precip. (in.)	1.38	2.09	1.11	1.76	2.17	4.29	3.36	2.41	2.85	2.52	3.38	1.65	4.29
Days With ≥ 0.1" Precipitation	7	7	8	8	8	8	7	7	9	10	10	9	98
Days With ≥ 0.5" Precipitation	1	1	2	2	2	2	3	3	4	4	3	2	29
Days With ≥ 1.0" Precipitation	0	0	0	0	1	1	1	1	1	1	1	0	7
Mean Snowfall (in.)	21.2	14.0	12.7	2.7	0.4	0.0	0.0	0.0	trace	0.4	8.7	24.4	84.5
Maximum Snow Depth (in.)	23	22	17	9	na	0	0	0	trace	na	11	25	na
Days With ≥ 1.0" Snow Depth	25	20	12	1	0	0	0	0	0	0	5	17	80

Whitehall *Washington County*   Elevation: 119 ft.   Latitude: 43° 33' N   Longitude: 73° 24' W

	JAN	FEB	MAR	APR	MAY	JUN	JUL	AUG	SEP	OCT	NOV	DEC	YEAR
Mean Maximum Temp. (°F)	30.1	34.4	44.3	58.6	70.8	79.7	84.0	81.8	73.1	60.6	47.5	35.1	58.3
Mean Temp. (°F)	21.0	24.1	34.1	47.5	59.1	68.2	72.6	70.9	62.4	50.6	39.7	27.4	48.1
Mean Minimum Temp. (°F)	11.8	13.7	23.9	36.2	47.0	56.6	61.2	60.1	51.7	40.6	31.8	19.7	37.9
Extreme Maximum Temp. (°F)	64	63	84	94	92	102	100	96	94	83	75	68	102
Extreme Minimum Temp. (°F)	-36	-33	-14	13	23	36	45	37	28	19	4	-25	-36
Days Maximum Temp. ≥ 90°F	0	0	0	0	0	3	4	3	0	0	0	0	10
Days Maximum Temp. ≤ 32°F	17	11	4	0	0	0	0	0	0	0	1	12	45
Days Minimum Temp. ≤ 32°F	29	26	24	11	1	0	0	0	0	6	17	27	141
Days Minimum Temp. ≤ 0°F	7	5	1	0	0	0	0	0	0	0	0	2	15
Heating Degree Days (base 65°F)	1,360	1,150	952	523	204	38	3	13	132	442	755	1,158	6,730
Cooling Degree Days (base 65°F)	0	0	0	5	29	141	246	204	62	3	0	0	690
Mean Precipitation (in.)	3.01	2.52	2.95	3.22	3.67	3.89	4.46	4.16	3.68	3.72	3.55	3.22	42.05
Extreme Maximum Daily Precip. (in.)	1.96	2.40	2.02	2.23	1.85	2.96	3.45	4.01	4.25	2.62	2.59	2.89	4.25
Days With ≥ 0.1" Precipitation	6	5	6	7	8	7	7	7	6	7	7	6	79
Days With ≥ 0.5" Precipitation	2	2	2	2	2	3	3	3	2	2	3	2	28
Days With ≥ 1.0" Precipitation	1	0	1	1	1	1	1	1	1	1	1	1	11
Mean Snowfall (in.)	16.6	12.0	12.5	2.1	0.0	0.0	0.0	0.0	0.0	trace	2.7	13.6	59.5
Maximum Snow Depth (in.)	na	na	na	2	0	0	0	0	0	na	na	na	na
Days With ≥ 1.0" Snow Depth	na	na	na	0	0	0	0	0	0	0	0	na	na

Yorktown Heights 1 W *Westchester County*   Elevation: 669 ft.   Latitude: 41° 16' N   Longitude: 73° 48' W

	JAN	FEB	MAR	APR	MAY	JUN	JUL	AUG	SEP	OCT	NOV	DEC	YEAR
Mean Maximum Temp. (°F)	34.5	38.4	46.8	59.1	69.4	77.5	82.0	80.7	73.5	62.1	51.2	39.6	59.6
Mean Temp. (°F)	26.6	29.7	37.5	49.2	59.2	67.9	72.7	71.4	63.9	52.6	43.1	32.3	50.5
Mean Minimum Temp. (°F)	18.7	21.0	28.2	39.2	48.8	58.2	63.3	62.1	54.4	43.1	35.0	24.9	41.4
Extreme Maximum Temp. (°F)	67	73	85	95	94	95	100	100	95	87	78	73	100
Extreme Minimum Temp. (°F)	-15	-5	0	14	33	39	49	39	32	25	13	-9	-15
Days Maximum Temp. ≥ 90°F	0	0	0	0	0	2	3	2	1	0	0	0	8
Days Maximum Temp. ≤ 32°F	13	8	3	0	0	0	0	0	0	0	1	7	32
Days Minimum Temp. ≤ 32°F	28	25	21	5	0	0	0	0	0	3	12	25	119
Days Minimum Temp. ≤ 0°F	2	0	0	0	0	0	0	0	0	0	0	0	2
Heating Degree Days (base 65°F)	1,183	991	846	474	208	43	4	11	96	385	650	1,008	5,899
Cooling Degree Days (base 65°F)	0	0	1	6	33	136	249	217	71	7	0	0	720
Mean Precipitation (in.)	3.59	2.97	3.96	4.60	4.35	4.76	4.82	4.41	4.53	4.53	4.39	3.88	50.79
Extreme Maximum Daily Precip. (in.)	2.48	2.22	4.60	5.15	3.35	2.82	3.44	4.04	10.95	4.64	2.97	3.00	10.95
Days With ≥ 0.1" Precipitation	7	6	7	8	8	8	7	7	6	6	7	6	83
Days With ≥ 0.5" Precipitation	3	2	3	3	3	3	3	3	3	3	3	3	35
Days With ≥ 1.0" Precipitation	1	1	1	1	1	1	2	1	1	1	1	1	13
Mean Snowfall (in.)	11.0	10.3	7.7	2.1	0.0	0.0	0.0	0.0	0.0	trace	1.3	7.6	40.0
Maximum Snow Depth (in.)	29	29	19	17	0	0	0	0	0	trace	5	15	29
Days With ≥ 1.0" Snow Depth	18	15	9	1	0	0	0	0	0	0	1	10	54

The period of record for all cooperative weather station data is 1980 – 2009. See User Guide for detailed explanation of data.

New York Weather Station Rankings

Annual Extreme Maximum Temperature

Highest			Lowest		
Rank	Station Name	°F	Rank	Station Name	°F
1	Mineola	105	1	Indian Lake 2 SW	91
2	Dobbs Ferry Ardsley	104	2	Morrisville 5 SW	92
2	New York Laguardia Arpt	104	3	Tully Heiberg Forest	93
4	New York Central Park Observ	103	4	Boonville 2 SSW	94
4	New York Ave V Brooklyn	103	4	Grafton	94
4	Wantagh Cedar Creek	103	6	Conklingville Dam	95
7	Bridgehampton	102	6	Wales	95
7	Islip-Macarthur Arpt	102	8	Dannemora	96
7	New York J F Kennedy Int'l Arpt	102	9	Allegany State Park	97
7	Whitehall	102	9	Buffalo Greater Buffalo Int'l	97
11	Albion 2 NE	101	9	Canton 4 SE	97
11	Aurora Research Farm	101	9	Delhi 2 SE	97
11	Bath	101	9	Lowville	97
11	Middletown 2 NW	101	9	Utica Oneida County Arpt	97
11	Syracuse Hancock Int'l Arpt	101	15	Alfred	98
11	Troy Lock and Dam	101	15	Binghamton Edwin A Link Field	98
17	Alcove Dam	100	15	Gouverneur 3 NW	98
17	Chazy	100	15	Ithaca Cornell Univ	98
17	Riverhead Research Farm	100	15	Peru 2 WSW	98
17	Valatie 1 N	100	15	Rochester Intl Arpt	98
17	Yorktown Heights 1 W	100	21	Albany County Arpt	99
22	Albany County Arpt	99	21	Avon	99
22	Avon	99	21	Westfield 2 SSE	99
22	Westfield 2 SSE	99	24	Alcove Dam	100
25	Alfred	98	24	Chazy	100

Annual Mean Maximum Temperature

Highest			Lowest		
Rank	Station Name	°F	Rank	Station Name	°F
1	Dobbs Ferry Ardsley	62.9	1	Indian Lake 2 SW	51.0
2	New York Central Park Observ	62.7	2	Boonville 2 SSW	51.1
3	New York Laguardia Arpt	62.5	3	Tully Heiberg Forest	52.3
4	New York Ave V Brooklyn	62.4	4	Dannemora	53.1
5	Riverhead Research Farm	62.1	5	Lowville	53.2
6	Mineola	61.9	6	Canton 4 SE	54.0
7	New York J F Kennedy Int'l Arpt	61.5	7	Morrisville 5 SW	54.3
8	Islip-Macarthur Arpt	60.8	8	Grafton	54.4
8	Middletown 2 NW	60.8	9	Binghamton Edwin A Link Field	54.9
10	Wantagh Cedar Creek	60.2	9	Conklingville Dam	54.9
11	Bridgehampton	59.8	11	Chazy	55.1
12	Yorktown Heights 1 W	59.6	11	Gouverneur 3 NW	55.1
13	Troy Lock and Dam	58.9	13	Allegany State Park	55.2
14	Valatie 1 N	58.4	13	Wales	55.2
15	Whitehall	58.3	15	Utica Oneida County Arpt	55.7
16	Albion 2 NE	58.1	16	Peru 2 WSW	55.9
17	Albany County Arpt	58.0	17	Ithaca Cornell Univ	56.2
18	Avon	57.6	18	Delhi 2 SE	56.3
18	Syracuse Hancock Int'l Arpt	57.6	19	Buffalo Greater Buffalo Int'l	56.6
20	Aurora Research Farm	57.3	20	Alcove Dam	56.7
20	Rochester Intl Arpt	57.3	21	Alfred	56.9
22	Bath	57.1	22	Bath	57.1
22	Westfield 2 SSE	57.1	22	Westfield 2 SSE	57.1
24	Alfred	56.9	24	Aurora Research Farm	57.3
25	Alcove Dam	56.7	24	Rochester Intl Arpt	57.3

Rankings include 25 highest/lowest stations. If state has less than 25 stations, all stations are included. The period of record is 1980–2009. See User Guide for detailed explanation of data.

Annual Mean Temperature

	Highest			Lowest	
Rank	Station Name	°F	Rank	Station Name	°F
1	New York Laguardia Arpt	55.6	1	Indian Lake 2 SW	40.7
2	New York Central Park Observ	55.3	2	Boonville 2 SSW	42.4
2	New York Ave V Brooklyn	55.3	3	Lowville	43.3
4	New York J F Kennedy Int'l Arpt	54.4	4	Tully Heiberg Forest	43.5
5	Mineola	53.7	5	Canton 4 SE	43.8
6	Riverhead Research Farm	53.6	6	Dannemora	43.9
7	Dobbs Ferry Ardsley	53.2	7	Gouverneur 3 NW	44.0
7	Wantagh Cedar Creek	53.2	8	Allegany State Park	44.6
9	Islip-Macarthur Arpt	52.6	8	Morrisville 5 SW	44.6
10	Bridgehampton	51.3	10	Delhi 2 SE	44.8
11	Middletown 2 NW	51.0	11	Chazy	45.1
12	Yorktown Heights 1 W	50.5	11	Conklingville Dam	45.1
13	Westfield 2 SSE	49.4	13	Alfred	45.2
14	Albion 2 NE	49.1	14	Grafton	45.3
14	Troy Lock and Dam	49.1	15	Bath	45.6
16	Buffalo Greater Buffalo Int'l	48.5	15	Peru 2 WSW	45.6
17	Rochester Intl Arpt	48.3	17	Wales	45.8
18	Albany County Arpt	48.2	18	Alcove Dam	46.1
18	Aurora Research Farm	48.2	19	Binghamton Edwin A Link Field	46.5
18	Syracuse Hancock Int'l Arpt	48.2	19	Ithaca Cornell Univ	46.5
21	Whitehall	48.1	21	Utica Oneida County Arpt	46.7
22	Valatie 1 N	47.8	22	Avon	47.7
23	Avon	47.7	23	Valatie 1 N	47.8
24	Utica Oneida County Arpt	46.7	24	Whitehall	48.1
25	Binghamton Edwin A Link Field	46.5	25	Albany County Arpt	48.2

Annual Mean Minimum Temperature

	Highest			Lowest	
Rank	Station Name	°F	Rank	Station Name	°F
1	New York Laguardia Arpt	48.7	1	Indian Lake 2 SW	30.3
2	New York Ave V Brooklyn	48.2	2	Gouverneur 3 NW	32.8
3	New York Central Park Observ	47.8	3	Lowville	33.3
4	New York J F Kennedy Int'l Arpt	47.2	4	Delhi 2 SE	33.4
5	Wantagh Cedar Creek	46.1	5	Alfred	33.5
6	Mineola	45.4	6	Boonville 2 SSW	33.6
7	Riverhead Research Farm	45.0	6	Canton 4 SE	33.6
8	Islip-Macarthur Arpt	44.3	8	Allegany State Park	34.0
9	Dobbs Ferry Ardsley	43.4	9	Bath	34.1
10	Bridgehampton	42.7	10	Dannemora	34.7
11	Westfield 2 SSE	41.6	10	Tully Heiberg Forest	34.7
12	Yorktown Heights 1 W	41.4	12	Morrisville 5 SW	34.9
13	Middletown 2 NW	41.2	13	Chazy	35.1
14	Buffalo Greater Buffalo Int'l	40.3	14	Conklingville Dam	35.3
15	Albion 2 NE	40.1	14	Peru 2 WSW	35.3
16	Rochester Intl Arpt	39.3	16	Alcove Dam	35.5
17	Troy Lock and Dam	39.2	17	Grafton	36.2
18	Aurora Research Farm	39.1	18	Wales	36.3
19	Syracuse Hancock Int'l Arpt	38.7	19	Ithaca Cornell Univ	36.6
20	Albany County Arpt	38.3	20	Valatie 1 N	37.1
21	Binghamton Edwin A Link Field	38.1	21	Utica Oneida County Arpt	37.6
22	Whitehall	37.9	22	Avon	37.8
23	Avon	37.8	23	Whitehall	37.9
24	Utica Oneida County Arpt	37.6	24	Binghamton Edwin A Link Field	38.1
25	Valatie 1 N	37.1	25	Albany County Arpt	38.3

Rankings include 25 highest/lowest stations. If state has less than 25 stations, all stations are included. The period of record is 1980–2009. See User Guide for detailed explanation of data.

Annual Extreme Minimum Temperature

Highest				Lowest		
Rank	Station Name	°F		Rank	Station Name	°F
1	New York Central Park Observ	-2		1	Gouverneur 3 NW	-45
1	New York J F Kennedy Int'l Arpt	-2		2	Chazy	-44
3	New York Laguardia Arpt	-3		3	Canton 4 SE	-40
3	Wantagh Cedar Creek	-3		4	Whitehall	-36
5	Mineola	-4		5	Indian Lake 2 SW	-35
5	New York Ave V Brooklyn	*-4*		5	Lowville	-35
7	Islip-Macarthur Arpt	*-7*		7	Dannemora	-34
8	Riverhead Research Farm	-8		7	Peru 2 WSW	-34
9	Dobbs Ferry Ardsley	-10		9	Boonville 2 SSW	-33
10	Bridgehampton	-11		10	Delhi 2 SE	-32
11	Albion 2 NE	-15		11	Morrisville 5 SW	*-30*
11	Yorktown Heights 1 W	-15		12	Alcove Dam	-29
13	Buffalo Greater Buffalo Int'l	-16		12	Conklingville Dam	-29
13	Westfield 2 SSE	*-16*		12	Tully Heiberg Forest	*-29*
15	Rochester Intl Arpt	-17		15	Utica Oneida County Arpt	*-27*
16	Binghamton Edwin A Link Field	-18		16	Grafton	*-26*
17	Wales	*-19*		17	Alfred	-25
18	Aurora Research Farm	-21		17	Syracuse Hancock Int'l Arpt	-25
19	Allegany State Park	*-22*		17	Valatie 1 N	*-25*
20	Albany County Arpt	-23		20	Avon	-24
20	Middletown 2 NW	-23		20	Bath	*-24*
20	Troy Lock and Dam	-23		20	Ithaca Cornell Univ	-24
23	Avon	-24		23	Albany County Arpt	-23
23	Bath	*-24*		23	Middletown 2 NW	-23
23	Ithaca Cornell Univ	-24		23	Troy Lock and Dam	-23

July Mean Maximum Temperature

Highest				Lowest		
Rank	Station Name	°F		Rank	Station Name	°F
1	Dobbs Ferry Ardsley	85.2		1	Indian Lake 2 SW	74.2
2	New York Laguardia Arpt	85.0		2	Boonville 2 SSW	74.9
3	New York Central Park Observ	84.8		3	Tully Heiberg Forest	75.9
4	New York Ave V Brooklyn	84.5		4	Wales	*77.4*
5	Riverhead Research Farm	84.0		5	Morrisville 5 SW	*77.5*
5	Whitehall	84.0		6	Allegany State Park	77.9
7	Mineola	83.7		6	Grafton	*77.9*
8	Troy Lock and Dam	83.5		6	Lowville	77.9
9	Middletown 2 NW	83.4		9	Dannemora	78.0
10	New York J F Kennedy Int'l Arpt	82.9		10	Conklingville Dam	*78.3*
11	Albany County Arpt	82.3		11	Binghamton Edwin A Link Field	78.4
12	Valatie 1 N	*82.2*		12	Canton 4 SE	79.0
13	Albion 2 NE	82.1		13	Delhi 2 SE	79.2
14	Islip-Macarthur Arpt	*82.0*		14	Ithaca Cornell Univ	79.5
14	Yorktown Heights 1 W	82.0		15	Alcove Dam	80.0
16	Syracuse Hancock Int'l Arpt	81.7		16	Alfred	80.1
17	Peru 2 WSW	81.4		16	Buffalo Greater Buffalo Int'l	80.1
17	Wantagh Cedar Creek	81.4		16	Gouverneur 3 NW	80.1
19	Aurora Research Farm	81.3		19	Westfield 2 SSE	*80.3*
19	Avon	81.3		20	Chazy	80.4
21	Rochester Intl Arpt	81.2		20	Utica Oneida County Arpt	80.4
22	Bridgehampton	80.9		22	Bath	*80.7*
23	Bath	*80.7*		23	Bridgehampton	80.9
24	Chazy	80.4		24	Rochester Intl Arpt	81.2
24	Utica Oneida County Arpt	80.4		25	Aurora Research Farm	81.3

Rankings include 25 highest/lowest stations. If state has less than 25 stations, all stations are included. The period of record is 1980–2009. See User Guide for detailed explanation of data.

January Mean Minimum Temperature

Highest			Lowest		
Rank	Station Name	°F	Rank	Station Name	°F
1	New York Laguardia Arpt	27.4	1	Indian Lake 2 SW	5.0
2	New York Ave V Brooklyn	27.2	2	Canton 4 SE	5.3
3	New York Central Park Observ	26.9	3	Gouverneur 3 NW	5.7
4	New York J F Kennedy Int'l Arpt	26.3	4	Lowville	7.2
5	Wantagh Cedar Creek	26.2	5	Chazy	8.0
6	Mineola	25.7	6	Dannemora	8.1
7	Riverhead Research Farm	25.0	7	Boonville 2 SSW	8.3
8	Islip-Macarthur Arpt	24.4	8	Peru 2 WSW	9.2
9	Bridgehampton	23.2	9	Conklingville Dam	9.4
10	Dobbs Ferry Ardsley	23.1	10	Delhi 2 SE	10.6
11	Westfield 2 SSE	19.9	11	Morrisville 5 SW	11.4
12	Buffalo Greater Buffalo Int'l	18.8	12	Alcove Dam	11.6
13	Yorktown Heights 1 W	18.7	13	Tully Heiberg Forest	11.7
14	Middletown 2 NW	18.5	14	Whitehall	11.8
15	Albion 2 NE	18.4	15	Grafton	12.1
16	Rochester Intl Arpt	17.8	16	Alfred	12.7
17	Aurora Research Farm	16.9	16	Bath	12.7
18	Avon	16.7	18	Valatie 1 N	13.0
19	Wales	15.9	19	Allegany State Park	13.4
20	Binghamton Edwin A Link Field	15.8	20	Utica Oneida County Arpt	14.3
20	Syracuse Hancock Int'l Arpt	15.8	21	Albany County Arpt	14.5
22	Ithaca Cornell Univ	14.7	22	Troy Lock and Dam	14.6
23	Troy Lock and Dam	14.6	23	Ithaca Cornell Univ	14.7
24	Albany County Arpt	14.5	24	Binghamton Edwin A Link Field	15.8
25	Utica Oneida County Arpt	14.3	24	Syracuse Hancock Int'l Arpt	15.8

Number of Days Annually Maximum Temperature ≥ 90°F

Highest			Lowest		
Rank	Station Name	Days	Rank	Station Name	Days
1	Dobbs Ferry Ardsley	18	1	Boonville 2 SSW	0
1	New York Laguardia Arpt	18	1	Grafton	0
3	New York Central Park Observ	17	1	Indian Lake 2 SW	0
4	Mineola	15	1	Morrisville 5 SW	0
4	New York Ave V Brooklyn	15	1	Tully Heiberg Forest	0
6	Troy Lock and Dam	13	1	Wales	0
7	Riverhead Research Farm	11	7	Allegany State Park	1
8	Middletown 2 NW	10	7	Conklingville Dam	1
8	New York J F Kennedy Int'l Arpt	10	9	Binghamton Edwin A Link Field	2
8	Valatie 1 N	10	9	Canton 4 SE	2
8	Whitehall	10	9	Dannemora	2
12	Aurora Research Farm	9	12	Buffalo Greater Buffalo Int'l	3
13	Albany County Arpt	8	12	Chazy	3
13	Albion 2 NE	8	12	Delhi 2 SE	3
13	Islip-Macarthur Arpt	8	12	Gouverneur 3 NW	3
13	Syracuse Hancock Int'l Arpt	8	12	Lowville	3
13	Yorktown Heights 1 W	8	17	Alfred	4
18	Avon	7	17	Ithaca Cornell Univ	4
19	Bath	6	17	Utica Oneida County Arpt	4
19	Peru 2 WSW	6	20	Alcove Dam	5
19	Rochester Intl Arpt	6	20	Bridgehampton	5
19	Wantagh Cedar Creek	6	20	Westfield 2 SSE	5
23	Alcove Dam	5	23	Bath	6
23	Bridgehampton	5	23	Peru 2 WSW	6
23	Westfield 2 SSE	5	23	Rochester Intl Arpt	6

Rankings include 25 highest/lowest stations. If state has less than 25 stations, all stations are included. The period of record is 1980–2009. See User Guide for detailed explanation of data.

Number of Days Annually Maximum Temperature ≤ 32°F

	Highest			Lowest	
Rank	Station Name	Days	Rank	Station Name	Days
1	Boonville 2 SSW	82	1	New York J F Kennedy Int'l Arpt	15
2	Indian Lake 2 SW	75	1	Riverhead Research Farm	15
3	Dannemora	73	3	Mineola	16
4	Tully Heiberg Forest	*72*	3	New York Ave V Brooklyn	*16*
5	Lowville	68	5	Bridgehampton	17
6	Canton 4 SE	66	5	Dobbs Ferry Ardsley	17
7	Grafton	62	5	Islip-Macarthur Arpt	*17*
7	Morrisville 5 SW	62	5	New York Central Park Observ	17
9	Gouverneur 3 NW	61	9	New York Laguardia Arpt	18
10	Chazy	60	9	Wantagh Cedar Creek	18
11	Peru 2 WSW	59	11	Middletown 2 NW	28
12	Binghamton Edwin A Link Field	58	12	Yorktown Heights 1 W	32
13	Allegany State Park	56	13	Troy Lock and Dam	40
13	Wales	*56*	13	Valatie 1 N	*40*
15	Utica Oneida County Arpt	*55*	15	Albany County Arpt	43
16	Ithaca Cornell Univ	52	16	Westfield 2 SSE	*44*
17	Buffalo Greater Buffalo Int'l	51	17	Whitehall	45
18	Alfred	48	18	Albion 2 NE	46
18	Conklingville Dam	48	18	Aurora Research Farm	46
18	Delhi 2 SE	48	18	Avon	46
18	Syracuse Hancock Int'l Arpt	48	18	Bath	*46*
22	Alcove Dam	47	18	Rochester Intl Arpt	46
23	Albion 2 NE	46	23	Alcove Dam	47
23	Aurora Research Farm	46	24	Alfred	48
23	Avon	46	24	Conklingville Dam	48

Number of Days Annually Minimum Temperature ≤ 32°F

	Highest			Lowest	
Rank	Station Name	Days	Rank	Station Name	Days
1	Indian Lake 2 SW	186	1	New York Laguardia Arpt	67
2	Alfred	170	2	New York Ave V Brooklyn	*69*
2	Delhi 2 SE	170	3	New York Central Park Observ	70
4	Bath	*169*	4	New York J F Kennedy Int'l Arpt	74
5	Boonville 2 SSW	168	5	Mineola	82
6	Lowville	167	6	Wantagh Cedar Creek	83
7	Gouverneur 3 NW	166	7	Riverhead Research Farm	92
8	Tully Heiberg Forest	*164*	8	Islip-Macarthur Arpt	*101*
9	Allegany State Park	163	9	Dobbs Ferry Ardsley	106
10	Canton 4 SE	162	10	Bridgehampton	109
11	Alcove Dam	160	11	Yorktown Heights 1 W	119
11	Dannemora	160	12	Westfield 2 SSE	*120*
13	Morrisville 5 SW	*157*	13	Middletown 2 NW	121
14	Peru 2 WSW	154	14	Buffalo Greater Buffalo Int'l	125
15	Chazy	153	15	Albion 2 NE	129
15	Grafton	*153*	16	Rochester Intl Arpt	131
15	Wales	*153*	17	Aurora Research Farm	132
18	Ithaca Cornell Univ	150	18	Troy Lock and Dam	133
19	Valatie 1 N	*148*	19	Syracuse Hancock Int'l Arpt	134
20	Conklingville Dam	147	20	Utica Oneida County Arpt	*140*
21	Avon	143	21	Albany County Arpt	141
22	Binghamton Edwin A Link Field	142	21	Whitehall	141
23	Albany County Arpt	141	23	Binghamton Edwin A Link Field	142
23	Whitehall	141	24	Avon	143
25	Utica Oneida County Arpt	*140*	25	Conklingville Dam	147

Rankings include 25 highest/lowest stations. If state has less than 25 stations, all stations are included. The period of record is 1980–2009. See User Guide for detailed explanation of data.

Number of Days Annually Minimum Temperature ≤ 0°F

	Highest			Lowest	
Rank	Station Name	Days	Rank	Station Name	Days
1	Indian Lake 2 SW	34	1	Bridgehampton	0
2	Gouverneur 3 NW	32	1	Islip-Macarthur Arpt	0
3	Canton 4 SE	31	1	Mineola	0
4	Lowville	27	1	New York Central Park Observ	0
5	Chazy	25	1	New York J F Kennedy Int'l Arpt	0
6	Boonville 2 SSW	23	1	New York Laguardia Arpt	0
7	Dannemora	21	1	New York Ave V Brooklyn	0
8	Peru 2 WSW	20	1	Riverhead Research Farm	0
9	Delhi 2 SE	18	1	Wantagh Cedar Creek	0
10	Conklingville Dam	17	10	Dobbs Ferry Ardsley	1
11	Morrisville 5 SW	16	11	Westfield 2 SSE	2
12	Alfred	15	11	Yorktown Heights 1 W	2
12	Whitehall	15	13	Albion 2 NE	3
14	Tully Heiberg Forest	14	13	Middletown 2 NW	3
15	Allegany State Park	13	15	Buffalo Greater Buffalo Int'l	4
15	Grafton	13	15	Rochester Intl Arpt	4
17	Alcove Dam	12	17	Aurora Research Farm	5
17	Bath	12	17	Binghamton Edwin A Link Field	5
19	Ithaca Cornell Univ	11	19	Avon	8
19	Utica Oneida County Arpt	11	19	Syracuse Hancock Int'l Arpt	8
19	Valatie 1 N	11	21	Albany County Arpt	9
22	Wales	10	21	Troy Lock and Dam	9
23	Albany County Arpt	9	23	Wales	10
23	Troy Lock and Dam	9	24	Ithaca Cornell Univ	11
25	Avon	8	24	Utica Oneida County Arpt	11

Number of Annual Heating Degree Days

	Highest			Lowest	
Rank	Station Name	Num.	Rank	Station Name	Num.
1	Indian Lake 2 SW	8,896	1	New York Laguardia Arpt	4,566
2	Boonville 2 SSW	8,369	2	New York Ave V Brooklyn	4,621
3	Lowville	8,133	3	New York Central Park Observ	4,622
4	Canton 4 SE	8,035	4	New York J F Kennedy Int'l Arpt	4,796
5	Tully Heiberg Forest	8,014	5	Mineola	4,931
6	Dannemora	7,933	6	Riverhead Research Farm	4,965
7	Gouverneur 3 NW	7,930	7	Wantagh Cedar Creek	5,083
8	Morrisville 5 SW	7,601	8	Dobbs Ferry Ardsley	5,140
9	Chazy	7,584	9	Islip-Macarthur Arpt	5,261
10	Allegany State Park	7,567	10	Bridgehampton	5,523
11	Delhi 2 SE	7,542	11	Middletown 2 NW	5,773
12	Conklingville Dam	7,483	12	Yorktown Heights 1 W	5,899
13	Peru 2 WSW	7,450	13	Westfield 2 SSE	6,263
14	Alfred	7,416	14	Albion 2 NE	6,365
15	Grafton	7,406	15	Troy Lock and Dam	6,422
16	Bath	7,301	16	Buffalo Greater Buffalo Int'l	6,508
17	Wales	7,242	17	Rochester Intl Arpt	6,553
18	Alcove Dam	7,190	18	Syracuse Hancock Int'l Arpt	6,618
19	Ithaca Cornell Univ	7,090	19	Aurora Research Farm	6,633
20	Binghamton Edwin A Link Field	7,060	20	Albany County Arpt	6,638
21	Utica Oneida County Arpt	7,059	21	Whitehall	6,730
22	Valatie 1 N	6,747	22	Avon	6,732
23	Avon	6,732	23	Valatie 1 N	6,747
24	Whitehall	6,730	24	Utica Oneida County Arpt	7,059
25	Albany County Arpt	6,638	25	Binghamton Edwin A Link Field	7,060

Rankings include 25 highest/lowest stations. If state has less than 25 stations, all stations are included. The period of record is 1980–2009. See User Guide for detailed explanation of data.

Number of Annual Cooling Degree Days

	Highest			Lowest	
Rank	Station Name	Num.	Rank	Station Name	Num.
1	New York Laguardia Arpt	1,262	1	Indian Lake 2 SW	140
2	New York Ave V Brooklyn	*1,187*	2	Boonville 2 SSW	230
3	New York Central Park Observ	1,184	3	Allegany State Park	*244*
4	New York J F Kennedy Int'l Arpt	1,026	4	Tully Heiberg Forest	*272*
5	Dobbs Ferry Ardsley	935	5	Morrisville 5 SW	*283*
6	Mineola	918	6	Delhi 2 SE	293
7	Riverhead Research Farm	914	7	Alfred	294
8	Wantagh Cedar Creek	878	8	Lowville	311
9	Islip-Macarthur Arpt	*839*	9	Grafton	*335*
10	Middletown 2 NW	778	10	Conklingville Dam	*339*
11	Troy Lock and Dam	733	11	Wales	*345*
12	Yorktown Heights 1 W	720	12	Bath	*347*
13	Whitehall	690	12	Dannemora	347
14	Albion 2 NE	669	14	Gouverneur 3 NW	364
15	Westfield 2 SSE	*662*	15	Canton 4 SE	410
16	Bridgehampton	632	16	Alcove Dam	412
17	Aurora Research Farm	615	17	Binghamton Edwin A Link Field	426
18	Albany County Arpt	603	18	Ithaca Cornell Univ	438
19	Syracuse Hancock Int'l Arpt	590	19	Chazy	441
20	Buffalo Greater Buffalo Int'l	582	20	Peru 2 WSW	475
21	Rochester Intl Arpt	581	21	Utica Oneida County Arpt	*494*
22	Valatie 1 N	*561*	22	Avon	533
23	Avon	533	23	Valatie 1 N	*561*
24	Utica Oneida County Arpt	*494*	24	Rochester Intl Arpt	581
25	Peru 2 WSW	475	25	Buffalo Greater Buffalo Int'l	582

Annual Precipitation

	Highest			Lowest	
Rank	Station Name	Inches	Rank	Station Name	Inches
1	Boonville 2 SSW	58.08	1	Peru 2 WSW	30.72
2	Dobbs Ferry Ardsley	51.49	2	Bath	*31.24*
3	Yorktown Heights 1 W	50.79	3	Avon	31.99
4	Bridgehampton	49.65	4	Rochester Intl Arpt	34.12
5	New York Central Park Observ	49.08	5	Albion 2 NE	35.55
6	Riverhead Research Farm	47.25	6	Aurora Research Farm	36.01
7	Islip-Macarthur Arpt	*46.53*	7	Canton 4 SE	36.64
8	Mineola	46.08	8	Ithaca Cornell Univ	36.78
9	Delhi 2 SE	45.98	9	Gouverneur 3 NW	37.32
10	New York Ave V Brooklyn	*45.96*	10	Alfred	37.49
11	Grafton	*45.91*	11	Syracuse Hancock Int'l Arpt	37.90
12	Tully Heiberg Forest	*45.74*	12	Albany County Arpt	39.14
13	Morrisville 5 SW	45.56	12	Binghamton Edwin A Link Field	39.14
14	Conklingville Dam	45.16	14	Troy Lock and Dam	39.46
15	New York Laguardia Arpt	44.66	15	Indian Lake 2 SW	40.19
16	Westfield 2 SSE	*44.59*	16	Buffalo Greater Buffalo Int'l	40.49
17	Allegany State Park	44.47	17	Alcove Dam	40.56
18	Middletown 2 NW	43.36	18	Dannemora	40.93
19	Wales	*42.99*	19	Valatie 1 N	*40.99*
20	Utica Oneida County Arpt	*42.90*	20	Lowville	41.24
21	New York J F Kennedy Int'l Arpt	42.64	21	Whitehall	42.05
22	Wantagh Cedar Creek	42.40	22	Wantagh Cedar Creek	42.40
23	Whitehall	42.05	23	New York J F Kennedy Int'l Arpt	42.64
24	Lowville	41.24	24	Utica Oneida County Arpt	*42.90*
25	Valatie 1 N	*40.99*	25	Wales	*42.99*

Rankings include 25 highest/lowest stations. If state has less than 25 stations, all stations are included. The period of record is 1980–2009. See User Guide for detailed explanation of data.

Annual Extreme Maximum Daily Precipitation

	Highest			Lowest	
Rank	Station Name	Inches	Rank	Station Name	Inches
1	Yorktown Heights 1 W	10.95	1	Troy Lock and Dam	3.00
2	Dobbs Ferry Ardsley	7.62	2	Aurora Research Farm	3.03
3	New York Central Park Observ	7.56	3	Alfred	3.33
4	Bridgehampton	7.04	3	Rochester Intl Arpt	3.33
5	Alcove Dam	6.89	5	Indian Lake 2 SW	3.43
6	Islip-Macarthur Arpt	6.74	6	Albion 2 NE	3.79
7	New York Laguardia Arpt	6.69	7	Allegany State Park	4.00
8	Riverhead Research Farm	6.34	8	Conklingville Dam	4.01
9	New York J F Kennedy Int'l Arpt	6.27	9	Binghamton Edwin A Link Field	4.05
10	Albany County Arpt	5.60	10	Canton 4 SE	4.10
11	New York Ave V Brooklyn	5.46	11	Morrisville 5 SW	4.11
12	Wantagh Cedar Creek	5.43	12	Utica Oneida County Arpt	4.14
13	Wales	5.33	13	Whitehall	4.25
14	Avon	5.20	14	Syracuse Hancock Int'l Arpt	4.29
15	Valatie 1 N	5.10	14	Westfield 2 SSE	4.29
16	Ithaca Cornell Univ	5.08	16	Mineola	4.30
17	Buffalo Greater Buffalo Int'l	5.01	17	Delhi 2 SE	4.49
18	Middletown 2 NW	5.00	18	Gouverneur 3 NW	4.51
19	Tully Heiberg Forest	4.98	19	Dannemora	4.55
20	Boonville 2 SSW	4.86	20	Bath	4.67
21	Peru 2 WSW	4.80	21	Grafton	4.75
22	Lowville	4.78	22	Lowville	4.78
23	Grafton	4.75	23	Peru 2 WSW	4.80
24	Bath	4.67	24	Boonville 2 SSW	4.86
25	Dannemora	4.55	25	Tully Heiberg Forest	4.98

Number of Days Annually With ≥ 0.1 Inches of Precipitation

	Highest			Lowest	
Rank	Station Name	Days	Rank	Station Name	Days
1	Boonville 2 SSW	116	1	Chazy	57
2	Allegany State Park	103	2	Peru 2 WSW	66
2	Morrisville 5 SW	103	3	Bath	71
2	Tully Heiberg Forest	103	3	Wantagh Cedar Creek	71
2	Wales	103	5	New York J F Kennedy Int'l Arpt	72
6	Westfield 2 SSE	98	6	Mineola	74
7	Dannemora	97	7	Avon	75
7	Utica Oneida County Arpt	97	7	New York Laguardia Arpt	75
9	Grafton	96	9	Alcove Dam	76
10	Buffalo Greater Buffalo Int'l	95	10	Islip-Macarthur Arpt	77
11	Delhi 2 SE	94	10	Middletown 2 NW	77
11	Lowville	94	10	New York Ave V Brooklyn	77
13	Syracuse Hancock Int'l Arpt	90	13	Bridgehampton	78
14	Alfred	88	13	New York Central Park Observ	78
14	Indian Lake 2 SW	88	13	Riverhead Research Farm	78
16	Albion 2 NE	87	13	Troy Lock and Dam	78
17	Binghamton Edwin A Link Field	84	17	Whitehall	79
17	Gouverneur 3 NW	84	18	Rochester Intl Arpt	80
17	Ithaca Cornell Univ	84	18	Valatie 1 N	80
20	Canton 4 SE	83	20	Albany County Arpt	81
20	Conklingville Dam	83	20	Dobbs Ferry Ardsley	81
20	Yorktown Heights 1 W	83	22	Aurora Research Farm	82
23	Aurora Research Farm	82	23	Canton 4 SE	83
24	Albany County Arpt	81	23	Conklingville Dam	83
24	Dobbs Ferry Ardsley	81	23	Yorktown Heights 1 W	83

Rankings include 25 highest/lowest stations. If state has less than 25 stations, all stations are included. The period of record is 1980–2009. See User Guide for detailed explanation of data.

Number of Days Annually With ≥ 0.5 Inches of Precipitation

Highest				Lowest		
Rank	**Station Name**	**Days**		**Rank**	**Station Name**	**Days**
1	Boonville 2 SSW	37		1	Bath	*18*
2	Dobbs Ferry Ardsley	35		1	Chazy	*18*
2	New York Central Park Observ	35		3	Avon	19
2	Yorktown Heights 1 W	35		4	Rochester Intl Arpt	20
5	Riverhead Research Farm	34		5	Albion 2 NE	21
6	Grafton	*33*		5	Aurora Research Farm	21
6	Mineola	33		5	Canton 4 SE	21
8	Bridgehampton	32		5	Ithaca Cornell Univ	21
8	Islip-Macarthur Arpt	*32*		5	Peru 2 WSW	21
8	Middletown 2 NW	32		10	Gouverneur 3 NW	22
8	New York Laguardia Arpt	32		11	Alfred	23
8	New York Ave V Brooklyn	*32*		11	Syracuse Hancock Int'l Arpt	23
13	New York J F Kennedy Int'l Arpt	31		13	Binghamton Edwin A Link Field	24
14	Delhi 2 SE	30		13	Buffalo Greater Buffalo Int'l	24
15	Conklingville Dam	29		15	Indian Lake 2 SW	25
15	Valatie 1 N	*29*		15	Lowville	25
15	Wales	*29*		15	Utica Oneida County Arpt	*25*
15	Westfield 2 SSE	*29*		18	Albany County Arpt	26
19	Alcove Dam	28		18	Allegany State Park	26
19	Morrisville 5 SW	28		20	Dannemora	27
19	Wantagh Cedar Creek	28		20	Troy Lock and Dam	27
19	Whitehall	28		20	Tully Heiberg Forest	*27*
23	Dannemora	27		23	Alcove Dam	28
23	Troy Lock and Dam	27		23	Morrisville 5 SW	28
23	Tully Heiberg Forest	*27*		23	Wantagh Cedar Creek	28

Number of Days Annually With ≥ 1.0 Inches of Precipitation

Highest				Lowest		
Rank	**Station Name**	**Days**		**Rank**	**Station Name**	**Days**
1	Boonville 2 SSW	13		1	Bath	*3*
1	Dobbs Ferry Ardsley	13		2	Avon	4
1	New York Ave V Brooklyn	*13*		2	Canton 4 SE	4
1	Yorktown Heights 1 W	13		2	Rochester Intl Arpt	4
5	Bridgehampton	12		2	Syracuse Hancock Int'l Arpt	4
5	Conklingville Dam	12		6	Albion 2 NE	5
5	Islip-Macarthur Arpt	*12*		6	Allegany State Park	5
5	Mineola	12		6	Aurora Research Farm	5
5	New York Central Park Observ	12		6	Chazy	*5*
5	New York J F Kennedy Int'l Arpt	12		6	Ithaca Cornell Univ	5
5	New York Laguardia Arpt	12		6	Wales	*5*
5	Riverhead Research Farm	12		12	Alfred	6
13	Wantagh Cedar Creek	11		12	Dannemora	6
13	Whitehall	11		12	Gouverneur 3 NW	6
15	Alcove Dam	10		12	Peru 2 WSW	6
15	Grafton	*10*		16	Buffalo Greater Buffalo Int'l	7
15	Middletown 2 NW	10		16	Morrisville 5 SW	7
18	Indian Lake 2 SW	9		16	Westfield 2 SSE	*7*
18	Troy Lock and Dam	9		19	Albany County Arpt	8
18	Valatie 1 N	*9*		19	Binghamton Edwin A Link Field	8
21	Albany County Arpt	8		19	Delhi 2 SE	8
21	Binghamton Edwin A Link Field	8		19	Lowville	8
21	Delhi 2 SE	8		19	Tully Heiberg Forest	*8*
21	Lowville	8		19	Utica Oneida County Arpt	*8*
21	Tully Heiberg Forest	*8*		25	Indian Lake 2 SW	9

Rankings include 25 highest/lowest stations. If state has less than 25 stations, all stations are included. The period of record is 1980–2009. See User Guide for detailed explanation of data.

Annual Snowfall

Highest			Lowest		
Rank	Station Name	Inches	Rank	Station Name	Inches
1	Boonville 2 SSW	197.5	1	Mineola	19.8
2	Syracuse Hancock Int'l Arpt	124.5	2	New York Ave V Brooklyn	*22.3*
3	Morrisville 5 SW	124.1	3	New York J F Kennedy Int'l Arpt	22.7
4	Lowville	121.4	4	New York Central Park Observ	23.6
5	Tully Heiberg Forest	*115.8*	5	New York Laguardia Arpt	25.9
6	Wales	*110.8*	6	Bridgehampton	26.5
7	Rochester Intl Arpt	99.4	7	Riverhead Research Farm	27.0
8	Buffalo Greater Buffalo Int'l	94.0	8	Dobbs Ferry Ardsley	30.6
9	Alfred	87.6	9	Troy Lock and Dam	38.6
10	Gouverneur 3 NW	84.6	10	Yorktown Heights 1 W	40.0
11	Westfield 2 SSE	*84.5*	11	Valatie 1 N	*41.4*
12	Grafton	*83.2*	12	Bath	*44.8*
13	Binghamton Edwin A Link Field	82.8	13	Avon	51.9
14	Canton 4 SE	77.9	14	Peru 2 WSW	52.0
15	Conklingville Dam	70.4	15	Chazy	*56.6*
16	Albion 2 NE	66.4	16	Aurora Research Farm	58.9
17	Delhi 2 SE	65.4	17	Whitehall	59.5
18	Ithaca Cornell Univ	63.9	18	Albany County Arpt	60.2
19	Albany County Arpt	60.2	19	Ithaca Cornell Univ	63.9
20	Whitehall	59.5	20	Delhi 2 SE	65.4
21	Aurora Research Farm	58.9	21	Albion 2 NE	66.4
22	Chazy	*56.6*	22	Conklingville Dam	70.4
23	Peru 2 WSW	52.0	23	Canton 4 SE	77.9
24	Avon	51.9	24	Binghamton Edwin A Link Field	82.8
25	Bath	*44.8*	25	Grafton	*83.2*

Annual Maximum Snow Depth

Highest			Lowest		
Rank	Station Name	Inches	Rank	Station Name	Inches
1	Tully Heiberg Forest	*60*	1	Mineola	20
2	Boonville 2 SSW	57	1	Riverhead Research Farm	20
3	Morrisville 5 SW	51	3	New York Ave V Brooklyn	*23*
4	Chazy	*50*	4	Allegany State Park	25
5	Conklingville Dam	45	4	New York Laguardia Arpt	25
6	Buffalo Greater Buffalo Int'l	44	6	Dobbs Ferry Ardsley	26
7	Aurora Research Farm	43	7	Avon	27
8	Troy Lock and Dam	39	7	Bridgehampton	27
9	Canton 4 SE	38	9	Albany County Arpt	28
10	Grafton	*37*	9	Ithaca Cornell Univ	28
11	Bath	*36*	9	New York J F Kennedy Int'l Arpt	28
12	Binghamton Edwin A Link Field	35	12	Yorktown Heights 1 W	29
12	Syracuse Hancock Int'l Arpt	35	13	Albion 2 NE	30
14	Rochester Intl Arpt	34	13	Gouverneur 3 NW	30
14	Wales	*34*	15	Delhi 2 SE	31
16	Lowville	33	16	Lowville	33
16	Valatie 1 N	*33*	16	Valatie 1 N	*33*
18	Delhi 2 SE	31	18	Rochester Intl Arpt	34
19	Albion 2 NE	30	18	Wales	*34*
19	Gouverneur 3 NW	30	20	Binghamton Edwin A Link Field	35
21	Yorktown Heights 1 W	29	20	Syracuse Hancock Int'l Arpt	35
22	Albany County Arpt	28	22	Bath	*36*
22	Ithaca Cornell Univ	28	23	Grafton	*37*
22	New York J F Kennedy Int'l Arpt	28	24	Canton 4 SE	38
25	Avon	27	25	Troy Lock and Dam	39

Rankings include 25 highest/lowest stations. If state has less than 25 stations, all stations are included. The period of record is 1980–2009. See User Guide for detailed explanation of data.

Number of Days Annually With ≥ 1.0 Inch Snow Depth

	Highest			Lowest	
Rank	Station Name	Days	Rank	Station Name	Days
1	Boonville 2 SSW	134	1	Mineola	18
2	Tully Heiberg Forest	*124*	1	New York J F Kennedy Int'l Arpt	18
3	Morrisville 5 SW	115	1	New York Ave V Brooklyn	*18*
4	Lowville	107	4	New York Laguardia Arpt	19
5	Gouverneur 3 NW	97	5	Bridgehampton	20
6	Allegany State Park	95	6	Riverhead Research Farm	21
7	Conklingville Dam	94	7	Dobbs Ferry Ardsley	34
7	Grafton	*94*	8	Albion 2 NE	47
9	Wales	*93*	9	Valatie 1 N	*53*
10	Canton 4 SE	92	10	Yorktown Heights 1 W	54
11	Chazy	*81*	11	Troy Lock and Dam	55
12	Westfield 2 SSE	*80*	12	Albany County Arpt	59
13	Binghamton Edwin A Link Field	79	13	Bath	*67*
14	Delhi 2 SE	78	14	Avon	70
14	Syracuse Hancock Int'l Arpt	78	15	Aurora Research Farm	71
16	Ithaca Cornell Univ	74	15	Buffalo Greater Buffalo Int'l	71
17	Rochester Intl Arpt	73	17	Rochester Intl Arpt	73
18	Aurora Research Farm	71	18	Ithaca Cornell Univ	74
18	Buffalo Greater Buffalo Int'l	71	19	Delhi 2 SE	78
20	Avon	70	19	Syracuse Hancock Int'l Arpt	78
21	Bath	*67*	21	Binghamton Edwin A Link Field	79
22	Albany County Arpt	59	22	Westfield 2 SSE	*80*
23	Troy Lock and Dam	55	23	Chazy	*81*
24	Yorktown Heights 1 W	54	24	Canton 4 SE	92
25	Valatie 1 N	*53*	25	Wales	*93*

Rankings include 25 highest/lowest stations. If state has less than 25 stations, all stations are included. The period of record is 1980–2009. See User Guide for detailed explanation of data.

Significant Storm Events in New York: 2000 – 2009

Location or County	Date	Type	Mag.	Deaths	Injuries	Property Damage ($mil.)	Crop Damage ($mil.)
Buffalo Metro Area, Western Southern Tier	11/20/00	Heavy Snow	na	0	0	46.5	0.0
New York City Metro Area	02/17/03	Heavy Snow	na	0	0	20.0	0.0
Northwest New York	04/04/03	Ice Storm	na	1	0	28.5	8.5
Northwestern Central New York	04/04/03	Ice Storm	na	0	0	28.5	0.0
Broome	06/13/03	Flash Flood	na	5	0	0.1	0.0
Sullivan	08/30/04	Flash Flood	na	0	0	20.0	0.0
Delaware	06/27/06	Flash Flood	na	2	0	250.0	0.0
Broome	06/27/06	Flash Flood	na	0	0	200.0	0.0
Tioga	06/27/06	Flash Flood	na	0	0	100.0	0.0
Sullivan	06/27/06	Flash Flood	na	1	0	100.0	0.0
Oneida	06/27/06	Flash Flood	na	0	0	50.0	0.0
Chenango	06/27/06	Flood	na	0	0	50.0	0.0
Otsego	06/27/06	Flash Flood	na	0	0	50.0	0.0
Broome	06/27/06	Flood	na	0	0	50.0	0.0
Chenango	06/27/06	Flash Flood	na	1	0	50.0	0.0
Madison	06/27/06	Flash Flood	na	0	0	25.0	0.0
Southeast New York	08/01/06	Excessive Heat	na	42	0	0.0	0.0
Southwest Suffolk County	04/16/07	Coastal Flood	na	0	0	26.0	0.0
Delaware	06/19/07	Flash Flood	na	4	0	30.0	0.0
Cattaraugus	08/09/09	Flash Flood	na	1	1	45.0	0.0
Chautauqua	08/09/09	Flash Flood	na	0	0	30.0	0.0
Jefferson and Lewis Counties	12/09/09	High Wind	58 mph	0	0	100.0	0.0

Note: Deaths, injuries, and damages are date and location specific.

Grey House Publishing

Grey House Publishing

2017 Title List
Visit www.GreyHouse.com for Product Information, Table of Contents, and Sample Pages.

General Reference
An African Biographical Dictionary
America's College Museums
American Environmental Leaders: From Colonial Times to the Present
Encyclopedia of African-American Writing
Encyclopedia of Constitutional Amendments
An Encyclopedia of Human Rights in the United States
Encyclopedia of Invasions & Conquests
Encyclopedia of Prisoners of War & Internment
Encyclopedia of Religion & Law in America
Encyclopedia of Rural America
Encyclopedia of the Continental Congress
Encyclopedia of the United States Cabinet, 1789-2010
Encyclopedia of War Journalism
Encyclopedia of Warrior Peoples & Fighting Groups
The Environmental Debate: A Documentary History
The Evolution Wars: A Guide to the Debates
From Suffrage to the Senate: America's Political Women
Gun Debate: An Encyclopedia of Gun Control & Gun Rights
Political Corruption in America
Privacy Rights in the Digital Era
The Religious Right: A Reference Handbook
Speakers of the House of Representatives, 1789-2009
This is Who We Were: 1880-1900
This is Who We Were: A Companion to the 1940 Census
This is Who We Were: In the 1900s
This is Who We Were: In the 1910s
This is Who We Were: In the 1920s
This is Who We Were: In the 1940s
This is Who We Were: In the 1950s
This is Who We Were: In the 1960s
This is Who We Were: In the 1970s
This is Who We Were: In the 1980s
This is Who We Were: In the 1990s
U.S. Land & Natural Resource Policy
The Value of a Dollar 1600-1865: Colonial Era to the Civil War
The Value of a Dollar: 1860-2014
Working Americans 1770-1869 Vol. IX: Revolutionary War to the Civil War
Working Americans 1880-1999 Vol. I: The Working Class
Working Americans 1880-1999 Vol. II: The Middle Class
Working Americans 1880-1999 Vol. III: The Upper Class
Working Americans 1880-1999 Vol. IV: Their Children
Working Americans 1880-2015 Vol. V: Americans At War
Working Americans 1880-2005 Vol. VI: Women at Work
Working Americans 1880-2006 Vol. VII: Social Movements
Working Americans 1880-2007 Vol. VIII: Immigrants
Working Americans 1880-2009 Vol. X: Sports & Recreation
Working Americans 1880-2010 Vol. XI: Inventors & Entrepreneurs
Working Americans 1880-2011 Vol. XII: Our History through Music
Working Americans 1880-2012 Vol. XIII: Education & Educators
Working Americans 1880-2016 Vol. XIV: Industry Through the Ages
World Cultural Leaders of the 20th & 21st Centuries

Education Information
Charter School Movement
Comparative Guide to American Elementary & Secondary Schools
Complete Learning Disabilities Directory
Educators Resource Directory
Special Education: Policy and Curriculum Development

Health Information
Comparative Guide to American Hospitals
Complete Directory for Pediatric Disorders
Complete Directory for People with Chronic Illness
Complete Directory for People with Disabilities
Complete Mental Health Directory
Diabetes in America: Analysis of an Epidemic
Directory of Health Care Group Purchasing Organizations
HMO/PPO Directory
Medical Device Market Place
Older Americans Information Directory

Business Information
Complete Television, Radio & Cable Industry Directory
Directory of Business Information Resources
Directory of Mail Order Catalogs

Directory of Venture Capital & Private Equity Firms
Environmental Resource Handbook
Food & Beverage Market Place
Grey House Homeland Security Directory
Grey House Performing Arts Directory
Grey House Safety & Security Directory
Hudson's Washington News Media Contacts Directory
New York State Directory
Sports Market Place Directory

Statistics & Demographics
American Tally
America's Top-Rated Cities
America's Top-Rated Smaller Cities
Ancestry & Ethnicity in America
The Asian Databook
Comparative Guide to American Suburbs
The Hispanic Databook
Profiles of America
"Profiles of" Series – State Handbooks
Weather America

Financial Ratings Series
TheStreet Ratings' Guide to Bond & Money Market Mutual Funds
TheStreet Ratings' Guide to Common Stocks
TheStreet Ratings' Guide to Exchange-Traded Funds
TheStreet Ratings' Guide to Stock Mutual Funds
TheStreet Ratings' Ultimate Guided Tour of Stock Investing
Weiss Ratings' Consumer Guides
Weiss Ratings' Financial Literary Basic Guides
Weiss Ratings' Guide to Banks
Weiss Ratings' Guide to Credit Unions
Weiss Ratings' Guide to Health Insurers
Weiss Ratings' Guide to Life & Annuity Insurers
Weiss Ratings' Guide to Property & Casualty Insurers

Bowker's Books In Print® Titles
American Book Publishing Record® Annual
American Book Publishing Record® Monthly
Books In Print®
Books In Print® Supplement
Books Out Loud™
Bowker's Complete Video Directory™
Children's Books In Print®
El-Hi Textbooks & Serials In Print®
Forthcoming Books®
Law Books & Serials In Print™
Medical & Health Care Books In Print™
Publishers, Distributors & Wholesalers of the US™
Subject Guide to Books In Print®
Subject Guide to Children's Books In Print®

Canadian General Reference
Associations Canada
Canadian Almanac & Directory
Canadian Environmental Resource Guide
Canadian Parliamentary Guide
Canadian Venture Capital & Private Equity Firms
Financial Post Directory of Directors
Financial Services Canada
Governments Canada
Health Guide Canada
The History of Canada
Libraries Canada
Major Canadian Cities

2017 Title List

Visit **www.SalemPress.com** for Product Information, Table of Contents, and Sample Pages.

Science, Careers & Mathematics
Ancient Creatures
Applied Science
Applied Science: Engineering & Mathematics
Applied Science: Science & Medicine
Applied Science: Technology
Biomes and Ecosystems
Careers in The Arts: Fine, Performing & Visual
Careers in Building Construction
Careers in Business
Careers in Chemistry
Careers in Communications & Media
Careers in Environment & Conservation
Careers in Financial Services
Careers in Healthcare
Careers in Hospitality & Tourism
Careers in Human Services
Careers in Law, Criminal Justice & Emergency Services
Careers in Manufacturing
Careers in Overseas Jobs
Careers in Physics
Careers in Sales, Insurance & Real Estate
Careers in Science & Engineering
Careers in Sports & Fitness
Careers in Technology Services & Repair
Computer Technology Innovators
Contemporary Biographies in Business
Contemporary Biographies in Chemistry
Contemporary Biographies in Communications & Media
Contemporary Biographies in Environment & Conservation
Contemporary Biographies in Healthcare
Contemporary Biographies in Hospitality & Tourism
Contemporary Biographies in Law & Criminal Justice
Contemporary Biographies in Physics
Earth Science
Earth Science: Earth Materials & Resources
Earth Science: Earth's Surface and History
Earth Science: Physics & Chemistry of the Earth
Earth Science: Weather, Water & Atmosphere
Encyclopedia of Energy
Encyclopedia of Environmental Issues
Encyclopedia of Environmental Issues: Atmosphere and Air Pollution
Encyclopedia of Environmental Issues: Ecology and Ecosystems
Encyclopedia of Environmental Issues: Energy and Energy Use
Encyclopedia of Environmental Issues: Policy and Activism
Encyclopedia of Environmental Issues: Preservation/Wilderness Issues
Encyclopedia of Environmental Issues: Water and Water Pollution
Encyclopedia of Global Resources
Encyclopedia of Global Warming
Encyclopedia of Mathematics & Society
Encyclopedia of Mathematics & Society: Engineering, Tech, Medicine
Encyclopedia of Mathematics & Society: Great Mathematicians
Encyclopedia of Mathematics & Society: Math & Social Sciences
Encyclopedia of Mathematics & Society: Math Development/Concepts
Encyclopedia of Mathematics & Society: Math in Culture & Society
Encyclopedia of Mathematics & Society: Space, Science, Environment
Encyclopedia of the Ancient World
Forensic Science
Geography Basics
Internet Innovators
Inventions and Inventors
Magill's Encyclopedia of Science: Animal Life
Magill's Encyclopedia of Science: Plant life
Notable Natural Disasters
Principles of Astronomy
Principles of Biology
Principles of Chemistry
Principles of Physical Science
Principles of Physics
Principles of Research Methods
Principles of Sustainability
Science and Scientists
Solar System
Solar System: Great Astronomers
Solar System: Study of the Universe
Solar System: The Inner Planets
Solar System: The Moon and Other Small Bodies

Solar System: The Outer Planets
Solar System: The Sun and Other Stars
World Geography

Literature
American Ethnic Writers
Classics of Science Fiction & Fantasy Literature
Critical Approaches: Feminist
Critical Approaches: Multicultural
Critical Approaches: Moral
Critical Approaches: Psychological
Critical Insights: Authors
Critical Insights: Film
Critical Insights: Literary Collection Bundles
Critical Insights: Themes
Critical Insights: Works
Critical Survey of Drama
Critical Survey of Graphic Novels: Heroes & Super Heroes
Critical Survey of Graphic Novels: History, Theme & Technique
Critical Survey of Graphic Novels: Independents/Underground Classics
Critical Survey of Graphic Novels: Manga
Critical Survey of Long Fiction
Critical Survey of Mystery & Detective Fiction
Critical Survey of Mythology and Folklore: Heroes and Heroines
Critical Survey of Mythology and Folklore: Love, Sexuality & Desire
Critical Survey of Mythology and Folklore: World Mythology
Critical Survey of Poetry
Critical Survey of Poetry: American Poets
Critical Survey of Poetry: British, Irish & Commonwealth Poets
Critical Survey of Poetry: Cumulative Index
Critical Survey of Poetry: European Poets
Critical Survey of Poetry: Topical Essays
Critical Survey of Poetry: World Poets
Critical Survey of Science Fiction & Fantasy
Critical Survey of Shakespeare's Plays
Critical Survey of Shakespeare's Sonnets
Critical Survey of Short Fiction
Critical Survey of Short Fiction: American Writers
Critical Survey of Short Fiction: British, Irish, Commonwealth Writers
Critical Survey of Short Fiction: Cumulative Index
Critical Survey of Short Fiction: European Writers
Critical Survey of Short Fiction: Topical Essays
Critical Survey of Short Fiction: World Writers
Critical Survey of World Literature
Critical Survey of Young Adult Literature
Cyclopedia of Literary Characters
Cyclopedia of Literary Places
Holocaust Literature
Introduction to Literary Context: American Poetry of the 20th Century
Introduction to Literary Context: American Post-Modernist Novels
Introduction to Literary Context: American Short Fiction
Introduction to Literary Context: English Literature
Introduction to Literary Context: Plays
Introduction to Literary Context: World Literature
Magill's Literary Annual 2015
Magill's Survey of American Literature
Magill's Survey of World Literature
Masterplots
Masterplots II: African American Literature
Masterplots II: American Fiction Series
Masterplots II: British & Commonwealth Fiction Series
Masterplots II: Christian Literature
Masterplots II: Drama Series
Masterplots II: Juvenile & Young Adult Literature, Supplement
Masterplots II: Nonfiction Series
Masterplots II: Poetry Series
Masterplots II: Short Story Series
Masterplots II: Women's Literature Series
Notable African American Writers
Notable American Novelists
Notable Playwrights
Notable Poets
Recommended Reading: 600 Classics Reviewed
Short Story Writers

Grey House Publishing | Salem Press | H.W. Wilson | 4919 Route, 22 PO Box 56, Amenia NY 12501-0056

History and Social Science

The 2000s in America
50 States
African American History
Agriculture in History
American First Ladies
American Heroes
American Indian Culture
American Indian History
American Indian Tribes
American Presidents
American Villains
America's Historic Sites
Ancient Greece
The Bill of Rights
The Civil Rights Movement
The Cold War
Countries, Peoples & Cultures
Countries, Peoples & Cultures: Central & South America
Countries, Peoples & Cultures: Central, South & Southeast Asia
Countries, Peoples & Cultures: East & South Africa
Countries, Peoples & Cultures: East Asia & the Pacific
Countries, Peoples & Cultures: Eastern Europe
Countries, Peoples & Cultures: Middle East & North Africa
Countries, Peoples & Cultures: North America & the Caribbean
Countries, Peoples & Cultures: West & Central Africa
Countries, Peoples & Cultures: Western Europe
Defining Documents: American Revolution
Defining Documents: American West
Defining Documents: Ancient World
Defining Documents: Civil Rights
Defining Documents: Civil War
Defining Documents: Court Cases
Defining Documents: Dissent & Protest
Defining Documents: Emergence of Modern America
Defining Documents: Exploration & Colonial America
Defining Documents: Immigration & Immigrant Communities
Defining Documents: Manifest Destiny
Defining Documents: Middle Ages
Defining Documents: Nationalism & Populism
Defining Documents: Native Americans
Defining Documents: Postwar 1940s
Defining Documents: Reconstruction
Defining Documents: Renaissance & Early Modern Era
Defining Documents: 1920s
Defining Documents: 1930s
Defining Documents: 1950s
Defining Documents: 1960s
Defining Documents: 1970s
Defining Documents: The 17th Century
Defining Documents: The 18th Century
Defining Documents: Vietnam War
Defining Documents: Women
Defining Documents: World War I
Defining Documents: World War II
The Eighties in America
Encyclopedia of American Immigration
Encyclopedia of Flight
Encyclopedia of the Ancient World
Fashion Innovators
The Fifties in America
The Forties in America
Great Athletes
Great Athletes: Baseball
Great Athletes: Basketball
Great Athletes: Boxing & Soccer
Great Athletes: Cumulative Index
Great Athletes: Football
Great Athletes: Golf & Tennis
Great Athletes: Olympics
Great Athletes: Racing & Individual Sports
Great Events from History: 17th Century
Great Events from History: 18th Century
Great Events from History: 19th Century
Great Events from History: 20th Century (1901-1940)
Great Events from History: 20th Century (1941-1970)

Great Events from History: 20th Century (1971-2000)
Great Events from History: 21st Century (2000-2016)
Great Events from History: African American History
Great Events from History: Cumulative Indexes
Great Events from History: LGBTG
Great Events from History: Middle Ages
Great Events from History: Modern Scandals
Great Events from History: Renaissance & Early Modern Era
Great Lives from History: 17th Century
Great Lives from History: 18th Century
Great Lives from History: 19th Century
Great Lives from History: 20th Century
Great Lives from History: 21st Century (2000-2016)
Great Lives from History: American Women
Great Lives from History: Ancient World
Great Lives from History: Asian & Pacific Islander Americans
Great Lives from History: Cumulative Indexes
Great Lives from History: Incredibly Wealthy
Great Lives from History: Inventors & Inventions
Great Lives from History: Jewish Americans
Great Lives from History: Latinos
Great Lives from History: Notorious Lives
Great Lives from History: Renaissance & Early Modern Era
Great Lives from History: Scientists & Science
Historical Encyclopedia of American Business
Issues in U.S. Immigration
Magill's Guide to Military History
Milestone Documents in African American History
Milestone Documents in American History
Milestone Documents in World History
Milestone Documents of American Leaders
Milestone Documents of World Religions
Music Innovators
Musicians & Composers 20th Century
The Nineties in America
The Seventies in America
The Sixties in America
Survey of American Industry and Careers
The Thirties in America
The Twenties in America
United States at War
U.S. Court Cases
U.S. Government Leaders
U.S. Laws, Acts, and Treaties
U.S. Legal System
U.S. Supreme Court
Weapons and Warfare
World Conflicts: Asia and the Middle East

Health

Addictions & Substance Abuse
Adolescent Health & Wellness
Cancer
Complementary & Alternative Medicine
Community & Family Health
Genetics & Inherited Conditions
Health Issues
Infectious Diseases & Conditions
Magill's Medical Guide
Nutrition
Nursing
Psychology & Behavioral Health
Psychology Basics

Grey House Publishing | Salem Press | H.W. Wilson | 4919 Route, 22 PO Box 56, Amenia NY 12501-0056

Current Biography
Current Biography Cumulative Index 1946-2013
Current Biography Monthly Magazine
Current Biography Yearbook: 2003
Current Biography Yearbook: 2004
Current Biography Yearbook: 2005
Current Biography Yearbook: 2006
Current Biography Yearbook: 2007
Current Biography Yearbook: 2008
Current Biography Yearbook: 2009
Current Biography Yearbook: 2010
Current Biography Yearbook: 2011
Current Biography Yearbook: 2012
Current Biography Yearbook: 2013
Current Biography Yearbook: 2014
Current Biography Yearbook: 2015
Current Biography Yearbook: 2016

Core Collections
Children's Core Collection
Fiction Core Collection
Graphic Novels Core Collection
Middle & Junior High School Core
Public Library Core Collection: Nonfiction
Senior High Core Collection
Young Adult Fiction Core Collection

The Reference Shelf
Aging in America
American Military Presence Overseas
The Arab Spring
The Brain
The Business of Food
Campaign Trends & Election Law
Conspiracy Theories
The Digital Age
Dinosaurs
Embracing New Paradigms in Education
Faith & Science
Families: Traditional and New Structures
The Future of U.S. Economic Relations: Mexico, Cuba, and Venezuela
Global Climate Change
Graphic Novels and Comic Books
Guns in America
Immigration
Immigration in the U.S.
Internet Abuses & Privacy Rights
Internet Safety
LGBTQ in the 21st Century
Marijuana Reform
The News and its Future
The Paranormal
Politics of the Ocean
Prescription Drug Abuse
Racial Tension in a "Postracial" Age
Reality Television
Representative American Speeches: 2008-2009
Representative American Speeches: 2009-2010
Representative American Speeches: 2010-2011
Representative American Speeches: 2011-2012
Representative American Speeches: 2012-2013
Representative American Speeches: 2013-2014
Representative American Speeches: 2014-2015
Representative American Speeches: 2015-2016
Representative American Speeches: 2016-2017
Rethinking Work
Revisiting Gender
Robotics
Russia
Social Networking
Social Services for the Poor
Space Exploration & Development
Sports in America

The Supreme Court
The Transformation of American Cities
U.S. Infrastructure
U.S. National Debate Topic: Educational Reform
U.S. National Debate Topic: Surveillance
U.S. National Debate Topic: The Ocean
U.S. National Debate Topic: Transportation Infrastructure
Whistleblowers

Readers' Guide
Abridged Readers' Guide to Periodical Literature
Readers' Guide to Periodical Literature

Indexes
Index to Legal Periodicals & Books
Short Story Index
Book Review Digest

Sears List
Sears List of Subject Headings
Sears: Lista de Encabezamientos de Materia

Facts About Series
Facts About American Immigration
Facts About China
Facts About the 20th Century
Facts About the Presidents
Facts About the World's Languages

Nobel Prize Winners
Nobel Prize Winners: 1901-1986
Nobel Prize Winners: 1987-1991
Nobel Prize Winners: 1992-1996
Nobel Prize Winners: 1997-2001

World Authors
World Authors: 1995-2000
World Authors: 2000-2005

Famous First Facts
Famous First Facts
Famous First Facts About American Politics
Famous First Facts About Sports
Famous First Facts About the Environment
Famous First Facts: International Edition

American Book of Days
The American Book of Days
The International Book of Days

Monographs
American Reformers
The Barnhart Dictionary of Etymology
Celebrate the World
Guide to the Ancient World
Indexing from A to Z
The Poetry Break
Radical Change: Books for Youth in a Digital Age

Wilson Chronology
Wilson Chronology of Asia and the Pacific
Wilson Chronology of Human Rights
Wilson Chronology of Ideas
Wilson Chronology of the Arts
Wilson Chronology of the World's Religions
Wilson Chronology of Women's Achievements

Grey House Publishing | Salem Press | H.W. Wilson | 4919 Route, 22 PO Box 56, Amenia NY 12501-0056